FINANCIAL POST

FPsurvey
Predecessor & Defunct

Additional Publications
For more detailed information, see the back of the book.

CANADIAN ALMANAC & DIRECTORY 2025
Répertoire et almanach canadien
2,348 pages, 8 ½ x 11, Hardcover
178th edition, December 2024
ISBN 978-1-63700-912-3
ISSN 0068-8193
A combination of textual material, charts, colour photographs and directory listings, the *Canadian Almanac & Directory* provides the most comprehensive picture of Canada, from physical attributes to economic and business summaries to leisure and recreation.

CANADIAN WHO'S WHO 2025
1,200 pages, 8 3/8 x 10 7/8, Hardcover
December 2024
ISBN 978-1-63700-922-2
ISSN 0068-9963
Published for over 100 years, this authoritative annual publication offers access to the top 10,000 notable Canadians in all walks of life, including details such as date and place of birth, education, family details, career information, memberships, creative works, honours, languages, and awards, together with full addresses. Included are outstanding Canadians from business, academia, politics, sports, the arts and sciences, and more, selected because of the positions they hold in Canadian society, or because of the contributions they have made to Canada.

FINANCIAL POST DIRECTORY OF DIRECTORS 2025
Répertoire des administrateurs
1,751 pages, 5 7/8 x 9, Hardcover
78th edition, September 2024
ISBN 978-1-63700-924-6
ISSN 0071-5042
Published biennially and annually since 1931, this comprehensive resource offers readers access to approximately 16,600 executive contacts from Canada's top 1,400 corporations. The directory provides a definitive list of directorships and offices held by noteworthy Canadian business people, as well as details on prominent Canadian companies (both public and private), including company name, contact information and the names of executive officers and directors. Includes all-new front matter and three indexes.

CANADIAN PARLIAMENTARY GUIDE 2025
Guide parlementaire canadien
1,310 pages, 6 x 9, Hardcover
159th edition, April 2025
ISBN 979-8-89179-345-3
ISSN 0315-6168
Published annually since before Confederation, this indispensable guide to government in Canada provides information on federal and provincial governments, with biographical sketches of government members, descriptions of government institutions, and historical text and charts. With significant bilingual sections, the Guide covers elections from Confederation to the present, including the most recent provincial elections.

ASSOCIATIONS CANADA 2025
Associations du Canada
2,130 pages, 8 ½ x 11, Softcover
46th edition, February 2025
ISBN 979-8-89179-341-5
ISSN 1186-9798
Over 20,200 entries profile Canadian and international organizations active in Canada. Over 2,000 subject classifications index activities, professions and interests served by associations. Includes listings of NGOs, institutes, coalitions, social agencies, federations, foundations, trade unions, fraternal orders, and political parties. Fully indexed by subject, acronym, budget, conference, executive name, geographic location, mailing list availability, and registered charitable organization.

FINANCIAL SERVICES CANADA 2025-2026
Services financiers au Canada
1,400 pages, 8 ½ x 11, Softcover
26th edition, May 2025
ISBN 979-8-89179-343-9
ISSN 1484-2408
This directory of Canadian financial institutions and organizations includes banks and depository institutions, non-depository institutions, investment management firms, financial planners, insurance companies, accountants, major law firms, major corporations, associations, and financial technology companies. Fully indexed.

LIBRARIES CANADA 2025-2026
Bibliothèques Canada
922 pages, 8 ½ x 11, Softcover
38th edition, July 2025
ISBN 979-1-89179-365-1
ISSN 1920-2849
Libraries Canada offers comprehensive information on Canadian libraries, resource centres, business information centres, professional associations, regional library systems, archives, library schools, government libraries, and library technical programs.

MAJOR CANADIAN CITIES: COMPARED & RANKED
Comparaison et classement des principales villes canadiennes
1,372 pages, 8 ½ x 11, Softcover
2nd edition, January 2024
ISBN 978-8-89179-049-0
This second edition has been completely revised with 2021 census data, including new tables and a refreshed layout. It provides an in-depth comparison and analysis of the 50 most populated cities in Canada.

CANADIAN ENVIRONMENTAL RESOURCE GUIDE 2024-2025
Guide des ressources environnementales canadiennes
860 pages, 8 ½ x 11, Softcover
26th edition, May 2024
ISBN 978-1-63700-914-7
ISSN 1484-2408
Canada's most complete national listing of environmental organizations, product and service companies and governmental bodies, all indexed and categorized for quick and easy reference. Also included is the Environmental Update, with recent events, maps, rankings, statistics, and trade shows and conferences. The online version features even more content, including associations, special libraries, and federal/provincial government information.

FINANCIAL POST

FPsurvey
Predecessor & Defunct
2025
41st Edition

GREY HOUSE PUBLISHING CANADA

Grey House Publishing Canada
PUBLISHER: Leslie Mackenzie
GENERAL MANAGER: Bryon Moore

Grey House Publishing
EDITORIAL DIRECTOR: Stuart Paterson
SENIOR VICE PRESIDENT, MARKETING: Jessica Moody

Grey House Publishing Canada
3 - 1500 Upper Middle Road, P.O. Box 76017
Oakville, ON L6M 3H5
866-433-4739
FAX 416-644-1904
www.greyhouse.ca
e-mail: info@greyhouse.ca

© 2025, Postmedia Network Inc.
365 Bloor St. East
Toronto, ON M4W 3L4
Email: fpadvisor@postmedia.com
legacy-fpadvisor.financialpost.com

Text © 2025 by Postmedia Network Inc.
Cover Art, Title Pages, Additional Publications and Backmatter © 2025 by Grey House Publishing Canada Inc.
Texte © 2025 par Postmedia Network Inc.
Couverture, pages de titre, publications supplémentaires et publicités © 2025 par Grey House Publishing Canada Inc.

Published in print form by Grey House Publishing Canada Inc. under exclusive license from Postmedia Network Inc.
All rights reserved.
Publié sous forme imprimé par Grey House Publishing Canada Inc. sous licence exclusive de Postmedia Network Inc.
Tous droits réservés.

Printed in Canada by Marquis Book Printing Inc.

41st edition published 2025
ISBN: 979-8-89179-357-6
ISSN: 1486-4916

Cataloguing in Publication Data is available from Libraries and Archives Canada.

Introduction

Welcome to **FP Survey - Predecessor & Defunct,** the comprehensive collection of corporate changes which have occurred over the years since 1929 when Financial Post first began its coverage of the Canadian corporate landscape.

First published under separate cover in 1981 as **The Financial Post Survey of Predecessor & Defunct Companies,** this book is a cumulative record of Canadian corporate changes which have occurred over time. As always, the universe of currently active public companies are recorded, in detail, in current editions of **FP Survey - Industrials** and **FP Survey - Mines & Energy**. All current editions in the FP Survey series are published by Grey House Publishing Canada.

Many factors contribute to the numerous changes recorded. Effective dates of these changes often reflect those provided by the stock exchanges or legal dates rather than shareholder or Corporate Registry approval dates. This volume contains details on corporate changes including:

- Amalgamations and mergers
- Acquisitions through purchase offers or share exchanges
- Incorporation changes
- Many once-public companies that no longer exist; others that are inactive shells
- Name changes
- Privatizations through share buy-backs and redemptions
- Receiverships
- Reorganizations
- Reverse takeovers

Information covering such corporate changes for public companies is detailed in this volume. The companies are listed alphabetically and, where available, the description includes the provincial or federal incorporation and date of the charter. The exchange basis of new shares for old is recorded. The solid square which may appear in an entry ■ denotes that subsequent information for the company name shown in the entry is available elsewhere in this book. Multiple corporate actions on each company are dated and grouped under a single company header in chronological order for ease of reading and referencing. Where current information is available on the company or in one of the FP Survey coverages, a note is indicated.

Details of asset distribution on companies being wound up or liquidated are also recorded. Companies for which charters have been cancelled or have been struck off provincial registers are included.

The source of this information is normally the gazettes or bulletins published by the federal or provincial governments. Such companies are not necessarily wound up or dissolved. Under certain circumstances the companies may apply to revive their charter. The time allowed for reinstatement varies from province to province. Further information on the status of specific companies may be obtained from the federal or provincial government under whose jurisdiction the incorporation was granted. Queries should be directed to the government departments listed on page 6.

Coverages are being added continuously to **FP Survey - Predecessor & Defunct** as corporate changes occur. We appreciate your input. If you would like to share your information with us, submit a correction, clarification or improvement, please feel free to contact our office.

Toronto, August 27, 2025

GOVERNMENT DEPARTMENTS

The following is a list of the federal and provincial government departments from which information on the status of companies may be obtained. A modest fee may be charged for such information.

FEDERAL
Corporations Canada
C.D. Howe Building
235 Queen Street
Ottawa, ON K1A 0H5
Telephone: (613) 941-9042
Toll-free: 1-866-333-5556
www.canada.ca/en/services/
business/federal-corporations
Email: corporationscanada@ic.gc.ca

ALBERTA
Service Alberta
Corporate Registry
Mezzanine Floor
John E. Brownlee Building
10365 97 Street
Edmonton, AB T5J 3W7
Telephone: (780) 427-7013
www.alberta.ca/service-alberta
Email: cr@gov.ab.ca

BRITISH COLUMBIA
BC Registry Services
Corporate Registry
200-940 Blanshard Street
PO Box 9431 Stn. Prov. Govt.
Victoria, BC V8W 9V3
Telephone: (250) 387-7848
Toll-free: 1-877-526-1526
www.bcregistryservices.gov.bc.ca
Email: bcregistries@gov.bc.ca
Also available through BC OnLine:
www.corporateonline.gov.bc.ca
Email: bconline@gov.bc.ca
Toll-free: 1-800-663-6102

MANITOBA
Entrepreneurship Manitoba Companies Office
Woodsworth Building
1010-405 Broadway Avenue
Winnipeg, MB R3C 3L6
Telephone: (204) 945-2500
Toll-free: 1-888-246-8353
www.companiesoffice.gov.mb.ca
Email: companies@gov.mb.ca

NEW BRUNSWICK
Service New Brunswick
Corporate Registry
432 Queen Street
PO Box 1998
Fredericton, NB E3B 5G4
Telephone: (506) 453-2703
Fax: (506) 453-2613
www.snb.ca/corporateregistry
Email: cr-rc@snb.ca

NEWFOUNDLAND & LABRADOR
Service NL
Registry of Companies
Commercial Registrations Division
Confederation Building, 10th Floor East Block
PO Box 8700
St. John's, NL A1B 4J6
Telephone: (709) 729-3317
Fax: (709) 729-0232
www.gov.nl.ca/snl/registries/companies-2
Email: servicenlinfo@gov.nl.ca

NORTHWEST TERRITORIES
Department of Justice
Corporate Registries
Stuart M. Hodgson Building
100-5009 49th Street
PO Box 1320
Yellowknife, NT X1A 2L9
Telephone: (867) 767-9304
Toll-free: (877) 743-3302
Fax: (867) 873-0243
www.justice.gov.nt.ca/en/corporate-registry-searches
Email: corporateregistries@gov.nt.ca

NOVA SCOTIA
Service Nova Scotia
Registry of Joint Stock Companies
Maritime Centre
900-1505 Barrington Street North
PO Box 1529
Halifax, NS B3J 2Y4
Telephone: (902) 424-7770
Toll-free: 1-800-225-8227
Fax: (902) 424-4633
www.novascotia.ca/sns/access/business/
registry-joint-stock-companies
Email: rjsc@novascotia.ca

NUNAVUT
Department of Justice
Legal Registries Division
PO Box 1000, Stn. 570
Iqaluit, NU X0A 0H0
Telephone: (867) 975-6590
Fax: (867) 975-6594
www.nunavutlegalregistries.ca
Email: corporatesearches@gov.nu.ca

ONTARIO
Ministry of Government & Consumer Services
ServiceOntario
200-393 University Avenue
Toronto, ON M5G 2M2
Telephone: (416) 212-8888
Toll-free: 1-888-745-8888
www.ontario.ca/page/business-services

OnCorp Direct Inc.
Telephone: (416) 964-2677
Toll-free: 1-800-461-7772
www.oncorp.com

ESC Corporate Services Ltd.
Telephone: (416) 595-7177
Toll-free: 1-800-668-8208
www.eservicecorp.ca

PRINCE EDWARD ISLAND
Consumer, Corporate and Insurance Division
Shaw Building South
100-105 Rochford Street
PO Box 2000
Charlottetown, PE C1A 7N8
Telephone: (902) 368-4550
Fax: (902) 368-5283
www.princeedwardisland.ca/en/feature/
pei-business-corporate-registry
Email: ccs@gov.pe.ca

QUEBEC
Revenu Québec
Direction du Registraire des entreprises
787 boulevard Lebourgneuf
CP 1364
Québec, QC G1K 9B3
Telephone: (418) 644-0075
Toll-free: 1-800-644-0075
www.registreentreprises.gouv.qc.ca
Email: registre@servicequebec.gouv.qc.ca

SASKATCHEWAN
Department of Justice
Corporate Registry
1301 1st Avenue
Regina, SK S4R 8H2
Toll-free: 1-866-275-4721
Fax: (306) 787-8999
www.isc.ca/corporateregistry
Email: corporateregistry@isc.ca

YUKON
Yukon Corporate Registries
Government of Yukon Administration Building
100-307 Black Street
Box 2703 (C-6)
Whitehorse, YT Y1A 2C6
Telephone: (867) 667-5314
Toll-free: 1-800-661-0408
www.ycor-reey.gov.yk.ca/corp
Email: corporateaffairs@gov.yk.ca

A

A & A Foods Ltd. (B.C. Jan. 16, 1976)
Aug. 5, 1997 – Name changed to A & A International Industries Inc.; basis 1 new for 5 old shs. ∎

A & A International Industries Inc. (B.C. Jan. 16, 1976)
Oct. 3, 2003 – Dissolved and struck from register.

A & E Capital Funding Inc. (Can. Nov. 8, 1979)
Oct. 18, 2005 – Name changed to E & E Capital Funding Inc. ∎

A B S Resources Ltd. (B.C. 1983)
Feb. 14, 1989 – Name changed to ABS Technology Ltd. ∎

A Buck or Two Stores Corporation (Ont. July 9, 1993)
Apr. 3, 1995 – Name changed to Denninghouse Inc. ∎

A. E. LePage Capital Properties (Ont. 1982)
Apr. 17, 1985 – Name changed to Royal LePage Capital Properties. ∎

A. L. Green Ltd. (Que. 1972 amalg.)
Oct. 28, 1975 – Acquired by Metropolitan Stores of Canada Ltd. following an offer to buy shs. for $1.75 each.

A. L. Van Houtte Ltée (Can. Mar. 25, 1980)
Oct. 30, 2000 – Name changed to Van Houtte Inc. ∎

A-Labs Capital I Corp. (Can. Mar. 6, 2018)
Dec. 23, 2020 – Name changed to Banxa Holdings Inc. and continued into British Columbia pursuant to Qualifying Transaction reverse takeover acquisition of BTC Corporation Holdings Pty Ltd.; basis 1 new for 4.66667 old shs. (see FPsurvey - Industrials)

A-Labs Capital V Corp. (Can. Nov. 29, 2018)
Mar. 1, 2024 – Name changed to Alterego Ventures 24 Corp. (see FPsurvey - Industrials)

A. Lambert International Inc. (Que. June 26, 1985)
Oct. 1988 – All o/s shs. acquired under mgmt. buyout; basis approx. $3.00 per sh.

A Little Reminder (ALR) Inc. (Wyo. July 31, 1998)
Apr. 30, 1999 – Name changed to ALR Technologies Inc.

A-1 Resources Ltd. (B.C. 1986)
Aug. 29, 1988 – Name changed to Canadian Transtech Industries Ltd. ∎

A-1 Steel and Iron Foundry (Vancouver) Ltd. (B.C. 1963)
Dec. 23, 1975 – Amalgamated with Ardiem Holdings Ltd. (5 for 1), E. C. Warner Investments Ltd. (1 for 1) and Harbour Ferries Ltd. (1 for 3) to form The Ardiem Industrial Corp.; basis 10 new for 1 old sh. (see The Ardiem Industrial Corporation)

A 77 Capital Inc. (Que. Dec. 9, 2003)
Dec. 23, 2004 – Formed Amadeus International Inc. in Quebec following Qualifying Transaction amalgamation with Amadeus International Inc. (deemed acquiror) and 9106-5086 Québec Inc. ∎

A&B Geoscience Corporation (B.C. July 13, 1987)
Apr. 11, 1995 – Continued into Anguilla.
June 18, 2003 – Name changed to Arawak Energy Corporation. ∎

A2 Acquisition Corp. (Alta. Feb. 2, 2015)
Mar. 3, 2017 – Name changed to Medicenna Therapeutics Corp. following reverse takeover acquisition of Medicenna Therapeutics Inc.; basis 1 new for 14 old shs. (see FPsurvey - Industrials)

A2Z Smart Technologies Corp. (B.C. Jan. 15, 2018)
July 31, 2024 – Name changed to A2Z Cust2Mate Solutions Corp. (see FPsurvey - Industrials)

AACE Environmental Services Inc. (Alta. Feb. 14, 1994)
Feb. 24, 1997 – Formed Enviro FX Inc. in Alberta on reverse takeover acquisition of and amalgamation with Lakewood Bio-Remediation Inc.; basis 1 new for 1 Lakewood sh. and 1 new for 2.1 AACE shs. ∎

AADCO Automotive Inc. (Alta. Aug. 28, 1997)
Jan. 2, 2008 – Name changed to Royce Resources Corp.; basis 1 new for 5 old shs. ∎

AADCO industries.com inc. (Alta. Aug. 28, 1997)
Feb. 18, 2002 – Name changed to AADCO Automotive Inc. ∎

AADirection Capital Corp. (B.C. Dec. 1, 2020)
Oct. 26, 2023 – Name changed to Centenario Gold Corp. pursuant to the Qualifying Transaction reverse takeover acquisition of (old) Centenario Gold Corp. and concurrent amalgamation of (old) Centenario with wholly owned 1403285 B.C. Ltd. (and continued under the 1403285 B.C. name). (see FPsurvey - Mines & Energy)

AAER Inc. (Can. June 18, 2003)
Aug. 20, 2010 – Pursuant to plan of reorganization and compromise under the Companies' Creditors Arrangement Act, (i) majority of assets were sold to Pioneer Wind Energy Systems, Inc., a wholly owned subsid. of Pioneer Power Solutions, Inc. for $450,000, (ii) some deposits on inventory and prepaid expenses were sold to Global Casting Inc. for $280,000 and (iii) subscription by Pioneer Wind Energy Holdings Inc., a wholly owned subsid. of Pioneer Power Solutions, Inc., for new shs. of AAER for $450,000, proceeds of which were distributed to AAER's creditors; shldrs. received nothing and Pioneer Power become the sole shldr.

AAI Industries Inc. (Ont. Dec. 12, 1986)
May 11, 1990 – Name changed to Bridgebank Capital Inc. ∎

AAJ Capital 1 Corp. (B.C. May 30, 2017)
Jan. 15, 2019 – Name changed to PharmaCielo Ltd. pursuant to Qualifying Transaction reverse takeover acquisition of private Toronto, Ont.-based (old) PharmaCielo Ltd. on a share-for-share basis (post-consolidation); basis 1 new for 11.94 old shs. (see FPsurvey - Industrials)

AAJ Capital 2 Corp. (B.C. Jan. 28, 2019)
Sept. 29, 2021 – Name changed to TUT Fitness Group Inc. pursuant to the Qualifying Transaction reverse takeover acquisition of TUT Fitness Group Limited; basis 1 new for 2 old shs. (see FPsurvey - Industrials)

AAN Ventures Inc. (B.C. Jan. 30, 2006)
June 7, 2017 – Name changed to Parana Copper Corporation; basis 1 new for 1.5 old shs. ∎

AAO Aquaculture International Corp. (B.C. 1986)
Dec. 3, 1993 – Dissolved and struck off register.

A&W Revenue Royalties Income Fund (B.C. Dec. 18, 2001)
Oct. 18, 2024 – All o/s trust units not already held acquired by A&W Food Services Canada Inc.; basis (i) $37 in cash; or (ii) one A&W Food Services sh.; or (iii) a combination of 32.54277% of the cash consideration (being $12.040825) and 67.45723% of the share consideration (being 0.6745723 of Food Service sh.) for 1 A&W Revenue Royalties trust unit.

A.B.C. Energy Ltd. (B.C. 1979)
July 6, 1982 – Name changed to St. Clair Resources Ltd.; basis 1 new for 3 old shs. ∎

ABC Mining Ventures Inc. (B.C. Apr. 28, 2006)
Oct. 11, 2007 – Name changed to Dundee Mines Ltd. ∎

ABC Technologies Holdings Inc. (Ont. Jan. 11, 2016)
Dec. 18, 2018 – Continued into British Columbia.
Oct. 30, 2023 – All o/s shs. not already owned acquired by AP IX Alpha Holdings (Lux) S.à.r.l. and Oaktree Capital Management, L.P.; basis Cdn$6.75 cash per sh.

ABC Technologies Inc. (B.C. 1973)
Nov. 4, 1993 – Delisted from the Vancouver Stock Exchange. Subsequently dissolved and struck from register.

ABDA International Holdings Corp. (B.C. 1982)
Feb. 25, 1994 – Dissolved and struck off register.

ABE Resources Inc. (Can. Apr. 7, 1996)
Mar. 27, 2018 – Name changed to Vision Lithium Inc. (see FPsurvey - Mines & Energy)

ABI Capital Corp. (Alta. July 18, 2000)
Apr. 9, 2002 – Name changed to Automated Benefits Corp. following Qualifying Transaction reverse takeover acquisition of Automated Benefits Inc. ∎

ABL Canada Inc. (Can. June 3, 1992)
Oct. 23, 2000 – Name changed to AldeaVision Inc. ∎

ABM Gold Corp. (B.C. 1986)
1989 – Continued into Ontario.
June 1, 1990 – Name changed to NorthWest Gold Corp. ∎

ABN Bank Canada (Ont. July 31, 1981)
Feb. 1, 1991 – Name changed to ABN AMRO Bank Canada.

ABS Technology Ltd. (B.C. 1983)
May 3, 1989 – Continued into Canada.
May 28, 1991 – Name changed to Darius Technology Ltd. ∎

ABX Resources Inc. (Alta. May 28, 1996)
Oct. 14, 2003 – Name changed to Expedition Energy Inc. following Qualifying Transaction reverse takeover acquisition of Expedition Energy Ltd.; basis 1 new for 5 old shs. ∎

ABcann Global Corporation (Can. Apr. 12, 2007)
Aug. 7, 2018 – Name changed to VIVO Cannabis Inc. ∎

AC Energy Inc. (Alta. Sept. 30, 1996)
Oct. 9, 2003 – Placed into receivership. No trustee appointed.

A.C. Global Capital Corp. (B.C. July 8, 1999)
Nov. 14, 2002 – Amalgamated with Arsenal Capital Inc., constituting A.C. Global's Qualifying Transaction, to form Arsenal Energy Inc.; basis 0.8 Arsenal Energy com. shs. for either 1 Arsenal Capital com. sh. or 1 A.C. Global com. sh. (see Arsenal Energy Inc.)

ACC TelEnterprises Ltd. (Ont. May 3, 1993)
Jan. 6, 1997 – Amalgamated with ACC Acquisition Corp., a wholly owned subsid. of parent ACC Corp. of Rochester, N.Y.; basis 1 special sh. for 1 ACC TelEnterprises com. sh. redeemed for $21.50 per sh.

ACCUM Therapeutics Inc. (Que. July 18, 2017)
Mar. 26, 2020 – Name changed to Defence Therapeutics Inc. and continued into British Columbia. (see FPsurvey - Industrials)

ACD Systems International Inc. (Alta. Jan. 21, 1999)
Feb. 21, 2006 – Continued into British Columbia.
Mar. 26, 2007 – Acquired by 0770303 B.C. Ltd., a company formed by 3 ACD Systems shldrs. holding a combined 52.5% interest in ACD Systems; basis $0.575 per sh.

ACDS Graphic System Inc. (Can. Sept. 9, 1983)
May 6, 2004 – Dissolved.

ACE Aviation Holdings Inc. (Can. June 29, 2004)
June 28, 2012 – All officers and directors resigned. Ernst & Young Inc. appointed liquidator.
May 26, 2015 – Initial distribution of $3.5411382 cash per sh. to shldrs. of record May 26, 2015, payable June 2, 2015.
June 22, 2016 – Distribution of approx. 36¢ cash per sh. to shldrs. of record June 14, 2016, payable June 22, 2016.
Mar. 13, 2024 – Final distrib. of 16¢ cash per sh. payable to shldrs. of record Mar. 5, 2024.
Mar. 15, 2024 – Voluntarily dissolved.

ACE/Security Laminates Corporation (Can. Sept. 28, 1998)
Nov. 12, 2011 – Dissolved.

ACFAW.COM Inc. (Can. June 21, 2002)
May 4, 2010 – Name changed to St-Georges Platinum and Base Metals Inc. following acquisition of Villebon property from St-Georges Minerals Ltd.; basis 1 new for 2 old shs. ■

ACL International Ltd. (Alta. Feb. 28, 1999 amalg.)
Feb. 15, 2017 – Name changed to Bow Energy Ltd. ■

ACME Lithium Inc. (B.C. Jan. 31, 2017)
Apr. 28, 2025 – Name changed to Surface Metals Inc.; basis 1 new for 3 old shs. (see FPsurvey - Mines & Energy)

ACME Resources Corp. (Ont. Sept. 1, 2009)
Dec. 10, 2018 – Name changed to Rapid Dose Therapeutics Corp. following reverse takeover acquisition of Rapid Dose Therapeutics Inc. (see FPsurvey - Industrials)

ACP Ace Venture Corporation (Yuk. Apr. 28, 2000)
Feb. 10, 2005 – Formed Cantronic Systems Inc. in British Columbia on Qualifying Transaction amalgamation with Cantronic Systems Inc., constituting a reverse takeover by Cantronic. ■

ACREX Ventures Ltd. (B.C. Aug. 1, 1969)
July 10, 2014 – Name changed to Alba Minerals Ltd.; basis 1 new for 5 old shs. ■

ACS Freezers Income Trust (Ont. Feb. 25, 1997)
July 11, 2001 – Name changed to Atlas Cold Storage Income Trust. ■

ACS Media Income Fund (Ont. Mar. 5, 2003)
Nov. 23, 2006 – Redeemed following sale of the fund's operating business to Pendo Acquisition ULC for $9.40 per unit.

ACSI-BIOREX Inc. (Can. Jan. 1, 1989 amalg.)
Oct. 18, 1993 – Dissolved.

ACSI Group Ltd. (Can. June 28, 1976)
Jan. 1, 1989 – Formed ACSI-BIOREX Inc. in Canada on amalgamation with Biorex Groupe-Conseil Inc. ■

ACT Aurora Control Technologies Corp. (B.C. Oct. 26, 2006)
May 28, 2015 – Name changed to Aurora Solar Technologies Inc. (see FPsurvey - Industrials)

A.C.T. Industrial Corporation (B.C. May 9, 1983)
July 6, 2000 – Name changed to Rhona Online.Com Inc. ■

ACTIVEnergy Income Fund (Alta. Oct. 27, 2004)
June 5, 2017 – Converted into an open-ended mutual fund; basis 1 series F unit for 1 fund unit.

ACT360 Solutions Ltd. (B.C. July 25, 2000)
June 2, 2016 – Name changed to Kona Bay Technologies Inc.; basis 1 new for 10 old shs. ■

AD OPT Technologies Inc. (Can. June 1, 1994)
Nov. 19, 2004 – Acquired indirectly by Kronos Incorporated for $6.25 per sh.

ADAM Technologies, Inc. (Alta. Apr. 2, 1993)
Jan. 11, 2001 – Name changed to Nucontex Corporation and continued into Ontario. ■

ADB Systems International Inc. (Ont. Nov. 28, 1983)
Nov. 5, 2002 – Name changed to ADB Systems International Ltd. pursuant to reorganization whereby shs. of the co. were exchanged for shs. of ADB Systems International Ltd. and ADB Systems International Inc. became a wholly owned subsid. ■

ADB Systems International Ltd. (Ont. Nov. 28, 1983)
July 18, 2006 – Name changed to Northcore Technologies Inc. ■

ADEX Mining Corp. (Ont. Dec. 31, 1992 amalg.)
July 19, 1996 – Name changed to Adex Mining Inc.; basis 1 new for 5 old shs. (see FPsurvey - Mines & Energy)

ADI Technologies, Inc. (B.C. Mar. 31, 1983)
Dec. 5, 2005 – Struck from registry and dissolved.

ADL Ventures Inc. (B.C. Feb. 27, 2018)
June 12, 2020 – Name changed to The Real Brokerage Inc. pursuant to Qualifying Transaction reverse takeover acquisition of Real Technology Broker Ltd. (see FPsurvey - Industrials)

ADR Capital Corp. (B.C. Apr. 20, 2011)
Feb. 13, 2013 – Name changed to Delta Gold Corporation pursuant to Qualifying Transaction reverse takeover acquisition of Delta Gold Inc. ■

ADR Explorations Ltd. (Ont. Aug. 12, 1997)
Aug. 30, 2000 – Formed cs-live.com inc. in Ontario on amalgamation with cs-live.com inc. ■

ADR Global Enterprises Ltd. (B.C. Feb. 4, 2000)
Dec. 12, 2002 – Name changed to Sonic Environmental Solutions Inc. following Qualifying Transaction acquisition of Sonic Energy Systems Inc. ■

ADS associés ltée (Can. June 13, 1978)
July 31, 1996 – Name changed to ADS inc.; basis 2 new for 1 old sh. ■

ADS inc. (Can. June 13, 1978)
Mar. 3, 2009 – Privatized. Shldrs. received 1 4076508 Canada Inc. redeem. pref. sh. for 1 ADS cl. A mutiple vtg. sh., immediately redeemed for 90¢ per sh.

ADSL Holdings Inc. (B.C. June 1, 2015)
Dec. 27, 2024 – Voluntarily delisted from Cboe. First distrib. of $0.053 cash per sh. to shldrs. of record Dec. 19, 2024.
Mar. 28, 2025 – Voluntarily dissolved.

ADT Finance Inc. (Can. Nov. 7, 1990)
June 30, 1995 – All o/s non-vtg. ser.A exch. shs. redeemed; basis 1 ADT Limited com. sh. for 1 ser.A exch. sh.

AEC Pipelines, L.P. (Alta. Dec. 20, 1996)
Sept. 21, 2000 – All o/s cl. A limited partnership units acquired by Alberta Energy Company Ltd.; basis 0.1552 Alberta Energy com. shs. for 1 AEC cl. A unit. (see Alberta Energy Company Ltd.)

AEC Power Ltd. (Alta. 1975)
Oct. 9, 1996 – TransAlta Energy Corporation acquired remaining two-thirds interest from Alberta Energy Company Ltd. for $32.6 million, and an additional $66.7 million to assume and retire existing o/s debt.

AEGIS Energy Ltd. (Alta. May 26, 1997)
July 7, 2000 – Amalgamated with Plexus Energy Ltd. (1 for 2.8225) and Peregrine Oil and Gas Ltd. (1 for 3.6474) to form Surge Petroleum Inc.; basis 1 Surge cl. A com. sh. for 3.3 AEGIS com. shs. (see Surge Petroleum Inc.)

AEX Gold Inc. (Can. Feb. 22, 2017)
July 12, 2022 – Name changed to Amaroq Minerals Ltd. ■

AEX Minerals Corporation (B.C. 1929)
May 4, 1972 – Dissolved.
Nov. 7, 1973 – Revived as AEX Minerals Corporation.
Dec. 5, 1975 – Name changed to Canadian Natural Resources Limited. ■

AF1 Capital Corp. (B.C. Mar. 19, 2018)
Dec. 4, 2020 – Name changed to PureK Holdings Corp. pursuant to Qualifying Transaction acquisition of 50.1% interest in PureKana, LLC; basis 1 new for 40 old shs. ■

AFC Energy Corporation (B.C. Dec. 12, 1977)
May 6, 1988 – Dissolved and struck off register.

AFF Automated Fast Foods Ltd. (B.C. Apr. 18, 1986)
July 31, 1998 – Name changed to Brier Resources Corporation. ■

AFG Flameguard Ltd. (Can. Oct. 12, 2011 amalg.)
Nov. 8, 2015 – Dissolved and struck from register.

AFL Capital Ventures Inc. (Yuk. Sept. 14, 2001)
Jan. 17, 2005 – Continued into Canada.
Jan. 18, 2005 – Name changed to Grey Horse Capital Corporation. ■

AFM Hospitality Corporation (Ont. 1908)
Sept. 18, 2003 – Continued into Canada.
Apr. 29, 2005 – Placed into receivership. Mintz & Partners Limited appointed receiver.

AFS Energy Inc. (Alta. Feb. 27, 1997)
June 1, 2005 – Name changed to Flagship Energy Inc. following reverse takeover acquisition of oil and gas interests in the Medicine Lodge area of Alberta; basis 0.06668831 cl. A shs. and 0.01500487 cl. B shs. for 1 com. sh. ■

AGC Americas Gold Corp. (B.C. May 23, 1986)
Sept. 1999 – Continued into Yukon.
Oct. 7, 1999 – Name changed to Timebeat.com Enterprises Inc. ■

A.G.F. Management Limited (Ont. Feb. 2, 1960)
Dec. 2, 1994 – Name changed to AGF Management Limited. (see FPsurvey - Industrials)

AGF Master Limited Partnership (Ont. Jan. 23, 1998 amalg.)
Nov. 6, 2012 – Dissolved for 2¢ per unit.

AGIP Resources Ltd. (Can. 1988 amalg.)
Sept. 28, 1992 – Name changed to Cameco Resources Ltd. ■

AGM Capital Corp. (B.C. Aug. 21, 1969)
July 13, 1993 – Continued into Yukon.
Sept. 24, 1993 – Name changed to Dueling Grounds Thoroughbred Racing Corporation; basis 1 new for 1 old sh. ■

AGRA Inc. (Can. Jan. 5, 1977)
Apr. 24, 2000 – Acquired by British-based AMEC plc; basis either 3.053 AMEC ord. shs. or Cdn$16 for 1 AGRA sh.

AGRA Industries Limited (Sask. Nov. 7, 1960)
Jan. 5, 1977 – Continued into Canada.
Jan. 9, 1997 – Name changed to AGRA Inc. ■

AGT Data Systems Limited (Can. 1967)
1974 – Over 98% of all o/s shs. acquired by Multiple Access Ltd.; basis 1 Multiple Access sh. for 3.5 AGT shs. (see Multiple Access Limited)

AGT Food and Ingredients Inc. (Ont. July 2, 2009)
Apr. 18, 2019 – Privatized; basis $18 cash per com. sh.

AGX Resources Corp. (B.C. Apr. 10, 1985)
May 22, 1996 – Continued into Yukon.
Nov. 26, 1999 – Name changed to Consolidated AGX Resources Corp.; basis 1 new for 4 old shs. ■

A.H.A. Automotive Technologies Corporation (Ont. Apr. 2, 1984 amalg.)
Jan. 4, 1990 – Ernst & Young Inc. of Toronto appointed receiver.
Mar. 31, 1990 – Inventory liquidated. Nothing left for preferred or unsecured creditors and shldrs.

The AHL Group Ltd. (Ont. 1944)
Aug. 16, 1985 – All o/s X and Y shs. acquired by Ivaco Inc.; basis 24 series E preferred and 30.24 cl. A com. shs. of Ivaco for 100 old shs.

AHT Corporation (Alta. Aug. 10, 1993)
July 12, 2001 – Name changed to SIMSMART Inc. and continued into Canada. ■

AI Centrix Resource Holdings Inc. (B.C. Feb. 19, 2021)
June 19, 2023 – Name changed to Resource Centrix Holdings Inc. (see FPsurvey - Mines & Energy)

AI Centrix Technologies Corp. (B.C. Feb. 19, 2021)
June 23, 2022 – Name changed to AI Centrix Resource Holdings Inc. ■

A.I. Software Inc. (B.C. Sept. 2, 1983)
July 2, 1996 – Name changed to Network Gaming International Corp. ■

AIC Diversified Canada Split Corp. (Alta. Jan. 1, 1999)
June 30, 2009 – All o/s shs. redeemed for $0.745601 per pref. sh. and $0.560658 per capital sh.

AIC Global Financial Split Corp. (Ont. Mar. 25, 2004)
June 1, 2011 – Terminated; basis $10 per pref. sh. and $0.0643 per cl.A sh.

AIC International Resources Corporation (B.C. Sept. 25, 1979)
Feb. 20, 1998 – Delisted from the Vancouver Stock Exchange. Subsequently struck from register and dissolved.

AIL Absorbent Industries Ltd. (B.C. 1986)
Feb. 28, 1992 – Dissolved and struck off register.

A.I.L. Alberta Investments Ltd. (Alta. 1982)
Oct. 15, 1987 – Amalgamated into The Churchill Corporation. Shldrs. received $10.50 per sh. or one cl. A sh. and $1,050 principal amt. of convertible debs. of Churchill.

AIM Health Group Inc. (Ont. July 13, 2005)
Sept. 6, 2011 – Privatized at 25¢ per sh.

AIM Medical Technologies Inc. (Alta. Jan. 24, 1994)
June 12, 1995 – Name changed to PLM Group Ltd.; basis 1 new for 2 old shs. ■

AIM Safety Company Inc. (B.C. June 24, 1983)
Jan. 29, 1999 – Name changed to AimGlobal Technologies Company Inc. ■

AIM1 Ventures Inc. (Ont. Mar. 30, 2017)
June 11, 2018 – Name changed to James E. Wagner Cultivation Corporation following Qualifying Transaction reverse takeover acquisition of James E. Wagner Cultivation Ltd.; basis 1 new for 4.847528 old shs. ■

AIM2 Ventures Inc. (Ont. Oct. 31, 2017)
Sept. 14, 2018 – Name changed to Canopy Rivers Inc. following Qualifying Transaction reverse takeover acquisition of Canopy Rivers Corporation, completed by way of an amalgamation of Canopy Rivers and a wholly owned subsidiary of AIM2.; basis 1 new for 26.565 old shs. ■

AIM3 Ventures Inc. (Ont. Feb. 20, 2018)
May 13, 2020 – Name changed to Vox Royalty Corp. pursuant to Qualifying Transaction reverse takeover acquisition of SilverStream SEZC; basis 1 new for 13.3125 old shs. ■

AIM4 Ventures Inc. (Ont. Nov. 29, 2018)
Dec. 23, 2020 – Name changed to Think Research Corporation pursuant to the Qualifying Transaction reverse takeover acquisition of TRC Management Holdings Corp.; basis 1 new for 24.76125 old shs. ■

AIMS Biotech Corporation (B.C. Nov. 10, 1981)
Mar. 28, 1991 – Dissolved and struck off register. (see The Bullet Group, Inc.)

AISI Research Corp. (B.C. 1986)
Jan. 15, 1993 – Dissolved and struck off register.

AIT Advanced Information Technologies Corporation (Can. Sept. 17, 1973)
July 23, 2002 – Amalgamated with 4081803 Canada Inc. wholly owned subsid. of Minnesota-based 3M Canada Company; basis $2.88 per sh.

AJ Perron Gold Corp. (Ont. Jan. 13, 1989 amalg.)
Mar. 27, 2000 – Struck off register.

AJA Health and Wellness Inc. (B.C. July 16, 2010 amalg.)
Sept. 18, 2024 – Continued into Alberta. (see FPsurvey - Industrials)

AJA Ventures Inc. (B.C. Feb. 11, 2020)
Aug. 29, 2023 – Name changed to Midori Carbon Inc. ■

AKA Ventures Inc. (B.C. Oct. 21, 1980)
Sept. 7, 2012 – Name changed to Phoenix Copper Corporation. ■

ALBA Petroleum Corporation (Ont. 1978)
Jan. 10, 1991 – Acquired by ALBERTA Oil and Gas Limited; basis 1 com. sh. for 2.15 cl. A com. shs. (see Alberta Oil and Gas Limited)

ALBERTA Oil and Gas Limited (Alta. Mar. 25, 1986)
Jan. 1, 1991 – Name changed to Alberta Oil and Gas Limited following amalgamation with 418871 Alberta Ltd. ■

ALDA Pharmaceuticals Corp. (B.C. May 30, 2000)
July 26, 2013 – Name changed to Nuva Pharmaceuticals Inc. ■

A.L.I. Technologies Inc. (B.C. Apr. 11, 1988)
Sept. 12, 2002 – Acquired by wholly owned Canadian subsid. of US-based McKesson Corporation; basis $43.50 per sh.

ALN Resources Corporation (Okla. Oct. 18, 1990 amalg.)
Jan. 4, 1993 – Name changed to American Natural Energy Corporation; basis 1 new for 10 old shs. ■

ALQ Gold Corp. (B.C. Feb. 25, 1985)
Oct. 30, 2018 – Name changed to Green Axis Capital Corp.; basis 1 new for 2 old shs. ■

ALX Resources Corp. (B.C. Oct. 11, 2007)
Jan. 2, 2025 – Acquired by Greenridge Exploration Inc.; basis 0.045 Greenridge shs. for 1 ALX Resources sh.

ALX Uranium Corp. (B.C. Oct. 11, 2007)
Jan. 13, 2020 – Name changed to ALX Resources Corp. ■

AM Gold Inc. (B.C. Aug. 25, 1970)
Aug. 30, 2016 – Privatized via acquisition by holding company 1079170 B.C. Ltd., controlled by CEO & dir. John Fiorino; basis 17¢ cash per sh. ■

AM Technologies Limited (Alta. Mar. 11, 1997)
June 21, 2002 – Name changed to Moncoa Corporation and continued into Canada following reverse takeover acquisition of Moncoa Medical Research Inc.; basis 1 new for 4 old shs. ■

AMCA International Limited (Can. July 30, 1912; via Dominion charter)
June 4, 1990 – Name changed to United Dominion Industries Limited; basis 1 new for 5 old shs. ■

AMD Resources Corporation (B.C. Sept. 23, 1965)
Apr. 24, 1992 – Name changed to Halo Gaming Corporation. ■

AME Limited (Ont. 1960)
Oct. 7, 1993 – Amalgamated with 1040908 Ontario Inc., a wholly owned subsid. of Kassner Investment Corporation Limited, for $2.85 per sh.

AME Resource Capital Corp. (B.C. June 1, 1964)
Sept. 1, 1999 – Succeeded by Western Pacific Trust Company following acquisition of AME Resource Capital (renamed Western Equity Loans Ltd.) by Western Pacific Trust Company; basis 1 new for 4 old shs. (see FPsurvey - Industrials)

AMERI Holdings, Inc. (Del. July 27, 1994)
Dec. 31, 2020 – Name changed to Enveric Biosciences, Inc.; basis 1 new for 4 old shs.

AMG Bioenergy Resources Holdings Ltd. (Alta. Dec. 15, 2006)
June 2, 2018 – Struck from registry.

AMG Oil Ltd. (Nev. Feb. 20, 1997)
Nov. 25, 2008 – Continued into Canada.
Dec. 17, 2009 – Name changed to Adira Energy Ltd. following reverse takeover acquisiton of Adira Energy Corp. ■

AMI Resources Inc. (B.C. Dec. 29, 1980)
Jan. 19, 2017 – Name changed to Ashanti Sankofa Inc. (see FPsurvey - Mines & Energy)

AMJ Campbell Inc. (Ont. Sept. 11, 1992)
Mar. 17, 2003 – Acquired by AMJ Management Acquisition Inc. wholly owned subsid. of 2015825 Ontario Inc.; basis $2.30 per sh.

AML International Inc. (Ont. May 14, 1981)
Jan. 3, 1995 – Delisted CDN. Subsequently struck from register and dissolved.

AMN Capital Corp. (B.C. Dec. 20, 2010)
Dec. 23, 2011 – Name changed to Altan Rio Minerals Limited pursuant to Qualifying Transaction reverse takeover acquisition of Altan Rio Minerals Limited; basis 1 new for 1.66665 old shs. ■

AMP Alternative Medical Products Inc. (B.C. Apr. 16, 2014)
Nov. 8, 2021 – Name changed to Greenrise Global Brands Inc. (see FPsurvey - Industrials)

A.M.P. Explorations & Mining Co. Ltd. (B.C. May 14, 1969)
May 27, 1991 – Name changed to Silverstone Resources Ltd.; basis 1 new for 3 old shs. ■

AMP German Cannabis Group Inc. (B.C. Apr. 16, 2014)
Jan. 29, 2021 – Name changed to AMP Alternative Medical Products Inc. ■

A.M.R. Corporate Group Ltd. (B.C. Feb. 22, 1984)
Dec. 3, 1998 – Name changed to Consolidated A.M.R. Corporate Ltd.; basis 1 new for 4 old shs. ■

AMR Technologies Inc. (Can. Aug. 8, 1994)
Apr. 28, 2006 – Name changed to Neo Material Technologies Inc. ■

AMS Homecare Inc. (B.C. Mar. 5, 1981)
Dec. 5, 2011 – Dissolved and struck from the register.

AMT Environmental Products Inc. (B.C. Dec. 4, 1986)
Feb. 26, 1997 – Continued into Nevada.
Feb. 27, 1997 – Name changed to Polymer Solutions, Inc.; basis 1 new for 3 old shs. ■

AMT Fine Foods Ltd. (Ont. Jan. 26, 1983)
Jan. 28, 2003 – Name changed to The Skor Food Group Inc. pursuant to reverse takeover acquisition of Derry Foods Limited; basis 1 new for 10 old shs. ■

AMT International Mining Corporation (Ont. Sept. 6, 1994)
Oct. 25, 2013 – Filed for bankruptcy. Richter Advisory Group Inc. appointed trustee.
May 5, 2015 – Final distrib. made the creditors. No distrib. made to shldrs.
Apr. 2017 – Trustee, Richter Advisory Group Inc., was discharged.

AMV Capital Corporation (B.C. Jan. 31, 2019)
Dec. 29, 2022 – Name changed to Abasca Resources Inc. pursuant to the reverse takeover acquisition of the Key Lake South uranium project in the southeastern Athabasca Basin area of northern Saskatchewan. (see FPsurvey - Mines & Energy)

AMVESCAP Inc. (N.S. June 1, 1997)
May 29, 2007 – Name changed to INVESCO Inc. ■

ANC Capital Ventures Inc. (B.C. Mar. 11, 2019)
July 6, 2022 – Name changed to VIP Entertainment Technologies Inc. pursuant to the Qualifying Transaction reverse takeover acquisition of VIP Entertainment Group Inc. (see FPsurvey - Industrials)

ANGOSS Software Corporation (Ont. Sept. 17, 1986 amalg.)
Apr. 30, 2013 – Acquired by Peterson Partners, Inc. for $0.525 per sh.

ANZ Bank Canada (Can. 1982)
Apr. 30, 1993 – Amalgamated with Hongkong Bank of Canada. (see Hongkong Bank of Canada)

APAC Minerals Inc. (B.C. Sept. 9, 1996)
Mar. 17, 2005 – Name changed to Golden China Resources Corporation and continued into Canada following reverse takeover acquisition of and amalgamation with Golden China Inc. by wholly owned 6334938 Canada Inc. ■

APAC Resources Inc. (B.C. May 31, 2011)
Jan. 11, 2018 – Name changed to XORTX Therapeutics Inc. following reverse takeover acquisition of XORTX Pharma Corp. (see FPsurvey - Industrials)

APAC Telecommunications Corporation (B.C. June 13, 1972)
Nov. 14, 2003 – Dissolved and struck from register.

APC Ventures, Inc. (Wash. July 23, 1987)
Feb. 29, 1996 – Name changed to Yukon Gold Corporation. ■

APEX Land Corporation (Alta. Dec. 7, 1988)
Nov. 3, 1999 – Name changed to The Apex Corporation. ■

APF Energy Trust (Alta. Oct. 10, 1996)
June 28, 2005 – Business combination with StarPoint Energy Trust to continue with the name StarPoint Energy Trust; basis 0.63 new StarPoint unit for 1 old APF unit. Also the old 9.4% APF conv. debs. were exchanged for new 9.4% StarPoint conv. debs. with a revised conversion rate of 59.95 new StarPoint units for $1,000 principal amt. from 88.8889 old APF units. (see StarPoint Energy Trust)

API Electronics Group Corp. (Ont. May 14, 1985)
Nov. 7, 2006 – Acquired by Delaware-based Rubincon Ventures, Inc. (renamed API Nanotronics Corp.); basis 1 API Nanotronics sh. for 10 API Electronics shs.

API Electronics Group Inc. (Ont. May 14, 1985)
Sept. 15, 2004 – Name changed to API Electronics Group Corp.; basis 1 new for 10 old shs. ■

APIC Petroleum Corporation (Del. July 21, 1998 amalg.)
Dec. 24, 2012 – Acquired by Longreach Oil and Gas Limited; basis 1 Longreach for 5.3846 APIC shs. (see Longreach Oil and Gas Limited)

APP Applied Polymer Products Inc. (Can. Feb. 23, 1987)
July 31, 1989 – Receiver Coopers & Lybrand of Edmonton, Alta., appointed.
Apr. 1990 – Certain assets sold to Agra Industries Limited.
May 1992 – No longer a going concern and remaining assets liquidated; there was no distribution to shldrs.
Oct. 31, 1996 – Dissolved.

APPx Crypto Technologies Inc. (B.C. Oct. 30, 2014)
Oct. 24, 2018 – Name changed to APPx Group Holdings Inc. ■

APPx Group Holdings Inc. (B.C. Oct. 30, 2014)
Mar. 6, 2019 – Name changed to Softlab9 Software Solutions Inc.; basis 1 new for 1.5 old shs. ■

APS Services Inc. (Alta. Aug. 9, 1993)
Feb. 2, 2002 – Struck from registry and dissolved.

AQM Copper Inc. (B.C. Mar. 23, 2005)
Jan. 17, 2017 – Acquired by Teck Resources Limited; basis 23¢ cash per sh.

ARC Energy Trust (Alta. May 7, 1996)
Dec. 31, 2010 – Succeeded by ARC Resources Ltd. pursuant to plan of arrangement whereby ARC Resources Ltd. was formed to facilitate the conversion of the trust into a corporation and the trust was subsequently dissolved. (see FPsurvey - Mines & Energy)

ARC International Corporation (Ont. Apr. 30, 1976)
Apr. 2000 – Three of the company's indirectly wholly owned subsidiaries received demands for repayment from their lenders of amounts owing under credit facilities.
May 2000 – Deloitte & Touche Inc. was appointed receiver of IcePro Canada Inc. (indirect wholly owned subsidiary) by HSBC Bank Canada. IcePro International Inc. and C.W. Davis Supply, Inc. (indirect wholly owned subsidiaries) were also in default on their credit facilities with HSBC Bank USA which were guaranteed by the company. Subsequently all the assets of IcePro International and its subsidiaries were liquidated by HSBC Bank USA leaving a balance owing of US$740,000. HSBC Bank USA then instituted an action against the company for recovery of the amount owing.
Oct. 2000 – Toronto-based RSM Richter (formerly Richter & Partners Inc.) was appointed receiver and manager of the assets, property and undertakings of ARC Sports.
Dec. 7, 2000 – ARC Sports made an assignment into bankruptcy.
Jan. 18, 2001 – Buckingham Sports Properties Company acquired from the receiver three of the company's ice rinks in the Toronto area (Chesswood, the Westwood and the ARC Skating Academy) for US$12,500,000 in cash. Subsequently the remaining assets and subsidiaries were sold.
Jan. 2004 – Receiver discharged. There were no funds available for distribution to shldrs.

A.R.C. Resins International Corp. (B.C. Oct. 22, 1984)
Dec. 28, 2000 – Acquired by indirect wholly owned subsid. of Tembec Inc. for $0.40 per sh. (see Tembec Inc.)

ARC Resources Ltd. (Alta. Jan. 22, 1996)
Jan. 6, 2011 – All exch. shs. redeemed for parent ARC Resources Ltd. (formerly ARC Energy Trust) com. shs following conversion of ARC Energy Trust into a corporation; basis 1 new ARC Resources com. sh. for 1 old ARC Resources 2.89162 exch. shs.

ARC STRATEGIC Energy Fund (Alta. Apr. 9, 1998)
Oct. 26, 2001 – All assets acquired by fund manager ARC Energy Management Ltd. plus original termination date moved forward from May 2008; initial distribution of $2.80 per unit, final distribution to be made at year-end.

ARCA Explorations Inc. (Can. Dec. 20, 1996)
Aug. 26, 2004 – Name changed to Pro-Spect-Or Resources Inc.; basis 1 new for 8 old shs. ■

AREV Brands International Ltd. (B.C. June 30, 2016)
Mar. 19, 2020 – Name changed to AREV NanoTech Brands Inc.; basis 1 new for 6 old shs. ■

AREV NanoTech Brands Inc. (B.C. June 30, 2016)
Aug. 11, 2021 – Name changed to AREV Life Sciences Global Corp. (see FPsurvey - Industrials)

AREV Nutrition Sciences Inc. (B.C. June 30, 2016)
Sept. 12, 2018 – Name changed to AREV Brands International Ltd. ■

AREVA Resources Canada Inc. (Can. Mar. 6, 1973)
Feb. 16, 2018 – Name changed to Orano Canada Inc.

ARHT Media Inc. (Ont. Oct. 2, 1987)
Oct. 4, 2024 – Filed for bankruptcy under the Bankruptcy and Insolvency Act (BIA) and MNP Ltd. was appointed trustee. All officers and directors resigned.

ARI Automated Recycling Inc. (B.C. July 25, 1984)
Nov. 1, 1994 – Name changed to Envipco Automated Recycling Inc.; basis 1 new for 5 old shs. ■

ARISE Technologies Corporation (Can. June 30, 2003 amalg.)
Mar. 2, 2012 – Substantially all assets acquired by Salamon Group Inc. pursuant to Bankruptcy and Insolvency Act proposal.
Apr. 11, 2012 – Assigned into bankruptcy. PricewaterhouseCoopers Inc. appointed trustee. No funds available for shldrs.

ART Advanced Research Technologies Inc. (Can. July 13, 1993)
Dec. 14, 2008 – Acquired by Dorsky Worldwide Corp. pursuant to a court-approved restructuring under the Bankruptcy and Insolvency Act (Canada). Secured and unsecured creditors received payment but there were no distributions to shldrs. as all o/s common and preferred shares were cancelled.

ASB Capital Inc. (B.C. July 18, 2011)
June 12, 2019 – Name changed to Else Nutrition Holdings Inc. pursuant to Qualifying Transaction reverse takeover acquisition of Else Nutrition GH Ltd.; basis 1 new for 5 old shs. (see FPsurvey - Industrials)

ASC Avcan Systems Corporation (B.C. Jan. 1, 1983 amalg.)
Sept. 7, 2001 – Name changed to Avcan Systems Inc.; basis 1 new for 10 old shs. ■

ASC Industries Ltd. (B.C. Aug. 25, 1970)
Nov. 24, 2004 – Name changed to Acero-Martin Exploration Inc. ■

ASI Internet Inc. (Ont. Dec. 12, 1995)
Dec. 14, 1999 – Formed Hip Interactive Corp. in Ontario on amalgamation with Hip Interactive Corp.; basis 1 new for 1.7075 old shs. ■

ASP123.com Systems Inc. (B.C. May 17, 1985)
Aug. 28, 2006 – Dissolved and struck from register.

ASTAware Technologies Inc. (Ont. Feb. 22, 1988)
Jan. 8, 2007 – Dissolved and struck from register.

AT Plastics Inc. (Ont. Mar. 14, 1989)
Aug. 7, 2003 – Amalgamated with Acetex Corporation; basis 1 Acetex sh. for 6 AT Plastics shs. (see Acetex Corporation)

AT&T Canada Inc. (Can. July 14, 1997)
June 26, 2003 – Name changed to Allstream Inc.; basis 1 new cl. A for 1 old cl. A sh. and 1 new cl. B for 1 old cl. B sh. ■

ATAC Resources Ltd. (B.C. Oct. 15, 1998)
July 11, 2023 – Acquired by Hecla Mining Company; basis (i) 0.0166 Hecla com. shs. plus (ii) 0.100 Cascadia Mineral Ltd. shs. for 1 ATAC Resources sh.

ATC Environmental Group Inc. (Alta. Dec. 31, 1993 amalg.)
Oct. 9, 2001 – Name changed to ATC Petroleum Services International Inc. ■

ATC Petroleum Services International Inc. (Alta. Dec. 31, 2001 amalg.)
Feb. 3, 2004 – Name changed to Tiger Pacific Mining Corp.; basis 1 new for 9 old shs. ■

ATC Technologies Corporation (B.C. Dec. 23, 1996)
July 11, 2005 – Dissolved and struck from register.

ATCO Industries Ltd. (Alta. Aug. 31, 1962)
Sept. 13, 1978 – Name changed to ATCO Ltd. (see FPsurvey - Mines & Energy; FPsurvey - Industrials)

ATCOR Resources Ltd. (Can. Nov. 23, 1990 amalg.)
Feb. 7, 1996 – All o/s cl. A non vtg. shs. and all cl. B com. shs. acquired by Forest Oil Corporation; basis $4.88 per sh.

A.T.H. Fund Inc. (B.C. June 22, 1973)
Nov. 12, 1993 – Dissolved and struck off register.

ATI Corporation (Ont. Feb. 16, 1962)
June 30, 1999 – Name changed to Prairie Capital Inc. ■

ATI Technologies Inc. (Ont. Aug. 20, 1985)
Oct. 25, 2006 – Plan of Arrangement acquisition by Advanced Micro Devices, Inc.; basis either US$16.40 and calculated incremental amount, or a share consideration for 1 old ATI sh.

ATS Andlauer Income Fund (Ont. Aug. 22, 2005)
Dec. 12, 2008 – Acquired by 2186940 Ontario Inc., a wholly owned subsid. of Andlauer Management Group Inc., for $10.75 per trust unit.

ATS Automation Tooling Systems Inc. (Ont. July 31, 1992 amalg.)
Name changed to ATS Corporation. (see FPsurvey - Industrials)

ATS Wheel Inc. (B.C. May 13, 1985)
July 20, 1998 – Name changed to JSS Resources Inc. ■

ATTN Aveca Entertainment Corporation (Can. Nov. 27, 1986 amalg.)
June 10, 1993 – Name changed to American Transportation Television Network, Inc.; basis 1 new for 3 old shs. ■

ATW Gold Corp. (B.C. Mar. 7, 2005)
Jan. 14, 2011 – Name changed to Redhill Resources Corp. ■

ATW Tech Inc. (Can. Nov. 5, 2007)
July 4, 2024 – Voluntarily filed for bankruptcy and Bresse Syndics Inc. appointed trustee. All officers and directors resigned.

ATW Venture Corp. (B.C. Mar. 7, 2005)
Oct. 21, 2008 – Name changed to ATW Gold Corp. ■

A2Z Technologies Canada Corp. (B.C. Jan. 15, 2018)
July 27, 2020 – Name changed to A2Z Smart Technologies Corp. ■

AUX Resources Corporation (B.C. Jan. 15, 1980)
July 20, 2021 – Amalgamated with 1302668 B.C. Ltd, a wholly owned subsid. of Scottie Resources Corp., to form AUX Resources Limited; basis 1 Scottie sh. for 1 AUX Resources sh.

A. V. Roe Canada Limited (Can. Sept. 1, 1945; via letters patent)
May 1, 1962 – Name changed to Hawker Siddeley Canada Ltd. ■

AVC Venture Capital Corp. (B.C. Apr. 14, 1999)
Aug. 21, 2006 – Dissolved.
Dec. 11, 2007 – Reinstated under provisions of the BCBCA.
June 15, 2012 – Name changed to Lateral Gold Corp. pursuant to Qualifying Transaction acquisition of Chilko property from Alto Ventures Ltd. ■

AVI Software Inc. (Can. 1986)
June 18, 2002 – Acquired by COGNICASE Inc.; basis either $0.675 plus 0.0668316 new COGNICASE com. sh., or 0.1336633 new COGNICASE com. sh. (see COGNICASE Inc.)

AVL Information Systems Inc. (Ont. 1927)
Aug. 12, 1996 – Name changed to AVL Information Systems Ltd.; basis 1 new for 5 old shs. ■

AVL Information Systems Ltd. (Ont. 1927)
Apr. 4, 2003 – Name changed to AVL Ventures Inc.; basis 1 new for 10 old shs. ■

AVL Ventures Inc. (Ont. 1927)
Feb. 24, 2014 – Dissolved and struck from register.

AVVA Technologies, Inc. (Alta. Nov. 16, 1993)
Oct. 1, 2003 – Amalgamated with Carmanah Technologies Corporation and 1057614 Alberta Ltd. (wholly owned by Carmanah); basis 1 Carmanah sh. for 8 AVVA shs. (see Carmanah Technologies Corporation)

A. W. White Mica Ltd. (Ont. 1942)
Mar. 14, 1978 – Charter cancelled.

AWG American-WestJava Gold Corp. (Ont. July 13, 1936)
Jan. 4, 1995 – Continued into British Columbia.
Sept. 28, 1995 – Name changed to AWG American-WestJava Inc.; basis 1 new for 10 old shs. ■

AWG American-WestJava Inc. (B.C. Jan. 4, 1995)
Oct. 11, 1995 – Continued into Ontario.
May 3, 1996 – Name changed to Kalimantan Gold Corporation following amalgamation of wholly owned 1170295 Ontario Limited with Kalimantan Minerals Ltd.; basis 1 new for 3 old shs. ■

AX1 Capital Corp. (B.C. Oct. 10, 2017)
Mar. 26, 2019 – Name changed to Luxxfolio Holdings Inc. pursuant to the reverse takeover acquisition of Luxxfolio Network Inc. (see FPsurvey - Industrials)

AXE Exploration Inc. (Can. Oct. 17, 2007)
Nov. 23, 2018 – Name changed to Terranueva Corporation pursuant to reverse takeover acquisition of Terranueva Pharma Corporation; basis 1 new for 16 old shs. (see FPsurvey - Industrials)

AXEA Capital Corp. (B.C. Jan. 4, 2008)
Oct. 22, 2012 – Name changed to MCW Enterprises Ltd. pursuant to Qualifying Transaction amalgamation of MCW Energy Group Limited (deemed acquiror) with wholly owned 665615 N.B. Ltd.; basis 1 new for 6 old shs. ■

AXEA Energy Inc. (B.C. Apr. 5, 2007)
Apr. 15, 2009 – Name changed to AgriMarine Holdings Inc. on Qualifying Transaction reverse takeover acquisition of AgriMarine Industries Inc. and amalgamation of AgriMarine Industries Inc. with wholly owned subsid. AXEA Holdings Ltd. ■

AXQP Inc. (Alta. May 26, 1987)
Oct. 7, 2009 – Name changed to Canamex Silver Corp. and continued into British Columbia. ■

AXR Resources Ltd. (Ont. July 4, 1988 amalg.)
Jan. 3, 1989 – Amalgamated with Mary Ellen Resources Ltd. (1 for 6) and Lenora Exploration Ltd. (1 for 4) to form a new co. named Greater Lenora Resources Corp.; basis 1 new for 5 old shs. (see Greater Lenora Resources Corp.)

AXS Blockchain Solutions Inc. (B.C. June 11, 2010)
Aug. 20, 2018 – Name changed to LiteLink Technologies Inc. ■

AXXENT Inc. (Ont. Feb. 2, 1999)
Apr. 23, 2001 – General Electric Capital Canada Inc. (GECC), the company's main lender, applied to the Ontario Superior Court of Justice for an order placing the company under the Bankruptcy and Insolvency Act and Toronto-based PricewaterhouseCoopers Inc. was appointed interim receiver. All officers and directors of the company and wholly owned AXXENT Corp. resigned.
July 2001 – TELUS Corporation acquired the majority of the company's Quebec-based assets from the interim receiver for an undisclosed amount.
Nov. 23, 2001 – Interim receiver had collected approximately $19,000,000 of accounts receivable and asset sales had resulted in net realizations of approximately $23,500,000. A distribution of $17,000,000 was paid to GECC.
Nov. 22, 2004 – Receiver discharged. There were no funds available for distribution to unsecured creditors or shldrs.

AZ Mining Inc. (B.C. Aug. 20, 1998)
Oct. 28, 2015 – Name changed to Arizona Mining Inc. ■

AZCAR Technologies Incorporated (Ont. Feb. 13, 1975)
Mar. 23, 2011 – All directors resigned. Patrick W. Carothers appointed chief liquidation officer.

Aabaab Uranium Mines Ltd. (B.C. 1969)
Jan. 1975 – Charter cancelled.

Aabbax International Financial Corp. (B.C. Aug. 6, 1985)
Nov. 17, 1995 – Delisted from the Vancouver Stock Exchange. Subsequently struck from register and dissolved.

Aabco Oil & Gas Inc. (B.C. Dec. 3, 1980)
Sept. 2, 1987 – Name changed to Aabco Ventures Inc. ■

Aabco Ventures Inc. (B.C. Dec. 3, 1980)
May 8, 1998 – Dissolved and struck off register.

Aabro Mining & Oils Ltd. (Alta. 1954)
Aug. 1975 – Charter cancelled.

Aalenian Resources Ltd. (B.C. June 25, 1963)
July 21, 1977 – Name changed to Silverado Mines Ltd.; basis 1 new for 3 old shs. ■

Aard-Ri International Inc. (Alta. Nov. 2, 1987)
July 18, 1991 – Name changed to 7 Crowns Corporation. ■

Aardmore Holdings Inc. (Alta. Aug. 9, 1982)
July 30, 1984 – Name changed to Enercan Group Inc. and continued into Ontario following reverse takeover acquisition of Enercan Inc. (see FPsurvey - Industrials)

Aardvark Capital Corp. (Ont. Jan. 29, 2021)
Apr. 14, 2022 – Name changed to Paycore Minerals Inc. pursuant to the Qualifying Transaction reverse takeover acquisition of 2766604 Ontario Ltd.; basis 1 new for 5 old shs. ■

Aardvark 2 Capital Corp. (Ont. Dec. 10, 2021)
Dec. 12, 2024 – Name changed to Nuvau Minerals Inc. pursuant to the Qualifying Transaction reverse takeover acquisition of Nuvau Minerals Inc.; basis 1 new for 7.2 old shs. (see FPsurvey - Mines & Energy)

Aardvark Ventures Inc. (B.C. July 19, 2001)
June 21, 2023 – Name changed to Mabel Ventures Inc. pursuant to the reverse takeover acquisition of private 1355638 B.C. Ltd. and concurrent amalgamation of 1355638 B.C. with wholly owned 1359787 B.C. Ltd. (and continued as Mabel Holdings Inc.). (see FPsurvey - Mines & Energy)

Aarn Exploration & Development Co. Ltd. (B.C. 1969)
Sept. 14, 1971 – Name changed to Century Interplex Corp. ■

Aaron Mines Ltd. (B.C. 1969)
Oct. 2, 1992 – Dissolved and struck off register.

Aaron Mining Ltd. (B.C. 1969)
Aug. 8, 1987 – Name changed to Aaron Mines Ltd. ■

Aaron Oil Corporation (Alta. Mar. 4, 1987)
July 11, 1995 – Name changed to Altmark Energy Inc.; basis 1 new for 1 old sh. ■

Aastra Technologies Inc. (Can. Apr. 6, 1995)
May 26, 1997 – Name changed to Aastra Technologies Limited; basis 1 new for 6 old shs. ■

Aastra Technologies Limited (Can. Apr. 6, 1995)
Feb. 5, 2014 – Acquired by Mitel Networks Corporation; basis 3.6 Mitel shs. and US$6.52 cash for 1 old Aastra sh.

Aatra Resources Ltd. (B.C. 1984)
Aug. 25, 1995 – Dissolved and struck off register.

Aavdex Corporation (Ont. June 17, 1983)
Nov. 16, 2005 – Name changed to Richmond Minerals Inc. (see FPsurvey - Mines & Energy)

Abac Resources Ltd. (B.C. Mar. 14, 1986)
Dec. 29, 1992 – Name changed to Quality Learning Systems (International) Inc.; basis 1 new for 5 old shs. ■

Abaca Mining Ltd. (B.C. 1967)
Jan. 15, 1974 – Name changed to Abaca Resource Industries Inc. ■

Abaca Resource Industries Inc. (B.C. 1967)
Aug. 1978 – Name changed to Corpac Minerals Ltd.; basis 1 new for 4 old shs. (see FPsurvey - Mines & Energy)

Abaca Resources Ltd. (B.C. 1983)
Jan. 20, 1984 – Name changed to Reba Resources Ltd. (see FPsurvey - Mines & Energy)

Abacan Resource Corporation (B.C. Dec. 31, 1982)
Aug. 31, 1984 – Continued into Alberta.
Mar. 3, 2000 – Declared bankruptcy. KPMG Inc. appointed trustee.

Abacan Resource Corporation (Alta. Aug. 31, 1984)
Feb. 10, 1995 – Amalgamated with Canadian Angus Resources Ltd. (0.30 for 1), Canadian Industrial Minerals Corp. (0.51 for 1), Canstar Ventures Corp. (0.45 for 1) and Profile Capital Corporation (0.23 for 1) to form a new co. also named Abacan Resource Corporation; basis 1 new for 1 old sh. (see Abacan Resource Corporation)

Abaco Gold Mines Ltd. (Man. June 1937)
1953 – Charter cancelled.

Abacon Developments Ltd. (Ont. 1945)
1967 – Charter cancelled.

Abacus Accounting Systems Inc. (Alta. Dec. 6, 1991)
Aug. 27, 1996 – Name changed to Abacus Software Group Inc. ■

Abacus Cities Ltd. (Alta. 1970)
May 11, 1979 – Placed into receivership. KPMG Inc. of Toronto, Ont. was appointed trustee.
Apr. 1, 1981 – Declared bankrupt on Apr. 1, 1981.
June 25, 1996 – Receiver discharged.
1999 – Two dividends totaling 48¢ were paid to unsecured creditors. A final dividend was paid in 1999.
June 1, 2000 – Trustee discharged. No distributions made to shldrs.

Abacus Health Products, Inc. (Ont. Oct. 30, 1996 amalg.)
June 12, 2020 – Acquired by Charlotte's Web Holdings, Inc.; basis 0.85 Charlotte's Web com. shs. for 1 Abacus Health sub. vtg. sh.
Aug. 24, 2020 – Name changed to Abacus Products, Inc. and continued into British Columbia.

Abacus Minerals Corporation (B.C. Oct. 17, 1983)
Apr. 23, 2001 – Name changed to Abacus Mining & Exploration Corporation; basis 1 new for 10 old shs. (see FPsurvey - Mines & Energy)

Abacus Mines & Realty Ltd. (Ont. 1945)
Mar. 21, 1963 – Name changed to Abacon Developments Ltd.; basis 1 new for 10 old shs. ■

Abacus Mines Ltd. (Ont. 1945)
1962 – Name changed to Abacus Mines & Realty Ltd. ■

Abacus Software Group Inc. (Alta. Dec. 6, 1991)
Aug. 1998 – PricewaterhouseCoopers Inc. was appointed receiver and manager. Funds from the sale of the Abacus II technology were used to repay debt owed by the company to CTQC Alberta Fund No. 1 Inc. There were no funds available for distribution to creditors or shldrs.
May 1, 2002 – Receiver discharged.

Abaddon Resources Inc. (B.C. Sept. 30, 1982 amalg.)
Dec. 28, 2000 – Name changed to Consolidated Abaddon Resources Inc.; basis 1 new for 10 old shs. ■

Abadex Mines Ltd. (Que. 1952)
June 1974 – Charter cancelled.

Abagold Resources Inc. (Ont. 1980)
Feb. 29, 1988 – Merged into Anchor Machine and Manufacturing Ltd.

Abalard Gold Mines Ltd. (Ont. 1946)
Nov. 1977 – Charter cancelled.

Abalone Resources Inc. (B.C. 1986)
Aug. 5, 1988 – Name changed to AAO Aquaculture International Corp. ■

Abangarez Mines Ltd. (Ont. 1945)
Charter cancelled.

Abaska Mining Co. Ltd. (Ont. 1955)
Aug. 1957 – Acquired by Continental Consolidated Mines & Oils Corp. Ltd.; basis 1 new for 10 old shs. (see Continental Consolidated Mines & Oils Corp. Ltd.)
1957 – Continued into Saskatchewan. (see Continental Consolidated Mines & Oils Corp. Ltd.)

Abaska Uranium Mines Ltd. (Ont. 1955)
Jan. 1956 – Name changed to Abaska Mining Co. Ltd. ■

Abaterra Energy Ltd. (B.C. July 2, 1981)
Mar. 9, 1989 – Name changed to Simba Oils Ltd. and continued into Alberta; basis unknown. ■

Abaton Resources Ltd. (B.C. 1980)
Apr. 30, 1987 – Amalgamated with International Gravis Computer Technology Inc. (1 for 3) to form Advanced Gravis Computer Technology Ltd.; basis 1 new for 1 old sh. (see Advanced Gravis Computer Technology Ltd.)

Abattis Biologix Corporation (B.C. June 30, 1997)
Sept. 11, 2012 – Name changed to Abattis Bioceuticals Corp.; basis 1 new for 5 old shs. (see FPsurvey - Industrials)

Abba Medix Group Inc. (Can. Mar. 31, 1995)
Nov. 7, 2016 – Name changed to Canada House Wellness Group Inc. following reverse takeover acquisition of 672800 N.B. Inc. (dba Marijuana for Trauma Inc.) [deemed acquiror] and acquisition of The Longevity Project Corp.; basis 1 new for 1.5 old shs. ■

Abbastar Holdings Ltd. (B.C. Apr. 13, 1992)
May 31, 2007 – Name changed to Abbastar Uranium Corp. ■

Abbastar Resources Corp. (B.C. Apr. 13, 1992)
July 26, 2013 – Name changed to Glenmark Capital Corp.; basis 4 new for 1 old sh. ■

Abbastar Uranium Corp. (B.C. Apr. 13, 1992)
July 28, 2009 – Name changed to Abbastar Resources Corp. ■

Abbeville Gold Mines Ltd. (Que. 1937)
1943 – Acquired by Toburn Gold Mines Ltd. No equity for Abbeville shldrs.

Abbey Exploration Inc. (Can. Dec. 13, 1985)
May 6, 2004 – Dissolved.

Abbey Glen Property Corporation (Ont. 1974 amalg.)
Mar. 1, 1977 – All o/s com. shs. acquired by Genstar Ltd. Control of co. acquired through purch. of 62.5% of com. stk. in July 1976, at $6.75 per sh.; subsequently reclassified as cl. A special shs., and all those not held by Genstar were redeemed at $6.75 per sh. or converted to Genstar ser. D pref.; basis 3 shs. Genstar for 10 shs. of Abbey Glen.

Abbey Life Insurance Company of Canada (Ont. 1963)
July 1, 1994 – Name changed to ITT Hartford Life Insurance Company of Canada. ■

Abbey Woods Developments Ltd. (B.C. May 17, 1985)
Aug. 17, 2000 – Acquired by AWD Acquisition Ltd., a wholly owned subsid. of Westbank Holdings Ltd., for 67¢ per sh.

Abbican Mines Ltd. (Ont. 1944)
Sept. 28, 1964 – Dissolved.

Abbot Energy Corporation (B.C. Apr. 27, 1981)
Aug. 21, 1989 – Continued into Delaware.
Sept. 3, 1992 – Name changed to Dale Energy Corporation.

Abby Energy Corporation (B.C. Apr. 16, 1980)
Jan. 12, 1984 – Name changed to Abby Investment Corporation. ■

Abby Investment Corporation (B.C. Apr. 16, 1980)
Apr. 6, 1988 – Name changed to Eagle Industries Ltd.; basis 1 new for 5 old shs. ■

Abcana Capital Inc. (B.C. Apr. 19, 2010)
Dec. 7, 2017 – Name changed to Casa Minerals Inc. pursuant to Qualifying Transaction reverse takeover acquisition of (old) Casa Minerals Inc. (see FPsurvey - Mines & Energy)

Abco Mining Ltd. (B.C. 1968)
Feb. 22, 1971 – Name changed to Aselo Industries Ltd. ■

Abconore Uranium Mines Ltd. (Ont. 1955)
1960 – Charter cancelled.

Abcourt Metals Inc. (Que. Jan. 11, 1971 amalg.)
Jan. 1980 – Name changed to Les Mines d'Argent Abcourt Inc. ■

Abel-Black Corporation Limited (Ont. 1969)
June 29, 1971 – Name changed to Black Photo Corporation Limited. ■

Abella Resources Ltd. (B.C. 1970)
Feb. 14, 1986 – Struck off register.

Aben Minerals Ltd. (B.C. Sept. 30, 1982 amalg.)
May 5, 2025 – Name changed to Aben Gold Corp. (see FPsurvey - Mines & Energy)

Aben Resources Ltd. (B.C. Sept. 30, 1982 amalg.)
Feb. 21, 2023 – Name changed to Aben Minerals Ltd.; basis 1 new for 10 old shs. ■

Abenakis Mines Ltd. (Ont. 1944)
May 1958 – Charter cancelled.

Abenteuer Resources Corp. (Alta. Nov. 20, 2000)
Dec. 31, 2010 – Continued into British Columbia.
Apr. 27, 2017 – Name changed to Volt Energy Corp. ■

Aber Diamond Corporation (B.C. Apr. 19, 1994 amalg.)
July 12, 2002 – Continued into Canada.
Nov. 19, 2007 – Name changed to Harry Winston Diamond Corporation. ■

Aber Resources Ltd. (B.C. 1980)
Apr. 25, 1994 – Amalgamated with Commonwealth Gold Corporation to form new co. with same name Aber Resources Ltd.; basis 1 new for 3 Commonwealth shs. and 1 new for 1 Aber sh. (see Aber Resources Ltd.)

Aber Resources Ltd. (B.C. Apr. 19, 1994 amalg.)
Aug. 18, 2000 – Name changed to Aber Diamond Corporation. ■

Aberdeen Asia-Pacific Income Investment Company Limited (Singapore Apr. 15, 1986)
Dec. 17, 2021 – Name changed to abrdn Asia-Pacific Income Fund VCC. (see FPsurvey - Industrials)

Aberdeen G7 Trust (Ont. Jan. 24, 2002)
Dec. 31, 2008 – Disolved and fund units redeemed for undisclosed amount.

Aberdeen International Inc. (Yuk. Sept. 8, 2000)
July 4, 2006 – Continued into Ontario. (see FPsurvey - Mines & Energy; FPsurvey - Industrials)

Aberdeen Minerals Limited (B.C. May 19, 1965)
Oct. 9, 1987 – Dissolved and struck off register.

Aberdeen Minerals Ltd. (Alta. 1966)
Mar. 6, 1970 – Name changed to Pistol Bay Mining Company Ltd. ■

Aberdeen SCOTS Trust (Ont. June 18, 2001)
June 1, 2009 – Liquidated for $23.58 per unit.

Aberdoon Mines Ltd. (Ont. 1955)
Apr. 1975 – Charter cancelled.

Aberford Resources Ltd. (Alta. 1981)
1982 – Amalgamated in Canada to continue with same name. (see Encor Energy Corporation Inc.)
Mar. 17, 1987 – Acquired by Encor Energy Corporation Inc. through a sh. exchange and subsequent amalgamation. Holders of Aberford com. shs. received 0.725 Encor com. shs. and 0.3 Abermin Corporation com. shs. for each Aberford com. sh. Encor also issued $30,469,920 of 6.5% jr. pref. shs. ser. M and 3,087,084 Encor 1988 Abermin warrants in exchange for $40,092,000 of Aberford 9% conv. subord. debs. The $9,908,000 of Aberford 9% conv. subord. debs. not exchanged became Encor 9% conv. subord. debs. Encor also took over $122,400,000 in bank obligations of Aberford. (see Encor Energy Corporation Inc.)

Abermin Corporation (Can. 1985)
June 1991 – Declared bankrupt on Mar. 22, 1990, and Deloitte & Touche of Vancouver was appointed trustee. All assets were liquidated, secured creditors received a small dividend (approx. 40¢ on the dollar) and shldrs. received no distribution.
Apr. 28, 2006 – Dissolved and struck from register.

Abeta Mining Corporation Limited (Que. 1954)
Aug. 30, 1978 – Wound up. Assets sold to Ateba Mines Inc. on May 7, 1977.

Abex Mines Ltd. (Ont. 1951)
Feb. 22, 1977 – Amalgamated with Pickle Crow Explorations Ltd. (1 for 5), Cariboo-Bell Copper Mines Ltd. (1 for 9), Beacon Mining Co. Ltd. (1 for 40) and Highland Mercury Mines Ltd. (1 for 5) to form Highland-Crow Resources Ltd.; basis 1 new for 50 old shs.

Abidonne Oils Ltd. (Alta. 1966)
1972 – Merged with Ulster Petroleums Ltd. (1 for 1) in January 1970; basis 2 new Ulster sh. for 3 old Abidonne shs. Charter cancelled.

Abigail Capital Corporation (B.C. Nov. 5, 2018)
July 9, 2021 – Name changed to OverActive Media Corp. pursuant to the Qualifying Transaction reverse takeover acquisition of (old) OverActive Media Corp. and concurrent amalgamation of (old) OverActive with wholly owned 13016838 Canada Inc. (and continued as OverActive Media Holdings Corp.); basis 1 new for 9 old shs. (see FPsurvey - Industrials)

Abila Mines Ltd. (Ont. 1955)
Oct. 5, 1959 – Dissolved.

Abilee Mines Ltd. (Ont. 1949)
1953 – Charter cancelled; assets distributed.

Abingdon Exploration Ltd. (Alta. Apr. 2, 1998)
Dec. 19, 2002 – Acquired by Drilcorp Energy Ltd.; basis 0.4 new Drilcorp com. sh. for 1 old Abingdon com. sh. (see Drilcorp Energy Ltd.)

Abington Ventures Inc. (B.C. June 10, 1999)
Oct. 6, 2009 – Name changed to Abington Resources Ltd.; basis 1 new for 6 old shs. (see FPsurvey - Mines & Energy)

Abino Gold Mines Limited (Ont. 1939)
July 22, 1982 – Amalgamated with Clicker Red Lake Mines Limited (1 for 18.23), Commander Red Lake Mines Limited (1 for 30.82), Dorion Red Lake Mines Limited (1 for 15.59), Duchesne Red Lake Mines Limited (1 for 10.57), Forsyth Mines Limited (1 for 6.38), Goldquest Explorations Corp. (1 for 1.26), Inore Gold Mines Limited (1 for 9.9), Laddie Gold Mines Limited (1 for 15.22) and Rowan Gold Mines Limited (1 for 4.91) to form Goldquest Exploration Inc.; basis 1 new for 12.94 old shs.

Abior Exploration Inc. (Can. Feb. 22, 1984)
Oct. 27, 1993 – Name changed to Diabior Explorations Inc.; basis 1 new for 3 old shs. ■

Abitca Corporation Ltd. (Can. 1951)
Mar. 1963 – Reported to be in bankruptcy. No recent report.

Abitca Lumber & Timber Corp. Ltd. (Can. 1951)
June 1959 – Name changed to Abitca Corporation Ltd. ■

Abitex Resources Inc. (Can. Apr. 7, 1996)
Apr. 16, 2013 – Name changed to ABE Resources Inc.; basis 1 new for 10 old shs. ■

Abitibi Asbestos Mining Company Limited (Que. June 21, 1966)
Sept. 17, 1985 – Name changed to Imco Resources Ltd. ■

Abitibi-Consolidated Inc. (Can. May 30, 1997)
Oct. 29, 2007 – Merged with Bowater Incorporated to form AbitibiBowater Inc.; basis 0.06261 AbitibiBowater sh. for 1 Abitibi-Consolidated sh. (see AbitibiBowater Inc.)

Abitibi Copper Mines Ltd. (Ont. Aug. 27, 1962)
Jan. 27, 1983 – Name changed to Abitibi Resources Ltd. (Les Ressources Abitibi Limitée); basis 1 new for 3 old shs. ■

Abitibi Metals Mines Ltd. (Que. July 12, 1951)
Dec. 1, 1989 – Name changed to Concorde Exploration Ltd.; basis 1 new for 15 old shs. ■

Abitibi Mining Corp. (B.C. June 16, 1983)
Dec. 1, 2014 – Dissolved.

Abitibi Paper Company Ltd. (Can. Feb. 9, 1914; via Dominion charter)
Oct. 15, 1979 – Name changed to Abitibi-Price Inc. ■

Abitibi Power & Paper Company Limited (Can. Feb. 9, 1914; via Dominion charter)
Dec. 1, 1965 – Name changed to Abitibi Paper Company Ltd. ■

Abitibi-Price Inc. (Can. Feb. 9, 1914; via Dominion charter)
May 30, 1997 – Amalgamated with Stone-Consolidated Corporation (1.0062 for 1) to form Abitibi-Consolidated Inc.; basis 1 new for 1 old sh. (see Abitibi-Consolidated Inc.)

Abitibi Resources Ltd. (Ont. Aug. 27, 1962)
June 14, 1989 – Name changed to Consolidated Abitibi Resources Ltd. following amalgamation with Mid-Canada Gold and Copper Mines Limited (1 for 1) and Pioneer Resources (Canada) Ltd. (1 for 1); basis 1 new for 5.7903 old shs. ■

Abitibi Royalties Inc. (B.C. Feb. 18, 2010)
Nov. 8, 2021 – Acquired by Gold Royalty corp.; basis 4.6119 Gold Royalty shs. for 1 Abitibi Royalty sh.

Abitibi Silver Mining Corp. (Que. 1968)
1971 – Merged into Abcourt Metals Inc.; basis 3 new for 5 old shs.

Abitibi Telephone Inc. (Que. 1956)
1966 – Northern Telephone Ltd., which held majority interest, acquired remaining interest.

Abitibi Ventures Ltd. (Que. 1945)
Apr. 1975 – Charter surrendered.

AbitibiBowater Inc. (Del. Jan. 25, 2007)
May 28, 2012 – Name changed to Resolute Forest Products Inc. ■

Able Explorations Ltd. (B.C. July 2, 1965)
July 3, 1979 – Name changed to Arrowhead Resources Ltd. ■

Able Land & Minerals Ltd. (Ont. 1959)
Jan. 10, 1968 – Dissolved. Prior to dissolution, assets exchanged for shs. of Canaveral International Inc.; basis 1 new for 20 old shs.

Ablevest Holdings Ltd. (Alta. Sept. 18, 1992)
Sept. 8, 1998 – Amalgamated with Temba Resources Ltd. (1 for 5) to form a new co. Westlinks Resources Ltd.; basis 1 new for 31.25 old shs. (see Westlinks Resources Ltd.)

Abo Oil Corporation (B.C. Aug. 6, 1981)
Feb. 11, 1986 – Name changed to Abo Resource Corp. ■

Abo Resource Corp. (B.C. Aug. 6, 1981)
June 23, 1995 – Name changed to Puma Minerals Corp. ■

Abode Mortgage Holdings Corp. (B.C. Oct. 10, 1986)
Aug. 19, 2013 – Name changed to Ayubowan Capital Ltd.; basis 1 new for 100 old shs. ■

Abound Gold Mines Ltd. (Ont. 1945)
1955 – Charter cancelled.

AbraPlata Resource Corp. (B.C. Feb. 27, 2017)
Mar. 9, 2021 – Name changed to AbraSilver Resource Corp. (see FPsurvey - Mines & Energy)

Abremor Metal Mines Ltd. (Ont. 1946)
1955 – Charter cancelled.

Abron Mines Ltd. (Que. 1946)
Jan. 1958 – Name changed to Mid-Bachelor Mines Ltd. ■

Absam Mines Ltd. (unknown)
Aug. 1974 – Charter cancelled.

Absolut Resources Corp. (Alta. Mar. 19, 1993)
Mar. 14, 2003 – Continued into Yukon.
Apr. 1, 2008 – Formed Absolut Resources Inc. in Yukon on amalgamation with 41310 Yukon Inc., a wholly owned subsid. Aquiline Resources Inc.; basis 1 Aquiline sh. for 9 Absolut shs.

Absolute Software Corporation (B.C. Nov. 24, 1993)
July 31, 2023 – Acquired by Crosspoint Capital Partners, L.P.; basis US$11.50 cash per sh.

Absorptive Technology Inc. (B.C. May 13, 1983)
Dec. 18, 1990 – Name changed to International Absorbents Inc.; basis 1 new for 5 old shs. ■

Abstract Enterprises Corp. (B.C. May 27, 1987)
Aug. 22, 2005 – Dissolved and struck from register.

Abuck Gold Mines Ltd. (Ont. 1944)
1955 – Charter cancelled.

Abundant Solar Energy Inc. (Ont. Sept. 23, 2013)
Oct. 7, 2022 – Name changed to SolarBank Corporation. ■

Abuy Gold Mines Ltd. (Ont. 1945)
Mar. 10, 1958 – Dissolved.

Acacia Capital Corporation (Yuk. Apr. 12, 2000)
Mar. 1, 2006 – Dissolved and struck off register.

Acacia Mineral Development Corporation Ltd. (B.C. Sept. 23, 1965)
Sept. 25, 1989 – Name changed to AMD Resources Corporation; basis 1 new for 5 old shs. ■

Acadamax Ventures Inc. (B.C. Apr. 19, 1972)
Nov. 6, 1997 – Continued into Bermuda.
Dec. 10, 1997 – Name changed to XMP Mining Limited. ■

Academy Capital Corp. (Ont. Apr. 5, 2004)
Jan. 18, 2006 – Name changed to Baymount Incorporated. (see FPsurvey - Industrials)

Academy Explorations Limited (Ont. July 20, 1970)
Nov. 26, 2018 – Name changed to Dixie Brands Inc. following reverse takeover acquisition of Dixie Brands, Inc. and concurrent amalgamation of (old) Dixie with wholly owned Dixie Brands Acquisition Inc. with (old) Dixie being renamed Dixie Brands (USA) Inc.; basis 1 new for 4 old shs. ■

Academy Metals Inc. (B.C. May 24, 2006)
Oct. 28, 2022 – Name changed to Bedford Metals Corp. (see FPsurvey - Mines & Energy)

Academy Resources Ltd. (B.C. Apr. 19, 1972)
Dec. 2, 1994 – Name changed to Acadamax Ventures Inc.; basis 1 new for 4 old shs. ■

Academy Ventures Inc. (B.C. July 8, 2003)
Dec. 5, 2008 – Name changed to First Bauxite Corporation; basis 2 new for 1 old sh. ∎

Acadia-Atlantic Sugar Refineries Limited (Ont. 1939)
Apr. 1962 – Name changed to Atlantic Sugar Refineries Co. Limited. ∎

Acadia Mineral Ventures Limited (N.S. Nov. 4, 1981)
Apr. 21, 1987 – Continued into Canada.
July 12, 1996 – Name changed to Acadia Minerals Corp.; basis 1 new for 10 old shs. ∎

Acadia Minerals Corp. (Can. Apr. 21, 1987)
Dec. 22, 1997 – Name changed to Acadia Minerals Limited. ∎

Acadia Minerals Limited (Can. Apr. 21, 1987)
May 16, 2001 – Formed Lydia Diamond Exploration of Canada Ltd. in Ontario on amalgamation with Lydia Consolidated Diamond Mines of Canada Ltd., constituting a reverse takeover by Lydia. (see FPsurvey - Mines & Energy)

Acadia Resources Corp. (B.C. Feb. 7, 2011)
Sept. 23, 2013 – Name changed to Horizon Petroleum plc and continued into Jersey. ∎

Acadia Sugar Refining Co. Ltd. (Ont. 1939)
June 1945 – Name changed to Acadia-Atlantic Sugar Refineries Limited. ∎

Acadia Trust Company (Can. - unspecified)
Aug. 1961 – Acquired by Montreal Trust Co.; basis 1 1/5 sh. Montreal Trust sh. plus $5.00 for 1 Acadia sh.

Acadia Uranium Mines Limited (Ont. 1942)
Mar. 1976 – Charter cancelled.

Acadian Gold Corporation (Can. Mar. 14, 2003)
June 28, 2007 – Name changed to Acadian Mining Corporation. ∎

Acadian Mining Corporation (Can. Mar. 14, 2003)
Oct. 22, 2013 – Acquired by LionGold Corp. Ltd. for 12¢ per sh.

Acadian Timber Income Fund (Ont. Dec. 15, 2005)
Jan. 1, 2010 – Converted into Acadian Timber Corp. (formerly CellFor Inc.) following transaction with 7273126 Canada Inc. (renamed CellFor Inc.); basis 1 Acadian Timber sh. for 1 Acadian Timber Income fund unit and 1 new CellFor sh. for 1 old CellFor sh.

Acana Capital Corp. (B.C. June 18, 2007)
May 28, 2015 – Name changed to Mag One Products Inc. ∎

Acana Capital Corp. (B.C. Oct. 17, 2014)
Nov. 30, 2017 – Name changed to BIG Blockchain Intelligence Group Inc. following reverse takeover acquisition of Blockchain Technology Group Inc. ∎

Acano Explorations Ltd. (B.C. 1974 amalg.)
July 30, 1976 – Name changed to Onaca Explorations Limited; basis 1 new for 5 old shs. ∎

Acanthus Real Estate Corporation (Ont. June 17, 1996)
Oct. 2, 1997 – Continued into Canada.
Oct. 11, 2000 – All o/s com. shs. acquired by Acadim Inc., a subsid. of Cadim Inc.; basis $9.40 per sh.

Acaplomo Mining & Development Co. Ltd. (B.C. Nov. 14, 1967)
June 15, 1979 – Name changed to Phillips Equity Corporation. ∎

Acara Rouyn Mines Ltd. (Ont. 1944)
Sept. 17, 1962 – Charter cancelled.

Acasta Enterprises Inc. (Ont. June 19, 2015)
Aug. 21, 2020 – Name changed to Apollo Healthcare Corp. ∎

Acasti Pharma Inc. (Que. Feb. 1, 2002)
Oct. 1, 2024 – Continued into British Columbia.
Oct. 7, 2024 – Continued into Delaware.
Oct. 28, 2024 – Name changed to Grace Therapeutics, Inc.

Accel Financial Group Ltd. (Alta. Dec. 21, 1995)
Apr. 22, 1999 – Amalgamated with 803685 Alberta Ltd., a wholly owned subsid. of T&W Financial Services Company L.L.C.; basis 1 cl. A redeem. pref. sh. (immediately redeem. for $2.50) for 1 com. sh.

Accelerator Capital Corporation (B.C. Feb. 5, 2008)
May 14, 2009 – Name changed to Oceanside Capital Corp. ∎

Acceleware Corp. (Alta. Aug. 6, 2004)
Apr. 26, 2011 – Succeeded by Acceleware Ltd. pursuant to a plan of arrangement whereby all assets and liabilities, with the exception of certain tax assets, were transferred to the new company. (see FPsurvey - Mines & Energy; FPsurvey - Industrials)

Accelio Corporation (Can. June 10, 1982)
Apr. 16, 2002 – Plan of Arrangement with California-based Adobe Systems Incorporated; basis 0.072573 new Adobe shs. for 1 old Accelio sh.

AccelRate Power Systems Inc. (B.C. Oct. 25, 1989)
June 20, 2011 – Name changed to Goldstrike Resources Ltd. following acquisition of Lucky Strike property option. ∎

Accend Capital Corporation (B.C. Dec. 3, 2007)
Nov. 29, 2017 – Name changed to M2 Cobalt Corp. ∎

Accent Resources Ltd. (B.C. 1966)
Mar. 10, 1975 – Name changed to Midas Resources Limited; basis 1 new for 3 old shs. ∎

Access ATM Network Inc. (Can. Oct. 2, 1984 amalg.)
Dec. 29, 1987 – Name changed to Ancom ATM International Inc. and continued into Ontario; basis 1 new for 3 old shs. ∎

Access Banking Network Inc. (Can. Oct. 2, 1984 amalg.)
May 24, 1985 – Name changed to Access ATM Network Inc.; basis 1 new for 10 old shs. ∎

Access Resources Ltd. (B.C. Jan. 26, 1968)
Aug. 22, 1986 – Dissolved and struck off register.

Access Technologies Inc. (B.C. 1980)
Apr. 24, 1992 – Dissolved and struck off register.

Access West Capital Corp. (B.C. Mar. 29, 2000)
June 20, 2002 – Name changed to Journey Unlimited Omni Brand Corporation following Qualifying Transaction acquisition of Journey Unlimited Equipment Inc. ∎

Acclaim Energy Trust (Alta. Apr. 20, 1994)
Jan. 5, 2006 – Formed Canetic Resources Trust in Alberta on amalgamation with StarPoint Energy Trust (1 for 1); basis 0.8333 Canetic trust units plus 0.0833 com. shs. and 0.0175 wts. of new exploration co. TriStar Oil & Gas Ltd. for 1 Acclaim unit. ∎

Acclaim Energy Trust (Alta. Jan. 10, 1997)
Oct. 1, 2002 – Acquired Ketch Energy Ltd., constituting a reverse takeover by Ketch Energy to continue under the name Acclaim Energy Trust; basis 1.15 Acclaim trust units for 1 Ketch Energy sh., plus 1 Ketch Resources sh. for 3 Ketch Energy shs. (see Acclaim Energy Trust)

Accord Capital Corporation (Alta. Sept. 1, 1989 amalg.)
Dec. 17, 1991 – Name changed to Consolidated Accord Capital Corporation; basis 1 new for 5 old shs. ∎

Accord Resources Inc. (Ont. 1982)
Jan. 9, 1996 – Name changed to International Accord Inc.; basis 1 new for 5 old shs. (see FPsurvey - Industrials)

Accra Explorations Ltd. (Ont. 1935)
May 24, 1972 – Amalgamated to form Xtra Developments Inc.; basis 1 new for 8 old shs. (see Xtra Developments Inc.)

Accra Industries Ltd. (B.C. 1969)
Mar. 31, 1983 – Charter cancelled.

Accrete Energy Inc. (Alta. Apr. 5, 2004)
Oct. 17, 2008 – Acquired by Pengrowth Energy Trust; basis 0.273 Pengrowth trust units plus 0.25 Argosy Energy Inc. shs. for 1 Accrete sh.

Accretive Flow-Through (2005) Limited Partnership (Alta. June 15, 2005)
July 10, 2008 – Liquidated for $1.5195 per unit and dissolved.

Accu-Chem Laboratories International Ltd. (B.C. Dec. 23, 1983)
May 14, 2012 – Dissolved and struck from register.

Accugraph Corporation (Ont. Sept. 13, 1976)
May 9, 1984 – Continued into Canada. (see Architel Systems Corporation)
Sept. 1, 1985 – Amalgamated with Cymbol Cybernetics Corporation to continue as Accugraph Corporation. (see Architel Systems Corporation)
June 30, 1998 – Amalgamated with a wholly owned subsid. of Architel Systems Corporation; basis 0.0833 Architel shs. for 1 Accugraph cl. A sh. (see Architel Systems Corporation)

Accura Resources Inc. (B.C. Apr. 9, 1987)
July 20, 1994 – Name changed to CT & T Telecommunications Inc. ∎

Ace Developments Ltd. (B.C. May 17, 1985)
Aug. 12, 1999 – Name changed to ASP123.com Systems Inc.; basis 1 new for 4 old shs. ∎

Ace Mining Co. Ltd. (B.C. 1952)
1969 – Merged into Avino Mines & Resources Ltd.; basis 1 new for 2 old shs.

Ace Oils, Ltd. (Can. 1926)
Acquired by Commonwealth Petroleum Services Ltd. (see Commonwealth Petroleum, Limited)

Ace Yellowknife Mines Ltd. (Ont. 1944)
Nov. 3, 1966 – Dissolved.

Acepharm Inc. (Alta. July 19, 1988)
Mar. 31, 1999 – Dissolved and struck from register.

Acero-Martin Exploration Inc. (B.C. Aug. 25, 1970)
June 8, 2010 – Name changed to AM Gold Inc. ∎

Acerus Pharmaceuticals Corporation (Ont. July 15, 2009)
July 10, 2023 – Acquired by First Generation Capital Inc. under the Companies' Creditors Arrangement Act. All o/s com. shs. were cancelled without consideration.

Acetex Corporation (Alta. Dec. 1, 1994)
July 22, 2005 – Plan of Arrangement acquisition by Celanese Corporation; basis Cdn$9.00 per sh.

Achates Resources Ltd. (B.C. Sept. 29, 1982)
Mar. 31, 1995 – Continued into Canada.
Apr. 18, 1995 – Name changed to Greenhope Resources Inc.; basis 1 new for 5 old shs. ∎

Acheron Mines Ltd. (B.C. 1968)
June 1, 1976 – Name changed to Pan Acheron Resources Ltd.; basis 1 new for 4 old shs. ∎

Acheron Resources Ltd. (B.C. Sept. 30, 1982 amalg.)
Sept. 12, 1994 – Name changed to Abaddon Resources Inc.; basis 1 new for 9 old shs. ∎

Achieva Development Corp. (B.C. Jan. 10, 1986)
July 9, 2008 – Name changed to Angus Ventures Corp.; basis 1 new for 4 old shs. ∎

Achievers Media Corporation (B.C. Apr. 16, 1987)
July 28, 1988 – Continued into Canada.
Nov. 6, 1992 – Name changed to The Achievers Training Group Inc.; basis 1 new for 5 old shs. ∎

The Achievers Training Group Inc. (Can. July 28, 1988)
May 5, 1993 – Continued into British Columbia.
June 21, 1993 – Name changed to Rockwealth International Resource Corp. ∎

Achilles Resources Ltd. (B.C. 1980)
Aug. 1, 1990 – Amalgamated with Golden Iskut Resources Incorporated (1 for 8), International Phoenix Energy Corporation (1 for 8) and Interstate Energy Corp. (1 for 14) to form a new co. Aegis Resources Ltd.; basis 1 new for 4.5 old shs. (see Aegis Resources Ltd.)

Acier Leroux inc. (Que. Apr. 19, 1928)
July 28, 2003 – Acquired by wholly owned subsid. of Russel Metals Inc.; basis either $6.30 or 1.2353 Russel shs., or combination of $4.60 plus 0.333 Russel shs. for either 1 Leroux cl. A or cl. B. sh.

Ackerman Gold Mines, Ltd. (Ont. 1937)
Mar. 1958 – Dissolved.

Acklands Limited (Man. 1905)
Nov. 30, 1996 – Continued into Canada.
Oct. 14, 1997 – Name changed to Acktion Corporation. ∎

Ackroo Inc. (Can. May 16, 2000)
Apr. 3, 2025 – Acquired by Paystone Inc.; basis 15¢ cash per sh.

Acktion Corporation (Can. Nov. 30, 1996)
Aug. 2, 2002 – Name changed to Morguard Corporation. ∎

Acmac Mining Corporation Ltd. (Ont. 1954)
Apr. 2, 1962 – Dissolved.

Acme Capital Corporation (Alta. Jan. 25, 2011)
Mar. 22, 2013 – Continued into Ontario.
Apr. 1, 2013 – Name changed to Pivot Technology Solutions, Inc. pursuant to Qualifying Transaction reverse takeover acquisition of Pivot Acquisition Corp.; basis 1 new for 8 old shs. ∎

Acme Farmers Dairy, Ltd. (Can. 1925)
1943 – Acquired by Dominion Dairies Ltd.; basis $25, $75 in 6% gen. mtge. bonds and 1.5 shs. for each $100 par pref. sh. of Acme.

Acme Gas and Oil Co. Limited (Ont. 1929)
Feb. 14, 1978 – Charter cancelled.

Acme Glove & Apparel Ltd. (Can. 1929)
July 1954 – Adjudged bankrupt.
Feb. 7, 1956 – Distribution made to 1st mtge. bondholders of $24.66 per $100 principal amount.
June 21, 1967 – Final distribution made to 1st mtge. bondholders of $0.46 per $100 principal amount.

Acme Glove Works Ltd. (Can. 1929)
Jan. 27, 1953 – Name changed to Acme Glove & Apparel Ltd. ∎

Acme Gold Company Limited (B.C. Sept. 25, 2020)
Apr. 9, 2025 – Name changed to BluEnergies Ltd. the reverse takeover acquisition of Canadian Global Energy Corp; basis 1 new for 2 old shs. (see FPsurvey - Mines & Energy)

Acme Investments Ltd. (Alta. 1954)
1969 – Amalgamated in Alberta to continue with same name.
July 26, 1974 – Name changed to Compass Investments of Alberta Limited. ∎

Acme Molybdenite Mining Co. Ltd. (Que. 1952)
Feb. 1976 – Charter cancelled.

Acme Oil Co. Ltd. (unknown)
1915 – Merged with Alberta Pacific Consolidated Oils, Ltd.; basis 1 new for 2 old shs.

Acme Resources Inc. (B.C. July 10, 1978)
Mar. 1, 2017 – Name changed to Affinity Metals Corp. (see FPsurvey - Mines & Energy)

Aconic Mining Corp. (Que. 1952)
June 1, 1974 – Charter cancelled.

Acorn Income Corp. (Alta. Jan. 10, 1997)
July 18, 2014 – Wound up. Distribution of $0.316 cash per sh.

Acorn Minerals Ltd. (Ont. 1938)
Nov. 1952 – Name changed to Spearhead Exploration Ltd. ∎

Acorn Resources Ltd. (B.C. 1979)
July 23, 1990 – Name changed to Consolidated Acorn Resources Ltd.; basis 1 new for 5 old shs. ∎

Acqualin Resources Ltd. (B.C. Sept. 24, 1982)
Oct. 22, 1985 – Name changed to Cobra Enterprises Ltd. ∎

Acquest Enterprises Ltd. (B.C. Apr. 28, 1983)
Sept. 27, 1991 – Dissolved and struck off register.

Acquisicorp Capital Ltd. (B.C. Aug. 15, 1985)
Jan. 22, 1993 – Dissolved and struck off register.

Acquisitor Mines Ltd. (B.C. 1984)
Jan. 29, 1987 – Continued into Canada.
May 2, 2002 – Dissolved.

Acreage Holdings, Inc. (B.C. Nov. 9, 2018)
Dec. 10, 2024 – Acquired by Canopy Growth Corporation through Canopy USA, LLC ; basis 0.045 Canopy Growth shs. for 1 Acreage cl. D subord. vtg. sh.

Acres Limited (Ont. 1964)
1975 – All o/s pref. and com. shs. acquired by Traders Group Limited; basis: pref., sh.-for-sh.; com., 3 cl. A Traders plus $5.00 for each 5 shs. held. Acres subsequently changed its name to Traders Finance Corporation (1976) Limited.

Acro Energy Technologies Corp. (B.C. Oct. 25, 2007)
Apr. 11, 2012 – Amalgamated into Lonestar Renewable Technologies Acquisition Corp., a wholly owned subsid. of Lonestar Renewable Technologies Corp.; basis US$0.04 cash per sh.

Acroil Petroleums Limited (Alta. 1951)
1964 – Name changed to Acroll Oil & Gas Ltd.; basis 1 new for 10 old shs. ∎

Acroll Oil & Gas Ltd. (Alta. 1951)
Dec. 8, 1977 – Name changed to Acroll Petroleums Ltd.; basis 1 new for 4 old shs. ∎

Acroll Petroleums Ltd. (Alta. 1951)
Nov. 1, 1982 – Amalgamated with Trans-Canada Resources Ltd. and 2 other cos. to form new co. also known as Trans-Canada Resources Ltd.; basis 1 cl. A sh. for each 2.3 old com. shs.

ActFit.com Inc. (Ont. Apr. 20, 1964)
Dec. 27, 2001 – Name changed to Telum International Corporation. ∎

Actidev Inc. (Que. May 1, 1988 amalg.)
Dec. 15, 1994 – Name changed to Alimentation Couche-Tard Inc. (see FPsurvey - Industrials)

Action Energy Inc. (Alta. Apr. 8, 1992)
Oct. 29, 2009 – Placed into receivership and Ernst & Young Inc. appointed receiver. All officers and directors resigned.
Nov. 2009 – Majority of assets sold to Westfire Energy Ltd. for $30,000,000.
Mar. 2010 – Assets in the Red Willow, Galahad and Killam areas of Alberta were sold to Cutpick Energy Inc. for $250,000.
Apr. 2010 – Remaining assets were sold to Sandbox Energy Corp. for a nominal amount.
July 2, 2010 – Struck from registry.
Oct. 2010 – Secured creditor paid $29,000,000 of the $32,000,000 owed. Insufficient funds for payment to unsecured creditors or shldrs. Ernst & Young Inc. discharged as receiver.

Action Exploration Ltd. (unknown)
May 1, 1972 – Amalgamated with 2 other cos. to form Action Minerals Ltd.

Action Minerals Inc. (B.C. Mar. 27, 1980)
Feb. 5, 2009 – Name changed to Aroway Minerals Inc.; basis 1 new for 40 old shs. ∎

Action Minerals Ltd. (B.C. 1972 amalg.)
Mar. 1974 – Name changed to Action Resources Ltd.; basis 1 new for 3 old shs. ∎

Action Resources Ltd. (B.C. 1972 amalg.)
1983 – Assets acquired by Interaction Resources Ltd.
Oct. 23, 1984 – Dissolved and struck off register upon application by Touche Ross Limited, liquidator.

Action Traders Inc. (Ont. Feb. 16, 1962)
June 21, 1988 – Name changed to ATI Corporation. ∎

Active Assets & Associates Inc. (B.C. Apr. 30, 1993)
May 16, 2002 – Name changed to Focus Ventures Ltd.; basis 1 new for 10 old shs. ∎

Active Control Technology Inc. (Ont. Apr. 1, 1997 amalg.)
Aug. 8, 2014 – Privatized by way of amalgamation with 2421987 Ontario Limited for 3¢ per com. sh. and 3¢ per 1,333.4 wts.

Active Growth Capital Inc. (Ont. July 19, 2007)
Dec. 6, 2016 – Name changed to Quantum Numbers Corp. ∎

Active Mines Ltd. (Ont. 1951)
Dec. 1972 – Amalgamated with Power Mines Ltd. (1 for 6) and Eclipse Metals Limited (1 for 2) to form Power Explorations & Holdings Limited; basis 1 new for 2 old shs.

Actoma Resources Ltd. (B.C. 1980)
Mar. 5, 1993 – Dissolved and struck off register.

Acton Limestone Quarries Limited (Ont. 1962)
Nov. 29, 1967 – Merged with Industrial Minerals of Canada Limited; basis 1 new for 100 old shs.

Actus Minerals Corp. (B.C. May 9, 2006)
Sept. 26, 2014 – Name changed to Arak Resources Ltd.; basis 1 new for 5 old shs. ∎

Acuity All Cap & Income Trust (Ont. Apr. 29, 2004)
Dec. 31, 2007 – Amalgamated with Acuity Diversified Total Return Trust, Acuity Multi-Cap Total Return Trust and Acuity Growth & Income Trust to continue under the Acuity Growth name; basis units of Acuity Growth based on an exchange ratio calculated on the relative net asset value of Acuity All-Cap and Acuity Growth. (see Acuity Growth & Income Trust)

Acuity Diversified Total Return Trust (Ont. Jan. 30, 2006)
Dec. 31, 2007 – Amalgamated with Acuity All Cap & Income Trust, Acuity Multi-Cap Total Return Trust and Acuity Growth & Income Trust to continue under the Acuity Growth name; basis 0.901164, 0.689882 and 0.686986 trust units, respectively, units of Acuity Growth based on an exchange ratio calculated on the relative

net asset value of Acuity Diversified and Acuity Growth. (see Acuity Growth & Income Trust)

Acuity Focused Total Return Trust (Ont. Jan. 28, 2005)
July 4, 2011 – Merged into Acuity Growth and Income Fund (an open-ended fund); basis net asset value per sh.

Acuity Growth & Income Trust (Ont. Nov. 27, 2003)
July 4, 2011 – Merged into Acuity Growth and Income Fund (an open-ended fund); basis net asset value per sh.

Acuity Multi-Cap Total Return Trust (Ont. Sept. 28, 2005)
Dec. 31, 2007 – Amalgamated with Acuity All Cap & Income Trust, Acuity Diversified Total Return Trust and Acuity Growth & Income Trust to continue under the Acuity Growth name; basis units of Acuity Growth based on an exchange ratio calculated on the relative net asset value of Acuity Multi-Cap and Acuity Growth. (see Acuity Growth & Income Trust)

Acuity Small Cap Corporation (Ont. June 6, 2007)
July 4, 2011 – Merged into Acuity Canadian Small Cap Fund (an open-ended fund); basis net asset value per sh.

AcuityAds Holdings Inc. (Can. June 28, 2011)
June 14, 2023 – Name changed to illumin Holdings Inc. (see FPsurvey - Industrials)

Acuma International Inc. (Alta. 1981)
Feb. 29, 1996 – Filed an assignment into bankruptcy and Perry Kreiger & Associates Inc. of Toronto was appointed trustee.
Apr. 1997 – All the assets had been sold and preferred creditors had been paid in full. A lawsuit for a defaulted promissory note was pending.
May 2003 – Litigation resolved as all parties agreed to drop their counter suits and no monies were distributed.
Sept. 1, 2003 – Trustee discharged. No distributions made to shldrs.

Acumen Technologies Inc. (Alta. Nov. 21, 1986)
Mar. 6, 1989 – Name changed to Polyair Tires Inc. ■

Acunet Corporation (Del. 1987)
Mar. 13, 1995 – Name changed to Corsaire Snowboard Incorporated; basis 1 new for 100 old shs.

AcuVision Systems Inc. (B.C. Aug. 26, 1983)
Aug. 27, 1991 – Name changed to International AcuVision Systems, Inc.; basis 1 new for 5 old shs. ■

Ad Astra Minerals Ltd. (Can. 1947)
May 1965 – Name changed to Ad Astra Minerals (1965) Ltd.; basis 1 new for 10 old shs. ■

Ad Astra Minerals (1965) Ltd. (Can. 1947)
Aug. 1965 – Name changed to Consolidated Ad Astra Minerals Ltd. ■

Ad Com Marketing Inc. (B.C. Aug. 31, 1979)
Jan. 10, 1990 – Delisted from the Vancouver Stock Exchange. Subsequently dissolved.

Ad-Dome International Limited (B.C. Dec. 23, 1983)
Mar. 1, 1998 – Delisted from the Vancouver Stock Exchange. Subsequently struck from register and dissolved.

Ada Explorations Ltd. (Ont. 1965)
1967 – Merged into Drope Lake Explorations Ltd.; basis 1 new for 4 old shs.

Adagio Capital Inc. (B.C. Mar. 25, 2021)
Mar. 13, 2024 – Name changed to AGEDB Technology Ltd. pursuant to the Qualifying Transaction reverse takeover acquisition of Advanced Graph Enterprise Database Inc. (AGEDB) and concurrent amalgamation of AGEDB with wholly owned 1441651 B.C. Ltd. (see FPsurvey - Industrials)

Adagio Investments Inc. (B.C. Mar. 27, 1984)
July 1992 – Coopers & Lybrand, Vancouver, was appointed receiver-manager following several rejected proposals to refinance the company's borrowings with Standard Chartered Bank.
May 1993 – Most of the assets and inventories of Adagio Enterprises Ltd., the co.'s main operating subsid., were sold. Secured creditors suffered a shortfall, and there were no funds available for distribution to unsecured creditors or shldrs.
Sept. 8, 1995 – Dissolved and struck off register.

Adaltis Inc. (Can. June 12, 1987)
Jan. 1, 1999 – Amalgamated in Canada to continue with same name.
Aug. 4, 2009 – Placed into bankruptcy. RSM Richter Inc. appointed trustee.

Adamas Resources Corp. (B.C. May 17, 1966)
Aug. 26, 2002 – Name changed to Britannica Resources Corp.; basis 1 new for 9.5 old shs. ■

Adamas Resources Inc. (Alta. June 5, 1987)
Mar. 1, 1989 – Name changed to Zeacan Products Ltd. ■

Adams Exploration Ltd. (B.C. 1980)
Nov. 4, 1994 – Dissolved and struck off register.

Adams Lake Mining Ltd. (B.C. 1972)
Dec. 10, 1983 – Dissolved.

Adams Silver Resources Inc. (B.C. 1980)
Apr. 21, 1986 – Name changed to Adams Exploration Ltd. ■

Adamus Resources Limited (W.A. Sept. 20, 2000)
Dec. 6, 2011 – Acquired by Endeavour Mining Corporation; basis 0.285 Endeavour com. shs. for 1 Adamus ord. sh. (see Endeavour Mining Corporation)

Adanac Gold Corp. (B.C. Apr. 21, 1992)
Nov. 4, 2004 – Name changed to Adanac Moly Corp. ■

Adanac Mining and Exploration Ltd. (B.C. June 2, 1966)
Apr. 13, 1995 – Amalgamated with Bell Molybdenum Mines Ltd. (1 new for 1 old sh.) to form Bell Molybdenum Mines Inc.; basis 1 new for 1 old sh. (see Bell Molybdenum Mines Inc.)

Adanac Moly Corp. (B.C. Apr. 21, 1992)
Nov. 6, 2006 – Name changed to Adanac Molybdenum Corporation. ■

Adanac Molybdenum Corporation (B.C. Apr. 21, 1992)
Dec. 17, 2015 – Acquired by Whitebox Advisors, LLC; basis $0.1837 cash per com. sh. including return of capital.

Adanac-Quebec Mines Ltd. (Ont. 1935)
Dec. 3, 1962 – Dissolved.

Adaptive Marketing Solutions Inc. (B.C. Apr. 28, 1988)
Jan. 18, 2002 – Name changed to Permission Marketing Solutions Inc.; basis 1 new for 2 old shs. ■

Adaptive Technologies (Canada) Inc. (B.C. Apr. 20, 1983)
July 6, 1988 – Delisted from the Vancouver Stock Exchange. Subsequently dissolved for failure to file and struck from register.

Adaptronix Technologies Limited (Ont. July 24, 1980)
Oct. 9, 1984 – Name changed to Pure Energy Resources Inc. ■

Adar Resources Ltd. (B.C. Feb. 14, 1972)
Apr. 29, 1980 – Name changed to Northern Engineered Gold Resources Ltd. ■

Adastra Labs Holdings Ltd. (B.C. Oct. 14, 1987)
Mar. 19, 2021 – Name changed to Phyto Extractions Inc.; basis 1 new for 3 old shs. ■

Adastra Minerals Inc. (Yuk. Aug. 11, 1995)
Aug. 15, 2006 – Acquired by First Quantum Minerals Ltd.; basis either Cdn$2.92 for 1 Adastra sh., or 1 First Quantum sh. plus Cdn$0.265 for 14.76 Adastra shs.

Adastral Resources Ltd. (B.C. Nov. 15, 1971)
July 9, 1996 – Name changed to Diagem International Resource Corp. ■

Adco Silver Mines Ltd. (B.C. 1969)
Feb. 1975 – Charter cancelled.

Adcore Capital Inc. (B.C. Oct. 19, 2007)
Aug. 13, 2010 – Name changed to Wind River Energy Corp. pursuant to Qualifying Transaction acquisition of Day Butte and Meadow Draw properties from Equinox Resources LLC. ■

Adda Minerals Company Limited (B.C. Aug. 14, 1985)
Jan. 18, 1996 – Name changed to Adda Resources Ltd. ■

Adda Resources Ltd. (B.C. Aug. 14, 1985)
Jan. 17, 2003 – Struck from register and dissolved.
Sept. 20, 2004 – Restored to register.
May 21, 2007 – Struck from register and dissolved.

Addax Petroleum Corporation (Can. Sept. 6, 2005)
Oct. 6, 2009 – Acquired by Mirror Lake Oil and Gas Company Limited, an indirect wholly owned subsid. of Sinopec International Petroleum Exploration and Production Corporation, for Cdn$52.80 per sh.

Added Capital Corp. (Alta. Aug. 24, 2005)
Oct. 10, 2008 – Continued into Ontario.
Oct. 30, 2008 – Name changed to Lakeside Steel Inc. ■

Added Capital Inc. (Ont. Oct. 7, 1988)
Apr. 24, 2020 – Name changed to Red Light Holland Corp. pursuant to reverse takeover acquisition of Red Light Holland Financing Inc. and Red Light Holland Debt Inc. (see FPsurvey - Industrials)

Addenda Capital Inc. (Que. July 5, 1996)
Apr. 24, 2008 – All shs. except those held by 9192-8192 Quebec Inc., a subsid. of The Co-operators Group Limited, exchanged for redeemable Amalco pref. shs. on a sh.-for-sh. basis following amalgamation with 9192-8192 Quebec Inc. Amalco pref. shs. subsequently redeemed for $26.50 per sh.

Addington Mines Ltd. (Ont. Feb. 12, 1936)
Dec. 1969 – Dissolved.

Addwest Minerals International, Ltd. (B.C. Mar. 14, 1966)
Aug. 26, 2013 – Dissolved and struck from register.

Adecka Factors Inc. (Alta. 1986)
Mar. 1, 1989 – Struck off register.

Adelaide Mining Ltd. (Ont. 1943)
Nov. 28, 1973 – Dissolved.

Adelaide Properties (London) Limited (Ont. 1955)
1976 – Acquired by Canadian Linen Supply Ontario Ltd. of Toronto.

Adele Malartic Mines Ltd. (Ont. 1945)
May 26, 1958 – Dissolved.

Adelemont Gold Mines Ltd. (Ont. 1945)
Sept. 1975 – Charter cancelled.

Adelina Resources Ltd. (Alta. 1979)
June 1, 1987 – Struck off register.

Adeline Lake Gold Mines (Can. Dec. 29, 1934)
1945 – Assets acquired by Horne Fault Mines Ltd.; basis 1 new for 7 old shs. (see Horne Fault Mines Limited)

Adent Capital Corp. (B.C. May 16, 2012)
Mar. 5, 2018 – Name changed to Khiron Life Sciences Corp. pursuant to Qualifying Transaction reverse takeover acquisition of (old) Khiron Life Sciences Corp.; basis 1 new for 8 old shs. (see FPsurvey - Industrials)

Adeona Pharmaceuticals, Inc. (Wyo. Sept. 30, 1992)
Oct. 15, 2009 – Continued into Nevada.
Feb. 15, 2012 – Name changed to Synthetic Biologics, Inc. ∎

Adeptron Technologies Corporation (Alta. Jan. 1, 2003 amalg.)
Mar. 20, 2012 – Formed Artaflex Inc. in Ontario pursuant to amalgamation with (old) Artaflex Inc. (deemed acquiror); basis 1 new for 25 old shs. ∎

Adera Financial Corp. Ltd. (B.C. 1971)
Aug. 20, 1987 – Name changed to Pacific Adera Financial Corp.; basis 1 new for 2 old shs. ∎

Adera Mining Ltd. (B.C. 1964)
Aug. 3, 1972 – Name changed to Western Adera Ltd.; basis 1 new for 4 old shs. ∎

Adesso Corporation (Alta. Jan. 22, 1993)
Apr. 1, 1994 – Name changed to Ryan Energy Technologies Inc. following acquisition of and subsequent amalgamation with Ryan Energy Technologies Inc. ∎

Adherex Technologies Inc. (Can. Aug. 14, 1998)
Aug. 25, 2011 – Continued into British Columbia.
Sept. 3, 2014 – Name changed to Fennec Pharmaceuticals Inc.; basis 1 new for 3 old shs. (see FPsurvey - Industrials)

Adian Gold Mines Ltd. (Ont. 1944)
Apr. 19, 1949 – Charter cancelled; assets distributed on basis of 1.2¢ per sh.

Adikann Goldfields Ltd. (B.C. Apr. 7, 1981)
May 3, 1999 – Name changed to Harben Industries Ltd.; basis 1 new for 20 old shs. ∎

Adira Energy Ltd. (Can. Nov. 25, 2008)
Apr. 19, 2018 – Name changed to Empower Clinics Inc. following the reverse takeover acquisition of SMAART Holdings Inc.; basis 1 new for 6.726254 old shs. (see FPsurvey - Industrials)

Adit EdTech Acquisition Corp. (Del. Oct. 15, 2020)
Dec. 29, 2023 – Name changed to GRIID Infrastructure Inc. pursuant to reverse takeover acquisition of Griid Holdco LLC. ∎

Adjustable Rate MBS Trust (Ont. May 27, 2005)
July 3, 2009 – Merged into Claymore Global Monthly Advantaged Dividend ETF; basis 1.6015 Claymore Global advisor cl. units for 1 Adjustable Rate MBS trust unit.

Administration and Trust Company (Société d'Administration et le Fiducie) (unknown 1902)
Dec. 1970 – Merged with Trust General du Canada; basis 4 new for 3 old shs.

Admiral Bay Resources Inc. (B.C. Sept. 3, 1987)
Sept. 23, 2019 – Name changed to Cultivar Holdings Inc. pursuant to the reverse takeover acquisition of Cultivar Holdings Ltd. ∎

Admiral Mines Ltd. (B.C. Mar. 20, 1964)
Aug. 14, 1986 – Name changed to Camino Resources Ltd.; basis 1 new for 2 old shs. ∎

Admiral Natural Gas Ltd. (Alta. 1951)
June 11, 1952 – Name changed to Westonian Petroleums Ltd. ∎

Admiral Oils Ltd. (Can. 1926)
Apr. 8, 1952 – Name changed to Canadian Admiral Oils Ltd.; basis 1 new for 3 old shs. ∎

Admiral Sanitation Inc. (Ont. Oct. 5, 1992)
Nov. 12, 1998 – Name changed to Admiral Inc. following amalgamation with wholly owned Admiral Inc.; basis 1 new for 1 old sh. (see FPsurvey - Industrials)

Admiral Yellowknife Mines Ltd. (Ont. 1954)
Nov. 7, 1978 – Dissolved.

Adnaron Copper Corp. Ltd. (Que. 1942)
1955 – Sold property for $15,000 and 75,000 shs. Fontana Mines (1945); and 75,000 shs. Pitt Gold Mining Co. Ltd. (see Pitt Gold Mining Co. Ltd.)

Adnaron Resources Inc. (B.C. Apr. 26, 1984)
Apr. 3, 1987 – Delisted from the Vancouver Stock Exchange. Subsequently dissolved.

Adnew Silver-Cobalt Mines Ltd. (Ont. 1948)
May 1960 – Charter cancelled.

Adnor Mines Limited (Que. 1951)
June 18, 1977 – Dissolved.

Adobe Resources Ltd. (Alta. Apr. 10, 1989)
Mar. 10, 1998 – Amalgamated with BriAlto Energy Corporation (1 new cl. A for 1 cl. A; 1 new cl. B for 1 cl. B sh.) to continue under the BriAlto name; basis 0.20 of a cl. A com. sh. of BriAlto for 1 com. sh. of Adobe. (see BriAlto Energy Corporation)

Adobe Ventures Inc. (B.C. June 1, 1995)
Oct. 27, 2005 – Name changed to Coalcorp Mining Inc. ∎

Adonis Mines Ltd. (B.C. Nov. 20, 1968)
Feb. 16, 1977 – Name changed to Global Energy Corporation; basis 1 new for 5 old shs. ∎

Adonos Resources Inc. (B.C. Mar. 30, 1989)
Dec. 31, 1992 – Amalgamated with Bellex Mining Corp. to form ADEX Mining Corp.; basis 1 new for 4.333 Bellex shs. and 1 new for 1 Adonos sh. (see ADEX Mining Corp.)

Adore Resources Ltd. (B.C. Aug. 9, 1984)
Oct. 14, 1986 – Name changed to Krieger Data International Corp. ∎

Adrian Mining Corp. Ltd. (Ont. 1956)
Feb. 1960 – Charter cancelled.

Adrian Resources Ltd. (B.C. Oct. 10, 1985)
Oct. 12, 2004 – Name changed to Petaquilla Minerals Ltd. (see FPsurvey - Mines & Energy)

Adriana Resources Inc. (Can. May 21, 2002)
Feb. 9, 2017 – Name changed to Sprott Resource Holdings Inc. following reverse takeover acquisition of Sprott Resource Corp. ∎

Adriana Ventures Inc. (Can. May 21, 2002)
Aug. 8, 2005 – Name changed to Adriana Resources Inc. following reverse takeover acquisition of 5050 Nunavut Ltd. ∎

Adriatic Resources Corporation (B.C. Sept. 25, 1979)
Nov. 26, 1987 – Name changed to AIC International Resources Corporation; basis 1 new for 5 old shs. ∎

Adroit Resources Inc. (B.C. May 28, 1993)
Nov. 9, 2015 – Name changed to iMetal Resources Inc.; basis 1 new for 10 old shs. (see FPsurvey - Mines & Energy)

Adsure Inc. (Can. Apr. 2, 1998)
Dec. 11, 2000 – Name changed to iForum Financial Network Inc. ∎

Adulis Minerals Corp. (Alta. July 18, 1985)
Apr. 30, 2001 – Name changed to Adulis Resources Inc.; basis 1 new for 4 old shs. ∎

Adulis Resources Inc. (Alta. July 18, 1985)
Oct. 14, 2005 – Name changed to Solana Resources Limited. ∎

Advance Environmental International Inc. (Ont. Nov. 28, 1983)
Aug. 21, 1989 – Name changed to Advance Realty Corporation. ∎

Advance Gold Corp. (B.C. Apr. 4, 2007)
Dec. 13, 2021 – Name changed to Advance Lithium Corp. (see FPsurvey - Mines & Energy)

Advance Multimedia Corporation (Alta. May 7, 1993)
Apr. 22, 1996 – Name changed to DiscoverWare Inc. ∎

Advance Murgor Explorations Limited (Ont. May 22, 1969)
July 19, 1985 – Name changed to Murgor Resources Inc.; basis 1 new for 2 old shs. ∎

Advance Realty Corporation (Ont. Nov. 28, 1983)
June 8, 1993 – Name changed to First Advance Capital Corporation; basis 1 new for 4 old shs. ∎

Advance Red Lake Gold Mines Inc. (Ont. July 13, 1936)
Dec. 8, 1989 – Name changed to Titan Empire Inc.; basis 0.2 subord. vtg. for 1 com sh. ∎

Advance Red Lake Gold Mines Limited (Ont. July 13, 1936)
Feb. 25, 1988 – Name changed to Advance Red Lake Gold Mines Inc.; basis 1 new for 4 old shs. ∎

Advance Red Lake Gold Mines Limited (Ont. 1936)
Sept. 5, 1979 – Dissolved; revived Sept. 4, 1981.

Advance Sports Medicine Corporation (Alta. July 9, 1986)
Sept. 18, 1995 – Name changed to Indo Pacific Resources Ltd.; basis 1 new for 5 old shs. ∎

Advance Tire Systems Inc. (B.C. May 13, 1985)
Nov. 17, 1993 – Name changed to ATS Wheel Inc.; basis 1 new for 5 old shs. ∎

Advance United Holdings Inc. (B.C. May 28, 2020)
Mar. 8, 2022 – Continued into Ontario.
Sept. 25, 2023 – Name changed to Advanced Gold Exploration Inc. (see FPsurvey - Mines & Energy)

Advanced Aero-Wing Systems Corporation (B.C. 1983)
Oct. 27, 1989 – Dissolved.

Advanced Ecology Systems Corp. (B.C. 1979)
Jan. 9, 1990 – Name changed to Consolidated Advanced Ecology Corp.; basis 1 new for 3 old shs. ∎

Advanced Electronic Systems Ltd. (Ont. June 14, 1988)
July 12, 1989 – Name changed to Mobile Computing Corporation. ∎

Advanced Explorations Inc. (Ont. Jan. 27, 1944)
July 10, 2015 – Filed a notice of intention to make a proposal under the Bankruptcy and Insolvency Act (BIA). Macpherson & Associates Inc. appointed proposal trustee.
Jan. 21, 2019 – Dissolved and struck from register.

Advanced Fiber Technologies (AFT) Income Fund (Que. Feb. 12, 2002)
Mar. 29, 2006 – Acquired by Aikawa Iron Works Co. for $3.00 per unit.

Advanced Gravis Computer Technology Ltd. (B.C. Apr. 30, 1987 amalg.)
Jan. 24, 1997 – Acquired by Pyramid Acquisition Corp., a wholly owned subsid. of American Brands Inc., for 50¢ per sh.

Advanced Growth Systems Inc. (B.C. 1966)
May 28, 1993 – Dissolved and struck off register.

Advanced Industrial Minerals, Inc. (Del. Oct. 17, 1989)
May 3, 1995 – Formed AIM Group, Inc. in Delaware on amalgamation with Heatshield Technologies Inc.; basis 0.808902 new for 1 Heatshield sh. and 0.426825 new for 1 Advanced Industrial sh.

Advanced Material Resources Limited (Alta. Sept. 11, 1986)
Aug. 8, 1994 – Continued into Canada.
June 10, 1998 – Name changed to AMR Technologies Inc. ∎

Advanced Primary Minerals Corporation (Ont. Sept. 27, 2002)
Nov. 9, 2012 – Formed Morien Resources Corp. in Ontario following reverse takeover acquisition of and amalgamation with Erdene Resources Inc. (deemed acquiror); basis 1 new for 7.85 old shs. (see FPsurvey - Mines & Energy)

Advanced Projects Ltd. (B.C. Mar. 20, 1964)
May 23, 2001 – Name changed to Skye Resources Inc.; basis 1 new for 5 old shs. ∎

Advanced Pultrusion Technologies Inc. (Ont. 1951)
Jan. 22, 2007 – Dissolved and struck from register.

Advanced Recruitment Technologies Inc. (Ont. Mar. 2, 1988)
June 12, 1995 – Name changed to Canadian States Gas Ltd. ∎

Advanced Sensing Systems Inc. (Alta. Mar. 3, 2000)
Dec. 1, 2000 – Continued into Canada.
Dec. 20, 2000 – Name changed to IROC Systems Corp.; basis 1 new for 2 old shs. ∎

Advanced Vision Systems Corp. (Alta. Aug. 29, 1995)
Aug. 27, 2010 – Name changed to Windamere Ventures Ltd. and continued into British Columbia; basis 1 new for 4 old shs. ∎

Advantage Capital Corp. (Alta. July 19, 1988)
Sept. 29, 1992 – Name changed to Acepharm Inc. ∎

Advantage Energy Income Fund (Alta. Apr. 17, 2001)
July 14, 2009 – Converted into Advantage Oil & Gas Ltd.; basis 1 Advantage Oil com. sh. for 1 Advantage Energy trust unit. Subsequently dissolved. (see Advantage Oil & Gas Ltd.)

Advantage Entertainment, Incorporated (Colo. 1986)
Jan. 15, 1990 – Name changed to Advantage Life Products, Inc.

Advantage Lithium Corp. (B.C. Mar. 1, 2007)
Apr. 22, 2020 – All o/s com. shs. not already held acquired by Orocobre Limited; basis 0.142 Orocobre ordinary shs. for 1 Advantage Lithium com. sh. (see Orocobre Limited)
Name changed to A.C.N. 646 148 754 Pty Ltd. (see Orocobre Limited)

Advantage Oil & Gas Ltd. (Alta. Dec. 6, 1994 amalg.)
Sept. 5, 2007 – Amalgamated in Alberta to continue with same name.
May 18, 2021 – Name changed to Advantage Energy Ltd. (see FPsurvey - Mines & Energy; FPsurvey - Industrials)

Advantage Wallsystems Inc. (Alta. Sept. 12, 1997)
May 6, 2003 – Plan of Arrangement with PFB Corporation; basis 1 new PFB sh. for 50 old Advantage shs. (see PFB Corporation)

Advantaged Canadian High Yield Bond Fund (Ont. Mar. 7, 2011)
Dec. 30, 2019 – Terminated; basis $7.34 cash per cl. A unit.

Advantaged Preferred Share Trust (Ont. May 24, 2006)
May 31, 2016 – Terminated. Distribution to unitholders of record May 31, 2016, made June 13, 2016; basis unknown.

AdvantEdge International Inc. (Alta. Oct. 1, 1993)
May 2, 2003 – Dissolved and struck from registry.

Advantex Marketing International Inc. (Ont. Aug. 29, 1978 amalg.)
Feb. 10, 1994 – Amalgamated with parent Samplex Inc. and 1047286 Ontario Inc. to form new co. with same name Advantex Marketing International Inc. (see FPsurvey - Industrials)

AdvanteXCEL.com Communications Corp. (Ont. Aug. 9, 1983)
Aug. 15, 2005 – Dissolved and struck from register.

Advanz Pharma Corp. (Can. June 22, 2018)
Jan. 1, 2020 – Continued into Jersey.
Jan. 20, 2020 – Name changed to Advanz Pharma Corp. Limited.

Advectus Life Sciences Inc. (B.C. Sept. 22, 1981)
Jan. 7, 2008 – Dissolved and struck from register.

Advent Communications Corp. (B.C. Feb. 14, 1984)
Aug. 19, 2003 – Name changed to Advent Wireless Inc.; basis 1 new for 3 old shs. ∎

Advent Developments Inc. (B.C. 1964)
Mar. 27, 1981 – Dissolved.

Advent Energy Capital Inc. (Alta. Nov. 16, 2000)
Apr. 1, 2004 – Amalgamated with Thrust Capital Corp., Xceleron Inc. and Zaio Canada Inc. to form Zaio Corporation, constituting a reverse takeover by Zaio Canada; basis 1 new for 1 Thrust sh., 0.6 new for 1 Xceleron sh., 1 new for 1 Zaio Canada sh. and 0.45 new for 1 Advent sh. Advent Energy, Thrust Capital and Xceleron were all Capital Pool Companies and the amalgamation constituted their Qualifying Transaction.

Advent Wireless Inc. (B.C. Feb. 14, 1984)
Mar. 23, 2017 – Name changed to Advent-AWI Holdings Inc. (see FPsurvey - Industrials)

Adventura Energy Corp. (B.C. Sept. 13, 1979)
Nov. 21, 1986 – Delisted from the Vancouver Stock Exchange. Subsequently dissolved for failure to file and struck from register.

Adventure Capital Corporation (Alta. July 27, 1993)
Oct. 21, 1994 – Name changed to HealthCare Capital Corp. ∎

Adventure Electronics Inc. (Can. Apr. 19, 1989)
Sept. 1, 1994 – Amalgamated in Canada to continue with same name.
Nov. 16, 1998 – Made an assignment into bankruptcy and Ernst & Young Inc. of Montreal, Que., was appointed receiver/trustee.
June 2002 – Liquidation of the company's assets was complete and secured creditors suffered a shortfall. There were no funds available for distribution to unsecured creditors or shldrs.
Sept. 1, 2002 – Ernst & Young were discharged as receiver/trustee.
June 10, 2004 – Dissolved and struck from register.

Adventure Gold Inc. (Can. Feb. 9, 2007)
June 14, 2016 – Acquired by Probe Metals Inc.; basis 0.39 Probe com. shs. for 1 Adventure com. sh.

Adventure Vehicle Dynamics Inc. (B.C. 1987)
May 13, 1994 – Dissolved and struck off register.

AdventurX.com, Inc. (Alta. Jan. 19, 1996)
Nov. 5, 1999 – Name changed to Nettron.Com, Inc. ∎

Adventus Mining Corporation (Can. Oct. 24, 2016)
Aug. 7, 2024 – Acquired by Silvercorp Metals Inc.; basis 0.1015 Silvercorp shs. for 1 Adventus sh.

Adventus Zinc Corporation (Can. Oct. 24, 2016)
June 12, 2019 – Name changed to Adventus Mining Corporation. ∎

Advitech Inc. (Can. June 30, 2004 amalg.)
Oct. 14, 2011 – Name changed to Botaneco Corp. pursuant to acquisition of Natunola Health Biosciences Inc.; basis 1 new for 4 old shs. ∎

Advocat Inc. (Del. Jan. 31, 1994)
Mar. 18, 2013 – Name changed to Diversicare Healthcare Services Inc.

Advocate Mines Limited (Ont. 1954)
Sept. 1982 – Company's Baie Verte, Nfld. mine was expropriated by the Government of Newfoundland. Liquidation payouts have been made, and bank loans paid out. Third party unsecured creditors received $1.00

on the dollar plus interest. There was no distribution available to shldrs.
Nov. 23, 1994 – Receiver discharged.

AdWall Capital Corp. (Alta. Oct. 18, 1994)
Aug. 6, 1998 – Continued into Wyoming.

Aegean Explorations Inc. (unknown)
June 1, 1977 – Amalgamated with La Teko Resources Ltd. to continue as La Teko Resources Ltd.

Aegean Gold Inc. (Yuk. Aug. 29, 1996)
Dec. 9, 1999 – Name changed to Aegean International Gold Inc.; basis 1 new for 2 old shs. ∎

Aegean International Gold Inc. (Yuk. Aug. 29, 1996)
Oct. 20, 2003 – Name changed to MinRes Resources Inc.; basis 1 new for 10 old shs. ∎

Aegean Metals Group Inc. (B.C. Mar. 19, 2008)
Jan. 21, 2015 – Acquired by Mariana Resources Limited; basis 1.902 Mariana ord. shs. for 1 Aegean com. sh. (see Mariana Resources Limited)

Aegean Resources Corporation (B.C. Nov. 20, 1978)
July 5, 1985 – Name changed to Realsearch International Systems Corporation; basis 1 new for 2.5 old shs. ∎

Aegis Development Corporation (Alta. May 26, 1997)
July 27, 1998 – Name changed to AEGIS Energy Ltd. ∎

Aegis Investment Management (Golf) Inc. (B.C. Oct. 6, 2006)
May 27, 2011 – Filed for bankruptcy. Boale, Wood & Company Ltd. was appointed trustee.
Mar. 25, 2013 – Dissolved and struck from register.

Aegis Resources Ltd. (B.C. 1982)
Apr. 7, 1986 – Name changed to Louisiana Mining Corporation (not to be confused with co. created by amalg. - B.C. 1990). (see FPsurvey - Mines & Energy)

Aegis Resources Ltd. (B.C. Aug. 1, 1990 amalg.)
Mar. 17, 1993 – Name changed to New Aegis Resources Ltd.; basis 1 new for 7 old shs. ∎

Aeon Ventures Ltd. (B.C. May 4, 1984)
June 28, 2004 – Name changed to Statesman Resources Ltd.; basis 1 new for 3 old shs. ∎

Aero Energy Ltd. (B.C. 1979)
1983 – Placed into receivership.
May 16, 1986 – Struck off register. Nothing left for shldrs.

Aero Mining Corp. (Que. 1955)
1960 – Assets acquired by Chess Mining Corp. Charter surrendered.

Aerocast Inc. (Can. Feb. 7, 2006)
Dec. 16, 2014 – Dissolved and struck from register.

AeroMechanical Services Ltd. (Can. Feb. 28, 2003 amalg.)
May 17, 2012 – Name changed to FLYHT Aerospace Solutions Ltd. ∎

Groupe Aeroplan Inc. (Can. May 5, 2008)
May 4, 2012 – Name changed to Aimia Inc. (see FPsurvey - Industrials)

Aeroplan Income Fund (Ont. May 12, 2005)
June 27, 2008 – Converted into Groupe Aeroplan Inc.; basis 1 com. sh. for 1 fund unit. (see Groupe Aeroplan Inc.)
Dec. 30, 2008 – Dissolved. (see Groupe Aeroplan Inc.)

Aeroquest International Limited (Ont. Oct. 27, 2004)
May 16, 2012 – Acquired by Geotech Ltd. for 15¢ per sh.

AEterna Laboratories Inc. (Can. Sept. 12, 1990)
June 3, 2004 – Name changed to Aeterna Zentaris Inc.; basis 1 com. for 1 subord. vtg. sh. ∎

Aeterna Zentaris Inc. (Can. Sept. 12, 1990)
Aug. 6, 2024 – Name changed to COSCIENS Biopharma Inc. (see FPsurvey - Industrials)

Aethon Minerals Corporation (B.C. May 12, 2016)
Dec. 20, 2019 – Acquired by AbraPlata Resource Corp.;
basis 3.75 AbraPlata com. shs. for 1 Aethon com. sh.

Aetna Gold Mines (Ont. 1918)
Mar. 1934 – Charter cancelled.

Aetna-Goldale Investments Limited (B.C. 1933)
Oct. 12, 1977 – Continued into Ontario.
1977 – Name changed to Goldale Investments Limited;
basis 1 new cl. B voting and 4 cl. A non-voting shs. for 1
old com. sh. ■

Aetna Investment Corporation Ltd. (B.C. 1933)
Aug. 2, 1972 – Name changed to Aetna-Goldale
Investments Limited. ■

Aetna Life Insurance Company of Canada (Ont. Aug.
7, 1889)
Sept. 30, 1993 – All o/s pfd. shs. redeemed; basis $25
per sh. plus all accrued and unpaid cum. dividends.
Oct. 1, 1999 – Acquired by John Hancock Canada, a
wholly owned subsid. of The Maritime Life Assurance
Company; basis 1 Maritime sh. for 1 Aetna sh.

Aetna Mines Ltd. (Ont. 1938)
Mar. 25, 1965 – Reported that shldrs. received 1 sh.
Norstar Lake Mines for each Aetna sh. held. Dissolved.

Afcan Mining Corporation (Que. Aug. 21, 1984)
Sept. 19, 2005 – Acquired by Eldorado Gold Corporation;
basis 1 Eldorado sh. for 6.5 Afcan shs.

Afexa Life Sciences Inc. (Alta. June 30, 1998 amalg.)
Dec. 14, 2011 – Amalgamated with 1625907 Alberta Ltd.,
wholly owned subsid. of Valeant Pharmaceuticals
International, Inc., for Cdn$0.85 per sh. (see Valeant
Pharmaceuticals International, Inc.)
Dec. 29, 2011 – Continued into Canada. (see Valeant
Pharmaceuticals International, Inc.)

Afferro Mining Inc. (B.C. July 27, 2004)
Dec. 20, 2013 – Acquired by International Mining and
Infrastructure Corporation plc for £0.80 plus a two-year
convertible loan note of £0.40.

Affiliated Lithium Mines Ltd. (Ont. 1956)
1966 – Charter cancelled.

Affinitek Corp. (Alta. Mar. 11, 1996)
Feb. 11, 2000 – Name changed to MediaNet
Communications Corp. ■

Affinor Resources Inc. (Can. Aug. 27, 1996)
May 29, 2014 – Name changed to Affinor Growers Inc.
(see FPsurvey - Industrials)

Affirm Capital Inc. (Alta. Oct. 1, 2001)
July 6, 2005 – Qualifying Transaction Plan of
Arrangement to convert company to a new company
named Canadian Equipment Rental Fund Limited
Partnership (LP) following purchase of 4-Way Equipment
Rentals Ltd.; basis 0.18117 new LP unit for 1 old Affirm
sh. (see Canadian Equipment Rental Fund Limited
Partnership)

Afford-A-Home Ind. Corp. (Alta. Mar. 27, 1987)
Aug. 17, 1988 – Name changed to Rawlins Industries
Inc.; basis 1 new for 5 old shs. ■

Afitex Financial Services Inc. (Ont. Mar. 9, 1981)
Oct. 13, 2000 – Delisted from the Canadian Dealing
Network. Subsequently struck from register and dissolved.

Afrasia Mineral Fields Inc. (B.C. June 24, 1986)
Jan. 24, 2017 – Name changed to Westbay Ventures
Inc.; basis 1 new for 4 old shs. ■

Africa Diamond Holdings Ltd. (Alta. Mar. 25, 1986)
Mar. 12, 2004 – Name changed to Sierra Leone Diamond
Company Limited and continued into Bermuda.

Africa Hydrocarbons Inc. (B.C. Apr. 11, 1983)
Apr. 25, 2013 – Continued into Alberta.
May 25, 2018 – Name changed to BlockchainK2 Corp.
(see FPsurvey - Industrials)

Africa Oil Corp. (B.C. Mar. 29, 1993)
May 14, 2025 – Name changed to Meren Energy Inc.
(see FPsurvey - Mines & Energy)

Africa West Minerals Corp. (B.C. Apr. 4, 2007)
May 3, 2010 – Name changed to Advance Gold Corp.;
basis 1 new for 2 old shs. ■

African Aura Mining Inc. (B.C. July 27, 2004)
Apr. 13, 2011 – Name changed to Afferro Mining Inc. ■

African Aura Resources Limited (British Virgin Islands
Aug. 10, 1998)
Oct. 14, 2009 – Formed Manaar Limited on amalgamation
with Manaar Limited, a wholly owned subsidiary of Mano
River Resources Inc. which then changed its name to
African Aura Mining Inc.; basis 1.57 Mano shs. for 1
African Aura sh. (see African Aura Mining Inc.)

African Energy Metals Inc. (B.C. Mar. 27, 2007)
Apr. 11, 2025 – Name changed to Magma Silver Corp.
(see FPsurvey - Mines & Energy)

African Gemstones Limited (B.C. July 24, 1987)
Feb. 16, 2009 – Dissolved and struck from register.

African Gold Group Inc. (Ont. Mar. 10, 2004 amalg.)
June 13, 2022 – Name changed to Toubani Resources
Inc.; basis 1 new for 3 old shs. ■

African Metals Corporation (Yuk. Nov. 19, 1997)
Jan. 4, 2005 – Continued into British Columbia.
Nov. 23, 2021 – Name changed to AFR NuVenture
Resources Inc. (see FPsurvey - Mines & Energy)

African Queen Mines Ltd. (B.C. Apr. 30, 2008)
Mar. 22, 2018 – Name changed to Desert Mountain
Energy Corp.; basis 1 new for 4 old shs. (see FPsurvey
- Mines & Energy; FPsurvey - Industrials)

African Selection Mining Corporation (Ont. Nov. 21,
1997 amalg.)
Apr. 23, 1998 – Continued into Yukon.
Sept. 3, 2008 – Dissolved and struck off register.

African Sky Communications Incorporated (Alta. June
20, 1994)
Dec. 2, 2004 – Struck from registry and dissolved.

Africana Mining Co. Ltd. (Que. 1965)
1969 – Name changed to Panacan Resources Ltd. ■

Africo Resources Ltd. (Can. July 4, 2006)
July 11, 2016 – Acquired by Camrose Resources Limited
for Cdn$1.00 per sh.

AfriOre Limited (Can. May 25, 1995)
July 30, 1997 – Continued into New Brunswick.
July 31, 2001 – Continued into Barbados.
June 15, 2005 – Continued into British Virgin Islands.
Feb. 16, 2007 – Acquired by Lonmin plc for $8.75 per sh.

Afton Food Group Ltd. (Ont. 1982)
Mar. 1, 2005 – Placed into receivership. Zeifman Partners
Inc. was appointed receiver.
Oct. 4, 2006 – Assets acquired by Chairman's Brand
Corporation for an undisclosed amount.
June 25, 2007 – Delisted from the Vancouver Stock
Exchange. Subsequently dissolved.

Afton Mines Ltd. (Ont. 1927)
1957 – Charter cancelled. (Not to be confused with co.
of same name; B.C. inc. 1965.)

Afton Mines Ltd. (B.C. 1965)
1981 – Acquired by Teck Corporation; basis $55 or one
$55 series C convert. pref. sh. of Teck for each Afton sh.
Teck's series C pref. shs. convert. into 2.5 Tech cl. B
com. shs. until June 30, 1986; thereafter into 2.3 Teck cl.
B com. shs. until Dec. 31, 1991. (see Teck Corporation)

Ag Armeno Mines and Minerals Inc. (B.C. Aug. 24,
1984)
Apr. 25, 2000 – Name changed to Golden Nugget
Exploration Inc.; basis 1 new for 15 old shs. ■

Ag Growth Income Fund (Ont. Mar. 24, 2004)
June 8, 2009 – Converted into a corp. pursuant to plan
of arrangement with Benachee Resources Inc., whereby
Ag Growth Fund became a wholly owned subsid. of
Benachee and Benachee Resources Inc. changed its
name to Ag Growth International Inc.; basis 1 Benachee
sh. for 1 Ag Growth fund unit or 1 cl. B exch. L.P. unit.

Ag Growth Industries Inc. (Alta. Nov. 7, 1996)
July 12, 2000 – Amalgamated with 875056 Alberta Ltd.;
basis 1 cl. A or 1 cl. B pfd. sh. of amalg. co. for 1 Ag
Growth com. sh. Each cl. A and cl. B sh. redeemable at
$1.25 per sh. Also 1 cl. C or 1 cl. D pfd. sh. of amalg. co.
for 1 series 1 pfd. sh. of Ag Growth. Each cl. C or cl. D
sh. redeemable at $1.50 per sh. The company will be a
private company.

Aga of Canada Ltd. (Ont. 1960)
1965 – Name changed to K. B. & G. Metal Products Ltd. ■

Aga Steel Radiators of Canada Ltd. (Ont. 1960)
Oct. 5, 1960 – Name changed to Aga of Canada Ltd. ■

Agarwal Resources Ltd. (B.C. June 24, 1977)
Oct. 1, 1997 – Name changed to Consolidated Agarwal
Resources Ltd.; basis 1 new for 3 old shs. ■

Agassiz Mines Ltd. (Man. Apr. 29, 1955)
Oct. 1969 – Name changed to Royal Agassiz Mines Ltd.;
basis 1 new for 3 old shs. ■

Agassiz Resources Ltd. (Man. Apr. 29, 1955)
July 29, 1991 – Declared bankrupt. Coopers & Lybrand
of Toronto appointed receiver.
June 13, 1994 – All assets sold for the compensation of
the secured creditors. Preferred creditors received a
nominal divd. but there was no distribution to shldrs.

Agate Bay Resources Ltd. (B.C. Mar. 23, 1967)
Apr. 14, 1998 – Name changed to Geodex Minerals Ltd.;
basis 1 new for 4 old shs. ■

Agau Resources, Inc. (Alta. Apr. 9, 1996)
Aug. 17, 2021 – Continued into Ontario.
Oct. 14, 2021 – Name changed to The Well Told
Company Inc. pursuant to the reverse takeover acquisition
of Well Told Inc. and concurrent amalgamation of Well
Told with wholly owned 2835270 Ontario Inc.; basis 1
new for 81.42 old shs. (see FPsurvey - Industrials)

Agave Silver Corp. (B.C. Oct. 12, 1966)
Dec. 20, 2016 – Name changed to First Energy Metals
Limited. ■

Agellan Commercial Real Estate Investment Trust
(Ont. Nov. 1, 2012)
Feb. 22, 2019 – All o/s trust units not already held
acquired by Elad Genesis Limited Partnership, an affiliate
of El-Ad Group, Ltd.; basis $14.25 cash per trust unit.

Agena Mines Ltd. (B.C. Jan. 1, 1968)
Sept. 13, 1968 – Name changed to Helgena Mines Ltd. ■

Agena Mining Co. Ltd. (Ont. 1966)
Sept. 1972 – Charter cancelled.

Aggressive Mining Limited (Ont. 1967)
Aug. 19, 1988 – Name changed to Sound Capital Inc. ■

Agincourt Explorations Inc. (B.C. Apr. 10, 1985)
Nov. 29, 1995 – Name changed to AGX Resources
Corp. ■

Agio Resources Corporation (B.C. 1968)
Dec. 18, 1992 – Dissolved and struck off register.

AgJunction Inc. (Alta. July 31, 1990)
Dec. 9, 2021 – Acquired by Kubota Corporation; basis
Cdn$0.75 cash per sh.

Agnew-Surpass Shoe Stores, Limited (Can. 1928)
Nov. 1961 – Acquired by Genesco Inc. of Nashville,
Tenn., for $24.25 per sh.

Agnico-Eagle Mines Limited (Ont. June 1, 1972 amalg.)
Apr. 26, 2013 – Name changed to Agnico Eagle Mines Limited. (see FPsurvey - Mines & Energy)

Agnico Mines Limited (Ont. Jan. 21, 1953)
June 1, 1972 – Merged with Eagle Gold Mines Limited to form Agnico-Eagle Mines Limited.

Agra Vegetable Oil Products Ltd. (Sask. Nov. 7, 1960)
Jan. 26, 1970 – Name changed to AGRA Industries Limited. ■

Agra Ventures Ltd. (B.C. June 24, 2004)
Aug. 2, 2023 – Name changed to Digicann Ventures Inc.; basis 1 new for 25 old shs. (see FPsurvey - Mines & Energy; FPsurvey - Industrials)

AgraFlora Organics International Inc. (B.C. June 24, 2004)
July 28, 2021 – Name changed to Agra Ventures Ltd. ■

Agratec Industries Ltd. (Alta. Aug. 1, 1966)
Sept. 20, 1971 – Name changed to Foremost International Industries Ltd. ■

Agricola Mines Ltd. (B.C. 1967)
Dec. 1974 – Charter cancelled.

Agricore United (Can. Dec. 17, 1992; via United Grain Growers Act)
June 19, 2007 – Acquired by Saskatchewan Wheat Pool Inc.; basis $20.50 per com. sh. and $24 plus accr. and unpaid divds. of $0.5781 per pref. sh. (see Saskatchewan Wheat Pool Inc.)

AgriMarine Holdings Inc. (B.C. Apr. 5, 2007)
May 21, 2015 – Privatized by way of amalgamation with a wholly owned subsidiary of major shareholder Dundee Agricultural Corporation (DAC). All common shares of the company, other than those held by DAC and its parent Dundee Corporation, were redeemed for 3¢ per share and delisted from the CSE on May 25, 2015.

AgriMinco Corp. (Ont. Mar. 9, 2011 amalg.)
July 9, 2018 – Certificate of incorporation cancelled and dissolved.

Agritech Capital Inc. (Que. Mar. 24, 2005)
June 30, 2009 – Formed Pigboss Follow-up Growth Inc. in Quebec following reverse takeover acquisition of and amalgamation with Pigboss Follow-up Growth Inc. ■

Agritek Bio Ingredients Corporation (Can. Dec. 15, 1992 amalg.)
Nov. 25, 1999 – Name changed to Innovium Capital Corp. ■

Agrium Inc. (Can. Dec. 21, 1992)
Jan. 2, 2018 – Merged with Potash Corporation of Saskatchewan Inc. under a new parent company, Nutrien Ltd.; basis 40 Nutrien shs. for 1 Potash sh. and 2.23 Nutrien shs. for 1 Agrium sh.
Oct. 18, 2022 – Name changed to Nutrien (Canada) Holdings ULC.

Agro International Holdings Inc. (B.C. Oct. 11, 1985)
May 28, 2004 – Name changed to HOST International Holdings Inc. pursuant to reverse takeover aquisition of Hubei Hualong Oilseed Science & Technology Co. Ltd. ■

Agro Pacific Industries Ltd. (B.C. Nov. 1, 1997)
May 21, 2002 – Continued into Canada.
July 26, 2004 – Name changed to Adriana Ventures Inc.; basis 1 new for 10 old shs. ■

AgroCultures Biotechnologies Inc. (Can. July 22, 1992)
Nov. 22, 1995 – Name changed to Nexia Biotechnologies Inc. ■

Agromex Inc. (Que. 1986)
Mar. 19, 1999 – All o/s subord. vtg. shs. repurchased for $0.096 per sh.

Agropur, coopérative agro-alimentaire (Que. Aug. 29, 1938)
Oct. 26, 2000 – Name changed to Agropur coopérative and continued into Canada.

Agrotech Greenhouses Inc. (B.C. Oct. 31, 1984)
Apr. 30, 2010 – Name changed to Archer Petroleum Corp. pursuant to acquisition of 0856348 B.C. Ltd., which became a wholly owned subsid.; basis 1 new for 3 old shs. ■

Agtech Income Fund (Ont. June 25, 2004)
Dec. 7, 2007 – Name changed to Alliance Grain Traders Income Fund. ■

Aguila American Gold Limited (B.C. Jan. 14, 2008)
Dec. 3, 2021 – Name changed to Aguila Copper Corp. ■

Aguila American Resources Ltd. (Bahamas Mar. 21, 1997)
Jan. 14, 2008 – Continued into British Columbia.
May 26, 2011 – Name changed to Aguila American Gold Limited. ■

Aguila Copper Corp. (B.C. Jan. 14, 2008)
Oct. 20, 2022 – Name changed to T2 Metals Corp. (see FPsurvey - Mines & Energy)

Ahed Corporation (Ont. Feb. 6, 1969)
July 30, 1987 – Name changed to ECO Corporation. ■

Ahed Music Corporation Limited (Ont. Feb. 6, 1969)
June 23, 1978 – Name changed to Ahed Corporation. ■

Aida Minerals Corp. (B.C. Sept. 10, 2013)
Feb. 2, 2018 – Name changed to BLOK Technologies Inc. following acquisition of 10375977 Canada Inc. (dba Greenstream). ■

Aigner Holdings Ltd. (B.C. 1976)
Jan. 21, 1994 – Dissolved and struck off register.

Aiguebelle Goldfields Ltd. (Ont. 1945)
1968 – Charter cancelled.

Aiguebelle Resources Inc. (Que. 1980)
Feb. 13, 1987 – Amalgamated with a subsid. of Cambior Inc.; basis 1 pref. sh. for each Aiguebelle held. On Feb. 16, 1987, pref. shs. of amalg. co. were redeemed at $1.158 per sh. (see Cambior Inc.)

Aiken Red Lake Gold Mines Ltd. (Ont. 1945)
1965 – Merged into Aiken-Russet Red Lake Mines Ltd.; basis 1 new for 2 old shs. (see Aiken-Russet Red Lake Mines Limited)

Aiken-Russet Red Lake Mines Limited (Ont. 1965)
Dec. 30, 1985 – Amalgamated with several other cos. to form Canhorn Mining Corporation; basis 1 new for 35.67 old shs. (see Canhorn Mining Corporation)

Aileron Ventures Limited (Alta. May 31, 2010)
Dec. 2, 2016 – Name changed to Integrated Energy Storage Corp. and continued into Canada. ■

Groupe Les Ailes de la Mode Inc. (Can. July 24, 1978)
Jan. 24, 2006 – Name changed to Groupe Bikini Village Inc. ■

Aim Explorations Ltd. (B.C. Apr. 18, 2011)
Feb. 8, 2018 – Name changed to DMG Blockchain Solutions Inc. pursuant to Qualifying Transaction reverse takeover acquisition of and amalgamation of (old) DMG Blockchain Solutions Inc. with a wholly owned subsidiary. (see FPsurvey - Industrials)

Aimco Industries Ltd. (Ont. 1965)
Apr. 1972 – International Telephone and Telegraph Corporation (ITT) of New York acquired over 99% of the co.'s o/s shs. by; basis 0.2977 ITT sh. for each Aimco sh. held. All o/s 7.5% conv. s.f. debs., ser. 4, retired by January 1972.

AimGlobal Technologies Company Inc. (B.C. June 24, 1983)
Dec. 12, 2005 – Dissolved and struck from register.

Aiml Resources Inc. (B.C. Nov. 5, 2009)
Nov. 6, 2020 – Name changed to AI/ML Innovations Inc. (see FPsurvey - Industrials)

Ainsmore Consolidated Mines Ltd. (Ont. 1942)
1954 – Wound up.

Ainsworth Base Metals Ltd. (B.C. 1951)
Dec. 1957 – Name changed to New Ainsworth Base Metals Ltd.; basis 1 new for 3 old shs. ■

Ainsworth Base Metals Ltd. (B.C. 1951)
1957 – Name changed to New Ainsworth Base Metals Ltd.; basis 1 new for 3 old shs.

Ainsworth Lumber Co. Ltd. (B.C. Mar. 31, 1993)
July 24, 2008 – Continued into Canada. (see Norbord Inc.)
May 2013 – Continued into British Columbia. (see Norbord Inc.)
Apr. 6, 2015 – All o/s shs. acquired by Norbord Inc.; basis 0.1321 Norbord com. shs. for 1 Ainsworth com. sh. (see Norbord Inc.)

Ainsworth Mines Ltd. (Ont. Aug. 17, 1936)
1951 – Charter cancelled.

Ainsworth Oils, Limited (Can. Mar. 1926)
June 14, 1927 – Name changed to Commonwealth Petroleum, Limited. ■

Ainsworth Resources Ltd. (B.C. 1979)
Apr. 4, 1985 – Struck off register.

Aintree Resources Inc. (B.C. Sept. 24, 2009)
Jan. 8, 2018 – Name changed to Viva Gold Corp. (see FPsurvey - Mines & Energy)

Aintree Resources Ltd. (B.C. May 22, 1986)
Apr. 27, 1994 – Name changed to ICCI Integrated Credit and Commerce Inc. ■

Air Canada (Can. Apr. 10, 1937; via Special Act of Parliament)
Feb. 28, 1978 – Continued into Canada; via The Air Canada Act - 1977. (see ACE Aviation Holdings Inc.)
Aug. 25, 1988 – Continued into Canada; via The Air Canada Public Participation Act. (see ACE Aviation Holdings Inc.)
Nov. 18, 2004 – Plan of Arrangement restructuring following emergence from Companies' Creditors Arrangement Act protection to continue as a new company named ACE Aviation Holdings Inc.; basis either 1 new voting ACE sh. or 1 new variable voting ACE sh. for 11,894 old Air Canada com. shs. Re-listed on TSX effective Nov. 24, 2006. (see FPsurvey - Industrials) (see ACE Aviation Holdings Inc.)

Air Niagara Express Inc. (Can. July 21, 1978)
Dec. 23, 2002 – Dissolved.

Air Systems Plus Corp. (Ont. 1975)
July 21, 1993 – Name changed to Sales Initiatives International Inc. ■

Airanium Surveys Limited (Sask. 1954)
Mar. 28, 1983 – Amalgamated with Dee Explorations (1982) Ltd.

Airbomb.com Marketing Ltd. (B.C. Jan. 22, 1987)
May 9, 2000 – Continued into Delaware.
May 15, 2000 – Name changed to Airbomb.com Inc.

Airborne Data Marketing Ltd. (B.C. June 16, 1964)
Sept. 11, 1987 – Name changed to International Airborne Systems Corp.; basis 1 new for 2 old shs. ■

Airedale Financial Corp. (B.C. Sept. 2, 1998)
Jan. 23, 2004 – Transaction with Jet Gold Corp. to acquire 2,312,500 Jet units (1 common share & ½ warrant) at 13¢ per unit and distribute the units to shldrs. and

subsequent wind-up represented the company's Qualifying Transaction. (see Jet Gold Corp.)

Airesurf Networks Holdings Inc. (Ont. Sept. 17, 2003)
Oct. 31, 2016 – Amalgamated with 2532314 Ontario Ltd., a wholly owned subsid. of IsoEnergy Ltd., to form IsoOre Ltd.; basis 0.020833 IsoEnergy com. shs. for 1 Airesurf sh.

Airgen Corporation (Alta. July 4, 1994)
June 9, 1998 – KPMG Inc. of Calgary was appointed receiver for the company and its subsidiaries.
Aug. 1, 2000 – Receiver discharged. There were no distributions to creditors or shldrs.

AirIQ Inc. (B.C. May 1, 1991)
Jan. 31, 2003 – Continued into Canada. (see FPsurvey - Industrials)

Airline Training International Ltd. (Alta. Sept. 30, 1998)
June 30, 2003 – Declared bankruptcy. Mintz & Partners Limited was appointed trustee.
Mar. 2, 2005 – Struck from registry and dissolved.

Airmaque Explorers Ltd. (Ont. 1959)
Aug. 1972 – Charter cancelled.

Airmar Red Lake Mines Ltd. (Ont. 1946)
Dec. 1970 – Charter cancelled.

Airnorth Mines Ltd. (Ont. 1961)
Nov. 2, 1976 – Dissolved.

AirPro Industries Inc. (B.C. Mar. 12, 1980)
May 8, 1995 – Name changed to Camelot Industries Inc.; basis 1 new for 4.7 old shs. ■

Airscrew-Weyroc Canada Ltd. (Can. 1969)
May 27, 1975 – Name changed to Northwood Panelboard Limited. ■

Airth Mining Co. Ltd. (Alta. 1970)
Mar. 31, 1977 – Charter cancelled.

AirWorks Media Incorporated (Alta. Nov. 30, 1987)
May 2, 2002 – Struck from registry and dissolved.

Airworks Media Services Ltd. (Alta. Nov. 30, 1987)
Oct. 31, 1996 – Name changed to AirWorks Media Incorporated. ■

Aitchison Capital Inc. (B.C. June 24, 1999)
June 20, 2002 – Name changed to TransGlobe Internet and Telecom Co., Ltd. following Qualifying Transaction reverse takeover acquisition of TransGlobe Internet & Telecom Co. Ltd. ■

Aitec Capital Corp. (Alta. Mar. 16, 1995)
Mar. 15, 2000 – Formed Infiniti Resources International Ltd. in Alberta on Major Transaction acquisition of Infiniti Resources International Ltd. and all assets of Infiniti Resources Limited Partnership and subsequent amalgamation with Infiniti Resources International; basis 1 new for 3 old shs. ■

Aitec Development Corp. (B.C. Sept. 19, 1984)
Oct. 13, 1988 – Name changed to Frozya Industries Inc. ■

Ajax Mercury Mines Limited (B.C. Jan. 26, 1966)
July 2, 1971 – Name changed to Ajax Resources Limited. ■

Ajax Minerals Limited (Ont. 1947)
Feb. 14, 1978 – Dissolved.

Ajax Oil and Gas Co. Ltd. (unknown)
1946 – Assets sold; shldrs. received $2.2395 per sh.

Ajax Resources Limited (B.C. Jan. 26, 1966)
Apr. 6, 1973 – Name changed to Pan-Ajax Resources Ltd. ■

Ajax Resources Ltd. (B.C. 1971)
Oct. 22, 1993 – Dissolved and struck off register.

Ajax Tungsten and Molybdenite Mines Ltd. (Ont. 1942)
1942 – Property acquired by Buckhorn Mines Ltd.

Ajay Resources Inc. (B.C. Feb. 13, 1980)
Nov. 16, 1987 – Delisted from the Vancouver Stock Exchange. Subsequently dissolved.

Akademia Enterprises Inc. (Alta. 1987)
Nov. 1, 1997 – Struck off register.

Akaitcho Yellowknife Gold Mines Limited (Ont. Jan. 30, 1945)
July 25, 1991 – Amalgamated with Royal Oak Resources Ltd. (5 for 6), Pamour Inc. (3 for 4), Giant Yellowknife Mines Limited (13 for 2) and Pamorex Minerals Inc. (3 for 5) to form a new co. named Royal Oak Mines Inc.; basis 3 new Royal Oak for 5 old Akaitcho shs. (see Royal Oak Mines Inc.)

Akasaba Gold Mines Ltd. (Ont. 1969)
Mar. 17, 1976 – Name changed to Akasaba Resources Ltd. ■

Akasaba Resources Ltd. (Ont. 1969)
Mar. 22, 1979 – Name changed to Sion Resources Ltd. ■

Akash Ventures Inc. (B.C. May 13, 1981)
Dec. 8, 1999 – Name changed to International Akash Ventures Inc.; basis 1 new for 3 old shs. ■

Akela Pharma Inc. (Can. May 9, 2002)
Feb. 11, 2014 – Dissolved and struck from register.

Akers Medical Technology Ltd. (Can. Aug. 30, 1946)
Oct. 26, 1994 – Name changed to Digital Fusion Multimedia Corp.; basis 1 new for 5 old shs. ■

Akiko Gold Resources Ltd. (B.C. Nov. 9, 1992 amalg.)
July 30, 1997 – Name changed to Prospex Mining Inc. and continued into Yukon. ■

Akiko-Lori Gold Resources Ltd. (B.C. 1982)
Jan. 16, 1991 – Amalgamated with Santa Marina Gold Ltd. (1 for 9) to form a new company also named Akiko-Lori Gold Resources Ltd.; basis 1 new for 1 old sh.
Nov. 9, 1992 – Amalgamated with Omega Gold Corporation (1 for 2.5) to form a new co. named Akiko Gold Resources Ltd.; basis 1 new for 1 old sh.

Akrokeri-Ashanti Gold Mines Inc. (Ont. July 7, 1995 amalg.)
Feb. 16, 2004 – All shares and intercompany debt of Ghanaian subsidiary Canadiana Gold Resources Limited were sold to Xtra-Gold Resources Corp. for US$25,000.
Mar. 2004 – Bonte Gold Mines Limited was petitioned by the co. into official liquidation in Ghana after producing less gold than forecasted. Bonte had received a letter of demand from its largest creditor for US$3,400,000 and was unable to meet this demand. The liquidation was supervised by the Ghanaian Registrar of Companies.
May 14, 2004 – All officers and directors resigned and the company ceased operations.
Dec. 22, 2004 – Xtra-Gold Resources Corp. acquired 90% interest in subsidiary Goldenrae Mining Company Limited and 18% secured notes and 14% convertible subordinate debentures for 2,698,350 restricted shares of Xtra-Gold.
June 20, 2006 – Duguay & Ringler Group of Companies reported that the company was bankrupt. There were no funds available for creditors or shldrs.

Akumin Inc. (Ont. Aug. 12, 2015 amalg.)
Sept. 30, 2022 – Continued into Delaware.
Feb. 6, 2024 – Privatized pursuant to a Chapter 11 plan of financial restructuring under which Stonepeak Partners L.P. acquired the company's com. shs. for US$25,000,000 cash which would be distributed to shldrs. on a pro rata basis.

Alabama Graphite Corp. (B.C. Apr. 13, 2006)
Apr. 23, 2018 – Acquired by Westwater Resources, Inc.; basis 0.08 Westwater com. shs. for 1 Alabama com. sh.

Alacer Gold Corp. (Yuk. Jan. 14, 1998)
Sept. 16, 2020 – Acquired by SSR Mining Inc.; basis 0.3246 SSR com. shs. for each Alacer sh.

Aladdin-Chibougamau Mines Limited (Ont. 1946)
Jan. 4, 1960 – Dissolved.

Aladdin-Groundhog Mines Ltd. (Ont. 1946)
Apr. 1956 – Name changed to Aladdin-Chibougamau Mines Limited. ■

Aladdin Oils Ltd. (unknown)
1929 – Acquired by Alberta Superior Oils Ltd.

Aladdin Resources Corp. (B.C. Dec. 6, 1988)
Jan. 27, 2004 – Name changed to Gold Point Exploration Ltd. ■

Aladin International Inc. (Ont. Aug. 1, 1975)
Sept. 5, 1990 – Delisted from the Alberta Stock Exchange. Subsequently struck from register and dissolved.

Aladin Minerals Limited (Ont. Aug. 1, 1975)
Oct. 17, 1986 – Name changed to Aladin International Inc. ■

Alakon Metals Ltd. (B.C. 1959)
Mar. 8, 1974 – Name changed to Gold Valley Resources Ltd.; basis 1 new for 5 old shs. ■

Alamac Mines Ltd. (Que. 1927)
1963 – Charter cancelled.

Alamar Industries Limited (Ont. Apr. 26, 1966)
July 1978 – Name changed to Ascot Energy Corporation of Canada Limited; basis 6 new for 1 old sh. ■

Alamar Mines Ltd. (Ont. Apr. 26, 1966)
Sept. 15, 1977 – Name changed to Alamar Industries Limited; basis 1 new for 30 old shs. ■

Alamo Developments Ltd. (B.C. 1980)
Jan. 14, 1988 – Name changed to United Beverages Limited. ■

Alamo Silver Lead Mining Co. Ltd. (Ont. 1948)
1951 – Charter cancelled.

Alamos Gold Inc. (B.C. Feb. 21, 2003 amalg.)
July 6, 2015 – Amalgamated with AuRico Gold Inc. (deemed acquiror) to continue as new Alamos Gold Inc. (Amalco) pursuant to plan of arrangement; basis (i) 1 Amalco cl. A sh. and 0.4397 AuRico Metals Inc. com. shs. plus US$0.0001 for 1 Alamos Gold Inc. com. sh. (ii) 1 Amalco cl. A purchase wt. for 1 old Alamos Gold Inc. sh. purchase wt. (iii) 0.5046 Amalco cl. A shs. plus 0.2219 AuRico Metal Inc. com. shs. for 1 AuRico Gold com. sh.

Alamos Minerals Ltd. (B.C. Jan. 11, 1996)
Feb. 21, 2003 – Formed Alamos Gold Inc. in British Columbia on amalgamation with National Gold Corporation with Alamos Minerals the deemed acquiror; basis 1 new for 2.352 National Gold shs. and 1 new for 2 Alamos Minerals shs. ■

Alamos Mines Ltd. (B.C. 1956)
July 17, 1969 – Dissolved.

Alana Mines Ltd. (Ont. 1949)
June 9, 1958 – Charter cancelled.

Alanda Energy Corp. (B.C. 1980)
May 10, 1985 – Struck off register.

Alange Energy Corp. (B.C. May 3, 1966)
July 19, 2011 – Name changed to PetroMagdalena Energy Corp.; basis 1 new for 7 old shs. ■

Alantra Venture Corp. (B.C. Mar. 20, 1978)
Aug. 14, 2006 – Struck from registry and dissolved.

Alaris Royalty Corp. (Can. May 23, 2006)
Sept. 4, 2020 – Succeeded by Alaris Equity Partners Income Trust pursuant to plan of arrangement whereby Alaris Equity Partners Income Trust was formed to facilitate the conversion of the corporation into an income trust. (see FPsurvey - Industrials)

Alarmforce Industries Inc. (Can. Nov. 16, 1988)
Jan. 9, 2018 – Acquired by BCE Inc.; basis (i) $16.00 cash per Alarmforce sh. or (ii) 0.2597 BCE com. shs. plus $0.01 cash for 1 Alarmforce sh.

Alascan Oil & Gas Ltd. (B.C.)
Sept. 19, 1968 – Dissolved.

Alaska Apollo Gold Mines Ltd. (B.C. Jan. 31, 1979)
Oct. 14, 1992 – Name changed to Alaska Apollo Resources Inc.; basis 1 new for 15 old shs. ■

Alaska Apollo Resources Inc. (B.C. Jan. 31, 1979)
June 29, 1998 – Name changed to Daugherty Resources Inc.; basis 1 new for 5 old shs. ■

Alaska-Canadian Mining and Exploration Co. Ltd. (Ont. 1958)
Aug. 3, 1964 – Charter cancelled.

Alaska Kenai Oils Ltd. (B.C. 1965)
Feb. 13, 1976 – Name changed to Kenai Oils Ltd. (see FPsurvey - Mines & Energy)

Alaska Mines and Minerals Inc. (Alaska 1951)
Nov. 1977 – Dissolved.

Alaska Pine and Cellulose Ltd. (Can. 1925)
1957 – Subsid. of Rayonier Inc., which holds all but 291 of the 100,000 o/s com. shs. Control was sold to latter by Abitibi Paper Company Ltd. and Koerner interests in 1954, and minority int. retained by these cos. was exchanged on basis of 12.5 shs. Rayonier com. for each sh. Alaska Pine.

Alaska-Yukon Pipelines Ltd. (Can. 1957)
Dec. 16, 1980 – Dissolved.

Alaska-Yukon Refiners & Distributors Ltd. (Alta. 1937)
Nov. 15, 1978 – Struck off register.

Alaskagold Mines Inc. (B.C. Sept. 28, 1979)
Sept. 19, 2005 – Dissolved and struck from registry.

Alaskon Resources Ltd. (B.C. Apr. 12, 1983)
June 7, 1993 – Name changed to El Bravo Gold Mining Ltd.; basis 1 new for 5 old shs. ■

Alawas Gold Corporation (B.C. 1984 amalg.)
Apr. 7, 1989 – Amalgamated with Kaaba Resources Inc. to form a new co. also known as Kaaba Resources Inc.; basis 1 new for 1 old sh. (see Kaaba Resources Inc.)

Alba Explorations Ltd. (Ont. 1935)
Nov. 1962 – Name changed to Accra Explorations Ltd.; basis 1 new for 4 old shs. ■

Alba Minerals Ltd. (B.C. Aug. 1, 1969)
Apr. 13, 2020 – Name changed to Caelan Capital Inc.; basis 1 new for 10 old shs. ■

Alban Explorations Ltd. (B.C. June 25, 1969)
May 19, 1994 – Name changed to Pacific Amber Resources Ltd.; basis 1 new for 5 old shs. ■

The Albany Corporation (Alta. 1980)
Aug. 17, 1993 – Name changed to LifeSpace Environmental Walls Inc. following amalgamation with a private co. named LifeSpace Environmental Walls Inc.; basis 21 new for 1,000 old shs. ■

Albany Oil & Gas Ltd. (Man. 1944)
1980 – Continued into Alberta.
May 17, 1988 – Name changed to The Albany Corporation. ■

Albany Resources Ltd. (B.C. May 31, 1979)
Dec. 14, 1993 – Continued into Yukon.
Apr. 7, 1995 – Name changed to International Albany Resources Ltd.; basis 1 new for 7 old shs. ■

Albany River Gold Mines Ltd. (Ont. July 16, 1938)
1945 – Acquired by Pickle Crow Gold Mines Ltd.; basis 1 new for 10 old shs. (see Pickle Crow Gold Mines Ltd.)

Albarmont Inc. (Que. 1971)
1985 – Name changed to Albarmont (1985) Inc.; basis 1 new for 3 old shs. (see FPsurvey - Mines & Energy)

Albarmont Mines Corporation (Que. 1971)
Name changed to Albarmont Inc. ■

Albarton Technologies Inc. (Alta. June 24, 1987)
Dec. 2, 2000 – Struck from registry and dissolved.

Albatros Gold Mines Ltd. (Que. 1956)
Aug. 17, 1985 – Charter cancelled.

Albedena Oils Ltd. (Alta. 1951)
Dec. 28, 1968 – Name changed to Nitracell Canada Ltd. ■

Albermont Petroleums Limited (Ont. 1951)
1956 – Acquired by Western Decalta Petroleum Ltd.; basis 1 new for 2 old shs. Co. notes also exchanged for Decalta notes par-for-par.

Alberni Mines Ltd. (B.C. 1964)
Feb. 2, 1983 – Struck off register.

Albert Mining Inc. (Can. Feb. 23, 1996)
Oct. 10, 2019 – Name changed to Windfall Geotek Inc. (see FPsurvey - Mines & Energy; FPsurvey - Industrials)

Alberta Central Developments Ltd. (unknown 1951)
1956 – Merged into Alscope Explorations Ltd.; basis 1 new for 2 old shs.

Alberta Central Oil Holdings Ltd. (unknown 1951)
Name changed to Alberta Central Developments Ltd. ■

Alberta Clipper Energy Inc. (Alta. June 3, 2005)
June 9, 2009 – Acquired by NAL Oil & Gas Trust; basis 0.078875 NAL Oil & Gas trust units for 1 Alberta Clipper com. sh. (see NAL Oil & Gas Trust)

Alberta Consolidated Gas Utilities Ltd. (Can. 1950)
May 20, 1954 – Name changed to Great Northern Gas Utilities Ltd. ■

Alberta Copper & Resources Ltd. (B.C. 1969)
1972 – Merged into Alberta Petroleums & Resources Ltd.; basis 1 new for 3 old shs. (see Alberta Petroleum & Resources Ltd.)

Alberta Diamondfields Inc. (Alta. Apr. 4, 1990)
Aug. 21, 2002 – Name changed to Delray Ventures Inc.; basis 1 new for 4 old shs. ■

Alberta Distillers Limited (Alta. 1946)
1964 – Acquired by National Distillers and Chemical Corp. of New York for $4.00 per sh. Holders of sh. purch. warr. received $1.00 for each sh. which would have been issuable through exercise of warr., upon surrender.

Alberta Eastern Gas Ltd. (Alta. 1968)
Oct. 31, 1976 – Approx. 99% of o/s shs. acquired by Ocelot Industries Ltd.; basis $9.00 plus one cl. B sh. of Ocelot for each sh. held. By July 1978 all remaining shs. were acquired. (see Ocelot Industries Ltd.)

Alberta Energy Company Ltd. (Alta. Sept. 18, 1973)
Apr. 8, 2002 – Amalgamated with PanCanadian Energy Corporation to form EnCana Corporation; basis 1.472 EnCana shs. for 1 Alberta Energy sh. (see Encana Corporation)

Alberta Fidelity Trust Co. (Alta. 1912)
Jan. 1969 – Assets and liabs. acquired by North West Trust Co.; basis 36,564 pref. shs. and 8,580 cl. A shs.

Alberta Focused Income & Growth Fund (Alta. Mar. 30, 2006)
Oct. 29, 2007 – Acquired by ACTIVEnergy Income Fund; basis 0.78214715 ACTIVEnergy unit for 1 Alberta Focused unit.

Alberta Gas Trunk Line Company Limited (Alta. 1954)
Sept. 1, 1980 – Name changed to NOVA, AN ALBERTA CORPORATION. ■

The Alberta Government Telephones Commission (Alta. 1906)
Oct. 1990 – Privatized with all of the assets, including all the o/s shs. in subsids., being transferred to a newly-formed mgmt. holding co., TELUS Corporation.

Alberta Gypsum Ltd. (Alta. Feb. 7, 1967)
Apr. 3, 1984 – Name changed to Alberta Pacific Gold Corporation. ■

Alberta Hotel Development Corp. (Alta. 1989)
Dec. 31, 1993 – Formed FirstEnergy Capital Corp. on amalgamation with FirstEnergy Capital Corp., subsequently became private; basis unknown. ■

Alberta Hotels & Resorts Inc. (Alta. Nov. 14, 1996)
June 5, 2002 – Amalgamated with private Alberta-based Canadian Destination Properties Inc.; basis 1 new Canadian Destination sh. for 5 old Alberta Hotels com. shs.

Alberta Leaseholds (Diversified) Limited (unknown)
1958 – In voluntary liquidation.

Alberta Minerals Limited (Alta. 1951)
Sept. 25, 1952 – Name changed to Pathfinder Leaseholds Limited. ■

Alberta Natural Gas Company Ltd. (Can. June 1, 1950; via Special Act of Parliament)
Mar. 28, 1996 – Acquired by TransCanada PipeLines Limited; basis $26.25 or 1.3588 TransCanada shs. for 1 Alberta Natural Gas sh. (see TransCanada PipeLines Limited)

Alberta Oil and Gas Limited (Alta. Mar. 25, 1986)
Dec. 1, 1997 – Name changed to Alberta Oil and Gas Petroleum Corp.; basis 1 new for 10 old shs. ■

Alberta Oil and Gas Petroleum Corp. (Alta. Mar. 25, 1986)
Apr. 23, 1998 – Formed Edge Energy Inc. pursuant to plan of arrangement amalgamation with Cairo Energy Inc., 763375 Alberta Ltd., 763387 Alberta Ltd. and 771988 Alberta Ltd.; basis 1 new for 3 old shs. ■

Alberta Oil Leaseholds Ltd. (Ont. May 14, 1949)
1952 – Assets acquired by West Plains Oil Resources Ltd.; basis 1 new for 3 old shs.

Alberta Oilsands Inc. (Alta. Dec. 5, 2003)
Dec. 6, 2016 – Formed Marquee Energy Ltd. in Alberta following reverse takeover acquisition of and amalgamation with (old) Marquee Energy Ltd. ■

Alberta Pacific Consolidated Oils, Limited (Alta. July 1914)
Mar. 8, 1965 – Merged with Canadian Industrial Gas & Oil Ltd.; basis 1 new for 13.7 old shs. (see Canadian Industrial Gas & Oil Ltd.)

Alberta Pacific Gold Corporation (Alta. Feb. 7, 1967)
Dec. 4, 1986 – Name changed to Golden Pacific Resources Inc. ■

Alberta Pacific Grain, Ltd. (Can. 1943)
June 6, 1967 – Assets merged with Federal Grain, Limited and its subsids. under agreement dated.

Alberta Pacific Leasing Corp. (Alta. Nov. 27, 1986)
July 18, 1989 – Name changed to Envirodyne International Inc. ■

Alberta Pacific Oil Co. Ltd. (unknown)
Merged with Alberta Pacific Consolidated Oils, Limited; basis 1 new for 1 old sh. (see Alberta Pacific Consolidated Oils, Limited)

Alberta Petroleum & Resources Ltd. (B.C. 1972 amalg.)
1977 – Acquired by Plains Investment Ltd.

Alberta Petroleum Co. Ltd. (unknown)
1914 – Acquired by Alberta Petroleum Consolidated Ltd.; basis 1 new for 1 old sh. (see Alberta Petroleum Consolidated Ltd.)

Alberta Petroleum Consolidated Ltd. (Alta. 1914)
1929 – In liquidation.
Mar. 15, 1941 – Dissolved and struck off register.

Alberta Phoenix Tube & Pipe Ltd. (Alta. 1955)
1967 – Name changed to Canadian Phoenix Steel & Pipe Ltd.

Alberta Power Limited (Can. 1971)
Apr. 1987 – No longer a public company effective.

Alberta Resource Capital Corporation (Alta. Aug. 30, 1985)
Feb. 1, 1999 – Struck off register.

Alberta Revenue Property Corporation (Alta. 1986)
July 17, 1991 – Acquired by 423187 Alberta Ltd., a wholly owned subsid. of Plaser Light Corporation; basis 0.0421 Plaser Light shs. for 1 Alberta Revenue Property sh. (see Plaser Light Corporation)

Alberta Royalties Syndicate (unknown)
Feb. 1954 – Acquired by Canadian Pipe Lines Producers Ltd. for 57,395 shs. (see Canadian Pipe Lines Producers Ltd.)

Alberta Skilift Ltd. (Alta. 1960)
1971 – Wound up.

Alberta Southern Oil Co., Ltd. (unknown)
1921 – Acquired by Southern Alberta Oils, Ltd.; basis 2 new for 1 old sh.

Alberta Star Development Corp. (Alta. Sept. 6, 1996)
July 15, 2015 – Name changed to Elysee Development Corp. (see FPsurvey - Industrials)

Alberta Star Mining Corp. (Alta. Sept. 6, 1996)
Sept. 20, 2001 – Name changed to Alberta Star Development Corp.; basis 1 new for 5 old shs. ■

Alberta Surface Systems Ltd. (Alta. Feb. 22, 1993)
July 14, 1999 – Name changed to MSI Energy Services Inc.; basis 1 new for 10 old shs. ■

Alberta Waste Resources & Energy Corporation (Alta. Nov. 8, 1993)
Mar. 1, 2000 – Struck from registry and dissolved.

Alberta Waters International Inc. (Alta. May 27, 1986)
Mar. 6, 1995 – Name changed to Loma Petroleum Resources Ltd.; basis 1 new for 4 old shs. ■

Albertan Federated Oils, Ltd. (Alta. Apr. 1930)
Struck off register.

Albertawest Forest Products Corporation Ltd. (Can. - unspecified)
June 1965 – Placed into voluntary liquidation.
Apr. 1966 – Alberta Supreme Court authorized distribution of $1,581,673 to registered shldrs. (approx. $1.10 per share).
Jan. 25, 1967 – Final distribution made.

Albertech Industries Ltd. (Alta. 1984)
May 1, 1994 – Dissolved and struck off register.

Albeta Mines Ltd. (B.C. 1961)
Mar. 1978 – R. W. Denson, liquidator, 759 Courtney St., Box 962, Victoria, B.C. Placed in voluntary liquidation. Assets reported distributed to shldrs.

Albion Pershing Gold Mines (Ont. 1945)
1954 – Name changed to Endeavor Mining Corp. Ltd.; basis 1 new for 1 old sh. ■

Albion Petroleum Ltd. (Alta. Apr. 4, 2005)
Mar. 30, 2015 – Name changed to First Mining Finance Corp. and continued into British Columbia following Qualifying Transaction reverse takeover acquisition of Sundance Minerals Ltd. (renamed KCP Minerals Inc.); basis 1 new for 4 old shs. ■

Albury Resources Ltd. (Alta. Apr. 9, 1980)
Sept. 25, 2009 – All assets were transferred to newly incorporated Albury Energy Ltd. Shldrs. received 1 Albury Energy sh. for each sh. held. Subsequently dissolved.

Alcan Aluminium Limited (Can. June 3, 1902)
Mar. 1, 2001 – Name changed to Alcan Inc. ■

Alcan Inc. (Can. June 3, 1902)
Nov. 16, 2007 – Acquired by Rio Tinto plc for US$101 per sh.
Jan. 1, 2008 – Name changed to Rio Tinto Alcan Inc.

Alcan Yellowknife Gold Mines Ltd. (Ont. 1944)
Sept. 1957 – Charter cancelled.

Alcanna Inc. (Can. Nov. 8, 2010)
Apr. 4, 2022 – Acquired by Sundial Growers Inc.; basis 8.85 Sundial shs. plus $1.50 cash for 1 Alcanna sh. (see Sundial Growers Inc.)

Alcanta International Education Ltd. (Cayman Islands Mar. 26, 1999)
Jan. 17, 2001 – Name changed to Access International Education Ltd.

Alcatel Canada Inc. (Can. June 6, 1986)
July 29, 2005 – All exch. shs. redeemed; basis 1 new Alcatel American Depositary Receipt (ADS) for 1 old exch. sh.
Jan. 1, 2007 – Name changed to Alcatel-Lucent Canada Inc.

Alcatel Networks Corporation (Can. June 6, 1986)
Oct. 5, 2000 – Name changed to Alcatel Canada Inc. ■

Alchemist Mining Inc. (B.C. Oct. 22, 2010)
Aug. 15, 2023 – Name changed to Lithos Energy Ltd. pursuant to the acquisition of Aqueous Resources LLC. ■

Alchemy Ventures Ltd. (B.C. May 17, 1984)
Jan. 22, 2004 – Name changed to i-minerals inc. and continued into Canada. ■

Alchib Developments Ltd. (Ont. 1969 amalg.)
Oct. 23, 1978 – Amalgamated with Kallio Iron Mines Ltd. (1 for 5) to form Kalrock Developments Ltd.; basis 1 new for 3 old shs.

Alcide Porcupine Mines Ltd. (Ont. 1939)
1957 – Charter cancelled.

Alcina Development Corporation (B.C. Apr. 11, 1962)
Apr. 7, 1986 – Delisted from the Vancouver Stock Exchange. Subsequently dissolved.

Alclare Resources Inc. (B.C. June 13, 1980)
Jan. 21, 1987 – Name changed to Chesapeake Computer Systems Inc. ■

Alcona Mines Ltd. (Ont. 1936)
May 16, 1975 – Charter cancelled.

Alcor Financial Corporation (Alta. 1989)
Jan. 31, 1992 – Amalgamated into Renoir Water Inc.; basis 2 shs. Renoir for each 1 com. sh. of Alcor. (see Renoir Water Inc.)

Alcor Minerals Ltd. (Alta. 1970)
July 4, 1974 – Name changed to Consolidated Alcor Resources Ltd.; basis 1 new for 5 old shs. ■

Alcor Resources Ltd. (B.C. Apr. 19, 1973)
June 16, 2008 – Name changed to Balto Resources Ltd. (see FPsurvey - Mines & Energy)

Alcourt Mines Limited (Ont. 1955)
Nov. 1972 – Charter cancelled.

Alcum Mining Ltd (B.C. 1975)
June 3, 1981 – Name changed to Code Petroleum Ltd. ■

Alda Industries Corporation (B.C. Nov. 23, 1983)
July 14, 1999 – Name changed to Crux Industries, Inc.; basis 1 new for 6 old shs. ■

Alda Mines Ltd. (B.C. 1967)
Mar. 18, 1977 – Dissolved.

Aldage Mines Ltd. (Ont. 1962)
1969 – Merged into Alchib Developments Ltd.; basis 9 new for 100 old shs.

AldeaVision Inc. (Can. June 3, 1992)
Oct. 4, 2006 – Name changed to AldeaVision Solutions Inc. following transfer of assets to newly created subsidiary AldeaVision Solutions Inc. following recapitalization and reorganization; basis 1 AldeaVision Solutions sh. and 0.0118737 VGS Seismic Canada Inc. cl. A shs. for 1 AldeaVision sh. ■

AldeaVision Solutions Inc. (Can. July 26, 2006)
Mar. 22, 2010 – Name changed to Aldea Solutions Inc. (see FPsurvey - Industrials)

Alder Resources Ltd. (B.C. Aug. 4, 2006)
Mar. 25, 2013 – Continued into Ontario. (see Rosita Mining Corporation)
July 28, 2015 – Acquired by Midlands Minerals Corporation; basis 1.81 Midlands com. shs. for 1 Alder com. sh. Subsequently, Midlands changed its name to Rosita Mining Corporation following a consolidation of its share 1 for 10. (see Rosita Mining Corporation)

Aldermac Copper Corporation Ltd. (Can. 1936)
Dec. 16, 1980 – Assets seized for bondholders following default of principal and interest of 5% bonds due Jan. 2, 1946. Payments made to secured creditors; nothing for common shldrs. Company dissolved.

Alderon Iron Ore Corp. (B.C. Mar. 21, 1978)
June 17, 2020 – Placed into receivership and Deloitte Restructuring Inc. appointed receiver. All officers and directors resigned.
Apr. 1, 2021 – Certain assets sold to Quebec Iron Ore Inc. and 12364042 Canada Inc. for an undisclosed amount. Monies used to repay indebtedness to Sprott Private Resources Lending (Collector), LP, with monies available for distrib. to creditors and shldrs.
Apr. 22, 2024 – Dissolved for failure to file and struck from registry.

Alderon Resource Corp. (B.C. Mar. 21, 1978)
Oct. 5, 2011 – Name changed to Alderon Iron Ore Corp. ■

Aldershot Resources Ltd. (Alta. Sept. 23, 1985)
Aug. 12, 1988 – Formed Eagle Lake Explorations Ltd. in Alberta on amalgamation with Eagle Lake Resources Ltd. ■

Aldershot Resources Ltd. (B.C. Sept. 8, 1987)
Jan. 4, 2019 – Continued into Alberta.
Jan. 7, 2019 – Name changed to Solo Growth Corp. ■

Aldever Resources Inc. (B.C. Apr. 13, 1992)
Feb. 13, 2020 – Name changed to Kiplin Metals Inc.; basis 1 new for 2.5 old shs. (see FPsurvey - Mines & Energy)

Aldfield Mining Corp. Ltd. (Que. 1955)
Mar. 1976 – Charter cancelled.

Aldina-Leduc Oil Company Limited (Alta. 1949)
Apr. 17, 1961 – Name changed to Norsul Oil & Mining Limited; basis 1 new for 10 old shs. ■

Aldona Mines Ltd. (Que. 1942)
Aug. 30, 1994 – Name changed to Aldona Resources Ltd. ■

Aldona Resources Ltd. (Que. 1942)
July 10, 1995 – Name changed to TCF Energy Inc.; basis 1 new for 10 old shs. ■

Aldor Exploration and Development Co. Ltd. (Ont. 1958)
1962 – Merged into Aldage Mines Ltd.

Aldred Investment Corp. (Canada) (Que. 1927)
1942 – First and final distribution made by Montreal Trust Co. as follows: for each $500 of debenture, $149.023, 2

shs. Quebec Power Co. and 4 shs. Shawinigan Water and Power Co.
May 1945 – Charter surrendered.

Aldrich Mining & Milling Co. Ltd. (Ont. 1944)
Nov. 21, 1955 – Dissolved.

Aldridge Minerals Inc. (B.C. June 6, 1994)
Dec. 27, 2018 – Acquired by Virtus Mining Ltd. (other than the 43.6% already held by Virtus); basis Cdn$0.10 per share.

Aldridge Resources Ltd. (B.C. June 6, 1994)
Apr. 21, 2004 – Name changed to Aldridge Minerals Inc.; basis 1 new for 4 old shs. ■

Aldrin Resource Corp. (B.C. Dec. 14, 2005)
Dec. 2, 2016 – Name changed to Power Metals Corp. (see FPsurvey - Mines & Energy)

Aldu Mines Ltd. (Ont. 1948)
1951 – Charter cancelled.

Aleafia Health Inc. (B.C. Feb. 2, 2007)
June 27, 2018 – Continued into Ontario.
Jan. 12, 2024 – Acquisition of certain assets by Red White & Bloom Brands Inc. for total consideration of $31,667,700. All issued and o/s shs. of the company were cancelled without consideration.
Mar. 1, 2024 – Assigned into bankruptcy and KSV Restructuring Inc. appointed trustee following termination of proceedings under the Companies' Creditor Arrangement Act (CCAA).

Aleeyah Capital Corp. (B.C. May 18, 2011)
July 24, 2012 – Name changed to Kesselrun Resources Ltd. pursuant to Qualifying Transaction acquisition of Bluffpoint gold project option agreement. (see FPsurvey - Mines & Energy)

Alegria Capital Inc. (Alta. May 14, 2003)
Apr. 23, 2004 – Continued into Alberta.
June 8, 2004 – Formed Pilot Energy Ltd. following Qualifying Transaction reverse takeover acquisition of and merger with Zidane Energy Inc. (private co.) for 9,746,547 Pilot com. shs. plus 1,600,000 wts. ■

Alegro Health Corp. (Can. Feb. 2, 2001)
Sept. 1, 2009 – Name changed to Centric Health Corporation. ■

Alert B&C Corporation (Can. Oct. 6, 1995)
Nov. 27, 2011 – Dissolved and struck from register.

Alert Care Corporation (Ont. Oct. 17, 1979)
Jan. 26, 2000 – Acquired by Alert Acquisition Corp.; basis $1.70 or 1 Alert Acquisition sh. for 1 Alert Care sh.

Aleta Resource Industries Ltd. (B.C. Jan. 26, 1966)
Sept. 12, 1984 – Name changed to Mandarin Capital Corporation. ■

Alewco Gold Mines Ltd. (Ont. May 5, 1937)
Liquidated.

Alexa Ventures Inc. (B.C. Sept. 8, 1986)
Nov. 26, 1999 – Name changed to Eiger Technology, Inc. ■

Alexander Energy Ltd. (Alta. Dec. 12, 1988)
Feb. 24, 2014 – Name changed to Spartan Energy Corp. pursuant to acquisition of Renegade Petroleum Ltd.; basis 1 new for 4 old shs. ■

Alexander News Corp. (Alta. June 20, 1994)
Jan. 25, 1996 – Name changed to Alexander News International Inc.; basis 1 new for 5 old shs. ■

Alexander News International Inc. (Alta. June 20, 1994)
Oct. 29, 1998 – Name changed to Alexander Resources International Inc. ■

Alexander Nubia International Inc. (Can. Apr. 30, 2008)
June 26, 2016 – Name changed to Aton Resources Inc. and continued into British Columbia. (see FPsurvey - Mines & Energy)

Alexander Red Lake Mines Ltd. (Ont. 1945)
Jan. 1977 – Name changed to Senlac Resources Inc.; basis 1 new for 10 old shs. ■

Alexander Resources International Inc. (Alta. June 20, 1994)
Apr. 28, 2000 – Name changed to African Sky Communications Incorporated. ■

Alexander Touche Insurance Inc. (Bermuda Nov. 21, 1985)
Sept. 29, 1995 – Acquired by Merchant Private Limited for $3.50 per sh. (see Merchant Private Limited)

Alexandra Capital Corp. (B.C. Oct. 17, 2011)
Oct. 30, 2018 – Name changed to Plymouth Rock Technologies Inc. following acquisition of (old) Plymouth Rock Technologies Inc. ■

Alexandria Minerals Corporation (Can. May 27, 2002)
Aug. 6, 2019 – Acquired by O3 Mining Inc.; basis 0.018041 O3 Mining com. shs. for 1 Alexandria sh. (see O3 Mining Inc.)

Alexco Resource Corp. (Yuk. Dec. 3, 2004)
Dec. 28, 2007 – Continued into British Columbia.
Sept. 12, 2022 – Acquired by Hecla Mining Company; basis 0.166 Hecla com. shs. for each com. sh. held valued at US$0.47 per sh.

Alexis Minerals Corporation (B.C. Aug. 8, 1988)
Feb. 16, 2004 – Continued into Ontario.
July 5, 2012 – Name changed to QMX Gold Corporation; basis 1 new for 20 old shs. ■

Alexis Nihon Finance Inc. (Que. 1974)
Apr. 24, 1991 – All 7.40% cum. redeem. pref. shs., ser. 1 redeemed for $25 plus dividends of $0.4625 per sh. payable to record holders of Mar. 31, 1991.

Alexis Nihon Real Estate Investment Trust (Que. Oct. 18, 2002)
May 24, 2007 – Acquired by Homburg Invest Inc. for $18.60 per unit. (see Homburg Invest Inc.)
July 2007 – Name changed to Homburg Real Estate Investment Trust. (see Homburg Invest Inc.)

Alexis Resources Ltd. (B.C. Aug. 8, 1988)
May 22, 2003 – Name changed to Alexis Minerals Corporation; basis 1 new for 3 old shs. ■

Alfred Lambert Inc. (Que. 1937)
July 31, 1973 – All o/s cl. A and cl. B shs. acquired by F.I.C. Fund Inc.; basis $25 per cl. A sh. Name subsequently changed to Famcorp Inc. effective June 26, 1985.

Alfred Lambert (1985) Inc. (Que. 1937)
June 26, 1985 – Name changed to A. Lambert International Inc. and continued into Quebec following reorganization of assets with parent co. Famcorp Inc. ■

Alfreida Nickel Mines Ltd. (Ont. 1957)
1966 – Charter cancelled.

Algae Biosciences Corporation (Alta. Jan. 3, 2008)
July 2, 2015 – Dissolved and struck from registry.

Algear Development Corporation (Can. Mar. 24, 1987)
Dec. 1, 1995 – Dissolved.

Algène Biotechnologies Corporation (Que. July 29, 1991)
May 1, 1996 – Continued into Quebec amalg.
July 6, 1999 – Name changed to SignalGene Inc.; basis 1 new com. for 1 old cl. B subord. vtg. sh. ■

Alger Gold Mines Ltd. (Ont. 1945)
1948 – Name changed to New Alger Mines Ltd.; basis 1 new for 3 old shs. ■

Algo Group Inc. (Can. June 25, 1954)
Dec. 10, 2011 – Dissolved and struck from register.

Algo Resources Ltd. (B.C. 1981)
Oct. 1, 1993 – Dissolved and struck off register.

Algold Resources Ltd. (Can. Feb. 23, 2011)
June 18, 2021 – Acquired by Aya Gold & Silver Inc.; basis 1 redeem. sh. for 1 Algold com. sh., redeemed for 1 Aya com. sh.

Algom Uranium Mines Ltd. (Ont. 1953)
1960 – Merged into Rio Algom Mines Limited; basis 165 new for 100 old shs.

The Algoma Central and Hudson Bay Railway Company (Can. Aug. 11, 1899; via Special Act of Parliament)
June 30, 1965 – Name changed to Algoma Central Railway. ■

Algoma Central Railway (Can. Aug. 11, 1899; via Special Act of Parliament)
Oct. 24, 1990 – Name changed to Algoma Central Corporation. (see FPsurvey - Industrials)

Algoma Central Railway Company (Can. Aug. 11, 1899; via Special Act of Parliament)
1901 – Name changed to The Algoma Central and Hudson Bay Railway Company. ■

Algoma Consolidated Trust (Can. - unspecified)
Apr. 22, 1957 – Interim distribution of $75 per whole unit made.
Jan. 23, 1961 – Second and final distribution of $61 per whole unit made.

Algoma Copper Mines Ltd. (Ont. Mar. 1942)
July 11, 1944 – Name changed to Bi-Ore Mines Ltd. ■

Algoma Exploration Co. Ltd. (Ont. 1925)
June 17, 1963 – Dissolved.

Algoma Finance Corp. (Ont. 1992)
Aug. 9, 1995 – Amalgamated with 125783 Ontario Inc., a wholly owned subsid. of Algoma Steel Inc.; basis (A) $24 plus an accrued divid. of $0.269 for each 5.50% pref. sh., (B) a percentage in cash, on the basis of $24, with the balance of the pref. shs. exchg'd on the basis of 2.75 Algoma Steel com. shs. plus a contingent value right for 1 old pref. sh., (C) 2.75 new Algoma Steel com. shs. plus a contingent value right for 1 old pref. sh. (see Algoma Steel Inc.)

Algoma Galena Co. Ltd. (Que. 1937)
Feb. 1973 – Charter cancelled.

Algoma Mining and Finance Ltd. (Ont. Mar. 19, 1928)
Dec. 18, 1936 – Merged into Maralgo Mines Limited; basis 1 new for 4 old shs. (see Maralgo Mines Limited)

Algoma Steel Company Limited (Ont. May 10, 1901)
July 1912 – Succeeded by Algoma Steel Coroporation. ■

Algoma Steel Coroporation (Ont. May 10, 1901)
Dec. 12, 1934 – Succeeded by The Algoma Steel Corporation, Limited. ■

The Algoma Steel Corporation, Limited (Ont. Dec. 12, 1934)
Oct. 15, 1988 – Acquired by Dofasco Inc.; basis $26.50 or 0.92 of a Dofasco sh. for 1 com. sh. and $26.25 or 0.91 of a Dofasco sh. for 1 cl. B pref. sh.
June 1, 1992 – Succeeded by Algoma Steel Inc. ■

Algoma Steel Inc. (Ont. June 1, 1992)
July 9, 1992 – All o/s The Algoma Steel Corporation, Limited pref. shs. ser. A shs. converted into 1.08620391531 com. shs. of Algoma Steel Inc. and all o/s pref. shs. ser. B converted into 1.11073146025 com. shs. of Algoma Steel Inc.
June 21, 2007 – Acquired by Essar Global Limited, a wholly owned subsid. of Essar Steel Holdings Limited; basis $56 per sh.
June 23, 2008 – Name changed to Essar Steel Algoma Inc. ■

Algoma Summit Gold Mines Ltd. (Ont. May 1934)
1939 – Name changed to Magino Gold Mines Ltd. and continued into Ontario. ■

Algonkian Uranium Corp. Ltd. (Ont. 1948)
1956 – Charter cancelled.

Algonquin Building Credits Limited (Ont. May 7, 1957)
Dec. 3, 1976 – Name changed to Algonquin Mercantile Corporation. ■

Algonquin Mercantile Corporation (Ont. May 7, 1957)
July 3, 2001 – Name changed to Automodular Corporation. ■

Algonquin Minerals Inc. (B.C. 1984)
June 2, 1992 – Name changed to Asean Holdings Inc.; basis 1 new for 3 old shs. (see FPsurvey - Industrials)

Algonquin Oil & Gas Limited (Alta. July 1, 1998 amalg.)
Mar. 8, 2012 – Name changed to PetroShale Inc. following reverse takeover acquisition of Mondak Petroleum Inc.; basis 1 new for 10 old shs. ■

Algonquin Petroleum Corporation (Alta. 1959)
July 1, 1998 – Amalgamated in Alberta to continue with same name.
Apr. 10, 2000 – Name changed to Algonquin Oil & Gas Limited; basis 1 new for 4 old shs. ■

Algonquin Power Income Fund (Ont. Sept. 8, 1997)
Oct. 29, 2009 – Converted into a corp. by way of plan of arrangement with Hydrogenics Corporation whereby Hydrogenics changed its name to Algonquin Power & Utilities Corp. (APUC), resulting in the fund becoming a wholly owned subsidiary; basis 1 APUC sh. for 1 Algonquin Power trust unit. All Hydrogenics assets and liabilities were transferred (except tax assets) to newly formed publicly listed Hydrogenics Corporation. Hydrogenics shldrs. exchanged shs. on a 1-for-1 basis for shs. of new Hydrogenics.
Mar. 4, 2010 – Name changed to Algonquin Power Co.

Algood Gold Mines Ltd. (unknown)
Mar. 1960 – Received 1 sh. Don Cameron Exploration Co. Ltd., for each 10 shs. Algood. Charter surrendered.

Algorithm Media Inc. (B.C. Oct. 23, 1987)
Dec. 18, 2009 – Name changed to Avere Energy Inc.; basis 1 new for 2 old shs. ■

Algray Mines (Québec) Ltd. (Ont. Nov. 1933)
1946 – Acquired by Beauchance Mines Ltd. for 1,000,000 shs.
1948 – Charter surrendered.

Algro Uranium Mines Ltd. (Ont. 1955)
Sept. 23, 1963 – Dissolved.

Aliant Inc. (Can. Mar. 9, 1999)
July 10, 2006 – Plan of Arrangement conversion into a new income trust named Bell Aliant Regional Communications Income Fund; basis 1 new Bell Aliant unit for 1 old Aliant com. sh. (see Bell Aliant Regional Communications Income Fund)

Alianza Holdings Ltd. (Ont. Apr. 24, 1996)
Apr. 30, 2015 – Acquired by Tarsis Resources Ltd. (renamed Alianza Minerals Ltd.); basis 1 Tarsis sh. for 1 Estrella sh.

Alianza Minerals Ltd. (B.C. Apr. 25, 2008)
Aug. 14, 2023 – Name changed to Silver North Resources Ltd.; basis 1 new for 5 old shs. (see FPsurvey - Mines & Energy)

Alias Research Inc. (Ont.)
June 16, 1995 – Merged into Silicon Graphics, Inc.; basis 0.90 new com. Silicon sh. for 1 com. Alias sh.

Alibaba Innovations Corp. (B.C. Sept. 19, 2013)
Nov. 3, 2016 – Name changed to Supreme Metals Corp. ■

Alice Arm Mines Ltd. (B.C. 1951)
1955 – Name changed to Frontier Exploration Ltd. ■

Alice Arm Mining Ltd. (B.C. Apr. 9, 1965)
Jan. 20, 1975 – Name changed to New Congress Resources Ltd.; basis 1 new for 5 old shs. ■

Alice Arm Molybdenum Co. Ltd. (B.C. Apr. 9, 1965)
Oct. 21, 1965 – Name changed to Alice Arm Mining Ltd. ■

Alice Lake Mines Ltd. (B.C. Sept. 28, 1955)
Oct. 29, 1993 – Name changed to Consolidated Alice Lake Mines Limited; basis 1 new for 4.5 old shs. ■

Alida Oil Co. Limited (Alta. 1955)
1958 – Name changed to Lobitos Oilfields Canada Ltd. ■

Alignvest Acquisition II Corporation (Ont. Feb. 28, 2017)
Dec. 5, 2019 – Continued into Bermuda.
Dec. 9, 2019 – Name changed to Sagicor Financial Company Ltd. pursuant to the Qualifying Acquisition of Sagicor Financial Corporation Limited. (see FPsurvey - Industrials)

Alignvest Acquisition Corporation (Ont. May 11, 2015)
Feb. 7, 2017 – Name changed to Trilogy International Partners Inc. pursuant to the Qualifying Acquisition of Trilogy International Partners LLC. Continued into British Columbia. ■

Aligro Inc. (Can. 1973)
Nov. 14, 1986 – Acquired by Steinberg Inc. for approx. 114,000,000 shs. consisting of 2,585,945 non-vtg. cl. A shs. and 5,171,890 conv. 4th pref. ser. 1 shs. (see Steinberg Inc.)

Alimentation Couche-Tard Inc. (Can. 1986)
June 22, 1994 – Acquired by Actidev Inc.; basis $3.00 or 1.48 Actidev shs. for 1 Alimentation Couche-Tard sh. (see Actidev Inc.)

Alina International Industries Ltd. (B.C. Mar. 14, 1966)
May 30, 1997 – Name changed to Addwest Minerals International, Ltd.; basis 1 new for 10 old shs. ■

Alina Mines and Oils Ltd. (B.C. Mar. 14, 1966)
Jan. 26, 1972 – Name changed to Alina International Industries Ltd. ■

Alinghi Minerals Inc. (B.C. Mar. 20, 1989)
Apr. 5, 2006 – Name changed to Dorex Minerals Inc. ■

Alio Gold Inc. (B.C. Mar. 17, 2005)
July 6, 2020 – Acquired by Argonaut Gold Inc.; basis 0.67 Argonaut shs. for 1 Alio Gold sh. (see Argonaut Gold Inc.)

Alit-El Mines Ltd. (Ont. 1968)
Feb. 20, 1980 – Dissolved.

Alita Resources Ltd. (B.C. July 5, 2009)
Aug. 1, 2014 – Name changed to Nexus Gold Corp. following the reverse takeover acquisition of Columbia Star Resources Corp. (see FPsurvey - Mines & Energy)

Alive International Inc. (Ont. July 15, 1994)
Mar. 22, 2004 – Name changed to Simberi Gold Corporation following amalgamation of wholly owned PNG Pacific Resources Inc. with 2034879 Ontario Limited, constituting a reverse takeover by 2034879 Ontario Limited. ■

Alix Resources Corp. (B.C. Dec. 5, 2007)
Dec. 6, 2017 – Name changed to Infinite Lithium Corp. ■

Aljema Rush Lake Mines Ltd. (Ont. 1946)
Feb. 1951 – Charter cancelled.

AlkaLi3 Resources Inc. (Alta. Jan. 24, 2008)
June 12, 2019 – Formed Loop Insights Inc. in British Columbia pursuant to the reverse takeover of and amalgamation with (old) Loop Insights Inc. ■

Alkaline Fuel Cell Power Corp. (B.C. Mar. 7, 1987)
May 4, 2023 – Name changed to Cleantech Power Corp. (see FPsurvey - Industrials)

Alkenore-Buffalo Gold Mines Ltd. (Ont. 1937)
1957 – Charter cancelled.

Alkey Industries Ltd. (B.C. 1964)
Oct. 24, 1983 – Name changed to American Volcano Minerals Corp. ■

All-Can Holdings Ltd. (B.C. 1965)
1979 – Placed into receivership. All assets sold for approx. $2.5 million to satisfy secured creditors. No distribution made to shldrs.
1981 – Receiver discharged.

All-Canadian Common Stock Trustee Shares Series A (Can. - unspecified 1930; via trust agreement)
Nov. 1, 1940 – Formed to hold a portfolio of Canadian common stocks for a ten-year term. Pd. dividends in each year. Terminated on maturity date.
Jan. 1, 1941 – Shs. redeemed at $10.7036 per sh.

All in West! Capital Corporation (Can. Aug. 16, 2005)
Aug. 16, 2017 – PricewaterhouseCoopers Inc. in the capacity of receiver for wholly owned All in West! Grande Cache I Ltd. and All in West! Grande Cache II Ltd. received approval from the court for the sale of the last remaining assets of the company. The company intends to allow its corporate registry to expire.
June 15, 2019 – Dissolved and struck from registry.

All-North Resources Ltd. (B.C. Aug. 8, 1988 amalg.)
July 10, 1996 – Name changed to International All-North Resources Ltd.; basis 1 new for 5 old shs. ■

All Quotes Data Ltd. (B.C. Aug. 4, 1989)
Mar. 8, 1995 – Name changed to AmCan Minerals Limited. (see FPsurvey - Mines & Energy)

All-Star Resources Ltd. (B.C. July 5, 1974)
Mar. 4, 1991 – Delisted from the Vancouver Stock Exchange. Subsequently dissolved.

Allan Resources Inc. (B.C. Aug. 25, 1988)
Feb. 8, 1996 – Name changed to Fortress Financial Corporation. ■

Allana Potash Corp. (Ont. Dec. 21, 2007)
June 25, 2015 – Acquired by Israel Chemicals Ltd. for 50¢ per sh.

Allana Resources Inc. (Alta. Dec. 4, 1995)
Dec. 21, 2007 – Continued into Ontario.
Jan. 14, 2010 – Name changed to Allana Potash Corp. ■

Allanco Iolite Monitor Corporation (B.C. June 24, 1983)
Jan. 16, 1989 – Name changed to AIM Safety Company Inc.; basis 1 new for 5 old shs. ■

Allante Resources Ltd. (B.C. June 16, 2006)
Jan. 12, 2021 – Name changed to World Copper Ltd. pursuant to the Qualifying Transaction reverse takeover acquisition of (old) World Copper Ltd. (concurrently renamed 1188893 B.C. Ltd.). (see FPsurvey - Mines & Energy)

Allarco Developments Ltd. (Alta. 1954)
Jan. 2, 1981 – Merged into Carma Developments Ltd. Carma purchased 51% int. from Cathton Holdings Ltd. at a price of $140 per sh. in November 1980, and subsequently offered remaining shldrs. $141 per sh. or 8.5 cl. A conv. shs. of Carma for 1 old Allarco sh.

Allard Bay Mines Ltd. (Que. 1958)
Nov. 1973 – Charter cancelled.

Allard River Mines Ltd. (Ont. 1956)
Apr. 2, 1969 – Charter cancelled.

Allbanc Split Corp. (Ont. Dec. 17, 1997)
Mar. 12, 2018 – Redeemed; basis $31.64 cash per cl. C pref. sh. and $75.7558 cash per cl. A capital sh.

Allbanc Split Corp. II (Ont. Dec. 7, 2005)
Mar. 1, 2021 – Redeemed; basis $25.67 cash per cl. A preferred shs. and $28.7955 cash per cl. B, ser, 2 preferred shs.

Allcop Mines Ltd. (Ont. 1956)
Oct. 24, 1973 – Charter cancelled.

Allcorp United Inc. (Ont. Sept. 29, 1975 amalg.)
Oct. 17, 1997 – Name changed to Ntex Incorporated following acquisition of Ntex Corporation; basis 1 new com. for 18 old com. or cl. A shs. ∎

Allegheny Enterprises Ltd. (Alta. Dec. 21, 1987)
Mar. 4, 1991 – Name changed to Allegheny Mines Corporation. ∎

Allegheny Mines Corporation (Alta. Dec. 21, 1987)
July 20, 1999 – Delisted from the Alberta Stock Exchange. Subsequently struck from register and dissolved.

Allegheny Mining & Explorations Co. Limited (Ont. 1964)
Mar. 1973 – Charter cancelled.

Allegiance Equity Corporation (Ont. Apr. 2, 1974)
Dec. 16, 2014 – Name changed to The Canadian Bioceutical Corporation. ∎

Allegiant Technologies Inc. (unknown Dec. 28, 1993)
Mar. 23, 1994 – Continued into Washington.
July 21, 1998 – Name changed to Shampan, Lamport Holdings Limited; basis 1 new for 4 old shs.

Allegro Property Inc. (B.C. Mar. 19, 1984)
July 5, 2000 – Name changed to Valdor Fiber Optics Inc. ∎

Allelix Biopharmaceuticals Inc. (Can. Aug. 21, 1981)
Dec. 29, 1999 – Formed NPS Allelix Corporation following acquisition by NPS Allelix Inc., a wholly owned subsid. of U.S.-based NPS Pharmaceuticals, Inc.; basis 0.3238 new NPS Allelix exch. sh. for 1 old Allelix com. sh.

Allen Berg Racing Ltd. (Alta. 1987)
June 1, 1993 – Dissolved and struck off register.

Allen-Vanguard Corporation (Ont. Nov. 17, 2003 amalg.)
Dec. 2009 – Commenced a Court-supervised process under the Companies' Creditors Arrangement Act (CCAA) for creditor and Court approval of a recapitalization transaction, and Deloitte & Touche Inc. was appointed monitor. Court approval was received on Dec. 16 and the recapitalization transaction was completed on Dec. 18. Under the transaction, Contagion AV Investments LLC, an affiliate of Versa Capital Management, Inc., became the new owner of the company. All com. shs. were cancelled and no distributions were made to shldrs.

Allenbee Petroleums Ltd. (Can. Mar. 12, 1948)
1951 – Acquired by Consolidated Allenbee Oil and Gas Co. Ltd.; basis 3 new for 5 old shs.

Alliance Atlantis Communications Inc. (Can. June 27, 1985)
Aug. 17, 2007 – Acquired by CanWest Global Communications Corp. and Goldman Sachs Capital Partners; basis $53 per cl. A and cl. B sh. (see Canwest Global Communications Corp.)

Alliance Building Corporation Limited (Ont. 1962)
Sept. 1978 – Amalgamated with 391314 Ontario Ltd. to continue under name of Alliance Building Corp. Ltd. Com. shldrs. received cl. C pref. shs. on sh.-for-sh. basis; subsequently redeemed at $5.25 per sh. All o/s warr. exercised prior to amalg.

Alliance Communications Corporation (Can. June 27, 1985)
Sept. 23, 1998 – Formed Alliance Atlantis Communications Inc. following merger with Atlantis Communications Inc. ∎

Alliance Credit Corporation (Que. 1955)
Apr. 18, 1977 – Assets liquidated: Montreal Trust Co., 777 Dorchester Blvd. W., Montreal, Que., trustee. The following partial payts. were made on the reducing balance to the secured noteholders: 30% on Oct. 31, 1967; 25% on Dec. 15, 1967; 30% on Feb. 29, 1968; 30% on Apr. 30, 1968; 40% on July 31, 1968; 30% on Nov. 29, 1968; 30% on Mar. 31, 1969; 40% on June 30, 1969. The payments made Feb. 21, 1972, plus 10th and final payment July 10, 1972, brought total payments to 100%

of princ. and int. on notes and coupons, plus a portion of the prem. and int. thereon per settlement authorized Mar. 1, 1972. Trust General du Canada, 10 ouest, rue Saint-Jacques, Montreal, Que., trustee for secured deb. holders made pay. of 12% on Mar. 15, 1971, 14% on Jan. 14, 1972, 25% on Sept. 15, 1972, 14% on Nov. 1, 1973, 8% on Dec. 17, 1974, and final paymt. of 7.03% on Apr. 18, 1977.

Alliance Energy Inc. (Alta. Feb. 3, 1992)
Apr. 25, 2001 – Acquired by APF Energy Inc.; basis $2.02 or 0.201 new APF trust unit for 1 old Alliance com. sh. (see APF Energy Trust)

Alliance Financing Group Inc. (Ont. Jan. 31, 2000)
Nov. 30, 2010 – Name changed to Stream Ventures Inc.; basis 1 new for 3 old shs. ∎

Alliance Forest Products Inc. (Can. Mar. 11, 1994)
Sept. 25, 2001 – Formed Bowater Canadian Forest Products Inc. pursuant to plan of arrangement with U.S.-based Bowater Incorporated; basis $13 plus either 0.166 exch. shs. of Bowater Canada Inc. or 0.166 com. shs. of Bowater Incorporated. ∎

Alliance Grain Traders Income Fund (Ont. June 25, 2004)
Sept. 18, 2009 – Converted into a corporation pursuant to plan of arrangement with wholly owned Alliance Grain Traders Inc.(AGTI); basis 1 AGTI com. sh. for 1 Alliance Grain Traders trust unit and 1 AGTI com. sh. for 1 Alliance Pulse Processors Inc. exch. sh. Subsequently dissolved. (see Alliance Grain Traders Inc.)

Alliance Grain Traders Inc. (Ont. July 2, 2009)
Oct. 3, 2014 – Name changed to AGT Food and Ingredients Inc. ∎

Alliance Mining and Securities Ltd. (Can. 1930)
1945 – No report.

Alliance Mining Corp. (Can. Feb. 3, 2002)
Oct. 12, 2018 – Continued into British Columbia. (see FPsurvey - Mines & Energy)

Alliance Pacific Gold Corp. (Yuk. June 12, 1997)
Sept. 24, 1998 – Name changed to International Alliance Resources Inc.; basis 1 new for 15 old shs. ∎

Alliance Resources Ltd. (B.C. Aug. 1, 1969)
Oct. 19, 1993 – Name changed to ACREX Ventures Ltd.; basis 1 new for 5 old shs. ∎

Alliance Split Income Trust (Ont. Apr. 15, 2004)
Aug. 5, 2008 – Together with Diversified Income Trust II, merged with Premier Value Income Trust to continue as Premier Value Income Trust; basis Alliance Split Income Trust (1.5814554810-for-1) and Diversified Income Trust II (1.1864599-for-1). (see Premier Value Income Trust)

Alliance Uranium Mines Ltd. (Ont. 1953)
June 1, 1959 – Dissolved.

AlliancePharma Inc. (Que. Mar. 5, 2008)
Feb. 1, 2017 – Name changed to KDA Group Inc. (see FPsurvey - Industrials)

Allican Resources Inc. (Can. Apr. 1, 1995 amalg.)
Mar. 12, 2007 – Dissolved.

Allied Cellular Systems Limited (B.C. Sept. 8, 1986)
May 4, 1993 – Delisted from the Vancouver Stock Exchange. Subsequently dissolved and struck from register.

Allied Chemical Corporation (N.Y. 1920)
Apr. 28, 1981 – Name changed to Allied Corporation. ∎

Allied Consolidated Energy Inc. (Alta. Feb. 27, 1998)
May 10, 1999 – Name changed to Allied Oil & Gas Corp.; basis 1 new for 5 old shs. ∎

Allied Copper Corp. (Ont. July 7, 1997)
Apr. 27, 2023 – Name changed to Volt Lithium Corp. ∎

Allied Corporation (N.Y. 1920)
Sept. 19, 1985 – Formed Allied-Signal Inc. in Delaware on amalgamation with The Signal Companies, Inc.; basis 1 new for 1 old sh. ∎

Allied Critical Metals Inc. (B.C. Dec. 1, 2014)
Continued into Cayman Islands. (see FPsurvey - Mines & Energy)

Allied Environmental Services Corporation (B.C. June 23, 1983)
Aug. 21, 1991 – Name changed to Philip Environmental Services (B.C.) Inc. ∎

Allied Equities Ltd. (Alta. June 3, 1987)
Nov. 16, 2022 – Struck from registry and dissolved.

Allied Gold Limited (Australia May 26, 2003)
June 30, 2011 – Name changed to Allied Gold Mining plc; basis 1 new for 6 old shs. ∎

Allied Gold Mining plc (U.K. Mar. 7, 2011)
Sept. 10, 2012 – Acquired by St Barbara Limited for A$1.025 plus 0.8 St Barbara shs. for 1 Allied Gold sh.

Allied Hotel Properties Inc. (B.C. Aug. 31, 1982)
Dec. 22, 2021 – Privatized via acquisition of all o/s shs. not already held acquired by Allied Holdings Ltd., a company owned by Peter Y. L. Eng, the company's CEO for 28¢ cash per sh.

Allied Investors Syndicate Limited (Bahamas 1967)
1971 – Name changed to A.I.S. Resources Limited. (see FPsurvey - Mines & Energy)

Allied Lithium & Minerals Co. Ltd. (unknown)
1965 – Declared defunct.

Allied-Lyons PLC (U.K. 1961)
Mar. 8, 1996 – Name changed to Allied Domecq PLC.

Allied Mines Ltd. (B.C. 1952)
May 1972 – Charter cancelled.
July 1973 – Charter revived.
1973 – Name changed to Allied Resources Ltd. ∎

Allied Mining & Development Co. Ltd. (B.C. 1940)
1952 – Acquired by Allied Mines Ltd. (see Allied Mines Ltd.)

Allied Mining Corporation (Que. 1950)
June 28, 1973 – Merged with United Asbestos Corp. Ltd. to form United Asbestos Inc.

Allied Nevada Gold Corp. (Del. Oct. 14, 2006)
Oct. 9, 2015 – Name changed to Hycroft Mining Corporation.

Allied Northern Capital Corporation (Ont. 1988)
Nov. 9, 2010 – Name changed to Shoal Point Energy Ltd. pursuant to amalgamation of wholly owned subsid. of Allied Northern with Shoal Point Energy Ltd., which constituted a reverse takeover of Allied Northern by Shoal Point. (see FPsurvey - Mines & Energy)

Allied Northern Resources Ltd. (Ont. 1988)
Jan. 9, 2009 – Name changed to Allied Northern Capital Corporation. ∎

Allied Oil & Gas Corp. (Alta. Feb. 27, 1998)
Feb. 1, 2002 – Amalgamated with 942235 Alberta Ltd., an indirect wholly owned subsid. of the City of Medicine Hat; basis $2.65 per sh.

Allied Oil Producers Ltd. (Alta. 1940)
1951 – Acquired by Canadian Atlantic Oil Co. Ltd.; basis 1 new for 6 old shs. (see Canadian Atlantic Oil Co. Ltd.)

Allied Pacific Properties and Hotels Ltd. (B.C. Apr. 7, 1983)
Apr. 1, 2008 – All shs. except those held by Allied Holdings Ltd. exchanged for redeemable Amalco pref. shs. on a sh.-for-sh. basis following amalgamation with Allied Holdings Ltd. Amalco pref. shs. subsequently redeemed for $0.125 per sh.

Allied Petroleum Inc. (Alta. Feb. 27, 1998)
Nov. 27, 1998 – Name changed to Allied Consolidated Energy Inc. following acquisition of the assets of NCE Oil & Gas Income Property Fund and NCE Income Resources Corp.; basis 1 new for 2 old shs. ■

Allied Petroleum of Canada Ltd. (Ont. 1948)
1965 – Charter cancelled.

Allied Pitch-Ore Mines Ltd. (Ont. 1949)
May 1972 – Charter cancelled.

Allied Resources Inc. (W.Va. Apr. 15, 1979)
Feb. 26, 2002 – Continued into Nevada.

Allied Resources Ltd. (B.C. 1952)
Dec. 1978 – Charter cancelled.

Allied Roxana Minerals Ltd. (Alta. 1936)
Feb. 25, 1974 – Merged into Cavalier Energy Inc.; basis 1 new for 3.54 old shs.

Allied-Signal Inc. (Del. Sept. 19, 1985 amalg.)
Dec. 2, 1999 – Name changed to Honeywell International Inc.; basis 1 new for 1 old sh. ■

Allied Strategies Inc. (B.C. Oct. 23, 1984)
May 29, 1996 – Name changed to Sleeman Breweries Ltd.; basis 1 new for 5 old shs. ■

Allied Telemedia Limited (Ont. 1944)
Mar. 16, 1976 – Dissolved.

Allied Towers Merchants Limited (Ont. 1962)
Apr. 1967 – Acquired by Oshawa Wholesale Limited; basis 3 Oshawa cl. A shs. for 10 Allied Towers 6% pref. shs.; 1 Oshawa cl. A sh. for 13 Allied Towers com. shs. and 1 Oshawa cl. A sh. for 17 Allied Towers com. shs. represented by voting trust certificate. (see Oshawa Wholesale Limited)

Allied Venture Properties Limited (Alta. Apr. 9, 1974 amalg.)
Aug. 1, 1978 – Name changed to Buckingham International Holdings Ltd.; basis unknown. ■

Allison Pass Mining Ltd. (B.C. 1965)
Sept. 23, 1974 – Dissolved and struck off register.

Allkem Limited (Australia Jan. 20, 2005)
Jan. 8, 2024 – Acquired by Arcadium Lithium plc; basis 1 Arcadium Lithium CDI for 1 Allkem ord. sh.

Allman Technologies Inc. (Can. May 11, 2005)
Apr. 27, 2009 – Name changed to Avaranta Resources Ltd. ■

Allmed International Investments Corp. (B.C. Nov. 20, 1978)
Feb. 7, 1997 – Name changed to Ecoprogress Canada Holdings Inc. ■

Allmetal Mines Ltd. (Ont. 1943)
Charter cancelled.

Allnet Secom Inc. (Alta. Aug. 20, 1997)
Feb. 2, 2012 – Struck from registry and dissolved.

Allon Therapeutics Inc. (Can. June 28, 2002)
July 16, 2013 – Acquired by Paladin Labs Inc. pursuant to a proposal under the Bankruptcy and Insolvency Act; basis $900,000 cash payment and redemption of all o/s shs. for $1.00 cash.
May 7, 2015 – Voluntarily dissolved.

Allore Rouyn Metals Corp. Ltd. (Ont. 1946)
1957 – Charter cancelled.

Alloy Capital Corp. (Alta. Nov. 13, 2007)
Dec. 20, 2010 – Name changed to Mkango Resources Inc. pursuant to Qualifying Transaction reverse takeover acquisition of Lancaster Exploration Limited; basis 1 new for 2.5 old shs. (see FPsurvey - Mines & Energy)

Alloycorp Mining Inc. (B.C. Feb. 2, 2006)
Aug. 10, 2016 – Privatized via amalgamation with 1080224 B.C. Ltd., wholly owned by Resource Capital Fund IV L.P. and Resource Capital Fund VI L.P., to continue under the Alloycorp name; basis 5¢ cash per sh.

Allrich Energy Group Inc. (Alta. Nov. 18, 1993)
Aug. 2, 1996 – Name changed to AltaRex Corp. following Qualifying Transaction reverse takeover acquisition of AltaRex Inc. ■

Allseasons Building Products Inc. (Alta. Feb. 3, 1995)
Oct. 6, 2000 – Formed Gemini Corporation in Alberta on amalgamation with Gemini Engineering Inc. and Kinetic Projects Inc. ■

Allstate Mining Corp. Ltd. (Ont. 1954)
Sept. 23, 1963 – Charter cancelled.

Allstate Uranium Corp. Ltd. (Ont. 1954)
Oct. 1959 – Name changed to Allstate Mining Corp. Ltd. ■

Allstream Inc. (Can. July 14, 1997)
June 4, 2004 – Plan of Arrangement acquisition by Manitoba Telecom Services Inc.; basis $23 and either 1.0909 new Telecom com. shs. or 1.0909 new Telecom cl. B pfce shs. for 1 cl. A or cl. B Allstream sh. (see Manitoba Telecom Services Inc.)
Name changed to Zayo Canada Inc. (see Manitoba Telecom Services Inc.)

Allure Industries Corporation (B.C. June 23, 1983)
Aug. 29, 1990 – Name changed to Allied Environmental Services Corporation; basis 1 new for 4 old shs. ■

Allure Resource Corporation (B.C. June 23, 1983)
Aug. 6, 1987 – Name changed to Allure Industries Corporation. ■

Allwest Industries Ltd. (B.C. 1966)
1982 – Placed into receivership and declared bankrupt. No distribution to unsecured creditors or shldrs.

Allyn Resources, Inc. (Alta. Nov. 19, 1987)
Nov. 18, 2004 – Continued into British Columbia.
Jan. 14, 2008 – Name changed to Troy Energy Corp.; basis 1 new for 5 old shs. ■

Alma Industries Inc. (Alta. 1981)
Sept. 1, 1989 – Name changed to Dynamax Petrochemical Corporation; basis 1 new for 3 old shs. ■

Alma Oil & Gas Ltd. (Alta. Aug. 22, 1994)
Feb. 16, 2000 – Amalgamation of Alma Oil & Gas with 854139 Alberta Ltd., a wholly owned subsid. of Hornet Energy Ltd.; basis 0.1613 Hornet shs. for 1 com. sh. Alma. (see Hornet Energy Ltd.)

Alma Resources Ltd. (B.C. Nov. 3, 1993)
May 15, 2008 – Name changed to Remstar Resources Ltd. ■

Almada Explorations Ltd. (Ont. 1966)
Apr. 1975 – Charter cancelled.

Almaden Resources Corporation (B.C. Sept. 25, 1980)
Dec. 31, 2001 – Amalgamated with Fairfield Minerals Ltd. to form Almaden Minerals Ltd.; basis 1 new for 1 Fairfield sh. and 0.77 new for 1 Almaden Resources sh. (see Almaden Minerals Ltd.)

Almadex Minerals Limited (B.C. Apr. 10, 2015)
May 18, 2018 – Name changed to Azucar Minerals Ltd. (see FPsurvey - Mines & Energy)

Almahust Energy Corp. (B.C. May 5, 1972)
Jan. 17, 1984 – Name changed to Canadian Entech Research Corp. ■

Almar Mining Corp. Ltd. (Que. 1956)
Nov. 4, 1978 – Charter cancelled.

Almarco Industries Ltd. (Alta. Sept. 27, 1954)
Mar. 13, 1999 – Struck off register.

Almark Capital Ltd. (Alta. 1974)
Feb. 1, 1992 – Formed Bioniche Inc. in Canada on amalgamation with two of Vetrepharm Inc.'s wholly owned subsidiaries, Bioniche Inc. and Caneire (Canada) Inc.; basis 1 new for 4 old shs. ■

Almark Resources Ltd. (Alta. 1974)
July 14, 1986 – Name changed to Almark Capital Ltd. ■

Almaza Mining Co. Ltd. (B.C. 1969)
Apr. 1975 – Charter cancelled.

Almine Resources Ltd. (B.C. 1980)
Aug. 18, 1989 – Dissolved.

Alminex Limited (Can. 1951)
Dec. 1, 1977 – Acquired by Canadian Superior Oil Ltd.; basis $7.00 plus 1/13 of a Canadian Superior sh. for 1 Alminex sh. (see Canadian Superior Oil Ltd.)

Alminister Oils Ltd. (Ont. 1948)
Aug. 1957 – Amalgamated with Continental Consolidated Mines & Oils Corp. Ltd.; basis 1 new for 10 old shs. (see Continental Consolidated Mines & Oils Corp. Ltd.)

Almo Capital Corp. (B.C. Apr. 16, 1999)
July 27, 2016 – Name changed to Blackrock Gold Corp. ■

Almont Capital Corp. (Alta. May 4, 2000)
Oct. 26, 2001 – Continued into Canada.
Dec. 24, 2001 – Name changed to Biophage Pharma Inc. on Qualifying Transaction reverse takeover acquisition of Biophage Inc. (see FPsurvey - Industrials)

Almonty Industries Inc. (B.C. Sept. 28, 2009)
Mar. 27, 2012 – Continued into Canada. (see FPsurvey - Mines & Energy)

Almore Explorations Ltd. (Ont. 1970)
Oct. 1973 – Amalgamated with 3 other cos. to form Tri-Bridge Consolidated Gold Mines Ltd.; basis 1 new for 10 old shs.

Almos Mines Limited (Ont. 1970)
Feb. 4, 1977 – Dissolved.

Aloak Corp. (Alta. Oct. 10, 1986)
June 22, 2006 – Name changed to Okalla Corp. ■

Alona Uranium Mines Ltd. (Ont. 1948)
Dec. 7, 1959 – Charter cancelled.

Alopex Gold Inc. (Can. Feb. 22, 2017)
June 8, 2018 – Name changed to AEX Gold Inc. ■

Alotta Resources Ltd. (B.C. 1983)
Apr. 2, 2007 – Struck from register and dissolved.

Alouette Mines Limited (Que. 1954)
Nov. 1972 – Charter cancelled.

Alouette Uranium & Copper Mines Inc. (Que. 1954)
1956 – Name changed to Alouette Mines Limited. ■

Alouettes 1974 Capital Inc. (Alta. Sept. 13, 2000)
Dec. 31, 2001 – Formed Caxton Group Inc. in Ontario following Qualifying Transaction reverse takeover acquisition of and amalgamation with Caxton Group Inc. ■

Alpa Industries Ltd. (Ont. 1969)
Mar. 1975 – Amalgamated with Desatoya Ltd., a subsid. of Reed Paper Ltd., to form Reed Lumber Co. Ltd. Shldrs. entitled to pref. shs. of the amalg. co. on a sh.-for-sh. basis; new shs. subsequently redeemed at $12 per sh.

Alpaka Resources Corp. (Can. May 6, 1987)
July 12, 2004 – Dissolved.

Alpetro Resources Ltd. (Alta. Oct. 6, 1994)
Dec. 6, 2011 – Privatized at 39¢ per sh.

Alpha Aracon Radio Electronics Limited (Ont. 1940)
July 1965 – Placed into receivership, following withdrawal of bank line of credit. Receiver: Clarkson Co.
July 1966 – Assets sold by auction.

Alpha Communications Corp. (Ont. Apr. 22, 1998)
Sept. 1, 2000 – Name changed to Lingo Media Inc. ■

Alpha Copper Corp. (B.C. Mar. 29, 2018)
Feb. 18, 2025 – Name changed to Star Copper Corp. (see FPsurvey - Mines & Energy)

Alpha Esports Inc. (B.C. Mar. 1, 2019)
Dec. 1, 2020 – Name changed to Alpha Esports Tech Inc. ■

Alpha Esports Tech Inc. (B.C. Mar. 1, 2019)
Jan. 11, 2022 – Name changed to Alpha Metaverse Technologies Inc. ■

Alpha Exploration Inc. (B.C. Sept. 27, 2013)
Sept. 28, 2014 – Acquired by Lakeland Resources Inc. (renamed ALX Uranium Corp.); basis 0.5 ALX Uranium com. sh. for 1 Alpha sh. (see ALX Uranium Corp.)

Alpha Gold Corp. (B.C. Feb. 25, 1985)
Aug. 20, 2013 – Name changed to ALQ Gold Corp.; basis 1 new for 10 old shs. ■

Alpha-Larder Mines Ltd. (Ont. 1938)
1957 – Charter cancelled.

Alpha Lithium Corporation (B.C. Oct. 1, 2009)
Dec. 21, 2023 – Acquired by Tecpetrol Investments S.L.; basis $1.48 cash per sh.

Alpha Metaverse Technologies Inc. (B.C. Mar. 1, 2019)
June 15, 2023 – Name changed to AlphaGen Intelligence Corp. (see FPsurvey - Industrials)

Alpha Minerals Inc. (Alta. July 19, 2000)
Dec. 6, 2013 – Acquired by Fission Uranium Corp.; basis 5.725 shs. of Fission and 0.5 shs. of Alpha Exploration for 1 Alpha Minerals sh. (see Fission Uranium Corp.)
Apr. 1, 2014 – Amalgamated with Fission Uranium Corp. (see Fission Uranium Corp.)

Alpha Mines Ltd. (B.C.)
Feb. 1977 – Dissolved.

Alpha North Esports & Entertainment Inc. (B.C. Mar. 1, 2019)
Aug. 19, 2020 – Name changed to Alpha Esports Inc. ■

Alpha-Omega Industries Inc. (B.C. Mar. 20, 1981)
Aug. 9, 1991 – Dissolved and struck off register.

Alpha-Omega Resources Corporation (B.C. Mar. 20, 1981)
Sept. 18, 1985 – Name changed to Alpha-Omega Industries Inc. ■

Alpha One Corporation (Ont. June 18, 2002)
Apr. 27, 2011 – Formed Solvista Gold Corporation in Ontario following Qualifying Transaction amalgamation with Solvista Gold Corporation; basis 1 new sh. for 1 Solvista sh. and 0.470588 new shs. for 1 Alpha One sh. ■

Alpha Peak Capital Inc. (B.C. June 23, 2015 amalg.; other amalgamating entity was 1016772 B.C. Ltd)
Sept. 5, 2023 – Name changed to Fiddlehead Resources Corp. ■

Alpha Peak Leisure Inc. (B.C. June 24, 2011)
June 23, 2015 – Amalgamated in British Columbia to continue with same name; other amalgamating entity was 1016772 B.C. Ltd.
Apr. 20, 2021 – Voluntarily delisted.
May 3, 2021 – Name changed to Alpha Peak Capital Inc.; basis 1 new for 10 old shs. ■

Alpha Ventures Inc. (Alta. Apr. 22, 1996)
Apr. 22, 1998 – Continued into Ontario.
Aug. 28, 1998 – Name changed to Alpha Communications Corp. ■

Alpha Yellowknife Gold Mines Ltd. (Ont. 1945)
June 1953 – Charter cancelled.

Alphamin Resources Corp. (B.C. Aug. 12, 1981)
Sept. 30, 2014 – Continued into Mauritius. (see FPsurvey - Mines & Energy)

Alphanco Venture Corp. (B.C. Aug. 1, 2018)
June 14, 2021 – Continued into Alberta.
July 12, 2021 – Name changed to Marvel Biosciences Corp. pursuant to the Qualifying Transaction reverse takeover acquisition of Marvel Biotechnology Inc., and concurrent amalgamation of (old) Marvel with wholly owned 2306696 Alberta Ltd. (see FPsurvey - Industrials)

AlphaNet Telecom Inc. (Ont. May 4, 1990)
Feb. 8, 1999 – Declared bankrupt and all directors had resigned. PricewaterhouseCoopers Inc. of Toronto was appointed trustee. Distributions were made to employees, secured and unsecured creditors but no funds were available for shldrs.
July 4, 2005 – Trustee discharged.

Alpine Exploration Corporation (B.C. May 12, 1980)
Nov. 19, 1997 – Name changed to Shiega Resources Corporation and continued into Yukon. ■

Alpine Oil Services Corporation (Alta. Aug. 22, 1989)
Aug. 21, 2000 – Following Plan of Arrangement with U.S.-based Weatherford International, Inc. all com. shs. were acquired in exchange for 0.039 of an exchangeable sh. of Weatherford Oil Services, Inc. or 0.039 of a Weatherford International common share for each Alpine com. sh. held. (see Weatherford Oil Services, Inc.)

Alpine Silver Ltd. (B.C. 1978)
Dec. 13, 1984 – Name changed to High Level Resources Ltd. ■

Alpine Subsurface Electronics Inc. (Alta. Aug. 22, 1989)
Mar. 1, 1994 – Name changed to Alpine Oil Services Corporation. ■

Alquin Mines Ltd. (B.C. 1966)
1969 – Name changed to Alquin Pacific Ltd. ■

Alquin Pacific Ltd. (B.C. 1966)
Oct. 15, 1974 – Dissolved.

Alrose Mining Co. Ltd. (Ont. 1959)
May 1980 – Charter cancelled.

Alsab Mines Ltd. (Que. 1957)
Feb. 15, 1975 – Charter cancelled.

The Alschbach Gold Mining Company, Limited (Ont. Aug. 28, 1922)
Feb. 25, 1985 – Name changed to Hispyke Explorations Inc. ■

Alschbach Kirkland Gold Mines Ltd. (Ont. 1937)
1944 – Name changed to Mylake Mines Ltd. ■

Alscope Consolidated Ltd. (Alta. Sept. 27, 1954)
Aug. 13, 1976 – Name changed to Almarco Industries Ltd.; basis 1 new for 10 old shs. ■

Alscope Explorations Ltd. (Alta. Sept. 27, 1954)
July 4, 1961 – Name changed to Alscope Consolidated Ltd.; basis 1 new for 7 old shs. ■

Alset Capital Inc. (B.C. Jan. 27, 2009)
Aug. 23, 2024 – Name changed to Alset AI Ventures Inc. (see FPsurvey - Industrials)

Alset Energy Corp. (B.C. July 10, 2003)
May 4, 2017 – Name changed to Alset Minerals Corp. ■

Alset Minerals Corp. (B.C. July 10, 2003)
Aug. 22, 2018 – Name changed to OrganiMax Nutrient Corp. ■

Alsof Mines Ltd. (Ont. 1957)
Aug. 1972 – Charter cancelled.

Alster Energy Ltd. (B.C. Dec. 22, 1980)
Oct. 21, 1983 – Name changed to New Alster Energy Ltd. ■

Alston Energy Inc. (Alta. Dec. 8, 2011)
July 25, 2012 – Amalgamated with CanRock Energy Corp., constituting a reverse takeover by CanRock Energy Corp., basis 1 new for 1 old sh. and 2.321 new for 1 CanRock sh. (see Alston Energy Inc.)

Alston Energy Inc. (Alta. July 17, 2012 amalg.)
May 9, 2014 – Placed into receivership and all officers and directors resigned. Alvarez and Marsal Canada Inc. appointed receiver.
Aug. 2014 – Sale of Pembina and minor properties completed for $469,480.
May 15, 2015 – Sale of Provost properties completed for $1,240,000.
May 23, 2015 – Alvarez and Marsal Canada discharged as monitor. No funds available for distribution to shldrs.

Alston Ventures Inc. (B.C. Nov. 1, 2007)
Dec. 8, 2011 – Name changed to Alston Energy Inc. and continued into Alberta. ■

Alta Explorations Inc. (B.C. May 13, 1981)
Mar. 15, 1994 – Name changed to Akash Ventures Inc.; basis 1 new for 5 old shs. ■

Alta Genetics Inc. (Can. Dec. 31, 1987 amalg.)
Aug. 3, 2000 – Going private transaction; basis $4.00 per com. sh.

Alta-Kor Inc. (Alta. Oct. 28, 1994)
Dec. 1999 – HSBC Bank Canada demanded payment of approx. $2,300,000 owed to HSBC as of Nov. 9, 1999.
Mar. 24, 2000 – Sought protection under the Companies' Creditor Arrangement Act (CCAA) which was terminated and PricewaterhouseCoopers in Edmonton, Alta., was appointed receiver.
2002 – All assets sold and a partial distribution was made to secured creditors.
June 30, 2003 – Receiver discharged. There were no funds available for distribution to shldrs.

Alta Mines Ltd. (Que. 1945)
May 12, 1959 – Name changed to Carbec Mines Ltd. ■

Alta Mira Energy Corp. (Alta. 1987)
Aug. 9, 1988 – Name changed to Miralta Energy Corp.; basis 1 new for 4 old shs. ■

Alta Natural Herbs & Supplements Ltd. (Alta. July 12, 1993)
June 21, 2019 – Name changed to Genix Pharmaceuticals Corporation. (see FPsurvey - Industrials)

Alta Pacific Capital Corp. (Alta. Nov. 23, 1993)
Dec. 14, 1999 – Name changed to Conquistador Resources Ltd.; basis 1 new for 5 old shs. ■

Alta Petroleum Ltd. (Alta. Nov. 16, 1977)
Apr. 4, 200 – Acquired by CanEuro Resources Ltd.; basis 0.8 CanEuro shs. for 1 Alta sh. (see CanEuro Resources Ltd.)

Alta Terra Ventures Corp. (Alta. June 5, 1998 amalg.)
Dec. 2, 2005 – Dissolved and struck from registry.

Alta Ventures Inc. (B.C. May 4, 1987)
Mar. 5, 1992 – Name changed to International Bio Waste Systems Inc. ■

Alta Vista Ventures Ltd. (B.C. July 23, 1980)
May 17, 2017 – Name changed to Global UAV Technologies Ltd. (see FPsurvey - Industrials)

AltaCanada Energy Corp. (Alta. Nov. 12, 1997)
Feb. 28, 2011 – Name changed to Montana Exploration Corp.; basis 1 new for 10 old shs. (see FPsurvey - Mines & Energy)

Altachem Pharma Ltd. (Alta. Dec. 16, 1996)
Oct. 5, 2005 – Name changed to Quest PharmaTech Inc. (see FPsurvey - Industrials)

AltaGas Canada Inc. (Can. Oct. 27, 2011)
Apr. 2, 2020 – Acquired by the Public Sector Pension Investment Board and the Alberta Teachers' Retirement Fund Board; basis $33.50 cash per sh.
Apr. 2, 2020 – Name changed to TriSummit Utilities Inc.

AltaGas Income Trust (Alta. May 1, 2004)
July 1, 2010 – Succeeded by AltaGas Ltd. pursuant to plan of arrangement whereby AltaGas Ltd. was formed to facilitate the conversion of the trust into a corporation and the trust was subsequently dissolved. (see FPsurvey - Mines & Energy; FPsurvey - Industrials)

AltaGas Services Inc. (Can. Aug. 30, 1993)
May 5, 2004 – Plan of Arrangement to convert company to a new income trust named AltaGas Income Trust; basis 1 new trust unit for 1 com. sh. (see AltaGas Income Trust)

AltaGas Utility Group Inc. (Can. July 6, 2005)
Oct. 15, 2009 – Acquired by AltaGas Holdings #3 Inc., an indirect wholly owned subsid. of AltaGas Income Trust, for $10.50 per sh. (see AltaGas Income Trust)

Altagem Resources Inc. (Alta. Aug. 15, 1995)
Feb. 2, 2016 – Struck from registry and dissolved.

Altair Gold Inc. (B.C. Nov. 17, 2005)
June 2, 2016 – Name changed to Altair Resources Inc. (see FPsurvey - Mines & Energy)

Altair International Gold Inc. (Ont. Apr. 1973)
Dec. 27, 1996 – Name changed to Altair International, Inc. ∎

Altair International, Inc. (Ont. Apr. 1973)
July 17, 2002 – Name changed to Altair Nanotechnologies Inc. and continued into Canada. ∎

Altair Mining Corporation Ltd. (N.P.L.) (B.C. Aug. 25, 1967)
Apr. 19, 1972 – Name changed to Consolidated Altair Developments Ltd.; basis 1 new for 4 old shs. ∎

Altair Nanotechnologies Inc. (Can. July 17, 2002)
May 15, 2012 – Continued into Delaware.

Altair Ventures Incorporated (B.C. Nov. 17, 2005)
Sept. 10, 2012 – Name changed to Altair Gold Inc. ∎

Altaley Mining Corporation (B.C. Apr. 11, 1986)
Mar. 21, 2023 – Name changed to Luca Mining Corp. (see FPsurvey - Mines & Energy)

Altan Nevada Minerals Limited (B.C. Apr. 4, 2008)
Oct. 20, 2023 – Name changed to Helius Minerals Limited. (see FPsurvey - Mines & Energy)

Altan Rio Minerals Limited (B.C. Dec. 20, 2010)
July 21, 2023 – Name changed to Golden Horse Minerals Limited. (see FPsurvey - Mines & Energy)

AltaQuest Energy Corporation (Alta. Mar. 28, 1996)
July 6, 2000 – Name changed to Chain Energy Corporation. ∎

Altar Gold & Resources Ltd. (B.C. 1979)
July 10, 1989 – Name changed to Northern Dancer Resources Ltd. ∎

AltaRex Corp. (Alta. Nov. 18, 1993)
May 31, 1997 – Amalgamated in Alberta to continue with same name.
Feb. 6, 2004 – Name changed to Twin Butte Energy Ltd. pursuant to plan of arrangement with AltaRex Medical Corp. (Medical) and Nova Bancorp Investments Ltd.; basis (i) more than 1,000 shs. - 1 Twin Butte sh. plus 10 Medical shs. for 10 AltaRex Corp. shs., (ii) 151 to 1,000 shs. - 5¢ plus 1 Medical sh. for 1 AltaRex Corp. sh. or (iii) less than 150 shs. - 65¢ cash for 1 AltaRex Corp. sh. ∎

AltaRex Medical Corp. (Alta. Dec. 8, 2003)
Dec. 15, 2004 – Plan of Arrangement amalgamation with ViRexx Medical Corp. to continue with the name ViRexx Medical Corp.; basis 1 new ViRexx sh. for 2 old AltaRex shs. (see ViRexx Medical Corp.)

Altarich Energy Inc. (Alta. Aug. 19, 1993)
Sept. 26, 1996 – Name changed to Millennium Communications Inc. following Qualifying Transaction acquisition of Cyphertech Systems (Canada) Inc.; basis 1 new for 1 old sh. ∎

Altaur Gold Explorations Inc. (Ont. Dec. 19, 1996 amalg.)
Feb. 13, 2006 – Certificate of incorporation cancelled and dissolved.

Altavista Mines Inc. (Can. Feb. 17, 1995)
July 26, 2000 – Name changed to Jitec Inc.; basis 1 new for 4 old shs. ∎

Altech Resource Services Ltd. (Alta. 1986)
Apr. 10, 1990 – Acquired by Canadian Fracmaster Ltd. for $0.485 per sh. (see Canadian Fracmaster Ltd.)

Altek Power Corporation (B.C. Jan. 27, 1986 amalg.)
July 15, 2013 – Dissolved and struck from register.

Alter NRG Corp. (Alta. Feb. 20, 2007)
Sept. 2, 2015 – Acquired by 1030629 B.C. Ltd., a wholly owned subsid. of Sunshine Kaidi New Energy Group Co., Ltd.; basis $5.00 cash per sh.

Altera Resources Inc. (B.C. Aug. 31, 1979)
Mar. 29, 1985 – Name changed to Ad Com Marketing Inc.; basis 1 new for 3 old shs. ∎

Alterio Resources Limited (Alta. 1987)
Jan. 4, 1991 – Amalgamated with Paragon Petroleum Limited (basis 1 new for 1 old sh.) and PPC Oil & Gas Corp. (basis 1 new for 2 old shs.) to form Paragon Petroleum Corporation; basis 1 new for 22 old shs. (see Paragon Petroleum Corporation)

Alternate Health Corp. (B.C. Oct. 26, 2014)
Jan. 29, 2024 – Struck from register and dissolved.

Alternative Earth Resources Inc. (B.C. Apr. 13, 1995)
Sept. 28, 2016 – Name changed to Black Sea Copper & Gold Corp. pursuant to the reverse takeover acquisition of (old) Black Sea Copper & Gold Corp.; basis 1 new for 1.24 old shs. ∎

Alternative Fuel Systems (2004) Inc. (Alta. Oct. 19, 2000)
June 7, 2011 – Acquired by AFS Acquisition Co. Inc., a wholly owned subsid. of Fuel Systems Solutions, Inc., for 50¢ per sh.

Alternative Fuel Systems Inc. (Alta. Feb. 27, 1997)
Aug. 4, 2004 – Name changed to AFS Energy Inc. pursuant to plan of arrangement under the Companies' Creditors Arrangement Act whereby the co.'s natural gas engine equipment business was transferred to a new co., Alternative Fuel Systems (2004) Inc., at fair market value of $1,400,000 and spun off; 90% of the new co. shs. were distributed to creditors and 10% to shldrs.; basis 1 new for 5 old shs. ∎

Altero Technologies Inc. (B.C. 1986)
June 10, 1994 – Dissolved and struck off register.

Alterra Power Corp. (B.C. Jan. 22, 2008)
Feb. 8, 2018 – Acquired by Innergex Renewable Energy Inc.; basis (i) 0.5563 Innergex com. shs., or (ii) Cdn$8.25 cash for 1 Alterra sh. (see Innergex Renewable Energy Inc.)

Alterra Resources Inc. (Ont.)
Jan. 8, 2008 – Dissolved and incorporation certificate cancelled.

Alterrus Systems Inc. (Alta. Jan. 19, 1996)
Jan. 21, 2014 – Filed for bankruptcy. The Bowra Group Inc. appointed trustee.

Altex Oils Ltd. (Alta. 1951)
1958 – Acquired by New Superior Oils of Canada Ltd; basis 1 new for 7.5 old shs.
1961 – Struck off register.

Altex Resources Ltd. (Alta. June 26, 1979)
Jan. 5, 1993 – Acquired by ATCOR Resources Ltd.; basis 1 ATCOR cl. A non-vtg. sh. for 2.475 Altex com. shs. (see ATCOR Resources Ltd.)

Altima Resources Ltd. (B.C. Nov. 14, 2003)
Dec. 6, 2024 – Name changed to Altima Energy Inc. (see FPsurvey - Mines & Energy)

Altina Capital Corp. (B.C. Aug. 23, 2019)
May 9, 2025 – Name changed to Aeonian Resources Corp. pursuant to the Qualifying Transaction reverse takeover acquisition of Aeonian Resources Ltd. (see FPsurvey - Mines & Energy)

Altiplano Minerals Ltd. (Alta. Mar. 5, 2010)
Nov. 10, 2010 – Continued into British Columbia.
June 6, 2018 – Name changed to Altiplano Metals Inc. (see FPsurvey - Mines & Energy)

Altitude Resources Inc. (Ont. Jan. 19, 2011)
Mar. 25, 2019 – Name changed to Vibe Bioscience Ltd. pursuant to the reverse takeover acquisition of Vibe Bioscience Corporation; basis 1 new for 12 old shs. ∎

Altitude Venture Capital Corp. (Can. June 19, 1998)
Dec. 27, 2000 – Name changed to D-BOX Technologies Inc. (see FPsurvey - Industrials)

Altius Renewable Royalties Corp. (Alta. Nov. 13, 2018)
Dec. 9, 2024 – All o/s shs., other than those held by Altius Minerals Corporation, acquired by Royal Aggregator LP; basis Cdn$12 cash per sh.

Altmark Energy Inc. (Alta. Mar. 4, 1987)
Mar. 20, 1997 – Amalgamated with 716881 Alberta Ltd., a wholly owned subsid. of Purcell Energy Ltd.; basis 0.6 Purcell shs. for 1 Altmark sh. (see Purcell Energy Ltd.)

Alto Explorations Ltd. (B.C. 1975)
Dec. 19, 1985 – Name changed to General Western Industries Ltd. ∎

Alto Industries Inc. (B.C. June 6, 1987)
Apr. 7, 1997 – Name changed to Alto Minerals Inc. ∎

Alto Minerals Inc. (B.C. June 6, 1987)
Apr. 19, 2002 – Name changed to Alto Ventures Ltd.; basis 1 new for 3.5 old shs. ∎

Alto Ventures Ltd. (B.C. June 6, 1987)
Sept. 22, 2020 – Name changed to Big Ridge Gold Corp. (see FPsurvey - Mines & Energy)

Altomac Uranium Mines Ltd. (Ont. 1953)
Sept. 21, 1959 – Dissolved.

The Alton Corporation (Ont. 1945)
1985 – Amalgamated with International Kenergy Resource Corporation to form Interquest Resources Corporation; basis 1 new for 1 old sh.

Alton Oils Ltd. (unknown)
Dec. 1952 – Assets sold to Triad Oil Co. Ltd.; basis 12 new for 1 old sh.
Feb. 24, 1953 – All o/s 4% debs. redeemed at par.

Altoro Gold Corp. (B.C. Mar. 7, 1979)
Oct. 18, 2000 – Acquired by Solitario Resources Corporation; basis 1 Solitario sh. for 3 Altoro shs.

Altra Ventures Inc. (B.C. Mar. 22, 1988)
Jan. 23, 1996 – Name changed to Odin Mining and Exploration Ltd.; basis 2 new for 3 old shs. ∎

Altum Resource Corp. (B.C. Feb. 20, 2019)
July 3, 2020 – Name changed to GoldHaven Resources Corp. (see FPsurvey - Mines & Energy)

Altura Energy Inc. (Alta. June 8, 2007)
Oct. 15, 2021 – Name changed to Tenaz Energy Corp. (see FPsurvey - Mines & Energy)

Altura Gold Mines Ltd. (Ont. Nov. 6, 1936)
Sept. 23, 1963 – Dissolved.

Altus Group Income Fund (Ont. Apr. 10, 2005)
Jan. 1, 2011 – Succeeded by Altus Group Limited pursuant to plan of arrangement whereby Altus Group Limited was formed to facilitate the conversion of the fund into a corporation and the fund was subsequently dissolved. (see FPsurvey - Industrials)

Altus Resources plc (U.K. Apr. 28, 2017)
Aug. 18, 2022 – Acquired by Elemental Royalties Corp.; basis 0.594 Elemental shs. for 1 Altus sh.
Dec. 2, 2022 – Name changed to Altus Strategies Limited.

Altus Strategies plc (U.K. Apr. 28, 2017)
June 6, 2017 – Name changed to Altus Resources plc. ■

Alubec Industries Inc. (Can. 1983)
Mar. 29, 1993 – Amalgamated into Holopak Technologies Inc. All o/s shs. of Alubec were exchanged for $5,190,243 and 223,000 com. shs. of Holopak.

Aludra Software Inc. (Ont. June 24, 1997)
Feb. 4, 2000 – Name changed to Aludra Inc. (see FPsurvey - Industrials)

Alumax Inc. (Del. Oct. 17, 1973)
Aug. 18, 1998 – Acquired by Aluminum Company of America of Pennsylvania; basis 0.6975 Aluminum shs. for 1 Alumax sh.

Aluminium Limited (Can. June 3, 1902)
Apr. 28, 1966 – Name changed to Alcan Aluminium Limited. ■

Aluminum Company of Canada, Ltd. (Can. 1902)
Apr. 23, 1987 – Shldrs. of Alcan Aluminium Limited (the parent co.) approved a sh. for sh. exchange, making Aluminum Co. of Canada, Ltd. the parent company of the Alcan Group. As part of the reorganization, the company's name has changed to Alcan Aluminium Limited, and now acts as both the parent holding company for the Alcan group, and the principal operating company in the group. (see Alcan Aluminium Limited)

Alur Mines Ltd. (Ont. 1949)
Dec. 22, 1958 – Dissolved.

Alvear Technologies Inc. (Alta. May 24, 1996)
Apr. 20, 1998 – Formed Nortech Geomatics International Inc. following merger with Nortech Geomatics Inc.; basis 1 new for 2 old shs. ■

Alvija Mines Ltd. (B.C. 1967)
Sept. 15, 1976 – Name changed to Paulson Mines Ltd.; basis 1 new for 4 old shs. ■

Alvopetro Inc. (Alta. Jan. 15, 2007)
Nov. 19, 2013 – Name changed to Fortaleza Energy Inc. following the sale of its interests in Brazilian petroleum assets. ■

Alwin Mining Co. Ltd. (B.C. 1964)
Nov. 1973 – Name changed to Advent Developments Inc.; basis 1 new for 5 old shs. ■

Alwyn Porcupine Mines Ltd. (Ont. 1945)
Nov. 8, 1977 – Dissolved.

Alya Ventures Ltd. (B.C. Jan. 21, 2010)
Mar. 6, 2012 – Name changed to Snipp Interactive Inc. pursuant to Qualifying Transaction acquisition of Consumer Impulse, Inc. (see FPsurvey - Industrials)

Alyattes Enterprises Inc. (Ont. July 5, 1996)
Feb. 1, 2007 – Name changed to Wedge Energy International Inc. pursuant to amalgamation of wholly owned 1272639 Alberta Ltd. with Wedge Energy Inc., constituting a reverse takeover by Wedge; basis 1 Alyattes sh. for 1 Wedge sh. Subsequently, Alyattes com. shs. were consolidated on a 3-for-4 basis. ■

Alyattes Resources Inc. (Ont. July 5, 1996)
June 28, 1999 – Name changed to Alyattes Enterprises Inc. ■

Alyson Holdings Ltd. (Alta. 1987)
Apr. 15, 1993 – Name changed to Continental Waste Conversion Inc. ■

Am-Can Productions Limited (Ont. 1964)
1968 – Charter cancelled.

Amadeus International Inc. (Que. Dec. 23, 2004 amalg.)
Nov. 16, 2015 – Struck from registry.

Amadeus Resources Inc. (B.C. Feb. 19, 1969)
July 10, 1987 – Dissolved and struck off register. (see Petrocel Industries Inc.)

Amador Gold Corp. (B.C. Oct. 24, 1980)
Oct. 30, 2018 – Name changed to Mene Inc. and continued into Ontario pursuant to reverse takeover acquisition of (old) Mene Inc. (see FPsurvey - Industrials)

Amagami Mines Ltd. (Ont. 1960)
June 30, 1980 – Amalgamated with Pyx Explorations Limited.

Amalfi Capital Corporation (Alta. Sept. 17, 2007)
Aug. 10, 2010 – Continued into Ontario.
Aug. 24, 2010 – Name changed to Royal Coal Corp. pursuant to the Qualifying Transaction reverse takeover acquisition of CDR Minerals Inc. and concurrent amalgamation of CDR with a wholly owned subsidiary (and continued as CDR Coal Limited and subsequently renamed Royal Coal Limited); basis 1 new for 2 old shs. ■

Amalgamated Beau-Belle Mines Ltd. (Ont. 1961)
Mar. 1, 1982 – Dissolved.

Amalgamated Bonanza Petroleum Ltd. (Alta. 1974 amalg.)
Dec. 7, 1979 – Merged with Gulf Canada Western Ltd., a subsid. of Gulf Canada Limited; basis $30 or 1 new for 2.82 old shs.

Amalgamated CanGold Inc. (Ont. July 25, 1995)
Jan. 1, 1996 – Formed Central Asia Goldfields Corporation in Ontario on amalgamation with Kazakstan Goldfields Corporation, constituting a reverse takeover by Kazakstan. ■

Amalgamated Chibougamau Gold Mines Ltd. (Que. 1946)
Dec. 23, 1972 – Dissolved.

Amalgamated Electric Corp. Ltd (Can. 1929)
May 1955 – 99% of com. shs. acquired by The General Electric Co. Ltd. of England. Controlling interest previously held by Northern Electric Co. Ltd., was sold to A. L. Mailman and J. L. Mailman in 1952 at $20 per sh. Minority shldrs. were at that time given opportunity to sell their shs. at the same price.

Amalgamated General Resources Ltd. (B.C. 1969)
Aug. 26, 1983 – Dissolved and struck off register.

Amalgamated Gold Fields Corp. Ltd. (Can. 1933)
Sold property to Headwater Mines Ltd. for undisclosed sh. int. Charter surrendered. (see Headwater Mines Ltd.)

Amalgamated Income Limited Partnership (B.C. Nov. 18, 1994)
Sept. 1, 2010 – Liquidated for $1.46 per sh.

Amalgamated Kirkland Mines Ltd. (Ont. July 10, 1939)
1971 – Assets acquired by Mayfield Explorations & Developments Limited.

Amalgamated Knee Lake Mines Ltd. (Man. 1947)
Apr. 1976 – Charter cancelled.

Amalgamated Larder Mines Limited (Ont. Oct. 27, 1941)
July 1980 – Name changed to Larder Resources Inc.; basis 1 new for 2 old shs. ■

Amalgamated Mines and Minerals Corp. (Que. 1951)
Sept. 2, 1978 – Charter cancelled.

Amalgamated Mining Development Ltd. (Que. 1959)
Jan. 15, 1985 – Formed Amalgamated Mining Western Ltd. on amalgamation with Amalgamated Mining Western Ltd.; basis 1 new for 1 old sh. ■

Amalgamated Mining Western Ltd. (Que. 1959)
July 12, 1994 – Name changed to Westall Resources Ltd.; basis 1 new for 3 old shs. (see FPsurvey - Mines & Energy)

Amalgamated Oil Co. Ltd. (B.C. 1918)
1950 – Name changed to Amalgamated Oil Co. (1950) Ltd.; basis 1 new for 5 old shs.

Amalgamated Oils Ltd. (Alta. 1941)
May 1955 – Liquidation payments totaling 50¢ per sh. made January 1944 to May 1955.
Oct. 15, 1958 – Sold to Western Decalta Petroleum Ltd. in 1958. Final distribution to shldrs. of 6 2/3¢ per sh.

Amalgamated Properties Limited (Can. 1961)
1979 – Amalgamated with Westburg Investments Ltd. to form Greenland Properties Ltd.; basis 1 new for 500 old shs. Privately held.

Amalgamated Rare Earth Mines Ltd. (Ont. 1957)
June 28, 1979 – Name changed to Rare Earth Resources Limited; basis 1 new for 5 old shs. ■

Amalgamated Resources Ltd. (Yuk. May 20, 1958)
May 1, 1974 – Name changed to Great Bear Mining Ltd.; basis 1 new for 5 old shs. ■

Amalta Oils & Minerals Limited (Alta. 1952)
Nov. 20, 1981 – Name changed to Paracorp Ltd. ■

Amalta Oils Limited (Alta. 1952)
July 4, 1966 – Name changed to Amalta Oils & Minerals Limited; basis 1 new for 5 old shs. ■

Amana Copper Ltd. (B.C. Feb. 4, 2011)
Oct. 27, 2015 – Name changed to International Wastewater Systems Inc. following reverse takeover acquisition of International Wastewater Heat Exchange Systems Inc. ■

Amanda Mines Ltd. (Man. 1943)
May 1956 – Name changed to Explorers Alliance Ltd. ■

Amanda Resources Ltd. (B.C. 1986)
Mar. 5, 1993 – Dissolved and struck off register.

Amanta Resources Ltd. (Wyo. Jan. 29, 1999)
Oct. 19, 2004 – Continued into British Columbia. (see FPsurvey - Mines & Energy)

Amar Ventures Inc. (B.C. Sept. 15, 1987)
Feb. 23, 1995 – Continued into Canada.
Mar. 3, 2003 – Dissolved.

Amarado Resources Ltd. (B.C. July 11, 1986)
May 25, 1995 – Continued into Canada.
Aug. 29, 1995 – Name changed to AfriOre Limited; basis 1 new for 2.5 old shs. ■

Amarillo Enterprises Inc. (Ont. Dec. 12, 1986)
June 23, 1988 – Continued into Alberta.
Aug. 15, 1988 – Name changed to Cromwell Resources Limited; basis 1 new for 4 old shs. (see FPsurvey - Mines & Energy)

Amarillo Gold Corporation (B.C. Jan. 18, 1983)
Apr. 7, 2022 – Acquired Hochschild Mining plc; basis Cdn$0.40 cash plus 1 Lavras Gold Corp. com, sh. for 1 Amarillo Gold sh.

Amark Explorations Ltd. (B.C. 1978)
Mar. 13, 1987 – Name changed to O.E.X. Electromagnetic Inc. (see FPsurvey - Industrials)

Amarok Energy Inc. (Alta. Aug. 22, 2012 amalg.)
June 16, 2014 – Name changed to Powder Mountain Energy Ltd.; basis 1 new for 5 old shs. ■

Amaroq Minerals Ltd. (Can. Feb. 22, 2017)
July 15, 2025 – Name changed to Amaroq Ltd. (see FPsurvey - Mines & Energy)

Amaryllis Ventures Ltd. (B.C. Feb. 2, 2006)
June 11, 2007 – Name changed to Avanti Mining Inc. ■

Amato Exploration Ltd. (B.C. Feb. 26, 2007)
Feb. 16, 2018 – Name changed to Aurora Royalties Inc. (see FPsurvey - Mines & Energy)

Amax Athabaska Uranium Mines Ltd. (Ont. 1949)
1954 – Merged into Pardee Amalgamated Mines Ltd.; basis 1 new for 5 old shs.

Amax Gold Inc. (Del. Apr. 1, 1987)
June 2, 1998 – Amalgamated with Kinross Gold Corporation; basis 0.8004 Kinross shs. for 1 Amax sh.

Amaya Gaming Group Inc. (Que. Jan. 30, 2004)
Nov. 28, 2014 – Name changed to Amaya Inc. ■

Amaya Inc. (Que. Jan. 30, 2004)
Aug. 1, 2017 – Name changed to The Stars Group Inc. and continued into Ontario. ■

Amazon Mining Holding plc (U.K. Aug. 14, 2006)
Apr. 26, 2011 – Name changed to Verde Potash plc. ■

Amazon Petroleum Corp. (B.C. June 9, 1981)
Feb. 24, 1992 – Name changed to Brigadier Resources Ltd.; basis 1 new for 3.5 old shs. ■

Ambari Brands Inc. (B.C. June 20, 2019)
July 24, 2024 – Name changed to Trilogy AI Corp. ■

Ambassador Development Corporation of Canada Ltd. (B.C. 1966)
June 1, 1978 – Amalgamated with 2 other cos. to form Ambassador Industries Ltd.; basis 1 new for 4 old shs.

Ambassador Industries Ltd. (B.C. June 1, 1978)
Apr. 22, 1997 – Name changed to Barrier Mining Corp.; basis 4 new for 1 old sh. ■

Ambassador Mines Ltd. (B.C. 1965)
June 8, 1973 – Name changed to Petrowest Resources Ltd.; basis 1 new for 5 old shs. ■

Ambassador Mining Developments Ltd. (Ont. 1960)
1970 – Name changed to New Ambassador Developments Ltd.; basis 1 new for 10 old shs. ■

Amber Energy Inc. (Alta. Dec. 1, 1992)
Nov. 23, 1998 – All o/s com. shs. acquired by Alberta Energy Company Ltd.; basis $7.50 per sh. or 0.225 of a com. sh. of Alberta Energy for 1 com. sh. of Amber. (see Alberta Energy Company Ltd.)

Amber Mining and Exploration Ltd. (Ont. 1944)
1953 – Charter cancelled.

Amber Resources Limited (B.C. Feb. 12, 1970)
Dec. 24, 1979 – Name changed to Banner Resources Ltd. ■

Ambergate Explorations Inc. (B.C. Feb. 27, 1987 amalg.)
Aug. 15, 1994 – Amalgamated with Kenrich Mining Corporation. (see Kenrich Mining Corporation)

Amberhill Mining Explorations Ltd. (B.C. 1980)
Oct. 25, 1982 – Name changed to Amberhill Petroleums Limited. ■

Amberhill Petroleums Limited (B.C. 1980)
Sept. 29, 1989 – Dissolved.

Amberquest Resources Ltd. (B.C. 1982)
Dec. 9, 1988 – Continued into Canada.
July 12, 2004 – Dissolved.

Ambis Mines Ltd. (Ont. 1958)
Sept. 22, 1966 – Dissolved.

Amble Green Ventures Inc. (B.C. 1981)
June 23, 1993 – Name changed to Western Logic Technologies Inc.; basis 1 new for 2 old shs. ■

Amble Resources Limited (B.C. 1980)
Oct. 17, 1986 – Acquired by Valar Resources Ltd.; basis 1 new for 3 old shs. (see Valar Resources Ltd.)

Amblin Resources Inc. (Alta. June 11, 1996)
Jan. 15, 2002 – Name changed to Amblin Technologies Inc.; basis 1 new for 5 old shs. ■

Amblin Technologies Inc. (Alta. June 11, 1996)
Dec. 2, 2004 – Struck from registry and dissolved.

Ambrex Mining Corporation (Ont. Aug. 21, 1995 amalg.)
June 14, 1999 – Continued into Alberta.
Sept. 15, 1999 – Name changed to Karmin Exploration Inc.; basis 1 new for 3 old shs. ■

Ambrilia Biopharma Inc. (Can. Apr. 2, 2001)
Apr. 8, 2011 – Filed for bankruptcy. Raymond Chabot inc. appointed trustee.

Amca Industries Ltd. (B.C. 1966)
Nov. 20, 1980 – Name changed to Amca Resources Ltd. ■

Amca Resources Ltd. (B.C. 1966)
July 16, 1993 – Dissolved and struck off register.

Amcan Cyphermaster Ltd. (B.C. 1984)
Apr. 14, 1988 – Acquired by Aura Systems Inc., a Delaware corporation; basis 1 new for 1 old sh.

Amcan Industries Corporation (Ont. 1918)
Mar. 18, 1982 – Placed into receivership. Proceeds from sale of assets insufficient to meet demands of secured creditors. No distribution to unsecured creditors or shldrs.

Amcan Insurance Services Inc. (Alta. 1987)
1992 – In receivership and Dunwoody Ltd. (Calgary) appointed receiver.
May 1993 – Secured creditors had been paid, but suffered a shortfall. The unsecured creditors received a small distribution, but there was nothing left for shldrs.
Dec. 1, 1994 – Receiver discharged.

Amcana Gold Mines Ltd. (B.C. 1960)
June 28, 1973 – Dissolved.

Amco Industrial Holdings Limited (Ont. 1954)
Nov. 4, 1985 – Name changed to International Amco Corporation; basis 1 new for 5 old shs. ■

Amcomri Entertainment Inc. (B.C. June 1, 2015)
Oct. 18, 2024 – Name changed to ADSL Holdings Inc. ■

Amcorp Industries Inc. (B.C. Mar. 24, 1966)
May 17, 1996 – Name changed to Molycor Gold Corporation. ■

Amera Industries Corp. (B.C. Sept. 17, 1979)
Feb. 10, 1995 – Name changed to International Amera Industries Corp.; basis 1 new for 8 old shs. ■

Amera Resources Corporation (B.C. Apr. 11, 2000)
Dec. 23, 2008 – Name changed to Panthera Exploration Inc.; basis 1 new for 10 old shs. ■

Ameracrude International Inc. (Ont. Oct. 22, 1976 amalg.)
Aug. 3, 1983 – Name changed to The Canadian Games Network Inc. ■

Ameracrude Resources Inc. (B.C. Feb. 18, 1980)
Oct. 28, 1981 – Name changed to Camino Energy Corp. ■

Amerada Hess Corporation (Del. 1920)
May 9, 2006 – Name changed to Hess Corporation.

Ameranium Mines Ltd. (Ont. 1949)
June 29, 1972 – Name changed to Jamestown Explorations Inc.; basis 1 new for 8 old shs. ■

Ameratech Systems Corporation (B.C. Dec. 5, 1979)
Aug. 26, 2013 – Dissolved and struck from register.

Amercoeur Energy (Canada) Ltd. (Ont. Oct. 28, 1974)
July 18, 1990 – Delisted from the Alberta Stock Exchange. Subsequently dissolved and charter cancelled.

Amerel Mining Co. Ltd. (Ont. 1960)
1969 – Assets sold to Twentieth Century Explorations Ltd.; basis 1 new for 20 old shs.

Amerex Development Corp. (B.C. Mar. 31, 1969)
Aug. 22, 1986 – Dissolved and struck off register.

Ameri-Can Agri Co. Inc. (B.C. Oct. 17, 2014)
Feb. 1, 2016 – Name changed to Acana Capital Corp. ■

Americ Mines Ltd. (Que. 1956)
Jan. 21, 1986 – Name changed to Novamin Inc.; basis 1 new for 8 old shs. ■

Americ Resources Corp. (B.C. May 25, 1983)
Apr. 27, 2001 – Name changed to Rolland Virtual Business Systems Ltd. following reverse takeover acquisition of Rolland Virtual Business Systems (Quebec) Ltd. ■

America Mineral Fields Inc. (B.C. Nov. 16, 1979)
Aug. 11, 1995 – Continued into Yukon.
May 17, 2004 – Name changed to Adastra Minerals Inc. ■

America West Capital Corp. (B.C. June 1, 1964)
Mar. 7, 1997 – Name changed to AME Resource Capital Corp. ■

American Agri-Technology Corporation (Can. Sept. 28, 1983)
June 10, 2004 – Struck from register and dissolved.

American Aquatech Inc. (B.C. 1981)
May 30, 1984 – Name changed to American Aquatech International Inc. ■

American Aquatech International Inc. (B.C. 1981)
Oct. 9, 1992 – Dissolved and struck off register.

American Barrick Resources Corporation (Ont. July 14, 1984 amalg.)
Jan. 1, 1995 – Name changed to Barrick Gold Corporation following amalgamation with a wholly owned subsidiary. ■

American Battery Metals Corp. (B.C. Mar. 2, 2017)
May 21, 2020 – Name changed to FenixOro Gold Corp. (see FPsurvey - Mines & Energy)

American Biodynamics Inc. (B.C. 1984)
1992 – Continued into Wyoming.

American Bonanza Gold Corp. (B.C. Dec. 10, 2004)
July 8, 2014 – Acquired by Kerr Mines Inc.; basis 0.53 Kerr com. shs. for 1 American Bonanza com. sh. (see Kerr Mines Inc.)

American Bonanza Gold Mining Corp. (B.C. July 19, 1994)
Mar. 30, 2005 – Succeeded by American Bonanza Gold Corp. pursuant to plan of arrangement acquisition of International Taurus Resources Inc. and the co. by newly incorporated wholly owned American Bonanza Gold Corp. (ABGC); basis 0.2 ABGC shs. for 1 International Taurus sh. and 0.25 ABGC shs. for 1 American Bonanza Gold Mining Corp. sh.

American Budgetel Inc. (B.C. 1983)
Jan. 26, 1989 – Name changed to ISO Ventures Inc.; basis 1 new for 5 old shs. ■

American Bullion Minerals Ltd. (B.C. June 11, 1987)
June 16, 2011 – Remaining 47.7% interest acquired by Red Chris Development Company Ltd., a wholly owned subsid. of Imperial Metals Corporation, for $2.45 per share.

American Can Canada Inc. (Can. 1887)
1984 – Amalgamated in Ontario to continue with same name.
Dec. 31, 1986 – Name changed to Onex Packaging Inc. ■

American Canadian Systems Inc. (B.C. July 2, 1980)
Apr. 3, 1991 – Name changed to Maxcard Systems International Inc. (see FPsurvey - Industrials)

American-Canadian Uranium Co. Ltd. (Del. 1949)
Feb. 1953 – Name changed to Athabasca Uranium Mines Ltd. ■

American Chibougamau Mines Ltd. (Que. 1956)
Oct. 1974 – Charter cancelled.

American Chromium Limited (Alta. 1981 amalg.)
Jan. 30, 1992 – Amalgamated with Courageous Exploration Inc. to form Rhonda Mining Corporation; basis 1 new for 10 Courageous shs. and 1 new for 10 American Chromium cl. A or cl. B shs. (see Rhonda Mining Corporation)

American Comstock Exploration Ltd. (B.C. Sept. 18, 1985)
Jan. 9, 1998 – Name changed to International Comstock Exploration Ltd.; basis 1 new for 5 old shs. ■

American Consolidated Minerals Corp. (B.C. Jan. 30, 2009 amalg.)
Dec. 4, 2014 – Acquired by Starcore International Mines Ltd.; basis 1 Starcore com. sh. for 3 American Consolidated com. shs.

American Copper and Smelting Ltd. (Can. 1968)
Dec. 16, 1980 – Dissolved.

American Copper Corp. (Yuk. Aug. 7, 1998)
July 29, 1999 – Name changed to E-Phoria Online Systems Inc. ■

American Copper Corporation (B.C. Jan. 27, 2006)
Jan. 30, 2009 – Formed American Consolidated Minerals Corp. in British Columbia on amalgamation with Golden Oasis Exploration Corp. and Lebon Gold Mines Limited; basis 1 new for 1 Golden Oasis sh., 1.2 new for 1 Lebon Gold sh. and 1 new for 1 American Copper sh. ■

American Coppermine Resources Limited (Alta. Mar. 27, 1987)
Feb. 4, 1997 – Name changed to Carleton Resources Corporation; basis 1 new for 3.2 old shs. ■

American Core Sectors Dividend Fund (Alta. Nov. 28, 2013)
June 11, 2019 – Converted into an exchange-traded fund; basis 1 new ETF sh. for 1 old trust unit.

American Creek Resources Ltd. (B.C. Feb. 12, 2004)
Aug. 26, 2005 – Continued into Alberta.
Dec. 11, 2018 – Continued into British Columbia. (see FPsurvey - Mines & Energy)

American CuMo Mining Corporation (B.C. 1971)
May 16, 2022 – Name changed to Multi-Metal Development Ltd. (see FPsurvey - Mines & Energy)

American Daleco Technologies Corp. (B.C. 1985)
Oct. 20, 1987 – Name changed to International Daleco Technologies Corp. and continued into California; basis 1 new for 3 old shs.

American Digital Industries Ltd. (B.C. Feb. 2, 1981)
June 21, 1991 – Dissolved and struck off register.

American Eagle Petroleums Ltd. (Sask. Aug. 24, 1954)
June 25, 1980 – Continued into Canada. (see CS Resources Limited)
June 1, 1982 – Continued into Alberta. (see CS Resources Limited)
Aug. 5, 1993 – Acquired by CS Resources Limited; basis 2 CS shs., 1.6 CS wts. and $12.50 for 100 American Eagle shs. (see CS Resources Limited)

American Eco Corporation (Ont. Feb. 6, 1969)
Aug. 2000 – Filed for protection under Chapter 11 of the United States Bankruptcy Code and under the Companies Creditors Arrangement Act. Texas-based BDO Seidman, LLP was appointed as financial advisors. In Canada, PricewaterhouseCoopers Inc. was appointed as monitor.
Oct. 30, 2000 – Certain of the company's assets had been sold and the net proceeds applied to outstanding debts. The company intended to dispose of additional assets but did not anticipate that the net proceeds would be sufficient enough to permit any distribution to shldrs.
Apr. 2002 – Hearing date had been obtained for an amended plan of liquidation. shldrs. had been deemed to reject the plan, or, are unimpaired, and their votes were not being solicited. New-York based Bankruptcy Services, LLP was handling the balloting and held copies of the amended plan of liquidation.

American Energy Corporation (B.C. 1982 amalg.)
June 1, 1984 – Name changed to Nickling Resources Inc.; basis 1 new for 5 old shs. ■

American Environmental Enterprises Corporation (Alta. 1985)
Mar. 1, 1992 – Struck off register.

American Ethanol (International) Corporation (Can. Sept. 28, 1983)
Aug. 19, 1996 – Name changed to American Agri-Technology Corporation. ■

American Exploration Corp. (Alta. Nov. 17, 1980)
Aug. 25, 1993 – Name changed to Asia Minerals Corp. ■

American Fibre Corporation (B.C. Sept. 14, 1983)
July 25, 1994 – Amalgamated with Heritage Petroleums Inc. to form Heritage American Resource Corp.; basis 1 new for 7 Heritage Petroleums shs. and 1 new for 8 American Fibre shs. (see Heritage American Resource Corp.)

American Fluorite Corporation (B.C. Dec. 12, 1977)
Mar. 21, 1983 – Name changed to AFC Energy Corporation. ■

American Frontier Mining & Refining Co. Ltd. (Ont. 1957)
Jan. 14, 1963 – Dissolved.

American Future Fuel Corporation (B.C. Mar. 3, 2015)
June 28, 2024 – Acquired by Premier American Uranium Inc.; basis 0.17 Premier American shs. for 1 American Future sh.

American Gem Corporation (Ont. Oct. 7, 1988)
Oct. 27, 1999 – Name changed to Digital Gem Corporation. ■

American Girl Resources Inc. (B.C. Sept. 4, 1986)
Apr. 1, 1991 – Name changed to T.K.O. Resources Inc.; basis 1 new for 2.5 old shs. ■

American Gold Capital Corporation (Alta. Oct. 30, 1995)
Oct. 17, 2001 – Continued into Cayman Islands.
Feb. 23, 2007 – Plan of Arrangement acquisition by Chesapeake Gold Corp.; basis 0.29 new Chesapeake com. sh. plus 0.029 new Chesapeake series 1 cl. A restricted vtg. sh. for 1 old American Gold com. sh. Also 0.29 new Chesapeake com. sh. purchase wt. for 1 old American Gold wt. (previously received as 0.5 new wt. for 1 com. sh.).

American Helium Inc. (B.C. Aug. 15, 2013)
May 25, 2022 – Name changed to Auscan Resources Inc.; basis 1 new for 3 old shs. (see FPsurvey - Mines & Energy)

American Highland Mining Corp. (B.C. Nov. 23, 1983)
Feb. 26, 1992 – Name changed to Cryocon Containers Inc. ■

American Income Trust (Ont. June 8, 1999)
June 19, 2006 – Merger involving AmeriStar RSP Income Trust (0.608722 for 1) and Income Financial Trust; basis

0.493092 new Income Financial unit for 1 old American Income unit

American Insulock Inc. (B.C. Oct. 19, 1984)
Sept. 20, 2010 – Name changed to Lexicon Building Systems Ltd. ■

American Investment Capital Corporation (Alta. 1986)
June 13, 1991 – Name changed to Westland Investment Corporation; basis 1 new for 2 old shs. ■

American Lead Silver Mines Ltd. (B.C. 1948)
Jan. 16, 1964 – Dissolved.

American Leduc Petroleums Limited (Alta. Sept. 6, 1947)
Oct. 21, 2003 – Merged with 1063339 Alberta Ltd., a wholly owned subsid. of Veteran Resources Inc.; basis $0.23 per sh. (see Veteran Resources Inc.)

American Lithium Company Ltd. (Que. 1954)
Aug. 26, 1972 – Dissolved.

American Manganese Inc. (B.C. July 8, 1987)
Oct. 3, 2022 – Name changed to RecycLiCo Battery Materials Inc. (see FPsurvey - Industrials)

American Manor Corp. (Can. Dec. 12, 1990 amalg.)
Aug. 10, 2000 – Name changed to American Manor Enterprises Inc.; basis 1 new for 2 old shs. ■

American Manor Enterprises Inc. (Can. Dec. 12, 1990 amalg.)
Oct. 25, 2006 – Name changed to Overland Realty Limited. ■

American Medical Technologies, Inc. (B.C. 1984)
1987 – Continued into Delaware.
Sept. 22, 1997 – Name changed to Tidel Technologies Inc.

American Metal Climax, Inc. (N.Y. 1887)
July 1, 1974 – Name changed to AMAX Inc.

American Metropolitan Enterprises Limited (Ont. 1960)
July 26, 1972 – Name changed to AME Limited. ■

American Microlink Inc. (B.C. Apr. 19, 1983)
June 27, 1985 – Name changed to International Union Resources Inc.; basis 1 new for 3 old shs. ■

American Mines & Minerals Ltd. (Que. 1956)
Feb. 1974 – Charter cancelled.

American Natural Energy Corporation (Okla. Oct. 18, 1990 amalg.)
July 20, 1994 – Amalgamated with Alexander Energy Corporation to form new co. with same name Alexander Energy Corporation; basis 1.62 new for 1 old sh.

American Nepheline Ltd. (Ont. 1945)
1961 – Name changed to Industrial Minerals of Canada Ltd.; basis 1 new for 10 old shs. ■

American Nevada Gold Corp. (B.C. May 12, 1987)
Aug. 6, 2004 – Name changed to Northern Canadian Minerals Inc.; basis 1 new for 5 old shs. ■

American Nortel Communications Inc. (B.C. 1979)
Feb. 9, 1993 – Continued into Wyoming.

American Oakwood Energy Ltd. (Alta. Nov. 17, 1980)
Oct. 29, 1986 – Name changed to American Ore Ltd. ■

American Ore Ltd. (Alta. Nov. 17, 1980)
Apr. 14, 1992 – Name changed to American Exploration Corp.; basis 1 new for 5 old shs. ■

American Pacific Exploration Ltd. (B.C. 1960)
May 15, 1969 – Struck off register.

American Pacific Minerals Ltd. (B.C. Oct. 1981 amalg.)
2000 – Continued into Delaware.

American Pacific Mining Company Inc. (B.C. 1983)
1988 – Continued into Canada. (see Breakwater Resources Ltd.)
Mar. 19, 1990 – Amalgamated with Breakwater Resources Ltd.; basis 3 new for 1 old sh. (see Breakwater Resources Ltd.)

American Petroleum Industries Canada Ltd. (Alta. 1952)
Struck off register.

American Platinum Inc. (B.C. 1980)
Sept. 3, 1993 – Dissolved and struck off register.

American Potash Corp. (B.C. June 5, 2006)
Jan. 22, 2018 – Name changed to New Tech Lithium Corp. ■

American Potash Corp. (B.C. June 5, 2006)
Dec. 20, 2024 – Name changed to American Critical Minerals Corp.; basis 1 new for 2.5 old shs. (see FPsurvey - Mines & Energy)

American Power & Waste Management Ltd. (B.C. June 14, 1988 amalg.)
Apr. 4, 1996 – Name changed to Columbia Fuels Inc. following reverse takeover acquisition of Columbia Fuels Inc.; basis 1 new for 5 old shs. ■

American Pyramid Resources Inc. (B.C. June 8, 1979 amalg.)
Nov. 6, 1987 – Delisted from the Vancouver Stock Exchange. Subsequently dissolved for failure to file.

American Reserve Energy Corporation (Alta. May 10, 2001)
May 28, 2003 – Name changed to bcMetals Corporation following Qualifying Transaction acquisition of Red Chris Development Company Ltd. for total consideration of 2,000,000 com. shs. ■

American Reserve Mining Corporation (B.C. Dec. 29, 1980)
Dec. 21, 1994 – Name changed to AMI Resources Inc.; basis 1 new for 16 old shs. ■

American Resource Corporation (Alta. May 2, 1994)
Nov. 2, 2007 – Dissolved and struck from registry.

American Sensors Inc. (Ont. May 13, 1993)
Mar. 1997 – Together with subsid. American Sensors Electronics Inc. (ASEI), applied for and were granted protection under the Companies' Creditors Arrangement Act. Coopers & Lybrand Limited was appointed monitor.
Sept. 1997 – Both the co. and ASEI were placed into receivership and Toronto-based Mandelbaum Spergel Inc. was appointed receiver. The court also approved the sale of certain assets of the co. and ASEI to North American Detectors Inc. for US$14,000,000 and 3,500,000 special warrants. The co. was also placed into bankruptcy and Mandelbaum Spergel was appointed trustee.
June 2002 – All known secured creditors had been paid.
June 1, 2004 – Trustee has kept the file open should there be any additional claims. There would not be sufficient funds for any distributions to unsecured creditors or shldrs.

American Sidewinder Oil Corporation (B.C. July 31, 1985)
Nov. 23, 1992 – Name changed to Texas Sidewinder Oil Corporation; basis 1 new for 3 old shs. ■

American Standard Mines Ltd. (B.C. Jan. 13, 1960)
1960 – Name changed to Consolidated Standard Mines Ltd.; basis 1 new for 3 old shs. ■

American Technology & Information Inc. (B.C. June 27, 1966)
Feb. 24, 1989 – Dissolved and struck off register.

American Telecommunications Corporation (B.C. 1979)
Dec. 31, 1990 – Name changed to ATC Inc. and continued into Delaware.

American Telesource International Inc. (Ont. May 26, 1994 amalg.)
May 22, 1998 – All o/s com. shs. exchanged for shares of American TeleSource International, Inc., a Delaware corporation; basis 1 com. sh. for 1 com. sh. Co. now a wholly owned subsid. of American TeleSource - Delaware.

American Transportation Television Network, Inc. (Can. Nov. 27, 1986 amalg.)
July 7, 1997 – Dissolved.

American Uranium Ltd. (B.C. 1967)
July 1972 – Name changed to Sonic Drying Systems Ltd.; basis 1 new for 3 old shs. ■

American Uranium Mining Corporation (B.C. June 24, 1985)
Sept. 18, 2020 – Name changed to Optimus Gold Corp. (see FPsurvey - Mines & Energy)

American Vanadium Corp. (Can. Mar. 2, 2006)
July 20, 2017 – Name changed to Monitor Ventures Inc.; basis 1 new for 25 old shs. ■

American Ventures Inc. (B.C. Sept. 2, 1987)
Apr. 1, 1992 – Name changed to Asha Ventures Inc.; basis 1 new for 3 old shs. ■

American Volcano Minerals Corp. (B.C. 1964)
Oct. 9, 1986 – Name changed to Genco Industries Inc. ■

American Wellhead Services Inc. (B.C. Mar. 11, 1983)
May 13, 1994 – Name changed to Coronado Resources Inc.; basis 1 new for 2 old shs. ■

American Westwater Technology Group Ltd. (B.C. 1983)
Nov. 12, 1993 – Dissolved and struck off register.

American Wild Woodland Ginseng Corp. (Can. Jan. 30, 1995)
July 6, 2006 – Dissolved.

American Wireless Corp. (Alta. Feb. 15, 1996)
Aug. 2, 2009 – Struck from registry and dissolved.

American Wollastonite Mining Corp. (B.C. Sept. 26, 1988)
Apr. 25, 1997 – Name changed to Previa Resources Ltd.; basis 1 new for 6.7 old shs. ■

American Yellowknife Exploration Co. Ltd. (Alta. 1944)
Feb. 5, 1945 – Name changed to American Yellowknife Gold Mines Ltd. and continued into Ontario; basis 1,200 new for 1 old sh. ■

American Yellowknife Gold Mines Ltd. (Ont. Feb. 5, 1945)
Mar. 1952 – Name changed to American Yellowknife Mines Ltd. ■

American Yellowknife Mines Ltd. (Ont. Feb. 5, 1945)
Aug. 1954 – Name changed to Rayrock Mines Limited; basis 1 new for 4 old shs. ■

Americanadian Mining and Exploration Co. Limited (Ont. 1928)
Aug. 9, 1972 – Dissolved.

Americas Bullion Royalty Corp. (Bermuda Aug. 20, 2012)
Apr. 17, 2014 – Succeeded by Till Capital Ltd. following the acquisition of Americas Bullion Royalty Corp. (predecessor public company) with Americas Bullion the deemed acquiror; basis 1 new for 100 old shs. ■

Americas Petrogas Inc. (Alta. Aug. 22, 2008 amalg.)
Aug. 9, 2016 – Name changed to GrowMax Resources Corp. ■

Americas Silver Corp. (Can. May 12, 1998)
Sept. 3, 2019 – Name changed to Americas Gold and Silver Corporation. (see FPsurvey - Mines & Energy)

Ameridex Minerals Corp. (B.C. July 8, 1987)
Sept. 13, 2006 – Name changed to Rocher Deboule Minerals Corp. ■

Ameridian Ventures Inc. (B.C. Apr. 18, 1988)
May 9, 2005 – Dissolved and struck from register.

Ameriplas Holdings Ltd. (Can. Sept. 26, 2003)
July 13, 2010 – Name changed to Downtown Industries Ltd.; basis 1 new for 20 old shs. ■

AmeriStar RSP Income Trust (Ont. Dec. 7, 1999)
June 19, 2006 – Merger involving American Income Trust (0.493092 for 1) and Income Financial Trust; basis 0.608722 new Income Financial unit for 1 old AmeriStar unit.

Ameritel Management, Inc. (B.C. 1980)
June 4, 1992 – Acquired by WCT Communications, Inc.; basis 1 WCT sh. for 3 Ameritel shs.

Ameritex Resources Ltd. (B.C. 1983)
Aug. 28, 1992 – Dissolved and struck off register.

Amerix Precious Metals Corporation (Ont. May 31, 2004)
Dec. 22, 2014 – Name changed to Eagle Graphite Incorporated; basis 1 new for 20 old shs. ■

Ameroil Energy Corporation (B.C. 1979)
Aug. 1989 – Continued into Alberta.
Oct. 18, 1990 – Amalgamated in Oklahoma to continue with same name.
Nov. 7, 1990 – Name changed to ALN Resources Corporation following amalgamation with wholly owned ALN Resources Corporation. ■

Amerpro Industries Inc. (Alta. May 30, 1988)
Mar. 6, 2009 – Name changed to Amerpro Resources Inc. and continued into British Columbia; basis 1 new for 5 old shs. ■

Amerpro Resources Inc. (B.C. Mar. 6, 2009)
Oct. 14, 2009 – Name changed to Electric Metals Inc. ■

Amertek Inc. (Can. Jan. 1, 1985 amalg.)
June 27, 1989 – Continued into Ontario.

Ametal Mining Corp. (Que. 1955)
Oct. 1974 – Charter cancelled.

Amex Ventures Inc. (B.C. July 30, 1998)
July 31, 2001 – Name changed to Global SortWeb.com Inc. followed by the Aug. 7, 2001, Qualifying Transaction acquisition of Monetary Capital Corporation; basis 4 new for 1 old sh. ■

Amflo Petroleum Corporation (B.C. 1970)
1980 – Acquired by American Fluorite Corporation; basis 3 American Fluorite shs. for 4 Amflo shs. (see American Fluorite Corporation)

Amhawk Resource Corp. (B.C. 1980)
May 27, 1987 – Name changed to Consolidated Amhawk Enterprises Ltd.; basis 1 new for 4 old shs. ■

Amherst Industries Inc. (unknown Mar. 1, 1974)
Dec. 1979 – Continued into Ontario.
Apr. 16, 1997 – Acquired by JELD-WIN of Canada, Ltd. for $1.654 per cl. A sh. and $1,000 per cl. B sh.

Amherst Woodworking Ltd. (unknown)
Mar. 1, 1974 – Amalgamated with Conduits Amherst Ltd.; basis 7.16 new for 1 old sh.

Amic Mica Mines Ltd. (Que. 1943)
Name changed to Mica Company of Canada Ltd.

Amica Mature Lifestyles Inc. (Can. Dec. 7, 1998)
Dec. 23, 2015 – Acquired by a wholly owned subsid. of BayBridge Seniors Housing Inc. for $18.75 per sh.

Amichi Gold Mines Ltd. (Ont. 1947)
Nov. 1958 – Charter cancelled.

Amicus Capital Corp. (B.C. May 31, 2007)
Nov. 21, 2008 – Name changed to Polo Biology Global Group Corporation pursuant to Qualifying Transaction reverse takeover acquisition of Rainbow Trend Limited; basis 1 new for 1.1538 old shs. ■

Amigo Mines Ltd. (Que. 1968)
Mar. 14, 1981 – Charter cancelled.

Amigo Silver Mines Ltd. (B.C. 1969)
Oct. 2, 1992 – Dissolved and struck off register.

Amint Investments Ltd. (Alta. 1987)
Oct. 1, 1991 – Struck off register.

Amir Mines Ltd. (B.C. Nov. 16, 1982)
Dec. 5, 1988 – Amalgamated with Bema International Resources Inc. (1 for 1) and Normine Resources Ltd. (1 for 2) to form Bema Gold Corporation; basis 1 new for 1 old sh. (see Bema Gold Corporation)

Amir Ventures Corp. (B.C. Nov. 16, 1979)
Aug. 8, 1995 – Name changed to America Mineral Fields Inc.; basis 3 new for 2 old shs. ■

Les Industries Amisco Ltée (Que. Feb. 9, 1954)
Mar. 4, 2009 – Privatized. Shldrs. received 1 Gestion Martin Poitras Inc. redeem. pref. sh. for 1 Les Industries Amisco sh., immediately redeemed for $1.75 per sh.

Amisk Inc. (Que. Dec. 27, 1979)
Nov. 30, 2007 – Acquired by Pan-O-Lac-Ltee. for $7,021,028.

Amisk Regional Investment Inc. (Que. Dec. 27, 1979)
Dec. 24, 1997 – Name changed to Amisk Inc. ■

Amlartic Gold Mines Ltd. (Ont. 1945)
Nov. 1973 – Charter cancelled.

Amm Gold Mines Ltd. (Ont. 1936)
Mar. 10, 1958 – Charter cancelled.

Ammonite Energy Ltd. (Alta. Mar. 28, 2006)
Dec. 15, 2009 – Acquired by Novus Energy Inc.; basis 0.825 Novus com. shs. for 1 Ammonite sh. (see Novus Energy Inc.)

Amoco Canada Petroleum Company (Can. 1969)
Jan. 7, 1992 – All o/s 13.5% junior notes (U.S.) redeemed at US$1,617,53 per $1,000 principal amount.
Sept. 1, 1995 – All o/s 7.375% U.S. debentures redeemed at US$1,022.10 per $1,000 principal amount.
Aug. 14, 2000 – Name changed to BP Canada Energy Company.

Amoco Corporation (Ind. 1889)
Jan. 4, 1999 – Amalgamated with The British Petroleum Company plc to form BP Amoco plc; basis 3.97 new ADS of BP Amoco for 1 com. sh. of Amoco. (see BP Amoco p.l.c.)

Amoil Petroleums Inc. (Alta. May 17, 1994 amalg.)
Jan. 23, 1997 – Name changed to Amoil Resources Inc.; basis 1 new for 3 old shs. ■

Amoil Resources Inc. (Alta. May 17, 1994 amalg.)
Dec. 8, 2000 – Name changed to River Valley Energy Services Corporation. ■

Amok Ltd. (Can. 1967)
Jan. 1, 1993 – Amalgamated with Cogema Canada Ltd. to form Cogema Canada Ltd. (see Cogema Canada Limited)

Amorada Gold Mines Ltd. (Ont. 1935)
Jan. 12, 1959 – Dissolved.

Amore Minerals Inc. (B.C. 1977)
Oct. 3, 1980 – Name changed to Amore Resources Inc. ■

Amore Resources Inc. (B.C. 1977)
July 31, 1984 – Name changed to Freeway Resources Ltd.; basis 1 new for 5 old shs. ■

Amorfix Life Sciences Ltd. (Can. Sept. 20, 2005 amalg.)
July 8, 2015 – Name changed to ProMIS Neurosciences Inc. ■

Amos Lithium Corp. (Que. 1955)
1958 – Name changed to Indian Chemical & Exploration Co. ■

Amos Mines Limited (Que. 1970)
Apr. 21, 1982 – Charter cancelled after sales of assets to Jonpol Explorations for 706,940 Jonpol shs., which were distributed to shldrs.; basis 1 new for 7.5 old shs. ■

Ampac Petroleum Resources Inc. (B.C. June 5, 1984)
Oct. 16, 1987 – Name changed to W.I. Wheels International Ltd. ■

Amparo Development Corp. (B.C. 1965)
Feb. 2, 1983 – Struck off register.

Amphi Gold Properties Ltd. (Que. 1937)
Charter cancelled.

Amplus Technologies Corporation (Alta. Aug. 10, 1993)
Oct. 24, 1995 – Name changed to Applied High Technology AHT Corporation. ■

Amporco Mining and Development Co. Ltd. (Ont. 1942)
1957 – Charter cancelled.

Amseco Exploration Ltd. (Can. July 19, 1984 amalg.)
Nov. 18, 2024 – Name changed to Canadian Gold Resources Ltd. pursuant to the reverse takeover acquisition of Canadian Gold Resources Ltd. (concurrently renamed 14697952 Canada Inc.); basis 1 new for 5 old shs. (see FPsurvey - Mines & Energy)

The Amseco Mining Corporation Ltd. (Can. July 19, 1984 amalg.)
Jan. 17, 2006 – Name changed to Amseco Exploration Ltd. ■

Amshaw Porcupine Mines, Ltd. (Ont. 1946)
1957 – Charter cancelled.

Amstar American Petroleum Corp. (B.C. 1981)
Apr. 30, 1985 – Name changed to Amstar Venture Corp. ■

Amstar Venture Corp. (B.C. 1981)
Feb. 23, 1989 – Name changed to Golden-Tonkin Resources Ltd.; basis 1 new for 5 old shs. ■

Amswiss Holdings Ltd. (Can. 1984)
Apr. 9, 1987 – Name changed to Lifequest International Inc.; basis 1 new for 14.8 old shs. ■

Amswiss Pharmaceuticals Inc. (Can. June 3, 1987)
Mar. 5, 1990 – Name changed to Amswiss Scientific Inc.; basis 1 new for 5 old shs. ■

Amswiss Scientific Inc. (Can. June 3, 1987)
Mar. 2, 2010 – Dissolved.

Amtelecom Group Inc. (Ont. Apr. 13, 1984)
Apr. 9, 2003 – Name changed to Century II Holdings Inc. ■

Amtelecom Income Fund (Ont. Jan. 14, 2003)
June 1, 2007 – Acquired by 3191293 Nova Scotia Limited, a subsidiary of Bragg Communications Incorporated; basis $14.25 per unit.

Amtelecom Inc. (Ont. 1928)
Apr. 18, 1984 – Succeeded by Amtelecom Group Inc. pursuant to plan of arrangement to facilitate a restructuring whereby Amtelecom Group Inc. was incorporated to become the parent of Amtelecom Inc. ■

Amtronics Enterprises Ltd. (B.C. 1986)
Sept. 12, 2005 – Dissolved and struck from register.

Amulet Gold Mines Ltd. (Que.)
Nov. 23, 1927 – Continued into Canada.
1927 – Name changed to Amulet Mines Ltd.; basis 1 new for 1 old sh. ■

Amulet Mines Ltd. (Can. Nov. 23, 1927)
1933 – Formed Waite Amulet Mines Ltd.; basis 1 new for 3 old shs.

Amulet Resources Corporation (B.C. June 25, 1986)
June 11, 1990 – Name changed to Golden Unicorn Mining Corporation; basis 1 new for 3 old shs. ■

Amurex Oil Company (Del. 1951)
Dec. 1961 – Merged with Murphy-Canada Oil Co. to form Murphy Oil Co. Ltd.; basis 1 new Murphy sh. for 1 old Amurex cl. A sh.

Amusecor Inc. (Que. 1968)
1983 – Continued into Canada.
Feb. 9, 1987 – Name changed to Alubec Industries Inc. ■

Amusements International Ltd. (Alta. Jan. 27, 1986)
July 26, 2005 – Name changed to BlueGrouse Seismic Solutions Ltd. pursuant to reverse takeover acquisition of Blue Grouse Seismic Solutions Ltd. effective Apr. 26, 2005; basis 1 new for 15 old shs. ■

AmWolf Capital Corp. (B.C. Apr. 23, 2018)
Jan. 28, 2021 – Name changed to Pontus Protein Ltd. pursuant to the Qualifying Transaction reverse takeover acquisition of Pontus Water Lentils Ltd. and concurrent amalgamation of Pontus Water with wholly owned 1253044 B.C. Ltd. (and continued as 42 Protein Corp.). (see FPsurvey - Industrials)

Amy Yellowknife Mines Ltd. (Ont. 1954)
Sept. 1962 – Dissolved.

Ana Lake Mining Ltd. (B.C. Dec. 6, 1968)
May 2, 1980 – Name changed to Archer Minerals Inc. ■

Ana Uranium Mines Ltd. (Ont. 1948)
Sept. 21, 1959 – Charter cancelled.

Anabar Mining and Development Co. Ltd. (Ont. 1953)
Nov. 1973 – Charter cancelled.

Anabie Gold Mines Ltd. (Ont. 1944)
1955 – Charter cancelled.

Anacon Extension Ltd. (Que. 1950)
1952 – Name changed to Anthonian Mining Corp. Ltd. ■

Anacon Lead Mines Ltd. (Ont. 1948)
1964 – Name changed to Key Anacon Mines Limited; basis 1 new for 3 old shs. ■

Anaconda Gold Corp. (Ont. July 22, 2002)
Apr. 18, 2007 – Name changed to Anaconda Mining Inc. following reverse takeover acquisition of Colorado Minerals Inc.; basis 1 new for 2 old shs. ■

Anaconda Mining Inc. (Ont. July 22, 2002)
May 12, 2022 – Name changed to Signal Gold Inc. ■

Anaconda Oil Co., Ltd. (Can. Apr. 14, 1926)
Oct. 1952 – Name changed to Canadian Anaconda Oils Ltd. ■

Anaconda Petroleum Ltd. (Can. Apr. 14, 1926)
Jan. 1971 – Name changed to Zebedee Oil Limited. ■

Anaconda Uranium Corporation (B.C. Apr. 12, 1994)
July 22, 2002 – Continued into Ontario.
Aug. 16, 2002 – Name changed to Anaconda Gold Corp.; basis 1 new for 3 old shs. ■

Anacondo Explorations Inc. (B.C. Dec. 22, 1980)
Sept. 16, 1992 – Name changed to O-Tech Ventures Corporation. ■

Anacortes Mining Corp. (B.C. Mar. 15, 2018)
July 4, 2023 – Acquired by Steppe Gold Ltd.; basis 0.4532 Steppe shs. for 1 Anacortes sh.

Anacott Acquisition Corporation (Can. Sept. 24, 2020)
Mar. 19, 2024 – Name changed to Ramp Metals Inc. following Qualifying Transaction amalgamation of (old) Ramp Metals Inc. with 1429494 B.C. Ltd, a wholly owned

subsidiary of Anacott Acquisition Corporation, constituting a reverse takeover by (old) Ramp Metals. (see FPsurvey - Mines & Energy)

Anadime Corporation (Alta. June 18, 1986)
Aug. 24, 2001 – Acquired by Newalta Corporation; basis 1 Newalta sh. for 6 Anadime shs. (see Newalta Corporation)

Anaergia Inc. (Can. Sept. 3, 2010)
Dec. 21, 2018 – Continued into British Columbia. (see FPsurvey - Industrials)

Analytical Software, Inc. (B.C. Aug. 19, 1998)
May 31, 2002 – Delisted from the TSX-Venture Exchange. Subsequently struck from register and dissolved.

AnalytixInsight Inc. (Man. Oct. 1, 1999)
Aug. 18, 2014 – Continued into Ontario. (see FPsurvey - Industrials)

Ananda Capital Corp. (Alta. Aug. 1, 2007)
Oct. 6, 2010 – Name changed to Colonial Coal International Corp. pursuant to reverse takeover acquisition of Colonial Coal Corporation by way of amalgamation between its wholly owned subsid. and Colonial constituting Ananda's Qualifying Transaction; basis 1 new for 2 old shs. (see FPsurvey - Mines & Energy)

Anarchist Mountain Resources Ltd. (B.C. Dec. 21, 1979)
Sept. 16, 1982 – Name changed to Cent-Ram Development Corp. ∎

Anatole Resources Limited (Ont. 1972)
Apr. 2, 1985 – Charter cancelled.

Anatolia Energy Corp. (Can. Sept. 25, 1995)
July 2, 2013 – Acquired by Cub Energy Inc.; basis 0.106 Cub shs. for 1 Anatolia sh. (see Cub Energy Inc.)

Anatolia Minerals Development Limited (Yuk. Jan. 14, 1998)
Feb. 23, 2011 – Name changed to Alacer Gold Corp. ∎

Anchor Capital Corporation (Alta. Feb. 20, 2014)
May 31, 2019 – Name changed to Spyder Cannabis Inc. pursuant to Qualifying Transaction reverse takeover acquisition of Spyder Vapes Inc. ∎

Anchor Gold Corp. (B.C. 1983)
Apr. 30, 1993 – Dissolved and struck off register.

Anchor Lamina Inc. (Ont. 1960)
Aug. 18, 1997 – Acquired by AKC Acquisition Corp., a wholly owned subsid. of Harrowston Inc., for $8.00 per sh.

Anchor Machine & Manufacturing Limited (Ont. 1960)
Mar. 26, 1991 – Name changed to Anchor Lamina Inc. ∎

Anchor Mines Ltd. (B.C. 1967)
Jan. 26, 1976 – Name changed to Eltron Security Systems Corp.; basis 1 new for 5 old shs. ∎

Anchor Petroleum Corp. (B.C. June 25, 1969)
May 30, 1983 – Name changed to Logo Resources Ltd.; basis 1 new for 5 old shs. ∎

Anchor Petroleums Limited (Ont. 1949)
May 1972 – Charter cancelled.

Anchor-Takla Mines Ltd. (B.C. 1968)
Apr. 1977 – Charter cancelled.

Anco Exploration Ltd. (Alta. 1968)
June 1970 – Acquired by T.C. Explorations Ltd.; basis 3 new for 1 old sh. and wts.

Ancom ATM International Inc. (Ont. Dec. 29, 1987)
Feb. 1991 – Placed into receivership.
May 1993 – All assets liquidated. Secured, unsecured and pfd. creditors suffered a shortfall and there was no distribution to shldrs.
July 1, 1993 – Trustee discharged.

Ancon Mining & Exploration Ltd. (Ont. 1945)
Sept. 1956 – Charter cancelled.

Anconia Resources Corp. (Ont. Mar. 22, 1962)
Oct. 1, 2020 – Name changed to Omai Gold Mines Corp. pursuant to the reverse takeover acquisition of Avalon Investment Holdings Ltd., and concurrent amalgamation of Avalon with a wholly owned subsidiary to continue as Omai Gold Mines Barbados Corp.; basis 1 new for 15 old shs. (see FPsurvey - Mines & Energy)

Ancroft Place Limited (Ont. 1926)
June 1972 – Following sale of its Toronto-held real estate properties assets distributed by means of divds. to shldrs. Final distribution of 60¢ per sh. made Aug. 29, 1977 and co. subsequently was dissolved.

Andacollo Mining Co. Ltd. (Ont. 1958)
Mar. 1976 – Charter cancelled.

Andar Gold Mines Ltd. (Ont. 1944)
Sept. 17, 1962 – Charter cancelled.

Andaurex Capital Resources Inc. (B.C. Jan. 22, 1980)
Aug. 31, 1995 – Name changed to Andaurex Industries Inc. ∎

Andaurex Industries Inc. (B.C. Jan. 22, 1980)
Dec. 6, 2006 – Formed San Anton Resource Corporation in Canada on amalgamation with Kings Minerals Canada Inc., constituting a reverse takeover by Kings Minerals Canada. Prior to amalgamation, all shs. of Kings-San Anton S.A. de C.V. were transferred to Kings Minerals Canada, which together with Kings-San Anton were wholly owned subsids. of Australia-based Kings Minerals NL. ∎

Andaurex Resources Inc. (B.C. Jan. 22, 1980)
Dec. 2, 1992 – Name changed to Andaurex Capital Resources Inc. ∎

Andean American Gold Corp. (B.C. Jan. 14, 1981)
Oct. 2, 2012 – Acquired by Lupaka Gold Corp.; 0.245 Lupaka com. shs. for 1 Andean com. sh.

Andean American Mining Corp. (B.C. Jan. 14, 1981)
Sept. 7, 2010 – Name changed to Andean American Gold Corp. ∎

Andean Precious Metals Corp. (B.C. Oct. 23, 2018)
Mar. 8, 2024 – Continued into Ontario. (see FPsurvey - Industrials)

Andean Resources Limited (Australia June 20, 1994)
Dec. 10, 2010 – Acquired by Goldcorp Inc.; basis either Cdn$6.50 or 0.14 Goldcorp shs. for 1 Andean Resources sh. (see Goldcorp Inc.)

AndeanGold Ltd. (B.C. Feb. 28, 2006)
Aug. 29, 2022 – Struck from register and dissolved.

Andele Capital Corporation (B.C. July 12, 2010)
Jan. 3, 2012 – Name changed to Network Media Group Inc. pursuant to Qualifying Transaction reverse takeover acquisition of Network Entertainment Inc. (see FPsurvey - Industrials)

Anderado Resources Inc. (B.C. Jan. 22, 1980)
Nov. 1980 – Name changed to Andaurex Resources Inc. ∎

Anderson Energy Inc. (Alta. Nov. 26, 2014)
Nov. 7, 2016 – Formed InPlay Oil Corp. in Alberta following the reverse takeover of and subsequent amalgamation with (old) InPlay Oil Corp. (see FPsurvey - Mines & Energy)

Anderson Energy Ltd. (Alta. Jan. 30, 2002)
Jan. 27, 2015 – Succeeded by Anderson Energy Inc. ∎

Anderson Exploration Ltd. (Can. Oct. 1, 1982 amalg.)
Oct. 18, 2001 – Acquired by Devon Acquisition Corporation, an indirect subsid. of Oklahoma-based Devon Energy Corporation, and amalgamated to form new co. with same name Anderson Exploration Ltd.; basis $40 per com. sh.
Oct. 25, 2001 – Name changed to Devon Canada Corporation and continued into Alberta.

Andes Mining & Exploration Co. Ltd. (B.C.)
June 27, 1977 – Dissolved.

Andex Mines Ltd. (B.C. 1966)
Dec. 8, 1983 – Name changed to Consolidated Andex Resources Ltd.; basis 1 new for 4 old shs. ∎

Andina Development Corporation (Alta. Mar. 26, 1996)
July 6, 2001 – Name changed to Carmanah Technologies Corporation pursuant to reverse takeover acquisition of Carmanah Technologies Inc.; basis 1 new for 1.5 old shs. ∎

Andina Minerals Inc. (Alta. Jan. 23, 2001)
Feb. 25, 2013 – Acquired by Hochschild Mining plc for $0.80 per sh.

Andman Porcupine Gold Mines Ltd. (Ont. 1944)
Feb. 1952 – Charter cancelled.

Andor Mining Inc. (Ont. Jan. 4, 2011)
Feb. 13, 2013 – Name changed to Trident Gold Corp. pursuant to Qualifying Transaction reverse takeover acquisition of Trident Gold Corp.; basis 1 new for 4.5455 old shs. ∎

Andover Mining & Exploration Ltd. (Ont. Sept. 19, 1958)
Feb. 15, 1971 – Name changed to Andover Resources Limited; basis 1 new for 5 old shs. ∎

Andover Mining Corp. (B.C. Feb. 12, 2003)
Feb. 12, 2014 – Deemed bankrupt. Grant Thornton Limited appointed trustee.
Dec. 4, 2014 – Grant Thornton Limited, trustee in bankruptcy, agreed to Enirgi Group Corporation paying $1,000,000 cash to purchase (i) all outstanding shares of Andover (Alaska) Inc., (ii) 61,089,050 common shares in Chief Consolidated Mining Company, and (iii) an inter-company loan advanced by Andover Mining Corp. to Chief Consolidated in the principal amount of US$2,394,810 plus accrued interest.
Mar. 2015 – Grant Thornton completed the sale of the company's material assets to Enirgi Group Corporation. Net proceeds to be distributed to the company's creditors.
Oct. 31, 2017 – Struck from the registry and dissolved.

Andover Resources Limited (Ont. Sept. 19, 1958)
1975 – Charter cancelled.
Sept. 27, 1977 – Charter revived.
1987 – Name changed to Andover Telecommunications Inc. ∎

Andover Telecommunications Inc. (Ont. Sept. 19, 1958)
June 1, 1989 – Name changed to Kennecom Inc. ∎

Andover Ventures Inc. (B.C. Feb. 12, 2003)
Jan. 6, 2012 – Name changed to Andover Mining Corp. ∎

Andowan Mines Ltd. (Ont. 1939)
Mar. 31, 1981 – Charter cancelled.

Andreane Mining Resources Inc. (Can. May 16, 1985)
May 6, 2004 – Dissolved.

Andrés Wines Ltd. (Can. Apr. 7, 1965)
Sept. 20, 2006 – Name changed to Andrew Peller Limited; basis 3 new for 1 old sh. (see FPsurvey - Industrials)

Andrew Wolf Cellars Ltd. (Alta. July 21, 1977)
Aug. 20, 1999 – Formed Celebration Cellars Ltd. in Alberta on amalgamation with 825691 Alberta Ltd. (deemed acquiror); basis 1 new for 1 825691 Alberta sh. and 1 new for 5 Andrew Wolf shs. ∎

Andrew Yellowknife Mines Ltd. (Ont. 1945)
1954 – Merged into Pardee Amalgamated Mines Ltd.; basis 1 new for 5 old shs.

Andria Resources Inc. (B.C. 1981)
Sept. 24, 1993 – Dissolved and struck off register.

Androck Inc. (Ont. Jan. 31, 1984 amalg.)
Nov. 7, 1985 – Name changed to Autrex Inc. ■

Andromed Inc. (Que. July 14, 1997)
May 23, 2006 – Name changed to Sonomed Inc. ■

Andromeda Ventures Inc. (B.C. 1987)
Dec. 4, 1992 – Dissolved and struck off register.

Androne Resources Ltd. (B.C. 1978)
Sept. 1, 1988 – Amalgamated into Pezgold Resource Corporation; basis 1 new for 1 old sh. (see Pezgold Resource Corporation)

Andy Yellowknife Mines Ltd. (Ont. 1946)
1952 – Charter cancelled.

Andyne Computing Limited (Ont. Nov. 26, 1976)
Jan. 14, 1998 – Acquired by Hummingbird Communications Ltd.; basis 0.18745 Hummingbird shs. for 1 Andyne sh. (see Hummingbird Communications Ltd.)

Anergy Capital Inc. (B.C. May 14, 2008)
Feb. 17, 2015 – Continued into Canada.
Feb. 24, 2015 – Name changed to Kraken Sonar Inc.; basis 1 new for 2.25 old shs. ■

Anexco Resources Ltd. (B.C. Mar. 1, 2006)
Nov. 4, 2014 – Name changed to Kaneh Bosm Biotechnology Inc. ■

Anfield Gold Corp. (B.C. May 13, 2005)
Dec. 22, 2017 – Acquired by Trek Mining Inc.; basis 0.407 Trek shares for each Anfield share. (see Equinox Gold Corp.)

Anfield Nickel Corp. (B.C. May 13, 2005)
May 10, 2016 – Name changed to Anfield Gold Corp. following the acquisition of Magellan Minerals Ltd. ■

Anfield Resources Inc. (B.C. Sept. 12, 1986)
Dec. 27, 2017 – Name changed to Anfield Energy Inc.; basis 1 new for 10 old shs. (see FPsurvey - Mines & Energy)

Anfield Ventures Inc. (B.C. May 13, 2005)
Aug. 18, 2009 – Name changed to Anfield Nickel Corp. ■

Angel Bioventures Inc. (Alta. Aug. 31, 1993)
Feb. 27, 2017 – Continued into British Columbia.
Mar. 28, 2017 – Name changed to AbraPlata Resource Corp. pursuant to reverse takeover acquisition of Huayra Minerals Corp.; basis 5 new for 1 old sh. ■

Angel Gold Corp. (B.C. Aug. 8, 1988 amalg.)
Dec. 19, 2022 – Name changed to Eon Lithium Corp. (see FPsurvey - Mines & Energy)

Angelus Explorations Inc. (Ont. 1947)
Nov. 28, 1978 – Dissolved.

Angelus Petroleums Ltd. (Ont. 1947)
Nov. 22, 1965 – Name changed to Angelus Petroleums (1965) Limited; basis 1 new for 5 old shs. ■

Angelus Petroleums (1965) Limited (Ont. 1947)
Name changed to Angelus Explorations Inc. ■

Angelwest Capital Corp. (B.C. Oct. 26, 2007)
Oct. 29, 2009 – Name changed to GreenAngel Energy Corp. pursuant to Qualifying Transaction acquisition of equity interests in six private green technology companies. ■

Angiotech Pharmaceuticals, Inc. (B.C. Oct. 21, 1989)
May 12, 2011 – Plan of compromise completed under Companies' Creditors Arrangement Act under which the US$250,000,000 7.75% sr. subordinate notes were cancelled and eliminated in exchange for issuance of 12,500,000 new com. shs.; sr. floating rate notes due 2013 were exchanged for new sr. secured floating rate

notes; and all o/s com. shs. were cancelled without consideration.

Angkor Gold Corp. (B.C. Oct. 16, 2008)
Sept. 5, 2019 – Name changed to Angkor Resources Corp. (see FPsurvey - Mines & Energy)

Angle Energy Inc. (Alta. Jan. 23, 2004)
Dec. 17, 2013 – Acquired by Bellatrix Exploration Ltd.; basis either i) $3.85 or ii) 0.4734 Bellatrix com. shs. for 1 Angle com. sh. (see Bellatrix Exploration Ltd.)

Angle Resources Ltd. (B.C. 1975)
Jan. 1, 1988 – Amalgamated with Silver Cloud Mines Ltd. (1 for 3) to continue as Angle Resources Ltd.; basis 1 new for 1 old sh. (see Nexus Resource Corporation)
May 5, 1988 – Amalgamated with Reward Resources Ltd. (1 for 3) and Nexus Resources Corporation (1 for 1) to form a new co. also named Nexus Resources Corporation; basis 0.89 new for 1 old sh. (see Nexus Resource Corporation)

Anglin-Norcross Corp. Ltd. (Can. 1931)
Sept. 1967 – Private co. Placed into bankruptcy.

Anglo Aluminum Corp. (B.C. Mar. 7, 1980)
July 12, 2013 – Name changed to Navasota Resources Inc.; basis 1 new for 10 old shs. ■

Anglo American Corporation of Canada Limited (Can. 1965)
1979 – Continued into Ontario.
June 18, 1981 – Name changed to Minorco Canada Limited. ■

Anglo American Exploration Ltd. (Alta. 1952)
June 8, 1962 – Shldrs. received 1 Norcan Oils Ltd. sh. for each Anglo sh. held; then British American Oil purchased all o/s Anglo American shs. at $6.00 per sh.

Anglo-American Mines Ltd. (Que. 1956)
Nov. 11, 1978 – Charter cancelled.

Anglo American Molybdenite Mining Corp. (Que. 1959)
1968 – Name changed to Cadillac Moly Mines Ltd.; basis 1 new debs. for 5 old shs. Anglo American 6.5% debs. converted to Cadillac Moly 7% income debs., dollar-for-dollar basis. ■

Anglo-American Nickel Mining Corp. Ltd. (Ont. 1965)
May 1976 – Charter cancelled.

Anglo American Resources Inc. (B.C. 1987)
Nov. 26, 1993 – Dissolved and struck off register.

Anglo-Andean Explorations, Inc. (B.C. July 29, 1983)
May 20, 1994 – Continued into Canada.
May 15, 2006 – Dissolved.

Anglo-Canadian Gas Corp. (B.C. June 8, 1987)
Jan. 20, 2011 – Name changed to Jager Metal Corp.; basis 1 new for 4 old shs. ■

Anglo-Canadian Mining Corp. (B.C. Oct. 5, 1979)
Aug. 30, 2017 – Name changed to Canada One Mining Corp. (see FPsurvey - Mines & Energy)

Anglo Canadian Mining Corporation (B.C. 1979)
Jan. 11, 1989 – Continued into Canada.
July 28, 1997 – Dissolved and struck from register.

Anglo-Canadian Oil Company Limited (Alta. 1934)
1955 – Sold to Canadian Oil Companies Ltd.; basis $2.75 and 1/7th Canadian Oil sh. for each Anglo-Canadian sh.

Anglo Canadian Oil Corp. (Alta. July 14, 2008 amalg.)
Dec. 31, 2012 – Formed Tallgrass Energy Corp. in Alberta on amalgamation with (old) Tallgrass Energy Corp.; basis 1 new for 14.4887 old shs. ■

Anglo-Canadian Oils Ltd. (Man. 1939)
1966 – Acquired by British American Oil Co. Ltd.; basis 3 new for 1 old sh.

Anglo-Canadian Pulp and Paper Mills, Limited (Que. 1924)
Jan. 27, 1975 – Remaining 18.3% interest acquired by Reed Paper Ltd.; basis 1 Reed Paper $2.00 cum. conv. pref. sh. for 1 Anglo-Canadian Pulp sh.

Anglo-Canadian Uranium Corp. (B.C. Oct. 5, 1979)
Aug. 29, 2011 – Name changed to Anglo-Canadian Mining Corp. ■

Anglo Dominion Gold Exploration Limited (Ont. Dec. 2, 1944)
Sept. 21, 1993 – Amalgamated with Coniagas Mines, Limited, Garrison Creek Consolidated Mines Ltd. and Quebec Sturgeon River Mines Limited to form QSR Limited; basis 32 new for 100 Coniagas shs., 7 new for 1,000 Garrison shs., 20 new for 100 Quebec Sturgeon shs. and 18 new for 100 Anglo Dominion shs. (see QSR Limited)

Anglo-Huronian Ltd. (Ont. 1933)
Nov. 18, 1963 – Merged with Kerr-Addison Gold Mines Ltd. (1 for 1) and Bouzan Mines Ltd. (1 for 10) to form a new co. named Kerr Addison Mines Limited; basis 8 new for 5 old shs. (see Kerr Addison Mines Limited)

Anglo Keno Developments Ltd. (Ont. 1934)
1977 – Name changed to Lumsden Building Corp. Inc.

Anglo Minerals Ltd. (Alta. Oct. 11, 1994)
Feb. 29, 2008 – Name changed to Anglo Potash Ltd. ■

Anglo Murmont Mining Corp. Ltd. (Sask. 1959)
Sept. 1961 – Struck off register.

Anglo-Norwegian Holdings Ltd. (Que. 1929)
Dec. 1954 – Name changed to Anglo-Scandinavian Investment Corporation of Canada.

Anglo Pacific Developments Ltd. (Alta. May 17, 1988)
Oct. 21, 1991 – Name changed to Farm Energy Corporation. ■

Anglo-Pacific Explorations Ltd. (B.C. 1963)
Feb. 4, 1983 – Dissolved.

Anglo Pacific Group plc (U.K. Feb. 7, 1967)
Oct. 6, 2022 – Name changed to Ecora Resources plc. (see FPsurvey - Mines & Energy)

Anglo Porcupine Gold Mines, Limited (Ont. May 17, 1922)
Apr. 30, 1996 – Name changed to Control Advancements Inc.; basis 1 new for 5 old shs. ■

Anglo Potash Ltd. (Alta. Oct. 11, 1994)
July 14, 2008 – Acquired by BHP Billiton Limited for $8.15 per sh.

Anglo-Rouyn Mines Limited (Ont. 1939)
Aug. 31, 1973 – Amalgamated with 251799 Investments Ltd. to form Canadian Memorial Services Ltd.; basis 1 new for 4 old shs. (see Canadian Memorial Services Limited)

Anglo Swiss Industries Inc. (B.C. Feb. 3, 1966)
Nov. 28, 1997 – Succeeded by Anglo Swiss Resources Inc. pursuant to plan of arrangement reorganization whereby wholly owned Canadian Sapphire Corp. completed a share-for-share exchange to became parent of Anglo Swiss Industries. ■

Anglo Swiss Mining Corporation (B.C. Feb. 3, 1966)
May 1, 1992 – Name changed to Anglo Swiss Industries Inc.; basis 1 new for 15 old shs. ■

Anglo Swiss Resources Inc. (Can. June 27, 1995)
June 19, 2014 – Name changed to Gungnir Resources Inc.; basis 1 new for 5 old shs. (see FPsurvey - Mines & Energy)

Anglo United Development Corporation Limited (Ont. 1942)
Nov. 28, 1986 – Acquired by Anglo United plc of London, England for $0.53 per sh.

Anglo Western Minerals Ltd. (B.C. 1955)
July 29, 1977 – Name changed to Anglo Western Petroleums Ltd.; basis 1 new for 4 old shs. ∎

Anglo Western Oil & Gas Ltd. (B.C. 1955)
July 26, 1961 – Name changed to Anglo Western Petroleums Ltd.; basis 1 new for 10 old shs. ∎

Anglo-Western Oils Ltd. (Can. 1930)
Liquidated on behalf of debenture holders.

Anglo Western Petroleums Ltd. (B.C. 1955)
Apr. 14, 1966 – Name changed to Anglo Western Minerals Ltd. ∎

Anglo Western Petroleums Ltd. (B.C. 1955)
May 31, 1991 – Dissolved and struck off register.

Angold Resources Ltd. (B.C. Oct. 22, 2012)
Feb. 13, 2024 – Name changed to Aero Energy Limited. (see FPsurvey - Mines & Energy)

The Angot Group Limited (Ont. 1963)
Apr. 1, 1979 – Name changed to Hawklin Industries Inc.; basis 1 new for 5 old shs. ∎

Angus Gold Inc. (B.C. Sept. 28, 2010)
July 2, 2025 – Acquired by Wesdome Gold Mines; basis 0.0095946645367412 Wesdome shs. plus 62¢ cash per sh. for 1 Angus Gold sh.

Angus Mines Limited (Que. 1947)
1951 – Wound up. No equity for shldrs.

Angus Mining Inc. (Ont. Apr. 20, 2010)
Jan. 25, 2021 – Name changed to Waverley Resources Ltd.; basis 1 new for 10 old shs. (see FPsurvey - Mines & Energy)

Angus Mining (Namibia) Inc. (Ont. Apr. 20, 2010)
July 16, 2012 – Name changed to Angus Mining Inc. ∎

Angus Oils, Limited (Can. Apr. 1926)
Taken over by Albertan Federated Oils, Ltd.; basis sh. for sh.

Angus Petroleums Ltd. (Alta. Apr. 9, 1951)
1959 – Struck off register.

Angus Resources Inc. (B.C. Jan. 15, 2008)
July 19, 2010 – Name changed to Batero Gold Corp. pursuant to Qualifying Transaction acquisition of Bahia Bonita Properties S.A. (see FPsurvey - Mines & Energy)

Angus Resources Limited (B.C. Feb. 12, 1970)
May 31, 1988 – Name changed to Canadian Angus Resources Ltd.; basis 1 new for 2 old shs. ∎

Angus River Mines Ltd. (B.C. 1951)
July 1969 – Assets acquired by Abco Mining Ltd. on a sh.-for-sh. basis. (see Abco Mining Ltd.)

Angus Ventures Corp. (B.C. Jan. 10, 1986)
July 13, 2009 – Name changed to Encanto Potash Corp. pursuant to reverse takeover acquisition of Encanto Potash Corp. and subsequent amalgamation of Encanto with wholly owned Encanto Holdings Ltd. (see FPsurvey - Mines & Energy)

Angus Ventures Inc. (B.C. Sept. 28, 2010)
Sept. 18, 2020 – Name changed to Angus Gold Inc. ∎

Animacis Technologies Inc. (Can. Oct. 28, 1998)
Sept. 19, 2003 – Dissolved.

Animas Resources Ltd. (B.C. June 29, 2006)
Apr. 24, 2014 – All o/s com. shs. not already held acquired by GoGold Resources Inc.; basis 0.0851 GoGold com. shs. plus 7¢ cash per sh. for 1 Animas com. sh.

Animatronix Entertainment Corporation (Yuk. July 9, 1992)
July 13, 1995 – Name changed to Creative Entertainment Technologies, Inc. ∎

Anina Resources Ltd. (B.C. Nov. 1984)
Aug. 1987 – Continued into Wyoming.
Sept. 9, 1987 – Name changed to ImmuDyne Inc. following acquisition of Immudyne, Inc. of Texas.

Anita Resources Inc. (B.C. Sept. 19, 1980)
June 25, 1984 – Name changed to Pluton Resource Corporation; basis 1 new for 2.5 old shs. ∎

Anitech Enterprises Inc. (Alta. Apr. 4, 1986)
Dec. 6, 1991 – Continued into British Columbia.
Mar. 30, 2006 – Formed IPICO Inc. in Ontario on amalgamation with AMtag ID Inc., constituting a reverse takeover by AMtag; basis 1 new for 1 AMtag sh. and 1 new for 191.6049 Anitech sh. ∎

Ankeno Mines Ltd. (Ont. May 2, 1944)
1955 – Name changed to Bankeno Mines Limited; basis 1 new for 5 old shs. ∎

Ankh Capital Inc. (B.C. Nov. 30, 2020)
Mar. 12, 2024 – Name changed to Quetzal Copper Corp. following Qualifying Transaction amalgamation of Quetzal Copper Limited with 1415994 B.C. Ltd., a wholly owned subsidiary of Ankh Capital, constituting a reverse takeover by Quetzal Copper Limited. (see FPsurvey - Mines & Energy)

Ann Arbor Bio-Image Systems Ltd. (B.C. 1983)
Sept. 8, 1986 – Name changed to Promethean Technologies Inc. (see FPsurvey - Industrials)

Annabel Gold Mines Inc. (B.C. Nov. 10, 1988)
Mar. 2, 1994 – Name changed to Carissa Mining Corporation. ∎

Annabelle Inc. (Que. Jan. 31, 1973)
Apr. 14, 2000 – Name changed to Waitsfield Capital Inc.; basis 1 new cl. A for 1 old cl. A sh. and 1 new cl. B for 1 old cl. B sh. ∎

Annamaque Mines Ltd. (Ont. 1943)
Mar. 1965 – Name changed to Adelaide Mining Ltd.; basis 1 new for 6 old shs. ∎

Annax Ventures Inc. (B.C. Feb. 10, 1987)
Sept. 28, 1995 – Name changed to International Annax Ventures Inc.; basis 1 new for 3 old shs. ∎

Annco Mines Ltd. (Ont. 1963)
Jan. 1, 1989 – Amalgamated with Wilanour Resources Limited and Wilmar Mines Ltd. to form Wilanour Resources Limited; basis 1 new for 1 Wilanour sh., 1 new for 2.4 Wilmar shs. and 1 new for 5.1 Annco shs. (see Wilanour Resources Limited)

Annex Exploration Corp. (B.C. Mar. 8, 1983)
Mar. 29, 1994 – Name changed to Redhawk Resources, Inc.; basis 1 new for 3 old shs. ∎

Annie Lake Mines (B.C. 1979)
Apr. 30, 1984 – Name changed to Cheryl Resources Inc.; basis 1 new for 5 old shs. ∎

Annis Mines Ltd. (B.C. 1964)
Sept. 3, 1974 – Dissolved and struck off register.

Annisquam Art Company Ltd. (B.C. June 5, 1984)
July 18, 1994 – Name changed to PHL Pinnacle Holdings Inc. ∎

Annmar Mining Ltd. (B.C. 1967)
Mar. 1972 – Name changed to Abaca Mining Ltd.; basis 1 new for 10 old shs. ∎

Annova Business Group Inc. (B.C. Nov. 17, 1986)
Nov. 27, 1998 – Name changed to Capital Alliance Group Inc.; basis 1 new for 2 old shs. ∎

Annova International Holdings Corp. (B.C. Nov. 17, 1986)
Apr. 27, 1995 – Name changed to Annova Business Group Inc.; basis 1 new for 4 old shs. ∎

Anoda Nickel Ltd. (B.C. Feb. 20, 1911)
Jan. 3, 1974 – Name changed to Trans Pacific Ventures Ltd. ∎

Anodor Minerals Inc. (Can. Aug. 9, 1984)
Mar. 13, 1991 – Name changed to Nora Exploration Inc.; basis 1 new for 4 old shs. ∎

Anoki Gold Mines Ltd. (Ont. 1938)
1965 – Assets acquired by Queenston Gold Mines; basis 1 new for 12 old shs. Charter cancelled.

Anomaly No. 4 Mines Ltd. (Ont. 1959)
1961 – Name changed to McAdam Mining Corporation Limited. ∎

Anooraq Resources Corporation (B.C. Apr. 19, 1983)
May 14, 2012 – Name changed to Atlatsa Resources Corporation. ∎

Anorak Capital Corp. (Alta. Nov. 4, 1996)
Dec. 3, 1997 – Name changed to Total Energy Services Ltd. ∎

AnorMED, Inc. (Can. Jan. 5, 1996)
Nov. 8, 2006 – Acquired indirectly by U.S.-based Genzyme Corporation for Cdn$13.50 per sh.

Ansar Financial and Development Corporation (Ont. Jan. 29, 2008)
Mar. 29, 2022 – Voluntarily delisted. (see FPsurvey - Industrials)

Ansco Resources B.C. Ltd. (B.C. Sept. 13, 1982)
May 15, 1989 – Name changed to Sunstate Resources Ltd.; basis 1 new for 3 old shs. ∎

Ansel Capital Corporation (Alta. Mar. 7, 1995)
Mar. 4, 1997 – Name changed to DeTECH Corporation. ∎

Ansell Capital Corp. (B.C. July 26, 2006)
Nov. 25, 2014 – Name changed to BriaCell Therapeutics Corp. following the reverse takeover acquisition of (old) BriaCell Therapeutics Corp.; basis 1 new for 3.25 old shs. (see FPsurvey - Industrials)

Ansell Lake Resources Ltd. (Ont. Nov. 5, 1987)
Aug. 7, 1996 – Formed Diversafile International Inc. in Ontario on amalgamation with Diversafile International Ltd., constituting a reverse takeover by Diversafile; basis 1 new for 5 old shs. ∎

Ansil Mines Ltd. (Ont. Nov. 26, 1945)
Dec. 29, 1981 – Name changed to Ansil Resources Ltd.; basis 1 new for 5 old shs. ∎

Ansil Resources Ltd. (Ont. Nov. 26, 1945)
Jan. 1, 2013 – Amalgamated with Jubliee Gold Inc. and Micron Gold Inc. to form Jubliee Gold Exploration Ltd.; basis 0.221 Jubliee Exploration com. shs. for 1 Jubliee Gold sh.; 1.035 Jubliee Exploration com. shs. for 1 Micron Gold sh.; and 0.551 Jubliee Exploration com. shs. for 1 Ansil sh.

Ansley Gold Mines Ltd. (Ont. May 2, 1944)
1949 – Name changed to Consolidated Ansley Gold Mines Ltd.; basis 1 new for 3 old shs. ∎

Anson-Cartwright Mines Ltd. (Ont. 1945)
Oct. 1977 – Charter cancelled.

Anson Petroleums Ltd. (Can. Apr. 1950)
May 1952 – Assets acquired by Bailey Selburn Oil & Gas Ltd.; basis 1 Bailey cl. A for 10 old shs.

Anstruther Rare Metals Ltd. (Ont. 1955)
May 13, 1965 – Dissolved.

Ansue Capital Corp. (B.C. Dec. 3, 2009)
Aug. 25, 2011 – Name changed to Caracara Silver Inc. pursuant to Qualifying Transaction reverse takeover acquisition of (old) Caracara Silver Inc.; basis 1 new for 3 old shs. ∎

Antalis Ventures Corp. (B.C. Feb. 13, 2018)
July 28, 2022 – Name changed to Plantify Foods, Inc. pursuant to the Qualifying Transaction reverse takeover acquisition of private Israel-based Peas of Bean Ltd. (POB) and concurrent amalgamation of POB with wholly owned 1372632 B.C. Ltd. (see FPsurvey - Industrials)

Antam Resources International Ltd. (Yuk. Sept. 9, 1997)
June 8, 1999 – Name changed to International Antam Resources Ltd.; basis 1 new for 7 old shs. ■

Antamena Capital Corp. (B.C. Mar. 28, 2007)
Sept. 3, 2008 – Name changed to Xtierra Inc. following Qualifying Transaction amalgamation of Orca Minerals Limited with a wholly owned subsid. of Antamena, constituting a reverse takeover by Orca; basis 1 new for 2 old shs. ■

Antares Minerals Inc. (Alta. Sept. 24, 2004)
Dec. 21, 2010 – Acquired indirectly by First Quantum Minerals Ltd.; basis $6.35 or 0.07619 First Quantum shs. plus 0.4505 newly formed Regulus Resources Inc. shs. for 1 Antares Minerals sh.

Antares Mining and Exploration Corporation (Ont. Sept. 8, 1993 amalg.)
Sept. 3, 1999 – Name changed to Caussa Capital Corporation. ■

Antares Oil & Gas Ltd. (Alta. 1971)
Apr. 1980 – Liquidated into Gulch Resources Ltd., which in 1979 had acquired 99% int. under a $2.00 per sh. purchase offer.

Antarex Metals Ltd. (Alta. Sept. 3, 1997)
Aug. 22, 2001 – Name changed to International Antarex Metals Ltd.; basis 1 new for 5 old shs. ■

Antelope Resources Inc. (Ont. Feb. 28, 1989 amalg.)
Oct. 15, 1994 – Dissolved.

Antelope Resources Limited (B.C. 1973)
Feb. 28, 1989 – Formed Antelope Resources Inc. in Ontario on amalgamation with Miles (Red Lake) Mines Ltd. ■

Antera Ventures I Corp. (B.C. June 20, 2018)
Dec. 8, 2020 – Name changed to Wishpond Technologies Ltd. pursuant to Qualifying Transaction reverse takeover acquisition of (old) Wishpond Technologies Ltd.; basis 1 new for 4.6467206 old shs. (see FPsurvey - Industrials)

Anterra Corporation (Alta. Mar. 22, 2000)
May 1, 2007 – Formed Anterra Energy Inc. in Alberta on amalgamation with Resolve Energy Inc. with Anterra the deemed acquiror; basis 1 new cl. A and cl. B sh. for 1 Resolve com. sh. and 0.5714285 new cl. A and 0.0132 cl. B shs. for 1 Anterra Corp. com. sh. ■

Anterra Energy Inc. (Alta. May 1, 2007 amalg.)
June 7, 2017 – PricewaterhouseCoopers Inc. appointed receiver. All directors resigned.
Aug. 1, 2017 – Assigned into bankruptcy. PricewaterhouseCoopers Inc. appointed trustee and all officers resigned.

Anthem Properties Corp. (B.C. July 18, 1997)
July 31, 2003 – Name changed to Anthem Works Ltd. ■

Anthem Resources Inc. (B.C. May 21, 2009)
July 24, 2015 – Acquired by Boss Power Corp.; basis 0.75 Boss com. shs. for 1 Anthem sh.

Anthem United Inc. (B.C. Jan. 14, 2011)
Oct. 7, 2016 – Acquired by Lowell Copper Ltd. (renamed JDL Gold Corp); basis 0.774 Lowell com. shs. for 1 Anthem sh. (see JDL Gold Corp.)

Anthem Ventures Capital Corp. (B.C. Apr. 3, 2007)
May 28, 2010 – Name changed to West Kirkland Mining Inc. pursuant to Qualifying Transaction reverse takeover acquisition of West Kirkland Mining Inc. ■

Anthem Works Ltd. (B.C. July 18, 1997)
May 13, 2004 – Continued into Canada.
June 4, 2004 – Going private transaction via acquisition by Anthem Acquisition Ltd. for $14.50 per sh.

The Anthes-Imperial Company Limited (Can. 1949)
Apr. 1962 – Name changed to Anthes Imperial Limited. ■

Anthes Imperial Limited (Can. 1949)
1968 – Molson Industries Ltd. acquired 99.9% of the o/s cl. A and cl. B shs.; basis 1.7 Molson cl. A sh. and $3.00 for each Anthes cl. A sh., 1.7 Molson cl. C sh. and $3.00 for each Anthes cl. B sh.

Anthes Industries Inc. (Can. Mar. 26, 1981)
Jan. 11, 1993 – Amalgamated with wholly owned Patheon Group Inc. to form new co. with same name Anthes Industries Inc.
May 12, 1993 – Name changed to Patheon Inc. ■

Anthex Industries Inc. (Ont. 1954)
Aug. 2, 1974 – Name changed to Anthex Industries Ltd.; basis 1 new for 3 old shs. ■

Anthex Industries Ltd. (Ont. 1954)
Jan. 16, 1984 – Charter cancelled.

Anthian Resource Corp. (B.C. Apr. 6, 1990)
June 19, 1997 – Continued into Canada.
Aug. 18, 2000 – Name changed to Sudamet Ventures Inc.; basis 1 new for 10 old shs. ■

Anthonian Mining Corp. Ltd. (Que. 1950)
May 8, 1982 – Charter cancelled.

Anthony Clark International Insurance Brokers Ltd. (Can. Apr. 1, 1996 amalg.)
Feb. 28, 1999 – Amalgamated in Alberta to continue with same name.
May 1, 2014 – Name changed to ACL International Ltd. ■

Antibe Therapeutics Inc. (Ont. May 5, 2009)
Apr. 22, 2024 – Placed into receivership and FTI Consulting Canada Inc. appointed receiver.

Antibi Gold Mines Ltd. (Ont. 1946)
1952 – Charter cancelled.

Anticline Petroleums Ltd. (unknown)
Dec. 31, 1968 – Merged with Excel Petroleums Ltd.; basis 1 new for 6 old shs.

Antigua Enterprises Inc. (B.C. Dec. 9, 1986)
July 17, 1998 – Continued into Yukon.
May 3, 2010 – Amalgamated with 44106 Yukon Inc., a wholly owned subsid. of Ashley NA, LLC, for US$0.31 per sh.

Antilles Resources Ltd. (B.C. Dec. 19, 1986)
Sept. 27, 1996 – Name changed to Golden Palm Resources Ltd.; basis 1 new for 5 old shs. ■

Antimony Gold Mining & Smelting Corp. Ltd. (Ont. 1948)
Mar. 1958 – Charter cancelled.

Antinouri Lake Mining Co. Ltd. (unknown)
Aug. 17, 1954 – Assets acquired by Baranouri Uranium Mines Ltd.; basis 10 new for 1 old sh.

Antioquia Gold Inc. (Ont. Apr. 25, 1997 amalg.)
Mar. 31, 2009 – Continued into Alberta.
Mar. 24, 2016 – Continued into British Columbia. (see FPsurvey - Mines & Energy)

Antipodes Gold Limited (B.C. Mar. 23, 1989)
Feb. 24, 2017 – Name changed to Chatham Rock Phosphate Limited following reverse takeover acquisition of Chatham Rock Phosphate (NZ) Limited (formerly known as (old) Chatham Rock Phosphate Limited); basis 1 new for 10 old shs. (see FPsurvey - Mines & Energy)

Antler Creek Energy Corp. (Alta. May 31, 2009 amalg.)
July 29, 2010 – Name changed to Pinecrest Energy Inc. ■

Antler Gold Mines Ltd. (Ont. 1934)
1949 – Charter cancelled.

Antler Hill Mining Ltd. (Alta. Sept. 11, 2009)
Apr. 29, 2021 – Continued into British Columbia. (see FPsurvey - Mines & Energy)

Antler Hill Oil & Gas Ltd. (Alta. Sept. 11, 2009)
June 29, 2017 – Name changed to Antler Hill Mining Ltd. ■

Antofagasta Gold Inc. (B.C. Aug. 27, 2010)
Feb. 12, 2013 – Continued into Ontario.
Nov. 25, 2013 – Name changed to Arena Minerals Inc. ■

Antoine Silver Mines Ltd. (B.C. 1964)
Oct. 1974 – Charter cancelled.

Antoinette Lake Mines Ltd. (Ont. 1949)
Jan. 9, 1980 – Charter cancelled.

Antone Petroleums Ltd. (Ont. 1952)
1955 – Purchased by American Leduc Petroleums Ltd.; basis 1 new for 3 old shs. Charter surrendered.

Antony Gas & Oil Explorations Limited (Ont. 1954)
June 27, 1973 – Name changed to Anthex Industries Inc. ■

Antony Resources Inc. (B.C. June 16, 1987)
Jan. 3, 1990 – Name changed to Sidewinder Conversions International Inc. following reverse takeover acquisition of Sidewinder Conversions Ltd. ■

Antrex Holdings Corp. (Ont. Apr. 29, 1983)
Feb. 23, 1995 – Name changed to Medican Pharma International Inc. ■

Antrim Energy Inc. (Alta. Sept. 29, 1999 amalg.)
Apr. 26, 2017 – Voluntarily dissolved.

Antrim Resources Inc. (B.C. Apr. 11, 1986)
Sept. 30, 1994 – Struck from registry and dissolved.

Antrim Resources Ltd. (B.C. 1978)
Jan. 31, 1984 – Name changed to Kenridge Mineral Corporation. ■

Anuk River Mines Ltd. (B.C. 1965)
Jan. 1973 – Wound up. Distribution of World Petroleum shs. made to Anuk shldrs.; basis 1 World Petroleum sh. for 10 Anuk shs.

Anuwon Uranium Mines Ltd. (Ont. 1953)
Mar. 1976 – Charter cancelled.

Anvil Mining Corporation Limited (B.C. 1965)
1974 – Name changed to Cyprus Anvil Mining Corporation. ■

Anvil Mining Limited (N.W.T. Jan. 8, 2004)
Mar. 20, 2012 – Acquired by Minmetals Resources Limited for Cdn$8.00 per sh.

Anvil Porcupine Gold Mines Ltd. (Ont. 1945)
1954 – Name changed to Burrex Mines Ltd. ■

Anvil Range Mining Corporation (Can. Feb. 2, 1994)
Jan. 16, 1998 – Granted protection under the Companies' Creditors Arrangement Act (CCAA) which was subsequently extended to Mar. 25, 1998. The co. was authorized by the Ontario court to pay amounts owing totaling $1,300,000 to its Yukon-based employees due to the shutdown of the Faro mine.
Apr. 21, 1998 – Court appointed Deloitte & Touche Inc. in Toronto, Ont., as interim receiver. By January 1999, the co. had been placed into receivership and Deloitte & Touche was appointed receiver. During 1999 and 2000, the receiver presented in court a Plan of Arrangement under the CCAA which was accepted by secured creditors who would benefit in the distribution of about $9,000,000. The Faro mine, leases and claims, the mill and milling structures were included in the Plan which was approved by the court.
May 1, 2003 – Appeal by unsecured debenture holders heard at a hearing in March 2002 was denied and the

monies approved under the Plan was distributed to secured creditors. There were no distributions to shldrs. The receiver would continue to manage the environmental aspects of the Faro mine site as outlined in Plan of Arrangement.

Anvil Resources Ltd. (B.C. Aug. 19, 1966)
July 24, 2003 – Name changed to Geocore Exploration Inc.; basis 1 new for 10 old shs. ■

Anzex Resources Ltd. (Yuk. Feb. 24, 1997)
Dec. 23, 2003 – Name changed to Helena Resources Limited; basis 1 new for 8 old shs. ■

Apamag Mines Ltd. (Ont. 1954)
Aug. 24, 1964 – Dissolved.

Apella Resources Inc. (B.C. Oct. 23, 1980)
May 28, 2012 – Name changed to PacificOre Mining Corp. ■

Apex Capital Corp. (Alta. Sept. 15, 2004)
July 14, 2008 – Formed Traxion Energy Inc. in Alberta on amalgamation with wholly owned Traxion Energy Inc. ■

Apex Consolidated Resources Ltd. (Ont. 1945)
May 1959 – Name changed to Abacus Mines Ltd.; basis 1 new for 6 old shs. ■

The Apex Corporation (Alta. Dec. 7, 1988)
Nov. 13, 2001 – Acquired by Bentall Corporation, a wholly owned subsid. of SITQ Vancouver Inc.; basis $2.60 per cl. A com. sh.

Apex Energy Corp. (B.C. Feb. 11, 1981)
Mar. 3, 1995 – Name changed to Nu-Apex Energy Corp.; basis 1 new for 4 old shs. ■

Apex Exploration & Mining Co. Ltd. (B.C. 1965)
Sept. 1974 – Charter cancelled.

Apex Gold Mines Ltd. (B.C. Jan. 25, 1935)
1957 – Placed into voluntary liquidation and assets distributed. Shldrs. received 1 Woodgreen Copper Mines sh. for 10 old Apex shs.

Apex Oils & Mines Ltd. (Ont. 1923)
1945 – Merged into Apex Consolidated Resources Ltd.; basis 1 new for 2.5 old shs. (see Apex Consolidated Resources Ltd.)

Apex Oils Ltd. (B.C. 1929)
1941 – Acquired by Vermillion Consolidated Oils Ltd. for 300,000 shs.

Apex Resorts Corporation (B.C. Feb. 22, 1984)
Nov. 12, 1996 – Name changed to A.M.R. Corporate Group Ltd.; basis 1 new for 10 old shs. ■

Aphelion Capital Corp. (B.C. Jan. 10, 2019)
Dec. 24, 2021 – Name changed to Edge Total Intelligence Inc. pursuant to the Qualifying Transaction reverse takeover acquisition of (old) Edge Technologies, Inc. (see FPsurvey - Industrials)

Aphria Inc. (Ont. Dec. 1, 2014)
May 5, 2021 – Acquired by Tilray, Inc.; basis 0.831 Tilray shs. for 1 Aphria sh. (see Tilray, Inc.)

Aphria International Inc. (Ont. July 17, 2015)
Mar. 28, 2018 – All o/s com. shs. not already held acquired by Aphria Inc.; basis 62¢ cash and 0.3545 Aphria com. shs. for 1 Nuuvera com. sh.

Apiva Ventures Limited (B.C. June 20, 1980)
Aug. 13, 2008 – Name changed to Mark One Global Industries, Inc. ■

Apiva.com Web Corporation (B.C. June 20, 1980)
Dec. 18, 2001 – Name changed to Apiva Ventures Limited. ■

Apivio Systems Inc. (B.C. Sept. 11, 2013 amalg.)
July 20, 2017 – All o/s shs. not already held acquired by 1101324 B.C. Ltd., a wholly owned subsid. of Nuri Telecom Company Limited; basis 45¢ cash per sh.

Apogee Minerals Ltd. (B.C. May 25, 1987)
Jan. 21, 2005 – Continued into Ontario.
Mar. 28, 2011 – Name changed to Apogee Silver Ltd. ■

Apogee Opportunities Inc. (Ont. Jan. 21, 2005)
Sept. 28, 2018 – Name changed to Halo Labs Inc. following reverse takeover acquisition of ANM, Inc. (dba Halo Labs) and concurrent amalgamation of Halo Labs with a wholly owned subsidiary of the company. ■

Apogee Silver Ltd. (Ont. Jan. 21, 2005)
Sept. 16, 2016 – Name changed to Apogee Opportunities Inc. ■

Apoka Capital Corporation (B.C. Nov. 26, 2007)
Oct. 29, 2008 – Name changed to Mala Noche Resources Corp. following Qualifying Transaction reverse takeover acquisition of Mala Noche Resources Corp. ■

Apollo Development Inc. (B.C. May 15, 1990)
Dec. 17, 1996 – Formed Sedna Geotech Inc. in Yukon on amalgamation with Sedna Geotech Inc., a wholly owned subsid. of Sedna Holdings Ltd.; basis 1 new for 1.1865 Sedna shs. and 1 new for 2 old Apollo sh. ■

Apollo Gas Income Fund (Ont. Feb. 26, 1998)
Feb. 1, 2001 – Wound up. Distribution totaled $1.74 per sh.

Apollo Gold & Silver Corp. (B.C. Nov. 4, 2010)
Sept. 10, 2021 – Name changed to Apollo Silver Corp. (see FPsurvey - Mines & Energy)

Apollo Gold Corporation (Ont. June 25, 2002 amalg.)
May 2003 – Continued into Yukon.
June 28, 2010 – Name changed to Brigus Gold Corp. following amalgamation of Linear Gold Corp. with a wholly owned subsid. of Apollo (deemed acquiror); basis 1 new for 4 old shs. ■

Apollo Gold Corp. (B.C. Nov. 4, 2010)
Jan. 8, 2021 – Name changed to Apollo Gold & Silver Corp. ■

Apollo Healthcare Corp. (Ont. June 19, 2015)
Jan. 12, 2022 – Acquired by Anjac SAS; basis $4.50 cash per cl. B sh.

Apollo Porcupine Mines Ltd. (Ont. 1946)
Apr. 1, 1965 – Dissolved.

Apolo II Acquisition Corp. (Ont. Dec. 15, 2017)
Nov. 12, 2019 – Name changed to Terrace Global Inc. pursuant to Qualifying Transaction reverse takeover acquisition of Terrace Inc. ■

Apolo III Acquisition Corp. (Ont. Jan. 19, 2018)
May 31, 2021 – Name changed to Playmaker Capital Inc. pursuant to the Qualifying Transaction reverse takeover acquisition of (old) Playmaker Capital Inc., with (old) Playmaker amalgamating with wholly owned 2830125 Ontario Inc. and then concurrently amalgamated into the company.; basis 1 new for 4.54 old shs. ■

Apolo Acquisition Corp. (Ont. May 18, 2017)
Jan. 25, 2018 – Name changed to CryptoGlobal Corp. following Qualifying Transaction reverse takeover acquisition of CryptoGlobal Inc.; basis 1 new for 3.938 old shs. ■

Apoquindo Minerals Inc. (B.C. Mar. 23, 2005)
June 11, 2010 – Name changed to AQM Copper Inc. ■

Ressources Appalaches inc. (Que. Sept. 23, 1993)
Jan. 20, 2015 – Placed into receivership. Ernst & Young Inc. appointed receiver and all officers and directors resigned.
Aug. 2016 – Assets sold to Maritime Dufferin Gold Corp. for a credit bid of US$10,000,000. Distribution to secured creditors ranking in priority to be discharged from cash proceeds of Cdn$335,000. No funds available for distribution to shldrs.
Sept. 22, 2016 – Ernst & Young Inc. discharged as receiver.
July 19, 2017 – Struck from registry.

Appareo Software Inc. (B.C. Apr. 29, 1982)
Sept. 29, 2004 – Name changed to Cellstop Systems Inc. following June 1, 2004, reverse takeover acquisition of CellStop International Limited. ■

Appature Mobile Applications Inc. (B.C. Oct. 30, 2014)
Mar. 27, 2018 – Name changed to APPx Crypto Technologies Inc. ■

Appia Energy Corp. (Can. Aug. 24, 2007)
Oct. 15, 2021 – Name changed to Appia Rare Earths & Uranium Corp. (see FPsurvey - Mines & Energy)

Appian Energy Corporation (B.C. 1980)
Dec. 21, 1981 – By agreement dated co. amalgamated with Tiber Resources Ltd. to form Tiber Energy Corporation; basis 1 new for 8 old shs.

Appian Resources Ltd. (B.C. Sept. 6, 1989 amalg.)
May 4, 1992 – Name changed to Sultan Minerals Inc.; basis 1 new for 4 old shs. ■

Appili Therapeutics Inc. (N.S. May 7, 2015)
Nov. 15, 2018 – Continued into Canada. (see FPsurvey - Industrials)

Applause Corporation (Alta. Jan. 28, 1994)
Oct. 2, 2003 – Struck from registry and dissolved.

Apple Capital Inc. (B.C. Apr. 16, 2007)
July 15, 2016 – Name changed to YDreams Global Interactive Technologies Inc. pursuant to reverse takeover acquisition of YDreams Brazil S.A. ■

Appleton Exploration Inc. (B.C. June 23, 2006)
June 1, 2012 – Name changed to Cornerstone Metals Inc.; basis 1 new for 5 old shs. ■

Applied Carbon Technology, Inc. (Ont. July 11, 1985)
July 14, 2000 – Name changed to Merchant Capital Group Incorporated; basis 1 new for 7 old shs. ■

Applied Energy Inc. (B.C. 1984)
July 21, 1995 – Dissolved and struck off register.

Applied Gaming Solutions of Canada Inc. (Alta. Oct. 13, 1995)
Nov. 14, 2002 – Name changed to Pacific Lottery Corporation; basis 1 new for 10 old shs. ■

Applied High Technology AHT Corporation (Alta. Aug. 10, 1993)
Mar. 12, 1999 – Name changed to AHT Corporation; basis 1 new for 10 old shs. ■

Applied Inventions Management Corporation (Ont. July 12, 1989)
July 8, 1992 – Name changed to Applied Inventions Management Inc.; basis 1 new for 4.8 old shs. ■

Applied Inventions Management Corp. (Ont. July 12, 1989)
Nov. 9, 2018 – Continued into British Columbia.
Nov. 14, 2018 – Name changed to Acreage Holdings, Inc. following reverse takeover acquisition of High Street Capital Partners, LLC (dba Acreage Holdings). ■

Applied Inventions Management Inc. (Ont. July 12, 1989)
Aug. 29, 2014 – Name changed to Applied Inventions Management Corp.; basis 1 new for 3 old shs. ■

Applied Terravision Systems Inc. (Alta. Sept. 11, 1978)
Apr. 3, 2002 – Amalgamated with Cognicase Acquisition II Corp. to become a wholly owned subsid. of COGNICASE Inc.; basis either 1 new amalco pref. sh. plus 0.105 COGNICASE com. shs., or 0.147574 COGNICASE com. shs. for 1 Applied Terravision com. sh. (see COGNICASE Inc.)

Appreciated Media Holdings Inc. (B.C. June 1, 2015)
Jan. 7, 2022 – Name changed to Amcomri Entertainment Inc. pursuant to the reverse takeover acquisition of Trinity Pictures Distribution Limited.; basis 1 new for 25 old shs. ■

Approach Resources Ltd. (B.C. Aug. 4, 1986)
Apr. 26, 1994 – Name changed to Future Media Technologies Corp. ∎

AppsVillage Australia Limited (Australia June 1, 2018)
Jan. 31, 2022 – Name changed to AdRabbit Limited. (see FPsurvey - Industrials)

Apsley Management Group Inc. (Alta. Aug. 17, 2000)
Apr. 25, 2003 – Name changed to Resverlogix Corp. following Qualifying Transaction acquisition of Resverlogix Inc. (see FPsurvey - Industrials)

Apteryx Imaging Inc. (B.C. Apr. 9, 2010)
Aug. 14, 2020 – Acquired by PDDS Buyer, LLC; basis Cdn$0.65 cash per sh.

Aptilon Corporation (Can. Apr. 1, 2005)
June 20, 2014 – Name changed to DMD Digital Health Connections Group Inc. ∎

Aqua-Aurum Mining Co. Ltd. (B.C. 1966)
Dec. 1974 – Charter cancelled.

Aqua Capital Corp. (B.C. Mar. 21, 2000)
May 15, 2002 – Name changed to Texada Software Inc. following Qualifying Transaction reverse takeover acquisition of RentOnTheDot Inc. ∎

Aqua Mining Corp. Ltd. (Que. 1961)
Nov. 1974 – Charter cancelled.

Aqua 1 Beverage Company, Inc. (B.C. Oct. 6, 1986)
Sept. 11, 2003 – Name changed to PowerNova Technologies Corporation following reverse takeover acquisition of Hydrogen Production Technologies Corporation. ∎

Aqua Pura Technologies Inc. (Alta. 1979)
Dec. 1, 1993 – Dissolved and struck off register.

Aqua-Pure Ventures Inc. (B.C. Aug. 24, 1992)
Nov. 13, 2001 – Continued into Alberta.
Aug. 18, 2015 – Placed into receivership. Grant Thornton Limited appointed receiver.
Nov. 2015 – All assets were sold. Under the purchase agreement a debt purchase provided for conversion of $7,260,000 of Hallmark Resources Ltd. and noteholders debt at a ratio of US$1.00 of debt for 0.70 class B units of the prospective purchaser. Secured creditor Agriculture Financials Services Corporation was repaid in full, with remaining monies being paid to other would be secured creditors who would suffer a short-fall. No monies would be available for shldrs.
Dec. 2016 – Remaining monies distrib. to secured creditors.
July 2, 2017 – Struck from registry and dissolved.

Aquablast Inc. (Ont. 1944)
1980 – Placed into bankruptcy in 1974. No distribution made to creditors. Trustee discharged.

Aquacare International Ltd. (B.C. 1966)
Jan. 31, 1977 – Dissolved.

AquaGold Resources Incorporated (Ont. Sept. 16, 1985)
Jan. 19, 1989 – Continued into Canada.
Nov. 17, 1992 – Name changed to Atlantic Industrial Minerals Incorporated. ∎

Aquamin Resources Inc. (B.C. Feb. 15, 1971)
May 10, 1994 – Name changed to Peruvian Gold Limited. ∎

Aquarius AI Inc. (B.C. Jan. 26, 2018 amalg.)
Mar. 27, 2023 – Name changed to P2Earn Inc.; basis 1 new for 4 old shs. (see FPsurvey - Industrials)

Aquarius Capital Corp. (Ont. Aug. 7, 2007)
May 31, 2011 – Name changed to China Green Star Agricultural Corporation pursuant to Qualifying Transaction reverse takeover acquisition of Sino Elite Group Limited; basis 1 new for 10 old shs. ∎

Aquarius Coatings Inc. (Ont. Dec. 12, 1986)
Feb. 24, 2017 – Name changed to Aquarius Surgical Technologies Inc. pursuant to acquisition of Surgical Lasers Inc.; basis 1 new for 20 old shs. (see FPsurvey - Industrials)

Aquarius Mines Ltd. (Que. 1971)
Feb. 1974 – Charter cancelled.

Aquarius Porcupine Gold Mines Ltd. (Ont. 1936)
1954 – Merged into Pardee Amalgamated Mines Ltd.; basis 1 new for 5 old shs.

Aquarius Seafarms Ltd. (B.C. 1985)
July 1990 – Receiver-manager appointed.
Aug. 31, 1990 – All assets liquidated. Secured creditors received partial repayment (approx. $2,000,000) while unsecured and preferred creditors and shldrs. received nothing.
Apr. 23, 1993 – Dissolved and struck off register.

Aquarius Ventures Inc. (B.C. Feb. 8, 1983)
Oct. 30, 2000 – Name changed to Citotech Systems Inc. following acquisition by Citotech Systems Inc. upon which Aquarius became a wholly owned subsid. of Citotech. ∎

Aquasol International Group Inc. (Alta. Apr. 28, 1987)
Oct. 5, 1999 – Struck off register.

Aquatech Systems Inc. (B.C. 1986)
Dec. 8, 1995 – Dissolved and struck off register.

Aquaterre Mineral Development Ltd. (B.C. May 11, 1993)
Oct. 23, 1997 – Name changed to Quaterra Resources Inc.; basis 1 new for 5 old shs. ∎

Aquatex Corporation (Alta. Oct. 21, 1992)
Aug. 10, 1998 – Deemed bankrupt.

Aquazoom Hydropower Solutions Inc. (B.C. Mar. 11, 2021)
Oct. 23, 2023 – Name changed to StickIt Technologies Inc. pursuant to the reverse takeover acquisition of StickIt Ltd. and concurrent amalgamation of StickIt with wholly owned Aquazoom Merger Ltd. (see FPsurvey - Industrials)

Aqueous Capital Corp. (Alta. Nov. 20, 2006)
Apr. 5, 2010 – Name changed to Stoneset Equity Development Corp. following amalgamation on Feb. 18, 2010, of wholly owned subsid. 1485359 Alberta Ltd. and Stoneset Equities Ltd. with Stoneset the deemed acquiror; basis 0.382556534 new shs. for 1 Stoneset Equities Ltd. sh. and 1 new for 1 Aqueous sh. ∎

Aquest Energy Ltd. (Alta. July 18, 2002)
Sept. 7, 2005 – Plan of Arrangement acquisition by Anderson Energy Ltd.; basis 0.31 new Anderson sh. for 1 old Aquest sh. (see Anderson Energy Ltd.)

Aquest Explorations Ltd. (B.C. Mar. 6, 1987)
July 18, 2002 – Continued into Alberta.
Feb. 3, 2004 – Name changed to Aquest Energy Ltd. following reverse takeover acquisition of Eravista Energy Corp.; basis 1 new for 4 old shs. ∎

Aquest Minerals Corporation (B.C. Mar. 6, 1987)
Jan. 8, 2002 – Name changed to Aquest Explorations Ltd.; basis 1 new for 10 old shs. ∎

Aquifer Springs Ltd. (Alta. Oct. 7, 1993)
May 6, 1996 – Name changed to Arrowhead Water Products Ltd. ∎

Aquila Energy Corp. (B.C. Nov. 25, 1987)
Oct. 3, 2005 – Dissolved and struck from register.
Jan. 18, 2008 – Restored to register.
May 13, 2013 – Dissolved and struck from register.

Aquila Networks Canada (British Columbia) Ltd. (B.C. May 8, 1897)
June 1, 2004 – Name changed to FortisBC Inc.

Aquila Resources Inc. (Ont. Feb. 12, 1997)
Dec. 15, 2021 – Acquired by Gold Resource Corporation; basis 0.0399 Gold Resource shs. for 1 Aquila sh.

Aquila Resources Ltd. (B.C. Nov. 25, 1987)
Mar. 8, 1995 – Name changed to Aquila Energy Corp.; basis 1 new for 2 old shs. ∎

Aquiline Resources Inc. (B.C. May 3, 1988)
Jan. 26, 2010 – Acquired by Pan American Silver Corp.; basis 0.2495 Pan American sh. plus 0.1 Pan American wt. for 1 Aquiline sh.

Aquilium Software Corporation (Can. Jan. 13, 1994)
Mar. 5, 2001 – Formed MDR Switchview Global Networks Inc. on amalgamation with MDR Technologies Inc., Switchview Inc. and Netperforms Corp.; basis 0.034 net old Aquilium com. shs. for 1 new MDR Switchview com. sh. ∎

Aquitaine Company of Canada Ltd. (Can. 1963)
June 26, 1981 – Canada Development Corporation purchased 74.8% interest held by Société Nationale Elf Acquitaine for $1,208,100,000.
Oct. 1981 – Canada Development Corporation acquired the balance for $407,400 from public shldrs.

Arabee Oil and Gas Co. Ltd. (B.C. 1952)
Dec. 1957 – Name changed to Arawain Producers Limited; basis 1 new for 5 old shs. ∎

Arabesque Resources Ltd. (B.C. Oct. 5, 1979)
Nov. 7, 1988 – Delisted Vancouver Stock Exchange. Subsequently struck from register and dissolved.

Aragon Explorations Ltd. (B.C. 1969)
Mar. 31, 1983 – Struck off register.

Arak Resources Ltd. (B.C. May 9, 2006)
Mar. 31, 2017 – Name changed to Cobalt 27 Capital Corp.; basis 3 new for 1 old sh. ∎

Arakis Capital Corporation (B.C. Sept. 12, 1986)
Jan. 14, 1991 – Name changed to Arakis Energy Corporation. ∎

Arakis Energy Corporation (B.C. Sept. 12, 1986)
Apr. 29, 1996 – Continued into Alberta. (see Talisman Energy Inc.)
Oct. 9, 1998 – Acquired by Talisman Energy Inc.; basis 1 Talisman sh. for 10 Arakis shs. (see Talisman Energy Inc.)

Arakis Mining Corporation (B.C. Sept. 12, 1986)
Oct. 17, 1988 – Name changed to Arakis Capital Corporation. ∎

Aralez Pharmaceuticals Inc. (B.C. Dec. 2, 2015)
Aug. 10, 2018 – The company and its subsidiary, Aralez Pharmaceuticals Canada Inc. commenced voluntary restructuring proceeding under the Companies' Creditors Arrangement Act (CCAA). Subsidiaries incorporated in the U.S. and Ireland (Aralez Pharmaceuticals US Inc., Aralez Pharmaceuticals Management Inc., POZEN Inc., Aralez Pharmaceuticals R&D Inc., Halton Laboratories LLC, Aralez Pharmaceuticals Holdings Limited and Aralez Pharmaceuticals Trading DAC) filed voluntary petitions for relief under Chapter 11 of the U.S. Bankruptcy Court.
Feb. 5, 2019 – Name changed to Old API Wind-down Ltd. ∎

Aramis Ventures Inc. (B.C. Aug. 29, 1988)
Mar. 31, 1994 – Name changed to Newera Capital Corporation. ∎

Aran Oil & Gas Ltd. (Alta. 1976)
Oct. 5, 1979 – Name changed to Canadian Aran Petroleums Ltd.; basis 1 new for 4 old shs. ∎

Aranjin Resources Ltd. (B.C. Nov. 14, 2012)
Aug. 14, 2025 – Name changed to Trinity One Metals Ltd. (see FPsurvey - Mines & Energy)

Aranka Gold Inc. (Ont. Feb. 18, 1953)
Jan. 29, 2009 – Acquired by Guyana Goldfields Inc.; basis 1 Guyana sh. for 3.25 Aranka shs.

Aranlee Resources Ltd. (B.C. Oct. 7, 1986)
Nov. 15, 1996 – Continued into Yukon.
Oct. 5, 1998 – Name changed to Southern Metals Corporation; basis 1 new for 7 old shs. ■

Arapaho Capital Corp. (B.C. Apr. 17, 1998)
Dec. 8, 2009 – Continued into Ontario.
Dec. 9, 2009 – Name changed to Malbex Resources Inc. following amalgamation of wholly owned 2206833 Ontario Inc. and Malbex Resources Inc., contituting a reverse takeover by Malbex whereby Malbex shldrs. received 1 Arapaho sh. for every 1.5 Malbex shs. held. ■

Arapahoe Energy Corporation (Alta. Jan. 14, 1997)
Feb. 24, 2004 – Amalgamated in Alberta to continue with same name.
Jan. 7, 2008 – Name changed to Canadian Phoenix Resources Corp. ■

Arapahoe Mining Corp. (B.C. Mar. 16, 1966)
May 6, 1996 – Name changed to Salus Resource Corp.; basis 1 new for 5 old shs. ■

Arauco Resources Corporation (B.C. Oct. 3, 1991)
Aug. 13, 1997 – Name changed to Kit Resources Ltd. and continued into Canada. ■

Arawain Producers Limited (B.C. 1952)
Mar. 1961 – Acquired by Western Allenbee Oil & Gas Co. Ltd.; basis 1 new for 2 old shs.

Arawak Energy Corporation (Anguilla Apr. 11, 1995)
Apr. 24, 2008 – Continued into Jersey.
June 3, 2008 – Name changed to Arawak Energy Limited. ■

Arawak Energy Limited (Jersey Apr. 24, 2008)
Apr. 15, 2009 – Acquired by Rosco S.A., a subsid. of Vitol Holding B.V., for $1.00 per sh.

Arawak Mines Ltd. (Ont. 1967)
Jan. 28, 1976 – Amalgamated to form Gerrard Realty Incorporated; basis 1 new for 90 old shs.

Arbade Gold Mines Ltd. (Ont. 1933)
Mar. 2, 1950 – Charter cancelled.

Arbatax International Inc. (Can. June 28, 1951; via letters patent)
Aug. 6, 1996 – Continued into Yukon.
Mar. 3, 1997 – Name changed to MFC Bancorp Ltd. ■

Arbec Forest Products Inc. (Can. Nov. 22, 1993)
May 31, 2006 – Acquired by Jolina Capital Inc. for $0.35 per sh.

Arbitrage Exploration Inc. (Ont. 1955)
Sept. 19, 2016 – Name changed to Argo Gold Inc. (see FPsurvey - Mines & Energy)

Arbor Capital Inc. (Ont. Aug. 31, 1973 amalg.)
Apr. 7, 1994 – Name changed to Arbor Memorial Services Inc. ■

Arbor Capital Resources Inc. (Ont. Aug. 31, 1973 amalg.)
Nov. 1, 1978 – Amalgamated with 35560 Ontario Limited to continue under the Arbor Capital name.
Mar. 14, 1986 – Name changed to Arbor Capital Inc. ■

Arbor Memorial Services Inc. (Ont. Aug. 31, 1973 amalg.)
Nov. 28, 2012 – Privatized for $32 per cl. A vtg. and cl. B non-vtg. sh.

Arbor Resources Inc. (B.C. Aug. 23, 1978)
Jan. 24, 1996 – Name changed to Klondike Gold Corp.; basis 1 new for 10 old shs. (see FPsurvey - Mines & Energy)

ArborScience Inc. (Ont. Sept. 30, 1996)
Feb. 2, 2001 – Notice to enforce a security for payment of the outstanding debenture received from the debenture holder.
Feb. 5, 2001 – Debenture holder served the co. with a proposal to accept collateral in satisfaction of the obligations secured.
May 17, 2001 – Debenture holder exercised his rights to repayment of the debenture and assumed title to all the co.'s assets in lieu of cash repayment, leaving the co. no longer solvent and all directors and officers resigned. No funds would be available for distribution to shldrs.

Arbour Energy Inc. (Alta. Apr. 9, 2001)
Oct. 2, 2011 – Struck from registry and dissolved.

Arbutus Food Corporation (B.C. Aug. 22, 1986)
Feb. 20, 1992 – Name changed to Sabre Marketing Corporation. ■

Arc Home Entertainment Diversified Ltd. (Ont. Feb. 6, 1969)
June 1970 – Name changed to Ahed Music Corporation Limited. ■

Arc Pacific Metals Ltd. (B.C. Aug. 25, 1987)
Mar. 6, 2000 – Name changed to Rampart Ventures Ltd.; basis 1 new for 3 old shs. ■

Arc Resources Ltd. (B.C. 1972)
Sept. 11, 1978 – Dissolved.

Arcadia Coal Co., Ltd. (Alta. Mar. 1929)
1931 – Dissolved and struck off register.

Arcadia Explorations Ltd. (B.C. 1967)
Aug. 11, 1983 – Name changed to New Arcadia Explorations Ltd. (N.P.L.); basis 1 new for 4 old shs. ■

Arcadia Minerals Limited (Que. 1953)
Apr. 30, 1971 – Share split; basis 1 new for 5 old shs.
Oct. 1974 – Charter cancelled.
May 1975 – Charter revived.
Sept. 1976 – In receivership.

Arcadia Mining Co. Ltd. (B.C.)
June 9, 1960 – Dissolved and struck off register.

Arcadia Nickel Corp. Ltd. (Que. 1953)
1959 – Name changed to Associated Arcadia Nickel Corp. Ltd. (1 new for 2 old), 6% 1st mtge. bonds replaced by Associated Arcadia 6% 1st. mtge. bonds, dollar for dollar and creditors received 10¢ cash and 90¢ in conv. gen. mtge. debs. of Associated Arcadia for each dollar owing to them. ■

Arcamatrix Corporation (Ont. Sept. 21, 1998)
Feb. 4, 2008 – Certificate of incorporation cancelled and dissolved.

Arcan Corp. Ltd. (Ont. 1937)
Oct. 24, 1973 – Dissolved.

Arcan Resources Ltd. (Alta. Jan. 1, 2007 amalg.)
June 8, 2015 – Acquired by Aspenleaf Energy Limited for 11¢ per sh.

Arcanna Industries Corp. (B.C. 1966)
Dec. 21, 1993 – Name changed to Mercana Industries Ltd. following amalgamation with Mercana Medical Supplies Ltd.; basis 1.34 new for 1 old sh. ■

Arcap Diversified Inc. (Ont. 1960)
Oct. 9, 1982 – Name changed to First United Capital Corp.; basis 1 new for 5 old shs. ■

Arcata Resources Corp. (Yuk. Oct. 4, 1999)
May 14, 2003 – Name changed to Goldrush Resources Ltd.; basis 1 new for 2 old shs. ■

Arch Development Corporation (B.C. Feb. 2, 1981)
June 3, 1988 – Name changed to American Digital Industries Ltd. ■

Archangel Diamond Corporation (B.C. July 3, 1987)
Sept. 16, 1996 – Continued into Yukon.
June 7, 2010 – Voluntarily dissolved.

Archean Oil Limited (Australia 1969)
Jan. 19, 1983 – Name changed to Tri-Arc Energy Limited.

Archean Star Resources Inc. (B.C. Oct. 29, 2009)
Jan. 28, 2011 – Amalgamated in British Columbia to continue with same name.
Feb. 5, 2014 – Name changed to Transatlantic Mining Corp. (see FPsurvey - Mines & Energy)

Archer Communications Inc. (B.C. Dec. 6, 1968)
July 10, 1990 – Continued into Alberta.
July 27, 1993 – Name changed to QSound Labs, Inc. (see FPsurvey - Industrials)

Archer Exploration Corp. (B.C. Oct. 26, 2018)
Apr. 26, 2024 – Name changed to NorthX Nickel Corp.; basis 1 new for 6 old shs. (see FPsurvey - Mines & Energy)

Archer International Developments Ltd. (B.C. Dec. 6, 1968)
Apr. 28, 1989 – Name changed to Archer Communications Inc. ■

Archer Minerals Inc. (B.C. Dec. 6, 1968)
Dec. 17, 1986 – Name changed to Archer International Developments Ltd. ■

Archer Petroleum Corp. (B.C. Oct. 31, 1984)
Nov. 9, 2017 – Name changed to Atlas Engineered Products Ltd. pursuant to the reverse takeover acquisition of (old) Atlas Engineered Products Ltd. (see FPsurvey - Industrials)

Archer Resources Ltd. (Alta. May 16, 1989)
Apr. 27, 1998 – Acquired by Dominion Acquisition Inc., a wholly owned subsid. of Dominion Energy Inc. of Richmond, Va., for $7.60 per sh.

Architectural Ceramic Developments Company Limited (Ont. 1960)
Dec. 1962 – Name changed to Western Heritage Properties Ltd. ■

Architel Systems Corporation (Can. Aug. 9, 1984)
July 6, 2000 – Acquired by Nortel Networks Corporation; basis 0.38682 Nortel com. shs. for 1 Architel com. sh. Originally incorporated in Ontario Mar. 7, 1984. (see Nortel Networks Corporation)

Arcis Corporation (Alta. Sept. 12, 1996)
Mar. 2, 2004 – Privatized at $1.26 per sh.

Arcland Resources Inc. (B.C. June 11, 1987)
Continued into Cayman Islands. (see FPsurvey - Mines & Energy)

Arco Resources Corp. (B.C. Mar. 13, 2006)
Mar. 12, 2018 – Name changed to Cannex Capital Holdings Inc. following amalgamation of a wholly owned subsidiary of Arco with Cannex Capital Group Inc., constituting a reverse takeover by Cannex. ■

Arcom Systems Ltd. (B.C.)
Oct. 24, 1972 – Name changed to Arcom Systems Manufacturing Ltd. ■

Arcom Systems Manufacturing Ltd. (B.C.)
Nov. 18, 1983 – Struck off register.

ArcPacific Resources Corp. (B.C. Feb. 1, 2011)
May 15, 2023 – Name changed to Avante Mining Corp. ■

Arctic Fox Interactive Ltd. (B.C. Feb. 19, 2013)
Nov. 23, 2020 – Name changed to Arctic Fox Ventures Inc. ■

Arctic Fox Minerals Corp. (Ont. Mar. 23, 2018)
Mar. 6, 2023 – Name changed to Collective Metals Inc.; basis 1 new for 10 old shs. (see FPsurvey - Mines & Energy)

Arctic Fox Ventures Inc. (B.C. Feb. 19, 2013)
Mar. 24, 2023 – Name changed to Arctic Fox Lithium
Corp. (see FPsurvey - Mines & Energy)

Arctic Glacier Income Fund (Alta. Jan. 22, 2002)
Jan. 22, 2015 – Initial distrib. of US$0.155570 per unit
was paid to unitholders of record Dec. 18, 2014.
Nov. 15, 2019 – Interim distrib. of Cdn$0.042818335 cash
per unit payable to unithldrs. of record Nov. 15, 2019, on
Dec. 6, 2019.
Sept. 11, 2020 – Interim distrib. of Cdn$0.01427278 cash
per unit payable to unithldrs. of record Aug. 17, 2020.
Nov. 7, 2022 – Final distrib. of Cdn$0.00549502 cash per
unit payable to unithldrs. of record Oct. 14, 2022.

Arctic Gold & Silver Mines Ltd. (B.C. Oct. 14, 1964)
Aug. 27, 1979 – Name changed to Azam Energy
Corporation; basis 1 new for 10 old shs. ■

The Arctic Group Inc. (Alta. Mar. 1, 1996)
Mar. 22, 2002 – Plan of Arrangement to reorganize
company into an income fund trust known as Arctic
Glacier Income Fund; basis 1 new Arctic Glacier trust
unit for 6 old Arctic Group com. shs. (see Arctic Glacier
Income Fund)

Arctic Hunter Energy Inc. (B.C. Feb. 21, 2006)
Jan. 12, 2021 – Name changed to Trans Canada Gold
Corp. (see FPsurvey - Mines & Energy)

Arctic Hunter Uranium Inc. (B.C. Feb. 21, 2006)
Dec. 15, 2011 – Name changed to Arctic Hunter Energy
Inc. ■

Arctic Mining & Exploration Limited (B.C. Oct. 14,
1964)
Feb. 8, 1968 – Name changed to Arctic Gold & Silver
Mines Ltd. ■

Arctic Red Resources Corp. (B.C. 1980)
Jan. 31, 1991 – Name changed to Chuska Resources
Corporation; basis 1 new for 10 old shs. ■

Arctic Star Diamond Corp. (Can. Jan. 5, 2001)
July 8, 2011 – Name changed to Arctic Star Exploration
Corp.; basis 1 new for 12 old shs. (see FPsurvey - Mines
& Energy)

Arctic Wings Limited (unknown)
1956 – Acquired by Transair Ltd.

Arctic Yellowknife Mines Limited (Ont. 1938)
Nov. 8, 1977 – Dissolved.

Arctos Petroleum Corp. (Alta. Sept. 30, 2004 amalg.)
Nov. 12, 2007 – Name changed to Stetson Oil and Gas
Ltd.; basis 1 new for 10 old shs. ■

Arcturus Growthstar Technologies Inc. (B.C. May 31,
1984)
Feb. 2, 2017 – Name changed to Future Farm
Technologies Inc. ■

Arcturus Resources Ltd. (B.C. Sept. 5, 1980)
Dec. 19, 2000 – Name changed to Arcturus Ventures
Inc.; basis 1 new for 5 old shs. ■

Arcturus Ventures Inc. (B.C. Sept. 5, 1980)
Oct. 22, 2019 – Name changed to OjO Electric Corp.
following reverse takeover acquisition of OjO Electric,
LLC. ■

Ardel Explorations Ltd. (Ont. 1970)
Nov. 1977 – Charter cancelled.

Ardell Mines Ltd. (Ont. 1947)
1957 – Charter cancelled.

Arden Holdings Inc. (Que. Apr. 18, 1980)
Feb. 15, 2002 – Privatized at $8.00 per sh.

Ardiem Holdings Ltd. (B.C. 1965)
Dec. 23, 1975 – Amalgamated with A1 Steel & Iron
Foundry (Vancouver) Ltd. (10-for-1), E. C. Warner
Investments Ltd. (sh-for-sh) and Harbour Ferries Ltd.

(1-for-3) to form The Ardiem Industrial Corp.; basis 5 new
for 1 old sh.

The Ardiem Industrial Corporation (B.C. 1975 amalg.)
Feb. 1983 – Declared bankrupt. Assets sold. No
distribution to shldrs.

Ardmore Gold Mines Ltd. (Ont. Nov. 14, 1936)
1955 – Charter cancelled.

Ardo Mines Inc. (B.C. June 14, 1968)
Oct. 19, 1976 – Name changed to Arex Resources Inc.;
basis 1 new for 5 old shs. ■

Ardo Mines Ltd. (B.C. June 14, 1968)
June 19, 1975 – Name changed to Ardo Mines Inc. ■

Ardonblue Ventures Inc. (B.C. Jan. 6, 2006)
Oct. 23, 2017 – Name changed to Juggernaut Exploration
Ltd. (see FPsurvey - Mines & Energy)

Area Mines Ltd. (Ont. 1925)
Apr. 1, 1971 – Acquired by Teck Corporation Limited;
basis 1 Teck cl. B sh. for 3 Area shs. (see Teck
Corporation Limited)

Arehada Mining Limited (Ont. June 7, 2005)
Aug. 17, 2016 – Undergoing voluntary dissolution; interim
distrib. of 4¢ cash per sh. to shldrs. of record Aug. 8,
2016.
May 10, 2019 – Second interim distrib. of 2¢ cash per sh.
to shldrs. of record Apr. 29, 2019, payable on May 10,
2019.
Feb. 10, 2023 – Court order for winding up and liquidating
the company granted. Albert Gelman Inc. appointed
liquidator.
Sept. 21, 2023 – Deemed insolvent and assigned into
bankruptcy. Albert Gelman Inc. appointed trustee.

Ressources Arena Gold inc. (Can. Apr. 24, 1996)
Jan. 6, 2004 – Dissolved.

Arena Minerals Inc. (Ont. Feb. 12, 2013)
Apr. 24, 2023 – All o/s shs. not already held acquired by
Lithium Americas Corp.; basis 0.0226 Lithium Americas
shs. and $0.0001 cash per 1 Arena Minerals sh. (see
Lithium Americas Corp.)

Arequipa Resources Ltd. (B.C. Feb. 13, 1984)
Oct. 25, 1996 – Acquired by Barrick Gold Corporation;
basis (i) $30 per sh. or (ii) 50¢ cash and 0.79 Barrick com.
shs. for 1 Arequipa com. sh. (see Barrick Gold
Corporation)

Arex Resources Inc. (B.C. June 14, 1968)
Jan. 15, 1980 – Name changed to Ohio Resources
Corporation; basis 1 new for 3 old shs. ■

Argcen Holdings Inc. (Can. 1919)
Sept. 17, 1985 – Formed Hollinger Inc. in Canada on
amalgamation with Hollinger Argus Limited (2.5 for 1)
and Labmin Resources Limited (3.5 for 1). ■

Argent Energy Trust (Alta. Jan. 31, 2012)
Feb. 2016 – Filed for protection under the Companies'
Creditors Arrangement Act (CCAA) and FTI Consulting
Canada Ltd. was appointed monitor.
May 2016 – Substantially all the assets were sold to BXP
Partners IV, LP. Proceeds received were insufficient to
provide funds for distrib. to unithldrs. or debentureholders.
Aug. 30, 2016 – Stay under CCAA for the trust and Argent
Canada (Holdings) Inc. was terminated resulting in an
assignment into bankruptcy. FTI Consulting Canada Inc.
was appointed trustee.

Argent Mining Corp. (B.C. Sept. 3, 1985)
June 21, 2007 – Name changed to Avion Resources
Corp.; basis 1 new for 3 old shs. ■

Argent Resources Ltd. (B.C. Sept. 3, 1985)
Apr. 7, 2006 – Name changed to Argent Mining Corp.;
basis 1 new for 3 old shs. ■

Argenta Oil & Gas Inc. (Ont. Sept. 21, 2005)
Nov. 22, 2006 – Continued into Canada.
Jan. 11, 2010 – Name changed to Azabache Energy Inc.;
basis 1 new for 5 old shs. ■

Argenta Resources Ltd (B.C. Aug. 24, 1979)
Apr. 4, 1987 – Name changed to Argenta Systems Inc. ■

Argenta Systems Inc. (B.C. Aug. 24, 1979)
Mar. 6, 2000 – Name changed to Illusion Systems Inc.;
basis 1 new for 2 old shs. ■

Argentex Mining Corporation (Del. Nov. 5, 2007)
June 3, 2011 – Continued into Nevada.
June 8, 2011 – Continued into British Columbia.
Aug. 22, 2016 – Acquired by Austral Gold Limited; basis
0.564676 Austral com. shs. for 1 Argentex com. sh.

Argentex Resources Exploration Corp. (Ont. 1980)
July 4, 1988 – Formed AXR Resources Ltd. in Ontario
on amalgamation with Sholia Resources Ltd. (1 for 5);
basis 1 new for 4 old shs. ■

Argentia Mines Ltd. (B.C. 1967)
Feb. 2, 1983 – Struck off register.

Argentina Gold Corp. (B.C. Oct. 14, 1981)
Feb. 3, 1995 – Continued into Canada.
Apr. 30, 1999 – Acquired by Homestake Mining Company;
basis 0.545 Homestake shs. for 1 Argentina sh.

Argentium Resources Inc. (Can. Aug. 11, 2011 amalg.)
Aug. 24, 2015 – Name changed to Northern Sphere
Mining Corp.; basis 1 new for 20 old shs. (see FPsurvey
- Mines & Energy; FPsurvey - Industrials)

Argentor Resources Ltd. (B.C. Nov. 27, 2004)
Jan. 11, 2006 – Name changed to Jantar Resources
Ltd. ■

Argex Mining Inc. (Can. Mar. 17, 2005)
July 20, 2012 – Name changed to Argex Titanium Inc. ■

Argex Silver Capital Inc. (Can. Mar. 17, 2005)
July 28, 2010 – Name changed to Argex Mining Inc. ■

Argex Titanium Inc. (Can. Mar. 17, 2005)
June 18, 2019 – Deemed insolvent. Notice filed to make
a proposal under the Bankruptcy and Insolvency Act
(BIA). PricewaterhouseCoopers Inc. was appointed
proposal trustee.
Dec. 5, 2019 – Reorganization proposal was accepted
by the majority of creditors. Under the proposal, secured
creditors will be paid in full and unsecured creditors to
receive distributions on a pro rata basis. All o/s shs. to
be redeemed for cancellation.
Jan. 14, 2020 – Court order was issued approving and
ratifying the proposal. All o/s shs. converted into
redeemable shs. immediately redeemed for $1 cash per
sh. All directors deemed to have resigned.

Argo Development Corp. (B.C. 1979)
Nov. 9, 1989 – Amalgamated with Exador Resources Inc.
(1 for 13) and Cheryl Resources Inc. (1 for 2) to form
Tymar Resources Inc.; basis 1 new for 2.5 old shs. (see
Tymar Resources Inc.)

Argo Energy Ltd. (Can. Feb. 23, 1995)
Apr. 26, 2005 – Plan of Arrangement with Lightning
Energy Ltd. (0.25 and 0.25 for 1) to convert company into
a new income trust named Sequoia Oil & Gas Trust and
a new exploration company named White Fire Energy
Ltd.; basis 0.17125 Sequoia trust units and 0.17125 White
Fire com. shs. for 1 Argo com. sh. (see Sequoia Oil &
Gas Trust; White Fire Energy Ltd.)

Argo Gold Mining Inc. (B.C. Apr. 22, 1977)
June 2, 1981 – Amalgamated with Pegasus Explorations
Ltd. to form Pegasus Gold Ltd.; basis 1.1 new for 1 old
sh. (see Pegasus Gold Ltd.)

Argo Living Soils Corp. (B.C. Mar. 14, 2018)
July 8, 2025 – Name changed to Argo Graphene
Solutions Corp. (see FPsurvey - Industrials)

Argo Petroleum Ltd. (Alta. 1967)
June 21, 1976 – Charter revived.
July 26, 1976 – Name changed to Argo Developments Ltd.

Argoma Uranium Mines Ltd. (Ont. 1955)
Oct. 5, 1959 – Dissolved.

Argon Electric Welding Co. Ltd. (Can. 1956)
May 1959 – Name changed to Argon Welding Industries Ltd. ■

Argon Welding Industries Ltd. (Can. 1956)
Dec. 16, 1980 – Dissolved.

Argonaut Gold Inc. (Ont. Apr. 3, 2007)
July 17, 2024 – Acquired by Alamos Gold Inc.; basis 0.0185 Alamos cl. A shs. plus 0.1 Florida Canyon shs. for 1 Argonaut sh.

Argonaut Gold Ltd. (Ont. Apr. 3, 2007)
Oct. 1, 2010 – Name changed to Argonaut Gold Inc. pursuant to vertical amalgamation with wholly owned Argonaut Gold Inc. ■

Argonaut Investment Corp. (Alta. Jan. 9, 1987)
Oct. 24, 1990 – Name changed to Spray-Air International, Inc.; basis 1 new for 3 old shs. ■

Argonaut Mines Ltd. (B.C. 1969)
1971 – Merged into Granite Mountain Mines Ltd. on sh.-for-sh. basis; except for vendor shs. which were exchanged 2 new for 3 old shs.

Argonaut Resources Ltd. (B.C. 1981)
July 28, 1989 – Name changed to P.D.C. Industrial Coatings Inc. and continued into Canada; basis 1 new for 2 old shs. ■

Argonaut Yellowknife Mines Ltd. (Ont. 1944)
1956 – Charter cancelled.

Argonauts Group Ltd. (Alta. Mar. 29, 1995)
June 7, 2002 – Formed Cequel Energy Inc. on amalgamation with subsid. Chain Energy Corporation. ■

Argonex International Ltd. (B.C. Feb. 7, 1984)
Jan. 9, 1989 – Delisted from the Vancouver Stock Exchange. Subsequently struck from register and dissolved.

Argosy Capital Corporation (Ont. 1939)
Jan. 28, 2008 – Certificate of incorporation cancelled and dissolved.

Argosy Energy Inc. (Alta. June 6, 2008)
May 30, 2013 – Placed into receivership. FTI Consulting Canada Inc. appointed receiver and manager. All officers and directors resigned.

Argosy Finance Company Limited (Ont. 1967)
Aug. 1979 – Name changed to Argosy Financial Group of Canada Limited. ■

Argosy Financial Group of Canada Limited (Ont. 1967)
Mar. 19, 1980 – Placed into receivership. Laventhol & Howarth Ltd. of Toronto appointed interim receiver manager..

Argosy Gold Mines Ltd. (Ont. May 2, 1935)
1938 – Name changed to Jason Mines Ltd.; basis 1 new for 5 old shs. ■

Argosy Minerals Inc. (Yuk. June 17, 1997)
May 26, 2005 – Continued into British Columbia.
Jan. 18, 2011 – Name changed to Argosy Minerals Limited and continued into Australia.

Argosy Mining Corp. (B.C. July 12, 1988)
Aug. 12, 1997 – Continued into Yukon. (see Argosy Minerals Inc.)
May 10, 1999 – Amalgamated into Calliope Metals Corporation; basis 0.6 Calliope shs. for 1 Argosy sh. (see Argosy Minerals Inc.)

Argosy Mining Corporation Limited (Ont. 1939)
Mar. 29, 1989 – Name changed to Argosy Capital Corporation. ■

Argosy Resources Corporation (B.C. June 5, 1981)
Oct. 24, 1991 – Name changed to Motion Works Corporation. ■

Argrel Resources Ltd. (B.C. 1979)
Nov. 5, 1993 – Dissolved and struck off register.

Argus Consolidated Mines Ltd. (B.C. 1954)
1957 – Name changed to Cassiar Copperfields Ltd.; basis 1 new for 2.5 old shs. ■

Argus Corporation Limited (Ont. Sept. 24, 1945)
Dec. 11, 1985 – Amalgamated in Canada to continue with same name.
Dec. 24, 1990 – Continued into Canada.
May 18, 2005 – Placed into receivership. RSM Richter Inc. appointed receiver and monitor.

Argus Metals Corp. (B.C. May 14, 1981)
Dec. 7, 2017 – Name changed to ePower Metals Inc. ■

Argus Resources Ltd. (Ont. 1969)
Oct. 4, 1979 – Continued into Alberta.
Oct. 2, 2006 – Struck from registry and dissolved.

Argyle Ventures Inc. (B.C. July 29, 1983)
May 11, 1994 – Name changed to Anglo-Andean Explorations, Inc. ■

Argyll Energy Corporation (Ont. Oct. 20, 1961)
June 1990 – Placed into receivership. Coopers & Lybrand (Calgary) appointed receiver.
May 1992 – All assets liquidated. No distribution to unsecured creditors or shldrs.

Argyll Gold Mines Limited (Ont. 1946)
Mar. 1976 – Charter cancelled.

Argyll Resources Ltd. (B.C. 1978)
June 30, 1983 – Amalgamated with wholly owned subsid. of Argyll Energy Corporation. Shldrs., other than Argyll Energy which held 51% int., received 1,717,310 cl. A shs. of Argyll Energy (1 for 1).

Arian Resources Corporation (Ont. Aug. 9, 1990)
Nov. 5, 1995 – Continued into New Brunswick. (see Bema Gold Corporation)
July 8, 1998 – Merged with a wholly owned subsid. of Bema Gold Corporation; basis 1 Bema sh. for 3.3 Arian shs. (see Bema Gold Corporation)

Arian Resources Corp. (B.C. Jan. 24, 2007)
July 9, 2018 – Struck from register and dissolved.

Arian Silver Corporation (B.C. May 4, 2004)
May 24, 2006 – Continued into British Virgin Islands.

Ariane Gold Corp. (Can. Mar. 6, 2002)
Nov. 28, 2003 – Plan of Arrangement with Cambior Inc.; basis 0.3436 Cambior shs. for 1 Ariane sh. (see Cambior Inc.)

Arianne Resources Inc. (Que. Dec. 14, 1959)
July 5, 2013 – Name changed to Arianne Phosphate Inc. (see FPsurvey - Mines & Energy)

Ariel Resources Ltd. (B.C. July 18, 1986)
Aug. 14, 2002 – Continued into Wyoming.

Aries Copper Mines Ltd. (Ont. 1955)
Apr. 1, 1965 – Dissolved.

Aries Resource Corp. (B.C. Mar. 21, 1978)
Sept. 24, 2008 – Name changed to Alderon Resource Corp.; basis 1 new for 10 old shs. ■

Aries Resources Inc. (Yuk. May 20, 1958)
May 19, 1999 – Name changed to Total Global Ventures Inc. and continued into British Columbia following reverse takeover acquisition of Golden Leaf Development Trust, Thompson & Redford Holdings Ltd., Golden Leaf Development Company and 535535 B.C. Ltd. ■

Aries Uranium Mines Ltd. (Ont. 1955)
1955 – Name changed to Aries Copper Mines Ltd. and continued into Ontario. ■

Arimathaea Resources Inc. (B.C. 1980)
June 29, 1992 – Continued into Bermuda.
1992 – Amalgamated with a Bermuda corporation to form The Van Diemen's Land Company Ltd.

Arimetco International Inc. (Can. Sept. 28, 1984)
May 6, 2004 – Dissolved.

Arimex Mining Corp. (B.C. May 30, 1986)
Feb. 22, 1999 – Name changed to International Arimex Resources Inc.; basis 1 new for 4 old shs. ■

Aris Canada Ltd. (Alta. June 8, 1994)
Jan. 10, 2003 – Company's controlling shldr., Aris Vision, Inc., applied to the Court of Queen's Bench of Alberta for the appointment of Calgary-based Ernst & Young Inc. as receiver/manager of the assets and undertaking of the company. The appointment became effective and all the directors resigned.
Nov. 1, 2004 – Receiver discharged. There were no distributions made to shldrs.

Aris Gold Corporation (Yuk. June 12, 1997)
Sept. 28, 2022 – Acquired by GCM Mining Corp. (renamed Aris Mining Corporation); basis 0.05 GCM Mining shs. for 1 Aris Gold sh.
Sept. 28, 2022 – Name changed to Aris Mining Holdings Corp.

Arista Exploration Limited (Ont. 1955)
Oct. 31, 1984 – Filed for dissolution.

Arista Resources Inc. (B.C. Sept. 10, 1987)
Jan. 15, 1996 – Name changed to Patricia Mines Inc.; basis 1 new for 3 old shs. ■

Arius Research Inc. (Ont. Aug. 11, 1999)
Sept. 26, 2008 – Acquired by 2179511 Ontario Ltd., a direct wholly owned subsid. of F.Hoffmann-LaRoche Ltd., for $2.44 per sh.

Arius3D Corp. (Ont. May 30, 2007)
Oct. 25, 2013 – Certain intellectual properly and physical assets were acquired by Arius Technology Corp. for an undisclosed amount.

Arivaca Silver Mines Ltd. (B.C. 1979)
Mar. 1, 1989 – Delisted from the Vancouver Stock Exchange. Subsequently dissolved for failure to file.

Arizako Mines Ltd. (B.C. 1961)
Oct. 22, 1984 – Amalgamated into Goldrich Resources Inc.

Arizona Gold Corp. (Can. Nov. 9, 1987)
Sept. 8, 2021 – Name changed to Sabre Gold Mines Corp. pursuant to the acquisition of Golden Predator Mining Corp. ■

Arizona Golden Pacific Resources Ltd. (B.C. 1983)
Dec. 4, 1992 – Dissolved and struck off register.

Arizona Jojoba, Inc. (B.C. 1985)
May 29, 1992 – Dissolved and struck off register.

Arizona Mining Inc. (B.C. Aug. 20, 1998)
Aug. 13, 2018 – All o/s com. shs. not already held acquired by South32 Limited; basis Cdn$6.20 cash per com. sh.

Arizona Silver Corporation (B.C. Aug. 25, 1970)
June 6, 1995 – Name changed to ASC Industries Ltd.; basis 1 new for 10 old shs. ■

Arizona Silver Corporation (N.P.L.) (B.C. Aug. 25, 1970)
July 23, 1979 – Name changed to Arizona Silver Corporation following conversion from a non-personal liability co. to a limited co. ■

Arizona Silver Exploration Inc. (B.C. May 12, 2011)
Sept. 22, 2023 – Name changed to Arizona Gold & Silver Inc. (see FPsurvey - Mines & Energy)

Arizona Star Resource Corp. (B.C. Feb. 3, 1986)
Mar. 14, 2008 – Acquired by Barrick Gold Corporation for $18 per sh.

Arizuma Silver Inc. (Ont. Dec. 12, 1995)
Oct. 13, 1999 – Name changed to ASI Internet Inc.; basis 1 new for 3 old shs. ■

Arjam Pacific Ltd. (B.C. 1966)
Feb. 2, 1983 – Struck off register.

Arjon Enterprises Inc. (Ont. 1937)
June 14, 1996 – Formed Cotton Cotton Valley Resources Corporation in Ontario pursuant to reverse takeover acquisition of and amalgamation with Cotton Valley Energy Limited; basis 1 new for 3 old shs. ■

Arjon Gold Mines Ltd. (Ont. 1937)
Aug. 3, 1995 – Name changed to Arjon Enterprises Inc.; basis 1 new for 10 old shs. ■

Ark Energy Ltd. (B.C. 1966)
June 27, 1990 – Name changed to Arcanna Industries Corp.; basis 1 new for 5 old shs. ■

Ark Explorations Ltd. (Ont. 1970)
Jan. 1977 – Amalgamated with 5 other cos. to form Ranchmen's Resources (1976) Ltd.; basis 1 new cl. A sh. for 13 old shs.

Ark La Tex Industries Ltd. (B.C. Dec. 13, 1978)
June 17, 1992 – Name changed to Landstar Properties Inc.; basis 1 new for 7 old shs. ■

Arkadia Capital Corp. (Alta. July 18, 2011)
Jan. 2, 2024 – Struck from registry and dissolved,

Arken Gold Mines Ltd. (Ont. 1944)
May 30, 1960 – Dissolved.

Arkona Resources Inc. (B.C. Mar. 27, 1980)
Aug. 11, 2004 – Name changed to Action Minerals Inc.; basis 1 new for 3 old shs. ■

Arling Resources Ltd. (B.C. 1985)
Dec. 7, 1995 – Name changed to ID Internet Direct Ltd. ■

Arlington Oil & Gas Ltd. (Yuk. June 27, 2001)
Mar. 12, 2003 – Name changed to Cypress Hills Resource Corp.; basis 1 new for 4 old shs. ■

Arlington Resources Inc. (Ont. Jan. 21, 1997)
Oct. 21, 2014 – Certificate of incorporation cancelled and dissolved.

Arlington Silver Mines Ltd. (B.C. 1952)
Dec. 13, 1969 – Name changed to Western Arlington Resources Ltd. ■

Arlington Ventures Ltd. (B.C. Apr. 14, 1983)
June 27, 2001 – Name changed to Arlington Oil & Gas Ltd. and continued into Yukon. ■

Arlo Resources Ltd. (B.C. Oct. 3, 1990)
Jan. 27, 1995 – Continued into Yukon.
June 8, 1998 – Name changed to International Arlo Resources Ltd.; basis 1 new for 5 old shs. ■

Armada Data Corporation (B.C. June 17, 1999)
Oct. 31, 2024 – All o/s com. shs. not already held acquired via amalgamation with 1498798 B.C. Ltd.; basis 1 redeem. pref. sh. for 1 Armada Data com. shs. immediately redeemed 4¢ cash per redeem. pref. sh.

Armada Explorations Ltd. (B.C. 1968)
Mar. 1973 – Amalgamated with 2 other cos. to continue with the same name Armada Explorations Ltd.; basis 1 new for 6.6 old shs.
May 1973 – Amalgamated with 2 other cos. to form Shelter Petroleums Ltd.
1973 – Amalgamated in British Columbia to continue with same name.

Armada Financial Corporation (Alta. Jan. 13, 1988)
Jan. 6, 1994 – Name changed to Armada Gold Corporation following reverse takeover by Trans Pacific Resources Group Ltd.; basis 1 new for 4 old shs. ■

Armada Gold and Minerals Ltd. (B.C. June 24, 1987)
Mar. 4, 1992 – Name changed to Armada Mercantile Ltd. (see FPsurvey - Industrials)

Armada Gold Corporation (Alta. Jan. 13, 1988)
July 5, 1996 – Continued into Yukon. (see FPsurvey - Mines & Energy)

Armada Porcupine Mines Ltd. (Ont. 1944)
1955 – Charter cancelled.

Armbro Enterprises Inc. (Can. Jan. 14, 1957)
June 28, 2001 – Name changed to Aecon Group Inc. (see FPsurvey - Industrials)

Armco Capital Corp. (Alta. July 7, 1997)
June 7, 2005 – Going private transaction via amalgamation with 1162812 Alberta Ltd., wholly owned subsid. of 3099477 Nova Scotia Limited; basis $1.09 per sh.

Armenex Resources Canada Inc. (B.C. May 27, 1980)
Aug. 31, 1994 – Name changed to Ecuadorean Copperfields Inc.; basis 1 new for 5 old shs. ■

Armenian Express Canada Inc. (B.C. May 27, 1980)
July 4, 1990 – Name changed to Armenex Resources Canada Inc.; basis 1 new for 5 old shs. ■

Armeno Resources Inc. (B.C. Aug. 24, 1984)
May 25, 1992 – Name changed to Ag Armeno Mines and Minerals Inc.; basis 1 new for 10 old shs. ■

Armistice Gold Mines Ltd. (Ont. 1937)
1954 – Merged into Pardee Amalgamated Mines Ltd.; basis 2 new for 15 old shs.

Armistice Resources Corp. (Can. Nov. 9, 1987)
Jan. 7, 2014 – Name changed to Kerr Mines Inc. ■

Armistice Resources Ltd. (Ont. June 29, 1984)
Nov. 9, 1987 – Continued into Canada.
Apr. 28, 2006 – Name changed to Armistice Resources Corp.; basis 1 new for 4 old shs. ■

Armont Gold Mines Ltd. (Ont. 1936)
1958 – Charter cancelled.

Armor Development Corporation (B.C. Nov. 14, 1967)
Apr. 6, 1990 – Dissolved and struck off register.

Armor Resources Ltd. (B.C. 1979)
Nov. 1, 1982 – Amalgamated with New Penn Energy Corporation, Justen Resources Ltd. and Prospect Energy Corporation to form a new co. also known as New Penn Energy Corporation; basis 1 new for 12 old shs.

Armore Mines Ltd. (B.C. 1949)
June 1973 – Name changed to Marcana Resources Ltd.; basis 1 new for 3 old shs. ■

Armour Uranium & Copper Mines, Ltd. (Ont. 1950)
Apr. 1958 – Charter cancelled.

Armsher Resources Inc. (Ont. 1987)
Jan. 5, 1990 – Name changed to Future Avenir Corp.; basis 0.2 new cl. A sub. vtg. and 1 new cl. B multi-vtg. for 1 old com. sh. ■

Armstrong Corporation (Ont. Jan. 26, 1999 amalg.)
Mar. 13, 2003 – Petitioned into bankruptcy. Deloitte & Touche Inc. in Toronto was appointed receiver manager of the assets of Armstrong.

Armstrong Housing Industries Ltd. (Ont. 1946)
Feb. 4, 1954 – Charter cancelled.

Armtec Infrastructure Income Fund (Ont. June 15, 2004)
Jan. 1, 2011 – Succeeded by Armtec Infrastructure Inc. pursuant to plan of arrangement whereby Armtec

Infrastructure Inc. was formed to facilitate the conversion of the fund into a corporation and the fund was subsequently dissolved. ■

Armtec Infrastructure Inc. (Ont. May 5, 2010)
June 17, 2015 – Name changed to 2242749 Ontario Limited. ■

Arncoeur Gold Mines Ltd. (Que. 1936)
June 1973 – Charter cancelled.

Arnhem Resources Inc. (B.C. Oct. 6, 1982)
May 24, 1985 – Name changed to Duck Book Communications Limited; basis 5 new for 1 old sh. ■

Arno Mines Ltd. (Ont. 1927)
June 30, 1980 – Dissolved.

Arnora Gold Mines Ltd. (Que. 1947)
1951 – Name changed to Arnora Sulphur Mining Corp. ■

Arnora Sulphur Mining Corp. (Que. 1947)
Aug. 1973 – Charter cancelled.

Arntfield Gold Mines Ltd. (Que. 1925)
1944 – Name changed to Arntfield Mining Corp. Ltd.; basis 1 new for 4 old shs. ■

Arntfield Mining Corp. Ltd. (Que. 1925)
1947 – Name changed to New Arntfield Mines Ltd.; basis 1 new for 2 old shs. ■

Arodien Resources Ltd. (B.C. 1969)
Mar. 28, 1978 – Name changed to Manchester Oil Corporation; basis 1 new for 4 old shs. ■

Aronos Multinational Inc. (Ont. Apr. 28, 1966)
Nov. 4, 1996 – Name changed to RDG Minerals Inc. ■

Aroway Minerals Inc. (B.C. Mar. 27, 1980)
Feb. 4, 2011 – Name changed to Aroway Energy Inc. (see FPsurvey - Mines & Energy)

ArPetrol Ltd. (Alta. Mar. 18, 2011)
Dec. 19, 2016 – Completed second distribution of 16¢ cash per sh. following an initial distribution of 40¢ cash per sh. made to shldrs. of record Sept. 12, 2016.
Dec. 20, 2016 – Voluntarily dissolved.

Arrabbiata Capital Corp. (B.C. June 23, 2000)
Jan. 5, 2007 – Continued into Ontario.
Jan. 8, 2007 – Name changed to Olivut Resources Ltd. following Qualifying Transaction amalgamation of Olivut Investments Ltd. with a wholly owned subsid. of Arrabbiata, constituting a reverse takeover by Olivut Investments; basis 1.558 new for 1 old sh. (see FPsurvey - Mines & Energy)

Arris Holdings Inc. (B.C. Oct. 30, 2009)
Mar. 25, 2014 – Name changed to Global Hemp Group Inc. (see FPsurvey - Industrials)

Arris Resources Inc. (B.C. Sept. 15, 1987)
Dec. 21, 2009 – Name changed to RTN Stealth Software Inc. pursuant to transaction with wholly owned subsids. CLI Resources Inc., QMI Seismic Inc. and Arris Holdings Inc.; basis 5 RTN shs, 1 CLI sh., 1 QMI sh. and 1 Arris Holdings sh. for 1 Arris Resources sh. ■

Arriscraft International Income Fund (Ont. Oct. 28, 2004)
July 23, 2007 – Assets acquired by General Shale Brick Inc.; trust units redeemed on July 24, 2007, for $7.85 per unit.

Arrival Energy Ltd. (Alta. Nov. 12, 1996)
Aug. 10, 2000 – Amalgamated with 859964 Alberta Ltd., a wholly owned subsid. of Chain Energy Corporation; basis 1.2846 Chain com. shs. for 1 Arrival cl. A sh. and 3.2114 Chain com. shs. for 1 Arrival cl. B sh. (see Chain Energy Corporation)

Arrow-Can Natural Gas Ltd. (B.C. 1969)
1977 – Acquired by Christal Natural Gas & Minerals Ltd.; basis 1 pref. sh. $5.00 par for 8.33 Arrow-Can shs.

Arrow Energy Ltd. (Alta. May 3, 2004 amalg.)
Nov. 2, 2009 – Name changed to Kallisto Energy Corp.; basis 1 new for 4 old shs. ■

Arrow-Marjon Oils Ltd (Alta. 1943)
1945 – Assets transferred to Arrow Oil Co. Ltd. for 2,000,000 shs.

Arrow Oil Co. Ltd. (Alta. Sept. 20, 1944)
1959 – Struck off register.

Arrow Tungsten Mines Ltd. (Ont. 1951)
Mar. 1976 – Charter cancelled.

Arrowfield Resources Ltd. (B.C. May 30, 1980)
Apr. 27, 1992 – Name changed to ITL Capital Corporation; basis 1 new for 2 old shs. ■

Arrowhead Gold Corp. (B.C. Nov. 16, 2006)
July 7, 2016 – Name changed to Kontrol Energy Corp.; basis 1 new for 6 old shs. ■

Arrowhead Gold Mines Ltd. (Que. 1934)
May 1988 – Amalgamated with Quebec Cobalt & Exploration Ltd.

Arrowhead Minerals Corporation (B.C. July 2, 1965)
Oct. 28, 1999 – Name changed to Gemini Energy Corp.; basis 1 new for 10 old shs. ■

Arrowhead Resources Ltd. (B.C, July 2, 1965)
Aug. 23, 1995 – Name changed to Double Arrow Oil & Gas Ltd.; basis 1 new for 10 old shs. ■

Arrowhead Water Products Ltd. (Alta. Oct. 7, 1993)
May 8, 2014 – Continued into British Columbia.
May 9, 2014 – Name changed to Captiva Verde Industries Ltd. ■

Arrowlink Corp. (Ont. Feb. 18, 1976)
May 17, 1996 – Name changed to Triarx Gold Corporation. ■

Arrowsmith Properties Limited (Alta. Apr. 9, 1998)
July 28, 2000 – Name changed to North Shore Mercantile Corporation and continued into Canada. ■

Arrowstar Resources Ltd. (B.C. Oct. 14, 1987)
Dec. 19, 2019 – Name changed to Adastra Labs Holdings Ltd. pursuant to reverse takeover acquisition of (old) Adastra Labs Holdings Ltd. (renamed Adastra Labs Holdings (2019) Ltd.). ■

Arsenal Capital Inc. (Alta. Aug. 3, 2000)
Nov. 14, 2002 – Formed Arsenal Energy Inc. in Alberta on Qualifying Transaction amalgamation with A.C. Global Capital Corp.; basis 0.8 Arsenal Energy com. sh. for either 1 Arsenal Capital com. sh. or 1 A.C. Global com. sh. ■

Arsenal Energy Inc. (Alta. Nov. 14, 2002 amalg.)
Sept. 16, 2016 – Amalgamated with Lone Pine Resources Canada Ltd., an indirect wholly owned subsid. of Prairie Provident Resources Inc.; basis 1.1417218 Prairie Provident com. shs. for 1 Arsenal com. sh.

Art In Motion Income Fund (B.C. June 1, 2004)
Sept. 29, 2008 – Acquired by Clarke Inc. for 75¢ per unit.

The Art of Animation Galleries Ltd. (Alta. Dec. 22, 1992)
Feb. 1, 1999 – Struck from registry and dissolved.

The Art Vault International Limited (Ont. Apr. 10, 2000)
Mar. 13, 2001 – Together with subsid. The Art Vault Limited, filed an assignment into bankruptcy. Toronto-based Schwartz Levitsky Feldman Inc. appointed trustee.
June 14, 2002 – Trustee discharged.

Arta Enterprises Inc. (Alta. Nov. 2, 2000)
July 19, 2002 – Formed Committee Bay Resources Ltd. in Alberta on Qualifying Transaction amalgamation with Committee Bay Resources Ltd. ■

Artaflex Inc. (Ont. Mar. 20, 2012 amalg.)
Apr. 30, 2013 – Privatized via a 1-for-2,500,000 sh. consolidation; basis Cdn$0.05 cash per sh.

Arteco Mortgage Investment Company (Can. 1974)
July 1, 1979 – Royal Trustco Limited acquired the remaining 90.1% int. in co., making it a wholly owned subsid. Company's name was subsequently changed to Royal Trustco Mortgage Company.

Artek Exploration Ltd. (Alta. Jan. 14, 2010 amalg.)
Apr. 16, 2015 – Name changed to Kelt Exploration (LNG) Ltd. ■

Artemis U.S. Capital Appreciation Fund (Ont. Feb. 25, 2011)
Feb. 24, 2015 – Terminated. All cl. A and cl. F units redeemed at $12.5808 per unit on Mar. 9, 2015.

Artemis Ventures Inc. (B.C. Mar. 25, 1981)
Jan. 4, 1999 – Name changed to Paradym Ventures Inc.; basis 2 new for 3 old shs. ■

Artesian Petroleum Corporation (B.C. Mar. 31, 1981)
Nov. 21, 1986 – Delisted Vancouver Stock Exchange. Subsequently struck from register and dissolved.

Artevo Corporation (Alta. Feb. 9, 2007)
May 30, 2008 – Amalgamated in Alberta to continue with same name.
Dec. 18, 2009 – Filed for bankruptcy. All directors resigned.

Artex Holdings & Explorations Ltd. (Ont. 1968)
July 1970 – Co-amalgamated with Boeing Holdings & Explorations Ltd.

Artex Mines Ltd. (Ont. 1968)
Name changed to Artex Holdings & Explorations Ltd.; basis 1 new for 2 old shs. ■

Artgallerylive.com Management Ltd. (B.C. Apr. 28, 1988)
Jan. 18, 2001 – Name changed to Adaptive Marketing Solutions Inc.; basis 1 new for 15 old shs. ■

Artha Resources Corporation (B.C. Jan. 9, 2006)
June 9, 2015 – Name changed to Centenera Mining Corp. following reverse takeover acquisition of Cardero Argentina S.A. ■

Arthurian Resources Ltd. (B.C. June 29, 1981)
Dec. 16, 1991 – Name changed to Pacific Copperfields Inc.; basis 1 new for 3 old shs. ■

Arthurs-Jones Inc. (Ont. Mar. 19, 1956)
Sept. 23, 1998 – Name changed to Invesprint Corporation. ■

Artillery Resources Ltd. (B.C. 1979)
Dec. 3, 1984 – Name changed to Ferber Mining Corp.; basis 1 new for 5 old shs. (see FPsurvey - Mines & Energy)

Artina Resources Ltd. (B.C. June 27, 1983)
May 16, 2000 – Name changed to Prophecy Entertainment Inc. ■

Artisan Corporation (Alta. Sept. 30, 1988)
May 27, 1998 – Acquired by Ensign Resource Service Group Inc.; basis (i) $10.50, (ii) 0.3415 Ensign shs. for 1 Artisan sh. or (iii) a combination thereof, subject to certain restrictions on the number of shs. issued or cash paid. (see Ensign Resource Service Group Inc.)

Artisan Drilling Ltd. (Alta. Sept. 30, 1988)
June 22, 1995 – Name changed to Artisan Corporation. ■

Artisan Energy Corporation (Alta. Nov. 1, 2010)
June 22, 2016 – Filed for bankruptcy. Faber Inc. was appointed trustee and all officers and directors resigned.
Mar. 2, 2018 – Struck from registry and dissolved.

Artistic Photo Plate Creations, Inc. (Wash. July 23, 1987)
Feb. 2, 1995 – Name changed to APC Ventures, Inc.; basis 1 new for 10 old shs. ■

Artopex International Inc. (Can. 1969)
Dec. 3, 1992 – Declared bankrupt. Liabs. amounted to $12,934,904, and the co. had no liquid assets. No distribution available for creditors or shldrs.

ArtQuest International Alliances Inc. (Que. Nov. 7, 1997)
July 20, 2016 – Struck from registry.

Aruma Ventures Inc. (B.C. Jan. 27, 1966)
Sept. 7, 1999 – Name changed to dot.com Technologies Inc.; basis 1 new for 2 old shs. ■

Arura Pharma Inc. (Can. June 28, 2007 amalg.)
July 20, 2011 – Dissolved and struck from register.

Arvida Exploration Ltd. (B.C. Mar. 17, 1981)
May 11, 1995 – Name changed to Jade International Industrial Group Inc.

Arwick International Resources Ltd. (B.C. 1979)
May 13, 1992 – Name changed to Gincho International Ventures Inc.; basis 1 new for 3 old shs. ■

Asamera Inc. (Can. 1925)
Aug. 5, 1988 – Acquired by Gulf Canada Resources Ltd.; basis 0.6397 Gulf shs. for 1 Asamera com. sh., or $11.75 and 1.4060 Gulf shs. for 1 Asamera 8% ser. C 2nd pref. sh., or $26.10 per Asamera sh. plus accr. divds., and 35¢ per Asamera wt. (see Gulf Canada Resources Limited)

Asamera Minerals Inc. (Ont. May 25, 1981)
May 4, 1987 – Continued into Canada.
Aug. 4, 1992 – All o/s shs. redeemed following amalgamation with a wholly owned subsid. of Asamera Inc.; basis $1.40 per com. sh.

Asamera Oil Corporation Ltd. (Can. 1925)
Sept. 30, 1980 – Name changed to Asamera Inc. ■

Asanko Gold Inc. (B.C. Sept. 23, 1999)
Apr. 30, 2020 – Name changed to Galiano Gold Inc. (see FPsurvey - Mines & Energy)

Asantae Holdings International Inc. (B.C. Jan. 31, 2006)
May 31, 2013 – Name changed to Avidus Management Group Inc. ■

Asbestos Lloyd Mines Limited (Ont. 1953)
Dec. 8, 1989 – Dissolved.

Ascalade Communications Inc. (B.C. Nov. 2, 2004)
Mar. 3, 2008 – Filed for protection under the Companies' Creditors Arrangement Act (CCAA) and Deloitte & Touche Inc. was appointed monitor.
Apr. 29, 2008 – Monitor filed under Chapter 15 of the U.S. Bankruptcy code seeking a stay in proceedings by creditors in the U.S.
May 14, 2008 – Deloitte & Touche Hong Kong appointed administrators of the scheme of arrangement filed by wholly owned Ascalade Communications Limited (ACL) which would involve the winding up of ACL and sale of assets located in the Peoples Republic of China.
Nov. 2008 – Interim distribution equivalent to 80% for each proven dollar of claim was made to proven creditors.
Dec. 31, 2008 – Remaining directors resigned.
Dec. 3, 2009 – Final distribution of the remaining 20% to proven creditors was paid.
Dec. 22, 2009 – Return of capital of Cdn$0.159 per com. sh. paid to all shldrs. of record Dec. 8, 2009. Deloitte & Touche was discharged as monitor.

Ascan Resources Ltd. (B.C. Dec. 20, 1971)
June 1973 – Name changed to Synergy Resources Ltd.; basis 1 new for 2 old shs. ■

Ascend Wellness Holdings, LLC (Del. May 15, 2018)
Apr. 22, 2021 – Name changed to Ascend Wellness Holdings, Inc. (see FPsurvey - Industrials)

Ascendant Copper Corporation (B.C. May 5, 2004)
July 3, 2008 – Name changed to Copper Mesa Mining Corporation. ■

Ascendant Resources Inc. (Ont. Oct. 24, 2011)
May 22, 2025 – All o/s shs. not already held acquired by Cerrado Gold Inc.; basis 0.1282 Cerrado shs. for 1 Ascendant sh.

Ascent Industries Corp. (B.C. Aug. 9, 2018 amalg.)
May 15, 2020 – Name changed to Luff Enterprises Ltd. ■

Ascentex Energy, Inc. (Alta. Apr. 14, 1987)
Mar. 3, 1997 – Name changed to Bonavista Petroleum Ltd.; basis 1 new for 3 old shs. ■

Ascentex Resources Ltd. (Alta. Apr. 14, 1987)
Jan. 17, 1992 – Name changed to Ascentex Energy, Inc.; basis 1 new for 5 old shs. ■

Ascopex Exploration Ltd. (Que. 1970)
May 25, 1985 – Charter cancelled.

Ascot Energy Corporation of Canada Limited (Ont. Apr. 26, 1966)
Oct. 29, 1981 – Name changed to Crosscut Explorations Inc. ■

Ascot Energy Resources Ltd. (Alta. Mar. 30, 1978)
Oct. 16, 2002 – Name changed to Great Northern Exploration Ltd. following reverse takeover acquisition of Great Northern Exploration Ltd. (1 for 6.5); basis 1 new for 5 old shs. ■

Ascot Investment Corporation (B.C. Feb. 3, 1987 amalg.)
Aug. 3, 1990 – Name changed to Pacific Western Investments Inc.; basis 1 new for 6 old shs. ■

Ascot Metals Corp. Ltd. (Que. 1949)
1956 – Name changed to Quebec Ascot Copper Corp. Ltd.; basis 1 new for 3 old shs. ■

The Ascot Petroleum Corporation (B.C. 1975)
Feb. 8, 1982 – Amalgamated with Canalta Resources Ltd. (0.3 for 1) and Sweetwater Petroleum Corporation (0.65 for 1) to form a new company named Consolidated Ascot Petroleum Corporation; basis 0.85 new for 1 old sh. (see Consolidated Ascot Petroleum Corporation)

Asea Brown Boveri Inc. (Can. Jan. 1, 1988 amalg.)
Dec. 23, 1999 – Name changed to ABB Inc.

Asea Inc. (Can. Dec. 31, 1982)
Jan. 1, 1988 – Formed Asea Brown Boveri Inc. in Canada on amalgamation with BBC Brown Boveri Canada Inc. ■

Asean Cybernetics Inc. (B.C. Jan. 7, 2000)
July 28, 2003 – Acquired by TransGlobe Internet and Telecom Co. Ltd.; basis 0.3175 TransGlobe com. shs. plus 0.3175 TransGlobe wts. (exercisable at 55¢ in year one and 62¢ in year two) for 1 Asean com. sh. (see TransGlobe Internet and Telecom Co., Ltd.)

Asean Energy Corp. (B.C. Jan. 14, 1981)
Aug. 20, 2015 – Name changed to Genovation Capital Corp. following reverse takeover acquisition of Valens Agritech Ltd. ■

Aselo Industries Ltd. (B.C. 1968)
Apr. 14, 1980 – Name changed to Fairmont Gas & Oil Corporation. ■

Asfe Mines Ltd. (Ont. 1951)
Sept. 21, 1959 – Dissolved.

Ash Temple Limited (Ont. 1950)
Dec. 31, 1981 – Private co. All o/s 6.5% secured debentures retired.

Ash Yellowknife Mines Ltd. (Can. 1946)
Charter cancelled.

Asha Ventures Inc. (B.C. Sept. 2, 1987)
Sept. 28, 1992 – Name changed to Cost Miser Coupons (International) Inc. ■

Ashanti Gold Corp. (B.C. Dec. 16, 1993)
Oct. 2, 2019 – Acquired by Desert Gold Ventures Inc. via a three-cornered amalgamation; basis 0.2857 Desert Gold com. shs. for each com. sh. held.

Ashburton Oil Ltd. (B.C. Feb. 25, 1981)
Apr. 18, 2006 – Dissolved and struck from register.

Ashburton Ventures Inc. (B.C. Nov. 10, 2006)
June 8, 2018 – Name changed to Progressive Planet Solutions Inc. (see FPsurvey - Mines & Energy; FPsurvey - Industrials)

Ashcroft Resources Ltd. (B.C. Mar. 12, 1965)
Dec. 5, 1986 – Name changed to Tchaikazan Enterprises Inc.; basis 1 new for 4 old shs. ■

Ashdod Systems Ltd. (Alta. Oct. 23, 1996)
Jan. 6, 2000 – Name changed to TER Thermal Retrieval Systems Ltd. ■

Asher Gold Mines Ltd. (Ont. 1945)
Mar. 4, 1965 – Dissolved.

Asher Resources Corporation (B.C. Feb. 2, 2011)
June 6, 2016 – Name changed to Drone Delivery Canada Corp. following reverse takeover acquisition of Drone Delivery Canada Inc.; basis 1 new for 4 old shs. ■

Ashgrove Energy Limited (N.S. Feb. 13, 1987)
Aug. 29, 1995 – Name changed to Search Energy Inc.; basis 1 new for 1 old sh. ■

Ashgrove Resources Limited (N.S. Feb. 13, 1987)
Aug. 19, 1993 – Name changed to Ashgrove Energy Limited; basis 1 new for 6 old shs. ■

Ashland Canadian Oils Ltd. (Can. 1951)
Sept. 9, 1970 – Name changed to Canadian Ashland Exploration Ltd. following acquisition by Ashland Oil Canada Limited.

Ashland Oil Canada Limited (Alta. 1957)
Mar. 1979 – Name changed to Kaiser Petroleum Ltd. following acquisition by Kaiser Resources Ltd. for $33.50 per sh.

Ashlar Financial Services Corp. (B.C. Apr. 18, 1986)
Sept. 26, 2003 – Dissolved and stuck from register.

Ashley Gold and Oil Minerals Limited (Ont. 1931)
May 17, 1949 – Name changed to Western Ashley Minerals Limited; basis 1 new for 4 old shs. ■

Ashloo Gold Mines Ltd. (B.C. 1936)
1948 – Struck off register.

Ashlu Exploration Ltd. (Alta. 1976)
July 10, 1987 – Name changed to Rhodes Energy Corporation; basis 1 new for 10 old shs. ■

Ashlu Gold Mines Limited (Alta. 1976)
Aug. 1979 – Name changed to Ashlu Exploration Ltd. ■

Ashmont Petroleums Ltd. (Alta. 1950)
1954 – Acquired by Pathfinder Petroleums Ltd.; basis 1 new for 2 old shs.

Ashmore Gold Mines Ltd. (Ont. 1968)
Dec. 1968 – Name changed to Murray Watts Explorations Ltd. ■

Ashnola Mining Co. Ltd. (B.C. May 26, 1978)
June 1, 1988 – Name changed to Tower Hill Mines Ltd.; basis 1.7 new for 1 old sh. ■

Ashton Long Lac Gold Mines Ltd. (Ont. 1936)
Feb. 1951 – Charter cancelled.

Ashton Mining of Canada Inc. (Can. July 29, 1993)
Jan. 19, 2007 – Amalgamated with a wholly owned subsid. of Stornoway Diamond Corporation; basis $1.25 per sh., or 1 Stornoway com. sh. plus 1 pref. sh. immediately redeem. for 1¢ cash, for 1 Ashton com. sh. (see Stornoway Diamond Corporation)

Asia Bio-Chem Group Corp. (B.C. Oct. 5, 2005)
Sept. 2, 2019 – Struck from registry and dissolved.

Asia Cannabis Corp. (Alta. Dec. 19, 2017)
Apr. 16, 2020 – Name changed to Asia Green Biotechnology Corp. (see FPsurvey - Industrials)

Asia Gold Corp. (B.C. Feb. 14, 2002)
Nov. 4, 2002 – Continued into Canada.
May 29, 2007 – Name changed to SouthGobi Energy Resources Ltd. and continued into British Columbia. ■

Asia Media Group Corporation (Ont. 1969)
Nov. 2006 – Voluntarily dissolved.

Asia Minerals Corp. (Alta. Nov. 17, 1980)
July 19, 1994 – Continued into British Columbia.
Oct. 16, 2000 – Name changed to American Bonanza Gold Mining Corp. ■

Asia Now Resources Corp. (Ont. Feb. 17, 2004)
Aug. 14, 2015 – Placed into receivership. Crowe Soberman Inc. appointed receiver and all officers and directors resigned.

Asia Pacific Capital Corporation (Can. Aug. 21, 1985)
June 6, 1989 – Name changed to Asiatel Media Corporation; basis 1 new for 4 old shs. ■

Asia Pacific Concrete Inc. (Alta. Mar. 19, 1996)
June 19, 2000 – Name changed to IVG Corporation. ■

Asia-Pacific Resources Ltd. (B.C. Jan. 29, 1986)
Sept. 22, 1995 – Name changed to Asia Pacific Resources Ltd. ■

Asia Pacific Resources Ltd. (B.C. Jan. 29, 1986)
Apr. 2, 2002 – Continued into New Brunswick.
Aug. 16, 2006 – Acquired by Italian-Thai Development Public Company Limited for $0.1425 per sh.

Asia Packaging Group Inc. (B.C. Jan. 25, 2010)
July 25, 2017 – Dissolved and struck from register.

Asia Sapphires Limited (Yuk. June 29, 1998)
July 5, 2003 – Dissolved.

Asiamerica Equities Ltd. (Wash. July 1, 1968)
Dec. 31, 1991 – Name changed to Mercer International Inc. ■

Asiamerica Holdings Ltd. (B.C. 1980)
Nov. 17, 1989 – Name changed to Stone Mark Capital Inc. ■

Asiamet Resources Limited (Bermuda Oct. 7, 1997)
Mar. 1, 2017 – Voluntarily delisted.

Asian Canadian Resources Ltd. (B.C. 1983)
July 4, 1990 – Name changed to Victorian Enuretic Services Ltd.; basis 1 new for 4.2 old shs. ■

Asian Mineral Resources Limited (New Zealand Nov. 17, 1988)
Dec. 31, 2004 – Continued into British Columbia.
Sept. 9, 2020 – Name changed to Decklar Resources Inc. (see FPsurvey - Mines & Energy)

Asian Resource Global Strategies Inc. (Ont. Aug. 2, 2007)
Dec. 29, 2010 – Name changed to Nesscap Energy Inc. pursuant to Qualifying Transaction reverse takeover acquisition of Nesscap, Inc. subsequently completed on Jan. 21, 2011. ■

Asiatel Media Corporation (Can. Aug. 21, 1985)
Aug. 30, 1991 – Name changed to Consolidated Asiatel Resources Ltd.; basis 1 new for 5 old shs. ■

Asitka Resource Corporation (B.C. Dec. 13, 1982)
Nov. 7, 1989 – Name changed to Orenda Forest Products Ltd. ◼

Asnazu Gold Dredging Ltd. (B.C. 1934)
Sept. 22, 1959 – Wound up. Total distribution of $0.99365 per sh.

Aspen Energy Corp. (Alta. Dec. 7, 1987)
May 5, 2003 – Name changed to Aspen Resources Corp.; basis 1 new for 8 old shs. ◼

Aspen Explorations Inc. (Ont. 1974)
May 25, 1979 – Name changed to Geolex Resources Ltd.; basis 1 new for 2 old shs. ◼

Aspen Grove Copper Mines Ltd. (B.C. Nov. 21, 1963)
1965 – Name changed to Aspen Grove Mines Ltd. ◼

Aspen Grove Mines Ltd. (B.C. Nov. 21, 1963)
Mar. 25, 1986 – Name changed to Legion Resources Ltd. (not to be confused with Legion Resources Ltd. - Ont.). ◼

Aspen Manufacturing Industries Inc. (Ont. July 4, 1985)
June 1, 2015 – Dissolved and struck from registry.

Aspen Resources Corp. (Alta. Dec. 7, 1987)
Jan. 25, 1996 – Name changed to Aspen Energy Corp.; basis 1 new for 5 old shs. ◼

Aspen Resources Corp. (Alta. Dec. 7, 1987)
Mar. 15, 2006 – Privatized at 22¢ per sh.

Aspen Resources Corp. (B.C. Oct. 7, 2022)
May 30, 2023 – Name changed to Bayridge Resources Corp. (see FPsurvey - Mines & Energy)

Aspen Venture Capital Corporation (Alta. Dec. 2, 1993)
June 2, 2001 – Struck from registry and dissolved.

Aspire Capital Inc. (Alta. Apr. 23, 1998)
Apr. 25, 2007 – Name changed to Calstar Oil & Gas Ltd. ◼

Aspreva Pharmaceuticals Corporation (Can. Dec. 20, 2001)
Nov. 19, 2004 – Continued into British Columbia.
Jan. 8, 2008 – Acquired by Galenica AG for US$26 per sh.

Asquith Resources Inc. (Ont. Oct. 23, 1986)
Dec. 31, 1998 – Amalgamated in Ontario to continue with same name.
Nov. 21, 2001 – Continued into Canada.
Dec. 12, 2001 – Name changed to AXMIN Inc. following reverse takeover acquisition of AXMIN Limited. (see FPsurvey - Mines & Energy)

Assante Corporation (Can. Dec. 22, 1995)
Nov. 18, 2003 – Plan of Arrangement with CI Fund Management Inc. and Loring Ward International Ltd.; basis 1 Loring com. sh. plus either $8.25 or 0.61543 CI com. shs., or a combination of cash and CI shs. for 1 Assante com. sh. (see CI Financial Inc.)
June 30, 2006 – Name changed to Assante Wealth Management (Canada) Ltd. (see CI Financial Inc.)

Assembly Mines Limited (unknown)
Dec. 30, 1977 – Amalgamated with Murray Watts Explorations Ltd.

Asset/Repo Depo Inc (Can.)
Jan. 1, 2004 – Name changed to ASSET Inc.

Assiniboine Oils Ltd. (Alta.)
1961 – Struck off register. Assets absorbed by West Canadian Oil & Gas Ltd.

AssistGlobal Technologies Corp. (B.C. Sept. 15, 1987)
July 11, 2005 – Name changed to Bassett Ventures Inc.; basis 1 new for 4 old shs. ◼

Associated Arcadia Nickel Corp. Ltd. (Que. 1953)
Nov. 17, 1969 – Name changed to Arcadia Minerals Limited. ◼

Associated Brands Income Fund (Ont. Sept. 25, 2002)
May 11, 2007 – Acquired indirectly by TorQuest Partners Inc. for 82¢ per unit.

Associated Developments Ltd. (unknown 1951)
1963 – Assets acquired by New Associated Developments Ltd.; basis 1 new for 6 old shs. (see New Associated Developments Limited)

Associated Freezers Income Trust (Ont. Feb. 25, 1997)
Sept. 6, 2000 – Formed ACS Freezers Income Trust following merger with privately held Atlas Cold Storage Holdings Limited. ◼

Associated Porcupine Mines Ltd. (Ont. 1968 amalg.)
Feb. 28, 1989 – Acquired by American Reserve Mining Corporation; basis $5.00 per sh., 0.75 American Reserve com. shs. and 0.1875 American Reserve wts. to purchase 1 com. sh. at $2.25. (see American Reserve Mining Corporation)

Associated Recreation Corp. (Ont. Apr. 30, 1976)
Nov. 3, 1983 – Name changed to ARC International Corporation. ◼

Associated Standard Wire and Cable Ltd. (Ont. 1954)
June 1962 – Name changed to Industrial Wire & Cable Co. Ltd. ◼

Associates Acceptance Company Limited (Can. Aug. 27, 1954)
Apr. 29, 1977 – Name changed to Associates Capital Corporation. ◼

Associates Capital Corporation (Can. Aug. 27, 1954)
Mar. 27, 1984 – Dissolved.

Associates Capital Corporation of Canada (Can. Oct. 19, 1982)
June 11, 2003 – Name changed to Citigroup Finance Canada Inc. ◼

Associates Discount (Canada) Ltd. (Can. Aug. 27, 1954)
Sept. 15, 1962 – Name changed to Associates Acceptance Company Limited. ◼

Associates Oil & Gas Corp. (Alta. June 16, 1993)
Dec. 2, 2000 – Dissolved and struck from registry.

Astar Minerals Ltd. (B.C. July 19, 2011)
Dec. 29, 2017 – Name changed to FinCanna Capital Corp. pursuant to reverse takeover acquisition of private company FinCanna Capital Corp. and amalgamation of FinCanna with a wholly owned subsidiary of Astar. (see FPsurvey - Industrials)

Aster Mines Ltd. (Man. 1928)
Oct. 1934 – Charter cancelled.

Aster Ventures Corp. (B.C. Apr. 11, 1983)
Mar. 22, 2001 – Name changed to Knight Petroleum Corp.; basis 1 new for 2 old shs. ◼

Astic Ventures Inc. (B.C. 1983)
July 15, 1994 – Dissolved and struck off register.

Aston Hill Advantage Bond Fund (Ont. Jan. 12, 2009)
May 12, 2017 – Name changed to LOGiQ Advantage Bond Fund. ◼

Aston Hill Advantage Oil & Gas Income Fund (Ont. Feb. 24, 2005)
May 12, 2017 – Name changed to LOGiQ Advantage Oil & Gas Income Fund. ◼

Aston Hill Advantage VIP Income Fund (Ont. Jan. 1, 2006)
May 12, 2017 – Name changed to LOGiQ Advantage VIP Income Fund. ◼

Aston Hill Capital Growth Fund (Ont. Sept. 29, 2003)
May 6, 2011 – Converted from a closed end investment fund to an open-ended mutual fund.

Aston Hill Financial Inc. (Alta. June 16, 1993)
Dec. 14, 2016 – Name changed to LOGiQ Asset Management Inc. following acquisition of Front Street Capital 2004 and Tuscarora Capital Inc. ◼

Aston Hill Global Agribusiness Fund (Ont. Oct. 29, 2007)
Mar. 18, 2013 – Converted into an open-ended mutual fund.

Aston Hill Global Convertible Bond Fund (Ont. Nov. 23, 2009)
July 4, 2011 – Converted from a closed end to an open-ended fund

Aston Hill Global Uranium Fund Inc. (Ont. Apr. 19, 2007)
Apr. 5, 2013 – Merged into Aston Hill Global Resource & Infrastructure Fund.

Aston Hill Oil & Gas Income Fund (Ont. Sept. 28, 2004)
Sept. 1, 2015 – Converted into an open-ended mutual fund.

Aston Hill Senior Gold Producers Income Corp. (Ont. Dec. 9, 2010)
Apr. 5, 2013 – Merged into Aston Hill Global Resource & Infrastructure Fund.

Aston Hill VIP Income Fund (Ont. Oct. 25, 2001)
May 12, 2017 – Name changed to LOGiQ VIP Income Fund. ◼

Aston Resources Ltd. (B.C. Feb. 15, 1967)
June 13, 1996 – Name changed to Consolidated Aston Resources Ltd.; basis 1 new for 3 old shs. ◼

Aston Resources Limited (B.C. 1969)
June 27, 1977 – Name changed to New Aston Resources Inc.; basis 1 new for 5 old shs. ◼

Astonish Lake Uranium Mining Corp. Ltd. (Ont. 1966)
Mar. 1976 – Charter cancelled.

Astorand Mines Ltd. (Ont. 1945)
July 1951 – Charter cancelled.

Astoria Quebec Mines Ltd. (Que. Jan. 25, 1938)
1948 – Name changed to Consolidated Astoria Mines Ltd.; basis 1 new for 5 old shs. ◼

Astoria Rouyn Mines Ltd. (Que. Nov. 26, 1927)
Jan. 25, 1938 – Continued into Quebec.
1938 – Name changed to Astoria Quebec Mines Ltd.; basis 1 new for 2 old shs. ◼

Astorius Resources Ltd. (B.C. May 4, 2007)
Apr. 13, 2020 – Name changed to Kingman Minerals Ltd. (see FPsurvey - Mines & Energy)

Astound Incorporated (Ont. Apr. 23, 1996)
Mar. 28, 2001 – Acquired by France-based Genesys S.A. for US$7,000,000 plus exch. shs. which are exchangeable at option of holder into Genesys com. shs. on 1-for-1 basis.

Astra Finance Ltd. (British Virgin Islands Aug. 22, 1991)
Jan. 3, 1998 – All o/s ser. 1 pref. shs. redeemed for $25 plus accrued divd. of $0.75648952 per sh.

Astrabrun Mines Ltd. (Ont. 1953)
Mar. 1976 – Charter cancelled.

Astral Bellevue Pathe Inc. (Ont. Nov. 17, 1973)
Aug. 27, 1986 – Continued into Canada.
Sept. 10, 1990 – Name changed to Astral Inc. ◼

Astral Bellevue Pathe Limited (Ont. Nov. 17, 1973)
Sept. 19, 1980 – Name changed to Astral Bellevue Pathe Inc. ◼

Astral Communications Inc. (Can. Aug. 27, 1986)
Feb. 25, 2000 – Name changed to Astral Media Inc. ◼

Astral Communications Ltd. (Ont. 1971)
Nov. 17, 1973 – Amalgamated with Bellevue-Pathe Ltd. to form Astral Bellevue Pathe Limited.

Astral Inc. (Can. Aug. 27, 1986)
Sept. 4, 1992 – Name changed to Astral Communications Inc. ∎

Astral Media Inc. (Can. Aug. 27, 1986)
July 9, 2013 – Acquired by BCE Inc. for $50 and $54.83 per cl.A and cl.B, respectively.

Astral Mining & Resources Ltd. (Ont. 1947)
Oct. 1962 – Name changed to New Astral Mining & Resources Ltd. ∎

Astral Mining Corporation (B.C. Feb. 12, 2004)
Feb. 13, 2012 – Acquired by Orex Minerals Inc.; basis 0.0834 Orex shs. for 1 Astral Mining sh.

Astridon Development Corp. (B.C. 1986)
Mar. 25, 1994 – Dissolved and struck off register.

Astris Energi Inc. (Ont. Sept. 22, 1987)
Aug. 17, 2007 – Name changed to Carthew Bay Technologies Inc. (see FPsurvey - Industrials)

Astrix Networks Inc. (Alta. Oct. 29, 2013 amalg.)
July 22, 2015 – Name changed to Memex Inc. (see FPsurvey - Industrials)

Astron Resources Corporation (Yuk. June 16, 1999)
Nov. 16, 2006 – Name changed to Nevada Copper Corp. and continued into British Columbia following reverse takeover acquisition of 607792 British Columbia Ltd. ∎

Astur Gold Corp. (B.C. Dec. 12, 2007)
Oct. 13, 2016 – Name changed to Black Dragon Gold Corp. ∎

Astwood Park Resources Inc. (Ont. Sept. 22, 1987)
Nov. 7, 1989 – Name changed to International Eagle Tool Inc.; basis 1 new for 2 old shs. ∎

Atacama Copper Corporation (B.C. Apr. 8, 2020)
Aug. 26, 2024 – Name changed to Fuerte Metals Corporation. (see FPsurvey - Mines & Energy)

Atacama Minerals Corp. (Can. Aug. 8, 1997)
Jan. 30, 2012 – Name changed to Sirocco Mining Inc. pursuant to acquisition of Sirocco Gold Inc. ∎

Atacama Pacific Gold Corporation (Can. June 12, 2008)
July 27, 2018 – Amalgamate with Rio2 Limited to continue under the Rio2 name (new Rio2); basis 0.6601 new Rio2 com. shs. for 1 Atacama sh. and 0.6667 new Rio2 com. shs. for 1 old Rio2 com. sh.

Atacama Resources Ltd. (B.C. 1981)
Nov. 14, 1990 – Amalgamated with Kap Resources Ltd. to form new co. with same name Kap Resources Ltd.; basis 0.75 new for 1 Atacama sh. (see KAP Resources Ltd.)

Atapa Minerals Limited (Can. Aug. 31, 1989)
Aug. 15, 2006 – Dissolved.

Atcan Capital Corp. (Can. Jan. 21, 1987)
June 17, 2005 – Dissolved.

Atco Mining Inc. (B.C. Jan. 28, 2021)
July 7, 2025 – Name changed to SuperQ Quantum Computing Inc. following acquisition of quantum computing software platform known as Super; basis 1 new for 10 old shs. (see FPsurvey - Industrials)

Ateba Mines Inc. (Ont. May 6, 1977)
Feb. 1, 1988 – Amalgamated in Ontario to continue with same name.
Jan. 10, 2001 – Name changed to Ateba Technology & Environmental Inc.; basis 1 new for 3 old shs. ∎

Ateba Resources Inc. (Ont. Feb. 1, 1988 amalg.)
Feb. 26, 2021 – Name changed to Glow LifeTech Corp. pursuant to the reverse takeover acquisition of Glow

LifeTech Ltd. and concurrent amalgamation of Glow LifeTech with wholly owned 2760626 Ontario Inc.; basis 1 new for 1.5 old shs. (see FPsurvey - Industrials)

Ateba Technology & Environmental Inc. (Ont. Feb. 1, 1988 amalg.)
Oct. 16, 2008 – Name changed to Ateba Resources Inc.; basis 1 new for 5 old shs. ∎

Athabasca Exploration & Mining Ltd. (Alta. 1969)
Dec. 31, 1981 – Struck off register.

Athabasca Minerals Inc. (Alta. Dec. 31, 2006 amalg.)
Nov. 2023 – Filed a notice of intention under the Bankruptcy and Insolvency Act (Canada). KSV Restructuring Inc. was appointed as proposal trustee.
Apr. 26, 2024 – Pursuant to a restructuring transaction, Badger Mining Corporation acquired all the assets of the company for $29,200,000; the o/s com. shs. were exchanged for shs. in newly incorporated 2585929 Alberta Ltd. on a 1-for-1 basis and subsequently cancelled in exchange for 1 com. sh. of 2585929 Alberta; and 1,000 com. shs. were issued to Badger resulting in Badger being the sole shldr. of the company. The purchase price was transferred to 2585929 Alberta for the sole purpose of paying the company's obligations and liabilities to its secured and unsecured creditors. Following the discharge of said obligations and liabilities, any residual value will be distributed to the shldrs. of 2585929 Alberta.

Athabasca Nuclear Corp. (Alta. Aug. 31, 2011)
Nov. 10, 2015 – Continued into British Columbia.
June 10, 2016 – Name changed to Clean Commodities Corp. ∎

Athabasca Oil Sands Corp. (Alta. Aug. 23, 2006)
May 10, 2012 – Name changed to Athabasca Oil Corporation. (see FPsurvey - Mines & Energy)

Athabasca Oil Sands Trust (Alta. Oct. 5, 1995)
July 5, 2001 – Formed Canadian Oil Sands Trust in Alberta on amalgamation with Canadian Oil Sands Trust (old). ∎

Athabasca Potash Inc. (Sask. Apr. 10, 2006)
Mar. 25, 2010 – Acquired by BHP Billiton Canada Inc. for $8.35 per sh.

Athabasca Uranium Inc. (B.C. June 6, 2007)
Nov. 17, 2014 – Name changed to Atom Energy Inc. ∎

Athabasca Uranium Mines Ltd. (Del. 1949)
Assets acquired by Pippin Athabasca Uranium Mines Ltd.; basis 1 new for 1 old sh. (see Pippin Mining & Uranium Corp.)
Charter cancelled. (see Pippin Mining & Uranium Corp.)

Athabaska Gold Resources Ltd. (B.C. Mar. 17, 1987)
Sept. 17, 2007 – Dissolved and struck from register.
June 20, 2008 – Restored to registry.
Dec. 12, 2011 – Dissolved and stuck from register.

Athabaska Goldfields & Uranium Ltd. (Ont. 1946)
Dec. 2, 1970 – Dissolved.

Athabaska Research Mining Co. Ltd. (Ont. 1949)
Apr. 1965 – Dissolved.

Athalmer Mines Ltd. (B.C. 1952)
1953 – Name changed to Silver Prince Mines Ltd. ∎

Athena Gold Corporation (B.C. 1983)
Jan. 30, 1995 – Acquired by Miramar Mining Corporation; basis 1 Miramar sh. for 2.8 Athena shs. (see Miramar Mining Corporation)

Athena Gold Corporation (Del. Dec. 23, 2003)
Apr. 15, 2025 – Continued into British Columbia. (see FPsurvey - Mines & Energy)

Athena Mines Ltd. (B.C. 1969)
Aug. 13, 1975 – Name changed to Saturn Energy & Resources Ltd.; basis 1 new for 4 old shs. ∎

Athena Silver Corporation (Del. Dec. 23, 2003)
Jan. 21, 2021 – Name changed to Athena Gold Corporation. ∎

Athlodge Uranium Mines Ltd. (Ont. 1949)
Mar. 1962 – Charter cancelled.

Athlone Energy Ltd. (B.C. Sept. 5, 1986)
Sept. 19, 2008 – Acquired by Daylight Resources Trust for 85¢ per sh.

Athlone Minerals Ltd. (B.C. Sept. 5, 1986)
Feb. 14, 2005 – Name changed to Athlone Energy Ltd. ∎

Athlone Resources Ltd. (B.C. Sept. 5, 1986)
May 4, 1999 – Name changed to Athlone Minerals Ltd.; basis 1 new for 10 old shs. ∎

Athona Mines (1937) Ltd. (Ont. Mar. 3, 1937)
Nov. 29, 1954 – Name changed to New Athona Mines Ltd.; basis 1 new for 4 old shs. ∎

Atico Mining Corporation (Yuk. Apr. 15, 2010)
Oct. 17, 2011 – Continued into British Columbia. (see FPsurvey - Mines & Energy)

Atikokan Iron Co. Ltd. (Can.)
1941 – Liquidated and property taken over by Atikokan Mines Ltd.; basis 5 shs. for each $1,000 Atikokan Iron bond. (see Atikokan Mines Limited)

Atikokan Mines Limited (Ont. 1941)
July 30, 1979 – Charter cancelled.

Atikokan Resources Inc. (Ont. May 27, 1994)
July 10, 2006 – Name changed to Silvermet Inc. pursuant to reverse takeover acquisition of Silvermet Corporation; basis 1 new for 5 old shs. ∎

Atikwa Minerals Corporation (Ont. July 31, 2003)
Nov. 18, 2009 – Name changed to Atikwa Resources Inc. and continued into Alberta. ∎

Atikwa Resources Inc. (Alta. Nov. 18, 2009)
Jan. 31, 2014 – Placed into receivership. Alvarez & Marsal Canada Inc. appointed receiver.
Dec. 17, 2014 – The sales agreement entered into with McLand Resources Ltd. for the acquisition of the Albert and Saskatchewan properties was completed for an undisclosed amount.
Apr. 2015 – The sales agreement with Greenland Resources Inc. for the properties in Manitoba was completed for an undisclosed amount.
June 2015 – Secured creditor suffered a shortfall and there were no distrib. available for unsecured creditors or shldrs. The receiver was discharged.

Atkins & Durbrow Ltd. (B.C. 1941)
Oct. 19, 1990 – Amalgamated with parent company Transcontinental Resources Limited to form a private company known as Tatramar Holdings Ltd.; basis $2.50 per sh.

Atkinson Dredging Co. Ltd. (B.C. 1946)
1952 – Charter cancelled.

Atlanta Gold Corporation (B.C. Mar. 6, 1985)
Apr. 3, 1997 – Name changed to Twin Gold Corporation concurrent with acquisition of Voisey Bay Resources Inc. whereby Voisey Bay shareholders received 1.5 Twin Gold shs. for 1 Voisey Bay sh. ∎

Atlanta Mines Ltd. (Que. 1953)
1971 – Shs. were consolidated on a 1-for-2 basis and exchanged sh. for sh. for Albarmont Mines Corporation shs.

Atlantic Acceptance Corporation Limited (Ont. 1953)
July 1965 – In receivership.
Nov. 1980 – Final distribution of $6,900,000, about 12.5% of amt. owing, made to senior noteholders.

Atlantic Coast Copper Corporation Limited (Ont. 1956)
Jan. 11, 1999 – Privatized following amalgamation agreement with its affiliates, Northern Canada Mines, Limited, Key Anacon Mines Limited, First Maritime Mining

Corporation Limited and Hunter Brook Minerals Limited; basis $9.00 per sh.

Atlantic Energy Corporation (B.C. Sept. 30, 1981)
May 29, 1987 – Continued into Canada.
June 1, 1987 – Merged into Bowtex Energy Ltd.; basis unknown.

Atlantic Gold Corporation (B.C. July 24, 1986)
July 23, 2019 – Acquired by St Barbara Limited; basis $2.90 cash plus 0.05 Artemis Gold Inc. shs. for 1 Atlantic Gold sh.

Atlantic Gold Mines Limited (N.S. Mar. 11, 1974)
June 19, 1975 – Acquired by Midas Resources Limited. Subsequently in 1977, the exchange was reversed and the co. was released from all obligations and liabs. to Continental Silver Corp. (originally Midas).
July 26, 1994 – Continued into Canada.
Feb. 19, 1996 – Name changed to Delwood Capital Corporation Ltd. ■

Atlantic Goldfields Inc. (B.C. 1962)
Sept. 29, 1989 – Amalgamated with Norcast Corporation to continue as a new company also named Atlantic Goldfields Inc.
June 20, 1990 – Name changed to Dexus Inc.; basis 1 cl. A non-vtg. and 1 cl. B vtg. sh. for 10 old shs. ■

Atlantic Industrial Minerals Incorporated (Can. Jan. 19, 1989)
Apr. 23, 2021 – Name changed to Sylla Gold Corp.; basis 1 new for 5 old shs. (see FPsurvey - Mines & Energy)

Atlantic Nickel Mines Ltd. (Ont. Oct. 16, 1963)
June 27, 1983 – Name changed to Syngold Exploration Inc. ■

Atlantic Oil Co. Ltd. (unknown)
1951 – Acquired by Canadian Atlantic Oil Co. Ltd.; basis 1 new for 2 old shs. (see Canadian Atlantic Oil Co. Ltd.)

Atlantic Power Corporation (Ont. June 18, 2004)
July 8, 2005 – Continued into British Columbia.
May 18, 2021 – Acquired by I Squared Capital Advisors (US) LLC; basis US$3.03 cash per sh.

Atlantic Power Preferred Equity Ltd. (Alta. June 26, 1998)
May 18, 2021 – Acquired by I Squared Capital Advisors (US) LLC; basis $22.00 cash per pref. sh.

Atlantic Shopping Centres Limited (N.S. Feb. 4, 1964)
Aug. 29, 1989 – Acquired by Empire Company Limited; basis 0.9 Empire cl. A non-vtg. shs. for 1 cl. A or B sh. held. All 9.25% cum. redeem. retract. pref. shs. ser. 1 redeemed Dec. 30, 1996; basis $25 per sh. plus accr. and unpaid divd. of 38¢.
July 1, 2003 – Name changed to Crombie Properties Limited. ■

Atlantic Sugar Refineries Co. Limited (Ont. 1939)
June 29, 1973 – Amalgamated with The Glengair Group Limited to form Jannock Corporation Limited; basis 1 Jannock 6% cum. redeem. pref. 1st ser. sh., $100 par, for 1 Atlantic 5% cum. redeem. pref. sh., $100 par; 1 Jannock $1.20 cl. A sh. for 1 Atlantic cl. A sh.; and 1 Jannock special sh. for 1 Atlantic com. sh. (see Jannock Corporation Limited)

Atlantic Trust Company (N.S. 1974)
Jan. 16, 1981 – Name changed to Atlantic Trust Company of Canada and continued into Canada. ■

Atlantic Trust Company of Canada (Can. Jan. 16, 1981)
May 11, 1989 – Formed Prenor Trust Company of Canada in Canada. ■

Atlantic Ventures Ltd. (B.C. Aug. 27, 1979)
Feb. 27, 1981 – Name changed to South Atlantic Ventures Ltd. ■

Atlantic Wholesalers Limited (N.B. 1944)
Jan. 2, 1977 – Acquired by Loblaw Companies Limited.

Atlantique Video & Sound Inc. (Can. July 10, 1978)
June 13, 1990 – Declared bankrupt, Ernst & Young, Inc., of Montreal appointed trustee.
May 13, 1993 – All the assets of the company had been liquidated. The secured creditors suffered a shortfall and there were no distributions to unsecured creditors or shldrs.
July 25, 2000 – Trustee discharged.

Atlantis Communications Inc. (Ont. June 1, 1989)
Dec. 2, 1993 – Continued into Canada. (see Alliance Atlantis Communications Inc.)
Sept. 23, 1998 – Merged with Alliance Communications Corporation to continue as Alliance Atlantis Communications Inc.; basis 0.025 Alliance Atlantis cl. C special vtg. shs. for 1 Atlantis subord. vtg. sh., convertible into 20 Alliance Atlantis cl. B non-vtg. shs. for each cl. C sh. resulting in an exchange basis of 0.5 Alliance Atlantis cl. B non-vtg. shs. for 1 Atlantis subord. vtg. sh. (see Alliance Atlantis Communications Inc.)

Atlantis Development Corp. Ltd. (Alta. Oct. 7, 1950)
1952 – Assets sold to Triad Oil Co. Ltd.; basis 1 new for 2.5 old shs.

Atlantis Enterprises International Ltd. (B.C. Mar. 31, 1987)
Mar. 4, 1991 – Delisted from the Vancouver Stock Exchange. Subsequently struck from register and dissolved.

Atlantis Exploration Inc. (Can. Sept. 23, 1983)
Feb. 3, 2004 – Name changed to Noveko Echographs Inc. following reverse takeover acquisition of Noveko Echographs Inc.; basis 1 new for 3 old shs. ■

Atlantis International Ltd. (Alta. 1980)
July 19, 1988 – Name changed to Atlantis Resources Ltd. ■

Atlantis Mines Ltd. (B.C. 1968)
July 1977 – Dissolved.

Atlantis Resources International Ltd. (Alta. 1980)
Dec. 6, 1983 – Name changed to International Atlantis Resources Ltd.; basis 1 new for 4 old shs. ■

Atlantis Resources Ltd. (Alta. 1980)
Dec. 6, 1994 – Acquired by Grad & Walker Energy Corporation; basis 0.185 Grad shs. for 1 Atlantis sh.

Atlantis Submarines International, Inc. (Can. - unspecified)
Sept. 25, 1992 – Acquired by Atlantis Submarines (International Holdings), Inc.; basis unknown.

Atlantis Systems Corp. (Can. Feb. 16, 1994)
Jan. 2, 2014 – Acquired by Bluedrop Performance Learning Inc. for $0.0276 per sh.
Sept. 30, 2014 – Name changed to Bluedrop Training & Simulation Inc.

Atlas Acceptance Corporation Limited (Ont. 1950)
Apr. 15, 1972 – All o/s 6% secured notes, due Oct. 15, 1973, redeemed at par plus accr. int.

Atlas Blockchain Group Inc. (B.C. July 18, 2018)
Oct. 7, 2019 – Name changed to Isracann Biosciences Inc. pursuant to the acquisition of private (old) Isracann Biosciences Inc., a low-cost industrial-scale cannabis producer.; basis 1 new for 3 old shs. (see FPsurvey - Industrials)

Atlas Chibougamau Mines Ltd. (Ont. 1955)
Apr. 22, 1965 – Dissolved.

Atlas Cloud Enterprises Inc. (Alta. Jan. 21, 2010)
July 18, 2018 – Continued into British Columbia.
July 27, 2018 – Name changed to Atlas Blockchain Group Inc. ■

Atlas Cold Storage Income Trust (Ont. Feb. 25, 1997)
Nov. 3, 2006 – Acquired indirectly by Iceland-based Avion Group hf. for Cdn$7.50 per sh.

Atlas Cromwell Ltd. (Ont. June 30, 1998 amalg.)
May 2, 2006 – Continued into British Columbia.
July 24, 2006 – Name changed to Terrane Metals Corp. following reverse takeover acquisition of four mineral claims previously owned by Goldcorp Canada Ltd. ■

Atlas Cromwell Resources Limited (Alta. July 12, 1996)
Aug. 25, 1997 – Continued into Ontario.
June 30, 1998 – Formed Polycorp Inc. in Ontario on reverse takeover acquisition of and amalgamation with Polycorp Inc. ■

Atlas Energy Ltd. (Alta. Nov. 29, 2000 amalg.)
Jan. 2, 2007 – Amalgamated with Pearl Exploration and Production Ltd.; basis 0.82 Pearl shs. for 1 Atlas sh. (see Pearl Exploration and Production Ltd.)

The Atlas Exploration Co. Ltd. (B.C. 1965)
1981 – Dissolved. Co. distributed $3,000,000 to shldrs. following revival based on co. int. in predecessor to Pine Point Mines. Unclaimed assets reverted to Crown in 1989.

Atlas Explorations Limited (B.C. Nov. 9, 1965)
July 26, 1974 – Name changed to Cima Resources Limited; basis 1 new for 4 old shs. ■

Atlas Gypsum Corp. Ltd. (Ont. 1955)
Nov. 1961 – Charter cancelled.

Atlas Minerals Inc. (Alta. Nov. 9, 2007 amalg.)
Feb. 22, 2010 – Name changed to Cliffmont Resources Ltd. and continued into British Columbia; basis 1 new for 10 old shs. (see FPsurvey - Mines & Energy)

Atlas Mining Corp. Ltd. (B.C. 1953)
Mar. 1957 – Name changed to Tofino Mines Ltd. ■

Atlas Rainbow Mines Ltd. (Ont. 1969)
Mar. 1976 – Charter cancelled.

Atlas Star Corporation (Alta. Dec. 1, 1997)
July 2003 – Placed into receivership. KMPG Inc. appointed receiver and manager.

Atlas Steels Limited (Can. 1925)
1963 – Acquired by Rio Algom Limited. All o/s bonds redeemed and shldrs. of record Apr. 11 received $37.74 per sh. Atlas Steels Limited subsequently changed its name to Asco Welland. Charter surrendered..

Atlas Sulphur & Iron Co. Ltd. (Que. 1951)
June 26, 1963 – Name changed to International Atlas Development & Exploration Limited; basis 1 new for 15 old shs. ■

Atlas Telefilm Ltd. (Ont. 1944)
1964 – Name changed to Allied Telemedia Limited. ■

Atlas Uranium Corporation Limited (Alta. 1954)
1968 – Name changed to Aabro Mining & Oils Ltd. ■

Atlas Yellowknife Mines Ltd. (Ont. Jan. 4, 1945)
July 18, 1979 – Name changed to Atlas Yellowknife Resources Limited. ■

Atlas Yellowknife Resources Limited (Ont. Jan. 4, 1945)
Feb. 8, 1988 – Name changed to PanAtlas Energy Inc.; basis 1 new for 12 old shs. ■

Atlatsa Resources Corporation (B.C. Apr. 19, 1983)
Sept. 18, 2019 – Privatized; basis Cdn$0.09203 cash per com. sh.

Atlin Nickel Mines Ltd. (Ont. Feb. 13, 1957)
1965 – Name changed to Northern Union Mines Ltd.

Atlin-Ruffner Mines (B.C.) Ltd. (B.C. 1949)
1965 – Name changed to Armore Mines Ltd.; basis 1 new for 5 old shs. ■

Atlin-Ruffner Mines Ltd. (B.C. Mar. 11, 1920)
1949 – Assets acquired by Atlin-Ruffner Mines (B.C.) Ltd.; basis 1 new for 4 old shs.

Atlin-Yukon Mining Ltd. (unknown)
1969 – Assets acquired by Bathurst Norsemines Ltd.; basis 6 new for 10 old shs.

AtmanCo Inc. (Can. Nov. 5, 2007)
June 12, 2018 – Name changed to ATW Tech Inc. ■

Atna Resources Ltd. (B.C. May 30, 1984)
Oct. 19, 2016 – Liquidation Plan filed for distribution to holders of allowed administrative claims, allowed priority tax claims and allowed priority non-tax claims in a cash amount equal to the allowed amount of said claims or lesser amounts as agreed to by said claim holders. On the effective date of the plan, all officers and directors shall be terminated and deemed to have resigned and all existing equity interests will be cancelled and extinguished without further action. Additionally on the effective date, the company and all its subsids. will be deemed to have been liquidated.
Nov. 20, 2017 – Struck from register and dissolved.

Atocha Resources Inc. (B.C. Aug. 21, 2006)
Feb. 12, 2013 – Name changed to Durango Resources Inc.; basis 1 new for 20 old shs. ■

Atom Energy Inc. (B.C. June 6, 2007)
Aug. 26, 2019 – Name changed to Sixth Wave Innovations Inc. (see FPsurvey - Mines & Energy; FPsurvey - Industrials)

Atom Gold Mines Ltd. (Ont. 1945)
Sept. 18, 1961 – Dissolved.

Atomic Minerals Ltd. (B.C. Mar. 13, 2006)
May 11, 2009 – Name changed to Arco Resources Corp. ■

Atomic Mining Corp. (Que. 1955)
Sept. 23, 1965 – Declared bankrupt.

Atominerals Exploration Ltd. (Alta. 1954)
Sept. 1954 – Succeeded by Imperial Mines & Metals Ltd.; basis 1 new for 4 old shs. ■

Atrium Biotechnologies Inc. (Can. Dec. 10, 1999)
June 15, 2007 – Name changed to Atrium Innovations Inc. ■

Atrium Innovations Inc. (Can. Dec. 10, 1999)
Feb. 18, 2014 – Acquired by Acquisition Glacier Inc. and Acquisition Glacier II Inc., backed by Permira Advisers LLC, for Cdn$24 per Atrium sh.

Atrium Resources Ltd. (B.C. 1981)
July 9, 1992 – Name changed to McCulloch's Canadian Beverages Inc. ■

Attila Resources Inc. (B.C. Feb. 19, 1969)
Jan. 15, 1982 – Name changed to Amadeus Resources Inc. ■

Attila Resources Ltd. (B.C. Aug. 25, 1971)
Nov. 1974 – Name changed to Klondex Mines Ltd.; basis 1 new for 5 old shs. ■

Attock Energy Corporation (Alta. Feb. 1, 1991 amalg.)
Apr. 7, 1997 – Acquired by Cypress Energy Inc. for 83¢ per sh. (see Cypress Energy Inc.)

Attock Oil Corporation (Alta. Feb. 1, 1991 amalg.)
Aug. 14, 1995 – Name changed to Attock Energy Corporation; basis 1 new for 4 old shs. ■

Attwell Capital Inc. (Ont. Mar. 27, 2009)
Mar. 25, 2011 – Name changed to Citation Resources Inc. pursuant to acquisition of 60% interest in Eva Kitto property in Ontario; basis 1 new for 2.4 old shs. ■

Attwood Copper Mines Limited (Ont. 1951)
Mar. 16, 1973 – Dissolved.

Attwood Gold Corporation (B.C. July 25, 1977)
June 2, 2000 – Name changed to Dynasty Motorcar Corporation following reverse takeover acquisition of Dynasty Motorcar (Canada) Corporation; basis 1 new for 1 old sh. ■

Au Martinique Silver Inc. (Ont. July 12, 1988 amalg.)
Aug. 21, 2006 – Name changed to Aura Silver Resources Inc. and continued into Canada. ■

Au Resources Ltd. (B.C. July 20, 1981)
Sept. 21, 1994 – Name changed to Texas T Resources Inc.; basis 1 new for 5 old shs. ■

Auband Mines Ltd. (Ont. 1944)
Aug. 20, 1962 – Distribution of assets on basis of $5.00 and 88 free shs. and 466 pooled shs. of Band-Ore Gold Mines Ltd. for each 1,000 shs. held. Charter reported cancelled.

Aubay Uranium Mines Ltd. (Ont. 1955)
Jan. 1968 – Charter cancelled.

Aubelle Mines Ltd. (Ont. 1944)
1959 – Merged into Hydra Explorations Ltd.; basis 1 new for 25 old shs. (see Hydra Explorations Limited)

Auberges des Gouverneurs Inc. (Que. 1983)
July 24, 1996 – All o/s com. shs. repurchased; basis 1 special pref. sh. immediately redeemed for 10¢ per sh. for 1 com. sh. Co. now private.

Aubet Explorations Ltd. (Ont. Nov. 30, 1970 amalg.)
Aug. 25, 1999 – Name changed to Visa Gold Explorations Inc. ■

Aubet Resources Inc. (Ont. Nov. 30, 1970 amalg.)
June 3, 1995 – Charter cancelled.
Mar. 3, 1998 – Charter revived.
Sept. 30, 1998 – Name changed to Aubet Explorations Ltd.; basis 1 new for 2.74 old shs. ■

Auburn Mines Ltd. (Ont. 1944)
Nov. 18, 1958 – Charter cancelled.

Auckland Explorations Ltd. (B.C. Nov. 8, 1984)
Feb. 15, 1996 – Name changed to Coromandel Resources Ltd.; basis 1 new for 3 old shs. ■

Auconda Porcupine Gold Mines Ltd. (Ont. 1945)
May 1958 – Charter cancelled.

Aucourt Mines Ltd. (Ont. 1945)
Aug. 28, 1961 – Charter cancelled.

Audax Gas & Oil Ltd. (Alta. 1977)
1985 – Became a wholly owned subsid. of Financial Trustco Capital Ltd.; basis 1 Financial Trustco ser. 1 pref. sh. and ½ warrant for 12.2 Audax shs.
June 27, 1986 – Following Plan of Arrangement, each com. sh. of Financial Trustco Capital Ltd. was exchanged for 1 new com. sh. and 1 special sh. of Financial Trustco Capital Ltd. Each special sh. was then exchanged for 2 com. shs. of Audax Gas & Oil Ltd.
Apr. 30, 1992 – Placed into receivership. Assets sold with no distribution to shldrs.
Nov. 25, 1992 – Dissolved.

Audiotech Healthcare Corporation (Alta. Mar. 19, 1997)
May 2, 2008 – Continued into British Columbia.
Dec. 5, 2012 – Privatized at $0.35 per sh.

Audit Resources Inc. (Alta. 1985)
Jan. 1, 1989 – Struck off register.

Audley Gold Mines Ltd. (Ont. 1944)
Oct. 21, 1963 – Dissolved.

Audora Porcupine Mines Ltd. (Ont. 1944)
1950 – Charter cancelled.

Audre Recognition Systems Inc. (B.C. Aug. 10, 1983)
Aug. 31, 1995 – Delisted from the NYSE. Subsequently dissolved.

Audrey Capital Corporation (B.C. Mar. 9, 2021)
Mar. 7, 2024 – Name changed to Applied Graphite Technologies Corporation following Qualifying Transaction amalgamation of (old) Applied Graphite Technologies Corporation (AGT) with 1445056 B.C. Ltd., a wholly owned subsidiary of Audrey Capital Corporation, constituting a reverse takeover by (old) AGT. (see FPsurvey - Industrials)

Audrey Resources Inc. (Que. 1985)
Nov. 15, 1995 – Acquired by Cambior Inc.; basis $1.40 or 1 Cambior sh. for 10.5 Audrey shs. (see Cambior Inc.)

AuEx Ventures, Inc. (B.C. May 10, 2004)
Nov. 8, 2010 – Acquired by Fronteer Gold Inc.; basis Cdn$0.66, 0.645 Fronteer shs. and 0.5 Renaissance Gold, Inc. shs. for 1 AuEx sh. (see Fronteer Gold Inc.)

Aufron Mines Ltd. (Ont. 1946)
Sept. 1961 – Charter cancelled; co. dissolved.

Augdome Exploration Ltd. (Ont. 1955)
1966 – Name changed to Augdome Corporation Limited. (see FPsurvey - Mines & Energy)

Augen Capital Corp. (Alta. Apr. 16, 1997 amalg.)
Nov. 19, 2004 – Continued into Ontario.
Aug. 1, 2012 – Name changed to Gensource Capital Corporation. ■

Augen Gold Corp. (Ont. Aug. 11, 2006)
Oct. 31, 2011 – Acquired by Trelawney Mining and Exploration Inc.; basis 0.0862 Trelawney shs. for 1 Augen sh. (see Trelawney Mining and Exploration Inc.)
Dec. 5, 2011 – Formed Trelawney Augen Acquisition Corp. pursuant to amalgamation with Trelawney Mining and Exploration Acquisition Corp. (see Trelawney Mining and Exploration Inc.)

Auger Lake Mining Corp. (Que. 1955)
Sept. 4, 1976 – Charter cancelled.

Augite Porcupine Mines Ltd. (Ont. July 15, 1936)
1939 – All assets acquired by Aunor Gold Mines Ltd.; basis 1 new for 3 old shs.

Augmitto Explorations Limited (Ont. 1945)
Oct. 29, 1994 – Placed into receivership in March 1989. No distribution to shldrs. Dissolved.

August Metal Corporation (B.C. Jan. 6, 2006)
Nov. 20, 2013 – Name changed to Ardonblue Ventures Inc.; basis 1 new for 10 old shs. ■

August Petroleums Ltd. (B.C. 1973 amalg.)
Oct. 1976 – Name changed to Cheyenne Petroleum Corporation; basis 1 new for 5 old shs. ■

August Porcupine Mines Limited (Ont. 1945)
June 1987 – Amalgamated with Fechter Industries Inc. to form Magnipower Industries Inc.

Augusta Corporation (B.C. May 25, 1998)
Aug. 3, 2001 – Name changed to Canley Developments Inc.; basis 1 new for 15 old shs. ■

Augusta Gold Corporation (Can. Aug. 26, 1985)
Oct. 15, 1999 – Name changed to Pulse Data Inc.; basis 1 new for 2.5 old shs. ■

Augusta Industries Inc. (Del. Oct. 13, 1999)
Oct. 2, 2018 – Name changed to IntellaEquity Inc.; basis 1 new for 10 old shs. ■

Augusta Metals Incorporated (B.C. Mar. 23, 1984)
Sept. 14, 2000 – Name changed to CyberCom Systems Inc. ■

Augusta Natural Gas Limited (unknown)
Mar. 1969 – Acquired by Northern and Central Gas Corp. Ltd. for $3,250,000.

Augusta Resource Corporation (Ont. Jan. 14, 1937)
June 28, 1999 – Continued into Canada. (see HudBay Minerals Inc.)
Sept. 29, 2014 – All o/s com. shs. not already held acquired by HudBay Minerals Inc.; basis 0.315 HudBay

com. sh. and 0.17 wt. for 1 Augusta com. sh. (see HudBay Minerals Inc.)
Dec. 17, 2014 – Name changed to HudBay Arizona Corporation. (see HudBay Minerals Inc.)

Augusta Technologies Ltd. (Alta. Dec. 19, 1996)
Dec. 21, 1998 – Continued into Ontario.
Jan. 26, 1999 – Name changed to Danbel Industries Corporation; basis 1 new for 4 old shs. ■

Augustine Ventures Inc. (Ont. May 7, 1997 amalg.)
Feb. 7, 2017 – Acquired by Red Pine Exploration Inc.; basis 0.76 Red Pine com. shs. for 1 Augustine com. sh.

Augustus Exploration Ltd. (Ont. 1958)
May 4, 1967 – Amalgamated with The Canadian Faraday Corporation Ltd. (1 for 1) to form Consolidated Canadian Faraday Ltd.; basis 1 new for 5 old shs. ■

Augustus Resources Ltd. (B.C. Mar. 14, 1983)
Feb. 20, 1987 – Name changed to Croesus Resources Inc.; basis 1 new for 2 old shs. ■

Augyva Mining Resources Inc. (Can. Dec. 5, 1986)
Mar. 8, 2017 – Name changed to Automotive Finco Corp.; basis 1 new for 15 old shs. (see FPsurvey - Industrials)

Auka Capital Corp. (Alta. Aug. 5, 2021)
Mar. 5, 2025 – Name changed to Dr. Phone Fix Canada Corporation pursuant to the Qualifying Transaction reverse takeover acquisition of Dr. Phone Fix Canada Limited and concurrent amalgamation of (old) Dr. Phone with wholly owned 2629911 Alberta Inc. (see FPsurvey - Industrials)

Aukeko Gold Mines Ltd. (Ont. 1944)
Oct. 22, 1962 – Charter cancelled.

Aull Metal Mines Ltd. (Ont. 1951)
Feb. 1962 – Dissolved.

Aulore Gold Mines Ltd. (Ont. 1945)
Nov. 6, 1961 – Dissolved.

Ault Foods Limited (Can. June 4, 1993)
Aug. 8, 1997 – Acquired by Parmalat Food Inc., an indirectly held subsid. of Parmalat Finanziaria S.p.A. of Italy, for $34 per sh.

Aumac Explorations Ltd. (unknown)
1977 – Amalgamated with 4 other cos. to form Branly Enterprises Inc.; basis 3 new for 2 old shs.

Aumacho River Mines Ltd. (Ont. Aug. 25, 1947)
1962 – Name changed to Urban Quebec Mines Ltd.; basis 1 new for 3 old shs. ■

Aumaque Gold Mines Ltd. (Ont. Sept. 29, 1943)
1964 – Name changed to Bounty Exploration Limited; basis 1 new for 6.5 old shs. ■

Aumega Discoveries Ltd. (B.C. Mar. 28, 1980)
Jan. 10, 2007 – Name changed to Fortress Base Metals Corp.; basis 1 new for 5 old shs. ■

Aumento Capital II Corporation (Ont. Nov. 26, 2010)
Feb. 10, 2014 – Name changed to The Intertain Group Limited pursuant to Qualifying Transaction reverse takeover acquisition of Goldstar Acquistionco Inc.; basis 1 new for 20 old shs. ■

Aumento Capital III Corporation (Ont. May 5, 2011)
June 13, 2013 – Continued into Canada.
Aug. 1, 2013 – Formed EXO U Inc. in Canada on amalgamation with (old) EXO U Inc. (see FPsurvey - Industrials)

Aumento Capital IV Corporation (Ont. June 11, 2013)
Apr. 30, 2015 – Name changed to GreenSpace Brands Inc. pursuant to the Qualifying Transaction reverse takeover acquisition of Life Choices Natural Food Corp.; basis 1 new for 2 old shs. ■

Aumento Capital V Corporation (Ont. July 16, 2014)
Apr. 27, 2017 – Name changed to WeedMD Inc. following Qualifying Transaction reverse takeover acquisition of

WeedMD Rx Inc. and subsequent amalgamation with a wholly owned subsidiary. ■

Aumento Capital VI Corporation (Ont. Jan. 6, 2017)
Sept. 26, 2018 – Name changed to CryptoStar Corp. following Qualifying Transaction reverse takeover acquisition of CryptoStar Inc. and concurrent amalgamation of CryptoStar with wholly owned 2626694 Ontario Inc. (see FPsurvey - Industrials)

Aumento Capital VII Corporation (Ont. Dec. 13, 2017)
Dec. 7, 2020 – Name changed to Emerge Commerce Ltd. pursuant to the Qualifying Transaction reverse takeover acquisition of EMERGE Commerce Inc. and concurrent amalgamation of EMERGE with wholly owned 1260383 B.C. Ltd.; basis 1 new for 1.333333 old shs. (see FPsurvey - Industrials)

Aumento Capital VIII Corp. (Ont. Nov. 20, 2020)
Jan. 11, 2022 – Name changed to Eddy Smart Home Solutions Ltd. pursuant to the reverse takeover acquisition of (old) Eddy Smart Home Solutions Inc. (see FPsurvey - Industrials)

Aumento Capital IX Corp. (Ont. Feb. 16, 2021)
Jan. 13, 2022 – Name changed to Pluribus Technologies Corp. pursuant to the Qualifying Transaction reverse takeover acquisition of Pluribus Technologies Inc. and concurrent amalgamation of Pluribus with wholly owned 13515630 Canada Inc. (and continued as Pluribus Technologies Holdings Inc.).; basis 1 new for 7.94118 old shs. (see FPsurvey - Industrials)

Aumento Capital Corporation (Ont. Feb. 3, 2010)
May 26, 2011 – Name changed to Annidis Corporation pursuant to the June 9, 2011, Qualifying Transaction reverse takeover acquisition of Annidis Health Systems Corp. (see FPsurvey - Industrials)

Aumine Resources Ltd. (B.C. July 27, 1987)
Aug. 6, 1998 – Name changed to PetroReal Oil Corporation. ■

Aumisko Exploration Inc. (Can. Jan. 23, 1987)
Dec. 13, 1989 – Name changed to Granisko Resources Inc.; basis 1 new for 2 old shs. ■

Aumo Explorations Inc. (Ont. Dec. 15, 1980)
July 31, 1993 – Formed RTO Enterprises Inc. in Ontario on amalgamation with RTO Enterprises Inc. (deemed acquiror); basis 1 new for 4 old shs. ■

Aumo Porcupine Mines Ltd. (Ont. 1944)
Apr. 22, 1965 – Dissolved.

Aunite Mining Corp. Ltd. (Ont. 1943)
Mar. 2, 1959 – Charter cancelled.

Aunor Gold Mines Limited (Ont. 1939)
Nov. 18, 1972 – Acquired by Pamour Porcupine Mines, Ltd.; basis 1 new sh. plus 25¢ for 1 old sh.

Aunore Resources Inc. (Can. Mar. 13, 1984)
May 31, 1991 – Name changed to Denyvan Resources Inc.; basis 1 new for 7 old shs. ■

Aupan Red Lake Resources Ltd. (Can. June 22, 1983)
Oct. 30, 1995 – Dissolved.

Aur Resources Inc. (Can. Sept. 14, 1981)
Sept. 28, 2007 – Amalgamated with Teck Cominco Limited; basis Cdn$41 per sh. or 0.8749 Teck cl. B subord. vtg. sh. and Cdn$0.0001 per com. sh. for 1 Aur Resources com. sh. (see Teck Cominco Limited)

Aura Gold Inc. (Ont. July 12, 1946)
Apr. 20, 2006 – Continued into Canada.
Aug. 16, 2007 – Name changed to Aura Minerals Inc. ■

Aura Health Inc. (Ont. July 9, 2018)
Oct. 22, 2019 – Name changed to Pharmadrug Inc. (see FPsurvey - Industrials)

Aura Industries Inc. (B.C. Jan. 19, 1987)
July 25, 1991 – Name changed to Nycal (Canada) Inc. ■

Aura Minerals Inc. (Can. Apr. 20, 2006)
Dec. 30, 2016 – Continued into British Virgin Islands. (see FPsurvey - Mines & Energy)

Aura Resources Inc. (Can. Aug. 21, 2006)
July 28, 2020 – Continued into British Columbia.
Aug. 4, 2020 – Name changed to Gold79 Mines Ltd. ■

Aura Silver Resources Inc. (Can. Aug. 21, 2006)
Nov. 28, 2018 – Name changed to Aura Resources Inc.; basis 1 new for 5 old shs. ■

Auracle Resources Ltd. (B.C. Feb. 2, 2007)
June 16, 2015 – Name changed to Four River Ventures Ltd.; basis 1 new for 20 old shs. ■

Aurado Exploration Ltd. (Ont. Jan. 27, 1994)
Apr. 15, 2003 – Continued into New Brunswick.
July 30, 2003 – Name changed to Aurado Energy Inc. following acquisition of oil and gas operations in Kazakhstan. (see FPsurvey - Mines & Energy)

Auralee Gold Mines Ltd. (Ont. 1946)
1957 – Charter cancelled.

Auralite Investments Inc. (B.C. Mar. 24, 2017)
July 23, 2020 – Name changed to Myconic Capital Corp.; basis 1 new for 10 old shs. ■

Auramex Resource Corp. (B.C. Jan. 15, 1980)
July 8, 2020 – Name changed to AUX Resources Corporation. ■

Aurcana Corporation (Ont. Oct. 12, 1917)
Sept. 14, 1998 – Continued into Canada.
Aug. 21, 2020 – Name changed to Aurcana Silver Corporation and continued into British Columbia. (see FPsurvey - Mines & Energy)

AurCrest Gold Inc. (Ont. Sept. 7, 1982)
Apr. 22, 2022 – Name changed to Big Tree Carbon Inc. (see FPsurvey - Mines & Energy)

Aurea Mining Inc. (B.C. June 8, 1988)
July 4, 2008 – Acquired by Newstrike Capital Inc.; basis 1 Newstrike com. sh. for 5.5 Aurea shs.

Aurelian Resources Inc. (Can. Dec. 6, 2000)
Oct. 6, 2008 – Acquired by Kinross Gold Corporation; basis 0.317 Kinross com. shs. plus 0.1429 wts. for 1 Aurelian sh.

Aurelian Small Business Developers Ltd. (Ont. June 11, 1070)
Feb. 1, 1982 – Name changed to Aurelian Developers Ltd. (see FPsurvey - Industrials)

Aureus Mining Inc. (Can. Feb. 1, 2011)
Dec. 12, 2016 – Name changed to Avesoro Resources Inc. ■

Aureus Ventures Inc. (Can. July 8, 2004)
Aug. 17, 2006 – Name changed to Velo Energy Inc. following the May 31, 2006, Qualifying Transaction acquisition of Velo Energy Ltd. ■

Aurex Resources Corp. (B.C. Feb. 24, 1981)
Mar. 13, 1997 – Name changed to Cobre Mining Company Inc.; basis 1 new for 10 old shs. ■

Aurex Resources Inc. (B.C. 1985 amalg.)
July 22, 1986 – Amalgamated with 2 other cos. to form Galveston Resources Ltd.; basis 1 new for 3.5 old shs.

Augent Gold Corp. (B.C. July 13, 2011)
Mar. 10, 2014 – Name changed to Augent Resource Corp. ■

Augent Resource Corp. (B.C. July 13, 2011)
Sept. 22, 2016 – Name changed to First Cobalt Corp. ■

Auriac Mines Ltd. (Que. May 19, 1936)
1945 – Merged into Union Mining Corp.; basis 1 new for 3 old shs.

Auric Development Corp. (B.C. Aug. 9, 2007)
Jan. 4, 2011 – Name changed to First Mexican Gold Corp. pursuant to Qualifying Transaction reverse takeover acquisition of First Mexican Resources Inc.; basis 1 new for 1.1376 old shs. ■

Auric Mining Explorations Ltd. (Ont. 1952)
June 1960 – Distributed one sh. Vulcan Mines Ltd. for each Auric sh. held; dissolved.

Auric Resources Limited (Ont. Nov. 23, 1936)
Mar. 29, 1979 – Name changed to Chancellor Energy Resources Inc.; basis 1 new for 4 old shs. ■

Auric Resources Ltd. (Bermuda Oct. 12, 1995)
Nov. 1, 2001 – Name changed to Lalo Ventures Ltd. and continued into Yukon; basis 1 new for 10 old shs. ■

Auricle Biomedical Corporation (B.C. June 1, 2007)
Apr. 19, 2010 – Amalgamated with Decoury Capital Corp. and Transformative Ventures Ltd. to form Aztech Innovations Inc. which then acquired Aztech Associates Inc. by reverse takeover constituting the Qualifying Transaction for each of Decoury, Transformative and Auricle; basis 1 Aztech sh. for 1 Decoury sh., 0.667 Aztech shs. for 1 Transformative sh. and 0.667 Aztech shs. for 1 Auricle sh.

AuRico Gold Inc. (Que. Feb. 25, 1986)
Aug. 26, 2011 – Continued into Ontario.
July 2, 2015 – Formed Alamos Gold Inc. in Ontario on the basis of 1 new Alamos sh. and US$0.0001 cash for 1 old Alamos sh. and 0.5046 new Alamos sh. for 1 AuRico sh. (see FPsurvey - Mines & Energy)

AuRico Metals Inc. (Ont. May 7, 2015)
Jan. 10, 2018 – Acquired by Centerra Gold Inc.; basis Cdn$1.80 cash per sh.

Aurifer Capital Corp. (B.C. Nov. 6, 2006)
Dec. 1, 2008 – Name changed to Jaxon Minerals Inc. ■

Auriga Gold Corp. (Ont. Apr. 21, 2010)
June 25, 2014 – Name changed to Minnova Corp. (see FPsurvey - Mines & Energy)

Auriga Resources Limited (B.C. Oct. 23, 1986)
Mar. 29, 1996 – Dissolved and struck off register.

Auriga Yellowknife Mines Ltd. (Ont. 1945)
1947 – Sold assets to Aurlando Consolidated Mining Corp. Ltd.; basis 1 new for 5 old shs. (see Aurlando Consolidated Mining Corp. Ltd.)
Dec. 12, 1955 – Dissolved. (see Aurlando Consolidated Mining Corp. Ltd.)

Auriginor Exploration Inc. (B.C. Jan. 31, 1980)
Mar. 3, 1998 – Continued into Canada.
Apr. 15, 2005 – Dissolved.

Aurion Resources Ltd. (Alta. Apr. 6, 2006)
Aug. 10, 2018 – Continued into British Columbia. (see FPsurvey - Mines & Energy)

Aurizon Mines Ltd. (B.C. Aug. 31, 1988)
June 1, 2013 – Acquired by Hecla Mining Company; basis either (i) Cdn$4.75 or (ii) 0.9953 Hecla com. shs. for 1 Aurizon sh. and amalgamated with 0963708 B.C. Ltd. to continue as Aurizon Mines Ltd.
Aug. 23, 2013 – Name changed to Hecla Quebec Inc. and continued into Canada.

Aurlando Consolidated Mining Corp. Ltd. (Ont. 1947 amalg.)
1956 – Charter cancelled.

Aurlando Gold Mines Ltd. (Ont.)
1947 – Sold assets to Aurlando Consolidated Mining Corp. Ltd.; basis 1 new for 5 old shs. (see Aurlando Consolidated Mining Corp. Ltd.)

Aurlode Gold Mines Ltd. (Ont. 1945)
July 14, 1948 – Name changed to Embury Lake Mining Co. Ltd. ■

Aurlot Explorations Ltd. (Ont. Feb. 23, 1988)
Dec. 18, 1992 – Formed USA Tough Inc. in Ontario on amalgamation with 978656 Ontario Limited; basis 1 new for 1 978656 Ontario sh. and 1 new for 10 Aurlot shs. ■

Auro Resources Corp. (B.C. Apr. 29, 1987)
Aug. 23, 2013 – Name changed to Tesoro Minerals Corp.; basis 1 new for 10 old shs. (see FPsurvey - Mines & Energy)

Aurochs, société d'exploration minière inc. (Can. Oct. 23, 1986)
Jan. 9, 1996 – Dissolved.

Aurofina Resource Corporation (B.C. Dec. 13, 1982)
Sept. 16, 1983 – Name changed to Asitka Resource Corporation. ■

Aurogin Resources Ltd. (B.C. Jan. 14, 1986)
Jan. 8, 1998 – Continued into Canada.
Aug. 28, 2007 – Formed Castle Gold Corporation in Canada on amalgamation with Morgain Minerals Inc. with Aurogin the deemed acquiror; basis 1 new for 2 Morgain shs. and 1 new for 2 Aurogin shs. ■

Auromar Development Corporation (B.C. Aug. 20, 1987)
Oct. 1, 1996 – Acquired by Casmyn Corp.; basis 1 Casmyn sh. for 2.6 Auromar shs.

Aurora Corporation (Ont. Mar. 5, 1945)
Jan. 3, 1995 – Delisted CDN. Subsequently dissolved and charter cancelled.

Aurora Energy Fund Ltd. (Alta. 1977)
July 1982 – Acquired by Humboldt Energy Corporation; basis 2.1 new for 1 old sh. (see Humboldt Energy Corporation)

Aurora Energy Resources Inc. (N.L. June 8, 2005)
Apr. 22, 2009 – Amalgamated with 59801 Newfoundland & Labrador Inc., a wholly-owned subsid. of Fronteer Development Group Inc.; basis 0.825 Fronteer Development shs. for 1 Aurora Energy sh. (see Fronteer Development Group Inc.)

Aurora Financial Corp. Ltd. (B.C.)
Sept. 7, 1972 – Dissolved.

Aurora Gold Ltd. (Alta. 1987)
Nov. 21, 1991 – Amalgamated with Frobisher Resources Ltd. to form Canadian Frobisher Resources Ltd.; basis 1 new for 1 Frobisher sh. and 1 new for 6.25 Aurora shs. (see Canadian Frobisher Resources Ltd.)

Aurora Oil & Gas Limited (Australia June 17, 1975)
June 12, 2014 – Acquired by Baytex Energy Corp.; basis A$4.20 cash per sh.

Aurora Platinum Corp. (Yuk. Aug. 8, 2000)
July 5, 2005 – Acquired by FNX Mining Company Inc.; basis 0.1918 FNX shs. for 1 Aurora sh. (see FNX Mining Company Inc.)

Aurora Sky Ventures Corp. (B.C. Sept. 16, 2021)
July 25, 2024 – Name changed to Onco-Innovations Limited pursuant to the reverse takeover acquisition of Onco-Innovations Inc. (see FPsurvey - Industrials)

Aurora Uranium & Gold Mines Ltd. (Ont. 1944)
1954 – Merged into Pardee Amalgamated Mines Ltd.; basis 1 new for 5 old shs.

Aurquest Resources Inc. (Ont. Nov. 24, 1999)
Feb. 22, 2018 – Name changed to Xanthic Biopharma Inc. ■

Aurtec Inc. (Can. June 7, 1984)
July 13, 2011 – Dissolved.

Aurum Gold Mines Limited (Can. 1972)
Dec. 16, 1980 – Dissolved.

Aurum Lake Mining Corporation (B.C. June 2, 2021)
Apr. 25, 2024 – Continued into Cayman Islands. (see FPsurvey - Mines & Energy; FPsurvey - Industrials)

Aurun Mines Ltd. (Alta. 1981)
Aug. 1, 1991 – Struck off register.

Aurun Resources Limited (Alta. 1981)
May 1, 1981 – Name changed to Aurun Mines Ltd. ■

Aurus Mining Ltd. (B.C. 1968)
July 4, 1980 – Name changed to Aucan Resources Ltd.; basis 1 new for 5 old shs. (see FPsurvey - Mines & Energy)

Aurvista Gold Corporation (Ont. June 3, 2010)
June 22, 2011 – Continued into Canada.
Nov. 20, 2017 – Name changed to Maple Gold Mines Ltd. ■

Auryn Resources Inc. (B.C. June 9, 2008)
Oct. 8, 2020 – Name changed to Fury Gold Mines Limited pursuant to acquisition of Eastmain Resources Inc. and spin-out of Auryn's Peruvian assets into separate companies.; basis 0.675627 new for 1 old sh. (see FPsurvey - Mines & Energy)

Auryx Gold Corp. (B.C. Oct. 11, 2007)
Dec. 30, 2011 – Acquired by B2Gold Corp.; basis 0.23 B2Gold shs. plus $0.001 for 1 Auryx sh.

Ausable Mines Ltd. (Que. 1951)
Feb. 1974 – Charter cancelled.

Ausam Energy Corporation (Alta. July 10, 1997)
July 2, 2010 – Dissolved and struck from registry.

Ausex Capital Corp. (B.C. Aug. 31, 2007)
Nov. 3, 2009 – Amalgamated with Lumex Capital Corp. and Tasman Metals Ltd. (deemed acquiror) to form new co. also named Tasman Metals Ltd. constituting a Qualifying Transaction; basis 1.0806 new for 1 Lumex sh., 1 new for 1 Tasman sh. and 1 new for 1 Ausex sh (see Tasman Metals Ltd.)

Ausic Mining & Reduction Co. Ltd. (Ont. 1944)
1955 – Name changed to United Cobalt Mines Ltd.; basis 1 new for 2 old shs. ■

Ausnoram Holdings Limited (Ont. May 17, 1965)
Feb. 10, 2010 – Name changed to Batavia Energy Corp. pursuant to Mar. 11, 2010, reverse takeover acquisition of Batavia Energy Inc. which amalgamated with wholly owned Condelta Inc. ■

Auspex Gold Ltd. (B.C. Feb. 16, 1981)
Dec. 4, 1995 – Name changed to Auspex Minerals Ltd. ■

Auspex Minerals Ltd. (B.C. Feb. 16, 1981)
Apr. 21, 1999 – Amalgamated with International Vestor Resources Ltd. to form EuroZinc Mining Corporation; basis 1 new for 1 International Vestor sh. and 0.75 new for 1 Auspex sh. (see EuroZinc Mining Corporation)

Austar Resources Corporation (B.C. Nov. 1, 1990 amalg.)
Jan. 31, 1996 – Name changed to Austpro Energy Corporation; basis 1 new for 4 old shs. ■

Austin Developments Corp. (B.C. Apr. 17, 1979)
Dec. 11, 2009 – Name changed to Universal Wing Technologies Inc.; basis 1 new for 20 old shs. ■

Austin Mines Inc. (B.C. June 24, 1983)
Mar. 13, 1995 – Name changed to Nighthawk Resources Inc. and continued into Alberta. ■

Austin Petroleums Inc. (B.C. Oct. 17, 1979)
Mar. 3, 1980 – Name changed to Pipestone Petroleums Inc. ■

Austin Resources Inc. (B.C.)
Aug. 1984 – Acquired by Lincoln Resources Inc.; basis 2 Lincoln shs. for 3 Austin shs. (see Lincoln Resources Inc.)

Austin Resources Ltd. (Ont. Mar. 15, 2007)
Sept. 25, 2023 – Voluntarily delisted. (see FPsurvey - Mines & Energy)

Austonia Red Lake Mines Ltd. (Ont. 1947)
Dec. 10, 1962 – Dissolved.

Austpro Energy Corporation (B.C. Nov. 1, 1990 amalg.)
Aug. 25, 2021 – Name changed to WonderFi Technologies Inc. pursuant to the reverse takeover acquisition of DeFi Ventures Inc. and concurrent amalgmation of DeFi with wholly owned 1302107 B.C. Ltd. (and continued as WonderFi Digital Inc.).; basis 1 new for 8.727 old shs. (see FPsurvey - Industrials)

Austra Resources Corporation (B.C. 1972)
Nov. 2, 1990 – Amalgamated with Barkerville Mining Co. Ltd. (NPL) to form a new co. named Austar Resources Corporation; basis 1 new for 1 old sh. (see Austar Resources Corporation)

Austrak International Canada Corporation (Alta. 1986)
Dec. 1, 1994 – Struck off register.

Austral Pacific Energy Ltd. (Yuk. Sept. 25, 1997)
Oct. 16, 2006 – Continued into British Columbia.
Apr. 30, 2009 – Placed into receivership. New Zealand-based Gerry Rea Partners appointed receiver.
Apr. 16, 2012 – Dissolved and struck from register.

Australian Banc Capital Securities Trust (Ont. Nov. 23, 2010)
Feb. 4, 2016 – Merged into North American Financials Capital Securities Trust to continue as Global Capital Securities Trust; basis 0.413485 Global Capital cl. A units for 1 Australian Banc cl. A unit and 0.391346 Global Capital cl. F units for 1 Australian Banc cl. F unit. (see Global Capital Securities Trust)

Australian Banc Income Fund (Ont.)
Name changed to Purpose Global Financials Income Fund. ■

Australian Gold Mines Corporation (B.C. 1983)
Aug. 23, 1990 – Name changed to Blue Sun Resource Corporation. ■

Australian Goldfields Limited (B.C. Oct. 14, 2016)
May 16, 2022 – Name changed to Oz Lithium Corporation. ■

Australian Oilfields Pty. Ltd. (B.C. Oct. 29, 1981)
June 10, 1997 – Continued into Alberta.
Sept. 15, 1997 – Name changed to Equatorial Energy Inc. ■

Australian REIT Income Fund (Ont.)
Dec. 18, 2023 – Terminated, basis $7.5272 cash per cl. A unit and $10.2327 cash per cl. F unit.

Australian Solomons Gold Limited (Qld. June 10, 2004)
Jan. 29, 2010 – Acquired by Allied Gold Limited; basis 0.85 Allied Gold shs. for 1 Australian Solomons sh. (see Allied Gold Limited)

Austro-Can Exploration Ltd. (B.C. 1968)
Dec. 31, 1979 – Name changed to Agio Resources Corporation; basis 1 new for 2 old shs. ■

AuTECO Minerals Ltd (Australia Aug. 3, 2004)
Nov. 24, 2023 – Name changed to FireFly Metals Ltd. (see FPsurvey - Mines & Energy)

Ressources Autanabi Inc. (Can. Apr. 9, 1996)
May 15, 2006 – Dissolved.

Auterra Mines Ltd. (Ont. 1944)
Sept. 18, 1961 – Dissolved.

Auterra Ventures Inc. (B.C. Mar. 30, 1988)
Feb. 24, 2005 – Name changed to Global Hunter Corp. ■

Authentex Software Limited Partnership (Ont. Nov. 2, 1995)
Mar. 28, 2005 – Continued into Alberta.
June 29, 2005 – Name changed to Ophir Ventures Inc. following reorganization and asset exchange; basis 1 Ophir sh. for 1 Authentex limited partnership unit. ■

Auto Electric Service Company Limited (Ont. 1918)
Aug. 1, 1974 – Name changed to Autolec Inc. ■

Auto Fabric Products Co. Ltd. (Can. 1928)
May 1961 – Name changed to Autofab Limited. ■

Auto Group International Ltd. (Ont. 1982)
Jan. 3, 1995 – Delisted CDN. Subsequently certificate of incorporation cancelled and dissolved.

Auto-Marine Acceptance Corporation Ltd. (Can. - unspecified)
1967 – Acquired by Chieftain Development Co. Ltd.; basis 1 new for 4.1 old shs. (see Chieftain Development Co. Ltd.)

Auto Marine Electric Ltd. (B.C. 1949)
Jan. 3, 1991 – Amalgamated with 391728 B.C. Ltd., a wholly owned subsid. of UAP Inc., for $28 per sh. (see UAP Inc.)

Autobyte Systems Corporation (B.C. Jan. 20, 1969)
June 11, 1993 – Dissolved and struck off register.

Autobyte Technologies Inc. (B.C. Nov. 7, 1980)
Oct. 5, 1994 – Continued into Canada.
Mar. 2, 2004 – Dissolved and struck from register.

AutoCanada Income Fund (Alta. Jan. 4, 2006)
Dec. 31, 2009 – Converted into AutoCanada Inc.; basis 1 AutoCanada com. sh. for 1 trust unit and 1 AutoCanada com. sh. for 1 AutoCanada Limited Partnership exch. LP unit.

Autocrat Resources Ltd. (B.C. 1980)
June 14, 1984 – Name changed to Jack Criswell Resources Ltd.; basis 1 new for 5 old shs. ■

Autocrown Corporation Limited (Ont. Apr. 27, 1980 amalg.)
Oct. 1, 1990 – Formed Microbix Biosystems Inc. in Ontario on amalgamation with Microbix Biosystems Inc. (see FPsurvey - Industrials)

Autofab Limited (Can. 1928)
Dec. 8, 1963 – In liquidation. Assets acquired by Montreal group headed by Morris Goldsmith. No assets available for shldrs.

Autolec Inc. (Ont. 1918)
Sept. 29, 1975 – Sale of assets to Acklands Ltd.
Nov. 20, 1975 – Name changed to Centurion Equities Corporation. ■

Automated Benefits Corp. (Alta. July 15, 1999)
Sept. 24, 2012 – Name changed to Symbility Solutions Inc. ■

Automated Recycling Inc. (B.C. July 25, 1984)
Mar. 1, 2001 – Name changed to OceanLake Commerce Inc. ■

Automodular Corporation (Ont. May 7, 1957)
Jan. 1, 2008 – Amalgamated in Ontario to continue with same name.
Mar. 14, 2018 – Amalgamated with HLS Therapeutics Inc. to continue as HLS Therapeutics Inc.; basis 0.165834 new HLS com. sh. and 1 new HLS pref. sh. for 1 Automodular sh.

Automotive Hardware Limited (Ont. 1944)
May 1984 – Name changed to The AHL Group Ltd. ■

AutoPoint Inc. (Que. 1952)
Aug. 8, 1988 – Acquired by Groupe T.C.G. (Quebec) Inc.; basis unknown. (see Groupe T.C.G. (Québec) Inc.)

Autostock Inc. (Que. Dec. 31, 1983 amalg.)
Dec. 31, 1997 – Acquired by 3011652 Nova Scotia Limited, an indirect wholly owned subsid. of Belron International NV, for $5.50 per sh.

AutoTradeCenter Canada Ltd. (Alta. Nov. 3, 1995)
May 2, 2008 – Dissolved and struck from register.

Autovend Technology Corp. (Can. Feb. 26, 1985)
Mar. 13, 1992 – Dissolved and struck off register.

Autrex Inc. (Ont. Jan. 31, 1984 amalg.)
Oct. 25, 1999 – Formed Basis100 Inc. in Ontario on amalgamation with e-Net (Canada) Financial Services Ltd., constituting a reverse takeover by e-Net; basis 1 new for 9.64022 Autrex cl. A or cl. B shs. Autrex shldrs. also received a cash distribution of 40¢ per sh. ■

Autumn Industries Inc. (B.C. Jan. 27, 1986 amalg.)
Mar. 7, 2001 – Name changed to Altek Power Corporation. ■

Auxellence Health Corporation (B.C. Nov. 9, 2011)
Sept. 8, 2016 – Name changed to EVITRADE Health Systems Corp.; basis 1 new for 15 old shs. ■

Auxly Cannabis Group Inc. (B.C. Aug. 24, 1987)
May 20, 2021 – Continued into Ontario. (see FPsurvey - Industrials)

Ava Gold Mining Company Ltd. (Ont. 1950)
July 10, 1973 – Charter cancelled.

Ava Resources Corp. (Alta. Dec. 15, 1994)
Apr. 1, 2014 – Dissolved following Qualifying Transaction private placement subscription of 668,719 Tasman Metals Ltd. units at $1.10 per unit plus wts. exercisable at $1.50 per unit for a 3-year period and distribution of Tasman units to shareholders. (see Tasman Metals Ltd.)

Avagenesis Corp. (Alta. Dec. 21, 2012)
Dec. 31, 2016 – Formed Liberty Biopharma Inc. in British Columbia following amalgamation with Avapecia Life Sciences Corp. ■

Avala Resources Ltd. (B.C. July 29, 2010)
Apr. 13, 2016 – Acquired by Dundee Precious Metals Inc.; basis 0.044 Dundee com. shs. for 1 Avala com. sh.
Dec. 31, 2021 – Name changed to DPM Avala d.o.o.

Avalanche Capital Venture Inc. (Can. Dec. 22, 1995)
Mar. 17, 1998 – Name changed to Syncom Image Display Systems Inc. ■

Avalanche Industries Ltd. (B.C. 1976 amalg.)
June 11, 1986 – Name changed to CTG Compression Technology Group Inc.; basis 1 new for 4 old shs. ■

Avalanche Minerals Ltd. (Can. July 12, 1987)
July 3, 2008 – Name changed to OroAndes Resource Corp.; basis 1 new for 4 old shs. ■

Avalanche Networks Corporation (Can. July 12, 1987)
Sept. 14, 2007 – Name changed to Avalanche Minerals Ltd. ■

Avalard Mines Ltd. (Ont. 1936)
Apr. 1, 1954 – Charter cancelled.

Avalite Inc. (Alta. May 9, 2005)
June 30, 2010 – Formed Innovative Wireline Solutions Inc. in Alberta following reverse takeover acquisition of and subsequent amalgamation with True Production Services Inc.; basis 1 new for 1.875 old shs. ■

Avallin Mines Ltd. (B.C. 1955)
May 15, 1969 – Struck off register.

Avalon Blockchain Inc. (B.C. Feb. 15, 1985 amalg.)
Apr. 15, 2020 – Name changed to WSM Ventures Corp. (see FPsurvey - Industrials)

Avalon Rare Metals Inc. (B.C. July 24, 1991 amalg.)
Feb. 9, 2011 – Continued into Canada.
Feb. 24, 2016 – Name changed to Avalon Advanced Materials Inc. (see FPsurvey - Mines & Energy)

Avalon Resources Inc. (B.C. 1980)
June 12, 1989 – Name changed to Twin Tires Systems Inc.; basis 1 new for 5 old shs. ■

The Avalon Telephone Company Limited (N.L. May 31, 1919)
1962 – Over 99% of ord. shs. acquired by Bell Canada; basis 2 Bell com. shs. for 7 Avalon ord. shs.
Jan. 1, 1970 – Name changed to Newfoundland Telephone Company Limited. ■

Avalon Ventures Ltd. (B.C. July 24, 1991 amalg.)
Feb. 23, 2009 – Name changed to Avalon Rare Metals Inc. ■

Avalon Works Corp. (Can. Apr. 6, 2000)
Feb. 17, 2014 – Dissolved and struck from registry.
Nov. 9, 2018 – Certificate of revival issued.
Mar. 29, 2021 – Name changed to Founders Metals Inc. ■

Avance International Inc. (B.C. Sept. 14, 1964)
Oct. 21, 1999 – Name changed to Avance Venture Corp.; basis 1 new for 5 old shs. ■

Avance Venture Corp. (B.C. Sept. 14, 1964)
Feb. 9, 2004 – Name changed to Santa Cruz Ventures Inc.; basis 1 new for 10 old shs. ■

Avanco Capital Corp. (B.C. Apr. 6, 2016)
July 31, 2018 – Name changed to Hill Street Beverage Company Inc. following Qualifying Transaction reverse takeover acquisition of Hill Street Marketing Inc. by way of an amalgamation with a wholly owned subsidiary. ■

Avantage Link inc. (Can. Feb. 17, 1995)
Dec. 18, 2002 – In December the company filed a motion with the Québec Superior Court to authorize the sale of its assets to 4123654 Canada Inc. and court-authorized sale generated proceeds of $415,000 for the benefit of secured and unsecured creditors. Raymond Chabot Inc. was appointed as interim receiver with the power to sell the assets and all directors resigned.
Feb. 3, 2004 – Receiver discharged. There were no funds available for shldrs.

Avante Logixx Inc. (Ont. May 19, 2006)
June 1, 2023 – Name changed to Avante Corp. (see FPsurvey - Industrials)

Avante Mining Corp. (B.C. Feb. 1, 2011)
Apr. 10, 2024 – Name changed to First Atlantic Nickel Corp. (see FPsurvey - Mines & Energy)

Avante Security Corp. (Ont. May 19, 2006)
Oct. 13, 2010 – Name changed to Avante Logixx Inc. ■

Avanté Technologies Inc. (Alta. Jan. 30, 1996)
July 2, 2006 – Struck from the registry and dissolved.

Avantec Technologies Inc. (B.C. June 7, 1999)
Aug. 17, 2009 – Name changed to Harmony Gold Corp.; basis 1 new for 9 old shs. ■

Avanti Capital Corp. (Ont. Oct. 21, 1985)
Apr. 30, 1992 – Name changed to AvantiCorp International Inc.; basis 1 new for 5 old shs. ■

Avanti Energy Inc. (B.C. Mar. 7, 2011)
Aug. 22, 2022 – Name changed to Avanti Helium Corp. (see FPsurvey - Mines & Energy)

Avanti Mining Inc. (B.C. Feb. 2, 2006)
Dec. 1, 2014 – Name changed to Alloycorp Mining Inc. ■

Avanti Productions Inc. (B.C. Mar. 18, 1983)
Dec. 5, 1989 – Name changed to First Entertainment Corporation. ■

AvantiCorp International Inc. (Ont. Oct. 21, 1985)
Jan. 14, 1999 – Name changed to Micromem Technologies Inc. (see FPsurvey - Industrials)

Avapecia Life Sciences Corp. (B.C. Jan. 10, 2014)
Jan. 3, 2017 – Amalgamated with Avagenesis Corp. to form Liberty Biopharma Inc.; basis 1 Liberty com. sh. for 3 Avapecia com. shs. (see Liberty Biopharma Inc.)

Avaranta Resources Ltd. (Can. May 11, 2005)
Dec. 23, 2010 – Name changed to Evrim Resources Corp. pursuant to acquisition of Evrim Metals Corp. and amalgamation of Evrim with wholly owned 0893812 B.C. Ltd. ■

Avatar Energy Inc. (Que. 1970)
Dec. 4, 1996 – Amalgamated with 9038-2110 Quebec Inc., a wholly owned subsid. of Neutrino Resources Inc.; basis 0.38 new Neutrino sh. for 1 old Avatar sh.

Avatar Energy Ltd. (Alta. Nov. 5, 2009)
Feb. 4, 2013 – Placed into receivership and all officers and directors resigned. Ernst & Young Inc. appointed receiver.

Avatar Petroleum Inc. (B.C. Nov. 17, 1980)
July 4, 2003 – Plan of Arrangement with Viceroy Resource Corporation (1 for 3 plus 1 new ViceroyEx sh. for 10 old shs. and 1 new SpectrumGold sh. for 30 old shs), Arapaho Capital Corp. (863,857 shs. on sale of subsid.) and Quest Investment Corporation (1 for 1.0514) to continue as Quest Capital Corp. (formerly Viceroy); basis 0.2825 new Quest Capital cl. A sh. for 1 old Avatar com. sh. (see Quest Capital Corporation)

Avatar Resource Corporation (B.C. Dec. 2, 1965)
Dec. 21, 1993 – Name changed to Blackline Oil Corporation; basis 1 new for 5 old shs. ■

AvCan Global Systems Inc. (B.C. Jan. 1, 1983 amalg.)
Apr. 21, 1999 – Name changed to ASC Avcan Systems Corporation; basis 1 new for 4 old shs. ■

Avcan Systems Inc. (B.C. Jan. 1, 1983 amalg.)
Oct. 9, 2003 – Name changed to Optimal Geomatics Inc. and continued into Canada. ■

Avco Delta Corp. Canada Ltd. (Ont. 1954)
May 5, 1971 – Merged into Avco Financial Service Canada Limited.

Avcorp Industries Inc. (Can. Feb. 28, 1986 amalg.)
Nov. 10, 2022 – Acquired by Latécoère S.A.; basis 11¢ cash per sh.

Aveda Transportation and Energy Services Inc. (Alta. May 9, 2006)
June 11, 2018 – Acquired by Daseke, Inc.; basis (i) Cdn$0.90 (US$0.70) cash; or (ii) 0.0751 Daseke com. shs.; or (iii) a combination of both.

AvenEx Energy Corp. (Alta. Jan. 1, 2011; amalg.)
Apr. 4, 2013 – Amalgamated with Pace Oil and Gas Ltd. and Charger Energy Corp. to form Spyglass Resources Corp. with Pace Oil and Gas the deemed acquiror; basis 1.3 Spyglass shs. for 1 Pace sh., 0.18 Spyglass shs. for 1 Charger and 1 Spyglass sh. for 1 AvenEx sh. (see Spyglass Resources Corp.)

Avenir Diversified Income Trust (Alta. Sept. 24, 2002)
Jan. 1, 2011 – Succeeded by AvenEx Energy Corp. pursuant to plan of arrangement whereby AvenEx Energy Corp. was formed to facilitate the conversion of the trust into a corporation and the trust was subsequently dissolved. ■

Avenor Inc. (Can. Jan. 1, 1989 amalg.)
July 28, 1998 – Name changed to Bowater Pulp and Paper Canada Inc. following Qualifying Transaction acquisition of all o/s com. shs. by Bowater Canada Inc., a subsid. of Bowater Incorporated of Greenville, S.C.; basis $35 per share or 1 Bowater Canada Inc. exchangeable sh. for 1 Avenor sh. resulting in Avenor becoming a wholly owned subsid. ■

Aventine Ventures Inc. (B.C. Nov. 17, 1995)
Apr. 30, 2004 – Name changed to Pacific Northwest Partners Limited; basis 1 new for 5 old shs. ■

Aventura Energy Inc. (Alta. Oct. 8, 1993)
May 13, 2004 – Acquired by BG Canada Ltd. for $5.10 per sh.

Avenue Financial Corporation (Ont. May 30, 1997)
June 19, 2007 – Name changed to Mantis Mineral Corp. ■

Avenue Industries Inc. (B.C. Sept. 25, 1985)
Aug. 29, 1997 – Name changed to Black Tusk Energy Inc. ■

Avenue of America Recording Limited (Ont. 1971)
Oct. 18, 1978 – Dissolved.

Avenue Resources Inc. (B.C. Sept. 25, 1985)
July 29, 1992 – Name changed to Avenue Industries Inc. ■

Avenza Global Technologies Corp. (Ont. May 21, 1987)
May 26, 2000 – Placed into receivership and Mintz & Partners Limited of Toronto were appointed receiver and manager of the company and all its subsids.
July 1, 2000 – All the assets had been sold and there was a small distribution to secured creditors. There were no distributions made to unsecured creditors or to shldrs. and the receiver was discharged.

Avere Energy Inc. (B.C. Oct. 23, 1987)
Aug. 9, 2010 – Name changed to East West Petroleum Corp. (see FPsurvey - Mines & Energy)

Avery Resources Inc. (Alta. May 13, 1996)
July 22, 2008 – Name changed to Bengal Energy Ltd.; basis 1 new for 5 old shs. (see FPsurvey - Mines & Energy)

Avesoro Resources Inc. (Can. Feb. 1, 2011)
Jan. 8, 2020 – All o/s com. shs not already held acquired by Avesoro Jersey Limited; basis £1.00 cash per sh.

Avian Capital Inc. (B.C. Oct. 6, 2006)
Dec. 30, 2009 – Name changed to Aegis Investment Management (Golf) Inc. following Qualifying Transaction reverse takeover acquisition of Parmasters Golf Training Centers, Inc. which amalgamated with wholly owned Avian Acquisition Corp. to continue under the Parmasters name. ■

Aviator Petroleum Corp. (Alta. Feb. 1, 2005)
Oct. 13, 2006 – Formed Critical Outcome Technologies Inc. in Ontario on Qualifying Transaction amalgamation with Critical Outcome Technologies Inc. (deemed acquiror). ■

Avic Technologies Inc. (Alta. Apr. 26, 2000)
Sept. 13, 2002 – Name changed to Ginger Beef Corporation following Qualifying Transaction reverse takeover acquisition of Ginger Beef Express Ltd. ■

Avid Oil & Gas Ltd. (Alta. Jan. 13, 1997)
July 10, 2001 – Acquired by subsid. of Husky Energy Inc.; basis $5.85 for each Avid cl. A sh. and $10 for each Avid cl. B sh. (see Husky Energy Inc.)

Avidian Gold Corp. (B.C. Sept. 24, 2013)
Oct. 20, 2020 – Continued into Ontario. (see FPsurvey - Mines & Energy)

Avidus Management Group Inc. (B.C. Jan. 31, 2006)
July 18, 2017 – Struck from registry and dissolved.

Avigilon Corporation (Can. Oct. 22, 2004)
Apr. 3, 2018 – Acquired by Motorola Solutions, Inc.; basis Cdn$27 cash per sh.

Avigo Resources Corp. (Can. June 19, 1997)
Sept. 2, 2008 – Name changed to Carbon Friendly Solutions Inc. following reverse takeover acquisition of Carbon Friendly Solutions Inc. ■

Avila Ligneris Gold Mines Ltd. (Ont. 1945)
Sept. 18, 1961 – Dissolved.

Avilla International Explorations Ltd. (Can. 1971)
Aug. 10, 1984 – Dissolved.

Avillabona Mines Ltd. (Ont. 1945)
1959 – Merged into Hydra Explorations Ltd.; basis 1 new for 25 old shs.

Avinda Video Incorporated (Ont. 1983)
Oct. 1991 – Placed into receivership. Assets sold. Secured creditors were paid. No distribution to unsecured creditors or shldrs.
Apr. 1993 – Receiver discharged.
Nov. 14, 1994 – Dissolved.

Avino Mines & Resources Ltd. (B.C. May 15, 1969)
May 12, 1995 – Name changed to International Avino Mines Ltd.; basis 1 new for 5 old shs. ■

Avino Mines Ltd. (unknown)
1969 – Merged into Avino Mines & Resources Ltd.

Avion Gold Corporation (B.C. Sept. 3, 1985)
June 14, 2011 – Continued into Ontario. (see Endeavour Mining Corporation)
Oct. 23, 2012 – Acquired by Endeavour Mining Corporation; basis 0.365 Endeavour shs. for 1 Avion sh. (see Endeavour Mining Corporation)

Avion Resources Corp. (B.C. Sept. 3, 1985)
June 5, 2009 – Name changed to Avion Gold Corporation. ■

Avista Real Estate Investment Trust (Ont. May 12, 1997)
Nov. 16, 1999 – Amalgamated with Summit Real Estate Investment Trust to be known as Summit Real Estate Investment Trust; basis 0.8 tr. unit of Summit for 1 tr. unit of Avista. (see Summit Real Estate Investment Trust)

Aviva Petroleum Canada Inc. (Alta. June 30, 1990 amalg.)
Jan. 31, 1994 – Name changed to Pero Development Group Inc. ■

Aviva Resources Inc. (B.C. 1981)
Nov. 15, 1987 – Name changed to VSC Technology Inc. ■

Avivagen Inc. (Can. Aug. 4, 2005 amalg.)
Apr. 23, 2024 – Filed a voluntary assignment in bankruptcy and BDO Canada Limited appointed trustee.

Avnel Gold Mining Limited (Guernsey Feb. 18, 2005)
Sept. 18, 2017 – Acquired by Endeavour Mining Corporation; basis 0.0187 Endeavour shs. for each Avnel sh. held.

Avoca Mines Canada Limited (Ont. 1969)
Oct. 29, 1994 – Dissolved.

Avocet Ventures Inc. (B.C. Nov. 19, 1986)
Apr. 8, 1996 – Following Plan of Arrangement, Avocet created two new companies, Avocet Mining Canada Inc. (AM B.C.) and Avocet Mining PLC (AM U.K.). All o/s shs. of Avocet Ventures were then acquired by AM U.K. on a 1 for 1 basis. Canadian residents had the option to receive pfd. shs. of AM B.C., redeemable at any time by AM U.K.

Avola Industries Inc. (B.C. Jan. 15, 1980)
Jan. 17, 2003 – Name changed to Auramex Resource Corp.; basis 1 new for 3 old shs. ■

Avon Gold Mines Ltd. (Que. 1935)
Oct. 1973 – Charter cancelled.

Avon Resources Ltd. (B.C. 1972)
Dec. 27, 1974 – Acquired by Lori Explorations Ltd. Shs. of Lori issued at a deemed value of 15¢ per sh. (see Lori Explorations Ltd.)

Avondale Resources Inc. (B.C. Apr. 30, 1987)
Sept. 18, 1992 – Name changed to Portman Explorations Ltd.; basis 1 new for 10 old shs. ■

Avonlee Capital Corporation (Ont. Nov. 28, 1983)
May 29, 1996 – Name changed to Internet Liquidators International Inc.; basis 1 new for 2.5 old shs. ■

Avotus Corporation (Can. Jan. 13, 1994)
May 20, 2005 – Going private transaction; basis 1 new sh. for 1,850,000 old shs. New shs. represented a right to receive 25¢ per pre-consolidation sh.
Dec. 17, 2008 – Continued into Ontario.

Awakn Life Sciences Corp. (B.C. June 21, 2018)
May 28, 2025 – Acquired by Solvonis Therapeutics plc; basis 46.67 Solvonis ord. shs. for 1 Awakn Life com. sh.

Award Capital Corp. (Ont. Mar. 5, 2007)
July 23, 2009 – Name changed to SPoT Coffee (Canada) Ltd. following amalgamation of a wholly owned subsid. with SPoT Coffee (Canada) Inc., constituting a Qualifying Transaction reverse takeover acquisition of SPoT Coffee (Canada) Inc. (see FPsurvey - Industrials)

Award Resources Ltd. (B.C. Dec. 1, 1972)
June 14, 1990 – Name changed to Tomco Developments Inc.; basis 1 new for 3 old shs. ■

Awesome Resources Ltd. (B.C. Mar. 30, 1983)
June 9, 1987 – Name changed to Santiago Capital Corp. ■

Axagon Resources Ltd. (B.C. 1987)
Jan. 12, 1996 – Dissolved and struck off register.

Axcan Pharma Inc. (Can. May 6, 1982)
Feb. 26, 2008 – Acquired by Texas Pacific Group (TPG), through TPG Capital, L.P. for US$23.35 per sh.
May 4, 2011 – Name changed to Aptalis Pharma Inc.

AXcension Capital Corp. (Ont. June 11, 1996 amalg.)
Aug. 30, 1999 – Name changed to Caspian Oil Tools Limited and continued into Bermuda; basis 1 new for 4 old shs.

Axel Mines Ltd. (B.C. 1969)
Mar. 31, 1983 – Struck off register.

Axia Multimedia Corporation (Alta. Apr. 12, 1994)
Nov. 24, 1998 – Name changed to Axia NetMedia Corporation. ■

Axia NetMedia Corporation (Alta. Apr. 12, 1994)
Aug. 3, 2016 – Acquired by Digital Connection (Canada) Corp. for $4.25 per sh.

Axiom Capital Advisors Inc. (Alta. Jan. 28, 2020)
Oct. 24, 2023 – Name changed to Impact Analytics Inc. ■

Axiom Explorations Inc. (B.C. Feb. 7, 1984)
Oct. 3, 1985 – Name changed to Axiom International Development Corporation. ■

Axiom International Development Corporation (B.C. Feb. 7, 1984)
Mar. 4, 1992 – Delisted Vancouver Stock Exchange. Subsequently struck from registry and dissolved.

Axion Communications Inc. (B.C. Jan. 21, 1980)
Dec. 2, 2002 – Amalgamated with Technovision Systems, Inc.; basis 0.603 Technovision shs. for 1 Axion sh. (see Technovision Systems, Inc.)

Axios Mobile Assets Corp. (Ont. Sept. 25, 1998)
Feb. 24, 2017 – Placed into receivership by senior secured lender. B. Riley Farber Inc. (previously A. Farber and Partners Inc.) appointed receiver and all officers and directors resigned.
Aug. 2017 – Majority of the assets sold and distrib. made to senior secured lender. No monies available for distrib. to unsecured creditors or shldrs.
Apr. 10, 2018 – Receiver was discharged.

Axis Auto Finance Inc. (Can. July 9, 2008)
Dec. 12, 2024 – The automotive loan and lease receivables and related assets were sold for $78,300,000 resulting in repayment in full of the credit facilities and loans. The o/s debentures were repaid equivalent to 60% of the face value.
June 26, 2025 – Privatized via a 1-for-38,000,000 consolidation; all fractional shs. cancelled for no consideration.

Axis.Port Inc. (Alta. July 7, 1996)
Nov. 2, 2002 – Struck from registry.

Aydon Income Properties Inc. (B.C. Jan. 22, 2015 amalg.)
Jan. 19, 2018 – Name changed to The Delma Group Inc. and continued into Canada following the reverse takeover acquisition of the Delma Group of companies.; basis 1 new for 200 old shs. ■

Ayerok Petroleum Ltd. (B.C. Apr. 4, 1979)
May 12, 1987 – Name changed to Westrok Capital Inc. ■

Ayers Capital Corp. (B.C. June 18, 1998)
May 29, 2000 – Name changed to CHK Wireless Technologies Inc. ■

Aylen Capital Inc. (Can. Oct. 28, 2010)
Dec. 21, 2020 – Name changed to DeepSpatial Inc. pursuant to the reverse takeover acquisition of Loc8 Corp. (dba Deepspatial AI) and concurrent amalgamation of Loc8 with wholly owned 2774951 Ontario Limited (and continued as DeepSpatial (Ontario) Inc.). (see FPsurvey - Industrials)

Aylen Mines Ltd. (Ont. 1953)
Sept. 1959 – Charter cancelled.

Aylette Chibougamau Gold Mines Ltd. (Ont. 1946)
1956 – Charter cancelled.

Aylmer and Malahide Telephone Company, Limited (Ont. 1928)
June 30, 1978 – Name changed to Amtelecom Inc. ■

Aylmer Mines Ltd. (Que. June 4, 1963)
Mar. 10, 1997 – Name changed to Héron Exploration Inc. ■

Ayotte Music Inc. (Alta. Feb. 27, 1998 amalg.)
May 10, 2000 – Continued into Canada.
Nov. 12, 2002 – Name changed to Verb Exchange Inc. pursuant to reverse takeover acquisition of Verb Exchange Inc.; basis 1 new for 5 old shs. ■

Ayr Mines Limited (Can. Nov. 8, 1957)
June 26, 1974 – Shldrs. approved dissolution of co. and surrender of charter.
Sept. 7, 1976 – Dissolved and struck off register.

Ayr Strategies Inc. (B.C. May 24, 2019)
Feb. 12, 2021 – Name changed to Ayr Wellness Inc. (see FPsurvey - Industrials)

Ayrex Resources Ltd. (Alta. Jan. 22, 1985)
July 21, 2003 – Name changed to Yangarra Resources Inc.; basis 1 new for 4 old shs. ■

Ayrhart Mining Corp. Inc. (Que. 1972)
Apr. 1977 – Name changed to Meston Lake Resources Inc.

Ayubowan Capital Ltd. (B.C. Oct. 10, 1986)
June 13, 2017 – Name changed to Discovery Metals Corp. ■

Azabache Energy Inc. (Can. Nov. 22, 2006)
Sept. 23, 2017 – Dissolved and struck from register.

Azam Energy Corporation (B.C. Oct. 14, 1964)
Dec. 6, 1985 – Dissolved and struck off register.

Azarga Uranium Corp. (B.C. Feb. 10, 1984)
Jan. 6, 2022 – Acquired by enCore Energy Corp.; basis 0.375 enCore shs. for 1 Azarga sh.

Azco Mining, Inc. (B.C. Aug. 20, 1981)
July 31, 1992 – Continued into Delaware.

Azdak Resources Ltd. (Can. Mar. 24, 1987)
Dec. 5, 1988 – Name changed to Algear Development Corporation; basis 1 new for 5 old shs. ■

Azen Mines Ltd. (Ont. 1965)
Nov. 7, 1977 – Charter cancelled.

Azimuth Energy Inc. (Alta. Aug. 28, 1997)
Mar. 30, 1999 – Formed C-Tech Energy Services Inc. following Qualifying Transaction acquisition of C-Tech Oilwell Technologies Inc.; basis 1 new for 1 old sh. ∎

Azimuth Resources Limited (Australia Sept. 13, 1999)
July 19, 2013 – Acquired by Troy Resources Limited; basis 1 Troy sh. for 5.695 Azimuth shs.

Azincourt Resources Inc. (B.C. Apr. 7, 2011)
June 24, 2013 – Name changed to Azincourt Uranium Inc. ∎

Azincourt Uranium Inc. (B.C. Apr. 7, 2011)
Oct. 16, 2017 – Name changed to Azincourt Energy Corp. (see FPsurvey - Mines & Energy)

Azor Mines Ltd. (Ont. 1950)
June 1961 – Distributed 1 free sh. and 14 pooled shs. Cayzor Athabaska Mines for each sh. held; small cash distribution also made. Dissolved.

Azora Minerals Inc. (B.C. Jan. 1, 1980)
Sept. 22, 1989 – Name changed to International Azora Minerals Inc.; basis 1 new for 4 old shs. ∎

Aztec Exploration Ltd. (B.C. 1952)
Apr. 20, 1961 – Dissolved.

Aztec Mining Co. Ltd. (unknown)
Shldrs. received 1 sh. B.R.X. (1935) Consolidated Mines Ltd. for each 2 shs. held. Aztec Mining Co. Ltd. charter cancelled. (see B.R.X. (1935) Consolidated Mines Ltd.)

Aztec Resources Ltd. (Alta. May 5, 1980)
Sept. 12, 1994 – Amalgamated with International Oiltex Ltd. (1 for 4.8) to form a new co. also known as Aztec Resources Ltd.; basis 1 new for 1 old sh. (see Aztec Resources Ltd.)

Aztec Resources Ltd. (Alta. 1992 amalg.)
Feb. 24, 1997 – Amalgamated with Pursuit Resources Inc. (1 for 2.7) to form a new company known as Pursuit Resources Corp.; basis 0.25 new Pursuit com. sh. pur. wt. plus either 1 new Pursuit Corp. com. sh. or $2.70 for 1 old Aztec com. sh. (see Pursuit Resources Corp.)

Aztech New Media Corp. (Ont. Feb. 9, 1993)
Aug. 23, 2002 – Name changed to Star Navigation Systems Group Ltd. pursuant to reverse takeover acquisition of Star Navigation Systems Inc. and amalgamation of Star with a wholly owned subsidiary; basis 1 new for 13.790694 old shs. (see FPsurvey - Industrials)

Aztek Energy Ltd. (Alta. Sept. 30, 2005 amalg.)
Jan. 18, 2010 – Formed Spartan Exploration Ltd. in Alberta pursuant to acquisition by and amalgamation with Spartan Exploration Ltd.; basis 0.0805 Spartan shs. for 1 Aztek sh. ∎

Aztek Resource Development Inc. (B.C. July 11, 1979)
Dec. 28, 2015 – Dissolved and struck from register.

Aztek Technologies Inc. (B.C. July 11, 1979)
Nov. 19, 2004 – Name changed to Aztek Resource Development Inc.; basis 1 new for 3 old shs. ∎

The Azterra Corporation (Alta. Nov. 29, 1995)
July 2, 2003 – Dissolved and struck from registry.

Azul Ventures Inc. (Ont. Mar. 15, 2007)
Sept. 24, 2014 – Name changed to Austin Resources Ltd.; basis 1 new for 3 old shs. ∎

Azura Ventures Ltd. (N.B. May 22, 2009)
June 13, 2012 – Name changed to Excellium Inc. pursuant to Qualifying Transaction reverse takeover acquisition of Excellium Technologies Inc. ∎

Azure Dynamics Corporation (Alta. May 14, 1993)
Mar. 26, 2012 – Filed for protection under the Companies' Creditors Arrangement Act (CCAA) and Ernst & Young Inc. was appointed monitor.
Aug. 31, 2012 – Sale of the company's portfolio of patents and related rights and assets was completed and

distributions were made to inter-company borrowings and certain secured creditors. No distributions were expected to be made to unsecured creditors or shldrs.
Oct. 9, 2012 – A liquidation services agreement was entered into with Heritage Global Partners for the sale of the remaining assets.
Nov. 27, 2012 – Majority of the remaining inventory and equipment was sold via an on-line auction, with several sales transactions for the higher value inventory, equipment and software were entered into and completed. Net proceeds amounted to US$1,126,422.
Nov. 25, 2015 – The monitor was discharged.
Nov. 2, 2017 – Dissolved and struck from register.

Azure Resources Corporation (B.C. Sept. 18, 1984)
June 13, 2014 – Name changed to Panorama Petroleum Inc.; basis 1 new for 10 old shs. ∎

Azure Resources Corp. (B.C. Feb. 2, 1999)
Aug. 9, 2005 – Name changed to Pencari Mining Corporation; basis 1 new for 3.5 old shs. ∎

Azure Resources Ltd. (B.C. 1946)
Apr. 23, 1987 – Name changed to Consolidated Azure Resources Ltd.; basis 1 new for 4 old shs. ∎

Azzardo Game Acquisition Corp. (B.C. Sept. 19, 2013)
Dec. 17, 2014 – Name changed to Carlyle Entertainment Ltd. ∎

B

"B" Corp. (Ont. 1978)
May 25, 1992 – All o/s fully participating redeemable retractable preferred shs. called for redemption; basis $30 per sh. plus a dividend of 72.2¢ payable to holders of record at May 1, 1992. Co. subsequently dissolved, Oct. 29, 1994.

B-For-G Capital Inc. (Alta. May 26, 2004)
Dec. 31, 2004 – Name changed to Parkbridge Lifestyle Communities Inc. following reverse takeover acquisition of Parkbridge 2003 Limited Partnership; basis 1 new for 33.3333 old shs. ∎

B. Greening Wire Co. Ltd. (Can. 1923)
Dec. 20, 1961 – Name changed to Greening Industries Limited. ∎

B Split Corp. (Ont. Sept. 18, 1997)
Nov. 29, 2002 – Redeemed in full; basis $3.14 per Capital sh. and $25 per Preferred sh.

B Split II Corp. (Ont. Mar. 23, 2000)
June 2, 2010 – All o/s shs. redeemed for $9.75 per pref. sh. and $11.0074 per capital sh.

B52 Investments Inc. (Can. July 12, 2002)
Sept. 25, 2003 – Name changed to DEQ Systems Corp. following Qualifying Transaction reverse takeover acquisition of D.E.Q. Casinos Royalties Ltd. ∎

B.A. Copper Mines Limited (B.C. Apr. 17, 1973)
June 17, 1982 – Name changed to B.A. Resources Ltd. ∎

B.A. Resources Ltd. (B.C. Apr. 17, 1973)
Mar. 10, 1995 – Continued into Canada.
Oct. 24, 1995 – Name changed to United China International Enterprises Group Ltd. ∎

B.A.C.M. Industries Limited (Man. 1960)
May 1970 – The majority of the o/s shs. acquired by Genstar Limited; basis 2 Genstar shs. for 1 B.A.C.M. sh.

BAE Systems Canada Inc. (Can. 1903)
Apr. 24, 2001 – Acquired by ONCAP L.P. for $25.25 per sh.
June 1, 2001 – Name changed to CMC Electronics Inc.

BAM Investments Corp. (Ont. Mar. 30, 1988 amalg.)
June 10, 2013 – Name changed to Partners Value Fund Inc. ∎

BAM Split Corp. (Ont. July 12, 2001)
Aug. 28, 2013 – Name changed to Partners Value Split Corp. (see FPsurvey - Industrials)

B.A.S.M. Resources Corporation (Alta. Nov. 25, 1986)
Apr. 14, 1999 – Continued into New Brunswick.
June 8, 1999 – Name changed to Fiton Technologies Corp. following reverse takeover acquisition of JAIT Energy Resources Inc. ∎

B.A.T. Industries PLC (U.K. Sept. 29, 1902)
Sept. 8, 1998 – Name changed to British American Tobacco plc.

BB1 Acquisition Corp. (Ont. Mar. 2, 2018)
Feb. 22, 2021 – Name changed to Cerrado Gold Inc. pursuant to the Qualifying Transaction reverse takeover acquisition of (old) Cerrado Gold Inc. and concurrent amalgamation of (old) Cerrado with wholly owned 2787735 Ontario Inc., with (old) Cerrado then immediately amalgamated into the company; basis 1 new for 8.31 old shs. (see FPsurvey - Industrials)

BBC Capital Management Inc. (B.C. Feb. 18, 2004)
Sept. 13, 2005 – Name changed to Cornerstone Industries International Inc. following Qualifying Transaction reverse takeover acquisition of Cornerstone Granite and Marble Wholesale, Inc. ∎

BBC Mortgage Company (B.C. 1971)
June 1981 – All o/s $2.28 pfce. ser. A shs. exchanged for an equivalent amount of $2.28 pref. ser. A shs. of Bank of British Columbia.
Oct. 30, 1981 – Put into liquidation in compliance with the 1980 Bank Act. At that date, assets of co. (net of liabs.) were acquired by the Bank of British Columbia Mortgage Corp.

BBC Realty Investors Ltd. (B.C. 1973)
Nov. 22, 1984 – Trust merged with the Bank of British Columbia, following bank subscribing for 2,445,713 com. shs. to trust for $14,674,278. Unitholders other than the Bank of B.C. had their cl. B units reclassified as cl. A units, and then exchanged on the basis of one Bank of B.C. com. sh. plus 25 of each cl. A trust units. The trust was subsequently wound up with the assets distributed to the Bank of B.C.

BBC-RI Services Ltd. (Can. 1954)
Nov. 1984 – Incorporated to be the financing arm of BBC Realty Investors Ltd. Jointly owned by BBC Realty and the Bank of B.C. However, following merger of BBC Realty Investor Ltd. into the Bank of B.C. BBC-RI became a wholly owned non-reporting subsid. of the bank.

BBF Resources Inc. (Alta. Mar. 18, 1996)
July 25, 2005 – Name changed to Western Energy Services Corp. (see FPsurvey - Mines & Energy; FPsurvey - Industrials)

BBTV Holdings Inc. (B.C. July 17, 2019)
Nov. 30, 2023 – Continued into Canada.
Jan. 12, 2024 – Privatized via amalgamation with 15384150 Canada Inc., an entity owned by founder Shahrzad Rafati; basis $0.375 cash per subord. vtg. sh. and $100 per $1,000 principal amount of the o/s 7% unsecured convertible debs.

B.C. Alberta Oils Limited (B.C. May 3, 1929)
Jan. 1, 1948 – Charter cancelled.

B.C. Bancorp (Can. Dec. 14, 1966; via Bank Act)
Nov. 12, 1996 – Acquired by Canadian Western Bank; basis 40¢ or 0.035 Canadian Western shs. for 1 B.C. Bancorp sh. (see Canadian Western Bank)

B.C. Base Metal Developments Ltd. (B.C. 1956)
1958 – Assets sold to Trenton Petroleum & Mineral Corp.

The BC Bud Corporation (B.C. Aug. 11, 2000)
Mar. 19, 2025 – Name changed to Digital Commodities Capital Corp. (see FPsurvey - Industrials)

B.C.-Cal. Oil and Gas Ltd. (B.C.)
1960 – Struck off register.

B.C. Central Credit Union (B.C. May 25, 1944)
Jan. 1, 1996 – Name changed to Credit Union Central of British Columbia. ■

B.C. Coal Ltd. (B.C. July 31, 1967)
June 1983 – Name changed to Westar Mining Ltd. ■

BC Gas Inc. (B.C. June 4, 1952)
July 1, 1989 – Amalgamated with Inland Natural Gas Co. Ltd., Columbia Natural Gas Limited and Fort Nelson Gas Ltd. to form new co. with same name BC Gas Inc.
July 1, 1993 – Name changed to BC Gas Utility Ltd.; basis 1 new for 1 old sh. ■

BC Gas Inc. (B.C. Aug. 15, 1985)
May 5, 2003 – Name changed to Terasen Inc. ■

BC Gas Utility Ltd. (B.C. July 1, 1989 amalg.)
Oct. 31, 2000 – All o/s 6.32% cum. redeem. 1st pref. shs. redeemed for $25 per sh.
Apr. 25, 2003 – Name changed to Terasen Gas Inc. ■

B.C. Metal Mines Ltd. (B.C. 1951)
1956 – Assets acquired by Castle Oil & Gas Ltd.; basis 1 new for 15 old shs.

B.C. Mica Mines Ltd. (B.C.)
Dissolved.

B.C. Minerals and Resources Development Co. Ltd. (B.C. 1940)
Jan. 18, 1959 – Dissolved.

B.C. Montana Oil Wells, Ltd. (Mont. 1923)
Bondholders foreclosed; property sold. Distribution not known.

B.C. Nickel Mines Ltd. (B.C. 1929)
Jan. 1, 1938 – Name changed to Pacific Nickel Mines Ltd.; basis 1 new for 4 old shs. ■

B.C. Pacific Capital Corporation (Can. Jan. 30, 1981)
May 18, 1988 – Continued into British Columbia. (see Brookfield Asset Management Inc.)
Apr. 4, 2007 – Acquired by Brookfield Asset Management Inc. for $0.80 per sh. (see Brookfield Asset Management Inc.)

B.C. Peat Co. Ltd. (B.C. 1941)
Dec. 1947 – Name changed to Atkins & Durbrow Ltd. ■

B.C. Placer Mining & Refining Ltd. (B.C. 1961)
June 5, 1963 – Name changed to Sterling Silver Mines Ltd. ■

B.C. Rail Ltd. (B.C. 1969)
May 12, 1994 – All o/s $2.3125 cum. redeem. retract. first pref. shs. ser. A redeemed; basis $25 plus accr. and unpaid divid. of $0.45245 per sh.

B.C. Report Magazine Ltd. (B.C. Mar. 23, 1989)
Mar. 31, 2005 – Name changed to Glass Earth Limited following reverse takeover acquisition of Glass Earth Limited. ■

BC Sugar Refinery, Limited (Can. June 7, 1920; via Dominion charter)
Aug. 20, 1997 – Acquired by BCS acquisition Inc., an indirect subsid. of Onex Corporation, for $16.50 per sh.

BC TELECOM Inc (Can. Nov. 14, 1984)
Feb. 1, 1999 – Merged with TELUS Corporation (0.7773 new for 1 old sh.) to form BCT.TELUS Communications Inc.; basis 1 BCT.TELUS sh. for 1 BC TELECOM sh. (see BCT.TELUS Communications Inc.)

BC TEL (Can. Apr. 12, 1916; via Special Act of Parliament)
Oct. 18, 1999 – Name changed to TELUS Communications (BC) Inc.; basis 1 new for 1 old pfd. sh. ■

B.C. Timber Ltd. (B.C. 1964)
1984 – Name changed to Westar Timber Ltd. (see British Columbia Resources Investment Corporation)

B.C. Turf & Country Club Ltd. (B.C. 1945)
May 1966 – Name changed to B.C. Turf Ltd. ■

B.C. Turf Ltd. (B.C. 1945)
Dec. 22, 1978 – Amalgamated with J. Diamond and Sons Limited (a privately owned Vancouver company). Shldrs. received shs. of the amalgamated co., immediately redeemed at $7.00 per sh.

B.C. Yukon Exploration Co. Ltd. (B.C. 1966)
Jan. 1977 – Charter cancelled.

BCB Holdings Inc. (Alta. July 12, 1993)
Oct. 1, 1996 – Continued into Ontario.
Sept. 2, 1998 – Name changed to B.C.B. Voice Systems Inc.; basis 1 new for 10 old shs. ■

B.C.B. Voice Systems Inc. (Ont. Oct. 1, 1996)
Oct. 16, 2000 – Name changed to VoiceIQ Inc. ■

BCE Development Corporation (B.C. Nov. 19, 1964)
July 14, 1989 – Continued into Canada.
Aug. 19, 1991 – Name changed to BF Realty Holdings Limited. ■

BCE Emergis Inc. (Can. Dec. 11, 1986)
Dec. 3, 2004 – Name changed to Emergis Inc. ■

BCE Mobile Communications Inc. (Can. 1987)
Oct. 25, 1999 – Acquired by Bell Canada for $58.75 per sh. (see Bell Canada)

BCE Place Finance Corporation (Que. 1987)
June 3, 1994 – All o/s 7.375% pfd. ser. 1 shs. and 7.75% pfd. ser. 2 shs. acquired under a purchase obligation event by BF Realty Holdings Limited; basis $25.75 plus any accrued and unpaid dividends for 1 old ser. 1 sh. and $26 plus any accrued and unpaid dividends for 1 old ser. 2 sh.

BCED Capital 1 Corporation (Que. 1986)
Apr. 14, 1992 – Name changed to Brookfield Capital 1 Corporation. ■

BCGold Corp. (B.C. Feb. 10, 2006)
Mar. 16, 2017 – Name changed to Pan Andean Minerals Ltd. ■

BCI Management Ltd. (Can. Dec. 22, 1986 amalg.)
Sept. 23, 1993 – Name changed to Unicap Commercial Corp. ■

BCS Collaborative Solutions Inc. (B.C. Jan. 27, 1966)
Sept. 2, 2003 – Name changed to BCS Global Networks Inc.; basis 1 new for 3 old shs. ■

BCS Global Networks Inc. (B.C. Jan. 27, 1966)
Aug. 25, 2005 – Acquired by 2073832 Ontario Inc. for $0.20 per sh.

BCS Technology Inc. (B.C. Oct. 25, 1985)
May 31, 2000 – Delisted from the CDNX. Subsequently struck from register and dissolved.

BCT.TELUS Communications Inc. (B.C. Oct. 26, 1998)
May 8, 2000 – Name changed to TELUS Corporation. (see FPsurvey - Industrials)

BCU Industries Inc. (Can. July 28, 1987)
June 10, 2004 – Dissolved.

BCX Split Corp. (Ont. June 26, 2003)
Aug. 6, 2008 – All o/s cap. shs. & pref. shs. redeemed for $23.277 per cap. sh. & $15.71 per pref. sh.

BCY LifeSciences Inc. (B.C. Aug. 19, 1998)
Aug. 21, 2007 – Name changed to BCY Resources Inc. ■

BCY Resources Inc. (B.C. Aug. 19, 1998)
Mar. 16, 2011 – Name changed to Mexigold Corp.; basis 1 new for 4 old shs. ■

BCY Ventures Inc. (B.C. Aug. 19, 1998)
Jan. 4, 2001 – Name changed to BCY LifeSciences Inc. ■

B.D. Petroleums Ltd. (B.C.)
1958 – Struck off register.

BDC Industries Corp. (B.C. Mar. 18, 1981)
Sept. 4, 1986 – Name changed to The Jolt Beverage Company, Ltd. ■

BDG Pacific Resources Inc. (B.C. Oct. 2, 1985)
Sept. 29, 1999 – Name changed to Southern Nites Petroleum Corp.; basis 1 new for 4 old shs. ■

BDI Mining Corp. (Yuk. Dec. 6, 1995)
Mar. 31, 2005 – Continued into British Virgin Islands.

BDS Industries Inc. (Alta. 1988)
Aug. 30, 1990 – Name changed to New-View Industries Inc. ■

BEB Resources Ltd. (B.C. 1983)
May 10, 1984 – Name changed to Migent Software Corp. ■

BELLUS Health Inc. (Can. June 17, 1993)
June 30, 2022 – Acquired by GSK plc; basis US$14.75 cash per sh.

BENEV Capital Inc. (Can. July 29, 1992)
Sept. 26, 2014 – Name changed to Diversified Royalty Corp. ■

BF Minerals Ltd. (Ont. Feb. 7, 1984)
July 2, 2008 – Name changed to Mukuba Resources Limited. ■

BF Realty Holdings Limited (Can. July 14, 1989)
May 2, 2002 – Dissolved.
July 30, 2003 – Charter revived.
June 1, 2012 – Dissolved.

BF Royal Inc. (Que. 1967)
May 15, 1992 – All assets liquidated. No distribution to shldrs.

BFC Construction Corporation (Can. Jan. 10, 1978)
Jan. 13, 2000 – Acquired indirectly by Armbro Enterprises Inc. for $12.25 per sh. (see Armbro Enterprises Inc.)

BFD Industries Inc. (B.C. 1983)
July 13, 1994 – Continued into Wyoming.

BFI Canada Income Fund (Ont. Feb. 20, 2002)
Oct. 2, 2008 – Converted from an income fund to BFI Canada Ltd. (see BFI Canada Ltd.)

BFI Canada Ltd. (Ont. May 5, 2008)
June 1, 2009 – Name changed to IESI-BFC Ltd. ■

BFK Capital Corp. (Ont. Oct. 29, 2013)
Mar. 15, 2017 – Name changed to The Hydropothecary Corporation pursuant to Qualifying Transaction reverse takeover acquisition of (old) The Hydrothecary Corporation; basis 1 new for 1.5 old shs. ■

BFS Entertainment & Multimedia Limited (Ont. Feb. 4, 1980)
Mar. 10, 2016 – Filed for bankruptcy. The Fuller Landau Group Inc. was appointed trustee.

BG Advantaged Corporate Bond Fund (Ont. Jan. 29, 2004)
July 14, 2008 – Merged with Brompton Top 50 Compound Growth Fund, Brompton Advantaged Tracker Fund, BG Advantaged S&P/TSX Income Trust Index Fund and BG Advantaged Equal Weighted Income Fund to form Brompton Advantaged VIP Income Fund; basis BG Advantaged Corporate Bond (0.577987-for-1), Brompton Top 50 Compound Growth (0.692406-for-1), Brompton Advantaged Tracker (1-for-1), BG Advantaged S&P/TSX (1.139860-for-1) and BG Advantaged Equal Weighted (0.845594-for-1). Immediately prior to the merger, Brompton Advantaged Tracker Fund units were consolidated on a 1-for-1.615694 basis.

BG Advantaged Equal Weighted Income Fund (Ont. Sept. 26, 2003)
July 14, 2008 – Merged with BG Advantaged Corporate Bond Fund, Brompton Top 50 Compound Growth Fund, Brompton Advantaged Tracker Fund and BG Advantaged S&P/TSX Income Trust Index Fund to form Brompton Advantaged VIP Income Fund; basis BG Advantaged Equal Weighted (0.845594-for-1), BG Advantaged Corporate Bond (0.577987-for-1), Brompton Top 50 Compound Growth (0.692406-for-1), Brompton Advantaged Tracker (1-for-1) and BG Advantaged S&P/TSX (1.139860-for-1). Immediately prior to the merger, Brompton Advantaged Tracker Fund units were consolidated on a 1-for-1.615694 basis.

BG Advantaged S&P/TSX Income Trust Index Fund (Ont. Apr. 28, 2003)
July 14, 2008 – Merged with BG Advantaged Equal Weighted Income Fund, BG Advantaged Corporate Bond Fund, Brompton Top 50 Compound Growth Fund and Brompton Advantaged Tracker Fund to form Brompton Advantaged VIP Income Fund; basis BG Advantaged S&P/TSX (1.139860-for-1), BG Advantaged Equal Weighted (0.845594-for-1), BG Advantaged Corporate Bond (0.577987-for-1), Brompton Top 50 Compound Growth (0.692406-for-1) and Brompton Advantaged Tracker (1-for-1). Immediately prior to the merger, Brompton Advantaged Tracker Fund units were consolidated on a 1-for-1.615694 basis.

BG Baron Group Inc. (B.C. Apr. 24, 1987)
Oct. 25, 1999 – Name changed to Consolidated BG Baron Group Inc.; basis 1 new for 5 old shs. ■

BG Income + Growth Split Trust (Ont. Mar. 29, 2004)
July 7, 2008 – Together with Brompton Stable Income Fund, Brompton Equal Weight Income Fund, Business Trust Equal Weight Income Fund, BG Top 100 Equal Weighted Income Fund and Brompton Tracker Fund, each merged with Brompton VIP Income Fund to continue as Brompton VIP Income Fund; basis BG Income + Growth Split Trust (1.013-for-1), Brompton Stable Income (0.9652-for-1), Brompton Equal Weight (0.8583-for-1) and Business Trust Equal Weight (0.6919-for-1), BG Top 100 Equal Weighted (0.7364-for-1) and Brompton Tracker Fund (0.6664-for-1),

BG Top 100 Equal Weighted Income Fund (Ont. Oct. 28, 2004)
July 7, 2008 – Together with Brompton Tracker Fund, BG Income + Growth Split Trust, Brompton Stable Income Fund, Brompton Equal Weight Income Fund and Business Trust Equal Weight Income Fund, each merged with Brompton VIP Income Fund to continue as Brompton VIP Income Fund; basis BG Top 100 Equal Weighted (0.7364-for-1), Brompton Tracker Fund (0.6664-for-1), BG Income + Growth Split Trust (1.013-for-1), Brompton Stable Income (0.9652-for-1), Brompton Equal Weight (0.8583-for-1) and Business Trust Equal Weight (0.6919-for-1).

B.G.M. Diversified Energy Inc. (B.C. Aug. 30, 1965)
Sept. 12, 2005 – Dissolved and struck from registry.
Sept. 26, 2007 – Restored to registry. (see FPsurvey - Mines & Energy)

BGP Acquisition Corp. (B.C. May 22, 2020)
Mar. 1, 2023 – Name changed to CRAFT 1861 Global Holdings Inc. pursuant to the Qualifying Acquisition of Craft 1861 Global, Inc. ■

BGR Precious Metals Inc. (Can. Sept. 2, 1983 amalg.)
June 23, 1999 – Name changed to Dundee Precious Metals Inc. (see FPsurvey - Mines & Energy)

BHK Resources Inc. (B.C. Dec. 10, 2012)
Jan. 21, 2015 – Name changed to BHK Mining Corp. pursuant to Qualifying Transaction acquisition of Dome International Global Inc. (see FPsurvey - Mines & Energy)

BHP Diamonds Inc. (Can. 1995)
May 14, 1998 – Amalgamated with BHP Holdings Canada Inc. and BHP Minerals Canada Ltd. to continue under the same name BHP Diamonds Inc.

BHP Minerals Canada Ltd. (Del. Nov. 29, 1971)
May 14, 1998 – Amalgamated with BHP Holdings Canada Inc. and BHP Diamonds Inc. to continue under the BHP Diamonds Inc. name. (see BHP Diamonds Inc.)

BHP-Utah Mines Ltd. (Del. Nov. 29, 1971)
May 15, 1992 – Name changed to BHP Minerals Canada Ltd. ■

BHR Buffalo Head Resources Ltd. (B.C. Oct. 17, 1984)
July 3, 2008 – Name changed to White Tiger Mining Corp.; basis 1 new for 4 old shs. ■

B.I. Ventures Ltd. (B.C. 1983)
June 16, 1989 – Dissolved.

BICC Phillips Inc. (Can. Mar. 2, 1953; via Dominion charter)
Apr. 2, 1996 – Amalgamated with BICC Newco Amalgamation Inc., an indirect wholly owned subsid. of BICC plc, the majority shldr.; basis $10 per sh.

BIF Corporation Limited (Ont. 1960)
June 28, 1978 – Name changed to York Centre Corporation. ■

BIG Blockchain Intelligence Group Inc. (B.C. Oct. 17, 2014)
Oct. 4, 2019 – Name changed to BIGG Digital Assets Inc. (see FPsurvey - Industrials)

BII Enterprises Inc. (Ont. Jan. 14, 1960)
Sept. 2, 1993 – Name changed to OSF Inc. ■

B.I.M. Minerals Ltd. (Ont. 1952)
Aug. 1960 – Charter cancelled.

BIOX Corporation (Can. Mar. 1, 2010 amalg.)
Sept. 27, 2017 – All o/s shs. not already held acquired by CFFI Ventures Inc., a wholly owned subsid. of Clearwater Fine Foods Incorporated; basis $1.23 cash per sh.

BIP Investment Corporation (B.C. Aug. 31, 2018)
Dec. 5, 2024 – Privatized; all 4,000,000 sr. pref. shs. ser.1 redeemed at $26.75 per sh.

BIT Integration Technology Inc. (Alta. Oct. 25, 1994)
Sept. 21, 2000 – Name changed to SmartCardeSolutions.Com Ltd. ■

B.J. Coughlin Co. Limited (Can. Feb. 17, 1910; via letters patent)
Jan. 20, 1966 – Name changed to Wajax Limited. ■

BLF Real Estate Investment Trust (Que. June 14, 2013)
Aug. 12, 2014 – Acquired by 881723 Canada Inc.; basis $7.50 cash per trust unit.

BLOK Technologies Inc. (B.C. Sept. 10, 2013)
Apr. 21, 2025 – Struck from register and dissolved for failure to file.

BLVD Centers Corporation (B.C. June 7, 2013)
Feb. 12, 2019 – Name changed to Ventura Cannabis and Wellness Corp. ■

BM Diamondcorp Inc. (Yuk. Dec. 6, 1995)
July 26, 2004 – Name changed to BDI Mining Corp. ■

BM-RT Ltd. (Que. 1923)
Nov. 11, 1981 – Name changed to Bank of Montreal Realty Finance Ltd.

BM-RT Realty Investments (Ont. 1973)
Sept. 25, 1981 – The Bank of Montreal made an offer to unitholders, under which each unit was exchangeable for $10.33 principal amount of 11.75% debs. of Bank of Montreal Mortgage Corporation, guaranteed by the bank. Debentures matured in 1991 on basis of one sh. of the bank for each $33 principal amt. of debentures. the trust units were redeemed. Unitholders received the above plus an income distribution of 15.25¢ per unit. Name subsequently changed to BRMI Realty Investments.

BMA Mining Corporation (B.C. Sept. 22, 1983)
May 26, 1999 – Name changed to Dasher Energy Corp.; basis 1 new for 5 old shs. ■

BMB Capital Corp. (B.C. May 14, 2007)
Oct. 6, 2010 – Name changed to Maritime Resources Corp. pursuant Qualifying Transaction acquisition of 50% interest in Green Bay gold prospect from Commander Resources Ltd. (see FPsurvey - Mines & Energy)

BMB Compuscience Canada Ltd. (Ont. 1983)
Jan. 9, 1995 – Name changed to Systems Xcellence Inc. following reverse takeover acquisition of Systems Xcellence Ltd. ■

BMC Oil & Gas Inc. (B.C. 1979)
Oct. 22, 1982 – Amalgamated with Intercep Industries Ltd. (3 new for 2 old shs.) to form Intercep Resources Ltd.; basis 1 new for 1 old sh. (see Intercep Resources Ltd.)

BMD Enterprises Ltd. (B.C. Aug. 25, 1982)
July 3, 2002 – Delisted from the TSX-Venture Exchange. Subsequently struck and dissolved.

BMEX Gold Inc. (B.C. July 10, 2017)
Oct. 4, 2024 – Name changed to Route 109 Resources Inc. (see FPsurvey - Mines & Energy)

BMGB Capital Corp. (B.C. Apr. 21, 2018)
Name changed to NAVCO Pharmaceuticals Inc. pursuant to the Qualifying Transaction reverse takeover acquisition of NAVCO Pharmaceuticals Limited. (see FPsurvey - Industrials)

BMO NT Financial Corporation (Can. 1977)
Aug. 31, 1992 – All o/s cap. shs. redeemed as of for either a price per sh. equal to the net asset value of the co. (on Aug. 31, 1992), divided by the number of capital shs. then outstanding (expected to be equal to $22.50) or, 1 capital sh. plus $22.50 to purchase 1 common sh. of the Bank of Montreal.

BMO II Financial Corporation (Can. 1977)
Sept. 30, 1992 – All pref. shs. redeemed at $22.50 per sh.

BMONT Split Corp. (Ont. June 29, 2004)
Aug. 6, 2009 – Redeemed all o/s pref. shs. and cap. shs. for $27.45 and $12.6596 per sh., respectively.

BMP Technologies Ltd. (B.C. 1982)
May 26, 1988 – Name changed to Palomar Capital Corp. ■

BMR Gold Corporation (Alta. Jan. 26, 1987)
May 22, 1990 – Continued into British Columbia. (see FPsurvey - Mines & Energy)

BNK Petroleum Inc. (B.C. May 26, 2008)
Nov. 10, 2020 – Name changed to Kolibri Global Energy Inc. (see FPsurvey - Mines & Energy)

BNN Investments Ltd. (Ont. Mar. 30, 1988 amalg.)
July 5, 2006 – Name changed to BAM Investments Corp. ■

BNN Split Corp. (Ont. July 12, 2001)
Dec. 15, 2006 – Name changed to BAM Split Corp. ■

BNP Canada Inc. (Que. 1961)
Nov. 1, 1981 – Merged with Banque Nationale de Paris Canada under the latter name.

BNS Capital Trust (Ont. Feb. 25, 2000)
Jan. 3, 2011 – Redeemed all o/s BaTS at $1,000 per BaTS.

BNS Mortgage Corporation (Can. 1973)
Dec. 31, 1980 – Amalgamated with Scotia Covenants Mortgage Corporation to form Scotia Mortgage Corporation. Total of 61,105 com. shs. of co. with par value of $100 conv. into 305,525 shs. with par value of $20 of amalg. co.

BNS Split Corp. (Ont. June 14, 2002)
Aug. 2, 2007 – Redeemed; basis $23 per pref. sh. and $38.4892 per capital sh.

BNS Split Corp. II (Ont. Feb. 28, 2005)
Sept. 22, 2020 – Terminated; cl.A cap. shs. and cl.B pref. ser.2 shs. redeemed at $14.4828 and $19.71 per sh., respectively.

BNT Ltd. (B.C. 1961)
Apr. 20, 1995 – All o/s cap. shs. and equity dividend shs. redeemed; basis $15.55 per capital sh. and $27.50 per equity dividend sh.

B.O.C. of Canada Limited (Can. - unspecified)
Nov. 1963 – Name changed to Great Plains Petroleums Limited following acquisition by Great Plains Development Company of Canada, Ltd.

BOE Capital Corp. (B.C. June 6, 2007)
July 21, 2010 – Name changed to Athabasca Uranium Inc. pursuant to Qualifying Transaction acquisition of option to acquire 50% interest in McCarthy uranium prospect in Saskatchewan. ■

BOVAR Inc. (Alta. June 1, 1977)
May 31, 2002 – Amalgamated in Alberta to continue with same name.
May 27, 2003 – Name changed to Orbus Pharma Inc. (see FPsurvey - Industrials)

BP Amoco p.l.c. (U.K. Dec. 31, 1998 amalg.)
May 1, 2001 – Name changed to BP plc.

BP Canada Inc. (Can. Apr. 27, 1979)
Feb. 28, 1983 – Name changed to BP Resources Canada Limited; basis 1 sh. of BP Resources Canada Limited and 1 cl. B and 3 cl. A shs. of B.P. Refining and Marketing Canada Limited for 1 old sh., following payment of $8.35 cash divd. ■

BP Canada Inc. (Can. Dec. 14, 1982)
Dec. 31, 1992 – Name changed to Talisman Energy Inc. ■

BP Canada Limited (Ont. Dec. 17, 1925)
Apr. 27, 1979 – Name changed to BP Canada Inc. and continued into Canada. ■

BP Canada (1969) Ltd. (Can. 1957)
1971 – Merged with Supertest Petroleum Corporation Limited into BP Canada Limited.

BP Oil & Gas Ltd. (Alta. 1951)
Oct. 18, 1972 – Amalgamated into BP Canada Limited; basis 1 new for 2.5 old shs. (see BP Canada Limited)

B.P. Refining and Marketing Canada Ltd. (Can. 1982)
Mar. 31, 1983 – All o/s cl. A shs. acquired under $1.23 per sh. takeover offer by Petro-Canada. All shs. not tendered were redeemed for cash. Non-voting cl. B shs. to be purchased in 1984-85 at $12.414 per sh.

BP Resources Canada Limited (Can. Dec. 14, 1982)
May 29, 1984 – Name changed to BP Canada Inc. ■

BP Tanker Finance Canada Limited (Can. 1965)
Feb. 27, 1986 – Shldrs. authorized an application for the dissolution of the corporation. All o/s 6.25% s.f. debs. ser. A were redeemed by the corporation effective Oct. 1, 1985.
Mar. 31, 1986 – Ceased to exist as a legal entity.

BPG Metals Corp. (B.C. Jan. 1, 2022)
May 19, 2022 – Name changed to Bravo Mining Corp. (see FPsurvey - Mines & Energy)

BPGM Metals Corp. (B.C. Jan. 1, 2022)
Jan. 5, 2022 – Name changed to BPG Metals Corp. ■

BPI Canadian Opportunities II Fund (Ont. Dec. 16, 1996)
Dec. 22, 1998 – Name changed to BPI Global Opportunities II Fund. ■

BPI Energy Holdings, Inc. (B.C. Aug. 15, 1980)
Feb. 4, 2013 – Dissolved and struck from registry.

BPI Financial Corporation (Can. Jan. 29, 1993)
Aug. 25, 1999 – All o/s com. shs. acquired by C.I. Fund Management Inc.; basis $5.00 in cash or 0.25 of a new C.I. com. sh. for 1 old BPI sh. (see C.I. Fund Management Inc.)

BPI Global Opportunities II Fund (Ont. Dec. 16, 1996)
Apr. 27, 2005 – Name changed to CI Global Opportunities II Fund. ■

BPI Industries Inc. (B.C. Aug. 15, 1980)
Feb. 10, 2006 – Name changed to BPI Energy Holdings, Inc. ■

B.P.I. Resources Ltd. (B.C. 1969)
1983 – Amalgamated in British Columbia to continue with same name.
Feb. 15, 1985 – Name changed to Brent Resources Group Ltd. ■

BPLI Holdings Inc. (Can. Mar. 28, 2019)
Apr. 20, 2021 – Privatized via the acquisition of all the o/s shs. not already held by Rizbollo Holding Limited and Name 3 Capital Inc.; basis 23¢ cash per sh.

BPO Properties Ltd. (Can. Nov. 3, 1978 amalg.)
May 2, 2013 – All pref. ser. G, J and M shs. exchanged for Brookfield Office Properties Inc. cl. AAA pref. ser. V, W and Y shs., respectively, on a share-for-share basis.

BQ Metals Corp. (B.C. Feb. 4, 2008)
Apr. 18, 2018 – Name changed to BeMetals Corp. (see FPsurvey - Mines & Energy)

B.R. Resources Ltd. (B.C. 1966)
Feb. 2, 1983 – Struck off register.

BRANCHEZ-VOUS! inc. (Can. Apr. 7, 2000)
June 9, 2009 – Name changed to BV! Media Inc. ■

BRC Development Corporation (Ont. Aug. 7, 1990)
Aug. 11, 2004 – Continued into Canada.
Aug. 13, 2004 – Name changed to BRC Diamond Corporation. ■

BRC Diamond Corporation (Can. Aug. 11, 2004)
Feb. 11, 2008 – Name changed to BRC DiamondCore Ltd. pursuant to acquisition of Diamond Core Resources (Pty) Limited. ■

BRC DiamondCore Ltd. (Can. Aug. 11, 2004)
June 27, 2011 – Name changed to Delrand Resources Limited; basis 1 new for 2 old shs. ■

BRL Enterprises Inc. (B.C. Apr. 2, 1931)
July 3, 1998 – Amalgamated with a wholly owned subsid. of B.C. Pacific Capital Corporation; basis 1 new redeem. pref. sh. for 1 com. sh. immediately redeemed for $6.75.

BRM Capital Corporation (Alta. July 20, 1990)
Mar. 30, 2001 – Name changed to Cartier Partners Financial Group Inc. ■

BRS Ventures Ltd. (B.C. June 8, 2007)
Sept. 1, 2016 – Name changed to Silver One Resources Inc.; basis 3 new for 1 old sh. (see FPsurvey - Mines & Energy)

BRX Mining & Petroleum Ltd. (B.C. 1979)
Feb. 22, 1985 – Name changed to Consolidated BRX Mining & Petroleum Ltd.; basis 1 new for 4 old shs. ■

B.R.X. (1935) Consolidated Mines Ltd. (B.C. 1935)
Dec. 1971 – Dissolved.

BSM Technologies Inc. (Ont. Oct. 14, 1999)
June 5, 2019 – All o/s com. shs. not already held acquired by Geotab Inc.; basis $1.40 cash per sh.

B.T. Gold Explorations Ltd. (B.C. 1981)
Sept. 25, 1987 – Dissolved.

BTL Group Ltd. (Alta. Mar. 28, 2011)
Jan. 10, 2019 – Name changed to Interbit Ltd. ■

BTU Capital Corp. (B.C. Aug. 28, 2008)
Aug. 29, 2017 – Name changed to BTU Metals Corp. (see FPsurvey - Mines & Energy)

B2B Solutions Inc. (B.C. Jan. 10, 2000)
Aug. 12, 2004 – Name changed to Timer Explorations Inc. pursuant to Qualifying Transaction acquisition of 56 mineral claims in British Columbia. ■

B2B Trust (Can. Jan. 1, 1991)
June 9, 2004 – Amalgamated with LBC AcquisitionCo Inc., wholly owned subsid. of Laurentian Bank of Canada; basis $9.50 per sh.
July 7, 2012 – Name changed to B2B Bank.

BUS Systems Inc. (Can. Nov. 9, 2005)
Dec. 29, 2008 – Name changed to SUB Capital Inc. ■

BV! Media Inc. (Can. Apr. 7, 2000)
Oct. 6, 2010 – Amalgamated with 7557175 Canada Inc., a wholly owned subsid. of Rogers Media Inc., for 40¢ per sh.

BW Technologies Ltd. (Alta. July 28, 1961)
June 17, 2004 – Acquired by First Technology Acquisition Canada Inc. for $36 per sh.

BWI Resources Limited (B.C. Aug. 25, 1987)
Jan. 2, 2001 – Name changed to Penteco Resources Ltd.; basis 1 new for 4 old shs. ■

B.X. Development Ltd. (B.C. 1956)
Aug. 31, 1981 – Amalgamated into Brent Petroleum Industries Ltd.; basis 1 com. sh. or 0.5 com. sh. and 0.5 pref. sh. for 1 old sh.

BXL Energy Ltd. (Alta. Feb. 9, 1995)
June 26, 2001 – Acquired by Viking Energy Royalty Trust; basis 0.333 Viking trust units or $1.12335 plus 0.20852 Viking trust units for 1 BXL sh. (see Viking Energy Royalty Trust)

BY & G Ventures Corp. (B.C. July 30, 1970)
Nov. 19, 1997 – Name changed to Load Resources Ltd.; basis 1 new for 4 old shs. ■

B.Y.G. Natural Resources Inc. (Ont. Apr. 1, 1969 amalg.)
Apr. 6, 2004 – PricewaterhouseCoopers Inc. appointed interim receiver and receiver-manager.
Feb. 22, 2007 – PricewaterhouseCoopers appointed trustee in bankruptcy.
2011 – By November, assets consisting of mineral claims and leases were sold. Funds totaling $2.77 million were distributed to secured creditors.
Aug. 26, 2014 – PricewaterhouseCoopers as bankruptcy trustee was discharged.
May 24, 2016 – Yukon court granted an order approving the Proposal Solicitation Procedure (PSP) for the purchase of remaining assets and remediation work on the Mount Nansen mine.
May 6, 2019 – Court approval received for the sale of the Mount Nansen mine site to Alexco Environmental Group Inc. and JDS Energy & Mining Inc.

BYND Cannasoft Enterprises Inc. (B.C. Mar. 29, 2021 amalg.)
July 22, 2024 – Name changed to Femto Technologies Inc. (see FPsurvey - Industrials)

B2Gold Back River Corp. (B.C. June 7, 1966)
Apr. 24, 2023 – Acquired by B2Gold Corp.; basis 0.3867 B2Gold shs. for 1 Sabina Gold sh.

Ba Ba Capital Inc. (Ont. Dec. 30, 1985)
May 11, 2016 – Name changed to Imex Systems Inc. following reverse takeover acquisition of (old) Imex Systems Inc.; basis 1 new for 11 old shs. (see FPsurvey - Industrials)

Bab-Sol Resource Explorations Ltd. (Ont. 1978)
Oct. 14, 1983 – Name changed to HWI Industries Inc.; basis 1 new for 6 old shs. ■

Babine International Resources Ltd. (B.C. 1967)
Dec. 1, 1972 – Amalgamated with Molymine Explorations Ltd. (1 for 9) to form Seneca Developments Ltd.; basis 1 new Seneca sh. for 6 old Babine shs.

Babine Lake Mines Ltd. (B.C. 1966)
Mar. 1970 – Name changed to Cyclone Mining Co. Ltd. ■

Babykins International Inc. (B.C. 1987)
July 1992 – Declared bankruptcy, and Manning Jamison Ltd. appointed receiver.
May 1993 – All assets sold. The secured creditors suffered a shortfall, and there was no distribution to unsecured creditors or shrlders.
Dec. 23, 1993 – Receiver discharged.
Apr. 13, 1995 – Dissolved and struck off register.

Babykins Products Canada Ltd. (B.C. 1987)
Oct. 10, 1990 – Name changed to Babykins International Inc. ■

Babyland Industries Inc. (B.C. Sept. 27, 1988)
Mar. 31, 1995 – Dissolved and struck off register.

Babylon Minerals Inc. (Ont. 1974)
Nov. 1978 – Amalgamated with Oxford Mines Limited, Solvang Explorations Limited, Firebird Petroleums Limited and Drayton Petroleum Limited to form Bab-Sol Resource Exploration Ltd.

Babylon Technologies Inc. (Alta. Apr. 30, 1999)
Oct. 2, 2006 – Struck from the registry and dissolved.

Baca Resources Ltd. (Alta. Nov. 1, 1985 amalg.)
July 11, 1994 – Name changed to CORDEX Petroleums Inc. ■

Bacanora Minerals Ltd. (Alta. Sept. 29, 2008)
Mar. 26, 2018 – Acquired by Bacanora Lithium plc; basis 1 new Bacanora Lithium ordinary sh. for 1 Bacanora com. sh.

Bachelor Lake Gold Mines Inc. (Que. Mar. 7, 1980)
June 22, 1994 – Amalgamated with Espalau Mining Corporation to form new co. with same name Espalau Mining Corporation; basis 1 Espalau sh. for 15 Bachelor shs. (see Espalau Mining Corporation)

Bachelor Lake Gold Mines Ltd. (Ont. 1947)
Jan. 5, 1970 – Charter cancelled.

Backer Petroleum Corp. (B.C. Dec. 30, 1988 amalg.)
Oct. 29, 1997 – Continued into Alberta. (see Allied Oil & Gas Corp.)
Sept. 18, 2000 – Amalgamated with wholly owned subsid. of Allied Oil & Gas Corp. for $1.75 per sh. (see Allied Oil & Gas Corp.)

Backer Resources Ltd. (B.C. 1972)
Jan. 3, 1989 – Amalgamated with Gallahad Petroleum Ltd. to form Backer Petroleum Corp.; basis 1 cl. A sh. for 1 cl. A sh. and 1 new cl. B sh. for 1 cl. B sh. (see Backer Petroleum Corp.)

Bacola Mining Explorations Ltd. (Ont. 1945)
Nov. 27, 1961 – Charter cancelled.

BacTech Enviromet Corporation (Can. Feb. 13, 1997)
Jan. 22, 2004 – Name changed to BacTech Mining Corporation. ■

BacTech Metallurgical Solutions Ltd. (Can. Feb. 13, 1997)
May 19, 2000 – Name changed to BacTech Enviromet Corporation. ■

BacTech Mining Corporation (Can. Feb. 13, 1997)
Dec. 2, 2010 – Name changed to REBgold Corporation pursuant to plan of arrangement whereby co. spun off certain assets to newly created BacTech Environmental Corporation. ■

Bad Boy Appliances and Furniture Limited (Can. 1968 amalg.)
Aug. 18, 1977 – Placed into receivership. Price Waterhouse Limited appointed receiver. No assets were available for unsecured claims or contingent liabs.

Baden Explorations Limited (B.C. July 21, 1980)
July 7, 1988 – Name changed to Reymont Gold Mines Ltd. and continued into Canada; basis 1 new for 10 old shs. ■

Baden Gold Mines Ltd. (Ont. 1935)
Oct. 22, 1962 – Dissolved.

Baden Resources Inc. (B.C. Jan. 19, 2020)
Mar. 2, 2023 – Name changed to NorthStar Gaming Holdings Inc. pursuant to the reverse takeover acquisition of NorthStar Gaming Inc.; basis 1 new for 3.333333 old shs. ■

Baden Technologies Inc. (Alta. Feb. 29, 2000)
July 23, 2010 – Name changed to FSI Energy Services Inc. ■

Badger Daylighting Inc. (Alta. Jan. 3, 1992)
Apr. 5, 2004 – Converted to an income trust named Badger Income Fund; basis 1 trust unit for 2 Badger com. shs.

Badger Daylighting Ltd. (Alta. Apr. 27, 2010)
May 5, 2021 – Name changed to Badger Infrastructure Solutions Ltd. (see FPsurvey - Mines & Energy; FPsurvey - Industrials)

Badger Income Fund (Alta. Mar. 31, 2004)
Dec. 31, 2010 – Succeeded by Badger Daylighting Ltd. pursuant to plan of arrangement whereby Badger Daylighting Ltd. was formed to facilitate the conversion of the fund into a corporation and the fund was subsequently dissolved. ■

Baetis Ventures Ltd. (B.C. Nov. 2, 2016)
Nov. 6, 2018 – Name changed to RE Royalties Ltd. pursuant to Qualifying Transaction reverse takeover acquisition of (old) RE Royalties Ltd.; basis 1 new for 3 old shs. (see FPsurvey - Mines & Energy; FPsurvey - Industrials)

Baffinland Iron Mines Corporation (Ont. Mar. 10, 1986)
Apr. 1, 2011 – Acquired by 1843208 Ontario Inc. for $1.50 per sh., 2007 wts. for 10¢ per wt. and 2009 wts. for 80¢ per wt.

Baffinland Iron Mines Ltd. (Ont. Feb. 18, 1963)
Feb. 10, 2004 – Acquired by Glimmer Resources Inc. (subsequently renamed Baffinland Iron Mines Corporation) in reverse takeover transaction. (see Baffinland Iron Mines Corporation)

Bagamac Mines Ltd. (Ont. 1926)
1956 – Name changed to Tribag Mining Co., Ltd.; basis 1 new for 5 old shs. ■

Baghdad Gold Mines Ltd. (Ont. 1937)
1938 – Name changed to Baghdad-Larder Mines Ltd. ■

Baghdad-Larder Mines Ltd. (Ont. 1937)
Mar. 1962 – Charter cancelled.

Baha Resources Ltd. (B.C. 1983)
Apr. 16, 1993 – Dissolved and struck off register.

Bahama Resources Ltd. (B.C. Dec. 15, 1980)
July 3, 1986 – Name changed to American Lightwave Corp.; basis 1 new for 10 old shs. (see FPsurvey - Industrials)

Bahamas-Caribbean Development Corporation Limited (Ont. 1962)
Mar. 24, 1972 – Name changed to Oceanus Industries (Bahamas) Ltd.; basis 1 new for 20 old shs. ■

Bahn Foods Inc. (B.C. Mar. 10, 1980)
Oct. 21, 1996 – Name changed to Consolidated Bahn Foods Inc.; basis 1 new for 10 old shs. ■

Baikal Forest Corp. (B.C. Sept. 18, 2007)
July 14, 2014 – All o/s com. shs. not already held acquired by Far East Forest Industry Inc.; basis 1 cl. A pref. sh. redeemed for Cdn$0.40 cash per sh. for 1 Baikal Forest com. sh.

Bailey Selburn Oil & Gas Ltd. (Can. 1952)
1962 – Acquired by Pacific Petroleums Ltd.; basis 4 Pacific shs. for 5 cl. A shs., and $5.00 or 5 Pacific shs. for 14 cl. B shs. (see Pacific Petroleums Ltd.)

Bainbridge Minerals Ltd. (B.C. Feb. 1, 1983)
Jan. 16, 2017 – Struck from registry and dissolved.

Baitex Medical Technologies Inc. (Ont. Apr. 12, 1984)
Nov. 10, 1994 – Name changed to Stockguard Corporation; basis 1 new for 10 old shs. ■

Baiville Gold Mines Ltd. (Ont. 1945)
Jan. 6, 1971 – Dissolved.

Baja Gold, Inc. (B.C. Nov. 9, 1989 amalg.)
May 31, 1996 – Amalgamated with Loki Gold Corporation to form VLB Resource Corporation which then was acquired by Viceroy Resource Corporation; basis 0.297 Viceroy shs. for 1 Baja sh.

Baja Mining Corp. (B.C. July 15, 1985)
Oct. 17, 2016 – Name changed to Camrova Resources Inc.; basis 1 new for 20 old shs. ■

BakBone Software Incorporated (Alta. Dec. 2, 1992)
Aug. 11, 2003 – Continued into Canada.
Jan. 14, 2011 – Acquired by Quest Software, Inc.; basis US$0.33 per com. sh. and US$1.29 per ser. A pref. sh.

Baker Gold Ltd. (B.C. 1979)
Mar. 20, 1985 – Amalgamated with U.S. Precious Metals, Inc.; basis 1 new for 1 old sh.

Baker Mining and Milling Co. (unknown)
Name changed to Baker Talc Limited; basis 50 new for 1 old pref. sh., and 5 new for 1 old com. sh.
1952 – Continued into Quebec. ■

Baker Talc Limited (Que. 1952)
1978 – Name changed to Bakertalc Inc. ■

Bakertalc Inc. (Que. 1952)
Aug. 11, 1987 – Continued into Quebec.
Jan. 24, 1995 – Name changed to Palace Explorations Inc. ■

Bakra Resources Ltd. (B.C. Dec. 8, 1986)
June 13, 1994 – Name changed to Northpoint Resources Ltd.; basis 1 new for 4.5 old shs. ■

Bakrie Minarak Energy Inc. (Alta. July 18, 1994)
May 24, 2000 – Name changed to Pertacal Energy Inc. ■

Balaclava Industries Ltd. (B.C. Mar. 25, 1983)
Nov. 8, 1996 – Name changed to Balaclava Mines Inc. ■

Balaclava Mines Inc. (B.C. Mar. 25, 1983)
June 7, 2001 – Name changed to Pillar Resources Inc.; basis 1 new for 10 old shs. ■

Balance Resources Ltd. (B.C. Oct. 4, 1984)
Feb. 1, 1991 – Name changed to International Topaz Business Development Corp. ■

Balboa Explorations Ltd. (Ont. 1944)
1946 – Acquired by Cortez Explorations Ltd. (see Cortez Explorations Ltd.)

Balboa Mining & Investments Limited (Ont. 1968)
Feb. 20, 1980 – Dissolved.

Balco Forest Products Ltd. (B.C. 1968)
Apr. 1972 – Name changed to Balco Industries Ltd. ■

Balco Industries Ltd. (B.C. 1968)
July 1987 – Acquired by Timber Investment Ltd.

Balcor Resources Corp. (B.C. July 20, 1979)
Feb. 12, 1990 – Name changed to Preston Resource Corp.; basis 1 new for 10 old shs. ∎

Bald Eagle Explorations Inc. (Ont. Mar. 9, 1979)
May 2, 1983 – Name changed to Consolidated Bald Eagle Explorations Inc.; basis 1 new for 8 old shs. ∎

Bald Eagle Gold Corp. (Ont. Jan. 25, 2018)
Aug. 18, 2022 – Name changed to Hercules Silver Corp. ∎

Bald Eagle Golf Corp. (Man. May 10, 2000)
Nov. 17, 2004 – Delisted TSX-Venture. Subsequently struck from register and dissolved.

Baldonnel Oil & Gas Ltd. (unknown)
1967 – Assets acquired by Pinnacle Petroleums Ltd. for 250,000 shs. (approximately 1 new for 6.8 old shs.).

Baldwin Hotels Limited (B.C. June 30, 1971)
Nov. 20, 1987 – Dissolved and struck off register.

Baldwin-Kirkland Gold Mines Ltd. (Ont. 1936)
1946 – Property sold to Baldwin Consolidated Mines Ltd.; basis 1 new for 10 old shs. Charter cancelled in 1947.

Balfour Mining Ltd. (B.C. 1969)
Jan. 1978 – Name changed to International Balfour Resources Ltd.; basis 1 new for 5 old shs. ∎

Bali Explorations Ltd. (B.C. 1971)
Sept. 16, 1983 – Struck off register.

Ballad Enterprises Ltd. (B.C. Aug. 22, 1967)
Nov. 16, 2001 – Name changed to Ballad Ventures Ltd.; basis 1 new for 3 old shs. ∎

Ballad Gold & Silver Ltd. (B.C. Aug. 22, 1967)
Jan. 14, 2009 – Name changed to Goldbank Mining Corporation; basis 1 new for 4 old shs. (see FPsurvey - Mines & Energy)

Ballad Ventures Ltd. (B.C. Aug. 22, 1967)
July 21, 2003 – Name changed to Ballad Gold & Silver Ltd.; basis 1 new for 2 old shs. ∎

Ballantyne Long Lac Mines Ltd. (Ont. 1934)
1957 – Charter cancelled.

Ballard Oil & Gas Limited (Alta. 1952)
Nov. 1, 1989 – Dissolved and struck off register.

Ballard Power Systems Inc. (Can. May 30, 1989)
Dec. 31, 2000 – Succeeded by Superior Plus Corp. pursuant to plan of arrangement to convert Superior Plus Income Fund (SPIF) to a corp. resulting in SPIF's wholly owned subsids. Superior Plus Limited Partnership and Superior Plus General Partner Inc. becoming wholly owned subsids. of Superior Plus Corp., with trust units of SPIF exchanged for common shares of Superior Plus Corp. on a 1-for-1 basis. All assets and liabilities of (old) Ballard Power Systems Inc. were transferred to (new) Ballard Power Systems Inc. which was spun out as a new public entity on a sh.-for-sh. basis. (see FPsurvey - Industrials)

Ballatar Explorations Ltd. (B.C. June 16, 1987)
Aug. 15, 1995 – Name changed to International Ballater Resources Inc.; basis 1 new for 7 old shs. ∎

Ballinderry Explorations Ltd. (B.C. June 2, 1969)
May 24, 1978 – Name changed to Prairie Pacific Energy Corporation; basis 1 new for 5 old shs. ∎

Ballinderry Royalties Corporation Ltd. (unknown)
1969 – Merged with Magnet Explorations Ltd. (1 for 3) to continue under the new name Ballinderry Explorations Ltd. effective Sept. 26.

Ballistic Energy Corporation (Alta. Mar. 12, 1992)
June 19, 1996 – All o/s com. shs. acquired by Stampeder Exploration Ltd.; basis $5.00 per sh. (see Stampeder Exploration Ltd.)

Balloch Resources Ltd. (Bermuda Oct. 6, 1996)
Nov. 30, 2005 – Name changed to Katanga Mining Limited. ∎

Ballyliffin Capital Corp. (Alta. June 22, 2006)
July 13, 2015 – Dissolved following Qualifying Transaction private placement subscription of 6,567,600 (post-consol. 1:5) Ironside Resources Inc. com. shs. at $0.0125 per sh. and distribution of Ironside shs. to shldrs. (see Ironside Resources Inc.)

Balmoral Capital Corp. (Alta. May 4, 1998)
Oct. 15, 1999 – Name changed to Commercial Consolidators Corp.; basis 1 new for 3 old shs. ∎

Balmoral Porcupine Gold Mines Ltd. (Ont. 1945)
1955 – Charter cancelled.

Balmoral Resources Ltd. (B.C. Jan. 24, 1983)
May 26, 2020 – Acquired by Wallbridge Mining Company Limited; basis 0.71 Wallbridge shs. for 1 Balmoral sh.

Baloil Lassiter Petroleum Ltd. (Alta. 1971 amalg.)
Sept. 8, 1989 – Name changed to Baloil Resources Ltd. ∎

Baloil Resources Ltd. (Alta. 1971 amalg.)
Aug. 11, 1993 – Acquired by Tanner Arctic Enterprises Ltd.; basis 1 Tanner Arctic sh. for 4.155 Baloil com. shs. and 0.4155 Baloil pfd. shs. (see Kuma Resources Ltd.)

Balsam Resources Inc. (B.C. Jan. 15, 1979)
Jan. 18, 1990 – Name changed to Consolidated Balsam Resources Inc.; basis 1 new for 2 old shs. ∎

Balsam Technologies Corp. (B.C. July 28, 2016 amalg.)
Sept. 21, 2021 – Name changed to Blender Bites Limited following reverse takeover acquisition of Blender Bites Incorporated. (see FPsurvey - Industrials)

Balsam Ventures Inc. (B.C. Mar. 13, 2000)
Nov. 12, 2003 – Name changed to Staccato Gold Resources Ltd. following Qualifying Transaction agreement with Band-Ore Resources Ltd. to acquire interest in claims and a mineral lease in the Thunder Bay area of northern Ontario. ∎

Baltac Oils Ltd. (Can. 1928)
1957 – Struck off register.

Baltic Mines Ltd. (Ont. 1947)
Apr. 15, 1963 – Dissolved.

Baltic Resources Inc. (Alta. Aug. 27, 1996)
Mar. 10, 2008 – Amalgamated in Alberta to continue with same name. (see PhosCan Chemical Corp.)
Mar. 17, 2008 – All o/s assets except the Martison phosphate property transferred to newly formed subsidiary Canadian Orebodies Inc. and then amalgamated with 1366825 Alberta Ltd., a wholly owned subsid. of PhosCan Chemical Corp.; basis 1.4 PhosCan com. shs. and 1 Canadian Orebodies com. sh. for 1 Baltic com. sh. Subsequently, Canadian Orebodies listed on the TSX. (see PhosCan Chemical Corp.)

Bam Bam Resources Corp. (B.C. Mar. 10, 2017)
May 31, 2022 – Name changed to Majuba Hill Copper Corp.; basis 1 new for 10 old shs. ∎

Bama Gold Corp. (B.C. Mar. 14, 2008)
June 9, 2016 – Name changed to Whattozee Networks Inc.; basis 1 new for 3 old shs. ∎

Bambi Mines Ltd. (Ont. 1945)
May 15, 1974 – Dissolved.

Bamboo Creek Gold Mines Ltd. (Ont. 1969)
Oct. 1972 – Charter cancelled.

Bamco Minerals Corp. (Alta. Nov. 23, 1993)
Feb. 1, 1996 – Name changed to Signet Industries Ltd. ∎

Bamex Mines Ltd. (Que. 1972)
Jan. 1980 – Declared bankruptcy.

Bamoos Lake Mines Ltd. (Ont. 1954)
Sept. 1959 – Dissolved.

Banbury Gold Mines Ltd. (B.C. Nov. 6, 1978)
July 6, 1992 – Name changed to Enerwaste Minerals Corp.; basis 1 new for 4 old shs. ∎

Banca Commerciale Italiana of Canada (Can. Oct. 8, 1981)
Nov. 14, 2001 – Name changed to IntesaBci Canada. ∎

Banca Mining & Exploration Ltd. (Ont. 1943)
Nov. 1954 – Charter cancelled.

Banco Central of Canada (Can. 1982)
Sept. 22, 1992 – Name changed to Banco Central Hispano - Canada following the October 1991 merger of parent bank Banco Central S.A. with Banco Hispanoamericano S.A.

Banco Central S.A. (Spain 1919)
Dec. 27, 1991 – Amalgamated in Spain to continue with same name.
June 23, 1992 – Name changed to Banco Central Hispanoamericano, S.A.

Banco Finance Ltd. (B.C. June 9, 1955)
1978 – Name changed to First Western Capital Ltd.

Banco Resources Ltd. (B.C. 1983)
Apr. 16, 1992 – Dissolved and struck off register.

Bancorp Financial Group Inc. (B.C. Oct. 11, 1996)
Sept. 4, 2003 – Going private transaction via amalgamation with Rivera Enterprises Ltd. All o/s com. shs. exchanged for redeemable pref. shs. redeemed at 12¢ per sh. on Sept. 11, 2003.

Bancroft Mica & Stone Products Syndicate Ltd. (Ont. 1944)
1953 – Charter cancelled.

The Bancroft Mines Ltd. (Ont. 1955)
July 27, 1976 – Charter cancelled.

Bancroft Uranium Mines Ltd. (Ont. 1955)
Nov. 12, 1971 – Name changed to The Bancroft Mines Ltd. ∎

Bancshare Portfolio Corp. (Ont. 1958)
Oct. 1, 1992 – All o/s partic. retract. pref. shs. redeemed for $21.50 per sh. plus an amount equal to all dividends accrued and unpaid up to but not including Oct. 1.
June 30, 1999 – Dissolved and struck off register.

Band-Ore Gold Mines Limited (Ont. Mar. 18, 1946)
Feb. 10, 1992 – Name changed to Band-Ore Resources Ltd.; basis 1 new for 2 old shs. ∎

Band-Ore Resources Ltd. (Ont. Mar. 18, 1946)
Aug. 30, 2006 – Continued into British Columbia. (see West Timmins Mining Inc.)
Sept. 18, 2006 – Amalgamated with Sydney Resource Corporation to form West Timmins Mining Inc.; basis 1 West Timmins sh. for 1 Sydney sh. and 0.9 West Timmins shs. for 1 Band-Ore sh. (see West Timmins Mining Inc.)

Bandera Gold Ltd. (Alta. Nov. 23, 1993)
July 9, 2018 – Name changed to Jaeger Resources Corp. (see FPsurvey - Mines & Energy)

Bandini Petroleum Co. (unknown)
1959 – Acquired by Westates Petroleum Co.

Bando Oil & Minerals Corp. (Que. Feb. 4, 1958)
1958 – Name changed to Vanguard Explorations Ltd. ∎

Bandolac Mining Company, Limited (Ont. Sept. 17, 1940)
Oct. 29, 2008 – Name changed to Schyan Exploration Inc. ∎

Bandon Capital Corp. (Alta. Oct. 27, 2004)
June 15, 2007 – Name changed to Bandon Capital Resources Ltd. ∎

Bandon Capital Resources Ltd. (Alta. Oct. 27, 2004)
Nov. 11, 2008 – Name changed to Kierland Resources Ltd. ∎

Bandowan Mines Ltd. (Ont. 1955)
1958 – Acquired by Vanguard Explorations Ltd.; basis 1 new for 1 old sh. (see Vanguard Explorations Ltd.)

Banff Brewery Corporation (Alta. Nov. 25, 1993)
Sept. 22, 1999 – Name changed to Peak Brewing Group Inc.; basis 1 new for 5 old shs. ■

Banff Brewing Capital Corp. (Alta. Nov. 25, 1993)
May 5, 1995 – Name changed to Banff Brewery Corporation. ■

Banff Mines Ltd. (B.C. 1961)
June 8, 1972 – Dissolved and struck off register.

Banff Oil Ltd. (Alta. 1951)
Dec. 1970 – Amalgamated into Aquitaine Co. of Canada Ltd.; basis 0.52 new for 1 old sh.

Banff Resources Ltd. (B.C. July 17, 1984)
Mar. 6, 1996 – Continued into Yukon.
Jan. 26, 2007 – Dissolved and struck off register.

Banister Continental Ltd. (Alta. Nov. 27, 1968)
Jan. 10, 1978 – Continued into Canada.
Aug. 27, 1990 – Name changed to Banister Inc. ■

Banister Foundation Inc. (Can. Jan. 10, 1978)
June 10, 1997 – Name changed to BFC Construction Corporation. ■

Banister Inc. (Can. Jan. 10, 1978)
June 13, 1994 – Name changed to Banister Foundation Inc.; basis 1 new for 1 old sh. ■

Bank Hapoalim (Canada) (Can. 1982)
Jan. 1, 1995 – Amalgamated with Republic National Bank of New York (Canada).

Bank of Alberta (Can. Mar. 22, 1984)
Nov. 1, 1987 – Formed Canadian Western Bank in Canada on amalgamation with Western & Pacific Bank of Canada. ■

Bank of Boston Canada (Can. May 27, 1982)
July 31, 1996 – Ceased operations in Canada.

Bank of British Columbia (Can. Dec. 14, 1966; via Bank Act)
Apr. 9, 1987 – Name changed to B.C. Bancorp following sale agreement with the Hongkong Bank of Canada. Under the sale agreement, 98.6% of the bank's assets and substantially all of its liabilities were sold for net proceeds of $63,535,000. ■

Bank of Credit and Commerce Canada (Can. 1982)
July 5, 1991 – Bank placed under liquidation after the Office of the Superintendent of Financial Institutions Canada seized control of the assets.
Sept. 6, 1991 – The Canada Deposit Insurance Corporation paid out $22,500,000 to depositors.
Sept. 23, 1991 – By an order the Superior Court of Quebec ordered that the bank be wound up and appointed Toronto-based Deloitte & Touche Inc. as permanent liquidator.
Dec. 31, 2000 – Liquidator paid out a dividend of $0.892 on the dollar to all creditors of record.
Mar. 17, 2003 – Bank placed under liquidation after the Office of the Superintendent of Financial Institutions Canada seized control of the assets on July 5, 1991. The Canada Deposit Insurance Corporation paid out $22,500,000 to depositors on Sept. 6, 1991. By an order dated Sept. 23, 1991, the Superior Court of Quebec ordered that the bank be wound up and appointed Toronto-based Deloitte & Touche Inc. as permanent liquidator. By Dec. 31, 2000, the liquidator had paid out a dividend of $0.892 on the dollar to all creditors of record. On Mar. 19, 2003, the liquidator sent a letter to all claimants, enclosing the final dividend and informing them that on Mar. 17, 2003, the Superior Court of Quebec had approved the final dividend payment to all claimants of record and released and discharged the liquidator as permanent liquidator of the bank.
Mar. 19, 2003 – Liquidator sent a letter to all claimants, enclosing the final dividend and informing them that on

Mar. 17, 2003, the Superior Court of Quebec had approved the final dividend payment to all claimants of record and released and discharged the liquidator as permanent liquidator of the bank.

Bank of Montreal (Can. May 18, 1822)
1871 – Continued into Canada; via Bank Act. (see FPsurvey - Industrials)

Bank of Montreal Mortgage Corporation (Ont. 1970)
1981 – Continued into Canada.

Bank of Montreal Realty Inc. (Can. 1956)
Apr. 30, 1993 – Dissolved.

The Bank of Nova Scotia (N.S. Mar. 30, 1832)
1871 – Continued into Canada; via Bank Act. (see FPsurvey - Industrials)

The Bank of Tokyo Canada (Can. July 30, 1981)
Apr. 1, 1996 – Formed Bank of Tokyo-Mitsubishi UFJ (Canada) in Canada following formation of Bank of Tokyo-Mitsubishi (Canada) following amalgamation with Mitsubishi Bank of Canada. ■

Bank of Tokyo-Mitsubishi UFJ (Canada) (Can. Apr. 1, 1996 amalg.)
Apr. 1, 2018 – Name changed to MUFG Bank, Ltd., Canada Branch.

The Bank of Toronto (Can. Mar. 18, 1855)
Feb. 1, 1955 – Amalgamated with The Dominion Bank to form The Toronto-Dominion Bank; basis 4 new for 3 old shs.

Bank of Western Canada (Can. 1966)
Sept. 14, 1967 – Winding up approved by shldrs.
Nov. 15, 1971 – Payments to shldrs. as follows: $13 per sh., Feb. 1, 1968; $1.00 per sh., Apr. 30, 1969; 50¢ per sh., Mar. 31, 1970, and final payment of 30.7¢ per sh., Nov. 15, 1971.

Bankeno Mines Limited (Ont. May 2, 1944)
Jan. 19, 1979 – Continued into Alberta.
Jan. 19, 1987 – Formed Bankeno Resources Limited in Alberta on amalgamation with subsid. Bankeno Resources Ltd. ■

Bankeno Resources Limited (Alta. Jan. 19, 1987 amalg.)
July 30, 1990 – Acquired by North Canadian Oils Limited for $4.25 per sh. (see North Canadian Oils Limited)

Bankers Cobalt Corp. (B.C. Mar. 27, 2007)
Aug. 26, 2020 – Name changed to Central African Gold Inc. ■

Bankers Petroleum Ltd. (B.C. June 24, 2004)
Oct. 5, 2016 – Acquired by Geo-Jade Petroleum Corporation; basis Cdn$2.20 cash per sh.

Bankers Petroleums (1975) Ltd. (Alta. 1952)
Feb. 1, 1989 – Struck off register.

Bankfield Consolidated Mines Ltd. (Ont. Aug. 6, 1936)
Mar. 1976 – Charter cancelled.

Bankfield Gold Mines Ltd. (Ont. Apr. 18, 1934)
1936 – Name changed to Bankfield Consolidated Mines Ltd.; basis 2 new for 3 old shs. ■

Bankit Resource Corp. (B.C. 1981)
Oct. 8, 1993 – Dissolved and struck off register.

Bankmont Realty Company Limited (Can. 1956)
Mar. 31, 1981 – Name changed to Bank of Montreal Realty Inc. ■

Banks Energy Inc. (Yuk. Apr. 6, 1998)
Nov. 7, 2005 – Acquired by Arapahoe Energy Corporation; basis 0.5 Arapahoe shs. for 1 Banks sh. (see Arapahoe Energy Corporation)

Banks Island Gold Ltd. (B.C. Jan. 18, 2011)
Jan. 8, 2016 – Filed for bankruptcy. D. Manning & Associates Inc. appointed trustee.
Jan. 15, 2016 – Placed into receivership and FTI Consulting Canada Inc. appointed receiver.
Dec. 2018 – Asset purchase agreement with MCC Non Ferrous Trading Inc., the company's secured debt holder, was completed. Monies received not sufficient for any distrib. to shldrs. or unsecured creditors. FTI Consulting Canada was discharged as receiver and manager.
Aug. 15, 2022 – Struck from register and dissolved.

Banks Island Gold Mines Ltd. (B.C. Mar. 20, 1964)
1965 – Name changed to War Eagle Resources Ltd. ■

Banks Ventures Ltd. (Yuk. Apr. 6, 1998)
July 26, 2004 – Name changed to Banks Energy Inc. ■

Banner Entertainment Inc. (B.C. Nov. 24, 1980)
June 15, 1990 – Name changed to Windsor Court Holdings Inc.; basis 1 new for 5 old shs. ■

Banner Industries Inc. (B.C. Nov. 24, 1980)
Sept. 25, 1987 – Name changed to Banner Entertainment Inc. ■

Banner Mining Corporation (B.C. 1979)
May 23, 2003 – Dissolved and struck from register.

Banner Petroleum Corp. Ltd. (unknown 1951)
1953 – Acquired by Consolidated Mic-Mac Oils Ltd.; basis 1 new for 5.5 old shs.

Banner Porcupine Mines Ltd. (Ont. 1945)
Apr. 26, 1983 – Amalgamated (1 new for 10 old shs.) with Broulan Reef Mines Limited and Hugh-Pam Porcupine Mines Ltd. to form Broulan Resources Inc.

Banner Resources Ltd. (B.C. Feb. 12, 1970)
Nov. 28, 1983 – Name changed to Angus Resources Limited; basis 1 new for 10 old shs. ■

Bannerman Resources Limited (Australia Feb. 18, 2005)
May 11, 2016 – Voluntarily delisted from TSX; continued to trade on Australian Securities Exchange and Namibian Stock Exchange.

Bannockburn Resources Inc. (Colo. July 31, 1981)
Feb. 25, 2004 – Continued into Wyoming.
Apr. 2, 2004 – Name changed to Bannockburn Resources Limited; basis 1 new for 4 old shs. ■

Bannockburn Resources Ltd. (Alta. 1981)
July 1, 1987 – Struck off register.

Bannockburn Resources Limited (Wyo. Feb. 25, 2004)
Aug. 12, 2004 – Continued into British Columbia.
Aug. 14, 2007 – Name changed to Lucara Diamond Corp.; basis 5 new for 1 old sh. (see FPsurvey - Mines & Energy; FPsurvey - Industrials)

Banque Canadienne Nationale (Can. - unspecified 1873)
Oct. 1979 – Amalgamated with La Banque Provinciale du Canada to form National Bank of Canada.

La Banque d'Economie de Québec (Can. 1872)
Nov. 9, 1969 – Name changed to La Banque Populaire. ■

La Banque Populaire (Can. 1872)
Aug. 1970 – Amalgamated into La Banque Provinciale du Canada; basis 7 new for 10 old shs.

La Banque Provinciale du Canada (Can. - unspecified July 1900)
Aug. 1970 – Merged with La Banque Populaire on a sh.-for-sh. basis, continuing as La Banque Provinciale du Canada.
Oct. 1979 – Amalgamated with Banque Canadienne Nationale to form National Bank of Canada.

Banqwest Resources Ltd. (B.C. 1953)
Oct. 3, 1986 – Name changed to Universal Pre-Vent Inc.; basis 1 new for 5 old shs. ■

Banro Capital Group Inc. (Ont. Mar. 9, 1965)
Jan. 9, 1990 – Name changed to International Infopet Systems Ltd. ∎

Banro Corporation (Ont. Oct. 24, 1996)
Apr. 2, 2004 – Continued into Canada.
Dec. 22, 2017 – Commenced restructuring proceedings under the Companies' Creditors Arrangement Act (CCAA). FTI Consulting Canada Inc. was appointed monitor.
Mar. 28, 2018 – Court approval for the plan of compromise and reorganization was received. Under the plan obligations under the secured notes, the Dore loan and the Namoya Forward II agreement would be exchanged for new equity; current equity holders of the company would have their interests extinguished without compensation resulting in the company becoming a wholly owned, indirect subsidiary of a newly incorporated Cayman Island company; and unsecured creditors would receive a pro rata share of the unsecured cash pool.
May 3, 2018 – The court approved plan of compromise and reorganization was completed and all existing equity and any equity related claims were cancelled without compensation.

Banro International Capital Inc. (Can. May 3, 1994)
May 14, 1996 – Name changed to Banro Resource Corporation. ∎

Banro Resource Corporation (Can. May 3, 1994)
Oct. 24, 1996 – Continued into Ontario.
Jan. 22, 2001 – Name changed to Banro Corporation; basis 1 new for 3 old shs. ∎

Banyan Coast Capital Corp. (Alta. July 26, 2010)
Feb. 19, 2013 – Name changed to Banyan Gold Corp. pursuant to Qualifying Transaction acquisition of gold-base metal properties. (see FPsurvey - Mines & Energy)

Banyan Industries International Inc. (B.C. Dec. 28, 1973)
Nov. 19, 1991 – Name changed to The Incentive Design Group Ltd. ∎

Bar-Le-duc Chibougamau Mines Ltd. (Ont. 1950)
June 1962 – Charter cancelled.

Bar-Fin Mining Corporation Ltd. (Ont. 1952)
Aug. 1960 – Charter cancelled.

Bar-Lan Gold Mines Ltd. (Ont. 1945)
1957 – Acquired by Gibson Mines Ltd.; basis 1 new for 6 old shs.

Bar-Manitou Mines Ltd. (Que. 1950)
Aug. 1972 – Charter cancelled.

Bar Metals Mines Ltd. (Que. 1951)
Sept. 2, 1978 – Charter cancelled.

Bar Resources Limited (Ont. Feb. 9, 1956)
Feb. 6, 1995 – Name changed to Southern Bar Minerals Corporation; basis 1 new for 3.5 old shs. ∎

Baraca Mines Ltd. (Que. 1956)
Mar. 23, 1959 – Absorbed by Roberval Mining Corp.; basis 1 new for 4 old shs.

Baradero Resources Limited (Yuk. Sept. 25, 2001)
Nov. 23, 2004 – Continued into British Columbia.
Sept. 15, 2005 – Name changed to Centrasia Mining Corp. following reverse takeover acquisition of 0724000 B.C. Ltd. ∎

Barandium Resources Limited (B.C. 1987)
Mar. 14, 1990 – Name changed to IGC International Golf Corporation. ∎

Baranouri Minerals Ltd. (Ont. 1954)
1960 – Acquired by The Mineral Exploration Corp. Ltd.; basis 1 new for 3 old shs.

Baranouri Uranium Mines Ltd. (Ont. 1954)
1959 – Name changed to Baranouri Minerals Ltd. ∎

Barbados Gold Mines Ltd. (Ont. 1945)
Aug. 1960 – Charter cancelled.

Barbana Mining Corp. Ltd. (Ont. 1946)
1956 – Charter cancelled.

Barbary Gold Mines Ltd. (Ont. 1946)
Oct. 5, 1959 – Charter cancelled.

Barbecon Inc. (Ont. 1978 amalg.)
Apr. 1, 1985 – Acquired by Abitibi-Price Inc. for $11.50 or 1 Abitibi-Price $0.94 series F pref. sh. for each Barbecon cl. A or B sh. (see Abitibi-Price Inc.)

Barber-Ellis of Canada, Ltd. (Ont. 1931)
June 1, 1978 – Merged with wholly owned subsid., Gage Envelopes Ltd., to form a new co. Barbecon Inc. First pref. shs. of Barber exch. for first pref. shs. of Barbecon Cl. A & B shs. of Barber exch. for com. shs. of Barbecon.

Barber-Larder Gold Mines Ltd. (Ont. 1937)
Apr. 1942 – Name changed to New Barber-Larder Mines Ltd. ∎

Barbi Lake Copper Mines Ltd. (Ont. Feb. 9, 1956)
July 24, 1978 – Name changed to Bar Resources Limited. ∎

Barbican Financial Corp. (B.C. 1983)
Sept. 24, 2007 – Struck from register and dissolved.

Barbour, G. E. Company Limited (N.B. 1905)
Nov. 14, 1988 – Name changed to G. E. Barbour Inc.

Barcan Communications Inc. (Can. July 16, 1987 amalg.)
June 4, 1997 – Dissolved.

Barcelona Traction, Light & Power Co. (Can. 1911)
Dec. 16, 1980 – Dissolved.

Barclay Oil Co. Ltd. (Ont. 1952)
Mar. 8, 1954 – Name changed to Claybar Uranium & Oil Ltd. ∎

Barclay Oils Ltd. (Sask.)
1960 – Struck off register.

Barclay Resources Ltd. (Alta. 1952)
May 22, 1981 – Name changed to 14943 Alberta Ltd. ∎

Barclay Resources Ltd. (B.C. 1977)
Feb. 10, 1978 – Name changed to Bute Resources Inc. ∎

Barclays Advantaged Corporate Bond Fund (Ont. Jan. 29, 2004)
Nov. 1, 2006 – Name changed to BG Advantaged Corporate Bond Fund. ∎

Barclays Advantaged Equal Weighted Income Fund (Ont. Sept. 26, 2003)
Nov. 1, 2006 – Name changed to BG Advantaged Equal Weighted Income Fund. ∎

Barclays Advantaged S&P/TSX Income Trust Index Fund (Ont. Apr. 28, 2003)
Nov. 1, 2006 – Name changed to BG Advantaged S&P/TSX Income Trust Index Fund. ∎

Barclays Bank of Canada (Can. 1981)
Aug. 31, 1996 – Amalgamated with Hongkong Bank of Canada.

Barclays Income + Growth Split Trust (Ont. Mar. 29, 2004)
Nov. 1, 2006 – Name changed to BG Income + Growth Split Trust. ∎

Barclays Top 100 Equal Weighted Income Fund (Ont. Oct. 28, 2004)
Nov. 1, 2006 – Name changed to BG Top 100 Equal Weighted Income Fund. ∎

BarCode Holdings Limited (Alta. May 12, 1998)
May 27, 2005 – Name changed to iSCOPE INC. following acquisition of all of the assets of Sobrema (3841031 Canada Inc.). ∎

Bard Mining Corp. Ltd. (unknown)
1960 – Charter cancelled.

Bard Silver & Gold Ltd. (B.C. May 7, 1981)
May 14, 1999 – Name changed to Consolidated Bard Silver & Gold Ltd.; basis 1 new for 5 old shs. ∎

Bard Ventures Ltd. (B.C. May 7, 1981)
Oct. 14, 2020 – Name changed to St. James Gold Corp. (see FPsurvey - Mines & Energy)

Bardine Oils Ltd. (B.C. 1975)
July 24, 1992 – Dissolved and struck off register.

Bardyke Mines Ltd. (Ont. 1956)
Nov. 2, 1981 – Dissolved.

Barel Duc Mines Ltd. (Ont. 1950)
1953 – Name changed to Bar-Le-duc Chibougamau Mines Ltd. ∎

Baretta Mining Corporation Ltd. (Alta. 1976)
Oct. 23, 1981 – Amalgamated into American Chromium Limited; basis 1 cl. A voting sh. and 1 cl. B non-voting sh. for 1 old sh.

Barexor Minerals Inc. (Que. May 5, 1966)
May 5, 2000 – Struck off register.

Bargis Mines Limited (Ont. 1951)
Dec. 1957 – Charter cancelled.

Bargold Mines Limited (Ont. Aug. 8, 1945)
Jan. 2, 1970 – Name changed to Ontex Mining Limited; basis 1 new for 4 old shs. ∎

Bargold Resources Ltd. (B.C. May 14, 1996)
Nov. 7, 2000 – Name changed to Indusmin Energy Corporation and continued into Yukon. ∎

Barima Exploration Co. Ltd. (Ont. 1946)
1949 – Voluntarily liquidated. Charter surrendered.

Barima Minerals Ltd. (Ont. 1947)
Feb. 14, 1973 – Dissolved.

Barisan Gold Corporation (B.C. Jan. 25, 2011)
May 2, 2017 – Name changed to Lithion Energy Corp. following acquisition of Railroad Valley and Black Canyon lithium prospects in Nevada and Arizona, respectively; basis 1 new for 5 old shs. ∎

Barker Minerals Ltd. (B.C. Nov. 5, 1993)
Aug. 1, 2000 – Amalgamated in British Columbia to continue with same name. (see FPsurvey - Mines & Energy)

Barker Resources Ltd. (B.C. Jan. 8, 1973)
July 26, 1977 – Name changed to Nortek Engines Ltd. ∎

Barker's Bakeries, Ltd. (Ont. 1930)
July 31, 1945 – Shldrs. approved sale of co. to Canadian Food Products Ltd. for $506,215, and distribution of proceeds; basis $51.25 per sh. to pref. shldrs. and $5.00 per sh. to com.

Barkerville Gold Mines Ltd. (B.C. Feb. 12, 1970)
Nov. 25, 2019 – All o/s com. shs. not already held acquired by Osisko Gold Royalties Ltd.; basis 0.0357 Osisko com. shs. for 1 Barkerville com. sh. (see Osisko Gold Royalties Ltd.)

Barkerville Mining Co. Ltd. (NPL) (B.C. 1945)
Nov. 2, 1990 – Amalgamated with Austra Resources Corporation to form a new co. named Austar Resources Corporation; basis 1 new for 4 old shs. (see Austar Resources Corporation)

Barkhor Resources Inc. (B.C. Aug. 19, 1985)
Dec. 1, 1998 – Name changed to Latigo Resources Inc.; basis 1 new for 5 old shs. ∎

Barkley Valley Mines Ltd. (B.C. 1961)
July 22, 1974 – Struck off register.

Barksdale Capital Corp. (B.C. Jan. 13, 1981)
Mar. 3, 2020 – Name changed to Barksdale Resources Corp. (see FPsurvey - Mines & Energy)

Barmont Mines Ltd. (Que. 1946)
Oct. 1973 – Charter cancelled.

Barnat Mines Ltd. (Que. 1948)
Mar. 31, 1970 – Assets sold to Lake Shore Mines Ltd.; basis 1 new for 5 old shs.

Barolo Ventures Corp. (B.C. June 13, 2006)
Nov. 23, 2020 – Name changed to Osisko Development Corp. pursuant to reverse takeover acquisition of mineral interests and portfolio of marketable securities from Osisko Gold Royalties Ltd.; basis 1 new for 60 old shs. ∎

Baron Gold Corp. (B.C. Apr. 24, 1987)
Mar. 20, 1998 – Name changed to BG Baron Group Inc. ∎

Barons Oil Limited (Alta. Feb. 28, 1950)
Jan. 1, 1974 – Mineral Resources International Limited acquired 70% interest in 1988 for $24,400,000 through a cash takeover offer. Subsequently amalgamated with a wholly owned subsid. of Mineral Resources to continue as Barons Oil Limited which became 85% owned on the transfer of Mineral Resources oil and gas assets. (see Conwest Exploration Company Limited)
June 3, 1990 – Amalgamated with 413749 Alberta Limited, a wholly owned subsidiary of Conwest Exploration Company Limited; basis 1 cl. B sh. of Conwest for each 4 com. shs. of Barons. (see Conwest Exploration Company Limited)

Baroque Resources Ltd. (B.C. May 19, 1981)
Feb. 9, 1990 – Name changed to Greenfields Industries Inc.; basis 1 new for 5 old shs. ∎

Barra Resources Inc. (Alta. Jan. 3, 1997)
July 30, 1999 – All o/s com. shs. acquired by Gentry Resources Ltd.; basis 0.381 Gentry com. shs. for 1 Barra sh. (see Gentry Resources Ltd.)

Barracuda Resources Ltd. (B.C. 1983)
July 18, 1985 – Name changed to International Laser Tech Inc. ∎

Barramundi Gold Ltd. (B.C. June 20, 1995)
Feb. 2, 1996 – Continued into Yukon.
Sept. 27, 2002 – Continued into Canada.
Nov. 12, 2002 – Name changed to PacRim Resources Ltd.; basis 1 new for 10 old shs. ∎

Barranco Resources Corp. (B.C. Mar. 2, 2011)
Oct. 30, 2012 – Name changed to Goldeneye Resources Corp. pursuant to Qualifying Transaction acquisition of Goldeneye Resources Inc. (see FPsurvey - Mines & Energy)

Barrentier Mines Ltd. (unknown)
Aug. 17, 1954 – Assets acquired by Baranouri Uranium Mines Ltd.; basis 1 new for 10 old shs.

Barrian Mining Corp. (B.C. Apr. 27, 2018)
June 2, 2020 – Name changed to New Placer Dome Gold Corp.; basis 1 new for 2 old shs. ∎

The Barrick-Cullaton Gold Trust (Ont. 1984)
July 29, 1985 – Name changed to The Renabie Gold Trust. ∎

Barrick Gold Corporation (Ont. July 14, 1984 amalg.)
Nov. 27, 2018 – Continued into British Columbia.
May 6, 2025 – Name changed to Barrick Mining Corporation. (see FPsurvey - Mines & Energy)

Barrick Gold Inc. (Ont. Jan. 1, 1999)
Mar. 2, 2009 – Acquired by Barrick Gold Corporation; basis 0.53 Barrick shs. for 1 Barrick Gold exch. sh.

Barrick Resources Corporation (Ont. May 1, 1983 amalg.)
July 14, 1984 – Amalgamated with Camflo Mines Limited and Bob-Clare Investments Limited to form new co. with same name Barrick Resources Corporation; basis 7 new for 1 Camflo shs., 1 new for 1 Bob-Clare sh. and 1 new for 1 Barrick sh.
Dec. 9, 1985 – Name changed to American Barrick Resources Corporation; basis 1 new for 5 old shs. ∎

Barrier Mining Corp. (B.C. June 1, 1978)
May 31, 2001 – Delisted from the CDN. Subsequently struck from register and dissolved.

Barrier Reef Resources Ltd. (B.C. 1972 amalg.)
Sept. 18, 1984 – Name changed to Consolidated Barrier Reef Resources Ltd.; basis 1 new for 5 old shs. ∎

Barrier Technology Inc. (B.C. July 10, 1986)
Mar. 11, 1996 – Name changed to International Barrier Technology Inc.; basis 1 new for 10 old shs. ∎

Barriere Explorations Ltd. (B.C. July 22, 1966)
Dec. 12, 1974 – CTO issued by the BCSC. Subsequently dissolved,

Barriere Lake Minerals Ltd. (B.C. 1962)
July 1972 – Name changed to Geneva Resources Ltd. ∎

Barriere Lake Mines Ltd. (B.C. 1962)
1967 – Name changed to Barriere Lake Minerals Ltd.; basis 1 new for 10 old shs. ∎

Barrincorp Industries Inc. (Ont. 1986 amalg.)
Nov. 30, 1989 – Acquired by DBC Acquisition Corp., an affiliate of Dent & Company Inc. for $5.55 per sh.

Barringham Rubber & Plastics Ltd. (Ont. 1938)
1952 – Acquired by Monsanto Canada Ltd., which purchased all o/s shs.

Barringham Rubber Co. Ltd. (Ont. 1938)
Dec. 1946 – Name changed to Barringham Rubber & Plastics Ltd. ∎

Barrington Enterprises Limited (Alta. Apr. 23, 1987)
Sept. 16, 1994 – Name changed to Phonettix Intelecom Ltd.; basis 1 new for 4 old shs. ∎

Barrington Exploration Corporation Limited (Ont. 1964)
Mar. 1976 – Charter cancelled.

Barrington Lake Copper Mines Ltd. (Ont. 1946)
June 1955 – Wound up with distribution of assets to shldrs.

Barrington Petroleum Ltd. (B.C. July 27, 1982)
Aug. 16, 1985 – Continued into Alberta. (see Petrobank Energy and Resources Ltd.)
Aug. 21, 2001 – Amalgamated with Petrobank Energy and Resources Ltd.; basis $0.70 or 0.333 Petrobank shs. for 1 Barrington sh. Also $1,000 principal Barrington notes exchanged for $950 unsecured 9% subord. Petrobank notes maturing July 21, 2006; also 1 Petrobank wt. exercisable at $915 per wt. into $1,000 Petrobank notes until Sept. 17, 2001; and wts. to purchase up to 60 Petrobank com. shs. at $2.50 before Sept. 18, 2003. (see Petrobank Energy and Resources Ltd.)

Barrington Properties Ltd. (B.C. July 27, 1982)
Nov. 27, 1984 – Name changed to Barrington Petroleum Ltd. ∎

Barrington Properties Limited (Alta. Apr. 23, 1987)
Apr. 11, 1988 – Name changed to Barrington Enterprises Limited. ∎

Barris Klein Holdings Inc. (Ont. Apr. 29, 1980)
Mar. 15, 1991 – Name changed to London Strauss Capital Corp.; basis 1 new for 9 old shs. ∎

Barron Hunter Hargrave Strategic Resources Inc. (Can. Mar. 14, 1985 amalg.)
Sept. 11, 1985 – Amalgamated with Beaver Energy Resources Inc. to form new co. with same name Barron Hunter Hargrave Strategic Resources Inc.; basis 1 new for 3 Beaver shs.
Aug. 5, 1997 – Dissolved.

Barry Copper Mines Ltd. (Que. 1955)
Nov. 4, 1978 – Charter cancelled.

Barsand Resources Inc. (B.C. Jan. 7, 1981)
Aug. 30, 1990 – Name changed to Harvest-Spring Nutritional Systems (1981) Corporation following takeover bid of Harvest-Spring Nutritional Systems Inc. ∎

Barsele Minerals Corp. (B.C. Feb. 20, 2013)
Mar. 20, 2024 – Name changed to First Nordic Metals Corp. (see FPsurvey - Mines & Energy)

Bart Mines Ltd. (B.C. Sept. 23, 1969)
Apr. 22, 1983 – Dissolved and struck off register.

Bart Resources Ltd. (B.C. 1983)
May 12, 1988 – Name changed to Thermo Tech International Inc. pursuant to reverse takeover acquisition of H.A. Thermal Ltd. ∎

Bartaco Industries Limited (Ont. 1961)
Apr. 30, 1978 – Name changed to Redlaw Industries Inc. and continued into Ontario. (see FPsurvey - Industrials)

Bartizan Capital Corporation (Alta. June 11, 1998 amalg.)
Sept. 16, 2002 – Made an assignment into bankruptcy due to numerous creditor claims. Alger & Associates Inc. of Calgary appointed trustee.
June 2004 – All assets sold and no funds were available for shldrs.
Sept. 26, 2006 – Trustee had received provable claims totaling $1,764,595 with known claims totaling $14,234,403, while the company's assets totaled $2,823,626. At the meeting of creditors, the trustee received permission to sell the condominium project located in Regina, Sask., for $1,150,000 and was scheduled to close in December 2002. Proceeds, net of mortgage and costs, were expected to be between $200,000 and $250,000.
2006 – Trustee discharged.

Barton Bay Resources Inc. (Ont. May 7, 1997)
Sept. 29, 2007 – Dissolved and certificate of incorporation cancelled.

Barvallee Mines Limited (Que. 1951)
1971 – Shs. consolidated; basis 1 new for 5 old shs. New shs. exch. for Albarmont Mines Corp. shs.

Barvin Mines Ltd. (Que. 1951)
May 1974 – Charter cancelled.

Barvue Mines Ltd. (Ont. 1950)
1957 – Name changed to Manitou-Barvue Mines Limited; basis 1 new for 10 old shs. ∎

Barymin Co. Ltd. (Ont. 1934)
1961 – Each shldr. entitled to receive $2.00 and 1 new sh. of Barymin Explorations Ltd. for 1 old sh. distributed Barex Trust certificates to shldrs.; basis 1 new for 1 old sh.

Barytex Resources Corp. (B.C. July 12, 1965)
Nov. 23, 1992 – Name changed to International Barytex Resources Ltd.; basis 1 new for 4 old shs. ∎

Basaba Enterprises Inc. (B.C. 1985)
May 8, 1992 – Dissolved and struck off register.

Basalt Bay Mines Ltd. (Ont. 1949)
May 1976 – Charter cancelled.

Basalt Uranium and Exploration Co. (Ont. 1949)
1955 – Name changed to Basalt Bay Mines Ltd.; basis 1 new for 2 old shs. ∎

Basco Oil & Gas Co. Ltd. (B.C. 1952)
1959 – Acquired by Provo Gas Producers Ltd.; basis 1 new for 3 old shs.

Base Metals Mining Corp. Ltd. (Can. 1929)
Dec. 15, 1980 – Dissolved for failure to file continuance prior to.

Base Oil & Gas Ltd. (Alta. Mar. 28, 2006)
Sept. 20, 2011 – Name changed to Marquee Petroleum Ltd. ■

Baseline Mines Ltd. (Ont. 1954)
May 13, 1970 – Charter cancelled.

Bashaw Capital Corp. (Can. Dec. 13, 2004)
June 13, 2005 – Wholly owned subsid. amalgamated with Dynamite Resources Ltd., constituting Bashaw's Qualifying Transaction and a reverse takeover by Dynamite.
Mar. 27, 2006 – Name changed to Dynamite Resources Ltd. ■

Bashaw Holdings Ltd. (Alta. Dec. 2, 1993)
July 4, 1995 – Name changed to BlueStar Battery Systems International Corp. ■

Bashaw Leduc Oil & Gas Ltd. (Alta. 1951)
June 12, 1979 – Name changed to Canadian Bashaw Leduc Oil & Gas Limited; basis 1 new for 5 old shs. ■

Basic Lead & Zinc Mines Ltd. (Ont. 1958)
Sept. 2, 1963 – Dissolved.

Basic Minerals Ltd. (Sask. 1956)
1958 – Name changed to Basic Lead & Zinc Mines Ltd. and continued into Ontario. ■

Basic Realty Investment Corporation (Alta. May 8, 1996)
Oct. 23, 2000 – Name changed to Uni-Invest Ltd. following reverse takeover acquisition of Uni-Invest Canada Ltd.; basis 1 new for 5 old shs. ■

Basic Resources International Limited (Ont. 1968)
July 31, 1972 – All assets and undertakings sold to Basic Resources International S.A. of Luxembourg; basis 1 new for 1 old sh. (see Basic Resources International S.A.)

Basic Resources International S.A. (Luxembourg)
Jan. 9, 1984 – Name changed to Brisa International S.A.; basis 1 new for 10 old shs. ■

BasicGov Systems, Inc. (B.C. Feb. 3, 1988)
Sept. 30, 2010 – Name changed to Pedro Resources Ltd. pursuant to sale of all non-cash assets and the name BasicGov Systems, Inc. to 0887901 B.C. Ltd., a wholly owned subsid. of Pender Growth Fund (VCC) Inc. (see FPsurvey - Mines & Energy)

Basin-Jib Gold Mines Inc. (Ont. 1955)
1955 – Assets acquired by Basin-Jib Mines Ltd.

Basin Pete Resources Ltd. (B.C. 1981)
May 1, 1987 – Name changed to Gametek Systems Inc. (see FPsurvey - Industrials)

Basin Petroleum Ltd. (Ont. Feb. 1, 1950)
1961 – Acquired by Basin Oil Exploration Ltd.; basis 1 new for 20 old shs. (see Basin Oil Exploration Ltd.)

Basinview Energy Inc. (Alta. July 31, 1997)
Mar. 14, 2001 – Acquired by 905948 Alberta Ltd., wholly owned subsid. of Danoil Energy Ltd.; basis $1.15 per sh. (see Danoil Energy Ltd.)

Basinview Energy Limited (Alta. July 31, 1997)
Feb. 10, 2000 – Name changed to Basinview Energy Inc.; basis 1 new for 2 old shs. ■

Basis100 Inc. (Ont. Oct. 25, 1999 amalg.)
Sept. 8, 2004 – Amalgamated with indirect subsid. of First American Real Estate Solutions LLC; basis 1 redeemable pfd. sh. (immediately redeemed at $1.00 per sh.) for 1 Basis100 com. sh.

Baska Uranium Mines Ltd. (Sask. May 17, 1949)
1966 – Name changed to Norbaska Mines Limited; basis 1 new for 5 old shs. ■

Baslen Petroleums Limited (Ont. Dec. 11, 1964)
Sept. 25, 1972 – Name changed to International Baslen Enterprises Limited; basis 1 new for 4 old shs. (see FPsurvey - Mines & Energy)

Bass Capital Corp. (Alta. Nov. 16, 1995)
Jan. 19, 1998 – Name changed to Shear Minerals Ltd. following acquisition of 974134 N.W.T. Limited. ■

Bassett Ventures Inc. (B.C. Sept. 15, 1987)
June 25, 2007 – Name changed to Arris Resources Inc. ■

Bassique Mines Ltd. (Ont. 1946)
Aug. 1960 – Charter cancelled.

Bastien Inc. (Que. 1960)
Mar. 23, 1990 – Liquidation of assets began Mar. 23, 1990 and by completed. Nothing left for shldrs.

Bastion Resources Ltd. (B.C. Dec. 4, 2009)
May 23, 2012 – Name changed to Pan American Fertilizer Corp. pursuant to the amalgamation of Acclaro Mining Corporation with a wholly owned subsidiary of Bastion, constituting a reverse takeover by Acclaro; basis 1 new for 2.5 old shs. ■

Bastion Square Partners Inc. (B.C. Feb. 24, 2021)
Apr. 14, 2023 – Name changed to Aluula Composites Inc. pursuant to the Qualifying Transaction reverse takeover acquisition of (old) Aluula Composites Inc. (see FPsurvey - Industrials)

Bata Petroleums Ltd. (Sask. 1943)
Apr. 15, 1965 – Name changed to Bata Resources Ltd.; basis 1 new for 6 old shs. ■

Bata Resources Ltd. (Sask. 1943)
Dec. 1968 – Amalgamated with Stampede Oils Limited (2 new for 1 old) and Galaxy Copper Ltd. (2 new for 5 old) to form United Bata Resources Ltd.; basis 1 new for 1 old sh. (see United Bata Resources Limited)

Batavia Energy Corp. (Ont. May 17, 1965)
Feb. 18, 2011 – Name changed to Victory Gold Mines Inc. ■

Batch-River Gold Mines Ltd. (Ont. 1947)
Feb. 14, 1973 – Dissolved.

Batchawana Mines Ltd. (Ont. 1964)
July 1967 – Charter cancelled.

Batchawana Uranium Mines Ltd. (Ont. 1949)
Sept. 1961 – Charter cancelled.

Bates & Innes, Limited (Can. 1920)
Aug. 15, 1963 – Placed into bankruptcy. No distribution to shldrs.

Bathrooms Beautiful Canada Ltd. (Can. 1984)
Dec. 9, 1988 – Declared bankruptcy.
June 6, 1991 – All assets sold, all creditors paid and the co. was wound up.

Bathurst Gold Mines Ltd. (Ont. Apr. 20, 1934)
Feb. 25, 1937 – Shs. exchanged (1 new for 8 old) for Gleemar Gold Mines Ltd. (see Gleemar Gold Mines Ltd.)

Bathurst Inlet Mining Corporation Ltd. (B.C. 1968)
1969 – Assets acquired by Bathurst Norsemines Ltd.; basis 12 new for 10 old shs.

Bathurst Mining Corp. Ltd. (N.B. 1952)
1955 – Merged into Maritimes Mining Corp. Ltd.

Bathurst Norsemines Ltd. (B.C. Dec. 24, 1969)
Aug. 22, 1986 – Name changed to Etruscan Enterprises Limited; basis 1 new for 3 old shs. ■

Bathurst Paper Limited (Can. Feb. 3, 1928)
Dec. 30, 1988 – Dissolved.

Bathurst Power & Paper Co. Ltd. (Can. Feb. 3, 1928)
Mar. 31, 1965 – Name changed to Bathurst Paper Limited. ■

Bathwick Mines Ltd. (Ont. 1951)
1954 – Name changed to Farcroft Mines Ltd. ■

Batiscam Mines Ltd. (Ont. 1950)
1951 – Name changed to Dovercourt Mines Ltd. ■

Baton Broadcasting Incorporated (Ont. Aug. 11, 1971)
Jan. 4, 1999 – Name changed to CTV Inc. ■

Batorie Mines Ltd. (Ont. 1945)
Oct. 7, 1946 – Placed into bankruptcy.
1948 – Interim divd. of 5¢ on the dollar paid to creditors. Final divd. of 29.71¢ on dollar paid in 1948.

Battery & Wireless Solutions Inc. (Alta. Dec. 16, 1993)
June 2, 2008 – Struck from register and dissolved.

Battery Elements Corp. (B.C. Sept. 2, 2020)
June 29, 2022 – Name changed to Molten Metals Corp. (see FPsurvey - Mines & Energy)

Battery Metals Royalties Corp. (B.C. July 9, 2021)
Sept. 26, 2022 – Name changed to Oracle Commodity Holding Corp. (see FPsurvey - Mines & Energy; FPsurvey - Industrials)

Battery One, Inc. (Alta. Dec. 15, 1986)
Nov. 4, 1996 – Name changed to Power Plus Corporation; basis 1 new com. plus 1 rt. for 20 old com. shs. ■

Battery One-Stop Inc. (Alta. Dec. 15, 1986)
Dec. 29, 1994 – Name changed to Battery One, Inc. ■

Battery Road Capital Corp. (Can. Apr. 20, 2018)
Oct. 21, 2021 – Name changed to E-Tech Resources Inc. pursuant to the Qualifying Transaction acquisition of E-Tech Kalapuse Mining (Pty) Ltd.; basis 2 new for 1 old sh. (see FPsurvey - Mines & Energy)

Battery Technologies Inc. (Ont. Dec. 3, 1986)
Sept. 15, 1988 – Amalgamated in Ontario to continue with same name. (see FPsurvey - Industrials)

BatteryOne Royalty Corp. (B.C. July 20, 2018)
June 9, 2019 – Name changed to Nova Royalty Corp. ■

Battle Creek Developments Ltd. (Can. Apr. 29, 1987)
Mar. 31, 1988 – Continued into Canada. (see Strike Energy Inc.)
July 6, 1994 – Amalgamated with Strike Energy Inc. to form Strike Energy Inc.; basis 1.2 new for 1 Battle sh. (see Strike Energy Inc.)

Battle Energy Corp. (B.C. 1980)
Dec. 31, 1986 – Amalgamated with Tri-Star Resources Ltd. (1 for 5) to form United Tri-Star Resources Ltd.; basis 1 new for 21.35 old shs.

Battle Mountain Canada Ltd. (Ont. Dec. 31, 1968)
Jan. 11, 2001 – Plan of Arrangement with parent Battle Mountain Gold Company and Newmont Mining Corporation; basis 0.105 Newmont shs. exchanged for 1 old Battle Mountain Canada exch. sh.

Battle Mountain Gold Inc. (B.C. Aug. 20, 1979)
June 15, 2017 – All o/s com. shs. not already held acquired by Gold Standard Ventures Corp.; basis 0.1891 Gold Standard com. shs. plus 8¢ cash for 1 Battle Mountain sh. (see Gold Standard Ventures Corp.)

Battle North Gold Corporation (B.C. Mar. 4, 1996)
May 21, 2021 – Acquired by Evolution Mining Limited; basis $2.65 cash per sh.

Battle Plains Petroleum Limited (Ont. 1952)
Feb. 1954 – Assets acquired by Oil Selections Ltd.

Battle View Oils Ltd. (Ont. 1937)
1941 – Acquired by Vermillion Consolidated Oils Ltd.; basis 139 new for 1,000 old shs. (see Vermillion Consolidated Oils Limited)

Battlecreek Mines Ltd. (unknown)
Sept. 1974 – Name changed to Battlecreek Resources Ltd. ■

Battlecreek Resources Ltd. (unknown)
Address & status unknown.

Battlefield Minerals Corporation (Yuk. Dec. 6, 1995)
Nov. 21, 2001 – Name changed to BM Diamondcorp Inc.; basis 1 new for 7 old shs. ■

Battleford Capital Inc. (Alta. Jan. 5, 2005)
Nov. 18, 2005 – Formed Sahara Energy Ltd. in Alberta on Qualifying Transaction amalgamation with Captain Energy Inc. with Battleford the deemed acquiror. ■

Battrix Investments Ltd. (Alta. Mar. 15, 1984)
Mar. 9, 2004 – Name changed to MaxxCapp Corporation; basis 1 new for 2 old shs. ■

Bauer Performance Sports Ltd. (B.C. Dec. 2, 2010)
June 19, 2014 – Name changed to Performance Sports Group Ltd. ■

Bavarian Lion Industries Ltd. (B.C. Dec. 6, 1984)
Nov. 25, 1991 – Name changed to First West Canada Capital Corporation. ■

Baxter Energy Systems Corporation (unknown)
Dec. 31, 1981 – Amalgamated with Baxter Resources Corporation to form Baxter Technologies Corporation.

Baxter Resources Corporation (Ont. 1972 amalg.)
Dec. 31, 1981 – Amalgamated with Baxter Energy Systems Corporation to form Baxter Technologies Corporation.

Baxter Technologies Corporation (Can. 1981 amalg.)
June 27, 1985 – Name changed to Standard-Modern Technologies Corporation. ■

Bay-Adelaide Garage Ltd. (Can. - unspecified)
May 1968 – All bonds redeemed and $55 per sh. was distributed.
1969 – Wound up. Final pay. of approx. $19 per sh. made.

Bay Ann Resources Inc. (B.C. Mar. 19, 1980)
May 23, 1985 – Name changed to Zorah Media Corporation. ■

Bay Copper Mines Limited (Can. Dec. 8, 1955)
Dec. 31, 1984 – Wound up. Dissolved on Jan. 29, 1985.

Bay Equities Inc. (Alta. July 19, 1999)
Sept. 10, 2007 – Acquired by 1289167 Alberta Ltd.; basis 1 ser. A pref. sh. for 1 com. sh. redeemable for $0.32.

Bay Lake Gold Mines Ltd. (Ont. 1948)
Jan. 27, 1966 – Charter cancelled.

Bay Mills Limited (Can. 1944)
July 1987 – All o/s shs. acquired following an offer of $13 per sh. by CertainTeed Corp. for all shs. not already held.

Bay Resources Ltd. (B.C. 1986)
Apr. 19, 1990 – Name changed to Frecom Communications Company Inc. ■

Bay Ressources et Services Inc. (Que. 1960)
Jan. 2, 1992 – Amalgamated with Exploration Duverny Inc. (1 for 3.71), Monique Exploration Inc. (1 for 5.35) and private co. Ste-Geneviève Explorations (1991) Inc. to form a new co. named SEG Exploration Inc.; basis 1 new SEG sh. for 5.24 old Bay shs. (see SEG Exploration Inc.)

Bay Roc Mining Co. Ltd. (Ont. 1973)
Jan. 2, 1975 – Merged into Sandhurst Mines Ltd.; basis 1 new for 8 old shs.

Bay Street Systems Ltd. (B.C. Dec. 16, 1983)
Aug. 17, 1993 – Name changed to Pacific Bay Street Systems Ltd.; basis 1 new for 5 old shs. ■

Bay Talent Group Inc. (B.C. Jan. 10, 2018)
Apr. 21, 2020 – Name changed to Hire Technologies Inc. (see FPsurvey - Industrials)

Baycourse Mines Ltd. (Ont. 1955)
1964 – Name changed to Prairie Potash Mines Ltd.

Bayfield Petroleum Company Limited (Ont. 1953)
Oct. 5, 1959 – Dissolved.

Bayfield Ventures Corp. (B.C. Dec. 8, 1986)
Jan. 5, 2015 – Acquired by New Gold Inc.; basis 0.0477 Bayfield com. shs. for 1 Bayfield com. sh.
Jan. 5, 2015 – Name changed to New Gold Bayfield Corp.

Bayfor Corporation Inc. (Ont. 1972 amalg.)
Feb. 20, 1980 – Dissolved.

Bayland Mines Ltd. (B.C. 1967)
Mar. 13, 1970 – Name changed to Texacal Resources Ltd. ■

Bayonne Mine Ltd. (B.C. 1962)
Sept. 14, 1972 – Dissolved and struck off register.

Bayou Bend Petroleum Ltd. (B.C. Dec. 29, 2006)
Oct. 21, 2009 – Name changed to ShaMaran Petroleum Corp. (see FPsurvey - Mines & Energy)

Bayridge Developments Ltd. (B.C. July 15, 1986)
Dec. 15, 1995 – Dissolved and struck off register.

Bayshore Floating Rate Senior Loan Fund (Ont. Mar. 30, 2005)
Mar. 26, 2009 – Liquidated.

Bayshore Petroleum Corp. (Alta. Oct. 22, 2003)
Feb. 18, 2022 – Name changed to Infinitum Copper Corp. pursuant to the reverse takeover acquisition of (old) Infinitum Copper Corp. (renamed Infinitum Copper Mining Corp.); basis 1 new for 20 old shs. ■

Bayside Capital Corporation (Alta. Dec. 22, 1994)
June 18, 1997 – Formed Pearl River Holdings Limited in Canada following reverse takeover acquisition of and amalgamation with Pearl River Holdings Limited; basis 1 new for 2 old shs. (see FPsurvey - Industrials)

Baystate Developments Ltd. (Ont. 1965)
July 1969 – Amalgamated with Select Leased Property Finance Ltd. to form Select Properties Ltd.; basis 21 new for 2 old shs.

Bayswater Uranium Corporation (B.C. Aug. 15, 2006 amalg.)
July 24, 2007 – Amalgamated with wholly owned subsid. of Kilgore Minerals Ltd. to form Bayswater Holdings Inc. and Kilgore changed its name to Bayswater Uranium Corporation; basis 1.25 new for 1 Kilgore sh. and 1 new for 1 Bayswater sh.
June 12, 2018 – Name changed to Green Thumb Industries Inc. following reverse takeover acquisition of VCP23, LLC.; basis 1 new for 10 old shs. (see FPsurvey - Industrials)

Bayswater Ventures Corp. (B.C. June 26, 1979)
Aug. 15, 2006 – Formed Bayswater Uranium Corporation in British Columbia on amalgamation with Pathfinder Resources Ltd. with Bayswater the deemed acquiror; basis 0.588 new for 1 Pathfinder sh. and 1 new for 1 Bayswater sh. ■

Baytex Energy Ltd. (Alta. June 3, 1993)
Oct. 29, 1997 – Merged with Dorset Exploration Ltd. (0.48 for 1) to form a new company also known as Baytex Energy Ltd.; basis 1 new Baytex for 1 old Baytex sh. (see Baytex Energy Ltd.)

Baytex Energy Ltd. (Alta. June 3, 1993)
Oct. 21, 1997 – Amalgamated in Alberta to continue with same name. (see Baytex Energy Trust)
Sept. 8, 2003 – Converted into Baytex Energy Trust with new company Crew Energy Inc.; basis either a) 1 new trust unit plus 1/3 new Crew sh., or b) 1 new Baytex Acquisition Corp. exch. sh. plus 1/3 new Crew sh., or c) a combination thereof. (see Baytex Energy Trust)

Baytex Energy Trust (Alta. July 24, 2003)
Dec. 31, 2010 – Succeeded by Baytex Energy Corp. pursuant to plan of arrangement whereby Baytex Energy Corp. was formed to facilitate the conversion of the trust into a corporation and the trust was subsequently dissolved. (see FPsurvey - Mines & Energy)

Bayview M Company Limited (Ont. 1953)
Oct. 5, 1959 – Dissolved.

Bayview Public Ventures Inc. (Ont. Dec. 21, 2005)
Sept. 22, 2008 – Name changed to Catch the Wind Ltd. and continued into Delaware pursuant to Qualifying Transaction reverse takeover acquisition of Catch the Wind, Inc.; basis 1 new for 4.99 old shs. ■

Bayview Red Lake Gold Mines Ltd. (Ont. 1944)
1947 – Assets acquired by Red Poplar Gold Mines Ltd.; basis 1 new for 3 old shs.

Bayview Resources Ltd. (B.C. 1980)
May 29, 1984 – Name changed to Alamo Developments Ltd.; basis 1 new for 2 old shs. ■

BayWest Capital Equities Corp. (Can. Dec. 10, 1981)
May 10, 1990 – Name changed to Diversified Baywest Capital Corp.; basis 1 new for 7.5 old shs. ■

Baz Resources Inc. (B.C. 1983)
Apr. 2, 1985 – Name changed to Chopp Computer Corporation Inc. ■

Bazeldo Mines Ltd. (Ont. 1963)
Oct. 20, 1977 – Dissolved.

Bazooka Mines Ltd. (Que. 1945)
Dec. 1979 – Charter cancelled.

bcMetals Corporation (Alta. May 10, 2001)
Mar. 21, 2007 – Acquired indirectly by Imperial Metals Corporation; basis $1.70 per sh. plus $0.02 for any options and warrants still outstanding.

Beach Gold Mines Ltd. (B.C. 1972)
May 17, 1983 – Name changed to Perron Gold Mines Ltd.; basis 1 new for 2 old shs. ■

Beacher Oil and Gas Ltd. (unknown)
1955 – Liquidated.

Beacon Acquisition Partners Inc. (Can. Mar. 13, 2007)
Jan. 9, 2017 – Dissolved and struck from register.

Beacon Energy Corporation (Alta. 1989)
Nov. 14, 1990 – Amalgamated with Copperwood Exploration Ltd. (0.6083 for 1) to form a new co. named Consolidated Beacon Resources Ltd.; basis 0.5348 new for 1 old sh. (see Consolidated Beacon Resources Ltd.)

Beacon Mining Co. Ltd. (Que. 1941)
Feb. 22, 1977 – Amalgamated with Pickle Crow Explorations Ltd. (1 for 5), Cariboo-Bell Copper Mines Ltd. (1 for 9), Abex Mines Ltd. (1 for 50) and Highland Mercury Mines Ltd. (1 for 5) to form Highland-Crow Resources Ltd.; basis 1 new for 40 old shs.

Beacon Natural Gas Synd. (unknown 1933)
Oct. 1, 1946 – Wound up. Property sold to Perry L. Jackson, Dunnville, Ont.

Beacon Petroleums Ltd. (Alta. 1937)
Jan. 1961 – Name changed to Beacon Placers Ltd.; basis 1 new for 10 old shs. ■

Beacon Placers Ltd. (Alta. 1937)
Oct. 31, 1968 – Struck off register.

Beacon Resources Inc. (Alta. Jan. 16, 2002)
Sept. 2, 2016 – Struck from the registry and dissolved.

BeaconEye Inc. (Can. Nov. 21, 1995)
Apr. 28, 1998 – Acquired by TLC The Laser Center Inc. for $1.50 per sh. (see TLC The Laser Center Inc.)

Beamscope Canada Inc. (Ont. May 7, 1982)
Sept. 2000 – Sold its computer hardware and software division assets to Ingram Micro Inc. for approx. $20,000,000.
Oct. 2000 – Prior agreement to sell the video entertainment and Laing branded products businesses to Navarre Corporation was terminated.
Nov. 15, 2000 – Granted a stay under the CCAA and Ernst & Young Inc. was appointed monitor. The stay was extended several times to Mar. 16, 2001.
Dec. 2000 – Sold certain assets of its direct-to-home Bell ExpressVu satellite system distribution business to Jonic International Inc. for approx. $30,000,000.
Mar. 15, 2001 – All directors and officers had resigned and the principal secured lender applied to the Ontario Superior Court to appoint a receiver.
Mar. 19, 2001 – Court appointed Ernst & Young Inc. as the receiver/manager.
May 2005 – No funds available for shldrs.
Oct. 13, 2005 – Receiver discharged.

Beanland Mining Co. Ltd. (Ont. 1937)
1950 – Name changed to Clenor Mining Company Ltd.; basis 1 new for 2 old shs. ■

Beano Gold Mines Ltd. (B.C. 1938)
Oct. 1956 – Charter cancelled.

Beanstalk Capital Corporation (B.C. July 6, 2000)
Sept. 5, 2002 – Name changed to Compliance Energy Corporation following Qualifying Transaction reverse takeover acquisition of Compliance Coal Corporation; basis 1 new for 2 old shs. ■

Beanstalk Capital Inc. (B.C. June 12, 2008)
July 27, 2011 – Name changed to Gold Mountain Mining Corp. pursuant to Qualifying Transaction acquisition of Elk gold prospect. ■

Beanstalk Capital Ltd. (B.C. Apr. 20, 2006)
Dec. 31, 2007 – Name changed to iCo Therapeutics Inc. following Qualifying Transaction reverse takeover acquisition of iCo Therapeutics Inc. and amalgamation of iCo with wholly owned 4448073 Canada Inc. (renamed iCology Corporation); basis 1 new for 2.8 old shs. ■

Bear Creek Energy Ltd. (Alta. Jan. 12, 1995)
Jan. 20, 2005 – Plan of Arrangement with Ketch Resources Ltd. to convert to a new income trust named Ketch Resources Trust and 2 new exploration cos. named Kereco Energy Ltd. and Bear Ridge Resources Ltd.; basis 0.5 new trust unit plus, either 0.2 new Kereco sh. or $0.54 plus, either 0.2 new Bear Ridge sh. or $0.245 for 1 old Bear Creek cl. A com. sh. (see Bear Ridge Resources Ltd.; Kereco Energy Ltd.; Ketch Resources Trust)

Bear Creek Gold Mines Ltd. (Que. 1971)
Sept. 22, 1972 – Name changed to International Video Cassette Systems Inc.

Bear Creek Mining Corporation (Yuk. Nov. 14, 2002)
July 16, 2004 – Continued into British Columbia. (see FPsurvey - Mines & Energy)

Bear Exploration & Radium Ltd. (Ont. June 6, 1932)
1948 – Merged assets with Yellowknife Gold Mines Ltd. to form Yellowknife Bear Mines Limited; basis 6 new for 10 old shs. (see Yellowknife Bear Mines Limited) Wound up. (see Yellowknife Bear Mines Limited)

Bear International Industries Ltd. (B.C. 1961)
Feb. 1972 – Name changed to Consolidated Bear Industries Ltd.; basis 1 new for 5 old shs. ■

Bear Lake Gold Ltd. (Ont. July 19, 1996)
May 27, 2014 – Acquired by Kerr Mines Inc.; basis 1.4 Kerr units (1 com. sh. & ½ wt.) for 1 Bear Lake sh. (see Arizona Gold Corp.)
Sept. 2, 2021 – Name changed to Bear Creek Gold Ltd. (see Arizona Gold Corp.)

Bear Lake Mines Ltd. (Can. 1928)
Dec. 16, 1980 – Dissolved for failure to file articles of continuance.

Bear Lake Resources Ltd. (B.C. May 13, 1985)
Apr. 17, 1990 – Name changed to Consolidated Bear Lake Resources Ltd.; basis 1 new for 3 old shs. ■

Bear Ridge Resources Ltd. (Alta. Dec. 14, 2004)
Aug. 24, 2007 – Acquired by Sabretooth Energy Ltd.; basis 0.525 Sabretooth com. sh. or 0.282 Sabretooth com. sh. plus $0.973 for each Bear com. sh. (see Sabretooth Energy Ltd.)

Bearcat Explorations Ltd. (B.C. 1969)
Aug. 22, 1979 – Continued into Alberta.
Aug. 23, 2004 – PricewaterhouseCoopers Inc. was appointed receiver, manager and trustee.
Jan. 12, 2006 – PricewaterhouseCoopers received approval from the Alberta court for the sale of all the assets. There would be no distrib. to creditors or shldrs.

Beardmore Resources Ltd. (B.C. 1986)
Aug. 27, 1993 – Dissolved and struck off register.

Bearing Lithium Corp. (B.C. Jan. 13, 2011)
Dec. 28, 2022 – Acquired by Lithium Power International Limited; basis 0.7 Lithium Power ordinary shs. for 1 Bearing com. sh.

Bearing Power (Canada) Limited (Ont. 1992 amalg.)
May 12, 1998 – Acquired by Wajax Industrial Components Ltd., a subsid. of Wajax Limited, for $1.40 per sh. (see Wajax Limited)

Bearing Resources Ltd. (B.C. Jan. 13, 2011)
May 10, 2017 – Name changed to Bearing Lithium Corp. ■

Bearn Gold Mines Ltd. (Que. 1950)
Aug. 26, 1978 – Charter cancelled.

Beartooth Platinum Corporation (Yuk. Aug. 17, 2001)
July 19, 2004 – Continued into Ontario.
July 17, 2009 – Formed Kria Resources Ltd. in Ontario pursuant to reverse takeover acquisition of and amalgamation with Kria Resources Inc.; basis 1 new for 20 old shs. ■

Beatrice Mining Co. Ltd. (B.C. 1954)
Apr. 2, 1964 – Dissolved.

Beatrice Red Lake Mines Ltd. (Ont. 1945)
1962 – Name changed to Interprovincial Dredging & Mining Co. Ltd.; basis 1 new for 5 old shs. ■

Beatrix Ventures Inc. (B.C. Oct. 28, 2009)
Sept. 11, 2013 – Name changed to Emerge Resources Corp. ■

Beattie-Duquesne Mines Ltd. (Que. 1951)
June 1972 – Name changed to Donchester-Duquesne Mines Ltd.; basis 1 new for 20 old shs. ■

Beattie Gold Mines Ltd. (Can. Dec. 28, 1931)
1937 – Continued into Quebec.
Sept. 1946 – Name changed to Consolidated Beattie Mines Ltd.; basis 1 new for 2 old shs. ■

Beatty Bros. Limited (Can. 1912)
June 16, 1970 – Amalgamated with its 69% owned subsid. GSW Limited to continue as GSW Limited; basis 10 com. shs. of Beatty for 11 cl. A com. and 22 cl. B com. shs. of GSW.

Beau Canada Exploration Ltd. (Can. May 14, 1981)
Nov. 4, 1993 – Amalgamated with Belmoral Mines Ltd. to form new co. with same name Beau Canada Exploration Ltd.; basis 1 new for 18.75 Belmoral shs. and 1 new for 1 Beau sh. (see Beau Canada Exploration Ltd.)

Beau Canada Exploration Ltd. (Can. May 14, 1981)
Nov. 13, 2000 – Acquired by Murphy Acquisition Corp., a wholly owned subsid. of U.S.-based Murphy Oil Corporation, for $2.15 per sh.

Beau Chibougamau Mines Ltd. (Ont. 1950)
1961 – Merged into Amalgamated Beau-Belle Mines Ltd.

Beau Pete Gold Mines Ltd. (Ont. 1944)
May 1958 – Charter cancelled.

Beau Pre Explorations Ltd. (B.C. Jan. 3, 1980)
June 30, 2008 – Dissolved and struck from register.

Beau Rand Gold Mines Ltd. (Ont. 1946)
Aug. 18, 1958 – Charter cancelled.

Beau Val Mines Ltd. (B.C. Mar. 30, 1983)
Jan. 16, 1991 – Name changed to Bullion Reef Resources Ltd.; basis 1 new for 3 old shs. ■

Beaubran Canagex Inc. (P.E.I. 1947)
Dec. 28, 1984 – Name changed to Beaubran Inc. ■

Beaubran Corporation (P.E.I. 1947)
Apr. 30, 1980 – Name changed to Beaubran Canagex Inc. following acquisition of the net assets of Canadgex Fund for 1,838,108 shs. ■

Beaubran Inc. (P.E.I. 1947)
Jan. 27, 1986 – Name changed to Timvest Growth Fund Inc. ■

Beaucage Mines Ltd. (Ont. 1953)
1958 – Name changed to Nova Beaucage Mines Limited; basis 1 new for 5 old shs. ■

Beaucamp Yellowknife Mines Ltd. (Ont. 1945)
1947 – Sold assets to Aurlando Consolidated Mining Corp. Ltd.; basis 1 new for 5 old shs.
Mar. 1957 – Charter cancelled.

Beauce Investments inc. (Que. Sept. 24, 2004)
Sept. 20, 2005 – Formed Novik Inc. in Quebec pursuant to Qualifying Transaction reverse takeover acquisition of and amalgamation with Novik Inc. ■

Beauchamps Exploration Inc. (B.C. Nov. 17, 1986)
Sept. 19, 2003 – Struck from the register and dissolved for failure to file.

Beauchance Mines Ltd. (Ont. 1945)
Oct. 11, 1965 – Dissolved.

Beauchastel Copper Mines Ltd. (Que. June 1, 1967)
Feb. 14, 2016 – Struck from registry and dissolved.

Beaucoeur Yellowknife Mines Ltd. (Ont. 1946)
Nov. 1961 – Charter cancelled.

Beaucoup Resources Ltd. (B.C. Apr. 8, 1981)
July 28, 1987 – Continued into Canada.
Sept. 13, 1988 – Name changed to BCU Industries Inc. ■

Beaucourt Gold Mines (Que. 1936)
June 1948 – Shldrs. received 52 shs. Beaucon Mining Co. for each 100 shs. Beaucourt. Charter surrendered February 1950.

Beaudega Mines Ltd (Ont. 1943)
Nov. 1961 – Charter cancelled.

Beaudelaire Mines Ltd. (Ont. 1945)
1961 – Charter cancelled.

Beaufield Consolidated Resources Inc. (B.C. May 6, 1980)
May 25, 2006 – Name changed to Beaufield Resources Inc.; basis 1 new for 10 old shs. ■

Beaufield Resources Inc. (B.C. May 6, 1980)
Oct. 14, 1992 – Name changed to Beaufield Consolidated Resources Inc.; basis 1 new for 10 old shs. ■

Beaufield Resources Inc. (B.C. May 6, 1980)
Apr. 4, 2013 – Continued into Canada. (see Osisko Mining Inc.)
Oct. 23, 2018 – Acquired by Osisko Mining Inc.; basis 0.0482 Osisko com. shs. for 1 Beaufield com. sh. (see Osisko Mining Inc.)
Dec. 20, 2018 – Continued into Ontario. (see Osisko Mining Inc.)

Beaufor Mining Corp. (Que. July 1935)
1939 – Merged into Cournor Mining Co. Ltd.; basis 74 new for 100 old shs.

Beaufort Energy Limited (B.C. Apr. 20, 1979)
Feb. 13, 1998 – Name changed to Venstone Ventures Corp.; basis 1 new for 3 old shs. ■

Beaufort Exploration Limited (Can. 1977)
Dec. 17, 1996 – All o/s cl. A com. and cl. A pref. shs. acquired by Equisure Financial Network Inc.; basis $0.5266567 per cl. A com. or cl. A pref. sh. (see Equisure Financial Network Inc.)

Beaufort Hills Resources Inc. (Ont. July 17, 1998 amalg.)
Nov. 11, 1999 – Name changed to InterRent Properties Ltd. following reverse takeover acquisition of InterRent Properties Inc.; basis 1 new for 3 old shs. ■

Beaufort Petroleum Investment Limited (Can. Dec. 13, 1978)
Feb. 22, 1996 – Name changed to gronArctic Energy Inc. ■

Beauharnois Light, Heat & Power Company (Que. 1904)
Apr. 5, 1944 – Properties were expropriated by the Province of Quebec and control was taken over by Quebec-Hydro.
Mar. 1, 1947 – Bonds redeemed.
Mar. 16, 1953 – Arbitration board awarded shldrs. $15,502,909 plus int. from Apr. 15, 1944, to May 1953 (aggregating $31.49 per sh.), less expenses of 5.28¢ per sh. Payment made through Montreal Trust Company of Montreal. Unconverted shs. of Beauharnois Power Corp. (exchanged in 1940; basis 1 new for 2 com., or 1 new for 2 cl. A), could also be cashed.

Beaulieu Yellowknife Mines Limited (Ont. 1945)
1949 – Name changed to Consolidated Beaulieu Mines Ltd.; basis 1 new for 5 old shs. ■

Beaument Oils, Ltd. (Can. 1929)
Assets sold to Gold Standard Oils for 145,000 shs.

Beaumont Mining Corp. Ltd. (Que. 1954)
Aug. 1973 – Charter cancelled.

Beaumont Resources Ltd. (B.C. Feb. 20, 1961)
June 1973 – Name changed to Consolidated Beaumont Resources Ltd.; basis 1 new for 5 old shs. ■

Beaumont Select Corporations Inc. (Alta. Dec. 19, 1986)
Oct. 21, 2014 – Privatized; basis $2.05 cash per cl. A sh.

Beaunorm Mines Ltd. (Ont. 1946)
Mar. 11, 1957 – Charter cancelled.

Beaupas Mines Ltd. (Que. 1951)
Aug. 13, 1977 – Dissolved.

Beauport Goldfields Ltd. (Ont. 1949)
Mar. 1960 – Charter cancelled.

Beauport Holdings Ltd. (Can. 1957)
Mar. 20, 1972 – Name changed to Beauport Investors Ltd.; basis 1 new for 5 old shs. ■

Beauport Investors Ltd. (Can. 1957)
Dec. 16, 1980 – Dissolved.

Beaupre Base Metals Mines Ltd. (Ont. 1950)
Oct. 15, 1969 – Charter cancelled.

Beauregard Yellowknife Mines Ltd. (Ont. 1945)
Apr. 9, 1953 – Charter cancelled.

Beauriv Yellowknife Mines Ltd. (Ont. 1945)
Apr. 21, 1958 – Charter cancelled.

Beauty Counselors International Inc. (Ont. Aug. 30, 1945)
Jan. 12, 1989 – Name changed to Century Technologies Inc.; basis 1 new for 5 old shs. ■

Beauty Counselors of Canada Ltd. (Can. 1938)
May 22, 1968 – Acquired by Dart Industries Inc. for US$5.12 per sh. Name subsequently changed to Beauty Counselors International Inc.

Beauverny Gold Mines Ltd. (Que. 1945)
Dec. 15, 1959 – Charter cancelled.

Beaver Air Conditioning Ltd. (Ont. 1960)
1969 – Amalgamated to form Beaver Engineering Ltd.

Beaver Energy Resources Inc. (Can. 1977)
Sept. 11, 1985 – Amalgamated with Barron Hunter Hargrave Strategic Resources Inc. to continue under the Barron Hunter name; basis 1 new for 3 old sh. (see Barron Hunter Hargrave Strategic Resources Inc.)

Beaver Engineering Limited (Ont. 1969 amalg.)
Mar. 1, 1978 – Amalgamated with Beaver Executive Holdings Ltd. to form Beaver Engineering Ltd. Shs. not tendered under the original offer of $6.25 per sh. were converted into special shs. subsequently called for redemption at $6.25 per sh., on Mar. 9, 1978.

Beaver Gold Resources Inc. (B.C. Apr. 25, 1978)
Sept. 9, 1982 – Name changed to Beaver Resources Inc. ■

Beaver Hill Lake Uranium Mines Limited (Ont. 1973)
Apr. 10, 1976 – Amalgamated with New Force Crag Mines Limited (1 for 1) and Crow River Gold Mines Inc. (0.6 for 1) to continue as New Force Crag Mines Limited; basis 0.75 new for 1 old sh.

Beaver Lake Energy Corporation (Ont. July 12, 1991)
Feb. 23, 1993 – Continued into Alberta.
Apr. 1, 1996 – Formed Beaver Lake Resources Corporation on amalgamation with wholly owned CAPCO Resource Properties Ltd. ■

Beaver Lake Resources Corporation (Alta. Feb. 23, 1993)
Sept. 13, 1999 – All o/s com. shs. acquired by Greka Energy Corporation; basis 1 Greka Energy sh. for 74.4 Beaver shs.

Beaver Lodge Mines Ltd. (B.C. 1951)
Oct. 1962 – Name changed to Western Beaver Lodge Mines Ltd.; basis 1 new for 3 old shs. ■

Beaver Lodge Uranium Mines Ltd. (B.C. 1951)
Apr. 1959 – Name changed to Beaver Lodge Mines Ltd. ■

Beaver Mines Ltd. (B.C. 1966)
Jan. 31, 1977 – Dissolved.

Beaver Mining Corp. (Que. 1971)
Dec. 1977 – Charter cancelled.

Beaver Oil & Gas Ltd. (unknown)
Aug. 1953 – Assets acquired by Castle Oil & Gas Ltd., for 652,345 shs.

Beaver Resources Inc. (B.C. Apr. 25, 1978)
July 6, 1992 – Delisted from the Toronto Stock Exchange. Subsequently struck from register and dissolved.

Beaver Silver Mines, Ltd. (B.C. 1926)
1943 – Liquidating divd. of 3¢ per sh. paid.
Jan. 21, 1965 – Struck off register.

Beaverbridge Mines Ltd. (Ont. 1965)
Mar. 1976 – Charter cancelled.

Beaverhead Resources Ltd. (Alta. 1979)
1980 – Continued into British Columbia.
Dec. 31, 1986 – Amalgamated with 3 other cos. to form International Interlake Industries Inc.; basis 1 new for 11.95 old shs.

Beaverhouse Lake Gold Mines Ltd. (Ont. 1935)
1950 – Name changed to Lake Beaverhouse Mines Ltd.; basis 2 new for 5 old shs. ■

Beavermouth Dredging Co. Ltd. (B.C. 1946)
1950 – Dissolved.

Beck Electric Manufacturing Company Limited (Ont. Oct. 26, 1954)
Aug. 28, 1972 – Name changed to Noma Industries Limited. ■

Becker Gold Mines Ltd. (Ont. Nov. 30, 1944)
Jan. 15, 2007 – Continued into British Columbia.
Jan. 6, 2012 – Name changed to Sonoro Metals Corp. ■

The Becker Milk Company Limited (Ont. Feb. 20, 1957)
May 1, 1988 – Amalgamated in Ontario to continue with same name. (see FPsurvey - Industrials)

Beckett Technologies Corp. (Ont. May 10, 1994)
June 12, 1998 – Equipment and intellectual property assets acquired by Fort James Corporation for an undisclosed amount. (see FPsurvey - Industrials)

Becnite Mines Ltd. (Ont. 1949)
Feb. 1958 – Charter cancelled.

Bedford Capital Financial Corp. (Liberia May 1, 1984)
June 26, 1998 – All o/s cl. B subord. vtg. shs. redeemed for $2.75 per sh.

Bedford Porcupine Gold Mines Ltd. (Ont. 1940)
1951 – Charter cancelled.

Bedford Software Limited (B.C. Oct. 2, 1983)
July 7, 1989 – Name changed to Stratford Software Corporation. ■

Bedrocan Cannabis Corp. (Ont. Sept. 11, 2012)
Sept. 1, 2015 – Acquired by Tweed Marijuana Inc.; basis 0.465 Tweed com. shs. for 1 Bedrocan sh. (see Tweed Marijuana Inc.)

Bedrock Resources Ltd. (B.C. 1982)
Dec. 31, 1984 – Name changed to Talemon Investments Ltd. ■

Bee & Vee Gold Mines Ltd. (Can. 1936)
Dec. 16, 1980 – Dissolved.

Bee Lake Mines Ltd. (Ont. 1945)
1952 – Charter cancelled; no equity.

Beech Petroleum Corp. (B.C. 1978)
July 6, 1979 – Name changed to Pilgrim Petroleum Inc. ■

Beecher Energy, Ltd. (B.C. Oct. 30, 1987)
Dec. 4, 1995 – Name changed to Rising Phoenix Development Group Ltd. ■

Beermaster Distributors Ltd. (B.C. 1959)
Mar. 1977 – Name changed to Sunatco Development Corporation; basis 1 new for 5 old shs. ■

Beetz Explorations Limited (Ont. 1977)
Dec. 5, 1980 – Amalgamated with Goldsec Explorations Ltd. to form Consolidated Goldsec Explorations Ltd.; basis 1 new for 5 old shs.

Begama Technologies Inc. (Can. Jan. 11, 2002)
Jan. 13, 2003 – Name changed to Victhom Human Bionics Inc. following Qualifying Transaction acquisition of Victhom Corporation. ■

Behaviour Communications Inc. (Can. Aug. 16, 1993)
Dec. 4, 2000 – Name changed to MDP Worldwide Entertainment Inc. ■

Beijing Marvel Cleansing Supplies Co. Ltd. (B.C. Dec. 31, 1986)
Feb. 4, 2009 – Name changed to Brand Marvel Worldwide Consumer Products Corporation. ■

Beirut Mining Co. Ltd. (Ont. 1953)
Mar. 1959 – Dissolved.

Bekeen Computer Corp. (Ont. 1962)
Jan. 3, 1995 – Delisted from the CDN. Subsequently dissolved and charter cancelled.

Bel-Air Resources Ltd. (B.C. Jan. 21, 1980)
Aug. 22, 1985 – Name changed to Consolidated Bel-Air Resources Ltd.; basis 1 new for 4 old shs. ∎

Bel Pac Industries Ltd. (B.C. 1983)
Nov. 5, 1993 – Dissolved and struck off register.

BelAir Energy Corporation (Alta. Oct. 31, 1997 amalg.)
Sept. 9, 2003 – Plan of Arrangement acquisition by Purcell Energy Ltd.; basis $0.10 plus 0.354 new Purcell com. sh. for 1 old BelAir com. sh. (see Purcell Energy Ltd.)

Belair Mines Inc. (Que. 1971)
Aug. 17, 1985 – Charter cancelled.

Belcarra Explorations Ltd. (B.C. 1966)
Apr. 4, 1978 – Name changed to Karin Lake Explorations Ltd.; basis 1 new for 5 old shs. (see FPsurvey - Mines & Energy)

Belcarra Motors Corp. (B.C. June 24, 1986)
Sept. 10, 1997 – Name changed to Predator Ventures Ltd. ∎

Belcarra Resources Ltd. (B.C. June 24, 1986)
Oct. 5, 1994 – Name changed to Belcarra Motors Corp. ∎

Belcher Iron Ores Ltd. (Ont. 1953)
1955 – Name changed to Vulcan Mines Ltd. ∎

Belcher Mining Corporation Ltd. (Ont. Nov. 4, 1932)
1970 – Merged into Little Long Lac Mines Ltd.; basis 2 new for 9 old shs.

Belcher's Island Iron Mines Ltd. (unknown)
Aug. 1965 – Charter cancelled.

Belcourt Gold Mines Ltd. (Que. 1946)
May 1974 – Charter cancelled.

Belcroft Radium Mines Ltd. (Ont. 1926)
Feb. 25, 1965 – Dissolved.

Belding-Corticelli Inc. (Can. 1911)
Apr. 22, 1982 – Placed into receivership.
Aug. 17, 1982 – Name changed to Marlen Univest Inc. ∎

Belding-Corticelli Limited (Can. 1911)
Aug. 1, 1979 – Name changed to Belding-Corticelli Inc. ∎

Beleave Inc. (Ont. Jan. 31, 2000)
Aug. 2020 – Assets in London, Ont., sold and proceeds used to repay secured creditors in full.
Oct. 2020 – Sale of substantially all of the assets to Wayne Patrick Consumer Products Ltd. was completed. Assets included sale of the shs. of wholly owned 9334416 Canada Inc., holder of the brands and the Medi-Green and My-Grow operations, and the shs. of wholly owned Beleave Kannabis Abbotsford Inc., holder of the cannabis licenses.
Nov. 30, 2020 – Proceedings under the Companies' Creditors Arrangement Act (CCAA) were terminated.
Jan. 19, 2021 – Filed for bankruptcy and Grant Thornton Limited was appointed trustee.

Belec Courville Mines Ltd. (Ont. 1945)
Sept. 1962 – Dissolved.

Belfast Mines Ltd. (Ont. 1945)
1964 – Assets acquired by Goldale Ltd.; basis 1 new for 10 old shs.

Belfast Petroleum Inc. (Alta. Sept. 14, 1993)
Aug. 17, 2000 – Acquired by Merit Energy Ltd.; basis 0.2667 Merit shs. for 1 Belfast sh. (see Merit Energy Ltd.)

Belgium Glove & Hosiery Co. of Canada Ltd. (Can. 1945)
Jan. 1951 – Name changed to Belgium Stores Ltd. ∎

Belgium Standard Limited (Can. 1945)
Jan. 1, 1985 – Amalgamated in Canada to continue with same name.
Nov. 12, 1985 – Name changed to Amertek Inc. ∎

Belgium Stores Ltd. (Can. 1945)
Apr. 1965 – Name changed to Belgium Standard Limited. ∎

Belgold Mines Ltd. (Ont. 1944)
1957 – Charter cancelled.

Belgravia Capital International Inc. (Can. Nov. 8, 2002)
Dec. 20, 2019 – Name changed to Belgravia Hartford Capital Inc. and continued into British Columbia. (see FPsurvey - Industrials)

Belinda Mines Ltd. (B.C. 1980)
May 25, 1982 – Name changed to Goldfever Resources Ltd. ∎

Belkin Inc. (B.C. 1949)
Mar. 1987 – All o/s shs. acquired at $23.50 per sh. by Paperboard Industries Corporation Inc.

Belkor Mines Ltd. (Ont. 1948)
1955 – Charter cancelled.

Bell Aliant Inc. (Ont. Apr. 30, 2010)
Nov. 3, 2014 – Acquired by BCE Inc.; basis either (i) $31.00, (ii) 0.6371 BCE com. shs. or (iii) $7.75 plus 0.4778 BCE com. shs. for 1 Bell Aliant com. sh.
Dec. 31, 2014 – Dissolved.

Bell Aliant Preferred Equity Inc. (Can. Jan. 31, 2011)
Nov. 4, 2014 – Amalgamated with 9034749 Canada Limited, a wholly owned subsid. of BCE Inc. to form a new co. with the same name Bell Aliant Preferred Equity Inc. and became a wholly owned subsid. of BCE Inc.; basis (i) 1 BCE ser. AM pref. sh. for 1 old Bell Aliant ser. A pref. sh. (ii) 1 BCE ser. AO pref. sh. for 1 old Bell Aliant ser. C pref. sh. (iii) 1 BCE ser. AQ pref. sh. for 1 old Bell Aliant ser. E pref. sh.

Bell Aliant Regional Communications Income Fund (Ont. Mar. 30, 2006)
Jan. 1, 2011 – Succeeded by Bell Aliant Inc. pursuant to plan of arrangement whereby Bell Aliant Inc. was formed to facilitate the conversion of the fund into a corporation and the fund was subsequently dissolved. ∎

Bell Canada (Can. Apr. 29, 1880; via Special Act of Parliament)
Jan. 31, 2007 – All o/s cl. A pref. shs. ser. 15, 16, 17, 18 and 19 were exchanged for 1st pref. ser. AE, AF, AG, AH and AI shs. of BCE Inc., on a 1-for-1 basis. Cl. A pref. shldrs. also received a special divid. of $0.20 per sh.

Bell Canada Enterprises Inc. (Can. Feb. 26, 1970)
Jan. 1, 1988 – Name changed to BCE Inc. (see FPsurvey - Industrials)

Bell Canada International Inc. (Can. Jan. 18, 1985)
Aug. 15, 2007 – Dissolved.

Bell Channel Mines Limited (Ont. Sept. 25, 1958)
Jan. 31, 1989 – Dissolved and struck off register.

Bell Coast Capital Corp. (B.C. July 23, 1981)
Mar. 22, 2005 – Name changed to Uranium Power Corp. ∎

Bell Earth Sciences Inc. (B.C. Apr. 12, 1995)
Mar. 1, 1999 – Delisted from the Vancouver Stock Exchange. Subsequently dissolved for failure to file.

Bell Knit Industries Limited (Can. 1915)
1983 – Distribution of approx. 80¢ per sh. made to shldrs. as part of dissolution process. Co. subsequently dissolved.

Bell MTS Inc. (Man. Aug. 3, 2004 amalg.)
Mar. 21, 2017 – Acquired by BCE Inc.; basis $40 cash or 0.6756 BCE com. shs. for 1 Manitoba Telecom sh.

Bell Manitou Gold Mine Ltd. (Que. 1945)
Aug. 5, 1978 – Charter cancelled.

Bell Mines, Ltd. (B.C. 1930)
May 13, 1936 – Merged into Highland-Bell Ltd.; basis 11 new for 1 old sh. (see Highland-Bell Ltd.)

Bell Molybdenum Mines Inc. (B.C. Apr. 12, 1995)
Aug. 11, 1997 – Name changed to Bell Earth Sciences Inc. ∎

Bell Molybdenum Mines Ltd. (B.C. Sept. 30, 1966)
Apr. 13, 1995 – Amalgamated with Adanac Mining and Exploration Ltd. to form Bell Molybdenum Mines Inc.; basis 1 new for 1 Bell sh. (see Bell Molybdenum Mines Inc.)

Bell Nordiq Group Inc. (Que. June 1, 1976)
June 30, 2006 – Redeemed ser. 8 pref. shs. for $25 plus accr. divd. of $0.359375 per sh.

Bell Nordiq Income Fund (Que. Mar. 5, 2002)
Jan. 31, 2007 – Privatized by Bell Aliant Regional Communications Income Fund; basis 0.4113 new Bell Aliant unit for 1 old Bell Nordiq unit. Also received $4.00 per unit as special distribution. (see Bell Aliant Regional Communications Income Fund)

Bell Resources Corporation (B.C. Apr. 29, 1991)
Apr. 22, 2008 – Name changed to Bell Copper Corporation following acquisition of Grandcru Resources Corporation (0.25 for 1) and private co. Rogue River Resources Corp. (1.8 for 1); basis 1 new for 2 old shs. (see FPsurvey - Mines & Energy)

Bell Syndicate No. 2 (unknown)
1929 – Taken over by Alberta Superior Oils Ltd.

The Bell Telephone Company of Canada (Can. Apr. 29, 1880; via Special Act of Parliament)
Apr. 28, 1983 – All o/s com. shs. exchanged for com. shs. of Bell Canada Enterprises Inc., on a 1-for-1 basis.
Jan. 1, 1987 – Name changed to Bell Canada. ∎

Bella Resources Inc. (Alta. Aug. 31, 1993)
Aug. 28, 2013 – Name changed to Angel Bioventures Inc.; basis 1 new for 4 old shs. ∎

Bellabon Resources Corp. (B.C. 1983)
Sept. 18, 1992 – Dissolved and struck off register.

Bellair Ventures Inc. (Can. Aug. 22, 2008)
July 15, 2013 – Name changed to Sustainco Inc. ∎

Bellamont Exploration Ltd. (Alta. May 29, 2006)
Mar. 28, 2012 – Acquired by Storm Resources Ltd.; basis either 56¢, 0.1445 Storm shs., or a combination thereof for 1 Bellamont sh. (see Storm Resources Ltd.)

Bellator Exploration Inc. (Alta. Jan. 29, 1987)
May 31, 2000 – Acquired by Baytex Energy Ltd.; basis 75¢ plus 0.165 Baytex shs. for 1 Bellator sh.

Bellatrix Exploration Ltd. (Alta. Nov. 1, 2009 amalg.)
June 4, 2019 – Continued into Canada.
Oct. 2, 2019 – Filed for protection under the Companies' Creditor Arrangement Act (CCAA). PricewaterhouseCoopers Inc. was appointed monitor.
May 29, 2020 – Substantially all assets sold to Return Energy Inc. (renamed Spartan Delta Corp.) for $102,000,000 including certain liabilities of $14,800,000. Proceeds were not sufficient to repay first lien lenders, or second lien and third lien noteholders in full. No distributions expected for shldrs.
June 2020 – Deemed insolvent and winding-up the business in accordance with CCAA proceedings.
Aug. 9, 2022 – Certain assets and existing liabilities transferred to 2350810 Alberta Ltd., a wholly owned subsid.; Spartan Delta Corp. acquired 1,000 new com. shs. and all other existing equity securities were cancelled for no consideration; net proceeds to be distributed to holders of the company's second lien notes; no distributions for holders of the third lien notes or unsecured creditors; and the company was dissolved.

Bellco Energy Corp. (B.C. 1983)
Aug. 14, 1987 – Name changed to Ocutech Canada Inc. ∎

Belle Aire Explorations Limited (Ont. Aug. 29, 1978 amalg.)
Sept. 22, 1982 – Name changed to Sprint Resources Ltd. ∎

Belle-Aura Mines Ltd. (Que. 1944)
May 18, 1974 – Dissolved.

Belle-Bry Yellowknife Mines Ltd. (Ont. 1944)
1954 – Merged into Pardee Amalgamated Mines Ltd.; basis 1 new for 5 old shs.

Belle Chibougamau Mines Ltd. (Ont. 1949)
1961 – Merged into Amalgamated Beau-Belle Mines Ltd.; basis 1 new for 3 old shs.

Belle Lorrain Mines Ltd. (Ont. 1930)
1930 – Charter cancelled.

Belle River Petroleums Ltd. (Ont. 1972)
Aug. 1973 – Amalgamated with 2 other cos. to form Consolidated Midvale Explorations Ltd.; basis 1 new for 18 Belle River shs. (see Consolidated Midvale Explorations Ltd.)

Belle Tahsis Mines Ltd. (B.C. 1957)
Oct. 1966 – Name changed to Bellex Mines Ltd. ■

Bellegrand Mines Ltd. (Ont. 1944)
1952 – Charter cancelled.

Bellekeno Mines Ltd. (Ont. 1950)
1955 – Name changed to Consolidated Bellekeno Mines Ltd.; basis 1 new for 3 old shs. ■

Bellemac Mud Lake Mines Ltd. (Ont. 1944)
Sept. 17, 1962 – Charter cancelled.

Belleterre Mines Ltd. (Ont. May 19, 1936)
1937 – Name changed to Belleterre Quebec Mines Ltd.

Bellevue Capital Corp. (Alta. June 21, 1996)
July 4, 2005 – Name changed to CMC Metals Ltd. and continued into British Columbia; basis 1 new for 2 old shs. ■

Bellevue Gold Mines Ltd. (Ont. 1945)
1969 – Charter cancelled.

Bellevue Oil and Minerals Ltd. (B.C. 1983)
Oct. 3, 1984 – Formed Bellevue Ventures Ltd. in British Columbia Formed Bellevue Ventures Ltd. following amalgamation with Royce Ventures Ltd. ■

Bellevue Resources Ltd. (Alta. May 4, 1993)
Sept. 29, 1995 – Acquired by Elk Point Resources Inc.; basis 0.2935 Elk Point shs. for 1 Bellevue sh. (see Elk Point Resources Inc.)

Bellevue Ventures Ltd. (B.C. Oct. 3, 1984 amalg.)
Feb. 7, 1985 – Name changed to International Bellevue Ventures Ltd.; basis 1 new for 3 old shs. ■

Bellex Mines Ltd. (B.C. 1957)
Dec. 18, 1978 – Dissolved.

Bellex Mining Corp. (B.C. 1988)
Dec. 31, 1992 – Amalgamated with Adonos Resources Inc. to form ADEX Mining Corp.; basis 1 new for 4.333 Adonos shs. and 1 new for 1 Bellex sh.

Bellezone Mines Ltd. (Ont. 1944)
Nov. 19, 1956 – Charter cancelled.

Bellhaven Copper & Gold Inc. (B.C. Apr. 8, 1980)
May 31, 2017 – Acquired by GoldMining Inc.; basis 0.25 GoldMining com. shs. for 1 Bellhaven com. sh.

Bellhaven Ventures Inc. (B.C. Apr. 8, 1980)
Oct. 6, 2006 – Name changed to Bellhaven Copper & Gold Inc. ■

Bellkurt Exploration & Development Ltd. (B.C. 1974)
Aug. 1979 – Name changed to Plymouth Oil & Gas Corp. ■

Bellore Mines Ltd. (B.C. 1949)
1952 – Dissolved and struck off register.

Bellren Mining Corp. Ltd. (Que. 1952)
Sept. 2, 1978 – Charter cancelled.

Bellringer Resources Ltd. (Alta. May 27, 1987)
Nov. 2, 2000 – Struck off register.

BellRock Brands Inc. (Ont. July 20, 1970)
Oct. 31, 2020 – Continued into British Columbia. (see FPsurvey - Mines & Energy)

Belltech Ventures Ltd. (B.C. Feb. 16, 2000)
Nov. 1, 2004 – Formed Welichem Biotech Inc. in British Columbia following Qualifying Transaction amalgamation with Welichem Biotech Inc., constituting a reverse takeover by Welichem. ■

Bellwether Capital Corp. (B.C. Aug. 17, 1998)
Mar. 19, 2001 – Name changed to FirstWeb Internet Solutions Inc.; basis 1 new for 3 old shs. ■

Bellwether Resources Ltd. (B.C. June 3, 1987)
Mar. 20, 1992 – Name changed to Eurocontrol Technics Inc.; basis 1 new for 3 old shs. ■

Belmine Exploration Ltd. (Ont. 1956)
Mar. 1976 – Charter cancelled.

Belmont Mining & Exploration Co. Ltd. (Que. 1950)
1959 – Assets acquired by Amalgamated Mining Development Corporation; basis 1 new for 4 old shs.

Belmont-Tonopah Explorations Limited (B.C. 1981)
May 18, 1983 – Name changed to B.T. Gold Explorations Ltd. ■

Belmoral Mines Ltd. (B.C. Aug. 19, 1968)
Dec. 20, 1985 – Continued into Canada. (see Beau Canada Exploration Ltd.)
Nov. 4, 1993 – Amalgamated with Beau Canada Exploration Ltd. (1 for 1) to form a new co. also named Beau Canada Exploration Ltd.; basis 1 new for 18.75 old shs. (see Beau Canada Exploration Ltd.)

Belore Mines Limited (Ont. 1968)
July 17, 1998 – Formed Golden Hart Exploration Inc. in Ontario on amalgamation with Golden Hart Exploration Inc. (1 for 1); basis 1 new for 5 old shs. ■

Belra Explorations Ltd. (Ont. 1968)
May 14, 1975 – Charter cancelled.

Belrosa Mines Ltd. (Ont. 1944)
1960 – Charter cancelled.

Beltec Enterprises Ltd. (B.C. Jan. 22, 1987)
Oct. 2, 1992 – Name changed to First Choice Industries Ltd.; basis 1 new for 2.5 old shs. ■

BelTeco Holdings Inc. (Can. - unspecified)
Nov. 26, 1994 – Charter cancelled and co. dissolved.

Belvedere Copper Corp. Ltd. (Que. 1952)
June 1974 – Charter cancelled.

Belvedere Resources Ltd. (B.C. Sept. 23, 1991)
Oct. 30, 2018 – Name changed to Helix Applications Inc. ■

Belville Zinc and Copper Mines Ltd. (Que. 1951)
Sept. 2, 1978 – Charter cancelled.

Belzberg Financial Markets & News International Inc. (Ont. Nov. 30, 1993)
July 14, 2000 – Name changed to Belzberg Technologies Inc.; basis 5 new for 1 old sh. ■

Belzberg Technologies Inc. (Ont. Nov. 30, 1993)
Apr. 13, 2011 – Name changed to Frontline Technologies Inc. pursuant to acquisition of Frontline Technologies Corp. ■

Bema Gold Corporation (B.C. Dec. 5, 1988 amalg.)
July 19, 2002 – Continued into Canada.
Feb. 27, 2007 – Acquired by Kinross Gold Corporation; basis 0.4447 Kinross sh. plus $0.01 for 1 Bema sh.
Mar. 2, 2007 – Name changed to EastWest Gold Corporation.

Bema International Resources Inc. (B.C. Jan. 13, 1986)
Dec. 5, 1988 – Formed Bema Gold Corporation in British Columbia on amalgamation with Amir Mines Ltd. (1 for 1) and Normine Resources Ltd. (1 for 2).; basis 1 new for 1 old sh. ■

Ben-Abraham Technologies Inc. (Wyo. Dec. 19, 1996 amalg.)
Dec. 17, 1999 – Name changed to BioSante Pharmaceuticals, Inc. ■

Ben Natural Gas Co., Ltd. (Ont. 1934)
Liquidated; Crown Trust Co., Brantford, liquidator.

Benachee Resources Inc. (Can. Jan. 1, 2001 amalg.)
June 3, 2009 – Name changed to Ag Growth International Inc. (see FPsurvey - Industrials)

Benchmark Botanics Inc. (Alta. Nov. 23, 2009)
Nov. 1, 2021 – Name changed to Craftport Cannabis Corp.; basis 1 new for 10 old shs. (see FPsurvey - Industrials)

Benchmark Energy Corp. (Can. Sept. 25, 1995)
Oct. 29, 2010 – Name changed to Bolivar Energy Corp. following Sept. 17, 2010, amalgamation of Bolivar Energy Inc. (deemed acquiror) with wholly owned Benchmark Colombia Acquisition Corp. ■

Benchmark Metals Inc. (B.C. Nov. 9, 2010)
Aug. 23, 2023 – Name changed to Thesis Gold Inc. pursuant to the acquisition of (old) Thesis Gold Inc. (concurrently renamed Thesis Gold (Holdings) Inc.); basis 1 new for 2.6 old shs. (see FPsurvey - Mines & Energy)

Bencorp Industries Ltd. (Can. Nov. 21, 1977)
Apr. 3, 1984 – Name changed to Doverton Oils Ltd. ■

Bencrest Mines Ltd. (B.C. 1969)
Aug. 22, 1977 – Dissolved.

Beneficial Finance Co. of Canada (Can. 1933)
Sept. 1983 – Acquired by Beneficial Canada Inc. and subsequently dissolved and assets transferred to Beneficial Canada.

Benem Ventures Inc. (Alta. Sept. 22, 2000)
May 20, 2008 – Name changed to Velocity Minerals Ltd. following reverse takeover acquisition of Velocity Exploration Ltd. (see FPsurvey - Mines & Energy)

Beneventum Mining Co. Ltd. (Alta. 1956)
May 15, 1972 – Struck off register.

Bengal Development Corp. Ltd. (Ont. 1959)
May 25, 1967 – Dissolved.

Benjamin Hill Mining Corp. (B.C. Aug. 21, 2014)
Apr. 22, 2024 – Name changed to Forge Resources Corp. (see FPsurvey - Mines & Energy)

Benjoe Mines Limited (Ont. 1968)
1970 – Name changed to Medipak Corporation Ltd. ■

Benmac Explorations Ltd. (Ont. 1964)
1967 – Merged into Drope Lake Explorations Ltd.; basis 1 new for 5 old shs.

Benn Explorations Ltd. (B.C. 1966)
Jan. 23, 1978 – Name changed to Allwest Industries Ltd. ■

Bennett Environmental Inc. (Can. July 29, 1992)
June 28, 2012 – Name changed to BENEV Capital Inc. ■

Benpel Industries Ltd. (B.C. Dec. 11, 1970)
Nov. 26, 1982 – Name changed to Palmer Industries Ltd. ■

Benroy Gold Mines Ltd. (Ont. 1947)
Nov. 9, 1964 – Dissolved.

Benson & Hedges (Canada) Inc. (Can. 1934)
Dec. 19, 1986 – This wholly owned subsidiary of Phillip Morris Inc. amalgamated with a wholly owned subsidiary of Rothmans of Pall Mall Limited to form a joint subsidiary,

Rothmans, Benson & Hedges Inc. which was 60% owned by Rothmans Inc. and 40% by Phillip Morris.

Benson & Hedges (Canada) Limited (Can. 1934)
Apr. 24, 1979 – Name changed to Benson & Hedges (Canada) Inc. ∎

Benson Industries Ltd. (B.C. 1967)
Nov. 21, 1977 – Continued into Canada.
1977 – Name changed to Bencorp Industries Ltd. ∎

Benson Mines Ltd. (B.C. May 29, 1963)
Oct. 4, 1982 – Name changed to Can Am Gold Resources Ltd.; basis 1 new for 4 old shs. ∎

Benson Petroleum Ltd. (Alta. Dec. 31, 1986)
Dec. 31, 1989 – Amalgamated in Alberta to continue with same name. (see Southward Energy Ltd.)
Dec. 31, 1995 – Amalgamated in Alberta to continue with same name. (see Southward Energy Ltd.)
Mar. 20, 2001 – Acquired by 896543 Alberta Ltd., a wholly owned subsid. of Southward Energy Ltd., for $3.05 per sh. (see Southward Energy Ltd.)

Bentall Capital Corporation (B.C. 1958)
Feb. 23, 1989 – Became private following redemption of 9% pref. shs. at $25.50 plus 33.75¢ per sh. accr. divd.

Bentall Corporation (Can. Sept. 7, 1990)
Apr. 4, 2001 – Acquired by SITQ Acquisition Inc., an indirect subsid. of SITQ Vancouver Inc.; basis $20 per sh.

Bentech Industries Inc. (B.C. 1984)
June 18, 1993 – Dissolved and struck off register.

Bentibo Mines Ltd. (Ont. 1947)
1953 – Charter cancelled.

Bentley Resources Ltd. (B.C. Mar. 12, 1970)
Mar. 4, 1991 – Delisted from the Vancouver Stock Exchange. Subsequently dissolved and struck from register.

Bentley's Limited (N.S. 1953)
1988 – All pref. shs. redeemed during; basis $124 per sh. including all accrued and unpaid div. Now private.

Benton-Brausche Oil Corp. Ltd. (Alta.)
1958 – Struck off register.

Benton Capital Corp. (B.C. July 10, 2003)
Apr. 28, 2016 – Name changed to Alset Energy Corp. ∎

Benton Resources Corp. (B.C. July 10, 2003)
Aug. 1, 2012 – Name changed to Benton Capital Corp. ∎

Benton Resources Ltd. (B.C. 1987)
Dec. 2, 1994 – Dissolved and struck off register.

Benvan Holdings Inc. (Ont. Apr. 20, 1964)
Dec. 27, 1991 – Name changed to Osgoode Holdings Inc.; basis 1 new for 10 old shs. ∎

Benvan Mines Limited (Ont. Apr. 20, 1964)
July 10, 1975 – Name changed to Howie Controls (Canada) Limited. ∎

Benvest Capital Inc. (Can. Oct. 10, 1985)
May 2, 2005 – Converted into Benvest New Look Income Fund; basis either 1 Benvest New Look trust unit or 1 New Look AcquisitionCo Inc. exch. sh. for 1 Benvest Capital sh. (see Benvest New Look Income Fund)

Benvest New Look Income Fund (Ont. May 1, 2005)
Mar. 4, 2010 – Converted into a corp. New Look Eyewear Inc. (formerly Sonomax Hearing Healthcare Inc.); basis 1 New Look sh. for 1 Benvest New Look fund unit and 1 Sonomax Technologies Inc. sh. for 1 Sonomax Hearing sh. (see New Look Eyewear Inc.)

Benz Capital Corp. (B.C. Nov. 9, 2011)
Jan. 28, 2015 – Name changed to Benz Mining Corp. (see FPsurvey - Mines & Energy)

Benz Capital Corp. (B.C. Feb. 8, 2021)
July 25, 2023 – Name changed to Avaron Mining Corp. (see FPsurvey - Mines & Energy)

Benz Energy Ltd. (Yuk. Apr. 7, 1992)
May 20, 1999 – Continued into Delaware.
June 24, 1999 – Name changed to Benz Energy Inc.

Benz Equities Ltd. (B.C. Feb. 9, 1981)
Apr. 7, 1992 – Continued into Yukon.
July 2, 1997 – Name changed to Benz Energy Ltd. following reverse takeover acquisition of Texstar Petroleum Inc. ∎

Benz Gold Resources Ltd. (B.C. Feb. 9, 1981)
Mar. 1, 1990 – Name changed to Benz Equities Ltd. ∎

Benzac Gold Mines Ltd. (Ont. 1945)
Mar. 11, 1957 – Charter cancelled.

Benzai Capital Corp. (B.C. Jan. 16, 2007)
Feb. 11, 2013 – Name changed to Redline Resources Inc.; basis 1 new for 2 old shs. ∎

Ber Resources Ltd. (B.C. 1984)
Mar. 26, 1993 – Dissolved and struck off register.

Berens Energy Ltd. (Alta. Nov. 19, 2003 amalg.)
Mar. 3, 2010 – Acquired by PetroBakken Energy Ltd. by way of amalgamation with PetroBakken Acquisition Ltd. for $2.70 per sh. (see PetroBakken Energy Ltd.)

Berens River Mines Ltd. (Ont. 1936)
1957 – Charter cancelled; distribution on basis of $1.06 and 0.333 sh. of Sunshine Lardeau Mines Ltd. for each sh. of Berens.

Beretta Resource Corp. (B.C. 1983)
Apr. 24, 1992 – Name changed to Optimark Data Systems Inc. ∎

Berglynn Resources Inc. (B.C. Mar. 27, 1980)
Mar. 11, 1992 – Name changed to Arkona Resources Inc.; basis 1 new for 2 old shs. ∎

Beringer Gold Corp. (B.C. May 26, 1986)
Nov. 17, 1997 – Amalgamated with Lions Gate Entertainment Corp.; basis 1 Lions Gate sh. for 10 Beringer Gold shs. (see Lions Gate Entertainment Corp.)

Berkana Energy Corp. (Alta. Feb. 22, 1993)
Jan. 23, 2008 – Acquired by Quatro Resources Inc. for $1.96 per cl. A sh.

Berkdale Mines Ltd. (Ont. 1973)
1975 – Amalgamated with 3 other cos. to form Berkwater Explorations Limited; basis 1.2 new for 1 old sh.

Berkeley Capital Corp. I (Ont. June 12, 2007)
Apr. 1, 2008 – Formed iLOOKABOUT Corp. in Ontario following Qualifying Transaction amalgamation with iLOOKABOUT Holdings Inc., constituting a reverse takeover by iLOOKABOUT; basis 1 new for 1 iLOOKABOUT sh. and 0.2083 new for 1 Berkeley sh. ∎

Berkeley Capital Corp. II (Ont. June 12, 2007)
June 17, 2009 – Completed private placement investment in Med BioGene Inc., which constituted Berkeley's Qualifying Transaction; basis 1 Med BioGene sh. for 0.7052 Berkeley shs. plus 0.3526 wts. Subsequently dissolved. (see Med BioGene Inc.)

Berkeley Mines Limited (Ont. 1963)
Sept. 3, 1994 – Dissolved.

Berkley Oil and Gas Ltd. (Alta. 1964)
1971 – Merged into Page Petroleum Ltd.; basis 1 new for 2 old shs.

Berkley Petroleum Corp. (Alta. Sept. 18, 1992)
Mar. 19, 2001 – Acquired by Anadarko Canada Acquisition Corporation, an indirect wholly owned subsid. of Houston-based Anadarko Petroleum Corporation, for $11.40 per sh.

Berkley Resources Inc. (B.C. Jan. 29, 1974)
July 18, 1986 – Amalgamated with Fortune Island Mines Ltd. (1 for 6) and Kerry Mining Ltd. (1 for 1) to continue with the same name Berkley Resources Inc.
Apr. 16, 2012 – Name changed to Berkley Renewables Inc.; basis 1 new for 10 old shs. (see FPsurvey - Mines & Energy; FPsurvey - Industrials)

Berkley Wallcoverings Inc. (Que. 1979)
Nov. 28, 1990 – All o/s shs. not already held acquired by WCA Canada Inc.; basis $6.35 per sh.

Berkshire Capital Corp. (Alta. Nov. 5, 1998)
Apr. 29, 2003 – Name changed to Minaean International Corp. pursuant to Qualifying Transaction reverse takeover acquisition of Minaean Venture Inc. ∎

Berkshire Griffin Inc. (Ont. Sept. 28, 1987)
July 31, 2009 – Formed China Wind Power International Corp. in Ontario on amalgamation with China Wind Power International Corp., constituting a reverse takeover by China Wind Power; basis 1 new sh. for 1 China Wind Power sh. and 1 new sh. for 16.51 Berkshire shs. ∎

Berkshire International Mining Ltd. (B.C. Mar. 8, 1978)
Jan. 24, 2002 – Name changed to Tyner Resources Ltd.; basis 1 new for 10 old shs. (see FPsurvey - Mines & Energy)

Berkwater Explorations Limited (Ont. 1975 amalg.)
1977 – Amalgamated with 4 other cos. to form Branly Enterprises Inc.; basis 13 new for 25 old shs.

Berkwood Resources Ltd. (B.C. Jan. 15, 1979)
Aug. 28, 2020 – Name changed to Goldcore Resources Ltd.; basis 1 new for 4 old shs. ∎

Berland Resources Ltd. (B.C. Oct. 24, 1997)
June 7, 2002 – Name changed to Lithic Resources Ltd. and continued into Canada; basis 1 new for 2 old shs. ∎

Berle Oil Corporation (B.C. Oct. 17, 1980)
May 31, 1983 – Name changed to Berle Resources Ltd. ∎

Berle Resources Ltd. (B.C. Oct. 17, 1980)
Aug. 6, 1987 – Name changed to Eagle Pass Resources Ltd.; basis 1 new for 5 old shs. ∎

Bermead Mining Corp. Ltd. (Ont. 1951)
Feb. 12, 2007 – Certificate of incorporation cancelled and company dissolved.

Bermont Mines Ltd. (Que. 1962)
Oct. 21, 1970 – Name changed to Atlantic Tungsten Corp. Ltd. (see FPsurvey - Mines & Energy)

Bermor Porcupine Gold Mines Ltd. (Ont. 1945)
Jan. 28, 1957 – Dissolved.

Bermuda Resources Ltd. (B.C. 1980)
Sept. 1, 1988 – Name changed to Ameritel Management, Inc. ∎

Bermuda-Schwortz Industries Inc. (Can. 1984)
Oct. 26, 1986 – Ceased operations.

Bern-Or Mines Ltd. (Que. 1961)
Mar. 22, 1986 – Charter cancelled.

Bern Resources Ltd. (B.C. Oct. 1, 1979)
Mar. 18, 1985 – Name changed to Pachena Industries Ltd. ∎

Bernack Coppermine Exploration Ltd. (Ont.)
1978 – Charter cancelled.

The Bernhardt Gold Mines Ltd. (unknown)
Feb. 18, 1963 – Dissolved.

Berry Creek Petroleums Ltd. (Alta. 1946)
Nov. 16, 1967 – Struck off register.

Bersimis Mining Co. (Que. 1953)
1976 – Name changed to Reed Mines Ltd.

Berton Gold Mines Ltd. (B.C. 1945)
Aug. 6, 1974 – Struck off register.

Berton Industries Limited (B.C. 1968)
1971 – Name changed to British Western Industries Limited. ■

Bertram Porcupine Mines Ltd. (Ont. 1945)
Feb. 1958 – Charter cancelled.

Berwick Retirement Communities Ltd. (Alta. May 18, 1988)
Nov. 9, 2005 – Privatized at $1.13 per sh.

Berwind Capital Corp. (Alta. Oct. 1, 1997)
Oct. 3, 2000 – Formed Sams Online Inc. in Ontario following Qualifying Transaction reverse takeover acquisition of and amalgamation with SamsCD.com Inc.; basis 1.82 new for 1 old sh. ■

Bespoke Capital Acquisition Corp. (B.C. July 8, 2019)
June 7, 2021 – Name changed to Vintage Wine Estates, Inc. and continued into Nevada pursuant to the Qualifying Acquisition of (old) Vintage Wine Estates, Inc. (VWE) and concurrent amalgamation of (old) VWE with wholly owned VWE Acquisition Sub Inc.

Besra Gold Inc. (Can. July 13, 2006)
Oct. 2015 – Filed a notice to make a proposal under the Bankruptcy and Insolvency Act (BIA) and MNP Ltd. named as proposal trustee.
Apr. 2016 – Creditors voted to accept the amended proposal which comprised: (i) an option to receive 3.25% of said creditor's proved claim in cash and the remaining 96.75% in the form of a new note; (ii) an option to receive 70% of said creditor's proven claims in com. shs. and the remaining 30% in the form of a new warrants; (iii) an option to divide said creditor's proven claim equally between options (i) and (ii); and (iv) an option of a convenience cash payment equal to the lesser of $3,000 and said creditor's proven claim which represents the default option for any creditor failing to make an election.
May 17, 2016 – Court approval was received for the restructuring proposal.
Nov. 2016 – Pursuant to a securities purchase agreement, Pangaea Holdings Limited was issued a secured convertible note due Nov. 17, 2021, convertible into com. shs. at a price of Cdn$0.01 per sh. and 1/3 of a warrant to purchase 333,333,333 com. shs. at an exercise price of Cdn$0.02 per sh. for a 5-year period. Cash proceeds from the financing used to settle the cash portion of claims and expenses incurred under the BIA proceedings.
Apr. 2017 – Distributions made to creditors and proposal trustee discharged. (see FPsurvey - Mines & Energy)

Best-Ore Mines Ltd. (Ont. 1947)
Nov. 19, 1956 – Charter cancelled.

Best Pacific Resources Ltd. (Alta. Sept. 20, 1989)
Dec. 11, 2002 – Acquired by Advantage Oil & Gas Ltd., wholly owned subsid. of Advantage Energy Income Fund; basis $1.25 per sh. (see Advantage Energy Income Fund)

Best Resources Inc. (B.C. 1983)
June 13, 1985 – Name changed to Cariana International Industries Inc. ■

Bestar inc. (Que. Jan. 22, 1964)
Jan. 12, 2015 – Privatized; basis 18¢ per com. sh. and $1.50 per cl. B pref. sh.

Bestquipt Sports Inc. (Ont. July 25, 1965)
Aug. 29, 2000 – Name changed to Big Hammer Group Inc. pursuant to reverse takeover acquisition of Big Hammer Interactive Ltd. and 1418963 Ontario Inc.; basis 1 new for 4 old shs. ■

Beta Brands Incorporated (Alta. 1986)
Dec. 29, 2003 – Liquidated following foreclosure on senior debt. Company dissolved.

Beta Gamma Exploration and Development Ltd. (Sask. 1949)
Mar. 1969 – Sold to General Petroleums Drilling Ltd. at 11¢ per sh.

Beta Gamma Mines Ltd. (Sask. 1949)
1956 – Name changed to Consolidated Beta Gamma Mines Ltd.; basis 1 new for 3 old shs. ■

Beta Minerals Inc. (Ont. Sept. 27, 2002)
Mar. 6, 2009 – Name changed to Advanced Primary Minerals Corporation following reverse takeover acquisition of Erdene Materials Corporation. ■

Betacom Corporation (Ont. May 17, 1922)
Dec. 2003 – Declared bankruptcy. (see FPsurvey - Industrials)

Bethel Gold Mines Ltd. (Ont. 1938)
1958 – Charter cancelled.

Bethex Explorations Ltd. (B.C. 1965)
Jan. 23, 1969 – In voluntary liquidation. Shldrs. received 17.4 shs. Valley Copper Mines Ltd. and 3 shs. Bethlehem Copper Corp. Ltd. for each 100 Bethex shs.

Bethlehem Copper Corporation (B.C. 1955)
July 31, 1981 – Amalgamated with Worwil Investments Inc., a wholly owned subsid. of Cominco Ltd. Minority shldrs. received one pref. sh. of amalgamated co. for each sh. held. Pref. shs. were immediately redeemed at $37.50 per sh. (see Cominco Ltd.)

Bethlehem Resources Corporation (B.C. 1982)
Mar. 7, 1995 – Amalgamated with 479392 B.C. Ltd., a wholly owned subsid. of Imperial Metals Corporation; basis 1 Imperial sh. for 3 Bethlehem shs. or $0.50 for each Bethlehem sh. held.
Dec. 29, 1995 – Dissolved and struck off register.

Bethpage Capital Corp. (B.C. May 13, 2010)
June 7, 2019 – Name changed to GreenStar Biosciences Corp. pursuant to reverse takeover acquisition of GreenStar Biosciences Inc.; basis 1 new for 2 old shs. ■

Bethsaida Copper Mines Ltd. (B.C. 1956)
1963 – Name changed to New Bethsaida Mines Limited. ■

Betina Resources Inc. (B.C. Mar. 16, 1966)
July 28, 1983 – Name changed to Nevcal Resources Ltd.; basis 1 new for 4 old shs. ■

Better Business Communications Inc. (Can. 1947)
Sept. 14, 1988 – Acquired by MH Acquisition Limited, a wholly owned subsid. of Maclean Hunter Limited, for $3.00 per sh. (see Maclean Hunter Limited)

Better Resources Limited (B.C. May 14, 1981)
Oct. 19, 2005 – Name changed to Bluerock Resources Ltd.; basis 1 new for 3 old shs. ■

betterU Education Corp. (B.C. Aug. 1, 2009 amalg.)
Oct. 13, 2017 – Continued into Canada.
Sept. 14, 2023 – Dissolved and struck from register.

Beulah Yellowknife Mines Ltd. (Ont. 1944)
1951 – Name changed to Fab Metal Mines Ltd. ■

Bev-Cal Mines Ltd. (B.C. 1963)
July 8, 1975 – Name changed to New Chemcrude Resources Ltd. ■

BevCanna Enterprises Inc. (B.C. July 13, 2017)
Oct. 18, 2024 – Name changed to Forte Group Holdings Inc. (see FPsurvey - Industrials)

Bevco Mines Ltd. (B.C. 1968)
1974 – Acquired by Nor-Can Minerals Ltd.; basis 1 new for 2 old shs.

Bevcon Mines Ltd. (Que. 1944)
1965 – Merged into Malartic Gold Fields (Quebec) Limited; basis 1 new for 10 old shs.

Bevcourt Gold Mines Ltd. (Que. 1944)
1955 – Name changed to Bevcon Mines Ltd.; basis 1 new for 7 old shs. ■

Beverly Development Inc. (B.C. 1985)
May 8, 1989 – Continued into Canada.
June 2, 1997 – Dissolved and struck from register.

Beverly Glen Capital Corp. (Ont. Apr. 5, 1984)
Dec. 7, 1999 – Name changed to Phonetime Inc. ■

Beverly Mines Limited (B.C. 1937)
Sept. 20, 1985 – Struck off register.

Bevo Agro Inc. (B.C. July 9, 1985)
Jan. 8, 2019 – Name changed to Zenabis Global Inc. pursuant to the reverse takeover acquisition of Sun Pharm Investments Ltd. and concurrent amalgamation with a wholly owned subsidiary of Bevo. ■

Bexar Ventures Inc. (B.C. Jan. 31, 2017)
Sept. 24, 2021 – Name changed to Immutable Holdings Inc. pursuant to the reverse takeover acquisition of (old) Immutable Holdings Inc.; basis 1 new for 12.4346 old shs. (see FPsurvey - Industrials)

Bexhill Gold Mines Ltd. (Ont. Jan. 1937)
Dec. 1954 – Charter cancelled.

Beyond Medical Technologies Inc. (B.C. Nov. 29, 2006)
July 15, 2025 – Name changed to Republic Technologies Inc. (see FPsurvey - Industrials)

Beyond Minerals Inc. (Can. Oct. 8, 2019)
May 15, 2023 – Name changed to Beyond Lithium Inc. (see FPsurvey - Mines & Energy)

Bi-Optic Ventures Inc. (B.C. May 31, 1984)
Feb. 11, 2016 – Name changed to Arcturus Growthstar Technologies Inc. ■

Bi-Ore Mines Ltd. (Ont. Mar. 1942)
1954 – Acquired by Consolidated Bi-Ore Mines Ltd.; basis 1 new for 5 old shs. (see Consolidated Bi-Ore Mines Ltd.)

Bi-Petro Resources Inc. (B.C. 1985)
May 28, 1993 – Dissolved and struck off register.

Bianca Resources Ltd. (B.C. 1974)
Nov. 18, 1981 – Acquired by Action Resources Ltd.; basis 1.5 new Action shs. for 1 old Bianca sh. (see Action Resources Ltd.)

Bibis Yukon Mines Ltd. (Ont. Dec. 18, 1950 amalg.)
Mar. 5, 1965 – Name changed to International Bibis Tin Mines Ltd.; basis 1 new for 5 old shs. ■

Bice Ventures Corp. (B.C. May 13, 1996)
Sept. 24, 1999 – Name changed to Pol-Invest Holdings Ltd.; basis 1 new for 3 old shs. ■

Bicer Medical Systems Ltd. (B.C. 1986)
Oct. 14, 1994 – Dissolved and struck off register.

Bickle Seagrave Limited (Ont. 1946)
1956 – In bankruptcy; Guaranty Trust Co. of Canada, Toronto, appointed trustee. Properties sold, and balance after prior claims paid to holders of 5.5% 1st mtge. bds. due Apr. 1, 1972, who received $71.15 per $100 par value.

Bicks of Canada Ltd. (Ont. 1956)
1966 – All o/s com. shs. acquired by Robin Hood Flour Mills Ltd. through offer at $16.50 per sh. Term debt assumed by Robin Hood.

Bicroft Uranium Mines Ltd. (Ont. 1955)
1961 – Merged into Macassa Gold Mines Ltd.; basis 1 new for 5 old shs.

Bid.Com International Inc. (Ont. Nov. 28, 1983)
Oct. 18, 2001 – Name changed to ADB Systems International Inc. following acquisition of a Norwegian company; basis 1 new for 2 old shs. ■

Bidcop Mines Ltd. (Ont. Nov. 27, 1923)
1969 – Name changed to Consolidated Bidcop Mines Ltd.; basis 1 new for 4 old shs. ■

BidCrawler.com Online Inc. (B.C. June 27, 1974)
Aug. 21, 2001 – Name changed to TradeRadius Online Inc.; basis 1 new for 4 old shs. ■

Bidd Consolidated Mines Ltd. (Ont. 1946)
Apr. 1958 – Charter cancelled.

Bidd Yellowknife Exploration Co. Ltd. (Ont. 1945)
1946 – Name changed to Bidd Consolidated Mines Ltd. and continued into Ontario; basis 1 new for 20 old shs. ■

Bidgood Consolidated Mines, Ltd. (Ont. Nov. 27, 1923)
1933 – Name changed to Bidgood Kirkland Gold Mines Ltd.; basis 1 new for 12 old shs. ■

Bidgood Kirkland Gold Mines Ltd. (Ont. Nov. 27, 1923)
Apr. 1956 – Name changed to Bidcop Mines Ltd.; basis 1 new for 5 old shs. ■

Bidgood Mines, Ltd. (Ont. Nov. 27, 1923)
1924 – Name changed to Bidgood Consolidated Mines, Ltd.; basis 1 new for 2 old shs. ■

Bidlamaque Gold Mines Ltd. (Que. 1934)
1944 – Continued into Ontario.
1945 – Name changed to New Bidlamaque Gold Mines Limited; basis 1 new for 2 old shs. ■

Big I Developments Ltd. (B.C. June 17, 1981)
May 19, 1998 – Name changed to Nustar Resources Inc.; basis 1 new for 5 old shs. ■

Big Agaunico Mines Ltd. (Ont. 1952)
1964 – Merged into Consolidated Professor Mines Ltd.; basis 1 new for 5 old shs. (see Consolidated Professor Mines Limited)

Big Bank Big Oil Split Corp. (Ont. Apr. 27, 2006)
Dec. 30, 2016 – Mandatory redemption; basis $7.589323 cash per cl. A capital shs. and $10 cash per cl. A pref. shs.

Big Bar Gold Corporation (B.C. Dec. 10, 1980)
Oct. 19, 2007 – Name changed to Big Bar Resources Corporation. ■

Big Bar Resources Corporation (B.C. Dec. 10, 1980)
Sept. 23, 2016 – Name changed to CVR Medical Corp. following purchase of patents relating to a diagnostic device. (see FPsurvey - Industrials)

Big Bear Exploration Ltd. (Alta. Apr. 11, 1996)
Feb. 8, 2000 – Acquired by Avid Oil & Gas Ltd.; basis 1 Avid sh. for 15 Big Bear shs. (see Avid Oil & Gas Ltd.)

Big Bear Oil and Gas Ltd. (Alta. June 20, 1996)
Dec. 31, 1996 – Formed Renata Resources Inc. in Alberta following acquisition of all o/s shs. of Renata Resources Inc., a private company; basis 1 new for 1 old sh. ■

Big Ben Resources Inc. (B.C. Mar. 4, 1983)
May 19, 1993 – Name changed to M.I.T. Ventures Corp.; basis 1 new for 3.5 old shs. ■

Big Blackfoot Resources Ltd. (Alta. Mar. 18, 1996)
Oct. 21, 2002 – Name changed to BBF Resources Inc.; basis 1 new for 2 old shs. ■

Big Cat Mines Ltd. (B.C. 1969)
June 13, 1977 – Dissolved.

Big Creek Resources Ltd. (B.C. 1985)
Dec. 1, 1992 – Amalgamated with Pacific Sentinel Gold Corp. to form new co. with same name Pacific Sentinel Gold Corp.; basis 1 new for 1 Pacific Sentinel sh. and 1 new for 1 Big Creek sh. (see Pacific Sentinel Gold Corp.)

Big Dan Mines Ltd. (Ont. 1948)
May 16, 1960 – Dissolved.

Big Divide Gold Mines Ltd. (Ont. 1934)
Feb. 1960 – Charter cancelled.

Big Dougie Capital Corp. (Alta. Dec. 14, 2017)
Nov. 13, 2020 – Name changed to Stuve Gold Corp. following the Qualifying Transaction reverse takeover of a 99.9% interest in Compania Recursos Andina Limitada; basis 1 new for 3 old shs. (see FPsurvey - Mines & Energy)

Big Dyke Consolidated Gold Mines (Ont. 1922)
1955 – Charter cancelled.

Big 8 Split Inc. (Ont. June 26, 2003)
Dec. 14, 2018 – Fund matured; basis $10 per cl. D pref. sh. and $16.56 per cl. D capital sh.

Big Five Capital Corp. (Alta. May 6, 2011)
Oct. 25, 2013 – Formed Lorne Park Capital Partners Inc. in Ontario pursuant to Qualifying Transaction amalgamation with Bellwether Asset Management Inc. (deemed acquiror); basis 1 new for 2 old shs. (see FPsurvey - Industrials)

Big Four Silver Mines Ltd. (B.C. 1946)
1952 – Assets sold to Cassiar Consolidated Mines Ltd.; basis 1 new for 4 old shs. (see Cassiar Consolidated Mines Limited)

Big Game Mines Ltd. (Ont. 1944)
Aug. 26, 1957 – Merged into Consolidated Frederick Mines Ltd. Big Game shs. entitled to equivalent of $1.54 per 11 old shs. (see Consolidated Frederick Mines Ltd.)

Big Glen Mines Ltd. (Ont. 1954)
July 9, 1969 – Charter cancelled.

Big Hammer Group Inc. (Ont. July 25, 1965)
Jan. 22, 2007 – Dissolved and struck from register.

Big Herb Lake Mining & Exploration Ltd. (Ont. 1947)
Mar. 1976 – Charter cancelled.

Big Horn Petroleums Limited (B.C.)
May 7, 1970 – Dissolved.

Big Horn Resources Ltd. (Can. Sept. 9, 1982)
Sept. 17, 2001 – Acquired by Westlinks Resources Ltd. through amalgamation of Big Horn and 3779041 Canada Ltd., a wholly owned subsid. of Westlinks; basis (I) 1 spec. sh. of the amalgamated company immed. redeem. for 22¢ cash and 0.74 Westlinks 1st pref. ser.1 shs. for 1 Big Horn com. sh., or (ii) 0.1905 Westlinks com. shs. for 1 Big Horn com. sh. (see Westlinks Resources Ltd.)

The Big I Mines Ltd. (B.C. 1959)
Nov. 5, 1993 – Dissolved and struck off register.

Big Inch Pipe Corp. Ltd. (Alta. 1959)
Oct. 1961 – Alberta Phoenix Tube & Pipe Ltd. offered $825 plus accr. int. for $1,000 6% 2nd mtge. bonds; $1,150 for each unit of $1,000 6% 2nd mtge. bonds and 25 com. shs.; $725 for each $1,000 6% gen. mtge. bonds; $1,375 for each unit of $1,000 6% gen. mtge. bond and 50 com. shs.; and $13 for each com. sh.

Big Island Copper Mines Ltd. (Ont. 1951)
Apr. 1959 – Charter cancelled.

Big Jackpot Mines Ltd. (Ont. 1952)
July 1973 – Charter cancelled.

Big Jim Gold Mines Ltd. (B.C. 1945)
1952 – Charter cancelled.

Big Joe Gold Mines Ltd. (Ont. 1945)
1955 – Name changed to Big Joe Mines Ltd. ■

Big Joe Mines Ltd. (Ont. 1945)
Nov. 11, 1965 – Charter cancelled.

Big Lake Mines Ltd. (B.C. 1965)
Feb. 25, 1983 – Struck off register.

Big Long Lac Gold Mining Co. Ltd. (Ont. 1933)
Dec. 8, 1988 – Name changed to Commstar Ltd. ■

Big M Petroleum Inc. (B.C. Mar. 31, 1981)
Aug. 17, 1990 – Name changed to Big M Resources Ltd. ■

Big M Resources Ltd. (B.C. Mar. 31, 1981)
July 17, 1992 – Name changed to Nickelodeon Minerals Inc.; basis 1 new for 3 old shs. ■

Big Missouri Mines Corp. Ltd. (Que. 1933)
July 1972 – Charter cancelled.

Big Mojo Capital Inc. (B.C. Apr. 30, 2009)
Jan. 8, 2013 – Name changed to CapGain Properties Inc. pursuant to Qualifying Transaction reverse takeover acquisition of (private) CapGain Properties Inc. ■

Big Nama Creek Mines Ltd. (Ont. 1954)
July 1977 – Name changed to York Consolidated Exploration Limited; basis 1 new for 2 old shs. ■

Big Nell Mines Ltd. (Que. Nov. 21, 1956)
Mar. 15, 1986 – Charter cancelled.
Oct. 15, 1996 – Charter revived.
Dec. 18, 1997 – Formed EP 2000 Conservation Inc. in Quebec on amalgamation with 9047-6094 Québec Inc.; basis 1 new for 3 old shs. ■

Big North Capital Inc. (B.C. Oct. 30, 2007)
Apr. 9, 2012 – Name changed to Big North Graphite Corp. ■

Big North Graphite Corp. (B.C. Oct. 30, 2007)
Nov. 24, 2016 – Name changed to Cobaltech Mining Inc. ■

Big Picture Multimedia Inc. (Alta. July 18, 1997)
Oct. 5, 1998 – Name changed to Big Picture Technologies Inc. ■

Big Picture Technologies Inc. (Alta. July 18, 1997)
July 12, 2001 – Company's board of directors voted to place the company into voluntary receivership at the direction of Network Capital Inc., a secured creditor and Calgary-based Arthur Anderson Inc. was appointed receiver/manager.
June 1, 2002 – All assets sold and the receiver (Deloitte & Touche) had been discharged. Secured creditors suffered a shortfall. There were no distributions made to unsecured creditors or shldrs.

Big Red Diamond Corporation (Ont. Dec. 17, 1999)
May 14, 2003 – Continued into Canada.
July 28, 2011 – Name changed to Northcore Resources Inc. (see FPsurvey - Mines & Energy)

Big Red Mining Corp. (B.C. Oct. 18, 2020)
Mar. 26, 2025 – Name changed to Antimony Resources Corp. (see FPsurvey - Mines & Energy)

Big Rock Brewery Income Trust (Alta. Nov. 18, 2002)
Jan. 7, 2011 – Succeeded by Big Rock Brewery Inc. pursuant to plan of arrangement whereby Big Rock Brewery Inc. was formed to facilitate the conversion of the trust into a corporation and the trust was subsequently dissolved. (see FPsurvey - Industrials)

Big Rock Brewery Ltd. (Alta. Sept. 24, 1984)
Jan. 15, 2003 – Converted into Big Rock Brewery Income Trust; basis 1 trust unit for 1 com. sh.

Big Rock Gold Ltd. (B.C. Oct. 15, 1986)
Apr. 5, 1988 – Name changed to International Cruiseshipcenters Corp. ■

Big Rock Labs Inc. (B.C. Apr. 4, 2014)
Nov. 21, 2017 – Name changed to Blox Labs Inc.; basis 1 new for 2 old shs. ■

Big Sandy Gold Mines Ltd. (Ont. 1947)
Jan. 4, 1960 – Charter cancelled.

Big Scoop Industries Ltd. (unknown)
June 9, 1972 – By an amended agreement dated Key Industries Ltd. acquired all o/s shs. of co. as follows: 1,033,333 escrowed shs. on basis of 2 sh. of Key for 4 shs. held; 234,000 pooled shs. on basis of 2 shs. of Key for 3 shs. held; and 102,700 shs. on basis of 3 Key shs. for each sh. held. Key Industries also offered a total of 66,667 shs. for conversion of co. debs.

Big Sky Petroleum Corporation (B.C. July 6, 2009)
Oct. 28, 2020 – Name changed to Pure Extracts Technologies Corp. pursuant to the reverse takeover acquisition of Pure Extracts Technologies Inc. and concurrent amalgamation of Pure Extracts with wholly owned 1270233 B.C. Ltd. (and continued as Pure Extracts

Manufacturing Corp.).; basis 1 new for 6 old shs. (see FPsurvey - Industrials)

Big Star Energy Inc. (B.C. June 11, 1987)
Feb. 19, 2004 – Name changed to Arcland Resources Inc.; basis 1 new for 6 old shs. ■

Big Stick Media Corporation (Ont. Sept. 25, 1995 amalg.)
July 21, 2010 – Privatized by way of amalg. with 2242823 Ontario Incorporated; basis 1 redeemable pref. sh. for 1 Big Stick com. sh. immediately redeemed for 10¢.

Big Strike Resources Ltd. (B.C. 1987)
Mar. 5, 1993 – Dissolved and struck off register.

Big Town Copper Mines Ltd. (Que. 1954 amalg.)
June 30, 1993 – Amalgamated with Pershing-Manitou Gold Mines Ltd./Société Minière Pershing-Manitou Ltée and Eastville Gold Mines Ltd./Société Minière Esteville Ltée to form Société Minière Pershing Manitou Ltée; basis 1 new for 1 Pershing-Manitou sh., 1 new for 5 Eastville shs. and 1 new for 2 Big Town shs.

Big Valley Resources Inc. (B.C. July 17, 1985)
Sept. 9, 2003 – Name changed to Consolidated Big Valley Resources Inc.; basis 1 new for 10 old shs. ■

Big Wind Capital Inc. (B.C. June 30, 2005)
Feb. 14, 2018 – Name changed to Hilltop Cybersecurity Inc. following acquisition of 25% interest in Hill Top Security, Inc. ■

Bighart Oil and Gas Ltd. (Alta. 1979 amalg.)
Oct. 1, 1982 – Amalgamated with a wholly owned subsid. of British Columbia Resources Investment Corporation (253754 Alberta Ltd.) to form Westar Petroleum Ltd.

Bighorn Development Corporation (B.C. 1979)
Dec. 16, 1994 – Dissolved and struck off register.

Bighorn Petroleum Ltd. (B.C. May 14, 1981)
May 7, 2009 – Name changed to Sunset Pacific Petroleum Ltd.; basis 1 new for 10 old shs. (see FPsurvey - Mines & Energy)

Bigknowledge Enterprises Inc. (Que. Sept. 24, 2004)
Dec. 6, 2005 – Made an assignment in bankruptcy under the Bankruptcy and Insolvency Act (BIA). Ernst & Young Inc. appointed trustee. All officers and directors resigned Nov. 30, 2005.
Feb. 21, 2017 – Struck from register and dissolved.

Bignell Chibougamau Exploration Ltd. (Que. 1964)
Aug. 30, 1973 – Operations suspended.

BigSky Resources Corp. (B.C. Nov. 4, 1996)
Nov. 27, 1996 – Continued into Yukon.
Sept. 18, 2000 – Name changed to International BigSky Resources Corp.; basis 1 new for 8 old shs. ■

Bigstack Opportunities I Inc. (Ont. Nov. 25, 2020)
May 16, 2025 – Name changed to Reeflex Solutions Inc. pursuant to the Qualifying Transaction reverse takeover acquisition of Reeflex Coil Solutions Inc. (see FPsurvey - Mines & Energy; FPsurvey - Industrials)

Bigstone Minerals Ltd. (B.C. May 17, 1966)
Aug. 30, 1993 – Name changed to Adamas Resources Corp.; basis 1 new for 5 old shs. ■

Bijou Mines & Oils Ltd. (Ont. June 17, 1974)
Aug. 20, 1985 – Name changed to Bijou Resource Corporation; basis 1 new for 4 old shs. ■

Bijou Resource Corporation (Ont. June 17, 1974)
Sept. 11, 1998 – Name changed to Kingscross Communities Incorporated following acquisition of Kingscross Developments Incorporated; basis 1 new for 5 old shs. ■

Bikestar Inc. (Alta. Jan. 19, 1996)
Aug. 23, 1999 – Name changed to AdventurX.com, Inc.; basis 1 new for 5 old shs. ■

Groupe Bikini Village Inc. (Can. July 24, 1978)
June 23, 2015 – On Mar. 31, 2015, substantially all assets were sold to Boutique La Vie en Rose Inc. with net proceeds distributed to creditors. On May 15, 2015, certificate of amendment issued by Industry Canada for the redesignation of all o/s com. shs. as redeemable com. shs. pursuant to a proposal in bankruptcy approved on May 14, 2015, by creditors. On May 28, 2015, Boutique La Vie en Rose Inc. subscribed for 1 com. sh. for $1 cash resulting in all o/s redeemable com. shs. being redeemed for nil consideration. No funds were available for com. shldrs.

Billikin Resources Inc. (B.C. Mar. 26, 1981)
Mar. 28, 1991 – Name changed to Cora Resources Ltd.; basis 1 new for 4 old shs. ■

Billy Goat Brands Ltd. (B.C. Sept. 22, 2020)
Sept. 12, 2022 – Name changed to GOAT Industries Ltd. (see FPsurvey - Mines & Energy; FPsurvey - Industrials)

Billy Goat Creek Mines Ltd. (B.C. 1970)
May 14, 1976 – Name changed to Circle Builders Corporation; basis 1 new for 4 old shs. ■

Biloxi Yellowknife Mines Ltd. (Ont. 1946)
Jan. 14, 1954 – Charter cancelled.

Biltaurum Mines Ltd. (Ont. 1949)
Apr. 1, 1965 – Dissolved.

Biltmore Hats Limited (Can. 1929)
July 6, 1973 – Name changed to Biltmore Industries Limited. ■

Biltmore Industries Limited (Can. 1929)
Apr. 13, 1982 – Filed voluntary assignment into bankruptcy. Preferred creditors pd. in full, leaving balance of $289,663 to cover claims of unsec. creditors totaling $5,265,600.
Aug. 29, 1984 – Notice of final divd. to unsec. creditors of 5.5¢ on the dollar. Nothing avail. for pref. or com. shldrs.

Biltrite Nightingale Inc. (Que. 1958)
Sept. 1988 – Acquired by Canam Manac Group Inc. (see The Canam Manac Group Inc.)

Bingo.com, Inc. (Fla. Jan. 12, 1987)
Apr. 7, 2005 – Succeeded by Bingo.com, Ltd. following merger into Anguilla incorporated parent company. ■

Bingo.com, Ltd. (Anguilla Sept. 30, 2004)
Jan. 22, 2015 – Name changed to Shoal Games Ltd. ■

Binoptic International Corporation (Alta. Jan. 13, 1987)
Mar. 22, 1994 – Continued into Delaware.

Binscarth PVC Ventures Inc. (Ont. Mar. 4, 2004)
July 13, 2005 – Name changed to DoveCorp Enterprises Inc. following Qualifying Transaction acquisition of Dove Corp. for total consideration of 40,000,000 com. shs. ■

Bio Angel 1 Corporation (Can. May 20, 2003)
Feb. 3, 2005 – Name changed to Omnitech Consultant Group Inc. following Qualifying Transaction reverse takeover acquisition of Omnitech Consultant Group Inc.; basis 1 new for 3.5 old shs. ■

Bio-Extraction Inc. (Ont. Mar. 16, 2006)
Dec. 30, 2009 – Name changed to BioExx Specialty Proteins Ltd. ■

Bio 1 Inc. (Can. Dec. 6, 2000)
June 2, 2003 – Name changed to Aurelian Resources Inc. following Qualifying Transaction reverse takeover acquisition of Aurelian Resources Corporation Ltd. ■

Bio-Vita Inc. (Que. 1967)
Aug. 1977 – Placed into bankruptcy on Nov. 29, 1973; charter cancelled. Payment made to one preferred claim in the Province of Quebec; divd. of 10% made to unsecured creditors.

BioAB Strategies Ltd. (B.C. Feb. 11, 2014)
Dec. 19, 2014 – Name changed to Invictus MD Strategies Corp. following acquisition of Greener Pastures Marihuana Dispensary Ltd. ■

BioAnalogics Systems, Inc. (B.C. Aug. 5, 1987)
Mar. 13, 1992 – Continued into Wyoming.
Nov. 5, 1992 – Continued into Oregon.
Aug. 16, 1993 – Name changed to International BioAnalogics Systems, Inc.; basis 1 new for 3 old shs. ■

BioCapital Investments Limited Partnership (Que. May 8, 1997)
Apr. 16, 2001 – Privatized; basis 1.156 units of mutual fund (created to hold all BioCapital units) plus $5.20 for 1 BioCapital unit, valued at approx. $16.76.

BioChem Pharma Inc. (Que. Dec. 14, 1972)
May 14, 2001 – Amalgamated with Shire Pharmaceuticals Group plc,; basis either 2.2757 Shire ord. shs., 0.7586 Shire Acquisition Inc. exch. shs., 0.7586 Shire ADS, or a combination of the three options for 1 BioChem sh. Each exch. sh. is exch. into 3 Shire ord. shs. or 1 Shire ADS.

Biocoll Medical Corp. (B.C. Dec. 4, 1980)
Aug. 12, 1997 – Name changed to GenSci Regeneration Sciences Inc. following amalgamation with wholly owned Osteopharm Limited; basis 1 new for 1 old sh. ■

BioDE Ventures Ltd. (B.C. Feb. 12, 2014)
Aug. 16, 2017 – Name changed to Exro Technologies Inc. following reverse takeover acquisition of (old) Exro Technologies Inc. and concurrent amalgamation of (old) Exro with wholly owned 1089001 B.C. Ltd. (see FPsurvey - Industrials)

Bioenvelop Technologies Corporation (Can. Mar. 11, 1998)
Aug. 17, 2006 – Filed a proposal under the Bankruptcy and Insolvency Act. André Giroux Conseils Inc. was appointed trustee in bankruptcy.

BioExx Specialty Proteins Ltd. (Ont. Mar. 16, 2006)
Oct. 1, 2013 – Filed for protection under the Companies' Creditors Arrangement Act (CCAA) and BDO Canada Limited was appointed monitor.
Oct. 11, 2013 – Court approval for varying of the initial stay order was received allowing secured creditor, Romspen Investment Corporation, to initiate foreclosure action over property in the North Corman Industrial Park, Saskatoon, Sask., and for Romspen and/or secured creditor Ag-West Bio Inc. to issue notices of sale in respect to unsold equipment currently or formerly located in the Saskatoon facility and for all of the company's patents, patents pending and propriety technologies (intellectual property).
Nov. 15, 2013 – The sale of the Saskatchewan assets to 508572 Alberta Ltd. was completed and distributions were subsequently made amounting to $5,333,624 to Romspen and $213,896 to Ag-West.
Jan. 15, 2014 – Court approval was received for the sale of the company's intellectual property to Siebte PMI Verwaltungs GmbH, the proceeds of which would not be sufficient to satisfy in full the claim of the debentureholders. No distributions were to be made to shlders.
Apr. 23, 2014 – BDO Canada Limited was discharged as monitor, (see FPsurvey - Industrials)

BIOflex Technologies Inc. (Can. July 19, 2012)
Dec. 18, 2015 – Name changed to Relevium Technologies Inc. ■

Bioflow Environmental Technologies Inc. (B.C. May 4, 1987)
Oct. 31, 1996 – Name changed to Strategic Merchant Bancorp Ltd. pursuant to plan of arrangement whereby newly incorporated Strategic Merchant Bancorp Ltd. acquired the co., Pacific Growth Ventures Ltd. and Strategic Equity Growth Fund (VCC) Ltd.; basis 1 new for 3 Bioflow shs., 2.81 new for 1 Pacific Growth sh. and 1.85 new for 1 Strategic Equity sh. ■

BioForest Pacific Inc. (Ont. Oct. 16, 1995)
Apr. 15, 2003 – Name changed to Byron Resources Inc.; basis 1 new for 140 old shs. ∎

Biogenetic Technologies Inc. (Ont. 1955)
1994 – Continued into Nevada.

BioHEP Technologies Ltd. (B.C. Feb. 11, 2014)
June 21, 2021 – Name changed to Next Hydrogen Solutions Inc. pursuant to the reverse takeover acquisition of Next Hydrogen Corporation. (see FPsurvey - Industrials)

Bioject Medical Systems Ltd. (B.C. Feb. 14, 1985)
Dec. 17, 1992 – Acquired by Bioject Medical Technologies, Inc.; basis unknown.

BioLink Corp. (Ont. Mar. 18, 1997 amalg.)
Mar. 31, 2000 – Name changed to First Empire Entertainment.com Inc.; basis 1 new for 4 old shs. ∎

Biologix (B.C.) Ltd. (B.C. Feb. 18, 1966)
May 1, 1998 – Name changed to Biologix International Ltd. (see FPsurvey - Industrials)

BioMS Medical Corp. (Alta. July 31, 2001)
July 8, 2010 – Name changed to Medwell Capital Corp. ∎

Biomax Technologies Inc. (B.C. Mar. 25, 1999 amalg.)
June 25, 2012 – Dissolved and struck from register.

Biomerge Industries Ltd. (B.C. Nov. 2, 1990 amalg.)
Apr. 15, 2009 – Continued into Alberta.
May 27, 2009 – Name changed to Total Energy Services Inc. pursuant to plan of arrangement to convert Total Energy Services Trust (TEST) to a corp. resulting in TEST becoming a wholly owned subsid. of Total Energy Services Inc. (TESI); basis 1 TESI sh. for 1 TEST trust unit, $0.00282 plus 0.000237 TESI shs. for 1 Biomerge vtg. sh. and $0.00389 for 1 Biomerge non-vtg. sh. (see FPsurvey - Mines & Energy; FPsurvey - Industrials)

Biomet Technology Inc. (B.C. Mar. 24, 1960)
Dec. 2, 1994 – Dissolved and struck off register.

Biometric Security Corp. (Wyo. Nov. 10, 1998)
Dec. 29, 1999 – Name changed to Safeguard Biometric Corp.; basis 1 new for 5 old shs. ∎

Biomin Therapeutic Corporation (B.C. Aug. 17, 1987)
Nov. 6, 1996 – Name changed to Pharmex Industries Inc. ∎

Biomind Labs Inc. (Alta. Mar. 29, 2005)
July 15, 2021 – Continued into Ontario. (see FPsurvey - Industrials)

Biomira Inc. (Can. Aug. 23, 1985)
Dec. 10, 2007 – Formed Oncothyreon Inc. following reconstitution into an indirect wholly owned subsid. of Oncothyreon Inc., originally incorporated as Biomira Corporation in Delaware on Sept. 7, 2007, and changed its name to Oncothyreon on Sept. 27, 2007; basis 1 new for 6 old shs. ∎

bioMmune Technologies Inc. (B.C. Jan. 28, 2011)
Mar. 30, 2017 – Name changed to Pascal Biosciences Inc. ∎

Bionaire Inc. (Can. 1977)
Apr. 9, 1996 – Acquired by RC Acquisition Inc., an indirect wholly owned Cdn. subsid. of The Rival Company, for $2.25 per sh.

Bionic Enterprises, Inc. (B.C. Feb. 28, 1986)
Aug. 31, 1994 – Name changed to Hymex Diamond Corp. following reverse takeover acquisition of 85% interest in Hymex Guinea S.A. ∎

Bioniche Inc. (Can. Feb. 1, 1992 amalg.)
Sept. 1, 1999 – Formed Bioniche Life Sciences Inc. in Canada on amalgamation with Renaissance Life Sciences Inc. (formerly Vetrepharm Inc.) and Vetrepharm Animal Health Inc.; basis 1,124.6 new com. shs. for 1 Renaissance com. sh., 1 new ser. 1 pref. sh. for 1

Renaissance cl. A special sh., 0.726 new for 1 Vetrepharm sh. and 0.2 new for 1 Bioniche sh. ∎

Bioniche Life Sciences Inc. (Can. Sept. 1, 1999 amalg.)
Nov. 24, 2014 – Name changed to Telesta Therapeutics Inc. ∎

Biopac Industries Inc. (B.C. Aug. 15, 1980)
Jan. 18, 1995 – Name changed to BPI Industries Inc.; basis 1 new for 4 old shs. ∎

Biopat Capital Inc. (Can. Feb. 7, 1996)
Dec. 4, 1997 – Name changed to Colt Energy Inc.; basis 1 new for 1 old sh. ∎

Biopotential Capital Inc. (Can. Jan. 9, 2004)
July 18, 2005 – Name changed to Osta Biotechnologies Inc. following Qualifying Transaction reverse takeover acquisition of Osta BioPharma Inc. ∎

Biorex Groupe-Conseil Inc. (Can. Feb. 21, 1978)
Jan. 1, 1989 – Amalgamated with ACSI Group Ltd. to form ACSI-BIOREX Inc. (see ACSI-BIOREX Inc.)

BioSante Pharmaceuticals, Inc. (Wyo. Dec. 19, 1996 amalg.)
Continued into Delaware.
July 18, 2013 – Name changed to ANI Pharmaceuticals, Inc.

Bioscrypt Inc. (Can. June 25, 1987)
Mar. 7, 2008 – Acquired by L-1 Identity Solutions, Inc.; basis 0.0324 L-1 shs. for 1 Bioscrypt sh.

Biosign Technologies Inc. (Ont. July 14, 2006 amalg.)
Apr. 7, 2017 – Certificate of incorporation cancelled and dissolved.

BioSource Industries Inc. (B.C. May 26, 1989)
May 19, 1993 – Formed BioSource International, Inc. in Delaware on amalgamation with TAGO Immunoligicals, Inc., constituting a Pooling of Interests.

BioSyntech, Inc. (Nev. Dec. 14, 1994)
Mar. 28, 2006 – Continued into Canada.
Sept. 10, 2010 – Placed into bankruptcy and PricewaterhouseCoopers Inc. was appointed trustee. All assets were sold and no distributions were available for shldrs.
Feb. 7, 2013 – Dissolved and struck from register.

Biotech Electronics Ltd. (Can. 1977)
Jan. 3, 1989 – Name changed to Bionaire Inc. ∎

Biotech Holdings Ltd. (Alta. Aug. 20, 1993)
Nov. 6, 2009 – Deemed bankrupt; Abakhan & Associated Inc. appointed trustee.

Biotech Medical Sciences Inc. (Alta. Nov. 12, 2001)
Jan. 6, 2005 – Amalgamated with Entech Investments Inc. (1 for 1) to continue with a new name CAPVEST Income Corp.; basis 0.88 new CAPVEST sh. for 1 old Biotech sh. (see CAPVEST Income Corp.)

Biotechna Environmental Limited (Alta. Mar. 13, 1967)
Sept. 13, 1996 – Name changed to Biotechna Environmental Technologies Corporation; basis 1 new for 15 old shs. ∎

Biotechna Environmental Technologies Corporation (Alta. Mar. 13, 1967)
May 8, 1998 – Continued into Anguilla.

BioteQ Environmental Technologies Inc. (B.C. Feb. 17, 1999)
Mar. 1, 2017 – Name changed to BQE Water Inc. (see FPsurvey - Industrials)

Biotonix (2010) Inc. (Can. Nov. 5, 2007)
Oct. 18, 2012 – Name changed to AtmanCo Inc. following reverse takeover acquisition of Atman Co.; basis 1 new for 2 old shs. ∎

Biovail Corporation (Ont. Mar. 29, 1994 amalg.)
June 29, 2005 – Continued into Canada.
Sept. 28, 2010 – Name changed to Valeant Pharmaceuticals International, Inc. pursuant to acquisition of (old) Valeant Pharmaceuticals International, Inc. and amalgamation of old Valeant with a wholly owned subsid. of Biovail Corporation. ∎

Biovail Corporation International (Ont. Mar. 29, 1994 amalg.)
Mar. 16, 2000 – Name changed to Biovail Corporation. ∎

Biovest Corp. I (Can. Aug. 27, 2009)
Mar. 11, 2013 – Name changed to Magor Corporation pursuant to Qualifying Transaction reverse takeover acquisition of Magor Communications Corp. (see FPsurvey - Industrials)

BioWest Therapeutics Inc. (B.C. Feb. 12, 2010)
Aug. 22, 2011 – Name changed to Carrus Capital Corporation. ∎

Bioxel Pharma Inc. (Can. July 13, 1995)
Apr. 30, 2009 – Declared bankrupt. No funds available for shldrs.

Birch Bay Gold Mines Ltd. (Ont. 1934)
1958 – Charter cancelled.

Birch Capital Inc. (Ont. Mar. 21, 1988)
Apr. 2, 1996 – Name changed to Breckenridge Technologies Inc. ∎

Birch Hill Gold Corp. (B.C. June 1, 2006)
June 3, 2014 – Formed Coldstream Mineral Ventures Corp. in British Columbia on amalgamation with 0996623 B.C. Ltd., a wholly owned subsid. of Canoe Mining Ventures Corp.; basis 1 Canoe com. sh. for 2.5 Birch com. shs.

Birch Lake Capital Inc. (Alta. Dec. 5, 2007)
Oct. 27, 2010 – Name changed to Birch Lake Energy Inc. pursuant to Qualifying Transaction acquisition of Canadian Rigger Energy Inc. ∎

Birch Lake Energy Inc. (Alta. Dec. 5, 2007)
June 2, 2018 – Struck from registry and dissolved.

Birch Mountain Resources Ltd. (Alta. Oct. 25, 1994)
Dec. 31, 1995 – Amalgamated in Alberta to continue with same name.
Nov. 5, 2008 – Placed into receivership by principal secured creditor. PricewaterhouseCoopers Inc. appointed receiver.
June 7, 2013 – Struck from registry and dissolved.

Birch Point Mines Ltd. (Ont. 1965)
1967 – Merged into the Great Molly Explorations and Enterprises Ltd.; basis 1 new for 4 old shs.

Birchcliff Energy Ltd. (Alta. Jan. 18, 2005 amalg.)
May 31, 2005 – Amalgamated with Veracel Inc. pursuant to a plan of arrangement to form new co. with same name Birchcliff Energy Ltd. (see FPsurvey - Mines & Energy)

Birchpoint Capital Inc. (Alta. Aug. 19, 2005)
Oct. 10, 2006 – Name changed to Ucore Uranium Inc. following Qualifying Transaction acquisition of Hot Rock Uranium Corp.; basis 2 new for 1 old sh. ∎

Birchtree Investments Inc. (B.C. Feb. 2, 2021)
July 14, 2021 – Name changed to Birchtree Investments Ltd. (see FPsurvey - Industrials)

Birchtree Mines Ltd. (Man. 1958)
Jan. 24, 1964 – Dissolved.

Birchwood Ventures Ltd. (B.C. Jan. 25, 1980)
Sept. 30, 1997 – Name changed to Oromin Explorations Ltd.; basis 1 new for 5 old shs. ∎

Bird Construction Company Limited (Sask. Feb. 15, 1930)
Feb. 27, 2006 – Converted into Bird Construction Income Fund; basis 3 Bird Construction trust units for 1 Bird Construction com. sh.

Bird Construction Income Fund (Ont. Jan. 1, 2006)
Jan. 1, 2011 – Succeeded by Bird Construction Inc. pursuant to plan of arrangement whereby Bird Construction Inc. was formed to facilitate the conversion of the fund into a corporation and the fund was subsequently wound up. (see FPsurvey - Industrials)

Bird River Chromite Mines (Man. Mar. 7, 1958)
July 19, 1989 – Name changed to Bird River Mines Co. Ltd. ■

Bird River Mines Co. Ltd. (Man. Mar. 7, 1958)
Feb. 13, 2001 – Name changed to Bird River Mines Inc. ■

Bird River Mines Inc. (Man. Mar. 7, 1958)
Feb. 7, 2011 – Name changed to Bird River Resources Inc. (see FPsurvey - Mines & Energy; FPsurvey - Industrials)

Birim Goldfields Inc. (Ont. July 29, 1980 amalg.)
Mar. 31, 1996 – Amalgamated in Ontario to continue with same name. (see Volta Resources Inc.)
Apr. 3, 2008 – Amalgamated with Goldcrest Resources Ltd. to form Volta Resources Inc.; basis 1 Volta com. sh. for 2.6 Birim com. shs. (see Volta Resources Inc.)

Birka Capital Corp. (Alta. Oct. 2, 1995)
Mar. 30, 1998 – Formed Qnetix Inc. following acquisition of Qnetix Computer Consultants Inc.; basis 1 new for 1 old sh. ■

Birks & Mayors Inc. (Can. 1879)
Oct. 1, 2013 – Name changed to Birks Group Inc. (see FPsurvey - Industrials)

Biroco Kirkland Mines Limited (Ont. Feb. 11, 1944)
Mar. 7, 1996 – Formed Inter.tain.net Inc. in Ontario on amalgamation with Inter.tain.net Inc.; basis 1 pref. sh. for 1 com. sh. redeemed for 10¢ per sh. ■

Biron Bay Gold Mines Limited (Ont. May 7, 1946)
Mar. 1981 – Name changed to Biron Bay Resources Limited; basis 1 new for 5 old shs. ■

Biron Bay Resources Limited (Ont. May 7, 1946)
May 1, 1997 – Formed Royal Ecoproducts Limited in Ontario on amalgamation with Royal Ecoproducts Ltd., constituting a reverse takeover by Royal Ecoproducts; basis 1 new subord. vtg. for 2.92 old com. shs. ■

Bishop Capital Corporation (B.C. Oct. 1, 1992)
Feb. 27, 1996 – Name changed to Bishop Resources Inc. and continued into Alberta. ■

Bishop Gold Inc. (Alta. Feb. 27, 1996)
Sept. 19, 2006 – Continued into British Columbia.
Nov. 20, 2007 – Name changed to First Pursuit Ventures Ltd.; basis 1 new for 20 old shs. ■

Bishop Mines Ltd. (B.C. 1976)
Oct. 12, 1982 – Name changed to Bishop Resources Development Ltd. (see FPsurvey - Mines & Energy)

Bishop Resources Inc. (Alta. Feb. 27, 1996)
Aug. 19, 2004 – Name changed to Bishop Gold Inc.; basis 1 new for 3 old shs. ■

Bishop Resources International Exploration Inc. (Que. June 10, 1950)
Nov. 30, 1995 – Name changed to Caldera Resources Inc.; basis 1 new for 10 old shs. ■

Bishu Mines Ltd. (Ont. 1945)
June 3, 1963 – Dissolved.

Bismillah Ventures Inc. (B.C. May 31, 1984)
Nov. 10, 1997 – Name changed to Royal Rock Ventures Inc.; basis 1 new for 5 old shs. ■

Bison Gold Exploration Inc. (Ont. Dec. 23, 2005 amalg.)
May 11, 2009 – Name changed to Bison Gold Resources Inc.; basis 1 new for 3 old shs. ■

Bison Gold Resources Inc. (Ont. Dec. 23, 2005 amalg.)
Oct. 23, 2017 – Acquired by Klondex Mines Ltd.; basis 0.1242 Klondex shs. for 1 Bison Gold sh. (see Klondex Mines Ltd.)

Bison Petroleum & Minerals Limited (Ont. 1960)
Dec. 12, 1987 – Name changed to United Bison Resources Limited. ■

Bison Petroleums Ltd. (Ont. Mar. 2, 1950)
1954 – Acquired by Saskalon Uranium & Oils Ltd.; basis 1 new for 5 old shs.

Bison Resources Ltd. (Alta. May 7, 1997)
Jan. 5, 2006 – Plan of Arrangement acquisition by Mission Oil & Gas Inc.; basis either $8.65, or 1.0949 new Mission shs., or $6.055 plus 0.3284 new Mission sh. for 1 old Bison sh. (see Mission Oil & Gas Inc.)

Bissett & Associates Investment Management Ltd. (Alta. Aug. 14, 1981)
Oct. 4, 2000 – Acquired by Templeton Management Limited, a wholly owned subsid. of California-based Franklin Resources, Inc., for $20.50 per sh. Name changed to Bissett Investment Management Ltd.

Bissett Gold Mines Ltd. (Man. Feb. 25, 1936)
May 1972 – Charter cancelled.

Bitcoin Treasury Corporation (B.C. July 27, 2021)
Jan. 21, 2025 – Continued into Alberta. (see FPsurvey - Industrials)

Bitcoin Trust (Ont. Jan. 12, 2021)
May 6, 2021 – Converted from a closed end fund to Ninepoint Bitcoin ETF, an exchange traded fund. (see Ninepoint Bitcoin ETF)

Bitec Development Corporation (B.C. 1980)
Mar. 31, 1994 – Dissolved and struck off register.

Bitech Corporation (Ont. Mar. 7, 1956)
Nov. 20, 1996 – Name changed to Bitech Petroleum Corporation and continued into Canada; basis 1 new for 15 old shs. ■

Bitech Energy Resources Limited (Ont. Mar. 7, 1956)
Aug. 11, 1989 – Name changed to Bitech Corporation. ■

Bitech Petroleum Corporation (Can. Nov. 20, 1996)
Oct. 5, 2001 – Acquired by LUKOIL Overseas Holding Ltd., for $1.55 per sh.

BitGold Inc. (Can. Apr. 29, 2015 amalg.)
July 30, 2015 – Name changed to GoldMoney Inc. ■

Bitumen Capital Inc. (Can. Mar. 17, 2006)
Oct. 11, 2017 – Name changed to Goliath Resources Limited following Qualifying Transaction reverse takeover acquistion of (old) Goliath Resources Limited and concurrent amalgamation of (old) Goliath with wholly owned 2590005 Ontario Inc.; basis 1 new for 1.67 old shs. (see FPsurvey - Mines & Energy)

Bizmac Mines Ltd. (Ont. 1956)
1959 – Name changed to Waco Petroleums Ltd. ■

Black Bay Uranium Ltd. (Alta. 1953)
June 1974 – Name changed to New Black Bay Minerals Ltd.; basis 1 new for 200 old shs. ■

Black Bear Oil & Gas Co. Ltd. (Ont. 1931)
1960 – Wound up.

Black Birch Capital Acquisition I Corp. (Ont. Jan. 26, 2009)
Sept. 20, 2011 – Name changed to Oremex Gold Inc. pursuant to Qualifying Transaction acquisiton of gold prospects from Oremex Resources Inc. (see FPsurvey - Mines & Energy)

Black Birch Capital Acquisition II Corp. (Can. Nov. 3, 2009)
June 14, 2013 – Name changed to Chinapintza Mining Corp. and continued into British Columbia pursuant to Qualifying Transaction reverse takeover acquisition of Guangshou Ecuador Mineral Ltd. and amalgamation of Guangshou Ecuador with wholly owned 0964675 B.C. Ltd. ■

Black Birch Capital Acquisition III Corp. (Can. Sept. 24, 2012)
July 28, 2017 – Continued into British Columbia.
June 12, 2018 – Name changed to GTEC Holdings Ltd. following Qualifying Transaction reverse takeover acquisition of GreenTec Holdings Ltd. and concurrent amalgamation of GreenTec with wholly owned 1155425 B.C. Ltd.; basis 1 new for 12 old shs. ■

Black Bourgon Mines Ltd. (Ont. 1953)
Jan. 20, 1964 – Dissolved.

Black Bull Resources Inc. (Alta. July 18, 1997)
June 12, 2008 – Continued into Canada.
Sept. 16, 2019 – Name changed to Magnetic North Acquisition Corp. (see FPsurvey - Mines & Energy; FPsurvey - Industrials)

Black Canyon Resources Inc. (Alta. Feb. 17, 1994)
Aug. 23, 1999 – Amalgamated with Eden Exploration Ltd. (0.122642 for 1) and 836296 Alberta Ltd. (wholly owned subsid. of Brandon Energy Ltd.) to form Cannon Oil & Gas Ltd.; basis 0.210526 Cannon shs. for 1 Black Canyon sh. (see Cannon Oil & Gas Ltd.)

Black Cliff Mines Limited (Ont. Nov. 25, 1955)
July 28, 1992 – Name changed to Altai Resources Inc. (see FPsurvey - Mines & Energy)

Black Creek Gold Mines Ltd. (Ont. 1945)
1968 – Charter cancelled.

Black Cricket Mines Ltd. (Ont. 1968)
Mar. 1976 – Charter cancelled.

Black Crow Mines Ltd. (Ont. 1947)
Feb. 11, 1965 – Charter cancelled.

Black Diamond Income Fund (Alta. Aug. 16, 2006)
Dec. 31, 2009 – Converted into Black Diamond Group Limited; basis 1 Black Diamond Group sh. for 1 Black Diamond Income trust unit.

Black Diamond Industries Ltd. (Alta. May 20, 1987)
Sept. 7, 1988 – Name changed to RPV Industries (Canada) Inc. ■

Black Diamond Resources Ltd. (B.C. 1948)
Dec. 11, 1986 – Formed Com-Air Containers (Canada) Inc. in British Columbia following amalgamation. ■

Black Diamond Tungsten Limited (B.C. 1951)
Dec. 1960 – Dissolved.

Black Dragon Gold Corp. (B.C. Dec. 12, 2007)
Mar. 1, 2019 – Voluntarily delisted from TSX-Venture Exchange; will continue to trade on Australian Securities Exchange (ASX). (see FPsurvey - Mines & Energy)

Black Eagle Exploration Co. Ltd. (Alta.)
1960 – Struck off register.

Black Giant Mines Ltd. (B.C. Apr. 11, 1962)
July 30, 1984 – Name changed to Alcina Development Corporation; basis 1 new for 5 old shs. ■

Black Gold Mines Ltd. (Ont. 1933)
Apr. 1958 – Charter cancelled.

Black Gold Oil & Gas Ltd. (Alta. 1988 amalg.)
Sept. 21, 1990 – Acquired by Intensity Resources Ltd.; basis 0.34418 Intensity shs. for 1 Black Gold sh. (see Intensity Resources Ltd.)

Black Gold Petroleums Ltd. (unknown)
Succeeded by Aztec Exploration Ltd. (see Aztec Exploration Ltd.)

Black Gold Resources (1973) Ltd. (Alta. 1966)
Aug. 29, 1980 – Amalgamated into Black Gold Oil & Gas Ltd.; basis 1 new for 1 old sh.

Black Gregor Explorations Ltd. (Ont. June 17, 1983)
Aug. 11, 1993 – Name changed to Gregor Goldfields Corp.; basis 1 new for 4 old shs. ■

Black Hat Capital Inc. (Alta. Apr. 29, 2004)
Apr. 10, 2007 – Name changed to Castle Resources Inc. following Qualifying Transaction acquisition of 312 hectares of mineral exploration properties in Zacatecas, Mexico. ■

Black Hawk Mining Inc. (Que. May 20, 1960)
Oct. 17, 2003 – Formed Glencairn Gold Corporation following reverse takeover acquisition of Glencairn Gold Corporation and amalgamation with a wholly owned subsidiary of Glencairn; basis 1 new for 3 old shs. ■

Black Hawk Mining Ltd. (Que. May 20, 1960)
Aug. 8, 1981 – Name changed to Black Hawk Mining Inc. ■

Black Hawk Porcupine Mines Ltd. (Ont. 1945)
Jan. 21, 1957 – Dissolved.

Black Hill Nickel Mines Limited (Ont. 1964)
Dec. 29, 2000 – Dissolved.

Black Hill Resources Ltd. (B.C. June 20, 1983)
Apr. 17, 1985 – Name changed to Texcan Technology Corp. ■

Black Isle Resources Corporation (B.C. Mar. 7, 1987)
Dec. 3, 2018 – Voluntarily delisted.
June 24, 2021 – Name changed to Alkaline Fuel Cell Power Corp. ■

Black Jade Resources Ltd. (B.C. 1983)
1985 – Name changed to International Magnetics Corporation. ■

Black Label Resources Inc. (B.C. Nov. 7, 1980)
June 3, 1992 – Name changed to Autobyte Technologies Inc. ■

Black Lake Uranium Mines Ltd. (Ont. 1948)
Nov. 5, 1962 – Dissolved.

Black Lion Capital Corp. (B.C. Jan. 7, 2015)
Apr. 13, 2021 – Name changed to Globally Local Technologies Inc. pursuant to the Qualifying Transaction reverse takeover acquisition of 2204901 Ontario Inc. (dba Globally Local) and concurrent amalgamation of Globally Local with wholly owned 2801318 Ontario Ltd.; basis 1 now for 2.5 old shs. ■

Black Marlin Energy Corp. (B.C. Dec. 5, 1980)
Nov. 21, 1986 – Delisted from the Vancouver Stock Exchange. Subsequently dissolved for failure to file and struck from register.

Black Marlin Energy Holdings Limited (British Virgin Islands Mar. 22, 2010)
Oct. 12, 2010 – Acquired by Afren plc; basis 0.3647 Afren shs. for 1 Black Martin sh.

Black Mountain Capital Corporation (Yuk. Dec. 28, 2001)
Nov. 20, 2007 – Name changed to Grand Peak Capital Corp.; basis 1 new for 5 old shs. (see FPsurvey - Industrials)

Black Mountain Gold USA Corp. (B.C. July 21, 2015)
Jan. 25, 2023 – Name changed to Millennial Potash Corp. (see FPsurvey - Mines & Energy)

Black Mountain Minerals Inc. (Ont. May 7, 1997 amalg.)
Nov. 30, 2006 – Name changed to Augustine Ventures Inc. ■

Black Oil Co. Ltd. (Alta.)
1958 – Struck off register.

Black Owl Resources Ltd. (B.C. May 5, 1966)
Dec. 14, 1990 – Dissolved and struck off register.

Black Panther Mining Corp. (B.C. Nov. 21, 1983)
June 19, 2015 – Name changed to Canadian International Pharma Corp. following reorganization into a generic drug manufacturing and distribution company. ■

Black Pearl Minerals Consolidated Inc. (Ont. July 17, 1995 amalg.)
Jan. 19, 2009 – Name changed to Canada Lithium Corp. ■

Black Pearl Minerals Inc. (Ont. July 17, 1995 amalg.)
July 20, 2000 – Name changed to Black Pearl Minerals Consolidated Inc.; basis 1 new for 5 old shs. ■

Black Pearl Petroleums Ltd. (B.C. Nov. 16, 1979)
Aug. 2, 1983 – Name changed to Signet Resources Inc. ■

Black Pearl Resources Ltd. (B.C. 1984)
Feb. 11, 1987 – Name changed to Wizan Productions Inc. under amalgamation agreement. ■

Black Petrol Operators Ltd. (Alta.)
1958 – Struck off register.

Black Photo Corporation Limited (Ont. 1969)
May 23, 1985 – All o/s com. shs. acquired by Scotts Hospitality Inc.; basis $22 per sh. (see Scott's Hospitality Inc.)

Black Point Capital Inc. (Can. Mar. 5, 2004)
Apr. 29, 2005 – Formed Mistral Pharma Inc. in Canada on Qualifying Transaction amalgamation with Mistral Pharma Inc. for 35,858,655 com. shs. at a deemed price of $0.20 per sh. ■

Black Point Resources Ltd. (B.C. 1994)
Jan. 12, 1995 – Continued into Ontario. (see The InfoUtility Corporation)
June 15, 2000 – Amalgamated with The InfoUtility Corporation (1 for 1) to continue as a new company named The InfoUtility Corporation; basis 1 new InfoUtility sh. for 4 old Black Point shs. (see The InfoUtility Corporation)

Black River Mining Ltd. (Que. Feb. 16, 1945)
1968 – Name changed to Menorah Mines Ltd.; basis 1 new for 3 old shs. ■

Black Rock Nevada Mines Ltd. (B.C. July 12, 1988)
July 26, 1993 – Name changed to Argosy Mining Corp.; basis 1 new for 2 old shs. ■

Black Sea Copper & Gold Corp. (B.C. Apr. 13, 1995)
Feb. 21, 2019 – Name changed to QX Metals Corp.; basis 1 new for 3 old shs. ■

Black Sea Energy Ltd. (Yuk. Feb. 21, 1995)
June 24, 1999 – Name changed to Ivanhoe Energy Inc. ■

Black Sheep Ventures Inc. (B.C. 1979)
July 11, 1985 – Name changed to Ameroil Energy Corporation. ■

Black Shield Metals Corp. (B.C. Oct. 13, 2017)
Oct. 27, 2021 – Name changed to Basin Uranium Corp. (see FPsurvey - Mines & Energy)

Black Smoker Ventures Inc. (B.C. Jan. 27, 2009)
Nov. 30, 2012 – Name changed to Jager Resources Inc.; basis 1 new for 13 old shs. ■

Black Sparrow Capital Corp. (Alta. June 22, 2011)
Dec. 1, 2014 – Name changed to Aphria Inc. and continued into Ontario following Qualifying Transaction reverse takeover acquisition of Pure Natures Wellness Inc.; basis 1 new for 10 old shs. ■

Black Springs Capital Corp. (Que. Mar. 24, 2014 amalg.)
Mar. 24, 2017 – Formed Kintavar Exploration Inc. in Quebec following Qualifying Transaction amalgamation with Groupe Ressources Geomines Inc.; basis 1 new for 2 old shs. (see FPsurvey - Mines & Energy)

Black Sturgeon Mines Ltd. (Ont. 1946)
1954 – Charter cancelled.

Black Swan Gold Mines Ltd. (B.C. June 24, 1983)
Nov. 1, 1999 – Name changed to Black Swan Resources Ltd. ■

Black Swan Resources Ltd. (B.C. June 24, 1983)
Feb. 5, 2001 – Continued into Yukon.
Oct. 8, 2003 – Name changed to Brazilian Diamonds Limited. ■

Black Thunder Petroleum Corporation (B.C. Aug. 13, 1969)
June 28, 1990 – Name changed to Conley Resources Corp.; basis 1 new for 5 old shs. ■

Black Tusk Energy Inc. (B.C. Sept. 25, 1985)
Nov. 6, 2006 – Dissolved and struck from register.

Black Tusk Resources Inc. (B.C. Nov. 18, 2016)
Mar. 1, 2023 – Name changed to Q Battery Metals Corp. ■

Black Widow Resources Inc. (Can. Jan. 20, 2011)
Sept. 30, 2016 – Name changed to BWR Exploration Inc. (see FPsurvey - Mines & Energy)

Blackberry Gold Resources Inc. (B.C. 1979)
May 1, 1992 – Dissolved and struck off register.

Blackbird Energy Inc. (B.C. Sept. 21, 2006)
Jan. 4, 2019 – Formed Pipestone Energy Corp. in Alberta pursuant to the reverse takeover acquisition of and amalgamation with Pipeline Oil Corp. (deemed acquiror); basis 1 new com. sh. for 10 Blackbird com. shs. and 0.05996 new com. shs. for 1 (old) Pipeline com. sh. ■

Blackbird Investments Inc. (B.C. Sept. 21, 2006)
Mar. 25, 2010 – Name changed to Blackbird Energy Inc. ■

Blackbridge Capital Corporation (B.C. Feb. 11, 1981)
Nov. 1, 1994 – Name changed to Rupert Resources Ltd. (see FPsurvey - Mines & Energy)

Blackburn-Pattison Mines Ltd. (Ont. 1935)
Mar. 4, 1965 – Dissolved.

Blackburn Ventures Corp. (B.C. Aug. 17, 2006)
Dec. 22, 2009 – Name changed to Morumbi Oil & Gas Inc. and continued into Alberta pursuant to Qualifying Transaction reverse takeover acquisition of Morumbi Capital Corp. ■

Blackchain Solutions Inc. (B.C. July 10, 2007)
Sept. 25, 2018 – Name changed to Trackloop Analytics Corp.; basis 1 new for 2 old shs. ■

Blackdog Resources Ltd. (Alta. Jan. 12, 2006 amalg.)
Nov. 4, 2014 – Name changed to StonePoint Energy Inc. ■

Blackdome Exploration Ltd. (B.C. 1978)
Apr. 8, 1986 – Name changed to Blackdome Mining Corporation. ■

Blackdome Mining Corporation (B.C. 1978)
Aug. 15, 1989 – Acquired by a wholly owned subsid. of MinVen Gold Corporation; basis 1 MinVen sh. for 1 Blackdome sh. with an additional consideration valued at $0.425 per Blackdome sh. (see MinVen Gold Corporation)

Blackeagle Development Corp. (B.C. Feb. 14, 2011)
June 29, 2016 – Name changed to EVI Global Group Developments Corp. ■

Blackhawk Resource Corp. (Alta. Mar. 25, 1986)
Mar. 5, 2020 – Continued into British Columbia.
Mar. 11, 2020 – Name changed to Blackhawk Growth Corp. (see FPsurvey - Industrials)

Blackheath Resources Inc. (B.C. May 2, 2011)
June 1, 2021 – Name changed to Green Impact Partners Inc. pursuant to reverse takeover acquisition of certain

clean energy assets, renewable natural gas development projects and solids recycling facilities from Wolverine Energy and Infrastructure Inc.; basis 1 new for 48.42 old shs. (see FPsurvey - Industrials)

BlackIce Enterprise Risk Management Inc. (B.C. July 10, 2007)
Dec. 28, 2017 – Name changed to Blackchain Solutions Inc. ■

BlackLine GPS Corp. (Alta. Oct. 11, 2006)
July 7, 2015 – Name changed to Blackline Safety Corp. (see FPsurvey - Industrials)

Blackline Oil Corporation (B.C. Dec. 2, 1965)
Feb. 19, 2001 – Name changed to Resourcexplorer Inc. and continued into Alberta following agreement with INToo Software Corporation to purchase software application and other assets. ■

Blackline Resource Corporation Ltd. (B.C. 1971)
Mar. 1973 – Amalgamated with Core Management Ltd. to continue as Blackline Resource Corporation Ltd.; basis 1 new Blackline sh. for each 2.37 old Blackline shs.
July 1973 – Amalgamated with Shelter Petroleums Ltd. to form Groundstar Petroleums Ltd.
1973 – Amalgamated in British Columbia to continue with same name.

Blackmist Resources Inc. (B.C. May 23, 1972)
Jan. 18, 1985 – Name changed to Stray Horse Resources Inc.; basis 1 new for 5 old shs. ■

BlackPearl Resource Inc. (Can. July 10, 2002)
Dec. 18, 2018 – Acquired by International Petroleum Corp. (IPC); basis 0.22 IPC com. shs. for 1 BlackPearl sh.

Blackpool Exploration Ltd. (Alta. Dec. 3, 1992)
Apr. 1, 2008 – Formed Western Canada Energy Ltd. in Alberta on amalgamation with Westbow Energy Inc. with Blackpool the deemed acquiror; basis 1 new for 1 Westbow sh. and 1 new for 2.1739 Blackpool shs. ■

Blackridge Holdings, Inc. (Alta. Oct. 22, 1993)
May 3, 1995 – Name changed to Lifestart Multimedia Corp. ■

Blackrock Gold Corp. (B.C. Apr. 16, 1999)
Mar. 17, 2021 – Name changed to Blackrock Silver Corp. (see FPsurvey - Mines & Energy)

BlackRock Silver Bullion Trust (Ont.)
Nov. 5, 2012 – Name changed to iShares Silver Bullion Fund pursuant to conversion from a closed-end fund into an exchange-traded fund. ■

BlackRock Ventures Inc. (Can. May 16, 1996)
July 11, 2006 – Acquired by BR Oil Sands Corporation, a wholly owned subsid. of Shell Canada Limited; basis $24 per sh. (see Shell Canada Limited)

Blackrun Minerals Inc. (B.C. June 19, 1991 amalg.)
Mar. 29, 2000 – Name changed to Diversified Industries Ltd. ■

Blackrun Ventures Inc. (B.C. June 19, 1991 amalg.)
June 10, 1999 – Name changed to Blackrun Minerals Inc.; basis 1 new for 4 old shs. ■

Blackstone Resources Inc. (B.C. June 6, 1985)
Apr. 23, 2001 – Name changed to Blackstone Ventures Inc.; basis 1 new for 2.5 old shs. ■

Blackstone Ventures Inc. (B.C. June 6, 1985)
Dec. 23, 2015 – Name changed to Lattice Biologics Ltd. following reverse takeover acquisition of Lattice Biologics Inc.; basis 1 new for 3 old shs. ■

Blackstrap Capital Corporation (Can. Aug. 29, 1989)
Sept. 16, 1999 – Name changed to Blackstrap Hospitality Corporation. ■

Blackstrap Hospitality Corporation (Can. Aug. 29, 1989)
May 18, 2005 – Amalgamated with 6358842 Canada Ltd.; basis 1 redeemable amalco. pfd. sh. for 1 old Blackstrap com. sh. The pfd. shs. immediately redeemed for $0.30 per sh.

Blackstream Energy Corporation (B.C. Feb. 21, 2006)
Oct. 11, 2013 – Name changed to SunOil Ltd. (see FPsurvey - Mines & Energy)

BlackWatch Energy Services Corp. (Alta. Oct. 14, 2008)
June 15, 2010 – Name changed to Calmena Energy Services Inc. ■

BlackWatch Energy Services Trust (Alta. June 23, 2006)
Jan. 7, 2009 – Converted into BlackWatch Energy Services Corp. (see BlackWatch Energy Services Corp.)

Blackwater Capital Corp. (Alta. Oct. 4, 2007)
Mar. 11, 2010 – Together with Latigo Capital Corporation, Warnic 1 Enterprises Ltd.and Valentine Ventures Corp. (Capital Pool Companies) amalgamated with Cumberland Oil & Gas Ltd. constituting Capital Pool Companies' Qualifying Transaction to form Cumberland Oil & Gas Ltd; basis Blackwater (0.2875-for-1), Latigo (0.3879-for-1), Warnic (0.3032-for-1), Valentine (0.3474-for-1) and Cumberland (1-for-1). (see Cumberland Oil & Gas Ltd.)

Blackwater Gold Corporation (B.C. Sept. 14, 1979)
Mar. 20, 2002 – Name changed to Bonaventure Enterprises Inc.; basis 1 new for 3 old shs. ■

Blackwater Mines Ltd. (Ont. 1971)
Aug. 11, 1972 – Amalgamated into Staple Mining Co. Ltd.; basis 1 new for 4.5 old shs.

Blackwell Capital Inc. (Alta. Aug. 26, 1999)
July 4, 2001 – Name changed to WellPoint Systems Inc. ■

Blackwolf Copper and Gold Ltd. (B.C. Nov. 16, 2009)
July 5, 2024 – Acquired by Treasury Metals Inc.; basis 0.607 Treasury shs. for 1 Blackwolf Copper sh. (see Treasury Metals Inc.)

Blackwood Hodge (Canada) Limited (Can. 1953)
June 30, 1987 – All o/s com. shs. not already held acquired by Blackwood Hodge p.l.c., through wholly owned Blackall of the o/s com. shs. that it did not already own at $13 per sh.

Blade Yellowknife Gold Mines Ltd. (Ont. 1945)
1954 – Charter cancelled.

Blairdon Gold Mines Ltd. (Ont. 1943)
1955 – Charter cancelled.

Blake-Chibougamau Mining Corp. (unknown)
1966 – Liquidated. Distributed to shldrs. $155,000 and 550,000 shs. Merrill Island Mining Corp.

Blake Mineral Resources Ltd. (Can. Apr. 5, 1954)
Oct. 1979 – Name changed to Blake Resources Ltd. ■

Blake Resources Ltd. (Can. Apr. 5, 1954)
May 2, 2002 – Dissolved.

Blamor Mines Limited (Ont. 1955)
Oct. 24, 1973 – Dissolved.

Blanchard Gold Mines Ltd. (Ont. 1945)
1954 – Charter cancelled.

Blandings Capital Limited (Alta. Dec. 15, 2006)
Apr. 26, 2010 – Name changed to AMG Bioenergy Resources Holdings Ltd. pursuant to Qualifying Transaction reverse takeover acquisition of AMG Bioenergy Resources Group Ltd. ■

Blanton Resources Corp. (B.C. Dec. 17, 2019)
Dec. 8, 2023 – Name changed to American Salars Lithium Inc. (see FPsurvey - Mines & Energy)

Blazedale Resources Inc. (Ont. 1983)
Mar. 31, 1986 – Amalgamated with Southern Eagle Petroleum Inc. and Alpha Energy Holdings to form Southern Eagle Petroleum Corp. Each 100 com. shs. of co. converted into 50 com. shs., 50 cl. A non-voting shs. and 100 pfce. shs. of the new co. (see Southern Eagle Petroleum Corp.)

Blind Creek Resources Ltd. (B.C. May 31, 2004)
Dec. 10, 2020 – Name changed to Blende Silver Corp. (see FPsurvey - Mines & Energy)

Blind River Uranium Mines Ltd. (Ont. 1954)
Aug. 1966 – Charter cancelled.

Bling Capital Corp. (Alta. Apr. 12, 2007)
June 28, 2010 – Name changed to Kestrel Gold Inc. following Qualifying Transaction acquisition of Toe property in the Yukon from BCGold Corp. (see FPsurvey - Mines & Energy)

Blingold Corp. (Ont. Sept. 14, 2020)
July 12, 2021 – Name changed to Caprock Mining Corp. (see FPsurvey - Mines & Energy)

Blis International Inc. (Alta. June 13, 1986)
Jan. 16, 1995 – Name changed to Millennia Foods Inc. ■

BlissCo Cannabis Corp. (B.C. Jan. 13, 1981)
July 15, 2019 – All o/s shs. not already held acquired by The Supreme Cannabis Company; basis 0.24 Supreme com. shs. 1 BlissCo com. sh. (see The Supreme Cannabis Company, Inc.)

Blizzard Energy Inc. (Alta. Dec. 19, 2002)
Aug. 3, 2005 – Plan of Arrangement with Shiningbank Energy Income Fund, Shiningbank Energy Ltd., Zenas Energy Corp. and Zenas Finance Corp.; basis 0.0777 new Shiningbank unit, plus 0.166 new Zenas com. sh., plus 1 new Zenas wt., plus $0.4097 for 1 old Blizzard com. sh. (see Shiningbank Energy Income Fund; Zenas Energy Corp.)

Blizzard Resources Ltd. (B.C. Apr. 18, 1979)
Dec. 5, 1986 – Dissolved and struck off register.

Block X Capital Corp. (B.C. Mar. 28, 1980)
Mar. 30, 2020 – Name changed to Brand X Lifestyle Corp.; basis 1 new for 2 old shs. ■

Block Bros. Industries Ltd. (B.C. 1962)
Mar. 15, 1982 – Controlling int. acquired by Olympia & York Developments Ltd. through purchase offer of $9.00 per sh. which extended from June 23, 1978, to Sept. 15, 1978. Subsequently co. became a wholly owned subsid. of Olympia & York following redemption of all remaining publicly held shs. Shldrs. received either $26,800 per sh. on date of redemption, or at their election, $27,500 per sh. on Mar. 15, 1982.

Block One Capital Inc. (B.C. Feb. 14, 2017)
Apr. 24, 2020 – Name changed to ESG Global Impact Capital Inc.; basis 1 new for 3 old shs. ■

Blockchain Foundry Inc. (B.C. Feb. 12, 2008)
Nov. 8, 2022 – Acquired by WonderFi Technologies Inc.; basis 0.2155 WonderFi shs. for 1 Blockchain sh.

Blockchain Holdings Ltd. (British Virgin Islands Dec. 18, 2013)
June 19, 2020 – Name changed to TraceSafe Inc. ■

Blockchain Power Trust (Ont. Feb. 3, 2014)
Oct. 4, 2019 – Name changed to Jade Power Trust. (see FPsurvey - Industrials)

Blockstrain Technology Corp. (B.C. Oct. 19, 2011)
Apr. 24, 2019 – Name changed to TruTrace Technologies Inc. (see FPsurvey - Industrials)

BlockTech Ventures Inc. (B.C. Aug. 21, 2017)
Aug. 13, 2018 – Name changed to Northstar Venture Technologies Inc. ■

Blocplay Entertainment Inc. (B.C. Oct. 30, 2014)
May 3, 2021 – Name changed to Playground Ventures Inc. (see FPsurvey - Industrials) ■

Blond Bear Holdings Inc. (Alta. July 18, 1996)
June 12, 2002 – Name changed to Grey Island Systems International Inc. following Qualifying Transaction reverse takeover acquisition of Grey Island Systems Inc.; basis 1 new for 4 old shs. ■

Blondeau Mines Ltd. (Ont. 1952)
1963 – Name changed to New Blondeau Nickel Mines Ltd.; basis 1 new for 2 old shs. ■

Blondeau Nickel Mines Ltd. (Ont. 1952)
1960 – Name changed to Blondeau Mines Ltd. ■

Blondor Quebec Mines, Limited (Ont. 1943)
Apr. 1, 1963 – Dissolved.

Bloom Health Partners Inc. (B.C. Nov. 22, 2011)
Jan. 3, 2023 – Petitioned into receivership and BDO Canada Limited appointed receiver.

Bloom Income & Growth Canadian Fund (Ont. Sept. 29, 2011)
Oct. 26, 2015 – Merged into Bloom Select Income Fund (Select); basis 0.693093575 Select trust units for 1 Bloom Income trust unit. (see Bloom Select Income Fund)

Bloom Lake Consolidated Mines Ltd. (Ont. 1925)
1944 – Assets acquired by Culver Gold Mines for 1,000,000 Culver shs.

Bloom Select Income Fund (Ont. Mar. 22, 2012)
Mar. 6, 2025 – Terminated; basis $7.9902 cash per fund unit.

Bloom U.S. Advantaged Income & Growth Fund (Ont.)
May 9, 2013 – Name changed to Bloom U.S. Income & Growth Fund. ■

Bloom U.S. Income & Growth Fund (Ont.)
Nov. 9, 2021 – Terminated; distrib. of pro rata share of net assets paid on or before Nov. 18, 2021.

Blouin Lake Gold Mines Ltd. (Can. 1934)
1960 – Wound up.

Blox Labs Inc. (B.C. Apr. 4, 2014)
Sept. 9, 2019 – Name changed to Sire Bioscience Inc. pursuant to the reverse takeover acquisition of Best Cannabis Products Inc. ■

Blue Bay Capital Inc. (B.C. Apr. 11, 2017)
Oct. 31, 2018 – Name changed to Specialty Liquid Transportation Corp. following Qualifying Transaction reverse takeover acquisition of (old) Specialty Liquid Transportation Corp.; basis 1 new for 2 old shs. ■

Blue Bonnets Raceway Inc. (Que. 1958)
June 7, 1972 – Acquired by Campeau Corporation for $3.00 per sh. (see Campeau Corporation)
1973 – Charter cancelled. (see Campeau Corporation)

Blue-Chip Gold Mines Ltd. (Ont. 1945)
Dec. 3, 1962 – Dissolved.

Blue Chip Petroleums Ltd. (Alta.)
1960 – Struck off register.

Blue-Chip Yellowknife Mines Ltd. (Ont. 1945)
May 1945 – Name changed to Blue-Chip Gold Mines Ltd. ■

Blue Cove Capital Corp. (B.C. Oct. 23, 2007)
Apr. 18, 2011 – Name changed to CuOro Resources Corp. pursuant to Qualifying Transaction acquisition of Colombian copper and gold prospects. ■

Blue Crown Petroleums Ltd. (Alta. 1951)
1968 – Acquired by Blue Crown, Inc.

Blue Desert Mining Inc. (B.C. Apr. 13, 1995)
May 25, 2000 – Name changed to Canada Fluorspar Inc.; basis 1 new for 3 old shs. ■

Blue Diamond Energy Resources Inc. (B.C. 1979)
Dec. 15, 1988 – Name changed to Nippon Investments Corp.; basis 1 new for 5 old shs. ■

Blue Diamond Mining Corporation (B.C. Oct. 4, 1989)
June 7, 2010 – Name changed to Colossal Resources Corp.; basis 1 new for 25 old shs. ■

Blue Emerald Resources Inc. (B.C. July 21, 1987)
Jan. 17, 2003 – Name changed to Saville Resources Inc.; basis 1 new for 15 old shs. ■

Blue Fyre One Inc. (Can. May 10, 2004)
Sept. 8, 2006 – Formed Soltoro Ltd. in Canada on Qualifying Transaction amalgamation with Soltoro Ltd. (deemed acquiror). ■

Blue Gayle Mines Ltd. (unknown)
1967 – Acquired by Norco Resources Ltd. (see Northern Coal Mines Ltd.)

Blue Gold International Inc. (Ont. 1968)
Dec. 29, 2004 – Struck from registry and dissolved.

Blue Gold Mining Inc. (B.C. June 18, 2009)
Dec. 18, 2012 – Acquired by Riverstone Resources Inc.; basis 0.801 Riverstone shs. for 1 Blue Gold sh. (see Riverstone Resources Inc.)

Blue Gold Resources Ltd. (B.C. Apr. 7, 1986)
Aug. 15, 1994 – Name changed to International Blue Gold Corp.; basis 1 new for 3 old shs. ■

Blue Gold Water Technologies Ltd. (B.C. June 20, 2006)
Oct. 1, 2013 – Name changed to Nanostruck Technologies Inc. ■

Blue Gulch Explorations Ltd. (B.C. Oct. 7, 1968)
May 10, 1973 – Name changed to Pacific Resources Development Ltd. ■

Blue Heaven Resources Corp. (Ont. Jan. 1, 1989)
July 19, 1995 – Name changed to Hydra Corp.; basis 1 new for 12 old shs. ■

Blue Heron Financial Corporation (Ont. May 30, 1997)
June 21, 2002 – Name changed to Avenue Financial Corporation; basis 1 new for 2 old shs. ■

Blue Horizon Industries Inc. (Alta. Jan. 27, 1995)
July 2, 2017 – Struck from registry.

Blue Ice Minerals Limited (Alta. Aug. 31, 1996 amalg.)
Nov. 28, 2001 – Name changed to Monroe Minerals Inc.; basis 1 new for 3 old shs. ■

Blue Jay Gold Mining Co. Limited (B.C. 1928)
Dec. 3, 1931 – Dissolved.

Blue Jay Long Lac Gold Mines (1938) Ltd. (Ont. 1938)
1952 – Charter cancelled.

Blue Lagoon Ventures Inc. (B.C. Jan. 29, 1986)
Dec. 8, 2004 – Name changed to VMX Resources Inc.; basis 1 new for 4 old shs. ■

Blue Lake Resources Ltd. (B.C. 1983)
Jan. 21, 1986 – Name changed to Lake Ventures Ltd. ■

Blue Lightning Ventures Inc. (B.C. Feb. 6, 1986)
Apr. 29, 2005 – Name changed to Universal Uranium Ltd. ■

Blue Moon Zinc Corp. (B.C. Jan. 15, 2007)
Apr. 14, 2021 – Name changed to Blue Moon Metals Inc. (see FPsurvey - Mines & Energy)

Blue Mountain Beverages Inc. (Ont. 1970)
Apr. 10, 2017 – Certificate of incorporation cancelled and company dissolved.

Blue Mountain Energy Ltd. (Alta. May 26, 1993)
Nov. 1, 2006 – Name changed to Trilogy Blue Mountain Ltd. following acquisition by Trilogy Energy Trust for $5.50 per sh. (see Trilogy Energy Trust)

Blue Mountain Resources Ltd. (Alta. May 26, 1993)
July 22, 2002 – Name changed to Blue Mountain Energy Ltd.; basis 1 new for 12.5 old shs. ■

Blue Note Metals Inc. (Can. Feb. 20, 2002)
Oct. 4, 2006 – Name changed to Blue Note Mining Inc. ■

Blue Note Mining Inc. (Can. Feb. 20, 2002)
May 22, 2013 – Filed a notice of intention to make a proposal under the Bankruptcy and Insolvency Act.
Nov. 22, 2013 – Filed for bankruptcy. PricewaterhouseCoopers Inc. appointed trustee and all officers and directors resigned.

Blue Parrot Energy Inc. (B.C. June 17, 1998 amalg.)
May 19, 2009 – Name changed to Ria Resources Corp.; basis 1 new for 20 old shs. ■

Blue Pearl Mining Ltd. (Ont. July 1, 1999)
May 15, 2007 – Name changed to Thompson Creek Metals Company Inc. ■

Blue Power Energy Corporation (Ont. June 17, 1985)
Apr. 20, 2006 – Name changed to Cadillac Ventures Inc.; basis 1 new for 5 old shs. (see FPsurvey - Mines & Energy)

Blue Quill Oil Co. Ltd. (Alta.)
1960 – Struck off register.

Blue Range Energy Corporation (Alta. June 4, 1986)
June 8, 1990 – Name changed to Blue Range Resource Corporation; basis 1 new for 8 old shs. ■

Blue Range Resource Corporation (Alta. June 4, 1986)
Feb. 17, 1999 – Acquired by Big Bear Exploration Ltd.; basis 11 Big Bear shs. for 1 Blue Range sh. (see Big Bear Exploration Ltd.)

Blue Regal Resources Ltd. (Ont. July 30, 1987)
Jan. 16, 1996 – Formed Unique Capital Corporation in Ontario on amalgamation with 1148929 Ontario Inc. ■

Blue Rhino Capital Corp. (B.C. Feb. 6, 2019)
July 30, 2021 – Name changed to ZEB Nickel Corp. pursuant to the Qualifying Transaction reverse takeover acquisition of Zebediela Nickel Company (Pty) Ltd.; basis 1 new for 2.3 old shs. (see FPsurvey - Mines & Energy)

Blue Ribbon Capital Corporation (Ont. Sept. 12, 2006)
Apr. 21, 2009 – Name changed to Kilo Goldmines Ltd. following Qualifying Transaction reverse takeover acqustion of Kilo Goldmines Inc. and amalgamation of Kilo with a wholly owned subsidiary; basis 1 new for 4 old shs. ■

Blue Ribbon Corp. Ltd. (Can. 1930)
1959 – Offer to acquire all o/s pref. and com. shs. made by Brooke Bond Canada (1959) Ltd.; basis $61.25 plus accr. divds. (total $62.08) for each pref. and $20 for each com. sh. Co. wound up.

Blue Ribbon Resources Ltd. (B.C. Oct. 4, 1989)
Mar. 9, 1998 – Name changed to New Blue Ribbon Resources Ltd.; basis 1 new for 5 old shs. ■

Blue Ridge Resources Ltd. (B.C. 1984)
July 13, 1988 – Name changed to International Trans Asia Trading Corp. ■

Blue River Mines Ltd. (Alta. 1986)
Oct. 2, 1989 – Name changed to Techmin Canada Ltd. ■

Blue Rock Cerium Mines Ltd. (Ont. 1952)
1956 – Name changed to Rare Earth Mining Co. Ltd. ■

Blue Sky Energy Inc. (Ont. Sept. 27, 2013)
Apr. 5, 2022 – Name changed to EV Technology Group Ltd. pursuant to the reverse takeover acquisition of EV

Technology Group Inc.; basis 1 new for 4 old shs. (see FPsurvey - Industrials)

Blue Sky Global Energy Corp. (Ont. Jan. 21, 2005)
May 28, 2024 – Continued into Alberta. (see FPsurvey - Mines & Energy)

Blue Sky Resources Ltd. (B.C. Jan. 21, 1980)
Feb. 28, 1996 – Name changed to Axion Communications Inc. ∎

Blue Sky Resources Ltd. (Alta. June 8, 1999)
Feb. 5, 2001 – Acquired by Fossil Bay Resources Ltd.; basis $0.34 per sh. Not to be confused with different company incorporated in B.C. (see Fossil Bay Resources Ltd.)

Blue Star Investment Limited (B.C. 1983)
June 19, 1992 – Dissolved and struck off register.

Blue Star Mines Ltd. (Ont. 1936)
Feb. 1952 – Charter cancelled.

Blue Star Mines Ltd. (B.C. 1957)
1978 – All assets sold to David Minerals.
Nov. 3, 1980 – Struck off register.

Blue Sun Resource Corporation (B.C. 1983)
Dec. 16, 1991 – Name changed to International Blue Sun Resource Corporation; basis 1 new for 3 old shs. ∎

Blue Thunder Mining Inc. (Ont. Apr. 28, 2017)
July 5, 2024 – Name changed to Mines D'or Orbec Inc. (see FPsurvey - Mines & Energy)

Blue Top Brewing Co. Ltd. (Can. 1927)
Apr. 1952 – Name changed to Ranger Brewing Company Ltd. ∎

Blue Tree Wireless Data Inc. (Can. Nov. 14, 2001)
Nov. 13, 2007 – Acquired by Sixnet Holdings, LLC for 21¢ per sh.

Blue Vista Enterprises Ltd. (Ont. 1974)
Dissolved.

Blue Vista Technologies Inc. (Ont. 1955)
Dec. 17, 2014 – Name changed to Arbitrage Exploration Inc.; basis 1 new for 4 old shs. ∎

Blue Zen Memorial Parks Inc. (Can. Aug. 11, 1994)
Aug. 25, 2024 – Dissolved for non-compliance.

BlueBird Battery Metals Inc. (B.C. Mar. 31, 2011)
Sept. 17, 2020 – Name changed to Huntsman Exploration Inc.; basis 1 new for 2 old shs. (see FPsurvey - Mines & Energy)

Bluebird Explorations Ltd. (B.C. Jan. 15, 1979)
Oct. 24, 1995 – Name changed to Spire Ventures Ltd.; basis 1 new for 4 old shs. ∎

Bluebird Minerals Ltd. (Alta. Aug. 31, 1996 amalg.)
Nov. 10, 1999 – Name changed to Blue Ice Minerals Limited; basis 1 new for 3 old shs. ∎

Bluebird Mines Ltd. (B.C. 1928)
Assets sold to Bluebird Slocan Mines Ltd. (see Bluebird Slocan Mines Ltd.)

Bluebird Slocan Mines Ltd. (B.C. 1951)
May 1958 – Charter cancelled.

Bluecap Mining Corp. (B.C. Feb. 5, 2021)
Mar. 6, 2024 – Name changed to Trimera Metals Corp. (see FPsurvey - Mines & Energy)

Bluedrop Performance Learning Inc. (N.L. Jan. 26, 2012)
Mar. 28, 2019 – Continued into Canada.
Mar. 16, 2020 – Name changed to BPLI Holdings Inc. ∎

Bluefire Mining Corp. (B.C. Mar. 17, 2011)
Feb. 17, 2016 – Name changed to Royalty North Partners Ltd. ∎

Bluegrass Petroleum Inc. (B.C. 1980)
Nov. 12, 1985 – Name changed to Superburn Systems Ltd. ∎

Bluegrass Raymond Mines Ltd. (Ont. 1944)
Nov. 1944 – Name changed to Bluegrass Uranium Mines Ltd. ∎

Bluegrass Uranium Mines Ltd. (Ont. 1944)
May 18, 1976 – Charter cancelled.

BlueGrouse Seismic Solutions Ltd. (Alta. July 14, 2005)
May 18, 2007 – Acquired by Divestco Inc.; basis 0.3125 Divestco shs. for 1 BlueGrouse sh. (see Divestco Inc.)

Blueland Capital Inc. (Alta. Jan. 4, 2000)
Jan. 31, 2003 – Continued into Canada.
Feb. 25, 2003 – Name changed to Nicer Canada Corp. following Qualifying Transaction reverse takeover acquisition of Nicer Canada Corp. ∎

Bluemount Resources Ltd. (Alta. 1969)
Jan. 4, 1977 – Amalgamated with several other cos. to form Ranchmen's Resources (1976) Ltd.; basis 2 cl. A for 3 com. shs.

Bluenose Gold Corp. (Yuk. June 12, 1997)
Feb. 24, 2020 – Name changed to Caldas Gold Corp. following reverse takeover acquisition of Medoro Resources Colombia Inc. (concurrently renamed Caldas Gold Colombia Inc.), which was facilitated through the acquisition of Medoro's parent Caldas Finance Corp.; basis 1 new for 10 old shs. ∎

Bluenose Pershing Mines Ltd. (Ont. 1944)
Dec. 3, 1962 – Dissolved.

BlueOcean NutraSciences Inc. (Ont. Sept. 17, 2010)
Apr. 12, 2018 – Name changed to CO2 Gro Inc. (see FPsurvey - Industrials)

BluePoint Data Storage, Inc. (Yuk. Sept. 14, 1993)
July 27, 2009 – Name changed to BluePoint Data, Inc. (see FPsurvey - Industrials)

Bluerock Acquisition Corp. (B.C. Jan. 14, 2008)
Dec. 14, 2009 – Acquired by PetroKamchatka Plc; basis 0.46837 PetroKamchatka shs. for 1 Bluerock sh. (see PetroKamchatka Plc)

Bluerock Resources Ltd. (B.C. May 14, 1981)
May 7, 2009 – Name changed to Argus Metals Corp.; basis 1 new for 15 old shs. ∎

Bluerock Ventures Corp. (B.C. Feb. 3, 2011)
Dec. 9, 2020 – Name changed to Tombill Mines Limited pursuant to the Qualifying Transaction reverse takeover acquisition of (old) Tombill Mines Limited and concurrent amalgamation of (old) Tombill with wholly owned Tombill Exploration Ltd. (and continued as Tombill Exploration Ltd.). ∎

BlueRush Media Group Corp. (Ont. Apr. 6, 2004)
Apr. 30, 2018 – Name changed to BlueRush Inc. (see FPsurvey - Industrials)

Bluesky Industries Inc. (Alta. June 2, 1988)
Sept. 17, 1991 – Name changed to Firelight Corporation; basis 1 new for 3 old shs. ∎

Bluesky Oil & Gas Ltd. (B.C. Dec. 8, 1979 amalg.)
Oct. 27, 1980 – Continued into Alberta.
Oct. 16, 1986 – Name changed to Mark Resources Inc.; basis 1 new for 3 old shs. ∎

BlueStar Battery Systems International Corp. (Alta. Dec. 2, 1993)
May 2001 – Company in default on its loan with Lumina Group, LLC.
June 29, 2001 – Lumina Group, LLC, as secured creditor, requested in June that the company sell all of its assets to reduce its indebtedness. At the public auction held the company sold the assets of wholly owned BlueStar Systems U.S.A. Inc. to Indiana-based Advanced Power Systems for US$1,200,000. Lumina LLC acquired the

assets of wholly owned BlueStar Systems Canada Corp. and BlueStar Systems Group, Inc. by crediting US$200,000 and US$60,000, respectively, against the US$1,550,000 outstanding indebtness owed to Lumina. The liquidation of the assets did not satisfy the indebtedness and there were no distributions made to the remaining creditors or shldrs. The company ceased operations.

Bluestone Resources Inc. (B.C. June 13, 2005)
Jan. 15, 2025 – Acquired by Aura Minerals Inc.; basis (i) Cdn$0.287 cash, or (ii) 0.0183 Aura shs. for 1 Bluestone sh.

Bluewater Oil & Gas Limited (Ont. 1956)
1972 – Continued into Alberta.
Jan. 11, 1985 – Acquired by Laramide Exploration, Inc. for US$6.00 per sh.

BluKnight Aquafarms Inc. (B.C. June 19, 2015)
Oct. 8, 2021 – Name changed to Looking Glass Labs Ltd. following the acquisition of HOK Technologies Inc. (dba House of Kibaa). ∎

Bluma Wellness Inc. (B.C. May 22, 2020)
Apr. 19, 2021 – Acquired by Cresco Labs Inc.; basis 0.0859 Cresco Labs shs. for 1 Bluma sh.

BluMont Capital Inc. (Ont. June 30, 2003)
Mar. 12, 2007 – Acquired by Integrated Asset Management Corp. following amalgamation agreement; basis 1 new Integrated Asset sh. for 2.8 old BluMont shs. (see Integrated Asset Management Corp.)

BluMont Man Alternative Yield Fund (Ont. Feb. 20, 2006)
Aug. 27, 2007 – Trust units redeemed for $8.9403499 per unit.

BluMont Strategic Partners Hedge Fund (Ont. Apr. 29, 2002)
Jan. 2, 2007 – Amalgamated into BluMont Canadian Opportunities Fund; basis 1 new for 1 old unit.

blutip Power Technologies Ltd. (Alta. Mar. 29, 2004 amalg.)
Feb. 28, 2012 – Placed into receivership. Duff & Phelps Canada Restructuring Inc. appointed receiver.
May 3, 2012 – Company's business and substantially all assets were sold on a going concern basis to 663447 N.B. Inc., an assignee of the secured lender. No funds available for unsecured creditors or shareholders.
July 4, 2012 – Receiver was discharged.

Blythwood Consolidated Resources Ltd. (Ont. 1974)
Mar. 11, 1986 – Name changed to First City Gold Corporation. ∎

Blythwood Mining Limited (Ont. 1974)
1983 – Name changed to Blythwood Consolidated Resources Ltd.; basis 1 new for 3 old shs. ∎

BnSellit Technology Inc. (Alta. Feb. 4, 2021)
Oct. 25, 2023 – Name changed to Metaguest.AI Incorporated. (see FPsurvey - Industrials)

Boardwalk Equities Inc. (Alta. July 14, 1993)
May 5, 2004 – Plan of Arrangement to convert company to a new income trust named Boardwalk Real Estate Investment Trust; basis 1 new trust unit for 1 com. sh.

Boat Rocker Media Inc. (Ont. Jan. 29, 2003)
Aug. 1, 2025 – Name changed to Blue Ant Media Corporation pursuant to the reverse takeover acquisition of Blue Ant Media Inc.; basis 1 new for 10 old shs. (see FPsurvey - Industrials)

Bobby Cadillac's Food Corporation (B.C. Mar. 30, 1983)
Apr. 24, 1996 – Formed Immune Network Research Ltd. in British Columbia on amalgamation with Immune Network Research Ltd.; basis 2 new for 3 old shs. ∎

Bobcam Mines Ltd. (Ont. 1949)
Dec. 3, 1962 – Dissolved.

Bobjo Mines Ltd. (Ont. 1928)
1956 – Name changed to R. J. Jowsey Mining Co. Ltd.; basis 1 new for 3 old shs. ■

Bobs Lake Gold Mines Ltd. (Ont. 1945)
July 7, 1952 – Name changed to New Bobs Lake Gold Mines Ltd. ■

Boca Resources Ltd. (Alta. 1980)
Dec. 12, 1987 – Formed Canadian Fortune Resources Inc. in Alberta on amalgamation with Dixalta Investments Ltd. ■

Bocabois Gold Mines Ltd. (Ont. 1946)
1970 – Charter cancelled.

Groupe Bocenor BF Inc. (Que. July 7, 1976; via letters patent)
June 15, 1990 – Name changed to Groupe Bocenor Inc. ■

Groupe Bocenor Inc. (Que. July 7, 1976; via letters patent)
July 17, 2007 – Name changed to GBO Inc. ■

Boch & Limoges Limited (B.C. Jan. 22, 1981)
July 21, 1994 – Name changed to Vannessa Ventures Ltd.; basis 1 new for 2.2 old shs. ■

Bochawna Copper Mines Limited (Ont. Dec. 12, 1967)
Dec. 6, 1996 – Name changed to Gold Coral Resources Inc. ■

Bock et Frère Ltée (Que. 1965)
Aug. 1972 – All pref. shs. redeemed at $21 per sh.

Bodega Ventures Inc. (Alta. Nov. 24, 1986)
Oct. 29, 1993 – Name changed to Leader Oil & Gas Ltd.; basis 1 new for 4 old shs. ■

Bodi-Gard Canada Limited (Can. 1962 amalg.)
Dec. 8, 1977 – Amalgamated with B.C.I. Furniture to form Bodi-Gard Canada (1977) Limited, a private co. An offer of $2.25 per sh. was made to co.'s minority shldrs.

Boeing Holdings & Explorations Ltd. (Ont. 1968)
Jan. 1972 – Name changed to Consolidated Boeing Holdings & Explorations Ltd.; basis 1 new for 2 old shs. ■

Boeing Mines Ltd. (Ont. 1966)
1968 – Merged into Boeing Holdings & Explorations Ltd.; basis 1 new for 3 old shs.

Bois Franc Royal Ltée (Que. 1967)
Sept. 20, 1991 – Name changed to BF Royal Inc. ■

Boischatel-Rouyn Development Co. Ltd. (Ont. 1926)
1927 – No report since issue of 12 shs. Thormoor Copper Mines Ltd. for each co. sh. held.

Boise Creek Resources Ltd. (B.C. 1983)
July 28, 1995 – Dissolved and struck off register.

Boise Yellowknife Mines Ltd. (Ont. 1945)
Mar. 1979 – Charter cancelled.

Bol Energy Ltd. (Alta. 1985)
Mar. 13, 1987 – Name changed to American Environmental Enterprises Corporation. ■

Bolands Limited (Can. - unspecified)
Nov. 1968 – Acquired by Oshawa Wholesale Limited for $600,000 and 76,340 cl. A shs. (see Oshawa Wholesale Limited)

Bolcar Energie Inc. (Can. June 18, 2003)
Nov. 7, 2006 – Name changed to AAER Inc. ■

Bold Capital Enterprises Ltd. (Can. May 16, 2018)
Sept. 23, 2024 – Name changed to Stardust Solar Energy Inc. pursuant to the Qualifying Transaction reverse takeover acquisition of Stardust Solar Holdings Inc. (see FPsurvey - Industrials)

Bold Ventures Inc. (B.C. June 8, 1989)
Aug. 31, 2010 – Continued into Ontario. (see FPsurvey - Mines & Energy)

Bolero Mines Limited (B.C. 1971)
Mar. 6, 1984 – Name changed to Michael Resources Ltd.; basis 1 new for 5 old shs. ■

Bolero Resources Corp. (Ont. Sept. 19, 2007)
Oct. 5, 2012 – Name changed to Canada Carbon Inc. (see FPsurvey - Mines & Energy)

Bolero Resources Inc. (B.C. Aug. 13, 1985)
Feb. 12, 1992 – Name changed to United Bolero Development Corp.; basis 1 new for 3 old shs. ■

Bolgo Gold Mines Ltd. (Que. 1949)
Aug. 1974 – Charter cancelled.

Boliden Limited (Can. Apr. 18, 1997)
Nov. 30, 2001 – Continued into Sweden.
Dec. 4, 2001 – Plan of Arrangement with wholly owned subsid. Boliden Redomiciliation Inc. and Sweden-based Boliden AB; basis 1 new Boliden AB ordinary sh. for 20 old Boliden com. shs.

Bolivar Energy Corp. (Can. Sept. 25, 1995)
Dec. 5, 2011 – Name changed to Anatolia Energy Corp. pursuant to the amalgamation of Anatolia Energy Inc. (deemed acquiror) with wholly owned 1629683 Alberta Ltd.; basis 1 new for 20 old shs. ■

Bolivar Gold Corp. (Yuk. June 19, 1997)
Mar. 6, 2006 – Plan of Arrangement amalgamation with wholly owned subsid. of Gold Fields Limited; basis $3.20 per com. sh., $2.20 per regular wt., $1.65 per A wt. and $1.00 per B wt.

Bolivar Goldfields Ltd. (Yuk. Sept. 14, 1993)
Feb. 8, 2001 – Name changed to Storage @ccess Technologies Inc. on acquisition of Storage Access Inc. ■

Bolivar Mines Ltd. (Ont. 1948)
Sept. 1955 – Charter cancelled.

Bolivian Gold Mines Limited (Ont. 1973)
July 27, 1976 – Charter cancelled.

Bolt Energy Ltd. (Alta. Feb. 7, 1996)
Sept. 25, 2002 – Acquired by Blue Mountain Energy Ltd.; basis 0.3125 new Blue Mountain com. sh. for 1 old Bolt com. sh. (see Blue Mountain Energy Ltd.)

Boltons Capital Corp. (Alta. Sept. 1, 1996)
May 8, 1997 – Continued into Yukon.
Feb. 5, 2003 – Name changed to Valterra Wines Ltd.; basis 1 new for 10 old shs. ■

Bomac Batten Limited (Can. Jan. 9, 1931)
Apr. 25, 1984 – Name changed to Principal Neo-Tech Inc.; basis 3 new for 1 old sh. ■

Bomaque Mines Ltd. (Ont. 1945)
1956 – Charter cancelled.

Bomarc Mining Co. Ltd. (B.C. 1967)
1970 – Amalgamated with Anglo Northern Mines to form Anglo-Bomarc Mines Ltd.

Bomax Resource Corp. (B.C. Dec. 14, 1982 amalg.)
Jan. 15, 2007 – Dissolved and struck from register.

Bombardier Limited (Can. 1954)
1976 – Acquired by MLW-Worthington Ltd. effective; basis 1 new MLW com. sh. for 5.25 old cl. A com. shs. or 5.25 old cl. B com. shs.

Bombardier-MLW Ltd. (Can. June 19, 1902; via letters patent)
June 23, 1978 – Name changed to Bombardier Inc. (see FPsurvey - Industrials)

Bombay Explorations Inc. (Ont. 1971)
July 1978 – Charter cancelled.

Bomem Inc. (Que. 1973)
Oct. 17, 1990 – Acquired by Mannesmann AG of Dusseldorf, Germany, for $1.25 per sh.

Bon Ton Silver Mines Ltd. (B.C. 1961)
July 22, 1974 – Dissolved and struck off register.

Bon-Val Mines Ltd. (B.C. 1967)
Aug. 1978 – Name changed to Cameron Resources Ltd. ■

Bonanza Blue Corp. (Ont. Aug. 19, 1985)
Dec. 5, 2016 – Name changed to CannaRoyalty Corp. pursuant to reverse takeover acquisition of Cannabis Royalties & Holdings Corp.; basis 1 new for 5 old shs. ■

Bonanza Explorations Inc. (B.C. May 10, 1967)
May 29, 2002 – Name changed to Bonanza Resources Corporation; basis 1 new for 3 old shs. ■

Bonanza Explorations Ltd. (B.C. 1964)
July 1971 – Name changed to Panama Mines Ltd. ■

Bonanza International Petroleums Limited (Alta. 1969)
Apr. 1974 – Amalgamated with Canadian Bonanza Petroleums Limited to form Amalgamated Bonanza Petroleum Ltd.; basis 4 new for 5 old Bonanza Int'l shs. (see Amalgamated Bonanza Petroleum Ltd.)

Bonanza Metals Inc. (Que. Mar. 27, 1986)
Aug. 26, 1992 – Name changed to Consolidated Bonanza Metals Inc.; basis 1 new for 5 old shs. ■

Bonanza Oil & Gas Ltd. (Alta. 1978)
Oct. 21, 1983 – Amalgamated with a wholly owned subsid. of Canusa Energy Ltd. to continue with the same name Bonanza Oil & Gas Ltd.; basis 1.75 new for 1 old sh. Subsequently controlling interest changed to Poco Petroleums Ltd. in 1987 through an asset/share transaction. (see Poco Petroleums Ltd.)
Jan. 1, 1992 – Acquired by Poco Petroleums Ltd. for 60¢ per sh. (see Poco Petroleums Ltd.)

Bonanza Red Lake Explorations Inc. (Ont. Sept. 22, 1978)
Oct. 12, 2000 – Name changed to Eugenic Corp.; basis 1 new for 3 old shs. ■

Bonanza Resources Corporation (B.C. May 10, 1967)
Feb. 18, 2011 – Name changed to BRS Resources Ltd. (see FPsurvey - Mines & Energy)

Bonanza Resources Ltd. (B.C. 1980)
1983 – Continued into Alberta.
Jan. 15, 1987 – Name changed to CanCapital Corporation. ■

Bonanza Silver Corporation (B.C. May 10, 1967)
Sept. 7, 2001 – Name changed to Bonanza Explorations Inc.; basis 1 new for 3 old shs. ■

Bonaparte Capital Corp. (B.C. July 10, 2007)
Aug. 11, 2010 – Name changed to Bonaparte Resources Inc. ■

Bonaparte Resources Inc. (B.C. 1981)
July 1984 – Acquired by Veronex Resources Ltd.; basis 1 Veronex sh. for 3 Bonaparte shs. (see Veronex Resources Ltd.)

Bonaparte Resources Inc. (B.C. July 10, 2007)
June 4, 2014 – Name changed to BlackIce Enterprise Risk Management Inc. ■

Bonar Inc. (Can. 1979)
Oct. 13, 1995 – Acquired by Low & Bonar Canada Inc. for $38 per sh.

Bonaventure Enterprises Inc. (B.C. Sept. 14, 1979)
Mar. 3, 2011 – Name changed to Iconic Minerals Ltd.; basis 1 new for 10 old shs. (see FPsurvey - Mines & Energy)

Bonaventure Mining Ltd. (Que. Feb. 28, 1967)
Aug. 27, 1978 – Charter cancelled.
June 19, 1996 – Charter revived.
Oct. 4, 1996 – Name changed to Venturbon Enterprises Inc. ■

Bonaventure Resources Ltd. (B.C. Sept. 18, 1985)
Feb. 21, 2003 – Struck from register and dissolved.

Bonaventure Technologies Inc. (Ont. 1931)
Sept. 23, 1983 – Continued into Canada - unspecified.
May 21, 2008 – Dissolved and struck from register.

Bonaventure Uranium Mines Ltd. (Que. 1954)
Nov. 18, 1978 – Charter cancelled.

Bonavista Energy Corporation (Alta. Dec. 31, 2010; amalg.)
July 31, 2020 – Continued into Canada.
Sept. 13, 2020 – All o/s shs. not already held acquired by G2S2 Capital Inc.; basis 5¢ cash per com. sh.
Nov. 6, 2020 – Continued into Alberta.

Bonavista Energy Trust (Alta. May 22, 2003)
Dec. 31, 2010 – Succeeded by Bonavista Energy Corporation pursuant to plan of arrangement whereby Bonavista Energy Corporation was formed to facilitate the conversion of the trust into a corporation and the trust was subsequently dissolved. ■

Bonavista Mining Corporation Ltd. (B.C. 1972)
July 1976 – Amalgamated into Eaton Mining & Exploration Co. Ltd.

Bonavista Petroleum Ltd. (Alta. Apr. 14, 1987)
July 7, 2003 – Converted into an income trust named Bonavista Energy Trust and a new junior exploration company named NuVista Energy Ltd.; basis 1 NuVista com. sh. and 2 Bonavista trust units, or 1 NuVista com. sh. and 2 ser. A exch. shs. of Bonavista Acquisition Corp., or 1 right to purchase NuVista com. sh. at $2.00 per sh. plus 2 exch. shs. for 1 Bonavista Petroleum com. sh.

Bond Street Transfer Corporation (B.C. 1974)
May 12, 1978 – Name changed to Cumo Resources Ltd. ■

Bondell Industries Inc. (B.C. 1981)
Dec. 29, 1993 – Name changed to Rift Resources Ltd.; basis 1 new for 3 old shs. ■

Bondell Resources Inc. (B.C. 1981)
May 12, 1987 – Name changed to Bondell Industries Inc. ■

Bonetal Gold Mines Ltd. (Ont. Nov. 10, 1936)
1951 – Acquired by Broulan Reef Mines Ltd.; basis 1 new for 2 old shs.

Bonfield Mines Ltd. (Ont. 1943)
Jan. 1958 – Charter cancelled.

Bonita Capital Corporation (Alta. May 11, 2004)
Mar. 21, 2005 – Continued into Canada.
Apr. 4, 2005 – Name changed to Palmarejo Gold Corporation following Qualifying Transaction acquisition of a gold-silver property in Mexico from Bolnisi Gold NL and Palmarejo Acquisition Corporation. ■

Bonkers Indoor Playgrounds Inc. (Alta. May 12, 1993)
Sept. 30, 1998 – Name changed to Bonkers Ventures Inc.; basis 1 new for 5 old shs. ■

Bonkers Ventures Inc. (Alta. May 12, 1993)
Nov. 2, 2015 – Dissolved and struck from register.

Bonmartic Mines Ltd. (Ont. 1946)
Mar. 10, 1958 – Dissolved.

Bonn Energy Corporation (Can. 1978)
Oct. 20, 1982 – Acquired by Turner Valley Financial Ltd. (see Turner Valley Financial Ltd.)

Bonne Bay Mines Ltd. (Ont. 1956)
May 18, 1976 – Charter cancelled.

Bonnet Mines Ltd. (B.C. 1967)
Aug. 1971 – Name changed to Bon-Val Mines Ltd. ■

Bonnet Plume River Mines Ltd. (B.C. 1966)
Apr. 1977 – Charter cancelled.

Bonnett's Energy Corp. (Alta. May 20, 2011)
Nov. 11, 2013 – Acquired by BEC Acquisition Ltd., a wholly owned subsid. of Mill City Capital, L.P., for $7.08 cash per sh.

Bonnett's Energy Services Trust (Alta. Aug. 12, 2005)
June 30, 2011 – Succeeded by Bonnett's Energy Corp. pursuant to plan of arrangement whereby Bonnett's Energy Corp. was formed to facilitate the conversion of the trust into a corporation and the trust was subsequently dissolved. ■

Bonnevier Mines Ltd. (B.C. 1959)
Jan. 14, 1983 – Struck off register.

Bonnie Gold Mines Ltd. (Ont. 1952)
May 27, 1965 – Charter cancelled.

Bonnyville Oil & Refining Corp. (Que. 1954)
May 15, 1962 – Name changed to Consolidated Bonnyville Ltd.; basis 1 new for 10 old shs. ■

Bonore Gold Mines Ltd. (Ont. 1945)
1955 – Charter cancelled.

Bonsecour Mines Ltd. (Ont. 1944)
1954 – Charter cancelled.

Bontan Corporation Inc. (Ont. Apr. 9, 1973)
July 5, 2013 – Name changed to Portage Biotech Inc. and continued into British Virgin Islands.

Bontera Mining Corp. Ltd. (Ont. 1944)
1957 – Charter cancelled.

Bonterra Energy Corp. (Alta. Feb. 17, 1998)
July 4, 2001 – Plan of Arrangement with Bonterra Acquisition Corp. and Bonterra Energy Income Trust; basis 1 new Bonterra Energy trust unit for 4 old Bonterra Energy Corp. com. shs.

Bonterra Energy Income Trust (Alta. May 15, 2001)
Nov. 12, 2008 – Converted to Bonterra Oil & Gas Ltd. (formerly SRX Post Holdings Inc.); basis 1 Bonterra Oil sh. for 1 Bonterra Energy trust unit. (see Bonterra Energy Corp.)
Jan. 1, 2010 – Dissolved pursuant internal reorganization of Bonterra Oil & Gas Ltd. (see Bonterra Energy Corp.)

Bonterra Energy Income Trust (Alta. July 1, 2001)
Feb. 7, 2002 – Merged with Comstate Resources Income Trust; basis 0.885 new Comstate trust unit for 1 old Bonterra trust unit. (see Bonterra Energy Income Trust)

Bonterra Oil & Gas Ltd. (Can. Feb. 17, 1981)
Jan. 1, 2010 – Formed Bonterra Energy Corp. in Canada on amalgamation with wholly owned subsid. also named Bonterra Energy Corp. (see FPsurvey - Mines & Energy)

Bonus Petroleum Corp. (B.C. Dec. 5, 1980)
Nov. 17, 1988 – Continued into Canada.
June 6, 1996 – Name changed to Bonus Resource Services Corp.; basis 1 new for 1 old sh. ■

Bonus Resource Services Corp. (Can. Nov. 17, 1988)
May 15, 2001 – Name changed to Enserco Energy Service Company Inc.; basis 1 new for 4 old shs. ■

Bonus Resources Ltd. (B.C. 1972)
Aug. 23, 1973 – Name changed to Santa Sarita Mining Company Limited. ■

Bonville Gold Mines Ltd. (Ont. 1945)
1959 – Merged into Hydra Explorations Ltd.; basis 1 new for 25 old shs.

Bonwitha Mining Co. Ltd. (Ont. 1960)
Jan. 1971 – Charter cancelled.

Booker Gold Explorations Ltd. (B.C. Feb. 18, 1983)
Feb. 8, 2000 – Name changed to Pacific Booker Minerals Inc.; basis 1 new for 5 old shs. (see FPsurvey - Mines & Energy)

bookfortravel.com Inc. (Alta. Sept. 25, 1995)
Dec. 2, 2004 – Dissolved and struck from register.

Book4golf.com Corporation (Can. Sept. 22, 1999 amalg.)
May 26, 2004 – Name changed to B-For-G Capital Inc. and continued into Alberta pursuant to plan of arrangement; basis 1 new for 3 old shs. ■

Boom Capital Corporation (Alta. Apr. 21, 1997)
Nov. 18, 1999 – Formed Ranchero Oil & Gas Ltd. in Alberta on Major Transaction amalgamation with Ranchero Oil & Gas Ltd.; basis 1 new for 1 Ranchero sh. and 0.4009 new for 1 Boom sh. ■

Boomerang Resources Inc. (Alta. Feb. 3, 1989)
June 30, 1994 – Amalgamated with 599045 Alberta Ltd. and Laurasia Resources Limited (1 for 1) to continue as Laurasia Resources Limited; basis 2.8 new Laurasia shs. for 1 old Boomerang sh. (see Laurasia Resources Limited)

Boomerang Tracking Inc. (Can. Jan. 22, 1997)
Nov. 2, 2004 – Acquired indirectly by LoJack Corporation; basis either Cdn$2.95, or LoJack Exchangeco exch. shs. or interim notes in the exchange ratio of 0.2192, or a combination thereof for 1 old Boomerang cl. A sh.

Boot Hill Mines (Ont. 1946)
1947 – Name changed to Boulder Gold Mines Ltd. ■

Boots Drug Stores (Canada) Ltd. (unknown)
Nov. 1983 – Boots Drug Stores (Holdings) Ltd., the parent co., made an offer for all o/s pref. shs. at $64.50 per sh. Offer expired Dec. 7, 1983. Subsequently, all pref. shs. not tendered were purchased under section 199 of the C.B.C.A.

Boralex Energy Corporation (Can. Nov. 9, 1982)
May 28, 1984 – Name changed to Boralex Inc. (see FPsurvey - Mines & Energy; FPsurvey - Industrials)

Boralex Power Income Fund (Que. Dec. 20, 2001)
Nov. 3, 2010 – Acquired by 7596740 Canada Inc., an indirect wholly owned subsid. of Boralex Inc.; basis 1 redeemable pref. sh. for 1 Boralex Power unit, immediately redeemed for $5.00, or 0.05 of a $100 6.75% Boralex Inc. deb. for 1 Boralex Power unit.

Boram Oil Ltd. (B.C. 1980)
Apr. 16, 1984 – Name changed to Can-Tel Communications Inc. ■

Boraway Mines Ltd. (B.C. July 2, 1965)
Mar. 10, 1972 – Name changed to Able Explorations Ltd. ■

Borcan Resources Ltd. (B.C. Apr. 7, 1978)
Feb. 27, 1985 – Name changed to Le Groupe Opus Communications Inc. ■

Bordeaux Energy Inc. (Ont. Mar. 15, 1979 amalg.)
Dec. 12, 2007 – Continued into British Columbia.
Nov. 10, 2008 – Name changed to Enterprise Energy Resources Ltd.; basis 1 new for 30 old shs. ■

Bordeaux Resources Ltd. (B.C. Apr. 25, 1984)
Sept. 3, 1992 – Name changed to Visionary Industries Ltd.; basis 1 new for 2.5 old shs. ■

Border Capital Corp. (Alta. Feb. 16, 1996)
Sept. 27, 2000 – Name changed to iTV Games, Inc. (see FPsurvey - Industrials)

Border Malartic Gold Mines Ltd. (Ont. 1944)
1954 – Merged into Pardee Amalgamated Mines Ltd.; basis 1 new for 50 old shs.

Border Oils Incorporated (B.C.)
1950 – Reported to be out of existence. Assets sold to Canamont Oil Co. of Columbia Falls, Montana.

Border Petroleum Corp. (Alta. June 15, 2010)
Mar. 24, 2014 – Name changed to Border Petroleum Limited; basis 1 new for 10 old shs. (see FPsurvey - Mines & Energy)

Border Petroleum Inc. (B.C. May 29, 1985)
June 15, 2010 – Continued into Alberta.
Sept. 14, 2010 – Name changed to Border Petroleum Corp.; basis 1 new for 4 old shs. ■

Border Petroleums Ltd. (Alta. Apr. 26, 1937)
In liquidation; The Security Trust Co. Ltd., liquidator, 209-8th Ave. W., Calgary, Alta.

Bordessa Mines Ltd. (Ont. 1945)
1947 – Formed Aurlando Consolidated Mining Corp. Ltd. in Ontario following merger of Auriga Yellowknife Mines Ltd., Aurlando Gold Mines Ltd., Beaucamp Yellowknife Mines Ltd., Cabala Yellowknife Mines Ltd., Bordessa Mines Ltd. and Larbel Gold Mines Ltd.; basis 1 new for 5 old shs. ■

Bordulac Mines Ltd. (Ont. 1945)
1963 – Name changed to North Bordulac Mines Ltd.; basis 1 new for 4 old shs. ■

Bordun Ltd. (Que. Dec. 1, 1970)
May 10, 2002 – Struck off register.

Bordun Mining Corp. Ltd. (Ont. 1962)
Oct. 26, 1973 – All assets and liabs. acquired by Bordun Mining (Quebec) Ltd. in 1971. Dissolved.

Bordun Mining (Quebec) Ltd. (Que. Dec. 1, 1970)
Oct. 4, 1996 – Name changed to Bordun Ltd. ■

Boreal Exploration Inc. (Que. May 25, 1981)
Jan. 8, 2001 – Name changed to TGW Corp. Inc.; basis 1 new for 5.4567089 old shs. ■

Boreal Metals Corp. (B.C. Dec. 31, 2013)
Oct. 21, 2020 – Name changed to Norden Crown Metals Corporation. ■

Boreal Rare Metals Ltd. (Can. 1951)
1957 – Assets acquired by Beauport Holdings Ltd.; basis 1 new for $1.00 of debt.

Borealis Exploration Limited (Can. Aug. 26, 1968)
Oct. 19, 1998 – Continued into United Kingdom.

Borealis Retail Real Estate Investment Trust (Ont. Mar. 28, 2003)
May 17, 2005 – Name changed to Primaris Retail Real Estate Investment Trust. ■

Boreas Mines Ltd. (Alta. 1955)
1959 – Name changed to Expander Mines & Petroleums Ltd. ■

Boreas (Yellowknife) Gold Mines Ltd. (Alta. 1955)
1956 – Name changed to Boreas Mines Ltd. ■

Borkin Industries Corp. (B.C. May 18, 1983)
Mar. 2, 1988 – Delisted from the Vancouver Stock Exchange. Subsequently dissolved for failure to file.

Borneo Gold Corporation (B.C. Apr. 29, 1987)
Jan. 4, 2000 – Name changed to Nexttrip.com Travel Inc. ■

Bornite Mines Ltd. (Que. 1955)
1966 – Name changed to Rouyn Exploration Ltd.; basis 1 new for 3 old shs.

Bornite Ridge Mines Ltd. (B.C. 1964)
Jan. 1971 – Name changed to International Bornite Mines Ltd.; basis 1 new for 5 old shs. ■

Boron Chemicals International Ltd. (B.C. June 10, 1987)
Aug. 8, 1997 – Name changed to Atacama Minerals Corp. and continued into Canada. ■

Boros Chibougamau Mines Ltd. (Ont. 1955)
Dec. 21, 1964 – Charter cancelled.

Boru Mining Ltd. (B.C. 1972)
July 30, 1976 – Name changed to Gallahad Petroleum Ltd.; basis 1 new for 5 old shs. ■

Boss Energy Ltd. (Alta. 1980)
Nov. 2, 1995 – Amalgamated with 3177319 Canada Inc., a wholly owned subsid. of Canadian Leader Energy Inc.; basis 1 new for 3.8 Boss Energy shs. (see Canadian Leader Energy Inc.)

Boss Gold Corp. (B.C. Mar. 26, 1981)
July 11, 2005 – Name changed to Boss Gold International Corp.; basis 1 new for 3 old shs. ■

Boss Gold International Corp. (B.C. Mar. 26, 1981)
June 15, 2007 – Name changed to Boss Power Corp. ■

Boss Power Corp. (B.C. Mar. 26, 1981)
July 21, 2015 – Name changed to Eros Resources Corp. following reverse takeover acquisition of Anthem Resources Inc. ■

Boston Bay Mines Ltd. (Que. Nov. 8, 1971)
May 2, 2003 – Struck off register.

Boston Development Corp. (Alta. Oct. 28, 1996)
Feb. 21, 2003 – Acquired by private co. 101037490 Saskatchewan Ltd. for $0.40 per sh.

Boston Financial Group Inc. (Alta. 1986)
Nov. 28, 1991 – Name changed to H. Jager Developments Inc. pursuant to reverse takeover acquisition of Harvey Jager Holdings Ltd.; basis 1 new for 10 old shs. ■

Boston Molybdenum Mines Ltd. (Ont. 1960)
Apr. 12, 1972 – Dissolved.

Boswell International Technologies Ltd. (B.C. June 18, 1982)
June 12, 1996 – Delisted from the Vancouver Stock Exchange. Subsequently dissolved for failure to file and struck from register.

Boswell River Mines Ltd. (B.C. 1966)
Sept. 1972 – Name changed to B.R. Resources Ltd., basis 1 new for 5 old shs. ■

Botaneco Corp. (Can. June 30, 2004 amalg.)
July 9, 2013 – Name changed to Natunola AgriTech Inc. ■

Botex Industries Corp. (B.C. Apr. 11, 1983)
Aug. 3, 2001 – Name changed to Radical Elastomers Inc. ■

Botswana Diamondfields Incorporated (B.C. June 29, 1981)
Jan. 14, 2000 – Acquired by Crew Development Corp.; basis 2 Crew shs. for 3 Botswana shs. (see Crew Development Corporation)

Bouchard-Clericy Gold Mines Ltd. (Ont. 1945)
1945 – Name changed to Bouchard Gold Mines Ltd. and continued into Ontario; basis 1 new for 2 old shs. ■

Bouchard Gold Mines Ltd. (Ont. 1945)
Jan. 1958 – Charter cancelled.

Bougainville Ventures Inc. (B.C. Apr. 29, 2014)
Oct. 25, 2019 – Name changed to Primo Nutraceuitcals Inc. (see FPsurvey - Industrials)

Boulder Creek Mines Ltd. (Alta. 1966)
Apr. 1978 – Charter cancelled.

Boulder Energy Ltd. (Alta. Dec. 19, 2014)
Apr. 18, 2016 – Privatized by amalgamation with 1951556 Alberta Ltd., a portfolio company of ARC Energy Fund 8, to continue as Boulder Energy Ltd.; basis $2.59 cash per sh.

Boulder Gold Mines Ltd. (Ont. 1946)
Apr. 9, 1966 – Dissolved.

Boulder Hill Mines Ltd. (Ont. 1945)
1948 – Acquired by Boulder Gold Mines Ltd.; basis 1 new for 3 old shs. (see Boulder Gold Mines Ltd.)

Boulder Mining Corporation (Ont. Dec. 1, 1988 amalg.)
Jan. 2, 2007 – Continued into British Columbia.
Jan. 9, 2007 – Name changed to Opal Energy Corp. ■

Boulder Mountain Resources Ltd. (B.C. 1982)
Nov. 5, 1987 – Name changed to Consolidated Boulder Mountain Resources Ltd.; basis 1 new for 5 old shs. ■

Boulevard Capital Ltd. (B.C. June 3, 1988)
June 28, 2001 – Name changed to Urban Communications Inc. ■

Boulevard Industrial Real Estate Investment Trust (Ont. Jan. 30, 2014)
Oct. 5, 2015 – Acquired by PRO Real Estate Investment Trust; basis 0.04651 PRO REIT tr. units for 1 Boulevard tr. unit.

Boundary Creek Resources Ltd. (Alta. June 15, 1999)
Sept. 6, 2002 – Acquired by Bow Valley Energy Ltd.; basis $2.40 or 1.5 Bow Valley cl. A shs. or a combination thereof for 1 Boundary Creek com. sh. (see Bow Valley Energy Ltd.)

Boundary Exploration Limited (B.C. 1966)
Aug. 22, 1974 – Name changed to Consolidated Boundary Exploration Limited; basis 1 new for 3 old shs. ■

Boundary Gold Corp. (B.C. 1966)
Mar. 25, 1994 – Dissolved and struck off register.

Bounty Consolidated Mines, Limited (Ont. Aug. 10, 1939)
July 21, 1949 – Charter cancelled.

Bounty Exploration Limited (Ont. Sept. 29, 1943)
Jan. 15, 1974 – Name changed to Gulfstream Resources Canada Limited. ■

Bounty Resources Inc. (B.C. 1979)
Apr. 20, 1982 – Name changed to Starlight Energy Corporation; basis 1 new for 3 old shs. ■

Bourbeau Lake Mines Ltd. (Que. 1945)
Oct. 9, 1982 – Charter cancelled.

Bourbon Mines Ltd. (Ont. 1945)
1956 – Charter cancelled.

Bourbon Mining Co. Ltd. (Que. 1959)
Nov. 18, 1978 – Charter cancelled.

Bouscadillac Gold Mines Ltd. (Ont. July 2, 1936)
1958 – Merged into Cadamet Mines Ltd.; basis 1 new for 4 old shs.

Bousquet Gold Mines Ltd. (Ont. 1920)
Dec. 31, 1962 – Dissolved.

Boutin Resources Inc. (Ont. Mar. 4, 1975)
Mar. 25, 1980 – Name changed to Cleyo Resources Inc. ■

Bouzan Gold Mines Ltd. (Ont. 1945)
1955 – Name changed to Bouzan Mines Ltd. ■

Bouzan Mines Ltd. (Ont. 1945)
Nov. 18, 1963 – Merged with Kerr-Addison Gold Mines Ltd. (1 for 1) and Anglo-Huronian Ltd. (8 for 5) to form a new co. named Kerr Addison Mines Ltd.; basis 1 new for 10 old shs. (see Kerr Addison Mines Limited)

Boville Resources Ltd. (B.C. Aug. 14, 1979)
Nov. 18, 1983 – Name changed to Torhsen Energy Corporation. ■

Bovinex Farms Limited (Can. 1971)
1978 – Stated to be inactive.

Bovis Corporation Limited (Ont. 1960 amalg.)
June 15, 1979 – Amalgamated with certain no. of its subsids. and Peel-Elder Developments Ltd. to form Kesmark Construction Ltd., a private co. Com. shs. of co. exch. for pref. shs. of new co., and subsequently red. at 75¢ per sh.

Bow Energy Ltd. (Alta. Feb. 28, 1999 amalg.)
Mar. 8, 2018 – Acquired by Petrolia Energy Corporation; basis 1.15 Petrolia shs. for 1 Bow Energy sh.

Bow Flex, Inc. (Wash. Jan. 28, 1993)
June 17, 1998 – Name changed to Direct Focus Inc. ■

Bow Island Drilling Canada Ltd. (Ont. 1953)
Sept. 1974 – Acquired by Thomson Industries Limited. (see Thomson Industries Limited)

Bow River Exploration Ltd. (Alta. Oct. 8, 1986)
Apr. 2, 2005 – Struck from registry and dissolved.

Bow River Resources Ltd. (B.C. July 19, 1965)
Feb. 8, 1979 – Name changed to Suneva Resources Limited; basis 1 new for 3 old shs. ■

The Bow Valley Brewing Company Ltd. (Alta. Jan. 28, 1993)
Oct. 6, 1999 – All o/s cl. A shs. acquired by Peak Brewing Group Inc.; basis 0.1656 new sh. Peak for 1 old Bow Valley cl. A sh. (see Peak Brewing Group Inc.)

Bow Valley Energy Inc. (Alta. Feb. 16, 1950)
Aug. 15, 1994 – All o/s com. and cl. Z shs. acquired by Talisman Energy Inc.; basis: (1) 0.54982 Talisman sh. for 1 com. sh. or $14.3846 per sh.; (2) 0.58721 Talisman sh. for 1 old $0.56 cum. redeem. convert. cl. Z pref. sh. or $15.3628 per sh. The $2.05 cum. redeem. cl. D pref. shs., ser. 1 shares were subsequently redeemed Sept. 15, 1994 at $25 per sh. plus accrued and unpaid dividends of $0.4241; and US$2 cum. redeem. cl. D pref. shs., ser. 2 at US$25 plus accrued and unpaid dividends of US$0.4137. (see Talisman Energy Inc.)

Bow Valley Energy Ltd. (Alta. June 27, 1996)
May 6, 2009 – Acquired by Dana Petroleum plc for 50¢ per sh.

Bow Valley Forest Products Limited (Alta. June 3, 1996)
July 21, 1998 – Name changed to Flowing Energy Corporation following acquisition of Flowing Energy Inc.; basis 1 new for 1 old sh. ■

Bow Valley Industries Ltd. (Alta. Feb. 16, 1950)
June 7, 1993 – Name changed to Bow Valley Energy Inc. ■

Bow Valley Resource Services Ltd. (Alta. June 1, 1977)
May 26, 1989 – Name changed to BOVAR Inc.; basis 1 new for 10 old shs. ■

Bowater Canada Inc. (Can. Apr. 15, 1998)
Oct. 29, 2007 – Name changed to AbitibiBowater Canada Inc.; basis 0.52 new for 1 old sh. (see FPsurvey - Industrials)

Bowater Canadian Forest Products Inc. (Can. Mar. 11, 1994)
Jan. 1, 2002 – Amalgamated with Bowater Pulp and Paper Canada Inc. to form a new company also known as Bowater Canadian Forest Products Inc. (see Bowater Canada Inc.)

Bowater Corporation of North America Ltd. (Can. 1952)
Oct. 20, 1964 – All o/s 5% and 5.5% pref. shs., $50 par, redeemed at $52.029 per sh. (incl. accr. divd. of 0.129¢), and $51.642 per sh. (incl. accr. divd. of 0.142¢), respectively. The co. was reorganized to form Bowater

Canadian Corp. and Bowaters United States Corp., both wholly owned subsids. of Bowater Paper Corporation Limited of Great Britain.

Bowater Incorporated (Del. Aug. 28, 1964)
Oct. 29, 2007 – Name changed to AbitibiBowater Inc. pursuant to plan of merger with Abitibi-Consolidated Inc. with each becoming a wholly owned subsid. of AbitibiBowater; basis 0.06261 new for 1 Abitibi-Consolidated sh. and 0.52 new for 1 Bowater sh. ■

Bowater Paper Corporation Limited (U.K. 1923)
1972 – Name changed to The Bowater Corporation Limited.

Bowater Pulp and Paper Canada Inc. (Can. Jan. 1, 1989 amalg.)
Jan. 1, 2002 – All o/s 7.50% convert. unsecured subord. debs. redeemed effective Feb. 15, 1999; basis $100.143836 (including accr. and unpaid divd. of 0.143836) for 1 sh. Co. now private. Amalgamated with Bowater Canadian Forest Products Inc. to form a new company also known as Bowater Canadian Forest Products Inc. (see Bowater Canada Inc.)

Bowaters Mersey Paper Company Limited (N.S. 1956)
Oct. 16, 1975 – Name changed to Bowater Mersey Paper Company Limited.

Bowes Company, Limited (Can. 1919)
Oct. 31, 1972 – Acquired by George Weston Limited for $27.50 per sh.

Bowes Gold Mines Ltd. (Que. Apr. 1, 1936)
1945 – Sold property to Dovercliff Gold Mines for 1,500,000 shs. of which 1,100,000 shs. to be distributed to shldrs. on sh.-for-sh. basis leaving balance of 400,000 shs. in Bowes treasury. No record of distribution being made.

Bowes Lyon Resources Ltd. (B.C. 1983)
July 24, 1992 – Dissolved and struck off register.

Bowie Yellowknife Mines, Ltd. (Ont. 1945)
1955 – Charter cancelled.

Bowler Patents Limited (B.C.)
Dec. 30, 1948 – Charter cancelled.

Bowmore Exploration Ltd. (Alta. May 10, 2000)
May 23, 2017 – Continued into British Columbia.
June 26, 2017 – Name changed to Osisko Metals Incorporated; basis 1 new for 3 old shs. ■

Bowood Energy Inc. (Can. Sept. 8, 1994)
Aug. 22, 2012 – Name changed to LGX Oil + Gas Inc.; basis 1 new for 20 old shs. ■

Bowram Energy Inc. (B.C. Apr. 10, 2006)
June 15, 2009 – Together with Woodbridge Energy Ltd., Fortriu Capital Corp. and Chinook Capital Corp., exchanged their respective net cash for shares of Terrace Resources Inc., all Capital Pool Companies, and each of Woodbridge, Fortriu, Chinook and Bowram, subsequently dissolved; basis 1 Terrace sh. for 0.43 Woodbridge shs., 1 Terrace sh. for 0.55 Fortriu shs., 1 Terrace sh. for 0.56 Chinook shs. and 1 Terrace sh. for 0.53 Bowram shs. (see Terrace Resources Inc.)

Bowridge Resource Group Inc. (Alta. Mar. 9, 1993)
Nov. 15, 2001 – All o/s com. shs. acquired by private, Calgary-based ESI Energy Services Inc.; basis $1.15 per sh.

Bowser Resources Ltd. (B.C. 1969)
July 18, 1977 – Dissolved.

Bowsinque Mines Ltd. (Ont. 1945)
Oct. 5, 1959 – Dissolved.

Bowtex Energy (Canada) Corporation (Can. 1986)
Oct. 21, 1993 – Name changed to Luscar Oil and Gas Ltd. and continued into Alberta. ■

Boxada Mines Ltd. (Ont. 1944)
1946 – Assets acquired by Argyll Gold Mines Ltd.; basis 6 new for 1 old sh.

Boxxer Gold Corp. (Alta. May 9, 1996)
Dec. 18, 2014 – Name changed to ExGen Resources Inc. ■

Boycon Pershing Gold Mines Ltd. (Ont. 1945)
1950 – Name changed to Keyboycon Mines Ltd.; basis 1 new for 4 old shs. ■

Boyd & Sohlman Ltd. (Ont. 1956)
Aug. 30, 1969 – Amalgamated with 3 other cos. to form Headway Corp. Ltd.

Boyd Group Income Fund (Man. Dec. 16, 2002)
Jan. 2, 2020 – Succeeded by Boyd Group Services Inc. pursuant to plan of arrangement whereby Boyd Group Services Inc. was formed to facilitate the conversion of the income fund into a corporation. (see FPsurvey - Industrials)

The Boyd Group Inc. (Man. Sept. 3, 1997)
Feb. 28, 2003 – Converted into an income trust named Boyd Group Income Fund; basis 0.1624 trust units plus 0.0876 Boyd Group Holdings Inc. cl. A com. shs. for 1 cl. A restricted voting sh.

Boyles Bros. Drilling Company Ltd. (B.C. 1926)
1966 – Acquired by Inspiration Limited, through offer of three $1.50 cum. conv. pref. shs., $25 par and a $25 5% note for each 7 cl. A shs. of Boyles Bros.; and 4 com. shs., a non-int.-bearing $11 note plus $1.00 for each cl. B sh. of Boyles Bros.

Boymar Gold Mines Ltd. (Ont. 1948)
1960 – Name changed to Marboy Mines Ltd.; basis 1 new for 5 old shs. ■

Boyuan Construction Group, Inc. (Can. May 4, 2007)
Aug. 28, 2020 – Privatized via a 1-for-8,000,000 consolidation; basis Cdn$0.50 cash per pre-consolidated sh.

Brabar Metals & Holdings Ltd. (Ont. 1962)
Feb. 20, 1980 – Dissolved.

Brabar Mines Ltd. (Ont. 1962)
Dec. 22, 1970 – Name changed to Brabar Metals & Holdings Ltd. ■

Brabeia Inc. (B.C. Jan. 16, 2007)
Feb. 25, 2016 – Name changed to Seahawk Ventures Inc. ■

Brace Resources Ltd. (B.C. May 17, 1966)
May 11, 1988 – Name changed to International Brace Resources Inc.; basis 1 new for 2 old shs. ■

Bracell Petroleums Limited (Alta. 1967)
1973 – Murphy Oil Company Ltd. acquired all o/s shs. at $3.00 per sh. Subsequently, co. placed in voluntary liquidation.

Bracemac Mines Ltd. (Ont. 1965)
Nov. 9, 1976 – Charter cancelled.

Brachium Capital Corp. (B.C. Mar. 4, 2019)
Dec. 9, 2020 – Name changed to WeCommerce Holdings Ltd. pursuant to the Qualifying Transaction reverse takeover acquisition of (old) WeCommerce Holdings Ltd., which was concurrently amalgamated into the company; basis 1 new for 36.9763 old shs. ■

Bracknell Corporation (Alta. May 19, 1965)
May 17, 1989 – Continued into Ontario.
Nov. 1, 2002 – All directors resigned. Co. never petitioned into bankruptcy. Lending group liquidated assets, proceeds unknown. No distributions available for shldrs.

Bracknell Resources Ltd. (Alta. May 19, 1965)
Jan. 26, 1989 – Name changed to Bracknell Corporation. ■

Braco Resources Ltd. (Alta. May 16, 1986)
Sept. 16, 1994 – Amalgamated with Yogen Fruz Canada Inc. and 1075296 Ontario Inc. to form a new co. known as Yogen Fruz World-Wide Inc.; basis 1 new for 13.9 old shs. Also continued into Ontario on Sept. 2, 1994. (see Yogen Fruz World-Wide Incorporated)

Bradbury International Equities Ltd. (B.C. Feb. 13, 1980)
Oct. 5, 1998 – Name changed to Consolidated Bradbury International Equities Ltd.; basis 1 new for 10 old shs. ■

Bradda Head Lithium Limited (British Virgin Islands Oct. 28, 2009)
Oct. 25, 2024 – Voluntarily delisted from the TSX Venture Exchange.

Braddick Resources Ltd. (B.C. Oct. 14, 1993)
July 8, 2002 – Name changed to Kingsman Resources Inc.; basis 1 new for 7 old shs. ■

Braden-Burry Expediting Ltd. (N.W.T. Oct. 31, 1997 amalg.)
Nov. 3, 2004 – Privatized via amalgamation with 5209 NWT Acquisition Co. Ltd. wholly owned subsid. of Stewart Holdings Ltd.; basis 1 new pfd. sh. for 1 com. sh. Preferred shs. immediately redeemed for $0.35 per sh.

Brades Resource Corp. (B.C. Sept. 20, 2006)
May 12, 2015 – Name changed to Canex Energy Corp.; basis 1 new for 3 old shs. ■

Bradex Mines Ltd. (Ont. 1965)
May 18, 1976 – Charter cancelled.

Bradian Mines Ltd. (B.C. 1934)
1935 – Acquired by Bralorne Mines Ltd.; basis 1 new for 2 old shs.

Brading Breweries Limited (Ont. 1914)
Dec. 1970 – Charter cancelled.

Bradley Copper Ltd. (B.C.)
Sept. 19, 1977 – Dissolved.

Bradmer Pharmaceuticals Inc. (Ont. June 16, 2005)
Feb. 10, 2006 – Amalgamated in Ontario to continue with same name.
Aug. 1, 2018 – Name changed to Galaxy Digital Holdings Ltd. and continued into Cayman Islands pursuant to plan of arrangement reverse takeover acquisition of First Coin Capital Corp. and Galaxy Digital LP.; basis 1 new for 126.38 old shs. ■

Bradner Resources Ltd. (B.C. June 22, 1983)
Dec. 14, 1999 – Name changed to Bradner Ventures Ltd.; basis 1 new for 7 old shs. ■

Bradner Ventures Ltd. (B.C. June 22, 1983)
Nov. 17, 2009 – Name changed to HIP Energy Corporation; basis 1 new for 5 old shs. ■

Bradnor Gold Mines Ltd. (Ont. 1944)
Name changed to Bradnor Malartic Mines Ltd. ■

Bradnor Malartic Mines Ltd. (Ont. 1944)
1958 – Charter cancelled.

Bradstone Capital Corp. (Ont. Apr. 18, 1997)
Apr. 25, 2019 – Name changed to Bucephalus Capital Corp. ■

Bradstone Equity Partners, Inc. (Alta. Feb. 14, 1992)
July 4, 2002 – Formed Quest Investment Corporation in British Columbia on amalgamation with Glenex Industries Inc. (1 cl. A subord. vtg. for 2.268), Peruvian Gold Limited (1 cl. A subord. vtg. for 1.7156) and Stockscape.com Technologies Inc. (1 cl. A subord. vtg. for 4.1387). ■

Bradsue Resources Ltd. (B.C. Mar. 17, 1980)
Aug. 27, 1993 – Name changed to E.T.C. Industries Ltd. ■

Brady Cross Lake Silver Mines Ltd. (Ont. 1949)
July 27, 1976 – Charter cancelled.

Brae-Breest Gold Mines Ltd. (Ont. 1936)
1953 – Name changed to Brae-Breest Uranium Mines & Metals Ltd. ■

Brae-Breest Uranium Mines & Metals Ltd. (Ont. 1936)
Dec. 1, 1958 – Dissolved.

Braegan Energy Ltd. (Alta. Oct. 10, 1996)
May 17, 2000 – Acquired by Sunfire Energy Corporation for 62¢ per sh. (see Sunfire Energy Corporation)

Braemar Petroleum Ltd. (Alta. 1951)
May 13, 1973 – Struck off register.

Braemount Resources Ltd. (Alta. May 27, 1987)
May 28, 1993 – Continued into British Columbia.
July 28, 1993 – Name changed to Lumby Resources Corporation; basis 1 new for 2 old shs. ■

Braeswood Explorations Limited (Ont. Sept. 18, 1980)
July 9, 1987 – Name changed to Medmerica Incorporated. ■

Braeval Mining Corporation (Ont. Feb. 26, 2010)
Apr. 22, 2014 – Name changed to Oban Mining Corporation following amalg. of wholly owned 2407574 Ontario Inc. and Oban Exploration Limited (deemed acquiror); basis 0.914 Oban Mining com. shs. for 1 old Oban Exploration sh. and 1 Oban Mining sh. for 3.14 old Braval Mining sh. ■

Brafor Capital Corporation Limited (Can. June 21, 1968)
Dec. 1979 – Name changed to Sonor Petroleum Corporation. ■

Bragus Mines Ltd. (Ont. 1964)
1972 – Dissolved.

Brahma Resources Inc. (B.C. June 10, 1983)
Feb. 3, 1988 – Continued into Canada.
Oct. 19, 1999 – Dissolved for non-compliance.

Braiden Resources Ltd. (B.C. Aug. 23, 1988 amalg.)
June 14, 2002 – Name changed to Pure Pioneer Ventures Ltd.; basis 1 new for 5 old shs. ■

Braingrid Limited (Ont. Oct. 26, 1988)
Aug. 11, 2021 – Name changed to Tony G Co-Investment Holdings Ltd. ■

Brainhunter Inc. (Ont. June 21, 2002)
Feb. 2010 – Under bidding process of the Companies' Creditors Arrangement Act (CCAA), acquired by Zylog Systems Ltd. No funds available for distrib. to shldrs.

Brainium Technologies Inc. (B.C. Apr. 21, 1988)
Oct. 2007 – Dissolved and struck from register.

Brake Check Canada Inc. (Can. 1987)
Mar. 15, 1991 – Entered receivership.
Apr. 4, 1991 – Declared bankruptcy. Coopers & Lybrand Limited (Edmonton) appointed receiver.
June 1991 – All assets sold. Secured creditors suffered a shortfall and no distribution made to unsecured creditors and shldrs.
Dec. 21, 1994 – Receiver-Manager discharged.
Mar. 8, 1995 – Trustee in bankruptcy discharged.

Brakpan Ventures Corp. (B.C. Nov. 17, 2014)
Mar. 29, 2017 – Name changed to International Cobalt Corp. ■

Bralorne Can-Fer Resources Ltd. (B.C. Apr. 2, 1931)
May 29, 1972 – Name changed to Bralorne Resources Limited. ■

Bralorne Gold Mines Ltd. (B.C. July 10, 1992)
Oct. 21, 2014 – All o/s com. shs. not already held acquired by Avino Silver & Gold Mines Ltd.: basis 0.14 Avino com. shs. for 1 Bralorne com. sh.

Bralorne Mines Limited (B.C. Apr. 2, 1931)
1959 – Name changed to Bralorne Pioneer Mines Ltd. following acquisition of Pioneer Gold Mines of B.C. Limited. ■

Bralorne-Pioneer Gold Mines Ltd. (B.C. July 10, 1992)
Aug. 24, 2004 – Name changed to Bralorne Gold Mines Ltd.; basis 1 new for 10 old shs. ■

Bralorne Pioneer Mines Ltd. (B.C. Apr. 2, 1931)
Dec. 2, 1969 – Name changed to Bralorne Can-Fer Resources Ltd. ■

Bralorne Resources Limited (B.C. Apr. 2, 1931)
Nov. 27, 1990 – Name changed to BRL Enterprises Inc.; basis 1 new for 25 old shs. ■

Bralsaman Petroleums Limited (B.C. 1952)
Jan. 1981 – Merged with Ranger Oil Limited. Com. shs. of co. (98.9% owned by Ranger) converted to pref. shs. and redeemed on Aug. 15, 1980 at $7.36 per sh. Co. dissolved.

Bramalea Consolidated Developments Limited (Ont. Dec. 11, 1957)
June 7, 1976 – Name changed to Bramalea Limited. ■

Bramalea Inc. (Ont. Dec. 11, 1957)
Apr. 26, 1995 – Petitioned into bankruptcy and declared bankrupt. Ernst & Young in Toronto appointed trustee. Properties returned to lenders and Bramalea Homes Texas Inc. sold for an undisclosed amount.
May 1996 – Montreal Trust Company of Canada, trustee for the debentureholders, announced that an initial distribution of $54.6 million or 27.3¢ per dollar of principal, would be made to debentureholders of record on June 10, 1996.
Sept. 1, 1997 – Trustee discharged and there was no distribution made to unsecured creditors or shldrs.

Bramalea Limited (Ont. Dec. 11, 1957)
Aug. 8, 1994 – Name changed to Bramalea Inc.; basis 1 new for 20 old shs. ■

Bramalea Properties Inc. (Ont. 1982 amalg.)
Mar. 23, 1992 – All o/s 9 3/4% cumulative redeemable retractable 1st pref. shs. ser. 1, redeemed; basis $25 plus a dividend of $0.555804 per sh.

Bramar Industries Corp. (Alta. Nov. 5, 1996)
May 2, 2004 – Dissolved and struck from register.

Brameda Resources Limited (B.C. 1968)
Feb. 1979 – Amalgamated with The Yukon Consolidated Gold Corporation Limited to become Brameda-Yukon Limited, wholly owned subsid. of Teck Corporation; basis 1 cl. B com. sh. of Teck for 5 old Brameda shs.

Braminco Enterprises Inc. (Ont. 1946)
June 27, 1995 – Amalgamated with Q-Zar (Canada) Limited a wholly owned subsid. of Q-Zar Inc.; basis 1 new for 6 old shs. (see Q-Zar Inc.)

Braminco Mines Limited (Ont. 1946)
May 10, 1995 – Name changed to Braminco Enterprises Inc. ■

Bramond Mines Ltd. (Ont. 1964)
1972 – Dissolved.

Brampton Brick Limited (Ont. Jan. 21, 1950)
June 23, 2021 – Amalgamated in Ontario to continue with same name.
June 25, 2021 – All o/s cl. A shs. not already held acquired by BBL Acquisitions Inc.; basis 1 redeem. BBL pref. sh. for 1 Brampton Brick cl.A sh., redeemable for $12 cash per pref. sh.

Brana Oil & Gas Ltd. (Alta. Sept. 23, 1982)
Mar. 1, 1993 – Struck off register.

Branbury Explorations Limited (Ont. Dec. 2, 1980)
Dec. 19, 1986 – Amalgamated in Ontario to continue with same name.
Mar. 2, 1987 – Name changed to MDC Corporation following consolidation of com. shs. on a 1-for-20 basis

and subdividing each such sh. into 0.75 cl. A shs. and 0.25 cl. B shs. ∎

Branco Resources Ltd. (B.C. Jan. 23, 2012)
Mar. 17, 2016 – Name changed to Candelaria Mining Corp. following Qualifying Transaction acquisition of 60% interest in Minera Apolo, S.A. de C.V. (see FPsurvey - Mines & Energy)

Brand X Lifestyle Corp. (B.C. Mar. 28, 1980)
May 21, 2021 – Name changed to Canadian Nexus Team Ventures Corp. ∎

Brand and Millen Limited (Ont. 1946)
Oct. 1951 – Declared bankrupt. Secured and pref. creditors paid in full; unsecured creditors received 52.6% of their claims; no assets available for shldrs.

Brand Leaders Income Fund (Ont. June 29, 2011)
Mar. 16, 2022 – Terminated: basis $11.7136 cash per fund unit payable Mar. 22, 2022.

Brand Leaders Plus Income Fund (Ont. May 28, 2014)
Oct. 24, 2014 – Converted to an exchange-traded fund.

Brand Marvel Worldwide Consumer Products Corporation (B.C. Dec. 31, 1986)
Dec. 2018 – Dissolved and struck from registry.

Brandale Food Services Inc. (Can. May 13, 1994)
Feb. 3, 1999 – Name changed to Villaret Resources Ltd. ∎

Brandenburg Energy Corp. (B.C. Nov. 1, 2007)
Aug. 26, 2021 – Name changed to CoinAnalyst Corp. pursuant to the reverse takeover acquisition of Germany-based Coin Analyst UG. (see FPsurvey - Industrials)

Brandenburg Metals Corp. (B.C. Nov. 1, 2007)
July 14, 2011 – Name changed to Brandenburg Energy Corp. ∎

BrandEra Inc. (Ont. Aug. 15, 1995 amalg.)
May 7, 2002 – Name changed to National Construction Inc. following reverse takeover acquisition of National Construction Group Inc. ∎

BrandEra.Com Inc. (Ont. Aug. 15, 1995 amalg.)
Apr. 23, 2001 – Name changed to BrandEra Inc.; basis 1 new for 10 old shs. ∎

Brandevor Enterprises Ltd. (B.C. Oct. 21, 1985)
Apr. 1, 1999 – Delisted from the Toronto Stock Exchange. Subsequently struck from register and dissolved.

Brandgamz Marketing Inc. (Can. Feb. 17, 2006)
Dec. 15, 2012 – Dissolved and struck from register.

Brandi-Ridge Resources Ltd. (Ont. 1980)
Feb. 11, 1986 – Name changed to Mintron Enterprises Ltd. (see FPsurvey - Industrials)

Brandon Energy Ltd. (Alta. Aug. 8, 1995)
Aug. 23, 1999 – Merged with Cannon Resources Ltd.; basis Brandon to receive 712,368 com. shs. of Cannon valued at $1.06 per sh. (see Cannon Oil & Gas Ltd.)

Brandon Gold Corporation (B.C. Mar. 16, 1966)
Sept. 16, 1999 – Name changed to Redmond Ventures Corp.; basis 1 new for 2 old shs. ∎

Brandram-Henderson Limited (Can. 1906)
Jan. 1960 – Canadian Industries Limited acquired o/s com. shs. at $28.84 per sh.

Brandselite International Corporation (Ont. July 30, 1984)
Aug. 17, 2001 – Laurentian Bank of Canada, the primary secured creditor, demanded repayment of all o/s loans owed, totaling US$1,661,526.
Sept. 2001 – Filed a Notice of Intention To Make a Proposal under the Bankruptcy and Insolvency Act allowing the company 30 days to facilitate restructuring.

In October 2001, an extension was granted to Nov. 16, 2001.
Nov. 27, 2001 – Laurentian Bank placed A. Farber & Partners Inc. as receiver to liquidate the company's remaining assets. A further extension was granted until Dec. 21, 2001.
May 29, 2006 – Receiver noted that the administration of the receivership had been concluded and no further recoveries were anticipated. All proceeds of the liquidation went to Laurentian Bank of Canada. There were no funds available for other creditors or shldrs.

Brandy Resources Inc. (B.C. Sept. 26, 1979)
Sept. 5, 1984 – Name changed to Vital Pacific Resources Ltd. following acquisition of Vital Resources Limited; basis 1 new for 2 old shs. ∎

Braner Resources Inc. (B.C. Apr. 3, 1987)
Feb. 14, 1992 – Name changed to Consolidated Braner Ventures Inc.; basis 1 new for 3 old shs. ∎

Branly Enterprises Inc. (Ont. 1977 amalg.)
1983 – Charter cancelled and revived.
Feb. 1984 – Name changed to Consolidated Branly Resources Inc.; basis 1 new for 6 old shs. ∎

Branta Explorations Ltd. (B.C. 1967)
Feb. 25, 1983 – Struck off register.

Brantford Cordage Co. Ltd. (Can. 1924)
1958 – Interests associated with Trafalgar Investments Ltd. acquired over 90% of the stk. of the co. through purch. of all o/s cl. A and B shs. at $24 per sh.

Brantford Roofing Company, Limited (Can. 1928)
1953 – All o/s cl. A and B shs. acquired by Domtar Limited at $18.50 per sh.

Brantford Trailer & Body Ltd. (Ont. 1957)
1968 – Ceased operations when assets and operations purchased by Canadian Trailmobile Ltd. from Nova Industrial Corp.

Bras d'Or Coal Co. Ltd. (unknown)
1969 – Operations ceased. Co. out of business.

Bras d'Or Mines Ltd. (Que. 1974)
Oct. 24, 1985 – Under amalgamation agreement dated shs. of co. exchanged for shs. of Belmoral Mines Ltd.; basis 1 new for 1.5 old shs.

Brascade Corporation (Can. Sept. 13, 2004 amalg.)
Dec. 13, 2006 – Continued into Ontario.
Jan. 1, 2007 – Amalgamated with Diversified Canadian Financial II Corp. (DCF II) and Diversified Canadian Holdings Inc. (DCHI) to form new co. with same name Brascade Corporation. A total of 522,486 cl. 1 sr. pref. ser. B shs. of Brascade and 3,865,812 cl. A pref. shs. of DCF II were redeemed at Cdn$40 and Cdn$25 per sh., respectively; 3,581,677 cl. 1 sr. pref. ser. B shs. of Brascade held by DCF II and DCHI were cancelled; and the remaining 1,160,375 Brascade pref. shs. and 4,134,188 cl. A pref. shs. of DCF II were exchanged for new ser. A sr. pref. shs. at the conversion rate of 1.6 and 1.0 per sh., respectively.
Nov. 27, 2007 – Name changed to Brookfield Investments Corporation. (see FPsurvey - Industrials)

Brascade Resources Inc. (Ont. 1975)
July 24, 1981 – Continued into Canada.
Sept. 13, 2004 – Formed Brascade Corporation in Canada on amalgamation with a wholly owned subsid. of Brascan Corporation; basis 1 Brascade Corporation cl.1 series B pfd. sh. for 1 Brascade Resources series B pfd. sh. ∎

Brascan Adjustable Rate Trust I (Ont. July 28, 2005)
Aug. 15, 2008 – Final distribution of $0.03 per trust unit was paid to unitholders of record July 31, 2008, following termination of the trust on Aug. 1, 2008.

Brascan Corporation (Ont. Aug. 1, 1997 amalg.)
Nov. 15, 2005 – Name changed to Brookfield Asset Management Inc. ∎

Brascan Financial Corporation (Ont. Feb. 8, 1994)
Dec. 31, 2004 – Amalgamated with Trilon Holdings Inc. to continue as 1644036 Ontario Limited; basis unknown.

Brascan Gold Inc. (B.C. July 6, 2018)
Apr. 3, 2023 – Name changed to Brascan Resources Inc. ∎

Brascan Limited (Can. July 12, 1912; via letters patent)
Aug. 11, 1997 – Amalgamated with The Edper Group Limited to form EdperBrascan Corporation; basis (i) 1.5 new cl. A ltd. vtg. shs. of EdperBrascan for 1 cl. A sh. of Brascan; (ii) 1 new cl. A pref. sh., ser. 4 of EdperBrascan for 1 old fltg. rate redeem. 1981 pref. shs., ser. D of Brascan; (iii) 1 new cl. A pref. sh., ser. 6 of EdperBrascan for 1 old $1.875 1981 pref. sh., ser. F of Brascan; and (iv) 1 new cl. A pref. sh., ser. 8 of EdperBrascan for 1 old cum. redeem. 1981 pref. sh., ser. J of Brascan. (see EdperBrascan Corporation)

Brascan Power Inc. (Ont. Oct. 17, 1969)
Jan. 27, 2006 – Name changed to Brookfield Power Inc. ∎

Brascan Resources Inc. (B.C. July 6, 2018)
Sept. 21, 2023 – Name changed to Nordique Resources Inc.; basis 1 new for 10 old shs. (see FPsurvey - Mines & Energy)

Brascan SoundVest Diversified Income Fund (Ont. Oct. 30, 2003)
Jan. 1, 2010 – Merged together with Brascan SoundVest Total Return Fund (BSTR) into Brookfield Soundvest Equity Fund (formerly Brascan SoundVest Focused Business Trust); basis 1.256327 Brookfield trust units for 1 BSTR trust unit and 1.655611 Brookfield trust units for 1 old trust unit. (see Brookfield Soundvest Equity Fund)

Brascan SoundVest Focused Business Trust (Ont. Sept. 28, 2005)
Jan. 1, 2010 – Name changed to Brookfield Soundvest Equity Fund following merger with Brascan SoundVest Total Return Fund (BSTR) and Brascan SoundVest Diversified Income Fund (BSDI); basis 1.256327 Brookfield trust units for 1 BSTR trust unit and 1.655611 Brookfield trust units for 1 BSDI trust unit. ∎

Brascan SoundVest Rising Distribution Split Trust (Ont. Feb. 25, 2005)
Apr. 30, 2010 – Name changed to Brookfield SoundVest Split Trust. ∎

Brascan SoundVest Total Return Fund (Ont. Sept. 29, 2004)
Jan. 1, 2010 – Merged together with Brascan SoundVest Diversified Income Fund (BSDI) into Brookfield Soundvest Equity Fund (formerly Bascan SoundVest Focused Business Trust); basis 1.655611 Brookfield trust units for 1 BSDI trust unit and 1.256327 Brookfield trust units for 1 old trust unit. (see Brookfield Soundvest Equity Fund)

Brasil Gold Resources Ltd. (B.C. July 25, 1984)
Oct. 5, 1990 – Name changed to ARI Automated Recycling Inc. ∎

Brasilca Mining Corporation (B.C. Aug. 20, 1987)
Mar. 19, 2012 – Struck from registry and dissolved.

Brass Capital Corp. (Alta. Nov. 6, 2007)
Nov. 2, 2009 – Name changed to Heatherdale Resources Ltd. pursuant to Qualifying Transaction reverse takeover acquisition of Heatherdale Resources Ltd.; basis 1 new for 2.5 old shs. ∎

Brass Ring Resources Inc. (B.C. Apr. 15, 1980)
Dec. 30, 1987 – Name changed to Oneida Resources Inc.; basis 1 new for 5 old shs. (see FPsurvey - Mines & Energy)

La Brasserie O'Malley de Québec Ltée (Que. 1963)
Aug. 19, 1966 – Placed into bankruptcy. No further report.

Brassneck Capital Corp. (Alta. June 18, 2015)
Aug. 30, 2017 – Name changed to National Access Cannabis Corp. following Qualifying Transaction reverse takeover acquisition of (old) National Access Cannabis

Corp. (NAC) and concurrent amalgamation of (old) NAC with wholly owned 1119622 B.C. Ltd.; basis 1.205 new for 1 old sh. ■

Brattle Street Investment Corp. (B.C. July 7, 2010)
Dec. 15, 2020 – Name changed to Salona Global Medical Device Corporation; basis 1 new for 1.3568521 old shs. ■

Brauch Database Systems, Inc. (Ont. Jan. 7, 2000 amalg.)
June 2003 – Wound up; basis unknown.

Bravada Gold Corporation (B.C. Sept. 4, 2009)
Jan. 7, 2011 – Amalgamated in British Columbia to continue with same name. (see FPsurvey - Mines & Energy)

Braveheart Resources Inc. (Ont. Oct. 13, 2009)
Jan. 19, 2023 – Name changed to Canadian Critical Minerals Inc. (see FPsurvey - Mines & Energy)

Bravo Gold Corp. (B.C. July 18, 1983)
Apr. 16, 2012 – Name changed to Homestake Resource Corporation; basis 1 new for 10 old shs. ■

Bravo Gold Inc. (B.C. July 18, 1983)
Sept. 22, 1998 – Name changed to International Bravo Resource Corporation; basis 1 new for 2 old shs. ■

Bravo Resource Partners Ltd. (Yuk. Jan. 21, 2000)
Aug. 1, 2012 – Dissolved and struck from register.

Bravo Resources Inc. (B.C. Nov. 14, 1986)
May 6, 1994 – Name changed to Oro Bravo Resources Ltd.; basis 1 new for 3.5 old shs. ■

Bravo Venture Group Inc. (B.C. July 18, 1983)
Feb. 22, 2010 – Name changed to Bravo Gold Corp. ■

Bravo Yellowknife Mines Ltd. (Ont. 1944)
Nov. 5, 1956 – Dissolved.

Bravura Ventures Corp. (B.C. Aug. 6, 2010)
Nov. 7, 2017 – Name changed to Quantum Cobalt Corp. ■

BrazAlta Resources Corp. (Alta. Nov. 24, 2004)
Feb. 13, 2009 – Name changed to Canacol Energy Ltd. (see FPsurvey - Mines & Energy)

Brazauro Resources Corporation (B.C. Mar. 12, 1986)
July 21, 2010 – Acquired by Eldorado Gold Corporation; basis 0.0675 Eldorado shs. plus 0.33 TriStar Gold Inc. shs., a newly incorporated public co.

Brazil Resources Inc. (B.C. Sept. 9, 2009)
Dec. 6, 2016 – Continued into Canada.
Dec. 7, 2016 – Name changed to GoldMining Inc. (see FPsurvey - Mines & Energy)

Brazilian Development Co. Ltd. (B.C. 1970)
Jan. 26, 1972 – Name changed to Minto Mining Ltd. ■

Brazilian Diamonds Limited (Yuk. Feb. 5, 2001)
Nov. 19, 2003 – Continued into British Columbia.
July 18, 2011 – Name changed to Kincora Copper Limited pursuant to reverse takeover acquisition of Kincora Group Limited. (see FPsurvey - Mines & Energy)

Brazilian Gold Corporation (B.C. Aug. 23, 2007)
Nov. 25, 2013 – Acquired by Brazil Resources Inc.; basis 0.172 Brazil Resources shs. for 1 Brazilian Gold sh. (see Brazil Resources Inc.)

Brazilian Goldfields Ltd. (Bahamas Mar. 21, 1997)
Nov. 27, 1998 – Name changed to Brazilian International Goldfields Limited; basis 1 new for 4 old shs. ■

Brazilian International Goldfields Limited (Bahamas Mar. 21, 1997)
Mar. 2, 2002 – Name changed to Aguila American Resources Ltd.; basis 1 new for 20 old shs. ■

Brazilian Light and Power Company Limited (Can. July 12, 1912; via letters patent)
June 23, 1969 – Name changed to Brascan Limited. ■

Brazilian Traction, Light and Power Company, Limited (Can. July 12, 1912; via letters patent)
July 4, 1966 – Name changed to Brazilian Light and Power Company Limited. ■

BrazMin Corp. (British Virgin Islands Apr. 5, 2005 amalg.)
July 9, 2007 – Name changed to Talon Metals Corp. ■

Brazos Pacific Corporation (B.C. Dec. 6, 1978)
Nov. 8, 1994 – Name changed to S.T.A. Resources Corporation; basis 1 new for 5 old shs. ■

Brazos Petroleum Corporation (B.C. Dec. 6, 1978)
Apr. 17, 1990 – Name changed to Brazos Pacific Corporation. ■

Bre-X Minerals Ltd. (Alta. May 30, 1988)
Mar. 26, 1997 – Held rights to develop the Busang property in Indonesia, on which it had reported a major gold discovery. Freeport-McMoRan Copper and Gold Inc., joint venturer, developer and operator of the Busang project, announced that after its due diligence review of Busang, it had found only 'insignificant' traces of gold.
May 4, 1997 – Strathcona Mineral Services Limited, an independent auditor, confirmed findings.
May 7, 1997 – Indonesian gov't transferred all leases held by Bre-X to state-owned PT Aneka Tambang.
May 8, 1997 – Members of the Bre-X Minerals Group announced that they had sought and received court protection under the Companies' Creditors Arrangement Act and the Alberta and C.B.C.A. Several lawsuits were launched against Bre-X, Bresea Resources Ltd. (held 22.36% interest at Oct. 16, 1996) and other defendants claiming in excess of $3,000,000,000 in damages. Subsequently the Court of Queen's Bench of Alberta appointed PricewaterhouseCoopers Inc. (PWC) as interim receiver and manager.
May 1, 2002 – An amended settlement agreement was entered into to settle all claims, other than trade creditors, for claims issued 12 mths. prior to the agreement date. Under the agreement, Bresea's obligation was to pay $9,000,000 to Bre-X's trustee and to transfer to Bre-X the 49,000,000 Bre-X com. shs. issued to Bresea. These monies and Bre-X shs. would be held by PWC pending completion or termination of the agreement. Also Bresea would receive for cancellation 800,000 of its own com. shs. held by Bre-X and Bresea would be released from all claims by Bre-X and its past and present shldrs. Completion of the agreement was subject to several conditions, including approval of the courts in Alberta, Ontario and Texas. The termination date, originally July 31, 2002, was extended indefinitely by the Alberta court following approval by the courts of Alberta and Ontario but not Texas.
Sept. 30, 2004 – Agreement closed following approval by the court in Texas.
Feb. 4, 2005 – Bresea (renamed Sasamat Capital Corporation in Aug. 2001) had all claims against it settled. Terms included the release of 49,000,000 Bre-X shs. and $9,040,000 ($40,000 int.) to PWC, the repurchase of 800,000 Bresea shs. from PWC and the return to Bresea of certain escrowed funds valued at approx. $483,500. Also Bresea issued to PWC 655,184 fully paid and non-assessable com. shs. representing 10% of Bresea's outstanding capital. The 10% equity pool was to be distributed by a professional trustee who would process and adjudicate the submitted claims and take custody of the pool from PWC. There were no distributions available for shldrs.

Brea Resources Corp. (Can. Aug. 10, 2010)
Sept. 10, 2012 – Name changed to Goldstream Minerals Inc. following reverse takeover acquisition of Goldstream Exploration Ltd. and subsequent amalgamation of Goldstream with a wholly owned subsidiary; basis 1 new for 2.5 old shs. ■

Bread Basket International Ltd. (Que. 1971)
Dec. 22, 1973 – Charter cancelled.

Breaker Energy Ltd. (Alta. Mar. 8, 2004)
Dec. 11, 2009 – Formed NAL Petroleum (BEL) Ltd. in Alberta on amalgamation with 1494705 Alberta Ltd., a wholly owned subsid. of NAL Oil & Gas Trust; basis 0.475 NAL trust units for 1 Breaker sh. ■

Breaking Data Corp. (Can. Mar. 17, 2004)
Dec. 27, 2018 – Name changed to Bragg Gaming Group Inc. (see FPsurvey - Industrials)

Breaking Point Developments Inc. (Alta. Aug. 7, 2007)
Feb. 2, 2016 – Struck from registry and dissolved.

Breakwater Resources Ltd. (B.C. Oct. 15, 1979)
May 11, 1992 – Continued into Canada.
Sept. 8, 2011 – Acquired by a wholly owned subsid. of Nyrstar NV for $7.00 per sh.
Sept. 28, 2011 – Continued into British Columbia.

Brears Trucking Ltd. (Alta. Aug. 20, 1997)
June 8, 2000 – Name changed to Allnet Secom Inc. on Qualifying Transaction reverse takeover acquisition of Allnet Secom Corp. ■

Breathtec Biomedical, Inc. (B.C. Apr. 10, 2015)
Feb. 19, 2019 – Name changed to Algernon Pharmaceuticals Inc. (see FPsurvey - Industrials)

Breckenridge Minerals Inc. (Ont. Mar. 21, 1988)
June 7, 2005 – Name changed to WavePower Systems International Inc. following acquisition of WavePower Systems Inc.; basis 1 new for 4 old shs. ■

Breckenridge Resources Ltd. (B.C. Apr. 26, 1984)
Sept. 25, 2003 – Name changed to GTO Resources Inc.; basis 1 new for 16 old shs. ■

Breckenridge Technologies Inc. (Ont. Mar. 21, 1988)
Oct. 23, 1996 – Name changed to Breckenridge Minerals Inc. ■

Breezy Lake Gold Mining Co. Ltd. (Ont. 1948)
1970 – Charter cancelled.

Bren-Mar Minerals Ltd. (B.C. Jan. 17, 1983)
Sept. 22, 2000 – Name changed to Canadian Metals Exploration Ltd. ■

Bren-Mar Resources Ltd. (B.C. Jan. 17, 1983)
Mar. 15, 2000 – Name changed to Bren-Mar Minerals Ltd.; basis 1 new for 5 old shs. ■

Brenbar Mines Limited (Ont. 1945)
Jan. 1, 2011 – Amalgamated with Concopper Enterprises Inc. and Mirado Nickel Mines Limited to form Micon Gold Inc.; basis 1.0200 Micon Gold cl A. shs. for 1 Concopper cl. A sh. and 0.3116 Micon Gold cl. B shs. for 1 Concopper cl. B sh.; 0.4185 Micon Gold cl. A shs. for 1 Mirado sh.; and 0.0363 Micon Gold cl. A shs. for 1 Brenbar sh.

Brenda Mines Ltd. (B.C. Oct. 25, 1955)
May 2, 1996 – All o/s com. shs. not already held acquired by Noranda Inc.; basis $21 per sh. (see Noranda Inc.)

Brenda Yellowknife Mines Limited (Ont. 1945)
1952 – Charter cancelled.

Brendex Resources Ltd. (B.C. 1962)
Feb. 4, 1983 – Struck off register.

Brendon Resources Ltd. (B.C. 1962)
July 27, 1976 – Name changed to Brendex Resources Ltd.; basis 1 new for 5 old shs. ■

Brenmac Mines Ltd. (B.C. 1965)
Nov. 4, 1975 – Name changed to International Brenmac Development Corp.; basis 1 new for 5 old shs. ■

Brenmore Quebec Mines Ltd. (Que. 1938)
Dec. 29, 1979 – Dissolved.

Brenna Resources Ltd. (B.C. Feb. 26, 1987)
May 20, 1999 – Name changed to Clearview Mineral Resources Corp.; basis 1 new for 10 old shs. ■

Brennan & Kenty Bros. Prospecting Co. Ltd. (Ont. 1934)
1953 – Charter cancelled.

Brent Explorations Ltd. (B.C. 1969)
Aug. 27, 1979 – Name changed to Brent Petroleum Industries, Ltd. ■

Brent Petroleum Industries, Ltd. (B.C. 1969)
May 20, 1983 – Name changed to B.P.I. Resources Ltd.; basis 1 new for 5 old shs. ■

Brent Resources Group Ltd. (B.C. 1983 amalg.)
Feb. 28, 1992 – Dissolved and struck off register.

Brentwood Resources Ltd. (B.C. 1983)
Nov. 7, 1986 – Name changed to Maverick Naturalite Beef Corporation. ■

Brenwest Mining Limited (B.C. Feb. 22, 1980)
Mar. 1, 1990 – Name changed to Ridgeway Petroleum Corp.; basis 1 new for 3 old shs. ■

Brenzac Development Corporation (B.C. Apr. 29, 1987)
Apr. 20, 1993 – Name changed to Consolidated Brenzac Development Corporation; basis 1 new for 3 old shs. ■

Bresea Resources Ltd. (Alta. Oct. 31, 1980)
May 6, 1983 – Continued into British Columbia.
Feb. 26, 1990 – Continued into Canada.
Aug. 23, 2001 – Name changed to Sasamat Capital Corporation; basis 1 new for 10 old shs. ■

Brett Explorations Ltd. (B.C. Jan. 9, 1967)
1968 – Name changed to Brettland Mines Ltd. ■

Brett Oil & Gas Ltd. (unknown)
1964 – Acquired by Calmar West Oils Ltd. for 2,000,000 shs. (see Calmar West Oils Ltd.)

Brett Oils Ltd. (Alta. 1948)
1978 – Name changed to Bro Resources Ltd.; basis 1 new for 5 old shs. ■

Brett Resources Inc. (B.C. Sept. 11, 1986)
Aug. 25, 2010 – Acquired by Osisko Mining Corp.; basis 0.34 Osisko shs. plus $0.0001 for 1 Brett sh. (see Osisko Mining Corporation)
Oct. 6, 2010 – Name changed to Osisko Hammond Reef Gold Ltd. (see Osisko Mining Corporation)

Brett Trethewey Mines Ltd. (Ont. Oct. 18, 1927)
Wound up. Shldrs. entitled to distribution of 0.1¢ per sh. ■

Brettland Mines Ltd. (B.C. Jan. 9, 1967)
Mar. 26, 1974 – Name changed to Valdez Resource Industries Ltd.; basis 1 new for 5 old shs. ■

Bretton Mines Ltd. (Ont. 1945)
Mar. 1976 – Charter cancelled.

Bretton Red Lake Gold Mines Ltd. (Ont. 1945)
1958 – Name changed to Bretton Mines Ltd. ■

The Bretton Resource Corporation (Alta. July 6, 1954)
Jan. 30, 1992 – Name changed to Suncrest Capital Corporation; basis 1 new for 2 old shs. ■

Bretzin Lead Silver Mines Ltd. (Ont. 1948)
1949 – Name changed to Bretzin Mines Ltd.

Brew Kettle Corporation (Ont. Aug. 21, 1992)
Oct. 13, 1995 – Name changed to Lago Resources Ltd.; basis 1 new for 7 old shs. ■

Brewbac Resources Inc. (Ont. 1986)
Feb. 28, 1994 – Charter cancelled and co. dissolved.

Brewers & Distillers of Vancouver Limited (Can. 1923)
Feb. 1959 – Name changed to Western Canada Breweries Limited. ■

Brewis Red Lake Mines Ltd. (Ont. 1945)
Jan. 21, 1955 – Name changed to DeCoursey-Brewis Minerals Ltd.; basis 1 new for 8 old shs. ■

Brewmaster Systems Ltd. (B.C. 1983)
1987 – Amalgamated (1 new for 5 old shs.) with Jolt Beverage Company, Ltd. (1 for 1) and Interbev Packaging Corp. The basis of the amal. was 5 shs. of Brewmaster for one sh. of Jolt Beverage and 2 shs. of Interbev for one sh. of Jolt Beverage. Brewmaster is now a division of the Jolt Beverage Company, Ltd.

Brewster Lake Mines Ltd. (B.C. Oct. 25, 1968)
Sept. 2, 1976 – Name changed to Mace Technology Inc.; basis 1 new for 5 old shs. ■

Brex Exploration Inc. (Can. June 2, 1986)
Nov. 6, 2008 – Dissolved.

BriAlto Energy Corporation (Alta. Jan. 27, 1994)
Sept. 20, 1999 – Name changed to Highland Energy Inc. following reverse takeover acquisition of Highland Energy Ltd. ■

Brian Mines Ltd. (Man. 1959)
1968 – Charter cancelled.

Briana Bio-Tech Inc. (B.C. Feb. 20, 1986)
Feb. 22, 1999 – Filed a Notice of Intention To Make a Proposal under the Bankruptcy and Insolvency Act.
Apr. 27, 1999 – Deemed bankrupt as its proposal was rejected by creditors. David Azoulay et Associés Inc. was appointed trustee.
June 2002 – All assets sold except for a participating interest in a U.S. company, the value of which remained uncertain.
June 1, 2004 – Trustee discharged and there were no funds available for distribution to shldrs.

Briana Resources Ltd. (B.C. Feb. 20, 1986)
Sept. 25, 1990 – Name changed to Briana Bio-Tech Inc. ■

Briar-Court Mines Ltd (Ont. 1965)
Mar. 1976 – Charter cancelled.

Briar Glen Developments Corporation (B.C. Dec. 22, 1986)
Sept. 7, 1994 – Name changed to Innova Technologies Corp.; basis 1 new for 2 old shs. ■

Brican Resources Ltd. (B.C. Apr. 6, 1976)
May 6, 1991 – Name changed to International Brican Resources Ltd.; basis 1 new for 3 old shs. ■

Bricana Explorations Ltd. (Ont. 1963)
June 1982 – Charter cancelled Mar. 14, 1978; revived Feb. 6, 1980. Notice given of company's intention to dissolve and distribute assets amongst its shldrs.

Brick Brewing Co. Limited (Ont. Feb. 20, 1984)
June 12, 2019 – Name changed to Waterloo Brewing Ltd. ■

The Brick Group Income Fund (Alta. May 25, 2004)
Dec. 30, 2010 – Succeeded by The Brick Ltd. pursuant to plan of arrangement whereby The Brick Ltd. was formed to facilitate the conversion of the fund into a corporation and the fund was subsequently dissolved. ■

The Brick Ltd. (Can. Sept. 24, 2010)
Apr. 2, 2013 – Acquired by Leon's Furniture Limited; basis either $5.40 or 0.0054 3% Leon's deb. for 1 The Brick sh.

Bricol Capital Corp. (Alta. Sept. 2, 1999)
Mar. 18, 2011 – Name changed to QSolar Limited pursuant to reverse takeover acquisition of QSolar Ltd.; basis 1 new for 2 old shs. (see FPsurvey - Industrials)

Bridge & Tank Company of Canada Limited (Ont. 1954)
May 1, 1979 – Amalgamated with a subsid. of York Steel Construction Limited; basis 1 redeem. special sh. for 1 com. sh. (special shs. subsequently redeemed at $7.20 per sh.). Pfce. shs. redeemed prior to amalg. on Apr. 20, 1979.

Bridge Echo Lake Mines (Ont. 1950)
Nov. 1963 – Charter cancelled.

Bridge Hill Mines Ltd. (Ont. 1971)
Mar. 1976 – Charter cancelled.

Bridge Integrated Technologies Inc. (Ont. Nov. 12, 1981)
Jan. 3, 1995 – Delisted from the CDN. Subsequently dissolved.

Bridge Resources Corp. (Alta. July 21, 2006)
Apr. 24, 2012 – Name changed to Idaho Natural Resources Corp.; basis 1 new for 100 old shs. ■

Bridge Resources Ltd. (B.C. Feb. 11, 1980)
Aug. 21, 1984 – Name changed to Ravenroc Resources Ltd.; basis 1 new for 3 old shs. ■

Bridge River Consolidated Mines Ltd. (B.C. 1928)
Sept. 1958 – Name changed to Bridge River United Mines Ltd.; basis 1 new for 10 old shs. ■

Bridge River Development Corp. (B.C. 1979)
Jan. 13, 1995 – Dissolved and struck off register.

Bridge River Noel Gold Mines Limited (unknown)
Oct. 23, 1958 – Dissolved.

Bridge River United Mines Ltd. (B.C. 1928)
Dec. 1970 – Name changed to International Space Modules Ltd. ■

Bridgebank Capital Inc. (Ont. Dec. 12, 1986)
Sept. 28, 1992 – Name changed to Aquarius Coatings Inc.; basis 1 new for 10 old shs. ■

Bridgedan Equities Inc. (Alta. Jan. 7, 1987)
Oct. 30, 1989 – Name changed to Everlast Filtration Systems Inc. ■

Bridgeland Explorations Ltd. (Ont. 1962)
May 4, 1967 – Dissolved.

BridgePoint International inc. (Que. May 28, 1962; via letters patent)
Nov. 3, 2003 – Privatized. BridgePoint shldrs. received 4,500,000 units (1 com. sh. & 1/2 wt.) of Afcan Mining Corporation held by the company; basis 0.078 Afcan units for 1 BridgePoint cl. A sh.

Bridgeport Ventures Inc. (Ont. May 10, 2007)
Dec. 4, 2012 – Name changed to Premier Royalty Inc. following acquisition of Premier Royalty Corporation; basis 1 new for 4 old shs. ■

Bridger Petroleum Corporation Ltd. (Alta. 1971)
June 1978 – Home Oil Co. Ltd. acquired all o/s shs. at $12.60 per sh. (see Home Oil Company Limited)

Bridger Resources Inc. (B.C. Oct. 2, 1985)
Aug. 20, 1993 – Name changed to BDG Pacific Resources Inc.; basis 1 new for 3 old shs. ■

Bridges Energy Inc. (Alta. Feb. 1, 1988 amalg.)
Aug. 1, 1995 – Struck off register.

The Bridges Initiatives Inc. (Alta. Mar. 10, 1994)
May 18, 1999 – Name changed to Bridges.com Inc. ■

Bridges Transitions Inc. (Alta. Mar. 10, 1994)
July 25, 2006 – Plan of Arrangement acquisition by 1239381 Alberta Inc.; basis $0.98 per sh.

Bridges.com Inc. (Alta. Mar. 10, 1994)
July 7, 2004 – Name changed to Bridges Transitions Inc. ■

Bridgetown Energy Corporation (Alta. Oct. 6, 1994)
Aug. 15, 2001 – Acquired by Olympia Energy Inc. for $1.95 per sh. (see Olympia Energy Inc.)

Bridgewater Systems Corporation (Can. Apr. 3, 1997)
Aug. 19, 2011 – Acquired by Amdocs Limited for $8.20 per sh.

Bridgewest Development Corporation (B.C. Mar. 18, 1981)
Sept. 10, 1984 – Name changed to BDC Industries Corp.; basis 1 new for 5 old shs. ■

Brier Resources Corporation (B.C. Apr. 18, 1986)
Aug. 2, 2000 – Name changed to Ashlar Financial Services Corp. pursuant to acquisition of Ashlar Capital Corporation. ■

Brigade Resource Corp. (B.C. Oct. 9, 2014)
July 21, 2017 – Name changed to Green 2 Blue Energy Corp. pursuant to the reverse takeover acquisition of (old) Green 2 Blue Energy Corp. (concurrently renamed G2BE Canada Inc.). ■

Brigade Resources Inc. (B.C. 1979)
Dec. 8, 1987 – Amalgamated with International Wildrose Resources Ltd. (1 for 1), Consolidated Dakota Resources Ltd., (1 for 1) and Mac-Am Resources Corp. (1 for 1) to continue as Colossus Resource Equities Inc.; basis 1 new for 3 old shs.

Brigadier Capital Corporation (Alta. 1987)
May 1, 1995 – Name changed to Brigadier Venture Capital Corporation; basis 1 new for 8 old shs. ■

Brigadier Energy Inc. (Alta. 1987)
Mar. 17, 1999 – Acquired by Raider Resources Ltd.; basis 0.8 Raider shs. for 1 Brigadier sh. (see Raider Resources Ltd.)

Brigadier Gold Limited (Ont. Feb. 13, 1996)
June 19, 2020 – Continued into British Columbia.
May 23, 2024 – Name changed to Pace Metals Ltd.; basis 1 new for 30 old shs. ■

Brigadier Resources Ltd. (B.C. June 9, 1981)
Apr. 4, 1994 – Name changed to Parametric Ventures Inc.; basis 1 new for 3.3 old shs. ■

Brigadier Venture Capital Corporation (Alta. 1987)
July 31, 1997 – Name changed to Brigadier Energy Inc.; basis 1 new for 1 old sh. ■

Brigdon Resources Inc. (B.C. Jan. 8, 1973)
Mar. 1, 1999 – Name changed to Tikal Resources Inc.; basis 1 new com. for 1 old cl. A sh. ■

Briggand Energy Corp. (Alta. May 13, 1996)
Mar. 11, 1997 – Name changed to Canop Worldwide Corp. following acquisition of Canop International Resource Ventures Inc. ■

Bright Red Lake Mines Ltd. (Ont. 1944)
Oct. 18, 1978 – Charter cancelled.

Bright Star Metals Inc. (Alta. Nov. 28, 1994)
Mar. 12, 2001 – Name changed to Jasper Mining Corporation. ■

Bright Star Trio Mining Ltd. (B.C. 1963)
May 18, 1972 – Merged into Salem Mines Ltd.

Bright Star Ventures Corporation (Alta. Nov. 28, 1994)
Oct. 14, 1999 – Name changed to Bright Star Metals Inc. ■

Bright Star Ventures Ltd. (B.C. Dec. 22, 1980)
Jan. 22, 2007 – Dissolved and struck from register.

BrightPath Early Learning Inc. (Can. Apr. 1, 2005)
July 31, 2017 – Acquired by Busy Bees Holdings Limited; basis 80¢ cash per sh.

Brightwave Ventures Inc. (Can. Dec. 31, 1999)
May 20, 2003 – Formed SNB Capital Corp. in British Columbia on amalgamation with Stratos BioTechnologies Inc. and Nucleus BioScience Inc., with Brightwave the deemed acquiror; basis 0.3333 new for 1 Stratos sh., 0.3319 new for 1 Nucleus sh. and 0.3424 new for 1 Brightwave sh. ■

Brightwest Resource Explorations Inc. (Ont. 1987)
Sept. 9, 1994 – Name changed to CD ROM Network Corp.; basis 2 new for 3 old shs. (see FPsurvey - Industrials)

Brightwork Resources Inc. (B.C. June 8, 1988)
Jan. 6, 1992 – Name changed to Consolidated Brightwork Resources Inc.; basis 1 new for 2 old shs. ■

Brigus Gold Corp. (Yuk. May 2003)
June 9, 2011 – Continued into Canada. (see Primero Mining Corp.)
Mar. 11, 2014 – Amalgamated with wholly owned subsidiary of Primero Mining Corp.; basis $0.000001 cash, 0.175 Primero com. shs. and 0.1 newly incorporated Fortune Bay Corp. com. shs. for 1 Brigus com. sh. (see Primero Mining Corp.)

Brigus Gold ULC (Can. June 25, 2010 amalg.)
June 28, 2010 – Amalgamated with 1526735 Alberta ULC, a wholly owned subsid. of Apollo Gold Corporation (deemed acquiror); basis 5.4742 Apollo shs. for 1 Linear sh. Subsequently, Apollo changed its name to Brigus Gold Corp. and consolidated its shs. on a 1-for-4 basis. (see Brigus Gold Corp.)

Brikon Explorations Ltd. (B.C. 1954)
June 1979 – Charter cancelled.

Brilliant Mining Corp. (Alta. Oct. 1, 1998)
Nov. 24, 2011 – Name changed to Brilliant Resources Inc. ■

Brilliant Resources Inc. (Alta. Oct. 1, 1998)
June 25, 2015 – Name changed to FCF Capital Inc. ■

Brimac Development Corporation (Alta. Feb. 16, 1987)
Feb. 2, 1993 – Name changed to Wintertherm Corporation. ■

Brimm Energy Corp. (B.C. Apr. 16, 1991)
Aug. 29, 1994 – Continued into Canada.
Mar. 7, 1997 – Name changed to Odyssey Petroleum Corporation. ■

Brimstone Gold Corp. (Can. July 27, 1988)
Oct. 21, 1999 – Name changed to Foxpoint Resources Ltd.; basis 1 new for 15 old shs. ■

Brinco Limited (N.L. 1953)
May 29, 1986 – Merged with its parent co., Dorset Resources Ltd., to form Consolidated Brinco Limited. Each holder of 1000 or more cl. A com. shs. of Brinco received one cl. A com. sh. of the new co. and $1.00 for 10 old shs. (see Consolidated Brinco Limited)

Brinton Carpets Ltd. (unknown)
Nov. 1966 – Acquired by Armstrong Cork Canada Ltd. for $51 per sh.

Brinton-Peterboro Carpet Co. Ltd. (unknown)
June 24, 1963 – Name changed to Brinton Carpets Ltd. ■

Brio Gold Inc. (Ont. July 11, 2014)
May 28, 2018 – Acquired by Leagold Mining Corporation; basis 0.922 Leagold com. shs. plus 0.4 wt. for 1 Brio Gold com. sh. (see Leagold Mining Corporation)

Brio Industries Inc. (B.C. Feb. 4, 1986)
Oct. 25, 1999 – Name changed to Leading Brands, Inc. ■

Brionor Resources Inc. (Can. Sept. 8, 2009)
June 9, 2017 – Name changed to Magna Terra Minerals Inc. (see FPsurvey - Mines & Energy)

Brisa International S.A. (Luxembourg)
July 29, 1986 – Shldrs. passed a resolution to dissolve and voluntarily liquidate the company.
Aug. 29, 1986 – Shldrs. received nine ordinary shs. of Basic Resources International (Bahamas) Limited for each sh. of Brisa held.

Brisbane Capital Corp. (Yuk. Jan. 28, 1999)
Dec. 17, 2003 – Dissolved.

Brisbet Uranium Mines Ltd. (Ont. 1955)
Oct. 5, 1959 – Dissolved.

Briscoe Bryce Mines Ltd. (Ont. 1938)
1965 – Name changed to Geovolco Mining Ltd. ■

Brisio Innovations Inc. (B.C. Feb. 11, 2014)
Dec. 3, 2018 – Name changed to NameSilo Technologies Corp. (see FPsurvey - Industrials)

Bristol Developments Ltd. (B.C. 1967)
Aug. 22, 1977 – Dissolved.

Bristol Explorations Ltd. (B.C. June 24, 1986)
July 17, 1996 – Name changed to Afrasia Mineral Fields Inc.; basis 1 new for 2 old shs. ■

Bristol Mines (1946) Ltd. (B.C. 1946)
Sept. 1973 – Name changed to Camero Developments Ltd.; basis 1 new for 10 old shs. ■

Bristol Oils Limited (Ont. 1948)
1953 – Name changed to New Bristol Oils Limited; basis 1 new for 4 old shs. ■

Brit-Leduc Oils Ltd. (Ont. 1947)
Nov. 18, 1963 – Dissolved.

Britalta Petroleums Ltd. (B.C. 1949)
1962 – Assets acquired by Wilshire Oil Co. of Texas.

Britannia Gold Corp. (B.C. Jan. 15, 1979)
June 14, 1999 – Name changed to Britannia Minerals Corp.; basis 1 new for 7 old shs. ■

Britannia Minerals Corp. (B.C. Jan. 15, 1979)
Aug. 7, 2001 – Name changed to Nanotek Inc. ■

Britannia Mining & Smelting Co. Ltd. (B.C. 1908)
Liquidated. All assets transferred to Howe Sound Co., 500 Fifth Ave., New York.

Britannica House Trust (Ont. 1945)
Nov. 30, 1971 – Wound up and assets distributed.

Britannica Resources Corp. (B.C. May 17, 1966)
Oct. 8, 2013 – Name changed to Trinity Valley Energy Corp. ■

Britaura Porcupine Mines Ltd. (Ont. 1945)
June 4, 1958 – Name changed to Luckridge Phosphate Mines Ltd. ■

Britco Oils Limited (Ont. 1952)
Aug. 1957 – Acquired by Continental Consolidated Mines and Oils Corp. Ltd.; basis 1 new for 5 old shs. (see Continental Consolidated Mines & Oils Corp. Ltd.)

Britcol Entertainment Corporation Ltd. (B.C. 1971)
Dec. 18, 1978 – Dissolved.

Britcol Resource Development Ltd. (B.C. 1979)
June 16, 1987 – Name changed to Coldspring Resources Ltd. ■

British Alberta Petroleums Ltd. (Alta.)
1960 – Struck off register.

British American Bank Note Company Limited (Can. 1909)
Oct. 1, 1984 – All o/s com. shs. acquired by Bell Canada; basis 0.85 com. sh. of Bell Canada for 1 sh. British American Bank Note. (see The Bell Telephone Company of Canada)

British-American Construction & Materials Ltd. (Man. 1960)
Aug. 1967 – Name changed to B.A.C.M. Industries Limited. ■

The British American Oil Company Limited (Ont. 1906)
June 4, 1909 – Continued into Canada; via Dominion charter.
Jan. 1, 1969 – Name changed to Gulf Oil Canada Limited. ■

British American Royalties Ltd. (Ont.)
1954 – Wound up. No distribution reported.

British Canadian Lithium Mines Ltd. (unknown 1933)
1969 – Charter surrendered.

British Canadian Mines, Ltd. (Ont. 1922)
1936 – Assets acquired by Santa Fe Gold Mines Ltd. (see Santa Fe Gold Mines Ltd.)

British Canadian Resources Ltd. (Can. 1980)
Nov. 10, 1983 – Acquired by Westgrowth Petroleums Ltd. Shldrs. received 1 Westgrowth com. sh. and $1.20 or 2 Westgrowth com. shs., in each case with 0.5 Westgrowth ser. C pref. shs. and 0.5 wts. to purch. 1 Westgrowth sh. at $5.00 over a 3-year period.

British Canadian Trust Company (Can. - unspecified)
Jan. 1961 – Acquired by The Canada Trust Co. for $303 per sh.

British Columbia Electric Company Limited (B.C. 1926)
Aug. 1, 1961 – Expropriated by Govt. of B.C. Pref. shldrs. received divds. to final payments being 34¢ on the 4% shs., 19¢ on the 4.5% shs., 20¢ on the 4.5% shs., 41¢ on the 4 3/4% shs., 22¢ on the 5% shs., and 24¢ on the 5.5% shs. Pref. shs. then exchanged par-for-par through the Montreal Trust Co. for perpetual govt. guar. bds. bearing int. from at rates equal to divd. rates of pref. shs. exch.; and callable on same terms including redempt. prem. At holder's option, perpetual bds. were exch. prior to Aug. 1, 1962, for 25-yr. bds. maturing at par on Aug. 1, 1986, but otherwise bearing same terms and conditions as perpetual bds. Funded debt included $40,000,000 6% debs. conv. into com. shs. of B.C. Power Corp. at the curr. rate of 27 shs. per $1,000 deb. ($37.04 per sh.). These debentures were called for redemption on June 18, 1962, at 105.70 and accr. int. Other 1st mtge. bds. and debs. o/s were assumed by B.C. Hydro and Power Authority.

British Columbia Electric Power and Gas Co. Ltd. (B.C. 1926)
Dec. 17, 1946 – Name changed to British Columbia Electric Company Limited. ■

British Columbia Explorers (1953) Ltd. (B.C. 1953)
1961 – Liquidated. Distributed to minority shldrs. $2.25 and 7 free shs. Perlite Mining Corp. for each sh. held. Majority shldr. (Rio Tinto) received free and pooled shs. to extent of 6.36 Perlite shs. for 1 old sh. (see Perlite Mining Corp. Ltd.)

British Columbia Forest Products Limited (B.C. Jan. 31, 1946)
Dec. 30, 1971 – Amalgamated in British Columbia to continue with same name.
Sept. 14, 1988 – Formed Fletcher Challenge Canada Limited on amalgamation with Crown Forest Products Ltd. ■

British Columbia Lead & Zinc Mines Ltd. (Ont. 1937)
Nov. 1977 – Charter cancelled.

British Columbia Mineral Recoveries Ltd. (B.C. 1952)
1956 – Charter cancelled.

British Columbia Oil Lands Ltd. (B.C. 1972)
1976 – BP Exploration Canada Ltd. acquired all o/s shs. of the co. for $20 per sh.

British Columbia Packers Limited (Can. 1928)
Nov. 1, 1984 – Acquired by Weston Resources Ltd., a subsid. of George Weston Ltd., for $71.50 per cl. A sh. and $65 per cl. B sh.

British Columbia Power Corporation Ltd. (Can. 1928)
Sept. 1963 – Liquidated following purch. of its operating subsid., B.C. Electric Company, by Govt. of B.C. Final price agreed to by both parties, was $197,114,358.
1969 – Initial distribution to shldrs. was $18.70 per sh., of which 52.64208¢ subject to income tax, paid Dec. 30, 1961. Distribution of $25 per sh., of which 95¢ subject to income tax, paid Jan. 2, 1964; 50¢ per sh. paid Mar. 12, 1965; final distribution of 2.82¢ per sh. made in early 1969.

British Columbia Pulp & Paper Co. Ltd. (Can. 1925)
Apr. 1951 – Name changed to Alaska Pine and Cellulose Ltd. ■

British Columbia Resources Investment Corporation (B.C. Feb. 22, 1978)
Sept. 1, 1988 – Name changed to Westar Group Ltd. ■

British Columbia Telephone Company (Can. Apr. 12, 1916)
May 1, 1993 – Formed BC TELECOM Inc as the holding company and became a wholly owned subsidiary of BC TELECOM Inc with name changed to BC TEL; basis 1 BC TELECOM com. sh. for 1 British Columbia Telephone com. sh. All existing British Columbia Telephone pref. shs. were redesignated under the BC TEL name. ■

British Columbia Telephone Company (Can. Apr. 12, 1916; via Special Act of Parliament)
May 1, 1993 – Name changed to BC TEL. ■

British Controlled Oilfields Limited (Can. Jan. 15, 1918)
Nov. 22, 2019 – Commenced court-supervised liquidation and KPMG Inc. appointed liquidator.
Sept. 10, 2021 – KPMG as liquidator completed the distribution of the company's assets to shldrs. with satisfactory ownership claims. The unclaimed part of the company's assets were remitted to the Receiver General of Canada.
Nov. 19, 2021 – Voluntarily dissolved.

British Dominion Oil and Development Corporation Limited (Can. 1925)
May 1950 – Name changed to New British Dominion Oil Company Limited; basis 1 new for 3 old shs. ■

British Empire Oil Developments Ltd. (Alta. Jan. 16, 1948)
Dec. 30, 1950 – Taken over by Trans Empire Oils Ltd.; basis 1 new for 5 old shs.

British Gas plc (U.K. 1986)
Feb. 18, 1997 – Name changed to BG plc.

British Group Holdings Inc. (B.C. May 1, 1987)
Oct. 15, 1996 – Name changed to British Group Resources Ltd. ■

British Group Real Estate Corp. (B.C. May 1, 1987)
Dec. 14, 1999 – Name changed to British Group Realty Corporation; basis 1 new for 4 old shs. ■

British Group Realty Corporation (B.C. May 1, 1987)
Feb. 26, 2002 – Amalgamated with J. Block Acquisition Co. Ltd.; basis 1 J. Block redeem. pfce. sh. immediately redeemed for $1.80 per sh. Co. now private.

British Group Resources Ltd. (B.C. May 1, 1987)
Oct. 28, 1997 – Name changed to British Group Real Estate Corp. ■

British Industries Ltd. (B.C. May 1, 1987)
Apr. 16, 1992 – Name changed to British Group Holdings Inc. ■

British International Finance (Canada) Limited (Ont. 1960)
Aug. 15, 1972 – Name changed to BIF Corporation Limited. ■

British Lion Mines Ltd. (B.C. June 19, 1987)
Oct. 31, 1994 – Delisted from the Vancouver Stock Exchange. Subsequently struck from register and dissolved

British Manganese Mines Ltd. (Ont. 1941)
1957 – Charter cancelled.

British Matachewan Gold Mines Ltd. (Ont. Sept. 30, 1919)
1977 – Name changed to Saskuram Explorations Inc. ■

British Medical Services Limited (B.C. Aug. 25, 1982)
Oct. 5, 1990 – Name changed to BMD Enterprises Ltd.; basis 1 new for 3 old shs. ■

British Mortgage & Trust Company (Ont. 1877)
Sept. 30, 1965 – Merged with Victoria and Grey Trust Co.; basis 1 sh. Victoria and Grey for each 6 shs. British Mortgage.

British Newfoundland Corporation Ltd. (N.L. 1953)
June 30, 1971 – Name changed to Brinco Limited. ■

British Pacific Financial Inc. (B.C. 1984)
Aug. 10, 1988 – Name changed to Inter-Asia Equities Inc.; basis 1 new for 10 old shs. ■

British Pacific Investment Corporation (B.C. 1967)
Feb. 25, 1983 – Dissolved.

British Pacific Oils Ltd. (B.C. June 25, 1937)
Sept. 5, 1939 – Liquidated.

British Pacific Resources Ltd. (B.C. 1984)
Nov. 18, 1985 – Name changed to British Pacific Financial Inc. ■

British Petroleum Co. Ltd. (Ont. 1929)
July 21, 1930 – Dissolved.

British Petroleum Company of Canada Limited (Can. 1957)
1969 – Name changed to BP Canada (1969) Ltd. ■

The British Petroleum Company p.l.c. (U.K. 1909)
Dec. 31, 1998 – Formed BP Amoco p.l.c. in United Kingdom on amalgamation with Amoco Corporation; basis 3.97 new for 1 Amoco sh. and 1 new for 1 British Petroleum sh. ■

British Petroleums Limited (Can. 1923)
Mar. 23, 1957 – Name changed to Leamac Petroleums Limited. ■

British Rubber Co. of Canada Ltd. (Que. 1935)
June 30, 1948 – Name changed to Mailman Corp. Ltd. ■

British Silbak Premier Mines Ltd. (B.C. 1935)
July 22, 1987 – Name changed to Silbak Premier Mines Ltd. ■

British Ungava Explorations Ltd. (Que. 1961)
Jan. 1967 – Wound up and assets distributed.

British Western Industries Limited (B.C. 1968)
Dec. 14, 1978 – Charter cancelled. Amalg. with others into private co., Royal International Equities Ltd. Minority shldrs. pd. 55¢ per sh. for stk.

Britmont Mines Ltd. (Ont. 1959)
Mar. 1976 – Charter cancelled.

Britt-Malartic Gold Mines Ltd. (Ont. 1936)
Sept. 8, 1966 – Dissolved.

Britt Resources Ltd. (B.C. July 28, 1982)
July 15, 1992 – Name changed to La Cieba Minerals Corp.; basis 1 new for 3 old shs. ■

Brittany Capital Corporation (Alta. Jan. 6, 1987)
Aug. 21, 1997 – Name changed to Brittany Energy Inc.; basis 1 new for 1 old sh. ■

Brittany Energy Inc. (Alta. Jan. 6, 1987)
June 16, 1999 – Amalgamated with Uniglobe Ventures Ltd. and 825281 Alberta Ltd., a wholly owned subsid. of Diaz Resources Ltd., to form Diaz Energy Inc.; basis 0.85 new for 1 Uniglobe Ventures sh. and 0.75 new for 1 Brittany sh. (see Diaz Resources Ltd.)

Brixton Energy Corp. (B.C. June 19, 1980)
June 4, 2018 – Struck from registry and dissolved.

Briyante Software Corp. (B.C. June 29, 1983)
Nov. 26, 2003 – Plan of Arrangement acquisition by Imagis Technologies Inc.; basis 0.31111 post-cons. new Imagis (4.5 for 1) sh. for 1 old Briyante sh. (see Imagis Technologies Inc.)

Bro Resources Ltd. (Alta. 1948)
Oct. 8, 1981 – Continued into British Columbia.
Dec. 6, 1990 – Name changed to Canadian Quantum
Energy Corporation; basis 1 new for 5 old shs. ■

Broad Scope Developments Ltd. (Ont. 1968)
Mar. 1973 – Amalgamated with 2 other cos. to form
Newore Developments Ltd.; basis 1 new for 2 old shs.

Broadback Mines Ltd. (Ont. 1959)
Dec. 1968 – Charter cancelled.

Broadband Learning Corporation (Can. Oct. 5, 2004)
Feb. 11, 2012 – Dissolved and struck from register.

Broadcast Capital Corp. (Alta. Oct. 4, 2005)
Dec. 15, 2006 – Formed Pebble Creek Mining Ltd. in
British Columbia pursuant to reverse takeover acquisition
of and amalgamation with Pebble Creek Resource Ltd. ■

Broadlands Resources Ltd. (B.C. 1978)
Apr. 6, 1995 – Amalgamated with Shorewood Exploration
Ltd. to form International Broadlands Resources Ltd.;
basis 1 new for 1 Shorewood sh. and 1 new for 1
Broadlands sh. (see International Broadlands Resources
Ltd.)

Broadlands Resources Ltd. (B.C. Apr. 6, 1995 amalg.)
July 16, 2003 – Name changed to Pinnacle Mines Ltd.;
basis 1 new for 5 old shs. ■

Broadview Capital Corporation (Alta. July 29, 1999)
May 30, 2000 – Name changed to Broadview Press Inc.
following reverse takeover acquisition of Broadview Press
Ltd. ■

Broadview Gold Mines Ltd. (Ont. 1949)
1957 – Charter cancelled.

Broadview Press Inc. (Alta. July 29, 1999)
Mar. 24, 2010 – Privatized at 10¢ per sh.

Broadview Resources Inc. (Alta. 1987)
May 1, 1989 – Amalgamated with Stockmen Oil and Gas
Ltd. to form Prime Petroleum Corporation; basis 1 new
for 2 Stockmen shs. and 1 new for 3.5 Broadview shs.
(see Stockmen Oil and Gas Ltd.)

Broadwater Developments Inc. (B.C. Feb. 1, 1984)
Apr. 18, 2000 – Name changed to Wyn Developments
Inc.; basis 1 new for 3 old shs. ■

Broadway Beverages Ltd. (B.C. 1983)
Sept. 23, 1990 – Dissolved and struck off register.

Broadway Gold Mining Ltd. (B.C. July 26, 2010)
Feb. 27, 2020 – Name changed to Mind Medicine
(MindMed) Inc. pursuant to the reverse takeover
acquisition of private Reno, Nev.-based Mind Medicine,
Inc.; basis 1 new for 8 old shs. (see FPsurvey -
Industrials)

Broadway Petroleum Corp. Ltd. (B.C. 1953)
1958 – Struck off register.

Brobar Mines & Oils Ltd. (Ont. 1956)
Feb. 4, 1970 – Charter cancelled.

Brock Gold Mines Ltd. (Ont. May 4, 1938)
1946 – Acquired by Upper Canada Mines Ltd.; basis 1
new for 15 old shs. (see Upper Canada Mines Ltd.)

Brock Petroleums Limited (Can. 1929)
Dec. 17, 1958 – Dissolved.

Brocker Investments Ltd. (Alta. Nov. 23, 1993)
Jan. 8, 1999 – Name changed to Brocker Technology
Group Ltd. ■

Brocker Technology Group Ltd. (Alta. Nov. 23, 1993)
July 21, 2001 – Continued into New Brunswick.
June 26, 2003 – Name changed to Datec Group Ltd. ■

Brockton Capital Corp. (B.C. Feb. 8, 2000)
Mar. 6, 2007 – Name changed to MegaWest Energy
Corp. ■

Brockton Resources Inc. (B.C. Dec. 16, 1987)
Nov. 19, 1992 – Name changed to Chartwell Ventures
Ltd.; basis 1 new for 2 old shs. ■

Brockton Ventures Inc. (B.C. Jan. 26, 2018)
July 30, 2020 – Name changed to TGS Esports Inc.
pursuant to the Qualifying Transaction reverse takeover
of Myesports Ventures Ltd. and concurrent amalgamation
of Myesports with wholly owned 1231527 B.C. Ltd. (see
FPsurvey - Industrials)

Brockville Chemicals Limited (Can. 1959)
Oct. 1965 – Merged with Genstar Ltd.; basis 0.57 new
com. sh. Sogemines for each partic. pref. sh. Brockville
com. shldrs. received 1/10 of shs. received by pref.

Brohm Resources Inc. (B.C. 1983)
Aug. 12, 1988 – Merged with MFC Mining Finance
Corporation to form MinVen Gold Corporation; basis 1
new for 1 old sh. (see MinVen Gold Corporation)

Broken Hill Explorations Ltd. (Ont. 1970)
Mar. 1976 – Charter cancelled.

Brominco Inc. (Que. 1976)
May 17, 1985 – Acquired by Aur Resources Inc.; basis
2.5 new for 1 old sh. (see Aur Resources Inc.)

Bromley.Marr ECOS Inc. (Alta. Nov. 18, 1994)
Aug. 31, 1999 – All the directors of the company resigned
due to existing debt difficulties.
Sept. 2, 1999 – Placed into receivership and
Calgary-based Ernst & Young Inc. was appointed
receiver.
2001 – All assets liquidated and secured creditors
suffered a shortfall of about $10,000,000. There were no
funds available for distribution to unsecured creditors or
shldrs.
Feb. 1, 2002 – Receiver discharged.

Bromont Estate Inc. (Que. 1971)
May 28, 1979 – Amalgamated with other cos. to form
Desourdy Inc. Co. now private.

**Brompton Advantaged Equal Weight Oil & Gas
Income Fund** (Ont. Feb. 24, 2005)
June 24, 2008 – Name changed to Brompton Advantaged
Oil & Gas Income Fund. ■

Brompton Advantaged Oil & Gas Income Fund (Ont.
Feb. 24, 2005)
Sept. 9, 2011 – Name changed to Aston Hill Advantage
Oil & Gas Income Fund. ■

Brompton Advantaged Tracker Fund (Ont. Jan. 1,
2006)
July 14, 2008 – Name changed to Brompton Advantaged
VIP Income Fund following merger with Brompton Top
50 Compound Growth Fund (basis 0.692406-for-1), BG
Advantaged S&P/TSX Income Trust Index Fund (1-for-1),
BG Advantaged Equal Weighted Income Fund
(0.845594-for-1) and BG Advantaged Corporate Bond
Fund (0.577987-for-1). Brompton Advantaged Tracker
Fund units were consolidated on a 1-for-1.615694 basis. ■

Brompton Advantaged VIP Income Fund (Ont. Jan. 1,
2006)
Sept. 9, 2011 – Name changed to Aston Hill Advantage
VIP Income Fund. ■

Brompton Equal Weight Income Fund (Ont. May 16,
2003)
July 7, 2008 – Together with Business Trust Equal Weight
Income Fund, BG Top 100 Equal Weighted Income Fund,
Brompton Tracker Fund, BG Income + Growth Split Trust
and Brompton Stable Income Fund, each merged with
Brompton VIP Income Fund to continue as Brompton VIP
Income Fund; basis Brompton Equal Weight
(0.8583-for-1), Business Trust Equal Weight
(0.6919-for-1), BG Top 100 Equal Weighted
(0.7364-for-1), Brompton Tracker Fund (0.6664-for-1),
BG Income + Growth Split Trust (1.013-for-1) and
Brompton Stable Income (0.9652-for-1).

Brompton Equal Weight Oil & Gas Income Fund (Ont.
Sept. 28, 2004)
June 20, 2008 – Name changed to Brompton Oil & Gas
Income Fund. ■

Brompton Equity Split Corp. (Ont. Feb. 13, 2004)
May 24, 2011 – Amalgamated with Dividend Growth Split
Corp. (DGS); basis 1.493584 DGS cl. A shs. for 1
Brompton Equity cl. A sh. and 1 DGS pref. sh. for 1
Brompton Equity pref. sh.

Brompton MVP Income Fund (Ont. May 22, 2002)
Jan. 3, 2006 – Amalgamated with Brompton VIP Income
Fund; basis 1.07245 new VIP units for 1 old MVP unit.
(see Brompton VIP Income Fund)

Brompton Oil & Gas Income Fund (Ont. Sept. 28, 2004)
Sept. 9, 2011 – Name changed to Aston Hill Oil & Gas
Income Fund. ■

Brompton Oil Split Corp. (Ont. Dec. 30, 2014)
Dec. 14, 2023 – Name changed to Brompton Energy Split
Corp. (see FPsurvey - Industrials)

Brompton Property Group Inc. (Alta. Aug. 21, 1997)
Sept. 22, 2005 – Going private transaction; basis 54¢ per
sh.

Brompton Stable Income Fund (Ont. Oct. 1, 2002)
July 7, 2008 – Together with Brompton Equal Weight
Income Fund, Business Trust Equal Weight Income Fund,
BG Top 100 Equal Weighted Income Fund, Brompton
Tracker Fund and BG Income + Growth Split Trust, each
merged with Brompton VIP Income Fund to continue as
Brompton VIP Income Fund; basis Brompton Stable
Income (0.9652-for-1); Brompton Equal Weight
(0.8583-for-1), Business Trust Equal Weight
(0.6919-for-1), BG Top 100 Equal Weighted
(0.7364-for-1), Brompton Tracker Fund (0.6664-for-1)
and BG Income + Growth Split Trust (1.013-for-1).

Brompton Top 50 Compound Growth Fund (Ont. Jan.
8, 2006)
July 14, 2008 – Merged with Brompton Advantaged
Tracker, BG Advantaged S&P/TSX Income Trust Index
Fund, BG Advantaged Equal Weighted Income Fund and
BG Advantaged Corporate Bond Fund to form Brompton
Advantaged VIP Income Fund; basis Brompton Top 50
Compound Growth (0.692406-for-1), Brompton Advantage
Tracker (1-for-1), BG Advantaged S&P/TSX
(1.139860-for-1), BG Advantaged Equal Weighted
(0.845594-for-1) and BG Advantaged Corporate Bond
(0.577987-for-1) . Immediately prior to the merger,
Brompton Advantaged Tracker Fund units were
consolidated on a 1-for-1.615694 basis.

Brompton Tracker Fund (Ont. Jan. 26, 2005)
July 7, 2008 – Together with BG Income + Growth Split
Trust, Brompton Stable Income Fund, Brompton Equal
Weight Income Fund, Business Trust Equal Weight
Income Fund and BG Top 100 Equal Weighted Income
Fund, each merged with Brompton VIP Income Fund to
continue as Brompton VIP Income Fund; basis Brompton
Tracker Fund (0.6664-for-1), BG Income + Growth Split
Trust (1.013-for-1), Brompton Stable Income
(0.9652-for-1), Brompton Equal Weight (0.8583-for-1),
Business Trust Equal Weight (0.6919-for-1) and BG Top
100 Equal Weighted (0.7364-for-1).

Brompton VIP Income Fund (Ont. Oct. 25, 2001)
Sept. 9, 2011 – Name changed to Aston Hill VIP Income
Fund. ■

Brompton VIP Income Trust (Ont. Oct. 25, 2001)
Nov. 17, 2005 – Name changed to Brompton VIP Income
Fund. ■

Bronco Energy Ltd. (Alta. May 31, 2004)
Nov. 10, 2010 – Acquired by Legacy Oil + Gas Inc.; basis
0.0182 Legacy shs. for 1 Bronco sh. (see Legacy Oil +
Gas Inc.)

Bronco Petroleums Ltd. (B.C. Mar. 25, 1980)
Sept. 5, 1985 – Name changed to Quorum Resource
Corp.; basis 1 new for 7 old shs. ■

Brongniart Chibougamau Mines Ltd. (Ont. 1956)
Sept. 1960 – Charter cancelled.

Bronson Mines Ltd. (B.C. 1973)
July 1980 – Name changed to Goliath Gold Mines Ltd.; basis 1 new for 2 old shs. ■

Bronx Minerals Inc. (B.C. May 27, 1980)
Sept. 7, 1999 – Name changed to Las Vegas From Home.com Entertainment Inc. ■

Bronx Ventures Inc. (B.C. Aug. 24, 1984)
Mar. 19, 2007 – Name changed to Zab Resources Inc.; basis 50 new for 1 old sh. ■

Brookbank-Sturgeon Mines Ltd. (Ont. 1950)
June 1983 – Merged with Ontex Resources Limited.

Brooke Bond Canada Ltd. (Can. 1911)
Nov. 1969 – Name changed to Brooke Bond Foods Limited. ■

Brooke Bond Foods Limited (Can. 1911)
Feb. 29, 1980 – Name changed to Brooke Bond Inc. ■

Brooke Bond Inc. (Can. 1911)
Apr. 15, 1984 – Reverted to private co. status upon redemption of all o/s pref. stk. at $26.16 per sh.

Brooke Cadillac Gold Mines Ltd. (Que. 1937)
July 22, 1978 – Charter cancelled.

Brookemont Capital Inc. (B.C. Mar. 28, 2007)
Nov. 17, 2014 – Name changed to Turbo Capital Inc.; basis 1 new for 2 old shs. ■

Brookfield Asset Management Inc. (Ont. Aug. 1, 1997 amalg.)
Dec. 9, 2022 – Name changed to Brookfield Corporation. (see FPsurvey - Industrials)

Brookfield Asset Management Reinsurance Partners Ltd. (Bermuda Dec. 10, 2020)
Dec. 9, 2022 – Name changed to Brookfield Reinsurance Ltd. ■

Brookfield Canada Office Properties (Ont. Mar. 19, 2010)
July 5, 2017 – All o/s trust units not already held acquired by Brookfield Property Partners L.P.; basis $32.50 cash per trust unit.

Brookfield Capital 1 Corporation (Que. 1986)
May 11, 1994 – All o/s 7.25% cumu. redeem. retract. pfd. shs. ser. 1 redeemed for $25 plus $0.19 in accr. divds. per sh.

Brookfield Dairy Products Limited (N.S. Sept. 6, 1950)
1974 – Stated to be a division of Scotsburn Cooperative Services Ltd., Scotsburn, N.S.

Brookfield High Yield Strategic Income Fund (Ont. May 23, 2012)
June 22, 2017 – Terminated; distrib. of $8.03 per trust unit.

Brookfield Homes Ltd (Can. Mar. 30, 1953)
May 20, 1997 – Amalgamated with 3307328 Canada Limited, a wholly owned subsid. of Brookfield Properties Corporation (Properties); basis 1 com. sh. of Properties for 1.5 old com. sh. of Brookfield Homes; the 7% convertible sub. unsecured deb. convertible into com. shs. of Brookfield Properties on a 59.24 new com. shs. per $1,000 princ. amt. of debs. until Apr. 15, 2004; 1.2 new cl. AA pref. ser. E shs. of Properties for 1 old pref. ser. A sh. (see Brookfield Properties Corporation)

Brookfield New Horizons Income Fund (Ont. Mar. 1, 2011)
Aug. 1, 2017 – Terminated: basis 20¢ cash per trust unit.

Brookfield Office Properties Canada (Ont. Mar. 19, 2010)
Feb. 29, 2012 – Name changed to Brookfield Canada Office Properties. ■

Brookfield Office Properties Inc. (Can. Sept. 5, 1978)
June 9, 2014 – Acquired by Brookfield Property Partners L.P. (BPP) on the basis of US$20.34 cash, 1 non-vtg. unit of BPP or one unit of Brookfield Office Properties Exchange LP, a subsidiary of BPP, for each com. sh. held. Class AAA pfce. shs. ser. G, H, J and K could be retained or exchanged for Brookfield Property Split Corp. senior pfd. shs. ser. 1, 2, 3 and 4, respectively, on a 1-for-1 basis. (see FPsurvey - Industrials) (see Brookfield Property Partners L.P.)

Brookfield Power Inc. (Ont. Oct. 17, 1969)
Mar. 31, 2008 – Name changed to Brookfield Renewable Power Inc. (see Brookfield Asset Management Inc.)

Brookfield Properties Corporation (Can. Sept. 5, 1978)
May 9, 2011 – Name changed to Brookfield Office Properties Inc. ■

Brookfield Property Partners L.P. (Bermuda Jan. 3, 2013)
July 27, 2021 – All o/s limited partnership units not already held acquired by Brookfield Asset Management Inc.; basis (i) US$18.17 cash; or (ii) 0.4006 Brookfield Asset cl., A limited vtg. shs; or (iii) 0.7268 Brookfield Property pref. unit with a liquidation preference of US$25.00 per unit for 1 Brookfield Property limited partnership unit,

Brookfield Real Estate Services Fund (Ont. Jan. 3, 2003)
Dec. 31, 2010 – Succeeded by Brookfield Real Estate Services Inc. pursuant to plan of arrangement whereby Brookfield Real Estate Services Inc. was formed to facilitate the conversion of the fund into a corporation. ■

Brookfield Real Estate Services Inc. (Ont. Oct. 28, 2010)
May 27, 2019 – Name changed to Bridgemarq Real Estate Services Inc. (see FPsurvey - Industrials)

Brookfield Reinsurance Ltd. (Bermuda Dec. 10, 2020)
Sept. 4, 2024 – Name changed to Brookfield Wealth Solutions Ltd. (see FPsurvey - Industrials)

Brookfield Renewable Energy Partners L.P. (Bermuda June 27, 2011)
May 4, 2016 – Name changed to Brookfield Renewable Partners L.P. (see FPsurvey - Mines & Energy; FPsurvey - Industrials)

Brookfield Renewable Power Fund (Que. Sept. 14, 1999)
Nov. 30, 2011 – Acquired by Brookfield Renewable Energy Partners L.P. (BREP); basis 1 BREP LP unit for 1 trust unit or 1 exchangeable share of Great Lakes Power Holding Corporation and subsequently wound up.

Brookfield Residential Properties Inc. (Ont. Mar. 31, 2011)
Mar. 17, 2015 – Acquired by Brookfield Asset Management Inc. for US$24.25 per sh. (see Brookfield Asset Management Inc.)
Dec. 2, 2022 – Name changed to Brookfield Residential Properties ULC. (see Brookfield Asset Management Inc.)

Brookfield Select Opportunities Income Fund (Ont. Apr. 24, 2014)
Apr. 19, 2023 – Terminated; distrib. to unitholders on a pro rata basis of an amount equal to the fund's net asset value.

Brookfield Soundvest Equity Fund (Ont. Sept. 28, 2005)
Feb. 21, 2018 – Name changed to Soundvest Equity Fund. ■

Brookfield SoundVest Split Trust (Ont. Feb. 25, 2005)
Feb. 21, 2018 – Name changed to Soundvest Split Trust. ■

Brookings Resources Ltd. (B.C. Dec. 17, 1981)
June 24, 1993 – Name changed to Cognoscente Software International Inc. ■

Brookline Minerals Inc. (B.C. Jan. 31, 1979)
July 31, 1991 – Continued into Canada.
Dec. 15, 1995 – Name changed to Ventel, Inc. ■

Brookline Minerals Inc./Minearux Brookline Inc. (B.C. 1979)
Sept. 19, 1991 – Amalgamated with Golden Group Explorations Inc. to form a new co. with the same name Brookline Minerals Inc.; basis 1 new for 2.4 old shs. (see Brookline Minerals Inc.)

Brooklyn Energy Corporation (Alta. Jan. 23, 1979)
June 3, 2004 – Name changed to Lightning Energy Ltd. following reverse takeover acquisition of Lightning Energy Ltd.; basis either $2.10 cash or 0.42 new Lightning shs. for 1 old Brooklyn sh. ■

Brooklyn Resources Inc. (B.C. Jan. 18, 1988)
Apr. 14, 1992 – Name changed to Stafford Industries Ltd.; basis 1 new for 2.5 old shs. ■

Brooklyn-Stemwinder Gold Mines Ltd. (B.C. 1933)
June 1952 – Dissolved.

Brooklyn Ventures Corp. (B.C. Oct. 15, 2007)
June 4, 2009 – Name changed to World Famous Pizza Company Ltd. following Qualifying Transaction reverse takeover acquisition of CFGI Holdings Inc. (see FPsurvey - Industrials)

Brookmere Ventures Inc. (B.C. 1982)
July 13, 1984 – Name changed to Tegra Enterprises Inc. ■

Brooks Automation (Canada), Inc. (Can. Dec. 12, 1985)
July 23, 2004 – Called for redemption; basis 0.52 new Brooks Automation, Inc. sh. for 1 old Brooks Automation (Canada) exch. sh.

Brooks Distributors Inc. (Ont. 1987)
Aug. 21, 1995 – Formed Ambrex Mining Corporation in Ontario on amalgamation with Ambrex Mining Corporation. ■

Brooks God's Lake Gold Mines Ltd. (Can. Dec. 12, 1933)
1936 – Name changed to Brooks God's Lake Mines Ltd. and continued into Ontario; basis 200 new for 1 old sh. ■

Brooks God's Lake Mines Ltd. (Ont. 1936)
Aug. 15, 1960 – Charter cancelled.

Brooks-PRI Automation (Canada), Inc. (Can. Dec. 12, 1985)
Feb. 27, 2003 – Name changed to Brooks Automation (Canada), Inc.; basis 1 new exch. for 1 old exch. sh. ■

Brooks Resources Limited (B.C. Apr. 10, 1986)
Sept. 1, 1998 – Name changed to International Brooks Petroleum Ltd.; basis 1 new for 10 old shs. ■

Brookwater Ventures Inc. (B.C. Dec. 21, 2009)
Sept. 27, 2013 – Continued into Ontario.
July 15, 2016 – Name changed to Blue Sky Energy Inc. ■

Broome Capital Inc. (B.C. Mar. 7, 2012)
May 29, 2019 – Name changed to Pasha Brands Ltd. pursuant to the reverse takeover acquisition of (old) Pasha Brands Ltd. and concurrent amalgamation of (old) Pasha with wholly owned 1171298 B.C. Ltd. to form Pasha Brands Holdings Ltd.; basis 1 new for 2 old shs. ■

Broshier Porcupine Mines Ltd. (Ont. 1940)
Feb. 1967 – Charter cancelled.

Brosnan Canadian Mines Limited (Que. Apr. 29, 1953)
Dec. 1, 1980 – Name changed to Brosnan Mines Limited. ■

Brosnan Chibougamau Mines Limited (Que. Apr. 29, 1953)
Apr. 2, 1968 – Name changed to Brosnan Canadian Mines Limited; basis 1 new for 4 old shs. ■

Brosnan Mines Limited (Que. Apr. 29, 1953)
Sept. 24, 1985 – Name changed to Brosnor Exploration Inc.; basis 1 new for 5 old shs. ■

Brosnor Exploration Inc. (Que. Apr. 29, 1953)
Dec. 5, 1990 – Name changed to Loubel Exploration Inc.; basis 1 new for 7 old shs. ■

Broughton Copper Limited (Que. 1956)
July 15, 1968 – Dissolved.

Broulan Porcupine Mines Ltd. (Ont. Mar. 18, 1936)
June 1951 – Merged into Broulan Reef Mines Limited. (see Broulan Reef Mines Limited)

Broulan Reef Mines Limited (Ont. 1951)
Apr. 26, 1983 – Formed Broulan Resources Inc. in Ontario on amalgamation with Banner Porcupine Mines Ltd. and Hugh-Pam Porcupine Mines Ltd. ■

Broulan Resources Inc. (Ont. Apr. 26, 1983 amalg.)
Nov. 29, 1989 – Amalgamated with a wholly owned subsid. of Cabre Explorations Ltd.; basis 1 new for 2.3 old shs. (see Cabre Exploration Ltd.)

Brower Exploration Inc. (B.C. Nov. 9, 1966)
May 12, 1994 – Name changed to Stocker & Yale, Inc. following reverse takeover by Stocker & Yale, Inc.; basis 1 new for 5 old shs. ■

Brown Bear Petroleums Limited (B.C. 1970)
July 17, 1973 – Amalgamated with United Falcon Oils Ltd. to continue as Brown Bear Petroleums Limited in mid-1972. Subsequently amalgamated with 2 other cos. to form Aug. Petroleums Ltd.; basis 1 new for 1.65 shs. Brown Bear.

Brown Bousquet Mines Ltd. (Ont. 1928)
1947 – Assets acquired by Interprovincial Mining Corp. for 1,065,000 shs.

Brown Company (Me. 1888)
Apr. 1965 – Merged into new Delaware co., also called Brown Co.

Brown-McDade Mines Ltd. (Ont. 1946)
Mar. 26, 1987 – Name changed to QZZ Inc. following amalgamation with 66123 Ontario Ltd.; basis 1 new for 10 old shs. (see FPsurvey - Industrials)

Brown-Munro Gold Mines Ltd. (Ont. 1929)
June 15, 1964 – Charter cancelled.

Brown Oils Ltd. (unknown)
1956 – Acquired by Scurry-Rainbow Oil (Sask.) Ltd.; basis 6 new for 5 old shs.

Brown-Overton Mines Ltd. (B.C. 1968)
Aug. 21, 1974 – Name changed to Oxbow Resources Ltd.; basis 1 new for 3 old shs. ■

Browning Communications Canada Inc. (Ont. 1983)
Jan. 14, 1991 – Struck from register and dissolved.

Brownlee Gold Mines Ltd. (Que. Oct. 1925)
1927 – Name changed to Brownlee Mines Ltd.; basis 3 new for 5 old shs. ■

Brownlee Mines Ltd. (Que. Oct. 1925)
June 30, 1936 – Continued into Ontario.
1936 – Name changed to Brownlee Mines (1936) Ltd.; basis 1 new for 5 old shs. ■

Brownlee Mines (1936) Ltd. (Ont. June 30, 1936)
Jan. 1939 – Name changed to Joliet-Quebec Mines, Limited. ■

Brownstar Ventures Inc. (B.C. May 25, 2004)
Aug. 15, 2005 – Name changed to Longview Strategies Incorporated following Qualifying Transaction acquisition of 2,400,000 Tournigan Gold Corporation com. shs., 1,120,000 Finavera Ltd. ordinary shs., 1,120,000 Finavera Renewables Ltd. ordinary shs. and all o/s shs. of Vallambrosa Holdings Ltd. ■

Brownstone Energy Inc. (B.C. July 31, 1987)
Dec. 1, 2011 – Continued into Canada.
June 23, 2016 – Name changed to ThreeD Capital Inc.; basis 1 new for 10 old shs. (see FPsurvey - Mines & Energy; FPsurvey - Industrials)

Brownstone Investment Inc. (B.C. July 31, 1987)
Apr. 2, 1997 – Name changed to Brownstone Resources Inc. ■

Brownstone Resources Inc. (B.C. July 31, 1987)
Dec. 23, 2003 – Name changed to Brownstone Ventures Inc. ■

Brownstone Ventures Inc. (B.C. July 31, 1987)
Jan. 18, 2011 – Name changed to Brownstone Energy Inc. ■

Bruce Consolidated Gold Mines Ltd. (Man. 1919)
Dec. 8, 1959 – Charter cancelled.

Bruce Dolomite Ltd. (Ont. 1962)
Mar. 14, 1977 – Dissolved.

Bruce Lake Mines Ltd. (B.C.)
Aug. 1969 – Dissolved and struck off register.

Bruce-Presto Mines Ltd (Ont. 1955)
Feb. 3, 1969 – Placed into liquidation. No equity for shldrs.

Bruck Mills Limited (Can. 1921)
Feb. 19, 1979 – Acquired by Toyobo Co. Ltd. and Marubeni Corporation in 1976 and 1977 and subsequently sold to Consolidated Textile Mills. (see Consolidated Textile Mills Limited)

Bruck Silk Mills Ltd. (Can. 1921)
Feb. 1948 – Name changed to Bruck Mills Limited. ■

Brudertown Oils Ltd. (Alta. 1951)
1961 – Struck off register.

Bruell Consolidated Mines Ltd. (Ont. 1945)
Nov. 1957 – Charter cancelled.

Bruell Gold Mines (1936) Ltd. (Ont. 1936)
1957 – Charter cancelled.

Bruin Point Helium Corp. (B.C. Aug. 15, 2013)
May 11, 2018 – Name changed to American Helium Inc. ■

Bruin Yellowknife Gold Mines Ltd. (Ont. 1945)
1966 – Charter cancelled.

Bruncor Inc. (N.B. July 1, 1985)
June 1, 1999 – Amalgamated with Maritime Telegraph and Telephone Company Limited (MT&T), Island Telecom Inc. and NewTel Enterprises Limited to form Aliant Inc.; basis 1.667 new for 1 MT&T sh., 0.6015 new for 1 MT&T pref. sh., 1 new for 1 Island Telecom sh., 1.567 new for 1 NewTel sh. and 1.011 new for 1 Bruncor sh. (see Aliant Inc.)

Bruneau Minerals Inc. (Que. Dec. 14, 1959)
Feb. 28, 2003 – Name changed to Arianne Resources Inc. following reverse takeover acquisition of Arianne Resources Inc.; basis 1 new for 6 old shs. ■

Bruneau Mines Ltd. (Que. Dec. 14, 1959)
Mar. 26, 1970 – Name changed to Bruneau Mining Corporation (1970); basis 1 new for 3 old shs. ■

Bruneau Mining Corporation (Que. Dec. 14, 1959)
Jan. 8, 1993 – Name changed to Bruneau Minerals Inc.; basis 1 new for 6 old shs. ■

Bruneau Mining Corporation (1970) (Que. Dec. 14, 1959)
Feb. 26, 1975 – Name changed to Bruneau Mining Corporation. ■

Brunette Porcupine Gold Mines Ltd. (Ont. 1945)
1963 – Merged with Queensland Explorations Ltd. to form Queensland Acceptance Corporation Ltd.; basis 1 new for 10 old shs.

Brunex Gold Resources Ltd. (Ont. Jan. 6, 1987)
Feb. 10, 1995 – Name changed to RES International Inc. ■

Brunhurst Mines Ltd. (Ont. 1951)
1959 – Merged into Hydra Explorations Ltd.; basis 1 new for 25 old shs.

Bruno Mining Corp. (Que.)
Oct. 1974 – Charter cancelled.

Bruns-Mines Ltd. (N.B. 1953)
Nov. 11, 1981 – Charter cancelled.

Brunsman Mines Ltd. (Ont. 1943)
1959 – Merged into Hydra Explorations Ltd.; basis 1 new for 25 old shs.

Brunston Mining Co. Ltd. (Ont. July 6, 1945)
Sept. 19, 1956 – Name changed to Sunburst Exploration Limited; basis 1 new for 5 old shs. ■

Brunswick Mining and Smelting Corporation Limited (N.B. Oct. 31, 1952)
Oct. 6, 1995 – Acquired by Noranda Inc.; basis 0.5 Noranda shs. for 1 Brunswick Mining sh. (see Noranda Inc.)

Brunswick Quebec Development Ltd. (Que. 1952)
1957 – Name changed to Abadex Mines Ltd. ■

Brunswick Resources Inc. (Alta. June 15, 2006)
Aug. 10, 2021 – Name changed to Poko Innovations Inc. and continued into Canada pursuant to the reverse takeover acquisition of Poko Group Ltd.; basis 1 new for 5 old shs. ■

Bryant Resources Inc. (B.C. Dec. 17, 2007)
Oct. 4, 2013 – Name changed to Outrider Energy Corp. ■

Brycon Explorations Ltd. (B.C. 1965)
1971 – Name changed to Brycon Industries Ltd. ■

Brycon Industries Ltd. (B.C. 1965)
Sept. 9, 1972 – Struck off register.

Bryell Minerals Ltd. (B.C. 1968)
June 27, 1977 – Dissolved.

Bryhern Exploration, Development & Mining Ltd. (Ont. 1943)
1954 – Merged into Pardee Amalgamated Mines Ltd.; basis 2 new for 15 old shs.

Brymore Oil & Gas Ltd. (B.C. May 16, 1979)
Feb. 9, 1995 – Continued into Alberta.
May 30, 1996 – Name changed to BXL Energy Ltd.; basis 1 new for 1 old sh. ■

Bryndon Ventures Inc. (Alta. Nov. 6, 1985)
Mar. 22, 1995 – Name changed to Conqueror Holdings Ltd. and continued into British Columbia; basis 1 new for 5 old shs. ■

Bucan Mines Ltd. (Ont. 1948)
Nov. 6, 1961 – Charter cancelled.

Buccaneer Gold Corp. (Ont. Oct. 4, 2004)
Dec. 6, 2021 – Name changed to Strategic Minerals Europe Corp. pursuant to the reverse takeover acquisition of Strategic Minerals Europe Inc.; basis 1 new for 5 old shs. (see FPsurvey - Mines & Energy)

Buccaneer Mines Ltd. (B.C. 1939)
June 3, 1974 – Dissolved and struck off register.

Buccaneer Resources Ltd. (B.C. 1965)
Sept. 20, 1985 – Struck off register.

Bucephalus Capital Corp. (Ont. Apr. 18, 1997)
June 23, 2021 – Name changed to Prophecy DeFi Inc. pursuant to change in investment focus on Decentralized Finance. (see FPsurvey - Industrials)

Buchanan Mines Ltd. (Alta. 1964)
Dec. 2, 1971 – Amalgamated with Complex Ore Research and Development Ltd.; basis 1 new for 10 Buchanan shs.

Buchans Minerals Corporation (Alta. Apr. 1, 2002 amalg.)
July 18, 2013 – Acquired by Minco PLC; basis 0.826 Minco shs. for 1 Buchans sh. (see Minco plc)

Buchans Mining Co. Ltd. (N.L.)
Dec. 23, 1958 – Merged into American Smelting & Refining Co. (a US co.).

Buchans River Ltd. (N.L. May 13, 1996)
Aug. 6, 2008 – Acquired by Royal Roads Corp.; basis 1.55 Royal Roads com. shs. for 1 Buchans River sh.

Buck Lake Ventures Ltd. (B.C. Feb. 2, 1981)
May 11, 2006 – Name changed to Ultra Uranium Corp.; basis 1 new for 5 old shs. ■

Buckeye Energy Corporation (Yuk. May 24, 2000)
Feb. 24, 2004 – Name changed to Regal Energy Corp. and continued into Alberta following Qualifying Transaction acquisition of 665433 Alberta Ltd.; basis 1 new for 2 old shs. ■

Buckeye Explorations Ltd. (B.C. 1967)
Apr. 1977 – Charter cancelled.

Buckhaven Capital Corp. (B.C. Oct. 23, 2018)
Mar. 18, 2021 – Name changed to Andean Precious Metals Corp. pursuant to the Qualifying Transaction reverse takeover acquisition of 1254688 B.C. Ltd. and concurrent amalgamation of 1254688 B.C. with wholly owned 1271860 B.C. Ltd.; basis 1 new for 1.5 old shs. ■

Buckhill Minerals Ltd. (Ont. 1945)
Mar. 28, 1980 – Dissolved.

Buckhorn Mines Ltd. (Ont. 1942)
1956 – Charter cancelled.

Buckhorn Mines Ltd. (B.C. 1967)
May 5, 1982 – Dissolved.

Bucking Horse Energy Inc. (B.C. Apr. 28, 2006)
Oct. 3, 2022 – Struck from registry and dissolved.

Buckingham Asbestos Co. Ltd. (Que. 1952)
Jan. 1974 – Charter cancelled.

Buckingham International Holdings Ltd. (Alta. Apr. 9, 1974 amalg.)
Aug. 31, 1992 – Delisted from the CDN. Subsequently struck from the register and dissolved.

Buckles Algoma Uranium Mines Ltd. (Ont. 1954)
1956 – Assets acquired by Spanish American Mines Ltd.; basis 1 new for 5 old shs.

Buckley Oils Ltd. (Alta.)
1958 – Struck off register.

Budbois Gold Mines Ltd. (Ont. 1946)
Mar. 1976 – Charter cancelled.

Budco Mines Ltd. (Ont. 1945)
1956 – Charter cancelled.

The Budd Automotive Company of Canada Ltd. (Ont. Oct. 8, 1965)
Apr. 2, 1979 – Name changed to Budd Canada Inc. ■

Budd Canada Inc. (Ont. Oct. 8, 1965)
May 23, 2003 – Name changed to ThyssenKrupp Budd Canada Inc. ■

Buddha Resources Inc. (B.C. Apr. 7, 1986)
Nov. 3, 2008 – Struck from register and dissolved.

Buena Exploration Ltd. (B.C. Aug. 5, 1983)
June 19, 1986 – Name changed to Hagensborg Resources Ltd. ■

Buena Vista Mining Co., Ltd. (B.C. 1927)
Jan. 1953 – Liquidated.

Buf-Gaspe Mines Ltd. (Ont. 1954)
Dec. 1962 – Charter cancelled.

Buff-Ario Gold Mines, Ltd. (Ont. 1936)
Mar. 27, 1957 – Charter cancelled.

Buffadison Gold Mines Ltd. (Ont. 1945)
1962 – Name changed to United Buffadison Mines Ltd.; basis 1 new for 5 old shs. ■

Buffalo Ankerite Holdings Ltd. (Ont. Oct. 5, 1932)
July 21, 1964 – Name changed to Romfield Building Corporation Limited. ■

Buffalo Canadian Gold Mines Ltd. (Can. Aug. 6, 1931)
Aug. 1960 – Dissolved.

Buffalo Capital Inc. (Can. Dec. 14, 2016)
Oct. 24, 2017 – Formed Waverley Pharma Inc. in Canada pursuant to Qualifying Transaction amalgamation with (old) Waverley Pharma Inc. (deemed acquiror); basis 1 new com. sh. for 1 Buffalo com. sh. and 400,000 new com. shs. for 1 (old) Waverley com. sh. (see FPsurvey - Industrials)

Buffalo Coal Corp. (Ont. Oct. 17, 2006)
Apr. 24, 2023 – Privatized via a 1-for-60,000,000 consolidation; basis Cdn$0.01 cash per pre-consolidated sh.

Buffalo Diamonds Ltd. (Alta. Dec. 1, 1998 amalg.)
Feb. 17, 2003 – Name changed to Buffalo Gold Ltd.; basis 1 new for 10 old shs. ■

Buffalo Gas & Oil Corporation (Que. 1970)
1972 – Shldrs. approved winding up of co. and distribution of its assets, chiefly shs. in its subsid., Guernsey Petroleum Corp.

Buffalo Gold Ltd. (Alta. Dec. 1, 1998 amalg.)
June 2, 2012 – Dissolved and struck from register.

Buffalo Lake Mines Ltd. (B.C. 1966)
Apr. 1975 – Charter cancelled.

Buffalo Mines Ltd. (B.C. Dec. 16, 1993)
Mar. 19, 1999 – Name changed to Gulf Shores Resources Ltd. ■

Buffalo Oil Company Limited (Sask. Oct. 18, 1993 amalg.)
June 2004 – Continued into Alberta.
Dec. 31, 2004 – Formed The Buffalo Oil Corporation in Alberta following reverse takeover acquisition of Fogo Resources Inc.; basis 1 new for 5 old shs. ■

The Buffalo Oil Corporation (Alta. Dec. 31, 2004 amalg.)
Aug. 10, 2007 – Amalgamated with Choice Resources Corp. following reverse takeover acquisition by Choice to continue as Buffalo Resources Corp.; basis 1 Buffalo Resources sh. for 1 Buffalo Oil sh. and 0.474 Buffalo Resources sh. for 1 Choice sh. (see Buffalo Resources Corp.)

Buffalo Red Lake Mines Ltd. (Ont. 1928)
1969 – Name changed to Consolidated Buffalo Red Lake Mines Ltd.; basis 1 new for 4 old shs. ■

Buffalo Resources Corp. (Alta. Aug. 3, 2007 amalg.)
Oct. 19, 2009 – Acquired by Twin Butte Energy Ltd. pursuant to plan of arrangement; basis 0.7 Twin Butte shs for 1 Buffalo sh. (see Twin Butte Energy Ltd.)

Buffalo Resources Ltd. (B.C. Feb. 14, 1984)
Sept. 18, 1992 – Name changed to Kruger Explorations Ltd.; basis 1 new for 4 old shs. ■

Buffalo River Exploration Ltd. (Can. 1966)
Nov. 21, 1972 – Charter cancelled.

Buffalo Shepmac Gold Mines Ltd. (Can. 1937)
Dec. 16, 1980 – Dissolved.

Buffana Uranium Mines Ltd. (Ont. 1955)
1961 – Name changed to Le Mans Explorations Limited. ■

Buffonta Mines Ltd. (Ont. 1938)
May 1976 – Charter cancelled.

Buhler Industries Inc. (Can. Feb. 1, 1994 amalg.)
Apr. 1, 2025 – All o/s shs. not already held acquired by ASKO Sinai ve Teknoloji Uretim Sanayi Ticaret Anomin Sirketi; basis $7.30 cash per sh.

Build America Investment Grade Bond Fund (Ont. Dec. 28, 2009)
Mar. 2, 2015 – Converted into Aston Hill Corporate Bond Fund, an open-ended fund, on a unit-for-unit basis; unitholders received special cash distributions of $0.2028 per cl. A unit and $0.2247 per cl. F unit.

Builders Energy Services Trust (Alta. Nov. 29, 2004)
Apr. 10, 2008 – Acquired by Essential Energy Services Trust; basis 1.25 Essential trust units for 1 Builders trust unit.

Buildex Venture Capital Corporation (Can. July 12, 2010)
Nov. 8, 2011 – Name changed to Îledor Exploration Corporation pursuant to Qualifying Transaction acquistion of L'Îledor Exploration Inc. ■

Building Products Limited (Can. 1925)
July 1964 – Name changed to Probuild Proceeds Limited following sale of its assets (including the Building Products name) to Imperial Oil Limited for $1,900,000 cash. ■

Bulkley Silver Resources, Inc. (B.C. 1980)
Oct. 27, 1986 – Amalgamated with Cater Energy, Inc. to form Houston Metals Corporation; basis 1 new for 1.333 old shs.

Bull Explorations Limited (B.C. Feb. 11, 1981)
Oct. 28, 1982 – Name changed to Hardy International Developments Inc. ■

Bull Red Lake Gold Mines Ltd. (Ont. 1945)
Oct. 7, 1957 – Charter cancelled.

Bulldog Energy Inc. (Alta. July 3, 2001)
Dec. 2, 2005 – Plan of Arrangement acquisition by Crescent Point Energy Trust; initially 3.257 new cl. A shs. exchanged for 1 cl. B sh; then basis 0.13 new Crescent unit and 0.5 new Bulldog Resources Inc. for 1 old Bulldog Energy cl. A. sh. (see Bulldog Resources Inc.; Crescent Point Energy Trust)

Bulldog Explorations Ltd. (Alta. Dec. 21, 2007)
Feb. 13, 2013 – Name changed to Green Arrow Resources Inc. and continued into British Columbia. (see FPsurvey - Mines & Energy)

Bulldog Mines Ltd. (Ont. 1970)
Mar. 1976 – Charter cancelled.

Bulldog Resources Inc. (Alta. Oct. 24, 2005)
Feb. 12, 2008 – Acquired by TriStar Oil & Gas Ltd.; basis 0.59 TriStar com. shs. for 1 Bulldog com. sh.
Feb. 12, 2008 – Name changed to TriStar BR Inc.

Bulldog Yellowknife Gold Mines Ltd. (Ont. 1947)
1956 – Name changed to Taurcanis Mines Ltd.; basis 1 new for 4 old shs. ■

Bullet Energy Ltd. (B.C. Nov. 6, 1981)
Mar. 8, 1985 – Name changed to The Bullet Group, Inc. ■

Bullet Exploration Inc. (Ont. Apr. 12, 2013)
Apr. 29, 2021 – Continued into British Columbia. (see Gold79 Mines Ltd.)
Dec. 2, 2024 – Acquired by Gold79 Mines Ltd.; basis 1 Gold79 sh. for 3 Bullet shs. (see Gold79 Mines Ltd.)

The Bullet Group, Inc. (B.C. Nov. 6, 1981)
Aug. 6, 1992 – Name changed to Consolidated Bullet Group, Inc.; basis 1 new for 4 old shs. ■

Bullfrog Gold Corp. (Del. July 23, 2007)
Jan. 25, 2021 – Name changed to Augusta Gold Corp.; basis 1 new for 6 old shs. (see FPsurvey - Mines & Energy)

Bullion Mountain Mining Ltd. (B.C. 1965)
July 23, 1976 – Name changed to Northern Bullion (Keno) Ltd.; basis 1 new for 3 old shs. ■

Bullion Range Exploration Corp. (B.C. Sept. 18, 1984)
Aug. 9, 1991 – Name changed to Maximusic North American Corporation following acquisition of Maximusic North American Corporation. ■

Bullion Reef Resources Ltd. (B.C. Mar. 30, 1983)
Mar. 27, 1995 – Name changed to Consolidated Bullion Reef Resources Ltd.; basis 1 new for 6 old shs. ■

Bullman Minerals Inc. (B.C. Nov. 17, 2010)
May 14, 2019 – Amalgamated with 1173240 B.C. Ltd., a wholly owned subsid. of D&S International Investments Limited, to form a new company under the Bullman Minerals Inc. name (New Bullman); basis 1 New Bullman cl. A pref. shs. for 1 Old Bullman com. sh,., redeemed for 12¢ cash per sh.

Bullman Ventures Inc. (B.C. Nov. 17, 2010)
July 17, 2013 – Name changed to Bullman Minerals Inc. pursuant to Qualifying Transaction acquisition of Birimian Gold AS. ■

Bulloch's Limited (Man. 1946)
1969 – All o/s cl. B shs. were acquired by Inter-City Gas Limited; basis 1 sh. of Inter-City Gas for 3 shs. of Bullochs'.
July 9, 1971 – Name changed to Inter-City Manufacturing Limited. ■

Bulls Offering Corporation (Can. Mar. 13, 1995)
Dec. 29, 1998 – Name changed to Merrill Lynch Mortgage Loans Inc. ■

Bulolo Gold Dredging Ltd. (B.C. 1930)
1966 – Merged into Placer Development Ltd.; basis 2 new for 5 old shs.

Bunker Hill Extension Mines Ltd. (Can. Jan. 25, 1928; via Dominion charter)
Dec. 3, 1981 – Name changed to Bunker Hill Resources Inc.; basis 1 new for 5 old shs. ■

Bunker Hill Mining Company Inc. (B.C. 1987)
Nov. 12, 1993 – Dissolved and struck off register.

Bunker Hill Resources Inc. (Can. Jan. 25, 1928; via Dominion charter)
May 19, 1987 – Name changed to Zacherra Holdings Inc.; basis 1 new for 4 old shs. ■

Buntin Reid Paper Co. Limited (Ont. 1966)
1971 – Acquired by Domtar Limited for $15 per sh. (see Domtar Limited)

Bunyoro Resources Inc. (B.C. 1983)
Mar. 24, 1986 – Name changed to Friedrich Technologies Inc. ■

Bur-Ley Porcupine Gold Mines Ltd. (Ont. 1944)
Sept. 26, 1960 – Charter cancelled.

Burbank Minerals Ltd. (Ont. 1959)
Jan. 6, 1971 – Dissolved.

Burchell Lake Mines Ltd. (Ont. 1944)
Aug. 3, 1964 – Dissolved.

Burchill Road Mines Ltd. (N.B. 1957)
Reported no longer in operation.

Burco Consolidated Lead and Silver Mines Ltd. (Ont. 1943)
June 1949 – Name changed to Burco Consolidated Mines Ltd. ■

Burco Consolidated Mines Ltd. (Ont. 1943)
Mar. 4, 1963 – Dissolved.

Burco Mines Ltd. (Ont. 1943)
Mar. 1949 – Name changed to Burco Consolidated Lead and Silver Mines Ltd. ■

Burcon Capital Corp. (Yuk. Nov. 3, 1998)
Oct. 18, 1999 – Name changed to Burcon NutraScience Corporation. ■

Burcon Developments Ltd. (B.C. Mar. 22, 1983)
June 26, 1995 – Name changed to Burcon International Developments Ltd.; basis 1 new for 19.2 old shs. ■

Burcon International Developments Ltd. (B.C. Mar. 22, 1983)
June 27, 1995 – Continued into Yukon.
Aug. 1, 1997 – Name changed to BurCon Properties Limited. ■

Burcon NutraScience Corporation (Yuk. Nov. 3, 1998)
Sept. 25, 2020 – Continued into British Columbia. (see FPsurvey - Industrials)

BurCon Properties Limited (Yuk. June 27, 1995)
June 1, 1998 – Amalgamated with Oxford Properties Group Inc. and Concord Pacific Group Inc. to form new co. with same name Oxford Properties Group Inc.; basis 0.73977 Oxford shs. and 0.7 Concord shs. for 1 BurCon sh. (see Oxford Properties Group Inc.)

Burdett Resources Ltd. (B.C. Apr. 18, 1986)
Nov. 19, 1991 – Name changed to AFF Automated Fast Foods Ltd.; basis 1 new for 3 old shs. ■

Burdos Mines Ltd. (B.C. 1966)
1978 – Name changed to Pentagon Resources Ltd.; basis 1 new for 5 old shs. ■

Burge Lake Goldfields Ltd. (Que. 1949)
May 1974 – Charter cancelled.

Burgess Point Resources Inc. (Ont. June 23, 1977)
Jan. 14, 1994 – Name changed to Metallica Resources Inc.; basis 1 new for 7 old shs. ■

Burgess Yellowknife Kirkland Mines Ltd. (Ont. 1944)
Mar. 1955 – Charter cancelled.

Burin Equities Corporation (Alta. Apr. 4, 1996)
Apr. 25, 1997 – Name changed to Starlink Communications Corporation. ■

Burin Gold Corp. (Ont. Feb. 27, 2018)
May 19, 2021 – Continued into British Columbia.
Aug. 23, 2023 – Name changed to Infinico Metals Corp. (see FPsurvey - Mines & Energy)

Burkham Mines Ltd. (B.C. 1968)
1976 – Dissolved.

Burkina Capital Corp. (Can. May 1, 1996)
Apr. 27, 1999 – Name changed to Canada's Choice Spring Water, Inc. following Qualifying Transaction acquisition of Natural Source, Canada Spring Water, Inc. ■

Burland Realty and Equipment Limited (unknown)
Nov. 1968 – Amalgamated into Intermetco Limited. (see Intermetco Limited)

Burlington Gold Mines Ltd. (B.C. Aug. 30, 1965)
Sept. 26, 1985 – Name changed to B.G.M. Diversified Energy Inc.; basis 1 new for 5 old shs. ■

Burlington Mall and Place Bourrassa (Ont. Mar. 16, 2001)
June 15, 2006 – Name changed to Burlington Mall.

Burlington Mines & Enterprises Ltd. (B.C. Aug. 30, 1965)
June 12, 1974 – Name changed to Burlington Gold Mines Ltd.; basis 1 new for 2 old shs. ■

Burlington Mines Ltd. (B.C. Aug. 30, 1965)
Aug. 17, 1970 – Name changed to Burlington Mines & Enterprises Ltd. ■

Burlington Packaging Limited (Ont. Feb. 28, 1928)
Aug. 31, 1992 – Delisted from the CDN. Subsequently charter cancelled and dissolved.

Burlington Resources Canada Energy Ltd. (Alta. Nov. 1, 1979)
Sept. 17, 2001 – Amalgamated with Burlington Resources Canada Inc. to form Burlington Resources Canada Ltd.

Burlington Resources Canada Inc. (Alta. June 16, 1999)
Sept. 14, 2001 – All o/s exch. shs. called for early redemption by Burlington Resources Inc.; basis 1 new Burlington Resources com. sh. for 1 old Burlington Canada exch. sh. Common shs. of Burlington Resources Inc. listed on NYSE.

Burlington Steel Co. Ltd. (Ont. 1930)
1962 – Amalgamated with Slater Industries Limited to form Slater Steel Industries Limited. Shldrs. of Burlington Steel received 0.5 pref. sh. and 1 com. sh. of the new co. for 1 com. sh. (see Slater Steel Industries Ltd.)

Burma Dip Gold Mines Ltd. (Ont. Aug. 14, 1944)
1953 – Name changed to Eldrich Mines Ltd. ■

Burma Shore Mines Ltd. (Ont. 1955)
May 6, 1965 – Charter cancelled.

Burma Shore Uranium Mines Ltd. (Ont. 1955)
Apr. 1956 – Name changed to Burma Shore Mines Ltd. ■

Burmac Energy Corporation (B.C. Mar. 30, 1981)
Feb. 7, 1991 – Name changed to Bus Holdings Corp.; basis 1 new for 7 old shs. ■

Burmis Energy Inc. (Alta. Nov. 25, 2002)
June 10, 2008 – Acquired by Baytex Energy Trust; basis 0.1525 Baytex trust units for 1 Burmis com. sh.

Burnaby Paperboard Ltd. (B.C. 1927)
Dec. 1964 – Converted to a private co. and cl. A shs. delisted. The com. shs. and all but 1,105 cl. A shs. held by MacMillan Bloedel Limited.

Burnaby Venetian Blinds Limited (Man. 1944)
Sept. 23, 1970 – Name changed to Hunter Douglas Canada Limited. ■

Burndale Resources Ltd. (B.C. Nov. 8, 1984 amalg.)
Sept. 14, 1989 – Name changed to Tai Energy Resources Corporation. ■

Burner Exploration Ltd. (Alta. June 3, 1993)
June 3, 1998 – All o/s acquired by Berkley Petroleum Corp.; basis 0.071428 Berkley com. shs. for 1 Burner com. sh. and 1 Berkley wt. for 14 Burner wts. (see Berkley Petroleum Corp.)

Burnett Limited (Can. 1931)
1955 – An order of bankruptcy was issued against the company. Co. subsequently wound up and liquidators received their discharge.

Burns & Co. Ltd. (Can. 1928)
Apr. 1965 – Name changed to Burns Foods Limited. ■

Burns Foods Limited (Can. 1928)
Dec. 4, 1978 – Amalgamated with WCB Holdings Ltd., following that co.'s offer to acquire Burns shs. for $18 each. Shldrs. who did not accept offer were issued 1 pref. sh. of amalg. co. for each Burns sh. held. The pref. shs. were subsequently redeemed at $18 per sh. Company now private.

Burnt Island Gold Ltd. (B.C. 1980)
June 6, 1987 – Name changed to New Era Developments Ltd. ■

Burnt River Uranium (Mines Ltd.) (Ont. 1953)
1957 – Distribution of 4 shs. Cardiff Uranium Mines Ltd. made for each sh. held. Charter surrendered.

Burnt Sand Solutions Inc. (Alta. Dec. 22, 1994)
Mar. 12, 1998 – Continued into Canada.
Oct. 18, 1999 – Name changed to Burntsand Inc. ■

Burntsand Inc. (Can. Mar. 12, 1998)
June 1, 2010 – Acquired by Open Text Corporation by way of amalgamation with 7534213 Canada Inc., a wholly owned subsid. of Open Text, for 15¢ per sh.

Burrard Building Operations Ltd. (Can. - unspecified)
1969 – Acquired by Block Bros. Industries Ltd. for $1,930,000 and 16,000 shs. (prior to 3-for-1 stock split). (see Block Bros. Industries Ltd.)

Burrard Dry Dock Co. Ltd. (Can. 1921)
1972 – Acquired by Cornat Industries Limited following purch. offer of $10 per sh. (see Cornat Industries Limited)

Burrard Mortgage Investments Ltd. (B.C. Apr. 11, 1956)
1978 – Name changed to Canlan Investment Corporation. ■

Burrard Oils Ltd. (B.C.)
1957 – Struck off register.

Burrard Ventures Inc. (B.C. 1981)
Sept. 24, 1993 – Dissolved and struck off register.

Burrex Mines Ltd. (Ont. 1945)
Dec. 1973 – Name changed to Burrgold Mines Ltd.; basis 1 new for 3 old shs. ■

Burrgold Mines Ltd. (Ont. 1945)
Mar. 1977 – Charter cancelled.

Burro Creek Minerals Ltd. (B.C. 1987)
Oct. 1, 1993 – Dissolved and struck off register.

Burrows Lead Mines Limited (Ont. 1950)
Mar. 1959 – Charter cancelled.

Burscott Gold Mines Ltd. (Ont. 1944)
Jan. 1971 – Charter cancelled.

Burtho Gold Mines Ltd. (Man. 1947)
Jan. 30, 1959 – Charter cancelled.

Burton Mines Ltd. (Ont. 1943)
1956 – Charter cancelled.

Burvan Gold Mines Ltd. (Ont. Dec. 15, 1932)
Name changed to Lake Caswell Mines Ltd.
June 26, 1934 – Continued into Ontario. ■

Bus Holdings Corp. (B.C. Mar. 30, 1981)
Nov. 17, 1997 – Name changed to Savannah Ventures Ltd. ■

Bush Consolidated Goldmines Ltd. (Can. 1934)
1944 – Charter cancelled.

Bushman Resources Inc. (B.C. Mar. 11, 1994)
Aug. 8, 2005 – Struck from the registry and dissolved.

Bushmills Energy Corporation (Alta. Mar. 16, 2001)
Feb. 5, 2003 – Plan of Arrangement with Brooklyn Energy Corporation; basis either $0.96 or 1.2 new Brooklyn com. shs. or a combination thereof for 1 old Bushmills sh. (see Brooklyn Energy Corporation)

Bushnell Communications Ltd. (Ont. 1960)
Aug. 31, 1980 – Amalgamated with Standard Broadcasting Corporation Limited in August 1980, following purch. offer; basis $16 or 1.333 com. sh. Standard for each sh. held. all Bushnell shs. not tendered were cancelled and cash placed in trust for the shldr.

Bushnell T.V. Co. Limited (Ont. 1960)
July 1969 – Name changed to Bushnell Communications Ltd. ■

The Business, Engineering, Science & Technology Discoveries Fund Inc. (Ont. Nov. 21, 1996)
July 11, 2014 – Succeeded by Tier One Capital Limited Partnership following acquisition of the assets of the fund by Tier One. (see FPsurvey - Industrials)

Business Systems International Inc. (Alta. Jan. 30, 1992)
Jan. 30, 1995 – Coopers & Lybrand Limited, Vancouver, was appointed receiver following an order by the Supreme Court of British Columbia.
Apr. 19, 1995 – All the assets had been sold. The secured lender suffered a significant shortfall, and there was no distribution to unsecured creditors or shldrs.
May 24, 1995 – Receiver discharged.

Business Trust Equal Weight Income Fund (Ont. Sept. 25, 2003)
July 7, 2008 – Together with BG Top 100 Equal Weighted Income Fund, Brompton Tracker Fund, BG Income + Growth Split Trust, Brompton Stable Income Fund and Brompton Equal Weight Income Fund, each merged with Brompton VIP Income Fund to continue as Brompton VIP Income Fund; basis Business Trust Equal Weight (0.6919-for-1), BG Top 100 Equal Weighted (0.7364-for-1), Brompton Tracker Fund (0.6664-for-1), BG Income + Growth Split Trust (1.013-for-1), Brompton Stable Income Fund (0.9652-for-1) and Brompton Equal Weight (0.8583-for-1).

Bute Resources Inc. (B.C. 1977)
May 24, 1979 – Amalgamated with International Pyramid Mines Inc., and Gilford Resources Ltd. to form American Pyramid Resources Inc.; basis 1 new for 2 old shs.

Butec International Chemical Corp. (B.C. Nov. 29, 1965)
May 5, 1988 – Name changed to International Butec Industries Corp.; basis 1 new for 3 old shs. ■

Butler Developments Corp. (B.C. Feb. 27, 1987)
Feb. 12, 2009 – Name changed to Butler Resource Corp.; basis 1 new for 8 old shs. ■

Butler Mountain Minerals Corp. (B.C. Dec. 30, 1980)
May 17, 1991 – Dissolved and struck off register.

Butler Mountain Moly Corp. (B.C. Dec. 30, 1980)
Jan. 11, 1983 – Name changed to Butler Mountain Minerals Corp. ■

Butler Resource Corp. (B.C. Feb. 27, 1987)
Mar. 4, 2010 – Name changed to Quantum Rare Earth Developments Corp. ■

Butte Canyon Resources Incorporated (Ont. Aug. 16, 1985)
Feb. 6, 1989 – Name changed to Innovative Marketing & Technologies Corp.; basis 1 new for 6 old shs. ■

Butte Energy Inc. (Alta. Feb. 5, 1992)
June 19, 2018 – Continued into British Columbia.
Oct. 24, 2024 – Name changed to Argenta Silver Corp. (see FPsurvey - Industrials)

Butte Resources Limited (Can. Aug. 19, 1987)
Sept. 22, 1989 – Name changed to Kingtron International Inc.; basis 1 new for 4 old shs. ■

Butter Rock Resources Inc. (B.C. June 19, 1987)
Sept. 25, 1992 – Name changed to INN Investment News Network Ltd. ■

Butterfly Hosiery Co. Ltd. (Que. 1919)
1962 – Acquired by Belding-Corticelli Ltd. for $2.25 per sh.

The Buttle Lake Mining Co. Ltd. (B.C. 1962)
1970 – Merged into Stampede International Resources Ltd.

Buval Executive Mining Industries Ltd. (B.C. 1966)
Oct. 22, 1979 – Dissolved and struck off register.

Buxton Real Estate Ltd. (unknown)
1970 – Acquired by Medallion Mortgage Corp. Ltd. for cash and Medallion shs. valued at $1.65 per Buxton sh. (see Medallion Mortgage Corp. Ltd.)

BuzBuz Capital Corp. (Ont. Feb. 26, 2018)
Oct. 15, 2021 – Name changed to NuGen Medical Devices Inc. pursuant to the Qualifying Transaction reverse takeover acquisition of Inolife R&D Inc. (renamed EPG Global Ltd.); basis 1 new for 2 old shs. (see FPsurvey - Industrials)

Buzz Telecommunications Services Inc. (Can. July 9, 2004)
Jan. 21, 2014 – Name changed to Knowlton Capital Inc. ■

Byron Americor Inc. (Ont. Oct. 16, 1995)
Sept. 21, 2007 – Name changed to Ungava Mines Inc. (see FPsurvey - Mines & Energy)

Byron Global Corp. (Ont. Oct. 16, 1995)
July 30, 2007 – Name changed to Byron Americor Inc. ■

Byron Resources Inc. (B.C. Oct. 30, 1986)
Sept. 3, 1992 – Name changed to Select Ventures Inc.; basis 1 new for 3 old shs. ■

Byron Resources Inc. (Ont. Oct. 16, 1995)
July 9, 2004 – Name changed to Byron Global Corp.; basis 1 new for 10 old shs. ■

Bytec-Comterm Inc. (Can. July 2, 1970)
June 27, 1984 – Name changed to Comterm Inc. ■

C

C & C Industries Corporation Ltd. (Bermuda Sept. 3, 1996)
Jan. 11, 2008 – Name changed to Xenex Minerals Ltd.

C & C Yachts Limited (Ont. 1969)
Dec. 22, 1981 – Amalgamated with Deplax Holdings Ltd. shldrs. received on sh.-for-sh. basis pref. shs. of Deplax which were redeemed on Jan. 4, 1982, at $6.00 per sh.

C & E Furniture Industries Inc. (B.C. Apr. 6, 1976)
May 4, 1994 – Delisted from the Vancouver Stock Exchange. Subsequently dissolved for failure to file and struck from register.

C and S Petroleums Ltd. (Alta.)
1960 – Struck off register.

C Level II International Holding Inc. (Can. Jan. 8, 2007)
June 30, 2008 – Name changed to Canadian Oil Recovery & Remediation Enterprises Ltd. following Qualifying Transaction reverse takeover acquisition of Canadian Oil Recovery & Remediation Enterprises Inc.; basis 1 new for 3 old shs. ■

C Level III Inc. (Can. June 10, 2011)
Dec. 6, 2013 – Name changed to Canoe Mining Ventures Corp. pursuant to Qualifying Transaction reverse takeover acquisition of 2299895 Ontario Inc. (see FPsurvey - Mines & Energy)

C Level Bio International Holding Inc. (Can. Apr. 6, 2006)
Mar. 5, 2007 – Name changed to Nevada Exploration Inc. following Qualifying Transaction reverse takeover acquisition of 2107189 Ontario Inc.; basis 1 new for 2 old shs. ■

C-MAC Industries Inc. (Can. Oct. 7, 1985)
Dec. 4, 2001 – Plan of Arrangement with US-based Solectron Corporation; basis 1.755 new Solectron com. shs. or 1.755 new Solectron Global Services Canada Inc. exchangeable shs. or a combination thereof for 1 old C-MAC com. sh.

C Squared Developments Inc. (B.C. Dec. 12, 1985)
May 14, 2003 – Name changed to Dynasty Gold Corp. (see FPsurvey - Mines & Energy)

C-Tech Energy Services Inc. (Alta. Aug. 28, 1997)
June 27, 2005 – Acquired indirectly by Dover Corporation for $0.44 per sh.

C1 Energy Ltd. (Alta. Sept. 25, 2003)
Sept. 26, 2007 – Amalgamated with Penn West Energy Trust; basis $0.20 per com. sh. (see Penn West Energy Trust)

C2C Gold Corp. (B.C. July 19, 1999)
Jan. 10, 2024 – Name changed to C2C Metals Corp. ■

C2C Metals Corp. (B.C. July 19, 1999)
Nov. 4, 2024 – Name changed to Urano Energy Corp. (see FPsurvey - Mines & Energy)

C.A. Bancorp Canadian Realty Finance Corporation (Ont. Dec. 21, 2007)
May 12, 2011 – Name changed to NorRock Realty Finance Corporation following C.A. Bancorp Inc.'s sale of its interest in the company, which resulted in a change of control. ■

C.A. Bancorp Inc. (Alta. Mar. 29, 2005)
Sept. 26, 2014 – Name changed to Crosswinds Holdings Inc. ■

C. A. Pitts Engineering Construction Limited (Ont. 1965 amalg.)
Aug. 21, 1974 – Name changed to Pitts Engineering Construction Limited. ■

CAE Industries Ltd. (Can. Mar. 17, 1947)
Sept. 15, 1993 – Name changed to CAE Inc. (see FPsurvey - Industrials)

CAG Capital Inc. (Can. June 12, 2007)
Nov. 25, 2009 – Continued into British Columbia.
Apr. 19, 2010 – Name changed to Stellar Biotechnologies Inc. pursuant to Qualifying Transaction reverse takeover acquisition of Stellar Biotechnologies Inc. ■

CAI Capital Corporation (Can. Nov. 20, 1990)
Jan. 8, 2004 – Dissolved. No funds available to shldrs.

CANADIAN Financials & Utilities Split Corp. (Ont. Oct. 26, 2006)
Feb. 1, 2012 – All o/s shs. redeemed for $10.0361 per pref. sh. and $5.4248 per cl. A sh.

CANCRETE Environmental Solutions Inc. (Alta. Nov. 27, 1995)
Apr. 2, 2001 – Struck from registry and dissolved.

CANMARC Real Estate Investment Trust (Que. Mar. 30, 2010)
Mar. 6, 2012 – Acquired by a wholly owned subsid. of Cominar Real Estate Investment Trust; basis either $16.50 or 0.7607 Cominar trust units for 1 CANMARC trust unit. (see Cominar Real Estate Investment Trust)

CAPA Software Publishing Corporation (Sask. July 12, 1990 amalg.)
Mar. 6, 1995 – Struck from register.

CAPVEST Income Corp. (Alta. Jan. 1, 2005 amalg.)
Mar. 2, 2009 – Dissolved at 73¢ per sh.

C.A.T. Computer Assisted Training Software Inc. (Can. Oct. 11, 1989)
Feb. 26, 2003 – Dissolved and struck from register.

CAVU Energy Metals Corp. (B.C. July 22, 2020)
Dec. 20, 2022 – Acquired by Alpha Copper Corp.; basis 0.7 Alpha shs. for 1 CAVU Energy sh. (see Alpha Copper Corp.)

CAVU Mining Corp. (B.C. July 22, 2020)
May 20, 2022 – Name changed to CAVU Energy Metals Corp. ■

C&C Cosmeceuticals Corp. (B.C. July 20, 2011)
May 12, 2017 – Name changed to Eviana Health Corporation. (see FPsurvey - Industrials)

C&C Energia Ltd. (Alta. Feb. 28, 2005)
Jan. 4, 2013 – Acquired by Pacific Rubiales Energy Corp; basis 0.3528 Pacific Rubiales shs. and 1 Platino Energy Corp. sh. plus $0.001 for 1 C&C sh. (see Pacific Rubiales Energy Corp.; Platino Energy Corp.)

C&C Energy Canada Ltd. (Alta. Feb. 28, 2005)
May 25, 2010 – Name changed to C&C Energia Ltd. ■

CB Gold Inc. (B.C. Oct. 28, 2010 amalg.)
Mar. 6, 2017 – Name changed to Red Eagle Exploration Limited. ■

CB Pak Inc. (Man. 1962)
Jan. 18, 1984 – Continued into Canada.
Dec. 4, 1989 – Acquired by Stone-Consolidated Inc. of Chicago, Ill., for $11.25 per sh.

CB Resources Ltd. (B.C. Mar. 3, 2005)
Aug. 18, 2009 – Name changed to Next Gen Metals Inc.; basis 1 new for 7.5 old shs. ■

CB2 Insights Inc. (Can. Dec. 27, 2017)
Nov. 23, 2020 – Name changed to Skylight Health Group Inc. ■

CBB Capital Ltd. (Can. July 10, 1985)
Mar. 5, 1990 – Name changed to PIC Capital Inc.; basis 1 new for 5 old shs. ■

CBCI Telecom Inc. (Can. Feb. 27, 1995)
June 12, 1997 – Acquired by Tandberg Acquisitions Inc., a wholly owned subsid. of Tandberg ASA; basis $6.60 per sh.

CBD MED Research Corp. (B.C. Oct. 24, 2004)
Feb. 28, 2019 – Name changed to World Class Extractions Inc. pursuant to the three-cornered amalgamation of World Class Extractions Inc. with CBD Acquisition Corp., a wholly owned subsidiary of CBD MED.; basis 3 new for 1 old sh. ■

CBM Asia Development Corp. (B.C. Apr. 26, 2006)
Mar. 15, 2016 – Struck from registry and dissolved.

CBO Resources Corp. (B.C. Apr. 19, 1984 amalg.)
Sept. 25, 1998 – Dissolved and struck off register.

CBOC Continental Inc. (Can. Oct. 22, 1996)
Apr. 16, 2001 – Name changed to Coastal Group Inc.; basis 1 subord. vtg., 1 multiple vtg. and 1 divd. sh. for 1 com. sh. ■

CBR Gold Corp. (Alta. July 19, 2002 amalg.)
Apr. 15, 2010 – Name changed to Niblack Mineral Development Inc. following spin-off of Canadian and Australian gold assets to wholly owned North Country Gold Corp. (NCG). CBR shldrs. received shs. of NCG on a 1-for-1 basis and NCG became a publicly listed co. ■

CBR International Biotechnologies Corp. (B.C. Mar. 13, 1987)
Mar. 30, 1993 – Name changed to Newen Enterprises Inc.; basis 1 new for 6 old shs. ■

CBX Ventures Inc. (B.C. Nov. 3, 1993)
Dec. 5, 2005 – Name changed to Alma Resources Ltd.; basis 3 new for 1 old sh. ■

C.C.C. Coded Communications Corporation (B.C. Sept. 12, 1980)
Oct. 21, 1992 – Name changed to CCI Coded Communications, Inc.; basis 1 new for 3 old shs. ■

CCC International Trade Inc. (Alta. June 24, 1987)
Apr. 6, 1990 – Name changed to The Canin Industrial Group Inc.; basis 1 new for 2 old shs. ■

CCC Internet Solutions Inc. (B.C. June 17, 1999)
Jan. 26, 2004 – Name changed to Armada Data Corporation. ■

CCI Coded Communications, Inc. (B.C. Sept. 12, 1980)
Aug. 20, 1993 – Continued into Delaware.
Aug. 27, 1993 – Name changed to Coded Communications Corporation.

CCPC Biotech Inc. (Ont. Feb. 4, 2000)
Dec. 16, 2004 – Voluntarily liquidated and dissolved.

CCR Technologies Ltd. (Alta. May 10, 1995 amalg.)
Dec. 2, 2010 – Filed proposal in bankruptcy under the Bankruptcy and Insolvency Act (BIA) and Hardie & Kelly Inc. appointed proposal trustee.
Mar. 1, 2011 – Com. shs. were redesignated as redeem. shs. and were subsequently redeemed and cancelled; no payment was made to shldrs. Unsecured creditors received amounts ranging from 50% to 100% of their unsecured claims and secured creditors received new class B com. shs. On implementation of the BIA proposal, secured creditors acquired ownership and control of CCR and all of its consolidated operations.

CCS Capital Inc. (B.C. July 7, 2009)
Oct. 22, 2010 – Continued into Cayman Islands.
Oct. 25, 2010 – Name changed to China Health Labs & Diagnostics Ltd. pursuant to Qualifying Transaction reverse takeover acquisition of Whole Vision Limited. ■

CCS Corporation (Alta. Apr. 17, 2002)
Nov. 15, 2007 – Special distrib. of 0.07583 per trust unit paid to unitholders.
Nov. 19, 2007 – Privatized; basis $46 cash per trust unit or exchangeable sh. equivalent.
Mar. 14, 2012 – Name changed to Tervita Corporation. ■

CCS Income Trust (Alta. Apr. 17, 2002)
Nov. 14, 2007 – Succeeded by CCS Corporation pursuant to a going private transaction and conversion into a corporation whereby assets were sold to Red Sky Acquisition Corp. for $46 per trust unit and delisted on Nov. 19, 2007. ■

CCT Capital Ltd. (B.C. Apr. 13, 2006)
Oct. 24, 2014 – Name changed to Mezzi Holdings Inc. ■

CCW System Ltd. (B.C. 1981)
Aug. 11, 1995 – Dissolved and struck off register.

The C. D. Mining Co. Ltd. (B.C. 1939)
Aug. 23, 1982 – Dissolved.

CD Plus.com Ltd. (Ont. Sept. 24, 1993)
Feb. 7, 2001 – Court order granted protection under the Companies' Creditors Arrangement Act (CCAA) to the company, wholly owned CD Plus.com Inc. and its subsidiary, Rembrandt Holdings Ltd. Toronto-based RSM Richter (formerly Richter & Partners Inc.) was appointed the monitor under the order.
Mar. 23, 2001 – Superior Court of Ontario terminated proceedings under the CCAA, appointed an interim receiver over the assets, property and undertakings of the three companies. Substantially all of the assets of the two subsidiaries, namely the chain of CD Plus.com stores and the Internet site, were sold to Markham, Ont.-based Records on Wheels Limited for approximately $7,300,000. The three companies filed for bankruptcy and all directors and officers of the three companies resigned. RSM Richter was then appointed trustee in bankruptcy.
June 26, 2002 – By June all assets had been sold and the distribution of proceeds was completed. Some secured creditors suffered a shortfall and there were no funds available for unsecured creditors or shldrs. The trustee was discharged.

CDA International Inc. (Ont. Sept. 18, 1997)
Feb. 25, 2005 – Placed into bankruptcy. A. Farber & Partners Inc. was appointed trustee in bankruptcy.

CDC Life Sciences Inc. (Can. June 14, 1973)
July 4, 1988 – Name changed to Connaught BioSciences Inc. ■

CDG Investments Inc. (Alta. Oct. 12, 1979)
July 24, 2008 – Formed Preo Software Inc. in Alberta on amalgamation with Preo Software Inc., constituting a reverse takeover by Preo; basis 2 new for 1 Preo sh. and 1 new for 4 CDG shs. ■

CDI Education Corporation (Ont. June 15, 1999 amalg.)
Oct. 6, 2003 – Acquired indirectly by California-based Corinthian Colleges, Inc.; basis Cdn$4.33 per com. sh.

CDIS Software Inc. (B.C. June 22, 1973)
Mar. 6, 1989 – Name changed to International CDIS Software Inc.; basis 1 new for 8 old shs. ∎

CDK Services Ltd. (Alta. May 7, 1997)
July 7, 2005 – Name changed to EcoMax Energy Services Ltd. ∎

CDM Capital Corp. (Alta. May 7, 1997)
July 28, 1999 – Name changed to CDK Services Ltd. following Qualifying Transaction acquisition of Tega Supply Inc. ∎

CDN BVentures Ltd. (B.C. Oct. 30, 2014)
Mar. 21, 2017 – Name changed to Appature Mobile Applications Inc. ∎

CDN MSolar Corp. (B.C. Sept. 30, 2013 amalg.)
Feb. 5, 2019 – Name changed to Blueberries Medical Corp. following reverse takeover acquisition of Blueberries Cannabis Corp. and concurrent amalgamation of Blueberries Cannabis with wholly owned 2663895 Ontario Inc. (and continued as Blueberries Research Corp.). (see FPsurvey - Industrials)

CDP Computer Data Processors Ltd. (Alta. 1966)
Aug. 10, 1973 – Merged with Digitech Corp. Ltd. (13.32 new for 1 old sh.) and its subsid., Digital Technology (Calgary) Ltd., to form Digitech Ltd.; basis 1 new for 1 old sh.

CDR Resources Inc. (B.C. Sept. 22, 1967)
Feb. 8, 1991 – Dissolved and struck off register.

CDRH Limited (Can. 1927)
May 25, 1972 – Name changed to Foodex Systems Limited. ∎

CE Brands Inc. (Alta. Oct. 15, 2018)
Apr. 4, 2025 – Name changed to Vitalist Inc. (see FPsurvey - Mines & Energy)

CE Franklin Ltd. (Alta. 1975)
Jan. 1, 1996 – Amalgamated in Alberta to continue with same name.
July 25, 2012 – Acquired by National Oilwell Varco, Inc., through wholly owned NOV Distribution Services ULC, for $12.75 per sh.

C.E.L. Industries Ltd. (B.C. 1983)
July 20, 1995 – Name changed to Pan Smak Pizza Inc. (see FPsurvey - Industrials)

C.E.M. Centry Electronic Monitoring Corporation (Ont. Apr. 29, 1988)
May 25, 1989 – Continued into Alberta.
Mar. 27, 1997 – Continued into British Columbia.
Mar. 31, 1997 – Name changed to Metalex Ventures Ltd.; basis 1 new for 5.2 old shs. (see FPsurvey - Mines & Energy)

CERF Incorporated (Alta. Aug. 10, 2011)
June 22, 2016 – Name changed to Canadian Equipment Rentals Corp. ∎

CES Energy Solutions Corp. (Can. Nov. 13, 1986)
Nov. 13, 2020 – Continued into Alberta. (see FPsurvey - Mines & Energy; FPsurvey - Industrials)

CES Software plc (U.K. June 24, 2003)
Feb. 4, 2005 – Name changed to FUN Technologies plc. ∎

C88 Capital Corporation (Alta. Mar. 18, 2003)
Mar. 29, 2006 – Name changed to Kam and Ronson Media Group Inc. following Qualifying Transaction reverse takeover acquisition of Kam & Ronson Enterprise Company Limited. ∎

CFCF Inc. (Can. Nov. 24, 1978)
Mar. 31, 1997 – Amalgamated with 3242722 Canada Inc., a wholly owned subsid. of Le Groupe Vidéotron Ltée; basis $21.50 per sh. (see Le Groupe Vidéotron Ltée)

CFCN Communications Limited (Ont. 1971)
July 1, 1977 – Acquired by Maclean-Hunter Limited for $14 per sh. (see Maclean-Hunter Limited)

CFE Industries Inc. (Alta. Nov. 30, 1993)
Oct. 18, 2002 – Name changed to Commercial Solutions Inc. pursuant to reverse takeover acquisition of Commercial Bearing Service (1966) Ltd.; basis 1 new for 5 old shs. ∎

CFG Holdings Inc. (Alta. July 15, 2004 amalg.)
Apr. 19, 2007 – KPMG Inc. appointed liquidator.
Apr. 26, 2007 – Distrib. of $0.09307 per sh. was made to shldrs. of record Apr. 20, 2007. Secured creditors suffered a shortfall.
Oct. 15, 2008 – KMPG Inc. discharged as liquidator.
Oct. 22, 2008 – Dissolved by court order.

CFM Corporation (Ont. Feb. 13, 1992)
Apr. 15, 2005 – Amalgamated with 1650150 Ontario Inc., a subsid. of Ontario Teachers' Pension Plan Board; basis $1.50 per sh.

CFM International Inc. (Ont. Feb. 13, 1992)
May 6, 1996 – Name changed to CFM Majestic Inc. ∎

CFM Majestic Inc. (Ont. Feb. 13, 1992)
Mar. 4, 2002 – Name changed to CFM Corporation. ∎

CFS Group Inc. (Can. July 25, 1925)
Sept. 11, 2000 – Going private transaction via amalgamation with wholly owned subsid. of Ajawak Investments Ltd. Canadian residents received 1 cl. A pfce. sh. of amalco. for 1 com. sh. redeemable Oct. 1, 2005, for $3.00 per sh.; non-Canadian residents received 1 cl. B pfce sh. for 1 com. sh. redeemed immediately for $3.00 per sh.

CFS International Inc. (Alta. Jan. 18, 1964)
Jan. 18, 2006 – Amalgamated with wholly owned subsid. of controlling shldr. Ports International Enterprises Ltd.; basis $3.75 per sh.

CFS Refractories Inc. (Can. July 25, 1925)
June 22, 1987 – Name changed to CFS Group Inc. ∎

CGA Mining Limited (Australia Oct. 16, 1985)
Jan. 21, 2013 – Acquired by B2Gold Corp.; basis 0.74 B2Gold shs. for 1 CGA Mining sh.

CGC Inc. (Can. Jan. 1, 1985 amalg.)
Dec. 31, 1996 – Acquired by a subsid. of USG Corporation for $11 per sh.

C.G.C. Mines Ltd. (Ont. 1966)
1976 – Dissolved.

The CGI Group Inc. (Que. June 1976)
Dec. 16, 1998 – Name changed to CGI Group Inc. ∎

CGI Group Inc. (Que. Sept. 29, 1981)
Jan. 30, 2019 – Name changed to CGI Inc. (see FPsurvey - Industrials)

C.G.S. Technology Inc. (Alta. Oct. 21, 1996)
Jan. 29, 1998 – Name changed to ILI Technologies Group Inc. following acquisition of ILI Technologies Corp. ∎

CH Financial Corporation (B.C. 1986)
July 3, 1992 – Dissolved and struck off register.

CHC Helicopter Corporation (Can. Feb. 18, 1987)
Sept. 16, 2008 – Succeeded by CHC Helicopter S.A. following acquisition by 6922767 Holding, S.a.r.l., a wholly owned subsidiary of First Reserve Corporation, for $32.68 per cl. A and B sh.

CHC Realty Capital Corp. (Ont. Apr. 12, 2013)
Feb. 19, 2015 – Name changed to CHC Student Housing Corp.; basis 1 new for 85 old shs. ∎

CHC Student Housing Corp. (Ont. Apr. 12, 2013)
Mar. 25, 2021 – Name changed to Bullet Exploration Inc. pursuant to the reverse takeover acquisition of 2294253 Alberta Ltd. ∎

CHEQ-IT Ltd. (Alta. May 28, 1993)
Apr. 19, 2010 – Acquired by Tuscany International Drilling Inc.; basis 0.0265 Tuscany shs. for 1 CHEQ-IT sh.

CHK Wireless Technologies Inc. (B.C. June 18, 1998)
July 25, 2003 – Name changed to GridSense Systems Inc. ∎

C.H.S. Oil and Gas Ltd. (Ont. 1934)
1960 – Wound up.

CHUM Limited (Ont. Oct. 2, 1944)
Oct. 31, 2006 – Acquired by Bell Globemedia Inc., a wholly owned subsid. of BCE Inc.; basis $52.50 per com. sh. and $47.25 per cl. B sh.

C-I Credit Corp. Ltd. (Ont. Apr. 3, 1962)
Jan. 25, 1969 – Name changed to Realty Capital Corp., Limited; basis 2 new cl. A or com. for 1 old cl. A or com. sh. ∎

CI Financial Corp. (Ont. Nov. 12, 2008)
Aug. 15, 2025 – Acquired by Mubadala Capital; basis $32 cash per sh.

CI Financial Income Fund (Ont. May 18, 2006)
Jan. 5, 2009 – Converted into CI Financial Corp. and all units and exch. cl. B LP units of Canadian International LP redeemed for CI Financial Corp. com. shs. on a 1-for-1 basis. (see CI Financial Corp.)

CI Financial Inc. (Ont. Jan. 14, 1994)
July 5, 2006 – Plan of Arrangement to convert company into an income trust named CI Financial Income Fund; basis 1 new trust unit for 1 com. sh. (see CI Financial Income Fund)

CI First Asset U.S. & Canada LifeCo Income ETF (Ont. July 26, 2013)
Apr. 22, 2021 – Name changed to CI U.S. & Canada LifeCo Income ETF. ∎

C.I. Fund Management Inc. (Ont. Jan. 14, 1994)
Nov. 4, 2002 – Name changed to CI Fund Management Inc. ∎

CI Fund Management Inc. (Ont. Jan. 14, 1994)
Dec. 6, 2005 – Name changed to CI Financial Inc. ∎

CI Galaxy Bitcoin Fund (Ont. Dec. 4, 2020)
May 10, 2021 – Merged into CI Galaxy Bitcoin ETF; basis 2.336595 U.S.$ ETF units for 1 cl. A unit.

CI Global Opportunities II Fund (Ont. Dec. 16, 1996)
June 29, 2007 – Terminated; basis $8.4756 per unit.

CI Master Limited Partnership (Ont. Dec. 21, 1994)
Apr. 30, 2014 – Liquidated and dissolved. Distribution of $0.15 cash per limited partnership unit

CI U.S. & Canada LifeCo Income ETF (Ont. July 26, 2013)
Apr. 27, 2022 – Name changed to CI U.S. & Canada Lifeco Covered Call ETF.

CIBT Education Group Inc. (B.C. Nov. 17, 1986)
Apr. 17, 2023 – Name changed to Global Education Communities Corp. (see FPsurvey - Industrials)

CIC Canola Industries Canada Inc. (Alta. Mar. 23, 1990)
Nov. 6, 1996 – Name changed to Canadian Agra Foods Inc. ∎

CIC Capital Ltd. (Can. June 20, 2003)
Nov. 23, 2013 – Continued into British Columbia.
Nov. 24, 2014 – Name changed to CIC Capital Fund Ltd. (see FPsurvey - Mines & Energy)

CIC Energy Corp. (British Virgin Islands Mar. 10, 2005)
Mar. 14, 2006 – Amalgamated in British Virgin Islands to continue with same name.
Sept. 12, 2012 – Merged with Jindal (BVI) Ltd., a wholly owned subsid. of Jindal Steel & Power (Mauritius) Limited, for Cdn$2.00 per sh.

CIC Mining Resources Ltd. (Can. June 20, 2003)
May 31, 2013 – Name changed to CIC Capital Ltd. ■

CIIT Inc. (Can. 1929)
Jan. 17, 1992 – Acquired by CIIT acquisition Inc., an indirect subsid. of Société Parisienne d'Entreprises et de Participations, for $16.15 per com. sh. and $105 per 5% pfd. sh.

C-I-L Inc. (Can. 1954)
Apr. 22, 1988 – Amalgamated with ICI Investments Canada Inc., an indirect wholly owned subsid. of Imperial Chemical Industries plc, making it a wholly owned subsid. of Imperial Chemical plc; basis $47 per sh.

CIM International Group Inc. (Ont. Feb. 18, 2010)
July 28, 2022 – Delisted from the CSE. Subsequently the certificate of incorporation was cancelled.

CINAR Corporation (Can. Dec. 10, 1976)
Mar. 15, 2004 – Acquired by investor group comprised of Michael Hirsh, Toper Taylor, OMERS Merchant Banking Group and TD Capital Canadian Private Equity Partners; basis US$3.60 per sh. plus possible residual of 70% of net proceeds from litigation.

CINS Holding Corp. (Cayman Islands Aug. 3, 2007)
Aug. 20, 2015 – Name changed to Sino Rise Group Holding Corp.

C.I.S. Technologies, Inc. (B.C. 1983)
1989 – Continued into Delaware.

CIT Exchangeco Inc. (Can. Nov. 16, 1999 amalg.)
July 5, 2002 – Called for redemption by parent 3026192 Nova Scotia Company; basis 0.6907 new Tyco International Ltd. com. sh. for 1 old CIT exchangeable sh.

The CIT Group, Inc. (Del. 1908)
June 4, 2001 – Acquired by US-based Tyco International Ltd.; basis 0.6907 new Tyco com. sh. for 1 old CIT com. sh. Also 1 old CIT Exchangeco shs. exchangeable into 1 new Tyco com. sh.

CITCO Financial Corporation (Can. 1977)
Oct. 1988 – All o/s com. shs. held by CITCO Holdings Ltd. which acquired all o/s pref. shs. under a 75¢ per sh. offer.

CIX Split Corp. (Ont. Apr. 27, 2007)
Feb. 1, 2011 – Dissolved and redeemed all Priority Equity shs. and cl. A shs. for $10.00 and $7.1437 per sh., respectively.

CJHC Capital Ltd. (Alta. Apr. 25, 2002)
Jan. 21, 2004 – Name changed to Dragon-Tex (Group) Limited following Qualifying Transaction acquisition of South Champ Trading Limited. ■

CKD Ventures Ltd. (B.C. May 17, 1984)
May 14, 1999 – Name changed to Alchemy Ventures Ltd.; basis 1 new for 10 old shs. ■

C.K.P. Developments Ltd. (Can. 1911)
Oct. 1962 – Transferred assets and liabs. to C.K.P. Developments Inc.
1962 – C.K.P. Developments Inc., through an offer to shldrs., acquired 400,000 of its shs. at US$21 per sh.
Nov. 7, 1963 – Name changed to Deltona Corporation; basis 1 new for 1 old sh.

CKR Carbon Corporation (B.C. Dec. 22, 2011)
Dec. 5, 2016 – Continued into Ontario.
Dec. 22, 2017 – Name changed to Gratomic Inc. (see FPsurvey - Mines & Energy)

CL Systems Limited (Ont. Dec. 24, 1985)
Feb. 1, 1993 – All o/s cl. A pref. shs. acquired by Shaw Cablesystems Ltd. for $307,750,000. (see Shaw Cablesystems Ltd.)

CLEARLINK Capital Corporation (Ont. Jan. 30, 1984)
Mar. 8, 2006 – Name changed to Renasant Financial Partners Ltd. ■

CLI Resources Inc. (B.C. Oct. 16, 2009)
Mar. 22, 2011 – Name changed to Choice Gold Corp. ■

CLS Holdings USA, Inc. (Nev. Mar. 31, 2011)
July 11, 2025 – Privatized via a 1-for-4,000,000 sh. consolidation. Fractional shldrs. of record would receive US$0.037 cash per pre-consolidated sh.

CM NT Equity Corp. (Can. 1977)
Mar. 31, 1993 – All o/s shs. redeemed; basis 1 Canadian Imperial Bank of Commerce com. sh. less approx. $14 for 1 CM NT sh.

C.M. Oliver Inc. (Can. Apr. 10, 1997)
Feb. 22, 2000 – Name changed to Datawest Solutions Inc.; basis 1 new for 2 old shs. ■

CM Pref. Corp. (Ont. 1981)
Mar. 31, 1993 – All o/s shs. redeemed. Shrlders received the lesser of $14 per sh. and the net asset value of the co. divided by the number of pfd. shs. then o/s for 1 old pfd. sh.

CMA Capital Corporation (Alta. July 24, 1986)
May 5, 1995 – Continued into Canada.
Nov. 1, 1997 – Struck off register.

CMC Metals Ltd. (B.C. July 4, 2005)
Mar. 19, 2025 – Name changed to Walker Lane Resources Ltd. (see FPsurvey - Mines & Energy)

CME Resources Inc. (Ont. Mar. 1, 1939)
Oct. 9, 1986 – Name changed to CME Capital Inc. (see FPsurvey - Industrials)

CME Telemetrix Inc. (Ont. Apr. 27, 1978)
Aug. 24, 2004 – Name changed to NIR Diagnostics Inc. ■

CMJ Capital Inc. (Que. Mar. 26, 2004)
Feb. 11, 2005 – Formed Power Tech Corporation Inc. in Quebec following Qualifying Transaction reverse takeover acquisition of and amalgamation with Power Tech Corporation Inc. (see FPsurvey - Industrials)

CML Global Capital Ltd. (Can. June 19, 1992)
Jan. 7, 2005 – Acquired by 6223711 Canada Inc. for $2.10 per sh.

CML Healthcare Income Fund (Ont. Jan. 12, 2004)
Jan. 1, 2011 – Succeeded by CML HealthCare Inc. pursuant to plan of arrangement whereby CML Healthcare Inc. was formed to facilitate the conversion of the fund into a corporation and the fund was subsequently dissolved. ■

CML Healthcare Inc. (Ont. June 28, 1971)
Feb. 25, 2004 – Merged with Cipher Pharmaceuticals Inc. and CML Healthcare Income Fund; basis either 4 new fund units plus 1 new Cipher com. sh. plus $7.00 or 4 new exch. shs. exchangeable into 4 new fund units plus 1 new Cipher com. sh. plus $7.00 for 1 old CML Healthcare com. sh. (see CML Healthcare Income Fund)

CML HealthCare Inc. (Ont. Jan. 1, 2011; amalg.)
Oct. 3, 2013 – Acquired by LifeLabs Inc., owned by a unit of Ontario Municipal Employees Retirement System, for $10.75 per sh.

CML Industries Ltd. (Ont. Jan. 28, 1974)
Aug. 2, 2000 – Acquired by 1418245 Ontario Inc., a wholly owned subsid. of Supremex Inc., for $6.00 per sh.

CMP Gold Trust (Ont. Dec. 20, 2007)
Dec. 17, 2012 – Name changed to Goodman Gold Trust. ■

CMP 1988 Oil and Gas Development Limited Partnership (Alta. Oct. 22, 1987)
Jan. 14, 1994 – All o/s units exchanged for com. shs. of Clearport Petroleums Ltd.; basis 2.56613 com. shs. for 1 unit. (see Clearport Petroleums Ltd.)

CMP 1988 Oil & Gas Development Trust (Alta. 1987)
Jan. 14, 1994 – All o/s units exchanged for com. shs. of Clearport Petroleums Ltd.; basis 2.21081 com. shs. for 1 unit. (see Clearport Petroleums Ltd.)

CMP 1989 Oil and Gas Development Limited Partnership (Alta. Mar. 10, 1989)
Jan. 14, 1994 – All partnership units acquired by Clearport Petroleums Ltd.; basis 1.617 Clearport com. shs. for 1 CMP unit. (see Clearport Petroleums Ltd.)

CMP Resources Ltd. (Can. 1991)
June 3, 1993 – Amalgamated with Plexus Resources Corporation (1.8 new for 1 old sh.) to form a new co. known as Kinross Gold Corporation; basis 2.1 new for 1 old sh.

CMQ Resources Inc. (Alta. Jan. 29, 2004 amalg.)
July 25, 2014 – Privatized by Matco Investments Ltd. for 2¢ per sh.

CMYK Capital Inc. (B.C. Apr. 19, 2006)
Aug. 18, 2009 – Formed Paget Minerals Corp. in British Columbia pursuant to Qualifying Transaction reverse takeover acquisition of and amalgamation with Paget Minerals Corp.; basis 1 new for 2 old shs. ■

CNI Computer Networks International Ltd. (B.C. Oct. 3, 1985)
June 20, 1988 – Delisted from the Vancouver Stock Exchange. Subsequently dissolved for failure to file and struck from register.

CNR Capital Corporation (Ont. June 8, 2005)
Dec. 12, 2008 – Name changed to Argonaut Exploration Inc. pursuant to Qualifying Transaction reverse takeover acquisition of Argonaut Resources Inc. (see FPsurvey - Mines & Energy)

CNRP Mining Inc. (B.C. Sept. 15, 2011)
June 6, 2018 – Name changed to Integrated Cannabis Company Inc. following reverse takeover acquisition of 1127466 B.C. Ltd. ■

COGNICASE Inc. (Can. Oct. 3, 1991)
Jan. 27, 2003 – Acquired by CGI Group Inc.; basis either $4.50 or 0.6311 cl. A subord. sh. of CGI or a combination thereof for 1 old COGNICASE sh. (see CGI Group Inc.)

COIN HODL INC. (Ont. Dec. 8, 2009)
Apr. 27, 2021 – Name changed to Tokens.com Corp. pursuant to the reverse takeover acquisition of Tokens.com Inc. and concurrent amlgamation of Tokens.com Inc. with wholly owned 2821956 Ontario Inc. (and continued as Tokens.com Capital Corp.); basis 1 new for 11.9868 old shs. ■

COM DEV International Ltd. (Can. June 25, 1993)
Feb. 0, 2016 – Acquired by Honeywell International Inc. through its Canadian subsid. Honeywell Limited and data services business was spun out through exactEarth Ltd.; basis Cdn $5.125 and 0.19785 exactEarth com. shs., plus a second payment of Cdn $0.125 payable two weeks later, for 1 COM DEV com. sh.

COMPASS Income Fund (Ont. Mar. 27, 2002)
Mar. 22, 2017 – Merged into MINT Income Fund; basis 1.6928173 MINT trust units for 1 COMPASS fund unit.

CON-SPACE Communications Ltd. (B.C. Apr. 23, 1991)
Nov. 4, 2009 – Acquired by Turret Oy AB for 3¢ per sh. Co. now private.

CORDEX Petroleums Inc. (Alta. Nov. 1, 1985 amalg.)
June 2, 2001 – Struck from registry and dissolved.

CORE Technologies Inc. (Alta. Mar. 11, 1997)
Oct. 19, 1999 – Formed Image Sculpting International Inc.; basis 1 new for 10 old shs. ■

COSTA Energy Inc. (Alta. June 19, 2004)
Jan. 14, 2010 – Formed Artek Exploration Ltd. in Alberta pursuant to reverse takeover acquisition of and amalgamation with Artek Exploration Ltd. (deemed acquiror); basis 0.028947 new for 1 old sh. ■

CO2 Solution Inc. (Que. Nov. 19, 1997)
Nov. 23, 2011 – Name changed to CO2 Solutions Inc. (see FPsurvey - Industrials)

C1 Cablesystems Inc. (Can. Oct. 26, 1984)
Apr. 2, 1991 – Name changed to Regional Cablesystems Inc. ■

CP Ships Limited (Can. June 29, 2001)
Oct. 3, 2001 – Continued into New Brunswick.
Dec. 20, 2005 – Plan of Arrangement acquisition by German conglomerate TUI AG for US$21.50 per sh. and subsequent amalgamation with TUI's Hapag-Llyod division.

CPAC (Care) Holdings Ltd. (Can. May 24, 1995)
July 12, 2005 – Acquired indirectly by Chartwell Seniors Real Estate Investment Trust for $1.55 per sh. (see Chartwell Seniors Housing Real Estate Investment Trust)

CPC RG One Corp. (Ont. Sept. 26, 2014)
Jan. 16, 2015 – Name changed to RG One Corp. ■

CPI Plastics Group Limited (Ont. Sept. 7, 1972)
Jan. 8, 2009 – Placed into receivership. Deloitte & Touche Inc. appointed receiver.

CPI Preferred Equity Ltd. (Alta. June 26, 1998)
Feb. 7, 2012 – Name changed to Atlantic Power Preferred Equity Ltd. ■

CPII Inc. (Can. Dec. 8, 2004)
July 4, 2005 – Plan of Arrangement to convert company into a new company named Whiterock Real Estate Investment Trust plus the acquisition of a property in Prince Edward Island constitutes CPII's Qualifying Transaction; basis 1 new Whiterock unit for 5 old CPII com. shs.

CPL Capital Inc. (Alta. Feb. 15, 2001)
Dec. 19, 2002 – Name changed to CPL Technologies Inc. following Qualifying Transaction acquisition of CPL Informatique Inc. ■

CPL Long Term Care Real Estate Investment Trust (Ont. Feb. 20, 1997)
May 2, 2002 – Acquired by Retirement Residences Real Estate Investment Trust; basis 1.2 new Retirement Residences trust units for 1 old CPL trust unit. (see Retirement Residences Real Estate Investment Trust)

CPL Technologies Inc. (Alta. Feb. 15, 2001)
Sept. 1, 2003 – Continued into Canada.
Jan. 13, 2009 – Name changed to Intema Solutions Inc. ■

CPL Ventures Limited (B.C. Aug. 10, 1995)
Nov. 11, 1996 – Name changed to Manfrey Capital Corporation; basis 1 new for 2 old shs. ■

C.P.M. Technologies Inc. (Alta. May 23, 1996)
Aug. 18, 1998 – Name changed to Grace Resources Inc. ■

CPT Pemberton Technologies Ltd. (B.C. June 19, 1980)
Nov. 8, 1999 – Name changed to Pemberton Energy Ltd. ■

CPVC Blackcomb Inc. (Alta. July 26, 2005)
July 30, 2007 – Formed Prestige Telecom Inc. in Canada on Qualifying Transaction amalgamation with Prestige Telecom Ltd., constituting a reverse takeover by Prestige. ■

CPVC Bromont Inc. (Alta. June 7, 2007)
June 24, 2009 – Name changed to Pro-Trans Ventures Inc. following amalgamation of wholly owned 1468729 Alberta Ltd. with Pro-Trans Ventures Inc., whereby Pro-Trans shldrs. received 1.66 CPVC shs. for each Pro-Trans sh. held. (see FPsurvey - Industrials)

CPVC Financial Corporation (Alta. Nov. 7, 2006 amalg.)
May 6, 2009 – Privatized at $0.02 per sh.

CPVC Financial Inc. (Alta. Feb. 17, 1995)
Nov. 7, 2006 – Formed CPVC Financial Corporation in Alberta on amalgamation with CPVC Tremblant Inc. with CPVC Financial Inc. the deemed acquiror; basis 2.889 new for 1 CPVC Tremblant sh. and 1 new for 1 CPVC Financial Inc. sh. ■

CPVC Tremblant Inc. (Alta. Apr. 27, 2004)
Dec. 18, 2006 – Amalgamated with CPVC Financial Inc. (1 for 1), Extenway Solutions Inc. and Arura Pharma Inc. to continue with the new name CPVC Financial Corporation; basis 2.889 new CPVC Financial shs. for 1 old CPVC Tremblant sh. (see CPVC Financial Corporation)

CPX Industries Inc. (Ont. 1985)
June 1, 1996 – Formed Java Gold Corporation in Ontario on amalgamation with Java Gold Corporation (deemed acquiror); basis 1 new for 19 CPX com. or ser. A subord. vtg. shs. ■

CQI-Biomed International Inc. (Can. Sept. 1, 1995)
Dec. 31, 1999 – Formed Bio-Med Laboratories Inc. on amalgamation with 3547639 Canada Inc. (see FPsurvey - Industrials)

CR Capital Corp. (Ont. Dec. 13, 2002)
Sept. 21, 2020 – Name changed to Stone Gold Inc. ■

C.R. Provini Financial Services Corp. (B.C. Aug. 12, 1986)
Jan. 24, 1994 – Name changed to DataWave Vending Inc.; basis 1 new for 5 old shs. ■

CRA Phase II Ltd. (Can. May 16, 1997)
Nov. 2, 2005 – Dissolved.

CRAFT 1861 Global Holdings Inc. (B.C. May 22, 2020)
Aug. 1, 2024 – Privatized via acquisition by Nano Cures International, Inc.; basis 1 new Nano consideration sh. for 1 old CRAFT 1861 subord. vtg. and proportionate vtg. shs. with a deemed value of US$26.77.

CRH Medical Corporation (B.C. Apr. 12, 2001)
Apr. 23, 2021 – Acquired by WELL Health Technologies Corp.; basis US$4.00 cash per sh.

CRM Capital Inc. (Ont. Aug. 14, 1989)
Apr. 1, 1997 – Formed Active Control Technology Inc. in Ontario on amalgamation with Active Control Technology Inc. and U R Alert Systems Inc. (a wholly owned subsid. of Active Control), constituting a reverse takeover by Active Control; basis 2 new for 1 Active Control sh. and 0.5 new for 1 CRM sh.; basis 0.5 new for 1 old sh. ■

CRMnet.com Inc. (Ont. Jan. 27, 1944)
Feb. 25, 2005 – Name changed to Advanced Explorations Inc.; basis 1 new for 3 old shs. ■

CROPS Inc. (Yuk. Apr. 23, 2018)
Mar. 24, 2021 – Continued into British Columbia.
Apr. 7, 2021 – Name changed to Metallum Resources Inc. pursuant to acquisition of Pick Lake Mining Limited from Superior Lake Resources Mining Limited, constituting a reverse takeover by Superior Lake; basis 1 new for 10 old shs. ■

CRS II Preferred NT Trust (Ont. June 22, 1994)
Feb. 28, 2002 – Senior dividend units expired at redemption price of $25 (dividend $13.55 plus premium $11.45).

CRS III Deferred Preferred Trust (Ont. June 22, 1998)
May 23, 2003 – Redeemed in full at $33.34 per unit.

CRS Electronics Inc. (Can. Sept. 1, 2009 amalg.)
Oct. 22, 2015 – Placed into receivership. Link & Associates Inc. was appointed receiver.

CRS Preferred NT Ltd. (Ont. Aug. 18, 1993)
Jan. 16, 2001 – Called in full.

CRS Robotics Corporation (Ont. Feb. 17, 1981)
May 31, 2002 – Acquired by Thermo Acquisition Corporation, indirect wholly owned subsid. of Delaware-based Thermo Electron Corporation; basis $5.75 per sh.

CS Resources Limited (Can. Sept. 6, 1989 amalg.)
Oct. 31, 1990 – Amalgamated in Canada to continue with same name.
Aug. 1, 1993 – Amalgamated with American Eagle Petroleums Ltd. to form new co. with same name CS Resources Limited.
Aug. 13, 1997 – Acquired by PanCanadian Petroleum Limited for $16 per sh.

CSA Management Inc. (unknown 1968)
Nov. 5, 1993 – Continued into Ontario. (see Goldcorp Inc.)
Nov. 1, 2000 – Amalgamated with Goldcorp Inc. to continue with the Goldcorp name; basis 2.1 new Goldcorp com. shs. for 1 CSA cl. A sh. and 6 new Goldcorp com. shs. for 1 CSA cl. B sh. (see Goldcorp Inc.)

CSA Management Limited (Can. 1968)
Mar. 31, 1994 – Principal assets of the company were amalgamated with those of Goldcorp Inc. (1.4 for 1) and Dickenson Mines Limited (1 for 1) to form a new Goldcorp Inc., a new CSA Management Inc., and a new wholly owned company, Lexam Explorations Inc.; basis 1 new CSA cl. A sh. for 1 old CSA cl. A sh. and 1 new CSA cl. B sh. for 1 old CSA cl. B sh. Prior to amalgamation, CSA continued into Ontario effective Nov. 5, 1993. (see CSA Management Inc.)

CSA Minerals Corp. (Ont. 1971)
Sept. 30, 1985 – Formed Consolidated CSA Minerals Inc. in Canada on amalgamation with CSA Minerals Inc.; basis 1 new for 4 old shs. ■

CSCC Casino Software Corporation (B.C. Jan. 30, 1996)
Mar. 1, 1999 – Delisted from the Vancouver Stock Exchange. Subsequently struck from register and dissolved.

C.S.D. Securities Limited (Can. May 6, 1932)
Dec. 28, 2006 – Amalgamated with 4394291 Canada Inc. to continue as 4394291 Canada Inc.
Nov. 17, 2007 – 4394291 Canada dissolved and struck off register.

CSG Resources Ltd. (B.C. Apr. 28, 1988)
Sept. 22, 1999 – Name changed to Artgallerylive.com Management Ltd. ■

CSI Credit Systems International Inc. (B.C. Sept. 9, 1992)
Feb. 23, 2000 – Amalgamated with 583969 BC Ltd. a wholly owned subsid. of Royal Bank of Canada; basis 1 redeemable pfd. sh. of amalg. co. for each sh. held, then pfd. shs. redeemed immediately at $1.30 per sh. The co. was privatized. Subsequently name of amalgamated co. changed to Ernex Marketing Inc.

CSI Wireless Inc. (Alta. July 31, 1990)
May 9, 2007 – Name changed to Hemisphere GPS Inc. ■

CSM Systems Corp. (Alta. Mar. 7, 2000)
Sept. 16, 2014 – Name changed to Visionstate Corp. (see FPsurvey - Industrials)

CST Coldswitch Technologies Inc. (B.C. Sept. 6, 1988)
Aug. 16, 2001 – Name changed to Coldswitch Technologies Inc. ■

CSW Ventures Corp. (Alta. Mar. 16, 2000)
Nov. 12, 2001 – Formed Direct IT Canada Inc. following acquisition of and amalgamation with Applied Planning Systems Inc. and Direct IT Inc. ■

CT & T Telecommunications Inc. (B.C. Apr. 9, 1987)
Feb. 12, 1998 – Name changed to Global CT & T Telecommunications Inc.; basis 1 new for 4 old shs. ■

CT Developers Ltd. (Can. Apr. 1, 2011)
May 4, 2021 – Name changed to Magna Mining Inc. pursuant to the Qualifying Transaction reverse takeover acquisition of Magna Mining Corp. and concurrent amalgamation of Magna with wholly owned 2813443 Ontario Inc. (and continued as Magna Mining (Canada)

Corp.).; basis 1 new for 4 old shs. (see FPsurvey - Mines & Energy)

C.T. Exploranda Ltd. (B.C. 1969)
Mar. 31, 1986 – Name changed to Izone International Ltd. (see FPsurvey - Mines & Energy; FPsurvey - Industrials)

CT Financial Services Inc. (Ont. Sept. 21, 1987)
Nov. 5, 1987 – Continued into Canada.
Feb. 3, 2000 – Acquired by The Toronto-Dominion Bank for $67 per sh.

CTB Industries Inc. (Alta. Oct. 9, 1987)
Apr. 1, 1996 – Struck off register.

CTC Crown Technologies Corporation (Alta. Jan. 10, 1995)
July 1, 2000 – Struck off register.

CTF Technologies Inc. (Yuk. Apr. 3, 1998)
Aug. 11, 2008 – Continued into British Columbia.
July 11, 2012 – Acquired by FleetCor Technologies, Inc.; basis $3.08 cash per sh.

CTG Compression Technology Group Inc. (B.C. 1976 amalg.)
Sept. 2, 1994 – Dissolved and struck off register.

CTG Inc. (Ont. 1980)
Dec. 31, 1985 – All o/s com. shs. and wts. acquired by B.T. (Canada) Holdings Inc., a wholly owned subsid. of British Telecommunications PLC, at $5.25 per sh. and 90¢ per wt.

C.T.I. Technologies Corp. (B.C. Aug. 5, 1963)
Mar. 23, 1990 – Delisted from the Vancouver Stock Exchange. Subsequently struck from register and dissolved for failure to file.
Mar. 23, 1990 – Name changed to World Videophone Teleconferencing Technologies Ltd.

CTV Inc. (Ont. Aug. 11, 1971)
May 26, 2000 – Acquired by BCE Inc. for $38.50 per sh.

C2 Global Technologies Inc. (Fla. Apr. 21, 1983)
2011 – Name changed to Counsel RB Capital Inc. ■

C2C Gold Corporation Inc. (Que. Nov. 14, 1938)
Mar. 11, 2010 – Name changed to Key Gold Holding Inc.; basis 1 new for 10 old shs. ■

C2C Inc. (Que. Nov. 14, 1938)
Feb. 27, 2008 – Name changed to C2C Gold Corporation Inc. ■

C2C Industrial Properties Inc. (Ont. July 30, 2008)
July 23, 2013 – Formed DIR Industrial Properties Inc. in Ontario on amalgamation with Dundee Industrial Atlantic Acquisition Inc., a wholly owned subsid. of Dundee Industrial Real Estate Investment Trust; basis 1 pref. DIR sh. for 1 C2C com. sh., immediately redeemed for 0.4485 Dundee REIT units. (see Dundee Industrial Real Estate Investment Trust)

C2C Mining Corporation (Alta. Mar. 13, 1997)
Dec. 22, 2000 – Name changed to C2C Zeolite Corporation. ■

C2C Zeolite Corporation (Alta. Mar. 13, 1997)
Apr. 21, 2006 – Name changed to ZEOX Corporation. ■

CUP Capital Corp. (Ont. Dec. 9, 2014)
Mar. 22, 2018 – Name changed to GBLT Corp. ■

CUV Ventures Corp. (B.C. May 30, 1980)
Nov. 11, 2019 – Name changed to RevoluGROUP Canada Inc. (see FPsurvey - Industrials)

CV Technologies Inc. (Alta. Oct. 1, 1997 amalg.)
June 30, 1998 – Amalgamated with HerbTech Inc. (0.896 for 1) to form new co. with same name CV Technologies Inc.; basis 0.896 new for 1 HerbTech sh. and 1.561 new for 1 CV Technologies sh.
Apr. 3, 2009 – Name changed to Afexa Life Sciences Inc. ■

CVAC Industries, Inc. (B.C. Dec. 3, 1980)
Nov. 27, 1995 – Name changed to Saddlerock Resources, Inc.; basis 1 new for 4 old shs. ■

CVC Cayman Ventures Corp. (B.C. Mar. 11, 2009)
Apr. 3, 2013 – Name changed to Discovery Harbour Resources Corp. following reverse takeover acquisition of Discovery Harbour Resources Corp.; basis 1 new for 3 old shs. (see FPsurvey - Mines & Energy)

CVL Resources Ltd. (B.C. Sept. 19, 1979)
Feb. 4, 2002 – Name changed to Newport Exploration Ltd.; basis 1 new for 10 old shs. (see FPsurvey - Mines & Energy)

CVRD Inco Limited (Can. July 25, 1916; via Dominion charter)
Nov. 29, 2007 – Name changed to Vale Inco Limited. ■

CVTech Group Inc. (Can. Apr. 20, 2005 amalg.)
Sept. 11, 2014 – Name changed to NAPEC Inc. ■

CVW Cleantech Inc. (Can. Mar. 19, 2009)
July 21, 2025 – Name changed to CVW Sustainable Royalties Inc. (see FPsurvey - Mines & Energy; FPsurvey - Industrials)

CWC Energy Services Corp. (Alta. Sept. 1, 2005 amalg.)
Nov. 13, 2023 – Acquired by Precision Drilling Corporation; basis (i) 0.002124306 Precision shs.; or (ii) $0.196668 cash; or (c) a combination thereof for 1 CWC Energy sh.

CWC Well Services Corp. (Alta. Sept. 1, 2005 amalg.)
May 15, 2014 – Name changed to CWC Energy Services Corp. following acquisition of Ironhand Drilling Inc. ■

CWN Mining Acquisition Corp (Can. May 10, 2012)
Jan. 3, 2018 – Name changed to GCC Global Capital Corporation following change of business acquisition of an interest in New Age Developments Ltd. (see FPsurvey - Industrials)

CXW Capital Corp. (Alta. Jan. 19, 1998)
Dec. 9, 2002 – Continued into Ontario.
Jan. 30, 2003 – Name changed to RoaDor Industries Ltd. pursuant to Qualifying Transaction reverse takeover acquisition of Proplas Ltd. (see FPsurvey - Industrials)

CY Oriental Holdings Ltd. (B.C. Feb. 3, 2006)
Oct. 22, 2012 – Dissolved and struck from register.

CYGAM Energy Inc. (Alta. Apr. 12, 1996)
Apr. 2, 2015 – Voluntarily filed for bankruptcy. Hardie and Kelly Inc. appointed trustee and all officers and directors resigned.

CZM Capital Corp. (B.C. July 19, 1999)
Jan. 26, 2010 – Name changed to Taku Gold Corp.; basis 1 new for 3 old shs. ■

Caba Uranium Ltd. (B.C. 1954)
May 1958 – Charter cancelled.

Cabala Yellowknife Mines Ltd. (Ont. 1945)
1947 – Sold assets to Aurlando Consolidated Mining Corp. Ltd.; basis 1 new for 5 old shs. (see Aurlando Consolidated Mining Corp. Ltd.)

Cabanga Developments Ltd. (Ont. Aug. 20, 1945)
June 1958 – Name changed to Palliser Petroleums Limited. ■

Cabano Expéditex Incorporated (Que. Apr. 30, 1985)
Aug. 23, 1991 – Name changed to Cabano Transportation Group Inc. ■

Cabano Kingsway Inc. (Que. Apr. 30, 1985)
Apr. 29, 1999 – Name changed to TransForce Inc. ■

Cabano Transportation Group Inc. (Que. Apr. 30, 1985)
Jan. 26, 1996 – Name changed to Cabano Kingsway Inc. ■

Cabernet Capital Corp. (B.C. Mar. 24, 2017)
Sept. 7, 2018 – Name changed to Auralite Investments Inc. following Qualifying Transaction acquisition of a 5% interest in EVVO Labs Pte. Ltd. and convertible bonds of Fourth-Link Inc. ■

Cable Hydrocarbons Inc. (Alta. Sept. 12, 1985)
Dec. 23, 1986 – Name changed to Monte Carlo Gold Mines Ltd. ■

Cable Mines & Oils Ltd. (Que. 1950)
1967 – Merged into St. Fabien Copper Mines Ltd.

Cable Satisfaction International Inc. (Can. Dec. 28, 1978)
Dec. 18, 2003 – Filed for protection under the Companies' Creditors Arrangement Act. RSM Richter Inc. appointed monitor and interim receiver.
Aug. 1, 2006 – All o/s shs. cancelled and newly created com. shs. issued to Catalyst Fund Limited Partnership I (42% interest), rights to purchase com. shs. issued to creditors (28% interest) and com. shs. issued to creditors (30% interest) in full satisfaction of their claim against the company. Sale of wholly owned Cabovisão-Televasão por Cabo, S.A. to Cogeco Cable Inc. was completed. Net proceeds from the sale and reorganization was estimated at €20,000,000.
Sept. 22, 2006 – Distrib. was made to shldrs.
Sept. 26, 2007 – RSM Richter Inc. discharged as monitor and interim receiver.
July 16, 2011 – Dissolved.

Cablecasting Limited (Ont. 1969)
Mar. 1978 – All o/s pref. shs. not held by directors were redeemed at $9.00 per share and the company became private.

Cableshare Inc. (Ont. 1973)
Jan. 24, 1997 – Acquired by Source Media, Inc.; basis 1 Source Media sh. for 5.0156 Cableshare shs.

Cableshare Limited (Ont. 1973)
Dec. 18, 1981 – Name changed to Cableshare Inc. ■

Cabletel Communications Corp. (Ont. Oct. 19, 1985)
May 18, 2004 – Wound up following sale of last remaining operating business with distributions to secured creditors. There were no funds available for shldrs.

Cablevision Nationale Ltée (B.C. 1965)
1975 – Continued into Quebec.
Sept. 1984 – Name changed to Cablevision Vidéotron Ltée. ■

Cablevision Vidéotron Ltée (Que. 1975)
Sept. 1985 – Amalgamated with Vidéotron Ltée to form a new co. also know as Vidéotron Ltée.

Cabo Exploration Ventures Inc. (Yuk. Feb. 1, 1996)
July 8, 1998 – Name changed to Cabo Mining Corp.; basis 1 new for 5 old shs. ■

Cabo Mining Corp. (Yuk. Feb. 1, 1996)
Jan. 5, 2004 – Name changed to Cabo Mining Enterprises Corp.; basis 1 new for 5 old shs. ■

Cabo Mining Enterprises Corp. (Yuk. Feb. 1, 1996)
Jan. 12, 2006 – Name changed to Cabo Drilling Corp. (see FPsurvey - Mines & Energy)

Cabo Ventures Inc. (B.C. Feb. 7, 1984)
Feb. 1, 1996 – Name changed to Cabo Exploration Ventures Inc. and continued into Yukon. ■

Cabol Enterprises Ltd. (Ont. 1951)
July 1976 – Charter cancelled; no details of settlement.

Cabot Capital Corporation (Ont. 1987)
May 1991 – Acquired by Manulift Financial Holdings Limited for $3.60 per com. sh., $25 per pref. sh., $1.41 per 1993 wt. and $1.10 per 1995 wt.

Cabot Resources Corp. (B.C. 1986)
Aug. 16, 1993 – Amalgamated with Quinterra Resources Inc. (0.75 new for 1 old sh.) and the Emtech Group Ltd.

to form a new co. known as Emtech Technology Corporation; basis 1 new for 1 old sh. (see Emtech Technology Corporation)

Cabot Yellowknife Gold Mines Ltd. (Ont. 1945)
Sept. 1957 – Charter cancelled.

Cabre Capital Corp. (B.C. May 18, 2010)
June 6, 2011 – Name changed to Northcliff Resources Ltd. pursuant to Qualifying Transaction reverse takeover acquisition of (old) Northcliff Resources Ltd. and subsequent amalgamation of old Northcliff with a wholly owned subsid.; basis 1 new for 5 old shs. (see FPsurvey - Mines & Energy)

Cabre Exploration Ltd. (B.C. Sept. 16, 1980)
Jan. 1985 – Continued into Alberta. (see EnerMark Income Fund)
Jan. 10, 2001 – Acquired by EnerMark Income Fund; basis 3.25 EnerMark trust units plus 1 EnerMark warrant for 1 Cabre sh. (see EnerMark Income Fund)

Cabrillo Capital Corporation (Alta. Jan. 18, 1996)
Oct. 2, 1998 – Name changed to Indico Technologies Corporation following acquisition of Edge Medical, Inc. ■

Cache Bay (Chibougamau) Mines Ltd. (Que.)
1956 – Charter cancelled; distribution to shldrs. reported made of vendor shs. in Obalski (1945) Ltd.; basis 1 sh. Obalski for 5 shs. Cache Bay. (see Obalski (1945) Ltd.)

Cache d'Or Gold Mines Ltd. (Ont. 1937)
1957 – Charter cancelled.

Cache d'Or Resources Inc. (B.C. Jan. 31, 1980)
Dec. 29, 1989 – Name changed to Consolidated Cache d'Or Resources Inc.; basis 1 new for 5 old shs. ■

Cache Exploration Inc. (B.C. Oct. 3, 2005)
Aug. 18, 2011 – Continued into Canada.
June 8, 2020 – Continued into British Columbia. (see FPsurvey - Mines & Energy)

Cache Explorations Inc. (Can. 1983)
Oct. 20, 1995 – Acquired by 3172694 Canada Inc., a wholly owned subsid. of MSV Resources Inc.; basis 1 MSV sh. for 4 Cache shs. (see MSV Resources Inc.)

Cachet Communications Inc. (Alta. Apr. 14, 1994)
June 1, 2000 – Struck from register and dissolved.

Cachet Enterprises Corp. (B.C. Sept. 19, 1990)
Apr. 2, 2004 – Name changed to Gold Star Resources Corp. ■

Cactus West Explorations Ltd. (B.C. May 11, 1983)
Apr. 29, 1996 – Name changed to Cimarron Minerals Ltd.; basis 1 new for 5 old shs. ■

Cadamet Mines Ltd. (Ont. 1958)
1966 – Name changed to Terrex Mining Co. Ltd.; basis 1 new for 5 old shs. ■

Cadan Resources Corporation (B.C. Aug. 28, 2007)
Oct. 7, 2016 – Name changed to Rizal Resources Corporation. (see FPsurvey - Mines & Energy)

Cade Struktur Corporation (Yuk. July 27, 2001)
Oct. 23, 2006 – Acquired by KHD Humboldt Wedag International Ltd.; basis 0.0029163 KHD shs. for 1 Cade sh. (see KHD Humboldt Wedag International Ltd.)

Caden Capital Corp. (B.C. Mar. 7, 2018)
Sept. 28, 2022 – Name changed to Zefiro Methane Corp. pursuant to the reverse takeover acquisition of Zefiro Methane Operations Corp. (see FPsurvey - Mines & Energy)

Cadence Energy Inc. (Alta. Dec. 14, 2004)
Nov. 12, 2008 – Name changed to Barrick Energy Inc. following acquisition by Barrick Gold Corporation for $6.75 per sh.

Cadet Resources Ltd. (B.C. 1973)
Oct. 1979 – Charter cancelled.

Cadilartic Mines Ltd. (Ont. 1944)
Nov. 1954 – Charter cancelled.

Cadillac Development Corporation Limited (Ont. 1953)
May 31, 1974 – Amalgamated with Canadian Equity & Development Corporation Ltd., Canadian Equity & Development Company Ltd., Fairview Corporation (Ontario) Limited and 3 other cos. to form Cadillac Fairview Corporation; basis 1.2 new for 1 Canadian Equity & Development Co. Ltd. sh., 1 new for 1 post-split Fairview Corporation of Canada Limited sh. (1.4-for-1 on a pre-split basis) and 1 new for 1 Cadillac Development sh. Fairview shs. continued to trade after a 1.4-for-1 split. The final step of the merger was effected Feb. 29, 1976, when Cadillac Fairview (Ontario charter) and Fairview Corporation of Canada Limited (Dominion charter) amalgamated to form Cadillac Fairview Corporation.

Cadillac Fairview Corporation (Ont. May 31, 1974 amalg.)
Oct. 31, 1988 – Acquired by JMB Institutional Realty Corp. effective Nov. 2, 1987, at $34 per sh. and $26.95 per wt. Following the October 1988 redemption of preference shs. at $10 and second preference shares at $10.70 per sh. (together with accrued dividends), the company was privatized. Subsequently, the company went public again on Nov. 6, 1997.

Cadillac Fairview Corporation (Ont. May 31, 1974 amalg.)
Mar. 28, 2000 – Succeeded by The Cadillac Fairview Corporation Limited following plan of arrangement acquisition by 1384183 Ontario Inc., a wholly owned subsid. of Ontario Teachers' Pension Plan Board, for $34 per sh. 1384183 Ontario Inc. subsequently changed its name to The Cadillac Fairview Corporation Limited.

Cadillac Gold Field Ltd. (Ont. 1945)
Charter cancelled; no record of equity.

Cadillac Mining Corporation (Ont. July 10, 2006)
2007 – Continued into British Columbia.
Sept. 2, 2014 – Acquired by Pilot Gold Inc.; basis 0.12195 Pilot units (1 common share & 1 warrant) for 1 Cadillac com. sh. Each wt. is exercisable to purchase 1 Pilot com. sh. at $2.00 for two years.

Cadillac Moly Mines Ltd. (Que. 1959)
Dec. 1973 – Became insolvent June 24, 1970; all assets sold by the trustee. Holders of 7% prior lien ser. A bds. due Dec. 30, 1973, received principal in full and approx. 80% of int. arrears; holders of 7% conv. income debs., due Dec. 30, 1978, received nothing. The obligation for the $23,686 housing mtge. was transferred to Little Long Lac Mines (now LAC Minerals Ltd.) which bought some of the property. Charter cancelled.

Cadington Resources Ltd. (Ont. May 11, 1987 amalg.)
Dec. 24, 1994 – Dissolved.
Apr. 4, 1996 – Revived.
Aug. 25, 1997 – Formed Icelandic Gold Corporation in New Brunswick on amalgamation with Icelandic Gold Corporation, constituting a reverse takeover by Icelandic; basis 1 new for 1 Icelandic sh. and 1 new for 6 Cadington shs. ■

Cadiscor Resources Inc. (Can. Mar. 6, 2006)
May 28, 2009 – Acquired by North American Palladium Ltd.; basis 0.33 North American Palladium shs. for 1 Cadiscor sh.
Mar. 4, 2011 – Name changed to NAP Quebec Mines Ltd. ■

Cadman Resources Inc. (B.C. Nov. 13, 2007)
Apr. 11, 2014 – Name changed to Matica Graphite Inc. ■

Cadomin Capital Corporation (Ont. Dec. 6, 2006)
Nov. 30, 2012 – Voluntarily dissolved.

Cadorna Resources Inc. (Alta. Apr. 7, 1999)
May 31, 2001 – Name changed to Innicor Subsurface Technologies Inc. following reverse takeover acquisition of and subsequent amalgamation with Innicor Subsurface Technologies Inc. ■

Cadre Resources Ltd. (B.C. Mar. 1, 1988)
June 19, 1995 – Continued into Canada.
July 16, 2011 – Dissolved.

Caelan Capital Inc. (B.C. Aug. 1, 1969)
Nov. 4, 2020 – Name changed to CDN Maverick Capital Corp.; basis 1 new for 2 old shs. (see FPsurvey - Mines & Energy)

Caen Yellowknife Mines Ltd. (Ont. 1944)
Jan. 10, 1945 – Name changed to Cassidy Yellowknife Mines Ltd. ■

Caerus Resource Corporation (B.C. Aug. 8, 1988 amalg.)
Oct. 4, 2012 – Name changed to Angel Gold Corp. ■

Caesar Minerals Ltd. (Ont. 1956)
Feb. 20, 1980 – Dissolved.

Caesar Silver Mines Ltd. (B.C. 1967)
Mar. 1976 – Amalgamated with Norex Resources Ltd.

Caesars Developments Ltd. (B.C. Aug. 28, 1969)
June 1972 – Name changed to Rio Sierra Developments Ltd. ■

Caesars Explorations Inc. (B.C. Jan. 24, 1983)
Nov. 4, 2002 – Name changed to Great Southern Enterprises Corp. ■

Caesars Gold Ltd. (B.C. Jan. 24, 1983)
Aug. 13, 1999 – Name changed to Caesars Explorations Inc.; basis 1 new for 2 old shs. ■

Cagim Real Estate Corporation (Can. July 15, 1998)
June 1, 2010 – Acquired by BTB Real Estate Investment Trust for $1.05 per cl. A sh.

Caimito Gold Mines Ltd. (Man. 1940)
Mar. 5, 1979 – Dissolved.

Caio Capital Corporation (Alta. Dec. 15, 1986)
Mar. 30, 1988 – Name changed to Battery One-Stop Inc. ■

Cairn Mines Ltd. (B.C. 1967)
Nov. 17, 1975 – Dissolved.

Cairn Petroleums Ltd. (Alta. 1974)
1981 – Acquired by Dynamar Energy Limited. (see Dynamar Energy Limited)

Cairnglen Explorations Ltd. (Ont. 1969)
May 14, 1975 – Charter cancelled.

Cairo Resources Inc. (B.C. Feb. 8, 2010)
Oct. 8, 2021 – Name changed to Gladiator Metals Corp. pursuant to the Qualifying Transaction acquisition of Bangles Gold Pty Ltd. (see FPsurvey - Mines & Energy)

Caisse centrale Desjardins (Que. June 22, 1979)
Jan. 1, 2017 – Amalgamated with the Fédération des caisses Desjardins du Québec.

La Caisse d'Economie de Notre-Dame de Québec (Can. 1872)
July 1944 – Name changed to La Banque d'Economie de Québec. ■

CaiTerra International Energy Corporation (B.C. July 27, 2009)
Oct. 1, 2015 – Continued into Alberta.
Jan. 2, 2024 – Struck from registry and dissolved.

Caiystane Capital Corporation (Alta. Jan. 13, 1988)
Oct. 6, 1992 – Name changed to Armada Financial Corporation. ■

Cajun Oil & Gas Producers Inc. (B.C. June 6, 1987)
Jan. 21, 1994 – Name changed to Alto Industries Inc.; basis 1 new for 6 old shs. ■

Cajun Oils Ltd. (Alta.)
1958 – Struck off register.

Cal-Can Mines Ltd. (B.C. 1968)
Dec. 1974 – Charter cancelled.

Cal-Dataline Corporation (Ont. July 20, 1977)
Feb. 24, 1984 – Name changed to Lansview Resource Corporation; basis 3 new for 1 old sh. ■

Cal-Denver Resources Ltd. (B.C. Sept. 8, 1966)
Oct. 13, 1987 – Name changed to Carson Gold Corp.; basis 1 new for 2 old shs. ■

Cal Dynamics Corp. (B.C. June 22, 1978)
July 31, 1984 – Name changed to Ridgecrest Resources Ltd.; basis 1 new for 5 old shs. ■

Cal Dynamics Energy Corp. (B.C. June 22, 1978)
Jan. 10, 1984 – Name changed to Cal Dynamics Corp. ■

Cal Graphite Corporation (Ont. July 11, 1985)
July 12, 1993 – Name changed to Applied Carbon Technology, Inc. ■

Cal-Por Gold Mines Ltd. (Ont. 1937)
Jan. 23, 1956 – Charter cancelled.

Cal-Star Inc. (Wyo. Jan. 29, 1999)
July 13, 2004 – Name changed to Amanta Resources Ltd. ■

Cal-West Petroleums Ltd. (Alta. Oct. 14, 1970)
May 15, 1985 – Name changed to Legacy Petroleum Ltd.; basis 1 new for 5 old shs. ■

Cal-Williston Petroleums Ltd. (Alta.)
Feb. 1954 – Acquired by Canadian Pipe Lines Producers Ltd. for 125,000 shs. (see Canadian Pipe Lines Producers Ltd.)

Calabogie Asbestos Mining Co. Ltd. (Ont. 1947)
Mar. 1976 – Charter cancelled.

Calahoo Petroleum Ltd. (Alta. May 27, 1993)
June 15, 2000 – Acquired by Samson Canada, Ltd., a wholly owned subsid. of Samson Investment Company, for $2.90 per sh.

Calais Group Inc. (Alta. Sept. 30, 1998)
Jan. 10, 2000 – Name changed to Airline Training International Ltd. ■

Calais Resources Inc. (B.C. Dec. 30, 1986)
Oct. 9, 2019 – Name changed to Blackbear Natural Resources Ltd. (see FPsurvey - Mines & Energy)

Calais Resources Ltd. (Alta. 1980)
June 1985 – Acquired by Financial Trustco Capital Ltd. for 45¢ and 0.45 Financial Trustco first pref. shs. for 1 Calais sh.

Calalta Petroleums Ltd. (Alta. 1948)
1963 – Assets acquired by Plains Petroleums Ltd.

Calavan Gold Mines Ltd. (B.C. 1946)
Assets sold to Privateer Mines Ltd.; basis 1 new for 6 old shs. (see Privateer Mine Limited)

Calaveras Explorations Ltd. (B.C. Mar. 31, 1980)
Feb. 18, 1986 – Name changed to Cardinal Mineral Corporation Ltd.; basis 1 new for 2.5 old shs. ■

Calaveras Resource Corp. (B.C. Mar. 10, 2017)
Feb. 12, 2018 – Voluntarily delisted. (see FPsurvey - Mines & Energy)

Calcana Oil Co. Ltd. (Alta. 1951)
Aug. 31, 1981 – Struck off register.

Calcar Development Inc. (Ont. 1972)
Nov. 5, 1976 – Amalgamated with 7 other cos. to form Wolverine Developments Inc.

Calco Resources Inc. (B.C. Mar. 8, 1978)
Feb. 19, 1997 – Name changed to Berkshire International Mining Ltd.; basis 1 new for 10 old shs. ■

Calcorp Resources Limited (B.C. 1967)
Jan. 31, 1977 – Dissolved.

Caldas Gold Corp. (Yuk. June 12, 1997)
Feb. 8, 2021 – Name changed to Aris Gold Corporation. ■

Calder-Bousquet Gold Mines Ltd. (Ont. 1934)
1954 – Merged into Pardee Amalgamated Mines Ltd.; basis 1 new for 5 old shs.

Caldera Environmental Corporation (B.C. 1988)
Aug. 16, 1994 – Continued into Yukon.
June 26, 1996 – Name changed to Caldera Technologies Corporation; basis 1 new for 10 old shs. (see FPsurvey - Industrials)

Caldera Mines Limited (B.C. 1984)
Apr. 30, 1987 – Name changed to MTC Electronic Technologies Co. Ltd. ■

Caldera Resources Inc. (Que. June 10, 1950)
June 20, 2017 – Deleted from registry.

Caldera Resources Ltd. (B.C. 1988)
Dec. 2, 1992 – Name changed to Caldera Environmental Corporation. ■

Calderone Corporation (Ont. May 27, 1983)
July 19, 2000 – Name changed to Cardinal Factor Corp. following reverse takeover acquisition of Cardinal Factor Inc. ■

Caldwell Linen Mills Limited (Ont. 1923)
1956 – Acquired by Dominion Textile Ltd., through offer to buy 2nd pref. and com. shs. for $17.50 per sh.

Caldwell U.S. Dividend Advantage Fund (Ont. Apr. 29, 2015)
Nov. 5, 2018 – Converted to an open-ended mutual fund.

Caledon Mountain Estates Ltd. (Ont. 1969 amalg.)
Jan. 1974 – S. B. McLaughlin Associates Ltd. acquired 98% of o/s com. shs., 100% of o/s warrants and $843,500 principal amt. of debs. out of a total $883,000; basis 28 McLaughlin shs. for ea. 100 Caledon shs., $1.00 for each warr. and 7% McLaughlin 1989 debs. exchanged for Caledon debs. On this date the co. and a wholly owned subsid. of McLaughlin were amalgamated to form Caledon Mountain Recreational Properties Ltd.; the remaining 6,800 publicly held com. shs. were converted into new 1st pref. shs., and com. shs. held by McLaughlin were converted into new 2nd pref. shs. (both 6% cum. non-voting redeem.) both on 1-for-1 basis; warrants became new com. shs. on a 1-for-1 basis; and debentures, formerly convertible into old com. shs. at $6.00 were made convertible into 1st pfce. shs. of the new co. at $6.00 per sh.

Caledonia Mines Ltd. (B.C. 1958)
Nov. 1968 – Struck off register.

Caledonia Mining Corporation (B.C. Feb. 5, 1992)
Mar. 29, 1995 – Continued into Canada.
Mar. 21, 2016 – Name changed to Caledonia Mining Corporation Plc and continued into Jersey.

Caledonia Resource Ltd. (B.C. Feb. 15, 1967)
Feb. 3, 1988 – Name changed to Aston Resources Ltd. ■

Caledonian Collieries Ltd. (Alta. 1919)
Aug. 15, 1931 – Struck off register.

Caledonian Pacific Minerals N.L. (Australia Aug. 16, 1993)
July 27, 2000 – Name changed to Quadtel Limited.

Calex Resources Limited (Ont. 1959)
Mar. 17, 1969 – Name changed to Pango Gold Mines Ltd. ■

Calex Resources Ltd. (Alta. Oct. 18, 1989)
Oct. 25, 1994 – Amalgamated with Beau Canada Exploration Ltd.; basis 0.5132 new for 1 old sh. (see Beau Canada Exploration Ltd.)

Calfrac Well Services Ltd. (Alta. Mar. 24, 2004 amalg.)
Dec. 18, 2020 – Continued into Canada. (see FPsurvey - Mines & Energy; FPsurvey - Industrials)

Calgary Alberta Oil Co. Ltd. (unknown)
1914 – Acquired by Alberta Petroleum Consolidated Ltd.; basis 3 new for 1 old sh. (see Alberta Petroleum Consolidated Ltd.)

Calgary & Edmonton Corporation Limited (Can. 1929)
Jan. 1968 – Acquired by Canadian Superior Oil Ltd.; basis 1.16 new for 1 old sh. (see Canadian Superior Oil Ltd.)

Calgary Cable TV Limited (Alta. 1970)
Jan. 1, 1977 – Minority shldr. int. acquired by Cablecasting Limited, for total consideration of $2,518,161.

Calgary Centre Holdings Ltd. (Alta. 1985)
July 20, 1992 – All o/s 8.125% cum. red. retract. first pref. shs. ser. 1 redeemed; basis $25 per sh. plus all accrued and unpaid preferential dividends.

Calgary Collieries Ltd. (Alta.)
Feb. 29, 1932 – Struck off register.

Calgary Petroleum Products Co., Ltd. (unknown)
1921 – Taken over by Royalite Oil Company, Limited; basis one $25 Royalite sh. for 116.25 shs. Calgary Petrol. (see Royalite Oil Company, Limited)

Calgary Power Ltd. (Can. May 12, 1947)
June 1, 1981 – Name changed to TransAlta Utilities Corporation. ■

Calgroup Graphics Corporation Ltd. (Ont. 1968)
Apr. 27, 1992 – Charter cancelled.

Calian Technologies Ltd. (Can. Sept. 27, 1982)
Apr. 1, 2016 – Name changed to Calian Group Ltd. (see FPsurvey - Industrials)

Calian Technology Ltd. (Can. Sept. 27, 1982)
Mar. 28, 2005 – Name changed to Calian Technologies Ltd. ■

Calibre Energy Inc. (Alta. July 29, 1988)
Dec. 15, 1999 – Following Plan of Arrangement under Companies Creditors Arrangement Act, Northridge Canada (1998) Inc., the senior secured lender, purchased all properties and assets including subsid. Trego Energy Inc. for consideration sufficient to repay other creditors. Distribution to Calibre shldrs. was 1 Trego cl. B com. sh. for 56 old Calibre shs.

Calibre Mining Corp. (B.C. Jan. 15, 1969)
June 19, 2025 – Acquired by Equinox Gold Corp.; basis 0.35 Equinox shs. for 1 Calibre Mining sh.

Calibre Technologies Corporation (B.C. Oct. 23, 1986)
Dec. 10, 1996 – Delisted from the Vancouver Stock Exchange. Subsequently struck from register and dissolved.

Calico Resources Corp. (B.C. June 17, 1998)
July 8, 2016 – Acquired by Paramount Gold Nevada Corp.; basis 0.07 Paramount com. shs. for 1 Calico com. sh.

Calico Silver Mines Ltd. (B.C. Jan. 10, 1962)
Feb. 6, 1980 – Name changed to Sable Resources Ltd.; basis 1 new for 5 old shs. (see FPsurvey - Mines & Energy)

Caliente Capital Corp. (B.C. July 7, 1999)
Mar. 13, 2003 – Formed Webtech Wireless Inc. in Alberta following Qualifying Transaction amalgamation with (old) WebTech Wireless Inc., constituting a reverse takeover by WebTech; basis 1 new for 1 old sh. of each co. except for 12,500,000 WebTech cl. A shs. which were exchanged on a 1-for-1.19 basis. ■

Caliente Resources Ltd. (B.C. 1984)
Oct. 9, 1992 – Dissolved and struck off register.

Califfi Capital Corp. (B.C. Nov. 24, 2016)
Aug. 5, 2021 – Name changed to Bonanza Mining Corporation. (see FPsurvey - Industrials)

California Exploration Ltd. (Yuk. Sept. 25, 2001)
June 3, 2004 – Name changed to Baradero Resources Limited; basis 1 new for 4 old shs. ■

California Gold Mines Inc. (B.C. Feb. 25, 1983)
Mar. 5, 1993 – Delisted from the Vancouver Stock Exchange. Subsequently dissolved and struck from registry.

California Gold Mines Ltd. (B.C. 1969)
June 6, 1988 – Amalgamated with Centurion Minerals Ltd. to form Centurion Gold Ltd.; basis 1 new for 4 old shs.

California Gold Mining Inc. (Alta. Sept. 17, 1998)
June 3, 2016 – Continued into Ontario. (see Stratabound Minerals Corp.)
Aug. 17, 2021 – Acquired by Stratabound Minerals Corp.; basis 1 Stratabound sh. for 1 California Gold sh. (see Stratabound Minerals Corp.)

California Lake Mines Ltd. (N.B.)
1966 – Charter cancelled.

California Nanotechnologies Corp. (Alta. Mar. 19, 2002)
Feb. 26, 2024 – Continued into Ontario. (see FPsurvey - Industrials)

California Silver Ltd. (B.C. 1969)
May 15, 1986 – Name changed to California Gold Mines Ltd. ■

California Yellowknife Gold Mines Ltd. (Ont. 1945)
1954 – Charter cancelled.

Caliph Petroleums Limited (B.C. 1953)
Jan. 1956 – Name changed to Peace River Petroleums Ltd. ■

Calivada Resources Limited (B.C. May 9, 1967)
Dec. 18, 1978 – Dissolved.
Mar. 1979 – Revived.
June 25, 1979 – Name changed to Heritage Petroleums Inc.; basis 1 new for 3 old shs. ■

Calix Gold Mines Ltd. (B.C. 1963)
1966 – Name changed to Calix Mines Ltd. ■

Calix Mines Ltd. (B.C. 1963)
Aug. 3, 1972 – Name changed to Bev-Cal Mines Ltd.; basis 1 new for 8 old shs. ■

Call Genie Inc. (Alta. Aug. 17, 2004 amalg.)
Jan. 9, 2012 – Name changed to VoodooVox Inc. pursuant to acquisition of the assets of VoodooVox, Inc. ■

Call-Goma Uranium Mines Ltd. (Ont. 1955)
Mar. 1958 – Charter cancelled.

Call-Net Enterprises Inc. (Can. Jan. 13, 1986)
July 8, 2005 – Formed Rogers Telecom Holdings Inc. pursuant to plan of arrangement acquisition by Rogers Communications Inc.; basis 1 Rogers cl. B non-vtg. sh. for 4.25 Call-Net cl. B non-vtg. shs.

Call 900 Inc. (Alta. Nov. 26, 1987)
Aug. 3, 1995 – Name changed to Xentel Interactive Inc. ■

CallDirect Capital Corp. (Alta. Nov. 22, 1996)
May 23, 2000 – Name changed to Ocean Ventures Inc.; basis 1 new for 5 old shs. ■

Callex Enterprises Ltd. (B.C. July 14, 1982)
Oct. 6, 1988 – Name changed to Shephard Insurance Group Limited. ■

Callex Mineral Explorations Ltd. (B.C. July 14, 1982)
Oct. 29, 1985 – Name changed to Callex Enterprises Ltd. ■

Callidus Capital Corporation (Ont. Oct. 3, 2003)
Nov. 7, 2019 – All o/s com. shs. not already held acquired by Braslyn Ltd, excluding shs. held by certain investment funds managed by The Catalyst Group Inc., FigCorp Ltd., and James Riley; basis 75¢ cash per sh.

Callinan Flin-Flon Mines Ltd. (Man. May 6, 1927)
1956 – Name changed to Consolidated Callinan Flin Flon Mines Limited; basis 1 new for 2 old shs. ■

Callinan Mines Limited (Can. June 23, 1980)
July 14, 2011 – Name changed to Callinan Royalties Corporation. ■

Callinan Royalties Corporation (Can. June 23, 1980)
May 8, 2014 – Acquired by Altius Minerals Corporation; basis 0.163 Altius com. shs. plus $0.203 cash for 1 Callinan com. sh.

Calling Valley Oils Limited (Alta.)
1970 – Merged into Westburne Petroleum & Minerals Ltd.

Calliope Metals Corporation (Can. Sept. 24, 1987)
June 17, 1997 – Continued into Yukon.
May 7, 1999 – Name changed to Argosy Minerals Inc. following reverse takeover acquisition of Argosy Mining Corp. for 57,183,960 com. shs. ■

Callisto Resources Ltd. (Alta. June 3, 1993)
Feb. 5, 1997 – Amalgamated with 711960 Alberta Ltd., a wholly owned subsid. of Alma Oil & Gas Ltd.; basis 1 cl. A sh. of Alma for 6 com. shs. of Callisto. (see Alma Oil & Gas Ltd.)

Callitas Health Inc. (Alta. Nov. 26, 2014)
Dec. 9, 2021 – Delisted from the CSE. Subsequently stuck from registry and dissolved.

Calloway Properties Inc. (Alta. Dec. 20, 1996)
Feb. 18, 2004 – Plan of Arrangement to convert company into an investment trust named Calloway Real Estate Investment Trust; basis 1 new trust unit for 2 com. shs. (see Calloway Real Estate Investment Trust)

Calloway Real Estate Investment Trust (Alta. Dec. 4, 2001)
May 28, 2015 – Name changed to Smart Real Estate Investment Trust following acquisition of 22 SmartCentres retail properties and related intellectual property. ■

Calmar West Oils Ltd. (Alta. 1948)
June 1965 – Name changed to Brett Oils Ltd.; basis 1 new for 4 old shs. ■

Calmark Explorations Ltd. (B.C. 1968)
1969 – Name changed to Calmark Industries Limited. ■

Calmark Industries Limited (B.C. 1968)
July 1972 – Name changed to Metrosposal Industries Limited; basis 1 new for 5 old shs.

Calmena Energy Services Inc. (Alta. Oct. 14, 2008)
Jan. 21, 2015 – Placed into receivership by senior lender. Ernst & Young Inc. appointed receiver.
May 2015 – Assets in the U.S. sold for $1,600,000.
Oct. 2015 – Assets in Mexico sold for $5,800,000.
Dec. 2015 – Interim distrib. made to secured lender, HSBC Bank Canada, of $6,500,000. Monies collected from the sale of assets insufficient to repay debt owed to secured and unsecured lenders or for distrib. to shldrs.
Jan. 2, 2017 – Struck from registry and dissolved.
Feb. 2017 – Ernst & Young discharged as receiver in the Chapter 15 proceedings in the U.S.

Calmont Oils Limited (Can. Mar. 15, 1926)
Sept. 1953 – Assets acquired by Anglo-Canadian Oil Company Limited; basis 1 new for 42 old shs. (see Anglo-Canadian Oil Company Limited)

Calmor Iron Bay Mines Limited (Ont. 1954)
Dec. 31, 1978 – International Mogul Mines Limited acquired remaining o/s shs. not already held through merger of Calmor with International Mogul Mines (Ontario) Ltd., forming Calmor Iron Bay Mines (1978) Ltd. effective Dec. 1, 1978. Calmor shldrs. received a choice of com.

shs. of the amalg. co. to Nov. 29, 1978, or thereafter pref. shs. The pref. shs. were all called for redemption at $1.13 per sh.

Calmor Mines Ltd. (Ont. 1945)
1962 – Assets distributed on basis of 448 shs. Iron Bay Mines for each 1,000 shs. Calmor, plus 9¢ cash for each Calmor sh. Assets not claimed transferred to the Public Trustee, and charter surrendered.

Calneva Resources Ltd. (B.C. Jan. 19, 1987)
Sept. 1, 1994 – Name changed to International Calneva Gold Corp.; basis 1 new for 5 old shs. ■

Calnor Resources Ltd. (B.C. Dec. 2, 1935)
Aug. 23, 1991 – Name changed to Norcal Resources Ltd.; basis 1 new for 3 old shs. ■

Calnorth Oils Ltd. (Alta. 1947)
July 1956 – Name changed to Northcal Oils Ltd.; basis 1 new for 4 old shs. ■

Calode Uranium Mining Co. Ltd. (Ont. 1954)
Sept. 1961 – Charter cancelled.

Calona Wines Limited (unknown)
1971 – Acquired by Standard Brands (B.C.) Ltd. in 1971-72 for $8.00 per sh.

Calor Laterite Corporation (B.C. 1979)
Sept. 16, 1982 – Name changed to Interstrat Resources Inc. ■

Calotto Capital Inc. (Ont. Feb. 19, 2007)
Oct. 28, 2009 – Name changed to Hamilton Thorne Ltd. pursuant to Qualifyinig Transaction reverse takeover acquisition of Hamilton Thorne, Inc.; basis 1 new for 7.712255 old shs. ■

Calpetro Resources Inc. (B.C. Jan. 8, 1980)
July 18, 1984 – Name changed to Nucal Resources Ltd.; basis 1 new for 5 old shs. ■

Calpine Canada Holdings Ltd. (Alta. Feb. 21, 2001)
May 27, 2002 – Called for automatic early redemption; basis 1 new Calpine Corporation com. sh. exchanged for 1 old Calpine Canada exchangeable sh. Common shs. of Calpine Corporation listed on NYSE.

Calpine Natural Gas Trust (Alta. Aug. 22, 2003)
Feb. 2, 2005 – Amalgamated with Viking Energy Royalty Trust; basis 2 new Viking units for 1 old Calpine unit. (see Viking Energy Royalty Trust)

Calpine Power Income Fund (Alta. July 16, 2002)
Feb. 14, 2007 – Acquired by Harbinger Capital Partners Special Situations Fund L.P. and Harbinger Capital Partners Master Fund I, Ltd.; basis $13 per unit

Calpine Resources Incorporated (B.C. 1983)
Apr. 12, 1990 – Merged with Prime Resources Group Inc. to become a wholly owned subsid.; basis 1 new sh. and 0.5 wts. for 1 old sh. Each wt. and $5.25 entitled holder to purchase 1 new sh. of merged co. until Apr. 12, 1991. (see Prime Resources Group Inc.)

Calstar Oil & Gas Ltd. (Alta. Apr. 23, 1998)
Oct. 2, 2017 – Struck from registry and dissolved.

Calta Mines Ltd. (B.C. 1966)
1973 – Merged with Coronet Mines Ltd. into Coralta Resources Ltd.; basis 1 new for 2 old shs.

Caltec Investments Inc. (Alta. Feb. 4, 1987)
Aug. 8, 1997 – Struck off register.

Caltech Data Ltd. (B.C. Feb. 5, 1988 amalg.)
Sept. 14, 1994 – Name changed to Roraima Gold Corporation; basis 1 new for 2 old shs. ■

Calterra Freehold Ventures Inc. (Alta. Apr. 26, 1982)
June 29, 2006 – Name changed to West Africa Energy Inc. and continued into British Columbia following reverse takeover acquisition of Mali Oil Development S.A.R.L. plus all rights to one hydrocarbon exploration licence and one right to a licence in approval, all located in

southeastern Mali, West Africa; basis 1 West Africa sh. for 2 Calterra shs. ■

Calterra Resources Ltd. (Alta. Apr. 26, 1982)
Apr. 24, 2001 – Name changed to Calterra Freehold Ventures Inc. ■

Calto Industries Inc. (Alta. 1986)
Oct. 2, 2000 – Struck from registry.

Calto Resources Inc. (Alta. 1986)
Dec. 28, 1988 – Name changed to Calto Industries Inc. ■

Caltor Petroleums Ltd. (unknown)
July 2, 1979 – Acquired by Canadian Long Island Petroleums Ltd. (see Canadian Long Island Petroleums Ltd.)

Calumet Uranium Mines Ltd. (Que. 1953)
Jan. 1965 – Name changed to Atlanta Mines Ltd.; basis 1 new for 5 old shs. ■

Calvada Resources Inc. (B.C. 1986)
May 1, 1990 – Amalgamated with Consolidated Powergem Resource Corporation and Tamavack Resources Inc. to form Eurus Resource Corp.; basis 1 new for 7.5 old shs. (see Eurus Resource Corp.)

Calvalley Petroleum Inc. (Can. Dec. 1, 1995 amalg.)
Aug. 21, 1996 – Amalgamated with O.R.I. Energy Inc. (0.6886 new cl. A sh. for 1 cl. A sh.) to form a new co. also known as Calvalley Petroleum Inc.; basis 0.25 new cl. A sh. for 1 com. sh. (see Calvalley Petroleum Inc.)

Calvalley Petroleum Inc. (Can. July 1, 1996 amalg.)
May 12, 2015 – Dissolved pursuant to the plan of arrangement with Calvalley Energy Limited; basis either (i) US$0.807, (ii) 1 Calvalley Energy com. sh. or (iii) combination of thereof per Calvalley Petroleum sh.

Calvan Consolidated Oil & Gas Co. Ltd. (Can. 1951)
1961 – Assets sold to Canadian Fina Oil Ltd.; basis $4.59 per sh. for min. holdings and $2.89 for majority holdings (latter held by Canadian Petrofina Ltd.).

Calvan Petroleums Ltd. (Alta. 1948)
1951 – Acquired by Calvan Consolidated Oil & Gas Co. Ltd.

Calvert-Dale Estates Ltd. (Ont. Oct. 20, 1961)
June 2, 1983 – Name changed to Argyll Energy Corporation. ■

Calvert Gas & Oils Limited (Can. Feb. 14, 1928)
Aug. 8, 1985 – Name changed to Heenan Petroleum Limited; basis 1 new for 5 old shs. ■

Calvert Porcupine Mines Ltd. (Ont. June 12, 1936)
Charter cancelled.

Calvin Exploration & Development Corporation (Que. 1954)
Aug. 21, 1974 – Acquired by Calvin Oil Co. Ltd. (see Calvin Oil Co. Ltd.)

Calvin Oil Co. Ltd. (Alta.)
Mar. 15, 1977 – Dissolved.

Calvista Gold Corporation (Ont. Jan. 8, 2010)
Dec. 13, 2012 – Acquired by AUX Acquisition 3 S.A.R.L. for $1.10 per sh.

Calway Brook Mines Inc. (Ont. 1971)
Feb. 20, 1980 – Dissolved.

Calypso Acquisition Corp. (B.C. Dec. 1, 1967)
Sept. 21, 2007 – Name changed to Calypso Uranium Corp. ■

Calypso Developments Ltd. (B.C. Dec. 1, 1967)
Nov. 18, 2002 – Name changed to Calypso Acquisition Corp.; basis 1 new for 10 old shs. ■

Calypso Food & Beverage Co. Ltd. (Ont. 1960)
Oct. 2, 1962 – Name changed to Grissol Foods Limited. ■

Calypso Uranium Corp. (B.C. Dec. 1, 1967)
May 15, 2013 – Acquired by U308 Corp.; basis 0.4 U308 shs. for 1 Calypso sh. (see U3O8 Corp.)

Calyx Bio-Ventures Inc. (B.C. June 10, 2008)
Feb. 5, 2018 – Name changed to Calyx Ventures Inc. (see FPsurvey - Industrials)

Calyx Growth Corporation (B.C. Dec. 11, 2015)
Mar. 25, 2019 – Name changed to Vapen MJ Ventures Corporation. ■

Cam-Net Communications Network Inc. (B.C. Jan. 29, 1982)
Feb. 1, 1991 – Continued into Canada.
Nov. 24, 1997 – Name changed to Suncom Telecommunications Inc. ■

Camabie Mines Ltd. (Ont. 1943)
Nov. 28, 1973 – Dissolved.

Camador Mining & Exploration Co. Ltd. (Que. 1962)
Feb. 1980 – Charter cancelled.

Caman Gold Mines Ltd. (Ont. 1945)
1954 – Merged with other mining cos. to form Garrison Creek Consolidated Mines Ltd.; basis 1 new for 15 old shs.

Camarillo Oils Limited (Ont. 1952)
Feb. 11, 1971 – Charter cancelled.

Camas Resources Ltd. (B.C. Jan. 9, 1987)
Jan. 17, 1991 – Name changed to Merlin Resources Inc. ■

Camber Sports Inc. (Alta. Oct. 14, 1987)
Mar. 24, 1993 – Name changed to Zycom Corporation; basis 1 new for 3 old shs. ■

Camberly Energy Ltd. (Alta. Feb. 21, 1992)
Aug. 2, 2010 – Dissolved and struck from the registry.

Camberton Iron Explorations Ltd. (Ont. 1952)
Feb. 20, 1980 – Dissolved.

Cambiex Exploration Inc. (Que. Feb. 21, 1993)
July 17, 2000 – Name changed to Hope Bay Gold Corporation Inc. ■

Cambior Inc. (Que. Nov. 7, 1973)
Nov. 8, 2006 – Acquired by IAMGOLD Corporation; basis 0.42 IAMGOLD shs. for 1 Cambior sh.

Camborne Industries Ltd. (B.C. 1987)
July 19, 1990 – Name changed to Camborne Industries PLC and continued into United Kingdom; basis 1 new sh. plus £0.50 for 1 old sh. ■

Camborne Resources Ltd. (B.C. 1987)
May 23, 1989 – Name changed to Camborne Industries Ltd. ■

Cambri Mining & Development Ltd. (B.C.)
Sept. 1968 – Struck off register.

Cambria Gold Mines Ltd. (B.C. 1928)
1946 – In liquidation.
Jan. 2, 1964 – Dissolved.

Cambria Resources Limited (B.C. May 23, 1986)
Mar. 2, 1989 – Name changed to On Wah Investments Corp. ■

Cambrian Explorations Ltd. (B.C. 1968)
Dec. 18, 1978 – Dissolved.

Cambrian Mining Limited (B.C.)
July 2, 1954 – Dissolved and struck off register.

Cambridge BioChemics Inc. (B.C. Mar. 20, 1978)
June 23, 1993 – Name changed to Cambridge Softek Inc. ■

Cambridge Colleges Inc. (Alta. Jan. 25, 1996)
June 2, 2001 – Struck from registry and dissolved.

Cambridge Colleges Ltd. (Alta. Jan. 25, 1996)
Feb. 8, 1999 – Name changed to Cambridge Colleges Inc. ■

Cambridge Development Corporation (B.C. Mar. 18, 1981)
Oct. 28, 1983 – Name changed to Bridgewest Development Corporation. ■

Cambridge Environmental Systems Inc. (B.C. June 15, 1966)
Dec. 9, 1993 – Continued into Alberta.
Dec. 2, 2010 – Struck from registry and dissolved.

Cambridge Leaseholds Limited (Ont. 1960)
Sept. 19, 1975 – By July 15, 1975, Oxford Development Group Ltd. had acquired most of all o/s com. shs. for $22 per sh. Shs. were delisted as Oxford had acquired all but a small amount.

Cambridge Minerals Ltd. (Alta. Dec. 29, 1993)
July 28, 1999 – Name changed to Cambridge Ventures Ltd. ■

Cambridge Mines, Ltd. (B.C. June 15, 1966)
Feb. 17, 1976 – Name changed to United Cambridge Mines Limited; basis 1 new for 5 old shs. ■

Cambridge Mining Corp. Ltd. (Ont. 1961)
May 1976 – Charter cancelled.

Cambridge Oil & Gas Ltd. (Alta. May 12, 1993)
Mar. 10, 1995 – Formed Riata Resources Ltd. in Alberta on amalgamation with Riata Resources Ltd. (1 for 1); basis 0.2 new for 1 old sh. ■

Cambridge Oil Co. (unknown)
May 6, 1952 – Assets acquired by Bailey Selburn Oil & Gas Ltd.; basis 46 cl. A shs. of Bailey for 1 Cambridge unit.

Cambridge Resources Ltd. (B.C. Mar. 23, 1988)
Dec. 2, 1991 – Name changed to Selkirk Springs International Corporation. ■

Cambridge Shopping Centres Limited (Ont. Dec. 29, 1975)
Dec. 15, 2000 – Acquired by Ivanhoe Inc. for $12.50 per sh.

Cambridge Softek Inc. (B.C. Mar. 20, 1978)
Nov. 21, 1994 – Name changed to Alantra Venture Corp.; basis 1 new for 5 old shs. ■

Cambridge Ventures Corporation (Alta. June 5, 1986)
Oct. 18, 1989 – Name changed to Cartaway Container Corporation; basis 1 new for 3 old shs. ■

Cambridge Ventures Ltd. (Alta. Dec. 29, 1993)
Feb. 2, 2001 – Name changed to VRX WorldWide Inc. ■

Camco Inc. (Can. Dec. 6, 1976)
Oct. 4, 2005 – Formed Mabe Canada Inc. following acquisition by Mexico-based Controladora Mabe S.A. de C.V.; basis Cdn$3.52 per sh.

Camdeck Gold Mines Ltd. (Ont. 1944)
1954 – Name changed to Camdeck Mines Ltd. ■

Camdeck Mines Ltd. (Ont. 1944)
July 27, 1976 – Charter cancelled.

Camden Oil Corporation (B.C. Jan. 31, 1980)
Dec. 2, 1992 – Name changed to Maxwell Resources Inc. ■

Camdev Corporation (Ont. Jan. 3, 1978 amalg.)
July 30, 1997 – Name changed to O&Y Properties Corporation. ■

Cameco - A Canadian Mining & Energy Corporation (Can. June 19, 1987)
Nov. 1, 1990 – Name changed to Cameco Corporation. (see FPsurvey - Mines & Energy; FPsurvey - Industrials)

Cameco Resources Ltd. (Can. 1988 amalg.)
Jan. 1, 1997 – Merged into Cameco Corporation.

Camel Oil & Gas Ltd. (Alta. 1979)
Oct. 28, 1985 – Merged into Trans-Canada Resources Ltd. Each 10 com. shs. of Camel exch. for one cl. A voting sh. of Trans-Canada. Also, all o/s 11% ser. A convert. debs. of Camel exch. into cl. A voting shs. of Trans-Canada; basis 222.22 shs. for each $1,000 principal amt.

Camelion Development Corp. (Alta. 1986)
Dec. 21, 1989 – Formed Great Northern Gold Inc. in Alberta on amalgamation with Great Northern Gold Inc.; basis 1 new for 1 Great Northern sh. and 1 new for 3 Camelion shs. ■

Camelot Industries Inc. (B.C. Mar. 12, 1980)
July 15, 1996 – Formed DC DiagnostiCare Inc. in British Columbia on amalgamation with DC DiagnostiCare Inc.; basis 1 new for 1 DC DiagnostiCare sh. and 1 new for 1.68 Camelot shs. ■

Cameo Cobalt Corp. (B.C. Mar. 3, 1987)
Apr. 26, 2019 – Name changed to Cameo Industries Corp. ■

Cameo Industries Corp. (B.C. Mar. 3, 1987)
Dec. 14, 2020 – Name changed to Metallica Metals Corp. ■

Cameo Mining Corporation Ltd. (B.C. May 3, 1966)
Aug. 24, 1966 – Name changed to Fury Explorations Ltd. ■

Cameo Resources Corp. (B.C. Mar. 3, 1987)
May 3, 2018 – Name changed to Cameo Cobalt Corp.; basis 3 new for 1 old sh. ■

Camerina Petroleum Corp. (Del. 1959)
1966 – Acquired by Western Equities, Inc. of Houston, Tex., for US$2.60 per sh.

Camero Developments Ltd. (B.C. 1946)
Aug. 23, 1982 – Dissolved.

Camero Resource Industries Ltd. (B.C. Aug. 2, 1966)
Sept. 30, 1982 – Name changed to International Camero Resources Ltd.; basis 1 new for 3 old shs. ■

Cameron Petroleums, Ltd. (Can. May 8, 1929)
Reported amalgamated with Atlantic Keystone Petroleums, Ltd.

Cameron Resources Ltd. (B.C. 1967)
Feb. 15, 1983 – Name changed to Jafta International Inc. ■

Cametin Industries Ltd. (B.C. 1967)
July 31, 1978 – Dissolved.

Camex Energy Corp. (B.C. Dec. 1, 1967)
Feb. 20, 2018 – Name changed to Desert Lion Energy Inc. and continued into Ontario pursuant to reverse takeover acquisition of Desert Lion Energy Corp. by way of a three-cornered amalgamation of Desert Lion and a wholly owned subsidiary of the company; basis 1 new for 12.0258 old shs. ■

Camex Mines Ltd. (Ont. 1947)
1963 – Assets sold to Braminco Mines Ltd. for $3,500 and 118,270 Braminco shs. Distribution of 1 Braminco sh. for each 10 Camex shs. held.
Aug. 25, 1966 – Dissolved.

Camex Prospecting Trust (unknown)
1947 – All assets transferred to Camex Mines Ltd. Basis of distribution: 500 shs. Braminco; 250 shs. Baltic; 2,000 shs. Lochabie Mines; 2,000 shs. Camabie Mines, and 2,640 shs. Camex Mines for each unit held. (see Camex Mines Ltd.)

Camflo International Inc. (Yuk. July 4, 2001)
Sept. 30, 2004 – Formed Arctos Petroleum Corp. in Alberta on amalgamation with Spearhead Resources Inc.

with Camflo the deemed acquiror; basis 1 new for 1 Spearhead sh. and 3 new for 4 Camflo shs. ■

Camflo Mattagami Mines Ltd. (Ont. 1958)
1966 – Name changed to Camflo Mines Limited. ■

Camflo Mines Limited (Ont. 1958)
July 14, 1984 – Amalgamated with Bob-Clare Investments Limited and Barrick Resources Corporation to continue as Barrick Resources; basis 7 new for 1 old sh. (see Barrick Resources Corporation)

Camflo Resources Ltd. (Alta. Mar. 21, 1997)
July 4, 2001 – Continued into Yukon.
Nov. 22, 2001 – Name changed to Camflo International Inc.; basis 1 new for 9 old shs. ■

Camford Capital Corporation (B.C. 1979)
Mar. 20, 1992 – Dissolved and struck off register.

Camfrey Resources Ltd. (B.C. Feb. 4, 1986)
Mar. 17, 1993 – Name changed to Brio Industries Inc.; basis 1 new for 2.5 old shs. ■

Camigos Mines Ltd. (B.C.)
Apr. 1975 – Charter cancelled.

Camindex Mines Limited (Ont. June 15, 1933)
Jan. 22, 1990 – Acquired by MVP Capital Corp.; basis 1 MVP sh. for 6.66 Camindex shs. (see MVP Capital Corp.)

Camine Resources Inc. (Alta. Sept. 22, 1983)
May 10, 1994 – Name changed to Beckett Technologies Corp. and continued into Ontario. ■

Caminex Corporation Limited (unknown)
1955 – Continued (jurisdiction unknown).
Dec. 1960 – Reported wound up and distribution of 84.3¢ per sh. made.

Camino Energy Corp. (B.C. Feb. 18, 1980)
Apr. 1, 1985 – Delisted from the Vancouver Stock Exchange. Subsequently dissolved and struck from register.

Camino Gold Mines Limited (Ont. Sept. 25, 1972)
Feb. 15, 1985 – CTO issued. Subsequently dissolved and charter cancelled.

Camino Resources Ltd. (B.C. Mar. 20, 1964)
Mar. 8, 1991 – Name changed to Advanced Projects Ltd.; basis 1 new for 4 old shs. ■

Camisha Resources Corp. (B.C. Oct. 1, 2009)
Apr. 19, 2013 – Name changed to Prima Fluorspar Corp. pursuant to reverse takeover acquisition of Prima Fluorspar Corp. ■

Camlachie Oils Exploration Ltd. (Ont. Aug. 3, 1945)
Jan. 1951 – Inactive.

Camlaren Mines Ltd. (Can. 1973)
June 30, 1987 – Name changed to Stamford Bancorp Inc.; basis 1 new for 3 old shs. ■

Camnor Resources Ltd. (B.C. Sept. 20, 1970)
Oct. 30, 2000 – Name changed to Stornoway Ventures Ltd.; basis 1 new for 8 old shs. ■

Camont Mining & Exploration Co. Ltd. (Que. 1956)
Dec. 5, 1981 – Charter cancelled.

Camoose Mines Ltd. (Ont. 1952)
May 1957 – Absorbed by subsidiary, Camoose Uranium Mines of America, Inc.

Camp McKinney Gold Mines Ltd. (B.C. 1959)
1962 – Name changed to McKinney Gold Mines Ltd. ■

Campaign Mining Co. Ltd. (Ont. 1971)
July 1973 – Merged into Sloane Mining Co. Ltd.; basis 1 new for 5 old shs.

Campar Capital Corporation (Ont. Aug. 20, 2014)
Oct. 18, 2016 – Merged into Starlight U.S. Multi-Family (No. 5) Core Fund; basis 0.138164 Starlight 5 cl. A unit for 1 Campar com. sh.

Campbell Chibougamau Mines Ltd. (B.C. June 7, 1950)
Sept. 2, 1980 – Name changed to Campbell Resources Inc. ■

Campbell Island Mines and Exploration Limited (Ont. Nov. 21, 1945)
Mar. 31, 1958 – Name changed to New Campbell Island Mines Limited; basis 1 new for 4 old shs. ■

Campbell Red Lake Mines Limited (Ont. July 18, 1944)
Aug. 12, 1987 – Continued into Canada. (see Placer Dome Inc.)
Aug. 13, 1987 – Amalgamated with Dome Mines Limited (0.851 for 1) and Placer Development Limited (1 for 1) to form a new company named Placer Dome Inc.; basis 1.702 new Placer shs. for 1 old Campbell sh. (see Placer Dome Inc.)

Campbell Resources Inc. (B.C. June 7, 1950)
Sept. 8, 1982 – Continued into Canada.
May 12, 1983 – Amalgamated with GM Resources Limited (1 for 5), United Asbestos Inc. (0.3 com. plus 1 pfce. for 1) and Camchib Resources Inc. (0.6 for 1) to continue as a new company also known as Campbell Resources Inc.; basis 1 com. for 1 old sh.
Dec. 10, 2009 – Placed into receivership. PricewaterhouseCoopers Inc. appointed receiver.
2010 – Secured debt not already held acquired by Nuinsco Resources Limited and Ocean Partners Holdings Limited for $4,050,000.

Campbell Soup Company Limited (Can. Nov. 28, 1930)
Aug. 16, 1991 – Acquired by Campbell Soup Acquisition Corp. for $41 per sh.
Aug. 4, 2003 – Name changed to Campbell Company of Canada.

Campbell, Wyant & Cannon Foundry Co. (Mich. 1927)
1956 – Name changed to Ridgeway Corp. ■

Campeau Corporation (Ont. Oct. 1, 1973)
Jan. 3, 1978 – Amalgamated in Ontario to continue with same name.
Feb. 14, 1992 – Name changed to Camdev Corporation following reorganization; basis 1 com. for 50 ord. shs. plus 1 com. for each 25 ser. B, ser. C or ser. D. pfd. shs. ■

Camphor Ventures Inc. (B.C. May 9, 1986)
Apr. 30, 2007 – Acquired by Mountain Province Diamonds Inc.; basis 0.41 Mountain Province shs. for 1 Camphor sh.

Campion Resources Ltd. (Alta. June 1, 1994)
June 12, 2002 – Acquired by Progress Energy Ltd.; basis 0.4 new Progress com. sh. for 1 old Campion com. sh. (see Progress Energy Ltd.)

Campo United Petroleums Ltd. (Alta. 1952)
1962 – Struck off register.

Campton Gold Mines Ltd. (Ont. 1946)
1951 – Name changed to Cayzor Athabaska Mines Ltd. ■

Camray Mines Ltd. (Ont. 1948)
Dec. 20, 1965 – Dissolved.

Camreco Inc. (Ont. 1946)
Nov. 29, 1991 – Amalgamated with Environmental Technologies Investments Inc. to form a new co. Environmental Technologies International Inc.; 90% of the com. shs. exchanged for com. shs. of Goldlund Mines Limited on the basis of 1 Goldlund for 10 Camreco and 10% of the com. shs. exhanged for the com. shs. of Environmental Technologies on the basis of 1 Environmental for 2 Camreco shs. (see Environmental Technologies International Inc.)

Camrelco Resources Group Ltd. (B.C. 1967)
May 22, 1981 – Name changed to Canadian Beaver Resources Ltd.; basis 1 new for 4 old shs. ■

Camrex Resources Ltd. (Alta. Apr. 18, 1979)
Aug. 20, 1996 – Name changed to Crispin Energy Inc. ■

Camrock Mines Ltd. (Ont. 1940)
1956 – Charter cancelled.

Camrose Gold and Metals Ltd. (Ont. 1948)
1956 – Charter cancelled.

Camrova Resources Inc. (B.C. July 15, 1985)
May 8, 2023 – Dissolved for failure to file.

Camsell River Mines Ltd. (Ont. 1946)
1956 – Charter cancelled.

CamVec Corporation (Ont. Sept. 11, 1992)
Aug. 14, 2001 – Name changed to AMJ Campbell Inc. ■

Can-Albion Petroleums Ltd. (B.C. 1940)
Aug. 9, 1976 – Dissolved.

Can Am Gold Resources Ltd. (B.C. May 29, 1963)
Sept. 20, 1985 – Name changed to Golden Quail
Resources Ltd.; basis 1 new for 2 old shs. ■

Can Am Industries Corporation (B.C. 1979)
Apr. 5, 1990 – Name changed to Save-On Automotive
Industries Corporation; basis 1 new for 3 old shs. ■

Can-Amera Export Refining Company Ltd. (Alta. June
5, 1953)
June 11, 1985 – Name changed to Can-Amera Oil Sands
Inc. (see FPsurvey - Mines & Energy)

Can-Amera Oil Sands Development Ltd. (Alta. June
5, 1953)
July 29, 1963 – Name changed to Can-Amera Export
Refining Company Ltd. ■

Can-Ameri Agri Co. Inc. (B.C. Oct. 17, 2014)
Apr. 28, 2017 – Privatized via 1-for-1,000 consolidation;
holders of fractional shs. received 35¢ cash per sh.

Can-American Copper Ltd. (B.C. 1956)
1959 – Acquired by Eagle Plains Development Co.; basis
1 new for 5 old shs.

Can-American Natural Resources Ltd. (B.C.)
Sept. 27, 1976 – Dissolved.

Can-American Petroleums Ltd. (B.C.)
1969 – Name changed to Can-American Natural
Resources Ltd.; basis 1 new for 6 old shs. ■

Can-Banc NT Corp. (Ont. July 10, 1992)
Sept. 2, 2003 – Redeemed in full effective; basis - capital
shs. at $56.267073 per sh. and preferred shs. at $25.70
per sh.

Can-Base Industries Ltd. (B.C. 1965)
Dec. 18, 1978 – Charter cancelled.

Can-Chin Entertainment Group Co. Ltd. (B.C. Feb. 11,
2000)
Aug. 18, 2008 – Dissolved and struck from register.

Can-Co Explorations Ltd. (Alta. 1969)
1972 – Assets acquired by Nor-Can Minerals Ltd.; basis
1 new for 2 old shs.

Can-Con Enterprises and Explorations Limited (Ont.
Nov. 30, 1970 amalg.)
Mar. 1976 – Charter cancelled.
June 17, 1980 – Charter revived.
Sept. 8, 1981 – Name changed to Aubet Resources Inc. ■

Can-Erin Mines Limited (Ont. 1939)
Nov. 16, 1964 – Name changed to Argosy Mining
Corporation Limited; basis 1 new for 5 old shs. ■

Can-Ex Resources Ltd. (B.C. 1982)
Dec. 14, 1990 – Name changed to Kintana Resources
Ltd.; basis 1 new for 5 old shs. (see FPsurvey - Mines &
Energy)

Can-Fer Mines Ltd. (Ont. 1957)
Dec. 2, 1969 – Assets acquired by Bralorne Pioneer
Mines Ltd. Subsequently wound up.

Can-Financials Income Corp. (Ont. Dec. 21, 2010)
May 4, 2016 – Merged and amalgamated with First Asset
Fund Corp; basis 0.37989 First Asset MSCI Canada
Quality Index Class ETF shs. for 1 Can-Financials equity
sh. (see First Asset MSCI Canada Quality Index Class
ETF)

Can-Met Explorations Ltd. (Ont. 1944)
1960 – Merged into Denison Mines Ltd.; basis 1 new for
200 old shs.

Can-Nation Resources Ltd. (B.C. 1969)
Sept. 30, 1983 – Struck off register.

Can Pro Developments Ltd. (B.C. Mar. 1, 1988)
May 19, 1993 – Name changed to Cadre Resources Ltd.;
basis 1 new for 6 old shs. ■

Can-60 Income Corp. (Ont. Aug. 23, 2010)
Nov. 12, 2015 – Converted into a mutual fund corporation
from a closed-end fund.

Can-Tel Communications Inc. (B.C. 1980)
Sept. 30, 1986 – Name changed to Euro-Asia Capital
Ltd.; basis 1 new for 3 old shs. ■

Can-Trac Industries Ltd. (B.C. 1959)
Sept. 27, 1976 – Dissolved.

Can West Exploration Inc. (B.C. Jan. 5, 1987)
Oct. 13, 2000 – Name changed to Watch Resources Ltd.;
basis 1 new for 20 old shs. ■

Cana Telecommunications Inc. (B.C. Apr. 21, 1987)
May 4, 1993 – Name changed to Consolidated
Technologies Holdings Inc. and continued into British
Columbia pursuant to reverse takeover acquisition of Call
Detailed Recording Services; basis 0.782985 new for 1
old sh. ■

Cana Venture Capital Corp. (Alta. Feb. 25, 2011)
Mar. 14, 2014 – Amalgamated with 1710560 Alberta Ltd.,
a wholly owned subsid. of Arkadia Capital Corp., basis
0.60434 Arkadia com. shs. for 1 Cana sh. (see Arkadia
Capital Corp.)

Canaan Explorers Limited (Ont. 1974)
Feb. 20, 1980 – Dissolved.

Canabec Explorations Ltd. (Ont. Oct. 16, 1975)
Jan. 26, 1988 – Name changed to Canabec Industries
Ltd.; basis 1 new for 10 old shs. ■

Canabec Industries Ltd. (Ont. Oct. 16, 1975)
Dec. 15, 1988 – Name changed to Environmental
Technologies Investments Inc. following vertical
amalgamation with new subsids. Environmental
Technologies Investments Inc. and 761515 Ontario Inc. ■

Canabo Medical Inc. (B.C. Feb. 2, 2007)
Mar. 26, 2018 – Name changed to Aleafia Health Inc. ■

Canabrava Diamond Corporation (B.C. Sept. 30, 1994)
Nov. 28, 2003 – Acquired by Superior Diamonds Inc.;
basis 1 Superior Diamonds sh. for 2.5 Canabrava shs.
(see Superior Diamonds Inc.)

Canaccord Capital Inc. (B.C. Feb. 14, 1997)
Dec. 1, 2009 – Name changed to Canaccord Financial
Inc. ■

Canaccord Financial Inc. (B.C. Feb. 14, 1997)
Oct. 1, 2013 – Name changed to Canaccord Genuity
Group Inc. (see FPsurvey - Industrials)

Canaccord Genuity Acquisition Corp. (Ont. June 28,
2017)
Aug. 31, 2018 – Name changed to Spark Power Group
Inc. following Qualifying Transaction reverse takeover
acquisition of Spark Power Corp. ■

Canaccord Genuity G Ventures Corp. (Ont. Mar. 31,
2021)
Oct. 11, 2023 – All o/s cl. A restricted vtg. units (1 cl. A
restricted vtg. sh. and ½ warrant) were redeemed for
$3.08 cash for 1 restricted vtg. sh. and 3¢ cash for ½
warrant.

Canaccord Genuity Growth II Corp. (B.C. Mar. 13,
2019)
Apr. 23, 2021 – Name changed to Taiga Motors
Corporation pursuant to the Qualifying Acquisition of
Taiga Motors Inc. (TMI), and concurrent amalgamation
of TMI and wholly owned 9434-3399 Québec inc.; basis
1 new for 5 old shs. ■

Canaccord Genuity Growth Corp. (Ont. Aug. 13, 2018)
Apr. 26, 2019 – Name changed to Columbia Care Inc.
and continued into British Columbia pursuant to the
Qualifying Acquisition of Columbia Care LLC. ■

Canaco Mining Resources Ltd. (Can. Jan. 3, 1987)
Sept. 28, 1998 – Name changed to Canaco Resources
Ltd.; basis 1 new for 3 old shs. ■

Canaco Resources Inc. (Can. Jan. 3, 1987)
Apr. 9, 2013 – Name changed to Orca Gold Inc. following
reverse takeover acquisition of Shark Minerals Inc.; basis
1 new for 3 old shs. ■

Canaco Resources Ltd. (Can. Jan. 3, 1987)
Nov. 10, 2003 – Name changed to Canaco Resources
Inc.; basis 1 new for 10 old shs. ■

Canacord Resources Inc. (Can. 1986)
Sept. 11, 1989 – Acquired by Prime Resources
Corporation; basis 1 Prime sh. for 10 Canacord shs. (see
Prime Resources Corporation)

Canada & Dominion Sugar Company Limited (Can.
Dec. 24, 1930; via Dominion charter)
Jan. 12, 1973 – Name changed to Redpath Industries
Limited. ■

Canada Bread Co. Ltd. (Ont. June 9, 1911)
Oct. 15, 1969 – Name changed to Corporate Foods
Limited. ■

Canada Bread Company, Limited (Ont. June 9, 1911)
May 27, 2014 – Acquired by Grupo Bimbo, S.A.B. de
C.V.; basis $72 cash plus stub dividend of $0.437 per sh.

Canada Brokerlink Inc. (Alta. May 27, 1991)
Mar. 27, 2000 – All o/s com. shs. acquired by 866295
Alberta Ltd., a wholly owned subsid. of Allianz of Canada
Inc.; basis $1.20 per sh.
Jan. 1, 2020 – Name changed to Brokerlink Inc.

Canada Cartage Diversified Income Fund (Ont. Jan.
30, 2006)
July 6, 2007 – Acquired by Nautic Partners VI, LP for
$11.30 per fund unit.

Canada Cement Lafarge Ltd. (Can. Oct. 22, 1927; via
letters patent)
Jan. 1, 1988 – Name changed to Lafarge Canada Inc. ■

Canada Chibougamau Resources Ltd. (Que. 1952)
Oct. 28, 1978 – Charter cancelled.

Canada China Clay and Silica Ltd. (Can. 1941)
1950 – Charter cancelled.

Canada Coal Inc. (Ont. Feb. 23, 2012 amalg.)
Mar. 25, 2021 – Name changed to Ayurcann Holdings
Corp. pursuant to the reverse takeover acquisition of
Ayurcann Inc. and concurrent amalgamation of Ayurcann
with wholly owned 12487772 Canada Inc.; basis 1 new
for 2 old shs. (see FPsurvey - Industrials)

Canada Cobalt Works Inc. (Can. Apr. 29, 2005)
May 19, 2020 – Name changed to Canada Silver Cobalt
Works Inc. ■

Canada Computational Unlimited Corp. (Ont. May 7, 2008)
June 16, 2022 – Name changed to SATO Technologies Corp. (see FPsurvey - Industrials)

Canada Crushed & Cut Stone Ltd. (Ont. 1951)
Apr. 23, 1969 – Name changed to Steetley Industries Limited. ■

Canada Development Corporation (Can. 1971; via Act of Parliament)
Jan. 7, 1988 – Name changed to Polysar Energy & Chemical Corporation. ■

Canada Electric Co. Ltd. (N.S. 1889)
Jan. 1961 – Acquired by the Province of Nova Scotia for $100 per pref. sh. and $150 per com. sh.

Canada Fluorspar Inc. (B.C. Apr. 13, 1995)
Feb. 5, 2001 – Name changed to Continental Ridge Resources Inc. ■

Canada Fluorspar Inc. (Alta. Apr. 15, 2009 amalg.)
May 30, 2014 – Acquired by CF Acquisition Inc., an indirect wholly owned subsid. of Golden Gate Capital LLC; basis 35¢ cash per sh.

Canada Foils Limited (Ont. 1922)
Mar. 1969 – Con-Pack Ltd., a wholly owned subsid. of Imperial Tobacco Co. of Canada Ltd., sold its int. of 98% of the o/s cl. A and 99% of the o/s com. shs. of Canada Foils Ltd., to Aluminum Co. of Canada Ltd. Con-Pack had acquired shs. in 1965-66 under offer at $40 per cl. A sh. and $45 per com. sh.

Canada Forgings Limited (Can. 1912)
1976 – From 1975 to 1976, Toromont Industries acquired all o/s com. shs. for $17 per sh.

Canada Foundries & Forgings Ltd. (Can. 1912)
Dec. 1966 – Name changed to Canada Forgings Limited. ■

Canada Garnet Ltd. (Que. 1937)
Oct. 19, 1974 – Dissolved.

Canada Gas Corp. (B.C. Feb. 1, 1984)
Mar. 1, 2011 – Name changed to Canada Rare Earths Inc. ■

Canada Geothermal Oil Ltd. (Ont. 1944)
1975 – Placed into receivership.
Nov. 7, 1977 – Unsecured creditors paid 70.157¢ (less 2¢ levy) per dollar claimed.
Jan. 1980 – Payment of 1.153¢ per dollar claimed. Proposal subsequently completed.
Apr. 4, 1986 – Trustee (Clarkson Gordon in Calgary) discharged.

Canada Gold Corporation (B.C. Nov. 8, 1984)
July 11, 2013 – Name changed to Stem 7 Capital Inc. ■

Canada Graphite Mines Ltd. (Ont. 1962)
Nov. 1967 – Charter cancelled.

The Canada Guarantee Company (Can. 1851)
Feb. 17, 1881 – Name changed to The Guarantee Company of North America. ■

Canada Guiana Mines Ltd. (Ont. 1947)
May 1952 – Charter cancelled; $0.01 per sh. distributed.

Canada House Cannabis Group Inc. (Can. Mar. 31, 1995)
July 28, 2023 – Name changed to MTL Cannabis Corp. pursuant to the reverse takeover acquisition of Montréal Cannabis Médical Inc. (see FPsurvey - Industrials)

Canada House Wellness Group Inc. (Can. Mar. 31, 1995)
Aug. 23, 2022 – Name changed to Canada House Cannabis Group Inc.; basis 1 new for 30 old shs. ■

Canada Income Plus Fund (Ont. 1985)
Oct. 9, 1992 – Dissolved. Unitholders of record Sept. 30, 1992, received a proportionate share of net interest

income from July 1 to Sept. 30, 1992, and from Oct. 1 to Oct. 9, 1992. This payment could be given in cheque form, representing net asset value of units held, less a termination fee of 1% or net asset value of units could be transferred to a mutual fund managed by The Guardian Group of Funds Limited without any termination fee as long as securities purchased were held for a period of not less than 12 months from date of transfer.

Canada Iron Foundries, Limited (Can. Mar. 1915)
1968 – Name changed to Canron Limited. ■

Canada Iron Inc. (Ont. Feb. 15, 2007)
June 11, 2021 – Name changed to Humble & Fume Inc. following reverse takeover acquisition of Canada Iron Inc. by Humble & Fume Inc. ■

Canada-Israel Petroleums Ltd. (Ont. 1956)
1960 – Wound up.

Canada Jetlines Ltd. (Can. Feb. 28, 2017 amalg.)
Feb. 28, 2017 – Formed Canada Jetlines Operations Ltd. in Canada. ■

Canada Jetlines Ltd. (Can. Feb. 28, 2017)
June 23, 2020 – Name changed to Global Crossing Airlines Inc. and continued into British Columbia pursuant to reverse takeover acquisition of (old) Global Crossing Airlines, Inc.; basis 1 new for 10 old shs. ■

Canada Jetlines Operations Ltd. (Can. Feb. 28, 2017 amalg.)
Sept. 11, 2024 – Voluntarily assigned into bankruptcy. BDO Canada Limited appointed trustee.

Canada Kelp Co. Ltd. (Can. - unspecified 1946)
1967 – Made a voluntary assignment into bankruptcy, Nov. 24, 1948. Assets reported sold, liabs. paid, and distribution made among shldrs. Charter surrendered. Not to be confused with another co. of the same name, incorporated B.C.

Canada Kelp Co. Ltd. (B.C. 1967)
1969 – Placed into receivership; assets sold early 1973 to Equatorial Resources Ltd. for $100,000.

Canada Lease Financing Ltd. (Ont. 1969)
Mar. 29, 1989 – Placed into receivership on Mar. 29, 1989. All assets sold. Nothing left for shldrs.

The Canada Life Assurance Company (Can. 1849)
Jan. 1, 2020 – Formed by amalgamation of The Great-West Life Assurance Company, its wholly owned subsids. Canada Life Financial Corporation and London Insurance Group Inc, and their wholly owned subsids. The Canada Life Assurance Company and London Life Insurance Company.

Canada Life Financial Corporation (Can. June 21, 1999)
July 10, 2003 – All o/s com. shs. acquired by Great-West Lifeco Inc.; basis $44.50 cash per sh., or 1.78 4.8% Great-West pref. shs., or 1.78 5.9% Great-West pref. shs., or 1.1849 Great-West com. shs. (or a combination thereof) for 1 Canada Life com. sh.
Jan. 5, 2011 – All o/s ser. B pref. shs. redeemed at $25 per sh.
Jan. 1, 2020 – Amalgamated with The Great-West Life Assurance Company, London Life Insurance Company and wholly owned subsid. The Canada Life Assurance Company plus holding co. London Insurance Group Inc. to continue as The Canada Life Assurance Company.

Canada Lithium Corp. (Ont. July 17, 1995 amalg.)
Jan. 31, 2014 – Name changed to RB Energy Inc. and continued into Canada pursuant to acquisition of Sirocco Mining Inc.; basis 1 new for 3 old shs. ■

Canada Machinery Corporation, Ltd. (Can. 1910)
1975 – Acquired by Canadian Ingersoll-Rand Co. Ltd.; basis 7 shs. of U.S. parent of Canadian Ingersoll-Rand for 10 Canada Machinery shs.

Canada Malting Co. Limited (Can. Sept. 27, 1927; via Dominion charter)
Dec. 5, 1995 – Acquired by ConAgra Investments (CMA) Limited wholly owned subsid. of ConAgra, Inc.; basis $20.50 per sh.

Canada Northern Power Corporation Ltd. (Can. 1924)
Dec. 9, 1955 – Wound up. Shldrs. of record received shares of Northern Quebec Power Co. Ltd. on the basis of 1 1/16 com. shs. of Northern Quebec for each 2 shs. of Canada Northern held.

Canada Northwest Australia Oil N.L. (Wash. 1979)
Nov. 24, 1986 – Name changed to National Venture Corporation NL; basis 1 new for 4 old shs.

Canada Northwest Energy Limited (Can. Apr. 1, 1893; via Dominion charter)
Oct. 15, 1991 – Acquired by Sherritt Gordon Limited; basis 0.0516 new com. sh. for 1 com. sh., 0.96775 new com. sh. for 1 old 9% pfd. ser. B sh., 0.96775 new com. sh. for 1 old 7.75% pfd. ser. C sh. and 101.548 new com. shs. for 1 old 8% conv. sub. deb. (see Sherritt Gordon Limited)

Canada Northwest Land Limited (Can. Apr. 1, 1893; via Dominion charter)
Feb. 19, 1982 – Name changed to Canada Northwest Energy Limited. ■

Canada Oil Lands Ltd. (Alta. 1951)
1964 – Acquired by Great Plains Development Co. of Canada Ltd. in 1964-65 for $3.25 per sh.

Canada Orient Resources Inc. (B.C. July 30, 1987)
Apr. 17, 1991 – Name changed to Consolidated Canada Orient Resources Inc.; basis unknown. ■

Canada Pacific Capital Corp. (Ont. May 28, 2010)
July 4, 2014 – Dissolved following Qualifying Transaction private placement subscription of 5,800,000 units of Lakeside Minerals Inc. (1 com. sh. plus 1/2 wts.) at 5¢ per unit (with wts. exercisable at 10¢ per wt. for 3 yrs.) and distribution of Lakeside units to shareholders; basis 0.54976 Lakeside units for 1 Canada Pacific Capital sh. (see Lakeside Minerals Inc.)

Canada Packers Inc. (Can. Aug. 13, 1927; via Dominion charter)
July 8, 1991 – Name changed to Maple Leaf Foods Inc. ■

Canada Packers Limited (Can. Aug. 13, 1927; via Dominion charter)
Dec. 14, 1979 – Name changed to Canada Packers Inc. ■

Canada Paving & Supply Corp. Ltd. (Ont. 1928)
1946 – Early in 1946, 1st pref. shldrs. accepted offer of Sterling Construction Co. Ltd., Windsor, to purchase 19,846 o/s 1st pref. shs. at $8.00 per sh.
1957 – Wound up.

Canada Payphone Corporation (B.C. Mar. 30, 1983)
Oct. 4, 2004 – Acquired by Globalive Communications Inc. for 2¢ per sh.

Canada Permanent Mortgage Corporation (Can. July 10, 1899)
Dec. 31, 1985 – Acquired by Genstar Financial Corporation, a wholly owned subsid. of Genstar Corporation, in August 1981; basis $35 per com. sh. and $41.75 per ser. A pref. sh. Genstar Financial subsequently increased its ownership to 99.9% Subsequently, amalgamated with Canada Trustco Mortgage Company to form a new company also called Canada Trustco Mortgage Company; basis 0.52465 of a new for 1 old sh.

Canada Permanent Toronto General Trust Company (Can. Dec. 1, 1961 amalg.)
Aug. 21, 1963 – Name changed to Canada Permanent Trust Company. ■

Canada Permanent Trust Company (Can. 1913)
Dec. 1, 1961 – Formed Canada Permanent Toronto General Trust Company in Canada on amalgamation with

The Toronto General Trusts Corp.; basis 101 new for 25 old shs. ■

Canada Permanent Trust Company (Can. Dec. 1, 1961 amalg.)
Dec. 1, 1967 – Amalgamated with Eastern & Chartered Trust Co. (1 for 1) to continue as Canada Permanent Trust Company; basis 2.25 new for 1 old sh. (see Canada Permanent Mortgage Corporation)
Dec. 31, 1974 – Acquired by Canada Permanent Mortgage Corporation; basis 3 new Permanent Mortgage shs. for 1 old Permanent Trust sh. (see Canada Permanent Mortgage Corporation)

Canada Pyrite Mines Ltd. (Ont. 1952)
1957 – Name changed to Blondeau Nickel Mines Ltd. ■

Canada Radium Mines Ltd. (Ont. 1926)
Name changed to Belcroft Radium Mines Ltd. ■

Canada Rare Earths Inc. (B.C. Feb. 1, 1984)
Aug. 1, 2012 – Name changed to Canada Strategic Metals Inc. ■

Canada Renewable Bioenergy Corp. (Alta. Apr. 5, 2007)
Sept. 27, 2012 – Continued into British Columbia.
Jan. 29, 2024 – Dissolved for failure to file and struck from register.

Canada Safeway Limited (Can. 1929)
Dec. 1, 1986 – Controlling interest in Safeway Stores Inc., the parent co., was purch. by Kohlberg, Kravis and Roberts & Co. Subsequently, the public pref. shs. of Canada Safeway Ltd were purchased and redeemed. All o/s shs. of Canada Safeway are now privately held.

Canada Silver Cobalt Works Inc. (Can. Apr. 29, 2005)
Jan. 23, 2024 – Name changed to Nord Precious Metals Mining Inc. (see FPsurvey - Mines & Energy)

Canada Southern Oil & Refining Co. Ltd. (unknown)
In liquidation; Wm. Walsh, Calgary, liquidator.

Canada Southern Oils Ltd. (Can. 1951)
Apr. 20, 1954 – Name changed to Canada Southern Petroleum Ltd. following division into Canso Oil Producers Ltd., Canso Natural Gas Ltd. and Canada Southern Petroleum Ltd.; basis 4 Canso Oil, 5 Canso Gas and 8 Canada Southern Pet. shs. for 8 Canada Southern Oils shs. ■

Canada Southern Petroleum Ltd. (Can. Apr. 13, 1954)
June 4, 1980 – Continued into Nova Scotia. (see Canadian Oil Sands Trust)
Mar. 3, 2005 – Continued into Alberta. (see Canadian Oil Sands Trust)
Oct. 27, 2006 – Amalgamated with 2 wholly owned subsidiaries of Canadian Oil Sands Trust; basis US$13.10 per sh. (see Canadian Oil Sands Trust)

Canada Starch Co. Inc. (Can. Jan. 22, 1906)
Dec. 1950 – Corn Products Refining Co., U.S. acquired all but 100 shs. of the minority interest in 7% pref. stock at $140 per sh.
1954 – Corn Products Refining Co. made offer of $75 per sh. for com. shs.
1956 – Became a wholly owned subsid. of Corn Products Refining Co.
Dec. 31, 2005 – Name changed to Casco Inc.

Canada Steamship Lines, Limited (Can. 1913)
Nov. 1971 – Power Corp. of Canada, Ltd. offered to buy all o/s com. shs. not already held by it at $40 per sh. On Dec. 19, 1975, all o/s 5% pref. shs. called for redemption at $6.7165 per sh., which incl. unpaid divds. of 15.4¢ per sh. Effective Jan. 2, 1976, all assets, undertakings and liabs. transferred to Power Corp. of Canada, Ltd. (see Power Corporation of Canada, Limited)

Canada Strategic Metals Inc. (B.C. Feb. 1, 1984)
July 5, 2018 – Name changed to Quebec Precious Metals Corporation; basis 1 new for 4.16 old shs. ■

Canada Sugar Refining Co., Ltd. (unknown)
1930 – Merged to form Canada & Dominion Sugar Co., Ltd.

Canada 3000 Inc. (Alta. Oct. 16, 1995)
Nov. 1, 2001 – Together with subsids., Canada 3000 Airlines Limited and Royal Aviation Inc., made assignments in bankruptcy and Deloitte & Touche Inc. was appointed trustee. All directors and officers resigned.
Nov. 16, 2001 – Direct and indirect subsidiaries, Holiday Travel Consultants Ltd., Canada 3000 Airport Services Limited, Royal Handling Inc., Canada 3000 Sales Limited and C3 Leisure Limited, made voluntary assignments into bankruptcy and Toronto-based PricewaterhouseCoopers Inc. was appointed trustee.
Nov. 30, 2001 – PricewaterhouseCoopers Inc. was substituted as trustee in bankruptcy for the co., Canada 3000 Airlines Limited and Royal Aviation Inc.
Jan. 10, 2003 – Court approved certain funds on hand in Canada 3000 Sales Limited (Sales) to be deemed trust funds for the benefit of ticketholders with claims for unused travel services against Sales.
July 25, 2003 – Trustee issued a one-time distribution of 10¢ on the dollar to beneficiaries with proven claims.
May 19, 2004 – Trustee issued a final notice to beneficiaries that had not returned their statutory declaration which had to be returned within 30 days of the final notice. The 30-day notice expired on July 2, 2004, and no further claims can be made against the Canada 3000 Sales trust fund.
Sept. 22, 2004 – PricewaterhouseCoopers Inc. was discharged as trustee and there were no funds available for any further dividend payments to unsecured creditors or shldrs.

Canada Trust Income Investments (Can. Aug. 17, 1973)
Nov. 1, 2007 – Dissolved for $0.008874317 per trust unit.

Canada Trustco Mortgage Company (Can. 1864)
Dec. 31, 1985 – Amalgamated with Canada Permanent Mortgage Corporation to form new co. with same name Canada Trustco Mortgage Company.
Nov. 25, 1987 – All o/s com. shs. acquired by CT Financial Services Inc.; basis 3 CT shs. for 1 Canada Trustco sh. The company became a principal subsidiary of CT Financial Services Inc. but all o/s pref. shs. remained under the Canada Trustco Mortgage Company name.

Canada Tungsten Inc. (Ont. Jan. 1, 1993 amalg.)
Jan. 10, 1997 – Acquired by Aur Resources Inc.; basis 1 new Aur sh. for 4.5 old Canada Tungsten shs. (see Aur Resources Inc.)

Canada Tungsten Mining Corporation Limited (Ont. July 31, 1959)
Jan. 7, 1993 – Amalgamated with Minerex Resources Ltd. and Canamax Resources Inc. to form Canada Tungsten Inc.; basis 1 new for 0.5 Minerex shs., 1 new for 5 Canamax shs. and 1 new for 1 Canada Tungsten sh. (see Canada Tungsten Inc.)

Canada Varnish Co. Ltd. (Ont. 1924)
Feb. 1953 – Name changed to Canvar Industries Ltd. following sale of assets to new co. Canada Varnish Ltd. for $375,000, leaving the co. with $700,000 in cash or other liquid assets. ■

Canada Vinegars, Limited (Can. 1925)
Dec. 13, 1930 – Dissolved voluntarily.

Canada Vinegars Limited (Can. 1928)
May 1961 – National Trust Co. Ltd., acting for Cerebos (Canada) Ltd., offered to purch. all o/s shs. at $42.50 per sh.

Canada West Capital Corporation (Alta. Jan. 29, 1993)
Sept. 24, 1999 – Name changed to Insurcom Financial Corporation. ■

Canada West Capital Inc. (Ont. June 14, 1988)
Jan. 13, 2004 – Continued into Canada.
Feb. 10, 2006 – Continued into Alberta.
Feb. 14, 2006 – Name changed to Canadian Sub-Surface Energy Services Corp. following reverse takeover

acquisition of Canadian Sub-Surface Energy Services Inc.; basis 1 cl. A sh. for 7 com. shs. ■

Canada West Drilling Company Limited (Alta. 1948)
Nov. 30, 1964 – Dissolved and struck off register.

Canada West Technology Corporation (Alta. Jan. 29, 1987)
Nov. 1, 1993 – Name changed to Bellator Exploration Inc.; basis 1 new for 2 old shs. ■

Canada Wire & Cable Company, Limited (Ont. 1929)
1964 – Acquired by Noranda Mines Ltd. in 1964-65; basis $5.00 and 4 new Noranda shs. for 10 old Canada Wire cl. A or B shs.

Canada Zinc Metals Corp. (B.C. Feb. 10, 1988)
May 7, 2018 – Name changed to ZincX Resources Corp. (see FPsurvey - Mines & Energy)

Canada's Choice Spring Water, Inc. (Can. May 1, 1996)
Apr. 25, 2002 – Name changed to Echo Springs Water Corp.; basis 1 new for 20 old shs. ■

Canada's Pizza Delivery Corp. (Can. June 5, 1986)
Aug. 21, 2007 – Acquired by Roberto Ledeboer for 60¢ per sh.
July 13, 2010 – Continued into Alberta.

Canadex Resources Limited (Ont. Apr. 3, 1969)
Feb. 28, 2008 – Acquired by Student Transportation of America Ltd.; basis $5.72 per com. sh. and $1.00 per cl. A pref. sh.

Canadian Acceptance Corporation Limited (Can. 1922)
Dec. 1982 – The Royal Bank of Canada purchased all o/s shs. held by C.I.T. Financial Corp. of New York effective Dec. 31, 1981 for approx. $130 million, after co. had sold certain assets not involved with equipment financing and leasing operations. Amalgamated with The Royal Bank subsid., RoyLease Ltd. (see The Royal Bank of Canada)

Canadian Admiral Corporation Ltd. (Can. 1946)
Nov. 3, 1981 – Placed into receivership when co. bankers called in loans of approx. $40 million. (see Inglis Limited)
Nov. 23, 1981 – Declared bankrupt. (see Inglis Limited)
Mar. 26, 1982 – Inglis Limited purchased co. plants located in Mississauga and Cambridge, Ont. and Montmagny, Que., together with certain inventories and trademarks for approx. $35 million. (see Inglis Limited)

Canadian Admiral Oils Ltd. (Can. 1926)
1957 – Sold to Canadian Homestead Oils Ltd.; basis 1 new for 4 old shs.

Canadian Advantaged Convertibles Fund (Ont. Dec. 10, 2010)
Dec. 21, 2015 – Name changed to First Asset Canadian Convertibles Fund. ■

Canadian Affiliated Financial Corp. (unknown)
Mar. 1, 1975 – Amalgamated with Continental Discount Corp. on pooling of interest basis to form Canadian Financial Company.

Canadian Agra Foods Inc. (Alta. Mar. 23, 1990)
Apr. 16, 1999 – Unsuccessful in completing required refinancing within the time stipulated by the courts and the Bank of Nova Scotia. Thus, the bank obtained a court order and Toronto-based RSM Richter Inc. was appointed receiver.
May 1, 2004 – Receiver discharged. Secured creditors suffered a shortfall and there were no funds available for unsecured creditors or shldrs.

Canadian Agtechnology Partners Inc. (Alta. 1987)
Jan. 4, 1996 – Name changed to SportsMate International Inc. ■

Canadian Airlines Corporation (Alta. Feb. 22, 1956)
July 6, 2000 – Acquired by Air Canada for $2.00 per sh. (see Air Canada)

Canadian Airways Ltd. (Can. 1930)
1942 – Assets and undertakings acquired by Canadian Pacific Railway Co. and transferred to Canadian Pacific Air Lines, Limited.

Canadian All Metals Explorations Limited (Ont. Jan. 14, 1955)
Mar. 26, 1990 – Struck from register and dissolved.

Canadian Allied Property Investments Limited (B.C. 1962)
May 1975 – Laing Investments Ltd. of Vancouver, owned 90% of the com. shs. and offered to acquire remaining shs. at $12.50 per sh.

Canadian Alumina Corp. Ltd. (N.S. 1956)
1964 – Reported wound up.

Canadian Anaconda Oils Ltd. (Can. Apr. 14, 1926)
Mar. 25, 1957 – Name changed to Anaconda Petroleum Ltd.; basis 1 new for 5 old shs. ■

Canadian Angus Resources Ltd. (B.C. Feb. 12, 1970)
Aug. 29, 1988 – Continued into Alberta. (see Abacan Resource Corporation)
Feb. 10, 1995 – Amalgamated with Abacan Resource Corporation, Canadian Industrial Minerals Corp., Canstar Ventures Corp. and Profile Capital Corporation to form Abacan Resource Corporation; basis 1 new for 1 Abacan sh., 0.51 new for 1 Canadian Industrial sh., 0.45 new for 1 Canstar sh., 0.23 new for 1 Profile Capital sh. and 0.30 new for 1 Canadian Angus sh. (see Abacan Resource Corporation)

Canadian Aran Petroleums Ltd. (Alta. 1976)
July 14, 1981 – Name changed to Emir Oils Ltd. ■

Canadian Arctic Petroleums Ltd. (B.C. 1979)
June 16, 1995 – Continued into Alberta.
Sept. 17, 1996 – Name changed to Tekerra Gas Inc. following reverse takeover acquisition of Tekerra Gas Inc.; basis 1 new for 2 old shs. ■

Canadian Arena Company (Que. 1923)
Nov. 30, 1974 – Name changed to Carena-Bancorp Inc. ■

Canadian Arrow Mines Limited (Ont. Dec. 8, 1938)
Feb. 1, 2018 – Acquired by Tartisan Resources Corp.; basis 1 Tartisan sh. for 17.5 Canadian Arrow shs. (see Tartisan Resources Corp.)

Canadian Ashmont Oils Ltd. (Alta. 1953)
Sept. 30, 1958 – In voluntary liquidation in 1958; struck off register.

Canadian Astoria Minerals Ltd. (Que. Jan. 25, 1938)
1963 – Name changed to Les Mines Cam Limitée; basis 1 new for 4 old shs. ■

Canadian Atlantic Oil Co. Ltd. (Alta. Mar. 1, 1945)
1958 – Acquired by Pacific Petroleums Ltd.; basis 1 new for 3 old shs. (see Pacific Petroleums Ltd.)

Canadian-Australian Exploration Ltd. (Ont. Aug. 14, 1944)
1965 – Name changed to Win-Eldrich Mines Limited; basis 1 new for 5 old shs. (see FPsurvey - Mines & Energy)

Canadian-Australian Prospectors Inc. (Ont. 1972)
June 26, 1974 – Name changed to Gemex Minerals Inc. ■

Canadian Aviation Electronics Ltd. (Can. Mar. 17, 1947)
June 1965 – Name changed to CAE Industries Ltd. ■

Canadian Bakeries Ltd. (Can. 1952)
1963 – Maple Leaf Mills Limited acquired virtually all o/s shs. not already owned for $8.50 per sh.

Canadian Banc Capital Securities Trust (Ont. May 22, 2009)
Feb. 4, 2016 – Merged into North American Financials Capital Securities Trust to continue as Global Capital Securities Trust; basis 0.968751 Global Capital cl. A units for 1 Canadian Banc cl. A unit and 0.970716 Global Capital cl. F units for 1 Canadian Banc cl. F unit. (see Global Capital Securities Trust)

Canadian Banc Recovery Corp. (Ont. May 25, 2005)
Jan. 27, 2012 – Name changed to Canadian Banc Corp. (see FPsurvey - Industrials)

Canadian Bank Note Company, Limited (Can. Mar. 24, 1910)
Mar. 25, 1982 – Continued into Ontario.
July 20, 2004 – Amalgamated with 1621248 Ontario Inc. a company indirectly owned by Douglas R. Arends; basis $3.50 per sh.

The Canadian Bank of Commerce (Can. 1867)
June 1, 1961 – Merged with Imperial Bank of Canada to form the Canadian Imperial Bank of Commerce.

Canadian Barranca Corporation Ltd. (Alta. 1962)
Apr. 1, 1987 – Struck off register.

Canadian Barranca Mines Ltd. (Alta. 1962)
Aug. 1970 – Name changed to Canadian Barranca Corporation Ltd. ■

Canadian Bashaw Leduc Oil & Gas Limited (Alta. 1951)
June 23, 1987 – Formed Erskine Resources Corporation; basis 1 new for 8 old shs. ■

Canadian Beaver Resources Ltd. (B.C. 1967)
Dec. 30, 1994 – Dissolved and struck off register.

Canadian Belle Mining Co. Inc. (Wash. Dec. 26, 1936)
Feb. 1953 – Struck off register.

The Canadian Bioceutical Corporation (Ont. Apr. 2, 1974)
Nov. 6, 2017 – Name changed to MPX Bioceutical Corporation. ■

Canadian Black River Petroleum Ltd. (Ont. Apr. 30, 1989 amalg.)
Feb. 13, 1998 – Formed Uruguay Goldfields Inc. in Alberta on amalgamation with wholly owned 762577 Alberta Ltd. and Uruguay Goldfields Inc.; basis 1 new for 25 old shs. ■

Canadian Blackhawk Energy Inc. (Alta. Nov. 9, 1995)
Feb. 19, 2003 – Plan of Arrangement acquisition by TM Energy Ltd.; basis $0.01 per sh.

Canadian Bonanza Petroleums Limited (Alta. 1966)
Apr. 1974 – Amalgamated with Bonanza International Petroleums Limited to form Amalgamated Bonanza Petroleum Limited; basis 1 new for 2 old shs.

Canadian Brazos Oil Ltd. (B.C. Nov. 21, 1977)
Oct. 10, 1979 – Name changed to Stateside Energy Corporation. ■

Canadian Breweries Limited (Ont. Mar. 30, 1930)
Nov. 9, 1973 – Name changed to Carling O'Keefe Limited. ■

Canadian British Aluminium Company Limited (Que. 1955)
July 31, 1970 – Merged with CRM Capital Ltd. to form Canadian Reynolds Metals Company, Limited. Each cl. A sh. exch. for 1 pref. of new co. and each cl. B sh. exch. for 1 new com. sh.

Canadian British Empire Oil Co. Ltd. (Alta. 1949)
1958 – Acquired by Canadian Western Oil Co. Inc.; basis 1 new for 3 old shs. (see Canadian Western Oil Co. Inc.)

Canadian Cablesystems Limited (Can. Jan. 23, 1920)
Jan. 30, 1981 – Name changed to Rogers Cablesystems Inc. ■

Canadian Cadillac Gold Mines (Que. 1937)
July 22, 1978 – Charter cancelled.

Canadian Canners Limited (Can. 1923)
1975 – From 1974 to 1975, Del Monte Corporation purchased all o/s cl. A shs. for $12 per sh.
Jan. 1978 – Cl. A & B shs. converted to com. shs. Del Monte holds 99.7% of o/s shs.

Canadian Car & Foundry Co. Ltd. (Can. 1901)
June 1955 – All cl. A and ord. shs. acquired by A. V. Roe Canada Ltd. (now Hawker-Siddeley Canada Ltd.) for $30 per sh.

Canadian Cariboo Resources Ltd. (B.C. Sept. 4, 1985)
Feb. 3, 1995 – Dissolved and struck off register.

Canadian Celanese Limited (Can. 1926)
July 1, 1963 – Merged into Canadian Chemical Company, Limited; basis $50 or 6 shs. of Canadian Chemical for each sh. held. Subsequently, name of Canadian Chemical changed to Chemcell (1963) Limited on share for share basis. (see Canadian Chemical Company, Limited)

Canadian Cellulose Company, Limited (B.C. 1964)
1978 – On formation of British Columbia Resources Investment Corporation (BCRIC), 81% int. held by B.C. govt. was transferred to BCRIC.
1980 – British Columbia Resources Investment Corporation acquired all remaining o/s shs. for $15 per sh.
1981 – Name changed to B.C. Timber Ltd. ■

Canadian Central Holdings Ltd. (Can. 1962)
May 1971 – Wound up and charter cancelled. Full payment made to pref. noteholders; nothing to unsecured creditors or shldrs.

Canadian Charcoal Products Ltd. (Ont. 1952)
June 1959 – Bankrupt. Reported to be wound up; nothing available for shldrs. of either class.

Canadian Chemical & Cellulose Company Ltd. (Can. 1951)
1959 – Prior to windup and surrender of charter issued 1 sh. of Canadian Chemical Company, Limited and 1 sh. of Columbia Cellulose Company Limited for each co. sh.

Canadian Chemical Company, Limited (Alta. 1950)
July 1, 1963 – Merged with Canadian Celanese Limited to form Chemcell (1963) Limited. Com. shldrs. of Cdn Chemical received 1 com. sh. Chemcell for each sh. held. Debt issued by Cdn Chemical became obligations of Chemcell (1963) Limited, and wts. issued by Cdn Chemical conferred right to purch. shs. of Chemcell on same terms.

Canadian Chemical Reclaiming Ltd. (Alta. May 10, 1995 amalg.)
Jan. 12, 2000 – Name changed to CCR Technologies Ltd. ■

Canadian Chieftain Petroleums Ltd. (unknown)
1956 – Continued into Alberta.
Aug. 1962 – Acquired by Delhi-Taylor interests of Dallas, for $1.325 per sh.

Canadian Cliffs Ltd. (Can. 1941)
Apr. 1957 – Name changed to Albanel Minerals Ltd.

Canadian Collieries (Dunsmuir) Ltd. (Can. 1910)
Jan. 24, 1957 – Name changed to Canadian Collieries Resources Ltd. ■

Canadian Collieries Resources Ltd. (Can. 1910)
1964 – Weldwood of Canada Ltd. acquired all o/s com. shs. for $13 per sh.
Mar. 1966 – Name changed to Weldwood of Canada Sales Limited following integration with Weldwood. All o/s 5% cum. red. pref. shs., 1963 ser., redeemed at $20 per sh. plus accr. divds.

Canadian Colonial Airways Limited (Can. 1928)
June 30, 1946 – Operated air service between Montreal and New York. Co. lost its franchise, and sold all its equipment.
1946 – Participated in formation of Peruvian International Airways.
Mar. 14, 1949 – Peruvian International Airways went into receivership. Stated shs. of Cdn. Colonial have no value.

Canadian Commercial and Industrial Bank (Can. 1975)
Apr. 23, 1981 – Name changed to Canadian Commercial Bank. ■

Canadian Commercial Bank (Can. 1975)
Sept. 1985 – Placed into liquidation by the Bank of Canada. At the time of its collapse, the bank had liabs. in excess of $2.2 billion. Price Waterhouse Limited was appointed as liquidator of CCB.
Aug. 31, 1987 – According to Price Waterhouse's second annual report on the liquidation, more than $1.3 billion had been realized through the sale of assets, comprising more than 70% on the original assets taken under administration at Sept. 3, 1985. Distributions to the Bank of Canada, the only secured creditor, totalled more than $1.1 billion. There remained approx. $642 million of assets in the liquidation, most of which comprised loans to borrowers who were in various degrees of financial distress.
Aug. 31, 1988 – Liquidator expected to be able to commence payments to unsecured creditors.

Canadian Comstock Exploration Ltd. (B.C. Sept. 18, 1985)
June 7, 1995 – Name changed to American Comstock Exploration Ltd.; basis 1 new for 4 old shs. ■

Canadian Coniaurum Investments Limited (Ont. 1929)
Dec. 29, 1970 – Name changed to MTS International Services Limited following acquisition of MTS Holdings Limited and the MTS group of cos. for $2,500,000. ■

Canadian Conquest Exploration Inc. (Alta. Mar. 27, 1987)
May 10, 1999 – Acquired by Cypress Energy Inc.; basis 0.162 Cypress cl. A shs. for 1 Conquest com. sh. (see Cypress Energy Inc.)

Canadian Conquest Mines Ltd. (Ont. 1966)
Mar. 1976 – Charter cancelled.

Canadian Consolidated Felt Co., Ltd. (Can. 1910)
1940 – Dominion Rubber Co., Ltd., purch. assets for $50,000, cancelled $198,000 indebtedness and assumed all liabs. Co. wound up and charter surrendered.

Canadian Consolidated Grain Company Limited (Can. 1928)
Apr. 1959 – Wound up following sale of assets to United Grain Growers Ltd.

Canadian Continental Oil Corp. (B.C. Apr. 19, 1984 amalg.)
Mar. 25, 1987 – Name changed to CBO Resources Corp.; basis 1 new for 4 old shs. ■

Canadian Converters' Company, Limited (Can. 1906)
1973 – Declared bankrupt; sold to Val Royal Sportswear Mfg., Ltd., a wholly owned subsid. of Queenswear (Canada) Ltd.
Apr. 10, 1978 – Divd. of 5% paid to unsecured creditors.
May 1982 – Second and final distribution of approx. 21% paid.

Canadian Convertible Debenture Fund (Ont.)
Apr. 30, 2011 – Converted from a closed end fund to an open-ended mutual fund.

Canadian Convertibles Income Plus Fund (Ont. Feb. 23, 2011)
Apr. 14, 2011 – Name changed to Canadian Convertibles Plus Fund. ■

Canadian Convertibles Plus Fund (Ont. Feb. 23, 2011)
Sept. 20, 2019 – Terminated. Net assets distributed to unithldrs. on a pro rata basis and the fund was dissolved.

Canadian Corduroys Ltd. (Can. 1949)
Apr. 21, 1952 – Name changed to Verney-Corduroys Limited. ■

Canadian Corporate Management Company Limited (Can. 1965)
June 11, 1986 – Amalgamated with a wholly owned subsid. of Federal Industries Ltd. At the holder's option, each cl. X and Y sh. was exchangeable for two cl. A common shs. of Federal Industries. Alternatively, shldrs. received (1 for 1) preferred shs. which could, at the holder's option be redeemed or purchased by Federal, in either case at $31 per sh.

Canadian Cottons Limited (Can. 1892)
Sept. 1959 – Canadian Corporate Management Company Limited acquired all o/s com. shs. at $27 per sh. All o/s 5% pref. shs. were called for redemption in 1959, at $20 per sh. On Mar. 16, 1960, name was changed to Canman Industries Ltd.

Canadian Crew Energy Corporation (B.C. Mar. 31, 1980)
Mar. 21, 1997 – Name changed to Crew Development Corporation. ■

Canadian Crude Separators Inc. (Alta. Oct. 24, 1983)
May 27, 2002 – Converted into CCS Income Trust; basis either 1 CCS Income trust unit or 1 CCS Inc. exch. sh. or a combination thereof for 1 Canadian Crude sh. (see CCS Income Trust)

Canadian Curtiss-Wright, Limited (Ont. 1951)
May 31, 1985 – Name changed to Curtiss-Wright of Canada Limited; basis 1 new for 5 old shs. ■

Canadian Data Preserve, Inc. (B.C. June 11, 2010)
Mar. 14, 2018 – Name changed to AXS Blockchain Solutions Inc. pursuant to acquisition of blockchain assets from Blockcorp Sociedad Anonima and concurrent acquisition of Do Some Marketing Block Corp Canada Inc., which was acquired to hold the blockchain assets acquired by the company. ■

Canadian Decalta Gas & Oils Ltd. (Can. 1947)
Dec. 1955 – Name changed to Western Decalta Petroleum Limited; basis 1 new for 4 old shs. ■

Canadian Delhi Oil Ltd. (Can. 1950)
Jan. 5, 1972 – Name changed to CanDel Oil Ltd.; basis 1 new for 2 old shs. ■

Canadian Delhi Petroleum (unknown 1953)
Apr. 12, 1957 – Amalgamated with Canadian Delhi Oil Ltd.

Canadian Dental Partners Inc. (Alta. Mar. 5, 1997)
Mar. 22, 2001 – Name changed to International Health Partners Inc. ■

Canadian Devonian Petroleums Limited (Can. Sept. 24, 1951)
Sept. 12, 1963 – Formed Teck Corporation Limited in Ontario following merger with The Teck-Hughes Gold Mines Limited and Lamaque Gold Mines Ltd. ■

Canadian Drawn Steel Company, Limited (Can. 1916)
1961 – Acquired by The Steel Company of Canada, Limited; basis $18 per com. sh. and $13 per pref. sh. (see The Steel Company of Canada, Limited)

Canadian Dredge and Dock Co Ltd. (Can. 1927)
July 7, 1967 – Name changed to CDRH Limited. ■

Canadian Dutch Oils, Ltd. (Ont. 1923)
1960 – Wound up.

Canadian Dyno Mines Ltd. (Ont. 1941)
1968 – Merged into International Mogul Mines Limited; basis 10 new Mogul shs. for 67 old Dyno shs. (see International Mogul Mines Limited)

Canadian Eagle Exploration Inc. (Can. Aug. 6, 1986)
Oct. 4, 1993 – Dissolved and struck off register.

Canadian Eagle Explorations Ltd. (B.C. Jan. 20, 1981)
Feb. 1, 1993 – Name changed to Eaglecrest Explorations Ltd.; basis 1 new for 4 old shs. ■

Canadian Eagle Oil & Gas Ltd. (B.C. 1981)
Mar. 17, 1986 – Name changed to Lifestyle Beverage Corporation. ■

Canadian Eagle Oil Company Limited (Can. 1928)
July 1959 – Taken over by Royal Dutch and Shell Transport & Trading Co. Ltd.; basis 2 Royal Dutch and 3 Shell Transport shs. for each 12 Canadian shs.
Jan. 1960 – Charter surrendered.

Canadian Educational Courseware, Inc. (B.C. Jan. 5, 1987)
Aug. 28, 1997 – Name changed to Can West Exploration Inc. ■

Canadian 88 Energy Corp. (Can. Sept. 4, 1987)
May 29, 2003 – Name changed to Esprit Exploration Ltd. ■

Canadian Emjay Petroleums Ltd. (Alta. 1949)
1957 – Acquired by Consolidated Emjay Petroleums Ltd.; basis 1 new for 5 old shs. (see Consolidated Emjay Petroleums Ltd.)

Canadian Empire Exploration Corp. (B.C. Feb. 24, 1987)
Feb. 23, 2007 – Name changed to X-Terra Resources Corporation; basis 1 new for 10 old shs. ■

Canadian Energy Convertible Debenture Fund (Ont.)
July 4, 2011 – Converted into an open-ended mutual fund.

Canadian Energy Exploration Inc. (Alta. Jan. 1, 2010 amalg.)
Oct. 31, 2012 – Acquired by Standard Exploration Ltd.; basis 0.13986 Standard shs. for 1 Canadian Energy sh. (see Standard Exploration Ltd.)

Canadian Energy Materials Corp. (B.C. Mar. 2, 2006)
Feb. 3, 2020 – Name changed to Gambier Gold Corp. ■

Canadian Energy Services & Technology Corp. (Can. Nov. 13, 1986)
June 20, 2017 – Name changed to CES Energy Solutions Corp. ■

Canadian Energy Services Ltd. (B.C. 1977)
July 10, 1992 – Name changed to Industra Service Corporation. ■

Canadian Energy Services L.P. (Ont. Jan. 13, 2006)
Jan. 1, 2010 – Converted into Canadian Energy Services & Technology Corp. (CESTC) (formerly Nevaro Capital Corporation); basis 1 CESTC sh. for 1 LP unit. (see Canadian Energy Services & Technology Corp.)

Canadian Entech Research Corp. (B.C. May 5, 1972)
Mar. 31, 1995 – Name changed to Canadian Entech Resources Inc.; basis 1 new for 5 old shs. ■

Canadian Entech Resources Inc. (B.C. May 5, 1972)
July 18, 1996 – Name changed to H2O Entertainment Corp. following reverse takeover acquisition of H2O Entertainment Ltd. ■

Canadian Enterprise Development Corporation Limited (Can. 1962)
July 29, 1986 – Shldrs. passed a resolution authorizing the liquidation and dissolution of the company.

Canadian Equipment Rental Fund Limited Partnership (Alta. Jan. 21, 2005)
Oct. 1, 2011 – Succeeded by CERF Incorporated pursuant to plan of arrangement whereby CERF Incorporated was formed to facilitate the conversion of the limited partnership into a corporation. ■

Canadian Equipment Rentals Corp. (Alta. Aug. 10, 2011)
June 30, 2017 – Name changed to Zedcor Energy Inc. ■

Canadian Equity & Development Company Limited (Ont. 1953)
May 31, 1974 – Amalgamated with The Cadillac Fairview Corporation Limited; basis 1.2 new for 1 old sh.

Canadian Estate Land Corp. (Ont. 1965)
Mar. 16, 1988 – Name changed to Silversword Corporation. ∎

Canadian Everock Explorations Inc. (Ont. Sept. 27, 1999)
Nov. 6, 2002 – Name changed to Everock Inc. pursuant to reverse takeover acquisition of Cali-Gem Resources Inc.; basis 1 new for 9.5 old shs. ∎

Canadian Export Gas & Oil Ltd. (Alta. May 13, 1950)
Apr. 23, 1977 – Acquired by Canex Placer Ltd., a wholly owned subsidiary of Placer Development Ltd., for $6.45 per sh.

Canadian Export Gas Ltd. (Can. 1954)
1958 – Acquired by Canadian Prospect Ltd.; basis 2.5 new for 1 old sh. (see Canadian Export Gas & Oil Ltd.)

Canadian Express Limited (Ont. Mar. 30, 1988 amalg.)
Dec. 24, 1990 – Name changed to Consolidated Canadian Express Limited; basis 1 new for 20 old shs. ∎

Canadian Express Ltd. (Ont. Mar. 30, 1988 amalg.)
Sept. 17, 2001 – Name changed to BNN Investments Ltd.; basis 1 new for 10 old shs. ∎

Canadian Fairbanks-Morse Co. Ltd. (Can. 1905)
June 1963 – Name changed to Robert Morse Corp. Ltd. ∎

The Canadian Faraday Corporation Ltd. (Ont. 1949)
May 4, 1967 – Amalgamated with Augustus Exploration Ltd. (1 for 5) and purchased the assets of Metal Mines Ltd. to form Consolidated Canadian Faraday Ltd.; basis 1 new for 1 old sh.

Canadian Ferrite Corporation (B.C. 1981)
Jan. 24, 1986 – Name changed to Maghemite Inc. (see FPsurvey - Industrials)

Canadian Ferrites Corporation (B.C. 1981)
Aug. 24, 1984 – Name changed to Canadian Ferrite Corporation. ∎

Canadian Fiber Foods Inc. (B.C. July 30, 1986)
Mar. 31, 1995 – Name changed to Red Engine Resources Corporation; basis 1 new for 4.5 old shs. ∎

Canadian 50 Advantaged Preferred Share Fund (Ont. Apr. 24, 2012)
Dec. 22, 2017 – Merged with Redwood Canadian Preferred Share Fund, a mutual fund trust managed by Redwood Asset Management Inc.; basis 0.701142 ETF units per class A unit and 0.735713 ETF units per class F unit.

Canadian Finance & Investment Ltd. (Man. 1926)
Dec. 1966 – British International Finance (Canada) Limited acquired all the business, property and assets; basis 1 BIF cl. A sh. for each cl. A or com. sh. of Canadian Finance. Warrants were exchanged for wts. to purch. cl. A shs. of BIF.

Canadian Financial Company (Que. 1975)
Jan. 1, 1985 – Name changed to Canadian Financial Corporation.

Canadian Financial Dividend & Income Fund (Ont. Jan. 27, 2006)
Jan. 16, 2007 – Amalgamated with Canadian Financial Income Fund; basis 0.902969 new Candian Financial Income unit for 1 old Canadian Financial Dividend unit.

Canadian Financial Founders (Can. 1930)
Apr. 1944 – Dissolved. Distribution: Ser. C, 1934, 1.157¢; 1936, 12.528¢. Entirely liquidated and exch. for ser. D in 1936. Ser. D, 1934-39, $1.50.

Canadian Financial Holdings Corporation (Ont. May 27, 1983)
July 10, 1998 – Formed Calderone Corporation following reverse takeover acquisition of Calderone Brothers Inc.; basis 1 new for 10 old shs. ∎

Canadian Financial Services NT Corp. (Ont. Aug. 17, 2000)
Dec. 1, 2005 – Redeemed in full; basis capital shs. - $62.52452 per sh. and preferred shs. - $15 per sh.

Canadian First Financial Group Inc. (Ont. Aug. 2, 1995)
Aug. 9, 2002 – Acquired by Dundee Wealth Management Inc. for $1.26 per sh. (see Dundee Wealth Management Inc.)

Canadian First Mortgage Corporation (Ont. 1963)
Oct. 31, 1980 – Amalgamated into Victoria and Grey Trust Company; basis 2 new Victoria and Grey shs. for 1 old Canadian First Mortgage sh. (see Victoria and Grey Trust Co.)

Canadian Foreign Investment Corp. Ltd. (Can. 1924)
Nov. 1950 – Control of co. acquired through offer to shldrs. of $80 (Cdn) per sh. by Dr. J. J. Abdalla of Brazil.

Canadian Foremost Ltd. (Alta. Aug. 1, 1966)
July 15, 1994 – Name changed to Foremost Industries Inc. ∎

Canadian Fortune Oil Ltd. (Alta. 1949)
1971 – Merged into Page Petroleum Ltd.; basis 1 new for 14 old shs.

Canadian Fortune Resources Inc. (Alta. Dec. 12, 1987 amalg.)
June 3, 1991 – Amalgamated with Canadian Gold Mines Ltd. to form Consolidated Canadian Fortune Resources Inc.; basis 1 new for 1 Canadian Gold sh. and 1 new for 2 Canadian Fortune shs. (see Consolidated Canadian Fortune Resources Inc.)

Canadian Fortune Resources Inc. (Alta. 1991 amalg.)
Sept. 17, 1993 – Amalgamated with Devnic Energy Inc. (1 for 1.77) and Petrolia Oil & Gas Ltd. (1 for 1) to form a new co. named Fortune Energy Inc.; basis 1 new for 0.51 old shs. (see Fortune Energy Inc.)

Canadian Foundation Company Limited (Can. 1963)
July 1, 1987 – Became a subsid. of Banister Continental Ltd.

Canadian Foundation Company Limited (Can. 1963)
June 8, 1989 – Name changed to The Foundation Company of Canada Ltd. ∎

Canadian Fracmaster Ltd. (Can. Apr. 5, 1976)
July 17, 1998 – Name changed to Fracmaster Ltd. ∎

Canadian Frobisher Resources Ltd. (B.C. Nov. 21, 1991 amalg.)
Sept. 8, 1994 – Acquired by Orbit Oil & Gas Ltd.; basis 1.025 new Orbit sh. for 1 old Canadian Frobisher sh. (see Orbit Oil & Gas Ltd.)

Canadian Futurity Oils Ltd. (Alta. Nov. 1, 1985 amalg.)
Aug. 4, 1989 – Name changed to Baca Resources Ltd.; basis 1 new for 5 old shs. ∎

The Canadian Games Network Inc. (Ont. Oct. 22, 1976 amalg.)
Jan. 14, 1987 – Name changed to Northquest Ventures Inc.; basis 1 new for 3 old shs. ∎

Canadian Geary Mining Corporation Ltd (Ont. 1964)
Feb. 20, 1980 – Dissolved.

Canadian General Electric Co. Ltd. (Can. 1892)
June 1, 1987 – Name changed to General Electric Canada Inc. ∎

Canadian General Securities, Limited (Can. 1926)
Mar. 1988 – Became a wholly owned subsid. of Central Capital Corp.

Canadian Giant Exploration Limited (B.C. Oct. 2, 1979)
Mar. 6, 1995 – Delisted from the Vancouver Stock Exchange. Subsequently dissolved for failure to file.

Canadian Gift Sales Limited (Ont. 1956)
1964 – Placed into bankruptcy. Assets purch. by M. Goldsmith and Co.

Canadian Glacier Beverage Corporation (B.C. Mar. 23, 1988)
Aug. 26, 1997 – Name changed to Glacier Ventures International Corp.; basis 1 new for 5 old shs. ∎

Canadian Gold & Metals Mining Co. Ltd (Ont. 1938)
1966 – Charter cancelled.

Canadian Gold Hunter Corp. (B.C. Feb. 3, 1983)
Aug. 20, 2004 – Continued into Canada.
Sept. 22, 2009 – Name changed to NGEx Resources Inc. ∎

Canadian Gold Mines Ltd. (Man. Jan. 22, 1986 amalg.)
June 3, 1991 – Amalgamated with Canadian Fortune Resources Inc. to form a new co. known as Consolidated Canadian Fortune Resources Inc.; basis 1 new for 1 old sh. (see Consolidated Canadian Fortune Resources Inc.)

Canadian Gold Operators Ltd. (Que. Aug. 22, 1931)
Aug. 21, 1937 – Name changed to Kewagama Gold Mines (Québec) Ltd. and continued into Quebec following acquisition by Kewagama Gold Mines, an Ontario corporation, and the subsequent transfer to Kewagama Gold Mines (Québec) Ltd. in October 1936. ∎

Canadian Gold Resources Inc. (Ont. Sept. 25, 1979)
May 5, 1997 – Name changed to Strategic Vista International Inc. following reverse takeover acquisition of Strategic Vista Corp.; basis 1 new for 25 old shs. ∎

Canadian Goldale Corporation Limited (Ont. 1919)
Dec. 31, 1972 – Name changed to Hambro Canada (1972) Limited. ∎

Canadian Golden Dragon Resources Ltd. (B.C. June 22, 1990 amalg.)
Nov. 5, 2007 – Name changed to Trillium North Minerals Ltd. ∎

Canadian Golden Gate Oils Ltd. (Alta. 1953)
May 1971 – Name changed to Petroquest Ltd. ∎

Canadian Goodrich Co. Ltd. (Can. 1922)
1936 – Name changed to B.F. Goodrich Rubber Co. of Canada, Ltd.

Canadian Graphite Ltd. (B.C. 1983)
July 4, 1989 – Name changed to BFD Industries Inc. ∎

Canadian Gridoil Limited (Alta. 1957)
Sept. 11, 1970 – Name changed to Ashland Oil Canada Limited. ∎

Canadian Grizzly Bear Mines Inc. (Alta. 1987)
Feb. 1, 1993 – Dissolved and struck off register.

Canadian Gypsum Company, Limited (Can. Jan. 1, 1985 amalg.)
Nov. 11, 1987 – Name changed to CGC Inc. ∎

Canadian Hearing Care Incorporated (Alta. Mar. 19, 1997)
Apr. 7, 1998 – Name changed to Audiotech Healthcare Corporation; basis 1 new for 1 old sh. ∎

Canadian Helicopters Group Inc. (Can. May 7, 2010)
Sept. 25, 2012 – Name changed to HNZ Group Inc. ∎

Canadian Helicopters Income Fund (Que. July 25, 2005)
Jan. 4, 2011 – Succeeded by Canadian Helicopters Group Inc. pursuant to plan of arrangement whereby Canadian Helicopters Group Inc. was formed to facilitate the conversion of the fund into a corporation and the fund was subsequently dissolved. ∎

Canadian Hidrogas Resources Ltd. (B.C. 1964)
1979 – Stratfield Investments Ltd., a wholly owned subsid. of Norcen Energy Resources Limited, acquired all o/s shs. in 1979-80 at $15.50 per sh.

Canadian High Crest Oils Ltd. (Alta. 1949)
June 1, 1966 – Name changed to Canadian Tricentrol Oils Ltd.; basis 1 new for 10 old shs. ■

Canadian High Income Equity Fund (Ont. Jan. 27, 2010)
Aug. 16, 2024 – Terminated; final distrib. to be made on a pro rata basis.

Canadian High Point Mines Ltd. (Ont. 1965)
1968 – Assets sold to Mission Financial Corp. Ltd.; basis 0.01311 new for 1 old sh.

Canadian High Yield Focus Fund (Ont. May 25, 2011)
June 27, 2016 – Terminated and dissolved. Net assets distributed on a pro rata basis.

Canadian Home Shopping Network (CHSN) Ltd. (Can. Apr. 3, 1986)
Sept. 1, 1993 – Acquired by Rogers Communications Inc.; basis 89.5¢ for 1 CHSN sh. or 1 Rogers Communications cl. B non-vtg. sh. for 19.25 CHSN shs.

Canadian Homestead Oils Limite (Alta. Mar. 18, 1947)
Apr. 14, 1980 – Amalgamated with Inter-City Gas Limited to form Inter-City Gas Corporation (Inter-City); basis 1.4 new shs. of Inter-City for 1 old sh. of Homstead.

Canadian Hotel Income Properties Real Estate Investment Trust (B.C. Apr. 28, 1997)
Dec. 6, 2007 – Acquired by BFO Acquisition Limited Partnership for $19.10 per unit.

Canadian Hunter Exploration Ltd. (Alta. Dec. 31, 1998)
Dec. 7, 2001 – Acquired by Burlington Acquisition Corporation, indirect wholly owned subsid. of US-based Burlington Resources Inc.; basis $53 per com. sh.

Canadian Husky Oil Ltd. (Can. 1953)
Apr. 1963 – Name changed to Husky Oil Canada Ltd. ■

Canadian Hydro Developers, Inc. (Alta. July 21, 1987)
Nov. 9, 2009 – Acquired by 1478860 Alberta Ltd., a wholly owned subsid. of TransAlta Corporation, for $5.25 per sh.

Canadian Hydrocarbons Ltd. (Can. 1955)
Dec. 31, 1978 – All o/s com. shs. not already held acquired by Inter-City Gas Limited; basis 1.5 com. shs. Inter-City for each com. sh. held. All o/s 5.5% 1st pref. shs. called for redemption on Dec. 31, 1987 at $21 per sh.

Canadian Ice Machine Co. Ltd. (Can. 1913)
June 30, 1967 – Name changed to Cimco Limited. ■

Canadian Imperial Ginseng Products Ltd. (B.C. Apr. 6, 1989)
Dec. 4, 1995 – Name changed to Imperial Ginseng Products Ltd. (see FPsurvey - Industrials)

Canadian Imperial Mines Inc. (B.C. Sept. 18, 1987)
Dec. 15, 1994 – Name changed to Pacific Imperial Mines Inc.; basis 1 new for 2.5 old shs. (see FPsurvey - Mines & Energy)

Canadian Imperial Venture Corp. (B.C. Sept. 4, 1986)
Mar. 30, 2021 – Name changed to Ikanik Farms Inc. pursuant to the reverse takeover acquisition of (old) Ikänik Farms Inc., and concurrent amalgamation of (old) Ikänik Farms with wholly owned 11326937 Canada Inc. (continued as Cannus Partners Amalco 2019 Inc.); basis 1 new for 1.5579299 old shs. ■

Canadian Income Management Trust (Alta. Nov. 9, 2005)
Sept. 10, 2012 – All tr. units redeemed for $1.79 per unit.

Canadian Indoor Golf Inc. (Ont. Apr. 30, 1976)
Dec. 12, 1978 – Name changed to Associated Recreation Corp.; basis 1 new for 5 old shs. ■

Canadian Industrial Alcohol Co., Ltd. (Can. Sept. 30, 1924; via letters patent)
June 1, 1950 – Name changed to H. Corby Distillery Ltd. ■

Canadian Industrial Gas & Oil Ltd. (Alta. 1965)
Oct. 28, 1975 – Amalgamated with Northern & Central Gas Corp. Ltd. through a holding company formed to facilitate the merger, to form Norcen Energy Resources Limited. Basis: 7 Norcen com. for 10 CIGOL shs.; 1 Norcen $1.06 ser. A 1st pref. sh. for each Northern & Central $1.06 ser. A 2nd pref. sh.; 1 Norcen $1.50 ser. B 1st pref. sh. for each Northern & Central $1.50 ser. B 2nd pref. sh.; Northern & Central com. and jr. pref. shs. and warr. exch for like shs. or warr. of Norcen. The redeem. 1st pref. sh. of Northern & Central remained o/s. (see Norcen Energy Resources Limited)

Canadian Industrial Gas Ltd. (Ont. 1950)
1965 – Acquired by former subsid., Canadian Industrial Gas & Oil Ltd., in exch. for 458,765 pref. and 145,893 com. shs. of that co. The com. shs. 3,677,822 com. shs. of CIGO already owned by CIG were distributed to CIG shldrs. and the CIGO pref. shs. to holders of pref. shs. of CIG.

Canadian Industrial Minerals Corp. (B.C. Dec. 7, 1983)
Jan. 20, 1995 – Continued into Alberta. (see Abacan Resource Corporation)
Feb. 10, 1995 – Amalgamated with Abacan Resource Corporation, Canadian Angus Resources Ltd., Canstar Ventures Corp. and Profile Capital Corporation to form Abacan Resource Corporation; basis 1 new for 1 Abacan sh., 0.30 new for 1 Canadian Angus sh., 0.45 new for 1 Canstar sh., 0.23 new for 1 Profile sh. and 0.51 new for 1 Canadian Industrial sh. (see Abacan Resource Corporation)

Canadian Industrial Minerals Ltd. (N.S. May 12, 1941)
Charter cancelled.

Canadian Industries Limited (Can. 1954)
Jan. 1, 1980 – Name changed to C-I-L Inc. ■

Canadian Ingersoll-Rand Co. Ltd. (Can. 1912)
Oct. 5, 1961 – Acquired by Ingersoll-Rand Co. of New York for $60 per sh.

Canadian Insulock Corporation (B.C. Oct. 19, 1984)
Sept. 5, 1995 – Name changed to American Insulock Inc.; basis 1 new for 4 old shs. ■

Canadian International Investment Trust Limited (Can. 1929)
June 30, 1980 – Name changed to CIIT Inc. ■

Canadian International Minerals Inc. (B.C. Mar. 2, 2006)
Apr. 12, 2018 – Name changed to Canadian Energy Materials Corp. ■

Canadian International Paper Company (Can. 1916)
Oct. 1, 1981 – Formed CIP Inc. on amalgamation with various Canadian Pacific Enterprises Limited affiliates after acquisition from International Paper Company for $1.1 billion.

Canadian International Pharma Corp. (B.C. Nov. 21, 1983)
Jan. 29, 2021 – Name changed to VAR Resources Corp. ■

Canadian International Power Company Limited (Can. 1956)
Apr. 30, 1979 – Liquidated and charter surrendered on final disposition of shs. of The Barbados Light & Power Company Limited. Distribution of Assets: A liquidating distribution made Oct. 3, 1977, consisting of 1 sh. of Bolivian Power Co. and 1 American depository receipt of Compania de Alumbrado Electrico de San Salvador, S.A. for each 2 cl. A or B shs. held. Cash distribution of US$20 per cl. A sh. and $17 U.S. (tax-def.) per cl. B sh. made Nov. 3, 1977. Subsequently, US$0.60 per cl. A and US$0.51 (tax-def.) per cl. B sh. were distributed June 29, 1978; and US$0.75 per cl A and B sh. paid Jan. 15, 1979.

Final distribution for tax purposes made consisting of $0.25 per cl. A and B sh. plus 1 Trust Unit in Canadian International Power Company Liquidating Trust. This Trust was created to hold the remaining assets for the benefit of the shldrs. whose int. will be represented in Trust units.

Canadian Interurban Properties Limited (Ont. 1917)
Oct. 1, 1973 – Amalgamated with Campeau Corporation; basis 1 1st pref. sh. of the new co. for each ser. A pref. sh. of Canadian Interurban, and 0.333 pref. sh. of the new co. for each com. sh. (other than those held by Campeau Corporation) of Canadian Interurban.

Canadian Investment Grade Preferred Share Fund (Ont. Nov. 28, 2016)
Aug. 28, 2023 – Terminated. Redemption price equal to the net asset value per unit, payable to unitholders Sept. 1, 2023.

Canadian Investment Grade Preferred Share Fund (P2L) (Ont. Nov. 28, 2016)
Sept. 24, 2018 – Name changed to Canadian Investment Grade Preferred Share Fund. ■

Canadian Jamieson Mines Ltd. (Ont. 1964)
Oct. 20, 1972 – Name changed to Unicorp Financial Inc. ■

Canadian Javelin Foundries & Machine Works Ltd. (Can. June 28, 1951; via letters patent)
1954 – Name changed to Canadian Javelin Limited. ■

Canadian Javelin Limited (Can. June 28, 1951; via letters patent)
May 22, 1981 – Name changed to Javelin International Limited. ■

Canadian Jorex Limited (Ont. Feb. 28, 1968)
Oct. 30, 1984 – Continued into Canada. (see Cypress Energy Inc.)
Oct. 17, 1996 – Acquired by Cypress Energy Inc. for 72¢ per sh. (see Cypress Energy Inc.)

Canadian Keeley Mines Ltd. (Ont. 1959)
July 22, 1981 – Name changed to Keeley-Frontier Resources Limited; basis 1 new for 7 old shs. ■

Canadian Kinetics Corporation (Alta. Dec. 15, 1986)
June 1, 1995 – Dissolved and struck off register.

Canadian Kirkland Mines Ltd. (Ont. Dec. 17, 1927)
July 15, 1942 – Acquired by Amalgamated Kirkland Mines Ltd.; basis 1 new for 10 old shs. (see Amalgamated Kirkland Mines Ltd.)

Canadian Kodiak Refineries Ltd. (Alta. 1958)
Jan. 1963 – Name changed to Kodiak Petroleums Ltd.; basis 1 new for 3 old shs. ■

Canadian Leader Energy Inc. (Alta. Nov. 24, 1986)
May 20, 1997 – Formed Centurion Energy International Inc. in Alberta on amalgamation with Eagle Energy Corp.; basis 0.6 new for 1 Eagle sh. and 1 new for 0.5 Canadian Leader sh. ■

Canadian Lencourt Mines Limted (Que. 1945)
May 4, 1987 – Name changed to Lencourt Limited; basis 1 new for 5 old shs. (see FPsurvey - Mines & Energy)

Canadian Liberty Development Corp. (B.C. 1983)
Mar. 1, 1996 – Dissolved and struck off register.

Canadian Light & Power Company (Que. 1904)
June 1949 – Property and rights purchased by Quebec Hydro-Electric Commission.
Apr. 1954 – 5% 1st mtge. bds. o/s paid off at maturity on July 1, 1949. Initial distribution of $20 per sh. paid October 1949; $5.00 per sh. paid April 1951; final distribution of $1.67 per sh. made April 1954.

Canadian Lithium Mining Corp. Ltd. (Ont. 1954)
1958 – Merged into Aug.us Exploration Ltd.; basis 1 new for 4.5 old shs.

Canadian Locomotive Company Ltd. (Can. 1911)
July 26, 1965 – Name changed to Fairbanks Morse (Canada) Ltd. ■

Canadian Long Island Petroleums Ltd. (Alta. Jan. 10, 1949)
July 31, 1979 – Name changed to First Calgary Petroleums Ltd.; basis 1 new for 2 old shs. ■

Canadian Longhorn Petroleum Corp. (B.C. 1981)
July 3, 1984 – Name changed to Canadian Ferrites Corporation. ■

Canadian Lynx Petroleum Ltd. (B.C. Sept. 19, 1986)
Sept. 19, 1995 – Name changed to Tanganyika Oil Company Ltd. and continued into Canada. ■

Canadian Magnesite Mines Ltd. (Ont. Nov. 13, 1962)
Aug. 18, 1989 – Name changed to EQ Resources Ltd. ■

Canadian Majestic Resources Ltd. (Alta. 1987)
Dec. 30, 1988 – Acquired by Chancellor Energy Resources Inc.; basis 1 Majestic sh. for 1.45 Chancellor shs. (see Chancellor Energy Resources Inc.)

Canadian Malartic Gold Mines Limited (Can. May 17, 1933)
Dec. 30, 1976 – Acquired by Canray Resources Limited; basis 1 new Canray sh. for 4 old Malartic shs. (see Canray Resources Limited)

Canadian Manganese Mining Corporation Limited (Ont. 1953)
Mar. 1976 – Charter cancelled.

Canadian Maple Leaf Financial Corporation (Can. June 19, 1992)
Oct. 29, 1999 – Name changed to CML Global Capital Ltd. ■

Canadian Marconi Company (Can. 1903)
Mar. 7, 2000 – Name changed to BAE Systems Canada Inc. ■

Canadian Media Arts Capital Corporation (Alta. July 24, 1986)
Apr. 19, 1990 – Name changed to CMA Capital Corporation; basis 1 new for 2 old shs. ■

Canadian Medical Laboratories Limited (Ont. June 28, 1971)
Apr. 3, 2003 – Name changed to CML Healthcare Inc.; basis 1 new for 30 old shs. ■

Canadian Medical Legacy Corp. (B.C. May 11, 1990)
Oct. 16, 1998 – Name changed to Continental Home Healthcare Ltd. ■

Canadian Memorial Services Limited (Ont. Aug. 31, 1973 amalg.)
Apr. 21, 1975 – Name changed to Arbor Capital Resources Inc. ■

Canadian Merrill Ltd. (Que. 1950)
Apr. 1980 – Transfer of co. business to Francana Oil & Gas Ltd. Exch. basis 1.9 Francana shs. for 1 old Merrill sh. (see Francana Oil & Gas Ltd.)

Canadian Metals Exploration Ltd. (B.C. Jan. 17, 1983)
June 28, 2004 – Name changed to Hard Creek Nickel Corporation. ■

Canadian Microcool Corp. (B.C. 1985)
July 19, 1990 – Name changed to EI Environmental Engineering Concepts Ltd. ■

Canadian Minefinders Ltd. (Ont. 1960)
1969 – Assets sold to Twentieth Century Explorations Ltd.; basis 1 new for 1 old sh.

Canadian Mineral Corporation (B.C. May 9, 1975)
Apr. 12, 1983 – Name changed to Canadian-United Minerals, Inc.; basis 1 new for 5 old shs. ■

Canadian Mineral Equities Ltd. (Ont. Aug. 28, 1936)
Assets distributed to shldrs.; basis $8.565 per sh.

Canadian Minerals Ltd. (Alta. 1951)
Oct. 3, 1960 – Name changed to Canadian Minerals (1960) Ltd. ■

Canadian Minerals (1960) Ltd. (Alta. 1951)
Aug. 20, 1970 – Name changed to Canadian Minerals & Resources Ltd.

Canadian Mining & Exploration Co. (Ont. 1945)
Mar. 26, 1956 – Charter cancelled.

Canadian Mining Company Inc. (Alta. June 5, 1987)
Feb. 8, 2016 – Name changed to Canadian Zeolite Corp. and continued into British Columbia. ■

The Canadian Mining Company Ltd. (Alta. June 5, 1987)
Apr. 10, 2000 – Name changed to Zeo-Tech Enviro Corp. ■

Canadian Mining Corp. (B.C. Apr. 26, 2013)
July 18, 2018 – Name changed to Chemesis International Inc. following the reverse takeover acquisition of an interest in a cannabis business; basis 1 new for 2 old shs. ■

Canadian Mining Resources Inc. (Alta. Apr. 12, 1994)
June 28, 1995 – Name changed to Axia Multimedia Corporation pursuant to reverse takeover acquisition of Axia Multimedia Corporation; basis 1 new for 2 old shs. ■

Canadian Mr. Build Industries Inc. (B.C. 1986)
Feb. 18, 1992 – Name changed to SoCal Capital Corp. ■

Canadian Mono Mines Inc. (B.C. Mar. 13, 1981)
Feb. 27, 2013 – Dissolved and struck from register.

Canadian Motor Lamp Co. Ltd. (Can. 1927)
May 1955 – Dominion Forge & Stamping Co. Ltd. acquired all o/s com. shs. at $26 per sh. Dominion Forge was committed to sell all its shs. to Lyon Inc., a U.S. firm. Prior to offer, Dominion Forge held 71,000 shs. Converted to a private co. as of Jan. 1, 1957.

Canadian Mountain Minerals Ltd. (Alta. Aug. 25, 1995)
Apr. 22, 1998 – Amalgamated with 766002 Alberta Ltd., a wholly owned subsid. of Goldtex Resources Ltd.; basis 6 Goldtex shs. for 1 Canadian Mountain sh.

Canadian Natural Resources Limited (B.C. Nov. 7, 1973)
Jan. 6, 1982 – Continued into Alberta. (see FPsurvey - Mines & Energy)

Canadian Neuromed Clinics Limited (Ont. Sept. 10, 1987)
Jan. 27, 1993 – Name changed to Evans Health Group Limited. ■

Canadian Newnorth Resources Limited (Ont. 1945)
Nov. 26, 1994 – Charter cancelled and co. dissolved.

Canadian Newscope Resources Ltd. (Can. Sept. 13, 1984)
July 11, 1994 – Name changed to Newscope Resources Ltd. ■

Canadian Nexus Team Ventures Corp. (B.C. Mar. 28, 1980)
Mar. 11, 2025 – Name changed to Data Watts Partners Inc. (see FPsurvey - Mines & Energy; FPsurvey - Industrials)

Canadian Nisto Mines Limited (Ont. 1948)
Mar. 1976 – Charter cancelled.

Canadian North Inca Mines Ltd. (Ont. 1945)
Nov. 1968 – Name changed to Southmark Petroleum Limited. ■

Canadian Northcor Energy Inc. (Alta. Dec. 5, 1986)
Nov. 18, 1993 – Amalgamated with Kemano Resources Ltd. (0.9 for 1 com., plus 1 for 1 ser. 1 conv. pfd.) to form

new company Purcell Energy Ltd.; basis 1 new amalco. sh. for 1 old Canadian Northcor sh. (see Purcell Energy Ltd.)

Canadian Northstar Corporation (Alta. Jan. 11, 1978)
July 13, 2001 – Formed First Chicago Investment Corporation on amalgamation with First Chicago Investment Corporation; basis 1 new sub. vtg. sh. plus 0.25 new multiple vtg. sh. plus 1 new dividend sh. for 1 old Canadian Northstar com. sh. ■

Canadian Northwest Mines & Oils Ltd. (Ont. 1950)
Jan. 1968 – Charter cancelled.

Canadian Obas Oil Limited (Alta. May 19, 1965)
May 22, 1979 – Name changed to Rupertsland Resources Co. Ltd. ■

Canadian Occidental Petroleum Ltd. (Can. July 12, 1971 amalg.)
Nov. 10, 2000 – Name changed to Nexen Inc. ■

Canadian Oil & Gas Reserves Ltd. (Alta. 1952)
1956 – Acquired by Canadusa Oil & Gas Reserves Ltd.; basis 1 new for 5 old shs.

Canadian Oil Companies Limited (Ont. 1908)
Oct. 12, 1962 – Shell Investments Ltd. offered to purchase all o/s com. shs. on either of two bases, as follows: (1)for each Canadian Oil com. sh., $32.50 in cash plus one 5.5% cum. pref. conv. $20 par sh. of Shell Investments, from Oct. 1, 1963 to Sept. 30, 1972, into a depository cert. representing 0.25 cl. B com. sh. of Shell Canada Ltd. (2)for each Canadian Oil com. sh., the sum of $52.50 in cash plus a warrant entitling the holder to purch., from Oct. 1, 1963 to Sept. 30, 1972, a depository cert. representing 0.25 cl. B com. sh. of Shell Canada Ltd. at $20. Shell Investments acquired more than 99% of Cdn Oil com. shs. and by Jan. 10, 1963, had transfered them to the Hesper Oil Co. Ltd., a wholly owned subsid. of Shell Canada. Hesper and Cdn Oil were then merged into a new co., Canadian Oil Co. Ltd. All o/s 4% and 5% pref. shs. of Cdn Oil Companies were redeemed on Jan. 14, 1963, the 4% at $103 plus 16¢ per sh. accr. divid. and the 5% at $105 plus 20¢ per sh. accr. divid. The 8% pref. shs. were exchanged sh.-for-sh. for cl. A pref. of the new Cdn Oil Co., and Shell Canada offered to purch. the new stk. at $175 per sh. The $30,000,000 o/s 4% serial and s.f. debs. of Cdn Oil Companies were exch. at par for 4.25% ser. E debs. of Shell Canada. Holders of 21,495 com. shs. of Cdn Oil Companies who did not accept the purch. offer of Shell Investments received 6% cl. B pref. stk. of the new Cdn Oil Co. Shs. redeemed Mar. 11, 1963 at $52.50 per sh. plus accr. divid. of 35¢ per sh. Each cl. B pref. sh. carried a purch. warrant similar to those issued under the original offer of Shell Investments.

Canadian Oil Holdings, Ltd. (unknown)
1928 – Taken over by Mar-Jon Oil Co. Ltd.; basis 1 new for 4 old shs. (see Mar-Jon Oil Co. Ltd.)

Canadian Oil Recovery & Remediation Enterprises Ltd. (Can. Jan. 8, 2007)
Nov. 28, 2022 – Dissolved.

Canadian Oil Sands Limited (Alta. Dec. 31, 2010; amalg.)
Mar. 21, 2016 – Name changed to Suncor Energy Ventures Holding Corporation following acquisition by Suncor Energy Inc.; basis 0.28 Suncor com. shs. for 1 Canadian Oil Sands com. sh.

Canadian Oil Sands Trust (Alta. Apr. 19, 1996)
July 9, 2001 – Amalgamated with Athabasca Oil Sands Trust effectuve; basis 1 old Canadian Oil Sands trust unit for 1 new Athabasca Oil Sands trust unit. Subsequent to the amalgamation, Athabasca changed its name to Canadian Oil Sands Trust. (see Canadian Oil Sands Trust)

Canadian Oil Sands Trust (Alta. July 5, 2001 amalg.)
Dec. 31, 2010 – Succeeded by Canadian Oil Sands Limited pursuant to plan of arrangement whereby Canadian Oil Sands Limited was formed to facilitate the

conversion of the trust into a corporation and the trust was subsequently dissolved. ■

Canadian Oilfield Solutions Corp. (Alta. Apr. 1, 1999 amalg.)
June 9, 2014 – Name changed to Divergent Energy Services Corp. (see FPsurvey - Mines & Energy; FPsurvey - Industrials)

Canadian Orebodies Inc. (Alta. Jan. 10, 2008)
July 21, 2008 – Continued into Ontario.
May 20, 2020 – Name changed to Hemlo Explorers Inc.; basis 1 new for 3 old shs. ■

Canadian Oriental Holdings Ltd. (Ont. 1969)
Dec. 1974 – Name changed to Canalite Limited. ■

Canadian Overseas Exploration Corporation (B.C. Aug. 15, 1966)
May 21, 1992 – Continued into Canada.
Dec. 13, 2004 – Dissolved.

Canadian Pacer Petroleum Corporation (B.C. Apr. 1, 1981)
Oct. 30, 1989 – Name changed to Providence Innovations Inc. ■

Canadian Pacific Air Lines, Limited (Can. 1936)
Jan. 30, 1987 – Acquired by PWA Corporation (formerly Pacific Western Airlines Corporation) from Canadian Pacific Limited. (see Pacific Western Airlines Corporation)

Canadian Pacific Air Lines, Limited (Can. 1936)
Jan. 1, 1988 – Formed Canadian Airlines International Ltd. on amalgamation with Pacific Western Airlines Ltd. to become a wholly owned subsid. of PWA Corporation. (see PWA Corporation)

Canadian Pacific Enterprises Limited (Can. 1962)
Dec. 6, 1985 – Merged with Canadian Pacific Limited. Prior to merger, all o/s pref. shs. series B retired for $102.8 million plus accrued divds. Each com. sh. of Canadian Pacific Enterprises exchanged for 1.675 ordinary shs. of Canadian Pacific. (see Canadian Pacific Limited)

Canadian Pacific Forest Products Limited (Ont. Apr. 3, 1936)
Jan. 1, 1989 – Amalgamated in Canada to continue with same name.
Mar. 21, 1994 – Name changed to Avenor Inc. ■

Canadian Pacific Investments Limited (Can. 1962)
May 5, 1980 – Name changed to Canadian Pacific Enterprises Limited. ■

Canadian Pacific Limited (Can. Feb. 16, 1881; via Dominion charter)
Oct. 2, 2001 – Plan of Arrangement to establish 5 separate companies in place of 5 CP business divisions. Basis in each case for 1 old Canadian Pacific Limited com. sh. plus cash for any fractional shs.: (1) 0.684 PanCanadian Energy Corporation (formerly PanCanadian Petroleum Limited); (2) 0.50 Canadian Pacific Railway Limited; (3) 0.25 CP Ships Limited; (4) 0.25 Fairmont Hotels & Resorts Inc.; and (5) 0.166 Fording Inc. Also shldrs. of 5.65% cum. redeem. First Pfd. shs. Series A entitled to receive $26 plus $0.2361 in accrued and unpaid dividends (total $26.2361) for 1 old pfd. sh.

Canadian Pacific Lumber Ltd. (Alta. 1951)
May 1, 1982 – Struck off register.

Canadian Pacific Oil Co., Ltd. (unknown)
In liquidation; Edna H. Ward, Vancouver, B.C., liquidator.

Canadian Pacific Railway Company (Can. Feb. 16, 1881; via Dominion charter)
July 3, 1971 – Name changed to Canadian Pacific Limited. ■

Canadian Pacific Railway Limited (Can. June 22, 2001)
Apr. 14, 2023 – Name changed to Canadian Pacific Kansas City Limited. (see FPsurvey - Industrials)

Canadian Pacific Sulphur Mines Limited (Ont. 1968)
Dec. 1973 – Dissolved.

Canadian Palladium Resources Inc. (B.C. Aug. 26, 2005)
Dec. 13, 2023 – Name changed to Quest Critical Metals Inc. (see FPsurvey - Mines & Energy)

Canadian Patricia Exploration Ltd. (Ont. Sept. 20, 1984)
Apr. 30, 1993 – Name changed to In-Flight Phone Canada Inc.; basis 1 new for 10.2 old shs. ■

Canadian Pawnee Oil Corporation (B.C. Jan. 15, 1979)
Nov. 7, 1989 – Name changed to Britannia Gold Corp.; basis 1 new for 10 old shs. ■

Canadian Penn Grade Producers Ltd. (unknown)
1952 – Reported out of existence.

Canadian Petrofina Ltd. (Can. 1953)
1968 – Name changed to Petrofina Canada Ltd. ■

Canadian Petroleum Resources Synd. (unknown)
1914 – Acquired by Alberta Petroleum Consolidated Ltd. (see Alberta Petroleum Consolidated Ltd.)

Canadian Phoenix Resources Corp. (Alta. Feb. 24, 2004 amalg.)
Mar. 8, 2013 – Name changed to Knol Resources Corp.; basis 1 new for 10 old shs. ■

Canadian Pioneer Energy Inc. (Alta. Mar. 31, 1978)
Dec. 20, 1995 – Acquired by Cimarron Petroleum Ltd.; basis 1 Cimarron sh. for 32.34 Canadian Pioneer shs. (see Cimarron Petroleum Ltd.)

Canadian Pioneer Management Ltd. (Can. July 31, 1968)
Aug. 17, 1987 – Name changed to Pioneer LifeCo Inc.; basis 1 new for 10 old shs. ■

Canadian Pioneer Oils Ltd. (Alta. Mar. 31, 1978)
Oct. 26, 1987 – Name changed to Canadian Pioneer Energy Inc.; basis 1 new for 4 old shs. ■

Canadian Pipe Lines & Petroleums Ltd. (Alta. 1953)
May 1957 – Amalgamated into Scurry-Rainbow Oil Ltd. (see Scurry-Rainbow Oil Limited)

Canadian Pipe Lines Producers Ltd. (Alta. 1953)
June 19, 1954 – Name changed to Canadian Pipe Lines & Petroleums Ltd. ■

Canadian Platinum Corp. (Alta. Nov. 2, 2011 amalg.)
Jan. 25, 2019 – Name changed to Aurex Energy Corp.; basis 1 new for 26 old shs. (see FPsurvey - Mines & Energy)

Canadian Platinum Refineries Inc. (Alta. 1980)
Oct. 1, 1988 – Dissolved and struck off register.

Canadian Plywood Corporation Limited (B.C. 1964)
Apr. 1971 – Placed into receivership.
1972 – Assets sold to British Columbia Forest Products Ltd.

Canadian Ponderay Energy Limited (Alta. 1962)
Mar. 30, 1995 – Dissolved and struck off register.

Canadian Power & Paper Securities Ltd. (Can. 1952)
July 1968 – Amalgamated with Warnock Hersey International Ltd.; basis 2 com. shs. for 1 com. sh., and pref. sh.-for-sh.

Canadian Preferred Share Trust (Ont. June 22, 2015)
Mar. 31, 2020 – Terminated; net assets distrib. to unitholders on a pro rata basis.

Canadian Premium Resource Corporation (B.C. 1983)
July 7, 1987 – Amalgamated with Mahogany Minerals Resources Inc. to form Mahogany Minerals Resources Inc.; basis 1 1/9 new for 1 old sh.

Canadian Premium Sand Inc. (Ont. Sept. 21, 2005)
Feb. 25, 2019 – Continued into Canada. (see FPsurvey - Mines & Energy; FPsurvey - Industrials)

Canadian Premium Select Income Fund (Ont. Oct. 28, 2011)
Nov. 11, 2013 – Converted from a closed end to an open-ended fund.

Canadian Prodigy Capital Corporation (Can. May 9, 2005)
July 13, 2010 – Amalgamated with Investissement Fronsac Inc., a wholly owned subsid. of Fronsac Capital Inc., which constituted Canadian Prodigy's Qualifying Transaction; basis 1 Fronsac Capital sh. for 2 Canadian Prodigy shs. (see Fronsac Capital Inc.)

Canadian Programming Concepts Ltd. (Yuk. Nov. 29, 1993)
Oct. 1, 1996 – Name changed to GST Global Telecommunications Inc. ■

Canadian Propane Limited (Alta.)
1961 – All o/s shs. not already held acquired by Canadian Hydrocarbons Ltd., at $3.00 per sh. Warrants to buy shs. of Canadian Hydrocarbons at $10 per sh. were issued to shldrs. who accepted offer; basis 1 wt. for 3.333 shs. of Canadian Propane. All o/s 5.5% s.f. debs. called for redemp. at $102.

Canadian Prospect Ltd. (Alta. May 13, 1950)
June 1958 – Name changed to Canadian Export Gas & Oil Ltd. ■

Canadian Public Venture Capital I Inc. (Alta. Jan. 24, 2002)
June 21, 2004 – Formed NordTech Aerospace Inc. in Canada on Qualifying Transaction amalgamation with NordTech Aerospace Inc., constituting a reverse takeover by NordTech. ■

Canadian Public Venture Equities 1 Inc. (Alta. Jan. 25, 2001)
Nov. 17, 2003 – Formed Vanguard Response Systems Inc. in Ontario on Qualifying Transaction amalgamation with NBC Team Ltd., constituting a reverse takeover by NBC Team; basis 1 new for 3 old shs. ■

Canadian Public Venture Finance I Inc. (Alta. Oct. 3, 2003)
Sept. 13, 2005 – Formed Extenway Solutions Inc. in Canada on Qualifying Transaction amalgamation with Extenway Solutions Inc., constituting a reverse takeover by Extenway. ■

Canadian Quantum Energy Corporation (B.C. Oct. 8, 1981)
Aug. 20, 2018 – Struck from the registry and dissolved.
Nov. 6, 2018 – Restored to the registry.
May 22, 2023 – Dissolved for failure to file and struck from register.

Canadian REIT Income Fund (Ont.)
Oct. 2, 2013 – Merged into First Asset REIT Income Fund, an open-ended fund; basis 0.7811 First Asset cl. A units for 1 Canadian REIT unit.

Canadian Real Estate Investment Trust (Ont. Apr. 1, 1984)
May 8, 2018 – Acquired by Choice Properties Real Estate Investment Trust; basis (i) $53.75 cash; or (ii) 4.2835 Choice Properties units for 1 Canadian trust unit.

Canadian Realty Investors (Ont. 1973)
Jan. 21, 1982 – Crown Trust Company made offer for all o/s units; basis $80 and nine 14.5% pfce. shs. of $20 par value for each 40 units tendered. As of January 1982, over 91% of the units acquired. Remaining units acquired in mid-1982.

Canadian Refractories Limited (unknown)
1970 – Dresser Industries, Inc. of Dallas, Tex., offered to acquire shs. it did not already hold at $18 per sh.
Aug. 31, 1971 – Amalgamated with Dresser Industries Canada Ltd.

Canadian Reserve Gold Corporation (B.C. Jan. 18, 1979)
Apr. 17, 1996 – Name changed to Christina Gold Resources Ltd.; basis 1 new for 5 old shs. ■

Canadian Reserve Investors Limited (Ont. July 26, 1966)
Oct. 1972 – Name changed to Simcoe Erie Investors Limited; basis 1 new for 5 old shs. ■

Canadian Reserve Oil and Gas Ltd. (Alta. 1970)
July 29, 1983 – Amalgamated with Getty Oil Ltd.

Canadian Resource Opportunities Inc. (Alta. Feb. 4, 1986)
Jan. 10, 2003 – Amalgamated with LHS Management Ltd.; basis 1 new amalco pfd. sh. for 1 old Canadian Resource com. sh. Preferreds to be redeemed immediately for $0.10 per sh.

Canadian Resources House Limited (B.C. Jan. 19, 2000)
Jan. 26, 2007 – Name changed to Nu Energy Uranium Corporation. ■

Canadian Resources Income Trust (Ont. Nov. 28, 1996)
Dec. 7, 2018 – Terminated; basis $7.8109 cash per trust unit.

Canadian Resources Income Trust II (Ont. Feb. 7, 1997)
Apr. 9, 2002 – Amalgamated with Canadian Resources Income Trust (CaRIT); basis 1.1693 CaRIT trust units for 1 CaRIT II trust unit. (see Canadian Resources Income Trust)

Canadian Reynolds Metals Co. Ltd. (Que. 1970 amalg.)
Sept. 30, 1980 – All o/s pref. shs. redeemed at $20 per sh. All o/s com. shs. held by Reynolds Metals Co. of Richmond, Va.

Canadian Rock Gas Ltd. (unknown)
In voluntary liquidation; W. R. Watson, Vancouver, B.C., liquidator.

Canadian Rocky Mountain Properties Inc. (Alta. Aug. 7, 1996)
July 2002 – Continued into Canada.
Feb. 27, 2004 – Acquired by Parkbridge Limited Partnership for $2.00 per sh.

Canadian Roxana Resources Limited (B.C. 1985)
May 18, 1995 – Delisted from the Vancouver Stock Exchange. Subsequently dissolved for failure to file.

Canadian Roxy Petroleum Ltd. (Alta. Mar. 25, 1980)
Apr. 14, 1994 – Acquired by Numac Energy Inc. for $5.10 per sh. (see Numac Energy Inc.)

Canadian Royalties Inc. (Alta. July 6, 1998)
Nov. 27, 2002 – Continued into Canada.
Jan. 12, 2010 – Acquired by Jien Canada Mining Ltd. for 80¢ per sh.

Canadian Salt Company Limited (Can. 1950)
Dec. 22, 1977 – Acquired by Morton Industries of Canada Ltd. a wholly owned subsid. of Morton-Norwich Products, Inc.; basis $20 or pref. shs. redeemed immediately at $20 per sh.
Jan. 1, 2014 – Name changed to K+S Windsor Salt Ltd. ■

Canadian Satellite Communications Inc. (Can. Oct. 3, 1980)
Apr. 2, 2001 – Acquired by Shaw Communications Inc.; basis 0.90 Shaw cl. B shs. plus $0.01 for 1 Canadian Satellite com. sh.
Oct. 3, 2006 – Name changed to Shaw Satellite Services Inc.

Canadian Satellite Radio Holdings Inc. (Ont. July 31, 2002)
Jan. 15, 2013 – Name changed to Sirius XM Canada Holdings Inc. ■

Canadian Scenic Oils Ltd. (Alta. 1970 amalg.)
June 19, 1973 – Amalgamated with Conventures Limited; basis 1 Conventures sh. for 3 Scenic shs.

Canadian Scotia Ltd. (N.S. 1946)
1958 – Absorbed by Code Oil & Gas Ltd.; basis 1.5 new for 1 old sh.

Canadian Security Underwriters Ltd. (Ont. 1960)
1966 – Name changed to Canadian Security Management Ltd.

The Canadian Shield Fund (Ont. Sept. 29, 2009)
July 8, 2011 – Converted from a closed end fund to an open-ended fund.

Canadian Shield Resources Inc. (Ont. Apr. 24, 1996)
Mar. 12, 2009 – Name changed to Canadian Shield Resources Ltd.; basis 1 new for 20 old shs. ■

Canadian Shield Resources Ltd. (Ont. Apr. 24, 1996)
Aug. 6, 2010 – Name changed to Estrella Gold Corporation. ■

Canadian Siam Resources Ltd. (Ont. Apr. 26, 1972)
Apr. 9, 1985 – Struck from register and dissolved.

Canadian Silica Corp. Ltd. (Ont. 1948)
1965 – Merged into Industrial Minerals of Canada Ltd.; basis 1 new for 11 old shs.

Canadian Silk Products Corp. (Que. 1929)
1960 – Placed into receivership. Assets sold by Montreal Trust Co. on behalf of first mtge. bondhldrs.; proceeds insufficient to satisfy unsecured creditors.
1962 – New mgmt. announced incr. in cap. stk. approved, and name change proposed to Property & General Securities Corp. No subsequent report.

Canadian Solar Inc. (Ont. Oct. 22, 2001)
June 1, 2006 – Continued into Canada.
July 23, 2020 – Continued into British Columbia.
July 29, 2022 – Continued into Ontario. (see FPsurvey - Industrials)

Canadian Spirit Resources Inc. (B.C. Jan. 22, 1987)
May 25, 2012 – Continued into Alberta. (see FPsurvey - Mines & Energy)

Canadian Spooner Industries Corporation (Ont. Nov. 18, 1998)
Apr. 21, 2008 – Dissolved and struck from register.

Canadian Spooner Resources Inc. (Can. Mar. 26, 1926)
Mar. 6, 2006 – Dissolved.

Canadian-Star Industries Inc. (Alta. 1986)
Nov. 1, 1993 – Dissolved and struck off register.

Canadian States Gas Ltd. (Ont. Mar. 2, 1988)
Oct. 27, 1995 – Name changed to Canadian States Resources Inc.; basis 2 new for 1 old sh. ■

Canadian States Resources Inc. (Ont. Mar. 2, 1988)
July 7, 1997 – Name changed to High North Resources Inc. ■

Canadian Steel Ceilings Ltd. (Can. - unspecified 1952)
1967 – Acquired by Cresswell Roll Forming Co. Ltd.

Canadian Stevia Corporation (Alta. Dec. 13, 2002 amalg.)
June 2, 2006 – Dissolved and struck from register.

Canadian Strategic Holdings Ltd. (B.C. 1986)
Jan. 26, 1996 – Dissolved and struck off register.

Canadian Sub-Surface Energy Services Corp. (Alta. Feb. 10, 2006)
June 26, 2009 – Acquired by Pure Energy Services Ltd.; basis 0.3017 Pure Energy shs. for 1 Canadian Sub-Surface sh. (see Pure Energy Services Ltd.)

Canadian Sumner Iron Works Ltd. (Can. - unspecified)
1965 – Acquired by Canadian Aviation Electronics Ltd. for an undisclosed amount. (see CAE Industries Ltd.)

Canadian Superior Energy Inc. (Alta. Mar. 21, 1983)
June 3, 2010 – Name changed to Sonde Resources Corp.; basis 1 new for 5 old shs. ■

Canadian Superior Oil Ltd. (Can. 1943)
Oct. 4, 1979 – All o/s shs. not already held acquired by Superior Oil Company, a Nevada corporation, 1979-80; basis US$25 and 1.145 Superior shs. (adjusted for Oct. 22, 5-for-1 split) for 1 old Canadian Superior sh.

Canadian Superior Oil of California Ltd. (Can. 1943)
1961 – Name changed to Canadian Superior Oil Ltd. ■

Canadian Supreme Energy Ltd. (Alta. June 15, 1987)
Feb. 18, 1993 – Name changed to Multi-Energies Developments Ltd.; basis 1 new for 2 old shs. ■

Canadian Systems International Inc. (Alta. July 31, 1990)
Oct. 26, 1992 – Name changed to Communications Systems International Inc. ■

Canadian TALON Resources, Ltd. (Yuk. Oct. 10, 1996)
June 30, 1999 – Name changed to TALON International Energy Ltd. ■

Canadian Tarpoly Company Limited (Ont. 1969)
1987 – Name changed to Cantar Incorporated. ■

Canadian Terminal System, Ltd. (Can. 1928)
July 1951 – Winding up order granted.
Apr. 1964 – Reported first mtge. 6% income bds. due June 1, 1951, not red. ($2,884,900 o/s at May 31, 1951). Also o/s $91,603 deb. due June 1, 1936.

Canadian Thorium Corporation Limited (Ont. 1943)
Sept. 20, 1961 – Name changed to Quebec Mattagami Minerals Limited; basis 1 new for 4 old shs. ■

Canadian Tire Receivables Trust (Ont. Mar. 31, 1995)
June 30, 2003 – Name changed to Glacier Credit Card Trust.

Canadian Tokar Limited (Que. 1926)
1975 – Name changed to Interpublishing (Canada) Limited. ■

Canadian Trace Minerals Ltd. (B.C. 1977)
Nov. 23, 1993 – Dissolved. Shldrs. received 2 com. shs. of Mineral Life Corporation for 1 com. sh. of Canadian Trace.

Canadian Transtech Industries Ltd. (B.C. 1986)
June 19, 1992 – Dissolved and struck off register.

Canadian Tricentrol Oils Ltd. (Alta. 1949)
May 5, 1972 – All o/s shs. (other than those already owned) acquired by Tricentrol Oils Limited, a wholly owned subsid. of Tricentrol Limited, London, England; basis $15 per sh.

Canadian Turbo Inc. (Alta. Dec. 24, 1947)
May 6, 1992 – Acquired by 410336 B.C. Ltd. for $3.96 per sh.
Jan. 3, 1996 – Dissolved and struck off register.

Canadian-United Minerals, Inc. (B.C. May 9, 1975)
Sept. 10, 1990 – Name changed to Mansfield Minerals Inc.; basis 1 new for 5 old shs. ■

Canadian Utilities & Telecom Income Fund (Ont.)
July 7, 2021 – Merged into Mulvihill Premium Yield Fund; basis 0.943342 Mulvihill cl. A units for 1 Canadian Utilities trust unit.

Canadian Venture Corp. (B.C. Sept. 9, 1986)
July 27, 1990 – Name changed to Consolidated Canadian Venture Corp.; basis 1 new for 3 old shs. ■

Canadian Venture Opportunities Fund Ltd. (Can. Jan. 11, 1993)
Nov. 12, 1999 – Name changed to Dynamic Venture Opportunities Fund Ltd. ■

Canadian Vickers, Ltd. (Can. 1911)
Oct. 27, 1978 – Name changed to Vickers Canada Inc.

Canadian Wallpaper Manufacturers Limited (Can. 1927)
1973 – Acquired by subsid. of Reed Paper Group Canada Holdings Ltd. for $200 per sh.

Canadian Waste Services Inc. (Can. - unspecified)
Jan. 1, 2004 – Name changed to Waste Management of Canada Corporation.

Canadian Water Corporation (B.C. July 27, 1987)
Nov. 7, 1996 – Name changed to Aumine Resources Ltd.; basis 1 new for 10 old shs. ∎

Canadian West Resources Ltd. (B.C. Aug. 17, 1987)
Sept. 29, 1995 – Acquired by Cantrell Capital Corp.; basis 1 Cantrell sh. for 6 Canadian West shs. (see Cantrell Capital Corp.)

Canadian Western Bank (Can. Nov. 1, 1987 amalg.)
Feb. 5, 2025 – All o/s com. shs not already held acquired by National Bank of Canada; basis 0.45 National Bank shs. for 1 Canadian Western sh.

Canadian Western Gypsum Corp. Ltd. (B.C. 1958)
Name changed to United Gypsum Corp. Ltd.

Canadian Western Lumber Co. Ltd. (Can. 1910)
July 6, 1956 – Crown Zellerbach Corp. (U.S.) acquired about 96% of co. shs. in May 1953; basis 1 sh. Crown Zellerbach Corp. for 3 shs. Canadian Western. Crown Zellerbach Canada offered its com. stk. for Canadian Western shs.

Canadian Western Natural Gas Company Limited (Alta. July 19, 1911)
Dec. 30, 1996 – All o/s cum. redeem. pref. shs. 4% ser. and cum. redeem. pref. shs. 5.5% ser. called for redemption; basis for the 4% series: $20.60 plus accrued and unpaid dividends of $0.0636 per sh. and for the 5.5% series: $20.60 plus accrued and unpaid dividends of $0.0874 per sh.

The Canadian Western Natural Gas, Light, Heat and Power Company Limited (Alta. July 19, 1911)
June 19, 1947 – Name changed to Canadian Western Natural Gas Company Limited. ∎

Canadian Western Oil Co. Inc. (Del. 1957)
Dec. 1959 – Acquired by Western States Petroleum Co. Inc. (now Westates); basis 3 new for 4 old shs.

Canadian Westgrowth Ltd. (Alta. 1981)
Nov. 4, 1987 – Acquired by Ulster Petroleums Ltd. (see Ulster Petroleums Ltd.)

Canadian Williston Minerals Ltd. (Alta. 1951)
1966 – Merged into Canadian Gridoil Ltd.; basis 1 new for 6.25 old shs.

Canadian Wirebound Boxes, Ltd. (Ont. 1928)
1954 – All com. and 99.8% of cl. A shs. acquired by Bathurst Paper for $64 per sh.
Dec. 1957 – Name changed to Bathurst Containers Ltd.

Canadian Wireless Trust (Ont. Sept. 28, 2006)
Jan. 3, 2014 – All tr. units redeemed for $13.075 per unit and fund terminated.

Canadian World Fund Limited (Ont. Nov. 13, 1986)
May 8, 2018 – All o/s com. shs. not already held acquired by Third Canadian General Investment Trust Limited; basis $9.25 cash per sh.

Canadian Worldwide Energy Limited (Alta. Oct. 16, 1952)
Sept. 9, 1987 – Name changed to Triton Canada Resources Ltd. ∎

Canadian Zeolite Corp. (B.C. Feb. 8, 2016)
Mar. 6, 2018 – Name changed to International Zeolite Corp. (see FPsurvey - Mines & Energy; FPsurvey - Industrials)

Canadian Zeolite Ltd. (Alta. June 5, 1987)
Nov. 19, 1996 – Name changed to The Canadian Mining Company Ltd. ∎

Canadian Zinc Corporation (B.C. Dec. 16, 1965)
May 7, 2018 – Continued into British Columbia.
Sept. 6, 2018 – Succeeded by NorZinc Ltd. pursuant to plan of arrangement whereby wholly owned NorZinc Ltd. was formed to become parent company of Canadian Zinc Corporation. ∎

Canadiana Genetics Inc. (Alta. June 30, 1990 amalg.)
Jan. 1999 – Delisted Alberta Stock Exchange on Feb. 2, 1995. Subsequently struck from register and dissolved.

Canadianwide Properties Limited (Ont. 1955)
Name changed to Thorntowne Properties which operates as a private co.

Canadore Mines & Resources Ltd. (Que. 1957)
Jan. 13, 1979 – Charter cancelled.

Canadore Mining & Development Corp. (Que. 1957)
Sept. 1972 – Name changed to Canadore Mines & Resources Ltd.; basis 1 new for 2 old shs. ∎

CanaDream Corporation (Alta. May 27, 1997)
July 18, 2017 – All o/s com. shs. not already held acquired by ATL Canada Ltd., a wholly owned subsid. of Apollo Tourism & Leisure Ltd.; basis $1.85 cash per sh.

Canadusa Oil & Gas Reserves Ltd. (Alta. 1952)
1957 – Acquired by Titan Petroleum Corp. Ltd.; basis 1 new for 10 old shs. (see Titan Petroleum Corp. Ltd.)

Canaf Group Inc. (Alta. Mar. 27, 1996)
July 27, 2018 – Name changed to Canaf Investments Inc. (see FPsurvey - Mines & Energy)

CanAfrican Metals and Mining Ltd. (Alta. Mar. 27, 1996)
June 1, 2007 – Name changed to Canaf Group Inc. ∎

Canagau Mines Ltd. (Ont. 1936)
Mar. 1976 – Charter cancelled.

Canalands Energy Corporation (Can. 1980)
Apr. 1, 1983 – Amalgamated with Invermere Resources Ltd. (1 new for 1 old sh.) to form Canalands Resources Corporation; basis 1 new for 1 old sh.

Canalands Resources Corporation (Can. Jan. 26, 1981)
Apr. 1, 1983 – Amalgamated in Canada to continue with same name. (see FPsurvey - Mines & Energy)

Canalask Nickel Mines Ltd. (Ont. 1953)
1962 – Name changed to Northwest Canalask Nickel Mines Ltd.; basis 1 new for 4 old shs. ∎

Canalaska Developments Ltd. (B.C. 1968)
Jan. 1975 – Charter cancelled.

CanAlaska Resources Ltd. (B.C. May 22, 1985)
Sept. 15, 1993 – Name changed to International CanAlaska Resources Ltd.; basis 1 new for 4 old shs. ∎

CanAlaska Ventures Ltd. (B.C. May 22, 1985)
Oct. 11, 2006 – Name changed to CanAlaska Uranium Ltd. (see FPsurvey - Mines & Energy)

Canalite Limited (Ont. 1969)
Nov. 1977 – Charter cancelled.

Canalta Minerals Ltd. (Alta. Aug. 12, 1988 amalg.)
Nov. 14, 1994 – Name changed to New Energy West Corporation; basis 1 new for 1 old sh. ∎

Canalta Oil Co. Ltd. (Ont. 1948)
1959 – Struck off register.

Canalta Resources Ltd. (B.C. 1968)
Feb. 8, 1982 – Amalgamated with Sweetwater Petroleum (0.65 for 1) and The Ascot Petroleum Corporation (0.85 for 1) to form a new company named Consolidated Ascot Petroleum Corporation; basis 0.3 new for 1 old sh. (see Consolidated Ascot Petroleum Corporation)

Canalynda Copper Mines Ltd. (Ont. 1956)
Nov. 12, 1969 – Charter cancelled.

CanAm Coal Corp. (Alta. Oct. 24, 1994)
Apr. 2, 2017 – Dissolved and struck from registry.

Canam Copper Co. Ltd. (Can. 1950)
May 1966 – In voluntary liquidation. Shldrs. received 1 sh. Giant Mascot Mines Ltd. for 8 old shs. (see Giant Mascot Mines Ltd.)

Canam Development Co. Ltd. (Can. 1950)
Jan. 1951 – Name changed to Canam Copper Co. Ltd. ∎

Canam Group Inc. (Que. Jan. 1, 1997 amalg.)
July 6, 2017 – Privatized through the acquisition of all o/s shs. not already held by the Dutil family by Canaveral Acquisitions Inc. (a company owned by members of the Dutil family) and American Industrial Partner Capital Fund VI, L.P.; basis $12.30 cash per sh.

The Canam Manac Group Inc. (Que. Oct. 31, 1981)
Jan. 1, 1997 – Amalgamated in Quebec to continue with same name.
Jan. 4, 2005 – Name changed to Canam Group Inc. ∎

Canam Mining Corp. Ltd. (B.C. 1944)
Aug. 1, 1954 – Assets acquired by Canam Copper Co. Ltd. for 1,220,000 shs. (see Canam Copper Co. Ltd.)

Canamax Energy Ltd. (Alta. Feb. 2, 2007)
Jan. 20, 2016 – Acquired by Edge Natural Resources LLC; basis 67¢ cash per com. sh.

Canamax Resources Inc. (Can. Dec. 21, 1982)
Jan. 7, 1993 – Amalgamated with Minerex Resources Ltd. and Canada Tungsten Mining Corporation Limited to form Canada Tungsten Inc.; basis 1 new for 0.5 Minerex shs., 1 new for 1 Canada Tungsten sh. and 1 new for 5 Canamax shs. (see Canada Tungsten Inc.)

Canamed Ventures Ltd. (Alta. Oct. 19, 1995)
Feb. 27, 1998 – Formed VSM MedTech Ltd. following acquisition of all o/s shs. of VSM Technology Inc.; basis 1 new for 4 old shs. (see FPsurvey - Industrials)

Canamera Explorations Inc. (B.C. Mar. 22, 1983)
May 3, 1988 – Name changed to Wind River Resources Ltd.; basis 1 new for 3 old shs. ∎

CanAmerica Precious Metals Inc. (Alta. 1986)
Oct. 1, 1992 – Struck off register.

Canamerican Drilling Corp. Ltd. (Ont. 1959)
July 7, 1966 – Filed an assignment into bankruptcy.

Canamex Industries Ltd. (B.C. Apr. 25, 1977)
July 29, 1986 – Name changed to International Cablecasting Technologies Inc. ∎

Canamex Resources Corp. (B.C. Oct. 7, 2009)
Nov. 8, 2017 – Name changed to Canamex Gold Corp. (see FPsurvey - Mines & Energy)

Canamex Silver Corp. (B.C. Oct. 7, 2009)
Oct. 18, 2010 – Name changed to Canamex Resources Corp. ∎

Canamin Resources Ltd. (B.C. 1980)
Mar. 26, 1991 – Name changed to New Canamin Resources Ltd.; basis 1 new for 5 old shs. ∎

Canamiska Copper Mines Ltd. (Ont. 1956)
Aug. 22, 1973 – Charter cancelled.

Cananto Mines Ltd. (Ont. 1955)
1966 – Charter cancelled.

Canarama Limited (Sask. 1957)
Jan. 1963 – Western Heritage Ltd. acquired controlling interest in 1962 and offered $2.00 per pref. sh.; $1.00 per com. sh. and 10¢ per purch. warr. All o/s shs. acquired under offer.

Canarc Resource Corp. (B.C. Jan. 22, 1987)
Dec. 8, 2020 – Name changed to Canagold Resources Ltd.; basis 1 new for 5 old shs. (see FPsurvey - Mines & Energy)

Canarchon Holdings Limited (Ont. 1952)
Feb. 7, 1991 – Dissolved following sale of its wholly owned subsid., Canarchon U.K. Limited, to R.E.A. Holdings plc; basis 0.50 com. shs. R.E.A. Holdings for 200 or more old shs. or $2.899 Cdn. for less than 200 old shs.

Canarctic Resources Ltd. (B.C. July 18, 1967)
Feb. 25, 1972 – Name changed to Concept Resources Ltd.; basis 1 new for 10 old shs. ■

Canarctic Ventures Ltd. (B.C. 1978)
Feb. 21, 1985 – Name changed to Consolidated Canarctic Industries Ltd.; basis 1 new for 2.5 old shs. ■

Canard Resources Ltd. (Can. July 13, 1988)
Mar. 6, 2000 – Dissolved.

CanArgo Energy Inc. (Alta. 1983)
Aug. 12, 1998 – Acquired by Fountain Oil Incorporation; basis 0.8 Fountain Oil shs. for 1 CanArgo sh.

CanAsia Financial Inc. (Alta. June 26, 2008)
Feb. 15, 2019 – Name changed to Composite Alliance Group Inc. pursuant to reverse takeover acquisition of Techni Modul Engineering S.A.; basis 1 new for 5 old shs. (see FPsurvey - Industrials)

Canasia Industries Corporation (B.C. Apr. 15, 1981)
Jan. 22, 2013 – Name changed to Makena Resources Inc.; basis 1 new for 20 old shs. ■

Canaska Explorers Ltd. (Ont. 1945)
1956 – Charter cancelled.

Canaustra Gold Exploration Limited (Ont. 1974 amalg.)
Mar. 10, 1989 – Merged with Cliff Resources Corporation (1 new for 1 old sh.); basis 3 new for 4 old shs. (see Cliff Resources Corporation)

CanAustra Resources Inc. (Alta. Sept. 22, 1993)
Apr. 18, 2005 – Continued into Yukon.
Aug. 15, 2005 – Name changed to Oriental Minerals Inc.; basis 1 new for 2 old shs. ■

CanBaikal Resources Inc. (Alta. Aug. 14, 1996)
Feb. 4, 2002 – Acquired by C.B. Acquisition Ltd. for $0.38 per sh.

CanBanc 8 Income Corp. (Ont. Oct. 30, 2012)
May 4, 2016 – Merged and amalgamated with First Asset Fund Corp; basis 0.98557 First Asset CanBanc Income Class ETF shs. for 1 CanBanc 8 equity sh. (see First Asset CanBanc Income Class ETF)

CanBanc Income Corp. (Ont. June 28, 2010)
Sept. 24, 2015 – Converted from a closed-end fund into a mutual fund company known as First Asset CanBanc Income ETF; basis 1 First Asset CanBanc com. sh. for 1 CanBanc equity sh.

Canboro Natural Gas & Oil Co. Ltd. (Ont. 1936)
1960 – Wound up.

Canbra Foods Ltd. (Alta. Sept. 13, 1957)
Aug. 25, 1999 – Acquired by 830686 Alberta Ltd., a wholly owned subsid. of James Richardson International Limited, for $23 per sh.

Canbras Communications Corp. (B.C. Aug. 7, 1986)
June 22, 1998 – Continued into Canada.
May 30, 2007 – Dissolved; final distribution was $0.0993 per com. sh.

Canbridge Oil Exploration Ltd. (Ont. 1952)
Dec. 1970 – Merged into Thomson Drilling Company Limited; basis 1 new for 10 old shs.

Canbud Distribution Corporation (Can. Oct. 4, 2018)
Feb. 28, 2022 – Name changed to Steep Hill Inc. (see FPsurvey - Industrials)

Canby Resources Inc. (B.C. 1986)
June 15, 1988 – Name changed to Bicer Medical Systems Ltd. ■

Cancal Mines Ltd. (B.C. 1969)
June 30, 1981 – Name changed to Cancal Resources Ltd. ■

Cancal Resources Ltd. (B.C. 1969)
Jan. 10, 1986 – Struck off register.

Cancall Cellular Communications Inc. (B.C. 1985)
Oct. 31, 2003 – Dissolved and struck from register.

Cancana Resources Corp. (Alta. Feb. 13, 1980)
Aug. 12, 2015 – Continued into British Columbia. (see Meridian Mining S.E.)
Nov. 28, 2016 – Acquired by Meridian Mining S.E.; basis 0.4 Meridian com. shs. for 1 Cancana sh. (see Meridian Mining S.E.)

CanCap Preferred Corporation (Que. Oct. 21, 1996)
July 3, 2007 – All o/s 5.4% pref. shs. redeemed for $25 per sh.

CanCapital Corporation (Alta. 1983)
May 12, 1993 – Continued into British Columbia.
July 14, 1994 – Name changed to Prada Holdings Ltd.; basis 1 new for 4 old shs. ■

Cancen Oil Canada Inc. (B.C. Mar. 5, 2010)
July 29, 2013 – Name changed to Ceiba Energy Services Inc. ■

Canchrome Mines Inc. (Can. Oct. 5, 1989)
Nov. 3, 1995 – Name changed to Cancor Mines Inc. ■

Cancoil Integrated Services Inc. (Alta. May 6, 1997)
July 26, 2002 – Name changed to Technicoil Corporation. ■

Cancom Industries Inc. (B.C. May 4, 1984)
July 10, 1990 – Name changed to Strategic Technologies Inc.; basis 1 new for 3.5 old shs. ■

Cancom Ventures Inc. (Alta. Dec. 4, 1987)
Sept. 19, 1989 – Name changed to Multi-Corp Inc. ■

Cancor Mines Inc. (Can. Oct. 5, 1989)
May 29, 2014 – Acquired by Yorbeau Resources Inc.; basis 1 Yorbeau unit (1 com. sh. & ½ wt.) for 12 Cancor com. sh.

Cancorp Enterprises Incorporated (B.C. 1980)
Oct. 9, 1989 – Name changed to G.E.M. Environmental Management, Inc. ■

Cancorp Technologies Inc. (Alta. Feb. 17, 1988)
Aug. 1, 1992 – Dissolved and charter cancelled.
Mar. 13, 1995 – Restored to registry.
Aug. 2, 2007 – Struck from the registry and dissolved.

Candao Enterprises Inc. (B.C. Aug. 4, 1987)
Mar. 12, 2012 – Dissolved and struck from register.

Candax Energy Inc. (Ont. June 4, 2004)
July 6, 2011 – Continued into British Columbia.
Nov. 17, 2015 – Remaining 19.25% interest acquired by Geofinance N.V.; basis Cdn$0.002 cash per sh.

CanDel Oil Ltd. (Can. 1950)
Oct. 31, 1981 – Acquired by Sulpetro Limited effective Aug. 5, 1981; basis $44.50 per share. Subsequently amalgamated into Sulpetro. (see Sulpetro Limited)

Candela Resources Ltd. (B.C. June 11, 1987)
Apr. 3, 1998 – Name changed to New Candela Resources Ltd.; basis 1 new for 4 old shs. ■

Canden Capital Corp. (B.C. Mar. 13, 2000)
June 12, 2000 – Continued into Yukon.
May 25, 2004 – Name changed to Superior Canadian Resources Inc. following Qualifying Transaction acquisition of mineral claims from Silver Harbour Investments Inc. ■

Candente Copper Corp. (B.C. Mar. 9, 2007)
May 19, 2023 – Name changed to Alta Copper Corp.; basis 1 new for 4 old shs. (see FPsurvey - Mines & Energy)

Candente Gold Corp. (B.C. Apr. 24, 2009)
Jan. 19, 2021 – Name changed to Xali Gold Corp. (see FPsurvey - Mines & Energy)

Candente Resource Corp. (B.C. May 1, 1997)
Sept. 27, 2002 – Continued into Canada.
Mar. 9, 2007 – Continued into British Columbia.
Dec. 31, 2009 – Name changed to Candente Copper Corp. ■

Candid Quebec Mines Ltd. (Ont. 1946)
1956 – Charter cancelled.

Cando Capital Inc. (Alta. Dec. 3, 1996)
Nov. 10, 1999 – Name changed to Trius Investments Inc. ■

Candol Developments Ltd. (B.C. Feb. 25, 1985 amalg.)
Mar. 30, 1993 – Name changed to Terrastar Development Corporation; basis 1 new for 10 old shs. ■

Candoo Metals & Oils Ltd. (Ont. 1946)
Feb. 16, 1954 – Acquired by Cordon Cobalt Mines Ltd.; basis 1 new for 4 old shs. (see Cordon Cobalt Mines Ltd.)

Candor Ventures Corp. (Ont. Mar. 29, 1999)
Apr. 5, 2005 – Formed Canstar Resources Inc. in Ontario on amalgamation with Nustar Resources Inc. with Candor the deemed acquiror. (see FPsurvey - Mines & Energy)

CanDorado Mines Ltd. (B.C. Oct. 22, 1984)
Dec. 10, 1993 – Name changed to A.R.C. Resins International Corp.; basis 1 new for 3 old shs. ■

Candorado Operating Company Ltd. (B.C. Aug. 4, 1992)
Aug. 8, 2012 – Name changed to Sunrise Resources Ltd.; basis 1 new for 5 old shs. (see FPsurvey - Mines & Energy)

Candore Explorations Ltd. (Ont. May 18, 1945)
Mar. 14, 1978 – Charter cancelled.
Nov. 19, 1981 – Charter revived.
Dec. 30, 1987 – Amalgamated with Golden Crescent Explorations Inc. to form Golden Crescent Resources Corp.; basis unknown.

Candy Express Stores Ltd. (B.C. Oct. 7, 1986)
Sept. 21, 1993 – Name changed to Patriots Venture Group Ltd.; basis 1 new for 3 old shs. ■

Candy Investments Limited (Ont. May 2, 1968)
Sept. 13, 2005 – Voluntarily dissolved for $0.5358 per sh.

Candy Mines & Investments Ltd. (Ont. May 2, 1968)
Apr. 1972 – Name changed to Candy Investments Limited. ■

Candy Mines Ltd. (Ont. May 2, 1968)
Dec. 1969 – Name changed to Candy Mines & Investments Ltd. ■

Cane Consolidated Explorations Limited (Ont. Oct. 12, 1917)
July 7, 1983 – Name changed to Cane Resources Ltd. ■

Cane Corporation (Ont. Oct. 12, 1917)
July 22, 1996 – Name changed to Aurcana Corporation; basis 1 new for 2 old shs. ■

Cane Resources Ltd. (Ont. Oct. 12, 1917)
July 31, 1984 – Name changed to Cane Corporation; basis 1 new for 5 old shs. ■

Cane Silver Mines Ltd. (Ont. Oct. 12, 1917)
Aug. 1977 – Name changed to Cane Consolidated Explorations Limited; basis 1 new for 8 old shs. ■

Caneco Audio-Publishers Inc. (B.C. 1980)
Aug. 18, 1989 – Dissolved.

Caneco Resources Inc. (B.C. 1980)
Jan. 20, 1986 – Name changed to Caneco Audio-Publishers Inc. ■

CanElson Drilling Inc. (Alta. June 30, 2008)
Dec. 11, 2008 – Amalgamated in Alberta to continue with same name. (see Trinidad Drilling Ltd.)
Aug. 17, 2015 – Acquired by Trinidad Drilling Ltd.; basis (i) 1.0631 Trinidad com. shs. or (ii) $4.90 cash, subject to proration, for 1 CanElson com. sh. (see Trinidad Drilling Ltd.)

Caneonti Mines Ltd. (Ont. 1951)
May 1976 – Charter cancelled.

Canerex Mines Ltd. (B.C. 1971)
Mar. 1978 – Charter cancelled.

Canetic Resources Trust (Alta. Jan. 5, 2006 amalg.)
Jan. 16, 2008 – Amalgamated with Penn West Energy Trust; basis 0.515 Penn West trust units for 1 Canetic trust unit. (see Penn West Energy Trust)

CanEuro Resources Ltd. (Alta. July 7, 1987)
Feb. 7, 1991 – Amalgamated with Polo Petroleum Ltd. (1 for 1) to form a new company named Attock Oil Corporation; basis 1 com. sh. for 5 cl. A shs. (see Attock Oil Corporation)

Canex Energy Corp. (B.C. Sept. 20, 2006)
Jan. 23, 2020 – Name changed to SKRR Exploration Inc. (see FPsurvey - Mines & Energy)

Canex Energy Inc. (Alta. June 14, 1996)
June 8, 2006 – Plan of Arrangement agreement with Crescent Point Energy Trust (CPET), 1238363 Alberta Ltd., and Crescent Point Resources Ltd. to continue as a new company named Canext Energy Ltd.; basis either (a) $0.587 plus 0.1003 new CPET unit plus 0.5 new Canext com. sh. plus 0.1666 new Canext sh. purchase wt., or (b) if electing to exercise the new Canext wts., $0.4209 plus 0.1003 new CPET unit plus 0.6666 new Canext com. sh. for 1 old Canex com. sh. (see Canext Energy Ltd.; Crescent Point Energy Trust)

Canex Minerals Ltd. (Que. 1956)
Nov. 4, 1978 – Charter cancelled.

Canext Energy Ltd. (Alta. Apr. 6, 2006)
June 22, 2007 – Amalgamated in Alberta to continue with same name. (see TriOil Resources Ltd.)
Apr. 22, 2010 – Acquired by TriOil Resources Ltd. (formerly One Exploration Inc.); basis 0.1 TriOil shs. for 1 Canext sh. (see TriOil Resources Ltd.)

Canexus Corporation (Alta. Mar. 17, 2011)
Mar. 10, 2017 – Name changed to Chemtrade Electrochem Inc. ■

Canexus Income Fund (Alta. June 28, 2005)
July 8, 2011 – Succeeded by Canexus Corporation pursuant to plan of arrangement whereby Canexus Corporation was formed to facilitate the conversion of the fund into a corporation and the fund was subsequently dissolved. ■

Canfe Ventures Ltd. (B.C. Jan. 14, 2008)
Oct. 21, 2010 – Name changed to Golden Fame Resources Corp. pursuant to Qualifying Transaction acquisition of Fame Oriented Holdings Limited. ■

The CanFibre Group Ltd. (Ont. Aug. 1977)
Jan. 9, 2007 – Dissolved and struck from register.

Canfic Resources Ltd. (B.C. Mar. 10, 1980)
May 6, 1987 – Name changed to Delcorp Resources Inc.; basis 2 new for 5 old shs. ■

Canfic Silver Mines Ltd. (B.C. Mar. 10, 1980)
Sept. 3, 1981 – Name changed to Canfic Resources Ltd. ■

Canfield Financial Ltd. (Alta. Mar. 11, 1996)
July 28, 1998 – Name changed to Learnco International Inc. ■

Canfor Capital Limited (B.C. 1972)
Oct. 15, 1989 – All o/s sr. pref. shs. redeemed at $25 per sh.
Jan. 1, 1990 – Amalgamated with other subsids. and affil. cos. into Canadian Forest Products Ltd.

Canfor Investments Ltd. (B.C. 1975)
Nov. 1983 – Wholly owned subsid. of Canadian Forest Products Ltd. All o/s publicly held pref. shs. called for redemption.

Canfor Pulp Income Fund (Ont. Apr. 19, 2006)
Jan. 1, 2011 – Succeeded by Canfor Pulp Products Inc. pursuant to plan of arrangement whereby Canfor Pulp Products Inc. was formed to facilitate the conversion of the fund into a corporation and the fund was subsequently dissolved. (see FPsurvey - Industrials)

Canford Explorations Ltd. (B.C. 1958)
Mar. 1969 – Name changed to Consolidated Vigor Mines Ltd. ■

Cangene Corporation (Ont. Feb. 22, 1984)
Feb. 25, 2014 – Acquired by Emergent BioSolutions Inc. for US$3.24 per sh.

Cangold Limited (Yuk. Mar. 17, 1997)
Dec. 22, 2004 – Continued into British Columbia.
May 28, 2015 – Acquired by Great Panther Silver Limited; basis 0.05 Great Panther com.shs. for 1 Cangold sh.

Cangold Mining & Exploration Co. Ltd. (B.C. 1944)
Jan. 1957 – Charter cancelled.

CanGold Resources Inc. (B.C. Feb. 14, 1994 amalg.)
July 25, 1995 – Name changed to Amalgamated CanGold Inc. and continued into Ontario; basis 1 new for 10 old shs. ■

Canguard Health Technologies Inc. (B.C. Feb. 25, 1983)
July 16, 1993 – Name changed to Canguard Pharma Inc. ■

Canguard Pharma Inc. (B.C. Feb. 25, 1983)
Aug. 17, 1994 – Name changed to GeriatRx Pharmaceutical Corp.; basis 1 new for 5 old shs. ■

Canhart Mines Ltd. (Ont. 1960)
Mar. 25, 1980 – Dissolved.

Canhorn Chemical Corporation (Ont. Apr. 19, 1995)
June 8, 2005 – Amalgamated with Nayarit Gold Inc. to continue as a new company also named Nayarit Gold Inc.; basis 1 new for 1 old sh. (see Nayarit Gold Inc.)

Canhorn Mining Corporation (Ont. Dec. 30, 1985 amalg.)
Apr. 26, 1995 – Amalgamated with Initiative Explorations Inc. to form Canhorn Chemical Corporation; basis 0.45 new for 1 Initiative sh. and 0.5 new for 1 Canhorn sh. (see Canhorn Chemical Corporation)

CaNickel Mining Limited (B.C. June 23, 2011)
June 27, 2025 – Voluntarily delisted from the TSX-Venture Exchange. (see FPsurvey - Mines & Energy)

Canico Resource Corp. (B.C. Nov. 24, 1980)
Feb. 10, 2006 – Acquired by Companhia Vale do Rio Doce for $20.80 per sh.

The Canin Industrial Group Inc. (Alta. June 24, 1987)
Mar. 13, 1999 – Struck off register.

Canivate Growing Systems Ltd. (B.C. Dec. 22, 2017)
Nov. 22, 2019 – Name changed to AgriFORCE Growing Systems Ltd. (see FPsurvey - Industrials)

Canlan Ice Sports Corp. (B.C. Apr. 11, 1956)
Dec. 24, 2004 – Amalgamated with 3 of its wholly owned subsidiaries, Ice Sports Centre Etobicoke Inc., Adult "Safe-Hockey" Leagues Ltd. and O & O Development Corporation to form new co. with same name Canlan Ice Sports Corp.
Dec. 30, 2019 – Amalgamated in British Columbia to continue with same name. (see FPsurvey - Industrials)

Canlan Investment Corporation (B.C. Apr. 11, 1956)
Aug. 3, 1999 – Name changed to Canlan Ice Sports Corp. ■

Canley Developments Inc. (B.C. May 25, 1998)
July 3, 2003 – Name changed to Sargold Resource Corporation. ■

Canlorm Resources Inc. (Ont. Oct. 5, 1965)
Aug. 1, 1995 – Continued into British Columbia.
Aug. 29, 1995 – Formed Oroperu Resources Inc. in British Columbia on amalgamation with Oroperu Resources Inc., constituting a reverse takeover by Oroperu; basis 1 new for 1 Oroperu sh. and 1 new for 7 Canlorm shs. ■

Canmag Holdings Limited (Ont. 1962)
Feb. 8, 1974 – Name changed to Film Funding Corporation Limited.

Canman Industries Limited (Can. 1892)
Nov. 1, 1965 – Amalgamated with Canadian Management Company Ltd. and Canadian Corporate Management Co. Limited under the name of Canadian Corporate Management Company Limited; basis 3 com. shs. for 1 old sh.

Canmark International Resources Inc. (B.C. July 17, 1981)
Mar. 29, 2010 – Dissolved and struck from register.

Canmax Inc. (Wyo. Sept. 11, 1992)
Apr. 1, 1999 – Name changed to Ardis Telecom and Technologies Inc.

Canmet Resources Limited (B.C. July 3, 1987)
Aug. 5, 1994 – Name changed to Archangel Diamond Corporation. ■

Canmex Minerals Corporation (B.C. Mar. 29, 1993)
Aug. 20, 2007 – Name changed to Africa Oil Corp. ■

Canmine Resources Corporation (Ont. Oct. 29, 1980 amalg.)
Aug. 2, 2002 – Granted protection under the Companies' Creditors Arrangement Act (CCAA) in order to restructure its financial obligations. Several extensions followed. This protection order replaced a previous plan where the Canmine refinery assets and chemical operations were to be transferred to a U.S. reporting company while all exploration and development assets would be retained. The refinery was temporarily placed on a care and maintenance basis.
Feb. 26, 2003 – Protection order was lifted and PricewaterhouseCoopers was appointed receiver to liquidate assets. All officers and directors resigned.
Sept. 12, 2003 – PricewaterhouseCoopers sold 9 separate parcels of land. The senior secured creditor suffered a shortfall and there were no funds available for unsecured creditors or shldrs.
Apr. 17, 2006 – Receiver noted that the company was defunct and there were no funds with which to apply for discharge.

Canna-V-Cell Sciences Inc. (B.C. Apr. 19, 2013)
Mar. 31, 2020 – Name changed to BioHarvest Sciences Inc. pursuant to the reverse takeover acquisition of Israel-based BioHarvest Ltd. and concurrent amalgamation of BioHarvest with wholly owned BioFarming Ltd. (see FPsurvey - Industrials)

Cannabis Growth Opportunity Corporation (Can. Oct. 29, 2017)
Jan. 19, 2021 – Name changed to Plant-Based Investment Corp. (see FPsurvey - Industrials)

Cannabis One Holdings Inc. (B.C. July 16, 2007)
Aug. 19, 2020 – Name changed to INDVR Brands Inc. (see FPsurvey - Industrials)

Cannabis Strategies Acquisition Corp. (Ont. July 31, 2017)
May 24, 2019 – Name changed to Ayr Strategies Inc. and continued into British Columbia pursuant to the Qualifying Acquisition of Washoe Wellness, LLC, The Canopy NV, LLC, Sira Naturals, Inc., LivFree Wellness LLC and CannaPunch of Nevada LLC. ∎

Cannabis Technologies Inc. (B.C. May 19, 1981)
Oct. 6, 2014 – Name changed to InMed Pharmaceuticals Inc. (see FPsurvey - Industrials)

Cannabis Wheaton Income Corp. (B.C. Aug. 24, 1987)
June 8, 2018 – Name changed to Auxly Cannabis Group Inc. ∎

Cannabunker Development Corp. (B.C. Dec. 12, 2017)
Dec. 4, 2018 – Name changed to XPhyto Therapeutics Corp. ∎

CannaGlobe Therapeutics Corp. (B.C. June 27, 2018)
Jan. 28, 2019 – Name changed to E-Gaming Ventures Corp. ∎

CannaOne Technologies Inc. (B.C. Oct. 19, 2016)
Apr. 19, 2021 – Name changed to Lynx Global Digital Finance Corporation. (see FPsurvey - Industrials)

CannaRoyalty Corp. (Ont. Aug. 19, 1985)
Jan. 8, 2020 – Acquired by Cresco Labs Inc.; basis 0.8428 Cresco subord. vtg. shs. for each sh. held.

Cannasat Therapeutics Inc. (Can. Mar. 15, 2006 amalg.)
Apr. 27, 2010 – Name changed to Cynapsus Therapeutics Inc. ∎

Cannelle Exploration Ltd. (B.C. Feb. 24, 1987)
Feb. 1, 1996 – Name changed to RangeStar Telecommunications Ltd. ∎

Cannex Capital Holdings Inc. (B.C. Mar. 13, 2006)
July 31, 2019 – Succeeded by 4Front Ventures Corp. pursuant to the amalgamation of wholly owned 1196260 B.C. Ltd. and (old) 4Front Ventures Corp. (deemed acquiror) to form (new) 4Front Ventures (resulting issuer), and the concurrent voluntary dissolution of Cannex (predecessor public company); basis 1 (new) 4Front Ventures subord. vtg. sh. for each Cannex com. sh. and 1 (new) 4Front Ventures cl.B proportionate vtg. sh. for each 80 Cannex cl.A conv. rest. shs. ∎

CanniMed Therapeutics Inc. (Can. Oct. 31, 2016)
May 2, 2018 – Acquired by Aurora Cannabis Inc.; basis (i) 3.40 Aurora shs.; or (ii) $43 in cash, subject to pro ration; or (iii) any combination of Aurora shs. and cash based on a maximum of $43 cash per sh. for 1 CanniMed com. sh.

Cannon Explorations Ltd. (B.C. 1986)
Sept. 23, 1987 – Name changed to U.T. Technologies Limited. (see FPsurvey - Industrials)

Cannon Minerals Ltd. (B.C. May 11, 1984)
Dec. 23, 1985 – Name changed to Nevada Goldfields Corporation. ∎

Cannon Mines Limited (Ont. July 25, 1965)
Aug. 29, 1988 – Name changed to Dencal Development Corporation; basis 1 new for 4 old shs. ∎

Cannon Oil & Gas Ltd. (Alta. Aug. 1, 1999 amalg.)
Feb. 12, 2007 – Acquired by G2 Resources Inc.; basis 0.95 new G2 sh. for 1 old Cannon sh. (see G2 Resources Inc.)

Cannon Point Resources Ltd. (B.C. May 26, 1978)
Oct. 30, 2015 – Acquired by Northern Dynasty Minerals Ltd.; basis 0.376 Northern com. shs. for 1 Cannon com. sh.

Cannon Resources Ltd. (B.C. Mar. 8, 1971)
Nov. 18, 1983 – Name changed to Samson Gold Corporation; basis 1 new for 4 old shs. ∎

Cannoo Mines Ltd. (B.C. 1966)
1969 – Assets acquired by National Nickel Ltd.; basis 1 new for 2.2 old shs.

CannTrust Holdings Inc. (Ont. Mar. 16, 2015)
Mar. 31, 2020 – Filed for protection under the Companies' Creditors Arrangement Act (CCAA) and Ernst & Young Inc. was appointed proposal monitor. (see FPsurvey - Industrials)

Cannvas MedTech Inc. (B.C. June 23, 2017)
Aug. 14, 2019 – Name changed to Eurolife Brands Inc.; basis 4 new for 1 old sh. ∎

Canoe Canadian Diversified Income Fund (Ont. Dec. 21, 2011)
Apr. 20, 2016 – Merged into Canoe Equity Income Class, an unlisted open-end mutual fund; basis 0.960018708 Canoe Equity series Z shs. for 1 Canoe Canadian fund unit. Net asset value per series Z sh. at Apr. 22, 2016, was $10.

Canoe 'GO CANADA' Income Fund (Alta. Dec. 17, 2010)
Dec. 18, 2012 – Merged into Canoe 'GO CANADA!' Equity Income Class (an open-ended fund); basis 0.89 'GO CANADA!' equity ser. A shs. for 1 'GO CANADA' income unit.

Canoe Resources Ltd. (Can. July 7, 1988)
May 16, 2012 – Dissolved.

Canoe Strategic Resources Income Fund (Alta. Apr. 26, 2011)
Dec. 14, 2012 – Merged into Canoe 'GO CANADA!' Equity Income Class (an open-ended fund); basis 0.77 Canoe ' GO CANADA!' equity ser. A shs. for 1 Canoe strategic unit.

Canoe U.S. Strategic Yield Advantaged Fund (Ont. Apr. 28, 2011)
May 16, 2016 – Merged into Canoe North American Monthly Income Class, an unlisted open-ended mutual fund; basis 0.861303952 Canoe North ser. Z shs. for 1 Canoe U.S. class A unit and 1.087675081 Canoe North ser. Z. shs. for 1 Canoe U.S. class U unit.

Canoel International Energy Ltd. (B.C. Sept. 20, 2007)
Oct. 2, 2014 – Name changed to Zenith Energy Ltd. ∎

Canoil Exploration Corporation (B.C. Mar. 5, 1981)
Mar. 14, 2002 – Name changed to AMS Homecare Inc. following reverse takeover acquisition of 393231 B.C. Ltd. and Ambassador Holdings Incorporated. ∎

Canol Metal Mines Ltd. (Ont. 1958)
Mar. 1976 – Charter cancelled.

Canol Mines Limited (B.C. 1966)
Sept. 20, 1985 – Struck off register.

Canolan Resources Ltd. (Ont. May 11, 1979)
Oct. 28, 1985 – Name changed to NuCanolan Resources Ltd.; basis 1 new for 5 old shs. ∎

Canop Worldwide Corp. (Alta. May 13, 1996)
Sept. 25, 2002 – Name changed to Avery Resources Inc.; basis 1 new for 10 old shs. ∎

Canopy Rivers Inc. (Ont. Oct. 31, 2017)
Feb. 23, 2021 – Name changed to RIV Capital Inc. ∎

Canora Gold Mines Ltd. (Ont. 1938)
1957 – Charter cancelled.

Canorama Explorations Ltd. (Ont. 1944)
1963 – Name changed to Consolidated Canorama Explorations Ltd.; basis 1 new for 4 old shs. ∎

Canorex Development Ltd. (B.C. 1969)
Mar. 31, 1983 – Struck off register.

Canoro Resources Ltd. (B.C. Aug. 11, 1995 amalg.)
Oct. 16, 2001 – Continued into Alberta.
Continued into British Columbia.
Sept. 9, 2013 – Struck from register and dissolved.
Nov. 26, 2015 – Limited restoration.
Nov. 27, 2017 – Limited restoration expired and dissolved.

Canova Resources Ltd. (B.C. 1983)
Aug. 13, 1993 – Dissolved and struck off register.

Canpac Minerals Limited (Can. 1969)
Jan. 1, 1978 – Merged with Fording Coal Ltd. to form a new company under the name Fording Coal Ltd.

Canpac National Packaging Ltd. (Alta. Nov. 29, 1991)
May 2, 2002 – Struck from registry and dissolved.

Canperu Mining Corporation Ltd. (Ont. 1959)
May 6, 1965 – Dissolved.

Canplats Resources Corporation (B.C. Feb. 15, 1967)
Feb. 8, 2010 – Acquired by Goldcorp Inc.; basis $4.60 plus 1 Camino Minerals Corporation sh. for 1 Canplats Resources sh. (see Goldcorp Inc.)

CanQuest Resource Corporation (Ont. 1954)
1986 – Continued into Alberta.
May 2, 2003 – Struck from registry and dissolved.

Canray Resources Limited (Ont. Feb. 13, 1934)
Nov. 29, 1983 – Name changed to Exall Resources Limited; basis 1 new for 4 old shs. ∎

Canreos Minerals (1980) Limited (Can. July 8, 1980)
Dec. 6, 1995 – Dissolved.

Canrise Resources Ltd. (Alta. Sept. 11, 1992)
Aug. 6, 1998 – All o/s com. shs. acquired by Poco Petroleums Ltd.; basis 0.3845 of a com. sh. of Poco for 1 com. sh. of Canrise. (see Poco Petroleums Ltd.)

Canroc Oils Ltd. (Alta. 1952)
1958 – Struck off register.

CanRock Energy Corp. (Alta. Oct. 27, 2004)
July 17, 2012 – Formed Alston Energy Inc. in Alberta on amalgamation with (old) Alston Energy Inc., with CanRock the deemed acquiror. ∎

Canron Inc. (Can. Mar. 1915)
June 1, 1990 – All o/s shs. not already held acquired by Ivaco Inc. at $20.50 resulting in Canron becoming a wholly owned subsid. of Ivaco. (see Ivaco Inc.)

Canron Limited (Can. Mar. 1915)
May 23, 1978 – Name changed to Canron Inc. ∎

Canscope Mining Ltd. (Ont. 1961)
Mar. 1967 – Charter cancelled.

CanScot Resources Ltd. (Alta. Nov. 24, 1997)
Sept. 29, 2003 – Acquired by APF Energy Inc. and APF Energy Trust; basis $2.60 or 0.226 new APF trust unit or a combination thereof for 1 old CanScot com. sh. (see APF Energy Trust)

Cansel River Silver Mines Ltd. (Alta. Dec. 29, 1976)
Apr. 24, 1979 – Name changed to Cathedral Minerals Ltd. ∎

Canshore Exploration Limited (Can. Apr. 17, 1979)
May 6, 2004 – Dissolved.

Cansib Energy Inc. (B.C. Oct. 7, 1987)
Jan. 16, 2006 – Dissolved and struck from registry.

Cansil Consolidated Mines Ltd. (B.C. 1946)
1950 – Charter cancelled.

Canso Explorations Ltd. (B.C. Mar. 14, 1988)
Mar. 25, 1994 – Name changed to GéoNova Explorations Inc. ∎

Canso Mining Corp. (N.S. 1938)
Assets assumed on sh.-for-sh. basis by Canadian Alumina Corp. (see Canadian Alumina Corp. Ltd.)

Canso Natural Gas Ltd. (Can. 1954)
1958 – Acquired by United Canso Oil & Gas Ltd.; basis 1 new for 2 old shs.

Canso Oil Producers Ltd. (Can. 1954)
July 2, 1958 – Merged into United Canso Oil & Gas Ltd.; basis 1 new for 2 old shs.

Canso Select Opportunities Fund (Ont. Sept. 25, 2013)
Sept. 4, 2018 – Completed plan of arrangement restructuring with Canso Select Opportunities Corporation (New Canso); basis (i) 2 New Canso Select cl. A multi-vtg. shs. for 1 (old) Canso Select cl. A unit; or (ii) 2 New Canso Select cl. B subord.-vtg. shs. for 1 (old) Canso Select cl. F units.

Cansorb Industries Inc. (B.C. Dec. 18, 1985)
May 14, 2012 – Dissolved and struck from register.

Cansortium Inc. (Ont. Aug. 31, 2018)
Feb. 5, 2025 – Name changed to Fluent Corp. (see FPsurvey - Industrials)

Canspar Mines Ltd. (Ont. 1944)
1956 – Charter cancelled.

Canstar Sports Inc. (Can. Mar. 17, 1981)
Mar. 17, 1995 – Acquired by NIKE Acquisition Inc., a wholly owned subsid. of NIKE, Inc., for $27.50 per sh.

Canstar Ventures Corp. (Alta. Jan. 6, 1987)
Feb. 10, 1995 – Amalgamated with Canadian Angus Resources Ltd., Canadian Industrial Minerals Corp. and Profile Capital Corporation to form Abacan Resources Corporation; basis 0.30 new for 1 Canadian Angus sh., 0.51 new for 1 Canadian Industrial Minerals sh., 0.23 new for 1 Profile Capital sh. and 0.45 new for 1 Canstar Ventures sh. (see Abacan Resource Corporation)

Canstat Petroleum Corporation (B.C. Sept. 14, 1979)
May 29, 1989 – Name changed to International Canstat Petroleum Corporation; basis 1 new for 5 old shs. ∎

Cantar Incorporated (Ont. 1969)
1993 – Formed Cantar/Polyair Inc. in Ontario on amalgamation with Cantar Corporation and Polyair Corporation. ∎

Cantar/Polyair Inc. (Ont. 1993 amalg.)
Feb. 20, 1996 – Succeeded by Polyair Inter Pack Inc. pursuant to reorganization whereby Cantar/Polyair shs. were exchanged for Polyair Inter Pack shs. ∎

Cantech Ventures Inc. (B.C. Apr. 4, 1997)
Aug. 22, 2003 – Name changed to New Cantech Ventures Inc.; basis 1 new for 10 old shs. ∎

Canteen Services Limited (Can. 1948)
Feb. 1962 – Name changed to The Vendron Corporation Ltd. ∎

Canterbury Resources Inc. (B.C. 1983)
Aug. 17, 1990 – Dissolved and struck off register.

Canterra Development Corp. Ltd. (B.C. 1959)
Jan. 10, 1983 – Struck off register.

Canterra Energy Ltd. (Can. 1983 amalg.)
Oct. 19, 1988 – Acquired by Husky Oil Ltd. for $3.00 per sh. (see Husky Oil Ltd.)

Cantex Energy Corporation (B.C. 1977)
Apr. 29, 1994 – Dissolved and struck off register.

Cantex Energy Inc. (Ont. Dec. 18, 1984)
June 21, 2001 – Name changed to Outlook Resources Inc. (see FPsurvey - Industrials)

Cantol Diversified Ltd. (Que. Nov. 7, 1935)
Sept. 8, 1971 – Name changed to Cantol Limited. ∎

Cantol Limited (Que. Nov. 7, 1935)
Dec. 23, 2005 – Privatize for $3.65 per sh.

Canton Explorations Limited (Ont. 1972)
Nov. 22, 1974 – Amalgamated with Foxdale Mines Limited (1 for 7.5), Marquis Explorations Limited (1 for 2.5), Long Point Gas & Oil Incorporated (1 for 3), Darwin Mines Limited (1 for 1.5), Gold Acres Mines Limited (1 for 7), Home Mining Developments Limited (1 for 7) and Force Crag Mines Limited (1 for 4.5) to form New Force Crag Mines Limited; basis 1 new for 5.5 old shs.

Canton Ventures Ltd. (B.C. Feb. 6, 1984)
Mar. 1, 1993 – Name changed to Seacorp Capital Corporation pursuant to reverse takeover acquisition of Seacorp Technology Corporation. ∎

Cantrell Capital Corp. (B.C. Mar. 6, 1986)
Oct. 23, 2009 – Name changed to Petroamerica Oil Corp. pursuant to Qualifying Transaction reverse takeover acquisition of Imore, S.A. ∎

Cantrell Resources Ltd. (B.C. Mar. 6, 1986)
June 19, 1992 – Name changed to Cantrell Capital Corp. ∎

Cantrend Industries Limited (Can. 1911)
1974 – Wilgram Corp. Ltd. acquired 96.5% of all o/s shs. through an offer of $2.00 per cl. A and $1.00 per cl. B sh.

Cantrex Group Inc. (Que. 1982)
Nov. 2, 1989 – Name changed to BMTC Group Inc. (see FPsurvey - Industrials)

Cantrex Group Inc. (Que. Nov. 2, 1989)
Oct. 25, 1999 – All shs. acquired by Transamerica Commercial Finance Corp. of Canada; basis $5.00 per sh. Not to be confused with parent company also named Cantrex Group Inc. (Que 1982).

Cantri Mines Limited (Ont. 1935)
Nov. 30, 1970 – Amalgamated with Con-Key Mines Ltd. (1 for 10), Point West Explorations Ltd. (1 for 10), St. Anthony Mines Ltd. (1 for 30), Temanda Mines Ltd. (1 for 30) and Tinex Development & Exploration Ltd. (1 for 30) to form Can-Con Enterprises and Explorations Limited; basis 1 new for 10 old shs.

Cantronic Systems Inc. (B.C. Feb. 10, 2005 amalg.)
Dec. 1, 2006 – Amalgamated in British Columbia to continue with same name.
Feb. 4, 2013 – Privatized at 4¢ per sh.

Canty Gold Mines (1945) Ltd. (B.C. Feb. 17, 1937)
1953 – Assets acquired by Nighthawk Gold Mines Ltd.; basis 1 new for 2 old shs.

Canu Resources Limited (B.C. 1980)
Dec. 18, 1986 – Amalgamated (1 new for 2 old shs.) with Ican Resources Ltd. (1 for 1) to form Ican Minerals Ltd.

Canuba Manganese Mines Ltd. (Ont. 1953)
Sept. 8, 1966 – Dissolved.

Canuc Mines Ltd. (Ont. 1965)
June 27, 1980 – Name changed to Canuc Resources Inc. ∎

Canuc Resources Corporation (Ont. 1965)
Jan. 13, 1997 – Amalgamated with Nova Beaucage Resources Limited (1 for 3.65) to form a new co. also named Canuc Resources Corporation; basis 1 new Canuc sh. for 1 old sh.

Canuc Resources Inc. (Ont. 1965)
July 2, 1996 – Name changed to Canuc Resources Corporation; basis 1 new for 5 old shs. ∎

Canuck Explorers Ltd. (Ont. 1938)
Sept. 18, 1961 – Dissolved.

Canuck Freehold Royalties Ltd. (Alta. 1951)
Mar. 31, 1967 – Dissolved and struck off register.

Canuck Resources Corp. (B.C. June 5, 1981)
Dec. 14, 1990 – Name changed to Intertel Communications Inc. ∎

Canus Iron Co. Ltd. (Que. 1956)
Charter cancelled.

Canus Laboratories Ltd. (B.C. Apr. 7, 1981)
Mar. 20, 1990 – Delisted from the Vancouver Stock Exchange. Subsequently dissolved for failure to file and struck from register.

Canus Mines & Explorations Ltd. (Ont. 1945)
Oct. 1948 – Name changed to Canus Petroleum Corp. Ltd. ∎

Canus Petroleum Corp. Ltd. (Ont. 1945)
1966 – Wound up.

Canusa Cariboo Gold Mines Ltd. (B.C. 1937)
1956 – Name changed to Canusa Mines Ltd.; basis 1 new for 5 old shs. ∎

Canusa Energy Ltd. (B.C. 1980)
Oct. 7, 1983 – Name changed to Bonanza Resources Ltd. following amalgamation of Bonanza Oil & Gas Ltd. and Cherokee Resources Ltd. with wholly owned subsids. of Canusa.; basis 1 new for 2 old shs. ∎

Canusa Financial Corporation (B.C. 1986)
Nov. 1, 1989 – Name changed to Micro Concepts Inc. ∎

Canusa Mines Ltd. (B.C. 1937)
May 28, 1969 – Name changed to Interplex Mining & Industrial Ltd.; basis 1 new for 2 old shs. ∎

CanUtilities Holdings Ltd. (Alta. Mar. 13, 1981)
July 3, 2001 – Dissolved and wound up into ATCO Ltd. Also Series A, B and C preferred shares were redeemed at $25 per sh.

Canvar Industries Ltd. (Ont. 1924)
1953 – Court action by two large holders of pref. shs. contesting right of co. to acquire a new business without first retiring the pref. shares was settled out of court, said to be a basis of $22 a share.
1954 – Shldrs. protective committee agreed to co.'s redemp. offer of $23 per pref. sh.

Canvass Ventures Ltd. (B.C. Feb. 27, 2017)
June 4, 2019 – Name changed to Nanalysis Scientific Corp. pursuant to Qualifying Transaction reverse takeover acquisition of Nanalysis Corp.; basis 1 new for 4 old shs. (see FPsurvey - Industrials)

Canvedo Industries Ltd. (Ont. 1949)
June 29, 1973 – Name changed to Corporate Master Ltd.; basis 1 new for 5 old shs. ∎

Canvend Venture Capital Inc. (Alta. June 11, 1987)
Oct. 19, 1990 – Name changed to Serenpet Energy Inc.; basis 1 new for 4 old shs. ∎

CanWel Building Materials Group Ltd. (Can. May 11, 2010)
May 31, 2021 – Name changed to Doman Building Materials Group Ltd. (see FPsurvey - Industrials)

CanWel Building Materials Income Fund (Ont. Apr. 5, 2005)
Feb. 1, 2010 – Converted into CanWel Holdings Corporation and subsequently dissolved; basis 1 CanWel Holdings com. sh. for 1 CanWel Building fund unit and 1 CanWel Holdings com. sh. for 1 CanWel Holding Partnership cl. B exch. LP unit. (see CanWel Holdings Corporation)

CanWel Building Materials Ltd. (B.C. Nov. 24, 1988)
May 18, 2005 – Converted into an income fund named CanWel Building Materials Income Fund; basis 2 trust units for 1 com. sh.

CanWel Holdings Corporation (B.C. Dec. 11, 2009)
May 11, 2010 – Name changed to CanWel Building Materials Group Ltd. and continued into Canada. ∎

Canwest Financial Holdings Limited (Ont. 1968)
1980 – Continued into Canada.
Jan. 1984 – All o/s pref. shs. redeemed and co. thereafter became private.

Canwest Global Communications Corp. (Ont. June 14, 1979)
May 27, 1986 – Continued into Manitoba.
July 25, 1991 – Continued into Canada.
Apr. 26, 2010 – Publishing and digital media assets were acquired by Postmedia Network Canada Corp.
Oct. 27, 2010 – Name changed to 2737469 Canada Inc. following sale of broadcast assets to Shaw Communications Inc. ◼

CanWest InSureco Inc. (Ont. 1986)
Dec. 11, 1990 – Dissolved and struck off register.

CanWest MediaWorks Income Fund (Ont. July 5, 2005)
July 11, 2007 – Acquired by CanWest MediaWorks Limited Partnership whereby fund units were redeemed for $9.00 per unit.

CanWest Trustco Limited (Can. 1983)
Apr. 26, 1996 – Amalgamated with 3211827 Canada Ltd. (formerly CanWest Financial Corporation); basis 67.2 new cl. B pref. shs. for 1 cl. A com. sh. The cl. B pref. shs. immediately redeemed for $0.01 per sh.

Canwex Explorations Ltd. (B.C. 1966)
Feb. 25, 1983 – Struck off register.

CanXGold Mining Corp. (B.C. Jan. 9, 2004)
Nov. 20, 2023 – Placed into receivership by senior secured creditor. PricewaterhouseCoopers Inc. appointed receiver and all officers and directors resigned.

Canyon Cariboo Gold Mines Ltd. (B.C. 1946)
Apr. 11, 1957 – Charter cancelled.

Canyon City Explorations Ltd. (B.C. 1967)
Dec. 18, 1978 – Dissolved.

Canyon Copper Corp. (Nev. Jan. 21, 2000)
May 31, 2013 – Continued into British Columbia.
July 27, 2018 – Name changed to Searchlight Resources Inc. (see FPsurvey - Mines & Energy)

Canyon Copper Mines Ltd. (B.C. 1961)
July 22, 1974 – Charter cancelled.

Canyon Services Group Inc. (Alta. Apr. 8, 2004)
June 8, 2017 – Acquired by Trican Well Services Ltd.; basis 1.70 Trican shs. for 1 Canyon Service sh.

Canzac Mines Ltd. (B.C. 1964)
1969 – Assets acquired by Wollaston Lake Mines Ltd.; basis 1 new for 3 old shs.

Canzona Minerals Inc. (B.C. 1966)
Aug. 1, 1982 – Amalgamated with American Energy Corporation (1 for 1) and Heartland Oil & Gas Corporation (1 for 2) to form a new co. also named American Energy Corporation; basis 1 new for 4 old shs.

Cap-Ex Iron Ore Ltd. (Can. Feb. 27, 2007)
Nov. 3, 2016 – Name changed to ML Gold Corp. ◼

Cap-Ex Ventures Ltd. (Can. Feb. 27, 2007)
Mar. 20, 2013 – Name changed to Cap-Ex Iron Ore Ltd. ◼

Cap-Link Ventures Ltd. (Can. May 25, 2005)
Apr. 8, 2010 – Name changed to Petrodorado Energy Ltd. ◼

Capalta Inc. (Alta. Nov. 6, 2000)
Nov. 12, 2002 – Acquired by CDK Services Ltd. considered to be Capalta's Qualifying Transaction; basis 1 new CDK unit (1 CDK com. sh. plus 1 wt.) for 1 old Capalta com. sh. (see CDK Services Ltd.)

Capberta Enterprises Inc. (Alta. 1987)
Nov. 1, 1990 – Struck off register.

Capco Gas & Oil Co. Ltd. (B.C.)
1958 – Struck off register.

Capco Resources Ltd. (Alta. Dec. 15, 1986)
June 2, 2015 – Dissolved and struck from register.

Cape Breton Development Corporation (Can. 1967)
Dec. 31, 2009 – Name changed to Enterprise Cape Breton Corporation.

Cape Copper Mines Limited (Ont. 1951)
Aug. 29, 1960 – Charter cancelled.

Cape Resources Inc. (Ont. Apr. 18, 1978)
Oct. 2, 1986 – Name changed to The International Pagurian Corporation Limited following acquisition by The International Pagurian Corporation Limited; basis 1 new for 9 old shs. ◼

Capella Resources Limited (B.C. July 6, 1973)
Nov. 23, 1990 – Dissolved and struck off register.

Capella Resources Ltd. (B.C. Feb. 27, 1987)
May 16, 2012 – Name changed to Cerro Mining Corp.; basis 1 new for 6 old shs. ◼

Capeq Corporation (Alta. Apr. 7, 1993)
Oct. 5, 1999 – Struck from register.

Capewell Petroleum Corp. Ltd. (Ont. Jan. 26, 1949)
1954 – Taken over by Saskalon Uranium & Oils Ltd.; basis 1 new for 5 old shs.

CapGain Properties Inc. (B.C. Apr. 30, 2009)
Mar. 27, 2013 – Continued into Alberta.
Jan. 15, 2020 – Name changed to MAACKK Capital Corp. (see FPsurvey - Industrials)

Capgrow Inc. (Alta. Feb. 4, 1987)
July 25, 1995 – Name changed to Oakhill Communications Inc.; basis 1 new for 3 old shs. ◼

Capilano Explorations Ltd. (B.C. 1969)
Feb. 1975 – Charter cancelled.

Capilano International Inc. (Can. Feb. 11, 1991 amalg.)
Aug. 14, 1996 – Name changed to Kelman Technologies Inc. ◼

Capilano Oil Co. Ltd. (B.C.)
1957 – Struck off register.

Capital ABTB Inc. (Can. Sept. 8, 2005)
Oct. 3, 2006 – Converted into an income trust named BTB Real Estate Investment Trust following Qualifying Transaction acquisition of property in Laval, Québec; basis 1 new BTB unit for 1 old Capital sh.

Capital Alliance Group Inc. (B.C. Nov. 17, 1986)
Nov. 14, 2007 – Name changed to CIBT Education Group Inc. ◼

Capital BLF Inc. (Can. Mar. 30, 2007)
June 14, 2013 – Continued into Quebec.
Aug. 23, 2013 – Succeeded by BLF Real Estate Investment Trust pursuant to plan of arrangement whereby BLF Real Estate Investment Trust was formed to facilitate the conversion of the corporation into a trust. ◼

Capital Building Industries Ltd. (Ont. Feb. 16, 1962)
Apr. 28, 1969 – Name changed to Capital Diversified Industries Limited. ◼

Capital Cable TV Ltd. (Alta. Dec. 9, 1966)
Feb. 29, 1984 – Name changed to Shaw Cablesystems Ltd. ◼

Capital Charter Corp. (B.C. Nov. 27, 1998)
Mar. 24, 2000 – Name changed to Zconnexx Corporation pursuant to reverse takeover acquisition of Zconnexx Corporation. ◼

Capital DGMC Inc. (Can. Mar. 8, 2005)
Jan. 12, 2020 – Struck from register and dissolved.

Capital Desbog Inc. (Can. Jan. 12, 2005)
Apr. 18, 2006 – Name changed to HLT Energies 2006 Inc. following Qualifying Transaction reverse takeover acquisition of HLT Energies Inc. for 30¢ per sh. ◼

Capital Diagnostic Corporation (Ont. Sept. 22, 1987)
Mar. 13, 2006 – Certificate of incorporation cancelled and dissolved.

Capital Diversified Industries Limited (Ont. Feb. 16, 1962)
Dec. 13, 1977 – Name changed to Action Traders Inc. ◼

Capital Dynamics Limited (Can. Oct. 31, 1972)
Aug. 25, 1995 – Dissolved.

Capital Endeavors Corporation (B.C. Feb. 3, 1999)
Feb. 25, 2002 – Acquired by EMedia Networks International Corp. which constituted the Qualifying Transaction of Capital Endeavors; basis 1 new EMedia unit (1 com. sh. plus 1 wt.) for 2.042 old Capital Endeavors com. shs. (see EMedia Networks International Corporation)

Capital Environmental Resource Inc. (Ont. May 23, 1997)
Aug. 2, 2004 – Name changed to Waste Services, Inc. following reorganization to alter corporate structure. ◼

Capital Gains Income STREAMS Corporation (Ont. Jan. 8, 2001)
Dec. 4, 2013 – Merged into Dividend 15 Split Corp.; basis 1.22352296 cl A shs. and 1.22352296 pfd shs. of Dividend 15 for 1 Capital Gains capital sh.; and 0.19516249 cl A shs. and 0.19516249 pfd shs. of Dividend 15 for 1 Capital Gains equity sh.

Capital Gold Corporation (Nev. Feb. 1982)
Nov. 21, 2005 – Continued into Delaware. (see Gammon Gold Inc.)
Apr. 12, 2011 – Acquired by Gammon Gold Inc.; basis US$1.09 plus 0.5209 Gammon shs. for 1 Capital Gold sh. (see Gammon Gold Inc.)

Capital Leasing Corporation Ltd. (Ont. 1961)
1962 – Out of business; no known assets.

Capital L'Estérel Inc. (Can. Oct. 31, 2003)
Apr. 12, 2005 – Name changed to iseemedia inc. following Qualifying Transaction reverse takeover acquisition of Isee Media Inc.; basis 1 new for 3.847 old shs. ◼

Capital Lithium Mines Ltd. (Ont. 1955)
1959 – Acquired by Aug.us Exploration Ltd.; basis 1 new for 6 old shs.

Capital MLB inc. (Que. Oct. 26, 2007)
Sept. 9, 2010 – Dissolved following Qualifying Transaction private placement subscription of 4,900,000 units (1 com. sh. plus 0.5 wt.) at 10¢ per unit and distribution of Nuvolt units to shldrs.; basis 1.337 Nuvolt units for 1 Capital MLB sh. (see Nuvolt Corporation Inc.)

Capital Maniwaki Inc. (Can. Mar. 8, 2005)
Feb. 23, 2009 – Name changed to Capital Vtechlab Inc. ◼

Capital Markets West Inc. (Alta. 1988)
June 30, 1991 – Wound up and charter cancelled. Shldrs. received an initial cash distribution of 43¢ per sh. in January 1991, a pro rata distribution of shs. in two private firms, SPI Synthetic Peptides Inc. and Nichols Advanced Technology Inc., and a final distribution of 7¢ per sh.

Capital Nobel Inc. (Can. Mar. 7, 2012)
May 30, 2013 – Succeeded by Nobel Real Estate Investment Trust pursuant to plan of arrangement reorganization which constituted the company's Qualifying Transaction; basis 1 Nobel REIT trust unit for 1 Capital Nobel com. sh.

Capital One Venture Group I Ltd. (B.C. Sept. 2, 2020)
Apr. 30, 2021 – Name changed to Battery Elements Corp. ◼

Capital Power Income L.P. (Ont. Mar. 27, 1997)
Nov. 10, 2011 – Acquired by Atlantic Power Corporation for $19.40 or 1.3 Atlantic shs. for 1 Capital Power sh. (see Atlantic Power Corporation)
Feb. 1, 2012 – Name changed to Atlantic Power Limited Partnership. (see Atlantic Power Corporation)

Capital Reserve Inc. (B.C. 1983)
June 19, 1992 – Dissolved and struck off register.

Capital Rouyn Gold Mines Ltd. (Que. 1926)
Oct. 13, 1973 – Dissolved.

Capital St-Charles inc. (Can. May 20, 2004)
Apr. 20, 2005 – Formed CVTech Group Inc. in Canada pursuant to Qualifying Transaction reverse takeover acquisition of and amalgamation with CVTech Investment Inc. ■

Capital 3429 inc. (Can. Jan. 13, 2004)
Oct. 30, 2006 – Name changed to IMS Experts-Consultants inc. following Qualifying Transaction acquisition of IMS Experts-conseils inc. and Pasquin St-Jean et Associés inc. ■

Capital Valmoris Inc. (Can. Nov. 5, 2007)
Mar. 18, 2010 – Name changed to Biotonix (2010) Inc. pursuant to Qualifying Transaction acquisition of certain assets held by 32527326 Canada Inc. ■

Capital Vtechlab Inc. (Can. Mar. 8, 2005)
Nov. 3, 2011 – Name changed to Capital DGMC Inc. ■

Capital Wapiti Inc. (Can. Feb. 27, 2007)
June 20, 2008 – Name changed to Investus Real Estate Inc. ■

Capital Wire Cloth & Manufacturing Co. Ltd. (Ont. 1912)
Dec. 3, 1962 – Name changed to Capital Wire Cloth Limited. ■

Capital Wire Cloth Limited (Ont. 1912)
1964 – Appleton Wire Works Corp. of Wisconsin acquired over 90% of shs. at $12.50 per sh.

Capital.Com Incorporated (Alta. Jan. 24, 1997)
Dec. 19, 2000 – Formed Pethealth Inc. in Canada on amalgamation with Pethealth Inc., constituting a reverse takeover by Pethealth. ■

Capitan Mining Inc. (B.C. Oct. 30, 2019)
Mar. 23, 2023 – Name changed to Capitan Silver Corp. (see FPsurvey - Mines & Energy)

Capitol Energy Resources Ltd. (Alta. June 30, 1995)
June 21, 2007 – Acquired by Provident Energy Ltd., a wholly owned subsid. of Provident Energy Trust, for $8.16 per sh. (see Provident Energy Trust)

Capitol Petroleums Limited (Ont. 1949)
1952 – Acquired by Ellesmere Oil & Development Ltd.; basis 1 new for 10 old shs.

Capo Resources Ltd. (B.C. Nov. 14, 2005)
May 16, 2008 – Name changed to Laurentian Goldfields Ltd. following acquisition of private co. Laurentian Goldfields Ltd. ■

Capoose Minerals Incorporated (B.C. Aug. 5, 1980)
July 10, 1986 – Name changed to Tyler Resources Inc. ■

Capoose Mining Incorporated (B.C. Aug. 5, 1980)
Dec. 19, 1981 – Name changed to Capoose Minerals Incorporated; basis 1 new for 2 old shs. ■

Capps Gold Mine Ltd. (Ont. 1935)
1952 – Charter cancelled.

Capra Minerals Ltd. (Alta. May 15, 1990)
Apr. 20, 1994 – Name changed to Urban Resource Technologies Inc.; basis 1 new for 2 old shs. ■

CapRate Commercial Properties Inc. (Alta. July 18, 1997)
Sept. 19, 2005 – Dissolution in progress; initial distribution was $0.2166 per sh. and final distribution expected in early 2006.

Capri Gold Mines Ltd. (Que. 1945)
Charter cancelled.

Capri Mining Corporation Ltd. (B.C. 1966)
Feb. 25, 1983 – Struck off register.

Capri Resources Ltd. (B.C. June 20, 1980)
Dec. 30, 1987 – Name changed to International Capri Resources Ltd. ■

Caprice Business Development Canada Inc. (B.C. Nov. 29, 2018)
Apr. 17, 2020 – Name changed to Leaf Mobile Inc. pursuant to Qualifying Transaction reverse takeover acquisition of 1182533 B.C. Ltd. (dba Leaf Digital Studios). ■

Caprice-Greystoke Enterprises Ltd. (B.C. June 26, 1986)
Sept. 30, 1996 – Delisted from the Vancouver Stock Exchange. Subsequently struck from register and dissolved.

Caprice Resources Inc. (B.C. 1972)
Dec. 30, 1983 – Dissolved.

Capricorn Business Acquisitions Inc. (Ont. May 7, 2008)
Sept. 7, 2021 – Name changed to Canada Computational Unlimited Corp. pursuant to the Qualifying Transaction reverse takeover acquisition of Canada Computational Unlimited Inc. (dba CCU.ai) and concurrent amalgmation of CCU.ai with wholly owned 9442-4868 Québec Inc.; basis 1 new for 2.7 old shs. ■

Capricorn Resources Ltd. (B.C. 1981)
Nov. 12, 1993 – Dissolved and struck off register.

Caprive Industries and Resources Limited (Que. 1957)
Nov. 11, 1978 – Charter cancelled.

Caprive Oil & Gas Co. Ltd. (Que. 1957)
Nov. 25, 1970 – Name changed to Caprive Industries and Resources Limited. ■

Caprock Energy Ltd. (B.C. Nov. 5, 1982)
Sept. 14, 1989 – Name changed to Consolidated Caprock Resources Ltd.; basis 1 new for 5 old shs. ■

Capstock Financial Inc. (B.C. May 31, 2006)
June 8, 2012 – Name changed to Gespeg Copper Resources Inc. pursuant to Qualifying Transaction acquisition of mineral property from Kimpar Resources Inc. ■

Capstone Gold Corp. (B.C. July 17, 1987)
Feb. 13, 2006 – Name changed to Capstone Mining Corp. ■

Capstone Infrastructure Corporation (B.C. May 20, 2010)
May 5, 2016 – Acquired by London, U.K.-based iCon Infrastructure Partners III, L.P. for $4.90 per 1 Capstone Infrastructure com. sh. and 1 cl. B unit, respectively. The cl. A pref. shs. would continue to be listed until further notice. (see FPsurvey - Mines & Energy; FPsurvey - Industrials)

Capstone Mining Corp. (B.C. July 17, 1987)
Mar. 25, 2022 – Acquired by Mantos Copper (Bermuda) Limited (renamed Capstone Copper Corp.); basis 1 Mantos Copper sh. for 1 Capstone Mining sh.

Capstone Mining North Ltd. (Can. July 11, 2007)
Nov. 26, 2008 – Acquired by Capstone Mining Corp.; basis 1.566 Capstone shs. for 1 Sherwood sh.

Capstream Ventures Inc. (B.C. June 21, 2011)
Mar. 10, 2017 – Name changed to Axion Ventures Inc. (see FPsurvey - Industrials)

Capsule Technology Group Inc. (Ont. 1987)
Dec. 1, 1989 – Declared bankrupt and assets liquidated. Peat Marwick Throne Inc. appointed trustee. Nothing left for shldrs.

Captain Consolidated Resources Ltd. (Ont. 1945)
Oct. 3, 1990 – Name changed to International Captain Industries Corp.; basis 1 new for 5 old shs. ■

Captain Mines Ltd. (Ont. 1945)
Dec. 31, 1980 – Name changed to Captain Consolidated Resources Ltd. ■

Captain Yellowknife Gold Mines Ltd. (Ont. 1945)
Jan. 10, 1957 – Name changed to Captain Mines Ltd. ■

Captech Communication Inc. (Can. Mar. 17, 1994)
July 16, 1997 – Name changed to Captech Multicom Inc.; basis 1 new for 4 old shs. ■

Captech Multicom Inc. (Can. Mar. 17, 1994)
Sept. 19, 2005 – Dissolved.

Captiva Verde Industries Ltd. (B.C. May 8, 2014)
Oct. 21, 2019 – Dissolved and struck from registry.

Captiva Verde Land Corp. (B.C. Nov. 9, 2015)
May 21, 2021 – Name changed to Captiva Verde Wellness Corp. (see FPsurvey - Industrials)

Captive Air International Inc. (Can. Jan. 22, 1987)
Apr. 8, 1996 – Name changed to KIK Tire Technologies Inc.; basis 1 new for 5 old shs. ■

Capture.Net Technologies Inc. (Ont. July 7, 1997)
Mar. 5, 2003 – Name changed to Sea Green Capital Corp. ■

Cara Operations Limited (Ont. Nov. 29, 1961)
Apr. 1, 1991 – Amalgamated with wholly owned subsid. Vanchick Investments Limited to continue as Cara Operations Limited.
Feb. 26, 2004 – Amalgamated with 2034619 Ontario Inc. for $8.00 per sh. and privatized.
Dec. 31, 2014 – Amalgamated with Prime Restaurants Inc. to continue as Cara Operations Limited.
May 16, 2018 – Name changed to Recipe Unlimited Corporation. ■

Caracara Silver Inc. (B.C. Dec. 3, 2009)
Sept. 12, 2019 – Name changed to Xtraction Services Holdings Corp. pursuant to the reverse takeover acquisition of Xtraction Services, Inc.; basis 1 new for 6.262 old shs. ■

Carada Capital Corp. (Alta. June 5, 1986)
Dec. 9, 1991 – Name changed to Norlana Energy Inc. ■

Caradoc Ekfrid Telephone Company, Limited (Ont. 1907)
Dec. 31, 1977 – Amalgamated with Bell Canada and charter cancelled.

Caramat Gold Mines Ltd. (Ont. 1936)
1968 – Merged into Milestone Exploration Ltd.; basis 4,124 new for 1,000 old shs.

Caramora Porcupine Mines Ltd. (Ont. 1945)
Nov. 28, 1973 – Charter cancelled.

Carat Exploration Inc. (B.C. Oct. 16, 2003)
Apr. 12, 2010 – Name changed to Stronghold Metals Inc. ■

Caratel Limited (Ont. Dec. 27, 1945)
Aug. 27, 1992 – Name changed to Juritel Systems Inc.; basis 1 new for 6 old shs. ■

Caravan Energy Corporation (B.C. Oct. 21, 2020)
Oct. 26, 2023 – Name changed to Neotech Metals Corp. (see FPsurvey - Mines & Energy)

Caravan Oil & Gas Ltd. (Alta. Oct. 25, 1994)
Dec. 7, 2000 – Amalgamated with Ketch Energy Ltd.; basis 0.59 Ketch com. shs. or $2.00 for 1 old Caravan com. sh. (see Ketch Energy Ltd.)

Caravan Trailer Lodges of B.C. Ltd. (B.C. 1967)
Apr. 21, 1977 – Name changed to Caravan Development Corporation.

Caravan Trailer Lodges (St. Lawrence) Ltd. (Can. 1968)
1978 – Name changed to Trevista Estates Limited. ■

Caravelle Mines Limited (Ont. 1959)
Mar. 1976 – Charter cancelled.

Caravelle Resources, Ltd. (B.C. Mar. 1982)
Oct. 16, 1986 – Name changed to STN Shop Television Network, Ltd. ■

Carbec Mines Ltd. (Que. 1945)
Dec. 1969 – Assets sold to Triton Explorations Ltd.; basis 1 Triton sh. for 9 Carbec shs. (see Triton Explorations Ltd.)

Carben Energy Inc. (B.C. 1984)
Nov. 6, 1987 – Name changed to American Medical Technologies, Inc. ■

Carber Capital Corp. (Ont. Dec. 30, 1985)
Aug. 17, 2010 – Name changed to Ba Ba Capital Inc.; basis 1 new for 10 old shs. ■

Carbite Golf Inc. (B.C. July 2, 1985)
Oct. 12, 2001 – Continued into Yukon.
May 25, 2005 – Dissolved and struck off register.

Carbiz.com Inc. (Ont. Mar. 31, 1998)
Oct. 6, 2003 – Name changed to Carbiz Inc. (see FPsurvey - Industrials)

Carbon Friendly Solutions Inc. (Can. June 19, 1997)
July 22, 2013 – Name changed to MicroCoal Technologies Inc. ■

Carbon2Green Corporation (Can. Jan. 20, 2005)
Jan. 4, 2012 – Name changed to TomaGold Corporation; basis 1 new for 5 old shs. (see FPsurvey - Mines & Energy)

Carbonate Larder Mines Ltd. (Ont. 1943)
1968 – Charter cancelled.

Carbondale Oils Ltd. (Alta.)
1960 – Struck off register.

CarbonOne Technologies Inc. (Alta. Apr. 16, 2002)
Sept. 29, 2016 – Name changed to TekModo Industries Inc. following acquisition of TekModo group of companies. ■

Card Lake Copper Mines Ltd. (Ont. 1969)
Oct. 31, 1986 – Amalgamated with 2 private cos., Mission Harker Exploration Ltd. and Matona Resources Limited, to form Card Lake Resources Limited; basis 1 new for 5 old shs. (see Card Lake Resources Limited)

Card Lake Resources Limited (Ont. Oct. 31, 1986 amalg.)
Apr. 20, 1994 – Name changed to Franc-Or Resources Corporation; basis 1 new for 10 old shs. ■

Cardero Resource Corp. (B.C. Dec. 31, 1985)
Feb. 1, 2022 – Acquired by World Copper Ltd.; basis 0.200795 World Copper shs. for 1 Cardero sh.
Feb. 1, 2022 – Name changed to Zonia Holdings Corp.

Cardero Resources Ltd. (B.C. 1976)
May 11, 1983 – Name changed to International Cardero Resources Inc.; basis 1 new for 3 old shs. ■

Cardiff Corporation (Alta. 1986)
Jan. 1, 1996 – Dissolved and struck off register.

Cardiff Energy Corp. (B.C. Feb. 1, 2010)
July 19, 2017 – Name changed to Cheetah Canyon Resources Corp. ■

Cardiff Fluorite Mines Ltd. (Ont. 1943)
Mar. 31, 1953 – Name changed to Cardiff Uranium Mines Limited; basis 1 new for 1 old sh. ■

Cardiff Resources Inc. (Alta. July 21, 2001)
Mar. 29, 2004 – Formed Hy-Drive Technologies Ltd. in Alberta following Qualifying Transaction amalgamation with Fat Power Inc., constituting a reverse takeover by Fat Power; basis 1 new for 2.2 Fat Power shs. and 1 new for 1 Cardiff sh. ■

Cardiff Uranium Mines Limited (Ont. 1943)
Sept. 25, 1988 – Name changed to Insulblock Systems Inc.; basis 1 new for 4 old shs. ■

Cardiff Ventures Corporation (Alta. 1986)
Nov. 4, 1992 – Name changed to Cardiff Corporation; basis 1 new for 5 old shs. ■

Cardigan Capital Corp. (Alta. July 17, 1997)
Jan. 11, 1999 – Formed Icron Systems Inc. in Alberta on amalgamation with wholly owned Icron Technologies Corporation, acquired in December 1998. ■

Cardigan Development Company Ltd. (B.C. 1955)
July 16, 1975 – Name changed to United Cardigan Development Co. Ltd.; basis 1 new for 10 old shs.

Cardinal Capital Partners Inc. (Ont. Mar. 25, 1994 amalg.)
Jan. 19, 2021 – Name changed to Psyence Group Inc. pursuant to the reverse takeover acquisition of Mindhealth Biomed Corp. and concurrent amalgamation of Mindhealth with wholly owned 1264216 B.C. Ltd. (and continued as Psyence Biomed Corp.).; basis 1 new for 19.24 old shs. (see FPsurvey - Industrials)

Cardinal Factor Corp. (Ont. May 27, 1983)
Dec. 8, 2008 – Dissolved and struck from register.

Cardinal Mineral Corporation Ltd. (B.C. Mar. 31, 1980)
Nov. 8, 1990 – Name changed to Connecticut Development Corporation; basis 1 new for 3 old shs. ■

Cardinal Petroleums Ltd. (Ont. Mar. 22, 1948)
1951 – Taken over by Consolidated Allenbee Oil and Gas Co. Ltd.; basis 2 new for 5 old shs.

Cardinal Resources Limited (Australia Nov. 11, 2010)
Jan. 19, 2021 – Acquired by Shandong Gold Mining (HongKong) Co., Limited; basis A$1.00 cash per ordinary sh.

Cardinal Uranium & Copper Mines Inc. (Que. 1954)
Oct. 20, 1973 – Dissolved.

Cardinal Yellowknife Mines Ltd. (Ont. 1944)
Sept. 1957 – Charter cancelled.

CardioComm Solutions Inc. (B.C. Oct. 26, 1989)
Nov. 26, 2007 – Name changed to CardioComm Solutions, Inc.; basis 1 new for 5 old shs. (see FPsurvey - Industrials)

Cardiome Pharma Corp. (B.C. Dec. 12, 1986)
Mar. 8, 2002 – Continued into Canada.
May 17, 2018 – Succeeded by Correvio Pharma Corp. pursuant to plan of arrangement whereby Cipher Pharmaceuticals Inc. acquired the Canadian business portfolio of Cardiome Pharma Corp. ■

Cardwell Oil Corporation Ltd. (B.C. 1967)
1970 – Name changed to Cardwell Resources Ltd. ■

Cardwell Resources Ltd. (B.C. 1967)
July 28, 1980 – Charter cancelled.

Care Point Medical Centres Ltd. (B.C. Sept. 14, 1982)
Sept. 18, 1991 – Name changed to Consolidated Care Point Medical Centres Ltd.; basis 1 new for 8 old shs. ■

Care Veterinary Pharmaceuticals Ltd. (B.C. 1973)
Mar. 3, 2014 – Dissolved and struck from register.

Carebook Technologies Inc. (B.C. July 11, 2018)
Sept. 15, 2021 – Continued into Canada.
Feb. 26, 2025 – All o/s shs. not already held by UIL Limited; basis 10¢ cash per sh.

CareerExchange Interactive Corp. (B.C. Apr. 21, 1999)
June 20, 2005 – Name changed to Cytiva Software Inc. ■

Caren Oil & Gas Company Limited (unknown)
Mar. 1953 – Acquired by Ridgeway Petroleums Ltd. for 700,000 shs. (see Ridgeway Petroleums Ltd.)

Carena-Bancorp Holdings Inc. (Can. Sept. 5, 1978)
Mar. 31, 1989 – Name changed to Carena Developments Limited. ■

Carena-Bancorp Inc. (Que. 1923)
Jan. 29, 1979 – All o/s com. and pref. shs. exchanged for shs. of Carena-Bancorp Holdings Inc.; basis 1 new for 1 old sh.

Carena Developments Limited (Can. Sept. 5, 1978)
June 4, 1996 – Name changed to Brookfield Properties Corporation; basis 1 new for 5 old shs. ■

Carey-Canadian Mines, Ltd. (Can. 1955)
Aug. 31, 1978 – Amalgamated with Jim Walter Building Products Ltd. to form Carey Canada Inc.

Carfinco Financial Group Inc. (Alta. Sept. 28, 2011)
Mar. 10, 2015 – Acquired by Banco Santander, S.A. for $11.25 per sh.
Aug. 19, 2021 – Name changed to Santander Consumer Inc. ■

Carfinco Income Fund (Ont. Aug. 26, 2002)
Jan. 1, 2012 – Succeeded by Carfinco Financial Group Inc. pursuant to plan of arrangement whereby Carfinco Financial Group Inc. was formed to facilitate the conversion of the fund into a corporation. ■

Carfinco Inc. (Ont. Dec. 30, 1996)
Nov. 27, 2002 – Succeeded by Carfinco Income Fund pursuant to plan of arrangement whereby Carfinco Income Fund was formed to acquire the company; basis 1 new trust unit for 1 old com. sh. ■

Cargojet Income Fund (Ont. Apr. 25, 2005)
Jan. 1, 2011 – Succeeded by Cargojet Inc. pursuant to plan of arrangement whereby Cargojet Inc. was formed to facilitate the conversion of the fund into a corporation and fund was subsequently dissolved. (see FPsurvey - Industrials)

Cariana International Industries Inc. (B.C. 1983)
July 9, 1993 – Dissolved and struck off register.

Caribbean Diversified Investments, Inc. (B.C. May 10, 2011)
Apr. 27, 2015 – Dissolved and struck from register.

Caribbean Gold Mines Ltd. (Ont. 1947)
Nov. 25, 1970 – Dissolved.

Caribbean Resources Corp. (B.C. 1978)
Oct. 27, 1989 – Amalgamated with Exmar Resources Ltd. (0.5334 for 1), Mishi Lake Resources Inc. (1 principal escrow sh. for 1) and Mishibishu Resources Ltd. (0.6278 for 1) to form Mishibishu Gold Corporation; basis 0.4215 new Mishibishu Gold sh. for 1 old sh. (see Mishibishu Gold Corporation)

Caribbean Resources Corporation (B.C. Aug. 20, 1990)
Apr. 1, 2016 – Privatized; basis $0.0052 cash per sh.

Caribe Petroleums Inc. (B.C. 1981)
Apr. 6, 1989 – Name changed to Crio Group Developments Inc.; basis 1 new for 5 old shs. ■

CaribGold Resources Inc. (Ont. May 9, 1990)
Dec. 30, 2002 – Name changed to Unigold Inc. pursuant to amalgamation of wholly owned 6035442 Canada Inc. with Unigold Resources Inc., acquired by reverse

takeover, and distribution of common shares of newly formed Caribgold Minerals Inc. (to which assets other than marketable securities were transferred) to shldrs. as a stk. divd.; basis 1 new for 2 old shs. (see FPsurvey - Mines & Energy)

Caribia Oil & Gas Co. Ltd. (B.C.)
1959 – Struck off register.

Cariboo-Bell Copper Mines Ltd. (B.C. 1965)
Feb. 22, 1977 – Amalgamated with Pickle Crow Explorations Ltd. (1 for 5), Beacon Mining Co. Ltd. (1 for 40), Abex Mines Ltd. (1 for 50) and Highland Mercury Mines Ltd. (1 for 5) to form Highland-Crow Resources Ltd.; basis 1 new for 9 Cariboo shs.

Cariboo Crescent Gold Mines Ltd. (B.C. 1945)
Oct. 1949 – Dissolved.

Cariboo Diatomite Consolidated 1960 Ltd. (B.C. 1960)
May 23, 1986 – Struck off register.

Cariboo Diatomite Ltd. (B.C. 1960)
Oct. 28, 1977 – Name changed to Cariboo Diatomite Consolidated 1960 Ltd. ■

Cariboo Gold Fields Ltd. (B.C. May 9, 1986)
Jan. 31, 2011 – Struck from register and dissolved.
Oct. 26, 2011 – Limited restoration to register.
Oct. 27, 2013 – Limited restoration expired and dissolved.

Cariboo Gold Quartz Mining Co. Ltd. (B.C. 1927)
June 15, 1972 – Amalgamated into Coseka Resources Ltd.; basis 1 new for 1.8 Cariboo shs.

Cariboo Gold Sands Ltd. (B.C. 1947)
June 12, 1952 – Dissolved and struck off register.

Cariboo-Hudson Gold Mines Ltd. (B.C. Nov. 27, 1936)
1946 – Name changed to Cariboo-Hudson Gold Mines (1946) Ltd. and continued into British Columbia; basis 1 new for 4 old shs. ■

Cariboo-Hudson Gold Mines (1946) Ltd. (B.C. 1946)
Dec. 1971 – Charter cancelled.

Cariboo Minelands Ltd. (B.C. Feb. 15, 1965)
May 12, 1970 – Name changed to Equatorial Resources Limited. ■

Caribou Brewing Company Ltd. (B.C. 1956)
Jan. 1962 – Placed into bankruptcy. Plant at Prince George, B.C., sold for $150,000. Receiver, James Moynes. Cap. stk. o/s 500,000 n.p.v. shs. There were o/s $500,000 1st mtge. bds., due June 15, 1967, and $180,000 debs. due May 1, 1968. Trustee for bd. hldrs., The Canada Trust Co., Vancouver.

Caribou Copper Resources Ltd. (Ont. Feb. 27, 2007)
Dec. 20, 2011 – Name changed to Caribou King Resources Ltd. ■

Caribou King Resources Ltd. (Ont. Feb. 27, 2007)
Dec. 22, 2011 – Continued into British Columbia.
Nov. 9, 2015 – Name changed to CKR Carbon Corporation. ■

Caribou Mines Ltd. (N.B. 1957)
Reported no longer in operation.

Caribou Resources Corp. (Alta. Feb. 1, 1997)
July 31, 2007 – Name changed to JED Production Inc. pursuant to acquisition by JED Oil Inc.; basis 1 JED Oil sh. for 10 Caribou shs.

Caribou Resources Corp. (Alta. Feb. 24, 1997 amalg.)
May 24, 2004 – Completed acquisition of and substitutional listing for Rainmaker Ventures Ltd. (which see) which constituted Rainmaker's Qualifying Transaction; basis 1 Caribou sh. for 7.6943 Rainmaker shs.

Carina Mineral Resources Corp. (Sask. Dec. 14, 1982)
May 11, 1990 – Name changed to Consolidated Carina Resources Corp.; basis 1 new for 3 old shs. ■

Carinor Porcupine Mines Ltd. (Ont. 1945)
1949 – Charter cancelled.

Carissa Mining Corporation (B.C. Nov. 10, 1988)
Oct. 27, 1995 – Name changed to Rockwell Ventures Inc.; basis 1 new for 5 old shs. ■

Carium Mines Ltd. (unknown)
Mar. 1, 1965 – Charter cancelled; initial distribution of $1.50 per sh. Nov. 30, 1961 (of which 5¢ deemed divd. for tax purposes); final distribution of 24.6¢ per sh. made to holders of record Dec. 24, 1962 (all nontaxable).

Carl Capital Corp. (B.C. Jan. 17, 2014)
Oct. 28, 2015 – Name changed to Carl Data Solutions Inc. ■

Carl Creek Resources Ltd. (B.C. 1980)
Oct. 7, 1986 – Formed Tanqueray Resources Ltd. in Alberta on amalgamation with Tanqueray Resources Ltd.; basis 1 new sh. for 1 Tanqueray sh. and 1 new sh. for 4 Carl Creek shs. ■

Carl Data Solutions Inc. (B.C. Jan. 17, 2014)
Oct. 7, 2022 – Name changed to infinitii ai inc. (see FPsurvey - Industrials)

Carlaw Capital II Corp. (Ont. May 22, 2007)
Aug. 20, 2009 – Name changed to TrueContext Mobile Solutions Corporation pursuant to Qualifying Transaction reverse takeover acquisition of TrueContext Corporation. ■

Carlaw Capital III Corp. (Ont. Oct. 24, 2007)
Aug. 31, 2011 – Name changed to Galane Gold Ltd. pursuant to Qualifying Transaction reverse takeover acquisition of Galane Gold Mines Ltd. and subsequent amalgamation of Galane with wholly owned subsid. 2293748 Ontario Limited; basis 1 new for 4 old shs. ■

Carlaw Capital IV Inc. (Ont. Sept. 2, 2010)
Mar. 11, 2014 – Name changed to OneRoof Energy Group, Inc. following Qualifying Transaction reverse takeover acquisition of OneRoof Energy, Inc.; basis 1 new for 10 old shs. (see FPsurvey - Industrials)

Carlaw Capital V Corp. (Ont. Oct. 17, 2014)
June 28, 2018 – Name changed to Eve & Co Incorporated following Qualifying Transaction reverse takeover acquisition of 1600978 Ontario Inc. (Natural MedCo) by way of an amalgamation with a wholly owned subsidiary; basis 2 new for 1 old sh. ■

Carlaw Capital Corp. (Ont. Oct. 17, 2006)
Dec. 31, 2007 – Name changed to Nyah Resources Corp. following Qualifying Transaction reverse takeover acquisition of Nyah Resources Inc. by way of an amalgamation with a wholly owned subsidiary. ■

Carleton Oils Ltd. (Alta. 1951)
1960 – Acquired by Western Decalta Petroleum Ltd.; basis 1 new for 2 old shs.

Carleton Resources Corporation (Alta. Mar. 27, 1987)
Nov. 1, 1999 – Struck off register.

Carleton Royalties Ltd. (Alta. Mar. 20, 1934)
Charter cancelled.

Carlin Gold Company Inc. (Ont. Apr. 1973)
Mar. 23, 1994 – Name changed to Altair International Gold Inc.; basis 1 new for 3 old shs. ■

Carlin Gold Corporation (Can. Feb. 18, 1946)
Aug. 29, 2007 – Continued into British Columbia. (see FPsurvey - Mines & Energy)

Carlin Resources Corp. (Can. Feb. 18, 1946)
June 3, 1999 – Name changed to Consolidated Carlin Resources Corp.; basis 1 new for 5 old shs. ■

Carlin-Type Holdings Ltd. (B.C. Mar. 18, 2019)
Dec. 11, 2019 – Name changed to Ridgeline Minerals Corp. (see FPsurvey - Mines & Energy)

Carling Acceptance Limited (Can. 1964)
Dec. 16, 1980 – Dissolved.

Carling Breweries (Alberta) Limited (Alta.)
Wholly owned subsid. of Canadian Breweries Limited, which was invoked by provisions of Companies Act to buy small residual public interest.

Carling Copper Mines Ltd. (Ont. Jan. 23, 1970)
June 21, 1984 – Name changed to Carling Gold Resources Inc. ■

Carling Gold Resources Inc. (Ont. Jan. 23, 1970)
Dec. 14, 1994 – Name changed to Jourdan Resources Inc. and continued into Canada; basis 1 new for 3 old shs. ■

Carling O'Keefe Limited (Ont. Mar. 30, 1930)
Mar. 31, 1976 – Amalgamated in Ontario to continue with same name.
Sept. 22, 1987 – Formed Carling O'Keefe Breweries of Canada Limited following acquisition by and amalgamation with IXL Holdings Canada Inc. in April 1987; basis $18 per sh. On July 28, 1989, series A pref. shs. redeemed at $53 plus $0.16274 accr. divd. and series B pref. shs. at $52.50 plus $0.19603 accr. divd.

Carlisle Goldfields Limited (Ont. Mar. 15, 2005)
Jan. 11, 2016 – Acquired by Alamos Gold Inc.; basis 0.0942 com. Alamos shs. plus 0.0942 wts. for 1 Carlisle com. sh. Each wt. is exercisable at $10 per Alamos com. sh. for three years.

Carlmac Gold Mines Ltd. (Ont. 1945)
Jan. 1957 – Charter cancelled.

Carlmand Mines Ltd. (Ont. 1958)
May 7, 1969 – Charter cancelled.

Carlsbad Ventures Inc. (B.C. Sept. 22, 1986)
Aug. 10, 1994 – Name changed to Zeus Energy Corp.; basis 1 new for 5 old shs. ■

Carlson Mines Ltd. (Que. Sept. 9, 1937)
May 4, 2001 – Struck off register.

Carlton Explorations Ltd. (Ont. 1972)
Jan. 2, 1975 – Amalgamated into Sandhurst Mines Ltd.; basis 2 new for 11 old shs.

Carlton Trail Limited Partnership (Man. June 15, 1999)
Jan. 3, 2011 – All o/s cl. A units acquired by Westcan Investment Trust (WIT) and Calgary Capital Investment Trust (CCIT); basis $0.143, 1 WIT cl. A unit and 1 CCIT cl. A unit for 1 Carlton Trail unit.

Carlton's Cleaning Carousels Ltd. (B.C. 1961)
Apr. 24, 1985 – Voluntary liquidation completed. Payments of 5¢ per sh. made in 1978, and 4¢ per sh. in 1985.

The Carlyle Corporation (Alta. Nov. 29, 1995)
Dec. 10, 1997 – Name changed to The Azterra Corporation following reverse takeover acquisition of Azterra Development Corporation; basis 1 new for 2 old shs. ■

Carlyle Eagle Petroleum Ltd. (Alta. 1982 amalg.)
Dec. 12, 1983 – Name changed to Carlyle Energy Ltd. following reorganization first pref. shs. converted into cl. C pref. shs. and cl. A and B pref. shs. created. ■

Carlyle Energy Ltd. (Alta. 1982 amalg.)
Apr. 29, 1989 – Placed into receivership. Ernst & Young Inc. appointed receiver.
June 1990 – Balance of assets sold. Secured creditors suffered a shortfall and there was no distribution to shldrs.
May 6, 1994 – Receiver discharged.

Carlyle Entertainment Ltd. (B.C. Sept. 19, 2013)
Apr. 21, 2025 – Struck from register and dissolved for failure to file.

Carlyle Inc. (Alta. July 2, 1987)
July 7, 1995 – Name changed to D.C. Corrosion Corporation; basis 1 new for 5 old shs. ■

Carlyle Mines Ltd. (Que. 1946)
1961 – Charter cancelled.

Carlyle Mining Corp. (B.C. Jan. 24, 2007)
Mar. 6, 2009 – Name changed to Rugby Mining Limited following Qualifying Transaction option to earn 60% equity interest in Sunland Properties Limited. ■

Carlyle Petroleum Ltd. (Alta. 1979)
Jan. 6, 1982 – Amalgamated with Eagle Explorations Ltd. (private co.) to form new co. also known as Carlyle Petroleum Ltd.; basis 1 new for 4 old shs.

Carma Corporation (Alta. May 29, 1981)
Oct. 6, 2000 – Amalgamated with a wholly owned subsid. of Brookfield Properties Corporation; basis $5.75 or 1 Brookfield sh. for 3.75 Carma shs. (see Brookfield Properties Corporation)

Carma Developers Ltd. (Alta. 1958)
June 1984 – All publicly held 8.75% 1st pref. shs. converted into cl. A shs. of parent co., Carma Ltd.; basis 5 cl. A shs. for 1 old pref. sh.

Carma Financial Services Corporation (Ont. Apr. 23, 1997)
Mar. 16, 2005 – Formed Synergex Corporation in Ontario on amalgamation with Synergex Corporation (deemed acquiror). ■

Carma Ltd. (Ont. Nov. 2, 1959)
May 29, 1981 – Continued into Alberta.
Sept. 22, 1987 – Name changed to Consolidated Carma Corporation; basis 1 new for 10 old shs. ■

Carmac Resources Ltd. (B.C. Sept. 20, 1970)
May 14, 1992 – Name changed to Camnor Resources Ltd.; basis 1 new for 2 old shs. ■

Carman Mines Ltd. (Ont. 1936)
1945 – Absorbed by Carshaw Porcupine Gold Mines Ltd.; basis 1 new for 3 old shs. (see Carshaw Porcupine Gold Mines Ltd.)

Carmanah Resources Ltd. (Alta. Sept. 20, 1991)
Sept. 6, 2001 – Delisted from the Toronto Stock Exchange. Subsequently dissolved.

Carmanah Technologies Corporation (Alta. Mar. 26, 1996)
Aug. 24, 2009 – Continued into British Columbia.
Aug. 20, 2019 – All o/s com. shs, not already held acquire by CMH Acquisition Corp., an entity controlled by two former directors of the company; basis Cdn$7.35 cash per sh.

Carmax Explorations Ltd. (Can. June 16, 2000)
Sept. 2, 2010 – Name changed to Carmax Mining Corp.; basis 1 new for 10 old shs. ■

Carmax Mining Corp. (Can. June 16, 2000)
July 3, 2018 – Name changed to District Copper Corp. ■

Carmel Pershing Mines Ltd. (Ont. 1945)
1957 – Charter cancelled.

Carmel Resources Limited (B.C. 1983)
Dec. 10, 2012 – Struck from register and dissolved.

Carmelita Petroleum Ltd. (B.C. June 24, 1987)
Oct. 16, 1996 – Name changed to Carmelita Resources Limited. ■

Carmelita Resources Limited (B.C. June 24, 1987)
July 4, 2000 – Name changed to Pierre EnTerprises Ltd.; basis 1 new for 10 old shs. ■

Carmelo Capital Corp. (B.C. Nov. 7, 2017)
Dec. 20, 2023 – Name changed to Integral Metals Corp. (see FPsurvey - Mines & Energy)

Carmen Energy Inc. (Alta. Aug. 5, 2009)
July 24, 2013 – Name changed to Margaux Resources Ltd. ■

Carmont Mines Ltd. (Ont. 1969)
1971 – Assets sold to Avilla International Explorations Ltd.; basis 1 new for 3 old shs.

Carndesson Mines Ltd. (Ont. 1952)
Apr. 9, 1975 – Charter cancelled.

Carnegie Mines Limited (Can. 1948)
1958 – Name changed to Carnegie Mining Corporation Ltd.; basis 1 new for 6 old shs. ■

Carnegie Mining Corporation Ltd. (Can. 1948)
Jan. 1, 1985 – Amalgamated with Kam-Kotia Mines Limited; basis 1 new for 100 old shs., and subsequently exch. for Kam-Kotia stk. on basis of 20 Kam-Kotia shs. for 1 Carnegie sh. (see Kam-Kotia Mines Limited)

Carnegie Petroleum, Ltd. (Can. 1930)
Nov. 1943 – Reported to be wound up.

Carnes Creek Explorations Ltd. (B.C. 1966)
Feb. 6, 1991 – Name changed to Marathon Telecom Corporation; basis 1 new for 3 old shs. ■

Carnival Resources Ltd. (B.C. Mar. 4, 1987)
Aug. 8, 2003 – Struck from register and dissolved.

Carnkid Mines Ltd. (Ont. 1964)
1972 – Dissolved.

Carolian Systems International Inc. (Ont. June 1985 amalg.)
Jan. 18, 1990 – Name changed to Delrina Corporation. ■

Carolin Mines Ltd. (B.C. Feb. 3, 1966)
Feb. 1, 1990 – Name changed to Anglo Swiss Mining Corporation; basis 1 cl. A redesignated as 1 com. sh. ■

Carolina Capital Corp. (B.C. July 26, 2010)
Oct. 12, 2016 – Name changed to Broadway Gold Mining Ltd. to reflect the change of geographical location of its principal business activity to the gold and copper mining property acquired in Montana. ■

Carolina Gold Resources Ltd. (B.C. Feb. 13, 1987)
Oct. 8, 1992 – Name changed to Rutherford Ventures Corp.; basis 1 new for 2 old shs. ■

Caron Malartic Gold Mines Ltd. (Ont. 1944)
Jan. 14, 1963 – Dissolved.

Carpathian Gold Inc. (Can. Jan. 17, 2003)
Aug. 26, 2016 – Name changed to Euro Sun Mining Inc. (see FPsurvey - Mines & Energy)

Carpatsky Petroleum Inc. (Alta. May 17, 1995 amalg.)
Apr. 15, 2005 – Acquired by Cardinal Resources plc; basis 0.5 Cardinal ord. shs. for 1 Carpatsky com. sh.

Carpenter Lake Resources Ltd. (B.C. Feb. 12, 1970)
Feb. 21, 1992 – Name changed to Wayside Gold Mines Ltd.; basis 1 new for 4 old shs. ■

Carpentier Goldfields Ltd. (Que. 1946)
Sept. 1950 – Charter cancelled.

Carpincho Capital Corp. (Can. Apr. 26, 2002)
June 11, 2018 – Name changed to Planet 13 Holdings Inc. following reverse takeover acquisition of MM Development Company, Inc. ■

Carpita Corporation (Ont. 1984 amalg.)
June 1990 – Placed into receivership.
June 5, 1991 – 30 of the 50 carpet showrooms owned had been sold to Color Carpet Inc., the rest being closed. Creditors suffered shortfall and no distribution to shldrs.

Carrara Exploration Corp. (B.C. Dec. 15, 2014)
July 14, 2017 – Name changed to PreveCeutical Medical Inc. following reverse takeover acquisition of (old) PreveCeutical Medical Inc. and subsequent amalgamation with wholly owned 1110607 B.C. Ltd.; basis 1 new for 3 old shs. (see FPsurvey - Industrials)

Carravelle Mines Ltd. (Ont. 1959)
Nov. 13, 1969 – Name changed to Caravelle Mines Limited. ■

Carrera Resources Ltd. (B.C. 1982)
Apr. 25, 1986 – Name changed to Desen Computer Industries Inc. (see FPsurvey - Industrials)

Carriage Automotive Group Inc. (Ont. Apr. 22, 1986)
Feb. 16, 2000 – Name changed to cars4U.com Ltd. ■

Carrigan Industries Ltd. (B.C. 1971)
June 20, 1985 – Amalgamated with Armoloy Electrolytic (Canada) Limited to continue under the same name Carrigan Industries Ltd.; basis 1 com. sh. for 1 com. sh. or 5 new pref. shs. for 1 old pref. sh.
Dec. 9, 1991 – Dissolved and struck off register.

Carrington Acquisition Corp. (Alta. July 21, 2005)
Sept. 2, 2016 – Dissolved and struck from register.

Carrol & Reed Limited (Ont. 1968)
May 14, 1975 – Dissolved.

Carrus Capital Corporation (B.C. Feb. 12, 2010)
Oct. 5, 2017 – Name changed to Global Blockchain Technologies Corp. ■

cars4U.com Ltd. (Ont. Apr. 22, 1986)
Feb. 17, 2003 – Name changed to cars4U Ltd. ■

Carscor Porcupine Gold Mines Ltd. (Ont. 1945)
Jan. 1958 – Charter cancelled.

cars4U Ltd. (Ont. Apr. 22, 1986)
May 10, 2006 – Converted into Chesswood Income Fund; basis 1 Chesswood unit for 18.33 cars4U shs. (see Chesswood Income Fund)

Carshaw Porcupine Gold Mines Ltd. (Ont. 1945)
Aug. 1972 – Charter cancelled.

Carson Gold Corp. (B.C. Sept. 8, 1966)
Aug. 11, 1995 – Continued into Yukon.
Oct. 21, 1996 – Name changed to DiamondWorks Ltd. ■

Carta Resources Ltd. (B.C. Mar. 14, 1986)
Dec. 24, 1999 – Name changed to Earthramp.com Communications Inc. ■

Cartaway Container Corporation (Alta. June 5, 1986)
Apr. 24, 1996 – Name changed to Cartaway Resources Corporation. ■

Cartaway Resources Corporation (Alta. June 5, 1986)
Feb. 1, 2000 – Struck from registry and dissolved.

Cartier Iron Corporation (Ont. Nov. 1, 1985)
Nov. 15, 2022 – Name changed to Cartier Silver Corporation; basis 1 new for 5 old shs. (see FPsurvey - Mines & Energy)

Cartier-Malartic Gold Mines Ltd. (Que. 1927)
1958 – Assets acquired by Cartier Quebec Explorations Ltd.; basis 1 new for 5 old shs.

The Cartier Mining Co. Ltd. (Que. 1957)
Nov. 28, 1988 – Name changed to Quebec Cartier Mining Company. ■

Cartier Partners Financial Group Inc. (Alta. July 20, 1990)
Jan. 7, 2004 – Acquired by Dundee Wealth Management Inc. (DWM); basis 0.0121192 new DWM com. sh. plus either $0.54, or 0.071523 new DWM com. sh., or a combination thereof for 1 old Cartier com. sh. (see Dundee Wealth Management Inc.)

Cartier Quebec Explorations Limited (Ont. Mar. 8, 1957)
Sept. 17, 1980 – Name changed to Cartier Resources Inc. ■

Cartier Resources Inc. (Ont. Mar. 8, 1957)
Oct. 22, 1993 – Name changed to Rockabee Investments Inc.; basis 1 new for 10 old shs. ∎

Cartwright Capital Ltd. (Alta. Aug. 23, 1993)
May 20, 1998 – Name changed to Acer Capital Corp. following acquisition of Nu-Life Industries Inc. (see FPsurvey - Industrials)

Carube Copper Corp. (Ont. Mar. 29, 2010)
Aug. 10, 2020 – Name changed to C3 Metals Inc. (see FPsurvey - Mines & Energy)

Caruscan Corporation (Ont. 1961)
Nov. 27, 1985 – All o/s cl. A and cl. B shs. acquired by Crownx Inc. under offer dated. Holders of each cl. A or cl. B sh. offered either $2.40 or one-ninth of one non-voting cl. A sh. of Crownx.

Carval Mines Ltd. (B.C. 1967)
Dec. 1974 – Charter cancelled.

Carvelle Capital Inc. (Alta. Mar. 6, 2001)
Dec. 19, 2002 – Name changed to Lexoil Incorporated following Qualifying Transaction reverse takeover acquisition of Lexoil Inc. ∎

Carvern International Industries Ltd. (B.C. 1972)
Feb. 17, 1983 – Continued into Canada.
Dec. 26, 2015 – Dissolved and struck from register.

Casa Del Sol Capital Ltd. (Alta. July 10, 2003)
Oct. 28, 2005 – Name changed to Tiger-Cat Energy Ltd. pursuant to Qualifying Transaction acquisition of 1160837 Alberta Ltd. ∎

Casa Grande Energy & Mines Ltd. (B.C. 1981)
May 22, 1992 – Name changed to Medical Polymers Technologies, Inc. ∎

Casabar Resources Inc. (Ont. 1987)
Jan. 17, 1989 – Name changed to First Ontario Capital Inc. ∎

Casablanca Capital Corp. (Alta. Feb. 12, 2004)
May 30, 2005 – Name changed to Purepoint Uranium Group Inc. and continued into Canada pursuant to Qualifying Transaction reverse takeover acquisition of Purepoint Uranium Corporation. (see FPsurvey - Mines & Energy)

Casakirk Gold Mines Ltd. (Ont. 1936)
May 27, 1965 – Dissolved.

Casamiro Resource Corporation (B.C. Jan. 23, 1984)
July 28, 2008 – Struck from register and dissolved.
Apr. 9, 2010 – Limited restoration to the registry.
Oct. 10, 2012 – Struck from registry and dissolved on expiry of the limited restoration period.

Casau Exploration Ltd. (B.C. 1984)
Apr. 16, 1992 – Dissolved and struck off register.

Cascade Fertilizers Ltd. (Alta. Mar. 13, 1967)
Jan. 31, 1990 – All assets sold to Esso Chemical Canada, a division of Imperial Oil Limited; basis 1 cl. A voting sh. and 100 cl. C redeem. shs. of Imperial Oil for 1 com. sh. Cl. C redeem. shs. were redeemed for $0.01 per sh. Holders of the 10% convertible debentures received 100% of the principal amt. thereof plus interest to the date of redemption.
May 25, 1990 – Name changed to Verdant Valley Ventures Inc. ∎

Cascade Lode Mines Ltd. (B.C. 1952)
1962 – Name changed to Trans-Ore Mines Ltd.; basis 1 new for 5 old shs. ∎

Cascade Metals Inc. (Alta. Oct. 30, 1995)
Oct. 16, 2001 – Name changed to American Gold Capital Corporation. ∎

Cascade Minerals Inc. (B.C. Apr. 5, 2005)
Dec. 15, 2006 – Formed Finavera Renewables Inc. in British Columbia pursuant to Qualifying Transaction reverse takeover acquisition of Finavera Renewables Limited and amalgamation with Finavera Energy Canada Inc., a wholly owned subsid. of Finavera. ∎

Cascade Molybdenum Mines Ltd. (B.C. 1964)
1975 – Name changed to New Cascade Minerals Ltd.; basis 1 new for 100 old shs. ∎

Cascade Oil & Gas Ltd. (Alta. Dec. 23, 1986)
June 23, 1998 – Name changed to Grey Wolf Exploration Inc.; basis 1 new for 1 old sh. ∎

Cascade Pacific Resources Limited (Ont. Dec. 7, 1962)
June 22, 1984 – CTO issued. Subsequently dissolved and charter cancelled.

Cascadero Copper Corporation (Alta. Oct. 30, 2003)
June 3, 2004 – Continued into British Columbia. (see FPsurvey - Mines & Energy)

Cascades Paperboard International Inc. (Can. Dec. 28, 1978)
July 22, 1996 – Name changed to Paperboard Industries International Inc. ∎

Cascades S.A. (France)
2008 – Name changed to Cascades S.A.S.

Cascadia Blockchain Group Corp. (B.C. Nov. 10, 2011)
July 2, 2025 – Name changed to World Blockchain Corp. (see FPsurvey - Industrials)

Cascadia Brands Inc. (Can. Jan. 30, 1978)
Aug. 12, 1998 – Amalgamated with 3450163 Canada Inc. for $8.00 per sh. Co. now private.

Cascadia Consumer Electronics Corp. (B.C. Nov. 10, 2011)
Sept. 10, 2018 – Name changed to Cascadia Blockchain Group Corp. ∎

Cascadia International Resources Inc. (B.C. July 18, 1983)
Mar. 29, 2004 – Continued into Alberta.
Feb. 6, 2009 – Name changed to Cascadia Resources Inc.; basis 1 new for 3 old shs. ∎

Cascadia Mines & Resources Ltd. (B.C. 1971)
Dec. 27, 1989 – Name changed to Noble Metal Group Incorporated; basis 1 new for 5 old shs. (see FPsurvey - Mines & Energy)

Cascadia Resources Inc. (Alta. Mar. 29, 2004)
July 31, 2014 – Name changed to Kaymus Resources Inc.; basis 1 new for 5 old shs. (see FPsurvey - Mines & Energy)

Cascadia Resources Ltd. (B.C. 1971)
Nov. 24, 1980 – Name changed to Cascadia Mines & Resources Ltd. ∎

Cascadia Technologies Ltd. (B.C. Jan. 26, 1987)
Mar. 2, 1998 – Delisted from the Vancouver Stock Exchange. Subsequently struck from register and dissolved.

Case Resources Inc. (Alta. Mar. 12, 1993)
July 28, 2004 – Plan of Arrangement exchange with Fairborne Energy Ltd.; basis 0.0909 new Fairborne sh. for 1 old Case sh. (see Fairborne Energy Ltd.)

Casey Mines Inc. (Ont. 1971)
Feb. 20, 1980 – Dissolved.

Casgrain & Charbonneau Ltée (Que. 1950)
Feb. 1979 – Placed into receivership. No money available for secured creditors. Trustee-Jacques Franco, Maheux, Noiseux, Noiseux Inc., Montreal, Que.

Cash Canada Group Ltd. (Alta. May 27, 1988)
Dec. 29, 2009 – Filed for bankruptcy. Faber and Company Inc. appointed trustee. The first secured party, CashCo Financial Inc., completed foreclosure on all personal property of the company on Dec. 16, 2009.
Aug. 2, 2011 – Struck from register and dissolved.

Cash Canada Pawn Corp. (Alta. May 27, 1988)
Jan. 4, 1996 – Name changed to Cash Canada Group Ltd.; basis 1 new for 4 old shs. ∎

Cash Minerals Ltd. (B.C. Oct. 15, 1985)
June 14, 2006 – Continued into Ontario.
June 25, 2010 – Name changed to Pitchblack Resources Ltd.; basis 1 new for 20 old shs. ∎

Cash Resources Ltd. (B.C. Oct. 15, 1985)
May 7, 2001 – Name changed to Cash Minerals Ltd.; basis 1 new for 5 old shs. ∎

The Cash Store Australia Holdings Inc. (Ont. Jan. 31, 2008)
Mar. 6, 2009 – Amalgamated in Ontario to continue with same name. (see FPsurvey - Industrials)

The Cash Store Financial Services Inc. (Ont. Jan. 17, 2002 amalg.)
Apr. 14, 2014 – Filed for protection under the Companies' Creditors Arrangement Act and FTI Consulting Canada Inc. was appointed monitor. (see FPsurvey - Industrials)

Cashbox Ventures Ltd. (B.C. Apr. 3, 2018)
May 31, 2023 – Name changed to Volta Metals Ltd. pursuant to the reverse takeover acquisition of LiCAN Exploration Inc.; basis 1 new for 10 old shs. (see FPsurvey - Mines & Energy)

Casino Silver Mines Ltd. (B.C. 1965)
Mar. 4, 1993 – Amalgamated with Pacific Sentinel Gold Corp.; basis 0.75 new com. Pacific Sentinel sh. and 0.75 Pacific Sentinel warrant for 1.0 old Casino Silver shs. The exchange ratio is 3 units of Pacific Sentinel stock for 4 com. shs. of Casino. The warrants are non-transferable and exercisable for com. shs. of Pacific for $3.00 per sh. until May 31, 1993. (see Pacific Sentinel Gold Corp.)

Casmont Industries Ltd. (Can. 1911)
Jan. 1955 – All o/s pref. shs. redeemed at $110 per sh.
May 31, 1959 – Charter surrendered.

Cason Gold Mines Ltd. (Ont. 1946)
1949 – Name changed to Coulee Lead and Zinc Mines Ltd. ∎

Caspian Energy Inc. (Ont. Jan. 26, 1982)
Feb. 25, 2015 – Continued into British Columbia.
Oct. 12, 2018 – Privatized via a 1-for-90,000,000 consolidation; basis $0.01 cash per pre-consolidated com. sh.

M.L. Cass Petroleum Corporation (B.C. Mar. 28, 1983)
Sept. 22, 1994 – Continued into Alberta.
Sept. 2, 2011 – Struck from registry and dissolved.

Cassandra Resources Inc. (B.C. Jan. 21, 1987)
June 29, 1993 – Name changed to Consolidated Cassandra Resources Inc.; basis 1 new for 3 old shs. ∎

Cassete Mines Ltd. (Ont. 1967)
1969 – Amalgamated into Summit Explorations & Holdings; basis 1 new for 10 old shs.

Cassia Petroleum Corporation (B.C. Apr. 17, 1979)
Apr. 3, 1987 – Delisted Vancouver Stock Exchange. Subsequently struck from register and dissolved.

Cassiar Asbestos Corporation Limited (Can. 1951)
Aug. 1, 1980 – Name changed to Cassiar Resources Limited. ∎

Cassiar Consolidated Mines Limited (B.C. May 8, 1951)
Oct. 6, 1976 – Name changed to Pacific Cassiar Mines Ltd.; basis 1 new for 5 old shs. ∎

Cassiar Copperfields Ltd. (B.C. 1954)
Sept. 24, 1970 – Dissolved and struck off register.

Cassiar Magnesium Inc. (Ont. Sept. 23, 1968)
July 25, 2001 – Name changed to Cassiar Resources Inc. ∎

Cassiar Mines & Metals Inc. (Ont. Sept. 23, 1968)
May 9, 2000 – Name changed to Cassiar Magnesium Inc. ∎

Cassiar Mining Corporation (Can. 1951)
Nov. 7, 1988 – Continued into British Columbia.
Dec. 14, 1989 – Name changed to Princeton Mining Corporation; basis 1 new com. for 1 old com. sh. and 1 new com. for 2 old cl. B pref. shs. ∎

Cassiar Rainbow Gold Mines Ltd. (Ont. 1947)
Apr. 30, 1962 – Dissolved.

Cassiar Resources Inc. (Ont. Sept. 23, 1968)
Aug. 6, 2003 – Name changed to Troutline Investments Inc. ∎

Cassiar Resources Limited (Can. 1951)
1980 – Acquired by a unit of Brinco Limited for $16.15 a sh. Subsequently, in 1987, Brinco reduced its interest to 56% through public offering of shares. (see Dorset Resources Ltd.)

Cassiar Yukon Gold Mines Ltd. (B.C. 1950)
Dec. 1, 1960 – Dissolved.

Cassidy Gold Corp. (B.C. Nov. 26, 1984)
June 21, 2017 – Privatized; basis $0.005 cash per com. sh.

Cassidy Resources Ltd. (B.C. Apr. 14, 1978)
Nov. 3, 1989 – Name changed to Massif Minerals Corporation; basis 1 new for 2 old shs. ∎

Cassidy Yellowknife Mines Ltd. (Ont. 1944)
Nov. 1979 – Charter cancelled.

Cassidy's Limited (Can. 1911)
1952 – All o/s com. shs. acquired by Caradsco Ltd. for $12.25 per com. sh.
Apr. 8, 1953 – Name changed to Casmont Industries Ltd. ∎

Cassidy's Ltd. (Que. Feb. 17, 1953)
Dec. 21, 1999 – Placed into receivership. PricewaterhouseCoopers Inc. was appointed receiver. ∎

Cassowary Capital Corporation Limited (Alta. Jan. 31, 2018)
Oct. 21, 2020 – Name changed to Western Gold Exploration Ltd. pursuant to the Qualifying Transaction reverse takeover acquisition of (old) Western Gold Exploration Limited; basis 1 new for 2.5 old shs. (see FPsurvey - Mines & Energy)

Casteck Mines Ltd (Ont. 1947)
Jan. 12, 1959 – Dissolved.

Castello Business Systems Ltd. (B.C. July 18, 1986)
Oct. 16, 1995 – Continued into Ontario.
Mar. 10, 1997 – Name changed to Castello Casino Corp.; basis 1 new for 4 old shs. ∎

Castello Casino Corp. (Ont. Oct. 16, 1995)
Jan. 18, 2001 – Name changed to BioForest Pacific Inc. pursuant to reverse takeover acquisition of BioForest Investments Inc.; basis 1 new for 14 old shs. ∎

Castello Resources Ltd. (B.C. July 18, 1986)
Jan. 21, 1993 – Name changed to Castello Business Systems Ltd. ∎

Castillian Resources Corp. (B.C. Feb. 19, 1987)
June 28, 2013 – Name changed to Coastal Gold Corp. following acquisition of Ridgemont Iron Ore Corp. ∎

Castle Bay Enterprises Ltd. (B.C. Dec. 9, 1998)
May 22, 2002 – Formed Radiant Communications Corp. in Canada on Qualifying Transaction amalgamation with subsidiaries of Delaware-based Radiant Communications, Inc., constituting a reverse takeover by Radiant (dissolved May 23, 2002); basis 1 new for 18 old shs. ∎

Castle Capital Corp. (Alta. 1987)
Aug. 30, 1989 – Name changed to The Hewlyn Corporation; basis 1 new for 3.5 old shs. ∎

Castle Capital Inc. (Ont. Jan. 19, 1966)
Aug. 12, 1998 – Name changed to EnerVision Incorporated and continued into Nova Scotia; basis 1 new for 4 old shs. ∎

Castle Gold Corporation (Can. Aug. 28, 2007 amalg.)
Feb. 24, 2010 – Acquired by Argonaut Gold Ltd. for Cdn$1.29 per sh. (see Argonaut Gold Ltd.)

Castle-Leduc Petroleums Ltd. (Alta. 1952)
Aug. 17, 1953 – Name changed to Castle Oil & Gas Limited; basis 1 new for 8 old shs. ∎

Castle Metals Corporation (B.C. Feb. 19, 1987)
July 29, 2002 – Name changed to Castillian Resources Corp.; basis 1 new for 10 old shs. ∎

Castle Minerals Inc. (B.C. Feb. 19, 1987)
Jan. 27, 1995 – Name changed to Castle Rock Exploration Corp.; basis 1 new for 2 old shs. ∎

Castle Mountain Mining Company Limited (Ont. Dec. 16, 2009)
June 25, 2015 – Name changed to Newcastle Gold Ltd. ∎

Castle Oil & Gas Co. Ltd. (unknown)
Wound up. Not to be confused with Castle Oil & Gas Limited (1952) incorp.

Castle Oil & Gas Limited (Alta. 1952)
Dec. 1983 – Shs. consol.; basis 1 new for 50,000 old shs. Fractional holders pd. $5.143 for 1 old sh. Co. became a wholly owned subsid. of Canadian Hydrocarbons Ltd.

Castle Peak Mining Ltd. (B.C. June 3, 2009)
Feb. 9, 2022 – Name changed to Akwaaba Mining Ltd. (see FPsurvey - Mines & Energy)

Castle Resources Inc. (Alta. Apr. 29, 2004)
Aug. 12, 2011 – Continued into Ontario.
Jan. 8, 2018 – Privatized; basis 20¢ cash per sh.

Castle Rock Exploration Corp. (B.C. Feb. 19, 1987)
Aug. 24, 1998 – Name changed to Castle Metals Corporation; basis 1 new for 5 old shs. ∎

Castle Rock Petroleum Ltd. (Alta. Mar. 17, 2004)
Oct. 5, 2007 – Acquired by Arrow Energy Ltd.; basis 1 Arrow com. sh. for 5 Castle cl. A shs. and 1 Arrow com. sh. for 0.5 Castle cl. B sh. (see Arrow Energy Ltd.)

Castle Silver Resources Inc. (Can. Apr. 29, 2005)
Feb. 23, 2018 – Name changed to Canada Cobalt Works Inc. ∎

Castle Tin Mines Ltd. (Ont. 1965)
June 1968 – Absorbed by Pacific Asbestos Ltd.; basis 45 new for 100 old shs. (see Pacific Asbestos Ltd.)

Castle-Trethewey Mines Ltd. (Ont. 1922)
1959 – Absorbed by McIntyre Porcupine Mines Ltd.; basis $4.93 and 1 sh. McIntyre for 78 old shs.

Castlebar Silver & Cobalt Mines Ltd. (Ont. 1954)
Dec. 30, 1985 – Amalgamated with several other cos. to form Canhorn Mining Corporation; basis 1 new for 32.6 old shs.

CastleRock Capital Inc. (Alta. Jan. 23, 2001)
Feb. 28, 2003 – Name changed to CastleRock Resources Inc. following Qualifying Transaction reverse takeover acquisition of Quitovac Mining Company Limited. ∎

CastleRock Resources Inc. (Alta. Jan. 23, 2001)
Dec. 31, 2004 – Name changed to Andina Minerals Inc. pursuant to reverse takeover acquisition of Andina Minerals Inc. (subsequently renamed Andina Holdings Inc.); basis 1 new for 5 old shs. ∎

Castlestar Capital Developments Corp. (Ont. 1990 amalg.)
Nov. 11, 1993 – Name changed to Southern Frontier Resources Inc.; basis 1 new for 5 old shs. ∎

Castlewood Metals and Explorations Ltd. (Ont. Aug. 9, 1990)
Nov. 3, 1995 – Name changed to Arian Resources Corporation; basis 1 new for 7 old shs. ∎

Castleworth Ventures Inc. (B.C. Feb. 11, 1981)
Jan. 20, 2006 – Name changed to Pan-Nevada Gold Corporation. ∎

Castor Coal & Construction Co. (unknown)
1952 – Reported out of business.

Casummit Lake Mines Ltd. (Ont. 1964)
Apr. 20, 1980 – Dissolved.

Casurina Performance Fund (Ont. Apr. 16, 2002)
July 30, 2004 – Name changed to Front Street Performance Fund. ∎

Cat Lake Mines Ltd. (Ont. 1954)
Mar. 1973 – Assets acquired by Fundy Chemical International Ltd.; basis 1 new for 3.25 old shs.

Catalina Energy Corp. (B.C. May 20, 1988)
Feb. 14, 2011 – Name changed to Catalina Metals Corp.; basis 1 new for 3 old shs. ∎

Catalina Gold Corp. (B.C. Feb. 6, 2017)
Apr. 17, 2020 – Name changed to District Mines Ltd.; basis 1 new for 3 old shs. (see FPsurvey - Mines & Energy)

Catalina Metals Corp. (B.C. May 20, 1988)
June 28, 2012 – Name changed to True Grit Resources Ltd. ∎

Catalina Oils Ltd. (unknown)
1959 – Acquired by Pacific Petroleums Ltd.; basis 4 new for 31 old shs. (see Pacific Petroleums Ltd.)

Catalyst Copper Corp. (B.C. Sept. 16, 1983)
May 27, 2016 – Acquired by Newcastle Gold Ltd.; basis 1 com. Newcastle sh. for 1 Catalyst com. sh. (see Newcastle Gold Ltd.)

Catalyst Paper Corporation (Can. Sept. 1, 2001 amalg.)
Jan. 26, 2017 – All o/s com. shs. not already held by Oaktree Capital Management, L.P., Mudrick Capital Management, L.P. and Cyrus Capital Partners, L.P. acquired for Cdn$0.50 cash per sh.

Catalyst Ventures Corporation (B.C. July 14, 1987)
Feb. 23, 2000 – Name changed to International Catalyst Ventures Inc.; basis 1 new for 6 old shs. ∎

Catamaran Corporation (Yuk. June 27, 2007)
July 28, 2015 – Acquired by 1031387 B.C. Unlimited Liability Company, a wholly owned subsid. of UnitedHealth Group Incorporated for US$61.50 per sh.

Catapult Energy Limited Partnership I (Alta. Jan. 18, 2005)
Mar. 31, 2008 – Dissolved.

Cataraqui Gold Mines Ltd. (Ont. 1936)
1950 – Charter cancelled.

Catch the Wind Ltd. (Del. Sept. 22, 2008)
June 23, 2010 – Amalgamated with and into wholly owned Catch the Wind Holdings Ltd., an Arizona corporation, which on the same day changed its name to Catch the Wind Ltd. upon redomestication into Cayman Islands.
Nov. 7, 2012 – Name changed to BlueScout Technologies Ltd.; basis 1 new for 20 old shs.

Catear Resources Ltd. (Alta. 1982)
1984 – Continued into British Columbia.
Apr. 8, 1994 – Dissolved and struck off register.

Catelli Food Products Ltd. (Can. 1928)
1964 – All cl. A shs. acquired since by Lake of the Woods Milling Co. Ltd., wholly owned subsid. of Ogilvie Flour Mills Co. Ltd. at $40 a sh. All o/s cl. B shs. also held by Ogilvie.

Catelli Properties Limited (Ont. 1954)
1964 – Property sold and all o/s bonds and debs. retired.

Cater Energy, Inc. (B.C. 1968)
Oct. 27, 1986 – Formed Houston Metals Corporation in British Columbia on amalgamation with Bulkley Silver Resources, Inc.; basis 1 new for 2 old shs. ■

Catface Copper Mines Limited (Ont. June 1, 1963)
Aug. 28, 2006 – Continued into British Columbia. (see FPsurvey - Mines & Energy)

Cathay Energy Inc. (Alta. Aug. 13, 1997)
Feb. 2, 2006 – Struck from registry and dissolved.

Cathay Forest Products Corp. (Can. Sept. 30, 2004)
July 22, 2018 – Dissolved and struck from register.

Cathay Overseas Inc. (Alta. Apr. 2, 1993)
Oct. 5, 1999 – Dissolved and struck from register.

Cathedral Energy Services Income Trust (Alta. June 24, 2002)
Dec. 18, 2009 – Converted into Cathedral Energy Services Limited pursuant to reorganization with SemBioSys Genetics Ltd. and dissolved; basis 1 Cathedral sh. for 1 Cathedral trust unit and 1 new SemBioSys sh. for 1 old SemBioSys sh. (see Cathedral Energy Services Ltd.)

Cathedral Energy Services Ltd. (Alta. Oct. 6, 1994)
July 3, 2024 – Name changed to ACT Energy Technologies Ltd.; basis 1 new for 7 old shs. (see FPsurvey - Mines & Energy; FPsurvey - Industrials)

Cathedral Energy Services Ltd. (Alta. Oct. 30, 2000)
Aug. 2, 2002 – Converted into an income trust named Cathedral Energy Services Income Trust; basis 1 trust unit for 1 com. sh.

Cathedral Gold Corporation (Ont. Apr. 16, 1987)
June 16, 2000 – Amalgamated with DirectionalPlus Ltd., constituting a reverse takeover by DirectionalPlus, to form new co. with same name Cathedral Gold Corporation.
Oct. 30, 2000 – Continued into Alberta.
Nov. 6, 2000 – Name changed to Cathedral Energy Services Ltd.; basis 1 new for 5 old shs. ■

Cathedral Minerals Ltd. (Alta. Dec. 29, 1976)
July 18, 1979 – Amalgamated in British Columbia to continue with same name.
Jan. 1, 1983 – Formed Mintek Resources Ltd. in British Columbia on amalgamation with Dayton Creek Silver Mines Ltd.; basis 1 new for 3 old shs. ■

Cathroy Larder Mines Ltd. (Ont. 1943)
1976 – Dissolved.

Catlow Resources Ltd. (B.C. Feb. 20, 1980)
Mar. 2, 1988 – Delisted from the Vancouver Stock Exchange. Subsequently dissolved for failure to file.

Cats Eye Capital Corp. (B.C. Oct. 11, 2007)
Aug. 19, 2010 – Name changed to Lakeland Resources Inc. pursuant to Qualifying Transaction acquisition of Camlaren property from Triple Dragon Resources Inc. ■

Causeway Energy Corporation (Alta. July 9, 1997)
Aug. 30, 2001 – Amalgamated with Bushmills Energy Corporation and PanCanadian Petroleum Limited; basis $2.58 plus 0.2 Bushmills shs. for 1 Causeway sh. (see Bushmills Energy Corporation)

Caussa Capital Corporation (Ont. Sept. 8, 1993 amalg.)
Jan. 20, 2003 – Name changed to Rainbow Gold Ltd.; basis 1 new for 10 old shs. ■

Cautivo Mining Inc. (Ont. Dec. 6, 2016)
Jan. 29, 2020 – Privatized in a going private transaction by way of a consolidation squeeze-out resulting in all

com. shs. held by Arias Resource Capital Fund II L.P. and Arias Resource Capital Fund II (Mexico) L.P., with each former holder of a pre-cons. sh. entitled to receive 15¢ cash; basis 1 new for 2,228,612 old shs.

Cava Resources Inc. (Ont. July 7, 1997)
June 19, 2018 – Name changed to Gold Rush Cariboo Corp. ■

Cavalcade Petroleums Ltd. (Ont. 1946)
Nov. 1959 – Name changed to International Kingdom Mining & Exploration Ltd.; basis 1 new for 11 old shs. ■

Cavalier Copper Corp. Ltd. (B.C. 1957)
Sept. 1957 – Name changed to Torvan Mines Ltd. ■

Cavalier Energy Inc. (Ont. 1974 amalg.)
Feb. 7, 1978 – Name changed to Cavalier Energy Limited and continued into Alberta. ■

Cavalier Energy Limited (Alta. Feb. 7, 1978)
Oct. 24, 1988 – Acquired by Cavalier Capital Corporation for $9.25 per sh. ■

Cavalier Mining Corp. Ltd. (Ont. 1955)
Sept. 18, 1961 – Dissolved.

Cavalier Uranium Mines (Ont. 1955)
Dec. 1955 – Name changed to Cavalier Mining Corp. Ltd. ■

Cavan Ventures Inc. (B.C. Feb. 28, 2006)
Jan. 10, 2018 – Name changed to Vertical Exploration Inc. (see FPsurvey - Mines & Energy)

Cavan Yellowknife Mines Ltd. (Ont. 1945)
1955 – Charter cancelled.

Cavell Energy Corporation (Alta. June 8, 1994)
July 20, 2004 – Plan of Arrangement acquisition by Paramount Energy Trust; basis either $2.40 or 0.21145 new Paramount trust unit or a combination thereof for 1 old Cavell com. sh. (see Paramount Energy Trust)

Cavern Resources Ltd. (B.C. Apr. 25, 1983)
June 12, 1984 – Name changed to Southwest Technologies Inc. ■

Caxton Group Inc. (Ont. Dec. 31, 2001 amalg.)
July 3, 2002 – Name changed to Pareto Corporation. ■

Caycuse Copper Co. (B.C. 1956)
May 15, 1969 – Struck off register.

Cayden Resources Inc. (B.C. Sept. 10, 2008)
Dec. 1, 2014 – Acquired by Agnico Eagle Mines Limited; basis 0.09 Agnico com. shs. and Cdn$0.01 cash for 1 Cayden com. sh.

Cayenne Capital Corp. (B.C. Oct. 15, 2015)
June 3, 2019 – Wholly owned Lot 49 Capital Corp. spun-out to the company's shldrs.; basis 1 Lot 49 sh. for 1 Cayenne sh.
July 2, 2022 – Name changed to Reverend Mining Corp. (see FPsurvey - Mines & Energy)

Caymus Resources Inc. (B.C. Jan. 24, 2011)
Apr. 1, 2014 – Dissolved following Qualifying Transaction private placement subscription of 363,383 Tasman Metals Ltd. units at $1.10 per unit plus wts. exercisable at $1.50 per unit for a 3-year period and distribution of Tasman units to shareholders. (see Tasman Metals Ltd.)

Caymus Ventures Corp. (B.C. May 8, 1987)
July 8, 1996 – Name changed to West Dynamic Toll Road Ltd. ■

Cayo Resources Inc. (Alta. Dec. 22, 1987)
Nov. 20, 1997 – Amalgamated with Pure Gold Resources Inc. to form Pure Gold Minerals Inc.; basis 1 new for 5 Pure Gold Resources shs. and 3 new for 5 Cayo Resources shs. (see Pure Gold Minerals Inc.)

Cayuga Steamship Co. Ltd. (Ont. 1953)
Apr. 1960 – Filed for bankruptcy.
Dec. 2, 1969 – Assets sold. Creditors received distribution of 33.086¢ on $1. Nothing available for shldrs.

Cayzor Athabaska Mines Ltd. (Ont. 1946)
1957 – Name changed to New Cayzor Athabaska Mines Ltd. ■

Caza Gold Corp. (B.C. Nov. 15, 2007)
June 8, 2018 – Name changed to Hydro66 Holdings Corp. following reverse takeover acquisition of Arctic Blockhain Ltd. and concurrent amalgamation of Arctic with wholly owned 1166031 B.C. Ltd. to form Hydro66 Canada Ltd. ■

Caza Oil & Gas, Inc. (B.C. June 9, 2006)
May 17, 2016 – Privatized; basis US$0.00481 cash per sh. following 1-for-560,000,000 sh. cons.

Cazador Explorations Limited (B.C. 1987)
Nov. 8, 1993 – Amalgamated with Granduc Mines Limited to form Granduc Mining Corporation; basis 1 new for 1 Granduc Mines sh. and 0.6 new for 1 Cazador Explorations sh. (see Granduc Mining Corporation)

Cdn Oilfield Technologies & Solutions Corp. (Alta. Apr. 1, 1999 amalg.)
Oct. 3, 2012 – Name changed to Canadian Oilfield Solutions Corp. ■

Ceapro Inc. (Alta. Jan. 1, 1997 amalg.)
2002 – Continued into Canada. (see Aeterna Zentaris Inc.)
June 7, 2024 – Acquired by Aeterna Zentaris Inc.; basis 0.02360 Aeterna shs. for 1 Ceapro sh. (see Aeterna Zentaris Inc.)

Ceasar Resources Ltd. (B.C. Aug. 10, 1983)
Apr. 7, 1987 – Name changed to Audre Recognition Systems Inc. ■

Cedar Capital Corp. (Alta. Apr. 25, 1994)
Feb. 27, 2002 – Name changed to Vancan Capital Corp.; basis 1 new for 4 old shs. ■

Cedar City Mines Ltd. (B.C. 1971)
Jan. 1979 – Charter cancelled.

Cedar Corporation (Alta. Oct. 28, 1985)
Oct. 22, 1998 – Struck off register.

Cedar Group, Inc. (Del. Nov. 3, 1993)
Aug. 1, 1996 – Name changed to Dominion Bridge Corporation.

Cedar Mountain Exploration Inc. (Alta. Mar. 16, 2006)
Mar. 27, 2012 – Name changed to Graphite One Resources Inc. ■

Cedar Oils Limited (Alta. Oct. 24, 1950)
Oct. 28, 1985 – Continued into Alberta.
Jan. 26, 1990 – Name changed to Seneca Metal Products Ltd. ■

Cedar Rapids Mines Ltd. (Ont. 1945)
Aug. 1960 – Charter cancelled.

Cedar Ridge Explorations Ltd. (Ont. 1980)
Jan. 3, 1984 – Name changed to Brandi-Ridge Resources Ltd. ■

Cedara Software Corp. (Ont. Jan. 19, 1982)
June 1, 2005 – Amalgamated with Merge Technologies Incorporated; basis 0.587 Merge Technologies com. shs. or 0.587 Merge Cedara ExchangeCo Limited exch. shs. for 1 Cedara sh. (see Merge Cedara Exchange Co Limited)

Cedarmine Resources Inc. (Alta. 1987)
Aug. 2, 2001 – Struck from registry and dissolved.

Cedarmont Capital Corp. (B.C. Feb. 2, 2021)
Jan. 20, 2022 – Name changed to ShinyBud Corp. pursuant to the Qualifying Transaction reverse takeover

acquisition of Shiny Bud Inc. and Mihi Inc.; basis 1 new for 42.748 old shs. ∎

Cedarvale Mines Ltd. (Que. 1957)
Feb. 1985 – Charter cancelled.

Ceduna Capital Corp. (Yuk. Jan. 28, 1999)
Apr. 8, 2005 – Continued into British Columbia.
May 30, 2005 – Name changed to Titan Uranium Exploration Inc. following Qualifying Transaction purchase of option to acquire the Thelon uranium project in Nunavut; basis 1 new for 2 old shs. ∎

Ceiba Energy Services Inc. (B.C. Mar. 5, 2010)
Aug. 10, 2017 – Acquired by Secure Energy Service Inc.: basis (i) $0.205 cash; or (ii) 0.02115 Secure com. shs.; or (iii) a combination thereof for 1 Ceiba sh. (see Secure Energy Services Inc.)

Celanese Canada Inc. (Can. Jan. 26, 1926)
Sept. 7, 1999 – Acquired by Hoechst Aktiengesellschaft of Germany for $27.25 per share.

Celanese Canada Limited (Can. Jan. 26, 1926)
May 1, 1978 – Name changed to Celanese Canada Inc. ∎

Celebration Cellars Ltd. (Alta. Aug. 20, 1999 amalg.)
July 3, 2001 – Name changed to WNS Inc. following reverse takeover acquisition of WNS.com Inc. for 10¢ per sh. ∎

Celebrity Energy Corp. (B.C. 1980)
Feb. 27, 1995 – Name changed to Polar Bear Development Corp.; basis 1 new for 4 old shs. ∎

Celest Medichem Inc. (B.C. Mar. 20, 2000)
May 15, 2000 – Continued into Yukon.
Dec. 12, 2001 – Name changed to Kronofusion Technologies Inc. following Qualifying Transaction reverse takeover acquisition of Kronofusion.com Technologies Inc. ∎

Celestar Exploration Ltd. (Alta. Nov. 24, 1997)
July 5, 1999 – Name changed to CanScot Resources Ltd. following reverse takeover acquisition of CanScot Resources Ltd.; basis 1 new for 5 old shs. ∎

Celeste Copper Corporation (Alta. Apr. 27, 2007)
Nov. 29, 2012 – Name changed to Celeste Mining Corp. ∎

Celeste Mining Corp. (Alta. Apr. 27, 2007)
Jan. 2, 2017 – Struck from register and dissolved.

Celestial Energy Inc. (Alta. Mar. 31, 2005)
July 12, 2007 – Name changed to Primera Energy Resources Ltd. ∎

Celico Resources Ltd. (B.C. 1967)
June 5, 1992 – Dissolved and struck off register.

Celina Resources Inc. (Ont. July 24, 1980)
1983 – Name changed to Adaptronix Technologies Limited; basis 1 new for 10 old shs. ∎

Cell-Loc Inc. (Alta. June 30, 1995)
Dec. 2, 2003 – Name changed to Capitol Energy Resources Ltd. following change of business to oil and gas from technology effected with Cell-Loc Location Technologies Inc. and Capitol Energy Resources Investment Partnership; basis 0.5 Capitol shs. and 0.5 Cell-Loc Location shs. for 1 Cell-Loc Inc. sh. ∎

Cell-Loc Location Technologies Inc. (Alta. Oct. 29, 2003)
Nov. 30, 2011 – Succeeded by Times Three Wireless Inc. pursuant to corporate reorganization whereby all assets, liabilities and business of Cell-Loc including $900,000 net cash in non-dilutive financing were transferred to Times Three. ∎

Cellardor Mines Ltd. (B.C. 1955)
Aug. 1976 – Charter cancelled.

CellBoardcast Group Inc. (Alta. June 7, 1996)
July 29, 2020 – Name changed to Twenty20 Investments Inc. ∎

CellCube Energy Storage Systems Inc. (B.C. Dec. 8, 1986)
June 1, 2021 – Name changed to Saltbae Capital Corp. (see FPsurvey - Industrials)

Cellstop Systems Inc. (B.C. Apr. 29, 1982)
Dec. 30, 2020 – Name changed to General Gold Resources Inc. ∎

Celltech Media Inc. (Ont. July 5, 1985)
June 28, 1995 – Name changed to Smartel Communications Corporation; basis 1 com. for 5 cl. A subord. vtg. shs. ∎

Celta Development & Mining Co. Ltd. (Can. 1936)
Jan. 4, 1957 – Name changed to Dablon Mining Corp. Ltd. ∎

Celtic Exploration Ltd. (Alta. Apr. 16, 2002)
Mar. 1, 2013 – Acquired by ExxonMobil Canada Ltd. for $24.50 plus 0.5 Kelt com. shs. for 1 Celtic sh. ∎

Celtic Knitting Company, Limited (Can. 1920)
Nov. 1955 – Acquired by National Hosiery Mills Limited for $27 per sh. (see National Hosiery Mills Limited)

Celtic Minerals Ltd. (B.C. 1970)
Apr. 17, 1975 – Name changed to Citlec Minerals Ltd.; basis 1 new for 4 old shs. ∎

Celtic Petroleums Ltd. (unknown)
Bankrupt; shs. worthless.

Celtic Resources Ltd. (B.C. Apr. 29, 1983)
Feb. 11, 1992 – Name changed to U.R. Flowers Corporation. ∎

CenAlta Energy Services Inc. (Alta. Aug. 28, 1997)
Oct. 18, 2000 – Acquired by Precision Drilling Corporation; basis 0.1432 new Precision sh. for 1 old CenAlta sh. (see Precision Drilling Corporation)

Cenco Petroleum Ltd. (B.C. Sept. 15, 1987)
Aug. 7, 1996 – Name changed to IGC Internet Gaming Corporation; basis 1.5 new for 1 old sh. ∎

Cenco Technologies Corp. (Alta. Jan. 29, 1997)
Oct. 31, 1999 – Continued into Ontario.
July 4, 2000 – Name changed to CencoTech Inc. ∎

CencoTech Inc. (Ont. Oct. 31, 1999)
Nov. 1, 2016 – Name changed to NamSys Inc. (see FPsurvey - Industrials)

Cenex Limited (Ont. 1945)
Oct. 11, 1979 – In receivership.
Sept. 22, 1981 – Charter cancelled.

Cenit Corporation (Ont. July 7, 2004)
Jan. 18, 2012 – Name changed to Superior Copper Corporation. ∎

Ceno Energy Ltd. (Alta. June 18, 2014 amalg.)
Oct. 8, 2014 – Name changed to Vital Energy Inc. (see FPsurvey - Mines & Energy)

Cenosis inc. (Can. Oct. 15, 1993)
Feb. 18, 2003 – Planned to make a proposal to creditors under the Federal Bankruptcy and Insolvency Act. Raymond Chabot Inc. was appointed trustee.
Mar. 20, 2003 – Sought and obtained a 45-day extension from the Quebec Court.
Nov. 2003 – Creditors unanimously accepted the proposal to restructure. They had the option of receiving either 10¢ cash or one share for each $1.00 of debt held. The company also stated that it was pursuing discussions with potential business partners and buyers in order to merge with or to dispose of some of its remaining assets.
Apr. 27, 2006 – Trustee had filed a notice of default on the previously noted proposal because the company had failed to pay the amount of the proposal to the trustee.

There were no assets, following bank seizure, and the company was no longer in operation. There were no funds available for creditors or shldrs.

Cenovus Energy Inc. (Can.)
Nov. 30, 2009 – Amalgamated in Canada to continue with same name. (see FPsurvey - Mines & Energy)

Cenpro Technologies Inc. (Alta. Feb. 22, 1996)
Aug. 2, 2006 – Dissolved and struck from register.

Cent-Ram Development Corp. (B.C. Dec. 21, 1979)
Jan. 7, 1983 – Name changed to I.S.L. Industries Ltd. ∎

Centamin Egypt Limited (Australia Mar. 24, 1970)
Dec. 30, 2011 – Succeeded by Centamin plc. ∎

Centamin plc (Jersey Dec. 30, 2011)
Nov. 26, 2024 – Acquired by AngloGold Ashanti plc; basis US$0.125 cash and 0.06983 AngloGold shs. for 1 Centamin ordinary sh.

Centaur Resources Ltd. (B.C. Oct. 25, 1985)
June 7, 1990 – Name changed to Technologia Systems Corp.; basis 2 new for 1 old sh. ∎

Centenario Copper Corporation (B.C. Jan. 19, 2004)
Apr. 15, 2009 – Acquired by Quadra Mining Ltd.; basis 0.28 Quadra shs. for 1 Centenario sh. (see Quadra Mining Ltd.)

Centenera Mining Corp. (B.C. Jan. 9, 2006)
May 27, 2019 – Name changed to Latin Metals Inc.; basis 1 new for 4 old shs. (see FPsurvey - Mines & Energy)

Centennial Acquisitions Corp. (B.C. Apr. 12, 2016)
Aug. 12, 2016 – Name changed to StartMonday Technology Corp. pursuant to reverse takeover acquisition of StartMonday Holding B.V. (see FPsurvey - Industrials)

Centennial Minerals Ltd. (B.C. 1980)
1985 – Acquired by Pegasus Gold Inc.; basis 30 new com. shs. and 100 new warrants for 100 old shs. Each warrant entitled holders to purchase 1 Pegasus sh. for $14.57 to 1988. (see Pegasus Gold Inc.)

Centennial Mines Ltd. (B.C. 1956)
1962 – Acquired by Magnum Consolidated Mining Co. Ltd.; basis 1 new for 4 old shs. (see Magnum Consolidated Mining Co. Ltd.)

Centennial Mines Ltd. (N.B. 1967)
May 1972 – Charter cancelled.

Centennial Mortgage Corp. Ltd. (B.C. 1958)
1969 – Declared bankrupt. Proceeds from liquidation of assets not sufficient to cover claims of secured creditors.
1982 – Struck off register.

Centerplate, Inc. (Del. Nov. 21, 1995)
Jan. 29, 2009 – Amalgamated with KPLT Holdings, Inc. and KPLT Mergerco, Inc., affiliates of Kohlberg & Company, LLC, for US$0.01 per IDS.

Centex Mines Ltd. (B.C. 1966)
Jan. 1976 – Name changed to Centex Resource Industries Ltd. ∎

Centex Resource Industries Ltd. (B.C. 1966)
Feb. 25, 1983 – Struck off register.

Centillion Industries Inc. (Alta. Apr. 16, 2002)
May 29, 2007 – Name changed to Palo Duro Energy Inc. ∎

Centiva Capital Inc. (Can. May 18, 2006)
Sept. 30, 2011 – Name changed to Spackman Equities Group Inc. (see FPsurvey - Industrials)

Centpac Development Inc. (B.C. Nov. 27, 1973)
May 1, 1979 – Name changed to Tracer Resources Corporation. ∎

Centra Gas Manitoba Inc. (Man. 1953)
July 30, 1999 – Acquired by The Manitoba Hydro Electric Board (together with Minell Pipelines Ltd.) for total consideration of $245,000,000.

Centra Gas Ontario Inc. (Ont. May 6, 1954)
Sept. 15, 1997 – All o/s 7.85% cum. redeem. 2nd pref. ser. A shs. redeemed for $25 per sh. plus divds. All o/s 2.70% cum. redeem. 1st pref. 2nd ser. shs. redeemed for $50.50 per sh. plus divds. All o/s $2.60 cum. redeem. 1st pref. 1st ser. shs. redeemed effective Sept. 1, 1997, for $50.50 per sh. plus divds. (see Union Gas Limited)
Jan. 1, 1998 – Amalgamated with Union Gas Limited to continue the Ontario distribution operations as Union Gas Limited with headquarters in Chatham, Ont. The two companies had operated under a shared services arrangement since 1994 and both were subsidiaries of Westcoast Energy Inc. (see Union Gas Limited)

Central African Gold Inc. (B.C. Mar. 27, 2007)
Feb. 7, 2022 – Name changed to African Energy Metals Inc. ■

Central Alberta Well Services Corp. (Alta. Sept. 1, 2005 amalg.)
June 8, 2011 – Name changed to CWC Well Services Corp. ■

Central and Eastern Canada Mines (1958) Ltd. (Ont. 1958)
1970 – Charter cancelled.

Central and Eastern Trust Company (Can. 1976 amalg.)
Mar. 1, 1981 – Amalgamated with Federal Trust Co. to form Central Trust Company; basis 1 new for 1 old sh.

Central and Nova Scotia Trust Company (N.B. 1974 amalg.)
July 2, 1976 – Amalgamated with The Eastern Canada Savings and Loan Co. to form Central and Eastern Trust Company; basis 1 cl. A sh. of amalgamated co. for 1 old Central and Nova Scotia Trust sh.

Central Asbestos Mines Ltd. (Que. 1953)
Jan. 1974 – Charter cancelled.

Central Asia Gold Limited (Australia Oct. 16, 1985)
Dec. 19, 2006 – Name changed to CGA Mining Limited. ■

Central Asia Goldfields Corporation (Ont. Jan. 1, 1996 amalg.)
Dec. 17, 2007 – Certificate of incorporation cancelled and dissolved.

Central B.C. Exploration Ltd. (B.C. 1967)
May 10, 1985 – Struck off register.

Central Cadillac Consolidated Mines Ltd. (Que. 1939)
Jan. 1947 – Name changed to Consolidated Central Cadillac Mines Ltd.; basis 1 new for 1 old sh. ■

Central Cadillac Gold Mines Ltd. (Que. July 6, 1936)
1939 – Name changed to Central Cadillac Mines Ltd. and continued into Quebec; basis 1 new for 1 old sh. ■

Central Cadillac Mines Ltd. (Que. 1939)
Nov. 1946 – Name changed to Central Cadillac Consolidated Mines Ltd.; basis 2 new for 5 old shs. ■

Central Canada Foods Corporation (Que. Sept. 18, 1963)
June 5, 2007 – Name changed to Central Industries Corporation Inc. ■

Central Canada Investments Ltd. (Ont. 1951)
Nov. 1960 – Co. distributed all its assets rateably to shldrs. Charter surrendered.

Central Canada Loan and Savings Company (Can. 1898)
1951 – All assets (except $750,000) acquired by Central Canada Investments Ltd.; basis 1 pref. sh., $100 par, and 10 com. shs. plus $30 for each sh. of Central Cda. Loan.

Central Capital Corporation (Can. May 2, 1986)
Jan. 4, 1993 – Privatized whereby all o/s com. shs., cl. A subord. vtg. shs., 7.625% cum. redeem. retract. sr. pref. shs. ser. A., 7.625% cum. redeem. retract. sr. pref. shs. ser. B. and 7.625% cum. redeem. retract. sr. pref. shs. ser. C exchanged for new com. shs.; basis 1 new com. sh. for 63.079 old com. shs.; 1 new com. sh. for 63.079 old cl. A subord. vtg. shs. and 1 new com. sh. for 7.58 old 7.625% cum. redeem. retract. sr. pref. shs. ser. A, B & C.
Jan. 1, 1998 – Formed YMG Capital Management Inc. in Canada on reverse takeover acquisition of and amalgamation with Yield Management Group; basis 1 new for 5 old shs. ■

Central Cheam Copper Mines Ltd. (B.C.)
Apr. 2, 1970 – Struck off register.

Central Chibougamau Mines Ltd. (Que. 1952)
1953 – Name changed to Brunswick Quebec Development Ltd. ■

Central Covenants (Holdings) Ltd. (Can. 1963)
Mar. 11, 1975 – Name changed to Scotia Covenants Corporation. ■

Central Crude Ltd. (B.C. Oct. 21, 1980)
July 2, 1991 – Continued into Ontario.
Aug. 3, 1994 – Name changed to River Gold Mines Ltd. ■

Central-Del Rio Oils Limited (Alta. July 11, 1947)
Nov. 15, 1971 – Name changed to PanCanadian Petroleum Limited. ■

Central Duparquet Mines Ltd. (Que. 1940)
June 6, 1981 – Charter cancelled.

Central Dynamics Ltd. (Can. Mar. 21, 1958)
Feb. 3, 1988 – Formed International Datacasting Corporation on amalgamation with International Datacasting Corporation. ■

Central Explorers Inc. (Alta. Apr. 16, 1986)
Jan. 9, 1992 – Acquired by Poco Petroleums Ltd. for 35¢ per sh. (see Poco Petroleums Ltd.)

Central Fund of Canada Limited (Ont. Nov. 15, 1961)
Apr. 5, 1990 – Continued into Alberta.
Jan. 16, 2018 – Succeeded by Sprott Physical Gold and Silver Trust pursuant to plan of arrangement whereby Sprott Physical Gold and Silver Trust was formed to facilitate Sprott Inc.'s acquisition of common shares of Central Fund of Canada Limited (CFCL) and exchange of CFCL class A shares for trust units. (see FPsurvey - Mines & Energy; FPsurvey - Industrials)

Central Gas Utilities Ltd. (Alta. 1951)
Nov. 15, 1967 – Struck off register.

Central Gold-Trust (Ont. Apr. 28, 2003)
Jan. 19, 2009 – Name changed to Central GoldTrust. ■

Central GoldTrust (Ont. Apr. 28, 2003)
Jan. 20, 2016 – Acquired by Sprott Physical Gold Trust; basis 4.4108 Sprott PGT trust units for 1 Central Gold trust unit.

Central Guaranty Trust Company (Can. 1981 amalg.)
Dec. 31, 1992 – Placed into liquidation. Deloitte & Touche Inc. appointed liquidator.

Central Guaranty Trustco Limited (Ont. Oct. 19, 1984)
Sept. 1992 – Served with petition of bankruptcy by a party claiming to be a noteholder of the co.
Mar. 1993 – Ernst & Young Inc. in Toronto was appointed administrator, manager and receiver by the courts following Plan of Arrangement filed under the Companies' Creditors Arrangement Act.
Apr. 6, 1994 – Substantial portion of assets liquidated and unlikely that remaining assets once liquidated would be sufficient to pay the claims of creditors.
Sept. 30, 1999 – Liquidated and no distributions to creditors or shldrs.

Central Industries Corporation Inc. (Que. Sept. 18, 1963)
June 5, 2010 – Struck from register.

Central Interior Cablevision Ltd. (B.C. 1972)
May 1, 1989 – Acquired by Shaw Cablesystems Inc.

Central Lake Uranium Ltd. (Ont. 1953)
1955 – Amalgamated into Bicroft Uranium Mines Ltd.; basis 1 new for 2 old shs.

Central Leduc Oils Limited (Alta. July 11, 1947)
Mar. 15, 1957 – Name changed to Central-Del Rio Oils Limited following merger with Del Rio Producers Ltd. ■

Central Manitoba Mines Ltd. (Man. 1925)
1964 – Name changed to Consolidated Manitoba Mines Ltd.; basis 1 new for 5 old shs. ■

Central Matachewan Mining Corp. Ltd. (Ont. 1932)
1948 – Property sold to Richore Gold Mines Ltd. for approx. 802,000 pooled shs. (see Richore Gold Mines Ltd.)
June 13, 1955 – Charter cancelled. No equity for shldrs. (see Richore Gold Mines Ltd.)

Central Metal Mines Ltd. (Que. 1957)
Nov. 27, 1976 – Dissolved.

Central Minera Corp. (Yuk. Feb. 4, 1999)
May 2, 2012 – Dissolved.

Central Mining Co. Ltd. (B.C. 1949)
1952 – Charter cancelled.

Central Northern Airways Ltd. (Can. 1947)
1956 – Name changed to Transair Limited. ■

Central Oils Ltd. (Alta. 1932)
Out of business; no assets.

Central Ontario Savings & Loan Corporation (Ont. 1959)
Dec. 31, 1971 – Acquired by Ontario Trust Co.; basis approx. 1.2969 new for 1 old sh. (see Ontario Trust Co.)

Central Ontario Trust & Savings Corporation (Ont. 1964)
1969 – Acquired by Aetna Investment Corp. Ltd.; basis 0.666 new Aetna sh. plus $8.00 for 1 old sh. In 1971, Central Ontario Trust shs. acquired from Aetna by Central Ontario Savings & Loan Corp. on equivalent basis.

Central Patricia Gold Mines, Limited (Ont. 1931)
June 12, 1980 – Amalgamated with McVittie-Graham Mining Company Limited to form Central Patricia Limited; basis 1 new for 4 old shs.

Central Patricia Limited (Ont. 1931)
Aug. 20, 1982 – Amalgamated with Conwest Exploration Company Limited (1 new cl. A and cl. B for 1 cl. A and cl. B), International Mogul Mines Limited (2 new cl. B for 1 com. and 1 new ser. A pfd. for 1 old 6% 1st pfd.), Chimo Gold Mines Limited (either $2.20 or 0.3 new cl. B for 1 com.) and 465128 Ontario Limited (0.88 new cl. A for 1 com.) to form a new co. also named Conwest Exploration Company Limited; basis 1.1 new Conwest cl. B shs. for 1 old Central Patricia com. sh. (see Conwest Exploration Company Limited)

Central Porcupine Mines Ltd. (Ont. 1933)
1964 – Name changed to United Porcupine Mines Ltd.; basis 1 new for 4 old shs. ■

Central Porphyry Contacts Ltd. (Ont. 1934)
Dec. 9, 1970 – Dissolved.

Central Resources Corp. (B.C. June 6, 2007)
Sept. 30, 2014 – Name changed to Uranium Standard Resources Ltd. following reverse takeover acquisition of Canadian Uranium Corp. ■

Central Sudbury Lead-Zinc Mines Ltd. (Ont. 1948)
Mar. 12, 1957 – Name changed to Stackpool Mining Co. Ltd.; basis 1 new plus 2 cents cash for 20 old shs. ■

Central Sun Mining Inc. (Can. June 8, 2005)
Apr. 1, 2009 – Acquired by B2Gold Corp.; basis 1.28 B2Gold shs. for 1 Central Sun sh.

Central Swayze Gold Mines Ltd. (unknown)
July 1934 – Name changed to Tyche Long Lac Gold Mines Ltd. ■

Central Timmins Exploration Corp. (Can. Nov. 10, 2017)
Aug. 31, 2020 – Name changed to P2 Gold Inc. (see FPsurvey - Mines & Energy)

Central Trust Company (Can. 1981 amalg.)
Dec. 31, 1988 – Formed Central Guaranty Trust Company on amalgamation with Guaranty Trust Company of Canada, Yorkshire Trust Company and Nova Scotia Savings and Trust Company. ■

Central Trust Company of Canada (N.B. 1920)
Jan. 1, 1974 – Amalgamated with its 99%-owned subsid., The Nova Scotia Trust Co., to form Central and Nova Scotia Trust Co.

Central Turner Petroleums, Ltd. (unknown)
Oct. 1932 – Acquired by West Turner Petroleums, Ltd. (see West Turner Petroleums Ltd.)

Central Tyrrell Gold Mines Ltd. (Ont. 1932)
1957 – Charter cancelled.

Central Whitemud Oil Syndicate (unknown)
1956 – Reported dissolved.

Central Zeballos Gold Mines Ltd. (B.C. 1938)
Mar. 1957 – Wound up. Total distribution: 0.333¢ per sh.

Centram Exploration Ltd. (Alta. Oct. 24, 1996)
Sept. 7, 2007 – Continued into Canada.
Sept. 10, 2007 – Name changed to Pancontinental Uranium Corporation. ■

Centrasia Mining Corp. (B.C. Nov. 23, 2004)
Mar. 27, 2008 – Name changed to Kola Mining Corp. ■

Centre Hill Mines Ltd. (Ont. 1953)
1966 – Name changed to Munro Copper Mines Ltd.; basis 1 new for 2 old shs. ■

Centre Valley Petroleums Ltd. (Alta.)
1960 – Struck off register.

Centrefield Petroleums Ltd. (Ont. 1949)
1952 – Assets acquired by Ellesmere Oil & Development Ltd.; basis 1 new for 10 old shs. Ellesmere acquired by New Concord Development Corp. Ltd. and Centrefield subsequently name changed to New Concord; basis 1 new for 30 old shs.

Centrefund Realty Corporation (Ont. Nov. 10, 1993)
Sept. 20, 2001 – Name changed to First Capital Realty Inc. ■

Centremaque Gold Mines Limited (Que. Dec. 5, 1936)
Aug. 7, 1956 – Name changed to Norsyncomaque Mining Limited; basis 1 new for 4 old shs. ■

Centric Energy Corp. (B.C. June 29, 2006)
Feb. 23, 2011 – Acquired by Africa Oil Corp. for $0.0001 plus 0.3077 Africa Oil shs. for 1 Centric sh. (see Africa Oil Corp.)

Centric Health Corporation (Can. Feb. 2, 2001)
June 22, 2020 – Name changed to CareRx Corporation; basis 1 new for 20 old shs. (see FPsurvey - Industrials)

Centrinity Inc. (Can. Nov. 21, 1996)
Nov. 12, 2002 – Amalgamated with direct wholly owned subsid. of Open Text Corporation; basis 1 new Open Text pfd. sh. for 1 old Centrinity com. sh. Preferreds immediately redeemed for $1.26 per sh.

Centrix Yellowknife Mines Ltd. (Ont. 1947)
1955 – Charter cancelled.

Centron Equity Corp. Ltd. (Alta. 1964)
July 15, 1978 – Struck off register.

Centura Resources Inc. (B.C. June 9, 1981)
Feb. 14, 2005 – Name changed to Polar Resources Corporation; basis 1 new for 2 old shs. ■

Centurion Energy International Inc. (Alta. May 20, 1997 amalg.)
Jan. 12, 2007 – Acquired by Dana Gas PJSC for $12 per sh.

Centurion Equities Corporation (Ont. 1918)
May 1979 – Name changed to Amcan Industries Corporation. ■

Centurion Equities Ltd. (Alta. 1980)
Dec. 21, 1990 – Name changed to Fire Boss Services Ltd. ■

Centurion Exploration Inc. (B.C. 1980)
Dec. 23, 1982 – Amalgamated with International Trojan Exploration Inc. to continue as Centurion Exploration Inc.; basis 1 new for 1 old sh.
June 11, 1983 – Amalgamated with Beaver Resources Inc.; basis 1 new for 1 old sh.

Centurion Gold Ltd. (B.C. June 8, 1988 amalg.)
Aug. 23, 1991 – Amalgamated with U.S. Precious Metals, Inc. to form Siskon Gold Corporation; basis 2 new for 3 Centurion shs.

Centurion Minerals Ltd. (B.C. 1972)
June 8, 1988 – Formed Centurion Gold Ltd. in British Columbia on amalgamation with California Gold Mines Ltd. (1 for 4); basis 1 new for 1 old sh. ■

Centurion Mines Limited (Ont. 1958)
Nov. 13, 1969 – Merged into Caravelle Mines Ltd.; basis 1 new for 2 shs. Centurion.

Century Circuits Ltd. (Ont. May 27, 1983)
Feb. 11, 1998 – Name changed to Canadian Financial Holdings Corporation. ■

Century Consolidated Oils Ltd. (Man.)
1959 – Struck off register.

Century Energy Corporation (Ont. Mar. 28, 1967)
Apr. 8, 1997 – Name changed to Senternet Technologies Inc. ■

Century Energy Ltd. (Alta. May 3, 2006)
Oct. 20, 2016 – Continued into British Columbia.
Jan. 18, 2021 – Name changed to Parent Capital Corp.; basis 1 new for 10 old shs. (see FPsurvey - Mines & Energy)

Century Financial Capital Group Inc. (Ont. Nov. 1, 1998 amalg.)
May 24, 2018 – Name changed to FSD Pharma Inc. following reverse takeover acquistion of FV Pharma Inc. and concurrent amalgamation of FV Pharma with wholly owned 2620756 Ontario Inc. ■

Century Global Commodities Corporation (B.C. Oct. 17, 2014)
Feb. 1, 2016 – Continued into Cayman Islands. (see FPsurvey - Mines & Energy; FPsurvey - Industrials)

Century Gold Corp. (Can. Apr. 24, 1997)
July 6, 2001 – Name changed to Novra Technologies Inc. (see FPsurvey - Industrials)

Century Gold Placers Ltd. (B.C. 1958)
May 4, 1972 – Dissolved.

Century Interplex Corp. (B.C. 1969)
June 27, 1977 – Dissolved.

Century Iron Mines Corporation (Can. July 10, 2007)
Oct. 17, 2014 – Continued into British Columbia.
Nov. 16, 2015 – Name changed to Century Global Commodities Corporation. ■

Century Metals Inc. (B.C. Aug. 24, 2017)
June 3, 2020 – Name changed to Reyna Silver Corp. pursuant to reverse takeover acquisition of (old) Reyna Silver Corp.; basis 1 new for 6.4 old shs. ■

Century Mining Corporation (Yuk. Sept. 24, 2003)
July 22, 2004 – Continued into Canada. (see White Tiger Gold Ltd.)
Oct. 24, 2011 – Acquired by 7918534 Canada Inc., a wholly owned subsid. of White Tiger Gold Ltd.; basis 0.4 White Tiger shs. for 1 Century Mining sh. (see White Tiger Gold Ltd.)

Century Mining Corp. Ltd. (Que. 1936)
Feb. 1974 – Charter cancelled.

Century Oils Ltd. (Man. 1951)
1958 – Assets sold for 675,000 shs. of Oregon Natural Gas Reserves Ltd.
1960 – Liquidated.

Century Technologies Inc. (Ont. Aug. 30, 1945)
Jan. 3, 1995 – Delisted from the CDN. Subsequently charter cancelled and the company dissolved.

Century II Holdings Inc. (Ont. Apr. 13, 1984)
Nov. 5, 2007 – Acquired by TransForce Income Fund for $10.20 per sh.

Century Uranium Co. (unknown)
Formed Century Mining & Development Corp following merger of Ranger Lake Uranium Co. Ltd., Horseshoe Bend Uranium Co. and Century Uranium Corp.

Cepeda Minerals Inc. (B.C. 1955)
Oct. 31, 2003 – Struck from register and dissolved.

Cephalon Resource Corporation (Alta. Aug. 15, 1986)
Feb. 2, 2003 – Struck from registry and dissolved.

Cequel Energy Inc. (Alta. Mar. 29, 1995)
July 7, 2004 – Plan of Arrangement reorganization with Progress Energy Ltd. to create a new company named Progress Energy Trust. New companies ProEx Energy Ltd. and Cyries Energy Inc. were also created. Basis of Arrangement a) 0.695 new Progress Trust trust unit plus 0.139 new ProEx com. sh. plus 0.139 new Cyries com. sh., or b) 0.695 new Progress Energy exch. sh. plus 0.139 new ProEx com. sh. plus 0.139 new Cyries com. sh., or c) a combination of a) and b). (see Cyries Energy Inc.; ProEx Energy Ltd.; Progress Energy Trust)

Cequence Energy Ltd. (Alta. Sept. 29, 2005)
Sept. 28, 2020 – Recapitalization transaction and privatization under the Companies' Creditors Arrangement Act (CCAA) was completed. Pursuant to the CCAA plan, all o/s com. shs. were cancelled and extinguished without any consideration or other compensation.

Cerametal Industries Limited (Ont. 1954)
July 1963 – Assets were seized by a bank and sold to D.H.I. Ltd., Brantford, Ont.

Ceramic Protection Corporation (Alta. Nov. 1, 1995 amalg.)
July 31, 2008 – Continued into Delaware.
Aug. 8, 2008 – Name changed to Protective Products of America, Inc.

Cercal Minerals Corporation (Ont. June 1, 1993 amalg.)
May 30, 2005 – Certificate of incorporation cancelled and dissolved.

Ceres Acquisition Corp. (B.C. Jan. 29, 2020)
Dec. 19, 2022 – Winding up; basis US$10.00045 cash per cl. A restrictive vtg. sh.

Ceres Capital Corp. (Alta. June 5, 2006)
Oct. 1, 2009 – Name changed to Reliable Energy Ltd. ■

Ceres Global Ag Corp. (Ont. Nov. 1, 2007)
July 9, 2025 – Acquired by Bartlett Grain Company, LLC; basis US$4.50 cash per sh.

Ceres Resources Limited (Can. 1980)
Feb. 1, 1983 – Amalgamated with Talcorp Holdings Limited, a wholly owned subsid. of Talcorp Limited.

Shldrs. of Ceres received 0.5 com. sh. and one $3.00 convert. pfce. sh. of Talcorp for 1 com. sh.

Ceridian HCM Holding Inc. (Del. July 3, 2013)
Jan. 31, 2024 – Name changed to Dayforce, Inc. (see FPsurvey - Industrials)

Cerna Copper Mines Ltd. (B.C. 1952)
1969 – Shldrs. received 1 sh. Dison International Ltd. for each 4 shs. held under transfer of assets.

Cerro Mining Corp. (B.C. Feb. 27, 1987)
Mar. 4, 2022 – Name changed to Friday's Dog Holdings Inc. pursuant to the revere takeover acquisition of Friday's Dog Inc. (FDI) and concurrent amalgamation of wholly owned 1308821 B.C. Ltd. and FDI. ■

Cerro Mining Ltd. (B.C. 1950)
1969 – Name changed to Crownex International Ltd. ■

Cerro Resources NL (Australia Feb. 27, 1985)
June 4, 2013 – Acquired by Primero Mining Corp.; basis 0.023 Primero shs. for 1 Cerro sh. (see Primero Mining Corp.)

Certicom Corp. (Ont. Mar. 20, 1985)
Aug. 18, 1999 – Continued into Yukon. (see Research In Motion Limited)
Jan. 13, 2003 – Continued into Canada. (see Research In Motion Limited)
Mar. 26, 2009 – Acquired by Research in Motion Limited for $3.00 per sh. (see Research In Motion Limited)

Cerus Energy Group Ltd. (B.C. Feb. 5, 1996)
June 24, 2019 – Name changed to Camarico Investment Group Ltd. (see FPsurvey - Industrials)

Cervantes Capital Corp. (B.C. Oct. 26, 2014)
Dec. 21, 2018 – Name changed to Christina Lake Cannabis Corp. (see FPsurvey - Industrials)

Cervin Capital Corporation (Can. Jan. 22, 1997)
July 22, 1999 – Name changed to R.A.N.K.I.N. Technologies Inc.; basis 1 new cl. A for 1 old cl. A sh. ■

Cervus Corp. (Alta. Nov. 24, 1998)
Jan. 6, 2006 – Plan of Arrangement to convert company to an income fund named Proventure Income Fund; basis 1 new unit for 1 com. sh. (see Proventure Income Fund)

Cervus Equipment Corporation (Can. Aug. 9, 1999)
Oct. 26, 2021 – All o/s com. shs. not already owned acquired by Brandt Tractor Ltd.; basis $19.50 per sh.

Cervus Financial Group Inc. (Alta. July 15, 2004 amalg.)
June 8, 2006 – Filed for protection under the Companies' Creditors Arrangement Act and KPMG Inc. appointed as monitor.
July 7, 2006 – Shs. of wholly owned Cervus Financial Corp. were sold to a subsid. of Macquirie Bank Limited for $11,512,212.
Aug. 9, 2006 – Name changed to CFG Holdings Inc. ■

Cervus International Inc. (Alta. Nov. 24, 1998)
Apr. 11, 2000 – Name changed to Cervus Corp.; basis 1 new for 2 old shs. ■

Cervus LP (Alta. Mar. 14, 2003)
Oct. 27, 2009 – Converted into a corp. by way of plan of arrangement with Vasogen Inc. whereby Vasogen changed its name to Cervus Equipment Corporation, resulting in Cervus LP and Cervus GP Ltd. becoming wholly owned subsids.; basis 3 Cervus Equipment shs. for 2 Cervus LP units. All Vasogen assets and liabilities were transferred (except tax assets) along with $7,500,000 from Cervus LP, to a new subsid. 7231971 Canada Inc. which amalgamated to form publicly listed IntelliPharmaCeutics International Inc. Vasogen shldrs. exchanged shs. on a 1-for-1 basis for shs. of IntelliPharmaCeutics. (see Cervus Equipment Corporation)

Cessford Gas & Oil Corp. Ltd. (Ont. 1957)
Aug. 1957 – Name changed to Cessland Gas & Oil Corp. Ltd. ■

Cessland Corporation Limited (Ont. Mar. 15, 1962)
Aug. 8, 2005 – Certificate of incorporation cancelled and dissolved.

Cessland Gas & Oil Corp. Ltd. (Ont. 1957)
1962 – Merged to form Cessland Corporation Limited; basis 1 new for 2 old shs. (see Cessland Corporation Limited)

Cetec Engineering Company Inc. (B.C. Nov. 10, 1982)
Dec. 22, 1995 – Name changed to International Cetec Investments Inc.; basis 1 cl. A and 3 non-vtg. redeem. pref. shs. for 3 com. shs. ■

Chablis Resources Ltd. (B.C. Apr. 26, 1984)
Sept. 6, 1988 – Name changed to Westhill Resources Limited. ■

Chai Cha Na Mining Inc. (Can. Feb. 12, 2007)
Dec. 16, 2016 – Dissolved and struck from register.

Chai-Na-Ta Corp. (Can. Aug. 12, 1981)
July 30, 2012 – Liquidated; final distribution of $0.293 cash per com.sh.
Sept. 26, 2012 – Voluntarily dissolved.

Chai-Na-Ta Ginseng Products Limited (Can. Aug. 12, 1981)
May 9, 1994 – Name changed to Chai-Na-Ta Corp. ■

Chain Energy Corporation (Alta. Mar. 28, 1996)
May 6, 2002 – Acquired by Argonauts Group Ltd.; basis $1.00 or 0.44 new Argonauts Group sh. for 1 old Chain Energy sh. (see Argonauts Group Ltd.)

ChaiNode Opportunities Corp. (Alta. Jan. 19, 2018)
Dec. 12, 2019 – Continued into Canada.
Dec. 13, 2019 – Name changed to Dore Copper Mining Corp. following Qualifying Transaction reverse takeover of AmAuCu Mining Corporation and amalgamation of AmAuCu with wholly owned 11588915 Canada Inc.; basis 1 new for 10.8 old shs. ■

Chairman Capital Corp. (Ont. May 31, 2006)
Aug. 13, 2010 – Continued into Jersey.
Oct. 4, 2010 – Name changed to Longreach Oil and Gas Limited pursuant to Qualifying Transaction reverse takeover acquisition of Longreach Oil and Gas Ventures Limited; basis 1 new for 5 old shs. ■

Chalcor Mining Corp. Ltd. (Ont. 1945)
1956 – Charter cancelled.

Chalice Diamond Corp. (B.C. July 31, 2006)
June 30, 2011 – Name changed to La Ronge Gold Corp. ■

Chalice Mining Inc. (B.C. Apr. 20, 1982)
Jan. 27, 1999 – Name changed to International Chalice Resources Inc.; basis 1 new for 5 old shs. ■

Chalk Holdings Ltd. (B.C. 1961)
1978 – Placed into receivership.

Chalk Media Corp. (B.C. Feb. 22, 2002)
Feb. 3, 2009 – Acquired by Research in Motion Limited for $0.142 per sh.

Chalkis Yellowknife Mines Ltd. (Ont. 1946)
Jan. 6, 1971 – Dissolved.

Challenger Deep Capital Corp. (Alta. Nov. 20, 2007)
Sept. 16, 2010 – Name changed to Challenger Deep Resources Corp. ■

Challenger Deep Resources Corp. (Alta. Nov. 20, 2007)
Oct. 29, 2015 – Name changed to DeepMarkit Corp. (see FPsurvey - Industrials)

Challenger Development Corp. (B.C. Sept. 24, 1990)
Apr. 11, 2013 – Name changed to DGS Minerals Inc.; basis 1 new for 10 old shs. ■

Challenger Energy Corp. (Can. Dec. 1, 2005 amalg.)
Sept. 25, 2009 – Acquired by Canadian Superior Energy Inc.; basis 0.51 Canadian Superior shs. for 1 Challenger Energy sh. (see Canadian Superior Energy Inc.)

Challenger Explorations Ltd. (B.C. 1971)
Oct. 21, 1983 – Struck off register.

Challenger International Ltd. (Bermuda 1980)
Dec. 18, 1995 – Name changed to Intelect Communications Systems Limited. ■

Challenger International Services Ltd. (Alta. June 1978)
Dec. 14, 1984 – Reverted to private co. status following redemption of publicly held cl. A special shs. at $2.00 per sh.

Challenger Minerals Ltd. (B.C. Sept. 24, 1990)
Feb. 2, 2005 – Name changed to Challenger Development Corp.; basis 1 new for 4 old shs. ■

Challenger Mines Ltd. (B.C. 1960)
July 11, 1977 – Dissolved.

Chalmers Press Limited (Ont. 1946)
1952 – On petition of gen. mtge. bondhldrs., co. placed into receivership.

Chamaelo Energy Inc. (Alta. Apr. 5, 2004)
June 27, 2005 – Plan of Arrangement to convert company into an income trust named Vault Energy Trust and an exploration company named Chamaelo Exploration Ltd.; basis (1) 0.5 new trust unit of Trust or, 0.5 new exch. sh. of Trust or, a combination thereof plus (2) 0.2 new explor. company com. sh. or, $0.62, for 1 old Chamaelo com. sh. (see Chamaelo Exploration Ltd.; Vault Energy Trust)

Chamaelo Exploration Ltd. (Alta. Jan. 5, 2006)
Oct. 24, 2006 – Acquired by Kereco Energy Ltd.; basis 0.51 Kereco sh. for 1 Chamaelo sh.

Chamberlain Oil & Gas Ltd. (Alta. 1951)
1956 – Name changed to New Chamberlain Petroleums Ltd.; basis 1 new for 4 old shs. ■

Chambers Petroleum Co., Ltd. (Alta.)
1929 – Name changed to Montreal-Alberta Petroleums Ltd. and continued into Canada. ■

Champagne Capital Corp. (Alta. 1987)
Aug. 1, 1992 – Struck off register.

Champagne Resources Ltd. (B.C. Apr. 14, 1983)
Jan. 27, 1988 – Name changed to Pass Lake Resources Ltd.; basis 1 new for 2 old shs. ■

Champignon Brands Inc. (B.C. Mar. 26, 2019)
Apr. 29, 2021 – Name changed to Braxia Scientific Corp. pursuant to the reverse takeover acquisition of Altmed Capital Corp. (see FPsurvey - Industrials)

Champion Gold Resources Inc. (Ont. Apr. 11, 1985)
July 21, 2000 – Name changed to Champion Natural Health.com Inc.; basis 1 new for 5 old shs. ■

Champion Iron Mines Limited (Australia May 18, 2006)
Mar. 31, 2014 – Succeeded by Champion Iron Limited pursuant to arrangement agreement acquisition by Mamba Minerals Limited (subsequently renamed Champion Iron Limited), with Champion Iron Mines Limited the deemed acquiror; basis 0.7333333 new for 1 old sh. (see FPsurvey - Mines & Energy)

Champion Minerals Inc. (Australia May 18, 2006)
Aug. 30, 2012 – Name changed to Champion Iron Mines Limited. ■

Champion Natural Health.com Inc. (Ont. Apr. 11, 1985)
Oct. 13, 2006 – Name changed to Champion Minerals Inc.; basis 1 new for 6 old shs. ■

Champion Oil & Gas Corporation (B.C. Sept. 14, 1979)
Oct. 25, 1985 – Name changed to Winkelmann Countermeasures Inc.; basis 1 new for 4 old shs. ■

Champion Resources Inc. (B.C. Mar. 16, 1988)
Apr. 23, 2004 – Continued into Canada.
Apr. 27, 2004 – Name changed to Red Back Mining Inc. prior to May 3, 2004, reverse takeover acquisition of Red Back Mining NL; basis 1 new for 3 old shs. ■

Champion Road Machinery Limited (Can. 1875)
Jan. 1, 1994 – Amalgamated in Canada to continue with same name.
Apr. 15, 1997 – Acquired by VCE Acquisition Inc., a wholly owned Canadian subsid. of Volvo Construction Equipment Corporation, a wholly owned subsid. of AB Volvo of Sweden, for $15 per sh.
Jan. 1, 2001 – Name changed to Volvo Motor Graders Limited.

Champlain Forest Products Limited (Ont. 1970)
Oct. 1974 – Placed into receivership. Assets subsequently sold with no distribution made to unsecured creditors and equity holders. Co. subsequently dissolved.

Champlain Resources Inc. (Alta. Jan. 16, 2002)
Apr. 13, 2012 – Name changed to Beacon Resources Inc.; basis 1 new for 10 old shs. ■

Chan Yellowknife Gold Ltd. (Ont. 1938)
1960 – Charter cancelled.

Chance Mining and Exploration Company Limited (Ont. 1964)
July 3, 1996 – Name changed to East Indies Mining Corporation. ■

Chancellor Energy Resources Inc. (Ont. Nov. 23, 1936)
Apr. 3, 1996 – Acquired by HCO Energy Ltd.; basis 0.32 HCO Energy shs. for 1 Chancellor sh. (see HCO Energy Ltd.)

Chancellor Enterprises Holdings Inc. (Ont. July 27, 1987)
Jan. 1, 2004 – Formed Dynamic Fuel Systems Inc. in Ontario pursuant to reverse takeover acquisition of and amalgamation with Dynamic Fuel Systems Inc. ■

The Chancellor Group Ltd. (Ont. 1981)
Aug. 25, 1989 – Continued into Canada.
June 15, 1992 – Declared bankruptcy. KPMG Inc. was appointed trustee.

Chandalar Resources Ltd. (B.C. 1959)
Apr. 7, 1978 – Amalgamated with International Park West Financial Corp. Ltd. to continue under latter name.

Chandeleur Bay Production Company Ltd. (B.C. Mar. 11, 1987)
Feb. 11, 1999 – Name changed to Golden Raven Resources Ltd.; basis 1 new for 7 old shs. ■

Changfeng Energy Inc. (Can. Jan. 29, 2008 amalg.)
June 18, 2018 – Continued into British Columbia.
Apr. 12, 2019 – Name changed to CF Energy Corp. (see FPsurvey - Industrials)

Changyu Medtech Ltd. (B.C. Dec. 21, 2005)
June 2, 2014 – Dissolved and struck from register.

Channel Bar Mining Co. Ltd. (B.C. 1969)
July 25, 1986 – Struck off register.

Channel Copper Mines Limited (B.C. 1966)
Oct. 7, 1983 – Dissolved.

Channel Gold Resources Corp. (B.C. May 17, 1966)
1979 – Name changed to St. Elias Exploration Corporation; basis 1 new for 5 old shs. ■

Channel i Canada Inc. (Ont. July 6, 1945)
Dec. 7, 1999 – Name changed to Zaurak Capital Corp.; basis 1 new for 12 old shs. ■

Channel Resources Ltd. (B.C. Sept. 7, 1979)
Nov. 1, 1989 – Amalgamated with Que West Resources Ltd. to form new co. with same name Channel Resources Ltd.
Jan. 24, 2014 – Acquired by West African Resources Limited; basis 0.25 West African com. sh. plus 0.125 wt. for 1 Channel com. sh.

Chantrell Ventures Corp. (B.C. July 29, 2004)
June 28, 2019 – Continued into Ontario.
July 5, 2019 – Name changed to O3 Mining Inc. pursuant to reverse takeover acquisition of certain non-core assets from Osisko Mining Inc.; basis 1 new for 40 old shs. ■

Chap Mercantile Inc. (Alta. Aug. 23, 1994)
Dec. 8, 2004 – Name changed to Silver Wheaton Corp.; basis 1 new for 5 old shs. ■

Chaparral Gold Corp. (B.C. Sept. 16, 2013)
Feb. 23, 2015 – Acquired by Waterton Precious Metals Bid Corp., wholly owned subsid. of Waterton Precious Metals Fund II Cayman, LP; basis 61¢ cash per sh.

Chapel Bay Explorations Inc. (Ont. 1983)
Sept. 10, 1985 – Name changed to Chelsea Creek Resources Inc.; basis 1 new for 3 old shs. ■

Chapel Resources Inc. (B.C. 1983)
Sept. 3, 1987 – Name changed to Broadway Beverages Ltd. following reverse takeover acquisition of Broadway Beverages Ltd. ■

Chapleau Resources Ltd. (B.C. Oct. 31, 1983)
Sept. 2, 2009 – Acquired by Magellan Minerals Ltd.; basis 0.267 Magellan shs. for 1 Chapleau sh.

Chapparal Mines Ltd. (B.C. 1968)
1973 – Name changed to Chapparal Petroleums Limited. ■

Chapparal Petroleums Limited (B.C. 1968)
May 1974 – Name changed to Richdale Petroleums Limited; basis 1 new for 5 old shs. ■

Chappie-Mammoth Gold Mines Ltd. (Ont. 1934)
1945 – Acquired by South Shore Gold Mines Ltd.; basis 1 new for 15 old shs. (see South Shore Gold Mines Ltd.)

Chapters Inc. (Ont. Apr. 11, 1995 amalg.)
Aug. 16, 2001 – Formed Indigo Books & Music Inc. in Ontario on amalgamation with Indigo Books & Music, Inc. ■

Chapters Online Inc. (N.B. July 23, 1999)
Nov. 12, 2001 – All o/s shs. not already held acquired by Indigo Books & Music Inc.; basis 1 new Indigo sh. for 7.14 old Chapters shs. (see Indigo Books & Music Inc.)

Chaput Copper Mines Ltd. (Ont. 1943)
1957 – Charter cancelled.

Charan Industries Inc. (Can. 1979)
Jan. 1993 – Dissolved.

Charger Energy Corp. (Alta. Dec. 13, 2006)
Apr. 10, 2013 – Amalgamated with Pace Oil and Gas Ltd. and AvenEx Energy Corp. to form Spyglass Resources Corp. with Pace Oil and Gas the deemed acquiror; basis 1.3 Spyglass shs. for 1 Pace sh., 1 Spyglass sh. for 1 AvenEx and 0.18 Spyglass shs. for 1 Charger sh. (see Spyglass Resources Corp.)

Charger Energy Inc. (Alta. Jan. 14, 1997)
Apr. 15, 2003 – Name changed to Arapahoe Energy Corporation; basis 1 new for 10 old shs. ■

Charger Petroleums Inc. (Alta. Jan. 14, 1997)
Aug. 23, 1999 – Name changed to Charger Energy Inc. ■

Charger Resources Ltd. (B.C. May 28, 1980)
Dec. 21, 1984 – Name changed to Tantalus Resources Ltd.; basis 1 new for 5 old shs. ■

Chargold Resources Ltd. (B.C. Feb. 10, 1988)
May 2, 1996 – Name changed to International Chargold Resources Ltd.; basis 2 new for 1 old sh. ■

Chargood Gold Mines Ltd. (Ont. 1947)
1952 – Charter cancelled.

Chariot Resources Limited (Yuk. Nov. 12, 1996)
Oct. 28, 2004 – Continued into British Columbia.
June 15, 2010 – Acquired by China Sci-Tech Holdings Limited for 67¢ per sh.

Charityville.com International Inc. (Can. Dec. 29, 1982)
July 12, 2000 – Name changed to eNblast productions inc.; basis 1 new for 10 old shs. ■

Charlebois Lake Uranium Ltd. (Can. 1951)
1953 – Acquired by International Ranwick Ltd.; basis 1 new for 4 old shs. (see Consolidated Ranwick Uranium Mines Ltd.)

Charlemagne Oil & Gas Ltd. (B.C. 1981)
Feb. 22, 1984 – Name changed to Charlemagne Resources Ltd. ■

Charlemagne Resources Ltd. (B.C. 1981)
July 22, 1994 – Dissolved and struck off register.

Charles E. Frosst & Co. (Que. 1931)
1965 – All cl. A shs. acquired by Merck & Co. Inc. of Rahway, N.J., under offer of $30 per sh.

Charles Gurd & Co., Limited (Can. 1906)
1947 – Sold to Orange Crush Ltd. (now Crush International Ltd.) for $900,000; shldrs. received $17 per com. sh., which included a divd. of $2.00 per sh. Orange Crush previously controlled Gurd, having acquired 90% of o/s com. stk. under 1946 offer to exchange 2 pref. shs. Orange Crush for 3 com. shs. Gurd.

Charles Long Lac Gold Mines Ltd. (Ont. 1938)
Mar. 15, 1972 – Dissolved.

Charleston Resources Ltd. (B.C. 1969)
Jan. 6, 1988 – Name changed to Envipco Canada Western Inc.; basis 1 new for 4 old shs. ■

Charlie O. Beverages Ltd. (Man. July 5, 1976)
1987 – Continued into British Columbia.
Feb. 13, 1990 – Name changed to Charlie O. Company, Inc. and continued into Wyoming. ■

Charlie O. Company, Inc. (Wyo. Feb. 13, 1990)
Dec. 14, 1995 – Name changed to Sooner Holdings Inc.

Charlim Explorations Ltd. (Can. Aug. 3, 1979)
Oct. 28, 1994 – Created a subsid., Ressources Chastel Inc., to which the Beauchastel property was sold; shldrs. received 1 sh. of Chastel for 10 shs. of Charlim. (see Lithos Corporation)
Nov. 2, 1994 – Amalgamated with Wrightbar Mines Ltd and 3063780 Canada Inc., a wholly owned subsid. of Wrightbar, to form Lithos Corporation; basis 1 new for 2.6 Charlim shs. (see Lithos Corporation)

Charlor Explorations Ltd. (Ont. 1969)
May 30, 1973 – Name changed to Canadian Oriental Holdings Ltd. ■

Charlotte Mines Ltd. (Ont. 1963)
Dec. 5, 1973 – Dissolved.

Charlotte Resources Ltd. (B.C. Mar. 31, 1980)
Oct. 28, 1983 – Name changed to New Pioneer Explorations Ltd.; basis 1 new for 3 old shs. ■

Charlotte Resources Ltd. (B.C. May 16, 2006)
Dec. 24, 2018 – Dissolved and struck from register.

Charm Yellowknife Gold Mines Ltd. (Ont. 1945)
1952 – Charter cancelled.

Charrington Business Consultants Inc. (Ont. June 24, 1996)
Feb. 23, 2001 – Name changed to Digital Duplication Inc. following acquisition of Millennium Compact Disc Industries Inc.; basis 1 new for 3 old shs. ∎

Charta Mines Ltd. (B.C. 1969)
1972 – Merged with Westview Mining Co. Ltd. to continue as Charta Mines Ltd.; basis 2 new for 1 old free sh., and sh. for sh. for escrowed shs.

Charta Mines Ltd. (B.C. 1972 amalg.)
May 27, 1977 – Name changed to Windmill Enterprises Ltd.; basis 1 new for 4 old shs. ∎

Charter Credit Corporation (Que. 1961)
1969 – 99.7%-owned subsid. of Charter Industries Ltd., which acquired control through a sh.-for-sh. offer. (see Charter Industries (1982) Ltd.)

Charter Industries Ltd. (Can. Nov. 1982)
Mar. 4, 1994 – Acquired by International Factors Corp. for $15.60 per sh.

Charter Industries (1982) Ltd. (Que. 1968)
Nov. 1982 – Continued into Canada.
Aug. 18, 1986 – Name changed to Charter Industries Ltd. ∎

Charter Minerals Inc. (B.C. Mar. 20, 1978)
May 21, 1991 – Name changed to New Charter Minerals Inc.; basis 1 new for 2 old shs. ∎

Charter Oil Company Limited (B.C. June 22, 1950)
Sept. 10, 1985 – Name changed to Trans-Dominion Energy Corporation; basis 1 new for 3 old shs. ∎

Charter Real Estate Investment Trust (Ont. Mar. 27, 2007)
Nov. 3, 2010 – Name changed to Partners Real Estate Investment Trust. ∎

Charter Realty Holdings Ltd. (Alta. Apr. 29, 2005)
May 14, 2007 – Converted into an income trust named Charter Real Estate Investment Trust; basis 1 trust unit for 10 com. shs.

Chartered Trust Company (Can. 1905)
Nov. 30, 1963 – Amalgamated with The Eastern Trust Company to form Eastern & Chartered Trust Company; basis 11 new for 10 old shs.

Charterhall Oil Canada Ltd. (Alta. 1974)
Nov. 1, 1985 – Amalgamated into Charterhall North America PLC; basis 1 new for 4.5 old shs. or, 75¢ per 1 old sh.

Charterhouse Preferred Share Index Corporation (Ont. Sept. 22, 2004)
Jan. 30, 2009 – Merged into Jov Leon Frazer Preferred Equity Fund; basis 1.70389 Jov Leon cl. A units for 1 Charterhouse cl. A pref. sh.

Chartwell Seniors Housing Real Estate Investment Trust (Ont. July 7, 2003)
Jan. 11, 2013 – Name changed to Chartwell Retirement Residences. (see FPsurvey - Industrials)

Chartwell Technology Inc. (Alta. Dec. 18, 1995)
July 19, 2011 – Amalgamated with 1606148 Alberta Ltd., a wholly owned subsid. of Amaya Gaming Group Inc.; basis either (i) $0.875 plus 0.125 Amaya shs. or (ii) $0.62 plus 0.21 Amaya shs. for 1 Chartwell sh. (see Amaya Gaming Group Inc.)
July 2011 – Name changed to Amaya (Alberta) Inc. (see Amaya Gaming Group Inc.)

Chartwell Ventures Ltd. (B.C. Dec. 16, 1987)
Dec. 18, 1995 – Continued into Alberta.
Dec. 8, 1998 – Name changed to Chartwell Technology Inc. ∎

The Chase Manhattan Bank of Canada (Can. 1981)
Dec. 31, 2000 – Name changed to J.P. Morgan Chase Bank (Canada).

Chase Resource Corporation (B.C. May 23, 1986)
May 30, 1997 – Amalgamated in British Columbia to continue with same name.
Aug. 29, 2005 – Dissolved and struck from register.

Chataway Exploration Co. Ltd. (B.C. Sept. 27, 1962)
Aug. 11, 1973 – Name changed to Chatex Industries Ltd.; basis 1 new for 4 old shs. ∎

Chatco Steel Products Ltd. (Ont. 1940)
Sept. 23, 1957 – Declared bankrupt; Guaranty Trust Co. of Canada, receiver and manager. Bondhldrs. accepted offer of W. H. Olsen Manufacturing Co. Ltd., giving them 6% bonds in that co. equal to 50% of the princ. amt. of the Chatco bonds; and also possible small amts. of cash receivable from operations by trustee.

Château Construction Inc. (Que. 1973)
Mar. 5, 1981 – Declared bankrupt. No distribution made to unsecured creditors.

Chateau-Gai Wines Ltd. (Can. 1928)
Apr. 30, 1973 – Minority interest acquired by John Labatt Ltd. for $44.75 per sh. (see John Labatt Limited)

Château Stores of Canada Ltd. (Can. June 9, 1969)
July 6, 2000 – Name changed to Le Château Inc. (see FPsurvey - Industrials)

Chatelet Mines Ltd. (Que. 1951)
1964 – Charter cancelled.

Chatex Industries Ltd. (B.C. Sept. 27, 1962)
Feb. 1, 1978 – Name changed to Rhodes Resources Inc.; basis 1 new for 3 old shs. ∎

Chatham Malleable and Steel Products Ltd. (Ont. 1940)
1943 – Name changed to Chatco Steel Products Ltd. ∎

Chatham Resources Ltd. (B.C. 1966)
July 19, 1977 – Name changed to Westmount Resources Ltd.; basis 1 new for 4 old shs. ∎

Chatwood Resources Ltd. (B.C. 1980)
Nov. 10, 1988 – Name changed to Logicon Products Ltd.; basis 1 new for 3 old shs. ∎

Chatworth Resources Inc. (B.C. Aug. 11, 1980)
Dec. 14, 2005 – Amalgamated with ComWest Capital Corp. to form ComWest Enterprise Corp.; basis 0.3333 new cl. A plus 1 cl. B for 1 ComWest sh. and 0.3886 new cl. A or cl. B for 1 Chatworth sh. (see ComWest Enterprise Corp.)

Chauvco Resources Ltd. (Alta. Jan. 16, 1981)
Dec. 22, 1997 – Following Plan of Arrangement with Pioneer Natural Resources Company, each com. sh. exchanged for 1 com. sh. of Chauvco Resources International Ltd. and either (i) 0.493827 of a sh. of Pioneer Natural or (ii) 0.49387 of a Pioneer Natural Resources (Canada) exchangeable sh.

Chava Resources Ltd. (B.C. Nov. 13, 2007)
Nov. 20, 2009 – Name changed to Minaurum Gold Inc. (see FPsurvey - Mines & Energy)

Chavigny Gold Mines Ltd. (Que. 1946)
Sept. 1972 – Charter cancelled.

Chavin of Canada Limited (Ont. 1960)
July 25, 1986 – Amalgamated with Dominion Explorers Limited (1 for 1) to continue as Dominion Explorers Inc.; basis 1 new for 8 old shs.

Cheapside Natural Gas and Oil Co. Ltd. (Ont. 1906)
1960 – Wound up.

Chedabucto Mining Corp. Ltd. (Ont. 1955)
Dec. 12, 1960 – Dissolved.

Cheers International Telemarketing Limited (B.C. Nov. 23, 1983)
Feb. 23, 1990 – Name changed to American Highland Mining Corp.; basis 1 new for 2 old shs. ∎

Cheetah Canyon Resources Corp. (B.C. Feb. 1, 2010)
Mar. 4, 2024 – Struck from register and dissolved.

Cheetah Ventures Ltd. (B.C. Sept. 26, 1988)
Oct. 21, 2010 – Name changed to Emperor Minerals Ltd. ∎

Cheewhat Mining Ltd. (B.C.)
Mar. 18, 1983 – Struck off register.

Chelan Resources Inc. (B.C. 1986)
Aug. 13, 1993 – Dissolved and struck off register.

Chelik Resources Inc. (B.C. Aug. 11, 1986)
Mar. 7, 1989 – Name changed to High Desert Mineral Resources, Inc. ∎

Chellew Gold Mines Ltd. (Ont. 1944)
1955 – Name changed to Chellew Mines Ltd.; basis 1 new for 1 old sh. ∎

Chellew Mines Ltd. (Ont. 1944)
Apr. 30, 1969 – Charter cancelled.

Chelsea Acquisition Corporation (Alta. July 22, 2011)
Dec. 10, 2013 – Formed Pediapharm Inc. in Canada purusant to Qualifying Transaction reverse takeover acquisition of and amalgamation with (old) Pediapharm Inc.; basis 1 new for 3 old shs. ∎

Chelsea Creek Resources Inc. (Ont. 1983)
Dec. 12, 1987 – Name changed to Thunder Bumpers Corporation. ∎

Chelsea Mercantile Bancorp Ltd. (Alta. Sept. 3, 1993)
Mar. 2, 2001 – Struck from registry and dissolved.

Chelsea Minerals Corp. (B.C. 1987)
May 16, 2011 – Acquired by Sennen Resources Ltd.; basis 1 Sennen sh. for 2.5 Chelsea shs. (see Sennen Resources Ltd.)

Chelsea Resources Ltd. (Ont. 1977)
June 5, 1992 – Dissolved and struck off register.

Chemalloy Minerals Limited (Ont. Jan. 15, 1952; via letters patent)
Oct. 23, 1974 – Name changed to International Chemalloy Corporation; basis 1 new for 3 old shs. ∎

Chemaphor Inc. (Can. Aug. 4, 2005 amalg.)
May 25, 2012 – Name changed to Avivagen Inc. ∎

Chembond Limited (Ont. Oct. 4, 1977)
Jan. 25, 2002 – Acquired by Mapei Acquisition Inc. for $0.10 per sh.

Chemcell Limited (Can. Jan. 26, 1926)
Dec. 1971 – Name changed to Celanese Canada Limited. ∎

Chemcell (1963) Limited (Can. Jan. 26, 1926)
June 1966 – Name changed to Chemcell Limited. ∎

Chemesis International Inc. (B.C. Apr. 26, 2013)
Nov. 22, 2022 – Name changed to Refined Metals Corp. ∎

Chemical Bank of Canada (Can. May 28, 1974)
Nov. 1, 1996 – Amalgamated with The Chase Manhattan Bank of Canada.

Chemistree Technology Inc. (B.C. Mar. 14, 2008)
June 24, 2024 – Name changed to Waverunner Capital Inc.; basis 1 new for 10 old shs. (see FPsurvey - Industrials)

Chemtrade Electrochem Inc. (Alta. Mar. 17, 2011)
Mar. 14, 2017 – All o/s com. shs. acquired by a wholly owned subsid. of Chemtrade Logistics Income Fund; basis $1.65 cash per sh.

Cheney Mines Ltd. (unknown)
May 16, 1960 – Charter cancelled; cash distribution of 1.25¢ per sh.

Cheni Gold Mines Inc. (Can. Dec. 28, 1966)
Jan. 19, 1995 – Amalgamated with Meota Resources Corp. to form 2 new companies, one named Cheni Resources Inc. and the other Meota Resources Corp.; basis 1 Cheni Resources sh. plus 0.20 Meota cl. A shs. for 1 Cheni Gold sh. (see Meota Resources Corp.)

Cheni Resources Inc. (Can. Nov. 14, 1994)
Oct. 23, 2000 – Continued into Ontario.
Nov. 24, 2000 – Name changed to Rodin Communications Corporation. (see FPsurvey - Industrials)

Chennault Gold Mines Ltd. (Ont. 1945)
Nov. 6, 1952 – Charter cancelled.

Cherish Properties Inc. (unknown)
June 17, 1974 – Amalgamated with Unicorp Financial Inc. to form Unicorp Financial Corporation; basis 901,800 new for 1,670 old shs.

Cherokee Developments Ltd. (B.C. Apr. 8, 1975)
Nov. 5, 1982 – Name changed to International Cherokee Developments Ltd.; basis 1 new for 3 old shs. ■

Cherokee Gold Mines Limited (Ont. 1946)
July 27, 1959 – Dissolved.

Cherokee Resources Limited (Alta. 1979)
Oct. 21, 1983 – Amalgamated with a wholly owned subsid. of Canusa Energy Ltd.; basis 1.425 shs. plus wt. to purchase 0.625 com. sh. at $3.50 for 1 old sh.

Cherry Lake Mines Ltd. (Ont. 1946)
Apr. 1951 – Name changed to Norzinc Mines Ltd. ■

Cherry Lane Fashion Group (North America) Ltd. (B.C. June 22, 1978)
July 8, 1998 – Name changed to Maracote International Resources Inc. ■

Cherry Street Capital Inc. (Ont. June 5, 2017)
Mar. 15, 2021 – Name changed to Tribe Property Technologies Inc. pursuant to the reverse takeover acquisition of (old) Tribe Property Technologies Inc. and concurrent amalgamation of (old) Tribe with wholly owned 1283534 B.C. Ltd. (and continued as Tribe Property Holdings Inc.).; basis 1 new for 8.4488 old shs. (see FPsurvey - Industrials)

Cherryhill Resources Inc. (Alta. May 8, 1997)
Dec. 6, 2000 – Formed Daedalian eSolutions Inc. in Ontario on reverse takeover acquisition of and amalgamation with Daedalian Systems Group Inc.; basis 1 new for 3 old shs. ■

Cheryl Resources Inc. (B.C. 1979)
Nov. 9, 1989 – Amalgamated with Exador Resources Inc. (1 for 13) and Argo Development Corp. (1 for 2.5) to form a new co. named Tymar Resources Inc.; basis 1 new for 2 old shs. (see Tymar Resources Inc.)

Chesapeake Computer Systems Inc. (B.C. June 13, 1980)
Nov. 1, 1991 – Dissolved and struck off register.

Chesbar Chibougamau Mines Ltd. (Que. Apr. 5, 1956)
June 12, 1969 – Name changed to Chesbar Iron Powder Ltd.; basis 1 new for 5 old shs. ■

Chesbar Iron Powder Ltd. (Que. Apr. 5, 1956)
Mar. 28, 1973 – Name changed to Chesbar Resources Inc. ■

Chesbar Resources Inc. (Que. Apr. 5, 1956)
June 26, 2003 – Name changed to Jaguar Nickel Inc. ■

Chesgo Mines Ltd. (Ont. 1945)
June 3, 1965 – Charter cancelled.

Cheskirk Mines Ltd. (Ont. 1945)
1965 – Name changed to Green Point Mines Ltd.; basis 1 new for 5 old shs. ■

Cheslynn Mines Ltd. (Ont. 1945)
Sept. 1960 – Charter cancelled.

Chess Mining Corp. (Que. 1955)
Aug. 20, 1966 – Dissolved.

Chess Uranium Corp. Ltd. (Que. 1955)
1958 – Name changed to Chess Mining Corp. ■

Chessminster Group Limited (Can. 1984)
Nov. 9, 1989 – Formed Pyrok Group Plc following merger dated Aug. 22, 1989; basis 1 new for 1 old sh.

Chesstown Capital Inc. (Ont. Nov. 24, 2006)
Aug. 9, 2011 – Name changed to Falcon Gold Corp. ■

Chesswood Income Fund (Ont. Feb. 16, 2006)
Jan. 1, 2011 – Succeeded by Chesswood Group Limited pursuant to plan of arrangement whereby Chesswood Group Limited was formed to facilitate the conversion of the fund into a corporation and the fund was subsequently dissolved. (see FPsurvey - Industrials)

Chestermere Development Ltd. (Alta. 1953)
Oct. 15, 1960 – Struck off register.

Chesterville Larder Lake Gold Mining Co. Ltd. (Ont. 1907)
1946 – Name changed to Chesterville Mines Ltd. ■

Chesterville Mines Ltd. (Ont. 1907)
Nov. 9, 1976 – Charter cancelled.

Chetwynd Resources Inc. (Ont. 1986)
Sept. 3, 1994 – Dissolved.

Chevron Corporation (Del. 1926)
Oct. 10, 2001 – Name changed to ChevronTexaco Corporation. ■

ChevronTexaco Corporation (Del. 1926)
May 10, 2005 – Name changed to Chevron Corporation.

Chevy Development Corporation (B.C. Dec. 3, 1980)
Sept. 2, 1992 – Name changed to International Cargocare Incorporated. ■

Chevy Oil Corporation (B.C. Dec. 3, 1980)
July 2, 1985 – Name changed to Chevy Development Corporation. ■

Cheyenne Energy Inc. (Alta. Oct. 6, 1997)
Feb. 11, 2008 – Placed into receivership. RSM Richter Inc. appointed receiver.

Cheyenne Petroleum Corporation (B.C. 1973 amalg.)
May 27, 1985 – Continued into Canada.
May 2, 2002 – Struck from register and dissolved.

Chib-Kayrand Copper Mines Limited (Ont. 1937)
Nov. 24, 1981 – Amalgamated with Cinequity Corporation to continue under name of latter co.; basis 1 new for 5 Chib-Kayrand shs.

La-Chib Mines Ltd. (Ont. 1959)
Dec. 23, 1987 – Name changed to Lachib Development Corporation; basis 1 new for 10 old shs. ■

Chibex Ltd. (Que. 1970)
Jan. 25, 1986 – Charter cancelled.

Chiblow Mines Ltd. (Ont. 1964)
1969 – Merged into Alchib Developments Ltd.; basis 31 Alchib for 100 Chiblow shs.

Chibmac Mines Limited (Que. Mar. 23, 1936)
Nov. 7, 1952 – Acquired by Sulphur Converting Corp.; basis 1 new for 15 old shs.

Chibou-Wica Goldfields Ltd. (Ont. 1946)
1952 – Charter cancelled.

Chiboug Copper Corporation Ltd. (Que. Jan. 24, 1953)
Jan. 24, 1995 – Name changed to Guyana Goldfields Inc.; basis 1 new for 4 old shs. ■

Chibougamau-Brunswick Minerals Ltd. (N.B. 1956)
Dec. 1959 – Charter cancelled.

Chibougamau Explorers Ltd. (Que. 1950)
1956 – Assets acquired by Anacon Lead Mines Ltd.; basis 1 new for 3 old shs.

Chibougamau Jaculet Mines Ltd. (Ont. Feb. 18, 1932)
1960 – Acquired by Copper Rand Chibougamau Mines Ltd.; basis 1 new for 5 old shs. (see Copper Rand Chibougamau Mines Ltd.)

Chibougamau Mining & Smelting Co. Inc. (Que. 1953)
Oct. 25, 1978 – Name changed to Les Mines C.M. & S. Inc. ■

Chibougamau Smelter Inc. (Que. 1953)
1954 – Name changed to Chibougamau Mining & Smelting Co. Inc. ■

Chibtown Copper Corp. (Que. 1956)
Name changed to Rainbow Mines Limited; basis 1 new for 1 old sh. ■

Chicobi Lake Mines Limited (Ont. 1951)
July 19, 1982 – Dissolved.

Chief Mountain Oils Limited (Alta. 1948)
1971 – Wound up.

Chief Redwater Oils Ltd. (Ont. Oct. 6, 1948)
1952 – Assets sold to West Plains Resources Ltd.; basis 1 new for 5 old shs.

Chief Sioux Mining Company Ltd. (Ont. 1944)
1952 – Charter cancelled.

Chieftain Development Co. Ltd. (Alta. 1964)
Aug. 31, 1988 – All o/s com. shs. and wts. acquired by Alberta Energy Company Ltd. (see Alberta Energy Company Ltd.)

Chieftain International, Inc. (Alta. Nov. 23, 1988)
Feb. 22, 1989 – Amalgamated in Alberta to continue with same name.
Aug. 8, 2001 – Acquired by Hunt Oil Canadian Acquisition III Corporation, a wholly owned subsid. of Hunt Oil Corporation, for US$29 per sh.

Chieftain Metals Corp. (Ont. Apr. 10, 2013)
Sept. 6, 2016 – Placed into receivership and Grant Thornton Limited appointed receiver and manager.
Aug. 2017 – Amended proposal was court approved under which certain of the company's liabilities would be restructured through the distribution of a lump sum in the maximum aggregate amount of $150,000. Crown claims and preferred claims to be paid in full before any distributions of the net balance to the holders of ordinary claims, up to a maximum of 5¢ on the dollar.
Mar. 26, 2018 – Certificate of incorporation cancelled and company dissolved.
Oct. 2020 – Grant Thornton, as receiver, was discharged after no purchaser for the company's assets was found and was deemed in the best interest of stakeholders to terminate the receivership.

Chieftain Metals Inc. (Ont. Nov. 16, 2009)
May 22, 2013 – Succeeded by Chieftain Metals Corp. pursuant to plan of arrangement and reorganization. All assets were transferred to newly formed Chieftain Metals Corp. and Chieftain Metals Inc. became a wholly owned subsidiary of Chieftain Metals Corp. ■

Chieftain Pershing Gold Mines Ltd. (Ont. 1944)
1958 – Charter cancelled.

Chiefton Exploration Ltd. (B.C. 1952)
May 1958 – Dissolved.

Chilco Resources Ltd. (unknown)
Sept. 9, 1980 – Amalgamated with wholly owned subsid. of Bonanza Oil & Gas Ltd. Shldrs. of Chilco received $3.40 for each Chilco sh., or 1 Bonanza sh. for each 3.3 Chilco shs.

Chilcotin Silver Mines Ltd (B.C. 1968)
Jan. 1975 – Charter cancelled.

Childs Red Lake Gold Mines Ltd. (Ont. 1945)
Nov. 1959 – Charter cancelled.

Chilean Gold Ltd. (B.C. Nov. 7, 1996)
May 23, 2002 – Name changed to Earth Star Diamonds Ltd. ∎

Chilean Metals Inc. (B.C. Aug. 19, 1987)
July 12, 2021 – Name changed to Power Nickel Inc. ∎

Chillicopper Corporation Limited (Ont. 1950)
Nov. 7, 1976 – Dissolved.

Chilliwack Telephones Ltd. (B.C. 1928)
Aug. 1, 1954 – Assets acquired by British Columbia Telephone Co., Ltd. for $679,000. O/s 5% pref. shs. redeemed July 1954. All ord. shs. were owned by Anglo-Canadian Telephone Co.

Chimata Gold Corp. (B.C. Nov. 16, 2010)
Feb. 14, 2019 – Name changed to CAT Strategic Metals Corporation. (see FPsurvey - Mines & Energy)

Chimera Resources Ltd. (B.C. 1982)
Aug. 9, 1985 – Name changed to E.S.I. Industries Corp.; basis 1 new for 3 old shs. ∎

Chimney Creek-Fraser Placer Mines Ltd. (Ont. 1944)
1956 – Charter cancelled.

Chimo Gold Mines Limited (Ont. 1945)
Aug. 20, 1982 – Amalgamated with Conwest Exploration Company Limited (1 new cl. A and cl. B for 1 cl. A and cl. B), Central Patricia Limited (1.1 new cl. B for 1 com.), International Mogul Mines Limited (2 new cl. B for 1 com. and 1 new ser. A pfd. for 1 old 6% 1st pfd.) and 465128 Ontario Limited (0.88 new cl. A for 1 com.) to form a new co. also named Conwest Exploration Company Limited; basis either $2.20 or 0.3 new Conwest cl. B sh. for 1 old Chimo com. sh. (see Conwest Exploration Company Limited)

China Cellular Communications Corp. (B.C. June 24, 1986)
Dec. 9, 1993 – Name changed to China Jinrong Corp. ∎

China Clipper Gold Mines Ltd. (Ont. June 27, 1996)
Apr. 27, 2001 – Name changed to Kinloch Resources Inc.; basis 1 new for 13 old shs. ∎

China Coal Corporation (B.C. May 23, 2006)
Nov. 3, 2014 – Dissolved for failure to file and struck from register.

China Commercial Corporation Ltd. (B.C. Feb. 20, 1969)
July 13, 1984 – Dissolved and struck off register.

China Diamond Corp. (Yuk. Oct. 8, 1997)
Apr. 30, 2008 – Dissolved.

China Drill Corporation (B.C. June 28, 2007)
Dec. 3, 2008 – Name changed to Yalian Steel Corporation on Qualifying Transaction reverse takeover acquisition of 85% interest in Yangzhou Yalian Steel Pipe Co., Ltd. ∎

China 88 Capital Corp. (Alta. Sept. 15, 2009)
Nov. 24, 2011 – Name changed to GeoVenCap Inc.; basis 1 new for 5 old shs. ∎

China First Capital Corp. (B.C. 1981)
July 20, 1990 – Amalgamated with a numbered co., 174389 Canada Limited, (a wholly owned subsid. of Black Hawk Mining Inc.). (see Black Hawk Mining Inc.)

China Green Star Agricultural Corporation (Ont. Aug. 7, 2007)
July 5, 2013 – Name changed to GreenStar Agricultural Corporation. ∎

China Growth Capital Inc. (Can. June 12, 2007)
Apr. 15, 2008 – Name changed to CAG Capital Inc. ∎

China Growth Enterprises Corp. (B.C. 1987)
Feb. 27, 1996 – Name changed to TS Telecom Ltd. ∎

China Health Labs & Diagnostics Ltd. (Cayman Islands Oct. 22, 2010)
Jan. 13, 2014 – Acquired by Century Delight Investment Limited for $0.62 per sh.

China International Enterprises Inc. (Can. June 20, 2000)
Nov. 14, 2006 – Name changed to China Software Technology Group Co., Ltd. and continued into Delaware.

China Jinrong Corp. (B.C. June 24, 1986)
June 25, 1996 – Name changed to Rystar Development Ltd.; basis 1 new for 4 old shs. ∎

China Minerals Mining Corporation (B.C. Jan. 18, 2006)
Aug. 24, 2018 – Name changed to Wildsky Resources Inc. (see FPsurvey - Mines & Energy)

China One Corporation (Can. Jan. 24, 2007)
Dec. 2, 2008 – Continued into Cayman Islands.
Aug. 17, 2009 – Name changed to IND DairyTech Limited. ∎

China Opportunities Fund (Ont. Feb. 22, 1994)
Apr. 26, 1999 – All o/s units called for redemption; basis $15.92 per unit.

China Opportunity Inc. (Ont. July 24, 2007)
June 29, 2011 – Name changed to Gondwana Gold Inc. ∎

China Sea Resources Corporation (B.C. 1983)
Apr. 16, 1993 – Dissolved and struck off register.

China Select Capital Partners Corp. (B.C. Sept. 12, 2007)
Oct. 19, 2011 – Name changed to Urban Select Capital Corporation. ∎

China Ventures Inc. (B.C. Mar. 31, 2000 amalg.)
Dec. 16, 2004 – Name changed to China Education Resources Inc.; basis 1 new for 5 old shs. (see FPsurvey - Industrials)

China Wind Power International Corp. (Ont. July 31, 2009 amalg.)
Dec. 2016 – Distribution of $0.1314 cash per sh. to shldrs. of record Aug. 23, 2016.
Nov. 8, 2017 – Voluntarily dissolved and removed from register.

Chinacom Technologies Inc. (B.C. Apr. 12, 1998)
Apr. 26, 2002 – Qualifying Transaction Plan of Arrangement with Emercap Ventures Inc. (1 for 2.7173) and Syntegra Investment Corp. (1 for 4.2953) to continue as VendTek Systems Inc.; basis 1 new VendTek for 2 old Chinacom. shs. (see VendTek Systems Inc.)

Chinapintza Mining Corp. (B.C. June 14, 2013)
Oct. 30, 2020 – Name changed to Thesis Gold Inc. following acquisition of Ranch gold prospect. ∎

Chinook Capital Corp. (B.C. July 6, 2007)
June 15, 2009 – Together with Bowram Energy Inc., Woodbridge Energy Ltd. and Fortriu Capital Corp., exchanged their respective net cash for shares of Terrace Resources Inc., all Capital Pool Companies, and each of Chinook, Bowram, Woodbridge and Fortriu subsequently dissolved; basis 1 Terrace sh. for 0.53 Bowram shs., 1 Terrace sh. for 0.43 Woodbridge shs., 1 Terrace sh. for 0.55 Fortriu shs. and 1 Terrace sh. for 0.56 Chinook shs. (see Terrace Resources Inc.)

Chinook Energy Inc. (Alta. June 29, 2010 amalg.)
Apr. 23, 2020 – Acquired by Tourmaline Oil Corp.; basis $0.0675 cash per sh.

Chinook Energy Services Inc. (Alta. Jan. 3, 1997)
Nov. 8, 2002 – Name changed to Deep Resources Ltd. ∎

Chinook Oils Ltd. (unknown)
1947 – Assets taken over by Coastal Oils Ltd. (see Coastal Oils Ltd.)

Chinook Testing Inc. (Alta. Jan. 3, 1997)
Feb. 1, 2000 – Merged with Roth Radiography & Inspection Services Ltd. to continue with the same name Chinook Testing Inc. for total consideration of $4,800,000.
Oct. 22, 2001 – Name changed to Chinook Energy Services Inc.; basis 1 new for 5 old shs. ∎

Chinook Tyee Industry Limited (Alta. Jan. 30, 1997)
Apr. 16, 2014 – Continued into British Columbia.
Aug. 22, 2019 – Name changed to AMP German Cannabis Group Inc. ∎

Chip Mines Ltd. (Ont. 1954)
Aug. 9, 1972 – Charter cancelled.

Chipman Energy Ltd. (Que. 1970)
May 15, 1996 – Name changed to Avatar Energy Inc.; basis 1 new for 4.5 old shs. ∎

Chipman Lake Mines Ltd. (Ont. 1949)
Feb. 1971 – Sold assets to Chipman Mining and Energy Corporation Ltd.; basis 1 new for 7 old shs.

Chipman Lake Uranium Mines Ltd. (Ont. 1949)
Oct. 1951 – Name changed to Chipman Lake Mines Ltd. ∎

Chipman Mining and Energy Corporation Ltd. (Que. 1970)
Aug. 12, 1994 – Name changed to Chipman Energy Ltd. ∎

Chirripo Resources Inc. (Alta. May 27, 1997)
Mar. 7, 2006 – Acquired by Milagro Energy Inc.; basis 0.5 new Milagro sh. plus $0.50 for 1 old Chirripo sh.

Chisel Lake Mines Ltd. (Ont. 1957)
1965 – Name changed to File Lake Explorations Ltd. ∎

Chisholm Resources Inc. (B.C. Apr. 4, 1972)
Aug. 25, 1989 – Dissolved and struck off register.

ChitrChatr Communications Inc. (B.C. Aug. 22, 2013)
Feb. 4, 2019 – Dissolved and struck from registry.
Nov. 25, 2019 – Restored to registry.
Dec. 6, 2024 – Name changed to Kannika Resources Inc. (see FPsurvey - Industrials)

Chix Mining Corporation Limited (Que. 1971)
May 1980 – Charter cancelled.

Chlormet Technologies Inc. (B.C. June 24, 2004)
Nov. 13, 2015 – Name changed to PUF Ventures Inc. ∎

Chocolate Pix Corporation (Ont. 1985)
Apr. 7, 1994 – Name changed to CPX Industries Inc.; basis 1 new for 5 old com. shs. and 1 new for 10 old ser. A special subord. vtg. shs. ∎

Choice Consolidation Corp. (B.C. Jan. 16, 2021)
Aug. 18, 2022 – All o/s cl. A restricted vtg. shs. redeemed for US$10.0169 cash per sh.

Choice Foods Corporation (Alta. Mar. 25, 1986)
Feb. 20, 1995 – Name changed to White Swan Resources Inc.; basis 1 new for 10 old shs. ∎

Choice Gold Corp. (B.C. Oct. 16, 2009)
Oct. 21, 2014 – Formed Copperbank Resources Corp. in British Columbia following its amalgamation with 0999279 B.C. Ltd., a spin-off of International Enexco Limited and 1016777 B.C. Ltd., a spin-off Full Metals Minerals Ltd. ∎

Choice Resources Corp. (B.C. Mar. 9, 1977)
Sept. 29, 2004 – Continued into Alberta.
Aug. 3, 2007 – Formed Buffalo Resources Corp. in Alberta on amalgamation with The Buffalo Oil Corporation following reverse takeover acquisition of Buffalo Oil; basis 1 new for 1 Buffalo Oil sh. and 0.474 new for 1 Choice sh. ∎

Choice Software Systems Ltd. (Alta. July 18, 1985)
Oct. 30, 1995 – Name changed to Timbuktu Gold Corp.; basis 1 new for 4.56 old shs. ∎

ChondroGene Limited (Ont. Feb. 20, 1997)
Oct. 20, 2006 – Name changed to GeneNews Limited. ■

Chontor Mining Corp. Ltd. (Ont. 1955)
June 1970 – Name changed to Willand Publishing Ltd.

Choom Holdings Inc. (B.C. Sept. 18, 2006)
Sept. 28, 2022 – Filed an assignment under the
Bankruptcy and Insolvency Act. Ernst & Young Inc.
appointed trustee.

Chopp Computer Corporation Inc. (B.C. 1983)
Nov. 14, 1986 – Sullivan Computer Corp. of New York
acquired all shs. of the company. Sullivan subsequently
changed its name to CHoPP Computer Corporation,
obtained listing on NASDAQ and voluntarily delisted from
VSE.
Feb. 25, 1999 – Name changed to Ants Software.com;
basis 1 new for 1 old sh.

Chopper Mines Ltd. (B.C. Sept. 14, 1979)
Nov. 9, 1984 – Name changed to Dragoon Resources
Ltd.; basis 1 new for 5 old shs. ■

Christian Creek Mines Ltd. (B.C. 1966)
Dec. 1968 – Name changed to Canwex Explorations
Ltd. ■

Christie Base Metals Ltd. (Que. 1952)
Charter cancelled.

Christie Lake Mines Ltd. (Ont. 1956)
May 27, 1965 – Dissolved.

Christina Explorations Ltd. (B.C. June 23, 1987)
Aug. 3, 1990 – Name changed to I.E.S. Technologies
Corp. ■

Christina Gold Resources Ltd. (B.C. Jan. 18, 1979)
Dec. 11, 1998 – Name changed to Powerhouse Energy
Corp.; basis 1 new for 2 old shs. ■

Christina Lake Mines Ltd. (B.C. June 16, 1964)
Apr. 17, 1979 – Name changed to Christina Resources
Limited. ■

Christina Lake Mines Ltd. (B.C. 1964)
Dec. 6, 1976 – Charter cancelled; revived, date unknown.

Christina Resources Limited (B.C. June 16, 1964)
Feb. 12, 1986 – Name changed to Airborne Data
Marketing Ltd. ■

Christman-Deer Mining Co. Ltd. (Ont. 1956)
Apr. 1967 – Charter cancelled.

Christo Quebec Gold Mines Ltd. (Ont. 1945)
1954 – Merged into Pardee Amalgamated Mines Ltd.;
basis 2 new for 85 old shs.

Christopher James Gold Corp. (B.C. Oct. 27, 1989)
Nov. 16, 2010 – Name changed to Gunpoint Exploration
Ltd.; basis 1 new for 10 old shs. (see FPsurvey - Mines
& Energy)

Christopher Silver Mines Ltd. (Ont. 1950)
1959 – Assets acquired by Agnico Mines Limited; basis
1 new for 5 old shs. (see Agnico Mines Limited)

Chromasco Corp. Ltd. (Ont. 1941)
June 1, 1974 – Amalgamated with subsids., Light Alloys
Corp. Ltd., and Chromium Mining & Smelting Corp. Ltd.
to form Chromasco Ltd.; basis 8 new for 1 old sh.

Chromasco Limited (Ont. June 1, 1974 amalg.)
July 23, 1980 – Continued into Canada.
Jan. 20, 1984 – Name changed to Timminco Limited. ■

Chrome Capital Inc. (Alta. Oct. 4, 2006)
Dec. 23, 2009 – Formed Blacksteel Energy Inc. in Alberta
following Qualifying Transaction amalgamation of wholly
owned 1495021 Alberta Ltd. with Blacksteel Oil Sands
Inc., constituting a reverse takeover by Blacksteel Oil
Sands. Chrome changed its name to Blacksteel Energy
Inc. and subsequently amalgamated with wholly owned

Blacksteel Oil Sands; basis 1 Blacksteel Energy sh. for
5 Chrome shs. (see FPsurvey - Mines & Energy)

ChroMedX Corp. (Ont. Sept. 8, 2014)
July 9, 2018 – Name changed to Relay Medical Corp. ■

Chromex Nickel Mines Ltd. (Can. Jan. 26, 1966)
Oct. 3, 1994 – Amalgamated with Kleena Kleene Gold
Mines Ltd. to form Maiden Creek Mining Company Inc.;
basis 1 new for 1 Chromex sh.

Chromite Ltd. (Que. 1940)
Jan. 1961 – Reported wound up. Distribution of 39.065¢
per sh.

Chromium Mining & Smelting Corp. Ltd. (Ont. 1934)
June 1, 1974 – Amalgamated with Chromasco Corp. Ltd.
and subsid. to form Chromasco Ltd.

Chromos Capital Corp. (B.C. Nov. 19, 2020)
June 17, 2021 – Name changed to Verses Technologies
Inc. pursuant to the reverse takeover acquisition of (old)
Verses Technologies Incorporated and concurrent
amalgamation of (old) Verses with wholly owned 1288098
B.C. Ltd. (and continued as Verses Holdings Inc.). ■

Chromos Molecular Systems Inc. (B.C. Nov. 22, 1995)
June 30, 2008 – Dissolved following spin-off of assets to
Calyx Bio-Ventures Inc. and amalgamation of wholly
owned 0828688 B.C. Ltd. with Modatech Systems Inc.
to form CHR Investment Corporation. Each Chromo shldr.
received 0.1 Calyx com. shs. and 1 CHR cl. A pref. sh.

Chrysalis Capital III Corporation (Ont. Mar. 23, 2006)
Feb. 28, 2007 – Name changed to U.S. Silver Corporation
following Qualifying Transaction reverse takeover
acquisition of Delaware-incorporated U.S. Silver
Corporation (subsequently renamed United States Silver,
Inc.). ■

Chrysalis Capital IV Corporation (Can. Oct. 12, 2006)
Mar. 5, 2008 – Name changed to Homeland Energy
Group Ltd. following Qualifying Transaction acquisition
of Homeland Energy Corp.; basis 1 new for 2 old shs. ■

Chrysalis Capital V Corporation (Can. Feb. 8, 2007)
Nov. 14, 2008 – Name changed to Enssolutions Group
Inc. pursuant to Qualifying Transaction reverse takeover
acquisition of Enssolutions Ltd. and amalgamation with
wholly owned Chrysalis Capital V (ENS) Corporation on
Oct. 30, 2008, to continue as Enssolutions Ltd. ■

Chrysalis Capital VI Corporation (Can. July 11, 2007)
July 20, 2010 – Name changed to Exclamation
Investments Corporation pursuant to Qualifying
Transaction acquisition of Exclamation Investments
Corporation. (see FPsurvey - Industrials)

Chrysalis Capital VII Corporation (Can. Apr. 30, 2008)
Oct. 5, 2010 – Name changed to Alexander Nubia
International Inc. pursuant to Qualifying Transaction
reverse takeover acquisition of Alexander Nubia Inc. ■

Chrysalis Capital VIII Corporation (Can. Oct. 12, 2010)
Feb. 5, 2013 – Name changed to Spectra7 Microsystems
Inc. pursuant to Qualifying Transaction reverse takeover
acquisitions of Fresco Microchip Inc. (deemed acquiror)
and RedMere Technology Limited; basis 1 new for
3.86364 old shs. ■

Chrysalis Capital IX Corporation (Can. Sept. 17, 2013)
July 7, 2010 – Continued into British Columbia.
July 7, 2015 – Name changed to Inspira Financial Inc.
following reverse takeover acquisition of (old) Inspira
Financial Inc.; basis 1 new for 1.765 old shs. ■

Chrysalis Capital Corporation (Ont. Oct. 1, 2003)
June 17, 2005 – Name changed to PharmEng
International Inc. following Qualifying Transaction reverse
takeover acquisition of PharmEng Technology Inc.; basis
1 new for 1 old sh. ■

Chrysalis Capital II Corporation (Ont. June 18, 2004)
July 26, 2006 – Continued into Canada.
Aug. 1, 2006 – Name changed to Tangarine Payment
Solutions Corp. pursuant to the Aug. 1, 2006, Qualifying
Transaction reverse takeover acquisition of Tangarine
Concepts Corporation and amalgamation of Tangarine
Concepts with wholly owned 6583425 Canada Inc.; basis
1 new for 3 old shs. ■

Chrysler Canada Inc. (Can. June 17, 1925)
Feb. 4, 2015 – Name changed to FCA Canada Inc.

Chrysler Canada Ltd. (Can. June 17, 1925)
June 15, 1999 – Name changed to DaimlerChrysler
Canada Inc. ■

Chrysler Corporation (Del. 1925)
Nov. 13, 1998 – Amalgamated with Daimler-Benz AG to
form DaimlerChrysler AG; basis 1 new for 1 Daimler-Benz
sh. and 0.547 new ordinary shs. for 1 Chrysler com. sh.
(see Daimler AG)

Chrysler Credit Canada Ltd. (Can. Oct. 31, 1987)
Jan. 1, 2000 – Formed DaimlerChrysler Financial
Services (debis) Canada Inc. in Canada following merger
with Mercedes-Benz Credit of Canada Inc. ■

The Chrysler Mining Syndicate Limited (B.C.)
Nov. 13, 1930 – Struck off register.

Chrysos Capital Corporation (Can. Jan. 16, 2008)
Mar. 1, 2010 – Name changed to Frontline Gold
Corporation pursuant to Qualifying Transaction acquisition
of mineral properties of Merrex Gold Inc. and of Société
Touba Mining S.A.R.L. (see FPsurvey - Mines & Energy)

Chuan Hup Canada Limited (B.C. Feb. 22, 1983)
June 30, 1992 – Name changed to IGT International
Growth Technologies Inc.; basis 1 new for 4 old shs. ■

Chuco Gold Mines Ltd. (Ont. 1948)
May 11, 1957 – Charter cancelled.

Chudleigh Ventures Inc. (Ont. May 9, 2008)
Aug. 18, 2010 – Name changed to Xylitol Canada Inc.
following Apr. 22, 2010, Qualifying Transaction reverse
takeover acquisition of Sweet Diabetic Delight Foods
Inc. ■

Chukuni Gold Mines Ltd. (Ont. June 28, 1945)
Oct. 2, 1985 – Name changed to Chukuni Resources
Inc.; basis 1 new for 10 old shs. ■

Chukuni Resources Inc. (Ont. June 28, 1945)
Jan. 3, 1995 – Delisted from the CDN. Subsequently
dissolved and charter cancelled.

Churchill Copper Corp. Ltd. (B.C. 1964)
July 20, 1972 – Name changed to Consolidated Churchill
Copper Corporation Ltd.; basis 1 new for 10 old shs. ■

The Churchill Corporation (Alta. Aug. 31, 1981 amalg.)
Dec. 31, 1987 – Amalgamated in Alberta to continue with
same name.
May 22, 2014 – Name changed to Stuart Olson Inc. ■

Churchill Energy Inc. (B.C. Apr. 9, 1980)
Jan. 21, 1986 – Name changed to Consolidated Churchill
Enterprises Inc.; basis 1 new for 1.82 old shs. ■

Churchill Energy Inc. (Sask. July 23, 2003)
June 29, 2006 – Continued into Alberta. (see Zargon
Energy Trust)
Sept. 28, 2009 – Acquired by Zargon Energy Trust; basis
0.01363 Zargon trust units or 22¢ per sh. or a combination
thereof for 1 Churchill com. sh. (see Zargon Energy Trust)

Churchill Growth Industrial AA Communications Inc.
(Ont. July 3, 1986)
June 29, 1987 – Name changed to The Telecommerce
Corporation. ■

Churchill Petroleums Inc. (B.C. 1978)
Jan. 31, 1983 – Name changed to Packard Resources
Ltd. ■

Churchill Resources Ltd. (B.C. May 30, 1986)
Aug. 18, 1997 – Amalgamated with Greystar Resources Ltd. to form new co. with same name Greystar Resources Ltd.; basis 1 new for 1 Greystar sh. and 1.3 new for 1 Churchill sh. (see Greystar Resources Ltd.)

Churchill River Mines Ltd. (Ont. 1955)
July 5, 1956 – Name changed to Val Jon Explorations Ltd. ■

Churchill Sbec Ltd. (Alta. Aug. 31, 1981 amalg.)
July 30, 1985 – Name changed to The Churchill Corporation. ■

Chuska Resources Corporation (B.C. 1980)
Mar. 30, 1993 – Acquired by Harken Energy Corporation; basis 1.2618 Harken shs. for 1 Chuska sh.

Chutine Resources Ltd. (B.C. Mar. 6, 1981)
1988 – Continued into Ontario.
Mar. 15, 1995 – Name changed to International CHS Resource Corporation; basis 1 new for 10 old shs. ■

Chyka Mines Ltd. (Ont. 1954)
Sept. 28, 1964 – Charter cancelled.

Cibola Red Lake Mines Ltd. (Ont. 1946)
Nov. 6, 1961 – Charter cancelled.

Cicada Ventures Ltd. (B.C. June 10, 1980)
Sept. 23, 2019 – Name changed to Tymbal Resources Ltd.; basis 1 new for 10 old shs. ■

Ciclo Capital Ltd. (Can. Oct. 2, 1996)
June 1, 1999 – Amalgamated with Comoro Capital Ltd. to form new co. with same name Ciclo Capital Ltd.; basis 1 new for 5 Comoro shs. and 1 new for 1 Ciclo sh. (see Patent Enforcement and Royalties Limited)
June 28, 1999 – Continued into Ontario. (see Patent Enforcement and Royalties Limited)
July 22, 1999 – Amalgamated with Patent Enforcement and Royalties Ltd. to continue as a new company named Patent Enforcement and Royalties Limited; basis 1 new Patent Enforcement com. sh. for 1 old Ciclo com. sh. (see Patent Enforcement and Royalties Limited)

Cie-Nergy Ply-Foil Canada Inc. (Can. Nov. 1, 1990)
Sept. 8, 2013 – Dissolved.

La Cieba Minerals Corp. (B.C. July 28, 1982)
Sept. 25, 1995 – Continued into Canada.
Sept. 26, 1995 – Name changed to Lowell Petroleum Inc. ■

Cielo Gold Corp. (B.C. Feb. 2, 2011)
Aug. 14, 2013 – Name changed to Cielo Waste Solutions Corp. (see FPsurvey - Industrials)

Cierra Pacific Ventures Ltd. (B.C. May 3, 1966)
July 15, 2009 – Name changed to Alange Energy Corp. pursuant to reverse takeover acquisition of Alange, Corp.; basis 1 new for 3 old shs. ■

Ciesta Gold Exploration Ltd. (B.C. 1982)
May 23, 1985 – Name changed to Rough River Petroleum Corporation. (see FPsurvey - Mines & Energy)

Cigar Oil & Gas Ltd. (Alta. June 18, 1987)
Jan. 21, 2003 – Amalgamation with Manhattan Resources Ltd. to form Pivotal Energy Ltd.; basis 1 new for 7 Manhattan Resources shs. and 0.471429 new for 1 Cigar Oil sh. (see Pivotal Energy Ltd.)

Cima Resources Limited (B.C. Nov. 9, 1965)
May 22, 1984 – Name changed to Consolidated Cima Resources Limited; basis 1 new for 4 old shs. ■

Cimarron Minerals Ltd. (B.C. May 11, 1983)
May 1, 2000 – Name changed to DiscFactories Corporation; basis 1 new for 2 old shs. ■

Cimarron Petroleum Ltd. (Alta. Mar. 3, 1978)
Apr. 15, 1997 – Acquired by Newport Petroleum Corporation; basis 2.7 Newport shs. for 1 Cimarron sh. The acquisition was accounted for as a pooling of interests. Subsequently amalgamated on Jan. 1, 1998. (see Newport Petroleum Corporation)

Cimatec Environmental Engineering Inc. (Can. Dec. 18, 1992 amalg.)
June 23, 2011 – Dissolved and struck from the register.

Cimco Limited (Can. 1913)
1969 – Toromont Industrial Holdings Ltd. acquired a 99.6% voting int. in the co. during; subsequently acquired a total of 99.94% of the voting com. shs. and 97.41% of the non-voting cl. A shs.

Cimtek Integrated Manufacturing Technologies Inc. (B.C. Sept. 25, 1985)
Jan. 17, 1997 – Name changed to Jakarta Development Corp.; basis 1 new for 5 old shs. ■

Cinaport Acquisition Corp. (Ont. Mar. 29, 2011)
Sept. 30, 2014 – Name changed to Mettrum Health Corp. following Qualifying Transaction reverse takeover acquisition of Mettrum Ltd.; basis 1 new for 14.5625 old shs. ■

Cinaport Acquisition Corp. II (Ont. Dec. 12, 2017)
Feb. 12, 2019 – Continued into Canada.
Feb. 19, 2019 – Name changed to Fire & Flower Holdings Corp. pursuant to Qualifying Transaction reverse takeover acquisition of Fire & Flower Inc.; basis 1 new for 10.6481482 old shs. (see FPsurvey - Industrials)

Cinar Films Inc. (Can. Dec. 10, 1976)
Dec. 16, 1998 – Name changed to CINAR Corporation. ■

Cinch Energy Corp. (Alta. July 24, 1998)
July 18, 2011 – Acquired by Tourmaline Oil Corp.; basis 0.06366 Tourmaline shs. for 1 Cinch sh.

Cinch Lake Uranium Mines Ltd. (Ont. 1949)
1954 – Name changed to Lake Cinch Mines Ltd.; basis 1 new for 2 old shs. ■

Cincinnati Energy Corp. (Ont. 1935)
June 11, 1994 – Charter cancelled and co. dissolved.

Cincinnati-Porcupine Mines Ltd. (Ont. 1935)
Dec. 1980 – Name changed to Cincinnati Resources Inc. ■

Cincinnati Resources Inc. (Ont. 1935)
Jan. 19, 1983 – Name changed to Cincinnati Energy Corp.; basis 1 new for 5 old shs. ■

Cincoro Capital Corp. (B.C. May 29, 2006)
June 11, 2009 – Name changed to Scorpio Gold Corporation following Qualifying Transaction reverse takeover acquistion of (old) Scorpio Gold Corporation; basis 1 new for 3 old shs. (see FPsurvey - Mines & Energy)

Cinderella Gold Mines Ltd. (Ont. 1945)
May 27, 1965 – Dissolved.

Cindy Mae Resources Inc. (Ont. 1984)
Aug. 28, 1995 – Name changed to Woodview Corporation; basis 1 new for 4 old shs. ■

Cindy Mines Ltd. (B.C. 1966)
Oct. 1974 – Charter cancelled.

Cinema Internet Networks Inc. (Can. Dec. 27, 1985)
June 18, 2014 – Continued into British Columbia.
June 27, 2014 – Name changed to Quentin Ventures Ltd.; basis 1 new for 10 old shs. ■

Cinemage Capital Corp. (Alta. Apr. 29, 1998)
July 25, 2002 – Continued into Canada.
Aug. 16, 2002 – Name changed to Cinemage Corporation. ■

Cinemage Corporation (Can. July 25, 2002)
Dec. 8, 2008 – Name changed to Fibresources Corporation; basis 1 new for 5 old shs. ■

Cinémaison 3D inc. (Que. Dec. 19, 2005; amalg.)
May 31, 2006 – Name changed to SENSIO Technologies Inc. pursuant to Qualifying Transaction reverse takeover acquisition of Les Technologies Sensorielles inc. ■

Cinémas Unis Ltée (Que. 1924)
1981 – Famous Players Ltd., the parent co., was reorganized whereby the real estate and theatre operations were separated. Consequently, co. continued with the Quebec Realty operations and its name was changed to Les Immeubles Famous Players (Quebec) Inc. A new subsidiary, Cinemas Unis Inc., was established to carry out the Quebec theatre operations. Also all public shs. were redeemed.

Cineplex Corporation (Ont. Jan. 31, 1982 amalg.)
June 28, 1985 – Name changed to Cineplex Odeon Corporation. ■

Cineplex Galaxy Income Fund (Ont. Oct. 2, 2003)
Jan. 4, 2011 – Succeeded by Cineplex Inc. pursuant to plan of arrangement whereby Cineplex Inc. was formed to facilitate the conversion of the fund into a corporation and the fund was subsequently dissolved. (see FPsurvey - Industrials)

Cineplex Odeon Corporation (Ont. Jan. 31, 1982 amalg.)
May 15, 1998 – Formed Loews Cineplex Entertainment Corporation in Delaware pursuant to plan of arrangement with LTM Holdings Inc., wholly owned by Sony Pictures Entertainment Inc.; basis 1 new for 10 old shs.

Cinévision Ltée (Que. 1966)
Apr. 26, 1976 – Placed into bankruptcy. No information available regarding distribution of assets.

Cinnabar Peak Mines Ltd. (Alta. Oct. 4, 1968)
Sept. 19, 1994 – Name changed to Sierra Capital Corp. ■

Cinola Mines Ltd. (B.C. Feb. 7, 1962)
1972 – Name changed to Consolidated Cinola Mines Ltd.; basis 1 new for 2 old shs. ■

Cinram International Income Fund (Ont. Mar. 21, 2006)
June 25, 2012 – Filed for protection under the Companies' Creditors Arrangement Act (CCAA) and FTI Consulting Canada Inc. appointed monitor.
Aug. 31, 2012 – Sale of North American assets to an affiliate of Najafi Companies was completed. Proceeds to be distrib. to senior secured creditors; no funds available for shldrs.
Feb. 5, 2013 – Sale of European assets was completed.
Feb. 24, 2016 – FTI Consulting Canada Inc. as monitor was discharged and proceedings under the CCAA was terminated.

Cinram International Inc. (Can. July 28, 1969)
May 8, 2006 – Converted into Cinram International Income Fund; basis 1 trust unit for 1 com. sh.

Cinram Ltd. (Can. July 28, 1969)
June 30, 1997 – Name changed to Cinram International Inc. ■

Cintech Tele-Management Systems, Inc. (Ohio Mar. 20, 1987)
Jan. 15, 2001 – Name changed to Cintech Solutions, Inc.

Cinzano Limited (Can. 1927)
1960 – Acquired by Instituto Finanziano Industriale of Italy, through purchase of cl. A ord. shs. held by minority shldrs., at £1 12s 6d a sh. Subsequently o/s 5.5% pref. £1 par shs. red.

Cipher Resources Inc. (B.C. Mar. 20, 1989)
June 26, 2019 – Name changed to Empress Resources Corp. ■

Cipway Gold Mines Ltd. (Ont. 1944)
1961 – Charter cancelled.

Circa Enterprises Inc. (Alta. Feb. 29, 1988)
Apr. 19, 2023 – Acquired by Sicame Canada Holdings Inc., a wholly owned subsid. of Sicame Group SAS; basis $2.1173 cash per sh.

Circa Telecommunications Inc. (Can. May 31, 1985)
Feb. 29, 1988 – Continued into Alberta.
Nov. 2, 1994 – Name changed to Circa Enterprises Inc. ■

Circle Bar Knitting Co. Ltd. (Can. 1915)
Apr. 1964 – Name changed to Bell Knit Industries Limited; basis 5 Circle cl. A for 1 Bell com. sh. and 1 Circle com. for 2 Bell com. shs. ■

Circle Builders Corporation (B.C. 1970)
Aug. 9, 1977 – Name changed to Miromit Solar Corp. ■

Circle Energy Inc. (Alta. Mar. 11, 1994)
Dec. 3, 2001 – Acquired by Rider Resources Inc.; basis $0.48 per sh. or 0.42 new Rider com. sh. for 1 old Circle com. sh.

Circle Petroleum Ltd. (B.C.)
1958 – Struck off register.

Circle Yellowknife Mines Ltd. (Ont. 1946)
Dec. 1977 – Charter cancelled.

Circo Craft Co. Inc. (Que. Aug. 29, 1973)
Oct. 30, 1996 – Acquired by HMTF Canada Acquisition Inc., a subsid. of Hicks, Muse, Tate & Furst Incorporated, for $11 per sh.

Circuit World Corporation (Can. Apr. 18, 1983)
Aug. 30, 2003 – Amalgamated with Firan Technology Group Inc. (FTG) following the July 30, 2003, reverse takeover acquisition of FTG, to form new co. with same name Circuit World Corporation.
May 18, 2004 – Name changed to Firan Technology Group Corporation. (see FPsurvey - Industrials)

Circumpacific Energy Corporation (B.C. Oct. 14, 1987)
June 16, 1997 – Continued into Yukon.
June 2, 2006 – Continued into British Columbia.
Nov. 25, 2010 – Privatized for 18¢ per sh.

Cirque Energy Corp. (Alta. Jan. 5, 1994)
June 3, 1999 – Name changed to Tikal Resources Corp. following acquisition of Tikal Resources Inc. Tikal shldrs. received 1 Cirque sh. for each 3.6 Tikal shs. held. ■

Cirque Energy Ltd. (Alta. Jan. 5, 1994)
May 12, 1998 – Name changed to Cirque Energy Corp.; basis 1 new for 4 old shs. ■

Cirrus Energy Corporation (Alta. June 14, 2002)
Apr. 15, 2011 – Acquired by Oranje-Nassau Energie B.V. for $1.15 per sh.

Cirrus Gold Corp. (B.C. Feb. 5, 2020)
July 22, 2022 – Name changed to American Copper Development Corporation. (see FPsurvey - Mines & Energy)

Cisco Resources Ltd. (B.C. Mar. 12, 1980)
Aug. 9, 1988 – Name changed to Consolidated Cisco Resources Ltd.; basis 1 new for 2 old shs. ■

The Citadel Capital Corporation (Ont. 1987)
Dec. 23, 1992 – All o/s 1st pfd. ser. A shs. redeemed for $25 per sh. Co. now private.

Citadel Diversified Investment Trust (Ont. July 11, 1997)
Nov. 24, 2009 – Name changed to Blue Ribbon Income Fund pursuant to reorganization with Blue Ribbon Fund Management Ltd. as manager. (see FPsurvey - Industrials)

Citadel Gold Mines Inc. (Ont. Mar. 22, 1962)
June 15, 2011 – Name changed to Anconia Resources Corp. pursuant to reverse takeover acquisition of 2215107 Ontario Inc. which held a mineral prospect in Nunavut; basis 1 new for 5 old shs. ■

Citadel HYTES Fund (Alta. Feb. 27, 2001)
Dec. 3, 2009 – Merged (together with Citadel Premium Income Fund, Citadel S-1 Income Trust Fund, Citadel Stable S-1 Income Fund and Equal Weight Plus Fund) into Citadel Income Fund (formerly Crown Hill Fund); basis 1 Citadel Income unit for 1.1581 Citadel Premium units, 1 Citadel Income unit for 1.8629 Citadel S-1 units, 1 Citadel Income unit for 1.0765 Citadel Stable S-1 units, 1 Citadel Income unit for 0.8028 Equal Weight Plus units and 1 Citadel Income unit for 1.7545 Citadel HYTES units.

Citadel Income & Growth Fund (Alta. Aug. 21, 2003)
July 20, 2006 – Merged with Citadel Multi-Sector Income Fund and MYDAS Fund to continue as a new fund named Citadel Premium Income Fund; basis 0.945 Citadel Premium units plus $0.0708 special distribution for 1 Citadel Income unit. (see Citadel Premium Income Fund)

Citadel Mines Limited (Ont. 1966)
Mar. 1976 – Charter cancelled.

Citadel Multi-Sector Income Fund (Alta. Dec. 12, 2002)
July 20, 2006 – Merged with Citadel Income & Growth Fund and MYDAS Fund to continue as a new fund named Citadel Premium Income Fund; basis 0.976 new Citadel Premium unit plus $0.25 special distribution for 1 old Multi-Sector unit. (see Citadel Premium Income Fund)

Citadel Premium Income Fund (Alta. June 6, 2006)
Dec. 3, 2009 – Merged (together with Citadel S-1 Income Trust Fund, Citadel Stable S-1 Income Fund, Equal Weight Plus Fund and Citadel HYTES Fund) into Citadel Income Fund (formerly Crown Hill Fund); basis 1 Citadel Income unit for 1.8629 Citadel S-1 units, 1 Citadel Income unit for 1.0765 Citadel Stable S-1 units, 1 Citadel Income unit for 0.8028 Equal Weight Plus units, 1 Citadel Income unit for 1.7545 Citadel HYTES units and 1 Citadel Income unit for 1.1581 Citadel Premium units.

Citadel S-1 Income Trust Fund (Alta. Aug. 11, 2000)
Dec. 3, 2009 – Merged (together with Citadel Stable S-1 Income Fund, Equal Weight Plus Fund, Citadel HYTES Fund and Citadel Premium Income Fund) into Citadel Income Fund (formerly Crown Hill Fund); basis 1 Citadel Income unit for 1.0765 Citadel Stable S-1 units, 1 Citadel Income unit for 0.8028 Equal Weight Plus units, 1 Citadel Income unit for 1.7545 Citadel HYTES units, 1 Citadel Income unit for 1.1581 Citadel Premium units and 1 Citadel Income unit for 1.8629 Citadel S-1 units.

Citadel SMaRT Fund (Alta. July 19, 2001)
Mar. 28, 2012 – Merged into Energy Income Fund; basis $17.45 or 3.074 Energy Income Fund trust units for 1 Citadel SMaRT trust unit.

Citadel Stable S-1 Income Fund (Alta. Dec. 6, 2004)
Dec. 3, 2009 – Merged (together with Equal Weight Plus Fund, Citadel HYTES Fund, Citadel Premium Income Fund and Citadel S-1 Income Trust Fund) into Citadel Income Fund (formerly Crown Hill Fund); basis 1 Citadel Income unit for 0.8028 Equal Weight Plus units, 1 Citadel Income unit for 1.7545 Citadel HYTES units, 1 Citadel Income unit for 1.1581 Citadel Premium units, 1 Citadel Income unit for 1.8629 Citadel S-1 units and 1 Citadel Income unit for 1.0765 Citadel Stable S-1 units.

Citation Explorations Ltd. (B.C. Apr. 1, 1966)
Aug. 14, 1969 – Name changed to Citex Mines Ltd. ■

Citation Gold Corp. (B.C. June 10, 1983)
Sept. 11, 1992 – Name changed to Cogenix Power Corporation. ■

Citation Growth Corp. (B.C. Apr. 24, 2007)
Nov. 10, 2020 – Name changed to Fiore Cannabis Ltd. (see FPsurvey - Industrials)

Citation Mines Ltd. (B.C. 1956)
Jan. 27, 1966 – Charter cancelled.

Citation Oils Ltd. (Ont. May 14, 1949)
1955 – Assets acquired by Consolidated East Crest Oil Company Limited; basis 1 new for 4 old shs. (see Consolidated East Crest Oil Company Limited)

Citation Resources Inc. (B.C. Oct. 25, 1996)
Oct. 1, 2002 – Continued into Yukon.
Oct. 25, 2002 – Name changed to Macarthur Diamonds Limited; basis 2 new for 5 old shs. ■

Citation Resources Inc. (Ont. Mar. 27, 2009)
July 8, 2014 – Acquired by Inlet Resources Ltd.; basis 0.5 Inlet com. shs. for 1 Citation com. sh. (see Inlet Resources Ltd.)
July 8, 2014 – Name changed to Citation Minerals Inc. on amalgamation with 1001323 B.C. Ltd. (a wholly owned subsid. of Inlet Resources Ltd.). (see Inlet Resources Ltd.)

Citation Silver Mines Ltd. (B.C. 1966)
Oct. 1974 – Charter cancelled.

Citco Growth Investments Ltd. (B.C. May 31, 1969)
July 28, 2005 – Name changed to First Global Investments Inc. ■

Citex Mines Ltd. (B.C. Apr. 1, 1966)
June 30, 1975 – Name changed to Consolidated Citex Resources Inc.; basis 1 new for 5 old shs. ■

Citibank Canada (Can. Nov. 2, 1981 amalg.)
1987 – Amalgamated in Canada to continue with same name.

Citicorp (Del. Dec. 4, 1967)
Oct. 7, 1998 – Amalgamated with Travellers Group Inc. to form CitiGroup Inc.; basis 2.5 new for 1 Citicorp sh. (see Travelers Group Inc.)

Citigroup Finance Canada Inc. (Can. Oct. 19, 1982)
Oct. 30, 2017 – Continued into British Columbia.
Dec. 1, 2017 – Name changed to Citigroup Finance Canada ULC.

Citizen Stash Cannabis Corp. (Can. Sept. 20, 2017)
Nov. 8, 2021 – Acquired by The Valens Company Inc.; basis 0.1620 Valens com. shs. for 1 Citizen Stash sh. (see The Valens Company Inc.)

Citlec Minerals Ltd. (B.C. 1970)
Sept. 30, 1982 – Amalgamated with Cyclone Developments Ltd. and Pan Acheron Resources Ltd. to form Acheron Resources Ltd.; basis 1 new for 3 Cyclone shs., 1 new for 4 Pan Acheron shs. and 1 new for 2 Citlec shs.

Citotech Systems Inc. (Can. Aug. 31, 2000)
July 20, 2004 – Name changed to Smartcool Systems Inc.; basis 1 new for 3 old shs. (see FPsurvey - Industrials)

Citra-Lartic Mines Ltd. (Ont. 1943)
Sept. 1955 – Name changed to Consolidated Thor Mines Ltd.; basis 1 new for 5 old shs. ■

Citralam Malartic Mines Ltd. (Ont. 1943)
1950 – Name changed to Citra-Lartic Mines Ltd.; basis 1 new for 4 old shs. ■

Citrine Holdings Ltd. (B.C. June 5, 1984)
Jan. 25, 2010 – Dissolved and struck from the register.

City Gold Corporation (Can. Feb. 11, 1986)
Oct. 4, 1988 – Name changed to Extracare Corporation. ■

City Resources (Canada) Limited (B.C. Feb. 7, 1962)
Apr. 22, 1994 – Name changed to Misty Mountain Gold Limited. ■

City Savings & Trust Company (Alta. 1962)
Sept. 19, 1978 – Name changed to First City Trust Company. ■

Civeo Corporation (Del. Oct. 8, 2013)
July 17, 2015 – Continued into British Columbia. (see FPsurvey - Industrials)

Claddagh Gold Limited (Can. Aug. 9, 1989 amalg.)
Sept. 1, 2000 – Name changed to Resorts Unlimited Management Inc.; basis 1 new for 4 old shs. ■

Claiborne Industries Limited (Alta. 1940)
May 22, 1990 – Acquired by 172071 Canada Inc. for $12 per sh.

Claim Lake Resources Inc. (Ont. Apr. 15, 1997)
Mar. 7, 2005 – Name changed to Fort Chimo Minerals Inc. following acquisition of Medical Miners Business which includes mining properties in northern Quebec; basis 1 new for 2 old shs. ■

Claim Post Resources Inc. (Ont. Sept. 21, 2005)
Nov. 16, 2018 – Name changed to Canadian Premium Sand Inc.; basis 1 new for 15 old shs. ■

Claimer Resources Inc. (B.C. 1986)
Apr. 11, 1989 – Name changed to Canadian Strategic Holdings Ltd. ■

Claimstaker Resources Ltd. (B.C. Feb. 8, 1990)
Sept. 5, 2001 – Name changed to J-Pacific Gold Inc. ■

Clairtone Sound Corporation Limited (Ont. 1958)
1979 – Dissolved.

Clan Resources Ltd. (B.C. July 9, 1987)
Dec. 20, 2004 – Name changed to Energy Metals Corporation. ■

Clansman Mines Ltd. (Ont. 1911)
Dec. 1975 – Charter cancelled.

Clara Capital Corp. (Can. Apr. 15, 2021)
Oct. 12, 2023 – Name changed to Clara Technologies Corp. (see FPsurvey - Industrials)

Clarcan Petroleum Corporation (Tex. 1966)
Mar. 1974 – Merged into Ladd Petroleum Corp., a wholly owned subsid. of Utah International Inc. of San Francisco; basis 1 sh. Utah for 8 shs. Clarcan.

Claremont Mines Ltd. (Que. 1945)
Oct. 1972 – Charter cancelled. (Not to be confused with co. of same name, Ont. inc. 1974).

Claremont Mines Limited (Ont. 1974)
Feb. 19, 1987 – Name changed to Claremont Industries Inc. (see FPsurvey - Industrials)

Clarendon Gold Mines Ltd. (Ont. 1944)
1957 – Charter cancelled.

Clarepine Developments Ltd. (Alta. June 4, 1963)
Dec. 1, 1993 – Dissolved and struck off register.

Clarepine Industries Inc. (Alta. May 23, 1957)
Nov. 1, 1993 – Struck off register.

Clarepine Oil and Gas Limited (Alta. June 4, 1963)
May 14, 1970 – Name changed to Clarepine Developments Ltd. ■

Clarica Life Insurance Company (Can. 1878)
May 29, 2002 – All com. shs. acquired by Sun Life Financial Services of Canada Inc.; basis 1.5135 Sun Life shs. for 1 Clarica Life sh. Preferred shs. were still active. (see Sun Life Financial Services of Canada Inc.)
Dec. 31, 2002 – Amalgamated with Sun Life Assurance Company of Canada, a wholly owned subsidiary of Sun Life Financial Services of Canada Inc. (see Sun Life Financial Services of Canada Inc.)

Clarinet Resources Ltd. (B.C. 1979)
July 29, 1987 – Continued into Alberta.
Aug. 16, 1996 – Name changed to Symmetry Resources Inc.; basis 1 new for 4 old shs. ■

Clarington Corporation (Ont. Oct. 15, 2003)
Feb. 2, 2006 – Acquired by Industrial Alliance Insurance and Financial Services Inc. for $15 per sh. (see Industrial Alliance Insurance and Financial Services Inc.)

Clarington Diversified Income + Growth Fund (Ont. Oct. 28, 2004)
June 27, 2009 – Merged into IA Clarington Diversified Income Fund, an open-ended mutual fund.

Clarion Environmental Technologies, Inc. (B.C. Sept. 19, 1980)
July 14, 1998 – Name changed to Clarion Resources Ltd. ■

Clarion Petroleums Ltd. (unknown)
Dec. 1, 1981 – Acquired by Roxy Petroleum Ltd.; basis 2 com. shs. and 1 sh. purchase warrant of Roxy for each 2 Clarion shs. (see Roxy Petroleum Ltd.)

Clarion Resources Ltd. (B.C. Sept. 19, 1980)
Feb. 20, 2004 – Dissolved and struck from the register.

Clarity Gold Corp. (B.C. Sept. 11, 2019)
Dec. 15, 2022 – Name changed to Clarity Metals Corp. (see FPsurvey - Mines & Energy)

Clarity Telecom Networking Inc. (Alta. June 19, 2000)
Mar. 16, 2001 – Name changed to NTG Clarity Networks Inc. ■

Clark Canadian Exploration Co. (Tex. 1966)
1973 – Name changed to Clarcan Petroleum Corporation; basis 1 new for 4 old shs. ■

Clark Gold Mines Ltd. (Que. 1934)
Oct. 16, 1982 – Charter cancelled.

Clark Pharmaceutical Laboratories Ltd. (Ont. Aug. 22, 1983)
Nov. 14, 1990 – Name changed to Dimethaid Research Inc.; basis 1 Dimethaid sh. for either 4 Clark com. shs. or 4 Clark cl. A shs. ■

Clarkside Corporation Limited (Ont. 1955)
Jan. 1963 – Acquired by Monarch Investments Ltd. for $456,479. All o/s long term debt retired.

Clarmin Explorations Inc. (B.C. Oct. 13, 2016)
Nov. 4, 2020 – Name changed to Cybin Inc. and continued into Ontario following reverse takeover acquisition of Cybin Corp. and concurrent amalgamation of Cybin Corp. with wholly owned 2762898 Ontario Inc. (see FPsurvey - Industrials)

Clarnor Malartic Mines Ltd. (Ont. 1945)
Aug. 29, 1960 – Charter cancelled.

Clarocity Corporation (Alta. Feb. 20, 2004 amalg.)
June 11, 2019 – Placed into receivership and Hardie & Kelly Inc. was appointed receiver.

Clarry Gold Mines Ltd. (Ont. 1944)
Jan. 12, 1959 – Dissolved.

Clarus Corporation (Ont. July 7, 1927)
Nov. 1990 – Coopers & Lybrand in Toronto was appointed receiver-manager of the company's assets.
Dec. 1990 – Harding Carpets sold.
Dec. 1, 1997 – Continuous Color Coat Limited sold. Receiver discharged and the secured creditors suffered a shortfall. No distribution was made to unsecured creditors or shldrs.

Classic Developments Ltd. (B.C. 1964)
Aug. 1971 – Name changed to Premier Cablevision Limited. ■

Classic Gold Resources Limited (B.C. Feb. 24, 1988)
Aug. 1, 2005 – Struck from register and dissolved.

Classic Sturgeon Gold Mines Ltd. (Ont. 1938)
1956 – Charter cancelled.

Claude Lake Mines Ltd. (Que. 1947)
1961 – Charter cancelled.

Claude Neon Advertising, Limited (Can. Dec. 30, 1929)
Jan. 1973 – Acquired by Arizona-based Combined Communications Corp. for $18,320,239.
Apr. 15, 1973 – Name changed to Claude Neon Limited. ■

Claude Neon General Advertising, Ltd. (Can. Dec. 30, 1929)
Aug. 3, 1965 – Name changed to Claude Neon Advertising, Limited. ■

Claude Neon Limited (Can. Dec. 30, 1929)
Feb. 1, 1979 – Name changed to Mediacom Inc.

Claude Resources Inc. (Can. Mar. 26, 1980)
June 7, 2016 – Acquired by Silver Standard Resources Inc.; basis 0.185 Silver Standard com. shs. plus $0.001 cash for 1 Claude com. sh.
Aug. 1, 2017 – Name changed to SGO Mining Inc.

Claudio's Restaurant Group Inc. (Ont. 1975)
1988 – Continued into Alberta.
Oct. 1, 1989 – Amalgamated in Alberta to continue with same name.
Apr. 2, 2001 – Charter cancelled and co. dissolved.

Claverny Gold Mines Ltd. (Que. 1937)
Nov. 1972 – Charter cancelled.

Clavos Enterprises Inc. (Ont. 1945)
Oct. 23, 1997 – Formed Magnesium Alloy Corporation in Ontario on amalgamation with Magnesium Alloy Corporation (deemed acquiror); basis 1 new for 2 old shs. ■

Clavos Porcupine Mines Limited (Ont. 1945)
Feb. 5, 1997 – Name changed to Clavos Enterprises Inc.; basis 1 new for 2 old shs. ■

Claw Lake Gold Mines Ltd. (Ont. 1937)
Apr. 14, 1958 – Dissolved.

Claw Lake Molybdenum Mines Limited (Ont. 1965)
Mar. 1976 – Charter cancelled.

Claw Resources Ltd. (B.C. 1986)
Aug. 5, 1994 – Dissolved and struck off register.

Clay-Mill Technical Systems Inc. (Ont. 1977)
Jan. 12, 1990 – Deemed bankrupt and assets liquidated. Nothing left for shldrs.

Clay-Tech Industries Inc. (Alta. 1988)
Apr. 2003 – Distribution of $0.09 per sh. considered to be return of capital.
Feb. 2, 2004 – Wound up.

Claybar Uranium & Oil Ltd. (Ont. 1952)
Apr. 1965 – Name changed to Canbridge Oil Exploration Ltd. ■

Claymac Mines Limited (Ont. 1954)
Mar. 1976 – Charter cancelled.
Dec. 28, 1977 – Charter revived.
Feb. 18, 1980 – Name changed to Texcan Energy & Resources Inc. ■

Claymore Equal Weight Banc & Lifeco ETF (Ont. Apr. 5, 2007)
Mar. 29, 2012 – Name changed to iShares Equal Weight Banc & Lifeco Fund. ■

Claymore Equal Weight Banc & Lifeco Trust (Ont. Apr. 5, 2007)
Feb. 6, 2008 – Name changed to Claymore Equal Weight Banc & Lifeco ETF following conversion from a closed end fund to an exchange-traded fund. ■

Claymore Gold Bullion ETF (Ont. May 19, 2009)
Mar. 29, 2012 – Name changed to iShares Gold Bullion Fund. ■

Claymore Gold Bullion Trust (Ont. May 19, 2009)
Feb. 16, 2010 – Name changed to Claymore Gold Bullion ETF following conversion from a closed-end fund to an exchange-traded fund. ■

Claymore Resources Ltd. (B.C. July 20, 1970)
Apr. 19, 1989 – Name changed to New Claymore Resources Ltd.; basis 1 new for 4 old shs. ■

Claymore Silver Bullion Trust (Ont.)
Mar. 29, 2012 – Name changed to BlackRock Silver Bullion Trust. ■

Clayoquot Resources Ltd. (Alta. July 18, 1994)
Mar. 24, 1998 – Name changed to Bakrie Minarak Energy Inc. ■

Claytron Energy Corporation (B.C. 1969)
Dec. 31, 1986 – Amalgamated with 3 other cos. to form International Interlake Industries Inc.; basis 1 new for 23 old shs. (see International Interlake Industries Inc.)

Clean Commodities Corp. (B.C. Nov. 10, 2015)
Oct. 17, 2019 – Name changed to Dixie Gold Inc. (see FPsurvey - Mines & Energy)

Clean Earth Chemical Corp. (B.C. June 25, 2018)
Aug. 12, 2019 – Name changed to Temas Resources Corp. (see FPsurvey - Mines & Energy)

Clean Power Capital Corp. (B.C. Dec. 6, 2018)
June 10, 2021 – Name changed to PowerTap Hydrogen Capital Corp. (see FPsurvey - Industrials)

Clean Power Income Fund (Ont. Oct. 31, 2001)
June 29, 2007 – Acquired by Macquarie Power & Infrastructure Income Fund; basis 0.5581 new Macquarie trust unit for 1 old Clean Power unit plus 1 contingency value receipt which would entitle the holder to a cash payment of up to $0.19 per Clean Power unit. (see Macquarie Power & Infrastructure Income Fund)

Cleanfield Alternative Energy Inc. (B.C. June 2, 2004)
Feb. 10, 2009 – Continued into Ontario. (see FPsurvey - Industrials)

CleanSoils Limited Partnership (Ont. May 24, 1994)
Jan. 5, 1998 – All securities of CleanSoils Limited owned by the partnership, which represent all the assets of the partnership, distributed to its limited partners; basis 1 new special sh. of CleanSoils Limited for 1 cl. A unit of the partnership; 1 sh. pur. wt. for 1 cl. C unit of the partnership and $1.00 principal amt. of convert. debs. for 1 cl. D unit of the partnership. The Partnership will be dissolved.

Cleantech Capital Inc. (Ont. Oct. 3, 2013)
Mar. 31, 2016 – Name changed to Char Technologies Ltd. following Qualifying Transaction reverse takeover acquisition of Char Technologies Inc. (see FPsurvey - Industrials)

Clear Creek Placers Ltd. (Can. 1941)
Charter cancelled.

Clear Creek Resources Ltd. (B.C. July 8, 1987)
Jan. 10, 2000 – Name changed to Olympus Stone Inc. and continued into Yukon; basis 1 new for 3 old shs. ■

Clear Energy Inc. (Alta. Dec. 9, 2002)
Aug. 15, 2006 – Plan of Arrangement combination with NAV Energy Trust (renamed Sound Energy Trust) to continue as a new co. named Sure Energy Inc.; basis 0.5 new Sound trust unit, 0.1667 new Sure sh., plus 0.0425 new Sure wt. for 1 old Clear sh. (see Sound Energy Trust; Sure Energy Inc.)

Clear Lake Gold Mines Ltd. (Ont. 1937)
1956 – Charter cancelled.

Clear Mines Ltd. (B.C. Mar. 28, 1979)
Aug. 16, 1985 – Name changed to Redwood Resources Inc.; basis 1 new for 3.9 old shs. ■

Clear Mountain Resources Corp. (B.C. May 11, 2010)
Aug. 24, 2016 – Name changed to Patriot One Technologies Inc. following reverse takeover acquisition of (old) Patriot One Technologies Inc. ■

Clear Petroleums Ltd. (Alta. 1950)
1964 – Struck off register.

Clear Sky Lithium Corp. (B.C. June 25, 2018)
Jan. 30, 2023 – Name changed to POWR Lithium Corp. (see FPsurvey - Mines & Energy)

Clear View Ventures, Inc. (B.C. May 18, 1983)
Apr. 25, 1994 – Name changed to Turbodyne Technologies Inc. ■

Clearford Industries Inc. (Can. July 6, 2005)
June 27, 2014 – Name changed to Clearford Water Systems Inc. ■

Clearford Water Systems Inc. (Can. July 6, 2005)
Oct. 11, 2022 – Pursuant to restructuring under the Bankruptcy and Insolvency Act (Canada) all o/s com. shs. were consolidated on a 1-for-0.000001 basis and re-designated as redeemable shs. which were immediately redeemed for no consideration. Company now private.

ClearFrame Solutions Corp. (B.C. Nov. 4, 1986)
Feb. 25, 2013 – Name changed to Clear Gold Resources Inc. (see FPsurvey - Mines & Energy)

ClearFrame Solutions Inc. (B.C. Nov. 4, 1986)
May 2, 2005 – Name changed to ClearFrame Solutions Corp.; basis 1 new for 20 old shs. ■

Clearly Canadian Beverage Corporation (B.C. Mar. 18, 1981)
June 3, 2013 – Dissolved and struck from register.

Clearnet Communications Inc. (Ont. Jan. 16, 1984)
Oct. 20, 1994 – Continued into Canada.
Jan. 19, 2001 – Acquired by TELUS Corporation; basis $70 or 1.636 TELUS non-vtg. shs. for 1 Clearnet cl. A sh.

Clearport Petroleums Ltd. (Alta. Mar. 8, 1972)
July 7, 1995 – Amalgamated with a wholly owned subsid. of International Euromin Corporation to form Eurogas Corporation; basis 0.315 Eurogas shs. for 1 Clearport sh. (see Eurogas Corporation)

ClearStream Energy Services Inc. (Ont. Feb. 18, 2011)
Jan. 31, 2022 – Continued into Alberta.
Dec. 1, 2022 – Name changed to FLINT Corp. (see FPsurvey - Mines & Energy; FPsurvey - Industrials)

Clearview Mineral Resources Corp. (B.C. Feb. 26, 1987)
Oct. 4, 2004 – Name changed to Mineral Hill Industries Ltd.; basis 1 new for 10 old shs. (see FPsurvey - Mines & Energy)

Clearwater Seafoods Income Fund (Ont. June 5, 2002)
July 11, 2011 – Continued into Canada.
Oct. 3, 2011 – Succeeded by Clearwater Seafoods Incorporated pursuant to plan of arrangement whereby Clearwater Seafoods Incorporated was formed to facilitate the conversion of the fund into a corporation. ■

Clearwater Seafoods Incorporated (Can. July 11, 2011)
Jan. 27, 2021 – Acquired by 12385104 Canada Inc., a company jointly owned (50/50 basis) by FNC Holdings Limited Partnership, representing a coalition of Mi'kmaq First Nations, and Premium Brands Holdings Corporation; basis $8.25 cash per share.

Cleaver Lake Mines Ltd. (B.C. 1970)
Mar. 19, 1980 – Name changed to Lawrence Mining Corporation; basis 1 new for 5 old shs. ■

Clement Systems Inc. (Alta. Sept. 22, 1997)
Dec. 22, 2006 – Delisted from the TSX-Venture Exchange. Subsequently struck from registry and dissolved.

Clementia Pharmaceuticals Inc. (Can. Nov. 5, 2010)
Apr. 18, 2019 – Acquired by Ipsen S.A.; basis US$25 cash per sh.

Clemex Technologies Inc. (Can. Oct. 22, 1990)
Dec. 30, 2016 – Privatized via amalgamation with 9804064 Canada Inc.; basis 1 cl. A redeemable pref. sh. for 1 Clemex cl. A com. sh., redeemed for 20¢ cash.

Clemson Resources Corp. (Can. Oct. 6, 2004)
Oct. 22, 2012 – Continued into British Columbia.
Apr. 16, 2013 – Name changed to Oyster Oil and Gas Ltd. ■

Clenor Mining Company Ltd. (Ont. 1937)
Dec. 1970 – Charter cancelled.

Cleranda Copper Mines Ltd. (Ont. 1955)
May 15, 1974 – Dissolved.

Clericy Consolidated Mines Ltd. (Can. 1926)
Dec. 16, 1980 – Charter cancelled.

Clericy Mines Ltd. (Can. 1926)
1927 – Name changed to Clericy Consolidated Mines Ltd.; basis 2 new for 1 old sh. ■

Clermont Capital Inc. (B.C. Mar. 8, 2011)
Apr. 19, 2013 – Name changed to NexGen Energy Ltd. pursuant to Qualifying Transaction reverse takeover acquisition of (old) NexGen Energy Ltd.; basis 1 new for 2.35 old shs. (see FPsurvey - Mines & Energy)

Clerno Mines Ltd. (Can. 1936)
Nov. 22, 1960 – Distributed 1.32151¢ per sh. Charter surrendered.

Clero Mines Ltd. (Que. 1965)
Feb. 7, 1981 – Charter cancelled.

Cleveland Copper Corp. Ltd. (Que. 1955)
Jan. 20, 1965 – Name changed to Delta Minerals Corporation; basis 1 new for 4 old shs. ■

Cleveland Mining & Smelting Co. Ltd. (B.C. 1962)
Mar. 1972 – Name changed to Consolidated Cleveland Resources Ltd.; basis 1 new for 6 old shs. ■

Clever Leaves Holdings Inc. (B.C. July 23, 2020)
May 17, 2024 – Voluntarily delisted. (see FPsurvey - Industrials)

Cleyn & Tinker Inc. (Que. 1962)
July 1988 – Acquired by Innocan Inc.

Cleyn & Tinker Ltd. (Que. 1962)
1978 – Name changed to Cleyn & Tinker Inc. ■

Cleyo Resources Inc. (Ont. Mar. 4, 1975)
July 2, 1997 – Name changed to Eloro Resources Ltd. following acquisition of 1179421 Ontario Limited; basis 2 new for 3 old shs. (see FPsurvey - Mines & Energy)

Clicker Red Lake Mines Limited (Ont. 1945)
Dec. 7, 1977 – Charter cancelled.
Feb. 20, 1980 – Charter revived.
July 22, 1982 – Amalgamated with Abino Gold Mines Limited (1 for 12.94), Commander Red Lake Mines Limited (1 for 30.82), Dorion Red Lake Mines Limited (1 for 15.59), Duchesne Red Lake Mines Limited (1 for 10.57), Forsyth Mines Limited (1 for 6.38), Goldquest Explorations Corp. (1 for 1.26), Inore Gold Mines Limited (1 for 9.9), Laddie Gold Mines Limited (1 for 15.22), and Rowan Gold Mines Limited (1 for 4.91) to form Goldquest Exploration Inc.; basis 1 new for 18.23 old shs.

ClickHouse.com Online Inc. (B.C. Aug. 5, 1987)
Sept. 19, 2002 – Name changed to Windridge Technology Corp.; basis 1 new for 5 old shs. ■

Cliff Creek Resources Ltd. (Ont. Sept. 23, 1968)
1986 – Name changed to Cliff Resources Corporation. ■

Cliff Resources Corporation (Ont. Sept. 23, 1968)
Sept. 6, 1995 – Name changed to Mineral Resources Corporation. ■

Cliffcrest Keno Mines Ltd. (Ont. 1951)
Apr. 20, 1967 – Charter cancelled.

Clifford Gold Mines Ltd. (Ont. 1924)
Sept. 18, 1961 – Dissolved.

Cliffside Capital Ltd. (Ont. Oct. 22, 2013)
Sept. 18, 2024 – Acquired by Cliffside Ltd.; basis 10¢ cash per sh. Shldrs. who elected to receive com. shs. of Cliffside Ltd. receive an aggregate of 56,281 purchaser shs.

Cliffwood Capital Corp. (B.C. Sept. 5, 2018)
Mar. 10, 2021 – Name changed to Hypercharge Networks Corp. (see FPsurvey - Industrials)

Clifton Consolidated Mines Ltd. (Ont. Mar. 1924)
1957 – Charter cancelled.

Clifton Porcupine Mines (unknown)
Mar. 1924 – Name changed to Clifton Consolidated Mines Ltd. and continued into Ontario; basis 1 new for 2 old shs. ■

Clifton Resources Limited (B.C. 1980)
Jan. 31, 1990 – Name changed to Consolidated Clifton Resources Limited; basis 1 new for 5 old shs. ■

Clifton Star Resources Inc. (B.C. Apr. 30, 1981)
Apr. 12, 2016 – Acquired by First Mining Finance Corp.; basis 1 First Mining com. sh. for 1 Clifton Star com. sh.
Oct. 19, 2022 – Name changed to Duparquet Gold Mines Inc.

Climax Mines Ltd. (B.C. 1935)
May 1958 – Dissolved.

Climax Silver Mines Ltd. (Ont. 1946)
1981 – Charter cancelled.

Cline Development Corporation (B.C. Jan. 14, 1983)
Sept. 3, 1993 – Name changed to Consolidated Cline Development Corporation; basis 1 new for 5 old shs. ■

Cline Mining Corporation (B.C. Jan. 14, 1983)
July 8, 2015 – Recapitalized under Companies' Creditors Arrangement Act (CCAA) resulting in the cancellation of all o/s com. shs. FTI Consulting Canada Inc. was appointed CCAA monitor. Secured noteholders were issued new voting and non-voting com. shs.

Clinger Gold Mines Ltd. (Ont. 1945)
May 18, 1976 – Charter cancelled.

CliniChem Development Inc. (Can. Jan. 30, 1998)
Dec. 15, 2000 – All o/s cl. A shs. acquired by BioChem Pharma Inc.; basis $18.43 per sh. (see BioChem Pharma Inc.)

Clio Tools.Com Ltd. (Sask. Jan. 27, 1992)
Nov. 2, 2004 – Struck from registry and dissolved.

Clip Money Inc. (B.C. Feb. 23, 2021)
Mar. 8, 2022 – Continued into Canada.
July 4, 2024 – Continued into Ontario. (see FPsurvey - Industrials)

clipclop.com Enterprises Inc. (B.C. Aug. 9, 1984)
Sept. 12, 2001 – Name changed to Worldwide Technologies Inc.; basis 1 new for 7 old shs. ■

Clipper Minerals Ltd. (B.C. Dec. 4, 1980)
Dec. 9, 1991 – Name changed to Stormin Resources Inc.; basis 1 new for 2.7 old shs. ■

Clix-Athabasca Uranium Mines Ltd. (Ont. 1950)
1962 – Name changed to Tinex Development & Exploration Ltd.; basis 100 new for 375 old shs. ■

Clodan Gold Mines Ltd. (Ont. 1945)
Dec. 10, 1962 – Dissolved.

Clonus Corporation (Can. Dec. 29, 1982)
Jan. 16, 1998 – Name changed to San-Mar Environmental Corp. ■

Cloud Nine Education Group Ltd. (B.C. Apr. 14, 2015)
Mar. 17, 2021 – Name changed to Cloud Nine Web3 Technologies Inc. ■

Cloud Nine Web3 Technologies Inc. (B.C. Apr. 14, 2015)
May 12, 2023 – Name changed to Anonymous Intelligence Company Inc. (see FPsurvey - Industrials)

CloudBench Applications, Inc. (B.C. Feb. 3, 1988)
Dec. 24, 2009 – Name changed to BasicGov Systems, Inc. ■

Cloudbreak Resources Ltd. (Can. May 13, 1987)
Apr. 23, 2010 – Continued into British Columbia.
Dec. 14, 2010 – Name changed to Petro One Energy Corp. ■

CloudMD Software & Services Inc. (B.C. Sept. 19, 2013)
July 11, 2024 – Acquired by CPS Capital L.P.; basis 4¢ cash per sh.
Jan. 12, 2025 – Name changed to Kii Health Holdings Inc.

Clover Gold Mines Ltd. (Can. Mar. 29, 1934)
Charter cancelled.

Clover Gold Syndicate Ltd. (unknown)
Mar. 29, 1934 – Name changed to Clover Gold Mines Ltd. and continued into Canada. ■

Clover Leaf Capital Corp. (B.C. Mar. 2, 2021)
Oct. 31, 2023 – Name changed to North Shore Uranium Ltd. issued pursuant to the Qualifying Transaction reverse takeover acquisition of North Shore Energy Metals Ltd. (see FPsurvey - Mines & Energy)

Cloverdale Resources Ltd. (B.C. 1964)
Feb. 25, 1983 – Struck off register.

Club Mate Holdings Ltd. (B.C. Nov. 19, 1984)
Apr. 28, 1997 – Name changed to International Millennium Mining Corp.; basis 1 new for 5 old shs. ■

Club Monaco Inc. (Ont. Sept. 21, 1987)
Apr. 6, 1999 – Acquired by PRL Acquisition Corp., a wholly owned subsid. of Polo Ralph Lauren Corporation, for $13 per sh.

Clubine Comstock Gold Mines Ltd. (B.C. 1931)
June 1954 – Dissolved.

ClubLink Corporation (Ont. Dec. 31, 1993 amalg.)
Aug. 4, 2009 – Amalgamated with ClubLink Enterprises Limited (formerly Tri-White Corporation); basis 1.1 ClubLink Enterprises shs. for 1 ClubLink Corporation sh. (see ClubLink Enterprises Limited)

ClubLink Enterprises Limited (Can. Oct. 22, 1997)
May 16, 2014 – Name changed to TWC Enterprises Limited. (see FPsurvey - Industrials)

Clucas Booker Gold Mining Company Limited (Ont. 1936)
Mar. 15, 1978 – Charter cancelled.

Cluff Gold plc (U.K. Nov. 30, 2004)
Sept. 28, 2012 – Name changed to Amara Mining plc.

Cluny Capital Corp. (Ont. Aug. 11, 2011)
Apr. 15, 2021 – Name changed to The Good Shroom Co Inc. and continued into Canada pursuant to the Qualifying Transaction reverse takeover acquisition of Teonan Biomedical Inc., and concurrent amalgamation of Teonan Biomedical with a wholly owned subsidiary; basis 1 new for 3 old shs. ■

Cluny Gold Mines Ltd. (Ont. 1944)
June 1953 – Charter cancelled.

Clyde Aircraft Manufacturing Co. Ltd. (Ont. 1940)
Mar. 15, 1949 – Charter cancelled; distributions totaling $1.485 plus 77¢ return on capital (final distribution) pd. from Dec. 21, 1946 to.

Clyde Resources Inc. (B.C. 1983)
Nov. 10, 1994 – Dissolved and struck off register.

Clydesdale Capital Corp. (Alta. May 18, 1995)
Nov. 7, 1996 – Continued into Ontario.
Nov. 21, 1996 – Name changed to Dundee Realty Corporation. ■

Co-enerco Resources Ltd. (Can. July 9, 1982)
July 4, 1994 – Acquired by Pennzoil Canada, Inc. for $8.60 per com. sh. and $1,050 for each $1,000 principal amt. of 6% debentures. (see Pennzoil Company)

Co-Maxx Energy Group Inc. (Alta. Feb. 10, 1988 amalg.)
May 1, 1995 – Acquired by NuGas Limited; basis $2.25 or $1.25 plus 0.5 NuGas shs. or 1 NuGas sh. for 1 Co-Maxx sh. (see NuGas Limited)

Co-operators General Insurance Company (Can. 1946)
Feb. 17, 1983 – Amalgamated in Canada to continue with same name. (see FPsurvey - Industrials)

Co-Steel Inc. (Ont. Sept. 10, 1970)
Oct. 25, 2002 – Name changed to Gerdau Ameristeel Corporation following reverse takeover acquisition of Brazil-based Gerdau S.A.'s North American operations. ■

Coachlight Resources Ltd. (Alta. May 14, 1985)
July 23, 1998 – Amalgamated with 779780 Alberta Ltd., a wholly owned subsid. of Danoil Energy Ltd.; basis 0.375 of a Danoil com. sh. plus 1 subco special sh. redeemable for 15¢ cash for 1 old Coachlight sh. (see Danoil Energy Ltd.)

Coal Creek Energy Inc. (B.C. Mar. 2, 1981)
Nov. 18, 2003 – Name changed to Corex Gold Corporation. ■

Coalcorp Mining Inc. (B.C. June 1, 1995)
Sept. 29, 2011 – Name changed to Melior Resources Inc. ■

Coalspur Mines Limited (Australia Dec. 31, 1985)
May 14, 2015 – Acquired by KC Euroholdings S.A.R.L.; basis A$0.023 cash per ordinary sh.

Coast Breweries Limited (Can. 1928)
Dec. 15, 1954 – Name changed to Lucky Lager Breweries (1954) Ltd. ■

Coast Diamond Ventures Ltd. (B.C. Jan. 1, 1983 amalg.)
June 9, 1994 – Name changed to AvCan Global Systems Inc.; basis 1 new for 3 old shs. ■

Coast Explorations Ltd. (B.C. 1962)
Apr. 1975 – Charter cancelled.

Coast Falcon Resources Ltd. (B.C. July 7, 1992)
Sept. 11, 2000 – Name changed to Inside Holdings Inc.; basis 1 new for 10 old shs. ■

Coast Industrial Hi-Tech Fabricating Ltd. (B.C. June 24, 1985)
Mar. 21, 1994 – Name changed to Maximum Resources Inc. ■

Coast Interior Ventures Ltd. (B.C. 1970)
Aug. 13, 2007 – Dissolved and struck from register.

Coast Mountain Power Corp. (B.C. July 8, 1999)
Aug. 4, 2006 – Acquired by NovaGold Resources Inc.; basis 0.1245 NovaGold com. shs. for 1 Coast Mountain com. sh.
2006 – Name changed to NovaGreenPower Inc. ■

Coast Range Resources Ltd. (B.C. 1983)
Feb. 26, 1993 – Dissolved and struck off register.

Coast Silver Mines Ltd. (B.C. Apr. 30, 1963)
Apr. 6, 1972 – Name changed to Consolidated Coast Silver Mines Ltd.; basis 1 new for 7 old shs. ■

Coast To Coast Oil Holdings, Ltd. (Can. 1920)
1939 – In voluntary liquidation; $40,000 proceeds from sale of property distributed to shldrs.

Coast Wholesale Appliances Income Fund (Alta. Mar. 24, 2005)
Jan. 1, 2011 – Succeeded by Coast Wholesale Appliances Inc. pursuant to plan of arrangement whereby Coast Wholesale Appliances Inc. was formed to facilitate the conversion of the fund into a corporation and the fund was subsequently dissolved. ■

Coast Wholesale Appliances Inc. (Can. Apr. 30, 2010)
Sept. 3, 2014 – Privatized. All o/s com. shs. not already held acquired by CWAL Investments Ltd.; basis $4.65 cash per sh.
Sept. 22, 2017 – Continued into Alberta.

Coastal Contacts Inc. (Can. Dec. 14, 2000)
May 2, 2014 – Acquired by Essilor International S.A.; basis $12.45 cash per Coastal sh.

Coastal Energy Company (Cayman Islands May 26, 2004)
Jan. 22, 2014 – Acquired by Strategic Resources (Global) Limited, by way of amalgamation with its wholly owned subsid., Condor Acquisition (Cayman) Limited, for $19 per sh.

Coastal Gold Corp. (B.C. Feb. 19, 1987)
July 13, 2015 – Acquired by First Mining Finance Corp.; basis 0.1625 First Mining com. shs. for 1 Coastal Gold com. sh. (see First Mining Finance Corp.)

Coastal Group Inc. (Can. Oct. 22, 1996)
Aug. 30, 2002 – Formed Continental (CBOC) Corporation in Canada on amalgamation with Prairie Capital Inc; basis 1 new divd., 0.8 new subord. vtg. and 0.8 new multiple vtg. for 1 old divd., 1 old subord. vtg. and 1 old multiple vtg. sh. ■

Coastal Income Corp. (Can. Apr. 23, 2002)
Mar. 20, 2007 – All senior retractable pfd. shs. redeemed; basis $25.20 per sh. plus $0.31071 for accrued and unpaid dividends.

Coastal International Ltd. (Bermuda 1980)
Dec. 6, 1985 – Name changed to Challenger International Ltd. ■

Coastal Mining Ltd (Que. 1962)
1968 – Name changed to Torcan Explorations Ltd.; basis 1 new for 3 old shs. ■

Coastal Oils Ltd. (Alta. Aug. 25, 1944)
Dec. 15, 1972 – Shldrs. approved sale of assets to Home Oil Co. Ltd. (which owned 99.3% o/s shs.) for $71,700 and divd. pay. of $1.245 per sh. to holders of record Dec. 14, 1972. In voluntary liquidation; liquidator: W. H. Bonney, c/o MacLeod, Dixon, 555 Bentall Bldg., Calgary.

Coastal Plain Resources Ltd. (Alta. June 27, 1986)
May 17, 2000 – Wound up.

Coastal Value Fund Inc. (Ont. Sept. 27, 2002)
Feb. 21, 2007 – Redeemed at $25.20 per pfd. sh. plus $0.2125 for accrued and unpaid dividends.

Coastline Petroleum Ltd. (B.C. Aug. 12, 1981)
Mar. 29, 1988 – Name changed to Coastline Resources Ltd. ■

Coastline Resources Ltd. (B.C. Aug. 12, 1981)
Apr. 13, 1992 – Name changed to REMCO Environmental Services Ltd. ■

Coastoro Resources Ltd. (B.C. 1981)
Nov. 10, 1988 – Merged with T & H Resources Ltd.; basis 0.5 new for 1 old sh.

Coastport Capital Inc. (Alta. Apr. 14, 2000)
June 1, 2005 – Continued into British Columbia.
Aug. 30, 2010 – Name changed to Donnybrook Energy Inc. and continued into Alberta. ■

Cob-Sil-Ore Mines Ltd. (Ont. 1950)
Jan. 1959 – Name changed to Norbank Explorations Ltd. ■

Cobagold Mines Ltd. (Ont. 1936)
1951 – Charter cancelled.

Cobalt Badger Silver Mines Ltd. (Ont. 1950)
May 1958 – Charter cancelled.

Cobalt Blockchain Inc. (Ont. May 23, 1980)
Nov. 1, 2021 – Name changed to Enerev5 Metals Inc. (see FPsurvey - Mines & Energy)

Cobalt Chemicals Ltd. (Ont. 1939)
Nov. 1954 – Acquired by Quebec Metallurgical Industries Ltd.; basis 1 new for 5 old shs. (see Quebec Metallurgical Industries Ltd.)

Cobalt Coal Corp. (Alta. Oct. 1, 2009 amalg.)
July 8, 2011 – Name changed to Cobalt Coal Ltd.; basis 1 new for 10 old shs. ■

Cobalt Coal Ltd. (Alta. Oct. 1, 2009 amalg.)
Apr. 2, 2016 – Struck from the registry and dissolved.

Cobalt Consolidated Mining Corp. Ltd. (Ont. Jan. 21, 1953)
Oct. 1957 – Name changed to Agnico Mines Limited; basis 1 new for 3.5 old shs. ■

Cobalt Contact Mines Ltd. (Ont. Mar. 1, 1925)
Dec. 21, 1936 – Continued into Quebec.
1936 – Name changed to York Bousquet Gold Mines Ltd.; basis 1 new for 10 old shs. ■

Cobalt Energy Ltd. (Alta. Nov. 9, 2005)
July 10, 2009 – Acquired by Bonterra Oil & Gas Ltd.; basis 0.011875 Bonterra shs. for 1 Cobalt cl. A sh. and 0.11875 Bonterra shs. for 1 Cobalt cl. B sh. (see Bonterra Oil & Gas Ltd.)

The Cobalt-Frontenac Mining Co. Ltd. (Ont. 1910)
1955 – Charter cancelled.

Cobalt Leith Mines Ltd. (Ont. 1956)
Jan. 1959 – Name changed to North Tech Exploration Ltd. ■

Cobalt Lode Silver Mines (Ont. 1949)
Jan. 21, 1953 – Continued into Ontario.
Jan. 1953 – Name changed to Cobalt Consolidated Mining Corp. Ltd.; basis 1 new for 8 old com. or 5 pref. shs. ■

Cobalt Power Group Inc. (B.C. Dec. 14, 2009)
Feb. 8, 2019 – Name changed to Power Group Projects Corp.; basis 1 new for 10 old shs. (see FPsurvey - Mines & Energy)

Cobalt Products Ltd. (Ont. 1938)
1967 – Merged into Resource Exploration & Development Co. Ltd.; basis 100 new for 91 old shs.

Cobalt 27 Capital Corp. (B.C. May 9, 2006)
Oct. 31, 2019 – All o/s com. shs. not already held acquired by Pala Investments Limited; basis $5.92 per sh., consisting of $4 in cash plus $1.92 in shs. of Nickel 28 Capital Corp. (renamed Conic Metals Corp.) for 1 Cobalt 27 sh.

Cobalt-Yellowknife Mines Ltd. (Can. 1946)
1949 – Name changed to Waddington Mining Corp. Ltd. ■

Cobaltech Mining Inc. (B.C. Oct. 30, 2007)
Dec. 5, 2017 – Acquired by First Cobalt Corp.; basis 0.2632 First Cobalt com. sh. for 1 Cobaltech sh. Name changed to CobalTech Mining Inc.

Cobatec Inc. (Ont. 1958)
Feb. 4, 2013 – Certificate of incorporation cancelled and dissolved.

Cobequid Life Sciences Inc. (N.S. 1985)
Sept. 23, 1992 – Continued into Canada.
June 22, 2000 – Acquired by 3723518 Canada Inc., an affiliate of Novartis Animal Health Inc., for $4 per sh.

Cobequid Resources Limited (N.S. 1985)
June 23, 1992 – Name changed to Cobequid Life Sciences Inc. ■

Cobi Foods Inc. (Ont. May 1, 1986 amalg.)
Oct. 12, 1995 – Acquired by Minas Group Limited for 37¢ per sh.

Cobil Uranium Mines Ltd. (Ont. 1953)
Mar. 1960 – Charter cancelled.

Cobra Enterprises Ltd. (B.C. Sept. 24, 1982)
Aug. 22, 1994 – Name changed to MVS Modular Vehicle Systems Ltd.; basis 1 new for 5 old shs. ■

Cobra Industries Inc. (Que. 1951)
June 1961 – Name changed to Dynamic Industries Inc. ■

Cobra Pacific Systems, Inc. (B.C. Sept. 24, 1982)
Feb. 16, 1998 – Name changed to Marathon Foods Inc. ■

Cobre Exploration Corp. (B.C. June 17, 1998)
Jan. 28, 2011 – Name changed to Calico Resources Corp. ■

Cobre Explorations Ltd. (B.C. Dec. 28, 1971)
Feb. 6, 1984 – Name changed to Mountain West Resources Inc. ■

Cobre Lake Uranium Mines (Ont. 1955)
1955 – Name changed to Oakwood Mines Ltd. and continued into Ontario. ■

Cobre Mining Company Inc. (B.C. Feb. 24, 1981)
Mar. 6, 1998 – All o/s com. shs. and ser. A and ser. B wts. acquired by Phelps Dodge Acquisition Corp., a indirect subsid. of Phelps Dodge Corporation of Phoenix, Arizona; basis US$3.85 for 1 com. sh. and US$0.10 for each ser. A and ser. B wts.

Cobriza Metals Corp. (B.C. May 16, 2011)
Sept. 13, 2013 – All o/s not held acquired by Candente Copper Corp.; basis 0.50 Candente shs. for 1 Cobriza sh. (see Candente Copper Corp.)

Coca-Cola Beverages Ltd. (Can. July 27, 1987)
Sept. 12, 1997 – Formed Coca-Cola Bottling Company in Canada following acquisition by Enterprises KOC Acquisitions Company, a wholly owned subsid. of Coca-Cola Enterprises Inc. of Atlanta, Ga., for $22 per sh. ■

Coca-Cola Bottling Company (Can. Sept. 12, 1997 amalg.)
Oct. 4, 2010 – Name changed to Coca-Cola Refreshments Canada Company.

Cocallen Porcupine Gold Mines Ltd. (Ont. 1946)
1956 – Charter cancelled.

Cochenour Marcus Gold Mines Ltd. (Ont. 1954)
1956 – Name changed to Consolidated Marcus Gold Mines Limited. ■

Cochenour Willans Gold Mines, Limited (Ont. Apr. 9, 1936)
Aug. 8, 1979 – Name changed to Wilanour Resources Limited; basis 1 new for 5 old shs. ■

Cochise Resources Inc. (Ont. Oct. 26, 1988)
Aug. 1, 2001 – Formed Neatt Corporation in Ontario on amalgamation with Neatt Corporation; basis 1 new for 20 old shs. ■

Cochrane-Dunlop Hardware Ltd. (Ont. 1909)
May 20, 1975 – Name changed to Cochrane-Dunlop Limited; basis 4 new com. for 1 old cl. A sh.; 6 new com. for 1 old com. sh. ■

Cochrane-Dunlop Limited (Ont. 1909)
Jan. 7, 1982 – Amalgamated with D. H. Frederick Holdings Limited to continue under the Cochrane-Dunlop Limited name. All o/s com. shs. exchanged into redeemable pfce. shs. of $10 par value which were redeemed at par on Jan. 8, 1982.
Dec. 1, 1987 – Placed into receivership and dissolved.

Cochrane Oil and Gas Ltd. (Alta. 1952)
Feb. 10, 1988 – Formed Co-Maxx Energy Group Inc. in Alberta on amalgamation with Maxxwell Energy Corp.; basis 1 new for 8 old shs. ■

Cockeram Red Lake Mines Ltd (Ont. 1927)
1948 – Name changed to Nova-Co Exploration Ltd.; basis 1 new for 3 old shs. ■

Cockfield, Brown & Company Limited (Can. 1928)
Oct. 3, 1979 – Name changed to Cockfield Brown Inc. ■

Cockfield Brown Inc. (Can. 1928)
May 1983 – Placed into receivership and PricewaterhouseCoopers Inc. (formerly Cooper & Lybrand) of Montreal was appointed receiver.
Mar. 1985 – Unsecured creditors were paid 58¢ on each dollar owed.
June 1987 – All preferred and secured creditors were repaid in full.
May 1989 – An additional 5¢ on each dollar owed was paid to unsecured creditors.
July 9, 1998 – Receiver was discharged and no further distribution was made to unsecured creditors or shldrs.
Jan. 2, 2003 – Dissolved.

Cockshutt Farm Equipment Ltd. (Can. 1911)
Feb. 1, 1962 – Sold its farm machinery division to The White Motor Co. Price included US$3,350,000 cash and $4,650,000 5.25% notes due to Feb. 1, 1966. Inventories amounting to $8,578,402 were consigned to The White Motor Co.
Feb. 8, 1962 – Name changed to C.K.P. Developments Ltd. ∎

Cockshutt Plow Co., Ltd. (Can. 1911)
Nov. 2, 1951 – Name changed to Cockshutt Farm Equipment Ltd. ∎

Coco Pool Corp. (B.C. Sept. 15, 2021)
Nov. 6, 2024 – Name changed to Viridian Metals Inc. pursuant to the Qualifying Transaction reverse takeover acquisition of Viridian Metals Corp.; basis 0.46 new for 1 old sh. (see FPsurvey - Mines & Energy)

Code Oil & Gas Ltd. (Alta.)
1965 – Struck off register.

Code Petroleum Ltd. (B.C. 1975)
Oct. 25, 1985 – Struck off register.

Codebase Ventures Inc. (B.C. Sept. 10, 2013)
Mar. 23, 2022 – Name changed to Cypher Metaverse Inc. (see FPsurvey - Industrials)

Codiac Development Company, Ltd. (N.B. 1961)
July 21, 1969 – Name changed to Copeland Process Limited. ∎

Codrington Resource Corporation (B.C. Jan. 15, 2007)
Nov. 23, 2015 – Name changed to NRG Metals Inc. ∎

The Codville Company, Ltd. (unknown 1905)
Acquired by Codville Distributors Ltd.

Cody-Reco Mines Ltd. (Ont. 1951)
1960 – Name changed to Vespar Mines Ltd.; basis 1 new for 3 old shs. ∎

Coeur d'Alene Mines Corporation (Idaho Nov. 1, 1928)
May 16, 2013 – Name changed to Coeur Mining, Inc. and continued into Delaware.

Coexco Petroleum Inc. (Alta. 1983)
Dec. 3, 1993 – Amalgamated with Shelter Oil & Gas Ltd. (1 for 4), Forewest Industries Ltd. (1 for 9.6526944) and Tesco Corporation to continue as Tesco Corporation; basis 1 new for 3.3139652 old shs. (see Tesco Corporation)

Coffee Tea or Me Cafe Inc. (Ont. Dec. 11, 1995)
Feb. 7, 2005 – Struck from register.

Coffin Mining Co. Ltd. (Can. July 2, 1932)
Oct. 3, 1934 – Continued into Quebec.
1934 – Name changed to Inspiration Mining & Development Co. Ltd. ∎

Cofiad Inc. (Que. 1953)
1968 – Liquidation of co. assets commenced
Dec. 15, 1976 – Distributions to ser. A noteholders were made as follows: 20% of total amount owned (incl. principal, premium and interest) on Jan. 31, 1971; 19% on Dec. 15, 1973; and a final payment of 7.08% on Apr. 2, 1980. Series A and C noteholders received a first and final payment of 10% of total amount owned on Dec. 15, 1976.

Cogas Energy Limited (B.C. 1964)
Jan. 17, 1995 – Amalgamated with 624151 Alberta Ltd., a wholly owned subsid. of Canadian Pioneer Energy Inc.; basis $5.95 per sh. for half of the com. sh. of Cogas tendered and 1.088 com. shs. of Canadian Pioneer for the other half sh. of Cogas tendered. (see Canadian Pioneer Energy Inc.)

Cogeco Cable Inc. (Can. Mar. 24, 1992)
Jan. 13, 2016 – Name changed to Cogeco Communications Inc. (see FPsurvey - Industrials)

Cogema Canada Limited (Can. Mar. 6, 1973)
Apr. 21, 1993 – Name changed to Cogema Resources Inc. ∎

Cogema Resources Inc. (Can. Mar. 6, 1973)
June 6, 2006 – Name changed to AREVA Resources Canada Inc. ∎

Cogenix Power Corporation (B.C. June 10, 1983)
July 25, 1996 – Name changed to Global Cogenix Industrial Corporation; basis 1 new for 5 old shs. ∎

Cogent Capital Corp. (Ont. Oct. 12, 1990)
Jan. 8, 2007 – Dissolved and struck from register.

Cogent Integrated Healthcare Solutions Corporation (Can. Dec. 4, 2003)
Jan. 17, 2007 – Name changed to The Silver Recycling Company Inc. ∎

Cogent Integrated Solutions Corporation (Can. Dec. 4, 2003)
Nov. 28, 2005 – Name changed to Cogent Integrated Healthcare Solutions Corporation; basis 1 new for 5 old shs. ∎

Cogesco Mining Resources Inc. (Can. 1985)
Aug. 4, 1987 – Name changed to Nova-Cogesco Resources Inc.; basis 1 new for 5 old sh. ∎

Cogient Corp. (Ont. Apr. 29, 1983)
Dec. 8, 2006 – Placed into receivership. Grant Thornton Limited appointed receiver.
Feb. 14, 2007 – Assets vested with trustee of debenture holders and to be distributed on a pro rata basis. No consideration available for shldrs.
Aug. 14, 2015 – Certificate of incorporation cancelled and dissolved.

Cogitore Resources Inc. (Ont. Dec. 13, 2002)
Mar. 26, 2015 – Name changed to CR Capital Corp. ∎

Cogivar Corporation (Can. Dec. 4, 2003)
Mar. 16, 2005 – Name changed to Kree Tech International Corporation following Qualifying Transaction reverse takeover acquisition of Kree Technologies Inc. ∎

Cognos Incorporated (Can. Dec. 23, 1969)
Feb. 4, 2008 – Acquired by International Business Machines Corporation for US$58 per sh.

Cognoscente Software International Inc. (B.C. Dec. 17, 1981)
Mar. 1, 1999 – Delisted from the Vancouver Stock Exchange. Subsequently struck from register and dissolved.

Coho Collective Kitchens Inc. (B.C. June 7, 2019)
May 22, 2024 – Name changed to Purebread Brands Inc. (see FPsurvey - Industrials)

Coho Resources Limited (Alta. May 9, 1980)
Oct. 5, 1993 – Amalgamated with Coho Resources Inc. to form Coho Energy, Inc.; basis 1 new for 1 Coho Resources Inc. sh. and 1 new for 3.85 Coho Resources Limited shs.

Coin Canyon Mines Ltd. (B.C. 1966)
Aug. 1971 – Amalgamated with Niseka Mining Ltd. to form Coseka Resources Ltd.; basis 1 sh. Coseka for 2 shs. of Coin.

Coin Explorations Ltd. (B.C. Mar. 16, 1966)
Dec. 20, 1972 – Name changed to Matador Developments Ltd. ∎

Coin Lake Gold Mines Limited (Ont. 1936)
Dec. 11, 1989 – Name changed to United Coin Mines Ltd.; basis 1 new for 2 old shs. ∎

CoinSmart Financial Inc. (B.C. Dec. 16, 1965)
July 10, 2023 – Acquired by WonderFi Technologies Inc.; basis 1.801462 WonderFi shs. for 1 CoinSmart sh.

Colabor Income Fund (Que. May 19, 2005)
Aug. 29, 2009 – Converted into Colabor Group Inc. following reorganization with ConjuChem Biotechnologies Inc. whereby Colabor Income Fund acquired ConjuChem for $5,000,000 to form ConjuChem Biotechnologies Inc. (new).

Colba.Net Telecom Inc. (Can. Feb. 5, 2004)
June 30, 2016 – Privatized; basis 1 new com. sh. for every 25,000,000 old com. shs. Fractional new com. shs. cancelled and consideration of 10¢ cash paid for each com. sh. that formed part of said fraction.

Colborne Natural Gas Ltd. (Ont. 1954)
Wound up.

Colby Mines Ltd. (B.C. Feb. 15, 1967)
Feb. 11, 1980 – Name changed to Colby Resources Corp. ∎

Colby Resources Corp. (B.C. Feb. 15, 1967)
Oct. 14, 1999 – Name changed to International Colby Resources Corp.; basis 1 new for 5 old shs. ∎

Colchester Mines Ltd. (N.L. 1966)
1975 – Charter cancelled.

Colchester Oil & Gas Co., Ltd. (unknown)
C/o Executors of estate, E. P. Rowe, 350 Bay St., Toronto. Stk. reported worthless.

Colchis Resources Ltd. (B.C. May 17, 1985)
Mar. 20, 1991 – Name changed to Northewan Minerals Corp.; basis 1 new for 5 old shs. ∎

Cold Creek Capital Inc. (Alta. Feb. 13, 2006)
Aug. 2, 2009 – Struck from registry and dissolved.

Cold Lake Pipe Line Company Limited (Alta. Oct. 16, 1952)
June 16, 1967 – Name changed to Worldwide Energy Company Ltd. ∎

Cold Lake Resources Inc. (B.C. 1978)
Dec. 11, 1985 – Name changed to FTI Foodtech International Inc. ∎

Coldspring Resources Ltd. (B.C. 1979)
July 14, 1989 – Name changed to Isleshaven Capital Corporation; basis 1 new for 10 old shs. ∎

Coldstream Copper Mines Ltd. (Ont. 1951)
1959 – Name changed to North Coldstream Mines Ltd.; basis 1 new for 4 old shs. ∎

Coldstream Mines Ltd. (Ont. 1972)
June 23, 1980 – Placed into receivership, Dec. 17, 1976. Rec. & mgr. Price Waterhouse, Box 51, Toronto-Dominion Centre, Toronto, Ont. M5K 1G1. International Mogul Mines Ltd. received $750,000 in settlement of a $4,500,000 debt in 1978. No further distributions expected. Charter cancelled.

Coldswitch Technologies Inc. (B.C. Sept. 6, 1988)
Aug. 9, 2002 – Name changed to Photon Control Inc. ∎

Colebucke Mines Ltd (Ont. 1947)
Acquired by Silverbucke Mines Ltd. date unknown; basis 1 new for 10 old shs. (see Silverbucke Mines Ltd.)

Coleco Industries, Inc. (Conn. 1961)
July 1988 – Filed for protection under the U.S. bankruptcy act.
1989 – Non-cash assets sold to a subsid. of Hasbro Inc.
Jan. 1, 1990 – Wound up with unsecured creditors receiving cash, warrants and shs. of Ranger Industries. Shldrs. received 1.125¢ per sh.

Coleman Collieries Limited (Alta. 1952)
Sept. 25, 1986 – All assets and liabs. assumed by Norcen Energy Resources Limited on Sept. 23, 1986. Co. dissolved. (see Norcen Energy Resources Limited)

Colena Mining Co. Ltd. (Ont.)
Apr. 2, 1969 – Charter cancelled.

Coleraine Asbestos Ltd. (Que. 1949)
Name changed to Coleraine Quebec Asbestos Ltd. ■

Coleraine Mining Resources Inc. (Que. Jan. 23, 1985)
Nov. 20, 2001 – Name changed to Amex Exploration Inc.; basis 1 new for 10 old shs. (see FPsurvey - Mines & Energy)

Coleraine Quebec Asbestos Ltd. (Que. 1949)
Dec. 23, 1972 – Dissolved.

Colerey Union Mines Ltd. (Ont. 1947)
Wound up.

Coles Book Stores Limited (Ont. 1960)
Aug. 31, 1978 – Acquired by Southam Press Limited for $23 per sh. (see Southam Press Limited)

Coleville Industries Ltd. (Alta. Jan. 23, 1987)
Oct. 27, 1993 – Name changed to Coleville Resources Limited; basis 1 new for 5 old shs. ■

Coleville Resources Limited (Alta. Jan. 23, 1987)
July 1, 2000 – Dissolved and struck from registry.

Colfax Energy Ltd. (Alta. Apr. 28, 1964)
July 5, 1988 – Name changed to Germain Industries Limited; basis 1 new for 8 old shs. ■

Colima Resources Limited (B.C. Mar. 2, 1984)
Apr. 27, 1990 – Name changed to Procordia Explorations Ltd.; basis 1 new for 2.5 old shs. ■

Colin Energy Corporation (Alta. Aug. 10, 1973 amalg.)
June 29, 1990 – Name changed to International Colin Energy Corporation; basis 1 new for 3 old shs. ■

Collart Gold Mines Ltd. (Ont. 1937)
1956 – Charter cancelled.

Colleen Copper Mines Ltd. (Ont. 1959)
Mar. 1976 – Charter cancelled.

College Plumbing Supplies Limited (Ont. 1953)
1977 – Placed into bankruptcy. Trustee: Touche Ross & Co., Toronto.
1980 – Taxation finalized with no distribution for unsecured creditors and shldrs.

Collicutt Energy Services Ltd. (Alta. Mar. 25, 1986)
Feb. 28, 2008 – Acquired by Finning International Inc.; basis $9.75 or 0.325 Finning com. shs. per Collicutt Energy com. sh. or a combination of both.

Collicutt Hanover Services Ltd. (Alta. Mar. 25, 1986)
Apr. 28, 2003 – Name changed to Collicutt Energy Services Ltd. ■

Collingwood Capital Corporation (B.C. July 14, 1982)
June 15, 2005 – Name changed to Rainy River Resources Ltd.; basis 4 new for 1 old sh. ■

Collingwood Energy Inc. (B.C. Aug. 20, 1979)
July 17, 1984 – Name changed to Collins Resources Ltd.; basis 1 new for 5 old shs. ■

Collingwood Terminals Ltd. (Ont. 1928)
Dec. 1973 – Name changed to Pemstar Holdings Ltd. ■

Collins Pacific Ltd. (B.C. 1944)
Oct. 23, 1958 – Struck off register.

Collins Resources Ltd. (B.C. Aug. 20, 1979)
June 25, 1992 – Name changed to Madison Enterprises Corp.; basis 1 new for 2.5 old shs. ■

Colloquium Capital Corp. (B.C. Mar. 23, 1998)
Feb. 25, 1999 – Name changed to Imagis Technologies Inc. following the Feb. 23, 1999, Qualifying Transaction reverse takeover acquisition of Imagis Cascade Technologies Inc. ■

Coloma Resources Limited (Ont. 1941)
July 31, 1988 – Formed FirstService Corporation in Ontario on amalgamation with FirstService Corporation. ■

Colomac Yellowknife Mines Ltd. (Ont. 1945)
1959 – Merged into Hydra Explorations Ltd.; basis 1 new for 25 old shs.

Colombia Crest Gold Corp. (B.C. Jan. 20, 1981)
Feb. 8, 2019 – Name changed to ATEX Resources Inc.; basis 1 new for 3 old shs. (see FPsurvey - Mines & Energy)

Colombia Goldfields Ltd. (Nev. Mar. 25, 2003)
July 31, 2006 – Continued into Delaware. (see Medoro Resources Ltd.)
Nov. 5, 2009 – Acquired by Medoro Resources Ltd.; basis 0.336 Medoro shs. plus 0.0108 Medoro wts. for 1 Colombia Goldfields sh. (see Medoro Resources Ltd.)

Colombian Mines Corporation (B.C. May 16, 2006)
Dec. 2, 2016 – Name changed to Newrange Gold Corp. ■

Colon Oil Co. Ltd. (Can. 1958)
1959 – Assets sold to Co. Shell de Venezuela Ltd.

Colonia Corporation (Alta. June 22, 1998)
Dec. 12, 2005 – Name changed to Colonia Energy Corp. ■

Colonia Energy Corp. (Alta. June 22, 1998)
Jan. 19, 2010 – Name changed to Renegade Petroleum Ltd.; basis 1 new for 10 old shs. ■

Colonial Asbestos Corp. (Ont. 1949)
1958 – Assets acquired by Normalloy Explorations Ltd. (see Normalloy Explorations Ltd.)

Colonial Natural Gas & Oil Co. Ltd. (Ont. Sept. 1932)
Aug. 1942 – Treleaven & Treleaven, of Hamilton, Ont., reported assets distributed.

Colonial Oil & Gas Limited (B.C. 1964)
Feb. 26, 1993 – Formed Cogas Energy Limited pursuant to plan of arrangement whereby Colonial com. shs. were deemed to be exchanged for Cogas com. shs.; basis 1 new for 2 old shs. ■

Colonial Steamships Ltd. (Can. 1933)
Dec. 1958 – Name changed to Scott Misener Steamships Limited. ■

Colonnade Capital Corp. (Ont. Apr. 3, 2008)
July 19, 2010 – Name changed to 3P International Energy Corp. ■

Colony Energy Ltd. (B.C. Oct. 29, 1984)
Apr. 11, 1996 – Continued into Alberta.
Feb. 28, 1998 – Name changed to Big Bear Exploration Ltd. following amalgamation with wholly owned Big Bear Exploration Ltd. ■

Colony Oil & Gas Co. Ltd. (Can. Feb. 6, 1936)
1949 – Assets acquired by Lloydminster Gas Co. for 110,000 shs. Struck off register.

Colony Pacific Explorations Ltd. (B.C. Nov. 26, 1979)
Mar. 30, 2001 – Amalgamated with 628916 Alberta Ltd. to form zed.i solutions inc.; basis 0.342 zed.i shs. for 1 Colony sh. (see zed.i solutions inc.)

Colony Resources Ltd. (unknown)
Sept. 1977 – Acquired by Gold Lake Resources Ltd. for $2,800,000 plus 200,000 Gold Lake shs. (see Gold Lake Resources Ltd.)

Color Your World, Inc. (Ont. 1955)
Oct. 24, 1984 – Color Tile, Inc. acquired 100% of o/s com. shs. at $25 per sh.

Colorado Resources Ltd. (B.C. Oct. 9, 2009)
Sept. 28, 2020 – Name changed to Questex Gold & Copper Ltd. ■

Colorfax International Inc. (B.C. 1978)
July 29, 1994 – Dissolved and struck off register.

Colortech Corporation (Ont. 1979)
July 23, 1996 – Acquired by Polyplast Muller Canada Inc., a wholly owned subsid. of Polyplast Muller GmbH, for $2.00 per sh.

Colossal Energy Inc. (B.C. Apr. 14, 1983)
Dec. 23, 1987 – Name changed to Consolidated Colossal Energy Inc.; basis 1 new for 2.5 old shs. ■

Colossal Resources Corp. (B.C. Oct. 4, 1989)
Dec. 13, 2012 – Name changed to Top Strike Resources Corp. and continued into Alberta. ■

Colossal Resources Corp. (B.C. Nov. 20, 1991)
Dissolved.

Colossus Minerals Inc. (Ont. Feb. 9, 2006)
Mar. 31, 2014 – Restructured under the Bankruptcy and Insolvency Act (BIA) pursuant to restructuring proposal resulting in consolidation of com. shs. on a 1-for-200 basis and the issuance of new com. shs. & new wts. to creditors. (see FPsurvey - Mines & Energy)

Colossus Nickel Development Ltd. (B.C. 1956)
Dec. 1959 – Name changed to Alamos Mines Ltd.; basis 1 new for 1 old sh. ■

Colossus Resource Equities Inc. (B.C. Dec. 8, 1987 amalg.)
Feb. 16, 1989 – Amalgamated with Delaware Resources Corporation to form Prime Resources Corporation; basis 1 new for 1 Delaware sh. and 1 new for 1 Colossus sh. (see Prime Resources Corporation)

Colours International Inc. (Ont. Feb. 9, 1983)
Jan. 3, 1995 – Delisted from the CDN. Subsequently struck from register and dissolved.

Colray Resources Inc. (Can. Sept. 28, 1983)
Mar. 1, 1994 – Name changed to American Ethanol (International) Corporation; basis 1 new for 10 old shs. ■

Colson Capital Corp. (Alta. Sept. 4, 2014)
May 31, 2021 – Name changed to Pathway Health Corp. pursuant to the Qualifying Transaction reverse takeover acquisition of (old) Pathway Health Corp. (renamed Pathway Health Services Corp.); basis 1 new for 2.941 old shs. ■

Colt Capital Corp. (Alta. Apr. 25, 2000)
May 15, 2006 – Continued into British Columbia.
July 18, 2007 – Name changed to Colt Resources Inc.; basis 1 new for 5 old shs. ■

Colt Energy Inc. (Can. Feb. 7, 1996)
Dec. 29, 1998 – Acquired by KeyWest Energy Corporation; basis 1 new KeyWest sh. for 1.68 old Colt shs. (see KeyWest Energy Corporation)

Colt Exploration Ltd. (Alta.)
1980 – Acquired by Golden Shamrock Resources Ltd.; basis 1.4 Shamrock shs. for 1 Colt sh. (see Golden Shamrock Resources Ltd.)

Colt Exploration Ltd. (B.C. June 10, 1982 amalg.)
Aug. 31, 1983 – Name changed to Colt Exploration (Western) Ltd. and continued into Alberta. ■

Colt Exploration (Western) Ltd. (Alta. Aug. 31, 1983)
Dec. 22, 1988 – Formed Stampede Oils Inc. on amalgamation with Stampede Oils Inc.; basis 1 new for 3 old shs. ■

Colt Resources Inc. (B.C. May 15, 2006)
Sept. 7, 2011 – Continued into Canada. (see FPsurvey - Mines & Energy)

Colt Resources Ltd. (B.C. 1972)
May 8, 1978 – Name changed to TransColt Resources Corporation; basis 1 new for 5 old shs. ■

Coltstar Ventures Inc. (B.C. June 19, 2007)
July 11, 2013 – Name changed to Metallis Resources Inc.; basis 1 new for 5 old shs. (see FPsurvey - Mines & Energy)

Columbia Beneficial Holdings Ltd. (B.C. 1964)
1972 – In voluntary liquidation. Liquidator: M. Donald Easton, 409 Granville St., Vancouver.
1973 – Distribution of assets (shs. of NWL Financial Corp. Ltd., now NW Financial Corp. Ltd., and some cash) on pro rata basis gave NWL Financial Corp. (majority shldr.) 807,998 shs., and minority shldrs. 194,150 shs. of NWL Financial.

Columbia Brewing Company Ltd. (B.C. 1950)
Sept. 30, 1974 – All o/s com. shs. acquired by John Labatt Ltd. at $5.00 per sh. and 1975. (see John Labatt Limited)

Columbia Care Inc. (B.C. Apr. 26, 2019)
Sept. 19, 2023 – Name changed to The Cannabist Company Holdings Inc. (see FPsurvey - Industrials)

Columbia Carpet Company Limited (B.C. 1946)
Aug. 25, 1960 – Dissolved and struck off register.

Columbia Cellulose Company Limited (B.C. 1946)
June 29, 1973 – All assets and liabs. excl. debt due Celanese Corp. transferred to wholly owned Canadian Cellulose Co., Ltd. Pref. shldrs. received 2 com. shs. of Cdn Cellulose for each pref. sh. held and com. shldrs., other than Celanese Corp., received one com. sh. of Cdn Cellulose for each com. sh. held. The balance of the com. shs. (approx. 79%) of Cdn Cellulose were issued to British Columbia Cellulose Co., a co. wholly owned by the Province of B.C. The pref. shldrs. also received a pay. of $1.80 on arrears on June 28, 1973. No payments made to the co. or to Celanese Corp. (which prev. held 91% of the co.'s o/s com. shs.) but both cos. were relieved of all obligations with respect to 1st mtge. bonds of the co. and bank debt of certain subsids. Cdn Cellulose issued 39,750 non-vtg. shs. to the co. as pay. for its deb.; these shs. were transferred to B.C. Cellulose.

Columbia Computing Services Ltd. (B.C. 1968)
Mar. 31, 1989 – Acquired by Hollis Investment Corporation, a wholly owned subsid. of Hollis plc; basis $5.75 per sh.

Columbia Copper Company Ltd. (B.C. Mar. 17, 1972)
Sept. 28, 2001 – Name changed to Kodiak Oil & Gas Corp. and continued into Yukon. ■

Columbia Copperfields Ltd. (B.C.)
1959 – Merged into Continental Consolidated Mines Ltd.

Columbia Explorations Ltd. (B.C. 1952)
1961 – Acquired by Imperial Metals & Power Ltd.; basis 1 new for 6 old shs.

Columbia Fuels Inc. (B.C. June 14, 1988 amalg.)
July 31, 1997 – Amalgamated in British Columbia to continue with same name.
Feb. 4, 1998 – Acquired by SNS Investment Inc. of British Columbia for 9¢ per sh.

The Columbia Gas System, Inc. (Del. 1926)
Jan. 20, 1998 – Name changed to Columbia Energy Group.

Columbia Gold Ltd. (B.C. 1951)
Jan. 1975 – Name changed to White Eagle Silver Mines, Limited. ■

Columbia Gold Mines Ltd. (B.C. Feb. 21, 1979)
May 12, 1999 – Name changed to Pacific Ridge Exploration Ltd.; basis 1 new for 3 old shs. (see FPsurvey - Mines & Energy)

Columbia Gypsum Co. Ltd. (B.C. 1954)
June 24, 1974 – Dissolved.

Columbia Lead & Zinc Mines Ltd. (B.C. 1951)
Mar. 1964 – Dissolved.

Columbia Leisure Corporation (B.C. 1964)
Nov. 3, 1995 – Dissolved and struck off register.

Columbia Metals Corporation Limited (Ont. 1945)
Oct. 18, 1978 – Charter cancelled.

Columbia Metals Corporation Limited (Ont. Mar. 7, 1949)
July 16, 2008 – Name changed to NWM Mining Corporation. ■

Columbia Metals Exploration Co. (Sask. 1954)
1965 – Name changed to Mid-Can Exploration Ltd. ■

Columbia Natural Gas & Oil Ltd. (Ont. 1934)
Sept. 28, 1946 – Assets sold and proceeds distributed.

Columbia Oil Co., Ltd. (unknown)
Acquired by Akamina Valley Oil Co., Ltd.; basis 1 new for 2 old shs.

Columbia Placers Ltd. (Can. Nov. 25, 1963)
1971 – Name changed to Maricana Enterprises Limited. ■

Columbia River Mines Ltd. (B.C. 1963)
June 27, 1973 – Name changed to Consolidated Columbia River Mines Ltd.; basis 1 new for 5 old shs. ■

Columbia Systems, Ltd. (B.C. 1975)
Nov. 23, 1984 – Charter cancelled.

Columbia Valley Mining & Development Ltd. (B.C. 1969)
July 11, 1977 – Dissolved.

Columbia Yukon Explorations Inc. (Alta. May 3, 1984)
Sept. 24, 2014 – Name changed to BC Moly Ltd. (see FPsurvey - Mines & Energy)

Columbia Yukon Resources Ltd. (Alta. May 3, 1984)
Dec. 4, 1998 – Name changed to Columbia Yukon Explorations Inc.; basis 1 new for 7 old shs. ■

Columbiere Mines Ltd. (Ont. 1952)
May 1971 – Charter cancelled.

Columbium Mining Products Ltd. (Que. 1956)
Oct. 1974 – Charter cancelled.

Columbus Copper Corporation (B.C. Jan. 4, 2005)
Oct. 6, 2015 – Acquired by Energulf Resources Inc.; basis 0.4937 Energulf com. shs. for 1 Columbus Copper sh.

Columbus Exploration Corporation (B.C. May 18, 2007)
Dec. 22, 2015 – Name changed to Organto Foods Inc. (see FPsurvey - Industrials)

Columbus Gold Corporation (Sask. May 14, 2003)
Dec. 20, 2004 – Continued into British Columbia.
June 5, 2020 – Name changed to Orea Mining Corp. ■

Columbus Silver Corporation (B.C. May 18, 2007)
Feb. 26, 2013 – Name changed to Columbus Exploration Corporation; basis 1 new for 4 old shs. ■

Columinda Metals Corporation Ltd. (Ont. 1952)
Sept. 19, 1960 – Charter cancelled.

Column Capital Corp. (B.C. Nov. 26, 2020)
Sept. 15, 2022 – Name changed to Largo Physical Vanadium Corp. pursuant to the Qualifying Transaction reverse takeover acquisition of (old) Largo Physical Vanadium Corp. [LPV] and concurrent amalgamation of (old) LPV with wholly owned 1356909 B.C. Ltd.; (old) LPV

was amalgamated into (new) LPV [the company].; basis 1 new for 7.547 old shs. (see FPsurvey - Mines & Energy)

Colvan Exploratons Ltd. (B.C. 1969)
Mar. 31, 1983 – Struck off register.

Com-Air Containers (Canada) Inc. (B.C. Dec. 11, 1986 amalg.)
June 19, 1992 – Charter cancelled and co. dissolved.

Com-Tron Systems Limited (Ont. 1967)
Mar. 5, 1975 – Charter cancelled.

Coma Lake Mines Ltd. (Ont. 1958)
May 27, 1965 – Dissolved.

Comac Food Group Inc. (Can. June 5, 1986)
Dec. 24, 2003 – Name changed to Canada's Pizza Delivery Corp. ■

Comamtech Inc. (Ont. Aug. 16, 2010)
June 15, 2011 – Name changed to DecisionPoint Systems, Inc. and continued into Delaware pursuant to reverse takeover acquisition of DecisionPoint Systems, Inc. and subsequent amalgamation of DecisionPoint with a wholly owned subsidiary of Comamtech.

Comanche Petroleums Inc. (B.C. 1979)
Oct. 18, 1989 – Name changed to Camford Capital Corporation; basis 1 new for 5 old shs. ■

Comaplex Minerals Corp. (Alta. Apr. 28, 1987)
July 2010 – Name changed to Meliadine Holdings Inc. pursuant to acquisition by Agnico-Eagle Mines Ltd.; basis 0.1576 Agnico-Eagle shs. plus 1 Geomark Exploration Ltd. for 1 Comaplex sh.

Comaplex Resources International Ltd. (B.C. 1968)
Dec. 8, 1993 – Acquired by Comstate Resources Ltd.; basis 0.35 Redfern Resources Ltd. shs. plus $2.35 or 1.6 Comstate shs. plus $1.20 for 1 Comaplex sh. (see Comstate Resources Ltd.)

Comara Mining & Milling Co. Ltd. (Ont. 1945)
1949 – Name changed to Columbia Metals Corporation Limited; basis 5 new pooled for 7 old shs. ■

Combine Drilling Company Limited (unknown)
1953 – All assets reported acquired by Thurston Developments Ltd.

Combined Engineered Products Ltd. (Can. 1945)
Dec. 3, 1974 – Name changed to Compro Limited. ■

Combined Enterprises Ltd. (Can. 1945)
Sept. 1962 – Name changed to Turnbull Elevator Ltd. ■

The Combined Larder Mines, Limited (Ont. Feb. 6, 1911)
Oct. 18, 1993 – Formed Buffalo Oil Company Limited in Saskatchewan; basis 1 new for 5 old shs. ■

Combined Logistics International Ltd. (Bahamas Sept. 10, 1997 amalg.)
Feb. 8, 2000 – Merged with Swedish-based private co. Wilson Logistics Group; basis US$0.33 per sh.

Combined Metal Mines Limited (Ont. Mar. 1, 1939)
Oct. 12, 1979 – Name changed to CME Resources Inc.; basis 1 new for 5 old shs. ■

Comco Mining and Smelting Corporation (B.C. Jan. 31, 1961)
Mar. 25, 1986 – Name changed to Quaker Resources Canada Ltd. ■

Comcorp Ventures Inc. (B.C. Aug. 20, 1998)
May 23, 2006 – Name changed to Wildcat Silver Corporation. ■

Comerica Bank Canada (Can. 1982)
May 5, 1986 – Bank sold a substantial amount of its loan assets to The Bank of Boston, Canada.
June 1987 – Bank ceased Canadian banking operations and in the process of winding up its operations in Canada.

Comet Drilling Ltd. (Alta. 1951)
Mar. 30, 1961 – Dissolved and struck off register.

Comet Duverny Gold Mines Ltd. (Que. 1945)
May 1974 – Charter cancelled.

Comet-Krain Mining Corp Ltd. (B.C. Jan. 1, 1950)
Aug. 1970 – Name changed to Comet Industries Ltd. (see FPsurvey - Mines & Energy; FPsurvey - Industrials)

Comet Mining Corp. Ltd. (B.C. 1964)
1964 – Merged into Comet-Krain Mining Corp. Ltd.

Comet Yellowknife Mines Ltd. (Ont. 1948)
Jan. 1950 – Charter cancelled; no equity.

Cominar Real Estate Investment Trust (Que. Mar. 31, 1998)
Mar. 3, 2022 – Acquired by a consortium consisting of Canderel Management Inc., FrontFour Capital Group LLC, Artis Real Estate Investment Trust, partnerships managed by Sandpiper Group and Koch Real Estate Investments LLC; basis $11.75 cash per trust unit.

Cominco Fertilizers Ltd. (Can. Dec. 21, 1992)
May 19, 1995 – Name changed to Agrium Inc. ■

Cominco Ltd. (Can. Jan. 9, 1906)
July 23, 2001 – Formed Teck Cominco Metals Ltd. pursuant to plan of arrangement acquisition by Teck Corporation; basis $6.00 plus 1.8 Teck cl. B sub-vtg. shs. for 1 Cominco sh. ■

Cominco Resources International Limited (B.C. Oct. 2, 1969)
May 5, 1987 – Continued into Canada. (see Cominco Ltd.)
June 2, 1995 – Acquired by Cominco Ltd.; basis 1 Cominco Ltd. sh. for 6.15 Cominco Resources shs. (see Cominco Ltd.)

Command Capital Inc. (Alta. May 23, 1997)
July 23, 1998 – Name changed to Military International Limited. ■

Command Drilling Corporation (Alta. Jan. 13, 2000)
Nov. 14, 2001 – Acquired by 19552 Yukon Inc., a wholly owned subsid. of Nabors Industries, Inc., for $3.40 per sh.

Command Oils Ltd. (Alta. 1937)
1962 – Assets sold to Commonwealth Petroleum Services Ltd.; basis 1 new for 8 old shs.

Command Performance Network Ltd. (Alta. Sept. 4, 1985)
Nov. 21, 1998 – Struck off register.

Command Post and Transfer Corporation (B.C. May 1, 1999 amalg.)
Aug. 1, 1999 – Amalgamated in Ontario to continue with same name.
May 20, 2004 – Acquired by Technicolor Creative Services Canada, Inc. for 4¢ per sh.

Command Resources Ltd. (B.C. 1966)
Dec. 20, 1974 – Name changed to Cordoba Developments Ltd.; basis 1 new for 2 old shs. ■

Commander Nickel Copper Mines Ltd. (unknown)
Name changed to Commander Resources Limited and continued into British Columbia.

Commander Red Lake Mines Limited (Ont. 1945)
July 22, 1982 – Amalgamated with Abino Gold Mines Limited (1 for 12.94), Clicker Red Lake Mines Limited (1 for 18.23), Dorian Red Lake Mines Limited (1 for 15.59), Duchesne Red Lake Mines Limited (1 for 10.57), Forsyth Mines Limited (1 for 6.38), Goldquest Explorations Corp. (1 for 1.26), Inore Gold Mines Limited (1 for 9.9), Laddie Gold Mines Limited (1 for 15.22) and Rowan Gold Mines Limited (1 for 4.91) to form Goldquest Exploration Inc.; basis 1 new for 30.82 old shs.

Commander Resources Ltd. (B.C. Mar. 30, 1983)
May 14, 1992 – Name changed to Commander Technologies Corp. ■

Commander Resources Ltd. (B.C. July 23, 1987)
June 3, 2025 – Acquired by Enduro Metals Corporation; basis 0.535 Enduro shs. for 1 Commander sh.

Commander Technologies Corp. (B.C. Mar. 30, 1983)
Sept. 12, 1995 – Name changed to SCS Solars Computing Systems Inc.; basis 1 new for 2 old shs. ■

Commando Gold Mines Ltd. (Que. Jan. 19, 1937)
May 1974 – Charter cancelled.

Commandor Mines Ltd. (Ont. 1936)
Charter cancelled.

Commerce Acquisition Corp. (Ont. Mar. 27, 2017)
May 24, 2019 – Name changed to Mimi's Rock Corp. pursuant to Qualifying Transaction reverse takeover acquisition of Mimi's Rock, Inc.; basis 1 new for 4 old shs. ■

Commerce Capital Corp. Ltd. (Can. 1970)
Jan. 1979 – Acquired by Eaton/Bay Financial Services effective for $9.00 per sh.

Commerce Capital Mortgage Corporation (Can. 1961)
Jan. 2, 1981 – Name changed to Eaton Bay Mortgage Corporation. ■

Commerce Capital Trust Company (Can. 1910)
Oct. 1980 – Name changed to Eaton Bay Trust Company (Alberta). ■

Commerce Nickel Mines Ltd. (Ont. 1965)
Sept. 5, 1979 – Charter cancelled.

Commerce Split Corp. (Ont. Nov. 27, 2006)
Mar. 26, 2010 – Succeeded by Original Commerce Split Fund pursuant to a capital reorganization whereby the assets of the company were allocated to two separate funds, Original Commerce Split Fund and New Commerce Split Fund. ■

Commerce - UD Inc. (Can. 1937)
Oct. 15, 1986 – All of the co's. public debt was redeemed.
Oct. 31, 1986 – All assets and liabs. assumed by the Canadian Imperial Bank of Commerce (the parent company), and a resolution was passed to voluntarily dissolve the co.

Commercial Acceptance Corporation Ltd. (Que. 1925)
1970 – Placed into bankruptcy
June 20, 1977 – Interim payment to ser. C, D, E and F secured notehldrs. of 12% on Aug. 2, 1971, and of 15.5% on Apr. 6, 1973; a final pay. of 12% made in December 1977. On the ser. B & C debs., a first and final pay. of 3.25% made June 20, 1977.

COmmercial and INdustrial Securities Income Trust (Ont. May 30, 2002)
Aug. 20, 2008 – Merged with Sentry Select Canadian Income Fund; basis 0.4438 Canadian Income Fund units for 1 COmmercial and INdustrial trust unit.

Commercial Consolidators Corp. (Alta. May 4, 1998)
Aug. 2, 2003 – Struck from registry.

Commercial Financial Corporation Limited (Ont. 1934)
1982 – Amalgamated in Ontario to continue with same name. (see Montreal Trustco Inc.)
Aug. 3, 1990 – Acquired by Montreal Trustco Inc. for $5.20 per sh. (see Montreal Trustco Inc.)

Commercial Industrial Minerals Limited (Ont. 1968)
Sept. 8, 1994 – Name changed to ICV Integrated Commercial Ventures Inc.; basis 1 new for 9 old shs. ■

Commercial Loan Co. Ltd. (Que. 1925)
1937 – Name changed to Commercial Acceptance Corporation Ltd. ■

Commercial Minerals Ltd. (Alta. Mar. 18, 1955)
1960 – Name changed to Commercial Oil and Gas Ltd.; basis 1 new for 10 old shs. ■

Commercial Oil & Gas Co., Ltd. (unknown)
Merged with Alberta Pacific Oil Co. Ltd.; basis 1 new for 2 old shs. (see Alberta Pacific Oil Co. Ltd.)

Commercial Oil and Gas Ltd. (Alta. Mar. 18, 1955)
Nov. 1, 1991 – Dissolved. All assets sold by a receiver appointed by the bank. Creditors suffered a shortfall and there was no distribution to the shldrs.

Commercial Oil & Gas Ltd. (Alta. 1955)
May 31, 1984 – Amalgamated (sh. for sh. for com. and pref. stocks) with Penstar Petroleum Ltd. to continue as Commercial Oil & Gas Ltd.

Commercial Oil Producers Ltd. (Alta. 1947)
1956 – Voluntarily liquidated.

Commercial Solutions Inc. (Alta. Nov. 30, 1993)
Feb. 6, 2014 – Acquired by Motion Industries (Canada), Inc., a wholly owned subsid. of Genuine Parts Company, for $1.07 per sh.

Commercial Uranium Ltd. (Alta. Mar. 18, 1955)
1955 – Name changed to Commercial Minerals Ltd. ■

Committee Bay Resources Ltd. (Alta. July 19, 2002 amalg.)
Mar. 2, 2009 – Name changed to CBR Gold Corp.; basis 1 new for 5 old shs. ■

Commodore Business Machines (Canada) Limited (Ont. 1958)
Aug. 17, 1976 – Name changed to Commodore International Limited.

Commodore Portable Typewriter Co. Ltd. (Ont. 1958)
Feb. 7, 1962 – Name changed to Commodore Business Machines (Canada) Limited. ■

Commoil Ltd. (Alta. 1936)
Dec. 28, 1962 – Assets sold to Commonwealth Petroleum Services Ltd. in 1962; basis 1 new for 1 old sh., plus a divd. of 7¢ per sh. to holders of record Dec. 28, 1962.

Commonwealth Acceptance Corp. Ltd. (B.C. 1947)
1969 – Declared bankrupt early. Harold Sigurdson, Vancouver, trustee.

Commonwealth Assisted Living Inc. (Alta. Nov. 12, 1996)
July 14, 1999 – Formed EnWave Corporation in Canada on amalgamation with DRI Dehydration Research Inc., constituting a reverse takeover by DRI; basis 1.86 new for 1 DRI sh. and 1 new for 1 Commonwealth sh. (see FPsurvey - Industrials)

Commonwealth Energy Corp. (Alta. Dec. 14, 1987)
June 29, 2001 – Acquired by Empire Energy Corp.; basis 1 Empire sh. for 6 Commonwealth shs.

Commonwealth Energy Inc. (Alta. June 24, 1986)
Feb. 8, 1996 – Name changed to Scimitar Hydrocarbons Corporation; basis 1 new for 1 old sh. ■

Commonwealth Exploration & Development Co. Ltd. (unknown)
1962 – Charter cancelled.

Commonwealth Gold Corporation (B.C. 1982)
Mar. 1, 1991 – Amalgamated with Golden Arrow Resources Inc. (1 for 3) and Yellow Band Resource Inc. (1 for 2) to form a new co. also named Commonwealth Gold Corporation; basis 1 new for 1 old sh. (see Commonwealth Gold Corporation)

Commonwealth Gold Corporation (B.C. Mar. 1, 1991 amalg.)
Apr. 25, 1994 – Amalgamated with Aber Resources Ltd. (1 for 1), to continue as Aber Resources Ltd.; basis 1 new for 3 old shs. (see Aber Resources Ltd.)

Commonwealth Holiday Inns of Canada Limited (Ont. 1964)
1979 – Scott's Restaurants Co. Limited acquired 99.5% of o/s com. shs. for $10 per sh. and offered $30 a sh. for all o/s pref. shs. Subsequently pref. shs. called for redempt. at $26.50 plus accr. divds. Plans to amalg. the 2 cos. were terminated in 1980. (see Scott's Restaurants Co. Limited)

Commonwealth International Corp. Ltd. (Can. 1933)
Apr. 16, 1974 – Name changed to Eaton Commonwealth Fund Ltd. ■

Commonwealth Minerals Ltd. (B.C. 1965)
Mar. 29, 1985 – Amalgamated with 3 other cos. to form Meridor Resources Limited; basis 0.14 new for 1 old sh.

Commonwealth Mining Corp. (Que. 1957)
Nov. 11, 1978 – Charter cancelled.

Commonwealth Mortgage & Savings Corp. (Ont. 1959)
Oct. 1963 – Name changed to Commonwealth Savings & Loan Corporation. ■

Commonwealth Petroleum, Limited (Can. Mar. 1926)
Nov. 25, 1959 – Name changed to Commonwealth Petroleum Services Ltd. ■

Commonwealth Petroleum Services Ltd. (Can. Mar. 1926)
1969 – Acquired by Westburne International Industries Ltd.; basis 2.5 new shs. plus $4.00 for 1 old sh. (see Westburne International Industries Ltd.)

Commonwealth Printing & Publishing Company Limited (B.C. 1933)
July 6, 1939 – Dissolved.

Commonwealth Richmond Properties Inc. (Ont. July 4, 1986)
Mar. 22, 1993 – Name changed to Empire Alliance Properties Inc.; basis 1 new for 16 old shs. (see FPsurvey - Industrials)

Commonwealth Savings & Loan Corporation (Ont. 1959)
June 4, 1970 – Name changed to Central Ontario Savings & Loan Corporation. ■

Commonwealth Trust Company (B.C. 1962)
1974 – Wound up and all creditors were paid by.

Commstar Ltd. (Ont. 1933)
July 6, 1998 – Acquired by Allied Cellular Technology Inc.; basis 1 Applied sh. for 3.62 Commstar shs.

Communications DVR Inc. (Can. Feb. 3, 2005)
Nov. 8, 2010 – Name changed to Exploration Aurtois Inc. ■

Communications Radiomutuel Inc. (Can. Sept. 1, 1985)
Dec. 16, 1987 – Name changed to Radiomutuel Inc. ■

Communications Systems International Inc. (Alta. July 31, 1990)
June 21, 2000 – Name changed to CSI Wireless Inc. ■

Communicorp Corporation (Ont. Nov. 28, 1989)
Sept. 23, 2004 – Dissolved and struck from register.

Community Gas Co. Ltd. (unknown)
May 15, 1941 – Liquidated.

Community Leaseholds Ltd. (unknown)
1965 – Acquired by Acroll Oil & Gas Ltd.; basis 35 new for 1 old sh.

Community Petroleums Ltd. (unknown)
1952 – Assets acquired by Peak Oils Ltd. for 568,000 shs.

Community Telephone Company Limited (Ont. 1955)
Nov. 18, 1968 – Distribution of 7.084 shs. of Continental for each 10 shs. of co. made. Also distribution of earned surplus made for each com. sh. held of co. Liab. for s.f. debs. assumed by Continental Telephone Holding Co.

Ltd., Que. Holders of sh. purch. warrs. could exercise same to Nov. 30, 1969.
1969 – Placed into liquidation. Pref. shs. redeemed at par for cash and/or com. shs. of Continental Telephone Corp.
Dec. 1, 1972 – All o/s 6.5% s.f. debs., ser. A, due 1978, were called for redemp. at 102% plus accr. int.

Comnetix Capital Corporation (Que. Dec. 1, 1999 amalg.)
Apr. 22, 2004 – Name changed to Comnetix Inc.; basis 1 new for 5 old shs. ■

Comnetix Inc. (Can. Mar. 29, 2004)
Feb. 23, 2007 – Plan of Arrangement acquisition by L-1 Identity Solutions, Inc.; basis US$1.17 per sh. ■

Comoro Capital Ltd. (Can. Dec. 18, 1995)
July 21, 1999 – Amalgamated with Ciclo Capital Ltd. (1 for 1) and Patent Enforcement and Royalties Limited; basis 1 Patent Enforcement sh. for 5 Comoro shs. (see Patent Enforcement and Royalties Limited)

Comox Resources Ltd. (B.C. Apr. 19, 1983)
Sept. 9, 1988 – Name changed to Pacific Comox Resources Ltd.; basis 1 new for 2 old shs. ■

Comp-Data International Inc. (B.C. May 27, 1980)
Oct. 5, 1987 – Name changed to Armenian Express Canada Inc. ■

Comp-U-Test Software Ltd. (B.C. 1988)
Dec. 17, 1990 – Name changed to Nucore Resources Ltd. ■

Compact Power Holdings Limited (Alta. Aug. 10, 1983)
Sept. 27, 2000 – Name changed to Exceed Capital Holdings Ltd. ■

Compagnie Agricole et Maraîchère de Sherrington (C.A.M.S.) Terres Noires Ltée (Que. Apr. 1, 1987)
Jan. 18, 1995 – Continued into Canada.
May 10, 1995 – Name changed to Rainmaker Digital Pictures Corp. following merger with a subsid. of Rainmaker Digital Pictures Corp.; basis 1 new for 2 old shs. ■

La Compagnie de Bois Nottaway Limitée (Que. 1950)
July 8, 1976 – Declared bankrupt.

La Compagnie du Téléphone Saguenay-Québec (Que. 1927)
1955 – Assets sold to Bell Telephone Co. of Canada. First mtge. bonds redeemed Dec. 1, 1954.

La Compagnie Foncière du Manitoba Ltée (Man. 1903)
Dec. 1967 – Amalgamated with Paris Canadian Investment Co. Ltd. to form La Compagnie Foncière du Manitoba (1967) Ltée.

La Compagnie Foncière du Manitoba (1967) Ltée (Man. Dec. 1967 amalg.)
Oct. 1, 1983 – Amalgamated with CIIT Inc. to continue as CIIT Inc.

La Compagnie Matco Mart Inc. (Que. Sept. 1, 1977)
Apr. 3, 1992 – Name changed to Matco Ravary Inc. ■

La Compagnie Minière De L'Ungava Ltée (Que. 1957)
Dec. 4, 1996 – Merged into Coretek Vencap Inc.; basis 1.5 new for 1 old sh. (see Ungava Minerals Corp.)

La Compagnie Minière Ligneris (Que. 1972)
June 18, 1977 – Dissolved.

Company's Coming Snack Bars Ltd. (Can. June 5, 1986)
July 20, 1990 – Name changed to Comac Food Group Inc. ■

CompAS Electronics Inc. (Can. June 15, 1993 amalg.)
Oct. 10, 1997 – Acquired by AIM Safety Company Inc.; basis 1 AIM sh. for 10 CompAS shs. (see AIM Safety Company Inc.)

Compass Investments of Alberta Limited (Alta. 1969 amalg.)
1978 – Paloma Petroleums Ltd. acquired 91.5% int. in 1975-76. Remaining int. acquired; basis 7.4 shs. of Paloma for 10 shs. of co. Amalgamated with parent co. in 1980.

Compass Petroleum Ltd. (Alta. Sept. 25, 2002)
Feb. 15, 2012 – Acquired by Whitecap Resources Inc.; basis either $1.60 or 0.205 Whitecap shs. for 1 Compass sh.

Compass Resources Ltd. (unknown)
1980 – Amalgamated with parent co., Paloma Resources.

Compass Resources Ltd. (B.C. Sept. 21, 1966)
June 9, 1993 – Name changed to United Compass Resources Ltd.; basis 1 new for 3 old shs. ■

Compel Capital Inc. (Ont. Dec. 20, 1945)
Apr. 7, 2021 – Name changed to ScreenPro Security Inc. following the reverse takeover acquisition of ScreenPro Security Ltd. ■

Compleat Health Corporation (B.C. 1983)
June 11, 1990 – Ceased operations.

Complex Minerals Corp. (Ont. Oct. 29, 1979)
Oct. 4, 2000 – Name changed to Ronin Resource Corp.; basis 1 new for 10 old shs. ■

Complex Ore Research and Development Ltd. (Alta. 1971)
Jan. 20, 1972 – Name changed to Cord International Minerals Ltd. ■

Compliance Energy Corporation (B.C. July 6, 2000)
Dec. 23, 2019 – Dissolved for failure to file and struck from register.

Comprehensive Medical Intelligence Inc. (Alta. May 30, 1997)
Oct. 30, 2001 – Formed RISE HealthWare Inc. in Alberta on amalgamation with 3161234 Manitoba Ltd. (operating as RISE HealthWare), constituting a reverse takeover by 3161234 Manitoba; basis 3 new for 1 3161234 Manitoba sh. and 1 new com. sh. plus 0.5 wts. for 3.5 Comprehensive Medical shs. ■

Compressario Corporation (Ont. Feb. 19, 2002 amalg.)
Aug. 25, 2010 – Certificate of incorporation cancelled and dissolved.

Compression & Encryption Technologies Inc. (Alta. Aug. 22, 1991)
May 2, 2003 – Struck from registry and dissolved.

Compression Technologies Inc. (Alta. Aug. 22, 1991)
Sept. 11, 1996 – Name changed to Compression & Encryption Technologies Inc.; basis 1 new for 5 old shs. ■

Compro Limited (Can. 1945)
Nov. 4, 1980 – All issued and o/s $1.10 conv. pref. shs., ser. A, called for redemption at $21.50 per sh. plus accrued divds. of 19.5¢ per sh. Co. is now private.

Comptec Industries Ltd. (B.C. Jan. 22, 1985)
May 9, 2000 – Name changed to Integrated Communications Industries Inc.; basis 1 new for 9 old shs. ■

Compton Explorations Ltd. (Ont. 1966)
1971 – Assets sold to Avilla International Explorations Ltd.; basis 2 new for 19 old shs.

Compton Petroleum Corporation (Alta. Oct. 15, 1992)
Sept. 14, 2012 – Acquired by MFC Industrial Ltd. for Cdn$1.25 per sh. (see MFC Industrial Ltd.)

Compu-Home Systems International Inc. (Ont. Feb. 18, 1976)
July 26, 1993 – Name changed to Arrowlink Corp. ■

Compu-Pour Industries Inc. (Alta. Jan. 30, 1992)
Oct. 22, 1993 – Name changed to Business Systems International Inc. ■

Compulsion River Mines Ltd. (Ont. 1968)
Feb. 26, 1998 – Dissolved.

CompuSoft Canada Inc. (Alta. Oct. 1, 1998 amalg.)
Apr. 19, 2001 – Name changed to TraceAbility Solutions Inc. (see FPsurvey - Industrials)

Computalog Gearhart Ltd. (Alta. Feb. 6, 1979 amalg.)
July 1, 1989 – Name changed to Computalog Ltd.

Computalog Ltd. (Alta. Feb. 6, 1979 amalg.)
Aug. 13, 1999 – Acquired by Precision Drilling Corporation; basis $9.00 or 0.38 Precision Drilling shs. for 1 Computalog sh. (see Precision Drilling Corporation)

Computalog Wireline Ltd. (Alta. Feb. 6, 1979 amalg.)
Aug. 22, 1980 – Name changed to Computalog Gearhart Ltd. ■

Computel Systems Ltd. (Can. 1967)
May 17, 1982 – Amalgamated with a wholly owned subsid. of Canada Systems Group Limited. Minority shldrs. received $16 per sh. while Royal Trustco Limited (which held 96% of the o/s shs. before the merger) received $8.50 per sh. and subsequently acquired a 25% int. in Canada Systems Group for approx. $13.8 million cash.

Computer Brokers of Canada Inc. (Ont. Mar. 9, 1993)
Apr. 19, 1995 – Name changed to Globelle Corporation. ■

Computer Innovations Distribution Inc. (Can. 1981 amalg.)
July 4, 1988 – Acquired by SHL Systemhouse Inc. for $3.60 per sh. (see SHL Systemhouse Inc.)

Computertime Network Corporation (Can. July 31, 1986 amalg.)
May 12, 1995 – Privatized at 75¢ per sh.

Computing Devices Canada Ltd. (Can. 1948)
1969 – All o/s Computing Devices (CDCI) shs. acquired by Minneapolis-based Control Data Corp. (renamed Ceridian Corp. in July 1992); basis 1 new Control Data sh. for 5 old CDCI shs.
Jan. 1, 2002 – Name changed to General Dynamics Canada Ltd. following acquisition by General Dynamics. ■

Computrex Centres Ltd. (B.C. Dec. 1, 1967)
Oct. 4, 2005 – Name changed to Camex Energy Corp. following acquisition of oil and gas interests in southern Alberta; basis 1 new for 2 old shs. ■

Comstate Resources Income Trust (Alta. May 15, 2001)
Feb. 7, 2002 – Name changed to Bonterra Energy Income Trust following reverse takeover acquisition of publicly listed Bonterra Energy Income Trust; basis 0.885 Comstate trust units for 1 Bonterra trust unit. ■

Comstate Resources Ltd. (B.C. Jan. 22, 1981)
July 4, 2001 – Converted into Comstate Resources Income Trust (CRIT) by way of acquisition by and amalgamation with Comstate Acquisition Corp., a wholly owned subsidiary of CRIT, to form new Comstate Resources Ltd., and shares of Comaplex Minerals Corp. held by the company distributed to shldrs.; basis 1 CRIT trust unit for 4 Comstate Resources Ltd. shs., plus 0.6 Comaplex Minerals Corp. com. shs. and 20¢ for 1 Comstate Resources Ltd. com. sh. (see Comstate Resources Income Trust)

Comstock Keno Mines Ltd. (Ont. Sept. 29, 1950; via letters patent)
Feb. 13, 1995 – Name changed to Thornbury Capital Corporation. ■

Comtech Capital Inc. (Alta. Dec. 21, 1995)
Dec. 12, 1997 – Name changed to Revere Communications Inc. ■

Comtech Group International Limited (Ont. June 15, 1946)
Dec. 1, 1981 – Continued into Canada.
Dec. 30, 1988 – Name changed to Postech Corporation. ■

Comtech Group Ltd. (Ont. 1968)
June 1969 – Acquired by Fibre Products of Canada Ltd.; basis 1.5 new com. shs. for 1 com. sh.

Comterm Inc. (Can. July 2, 1970)
Aug. 1, 1983 – Name changed to Bytec-Comterm Inc. ■

Comterm Inc. (Can. July 2, 1970)
Oct. 22, 1990 – Declared bankrupt. Information regarding distribution to shldrs. was not available.

Comterm Limited (Can. July 2, 1970)
May 6, 1981 – Name changed to Comterm Inc. ■

Comtron Enterprises Inc. (B.C. May 23, 1986)
Oct. 21, 1993 – Name changed to Olympic Resources Ltd.; basis 1 new for 3 old shs. ■

ComWest Capital Corp. (B.C. July 25, 1977)
Dec. 14, 2005 – Amalgamated with Chatworth Resources Inc. (0.3886 cl. A or 0.3886 cl. B for 1) to continue as a new company named ComWest Enterprise Corp.; basis 1 cl. B com. sh. plus 0.3333 new cl. A equity sh. for 1 com. sh. (see ComWest Enterprise Corp.)

ComWest Enterprise Corp. (B.C. Nov. 30, 2005 amalg.)
Aug. 1, 2014 – Name changed to Unisync Corp. (see FPsurvey - Industrials)

Con-Am Resources Ltd. (B.C. 1967)
Feb. 23, 1983 – Struck off register.

Con-Key Mines Ltd. (Ont. 1945)
Nov. 30, 1970 – Amalgamated with Cantri Mining Ltd. (1 for 10), Point West Explorations Ltd. (1 for 10), St. Anthony Mines Ltd. (1 for 30), Temanda Mines Ltd. (1 for 30) and Tinex Development & Exploration Ltd. (1 for 30) to form Can-Con Enterprises and Explorations Limited; basis 1 new for 10 old shs.

Con-Shawkey Gold Mines Ltd. (Ont. 1945)
1969 – Name changed to Kenn Holdings and Mining Ltd. ■

Cona Resources Ltd. (Alta. Nov. 18, 2009)
May 24, 2018 – All o/s com. shs. not already held acquired through certain affiliates of Waterous Energy Fund; basis $2.25 cash per sh.
Aug. 14, 2020 – Formed Strathcona Resources Ltd. following amalgmlation with Strath Resources Ltd. (see FPsurvey - Mines & Energy)

Conac Software Corporation (B.C. July 3, 1987)
Dec. 3, 2004 – Name changed to Lomiko Enterprises Ltd.; basis 1 new for 15 old shs. ■

Conagami Mines Ltd. (Ont. 1959)
1968 – Charter cancelled.

Conaldan Yellowknife Mines Ltd. (Ont. 1945)
1956 – Charter cancelled.

Conar Oil Ltd. (B.C. 1980)
Apr. 3, 1981 – Name changed to Southfork Energy Corporation. ■

Conbeau Resources Ltd. (B.C. Feb. 20, 1961)
Dec. 3, 1984 – Name changed to Inlet Resources Ltd.; basis 1 new for 7 old shs. ■

Concentrated Rare Earth Minerals Ltd. (Can. - unspecified)
Mar. 2, 1992 – Amalgamated with Enertex Developments Inc. (1 for 12.6), Goldmac Explorations Inc. (1 for 17.5), Norlode Resources Inc., Offset Natural Resources Ltd. (1 for 11), Preston Resources Ltd., Saranac Resources Ltd. and Uranex Resources Limited (1 for 13.5) to form a new co. named Marvas Developments Ltd.

Concept Industries Inc. (B.C. Aug. 4, 1987)
June 23, 2000 – Name changed to Concept Wireless Inc. ■

Concept Resources Ltd. (B.C. July 18, 1967)
Aug. 21, 1978 – Continued into Alberta.
Oct. 23, 1987 – Name changed to Skyline Natural Resources Ltd. ■

Concept Wireless Inc. (B.C. Aug. 4, 1987)
Feb. 27, 2003 – Name changed to Candao Enterprises Inc.; basis 1 new for 10 old shs. ■

Concert Industries Ltd. (B.C. Jan. 26, 1984)
Mar. 17, 1995 – Continued into Canada.
Dec. 31, 2004 – Implementation of a plan of compromise and arrangement following Companies' Creditors Arrangement Act was completed and all of the Canadian operating subsids. were acquired by Tricap Restructuring Fund. shldrs. received no distributions.

Concert Resources Inc. (B.C. Jan. 26, 1984)
Sept. 30, 1987 – Name changed to Concert Industries Ltd. ■

Concho Resources & Energy Inc. (Ont. Apr. 29, 1983)
Mar. 4, 1999 – Name changed to Tellerian Capital Corp. following reverse takeover acquisition of Klarinette Holdings Inc. for 2,768,232 units (1 com. sh. & 1 wt.). ■

Concopper Enterprises Inc. (Ont. Oct. 3, 1983)
Jan. 1, 2011 – Amalgamated with Mirado Nickel Mines Limited and Brenbar Mines Limited to form Micon Gold Inc.; basis 0.4185 Micon Gold cl. A shs. for 1 Mirado sh.; 0.0363 Micon Gold cl. A shs. for 1 Brenbar sh.; and basis 1.0200 Micon Gold cl A. shs. for 1 Concopper cl. A sh. and 0.3116 Micon Gold cl. B shs. for 1 Concopper cl. B sh.

Concopper Phosphate Inc. (Ont. Oct. 3, 1983)
Apr. 20, 1998 – Name changed to Concopper Enterprises Inc. ■

Concord Capital Corp. (Ont. Jan. 11, 1979 amalg.)
Feb. 7, 1994 – Struck from registry and dissolved.

Concord Development Corp. Ltd. (Ont. 1951)
1952 – Name changed to New Concord Development Corp. Ltd. ■

Concord Development Corporation Ltd. (B.C. 1968)
May 1985 – All publicly held pref. and com. shs. purchased by co. at an undisclosed price. there were 16 com. shldrs. and 2 pref. shldrs.

Concord Energy Corp. (B.C. Aug. 8, 1979)
Feb. 17, 1988 – Name changed to United Safety Technology Inc. ■

Concord Pacific Group Inc. (Yuk. Mar. 14, 1997)
June 17, 1998 – Continued into Canada.
Jan. 3, 2003 – Acquired by Adex Securities Inc. for $3.40 per sh.
Apr. 6, 2009 – Name changed to One West Holdings Ltd.

Concorde Exploration Ltd. (Que. July 12, 1951)
July 17, 1997 – Struck off register.

Concorde Explorations Limited (B.C. 1967)
Feb. 25, 1983 – Struck off register.

Concordia Healthcare Corp. (Ont. Jan. 20, 2010)
June 27, 2016 – Name changed to Concordia International Corp. ■

Concordia International Corp. (Ont. Jan. 20, 2010)
June 22, 2018 – Continued into Canada.
Dec. 3, 2018 – Name changed to Advanz Pharma Corp. ■

Concordia Resource Corp. (B.C. Mar. 21, 2006 amalg.)
Dec. 4, 2013 – Name changed to Kaizen Discovery Inc. following reverse takeover acquisition of certain assets from HPX TechCo Inc.; basis 1 new for 5 old shs. ■

Concourse Mines Ltd. (Ont. 1970)
Feb. 28, 1972 – Amalgamated with Coniston Copper Mines Ltd. and Gogama Minerals Ltd. to form Coniston Explorations & Holdings Ltd.; basis 1 new for 3 Concourse shs.

Condaka Metals Corp. (B.C. June 1, 1964)
Sept. 16, 1987 – Name changed to Dakon Metals Inc.; basis 1 new for 2 old shs. ∎

Condonna Uranium Mines (Ont. 1957)
Oct. 10, 1961 – Dissolved.

Condor Gold Corp. (Ont. June 19, 1997)
Jan. 11, 2016 – Dissolved and struck from register.

Condor Gold Fields Inc. (Can. May 13, 1987)
Nov. 8, 2002 – Name changed to Cloudbreak Resources Ltd.; basis 1 new for 16 old shs. ∎

Condor Gold Mines (1936) Ltd. (Ont. 1936)
Sept. 8, 1966 – Dissolved.

Condor Gold plc (U.K. Oct. 10, 2005)
Jan. 15, 2024 – Acquired by Metals Exploration plc; basis 4.0526 Metals ord. shs., £0.099 cash and 1 contingent value right for 1 Condor Gold ord. sh.

Condor International Resources Inc. (B.C. Nov. 16, 1986)
May 3, 1999 – Name changed to Northern Empire Minerals Ltd.; basis 1 new for 15 old shs. ∎

Condor Mines Ltd. (B.C. 1967)
May 1972 – Name changed to Corvus Mines Ltd.; basis 1 new for 4 old shs. ∎

Condor Petroleum Inc. (Alta. Oct. 20, 2006)
Aug. 16, 2010 – Amalgamated in Alberta to continue with same name.
June 9, 2022 – Name changed to Condor Energies Inc. (see FPsurvey - Mines & Energy)

Condor Precious Metals Inc. (B.C. Nov. 16, 1986)
Oct. 7, 1991 – Name changed to Condor International Resources Inc. ∎

Conduits-Amherst Limited (Ont. 1974 amalg.)
Mar. 14, 1983 – Aqua Gem Investments Ltd. acquired 82% of o/s com. shs. at $1.27 per sh. and made follow-up offer for remaining shs. at $1.30 per sh. to Oct. 14, 1984, when co. became privately held.

Conduits National Company, Limited (Ont. 1935)
Mar. 1974 – Amalgamated into Conduits-Amherst Ltd.; basis 3 new for 1 old sh.

Cone Mt. Mines Ltd. (B.C. 1969)
Nov. 23, 1978 – Name changed to Cancal Mines Ltd.; basis 1 new for 5 old shs. ∎

Conecho Mines Ltd. (Ont. 1950)
Aug. 26, 1957 – Merged into Consolidated Frederick Mines Ltd.; basis 2.40625¢ cash equivalent for each Conecho sh. (see Consolidated Frederick Mines Ltd.)

Conex Continental Inc. (Ont. July 23, 1984)
1998 – Continued into Delaware.
Mar. 5, 2001 – Name changed to Dominion International Investments Inc.

Conex Mining Co. Ltd. (Ont. 1955)
1972 – Charter cancelled.

Confederation Energy Corporation Limited (Alta. 1982 amalg.)
July 1, 1986 – Struck off register.

Confederation Minerals Ltd. (B.C. Nov. 3, 2005)
June 18, 2020 – Name changed to Trillium Gold Mines Inc. ∎

Confederation Mining Corp. Ltd. (Que. 1953)
Oct. 23, 1976 – Dissolved.

Confidata Resource Corp. (Alta. 1987)
May 2, 2003 – Struck from registry and dissolved.

Cong Industries Inc. (Ont. 1980)
Apr. 19, 1996 – Name changed to Outer Edge Inc. following amalgamation with Virtual Images (Canada) Inc. ∎

Congava Mines Ltd. (Que. 1957)
Dec. 30, 1960 – Charter cancelled.

Conger Feldspar Mining Co. Ltd. (Ont. 1945)
1956 – Charter cancelled.

Conger Lehigh Fuels Ltd. (Can. 1910)
July 1954 – Placed into liquidation. Distribution of $28.25 per sh. made.
Apr. 26, 1955 – Distribution of $3.00 per share made. $14.30 of total declared taxable income. Small final distribution reported to have been made.

Congress Gold Mines Ltd. (B.C. 1933)
June 1956 – Charter cancelled.

Congress Mining Corp. Ltd. (Ont. 1971)
Aug. 11, 1972 – Amalgamated into Staple Mining Co. Ltd.; basis 1 new for 4 old shs.

The Coniagas Mines, Limited (Ont. Nov. 24, 1906)
Sept. 21, 1993 – Amalgamated with Anglo Dominion Gold Exploration Limited (18 for 100), Garrison Creek Consolidated Mines Ltd. (7 for 1,000) and Quebec Sturgeon River Mines Limited (20 for 100) to form a new co. named QSR Limited; basis 32 new for 100 old shs. (see QSR Limited)

Coniagas Resources Limited (Ont. Sept. 8, 1993 amalg.)
July 23, 2009 – Name changed to Lithium One Inc. ∎

Coniaurum Holdings Ltd. (Ont. 1929)
May 1, 1967 – Name changed to Canadian Coniaurum Investment Limited.

Coniaurum Mines Ltd. (Ont. 1929)
Feb. 28, 1961 – Mining operations ceased and mining assets sold. Distributed 0.05 sh. of United Keno Hill Mines Ltd. and 0.2 sh. Carium Mines Ltd. for each Coniaurum sh. held.
1961 – Name changed to Coniaurum Holdings Ltd. ∎

Conic Metals Corp. (B.C. June 25, 2019)
Mar. 10, 2021 – Name changed to Nickel 28 Capital Corp. (see FPsurvey - Mines & Energy)

Conigo Mines Ltd. (Ont. Apr. 23, 1936)
Feb. 1971 – Assets sold to Amos Mines Ltd.

Conisil Mines Limited (Ont. Sept. 18, 1946)
Apr. 28, 1986 – Name changed to Conisil Resources Inc. ∎

Conisil Resources Inc. (Ont. Sept. 18, 1946)
Nov. 16, 1992 – Name changed to Human Resources for Growth Inc. ∎

Coniska Copper Mines Ltd. (Can. 1956)
Dec. 1960 – Wound up.

Coniston Capital Corporation (Can. July 31, 1968)
Aug. 10, 1995 – Continued into British Columbia.
Aug. 8, 1996 – Name changed to CPL Ventures Limited. ∎

Coniston Copper Mines Ltd. (Ont. 1969)
Feb. 28, 1972 – Amalgamated with Gogama Minerals Ltd. and Concourse Mines Ltd. to form Coniston Explorations & Holdings Ltd.; basis 1 new for 2.5 shs. of Coniston. (see Coniston Explorations & Holdings Ltd.)

Coniston Explorations & Holdings Ltd. (Ont. 1972 amalg.)
Mar. 14, 1978 – Charter cancelled.

Conjo Yellowknife Mines Ltd. (Ont. 1945)
Apr. 1957 – Charter cancelled.

ConjuChem Biotechnologies Inc. (Can. Feb. 1, 2006)
Aug. 28, 2009 – Name changed to Colabor Group Inc. pursuant to plan of arrangement resulting in Colabor Income Fund becoming a wholly owned subsid. of Colabor Group Inc., with trust units of Colabor Income Fund and exch. LP units of subsidiary Colabor Limited Partnership exchanged for common shares of Colabor Group Inc. on a 1-for-1 basis. All assets and liabilities of (old) ConjuChem Biotechnologies Inc. were transferred to (new) ConjuChem Biotechnologies Inc. which was spun out as a new public entity on a sh.-for-sh. basis. (see FPsurvey - Industrials)

ConjuChem Biotechnologies Inc. (Can. Aug. 25, 2009)
July 20, 2010 – Filed for bankruptcy. RSM Ritcher Inc. appointed trustee.
May 21, 2013 – Final distribution made. Secured creditors repaid in full; unsecured creditors suffered a shortfall. No distribution for shldrs. Application made for discharge.

ConjuChem Inc. (Que. Apr. 29, 1997)
May 23, 2006 – Name changed to ConjuChem Biotechnologies Inc. pursuant to plan of arrangement reorganization; basis 1 ConjuChem Biotechnologies sh. plus 1 6550568 Canada Inc. sh. for 1 ConjuChem sh. ∎

Conjuror Bay Mines Ltd. (B.C. 1967)
Dec. 24, 1974 – Name changed to Philco Resources Ltd.; basis 1 new for 2 old shs. ∎

Conlee Red Lake Gold Mines Ltd. (Ont. 1945)
1957 – Charter cancelled.

Conley Resources Corp. (B.C. Aug. 13, 1969)
Jan. 7, 1994 – Dissolved and struck off register.

Conmar Explorations Ltd. (Ont. 1944)
1973 – Charter surrendered.

The Conn Chem Group Ltd. (Can. Dec. 16, 1977)
Nov. 28, 1979 – Name changed to CCL Industries Inc. (see FPsurvey - Industrials)

Conn Chem Limited (Ont. Apr. 15, 1957)
Sept. 15, 1977 – TPC Packaging Corp. acquired 99.9% of o/s cl. A & B shs. at $10 per sh.
Dec. 16, 1977 – Continued into Canada.
Jan. 1, 1978 – Amalgamated with TPC Packaging Corp. to form Conn Chem Limited; basis $10 per sh.
May 25, 1978 – Name changed to The Conn Chem Group Ltd. ∎

Connacher Oil and Gas Limited (Alta. July 3, 1997 amalg.)
Mar. 30, 2015 – Continued into Canada.
Jan. 30, 2018 – Court approval was received for the granting of a bitumen royalty to Burgess Energy Holdings, LLC on all the lands containing bitumen together with the oil sands rights and interest owned by the company for an undisclosed cash consideration. Proceeds used to repay in full its US$16,521,164 interim revolving credit facility.
May 6, 2019 – Entered into an amended and restated support agreement with certain first lien lenders which hold 75% of the principal amount of debt outstanding and seeking court approval for the filing of a plan of compromise and arrangement under the CCAA. Under the amended 2019 CCAA plan, the company's creditors will not be paid in full and no value will accrue to the company's existing shldrs.and upon implementation of the 2019 CCAA plan, all outstanding shs. and options of the company will be cancelled for no consideration and without any vote of the existing shldrs.
July 16, 2019 – Received court approval for amended 2019 CCAA plan of compromise and arrangement under which the first lien credit holders will exchange obligations owed to them for 100% of the equity interests in the company and new senior secured debt.
Sept. 30, 2019 – Pursuant to the amended and restated plan of compromise, the first lien lenders acquired all of the company's share capital and all existing equity interests, including the company's com. shs., have been cancelled for no consideration.

Connaught BioSciences Inc. (Can. June 14, 1973)
Jan. 16, 1990 – Acquired by Institut Merieux S.A. of France for $37 per sh.

Connaught Ventures Inc. (B.C. Apr. 3, 2018)
Mar. 31, 2021 – Name changed to Principal Technologies Inc. (see FPsurvey - Industrials)

Connecticut Development Corporation (B.C. Mar. 31, 1980)
Apr. 16, 1999 – Name changed to Mira Properties Ltd.; basis 1 new for 6 old shs. ∎

Connetricia Gold Mines Ltd. (Ont. 1936)
1944 – Name changed to Connetricia Mines & Exploration Ltd. ∎

Connetricia Mines & Exploration Ltd. (Ont. 1936)
1953 – Charter cancelled.

Connor, Clark & Lunn Conservative Income & Growth Fund (Ont. Nov. 29, 2001)
June 1, 2012 – Converted from a closed-end to an opened-end fund.

Connor, Clark & Lunn Conservative Income Fund (Ont. Nov. 29, 2004)
Feb. 7, 2011 – Merged with Connor, Clark & Conservative Income & Growth Fund (CCP); basis 0.398816 CCP units for 1 Connor, Clark & Lunn unit. (see Connor, Clark & Lunn Conservative Income & Growth Fund)

Connor, Clark & Lunn Conservative Income Fund II (Ont. Sept. 29, 2005)
June 14, 2010 – Merged into Connor, Clark & Lunn Conservative Income & Growth Fund (previously Connor, Clark & Lunn PRINTS Trust); basis 0.369269324 Connor, Clark & Lunn Conservative Income & Growth Fund units for 1 Connor, Clark & Lunn Conservative Income Fund II unit. (see Connor, Clark & Lunn Conservative Income & Growth Fund)

Connor, Clark & Lunn Financial Opportunities Fund (Ont. June 28, 2007)
June 14, 2013 – Merged into Australian Banc Income Fund; basis 0.557596 Australian Banc cl. A and cl. F shs. for 1 Connor, Clark & Lunn cl. A and cl. F sh. (see Australian Banc Income Fund)

Connor, Clark & Lunn Global Financials Fund (Ont. Apr. 27, 2006)
Feb. 5, 2008 – Merged with Connor, Clark & Lunn Global Financials Fund II (GF2) basis 1.136 GF2 fund units for 1 Connor, Clark & Lunn Financials Fund (GF1) fund unit. (see Connor, Clark & Lunn Global Financials Fund II)

Connor, Clark & Lunn Global Financials Fund II (Ont. Feb. 27, 2007)
Oct. 5, 2011 – Merged with Focused Global Trends Fund (FTF); basis 0.872876 cl. A and 0.871693 cl. F units of FTF for 1 Connor, Clark & Lunn Global Financials Fund II (GFT) unit. (see Connor, Clark & Lunn Financial Opportunities Fund)

Connor, Clark & Lunn PRINTS Trust (Ont. Nov. 29, 2001)
June 14, 2010 – Name changed to Connor, Clark & Lunn Conservative Income & Growth Fund. ∎

Connor, Clark & Lunn ROC Pref Corp. (Can. Jan. 12, 2006)
Dec. 22, 2009 – Redeemed pref. shs. for $12.9841 per sh.

Connor, Clark & Lunn Real Return Income Fund (Ont. June 29, 2005)
Jan. 9, 2013 – Merged into ING Floating Rate Senior Loan Fund; basis 0.732842 ING cl. A units for 1 Connor, Clark & Lunn unit. (see ING Floating Rate Senior Loan Fund)

Connor, Clark & Lunn TIGERS Trust (Ont. Apr. 29, 2002)
Dec. 12, 2005 – Terminated; basis $17.5159 per unit.

Connor Clark Ltd. (Ont. 1985)
May 5, 1999 – Acquired by Royal Bank of Canada for $6.85 per cl. A sh.
Oct. 31, 2005 – Name changed to Conlark Inc.

Connors Bros. Income Fund (Ont. Sept. 24, 2001)
Nov. 21, 2008 – Acquired by Centre Partners Management, LLC for Cdn$8.50 per unit.

Connors Bros. Limited (N.B. 1923)
Nov. 1967 – George Weston Limited acquired 80% of the o/s cl. B vtg. shs.
Sept. 1970 – George Weston Limited acquired the remaining cl. B vtg. shs. Now a wholly owned subsid.
1982 – Amalgamated in New Brunswick to continue with same name.

Conoco Canada Resources Limited (Can. June 4, 1909; via Dominion charter)
Aug. 30, 2002 – Name changed to ConocoPhillips Canada Resources Corp. ∎

Conoco Silver Mines Ltd. (B.C. 1968)
Oct. 31, 1974 – Name changed to Canalta Resources Ltd.; basis 1 new for 5 old shs. ∎

ConocoPhillips Canada Resources Corp. (Can. June 4, 1909; via Dominion charter)
Jan. 5, 2010 – Continued into Alberta.

Conor Pacific Environmental Technologies Inc. (Alta. Sept. 18, 1987)
June 3, 2002 – Name changed to Conor Pacific Group Inc. ∎

Conor Pacific Group Inc. (Alta. Sept. 18, 1987)
Aug. 20, 2003 – Name changed to Precision Assessment Technology Corporation. (see FPsurvey - Industrials)

ConPac Resources Ltd. (B.C. 1978)
Apr. 9, 1987 – Continued into Canada.
Apr. 10, 1987 – Name changed to ConPak Seafoods Inc. ∎

ConPak Seafoods Inc. (Can. Apr. 9, 1987)
Oct. 1, 1990 – Amalgamated with operating companies Clarenville Ocean Products Limited and Peninsula Seafoods Limited to continue under the same name ConPak Seafoods Inc. (see FPsurvey - Industrials)

Conporec Inc. (Can. June 23, 2005 amalg.)
June 3, 2009 – Acquired by Solutions Développement Durable (SDD) inc.; basis $100 for 100 cl. A shs. Pursuant to Plan of Transaction and Arrangement under the Companies' Creditors Arrangement Act, all issued and o/s com. shs. were cancelled resulting in no funds available to shldrs.

Conqueror Holdings Ltd. (B.C. Mar. 22, 1995)
Aug. 9, 2000 – Amalgamated with wholly owned subsid. of Med Net International Ltd.; basis 0.085 Med Net shs. for 1 Conqueror sh.

Conquest Exploration Ltd. (B.C. Apr. 8, 1980)
Apr. 29, 1996 – Name changed to International Conquest Exploration Ltd.; basis 1 new for 3 old shs. ∎

Conquest Explorations Ltd. (Ont. 1956)
Sept. 22, 1966 – Dissolved.

Conquest Oil & Mining Ltd. (unknown)
1980 – Amalgamated with parent co., Paloma Petroleum Ltd.

Conquest Ventures Inc. (B.C. Apr. 8, 1980)
Nov. 26, 2003 – Name changed to Bellhaven Ventures Inc.; basis 1 new for 2 old shs. ∎

Conquest Yellowknife Resources Limited (Ont. Jan. 23, 1945)
Feb. 9, 2000 – Name changed to Conquest Resources Limited following reverse takeover acquisition of Baobab Minerals Inc.; basis 1 new for 4 old shs. (see FPsurvey - Mines & Energy)

Conquistador Mines Ltd. (B.C. Nov. 3, 1987 amalg.)
Aug. 6, 1997 – Continued into Yukon.
Jan. 30, 1998 – Amalgamated with Corona Goldfields Inc. to continue with the same name Conquistador Mines Ltd.
Dec. 14, 2001 – Name changed to Western Platinum Holdings Ltd.; basis 1 new for 5 old shs. ∎

Conquistador Mines Ltd. (Yuk. Aug. 6, 1997)
Feb. 2, 1998 – Amalgamated with Corona Goldfields Inc. (1.3 new for 1 old sh.) to continue as Conquistador Mines Ltd.; basis 1 new for 1 old sh.

Conquistador Resources Ltd. (Alta. Nov. 23, 1993)
Mar. 28, 2001 – Name changed to Bandera Gold Ltd.; basis 1 new for 2 old shs. ∎

Conrad Hanson Mines Ltd. (Ont. 1944)
1955 – Charter cancelled.

Conrex Corporation (Ont. Oct. 1, 1987 amalg.)
June 30, 1989 – Amalgamated with Falvo Estates Limited (1 for 1) to form Falvo Corporation; basis 1 new for 5 old shs. (see Falvo Corporation)

Conro Development Corporation Ltd. (Que. 1936)
Aug. 25, 1973 – Dissolved.

Conroyal Gold Mines Ltd. (Ont. 1926)
1937 – Property acquired by Kirkroyale Gold Mines Ltd.; basis 1 new for 3 old shs. (see Kirkroyale Gold Mines Ltd.)

Conroyal Mines Ltd. (Ont. 1926)
1929 – Name changed to Conroyal Gold Mines Ltd.; basis 1 new for 2 old shs. ∎

Conscience Capital Inc. (Can. June 8, 2018)
July 30, 2020 – Name changed to DGTL Holdings Inc. pursuant to Qualifying Transaction reverse takeover of Hashoff LLC. (see FPsurvey - Industrials)

Conscot Resources Ltd. (B.C. Nov. 17, 1982)
May 8, 1992 – Name changed to Masters Holdings Inc.; basis 1 new for 10 old shs. ∎

Conserve Energy Corporation (Alta. Aug. 20, 1993)
Mar. 18, 1996 – Name changed to Biotech Holdings Ltd.; basis 1 new for 2 old shs. ∎

Consolidated AGX Resources Corp. (Yuk. May 22, 1996)
July 9, 2007 – Continued into British Columbia.
July 17, 2007 – Name changed to Petro Rubiales Energy Corp. ∎

Consolidated Abaddon Resources Inc. (B.C. Sept. 30, 1982 amalg.)
Jan. 13, 2011 – Name changed to Aben Resources Ltd. ∎

Consolidated Abitibi Resources Ltd. (Ont. Aug. 27, 1962)
Dec. 24, 1999 – Acquired by Aur Resources Inc.; basis 1 Aur sh. for 22 Consolidated Abitibi shs. (see Aur Resources Inc.)

Consolidated Accord Capital Corporation (Alta. Sept. 1, 1989 amalg.)
June 14, 1996 – Formed Peak Energy Services Ltd. in Alberta on amalgamation with Burr Leasing Ltd. with Consolidated Accord the deemed acquiror. ∎

Consolidated Acorn Resources Ltd. (B.C. 1979)
Sept. 9, 1994 – Dissolved and struck off register.

Consolidated Ad Astra Minerals Ltd. (Can. 1947)
1989 – Dissolved.

Consolidated Advanced Ecology Corp. (B.C. 1979)
Oct. 29, 1993 – Dissolved and struck off register.

Consolidated African Mining Corporation (B.C. June 13, 1983)
Dec. 8, 1997 – Continued into Yukon.
Jan. 19, 2000 – Name changed to Excam Developments Inc.; basis 1 new for 10 old shs. ■

Consolidated Agarwal Resources Ltd. (B.C. June 24, 1977)
Jan. 13, 2005 – Voluntarily dissolved and distributed investment in private co. Norwood Resources Inc. to shrhldrs.; basis 1.133 new Norwood shs. and 0.353 new Norwood wts. for 1 old Cons. Agarwal sh. ■

Consolidated Alcor Resources Ltd. (Alta. 1970)
July 31, 1981 – Struck off register.

Consolidated Alice Lake Mines Limited (B.C. Sept. 28, 1955)
June 1, 1994 – Name changed to International Sales Information Systems Inc. ■

Consolidated Allenbee Oil & Gas Company Limited (Can. Jan. 8, 1952)
Apr. 6, 1960 – Name changed to Western Allenbee Oil & Gas Company Limited; basis 1 new for 4 old shs. ■

Consolidated Alliance Resources Corp. (B.C. Mar. 30, 1981)
July 9, 1999 – Name changed to Dyna Haul Corporation following acquisition of Dyna-Haul Ltd. ■

Consolidated Altair Developments Ltd. (B.C. Aug. 25, 1967)
Aug. 19, 1976 – Name changed to Super Scoop Ice-Cream Corporation; basis 1 new for 5 old shs. ■

Consolidated Amhawk Enterprises Ltd. (B.C. 1980)
Aug. 5, 1994 – Dissolved and struck off register.

Consolidated A.M.R. Corporate Ltd. (B.C. Feb. 22, 1984)
Oct. 18, 2000 – Name changed to Consolidated A.M.R. Development Corp.; basis 1 new for 5 old shs. ■

Consolidated A.M.R. Development Corp. (B.C. Feb. 22, 1984)
Jan. 9, 2002 – Name changed to West Hawk Development Corp.; basis 1 new for 3.3 old shs. ■

Consolidated Andex Resources Ltd. (B.C. 1966)
Sept. 24, 1993 – Dissolved and struck off register.

Consolidated Ansley Gold Mines Ltd. (Ont. May 2, 1944)
1950 – Name changed to Ankeno Mines Ltd.; basis 1 new for 3 old shs. ■

Consolidated Ascot Petroleum Corporation (B.C. 1982 amalg.)
Feb. 3, 1987 – Formed Ascot Investment Corporation in British Columbia on amalgamation with wholly owned 1514 Holdings Ltd.; basis 3 new com. and 1 new pref. for 1 old pref. and 1 new com. for 1 old com. sh. ■

Consolidated Ashley Minerals Limited (Ont. 1931)
Aug. 20, 1956 – Name changed to Daering Explorers Corporation Limited. ■

Consolidated Asiatel Resources Ltd. (Can. Aug. 21, 1985)
Dec. 2, 1994 – Continued into Yukon.
Dec. 21, 1994 – Name changed to Sino Foods Corp. ■

Consolidated Aston Resources Ltd. (B.C. Feb. 15, 1967)
Aug. 1, 2005 – Struck from registry and dissolved.

Consolidated Astoria Mines Ltd. (Que. Jan. 25, 1938)
1955 – Name changed to Canadian Astoria Minerals Ltd.; basis 1 new for 3 old shs. ■

Consolidated Azure Resources Ltd. (B.C. 1946)
Aug. 18, 1987 – Amalgamated in British Columbia to continue with same name.
Feb. 5, 1988 – Formed Caltech Data Ltd. in British Columbia on amalgamation with Caltech Industries Ltd. ■

Consolidated BRX Mining & Petroleum Ltd. (B.C. 1979)
Feb. 25, 1994 – Dissolved and struck off register.

Consolidated Bahn Foods Inc. (B.C. Mar. 10, 1980)
Apr. 28, 1997 – Creditors rejected a restructuring proposal and the company was placed into bankruptcy. Dudley W. Branch and Associated Inc. of Coquitlam, B.C., was appointed trustee.
Mar. 1998 – New proposal was made to settle creditors' claims by issuing a maximum of 100% of the o/s shares of the co., settling all debts.
July 20, 1999 – Court approved the proposal previously accepted by the co.'s creditors for issuance of 1,341,769 shs., which was all the issued and o/s shs. of the co., to settle debts totaling $621,133.
June 1, 2002 – Discharged from bankruptcy and Dudley W. Branch and Associates Inc. discharged as trustee. There were no distributions made to shldrs.

Consolidated Bakeries of Canada Limited (Can. 1928)
Mar. 1966 – Inter City Baking Co. Ltd., a subsid. of Ogilvie Flour Mills Co. Ltd., offered to purchase o/s shs. of Consolidated Bakeries at $8.00 per sh.

Consolidated Bald Eagle Explorations Inc. (Ont. Mar. 9, 1979)
Oct. 3, 1983 – Name changed to Megacard Technologies Inc. ■

Consolidated Balsam Resources Inc. (B.C. Jan. 15, 1979)
Oct. 1, 1991 – Name changed to Bluebird Explorations Ltd.; basis 1 new for 3 old shs. ■

Consolidated Bard Silver & Gold Ltd. (B.C. May 7, 1981)
May 15, 2000 – Name changed to Bard Ventures Ltd.; basis 1 new for 5 old shs. ■

Consolidated Barrier Reef Resources Ltd. (B.C. 1972 amalg.)
Apr. 8, 1986 – Name changed to MFC Mining Finance Corporation. ■

Consolidated-Bathurst (DG) Ltd. (Can. 1973)
May 15, 1978 – Amalgamated with Domglas Ltd. to form Domglas Inc. Minority shldrs. received pref. shs. of new co., redeemed at $20 per sh.

Consolidated-Bathurst Inc. (Can. 1931)
Apr. 3, 1989 – Acquired by Stone Container Corporation for $25 per A and B com. shs.

Consolidated-Bathurst Limited (Can. 1931)
Nov. 23, 1978 – Name changed to Consolidated-Bathurst Inc. ■

Consolidated Beacon Resources Ltd. (Alta. Oct. 11, 1990 amalg.)
July 23, 2009 – Continued into British Columbia.
July 24, 2009 – Name changed to Zone Resources Inc.; basis 1 new for 30 old shs. ■

Consolidated Bear Industries Ltd. (B.C. 1961)
June 30, 1978 – Amalgamated with The Resource Service Group Ltd.; basis 4 com. for 1 old sh.

Consolidated Bear Lake Resources Ltd. (B.C. May 13, 1985)
Nov. 29, 1990 – Name changed to Advance Tire Systems Inc. following reverse takeover acquisistion of Twin Tyres Holdings Ltd. of Australia. ■

Consolidated Beattie Mines Ltd. (Que. 1937)
Jan. 1, 1952 – Merged into Beattie-Duquesne Mines Ltd.; basis 2 new for 5 old shs. (see Beattie-Duquesne Mines Ltd.)

Consolidated Beaulieu Mines Ltd. (Ont. 1945)
Oct. 23, 1974 – Charter cancelled.

Consolidated Beaumont Resources Ltd. (B.C. Feb. 20, 1961)
Nov. 22, 1978 – Name changed to Conbeau Resources Ltd.; basis 1 new for 3 old shs. ■

Consolidated Bel-Air Resources Ltd. (B.C. Jan. 21, 1980)
Dec. 13, 1991 – Name changed to Blue Sky Resources Ltd.; basis 1 new for 3 old shs. ■

Consolidated Bellekeno Mines Ltd. (Ont. 1950)
Mar. 1976 – Charter cancelled.

Consolidated Beta Gamma Mines Ltd. (Sask. 1949)
Jan. 20, 1969 – Name changed to Beta Gamma Exploration and Development Ltd.; basis 1 new for 200 old shs. ■

Consolidated BG Baron Group Inc. (B.C. Apr. 24, 1987)
Apr. 3, 2000 – Name changed to In.Sync Industries Inc. ■

Consolidated Bi-Ore Mines Ltd. (Ont. 1954)
May 27, 1965 – Dissolved.

Consolidated Bidcop Mines Ltd. (Ont. Nov. 27, 1923)
Sept. 1970 – Name changed to Consolidated Bidcop Mining Corp. Ltd.; basis 1 new for 4 old shs. ■

Consolidated Bidcop Mining Corp. Ltd. (Ont. Nov. 27, 1923)
Aug. 9, 1974 – Name changed to Yorkshire Resources Limited; basis 1 new for 4 old shs. ■

Consolidated Big Valley Resources Inc. (B.C. July 17, 1985)
Jan. 31, 2007 – Name changed to Gold Bullion Development Corp. ■

Consolidated Boeing Holdings & Explorations Ltd. (Ont. July 20, 1970)
Apr. 1980 – Name changed to Academy Explorations Limited. ■

Consolidated Bonanza Metals Inc. (Que. Mar. 27, 1986)
Feb. 21, 1995 – Name changed to Mincor Resources Inc. ■

Consolidated Bonnyville Ltd. (Que. 1954)
Dec. 1963 – Acquired by Worldwide Energy Company Ltd.; basis 1 new for 2 old shs. (see Cold Lake Pipe Line Company Limited)

Consolidated Boulder Mountain Resources Ltd. (B.C. 1982)
Jan. 25, 1993 – Amalgamated with Consolidated Rich Coast Sulpher Ltd. to form Rich Coast Resources Ltd.; basis 1 new for 1 Consolidated Rich sh. and 1 new for 10 Consolidated Boulder shs. (see Rich Coast Resources Ltd.)

Consolidated Boundary Exploration Limited (B.C. 1966)
Mar. 7, 1989 – Name changed to Boundary Gold Corp.; basis 1 new for 5 old shs. ■

Consolidated Bradbury International Equities Ltd. (B.C. Feb. 13, 1980)
Apr. 17, 2001 – Name changed to Talus Ventures Corp.; basis 1 new for 4 old shs. ■

Consolidated Braner Ventures Inc. (B.C. Apr. 3, 1987)
May 13, 1994 – Name changed to Sunmakers Travel Group Inc. ■

Consolidated Brenzac Development Corporation (B.C. Apr. 29, 1987)
Apr. 16, 1996 – Name changed to Borneo Gold Corporation. ■

Consolidated Brewis Minerals Ltd. (Ont. 1945)
Apr. 25, 1977 – Name changed to Conbrew Resource Exploration Limited; basis 2 new for 3 old shs.

Consolidated Brightwork Resources Inc. (B.C. June 8, 1988)
Nov. 18, 1997 – Name changed to Petra Resource Corp. ■

Consolidated Brinco Limited (Can. Dec. 17, 1980)
Feb. 11, 1992 – Amalgamated with a wholly owned subsid. of Hillsborough Resources Limited; basis 1 new for 1.625 old shs. (see Hillsborough Resources Limited)

Consolidated Buffalo Red Lake Mines Ltd. (Ont. 1928)
Nov. 8, 1977 – Charter cancelled.

Consolidated Building Corporation Limited (Ont. 1957)
Dec. 1, 1978 – Amalgamated with Citrust Developments Limited, City Savings Nominees Ltd. and First City Investments Ltd. to form First City Developments Ltd. Minority shldrs. of Consolidated Building received 1 new cl. A cum. redeem. pref. sh. for each com. sh. held. Pref. shs. were redeemed on Feb. 1, 1979, for $4.75 per sh.
1978 – Continued into Alberta.

Consolidated Bullet Group, Inc. (B.C. Nov. 6, 1981)
Sept. 4, 1996 – Name changed to New Bullet Group Inc.; basis 1 new for 4.5 old shs. ■

Consolidated Bullion Reef Resources Ltd. (B.C. Mar. 30, 1983)
Mar. 8, 1996 – Name changed to Canada Payphone Corporation. ■

Consolidated Cache d'Or Resources Inc. (B.C. Jan. 31, 1980)
Mar. 19, 1993 – Name changed to Auriginor Exploration Inc. ■

Consolidated Callinan Flin Flon Mines Limited (Man. May 6, 1927)
June 23, 1980 – Continued into Canada.
Mar. 10, 1998 – Name changed to Callinan Mines Limited. ■

Consolidated Cambridge Mines Limited (B.C. June 15, 1966)
July 20, 1993 – Name changed to Cambridge Environmental Systems Inc. ■

Consolidated Canada Orient Resources Inc. (B.C. July 30, 1987)
Mar. 25, 1994 – Dissolved and struck off register. Note: dissolved under previous name, Canada Orient Resources Inc., as the British Columbia registry did not recognize the name change to Consolidated Canada Orient Resources Inc.

Consolidated Canadian Express Limited (Ont. Mar. 30, 1988 amalg.)
May 18, 2001 – Name changed to Canadian Express Ltd. ■

Consolidated Canadian Faraday Ltd. (Ont. May 4, 1967 amalg.)
July 11, 1983 – Name changed to Faraday Resources Inc. ■

Consolidated Canadian Fortune Resources Inc. (Alta. 1991 amalg.)
Mar. 15, 1993 – Name changed to Canadian Fortune Resources Inc. ■

Consolidated Canadian Venture Corp. (B.C. Sept. 9, 1986)
Mar. 31, 1995 – Continued into Cayman Islands.
July 14, 1995 – Name changed to Primeline Energy Holdings Inc.; basis 1 new for 3 old shs.

Consolidated Canarctic Industries Ltd. (B.C. 1978)
Nov. 1985 – Placed into receivership.
June 1, 1987 – Primary assets had been sold, and only the primary secured lender, The Bank of Montreal, had been compensated in full. Receivership was subsequently discharged.

Consolidated Candego Mines Ltd. (Ont. 1945)
1954 – Assets acquired by East MacDonald Mines Ltd.; basis 1 new for 5 old shs.

Consolidated Canorama Explorations Ltd. (Ont. 1944)
Feb. 20, 1980 – Charter cancelled; revived Aug. 6, 1981.

Consolidated Caprock Resources Ltd. (B.C. Nov. 5, 1982)
Mar. 12, 1993 – Name changed to Minco Mining & Metals Corporation; basis 1 new for 3 old shs. ■

Consolidated Care Point Medical Centres Ltd. (B.C. Sept. 14, 1982)
July 5, 2004 – Declared bankrupt. PricewaterhouseCoopers Inc. was appointed trustee.
Aug. 2004 – Pender Financial Group Corp. bought 10 of the 15 clinics and the Care Point name for $772,500. The remaining clinic were purchased by Trafalgar Health Clinics Ltd. for an undisclosed amount.
Nov. 6, 2006 – Dissolved and struck from register.

Consolidated Carina Resources Corp. (Sask. Dec. 14, 1982)
Sept. 22, 1995 – Name changed to United Carina Resources Corp.; basis 1 new for 4 old shs. ■

Consolidated Carlin Resources Corp. (Can. Feb. 18, 1946)
May 16, 2000 – Name changed to Carlin Gold Corporation; basis 1 new for 3 old shs. ■

Consolidated Carma Corporation (Alta. May 29, 1981)
May 15, 1996 – Name changed to Carma Corporation. ■

Consolidated Cassandra Resources Inc. (B.C. Jan. 21, 1987)
Sept. 14, 1993 – Name changed to Bolivar Goldfields Ltd. and continued into Yukon. ■

Consolidated Central Cadillac Mines Ltd. (Que. 1939)
July 1963 – Name changed to Novamines Corporation; basis 1 new for 4 old shs. ■

Consolidated Chibougamau Goldfields Ltd. (unknown)
1950 – Absorbed by Campbell Chibougamau Mines Ltd.; basis 1 new for 8 old shs. (see Campbell Chibougamau Mines Ltd.)

Consolidated Churchill Copper Corporation Ltd. (B.C. 1964)
1979 – Name changed to Lamaque Mining Company 1964 Limited following acquisition by Amalgamated Brenda-Yukon Limited; basis $2 per sh. ■

Consolidated Churchill Enterprises Inc. (B.C. Apr. 9, 1980)
Oct. 5, 1992 – Name changed to Samia Ventures Inc.; basis 1 new for 7 old shs. ■

Consolidated Cima Resources Limited (B.C. Nov. 9, 1965)
July 20, 1989 – Continued into Canada.
Aug. 15, 1989 – Name changed to Hankin Atlas Industries Limited. ■

Consolidated Cinola Mines Ltd. (B.C. Feb. 7, 1962)
Nov. 10, 1986 – Name changed to City Resources (Canada) Limited. ■

Consolidated Cisco Resources Ltd. (B.C. Mar. 12, 1980)
Aug. 8, 1991 – Name changed to Inca Gold Ltd.; basis 1 new for 1 old sh. ■

Consolidated Citex Resources Inc. (B.C. Apr. 1, 1966)
Dec. 11, 1978 – Dissolved.
June 28, 1979 – Revived.
July 19, 1979 – Name changed to Pacific Foam Form Inc.; basis 1 new for 5 old shs. ■

Consolidated Cleveland Resources Ltd. (B.C. 1962)
Feb. 4, 1983 – Struck off register.

Consolidated Clifton Resources Limited (B.C. 1980)
Sept. 27, 1990 – Name changed to Taina Developments Corporation. ■

Consolidated Cline Development Corporation (B.C. Jan. 14, 1983)
Nov. 29, 1996 – Name changed to Cline Mining Corporation. ■

Consolidated Coast Silver Mines Ltd. (B.C. Apr. 30, 1963)
Aug. 28, 1975 – Name changed to Newcoast Silver Mines Ltd.; basis 1 new for 5 old shs. ■

Consolidated Colossal Energy Inc. (B.C. Apr. 14, 1983)
May 2, 1988 – Name changed to Draco Gold Mines Inc. ■

Consolidated Columbia River Mines Ltd. (B.C. 1963)
Feb. 17, 1978 – Name changed to Ruth Vermont Mine Ltd. (N.P.L.); basis 1 new for 10 old shs. ■

Consolidated Computer Inc. (Ont. 1968)
Mar. 1984 – The Clarkson Co. appointed receiver/manager. Funds received from sale of assets were insufficient to pay unsecured creditors.

Consolidated Computer Services Limited (Ont. 1968)
1970 – Name changed to Consolidated Computer Inc. ■

Consolidated Consumer General Inc. (Ont. 1980)
Oct. 5, 1993 – Name changed to Cong Industries Inc.; basis 1 new for 2 old shs. ■

Consolidated Copper-Lode Developments Inc. (Ont. 1964)
Mar. 1, 1984 – Name changed to Norbeau Mines Inc. ■

Consolidated Copperstone Resources Corporation (B.C. May 10, 1967)
Mar. 14, 2000 – Name changed to Bonanza Silver Corporation. ■

Consolidated Cordasun Oils Ltd. (Ont. Dec. 16, 1948)
Jan. 1958 – Acquired by Okalta Oils Ltd.; basis 1 new for 10 old shs.

Consolidated Cottonballs Corporation (Alta. Oct. 9, 1987)
May 12, 1994 – Name changed to CTB Industries Inc.; basis 1 new for 9 old shs. ■

Consolidated Cove Resources Corporation (B.C. Apr. 6, 1981)
May 11, 1995 – Name changed to Derek Resources Corporation; basis 1 new for 4.6 old shs. ■

Consolidated Creameries, Ltd. (Ont. 1928)
Property sold; total of 25¢ per sh. distributed to pref. shldrs.

Consolidated CSA Minerals Inc. (Can. Sept. 30, 1985 amalg.)
Apr. 4, 1987 – Name changed to Pamorex Minerals Inc. ■

Consolidated Cyll Industries Limited (B.C. 1984)
Jan. 31, 1995 – Name changed to RW Packaging Ltd.; basis 1 new for 5 old shs. ■

Consolidated Cyn-Tech Ventures Ltd. (B.C. July 25, 1986)
June 27, 1996 – Name changed to Trans-Orient Petroleum Ltd.; basis 3 new for 1 old sh. ■

Consolidated Daering Enterprises & Mining Inc. (Ont. 1931)
Dec. 11, 1981 – Name changed to Sim-Tek Enterprises & Exploration Inc.; basis 1 new for 3 old shs. ■

Consolidated Dakota Resources Ltd. (B.C. 1979)
Dec. 8, 1987 – Amalgamated with International Wildrose Resources Ltd. (1 for 1), Brigade Resources Inc. (1 for 3) and Mac-Am Resources Corp. (1 for 1) to continue as Colossus Resource Equities Inc.; basis 1 new for 1 old sh.

Consolidated Dasher Resources Inc. (Ont. Dec. 19, 1980)
Apr. 16, 1993 – Name changed to Tm Technologies Corp. ■

Consolidated Deer Creek Resources Limited (Ont. Feb. 26, 1981)
Sept. 20, 1996 – Formed Montemor Resources Inc. in Ontario on amalgamation with 1169479 Ontario Inc., constituting a reverse takeover by 1169479 Ontario, basis 1 new for 1 1169479 Ontario sh. and 1 new for 3 Consolidated Deer Creek shs. ■

Consolidated Del Norte Ventures Inc. (B.C. Sept. 27, 1979)
Apr. 15, 1991 – Name changed to Idaho-Maryland Mining Corporation. ■

Consolidated Dencam Development Corporation (B.C. Sept. 12, 1986)
Mar. 13, 2009 – Name changed to Equinox Exploration Corp. ■

Consolidated Denison Mines Ltd. (Ont. 1936)
1960 – Merged into Denison Mines Limited.

Consolidated Diana Gold Mines Ltd. (Man. 1936)
Dec. 5, 1963 – Charter cancelled.

Consolidated Discovery Yellowknife Mines Ltd. (Ont. 1945)
1964 – Merged with Ormsby Mines Ltd. to form Discovery Mines Limited effective Mar. 5; basis 3 new for 5 old shs.

Consolidated Diversified Standard Industries Ltd. (Can. May 6, 1932)
Oct. 29, 1982 – Name changed to C.S.D. Securities Limited. ■

Consolidated Dixie Resources Inc. (Ont. June 30, 1987 amalg.)
Dec. 15, 1992 – Name changed to United Dixie Resources Inc.; basis 2 new for 5 old shs. ■

Consolidated DLP Limited (Can. 1969)
Dec. 16, 1980 – Dissolved.

Consolidated Dragon Oils Ltd. (Ont. 1950)
1965 – Assets acquired by Plains Petroleums Ltd.; basis 3 new for 2 old shs.

Consolidated Duquesne Mining Co. Ltd. (Que. Apr. 13, 1938)
Jan. 1, 1952 – Merged into Beattie-Duquesne Mines Ltd.; basis 2 new for 3 old shs. (see Beattie-Duquesne Mines Ltd.)

Consolidated Durham Mines & Resources Limited (Ont. 1945)
Mar. 15, 1984 – Formed Durham Resources Inc. in Ontario on amalgamation with Onaping Resources Limited; basis 1 new sub. vtg. for 2.25 old o/s com. shs. and 1 new wt. for 1 old wt. ■

Consolidated Earth Stewards Inc. (B.C. Nov. 21, 1983)
Aug. 29, 2002 – Name changed to Royal County Minerals Corp.; basis 1 new for 4 old shs. ■

Consolidated East Crest Oil Company Limited (Can. 1928)
Dec. 1971 – Acquired by Pan Ocean Oil Corporation; basis 15.06 new for 100 old shs. (see Pan Ocean Oil Corporation)

Consolidated Ecoprogress Technology Inc. (B.C. Nov. 20, 1978)
June 18, 2012 – Dissolved and struck from register. ■

Consolidated Emjay Petroleums Ltd. (unknown)
1959 – Charter cancelled.
Charter revived.
Name changed to New Emjay Petroleums Ltd.; basis 1 new for 200 old shs. ■

Consolidated Enfield Corporation (Ont. Apr. 6, 1984)
May 13, 2004 – Name changed to West Street Capital Corporation. ■

Consolidated Envirowaste Industries Inc. (B.C. Sept. 1, 1983)
Mar. 4, 2010 – Privatized at 14¢ per sh.

Consolidated Epix Technologies Limited (Yuk. Nov. 8, 1995)
Dec. 3, 2004 – Amalgamated with Saxon Energy Services Inc. to continue as a new company also named Saxon Energy Services Inc.; basis 1 new Saxon sh. for 3 old Consolidated Epix shs. (see Saxon Energy Services Inc.)
Dec. 13, 2004 – Continued into Alberta. (see Saxon Energy Services Inc.)

Consolidated Eskay Gold Corp. (B.C. July 17, 1984)
Apr. 8, 1993 – Name changed to dba Telecom Corporation. ■

Consolidated E.T.C. Industries Ltd. (B.C. Mar. 17, 1980)
July 25, 2003 – Name changed to Highbank Resources Ltd. ■

Consolidated Eurocan Ventures Ltd. (B.C. Feb. 20, 1978)
Apr. 19, 1994 – Continued into Canada.
Jan. 9, 1997 – Name changed to Tenke Mining Corp. ■

Consolidated Ewing Industries Inc. (B.C. June 10, 1980)
Apr. 26, 1999 – Name changed to Sirius Resources Ltd.; basis 1 new for 10 old shs. ■

Consolidated Excellerated Resources Inc. (B.C. Jan. 18, 1983)
Nov. 21, 2003 – Name changed to Amarillo Gold Corporation. ■

Consolidated Exploration & Mining Co. Ltd. (Que. 1957)
Nov. 11, 1978 – Charter cancelled.

Consolidated Explorer Petroleum Corporation (B.C. Sept. 16, 1950)
July 14, 1989 – Name changed to PEC Energy Corp. ■

Consolidated Fenimore Iron Mines Ltd. (Que. 1947)
July 17, 1972 – Name changed to New Fenimore Iron Mines Ltd.; basis 1 new for 200 old shs. ■

Consolidated First Northern Developments Inc. (B.C. Jan. 23, 1984)
Mar. 15, 1996 – Name changed to Golden Temple Mining Corp.; basis 1 new for 5 old shs. ■

Consolidated Five Star Resources Ltd. (Alta. Jan. 18, 1964)
Dec. 5, 1995 – Name changed to CFS International Inc. ■

Consolidated Fortress Resources Inc. (B.C. July 28, 1987 amalg.)
July 31, 2002 – Name changed to Fortress IT Corp. and continued into Canada. ■

Consolidated Fortune Channel Mines Ltd. (B.C. 1969)
Sept. 5, 1975 – Name changed to United Fortune Channel Mines Ltd.; basis 1 new for 5 old shs. ■

Consolidated Found Lake Gold Mines Ltd. (Ont. Feb. 27, 1937)
Charter cancelled.

Consolidated Frederick Mines Ltd. (Ont. 1956)
1962 – Distribution of 38.5¢ per sh. made. Charter surrendered, and co. wound up.

Consolidated Fredonia Resources Ltd. (B.C. May 21, 1980)
Oct. 11, 1985 – Name changed to Sun River Gold Corp. ■

Consolidated Fulbro Gold Mines Ltd. (Ont. Dec. 17, 1946)
Jan. 15, 1980 – Name changed to Sycon Energy Corporation. ■

Consolidated Gas-Ice (Canada) Ltd. (B.C. 1949)
Aug. 1959 – In bankruptcy.

Consolidated Gascome Oils Ltd. (Alta. Dec. 23, 1977)
Oct. 2, 1987 – Name changed to Reef Hydrocarbons Ltd. ■

Consolidated Gem Explorations Ltd. (B.C. 1962)
Jan. 1973 – Name changed to Brendon Resources Ltd.; basis 1 new for 5 old shs. ■

Consolidated Genco Industries Inc. (B.C. 1964)
Oct. 1, 1993 – Dissolved and struck off register.

Consolidated General Diamond Corporation (B.C. June 11, 1987)
Oct. 15, 2001 – Name changed to Exxel Energy Corp.; basis 1 new for 4 old shs. ■

Consolidated General Sea Harvest Corporation (B.C. 1983)
Oct. 22, 1993 – Dissolved and struck off register.

Consolidated General Western Industries Ltd. (B.C. 1975)
Dec. 3, 1991 – Name changed to Danco Industries Ltd.; basis 1 new for 10 old shs. ■

Consolidated Giant Metallics Mines Ltd. (B.C. 1964)
Sept. 25, 1978 – Dissolved.

Consolidated Gillies Lake Mines Ltd. (Ont. 1933)
1968 – Merged into Associated Porcupine Mines Ltd.; basis 1 new for 6.02936 old shs.

Consolidated Glass Industries Limited (Can. 1950)
Dec. 16, 1980 – All assets and liabs. acquired in 1965 by Glaverbel Canada Ltée for $1.50 per sh. Co. dissolved.

Consolidated Global Cable Systems, Inc. (B.C. 1987)
Jan. 19, 2010 – Name changed to Chelsea Minerals Corp. ■

Consolidated Global Diamond Corp. (B.C. Sept. 25, 1985)
Oct. 30, 2009 – Name changed to Gem International Resources Inc. ■

Consolidated Global Minerals Ltd. (Alta. July 24, 1989)
Mar. 31, 2006 – Continued into British Columbia.
Nov. 27, 2006 – Name changed to Global Minerals Ltd. ■

Consolidated Global Technologies Inc. (B.C. Jan. 13, 1981)
Dec. 17, 2003 – Name changed to Garnet Point Resources Corp. following reverse takeover acquisition of four Crown-granted mineral claims in Saskatchewan known as the Search River property. ■

Consolidated Gold City Mining Corporation (B.C. Oct. 27, 1994 amalg.)
Aug. 26, 1998 – Name changed to Gold City Industries Ltd.; basis 1 new for 7 old shs. ■

Consolidated Gold Hawk Resources Inc. (Ont. Mar. 10, 1980)
Sept. 4, 1985 – Continued into Canada.
June 10, 1998 – Name changed to Gold Hawk Resources Inc. ■

Consolidated Gold Standard Resources Inc. (B.C. 1981)
Dec. 1986 – Continued into Wyoming.
Jan. 18, 1988 – Name changed to Strategic Industries Inc.

Consolidated Gold Vessel Resources Inc. (Can. Aug. 26, 1985)
July 4, 1995 – Name changed to Golden Bear Minerals Inc. ■

Consolidated Gold Win Ventures Inc. (B.C. Oct. 2, 1984)
Apr. 9, 2009 – Name changed to Encore Renaissance Resources Corp. ■

Consolidated Goldbank Ventures Ltd. (Alta. Oct. 21, 1987)
Aug. 13, 2003 – Name changed to NEMI Northern Energy & Mining Inc. ■

Consolidated Golden Arrow Mines Ltd. (Ont. Dec. 8, 1938)
Mar. 1970 – Name changed to Canadian Arrow Mines Limited. ■

Consolidated Golden Lion Resources Ltd. (B.C. May 25, 1983)
Sept. 11, 1995 – Name changed to Americ Resources Corp.; basis 1 new for 4.5 old shs. ■

Consolidated Golden Pyramid Resources Inc. (B.C. May 18, 1983)
Dec. 14, 1993 – Name changed to Data Dial International Inc. ■

Consolidated Golden Thunder Resources Ltd. (B.C. June 7, 1983)
May 10, 2004 – Name changed to GHG Resources Limited. ■

Consolidated Golden Unicorn Mining Corporation (B.C. June 25, 1986)
Dec. 9, 1999 – Name changed to Kirkstone Ventures Ltd.; basis 1 new for 10 old shs. ■

Consolidated Goldfields of Manitoba Ltd. (Man. 1933)
Mar. 17, 1977 – Charter cancelled.

Consolidated Goldrite Mining Corp. (Can. Feb. 17, 1983)
Apr. 30, 1996 – Name changed to Bestar International Group Ltd. and continued into Cayman Islands.

Consolidated Goldstack International Resources Inc. (B.C. Aug. 29, 1979)
June 30, 1995 – Name changed to Zim-Gold Resources Ltd. ■

Consolidated Goldwest Resources Ltd. (B.C. Aug. 25, 1980)
Aug. 6, 1992 – Name changed to Tenby Developments Ltd.; basis 1 new for 7.5 old shs. ■

Consolidated Granby Resources Limited (B.C. 1982)
May 16, 1997 – Continued into Canada.
Nov. 6, 2000 – Name changed to CRA Phase II Ltd.; basis 1 new for 4 old shs. ■

Consolidated Grand National Resources Inc. (B.C. Nov. 25, 1980)
Nov. 28, 2000 – Name changed to First Star Innovations Inc. ■

Consolidated Grandview Inc. (Ont. Nov. 23, 1945)
July 6, 2004 – Name changed to Grandview Gold Inc.; basis 3 new for 1 sh. ■

Consolidated Grease Creek Petroleum Ltd. (B.C. 1937)
1957 – Acquired by Share Oils Ltd.; basis 1 new for 3 old shs. (see Share Oils Ltd.)

Consolidated Gulfside Resources Ltd. (B.C. Oct. 14, 1987)
Apr. 11, 2007 – Name changed to Gulfside Minerals Ltd. ■

Consolidated Guyana Mines Ltd. (Ont. 1946)
1957 – Name changed to Latin American Mines Ltd.; basis 1 new for 5 old shs. ■

Consolidated HCI Holdings Corporation (Can. Sept. 6, 1930)
Nov. 12, 2021 – Continued into British Columbia.
Nov. 15, 2021 – Name changed to Atmofizer Technologies Inc. pursuant to the reverse takeover acquisition of Vaxxinator USA LLC (dba Vaxxinator Enterprises Inc.).; basis 1 new for 24.691 old shs. (see FPsurvey - Industrials)

Consolidated H2O Entertainment Corp. (B.C. May 5, 1972)
July 30, 2007 – Name changed to Tri-River Ventures Inc. (see FPsurvey - Mines & Energy)

Consolidated Hale Resources Ltd. (B.C. 1980)
Jan. 21, 1994 – Name changed to Richco Investors Inc. ■

Consolidated Halliwell Ltd. (Que. 1933)
July 1969 – Name changed to International Halliwell Mines Ltd.; basis 1 new for 10 old shs. ■

Consolidated Halo Uranium Mines Ltd. (Ont. 1954)
Oct. 10, 1961 – Assets comprising shs. in Amalgamated Rare Earth Mines distributed to shldrs.; basis 9.5 shs. Amalgamated for 15 Consolidated Halo shs. Co. dissolved.

Consolidated Harpers Malartic Gold Mines Ltd. (Ont. 1949)
Mar. 1976 – Charter cancelled.

Consolidated HCO Energy Ltd. (Can. 1987)
July 27, 1993 – Name changed to HCO Energy Ltd. ■

Consolidated Heron Resources Ltd. (B.C. 1978)
Feb. 8, 1993 – Name changed to Fintra Ventures Ltd.; basis 1 new for 2 old shs. ■

Consolidated Homestake Mining & Development Co. Ltd. (B.C. 1921)
1927 – Name changed to Toric Mines Co. Ltd. ■

Consolidated Homestead Oil Co. Ltd. (Alta. Mar. 18, 1947)
1950 – Name changed to Western Homestead Oils Ltd.; basis 1 new for 4 old shs. ■

Consolidated Howey Gold Mines Ltd. (Ont. Mar. 12, 1926)
Apr. 7, 1960 – Name changed to Howey Consolidated Mines Ltd. ■

Consolidated Impact Resources Inc. (B.C. Apr. 17, 1969)
July 22, 1992 – Name changed to InContext Systems Inc. following acquisition of Incontext Corporation. ■

Consolidated Imperial Minerals Ltd. (Que. 1953)
Mar. 1, 1979 – Name changed to Consolidated Imperial Resources Limited (Ressources Consolidées Imperial Ltée); basis 1 new for 2 old shs. ■

Consolidated Imperial Resources Energy Ltd. (Que. 1953)
May 6, 1988 – Name changed to Consolidated Imperial Resources Inc.; basis 1 new for 4 old shs. (see FPsurvey - Mines & Energy)

Consolidated Imperial Resources Limited (Que. 1953)
Mar. 18, 1983 – Name changed to Consolidated Imperial Resources Energy Ltd. (Ressources Consolidées Impérial Energie Ltée); basis 1 new for 8 old shs. ■

Consolidated Indescor Corp. (B.C. Oct. 15, 1981)
Aug. 2, 1993 – Struck from registry and dissolved.

Consolidated Indore Uranium Mines Ltd. (Ont. 1947)
Apr. 1958 – Charter cancelled.
May 1958 – Assets sold to United Uranium Corp. Ltd.

Consolidated Inland Recovery Group Ltd. (B.C. 1980)
Sept. 24, 1993 – Dissolved and struck off register.

Consolidated International Petroleum Corporation (B.C. June 1, 1985 amalg.)
Apr. 30, 1986 – Name changed to International Petroleum Corporation. ■

Consolidated Interstat Ventures Inc. (B.C. Sept. 17, 1985)
Nov. 23, 1999 – Name changed to Diamcor Mining Inc. (see FPsurvey - Mines & Energy)

Consolidated JABA Inc. (Alta. Nov. 5, 1987)
Dec. 11, 2003 – Name changed to JABA Exploration Inc. ■

Consolidated Jalna Resources Limited (B.C. June 27, 1974)
Apr. 16, 1993 – Name changed to Jalna Mining Corp.; basis 1 new for 4 old shs. ■

Consolidated Kaitone Holdings Ltd. (B.C. Apr. 18, 1988)
May 8, 2003 – Name changed to Largo Resources Ltd.; basis 1 new for 3 old shs. ■

Consolidated Kalco Valley Mines Ltd. (B.C. May 17, 1966)
Nov. 27, 1979 – Name changed to Brace Resources Ltd. ■

Consolidated Kassan Resources Inc. (B.C. Apr. 30, 1987)
Jan. 16, 1995 – Name changed to East Africa Gold Corporation. ■

Consolidated Keld'Or Resources Inc. (B.C. May 17, 1984)
Mar. 18, 1994 – Name changed to CKD Ventures Ltd.; basis 1 new for 5 old shs. ■

Consolidated Key Oils Ltd. (B.C. 1955)
Dec. 1968 – Approx. 98% of o/s shs. acquired for cash in 1968 by Westburne Petroleum Services Ltd. Name of Consolidated Key Oils changed to Commonwealth Drilling (B.C.) Ltd.

Consolidated Knobby Lake Mines Limited (Can. July 19, 1956)
Sept. 23, 1988 – Name changed to Kancana Ventures Limited; basis 1 new for 3 old shs. ■

Consolidated Kookaburra Resources Ltd. (B.C. July 16, 2004)
Mar. 9, 2007 – Name changed to Salazar Resources Limited following reverse takeover acquisition of Curiming S.A. (see FPsurvey - Mines & Energy)

Consolidated Kronofusion Technologies Inc. (Yuk. May 15, 2000)
Sept. 22, 2004 – Name changed to JER Envirotech International Corp. following reverse takeover acquisition of JER Envirotech Ltd.; basis 1 new for 2 old shs. ■

Consolidated Kyle Resources Inc. (B.C. Oct. 21, 1980)
July 27, 1992 – Name changed to Zappa Resources Ltd.; basis 1 new for 3 old shs. ■

Consolidated Lebel Oro Mines Ltd. (Ont. Apr. 1920)
1952 – Name changed to Copper-Man Mines Ltd.; basis 1 new for 4 old shs. ■

Consolidated Lithium Corporation of Canada Ltd. (Que. 1955)
Mar. 14, 1981 – Charter cancelled.

Consolidated Lithograph Manufacturing Co. Ltd. (Can. 1926)
1953 – Acquired by Somerville Ltd. for $12.25 per sh.

Consolidated Logan Mines Ltd. (B.C. July 26, 1978)
Jan. 30, 2002 – Name changed to Logan Resources Ltd.; basis 1 new for 5 old shs. ■

Consolidated Lone Star Resource Corporation (B.C. 1980)
Mar. 4, 1994 – Dissolved and struck off register.

Consolidated Louanna Gold Mines Ltd. (Ont. 1963)
June 13, 2006 – Certificate of incorporation cancelled and dissolved.

Consolidated Madison Holdings Ltd. (B.C. 1984)
June 27, 1996 – Amalgamated with Future Avenir Corp. to form Ourominas Minerals Inc.; basis 0.9 Ourominas com. shs. for 1 Future Avenir cl. A subord. vtg. sh. plus 1 Ourominas com. sh. for 1 Future Avenir cl. B multiple vtg. sh. and 0.6 Ourominas com. shs. for 1 Consolidated Madison com. sh. (see Ourominas Minerals Inc.)

Consolidated Magna Ventures Ltd. (B.C. Dec. 23, 1983)
Jan. 10, 2002 – Name changed to Skinny Technologies Inc. ■

Consolidated Mango Resources Ltd. (B.C. Sept. 14, 1987)
Mar. 10, 2000 – Continued into Delaware.
Mar. 13, 2000 – Formed U.S. Cobalt Inc. pursuant to plan of arrangement acquisition of U.S. Cobalt Inc. ■

Consolidated Manitoba Mines Ltd. (Man. 1925)
Mar. 17, 1977 – Dissolved.

Consolidated Manitou Resources Inc. (B.C. May 9, 1983)
July 5, 1991 – Name changed to A.C.T. Industrial Corporation. ■

Consolidated Mann Oil Inc. (Can. Mar. 3, 1981)
Feb. 28, 1997 – Dissolved.

Consolidated Manus Industries Inc. (B.C. Sept. 30, 1967)
Feb. 8, 1996 – Name changed to Westmount Resources Ltd.; basis 1 new for 5 old shs. ■

Consolidated Maple Bay Copper Mines Limited (Ont. 1953)
Nov. 8, 1974 – Name changed to Yorkshire Copper Mines Limited. ■

Consolidated Marbenor Mines Limited (Ont. 1941)
Dec. 30, 1985 – Amalgamated with 3 other cos. to form Canhorn Mining Corporation; basis 1 new for 26.72 old shs.

Consolidated Marcus Gold Mines Limited (Ont. 1954)
July 12, 1988 – Formed Marcus Energy Inc. in Ontario on amalgamation. ■

Consolidated Marina Explorations Ltd. (B.C. June 9, 1987)
Feb. 25, 1994 – Name changed to Watson Bell Communications Inc. ■

Consolidated Matarrow Mines Ltd. (Ont. 1948)
June 1955 – Name changed to Jeanette Minerals Ltd.; basis 1 new for 3.5 old shs. ■

Consolidated Maybrun Mines Limited (Ont. 1953)
July 22, 1999 – Charter cancelled and co. dissolved.

Consolidated Maymac Petroleum Corporation (B.C. May 11, 1971)
July 7, 2000 – Continued into Yukon.
Jan. 16, 2003 – Name changed to Northern Star Mining Corp. ■

Consolidated McKinney Resources Inc. (B.C. July 11, 1979)
Dec. 9, 1996 – Name changed to Aztek Technologies Inc.; basis 1 new for 5 old shs. ■

Consolidated Mercantile Corporation (Ont. Aug. 12, 1940)
Oct. 22, 1998 – Name changed to Consolidated Mercantile Incorporated; basis 1 new for 2 old shs. ■

Consolidated Mercantile Incorporated (Ont. Aug. 12, 1940)
May 10, 2010 – Formed Genterra Capital Inc. in Ontario on amalgamation with Genterra Inc., with Consolidated Mercantile the deemed acquiror; basis 1 new sh. for 1 Consolidated Mercantile sh. and basis 1 new sh. for 3.6 Genterra shs. ■

Consolidated Mic Mac Oils Ltd. (Alta. 1953)
1963 – Acquired by Hudson's Bay Oil and Gas Company Limited; basis either $4.50 or 1 new Hudson's Bay sh. for 3.75 old Mic Mac shs. (see Hudson's Bay Oil and Gas Company Limited)

Consolidated Midvale Explorations Ltd. (Ont. 1973 amalg.)
1978 – Amalgamated with Lumsden Building Corp. Inc.; basis 1 sh. Lumsden for 6 shs. Consolidated.

Consolidated Minerva Gold Mines Ltd. (B.C. Jan. 14, 1981)
July 9, 1996 – Name changed to El Misti Gold Limited. ■

Consolidated Mining & Smelting Co. of Canada Ltd. (Can. Jan. 9, 1906)
May 16, 1966 – Name changed to Cominco Ltd. ■

Consolidated Mogador Mines Ltd. (Que. 1946)
Oct. 26, 1985 – Charter cancelled.

Consolidated Mogul Mines Ltd. (Ont. 1945)
1967 – Name changed to Mogul Mines Ltd. ■

Consolidated Monarch Metal Mines Ltd. (B.C. Feb. 18, 1966)
Nov. 15, 1977 – Name changed to San Rafael Resources Ltd.; basis 1 new for 3 old shs. ■

Consolidated Monpas Mines Limited (Que. 1946)
1971 – Shs. consol.; basis 3 new for 8 old shs. New shs. then exch. for Albarmont Mines Corp.

Consolidated Montclerg Mines Limited (Ont. 1939)
Nov. 25, 1986 – Name changed to Montclerg Resources Limited; basis 1 new for 5 old shs. ■

Consolidated Morrison Explorations, Limited (Ont. Apr. 1951)
Oct. 22, 1980 – Name changed to Morrison Petroleums Ltd. ■

Consolidated Mosher Mines Ltd. (Ont. 1950)
1967 – Merged into MacLeod Mosher Gold Mines Ltd.; basis 1 new for 3 old shs.

Consolidated Mt. Hyland Mines & Resources Ltd. (B.C. Sept. 14, 1964)
Jan. 2, 1976 – Name changed to Avance International Inc. ■

Consolidated Natural Gas Co., Ltd. (Ont. 1934)
Defunct; assets taken over by creditors.

Consolidated NBS Inc. (Can. 1983)
June 10, 1992 – Name changed to SBN Systems Inc. ■

Consolidated Negus Mines Ltd. (Ont. 1938)
June 26, 1973 – Assets sold to Gramara Mercantile Corp. Ltd.; basis 1 new for 20 old shs.
July 22, 1975 – Articles of dissolution filed.

Consolidated Nevada Goldfields Corporation (Can. Apr. 27, 1989)
May 14, 1998 – Name changed to Real del Monte Mining Corporation; basis 1 new for 10 old shs. ■

Consolidated New Pacific Ltd. (Ont. 1943)
Nov. 17, 1969 – Name changed to Conuco Limited. ■

Consolidated New Sage Resources Ltd. (B.C. Dec. 19, 1980)
Oct. 24, 2003 – Continued into Canada.
May 24, 2007 – Name changed to New Sage Energy Corp. ■

Consolidated Newen Enterprises Inc. (B.C. Mar. 13, 1987)
Apr. 7, 2003 – Name changed to North American Gold Inc.; basis 1 new for 5 old shs. ■

Consolidated Newgate Resources Ltd. (B.C. Apr. 22, 1986)
Jan. 17, 1996 – Name changed to Antler Resources Ltd.; basis 1 new for 12 old shs. (see Winspear Resources Ltd.)

Consolidated Newjay Resources Ltd. (B.C. July 31, 1979)
May 9, 1995 – Name changed to Indo-Pacific Energy Ltd. ■

Consolidated Niche Peripherals Inc. (B.C. May 22, 1986)
Apr. 18, 2001 – Delisted from CDNX, Subsequently struck from register and dissolved.

Consolidated Nicholson Mines Limited (Ont. Nov. 23, 1936)
Jan. 8, 1975 – Name changed to Auric Resources Limited; basis 1 new for 3 old shs. ■

Consolidated Nicola Goldfields Ltd. (B.C. 1937)
1956 – Charter cancelled.

Consolidated Nirvana Industries Ltd. (B.C. Mar. 7, 1980)
June 2, 1995 – Name changed to Navasota Resources Ltd.; basis 1 new for 3 old shs. ■

Consolidated Norex Resources Corp. (B.C. 1967)
May 14, 1992 – Acquired by Morgan Hydrocarbons Inc.; basis 1.225 Morgan shs. for 1 Norex sh. (see Morgan Hydrocarbons Inc.)

Consolidated Norsemont Ventures Ltd. (B.C. June 10, 1977)
Jan. 27, 2005 – Name changed to Norsemont Mining Inc. ■

Consolidated North Coast Industries Ltd. (B.C. Dec. 19, 1984)
Jan. 5, 1998 – Amalgamated with Pacific Sentinel Gold Corp. to form Great Basin Gold Ltd.; basis 1 new for 5 Pacific Sentinel shs. and 1 new for 1.6 Consolidated North Coast shs. (see Great Basin Gold Ltd.)

Consolidated Northland Mines Ltd. (Ont. Mar. 1940)
1965 – Merged into Crestland Mines Ltd.; basis 3 new for 5 old shs. (see Crestland Mines Ltd.)

Consolidated Northland Oils Limited (Alta. 1949)
Jan. 11, 1996 – Name changed to International Northland Resources Inc.; basis 1 new for 2 old shs. ■

Consolidated Novell Mines Ltd. (Ont. 1955)
Mar. 1976 – Charter cancelled.

Consolidated Nu-Media Industries Inc. (B.C. Oct. 20, 1986)
Oct. 8, 1997 – Name changed to Pan Asia Mining Corp. and continued into Yukon. ■

Consolidated Nu-Sky Exploration Inc. (B.C. July 15, 1986)
Feb. 28, 1995 – Amalgamated with its two wholly owned subsids., Nu-Sky Energy Inc. and Whirlwind Energy Ltd., to continue as Nu-Sky Energy Inc.
Feb. 28, 1995 – Continued into Alberta.
May 12, 1995 – Name changed to Nu-Sky Energy Inc. ■

Consolidated Oasis Resources Inc. (Can. Oct. 21, 1988)
Aug. 2, 2001 – Name changed to Oasis Diamond Exploration Inc. ■

Consolidated Oberg Industries Ltd. (B.C. 1965)
Jan. 16, 1997 – Name changed to Hytec Flow Systems, Inc. (see FPsurvey - Industrials)

Consolidated Odyssey Exploration Inc. (B.C. Aug. 19, 1994 amalg.)
Aug. 26, 2005 – Formed Odyssey Petroleum Corp. in British Columbia on acquistion of and amalgamation with U.S. Oil and Gas Resources Inc. ■

Consolidated Oil Co., Ltd. (unknown 1935)
In liquidation; H. D. Campbell, 812 Standard Bldg., Vancouver, liquidator.

Consolidated Ojibway Resources Ltd. (Que. Nov. 12, 1985)
Aug. 10, 1994 – Name changed to Diabex Resources Inc. ■

Consolidated Oka Sand & Gravel Co. Ltd. (Que. June 26, 1928)
Mar. 1955 – Name changed to McCord Street Sites Limited. ■

Consolidated Omab Enterprises Ltd. (B.C. Dec. 17, 1973)
Mar. 2, 1989 – Delisted from the Vancouver Stock Exchange. Subsequently struck from register and dissolved.

Consolidated Ontario Gold Mines Ltd. (Ont. 1933)
1940 – Dormant since 1935. Planned to wind up during.

Consolidated Ophir Ventures Inc. (Alta. Mar. 28, 2005)
Mar. 14, 2006 – Amalgamated with CIC Energy Corp.; basis 1 new CIC sh. for 1 old Consolidated Ophir sh. (see CIC Energy Corp.)

Consolidated Oriole Communications Inc. (B.C. May 23, 1972)
Mar. 26, 1996 – Name changed to Oriole Systems Inc. ■

Consolidated Orlac Mines Ltd. (Ont. 1944)
May 1956 – Name changed to Abbican Mines Ltd.; basis 1 new for 6 old shs. ■

Consolidated Orofino Resources Limited (Ont. 1945)
Mar. 8, 1983 – Name changed to Orofino Resources Limited. ■

Consolidated Ouro Brasil Ltd. (Yuk. Dec. 16, 1997)
Aug. 29, 2002 – Name changed to Superior Diamonds Inc. ■

Consolidated P P M Development Corp. (B.C. Sept. 25, 1985)
Apr. 23, 2004 – Name changed to Consolidated Global Diamond Corp. ■

Consolidated Pace II Industries Ltd. (B.C. Apr. 1, 1981)
June 18, 1988 – Name changed to Canadian Pacer Petroleum Corporation; basis 5 new for 1 old sh. ■

Consolidated Pacific Bay Minerals Ltd. (B.C. Dec. 16, 1983)
July 22, 2008 – Name changed to Pacific Bay Minerals Ltd. (see FPsurvey - Mines & Energy)

Consolidated Panther Mines Ltd. (Ont. 1960)
Mar. 31, 1988 – Name changed to Panthco Resources Inc.; basis 1 new for 3 old shs. ■

Consolidated Paper Corporation Limited (Can. 1931)
Oct. 1, 1967 – Name changed to Consolidated-Bathurst Limited. ■

Consolidated Parklane Resources Inc. (Alta. Mar. 9, 1988)
Apr. 15, 1991 – Continued into British Columbia.
Jan. 7, 1993 – Name changed to Micrologix Biotech Inc. following acquisition of Microtek Research and Development Ltd. and Micrologix International Ltd.; basis 1 new for 2 old shs. ■

Consolidated Payette International Resources Ltd. (B.C. 1967)
Apr. 28, 1976 – Name changed to Celico Resources Ltd. ■

Consolidated Paymaster Resources Ltd. (B.C. May 31, 1979)
July 5, 1988 – Name changed to Albany Resources Ltd.; basis 1 new for 4.5 old shs. ■

Consolidated Paytel Ltd. (B.C. Aug. 9, 1983)
June 1, 1994 – Name changed to Paytel Industries Ltd.; basis 1 new for 3 old shs. ■

Consolidated P.C.R. Industries Ltd. (B.C. Apr. 2, 1980)
Dec. 2, 1988 – Name changed to Oregon Resources Corp. ■

Consolidated Peak Oils Ltd. (Ont. 1946)
Mar. 4, 1960 – Acquired by Consolidated Allenbee Oil & Gas Company Limited; basis 1 new for 2 old shs.

Consolidated Pemberton Technologies Ltd. (B.C. June 19, 1980)
June 22, 1995 – Name changed to CPT Pemberton Technologies Ltd.; basis 1 new for 5 old shs. ■

Consolidated Peritronics Medical Inc. (B.C. 1981)
Nov. 15, 1996 – Name changed to Peritronics Medical, Ltd.; basis 1 new for 2 old shs. ■

Consolidated Pershcourt Mining Ltd. (Que. 1945)
1971 – Merged into Abcourt Metals Inc.; basis 1 new for 5 old shs.

Consolidated Petroquin Resources Limited (B.C. Jan. 12, 1979)
July 11, 2005 – Name changed to Xemplar Energy Corp. ■

Consolidated Phantom Industries Limited (Ont. 1928)
1967 – Released from receivership.
July 30, 1971 – Name changed to In.Mark Corporation. ■

Consolidated Pine Channel Gold Corp. (B.C. Mar. 24, 1987)
May 10, 2006 – Name changed to Star Uranium Corp. ■

Consolidated Pipe Lines Company (Can. 1955)
Sept. 14, 1988 – Acquired by Unigas Corporation for $12 per sh.

Consolidated Platinum Industries Inc. (B.C. Oct. 23, 1984)
May 25, 1993 – Name changed to Allied Strategies Inc. ■

Consolidated Player Resources Inc. (B.C. 1981)
Dec. 23, 1988 – Name changed to Epping Realty Corporation; basis 1 new for 3 old shs. ■

Consolidated PlenTech Electronics Inc. (B.C. 1981)
July 27, 2015 – Dissolved and struck from register.

Consolidated Pope Valley Holdings Ltd. (B.C. Mar. 24, 1986)
May 5, 1994 – Name changed to Da Capo Resources Ltd. ■

Consolidated Powergem Resource Corporation (B.C. 1980)
May 1, 1990 – Amalgamated with Tamavack Resources Inc. and Calvada Resources Inc. to form Eurus Resource Corp.; basis 1 new for 7.5 old shs. (see Eurus Resource Corp.)

Consolidated Press Limited (Can. 1929)
1957 – Acquired by Liberty of Canada Ltd. for $4.75 per cl. A sh. and $2.00 per cl. B sh.

Consolidated Professor Mines Limited (Ont. 1981)
May 27, 1996 – Acquired by Royal Oak Mines Inc. for 80¢ per sh. (see Royal Oak Mines Inc.)

Consolidated Properties Ltd. (Alta. Sept. 9, 1994)
Aug. 26, 1998 – Continued into Canada.
Jan. 28, 2005 – Plan of Arrangement amalgamation with Canadian Aspen Properties Ltd.; basis $2.75 for 1 old Cons. Properties sh.

Consolidated Proprietary Mines Holdings Ltd. (Ont. 1951)
Mar. 13, 1979 – Charter cancelled.

Consolidated Prudential Mines Ltd. (B.C. 1958)
Feb. 1972 – Merged into Davenport Oils & Mining Ltd.; basis 1 new for 2 old shs.

Consolidated Puma Minerals Corp. (B.C. Aug. 6, 1981)
Aug. 7, 2009 – Acquired by Sage Gold Inc.; basis 1.202 Sage shs. for 1 Consolidated Puma sh. (see Sage Gold Inc.)

Consolidated QData Systems Inc. (B.C. July 2, 1985)
Jan. 5, 1996 – Name changed to Carbite Golf Inc. ■

Consolidated Quebec Gold Mining & Metals Corp. (Que. 1933)
Mar. 1951 – Early in 1951, shldrs. received 16 $1.00 par 3% redeem. pref. shs. for each 100 old shs.; these pref. shs. were redeemed.
1963 – Name changed to Commercial Holdings & Metals Corp.; basis 1 new for 2 old shs.

Consolidated Quebec Smelting & Refining Ltd. (Que. 1947)
1968 – Name changed to Magnetics International Ltd. ■

Consolidated Quebec Yellowknife Mines Ltd. (Que. 1944)
May 1974 – Charter cancelled.

Consolidated Raindor Mines Ltd. (Ont. 1945)
July 27, 1976 – Charter cancelled.

Consolidated Rambler Mines Limited (Ont. 1961)
Jan. 28, 1999 – Acquired by Grand River Holdings Limited, a wholly owned subsid. of J.D. Irving, Limited, for $20.75 per sh.

Consolidated Ramrod Gold Corporation (B.C. Mar. 1, 1983 amalg.)
Dec. 14, 1989 – Amalgamated with Strongbow Resources Corporation to form new co. with same name Consolidated Ramrod Gold Corporation; basis 1 new for 1 Strongbow sh. and 1 new for 4.867 Consolidated Ramrod shs.
Apr. 9, 1996 – Name changed to Quest International Resources Corporation. ■

Consolidated Ranwick Uranium Mines Ltd. (Ont. 1949)
1955 – Name changed to International Ranwick Ltd. ■

Consolidated Rapid River Resources Ltd. (Alta. 1966)
Nov. 30, 1981 – Struck off register.

Consolidated Reactor Uranium Mines Ltd. (Ont. 1974 amalg.)
Oct. 23, 1987 – Name changed to Canaustra Gold Exploration Limited. ■

Consolidated Red Poplar Minerals Ltd. (Ont. 1947)
Oct. 1971 – Name changed to New Dimension Resources Ltd.; basis 1 new for 5 old shs. ■

Consolidated Redding Explorations Corporation (B.C. July 18, 1983)
June 20, 1996 – Name changed to Redex Gold Inc. ■

Consolidated Regal Resources Ltd. (B.C. Apr. 15, 1979)
Sept. 18, 1992 – Name changed to Fresco Developments Ltd.; basis 1 new for 2.5 old shs. ■

Consolidated Regcourt Mines Ltd. (Que. 1944)
1968 – Assets sold to Kelly Lake Nickel Mines Ltd.; basis 1 new for 10 old shs.

Consolidated Retail Solutions Inc. (B.C. Sept. 16, 1983)
July 18, 1994 – Name changed to Ventir Challenge Enterprises Ltd. ■

Consolidated Rexspar Minerals & Chemicals Limited (Ont. 1951)
Oct. 1, 1987 – Formed Conrex Corporation in Ontario on amalgamation with a private co. ■

Consolidated Rhodes Resources Inc. (B.C. Sept. 27, 1962)
Mar. 4, 1992 – Name changed to Fairhaven Resources Ltd.; basis 1 new for 5 old shs. ■

Consolidated Ribago Mines Ltd. (Ont. 1944)
Mar. 1976 – Charter cancelled.

Consolidated Rich Capital Corporation (B.C. 1983)
May 26, 2008 – Struck from registry and dissolved.

Consolidated Rich Coast Sulphur Ltd. (B.C. 1984)
Jan. 25, 1993 – Amalgamated with Consolidated Boulder Mountain Resources Ltd. to form Rich Coast Resources Ltd.; basis 1 new for 10 Consolidated Boulder shs. and 1 new for 1 Consolidated Rich sh. (see Rich Coast Resources Ltd.)

Consolidated Richland Mines Inc. (B.C. May 25, 1987)
Jan. 19, 1999 – Name changed to Apogee Minerals Ltd. ■

Consolidated Rideau Resources Corp. (B.C. May 16, 1979)
Feb. 1, 1995 – Name changed to Brymore Oil & Gas Ltd.; basis 1 new for 2 old shs. ■

Consolidated Rio Plata Resources Ltd. (B.C. Mar. 6, 1962)
Oct. 28, 1993 – Name changed to New Rio Resources Ltd.; basis 1 new for 4 old shs. ■

Consolidated Ripple Resources Ltd. (B.C. 1981)
Aug. 13, 1993 – Dissolved and struck off register.

Consolidated Rochette Mines Ltd. (Que. 1936)
Feb. 1955 – Name changed to Conro Development Corporation Ltd.; basis 1 new for 5 old shs. ■

Consolidated Royalgroup Inc. (Ont. Apr. 28, 1966)
Nov. 8, 1991 – Name changed to Aronos Multinational Inc. ■

Consolidated Ruskin Developments Ltd. (B.C. 1974)
Mar. 31, 1992 – Amalgamated with Solid Gold Capital Corp. to form new co. with same name Consolidated Ruskin Developments Ltd.; basis 1 new for 1.2 Solid Gold shs. and 1 new for 1 Consolidated Ruskin sh. (see Consolidated Ruskin Developments Ltd.)

Consolidated Ruskin Developments Ltd. (B.C. Mar. 31, 1992 amalg.)
Nov. 23, 1992 – Name changed to Leisureways Marketing Ltd. ■

Consolidated SYH Corporation (Ont. 1961)
Oct. 29, 1991 – Amalgamated with Newco, a wholly owned subsid. of The Woodbridge Company; basis 25¢ or 2.43 new wts. for 1 Consolidated SYH sh. Wts. entitle the holders to purchase 1 cl. A sub. vtg. sh. of Central Capital Corporation for $14 per sh. until Sept. 29, 1994.

Consolidated St. Simeon Mines Ltd. (Que. 1950)
May 1974 – Charter cancelled.

Consolidated Samarkand Resources Inc. (B.C. Apr. 11, 1986)
Oct. 15, 1999 – Name changed to Soho Resources Corp.; basis 1 new for 6 old shs. ■

Consolidated Sannorm Mines Ltd. (Ont. 1944)
Mar. 15, 1955 – Charter cancelled.

Consolidated Sarabat Gold Corporation (B.C. Apr. 28, 1988)
Nov. 20, 1998 – Name changed to CSG Resources Ltd.; basis 1 new for 3 old shs. ■

Consolidated Sasha Technology Ltd. (Can. Mar. 9, 1987)
May 6, 2004 – Dissolved.

Consolidated Sea Gold Corp. (B.C. July 26, 1979)
May 9, 1990 – Name changed to Sea Gold Resources Inc.; basis 1 new for 2 old shs. ■

Consolidated Serena Resources Ltd. (B.C. July 17, 1987)
Mar. 7, 2003 – Name changed to Capstone Gold Corp. ■

Consolidated Shasta Resources Inc. (B.C. Sept. 2, 1966)
Nov. 23, 1994 – Name changed to Lima Gold Corporation. ■

Consolidated Shoshoni Gold Inc. (B.C. Apr. 23, 1985)
Jan. 7, 2000 – Name changed to New Shoshoni Ventures Ltd.; basis 1 new for 10 old shs. ■

Consolidated Shunsby Mines Limited (Ont. Feb. 10, 1944)
June 25, 1975 – Name changed to MW Resources Limited; basis 1 new for 3 old shs. ■

Consolidated Silver Banner Mines Ltd. (Ont. 1950)
1955 – Acquired by Tecumseh Developments Ltd.; basis 1 new for 10 old shs. (see Tecumseh Developments Ltd.)

Consolidated Silver Belle Mines Ltd. (Ont. 1960)
June 27, 1966 – Amalgamated with Jayco Mines (1966) Ltd. to form Silver Belle Mines (1966) Ltd. (see Silver Belle Mines (1966) Ltd.)

Consolidated Silver Butte Mines Ltd. (B.C. Dec. 31, 1957)
July 31, 1989 – Name changed to Silver Butte Resources Ltd. ■

Consolidated Silver Ridge Mines Ltd. (B.C. Dec. 2, 1935)
Sept. 17, 1981 – Name changed to Northcal Resources Ltd. ■

Consolidated Silver Standard Mines Limited (B.C. Dec. 11, 1946)
Apr. 9, 1990 – Name changed to Silver Standard Resources Inc. ■

Consolidated Silver Tusk Mines Ltd. (B.C. 1976 amalg.)
Feb. 11, 2000 – Continued into Yukon.
May 20, 2005 – Dissolved and struck off register.

Consolidated Skeena Mines Ltd. (B.C. 1951)
Feb. 1969 – Merged into International Mariner Resources Ltd.; basis 1 new for 4.5 old shs., plus 1 ser. C sh. purch. warr. of Mariner for each 2 shs. received on exch. (see International Mariner Resources Ltd.)

Consolidated Spectra Ventures Ltd. (B.C. Oct. 16, 1984)
Dec. 27, 1996 – Name changed to Tiger International Resources Inc. (see FPsurvey - Mines & Energy)

Consolidated Spectrum Resources Ltd. (B.C. 1967)
Name changed to Spectrum Industrial Resources Ltd.; basis 1 new for 2 old shs. ■

Consolidated Spire Ventures Ltd. (B.C. Jan. 15, 1979)
Dec. 1, 2010 – Name changed to Berkwood Resources Ltd.; basis 1 new for 10 old shs. ■

Consolidated Standard Mines Ltd. (B.C. Jan. 13, 1960)
Apr. 15, 1975 – Name changed to Golden Standard Mines Ltd.; basis 1 new for 5 old shs. ■

Consolidated Stanford Corporation (Ont. Apr. 8, 1968)
Dec. 3, 2003 – Voluntarily wound up. Distributiion basis $0.39 per com. and cl. A sh.

Consolidated Stikine Silver Ltd. (B.C. 1963)
Sept. 20, 1989 – Name changed to Stikine Resources Ltd. ■

Consolidated Stone Industries Inc. (B.C. May 16, 1980)
Aug. 22, 2005 – Dissolved and struck from register.

Consolidated Strategic Metals Inc. (B.C. 1982)
Feb. 14, 1983 – Name changed to New Strategic Metals Inc.; basis 1 new for 4 old shs. ■

Consolidated Sudbury Basin Mines Ltd. (Ont. 1942)
June 30, 1960 – Amalgamated with Giant Yellowknife Gold Mines Limited to form Giant Yellowknife Mines Ltd.; basis 1 new for 25 old shs. (see Giant Yellowknife Mines Limited)

Consolidated Summit Mines Limited (Ont. 1962)
May 1, 1983 – Formed Barrick Resources Corporation in Ontario on amalgamation with Petronic Resources Ltd. and following the Apr. 28, 1983, acquisition of Barrick Petroleum Corporation; basis 1 new for 4 old shs. ■

Consolidated Suntec Ventures Limited (B.C. Jan. 27, 1986 amalg.)
Oct. 3, 1990 – Name changed to Vortex Energy Systems Inc. ■

Consolidated Taché Mines & Investments Ltd. (Que. 1951)
June 18, 1982 – Name changed to Taché Resources Inc. ■

Consolidated Takepoint Ventures Ltd. (Yuk. June 25, 2002)
Dec. 18, 2002 – Name changed to Lake Shore Gold Corp. pursuant to reverse takeover acquisition of Aurora Platinum Corp. ■

Consolidated Tako Resources Ltd. (B.C. Sept. 18, 1972)
Jan. 18, 2000 – Name changed to International Tako Industries Inc.; basis 1 new for 3.8 old shs. ■

Consolidated Talcorp Limited (Can. Dec. 1978 amalg.)
May 7, 1991 – Name changed to Sound Insight Enterprises Limited. ■

Consolidated Taywin Resources Ltd. (B.C. Nov. 15, 1972 amalg.)
Apr. 29, 1996 – Name changed to Inspiration Mining Corporation. ■

Consolidated T.C. Resources Ltd. (B.C. Apr. 24, 1987)
May 20, 1992 – Name changed to Cyclone Capital Corp. ■

Consolidated Team Resources Corp. (B.C. May 20, 1988)
June 28, 2000 – Name changed to QHR Technologies Inc. following reverse takeover acquisition of New Horizon Technologies Inc. ■

Consolidated Technologies Holdings Inc. (B.C. May 4, 1993)
Nov. 26, 2001 – Name changed to Tigertel Telecommunications Corp. and continued into British Columbia pursuant to reverse takeover acquisition of Tigertel Communications Inc. ■

Consolidated Texas Northern Minerals Limited (B.C. Dec. 23, 1980)
June 28, 2000 – Name changed to Rio Verde Industries Inc.; basis 1 new for 8 old shs. (see FPsurvey - Mines & Energy)

Consolidated Textile Mills Limited (Can. Apr. 30, 1946)
June 30, 1980 – Name changed to Consoltex Canada Inc. ■

Consolidated Thermo Tech International Inc. (B.C. 1983)
June 9, 1992 – Name changed to Thermo Tech Technologies Inc.; basis 1 new for 3 old shs. ■

Consolidated Thompson Iron Mines Limited (Can. July 1, 1989 amalg.)
May 16, 2011 – Acquired by Cliffs Natural Resources Inc. for $17.25 per sh.

Consolidated Thompson-Lundmark Gold Mines Limited (Can. Dec. 18, 1985 amalg.)
July 1, 1989 – Amalgamated with Québec Cobalt and Exploration Limited and Ghanorcan Resources Ltd. to form new co. with same name Consolidated

Thompson-Lundmark Gold Mines Limited; basis 1 new for 2 Québec Cobalt shs., 1 new for 2.1 Ghanorcan shs. and 1 new for 1 Consolidated Thompson-Lundmark sh.
Aug. 24, 2006 – Name changed to Consolidated Thompson Iron Mines Limited. ■

Consolidated Thor Mines Ltd. (Ont. 1943)
Jan. 18, 1957 – Name changed to Nealon Mines Ltd. ■

Consolidated Thunderbird Projects Ltd. (B.C. Dec. 16, 1965)
Aug. 16, 1999 – Name changed to Jenosys Enterprises Inc. ■

Consolidated Tonka Resources Inc. (Can. Jan. 14, 1972)
Nov. 26, 1993 – Name changed to South China Industries (Canada) Inc.; basis 1 subord. vtg. sh. for 2 com. shs. ■

Consolidated Top Gun Explorations Inc. (B.C. Nov. 20, 1986)
Sept. 13, 1993 – Name changed to Sterling Pacific Resources Inc. ■

Consolidated Topaz Exploration Ltd. (B.C. Feb. 21, 1983)
Aug. 6, 1991 – Name changed to Topaz Resources International Inc.; basis 1 new for 2 old shs. ■

Consolidated Topper Gold Corporation (B.C. Nov. 23, 1959)
Feb. 6, 2002 – Name changed to Topper Resources Inc. ■

Consolidated Toronto Development Corp. Ltd. (Ont. 1954)
1964 – Name changed to Great Northern Capital Corporation Limited. ■

Consolidated Tower Resources Ltd. (B.C. 1961)
Mar. 18, 1983 – Struck off register. ■

Consolidated TranDirect.com Technologies Inc. (B.C. June 14, 1985)
June 20, 2001 – Name changed to International Samuel Exploration Corp. ■

Consolidated Trans-Canada Resources Ltd. (Alta. 1984 amalg.)
Oct. 10, 1989 – Acquired by Ranchmen's Resources Ltd.; basis 0.69 new Ranchmen's shs. for 1 old Trans-Canada sh. (see Ranchmen's Resources Ltd.)

Consolidated Trillion Resources Ltd. (Alta. July 24, 1987)
Dec. 2, 2003 – Acquired by Viceroy Exploration Ltd.; basis 0.7 Viceroy shs. for 1 Consolidated Trillion sh. (see Viceroy Exploration Ltd.)

Consolidated Trilogy Ventures Ltd. (B.C. Apr. 3, 1986)
Dec. 22, 1998 – Name changed to Thyssen Mining Exploration Inc. ■

Consolidated Tungsten Mining Corp. of Canada Ltd. (Ont. Feb. 2, 1951)
1958 – Name changed to Mount Wright Iron Mines Company Limited; basis 1 new for 4 old shs. ■

Consolidated TVX Mining Corporation (Ont. Oct. 31, 1984)
Jan. 22, 1991 – Acquired by TVX Gold Inc. (see TVX Gold Inc.)

Consolidated United Safety Technology Inc. (B.C. Aug. 8, 1979)
Sept. 29, 1994 – Name changed to Genetronics Biomedical Ltd.; basis 1 new for 5.6 old shs. ■

Consolidated Uranium Corp. (Que. 1954)
Aug. 1957 – Acquired by Continental Consolidated Mines & Oils Corp. Ltd.; basis 1 new for 10 old shs. (see Continental Consolidated Mines & Oils Corp. Ltd.)

Consolidated Uranium Inc. (Ont. July 23, 2021)
Dec. 11, 2023 – All o/s shs. not already held acquired by IsoEnergy Ltd.; basis 0.500 IsoEnergy shs. for 1 Consolidated Uranium sh. ■

Consolidated Valley Ventures Ltd. (B.C. Sept. 19, 1979)
Mar. 12, 1997 – Name changed to CVL Resources Ltd. ■

Consolidated Van-City Marble Ltd. (B.C. 1987)
Jan. 23, 2004 – Dissolved and struck from register. ■

Consolidated Van-Tor Resources Ltd. (B.C. 1948)
Feb. 1971 – Merged with 4 other cos. into International Mariner Resources Ltd.; basis 2 shs. plus 1 cl. C warr. of Mariner for 18 shs. of Van-Tor. ■

Consolidated Vauze Mines Ltd. (Ont. 1944)
1961 – Assets acquired by Vauze Mines Ltd.

Consolidated Venturex Holdings Ltd. (B.C. Nov. 21, 1983)
May 24, 2007 – Name changed to Venturex Explorations Inc. ■

Consolidated Vigor Mines Ltd. (B.C. 1958)
Mar. 1973 – Charter cancelled.

Consolidated Virginia Mining Corp. (Que. 1947)
Aug. 1974 – Charter cancelled.

Consolidated Viscount Resources Ltd. (B.C. Mar. 9, 1977)
Feb. 20, 2001 – Name changed to Choice Resources Corp.; basis 1 new for 3 old shs. ■

Consolidated Wellington Resources Ltd. (B.C. June 20, 1953)
Sept. 24, 1987 – Name changed to First Hospitality (Canada) Corporation. ■

Consolidated West Hill Energy Inc. (Ont. June 17, 1964)
Nov. 21, 1997 – Formed African Selection Mining Corporation in Ontario on amalgamation with African Selection Mining Corporation; basis 1 new for 0.25 old shs. ■

Consolidated West Petroleum Limited (Ont. 1948)
Sept. 19, 1977 – Minority shldrs. received pref. shs. red. at $6.90 per sh. on amalg. with subsid. of Western Decalta Petroleum (1977) Ltd.

Consolidated Western and Pacific Resources Corp. (B.C. May 27, 1991 amalg.)
July 9, 1996 – Name changed to Synergy Resource Technologies Inc. ■

Consolidated Westrex Development Corp. (B.C. Aug. 29, 1979)
July 25, 1991 – Name changed to Westrex Energy Corp. ■

Consolidated Westview Resource Corp. (B.C. Feb. 25, 1986)
Nov. 23, 2017 – Name changed to Lithoquest Diamonds Inc. following reverse takeover acquisition of (old) Lithoquest Diamonds Inc. ■

Consolidated Woodgreen Mines Ltd. (Ont. 1948)
1964 – Name changed to Cumberland Mining Co. Ltd.; basis 1 new for 5 old shs. ■

Consolidated Woodjam Copper Corp. (B.C. July 20, 2011)
Dec. 15, 2022 – Acquired by Vizsla Copper Corp.; basis 0.307206085 Vizsla shs. for 1 Consolidated Woodjam sh.

Consolidated Yukeno Mines Ltd. (Ont. 1949)
1951 – Name changed to Yukeno Mines Ltd. and continued into Ontario; basis 1 new for 2 old shs. ■

Consolidated Yukon Minerals Corporation (Alta. 1986)
Oct. 1, 1994 – Dissolved and struck off register.

Consolitech Invest Corp. (Alta. Sept. 27, 1994)
July 19, 2001 – Name changed to HTN Inc. pursuant to reverse takeover acquisition of HTN (Ontario) Inc.; basis 1 new for 2 old shs. ■

Consoltex Canada Inc. (Can. Apr. 30, 1946)
June 27, 1991 – Acquired by CCI Acquisitions Inc. for $33 per sh.

Consoltex Group Inc. (Can. Sept. 16, 1992)
Dec. 16, 1999 – All o/s sub. vtg. shs. acquired by a subsid. of American Industrial Partners; basis Cdn$5.60 per sh.
Jan. 1, 2000 – Name changed to Consoltex Inc.

Consort Energy Corp. (B.C. Feb. 13, 1981)
Apr. 27, 1990 – Name changed to International Consort Industries Inc.; basis 1 new for 2 old shs. ■

Constantine Metal Resources Ltd. (B.C. Mar. 3, 2006)
Nov. 7, 2022 – Acquired by American Pacific Mining Corp.; basis 0.881 American Pacific shs. for 1 Constantine sh.

Consteel Explorations Ltd. (B.C. 1969)
June 27, 1977 – Dissolved.

Constellation Brands Canada, Inc. (Can. Sept. 7, 1993 amalg.)
Dec. 17, 2016 – Name changed to Arterra Wines Canada, Inc.

Constellation Capital Enterprises Inc. (Ont. June 30, 1989)
June 12, 1995 – Name changed to Raw Creek Resources Inc. ■

Constellation Copper Corporation (Can. June 21, 2002)
Dec. 23, 2008 – Filed for bankruptcy. Deloitte & Touche Inc. appointed trustee.

Constellation Oil & Gas Ltd. (Alta. Aug. 12, 1992)
May 31, 2000 – Name changed to International Sovereign Energy Corp.; basis 1 new for 5 old shs. ■

Consular-Harker Mines Ltd. (Ont. 1949)
Mar. 1969 – Charter cancelled.

Consumer Credit Corporation Limited (Ont. 1962)
Feb. 25, 1966 – Name changed to Glengair Group Ltd. following reorganization; basis 1 new for 1 old sh. Each $500 princ. amt. of Consumer 6.75% conv. sec. notes, ser. B, due June 15, 1966, exch. for $500 princ. amt. of 6.75% debs., ser. A, and 50 com. sh. of Glengair; each $500 princ. amt. of Consumer 6.75% sec. notes ser. C, due June 15, 1981, exch. for $500 princ. amt. of 6.75% debs., ser. A, and 45 com. sh. of Glengair; sh. purch warr. originally issued with sec. C notes, exch. for 10 com. sh. of Glengair for each 100 Consumer com. sh. called for by such warr.; each $100 princ. amt. of Consumer 5.5% conv. debs., due Nov. 15, 1978, exch. for $60 princ. amt. of 6.75% debs., ser. A, and 6 com. sh. of Glengair; 125,000 o/s 6.5% Consumer pref. shs. ser. A exch. for 250,000 Glengair com. shs. ■

Consumer General Inc. (Ont. 1980)
Mar. 4, 1993 – Name changed to Consolidated Consumer General Inc.; basis 1 new for 2 old shs. ■

Consumers Distributing Company Limited (Ont. 1956)
Dec. 16, 1987 – All o/s cl. A and sub. vtg. cl. B, not already owned, acquired by Loeb Inc., a wholly owned subsid. of Provigo Inc.; basis $5.50 per sh. (see Provigo Inc.)

Consumers' Gas Company (Can. 1848)
1954 – Continued into Ontario.
Apr. 9, 1980 – Name changed to Hiram Walker-Consumers Home Ltd. to reflect acquisition of Home Oil, Cygnus Corp. and Hiram Walker Gooderham Worts. ■

The Consumers' Gas Company Ltd. (Ont. Mar. 23, 1848)
July 25, 2002 – Name changed to Enbridge Gas Distribution Inc. ■

The Consumers' Gas Company Ltd. (Ont. 1848)
Mar. 15, 1991 – Acquired by British Gas Holdings (Canada) Limited for $34.265 per sh. On Mar. 10, 1992, an issue of 15% public float from parent British Gas plc was made and the instalment receipts began trading on the Toronto and Montreal stock exchanges. On June 30, 1994, IPL Energy purchased an 85% interest in The Consumers' Gas Company Ltd. from British Gas plc. Effective Dec. 13, 1996, IPL purchased the remaining 15% interest for $24 or $1.50 plus a fraction of an IPL Energy com. sh. having a value of $22.50. On July 5, 1999, all remaining o/s pref. shs. (group 1 ser. A, group 1 ser. B and group 2 ser. C) were redeemed for $101.060274, $101.060274 and $25.017671 per sh., respectively.

Consumers Glass Company Limited (Can. Oct. 4, 1917)
July 1, 1986 – Name changed to Consumers Packaging Inc. ■

Consumers Packaging Inc. (Can. Oct. 4, 1917)
May 23, 2001 – Order under the Companies' Creditors Arrangement Act (CCAA) obtained, staying proceedings against the co. until June 22, 2001. Toronto-based KPMG Inc. appointed monitor.
Apr. 30, 2002 – Filed an assignment into bankruptcy and KPMG Inc. was appointed trustee. All directors resigned. Virtually all of the co.'s Canadian and overseas assets were sold, satisfying most of the claims made by the secured creditors.
Dec. 20, 2002 – First interim cash dividend to unsecured creditors of 3.5¢ on the dollar was issued.
Jan. 22, 2003 – KPMG filed a proposal under the Bankruptcy and Insolvency Act (Canada) and a meeting of the creditors was held on Feb. 4, 2003. Under the proposal, the claims of the creditors would be settled for the remaining assets and a $30,000,000 face amount Recovery Note to be issued by the company; the company's capital stock would be reorganized whereby all the shares will be converted into one redeemable preferred share having an aggregate value of $1; and the company's bankruptcy would be annulled allowing OI Canada Holdings B.V. to acquire a restructured Consumers Packaging (which will be free and clear of any claims of the creditors other than the claims of KPMG under the recovery note). The amended proposal would provide for possible payments to the unsecured creditors of up to 9.1¢ on the dollar compared to 6.9¢ on the dollar in bankruptcy.
Apr. 29, 2003 – Restructured Consumers Packaging was continued under the Nova Scotia Companies Act. All the terms of the amended proposal were completed, annuling the bankruptcy. Remaining assets of the company were vested with KPMG and the company's common and preferred share capital was cancelled.
Apr. 30, 2003 – Consumers Packaging amalgamated with OI Canada to form Amalco. Future dividends were dependent on recoveries under the Recovery Note, repayable on a sharing formula of the net benefits derived from utilization of tax loss attributes held by Amalco. The Recovery Note expires in 10 years. It was unlikely that there would be monies available for distribution to shldrs. after unsecured creditors received 100% of their claims.

The Consumers' Waterheater Income Fund (Ont. Oct. 28, 2002)
Jan. 1, 2011 – Succeeded by Enercare Inc. pursuant to plan of arrangement whereby Enercare Inc. was formed to facilitate the conversion of the fund into a corporation and the fund was subsequently dissolved. ■

Contach Industries Inc. (Ont. Sept. 18, 1980)
Aug. 23, 1993 – Struck from registry and dissolved.

Contact Diamond Corporation (Ont. Feb. 11, 1999 amalg.)
Jan. 12, 2007 – Acquired by Stornoway Diamond Corporation; basis 0.36 new Stornoway sh. for 1 old Contact sh. (see Stornoway Diamond Corporation)

Contact Exploration Inc. (Alta. Sept. 1, 1995)
Dec. 19, 2014 – Formed Kicking Horse Energy Inc. in Alberta on amalgamation with Donnycreek Energy Inc., with Contact the deemed acquiror; basis 0.60 Kicking Horse shs. for 1 Donnycreek sh. and 0.075 Kicking Horse shs. for 1 Contact sh. ■

Contact Gold Corp. (Nev. June 7, 2017)
May 1, 2024 – Acquired by Orla Mining Ltd.; basis 0.0063 Orla shs. for 1 Contact Gold sh.

Contact Gold Mines Ltd. (Sask. Feb. 16, 1960)
July 7, 1969 – Name changed to Contact Ventures Ltd. ■

Contact Minerals Ltd. (Man. 1955)
Feb. 25, 1967 – Dissolved.

Contact Ventures Ltd. (Sask. Feb. 16, 1960)
Sept. 9, 1982 – Continued into Canada.
Apr. 15, 1988 – Name changed to West Pride Industries Corp.; basis 1 new for 4 old shs. ■

Contact Vet Inc. (Can. Oct. 19, 2020)
May 18, 2021 – Name changed to QNB Metals Inc. (see FPsurvey - Mines & Energy)

Contakt World Technologies Corp. (B.C. July 10, 2007)
Mar. 30, 2022 – Name changed to Infinity Stone Ventures Corp. (see FPsurvey - Mines & Energy)

Contec Innovations Inc. (B.C. Apr. 14, 2000)
Dec. 29, 2011 – Dissolved and struck from register.

Contender Resources Ltd. (B.C. Feb. 24, 1984)
July 14, 1986 – Name changed to Strategic Communications Ltd. ■

Contex Silver Mines Ltd. (B.C. 1968)
Name changed to Goldex Developments Ltd.

Context Energy Inc. (Alta. July 13, 1999)
Feb. 28, 2001 – Formed Ravenwood Resources Inc. in Alberta on amalgamation with Ravenwood Resources Inc., constituting a reverse takeover by Ravenwood; basis 4.25 new for 1 Ravenwood sh. and 1 new for 2 Context shs. ■

Conti-Mac Mines Ltd. (Ont. 1946)
May 1957 – Charter cancelled.

Contiki Resources Ltd. (B.C. Sept. 22, 1992)
Sept. 1, 1999 – Name changed to GoldenGoals.com Ventures Inc. following acquisition of Alternative Card Company Ltd. ■

Continent Group Inc. (Alta. Feb. 17, 1995)
May 26, 1999 – Name changed to POPi Group Inc. ■

Continent Resources Inc. (B.C. Nov. 8, 2005)
Jan. 12, 2006 – Continued into Alberta.
Aug. 18, 2008 – Continued into British Columbia.
Oct. 9, 2009 – Name changed to Copper One Inc. and continued into Canada. ■

Continental Bank Capital Corporation (Ont. 1981)
1981 – Name changed to Continental Bank Leasing Corporation and continued into Ontario. ■

Continental Bank Leasing Corporation (Ont. 1981)
Oct. 1986 – Sold to Central Capital Corporation by its parent company, the Continental Bank. The bank received secured notes and convertible debentures which it subsequently sold for $112,000,000. It retained transferable options to purch. up to 891,000 cl. A shs. of Central Capital Corporation for $19.625 per sh. up to Dec. 30, 1990.

Continental Bank of Canada (Can. July 14, 1977; via Bank Act)
Nov. 1, 1981 – Amalgamated in Canada to continue with same name.
Oct. 22, 1996 – Name changed to CBOC Continental Inc. and continued into Canada. ■

Continental (CBOC) Corporation (Can. Aug. 30, 2002 amalg.)
June 4, 2004 – Name changed to Stonington Capital Corporation. ■

Continental Can Company of Canada Limited (Can. 1935)
1977 – Name changed to The Continental Group of Canada Ltd. ■

Continental CareTech Corporation (Ont. June 1, 1965)
May 17, 1996 – Name changed to Corona Gold Corporation. ■

Continental Cash Technologies Corporation (Alta. Jan. 14, 1993)
July 7, 2004 – Continued into Ontario.
Dec. 29, 2004 – Name changed to Cenit Corporation. ■

Continental Cinch Mines Ltd. (B.C. 1959)
Nov. 1973 – Name changed to Gladiator Resources Ltd.; basis 1 new for 7 old shs. ■

Continental Conquest Capital Corp. (Ont. July 31, 1981)
Jan. 21, 1999 – Formed The Streetwear Corporation in Ontario following amalgamation with The Streetwear Corporation; basis 1 new for 1 old sh. ■

Continental Consolidated Mines & Oils Corp. Ltd. (Sask. 1957)
Sept. 22, 1961 – Struck off register.

Continental Consolidated Mines Ltd. (B.C. 1959)
1967 – Name changed to Continental Cinch Mines Ltd.; basis 1 new for 10 old shs. ■

Continental Copper Co. Ltd. (Can.)
Aug. 6, 1931 – Charter cancelled.

Continental Copper Corporation (B.C. May 29, 1984)
Oct. 23, 1997 – Name changed to Continental Energy Corporation. (see FPsurvey - Mines & Energy)

Continental Copper Mines Limited (Que. Nov. 14, 1938)
Apr. 4, 1996 – Name changed to Continental Resources Ltd. ■

Continental Datanet Inc. (B.C. 1982)
Mar. 19, 1993 – Dissolved and struck off register.

Continental Diamond Drilling & Exploration Co. Ltd. (Ont. 1945)
1949 – Name changed to Continental Exploration Ltd. ■

Continental Discount Corporation (Que. 1955)
Mar. 1, 1975 – Amalgamated with Canadian Affiliated Financial Corp. on a pooling of interest basis to form Canadian Financial Company.

Continental Exploration & Development Ltd. (Ont. July 23, 1984)
Aug. 8, 1996 – Name changed to Conex Continental Inc.; basis 1 new for 5 old shs. ■

Continental Exploration Ltd. (Ont. 1945)
1962 – Charter cancelled; shs. exch. into Canadian Faraday Ltd.; basis 1 new for 50 old shs.

Continental Fashion Group Inc. (Alta. June 1, 1990)
Sept. 5, 1996 – Formed Genoil Inc. in Canada on amalgamation with Genoil Inc.; basis 1 new for 1 Genoil sh. and 1 new for 10 Continental Fashion shs. (see FPsurvey - Mines & Energy; FPsurvey - Industrials)

Continental Gas Corporation Ltd. (Ont. 1931)
1958 – Wound up.

Continental Gold Corp. (B.C. 1987)
Jan. 15, 1991 – Acquired by Placer Dome Inc. for $20 per sh. (see Placer Dome Inc.)

Continental Gold Inc. (Ont. Apr. 27, 2015)
Mar. 9, 2020 – Acquired by 2727957 Ontario Inc., an indirect subsidiary of Zijin Mining Group Co., Ltd.; basis Cdn$5.50 cash per com. sh.

Continental Gold Limited (Bermuda Mar. 30, 2010 amalg.)
June 10, 2015 – Succeeded by Continental Gold Inc. pursuant to scheme of arrangement whereby wholly owned Continental Gold Inc. was formed to acquire Continental Gold Limited. ■

The Continental Group of Canada Ltd. (Can. 1935)
May 1, 1983 – All o/s com. shs. acquired by CCL Industries Inc.; basis 2,120,000 CCL cl. B non-vtg. shs. and 625,000 cl. A vtg. shs. of CCL. Name subsequently changed to Continental Can Canada Inc.

Continental Home Healthcare Ltd. (B.C. May 11, 1990)
Aug. 6, 2007 – Dissolved and struck from register.

Continental Illinois Bank (Canada) (Can. 1981)
1987 – Acquired by The Swiss Bank Corp.

Continental Iron & Titanium Mining Ltd. (Que. 1955)
June 29, 1960 – Name changed to Continental Titanium Corp. ■

Continental Kirkland Mines Ltd. (Ont. 1927)
Dec. 31, 1970 – Dissolved.

Continental Lead Mines Ltd. (Ont. 1946)
1949 – Continued into Ontario.
1956 – Charter cancelled.

Continental Loan Corp. (Que. 1955)
July 1960 – Name changed to Continental Discount Corporation. ■

Continental McKinney Mines Ltd. (B.C. 1959)
Dec. 31, 1972 – Name changed to Chandalar Resources Ltd.; basis 1 new for 10 old shs. ■

Continental Minerals Corporation (B.C. Feb. 7, 1962)
May 6, 2011 – Acquired by Jinchuan Group Ltd. for $2.60 per sh.

Continental Minerals Corporation (B.C. June 15, 1970)
Mar. 6, 1987 – Dissolved and struck off register.

Continental Mines Ltd. (Ont. 1922)
1927 – Assets sold to Continental Kirkland Mines Ltd.; basis 2 new for 10 old shs.

Continental Mining Corporation (unknown)
1959 – Merged into Continental Consolidated Mines Ltd.; basis 1 new for 3 old shs.

Continental Mining Exploration Ltd. (Ont. 1953)
1958 – Merged into Augustus Exploration Ltd. (see Augustus Exploration Ltd.)

Continental Nickel Limited (Can. Nov. 23, 2006)
Sept. 18, 2012 – Acquired by IMX Resources Limited; basis 3.7 ord. shs. plus 0.5 wts. of IMX for 1 Continental sh.

Continental Oil Co. of Canada Ltd. (Alta. 1936)
1951 – Name changed to New Continental Oil Company of Canada Limited; basis 1 new for 2 old shs. ■

Continental Pacific Resources Inc. (B.C. Aug. 20, 1986)
Jan. 23, 1998 – Name changed to Northern Continental Resources Inc.; basis 1 new for 8 old shs. ■

Continental Pharma Cryosan Inc. (Can. Apr. 10, 1972)
Aug. 29, 1995 – Name changed to IBEX Technologies Inc. ■

Continental Potash Corp. Ltd. (Ont. 1951)
Mar. 1976 – Charter cancelled.

Continental Precious Minerals Inc. (Ont. July 7, 1987 amalg.)
Mar. 2, 2020 – Name changed to Metamaterial Inc. pursuant to reverse takeover acquisition of Metamaterial Technologies Inc. ■

Continental Research & Development Ltd. (Alta. Jan. 16, 1956)
July 23, 1984 – Continued into Ontario.
Jan. 14, 1987 – Name changed to Continental Research Exploration & Development Ltd. ■

Continental Research Exploration & Development Ltd. (Ont. July 23, 1984)
Oct. 6, 1994 – Name changed to Continental Exploration & Development Ltd.; basis 2 new for 5 old shs. ■

Continental Resources Ltd. (Que. Nov. 14, 1938)
July 26, 2004 – Name changed to C2C Inc. pursuant to reverse takeover acquisition of claims and options on properties of 170364 Canada Inc. and Exploration Malartic-Sud Inc., respectively; basis 1 new for 3 old shs. ■

Continental Ridge Resources Inc. (B.C. Apr. 13, 1995)
May 13, 2003 – Name changed to Nevada Geothermal Power Inc. ■

Continental Silver Corp. (B.C. 1966)
June 27, 1985 – Amalgamated with Arizona Silver Corporation to continue under the latter name; basis 1 new for 2 old shs.

Continental Tin Mines Ltd. (Ont. 1943)
1944 – Name changed to Aldrich Mining & Milling Co. Ltd. and continued into Ontario. ■

Continental Titanium Corp. (Que. 1955)
Apr. 1974 – Charter cancelled.

Continental Tyre Ltd. (B.C. Dec. 15, 1986)
Nov. 22, 1991 – Dissolved. shldrs. to receive 0.25811698845 sh. of Export Tyre Holding Co. for each sh. of Continental held. (see Export Tyre Holding Co.)

Continental Uranium Corp. (Sask. 1954)
Aug. 1957 – Acquired by Continental Consolidated Mines & Oils Corp. Ltd.; basis 1 new for 10 old shs. (see Continental Consolidated Mines & Oils Corp. Ltd.)

Continental Utilities Ltd. (Alta. Jan. 16, 1956)
July 28, 1967 – Name changed to Continental Research & Development Ltd. ■

Continental Waste Conversion Inc. (Alta. 1987)
Oct. 9, 1997 – Name changed to EnviroPower Industries Inc. (see FPsurvey - Industrials)

Continuum Arts Inc. (B.C. Apr. 18, 1984)
May 13, 1999 – Name changed to Continuum Resources Ltd.; basis 1 new for 3 old shs. ■

Continuum Health Care Inc. (Alta. Dec. 21, 1999)
Dec. 18, 2009 – Privatized by way of amalgamation with Hallmark Properties Ltd. to continue as Hallmark Properties Ltd.; basis 1 Hallmark redeemable pref. sh. for 1 Continuum com. sh. immediately redeemed for 29¢ and 1 Hallmark ser. 1 pref. sh. for 1 Continuum pref. sh.

Continuum Resources Ltd. (B.C. Apr. 18, 1984)
Mar. 9, 2009 – Acquired by Fortuna Silver Mines Inc.; basis 0.0564 Fortuna Silver shs. for 1 Continuum Resources sh. (see Fortuna Silver Mines Inc.)

Contour Blind & Shade (Canada) Ltd. (Ont. 1966)
Apr. 26, 1983 – Continued into Canada.
Oct. 31, 1985 – Continued into British Columbia.
Dec. 17, 1991 – Name changed to Contour Consumer Products Inc. ■

Contour Consumer Products Inc. (B.C. Oct. 31, 1985)
Aug. 26, 1992 – Name changed to Home Products Inc.; basis 1 new for 5 old shs. (see FPsurvey - Industrials)

Contour Telecom Management Inc. (Can. May 17, 1996)
Aug. 27, 1999 – Name changed to TigerTel Inc. following acquisition of TigerTel Services Limited, a subsid. of Applied Cellular Technology Inc.; basis 1 new for 4 old shs. ■

Contrans Corp. (Ont. July 23, 1982)
July 23, 2002 – Converted into Contrans Income Fund; basis 4 Contrans Income subord. vtg. trust units for 1 Contrans Corp. cl. A subord. vtg. sh.

Contrans Group Inc. (Ont. Oct. 15, 2009)
Dec. 11, 2014 – Acquired by TransForce Inc. for $14.60 per class A & B sh. (see TransForce Inc.)

Contrans Income Fund (Ont. Apr. 16, 2002)
Dec. 3, 2009 – Converted into Contrans Group Inc. pursuant to plan of arrangement; basis (i) 1 Contrans Group cl. A subord. vtg. sh. for 1 Contrans Income Fund cl. A subord. vtg. unit, (ii) 1 Contrans Group cl. A subord. vtg. sh. for 1 cl. A limited partnership unit of Contrans Holding Limited Partnership, Contrans Services LP and Contrans Holding II LP and (iii) 1 Contrans Group cl. B multiple vtg. sh. for 1 cl. B limited partnership unit of Contrans Holding Limited Partnership, Contrans Services LP and Contrans Holding II LP. (see Contrans Group Inc.)

Contrarian Capital Corp. (Alta. Sept. 11, 1998)
Aug. 24, 1999 – Name changed to Octane Energy Services Ltd. following Qualifying Transaction acquisition of Hughes Oilfield Holdings Ltd. ■

Control Advancements Inc. (Ont. May 17, 1922)
Aug. 8, 2000 – Name changed to Betacom Corporation. ■

Control Data Corporation (Minn. 1957)
1968 – Continued into Delaware.
June 3, 1992 – Name changed to Ceridian Corporation.

Control Energy Corp. (B.C. 1980)
Mar. 26, 1993 – Dissolved and struck off register.

Control of Remote Embedded Technologies Inc. (Alta. Mar. 11, 1997)
Jan. 15, 1998 – Name changed to CORE Technologies Inc. ■

Control Science Corporation (Can. Oct. 21, 1987)
Aug. 12, 1996 – Name changed to Steppe Gold Resources Ltd. and continued into Yukon. ■

Controlled Environment Farming International Ltd. (B.C. 1965)
Oct. 9, 1987 – Name changed to International Controlled Investments Inc. ■

Controlled Foods International Ltd. (Del. 1969)
Sept. 1983 – All com. shs. acquired by Keg Restaurants Ltd., on the basis of either 1.125 cl. A non-voting shs. of Keg or $2.50 plus 0.666 cl. A sh. for each com. sh. of Controlled Foods. Cash was paid in lieu of fractional shs. in an amount equal to $4.50 multiplied by the fractional interest held. (see Keg Restaurants Ltd.)

Contwoyto Goldfields Limited (Alta. Sept. 13, 1983)
May 13, 1996 – Formed Corridor Resources Inc. in Alberta on amalgamation with Corridor Resources Inc.; basis 1 new for 5 old shs. ■

Conuco Limited (Ont. 1943)
1978 – Continued into Alberta.
1979 – Merged with 3 private cos., Caballero Explorations Ltd., Canada 91639 Ltd. and Exalta Petroleums Ltd., into Conuco Resources Limited (Alta. incorp); basis 1 new spec. sh. for 3 com. or pref. shs. of Conuco Ltd. Conuco Resources then merged into Brinco Limited; basis 1 com., 1 ser. A pref. and 1 ser. B pref. sh. of Brinco for 1 Conuco Resources spec. sh.

Convalo Health International, Corp. (B.C. June 7, 2013)
June 13, 2017 – Name changed to BLVD Centers Corporation. ■

Converge Technology Solutions Corp. (B.C. Jan. 4, 2018)
Dec. 15, 2020 – Continued into Canada.
Apr. 24, 2025 – Acquired by 16728421 Canada Inc. an affiliate of H.I.G. Capital, LLC and then merged with Mainline Information Systems, LLC, an existing H.I.G. portfolio company, to form Pellera Technologies; basis $6.00 in cash.
Apr. 28, 2025 – Continued into British Columbia.

Conversant Intellectual Property Management, Inc. (Can. Apr. 8, 2005)
Apr. 1, 2021 – Name changed to MOSAID Technologies Incorporated.

Convertible & Yield Advantage Trust (Ont. Sept. 24, 2003)
Oct. 31, 2013 – Redeemed. Net asset value $23.4459 per unit.

Convertible Debentures Income Fund (Ont. Dec. 29, 2010)
Apr. 20, 2016 – Merged into Canoe Canadian Asset Allocation Class, an unlisted open-end mutual fund; basis 0.746276976 Canoe series Z shs. for 1 Convertible Debentures trust unit. Net asset value per series Z sh. at Apr. 22, 2016, was $10.

Conveying Equipment Ltd. (Ont. 1937)
1958 – Charter surrendered.

Convoy Capital Corp. (Can. Jan. 8, 1952)
Sept. 24, 1992 – Name changed to Hariston Corporation; basis 1 new for 5 old shs. ■

Convoy Red Lake Mines Ltd. (Ont. 1945)
Aug. 29, 1960 – Charter cancelled.

Conway Gold Mines Ltd. (Que. 1944)
Apr. 28, 1961 – Properties taken over by Belleterre Quebec Mines as payment for debts. Charter surrendered.

Conway Resources Inc. (Que. June 10, 2005)
Oct. 25, 2013 – Filed for bankruptcy. Lemieux Nolet inc. appointed trustee.
Oct. 25, 2016 – Voluntarily dissolved.

Conwest Exploration Company Limited (Ont. 1938)
Aug. 20, 1982 – Amalgamated with Central Patricia Limited (1.1 new cl. B for 1 com.), International Mogul Mines Ltd. (2 new cl. B shs. for 1 com.), Chimo Gold Mines Limited (either $2.20 or 0.3 new cl. B sh. for 1 com. and 1 new ser. A pref. for 1 old 6% pref.) and 465128 Ontario Limited (0.88 new cl. A sh. for 1 com.) to continue as Conwest Exploration Company Limited; basis 1 cl. A sh. and cl. B sh. for 1 cl. A sh. and cl. B sh.
June 1, 1990 – Amalgamated with Mineral Resources International Limited (1 cl. B for each 2.35 old com. shs.) to continue as Conwest Exploration Company Limited; basis 1 cl. A sh. for 1 cl. A sh.; 1 new cl. B sh. for 1 cl. B sh. and 1 new 1st pref. sh. ser. 1 for 1 old 1st pref. sh. ser. D.
Aug. 23, 1991 – Continued into Alberta.
Feb. 5, 1996 – Acquired by Alberta Energy Company Limited; basis either $28 or 1.25 Alberta Energy shs. for 1 Conwest sh.

Cook Lake Gold Mines Ltd. (Ont. 1936)
Oct. 31, 1960 – Charter cancelled.

Cooksville Company, Limited (Can. 1918)
1953 – All o/s cl. A and B shs. acquired by Domtar Limited at $20 per cl. A and $15 per cl. B sh.

CoolBrands International Inc. (N.S. Mar. 18, 1998)
Mar. 27, 2006 – Continued into Canada.
Nov. 1, 2010 – Name changed to Swisher Hygiene Inc. and continued into Delaware pursuant to reverse takeover acquisition of Swisher International, Inc.

La Coop fédérée (Que. Dec. 29, 1922)
Feb. 27, 2020 – Name changed to Sollio Cooperative Group.

Cooper Canada Limited (Ont. 1945)
June 24, 1987 – All o/s com. shs. acquired by Charan Industries Inc. for $6.00 per sh. (see Charan Industries Inc.)

Cooper Lake Gold Mines Ltd. (Ont. 1945)
Apr. 1, 1963 – Dissolved.

Cooper Minerals Inc. (B.C. May 19, 1999)
May 28, 2012 – Name changed to United Coal Holdings Limited. ■

Cooper-Nanton Oil Co., Ltd. (Can. 1926)
1929 – Name changed to New Cooper-Nanton Oils, Ltd.; basis 1 East Crest Oil Co. Ltd. and 4 New Cooper for 4 old shs.

Cooper of Canada Limited (Ont. 1945)
June 1, 1977 – Name changed to Cooper Canada Limited. ■

Coopérative Agricole de Granby (Que. Aug. 29, 1938)
1979 – Name changed to Agropur, coopérative agro-alimentaire. ■

Cooperative Energy Development Corporation (Can. July 9, 1982)
May 30, 1991 – Name changed to Co-enerco Resources Ltd. ■

Coopérative fédérée de Québec (Que. Dec. 29, 1922)
Feb. 15, 1996 – All o/s first ranking ser. 1 pref. shs. redeemed; basis $25.75 per sh.
June 1, 2006 – Name changed to La Coop fédérée. ■

Coopers Park Corporation (Can. Dec. 9, 2004)
May 26, 2015 – Privatized; basis $1.62071 cash per com. sh.
Apr. 7, 2016 – Continued into British Columbia.

Cop-Ex Mining Corp. Ltd. (Can. 1946)
Aug. 25, 1981 – Name changed to Amalgamated Cop-Ex Resources Ltd.

Cop-Gold Explorers Ltd. (unknown)
Feb. 1973 – Charter cancelled.

Cop-Mac Mines Ltd. (B.C. 1967)
July 1973 – Name changed to Cametin Industries Ltd.; basis 1 new for 4 old shs. ■

Copa Mining Corporation Ltd. (Ont. 1949)
June 1961 – Name changed to Copa Petroleum.

Copconda Mines Limited (Ont. 1963)
July 23, 1979 – Name changed to Copconda Resources Inc. ■

Copconda Resources Inc. (Ont. 1963)
Oct. 1980 – Acquired by Copconda-York Resources Inc.; basis 2 Copconda-York shs. for 1 Copconda Resources sh.

Copconda York Resources Inc. (Can. 1980)
July 15, 1987 – Name changed to Pacvest Capital Inc. ■

Cope Lake Mines Ltd. (Ont. 1967)
Mar. 13, 1979 – Charter cancelled.

Copeland Flour Mills, Ltd. (Ont. 1920)
Apr. 1952 – All com. shs. acquired by Pillsbury Mills of U.S.
July 1, 1962 – All o/s pref. shs. redeemed at $45.88 per sh.

Copeland Process Limited (N.B. 1961)
1976 – Name changed to Copeland Systems Limited. ■

Copeland Resources Ltd. (B.C. June 15, 1987)
Oct. 23, 1991 – Name changed to Copeland Technologies Inc. ■

Copeland Systems Limited (N.B. 1961)
Jan. 1978 – Name changed to MSZ Resources Ltd. following acquisition by HCI Holdings Ltd. of 97% of the o/s shs., assets and operations of both cos. were consol. ■

Copeland Technologies Inc. (B.C. June 15, 1987)
Sept. 16, 1994 – Name changed to Golden Chief Resources Inc. ■

Copernic Business Solutions Inc. (Can. Aug. 26, 2004)
Oct. 13, 2004 – Name changed to Coveo Solutions Inc. (see FPsurvey - Industrials)

Copernic Inc. (Ont. July 5, 1985)
Nov. 16, 2010 – Acquired by N. Harris Computer Corporation, a wholly owned subsid. of Constellation Software Inc. pursuant to plan of arrangement whereby certain assets of Copernic and sale proceeds were transferred to newly incorporated Comamtech Inc.; basis 1 Comamtech sh. for 1 Copernic sh.

Copernican British Banks Fund (Ont. June 25, 2007)
Nov. 18, 2013 – Converted from a closed end to an open-ended fund.

Copernican International Financial Split Corp. (Ont. Jan. 24, 2007)
Nov. 29, 2013 – Terminated; all pfd. shs. redeemed for $6.375767 per pfd. sh. and no distribution for cl. A shs.

Copernican International Premium Dividend Fund (Ont. Apr. 27, 2007)
May 2, 2014 – Converted from closed-end to open-ended fund.

Copernican World Banks Income and Growth Trust (Ont. Feb. 27, 2006)
Dec. 13, 2010 – Merged into Global Banks Premium Income Trust; basis 0.879911 Global Banks Premium units for 1 Copernican World Banks unit. (see Global Banks Premium Income Trust)

Copernican World Banks Split Inc. (Ont. Sept. 26, 2006)
Nov. 29, 2013 – Terminated; all pfd. shs. redeemed for $4.698617 per pfd. sh. and no distribution for cl. A shs.

Copernican World Financial Infrastructure Trust (Ont. July 26, 2006)
Mar. 5, 2014 – Terminated; all units redeemed for $8.4192 per unit.

Copp Clark Limited (Ont. 1965 amalg.)
1984 – Amalgamated into Copp Clark Pitman Limited.

Copp Clark Pitman Limited (Ont. 1984 amalg.)
Dec. 1977 – Privatized.

Copp Clark Publishing Co. Ltd. (Ont. 1955)
Apr. 1965 – Amalgamated into Copp Clark Limited.

Copper Basin Mines Ltd. (B.C. 1946)
June 1974 – Charter cancelled.

Copper Belt Resources Ltd. (B.C. Mar. 3, 2005)
Aug. 11, 2008 – Name changed to CB Resources Ltd. ■

Copper Bounty Mines Ltd. (B.C. 1947)
June 7, 1983 – Name changed to Walmont Precious Metals Corp. and continued into Canada; basis 1 new for 4 old shs. ■

Copper-Can Developments Ltd. (B.C. 1963)
Dec. 20, 1968 – Name changed to SMI Processes Ltd.

Copper Canyon Resources Ltd. (Alta. Feb. 11, 2005)
May 24, 2011 – Amalgamated with NovaGold Resources Inc.; basis $0.001 plus 0.0735 NovaGold shs. for 1 Copper Canyon sh. plus 1 sh. of newly formed Omineca Mining and Metals Ltd. for 4 Copper Canyon shs.

Copper Cliff Consolidated Mining Corp. (Que. 1952)
1956 – Acquired by Copper Rand Chibougamau Mines Ltd.; basis 20 new for 40 old shs.

Copper Corporation of America (Que. 1967)
Feb. 1974 – Charter cancelled.

Copper Cowboy Resources Inc. (B.C. Apr. 26, 2007)
July 14, 2014 – Name changed to True Zone Resources Inc. ■

Copper Creek Gold Corp. (Can. Aug. 13, 1997)
Nov. 6, 2017 – Continued into British Columbia.
May 1, 2018 – Name changed to Surge Exploration Inc.; basis 2 new for 1 old sh. ■

Copper Creek Ventures Ltd. (B.C. June 19, 1987)
Aug. 13, 1997 – Continued into Canada.
July 26, 2010 – Name changed to Copper Creek Gold Corp. ■

Copper Dome Minerals Ltd. (Alta. 1969)
Feb. 8, 1972 – Name changed to Bonanza International Petroleums Limited. ■

Copper Dome Mines Ltd. (Alta. Apr. 22, 1994)
Nov. 2, 1998 – Continued into British Columbia.
Nov. 6, 1998 – Name changed to Dome Ventures Inc.; basis 1 new for 2 old shs. ■

Copper Fox Metals Inc. (Alta. Feb. 27, 2004)
July 15, 2010 – Continued into British Columbia. (see FPsurvey - Mines & Energy)

Copper Giant Mining Corp. Ltd. (B.C. 1966)
Nov. 1, 1981 – Amalgamated with Les Mines d'Or Thompson-Bousquet Ltée (5 for 4) and Silverstack Mines Ltd. (1 for 1) to form Long Lac Minerals Limited; basis 1 new for 4.5 old shs.

Copper Hill Corporation (Ont. May 13, 1936)
Feb. 13, 2004 – Name changed to Viking Gold Exploration Inc.; basis 1 new for 4 old shs. ■

Copper-Hill Mining Co. Ltd. (Ont. 1945)
Oct. 1956 – Charter cancelled.

Copper Horn Mining Ltd. (B.C. 1966)
Mar. 28, 1974 – Name changed to Hitec Development Corporation.

Copper Island Mines Ltd. (B.C. 1946)
1950 – Name changed to Pacific Base Metal Mines Ltd. ■

Copper Island Mining Co. Ltd. (unknown)
Aug. 1957 – Acquired by Continental Consolidated Mines & Oils Corp. Ltd.; basis 1 new for 5 old shs. (see Continental Consolidated Mines & Oils Corp. Ltd.)

Copper Jim Mines Ltd. (Ont. 1955)
July 27, 1976 – Charter cancelled.

Copper Keays Mines Ltd. (B.C. 1969)
Dec. 9, 1977 – Name changed to Lincoln Resources Inc. ■

Copper King Mines Ltd. (B.C. 1957)
1977 – Assets acquired by Proto Explorations & Holdings Inc.; basis 1 new for 7 old shs.

Copper Lake Explorations Ltd. (B.C. 1963)
Jan. 19, 1996 – Dissolved and struck off register.

Copper Lake Mines Ltd. (Ont. 1967)
Mar. 1979 – Charter cancelled.

Copper Lake Resources Ltd. (B.C. Oct. 17, 1984)
Jan. 20, 2022 – Continued into Ontario. (see FPsurvey - Mines & Energy)

Copper Leaf Mines Ltd. (B.C. 1956)
July 8, 1976 – Charter cancelled.

Copper-Lode Mines Ltd. (Ont. 1964)
June 6, 1977 – Name changed to Consolidated Copper-Lode Developments Inc.; basis 1 new for 10 old shs. ■

Copper-Man Mines Ltd. (Ont. Apr. 1920)
July 1974 – Net assets sold to Hartland Mines Ltd.; basis 1 sh. Hartland for each 3 shs. Copper-Man.

Copper Mesa Mining Corporation (B.C. May 5, 2004)
Feb. 17, 2025 – Struck from registry and dissolved for failure to file.

Copper Mountain Consolidated Limited (B.C. 1959)
Sept. 17, 1973 – Formed Rocky Mountain Trench Mines Ltd. in British Columbia on amalgamation with Rocky Mountain Trench Mines Ltd.; basis 1 new for 1 old sh. ■

Copper Mountain Mines Ltd. (B.C. 1959)
1962 – Name changed to Copper Mountain Consolidated Limited; basis 1 new for 5 old shs. ■

Copper Mountain Mines Ltd. (B.C. Aug. 27, 1997)
Mar. 31, 2000 – Amalgamated with International Skyline Gold Corporation to form new co. with same name Copper Mountain Mines Ltd.; basis 1 new for 8 International Skyline shs. and 4,247 new for 1 Copper Mountain sh.
July 26, 2000 – Name changed to China Ventures Inc. following acquisition of CEN China Education Network Ltd. ■

Copper Mountain Mining Corporation (B.C. Apr. 20, 2006)
June 22, 2023 – Acquired by Hudbay Minerals Inc.; basis 0.381 Hudbay shs. for 1 Copper Mountain sh.

Copper North Mining Corp. (B.C. Aug. 3, 2011)
Dec. 1, 2020 – All o/s com. shs. not already held acquired by Granite Creek Copper Ltd.; basis 1 Granite Creek sh. for 2.5 Copper North shs. (see Granite Creek Copper Ltd.)

Copper One Inc. (Can. Oct. 9, 2009)
Sept. 30, 2019 – Name changed to QuestCap Inc. ■

Copper Pass Mines Ltd. (Alta. 1966)
July 1, 1985 – Struck off register.

Copper Plate Mines Ltd. (B.C. 1969)
Mar. 1973 – Merged with Armada Explorations Ltd. and Solar Reef Petroleums Ltd. into Armada Explorations Ltd.; basis 1 new for 7.7 old shs.

Copper Prince Mines Ltd. (Ont. Feb. 5, 1951)
1981 – Name changed to Copper Prince Resources Inc. ■

Copper Prince Resources Inc. (Ont. Feb. 5, 1951)
Sept. 13, 1983 – Continued into British Columbia.
July 3, 1986 – Name changed to Churchill Growth Industrial AA Communications Inc. and continued into Ontario. ■

Copper Queen Explorations Ltd. (B.C. 1966)
May 1976 – Charter cancelled.

Copper Rand Chibougamau Mines Ltd. (Que. 1956)
1962 – Name changed to The Patino Mining Corporation and continued into Ontario; basis 1 new for 6.5 old shs. ■

Copper Reef Mines Ltd. (Ont. 1962 amalg.)
1967 – Charter cancelled.

Copper Reef Mines (1973) Ltd. (Man. Mar. 27, 1973)
Jan. 18, 2005 – Name changed to Copper Reef Mining Corporation. ■

Copper Reef Mining Corporation (Man. Mar. 27, 1973)
Aug. 19, 2020 – Name changed to Voyageur Mineral Explorers Corp. (see FPsurvey - Mines & Energy)

Copper Ridge Exploration Inc. (B.C. May 26, 2021)
Jan. 16, 2023 – Name changed to Norris Lithium Inc. ■

Copper Ridge Explorations Inc. (B.C. Aug. 19, 1983)
May 31, 2011 – Name changed to Redtail Metals Corp. ■

Copper Ridge Mines Ltd. (B.C. Feb. 27, 1951)
Feb. 27, 1982 – Name changed to Northern Copper Ridge Mines Ltd. ■

Copper Ridge Silver Zinc Mines Limited (B.C. Feb. 27, 1951)
May 2, 1962 – Name changed to Copper Ridge Mines Ltd.; basis 1 new for 4 old shs. ■

Copper Soo Mining Co. Ltd. (B.C. Feb. 20, 1961)
July 7, 1969 – Name changed to Beaumont Resources Ltd.; basis 1 new for 5 old shs. ■

Copper Stack Resources Ltd. (B.C. 1983)
May 29, 1990 – Name changed to Katlor Explorations Ltd.; basis 1 new for 4 old shs. ■

Copper States Resources Inc. (Alta. Mar. 27, 1987)
Aug. 26, 1996 – Name changed to American Coppermine Resources Limited; basis 1 new for 4 old shs. ■

Copper Town Mines Ltd. (B.C.)
June 1974 – Charter cancelled.

Copper Uranium Ltd. (Que. 1950)
May 1974 – Charter cancelled.

Copper Valley Mines Ltd. (Que. 1956)
Sept. 28, 1985 – Charter cancelled.

Copperbank Resources Corp. (B.C. Oct. 21, 2014 amalg.)
Apr. 19, 2022 – Name changed to Faraday Copper Corp. (see FPsurvey - Mines & Energy)

Coppercorp Ltd. (Ont. Aug. 30, 1951)
Mar. 14, 1989 – Struck from registry and dissolved.

Coppercrest Mines Ltd. (Ont. 1952)
1957 – Name changed to Peerless Canadian Explorations Ltd. ■

Copperfields Mining Corporation (Ont. 1954)
Aug. 29, 1983 – Amalgamated with Teck Corporation; basis 5 Teck cl. B com. shs. for 4 Copperfields shs. (see Teck Corporation)

Copperknife Mines Ltd. (B.C. 1966)
July 1973 – Charter cancelled.

Copperleaf Technologies Inc. (B.C.)
Feb. 18, 2004 – Continued into Canada.
Sept. 3, 2024 – Acquired by Industrial and Financial Systems, IFS AB; basis $12 cash per sh.
Jan. 1, 2025 – Continued into Ontario.

Copperquest Inc. (Ont. May 27, 1987)
June 5, 2000 – Name changed to Gastar Exploration Ltd. and continued into Alberta pursuant to reverse takeover acquisition of 1075191 Ontario Ltd.; basis 1 new for 6 old shs. ■

Copperstone Resources Corporation (B.C. May 10, 1967)
Dec. 10, 1998 – Name changed to Consolidated Copperstone Resources Corporation; basis 1 new for 4 old shs. ■

Copperstream-Frontenac Mines Ltd. (Ont. 1956)
Mar. 1976 – Charter cancelled.

Copperstream Mines Ltd. (Ont. 1956)
Feb. 1962 – Name changed to Copperstream-Frontenac Mines Ltd.; basis 1 new for 1 old sh. ■

Copperust Mines Ltd. (B.C. 1966)
Oct. 20, 1978 – Name changed to Ark Energy Ltd. ■

Copperville Mining Corp. Ltd. (Ont. 1966)
Mar. 1976 – Charter cancelled.

Copperwood Exploration Ltd. (Alta. 1986)
Nov. 14, 1990 – Amalgamated with Beacon Energy Corporation (0.5348 for 1) to form a new co. named Consolidated Beacon Resources Ltd.; basis 0.6083 new for 1 old sh. (see Consolidated Beacon Resources Ltd.)

Cor-O-Tex Industrial Minerals Ltd. (Ont. 1961)
Oct. 22, 1965 – Dissolved.

Cora Resources Ltd. (B.C. Mar. 26, 1981)
Nov. 19, 2003 – Name changed to Boss Gold Corp.; basis 1 new for 3 old shs. ■

Coral Energy Corp. (B.C. Jan. 22, 1981)
Oct. 16, 1987 – Name changed to Coral Gold Corporation. ■

Coral Gold Corporation (B.C. Jan. 22, 1981)
Sept. 14, 2004 – Name changed to Coral Gold Resources Ltd.; basis 1 new for 10 old shs. ■

Coral Gold Resources Ltd. (B.C. Jan. 22, 1981)
Nov. 23, 2020 – Acquired by Nomad Royalty Company Ltd.; basis 0.80 Nomad units (1 com. sh. & ½ wt.) plus 5¢ cash for 1 Coral Gold sh. (see Nomad Royalty Company Ltd.)

Coral Sea Petroleums Ltd. (Alta. June 28, 1994)
Sept. 3, 2008 – Name changed to Coral Sea Resources Inc.; basis 1 new for 10 old shs. ■

Coral Sea Resources Inc. (Alta. June 28, 1994)
Apr. 14, 2010 – Name changed to Sagres Energy Inc. pursuant to reverse takeover acquisition of Sagres Energy Inc. and amalgamation of Sagres with a wholly owned subsidiary. (see FPsurvey - Mines & Energy)

Coralta Resources Limited (B.C. 1973)
Jan. 1, 1987 – Struck from register.

Coranex Ltd. (unknown)
Nov. 1, 1978 – Dissolved.

Corazon Gold Corp. (B.C. June 4, 2007)
Dec. 4, 2017 – Name changed to NanoSphere Health Sciences Inc. following reverse takeover acquisition of NanoSphere Health Sciences LLC. (see FPsurvey - Industrials)

Corbal Capital Corp. (Ont. May 15, 2007)
Dec. 2, 2009 – Name changed to iSign Media Solutions Inc. pursuant to Qualifying Transaction reverse takeover acquisition of iSign Media Corporation. (see FPsurvey - Industrials)

Corbold Creek Development Inc. (Ont. 1974)
Nov. 5, 1976 – Amalgamated with 6 other cos. to form Wolverine Developments, Inc.; basis 1 new for 13 old shs.

Corby Distilleries Limited (Can. Sept. 30, 1924; via letters patent)
Nov. 7, 2013 – Name changed to Corby Spirit and Wine Limited. (see FPsurvey - Industrials)

Cord Developments Ltd. (B.C. 1972)
May 27, 1974 – Name changed to Beach Gold Mines Ltd. ■

Cord International Minerals Ltd. (Alta. 1971)
May 29, 1981 – Struck off register.

Cordal Resources Ltd. (B.C. Mar. 20, 1981 amalg.)
Nov. 4, 1999 – Name changed to Skyharbour Developments Ltd.; basis 1 new for 4 old shs. ■

Cordasun Petroleums Ltd. (Ont. Dec. 16, 1948)
1950 – Name changed to Consolidated Cordasun Oils Ltd. ■

Cordero Energy Inc. (Alta. Mar. 30, 2005)
Sept. 11, 2008 – Acquired by Ember Resources Inc.; basis 2.683 Ember com. shs. or $5.50 for 1 Cordero com. sh.

Cordex Venture Corporation (B.C. Mar. 9, 1987)
Jan. 7, 2000 – Formed Brauch Database Systems, Inc. in Ontario pursuant to reverse takeover acquisition of and amalgamation with Brauch Database Systems, Inc. ■

Cordiale Resources Inc. (B.C. Nov. 17, 1986)
June 22, 1989 – Name changed to Vioclone Biologicals Inc. ■

Cordoba Developments Ltd. (B.C. 1966)
Jan. 1977 – Name changed to Gold Cup Resources Ltd.; basis 1 new for 2 old shs. ■

Cordoba Mines Ltd. (Man. 1957)
1970 – Charter cancelled.

Cordon Cobalt Mines Ltd. (Ont. 1951)
Oct. 1959 – Charter cancelled.

Cordova Industries Ltd. (Alta. Sept. 22, 1999)
Sept. 26, 2003 – Continued into Canada.
Nov. 24, 2003 – Name changed to Ameriplas Holdings Ltd. following Qualifying Transaction reverse takeover acquisition of Ameriplas International Inc. ■

Cordwell International Developments Ltd. (Ont. July 21, 1950)
Nov. 28, 1973 – Dissolved.

Cordy Oilfield Services Inc. (Alta. Apr. 30, 1998)
Apr. 29, 2022 – Acquired by Vertex Resource Group Ltd. and subsequently amalg. with wholly owned Vertex Energy Services Ltd.; basis 0.081818 Vertex Resource shs. for 1 Cordy Oilfield sh.

Core Assets Corp. (B.C. Apr. 20, 2016)
June 4, 2025 – Name changed to Core Silver Corp.; basis 1 new for 10 old shs. (see FPsurvey - Mines & Energy)

Core Canadian Dividend Trust (Ont. Oct. 27, 2006)
July 6, 2021 – Merged into Mulvihill Premium Yield Field; basis 0.474274 Mulvihill cl. A units for 1 Core Canadian trust unit.

Core Energy Corp. (B.C. 1980)
July 22, 1988 – Name changed to Core Ventures Ltd. ■

Core Explorations Ltd. (Alta. July 4, 1972)
May 20, 1993 – Name changed to Kelsey's International Inc.; basis 1 new for 5 old shs. ■

Core Gold Inc. (B.C. Sept. 27, 2017)
May 20, 2020 – Privatized via a 1-for-75,000,000 consolidation. Minority shldrs. received 3.1 Titan Minerals Limited ordinary shs. for 1 Core Gold com. sh.

Core IncomePlus Fund (Ont. June 29, 2005)
Oct. 1, 2007 – Merged into YIELDPLUS Income Fund; basis 0.75597249 YIELDPLUS trust unit for 1 Core trust unit. (see YIELDPLUS Income Fund)

Core Management Ltd. (unknown)
Mar. 1973 – Amalgamated into Blackline Resource Corporation Ltd. under name of Blackline.

Core Ventures Ltd. (B.C. 1980)
Dec. 9, 1991 – Name changed to Encore Ventures Ltd.; basis 1 new for 5 old shs. ■

Corean Mines Ltd. (Alta. 1964)
Name changed to Buchanan Mines Ltd. ■

Coreco Inc. (Can. Mar. 29, 1979)
May 2, 2005 – Plan of Arrangement acquisition by DALSA Corporation; basis either $10, or 0.5207 new DALSA com. sh., or a combination thereof for 1 old Coreco sh. (see DALSA Corporation)

Corel Corporation (Can. May 29, 1985)
Sept. 2, 2003 – Acquired by U.S.-based Vector CC Acquisition Inc. for US$1.05 per sh.

Corel Corporation (Can. May 29, 1985)
Sept. 2, 2003 – Continued into Ontario.
Jan. 27, 2006 – Continued into Canada.
Jan. 29, 2010 – Acquired by Corel Holdings, L.P., an indirect controlled entity of Vector Capital Corporation for US$4.00 per sh.
Feb. 17, 2016 – Continued into British Columbia.

Corel Systems Corporation (Can. May 29, 1985)
July 20, 1992 – Name changed to Corel Corporation. ■

Coreland Capital Inc. (B.C. Apr. 3, 2008)
Mar. 17, 2011 – Name changed to Rathdowney Resources Ltd. pursuant to Qualifying Transaction reverse takeover acquisition of Rathdowney Resources Limited; basis 1 new for 5 old shs. (see FPsurvey - Mines & Energy)

Core.Mark International Inc. (B.C. Mar. 18, 1983)
June 14, 1984 – Continued into Canada.
Aug. 29, 1989 – Acquired by CMI Acquisition Corp. for $7.00 per com. sh. and $25.36125 per pref. sh.

Coretec Inc. (Ont. Feb. 25, 1980)
Dec. 31, 2009 – Acquired by DDi Corp. for 38¢ per sh.

Coretec Multimedia Inc. (Alta. Mar. 8, 1995)
Dec. 5, 1995 – Name changed to Totally Hip Software Inc. ■

Coretek Vencap Inc. (Can. Oct. 15, 1986)
Dec. 4, 1996 – Name changed to Ungava Minerals Corp.; basis 1 new for 10 old shs. ■

Corex Gold Corporation (B.C. Mar. 2, 1981)
Apr. 18, 2018 – Acquired by Minera Alamos Inc.; basis 0.95 Minera Alamos com. shs. for 1 Corex Gold. sh.

Corgemines Ltd. (Que. 1963)
Mar. 1975 – Charter cancelled.

Corinth Resources Ltd. (B.C. 1982)
Oct. 1, 1984 – Name changed to BMP Technologies Ltd. ■

Corinthian Resources Ltd. (B.C. Sept. 19, 1977)
Feb. 4, 1986 – Name changed to Pacific Basin Development Corporation. ■

Cork Exploration Inc. (Alta. Feb. 14, 2005)
Nov. 22, 2007 – Formed Profound Energy Inc. in Alberta following reverse takeover acquisition of and amalgamation with Profound Energy Ltd.; basis 1 new for 4 old shs. ■

Cork-Province Mines Ltd. (B.C. 1927)
1949 – Liquidated.

Corker Resources Inc. (Alta. Nov. 1, 1996)
July 15, 1999 – Name changed to TriQuest Energy Corp. ■

Corlac Oilfield Leasing Ltd. (Alta. Mar. 19, 1996)
Mar. 31, 2000 – Name changed to Enhanced Energy Services Ltd. ■

Cornat Industries Limited (B.C. Aug. 5, 1969)
July 1, 1978 – Formed Versatile Cornat Corporation in British Columbia on amalgamation with Versatile Manufacturing Ltd.; basis 1 new ser. A cum. redeem. pref. sh. for 1 Versatile Manufacturing sh. and 1 new for 1 Cornat sh. ■

Cornat Industries Limited (B.C. 1969)
July 1, 1978 – Amalgamated with Versatile Manufacturing Ltd. to form a new company named Versatile Cornat Corporation; basis 1 new Versatile Cornat sh. for 1 old Cornat sh. (see Versatile Cornat Corporation)

Corner Bay Minerals Inc. (Ont. Apr. 22, 1991 amalg.)
Mar. 1, 2001 – Name changed to Corner Bay Silver Inc. ■

Corner Bay Silver Inc. (Ont. Apr. 22, 1991 amalg.)
Feb. 25, 2003 – Acquired by Pan American Silver Corp.; basis 0.3846 Pan American shs. plus 0.1923 wts. for 1 Corner Bay sh.

Corner Properties Inc. (Ont. 1972)
Jan. 4, 1973 – Name changed to Equicorp Industries Limited. ■

Cornerstone Capital Resources Inc. (Alta. July 21, 1999)
Mar. 1, 2023 – All o/s shs. not already held acquired by SolGold plc; basis 15 SolGold ordinary shs. for 1 Cornerstone com. sh. (see SolGold plc)
2023 – Name changed to SolGold Canada Inc. (see SolGold plc)

Cornerstone Industrial Minerals Corporation (Ont. Aug. 7, 1986)
Mar. 19, 1999 – Acquired by 9071-6218 Quebec Inc., a wholly owned subsid. of Seven Peaks Mining, Inc., for 12¢ per sh.

Cornerstone Industries International Inc. (B.C. Feb. 18, 2004)
Aug. 25, 2008 – Dissolved and struck from register.

Cornerstone Innovations Inc. (Alta. July 12, 1996)
June 2, 1999 – Continued into Canada.
June 11, 1999 – Name changed to EXI Technologies Inc. ■

Cornerstone Metals Inc. (B.C. June 23, 2006)
Sept. 25, 2018 – Name changed to First Vanadium Corp. ■

Corniche Capital Inc. (Alta. Dec. 4, 1995)
Aug. 28, 2001 – Name changed to Printlux.com Inc.; basis 1 new for 2 old shs. ■

Corniche Industries Corp. (Can. July 17, 1987)
Nov. 2, 1995 – Dissolved.

Corniche Mineral & Processing Inc. (Can. July 17, 1987)
Nov. 10, 1989 – Name changed to Corniche Industries Corp. ■

Corniche Resources Ltd. (B.C. June 1, 1983)
Apr. 18, 1988 – Name changed to International Avalon Aircraft Inc.; basis 1 new for 10 old shs. ■

Corning Resources Ltd. (B.C. July 31, 1987)
Mar. 1, 1996 – Dissolved and struck off register.

Cornucopia Explorations Ltd. (B.C. May 25, 1960)
June 29, 1961 – Name changed to Hanna Gold Mines Ltd. ■

Cornucopia Gold Mines Ltd. (Utah 1977)
Aug. 19, 1987 – Name changed to Valley View Gold Mines Ltd. ■

Cornucopia Resources Ltd. (B.C. Nov. 14, 1985 amalg.)
July 9, 1999 – Name changed to Stockscape.com Technologies Inc. pursuant to reverse takeover acquisition of Stockscape.com Technologies (Canada) Ltd.; basis 1 new for 10 old shs. ■

Cornwall Petroleum & Resources Ltd. (B.C. Nov. 10, 1978)
Aug. 23, 1984 – Name changed to Rexplore Resources International Limited. ■

Coro Mining Corp. (B.C. Sept. 22, 2004)
May 27, 2020 – Name changed to Marimaca Copper Corp.; basis 1 new for 25 old shs. (see FPsurvey - Mines & Energy)

Corolla Resources Ltd. (B.C. Nov. 10, 1981)
Apr. 15, 1994 – Dissolved and struck off register.

Coromandel Resources Ltd. (B.C. Nov. 8, 1984)
May 5, 2000 – Name changed to International Coromandel Resources Ltd.; basis 1 new for 5 old shs. ■

Corona Corporation (Ont. July 1, 1988 amalg.)
June 12, 1991 – Name changed to International Corona Corporation; basis 1 new for 2 old shs. ■

Corona Gold Corporation (Ont. June 1, 1965)
June 10, 2002 – Formed Unisphere Waste Conversion Ltd. in Ontario pursuant to reverse takeover acquisition of and amalgamation with Unisphere Waste Conversion Ltd. ■

Corona Gold Corporation (Ont. May 28, 2002 amalg.)
Aug. 27, 2015 – Acquired by Oban Mining Corporation; basis 0.38355 (post consol.) Oban com. shs. for 1 Corona com. sh. (see Oban Mining Corporation)

Corona Gold Mines Ltd. (Man. 1945)
Dec. 5, 1963 – Charter cancelled.

Corona Investments Inc. (Alta. July 17, 1997)
Nov. 2, 2000 – Name changed to Payment Services Interactive Gateway Corp. ■

Corona Resources Ltd. (B.C. 1979)
June 23, 1982 – Name changed to International Corona Resources Ltd.; basis 1 new for 4 old shs. ■

Coronada Mines Ltd. (Man. 1957)
1957 – Name changed to Cordoba Mines Ltd. and continued into Manitoba. ■

Coronado Resources Inc. (B.C. Feb. 16, 1983)
Dec. 7, 1990 – Name changed to Iron King Mines Inc.; basis 1 new for 3 old shs. ■

Coronado Resources Inc. (B.C. Mar. 11, 1983)
Oct. 27, 1997 – Name changed to Habanero Resources Inc.; basis 1 new for 2 old shs. ■

Coronado Resources Ltd. (B.C. Sept. 22, 2004)
May 28, 2019 – Name changed to Interlapse Technologies Corp. ■

Coronation Allied Industries Ltd. (B.C. 1967)
Apr. 1977 – Dissolved.

Coronation Credit Corporation Limited (B.C. 1954)
Jan. 1979 – During the period of 1969-74, Cornat Industries Limited acquired 100% o/s com. and 98.2% o/s pref. shs. of the co. Basis: sh.-for-sh. to 1971; sh.-for-sh. plus pay. by shldr. of 50¢ cash to January 1974, and cash offer of $3.50 per com. and $1.55 per pref. sh. to November 1974. Coronation was sold by Cornat.

Coronation Gulf Mines Ltd. (B.C. 1967)
Sept. 1971 – Name changed to Coronation Allied Industries Ltd. ■

Coronation Minerals Inc. (Alta. Mar. 16, 1994)
Apr. 23, 2004 – Continued into Ontario.
Aug. 18, 2009 – Name changed to Guyana Precious Metals Inc. ■

Coronation Mortgage Co. Ltd. (B.C. 1954)
Jan. 1961 – Name changed to Coronation Credit Corporation Limited. ■

Coronation Resources (Canada) Inc. (Ont. Jan. 15, 1979)
Feb. 21, 1989 – Struck from register.

Coronation Royalties Limited (Alta. 1937)
1941 – Merged with 8 other cos. into Amalgamated Oils Limited; basis 95 new for 500 old shs.

Coronet Carpets Inc. (Can. 1986 amalg.)
Dec. 18, 1990 – Following reorganization and share consolidation all o/s shs. not held by Cambridge Holdings Inc. and William T. Bodenhamer were exchanged for $4.00 per sh. The company is now private.

Coronet Gold Mine Ltd. (Que. 1950)
May 1974 – Charter cancelled.

Coronet Housewares Inc. (Que. 1957)
1986 – Privatized.

Coronet Metals Inc. (B.C. Oct. 23, 1989)
June 1, 2018 – Name changed to MegumaGold Corp. (see FPsurvey - Mines & Energy)

Coronet Mines Ltd. (B.C. 1961)
1973 – Merged with Calta Mines Ltd. into Coralta Resources Ltd.; basis 1 new for 4 old shs.

Coronet Resources Ltd. (B.C. June 7, 1983)
Feb. 5, 1986 – Name changed to Thunder Engines Corporation. ■

Corpex (1977) Inc. (Que. 1957)
Mar. 30, 1979 – Liquidated by parent company, York Lambton Corporation Limited, and charter surrendered.

Corporate Catalyst Acquisition Inc. (Ont. Oct. 11, 2012)
June 8, 2018 – Name changed to Globalive Technology Inc. following Qualifying Transaction reverse takeover acquisition of Globalive Technology Partners Inc. (GTP) and concurrent amalgamation of GTP with wholly owned 2636513 Ontario Inc., which was then vertically amalgamated into the company.; basis 1 new for 6.66 old shs. ■

Corporate Foods Limited (Ont. June 9, 1911)
May 6, 1997 – Name changed to Canada Bread Company, Limited. ■

Corporate Master Ltd. (Ont. 1949)
Dec. 27, 1978 – Effective June 30, 1978 the com. shs. of the co. were converted into first pref. shs. which were subsequently redeemed.

Corporate Oil & Gas Ltd. (Man. July 5, 1976)
Dec. 9, 1987 – Name changed to Charlie O. Beverages Ltd. ■

Corporate Properties Limited (Ont. June 19, 1962)
Nov. 22, 2006 – Name changed to SeaMiles Limited. ■

Corporation d'Expansion Financière (Que. 1957)
1975 – All o/s com., pref. and special shs. acquired by York Lambton Corporation Limited; basis 4 York cl. B shs. for each Corpex com. sh., 5 York cl. A shs. plus $2.00 for each Corpex pref. sh., and 4 York cl. A shs. for each Corpex special sh. (see Corpex (1977) Inc.)
Nov. 2, 1977 – Merged with Simard-Beaudry Inc. to form Corpex (1977) Inc. (see Corpex (1977) Inc.)

Corporation Falconbridge Copper (Que. 1917)
May 26, 1987 – Name changed to Minnova Inc. ■

La Corporation Foncière de Montréal (Que. 1957)
Sept. 24, 1968 – Declared bankrupt. Trustee: Clarkson, Gordon & Co., Montreal. Trustee for secured note holders: Royal Trust Co.

Corptech Industries Inc. (B.C. Mar. 28, 1980)
July 15, 1992 – Name changed to Forefront Ventures Ltd.; basis 1 new for 4 old shs. ■

Corra Capital Corp. (B.C. May 12, 2000)
July 26, 2002 – Formed GATCO Technologies Inc. in Delaware following Qualifying Transaction reverse takeover acquisition of and amalgamation with Global American Technology Corp.

Correvio Pharma Corp. (Can. Mar. 7, 2018)
June 1, 2020 – Acquired by ADVANZ PHARMA Corp. Limited; basis US$0.42 cash per sh.

Corrida Oils Ltd. (Alta. Jan. 15, 1982)
1982 – Continued into British Columbia. (see Oakwood Petroleums Ltd.)
Nov. 21, 1985 – Acquired by Oakwood Petroleums Ltd. Shldrs. received 1 ser. D. Oakwood pref. sh. and 8 com. shs. Nucorr Petroleums Ltd. for each 60 shs. Corrida. (see Oakwood Petroleums Ltd.)

Corridor Resources Inc. (Alta. May 13, 1996 amalg.)
Mar. 4, 2020 – Name changed to Headwater Exploration Inc. (see FPsurvey - Mines & Energy)

Corrie Copper Ltd. (B.C. Mar. 30, 1971)
Mar. 14, 1984 – Name changed to Corrie Resources Ltd. ■

Corrie Resources Ltd. (B.C. Mar. 30, 1971)
Apr. 8, 1987 – Name changed to Golden Seven Industries Inc. ■

Corriente Resources Inc. (B.C. Feb. 16, 1983)
Aug. 5, 2010 – Acquired by CRCC-Tongguan Investment (Canada) Co., Ltd., a wholly owned subsid. of CRCC-Tongguan Investment Co., for $8.60 per sh.

Corrugated Paper Box Company, Limited (Can. 1928)
1954 – Hinde & Dauch Limited acquired all o/s com. stk. for $17 per sh.

Corsa Capital Ltd. (B.C. June 14, 2007)
Apr. 27, 2011 – Name changed to Corsa Coal Corp. ■

Corsa Coal Corp. (B.C. June 14, 2007)
June 27, 2011 – Continued into Canada. (see FPsurvey - Mines & Energy)

Corsair Exploration Inc. (Alta. Oct. 31, 1985 amalg.)
July 18, 2002 – Acquired by Northrock Resources Ltd. for $3.00 per sh. ■

Corsair Petroleum Inc. (Alta. Oct. 31, 1985 amalg.)
Feb. 6, 1996 – Name changed to Corsair Exploration Inc.; basis 1 new for 5 old shs. ■

Corsayre Capital Corporation (Alta. Sept. 13, 1995)
Oct. 1, 1997 – Formed CV Technologies Inc. in Alberta on Major Transaction amalgamation with CV Technologies Inc., constituting a reverse takeover by CV Technologies. ■

Corson Gold Mines Ltd. (Ont. 1937)
Nov. 1957 – Charter cancelled.

Corsurex Resource Corp. (B.C. Nov. 18, 2016)
Sept. 11, 2020 – Name changed to Gold Port Corporation; basis 1 new for 2 old shs. (see FPsurvey - Mines & Energy)

Cortex Business Solutions Inc. (Alta. Oct. 1, 1999)
Feb. 21, 2019 – Acquired by Drilling Info, Inc., a portfolio company of Genstar Capital Partners, LLC; basis $4.55 cash per sh.

Cortez Corporation (Alta. 1968)
June 2, 1986 – Name changed to Cortez International Ltd.; basis 1 new for 2 old shs. ■

Cortez Explorations Ltd. (Ont. 1946)
Sept. 27, 1957 – Name changed to Marpic Explorations Ltd. ■

Cortez Gold Corp. (B.C. Mar. 29, 2007)
Aug. 11, 2015 – Acquired by Starcore International Mines Ltd.; basis 3 Starcore shs. for 1 Cortez sh.

Cortez International Ltd. (Alta. 1968)
May 1, 1990 – Struck off register.

Cortez Resources Corp. (B.C. Mar. 29, 2007)
Sept. 18, 2009 – Name changed to Cortez Gold Corp. ■

Cortina Capital Corp. (Can. Sept. 11, 2015)
Oct. 20, 2017 – Name changed to Ecolomondo Corporation pursuant to Qualifying Transaction reverse takeover acquisition of private Saint-Laurent, Que.-based Ecolomondo Corporation Inc. on the basis of 5.5 Cortina common shares for each Ecolomondo share held. (see FPsurvey - Industrials)

Cortus Metals Inc. (B.C. June 25, 2018)
Feb. 12, 2024 – Name changed to Metalero Mining Corp.; basis 1 new for 15 old shs. (see FPsurvey - Mines & Energy)

Corum Resource Corp. (B.C. Feb. 19, 1988)
Aug. 19, 1999 – Name changed to El Nino Ventures Inc.; basis 1 new for 12 old shs. ■

Corus Entertainment Inc. (Can. Mar. 3, 1998)
Sept. 1, 1999 – Continued into Alberta. (see FPsurvey - Industrials)

Corval Resources Ltd. (N.P.L.) (B.C. Aug. 25, 1970)
May 3, 1977 – Name changed to Arizona Silver Corporation (N.P.L.); basis 1 new for 3 old shs. ■

Corvette Gold Mines Ltd. (Ont. 1927)
1976 – Amalgamated with 3 other cos. to form Berkwater Explorations Limited; basis 1.66 new for 1 old sh.

Corvette Petroleum Corporation (B.C. Nov. 14, 1967)
May 17, 1985 – Name changed to Armor Development Corporation; basis 1 new for 7 old shs. ■

Corvus Gold Inc. (B.C. Apr. 13, 2010)
Jan. 20, 2022 – All o/s shs. other than those already held acquired by AngloGold Ashanti Limited; basis Cdn$4.10 cash per sh.

Corvus Mines Ltd. (B.C. 1967)
Dec. 18, 1978 – Dissolved.

Corwin Gold Mines Ltd. (Can. 1933)
Dec. 1949 – Dissolved.

Coscan Development Corporation (Can. Mar. 30, 1953)
May 7, 1996 – Name changed to Brookfield Homes Ltd; basis 1 new for 5 old shs. ■

Coscient Group Inc. (Can. Feb. 15, 1989)
Jan. 25, 2000 – Name changed to Motion International Inc.; basis 1 new for 1 cl. A sh. ■

Coseka Resources Ltd. (B.C. 1971 amalg.)
June 15, 1972 – Amalgamated with Cariboo Gold Quartz Mining Co. Ltd. to form Coseka Resources Limited. (see Coseka Resources Limited)

Coseka Resources Limited (B.C. June 15, 1972 amalg.)
Jan. 14, 1991 – Acquired by North Canadian Oils Limited for 16¢ per sh. (see North Canadian Oils Limited)

Cosgrove-Moore Bindery Services Limited (Ont. Feb. 23, 1987)
June 2000 – Deemed bankrupt. Deloitte & Touche appointed trustee.

Cosmic Industries Ltd. (B.C. Feb. 23, 1970 amalg.)
July 22, 1988 – Dissolved and struck off register.

Cosmic-Lode Mines Ltd. (B.C. 1967)
1970 – Merged into Cosmic Nickel Mines Ltd.; basis 1 new for 10 old shs.

Cosmic Nickel Mines Ltd. (B.C. Feb. 23, 1970 amalg.)
June 5, 1972 – Name changed to New Cosmic Industries Ltd.; basis 1 new for 10 old shs. ■

Cosmo Capital Corp. (Alta. Oct. 12, 1999)
Dec. 17, 2004 – Name changed to Reco International Group Inc. (see FPsurvey - Industrials)

Cosmos Imperial Mills, Limited (Can. 1926)
Mar. 23, 1973 – Placed into bankruptcy.
July 10, 1975 – Token recovery of 13.6% paid to unsecured creditors.

Cosmos Resources Inc. (B.C. Apr. 26, 1971)
Nov. 16, 1990 – Delisted from the Vancouver Stock Exchange. Subsequently struck from register and dissolved.

Cossette Communication Group Inc. (Que. Mar. 23, 1999)
Feb. 18, 2009 – Name changed to Cossette Inc. ■

Cossette Inc. (Que. Mar. 23, 1999)
Dec. 30, 2009 – Privatized by way of amalgamation with 9209-6841 Québec Inc., a wholly owned subsid. of Mill Road Capital, Limited Partnership, for $8.10 per sh.

Cost Miser Coupons (International) Inc. (B.C. Sept. 2, 1987)
Feb. 24, 1994 – Name changed to Integrated Media Communications Inc.; basis 1 new for 5 old shs. ■

Costain Limited (Can. Mar. 30, 1953)
May 12, 1987 – Name changed to Coscan Development Corporation. ■

Costebel Mines Ltd. (unknown)
Aug. 1968 – Name changed to North Shore Uranium Corp. ■

Costigan Gold Corporation (Ont. 1962)
Mar. 27, 2006 – Certificate of incorporation cancelled and dissolved.

Cosworth Minerals Ltd. (Yuk. Mar. 30, 1998)
Feb. 13, 2002 – Name changed to Palcan Fuel Cells Ltd. pursuant to reverse takeover acquisition of Palcan Fuel Cells Ltd. ■

Cosworth Ventures Ltd. (B.C. June 9, 1987)
Mar. 30, 1998 – Name changed to Cosworth Minerals Ltd. and continued into Yukon. ■

Cotinga Pharmaceuticals Inc. (Ont. Oct. 13, 2006 amalg.)
Nov. 2, 2023 – Charter cancelled and removed from registry.

Cotley Mines Ltd. (Can. 1953)
July 1976 – Charter cancelled.

Cott Beverages Ltd. (Can. July 25, 1955)
July 3, 1991 – Name changed to Cott Corporation. ■

Cott Corporation (Can. July 25, 1955)
Mar. 2, 2020 – Name changed to Primo Water Corporation pursuant to acquisition of (old) Primo Water Corporation. ■

Cotton Valley Resources Corporation (Ont. June 14, 1996 amalg.)
Feb. 9, 1998 – Continued into Yukon.
May 12, 2000 – Name changed to Aspen Group Resources Corporation. (see FPsurvey - Mines & Energy)

Cotton Valley Resources Inc. (Ont. May 10, 1961)
Nov. 17, 1982 – Continued into British Columbia.
Dec. 17, 1984 – Name changed to Conscot Resources Ltd.; basis 1 new for 2 old shs. ■

Cottonballs Corporation (Alta. Oct. 9, 1987)
Feb. 7, 1992 – Name changed to Consolidated Cottonballs Corporation; basis 1 new for 7 old shs. ■

Cottonwood Placer Ltd. (B.C. 1960)
July 15, 1974 – Struck off register.

Cotwood Tertiary Mines Ltd. (Ont. 1941)
Dec. 1963 – Charter cancelled.

Coubran Resources Ltd. (Ont. Jan. 28, 2000)
Mar. 5, 2004 – Name changed to Sanu Resources Ltd. and continued into Canada. ■

Cougar Development Corporation Ltd. (Sask. 1955)
May 11, 1978 – Amalgamated with subsid. to form American Chromium Limited.

Cougar Minerals Corp. (Can. Apr. 21, 2004)
Jan. 11, 2016 – Continued into British Columbia.
May 25, 2016 – Name changed to TrackX Holdings Inc. following reverse takeover acquisition of TrackX, Inc.; basis 1 new for 2 old shs. (see FPsurvey - Industrials)

Couldrey Creek Oils Ltd. (B.C.)
Dec. 1939 – Name changed to Pinhorn Oils, Ltd.

Coulee Lead and Zinc Mines Ltd. (Ont. 1946)
Mar. 3, 1977 – Amalgamated with Headway Red Lake Gold Mines Ltd. (1 for 20) to form Wayfair Explorations Ltd.; basis 1 new for 10 old shs.

Coulee Ridge Capital Corp. (Alta. May 15, 1996)
Nov. 4, 1997 – Name changed to Del Roca Energy Inc. following reverse takeover acquisition of Del Roca Resources Ltd. ■

Coulson Consolidated Gold Mines, Ltd. (Ont. 1928)
1951 – Charter cancelled.

Counsel Corporation (Ont. Aug. 2, 1979)
Dec. 31, 1988 – Amalgamated in Ontario to continue with same name.
June 23, 2015 – Name changed to Street Capital Group Inc. ■

Counsel RB Capital Inc. (Fla. Apr. 21, 1983)
Aug. 22, 2013 – Name changed to Heritage Global Inc.

Counsel Real Estate Investment Trust (Ont. July 10, 1981)
July 21, 1995 – Name changed to RioCan Real Estate Investment Trust. (see FPsurvey - Industrials)

CounterPath Corporation (Nev. Apr. 18, 2003)
Mar. 3, 2021 – Acquired by Alianza, Inc.; basis US$3.49 cash per sh.

Countryside Power Income Fund (Ont. Feb. 16, 2004)
Aug. 17, 2007 – Acquired by Fort Chicago Energy Partners L.P.; basis $9.60 per trust unit and US$1,010 per US$1,000 of 6.25% exchangeable debentures. (see Fort Chicago Energy Partners L.P.)

County Capital One Ltd. (Can. Oct. 11, 2017)
May 27, 2019 – Name changed to Adcore Inc. Qualifying Transaction reverse takeover acquisition of Podium Advertising Technologies Ltd.; basis 1 new for 4.5738 old shs. (see FPsurvey - Industrials)

County Capital 2 Ltd. (B.C. Oct. 15, 2019)
Nov. 25, 2021 – Name changed to Givex Information Technology Group Limited pursuant to the Qualifying Transaction reverse takeover acquisition of Givex Corporation and concurrrent amalgamation of Givex with wholly owned County Subco Corp.; basis 1 new for 9.1871 old shs. ■

County Savings & Loan Corp. (Ont. 1964)
June 26, 1974 – Amalgamated with its subsid., Federal Trust & Savings Co., to form Federal Trust Company; basis 1 new for 1.5 old shs.

Courage Energy Inc. (Alta. Feb. 24, 1987)
June 29, 1990 – Amalgamated in Alberta to continue with same name.
Sept. 1, 1995 – Amalgamated in Alberta to continue with same name.
July 26, 2001 – Acquired by Samson Canada, Ltd., a wholly owned subsid. of Samson Investment Company, for $5.20 per sh.

Courageous Exploration Inc. (Alta. 1986)
Jan. 31, 1992 – Amalgamated with American Chromium Limited to form Rhonda Mining Corporation; basis 1 new for 10 American Chromium shs. and 1 new for 10 Courageous shs. (see Rhonda Mining Corporation)

Courageous Gold Mines Ltd. (Ont. 1944)
Apr. 20, 1963 – Dissolved.

Courier Explorations Ltd. (Ont. 1970)
Feb. 1972 – Amalgamated to form Proto Explorations & Holdings Inc.; basis 5 new for 23 old shs.

Cournor Mining Co. Ltd. (Que. Feb. 1, 1937)
1960 – Name changed to Courvan Mining Co. Ltd.; basis 1 new for 2 old shs. ■

Courtesy Oils Ltd. (Alta. 1953)
Feb. 28, 1957 – Struck off register.

Courtland Capital Corp. (B.C. July 25, 2007)
Dec. 10, 2009 – Name changed to ForceLogix Technologies Inc. pursuant to Qualifying Transaction reverse takeover acquisition of ForceLogix, Inc. ■

Courtland Capital Inc. (B.C. July 25, 2007)
June 5, 2018 – Name changed to Tree of Knowledge International Corp. following reverse takeover acquisition of Tree of Knowledge Inc.; basis 1 new for 49.16 old shs. ■

Courtmont Gold Mines Ltd. (Ont. 1945)
Nov. 26, 1969 – Charter cancelled.

Courtown Gold Mines Ltd. (Que. 1946)
1966 – Wound up.

Courvan Mining Co. Ltd. (Que. Feb. 1, 1937)
July 25, 2002 – Formed Rutter Technologies Inc. following reverse takeover acquisition of Rutter Technologies Inc.; basis 1 new for 3 old shs. ■

Courville Mines Ltd. (Que. 1944)
Mar. 1974 – Charter cancelled.

Cous Creek Copper Mines Ltd. (B.C. July 2, 1974)
Feb. 2, 1989 – Delisted from the Vancouver Stock Exchange. Subsequently dissolved for failure to file.

Coutts Pipe Line Co. Ltd. (Alta. 1932)
Jan. 6, 1943 – Struck off register.

Coutu Gold Mines Ltd. (Ont. 1958)
June 1972 – Charter cancelled.

The Jean Coutu Group (PJC) Inc. (Que. June 22, 1973)
May 15, 2018 – Acquired by METRO INC.; basis (i) $24.50 cash; or (ii) 0.61006 METRO com. sh. for 1 Jean Coutu cl. A subord. vtg. sh.

Couverden Point Resources Ltd. (B.C. June 27, 1988)
June 26, 1991 – Name changed to Kilkenney Resources Ltd.; basis 1 new for 2.5 old shs. ■

Couvrette & Provost Ltée (Que. Nov. 14, 1961)
July 10, 1970 – Name changed to Provigo Inc. ■

Cove Energy Corporation (B.C. Apr. 6, 1981)
May 12, 1988 – Name changed to Cove Resources Corporation. ■

Cove Resources Corporation (B.C. Apr. 6, 1981)
Aug. 11, 1992 – Name changed to Consolidated Cove Resources Corporation; basis 1 new for 5 old shs. ■

Cove Uranium Mines Ltd. (Ont. July 25, 1951)
Apr. 1, 1982 – CTO issued. Subsequently dissolved and charter cancelled.

Covenant Resources Ltd. (B.C. 1987)
July 15, 1991 – Amalgamated with El Condor Resources Ltd. (1 for 1) to form a new co. also named El Condor Resources Ltd.; basis 1 new for 1 old sh. (see El Condor Resources Ltd.)

Covenant Resources Ltd. (B.C. Feb. 23, 2007)
Dec. 13, 2010 – Name changed to Passport Energy Ltd. ■

Coventree Inc. (Ont. Mar. 2, 1998)
Feb. 15, 2012 – Commenced voluntary liquidation and KSV Advisory Inc. (formerly Duff & Phelps Canada Restructuring Inc.) was appointed liquidator.
May 4, 2012 – Distrib. of $2.94 cash and 0.175 Xceed Mortgage Corporation made to shldrs.
Dec. 2012 – Distrib. of 58¢ cash per sh. made to shldrs.
Jan. 16, 2018 – KSV Kofman was discharged as liquidator.
June 29, 2018 – Dissolved.

Coventry Charter Corporation (Yuk. May 24, 2000)
May 21, 2003 – Name changed to Monster Copper Corporation following Qualifying Transaction reverse takeover acquisition of Monster Copper Resources Inc.; basis 1 new for 2 old shs. ■

Coventry Gold Mines Ltd. (Ont. 1944)
May 1955 – Charter cancelled.

Coventry Resources Inc. (B.C. May 29, 1984)
May 25, 2016 – Name changed to Coventry Resources Limited and continued into Australia. ■

Coventry Resources Limited (Australia May 25, 2016)
Sept. 20, 2017 – Name changed to PolarX Limited.

Coventry Ventures Inc. (B.C. Feb. 15, 1984)
July 3, 1992 – Dissolved and struck off register.

Cover Technologies Inc. (B.C. June 18, 2007)
Aug. 3, 2023 – Name changed to PlasCred Circular Innovations Inc. pursuant to reverse takeover acquisition of PlasCred Inc.; basis 1 new for 2 old shs. (see FPsurvey - Industrials)

Covesco Capital Corporation (Ont. 1982 amalg.)
Aug. 14, 1996 – Formed Magra Computer Technologies Corp. in Ontario on amalgamation with Magra Computer Products Inc., 1069996 Ontario Inc. and 1069998 Ontario Inc., constituting a reverse takeover by Magra; basis 1 new com. for 1 old com. sh., 1 new com. for 1 old cl. A special sh., 1 new 1st pref. ser. A for 1 old 1st pref. ser. A sh., and 1 new ser. A sh. purch. wt. and 1 new com sh. for 1 old convert. note exercisable for 11¢ prior to Sept. 1, 1997, at $0.125 prior to Sept. 1, 1998, and at 15¢ prior to Sept. 1 1999. ■

Covik Development Corp. (B.C. Mar. 26, 1987)
Oct. 23, 2006 – Name changed to Monarch Energy Limited. ■

Covington Industries Limited (Ont. 1984)
Sept. 16, 1992 – Formed Covington International Limited on amalgamation with its owned subsid., Covington International Limited; basis 1 new for 2 old shs. ■

Covington International Limited (Ont. 1984)
Mar. 13, 2006 – Certificate of incorporation cancelled and dissolved.

Covington Springs Explorations Inc. (Ont. 1984)
Feb. 1988 – Name changed to Covington Industries Limited. ■

Covitec Group Inc. (Que. Mar. 11, 1986)
Feb. 8, 2001 – Acquired by Technicolour Canada Acquisition Corp. for 88¢ per sh.

Cowansville Capital Inc. (Can. Apr. 20, 2004)
Nov. 14, 2005 – Name changed to Malette Industries Inc. following Qualifying Transaction reverse takeover acquisition of Malette International Inc. for 10,000,000 com. shs.; basis 1 new for 3.571 old shs. ■

Cowichan Copper Co. Ltd. (B.C. 1952)
1968 – Name changed to Cerna Copper Mines Ltd.; basis 1 new for 5 old shs. ■

Cowl Limited (Can. 1971)
1974 – Budd Automotive Co. of Canada Ltd., through James B. Carter Ltd., acquired the assets of the co. for an undisclosed amount from the Manitoba Development Corp.

Coxe Commodity Strategy Fund (Ont. Apr. 30, 2008)
Oct. 7, 2016 – Amalgamated with Global Water Solutions Fund; class A unitholders received 1.183932 Global Water Solutions fund units for each unit held and class F unitholders received 1.302514 Global Water Solutions fund units for each unit held. (see Global Water Solutions Fund)

Coxe Global Agribusiness Income Fund (Ont.)
Oct. 19, 2016 – Terminated. Trust units redeemed for $7.8533 cash per unit.

Coxheath Gold Holdings Limited (N.S. Nov. 22, 1985 amalg.)
1990 – Placed into receivership and PricewaterhouseCoopers Inc. of Halifax was appointed receiver/manager.
Mar. 1994 – PricewaterhouseCoopers entered into an agreement with Tangier Mining Inc. to sell all the assets of Coxheath.
May 5, 1995 – Agreement closed in escrow. Secured creditors agreed to keep their existing security and would be paid out of the net operating profits.
Aug. 1995 – Declared bankrupt and there were no funds available for distribution to shldrs.
June 4, 2001 – Receiver discharged.

Coyotenet Communications Group Inc. (Alta. Jan. 31, 2002 amalg.)
Sept. 1, 2006 – Name changed to Magnate Ventures Inc. and continued into British Columbia; basis 1 new for 6.5 old shs. ■

Crack Resources Ltd. (B.C. 1980)
Oct. 14, 1994 – Dissolved and struck off register.

Crackerjack Capital Corporation (Can. June 5, 1986)
June 10, 1987 – Name changed to Company's Coming Snack Bars Ltd. ■

Crackingstone Mines Limited (Ont. 1952)
Nov. 1982 – Amalgamated with Sparton Mining and Development Limited to form Sparton Resources Inc.; basis 1 new for 1.4 old shs.

Cradgene Mining Corporation Ltd. (Ont. 1946)
1956 – Charter cancelled.

Cradle Mountain Canada Ltd. (Alta. June 27, 1988)
May 6, 1997 – Name changed to Upper Canada Gaming Corporation; basis 1 new for 5 old shs. ■

Craftech Manufacturing Inc. (Can. 1987)
Mar. 25, 1994 – Amalgamated with Shortline Investments Inc., Buhler Holdings Inc., and JBC Holdings Inc. to continue as Buhler Industries Inc.; basis 0.027412 cl. A com. shs. of Buhler for each sh. of Craftech held. (see Buhler Industries Inc.)

Craibbe-Fletcher Gold Mines Ltd. (Ont. 1944)
Dec. 30, 1994 – Amalgamated with 1094949 Ontario Limited, a wholly owned subsid. of Placer Dome Canada Limited; basis 1 Placer Dome cl. A pref. sh. for 1 Craibbe-Fletcher sh. Pref. shs. were immediately redeemed for 80¢ per sh,

The Craig Bit Company Limited (Ont. 1941)
1976 – More than 94% of o/s shs. acquired at $7.00 per sh. by Kennametal Inc. Co. subsequently became a wholly owned subsid. of Kennametal.

Craig Music & Entertainment Inc. (Man. July 5, 1999)
Mar. 28, 2002 – Privatized; basis $5.00 per sub. vtg. cl. A sh.

Craigmont Mines Limited (B.C. 1946)
May 31, 1985 – Acquired by M. Seven Industries for $1.27 per sh.

Crailar Technologies Inc. (B.C. Oct. 6, 1998)
July 5, 2016 – Assigned into bankruptcy and The Bowra Group Inc. was appointed trustee.

Cramac Resources Limited (Alta. 1974)
June 6, 1978 – Name changed to Surf Oils Ltd.; basis 1 new for 3 old shs. ■

Cran-Kor Metal Mines Ltd. (unknown)
1956 – Acquired by Valray Explorations Ltd.; basis 1 new for 3 old shs. (see Valray Explorations Ltd.)

Cranbourne Minerals Exploration & Development Co. Ltd. (Que. 1952)
July 22, 1966 – Name changed to Maclan Exploration Limited. ■

Crane Aviation Limited (Can. 1960)
June 1967 – Believed dissolved.

Crane Capital Corp. (B.C. Mar. 3, 2018)
Mar. 3, 2021 – Name changed to Lode Metals Corp. ■

Cranefield International Inc. (Can. Sept. 27, 1993)
Mar. 2, 2000 – Name changed to Thornecliff Ventures Limited; basis 1 new for 2 old shs. ■

Crangold Mines Ltd. (Man. Aug. 10, 1937)
1956 – Acquired by Valray Explorations Ltd.; basis 1 new for 4 old shs. (see Valray Explorations Ltd.)

Cranstown Capital Corp. (B.C. Feb. 2, 2021)
Mar. 20, 2025 – Name changed to J2 Metals Inc. pursuant to the Qualifying Transaction reverse takeover acquisition (old) J2 Metals Inc. (see FPsurvey - Mines & Energy)

Cranwell Oil Company Ltd. (Ont. 1983)
May 2, 1988 – Name changed to North American Resource Capital Limited. ■

Craven Resources Inc. (B.C. July 18, 1983)
Apr. 19, 1990 – Name changed to Craven Ventures Inc. ■

Craven Ventures Inc. (B.C. July 18, 1983)
Apr. 7, 1997 – Name changed to Cascadia International Resources Inc. ■

Crawford Allied Industries Limited (Ont. 1964)
May 1979 – Amalgamated with Superior Sand, Gravel and Suppliers Ltd. to form Superior Crawford Sand & Gravel Limited. Minority shldrs. received. $10.50 per sh.

Crawford-Ontario Sand & Gravel Ltd. (Ont. 1964)
1968 – Name changed to Crawford Allied Industries Limited. ■

Crazy Horse Industries Inc. (B.C. Nov. 3, 1993)
July 20, 1999 – Name changed to CBX Ventures Inc.; basis 1 new for 8 old shs. ■

Crazy Horse Resources Inc. (B.C. May 8, 2007)
June 8, 2017 – Name changed to Rockwealth Resources Corp.; basis 1 new for 10 old shs. ■

Cream Minerals Ltd. (B.C. Oct. 12, 1966)
Oct. 2, 2013 – Name changed to Agave Silver Corp.; basis 1 new for 10 old shs. ■

Cream Silver Mines Ltd. (B.C. Oct. 12, 1966)
Dec. 22, 1994 – Name changed to Cream Minerals Ltd.; basis 1 new for 5 old shs. ■

Creation Capital Corp. (B.C. Feb. 15, 2018)
June 3, 2019 – Name changed to Greenlane Renewables Inc. pursuant to Qualifying Transaction reverse takeover acquisition of PT Biogas Holdings Limited. (see FPsurvey - Industrials)

Creation Casinos Inc. (Alta. Oct. 22, 1997)
Dec. 16, 2004 – Continued into British Columbia.
July 22, 2008 – Name changed to Orca Power Corp.; basis 1 new for 2.5 old shs. ■

Creation Ventures Inc. (Alta. Oct. 22, 1997)
Nov. 20, 2003 – Name changed to Creation Casinos Inc. ■

Creative Entertainment Technologies, Inc. (Yuk. July 9, 1992)
May 17, 2005 – Dissolved and struck off register. ■

Creative Patents & Products Limited (Ont. 1970)
Mar. 14, 1978 – Charter cancelled.

Creative Products Inc. (B.C. 1983)
Mar. 5, 1993 – Dissolved and struck off register.

Creative Telefilms & Artists Ltd. (Ont. 1919)
July 1960 – Name changed to Seven Arts Productions Ltd. ■

Creator Capital Incorporated (B.C. Jan. 28, 1981)
Jan. 27, 1995 – Name changed to Sky Games International Ltd. ■

Credent Capital Corp. (B.C. Mar. 25, 2011)
Oct. 14, 2021 – Name changed to Good Gamer Entertainment Inc. pursuant to the Qualifying Transaction reverse takeover acquisition of Good Gamer Corp.; basis 1 new for 5 old shs. (see FPsurvey - Industrials)

Credico Inc. (Que. 1961)
1969 – Bankrupt and wound up. Full payments were made to secured notehldrs.; unsecured creditors received 38¢ on the dollar; nothing to shldrs.

Credit Acceptance Corp. Ltd. (B.C. 1947)
Mar. 1965 – Name changed to Commonwealth Acceptance Corp. Ltd. ■

Crédit Commercial de France (Canada) (Can. 1981)
July 1, 1990 – Amalgamated with Société Générale (Canada) to continue as Société Générale (Canada). (see Société Générale (Canada))

Crédit de l'Est Inc. (Que. 1955)
June 15, 1962 – Name changed to Alliance Credit Corporation. ■

Crédit Foncier (Que. 1880)
Sept. 1986 – Merged with Montreal Trustco.

Crédit Foncier Franco-Canadien (Que. 1880)
July 1, 1980 – Name changed to Crédit Foncier. ■

Crédit Industriel Desjardins Incorporated (Que. Sept. 1975)
Dec. 23, 1988 – Formed Desjardins Trustco Inc. on amalgamation with Fiducie Desjardins Inc. ■

Crédit Lyonnais Canada (Can. Jan. 1, 1982)
Mar. 19, 2001 – Amalgamated with HSBC Bank Canada via a payment of preferred shs. immediately redeemed for cash. (see HSBC Bank Canada)

Credit M.-G. Inc. (Que. 1960)
Feb. 1971 – Placed into liquidation as a result of default. Secured noteholders received payment of 5% of principal plus int.
1978 – Secured noteholders received a further payment of 85% of principal by 1978.

Crédit St-Laurent Inc. (Que. 1952)
Dec. 1968 – Entered voluntary liquidation. C/o Mercure, Béliveau, Gagnon, Martin & Perras, trustees, 804 Tour de la Bourse, Montréal, Que. Final payment of 15¢ per 1st pref. sh. pd. Oct. 15, 1968; 16¢ per 2nd pref. sh. pd. Aug. 1, 1968; and 3¢ per cl. A sh. pd. Aug. 1, 1968. Trustee for secured note and debhldrs. is General Trust of Canada.

Crédit Suisse Canada (Can. 1983)
Jan. 1, 1997 – Name changed to Crédit Suisse First Boston Canada.

Credit Union Central of British Columbia (B.C. May 25, 1944)
July 1, 2008 – Name changed to Central 1 Credit Union.

Credo Mining Ltd. (Que. 1964)
Mar. 1975 – Charter cancelled.

Cree Lake Mining Ltd. (B.C. May 30, 1966)
Jan. 2, 1980 – Name changed to Scarboro Resources Ltd. ■

Cree Lake Resources Corp. (Ont. Oct. 12, 1990)
May 5, 1997 – Name changed to Cogent Capital Corp. ■

Cree Mining Corp. Ltd. (Sask.)
Sept. 1964 – Struck off register.

Cree Oil of Canada Ltd. (Can. 1956)
1958 – Acquired by North Star Oil Ltd.; basis 1 cl. A or com. of North Star for 3 Cree; debs. exch. at par.

Creighton-Fairbanks Mines Ltd. (Ont. 1928)
1936 – Charter cancelled.

Creo Inc. (Can. May 30, 1985)
June 15, 2005 – Acquired by Eastman Kodak Company for US$16.50 per sh.

Creo Products Inc. (Can. May 30, 1985)
Feb. 20, 2002 – Name changed to Creo Inc. ■

Crescendo Capital Corp. (Ont. May 7, 1991 amalg.)
July 24, 1996 – Name changed to TragoeS Inc. ■

Crescent Creamery Co. Ltd. (Man. 1905)
1956 – Offer of $70 per sh. made for o/s pref. stk. through Royal Trust Co. Dominion Dairies, which previously held all com. stk., sold its int. to Modern Dairies Ltd. of Winnipeg.

Crescent Kirkland Gold Mines Ltd. (Ont. 1936)
Nov. 19, 1956 – Charter cancelled.

Crescent Mines Ltd. (B.C. 1968)
Aug. 16, 1985 – Name changed to Redwing Resources Inc.; basis 1 new for 4.3 old shs. ■

Crescent Point Energy Corp. (Alta. Aug. 1, 2006)
May 10, 2024 – Name changed to Veren Inc. ■

Crescent Point Energy Ltd. (Alta. June 20, 2001)
Sept. 10, 2003 – Reorganization with Tappit Resources Ltd. into Crescent Point Energy Trust and StarPoint Energy Ltd.; basis cl. A shs. (cl. B shs.) - 0.50 (0.75) new StarPoint com. sh. plus either a) 0.50 (0.75) new Crescent Point trust unit, or b) 0.50 (0.75) new Crescent Point Acquisition Ltd. exch. sh., or c) a combination thereof for 1 cl. A (cl. B) Crescent Point sh. (see Crescent Point Energy Trust)

Crescent Point Energy Trust (Alta. July 22, 2003)
July 7, 2009 – Converted into a corporation whereby Wild River Resources Ltd. completed the reverse takeover acquisition of the trust and Wild River changed its name to Crescent Point Energy Corp. (CPEC). Crescent Point Energy Trust (CPET) subsequently dissolved and unitholders received 1 CPEC com. sh. for 1 CPET trust unit. (see Crescent Point Energy Corp.)

Crescent Resources Corp. (B.C. May 29, 1984)
Jan. 8, 2013 – Name changed to Coventry Resources Inc. following reverse takeover acquisition of Coventry Resources Limited; basis 1 new for 5 old shs. ■

Creso Exploration Inc. (Ont. Aug. 25, 2004)
Sept. 29, 2010 – Continued into Canada.
Apr. 8, 2014 – Amalgamated with 8704996 Canada Inc., a wholly owned subsid. of Dundee Sustainable Technologies Inc.; basis 1 new Dundee Sustainable sub. vtg. sh. for 2 old Creso com. shs.

Cressy Gold Mines Ltd. (Ont. 1947)
Aug. 1958 – Charter cancelled.

Crest Petroleum Corp. (B.C. Jan. 24, 2012)
Oct. 21, 2016 – Name changed to GFG Resources Inc. following Qualifying Transaction reverse takeover acquisition of (old) GFG Resources Inc. (see FPsurvey - Mines & Energy)

Crest Resources Inc. (B.C. Nov. 23, 2017)
Sept. 9, 2024 – Name changed to Mineral Road Discovery Inc. (see FPsurvey - Mines & Energy)

Crest Resources Ltd. (B.C. July 2, 1986)
Mar. 23, 1992 – Name changed to Sentinel Resources Ltd.; basis 1 new for 3 old shs. ■

Crest Ventures Ltd. (B.C. 1955)
Apr. 1974 – Name changed to Van-Sea Resources Ltd.; basis 1 new for 3 old shs. ■

Crestar Energy Inc. (Can. Oct. 1, 1985)
Nov. 13, 2000 – Acquired by Gulf Canada Resources Ltd. for $3.25 plus 3.333 ordinary shs. of Gulf Canada. (see Gulf Canada Resources Limited)

Crestaurum Mines Ltd. (Ont. 1945)
1964 – Name changed to United Comstock Lode Mines Ltd. ■

Crestbrook Forest Industries Ltd. (B.C. June 30, 1965 amalg.)
Apr. 12, 1999 – Acquired by Tembec Inc.; basis 0.51298 Tembec cl. A shs. or $4.50 in cash for 1 Crestbrook sh. Crestbrook shldrs. also received a contingent value right entitling them to a one-time payment of up to $1.50 per sh. on Mar. 31, 2000, depending upon the 1999 average price of NBSK (northern bleached softwood kraft) pulp. (see Tembec Inc.)

Crestbrook Timber Limited (B.C. Nov. 22, 1955)
June 30, 1965 – Amalgamated in British Columbia to continue with same name.
Apr. 18, 1967 – Name changed to Crestbrook Forest Industries Ltd. ■

Crestfield Uranium Mines Ltd. (Ont. 1953)
Apr. 6, 1964 – Dissolved.

Crestland Mines Ltd. (Ont. 1965)
July 30, 1976 – Merged with 2 other cos. into Pyx Explorations Ltd.; basis 1 new for 15 old shs.

Creston Gold Mines Ltd. (B.C. 1946)
1947 – Name changed to Rossland Mines Ltd. ■

Creston Moly Corp. (B.C. Aug. 5, 1977)
June 21, 2011 – Acquired by Mercator Minerals Ltd.; basis 8¢ plus 0.15 Mercator shs. for 1 Creston sh. (see Mercator Minerals Ltd.)

Creststreet Power & Income Fund LP (Ont. Dec. 21, 2001)
July 11, 2008 – Redeemed all units and 7% and 8% debs. for $6.9150 per unit, $1,032.44 per $1,000 7% debs. and $1,062.33 per $1,000 8% debs. and dissolved.

Crestview Petroleum Corporation (Alta. July 31, 1992)
Apr. 3, 1995 – Amalgamated with 631388 Alberta Ltd., a wholly owned subsid. of Cube Energy Corp.; basis 1 new Cube sh. for 30 old Crestview shs. (see Cube Energy Corp.)

Crestwell Resources Inc. (B.C. July 25, 2011)
Oct. 17, 2016 – Name changed to Organic Garage Ltd. following reverse takeover acquisition of (old) Organic Garage Ltd.; basis 1 new for 4 old shs. ■

Crestwood Kitchens Limited (B.C. 1955)
1976 – Acquired by K. G. R. Holdings Ltd., owned by Fred Kruberg, for $2.65 per sh.

Cresval Capital Corp. (B.C. July 23, 2001)
Oct. 22, 2021 – Name changed to Transforma Resources Corporation; basis 1 new for 5 old shs. (see FPsurvey - Mines & Energy)

Creswell Mines Ltd. (Ont. 1964)
1973 – Name changed to Newcrest Developments Limited; basis 1 new for 5 old shs. ■

Crew Development Corporation (B.C. Mar. 31, 1980)
Jan. 28, 2000 – Continued into Yukon.
Jan. 26, 2004 – Name changed to Crew Gold Corporation. ■

Crew Energy Inc. (Alta. May 12, 2003)
Oct. 3, 2024 – Acquired by Tourmaline Oil Corp.; basis 0.114802 Tourmaline com. shs. for 1 Crew com. sh., which valued Crew at $6.73 per sh.

Crew Gold Corporation (Yuk. Jan. 28, 2000)
Jan. 19, 2011 – Acquired by Nord Gold (Yukon) Inc., a wholly owned subsid. of Nord Gold N.V., for US$4.65 per sh.

Crew Minerals Inc. (B.C. Jan. 29, 1986)
Apr. 20, 1988 – Name changed to Asia-Pacific Resources Ltd. ■

Crew Natural Resources Limited (B.C. Jan. 18, 1985)
Oct. 5, 1994 – Name changed to South Crofty Holdings Ltd.; basis 1 new for 2 old shs. ■

Crewe Mining and Development Co. Ltd. (Ont. 1947)
1958 – Charter cancelled.

Cricket Capital Corp. (B.C. June 5, 2006)
July 13, 2010 – Name changed to Cricket Resources Inc. pursuant to Qualifying Transaction acquisition of an option to acquire a 60% interest in the Forgan Lake Property owned by TNR Gold Corp. ■

Cricket Media Group Ltd. (Ont. July 26, 2011)
May 13, 2016 – Acquired by newly formed Cricket Acquisition Group, Inc., for Cdn$0.14 per each Cricket com. sh. and ser. A pref. sh.

Cricket Resources Inc. (B.C. June 5, 2006)
July 17, 2017 – Name changed to Eastern Zinc Corp.; basis 1 new for 10 old shs. ■

Crimson Falcon Capital Corp. (B.C. Sept. 1, 2009)
Oct. 20, 2011 – Name changed to Crimson Bioenergy Ltd. pursuant to Qualifying Transaction acquisition of CSQ Environmental Technologies Ltd. (see FPsurvey - Industrials)

Crimson Tide Resources Ltd. (B.C. Dec. 23, 1980)
Dec. 16, 1986 – Name changed to H.E.R.O. Industries Ltd. ■

Crimsonstar Mining Corporation (B.C. June 19, 1991 amalg.)
May 21, 1993 – Name changed to Mountain View Ventures Inc.; basis 1 new for 5 old shs. ■

Crimsonstar Resources Ltd. (Can. 1987)
June 19, 1991 – Amalgamated with Florin Resources Inc. (1 for 2.5) to form a new co. named Crimsonstar Mining Corporation; basis 1 new for 2 old shs. Also continued into Canada. (see Crimsonstar Mining Corporation)

Crio Group Developments Inc. (B.C. 1981)
Oct. 14, 1992 – Name changed to Tele Pacific International Communications Corp. ■

Crisan Resources Ltd. (B.C. Apr. 27, 1987)
Aug. 15, 1994 – Name changed to Starteck Industries Ltd.; basis 1 new for 3 old shs. ■

Crispin Energy Inc. (Alta. Apr. 18, 1979)
May 6, 2005 – Amalgamated with Pengrowth Corporation and Pengrowth Energy Trust; basis either 0.0512 Pengrowth cl. A trust units or 0.0725 Pengrowth cl. B trust units for 1 Crispin com. sh. (see Pengrowth Energy Trust)

Criss Creek Mines Ltd. (B.C. 1968)
Oct. 28, 1970 – Name changed to Topley Criss Mines Ltd. ■

Cristobal Resources Inc. (Que. Dec. 18, 1981)
Sept. 30, 1999 – Formed Netgraphe Inc.; basis 1 new for 3 old shs. ■

Criterion Business Trust TA Fund (Ont. Dec. 15, 2004)
Mar. 7, 2007 – Wound up; basis $6.27 per unit.

Criterion Dow Jones - AIG Commodity Index Fund (Ont. May 18, 2005)
May 31, 2006 – Converted into an open-ended mutual fund trust; basis 1 new class E unit for 1 old trust unit. Also delisted from TSX as part of mutualization.

Critical Capital Corporation (B.C. June 3, 2009)
Mar. 4, 2011 – Name changed to Castle Peak Mining Ltd. pursuant to Qualifying Transaction reverse takeover acquisition of Castle Peak Mining Ltd. ■

Critical Control Energy Services Corp. (Alta. Aug. 20, 1999 amalg.)
Mar. 1, 2019 – Voluntarily delisted from Toronto Stock Exchange (TSX).
June 5, 2019 – Privatized. All o/s com. shs. and pref. shs. not already held by 2209021 Ontario Inc. and Alykhan Mamdani redeemed for 8¢ cash per com. sh. and 42¢ cash per pref. sh.

Critical Elements Corporation (Can. Sept. 11, 2006)
June 19, 2019 – Name changed to Critical Elements Lithium Corporation. (see FPsurvey - Mines & Energy)

Critical Outcome Technologies Inc. (Ont. Oct. 13, 2006 amalg.)
Jan. 10, 2018 – Name changed to Cotinga Pharmaceuticals Inc. ■

CriticalControl Solutions Corp. (Alta. Aug. 20, 1999 amalg.)
June 23, 2015 – Name changed to Critical Control Energy Services Corp. ■

Crius Energy Trust (Ont. Sept. 7, 2012)
July 18, 2019 – Acquired by Vistra Energy Corp. and subsequently wound-up; basis Cdn$8.80 per trust unit.

Crocan Capital Corp. (B.C. Aug. 31, 2018)
Feb. 1, 2021 – Name changed to Gama Explorations Inc. ■

Crocodile Gold Corp. (Yuk. Aug. 25, 1997)
Dec. 7, 2009 – Continued into Ontario.
July 10, 2015 – Formed Newmarket Gold Inc. in Ontario on amalgamation with (old) Newmarket Gold Inc. pursuant to plan of arrangement with Crocodile the deemed acquiror; basis Cdn$0.37 or 0.2456 new Newmarket com.

shs. or a combination thereof for 1 Crocodile com. sh. and 0.2 new Newmarket com. shs. for 1 old Newmarket com. sh. ■

Crocotta Energy Inc. (Alta. Aug. 18, 2005)
Aug. 11, 2014 – Acquired by Long Run Exploration Ltd.; basis 0.415 Long Run com. shs., 1 Leucrotta Exploration Inc. com. sh. and 0.2 Leucrotta wts. for 1 Crocotta com. sh. (see Long Run Exploration Ltd.)

Croesus Gold Inc. (Ont. Nov. 21, 1995)
Nov. 17, 2006 – Continued into British Columbia.
June 23, 2008 – Name changed to Kenieba Goldfields Ltd. ■

Croesus Resources Inc. (B.C. Mar. 14, 1983)
Nov. 10, 1995 – Name changed to International Croesus Ventures Corp.; basis 1 new for 3.3 old shs. ■

Croft Uranium Mines Ltd. (Ont. 1954)
1955 – Merged into Bicroft Uranium Mines Ltd.; basis 1 new for 3 old shs.

Croinor Pershing Mines Ltd. (Que. 1944)
July 1972 – Charter cancelled.

Crombie Properties Limited (N.S. Feb. 4, 1964)
Jan. 25, 2006 – Name changed to ECL Properties Limited.

Cronin Babine Mines Ltd. (Ont. 1948)
1956 – Name changed to New Cronin Babine Mine Ltd.; basis 1 new for 5 old shs. ■

Cronos Group Inc. (Ont. Aug. 21, 2012)
July 9, 2020 – Continued into British Columbia. (see FPsurvey - Industrials)

Cronus Resources Ltd. (B.C. Aug. 5, 2005)
Nov. 23, 2009 – Continued into Ontario.
Mar. 30, 2010 – Formed Continental Gold Limited in Bermuda on amalgamation with Continental Gold Limited constituting a reverse takover by Continental; basis 1 new for 2.6973 Continental shs. and 1 new for 2.35712 Cronus shs. ■

Crop Infrastructure Corp. (B.C. May 31, 2011)
Jan. 16, 2020 – Name changed to Vert Infrastructure Ltd.; basis 1 new for 15 old shs. ■

Crosby Oil Corp. Ltd. (Ont. 1952)
Dec. 1957 – Dissolved.

Croskery Mines Ltd. (Ont. 1945)
1956 – Charter cancelled.

Cross Border Capital I Inc. (Ont. June 30, 2020)
July 7, 2022 – Name changed to SuperBuzz Inc. pursuant to the Qualifying Transaction reverse takeover acquisition of Israel-based Message Notify Ltd. (dba SuperBuzz). (see FPsurvey - Industrials)

Cross Border Capital Inc. (Alta. May 24, 2000)
Feb. 5, 2003 – Qualifying Transaction amalgamation with Cyan Corporation (0.697951 for 1) and Titan Digital Storage Corporation (1 for 1) to form a new company named Titan Digital Corporation; basis 1 new amalco. sh. for 1 old Cross Border com. sh. (see Titan Digital Corporation)

Cross Canada International Inc. (Ont. Jan. 13, 1972)
Nov. 11, 1998 – Name changed to Senator Minerals Inc.; basis 1 new for 10 old shs. ■

Cross Canada Resources Inc. (Ont. Jan. 13, 1972)
Nov. 13, 1995 – Name changed to Cross Canada International Inc.; basis 1 new for 10 old shs. ■

Cross Fault Gold Mines Ltd. (Ont. 1945)
1948 – Name changed to Cross Fault Mines Ltd. ■

Cross Fault Mines Ltd. (Ont. 1945)
Sept. 18, 1961 – Charter cancelled.

Cross Lake Minerals Ltd. (B.C. Aug. 17, 1987)
June 1, 2009 – Name changed to 0373849 B.C. Ltd. ■

Cross Lake Mining Co. Ltd. (Ont. 1955)
Sept. 1958 – Charter cancelled.

Cross Pacific Pearls Inc. (B.C. 1988)
Sept. 29, 1995 – Dissolved and struck off register.

Crosscourt Gold Mines Ltd. (Ont. 1941)
Apr. 11, 1955 – Charter cancelled.

Crosscut Explorations Inc. (Ont. Apr. 26, 1966)
Dec. 19, 1984 – Name changed to Renaissance Industrial Corp.; basis 1 new for 8 old shs. ■

Crossfield Capital Corp. (Alta. Feb. 12, 2004)
Sept. 22, 2005 – Name changed to Royal Laser Corp. following Qualifying Transaction acquisition of WAM Industries Ltd. and Royal Laser Mfg. Inc. ■

Crossfire Energy Services Inc. (Alta. Aug. 23, 2004 amalg.)
Feb. 20, 2008 – Placed into receivership by secured creditor. PricewaterhouseCoopers Inc. appointed receiver and all officers and directors resigned.
Apr. 28, 2008 – PricewaterhouseCoopers Inc. was appointed trustee in bankruptcy.
Feb. 2, 2010 – Dissolved and struck from register.
May 31, 2010 – PricewaterhouseCoopers Inc. was discharged as receiver. Secured creditor suffered a significant shortfall and no funds were available for unsecured creditors or shldrs.

Crossfire Holdings Inc. (Alta. Aug. 23, 2004 amalg.)
July 18, 2007 – Name changed to Crossfire Energy Services Inc. ■

Crosshair Energy Corporation (B.C. Sept. 2, 1966)
Sept. 23, 2013 – Name changed to Jet Metal Corp.; basis 1 new for 10 old shs. ■

Crosshair Exploration & Mining Corp. (B.C. Sept. 2, 1966)
Nov. 2, 2011 – Name changed to Crosshair Energy Corporation. ■

CrossKeys Systems Corporation (Can. Oct. 28, 1992)
Apr. 12, 2001 – Acquired by UK-based Orchestream Holdings plc; basis 0.453 ordinary shs. of Orchestream, or 0.453 Orchestream ADSs for 1 old CrossKeys sh.

Crossland Industries Corporation (B.C. Dec. 31, 1980)
Mar. 2, 1989 – Delisted from the Vancouver Stock Exchange. Subsequently dissolved for failure to file.

CrossOff Incorporated (N.S. Aug. 20, 1985)
June 22, 2006 – Name changed to Nexient Learning Inc. ■

Crossover Acquisitions Inc. (Ont. May 27, 2019)
Aug. 22, 2023 – Name changed to Resolute Resources Ltd. pursuant to the Qualifying Transaction reverse takeover acquisition of (old) Resolute Resources Ltd.; basis 1 new for 2 old shs. (see FPsurvey - Mines & Energy; FPsurvey - Industrials)

Crossroad Ventures Inc. (B.C. Mar. 15, 2000)
Jan. 8, 2003 – Acquired by Consolidated Goldbank Ventures Ltd.; basis 2 new Goldbank com. shs. for 3 old Crossroad com. shs.
Jan. 17, 2018 – Formed Neptune Dash Technologies Corp. on amalgamation with Neptune Dash Nodes Corp. (deemed acquiror). ■

Crossroads Explorations Inc. (Can. Sept. 3, 2003)
Apr. 13, 2007 – Name changed to New Horizon Uranium Corporation following reverse takeover acquisition of New Horizon Uranium Corporation. ■

Crosswinds Holdings Inc. (Alta. Mar. 29, 2005)
Dec. 18, 2019 – Distrib. of 10¢ cash paid to shldrs. of record Dec. 17, 2019.
July 14, 2021 – Name changed to Biomind Labs Inc. pursuant to the reverse takeover acquisition of Biomind Research Corp. and concurrent amalgamation of Biomind with wholly owned Crosswinds Mergersub Inc.; basis 1 new for 32.5 old shs. ■

Crow River Gold Mines Inc. (Ont. 1974)
Apr. 10, 1976 – Amalgamated with New Force Crag Mines Limited (1 for 1) and Beaver Hill Lake Uranium Mines Limited (0.75 for 1) to continue as New Force Crag Mines Limited; basis 0.6 new for 1 old sh.

Crowbank Mines Ltd. (Ont. 1944)
Jan. 1974 – Name changed to Patmore Developments Limited; basis 1 new for 10 old shs. ■

Crowder Communication Corporation (B.C. 1978)
Aug. 10, 1988 – Name changed to Sigmacom Systems Incorporated; basis 1 new for 5 old shs. ■

Crowduck Bay Mines Ltd. (Ont. 1972)
Nov. 1977 – Charter cancelled. Trustee discharged in 1978.

Crowflight Minerals Inc. (B.C. Jan. 11, 1937)
July 30, 2003 – Continued into Ontario.
June 23, 2011 – Name changed to CaNickel Mining Limited and continued into British Columbia. ■

Crown Butte Resources Ltd. (Can. Feb. 5, 1987)
May 14, 2003 – Voluntary liquidation. Distribution to shldrs. of record $0.1769 per com. sh.

Crown Cork and Seal Company, Limited (Ont. 1935)
Apr. 29, 1978 – Merged with Crown Cork Holdings Inc. and nine wholly owned subsids. Shldrs. received pref. shs. of the new co., subsequently red. at $280 per sh. All o/s shs. of amalg. co. now held by Crown Cork & Seal Co. Inc. of Philadelphia, parent of Crown Cork Holdings Inc.

Crown-Dominion Oil Company, Ltd. (Ont. 1928)
Feb. 1949 – Name changed to Reliance Petroleum Ltd. ■

Crown Forest Industries Limited (B.C. 1970 amalg.)
Feb. 19, 1988 – Amalgamated with British Columbia Forest Products Limited to form Fletcher Challenge Canada Limited. (see British Columbia Forest Products Limited)

Crown Gold Corporation (Can. Aug. 30, 2010 amalg.)
June 30, 2014 – Name changed to Crown Mining Corporation; basis 1 new for 10 old shs. ■

Crown Hill Dividend Fund (Ont. May 19, 2004)
Dec. 31, 2008 – Merged into MACCs Sustainable Yield Trust; basis 1.1742 MACCs units for 1 Crown unit. Subsequently MACCs changed its name to Crown Hill Fund. (see Crown Hill Fund)

Crown Hill Fund (Ont. Jan. 28, 2005)
Dec. 2, 2009 – Name changed to Citadel Income Fund pursuant to merger with Citadel Premium Income Fund, Citadel S-1 Income Trust Fund, Citadel Stable S-1 Income Fund, Citadel HYTES Fund and Equal Weight Plus Fund, with Crown Hill Fund the deemed acquiror. (see FPsurvey - Industrials)

Crown Life Insurance Company (Can. June 14, 1900; via Special Act of Parliament)
Dec. 20, 2001 – Insurance operations acquired by Canada Life Assurance Company effective Jan. 1, 1999. All common shares owned by HARO Financial Corporation and Extendicare Inc. Also all class I series A preferred shs. redeemed at $25 per sh. plus accrued dividend of $0.5503.
Oct. 30, 2012 – Amalgamated with The Canada Life Assurance Company to continue under The Canada Life Assurance Company name.

Crown Life Properties Inc. (Ont. 1980)
Feb. 10, 1992 – All o/s 7.375% Preferred Shares, Series 1 called for redemption; basis $25 plus accrued dividend of $0.2026 per sh.

Crown-Meakins Inc. (Ont. 1968)
Jan. 5, 1976 – Name changed to Medicorp Technology Ltd. ■

Crown Minerals Inc. (Can. June 11, 2007)
Aug. 30, 2010 – Formed Crown Gold Corporation in Canada on amalgamation with Gold Summit Corporation;

basis 1.65 new for 1 Gold Summit sh. and 1 new for 1 Crown Minerals sh. ■

Crown Mining and Refining Company Limited (Alta. 1947)
Feb. 14, 1953 – Struck off register.

Crown Mining Corporation (Can. Aug. 30, 2010 amalg.)
Apr. 8, 2021 – Name changed to US Copper Corp. (see FPsurvey - Mines & Energy)

Crown Point Exploration Ltd. (Alta. 1966)
1969 – In voluntary liquidation, with Guaranty Trust Co. appointed liquidator.
Aug. 31, 1982 – Struck off register.

Crown Point Ventures Ltd. (B.C. Mar. 16, 1966)
July 27, 2012 – Continued into Alberta.
July 31, 2012 – Name changed to Crown Point Energy Inc. (see FPsurvey - Mines & Energy)

Crown Silver Development Ltd. (B.C. 1950)
Name changed to Cerro Mining Ltd. prior to May 31, 1969; basis 1 new for 5 old shs. ■

Crown Silver Lead Mines Ltd. (B.C. 1950)
1954 – Name changed to Crown Silver Development Ltd. ■

Crown Yellowknife Mines Ltd. (Alta. 1947)
July 29, 1950 – Name changed to Crown Mining and Refining Company Limited. ■

Crown Zellerbach Canada Limited (B.C. 1970 amalg.)
Oct. 1, 1983 – Name changed to Crown Forest Industries Limited. ■

Crownbridge Copper Mines Ltd. (Ont. Oct. 7, 1963)
Mar. 1976 – Charter cancelled.
1977 – Charter revived.
Feb. 2, 1979 – Name changed to Crownbridge Industries Inc.; basis 1 new for 10 old shs. ■

Crownbridge Industries Inc. (Ont. Oct. 7, 1963)
July 21, 1997 – Struck from registry and dissolved.

Crownex International Ltd. (B.C. 1950)
Nov. 1971 – Name changed to Dison International Ltd.; basis 1 new for 5 old shs. ■

Crownia Holdings Ltd. (B.C. July 16, 2012)
Oct. 31, 2022 – Dissolved and struck from register.

CrownJoule Exploration Ltd. (Alta. Oct. 4, 1996)
July 14, 2000 – Acquired by BelAir Energy Corporation; basis 10¢ and 0.42 BelAir shs. for 1 CrownJoule sh. (see BelAir Energy Corporation)

Crownx Inc. (Can. Aug. 7, 1968; via Dominion charter)
Nov. 17, 1994 – Name changed to Extendicare Inc. ■

Crows Nest Industries Limited (Can. 1897)
Mar. 1, 1978 – Assets and operations acquired by Shell Canada Resources Limited, a wholly owned subsid. of Shell Canada Limited after 97% o/s com. and all o/s pref. shs. were tendered; basis $85 per com. and $77.28 per pref. sh. (see Shell Canada Limited)

Crow's Nest Pass Coal Company Ltd. (Can. 1897)
May 1965 – Name changed to Crows Nest Industries Limited. ■

Crowshore Gold Mines Ltd. (Ont. 1936)
May 1944 – Name changed to Crowshore Patricia Gold Mines Ltd. and continued into Ontario; basis 1 new for 2 old shs.

Crowshore Patricia Gold Mines Ltd. (Ont. May 1944)
Mar. 1955 – Name changed to Crowpat Minerals Ltd.; basis 1 new for 4 old shs.

Crowsnest Acquisition Corp. (Alta. Sept. 19, 2012)
Oct. 20, 2014 – Name changed to QE2 Acquisition Corp. following Qualifying Transaction reverse takeover acquisition of (old) QE2 Acquisition Corp. ■

Croydon Mercantile Corp. (B.C. Feb. 15, 1985 amalg.)
Nov. 20, 2015 – Name changed to World Mahjong Limited pursuant to reverse takeover acquisition of (old) World Mahjong Limited. ■

Croydon Mines Ltd. (B.C. June 25, 1963)
May 30, 1973 – Name changed to Aalenian Resources Ltd.; basis 1 new for 10 old shs. ■

Croydon Rouyn Mines Ltd. (Ont. 1945)
Aug. 28, 1980 – Amalgamated with Nuinsco Resources Limited to form a new co. under the same name of Nuinsco; basis 1 new for 150 old shs.
1980 – Continued into British Columbia.

Crude Oils Limited (Alta. 1938)
1970 – Merged into Westburne Petroleum & Minerals Ltd.

Cruiser Minerals Ltd. (B.C. Mar. 11, 1983)
Jan. 4, 1993 – Name changed to E.C.A. Technology Ltd. ■

Cruiser Oil & Gas Ltd. (Alta. Oct. 9, 1998)
Nov. 24, 2008 – Acquired by One Exploration Inc.; basis 0.0609 One Exploration shs. for 1 Cruiser sh.

Crusade Petroleum Corporation Limited (Alta. 1959)
Dec. 1971 – Acquired by Pan Ocean Oil Corp.; basis 6.6 new for 100 old shs.

Crusader Gold Corporation (B.C. 1981)
Nov. 13, 1992 – Name changed to Shorewood Explorations Ltd.; basis 1 new for 2.5 old shs. ■

Crusader Mines Ltd. (Ont. 1966)
Dec. 1973 – Charter cancelled.

Crusader Petroleums Ltd. (Ont. June 1947)
1951 – Assets acquired by Astral Mining & Resources Ltd. for 400,000 shs.

Crush International Limited (Ont. 1927)
Jan. 29, 1981 – Name changed to Great Pacific Industries Inc. ■

Crux Industries, Inc. (B.C. Nov. 23, 1983)
Nov. 17, 2005 – Name changed to Mont Blanc Resources Inc. ■

Cruz Capital Corp. (B.C. Mar. 28, 2007)
Feb. 23, 2017 – Name changed to Cruz Cobalt Corp. ■

Cruz Cobalt Corp. (B.C. Mar. 28, 2007)
Aug. 9, 2021 – Name changed to Cruz Battery Metals Corp. (see FPsurvey - Mines & Energy)

Cruz Silver Mines Inc. (Alta. 1983)
June 30, 1986 – Name changed to Gold Shield Exploration and Development Inc.; basis 1 new for 8 old shs. ■

CruzSur Energy Corp. (B.C. June 5, 2017)
Oct. 2, 2020 – Name changed to NGX Energy International Corp. ■

Cry Lake Minerals Ltd. (B.C. 1968)
Mar. 18, 1983 – Struck off register.

Cryderman Gold Inc. (B.C. Apr. 24, 1987)
Dec. 16, 1992 – Name changed to Softfund Capital Partners Inc. ■

Cryderman Gold Mines Ltd. (Man. 1934)
Dec. 1963 – Charter cancelled.

CryoCath Technologies Inc. (Que. Aug. 24, 1994)
Dec. 22, 2008 – Acquired by Medtronic Canada Acquisition Inc., an indirect wholly owned subsid. of Medtronic, Inc., for $8.75 per sh.

Cryocon Containers Inc. (B.C. Nov. 23, 1983)
June 17, 1993 – Name changed to Cryocon-Pacific Containers Inc.; basis 1 new for 5 old shs. ■

Cryocon-Pacific Containers Inc. (B.C. Nov. 23, 1983)
May 6, 1996 – Name changed to Alda Industries Corporation; basis 1 new for 2 old shs. ■

Cryopak Industries Inc. (B.C. Feb. 13, 1981)
Oct. 2006 – Placed into receivership by secured creditors. Deloitte & Touche LLP was appointed receiver and PricewaterhouseCoopers Inc. was appointed trustee in bankruptcy for wholly owned Cryopak Corporation Ltd.

Cryptanite Blockchain Technologies Corp. (B.C. June 24, 1986)
Oct. 24, 2019 – Name changed to Intellabridge Technology Corporation. (see FPsurvey - Industrials)

Cryptic Ventures Inc. (B.C. Jan. 26, 1987)
Nov. 21, 1996 – Name changed to Zen International Resources Ltd. and continued into Yukon; basis 1 new for 5 old shs. ■

Cryptobloc Technologies Corp. (B.C. Jan. 16, 2015)
Feb. 6, 2020 – Name changed to Global Elsimate Capital Corp. ■

Cryptoblox Technologies Inc. (B.C. Jan. 16, 2015)
Nov. 26, 2024 – Name changed to Dynamite Blockchain Corp. (see FPsurvey - Industrials)

Cryptobuyer Technologies Corp. (B.C. Feb. 18, 2017)
May 1, 2018 – Name changed to Digital Buyer Technologies Corp. ■

CryptoGlobal Corp. (Ont. May 18, 2017)
July 10, 2018 – Formed HyperBlock Inc. in Ontario pursuant to acquistion by and amalgamtion with HyperBlock Technologies Corp.; basis 0.4299 HyperBlock shs. for 1 CryptoGlobal sh. ■

Cryptologic Corp. (Alta. Sept. 11, 2014 amalg.)
May 28, 2021 – Name changed to Greenhawk Resources Inc. following the acquisition of RSG Mining Corp. (see FPsurvey - Mines & Energy)

CryptoLogic Exchange Corporation (Ont.)
Apr. 11, 2012 – Acquired by CryptoLogic Callco ULC; basis 1 CryptoLogic Limited ord. sh. for 1 CryptoLogic exch. sh. (see CryptoLogic Limited)

CryptoLogic Inc. (Ont. Mar. 7, 1996 amalg.)
June 1, 2007 – Acquired by CryptoLogic Limited (CryptoLogic Ireland); 1 CryptoLogic Ireland ordinary sh. or 1 CryptoLogic Exchange Corporation exchangeable sh. (see CryptoLogic Limited)

CryptoLogic Limited (Guernsey Apr. 13, 2007)
July 31, 2012 – Acquired by Amaya Gaming Group Inc. for US$2.535 per ord. sh. (see Amaya Gaming Group Inc.)

Crystal Bridge Enterprises Inc. (B.C. Nov. 15, 2017)
Mar. 31, 2021 – Name changed to Alpha Cognition Inc. pursuant to Qualifying Transaction reverse takeover acquisition of Alpha Cognition Inc. (renmaed Alpha Cognition Canada Inc.); basis 1 new for 7.14 old shs. (see FPsurvey - Industrials)

Crystal Comstock Mines Limited (Ont. 1973)
May 31, 1977 – Name changed to Edgewood Explorations Inc. ■

Crystal Exploration Inc. (B.C. Nov. 9, 2010)
May 29, 2018 – Name changed to Benchmark Metals Inc.; basis 1 new for 3 old shs. ■

Crystal Graphite Corporation (B.C. Nov. 27, 1979)
July 30, 2007 – Dissolved and stuck from register.

Crystal-Kirkland Mines Ltd. (unknown)
Nov. 30, 1964 – Charter cancelled.

Crystal Lake Mining Corporation (B.C. July 20, 2009)
July 3, 2020 – Name changed to Enduro Metals Corporation. (see FPsurvey - Mines & Energy)

Crystal Mountain Resources Ltd. (B.C. 1982)
Sept. 3, 1993 – Dissolved and struck off register.

Crystal Peak Minerals Inc. (Yuk. May 26, 2011)
Dec. 15, 2021 – Continued into British Columbia.
Dec. 22, 2021 – Name changed to Western Exploration Inc. pursuant to the reverse takeover acquisition of Western Exploration LLC; basis 1 new for 363.3 old shs. (see FPsurvey - Mines & Energy)

Crystal-Vintage Growth Corporation (Can. May 3, 2004)
Jan. 15, 2008 – Acquired by Mercator Transport Group Corporation; basis 1.25 Mercator shs. for 1 Crystal-Vintage sh. Subsequently dissolved. (see Mercator Transport Group Corporation)

Crystallex International Corporation (B.C. May 22, 1984)
Jan. 23, 1998 – Continued into Canada. (see FPsurvey - Mines & Energy)

cs-live.com inc. (Ont. Aug. 30, 2000 amalg.)
Jan. 17, 2002 – Name changed to Intelligent Web Technologies Inc. (see FPsurvey - Industrials)

Cub Aircraft Corp., Ltd. (Ont. 1937)
Mar. 1949 – Name changed to Transvision-Television (Canada) Ltd. ■

Cub Energy Inc. (Ont. Apr. 3, 2008)
Feb. 28, 2012 – Continued into Canada.
Dec. 30, 2022 – Name changed to Carcetti Capital Corp.; basis 1 new for 300 old shs. (see FPsurvey - Mines & Energy; FPsurvey - Industrials)

Cuba Ventures Corp. (B.C. May 30, 1980)
Mar. 1, 2018 – Name changed to CUV Ventures Corp. ■

Cubacan Exploration Inc. (Alta. Jan. 12, 1995)
July 2, 2004 – Dissolved and struck from registry.

Cubamina Ltd. (unknown 1954)
1957 – Merged into International Metal and Petroleum Corp.; basis 1 new for 2 old shs.

Cubar Uranium Mines Ltd. (Ont. 1953)
June 29, 1964 – Charter cancelled.

Cube Energy Corp. (B.C. Feb. 6, 1979)
Apr. 30, 1997 – Amalgamated with Barrington Petroleum Ltd.; basis $13 per sh. (see Barrington Petroleum Ltd.)

Cube Resources Ltd. (B.C. May 2, 1972)
Apr. 7, 1986 – Delisted Vancouver Stock Exchange. Subsequently struck from register and dissolved.

Cubix Investments Inc. (B.C. May 28, 1980)
Jan. 19, 2001 – Name changed to Cubix Investments Ltd. and continued into Bermuda. ■

Cubix Investments Ltd. (Bermuda Jan. 19, 2001)
Nov. 10, 2003 – Name changed to Q Investments Ltd.; basis 1 new for 10 old shs. ■

Cuda Capital Corp. (B.C. Jan. 6, 2006)
Nov. 24, 2009 – Name changed to August Metal Corporation; basis 1 new for 5 old shs. ■

Cuda Consolidated Inc. (Ont. Apr. 9, 1973)
Sept. 30, 1994 – Name changed to Foodquest Corp. ■

Cuda Oil and Gas Inc. (Que. Mar. 26, 1999)
Nov. 18, 2021 – Placed into receivership by the company's senior and subordinate secured lenders. FTI Consulting Canada Inc. was appointed receiver and all the officers and directors resigned.

Cue Capital Corp. (B.C. Feb. 22, 2006)
Oct. 19, 2007 – Name changed to Cue Resources Ltd. ■

Cue Resources Ltd. (B.C. Feb. 22, 2006)
Apr. 3, 2012 – Acquired by Uranium Energy Corp.; basis 0.0195 Uranium Energy shs. for 1 Cue Resources sh.

Cuervo Resources Inc. (Ont. Feb. 11, 2005)
June 9, 2015 – Certificate of incorporation cancelled and dissolved.

Cugold Ventures Inc. (B.C. May 25, 1987)
Dec. 6, 1999 – Name changed to Firestone Ventures Inc.; basis 1 new for 3 old shs. ■

Culada Asset Management, Inc. (Can. Jan. 19, 2015)
June 19, 2018 – Name changed to ApartmentLove Inc. (see FPsurvey - Industrials)

Culane Energy Corp. (Alta. June 19, 1996)
Aug. 2, 2011 – Acquired by Killam Acquisition Company Ltd. for $2.32 per sh.

Culinar Inc. (Que. 1947)
Sept. 15, 1999 – Acquired by Saputo Group Inc. for $282,200,000. (see Saputo Group Inc.)

Cullaton Lake Gold Mines Ltd. (Ont. 1980)
June 8, 1984 – Shs. exchanged for shs. of Royex Sturgex Mining Limited in connection with amalgamation approved by shldrs.; basis 3 Royex com. shs. and 1 convert. pref. sh. of Royex for each 11 Cullaton com. shs. held; and 1 Royex pref. sh. for 2 old Cullaton pref. shs.

Culmina Ventures Corp. (B.C. Mar. 25, 2019)
May 19, 2021 – Name changed to Telescope Innovations Corp. pursuant to the reverse takeover acquisition of ClearMynd Technology Solutions Corp. (see FPsurvey - Industrials)

Cultivar Holdings Inc. (B.C. Sept. 3, 1987)
Apr. 9, 2020 – Name changed to Predictmedix Inc. ■

Cultus Explorations Ltd. (Alta. May 27, 1963)
May 6, 1976 – Name changed to Newcan Minerals Limited; basis 1 new for 5 old shs. ■

Cultus Pacific N.L. (N.S.W. 1968)
1984 – Continued into Western Australia.
Jan. 30, 1986 – Name changed to Cultus Resources N.L.; basis 1 new for 8 old shs. ■

Cultus Resources N.L. (W.A. 1984)
July 1, 1989 – Name changed to Cultus Petroleum NL.

Culver Gold Mines Ltd. (Ont. 1943)
Oct. 1977 – Charter cancelled.

Cumberland Mining Co. Ltd. (Ont. 1948)
May 1976 – Charter cancelled.

Cumberland Oil & Gas Ltd. (Alta. Feb. 26, 2010 amalg.)
Oct. 15, 2012 – Acquired by Kallisto Energy Corp.; basis 0.9180 Kallisto shs. for 1 Cumberland sh. (see Kallisto Energy Corp.)

Cumberland Resources Ltd. (B.C. Dec. 4, 1979)
July 10, 2007 – Acquired by Agnico-Eagle Mines Limited; basis 0.185 new Agnico-Eagle sh. for 1 Cumberland sh. (see Agnico-Eagle Mines Limited)

Cumberland Resources Nickel Corp. (B.C. Feb. 16, 2022)
Jan. 24, 2025 – Name changed to Global Defence Metals Corp. ■

Cumbre Ventures Inc. (Ont. Apr. 12, 2006)
Nov. 9, 2007 – Formed Atlas Minerals Inc. in Alberta on Qualifying Transaction reverse takeover of and amalgamation with Atlas Minerals Inc. ■

Cumex Mines Ltd. (Que. 1967)
Aug. 27, 1968 – Name changed to Pacific Nickel Mines Ltd. ■

Cumo Resources Ltd. (B.C. 1974)
Mar. 19, 1993 – Dissolved and struck off register.

Cumont Mines Ltd. (B.C. 1965)
July 1974 – Merged with Nufort Resources Ltd. to form Nufort Resources Ltd.; basis 5 new for 6 old shs.

Cumulus Technology Ltd. (B.C. Jan. 25, 1985)
Dec. 12, 1994 – Delisted from the Toronto Stock Exchange. Subsequently struck from register and dissolved for failure to file.
Aug. 1, 1999 – Name changed to Cumulus Ventures Ltd.; basis 1 new for 7 old shs.

Cunigold Mines Ltd. (Ont. 1945)
Oct. 10, 1961 – Dissolved.

Cuniptau Mines Ltd. (Ont. Dec. 1933)
1943 – Name changed to Ontario Nickel Corp. Ltd; basis 1 new for 3 old shs. ■

Cunningham Lindsey Group Inc. (Can. Mar. 12, 1987)
Dec. 20, 2007 – Acquired by Fairfax Financial Holdings Limited for $3.20 per sh.

CuOro Resources Corp. (B.C. Oct. 23, 2007)
May 30, 2014 – Name changed to Rockshield Capital Corp. ■

Cup Lake Uranium Ltd. (B.C. 1969)
Dec. 30, 1970 – Name changed to Mara Lake Mines Ltd. ■

Cup Oil Limited (Alta. 1985)
Sept. 7, 1988 – Name changed to Cup Resources Inc.; basis 1 new for 4 old shs. (see FPsurvey - Mines & Energy)

Cupra Mines Ltd. (Que. 1961)
June 1, 1969 – Assets acquired by Quebec Lithium Corp. Cash consideration of $3,172,709 distributed to shldrs. (Sullivan Mines and Sullico Mines); co. subsequently wound up.

Curator Resources Ltd. (B.C. Feb. 3, 1983)
Oct. 8, 1985 – Name changed to International Curator Resources Ltd.; basis 1 new for 3 old shs. ■

Cure Capital Corp. (B.C. Mar. 7, 2018)
Oct. 8, 2019 – Name changed to Pinnacle North Gold Corp. ■

Curion Venture Corporation (B.C. Aug. 30, 1990)
Oct. 31, 2001 – Name changed to UC Resources Ltd.; basis 1 new for 5 old shs. ■

Curis Resources Ltd. (B.C. Jan. 31, 2011)
Nov. 25, 2014 – All o/s com. shs. not already held acquired by Taseko Mines Limited; basis 0.438 Taseko com shs. for 1 Curis sh.

Curlew Lake Resources Inc. (B.C. Jan. 15, 1987)
Nov. 24, 2017 – Name changed to C21 Investments Inc. (see FPsurvey - Industrials)

Curragh Inc. (Ont. Apr. 29, 1987)
Dec. 1993 – Late in 1993, the company's assets were placed into receivership and PricewaterhouseCoopers Inc. and KPMG Inc. were appointed as receivers. The Sä Dena Hes mine and the Stronsay development property were sold to a joint venture between Cominco Ltd., Teck Corporation, Korea Zinc Co. Ltd. and the Samsung Corporation.
Nov. 1994 – Faro and Westray properties and other certain assets were sold to Anvil Range Mining Corporation for $27,000,000.
Apr. 1, 1995 – All major assets had been sold and the receivers discharged. There were no distributions made to unsecured creditors or shldrs.

Curragh Resources Inc. (Ont. Apr. 29, 1987)
May 11, 1992 – Name changed to Curragh Inc. ■

Curran Bay Resource Ltd. (Ont. Dec. 7, 1983)
Aug. 18, 1993 – Amalgamated with Primrose Gold Resources Inc. to form new co. with same name Curran Bay Resource Ltd.
Aug. 23, 1993 – Amalgamated in Ontario to continue with same name.
May 15, 2003 – Name changed to Snackie Jack's Ltd. following reverse takeover acquisition of Snackie Jack's Ltd.; basis 1 new for 19 old shs. ■

Curran Bay Resource Ltd. (Ont. 1983)
Aug. 23, 1993 – Amalgamated with Primrose Gold Resources Inc. (1 for 1) to continue as Curran Bay Resource Ltd.; basis 1 new for 1 old sh.

CurrencyWorks Inc. (Nev. July 20, 2010)
Aug. 24, 2022 – Name changed to MetaWorks Platforms, Inc.

Current Technology Corporation (B.C. 1986)
May 13, 2004 – Continued into Canada.
Mar. 11, 2013 – Dissolved and struck from register.

Currie Mines Ltd. (Ont. 1956)
Dec. 24, 1962 – Charter cancelled.

Currie Rose Resources Inc. (Ont. Aug. 24, 1973)
May 20, 1980 – Continued into Canada.
Feb. 3, 2006 – Continued into British Columbia.
Oct. 18, 2023 – Name changed to Velox Energy Materials Inc. (see FPsurvey - Mines & Energy; FPsurvey - Industrials)

Curtiss-Wright of Canada Limited (Ont. 1951)
July 7, 1986 – Amalgamated with a wholly owned subsid. of Curtiss-Wright Corporation on June 30, 1986; basis 1 new pref. sh. for 1 com. sh. Pref. shs. were redeemed at $9.25 per sh.

Cusac Gold Mines Ltd. (B.C. Nov. 19, 1965)
Apr. 21, 2008 – Acquired by Hawthorne Gold Corp.; basis 1 Hawthorne sh. for 19 Cusac shs.

Cusac Industries Ltd. (B.C. Nov. 19, 1965)
Aug. 14, 1995 – Name changed to Cusac Gold Mines Ltd. ■

Cusco Mines Ltd. (Ont. Oct. 17, 1933)
1965 – Name changed to Probe Mines Limited; basis 1 new for 4 old shs. ■

Cusil Venture Corporation (B.C. Sept. 5, 1997)
July 3, 2003 – Name changed to Innexus Biotechnology Inc. following reverse takeover acquisition of Innexus Inc. ■

Cuspis Capital II Ltd. (Ont. Sept. 3, 2019)
Feb. 21, 2025 – Name changed to IC Group Holdings Inc. pursuant to the Qualifying Transaction reverse takeover acquisition of 11197894 Canada Ltd. (dba IC Group Inc.) and concurrent amalgamation of 11197894 Canada with wholly owned 16470734 Canada Inc.; basis 1 new for 4.3103 old shs. (see FPsurvey - Industrials)

Cuspis Capital III Ltd. (Ont. Sept. 3, 2019)
Feb. 9, 2024 – Name changed to Cytophage Technologies Ltd. pursuant to the Qualifying Transaction reverse takeover acquisition of Cytophage Technologies Inc.; basis 1 new for 4.1448 old shs. (see FPsurvey - Industrials)

Cuspis Capital Ltd. (Ont. Oct. 5, 2018)
Apr. 15, 2021 – Acquired by Graphene Manufacturing Group Ltd.; basis 0.403 Graphene ordinary shs. for 1 Cuspic com. sh.

Custer Resources Inc. (B.C. 1980)
June 1, 1982 – Amalgamated with Palliser Resources Inc. (1 for 1) and Tiger Oil Corp. (1 for 2.2) to form Palliser International Energy Inc.; basis 1 new for 2.5 Custer shs.

Custom Cryogenic Grinding Corporation (Alta. Oct. 16, 1961)
June 1998 – Acquired by Pavaco Plastics Incorporated for an undisclosed amount.

Custom Direct Income Fund (Ont. Mar. 18, 2003)
June 18, 2007 – All assets acquired by EdgeStone Capital Partners, L.P. with proceeds used to redeem trust units at $10.20 per unit. Custom Direct was subsequently wound up.

Custom Petroleum Corporation (Can. Oct. 14, 1980)
Dec. 5, 1995 – Dissolved.

Cutlass Explorations Ltd. (B.C. Aug. 1, 1969)
Apr. 27, 1977 – Name changed to Great Hercules Resources Inc.; basis 1 new for 5 old shs. ■

Cutlass Industries Corporation (B.C. Nov. 16, 1983)
Jan. 9, 1996 – Name changed to Triangle Industries Ltd.; basis 1 new for 4 old shs. ■

Cutlass Resources Ltd. (B.C. Nov. 16, 1983)
Mar. 4, 1985 – Name changed to Cutlass Industries Corporation. ■

Cutty Resources Inc. (B.C. Apr. 27, 1982)
Apr. 15, 1991 – Name changed to Hatco Capital Inc. ■

Cutwater Capital Corporation (Ont. Sept. 28, 2004)
Mar. 31, 2006 – Name changed to OutdoorPartner Media Corporation following Qualifying Transaction reverse takeover acquisition of OutdoorPartner Media Canada Inc.; basis 1 new for 4 old shs. ■

Cuvier Mines Inc. (Que. 1980)
July 19, 1988 – Amalgamated with a subsid. of Kam Creed Mines Ltd. to continue under the Kam Creed Mines name; basis 1 Kam Creed sh. for 2 Cuvier shs.

Cuvier Mines Ltd. (Que. 1946)
Jan. 1, 1980 – Amalgamated with Quebec Uranium Corporation to form Cuvier Mines Inc.; basis 1 new for 1 old sh.

Cyan Corporation (Alta. Oct. 21, 1997)
Feb. 5, 2003 – Amalgamated with Cross Border Capital Inc. and Titan Digital Storage Corporation to form Titan Digital Corporation, constituting Cyan's Qualifying Transaction; basis 1 new for 1 Cross Border sh., 1 new for 1 Titan Digital Storage sh. and 0.697951 new for 1 Cyan sh. (see Titan Digital Corporation)

Cyber Digital Video Services Ltd. (Ont. 1982)
June 24, 1996 – Name changed to Racad Technologies Ltd. pursuant to reverse takeover acquisition of Racad Group Inc.; basis 1 new for 10 old shs.

CyberCom Systems Inc. (B.C. Mar. 23, 1984)
Sept. 7, 2015 – Dissolved and struck from register.

Cyberion Networking Corp. (B.C. May 27, 1988)
Dec. 30, 1998 – Name changed to NexMedia Technologies Inc. ■

Cybermedix Inc. (Ont. 1978)
Oct. 20, 1989 – Acquired by COGECO Inc. for $14.30 per sh.
Oct. 1, 1994 – Dissolved.

Cybermind Group Inc. (Ont. 1946)
May 29, 1997 – Formed InterOil Corporation in New Brunswick on amalgamation with South Pacific InterOil Limited, constituting a reverse takeover by South Pacific. ■

Cyberplex Inc. (Ont. Sept. 20, 1995)
Jan. 1, 2000 – Amalgamated in Ontario to continue with same name.
June 13, 2013 – Name changed to EQ Inc. (see FPsurvey - Industrials)

Cycle Yellowknife Gold Mines Ltd. (Ont. 1937)
1955 – Charter cancelled.

Cyclical Split NT Corp. (Ont. Oct. 24, 2003)
Dec. 16, 2008 – Redeemed pref. and cap. shs. for $25 and $118.36821 per sh., respectively.

Cyclone Capital Corp. (B.C. Apr. 24, 1987)
June 4, 1996 – Name changed to Nikos Explorations Ltd.; basis 1 new for 5 old shs. ■

Cyclone Developments Ltd. (B.C. 1960)
Sept. 30, 1982 – Amalgamated with Citlec Minerals Ltd. (1 new for 2 old shs.) and Pan Acheron Resources Ltd. (1 new for 4 old shs.) to form Acheron Resources Ltd.; basis 1 new for 3 old shs.

Cyclone Mining Co. Ltd. (B.C. 1966)
Jan. 31, 1977 – Dissolved.

Cyclonic Investments Corporation (Can. Nov. 22, 1996)
Feb. 11, 1999 – Name changed to Imaflex Inc. following reverse takeover acquisition of (old) Imaflex Inc. (see FPsurvey - Industrials)

Cyclops Gas Syndicate (unknown)
1934 – Amalgamated with Regal Gas Syndicate to form Firelite Gas & Oil Co. Ltd.

Cyclops Mining Co. Ltd. (B.C. 1950)
July 1954 – Dissolved.

Cycomm International Inc. (Ont. 1968)
Oct. 14, 1995 – Continued into Wyoming.

Cygnal Technologies Corporation (Ont. Sept. 20, 1984)
Apr. 2, 2008 – Acquired by CYN Holdings, LLC following court-supervised restructuring.

Cygnus Corporation Limited (Can. 1964)
Dec. 21, 1979 – Amalgamated with Home Oil Company Limited and a wholly owned subsid. of Consumers' Gas to form new co. Home Oil Company Limited; basis $29.25 or 1.17 Consumers' Gas 7.5% conv. pref. shs. for 1 Cygnus sh. (see Home Oil Company Limited)

Cylinder Enterprises Limited (Alta. Aug. 3, 1995)
Feb. 16, 2000 – Name changed to Mondev Senior Living Inc. pursuant to reverse takeover acquisition of Mondev Senior Living Inc. ■

Cyll Industries Limited (B.C. 1984)
Dec. 22, 1988 – Name changed to Consolidated Cyll Industries Limited; basis 1 new for 3 old shs. ■

Cymat Corp. (Ont. June 30, 1998 amalg.)
Aug. 8, 2006 – Name changed to Cymat Technologies Ltd. pursuant to plan of arrangement whereby Cymat Corp. transferred to newly created Cymat Technologies Ltd. all assets and liabilities except future tax assets, plus $1,600,000 in cash. Cymat Corp. shldrs. received 1 Cymat Technologies sh. for each sh. held. (see FPsurvey - Industrials)

Cymbal Explorations Inc. (Ont. Oct. 29, 1979)
Mar. 1986 – Name changed to Cymbal Resource Corporation; basis 1 new for 5 old shs. ■

Cymbal Resource Corporation (Ont. Oct. 29, 1979)
Apr. 4, 1995 – Name changed to International Legacy Inc.; basis 0.2 subord. vtg. and 0.8 multiple vtg. for 1 com. sh. ■

Cymric Resources Limited (Can. Sept. 23, 1983 amalg.)
Dec. 20, 1988 – Name changed to The Rimoil Corporation; basis 1 new for 5 old shs. ■

Cyn-Tech Ventures Inc. (B.C. July 25, 1986)
June 29, 1995 – Name changed to Consolidated Cyn-Tech Ventures Ltd.; basis 1 new for 5 old shs. ■

Cynapsus Therapeutics Inc. (Can. Mar. 15, 2006 amalg.)
Oct. 24, 2014 – Acquired by Sunovion Pharmaceuticals Inc.; basis US$40.50 cash per sh.

Cyntar Ventures Inc. (B.C. July 18, 2017)
Mar. 24, 2021 – Name changed to Clearmind Medicine Inc. (see FPsurvey - Industrials)

Cyon Exploration Ltd. (B.C. May 20, 1988)
Sept. 13, 2021 – Name changed to Gold State Resources Inc. ■

Cypango Ventures Ltd. (Alta. Feb. 13, 1980)
Feb. 24, 2000 – Name changed to Techsite Strategies Corp.; basis 1 new for 10 old shs. ■

Cypherpunk Holdings Inc. (Ont. Oct. 1, 2002)
Sept. 12, 2024 – Name changed to Sol Strategies Inc. (see FPsurvey - Industrials)

Cypress Development Corp. (B.C. Oct. 24, 1995)
Jan. 30, 2023 – Name changed to Century Lithium Corp. (see FPsurvey - Mines & Energy)

Cypress Drilling Ltd. (Alta. Mar. 25, 1985)
June 17, 1987 – Name changed to Precision Drilling (1987) Ltd. following acquisition of a private co.; basis 1 new for 5 old shs. ∎

Cypress Energy Inc. (Alta. Nov. 16, 1995)
Apr. 11, 2001 – Acquired by and amalgamated with PrimeWest Oil & Gas Corp.; basis $14, 1.45 PrimeWest Energy Trust units or 1.45 PrimeWest Oil exch. shs. for 1 Cypress cl. A and cl. B sh. (see PrimeWest Energy Trust)

Cypress Hills Resource Corp. (Yuk. June 27, 2001)
July 26, 2005 – Continued into Alberta.
Apr. 9, 2021 – Continued into British Columbia. (see FPsurvey - Mines & Energy)

Cypress Minerals Corp. (B.C. Oct. 24, 1995)
Sept. 16, 1999 – Name changed to Cypress Development Corp.; basis 1 new for 9 old shs. ∎

Cypress Oil Company, Limited (Can. 1927)
1940 – Name changed to O.K. Copper Gold Mines Ltd. and continued into British Columbia. ∎

Cypress Petroleum Corp. (Sask. Aug. 23, 1991)
Oct. 24, 1995 – Continued into British Columbia.
Oct. 26, 1995 – Name changed to Cypress Minerals Corp. ∎

Cyprium Mining Corporation (Can. Feb. 17, 2005)
Feb. 2, 2019 – Dissolved.

Cyprus Anvil Mining Corporation (B.C. 1965)
1975 – Amalgamated in British Columbia to continue with same name. (see Amoco Canada Petroleum Company; Hudson's Bay Oil and Gas Company Limited)
June 1, 1981 – Acquired by Hudson's Bay Oil and Gas Company Limited for $44.25 per sh. (see Amoco Canada Petroleum Company; Hudson's Bay Oil and Gas Company Limited)

Cyprus Capital Corporation (Can. May 2, 1996)
Feb. 7, 2001 – Name changed to Everest Energy Corporation following Qualifying Transaction reverse takeover acquisition of Everest Energy Inc. ∎

Cyprus Mines Ltd. (Ont. 1945)
1968 – Name changed to Nemo Mines Ltd. ∎

Cyprus Resources Limited (B.C. 1957)
Feb. 28, 1977 – Name changed to Pacific Cypress Minerals Ltd. ∎

Cyrano Resources Inc. (B.C. Sept. 15, 1980)
Nov. 14, 1985 – Formed Cornucopia Resources Ltd. in British Columbia on amalgamation with Cornucopia Resources Ltd.; basis 1 new for 2 old shs. ∎

Cyries Energy Inc. (Alta. May 20, 2004)
Mar. 14, 2008 – Acquired by Iteration Energy Ltd.; basis 1.62 Iteration shs. for 1 Cyries sh. (see Iteration Energy Ltd.)
Jan. 1, 2010 – Amalgamated with Iteration Energy Ltd. (see Iteration Energy Ltd.)

Cyril Knight Prospecting Co. Ltd. (Can. 1928)
Charter cancelled.

Cyterra Capital Corp. (B.C. July 27, 2009)
Mar. 8, 2012 – Name changed to CaiTerra International Energy Corporation pursuant to Qualifying Transaction reverse takeover acquisition of West Pacific Petroleum Inc.'s 100% interests in the Lac La Biche and Amadou projects. ∎

Cytiva Software Inc. (B.C. Apr. 21, 1999)
Apr. 1, 2011 – Acquired by Taleo Corporation for 42¢ per sh.

Cytovax Biotechnologies Inc. (Can. Apr. 1, 1998)
Dec. 8, 2004 – Name changed to Millenium Biologix Corporation following reverse takeover acquisition of Millenium Biologix Inc. ∎

Cytrigen International Inc. (Ont. 1977)
Jan. 5, 1988 – Continued into Canada.
Dec. 9, 1999 – Dissolved and struck from register.

Czar Resources Ltd. (Alta. Apr. 11, 1974)
Dec. 6, 1995 – Acquired by Ranger Oil Limited for $1.55 per sh. (see Ranger Oil Limited)

D

D-Fense Capital ltée (Can. Feb. 17, 2005)
Apr. 19, 2013 – Name changed to Freyja Resources Inc. ∎

D2L Holdings Inc. (Ont. Jan. 2, 2011)
June 20, 2014 – Name changed to D2L Inc. and continued into Canada. (see FPsurvey - Industrials)

D. A. Stuart Ltd. (Ont. May 20, 1936)
Feb. 23, 1995 – Acquired by Werhahn International Inc. for $8.50 per sh.

D.A. Stuart Oil Co., Limited (Ont. May 20, 1936)
Oct. 20, 1986 – Name changed to D. A. Stuart Ltd. ∎

DALSA Corporation (Ont. Jan. 16, 1996)
Feb. 22, 2011 – Name changed to Teledyne DALSA, Inc. following acquisition by Teledyne Technologies Incorporated for $18.25 per sh.

D.A.S. Electronics Industries Inc. (Ont. Apr. 26, 1966)
Oct. 25, 1993 – Name changed to The Pace Corporation following reverse takeover acquisition of Pace Environs Inc.; basis 1 new for 25 old shs. ∎

DATA Group Ltd. (Ont. Mar. 7, 2011)
July 4, 2016 – Name changed to DATA Communications Management Corp.; basis 1 new for 100 old shs. (see FPsurvey - Industrials)

DC Acquisition Corp. (B.C. Nov. 28, 2017)
Oct. 20, 2020 – Name changed to Kiaro Holdings Corp. pursuant to the Qualifying Transaction reverse takeover acquisition of Kiaro Brands Inc. and concurrent amalgamation of Kiaro Brands with wholly owned 1251542 B.C. Ltd.; basis 1 new for 1.7142857 old shs. (see FPsurvey - Industrials)

D.C. Corrosion Corporation (Alta. July 2, 1987)
June 10, 1999 – Name changed to Total Telcom Inc. (see FPsurvey - Industrials)

DC DiagnostiCare Inc. (B.C. July 15, 1996 amalg.)
Mar. 13, 2002 – Acquired by Diagnosticare Acquisition Limited, a wholly owned subsid. of Canadian Medical Laboratories Limited, for 60¢ per sh. (see Canadian Medical Laboratories Limited)

DCB Capital Inc. (Que. Feb. 22, 2006)
Oct. 3, 2006 – Formed Opsens Inc. in Quebec following Qualifying Transaction reverse takeover acquisition of and amalgamation with Opsens inc. ∎

DCS International Systems Corporation (B.C. Jan. 12, 1987)
June 10, 1993 – Name changed to Step 2 Software Corporation; basis 1 new for 5 old shs. ∎

DDJ Canadian High Yield Fund (Ont. Aug. 15, 1997)
Nov. 28, 2005 – Name changed to DDJ High Yield Fund. ∎

DDJ High Yield Fund (Ont. Aug. 15, 1997)
Aug. 15, 2017 – Terminated; distribution of $10.450215 cash per trust unit.

DDJ U.S. High Yield Fund (Ont. Aug. 19, 2003)
May 25, 2006 – Redeemed for Cdn$8.6227 per unit.

DDS Wireless International Inc. (B.C. Sept. 28, 1987)
July 4, 2014 – Acquired by 0998556 B.C. Ltd., a wholly owned subsid. of Ghai Investments Ltd., for $2.25 per sh.

DEB Canadian Explorations 1977 (Can. - unspecified 1977)
Feb. 8, 1989 – All assets sold and the partnership dissolved.

DEB Canadian Explorations 1978 (Alta. Aug. 15, 1978)
Feb. 8, 1989 – All assets sold during 1988 and the limited partnership dissolved.

DEKALB Energy Company (Del. 1970)
May 17, 1995 – Merged into Apache Corporation of Houston, Tex.; basis 0.8764 Apache com. shs. for 1 DEKALB cl. B sh.

DEQ Systems Corp. (Can. July 12, 2002)
Jan. 24, 2017 – Acquired by Scientific Games Corporation; basis Cdn$0.38 cash per sh.

D.F.I. Ventures Ltd. (B.C. Apr. 28, 1986)
Jan. 17, 1989 – Name changed to National Quick Lube Ltd. pursuant to reverse takeover acquisition of National Quick Lube, Inc.; basis 1 new for 2 old shs. ∎

D.G. Jewellry of Canada Ltd. (Can. Jan. 21, 1979)
Apr. 18, 1988 – Continued into Ontario.
Aug. 11, 1999 – Name changed to D.G. Jewelry Inc.

DGE Technologies Corporation (Alta. 1987)
Dec. 3, 1990 – Name changed to DKW Systems Corporation. ∎

DGM Minerals Corp. (B.C. Sept. 21, 2010)
Apr. 24, 2014 – Name changed to Less Mess Storage Inc. pursuant to reverse takeover acquisiton of Krakowska House Sp.zo.o, Torunska House Sp.zo.o, Selvang Evropska Building a.s., City Self-Storage Sp.zo.o and City Self-Storage s.r.o.; basis 1 new for 12 old shs. ∎

DGS Minerals Inc. (B.C. Sept. 24, 1990)
Jan. 31, 2017 – Name changed to Dragon Legend Entertainment (Canada) Inc. pursuant to the reverse takeover acquisition of the assets of Dragon Legend Entertainment Inc. ∎

DH Corporation (Ont. Apr. 28, 2010)
June 16, 2017 – Amalgamated with Misys Limited an affiliate of Vista Equity Partners Management LLC; basis $25.50 cash per sh.

D. H. Howden & Co. Limited (Ont. 1907)
Aug. 14, 1987 – Acquired by Sodisco Inc. (see Sodisco Inc.; Unigesco Inc.)

DHX Media Ltd. (N.S. Feb. 12, 2004)
Apr. 25, 2006 – Continued into Canada.
Dec. 18, 2019 – Name changed to WildBrain Ltd. (see FPsurvey - Industrials)

D.K. Platinum Corporation (B.C. 1983)
Apr. 2, 1990 – Name changed to TEGL Systems Corporation. ∎

DKW Systems Corporation (Alta. 1987)
July 21, 1998 – Acquired by APG Solutions & Technology Inc. for 47¢ per sh.

DLP Diversified Ltd. (Can. 1969)
July 1971 – Name changed to Consolidated DLP Limited; basis 1 new for 2 old shs. ∎

DLP Resources (2020) Limited (Alta. Nov. 9, 2017)
Jan. 26, 2021 – Name changed to DLP Resources Inc. (see FPsurvey - Mines & Energy)

DLV Resources Ltd. (B.C. Nov. 27, 2017)
Dec. 29, 2022 – Name changed to West Red Lake Gold Mines Ltd. pursuant to the reverse takeover acquisition

of West Red Lake Gold Mines Inc. (see FPsurvey - Mines & Energy)

DMD Digital Health Connections Group Inc. (Can. Apr. 1, 2005)
Oct. 10, 2018 – Privatized via acquisition by 10653365 Canada Inc., a company controlled by insiders of DMD, and subsequent amalg. with DMD Connects Services Inc.; basis (i) 25¢ cash per com. sh., or (ii) 1 cl. B 10653365 Canada com. sh. for 1 DMD com. sh.
Oct. 11, 2018 – Name changed to DMDConnects Services Inc.

DMI Technology Inc. (Alta. Nov. 24, 1993)
May 2, 2009 – Struck from the registry and dissolved.

DMR Consulting Group Inc. (Can. Feb. 26, 1973)
2000 – Name changed to DMR Consulting Inc. ∎

DMR Consulting Inc. (Can. Feb. 26, 1973)
Apr. 1, 2002 – Name changed to Fujitsu Consulting Inc.

DMR Group Inc. (Can. Feb. 26, 1973)
Dec. 6, 1995 – Acquired by Amdahl Canada Acquisition Inc., a wholly owned subsid. of Amdahl Canada Limited, for $12.50 per sh.
Jan. 16, 1997 – Name changed to DMR Consulting Group Inc. ∎

DMR Resources Ltd. (Ont. 1981)
Oct. 20, 2008 – Dissolved.

DNI Holdings Inc. (B.C. 1967)
Sept. 3, 1993 – Dissolved and struck off register.

DOJA Cannabis Company Limited (B.C. Dec. 20, 2011)
Jan. 31, 2018 – Name changed to Hiku Brands Company Ltd. following acquisition of TS Brandco Holdings Inc. ∎

D1 Capital Corp. (B.C. Oct. 10, 2017)
Feb. 10, 2021 – Name changed to Gemina Laboratories Ltd. pursuant to the reverse takeover acquisition of Ecoscreen Solutions Inc. and concurrent amalgamation of Ecoscreen with wholly owned 1272305 B.C. Ltd. (see FPsurvey - Industrials)

DPC Biosciences Corporation (Ont. Sept. 25, 1995 amalg.)
Sept. 14, 2006 – Name changed to iGaming Corporation following acquisition of certain assets from Global Market Focus Inc. ∎

DPF India Opportunities Fund (Ont. July 13, 2007)
June 12, 2014 – Converted to an open-end mutual fund.

DPI Technologies Inc. (Can. Feb. 11, 1998)
Aug. 16, 1999 – Name changed to Dynex Power Inc. ∎

DPVC Inc. (Can. June 3, 2008)
Oct. 19, 2010 – Name changed to TitanStar Properties Inc. ∎

DRAXIS Health Inc. (Can. Oct. 13, 1987)
May 30, 2008 – Acquired by Jubilant Organosys Ltd. for US$6.00 per com. sh.

DRC Resources Corporation (B.C. Jan. 31, 1980)
June 1, 2005 – Name changed to New Gold Inc. (see FPsurvey - Mines & Energy)

DRG Inc. (Can. 1933)
1982 – Continued into British Columbia.
Aug. 14, 1987 – Delisted following acquisition of all o/s shs. by DRG plc, through an indirect wholly owned subsid. Shares acquired under purchase offer at $27 per share.

DRG Limited (Can. 1933)
Apr. 23, 1981 – Name changed to DRG Inc. ∎

DRM Ventures Inc. (Ont. Aug. 24, 2009)
Nov. 24, 2011 – Dissolved following Qualifying Transaction private placement purchase of 4,264,706 shs. of Patient Home Monitoring Corp.
Dec. 15, 2011 – Dissolved.

DRW Environmental Technologies Inc. (Alta. 1987)
Apr. 1, 1997 – Dissolved and struck from register.

DSI DataTech Systems Inc. (B.C. May 7, 1987)
May 14, 2001 – Continued into Canada.
July 6, 2005 – Dissolved and struck from register.

DTI Dental Technologies Inc. (B.C. May 30, 1997)
Sept. 26, 2006 – Acquired by 1252771 Alberta Ltd., an affiliate of HealthPointCapital, LLC; basis $1.60 per sh.

DTM Information Technology Group Inc. (Can. Dec. 1, 1993 amalg.)
Jan. 10, 2001 – Name changed to Nexxlink Technologies Inc. ∎

DTS Capital Corporation (Alta. Mar. 2, 1987)
May 16, 1990 – Name changed to Petroleum Capital Energy Inc.; basis 1 new for 5 old shs. ∎

DUSA Pharmaceuticals, Inc. (N.J. Feb. 21, 1991)
Dec. 21, 2012 – Acquired by Caraco Pharmaceutical Laboratories, Ltd. for US$8.00 per sh.

DV Resources Ltd. (Ont. Dec. 21, 1979 amalg.)
Nov. 27, 2017 – Name changed to DLV Resources Ltd. and continued into British Columbia. ∎

DVD Investments Limited (Ont. Feb. 10, 2005)
Oct. 22, 2007 – Name changed to Mooncor Oil & Gas Corp. following reverse takeover acquisition of Mooncor Energy Inc. ∎

DVR Resources Ltd. (B.C. Oct. 5, 1987)
June 14, 1993 – Name changed to Gresham Resources Inc.; basis 1 new for 4.5 old shs. ∎

DXI Capital Corp. (B.C. Aug. 16, 2005)
July 18, 2025 – Name changed to VVT Med Inc. pursuant to the reverse takeover acquisition of V.V.T. Med Ltd. and Exiteam Acquisition Corp.; basis 1 new for 4.67 old shs. (see FPsurvey - Industrials)

DXI Energy Inc. (B.C. Aug. 16, 2005)
Sept. 11, 2020 – Name changed to DXI Capital Corp.; basis 1 new for 100 old shs. ∎

DY 4 Systems Inc. (Ont. Oct. 9, 1979)
Dec. 19, 2000 – Acquired by C-Mac Industries Inc. for $17 per sh. (see C-MAC Industries Inc.)

Da Capo Resources Ltd. (B.C. Mar. 24, 1986)
Nov. 12, 1996 – Amalgamated with Granges Inc. (1 for 1) which continued with the new name Vista Gold Corp.; basis 1 new for 2 old shs. (see Vista Gold Corp.)

Da-Kerr-Ad Consolidated Mines Ltd. (Que. 1943)
May 1974 – Charter cancelled.

Dablon Mining Corp. Ltd. (Can. 1936)
Dec. 16, 1980 – Dissolved.

Dacha Capital Inc. (Can. Apr. 3, 1996)
Sept. 28, 2010 – Name changed to Dacha Strategic Metals Inc. ∎

Dacha Strategic Metals Inc. (Can. Apr. 3, 1996)
Aug. 20, 2014 – All com. shs. redeemed in exchange for 0.842 Merus Labs International Inc. com. shs. per 1 Dacha sh., equivalent to US$0.1777 per sh. Dacha would subsequently be wound up. (see Merus Labs International Inc.)

Dack Creek Mines Ltd. (Ont. 1943)
Nov. 5, 1962 – Dissolved.

Dadson Lake Chibougamau Mines Ltd. (Que. 1956)
1960 – Name changed to Saucon Development Corp. ∎

Daedalian eSolutions Inc. (Ont. Dec. 6, 2000 amalg.)
Jan. 31, 2002 – Acquired by wholly owned subsid. of TELUS Corporation for 17¢ payable in TELUS non-vtg. shs. for 1 Daedalian com. sh. Subsequently amalgamated on Jan. 31, 2002.

Daer Gold Mines Ltd. (B.C. Dec. 21, 1987)
Nov. 28, 1991 – Name changed to I.M.P.A.C.T. Minerals Inc. ∎

Daering Explorers Corporation Limited (Ont. 1931)
July 12, 1971 – Name changed to Consolidated Daering Enterprises & Mining Inc.; basis 1 new for 4 old shs. ∎

Dagilev Capital Corp. (B.C. Dec. 12, 2007)
June 4, 2010 – Name changed to Astur Gold Corp. following Qualifying Transaction acquisition of Exploraciones Mineras del Cantábrico, S.A. ∎

Dagobah Ventures Ltd. (B.C. Nov. 10, 2014)
July 10, 2018 – Name changed to Clear Blue Technologies International Inc. and continued into Ontario following reverse takeover acquistion of Clear Blue Technologies Inc. and amalgamation of Clear Blue Technologies with a wholly owned subsidiary of Dagobah Ventures Ltd. (see FPsurvey - Industrials)

Dai-Ichi Kangyo Bank (Canada) (Can. Jan. 21, 1982)
Nov. 1, 2000 – Amalgamated with The Industrial Bank of Japan (Canada) to form Mizuho Bank (Canada). (see Mizuho Bank (Canada))

Daimler AG (Germany May 6, 1998)
Feb. 1, 2022 – Name changed to Mercedes-Benz Group AG.

Daimler Resources Inc. (B.C. 1982)
May 27, 1994 – Dissolved and struck off register.

DaimlerChrysler Canada Inc. (Can. June 17, 1925)
Aug. 3, 2007 – Name changed to Chrysler Canada Inc. ∎

DaimlerChrysler Financial Services (debis) Canada Inc. (Can. Jan. 1, 2000 amalg.)
Dec. 2, 2002 – Name changed to DaimlerChrysler Services Canada Inc. ∎

DaimlerChrysler Services Canada Inc. (Can. Jan. 1, 2000 amalg.)
Jan. 1, 2006 – Name changed to DaimlerChrysler Financial Services Canada Inc.

Daine Mining Corp. Ltd. (Que. 1950)
1957 – Name changed to Cable Mines & Oils Ltd.; basis 1 new for 6 old shs. ∎

Dairy Barn Stores of Canada Limited (Que. 1971)
Nov. 3, 1973 – Charter cancelled.

Dairy Corporation of Canada, Ltd. (Ont. 1929)
Feb. 26, 1945 – Name changed to Silverwood Western Dairies Limited following acquisition of all o/s com. shs. by Silverwood Dairies, Limited; basis 1 new for 1 old sh. ∎

Daisyfresh Creations Inc. (Que. 1934)
1981 – Reverted private co. status.

Dajaty Mines Ltd. (Ont. 1945)
Oct. 2, 1968 – Dissolved.

Dajin Lithium Corp. (B.C. Aug. 5, 1987)
Jan. 13, 2022 – Formed HeliosX Technologies Corp. in British Columbia pursuant to amalgamation with HeliosX Corp. ∎

Dajin Resources Corp. (B.C. Aug. 5, 1987)
Jan. 20, 2020 – Name changed to Dajin Lithium Corp. ∎

Dakar Resource Corp. (B.C. Oct. 21, 2010)
Feb. 27, 2014 – Name changed to Jericho Oil Corporation. ∎

Dakon Metals Inc. (B.C. June 1, 1964)
Oct. 19, 1990 – Dissolved and struck off register.

Dakota Energy Corp. (B.C. 1979)
June 19, 1987 – Name changed to Consolidated Dakota Resources Ltd. ∎

Dakota Metals Corp. (B.C. June 1, 1964)
June 8, 1982 – Name changed to Condaka Metals Corp. ■

Dakota Mining Corporation (Can. Dec. 16, 1988)
Feb. 1999 – Defaulted on payments of interest on its 7.5% conv. debs.
May 1999 – Wholly owned USMX of Alaska, Inc., the company's sole producing subsid., voluntarily filed for reorganization under Chapter 11 of the U.S. Bankruptcy Code.
July 19, 1999 – Filed for bankruptcy under the Bankruptcy and Insolvency Act (Canada) following unsuccessful attempts to restructure its debt and to solicit new financing to facilitate the startup of mining operations. All directors resigned. Vancouver-based KPMG Inc. was appointed trustee.
May 27, 2003 – Trustee discharged. No distributions made to shldrs.

Dakota Resources Limited (Alta. Feb. 18, 1987)
June 3, 1998 – Name changed to Dynamix Corporation. ■

Dakota Silver Mines Ltd. (B.C. June 1, 1964)
Aug. 26, 1974 – Charter cancelled and co. dissolved.
Dec. 3, 1979 – Charter and company revived.
Feb. 21, 1980 – Name changed to Dakota Metals Corp. ■

Dal Duverny Gold Mines Limited (Ont. 1945)
1952 – Charter cancelled.

Dalby-Larder Gold Mines Ltd. (Can.)
1960 – Charter cancelled.

Dalco Petroleum Ltd. (Alta. May 31, 1979 amalg.)
Apr. 15, 1982 – Name changed to Dynex Petroleum Ltd. ■

Dale Estate Ltd. (Ont. Oct. 20, 1961)
Mar. 3, 1965 – Name changed to Calvert-Dale Estates Ltd. ■

Dale Gold Mines Ltd. (Ont. 1945)
Aug. 1961 – Charter cancelled.

Dale Mountain Mines Ltd. (Ont. 1957)
Dec. 28, 1964 – Charter cancelled.

Dale-Parizeau inc. (Can. Oct. 29, 1964; via Dominion charter)
Jan. 1, 1991 – Amalgamated with a wholly owned subsid. Dale & Company Ltd. to continue with the same name Dale-Parizeau inc.
Apr. 15, 1995 – All o/s pfd. ser. A shs. redeemed as of; basis $10 per sh. plus a premium of $0.60 plus an accrued dividend of $0.06. Co. now private.

Dale-Ross Holdings Limited (Can. Oct. 29, 1964; via Dominion charter)
Aug. 1980 – Sodarcan Limited, a private co. purchased over 90% of o/s com. shs. for $21 per sh. Remaining com. shs. acquired under provisions of the Companies Act.
May 27, 1986 – Name changed to Dale-Parizeau inc. following acquisition of Gerard-Parizeau. ■

Daleco Resources Corporation (Ont. Feb. 28, 1986)
Oct. 1, 1996 – Continued into Delaware.

Dalex Co. Limited (Ont. 1952)
Dec. 31, 1952 – Amalgamated with its wholly owned subsid. Dalex Industries Limited to continue under the same name; basis 1 cl. A sh. for 1 com. sh.

Dalex Mines Ltd. (B.C. 1966)
Jan. 17, 1977 – Dissolved.

Dalfen's Limited (Que. 1959)
Apr. 30, 1993 – All o/s shs. repurchased for $2.20 per sh. Co. now private.

Dalhart Beryllium Mines & Metals Ltd. (Ont. 1956)
1960 – Assets acquired by Canhart Mines Ltd.; basis 1 Canhart share for 10 Dalhart shs.

Dalhart Minerals Corp. Ltd. (Ont. 1956)
1957 – Name changed to Dalhart Beryllium Mines & Metals Ltd. ■

Dalhat Mines Ltd. (B.C.)
July 2, 1975 – Dissolved.

Dalier Resources Ltd. (Can. Apr. 26, 1926; via Dominion charter)
Oct. 25, 1994 – Name changed to Vescan Equities Inc. ■

Daljo Gold Mines Ltd. (Ont. 1946)
Dec. 1962 – Charter cancelled.

Dallas Enviro-Health Systems Ltd. (B.C. Dec. 23, 1983)
Jan. 16, 1996 – Name changed to Accu-Chem Laboratories International Ltd.; basis 1 new for 10 old shs. ■

Dallas Oil Co., Ltd. (unknown)
Aug. 1929 – Taken over by Calmont Oils, Ltd.; basis 1 new for 3 old shs. (see Calmont Oils Limited)

Dallas Petroleum Resources Inc. (Ont. May 14, 1981)
July 4, 1988 – Name changed to AML International Inc. ■

Dallas Yellowknife Gold Mines Ltd. (Ont. 1945)
1954 – Charter cancelled.

Dally Development Corp. (Ont. May 14, 1985)
July 7, 1993 – Name changed to TNK Resources Inc. ■

Dalmac Energy Inc. (Alta. July 23, 2003)
Jan. 27, 2020 – Placed into receivership by secured lender. The Bowra Group Inc. appointed receiver.

Dalmatian Resources Ltd. (B.C. June 26, 1979)
Feb. 18, 2002 – Name changed to Enwest Ventures Corp.; basis 1 new for 3 old shs. ■

Dalmys (Canada) Limited (Can. Aug. 5, 1971)
Mar. 7, 1996 – Following Plan of Arrangement and reorganization of share capital, all o/s com. and cl. C non-vtg. shs. converted into 1 redeem. pref. sh. immediately redeemed for 25¢ per sh. and became a unit of Reitmans (Canada) Ltd.

Dalpas Gold Mines Limited (Ont. 1947)
1952 – Charter cancelled.

Dalphine Enterprises Ltd. (B.C. Apr. 2, 1980)
Dec. 10, 1993 – Name changed to Inflazyme Pharmaceuticals Ltd. ■

Dalradian Resources Inc. (Ont. Mar. 27, 2009)
Sept. 10, 2018 – All com. shs. except those held by certain members of the Dalradian senior management team, Sean Roosen and Osisko Gold Royalties Ltd. were acquired by Orion Resource Partners (USA) LP, an affiliate of Orion Mine Finance; basis $1.47 cash per sh.

Dalray Yellowknife Gold Mines Ltd. (Ont. 1945)
1956 – Charter cancelled.

Dalton Development Ltd. (B.C. 1969)
Mar. 31, 1983 – Dissolved.

Dalton Enterprises Ltd. (B.C. 1983)
Jan. 17, 1995 – Continued into Wyoming.
Mar. 1, 1996 – Name changed to Dalton Specialties Ltd. and continued into Delaware.

Dalton Resources Ltd. (B.C. 1969)
May 24, 1973 – Name changed to Dalton Development Ltd. ■

Dalton Resources Ltd. (Alta. July 20, 1993)
Mar. 15, 1996 – Amalgamated with Piper Petroleums Ltd. (1 new for 3.5 old cl. A shs.) to form a new company also known as Dalton Resources Ltd.; basis 1 com. sh. for 1 com. sh. (see Dalton Resources Ltd.)

Dalton Resources Ltd. (Alta. Mar. 15, 1996)
Nov. 20, 2000 – Amalgamated with Tiverton Petroleums Ltd.; basis 0.78 new Tiverton sh. for 1 old Dalton sh. (see Tiverton Petroleums Ltd.)

Damara Gold Corp. (B.C. Aug. 1, 1989 amalg.)
July 18, 2024 – Name changed to Bronco Resources Corp.; basis 1 new for 4 old shs. (see FPsurvey - Mines & Energy)

Damascus Mines Limited (Ont. 1946)
Mar. 1960 – Dissolved.

Damascus Resources Ltd. (B.C. Apr. 5, 1968)
July 26, 1982 – Name changed to International Damascus Resources Ltd.; basis 1 new for 4 old shs. ■

Damian Capital Corp. (Alta. Feb. 17, 1995)
May 15, 2006 – Name changed to CPVC Financial Inc. ■

Damon Capital Corp. (B.C. May 12, 2011)
Nov. 16, 2016 – Name changed to Arizona Silver Exploration Inc. following Qualifying Transaction acquisition of Arizona Silver Corporation. ■

Dan Krech Productions Inc. (Ont. June 24, 1985)
July 1, 1996 – Continued into Nova Scotia. Name changed to IDT Entertainment Canada, Corp. ■

Danacore Industries Inc. (B.C. Jan. 10, 2018)
Dec. 20, 2019 – Name changed to Bay Talent Group Inc. pursuant to the Qualifying Transaction reverse takeover acquisition of (old) Bay Talent Group Inc. and concurrent amalgamation of (old) Bay Talent with wholly owned Danacore Acquisition Corp. (and continued as BTG Holdco Inc.); basis 1 new for 2 old shs. ■

Danaray Uranium Mines Ltd. (Ont. 1949)
Apr. 1, 1963 – Charter cancelled.

Danavation Technologies Corp. (B.C. June 4, 2007)
Oct. 20, 2022 – Continued into Ontario. (see FPsurvey - Industrials)

Danbel Industries Corporation (Ont. Dec. 21, 1998)
Dec. 16, 2011 – Name changed to Danbel Ventures Inc.; basis 1 new for 10 old shs. ■

Danbel Ventures Inc. (Ont. Dec. 21, 1998)
Apr. 20, 2017 – Name changed to Maricann Group Inc. ■

Danbus Memory Systems Incorporated (Calif. Aug. 11, 1988)
Jan. 6, 1989 – Name changed to Danbus Magnetic Systems, Inc.; basis 2 new for 1 old sh.

Danbus Resources Inc. (B.C. 1985)
Aug. 11, 1988 – Continued into California.
Aug. 12, 1988 – Formed Danbus Memory Systems Incorporated on amalgamation with Magnum Technology Corporation; basis 2 new for 1 old sh. ■

Dancap Resources Inc. (Alta. Apr. 8, 1994)
Sept. 19, 1997 – Name changed to Storm Energy Inc. following reverse takeover acquisition of Storm Energy Corporation; basis 2.13725 new for 1 old sh. ■

Dancer Energy & Resource Corp. (B.C. Feb. 26, 1981)
Apr. 3, 1987 – Delisted from the Vancouver Stock Exchange. Subsequently dissolved for failure to file and struck from register.

Dancing Star Resources Ltd. (B.C. Apr. 19, 1973)
July 9, 2003 – Name changed to Alcor Resources Ltd.; basis 1 new for 2 old shs. ■

Danco Industries Ltd. (B.C. 1975)
Oct. 27, 2008 – Dissolved and struck from register.

Dangerfield Resources Inc. (Alta. Oct. 23, 1986)
July 15, 1994 – Amalgamated with Remington Energy Ltd.; basis 75¢ plus 0.20 Remington shs., or 0.40 Remington shs. for 1 Dangerfield sh. (see Remington Energy Ltd.)

Daniel Diversified Ltd. (Ont. 1958)
Aug. 29, 1983 – Name changed to Kaolin of Canada Inc. (see FPsurvey - Mines & Energy)

Daniel Mining Co. Ltd. (Ont. 1958)
1969 – Name changed to Daniel Diversified Ltd. ■

Daniel Resources Inc. (Ont. 1982)
July 13, 1987 – Continued into Ontario.
July 23, 1993 – Name changed to Zlin Aerospace Inc. (see FPsurvey - Industrials)

Daniel Silver Mining Co. Ltd. (Ont. 1936)
July 2, 1957 – Charter cancelled.

Danier Leather Inc. (Ont. June 30, 1972)
Mar. 21, 2016 – Voluntarily filed for bankruptcy under the Bankruptcy and Insolvency Act (BIA). KSV Kofman Inc. appointed trustee and all officers and directors resigned.

Danis Quebec Gold Mines Ltd. (Ont. 1946)
Jan. 1957 – Charter cancelled.

Dankoe Mines Ltd. (B.C. Mar. 24, 1937)
Oct. 30, 1996 – Name changed to Emerald Dragon Mines Inc.; basis 1 new for 5 old shs. ■

Danlou Mines Ltd. (Ont. 1958)
Oct. 22, 1965 – Dissolved.

Danoil Energy Ltd. (Alta. Sept. 1, 1995 amalg.)
Apr. 20, 2001 – Formed Acclaim Energy Trust pursuant to plan of arrangement whereby Danoil amalgamated with Nevis Ltd., a wholly owned subsidiary of Western Facilities Fund, to form Acclaim Energy Inc. with Danoil the deemed acquiror and Western Facilities changed its name to Acclaim Energy Trust; basis 1 new trust unit for 14 Western Facilities trust units and 1 new trust unit for 1 Danoil cl. A com. sh. ■

Danra Resources Limited (Ont. 1984)
Mar. 27, 2006 – Certification of incorporation cancelled and dissolved.

Danrod Malartic Mines Ltd. (Ont. 1945)
1956 – Charter cancelled.

Danstar Mines Ltd. (B.C. Apr. 19, 1973)
May 4, 1983 – Name changed to Danstar Resources Ltd. ■

Danstar Resources Ltd. (B.C. Apr. 19, 1973)
May 21, 1992 – Name changed to Star Dance Resources Ltd.; basis 1 new for 4.4 old shs. ■

Dante Red Lake Gold Mines Ltd. (Ont. 1946)
Sept. 9, 1958 – Dissolved.

Danvers Resources Inc. (Ont. 1977)
Aug. 1987 – Name changed to Cytrigen International Inc. ■

Daon Centre Limited Partnership (B.C. 1979)
1987 – Dissolved.

Daon Development Corporation (B.C. Nov. 19, 1964)
Feb. 21, 1986 – Name changed to BCE Development Corporation. ■

d'Aragon Mines Ltd. (Ont. 1945)
June 6, 1978 – Name changed to Pennant Resources Ltd.; basis 1 new for 3 old shs. ■

d'Arcy Oil & Gas Ltd. (Ont. 1951)
1953 – Name changed to Lariat Exploration and Development Ltd. ■

Daren Industries Ltd. (B.C. July 11, 1986)
Feb. 2002 – Wholly owned Hanson Lake Sand Corp. was unable to make further payments under existing loan agreements and the company as guarantor of the loans received notice of intent to enforce the general security arrangements.
May 1, 2002 – Company and wholly owned Hanson Lake were placed into receivership and Calgary-based Ernst & Young Inc. was appointed receiver/manager.
May 13, 2003 – Ernst & Young was discharged as receiver. No information was available regarding distributions to creditors or shldrs.

Daren Resources Ltd. (B.C. July 11, 1986)
Dec. 2, 1999 – Name changed to Daren Industries Ltd.; basis 1 new for 3 old shs. ■

Darford International Inc. (Alta. June 16, 2008)
Oct. 24, 2012 – The Bowra Group Inc. appointed receiver by court order.
Dec. 2012 – Assets sold to CanAm Pet Treats Inc. for an undisclosed amount.
Jan. 2, 2017 – Dissolved and struck from registry.

Darien Business Development Corp. (Alta. Nov. 23, 2004)
Mar. 18, 2019 – Name changed to Vireo Health International, Inc. following reverse takeover acquisition of Vireo Health, Inc.; basis 1 new for 19.4024 old shs. ■

Darien Resource Development Corp. (B.C. Mar. 13, 2017)
Apr. 4, 2018 – Name changed to New Energy Metals Corp. (see FPsurvey - Mines & Energy)

Darius Technology Ltd. (Can. May 3, 1989)
Jan. 2, 2003 – Dissolved and struck from register.

Darkhawk Development Corporation Ltd. (B.C. 1968)
1982 – Acquired by Trans-Canada Resources Ltd. for $1.15 per sh.

Darkhawk Mines Ltd. (B.C. 1968)
Aug. 1972 – Name changed to Darkhawk Development Corporation Ltd. ■

Darkwater Mines Ltd. (Ont. 1935)
1958 – Dissolved. No equity to shldrs.

Darmac Gold Mines Ltd. (Ont. 1945)
Mar. 1958 – Charter cancelled.

Darnley Bay Resources Limited (Ont. Nov. 25, 1993)
Aug. 8, 2017 – Name changed to Pine Point Mining Limited. ■

Darsi Mines Ltd. (B.C. 1966)
Apr. 23, 1974 – Name changed to Dasher Development Corporation; basis 1 new for 3 old shs. ■

Dart Energy Inc. (Alta. Jan. 22, 1992)
Mar. 13, 1998 – Name changed to Eyelogic Systems Inc. following acquisition of Eyelogic Inc.; basis 1 new for 4 old shs. ■

Dart Mines Ltd. (Que. 1956)
Feb. 6, 1982 – Charter cancelled.

Dartmouth Porcupine Gold Mines Ltd. (Ont. 1940)
1949 – Placed into bankruptcy. No equity for shldrs.

Darva Resources & Development Ltd. (B.C. 1971)
Jan. 11, 1979 – Name changed to Eldorado Minerals & Petroleum Corp. ■

Darwin Capital Corp. (B.C. Mar. 2, 1999)
Oct. 18, 2000 – Name changed to Unilink Tele.com Inc. ■

Darwin Mines Limited (Ont. 1970)
Nov. 22, 1974 – Amalgamated with Foxdale Mines Limited (1 for 7.5), Canton Explorations Limited (1 for 5.5), Marquis Explorations Limited (1 for 2.5), Long Point Gas & Oil Incorporated (1 for 3), Gold Acres Mines Limited (1 for 7), Home Mining Developments Limited (1 for 7) and Force Crag Mines Limited (1 for 4.5) to form New Force Crag Mines Limited; basis 1 new for 1.5 old shs.

Darwin Resources Corp. (B.C. Aug. 23, 2011)
July 28, 2014 – Acquired by Tinka Resources Ltd.; basis 0.1818 Tinka com. shs. for 1 Darwin com. sh.

Dash Capital Corp. (Alta. Jan. 13, 2021)
Dec. 20, 2023 – Name changed to Simply Solventless Concentrates Ltd. pursuant to the Qualifying Transaction reverse takeover acquisition of (old) Simply Solventless Concentrates Ltd.; basis 1 new for 2 old shs. (see FPsurvey - Industrials)

Dash Lake Resources Ltd. (B.C. Oct. 10, 1980)
June 9, 1989 – Dissolved and struck off register.

Dasher Development Corporation (B.C. 1966)
Feb. 1977 – Name changed to Nightwatch Resources Inc.; basis 1 new for 3 old shs. ■

Dasher Energy Corp. (B.C. Sept. 22, 1983)
Oct. 3, 2002 – Name changed to Dasher Resources Corp. ■

Dasher Exploration Ltd. (B.C. Sept. 22, 1983)
June 27, 2005 – Name changed to New World Resource Corp. ■

Dasher Resources Corp. (B.C. Sept. 22, 1983)
Apr. 16, 2003 – Name changed to Dasher Exploration Ltd.; basis 1 new for 10 old shs. ■

Dasher Resources Ltd. (Ont. Dec. 19, 1980)
June 21, 1991 – Name changed to Consolidated Dasher Resources Inc.; basis 1 new for 4 old shs. ■

Dassen Gold Mines Ltd. (Ont. 1945)
1957 – Charter cancelled.

Dassen Gold Resources Ltd. (B.C. 1975)
Sept. 12, 2005 – Dissolved.

Dasserat Developments Corp. (B.C. July 24, 1987)
Apr. 8, 1994 – Name changed to Vantage Enterprises Corp.; basis 1 new for 4 old shs. ■

Dassoro Mines Ltd. (Ont. 1946)
1956 – Charter cancelled.

Dastur Gold Mines Limited (Ont. 1945)
Apr. 1958 – Charter cancelled.

Data Deposit Box Inc. (B.C. Sept. 16, 2014)
Apr. 7, 2020 – Acquired by HostPapa, Inc.; basis $0.012491639 cash per sh.

Data Dial International Inc. (B.C. May 18, 1983)
May 15, 1997 – Name changed to First Telecom Corporation; basis 1 new for 5 old shs. ■

Data Fortress Systems Group Ltd. (B.C. May 13, 1985)
Jan. 11, 2010 – Dissolved and struck from register.

Data Gathering Capital Corp. (Ont. Mar. 31, 1998)
Sept. 17, 1999 – Name changed to Carbiz.com Inc. ■

The Data Group Income Fund (Ont. Nov. 15, 2004)
Jan. 1, 2012 – Succeeded by Data Group Inc. pursuant to plan of arrangement whereby The Data Group Inc. was formed to facilitate the conversion of the fund into a corporation. ■

Data Group Inc. (Ont. Mar. 7, 2011)
Jan. 2, 2014 – Succeeded by DATA Group Ltd. pursuant to reorganization whereby Data Group Inc. amalgamated with wholly owned Data Group Ltd., The Fulfillment Solutions Advantage Inc. and FSA Datalytics Canada Inc. to form DATA Group Ltd.

Data Group Investments Ltd. (Alta. 1986)
May 1, 1991 – Struck off register.

Data Trax Systems Inc. (Alta. July 9, 1991)
May 25, 1998 – Name changed to Data Trax Systems Ltd.; basis 1 new for 10 old shs. (see FPsurvey - Industrials)

Datacom Wireless Corporation (Can. Dec. 31, 2000)
Sept. 30, 2009 – Amalgamated with a wholly owned subsid. of BSM Technologies Inc.; basis 4.2421 BSM shs. for 1 Datacom sh. (see BSM Technologies Inc.)

Datacrown Inc. (Can. 1979 amalg.)
Sept. 28, 1983 – 97.6% of o/s shs. (held by Crownx Inc.) acquired by Crowntek Inc. on sh.-for-sh. basis. Remaining 2.4% int. acquired at $14 per sh.

Datagram Inc. (Que. 1976)
July 21, 1988 – Acquired by Memotec Data Inc. for $4.00 per sh. (see Memotec Data Inc.)

Datalex Corp. (Can. Mar. 25, 1982)
Nov. 9, 2007 – Dissolved.

Dataline Inc. (Ont. 1968)
May 31, 1983 – Amalgamated with Canquote Inc., a private co., to continue as Dataline Inc. Each com. sh. exchanged for 1 cl. B special sh. of amalg. co. Cl. B special shs. were redeem. up to 60 days after amalg. at $10.50 per sh., or convert. into com. shs. of amalg. co. on sh.-for-sh. basis.

Dataline Systems Limited (Ont. 1968)
May 1, 1981 – Name changed to Dataline Inc. ■

Datalogger Inc. (Alta. Dec. 31, 1992)
Nov. 5, 1997 – Name changed to ICE Drilling Enterprises Inc. following reverse takeover acquisition of ICE Drilling Services Inc.; basis 1 new for 5 old shs. ■

Datamark Business Forms Ltd. (Can. Nov. 19, 1973)
Aug. 12, 1988 – Name changed to Datamark Inc. ■

Datamark Inc. (Can. Nov. 19, 1973)
Nov. 10, 1999 – Name changed to Datamark Systems Group Inc. ■

Datamark Systems Group Inc. (Can. Nov. 19, 1973)
June 13, 2007 – Acquired by Komunik Corporation and amalgamated; basis either i) cash $2.0275 for 1 com. sh. or ii) 1 new Komunik com. sh. for 1 old Datamark com. sh. or iii) combination thereof. (see Komunik Corporation)

DataMiners Capital Corp. (Alta. Oct. 1, 2013)
Aug. 28, 2019 – Name changed to Zoomd Technologies Ltd. pursuant to Qualifying Transaction reverse takeover acquisition of Zoomd Ltd.; basis 1 new for 2.5 old shs. (see FPsurvey - Industrials)

DataMirror Corporation (Ont. Nov. 19, 1993)
Feb. 1, 1996 – Amalgamated in Ontario to continue with same name.
Sept. 6, 2007 – Acquired by IBM Corp. for Cdn$27 per sh.

Datapro Ltd. (Ont. 1962)
Apr. 1974 – Name changed to Real Time Datapro Ltd. ■

Dataspan Technology Inc. (Alta. 1987)
Dec. 27, 1991 – Made an assignment into bankruptcy. Peat Marwick Thorne Inc., Calgary was appointed trustee.
Mar. 19, 1993 – Declared bankrupt. There was no distribution to shldrs.
Nov. 1, 1993 – Struck off register.

DataTech Systems Ltd. (B.C. 1968)
Nov. 28, 1994 – Amalgamated with a wholly owned subsid. of SHL Systemhouse Inc.; basis 90¢ per sh. or the equivalent in SHL shs. (see SHL Systemhouse Inc.)

DataTracker International Inc. (B.C. Feb. 25, 1983)
Feb. 4, 1991 – Name changed to California Gold Mines Inc. ■

DataWave Systems Inc. (B.C. Aug. 12, 1986)
Sept. 19, 2000 – Continued into Yukon.
Feb. 23, 2005 – Continued into Delaware.

DataWave Vending Inc. (B.C. Aug. 12, 1986)
Jan. 15, 1997 – Name changed to DataWave Systems Inc. ■

Datawest Solutions Inc. (Can. Apr. 10, 1997)
Nov. 3, 2004 – Acquired by Canadian subsid. of Open Solutions Inc.; basis Cdn$1.16 per com. sh. and Cdn$2.60 per pfd. sh.

DataWind Inc. (Can. Apr. 16, 2014)
Apr. 9, 2019 – Name changed to Jeotex Inc.; basis 1 new for 20 old shs. ■

Datec Group Ltd. (N.B. July 21, 2001)
Feb. 9, 2006 – Plan of Arrangement exchange with Elandia, Inc.; basis 0.2015 new Elandia sh. for 1 old Datec sh.

Datel Industries Inc. (B.C. 1983)
Sept. 3, 1993 – Dissolved and struck off register.

Dateland Capital Group Inc. (Alta. 1986)
Jan. 27, 1992 – Name changed to Austrak International Canada Corporation; basis 1 new for 2.5 old shs. ■

Datex Technologies Corporation (Can. May 18, 2004)
Mar. 24, 2011 – Privatized at 4¢ per sh.

Datinvest International Ltd. (B.C. May 1, 1987)
Aug. 12, 2021 – Name changed to Irwin Naturals Inc. pursuant to the reverse takeover acquisition of Irwin Naturals and GVB Biopharma; basis 1 new for 8.316 old shs. (see FPsurvey - Industrials)

Datumone Petroleum Ltd. (B.C. 1979)
Oct. 10, 1984 – Name changed to Mischief Enterprises Ltd.; basis 1 new for 5 old shs. ■

Daugherty Resources Inc. (B.C. Jan. 31, 1979)
June 28, 2004 – Name changed to NGAS Resources, Inc. ■

Dauntless Capital Corp. (B.C. Oct. 30, 2009)
Sept. 2, 2010 – Name changed to Tigris Uranium Corp. pursuant to Qualifying Transaction acquisition of option from NZ Uranium, LLC to acquire uranium properties in New Mexico. ■

Dauphin Iron Mines Ltd. (Que. 1958)
Dec. 1973 – Charter cancelled.

Daura Capital Corp. (B.C. Mar. 29, 2018)
Jan. 20, 2025 – Name changed to Daura Gold Corp. pursuant to the Qualifying Transaction acquisition of Estrella Gold S.A.C. (see FPsurvey - Mines & Energy)

Davenport Industries Ltd. (B.C. Feb. 28, 1972 amalg.)
Aug. 19, 1991 – Name changed to DVO Industries Ltd.; basis 1 new for 5 old shs. (see FPsurvey - Mines & Energy; FPsurvey - Industrials)

Davenport Oils and Mining Ltd. (B.C. Feb. 28, 1972 amalg.)
Aug. 7, 1973 – Name changed to Davenport Industries Ltd. ■

Daverich Minerals Ltd. (Ont. 1975)
Dec. 2, 1976 – Amalgamated with Forefront Uranium Mines Ltd. and Eldex Minerals Ltd. to form Forefront Consolidated Explorations Ltd.; basis 1 new for 2.75 old shs.

Davic Enterprises Incorporated (B.C. June 4, 1987)
Mar. 10, 1997 – Name changed to RBD Enterprises Inc.; basis 1 new for 5.5 old shs. ■

David & Frère, Ltée (Que. 1928)
1967 – During all o/s cl. B voting shs. acquired by Hershey Chocolate of Canada Ltd., a wholly owned subsid. of Hershey Chocolate Corp. All o/s cl. A shs. redeemed Aug. 21, at $50 per sh. plus declared but unpaid divds.

David Copperfield Explorations Ltd. (Ont. 1956)
July 13, 1962 – Dissolved.

David Minerals Ltd. (B.C. 1981 amalg.)
May 28, 1993 – Dissolved and struck off register.

Davidor Mines Ltd. (Ont. 1944)
Nov. 1973 – Charter cancelled.

Davidson Tisdale Ltd. (Ont. Apr. 17, 1945)
July 10, 2002 – Name changed to Northcott Gold Inc. ■

Davidson Tisdale Mines Limited (Ont. Apr. 17, 1945)
Aug. 26, 1992 – Name changed to Davidson Tisdale Ltd. ■

Davie Industries Inc. (Can. 1937)
Apr. 7, 2003 – Name changed to Davie Maritime Inc. ■

Davie Maritime Inc. (Can. 1937)
Oct. 16, 2006 – Name changed to 4008249 Canada Inc. ■

Davie Yards Inc. (Can. Sept. 12, 2006)
Feb. 25, 2010 – Filed for creditor protection under the Companies' Creditors Arrangement Act and Deloitte Restructuring Inc. was appointed monitor.
July 29, 2011 – Name changed to 4370422 Canada Inc. ■

Davies Irwin Ltd. (Que. May 24, 1955)
Sept. 1, 1972 – Name changed to Dilmont Inc. (see FPsurvey - Industrials)

Davies Petroleum Ltd. (unknown)
1952 – Assets acquired by New Davies Petroleums Ltd.

Davis + Henderson Corporation (Ont. Apr. 28, 2010)
May 4, 2014 – Name changed to DH Corporation. ■

Davis + Henderson Income Fund (Ont. Nov. 6, 2001)
Jan. 1, 2011 – Succeeded by Davis + Henderson Corporation pursuant to plan of arrangement whereby Davis + Henderson Corporation was formed to facilitate the conversion of the fund into a corporation and the fund was subsequently dissolved. ■

Davis Distributing & Vending Limited (Ont. May 26, 1953)
Jan. 23, 1973 – Name changed to Davis Distributing Limited. (see FPsurvey - Industrials)

Davis Industries Ltd. (Alta. 1968)
Feb. 1983 – Placed into receivership. Assets subsequently sold; no distribution to shldrs.

Davis-Keays Mining Co. Ltd. (B.C. 1967)
June 30, 1983 – Name changed to Davis-Keays Mining Ltd. (see FPsurvey - Mines & Energy)

Davis Leather Co., Ltd. (Can. 1931)
May 1959 – Name changed to Tancord Industries Ltd. ■

Davison Oil Ltd. (Can. 1952)
1954 – Taken over by Calvan Consolidated Oil & Gas Co. Ltd.; basis 1 new for 6 old shs.

Davnor Water Treatment Technologies Ltd. (Alta. July 26, 1995)
Jan. 2, 2006 – Dissolved and struck from register.

Davoil Natural Resources Limited (Alta. 1952)
Jan. 4, 1977 – Amalgamated with several other cos. to form Ranchmen's Resources (1976) Ltd.; basis 1 cl. A sh. for 6 com. shs.

Davolite Oil Co. Ltd. (Alta.)
1960 – Struck off register.

Davstar Industries Ltd. (Ont. 1985)
July 27, 1995 – Name changed to UROHEALTH Systems, Inc. and continued into Delaware. ■

Dawmac Mining & Oils Ltd. (unknown)
1957 – Merged into International Metal and Petroleum Corp.

Dawn Petroleums Ltd. (Alta. 1952)
Feb. 1972 – Dissolved. No distribution to shldrs.

Dawson Creek Capital Corp. (Alta. Feb. 14, 2006)
Dec. 12, 2007 – Continued into Jersey.
Dec. 27, 2007 – Name changed to Lydian International Limited pursuant to Qualifying Transaction reverse takeover acquisition of Lydian Resource Company Limited; basis 2 new for 3 old shs. ■

Dawson Developments Limited (B.C. Nov. 19, 1964)
Dec. 3, 1973 – Name changed to Daon Development Corporation. ■

Dawson Eldorado Gold Explorations Ltd. (B.C. 1979)
Aug. 30, 1985 – Continued into Canada.
Oct. 21, 1985 – Name changed to Dawson Eldorado Mines Ltd. following merger with wholly owned subsids. Silvercrest Resource Corporation, Ebony Resources Ltd. and Aerovan Transport Limited. ∎

Dawson Eldorado Mines Ltd. (Can. Aug. 30, 1985)
Mar. 6, 2000 – Dissolved.

Dawson Gold Corp. (B.C. Jan. 16, 2006)
Mar. 6, 2019 – Name changed to FluidOil Limited. ∎

Dawson Gold Mines Ltd. (Ont. Sept. 22, 1939)
1940 – Status unknown. No report since.

Dawson Housing Developments Ltd. (B.C. Nov. 19, 1964)
Nov. 14, 1968 – Name changed to Dawson Developments Limited. ∎

Dawson Range Mines Ltd. (N.P.L.) (B.C. Feb. 12, 1970)
Jan. 29, 1979 – Name changed to Carpenter Lake Resources Ltd.; basis 1 new for 5 old shs. ∎

Dawson-White Gold Mines Ltd. (Ont. Nov. 2, 1936)
Sept. 22, 1939 – Name changed to Dawson Gold Mines Ltd. and continued into Ontario. ∎

Dayak Goldfields Corporation (Ont. June 1, 1996 amalg.)
May 15, 1997 – Amalgamated with 1227035 Ontario Limited, a wholly owned subsid. of International Pursuit Corporation (Pursuit); basis 1.1 new com. shs. of Pursuit for 3 com. shs. of Dayak. (see International Pursuit Corporation)

Daybreak Energy Corporation (Alta. May 19, 2000)
Dec. 19, 2001 – Name changed to Result Energy Inc.; basis 1 new for 8 old shs. ∎

Daybreak Mining Corp. (1957) Ltd. (B.C. 1957)
Dec. 1971 – Struck off register.

Daybreak Resources Corporation (Alta. May 19, 2000)
July 12, 2000 – Name changed to Daybreak Energy Corporation. ∎

Day4 Energy Inc. (Yuk. June 28, 2000)
June 24, 2005 – Continued into Canada.
June 28, 2012 – Continued into British Columbia.
Aug. 28, 2012 – Name changed to 0944460 B.C. Ltd. following transfer of all business, assets and operations to a private company owned and controlled by two executives of the company for $500,000 cash and assumption of all liabilities. ∎

Dayjon Explorations and Holdings Ltd. (Ont. 1959)
Apr. 22, 1980 – Dissolved.

Dayjon Explorers Ltd. (Ont. 1959)
1963 – Name changed to Dayjon Explorations and Holdings Ltd. ∎

Daylight Energy Ltd. (Alta. May 7, 2010; amalg.)
Dec. 23, 2011 – Formed Sinopec Daylight Energy Ltd. in Alberta pursuant to amalgamation with 1635905 Alberta Ltd., a wholly owned subsid. of Sinopec International Petroleum Exploration and Production Corporation, which acquired Daylight Energy Ltd. for $10.08 per com. sh. ∎

Daylight Energy Trust (Alta. Sept. 10, 2004)
Sept. 26, 2006 – Name changed to Daylight Resources Trust following acquisition of Sequoia Oil & Gas Trust by Daylight Energy Trust and the transfer of assets of both Sequoia and Daylight Energy to Daylight Resources; basis 0.6642 Daylight Resources units plus 0.0417 new Trafalgar Energy Ltd. com. shs. and 0.0116 new Trafalgar warrants for 1 Daylight Energy trust unit. ∎

Daylight Resources Trust (Alta. Aug. 16, 2006)
May 7, 2010 – Succeeded by Daylight Energy Ltd. following conversion of Daylight Resources Trust into a corporation. ∎

The Daymond Co. Ltd. (Can. - unspecified)
1967 – Purchased by Canada & Dominion Sugar Co., Ltd.

Dayton Creek Silver Mines Ltd. (Alta. 1970)
Nov. 18, 1982 – Continued into British Columbia.
Jan. 1, 1983 – Amalgamated with Cathedral Minerals Ltd. to form Mintex Resources Ltd.; basis 1 new for 3 old shs.

Dayton Development Corp. (B.C. May 7, 1985)
Oct. 31, 1991 – Name changed to Dayton Mining Corporation. ∎

Dayton Mining Corporation (B.C. May 7, 1985)
Apr. 11, 2002 – Formed Pacific Rim Mining Corp. in British Columbia on amalgamation with Pacific Rim Mining Corp. with Dayton the deemed acquiror; basis 1 new for 1 Pacific Rim sh. and 1.76 new for 1 Dayton sh. ∎

Dayton-Porcupine Mines Limited (Ont. Feb. 9, 1937)
Nov. 15, 1982 – Name changed to Denom Resources Inc. ∎

Dayton Tire Canada Ltd. (Ont. 1899)
Nov. 1, 1978 – All assets transferred to wholly owned subsid. of Firestone Canada Inc. Charter surrendered.

Daytona Capital Corporation (Alta. Nov. 23, 1993)
Jan. 22, 2002 – Acquired by Hutchinson Acquisitions Corp. for $0.13 per sh.

Daytona Energy Corp. (B.C. Apr. 30, 1987)
Jan. 29, 1999 – Continued into Yukon.
Jan. 29, 2005 – Continued into British Columbia.
Feb. 2, 2007 – Continued into Alberta.
Sept. 1, 2010 – Name changed to Riata Resources Corp.; basis 1 new for 10 old shs. ∎

dba Telecom Corporation (B.C. July 17, 1984)
Sept. 17, 2004 – Name changed to Magnum Minerals Corp.; basis 1 new for 50 old shs. ∎

De Baca Resources Inc. (B.C. Sept. 14, 1982)
Nov. 13, 1985 – Name changed to Care Point Medical Centres Ltd. following amalgamation agreement in mid-1985. ∎

De Clerq Mining Limited (Que. 1946)
1950 – Charter cancelled.

The de Havilland Aircraft of Canada, Limited (Ont. 1928)
Jan. 31, 1986 – All o/s shs. acquired by The Boeing Company from Canada Development Investment Corporation for $90,000,000 cash and $65,000,000 in deferred payments, making de Havilland a division of Boeing Canada Limited.

De Lesseps Mining Corp. Ltd. (Que. 1965)
May 15, 1982 – Charter cancelled.

De Santis Gold Mining Co. Ltd. (Ont. May 21, 1928)
June 1935 – Name changed to De Santis Porcupine Mines Ltd.; basis 1 new for 2 old shs. ∎

De Ville Copper Mines Ltd. (Ont. 1953)
Apr. 8, 1970 – Charter cancelled.

Deadpool Capital Corp. (B.C. July 6, 2018)
Jan. 19, 2021 – Name changed to Revitalist Lifestyle and Wellness Ltd. (see FPsurvey - Industrials)

Deak International Resources Corporation (Ont. Jan. 13, 1989 amalg.)
Mar. 27, 1989 – Name changed to Deak Resources Corporation. ∎

Deak Resources Corporation (Ont. Jan. 13, 1989 amalg.)
Oct. 7, 1994 – Name changed to AJ Perron Gold Corp. ∎

Deal Capital Ltd. (B.C. June 29, 2006)
July 16, 2007 – Name changed to Animas Resources Ltd. ∎

Deal Pro Capital Corporation (Ont. June 11, 2021)
Mar. 26, 2024 – Name changed to Urban Infrastructure Group Inc. following Qualifying Transaction amalgamation of Urban Utilities Contractors Inc. (UUC) with 1000773456 Ontario Inc., a wholly owned subsidiary of Deal Pro Capital, constituting a reverse takeover by UUC. (see FPsurvey - Industrials)

Dealcheck.com Inc. (Ont. Apr. 9, 1973)
Apr. 21, 2003 – Name changed to Bontan Corporation Inc.; basis 1 new for 7 old shs. ∎

DealNet Capital Corp. (Ont. Nov. 22, 2000)
Nov. 30, 2020 – Acquired by Simply Green Home Services Inc.; basis 16¢ cash per sh.

Dean Lake Mines Ltd. (Que. 1972)
1978 – Wound up.
Mar. 30, 1979 – Shldrs. received 9.72¢ per sh., representing total distribution of assets.

Deane-Cadillac Mining Corp. (Que. Aug. 1936)
Charter cancelled.

Deans Geographics Ltd. (B.C. 1973)
Nov. 18, 1974 – Name changed to Deans Industries Ltd. ∎

Deans Industries Ltd. (B.C. 1973)
1976 – Name changed to International Geographics Ltd. ∎

Deans Knight Income and Growth Fund (Ont. Feb. 23, 2006)
Oct. 7, 2011 – Redeemed at $7.2830 per unit.

Deans Knight Income Corporation (B.C. Sept. 17, 1985)
Apr. 11, 2001 – Continued into Canada.
Apr. 16, 2014 – Privatized. Cash distribution of $9.75 per com. sh. to be distributed on Apr. 30, 2014.

Dearborn Uranium Ltd. (unknown)
Nov. 1977 – Reported defunct.

Dearborn Uranium Mines Limited (Ont. 1955)
Feb. 5, 1980 – Dissolved.

Dease-Lake Cassiar Mines Ltd. (Can. 1943)
July 1961 – Dissolved.

Death Valley Resources Ltd. (B.C. Oct. 5, 1987)
Apr. 12, 1989 – Name changed to DVR Resources Ltd. ∎

Deauville Explorations Ltd. (Ont. 1967)
1968 – Name changed to Deauville Holdings & Explorations Limited. ∎

Deauville Holdings & Explorations Limited (Ont. 1967)
Mar. 15, 1978 – Amalgamated with New Bedford Resources & Developments Limited; basis 1 new for 6 Deauville shs.

Deb Yellowknife Gold Mines Ltd. (Ont. 1945)
Nov. 7, 1955 – Charter cancelled.

Deban Mines Ltd. (Ont.)
Dec. 1960 – Charter cancelled.

Debhold (Canada) Limited (Ont. 1966)
Oct. 31, 1979 – Amalgamated into Anglo American Corporation of Canada Limited, along with two private cos. All o/s ser. A & B pref. shs. exchanged on sh.-for-sh. basis for ser. A & B pref. shs. of Anglo American.

Deburmac Gold Mines Limited (Ont. 1946)
Jan. 1958 – Charter cancelled.

Debut Diamonds Inc. (Ont. Oct. 18, 2007)
May 6, 2021 – Name changed to Wesana Health Holdings Inc. and continued into British Columbia pursuant to the reverse takeover acquisition of WeSana Health Inc.; basis 1 new for 28.1245577 old shs. (see FPsurvey - Mines & Energy)

Decade Explorations Limited (Ont. 1972)
Oct. 18, 1978 – Charter cancelled.

Decade International Development Ltd. (B.C. Apr. 24, 1972)
Apr. 11, 2002 – Name changed to Seymour Exploration Corp.; basis 1 new for 7 old shs. ■

Decalta Oils Limited (Can. 1947)
1952 – Name changed to Canadian Decalta Gas & Oils Ltd.; basis 1 new for 3 old shs. ■

Decarbonization Plus Acquisition Corporation IV (Cayman Islands Feb. 22, 2021)
Feb. 23, 2023 – Formed Hammerhead Energy Inc. ■

Decary Metals Inc. (unknown)
Jan. 31, 1952 – Continued into Quebec.
May 26, 1952 – Name changed to Empire Oil & Minerals Inc. ■

Decca Resources Limited (B.C. Feb. 18, 1965)
Nov. 8, 1977 – Name changed to Sceptre Resources Limited following acquisition of Sceptre Oils Ltd. ■

Decision Dynamics Technology Ltd. (Can. Nov. 18, 2003)
May 17, 2010 – Acquired by Acorn Energy, Inc.; basis 0.0162 Acorn shs. for 1 Decision Dynamics sh. ■

Decker Lake Mines Limited (B.C. 1970)
May 9, 1983 – Name changed to Decker Resources Ltd. ■

Decker Resources Ltd. (B.C. 1970)
Sept. 18, 1992 – Dissolved and struck off register. ■

Declan Cobalt Inc. (B.C. Aug. 26, 2005)
Feb. 22, 2019 – Name changed to 21C Metals Inc. ■

Declan Resources Inc. (B.C. Aug. 26, 2005)
Aug. 28, 2018 – Name changed to Declan Cobalt Inc. ■

Deco Plantminder Inc. (B.C. 1983)
Apr. 30, 1987 – Name changed to Canterbury Resources Inc.; basis 1 new for 3 old shs. ■

Decoma International Inc. (Ont. July 30, 1997)
Mar. 7, 2005 – All cl. A sub. vtg. shs. not already held acquired by Magna International Inc.; basis 0.1453 new Magna cl. A sub. vtg. sh. or $88.2856 per sh. for 1 old Decoma cl. A sub. vtg. sh. Also all o/s 6.5% conv. sub. Decoma debs. were exchanged for 6.5% conv. sub. Magna debs. which are convertible into Magna cl. A sub. vtg. shs. at $91.19 per sh. ■

Decourcy Capital Corp. (B.C. Mar. 7, 2007)
Apr. 19, 2010 – Amalgamated with Transformative Ventures Ltd. and Auricle Biomedical Corporation to form Aztech Innovations Inc. which then acquired Aztech Associates Inc. by reverse takeover constituting the Qualifying Transaction for each of Transformative, Auricle and Decourcy; basis 0.667 Aztech shs. for 1 Transformative sh., 0.667 Aztech shs. for 1 Auricle sh. and 1 Aztech sh. for 1 Decourcy sh. ■

DeCoursey-Brewis Minerals Ltd. (Ont. 1945)
Jan. 1964 – Name changed to Consolidated Brewis Minerals Ltd.; basis 1 new for 4 old shs. ■

Decoursey Mountain Mining Co. Inc. (Alaska 1951)
1958 – Name changed to Alaska Mines and Minerals Inc. ■

Dectron Internationale Inc. (Can. Mar. 30, 1998)
Aug. 26, 2008 – All o/s com. shs. not held acquired by newly formed co. by way of amalgamation with 6697007 Canada Inc. and 6996990 Canada Inc.; basis 1 pref. sh. for 1 com. sh. immediately redeemed for $4.20. ■

Dedicated Technologies Corporation (Ont. 1989)
Feb. 2, 1995 – Filed a Notice of Intention To Make a Proposal under the Bankruptcy and Insolvency Act (Canada). KPMG Inc., Ottawa, appointed receiver. (see AIT Advanced Information Technologies Corporation)
June 1, 1995 – All inventory, intangible and intellectual assets acquired by AIT Advanced Information Technologies Corporation of Ottawa for $850,000 and in August acquired all o/s shs. for 14.5¢ per sh. Secured creditors were paid in full and unsecured creditors received 90¢ on the dollar. (see AIT Advanced Information Technologies Corporation)
May 28, 1997 – Trustee discharged. (see AIT Advanced Information Technologies Corporation)

Deeded Royalties Ltd. (Ont. 1934)
1960 – Wound up.

Deena Energy Inc. (Can. Aug. 23, 1988)
Sept. 12, 2002 – Dissolved.

Deena Explorations Limited (Can. Aug. 23, 1988)
June 29, 1994 – Name changed to Deena Energy Inc.; basis 1 new for 4 old shs. ■

Deep Basin Energy Inc. (Alta. July 29, 1988)
July 15, 1997 – Name changed to Calibre Energy Inc. ■

Deep Basin Petroleum Corporation (Alta. July 29, 1988)
Sept. 28, 1995 – Name changed to Deep Basin Energy Inc.; basis 1 new for 4 old shs. ■

Deep Gulch Mines Ltd. (B.C. 1959)
1960 – Name changed to Copper Mountain Mines Ltd. ■

Deep Lake Gold Mines Ltd. (Ont. 1938)
Aug. 1957 – Charter cancelled.

Deep Oils Limited (Alta. 1938)
1970 – Merged into Westburne Petroleum & Minerals Ltd.

Deep Resources Ltd. (Alta. Jan. 3, 1997)
Aug. 1, 2006 – Plan of Arrangement acquisition by Choice Resources Corp.; basis 0.285714 new Choice sh. plus 0.1 new Choice warrant exercisable at $1.50 per sh. for 1 old Deep sh. (see Choice Resources Corp.)

Deep Rock Gold Mines Limited (Man. Mar. 10, 1920)
Nov. 10, 1937 – Charter cancelled.

Deep Shaft Technology International Incorporated (B.C. July 21, 1983)
Nov. 15, 1988 – Name changed to Noram Environmental Solutions Inc. ■

Deep South Petroleum Inc. (B.C. 1980)
Aug. 22, 1985 – Name changed to Gold Texas Resources Ltd.; basis 1 new for 2 old shs. ■

Deep-South Resources Inc. (B.C. Apr. 24, 1987)
Nov. 10, 2023 – Name changed to Koryx Copper Inc. (see FPsurvey - Mines & Energy)

DeepRock Minerals Inc. (B.C. Dec. 1, 2014)
Apr. 23, 2025 – Name changed to Allied Critical Metals Inc. pursuant to the reverse takeover acquisition of ACM Holdings Ltd. (formerly Allied Critical Metals Corp.); basis 1 new for 40 old shs. ■

Deepwell Energy Services Trust (Alta. Apr. 21, 2006)
June 9, 2010 – Succeeded by Palko Environmental Ltd. pursuant to plan of arrangement whereby Palko Environmental Ltd. was formed to facilitate the conversion of the trust into a corporation and the trust was subsequently dissolved. ■

Deer Creek Energy Limited (Alta. Oct. 1, 1996)
Dec. 14, 2005 – Amalgamated indirectly with Total E & P Canada Ltd.; basis $31 per sh.

Deer Creek Resources Limited (Ont. Feb. 26, 1981)
Nov. 21, 1986 – Name changed to Consolidated Deer Creek Resources Limited; basis 1 new for 4 old shs. ■

Deer Horn Capital Inc. (B.C. Aug. 7, 2014)
May 28, 2021 – Name changed to First Tellurium Corp. (see FPsurvey - Mines & Energy)

Deer Horn Metals Inc. (Can. Apr. 16, 2004)
Aug. 7, 2014 – Continued into British Columbia.
Oct. 7, 2014 – Name changed to Deer Horn Capital Inc. ■

Deer Horn Mines Limited (Ont. 1950)
Oct. 18, 1978 – Charter cancelled.

Deer Lake Mines Ltd. (B.C. 1973)
June 8, 1976 – Amalgamated with Nithex Exploration and Development Ltd. to form Nithex Exploration Ltd.

Deerbrook Investments Ltd. (Alta. Dec. 4, 1986)
Mar. 24, 1988 – Name changed to Liquidation World Inc. ■

Deerfoot Resources Inc. (Ont. 1927)
Dec. 14, 1989 – Name changed to Geneva Lake Minerals Corporation. ■

Deermont Oil & Gas Co. Ltd. (Ont. 1946)
Mar. 11, 1955 – Dissolved.

Deerpark Mines Ltd. (Ont. Dec. 23, 1964)
1970 – Name changed to Standard Nickel Mines Limited. ■

Deerpark Petroleums Ltd. (Ont. Dec. 23, 1964)
Name changed to Deerpark Mines Ltd. ■

DeeThree Exploration Inc. (Alta. Nov. 22, 2007)
Jan. 1, 2010 – Formed DeeThree Exploration Ltd. in Alberta following amalgamation with wholly owned DeeThree Exploration Ltd. ■

DeeThree Exploration Ltd. (Alta. Jan. 1, 2010 amalg.)
May 15, 2015 – Name changed to Granite Oil Corp. pursuant to a plan of arrangement whereby certain assets were spun out to Boulder Energy Ltd.; basis 1 new for 3 old shs. ■

Deex Resources Corp. (B.C. May 5, 1983 amalg.)
May 22, 1987 – Name changed to Seam Resources Corporation. (see FPsurvey - Mines & Energy)

DeFi Technologies Inc. (Ont. Nov. 3, 2009)
June 1, 2022 – Name changed to Valour Inc. ■

Defiance Capital Corp. (B.C. July 19, 2007)
June 27, 2011 – Name changed to Defiance Silver Corp. (see FPsurvey - Mines & Energy)

Defiance Mining Corporation (Can. June 25, 2003)
Sept. 9, 2004 – Plan of Arrangement with Rio Narcea Gold Mines, Ltd.; basis 1 new Rio Narcea sh. for 5.25 old Defiance shs. (see Rio Narcea Gold Mines, Ltd.)

Defiant Energy Corporation (Alta. Sept. 24, 1998)
Dec. 23, 2004 – Plan of Arrangement amalgamation with Defiant Resources Corporation, Advantage Energy Income Fund and Advantage Oil & Gas Ltd.; basis 0.1666 new Defiant Resources com. sh. plus, either 0.201373 new Advantage Energy trust unit or, 0.201373 new Advantage Oil exch. sh. or, $4.40 or, a combination thereof for 1 old Defiant Energy com. sh. (see Advantage Energy Income Fund; Defiant Resources Corporation)

Defiant Minerals Inc. (B.C. May 26, 1983)
Feb. 14, 1991 – Name changed to Hillestad Pharmaceuticals Inc. pursuant to reverse takeover acquisition of Hillestad International Inc. ■

Defiant Resources Corporation (Alta. Nov. 1, 2004)
Apr. 4, 2008 – Acquired by Profound Energy Inc.; basis 0.55 Profound com. shs. for 1 Defiant com. sh.

Definity Financial Corporation (Ont. June 30, 2021)
Jan. 1, 2024 – Continued into Canada. (see FPsurvey - Industrials)

Defor Chibougamau Mines Ltd. (Que. 1949)
May 1974 – Charter cancelled.

Defrostomatic Co. Limited (Que. 1957)
Oct. 1961 – Acquired by A. Belanger Ltée.

Dejour Energy Inc. (B.C. Aug. 16, 2005)
Oct. 27, 2015 – Name changed to DXI Energy Inc.; basis 1 new for 5 old shs. ■

Dejour Enterprises Ltd. (Ont. Mar. 29, 1968)
Aug. 16, 2005 – Continued into British Columbia.
Mar. 28, 2011 – Name changed to Dejour Energy Inc. ■

Dejour Mines Limited (Ont. Mar. 29, 1968)
Oct. 30, 2001 – Name changed to Dejour Enterprises Ltd.; basis 1 new for 15 old shs. ■

Del-Gold Mines Ltd. (Ont. 1946)
Mar. 1955 – Name changed to Siloro Mines Ltd. ■

Del Mar Energy Inc. (Alta. Oct. 8, 1993)
Mar. 22, 2000 – Name changed to Aventura Energy Inc.; basis 1 new for 3 old shs. ■

The Del Norte Chrome Corporation (B.C. Sept. 27, 1979)
Dec. 14, 1979 – Name changed to Del Norte Chrome Corporation. ■

Del Norte Chrome Corporation (B.C. Sept. 27, 1979)
Oct. 16, 1989 – Name changed to Consolidated Del Norte Ventures Inc.; basis 1 new for 5 old shs. ■

Del Rio International, a Resource and Technology Corporation (Alta. 1983)
June 3, 1994 – Name changed to Money Works Inc. ■

Del Rio Producers Ltd. (Alta. 1947)
Mar. 15, 1957 – Acquired by Central Leduc Oils Ltd.; basis 5 new for 7 old shs.

Del Rio Resources Ltd. (Alta. 1983)
Feb. 18, 1988 – Name changed to Del Rio International, a Resource and Technology Corporation; basis 2 new for 1 old sh. ■

Del Roca Energy Inc. (Alta. May 15, 1996)
Nov. 2, 1998 – Amalgamated with Tekerra Gas Inc. (0.6 new for 1 old) to form a new co. known as Del Roca Energy Ltd. (Del Roca); basis 0.29875 of a new sh. of Del Roca for 1 old sh. (see Del Roca Energy Ltd.)

Del Roca Energy Ltd. (Alta. Oct. 31, 1998)
Feb. 14, 2003 – Acquired by TUSK Energy Inc.; basis $0.64 or 0.25 new TUSK sh. or a combination thereof for 1 old Del Roca sh. (see TUSK Energy Inc.)

Delahey Consolidated Nickel Mines Limited (Ont. 1957)
Dec. 3, 1980 – Amalgamated with 3 other cos. to form Hoffman Exploration & Minerals Limited; basis 1 new for 1 old sh.

Delahey Lake Nickel Ltd. (Ont. 1956)
1967 – Merged into Delahey Consolidated Nickel Mines Ltd.; basis 10 new for 45 old shs.

Delandore Mines Ltd. (Ont. 1937)
1941 – Property taken over by Delandore Sulphur & Iron Mines Ltd. Charter surrendered.

Delandore Sulphur & Iron Mines Ltd. (Ont. 1941)
Jan. 1954 – Wound up, made a distribution of 1 sh. Atlas Sulphur and Iron Co. for each 6 shs. Delandore held.

Delaney Energy Services Corporation (Alta. Nov. 1, 1996)
June 28, 2001 – Acquired by Integrated Production Services Ltd. for $1.05 per sh. (see Integrated Production Services Ltd.)

Delano Technology Corporation (Ont. May 7, 1998)
Aug. 2, 2002 – Plan of Arrangement with US-based divine inc.; basis either 0.04748 new divine com. sh. or 0.04748 new divine exchangeable sh. for 1 old Delano com. sh.

Delavaco Residential Properties Corp. (Ont. Mar. 19, 2007)
July 26, 2016 – Name changed to Firm Capital American Realty Partners Corp. ■

Delaware Resources Corporation (B.C. Mar. 22, 1983)
Feb. 1, 1989 – Formed Prime Resources Corporation in British Columbia on amalgamation with Colossus

Resource Equities Inc. (1 for 1); basis 1 new for 1 old sh. ■

Delayed Data Communications Inc. (Ont. Sept. 24, 1986)
Jan. 18, 1996 – Continued into Canada.
Mar. 22, 1996 – Name changed to NSI Communications Inc. ■

Delbancor Industries Inc. (B.C. Apr. 17, 1957)
Mar. 16, 1998 – Delisted from the Vancouver Stock Exchange. Subsequently dissolved and struck from register.

Delbo Tungsten Mines Ltd. (B.C. 1953)
May 22, 1958 – Dissolved.

Delbridge Mines Limited (Ont. 1966)
July 4, 1990 – Formed Hoverspace International Corp. on amalgamation with Hoverspace Concepts Inc.; basis 1 new for 2 old shs. (see FPsurvey - Mines & Energy)

Delbrook Mines Ltd. (B.C. 1970)
Aug. 27, 1975 – Dissolved.

Delcairo Gold Mines Ltd. (Ont. 1936)
Aug. 7, 1956 – Dissolved.

Delcore Porcupine Mines Limited (Ont. 1944)
Nov. 28, 1973 – Dissolved.

Delcorp Resources Inc. (B.C. Mar. 10, 1980)
Nov. 20, 1990 – Name changed to Bahn Foods Inc. following reverse takeover acquisition of Bahn Foods Corporation; basis 1 new for 4 old shs. ■

d'Eldona Gold Mines Limited (Ont. 1944)
Oct. 5, 1984 – Formed d'Eldona Resources Ltd. in Ontario on amalgamation with Parapet Petroleum Inc. (1 for 13); basis 1 new for 2 old shs. ■

d'Eldona Resources Ltd. (Ont. Oct. 5, 1984 amalg.)
June 1, 1988 – Name changed to Western D'Eldona Resources Limited; basis 1 new for 3 old shs. ■

Delgratia Developments Ltd. (B.C. Feb. 14, 1984)
Apr. 18, 1995 – Name changed to Delgratia Mining Corporation. ■

Delgratia Mining Corporation (B.C. Feb. 14, 1984)
Feb. 4, 1999 – Continued into Yukon.
Feb. 10, 1999 – Name changed to Central Minera Corp. ■

Delhi Pacific Mines Limited (Ont. Sept. 5, 1934)
Dec. 19, 1980 – Name changed to Delhi Pacific Resources Ltd. ■

Delhi Pacific Resources Ltd. (Ont. Sept. 5, 1934)
July 4, 1986 – Delisted from the Toronto Stock Exchange. Subsequently voluntarily dissolved.

Delhi (Temagami) Gold Mines Ltd. (Ont. Sept. 5, 1934)
1951 – Name changed to New Delhi Mines Ltd.; basis 1 new for 4 old shs. ■

Delic Holdings Corp. (B.C. Nov. 17, 2005)
June 26, 2023 – Placed into receivership. Zeifman Partners Inc. appointed receiver and all officers and directors resigned.

Delic Holdings Inc. (B.C. Nov. 17, 2005)
Sept. 30, 2021 – Name changed to Delic Holdings Corp. ■

Delicious Alternative Desserts Ltd. (Alta. Apr. 5, 1994)
Mar. 2, 2004 – Dissolved and struck from registry.

Delicorp Foodservice Inc. (Ont. Mar. 4, 1983)
June 23, 1993 – Charter cancelled.
Aug. 9, 1995 – Charter revived.
Oct. 9, 1996 – Name changed to Noble House Communications Inc.; basis 1 new for 9 old shs. ■

Delivra Corp. (Ont. Oct. 21, 2013)
July 8, 2019 – Acquired by Harvest One Cannabis Inc.; basis 0.595 Harvest One shs. for 1 Delivra sh. (see Harvest One Cannabis Inc.)

Delkirk Mining Ltd. (B.C. 1966)
July 1972 – Name changed to Delkirk Resources Ltd. (see FPsurvey - Mines & Energy)

Dellaterra Resources Ltd. (B.C. Aug. 17, 1983)
June 25, 1992 – Name changed to United America Enterprises Ltd.; basis 1 new for 5 old shs. ■

The Delma Group Inc. (Can. Jan. 19, 2018)
Jan. 21, 2020 – Name changed to Emergia Inc. (see FPsurvey - Industrials)

Delmay Mining Corporation (Alta. Aug. 21, 1985)
Sept. 9, 1993 – Name changed to Delmay Energy Corporation.

Delmico Mines Ltd. (Ont. 1954)
Dec. 7, 1977 – Charter cancelled.

Delnaur Gold Mines Ltd. (Ont. 1940)
1968 – Merged into Associated Porcupine Mines Ltd.; basis 1 new for 143,658 old shs. (see Associated Porcupine Mines Ltd.)

Delnite Mines Ltd. (Ont. 1934)
July 1970 – Wound up. From 1960-1969, distributed total of $1.0575 per sh. and equivalent of 15¢ per sh. (comprising 10 shs. of Alminex Ltd., for 100 old Delnite shs.)

Delon Resources Corp. (B.C. Jan. 24, 2011)
Apr. 22, 2013 – Name changed to Gener8 Media Corp. following reverse takeover acquisition of Gener8 Digital Media Corp.; basis 1 new for 2 old shs. ■

Deloro Minerals Ltd. (Alta. Apr. 19, 1996)
Aug. 17, 2005 – Name changed to Deloro Resources Ltd.; basis 1 new for 2 old shs. ■

Deloro Resources Ltd. (Alta. Apr. 19, 1996)
Mar. 10, 2009 – Continued into British Columbia.
Feb. 4, 2014 – Continued into Saskatchewan. (see FPsurvey - Mines & Energy)

Delosha Porcupine Mines Ltd. (Ont. 1937)
Aug. 7, 1956 – Dissolved.

Delpet Resources Ltd. (Can. July 7, 1981)
June 6, 2000 – Name changed to HTI Ventures Corp. ■

Delphi Energy Corp. (Alta. June 19, 2003 amalg.)
Nov. 15, 2019 – Continued into Canada.
Apr. 14, 2020 – Filed for protection under the Companies' Creditors Arrangement Act (CCAA) and PricewaterhouseCoopers Inc. was appointed monitor.
Oct. 16, 2020 – Plan of compromise and arrangement completed under the CCAA under which all issued and o/s com. shs. were cancelled and extinguished for no consideration and without any return on capital. New cl. A com. shs. were issued to secured creditors and unsecured creditors with claims less than or equal to $5,000 were paid in full.
Dec. 18, 2020 – Name changed to Distinction Energy Corp. ■

Delpine Mines Ltd. (Ont. 1940)
Aug. 1957 – Charter cancelled.

Delrand Resources Limited (Can. Aug. 11, 2004)
June 16, 2017 – Name changed to KuuHubb Inc. pursuant to acquisition of KuuHubb Oy. (see FPsurvey - Industrials)

Delray Ventures Inc. (Alta. Apr. 4, 1990)
Aug. 8, 2008 – Name changed to Clydesdale Resources Inc. and continued into British Columbia. (see FPsurvey - Mines & Energy)

Delrey Metals Corp. (B.C. Oct. 18, 2017)
Feb. 18, 2020 – Name changed to Carlyle Commodities Corp.; basis 1 new for 7 old shs. (see FPsurvey - Mines & Energy)

Delrina Corporation (Ont. June 1985 amalg.)
Nov. 22, 2002 – Acquired by Symantec Corporation; basis 1 Symantec sh. for 1 Delrina exch. sh.

Delsohn Bathurst Mines Ltd. (Ont. 1953)
1962 – Charter cancelled.

Delta Acceptance Corp. Ltd. (Ont. 1954)
Nov. 1966 – Name changed to Avco Delta Corp. Canada Ltd. ■

Delta-Benco Limited (Ont. 1958)
Mar. 22, 1985 – Name changed to Delta Benco Inc. following acquisition by Triple Crown Electronics Inc.

Delta CleanTech Inc. (Alta. Dec. 22, 2020)
Mar. 24, 2025 – Name changed to Regenera Insights Inc. (see FPsurvey - Industrials)

Delta Credit Union (Can. - unspecified)
Jan. 1, 2000 – Merged with First Heritage Savings Credit Union to form First Heritage Delta Credit Union. (see First Heritage Delta Credit Union)

Delta Exploration Inc. (B.C. Mar. 6, 1987)
Feb. 4, 2009 – Acquired by Rockgate Capital Inc.; basis 0.5 Rockgate shs. for 1 Delta sh.

Delta Explorations Ltd. (B.C. 1966)
Feb. 25, 1983 – Struck off register.

Delta Gold Corporation (B.C. Apr. 20, 2011)
July 9, 2015 – Name changed to Mission Gold Ltd.; basis 1 new for 16 old shs. ■

Delta Gold Mining Corporation (B.C. Oct. 22, 1968)
May 30, 1997 – Amalgamated with Chase Resource Corporation; basis 1 Chase sh. for 2 Delta shs. (see Chase Resource Corporation)

Delta Hotels Limited (B.C. 1970)
1974 – Oxford Properties (B.C.) Limited acquired all o/s com., $0.12 pref. and unlisted cl. B pref. shs. for $4.50 per sh.

Delta International Industries Corp. (B.C. Mar. 6, 1987)
July 15, 2002 – Name changed to Delta Exploration Inc.; basis 1 new for 3 old shs. ■

Delta International Minerals Ltd. (B.C. 1969)
Feb. 10, 1975 – Charter cancelled.

Delta Minerals Corporation (Que. 1955)
Oct. 1974 – Charter cancelled.

Delta Mining Corporation Ltd. (Que. 1962)
1965 – Shs. exch. for Delta Minerals Corporation; basis 1 new pooled for 4 old pooled shs., and 1 new free for 2 old free shs. (see Delta Minerals Corporation)

Delta North Transportation Ltd. (Alta. Mar. 13, 1984)
Dec. 1993 – Voluntarily liquidated. All capital assets sold.
1994 – During 1994 redeemed 148,527 com. shs. at $2.00 per sh., 90,757 com. shs. at $5.00 per sh., and cancelled without payment 63,570 com. shs.
Oct. 31, 1995 – Dissolved and struck off register.

Delta Petroleum Corporation Ltd. (Alta. 1968)
1983 – Placed into receivership. Receiver/manager, Thorne Riddell Inc., Calgary, Alta., appointed.

Delta Refining Corporation (B.C. 1966)
May 6, 1983 – Declared bankrupt, Pannell Kerr Forester (formerly Campbell Sharp Limited) appointed trustee.
June 4, 1986 – Bulk of property liquidated.
Aug. 29, 1989 – Creditors expected to receive a partial compensation with no distrib. to com. shldrs.

Delta Star Resources Inc. (B.C. 1985)
Mar. 31, 1992 – Name changed to Accord Financial Corp. pursuant to reverse takeover acquisition of Accord Business Credit Inc.; basis 1 new for 5 old shs. (see FPsurvey - Industrials)

Delta Systems, Inc. (Miss. Mar. 17, 1990)
Jan. 14, 1993 – Continued into Arkansas.
June 2, 2005 – Continued into Canada.
Oct. 2, 2007 – Wholly owned U.S subsid., Delta Systems Inc., filed for Chapter 11 bankruptcy protection and all officers and directors resigned. No proceeds or income from bankruptcy proceedings were expected due to amounts owed by subsid. to secured and unsecured creditors.
June 29, 2011 – Dissolved.

Deltan Corporation Limited (Can. 1959)
Dec. 1977 – Acquired by Prudel Limited for $10 per sh. Subsequently, Deltan Corporation Limited, Prudel Limited and Deltan Realty Limited amalgamated to form new private co. Deltan Realty Limited.

Deltec International Limited (Ont. 1964)
1973 – All assets and liabs. transferred to a new English co. of same name and Cdn. co. dissolved. During all o/s com. shs. were exch. for ord. shs. and later exch. for ADRs (American Depository Receipts) of UK co.

Deltec Resources Ltd. (B.C. 1986)
Feb. 4, 1991 – Name changed to Pacific Titan Resource Corp.; basis 1 new for 2 old shs. ■

Deltona Industries Inc. (Ont. Sept. 19, 1958)
Jan. 22, 2007 – Certificate of incorporation cancelled and dissolved.

Delwin Mines Ltd. (Ont. 1937)
1962 – Charter cancelled.

Delwood Capital Corporation Ltd. (Can. July 26, 1994)
July 10, 1996 – Name changed to Indostar Gold Corp.; basis 2.5 new for 1 old cl. A subord. vtg. sh. and 2.5 new for 1 old cl. B multiple vtg. shs. ■

Delwood Porcupine Gold Mines Ltd. (Ont. 1936)
Aug. 1960 – Charter cancelled.

Demand Gold Ltd. (B.C. Nov. 4, 1986)
Mar. 3, 1999 – Name changed to Demand Ventures Ltd.; basis 1 new for 3 old shs. ■

Demand Technologies Ltd. (B.C. Nov. 4, 1986)
Jan. 25, 1995 – Name changed to Demand Gold Ltd. ■

Demand Ventures Ltd. (B.C. Nov. 4, 1986)
Aug. 1, 2000 – Name changed to Knexa.com Enterprises Inc. ■

Demcap Investments Inc. (Can. June 23, 2005)
July 3, 2007 – Formed iPerceptions Inc. in Canada on amalgamation with iPerceptions Inc. following June 29, 2007, Qualifying Transaction reverse takeover acquisition of iPerceptions Inc. ■

Demesne Resources Ltd. (B.C. Jan. 14, 2019)
Jan. 23, 2025 – Name changed to American Tungsten Corp. (see FPsurvey - Mines & Energy)

Demontigny Minerals Resources Inc. (Can. Dec. 27, 1985)
Aug. 27, 1997 – Dissolved.

Dempsey Cadillac Gold Mines Ltd. (Ont. 1936)
Dec. 1943 – Name changed to Dominion Malartic Gold Mines Ltd. ■

Dempsey Oils Limited (Alta. 1951)
1969 – Merged into General Petroleums Drilling Ltd.; basis 1 cl. B 7% pref. sh. of General for 1 sh. of Dempsey.

Dempster Explorations Ltd. (Ont. 1956)
Apr. 13, 1981 – Name changed to Tritex Petroleum Corp.; basis 1 new for 3 old shs. ■

Demsey Mines Ltd. (B.C. 1969)
Dec. 18, 1978 – Dissolved.

Denali Petroleums Ltd. (Can. Jan. 30, 1985)
Apr. 29, 1997 – Amalgamated with 3229211 Canada Ltd., a wholly owned subsid. of Windstar Energy Ltd.; basis 1

new sh. of Windstar for 1 old sh. of Denali. (see Windstar Energy Ltd.)

Denallan Gold Mines Ltd. (Ont. 1945)
Apr. 1958 – Charter cancelled.

Denar Mines Ltd. (B.C. Mar. 31, 1978)
Sept. 1, 1987 – Name changed to International Sinabarb Industries Ltd. ■

Denarius Silver Corp. (B.C. Apr. 8, 1981)
Feb. 1, 2022 – Name changed to Denarius Metals Corp. (see FPsurvey - Mines & Energy)

Denault Limitée (Que. 1934)
June 1969 – Acquired by Couvrette & Provost Ltée; basis 2 com. shs. of Couvrette for each cl. A or B sh. of Denault.

Denbridge Capital Corporation (Ont. Jan. 15, 1952; via letters patent)
Feb. 16, 1994 – Continued into Canada.
June 19, 2001 – Name changed to Atlantis Systems Corp.; basis 1 new for 40 old shs. ■

Denbros Mines Ltd. (Ont. Dec. 20, 1945)
1947 – Name changed to Slocan-Rambler Mines (1947) Ltd. ■

Denbury Resources Inc. (Can. Sept. 13, 1984)
Apr. 21, 1999 – Continued into Delaware.
Sept. 15, 2020 – Name changed to Denbury Inc.

Dencal Development Corporation (Ont. July 25, 1965)
Feb. 4, 1991 – Name changed to Bestquipt Sports Inc.; basis 1 new for 5 old shs. ■

Dencam Development Corporation (B.C. Sept. 12, 1986)
Jan. 19, 1994 – Name changed to Consolidated Dencam Development Corporation; basis 1 new for 2.5 old shs. ■

Dencroft Mines Ltd. (Ont. 1949)
Mar. 25, 1965 – Dissolved.

Denison Copper Mines Ltd. (Ont. 1928)
1936 – Assets acquired by Denison Nickel Mines Ltd.; basis 1 new for 2 old shs.

Denison Energy Inc. (Ont. Mar. 24, 1960)
Mar. 8, 2004 – Name changed to Denison Mines Inc. pursuant to reorganization whereby Denison Energy Inc. transferred its mining and environmental services businesses to wholly owned Denison Mines Inc. incorporated Sept. 25, 2003. Denison Energy shldrs. received Denison Mines shs. on a 1-for-1 basis. ■

Denison Energy Inc. (Ont. Feb. 12, 1973)
Mar. 24, 2004 – Formed Calfrac Well Services Ltd. in Alberta on reverse takeover acquisition of and amalgamation with Calfrac Well Services Ltd. Prior to the transaction, almost all of Denison's assets were transferred to 2 new cos. ■

Denison Mines Inc. (Ont. Sept. 25, 2003)
Dec. 7, 2006 – Acquired by International Uranium Corporation (renamed Denison Mines Corp.); basis 2.88 International Uranium shs. for 1 Denison Mines Inc. sh.

Denison Mines Limited (Ont. Mar. 24, 1960)
May 28, 2002 – Name changed to Denison Energy Inc.; basis 1 new for 20 old shs. ■

Denison Nickel Mines Ltd. (Ont. 1936)
1949 – Name changed to North Denison Mines Ltd.; basis 1 new for 4 old shs. ■

Denlake Mining Co. Ltd. (Ont. 1950)
Mar. 1958 – Charter cancelled.

Denninghouse Inc. (Ont. July 9, 1993)
Aug. 3, 2007 – Wound up. Assets and business sold off for undisclosed proceeds.

Dennisteel Corp. Ltd. (Ont. 1936)
Dec. 2, 1970 – Dissolved.

Denn'or Exploration Inc. (Que. Nov. 20, 1985)
Feb. 15, 1993 – Name changed to Sulliden Exploration Inc.; basis 1 new for 5 old shs. ■

Denom Resources Inc. (Ont. Feb. 9, 1937)
Apr. 26, 1983 – Continued into British Columbia.
Jan. 7, 1986 – Name changed to ITM Corporation and continued into Ontario. ■

Denore Mines Ltd. (Ont. 1966)
Mar. 1976 – Charter cancelled.

Denovo Capital Corp. (Alta. Apr. 27, 2010)
Sept. 19, 2011 – Continued into British Columbia.
Sept. 23, 2011 – Name changed to Horn Petroleum Corporation pursuant to Qualifying Transaction reverse takeover acquisition of Canmex Holdings (Bermuda) I Ltd., a wholly owned subsid. of Africa Oil Corp.; basis 0.65 new for 1 old sh. ■

DeNovo Corp. (Ont. Sept. 3, 1986)
Oct. 29, 1996 – Name changed to Princeton Media Group Inc.; basis 1 new for 20 old shs. ■

Denovo Gold Mines Ltd. (Ont. 1941)
1951 – Name changed to Denovo Mining Corp. Ltd. ■

Denovo Mining Corp. Ltd. (Ont. 1941)
Sept. 29, 1966 – Dissolved.

Denrow Mines Ltd. (Man. 1957)
Mar. 1, 1973 – Dissolved.

Denroy Manufacturing Corporation (Ont. Mar. 1, 1945)
June 14, 2005 – Name changed to Denroy Resources Corporation; basis 1 new for 35 old shs. ■

Denroy Resources Corporation (Ont. Mar. 1, 1945)
May 16, 2007 – Continued into Canada.
May 25, 2007 – Name changed to Nevoro Inc. ■

Denstone Minerals Ltd. (B.C. Apr. 10, 1997)
Feb. 4, 2000 – Name changed to Denstone Ventures Ltd.; basis 1 new for 7 old shs. ■

Denstone Resources Ltd. (B.C. Apr. 10, 1997)
Mar. 4, 1998 – Name changed to Denstone Minerals Ltd.; basis 1 new for 2 old shs. ■

Denstone Ventures Ltd. (B.C. Apr. 10, 1997)
Oct. 10, 2002 – Name changed to Mesa Resources Inc.; basis 1 new for 5 old shs. ■

Dentonia Mines Ltd. (Can. 1929)
1948 – Liquidated.

Dentonia Resources Ltd. (B.C. May 31, 1979)
May 27, 2024 – Dissolved for failure to file and struck from the register.

Denver Silver Inc. (B.C. 1978)
Sept. 12, 1984 – Name changed to Androne Resources Ltd.; basis 1 new for 4 old shs. ■

Denyvan Resources Inc. (Can. Mar. 13, 1984)
Jan. 27, 1995 – Amalgamated with Minorca Resources Ltd. and Orco Resources Inc. to form Minorca Resources Inc.; basis 1 new for 1 Minorca sh., 0.38 new for 1 Orco sh. and 0.92 new for 1 Denyvan sh. (see Minorca Resources Inc.)

Departure Bay Capital Corp. (B.C. Feb. 16, 2022)
July 16, 2025 – Name changed to Cheelcare Inc. pursuant to the Qualifying Transaction reverse takeover acquisition of 9302204 Canada Inc. (dba Cheelcare); basis 1 new for 3 old shs. (see FPsurvey - Industrials)

DePaul Capital Corporation (B.C. Nov. 7, 2011)
Dec. 4, 2014 – Name changed to Quadron Capital Corporation. ■

Deploy Technologies Inc. (Nev. Sept. 15, 2010)
Dec. 7, 2017 – Name changed to Body and Mind Inc.; basis 1 new for 3 old shs. (see FPsurvey - Industrials)

Depositors Mortgage Corporation (Que. 1960)
Oct. 19, 1973 – Company deemed to have made a statutory assignment, which was finalized; subsequently the trustee was discharged.
Apr. 23, 1975 – 77.5% of secured notes had been redeemed.

Deprenyl Animal Health, Inc. (U.S. July 19, 1990)
Dec. 5, 1996 – Merged with Deprenyl Animal Health, Inc. (Louisiana incorp.) and a wholly owned subsid. and by a plan of share exchange acquired by Draxis Health Inc.; basis 1.35 new com. sh. of Draxis for 1 com. sh. of Deprenyl Health (Louisiana). (see DRAXIS Health Inc.)

Deprenyl Research Limited (Can. Oct. 13, 1987)
June 9, 1994 – Name changed to DRAXIS Health Inc. ■

Deprenyl USA, Inc. (N.J. Feb. 21, 1991)
June 11, 1993 – Name changed to DUSA Pharmaceuticals, Inc. ■

Deragon Langlois Ltée (Can. 1983)
Dec. 11, 1989 – Name changed to Desjardins Deragon Langlois Ltd. ■

Deranco Mines Ltd. (Ont. 1958)
July 9, 1969 – Charter cancelled.

Derby Mines Ltd. (B.C. 1969)
June 1971 – Name changed to International Visual Systems Ltd. ■

Dercon Mines Ltd. (Ont. 1944)
Oct. 29, 1953 – Charter cancelled.

Dereham Gas & Oil Ltd. (Ont. 1937)
1945 – Assets sold to Queenston Gas & Oil Co. Ltd.

Derek Oil & Gas Corporation (B.C. Apr. 6, 1981)
July 2, 2013 – Name changed to Newcastle Energy Corp. ■

Derek Resources Corporation (B.C. Apr. 6, 1981)
Mar. 3, 2003 – Name changed to Derek Oil & Gas Corporation; basis 1 new for 3 old shs. ■

Derlak Enterprises Inc. (Ont. Nov. 7, 1991 amalg.)
Jan. 28, 2008 – Dissolved and struck from register.

Derlak Gold Inc. (Ont. Nov. 7, 1991 amalg.)
Sept. 9, 1998 – Name changed to Derlak Enterprises Inc. ■

Derlak Red Lake Gold Mines Ltd. (Ont. 1936)
Nov. 7, 1991 – Formed Derlak Gold Inc. in Ontario on amalgamation with Royado Mines Limted, a wholly owned subsid. of Mirado Nickel Mines Limited; basis 1 new for 4 old shs. ■

Derlan Industries Limited (Ont. Mar. 29, 1984)
Dec. 3, 2002 – Name changed to Northstar Aerospace Inc. ■

Derlan Manufacturing Inc. (Can. - unspecified)
Dec. 3, 2002 – Name changed to Northstar Aerospace (Canada) Inc.

Derogan Asbestos Corp. Ltd. (Que. 1952)
Aug. 1972 – Charter cancelled.

Derosier Nickel & Copper Mines Ltd. (Ont. 1952)
1954 – Merged into Temagami Mining Co. Ltd.; basis 1 new for 3 old shs.

Derrick Energy Corporation (Alta. Jan. 19, 1987)
July 13, 1999 – Acquired by Derrick Resources Inc., wholly owned unit of EnerMark Inc.; basis $5.00 and 1 new Derrick Resources sh. for 1 old Derrick Energy sh.

Derrick Oil and Gas Co. Ltd. (Ont. Nov. 5, 1951)
1955 – Reported inactive.

Derrick Oil & Gas Limited (Alta. Jan. 19, 1987)
Dec. 13, 1995 – Name changed to Derrick Energy Corporation; basis 1 new for 5 old shs. ■

Derrick Petroleum Corp. (B.C. Nov. 21, 1983)
Sept. 29, 1993 – Name changed to Earth Stewards, Inc. ■

Derrick Resources Inc. (Alta. Apr. 22, 1999)
July 12, 2001 – Acquired by EOG Resources Canada Inc. for $4.82 per sh.

Derry-Gold Resources Inc. (Ont. Sept. 28, 1987)
Jan. 18, 1993 – Name changed to Selby Green International Ltd.; basis 1 new for 10 old shs. ■

Des Barats Mining Co. Ltd. (Ont. 1955)
Nov. 11, 1965 – Charter cancelled.

The Descartes Systems Group Inc. (Ont. May 22, 1981)
July 5, 2006 – Continued into Canada. (see FPsurvey - Industrials)

Desco Energy Ltd. (Alta. June 23, 2005)
Jan. 9, 2007 – Amalgamated with Arcan Resources Ltd. (1 for 1) to continue as a new company named Arcan Resources Ltd.; basis 0.36231884 new Arcan sh. for 1 old Desco sh. (see Arcan Resources Ltd.)

Desco Exploration Ltd. (Alta. Apr. 16, 2002)
Oct. 7, 2002 – Name changed to Celtic Exploration Ltd. following Qualifying Transaction exchange with Jared Oils Ltd. of shares and cash for oil and gas assets. ■

Desco Mines Limited (Ont. 1951)
1953 – Charter cancelled.

Desco Resources Inc. (Alta. July 8, 2009)
July 8, 2010 – Formed Manitok Energy Inc. in Alberta pursuant to Qualifying Transaction acquisition of and amalgamation with Manitok Exploration Inc.; basis 1 new for 2.667 old shs. ■

Desco Resources Ltd. (Alta. Feb. 20, 1997)
Dec. 4, 1998 – Name changed to PEYTO Exploration & Development Corp. following Qualifying Transaction acquisition of a producing oil and gas property. ■

Descon Ventures Inc. (Alta. Nov. 21, 1996)
Feb. 2, 1999 – Name changed to Emercor Building Systems Ltd.; basis 1 new for 5 old shs. ■

Deseret Peak Mines Ltd. (B.C. 1966)
Nov. 25, 1974 – Struck off register.

Desert Gold Resources Inc. (B.C. Sept. 15, 1987)
July 7, 1993 – Name changed to Desert Holdings Inc.; basis 1 new for 3 old shs. ■

Desert Holdings Inc. (B.C. Sept. 15, 1987)
Feb. 11, 2003 – Name changed to Tinka Resources Limited; basis 1 new for 3 old shs. (see FPsurvey - Mines & Energy)

Desert Lion Energy Inc. (Ont. Feb. 20, 2018)
July 17, 2019 – Acquired by Lepidico Ltd.; basis 5.4 Lepidico ord. shs. for 1 Desert Lion com. sh.

Desert Rose Resources Inc. (B.C. 1977)
Jan. 16, 1989 – Continued into Delaware.
Jan. 24, 1989 – Name changed to QSA Technology, Inc.

Desert Star Resources Ltd. (B.C. Aug. 29, 1986)
Apr. 15, 2015 – Amalgamated with Providence Resources Corp. to form a new Desert Star Resources Ltd. (Amlaco); basis 0.4 Amalco com. shs. plus 0.4 Amalco wts. for 1 Providence com. sh. and 1 Amalco com. sh. for 1 (old) Desert Star Resources Ltd. Each purchased wts. is exercisable at 25¢ for a period of 2 yrs.
Dec. 21, 2017 – Name changed to Kutcho Copper Corp. (see FPsurvey - Mines & Energy)

Desert Sun Mining Corp. (B.C. May 21, 1980)
Apr. 7, 2006 – Acquired by Yamana Gold Inc.; basis 0.6 Yamana shs. for 1 Desert sh. (see Yamana Gold Inc.)

Designed Data (Canada) Inc. (B.C. Sept. 1, 1981)
May 3, 1990 – Name changed to Pier Mac Environment Management Inc.; basis 1 new for 3 old shs. ■

Desjardins Deragon Langlois Ltd. (Can. 1983)
Mar. 15, 1991 – Acquired by Corporation Desjardins de valeurs mobilières for 52¢ per sh.

Desjardins Financial Corporation Inc. (Que. Oct. 1, 1993)
Dec. 16, 2003 – Called for redemption; basis $25 plus $0.30978 accrued and unpaid dividends for 1 old Desjardins cl. A pfd. sh.

Desjardins Laurentian Financial Corporation (Que. Oct. 1, 1993)
July 13, 1995 – Name changed to Desjardins-Laurentian Financial Corporation. ■

Desjardins-Laurentian Financial Corporation (Que. Oct. 1, 1993)
May 15, 2003 – Name changed to Desjardins Financial Corporation Inc. ■

Desjardins Mines Limited (Que. 1937)
Aug. 2, 2012 – Continued into British Columbia.
Jan. 28, 2014 – Voluntarily dissolved.

Desjardins Trustco Inc. (Que. Sept. 1975)
Nov. 22, 1993 – Acquired by La Société Financière des caisses Desjardins Inc.; basis $2.00 per sh. for 90.4% of the o/s shs. revised to $2.25 per sh. for the remaining 9.6% o/s shs.

Desk Holdings Ltd. (B.C. Dec. 13, 2021)
June 10, 2022 – Name changed to Powerstone Metals Corp. ■

Desmarais Energy Corporation (Alta. June 24, 1994)
Jan. 2, 2017 – Struck off the registry and dissolved.

Desmeloizes Mining Corp. (unknown)
1953 – Sold property to Duvan Copper Co. Ltd.; basis 1 new escrowed sh. for 4 old shs. (see Duvan Copper Co. Ltd.)

Desmond Investments Ltd. (B.C. Mar. 25, 2011)
Feb. 7, 2017 – Name changed to DLC Holdings Corp. (see FPsurvey - Industrials)

Desmont Mining Corp. Ltd. (Ont. 1944)
Mar. 30, 1959 – Dissolved.

DeSoto Mines Ltd. (unknown)
1957 – Name changed to B.X. Mining Co. Ltd.

Desperado Resources Inc. (B.C. 1981)
Aug. 14, 1986 – Name changed to Skyway Resources Ltd. ■

Desrem Mining Syndicate Ltd. (Ont. 1947)
1953 – Charter cancelled.

Dessir Resources Ltd. (B.C. Feb. 3, 1988)
June 7, 1993 – Name changed to Taurus Exploration Ltd.; basis 1 new for 5 old shs. ■

Destaffany Tantalum Beryllium Mines Ltd. (Can. 1945)
All assets sold to Boreal Rare Metals Ltd. (see Boreal Rare Metals Ltd.)

Destination Resorts Inc. (Alta. Dec. 5, 1996)
Dec. 4, 2000 – All o/s com. shs. acquired by TGS Properties Ltd.; basis 0.575 of a new TGS com. sh. for 1 old Destination com. sh. All o/s 8% convert. sub. debs. redeemed on July 2, 2002; basis 149 com. shs. of Destination for each $1,000 principal converted which were then exchanged for 0.575 of a TGS com. sh. for 1 old Destination com. sh. (see TGS Properties Ltd.)

Destiny Hospitality Ltd. (Alta. Feb. 10, 1999)
May 16, 2003 – Amalgamated with Real Time Measurements Inc. deemed to be Destiny's Qualifying Transaction; basis 0.1149425 new Real Time sh. for 1 old Destiny sh.

Destiny Media Technologies Inc. (Colo. Aug. 24, 1998)
Oct. 8, 2014 – Continued into Nevada. (see FPsurvey - Industrials)

Destiny Resource Services Corp. (Alta. Apr. 7, 1993)
May 13, 2010 – Name changed to Logan International Inc. pursuant to reverse takeover acquisition of Logan Holdings, Inc. ■

Destiny Resources Ltd. (B.C. Nov. 6, 1978)
June 12, 1990 – Name changed to Double Down Resources Ltd.; basis 1 new for 7 old shs. ■

Destor-O'Hara Mines Ltd. (Ont. 1956)
Feb. 18, 1963 – Dissolved.

Destor Valley Gold Mines Ltd. (Que. 1944)
Charter cancelled.

Destorada Mines Ltd. (Ont. 1945)
Mar. 25, 1965 – Dissolved.

Destorbelle Mines Limited (Ont. Nov. 23, 1945)
Aug. 6, 2004 – Acquired by Excellon Resources Inc.; basis 60¢ plus 3.25 Excellon shs. for 1 Destorbelle sh.

Destron/IDI Inc. (Can. 1984)
Oct. 1, 1993 – Continued into Delaware.

Destron Technologies Inc. (Can. 1984)
May 20, 1986 – Name changed to International Destron Technologies Inc. ■

DeTECH Corporation (Alta. Mar. 7, 1995)
Aug. 2, 2006 – Dissolved and struck from register.

Detec Resources Ltd. (B.C. Oct. 16, 1997)
Oct. 19, 2000 – Name changed to Streamline Web Broadcasting Inc. ■

Detector Exploration Ltd. (Alta. Jan. 9, 1991)
Feb. 22, 2016 – Petitioned into receivership and Hardie & Kelly Inc. was appointed receiver. All officers and directors resigned.
July 2, 2018 – Struck from registry and dissolved.

Detector Resources Ltd. (Alta. Jan. 9, 1991)
July 19, 1999 – Name changed to Detector Exploration Ltd.; basis 1 new for 4 old shs. ■

Detomac Mines Ltd. (Ont. 1943)
Mar. 25, 1965 – Dissolved.

Detour Gold Corporation (Can. July 19, 2006)
Feb. 4, 2020 – Acquired by Kirkland Lake Gold Ltd.; basis 0.4343 Kirkland Lake com. shs. for 1 Detour Gold sh. (see Kirkland Lake Gold Ltd.)

Detroit International Bridge Company (Mich. 1927)
July 1979 – Merged with wholly owned subsid. of Central Cartage Co. (private co.). Minority shldrs. received $25 a sh. for 1 old sh.

Detta Minerals Limited (Ont. May 18, 1945)
Oct. 30, 1956 – Name changed to Candore Explorations Ltd.; basis 1 new for 6 old shs. ■

Detta Red Lake Mines, Limited (Ont. May 18, 1945)
July 19, 1950 – Name changed to Detta Minerals Limited. ■

Dev Investments Inc. (Alta. Nov. 7, 2000)
Mar. 2, 2004 – Name changed to Indicator Minerals Inc. following Qualifying Transaction acquisition of mineral interests. ■

Devco Enterprises Inc. (B.C. June 23, 1983)
Oct. 5, 1995 – Name changed to SBI Skin Biology Incorporated; basis 1 new for 4 old shs. ■

DevCorp Capital Inc. (Alta. Feb. 4, 2011)
Dec. 20, 2013 – Name changed to Great Prairie Energy Services Inc. following the Qualifying Transaction reverse takeover acquisition of Good to Go Rentals Ltd. and Neigum Hot Oilers Inc. ■

Develcon Electronics Ltd. (Sask. Aug. 15, 1974)
May 28, 1999 – Amalgamated with Vianet Technologies, Inc.; basis 0.0325203 Vianet shs. for 1 Develcon sh.

Developer Ventures Inc. (Alta. Sept. 21, 2000)
Feb. 4, 2002 – Name changed to DevStudios International Inc. following Qualifying Transaction acquisition of DevStudios Inc. ■

Developments by Jayman Inc. (Alta. Dec. 7, 1988)
July 2, 1991 – Name changed to APEX Land Corporation. ■

Developpement Minier Aurtec Inc. (Can. June 7, 1984)
Sept. 23, 1994 – Name changed to Aurtec Inc. ■

Deveron Resources Ltd. (Ont. Mar. 28, 2011)
July 12, 2016 – Name changed to Deveron UAS Corp. ■

Deveron UAS Corp. (Ont. Mar. 28, 2011)
Sept. 3, 2020 – Name changed to Deveron Corp. (see FPsurvey - Industrials)

Devil Lake Mines Ltd. (Ont.)
Mar. 26, 1969 – Charter cancelled.

Devil's Elbow Mines Ltd. (Ont. 1965)
1973 – Name changed to New Devil's Elbow Mines Ltd.; basis 1 new for 4 old shs. ■

Devin Energy Corporation (B.C. Jan. 21, 1987)
Aug. 17, 2020 – Dissolved for failure to file and struck from register.

Devine Entertainment Corporation (Ont. Sept. 20, 1982)
Feb. 22, 2011 – Dissolved and struck from register.

Devjo Industries Inc. (Ont. June 17, 1986)
Dec. 2, 2002 – Privatized at 50¢ per sh.

Devlan Exploration Company Ltd. (Alta. Sept. 18, 1992)
Nov. 3, 1998 – Name changed to Devlan Exploration Inc.; basis 1 new for 4 old shs. ■

Devlan Exploration Inc. (Alta. Sept. 18, 1992)
July 8, 2005 – Plan of Arrangement acquisition by Cyries Energy Inc.; basis 0.25 new Cyries sh. plus 0.5 new Dual Exploration Inc. sh. for 1 old Devlan sh. (see Cyries Energy Inc.; Dual Exploration Inc.)

Devnic Energy Inc. (Alta. 1987)
Sept. 17, 1993 – Amalgamated with Petrolia Oil & Gas Ltd. and Canadian Fortune Resource Inc. to form Fortune Energy Inc.; basis 1 new for 1 Petrolia sh., 1 new for 0.51 Canadian Fortune shs. and 1 new for 1.77 Devnic shs. (see Fortune Energy Inc.)

Devon-Leduc Oils Ltd. (Man. 1948)
Oct. 30, 1956 – Name changed to Devon-Palmer Oils Ltd. ■

Devon-Palmer Oils Ltd. (Man. 1948)
Mar. 1967 – Merged with Triad Oil Holdings Ltd. into Triad Oil Manitoba Ltd.; basis 1 old sh. for one 5.75% sh. of Triad Manitoba; latter red. on Apr. 30, 1967, at $2.25 per sh. plus accrued divds.

Devon Ventures Corporation (B.C. Nov. 30, 2001)
June 23, 2004 – Name changed to Pender Financial Group Corporation. ■

Devonion Resources Ltd. (B.C. 1980)
Sept. 1, 1987 – Name changed to Koba Capital Corporation; basis 1 new for 2.5 old shs. (see FPsurvey - Industrials)

Devonshire Gold Resources Inc. (Ont. Feb. 9, 1983)
June 1987 – Name changed to Colours International Inc. ■

Devonshire Resources Ltd. (B.C. Feb. 6, 2004)
Nov. 18, 2009 – Name changed to Gold Standard Ventures Corp.; basis 1 new for 4 old shs. ■

Devran Petroleum Ltd. (Can. Mar. 14, 1986 amalg.)
Dec. 11, 1995 – Name changed to Reserve Royalty Corporation following acquisition of Reserve Royalty Corporation. ■

DevStudios International Inc. (Alta. Sept. 21, 2000)
Mar. 2, 2020 – Struck from registry and dissolved.

Devtek Corporation (Ont. Nov. 12, 1981)
Sept. 12, 2000 – Acquired by Héroux Inc.; basis $3.50 or 0.833 Héroux shs. for 1 Devtek sh. (see Héroux Inc.)

DevvStream Holdings Inc. (B.C. Aug. 13, 2021)
Nov. 7, 2024 – Acquired by Focus Impact Acquisition Corp. (renamed DevvStream Corp.).

Dewey Oil and Gas Inc. (Ont. 1984)
Sept. 29, 1987 – Amalgamated with Southern Eagle Petroleum Corp. to form Southern Eagle Enterprises Inc.; basis 43 com. shs. and 75 cl. A non-voting shs. of new co. for each 100 old shs. of Dewey. (see Southern Eagle Enterprises Inc.)

Dewmella Inc. (Alta. July 9, 2003)
Nov. 19, 2004 – Name changed to Contact Image Corporation following Qualifying Transaction reverse takeover acquisition of Contact Image Group Inc. (see FPsurvey - Industrials)

Dewson Mines Limited (Ont. 1948)
Feb. 24, 1958 – Dissolved.

Dexit Inc. (Ont. Oct. 22, 2001)
Aug. 17, 2007 – Name changed to Hosted Data Transaction Solutions Inc. ∎

Dexleigh Corporation (Can. June 30, 1984 amalg.)
Feb. 9, 1999 – Privatized at $2.00 per sh.
June 27, 2005 – Continued into Ontario.

Dexter Red Lake Gold Mines Ltd. (Ont. 1944)
1950 – Charter cancelled; assets sold to Campbell Red Lake Mines. Distribution made of 1 Campbell sh. plus $0.17 for each 10 Dexter shs. (see Campbell Red Lake Mines Limited)

Dexton Technologies Corporation (B.C. Dec. 19, 1994)
Nov. 19, 2001 – Name changed to Strategem Capital Corporation. (see FPsurvey - Industrials)

Dexus Inc. (Ont. Sept. 29, 1989 amalg.)
June 30, 1993 – Acquired by Trimin Enterprises Inc.; basis 1.42 Trimin shs. for 1 Dexus cl. A non-vtg. sh. and 1 Dexus cl. B vtg. sh. (see Trimin Enterprises Inc.)

Dexx Corporation (Ont. Aug. 19, 1983)
Aug. 17, 2015 – Dissolved and struck from register.

Dexx Energy Corporation (B.C. 1969)
Apr. 8, 1993 – Delisted from the CDN. Subsequently dissolved and struck from register.

Dia Bras Exploration Inc. (Can. Apr. 11, 1996)
Dec. 7, 2012 – Name changed to Sierra Metals Inc. ∎

Dia-M Resources International Inc. (B.C. 1986)
Feb. 9, 1987 – Name changed to DiaEm Resources Ltd. ∎

Dia Met Minerals Ltd. (B.C. Mar. 28, 1983)
Nov. 2, 2001 – Amalgamated with Tortilla Acquisition Inc., an indirect wholly owned subsid. of BHP Limited, for $21 per cl. A and cl. B sh.

Diabex Resources Inc. (Que. Nov. 12, 1985)
Nov. 1, 1999 – Formed Metco Resources Inc. in Quebec on amalgamation with Mafricor Resources Inc. with Diabex the deemed acquiror; basis 1 new for 1 Mafricor sh. and 1 for 2 Diabex shs. ∎

Diabior Explorations Inc. (Can. Feb. 22, 1984)
June 3, 1996 – Amalgamated with Virginia Gold Mines Inc. (1 new for 1.22 old) to form a new co. also known as Virginia Gold Mines Inc.; basis 1 new for 2 old shs. and shldrs. of record as of May 31, 1996 also received 1 com. sh. of subsid. Abior Explorations for 10 com. Diabior shs. (see Virginia Gold Mines Inc.)

Diadem Mines Ltd. (Ont. 1946)
Mar. 25, 1965 – Dissolved.

DiaEm Resources Ltd. (B.C. 1986)
Aug. 23, 1988 – Dissolved.

Diagem Inc. (Can. Dec. 9, 2004)
Sept. 18, 2011 – Dissolved.

Diagem International Resource Corp. (B.C. Nov. 15, 1971)
Dec. 9, 2004 – Continued into Canada.
Apr. 21, 2005 – Name changed to Diagem Inc. ∎

DiagnoCure Inc. (Que. Dec. 8, 1994)
June 7, 2016 – In voluntary liquidation. PricewaterhouseCoopers Inc. appointed liquidator and all officers and directors resigned.
June 16, 2016 – Name changed to 9342-8530 Quebec inc. ∎

Dialogue Health Technologies Inc. (Can. July 5, 2016)
May 10, 2023 – Acquired by Sun Life Financial Inc.; basis $5.15 cash per sh.

Dialogue Technologies Inc. (Can. July 5, 2016)
Nov. 23, 2020 – Name changed to Dialogue Health Technologies Inc. ∎

DiaMedica Inc. (Man. Jan. 21, 2000)
Apr. 11, 2016 – Continued into Canada.
Dec. 29, 2016 – Name changed to DiaMedica Therapeutics Inc. ∎

DiaMedica Therapeutics Inc. (Can. Apr. 11, 2016)
May 31, 2019 – Continued into British Columbia. (see FPsurvey - Industrials)

Diamond Exploration Inc. (Ont. Jan. 28, 1994)
Oct. 29, 2009 – Name changed to Diamond International Exploration Inc. and continued into British Columbia. ∎

Diamond Fields International Ltd. (British Virgin Islands Mar. 8, 1996)
June 8, 1998 – Continued into Yukon.
Mar. 27, 2007 – Continued into British Columbia.
Dec. 7, 2017 – Name changed to Diamond Fields Resources Inc. ∎

Diamond Fields Resources Inc. (B.C. Feb. 13, 1987)
Aug. 22, 1996 – All o/s com. shs. acquired by Inco Limited; basis 1 old Diamond Fields com. sh. for (i) 0.557 of an Inco com. sh. or $26.39 (based on a value of $47.375 per Inco com. sh.); (ii) 0.091 of a new ser. of Inco 5.5% conver. pref. sh, ser. E with a liquidation value of US$50 each; (iii) 0.25 of a cl. VBN sh. and (iv) 1 promisory note, payable with 1 com. sh. of Diamond Fields International Ltd., holder of the diamond mining and exploration interests and related assets and liabs. (see Inco Limited)

Diamond Fields Resources Inc. (B.C. Mar. 27, 2007)
Jan. 30, 2023 – Name changed to DFR Gold Inc. (see FPsurvey - Mines & Energy)

Diamond Four Oil Limited (Alta. 1948)
Oct. 1, 1992 – Struck off register.

Diamond Frank Exploration Inc. (Can. Oct. 17, 2007)
Apr. 8, 2013 – Name changed to AXE Exploration Inc. ∎

Diamond Hawk Mining Corp. (Alta. Feb. 11, 2005 amalg.)
July 14, 2005 – Continued into British Columbia.
May 20, 2019 – Dissolved and struck from registry.
Nov. 14, 2022 – Restored to registry.
Nov. 14, 2022 – Name changed to 0730004 B.C. Ltd. (see FPsurvey - Mines & Energy)

Diamond International Exploration Inc. (B.C. Oct. 29, 2009)
Mar. 14, 2011 – Name changed to Northaven Resources Corp. ∎

Diamond International Industries Inc. (B.C. Sept. 29, 1980)
Dec. 2, 1999 – Name changed to Vault Systems Inc.; basis 1 new for 8 old shs. ∎

Diamond Oil & Gas Ltd. (unknown)
Oct. 1957 – Dissolved.

Diamond Resources Inc. (B.C. Sept. 29, 1980)
Aug. 10, 1989 – Name changed to Diamond International Industries Inc. ∎

Diamond Robinson Equities Ltd. (B.C. Aug. 15, 1989)
Nov. 8, 1996 – Continued into Yukon.
Nov. 12, 1996 – Name changed to Seahawk Minerals Ltd.; basis 1 new for 3.0712 old shs. ∎

Diamond Tree Energy Ltd. (Alta. June 9, 2000)
Oct. 17, 2007 – Acquired by Crocotta Energy Inc.; basis 0.9527 Crocotta com. sh. and 1 Upper Lake Oil and Gas Ltd. com. sh. for 1 Diamond Tree com. sh. (see Crocotta Energy Inc.; Upper Lake Oil and Gas Ltd.)

Diamondex Resources Ltd. (B.C. Feb. 18, 1999)
Dec. 9, 2009 – Name changed to Canterra Minerals Corporation; basis 1 new for 10 old shs. (see FPsurvey - Mines & Energy)

Diamonds North Resources Ltd. (B.C. Feb. 13, 2002)
Feb. 19, 2013 – Amalgamated with Uranium North Resources Corp. to form Adamera Minerals Corp.; basis 0.2 Adamera Minerals shs. for 1 Uranium North sh. and 0.1333 Adamera Minerals shs. for 1 Diamonds North sh.

DiamondWorks Ltd. (Yuk. Aug. 11, 1995)
June 22, 2004 – Name changed to Energem Resources Inc. ∎

Diana Explorations Ltd. (B.C. Apr. 13, 1966)
Nov. 9, 1982 – Formed Equus Petroleum Corporation in British Columbia on amalgamation with Arabian Petroleum Corporation and Persian Petroleum Corporation; basis 1 new for 1.5385 old shs. ∎

Diana Resources Ltd. (B.C. 1983)
Aug. 20, 1993 – Dissolved and struck off register.

Diane Mines Limited (Alta. 1988)
Oct. 1, 1992 – Dissolved and struck off register.

Dianor Resources Inc. (Que. July 20, 1987)
Sept. 3, 2015 – Placed into receivership. Richter Advisory Group Inc. appointed receiver.
Oct. 26, 2016 – Sales of assets was completed. Distrib. to be made to holders of gross overridging royalty amounting to $400,000. Secured creditor suffered a short-fall and no monies available for distrib. to lower-ranking secured creditors, unsecured creditors or shldrs.
Sept. 24, 2018 – Struck from register and dissolved.

Diasyn Technologies Limited (Can. Jan. 15, 1988)
July 27, 1993 – Amalgamated with Syntech Diamond Films Inc. to form Structured Biologicals Inc.; basis 1 new for 5 Syntech shs. and 1 new for 5 Diasyn shs. (see Structured Biologicals Inc.)

Diatec Resources Ltd. (B.C. 1980)
Oct. 6, 1989 – Delisted from the Vancouver Stock Exchange. Subsequently struck from register and dissolved for failure to file.

Diaterre Gold Mines Ltd. (Ont. 1944)
Aug. 7, 1956 – Dissolved.

Diaz Resources Ltd. (B.C. Nov. 3, 1986)
Apr. 14, 1998 – Continued into Alberta. (see Tuscany Energy Ltd.)
July 19, 2013 – Acquired by Tuscany Energy Ltd.; basis 0.31 Tuscany shs. for 1 Diaz sh. (see Tuscany Energy Ltd.)

Dibi Resources Inc. (B.C. 1983)
July 1985 – Amalgamated into Eden Roc Mineral Corp.; basis 1 sh. Eden Roc for each 5 shs. Dibi.

Dickenson Mines Limited (Ont. Oct. 11, 1960)
Mar. 31, 1994 – Principal assets of the company were amalgamated with those of Goldcorp Inc. (1.4 for 1) and CSA Management Limited (1 for 1) to form a new Goldcorp Inc., a new CSA Management Inc., and a new

wholly owned company, Lexam Explorations Inc.; basis 1 new Goldcorp cl. A sh. for 1 old Dickenson cl. A sh. and 1 new Goldcorp cl. B sh. for 1 old Dickenson cl. B sh. (see CSA Management Inc.; Goldcorp Inc.; Lexam Explorations Inc.)

Dickenson Mines Ltd. (Ont. 1960 amalg.)
Oct. 1980 – Amalgamated with Silvana Mines Inc. to continue under the Dickenson Mines Ltd. name; basis 1 cl. A & 1 new cl. B for 1 old sh. (see Dickenson Mines Limited)

Dickenson Red Lake Mines Ltd. (Ont. 1944)
1949 – Name changed to New Dickenson Mines Ltd.; basis 3 new for 10 old shs. ■

Dicon Systems Limited (Ont. 1974)
Nov. 29, 1991 – Name changed to Disys Corporation. ■

Dictator Mines Ltd. (B.C. 1969)
Apr. 15, 1983 – Struck off register.

Dictore Porcupine Gold Mines Ltd. (Ont. 1939)
Aug. 1957 – Charter cancelled.

Diepdaume Mines Limited (Can. Nov. 17, 1971)
May 16, 2023 – Dissolved for non-compliance.

Difference Capital Financial Inc. (Can. Jan. 14, 1972)
June 20, 2019 – Name changed to Mogo Inc. and continued into British Columbia pursuant to acquisition of Mogo Finance Technology Inc. (see FPsurvey - Industrials)

Difference Capital Funding Inc. (Can. Jan. 14, 1972)
June 13, 2013 – Name changed to Difference Capital Financial Inc.; basis 1 new for 10 old shs. ■

Digby Dome Mines Ltd., He (Ont. 1910)
1955 – Name changed to New Digby Dome Mines Ltd.; basis 1 new for 3 old shs. ■

Digger Resources Inc. (B.C. Dec. 31, 1985)
Nov. 13, 2017 – Struck from register and dissolved.

Digicon Inc. (Tex. 1965)
1969 – Continued into Delaware.
Aug. 30, 1996 – Name changed to Veritas DGC Inc. following acquisition by Veritas Energy Services Inc.

DigiCrypts Blockchain Solutions Inc. (Ont. Dec. 11, 1998)
May 20, 2021 – Name changed to DigiMax Global Inc. ■

Digifonica International Inc. (Alta. Nov. 23, 2004)
Dec. 10, 2013 – Name changed to Dominion Energy Inc. ■

Digihost Technology Inc. (B.C. Feb. 18, 2017)
Mar. 6, 2025 – Name changed to Digi Power X Inc. (see FPsurvey - Industrials)

DigiMax Global Inc. (Ont. Dec. 11, 1998)
Dec. 9, 2022 – Name changed to Spetz Inc. following acquisition of Spetz Tech Ltd. (see FPsurvey - Industrials)

Digital Artisans Guild Inc. (Alta. Dec. 14, 2000 amalg.)
May 2, 2003 – Dissolved and struck from register.

Digital Atheneum Technology Corporation (Can. July 21, 2000)
May 18, 2004 – Name changed to Nickel Petroleum Resources Ltd. following Qualifying Transaction acquisition of certain U.S. oil and gas exploration assets from Nickel Energy, LLC. ■

Digital Buyer Technologies Corp. (B.C. Feb. 18, 2017)
Aug. 31, 2021 – Name changed to Planet Based Foods Global Inc. pursuant to the reverse takeover acquisition of Planet Based Foods, Inc. and concurrent amalgamation of Planet Based with wholly owned DBT (USA) Corp. (see FPsurvey - Industrials)

Digital Composition Systems Ltd. (B.C. Jan. 12, 1987)
Mar. 1, 1990 – Name changed to DCS International Systems Corporation; basis 1 new for 5 old shs. ■

Digital Consumer Dividend Fund (Alta.)
Feb. 17, 2022 – Merged into Global Innovation Dividend Fund; basis 0.77032870 Global Innovation fund units for 1 Digital Consumer fund unit. (see Global Innovation Dividend Fund)

Digital Courier International Corporation (Alta. Nov. 30, 1993)
Sept. 25, 1998 – Placed into receivership June 17, 1998 and Grant Thorton Limited in B.C. appointed receiver-manager. all assets acquired by U.S. based Digital Generation Systems, Inc. for $13.5 million.

Digital Cybernet Corporation (Ont. Sept. 27, 1999)
Nov. 21, 2000 – Name changed to Canadian Everock Explorations Inc. ■

Digital Dispatch Systems Inc. (B.C. Sept. 28, 1987)
Mar. 18, 2008 – Name changed to DDS Wireless International Inc. ■

Digital Duplication Inc. (Ont. June 24, 1996)
Feb. 19, 2007 – Dissolved and struck from register.

Digital Fusion Multimedia Corp. (Can. Aug. 30, 1946)
Mar. 6, 2000 – Dissolved.

Digital Gem Corporation (Ont. Oct. 7, 1988)
Oct. 31, 2000 – Name changed to Northern Financial Corporation. ■

Digital Nervous Systems Inc. (Alta. July 19, 2000)
Aug. 26, 2003 – Qualifying Transaction acquisition by Battery & Wireless Solutions Inc. (BWS); basis 1 new BWS unit for 1 old Digital sh. One BWS unit equals 0.91081 BWS sh. plus 0.5 BWS wt. (entitling holder to purchase 1 BWS sh. at $0.40 in year one and at $0.50 in year two.). (see Battery & Wireless Solutions Inc.)

Digital Precision Imagery Corp. (Alta. Dec. 31, 1987)
Sept. 18, 1995 – Delisted from the Alberta Stock Exchange. Subsequently struck from register and dissolved.
Apr. 16, 1998 – Name changed to Alava Ventures Inc.; basis 1 new for 25 old shs.

Digital Processing Systems Inc. (Ont. Dec. 29, 1987)
Oct. 30, 2000 – All o/s com. shs. acquired by Leitch Technology Corporation; basis either $6.50 per sh.; the fraction of a Leitch sh. equal to a $6.50 dividend; or a combination thereof. (see Leitch Technology Corporation)

Digital Rooster.com Inc. (Ont. Jan. 16, 1984)
Dec. 2, 2002 – Name changed to Digital Rooster.com Ltd.; basis 1 new for 50 old shs. ■

Digital Rooster.com Ltd. (Ont. Jan. 16, 1984)
Feb. 1, 2005 – Name changed to Phinder Technologies Inc. ■

Digital Shelf Space Corp. (B.C. Dec. 11, 2009)
June 18, 2015 – Name changed to Movit Media Corp. ■

Digital Ventures Inc. (B.C. Feb. 11, 1981)
Jan. 4, 2002 – Name changed to Castleworth Ventures Inc.; basis 1 new for 2 old shs. ■

Digital World Trust (Ont. Feb. 15, 2000)
Aug. 5, 2005 – Name changed to Top 10 Canadian Financial Trust; basis 1 new for 5 old shs. ■

Digital Youth Network Corp. (Alta. Nov. 22, 1996)
May 2, 2010 – Dissolved and struck from register.

Digitech Ltd. (Alta. Aug. 10, 1973 amalg.)
Nov. 17, 1987 – Name changed to Colin Energy Corporation; basis 1 new for 5 old shs. ■

Dikor Mines Ltd. (Que. 1946)
Oct. 1957 – Charter cancelled.

Dimac Resources Corp. (B.C. 1979)
Feb. 14, 1986 – Struck off register.

Dimension Five Technologies Inc. (B.C. Jan. 10, 2018)
Apr. 23, 2021 – Name changed to Aduro Clean Technologies Inc. pursuant to the reverse takeover acquisition of Aduro Energy Inc.; basis 1 new for 3 old shs. (see FPsurvey - Industrials)

Dimension House International, Inc. (B.C. 1979)
June 6, 1990 – Name changed to PII Photovision International, Inc. ■

Dimensions West Energy Inc. (B.C. 1979)
July 11, 2005 – Dissolved and struck from register.

Dimensions West Marketing Inc. (B.C. 1979)
Nov. 14, 1997 – Name changed to Dimensions West Energy Inc. ■

Dimethaid Research Inc. (Ont. Aug. 22, 1983)
Oct. 31, 2005 – Name changed to Nuvo Research Inc. ■

Dimitra Developments Corp. (B.C. Apr. 21, 1986)
Aug. 23, 1996 – Name changed to Jeda Petroleum Ltd. ■

Ding How Mines Limited (Ont. 1946)
Apr. 30, 1982 – Name changed to Eramosa Technology Corporation. ■

Dingman Industries Inc. (Can. Mar. 6, 1989)
Dec. 13, 2004 – Dissolved.

Dino International Inc. (Ont. Aug. 16, 1985)
Jan. 3, 1995 – Delisted from the CDN. Subsequently dissolved.

Dinosaur Energy Ltd. (Alta. Dec. 16, 1993)
Dec. 23, 1996 – Name changed to Battery & Wireless Solutions Inc. following acquisition of Magnacharge Battery Corporation a B.C. corporation; basis 1 new for 1 old sh. ■

Dinwell Lac Gold Mines Ltd. (Ont. 1937)
1951 – Charter cancelled.

Dion Entertainment Corp. (Can. May 7, 1987)
2003 – Petitioned into receivership.

DionyMed Brands Inc. (B.C. Mar. 22, 2017)
Oct. 29, 2019 – Petitioned into receivership by the holder of the company's sr. secured credit facility following notice of default and demand for immediate payment of the US$24,810,682 owing under the credit facility. FTI Consulting Canada Inc. appointed receiver and all independent directors resigned.
Jan. 2020 – Assets sold. First secured creditor suffered a shortfall.
Mar. 10, 2020 – Delisted CSE.
Nov. 6, 2023 – Dissolved for failure to file.

Dioro Exploration NL (Australia Jan. 27, 1981)
Mar. 30, 2010 – Acquired by Avoca Resources Limited; basis 65¢ plus 0.35 Avoca shs. for 1 Dioro sh.

Diplomat Resources Inc. (B.C. May 14, 1981)
June 26, 1991 – Name changed to Sway Resources Inc.; basis 1 new for 4 old shs. ■

Direct Choice T.V. Inc. (B.C. Apr. 29, 1987)
Dec. 11, 1996 – Name changed to Star Choice Communications Inc. and continued into Canada. ■

Direct Communication Solutions, Inc. (Fla. Sept. 9, 2006)
Apr. 3, 2017 – Continued into Delaware. (see FPsurvey - Industrials)

Direct Energy (Ont. June 6, 1996)
Aug. 23, 2000 – All assets sold to British-based Centrica plc; basis $28.25 per trust unit and 11.5% convertible sub. debs. converted into trust units at $21.25 per trust unit and subsequently redeemed.

Direct Equity Corporation (Ont. 1981)
Oct. 1, 1993 – Formed Envirothermic Technologies Limited in Ontario on amalgamation with 989175 Ontario Limited and Envirothermic Technologies Limited; basis

1 new for 1 989175 Ontario sh., 1 new for 1 Envirothermic sh. and 1 new for 2 Direct Equity shs. ∎

Direct Focus Inc. (Wash. Jan. 28, 1993)
May 21, 2002 – Name changed to Nautilus Group Inc. ∎

Direct IT Canada Inc. (Alta. Mar. 16, 2000)
July 27, 2006 – Formed Rage Energy Ltd. in Alberta on amalgamation with 1208640 Alberta Inc., constituting a reverse takeover by 1208640 Alberta; basis 1 new for 2 old shs. (see FPsurvey - Mines & Energy)

DirectCash Income Fund (Alta. Nov. 2, 2004)
Dec. 31, 2010 – Succeeded by DirectCash Payments Inc. pursuant to plan of arrangement whereby DirectCash Payments Inc. was formed to facilitate the conversion of the fund into a corporation and the fund was subsequently dissolved. ∎

DirectCash Payments Inc. (Alta. Oct. 7, 2010)
Jan. 10, 2017 – Amalgamated with 1999162 Alberta ULC, indirect wholly owned subsid. of Cardtronics Holdings Limited, to form DirectCash Payments ULC; basis $19 cash per sh.
Jan. 10, 2017 – Name changed to DirectCash Payments ULC.

Director Oils, Limited (Can. Mar. 20, 1929)
1936 – Assets sold to Royalite Oil Company, Limited for 3,000 shs. (see Royalite Oil Company, Limited)

Disani Capital Corp. (Can. Feb. 20, 2004)
Nov. 26, 2014 – Name changed to NeutriSci International Inc. and continued into British Columbia following reverse takeover acquisition of (old) NeutriSci International Inc.; basis 1 new for 3 old shs. (see FPsurvey - Industrials)

DiscFactories Corporation (B.C. May 11, 1983)
Feb. 21, 2007 – Name changed to Excalibur Resources Ltd. ∎

DiscoverWare Inc. (Alta. May 7, 1993)
Mar. 5, 2001 – Placed into receivership. RSM Richter Inc. was appointed receiver and manager.

Discovery Acquisitions Inc. (Alta. Sept. 6, 1996)
Nov. 20, 2002 – Name changed to Vision HRM Software Inc.; basis 1 new for 3 old shs. ∎

Discovery Air Inc. (Ont. Nov. 12, 2004)
Mar. 27, 2006 – Continued into Canada.
May 30, 2017 – All o/s cl. A com. shs. not already held acquired by 10123200 Canada Inc., a wholly owned subsid. of an investment fund managed by Clairvest Group Inc.; basis 20¢ cash per sh.

Discovery Capital Corporation (B.C. July 28, 2000 amalg.)
Oct. 1, 2007 – Liquidated for $0.2354 per com. sh.

Discovery Distributing Corp. (B.C. Oct. 25, 1983)
July 28, 1993 – Name changed to Discovery Technologies Corp. ∎

Discovery Distributing Corp. (B.C. 1983)
May 3, 1991 – Amalgamated with Surecharge Industries Limited (1 new for 1 old sh.), Intermarc Distributing Corp. and 372604 B.C. Limited to continue under the Discovery Distributing Corp. name; basis 1 new for 1 old sh.

Discovery Gold Explorations Ltd. (B.C. Jan. 28, 1983)
Jan. 9, 1989 – Delisted from the Vancouver Stock Exchange. Subsequently struck from register and dissolved.

Discovery Lithium Inc. (B.C. Oct. 26, 2021)
Mar. 28, 2025 – Name changed to Discovery Energy Metals Corp. (see FPsurvey - Mines & Energy)

Discovery Metals Corp. (B.C. Oct. 10, 1986)
Apr. 14, 2021 – Name changed to Discovery Silver Corp. (see FPsurvey - Mines & Energy)

Discovery Mines Limited (Can. Jan. 7, 1982)
Mar. 1, 1987 – Formed Discovery West Corp. in Canada on amalgamation with Midcon Oil & Gas Ltd. (9 for 5) and

Yellowknife Bear Resources Inc. (1 for 1); basis 1 new for 1 old sh. ∎

Discovery One Investment Corp. (B.C. Feb. 14, 2018)
Oct. 20, 2021 – Name changed to Pathfinder Ventures Inc. pursuant the reverse takeover acquisition of Pacific Frontier Investments Inc. (PFI) and concurrent amalgamation of PFI and wholly owned 1231986 B.C. Ltd.; basis 1 new for 2.3 old shs. (see FPsurvey - Industrials)

Discovery PGM Exploration Ltd. (B.C. July 17, 1981)
June 16, 2008 – Acquired by Marathon PGM Corporation; basis 0.0794 Marathon com. shs. for 1 Discovery PGM com. sh.

Discovery Technologies Corp. (B.C. Oct. 25, 1983)
Mar. 5, 1996 – Delisted from the Vancouver Stock Exchange. Subsequently struck from register and dissolved.

Discovery Ventures Inc. (B.C. Oct. 13, 1999)
June 6, 2016 – Name changed to MX Gold Corp. (see FPsurvey - Mines & Energy; FPsurvey - Industrials)

Discovery West Corp. (Can. Mar. 1, 1987 amalg.)
May 30, 1997 – Acquired by Magin Energy Inc.; basis $2.56 or 0.9846 Magin shs. for 1 Discovery sh.

Discovery Yellowknife Mines Ltd. (Ont. 1945)
1952 – Name changed to Consolidated Discovery Yellowknife Mines Ltd.; basis 1 new for 2 old shs. ∎

Discreet Logic Inc. (Que. Sept. 10, 1991)
Mar. 17, 1999 – Acquired by Autodesk, Inc. of California; basis 0.33 Autodesk shs. for 1 Discreet sh.

Discrete TimeSystems, Inc. (B.C. Mar. 31, 1983)
Feb. 14, 1992 – Name changed to ADI Technologies, Inc.; basis 1 new for 25 old shs. ∎

Disher Steel Construction Co. Ltd. (Ont. 1923)
1955 – Canada Iron Foundries Ltd. purchased all o/s com. shs. at $13 per sh.

Disnat Investments Inc. (Can. 1982)
May 30, 1990 – Acquired by Corporation Desjardins de valeurs mobilières for $3.15 per sh.

Dison International Ltd. (B.C. 1950)
Sept. 20, 1983 – Struck off register.

Dispersion Technologies Inc. (B.C. Feb. 21, 2013)
Mar. 16, 2021 – Name changed to Spectrum Digital Holdings Inc. (see FPsurvey - Industrials)

Distillers Corporation-Seagrams Limited (Can. Mar. 2, 1928; via Dominion charter)
Jan. 20, 1975 – Name changed to The Seagram Company Ltd. ∎

Distinct Infrastructure Group Inc. (Alta. Sept. 19, 2012)
Mar. 11, 2019 – Placed into receivership, Deloitte Restructuring Inc. was appointed receiver and manager and all independent directors resigned. Secured bank lender was expected to suffer a shortfall and subordinate lender and shldrs. were not expected to see any distribution.

Distinction Energy Corp. (Can. Nov. 15, 2019)
Sept. 22, 2021 – All o/s shs. not already held acquired by Kiwetinohk Resources Corp., subsequently renamed Kiwetinohk Energy Corp.; basis 20 Kiwetinohk sh. for 1 Distinction sh.

District Copper Corp. (Can. June 16, 2000)
Feb. 1, 2021 – Continued into British Columbia. (see FPsurvey - Mines & Energy)

District Finance Corporation (Montreal) Ltd. (Que. 1953)
Apr. 1965 – Name changed to Cofiad Inc. ∎

District Trust Company (Ont. 1961)
Dec. 1, 1975 – Amalgamated with Shore to Shore Corporation Limited (1 cl. A or cl. B for 1) to continue with

the same name District Trust Company; basis 2 new for 1 old sh.
1982 – Operations were managed by the Sterling Trust Corporation over a five year period under an agreement.
1987 – Subsequent to the expiration of the agreement, the company was wound up.
Feb. 1992 – Liquidated. No distribution for shldrs. of cl. A or cl. B shs.

Disys Corporation (Ont. 1974)
July 24, 1996 – Formed Kasten Chase Applied Research Limited in Ontario on amalgamation with Kasten Chase Applied Research Limited and Kasten's parent Temple Ridge (1994) Limited, accounted as a Pooling of Interests. ∎

Ditek Software Corp. (Can. Oct. 2, 1985)
Mar. 17, 2000 – Name changed to Homeproject.com Inc. ∎

Ditem Explorations Inc. (Can. Nov. 26, 1993)
Sept. 28, 2019 – Struck from register and dissolved.

Divcom Lighting Inc. (Can. Mar. 17, 2004)
Jan. 13, 2012 – Dissolved and struck from register.

Divcom Technologies Inc. (Alta. Jan. 25, 1999)
Mar. 17, 2004 – Continued into Canada.
June 16, 2004 – Name changed to Divcom Lighting Inc. ∎

Diversafile International Inc. (Ont. Aug. 7, 1996 amalg.)
Nov. 15, 2010 – Dissolved and struck from register.

Diversaflow Corporation Ltd. (Alta. July 27, 1999)
May 18, 2006 – Name changed to Iplayco Corporation Ltd. ∎

Diverse Technology Investments Pty Ltd (Australia June 1, 2018)
Dec. 3, 2018 – Name changed to AppsVillage Australia Limited. ∎

Diversified Alpha Fund II (Ont. Sept. 27, 2011)
June 29, 2014 – Terminated and all o/s units redeemed. Distribution of $7.38 per unit representing liquid assets was paid on July 11, 2014, with net proceeds from illiquid assets to be distributed if and when received.

Diversified Baywest Capital Corp. (Can. Dec. 10, 1981)
Sept. 23, 1991 – Formed Nextwave Software Corporation in Canada on amalgamation with Nextwave Software Corporation; basis 1 new for 0.6 Nextwave shs. and 1 new for 1 Diversified Baywest sh. ∎

Diversified Canadian Financial II Corp. (Ont. Oct. 2, 2001)
Jan. 4, 2007 – Amalgamated with Brascade Corporation; basis either 1 new Brascade Class 1 Senior pfd. sh., Series A or $25 for 1 old Diversified cl. A pfd. sh. (see Brascade Corporation)

Diversified Cosmetics International Inc. (Alta. Feb. 4, 1987)
Aug. 2001 – Wound up and dissolved. The co. distributed to shldrs. of record Sept. 29, 1999, 1 B.C.-based I Crystal, Inc. sh. for 5.887 Diversified Cosmetics shs.

Diversified Credit Corporation Limited (Ont. 1946)
Jan. 31, 1981 – Became a private co.

Diversified Entertainment Inc. (B.C. 1983)
May 14, 1993 – Dissolved and struck off register.

Diversified Income Trust II (Ont. Oct. 30, 2002)
Aug. 5, 2008 – Together with Alliance Split Income Trust, merged with Premier Value Income Trust to continue as Premier Value Income Trust; basis Diversified Income Trust II (1.1864599-for-1) and Alliance Split Income Trust (1.5814554810-for-1). (see Premier Value Income Trust)

Diversified Industries Ltd. (B.C. June 19, 1991 amalg.)
Dec. 10, 2012 – Shares consolidated on a 1-for-25,000,000 basis; distrib. of $0.00071 per pre-consolidated sh.
July 11, 2013 – Voluntarily dissolved and removed from register.

Diversified Investment Grade Income Trust, Series 1 (Ont. Sept. 16, 2002)
Oct. 10, 2007 – All o/s trust units redeemed for $8.95 per trust unit.

Diversified Mines Ltd. (Ont. Apr. 1973)
Name changed to Tex-U.S. Oil & Gas Inc. ■

Diversified Mining Interests (Canada) Ltd. (Ont. 1945)
Mar. 1949 – Name changed to Progress Diversified Minerals Ltd.; basis 1 new for 2 old shs. ■

Diversified Monthly Income Corporation (Ont. July 14, 1994)
Sept. 30, 1999 – All o/s monthly divd. income shs. redeemed for $23.5337 per sh.

Diversified Preferred Foods Ltd. (B.C. 1981)
Jan. 18, 1990 – Name changed to Diversified Publishing Ltd. ■

Diversified Preferred Share Trust (Ont. Oct. 16, 2003)
May 13, 2012 – Converted from a closed-end to an open-ended fund.
May 24, 2013 – Name changed to Sentry Global Balanced Income Fund.

Diversified Private Equity Corp. (Alta. Nov. 27, 2006)
Mar. 16, 2012 – All o/s cl. A shs. redeemed for $4.5005414 per sh. Net asset value to be distributed to shareholders and co. to be wound up.

Diversified Publishing Ltd. (B.C. 1981)
July 9, 1993 – Dissolved and struck off register.

Diversified Royalty Corp. (Can. July 29, 1992)
Oct. 15, 2020 – Continued into British Columbia. (see FPsurvey - Industrials)

Diversified Technology Inc. (B.C. Mar. 31, 1983)
Feb. 16, 1988 – Name changed to Discrete TimeSystems, Inc. ■

Diversified Utility Trust (Ont. Dec. 21, 1998)
Apr. 12, 2004 – Redeemed in full; basis $28.89 per trust unit.

diversiGlobal Dividend Value Fund (Ont. May 30, 2006)
Mar. 17, 2010 – Merged with Dynamic Global Dividend Value Fund, an open-ended mutual fund.

Diversinet Corp. (Ont. Dec. 8, 1993 amalg.)
Oct. 18, 2013 – Commenced voluntary liquidation. Duff & Phelps Canada Restructuring Inc. appointed liquidator.
Dec. 16, 2014 – Final distribution of US$0.0806 per sh. made to shldrs. by way of capital return.
Jan. 27, 2015 – Duff & Phelps Canada Restructuring Inc. discharged as liquidators and the company dissolved.

diversiTrust Energy Income Fund (Ont. Nov. 29, 2004)
Mar. 19, 2010 – Together with diversiTrust Income+ Fund merged with Dynamic Energy Income Fund and Dynamic Strategic Yield Fund (open-ended funds), respectively, to continue as Dynamic Energy Income Fund; basis 1 Dynamic Energy ser. A unit for 1 diversiTrust Energy Income Fund unit and 1 Dynamic Energy ser. A unit for 1 diversiTrust Income+ Fund unit.

diversiTrust Income Fund (Ont. Oct. 29, 2002)
Mar. 17, 2010 – Merged (together with diversiTrust Stable Income Fund and diversiYield Income Fund) into Dynamic Strategic Yield Fund, an open-ended mutual fund.

diversiTrust Income+ Fund (Ont. Jan. 29, 2004)
Mar. 19, 2010 – Together with diversiTrust Energy Income Fund merged with Dynamic Strategic Yield Fund and Dynamic Energy Income Fund (open-ended funds), respectively, to continue as Dynamic Energy Income Fund; basis 1 Dynamic Energy ser. A unit for 1 diversiTrust Income+ Fund unit and 1 Dynamic Energy ser. A unit for 1 diversiTrust Energy Income Fund unit.

diversiTrust Stable Income Fund (Ont. Aug. 22, 2003)
Mar. 17, 2010 – Merged (together with diversiTrust Income Fund and diversiYield Income Fund) into Dynamic Strategic Yield Fund, an open-ended mutual fund.

Diversity Capital Corporation (Alta. Feb. 26, 1986)
Jan. 13, 1994 – Name changed to Diversity Corporation; basis 1 new for 10 old shs. ■

Diversity Corporation (Alta. Feb. 26, 1986)
Aug. 23, 2002 – Name changed to Pancontinental Energy Inc. pursuant to reverse takeover acquisition of Pancontinental Energy Limited; basis 1 new for 5 old shs. ■

diversiYield Income Fund (Ont. June 29, 2005)
Mar. 17, 2010 – Merged (together with diversiTrust Income Fund and diversiTrust Stable Income Fund) into Dynamic Strategic Yield Fund, an open-ended mutual fund.

Divestco Inc. (Alta. Sept. 23, 2003 amalg.)
June 14, 2019 – Voluntarily filed for bankruptcy and Grant Thornton Limited appointed trustee.

Dividend Growth Split Corp. (Ont. Sept. 25, 2007)
May 18, 2011 – Amalgamated in Ontario to continue with same name. (see FPsurvey - Industrials)

Divine Energy Inc. (Alta. June 7, 1996)
May 10, 2006 – Name changed to CellBoardcast Group Inc. ■

Dixie Brands Inc. (Ont. July 20, 1970)
Sept. 26, 2020 – Name changed to BellRock Brands Inc. pursuant to the reverse takeover acquisition of certain equity and debt interests of BR Brands, LLC, as well as certain assets and liabilities of BR Brands. ■

Dixie-Carolina Mining Corp. Ltd. (Ont. 1964)
July 27, 1976 – Charter cancelled.

Dixie Meadow Gold Mines Ltd. (Alta. 1974)
Dec. 8, 1981 – Name changed to Opact Energy Ltd. ■

Dixie Oil and Gas Corp. (Ont. 1980)
Aug. 31, 1987 – Amalgamated with Rockmere Lake Explorations Ltd. (0.6 for 1) and Oneida Energy & Resources Corp. (o.667 for 1) to form Consolidated Dixie Resources Inc.

Dizun International Enterprises Inc. (B.C. Nov. 22, 2011)
Nov. 17, 2020 – Name changed to Maitri Health Technologies Corp. pursuant to the reverse takeover acquisition of Maitri Health Corp. and concurrent amalgamation of Maitri with wholly owned 1264381 B.C. Ltd. (and continued as Maitri Holdings Corp.).; basis 1 new for 20 old shs. ■

Do-Mor Petroleums Ltd. (Alta. 1952)
1954 – Acquired by Nuco Petroleums Ltd.; basis 1 new for 10 old shs. (see Nuco Petroleums Ltd.)

Dobell Porcupine Mines Ltd. (unknown)
Mar. 18, 1963 – Dissolved.

Dobhai Ventures Inc. (B.C. Dec. 15, 2006)
Sept. 8, 2010 – Name changed to Formation Fluid Management Inc. ■

Dobie Mines Ltd. (Ont. 1911)
Dec. 9, 1970 – Letters Patent cancelled.

Dobrana Resources Ltd. (B.C. June 11, 1987)
Nov. 9, 1998 – Name changed to Big Star Energy Inc.; basis 1 new for 5 old shs. ■

Doca Capital Corp. (B.C. July 27, 2009)
Oct. 10, 2012 – Name changed to Great Northern Gold Exploration Corporation pursuant to Qualifying Transaction acquisition of Wekusko and Ferro properties. ■

Docana Oils & Mines Limited (Ont. 1949)
Apr. 9, 1975 – Dissolved.

Dr. A. W. Chase Medicine Co. Ltd. (Can. 1925)
1963 – Acquired by National Drug and Chemical Co. of Canada Ltd. for $7.00 per sh.

Docu-Fax International Inc. (Can. Feb. 9, 1981)
Sept. 20, 1994 – Name changed to International Telepresence (Canada) Inc.; basis 1 new for 5 old shs. ■

Docucorp Systems Inc. (Can. Mar. 3, 1988)
July 23, 1999 – Acquired by Citipost Corporation for 29¢ per sh.

Dodge Copper Mines Limited (Ont. 1952)
Mar. 1976 – Charter cancelled.

Dodge Oil Developments Ltd. (Alta.)
1958 – Struck off register.

Dofasco Inc. (Can. May 15, 1917 amalg.)
Mar. 31, 2006 – Acquired by Arcelor S.A. for Cdn$71 per sh. On May 15, 2007, 7.55% ser. B notes and 4.96% ser. A notes were redeemed for $104.384 per $100 par, respectively, plus accrued and unpaid int.

Dofor Inc. (Que. 1982)
June 1987 – During 1987, Société générale de financement du Québec purchased all the shs. it did not already own at $29.50 for pref. and $29 for com. shs. Dofor's shs. were delisted.

Dog River Mining Co. Ltd. (Alta. 1953)
Sept. 30, 1957 – Struck off register.

Dog'N Suds Food Services Ltd. (B.C. 1968)
Dec. 22, 1975 – Dissolved.

Dogpaw Gold Mines Ltd. (Ont. 1947)
1951 – Acquired by Falnora Gold Mines Ltd. on 1-for-5 sh. basis. (see Falnora Gold Mines Ltd.)

Dolce Enterprises Inc. (Alta. Feb. 14, 2006)
Dec. 15, 2006 – Formed Sinchao Metals Corp. in British Columbia on Qualifying Transaction amalgamation with Sinchao Metals Corp., constituting a reverse takeover by Sinchao; basis 1 new for 1 Sinchao sh. and 1 new for 6 Dolce shs. ■

Dolce Financial Corp. (Alta. Feb. 28, 2005)
Jan. 31, 2007 – Name changed to Seaway Energy Services Inc. following the Oct. 4, 2006, Qualifying Transaction reverse takeover acquisition of Seaway Project Management (1998) Ltd. ■

Dolly Resources Ltd. (B.C. 1960)
Mar. 1977 – Name changed to Dolly Varden Resources Limited. ■

Dolly Varden Minerals Inc. (Ont. Dec. 21, 1979 amalg.)
Nov. 23, 1992 – Name changed to New Dolly Varden Minerals Inc.; basis 1 new for 5 old shs. ■

Dolly Varden Mines Ltd. (B.C. 1960)
Feb. 24, 1976 – Name changed to Silver Dolly Resources Ltd.; basis 1 new for 4 old shs. ■

Dolly Varden Properties Ltd. (unknown)
Wound up voluntarily.

Dolly Varden Resources Inc. (Ont. Dec. 21, 1979 amalg.)
Jan. 31, 2012 – Name changed to DV Resources Ltd. ■

Dolly Varden Resources Limited (B.C. 1960)
Dec. 21, 1979 – Amalgamated with Yorkshire Resources Limited, Yorkshire Copper Mines Limited, Kitsault Silver Mines Ltd. and Copper Cliff Mines Ltd. to form Dolly Varden Minerals Inc.; basis 0.5024 new cl. A for 1 old sh. (see Dolly Varden Minerals Inc.)

Dolmac Mines Ltd. (Ont. 1954)
Dec. 12, 1978 – Amalgamated with 2 other cos. to form Junction Explorations Ltd.; basis 1 sh. Junction for 8 shs. Dolmac.

Dolomite Oils Ltd. (unknown)
Assets sold to Foothills Oil & Gas Co., Ltd.; basis 1 new for 16 old shs. (see Foothills Oil & Gas Ltd.)

Dolphin Explorations Ltd. (B.C. Sept. 29, 1982)
Oct. 7, 1988 – Continued into Ontario.
Feb. 18, 1994 – Name changed to American Gem Corporation; basis 1 new for 20 old shs. ■

Dolphin-Miller Mines Ltd. (Ont. 1944)
Dec. 1983 – Charter cancelled; shldrs. received shs. in Langis Silver & Cobalt Mining Co. Ltd. on a 1-for-1 basis.

Dolphin Quest Inc. (Ont. Sept. 30, 1996 amalg.)
Mar. 19, 1997 – Formed Naftex Energy Corporation in Ontario on amalgamation with Naftex Energy Corporation, constituting a reverse takeover by Naftex, and acquisition of Coplex (Egypt) Limited and Coplex (East Shabwa) Limited. ■

Dolphin Yellowknife Mines Ltd. (Ont. 1944)
1958 – Name changed to Dolphin-Miller Mines Ltd. ■

Dolsan Mines Ltd. (Que. 1937)
Mar. 1968 – Name changed to Consolidated Dolsan Mines Ltd. pursuant to reorganization (subsequently became inactive in 1977); basis 1 new for 5 old shs.

Doman Industries Limited (B.C. Apr. 18, 1955)
July 27, 2004 – Succeeded by Western Forest Products Inc. pursuant to restructuring plan whereby Western Forest Products became the new corporate parent of Doman's operations. (see FPsurvey - Industrials)

Domco Inc. (Can. Nov. 1, 1967 amalg.)
July 30, 1999 – Name changed to Domco Tarkett Inc. following acquisition of Tarkett North America Holding Inc. ■

Domco Industries Limited (Can. Sept. 29, 1919; via Dominion charter)
Nov. 1, 1967 – Amalgamated in Canada to continue with same name.
May 17, 1994 – Name changed to Domco Industries Ltd. ■

Domco Industries Ltd. (Can. Nov. 1, 1967 amalg.)
July 10, 1996 – Name changed to Domco Inc. ■

Domco Tarkett Inc. (Can. Nov. 1, 1967 amalg.)
Nov. 3, 2003 – Amalgamated with 4158148 Canada Inc.; basis 1 amalco redeemable preferred sh. for 1 Domco com. sh. Preferreds redeemed at $7.75 per sh.

Dome Babine Mines Ltd. (B.C. 1967)
Mar. 1970 – Name changed to Babine International Resources Ltd. ■

Dome Canada Limited (Alta. Dec. 30, 1958)
July 3, 1986 – Name changed to Encor Energy Corporation Ltd. ■

Dome Exploration (Western) Ltd. (Can. 1950)
1958 – Name changed to Dome Petroleum Limited. ■

Dome Extension Mines Co., Ltd. (unknown)
1920 – Acquired by Dome Mines Limited; basis 1 new and $0.25 for each 30 Dome Extension shs. (see Dome Mines Limited)

Dome Mines Limited (Can. July 7, 1923)
Aug. 13, 1987 – Amalgamated with Campbell Red Lake Mines (1.702 for 1) and Placer Development Limited (1 for 1) to form a new company named Placer Dome Inc.; basis 0.851 new for 1 old sh. Dome Mines Ltd. shldrs. hold approx. 37% of the amalg. co. (see Placer Dome Inc.)

Dome Mountain Resources Ltd. (Ont. 1981)
Nov. 6, 1996 – Name changed to DMR Resources Ltd.; basis 1 new for 3 old shs. ■

Dome Oils, Ltd. (Can. Apr. 1929)
Liquidated; Security Trust Co., Calgary, Alta., liquidator.

Dome Petroleum Limited (Can. 1950)
Sept. 1, 1988 – Merged with Amoco Canada Petroleum Company Limited. (see Amoco Canada Petroleum Company)

Dome Ventures Corporation (Del. Dec. 16, 1999)
May 4, 2010 – Acquired by Metalline Mining Company; basis 0.968818 Metalline shs. for 1 Dome sh. (see Metalline Mining Company)

Dome Ventures Inc. (B.C. Nov. 2, 1998)
Dec. 16, 1999 – Name changed to EComm Systems Corporation and continued into Delaware on reverse takeover acquisition of EComm Systems LLC. ■

Domego Resources Ltd. (B.C. 1978)
Oct. 19, 1987 – Continued into Canada.
Oct. 30, 1987 – Name changed to Polysteel Building Systems Ltd. ■

Domequity Growth & Calgary Ltd. (Can. 1951)
1980 – Continued into Alberta.
Dec. 20, 1991 – Formed Dominion Equity Resource Fund Inc. on amalgamation with Enerplus Energy Funds Ltd. and Enerplus Energy Funds II Ltd.

Domglas Ltd. (Can. 1913)
May 15, 1978 – Amalgamated with Consolidated-Bathurst (DG) Ltd. to form Domglas Inc. Under the amalgamation agreement all shs. held by the majority shldr., Consolidated-Bathurst, were cancelled, and remaining minority shs. were converted sh.-for-sh. into pref. shs. of Domglas Inc. Pref. shs. were called for redemption at $20 per sh. thereafter.

Domini Sportswear Ltd. (Can. Oct. 2, 1986)
Mar. 1991 – Declared bankrupt. Coopers & Lybrand of Calgary, Alta., appointed trustee.
May 1993 – All the assets had been sold. The secured creditors suffered a shortfall, and there was no distribution to unsecured creditors or shldrs.
Feb. 27, 1997 – Trustee discharged.

Dominican Mineral Resources Inc. (Alta. Oct. 24, 2012)
Feb. 27, 2017 – Name changed to Trojan Gold Inc. ■

Dominion Alloysteel Corp., Ltd. (Can. 1923)
Oct. 1948 – Liquidated.
July 10, 1950 – First and final distribution of 46¢ per pref. and com. sh. made.

Dominion Asbestos Mines Ltd. (Que. 1950)
1956 – Name changed to Daine Mining Corp. Ltd. ■

The Dominion Bank (Can. 1869)
Feb. 1, 1955 – Amalgamated with The Bank of Toronto to form The Toronto-Dominion Bank.

Dominion Bridge Company, Limited (Can. 1882)
June 1, 1981 – Name changed to AMCA International Limited. ■

Dominion Citrus & Drugs Ltd. (Ont. 1969 amalg.)
Jan. 23, 1983 – All o/s shs. acquired in October 1982 following an offer of $8.25 per share by Algonquin Mercantile Corporation. Shldrs. received either cash or preferred shares which were redeemed for $8.25 on Jan. 23, 1983. (see Algonquin Mercantile Corporation)

Dominion Citrus Company Limited (Ont. 1953)
Jan. 1969 – Amalgamated with 2 other cos. to form The Dominion Citrus & Drugs Ltd.

Dominion Citrus Income Fund (Ont. Nov. 21, 2005)
Aug. 23, 2016 – Assets sold to Dominion Holdings Corporation for $10,805,070; initial distribution of 48¢ per unit paid on Aug. 31, 2016, to shldrs. of record Aug. 26, 2016.

Dominion Citrus Limited (Ont. Jan. 27, 1992 amalg.)
Dec. 31, 2017 – Acquired by a subsid. of Dominion Holding Corporation; basis $1.75 cash per ser. A pref. sh.

Dominion Coal Company, Limited (N.S. 1893)
Sept. 19, 1975 – Dissolved. Interim distributions of assets made to pref. shldrs. consisting of $21 and $14 in September 1973 and 1974, respectively. Final distribution of $5.50 made.

Dominion Corset Company Limited (Que. 1934)
Oct. 1, 1976 – Name changed to Daisyfresh Creations Inc. ■

Dominion Dairies Limited (Can. 1943)
July 1, 1981 – 99.5% of o/s shs. acquired by John Labatt Ltd. through offer of $26.01 per sh. Shldrs. had option of receiving 1.04 cl. A conv. com. shs. of John Labatt for each sh. tendered in lieu of cash. (see John Labatt Limited)
Aug. 1981 – All o/s shs. not already held acquired by John Labatt Ltd. (see John Labatt Limited)

Dominion Diamond Corporation (Can. July 12, 2002)
Nov. 3, 2017 – Acquired by Northwest Acquisitions ULC; basis US$14.25 cash per sh.
Nov. 17, 2017 – Name changed to Dominion Diamond Mines ULC and continued into British Columbia.

Dominion Electric Power, Ltd. (Sask. 1928)
Dec. 31, 1946 – Taken over by Sask. early in 1945 by acquisition of all com. stk. for $450,000. O/s 6% cum. pref. shs. redeemed June 1, 1945, at 105. All o/s ($1,072,000) 4.5% 1st mtge. ser. bds. due 1964, redeemed in 1946 at 103. Completely absorbed by the Sask. Power Commission and ceased to exist as a separate company.

Dominion Electrohome Industries, Limited (Ont. Apr. 1, 1933)
June 6, 1967 – Name changed to Electrohome Limited. ■

Dominion Energy Corporation (B.C. 1968)
July 1, 1988 – Struck from register.

Dominion Energy Inc. (Alta. Nov. 23, 2004)
June 30, 2014 – Name changed to Dynamic Oil & Gas Exploration Inc. ■

Dominion Engineering Works Ltd. (Can. 1924)
Jan. 1962 – Acquired by Canadian General Electric Co. Original basis; 1 C.G.E. $1.25 pref. sh. plus $3.00 for each of the 625,000 com. shs. then o/s. Shs. deposited prior to Oct. 4, 1961, received reg. s.a. divd. of 50¢ per sh. paid by the co. on Nov. 1, 1961. On Jan. 22, 1962, Dom. Engineering paid a taxable stk. divd. of 1 com. sh. valued at $24.80 per sh. for each sh. held in order to capitalize its undistributed earnings. Thereafter; basis exch. offer was of 0.5 of 1 pref. sh. plus $1.50 for each Dom. Engineering share.

Dominion Equity Investments Ltd. (Can. 1951)
June 4, 1980 – Name changed to Domequity Growth & Calgary Ltd. ■

Dominion Explorers Inc. (Ont. July 19, 1985 amalg.)
July 26, 1986 – Amalgamated with Chavin of Canada Limited to form new co. with same name Dominion Explorers Inc.; basis 1 new for 8 Chavin shs. and 1 new for 1 Dominion sh. (see Dominion Explorers Inc.)
Jan. 9, 1995 – Amalgamated with Gobi Oil & Gas Ltd. (1 for 5.5) to continue as a new company also known as Dominion Explorers Inc.; basis 1 new sh. plus 1 participating rt. in Croinor Inc., a wholly owned subsid. of the co., for 12.5 old Dominion shs. Also continued into Alberta. (see Dominion Explorers Inc.)

Dominion Explorers Inc. (Alta. Dec. 31, 1994 amalg.)
Mar. 6, 1997 – Plan of Arrangement merger with Neutrino Resources Inc. to continue as a new company also known as Neutrino Resources Inc.; basis either 0.6 new Neutrino sh. or $1.25 for 1 old Dominion Explorers com. sh. (see Neutrino Resources Inc.)

Dominion Explorers Limited (Can. June 14, 1928)
July 19, 1985 – Formed Dominion Explorers Inc. in Ontario on amalgamation with NBU Mines Limited and Tex-Sol Explorations Limited; basis 1 new for 0.9 NBU shs., 1 new for 2.5 Tex-Sol shs. and 1 new for 1 Dominion sh. ■

Dominion Fabrics Limited (Ont. 1926)
1971 – Wabasso Inc. holds 96.3% of the o/s pref. shs. and 99.9% of the o/s com. shs. following an offer of $4.00 for each pref. or com. sh., plus the issue of 1 com. sh. of

Wabasso for each 10 Dominion Fabrics shs., whether pref. or com. Assets of co. and Dominion Yarns acquired and 1972 for approx. $2,325,000 net.

Dominion Fluoridators Ltd. (Ont. 1952)
Jan. 1965 – Placed into receivership on Sept. 4, 1963. Wound up. No distribution made.

Dominion Foils (Canada) Ltd. (Que. 1951)
Dec. 1, 1951 – Name changed to Aluminum Rolling Mills Limited.

Dominion Forge Ltd. (Ont. 1955)
1961 – Now a wholly owned subsidiary of Canadian Corporate Management Co. Ltd., which acquired o/s com. stk. Funded debt redeemed in 1965.

Dominion Foundries and Steel, Limited (Can. May 15, 1917 amalg.)
Oct. 6, 1980 – Name changed to Dofasco Inc. ■

Dominion Gas & Electric Co. (Del. 1930)
July 1, 1944 – All the assets were merged with International Utilities Corp. The 6.5% coll. trust bonds o/s with the public were redeemed May 15, 1944 at $101.

Dominion General Investment Corporation (Ont. Sept. 10, 2014)
July 29, 2016 – Name changed to Hampton Financial Corporation pursuant to Qualifying Transaction reverse takeover acquisition of Hampton Equity Partners Limited. ■

Dominion Glass Company Limited (Can. 1913)
Jan. 15, 1975 – Consolidated-Bathurst (DG) Limited, a wholly owned subsid. of Consolidated-Bathurst Limited, had acquired 95% of the com. and all o/s pref. through purch. offer of $14 per sh.
May 3, 1976 – Name changed to Domglas Ltd. ■

Dominion Jubilee Corporation Limited (Can. Apr. 2, 1969)
Aug. 28, 1997 – Dissolved.

Dominion Leaseholds Ltd. (Alta. 1951)
Sept. 1974 – Charter cancelled.

Dominion Lime Ltd. (Que. 1949)
Dec. 15, 1977 – Name changed to Domlim Inc. ■

The Dominion Linseed Oil Co. Ltd. (Can. 1903)
1957 – Name changed to Hart Battery Company (1957) Limited and continued into Canada. ■

Dominion Magnesium Limited (Ont. 1941)
Aug. 16, 1971 – Name changed to Chromasco Corp. Ltd. ■

Dominion Malartic Gold Mines Ltd. (Ont. 1936)
Dec. 2, 1963 – Dissolved.

Dominion Motors, Ltd. (Ont. 1931)
1944 – Balance of assets sold and winding-up of co. authorized by shldrs. No distribution to shldrs.

Dominion Natural Gas Co. Ltd. (Ont. Oct. 12, 1904)
1950 – Acquired by Union Gas Co. of Canada and Provincial Gas Co.

Dominion Nickel Mines Ltd. (B.C. 1968)
Feb. 25, 1983 – Struck off register.

Dominion Nickel Mining Corp. Ltd. (Ont. 1943)
1953 – Name changed to New Dominion Nickel Mines Ltd.; basis 1 new for 3 old shs. ■

Dominion Oil Co. Ltd. (Ont. 1907)
1958 – Wound up.

Dominion Oil Investments Ltd. (Alta. Feb. 4, 1991)
Aug. 2, 2003 – Struck from registry and dissolved.

Dominion Palace Pier Corp. Ltd. (Ont. 1927)
1941 – Name changed to Humber Amusement Pier Limited following acquisition of pier under development from receiver; nothing available for shdrs. ■

Dominion Road Machinery Co. Limited (Can. 1875)
May 24, 1977 – Name changed to Champion Road Machinery Limited. ■

Dominion Royalty Corp. Ltd. (Ont. 1934)
Oct. 20, 1976 – Amalgamated with 3 other cos. to form Ameracrude International Inc.; basis 1 new for 6.4 old shs.

Dominion Rubber Co. Ltd. (unknown)
1940 – Virtually all shs. held by U.S. parent, Uniroyal Inc.
1966 – Name changed to Uniroyal (1966) Ltd. ■

Dominion-Scottish Investments Limited (Can. May 2, 1929)
Jan. 15, 1988 – All o/s pref. shs. redeemed at $52.50 plus accr. divds. Subsequently, company was liquidated and all assets distributed to shldrs.
May 24, 1988 – Dissolved.

Dominion Securities Limited (Ont. 1949)
Mar. 31, 1988 – Name changed to RBC Dominion Securities Inc.; basis $7.67 cash and 0.5459 com. shs. of The Royal Bank of Canada for 1 old sh. Shs. were delisted on the same day and the company will no longer be reporting as a public company.

Dominion Steel and Coal Corporation, Limited (N.S. Jan. 1, 1928)
1969 – All o/s ord. shs. acquired by Sidbec for $11 per sh. Payment of princ. and int. of debs. unconditionally guaranteed by Sidbec (owned by Province of Quebec).

Dominion Stores Limited (Can. 1919)
Aug. 30, 1984 – Formed Argcen Holdings Inc. following corporate reorganization; basis 1 new for 1 old sh. ■

Dominion Structural Steel Limited (Can. 1930)
1954 – Canada Iron Foundries Ltd. purchased all o/s com. shs. for $42 per sh.
1961 – All 5% pref. shs. redeemed.

Dominion Sugar Co. Ltd. (unknown)
1930 – Merged to form Canada & Dominion Sugar Co., Ltd.

Dominion Tar & Chemical Co. Ltd. (Can. Jan. 17, 1929)
Apr. 1965 – Name changed to Domtar Limited. ■

Dominion Telegraph Securities, Ltd. (Ont. 1924)
1949 – Charter cancelled; telegraph system and lease sold to Canadian National Railways for $1,017,,900. Holders of 5.5% s.f. mtge. bds. received $103 plus int. on ser. A bds., and $106 plus int. on ser. B bds. Holders of $463,924 certificates of int. received $20.46 per $100 face value certificates.

Dominion Textile Company, Limited (Can. Dec. 9, 1922; via letters patent)
Sept. 17, 1969 – Name changed to Dominion Textile Limited. ■

Dominion Textile Inc. (Can. Dec. 9, 1922; via letters patent)
Jan. 21, 1998 – Acquired by DT Acquisition Inc., an affiliate of Polymer Group, Inc.; basis $11.75 per com. sh., $109.50 per 1st pref. sh. and $25 per 2nd pref. sh.

Dominion Textile Limited (Can. Dec. 9, 1922; via letters patent)
Jan. 1, 1979 – Name changed to Dominion Textile Inc. ■

Dominion Uranium Corporation (Que. 1954)
Oct. 10, 1973 – Dissolved.

Dominion Water Reserves Corp. (Can. July 31, 2020 amalg.)
Nov. 23, 2022 – Name changed to Prime Drink Group Corp. (see FPsurvey - Industrials)

Dominion Woollens and Worsteds Limited (Can. 1928)
1958 – Plant at Hespeler, Ont., sold to Silknit Ltd. for $380,000; distributed as part pay. to holders of 1st mtge. bds. No funds available for 5% s.f. debs.

Domlim Inc. (Que. 1949)
Dec. 31, 1980 – Merged into Graylim Inc., a private company; basis $30 per sh.

Domtar (Canada) Paper Inc. (B.C. Aug. 21, 2006)
June 3, 2014 – Redeemed; basis 1 Domtar Corporation com. sh. plus all declared and unpaid divd. for 1 Domtar (Canada) exch. sh. (see Domtar Corporation)

Domtar Corporation (Del. Aug. 16, 2006)
Dec. 2, 2021 – Acquired by Paper Excellence B.V.; basis US$55.50 cash per sh.

Domtar Inc. (Can. Dec. 31, 1977 amalg.)
Dec. 24, 2007 – All issued and o/s pref. shs acquired and subsequently privatized; basis 1 ser. A pref. sh. for $25 plus $0.4932 divd. and 1 ser. B pref. sh. for $25 plus $0.2466 divd.

Domtar Limited (Can. Jan. 17, 1929)
Dec. 31, 1977 – Formed Domtar Inc. in Canada on amalgamation with several subsids. ■

Don Barnes Ltd. (unknown)
1968 – Acquired by Bartaco Industries Ltd. in 1968-69.

Don Cameron Exploration Co. Ltd. (Ont. 1945)
1968 – Merged with other cos. to form Milestone Exploration Ltd.; basis 1,000 new for 8,177 old shs.

Don Henry Uranium Mines Ltd. (Ont. 1954)
June 3, 1963 – Dissolved.

Don Jon Mines Ltd. (Man. 1951)
Feb. 19, 1959 – Dissolved.

Don Martic Gold Mines Ltd. (Ont. Oct. 2, 1934)
June 1950 – Charter cancelled.

Don Oils Limited (Alta. 1949)
1958 – Struck off register.

Dona Patricia Gold Mines, Ltd. (Ont. 1936)
1956 – Charter cancelled.

Donabelle Mines Ltd. (Ont. 1944)
1957 – Charter cancelled.

Donalda Copper Mines Ltd. (Que. 1942)
1943 – Name changed to Donalda Mines Ltd. ■

Donalda Mines Ltd. (Que. 1942)
Jan. 15, 1972 – Name changed to Aldona Mines Ltd.; basis 1 new for 9 old shs. ■

Donard Gold Mines Ltd. (Ont. 1945)
1962 – Charter cancelled.

Donchester-Duquesne Mines Ltd. (Que. 1951)
Mar. 1973 – Assets acquired by Fundy Chemical International Ltd.; basis 1 new for 2 old shs.

Donchester Mines Ltd. (Can. June 5, 1933)
1941 – Acquired by Beattie Gold Mines Ltd.; basis approx. 1 new for 12 old shs. (see Beattie Gold Mines Ltd.)

Donegal Petroleums Limited (Ont. 1951)
1953 – Assets acquired by Lariat Exploration and Development Ltd.; basis 1 new for 2 old shs.

Donegal Resources Ltd. (B.C. 1977)
Mar. 1, 1984 – Name changed to Markway Resources Ltd.; basis 1 new for 5 old shs. ■

Donlee Manufacturing Industries Limited (Ont. 1968 amalg.)
Dec. 1977 – Became private when all shs. were tendered to purch. offer of $6.50 per sh.

Donmaque Gold Mines Ltd. (Ont. 1946)
Nov. 12, 1969 – Charter cancelled.

Donna Mines Ltd. (B.C. 1967)
Aug. 14, 1978 – Name changed to Oliver Resources Ltd.; basis 1 new for 5 old shs. ■

Donnacona Paper Co. Ltd. (Que. 1928)
Aug. 1952 – Howard Smith Paper Mills, which subsequently became a wholly owned subsid. of Dominion Tar & Chemical Co. Ltd., offered 1.25 Howard Smith shares for each Donnacona sh., thus acquiring 98.5% of o/s shs.
Nov. 1, 1962 – Special distribution of $52 per sh. was paid to shldrs. of record Oct. 12.
Nov. 27, 1962 – Shldrs. approved sale of Donnacona's assets to Dominion Tar & Chemical and winding up of the co.
Dec. 7, 1962 – Final distribution of $53 per sh. was made to shldrs. other than Dominion Tar.

Donnell & Mudge Ltd. (Ont. 1919)
June 1958 – Name changed to United Telefilms Ltd. ■

Donner Metals Ltd. (B.C. June 28, 2005)
Oct. 2, 2014 – Name changed to Sphinx Resources Ltd. (see FPsurvey - Mines & Energy)

Donner Minerals Ltd. (B.C. Apr. 25, 1966)
Aug. 16, 2005 – Name changed to Donner Petroleum Ltd. following reorganization into two units, a new mining company named Donner Metals Ltd. and the original renamed company which became a petroleum company; basis 1 Donner Metals sh. for 10 Donner Minerals shs. and 1 Donner Petroleum sh. for 40 Donner Minerals shs. ■

Donner Petroleum Ltd. (B.C. Apr. 25, 1966)
Aug. 18, 2005 – Continued into Alberta.
Jan. 1, 2007 – Name changed to Crocotta Energy Inc.; basis 1 new for 13.5135 old shs. ■

Donner Resources Ltd. (B.C. Apr. 25, 1966)
Nov. 7, 1997 – Name changed to Donner Minerals Ltd. ■

Donnybrook Energy Inc. (Alta. Aug. 30, 2010)
Oct. 28, 2014 – Name changed to Stonehaven Exploration Ltd.; basis 1 new for 40 old shs. ■

Donnybrook Resources Inc. (B.C. Apr. 17, 1986)
Aug. 13, 2003 – Name changed to Rodinia Minerals Inc.; basis 1 new for 5 old shs. ■

Donnycreek Energy Inc. (Alta. Sept. 1, 2011)
Dec. 24, 2014 – Amalgamated with Contact Exploration Inc. (deemed acquiror) to form Kicking Horse Energy Inc.; basis (i) 0.075 Kicking Horse com. shs for 1 Contact sh. (ii) 0.60 Kicking Horse com. shs for 1 Donnycreek com. sh.

Donohue Brothers Limited (Que. Mar. 30, 1920; via letters patent)
Sept. 1970 – Name changed to Donohue Company Limited. ■

Donohue Company Limited (Que. Mar. 30, 1920; via letters patent)
July 8, 1978 – Name changed to Donohue Inc. ■

Donohue Inc. (Que. Mar. 30, 1920; via letters patent)
June 26, 2000 – Acquired by Abitibi-Consolidated Inc.; basis $12 plus 1.8462 Abitibi-Consolidated shs. for 1 Donohue sh. (see Abitibi-Consolidated Inc.)

Donrand Mines Limited (Ont. Jan. 27, 1944)
Aug. 18, 2000 – Name changed to CRMnet.com Inc. following reverse takeover acquistion of Relationship Marketing Resources Inc.; basis 1 new for 2 old shs. ■

Dontrell Capital Ltd. (Can. Apr. 5, 1994)
Dec. 18, 1995 – Continued into Ontario.
Jan. 23, 1996 – Formed Mond Industries Inc. in Ontario on amalgamation with DiLillo Holdings Inc. and Mond Industries Inc. ■

Donway Explorations Limited (unknown)
Oct. 20, 1976 – Amalgamated with 3 other cos. to form Ameracrude International Inc.; basis 1 new for 10 old shs. ■

Doobah Mining Ltd. (B.C. 1972)
Mar. 23, 1984 – Struck off register.

Doonson Gold Mines Ltd. (Ont. 1945)
Mar. 11, 1957 – Charter cancelled.

d'Or Val Mines Ltd. (B.C. 1979)
Aug. 31, 1988 – Merged with Perron Gold Mines Ltd. following acquisition of all assets of Perron Gold Mines and d'Or Val Mines Ltd. by private co. Aurizon Mines Ltd.; basis 0.5 new shs. for 1 Perron sh. and 0.4167 new shs. for 1 d'Or Val sh. Prior to transfer of assets, Perron and d'Or Val were amalgamated as Amalgamated d'Or Val Perron Mines Ltd. and then dissolved. (see Aurizon Mines Ltd.)

Dora Explorations Ltd. (B.C. 1966)
Mar. 29, 1985 – Amalgamated with 3 other cos. to form Meridor Resources Limited; basis 0.2231 new for 1 old sh.

Dorado Industries Ltd. (Ont. 1969)
July 1974 – Merged into Reactor Industries Limited.

Dorado Resources Ltd. (B.C. Mar. 8, 1978)
May 5, 1987 – Name changed to International Dorado Resources Ltd.; basis 1 new for 4 old shs. ■

Dorado Uranium Ltd. (B.C. 1953)
May 1958 – Charter cancelled.

Dorado Uranium Mines Limited (Ont. 1969)
Apr. 1972 – Name changed to Dorado Industries Ltd. ■

Doral Mining Explorations Ltd. (Que. 1965)
Jan. 1974 – Charter cancelled.

Doramal Mines Limited (Ont. 1947)
Oct. 1949 – Charter cancelled; distribution of 0.5¢ per sh.

Dorato Resources Inc. (Wyo. Apr. 24, 1998)
Aug. 21, 2006 – Continued into British Columbia.
Oct. 23, 2013 – Name changed to Xiana Mining Inc.; basis 1 new for 20 old shs. (see FPsurvey - Mines & Energy)

Dorbaska Gold Mines Ltd. (Ont. 1944)
1957 – Charter cancelled.

Dorbrun Mines Ltd. (Can. 1946)
Nov. 1961 – Charter cancelled.

Dorchester Energy Inc. (Alta. Sept. 7, 1993)
Dec. 20, 2002 – Acquired by Celtic Exploration Ltd.; basis either 0.233 new Celtic com. sh., or $0.70, or a combination thereof for 1 old Dorchester com. sh. (see Celtic Exploration Ltd.)

Dorchester Hotels Inc. (B.C. 1974)
Mar. 1989 – Placed into bankruptcy.
June 5, 1992 – Dissolved and struck off register.

Dorchester Resources Inc. (Ont. Oct. 13, 1987)
Apr. 26, 1990 – Name changed to Xxpert Rental Tool Inc.; basis 1 new for 2 old shs. ■

Dorchester Resources Ltd. (B.C. May 25, 1960)
Dec. 20, 1976 – Name changed to Taurus Resources Limited. ■

Dore Copper Mining Corp. (Can. Dec. 12, 2019)
Feb. 3, 2025 – Acquired by Cygnus Metals Limited; basis 1.8297 Cygnus ord. shs. for 1 Dore Copper com. sh.

Dore Explorations Inc. (Ont. June 16, 1982)
Dec. 24, 1987 – Amalgamated with Norbaska Mines Limited to form Dore Norbaska Resources Inc.; basis 1 new for 1 old sh. (see Dore Norbaska Resources Inc.)

Dore Norbaska Resources Inc. (Ont. Nov. 2, 1987 amalg.)
Feb. 23, 1998 – Formed The Griffin Corporation in Ontario on amalgamation with Griffin Development & Management Corp, 1106256 Ontario Inc. and GRFN Real Estate Investment Corporation, constituting a reverse takeover by Griffin; basis 1 new for 25 old shs. ■

Doreva Gold Mines, Ltd. (Ont. May 27, 1936)
Mar. 1951 – Charter cancelled.

Dorex Minerals Inc. (B.C. Mar. 20, 1989)
Sept. 18, 2017 – Name changed to Cipher Resources Inc. ■

Dorion Red Lake Mines Limited (Ont. 1945)
July 22, 1982 – Amalgamated with Abino Gold Mines Limited (1 for 12.94), Clicker Red Lake Mines Limited (1 for 18.23), Commander Red Lake Mines Limited (1 for 30.82), Duchesne Red Lake Mines Limited (1 for 10.57), Forsyth Mines Limited (1 for 6.38), Goldquest Explorations Corp. (1 for 1.26), Inore Gold Mines Limited (1 for 9.9), Laddie Gold Mines Limited (1 for 15.22) and Rowan Gold Mines Limited (1 for 4.91) to form Goldquest Exploration Inc.; basis 1 new for 15.59 old shs.

Doris Yellowknife Gold Mines Ltd. (Ont. 1945)
1956 – Charter cancelled.

Dorita Silver Mines Ltd. (B.C. 1950)
Nov. 1, 1978 – Name changed to Liberty Petroleums Inc. ■

Dornoch International Inc. (B.C. 1967)
Apr. 28, 1988 – Name changed to DNI Holdings Inc. ■

Doron Explorations Inc. (B.C. Oct. 20, 1982)
Mar. 1, 1993 – Name changed to WEW Ventures Inc.; basis 1 new for 5 old shs. ■

Dorreen Gold Mines Ltd. (B.C. 1949)
1951 – Assets acquired by Dorreen Mines Ltd. for 1,200,000 shs., part pooled.

Dorreen Mines Ltd. (B.C. 1951)
1970 – Struck off register.

Dorrigo Energy Inc. (Alta. Apr. 15, 1993)
Feb. 10, 1995 – Amalgamated with 611903 Alberta Ltd., a wholly owned subsid. of Sunalta Energy Inc.; basis 1 sh. Sunalta for 2.5 shs. Dorrigo. (see Sunalta Energy Inc.)

Dorsay (Canada) Ltd. (unknown)
Oct. 1964 – Acquired by Montex Holdings Ltd. (see Montex Holdings Ltd.)

Dorsay Mines Ltd. (Ont. 1959)
1960 – Name changed to Lubec Lead Mines Ltd. ■

Dorset Exploration Ltd. (Alta. Jan. 12, 1988)
Oct. 29, 1997 – Amalgamated with Baytex Energy Ltd.; basis 0.48 Baytex cl. A shs. for 1 Dorset sh. (see Baytex Energy Ltd.)

Dorset Resources Ltd. (Can. Dec. 17, 1980)
May 20, 1986 – Name changed to Consolidated Brinco Limited following merger with its subsidiary, Brinco Limited; basis 1 new for 10 old shs. ■

Dortera Mines Ltd. (Ont. 1944)
Sept. 30, 1957 – Dissolved.

Dorvue Gold Mines Ltd. (Ont. 1947)
Feb. 14, 1973 – Dissolved.

dot.com Technologies Inc. (B.C. Jan. 27, 1966)
July 12, 2002 – Name changed to BCS Collaborative Solutions Inc. pursuant to reverse takeover acquisition of Broadband Collaborative Solutions Inc.; basis 1 new for 2 old shs. ■

Dotcom 2000 Inc. (Ont. Aug. 25, 1999 amalg.)
Jan. 10, 2002 – Name changed to Konexus Technologies Limited. ■

Double "A" Uranium, Mining & Development Co. Ltd. (Sask. 1954)
Sept. 1961 – Struck off register.

Double Arrow Oil & Gas Ltd. (B.C. July 2, 1965)
Dec. 2, 1996 – Name changed to Arrowhead Minerals Corporation. ■

Double Chance Resources Ltd. (B.C. Mar. 31, 1980)
Feb. 9, 1983 – Name changed to Calaveras Explorations Ltd. ■

Double Creek Mining Corporation (B.C. Sept. 23, 1987)
Aug. 17, 1998 – Name changed to Minaterra Minerals Ltd.; basis 1 new for 3 old shs. ■

Double Deuce Exploration Corp. (B.C. Aug. 25, 2021)
Mar. 17, 2025 – Name changed to Precore Gold Corp. (see FPsurvey - Mines & Energy)

Double Down Resources Ltd. (B.C. Nov. 6, 1978)
Dec. 22, 2000 – Formed Meteor Creek Resources Inc. in Ontario on reverse takeover acquisition of and amalgamation with Meteor Creek Resources Inc.; basis 1 new for 4 old shs. ■

Double Eagle Energy & Resources Ltd. (B.C. 1968)
May 4, 1984 – Name changed to Double Eagle Technology Ltd. ■

Double Eagle Entertainment Corp. (B.C. 1980)
Aug. 28, 2003 – Dissolved and struck from register. ■

Double Eagle Technology Ltd. (B.C. 1968)
1984 – Continued into Canada.
May 7, 1985 – Name changed to Chessminster Group Limited. ■

Double Impact Communications Corp. (Can. Sept. 8, 1994)
Aug. 20, 1998 – Name changed to Next Millennium Commercial Corp.; basis 1 new for 4 old shs. ■

Double Strike Mines Ltd. (Ont. 1946)
Apr. 1, 1965 – Dissolved.

DoubleLine Income Solutions Trust (Ont. Oct. 24, 2013)
Nov. 27, 2018 – Amalgamated with PineBridge Investment Grade Preferred Securities Fund to form BMO PineBridge Preferred Securities TACTIC™ Fund, an open-end daily redeemable mutual fund.

Doublestar Resources Ltd. (Yuk. Oct. 7, 1996)
Oct. 10, 2002 – Continued into British Columbia. (see Selkirk Metals Corp.)
Aug. 2, 2007 – Acquired by Selkirk Metals Corp.; basis 0.5 new Selkirk com. sh. for 1 old Doublestar cl. A sh. (see Selkirk Metals Corp.)

Doubleview Capital Corp. (B.C. Jan. 18, 2008)
May 7, 2020 – Name changed to Doubleview Gold Corp. (see FPsurvey - Mines & Energy)

Doucette Developments Corp. (B.C. Apr. 11, 1983)
Aug. 30, 1995 – Name changed to Traders International Franchise Systems Inc. ■

Dougall Gold Mines Ltd. (Ont. 1946)
May 19, 1958 – Dissolved.

Douglas Gold Mines Ltd. (B.C. 1961)
Dec. 18, 1969 – Struck off register.

Douglas Lake Mines Ltd. (Man. 1936)
Dec. 5, 1963 – Dissolved.

Douglas Leaseholds Limited (Ont. 1955)
Nov. 1, 1978 – In late 1978, approx. 95% of co.'s o/s com. shs. acquired by 389128 Ontario Ltd. (a wholly owned subsid of Chalet Oil Ltd.) through purchase offer of $5.34 per sh. Amalgamated with 392630 Ontario Ltd. (a subsid. of 389128 Ontario Ltd.).
Nov. 10, 1978 – All com. shs. held by minority shldrs. were redesignated as special shs. and were called for redemption at $5.34 per sh.

Dougron Gold Mines Ltd. (Ont. 1947)
Jan. 1975 – Charter cancelled.

Dove Lake Mines Ltd. (Ont. 1971)
Aug. 11, 1972 – Amalgamated into Staple Mining Co. Ltd.; basis 1 new for 5 old shs.

DoveCorp Enterprises Inc. (Ont. Mar. 4, 2004)
July 12, 2007 – Filed for protection under the Companies' Creditors Arrangement Act (CCAA) to initiate restructuring proceedings. RSM Richter Inc. appointed as monitor.
Oct. 10, 2007 – RSM Richter Inc. discharged as monitor. All assets sold as of Sept. 21, 2007, and operations terminated on Sept. 28, 2007. There were no distributions to shldrs. ■

Dover Development Corp. (Ont. July 28, 1987)
Oct. 16, 1992 – Name changed to Halozone Technologies Inc. following acquisition of all o/s com. shs. of Halozone Recycling Inc. ■

Dover Enterprises Ltd. (Alta. Jan. 30, 1987)
Mar. 1, 1999 – Struck from registry and dissolved. ■

Dover Industries Limited (Can. Mar. 27, 1940)
Feb. 10, 2009 – Acquired by Parrish & Heinbecker, Limited for $19.25 per sh.

Dovercliff Gold Mines Ltd. (Ont. 1944)
Nov. 1973 – Charter cancelled.

Dovercliff Minerals Ltd. (Ont. 1979)
Apr. 28, 1987 – Name changed to T.L.C. Properties Inc. following amalgamation with 701594 Ontario Limited. (see FPsurvey - Mines & Energy)

Dovercourt Mines Ltd. (Ont. 1950)
1965 – Charter cancelled.

Doverton Oils Ltd. (Can. Nov. 21, 1977)
Sept. 10, 1997 – Dissolved.

Dovetec Corporation (Ont. June 11, 1992 amalg.)
June 27, 2006 – Dissolved.

Dow Brewery Limited (Can. 1909)
June 1963 – Acquired by Canadian Breweries Limited for $60 a sh. (see Canadian Breweries Limited)

Down North Minerals Ltd. (Alta. 1957)
Apr. 1975 – Reported to be dissolved.

Down North Minerals Ltd. (B.C. 1968)
Sept. 1968 – Name changed to Northern Lights Minerals Ltd. ■

Downtown Industries Ltd. (Can. Sept. 26, 2003)
Nov. 4, 2010 – Name changed to Inform Resources Corp. and continued into British Columbia; basis 2 new for 1 old sh. ■

Doxa Energy Ltd. (B.C. Feb. 13, 2007)
Dec. 22, 2020 – Name changed to ProStar Holdings Inc. pursuant to reverse takeover acquisition of ProStar Geocorp Inc. and concurrent amalgamation of ProStar Geopcorp with wholly owned Doxa Merger Corp.; basis 1 new for 17 old shs. (see FPsurvey - Industrials)

Draco Gold Mines Inc. (B.C. Apr. 14, 1983)
June 29, 1990 – Continued into Alberta.
July 3, 1990 – Formed Stanford Energy Corporation on amalgamation with Stanford Energy Corporation; basis 1 new for 1 old sh. ■

Draco Mines Ltd. (Ont. 1945)
May 1949 – Charter cancelled.

DraftTeam Daily Fantasy Sports Corp. (B.C. June 17, 1998)
Oct. 5, 2015 – Name changed to Fantasy Aces Daily Fantasy Sports Corp. ■

DraftTeam Fantasy Sports Inc. (B.C. May 28, 2009)
Mar. 10, 2015 – Acquired by Sabre Graphite Corp.; basis 0.4667 Sabre com. sh. for 1 DraftTeam sh.

Dragon Capital Corporation (Ont. June 7, 2005)
June 27, 2007 – Name changed to Arehada Mining Limited following the Mar. 14, 2007, Qualifying Transaction reverse takeover acquisition of Arehada Mining Corporation. ■

Dragon Gem Corp. (B.C. Mar. 30, 1981)
Apr. 15, 1998 – Name changed to Consolidated Alliance Resources Corp.; basis 1 new for 3 old shs. ■

Dragon Legend Entertainment (Canada) Inc. (B.C. Sept. 24, 1990)
June 24, 2024 – Dissolved for failure to file.

Dragon Oils & Gas Ltd. (Ont. 1950)
Dec. 30, 1954 – Name changed to Consolidated Dragon Oils Ltd.; basis 1 new for 3 old shs. ■

Dragon Pharmaceutical, Inc. (Fla. Aug. 22, 1989)
July 28, 2010 – Privatized for US$0.82 per sh.

Dragon-Tex (Group) Limited (Alta. Apr. 25, 2002)
Apr. 28, 2006 – Formed Med BioGene Inc. in British Columbia pursuant to reverse takeover acquisition of Med BioGene Inc. and amalgamation with a wholly owned subsidiary of Med BioGene; basis 1 new for 2 old shs. ■

Dragonfly Capital Corp. (B.C. Mar. 19, 2010)
Aug. 2, 2022 – Name changed to Black Swan Graphene Inc. pursuant to the Qualifying Transaction reverse takeover acquisition of (old) Black Swan Graphite Inc. (see FPsurvey - Industrials)

Dragonfly Distributors Incorporated (B.C. Feb. 8, 1984)
Feb. 24, 1992 – Name changed to Nu-Lite Industries Ltd.; basis 1 new for 7 old shs. ■

DragonWave Inc. (Can. Feb. 24, 2000)
July 31, 2017 – Placed into receivership by senior lenders and KSV Kofman Inc. appointed receiver. All officers and directors resigned.
Oct. 25, 2017 – Assets and operations acquired by Transform-X, Inc. for an undisclosed amount. Senior lenders incurred a substantial shortfall; no distributions available for shldrs. ■

Dragoon Resources Ltd. (B.C. Sept. 14, 1979)
May 20, 1998 – Name changed to Seabridge Resources Inc.; basis 1 new for 10 old shs. ■

Draig Energy Ltd. (Alta. June 8, 1992)
July 24, 2000 – All o/s com. and First pfd. Series A shs. acquired by NAL Oil and Gas Trust; basis 0.2375 NAL trust units for each com. sh. and 0.125 NAL trust units for each pfd. sh. (see NAL Oil & Gas Trust)

Draig Resources Ltd. (Alta. June 8, 1992)
Aug. 15, 1997 – Name changed to Draig Energy Ltd.; basis 1 new for 2 old shs. ■

Drake Energy Ltd. (Alta. Jan. 28, 1994)
May 26, 2010 – Filed for bankruptcy under Bankruptcy and Insolvency Act. Ernest & Young appointed trustee.

Drake Environmental Recovery Ltd. (Alta. July 24, 1986)
Mar. 16, 1994 – Name changed to HydroMet Environmental Recovery Ltd. ■

Drake Pacific Enterprises Ltd. (Alta. Jan. 28, 1994)
Aug. 5, 2009 – Name changed to Drake Energy Ltd. ■

Drake Petroleums Ltd. (Alta. July 24, 1986)
July 26, 1993 – Name changed to Drake Environmental Recovery Ltd. ■

Drake Yellowknife Gold Mines Ltd. (Ont. 1944)
Sept. 1976 – Charter cancelled.

Drako Capital Corp. (Alta. Jan. 21, 2010)
Aug. 22, 2012 – Formed Amarok Energy Inc. in Alberta on amalgamation with Trilateral Energy Ltd. with Drako Capital the deemed acquiror; basis 0.6 new for 1 old sh. ■

Dramex Corporation (Can. 1986 amalg.)
Oct. 28, 1996 – All o/s cl. A shs. repurchased for $2.00 per sh. Co. now private.

Dransfield Mining Co. Ltd. (Ont. 1937)
1947 – Name changed to Foundation Consolidated Mines Ltd. ■

Draper Lake Frontenac Lead-Zinc Mines Ltd. (Ont. 1937)
1957 – Name changed to Lake Kingston Mines Ltd.; basis 3 new for 10 old shs. ∎

Draw International Resources Corporation (B.C. 1978)
Mar. 27, 1992 – Dissolved and struck off register.

Draw Resources Corporation (B.C. 1978)
Nov. 20, 1985 – Name changed to Draw International Resources Corporation; basis 4 new for 1 old sh. ∎

Drawson Red Lake Gold Mines Ltd. (Ont. 1946)
Nov. 10, 1966 – Dissolved.

Drayton Petroleum Limited (unknown)
Nov. 1978 – Amalgamated with Oxford Mines Limited, Babylon Minerals Inc., Solvang Explorations Limited and Firebird Petroleums Limited to form Bab-Sol Resource Explorations Limited; basis 1 new for 20 old shs. (see Bab-Sol Resource Explorations Ltd.)

Drayton Valley Hotel Co. Ltd. (Alta. 1954)
Name changed to Acme Investments Ltd. ∎

Drayton Valley Power Income Fund (Alta. Jan. 2, 1997)
Aug. 23, 2001 – Acquired by indirect subsid. of Algonquin Power Income Fund for $4.30 per sh. (see Algonquin Power Income Fund)

Dreadnought Investments Limited (Ont. 1963)
Apr. 25, 1988 – Name changed to Rothwell Industries Ltd.; basis 1 new for 2 old shs. ∎

Dream Global Real Estate Investment Trust (Ont. Apr. 21, 2011)
Dec. 12, 2019 – All assets and subsidiaries acquired by real estate funds managed by The Blackstone Group Inc.; basis $16.75 cash per trust unit.

Dream Hard Asset Alternatives Trust (Can. Apr. 28, 2014)
Oct. 26, 2020 – Name changed to Dream Impact Trust. (see FPsurvey - Industrials)

Dream Wizards Investments Ltd. (Can. Sept. 8, 2000)
Feb. 28, 2003 – Formed AeroMechanical Services Ltd. in Canada on Qualifying Transaction amalgamation with AeroMechanical Services Ltd., 883946 Alberta Ltd. and 883955 Alberta Ltd., constituting a reverse takeover by AeroMechanical. ∎

Dreamweaver Capital Corp. (B.C. May 23, 2007)
Nov. 26, 2009 – Name changed to NV Gold Corporation pursuant to Qualifying Transaction acquisition of NV Gold Corporation (USA). (see FPsurvey - Mines & Energy)

Dreco Energy Services Ltd. (Alta. Aug. 27, 1980)
Oct. 1, 1997 – Following Plan of Arrangement with National-Oilwell, Inc. of Houston, all o/s cl. A com. shs. exchanged for exchangeable shares; basis 0.9159 of an exchangeable sh. for 1 cl. A com. sh. Exchangeable shs. exchangeable at any time into 1 com. sh. of National-Oilwell, Inc.
Sept. 25, 2002 – Redeemed by US-based parent National Oilwell, Inc.; basis 1 new National Oilwell com. sh. for 1 old Dreco exchangeable sh.

Dresden Mines Ltd. (Ont. 1972)
1976 – Amalgamated with 3 other cos. to form Berkwater Explorations Ltd.; basis 1 new for 2 old shs.

Drexel Capital Corp. (B.C. June 18, 2009)
Apr. 25, 2011 – Name changed to Drexel Resources Ltd. pursuant to Qualifying Transaction acquisition of 60% interest in Titan property located near Atlin, B.C. ∎

Drexel Enterprise Corporation (B.C. Oct. 16, 1984)
June 28, 1993 – Name changed to Graffoto Industries Corporation; basis 1 new for 2 old shs. ∎

Drexel Resources Ltd. (B.C. June 18, 2009)
Aug. 23, 2011 – Name changed to Blue Gold Mining Inc. ∎

Drexore Developments Inc. (B.C. Feb. 7, 1984)
Nov. 2, 1989 – Name changed to Cabo Ventures Inc.; basis 1 new for 4 old shs. ∎

Drift Lake Resources Inc. (Ont. Sept. 7, 2006)
Oct. 12, 2011 – Name changed to Sintana Energy Inc. ∎

Driftwood Mines Ltd. (B.C. 1976)
Aug. 26, 1983 – Struck off register.

Drilcorp Energy Ltd. (Alta. Oct. 31, 1997)
June 13, 2006 – Acquired by Twin Butte Energy Ltd.; basis $0.60, or 0.5 new Twin Butte sh., or a combination thereof for 1 old Drilcorp sh. (see Twin Butte Energy Ltd.)

Drilcorp Slimhole Technologies Ltd. (Alta. Oct. 31, 1997)
Nov. 12, 1999 – Name changed to Drilcorp Energy Ltd. ∎

Drillers & Producers Ltd. (unknown)
1948 – Crown Trust Co., Calgary, was trustee for bdhldrs. Distribution of 44% of par made; further small payment likely.

Drillers Technology Corp. (Alta. Jan. 13, 1997)
Nov. 23, 2005 – Acquired by Saxon Energy Services Inc. for $1.85 per sh. (see Saxon Energy Services Inc.)

Drive Products Income Fund (Ont. May 1, 2006)
Nov. 18, 2010 – Acquired by 2256479 Ontario Inc. for $2.50 per unit.

Driven Capital Corp. (B.C. Nov. 25, 2009)
Apr. 23, 2014 – Name changed to Greenflag Ventures Inc.; basis 1 new for 10 old shs. ∎

Driver Development Corporation Limited (Alta. 1952)
1971 – In voluntary liquidation. New co., Delta Hotels Limited formed to acquire the assets; basis 5 shs. Driver for 1 sh. of Delta.

Driver Energy Services Inc. (Alta. July 5, 1999)
Nov. 24, 2003 – Name changed to Kodiak Energy Services Ltd. pursuant to reverse takeover acquisition of Kodiak Construction Ltd.; basis 1 new for 2 old shs. ∎

Driver Petroleums Limited (Alta. 1952)
1967 – Sold to Jack Crossi, Vancouver, B.C.
1968 – Name changed to Driver Development Corporation Limited. ∎

Dromedary Exploration Company Ltd. (B.C. Aug. 5, 1987)
Aug. 18, 1993 – Name changed to HEC Hitech Entertainment Corporation. ∎

Dromoland Development Corporation (B.C. 1980)
Nov. 8, 1984 – Formed Burndale Resources Ltd. in British Columbia on amalgamation with Graham Island Resources Ltd. ∎

Drone Acquisition Corp. (B.C. June 1, 2018)
Aug. 15, 2019 – Name changed to Draganfly Inc. pursuant reverse takeover acquisition of Draganfly Innovations Inc. (see FPsurvey - Industrials)

Drone Delivery Canada Corp. (B.C. Feb. 2, 2011)
Aug. 30, 2024 – Name changed to Volatus Aerospace Inc. following merger of equals business combination with Volatus Aerospace Corp. (see FPsurvey - Industrials)

Drope Lake Explorations Ltd. (Ont. 1967)
Dec. 22, 1970 – Name changed to Drope Lake Metals & Holdings Limited. ∎

Drope Lake Metals & Holdings Limited (Ont. 1967)
Feb. 1980 – Charter cancelled.

Droumaque Gold Mines Ltd. (Que. 1944)
Mar. 13, 1976 – Charter cancelled.

Drucox Petroleum Corporation (B.C. 1980)
Oct. 17, 1984 – Name changed to Marketfax Infoservices Ltd. ∎

Drude Uranium Mines Ltd. (Ont. 1955)
July 26, 1976 – Charter cancelled.

Drug Royalty Corporation Inc. (Can. Mar. 22, 1993)
May 2, 2002 – Acquired by DRC Acquisitionco Inc., a wholly owned subsid. of Inwest Investments Ltd.; basis $3.05 per sh.

Druk Capital Partners Inc. (B.C. Mar. 16, 2010)
Sept. 25, 2012 – Name changed to Falco Pacific Resource Group Inc. pursuant to Qualifying Transaction acquisition of gold-base metal properties. ∎

Drumetco Inc. (Que. 1964)
Jan. 10, 1975 – Declared bankrupt. Trustee - S. B. Freed.

Drummond Copper Corp. Ltd. (Que. 1953)
Sept. 30, 1978 – Charter cancelled.

Drummond Financial Corporation (Del. June 1, 1993)
July 2001 – Continued into Washington.

Drummond, McCall & Co., Limited (Ont. June 13, 1913)
Dec. 30, 1978 – Name changed to Drummond McCall Inc. and continued into Canada. ∎

Drummond McCall Inc. (Can. Dec. 30, 1978)
May 10, 1984 – Name changed to Marshall Drummond McCall Inc. ∎

Drummond Petroleum Ltd. (Alta. Oct. 6, 1977)
June 2, 1987 – Name changed to Excel Energy Inc.; basis 1 new for 10 old shs. ∎

Drummond Welding and Steel Works Ltd. (Que. 1950)
1975 – All o/s cl. A shs. acquired by Industries Drummond Ltée; basis $7.00 per sh. All o/s cl. B shs. previously held by Industries Drummond Ltée.

Dryad Mines Ltd. (B.C. 1969)
Aug. 18, 1975 – Dissolved.

Dryden Paper Company, Limited (Can. 1920)
1954 – Acquired by Anglo-Canadian Pulp and Paper Mills Ltd.; basis $35 plus 1 com. sh. of Anglo-Cdn. for each com. sh. of Dryden.

Dryden Resource Corporation (B.C. Feb. 4, 1981)
June 1, 1993 – Amalgamated with Stow Resources Ltd. to form Leicester Diamond Mines Ltd.; basis 1 new for 1 Stow sh. and 1 new for 1.55 Dryden shs. (see Leicester Diamond Mines Ltd.)

Du Pont Canada Inc. (Can. Nov. 18, 1910)
Aug. 6, 1993 – Name changed to DuPont Canada Inc. ∎

Du Pont Company of Canada (1956) Ltd. (Can. Nov. 18, 1910)
Dec. 31, 1958 – Name changed to Du Pont of Canada Ltd. ∎

Du Pont of Canada Ltd. (Can. Nov. 18, 1910)
June 1, 1979 – Name changed to Du Pont Canada Inc. ∎

Dual Dome Petroleums Ltd. (Alta.)
1960 – Struck off register.

Dual Exploration Inc. (Alta. Apr. 19, 2005)
Dec. 14, 2006 – Acquired by Cyries Energy Inc.; basis 0.167 new Cyries sh. for 1 old Dual sh. (see Cyries Energy Inc.)

Dual Resources Ltd. (B.C. Mar. 5, 1973)
Jan. 7, 1994 – Name changed to Serengeti Diamonds Ltd. ∎

DualEx Energy International Inc. (Alta. Mar. 20, 2006)
Dec. 20, 2016 – Name changed to Return Energy Inc; basis 1 new for 10 old shs. ∎

Dubar Exploration Ltd. (Man. 1954)
Dec. 1960 – Charter cancelled.

Dubenski Gold Mines Limited (Can. June 2, 1983)
Nov. 1, 1995 – Dissolved.

Dubuisson Goldfields Ltd. (Que. 1936)
June 22, 1973 – Name changed to Dubuisson Explorations Ltd.; basis 1 new for 20 old shs. (see FPsurvey - Mines & Energy)

Ducan Range Iron Mines Ltd. (Ont. 1956)
Aug. 15, 1979 – Name changed to Duncan Gold Resources Inc. ■

Duchesne Red Lake Mines Limited (Ont. 1946)
July 22, 1982 – Amalgamated with Abino Gold Mines Limited (1 for 12.94), Clicker Red Lake Mines Limited (1 for 18.23), Commander Red Lake Mines Limited (1 for 30.82), Dorion Red Lake Mines Limited (1 for 15.59), Forsyth Mines Limited (1 for 6.38), Goldquest Explorations Corp. (1 for 1.26), Inore Gold Mines Limited (1 for 9.9), Laddie Gold Mines Limited (1 for 15.22) and Rowan Gold Mines Limited (1 for 4.91) to form Goldquest Exploration Inc.; basis 1 new for 10.57 old shs.

Duck Book Communications Limited (B.C. Oct. 6, 1982)
Nov. 7, 1988 – Delisted from the Vancouver Stock Exchange. Subsequently dissolved for failure to file.

Duckhorn Ventures Ltd. (B.C. Mar. 25, 2019)
Mar. 16, 2022 – Name changed to Helium Evolution Incorporated pursuant the reverse takeover acquisition of (old) Helium Evolution Incorporated. (see FPsurvey - Mines & Energy)

Duckworth Capital Corp. (Can. May 1, 2017)
Feb. 21, 2019 – Name changed to GoldSpot Discoveries Corp. following Qualifying Transaction reverse takeover acquisition of (old) GoldSpot Discoveries Inc.; basis 1 new for 2 old shs. ■

Ducore Mines Ltd. (Ont. 1946)
1955 – Charter cancelled.

Ducros Mines Ltd. (Que. 1965)
June 1, 1976 – Merged into Brominco Inc.; basis 1 Brominco for 50 Ducros shs.

Duecritt Silver-Cobalt Mines Ltd. (Ont. 1942)
Name changed to Niki Silver-Cobalt Mines Ltd. ■

Dueling Grounds Entertainment Corporation (Yuk. July 13, 1993)
Dec. 20, 1995 – Continued into Delaware.

Dueling Grounds Thoroughbred Racing Corporation (Yuk. July 13, 1993)
Dec. 1, 1995 – Name changed to Dueling Grounds Entertainment Corporation; basis 1 new for 1 old sh. ■

Duffree Rouyn Gold Mines Ltd. (Ont. 1946)
Apr. 15, 1965 – Dissolved.

Duffy Lake Mines Ltd. (B.C. 1966)
Jan. 17, 1977 – Dissolved.

Dufort Capital Inc. (Can. Jan. 19, 2005)
Dec. 30, 2005 – Name changed to Odesia Group Inc. following Qualifying Transaction reverse takeover acquisition of Odesia Solutions Inc. ■

Dufresnoy Industrial Minerals Inc. (Que. May 25, 1981)
Jan. 14, 1997 – Name changed to Boreal Exploration Inc. ■

Dufresnoy Mines Ltd. (Ont. 1956)
Dec. 10, 1969 – Dissolved.

Dufresnoy, Société d'exploration minière inc. (Que. May 25, 1981)
Nov. 12, 1993 – Name changed to Dufresnoy Industrial Minerals Inc.; basis 1 new for 5 old shs. ■

Duft Biotech Capital Ltd. (B.C. May 30, 2000)
Nov. 26, 2003 – Name changed to ALDA Pharmaceuticals Corp. following Qualifying Transaction acquisition of substantially all assets of ALDA Pharmaceuticals, Inc. ■

Dugold Mining Co. Ltd. (Que. 1938)
1949 – Wound up.

Duke Capital Corp. (B.C. June 17, 1999)
Oct. 30, 2000 – Name changed to CCC Internet Solutions Inc. following Qualifying Transaction reverse takeover acquisition of CCC Internet Solutions Inc. ■

Duke Energy Canada Exchangeco Inc. (Can. Sept. 14, 2001)
Jan. 26, 2007 – Name changed to Spectra Energy Canada Exchangeco Inc. ■

Duke Energy Income Fund (Alta. Nov. 2, 2005)
Jan. 2, 2007 – Name changed to Spectra Energy Income Fund. ■

Duke Enterprises Ltd. (B.C. Dec. 16, 1983)
Aug. 21, 1992 – Name changed to Bay Street Systems Ltd. ■

Duke Minerals Ltd. (B.C. Dec. 16, 1983)
July 6, 1989 – Name changed to Duke Enterprises Ltd. ■

Dula Metals Corp. (Que. 1956)
Sept. 9, 1972 – Dissolved.

Dulac Chibougamau Mines Ltd. (Que. 1957)
Aug. 1972 – Charter cancelled.

Dulama Gold Mines Ltd. (Ont. Dec. 2, 1944)
May 29, 1950 – Name changed to Ladulama Gold Mines Ltd.; basis 1 new for 2 old shs. ■

Duluth Metals Limited (Ont. Mar. 8, 2005)
Jan. 23, 2015 – Acquired by a wholly owned subsid. of Autofagasta plc for 45¢ per sh.

Duluth Red Lake Gold Mines Ltd. (Ont. 1945)
Apr. 29, 1970 – Charter cancelled.

Dumac Mines Ltd. (B.C. 1947)
Apr. 11, 1957 – Charter cancelled.

Dumagami Mines Limited (Que. 1961)
Dec. 27, 1989 – Amalgamated with a subsid. of Agnico-Eagle Mines Limited; basis 1.7 Agnico-Eagle shs. for 1 Dumagami sh. (see Agnico-Eagle Mines Limited)

Dumar Gold Mines Ltd. (Ont. 1945)
Jan. 21, 1957 – Dissolved.

DuMaurier Mines and Holdings Ltd. (Ont. 1958)
Feb. 20, 1980 – Dissolved.

DuMaurier Mines Ltd. (Ont. 1958)
Aug. 1962 – Name changed to DuMaurier Mines and Holdings Ltd. ■

Dumico Gold Corp. (Que. Mar. 7, 1936)
May 1967 – Reported out of business.

Dumont Explorations Ltd. (B.C. 1961)
May 6, 1971 – Struck off register.

Dumont Nickel Corporation (N.P.L.) (Que. Sept. 22, 1954; via letters patent)
Feb. 12, 1997 – Name changed to Dumont Resources Inc. (co. never traded under this name); basis 1 new for 10 old shs. ■

Dumont Nickel Inc. (Que. July 30, 1998 amalg.)
May 11, 2010 – Name changed to DNI Metals Inc.; basis 1 new for 8 old shs. (see FPsurvey - Mines & Energy)

Dumont Resources Inc. (Que. Sept. 22, 1954; via letters patent)
July 30, 1998 – Formed Dumont Nickel Inc. in Quebec on amalgamation with Edgehill Partners Inc. (deemed acquiror); basis 2 new for 1 Edgehill sh. and 1.8 new for 5 Dumont Resources shs. ■

Dun Raven Mines Ltd. (Que. 1954)
May 1980 – Charter cancelled.

Dunav Resources Ltd. (B.C. Apr. 14, 2004)
Oct. 3, 2014 – Acquired by Avala Resources Ltd.; basis 1.0457 Avala com. shs. and 1.0457 wts. for 1 Dunav com. sh. and 1 wt., respectively.

Dunbar Capital Corp. (B.C. Oct. 19, 2017)
Dec. 31, 2018 – Name changed to Cannara Biotech Inc. pursuant to the Qualifying Transaction reverse takeover acquisition of (old) Cannara Biotech Inc. and concurrent amalgamation of (old) Cannara with wholly owned 11038427 Canada Inc. (see FPsurvey - Industrials)

Dunbar Metals Corp. (B.C. Feb. 1, 2023)
May 21, 2025 – Name changed to Kirkstone Metals Corp. (see FPsurvey - Mines & Energy)

Duncan Gold Resources Inc. (Ont. 1956)
June 12, 2006 – Certificate of incorporation cancelled and dissolved.

Duncan Ladue Mines Ltd. (B.C. 1964)
Sept. 3, 1974 – Dissolved and struck off register.

Duncan Park Holdings Corporation (Ont. Nov. 12, 1981)
May 13, 2019 – Voluntarily delisted.
July 13, 2020 – Name changed to Psyched Wellness Ltd. (see FPsurvey - Industrials)

Duncan Petroleums, Ltd. (Can. 1930)
Apr. 25, 1940 – Name changed to Brunswick Royalties Ltd.

Duncastle Gold Corp. (B.C. Apr. 28, 2006)
Feb. 25, 2015 – Name changed to Group Ten Metals Inc. ■

Dundarave Resources Incorporated (B.C. Sept. 17, 1984)
Feb. 4, 1993 – Name changed to SRR Mercantile Inc.; basis 1 new for 3.2 old shs. ■

Dundarave Resources Inc. (B.C. Sept. 8, 2004)
Mar. 5, 2015 – Name changed to Nano One Materials Corp. following reverse takeover acquisition of Perfect Lithium Corp.; basis 1 new for 2 old shs. (see FPsurvey - Industrials)

Dundee Acquisition Ltd. (Ont. Mar. 5, 2015)
Apr. 24, 2017 – All o/s class A restricted vtg. shs. redeemed for $10.04 cash per sh.

Dundee Bancorp Inc. (Ont. Nov. 2, 1984)
Dec. 21, 2004 – Name changed to Dundee Corporation. (see FPsurvey - Industrials)

Dundee Capital Inc. (Ont. 1987)
Apr. 21, 1993 – All o/s com. shs. repurchased for $7.45 per sh.

Dundee Capital Markets Inc. (Ont. Dec. 10, 2010)
Feb. 3, 2012 – Acquired by Dundee Corporation for $1.125 per sh.

Dundee Energy Limited (Can. Aug. 31, 1995 amalg.)
Mar. 27, 2019 – Filed an assignment under the Bankruptcy and Insolvency Act and MNP Ltd. appointed trustee.

Dundee Industrial Real Estate Investment Trust (Ont. July 20, 2012)
May 8, 2014 – Name changed to Dream Industrial Real Estate Investment Trust. (see FPsurvey - Industrials)

Dundee International Real Estate Investment Trust (Ont. Apr. 21, 2011)
May 12, 2014 – Name changed to Dream Global Real Estate Investment Trust. ■

Dundee Mines Ltd. (B.C. 1952)
May 3, 1973 – All assets acquired by Palliser Petroleums Limited; basis 1 new for 3 old shs.
Name changed to Yankee Girl Resources Corp.

Dundee Mines Ltd. (B.C. Apr. 28, 2006)
May 27, 2008 – Name changed to Duncastle Gold Corp. ■

Dundee-Palliser Resources Inc. (Ont. Aug. 20, 1945)
Apr. 1, 1996 – Formed Scorpion Minerals Inc. in Ontario on amalgamation with Scorpion Minerals Inc., constituting a reverse takeover by Scorpion (a newly incorporated

Canadian co. formed to acquire Scorpion Metals N.L., an Australian co.); basis 1 new for 30 old shs. ■

Dundee Petroleum Corp. (Alta. Aug. 17, 1995)
Sept. 22, 2000 – Acquired by 879575 Alberta Ltd., a wholly owned subsid. of the City of Medicine Hat (Alberta), for 40¢ per sh. ■

Dundee Real Estate Investment Trust (Ont. May 9, 2003)
May 13, 2014 – Name changed to Dream Office Real Estate Investment Trust. (see FPsurvey - Industrials)

Dundee Realty Corporation (Ont. Nov. 7, 1996)
June 30, 2003 – Converted into an investment trust named Dundee Real Estate Investment Trust (REIT); basis 1 Dundee REIT unit plus $3.00 for 1 Dundee Realty com. sh.
May 30, 2013 – Name changed to DREAM Asset Management Corporation.

Dundee Resources Corp. (B.C. May 18, 1983)
Jan. 20, 1993 – Name changed to Clear View Ventures, Inc.; basis 1 new for 5 old shs. ■

Dundee Wealth Management Inc. (Ont. Nov. 6, 1998)
June 28, 2007 – Name changed to DundeeWealth Inc. ■

DundeeWealth Inc. (Ont. Nov. 6, 1998)
Sept. 9, 2011 – All 1st pfce. ser. 1 shs. redeemed for $26.50 per sh. plus accrued and unpaid divds. and all com. shs. acquired by The Bank of Nova Scotia for $21 per sh.
Nov. 1, 2013 – Name changed to HollisWealth Inc. ■

Dune Mineral Corporation (B.C. Dec. 12, 1974)
May 20, 1980 – Name changed to Goldwinn Resources Ltd. ■

Dune Resources Limited (Alta. 1980)
Dec. 23, 1988 – Name changed to Robson Petroleum Ltd.; basis 1 new for 3 old shs. ■

Dunes Exploration Ltd. (Alta. May 21, 1993)
Nov. 2, 2014 – Dissolved and struck from register.

Dunford Rouyn Mines Ltd. (Ont. Feb. 16, 1937)
Distributed 1 Joliet-Quebec Mines, Limited sh. plus 2.18¢ for each 9 shs. held. Charter surrendered. (see Joliet-Quebec Mines, Limited)

Dunfrazier Gold Explorations Inc. (Ont. Nov. 14, 1983)
July 6, 1992 – Name changed to Interlock Consolidated Enterprises Inc. (see FPsurvey - Mines & Energy)

Dungannon Explorations Ltd. (B.C. 1975)
Aug. 9, 1989 – Formed Claddagh Gold Limited in Canada on amalgamation with Jamex Resources Ltd. ■

Dunhill Alberta Capital Corporation (Can. Dec. 11, 1986)
Aug. 10, 1989 – Name changed to Dunhill Industries Inc.; basis 1 new for 4 old shs. ■

Dunhill Development Corporation Ltd. (B.C. 1967)
Nov. 18, 1976 – Name changed to Housing Corporation of British Columbia.

Dunhill Industries Inc. (Can. Dec. 11, 1986)
June 7, 1991 – Name changed to Immedia Infomatic International Inc. following acquisition of Immedia Infomatic Inc.; basis 1 new for 1 old sh. ■

Dunlap Resources Ltd. (B.C. Sept. 15, 1993)
Feb. 11, 1997 – Continued into Yukon.
Feb. 13, 1997 – Name changed to International Dunlap Minerals Corporation. ■

Dunlop Canada Limited (Ont. 1899)
1974 – Name changed to Whitby Tire Ltd. ■

Dunlop Consolidated Mines Ltd. (Ont. 1927)
Dec. 1957 – Charter cancelled.

Dunlop Industries Inc. (Alta. 1984)
Feb. 1, 1994 – Dissolved and struck off register.

Dunlop Lake Uranium Mines Limited (Ont. 1973)
Feb. 20, 1974 – Name changed to Beaver Hill Lake Uranium Mines Limited. ■

Dunlop Mining Co. Ltd. (Man. 1966)
1971 – All assets acquired by Cadillac Explorations Ltd. for issuance of 525,000 shs.

Dunlop Tire & Rubber Goods Co. Ltd. (Ont. 1899)
1954 – Name changed to Dunlop Canada Limited. ■

Dunmar Mines Ltd. (Ont. 1946)
1954 – Merged into Garrison Creek Consolidated Mines Ltd.; basis 1 new for 15 old shs. ■

Dunmore Mines Ltd. (B.C. 1954)
Aug. 30, 1976 – Charter cancelled.

Dunn Yellowknife Mines Ltd. (Ont. 1945)
1952 – Charter cancelled.

Dunnedin Ventures Inc. (B.C. Jan. 12, 1987)
Apr. 1, 2020 – Name changed to Kodiak Copper Corp.; basis 1 new for 5 old shs. (see FPsurvey - Mines & Energy)

Dunoil Resources Ltd. (Alta. 1980)
June 26, 1986 – Name changed to Dune Resources Limited. ■

Dunraine Mines Limited (Can. July 6, 1942)
Feb. 6, 1990 – Name changed to International Dunraine Limited; basis 1 cl. A and 1 cl. B for 2 com. shs. ■

Dunsmuir Resources Ltd. (Can. July 30, 1987)
July 12, 2004 – Dissolved.

Dunsmuir Ventures Ltd. (B.C. May 11, 2000)
Jan. 18, 2006 – Succeeded by Peregrine Diamonds Ltd. following amalgamation of Dunsmuir with Peregrine Holdings Ltd., a wholly owned subsid. of Peregrine Diamonds Ltd. ■

Dunvegan Mines Limited (Ont. 1946)
Mar. 1976 – Charter cancelled.

Dunwell Mines Ltd. (B.C. 1922)
1939 – Bankrupt.
1948 – Property reverted to prov. govt. No equity for creditors or shldrs.

Duomalartic Gold Mines Ltd. (Ont. 1944)
Apr. 9, 1975 – Dissolved.

Duparquet Mining Co. Ltd. (Que. 1927)
Mar. 1976 – Charter cancelled.

Dupel Mines Ltd. (Bermuda)
1964 – Assets acquired by Goldale Ltd.; basis 1 new for 12.5 old shs.

DuPont Canada Inc. (Can. Nov. 18, 1910)
July 29, 2003 – Acquired by E.I. du Pont de Nemours and Company for Cdn$21.75 per cl. A sh.
Apr. 12, 2004 – Name changed to E.I. du Pont Canada Company.

Dupont Capital Inc. (Can. Feb. 24, 2003)
June 30, 2004 – Formed Advitech Inc. in Canada on Qualifying Transaction amalgamation with Advitech Solutions Inc., constituting a reverse takeover by Advitech; basis 5.8 new for 1 Advitech sh. and 1 new for 1 Dupont sh. ■

Dupont-Hodgson Gold Mines Ltd. (Ont. 1936)
Aug. 29, 1960 – Charter cancelled.

Duport Mining Company Limited (Ont. 1929)
Apr. 6, 1981 – All assets acquired by Consolidated Professor Mines Ltd.; basis 1 new for 2 old shs.

Dupresnoy Mines Ltd. (Que. 1944)
Mar. 1955 – Acquired by Lake Dufault Mines Ltd.; basis 1 new for 3.5 old shs.

Dupuis Frères, Limitée (Que. 1921)
Feb. 7, 1978 – Declared bankrupt. Proceeds from the sale of assets were not sufficient to cover the $11 million in secured debt.

Duquesne Mining Co. Ltd. (Que. Apr. 13, 1938)
May 22, 1948 – Name changed to Consolidated Duquesne Mining Co. Ltd.; basis 1 new for 3 old shs. ■

Duquesto Gold Mines Ltd. (Ont. 1945)
May 1958 – Charter cancelled.

Dura Products International Inc. (Ont. Aug. 19, 1983)
Jan. 15, 2004 – Name changed to Dexx Corporation; basis 1 new for 50 old shs. ■

Duran Gold Corp. (B.C. Mar. 5, 1997)
Aug. 10, 2000 – Name changed to Duran Ventures Inc.; basis 1 new for 2 old shs. ■

Duran Ventures Inc. (B.C. Mar. 5, 1997)
Oct. 30, 2008 – Continued into Canada.
Sept. 5, 2018 – Name changed to Peruvian Metals Corp. (see FPsurvey - Mines & Energy)

Durandel Minerals Corporation (Can. Sept. 24, 1987)
July 15, 1996 – Name changed to Calliope Metals Corporation; basis 1 new for 2 old shs. ■

Durango Capital Corp. (B.C. Aug. 16, 1996)
Apr. 6, 2009 – Name changed to Falkirk Resources Corp.; basis 1 new for 10 old shs. ■

Durango Resources Inc. (B.C. Aug. 21, 2006)
Mar. 17, 2025 – Name changed to Quantum Critical Metals Corp. (see FPsurvey - Mines & Energy)

Duranium Mines Ltd. (Ont. 1946)
Acquired by Continental Consolidated Mines & Oils Corp. Ltd.; basis 1 new for 10 old shs. (see Continental Consolidated Mines & Oils Corp. Ltd.)

Durecon Explorations Ltd. (Ont. 1954)
Apr. 8, 1965 – Dissolved.

Durex Mines Ltd. (Ont. 1946)
1956 – Charter cancelled.

Durga Resources Ltd. (Alta. June 22, 1987)
Oct. 6, 1993 – Name changed to Leader Mining Corporation. ■

Durham Capital Corp. (Alta. Oct. 14, 2005)
Dec. 31, 2006 – Formed Sikanni Services Ltd. in Alberta on Qualifying Transaction amalgamation with Sikanni Services Ltd., constituting a reverse takeover by Sikanni. ■

Durham Explorations Ltd. (Ont. 1945)
1959 – Name changed to Consolidated Durham Mines & Resources Limited; basis 1 new for 5 old shs. ■

Durham Red Lake Gold Mines Ltd. (Ont. 1945)
1954 – Name changed to Durham Explorations Ltd. ■

Durham Resources Inc. (Ont. Mar. 15, 1984 amalg.)
Apr. 21, 1987 – Name changed to Landmark Corporation. ■

Durham Resources Ltd. (B.C. 1979)
July 9, 1991 – Amalgamated with Edge Resources Ltd. (1 new for 2 old shs.) to form a new co. called Gothic Resources Inc. (Ressources Gothic Inc.); basis 1 new for 1.333 old shs. (see Gothic Resources Inc.)

Durkin Hayes Publishing Ltd. (Ont. Jan. 1, 1989 amalg.)
Oct. 30, 1998 – Name changed to IMARK Corporation; basis 1 new for 7 old shs. ■

Duro Metals Inc. (Alta. July 18, 2018)
Nov. 26, 2021 – Name changed to Torr Metals Inc. and continued into British Columbia pursuant to the Qualifying Transaction reverse takeover acquisition of 1306043 B.C. Ltd. and concurrent amalgamation of 1306043 B.C. with a wholly owned subsidiary.; basis 1 new for 1.4538 old shs. (see FPsurvey - Mines & Energy)

Durocher Uranium Company Ltd. (Alta. 1954)
May 7, 1974 – Name changed to Infrationics Industries Ltd. ■

Durum Cons. Energy Corp. (Yuk. Oct. 24, 1997)
June 12, 2002 – Name changed to TAG Oil Ltd. ■

Durum Energy Corp. (B.C. Dec. 12, 1990)
Oct. 24, 1997 – Continued into Yukon.
Oct. 27, 1998 – Name changed to Durum Cons. Energy Corp.; basis 1 new for 5 old shs. ■

Durvada Resources Ltd. (Alta. 1987)
May 21, 1992 – Following Plan of Arrangement shares exchanged for shares of Durga Resources Ltd.; basis 1.5 shs. of Durga for 1 sh. of Durvada. (see Durga Resources Ltd.)

DuSolo Fertilizers Inc. (Can. Mar. 11, 2004)
July 19, 2016 – Continued into British Columbia.
Dec. 18, 2017 – Name changed to Fengro Industries Corp. ■

Dustbane Enterprises Limited (Can. 1965)
June 1981 – Acquired by Montevilla Holdings Limited for $14.25 per sh.

Dusty Chief Mines Ltd. (B.C. 1969)
Jan. 31, 1977 – Dissolved.

Dusty Mac Mines Ltd. (B.C. Aug. 6, 1968)
May 21, 1992 – Name changed to International Dusty Mac Enterprises Ltd.; basis 1 new for 5 old shs. ■

Dusty Mac Oil and Gas Ltd. (B.C. Aug. 6, 1968)
Apr. 2, 1996 – Name changed to TransGlobe Energy Corporation. ■

Dutch Creek Resources Ltd. (B.C. 1987)
Apr. 1990 – Placed into receivership. Debenture holders seized assets. Nothing left for creditors and shldrs.
Oct. 1, 1993 – Dissolved and struck off register.

Duthie Mines (1946) Ltd. (B.C. 1946)
1951 – Charter cancelled.

Dutton Resources Ltd. (Ont. 1982)
Nov. 14, 1985 – Amalgamated with 6 other cos. to form Paladin Petroleum Corporation; basis 1 new for 5 old shs. ■

Duval Gold Mines Ltd. (Que. 1945)
May 11, 1974 – Dissolved.

Duvan Copper Co. Ltd. (Que. 1953)
Sept. 11, 1982 – Charter cancelled.

Duvay Gold Mines Limited (Ont. Nov. 21, 1944)
Mar. 28, 1952 – Name changed to Duvex Oils & Mines Limited; basis 1 new for 4 old shs. ■

Duvernay Oil Corp. (Alta. June 27, 2001)
Aug. 29, 2008 – Acquired by Royal Dutch Shell plc, through wholly owned Shell Canada Limited, for $83 per sh.

Duvex Oils & Mines Limited (Ont. Nov. 21, 1944)
Aug. 25, 1971 – Name changed to United Duvex Oils & Mines Ltd.; basis 1 new for 10 old shs. ■

Dwight Edwards (Canada) Ltd. (Can. 1940)
Apr. 27, 1955 – Name changed to Wingate Equipment Lessors Ltd.

Dye & Durham Corporation (B.C. July 18, 2005)
Nov. 8, 2017 – Continued into Ontario.

Dyke Lake Mines Ltd. (Ont. 1945)
Sept. 12, 1961 – Charter cancelled.

Dyke Mines Ltd. (B.C. 1971)
June 8, 1981 – Struck off register.

Dylex Diversified Limited (Can. 1928; via Dominion charter)
June 1972 – Name changed to Dylex Limited. ■

Dylex Diversified (1967) Ltd. (Can. 1928; via Dominion charter)
May 6, 1969 – Name changed to Dylex Diversified Limited. ■

Dylex Limited (Can. 1928; via Dominion charter)
May 17, 2001 – Acquired by Hardof World Group Inc.; basis $1.30 for 1 old Dylex com. sh. Subsequently legal action was undertaken in September 2001 against Dylex's former board of directors, certain of its senior officers and legal advisors and third parties. Legal proceedings were settled in February 2006 for the all-inclusive sum of $32,000,000 payable to trustee RSM Richter Inc. for distribution to Dylex's creditors and former employees, who will receive 60 to 63¢ on the dollar.

Dyna Gold Resources Inc. (B.C. 1967)
Dec. 13, 1991 – Dissolved and struck off register.

Dyna Haul Corporation (B.C. Mar. 30, 1981)
Apr. 26, 2000 – Wholly owned Dyna-Haul Ltd. received a notice of default from the Alberta Treasury Branch (ATB)
May 1, 2000 – Dyna-Haul Ltd. received a demand for payment of loans outstanding.
May 29, 2000 – Dyna-Haul Ltd., the company's principal asset, was placed into receivership and Edmonton-based KPMG Inc. was appointed receiver/manager by ATB. All of the directors resigned.
June 1, 2002 – KPMG was discharged and there was no information available regarding distributions to creditors or shldrs.

Dynacare Inc. (Ont. Sept. 8, 1981)
May 20, 1997 – All o/s sub. vtg. shs. exchanged for either 1 deemed dividend pref. sh., 1 capital pref. sh. or a combination of cap. pref. shs. and deemed div. pref. shs. for 1 old sub. vtg. sh. automatically redeemed for $6.45 per sh.
July 30, 2002 – Acquired by North Carolina-based Laboratory Corporation of America Holdings; basis US$11.50 plus 0.2328 new Laboratory Corporation com. sh.

Dynaco Resources Ltd. (B.C. 1965)
May 20, 1980 – Dissolved and struck off register.

Dynacor Gold Mines Inc. (Que. Dec. 15, 2006)
June 23, 2022 – Name changed to Dynacor Group Inc. (see FPsurvey - Mines & Energy)

Dynacor Mines Inc. (Que. Nov. 14, 1983)
July 17, 2007 – Name changed to Malaga Inc. (see FPsurvey - Mines & Energy)

Dynacore Enterprises Ltd. (B.C. 1965)
Feb. 9, 1971 – Name changed to Dynaco Resources Ltd.; basis 1 new for 3 old shs. ■

Dynacore Explorations Ltd. (B.C. 1965)
July 1967 – Name changed to Dynacore Enterprises Ltd.; basis 1 new for 1 old sh. ■

Dynalta Energy Corporation (Can. June 20, 1988)
June 7, 1993 – Amalgamated with Fossil Oil & Gas Limited; basis 1 Fossil Oil sh. for 18.8 Dynalta shs. or 1.88 Dynalta pref. shs. (see Fossil Oil & Gas Limited)

Dynalta Oil & Gas Co. Ltd. (Alta. 1959)
Dec. 1971 – Acquired by Pan Ocean Oil Corp.; basis 14.47 new for 100 old shs.

Dynamar Energy Limited (Alta. Aug. 8, 1977 amalg.)
May 16, 1989 – Placed into receivership, and Coopers & Lybrand Ltd. of Calgary, Alta., appointed receiver.

Dynamax Petrochemical Corporation (Alta. 1981)
Dec. 18, 1992 – Name changed to Wildrose Ventures Inc.; basis 1 new for 8 old shs. ■

Dynamic Capital Canada Corp (Sask. Feb. 7, 2001)
Nov. 10, 2004 – Name changed to Churchill Energy Inc. following Qualifying Transaction reverse takeover acquisition of Churchill Energy Inc.; basis 1 new for 5 old shs. ■

Dynamic Capital Corp. (Can. 1980)
1987 – Continued into Ontario.
June 28, 1990 – Name changed to Dundee Capital Inc.; basis 1 new com. and 0.25 wts. for 1 old com. or cl. A sh. ■

Dynamic Digital Depth Inc. (Alta. Feb. 4, 1987)
Jan. 3, 2002 – Acquired by DDD Group plc; basis 1 DDD sh. plus 1 wt. for 1 Dynamic sh.

Dynamic Fuel Systems Inc. (Ont. Jan. 1, 2004 amalg.)
Dec. 18, 2012 – Name changed to dynaCERT Inc. (see FPsurvey - Industrials)

Dynamic Industries Inc. (Que. 1951)
Feb. 1, 1980 – Placed into bankruptcy. Assets purchased by Pylonex Inc.

Dynamic Israel Growth Fund (Ont. Feb. 8, 1995)
June 1, 1998 – All o/s transferable non-redeem. units redeemed for the net asset value per unit making the fund an open end mutual fund.

Dynamic Mining Exploration Ltd. (Que. 1969)
Feb. 16, 1987 – Name changed to Dynamic Consolidated Resources Ltd.; basis 1 new for 8 old shs. (see FPsurvey - Mines & Energy)

Dynamic Oil & Gas Exploration Inc. (Alta. Nov. 23, 2004)
Mar. 14, 2017 – Name changed to Darien Business Development Corp.; basis 1 new for 10 old shs. ■

Dynamic Oil & Gas, Inc. (B.C. Mar. 27, 1979)
Oct. 5, 2005 – Acquired by Sequoia Oil & Gas Trust; basis $1.71 plus 1 Shellbridge Oil & Gas, Inc. sh. for 1 Dynamic sh. (see Sequoia Oil & Gas Trust; Shellbridge Oil & Gas, Inc.)

Dynamic Oil Limited (B.C. Mar. 27, 1979)
Sept. 21, 1998 – Name changed to Dynamic Oil & Gas, Inc. ■

Dynamic Petroleum Products Ltd. (Alta. 1952)
Dec. 1971 – Acquired by Pan Ocean Oil Corp.; basis 9.53 new for 100 old shs.

Dynamic Petroleums Ltd. (Alta. 1952)
1958 – Name changed to Dynamic Petroleum Products Ltd.; basis 1 new free for 4 old free shs.; 1 new escrowed for 13 old escrowed shs. ■

Dynamic Resources Corp. (Alta. May 21, 1993)
Feb. 15, 2011 – Name changed to Dunes Exploration Ltd.; basis 1 new for 40 old shs. ■

Dynamic Technologies Group Inc. (Alta. Jan. 18, 2005)
July 27, 2023 – Pursuant to a transaction under the Companies' Creditors Arrangement Act (CCAA) the purchaser, Promising Expert Limited, through a newly formed Canadian subsid., acquired 1 new cl. A com. sh. of the company for subscription price of $1.00. All other issued and outstanding equity of the company other than the new cl. A com. sh. were cancelled for no consideration, resulting in the purchaser owning 100% of the issued and outstanding equity securities of the company.

Dynamic Venture Opportunities Fund Ltd. (Can. Jan. 11, 1993)
Oct. 22, 2018 – Name changed to B.E.S.T. Venture Opportunities Fund Inc. (see FPsurvey - Industrials)

Dynamic Ventures Ltd. (Alta. May 21, 1993)
Mar. 5, 2004 – Name changed to Dynamic Resources Corp.; basis 1 new for 10 old shs. ■

Dynamite Resources Ltd. (B.C. June 13, 2005)
Aug. 17, 2007 – Amalgamated in Ontario to continue with same name. (see Avion Resources Corp.)
May 11, 2009 – Acquired by Avion Resources Corp.; basis 0.75 Avion shs. for 1 Dynamite sh. (see Avion Resources Corp.)

Dynamix Corporation (Alta. Feb. 18, 1987)
Oct. 2, 2004 – Struck from registry and dissolved.

Dynamo Capital Corp. (B.C. Jan. 18, 2018)
Nov. 17, 2021 – Name changed to CareSpan Health, Inc. pursuant to the Qualifying Transaction reverse takeover acquisition of CareSpan Holdings, Inc.; basis 1 new for 4.66667 old shs. (see FPsurvey - Industrials)

Dynamo Mines Ltd. (B.C. 1966)
Feb. 25, 1983 – Struck off register.

Dynamo Resources Ltd. (B.C. 1987)
Sept. 3, 1993 – Dissolved and struck off register.

DynaMotive Energy Systems Corporation (B.C. Apr. 11, 1991)
Jan. 7, 2013 – Struck from register and dissolved.
Apr. 1, 2014 – Restored to registry.
Sept. 27, 2016 – Struck from register and dissolved.

DynaMotive Technologies Corporation (B.C. Apr. 11, 1991)
Nov. 14, 2001 – Name changed to DynaMotive Energy Systems Corporation. ■

DynaQuip Incorporated (Can. May 28, 1981)
Oct. 25, 1984 – Name changed to Evertz Microsystems Inc. ■

Dynasearch Exploration Ltd. (unknown)
Aug. 8, 1977 – Amalgamated with Mymar Mining and Reduction Limited to form Dynamar Energy Limited; basis 1 new for 1.5 old shs.

Dynasty Components Inc. (Can. Oct. 14, 1983)
Nov. 30, 2001 – Obtained order from the Ontario Superior Court of Justice for protection under the Companies Creditors Arrangement Act (CCAA). Ottawa-based Deloitte & Touche Inc. was appointed monitor. The company also announced that wholly owned DCIenable Inc. filed an assignment into bankruptcy.
Dec. 2001 – Sought and obtained court order appointing Deloitte & Touche as interim receiver so they could assist in the operation of the business and, if required, effect a sale of the co.'s assets.
Feb. 2004 – Remaining directors resigned. Receiver was discharged and secured creditors suffered a shortfall. No funds were available for distribution to unsecured creditors or shldrs.
Apr. 15, 2005 – Dissolved.

Dynasty Explorations Ltd. (B.C. 1964)
Apr. 1975 – Amalgamated into Cyprus Anvil Mining Corporation.

Dynasty Gaming Inc. (Can. Aug. 11, 1994)
Dec. 30, 2010 – Name changed to Blue Zen Memorial Parks Inc. following reverse takeover acquisition of Blue Zen Memorial Park Ltd.; basis 1 new for 10 old shs. ■

Dynasty Metals & Mining Inc. (Yuk. June 28, 2000)
Sept. 27, 2017 – Continued into British Columbia.
Sept. 28, 2017 – Name changed to Core Gold Inc. ■

Dynasty Motorcar Corporation (B.C. July 25, 1977)
June 29, 2004 – Name changed to ComWest Capital Corp.; basis 1 new for 10 old shs. ■

Dynatec Corporation (Can. Oct. 31, 1995)
June 18, 2007 – Acquired by Sherritt International Corporation and FNX Mining Company Inc.; basis 0.19 new Sherritt com. shs. and 0.0634 new FNX com. shs. for 1 old Dynatec com. sh. (see FNX Mining Company Inc.; Sherritt International Corporation)

Dynetek Industries Ltd. (B.C. Jan. 18, 1990)
June 29, 1998 – Continued into Alberta.
Sept. 20, 2012 – Acquired by Luxfer Canada Limited, a wholly owned subsidiary of Luxfer Holdings PLC , for 24¢ per sh.

Dynex Petroleum Ltd. (Alta. May 31, 1979 amalg.)
Nov. 1, 1994 – Dissolved and struck off register.

Dynex Power Inc. (Can. Feb. 11, 1998)
Mar. 20, 2019 – All o/s com. shs. not already held acquired by Zhuzhou CRRC Times Electric Co., Ltd.; basis 65¢ cash per sh.

Dyno Mines Ltd. (Ont. 1941)
1956 – Name changed to Canadian Dyno Mines Ltd.; basis 1 new for 4 old shs. ■

Dyonix Greentree Technologies Inc. (B.C. 1979)
Mar. 2, 1990 – Dissolved.

E

E-Amigos.com Inc. (Alta. Mar. 17, 2000)
July 5, 2002 – Amalgamated with Sydenham Capital Inc. (1 for 1) and The Learning Library Inc. to form a new company also named The Learning Library Inc.; basis 0.66667 new Learning Library com. sh. for 1 old E-Amigos.com com. sh. (see The Learning Library Inc.)

E & E Capital Funding Inc. (Can. Nov. 8, 1979)
Jan. 9, 2006 – Amalgamated with Global (GMPC) Holdings Inc. to form GC-Global Capital Corp.; basis 0.3 new for 1 Global (GMPC) sh. and 1 new sub. vtg. sh. for 1 E & E Capital com. sh. (see GC-Global Capital Corp.)

E Automotive Inc. (Can. July 27, 2017)
May 24, 2023 – Voluntarily delisted. (see FPsurvey - Industrials)

E-Claim Solution Inc. (Can. Nov. 9, 2005)
Apr. 4, 2007 – Name changed to BUS Systems Inc. ■

E*Comnetrix Inc. (Can. June 20, 2000)
Aug. 8, 2002 – Name changed to Moving Bytes Inc. ■

E-Cruiter.com Inc. (Can. May 24, 1996)
Nov. 19, 2001 – Name changed to Workstream Inc.

E-Energy Ventures Inc. (B.C. Feb. 23, 1987)
June 15, 2020 – Dissolved and struck from registry.
Dec. 23, 2021 – Restored to registry. (see FPsurvey - Mines & Energy)

E-Gaming Ventures Corp. (B.C. June 27, 2018)
July 25, 2019 – Name changed to AMPD Ventures Inc. pursuant to the reverse takeover acquisition of AMPD Holdings Corp. (see FPsurvey - Industrials)

e-Manufacturing Networks Inc. (Alta. Nov. 19, 1996)
Aug. 2, 2003 – Struck from registry and dissolved.

e-minerals exploration corp. (Ont. Feb. 22, 1996)
Sept. 27, 2000 – Name changed to Eminator Capital Corp. ■

E-Phoria Online Systems Inc. (Yuk. Aug. 7, 1998)
Apr. 29, 2004 – Dissolved.
Feb. 13, 2006 – Revived.
Sept. 3, 2008 – Dissolved and struck off register.

e-Quisitions Inc. (Alta. May 5, 2000)
Sept. 1, 2005 – Formed Central Alberta Well Services Corp. in Alberta on amalgamation with Central Alberta Well Services Corp., constituting a reverse takeover by Central Alberta; basis 1 new for 1 Central Alberta sh. and 1 new for 20 e-Quisitions shs. ■

E-Tech Investments Inc. (Alta. Jan. 30, 1997)
Apr. 16, 1999 – Name changed to The Zone Entertainment Group, Inc. following acquistion of 527086 B.C. Ltd. ■

E-Tronics Inc. (Alta. May 16, 2000)
Oct. 28, 2002 – Name changed to Western Lakota Energy Services Inc. ■

E-Ventures Inc. (Ont. July 3, 1986)
Dec. 24, 2007 – Certificate of incorporation cancelled and dissolved.
Feb. 26, 2013 – Revived. (see FPsurvey - Industrials)

E-xact Transactions Ltd. (B.C. Aug. 13, 1998)
July 28, 1999 – Continued into Delaware.
Dec. 8, 2010 – Privatized at 40¢ per sh. with immediate cash payment of 15¢ per sh. plus 8% vendor take-back note of 25¢ per sh. payable over 5 years, or immediate cash payment of 30¢ per sh.

The E21 Group Inc. (Ont. Oct. 1, 1994)
Sept. 2, 2003 – Name changed to Green Environmental Technologies Inc.; basis 1 new for 3 old shs. (see FPsurvey - Industrials)

E3 Energy Inc. (Can. July 6, 1987 amalg.)
Jan. 14, 2005 – Amalgamated with StarPoint Energy Ltd. to form StarPoint Energy Trust; basis 0.25 new trust units or 0.25 StarPoint Energy Ltd. exch. shs. plus 0.1111 Mission Oil & Gas Inc. shs. for 1 StarPoint sh. and 0.11 new trust units or 0.11 StarPoint Energy Ltd. exch. shs. plus 0.0488 Mission Oil & Gas Inc. shs. for 1 E3 Energy sh. (see Mission Oil & Gas Inc.; StarPoint Energy Trust)

E3 Metals Corp. (B.C. Aug. 19, 1998)
July 7, 2022 – Name changed to E3 Lithium Ltd. (see FPsurvey - Mines & Energy)

E36 Capital Corp. (B.C. Mar. 6, 2019)
Feb. 23, 2021 – Name changed to Kalo Gold Holdings Corp. pursuant to the Qualifying Transaction reverse takeover acquisition of Kalo Gold Corp., and concurrent amalgamation of Kalo Gold Corp. with wholly owned 1266094 B.C. Ltd. to continue as Kalo Gold Corp. ■

E4 Energy Inc. (Alta. Dec. 1, 1983)
Feb. 12, 2008 – Acquired by Twin Butte Energy Ltd.; basis 0.3673 Twin Butte com. shs. for 1 E4 Energy com. sh.

E5 Resource Corporation (B.C. 1983)
Mar. 6, 1986 – Name changed to Enershare Technology Corporation. ■

EA Education Group Inc. (B.C. Nov. 17, 2006)
Aug. 17, 2015 – Continued into Canada.
Jan. 29, 2020 – Continued into British Columbia.
Feb. 6, 2020 – Name changed to TWX Group Holding Limited. (see FPsurvey - Industrials)

E. A. Viner Holdings Limited (Ont. Oct. 12, 1977)
June 28, 1988 – Name changed to Fahnestock Viner Holdings Inc. ■

EACOM Timber Corporation (B.C. Apr. 2, 1980)
Sept. 6, 2013 – All o/s not held acquired by Kelso & Company for 38¢ per sh.

EAGC Ventures Corp. (Ont. Feb. 23, 1988)
Feb. 18, 2003 – Plan of Arrangement to amalgamate with 151798 Ontario Inc., wholly owned subsid. of Bema Gold Corporation; basis 1 new Bema com. sh. for 1 old EAGC com. sh. (see Bema Gold Corporation)

EAV Ventures Corp. (B.C. Nov. 7, 1980)
Oct. 6, 1999 – Name changed to VendTek Systems Inc. ■

E.C. Auto Centres Inc. (B.C. Apr. 16, 1987)
Feb. 27, 1995 – Name changed to Python Oil & Gas Corporation; basis 1 new for 3.5 old shs. ■

E. C. Warner Investments Ltd. (B.C. 1964)
Dec. 23, 1975 – Amalgamated with A-1 Steel and Iron Foundry (Vancouver) Ltd. (10 for 1), Ardiem Holdings Ltd. (5 for 1) and Harbour Ferries Ltd. (1 for 3) to form The Ardiem Industrial Corp.; basis 1 new for 1 old sh.

E.C.A. Technology Ltd. (B.C. Mar. 11, 1983)
Sept. 30, 1997 – Name changed to Marine BioProducts International Corporation. ■

ECC Ventures 1 Corp. (B.C. Jan. 15, 2018)
Dec. 18, 2019 – Name changed to A2Z Technologies Canada Corp. pursuant to the Qualifying Transaction reverse takeover acquisition of an initial 99.46% interest in Israel-based A2Z Advanced Solutions Ltd.; basis 1 new for 1.4 old shs. ∎

ECC Ventures 2 Corp. (B.C. Jan. 15, 2018)
June 4, 2021 – Name changed to Infield Minerals Corp. pursuant to the Qualifying Transaction reverse takeover acquisition of based (old) Infield Minerals Corp., and concurrent amalgamation of (old) Infield and wholly owned 1276678 B.C. Ltd.; basis 1 new for 2.25 old shs. (see FPsurvey - Mines & Energy)

ECC Ventures 3 Corp. (B.C. Jan. 14, 2021)
Mar. 23, 2022 – Name changed to Sparx Technology Inc. pursuant to the Qualifying Transaction reverse takeover acquisition of (old) Sparx Technology Inc. and concurrent amalgamation of (old) Sparx with wholly owned 13255841 Canada Ltd. (and continued as Sparx Technology Corp.); basis 1.2 new for 1 old sh. ∎

ECL Enviroclean Ventures Ltd. (B.C. Jan. 1, 1984)
July 11, 2017 – Dissolved and struck from register.

ECLIPS Inc. (Alta. Sept. 23, 1992)
July 10, 2006 – Name changed to Cadillac Mining Corporation and continued into Ontario following reverse takeover acquisition of Cadillac West Exploration Inc.; basis 1 new for 8 old shs. ∎

E.C.M. Paytel Ltd. (B.C. Aug. 9, 1983)
Feb. 21, 1990 – Name changed to Consolidated Paytel Ltd.; basis 1 new for 10 old shs. ∎

ECO Corporation (Ont. Feb. 6, 1969)
Dec. 8, 1993 – Name changed to American Eco Corporation; basis 1 new for 10 old shs. ∎

ECU Silver Mining Inc. (Que. June 5, 1985)
Sept. 8, 2011 – Acquired by Golden Minerals Company for $0.000394 plus 0.05 Golden com. shs and 1 new wt. for 1 old wt exercisable for $19.00 per Golden sh.

E.D. Smith Income Fund (Ont. Apr. 29, 2005)
Oct. 18, 2007 – Acquired by TreeHouse Foods, Inc.; basis $9.055 cash per trust unit.
Oct. 30, 2007 – Final distrib. of $0.1206 cash per unit made to unitholders of record Oct. 15, 2007.

EDP Data Centres Ltd. (B.C. 1967)
Dec. 3, 1969 – Name changed to EDP Industries Limited. ∎

EDP Industries Limited (B.C. 1967)
Mar. 1975 – Name changed to EDP Industries (Western) Ltd.; basis 1 new for 40,000 old shs. Holders of less than 40,000 shs. will receive 5.6 cents per sh., thus making the co. private.

E.E.C. Marketing Corp. (B.C. Sept. 17, 1979)
Jan. 13, 1992 – Name changed to Amera Industries Corp. ∎

EEE Exploration Corp. (B.C. Nov. 11, 2014)
Sept. 21, 2022 – Name changed to Spod Lithium Corp. (see FPsurvey - Mines & Energy)

EEStor Corporation (Ont. Sept. 28, 2004)
Feb. 9, 2021 – Name changed to Fuelpositive Corporation. (see FPsurvey - Industrials)

EFH Holdings Inc. (Ont. Jan. 11, 2005 amalg.)
Aug. 23, 2021 – Name changed to ICPEI Holdings Inc. ∎

EFT Canada Inc. (Ont. May 1, 2006 amalg.)
Mar. 16, 2016 – Acquired by 1422748 Ontario Inc. (controlled by Jonathan Pasternak) for $0.105 per sh.

E.G. Capital Inc. (Ont. Aug. 15, 1995 amalg.)
Mar. 13, 2014 – Name changed to Quantum International Income Corp.; basis 1 new for 10 old shs. ∎

EGI Canada Corporation (Ont. June 12, 2000)
Dec. 21, 2005 – Acquired indirectly by E*TRADE Financial Corporation; basis 1 new E*TRADE com. sh. for 1 old EGI exch. sh.

EGI Financial Holdings Inc. (Ont. Jan. 11, 2005 amalg.)
May 25, 2015 – Name changed to Echelon Financial Holdings Inc. ∎

EI Environmental Engineering Concepts Ltd. (B.C. 1985)
Dec. 1, 2008 – Dissolved and struck from register.

EIS Capital Corp. (Alta. Oct. 23, 2009)
Aug. 2, 2011 – Name changed to Entrec Transportation Services Ltd. pursuant to Qualifying Transaction reverse takeover acquisition of Diamond B Transport Ltd., a wholly owned subsid. of Entrec Transportation Services Inc. ∎

E. J. Sharpe Instruments of Canada Limited (Ont. June 22, 1960)
June 2, 1964 – Name changed to Sharpe Instruments of Canada Limited. ∎

EKZ Investments Ltd. (Alta. May 16, 2000)
Dec. 20, 2000 – Name changed to E-Tronics Inc. ∎

E.L. Products Ltd. (B.C. 1930)
July 3, 1967 – Dissolved and struck off register.

ELAN Energy Inc. (Alta. Jan. 14, 1988 amalg.)
Oct. 17, 1997 – All o/s com. shs. acquired by Ranger Oil Limited; basis $10.55 or 0.72026 of a com. sh. of Ranger Oil for 1 com. sh. of ELAN or a combination thereof. (see Ranger Oil Limited)

ELE Capital Corporation (B.C. Dec. 19, 1994)
July 27, 2006 – Name changed to Lero Gold Corp. following reverse takeover acquisition of Tournon Finance Limited and certain assets from Oriel Resources plc. ∎

E.L.E. Energy Inc. (B.C. Aug. 21, 1972)
Nov. 12, 1992 – Name changed to Maple Leaf Springs Water Corporation following acquisition of Maple Leaf Springs Enterprises; basis 1 new for 4 old shs. ∎

ELI Eco Logic Inc. (Ont. Mar. 25, 1994 amalg.)
May 24, 2005 – Name changed to Global Development Resources, Inc.; basis 1 new for 5 old shs. ∎

E.L.M. Group Inc. (Alta. 1988)
July 9, 1992 – Name changed to Vivant Natural Spring Water, Inc.; basis 1 new for 2 old shs. ∎

EM Net Corp. (B.C. May 17, 1983)
Nov. 25, 1999 – Name changed to T & E Theatre.com Inc. and continued into Canada. ∎

EM Resources Inc. (Ont. Apr. 8, 2005)
July 15, 2011 – Name changed to Rio Verde Minerals Development Corp. and continued into British Virgin Islands. ∎

EMC Metals Corp. (B.C. July 17, 2006)
Nov. 28, 2014 – Name changed to Scandium International Mining Corp. (see FPsurvey - Mines & Energy)

EMED Mining Public Limited (Cyprus Sept. 17, 2004)
Oct. 19, 2015 – Name changed to Atalaya Mining plc; basis 1 new for 30 old shs.

EMG Capital Ltd. (Alta. Jan. 27, 1999)
Jan. 26, 2000 – Name changed to Electronics Manufacturing Group Inc. ∎

EMJ Data Systems Ltd. (Ont. July 20, 1979)
Dec. 3, 2004 – Amalgamated indirectly with Synnex Canada Ltd.; basis $6.60 per sh.

EMM Energy Inc. (Alta. Mar. 28, 2000)
June 22, 2010 – Formed SkyWest Energy Corp. in Alberta on amalgamation with (old) SkyWest Energy Corp., with SkyWest the deemed acquiror. ∎

EMR Microwave Technology Corporation (Alta. Oct. 20, 1987)
Nov. 2, 2005 – Dissolved.

EMS Systems Ltd. (B.C. 1968)
Jan. 15, 1993 – Dissolved and struck off register.

EMedia Networks International Corporation (B.C. May 27, 1999)
Jan. 29, 2014 – Privatized for $0.045 per sh.

ENERGY INDEXPLUS Dividend Fund (Alta. June 29, 2011)
June 17, 2015 – Merged into Middlefield Global Infrastructure Fund (open-ended fund); basis 0.52583938 ser. A units for 1 ENERGY trust unit.

ENERTEC Resource Services Inc. (Alta. Mar. 19, 1984)
Oct. 8, 1999 – All o/s com. shs. acquired by Veritas Energy Services; basis 0.345 cl. A exchangeable series 1 sh. of Veritas for 1 old ENERTEC com. sh. (see Veritas Energy Services Inc.)

ENPAR Technologies Inc. (Ont. Feb. 15, 1996)
Jan. 2, 2018 – Name changed to Current Water Technologies Inc. (see FPsurvey - Industrials)

ENSERCH Corporation (Tex. 1942)
June 14, 1999 – Name changed to TXU Gas Company.

ENTREC Corporation (Alta. Oct. 23, 2009)
May 15, 2020 – Filed for protection under the Companies' Creditors Arrangement (CCAA). Alvarez & Marsal Canada Inc. was appointed as monitor of the company in its CCAA proceedings.
Oct. 2020 – Sale of the Bonnyville and Fort McMurray, Alta., assets was completed in September and the liquidation of assets located in Grande Prairie and Whitecourt, Alta., was completed by Ritchie Bros. Auctioneers (Canada) Ltd. on Oct. 6 and 7. Miscellaneous equipment located in Grande Prairie that was excluded from the liquidation, as well as the trade name of Capstan and its website, were sold in September. Net proceeds to be used to pay down debt owed to secured creditors; com. sh. and unsecured convertible sub. debs. holders will not receive any payments or distributions.
Nov. 6, 2020 – Sale of substantially all of the U.S. assets to Prolift Rigging Company, LLC was completed for net proceeds of US$24,300,000. (see FPsurvey - Industrials)

EP 2000 Conservation Inc. (Que. Dec. 18, 1997 amalg.)
May 6, 2005 – Struck off register.

E.P.A. Enterprises Inc. (B.C. Jan. 9, 1987)
Apr. 9, 1998 – Name changed to Ecology Pure Air International, Inc.; basis 1 new com. and 1 new cl. 1 sh. pur. wt. of Ecology for 2 old com. shs. of E.P.A. (see FPsurvey - Industrials)

EPCOR Power Equity Ltd. (Alta. June 26, 1998)
Nov. 4, 2009 – Name changed to CPI Preferred Equity Ltd. following acquisition of EPCOR Utilities Inc.'s power generation assets and operations by Capital Power Corporation on July 1, 2009. ∎

EPCOR Power L.P. (Ont. Mar. 27, 1997)
Nov. 4, 2009 – Name changed to Capital Power Income L.P. following acquisition of EPCOR Utilities Inc.'s power generation assets and operations by Capital Power Corporation on July 1, 2009. ∎

EPCOR Preferred Equity Inc. (Alta. July 30, 2002)
Oct. 1, 2007 – All o/s cum. redeem. first pref. shs. series 1 redeemed for $25 per pref. sh.

EPI Environmental Technologies Inc. (B.C. Oct. 4, 2005)
Sept. 24, 2013 – Privatized at $0.23 per sh.

EPICentrix Technologies, Inc. (Yuk. Nov. 15, 1996)
July 5, 2004 – Name changed to Ventura Gold Corp. ∎

EPM Mining Ventures Inc. (Ont. Nov. 27, 1996 amalg.)
May 26, 2011 – Continued into Yukon.
June 25, 2015 – Name changed to Crystal Peak Minerals Inc. ∎

EPS Capital Corp. (B.C. Dec. 15, 1998)
July 31, 2001 – Name changed to BioMS Medical Corp. and continued into Alberta. ■

EQ Resources Ltd. (Ont. Nov. 13, 1962)
Nov. 23, 1998 – Formed Teton Petroleum Company in Delaware following amalgamation with American-Tyumen Exploration Company (deemed acquiror); basis 1.5 Teton shs. for 10 American-Tyumen shs. and 1 Teton sh. for 10 EQ shs. ■

ERA Carbon Offsets Ltd. (B.C. July 6, 2005)
Mar. 4, 2013 – Name changed to Offsetters Climate Solutions Inc. ■

ERG Resources Inc. (Que. Jan. 25, 1938)
Nov. 27, 1991 – Toronto-based KMPG Inc. was appointed receiver of certain assets of the company. All assets were sold resulting in a major shortfall for secured creditors; there were no distributions to unsecured creditors or shldrs.
Oct. 1, 2001 – Administration was complete and KPMG was discharged as receiver.

E.R.I. Explorations Inc. (Ont. 1971)
Mar. 1976 – Charter cancelled.

ERI Ventures Inc. (B.C. Dec. 7, 1983)
Sept. 9, 1997 – Name changed to Antam Resources International Ltd. and continued into Yukon. ■

ERL Resources Ltd. (B.C. 1972)
Dec. 16, 1980 – Name changed to Tenajon Silver Corp. ■

ESC Envirotech Systems Corporation (B.C. June 11, 1980)
Mar. 22, 1999 – Name changed to SWI Steelworks Inc.; basis 1 new for 10 old shs. ■

ESG Capital 1 Inc. (Ont. Mar. 8, 2021)
Apr. 19, 2023 – Name changed to Full Circle Lithium Corp. pursuant to the Qualifying Transaction reverse takeover acquisition of Full Circle Lithium Inc. and concurrent amalgamation of (old) Full Circle with wholly owned 1000412731 Ontario Inc. (and continued as Full Circle Canada Inc.); basis 1 new for 1.17 old shs. (see FPsurvey - Industrials)

ESG Global Impact Capital Inc. (B.C. Feb. 14, 2017)
June 29, 2023 – Name changed to AI Artificial Intelligence Ventures Inc. (see FPsurvey - Industrials)

ESI Energy Services Inc. (Alta. Feb. 22, 2001)
May 27, 2021 – Privatized via a 1-for-46,087,216 consolidation. All fractional shs. redeemed for 75¢ cash per sh. and then cancelled.

ESI Entertainment Systems Inc. (Can. Dec. 9, 1999)
Feb. 27, 2006 – Continued into British Columbia.
Nov. 1, 2013 – Acquired by Bastion Finance Corporation for $0.055 per sh.

E.S.I. Environmental Sensors Inc. (B.C. Apr. 8, 1981)
Aug. 31, 2020 – Name changed to ESV Resources Ltd.; basis 1 new for 7 old shs. ■

E.S.I. Industries Corp. (B.C. 1982)
Aug. 4, 1989 – Dissolved.

ESM Resources Ltd. (B.C. Nov. 7, 1980)
Dec. 10, 1998 – Name changed to EAV Ventures Corp.; basis 1 new for 5 old shs. ■

ESO Uranium Corp. (Alta. July 19, 2000)
Nov. 2, 2012 – Name changed to Alpha Minerals Inc.; basis 1 new for 10 old shs. ■

ESS Capital Inc. (Alta. Apr. 16, 2002)
Dec. 8, 2003 – Name changed to Centillion Industries Inc. pursuant to Qualifying Transaction acquisition of MPC Circuits Ltd. ■

ESTec Systems Corp. (B.C. 1975)
Dec. 19, 2005 – Continued into Alberta.
Dec. 20, 2016 – Privatized by CEO and major shareholder Anthony B. Nelson. Through a series of transactions, 2000285 Alberta Ltd., an entity controlled by Mr. Nelson, acquired all shares of ESTec held by minority shareholders for 12¢ per share and amalgamated with ESTec, which then was acquired by 2000067 Alberta Ltd., another entity controlled by Mr. Nelson.

ESV Resources Ltd. (B.C. Apr. 8, 1981)
Feb. 19, 2021 – Name changed to Denarius Silver Corp. pursuant to reverse takeover acquisition of 1255269 B.C. Ltd.., and purchase of Zancudo property from Gran Colombia Gold Corp., and concurrent amalgamation of 1255269 B.C. Ltd. and wholly owned 1270702 B.C. Ltd. ■

E79 Resources Corp. (B.C. Sept. 27, 2018)
Oct. 19, 2023 – Name changed to Serra Energy Metals Corp. (see FPsurvey - Mines & Energy)

ET 2000 Corp. (Ont. 1986)
Nov. 8, 1993 – Name changed to Nordic Lite Inc. ■

E.T.C. Industries Ltd. (B.C. Mar. 17, 1980)
Jan. 28, 2002 – Name changed to Consolidated E.T.C. Industries Ltd.; basis 1 new for 10 old shs. ■

ETC Transaction Corporation (Alta. Sept. 5, 1986)
May 7, 1997 – Name changed to Electronic Transmission Corporation and continued into Delaware.

ETS International, Inc. (Va. 1973)
Sept. 10, 1998 – Name changed to InfraCorps Inc.

EURO Ressources S.A. (France Apr. 20, 1993)
Feb. 27, 2024 – All o/s shs. not already held acquired by IAMGOLD Corporation; basis €3.50 cash per sh.

EV Ventures Inc. (B.C. Jan. 28, 2021)
Sept. 19, 2022 – Name changed to Atco Mining Inc. ■

EVEolution Ventures Inc. (B.C. Aug. 31, 1999)
Nov. 14, 2002 – Continued into Yukon.
Apr. 22, 2003 – Name changed to Bear Creek Mining Corporation following Qualifying Transaction reverse takeover acquisition of Bear Creek Mining Company. ■

EVI Global Group Developments Corp. (B.C. Feb. 14, 2011)
Mar. 15, 2019 – Name changed to StillCanna Inc. ■

EVITRADE Health Systems Corp. (B.C. Nov. 9, 2011)
May 1, 2019 – Name changed to Theramed Health Corporation. ■

EVP CPC Inc. (Ont. Oct. 4, 2021)
Apr. 25, 2023 – Name changed to EVP Capital Inc. ■

EVP Capital Inc. (Ont. Oct. 4, 2021)
Dec. 11, 2024 – Name changed to Sharp Therapeutics Corp. pursuant to the Qualifying Transaction reverse takeover acquisition of Sharp Edge Labs, Inc. (see FPsurvey - Industrials)

E.W.M.C. International Inc. (Ont. Oct. 31, 1987)
Sept. 27, 2001 – Name changed to Environmental Waste International Inc. ■

EXFO Electro-Optical Engineering Inc. (Can. Sept. 18, 1985)
Feb. 28, 2010 – Name changed to EXFO Inc. ■

EXFO Inc. (Can. Sept. 18, 1985)
Aug. 31, 2021 – Privatized via acquisition of all o/s subord. vtg. shs. not already held, by 11172239 Canada Inc., a company controlled by Germain Lamonde, founder of the company; basis US$6.25 cash per subord. vtg. sh.

EXI Technologies Inc. (Can. June 2, 1999)
Sept. 12, 2000 – Name changed to EXI Wireless Inc. ■

EXI Wireless Inc. (Can. June 2, 1999)
Apr. 4, 2005 – Acquired by Applied Digital Solutions, Inc.; basis 1 Applied Digital sh. for 3.0295 EXI Wireless shs.

EXMIN Resources Inc. (B.C. July 14, 2005)
Oct. 2, 2009 – Acquired by Dia Bras Exploration Inc.; basis 0.2040 Dia Bras shs. for 1 EXMIN sh. (see Dia Bras Exploration Inc.)

EXP Resources Ltd. (Alta. Jan. 25, 1988)
July 7, 2003 – Name changed to Maxim Resources Inc.; basis 1 new for 20 old shs. ■

EYEFI Group Technologies Inc. (B.C. Oct. 4, 2018)
Aug. 9, 2023 – Name changed to Sparc AI Inc. (see FPsurvey - Industrials)

EZ Ventures Ltd. (B.C. Feb. 8, 1983)
Oct. 5, 1987 – Name changed to Häglund Industries International Incorporated. ■

Eagle Ace Uranium Mines Ltd. (Ont. 1950)
1951 – Charter cancelled; assets distributed in 1951-52.

Eagle Asbestos Corp. Ltd. (B.C.)
May 15, 1969 – Struck off register.

Eagle Bay Mines Ltd. (B.C. Sept. 15, 1969)
May 28, 1973 – Name changed to Leisure Developments Ltd. ■

Eagle Bay Resources Corp. (B.C. Aug. 2, 2018)
May 1, 2024 – Name changed to Apex Critical Metals Corp. (see FPsurvey - Mines & Energy)

Eagle Crest Exploration Co. Ltd. (Ont. 1946)
1951 – Charter cancelled.

Eagle Energy Corp. (Alta. Sept. 13, 1985)
May 26, 1997 – Amalgamated with Canadian Leader Energy Inc. to form Centurion Energy International Inc.; basis 0.5 new for 1 Canadian Leader sh. and 0.6 new for 1 Eagle sh. (see Centurion Energy International Inc.)

Eagle Energy Inc. (Alta. Jan. 27, 2016)
Nov. 19, 2019 – Placed into receivership by secured lender and FTI Consulting Canada Inc. was appointed receiver. All officers and directors resigned.
June 30, 2020 – Proposal filed under the Bankruptcy and Insolvency Act was approved by the court. Under the proposal, all o/s com. shs. were redesignated as redeemable com. shs., redeemable for nil consideration and a new class of com. shs. issued to EEI Holdco, LLC in settlement of a portion of the amount owing to a secured creditor resulting in the company being a wholly owned subsid. of EEI Holdco.

Eagle Energy Trust (Alta. July 20, 2010)
Jan. 27, 2016 – Succeeded by Eagle Energy Inc. pursuant to plan of arrangement whereby Eagle Energy Inc. was formed (on amalgamation of Maple Leaf Royatlies Corp. and Eagle Newco Inc., a wholly owned subsid. of the trust) to facilitate conversion of the trust into a corporation; basis 1 new Eagle sh. for 1 EET trust unit and 0.0947 new Eagle shs. for 1 Maple Leaf sh. ■

Eagle Gold Mines Limited (Ont. Aug. 14, 1945)
June 1, 1972 – Merged with Agnico Mines Limited to form Agnico-Eagle Mines Limited; basis 1 new for 1 old sh.

Eagle Graphite Incorporated (Ont. May 31, 2004)
July 20, 2023 – Placed into receivership and FTI Consulting Canada Inc. appointed receiver.

Eagle Head Mines Ltd. (Ont. 1966)
1968 – Merged into Jubilant Eagle Holdings and Explorations Ltd.; basis 1 new for 5 old shs.

Eagle Hill Exploration Corporation (B.C. July 21, 2006)
Aug. 20, 2015 – Continued into Ontario. (see Oban Mining Corporation)
Aug. 27, 2015 – Acquired by Oban Mining Corporation; basis 0.5 (post consol.) Oban com. shs. plus 0.25 (post consol.) wts. for 1 Eagle com. sh. Each wt., is exercisable at 15¢ per share for three years. (see Oban Mining Corporation)

Eagle I Capital Corporation (B.C. Oct. 23, 2007)
Feb. 6, 2023 – Name changed to Weekapaug Lithium Limited pursuant to the reverse takeover acquisition of

Weekapaug Lithium Inc. and concurrent amalgamation of (old) Weekapaug with wholly owned 1000428387 Ontario Inc. (and continued as Weekapaug Lithium Subco Inc.). ■

Eagle Industries Limited (B.C. 1968)
Dec. 1972 – Acquired by Bralorne Resources Ltd. for $6.00 per sh.

Eagle Industries Ltd. (B.C. Apr. 16, 1980)
June 8, 1992 – Name changed to Innovative Waste Technologies Inc. (not to be confused with the co. of same name - 1968). ■

Eagle Lake Explorations Ltd. (Alta. Aug. 12, 1988 amalg.)
Dec. 16, 1991 – Name changed to Canalta Minerals Ltd.; basis 1 new for 5 old shs. ■

Eagle Mountain Gold Corp. (B.C. Oct. 16, 2003)
Mar. 4, 2014 – Amalgamated with 0987687 B.C. Ltd., a wholly owned subsid. of Goldsource Mines Inc.; basis 0.52763 Goldsource com. shs. for 1 Eagle Mountain sh. (see Goldsource Mines Inc.)

Eagle Mountain Trout Farms Ltd. (B.C. 1981)
Dec. 17, 1987 – Name changed to Preferred Foods Ltd. ■

Eagle Pass Resources Ltd. (B.C. Oct. 17, 1980)
Sept. 17, 1992 – Name changed to Starcore Resources Ltd.; basis 1 new for 3 old shs. ■

Eagle Plains Developments Ltd. (Yuk. 1958)
Oct. 31, 1961 – Struck off register.

Eagle Plains Resources Ltd. (Alta. Mar. 30, 1994)
May 12, 1999 – Amalgamated in Alberta to continue with same name. (see FPsurvey - Mines & Energy)

Eagle Precision Technologies Inc. (Ont. Feb. 27, 1959)
Nov. 19, 2003 – Going private transaction. Became a wholly owned subsid. of Canadian Imperial Bank of Commerce; basis $0.00118 per com. sh.

Eagle Resources Ltd. (B.C. 1975)
Sept. 1978 – Name changed to Bardine Oils Ltd. ■

Eagle Ridge Resources Ltd. (B.C. Nov. 10, 1981)
Sept. 12, 1986 – Name changed to AIMS Biotech Corporation. ■

Eagle River Mines Ltd. (B.C. Mar. 20, 1981 amalg.)
Jan. 29, 1985 – Name changed to Twin Eagle Resources Inc.; basis 1 new for 5 old shs. ■

Eagle Rock Exploration Ltd. (Alta. Mar. 4, 2002)
Nov. 16, 2009 – Name changed to Wild Stream Exploration Inc.; basis 1 new for 30 old shs. ■

Eagle Star Minerals Corp. (Can. Mar. 11, 2004)
Feb. 28, 2014 – Name changed to DuSolo Fertilizers Inc. ■

Eagle Star Petroleum Corp. (Can. Mar. 11, 2004)
July 6, 2010 – Name changed to Eagle Star Minerals Corp. ■

Eaglecrest Explorations Ltd. (B.C. Jan. 20, 1981)
Feb. 14, 2011 – Name changed to Colombia Crest Gold Corp. ■

Eagleford Energy Corp. (Ont. Nov. 30, 2009 amalg.)
Feb. 1, 2016 – Name changed to Intelligent Content Enterprises Inc.; basis 1 new for 10 old shs. ■

Eagleford Energy Inc. (Ont. Nov. 30, 2009 amalg.)
Aug. 25, 2014 – Name changed to Eagleford Energy Corp.; basis 1 new for 10 old shs. ■

Eaglelund Gold Mines Ltd. (Ont. 1950)
Oct. 21, 1963 – Dissolved.

Eaglestar Ventures Inc. (B.C. Jan. 19, 2006)
Dec. 5, 2006 – Name changed to Waratah Coal Inc. pursuant to Qualifying Transaction reverse takeover acquisition of Waratah Coal Pty Ltd. ■

Eaglet Mines Limited (Ont. 1972)
1978 – Continued into British Columbia.
May 27, 1994 – Dissolved and struck off register.

Eaglewood Energy Inc. (Alta. July 31, 1987 amalg.)
July 14, 2014 – Acquired by Transform Exploration Pty. Ltd.; basis 38¢ cash per sh.

Earl Gold Mines Ltd. (Ont. 1944)
1954 – Charter cancelled.

Earl Resources Limited (Cayman Islands July 17, 1998)
Feb. 7, 2018 – Continued into British Columbia.
June 29, 2022 – Name changed to Klimat X Developments Inc. ■

Earlcrest Resources Ltd. (B.C. 1959)
Dec. 1979 – Amalgamated with General Resources Limited to form Amalgamated General Resources Limited.

Early Bird Mines Limited (B.C. Sept. 20, 1965)
Oct. 17, 1983 – Name changed to Euro-American Financial Services Ltd. following acquisition of Euro-American Agencies Ltd. for 844,444 com. shs. valued at 45¢ each and 2,655,556 restricted com. shs. valued at 35¢ each; basis 1 new for 3 old shs. ■

Early Resources Ltd. (Alta. June 2, 1993)
Nov. 17, 1994 – Name changed to Lionheart Energy Corp.; basis 1 new for 10 old shs. ■

EarlyRain Inc. (Alta. Nov. 26, 1999)
2005 – Dissolved.

Earny Resources Ltd. (B.C. Feb. 9, 2011)
Feb. 28, 2019 – Name changed to Orchid Ventures, Inc. pursuant to the reverse takeover acquisition of CR International Inc. (see FPsurvey - Industrials)

Earth Alive Clean Technologies Inc. (Can. Apr. 10, 2014 amalg.)
Feb. 5, 2025 – Pursuant to a reverse vesting order under the Bankruptcy and Insolvency Act (Canada), 9530-8086 Québec Inc. subscribed for 1,000 new cl. A com. shs. of the company and all o/s shs. were cancelled for no consideration.

Earth Heat Resources Ltd. (B.C. Dec. 23, 2004)
May 17, 2013 – Name changed to Rampart Energy Limited. ■

Earth King Resources Inc. (B.C. Dec. 20, 1983)
Mar. 17, 1997 – Name changed to West African Gold Corp. and continued into Yukon. ■

Earth Star Diamonds Ltd. (B.C. Nov. 7, 1996)
Dec. 2, 2003 – Amalgamated with Poplar Resources Ltd. (1 for 10) to continue under the new name Nordic Diamonds Ltd.; basis 1 new Nordic sh. for 3 old Earth Star shs.

Earth Stewards, Inc. (B.C. Nov. 21, 1983)
July 17, 1997 – Name changed to Consolidated Earth Stewards Inc.; basis 1 new for 5 old shs. ■

EarthFirst Canada Inc. (Can. Dec. 8, 2004)
Mar. 2, 2010 – Amalgamated with Maxim Power Corp., pursuant to CCAA protection, no funds available for shldrs. (see Maxim Power Corp.)
Mar. 2, 2010 – Continued into Alberta. (see Maxim Power Corp.)

Earthquake Venture Capital Corporation (Can. June 23, 1998)
Aug. 11, 2000 – Name changed to Rutel Corporation. ■

Earthramp.com Communications Inc. (B.C. Mar. 14, 1986)
Jan. 16, 2002 – Continued into Alberta.
Sept. 18, 2007 – Name changed to Champlain Resources Inc. ■

EarthRenew Inc. (Ont. June 2, 2014)
Sept. 25, 2023 – Name changed to Replenish Nutrients Holding Corp. and continued into Alberta. (see FPsurvey - Industrials)

Earthwhile Developments Inc. (Alta. Sept. 1, 1994 amalg.)
Mar. 13, 1999 – Struck from registry and dissolved.

East Africa Gold Corporation (B.C. Apr. 30, 1987)
Aug. 23, 1996 – Continued into Yukon.
Aug. 31, 1999 – Amalgamated with Spinifex Gold NL of Australia; basis 1.63 new Spinifex shs. for 1 old East Africa Gold com. sh.

East Amphi Gold Mines Limited (Que. 1942)
June 6, 1981 – Charter cancelled.

East Asia Gold Corp. (Ont. Feb. 23, 1988)
May 28, 2001 – Name changed to EAGC Ventures Corp.; basis 1 new for 14 old shs. ■

East Asia Minerals Corporation (B.C. June 5, 1996)
Oct. 20, 2020 – Name changed to Baru Gold Corp. (see FPsurvey - Mines & Energy)

East Bay Copper Co. Ltd. (Can. Oct. 31, 1927)
1936 – Name changed to East Bay Gold Limited; basis 1 new for 3 old shs. ■

East Bay Gold Limited (Can. Oct. 31, 1927)
June 5, 1997 – Dissolved.

East Bay Mines of Red Lake Ltd. (Ont. 1928)
1945 – Acquired by Inore Gold Mines Ltd.; basis 1 new for 2 old shs. (see Inore Gold Mines Limited)

East Braintree Lithium Corp. Ltd. (Man. 1946)
Nov. 1961 – Charter cancelled.

East Coast Energy Ltd. (N.S. June 8, 1981)
Nov. 23, 1992 – Struck off register.

East Coast Investment Grade Income Fund (Ont. Apr. 26, 2012)
June 29, 2020 – Converted into an open-ended mutual fund; 1 ser. FD mutual fund unit for 1 East Coast trust unit.

East Cobalt Mines Ltd. (Ont. 1960)
Jan. 18, 1972 – Voluntarily dissolved. K. H. Bates, liquidator.

East Coppermine Exploration Co. Ltd. (Can. 1968)
1975 – Wound up.

East Crest Oil Company Limited (Can. 1928)
1953 – Name changed to Consolidated East Crest Oil Company Limited; basis 1 new for 10 old shs. ■

East Dalquier Gold Mines Ltd. (Que. 1944)
Aug. 5, 1978 – Charter cancelled.

East Energy Corp. (B.C. Sept. 26, 2005)
Dec. 16, 2009 – Name changed to Rare Earth Metals Inc. pursuant to amalgamation of a wholly owned subsid. with Rare Earth Metals Inc., constituting a reverse takeover by Rare Earth. ■

East Indies Mining Corporation (Ont. 1964)
Feb. 13, 1998 – Formed Falcon Well Services Ltd. in Canada on reverse takeover acquisition of and amalgamation with Falcon Well Services Ltd.; basis 27.42505 new for 1 Falcon cl. A com. sh. and 1 new for 1 East Indies Mining sh. ■

East Kootenay Power Company, Limited (Can. 1922)
1966 – Acquired by B.C. Hydro & Power Authority for $275 per pref. sh. and $29 per com. sh.; arrears on pref. shs. amounted to $175 per sh.

East-Leduc Oil Co. Ltd. (Alta. June 4, 1947)
Dec. 30, 1950 – Taken over by Trans Empire Oils Ltd.;
basis 1 new for 15 old shs.

East Long Uranium Mines Ltd. (Ont. 1955)
Oct. 21, 1963 – Dissolved.

East MacDonald Mines Ltd. (Que. 1952)
Oct. 23, 1982 – Charter cancelled.

East Malartic Mines Limited (Que. 1934)
Mar. 5, 1979 – Name changed to Les Mines-Est Malartic
Ltée. ■

East Manitou Mines Limited (Que. 1950)
Charter cancelled.

East Rim Nickel Mines Ltd. (Ont. 1950)
1954 – Name changed to Nickel Rim Mines Ltd.; basis 1
new for 2 old shs. (see FPsurvey - Mines & Energy)

East Rock Explorations Ltd. (Ont. 1970)
Aug. 11, 1972 – Amalgamated into Staple Mining Co.
Ltd.; basis 1 new for 4 old shs.

East Rouyn (Quebec) Ltd. (Que. 1937)
1947 – Charter cancelled; distribution equivalent to 78
shs. Rouyn Merger Gold Mines Ltd. per 100 old shs.

East Side Capital Inc. (Alta. Jan. 21, 2000)
Jan. 16, 2003 – Name changed to Redex Inc. following
Qualifying Transaction reverse takeover acquisition of
Société Immobilière Redex Ltée. ■

East Sullivan Mines Limited (Que. 1944)
July 1, 1983 – Amalgamated with Sullivan Mining Group
Ltd. to form Sullivan Mines Inc.; sh. for sh. basis.

East Trecesson Gold Mines Ltd. (Que. 1948)
Oct. 6, 1973 – Dissolved.

East Trinity Metals & Holdings Ltd. (Que. 1953)
Mar. 20, 1982 – Charter cancelled.

East Trinity Mining Corporation (Que. 1953)
1971 – Name changed to East Trinity Metals & Holdings
Ltd. ■

East Ventures Ltd. (Que. 1960)
Jan. 1974 – Charter cancelled.

East West Resource Corporation (B.C. 1979)
Dec. 11, 2005 – Continued into Ontario.
Feb. 5, 2010 – Name changed to Rainy Mountain Royalty
Corp. and continued in British Columbia following
private placement of 3,750,000 post-cons. com. shs. with
Rainy Mountain Capital Corp. which constituted Rainy
Mountain's Qualifying Transaction; basis 1 new for 5 old
shs. (see FPsurvey - Mines & Energy)

East West Resources Ltd. (Que. 1973)
1980 – Wound up.

East West Trade Finance Corp. (Can. July 6, 1987
amalg.)
Mar. 16, 1993 – Name changed to Mill City Gold Mining
Corp. ■

Eastbourne Credit Company Limited (Ont. 1963)
June 19, 1972 – Name changed to TDRI Limited. ■

Eastchester Mines Ltd. (Ont. 1945)
Jan. 1958 – Charter cancelled.

EastCoal Inc. (B.C. Dec. 15, 1986)
Aug. 27, 2021 – Name changed to CoTec Holdings Corp.
(see FPsurvey - Industrials)

EastCoast Energy Corporation (British Virgin Islands
Apr. 28, 2004)
Feb. 2, 2007 – Name changed to Orca Exploration Group
Inc. ■

Eastcourt Gold Mines Ltd. (Que. 1945)
Dec. 5, 1981 – Charter cancelled.

Easter Island Mines (unknown)
Jan. 15, 1963 – Dissolved.

Eastern & Chartered Trust Co. (Can. 1963)
Dec. 1, 1967 – Amalgamated with Canada Permanent
Trust Company (2.25 for 1) to continue with the name
Canada Permanent Trust Company; basis 1 new for 1
old sh. Canada Permanent Mortgage Corp. offered to
exchange 3 of its shs. for each new sh. until Feb. 29,
1968.

Eastern Asbestos Co. Ltd. (Que. 1952)
Oct. 1974 – Charter cancelled.

Eastern Bakeries Limited (N.B. 1935)
Sept. 1989 – Acquired by Corporate Foods Limited; basis
0.9 Corporate shs. for 1 Eastern sh. (see Corporate Foods
Limited)

Eastern Canada Coastal Steamships, Ltd. (N.B. 1929)
1947 – Reported out of business.

Eastern Canada Gas & Oil Ltd. (Que. 1954)
1960 – Name changed to Southern Exploration &
Development Corporation. ■

Eastern Canada Savings and Loan Company (Can.
1887)
July 2, 1976 – Amalgamated with Central and Nova Scotia
Trust Company to form Central and Eastern Trust
Company; basis 1 cl. A sh. for 1 old Eastern Canada sh.

Eastern Dairies, Limited (Can. 1926)
1943 – Acquired by Dominion Dairies Ltd.; basis equal
amount of 6% first mtge. bds. for old bds.; one 5% pref.
sh. and 3 com. shs. for 1 old pref. sh.; and 3 new com.
shs. for 20 old shs.

Eastern Goldfields Ltd. (Can. Oct. 15, 1986)
Oct. 12, 1993 – Name changed to Target Vanguard
Capital Inc.; basis 1 new for 2 old shs. ■

Eastern Leaseholds Inc. (B.C. 1979)
Mar. 5, 1984 – Name changed to GLF Technologies
(1979) Ltd. ■

Eastern Light & Power Company Limited (N.S. 1931)
Dec. 30, 1966 – All o/s pref. and com. shs. acquired by
the Nova Scotia Power Commission.

Eastern Lights Resources Ltd. (B.C. Feb. 11, 1981)
Jan. 9, 1989 – Delisted from the Vancouver Stock
Exchange. Subsequently struck from register and
dissolved.

Eastern Meridian Mining Corporation (Alta. Apr. 7,
1989)
Nov. 23, 2000 – Name changed to New Meridian Mining
Corp.; basis 1 new for 10 old shs. ■

Eastern Metals Corp. Ltd. (Que. 1951)
1959 – Name changed to Territory Mining Co. Ltd.; basis
1 new for 5 old shs. ■

Eastern Mines Ltd. (B.C. 1980)
Sept. 1, 1989 – Amalgamated with Gallant Gold Mines
Ltd., Silver Sceptre Resources Ltd. and Standard Gold
Mines Ltd. to form HLX Resources Limited; basis 0.2266
new for 1 Gallant Gold sh., 0.1204 new for 1 Silver
Sceptre sh., 0.2735 new for 1 Standard Gold sh. and
0.1519 new for 1 Eastern Mines sh. (see HLX Resources
Ltd.)

Eastern Mining & Smelting Corporation Ltd. (Que.
1953)
1958 – Name changed to Nickel Mining & Smelting Corp.;
basis 1 new for 2.75 old shs. ■

Eastern-Northern Explorations Ltd. (Ont. 1954)
July 8, 1965 – Dissolved.

Eastern Oil Ltd. (unknown)
1941 – Charter surrendered.

Eastern Opemiska Mines Ltd. (Que. 1956)
Nov. 4, 1978 – Charter cancelled.

Eastern Provincial Airways Limited (N.L. Mar. 8, 1949)
Nov. 12, 1980 – Name changed to Newfoundland Capital
Corporation Limited following reorganization; basis 1 new
cl. A and cl. B sh. for 1 old sh. ■

Eastern Smelting & Refining Co. Ltd. (Que. 1953)
1955 – Merged into Eastern Mining & Smelting Corp. Ltd.

Eastern Sound Co. Ltd. (unknown)
1969 – Acquired by Manoir Industries Ltd. for 100,000
com. shs. (see Manoir Industries Ltd.)

Eastern Stone Products Ltd. (Alta. Mar. 8, 1988)
July 7, 1995 – Continued into Ontario.
Aug. 18, 1995 – Name changed to Greenshield
Resources Inc.; basis 1 new for 10 old shs. ■

Eastern Trust Company (Can. 1893)
Nov. 30, 1963 – Amalgamated with Chartered Trust
Company to form Eastern & Chartered Trust Company.

Eastern Utilities Associates (P.E.I. 1940)
Apr. 16, 2000 – Acquired by National Grid plc for
US$31.459 per sh.

Eastern Zinc Corp. (B.C. June 5, 2006)
June 22, 2020 – Name changed to Major Precious Metals
Corp. ■

Eastlynn Mines Ltd. (Man. 1947)
Nov. 19, 1953 – Dissolved.

Eastmac Mines Ltd. (Que. 1946)
May 1974 – Charter cancelled.

Eastmain Resources Inc. (Ont. Apr. 28, 1982)
Oct. 13, 2020 – Acquired by Auryn Resources Inc.
(renamed Fury Gold Mines Limited); basis 0.116685115
post-consolidated Auryn com. shs. for 1 Eastmain sh.

Eastmaque Gold Mines Ltd. (B.C. Oct. 9, 1980)
Dec. 14, 1992 – Amalgamated with Equinox Resources
Ltd. (basis 1 new for 1 old sh.) to form a new co. also
known as Equinox Resources Ltd.; basis 1 com. sh. for
10 old shs. and 1 new com. sh. plus 1 new sh. purchase
warrant and 1 new cl. A series A production participating
preferred sh. for 2 old Eastmaque 8% convertible pref.
shs. (see Equinox Resources Ltd.)

Eastmin Resources Inc. (B.C. 1987)
Dec. 16, 1994 – Dissolved and struck off register.

Eastmont Gold Mines Limited (Ont. Sept. 17, 1986
amalg.)
Mar. 2, 1993 – Name changed to ANGOSS Software
Corporation; basis 1 new for 2 old shs. ■

Eastmont Holdings Ltd. (B.C. 1968)
Feb. 23, 1983 – Charter cancelled.

Eastmont Larder Lake Gold Mines Ltd. (Ont. Mar. 17,
1943)
Sept. 17, 1986 – Amalgamated with 677804 Ontario
Limited to form Eastmont Gold Mines Limited; basis 1
new for 10 old shs.

Easton Minerals Ltd. (B.C. Apr. 3, 1984)
Oct. 20, 2008 – Dissolved and struck from register.
Mar. 26, 2010 – Restored to register.
Sept. 21, 2015 – Dissolved and struck from register.

Eastview Mines Ltd. (Ont. 1945)
Jan. 31, 1979 – Charter cancelled.

Eastville Gold Mines Co. Ltd. (Que. 1945 amalg.)
June 30, 1993 – Amalgamated with Pershing-Manitou
Gold Mines Ltd./Société Minière Pershing-Manitou Ltée
and Big Town Copper Mines Ltd./Société Minière Grande
Ville Ltée to form Société Minière Pershing Manitou Ltée;
basis 1 new for 1 Pershing-Manitou sh., 1 new for 2 Big
Town shs. and 1 new for 5 Eastville shs.

Eastward Mines Ltd. (Ont. 1923)
1946 – Acquired by Upper Canada Mines Ltd.; basis 1
new for 8 old shs. (see Upper Canada Mines Ltd.)

Eastwebb Mines Ltd. (Ont. 1944)
Sept. 9, 1958 – Charter cancelled.

Eastwood Oil Co. Ltd. (Alta. 1959)
1960 – Acquired by Medallion Petroleums Ltd.; basis 9 new for 10 old shs.

Easy Street Adventures Inc. (Can. Mar. 4, 1992)
Jan. 2, 2003 – Dissolved.

Easy Washing Machine Co. Ltd. (Ont. 1934)
1958 – Acquired by General Steel Wares Ltd.; basis 1 sh. General Steel Wares plus $1.00 for each com. sh. of Easy. All o/s 5% pref. shs., $20 par, redeemed Oct. 10, 1963, at $21 per sh.

easyhome Ltd. (Ont. July 31, 1993 amalg.)
Sept. 14, 2015 – Name changed to goeasy Ltd. (see FPsurvey - Industrials)

EasyMed Services Inc. (B.C. May 19, 2009)
Oct. 21, 2013 – Name changed to EasyMed Technologies Inc.; basis 1 new for 5 old shs. ■

EasyMed Technologies Inc. (B.C. May 19, 2009)
Jan. 29, 2016 – Name changed to Easy Technologies Inc.; basis 1 new for 10 old shs. (see FPsurvey - Industrials)

Easynet Data Corporation (Ont. 1928)
Apr. 30, 1996 – Name changed to Vertigo 3D, Inc. ■

Eat & Beyond Global Holdings Inc. (B.C. Sept. 9, 2019)
June 17, 2025 – Name changed to Digital Asset Technologies Inc. (see FPsurvey - Industrials)

Eat Beyond Global Holdings Inc. (B.C. Sept. 9, 2019)
Mar. 29, 2022 – Name changed to Eat & Beyond Global Holdings Inc. ■

Eaton Bay Mortgage Corporation (Can. 1961)
Mar. 16, 1982 – Name changed to Seaway Mortgage Corporation. ■

Eaton Bay Trust Company (Can. 1982 amalg.)
Nov. 13, 1985 – Name changed to Eaton Trust Company. ■

Eaton Bay Trust Company (Alberta) (Can. 1910)
Dec. 31, 1982 – Amalgamated with its wholly owned subsid., East Bay Trust Company, to form a new co. also known as Eaton Bay Trust Company; basis 1 com. sh. for 1 com. sh. or 1 new pref. sh. for 1 old pref. sh.

Eaton Commonwealth Fund Ltd. (Can. 1933)
Apr. 12, 1978 – Name changed to Eaton Bay Commonwealth Fund Ltd.

Eaton Mining & Exploration Ltd. (B.C. 1979)
Feb. 24, 1982 – Name changed to Synco Development Corporation; basis 1 new for 4 old shs. (see FPsurvey - Mines & Energy)

Eaton Trust Company (Can. 1982 amalg.)
Feb. 12, 1988 – Amalgamated with Eaton Bay Holdings Limited and Laurentian Bank of Canada. Holders of series A preference shs. of Eaton Trust received cl. A series 3 preferred shs. of Laurentian Bank, sh.-for-sh.

Ebenezer Investments Ltd. (Alta. Nov. 19, 1993)
Oct. 31, 1996 – Name changed to Stealth Mining Corporation. ■

ebisdot.com inc. (Alta. Apr. 12, 2000)
Jan. 2, 2002 – Name changed to WorkGroup Designs Ltd. following Qualifying Transaction reverse takeover acquisition of WorkGroup Designs Inc. ■

Ebony Gold & Gas Inc. (B.C. Sept. 1, 1981)
Dec. 9, 1998 – Name changed to Running Foxes Petroleum Corp.; basis 1 new for 3 old shs. ■

Ebony Gold Corporation (B.C. Oct. 2, 1980)
June 24, 1993 – Name changed to Otis J. Exploration Corp.; basis 1 new for 5 old shs. ■

Ebor Uranium Mines Ltd. (Ont. 1954)
July 8, 1965 – Dissolved.

Ebully Inc. (Alta. Aug. 13, 1999)
May 1, 2004 – Wound up; basis $0.15 per sh. for non-insider shldrs. and $0.075 per sh. for insider shldrs.

Echelon Financial Holdings Inc. (Ont. Jan. 11, 2005 amalg.)
Dec. 14, 2020 – Name changed to EFH Holdings Inc. ■

Echelon Industries Inc. (Alta. Jan. 11, 1993)
Feb. 1, 1999 – Struck off register.

Echelon Petroleum Corp. (B.C. Dec. 17, 2009)
May 9, 2016 – Name changed to Trenchant Capital Corp. ■

Echo Bay Mines Ltd. (Alta. 1964)
Oct. 10, 1980 – Continued into Canada.
Feb. 6, 2003 – Business combination with Kinross Gold Corporation and TVX Gold Inc.; basis 0.1733 Kinross sh. for 1 Echo Bay sh.

Echo Bay Mining Ltd. (B.C. 1968)
Sept. 1972 – Name changed to Echo Industries Ltd. ■

Echo Downhole Technologies Inc. (Alta. Oct. 14, 1992)
Sept. 27, 1993 – Acquired by Alpine Subsurface Technologies Inc.; basis 1 Alpine sh. for 3 Echo shs. (see Alpine Subsurface Electronics Inc.)

Echo Energy Canada Inc. (Ont. Oct. 17, 1997)
Oct. 21, 2010 – Placed into receivership. KPMG Inc. appointed receiver.

Echo-Indin Mines Ltd. (Ont. 1945)
Sept. 18, 1961 – Charter cancelled.

Echo Industries Ltd. (B.C. 1968)
Sept. 13, 1977 – Charter cancelled.

Echo Mountain Resources Ltd. (B.C. Aug. 15, 1985)
June 15, 1988 – Name changed to Acquisicorp Capital Ltd.; basis 1 new for 10 old shs. ■

Echo Springs Water Corp. (Can. May 1, 1996)
Jan. 28, 2004 – Plan of Arrangement under Companies' Creditors Arrangement Act to permit CJC Bottling Limited to manage and control all business operations. The settlement fund allowed a maximum $500 payment per proven claim plus proportionate share in balance of fund.

Eclipse Capital Corporation (Ont. Sept. 2, 1983)
Nov. 14, 2003 – Acquired by Alert Care Corporation, a wholly owned subsid. of CSH Trust, for $4.73.

Eclipse Gold Mining Corporation (B.C. May 3, 2019)
Feb. 18, 2021 – Acquired by Northern Vertex Mining Corp.; basis 1.09 Northern Vertex shs. for 1 Eclipse sh. (see Northern Vertex Mining Corp.)

Eclipse Metals Limited (Ont. 1971)
1972 – Amalgamated with Power Mines Ltd. (1 for 6) and Active Mines Limited (1 for 2) to form a new co. Power Explorations & Holdings Limited in December; basis 1 new for 2 old shs.

Eclipse Mining Corp. (B.C. Aug. 11, 1980)
Dec. 28, 1990 – Dissolved and struck off register.

Eclipse Residential Mortgage Investment Corporation (Ont. Apr. 3, 2013)
May 24, 2019 – Voluntarily dissolving. First distrib. of $8.65 cash per sh. payable May 28, 2019, to shldrs. of record May 23, 2019.
Oct. 4, 2019 – Second and final distrib. of $1.03 cash per sh. payable Oct. 4, 2019, to shldrs. of record Sept. 30, 2019.
Oct. 7, 2019 – Dissolved and struck from register.

Eclund Gold Mines Ltd. (Ont. 1950)
Charter cancelled.

Eco-Dynamics Industries Inc. (Alta. Nov. 17, 1977)
May 1, 1997 – Struck off register.

eCobalt Solutions Inc. (B.C. June 13, 1988)
July 29, 2019 – Acquired by Jervois Mining Limited; basis 1.65 Jervois shs. for 1 eCobalt sh. (see Jervois Mining Limited)

EcoMax Energy Services Ltd. (Alta. May 7, 1997)
Oct. 5, 2011 – Name changed to Tasca Resources Ltd. and continued into British Columbia pursuant to acquisition of an option to earn 60% interest in the Acacia mineral prospect resulting in the reverse takeover by Tasca Resources Ltd. ■

EComm Systems Corporation (Del. Dec. 16, 1999)
Apr. 27, 2001 – Name changed to Dome Ventures Corporation. ■

EcomPark Inc. (Ont. Oct. 18, 1993)
Sept. 27, 2000 – Name changed to NAME Inc. ■

Econ Ventures Ltd. (B.C. Mar. 29, 1984)
July 13, 1995 – Continued into Canada.
Sept. 12, 2000 – Name changed to Richcor Resources Ltd.; basis 1 new for 10 old shs. ■

Econogreen Environmental Systems Ltd. (B.C. 1984)
June 28, 1995 – Name changed to Voisey Bay Resources Inc. ■

Economy Inns, Inc. (B.C. Oct. 27, 1971)
Oct. 16, 1985 – Name changed to Mintel International Development Corp. ■

Ecopia BioSciences Inc. (Can. Jan. 19, 1998)
Mar. 14, 2007 – Formed Thallion Pharmaceuticals Inc. in Canada on amalgamation with Caprion Pharmaceuticals Inc. with Ecopia the deemed acquiror; basis 1 new for 10 old shs. ■

Ecoprogress Canada Holdings Inc. (B.C. Nov. 20, 1978)
May 6, 1998 – Name changed to Consolidated Ecoprogress Technology Inc.; basis 1 new for 10 old shs. ■

Ecos Resources Limited (B.C. 1980)
July 30, 1993 – Dissolved and struck off register.

Ecosse Energy Corp. (Can. July 6, 2005)
June 17, 2015 – Dissolved and struck from register.

Ecstall Mining Co. Ltd. (B.C. 1951)
Aug. 31, 1960 – In voluntary liquidation. Assets taken over by parent co., Texas Gulf Sulpher Co., of New York.

Ecstall Mining Corporation (B.C. May 16, 1984)
Mar. 27, 2007 – Acquired by Mantle Resources Inc.; basis 0.41 new Mantle sh. for 1 old Ecstall sh. (see Mantle Resources Inc.)

Ecuador Gold and Copper Corp. (Alta. Mar. 7, 2008)
Nov. 1, 2016 – Acquired by Odin Mining and Exploration Ltd. (renamed Lumina Gold Corp.); basis 1.0433 Odin com. shs. for 1 Ecuador sh. (see Lumina Gold Corp.)

Ecuadorean Copperfields Inc. (B.C. May 27, 1980)
June 14, 1996 – Name changed to Bronx Minerals Inc.; basis 1 new for 3 old shs. ■

Ecuadorian Minerals Corporation (Yuk. Feb. 14, 1994)
Jan. 24, 2002 – Name changed to International Minerals Corporation. ■

EcuaGold Resources Ltd. (B.C. Feb. 28, 2006)
Oct. 14, 2008 – Name changed to AndeanGold Ltd. ■

eCycling Technologies Inc. (Alta. Dec. 3, 1996)
Oct. 18, 2007 – Name changed to Trius Investments Inc. ■

Ed. Hargreaves Kirkland Gold Mines Ltd. (Ont. July 1934)
1957 – Charter cancelled.

Edar Uranium Mines Ltd. (Ont. 1967)
Dec. 19, 1979 – Dissolved.

Edco Mining & Exploration Ltd. (N.B. 1954)
Dec. 7, 1966 – Charter cancelled.

Eddy Match Company, Limited (Can. 1927)
June 1, 1975 – All o/s com. shs. acquired by Warrington Products Ltd., through purch. offer made of $30 per sh. (see Warrington Products Limited)

Eddy Paper Company Limited (Can. 1946)
July 20, 1962 – All com. shs. acquired by George Weston Ltd. through offer made in 1962 of 1.5 cl. A shs. of Weston plus $1.50 for each Eddy com. sh. The $20 cl. A shs. of Eddy were called for redemption at $22.50 plus divd. of $0.10 per sh.

Eden Exploration Ltd. (Alta. Mar. 25, 1993)
Aug. 23, 1999 – Amalgamated with Black Canyon Resources Inc. (0.210526 for 1) and 836296 Alberta Ltd. (wholly owned subsid. of Brandon Energy Ltd.) to form Cannon Oil & Gas Ltd.; basis 0.122642 Cannon shs. for 1 Eden sh. (see Cannon Oil & Gas Ltd.)

Eden Industries International Ltd. (Ont. 1966)
Mar. 16, 1976 – Charter cancelled.

Eden Roc Mineral Corp. (Ont. 1935)
July 30, 1985 – Amalgamated with Dibi Resources Inc. to form new co. with same name Eden Roc Mineral Corp.
Dec. 11, 2017 – Dissolved and struck from registry.

Edena Mines Ltd. (Ont. 1926)
1944 – Dissolved.

Edenbridge Corp. (Ont. Dec. 23, 1996)
July 13, 1999 – Name changed to Integrated Asset Management Corp.; basis 1 new for 5 old shs. ■

Edge Energy Inc. (Alta. Mar. 25, 1986)
Aug. 23, 2000 – Acquired by Ventus Energy Ltd.; basis 0.375 Ventus shs. for 1 Edge sh. (see Ventus Energy Ltd.)

Edge Resources Inc. (Alta. July 23, 2009)
Apr. 29, 2016 – Placed into receivership. Grant Thornton Limited was appointed receiver and all officers and directors resigned.
Oct. 31, 2016 – Oil and gas properties in Alberta and Saskatchewan were sold. Net proceeds were distrib. to secured creditor. No proceeds available for distrib. to shldrs.
Feb. 2017 – Grant Thornton was discharged as receiver.
Mar. 2, 2018 – Struck from registry and dissolved.

Edge Resources Ltd. (B.C. 1983)
July 9, 1991 – Amalgamated with Durham Resources Ltd. (1 new for 1.333 old shs.) to form a new co. called Gothic Resources Inc. (Ressources Gothic Inc.); basis 1 new for 2 old shs. (see Gothic Resources Inc.)

Edgefront Real Estate Investment Trust (Ont. May 10, 2013)
Apr. 3, 2017 – Name changed to Nexus Real Estate Investment Trust pursuant to acquisition of Nobel Real Estate Investment Trust. ■

Edgefront Realty Corp. (Ont. July 30, 2012)
Jan. 13, 2014 – Succeeded by Edgefront Real Estate Investment Trust pursuant to plan of arrangement whereby Edgefront Real Estate Investment Trust was formed to facilitate the conversion of the corporation into a trust; basis 1 trust unit or class B LP unit of Edgefront Limited Partnership for 20 old shs. ■

Edgehill Mines Ltd. (Ont. 1947)
Dec. 1954 – Charter cancelled.

Edgemont Resources Corp. (B.C. 1980)
Aug. 21, 1992 – Dissolved and struck off register.

Edgewater Mining Co. Ltd. (B.C. July 18, 1967)
Feb. 6, 1970 – Name changed to Canarctic Resources Ltd. ■

Edgewater Petroleums Ltd. (Ont. 1962)
Dec. 6, 1972 – Charter cancelled.

Edgewater Porcupine Gold Mines Ltd. (Ont. 1944)
Nov. 6, 1961 – Dissolved.

Edgewater Resources Ltd. (B.C. 1983)
Dec. 8, 1986 – Name changed to MI Software Corporation. ■

Edgewood Explorations Inc. (Ont. 1973)
Nov. 9, 1978 – Amalgamated with Jaridge Explorations Inc. which continued as Jaridge Explorations Inc.; basis 1 new for 1.5 old shs. (see Jaridge Explorations Inc.)

Edifice Explorations Ltd. (Ont. Sept. 22, 1989)
June 11, 1996 – Formed Goldmint Explorations Ltd. in Ontario on amalgamation with 1170406 Ontario Limited (wholly owned by Goldbrook Explorations Inc.) and concurrent acquisition of Trip Line Mineral Development Inc. and Higley Flow Equities Ltd., constituting a reverse takeover by Trip Line; basis 2.5 new units (1 sh. & 1 wt.) for 1 1170406 Ontario sh. and 1 new sh. for 10 Edifice shs. ■

Edina International Ltd. (B.C. Apr. 4, 1972)
Mar. 13, 1981 – Name changed to Chisholm Resources Inc.; basis 1 new for 3 old shs. ■

Edina Resources Ltd. (B.C. Apr. 4, 1972)
July 20, 1973 – Name changed to Edina International Ltd. ■

Edinov Corporation (Can. May 15, 1989 amalg.)
Nov. 3, 1993 – Name changed to Cedar Group, Inc. and continued into Delaware. ■

Edinov Technologies Inc. (Can. May 15, 1989 amalg.)
Apr. 27, 1993 – Name changed to Edinov Corporation; basis 1 new for 5 old shs. ■

Edison Battery Metals Corp. (B.C. Nov. 8, 2009)
Nov. 24, 2021 – Name changed to Edison Lithium Corp. (see FPsurvey - Mines & Energy)

Edison Cobalt Corp. (B.C. Nov. 8, 2009)
July 30, 2021 – Name changed to Edison Battery Metals Corp. ■

eDispatch.com Wireless Data Inc. (B.C. May 1, 1991)
July 31, 2002 – Name changed to AirIQ Inc. ■

Edleun Group, Inc. (Can. Apr. 1, 2005)
Aug. 1, 2013 – Name changed to BrightPath Early Learning Inc. ■

Edlon Mines Ltd. (Ont. 1952)
Mar. 1, 1978 – Name changed to Petroline Explorers Inc. ■

Edmac Mines Ltd. (B.C. 1966)
Feb. 25, 1983 – Charter cancelled.

Edmonton Concrete Block Co. Ltd. (Alta. 1949)
Dec. 10, 1971 – Amalgamated with 5 other cos., to form Consolidated Concrete Ltd., a wholly owned subsid. of BACM Industries Ltd.

Edmonton International Industries Ltd. (Alta. 1965)
June 2, 2018 – Dissolved and struck from registry.

Edmor Mines Ltd. (Ont. 1944)
Oct. 7, 1957 – Dissolved.

Edna-Golden Horn Mines Ltd. (Man. 1946)
Dec. 19, 1962 – Charter cancelled.

Edomar Resources Inc. (Ont. Mar. 21, 1945)
Oct. 9, 1996 – Formed Kazakstan Goldfields Corporation in Ontario pursuant to reverse takeover acquisition of and amalgamation with 1173458 Ontario Limited; basis 1 new for 2.6 old shs. ■

Edoran Oil Corp. Ltd. (Alta. 1952)
1965 – Name changed to Kamalta Exploration Ltd.; basis 1 new for 5 old shs. ■

Edper Enterprises Ltd. (Can. Nov. 10, 1951)
1982 – Continued into Ontario.
June 8, 1995 – Name changed to HIL Corporation Limited. ■

The Edper Group Limited (Ont. Oct. 28, 1975)
Jan. 13, 1997 – Amalgamated with Hees International Bancorp Inc. to form new co. with same name The Edper Group Limited; basis 0.38 new cl. A sh. for 1 Edper cl. A non-vtg. sh. and 1 new instalment receipt for 1 Edper instalment receipt. (see The Edper Group Limited)

The Edper Group Limited (Ont. Dec. 31, 1996 amalg.)
Aug. 1, 1997 – Formed EdperBrascan Corporation in Ontario on amalgamation with Brascan Corporation; basis 1 new cl. A ltd. vtg. sh. for 1 old cl. A ltd. vtg. sh., 1 new cl. B ltd. vtg. sh. or 1 new cl. A ltd. vtg. sh. for 1 old cl. B ltd. vtg. sh., and 1 cl. A pref. sh. ser.1, 2 and 3 for 1 cl. A pref. sh. ser. D, E and G. ■

EdperBrascan Corporation (Ont. Aug. 1, 1997 amalg.)
May 3, 2000 – Name changed to Brascan Corporation. ■

Edross Consolidated Mines Ltd. (unknown)
Dec. 10, 1962 – Dissolved.

Educor International Inc. (Can. May 18, 1989)
July 20, 2000 – Name changed to LogicalOptions International Inc. ■

Edvan Oils Ltd. (B.C. 1947)
1970 – Name changed to Legend Explorations Ltd.; basis 1 new for 5 old shs. ■

Edward Lipsett (1930) Limited (B.C. 1930)
Jan. 11, 1965 – Name changed to E.L. Products Ltd. ■

Edwards Consolidated Mines Ltd. (Ont. 1938)
1955 – Charter cancelled.

Edwards Steel Fabricators Inc. (Ont. Nov. 8, 1985)
Sept. 1, 1989 – Placed into receivership; Arthur Andersen & Co. appointed receiver.
June 1, 1992 – All assets sold. Secured creditors suffered a shortfall and no distribution to unsecured creditors or shldrs.

Edwaska Gold Mines Ltd. (Ont. 1944)
Nov. 1959 – Charter cancelled.

Efficacious Elk Capital Corp. (B.C. May 22, 2018)
Mar. 15, 2022 – Name changed to MiMedia Holdings Inc. pursuant to the Qualifying Transaction reverse takeover acquisition of MiMedia Inc.; basis 0.52083 new for 1 old sh. (see FPsurvey - Industrials)

Egalite Ventures Ltd. (B.C. Mar. 7, 1979)
June 26, 1980 – Name changed to Glory Explorations Ltd.; basis 1 new for 3.5 old shs. ■

Ego Mines Ltd. (Ont. 1958)
June 16, 1978 – Name changed to Ego Resources Limited. ■

Ego Resources Limited (Ont. 1958)
Sept. 11, 1997 – Name changed to Cobatec Inc. ■

egX Group Inc. (B.C. Dec. 12, 1977)
May 14, 2012 – Dissolved and struck from register.

Eicon Technology Corporation (Can. Oct. 12, 1984)
Nov. 30, 2000 – All o/s com. shs. acquired by wholly owned subsid. of Denmark-based i-data international a-s; basis $5.00 per sh.

Eiger Technology, Inc. (B.C. Sept. 8, 1986)
Nov. 22, 2000 – Continued into Ontario.
June 24, 2008 – Name changed to Gamecorp Ltd.; basis 1 new for 10 old shs. ■

8 Crown Capital Corp. (B.C. Dec. 8, 1998)
Dec. 16, 1999 – Name changed to Starfire Technologies International Inc. ■

Eight Solutions Inc. (B.C. Jan. 24, 2011)
Aug. 22, 2022 – Dissolved and struck from register.

8859582 Canada Inc. (Can. Mar. 20, 2015)
May 27, 2015 – Name changed to Rx Drug Mart Inc. ■

888 China Holdings Limited (Yuk. Feb. 21, 1995)
June 3, 1996 – Name changed to Black Sea Energy Ltd. ■

88 Capital Corp. (B.C. Jan. 27, 2011)
Oct. 19, 2017 – Name changed to Golden Ridge Resources Ltd. following reverse takeover acquisition of (old) Golden Ridge Resources Ltd. (see FPsurvey - Mines & Energy)

Ekaton Energy Limited (Alta. 1983)
May 14, 1986 – Name changed to Ekaton Industries Inc. ■

Ekaton Industries Inc. (Alta. 1983)
Jan. 1, 1992 – Struck off register.

Ekersval Resources Ltd. (Ont. Feb. 18, 1988)
Oct. 13, 1992 – Name changed to maxill inc. following amalgamation with two wholly owned subsids.; basis 1 new for 3 old shs. ■

El Alamein Mines Ltd. (B.C. 1948)
Nov. 25, 1965 – Charter cancelled.

El-Bonanza Mining Corporation, Limited (Ont. Jan. 13, 1934)
Sept. 15, 1980 – Dissolved.
Dec. 9, 1980 – Revived.
Oct. 29, 1994 – Charter cancelled and co. dissolved.
Feb. 20, 1996 – Charter and company revived.
Apr. 23, 1999 – Name changed to Virgin Metals Inc. following acquisition of Virgin Metals (Canada) Limited. ■

El Bravo Gold Mining Ltd. (B.C. Apr. 12, 1983)
July 3, 1995 – Continued into Bermuda.
Dec. 17, 1997 – Name changed to El Bravo Resources International Ltd. ■

El Bravo Resources International Ltd. (Bermuda July 3, 1995)
Sept. 18, 2000 – Name changed to Tri-X International Ltd.; basis 1 new for 14 old shs.

El Callao Mining Corp. (B.C. July 4, 1986)
Aug. 20, 2004 – Plan of Arrangement acquisition by Crystallex International Corproation; basis 0.01818 new Crystallex sh. for 1 old El Callao sh. ■

El Camino Resources Inc. (B.C. 1983)
July 24, 1985 – Name changed to C.I.S. Technologies, Inc. ■

El Cap Gold Mines Ltd. (B.C. Aug. 23, 1983)
Sept. 4, 1996 – Name changed to Lakeland Royalty & Petroleum Corporation; basis 1 new for 3.7 old shs. ■

El Coco Explorations Ltd. (Ont. 1958)
May 31, 1971 – Sold assets and liabs. to El Coco Explorations (Quebec) Ltd. for 1,586,005 shs. (675,000 shs. escrowed)

El Coco Explorations Ltd. (B.C. 1975)
Aug. 7, 1984 – Name changed to Dassen Gold Resources Ltd. ■

El Coco Explorations (Quebec) Ltd. (Que. 1971)
1975 – Received 1,586,005 shs. of El Coco Explorations Ltd. (B.C. inc.) for sale of property.

El Condor Minerals Inc. (B.C. Aug. 4, 2010)
June 3, 2015 – Name changed to Worldwide Resources Corp. (see FPsurvey - Mines & Energy)

El Condor Resources Ltd. (B.C. 1986)
July 15, 1991 – Amalgamated with Covenant Resources Inc. (1 for 1) to continue as El Condor Resources Ltd.; basis 1 new for 1 old sh. (see El Condor Resources Ltd.)

El Condor Resources Ltd. (B.C. 1991 amalg.)
Jan. 15, 1996 – All o/s com. shs. acquired by Royal Oak Mines Inc.; basis 0.95 new com. sh. Royal Oak plus $2.00

in cash for 1 com. sh. El Condor. Subsequently dissolved Dec. 16, 1997. (see Royal Oak Mines Inc.)

El Dorado Systems (Canada) Inc. (B.C. Sept. 3, 1980)
Oct. 3, 1988 – Delisted from the Vancouver Stock Exchange. Subsequently struck from register and dissolved.

El Misti Gold Limited (B.C. Jan. 14, 1981)
Oct. 21, 1999 – Name changed to Andean American Mining Corp.; basis 1 new for 20 old shs. ■

El Nino Ventures Inc. (B.C. Feb. 19, 1988)
Dec. 30, 2022 – Name changed to MetalQuest Mining Inc.; basis 1 new for 2.5 old shs. (see FPsurvey - Mines & Energy)

El Paraiso Resources Limited (B.C. 1982)
Oct. 28, 1988 – Name changed to Commonwealth Gold Corporation. ■

El Paso Energy Corp. (B.C. Aug. 21, 1972)
July 26, 1984 – Name changed to E.L.E. Energy Inc.; basis 1 new for 2 old shs. ■

El Pen-Rey Mines Ltd. (Ont. 1944)
1950 – Name changed to El Pen-Rey Oil & Mines Ltd. ■

El Pen-Rey Oil & Mines Ltd. (Ont. 1944)
1961 – Wound up.

El Sol Gold Mines Ltd. (Ont. 1946)
1957 – Name changed to El Sol Mining Ltd. ■

El Sol Mining Ltd. (Ont. 1946)
1964 – Name changed to Tex-Sol Explorations Limited; basis 1 new for 5 old shs. ■

El Tigre Silver Corp. (Can. Dec. 10, 2007)
Nov. 25, 2015 – Acquired by Oceanus Resources Corporation; basis 0.2839 Oceanus com. sh. for 1 El Tigre com. sh. (see Oceanus Resources Corporation)

Elaine Red Lake Gold Mines Ltd. (Ont. 1946)
1947 – Name changed to Greenoaks Mines Ltd. ■

Elan Industries Inc. (B.C. June 1, 1982 amalg.)
Aug. 17, 1990 – Name changed to Trylox Environmental Corporation; basis 1 new for 4 old shs. ■

Elancra Mines Ltd. (Ont. 1949)
1957 – Charter cancelled.

Elar Mines Ltd. (Ont. 1972)
Aug. 6, 1975 – Dissolved.

Elcor Gold Mines Ltd. (Ont. 1945)
Apr. 1, 1963 – Dissolved.

Elcora Resources Corp. (Can. June 6, 2011)
Feb. 2, 2016 – Name changed to Elcora Advanced Materials Corp. (see FPsurvey - Mines & Energy)

Elder Gold Mines Ltd. (Ont. 1944)
1946 – Name changed to Elder Mines Ltd. ■

Elder Mines and Developments Limited (Ont. 1944)
1962 – Name changed to Elder-Peel Ltd. ■

Elder Mines Ltd. (Ont. 1944)
1959 – Name changed to Elder Mines and Developments Limited. ■

Elder-Peel Ltd. (Ont. 1944)
Dec. 1963 – Name changed to Peel-Elder Limited; basis 1 new for 10 old shs. ■

Elder-Red Lake Gold Mines Ltd. (Ont. 1936)
Name changed to Britt-Malartic Gold Mines Ltd. ■

Elder Technologies Limited (B.C. 1983)
Feb. 21, 1992 – Dissolved and struck off register.

Elders IXL Canada Inc. (Ont. 1956)
Feb. 4, 1991 – Name changed to Foster's Brewing Group Canada Inc.

Elders IXL Limited (Australia 1962)
Nov. 30, 1990 – Name changed to Foster's Brewing Group Limited.

Eldex Minerals Ltd. (Ont. 1975)
Dec. 2, 1976 – Amalgamated with 2 other cos. to form Forefront Consolidated Explorations Ltd.; basis 1 new for 3 old shs.

Eldon Resources Ltd. (B.C. Oct. 11, 1979)
Mar. 27, 1998 – Formed KSAT Satellite Networks Inc. following acquisition of Xenexi Telecommunications Development Inc.; basis 1 new for 3 old shs. ■

Eldona Gold Mines Ltd. (Ont. 1944)
1952 – Name changed to d'Eldona Gold Mines Limited; basis 1 new for 3 old shs. ■

Eldorado Corporation Ltd. (Bermuda Apr. 2, 1992)
Apr. 23, 1996 – Name changed to Eldorado Gold Corporation and continued into British Columbia. ■

Eldorado Explorations Ltd. (Man. July 5, 1976)
June 26, 1979 – Name changed to Corporate Oil & Gas Ltd. ■

Eldorado Gold Corporation (B.C. Apr. 23, 1996)
June 28, 1996 – Continued into Canada.
Nov. 9, 1996 – Amalgamated with HRC Development Corporation to form new co. with same name Eldorado Gold Corporation; basis 1 new for 2 HRC shs. and 1 new for 1 Eldorado sh.
Nov. 19, 1996 – Amalgamated in Canada to continue with same name. (see FPsurvey - Mines & Energy)

Eldorado Minerals & Petroleum Corp. (B.C. 1971)
1981 – Amalgamated in British Columbia to continue with same name.
May 28, 1993 – Dissolved and struck off register.

Eldorado Mining & Refining Ltd. (Ont. 1926)
Jan. 28, 1944 – Assets and liabs. expropriated by Canadian govt. Shldrs. received $1.35 per sh.

Eldrich Mines Ltd. (Ont. Aug. 14, 1944)
1963 – Name changed to Canadian-Australian Exploration Ltd. ■

Electra Energy Corporation (Alta. Aug. 6, 1992)
July 2, 2001 – Dissolved and struck from register.

Electra Gold Ltd. (B.C. Dec. 1, 1981 amalg.)
Feb. 2, 2015 – Name changed to Electra Stone Ltd. ■

Electra Mining Consolidated Ltd. (B.C. Dec. 1, 1981 amalg.)
Feb. 17, 1997 – Name changed to Electra Gold Ltd. ■

Electra North West Resources Ltd. (B.C. Dec. 1, 1981 amalg.)
Aug. 21, 1992 – Name changed to Electra Mining Consolidated Ltd.; basis 1 new for 5 old shs. ■

Electra Resources Corporation (B.C. 1978)
Dec. 31, 1981 – Amalgamated with Pacific North West Resources Ltd. to form Electra North West Resources Ltd.; sh. for sh. basis.

Electra Stone Ltd. (B.C. Dec. 1, 1981 amalg.)
May 18, 2020 – Dissolved and struck from register.

Electra Title Corporation (B.C. 1983)
Feb. 13, 1987 – Name changed to B.I. Ventures Ltd. ■

Electrameccanica Vehicles Corp. (B.C. Feb. 16, 2015)
Mar. 27, 2024 – Acquired by Xos Services, Inc.; basis 0.0143739 Xos shs. for 1 Electrameccanica sh.

The Electric Mail Company Inc. (B.C. Dec. 19, 1994)
Mar. 30, 2004 – Name changed to ELE Capital Corporation following sale of assets and operations to a

subsidiary of j2 Global Communications, Inc.; basis 1 new for 10 old shs. ∎

Electric Metals Inc. (B.C. Mar. 6, 2009)
Sept. 11, 2013 – Formed Moimstone Corporation in British Columbia pursuant to reverse takeover of and amalgamation with (old) Moimstone Corporation; basis 0.1 new com. shs. for 1 Electric com. sh. and 1 new com sh. for 1 (old) Moimstone com. sh. ∎

Electrical Mfg. Co. Ltd. (Que. 1945)
Feb. 11, 1960 – Name changed to Fleetwood Corporation. ∎

Electro-Knit Fabrics (Canada) Ltd. (Can. 1956)
Nov. 1980 – Name changed to Electro-Knit Fabrics Ltd. ∎

Electro-Knit Fabrics Ltd. (Can. 1956)
Dec. 1982 – Placed into receivership.
Apr. 20, 1983 – Declared bankrupt. No distribution made to unsecured creditors.

electroBusiness.com Inc. (Alta. Oct. 1, 1999)
May 25, 2007 – Name changed to Cortex Business Solutions Inc. ∎

Electrofuel Inc. (Ont. Sept. 24, 1996)
Aug. 13, 2002 – Name changed to Electrovaya Inc. (see FPsurvey - Industrials)

Electrohome Broadcasting Inc. (Ont. Mar. 31, 1998)
May 8, 2000 – All o/s cl. A and cl. B shs. acquired by 1406236 Ontario Inc.; basis $32.17 per sh.

Electrohome Limited (Ont. Apr. 1, 1933)
June 28, 1980 – Amalgamated in Ontario to continue with same name. (see Electrohome Limited)
May 1, 1988 – Amalgamated in Ontario to continue with same name. (see Electrohome Limited)
Apr. 1, 1998 – Plan of Arrangement with Baton Broadcasting Incorporated to transfer all shs. of Baton held by Electrohome Limited to a new company known as Electrohome Broadcasting Inc., splitting Electrohome Limited into 2 public companies, one retaining the Electrohome Limited name; basis (a) 1 cl. X sh. of new Electrohome Limited and 1 cl. X sh. of Electrohome Broadcasting for 1 cl. X sh. of old Electrohome Limited and (b) 1 cl. Y sh. of new Electrohome and 1 cl. Y sh. of Electrohome Broadcasting for 1 cl. Y sh. of old Electrohome Limited. (see Electrohome Limited)

Electrohome Limited (Ont. Apr. 1, 1933)
Oct. 1, 2008 – Liquidated, sold remaining assets consisting of 26.5% interest in Mechdyne Corporation back to Mechdyne for US$616,444 plus US$3,082,222 10-yr. 4.3% promissory note. John A. Pollock, Co.'s major shldr. purchased the 10-yr. note for US$2,934,592 to aid the final distribution to shldrs. Subsequently dissolved.

Electrolier Corporation (Que. 1961)
Dec. 7, 1965 – Acquired by Sylvania Electric (Canada) Ltd. through offer made to purch. all cl. A shs. at $14 Cdn per sh. Sylvania previously acquired all o/s cl. B shs. at $14 per sh.

Electromed Inc. (Que. Sept. 23, 1987)
Oct. 15, 2003 – Name changed to Evolved Digital Systems Inc.; basis 1 new for 8 old shs. ∎

Electronic Associates Ltd. (Ont. 1946)
Nov. 1, 1963 – Name changed to Electronic Associates of Canada Limited. ∎

Electronic Associates of Canada Limited (Ont. 1946)
Nov. 6, 1974 – Placed into receivership; assets sold to Sentrol Systems Ltd. No distribution expected for pref. or unsecured creditors or shldrs.

Electronics Manufacturing Group Inc. (Alta. Jan. 27, 1999)
Jan. 1, 2003 – Formed Adeptron Technologies Corporation in Alberta on amalgamation with wholly owned subsidiaries J.F.B. Technologies Inc. and Continuum Technologies Inc. ∎

Electrum Lake Gold Mines Ltd. (Ont. 1959)
Dec. 1966 – Charter cancelled.

Elegance Business Corporation (B.C. Jan. 4, 1984)
Jan. 9, 1989 – Delisted from the Vancouver Stock Exchange. Subsequently struck from register and dissolved.

Elektra Power Inc. (B.C. July 17, 1974)
Dec. 16, 1988 – Dissolved and struck off register.

Element Financial Corporation (Ont. Dec. 15, 2011 amalg.)
Oct. 3, 2016 – Name changed to Element Fleet Management Corp. pursuant to plan of arrangement whereby ECN Capital Corp. was spun off as a separate publicly traded company. (see FPsurvey - Industrials)

Element Nutritional Sciences Inc. (B.C. June 25, 2018)
Jan. 26, 2024 – Name changed to Promino Nutritional Sciences Inc. (see FPsurvey - Industrials)

Element 79 Capital Inc. (Can. Feb. 6, 2013)
Nov. 14, 2018 – Name changed to Mondias Natural Products Inc. following Qualifying Transaction reverse takeover acquisition of (old) Mondias Natural Products Inc.; basis 1 new for 1.5 old shs. ∎

Elemental Royalties Corp. (B.C. July 19, 2016)
Sept. 26, 2022 – Name changed to Elemental Altus Royalties Corp. (see FPsurvey - Mines & Energy)

Elephant Hill Capital Inc. (Alta. Jan. 15, 2018)
Dec. 7, 2020 – Name changed to Real Luck Group Ltd. pursuant to Qualifying Transaction reverse takeover acquisition of Esports Limited (dba Luckbox); basis 1 new for 4.2 old shs. (see FPsurvey - Industrials)

Elevation Capital Corp. (B.C. Dec. 11, 2012)
Apr. 22, 2016 – Voluntarily dissolved following Qualifying Transaction private placement acquisition of 2,800,000 units (1 com. sh. & ½ wt.) of Sora Capital Corp. at 17¢ per unit (with wts. exercisable at 20¢ per sh. for two years) and distribution of Sora units to shareholders. (see Sora Capital Corp.)

Elevation Technologies, Inc. (B.C. Jan. 3, 2019)
May 7, 2020 – Name changed to Hapbee Technologies, Inc. (see FPsurvey - Industrials)

Eleven Business Acquisitions Inc. (Can. May 17, 1984)
July 23, 1990 – Name changed to Ivana Capital Corporation. ∎

Elf Oil Exploration and Production Canada Ltd. (Can. 1963)
1976 – Acquired by Aquitaine Company of Canada Ltd. for 930,000 com. shs. of Aquitaine. (see Aquitaine Company of Canada Ltd.)

Elgin Mining Inc. (Ont. July 11, 2008)
Sept. 12, 2014 – Acquired by Mandalay Resources Corporation; basis either (i) Cdn$0.37 or (ii) 0.4111 Mandalay com. shs. for 1 Elgin com. sh.

Elgin Petroleum Corporation Limited (unknown)
1962 – Became a wholly owned subsid. of Rayrock Mines Ltd.

Elgin Producing Syndicate (Ont.)
1945 – Assets sold to Queenston Gas & Oil Co. Ltd.

Elgin Resources Inc. (Alta. Mar. 31, 1994)
Apr. 25, 2005 – Formed Eastern Platinum Limited in British Columbia on amalgamation with Jonpol Explorations Limited with Elgin the deemed acquiror; basis 1 new for 4 Jonpol shs. and 1 new for 1 Elgin sh. (see FPsurvey - Mines & Energy)

Elgo Mines Ltd. (Que. 1959)
May 8, 1982 – Charter cancelled.

Elissa Resources Ltd. (B.C. Oct. 7, 2007)
Feb. 17, 2016 – Name changed to NexOptic Technology Corp. (see FPsurvey - Industrials)

Elite Capital Corporation (Alta. Oct. 25, 2000)
Dec. 6, 2001 – Formed Elite Technical Inc. in Alberta pursuant to Qualifying Transaction reverse takeover acquisition of and amalgamation with Elite Technical Inc.; basis 1 new for 2 old shs. ∎

Elite Imaging Inc. (Ont. Aug. 12, 2015 amalg.)
Mar. 22, 2017 – Name changed to Akumin Inc. ∎

Elite Insurance Management Ltd. (B.C. 1979)
July 1, 1988 – Amalgamated with a subsidiary of Morgan Financial Corporation; basis 0.9 Morgan com. for 1 Elite com. sh. (see Morgan Financial Corporation)

Elite Real Estate Canada Inc. (Can. Jan. 22, 1990)
Mar. 21, 1995 – Name changed to Far Eastern Energy Corporation; basis 1 new for 4 old shs. ∎

Elite Resource Corp. (B.C. 1983)
Oct. 3, 1986 – Name changed to Myriad Concepts, Ltd.; basis 1 new for 2 old shs. (see FPsurvey - Industrials)

Elite Technical Inc. (Alta. Dec. 6, 2001 amalg.)
Nov. 10, 2005 – Declared bankruptcy. RSM Richter Inc. was appointed trustee.

Elizabeth Gold Mining Co., Ltd. (Ont. 1936)
1956 – Charter cancelled.

The Elk Creek Waterworks Company Limited (B.C. 1905)
1980 – New district of Chilliwack acquired all o/s com. shs. for $23 per sh.
Aug. 31, 1981 – All o/s s.f. bonds due 1983, redeemed at paid up value.

Elk Equities Inc. (Alta. June 9, 1997)
Aug. 9, 2002 – Name changed to Qeva Group Inc. ∎

Elk Lake Metals & Holdings Ltd. (Ont. 1958)
Feb. 1980 – Charter cancelled.

Elk Lake Mines Ltd. (Ont. 1958)
Dec. 22, 1970 – Name changed to Elk Lake Metals & Holdings Ltd. ∎

Elk Petroleums Ltd. (Ont. 1951)
1958 – Wound up.

Elk Point Game Ranching Corp. (Can. Sept. 10, 1987)
Nov. 9, 1993 – Name changed to Elk Point Resources Inc. ∎

Elk Point Resources Inc. (Can. Sept. 10, 1987)
Jan. 31, 2003 – All o/s com. shs. acquired by Acclaim Energy Trust; basis $3.70 in cash or 0.95 of an Acclaim trust unit or a comb. thereof plus one-half of a com. sh. of newly created Burmis Energy Inc. for 1 old Elk Point sh.

Elkhorn Gold Mining Corporation (B.C. Mar. 12, 1980)
Oct. 11, 2011 – Name changed to Tulloch Resources Ltd. ∎

Elkins Productions of Canada Ltd. (Ont. 1972)
June 1973 – Amalgamated with 2 other cos. to form Life Investors International Ltd.; basis 1 cl. B for 1 old spec. sh.; 1 new cl. A and 1 new com. for each 2 old com. shs. (see Life Investors International Limited)

Elks Inc. (Can. Aug. 17, 1981)
1991 – Declared bankrupt and Coopers & Lybrand (Toronto) appointed trustees in bankruptcy. Assets liquidated. No distribution to shldrs.
Sept. 3, 1994 – Dissolved.

Elks Stores Limited (Ont. Sept. 30, 1968 amalg.)
Aug. 17, 1981 – Name changed to Elks Inc. and continued into Canada. ∎

Elkwater Resources Ltd. (Alta. Mar. 29, 2000)
Feb. 25, 2015 – Name changed to Striker Exploration Corp.; basis 1 new for 20 old shs. ∎

Ella Resources Inc. (B.C. June 1, 1993 amalg.)
Jan. 25, 2001 – Name changed to Kinetic Energy Inc. following acquisitions of Reefex Corporation and 1272891 Ontario Inc. ■

Ellburn Porcupine Gold Mines Ltd. (Ont. 1944)
June 11, 1956 – Dissolved.

Ellen Gold Mines Ltd. (Ont. 1934)
Dec. 1957 – Charter cancelled.

Ellesmere Minerals Ltd. (Alta. Mar. 16, 1994)
Nov. 8, 2004 – Name changed to Matador Exploration Inc.; basis 1 new for 4 old shs. ■

Ellesmere Oil & Development Ltd. (unknown)
1952 – Acquired by New Concord Development Corp. Ltd.; basis 1 new for 3 old shs. (see New Concord Development Corp. Ltd.)

Ellios Resources Ltd. (B.C. Jan. 30, 1986)
Oct. 11, 1996 – Name changed to Fjordland Minerals Ltd. ■

Elliot Uranium Mines Ltd. (Ont. 1953)
1970 – Dissolved.

Ellis Oil Co., Ltd. (unknown)
1927 – Acquired by Spooner Oils Ltd.; basis 1 new for 3 old shs. (see Spooner Oils Ltd.)

Ellmargo Mining Co. Ltd. (Ont. 1950)
Nov. 1967 – Charter cancelled.

Elm Point Mines Ltd. (Ont. 1966)
1969 – Merged into Great Eagle Explorations and Holdings Ltd.; basis 1 new for 8 old shs.

Elm Tree Minerals Inc. (B.C. Dec. 4, 2006)
Aug. 23, 2013 – Name changed to Ximen Mining Corp. (see FPsurvey - Mines & Energy)

Elmac Malartic Mines Ltd. (Ont. 1945)
Nov. 9, 1976 – Charter cancelled.

Elmira Capital Inc. (B.C. Aug. 22, 2014)
May 12, 2023 – Name changed to Cameo Resources Inc. (see FPsurvey - Mines & Energy)

Elmont Gold Mines Ltd. (Ont. 1946)
1955 – Charter cancelled.

Elmont Industries Ltd. (B.C. 1980)
Sept. 23, 1983 – Merged into Kapok Tree Inns Corporation; basis 4.2 shs. of Elmont for 1 sh. of Kapok. Co. was subsequently wound up.

Elmos Gold Mines Ltd. (Ont. 1936)
1941 – Charter cancelled.

Elmridge Mines Ltd. (Ont. 1953)
1956 – Charter cancelled.

Elmwood Mines Ltd. (Ont. 1952)
1968 – Merged with other cos. to form Milestone Exploration Ltd.; basis 100 new for 1,390 old shs.

Elmwood Resources Limited (Ont. 1928)
July 1985 – Name changed to Easynet Data Corporation. ■

Elnido Mines Ltd. (unknown)
Mar. 1951 – Charter cancelled.

Eloda Corporation (Can. Oct. 3, 2005)
Oct. 19, 2009 – Name changed to 4404980 Canada Inc. following sale of all assets to Société en commandite Eloda. ■

Eloda 2006 Corporation (Can. Oct. 3, 2005)
Jan. 12, 2007 – Name changed to Eloda Corporation. ■

Elora Industries Ltd. (Can. 1928)
Ceased operations, approx. 1952.
June 1954 – Certain property and equipment of co. offered for sale, by the Industrial Development Bank, which had loaned co. $216,800.

Elrock Mining Corp. (Alta. 1953)
June 1956 – Name changed to Three Arrows Mining Explorations Ltd. ■

Elroy Gold Mines Ltd. (Ont. 1944)
Name changed to Belteco Kirkland Gold Mines Ltd.

Elson Energy Enterprises Ltd. (Alta. May 15, 2009)
Sept. 15, 2011 – Formed MATRRIX Energy Technologies Inc. in Alberta on Qualifying Transaction amalgamation with (old) MATRRIX Energy Technologies Inc. (deemed acquiror). ■

Eltron Energy Corporation (B.C. 1967)
Aug. 22, 2003 – Struck from register and dissolved.

Eltron Security Systems Corp. (B.C. 1967)
Nov. 28, 1980 – Name changed to Eltron Energy Corporation. ■

Elvir Gold Mines Ltd. (Ont. 1945)
1956 – Charter cancelled.

Elvue Mines Ltd. (Ont. 1956)
Oct. 19, 1967 – Dissolved.

Elwood Mining Exploration Co. (Que. 1956)
1959 – Merged into Amalgamated Mining Development Corp. Ltd.; basis 1 new for 6.5 old shs.

Ely Gold & Minerals Inc. (B.C. Nov. 2, 2005)
Nov. 22, 2017 – Name changed to Ely Gold Royalties Inc. ■

Ely Gold Royalties Inc. (B.C. Nov. 2, 2005)
Aug. 24, 2021 – Acquired by Gold Royalty Corp.; basis (i) 0.2450 Gold Royalty com. shs, plus $0.0001 cash; or (ii) 0.09916 Gold Royalty com. shs. plus $0.869053 cash for 1 Ely Gold sh.

Embassy Developments Ltd. (Alta. 1946)
Dec. 7, 1977 – Placed into liquidation.
Aug. 25, 1982 – Liquidator's final account filed.
Nov. 30, 1982 – Struck off register.

Embassy Mines Ltd. (Ont. 1956)
1960 – Assets acquired by Bison Petroleum and Minerals Ltd.; basis 1 new for 7 old shs.

Embassy Petroleums Ltd. (Can. 1923)
1974 – Merged into Cavalier Energy Inc.; basis 1 new for 3.54 old shs.

Embassy Resources Ltd. (Ont. 1983 amalg.)
1984 – Acquired by Unicorp Canada Corporation; basis 0.6 of one cl. A pfce. sh. series A for each sh. of Embassy held. (see Unicorp Canada Corporation)

Ember Resources Inc. (Alta. June 3, 2005)
June 17, 2011 – Acquired by an investor group led by Brookfield Special Situations Group, funds that are part of ARC Financial Corp. group and funds that are part of the KERN Partners Ltd. group for 50¢ per sh.

EmberClear Corp. (Alta. Feb. 17, 2004)
July 2016 – Proposal under the Bankruptcy and Insolvency Act was approved by the court under which operations and assets were transferred to Houston-based Ember Partners LP. Creditors to receive cash payment of US$0.10 on every US$1 of proven claim or note payable valued at US$0.70 on every US$1 of proven claim. No funds available for distribution to shldrs.
Nov. 10, 2016 – Dissolved and struck from register.

EmberClear Inc. (Alta. Feb. 17, 2004)
Dec. 29, 2010 – Name changed to EmberClear Corp. ■

Emblem Capital Inc. (Can. Sept. 11, 2003)
Apr. 26, 2007 – Name changed to SQI Diagnostics Inc. followed by Qualifying Transaction amalgamation of

wholly owned 6701914 Canada Inc. with umedik, Inc.; basis 1 new for 6 old shs. (see FPsurvey - Industrials)

Emblem Corp. (Can. Dec. 5, 2016)
Mar. 19, 2019 – Acquired by Aleafia Health Inc., following amalgamation with 11208578 Canada Inc., a wholly owned subsid. of Aleafia; basis 0.8377 Aleafia com. sh. for 1 Emblem sh. (see Aleafia Health Inc.)

Embury Lake Mining Co. Ltd. (Ont. 1945)
Nov. 27, 1961 – Dissolved.

Emco Limited (Ont. May 28, 1906; via letters patent)
Apr. 1, 1990 – Amalgamated in Ontario to continue with same name.
Jan. 1, 1993 – Amalgamated in Ontario to continue with same name.
May 9, 2003 – Acquired by 2022841 Ontario Inc. for $16.60 per sh. and $1,022.79 per $1,000 conv. deb.

Emerald Bay Energy Inc. (Alta. May 9, 1997)
Mar. 17, 2020 – Name changed to Nexera Energy Inc.; basis 1 new for 15 old shs. (see FPsurvey - Mines & Energy)

Emerald Dragon Mines Inc. (B.C. Mar. 24, 1937)
Aug. 29, 2003 – Struck from register and dissolved.

Emerald Gas Synd. (unknown)
1945 – Acquired by Queenston Gas & Oil Co. Ltd.

Emerald Glacier Mines Ltd. (B.C. 1947)
1957 – Acquired by Glacier Mining Ltd.; basis 1 new for 4 old shs. (see Glacier Explorers Ltd.)

Emerald Glacier Mines Ltd. (B.C. 1966)
Dec. 22, 1975 – Charter cancelled.

Emerald Health Therapeutics, Inc. (B.C. July 31, 2007)
Nov. 14, 2022 – Acquired by Skye Bioscience, Inc.; basis 1.95 Skye shs. for 1 Emerald Health sh.

Emerald Isle Resources Inc. (B.C. Nov. 20, 1980)
June 6, 2011 – Struck from registry and dissolved.
Jan. 3, 2013 – Restored to registry. (see FPsurvey - Mines & Energy)

Emerald Lake Mines Ltd. (Ont. 1965)
1969 – Amalgamated into Summit Exploration & Holdings; basis 1 new for 5 old shs.

Emerald Oils Ltd. (B.C.)
1958 – Struck off register.

Emerald Star Mining Explorations Ltd. (B.C. Nov. 7, 1980)
Mar. 28, 1996 – Name changed to ESM Resources Ltd.; basis 1 new for 3.5 old shs. ■

Emerald Ventures Inc. (B.C. May 17, 1984)
Apr. 3, 1992 – Name changed to Spatializer Audio Laboratories, Inc. and continued into Yukon. ■

Emerald Yellowknife Mines Ltd. (Ont. 1944)
1955 – Charter cancelled.

Emercap Ventures Inc. (B.C. Feb. 25, 2000)
Apr. 26, 2002 – Qualifying Transaction Plan of Arrangement with Syntegra Investment Corp. (1 for 4.2953) and Chinacom Technologies Inc. (1 for 2) to continue as VendTek Systems Inc.; basis 1 new VendTek for 2.7173 old Emercap shs. (see VendTek Systems Inc.)

Emercor Building Systems Ltd. (Alta. Nov. 21, 1996)
May 2, 2006 – Dissolved and struck from register.

Emerge Oil & Gas Inc. (Can. Dec. 24, 2003)
Aug. 18, 2008 – Continued into Alberta. (see Twin Butte Energy Ltd.)
Jan. 16, 2012 – Acquired by Twin Butte Energy Ltd.; basis 0.585 Twin Butte shs. for 1 Emerge sh. (see Twin Butte Energy Ltd.)

Emerge Resources Corp. (B.C. Oct. 28, 2009)
Feb. 29, 2016 – Name changed to Vaxil Bio Ltd. following reverse takeover acquisition of (old) Vaxil Bio Ltd.; basis 1 new for 2 old shs. (see FPsurvey - Industrials)

Emergence Resort Canada Inc. (Can. June 21, 2002)
June 3, 2009 – Name changed to ACFAW.COM Inc. pursuant to Qualifying Transaction reverse takeover acquisition of ACFAW.COM Inc. ■

EmerGeo Solutions Worldwide Inc. (B.C. Oct. 16, 1997)
Apr. 2, 2018 – Dissolved and struck from register.

Emerging Africa Gold (EAG) Inc. (Que. 1957)
May 31, 2002 – Amalgamated with wholly owned subsid. of Diagem International Resources Corp.; basis 1 Diagem sh. for 1 Emerging Africa sh. (see Diagem International Resource Corp.)

Emerging Alberta Resource Corp. (Alta. Oct. 24, 1989)
Aug. 1, 1995 – Name changed to Renfield Enterprises Inc. ■

Emerging Growth Technologies Inc. (B.C. 1987)
Apr. 23, 1996 – Name changed to Mandorin Goldfields Inc. ■

Emerging Ventures Corp. (B.C. Sept. 28, 1999)
Aug. 1, 2002 – Formed QGX Ltd. in Ontario on Qualifying Transaction amalgamation with Quincunx Gold Exploration Ltd., constituting a reverse takeover by Quincunx; basis 4 new com. shs., 1 new cl. A sh. sh., 1 new cl. B sh., 1 new cl. C sh. and 1 new cl. D sh. for each 8 Quincunx shs. and 1 new com. sh. for 2.5 Emerging Ventures sh. ■

Emergis Inc. (Can. Dec. 11, 1986)
Jan. 21, 2008 – Acquired by TELUS Corporation for $8.25 per sh.

Emergo Software Corp. (B.C. Jan. 12, 1987)
Apr. 17, 2000 – Name changed to eTVtech.com Communications Inc. ■

Emerick Resources Corp. (B.C. Aug. 19, 1966)
Dec. 17, 2012 – Name changed to Medgold Resources Corp. following reverse takeover acquisition of Medgold Resource Ltd. ■

Emerita Gold Corp. (B.C. Oct. 30, 2009)
Jan. 13, 2014 – Name changed to Emerita Resources Corp. (see FPsurvey - Mines & Energy)

Emerson Exploration Inc. (B.C. Feb. 10, 1988)
Sept. 16, 2005 – Name changed to GBS Gold International Inc. ■

Emgold Mining Corporation (B.C. Aug. 31, 1989 amalg.)
Mar. 2, 2022 – Name changed to Emergent Metals Corp.; basis 1 new for 10 old shs. (see FPsurvey - Mines & Energy)

Eminator Capital Corp. (Ont. Feb. 22, 1996)
Feb. 26, 2001 – Formed Internet Shopping Catalog Inc. in Ontario on amalgamation with Internet Shopping Catalog Inc., constituting a reverse takeover by Internet Shopping; basis 1 new for 1 Internet Shopping sh. and 0.1693218 new for 1 Eminator sh. (see FPsurvey - Industrials)

Eminence Capital I Inc. (Ont. Aug. 2, 2006)
Sept. 13, 2007 – Name changed to SonnenEnergy Corp. (see FPsurvey - Mines & Energy; FPsurvey - Industrials)

Eminence Capital II Inc. (Ont. Aug. 2, 2006)
May 31, 2010 – Name changed to Xmet Inc. pursuant to Qualifying Transaction acquisition of On-Strike Gold Inc. ■

Emir Oils Ltd. (Alta. 1976)
June 8, 1992 – Acquired by Renaissance Energy Ltd.; basis 70¢ per sh. or 0.0538 Renaissance shs. for 1 Emir sh. (see Renaissance Energy Ltd.)

Emjay Petroleums Ltd. (unknown)
1954 – Acquired by Canadian Emjay Petroleums Ltd.; basis 1 new for 3 old shs. (see Canadian Emjay Petroleums Ltd.)

Emo Mines Ltd. (Ont. 1954)
Aug. 25, 1966 – Dissolved.

eMobile Data Corporation (Yuk. Mar. 22, 2001)
Oct. 2, 2002 – Acquired by U.S.-based Itron, Inc. for US$0.268 per sh.

Emory Gold Mines Ltd. (Ont. 1945)
Mar. 30, 1959 – Dissolved.

Emperor Gold Corporation (B.C. Aug. 31, 1989 amalg.)
Aug. 1, 1997 – Name changed to Emgold Mining Corporation. ■

Emperor Minerals Ltd. (B.C. Sept. 26, 1988)
Aug. 24, 2012 – Name changed to Emperor Oil Ltd. (see FPsurvey - Mines & Energy)

Emperor Mines Ltd. (B.C. 1966)
June 1973 – Name changed to Taronga Resources Ltd.; basis 1 new for 5 old shs. ■

Empire Acceptance Corporation Limited (B.C. 1962)
1980 – All assets sold and distribution made to secured creditors in early 1980. No distribution for shldrs.

Empire Asbestos Ltd. (Que. 1952)
May 25, 1974 – Dissolved.

Empire Brass Mfg. Co. Ltd. (Ont. May 28, 1906; via letters patent)
Feb. 1957 – Name changed to Emco Limited. ■

Empire Capital Corp. (B.C. July 28, 2009)
July 26, 2011 – Continued into Canada.
Aug. 2, 2011 – Name changed to Zonte Metals Inc.; basis 2 new for 1 old sh. (see FPsurvey - Mines & Energy)

Empire Crude Oil Co. Ltd. (Alta. July 27, 1937)
Property taken over by Howey Syndicate.

Empire Development Co. Ltd. (B.C. Oct. 14, 1948)
Mar. 22, 1982 – CTO issued. Subsequently dissolved.

Empire Equity Corporation Inc. (Can. May 6, 1987)
July 30, 1996 – Name changed to Alpaka Resources Corp. ■

Empire Explorations Ltd. (unknown)
May 1956 – Acquired by Castle Oil & Gas Ltd.; basis 1 new for 10 old shs. (see Castle Oil & Gas Limited)

Empire Gold Mines Ltd. (Ont. Feb. 6, 1923)
1968 – Merged into Associated Porcupine Mines Ltd.; basis 1 new for 5.15633 old shs.

Empire Gold Resources Ltd. (B.C. Nov. 7, 1984)
Jan. 9, 1989 – Delisted from the Vancouver Stock Exchange. Subsequently struck from register and dissolved.

Empire Industries Ltd. (Alta. Jan. 18, 2005)
Mar. 1, 2021 – Name changed to Dynamic Technologies Group Inc. ■

Empire Information Ltd. (Ont. 1945)
Wound up. Nothing available for shldrs.

Empire Mercury Corporation Ltd. (B.C. July 12, 1965)
Dec. 17, 1970 – Name changed to Empire Metals Corporation Ltd. ■

Empire Metals Corp. (B.C. Feb. 2, 1981)
Aug. 7, 2025 – Name changed to Roland Mineral Enterprises Corp. (see FPsurvey - Mines & Energy)

Empire Metals Corporation Ltd. (B.C. July 12, 1965)
Jan. 23, 1976 – Name changed to Sovereign Metals Corporation Ltd.; basis 1 new for 5 old shs. ■

Empire Minerals Inc. (Que. Jan. 31, 1952)
May 8, 1982 – Charter cancelled.
Dec. 17, 1996 – Restored to registry.
Feb. 1, 2016 – Name changed to Empire Minerals Corporation Inc. (see FPsurvey - Mines & Energy)

Empire Mining Corporation (B.C. Jan. 4, 2005)
Jan. 10, 2013 – Name changed to Columbus Copper Corporation. ■

Empire Oil & Minerals Inc. (Que. Jan. 31, 1952)
Nov. 1965 – Name changed to Empire Minerals Inc.; basis 1 new for 3 old shs. ■

Empire Petroleums Limited (Alta. Mar. 2, 1943)
1953 – Acquired by Texas Calgary Co.; basis 1 new for 5 old shs.

Empire Resource Exploration Ltd. (Ont. 1979)
Oct. 24, 1983 – Name changed to Paramount Ventures Inc. ■

Empire Resources Inc. (B.C. Oct. 5, 1979)
Aug. 15, 1984 – Name changed to Arabesque Resources Ltd.; basis 1 new for 3 old shs. ■

Empire Rock Minerals Inc. (B.C. Feb. 2, 1981)
Feb. 2, 2017 – Name changed to Empire Metals Corp. ■

Empire Technologies Ltd. (B.C. Aug. 19, 1998)
Aug. 8, 2000 – Name changed to Analytical Software, Inc. ■

Empire Valley Gold Mines Ltd. (B.C. 1953)
Aug. 30, 1976 – Dissolved.

Empirical Inc. (Alta. May 29, 2000)
Nov. 2, 2010 – Dissolved and struck from register.

Empress Capital Corp. (B.C. Feb. 4, 1999)
May 19, 2000 – Name changed to Daybreak Resources Corporation and continued into Alberta. ■

Empress Consolidated Gold Mines, Ltd. (Ont. Nov. 18, 1936)
1956 – Charter cancelled.

Empress Gold Mines Ltd. (B.C. 1936)
1951 – Struck off register.

Empress Resources Corp. (B.C. Mar. 20, 1989)
July 8, 2020 – Acquired by Alto Ventures Ltd.; basis 1 Alto Ventures sh. and 0.08 com. shs. of newly incorporated Empress Royalty Corp. for 1 Empress Resource com. sh. (see Alto Ventures Ltd.)

Empyrean Diagnostics Ltd. (B.C. 1986)
Jan. 10, 1997 – Continued into Arizona.
Mar. 19, 1999 – Name changed to Empyrean Bioscience Inc.

Emrex Mining Ltd. (Ont. 1962)
Feb. 17, 1981 – Charter cancelled.

Emtech Ltd. (Bermuda June 14, 1994)
Aug. 2, 1996 – Name changed to Ashurst Technology Ltd.

Emtech Technology Corporation (N.B. Feb. 20, 1992)
Jan. 20, 1993 – Continued into Ontario. (see Emtech Ltd.)
July 29, 1993 – Amalgamated in British Columbia to continue with same name. (see Emtech Ltd.)
July 22, 1994 – All o/s com. shs. exchanged for units of Emtech Ltd.; basis 1 new unit (consisting of 1 com. sh. and 1 depository receipt) for 1 old sh. (see Emtech Ltd.)

En-Ola Explorations Ltd. (Que. 1963)
1974 – Charter cancelled.

En-R-Tech International Inc. (B.C. Aug. 7, 1991)
Nov. 16, 1993 – Name changed to International En-R-Tech Inc.; basis 2 new for 1 old sh. ■

EnQuest Energy Services Corp. (Alta. Apr. 29, 2008 amalg.)
Aug. 27, 2010 – Acquired by TFI Holdings Inc., a wholly owned subsid. of TransForce Inc., for Cdn$0.17 per sh. (see TransForce Inc.)

Enamel & Heating Products, Limited (Can. 1928)
Apr. 11, 1974 – Name changed to Enheat Limited. ■

eNblast productions inc. (Can. Dec. 29, 1982)
June 10, 2004 – Dissolved.

Enbridge Gas Distribution Inc. (Ont. Mar. 23, 1848)
Jan. 1, 2019 – Amalgamated with Union Gas Limited to form Enbridge Gas Inc.

Enbridge Income Fund (Alta. May 22, 2003)
Dec. 17, 2010 – Succeeded by Enbridge Income Fund Holdings Inc. pursuant to plan of arrangement whereby Enbridge Income Fund Holdings Inc. was formed to facilitate the conversion of the fund into a corporation. ■

Enbridge Income Fund Holdings Inc. (Alta. Mar. 26, 2010)
Nov. 12, 2018 – Voluntarily dissolved and all o/s com. shs. not already held acquired by Enbridge Inc.; basis 0.7350 Enbridge com. sh. plus 45¢ cash for 1 Income Fund sh.

Encal Energy Ltd. (Alta. Apr. 30, 1987)
Apr. 23, 2001 – Amalgamated with Calpine Corporation to form Calpine Canada Holdings Ltd.; basis 0.1493 Calpine Canada exch. shs. for 1 Encal sh.

Encana Corporation (Can. June 26, 2001)
Jan. 24, 2020 – Succeeded by Ovintiv Inc. pursuant to a plan of arrangement whereby Ovintiv Inc., a new Delaware incorporated company, acquired all of the common shares of Encana Corporation (renamed Ovintiv Canada ULC), resulting in Ovintiv Inc. becoming the parent company.; basis 1 new for 5 old shs. (see FPsurvey - Mines & Energy)

EnCap Investments Inc. (B.C. Aug. 11, 2008)
Feb. 15, 2012 – Name changed to LCTI Low Carbon Technologies International Inc. ■

Encom Environmental & Communications Systems Ltd. (B.C. Mar. 22, 1972)
Nov. 14, 1994 – Name changed to ST Systems Corp. following acquisition of 403930 Alberta Ltd. and Sable Technologies Inc.; basis 1 new for 5.5 old shs. ■

Encor Energy Corporation Inc. (Alta. Dec. 30, 1958)
Feb. 29, 1988 – Amalgamated with TCPL Energy Ltd., a wholly owned subsid. of TransCanada PipeLines Limited; basis $9.375 per sh. (see TransCanada PipeLines Limited)

Encor Energy Corporation Ltd. (Alta. Dec. 30, 1958)
Jan. 8, 1987 – Name changed to Encor Energy Corporation Inc. ■

Encor Inc. (Alta. Feb. 10, 1984)
May 27, 1993 – Acquired by Talisman Energy Inc.; basis 1 Talisman sh. for 30 Encor shs. and 1 Talisman 8.5% conv. deb. for 1 Encor 8.5% conv. deb. (see Talisman Energy Inc.)

Encore Products Inc. (B.C. 1983)
Nov. 13, 1992 – Dissolved and struck off register.

Encore Renaissance Resources Corp. (B.C. Oct. 2, 1984)
May 1, 2012 – Name changed to WestKam Gold Corp.; basis 1 new for 10 old shs. (see FPsurvey - Mines & Energy)

Encore Tickets Limited (Can. Dec. 11, 1986)
May 6, 2004 – Dissolved.

Encore Ventures Ltd. (B.C. 1980)
June 30, 1993 – Acquired by Prime International Corporation; basis 1 Prime sh. for 2.5 Encore shs.

Encounter Energy Inc. (Alta. May 19, 1998 amalg.)
Oct. 18, 2002 – Amalgamated with Impact Energy Inc.; basis 0.78 new Impact sh. for 1 old Encounter sh. (see Impact Energy Inc.)

Encounter Energy Resources Limited (Alta. 1980)
1984 – Virtually all o/s com. shs. acquired by Oakwood Petroleums Ltd. for total consideration (incl. costs of acquisition) of $8,556,000.

Encue Capital Corp. (Alta. June 15, 1992)
Feb. 17, 1997 – Name changed to Visionwall Incorporated; basis 1 cl. A for 1 com. sh. (see FPsurvey - Industrials)

Endako Mines Ltd. (B.C. 1962)
Feb. 22, 1971 – Amalgamated with Placer Development Ltd.; basis 1 new for 2 old shs.

Endatcom Ventures Corporation (B.C. May 18, 1983)
May 24, 1985 – Name changed to Borkin Industries Corp. ■

Endeavor Mining Corp. Ltd. (Ont. 1945)
Mar. 28, 1956 – Amalgamated into Mining Endeavor Co. Ltd.; basis 1 new for 1 old sh. (see Mining Endeavor Co. Ltd.)

Endeavour Financial Corporation (Cayman Islands July 25, 2002)
Sept. 14, 2010 – Name changed to Endeavour Mining Corporation. ■

Endeavour Gold Corp. (B.C. Mar. 11, 1981)
Sept. 13, 2004 – Name changed to Endeavour Silver Corp. (see FPsurvey - Mines & Energy)

Endeavour Mining Capital Corp. (Cayman Islands July 25, 2002)
July 25, 2008 – Name changed to Endeavour Financial Corporation. ■

Endeavour Mining Corporation (Cayman Islands July 25, 2002)
June 16, 2021 – Succeeded by Endeavour Mining plc pursuant to scheme of arrangement whereby common shares of Endeavour Mining Corporation were exchanged for ordinary shares of U.K. incorporated Endeavour Mining plc resulting in the latter becoming parent company. (see FPsurvey - Mines & Energy)

Endeavour Oil & Gas Ltd. (Alta. Jan. 12, 1995)
Oct. 18, 1995 – Name changed to Cubacan Exploration Inc.; basis 1 new for 1 old sh. ■

Endeavour Resources Inc. (Alta. Feb. 12, 1987)
Feb. 15, 2002 – Acquired by Aspen Group Resources Corporation; basis 0.2375 Aspen shs. plus 0.11875 wts. for 1 Endeavour sh.

Enderby Oils Ltd. (B.C.)
1958 – Struck off register.

Endev Energy Inc. (Alta. Aug. 1, 1996 amalg.)
July 28, 2008 – Acquired by Penn West Energy Trust; basis 0.041 Penn West trust units for 1 Endev Energy com. sh.

Endless Energy Corporation (Alta. Mar. 27, 1997)
Aug. 30, 2004 – Name changed to Marauder Resources East Coast Inc. pursuant to plan of arrangement whereby western Canadian oil and gas properties were sold and East Coast oil and gas properties acquired through acquisition of the remaining 51% interest in 1153845 Nova Scotia Limited from Marauder Resources Corp. ■

Endo International plc (Ireland Oct. 31, 2013)
Mar. 20, 2017 – Voluntarily delisted; will continue to trade on NASDAQ Global Select Market.
Aug. 16, 2022 – Filed for protection under Chapter 11 of the U.S. Bankruptcy Code.
Apr. 23, 2024 – Pursuant to a Plan of Reorganization, substantially all the assets of the company were transferred to various purchasers in the U.S., Canada and Luxembourg. All o/s equity interests were terminated and cancelled without any consideration and the company was dissolved.

Endocan Solutions Inc. (B.C. May 11, 2011)
Mar. 10, 2022 – Name changed to Nirvana Life Sciences Inc. pursuant to the reverse takeover acquisition of (old) Nirvana Life Sciences Inc. (concurrently renamed 1253766 B.C. Ltd.). (see FPsurvey - Industrials)

The Endurance Fund Corporation (Ont. June 21, 2004)
Feb. 20, 2008 – Name changed to Metals Creek Resources Corp. (see FPsurvey - Mines & Energy)

Endurance Gold Corporation (Can. Dec. 16, 2003)
Aug. 16, 2004 – Continued into British Columbia. (see FPsurvey - Mines & Energy)

Endurance Minerals Inc. (B.C. June 13, 1983)
Jan. 19, 1994 – Name changed to Takura Minerals Inc.; basis 1 new for 3 old shs. ■

Enercare Inc. (Can. Sept. 27, 2010)
Oct. 17, 2018 – Acquired by Brookfield Infrastructure Partners L.P. and its institutional partners; basis $29 cash per share.

Enerchem International Inc. (Alta. June 27, 1988)
June 16, 2010 – Acquired by Trinity Capital Partners Ltd. for $2.75 per sh.

EnerDynamic Hybrid Technologies Corp. (Ont. Apr. 28, 2010)
Jan. 12, 2022 – Name changed to Net Zero Renewable Energy Inc. ■

Enerflex Systems Income Fund (Alta. Aug. 22, 2006)
Feb. 26, 2010 – Acquired by Toromont Industries Ltd. and dissolved; basis either $14.25 per trust unit or 0.5382 Toromont shs. plus 5¢ per trust unit.

Enerflex Systems Ltd. (Alta. Apr. 21, 1980)
Apr. 17, 1986 – Continued into Canada.
Oct. 5, 2006 – Converted into an income trust named Enerflex Systems Income Fund; basis either 2 trust units, 2 Enerflex Holdings L.P. exch. units or 1 trust unit plus 1 L.P. exch. unit for 1 com. sh.

Enerfund (1987) Oil & Gas Limited Partnership (Alta. 1987)
Feb. 17, 1989 – Limited partners received at their option mutual fund shares of Enerplus Energy Funds Ltd. or their prorata share of the partnership assets.

Energas Resources Inc. (B.C. Nov. 23, 1987)
Apr. 2003 – Continued into Delaware.

Energem Resources Inc. (Yuk. Aug. 11, 1995)
July 21, 2005 – Continued into British Columbia.
Aug. 20, 2012 – Dissolved and struck from register.

Energentia Resources Inc. (B.C. Apr. 28, 2005)
May 7, 2008 – Acquired by Mega Uranium Ltd.; basis 1 Mega sh. for 10 Energentia shs.

Energizer Resources Inc. (Nev. Mar. 1, 2004)
May 14, 2008 – Continued into Minnesota.
Apr. 24, 2017 – Name changed to NextSource Materials Inc. ■

Energold Mining Ltd. (B.C. Apr. 3, 1973)
Sept. 30, 2005 – Name changed to Energold Drilling Corp. (see FPsurvey - Mines & Energy; FPsurvey - Industrials)

EnerGulf Resources Inc. (B.C. Jan. 30, 1981)
June 27, 2003 – Continued into Yukon.
Sept. 13, 2010 – Continued into British Columbia.
Jan. 8, 2024 – Dissolved.

Energy & Precious Metals Inc. (Ont. 1979)
Feb. 6, 1986 – Name changed to Colortech Corporation. ■

Energy & Resources (Cam) Limited (Que. Jan. 25, 1938)
Oct. 7, 1986 – Name changed to ERG Resources Inc. ■

Energy Credit Opportunities Income Fund (Ont. Apr. 29, 2015)
Feb. 14, 2018 – Converted to an open-end fund.

Energy Exploration Technologies Inc. (Nev. Sept. 27, 1994)
Oct. 24, 2003 – Continued into Alberta.
Sept. 22, 2008 – Name changed to NXT Energy Solutions Inc. (see FPsurvey - Mines & Energy; FPsurvey - Industrials)

Energy International Overseas Corp. (N.Y. 1974)
Mar. 26, 1996 – Name changed to Nova Continental Development Corp.

Energy Leaders Income Fund (Ont.)
Nov. 30, 2017 – Terminated. Distribution of $6.2537 per unit paid on or about Dec. 6, 2017.

Energy Leaders Plus Income Fund (Ont. Sept. 24, 2014)
Oct. 24, 2016 – Converted to an exchange traded fund.

Energy Metals Corporation (B.C. July 9, 1987)
Aug. 14, 2007 – Acquired by Uranium One Inc.; basis 1.15 Uranium One com. shs. for 1 Energy Metals com. sh.

Energy North Inc. (Alta. Feb. 3, 1994)
Aug. 5, 2004 – Plan of Arrangement exchange with Argo Energy Ltd. to continue as Argo Energy Ltd.; basis 0.3084 new Argo sh. for 1 old Energy North sh.

Energy Plus Income Trust (Alta. Sept. 23, 2004)
Oct. 7, 2010 – Merged into Energy Income Fund (ENI) (previously named Sustainable Production Energy Trust) ; basis 1 ENI trust unit for 1.2818 Energy Plus trust units.

Energy Power Systems Limited (Ont. Oct. 5, 1988)
Feb. 12, 2003 – Name changed to EnerNorth Industries Inc.; basis 1 new for 3 old shs. ■

Energy Savings Income Fund (Ont. Feb. 14, 2001)
June 1, 2009 – Name changed to Just Energy Income Fund. ■

Energy Split Corp. II Inc. (Que. Sept. 29, 2004)
Dec. 17, 2010 – Redeemed at $9.86 per capital yield sh. and $13.74 per ROC preferred sh.

Energy Split Corp. Inc. (Que. July 24, 2003)
Sept. 19, 2011 – Redeemed for $15.19 per capital yield sh. and $21 per cl. B pref. sh.

EnerMark Income Fund (Alta. July 7, 1986)
June 28, 2001 – Name changed to Enerplus Resources Fund pursuant to reverse takeover acquisition of Enerplus Resources Fund; basis 0.173 Enerplus unit for 1 EnerMark unit. ■

Enermet Resources Limited (Ont. 1961)
Feb. 24, 1986 – Charter cancelled.

EnerNorth Industries Inc. (Ont. Oct. 5, 1988)
Mar. 26, 2007 – Filed for bankruptcy. RSM Richter Inc. appointed trustee.
Mar. 26, 2008 – Majority of assets were sold and secured creditors were paid in full.
Feb. 10, 2011 – Trustee was discharged. Unsecured creditors suffered a shortfall and there were no funds available for shldrs.

Enerplus Corporation (Alta. Aug. 12, 2010)
June 4, 2024 – Acquired by Chord Energy Corporation; basis 0.10125 Chord shs. plus US$1.84 cash for 1 Enerplus sh.

Enerplus Resources Corporation (Alta. Aug. 16, 1985)
Nov. 1, 1994 – All o/s ser. G petroleum royalty units exchanged for ser. G trust units of Enerplus Resources Fund; basis 1 new trust unit for 1 old royalty unit.

Enerplus Resources Fund (Alta. July 7, 1986)
June 28, 2001 – Acquired by EnerMark Income Fund (subsequently renamed Enerplus Resources Fund); basis 1 EnerMark (renamed Enerplus) trust unit for 1 Enerplus trust unit. (see Enerplus Resources Fund)

Enerplus Resources Fund (Alta. July 7, 1986)
Jan. 1, 2011 – Succeeded by Enerplus Corporation pursuant to plan of arrangement whereby Enerplus Corporation was formed to facilitate the conversion of the fund into a corporation and the fund was subsequently dissolved. ■

Enershare Technology Corporation (Ont. May 17, 1985)
June 21, 2004 – Declared bankruptcy. Zeifman Partners Inc. was appointed trustee.

EnerSpar Corp. (Alta. June 27, 2011)
June 15, 2022 – Name changed to NurExone Biologic Inc. following reverse takeover acquisition of private Israel-based NurExone Biologic Ltd.; basis 1 new for 10 old shs. ■

Enerstar Resources Inc. (Alta. June 15, 1995)
Aug. 1, 1996 – Formed Net Shepherd Inc. in Alberta on reverse takeover acquisition of and amalgamation with Net Shepherd Inc. ■

Enerteck Energy Technologies Corporation (B.C. 1984)
May 13, 1994 – Dissolved and struck off register.

Enertex Developments Inc. (Ont. 1975)
Mar. 2, 1992 – Amalgamated with Concentrated Rare Earth Minerals Ltd., Goldmac Explorations Inc. (1 for 17.5), Norlode Resources Inc., Offset Natural Resources Ltd. (1 for 11), Preston Resources Ltd., Saranac Resources Ltd. and Uranex Resources Limited (1 for 13.5) to form a new co. named Marvas Developments Ltd.; basis 1 new for 12.6 old shs. (see Marvas Developments Ltd.)

EnerVest Diversified Income Trust (Alta. Aug. 5, 1997)
Nov. 6, 2013 – Name changed to Canoe EIT Income Fund. (see FPsurvey - Mines & Energy; FPsurvey - Industrials)

EnerVest Energy and Oil Sands Total Return Trust (Alta. Feb. 22, 2006)
Nov. 20, 2013 – Merged into Canoe Energy Income Fund, an open-ended fund; basis 0.76 Canoe Energy ser. A sh. for 1 EnerVest trust unit.

EnerVest FTS Limited Partnership 2001 (Alta. Jan. 31, 2001)
Dec. 4, 2003 – Dissolved following sale of all assets to EnerVest Natural Resources Fund Ltd., in exchange for mutual fund shares of EnerVest Natural.

EnerVision Incorporated (N.S. Aug. 12, 1998)
Sept. 29, 2004 – Name changed to The Helical Corporation Inc. ■

Enerwaste Minerals Corp. (B.C. Nov. 6, 1978)
Feb. 11, 1994 – Name changed to Universal Gun-Loc Industries Ltd. ■

Enex Mines Ltd. (N.P.L.) (B.C. Apr. 24, 1967)
Nov. 22, 1972 – Name changed to Enex Resources Limited. ■

Enex Resources Limited (B.C. Apr. 24, 1967)
Oct. 26, 1983 – Name changed to Enexco International Limited. ■

Enexco International Limited (B.C. Apr. 24, 1967)
Oct. 31, 1991 – Name changed to International Enexco Limited; basis 1 new for 5 old shs. ■

The Enfield Corporation Limited (Ont. Apr. 6, 1984)
July 9, 1990 – Name changed to Consolidated Enfield Corporation; basis 1 new for 5 old shs. ■

Enfield Resources Inc. (B.C. Mar. 21, 1978)
Sept. 27, 1989 – Name changed to Pacific Summa Capital Corp.; basis 1 new for 5 old shs. ■

Enforcer Gold Corp. (B.C. Aug. 18, 2010)
Oct. 29, 2019 – Name changed to Pasofino Gold Limited. (see FPsurvey - Mines & Energy)

Engagement Labs Inc. (Can. Nov. 26, 2007)
Mar. 4, 2022 – Acquired by DGTL Holdings Inc.; basis 0.1136 DGTL shs. for 1 Engagement Labs sh.

enGene Holdings Inc. (Can. Apr. 24, 2023)
Oct. 31, 2023 – Continued into British Columbia. (see FPsurvey - Industrials)

Engenuity Technologies Inc. (Can. Nov. 19, 1980)
June 4, 2007 – Amalgamated with 4341392 Canada Inc., a subsidiary of CAE Inc.; basis 1 new redeemable pfd. sh. for 1 old eNGENUITY com. sh. Preferreds were redeemed for $1.20 per sh.

Engine Gaming and Media, Inc. (B.C. Dec. 18, 2020)
Apr. 11, 2023 – Name changed to GameSquare Holdings, Inc. pursuant to the reverse takeover acquisition of Gamesquare Esports Inc.; basis 1 new for 4 old shs. ■

Engine Media Holdings, Inc. (Ont. Apr. 8, 2011)
Dec. 18, 2020 – Continued into British Columbia.
Oct. 19, 2021 – Name changed to Engine Gaming and Media, Inc. ■

Engineering Power Systems Group Inc. (Ont. Oct. 5, 1988)
Jan. 29, 1999 – Name changed to Engineering Power Systems Limited; basis 1 new for 4 old shs. ■

Engineering Power Systems Limited (Ont. Oct. 5, 1988)
Feb. 28, 2001 – Name changed to Energy Power Systems Limited; basis 1 new for 4 old shs. ■

Engineering.com Incorporated (Ont. Sept. 18, 2000 amalg.)
Jan. 2, 2014 – Privatized at 3¢ per sh. (prior to 1-for-350,000 sh. consolidation).

Englefield Resources Ltd. (B.C. Jan. 30, 1987)
Apr. 22, 1992 – Name changed to Valu Concepts International Corp. ■

EnGlobe Corp. (Can. Sept. 28, 2004)
Jan. 18, 2011 – Privatized at $0.265 per sh.

Enhanced Energy Services Ltd. (Alta. Mar. 19, 1996)
Mar. 12, 2001 – Name changed to EnSource Energy Services Inc.; basis 1 new for 4 old shs. ■

Enhanced Oil Resources Inc. (B.C. Feb. 22, 1980)
Aug. 16, 2016 – Name changed to Hunter Oil Corp. ■

Enheat Inc. (Can. 1928)
Aug. 31, 1988 – Acquired by Amherst Aerospace Inc.

Enheat Limited (Can. 1928)
June 9, 1980 – Name changed to Enheat Inc. ■

Ennisteel Corp. (Ont. Jan. 1, 1980)
Sept. 29, 1994 – Acquired by Acier Leroux Inc. for $1.16 per sh. (see Acier Leroux inc.)

Enrich Gold Mines Ltd. (Ont. 1944)
Mar. 6, 1950 – Assets acquired by Enrich Mines (1945) Ltd.; basis 25 new for 1 old sh. Charter surrendered.

Enrich Mines (1945) Ltd. (Ont. 1945)
Apr. 9, 1975 – Charter cancelled.

Enrich Ventures Ltd. (B.C. Jan. 9, 1979)
Oct. 10, 2005 – Dissolved and struck from register.

ens Bio Logicals inc. (Can. Dec. 28, 1978)
June 3, 1987 – Name changed to Enscor Inc. ■

Ensbrook Asbestos Corp. Ltd. (B.C. 1966)
Nov. 1968 – Name changed to Ensbrook Mines Ltd. ■

Ensbrook Mines Ltd. (B.C. 1966)
Jan. 31, 1977 – Dissolved.

Enscor Inc. (Can. Dec. 28, 1978)
June 2, 1998 – Name changed to The Rose Corporation. ■

Enseco Energy Services Corp. (Alta. Oct. 23, 2006 amalg.)
Oct. 14, 2015 – Placed into receivership and PricewaterhouseCoopers Inc. was appointed receiver. All officers and directors resigned.
Dec. 21, 2015 – Assigned into bankruptcy and PricewaterhouseCoopers named as trustee.
2016 – Court approval was received for the sale of fixed assets and equipment, of which two offers were closed by January 27. In March, the court approved the sale of the remaining assets. In August, following the distrib. of funds to the secured creditor, PricewaterhouseCooper was discharged as receiver and trustee in bankruptcy. No funds were available for unsecured creditors or shldrs.

Ensel Corporation (Alta. July 31, 1987 amalg.)
May 3, 2005 – Name changed to Surge Resources Inc. ■

Enserco Energy Service Company Inc. (Can. Nov. 17, 1988)
Apr. 30, 2002 – Acquired by Nabors Industries, Inc.; basis Cdn$15.6529 or 0.2377 Nabors exch. shs. for 1 Enserco com. sh. (see Nabors Exchangeco (Canada) Inc.)

EnServ Corporation (Alta. Mar. 6, 1986)
June 7, 1996 – Acquired by Precision Drilling Corporation; basis $17.50 or $2.03 plus 0.56357 Precision shs. for 1 EnServ sh. (see Precision Drilling Corporation)

Ensign Oils Limited (Alta. 1965)
1971 – Merged with Houston Oils Ltd.; basis 1 new for 1 old sh.

Ensign Resource Service Group Inc. (Alta. Mar. 31, 1987)
May 19, 2005 – Name changed to Ensign Energy Services Inc. (see FPsurvey - Mines & Energy; FPsurvey - Industrials)

EnSource Energy Services Inc. (Alta. Mar. 19, 1996)
July 23, 2002 – Acquired by Enerflex Systems Ltd.; basis 0.26 new Enerflex com. sh. for 1 old EnSource com. sh. (see Enerflex Systems Ltd.)

Enssolutions Group Inc. (Can. Feb. 8, 2007)
Mar. 17, 2023 – Dissolved.

Enstar Development Corporation (B.C. 1981)
Oct. 30, 1985 – Name changed to Mitek Industrial Corporation following reverse takeover by the Mitek Group. ■

Entec Systems Inc. (Alta. Oct. 5, 1987)
Apr. 2, 2002 – Struck from registry and dissolved.

Entech Investments Inc. (Alta. Nov. 12, 2001)
Jan. 1, 2005 – Formed CAPVEST Income Corp. in Alberta on amalgamation with Biotech Medical Sciences Inc. with Entech the deemed acquiror; basis 0.88 new for 1 Biotech sh. and 1 new for 1 Entech sh. ■

EnterCor Entertainment Corp. (Alta. Mar. 11, 1997)
Nov. 1, 2004 – Name changed to Entercor Resource Corp.; basis 1 new for 5 old shs. ■

Entercor Resource Corp. (Alta. Mar. 11, 1997)
Dec. 30, 2006 – Name changed to Ranger Ridge Resources Ltd. and continued into British Columbia. ■

Enterprise Capital Corporation (Alta. Mar. 7, 2008)
July 12, 2012 – Name changed to Ecuador Gold and Copper Corp. pursuant to Qualifying Transaction reverse takeover acquistion of Ecuador Capital Corp. and subsequent amalgamation of Ecuador Capital with a wholly owned subsid.; basis 1 new for 1.25 old shs. ■

Enterprise Development Corporation (B.C. 1972)
Mar. 14, 1984 – Name changed to Magenta Development Corporation; basis 1 new for 5 old shs. ■

Enterprise Energy Resources Ltd. (B.C. Dec. 12, 2007)
Aug. 21, 2013 – Acquired by LNG Energy Ltd. (basis 5 LNG shs. for 1 Enterprise sh.) and amalgamated with a wholly owned subsidiary of LNG Energy to form LNG Exploration Ltd. (see LNG Energy Ltd.)

Enterprise Mining Co. Ltd. (Que. 1955)
Oct. 12, 1974 – Dissolved.

Enterprise Oil Limited (Alta. Mar. 23, 2004)
May 30, 2007 – Name changed to Enterprise Oilfield Group, Inc. ■

Enterprise Oilfield Group, Inc. (Alta. Mar. 23, 2004)
July 30, 2012 – Name changed to Enterprise Group, Inc. (see FPsurvey - Mines & Energy; FPsurvey - Industrials)

Enterprise Resources Inc. (B.C. Dec. 7, 1983)
May 6, 1993 – Name changed to ERI Ventures Inc.; basis 1 new for 3 old shs. ■

Enterra Communications Inc. (Alta. Aug. 10, 1994)
Feb. 2, 2008 – Dissolved and struck from registry.

Enterra Energy Corp. (Alta. June 30, 1998)
Nov. 28, 2003 – Converted into an income trust named Enterra Energy Trust; basis 2 trust units, 2 exchangeable shs. or a combination thereof for 1 Enterra com. sh.
June 1, 2010 – Name changed to Equal Energy Holdings Ltd.

Enterra Energy Trust (Alta. Oct. 24, 2003)
June 1, 2010 – Succeeded by Equal Energy Ltd. pursuant to plan of arrangement whereby Equal Energy Ltd. was formed to facilitate the conversion of the trust into a corporation and Enterra subsequently dissolved. ■

Entertainment One Income Fund (Ont. Sept. 15, 2003)
Mar. 30, 2007 – Acquired by Entertainment One Ltd. (formerly Earl Street Capital Ltd.); basis Cdn$3.60 per unit.

Entertainment Parks International Corp. (Ont. Dec. 6, 1991)
May 4, 1994 – Name changed to Playdium Entertainment Corporation. ■

Entertainment Royalties Inc. (Alta. June 13, 2000)
Jan. 2, 2014 – Struck from registry and dissolved.

Entheos Capital Corporation (B.C. Aug. 11, 2000)
Name changed to The BC Bud Corporation pursuant to the reverse takeover acquisition of The BC Bud Corporation (renamed BC Bud Holdings Corp.). ■

Enthusiast Gaming Holdings Inc. (Ont. Feb. 27, 2017)
Sept. 5, 2019 – Acquired by J55 Capital Corp., basis 4.22 J55 common shares for each Enthusiast share held.
Sept. 6, 2019 – Name changed to Enthusiast Gaming Properties Inc.

Entourage Health Corp. (Ont. July 16, 2014)
Apr. 9, 2025 – Acquired by 1001095275 Ontario Inc,; basis $0.005 cash per sh.

Entourage Metals Ltd. (B.C. Apr. 26, 2010)
Mar. 2, 2016 – Name changed to Genesis Metals Corp.; basis 1 new for 1.5 old shs. ■

Entrec Transportation Services Ltd. (Alta. Oct. 23, 2009)
June 1, 2012 – Name changed to ENTREC Corporation. ■

Entrée Gold Inc. (B.C. July 19, 1995)
Jan. 22, 2003 – Continued into Yukon.
May 27, 2005 – Continued into British Columbia.
May 12, 2017 – Name changed to Entrée Resources Ltd. (see FPsurvey - Mines & Energy)

Entrée Resources Inc. (B.C. July 19, 1995)
Oct. 10, 2002 – Name changed to Entrée Gold Inc.; basis 1 new for 2 old shs. ■

Entreplex Technology Corporation (Alta. Aug. 13, 1999)
Oct. 6, 2000 – Name changed to Ivrnet Inc. ■

Envipco Automated Recycling Inc. (B.C. July 25, 1984)
Aug. 20, 1999 – Name changed to Automated Recycling Inc. ■

Envipco Canada Western Inc. (B.C. 1969)
Mar. 1, 1989 – Delisted from the Vancouver Stock Exchange. Subsequently dissolved and struck from register.

Enviro Energy Capital Corp. (B.C. Mar. 14, 2007)
Apr. 14, 2009 – Name changed to Silver Sun Resource Corp. ■

Enviro FX Inc. (Alta. Feb. 24, 1997 amalg.)
Jan. 26, 1999 – Name changed to Niaski Environmental Inc.; basis 1 new for 3 old shs. ■

Enviro Waste Technologies Inc. (Ont. June 10, 1953)
Mar. 11, 2002 – Amalgamated with First Canadian Gold Corporation Inc. (1 for 1) to continue as Compressario Corporation; basis 1 new Compressario for 5.45 old Enviro Waste shs. (see Compressario Corporation)

Envirodyne Industries Inc. (Alta. July 26, 1988)
Aug. 7, 1992 – Name changed to Telesis Industrial Group Inc.; basis 1 new for 6 old shs. ■

Envirodyne International Inc. (Alta. July 26, 1988)
Mar. 7, 1991 – Name changed to Envirodyne Industries Inc.; basis 1 new for 3 old shs. ■

EnviroLeach Technologies Inc. (Alta. Oct. 21, 2016)
Aug. 5, 2021 – Name changed to EnviroMetal Technologies Inc. (see FPsurvey - Mines & Energy)

Environmental Applied Research Technology House - EARTH (Canada) Corporation (Can. Mar. 25, 1993)
Nov. 4, 2005 – Name changed to TORR Canada Inc.; basis 1 new for 5 old shs. ■

Environmental Containment Systems Limited (Alta. Jan. 22, 1987)
Dec. 31, 1993 – Formed ATC Environmental Group Inc. in Alberta on amalgamation with Applied Technology Corporation Inc.; basis 1 new for 2 Applied Technology shs. and 1 new for 7 Environmental Containment shs. ■

Environmental Management Solutions Inc. (Alta. Aug. 31, 2000)
Sept. 28, 2004 – Continued into Canada.
Apr. 25, 2007 – Name changed to EnGlobe Corp. ■

Environmental Reclamation Inc. (Ont. Sept. 30, 1994 amalg.)
Mar. 20, 2006 – Struck from the register and dissolved.

Environmental Technologies Inc. (Alta. Sept. 28, 1987)
Oct. 2, 2002 – Struck from registry and dissolved.

Environmental Technologies International Inc. (Ont. Nov. 29, 1991 amalg.)
Apr. 24, 1998 – Name changed to Eco Technologies International Inc. pursuant to reverse takeover acquisition of Eco Environmental, Inc.; basis 1 new for 150 old shs. (see FPsurvey - Industrials)

Environmental Technologies Investments Inc. (Ont. Oct. 16, 1975)
Nov. 29, 1991 – Amalgamated with Camreco Inc. to form a new co. Environmental Technologies International Inc. (see Environmental Technologies International Inc.)

Environmental Waste International Inc. (Ont. Oct. 31, 1987)
Jan. 8, 2025 – All o/s shs. not already held acquired by Hydrotrux Group Ltd.; basis $0.0035 cash per sh.

Enviropave International Ltd. (Alta. May 29, 1996)
Jan. 1, 2011 – Name changed to Rockex Mining Corporation pursuant to reverse takeover acquisition of Rockex Limited and subsequent amalgamation of Rockex with wholly owned subsid. 1837427 Ontario Inc.; basis 1 new for 6 old shs. ■

Enviropro International Inc. (Ont. Oct. 12, 1990)
May 7, 2009 – Certificate of incorporation cancelled and dissolved.

Envirotek Remediation Inc. (B.C. Oct. 21, 1980)
Aug. 17, 2021 – Name changed to Homerun Resources Inc. (see FPsurvey - Mines & Energy)

Envirothermic Technologies Limited (Ont. Oct. 1, 1993 amalg.)
Sept. 30, 1994 – Amalgamated with Orizon Systems Inc. to form new co. with same name Envirothermic Technologies Limited.
June 22, 1998 – Name changed to Environmental Reclamation Inc. following reverse takeover acquisition of Environmental Reclamation, Inc. of Idaho; basis 1 new for 35 old shs. ■

Envirotrain Capital Corp. (Can. May 30, 2000)
June 30, 2001 – Formed Railpower Technologies Corp. in Canada on amalgamation with Railpower Technologies Inc., constituting a reverse takeover by Railpower. ■

Envirotreat Systems Inc. (B.C. Nov. 17, 1982)
Sept. 2, 1999 – Name changed to Treat Systems Inc.; basis 1 new for 25 old shs. ■

Envirowaste Industries Inc. (B.C. Sept. 1, 1983)
Mar. 24, 1992 – Name changed to Consolidated Envirowaste Industries Inc.; basis 1 new for 3 old shs. ■

Envision Credit Union (Can. - unspecified)
Jan. 1, 2010 – Merged with Valley First Credit Union to form First West Credit Union.

Envoy Capital Group Inc. (Ont. Dec. 5, 1997)
Dec. 19, 2011 – Formed Merus Labs International Inc. in British Columbia pursuant to amalgamation with (old) Merus Labs International Inc. with Envoy Capital the deemed acquiror. ■

Envoy Communications Group Inc. (B.C. Dec. 28, 1973)
Dec. 5, 1997 – Continued into Ontario.
Apr. 5, 2007 – Name changed to Envoy Capital Group Inc. ■

Envoy Resources Ltd. (B.C. 1972)
Apr. 23, 1979 – Name changed to ERL Resources Ltd.; basis 1 new for 3 old shs. ■

Enwest Ventures Corp. (B.C. June 26, 1979)
Feb. 25, 2003 – Name changed to Bayswater Ventures Corp.; basis 1 new for 3 old shs. ■

eOptimize Advanced Systems Inc. (B.C. Feb. 4, 1999)
Sept. 7, 2009 – Dissolved and struck from register.

ePals Corporation (Ont. July 26, 2011)
July 10, 2014 – Name changed to Cricket Media Group Ltd.; basis 1 new for 25 old shs. ■

Epic Beverages Ltd. (Alta. Feb. 16, 1993)
Aug. 1, 1999 – Struck from registry and dissolved.

Epic Data Inc. (B.C. Sept. 19, 1985)
July 6, 1992 – Name changed to Epic Data International Inc. ■

Epic Data International Inc. (B.C. Sept. 19, 1985)
July 3, 2013 – Acquired by Sylogist Ltd. for $5,000,000 cash, as well as $0.0001 cash per share. All of Epic Data's China-based operations and the $5,000,000 proceeds were transferred to newly formed Epic Fusion Corp.; basis 1 Epic Fusion sh. for 1 Epic Data sh.

Epic Energy Inc. (B.C. July 8, 1992)
Apr. 15, 1996 – Continued into Alberta.
Jan. 2, 2009 – Struck from registry and dissolved.

Epic Mines Ltd. (Ont. 1948)
Aug. 29, 1960 – Charter cancelled.

Epic Oil and Gas Ltd. (B.C. June 17, 1998 amalg.)
Apr. 11, 2003 – Name changed to Blue Parrot Energy Inc. pursuant to reverse takeover acquisition of Blue Parrot Resources Inc.; basis 1 new for 5 old shs. ■

Epic Resources (B.C.) Ltd. (B.C. Jan. 9, 1981)
June 17, 1998 – Amalgamated with Safari International Resources Ltd. to form Epic Oil and Gas Ltd.; basis 0.9 new for 1 Safari sh. and 1 new for 1 Epic Resources sh. (see Epic Oil and Gas Ltd.)

Epicore BioNetworks Inc. (Alta. Jan. 9, 1987)
Dec. 19, 2017 – Acquired by Neovia S.A.S.; basis Cdn$1.30 cash per sh.

Epicore Networks, Inc. (Alta. Jan. 9, 1987)
Aug. 28, 2000 – Name changed to Epicore BioNetworks Inc.; basis 1 new for 4 old shs. ■

Epicure Food Products, Inc. (B.C. Apr. 21, 1987)
Mar. 4, 1992 – Delisted from the Vancouver Stock Exchange. Subsequently dissolved.

Epitek International Inc. (Can. Dec. 9, 1981 amalg.)
Aug. 3, 1987 – Name changed to International Epitek Inc.; basis 1 new for 20 old shs. ■

Epix Technologies Limited (B.C. July 19, 1995)
Nov. 8, 1995 – Continued into Yukon.
Mar. 20, 2000 – Name changed to Consolidated Epix Technologies Limited; basis 1 new for 10 old shs. ■

Eplett Dairies Company Limited (Ont. June 17, 1949)
May 10, 1989 – All o/s com. and pref. shs. acquired by Beatrice Foods Inc., a subsid. of Onex Corporation; basis $1.30 for each com. sh. and $10 for each pref. sh.

Epoch Capital Corporation (B.C. 1977)
Oct. 28, 1996 – Amalgamated with Quest Capital Corporation to form new co. with same name Quest Capital Corporation; basis 0.85 new for 1 Quest Capital sh. (see Quest Capital Corporation)

ePower Metals Inc. (B.C. May 14, 1981)
Sept. 4, 2019 – Name changed to Prime Mining Corp.; basis 1 new for 2 old shs. (see FPsurvey - Mines & Energy)

Epping Realty Corporation (B.C. 1981)
July 16, 1993 – Dissolved and struck off register.

Epping Resources Ltd. (Ont. 1943)
Dec. 1, 1986 – Name changed to Tri-D Automotive Limited. ■

Eptheca Solutions Inc. (Can. Feb. 12, 2002)
Jan. 19, 2007 – Name changed to Intercable ICH Inc. (see FPsurvey - Industrials)

Equal Energy Ltd. (Alta. Apr. 8, 2010)
Aug. 1, 2014 – Acquired by Petroflow Energy Corporation; basis US$5.43 cash plus cash div. of US$0.05 per sh.

Equal Weight Plus Fund (Alta. Dec. 22, 2005)
Dec. 3, 2009 – Merged (together with Citadel HYTES Fund, Citadel Premium Income Fund, Citadel S-1 Income Trust Fund and Citadel Stable S-1 Income Fund) into Citadel Income Fund (formerly Crown Hill Fund); basis 1 Citadel Income unit for 1.7545 Citadel HYTES units, 1 Citadel Income unit for 1.1581 Citadel Premium units, 1 Citadel Income unit for 1.8629 Citadel S-1 units, 1 Citadel Income unit for 1.0765 Citadel Stable S-1 units and 1 Citadel Income unit for 0.8028 Equal Weight Plus units.

Equashare Management Corp. (Ont. July 3, 1986)
Feb. 29, 1996 – Name changed to Forest Hill Capital Corporation; basis 1 new for 40 old shs. (see FPsurvey - Industrials)

Equatorial Energy Inc. (Alta. June 10, 1997)
Nov. 20, 2002 – Name changed to Resolute Energy Inc. following reverse takeover acquisition of Resolute Energy Corporation. ■

Equatorial Resources Limited (B.C. Feb. 15, 1965)
Jan. 12, 1976 – Name changed to Intergold Resources Inc.; basis 1 new for 3 old shs. ■

eQube Gaming Limited (Hong Kong Aug. 4, 2011)
Aug. 23, 2021 – Voluntarily delisted and intents to dissolve.

Equess Communications Inc. (Alta. Feb. 6, 1997 amalg.)
June 2, 2003 – Dissolved and struck from register.

Equican Capital Corporation (B.C. 1987)
Aug. 23, 1995 – Name changed to Genterra Capital Corporation; basis 1 new cl. A sub. vtg. for 1 old cl. A sub. vtg. sh. and 1 new cl. B multiple vtg. for 1 old cl. B multiple vtg. sh. ■

Equican Industries Incorporated (Ont. 1972)
Jan. 16, 1978 – Name changed to Equican Ventures Ltd.; basis 1 new for 10 old shs. ■

Equican Ventures Corp. (B.C. 1987)
Jan. 27, 1988 – Name changed to Equican Capital Corporation; basis 1 new for 3 old shs. ■

Equican Ventures Inc. (Ont. 1972)
Dec. 4, 1987 – Amalgamated with Global International Energy Inc. (1 new for 1 old sh.), Southern Eagle Enterprises Inc. (23 new for 38 old shs.), Glenrealco Inc. (1,828,519 new for 200 old shs.) and Four Fifty Dobbie Inc. to form a new co. called Equican Ventures Corp.; basis 25 new for 8 old shs.

Equican Ventures Ltd. (Ont. 1972)
Jan. 16, 1979 – Name changed to Equican Ventures Inc. ■

Equicap Financial Corp. (B.C. Nov. 25, 1983)
Feb. 10, 2005 – Name changed to Zecotek Medical Systems Inc. ■

Equicorp Industries Limited (Ont. 1972)
1976 – Name changed to Equicorp Industries Incorporated.

Equifax Canada Inc. (Can. Dec. 31, 1989)
Dec. 17, 2012 – Name changed to Equifax Canada Co. and continued into Nova Scotia.

Equine Resources Ltd. (B.C. 1983)
Jan. 1, 1987 – Formed Western Canadian Mining Corporation in British Columbia on amalgamation with Western Canadian Mining Ltd.; basis 3 new for 10 old shs. ■

Equinox Copper Corp. (B.C. Sept. 12, 1986)
Sept. 23, 2013 – Name changed to Anfield Resources Inc.; basis 1 new for 10 old shs. ■

Equinox Entertainment Corp. (B.C. 1980)
Aug. 31, 1988 – Name changed to Cancorp Enterprises Incorporated. ■

Equinox Exploration Corp. (B.C. Sept. 12, 1986)
Feb. 1, 2013 – Name changed to Equinox Copper Corp. ■

Equinox Minerals Limited (Can. Jan. 19, 2004)
July 19, 2011 – Acquired by a wholly owned subsid. of Barrick Gold Corporation for Cdn$8.15 per sh. (see Barrick Gold Corporation)

Equinox Resources Ltd. (B.C. 1983)
Dec. 14, 1992 – Amalgamated with Eastmaque Gold Mines Ltd. to form new co. with same name Equinox Resources Ltd. (see Equinox Resources Ltd.)

Equinox Resources Ltd. (B.C. Dec. 8, 1992 amalg.)
Mar. 11, 1994 – Amalgamated with 1057451 Ontario Limited, a wholly owned subsid. of Hecla Mining Company; basis 0.30 com. shs. Hecla for each com. sh. Equinox; and unsec. sub. notes of Hecla in the principal amt. of $1.50 for each ser. A, cl. A Production Participating pfd. shs. of Equinox.

Equipements Denis Incorporated (Que. 1976)
Dec. 20, 1987 – Name changed to Le Groupe Equipements Denis Inc. / Denis Equipment Group Inc. ■

Equis Energy Corp. (Alta. Mar. 30, 1993)
Oct. 15, 1996 – Amalgamated with Magin Energy Inc. (1 for 1), Denergy Limited (1 for 1) and Magin Finance Corp.

to form a new co. also named Magin Energy Inc.; basis 1 new for 11 old shs. (see Magin Energy Inc.)

Equisure Financial Network Inc. (Ont. Apr. 24, 1961)
Feb. 12, 2001 – Acquired by 1440915 Ontario Inc., an associate of ING Canada Inc. for $7.00 per sh.

Equitable Group Inc. (Ont. Jan. 1, 2004)
June 6, 2022 – Name changed to EQB Inc. (see FPsurvey - Industrials)

Equitas Resources Corp. (B.C. Sept. 1, 1994)
Apr. 18, 2017 – Name changed to Altamira Gold Corp. (see FPsurvey - Mines & Energy)

Equitec Products Corp. (Alta. Oct. 20, 1987)
Apr. 9, 1999 – Struck from registry and dissolved.

EquiTech Corporation (Alta. June 23, 2000)
Dec. 2, 2010 – Dissolved and struck from register.

Equitorial Capital Corp. (B.C. Sept. 21, 2010)
July 4, 2013 – Name changed to Equitorial Exploration Corp. ■

Equitorial Exploration Corp. (B.C. Sept. 21, 2010)
Sept. 14, 2020 – Name changed to Lake Winn Resources Corp.; basis 1 new for 10 old shs. (see FPsurvey - Mines & Energy)

Equitrust Mortgage and Savings Corporation (Can. 1963)
Jan. 1, 1984 – Merged into First City Mortgage Company.

Equity Explorations Ltd. (Ont. Aug. 14, 1945)
1967 – Name changed to Eagle Gold Mines Limited; basis 1 new for 2 old shs. ■

Equity Financial Holdings Inc. (Can. Jan. 17, 2005)
Dec. 22, 2017 – Acquired by Smoothwater Capital Corporation; basis $10.25 cash per share.

Equity Investments Corp. (B.C. 1988)
Dec. 28, 1993 – Name changed to TelSoft Mobile Data Inc. ■

Equity Mining Capital Limited (B.C. 1968)
Apr. 20, 1976 – Amalgamated with S. G. Mining Inc. to form Equity Mining Corporation.

Equity Mining Corporation (B.C. 1976)
Feb. 13, 1979 – Amalgamated with Equity Silver Mines Limited, a wholly owned susbsid. of Placer Development Ltd. (subsequently Placer Dome Inc.), to form a new Equity Silver Mines Limited.

Equity Preservation Corp. (B.C. 1983)
July 1993 – Continued into Delaware.
Aug. 4, 1993 – Formed Brassie Golf Corporation on amalgamation with Brassie Golf Corporation.

Equity Reserve Corp. (B.C. 1986)
Feb. 14, 1994 – Amalgamated with Nova-Cogesco Resources Inc. (2 new for 5 old shs.), Orofino Resources Limited (1 new for 12 old shs.), and Hughes Lang Corporation (1 new com. sh. for 1 cl. A com. sh. or cl. B sub. vtg. sh.) to form a new co. known as CanGold Resources Inc.; basis 5 com. for 3 com. shs. and 1 new 7% pref. sh., ser. A for 1 old 7% pref. sh., ser. A. (see CanGold Resources Inc.)

Equity Silver Mines Limited (B.C. Feb. 13, 1979)
July 26, 1995 – All o/s shs. not already held acquired by Placer Dome Canada Inc., a subsid. of Placer Dome Inc.; basis 85¢ per sh. Equity Silver subsequently continued into Canada effective Dec. 12, 1995. (see Placer Dome Inc.)

Equity Standard Corporation (Ont. 1962)
Sept. 22, 1989 – Formed Bekeen Computer Corp. on amalgamation with Bekeen Computer Corp. ■

Equivest International Financial Corp. (B.C. Mar. 19, 1984)
Mar. 25, 1996 – Name changed to Allegro Property Inc. ■

Equus Energy Corporation (B.C. Nov. 9, 1982 amalg.)
Aug. 27, 2008 – Name changed to Habibi Resources Corporation. ■

Equus Industries Inc. (Ont. July 19, 1974)
Mar. 4, 1991 – Name changed to Eros Financial Investments Inc.; basis 1 new for 10 old shs. ■

Equus Petroleum Corporation (B.C. Nov. 9, 1982 amalg.)
Sept. 30, 1997 – Name changed to Nuequus Petroleum Corporation; basis 1 new for 5 old sh. ■

Era Resources Inc. (Can. Sept. 6, 2012)
June 15, 2017 – Privatized; basis 25¢ cash per sh.

Eracon Industries Inc. (B.C. Aug. 26, 1985)
June 2, 1993 – Name changed to ZComm Industries Inc. ■

Eramosa Technology Corporation (Ont. 1946)
May 29, 1987 – Amalgamated with Hammond Manufacturing Company Limited. Shs. were delisted on June 30, 1988.

Erdene Gold Inc. (Can. June 27, 2000)
May 29, 2008 – Name changed to Erdene Resource Development Corporation. (see FPsurvey - Mines & Energy)

eReservation Systems Corp. (B.C. June 17, 1998)
Oct. 25, 2007 – Name changed to Cobre Exploration Corp. ■

Erez Inc. (Alta. Nov. 7, 2000)
July 18, 2003 – Name changed to MCS Global Corp. ■

Ergo Ventures Inc. (Alta. Aug. 21, 2001)
Feb. 20, 2003 – Name changed to Ergoresearch Ltd. following Qualifying Transaction reverse takeover acquisition of Ergoresearch Inc. ■

Ergoresearch Ltd. (Alta. Aug. 21, 2001)
Feb. 16, 2018 – Continued into Canada.
Mar. 2, 2018 – Privatized; basis 1 redeemable pref. sh. for 1 Egoresearch com. sh., immediately redeemed for 30¢ cash per pref. sh.

Erica Resources Ltd. (B.C. 1972)
Dec. 9, 1983 – Struck off register.

Ericksen-Ashby Mines Ltd. (B.C. 1963)
Aug. 26, 1974 – Dissolved.

Erickson Gold Mines Ltd. (B.C. 1974 amalg.)
Dec. 6, 1985 – Name changed to Total Erickson Resources Ltd. ■

Erie Diversified Industries Limited (Ont. Aug. 12, 1940)
Aug. 10, 1973 – Name changed to Lambda Mercantile Corporation Ltd. ■

Erie Flooring and Wood Products Limited (Ont. Aug. 12, 1940)
Nov. 21, 1968 – Name changed to Erie Diversified Industries Limited; basis 1 new for 1 old sh. ■

Erie Gas Ltd. (Ont. 1931)
Wound up. No distribution to shldrs.

Erient Resources Inc. (B.C. Sept. 28, 1978)
Oct. 13, 1987 – Name changed to First Idaho Resources Inc.; basis 2 new for 1 old sh. ■

Erieshore Industries Ltd. (Ont. 1971 amalg.)
Oct. 29, 1980 – Amalgamated with Pensec Explorations Inc. and Portfield Industries Inc. to form Portfield Industries Inc.; basis 1 new for 4 old shs.

Erin Explorations Ltd. (B.C. 1966)
Name changed to Intercon Petroleum Inc. ■

Erin Kirkland Mines Ltd. (Ont. 1944)
Mar. 30, 1967 – Charter cancelled.

Erin Petroleums Ltd. (unknown)
1952 – Reported to be wound up.

Erin Ventures Inc. (Alta. July 19, 1993)
Dec. 15, 2017 – Continued into British Columbia.
Feb. 3, 2023 – Name changed to Boron One Holdings Inc. (see FPsurvey - Mines & Energy)

Erndale Mines Ltd. (Ont. 1947)
1949 – Name changed to Elancra Mines Ltd. and continued into Ontario; basis 1 new for 5 old shs. ■

Ernest Carriere Inc. (Que. 1959)
Formed under name of Ernest Carriere (1959) Inc. to acquire assets and liabs. of Ernest Carriere Inc. No public interest.

Eros Entertainment Inc. (Ont. July 19, 1974)
July 6, 1994 – Name changed to Flying Disc Entertainment Inc. ■

Eros Financial Investments Inc. (Ont. July 19, 1974)
June 2, 1992 – Name changed to Eros Entertainment Inc. ■

Eros Red Lake Mines Ltd. (Ont. 1958)
July 1976 – Charter cancelled.

Eros Resources Corp. (B.C. Mar. 26, 1981)
Apr. 21, 2025 – Name changed to Trident Resources Corp.; basis 1 new for 10 old shs. (see FPsurvey - Mines & Energy)

Eros Resources Ltd. (B.C. 1987)
Feb. 21, 1992 – Name changed to International Eros Holdings Ltd.; basis 1 new for 2 old shs. ■

Errowana Gold Mines Ltd. (Ont. 1938)
Sept. 30, 1957 – Charter cancelled.

Erskine Resources Corporation (Alta. 1951)
Nov. 9, 1988 – Acquired by Mark Resources Inc.; basis 1 Mark sh. for 2 Erskine shs. (see Mark Resources Inc.)

Esansee Explorations Ltd. (B.C. 1967)
Mar. 18, 1977 – Dissolved.

Escape Gold Inc. (Can. Mar. 16, 2000)
Nov. 15, 2011 – Name changed to Rio Silver Inc. (see FPsurvey - Mines & Energy)

Escape Group Inc. (Can. Mar. 16, 2000)
July 26, 2007 – Name changed to Escape Gold Inc. ■

Escape.Com Inc. (Can. Mar. 16, 2000)
Oct. 11, 2001 – Name changed to Escape Group Inc. following the Sept. 18, 2001, Qualifying Transaction reverse takeover acquisition of Creative Travel Adventures Ltd. ■

Escarpment Oils Limited (Ont.)
Dec. 12, 1960 – Dissolved.

Escudo Capital Corporation (B.C. Feb. 28, 2011)
May 2, 2013 – Name changed to Aston Bay Holdings Ltd. pursuant to Qualifying Transaction reverse takeover acquisition of Aston Bay Ventures Ltd. (see FPsurvey - Mines & Energy)

eShippers Management Ltd. (B.C. Aug. 4, 1992)
May 9, 2022 – Name changed to Resouro Gold Inc. pursuant to the reverse takeover acquisition of private Singapore-based ISON Mining Pte. Ltd.; basis 1 new for 2 old sh. ■

eShippers.com Management Ltd. (B.C. Aug. 4, 1992)
Feb. 28, 2003 – Name changed to eShippers Management Ltd.; basis 1 new for 10 old shs. ■

Eskay Gold Corp. (B.C. July 17, 1984)
Oct. 5, 1992 – Name changed to Consolidated Eskay Gold Corp.; basis 1 new for 1.8 old shs. ■

Esker Resources Ltd. (Alta. Mar. 13, 1981)
Feb. 18, 2002 – Acquired by Rider Resources Inc.; basis either $0.47 plus 0.24 new Rider sh. or 0.867 new Rider sh. for 1 old Esker sh.

Eskimo Copper Mines Ltd. (Ont. 1968)
Mar. 1976 – Charter cancelled.

Eskimo International Resources Ltd. (Can. Jan. 14, 1972)
Aug. 1972 – Name changed to Natalma Mines Limited. ■

Eskimo Resources Ltd. (B.C. Mar. 24, 1966)
Jan. 5, 1987 – Name changed to Ft. Lauderdale Resources Inc.; basis 1 new for 2 old shs. ■

Esmond Mills Limited (Que. 1930)
1953 – Private company since when all 5% of pref. stk. redeemed at $22.25 plus 25¢ accr. divds. All com. held by Beaton Manufacturing Co.

eSoft, Inc. (Colo. Mar. 3, 1984)
Feb. 17, 1998 – Continued into Delaware.

Espalau Inc. (Que. Aug. 30, 1980)
June 21, 1994 – Name changed to Espalau Mining Corporation. ■

Espalau Mining Corporation (Que. Aug. 30, 1980)
June 22, 1994 – Amalgamated with Bachelor Lake Gold Mines Inc. (1 new for 15 old shs.), to continue as Espalau Mining Corporation; basis 1 new for any old fractional sh. equal to or higher than 0.5 com. shs.

Espalau Mining Corporation (Que. Aug. 30, 1980)
Dec. 24, 1998 – Name changed to Ced-Or Corporation. (see FPsurvey - Industrials)

Esperanza Explorations Ltd. (B.C. Feb. 21, 1979)
Mar. 28, 1990 – Name changed to Columbia Gold Mines Ltd.; basis 1 new for 3 old shs. ■

Esperanza Mines Ltd. (B.C. 1927)
May 15, 1969 – Struck off register.

Esperanza Resources Corp. (B.C. Dec. 1, 1990 amalg.)
Sept. 3, 2013 – Acquired by 0975064 B.C. Ltd., a wholly owned subsid. of Alamos Gold Inc.; basis Cdn$0.85 plus 0.0625 Alamos wts.for 1 Esperanza sh. and 0.15 Alamos wts. for 1 Esperanza wt. (see Alamos Gold Inc.)

Esperanza Silver Corporation (B.C. Dec. 1, 1990 amalg.)
July 19, 2010 – Name changed to Esperanza Resources Corp. ■

Espial Group Inc. (Can. Apr. 25, 1997)
May 29, 2019 – Acquired by Enghouse Systems Limited; basis $1.57 cash per sh.

Espina Copper Developments Ltd. (B.C. 1972)
Sept. 13, 1977 – Name changed to Northern Espina Resources Ltd.; basis 1 new for 4 old shs. ■

Esplanade Centre Holdings Ltd. (B.C. 1986)
Nov. 15, 1989 – Acquired by Canlan Investment Corporation; basis 3 Canlan shs. for 4 Esplanade shs. (see Canlan Investment Corporation)

Espoir Exploration Corp. (Alta. Oct. 23, 2002)
Jan. 12, 2006 – Acquired by and merged into Rockyview Energy Inc.; basis following conversion of all cl. B shs. to cl. A shs., either $3.19 or 0.5148 Rockyview com. shs. for 1 Espoir cl. A sh. (see Rockyview Energy Inc.)

Esprit Energy Trust (Alta. Aug. 16, 2004)
Oct. 4, 2006 – Plan of Arrangement acquisition by Pengrowth Energy Trust; basis 0.53 new Pengrowth unit for 1 old Esprit unit. Also Pengrowth assumed the obligations of the 6.5% Esprit debs. (see Pengrowth Energy Trust)

Esprit Exploration Ltd. (Can. Sept. 4, 1987)
Oct. 5, 2004 – Converted into a new company named ProspEx Resources Ltd. and new income trust named Esprit Energy Trust; basis either $0.22, 0.25 cl. B trust unit and 0.20 new com. sh. or, $0.22 and 0.25 new exch. sh. for 1 Esprit Exploration com. sh.

Esprit Resources Ltd. (Alta. 1983)
June 20, 1990 – Amalgamated with Esprit Acquisition Corp., a wholly owned subsid. of American Eagle Petroleums Ltd. Shldrs. entitled to receive $0.40 per sh. of Esprit held. (see American Eagle Petroleums Ltd.)

Esrey Energy Ltd. (B.C. Feb. 24, 2000)
Oct. 16, 2017 – Name changed to Esrey Resources Ltd. (see FPsurvey - Mines & Energy)

Essar Steel Algoma Inc. (Ont. June 1, 1992)
Sept. 5, 2014 – Continued into Canada.
Dec. 3, 2018 – Name changed to Old Steelco Inc. following the acquisition of substantially all of the operating assets and liabilities of the company by Algoma Steel Holdings Inc.

Essence Biotechnologies Inc. (B.C. July 31, 1985)
Nov. 14, 1990 – Name changed to American Sidewinder Oil Corporation. ■

Essence Resources Inc. (B.C. July 31, 1985)
Jan. 11, 1988 – Name changed to Essence Biotechnologies Inc. ■

Essendon Solutions Inc. (Alta. July 19, 2000)
June 27, 2005 – Name changed to ESO Uranium Corp. ■

Essential Energy Services Ltd. (Alta. Feb. 26, 2010)
Nov. 16, 2023 – Acquired by and amalgamated with a wholly owned subsid. of Element Technical Services Inc.; basis 40¢ cash per sh.

Essential Energy Services Trust (Alta. Apr. 4, 2006)
May 5, 2010 – Succeeded by Essential Energy Services Ltd. pursuant to plan of arrangement whereby Essential Energy Services Ltd. was formed to facilitate the conversion of the trust into a corporation. ■

Essex Angel Capital Inc. (Can. Feb. 10, 2010)
Feb. 14, 2017 – Continued into British Columbia.
Nov. 9, 2017 – Name changed to Block One Capital Inc. ■

Essex Minerals Inc. (B.C. Nov. 19, 2012)
Aug. 25, 2023 – Name changed to Optegra Ventures Inc.; basis 1 new for 10 old shs. (see FPsurvey - Mines & Energy)

Essex Packers Ltd. (Ont. 1946)
1976 – Declared bankrupt with no distribution to shldrs. after liquidation.
1979 – Trustee in bankruptcy discharged.

Essex Petroleum Corporation (B.C. Jan. 24, 1980)
Nov. 18, 1985 – Name changed to Fibertech Industries Corp. ■

Essex Resource Corporation (B.C. Aug. 25, 1987)
Apr. 8, 2002 – Name changed to Maximus Ventures Ltd.; basis 1 new for 10 old shs. ■

Essor Exploration Inc. (Que. 1986)
June 3, 1991 – Name changed to Orco Resources Inc.; basis 1 new for 10 old shs. ■

Esstra Industries Corp. (B.C. Mar. 3, 1983)
May 7, 1993 – Continued into Alberta. (see Esstra Industries Inc.)
Sept. 3, 1997 – Separated into two new companies, Esstra Industries Inc. (New Esstra) and Antarex Metals Ltd.; basis 1 New Esstra com. sh. and 1 Antarex com. sh. for 1 Old Esstra com. sh. (see Esstra Industries Inc.)

Esstra Industries Inc. (Alta. Sept. 6, 1996)
Feb. 23, 2018 – Continued into British Columbia.
Sept. 27, 2024 – Name changed to Miivo Holdings Corp.; basis 2 new for 1 old sh. (see FPsurvey - Industrials)

eStation Network Services Inc. (Ont. Jan. 8, 1986)
Dec. 21, 2004 – Acquired by Threshold Financial Technologies Inc.; basis unknown.

eStation.com Inc. (Ont. Jan. 8, 1986)
Dec. 14, 2001 – Name changed to eStation Network Services Inc. ■

Estaurum Mines Ltd. (Can. Mar. 20, 1987)
July 22, 1991 – Name changed to Westaurum Industries Inc. ■

Estella Mines Ltd. (B.C. 1950)
1955 – Name changed to United Estella Mines Ltd.; basis 1 new for 5 old shs. ■

Esten Explorations Inc. (Ont. 1973)
Nov. 7, 1983 – Dissolved.

Ester Porcupine Gold Mines Ltd. (Ont. 1944)
May 1958 – Dissolved.

Estrella Gold Corporation (Ont. Apr. 24, 1996)
Apr. 14, 2015 – Name changed to Alianza Holdings Ltd. ■

Estrella International Energy Services Ltd. (Alta. Jan. 11, 2007)
Jan. 3, 2017 – Privatized; basis 19¢ cash per sh.

eTV Technology Inc. (B.C. Jan. 12, 1987)
Apr. 2, 2009 – Name changed to Ocean Park Ventures Corp.; basis 1 new for 4 old shs. ■

Etac Sales Ltd. (Can. July 9, 1975)
Mar. 28, 1994 – Placed into bankruptcy and Doane Raymond Limited of Toronto was appointed receiver and BDO Dunwoody was named as trustee.
May 1995 – All the assets had been sold and the company was in the process of being wound up.
Dec. 4, 2000 – Receiver discharged and the company was wound up. There were no distributions to creditors or shldrs.

Etana Technologies Corporation (B.C. Apr. 28, 1986)
July 29, 1991 – Name changed to TechTana Capital Ltd.; basis 1 new for 2 old shs. ■

Ethel Copper Mines Ltd. (Ont. 1952)
Dec. 12, 1955 – Dissolved.

Ethelda Red Lake Mines Ltd. (Ont. 1946)
1955 – Charter cancelled.

Ether Capital Corporation (Ont.)
June 18, 2024 – Converted into an exchange-traded-fund (ETF); basis 1 Purpose Ether Staking ETF sh. for 1 Ether Capital com. sh.

Ethicorp Resources Limited (Alta. Apr. 16, 1986)
Oct. 26, 1987 – Name changed to Central Explorers Inc.; basis 1 new for 3 old shs. ■

Ethiopian Potash Corp. (Ont. Mar. 9, 2011 amalg.)
July 15, 2013 – Name changed to AgriMinco Corp. ■

Ethos Capital Corp. (B.C. Mar. 12, 2007)
Apr. 4, 2012 – Name changed to Ethos Gold Corp. ■

Ethos Gold Corp. (B.C. Mar. 12, 2007)
Apr. 6, 2022 – Name changed to Prospector Metals Corp.; basis 1 new for 3 old shs. (see FPsurvey - Mines & Energy)

Etna Resources Inc. (B.C. Sept. 18, 2006)
Jan. 20, 2010 – Name changed to Pan American Lithium Corp. ■

Etrion Corporation (B.C. Sept. 10, 2009)
Aug. 24, 2021 – Return of capital distrib. of US$0.327 cash per sh. made to shldrs. of record Aug. 17, 2021.
Sept. 17, 2021 – Voluntarily delisted from TSX; continued to trade on NASDAQ Stockholm. (see FPsurvey - Mines & Energy; FPsurvey - Industrials)

Etruscan Enterprises Limited (B.C. Dec. 24, 1969)
Aug. 12, 1997 – Continued into Nova Scotia.
Sept. 11, 1997 – Name changed to Etruscan Resources Incorporated. ■

Etruscan Resources Incorporated (N.S. Aug. 12, 1997)
Sept. 15, 2010 – Amalgamated with 3246772 Nova Scotia Limited, a wholly owned subsid. of Endeavour Financial Corporation; basis Cdn$0.26 plus 0.0932 Endeavour shs. for 1 Etruscan sh. (see Endeavour Mining Corporation)
Dec. 8, 2010 – Name changed to Endeavour Resources Inc. (see Endeavour Mining Corporation)

eTVtech.com Communications Inc. (B.C. Jan. 12, 1987)
May 2, 2001 – Name changed to eTV Technology Inc. ■

Eugenic Corp. (Ont. Sept. 22, 1978)
Nov. 30, 2009 – Formed Eagleford Energy Inc. in Ontario on amalgamation with its wholly owned subsid. Eagleford Energy Inc. ■

Eurasia Gold Corp. (Alta. June 6, 1984)
Sept. 28, 1999 – Continued into Yukon.
May 23, 2006 – Name changed to Eurasia Gold Inc. and continued into Canada following reverse takeover acquisition of Kazakhstan-based JSC Charaltyn; basis 1 new for 10 old shs. ■

Eurasia Gold Inc. (Can. May 23, 2006)
Sept. 11, 2007 – Acquired by Kazakhmys plc, through wholly owned Kazakhmys Gold Inc.; basis Cdn$0.85 per com. sh.

Eurasian Minerals Inc. (Alta. May 13, 1996)
July 19, 2017 – Name changed to EMX Royalty Corporation. (see FPsurvey - Mines & Energy)

Eureka Corporation Ltd. (N.S. 1937)
1963 – Assets acquired by Silver Eureka Corp.; basis 1 new for 10 old shs.

Eureka Kirkland Gold Mines, Limited (Ont. 1922)
Feb. 21, 1955 – Dissolved.

Eureka 93 Inc. (Can. June 18, 2014)
Aug. 28, 2020 – Assigned into bankruptcy and Deloitte Restructuring Inc. appointed trustee.

Eureka Resources, Inc. (B.C. June 16, 1981)
May 9, 1990 – Amalgamated with Hawthorne Gold Corporation (0.2 for 1) to continue with the same name Eureka Resources, Inc.; basis 1 new for 1 old sh.
Oct. 30, 2018 – Name changed to Kore Mining Ltd. following reverse takeover acquisition of (old) Kore Mining Ltd. and concurrent amalgamation of (old) Kore with a wholly owned subsidiary of the company, with (old) Kore renamed 1065591 B.C. Ltd.; basis 1 new for 10 old shs. (see FPsurvey - Mines & Energy)

Euro-Ad Systems Inc. (B.C. Dec. 31, 1985)
July 3, 1997 – Name changed to Sun Devil Gold Corp.; basis 1 new for 2 old shs. ■

Euro-American Financial Services Ltd. (B.C. 1981)
Apr. 7, 1986 – Delisted from the Vancouver Stock Exchange. Subsequently struck from register and dissolved.

Euro-Asia Capital Ltd. (B.C. 1980)
Jan. 18, 1989 – Name changed to Asiamerica Holdings Ltd.; basis 1 new for 3 old shs. ■

Euro Asia Pay Holdings Inc. (B.C. Oct. 16, 2017)
June 1, 2022 – Name changed to Hero Innovation Group Inc. (see FPsurvey - Industrials)

Euro Banc Capital Securities Trust (Ont. May 28, 2014)
Feb. 4, 2016 – Merged into North American Financials Capital Securities Trust to continue as Global Capital Securities Trust; basis 0.382254 Global Capital cl. A units for 1 Euro Banc cl. A unit. (see Global Capital Securities Trust)

Euro-Nevada Mining Corporation Limited (Ont. Jan. 7, 1987)
Sept. 20, 1999 – Amalgamated with Franco-Nevada Mining Corporation; basis 0.77 Franco-Nevada shs. for 1 Euro-Nevada sh. (see Franco-Nevada Mining Corporation Limited)

Euro-Pacific Resource Group Inc. (B.C. Sept. 3, 1985)
May 21, 1996 – Name changed to Holt International Investments Ltd.; basis 1 new for 5 old shs. ■

Euro Petroleum Corp. (B.C. Sept. 19, 1983)
Feb. 19, 1991 – Name changed to Morgan Petroleum Inc.; basis 1 new for 5 old shs. ■

Eurocan Ventures Ltd. (B.C. Feb. 20, 1978)
Feb. 8, 1991 – Name changed to Consolidated Eurocan Ventures Ltd.; basis 1 new for 10 old shs. ■

Eurocontrol Technics Group Inc. (B.C. June 3, 1987)
Apr. 17, 2019 – Continued into Ontario.
Apr. 18, 2019 – Name changed to Talisker Resources Ltd.; basis 1 new for 4 old shs. (see FPsurvey - Mines & Energy)

Eurocontrol Technics Inc. (B.C. June 3, 1987)
Aug. 22, 2011 – Name changed to Eurocontrol Technics Group Inc. ■

Eurogas Corporation (Can. Apr. 28, 1989)
Aug. 31, 1995 – Amalgamated with Clearport Petroleums Ltd. to form Eurogas Corporation; basis 0.63 new for 1 Clearport sh. and 1 new for 2 Eurogas shs. (see Eurogas Corporation)

Eurogas Corporation (Can. Aug. 31, 1995 amalg.)
June 15, 2011 – Name changed to Dundee Energy Limited. ■

Eurogold Resources Inc. (B.C. May 29, 1986)
May 12, 1992 – Name changed to Superior Pipeline Corporation. ■

Eurolife Brands Inc. (B.C. June 23, 2017)
Dec. 4, 2020 – Name changed to Plant&Co. Brands Ltd. ■

Euromin Canada Ltd. (B.C. Feb. 16, 1983)
Apr. 28, 1989 – Continued into Canada.
June 3, 1994 – Name changed to International Euromin Corporation; basis 1 new for 5 old shs. ■

Europa Mines Inc. (Que. 1972)
Aug. 29, 1981 – Charter cancelled.

Europa Petroleum Ltd. (Alta. 1981)
Nov. 7, 1984 – Acquired by Orbit Oil & Gas Ltd.; basis 1 Orbit sh. for 5 Europa shs.

Europacific Metals Inc. (B.C. June 16, 2017)
Sept. 13, 2024 – Name changed to Ibero Mining Corp. (see FPsurvey - Mines & Energy)

Europe Blue-Chip Dividend & Growth Fund (Ont. Feb. 26, 2014)
Mar. 29, 2019 – Terminated; basis $7.1528 cash per trust unit.

European Commercial Real Estate Investment Trust (Ont. July 25, 2016)
Mar. 29, 2019 – Name changed to European Residential Real Estate Investment Trust following acquisition of a portfolio of multi-residential properties in the Netherlands. (see FPsurvey - Industrials)

European Commercial Real Estate Limited (Ont. July 25, 2016)
May 3, 2017 – Succeeded by European Commercial Real Estate Investment Trust pursuant to plan of arrangement whereby European Commercial Real Estate Investment Trust was formed to facilitate the conversion of the corporation into a trust; basis 1 new for 31.25 old shs. ■

European Dividend Growth Fund (Ont.)
Apr. 23, 2019 – Converted from a closed-end fund to an exchange trade fund.

European Energy Metals Corp. (B.C. Feb. 2, 2021)
Nov. 4, 2024 – Name changed to Grit Metals Corp. (see FPsurvey - Mines & Energy)

European Ferro Metals Ltd. (B.C. Dec. 31, 2013)
Nov. 7, 2016 – Name changed to Boreal Metals Corp. ■

European Focused Dividend Fund (Alta. Oct. 25, 2017)
July 14, 2020 – Merged into Global Dividend Growers Income Fund; basis 0.56876901 Global Dividend units for 1 European Focused fund unit. (see Global Dividend Growers Income Fund)

European Garnet Ltd. (B.C. Jan. 29, 1986)
Dec. 16, 1996 – Name changed to Indo Metals Ltd.; basis 1 new for 2 old shs. ■

European Gold Resources Inc. (Ont. Sept. 20, 1996 amalg.)
May 10, 2004 – Name changed to Galantas Gold Corporation. (see FPsurvey - Mines & Energy)

European Goldfields Limited (Yuk. Mar. 1, 2000)
Mar. 1, 2012 – Formed Eldorado Gold Yukon Corp. following acquisition by Eldorado Gold Corporation and subsequent amalgamation with newly incorporated wholly owned Eldorado Gold Yukon Corp.; basis 0.85 Eldorado shs. plus Cdn$0.0001 for 1 Eldorado Gold sh.

European Metals Corp. (Ont. Feb. 24, 2014 amalg.)
July 6, 2020 – Name changed to Gold'n Futures Mineral Corp. ■

European Minerals Corporation (Yuk. Nov. 1, 1995)
Apr. 8, 2005 – Continued into British Virgin Islands.
July 14, 2008 – Name changed to Orsu Metals Corporation. ■

European Mining Finance Limited (Bermuda 1988)
Jan. 19, 1998 – Name changed to Griffin Mining Limited.

European Original New York Seltzer Ltd. (B.C. 1983)
Apr. 26, 1988 – Dissolved.

European Premium Dividend Fund (Ont. Oct. 31, 2007)
Dec. 13, 2010 – Merged into Copernican International Premium Dividend Fund; basis 1.230920 Copernican International units for 1 European Premium unit. (see Copernican International Premium Dividend Fund)

European Strategic Balanced Fund (Ont. Apr. 29, 2014)
Jan. 9, 2017 – Terminated; basis $9.8814 cash per trust unit including $1.8018 in taxable capital gains.

European Technologies International Inc. (Alta. 1987)
June 1, 2001 – Name changed to Steely Group Inc.; basis 1 new for 15 old shs. ■

European Uranium Resources Ltd. (B.C. Mar. 27, 2008)
May 27, 2016 – Name changed to Azarga Metals Corp.; basis 1 new for 10 old shs. (see FPsurvey - Mines & Energy)

European Ventures Inc. (B.C. May 25, 1987)
Dec. 1, 1994 – Name changed to Cugold Ventures Inc.; basis 1 new for 4 old shs. ■

Europrime Capital Corporation (B.C. Sept. 15, 1986)
June 6, 1995 – Name changed to International Europrime Capital Corporation; basis 1 new for 25 old shs. ■

Eurotech Building Products Inc. (B.C. Mar. 25, 1981)
Sept. 15, 1992 – Name changed to Eurotech Technologies Inc.; basis 1 new for 2 old shs. ■

Eurotech Technologies Inc. (B.C. Mar. 25, 1981)
Apr. 29, 1996 – Name changed to Artemis Ventures Inc.; basis 1 new for 4 old shs. ■

Eurotin Inc. (Ont. July 31, 2008)
Oct. 25, 2021 – Name changed to Li-Metal Corp. pursuant to the reverse takeover acquisition of 2555663 Ontario Limited (dba Li-Metal) and concurrent amalgamation of Li-Metal with wholly owned 2848302 Ontario Inc. (and continued as Li-Metal North America Inc.); basis 1 new for 124.721682 old shs. ■

EuroZinc Mining Corporation (B.C. Apr. 21, 1999)
Oct. 31, 2006 – Plan of Arrangement amalgamation with Lundin Mining Corporation; basis 0.0952 new Lundin sh. plus $0.0001 for 1 old EuroZinc sh.

Eurus Resource Corp. (B.C. May 1, 1990 amalg.)
Oct. 2, 1995 – Acquired by Crystallex International Corp.; basis 0.15513146 Crystallex shs. and 0.15513146 Crystallex wts. for 1 Eurus sh.

Eva Lake Gold Mines Ltd. (Ont. 1936)
Aug. 18, 1958 – Dissolved.

Evangeline Financial Services Corporation (Can. Dec. 23, 1988 amalg.)
Dec. 1, 1999 – Name changed to Equisure Financial Management Limited.

Evangeline Gold and Copper Mines, Ltd. (N.S. 1927)
1934 – Name changed to Trinidad Mines, Gas & Oils, Ltd. ■

Evangeline Savings and Mortgage Company (Can. 1964)
Dec. 23, 1988 – Formed Evangeline Financial Services Corporation in Canada on amalgamation with Evangeline Financial Services Corporation. ■

Evans, Coleman & Gilley Brothers Limited (Can. 1928)
Sept. 19, 1957 – Amalgamated with British Columbia Cement Co. Ltd.

Evans Health Group Limited (Ont. Sept. 10, 1987)
June 29, 1994 – Formed FoxMeyer Canada Inc. in Ontario on amalgamation with FoxMeyer Canada Inc. ■

Eve & Co Incorporated (Ont. Oct. 17, 2014)
Mar. 25, 2022 – Filed for protection under the Companies' Creditors Arrangement Act (CCAA) and BDO Canada Limited was appointed monitor.
Nov. 25, 2022 – Sale of wholly owned Natural Medco Ltd. was completed. Monies received insufficent and secured debtors suffered a shortfall. No monies available for distrib. to unsecured creditors or shldrs.
Nov. 30, 2022 – The CCAA was terminated and BDO Canada was discharged as monitor. (see FPsurvey - Industrials)

Eveco Nickel Mines Ltd. (Ont. 1956)
Mar. 30, 1967 – Dissolved.

Evelynn Nickel Mines Ltd. (Ont. 1956)
1962 – Name changed to Hardiman Bay Mines Ltd. ■

Even Resources Ltd. (B.C. June 29, 1983)
Feb. 27, 1998 – Name changed to Plata Minerals Corp.; basis 1 new for 7 old shs. ■

Evenlode Gold Mines Ltd. (Can. Dec. 14, 1927)
1961 – Name changed to Evenlode Mines Limited. ■

Evenlode Mines Limited (Can. Dec. 14, 1927)
Aug. 31, 1987 – Dissolved.

Events International Holding Corporation (Can. Aug. 11, 1994)
Dec. 9, 2005 – Name changed to Dynasty Gaming Inc. ■

eVenture Capital Corp. (B.C. Feb. 24, 2000)
Nov. 28, 2006 – Name changed to Invicta Oil & Gas Ltd. following reverse takeover acquisition of a 15% interest in oil and gas leases in Texas; basis 1 new for 2 old shs. ■

Everbright Capital Corporation (Can. Nov. 15, 2004)
Sept. 14, 2013 – Dissolved and struck from registry.

Everclear Capital Ltd. (B.C. Jan. 23, 2008)
July 14, 2010 – Name changed to Avrupa Minerals Ltd. pursuant to Qualifying Transaction acquisition agreement with Metallica Mining ASA to acquire 90% of MAEPA Empreendimentos Mineiros e Participacoes Lda. and 92.5% of Innomatik Exploration Kosovo LLC. (see FPsurvey - Mines & Energy)

Everdeen Resources Ltd. (Ont. Feb. 10, 1986)
Mar. 22, 1994 – Formed Hendricks Minerals Canada Limited in Ontario on amalgamation with Hendricks Minerals Canada Limited; basis 1 new cl. A subord. vtg. for 1 old sh. ■

Eveready Income Fund (Alta. Aug. 18, 2004)
Jan. 7, 2009 – Converted into Eveready Inc.; basis 1 Eveready Inc. sh. for 5 Eveready Income trust units. (see Eveready Inc.)

Eveready Inc. (Alta. Oct. 27, 2008)
Aug. 6, 2009 – Acquired by Clean Harbors, Inc.; basis 0.1304 Clean Harbors shs. plus Cdn$3.30 for 1 Eveready sh.

Everest Energy Corporation (Can. May 2, 1996)
Dec. 21, 2005 – Continued into Alberta.
Feb. 6, 2006 – Name changed to Westbow Energy Inc. following reverse takeover acquisition of Westbow Energy Inc.; basis 10.13611 new for 1 Westbow sh. and 1 new for 9.7372 Everest shs. ■

Everest Equity Inc. (Alta. June 14, 1991)
Dec. 21, 1992 – Name changed to V.Fund Investments Limited. (see FPsurvey - Mines & Energy)

Everest Mines and Minerals Ltd. (B.C. Sept. 4, 1986)
Apr. 4, 2000 – Name changed to First Narrows Resources Corp.; basis 1 new for 10 old shs. ■

Everest Mining and Exploration Ltd. (Sask. 1966)
1970 – Name changed to Everest Resources Ltd. ■

Everest Resources Ltd. (Sask. 1966)
Sept. 1973 – Charter cancelled.

Everest Resources Ltd. (B.C. Jan. 31, 1983)
Sept. 27, 1989 – Name changed to Northfork Ventures Ltd.; basis 1 new for 3 old shs. ■

Everest Ventures Corp. (Alta. Jan. 11, 2007)
June 25, 2010 – Name changed to Estrella International Energy Services Ltd. pursuant to Qualifying Transaction reverse takeover acquisition of Estrella Overseas Limited; basis 1 new for 5.27625 old shs. ■

Everest Ventures Inc. (B.C. Apr. 23, 2007)
June 28, 2016 – Name changed to Halio Energy Inc. (see FPsurvey - Mines & Energy)

Everett Resources Ltd. (B.C. Dec. 4, 2006)
Mar. 20, 2012 – Name changed to Elm Tree Minerals Inc.; basis 1 new for 12 old shs. ■

Everfront Ventures Corp. (Ont. Apr. 11, 2011)
Sept. 27, 2017 – Name changed to DataMetrex AI Limited following Qualifying Transaction reverse takeover of Datametrex Limited and subsequent amalgamation of Datametrex with wholly owned Everfront Acquisition Corp,. (see FPsurvey - Industrials)

Evergold Resources Inc. (B.C. May 27, 1987)
Nov. 3, 1992 – Name changed to Westrend Natural Gas Inc.; basis 1 new for 5 old shs. ■

Evergreen Energy Resources Ltd. (Ont. June 3, 1955)
Aug. 9, 1984 – Name changed to Evergreen International Corp.; basis 1 new for 4 old shs. ■

Evergreen Gaming Corporation (B.C. Apr. 11, 1979)
Dec. 28, 2022 – Acquired by Maverick Gaming LLC; basis US$0.65 cash per sh.

Evergreen International Corp. (Ont. June 3, 1955)
Mar. 29, 1985 – Amalgamated with Villanova Natural Gas Corporation (1 for 2) to continue with the same name Evergreen International Corp.; basis 1 new for 1 old sh.
July 19, 1989 – Delisted from the Toronto Stock Exchange. Subsequently struck from register and dissolved.

Evergreen International Technology Inc. (B.C. Apr. 11, 1983)
Jan. 31, 1997 – Name changed to Jot-It! Software Corp. ■

Everlast Filtration Systems Inc. (Alta. Jan. 7, 1987)
Feb. 1, 1999 – Struck from registry and dissolved.

Evermount Ventures Inc. (B.C. Apr. 16, 2012)
July 19, 2021 – Name changed to OOOOO Entertainment Commerce Limited pursuant to the Qualifying Transaction reverse takeover acquisition of Video Commerce Group Ltd.; basis 1 new for 2 old shs. (see FPsurvey - Industrials)

Everock Inc. (Ont. Sept. 27, 1999)
Continued into Nevada.

Everton Resources Inc. (Alta. Nov. 7, 1996)
May 19, 2004 – Continued into Canada.
Sept. 15, 2020 – Name changed to Molecule Holdings Inc. pursuant to reverse takeover acquisition of private Lansdowne, Ont.-based Molecule Inc. on a post-consolidation share-for-share basis; basis 1 new for 10 old shs. (see FPsurvey - Industrials)

Evertz Microsystems Inc. (Can. May 28, 1981)
June 6, 1997 – Name changed to Evertz Technologies Limited. (see FPsurvey - Industrials)

EveryWare Development Canada Corp. (Can. Mar. 6, 1991)
July 15, 1997 – Merged with InContext Systems Inc. to form EveryWare Development Inc. (EveryWare); basis 1 new sh. of EveryWare for 10 com. shs. (see EveryWare Development Inc.)

EveryWare Development Inc. (Can. Mar. 6, 1991)
Dec. 17, 1998 – Acquired by Pervasive Acquisition Corporation, a wholly owned subsid. of Pervasive Software Inc. of Austin, Tex., for $1.20 per sh.

eVirus Software Corporation (B.C. Aug. 16, 1996)
Nov. 15, 2002 – Name changed to Durango Capital Corp. ■

Evolved Digital Systems Inc. (Que. Sept. 23, 1987)
Jan. 5, 2016 – Dissolved.

Evolving Gold Corp. (Can. June 19, 2003)
Mar. 3, 2015 – Continued into British Columbia.
May 24, 2022 – Name changed to Future Fuel Corporation pursuant to the reverse takeover acquisition of Elephant Capital Corp. ■

Evrim Resources Corp. (Can. May 11, 2005)
Jan. 6, 2011 – Continued into British Columbia.
Aug. 18, 2020 – Name changed to Orogen Royalties Inc. following acquisition of Renaissance Gold Inc. (see FPsurvey - Mines & Energy)

Ewing Oil Corporation (B.C. June 10, 1980)
Dec. 6, 1989 – Name changed to Consolidated Ewing Industries Inc.; basis 1 new for 5 old shs. ■

Ex Fund (A) Capital Corp. (B.C. Mar. 26, 1999)
July 28, 2000 – Formed Discovery Capital Corporation in British Columbia on Qualifying Transaction amalgamation with Discovery Capital Corporation; basis 1 new for 1 old sh. ■

Ex-Mother Lode Mines Ltd. (unknown)
1962 – Name changed to Opemisca Dufault Mines Ltd. and continued into Quebec; basis 1 new for 4 old shs. (see FPsurvey - Mines & Energy)

exactEarth Ltd. (Can. Aug. 11, 2006)
Dec. 3, 2021 – Acquired by Spire Global, Inc.; basis Cdn$2.5009 cash plus 0.1 Spire Global cl. A com. shs. for 1 exactEarth com. sh.

Exador Resources Inc. (Can. 1987)
Nov. 9, 1989 – Formed Tymar Resources Inc. in British Columbia on amalgamation with Cheryl Resources Inc. (1 for 2) and Argo Development Corp. (1 for 2.5); basis 1 new for 13 old shs. ■

Exall Energy Corporation (Ont. Sept. 15, 2006)
July 11, 2008 – Continued into Alberta.
Mar. 25, 2015 – Petitioned into receivership. MNP Ltd. appointed receiver and all officers and directors resigned.

Exall Resources Limited (Ont. Feb. 13, 1934)
Dec. 21, 2006 – Formed Gold Eagle Mines Ltd. in Ontario on amalgamation with wholly owned Gold Eagle Mines Limited; basis 0.5428 new for 1 old sh. Subsequently, wholly owned 2117523 Ontario Inc. amalgamated with Southern Star Resources Ltd. on a sh.-for-sh. basis, with Gold Eagle the deemed acquiror. ■

Exalt Capital Corp. (B.C. Feb. 20, 2017)
Aug. 23, 2018 – Name changed to Astron Connect Inc. pursuant to Qualifying Transaction reverse takeover acquisition of Sachiel Connect Inc. (see FPsurvey - Industrials)

ExAlta Energy Inc. (Alta. Mar. 15, 2002)
Jan. 23, 2008 – Acquired by Galleon Energy Inc.; basis 0.118 Galleon cl. A shs. for 1 ExAlta Energy com. sh. (see Galleon Energy Inc.)

Excalibur Development Ltd. (B.C. 1969)
Dec. 23, 1980 – Name changed to Excalibur Energy Corporation. ■

Excalibur Energy Corporation (B.C. 1969)
Sept. 18, 1981 – Dissolved.

Excalibur Exploration Ltd. (unknown)
Nov. 20, 1972 – Amalgamated with Metron Exploration Ltd. to form Dynasearch Exploration Ltd.

Excalibur Resources Ltd. (B.C. May 11, 1983)
Jan. 24, 2011 – Continued into Ontario.
Dec. 7, 2016 – Name changed to Metalla Royalty & Streaming Ltd.; basis 1 new for 3 old shs. (see FPsurvey - Mines & Energy)

Excam Developments Inc. (Yuk. Dec. 8, 1997)
Dec. 31, 2004 – Dissolved.

Excapsa Software Inc. (B.C. Apr. 28, 2004)
Feb. 28, 2005 – Continued into Canada.
May 21, 2013 – Dissolved and struck from register.

Exceed Capital Holdings Ltd. (Alta. Aug. 10, 1983)
July 16, 2007 – Name changed to Gallic Energy Ltd. ■

Exceed Energy Inc. (Alta. Mar. 25, 2003)
Dec. 24, 2009 – Acquired by WestFire Energy Ltd.; basis 0.01 WestFire shs. for 1 Exceed sh. (see WestFire Energy Ltd.)

Excel Energy Inc. (Alta. Oct. 6, 1977)
Aug. 2, 1995 – Acquired by Ranchmen's Resources Ltd.; basis 0.3 Ranchmen's shs. for 1 Excel sh. (see Ranchmen's Resources Ltd.)

Excel Gold Mining Inc. (Can. Feb. 12, 1990 amalg.)
Dec. 5, 2013 – Filed for protection under the Bankruptcy and Insolvency Act (BIA).
2014 – Subsequently André Allard & associés inc. appointed trustee under the BIA and a proposal was made to creditors which was accepted by said creditors in March 2014. Court approval was received Apr. 17, 2014. (see FPsurvey - Mines & Energy)

Excel India Growth & Income Fund (Ont. Apr. 23, 2015)
July 14, 2017 – Merged into Excel India Balanced Fund; basis 2.5005 Excel Balanced ser. X units plus final distrib. of 4¢ cash for 1 Excel India Growth tr. unit.

Excel India Trust (Ont. June 29, 2007)
July 28, 2010 – Voluntarily delisted pursuant to merger with Excel India Fund; basis 1 Excel India Fund ser.A unit for 1 trust unit.

Excel Latin America Bond Fund (Ont. May 30, 2012)
Sept. 3, 2015 – Merged into Excel High Income Fund (open-ended fund); basis 1 Excel High ser. F unit. for 1 Excel Latin cl. A unit.

Excel Latin America Bond Fund II (Ont. Apr. 23, 2013)
Sept. 3, 2015 – Merged into Excel High Income Fund (open-ended fund); basis 1 Excel High ser. F unit. for 1 Excel Latin cl. A unit.

Excel Petroleums Ltd. (Alta. 1959)
1969 – Name changed to Westburne Petroleum & Minerals Ltd. ■

Excel-Tech Ltd. (Can. May 29, 1981)
Dec. 3, 2007 – Acquired by Natus Medical Incorporated for $3.25 per sh.

Excel Transcontinental Corporation (Alta. May 11, 1988)
Nov. 1, 1996 – Dissolved and struck off register.

Excellerated Resources Inc. (B.C. Jan. 18, 1983)
Feb. 28, 2000 – Name changed to Consolidated Excellerated Resources Inc.; basis 1 new for 5.8 old shs. ■

Excellium Inc. (N.B. May 22, 2009)
Jan. 24, 2014 – Name changed to XL-ID Solutions Inc. ■

Excello Mines Ltd. (Ont. 1933)
Nov. 21, 1955 – Dissolved.

Excellon Resources Inc. (B.C. Mar. 4, 1987)
May 31, 2012 – Continued into Ontario. (see FPsurvey - Mines & Energy)

Excelsior Energy Limited (Alta. Sept. 6, 2006 amalg.)
Nov. 9, 2010 – Formed AOC (ELE) Corp. in Alberta on amalgamation with 1558693 Alberta Ltd., a wholly owned subsid. of Athabasca Oil Sands Corp.; basis 36¢ cash or 0.0347 Athabasca shs. for 1 Excelsior sh. (see Athabasca Oil Sands Corp.)

The Excelsior Life Insurance Company (Ont. Aug. 7, 1889)
Jan. 16, 1989 – Name changed to Aetna Life Insurance Company of Canada. ■

Excelsior Mines Ltd. (Ont. 1952)
July 1979 – Dissolved.

Excelsior Mining Corp. (B.C. June 9, 2005)
Nov. 14, 2024 – Name changed to Gunnison Copper Corp. (see FPsurvey - Mines & Energy)

Excelsior Oils, Ltd. (unknown)
Wound up.

Excelsior Refineries Ltd. (Alta. 1949)
Mar. 1958 – Richwell Petroleums Ltd. acquired all assets of Excelsior; basis 1 Richwell for 2 Excelsior shs.

Exceptional Technologies Fund 5 (VCC) Inc. (B.C. Dec. 17, 1997)
Apr. 13, 2007 – Dissolved via Plan of Liquidation. Final in-kind distribution was $0.53 per sh.

Exchange Income Corporation (Can. Jan. 24, 2002)
Mar. 31, 2009 – Continued into British Columbia.
June 4, 2009 – Continued into Canada. (see FPsurvey - Industrials)

The Exchange Industrial Group Inc. (Man. Sept. 27, 2002)
May 10, 2004 – Plan of Arrangement agreement with Perimeter Aviation Ltd. and Perimeter Airlines (Inland) Ltd. to form a new company named Exchange Industrial Income Fund. This transaction was considered to be the company's Qualifying Transaction. (see Exchange Industrial Income Fund)

Exchange Industrial Income Fund (Man. Mar. 22, 2004)
July 31, 2009 – Converted into newly incorporated Exchange Income Corporation; basis 1 Exchange Income com. sh. for 1 Exchange Industrial trust unit.

Exchange Resources Ltd. (Alta. Feb. 16, 1988)
Sept. 30, 1994 – Acquired by Mannville Oil & Gas Ltd. for $2.75 per sh. (see Mannville Oil & Gas Ltd.)

Exchequer Resource Corp. (Alta. Feb. 19, 2001)
Oct. 24, 2004 – Continued into British Columbia.
July 18, 2014 – Name changed to CBD MED Research Corp.; basis 1 new for 10 old shs. ■

Exclamation International Incorporated (Alta. Jan. 5, 1999)
Feb. 17, 2000 – Continued into Ontario.
July 16, 2002 – Name changed to Points International Ltd. ■

Exclusive Resources Ltd. (B.C. 1969)
Mar. 3, 1975 – Dissolved.

Exco Energy Ltd. (Can. May 23, 1984)
Jan. 2, 2003 – Dissolved.

Executive Explorations Ltd. (Ont. 1966)
1968 – Merged into Boeing Holdings & Explorations Ltd.; basis 1 new for 5 old shs.

Executive Inn Group Corporation (Can. July 7, 1997)
July 25, 2007 – Privatized all shs. redeemed at $0.97 per sh.

Exel Explorations Ltd. (B.C. 1969)
Nov. 1, 1977 – Name changed to Northern Lights Resources Ltd.; basis 1 new for 5 old shs. ■

Exelerate Health Inc. (B.C. May 8, 2018)
Feb. 19, 2019 – Name changed to Exelerate Capital Corp. (see FPsurvey - Industrials)

ExelTech Aerospace Inc. (Can. June 21, 2004 amalg.)
May 29, 2010 – Assigned into bankruptcy. RSM Richter Inc. appointed trustee.
June 2, 2010 – Petitioned into receivership. RSM Richter Inc. appointed receiver.
Dec. 6, 2012 – Final distribution to be made on or about Dec. 21, 2012. Secured creditors repaid in full; unsecured creditor suffered a shortfall. No distributions to shldrs. Application made for discharge of trustee.
Mar. 20, 2013 – Receiver was discharged.

Exeter Capital Corporation (Alta. 1987)
May 25, 1989 – Name changed to DGE Technologies Corporation; basis 1 new for 4 old shs. ■

Exeter Mines Ltd. (B.C. June 25, 1969)
May 30, 1975 – Name changed to Tinta Hill Mines Ltd.; basis 1 new for 5 old shs. ■

Exeter Mining Inc. (B.C. 1987)
Aug. 22, 1994 – Dissolved and struck off register.

Exeter Oil & Gas Limited (B.C. 1980)
Apr. 11, 2000 – Name changed to Terradyne Energy Corporation and continued into Alberta; basis 1 new for 3 old shs. ■

Exeter Resource Corporation (B.C. Feb. 10, 1984)
Aug. 9, 2017 – All o/s com. shs. not already held acquired by Goldcorp Inc.; basis 0.12 Goldcorp com. shs. for 1 Exeter sh. (see Goldcorp Inc.)

ExGen Resources Inc. (Alta. May 9, 1996)
Jan. 11, 2019 – Continued into British Columbia. (see FPsurvey - Mines & Energy)

Exile Resources Inc. (Can. Aug. 9, 2005)
July 30, 2012 – Name changed to Oando Energy Resources Inc.; basis 1 new for 16.28 old shs. ■

Exito Energy Inc. (Alta. Nov. 1, 2010)
Dec. 6, 2012 – Name changed to Artisan Energy Corporation pursuant to Qualifying Transaction reverse takeover acquisition of Bentley Oil & Gas Ltd.; basis 1 new for 2 old shs. ■

Exito Energy II Inc. (Alta. Nov. 11, 2010)
Jan. 26, 2018 – Formed Good Life Networks Inc. in British Columbia following Qualifying Transaction reverse takeover acquisition of and amalgamation with (old) Good Life Networks Inc.; basis 1 new for 2 old shs. ■

Exito Minerals Ltd. (B.C. Aug. 16, 1996)
Aug. 27, 1999 – Name changed to eVirus Software Corporation. ■

Exmar Resources Ltd. (B.C. 1983)
Oct. 27, 1989 – Amalgamated with Caribbean Resources Corp. (0.4215 for 1), Mishi Lake Resources Inc. (1 principal escrow sh. for 1) and Mishibishu Resources Ltd. (0.6278 for 1) to form Mishibishu Gold Corporation; basis 0.5334 new Mishibishi Gold sh. for 1 old sh. (see Mishibishu Gold Corporation)

Exmoor Oil & Gas Corporation (Can. Aug. 2, 1929; via letters patent)
Jan. 22, 1990 – Name changed to Koala Kreme Inc.; basis 1 new for 2 old shs. ■

Exmouth Capital Corp. (B.C. Nov. 6, 1998)
Dec. 22, 2003 – Transaction with PhotoChannel Networks Inc. (PNI) to acquire and distribute 2,450,000 PNI shs. to shldrs. Subsequent wind-up represented company's Qualifying Transaction. (see Photochannel Networks Inc.)

Exol Industries Inc. (B.C. July 30, 1970)
July 19, 1991 – Name changed to BY & G Ventures Corp.; basis 1 new for 3 old shs. ■

Exor Data Inc. (B.C. July 3, 1987)
Apr. 22, 1998 – Name changed to Conac Software Corporation following acquisition of The Conac Group Inc.; basis 1 new for 3 old shs. ■

Expanded Metal Corporation (Can. 1986 amalg.)
Jan. 17, 1990 – Name changed to Dramex Corporation. ■

Expander Mines & Petroleums Ltd. (Alta. 1955)
Nov. 28, 1973 – Name changed to Northrim Mines Ltd.; basis 1 new for 20 old shs. ■

Expatriate Resources Ltd. (B.C. May 21, 1993)
Dec. 20, 2004 – Name changed to Yukon Zinc Corporation pursuant to plan of arrangement to separate certain properties into a new co. named Pacifica Resources Ltd.; basis 1 Yukon Zinc sh. and 1 Pacifica sh. for 1 Expatriate sh. ■

Expedition Energy Inc. (Alta. May 28, 1996)
Nov. 6, 2007 – Acquired by Salvo Energy Corporation for $0.34 per sh.

Expedition Mining Inc. (B.C. Feb. 6, 1986)
Feb. 4, 2016 – Name changed to Imagin Medical Inc. following reverse takeover acquisition of BSS Life Science Inc. (see FPsurvey - Industrials)

Expeditor Resource Group Ltd. (B.C. Sept. 1, 1983)
Aug. 2, 1989 – Name changed to Mt. Expeditor Resources Ltd.; basis 1 new for 5 old shs. ■

Expense Management and Control, Inc. (Tex. 1985)
Mar. 23, 1990 – Name changed to Integrated Travel Systems, Inc. ■

Experion Holdings Ltd. (Can. Sept. 20, 2017)
June 14, 2021 – Name changed to Citizen Stash Cannabis Corp. ■

Explogas Inc. (Alta. Jan. 25, 1988)
Sept. 25, 1996 – Name changed to EXP Resources Ltd.; basis 1 new for 6 old shs. ■

Explogas Ltd. (Can. Apr. 4, 1996)
Jan. 18, 2001 – Name changed to MD Multimedia Inc. ■

Explor Resources Inc. (Alta. Apr. 4, 1990)
Dec. 30, 2019 – Amalgamated with 2227390 Alberta Ltd., a wholly owned subsid. of Galleon Gold Corp., to form GGO Gold Corp.; basis 0.5 Galleon Gold com. sh. for 1 Explor Resources sh.
Dec. 30, 2019 – Name changed to GGO Gold Corp.

Exploration Acabit Inc. (Que. Nov. 9, 1989 amalg.)
Aug. 22, 1996 – Name changed to Western Pacific Mining Exploration Inc. ■

Exploration Aiguebelle Inc. (Que. 1980)
Sept. 20, 1983 – Name changed to Aiguebelle Resources Inc. ■

Exploration Aster Inc. (Can. Apr. 11, 1986)
Nov. 3, 1989 – Name changed to Canspar Resources Inc.; basis 1 new for 10 old shs. (see FPsurvey - Mines & Energy)

Exploration Aurtois Inc. (Can. Feb. 3, 2005)
Mar. 7, 2023 – Dissolved for non-compliance.

Exploration Duverny Inc. (Que. Apr. 26, 1989)
Jan. 2, 1992 – Amalgamated with Bay Ressources et Services Inc. (1 for 5.24), Monique Exploration Inc. (1 for 5.35) and private co. Ste-Geneviève Explorations (1991) Inc. to form SEG Exploration Inc.; basis 1 SEG sh. for 3.71 Duverny shs. (see SEG Exploration Inc.)

Exploration Louphior Inc. (Can. 1987)
Feb. 12, 1990 – Formed Temisca Resources Inc. in Canada on amalgamation with 169457 Canada Inc.; basis 1 new for 1 169457 Canada sh. and 1 new for 4 Exploration Louphior shs. ■

Exploration Mirandor Inc. (Can. Jan. 22, 1987)
June 10, 2004 – Dissolved.

Exploration Monicor Inc. (Que. 1985)
Oct. 13, 1988 – Name changed to Monique Exploration Inc.; basis 1 new for 4 old shs. ■

Exploration Terrenex Inc. (Alta. Sept. 11, 1991 amalg.)
Nov. 16, 1993 – Name changed to Terrenex Ventures Inc.; basis 1 new for 10 old shs. ■

Exploration Trois-Dimensions Inc. (Can. Jan. 20, 1986)
Dec. 13, 1996 – Name changed to Tiaro Bay Resources Inc. (see FPsurvey - Mines & Energy)

Explorations Deux-Montagnes Inc. (Can. Jan. 6, 1987)
Sept. 10, 1990 – Name changed to Intermont Exploration Inc. ■

Explorations Mon-Dor Inc. (Que. Dec. 18, 1981)
Dec. 2, 1988 – Name changed to Cristobal Resources Inc.; basis 1 new for 10 old shs. ■

Explorator Resources Inc. (Alta. May 18, 2005)
June 22, 2007 – Continued into Ontario.
May 20, 2011 – Acquired by Sociedad Punta del Cobre S.A. for $0.685 per sh.

Explorer Flow-Through Limited Partnership (Ont. Nov. 27, 2003)
Feb. 15, 2006 – Dissolved with net asset value of $28.01 per unit.

Explorer Petroleum Corp. (B.C. Sept. 16, 1950)
Sept. 25, 1985 – Name changed to Consolidated Explorer Petroleum Corporation; basis 1 new for 5 old shs. ■

Explorers Alliance Ltd. (Man. 1943)
Dec. 1963 – Charter cancelled.

Explorex Capital Ltd. (B.C. Jan. 6, 2011)
June 11, 2012 – Name changed to Explorex Resources Inc. pursuant to Qualifying Transaction acquisition of mineral property option agreement. ■

Explorex Resources Inc. (B.C. Jan. 6, 2011)
Apr. 28, 2020 – Name changed to Raffles Financial Group Limited pursuant to reverse takeover acquisition of Raffles Financial Pte. Ltd.; basis 1 new for 25.94658 old shs. ■

Expo Iron Ltd. (Que. 1969)
Jan. 25, 1986 – Charter cancelled.

Expo Ungava Mines Ltd. (Ont. 1966)
July 29, 1980 – Amalgamated with Ron-Roy Uranium Mines Ltd. (1 for 5) to form Exroy Resources Ltd.; basis 1 new for 8 old shs. (see Exroy Resources Ltd.)

Export Development Corporation (Can. Oct. 1, 1969; via Export Development Act)
Dec. 21, 2001 – Name changed to Export Development Canada.

Export Nickel Corp. of Canada Ltd. (Ont. 1956)
Nov. 1961 – Charter cancelled.

Export Red Lake Gold Mines Ltd. (Ont. 1944)
1952 – Charter cancelled.

Export Tyre Holding Co. (Del. 1986)
Jan. 31, 1995 – Amalgamated with Arizona/Guam Investment Company; basis 1 new ser. B com. sh. for 1 com. sh. and 1 new ser. A pref. sh. for 1 old ser. A pref. sh.

Express Capital Corp. (B.C. Nov. 11, 2014)
Apr. 14, 2021 – Name changed to EEE Exploration Corp. ■

Express Resources Ltd. (B.C. Feb. 17, 1983)
June 27, 1988 – Name changed to First Star Energy Ltd.; basis 1 new for 2 old shs. ■

Exquisite Form Brassiere (Canada) Limited (Ont. 1949)
Apr. 20, 1983 – Placed into receivership. Assets liquidated and no distribution made to shldrs.

Exroy Resources Ltd. (Ont. July 29, 1980 amalg.)
Sept. 30, 1994 – Name changed to Birim Goldfields Inc. following reverse takeover acquisition of Birim Goldfields Ltd.; basis 1 new cl. A sh. and 1 wt. for 4 old com. shs. ■

Exshaw Oil Corporation (Alta. Oct. 13, 2006)
Nov. 8, 2019 – Name changed to Topaz Energy Corp. (see FPsurvey - Mines & Energy)

Extant Investments Inc. (B.C. July 27, 1979)
Nov. 14, 2001 – Name changed to Sydney Resource Corporation. ■

Extendicare (Canada) Limited (Can. Aug. 7, 1968; via Dominion charter)
Feb. 24, 1974 – Name changed to Extendicare Ltd. ■

Extendicare Inc. (Can. Aug. 7, 1968; via Dominion charter)
Nov. 10, 2006 – Converted into an income trust named Extendicare Real Estate Investment Trust (REIT). Basis for sub. voting shldrs.: 1 Assisted Living Concepts, Inc. sub. voting cl. A com. sh. plus either 1 REIT unit, or 1 cl. B Extendicare L.P. unit, or a combination thereof for 1 sub. voting sh. Basis for multiple voting shldrs.: 1 Assisted Living Concepts, Inc. multiple voting cl. B com. sh. plus either 1.075 REIT unit, or 1.075 Extendicare Holding Partnership L.P. unit, or a combination thereof, for 1 multiple voting sh.

Extendicare Ltd. (Can. Aug. 7, 1968; via Dominion charter)
Nov. 29, 1983 – Name changed to Crownx Inc. ■

Extendicare Real Estate Investment Trust (Ont. Sept. 11, 2006)
July 1, 2012 – Succeeded by Extendicare Inc. pursuant to plan of arrangement whereby Extendicare Inc. was formed to facilitate the conversion of the trust into a corporation. (see FPsurvey - Industrials)

Extension Oil Co. Ltd. (Alta. 1938)
1941 – Assets transferred to Extension Oil Royalties Ltd. Shldrs. received 1% net royalty in Extension No. 1 and in Extension No. 2 wells for 25,000 old shs.

Extenway Solutions Inc. (Can. Sept. 13, 2005 amalg.)
Apr. 13, 2016 – Deemed to have filed an assignment in bankruptcy. PricewaterhouseCoopers Inc. was appointed as trustee and all officers and directors resigned.

Exterior Petroleums Ltd. (Alta.)
1958 – Struck off register.

Extorre Gold Mines Limited (Can. Dec. 21, 2009)
Aug. 27, 2012 – Acquired by Yamana Gold Inc.; basis $3.50 cash and 0.0467 Yamana Gold com. shs. for each sh. held. (see Yamana Gold Inc.)

Extotal Resources Inc. (B.C. 1979)
Nov. 1, 1989 – Name changed to Luxor Resources Ltd.; basis 1 new for 2 old shs. ■

Extracare Corporation (Can. Feb. 11, 1986)
Aug. 2, 1995 – Name changed to South Pacific Resources Corp.; basis 1 new for 3 old shs. ■

Extract Resources Limited (Australia Sept. 1, 1992)
May 28, 2012 – Acquired by Taurus Mineral Limited for A$8.65 per ord. sh.

Extreme CCTV Inc. (Can. Mar. 16, 2001)
Mar. 7, 2008 – Acquired by Robert Bosch GmbH for $5.00 per sh.

Extreme Energy Corporation (Alta. Aug. 16, 1996)
May 6, 2005 – Plan of Arrangement acquisition by C1 Energy Ltd.; basis 0.22 new C1 sh. for 1 old Extreme sh. and 0.22 new C1 purchase wt. for 1 old Extreme purchase wt. (see C1 Energy Ltd.)

Extreme Technologies Inc. (B.C. July 7, 1989)
Dec. 5, 1995 – Name changed to PortaCom Wireless, Inc.; basis 1 new for 1 old sh. ■

Extreme Vehicle Battery Technologies Corp. (B.C. Jan. 16, 2015)
Mar. 3, 2022 – Name changed to Cryptoblox Technologies Inc. ■

Exxadon Technology Corporation (Ont. Oct. 31, 1987)
Dec. 3, 1996 – Name changed to E.W.M.C. International Inc. ■

Exxel Energy Corp. (B.C. June 11, 1987)
May 30, 2008 – Name changed to XXL Energy Corp.; basis 1 new for 20 old shs. (see FPsurvey - Mines & Energy)

Exxeter Resources Corp. (Can. Dec. 28, 1978)
Aug. 3, 1995 – Name changed to Exxeter Resources Inc. ■

Exxeter Resources Inc. (Can. Dec. 28, 1978)
July 26, 1996 – Name changed to Cable Satisfaction International Inc.; basis 1 new for 25 old shs. ■

Eyecarrot Innovations Corp. (B.C. Sept. 7, 2011)
June 30, 2020 – Name changed to Binovi Technologies Corp. (see FPsurvey - Industrials)

Eyelogic Systems Inc. (Alta. Jan. 22, 1992)
Sept. 15, 2016 – Initial distribution of 33¢ cash per sh. made on Dec. 21, 2015, with final distribution of 4¢ cash per sh.
Oct. 13, 2016 – Voluntarily liquidated and dissolved.

Eyetel Technologies, Inc. (B.C. 1984)
July 20, 1994 – Continued into Wyoming.

Ezekiel Explorations Ltd. (B.C. Feb. 24, 1981)
Dec. 11, 1991 – Name changed to Aurex Resources Corp.; basis 1 new for 5 old shs. ■

Ezenet Corp. (Alta. May 7, 1998)
Sept. 26, 2001 – Acquired by COGNICASE Acquisition Corp., a wholly owned subsid. of COGNICASE Inc.; basis (i) 1 COGNICASE pref. sh. redeemable for $3.16, (ii) 0.393 COGNICASE shs. or (iii) a combination thereof for 1 Ezenet sh. (see COGNICASE Inc.)

F

F and G Aluminum Storms Ltd. (Ont. 1958)
Mar. 1963 – Name changed to Genoco Aluminum Ltd. ■

FA Power Fund (Ont. May 23, 2000)
June 19, 2008 – Amalgamated with First Asset PowerGen Fund (PGT); basis 1.0527 PGT trust units for 1 FA Power trust unit.

FABI Ltd. (Can. Jan. 29, 1962)
June 1967 – Name changed to Sintra Ltd. ■

FACS Limited (Ont. 1967)
1972 – Wound up. No assets available for distribution.

FACS Records Storage Income Fund (B.C. Feb. 1, 1997)
Feb. 8, 2001 – Wound up. Final distribution of remaining proceeds was $8.0367 per unit.

FAM Real Estate Investment Trust (Ont. Aug. 27, 2012)
Mar. 16, 2015 – Name changed to Slate Office Real Estate Investment Trust. ■

FAS International Limited (Alta. Aug. 21, 1987)
Feb. 2, 2003 – Struck from registry and dissolved.

FAX Capital Corp. (Can. Mar. 1, 1978)
July 7, 2022 – All o/s shs. not already held acquired by Federated Capital Corp.; basis $5.18 cash per sub. vtg. sh.

FBA Ventures Ltd. (N.L. May 23, 1989)
Apr. 15, 1994 – Name changed to NexStar Automation, Inc. pursuant to reverse takeover acquisition of NexStar Corporation. ■

F.C. Financial Corp. (B.C. 1983)
Dec. 13, 1991 – Name changed to West F.C. Finance Corp.; basis 1 new for 10 old shs. ■

FCA International Ltd. (Can. Apr. 20, 1945)
June 10, 1998 – Acquired by FCA Acquisition Corporation, an affiliate of NCO Group, Inc., for $9.60 per sh.

FCE Canada Inc. (Alta. Sept. 11, 2003)
Aug. 20, 2004 – Formed FuelCell Energy, Ltd. following amalgamation into parent company FuelCell Energy, Inc. ■

FCF Capital Inc. (Alta. Oct. 1, 1998)
May 16, 2016 – Name changed to Founders Advantage Capital Corp.; basis 1 new for 15 old shs. ■

FCMI Financial Corporation (Ont. 1981)
Apr. 9, 1997 – Privatized at $4.60 per sh.

F.D.G. Mining Inc. (B.C. Apr. 10, 2007)
May 8, 2013 – Name changed to Tango Gold Mines Incorporated. ■

F.D.R. Explorations Ltd. (Ont. 1974)
July 6, 1976 – Amalgamated with other cos. to form Gambit Consolidated Explorations Ltd.; basis 1 new for 3 old shs.

FDX Corp. (Del. 1971)
Feb. 10, 2000 – Name changed to FedEx Corporation.

FE Battery Metals Corp. (B.C. Oct. 12, 1966)
Dec. 9, 2024 – Name changed to Linear Minerals Corp. (see FPsurvey - Mines & Energy)

FET Resources Ltd. (Alta. July 12, 2002)
Jan. 16, 2007 – Privatized by Focus Energy Trust; basis 1.473 new trust units for 1 old exch. sh. (see Focus Energy Trust)

FFC Equities Ltd. (B.C. July 24, 1986)
Oct. 8, 1993 – Continued into Alberta.
Feb. 1, 1994 – Name changed to Outrider Resources Ltd. ■

FG Acquisition Corp. (B.C. Oct. 25, 2021)
Sept. 25, 2024 – Name changed to Saltire Capital Ltd. pursuant to Qualifying Acquisition of Strong/MDI Screen Systems, Inc. (see FPsurvey - Industrials)

F H P Explorations Ltd. (B.C. 1965)
1966 – Name changed to Nelway Mines Ltd. ■

F.K.I. International Inc. (Que. Jan. 30, 1967)
June 20, 2017 – Struck from register and dissolved.

FLO Capital Inc. (Alta. Nov. 27, 1995)
Sept. 25, 1996 – Name changed to CANCRETE Environmental Solutions Inc.; basis 1 new for 1 old sh. ■

FLYHT Aerospace Solutions Ltd. (Can. Feb. 28, 2003 amalg.)
Dec. 30, 2024 – Acquired by Firan Technology Group Corp. via plan of arrangement; basis (i) 11.03¢ cash and 0.0333 Firan Technology com. shs.; (ii) 33.79¢ cash; or (iii) 0.0495 Firan Technology com. sh,

FM Resources Corp. (B.C. July 30, 1971)
Sept. 1, 2006 – Name changed to Strikewell Energy Corp. (see FPsurvey - Mines & Energy)

F M Resources Ltd. (B.C. Sept. 1, 1981)
Oct. 20, 1987 – Name changed to Designed Data (Canada) Inc. ■

FMF Capital Group Ltd. (Ont. Oct. 20, 2004)
May 18, 2007 – Amherst Capital, LLC appointed to act as trustee to liquidate remaining assets and wind down business operations of wholly owned FMF Capital, LLC. All officers and directors resigned. Proceeds from liquidation to be paid to creditors with no distrib. available for shldrs.
Aug. 1, 2008 – Dissolved and struck from register.

FMG Telecomputer Ltd. (Can. Apr. 5, 1983)
July 4, 1989 – Name changed to SOK Properties Ltd. ■

FMI Holdings Ltd. (B.C. Jan. 10, 2008)
Sept. 1, 2010 – Abakhan & Associates Inc. appointed liquidator. All officers and directors resigned.
Jan. 30, 2012 – All o/s com. shs. cancelled following the distribution of $0.5833 cash payable to shldrs. of record Jan. 18, 2012.

FMX Ventures Inc. (Ont. Sept. 23, 1935)
Dec. 5, 2011 – Name changed to Tolima Gold Inc. pursuant to reverse takeover transaction acquisition of Tolima Gold Corp.; basis 1 new for 2 old shs. ■

F. N. Burt Company, Limited (Ont. 1909)
Nov. 1938 – Amalgamated with Moore Corp., Ltd.; basis 1 cl. A sh. of Moore for 1 7% conv. pref. sh. of Burt and 3 com. shs. of Moore for 4 com. shs. of Burt.

FNI Fashion Network Inc. (B.C. Mar. 3, 1983)
Mar. 22, 1994 – Name changed to Gala-Bari International Inc.; basis 1 new for 5 old shs. ■

FNX Mining Company Inc. (Ont. June 26, 1984)
May 28, 2010 – Aquired by Quadra Mining Ltd.; basis $0.0001 plus 0.87 Quadra shs. for 1 FNX sh. (see Quadra FNX Mining Ltd.)

FOCH Consumer Electronics Corporation (B.C. Jan. 5, 1988)
Jan. 22, 1996 – Name changed to Hawkeye Gold Corporation; basis 1 new for 5 old shs. ■

F. P. Chapple Co. Ltd. (Ont. 1959)
1961 – Name changed to Frank Chapple Ltd. ■

FP Newspapers Income Fund (Ont. May 15, 2002)
Dec. 31, 2010 – Succeeded by FP Newspapers Inc. pursuant to plan of arrangement whereby FP Newspapers Inc. was formed to facilitate the conversion of the fund into a corporation and the fund was subsequently dissolved. (see FPsurvey - Industrials)

FP Resources Limited (N.L. Dec. 19, 1986)
Mar. 25, 2008 – Amalgamated with wholly owned 6916716 Canada Inc. to form new co. with same name FP Resources Limited, to carry on investment holding activities; basis 1 new com. sh. for 1,000 old com. shs. or 1 new pref. sh. for 1 com. sh. redeemable for $17.19.

FPE-Pioneer Electric Limited (Man. Jan. 15, 1946)
Nov. 30, 1972 – Name changed to Federal Pioneer Limited. ■

FPI Limited (Ont. Sept. 3, 1986 amalg.)
Dec. 19, 1986 – Continued into Newfoundland and Labrador.
Jan. 8, 2008 – Name changed to FP Resources Limited. ■

FPS Pharma Inc. (B.C. Sept. 1, 2004)
Jan. 16, 2017 – Name changed to Capha Pharmaceuticals Inc. (see FPsurvey - Industrials)

FRV Media Inc. (Can. Oct. 20, 1998)
Apr. 11, 2012 – Name changed to Global SeaFarms Corporation prior to reverse takeover acquisition of Global SeaFarms Group Inc.; basis 1 new for 50 old shs. ■

FSD Pharma Inc. (Ont. Nov. 1, 1998 amalg.)
Aug. 15, 2024 – Name changed to Quantum BioPharma Ltd.; basis 1 new for 65 old shs. (see FPsurvey - Industrials)

FSI Energy Group Inc. (Alta. Feb. 29, 2000)
Aug. 2, 2017 – Dissolved and struck from registry.

FSI Energy Services Inc. (Alta. Feb. 29, 2000)
June 6, 2012 – Name changed to FSI Energy Group Inc. ■

FSPI Technologies Corp. (Alta. Mar. 27, 1996)
Sept. 2, 2004 – Struck from the registry and dissolved.

FSR Industries Inc. (B.C. Nov. 21, 1983)
June 15, 1993 – Name changed to Syspower Multimedia Industries Inc. ■

FT Capital Ltd. (Alta. July 10, 1980 amalg.)
June 30, 2009 – Wound up and dissolved.

FTC Cards Inc. (B.C. Mar. 9, 2012)
May 4, 2022 – Name changed to Beyond Oil Ltd. pursuant to the reverse takeover acquisition of Beyond Oil Inc. (see FPsurvey - Industrials)

FTI Foodtech International Inc. (B.C. 1978)
Aug. 28, 2008 – Continued into Canada. (see FPsurvey - Industrials)

FTM Investment Corporation (Can. July 15, 1998)
Sept. 7, 2004 – Name changed to Cagim Real Estate Corporation following Qualifying Transaction acquisition of Edifice Centre d'Affaires Le Mesnil; basis 1 new for 5 old shs. ■

FTM Resources Inc. (Can. Mar. 2, 1983)
Feb. 27, 1985 – Name changed to First General Mine Management & Gold Corp.; basis 1 new for 2 old shs. ■

FUN Technologies Inc. (Can. Nov. 18, 2005)
Dec. 27, 2007 – Acquired by Liberty Media Corporation; basis £1.75 per sh.

FUN Technologies plc (U.K. June 24, 2003)
Mar. 8, 2006 – Scheme of Arrangement with UK-based Liberty Media Corporation to continue as a new company named FUN Technologies Inc.; basis 0.5453 new Fun Inc. sh. plus either 163.69 pence or C$3.290824 for 1 old FUN plc sh. (see FUN Technologies Inc.)

FVC First Venture Capital Corp. (B.C. Apr. 15, 1998)
Apr. 8, 1999 – Name changed to Lasik Vision Corporation following reverse takeover acquisition of Lasik Vision Canada Inc. ■

FW Omnimedia Corp. (Alta. Aug. 7, 1996)
Feb. 2, 2009 – Struck from registry and dissolved.

F.W. Woolworth Company (N.Y. 1911)
Aug. 7, 1989 – Name changed to Woolworth Corporation after becoming a wholly owned subsid. of Woolworth Corporation. ■

Fab Metal Mines Ltd (Ont. 1944)
Mar. 1976 – Charter cancelled.

Fabled Copper and Gold Corp. (B.C. Apr. 27, 2016)
June 16, 2021 – Name changed to Fabled Copper Corp. (see FPsurvey - Mines & Energy)

Fabled Copper Corp. (B.C. Dec. 15, 2014)
Oct. 19, 2020 – Name changed to Fabled Silver Gold Corp. (see FPsurvey - Mines & Energy)

Fabula Exploration Inc. (B.C. Dec. 11, 2015)
Dec. 31, 2018 – Name changed to Calyx Growth Corporation pursuant to the acquisition of New Gen Holdings Inc. ■

Facedrive Inc. (Alta. Jan. 18, 2018)
Dec. 31, 2019 – Continued into Ontario.
Oct. 4, 2022 – Name changed to Steer Technologies Inc. ■

Facet Energy Inc. (Alta. 1987)
Nov. 29, 1988 – Amalgamated with Raider Resources Inc. to continue as Raider Resources Inc.; basis 1 new for 1 old sh. (see Raider Resources Inc.)

Fahnestock Viner Holdings Inc. (Ont. Oct. 12, 1977)
Sept. 2, 2003 – Name changed to Oppenheimer Holdings Inc. ■

Fahrenheit Mining Co. Ltd. (Ont. 1946)
Feb. 14, 1973 – Dissolved.

Fair Harbour Mining Corporation (B.C. Dec. 9, 1986)
Dec. 16, 1991 – Name changed to Fair Resources Group Inc.; basis 1 new for 5 old shs. ■

Fair Oil and Gas Ltd. (Ont. 1948)
1960 – Struck off register.

Fair Resources Group Inc. (B.C. Dec. 9, 1986)
Dec. 2, 1992 – Name changed to Southhampton Enterprises Corp. ■

Fair Sky Resources Inc. (Alta. Mar. 21, 2006 amalg.)
Dec. 7, 2007 – Placed into receivership. Deloitte & Touche Inc. of Calgary, Alta., appointed interim receiver.

Fairbanks Gold Ltd. (B.C. 1988)
Feb. 3, 1992 – Acquired by Amax Gold Inc. through its wholly owned subsid., Amax Gold (B.C.) Ltd.; basis 2 Amax shs. and 1 wt. for 4 Fairbanks shs. (see Amax Gold Inc.)

Fairbanks Morse (Canada) Ltd. (Can. 1911)
Jan. 26, 1970 – Merged with Crucible Steel of Canada Ltd. into Colt Industries (Canada) Ltd. Colt Industries, Inc. then acquired all remaining public interest under its offer of $9.00 per sh.

Fairbanks Uranium Mines Ltd. (Ont. 1945)
Apr. 2, 1962 – Dissolved.

Fairbanks Yellowknife Gold Mines Ltd. (Ont. 1945)
July 16, 1952 – Name changed to Fairbanks Uranium Mines Ltd. ■

Fairborn Mines Ltd. (B.C. 1965)
July 26, 1976 – Dissolved.

Fairborne Energy Ltd. (Alta. Jan. 9, 2002)
July 7, 2003 – Amalgamated in Alberta to continue with same name.
Dec. 19, 2007 – Amalgamated in Alberta to continue with same name.
Jan. 9, 2013 – Name changed to Santonia Energy Inc. ■

Fairborne Energy Trust (Alta. Apr. 20, 2005)
Dec. 24, 2007 – Merged and amalgamated with Fairborne Energy Ltd.; basis 1 Fairborne Energy Trust exch. shs. for 1 Fairborne Energy Ltd. com. sh. (see Fairborne Energy Ltd.)

Fairchild Aircraft Limited (Can. 1929)
Voluntarily liquidated. Amount of $264,546 distributed to shldrs. at rate of $2.07 per sh. Sh. certs. cancelled.

Fairchild Gold Corporation (B.C. Apr. 12, 1977)
Dec. 7, 1990 – Name changed to First International Metals Corp.; basis 1 new for 3 old shs. ■

Fairchild Investments Inc. (B.C. July 26, 1979)
June 26, 1995 – Continued into Bermuda.
Sept. 7, 1995 – Name changed to Fairchild Investments Ltd. ■

Fairchild Investments Ltd. (Bermuda June 26, 1995)
Nov. 12, 2009 – Name changed to Stone Resources Limited.

Fairchild Lake Gold Mines Ltd. (Ont. 1950)
1958 – Charter cancelled.

Fairchild Resources Inc. (B.C. Apr. 12, 1977)
Nov. 18, 1988 – Name changed to Fairchild Gold Corporation. ■

Faircoff Athabasca Uranium Mines Ltd. (Ont. 1950)
Mar. 1976 – Charter cancelled.

Faircourt Income & Growth Split Trust (Ont. Oct. 29, 2004)
Nov. 1, 2010 – Merged into Faircourt Split Trust; basis 0.954377 Faircourt Split unit for 1 Faircourt Income unit and 1 Faircourt Split pfd. sh. for 1 Faircourt Income pfd. sh. (see Faircourt Split Trust)

Faircourt Income Split Trust (Ont. Feb. 14, 2003)
Feb. 2, 2007 – Merged into Income & Growth Split Trust (renamed Faircourt Income & Growth Split Trust); basis 1 new pfd. for 1 old pfd. and 0.60851 new unit for 1 old unit. (see Faircourt Income & Growth Split Trust)

Faircourt Split Five Trust (Ont. July 29, 2003)
Feb. 2, 2007 – Merged into Income & Growth Split Trust (renamed Faircourt Income & Growth Split Trust); basis 1 new pfd. sh. for 1 old pfd. sh. and 1.6547 new units for 1 old unit. (see Faircourt Income & Growth Split Trust)

Faircourt Split Seven Trust (Ont. Feb. 25, 2004)
Feb. 2, 2007 – Merged into Income & Growth Split Trust (renamed Faircourt Income & Growth Split Trust); basis 1 new pfd. sh. for 1 old pfd. sh. and 1.42055 new units for 1 old unit. (see Faircourt Income & Growth Split Trust)

Faircourt Split Trust (Ont. Feb. 27, 2006)
Dec. 8, 2023 – Terminated. Cash distrib. to be made on a pro rata basis.

Fairfax Africa Holdings Corporation (Can. Apr. 28, 2016)
Dec. 15, 2020 – Name changed to Helios Fairfax Partners Corporation. (see FPsurvey - Industrials)

Fairfax Bay Resources Inc. (Ont. Oct. 11, 1984)
Feb. 27, 1990 – Name changed to Zynex Corporation; basis 1 new for 3 old shs. ■

Fairfax Capital Inc. (B.C. Feb. 11, 2005)
Jan. 28, 2008 – Name changed to Free Energy International Inc. following Qualifying Transaction reverse takeover acquisition of Free Energy Solutions Inc. completed on Nov. 5, 2007. ■

Fairfax Mines Ltd. (Ont. 1947)
July 27, 1976 – Charter cancelled.

Fairfield Explorations Inc. (Can. Apr. 15, 1985)
Sept. 21, 1993 – Name changed to Fairstar Explorations Inc. ■

Fairfield Minerals Ltd. (B.C. Oct. 23, 1984)
Dec. 31, 2001 – Formed Almaden Minerals Ltd. in British Columbia on amalgamation with Almaden Resources Corporation (deemed acquiror); basis 0.77 new for 1 Almaden Resources sh. and 1 new for 1 Fairfield sh. (see FPsurvey - Mines & Energy)

Fairhaven Resources Ltd. (B.C. Sept. 27, 1962)
May 29, 2002 – Name changed to International Fairhaven Resources Ltd.; basis 1 new for 5 old shs. ■

Fairlady Energy Inc. (B.C. Feb. 8, 1980)
Feb. 10, 1988 – Continued into Canada.
July 5, 2017 – Voluntarily dissolved and struck from register.

Fairlane Oil & Gas Ltd. (Alta. Mar. 15, 1963)
1963 – Name changed to Numac Oil & Gas Ltd. ■

Fairlane Transportation Inc. (B.C. Jan. 18, 1983)
Oct. 21, 1998 – Name changed to Excellerated Resources Inc.; basis 1 new for 4 old shs. ■

Fairley Red Lake Gold Mines Ltd. (Ont. 1946)
Oct. 22, 1962 – Dissolved.

Fairline Energy Services Inc. (Can. June 29, 1995)
May 15, 2000 – Acquired by Wellco Energy Services; basis 1.5 Wellco shs. for 1 Fairline sh. (see Wellco Energy Services Inc.)

Fairline Financial International Corporation (Can. June 29, 1995)
June 3, 1998 – Name changed to Fairline Energy Services Inc.; basis 1 new for 1 old sh. ■

Fairmile Acquisitions Inc. (Can. May 27, 1987)
Mar. 7, 1996 – Name changed to Fairmile Gold Corporation. ■

Fairmile Gold Corporation (Can. May 27, 1987)
Sept. 19, 2000 – Name changed to Fairmile Goldtech Inc.; basis 1 new for 10 old shs. ■

Fairmile Goldtech Inc. (Can. May 27, 1987)
Feb. 23, 2005 – Continued into British Columbia.
Jan. 5, 2015 – Dissolved and struck from register.

Fairmont Gas & Oil Corporation (B.C. 1968)
May 23, 1984 – Name changed to Cater Energy, Inc.; basis 1 new for 5 old shs. ■

Fairmont Hotels & Resorts Inc. (Can. Nov. 27, 1989)
May 11, 2006 – Acquired by Kingdom Hotels International and Colony Capital, LLC for US$45 per sh.

Fairmont Resources Inc. (Alta. Feb. 12, 1987)
Jan. 8, 1996 – Name changed to Endeavour Resources Inc.; basis 1 new for 1 old sh. ■

Fairmont Resources Inc. (B.C. May 25, 2007)
June 11, 2020 – Name changed to i3 Interactive Inc. pursuant to reverse takeover acquisition of Influencers Interactive Inc. ■

Fairmount Energy Inc. (Can. Apr. 1, 2002)
Dec. 1, 2009 – Acquired by Delphi Energy Corp.; basis 0.3571 Delphi shs. for 1 Fairmount sh. (see Delphi Energy Corp.)

Fairmount Mining & Explorations Ltd. (Ont. 1969)
July 30, 1979 – Dissolved.

Fairquest Energy Limited (Alta. Mar. 7, 2005)
June 6, 2007 – Acquired by Fairborne Energy Trust; basis 0.39 trust unit of Fairborne Energy for 1 Fairquest Energy com. sh.
Feb. 14, 2008 – Dissolved.

Fairstar Explorations Inc. (Can. Apr. 15, 1985)
Aug. 18, 2005 – Formed FairWest Energy Corporation in Canada on amalgamation with Western Energy Corporation, constituting a reverse takeover by Western Energy; basis 1 new for 1 Western Energy sh. and 1 new for 6.7226 Fairstar shs. ■

Fairview Capital Corp. (Man. May 10, 2000)
June 15, 2001 – Name changed to Bald Eagle Golf Corp. ■

Fairview Corporation (Ontario) Limited (Ont. 1958)
May 31, 1974 – Amalgamated with Cadillac Development Corporation Limited, Canadian Equity & Development Corporation Ltd., Canadian Equity & Development Company Ltd. and 3 other cos. to form Cadillac Fairview Corporation; basis 1 new for 1 Cadillac Development sh., 1.2 new for 1 Canadian Equity & Development Co. Ltd. sh. and 1 new for 1 post-split Fairview Corporation of Canada Limited sh. (1.4-for-1 on a pre-split basis). Fairview shs. continued to trade after a 1.4-for-1 split. The final step of the merger was effected Feb. 29, 1976, when Cadillac Fairview (Ontario charter) and Fairview Corporation of Canada Limited (Dominion charter)

amalgamated to form Cadillac Fairview Corporation. (see Cadillac Fairview Corporation)

Fairview Mining Inc. (Ont. 1973)
Mar. 1, 1978 – Amalgamated with 3 other cos. to form Jaridge Explorations Inc.; basis 1 new for 4 old shs.

Fairway Automotive Industries Ltd. (Ont. 1959)
Mar. 18, 1988 – Name changed to Fairway Industries Ltd.; basis 1 new for 3 old shs. ■

Fairway Diversified Income and Growth Trust (Ont. Feb. 26, 2004)
Jan. 26, 2009 – Amalgamated into Crown Hill Fund; basis 1.30587 Crown Hill Fund units for 1 Fairway Diversified trust unit. (see Crown Hill Fund)

Fairway Flinflon Mines Ltd. (Ont. 1951)
Dec. 1970 – Charter cancelled.

Fairway Industries Ltd. (Ont. 1959)
Apr. 6, 1994 – Name changed to Pharmaglobe Inc.; basis 1 new for 3 old shs. (see FPsurvey - Industrials)

Fairway Investment Grade Income Fund (Ont. Feb. 25, 2005)
June 29, 2007 – Amalgamated with Global Preferred Securities Trust and subsequently merged into Fairway Diversified Income and Growth Trust; basis 0.678498 Fairway Diversified units for 1 Fairway Investment unit and 0.713949 Fairway Diversified units for 1 Global unit. (see Fairway Diversified Income and Growth Trust)

FairWest Energy Corporation (Can. Aug. 18, 2005 amalg.)
June 26, 2015 – Dissolved and struck from register,

Faith Mines Ltd. (Ont. May 14, 1985)
Feb. 4, 1986 – Continued into British Columbia.
Feb. 28, 1996 – Name changed to Panterra Minerals Inc.; basis 1 new for 10 old shs. ■

Faith Spring Venture Inc. (B.C. Oct. 26, 2011)
July 23, 2013 – Name changed to Viscount Mining Corp. pursuant to Qualifying Transaction reverse takeover acquisition of Viscount Mining Resources Ltd.; basis 1 new for 2 old shs. (see FPsurvey - Mines & Energy)

Fajana Resources Ltd. (Alta. 1987)
July 13, 1993 – Name changed to Kolvox Communications Inc.; basis 1 new for 1 old sh. ■

Falaise Lake Mines Ltd. (B.C. 1966)
Sept. 1973 – Name changed to Rosmac Mines Ltd.; basis 1 new for 5 old shs. ■

Falco Pacific Resource Group Inc. (B.C. Mar. 16, 2010)
July 24, 2014 – Name changed to Falco Resources Ltd. ■

Falco Resources Ltd. (B.C. Mar. 16, 2010)
June 15, 2015 – Continued into Canada. (see FPsurvey - Mines & Energy)

Falcon Explorations Ltd. (B.C. 1969)
Apr. 13, 1976 – Name changed to Bullseye Gas Corp.; basis 1 new for 5 old shs.

Falcon Gold Corp. (Ont. Nov. 24, 2006)
May 2, 2013 – Continued into British Columbia. (see FPsurvey - Mines & Energy)

Falcon Island Mining Co. Ltd. (Man. 1943)
1955 – Charter cancelled.

Falcon Lake Mining Corp. Ltd. (Ont. 1970)
May 1972 – Amalgamated into Bayfor Corp. Inc.; basis 1 new for 4 old shs.

Falcon Point Resources Ltd. (Ont. Mar. 15, 1979 amalg.)
July 20, 1998 – Name changed to Ontario Hose Specialties Inc. pursuant to reverse takeover acquisition of Ontario Hose Specialties Inc.; basis 1 new for 8 old shs. ■

Falcon Resources Inc. (B.C. Feb. 1980)
Jan. 31, 1986 – Name changed to International Falcon Resources Inc.; basis 2 new for 5 old shs. ■

Falcon Super Fax Graphics Inc. (Ont. May 29, 1987)
May 6, 1992 – Name changed to Falcon Group Ltd.; basis 2 new for 1 old sh. (see FPsurvey - Industrials)

Falcon Ventures Incorporated (B.C. Apr. 15, 1983)
June 26, 2008 – Name changed to Falcon Ventures International Inc. and continued into Alberta. ■

Falcon Ventures International Corp. (B.C. Apr. 15, 1983)
Dec. 24, 2002 – Name changed to Falcon Ventures Incorporated; basis 1 new for 10 old shs. ■

Falcon Ventures International Inc. (Alta. June 26, 2008)
Nov. 5, 2009 – Name changed to Firebird Resources Inc. and continued into British Columbia; basis 1 new for 5 old shs. ■

Falcon Well Services Ltd. (Can. Feb. 13, 1998 amalg.)
May 19, 1999 – Placed into receivership and Richer, Taylor & Allen Inc., of Calgary, Alta., was appointed receiver/manager. All of the assets were sold and the secured creditors suffered a shortfall. There were no funds available for distribution to unsecured creditors or shldrs.
Mar. 27, 2003 – Receiver discharged.

Falconbridge Copper Limited (Que. 1917)
Apr. 29, 1980 – Name changed to Corporation Falconbridge Copper. ■

Falconbridge Gold Corporation (Ont. Dec. 23, 1987)
Jan. 7, 1994 – Amalgamated with a wholly owned subsid. of Kinross Gold Corporation; basis 1 Kinross sh. for 1 Falconbridge sh.

Falconbridge Limited (Ont. Aug. 28, 1928)
June 22, 1994 – Amalgamated with Falconbridge Inc. and Trelleborg Mining Limited to form new co. with same name Falconbridge Limited. Previously, all o/s shs. were acquired by FL Acquisition Corp., jointly owned by Noranda Inc. and Trelleborg AB, effective Sept. 1989; basis $37 per sh.
June 30, 2005 – Remaining 41% interest acquired by Noranda Inc. and amalgamated to form new co. with same name Falconbridge Limited; basis 1.77 new Falconbridge (formerly Noranda) shs. for 1 old Falconbridge sh. Each Noranda pref. sh. or jr. pfce. sh. and old Falconbridge pref. sh. was converted into an equal number of pref. shs. or jr. pfce. shs. of the new Falconbridge Limited having the same attributes as before.

Falconbridge Limited (Ont. June 30, 2005 amalg.)
Nov. 1, 2006 – Com. shs. acquired by Swiss-based Xstrata plc for Cdn$62.50 per sh.
Oct. 24, 2007 – Name changed to Xstrata Canada Corporation. ■

Falconbridge Nickel Mines Ltd. (Ont. Aug. 28, 1928)
Apr. 20, 1982 – Name changed to Falconbridge Limited. ■

Falconcrest Resources Inc. (Ont. Jan. 27, 1986)
Aug. 21, 1998 – Formed SFP Communications Group Inc. following acquisition of Spencer Francey Peters Inc.; basis 1 new for 4 old shs. ■

Faldo Mines & Energy Corp. (Ont. Sept. 24, 1986)
May 19, 1992 – Name changed to Delayed Data Communications Inc.; basis 1 new for 3 old shs. ■

Faleck and Margolies Ltd. (Ont. 1977)
Apr. 20, 1990 – Delisted from the Alberta Stock Exchange. Subsequently dissolved.

Falgar Mining Corporation Ltd. (Ont. 1952)
1955 – Name changed to Sheraton Uranium Mines Ltd. ■

Falkirk Resources Corp. (B.C. Aug. 16, 1996)
June 26, 2013 – Name changed to Jemi Fibre Corp. following reverse takeover acquisition of Dual Enterprises Ltd.; basis 1 new for 10 old shs. ∎

Fall River Resources Ltd. (Alta. Feb. 5, 1998)
Dec. 23, 2004 – Continued into British Columbia.
Jan. 22, 2010 – Name changed to Earth Heat Resources Ltd. pursuant to Qualifying Transaction reverse takeover acquisition of Earth Heat Australia Pty Ltd. ∎

Fallinger Corporation (Que. 1971)
July 1976 – Name changed to Sogevex Inc. (see FPsurvey - Mines & Energy)

Fallinger Mining Corporation (Que. 1971)
Jan. 1973 – Name changed to Fallinger Corporation. ∎

Fallmac Nickel Mines Ltd. (Ont. 1952)
Mar. 1976 – Charter cancelled.

Falmouth Petroleum Ltd. (Can. Feb. 13, 1981)
Oct. 16, 1989 – Name changed to RoyShel Properties Ltd. ∎

Falnora Gold Mines Ltd. (Ont. 1950)
May 1967 – Charter cancelled.

Falvo Corporation (Ont. 1989 amalg.)
June 9, 1999 – Privatized; basis 1 cl. B sh. for 1 com. sh., redeemable for 92¢ per sh.

Falvo Estates Ltd. (Ont. Dec. 1, 1987 amalg.)
June 30, 1989 – Amalgamated with Conrex Corporation to form Falvo Corporation; basis 1 new for 5 Conrex shs. and 1 new for 1 Falvo Estates sh. (see Falvo Corporation)

Family Building Credits Ltd. (Can. 1953)
Dec. 1955 – Acquired by Interprovincial Building Credits Ltd.; basis 1 Interprovincial sh. for 3 Family shs.

Family Memorials Inc. (Ont. Feb. 26, 2002)
Dec. 16, 2012 – Continued into British Columbia.
Feb. 16, 2018 – Amalgamated with 1142431 B.C. Ltd.; basis 1 cl. A Amalco pref. sh. for 1 Family com. sh. immediately exchanged for 1 com. sh. of Thunder River Enerprises Inc. on a 1-for-1 basis.

Fan-Tan Mines Ltd. (B.C. 1966)
Oct. 1974 – Charter cancelled.

Fancamp Resources Ltd. (B.C. Jan. 16, 1986)
Nov. 4, 1999 – Name changed to Fancamp Exploration Ltd.; basis 1 new for 2 old shs. (see FPsurvey - Mines & Energy)

Fandom Sports Media Corp. (B.C. May 12, 2006)
Apr. 12, 2022 – Name changed to Fandifi Technology Corp. (see FPsurvey - Industrials)

Fanlogic Interactive Inc. (B.C. July 6, 2007)
Dec. 1, 2020 – Name changed to Health Logic Interactive Inc.; basis 1 new for 10 old shs. (see FPsurvey - Industrials)

Fano Mining & Exploration Inc. (Que. 1945)
May 27, 1971 – Name changed to Fanex Resources Ltd.; basis 1 new for 7 old shs.

Fano Uranium Mines Ltd. (Ont. 1954)
1956 – Acquired by Fano Mining & Exploration Inc. (see Fano Mining & Exploration Inc.)

FansUnite Entertainment Inc. (B.C. Nov. 9, 2018)
Aug. 22, 2024 – Voluntarily delisted.
Aug. 29, 2024 – Return of capital distrib. of $0.0725 cash per sh. payable to shldrs. of record Aug. 26, 2024. (see FPsurvey - Industrials)

Fantasy Aces Daily Fantasy Sports Corp. (B.C. June 17, 1998)
Dec. 3, 2018 – Dissolved and struck from register.

Fantasy Creations Limited (Ont. 1945)
1978 – Acquired by Sydney Fromer, pres., for $1.50 per sh.

Fantasy 6 Sports Inc. (B.C. Feb. 10, 2015)
June 9, 2017 – Name changed to Victory Square Technologies Inc. (see FPsurvey - Industrials)

Fantasy 360 Technologies Inc. (B.C. Nov. 16, 2016)
Feb. 3, 2022 – Name changed to XR Immersive Tech Inc. (see FPsurvey - Industrials)

Fantom Technologies Inc. (Ont. May 12, 1986)
Oct. 25, 2001 – Filed for protection under the Companies' Creditors Arrangement Act and all remaining officers and directors resigned.
Mar. 22, 2002 – Proceedings under the Companies' Creditors Arrangement Act were terminated and PricewaterhouseCoopers Inc. was appointed trustee in bankruptcy.

Far East Gold Inc. (Ont. Dec. 15, 1995 amalg.)
Apr. 21, 1997 – Acquired by KWG Resources Inc.; basis 1 KWG sh. plus 1/3 wts. for 2.68 Far East shs. (see KWG Resources Inc.)

Far East Minerals Ltd. (B.C. 1965)
Nov. 1979 – Charter cancelled.

Far East Resources Corporation (B.C. May 9, 1983)
Sept. 28, 1990 – Dissolved and struck off register.

Far Eastern Energy Corporation (Can. Jan. 22, 1990)
July 12, 2004 – Dissolved.

Far North Exploration Ltd. (Alta. 1955)
Dec. 1958 – Name changed to New Far North Exploration Ltd.; basis 1 new for 5 old shs. ∎

Far Resources Ltd. (B.C. July 7, 2005)
Jan. 7, 2022 – Name changed to Foremost Lithium Resource & Technology Ltd. ∎

Far West Industries Inc. (B.C. Aug. 12, 1981)
Nov. 13, 2003 – Plan of Arrangement with Digital Dispatch Systems Inc. (DDS); Ghai Investments Ltd. and 3776107 Canada Inc.; basis either 0.05 new DDS sh. or, $0.15 plus 1/40 new DDS sh. for 1 old Far West sh.

Far West Mining Ltd. (Alta. Aug. 25, 1994)
May 17, 2006 – Continued into British Columbia. (see Capstone Mining Corp.)
June 23, 2011 – Acquired by Capstone Mining Corp.; basis either (i) $9.19, (ii) 1.825 Capstone shs. plus $1.00 or (iii) 2.047 Capstone shs. plus $0.001 for 1 Far West sh. (see Capstone Mining Corp.)

Faraday Resources Inc. (Ont. May 4, 1967 amalg.)
Sept. 1, 1986 – Amalgamated with Marcon Canadian Holdings Inc. to form new co. with same name Faraday Resources Inc.; basis 1 new for 1 Faraday sh. (see Conwest Exploration Company Limited)
Sept. 3, 1993 – Acquired by Conwest Exploration Company Limited; basis 0.42 Conwest shs. for 1 Faraday sh. (see Conwest Exploration Company Limited)

Faraday Uranium Mines Ltd. (Ont. 1949)
1963 – Name changed to The Canadian Faraday Corporation Ltd.; basis 2 new for 5 old shs. ∎

Farallon Mining Ltd. (B.C. July 4, 1991)
Mar. 10, 2011 – Acquired by Nyrstar NV for Cdn$0.80 per sh.

Farallon Resources Ltd. (B.C. July 4, 1991)
June 16, 2009 – Name changed to Farallon Mining Ltd. ∎

Faraway Gold Mines Ltd. (B.C. 1984)
July 9, 1993 – Dissolved and struck off register.

Farboro Resources Inc. (Que. 1985)
Mar. 31, 1989 – Amalgamated with Oz Exploration Inc., Omega Exploration Inc., Norwood Exploration Inc., and Onyx Exploration Inc. to form Orient Resources Inc.

Farcroft Mines Ltd. (Ont. 1951)
Nov. 9, 1964 – Charter cancelled.

Fareport Capital Inc. (Ont. Apr. 17, 1997)
July 23, 2012 – Dissolved and struck from register.

Fargo Capital Corp. (B.C. Apr. 5, 2006)
July 16, 2007 – Name changed to Pacific Coast Nickel Corp. following Qualifying Transaction reverse takeover acquisition of Pacific Coast Nickel Corp. ∎

Fargo Oils Ltd. (Alta. 1950)
1968 – Merged into Reserve Oil and Gas Co.; basis 43 new for 100 old shs.

Fargo Resources Limited (B.C. Jan. 27, 1981)
Sept. 13, 1991 – Name changed to Lang Bay Resources Ltd.; basis 1 new for 4 old shs. ∎

The Farini Companies Inc. (Ont. Dec. 23, 1964)
Aug. 22, 2016 – Dissolved and struck from register.

The Farini Group Inc. (Ont. Dec. 23, 1964)
Sept. 11, 1997 – Name changed to The Farini Companies Inc.; basis 1 new for 10 old shs. ∎

Farm Energy Corporation (Alta. May 17, 1988)
Feb. 9, 2001 – Name changed to High Energy Ventures Inc. ∎

Farmers & Merchants Trust Company (Can. 1910)
Oct. 28, 1976 – Name changed to Commerce Capital Trust Company. ∎

Farmers & Merchants Trust Co. Ltd. (Can. 1910)
Apr. 3, 1975 – Name changed to Farmers & Merchants Trust Company. ∎

Farmers Edge Inc. (Man. Aug. 21, 2014 amalg.)
Aug. 15, 2022 – Continued into Canada.
Mar. 25, 2024 – All o/s shs. not already held acquired by Fairfax Financial Holdings Limited; basis 35¢ cash per sh.

Farmers Gas Company Limited (Ont. 1965)
Mar. 16, 1976 – Charter cancelled.

Farmers' Mutual Petroleums Ltd. (unknown)
1954 – Acquired by Canadian Pipe Lines & Petroleums Ltd.; basis 15 new for 16 old shs. (see Canadian Pipe Lines & Petroleums Ltd.)

Faro Petroleum Ltd. (Alta. May 19, 1994)
Oct. 7, 1997 – Name changed to Montauk Resource Corporation. (see FPsurvey - Mines & Energy)

Farrah Resources Ltd. (B.C. Apr. 29, 1977)
Sept. 26, 1988 – Dissolved and struck off register.

Farrell Oils Limited (Alta.)
1958 – Struck off register.

Farrell Rouyn Mines (Quebec) Ltd. (Que. 1937)
Jan. 12, 1959 – Dissolved.

Farwest Mining Ltd. (B.C. 1955)
Mar. 17, 1975 – Charter cancelled.

Farwest Tungsten Copper Mines Ltd. (B.C. 1955)
Apr. 1959 – Name changed to Farwest Mining Ltd. ∎

Fast Line Holding Inc. (B.C. Aug. 6, 2015 amalg.)
Oct. 23, 2023 – Dissolved for failure to file.

Fastfoot Industries Ltd. (B.C. June 13, 1995)
Dec. 14, 2001 – Name changed to Fab-Form Industries Ltd.; basis 1 new for 3 old shs. (see FPsurvey - Industrials)

Fastlane International Enterprises Inc. (B.C. 1983)
May 1993 – Continued into Wyoming.

Fasttask Technologies Inc. (B.C. Dec. 3, 2010)
June 1, 2021 – Name changed to Komo Plant Based Foods Inc. pursuant to the reverse takeover acquisition of Komo Plant Based Comfort Foods Inc. (Komo Comfort) and concurrent amalgamation of Komo Comfort and wholly owned 1285877 B.C. Ltd. (see FPsurvey - Industrials)

Fathom Oceanology Limited (Can. Dec. 6, 1968; via letters patent)
Nov. 24, 1989 – Acquired by Indal Limited, a wholly owned subsid. of RTZ Corp., PLC for $3.00 per sh.

Fatima Mining Co. Ltd. (Ont. 1956)
1964 – Name changed to Texmont Mines Ltd.; basis 1 new for 2 old shs. ■

Faulkenham Lake Gold Mines Ltd. (Ont. July 14, 1936)
1948 – Name changed to New Faulkenham Mines Ltd.; basis 1 new for 4 old shs. ■

Faustin Explorations Ltd. (Ont. 1947)
Sept. 15, 1960 – Charter cancelled.

Favourable Mines Ltd. (Ont. 1966)
1969 – Merged into Alchib Developments Ltd.; basis 12 new for 100 old shs.

Fawn Bay Development Ltd. (B.C. 1959)
Feb. 1973 – Name changed to Can-Trac Industries Ltd.; basis 1 new for 5 old shs. ■

Faymar Capital Corporation (Alta. July 29, 1996)
Oct. 30, 1997 – Name changed to Valu-net Corporation. ■

Feather Gold Resources Ltd. (B.C. Aug. 12, 1987)
Oct. 5, 1995 – Name changed to Sovereign Chief Ventures Ltd.; basis 1 new for 4.7 old shs. ■

Featherstone Resources Ltd. (B.C. June 14, 1977)
May 3, 2002 – Name changed to Newcastle Minerals Ltd.; basis 1 new for 3 old shs. ■

Feathertouch E-Comm Inc. (Can. Aug. 12, 1985)
June 10, 2004 – Dissolved.

Fecop Mines Ltd. (Ont. 1957)
1965 – Charter cancelled.

Fed-Med Services Corp. (Can. Sept. 10, 1987)
Dec. 5, 1990 – Name changed to Elk Point Game Ranching Corp. ■

Federal Business Development Bank (Can. Dec. 20, 1974)
July 13, 1995 – Name changed to Business Development Bank of Canada.

Federal Chibougamau Mines Ltd. (Ont. 1959)
1968 – Name changed to New Federal Chibougamau Mines Ltd.; basis 1 new for 10 old shs. ■

Federal Diversiplex Limited (Can. 1948)
Dec. 16, 1978 – Amalgamated into Hardee Farms International Ltd.; basis 3 new for 1 old Federal sh.

Federal Energy Corporation Limited (Alta. July 30, 1987)
Aug. 11, 1997 – Continued into British Columbia.
Aug. 18, 1997 – Name changed to Glenhaven Resources Inc. ■

Federal Express Corporation (Del. 1971)
Jan. 28, 1998 – Name changed to FDX Corp. ■

Federal Farms Limited (Can. 1948)
Nov. 1970 – Name changed to Federal Diversiplex Limited. ■

Federal Foundries & Steel Co. Ltd. (Ont. 1941)
1947 – Acquired by Quality Steels (Canada) Ltd.

Federal Gold Mines Ltd. (B.C. 1933)
1952 – Charter cancelled.

Federal Grain, Limited (Can. July 25, 1929; via Dominion charter)
Aug. 1, 1967 – Amalgamated in Canada to continue with same name.
Apr. 16, 1973 – Name changed to Federal Industries Ltd. ■

The Federal Group Inc. (Ont. 1963)
Oct. 15, 1994 – Dissolved and struck off register.

Federal Industries Ltd. (Can. Aug. 1, 1967 amalg.)
June 1, 1995 – Name changed to Russel Metals Inc. ■

Federal Kirkland Mines Ltd. (Alta. 1983)
Dec. 23, 1987 – Name changed to Coexco Petroleum Inc.; basis 1 new for 10 old shs. ■

Federal Kirkland Mining Co. Ltd. (Ont. Aug. 1927)
1958 – Merged into Cadamet Mines Ltd.; basis 1 new for 5 old shs.

Federal Metals Corporation (Que. 1952)
Aug. 1, 1978 – Amalgamated with Peninsula Metals Corp. to form Fedpen Ltée.

Federal Oil & Gas Corp. Ltd. (unknown)
Acquired by New Federal Oils, Ltd.; basis 1 new for 2 old shs.
1927 – Charter cancelled.

Federal Oils Limited (Alta. Aug. 24, 1937)
1950 – Assigned its holdings to Flock Oil & Gas Syndicate.

Federal Oils Syndicate No. 1 (unknown)
1966 – Sold to Darmac Oils Ltd. and dissolved.

Federal Pioneer Limited (Man. Jan. 15, 1946)
Jan. 27, 1978 – Continued into Canada.
May 18, 1990 – Acquired by Schneider Canada Inc. for $15 per sh.

Federal Trust & Savings Co. (Can. - unspecified)
June 26, 1974 – Amalgamated with subsid., County Savings & Loan Corp., to form Federal Trust Company.

Federal Trust Company (Ont. 1974 amalg.)
Mar. 1, 1981 – Central and Eastern Trust Company acquired 99.7% of o/s com. shs. in May 1980 for $5.00 million cash and $4.5 million in 7.5% cum. red. pref. shs. of Central and Eastern. co. amalg. with Central and Eastern Trust Company to form Central Trust Company. Shs. held by Central and Eastern Trust were cancelled and the remaining 3,295 shs. were converted into shs. of the new co. on basis of 1 new for 2 old shs.

Federal Trustco Inc. (Ont. Apr. 3, 1962)
July 1980 – Name changed to RealCap Holdings Limited. (see FPsurvey - Mines & Energy; FPsurvey - Industrials)

Federated Mining Corp. Ltd. (B.C. 1966)
1973 – Reported to be without material assets. Property sold 1973-74 for 1,160,006 shs. to Northrim Mines Ltd. to satisfy creditors and shldrs. Shldrs. received 1 sh. Northrim for 6.9484 old shs.; creditors received 1 sh. for $1.94 debt.

Federated Petroleums Ltd. (Alta. 1938)
1955 – Merged with Home Oil Co. Ltd.; basis 1 cl. A or B sh. Home for ea. 2 shs. Federated.

Fedora Industries Inc. (B.C. Jan. 22, 1987)
Feb. 22, 2000 – Name changed to Airbomb.com Marketing Ltd. ■

Fedpen Ltée (Que. Aug. 1, 1978 amalg.)
Feb. 17, 1997 – Name changed to Mafricor Resources Inc. ■

Feel Foods Ltd. (B.C. Aug. 13, 2014 amalg.)
May 17, 2022 – Name changed to Ultra Brands Ltd.; basis 1 new for 10 old shs. (see FPsurvey - Industrials)

Feel Good Cars Corporation (Ont. Sept. 28, 2004)
June 15, 2007 – Name changed to ZENN Motor Company Inc. ■

Felix Gold Mines Ltd. (Ont. 1946)
Dec. 9, 1957 – Dissolved.

Femco Mines Ltd. (Ont. Dec. 15, 1950)
July 8, 1965 – Dissolved.

Fenchurch Mining Co. Ltd. (B.C. 1957)
Aug. 1960 – Dissolved.

Fengro Industries Corp. (B.C. July 19, 2016)
July 27, 2020 – Name changed to Elemental Royalties Corp. pursuant to reverse takeover acquisition of Elemental Royalties Limited; basis 1 new for 209 old shs. ■

Fenimore Iron Mines Ltd. (Que. 1947)
Jan. 1955 – Name changed to Consolidated Fenimore Iron Mines Ltd.; basis 1 new for 7 old shs. ■

Fenix Mines Ltd. (B.C. 1966)
Oct. 1974 – Charter cancelled.

Fenway Resources Ltd. (B.C. Mar. 12, 1980)
June 1998 – Continued into Delaware.

Fera Plastics Ltd. (B.C. 1969)
Aug. 1983 – All o/s com. shs. acquired by private interests.

Feralco Industries Limited (Can. 1949)
Dec. 16, 1980 – Dissolved.

Ferguson Mines Ltd. (Ont. 1949)
May 6, 1965 – Dissolved.

Fermac Graphic Industries Limited (Ont. 1951)
Nov. 4, 1970 – Placed into bankruptcy Oct. 23, 1964. Subsequently dissolved.

Les Fermes Agrivest Inc. (Que. Apr. 24, 1987)
June 13, 1990 – Name changed to Les Investissements Embrygènes ltée. ■

Fermont Mines Ltd. (Ont.)
Apr. 9, 1969 – Charter cancelled.

Feromac Mines Ltd. (Ont. 1955)
Dec. 9, 1970 – Charter cancelled.

Feronia Inc. (Ont. Aug. 18, 2010)
Aug. 18, 2016 – Continued into British Columbia.
Nov. 23, 2020 – Deemed bankrupt following completion of sale and restructuring transaction under the Bankruptcy and Insolvency Act (BIA). Ernst & Young Inc. appointed trustee.

Ferro Iron Ore Corp. (B.C. Sept. 26, 2006)
June 14, 2013 – Continued into Ontario.
July 19, 2013 – Name changed to Wolf Resource Development Corp.; basis 1 new for 4 old shs. ■

Ferrous Iron Mines Limited (Ont. 1955)
Nov. 28, 1973 – Dissolved.

Ferrum Americas Mining Inc. (Can. Nov. 30, 2011 amalg.)
Mar. 14, 2016 – Name changed to Toachi Mining Inc.; basis 1 new for 5 old shs. ■

Fest Resources Corp. (B.C. June 15, 1980)
Oct. 2, 1992 – Name changed to Minvita Enterprises Ltd.; basis 1 new for 3 old shs. ■

Festino Venture Corp. (Alta. June 16, 2000)
Aug. 1, 2006 – Name changed to Maskal Energy Inc. following non-arm's length Qualifying Transaction acquisition of Malahat Oil & Gas Ltd. ■

Fiber Optic Systems Technology, Inc. (Del. Oct. 13, 1999)
Oct. 31, 2011 – Name changed to Augusta Industries Inc. ■

Fiberglas Canada Inc. (Can. 1939)
Oct. 31, 1989 – Amalgamated with a wholly owned subsid. of Owens-Corning Fiberglas Corporation. Co. now private.

Fiberoptic One Inc. (Can. Apr. 2, 2001)
Sept. 20, 2004 – Name changed to GlobeeCom International Inc. pursuant to Qualifying Transaction

acquisition of GlobeeCom International Inc. (subsequently renamed GlobeeCom Inc.). (see FPsurvey - Industrials)

FiberQuest Networks Corp. (B.C. July 5, 2000)
Aug. 7, 2001 – Name changed to StorageFlow Systems Corp. ■

Fibertech Industries Corp. (B.C. Jan. 24, 1980)
Aug. 11, 1989 – Name changed to Solar Pharmaceutical Ltd.; basis 1 new for 4 old shs. (see FPsurvey - Industrials)

Fibonacci Capital Corp. (B.C. Jan. 23, 2019)
Nov. 30, 2020 – Name changed to Levitee Labs Inc. (see FPsurvey - Industrials)

Fibre-Klad Industries Ltd. (Alta. Jan. 28, 1987)
May 16, 1994 – Amalgamated with Tanqueray Resources Ltd. to form new co. with same name Tanqueray Resources Ltd.; basis 0.94 new for 1 Fibre-Klad sh. (see Tanqueray Resources Ltd.)

Fibre Products of Canada Limited (Ont. June 15, 1946)
Nov. 1969 – Name changed to Comtech Group International Limited. ■

Fibrek Inc. (Can. Mar. 24, 2010)
Aug. 3, 2012 – Amalgamated with RFP Acquisition Inc., a wholly owned subsid. of Resolute Forest Products Inc.; basis either (i) Cdn$0.55 plus 0.0284 Resolute Forest shs., (ii) Cdn$1.00 or (iii) 0.0632 Resolute Forest shs. for 1 Fibrek sh. (see Resolute Forest Products Inc.)

Fibrequest International Ltd. (B.C. Aug. 9, 1983)
June 27, 1988 – Name changed to E.C.M. Paytel Ltd. ■

Fibres Armtex Inc. (Que. 1983)
Feb. 16, 1989 – Acquired by Fibres C.D.L. Inc.; basis unknown.

Fibresources Corporation (Can. July 25, 2002)
Feb. 11, 2020 – Continued into British Columbia.
Aug. 25, 2020 – Name changed to AJA Ventures Inc. ■

Fibreweld Industries Ltd. (B.C. 1946)
July 17, 1947 – Voluntary liquidation approved by shldrs. and co. wound up. Nothing available for shldrs.

Fiddlehead Resources Corp. (B.C. June 23, 2015 amalg.; other amalgamating entity was 1016772 B.C. Ltd)
Sept. 12, 2024 – Continued into Alberta. (see FPsurvey - Mines & Energy)

Fidelio Enterprises Corporation (Alta. 1986)
Sept. 11, 1991 – Formed Exploration Terrenex Inc. in Alberta on amalgamation with Terrenex Ventures Inc.; basis 6 new for 1 Terrenex sh. and 1 new for 1 Fidelio sh. ■

Fidelity Mining Investments Ltd. (Ont. 1958)
June 1974 – Name changed to New Fidelity Minerals Ltd. ■

Fidelity Mortgage and Savings Corporation (Can. 1963)
Dec. 30, 1977 – Name changed to Equitrust Mortgage and Savings Corporation. ■

Fidelity Mortgage Investments Ltd. (Man. 1964)
June 1968 – Private co. owned by Camwood Securities Ltd. All funded debt redeemed.

Fidelity Partnership 1993 (Ont. Dec. 23, 1992)
Dec. 30, 2005 – Dissolved following final distribution.

Fidelity Partnership 1994 (Ont. Dec. 22, 1993)
Mar. 30, 2007 – Dissolved.

Fidelity Partnership 1995 (Ont. Dec. 22, 1994)
Mar. 31, 2008 – Dissolved

Fidelity Partnership 1996 (Ont. Feb. 26, 1996)
Jan. 5, 2012 – Ceased operations on Dec. 31, 2011.
Apr. 2, 2012 – Dissolved.

The Fidelity Trust Company (Man. 1909)
1972 – Continued into Canada.
Dec. 31, 1980 – Amalgamated with its 99.9%-owned subsidiary, The Fort Garry Trust Company, and continued under the Fidelity Trust Co. name. Com. shldrs. received com. stk. of amalg. co. on a sh.-for-sh. basis. Pfce. stk. also exchanged on a sh.-for-sh. basis.

Fidelity Uranium Mines Ltd. (Alta. 1955)
Dec. 15, 1962 – Dissolved.

Fidinam Properties Inc. (Ont. 1982 amalg.)
Mar. 19, 1986 – All o/s com. shs. acquired by Bramalea Limited for approx. $171,000,000.
June 5, 1986 – Name changed to Bramalea Properties Inc. ■

Fidmor Mortgage Investors Corporation (Can. Dec. 31, 1973)
July 5, 1985 – Name changed to Security Home Mortgage Investment Corporation. ■

Fiducie Desjardins inc. (Que. Sept. 27, 1962; via letters patent)
Aug. 25, 2004 – Redemption of ser. 1 pref. shs.; basis $25 plus accr. and unpaid divd. of $0.07372 per sh.

Fiducie du Québec (Que. Sept. 27, 1962; via letters patent)
Sept. 28, 1988 – Name changed to Fiducie Desjardins inc. ■

Fiedmont Resources Ltd. (Ont. Mar. 2, 1988)
Nov. 17, 1992 – Name changed to Advanced Recruitment Technologies Inc.; basis 1 new for 5 old shs. ■

Field Explorations Ltd. (Ont. 1966)
1968 – Merged into Sakfield Mines & Investments Ltd.; basis 1 new for 3 old shs.

Field Petroleum Corp. (B.C. Dec. 1, 1980)
Apr. 12, 1990 – Name changed to L & D Property Operations (Canada) Ltd. ■

Field Trip Health Ltd. (Alta. Sept. 11, 1998)
Oct. 1, 2020 – Continued into Canada.
Aug. 11, 2022 – Name changed to Reunion Neuroscience Inc. following transfer of Field Trip Clinics business to newly incorporated wholly owned Field Trip Health & Wellness Ltd. and spin out of Field Trip H&W to shareholders.; basis 1 new for 5 old shs. ■

Fieldex Exploration Inc. (Can. May 29, 1985)
Aug. 10, 2020 – Name changed to Fokus Mining Corporation. (see FPsurvey - Mines & Energy)

Fields Stores Limited (B.C. 1948)
May 9, 1977 – All o/s com. shs. acquired by Zeller's Limited; basis 3 Zeller's shs. for 1 Fields sh.

Fiera High Income Trust (Ont. Sept. 4, 1997)
Nov. 12, 2012 – Dissolved for $9.0501 per tr. unit.

Fiera Sceptre Inc. (Ont. Nov. 22, 1955)
Apr. 16, 2012 – Name changed to Fiera Capital Corporation. (see FPsurvey - Industrials)

Fifth Avenue Ventures Corp. (B.C. 1979)
Nov. 15, 1990 – Name changed to Instar Energy Corp.; basis 1 new for 5 old shs. ■

Fifth Era Knowledge Inc. (Alta. July 22, 1999)
Sept. 25, 2003 – Name changed to Triton Capital Corporation; basis 1 new for 7 old shs. ■

Fifth Generation Systems Inc. (B.C. 1983)
June 4, 1986 – Name changed to China Sea Resources Corporation. ■

Fifty-Plus.Net International Inc. (Can. July 31, 1991)
July 1, 2008 – Formed ZoomerMedia Limited in Canada on amalgamation with wholly owned subsidiaries Fifty-Plus.Net Inc. and ZoomerMedia Limited (previously Kemur Publishing Co. Ltd.). ■

Figuery Gold Mines Ltd. (Ont. 1944)
Nov. 5, 1956 – Dissolved.

Filament Health Corp. (B.C. June 22, 2021 amalg.)
May 22, 2025 – Voluntarily delisted from the Cboe Canada Exchange. (see FPsurvey - Industrials)

File Lake Explorations Ltd. (Ont. 1957)
Mar. 1976 – Charter cancelled.

File Lake Gold Mines Ltd. (Man. 1938)
Mar. 5, 1979 – Dissolved.

Filion Gold Mines Ltd. (Ont. 1945)
1959 – Name changed to Teal Exploration Limited. ■

Filo Corp. (Can. May 12, 2016)
Jan. 20, 2025 – All o/s shs. not already held acquired by BHP Group Limited and Lundin Mining Corporation; basis (i) Cdn$33 cash; or (ii) 2.3578 Lundin Mining shs.; or (iii) a combination of cash and shs. for 1 Filo sh.

Filo Mining Corp. (Can. May 12, 2016)
June 23, 2023 – Name changed to Filo Corp. ■

Fin-Lan Copper Mines Ltd. (Ont. 1969)
Mar. 1976 – Charter cancelled.

Fin Resources Inc. (Ont. 1975)
July 7, 1987 – Amalgamated with Continental Precious Minerals Inc. to form a new co. with the same name Continental Precious Minerals Inc.; basis 1 new for 2 old shs.

Financial Collection Agencies Ltd. (Can. Apr. 20, 1945)
Oct. 17, 1977 – Name changed to FCA International Ltd. ■

Financial 15 Split Corp. II (Ont. Sept. 3, 2004)
Mar. 18, 2015 – Name changed to North American Financial 15 Split Corp. (see FPsurvey - Industrials)

Financial Models Company Inc. (Ont. Feb. 2, 1976)
Apr. 20, 2005 – Acquired indirectly by SS&C Technologies, Inc. for Cdn$17.70 per sh.

Financial Preferred Securities Corporation (Alta. Sept. 25, 2006)
June 14, 2012 – All o/s pfd. shs. redeemed for $13.72 per sh.

Financial Services Income STREAMS Corporation (Ont. June 13, 2000)
Feb. 2, 2011 – All capital yield and equity dividend shs. redeemed for $25 per sh. and $9.7723 per sh., respectively, and company dissolved.

Financial Trustco Capital Limited (Alta. July 10, 1980 amalg.)
July 25, 1989 – Name changed to FT Capital Ltd. ■

La Financière Coopérants Inc. (Que. 1987)
Mar. 13, 1992 – Liquidated for $2.00 per sh.

La Financière Entraide-Coopérants Inc. (Que. 1987)
May 7, 1990 – Name changed to La Financière Coopérants Inc. to reflect the takeover bid made by the Cooperants Group in July 1989. ■

Finavera Renewables Inc. (B.C. Dec. 15, 2006 amalg.)
Feb. 8, 2011 – Name changed to Finavera Wind Energy Inc. following reverse takeover acquisition of Finavera Renewables Limited; basis 1 new for 10 old shs. ■

Finavera Solar Energy Inc. (B.C. Dec. 15, 2006 amalg.)
Jan. 29, 2016 – Name changed to Solar Alliance Energy Inc. (see FPsurvey - Mines & Energy; FPsurvey - Industrials)

Finavera Wind Energy Inc. (B.C. Dec. 15, 2006 amalg.)
July 2, 2015 – Name changed to Finavera Solar Energy Inc. ■

Fincorp Capital Ltd. (Ont. Dec. 13, 1978 amalg.)
Sept. 4, 1991 – Placed into receivership and Orenstein & Partners of Toronto appointed receiver.
May 1, 1998 – Wound up and receiver discharged. Assets were foreclosed upon. Secured creditors suffered a shortfall and there was no distribution available for unsecured creditors or shldrs.

Find Energy Ltd. (Alta. Aug. 8, 1995)
Sept. 22, 2006 – Acquired indirectly by Shiningbank Energy Income Fund; basis 0.465 new Shiningbank unit for 1 old Find Energy sh. (see Shiningbank Energy Income Fund)

Findore Gold Resources Ltd. (Ont. June 19, 1997)
Nov. 3, 2000 – Name changed to Ripped Canada Artists Inc. ■

Findore Minerals Inc. (Ont. Dec. 18, 1984)
Jan. 16, 1998 – Name changed to Cantex Energy Inc. ■

Finlayson Enterprises Ltd. (Can. 1924)
Mar. 27, 1986 – Amalgamated with 147742 Canada Limited, its major shldr. to become a private co. Public shldrs. received preferred stk. (166 shs. for each common and 10 for each preferred held) which was subsequently redeemed at 10¢ per sh.

Finline Technologies Ltd. (Ont. Feb. 24, 1989)
Nov. 28, 2005 – Dissolved and struck from register.

Finnin Mining Co. Ltd. (Ont. 1959)
May 13, 1965 – Dissolved.

Finning Ltd. (Can. Oct. 8, 1986)
Apr. 25, 1997 – Name changed to Finning International Inc.; basis 2 new for 1 old sh. (see FPsurvey - Industrials)

Finning Tractor & Equipment Co. Ltd. (B.C. Jan. 4, 1933)
Oct. 8, 1986 – Continued into Canada.
Apr. 23, 1987 – Name changed to Finning Ltd. ■

Finor Exploration Inc. (Can. Nov. 23, 1984)
Apr. 24, 1989 – Declared bankrupt.

Finore Mining Inc. (B.C. Nov. 29, 2006)
Oct. 19, 2017 – Name changed to Micron Waste Technologies Inc. following acquisition of (old) Micron Waste Technologies Inc. by way of amalgamation of Micron Waste and a wholly owned subsidiary of Finore; basis 1 new for 2 old shs. ■

FinTech Services Ltd. (Alta. Mar. 1, 1993)
Aug. 13, 2001 – Name changed to FinTech Solutions Ltd.; basis 1 new com. for 1 old cl. A sh. ■

FinTech Solutions Ltd. (Alta. Mar. 1, 1993)
Aug. 15, 2002 – Name changed to Sylogist Inc. ■

Fintra Ventures Ltd. (B.C. 1978)
June 21, 1996 – Name changed to U.S. Diamond Corp. ■

Fintry Enterprises Inc. (B.C. Dec. 16, 1965)
Dec. 23, 2005 – Name changed to Mesa Uranium Corp. pursuant to reverse takeover acquisition of BZU Minerals Ltd.; basis 1 new for 2 old shs. ■

Fiore Exploration Ltd. (B.C. Mar. 31, 1988)
Sept. 25, 2017 – Succeeded by Fiore Gold Ltd. pursuant to arrangement agreement acquisition by GRP Minerals Corp. (renamed Fiore Gold Ltd.); basis 0.265 GRP shs. for 1 Fiore Exploration sh. ■

Fiore Gold Ltd. (B.C. Sept. 25, 2017)
Jan. 14, 2022 – Acquired by Calibre Mining Corp.; basis 0.994 Calibre shs. plus Cdn$0.10 cash for 1 Fiore sh. (see Calibre Mining Corp.)

Fiorentina Minerals Inc. (B.C. Nov. 24, 2017)
Sept. 23, 2020 – Name changed to Gold Basin Resources Corporation. (see FPsurvey - Mines & Energy)

Firan Corporation (Ont. Nov. 30, 1978 amalg.)
Dec. 1, 1993 – Amalgamated in Ontario to continue with same name.
Aug. 31, 1999 – Name changed to Glendale International Corp. ■

Firan-Glendale Corporation (Ont. July 30, 1954 amalg.)
Nov. 30, 1978 – Amalgamated in Ontario to continue with same name.
Apr. 14, 1982 – Name changed to Firan Corporation. ■

Fircrest Resources Ltd. (B.C. Apr. 7, 1986)
Oct. 30, 1991 – Name changed to NTC Capital Corporation; basis 1 new for 5 old shs. ■

Fire Boss Services Ltd. (Alta. 1980)
Mar. 3, 1994 – Name changed to Boss Energy Ltd. ■

Fire Cannabis Inc. (Can. May 29, 2017)
Nov. 26, 2018 – Name changed to SLANG Worldwide Inc. ■

Fire River Copper Mines Ltd. (Ont. 1956)
1959 – Name changed to Golden Algoma Mines Ltd. ■

Fire River Gold Corp. (Ont. Feb. 8, 1988)
Feb. 5, 1997 – Name changed to Kingly Enterprises Inc.; basis 1 new for 4 old shs. (see FPsurvey - Industrials)

Fire River Gold Corp. (B.C. Sept. 22, 1997)
June 30, 2021 – Name changed to Yumy Bear Goods Inc. pursuant to the reverse takeover acquisition of (old) Yumy Bear Goods Inc. and concurrent amalgamation of (old) Yumy Bear with and into wholly owned 1295304 B.C. Ltd.; basis 1 new for 3 old shs. ■

Fireball Resources Ltd. (B.C. 1984)
June 26, 1992 – Dissolved and struck off register.

Firebird Capital Partners Inc. (B.C. July 31, 2007)
Dec. 27, 2012 – Name changed to Firebird Energy Inc. ■

Firebird Energy Inc. (B.C. July 31, 2007)
Sept. 4, 2014 – Name changed to T-Bird Pharma Inc. following reverse takeover acquisition of Thunderbird Biomedical Inc.; basis 1 new for 15 old shs. ■

Firebird Petroleums Limited (Ont. 1975)
Nov. 1978 – Amalgamated with Oxford Mines Limited, Babylon Minerals Inc., Solvang Explorations Limited and Drayton Petroleum Limited to form Bab-Sol Resource Explorations Limited; basis 35 new for 100 old shs.

Firebird Resources Inc. (B.C. Nov. 5, 2009)
Feb. 12, 2020 – Name changed to Aiml Resources Inc.; basis 1 new for 10 old shs. ■

Fireco Sales Limited (Ont. 1951)
Dec. 31, 1981 – Officially declared bankrupt, in order that Brian Barr Holdings Ltd. could purchase assets of co. New co. formed to operate under same name. No distribution made to shldrs.

Firefly Mining Corporation Ltd. (Ont. 1968)
Mar. 1976 – Charter cancelled.

Firelight Corporation (Alta. June 2, 1988)
Dec. 2, 2010 – Dissolved and struck from registry.

Firesand Resources Ltd. (Ont. July 28, 1978)
Dec. 30, 1997 – Name changed to Talisman Enterprises Inc.; basis 1 new for 4.49 old shs. (see FPsurvey - Industrials)

Firespur Explorations Ltd. (Ont. July 28, 1978)
May 1, 1989 – Name changed to Firesand Resources Ltd.; basis 1 new for 1.5 old shs. ■

Firesteel Resources Inc. (Alta. Feb. 14, 1992)
Aug. 10, 2018 – Name changed to Nordic Gold Corp. ■

Firestone Petroleums Limited (Alta. 1936)
1941 – Merged with 8 other cos. into Amalgamated Oils Limited; basis 33 new for 500 old shs.

Firestone Ventures Inc. (B.C. May 25, 1987)
Oct. 5, 2005 – Continued into Alberta. (see FPsurvey - Mines & Energy)

Fireswirl Technologies Inc. (Alta. June 30, 2005)
Nov. 27, 2020 – Name changed to Pampa Metals Corporation following reverse takeover acquisition of West Pacific Ventures Corp. ■

Fireweed Zinc Ltd. (Yuk. Oct. 20, 2015)
June 30, 2022 – Name changed to Fireweed Metals Corp. (see FPsurvey - Mines & Energy)

Fireworks Entertainment Inc. (Ont. May 3, 1995)
Aug. 13, 1998 – All o/s cl. B sub. vtg. shs. aquired by CanWest Entertainment, a wholly owned subsid. of CanWest Global Communications Corp; basis $3.50 per sh. (see Canwest Global Communications Corp.)

Firm Capital American Realty Partners Corp. (Ont. Mar. 19, 2007)
Jan. 1, 2020 – Succeeded by Firm Capital American Realty Partners Trust pursuant to plan of arrangement whereby Firm Capital American Realty Partners Trust was formed to facilitate the conversion of the corporation into a trust. ■

Firm Capital American Realty Partners Trust (Ont. Oct. 15, 2019)
Sept. 21, 2020 – Name changed to Firm Capital Apartment Real Estate Investment Trust. (see FPsurvey - Mines & Energy)

Firm Capital Mortgage Investment Fund (Ont. July 13, 1999)
May 22, 2001 – Name changed to Firm Capital Mortgage Investment Trust. ■

Firm Capital Mortgage Investment Trust (Ont. July 13, 1999)
Jan. 1, 2011 – Succeeded by Firm Capital Mortgage Investment Corporation pursuant to plan of arrangement whereby Firm Capital Mortgage Investment Corporation was formed to facilitate the conversion of the trust into a corporation and the trust was subsequently dissolved. (see FPsurvey - Industrials)

First Advance Capital Corporation (Ont. Nov. 28, 1983)
Nov. 30, 1994 – Name changed to Avonlee Capital Corporation; basis 1 new for 3 old shs. ■

First Alberta Enterprise Corporation (Alta. Apr. 4, 1986)
Oct. 17, 1990 – Name changed to Anitech Enterprises Inc. ■

First All-Canadian Trustee Shares (1945 Fund)
(unknown 1931; via trust agreement)
Jan. 15, 1942 – Trust liquidated.

First American Capital Group Inc. (B.C. Jan. 27, 1984)
June 23, 1993 – Name changed to Rosetta Technologies Inc. following acquisition of Timespan Communications Corp.; shs. redesignated as com. shs. with a par value of $0.01 (U.S.). ■

First American Minerals Corporation (Ont. June 28, 1984 amalg.)
May 11, 1987 – Name changed to Multireal Properties Inc. ■

First American Mining Corporation (B.C. 1983)
May 5, 1988 – Continued into Wyoming.

First American Resources Ltd. (Ont. 1981)
June 28, 1984 – Amalgamated with First Ohio Explorations Inc. (1 new for 2.5 old shs.) to form First American Minerals Corporation; basis 1 new for 5 old shs.

First Americas Gold Corporation (B.C. Apr. 3, 2007)
Feb. 3, 2016 – Name changed to Intact Gold Corp. (see FPsurvey - Mines & Energy)

1st Anyox Resources Limited (B.C. Feb. 8, 1984)
Feb. 28, 2005 – Name changed to Victory Resources Corporation. ∎

The First Asia Income Fund (Ont. Apr. 28, 1997)
Oct. 8, 2003 – Name changed to Ravensource Fund. (see FPsurvey - Industrials)

First Asset Active Credit Fund (Ont. July 30, 2003)
Jan. 20, 2015 – Merged into First Asset Active Credit ETF; basis 1.10586 Cdn$ ETF com. units for 1 ser. A unit and 0.41337 US$ ETF com. units for 1 ser. B unit. (see First Asset Active Credit ETF)

First Asset/BlackRock North American Dividend Achievers Trust (Ont. Nov. 9, 2005)
Dec. 30, 2009 – Merged (together with First Asset Income & Growth Fund) into Criterion Global Dividend Fund; basis 1.01086 Criterion cl. D units for 1 Income & Growth unit and 0.73904 Criterion cl. D units for 1 Dividend Achievers unit

First Asset Canadian Convertibles Fund (Ont. Dec. 10, 2010)
Dec. 10, 2018 – Merged into First Asset Canadian Convertible Bond ETF; basis 0.677415 First Asset ETF units for 1 First Asset Cdn. Fund trust unit.

First Asset Canadian Dividend Opportunity Fund (Ont. Mar. 22, 2010)
Apr. 20, 2012 – Converted from a closed-end fund to an open-ended fund

First Asset Canadian Dividend Opportunity Fund II (Ont. Jan. 25, 2012)
Mar. 6, 2014 – Merged into First Asset Canadian Dividend Opportunity Fund (the mutual fund); basis 1 cl.X unit of mutual fund for 1 First Asset Canadian Dividend Opportunity Fund II unit.

First Asset Canadian REIT Income Fund (Ont. Oct. 28, 2004)
July 14, 2015 – Converted into an Exchange-Traded Fund and name changed to First Asset Canadian REIT ETF.

First Asset CanBanc Split Corp. (Ont. Sept. 5, 2008)
Jan. 18, 2016 – Redeemed; basis $10.0268 cash per pref. sh. and $30.1588 cash per cl. A sh.

First Asset Diversified Convertible Debenture Fund (Ont. Oct. 30, 2000)
Dec. 10, 2018 – Merged into First Asset Canadian Convertible Bond ETF: basis 1.413423 First Asset ETF units for 1 First Asset Fund trust unit.

First Asset Energy & Resource Fund (Ont. Aug. 9, 1996)
Aug. 1, 2017 – Terminated; basis $15.7407 cash per limited partnership unit.

First Asset Energy & Resource Income & Growth Fund (Ont. Nov. 12, 1997)
Oct. 5, 2007 – Acquired by First Asset Energy & Resource Fund (Fund I); basis 1.4819 Fund I trust units for 1 First Asset Energy & Resource Income & Growth Fund trust unit. (see First Asset Energy & Resource Fund)

First Asset Equal Weight Pipes & Power Income Fund (Ont. Jan. 27, 2005)
June 21, 2006 – Name changed to First Asset Pipes & Power Income Fund. ∎

First Asset Equal Weight REIT Income Fund (Ont. Oct. 28, 2004)
Aug. 31, 2007 – Name changed to First Asset REIT Income Fund. ∎

First Asset Equal Weight Small-Cap Income Fund (Ont. Apr. 7, 2005)
Sept. 29, 2006 – Merged into First Asset Equal Weight REIT Income Fund; basis 0.6581 new REIT unit for 1 old Small Cap unit. (see First Asset Equal Weight REIT Income Fund)

First Asset Global Infrastructure Fund (Ont. May 30, 2007)
Dec. 30, 2009 – Merged into Criterion Water Infrastructure Fund; basis 0.95348 Criterion cl. D units for 1 First Asset unit.

First Asset Hamilton Capital European Bank Fund (Ont. Oct. 29, 2014)
Apr. 25, 2016 – Converted from a closed-end fund to an exchange-fund under the name First Asset Global Financial Sector ETF.

First Asset Income & Growth Fund (Ont. Nov. 29, 2004)
Dec. 30, 2009 – Merged (together with First Asset/BlackRock North American Dividend Achievers Trust) into Criterion Global Dividend Fund; basis 1.01086 Criterion cl. D units for 1 Income & Growth unit and 0.73904 Criterion cl. D units for 1 Dividend Achievers unit

First Asset Morningstar U.S. Consumer Defensive Index Fund (Ont. Feb. 27, 2013)
Sept. 14, 2018 – Merged into First Asset MSCI USA Low Risk Weighted ETF; basis 0.562572 First Asset MSCI USA units for each unit held (see First Asset MSCI USA Low Risk Weighted ETF)

First Asset North American Convertibles Fund (Ont.)
Dec. 10, 2018 – Merged into First Asset Canadian Convertible Bond ETF; basis 0.765118 First Asset ETF units for 1 First Asset N.A. Fund trust unit.

First Asset Opportunity Fund (Ont. June 28, 1999)
Dec. 6, 2007 – All units terminated and redeemed; basis $2.06 per unit.

First Asset Pipes & Power Income Fund (Ont. Jan. 27, 2005)
Jan. 16, 2015 – Converted into closed-end fund, First Asset Active Utility & Infrastructure ETF; basis 1 new com. unit for 1 old tr. unit.

First Asset PowerGen Fund (Ont. Apr. 25, 2001)
Jan. 31, 2011 – Succeeded by Sprott Power Corp. pursuant to amalgamation of wholly owned 7707479 Canada Inc. with Sprott Power Corp.; basis 5.35402342 Sprott Power Corp. shs. for 1 First Asset PowerGen Fund unit. ∎

First Asset PowerGen Trust I (Ont. May 23, 2000)
Mar. 14, 2007 – Name changed to FA Power Fund. ∎

First Asset PowerGen Trust III (Ont. Apr. 25, 2001)
Mar. 14, 2007 – Name changed to First Asset PowerGen Fund. ∎

First Asset REIT Income Fund (Ont. Oct. 28, 2004)
June 22, 2012 – Name changed to First Asset Canadian REIT Income Fund. ∎

First Asset U.S. & Canada LifeCo Income ETF (Ont. July 26, 2013)
Apr. 29, 2019 – Name changed to CI First Asset U.S. & Canada LifeCo Income ETF. ∎

First Asset U.S. & Canada LifeCo Income Fund (Ont. July 26, 2013)
Sept. 3, 2014 – Converted into an exchange-traded-fund; basis 1 com. unit for 1 trust unit.
Sept. 3, 2014 – Name changed to First Asset U.S. & Canada LifeCo Income ETF. ∎

First Asset Yield Opportunity Trust (Ont. July 30, 2003)
Dec. 24, 2014 – Name changed to First Asset Active Credit Fund. ∎

First Au Strategies Corp. (Yuk. Mar. 17, 1997)
June 4, 2003 – Name changed to Cangold Limited. ∎

First Australia Prime Income Investment Company Limited (Singapore Apr. 15, 1986)
May 22, 2001 – Name changed to Aberdeen Asia-Pacific Income Investment Company Limited. ∎

First B Shares Inc. (Ont. Feb. 27, 1990)
Apr. 23, 1996 – All o/s units and equity divd. shs. redeemed for $50.8170 per unit and $26.5056 per equity divd. sh.

First Bauxite Corporation (B.C. July 8, 2003)
Jan. 3, 2019 – Privatized via a 1-for-100,000,000 sh. consolidation; basis Cdn$0.04 cash per com. sh.

First Calgary Petroleums Ltd. (Alta. Jan. 10, 1949)
Nov. 25, 2008 – Acquired by Eni S.p.A. for Cdn$3.60 per sh.

First Canada Financial Corp. (Alta. July 18, 1986)
June 4, 1996 – Name changed to Western Pacific Gold Inc.; basis 1 com. for 5 subord. vtg. shs. ∎

First Canadian Energy Corporation (B.C. 1981)
Mar. 2, 1988 – Delisted from the Vancouver Stock Exchange. Subsequently dissolved for failure to file and struck from register.

First Canadian Energy Ltd. (Alta. Feb. 7, 1996)
June 24, 2003 – Qualifying Transaction amalgamation with private company Northern Shield Resources Inc. (received 21,321,096 shs) to continue as a new company also known as Northern Shield Resources Inc. for total consideration of 3,400,000 new Northern Shield shs.

First Canadian Futures Inc. (Ont. 1985)
Mar. 1987 – Davidson Partners Ltd. purchased the remaining o/s common shs., making it a wholly owned subsid.

First Canadian Gold Corporation Inc. (Ont. July 19, 1972)
Feb. 19, 2002 – Formed Compressario Corporation in Ontario on amalgamation with Enviro Waste Technologies Inc. with First Canadian the deemed acquiror; basis 1 new for 5.45 Enviro shs. and 1 new for 1 First Canadian sh. ∎

First Canadian Investments Limited (Ont. 1970)
Mar. 31, 1981 – Name changed to Bank of Montreal Mortgage Corporation. ∎

First Capital Realty Inc. (Ont. Nov. 10, 1993)
Dec. 30, 2019 – Succeeded by First Capital Real Estate Investment Trust pursuant to plan of arrangement whereby First Capital Real Estate Investment Trust was formed to facilitate the conversion of the corporation into a trust. (see FPsurvey - Industrials)

First Castle Enterprises Inc. (B.C. Aug. 19, 1998)
Oct. 23, 2006 – Dissolved and struck from register.

1st Century Healthcare International Inc. (Alta. May 2, 1988)
July 5, 1994 – Delisted from the Alberta Stock Exchange. Subsequently struck from register and dissolved.
Oct. 11, 1995 – Name changed to Pura Vida International Corporation; basis 1 new for 4 old shs.

First Chartered Development Corporation (B.C. June 13, 1972)
Mar. 24, 1995 – Name changed to APAC Telecommunications Corporation following reverse takeover acquisition of Asia Pacific Telecommunications Corporation; basis 1 new for 2.3 old shs. ∎

First Chicago Investment Corporation (Alta. Jan. 11, 1978)
Mar. 15, 2004 – Name changed to Graystone Corporation; basis 9 new for 1 old sh. ∎

First China Investment Corp. (B.C. 1981)
Sept. 8, 1987 – Name changed to China First Capital Corp.; basis 1 new for 4 old shs. ∎

First Choice Industries Ltd. (B.C. Jan. 22, 1987)
Nov. 21, 2003 – Name changed to Glen Hawk Minerals Ltd.; basis 1 new for 2 old shs. ∎

First Choice Products Inc. (Alta. Oct. 1, 2008 amalg.)
July 4, 2016 – Voluntarily delisted from CSE. (see FPsurvey - Mines & Energy; FPsurvey - Industrials)

First City Financial Corporation Ltd. (B.C. Apr. 24, 1970)
Jan. 2, 1992 – Name changed to Harrowston Corporation and continued into Canada; basis 1 new cl. A for 1 old com. sh. and then consolidated on a 1-for-10 basis. ■

First City Gold Corporation (Ont. 1974)
Dec. 15, 1986 – Name changed to VenTech Healthcare Inc. ■

First City Trust Company (Alta. 1962)
July 10, 1992 – Acquired by North American Life Assurance Co.; basis $1.82 principal amt. of junior notes of North American Life for each ser. A pfd. sh. held, $1.81 principal amt. of junior notes of North American Life for each ser. B pfd. sh. held, and $1.34 principal amt. of junior notes of North American Life for each 8.75% cum. pfd. sh.

First City Trustco Inc. (B.C. July 29, 1981)
July 30, 1986 – Continued into Canada.
July 6, 1992 – Name changed to Talborne Capital Corporation. ■

First Class Entertainment and Filmworks Corporation (Alta. 1976)
May 1, 1990 – Struck off register.

First Cobalt Corp. (B.C. July 13, 2011)
Sept. 4, 2018 – Continued into Canada.
Dec. 7, 2021 – Name changed to Electra Battery Materials Corporation. (see FPsurvey - Mines & Energy)

First Commercial Financial Group Inc. (Alta. Apr. 18, 1986)
Sept. 28, 1989 – Name changed to Micron Metals Canada Corp. ■

First Consort Hotels & Inns Ltd. (B.C. 1988)
Oct. 22, 1993 – Dissolved and struck off register.

First Corporate Capital Inc. (Ont. 1987)
May 2, 1997 – Amalgamated with Genterra Capital Corporation and Mutec Equities Inc. to form Genterra Capital Corporation; basis 0.69 new cl. A shs. for 1 cl. A sh., 0.759 new cl. A shs. for 1 cl. B sh., and 0.69 new cl. A shs. for 1 cl. C sh. (see Genterra Capital Corporation)

First Devonian Explorations Ltd. (B.C. Feb. 6, 1979)
Jan. 4, 1989 – Name changed to Cube Energy Corp.; basis 1 new for 10 old shs. ■

First Division Ventures Inc. (B.C. Mar. 2, 2017)
Mar. 11, 2019 – Name changed to American Battery Metals Corp. ■

First Dynasty Industries Inc. (Can. Feb. 2, 1987)
Apr. 26, 1996 – Dissolved.

First Dynasty Mines Ltd. (Yuk. Aug. 11, 1994)
July 17, 2002 – Name changed to Sterlite Gold Ltd. ■

First Dynasty Ventures Inc. (Can. Oct. 7, 1983)
Oct. 28, 1986 – Name changed to Firstfund Capital (1986) Corp. ■

First Eastern Equities Inc. (Ont.)
July 4, 1994 – Dissolved.

First Eastern Gold Development Inc. (Ont. 1973)
Feb. 1980 – Charter cancelled.

First Eastern Property Development Inc. (Ont.)
July 29, 1988 – Name changed to First Eastern Equities Inc.; basis 1 new for 5 old shs. ■

First Echelon Ventures Inc. (B.C. Mar. 28, 1980)
Dec. 11, 2003 – Name changed to Aumega Discoveries Ltd.; basis 1 new for 4 old shs. ■

First Empire Corporation Inc. (Ont. Mar. 18, 1997 amalg.)
Nov. 1, 2004 – Name changed to Noble House Entertainment Inc.; basis 1 new for 2 old shs. ■

First Empire Entertainment.com Inc. (Ont. Mar. 18, 1997 amalg.)
Aug. 14, 2003 – Name changed to First Empire Corporation Inc.; basis 1 new for 2 old shs. ■

First Energy Metals Limited (B.C. Oct. 12, 1966)
Nov. 1, 2022 – Name changed to FE Battery Metals Corp.; basis 1 new for 3.8 old shs. ■

First Entertainment Corporation (B.C. Mar. 18, 1983)
May 2, 1990 – Name changed to International Avanti Productions Inc. ■

First Entertainment Corporation (B.C. Sept. 22, 1989)
July 12, 1996 – Name changed to MMX Ventures Inc.; basis 1 new for 5 old shs. ■

First Factor Developments Inc. (B.C. Apr. 20, 1979)
Aug. 14, 2007 – Name changed to Millrock Resources Inc. ■

First Fortune Investments Inc. (B.C. Mar. 19, 1980)
Sept. 18, 2007 – Name changed to Hansa Resources Limited. ■

First General Mine Management & Gold Corp. (Can. Mar. 2, 1983)
Dec. 21, 1989 – Name changed to Laser Magic International Inc. ■

First Generation Financial Group Ltd. (B.C. 1983)
Apr. 20, 1993 – Became a wholly owned subsid. of Canadian Maple Leaf Financial Corporation. Holders of com. shs. received 1 cl. 1 com. and 1 cl. B pref. sh. for each com. sh. held. Cl. 1 com. shs. exchanged (0.33 new for 1 old) for cl. A restricted vtg. shs. of Canadian Maple Leaf Financial Corporation. Cl. B pref. shs. redeemed for $0.08; 0.0973 com. shs. Katlor Explorations Ltd.; 0.0947 cl. A shs. Canadian Maple Leaf Financial Corporation and 0.0050 com. shs. North American Environmental Group Ltd. (see Canadian Maple Leaf Financial Corporation)

First Generation Resources Ltd. (B.C. 1983)
Oct. 9, 1991 – Name changed to First Generation Financial Group Ltd. ■

First Global Investments Inc. (B.C. May 31, 1989)
Oct. 1, 2021 – Voluntarily dissolved.

First Gold Exploration Inc. (Can. Sept. 11, 2006)
Feb. 18, 2011 – Name changed to Critical Elements Corporation. ■

First Gold Resources Corporation (B.C. June 13, 1995)
Oct. 25, 1999 – Name changed to Fastfoot Industries Ltd. ■

First Goldwater Resources Inc. (B.C. July 15, 1985)
July 20, 2004 – Name changed to Baja Mining Corp. following reverse takeover acquisition of Mintec International Corporation. ■

First Graphite Corp. (B.C. Aug. 29, 1986)
Jan. 18, 2013 – Name changed to Desert Star Resources Ltd.; basis 1 new for 2 old shs. ■

First Growth Holdings Ltd. (B.C. Jan. 25, 2011)
July 17, 2017 – Filed voluntary assignment in bankruptcy and Crowe MacKay & Company Ltd. appointed trustee.

First Guardian Petroleum Corporation (B.C. Apr. 11, 1986)
July 6, 1993 – Amalgamated with Tai Energy Resources Corporation to form Tai Energy Corporation; basis 0.489112 new for 1 Tai Energy Resources sh. and 0.157968 new for 1 First Guardian sh. (see Tai Energy Corporation)

First Gullane Capital Inc. (Can. May 9, 1994)
Jan. 2, 1996 – Formed Xinex Networks Inc. in Canada on amalgamation with Xinex Labs Inc., constituting a reverse takeover by Xinex; basis 0.77371 prcfl. and 1.12829 com. shs. for 1 Xinex cl. A com. sh., 1.6 pref. and 2.4 com. shs. for 1 Xinex cl. B com. sh., 1 com. sh. for 1 Xinex cl. C non-vtg. com. sh. and 1 com. sh. for 1 First Gullane com. sh. ■

First Harbour Enterprises Inc. (B.C. Feb. 4, 1999)
Oct. 17, 2005 – Dissolved and struck from register.

First Heritage Delta Credit Union (Can. - unspecified)
Aug. 1, 2001 – Name changed to Envision Credit Union. ■

First Heritage Savings Credit Union (unknown)
Jan. 1, 2000 – Merged with Delta Credit Union to form First Heritage Delta Credit Union. (see First Heritage Delta Credit Union)

First Hospitality (Canada) Corporation (B.C. June 20, 1953)
Nov. 5, 1991 – Name changed to Southern Pacific Development Corporation; basis 1 new for 5 old shs. ■

First Host Hotel Corp. (Alta. June 10, 1998)
Apr. 19, 2001 – Name changed to Vision SCMS Inc. following reverse takeover acquisition of Vision Logistics Group Inc. for 12,250,568 post-cons. com. shs. at 95¢ per sh.; basis 1 new for 10.473 old shs. (see FPsurvey - Industrials)

First Houston Oil & Minerals Ltd. (Alta. 1981)
May 1, 1985 – Struck off register.

First Idaho Resources Inc. (B.C. Sept. 28, 1978)
Nov. 24, 2023 – Voluntarily delisted.
Mar. 12, 2024 – Name changed to 0180791 B.C. Ltd. (see FPsurvey - Mines & Energy)

First Impression Singles Network Ltd. (B.C. June 23, 1987)
May 30, 1997 – Name changed to Global Explorations Corporation. ■

First Industrial Capital Corporation (Alta. Mar. 10, 1997)
Jan. 8, 2001 – Name changed to OnBus Technologies Inc. ■

First Integrated Enterprises Ltd. (Alta. Aug. 2, 2000)
Mar. 7, 2005 – Name changed to Kootenay Gold Inc. pursuant to Qualifying Transaction acquisition of Kootenay Gold Corp.; basis 1 new for 1 old sh. ■

First International Metals Corp. (B.C. Apr. 12, 1977)
July 17, 2000 – Name changed to Mill Bay Ventures Inc.; basis 1 new for 5 old shs. ■

First Ivana Technologies Ltd. (Can. May 17, 1984)
Apr. 6, 1993 – Name changed to Vitamed Biopharmaceuticals Ltd.; basis 1 new for 2 old shs. ■

First Labrador Acquisitions Inc. (Alta. May 8, 1996)
Oct. 23, 2003 – Name changed to Silver Spruce Resources Inc.; basis 1 new for 8 old shs. (see FPsurvey - Mines & Energy)

First Legacy Mining Corp. (B.C. Oct. 5, 2016)
Dec. 27, 2018 – Name changed to Defense Metals Corp. (see FPsurvey - Mines & Energy)

First Light Capital Corp. (B.C. Mar. 15, 2018)
Oct. 6, 2021 – Name changed to Anacortes Mining Corp. pursuant to the Qualifying Transaction reverse takeover acquisition of New Oroperu Resources Inc.; basis 1 new for 6 old shs. ■

First Lithium Resources Inc. (B.C. Sept. 1, 2005)
Oct. 11, 2012 – Name changed to Golden Virtue Resources Inc.; basis 1 new for 10 old shs. ■

First Majestic Resource Corp. (Yuk. Jan. 2, 2002)
Jan. 17, 2005 – Continued into British Columbia.
Nov. 22, 2006 – Name changed to First Majestic Silver Corp. (see FPsurvey - Mines & Energy)

First Manhattan Resources Corp. (B.C. Feb. 14, 1984)
June 27, 1990 – Name changed to Napier International Technologies Inc.; basis 3 new for 2 old shs. ■

First Marathon Inc. (Ont. 1982)
Aug. 17, 1999 – Acquired by National Bank of Canada; basis $26 or 1.3 National Bank shs. for 1 First Marathon sh.

First Maritime Mining Corporation Limited (N.B. 1955)
Jan. 11, 1999 – Privatized following amalgamation agreement with its affiliates, Northern Canada Mines, Limited, Atlantic Coast Copper Corporation Limited, Key Anacon Mines Limited and Hunter Brook Minerals Limited; basis $9.10 per sh.

First Medical Management Ltd. (B.C. 1973)
May 22, 1992 – Dissolved and struck off register.

The First Mercantile Currency Fund, Inc. (Ont. 1978)
June 30, 1999 – Converted from a closed-end fund to an open-ended fund.
Dec. 30, 2009 – Charter cancelled.

First Mexican Gold Corp. (B.C. Aug. 9, 2007)
July 8, 2020 – Name changed to QcX Gold Corp. (see FPsurvey - Mines & Energy)

First Mining Finance Corp. (B.C. Mar. 30, 2015)
Jan. 11, 2018 – Name changed to First Mining Gold Corp. (see FPsurvey - Mines & Energy)

1st Miracle Group, Inc. (Del. Mar. 23, 1998)
Nov. 12, 2001 – Name changed to Miracle Entertainment, Inc.; basis 1 new for 900 old shs.

First Mountain Exploration Inc. (Alta. Feb. 10, 2011)
July 5, 2016 – Name changed to Point Loma Resources Ltd. following reverse takeover acquisition of Point Loma Energy Ltd.; basis 1 new for 10 old shs. ■

First Mountain Exploration Ltd. (Alta. Feb. 10, 2011)
Sept. 2, 2014 – Name changed to First Mountain Exploration Inc. ■

First Munich Capital Ltd. (Ont. 1955)
Mar. 28, 1990 – Voluntarily dissolved.

First Narrows Resources Corp. (B.C. Sept. 4, 1986)
Mar. 16, 2009 – Dissolved and struck from register.

First National AlarmCap Income Fund (Alta. Feb. 24, 2005)
Sept. 26, 2011 – Acquired by Stanley Canada Corporation, a subsid. of Stanley Black & Decker, Inc., for $59,671,000.

First National Financial Income Fund (Ont. Apr. 19, 2006)
Jan. 1, 2011 – Succeeded by First National Financial Corporation pursuant to plan of arrangement whereby First National Financial Corporation was formed to facilitate the conversion of the fund into a corporation and the fund was subsequently dissolved. (see FPsurvey - Industrials)

First National Mortgage Investment Fund (Ont. Nov. 27, 2012)
Dec. 22, 2017 – Terminated; basis $9.33 cash per sh.

First National Mortgage (1962) Ltd. (B.C. 1962)
May 2, 1968 – Name changed to Block Bros. Industries Ltd. ■

First National Uranium Mines Limited (Ont. 1967)
June 26, 1973 – Assets sold to Gramara Mercantile Corp. Ltd.; basis 1 new for 10 old shs.
July 22, 1975 – Articles of dissolution filed.

First Nickel Inc. (Ont. Nov. 12, 2003)
Sept. 1, 2015 – Placed into receivership under the Bankruptcy and Insolvency Act. KSV Kofman Inc. appointed receiver. In September 2015, the Lockerby mine was abandoned.
Sept. 2016 – Secured creditors suffered a shortfall and no monies available for distrib. to shldrs. KSV Kofman as receiver was discharged.

First Northern Developments Inc. (B.C. Jan. 23, 1984)
Sept. 20, 1993 – Name changed to Consolidated First Northern Developments Inc.; basis 1 new for 2.65 old shs. ■

First Northern Exploration Ltd. (Can. 1965)
Dec. 16, 1980 – Dissolved.

First One Capital Inc. (Ont. Sept. 25, 2002)
Aug. 22, 2005 – Formed redCity Search Company Inc. in Ontario on Qualifying Transaction amalgamation with Red Media Corp., constituting a reverse takeover by Red Media; basis 1 new for 1 Red Media sh. and 0.37 new for 1 First One sh. ■

First Ontario Capital Inc. (Ont. 1987)
July 15, 1989 – Amalgamated with Lunel Enterprises Inc. to form a new co. also known as First Ontario Capital Inc.; basis 1 cl. A sh. for 1 cl. B sh., 1 new cl. B sh. for 1 cl. A sh. and 1 new sp. sh. for 1 old sp. sh.

First Ontario Capital Inc. (Ont. 1987)
Dec. 16, 1993 – Name changed to First Corporate Capital Inc. following amalgamation with 1040468 Ontario Limited. ■

First Orenda Mines Ltd. (Que. 1938)
June 1, 1976 – Merged into Brominco Inc.; basis 1 new for 100 old shs.

First Place Tower Inc. (Ont. Mar. 20, 1995)
Sept. 8, 1999 – All o/s units acquired by O & Y Properties Corporation; basis $40 per unit.
Name changed to First Place Tower Brookfield Properties Inc.

First Point Capital Corp. (Alta. Feb. 2, 1995)
Jan. 10, 1997 – Name changed to First Point Minerals Corp. ■

First Point Minerals Corp. (Alta. Feb. 2, 1995)
May 30, 2017 – Name changed to FPX Nickel Corp. (see FPsurvey - Mines & Energy)

First Potash Corp. (B.C. Sept. 18, 2006)
Mar. 5, 2015 – Dissolved and struck from register.
Oct. 23, 2020 – Restored to registry.
June 29, 2022 – Name changed to First Phosphate Corp. (see FPsurvey - Mines & Energy)

The First Preferred Trust (Ont. 1985)
Oct. 12, 1990 – All o/s cap. units redeemed; basis $25 per unit.

First Premium Income Trust (Ont. June 21, 1996)
July 2, 2010 – Merged into Premier Canadian Income Fund; basis 2.372708 Premier Canadian trust units for 1 First Premium trust unit. (see Premier Canadian Income Fund)

First Premium Oil & Gas Income Trust (Ont. Feb. 26, 1997)
Dec. 29, 2006 – Redeemed; basis $13.0153 per unit.

First Premium U.S. Income Trust (Ont. Jan. 22, 1997)
Dec. 2, 2005 – Change of business and capital restructuring then continued as Top 10 Split Trust; basis 1 Top 10 capital unit and 1 Top 10 preferred security for 1 First Premium unit (following 1-for-2.29810574 cons.). (see Top 10 Split Trust)

First Pursuit Ventures Ltd. (B.C. Sept. 19, 2006)
June 3, 2011 – Name changed to Silver Pursuit Resources Ltd. ■

First Quantum Minerals Ltd. (Yuk. July 18, 1996)
Aug. 11, 2003 – Continued into Canada.
June 3, 2005 – Continued into British Columbia. (see FPsurvey - Mines & Energy)

First Quantum Ventures Ltd. (B.C. Dec. 21, 1983)
July 18, 1996 – Name changed to First Quantum Minerals Ltd. and continued into Yukon. ■

First Responder Technologies Inc. (B.C. Jan. 27, 2017)
Feb. 21, 2024 – Name changed to Quebec Pegmatite Holdings Corp. pursuant to the reverse takeover acquisition of Quebec Pegmatite Corp. ■

First Royal Financial Corp. (Alta. 1987)
Mar. 2, 2004 – Dissolved and struck from registry.

First Sahara Energy Inc. (Ont. Mar. 11, 2003)
Nov. 26, 2014 – Name changed to M Pharmaceutical Inc. and continued into Alberta. ■

First Security Corporation (B.C. May 11, 1984)
Mar. 8, 1993 – Name changed to TeleLink Communications Corporation. ■

First Silver Reserve Inc. (B.C. July 28, 1987)
Sept. 18, 2006 – Plan of Arrangement acquisition by First Majestic Resource Corp.; basis either $2.165 per sh., or 1 new First Majestic sh. for 2 old First Silver shs. (see First Majestic Resource Corp.)

First Source Resources Inc. (B.C. Oct. 20, 2005)
Oct. 28, 2010 – Formed CB Gold Inc. in British Columbia pursuant to reverse takeover acquisiton of and amalgamation with CB Gold Inc.; basis 1 new for 4 old shs. ■

First Southern Resource Corp. (Ont. Apr. 29, 1983)
Apr. 16, 1993 – Name changed to Antrex Holdings Corp. ■

First Sports International Inc. (Ont. Dec. 18, 1992 amalg.)
July 17, 1995 – Formed Black Pearl Minerals Inc. in Ontario on amalgamation with 1131069 Ontario Ltd.; basis 1 new for 1 1131069 Ontario sh. and 1 new for 5 First Sports cl. A shs. ■

First Standard Mining Ltd. (B.C. Jan. 13, 1960)
July 16, 1993 – Name changed to First Standard Ventures Ltd. ■

First Standard Ventures Ltd. (B.C. Jan. 13, 1960)
Sept. 19, 1995 – Name changed to LRG Restaurant Group, Inc.; basis 1 new for 10 old shs. ■

First Star Capital Corporation (B.C. Feb. 17, 1983)
July 9, 1993 – Dissolved and struck off register.

First Star Energy Ltd. (B.C. Feb. 17, 1983)
Mar. 30, 1990 – Name changed to First Star Capital Corporation. ■

First Star Energy Ltd. (Alta. Feb. 22, 1993)
Aug. 14, 2000 – Name changed to Rosetta Exploration Inc.; basis 1 new for 5 old shs. ■

First Star Innovations Inc. (B.C. Nov. 25, 1980)
Dec. 16, 2003 – Name changed to First Star Resources Inc. ■

First Star Resources Inc. (B.C. Nov. 25, 1980)
May 14, 2015 – Dissolved and struck from register.

First Step Incorporated (Alta. Mar. 23, 1992)
Nov. 7, 2001 – Name changed to FootSource Inc. ■

First Step Ventures Corporation (B.C. Dec. 23, 1997)
July 31, 2003 – Name changed to Atikwa Minerals Corporation and continued into Ontario following Qualifying Transaction acquisition of Atikwa Minerals Limited; basis 1 new for 2 old shs. ■

First Strike Diamonds Inc. (Ont. Jan. 28, 1974)
Jan. 28, 2008 – Certificate of incorporation cancelled and dissolved.

First Telecom Corporation (B.C. May 18, 1983)
Mar. 13, 2002 – Name changed to Sunorca Development Corp.; basis 1 new for 3 old shs. ■

First Tiffany Resource Corporation (Alta. Mar. 7, 1966)
May 3, 1984 – Continued into Ontario.
Feb. 17, 2007 – Certificate of incorporation cancelled and dissolved.

First Toronto Capital Corporation (Ont. 1956)
Jan. 1, 1989 – Formed First Toronto Mining Corporation in Ontario on amalgamation with Pacvest Capital Inc. ■

First Toronto Mining Corporation (Ont. Jan. 1, 1989 amalg.)
July 6, 1993 – Bankrupt.
Sept. 3, 1994 – Dissolved. No funds available for distribution to shldrs.

First Tower Enterprises Inc. (B.C. Feb. 4, 1999)
Apr. 1, 2002 – Name changed to eOptimize Advanced Systems Inc. following Qualifying Transaction reverse takeover acquisition of eOptimize.com Inc.; basis 1 new for 2 old shs. ■

First Tridon Industries Inc. (B.C. Dec. 8, 1977)
July 5, 1993 – Name changed to O.J. Oil and Gas Corporation; basis 1 new for 5 old shs. ■

First Trimark Ventures Inc. (B.C. Mar. 3, 2000)
May 23, 2003 – Formed Lumina Copper Corp. following Qualifying Transaction reverse takeover acquisition of CRS Copper Resources Corp.; basis 1 new for 10 old shs. ■

First Triton Capital Corporation (Can. July 7, 1997)
Aug. 5, 1999 – Name changed to Executive Inn Group Corporation. ■

First Trust Advantaged Short Duration High Yield Bond Fund (Ont. Apr. 26, 2011)
Feb. 1, 2016 – Converted into an exchange traded fund and renamed First Trust Short Duration High Yield Bond ETF (CAD-Hedged); basis 0.5 advisor cl. units for 1 cl. A unit and 0.5 com. units for 1 cl. F unit.

First Trust Global DividendSeeker Fund (Ont. Jan. 30, 2014)
June 8, 2016 – Terminated; basis $6.5385 cash per cl. A unit and $8.5796 cash per cl. F unit.

First Trust/Highland Capital Floating Rate Income Fund (Ont. Jan. 27, 2005)
Aug. 14, 2009 – Merged into First Trust/Highland Capital Floating Rate Income Fund II; basis 0.449719 Income Fund II units for 1 unit. (see First Trust/Highland Capital Floating Rate Income Fund II)

First Trust/Highland Capital Floating Rate Income Fund II (Ont. May 16, 2005)
Mar. 14, 2011 – Liquidated for $1.58 per unit.

First Uranium Corporation (Ont. Sept. 22, 2005)
Dec. 15, 2006 – Continued into British Columbia. (see Algold Resources Ltd.)
June 13, 2012 – Continued into Ontario. (see Algold Resources Ltd.)
Dec. 23, 2013 – Acquired by Algold Resources Ltd. basis 0.0729849 Algold com. shs. plus 0.5 wts. (with wts. exercisable at 20¢ per wt. for a period of 18 mths.) for 1 First Uranium unit. (see Algold Resources Ltd.)

First Uranium Resources Ltd. (B.C. Dec. 14, 2016)
Feb. 27, 2024 – Name changed to Rua Gold Inc. pursuant to the reverse takeover acquisition of Reefton Goldfields Inc. (see FPsurvey - Mines & Energy)

First V Shares Inc. (Ont. July 5, 1991)
Oct. 27, 1993 – All o/s pfd. cl. 1 ser. A shs. redeemed or converted; basis 0.6849 com. shs. of Varity Corporation for 1 old pfd. sh. or redeemable at US$20 per sh.

First Vanadium Corp. (B.C. June 23, 2006)
July 6, 2021 – Name changed to Phenom Resources Corp. (see FPsurvey - Mines & Energy)

First Venture Capital Corporation (B.C. Oct. 18, 1999)
Nov. 5, 2003 – Name changed to First Venture Technologies Corp. following Qualifying Transaction acquisition of exclusive global licensing rights to a new yeast technology from the University of British Columbia. ■

First Venture Developments Ltd. (B.C. Aug. 24, 1987)
Dec. 3, 1998 – Name changed to Knightswood Financial Corp.; basis 1 new for 5 old shs. ■

First Venture Technologies Corp. (B.C. Oct. 18, 1999)
May 20, 2008 – Name changed to Functional Technologies Corp. ■

First West Canada Capital Corporation (B.C. Dec. 6, 1984)
Dec. 20, 1993 – Continued into Wyoming.
Jan. 14, 1994 – Formed Caring Products International, Inc. in Delaware; basis 1 new for 5 old shs.

First Western Communications Corp. (B.C. 1983)
Apr. 28, 1988 – Name changed to Galaxy Industries Ltd. ■

First Western Financial Ventures Inc. (Alta. June 9, 2006)
Apr. 6, 2009 – Acquired by Redcliffe Exploration Inc.; basis $0.125 or 0.39 Redcliffe Exploration shs. for 1 First Western Financial sh. (see Redcliffe Exploration Inc.)

First Western Minerals Inc. (B.C. Mar. 23, 1984)
July 4, 1997 – Name changed to Augusta Metals Incorporated. ■

First Western Resources Inc. (B.C. 1983)
Dec. 10, 1984 – Name changed to First Western Communications Corp. ■

First Yellowhead Equities Inc. (Alta. Jan. 20, 1998)
July 6, 2005 – Going private transaction; basis 1 new series A non-vtg. pfd. sh. for 1 com. sh. immediately redeemed for $2.50 per sh.

Firstbank Investments Limited (Ont. 1970)
Aug. 16, 1973 – Name changed to First Canadian Investments Limited. ■

FirstClass Systems Corporation (Alta. Feb. 9, 1987)
Oct. 1, 2001 – Name changed to Serebra Learning Corporation. ■

FirstEnergy Capital Corp. (Alta. 1989)
Sept. 29, 2016 – Continued into Canada.

Firstfund Capital (1986) Corp. (Can. Oct. 7, 1983)
Oct. 31, 1988 – Name changed to Consolidated Firstfund Capital Corp.; basis 1 new for 10 old shs. (see FPsurvey - Industrials)

FirstGrowth Capital Inc. (B.C. Feb. 10, 2005)
Aug. 17, 2007 – Name changed to FirstGrowth Exploration & Development Services Corp. ■

FirstGrowth Exploration & Development Services Corp. (B.C. Feb. 10, 2005)
Dec. 15, 2008 – Name changed to Kinetex Resources Corp. ■

Firstland Energy Limited (Alta. Aug. 25, 1995)
June 11, 2009 – Name changed to Traverse Energy Ltd. ■

Firstline Ventures Ltd. (B.C. May 4, 1984)
Nov. 18, 1999 – Name changed to Aeon Ventures Ltd.; basis 1 new for 2 old shs. ■

FirstMiss Gold Inc. (Nev. Aug. 1987)
June 25, 1996 – Name changed to Getchell Gold Corporation.

FirstService Corporation (Ont. July 31, 1988 amalg.)
June 1, 2015 – Name changed to Colliers International Group Inc. following spin-out of the Residential Real Estate Services and Property Services business segments to (new) FirstService Corporation. (see FPsurvey - Industrials)

FirstSmart Sensor Corp. (unknown Nov. 28, 1994)
Nov. 13, 1997 – Amalgamated in British Columbia to continue with same name.
Mar. 8, 2010 – Dissolved and struck from register.

FirstWeb Internet Solutions Inc. (B.C. Aug. 17, 1998)
Feb. 27, 2006 – Dissolved.
Nov. 15, 2007 – Restored to register.
Nov. 12, 2009 – Dissolved and struck from register.

Fischer & Porter (Canada) Limited (Can. Jan. 15, 1949)
Aug. 11, 1987 – Continued into Ontario.

Fish Creek Oil Co., Ltd. (B.C. 1914)
1960 – Struck off register.

Fish Lake Gold Mines Ltd. (unknown)
Sept. 16, 1933 – Name changed to South Tiblemont Mines, Limited. ■

Fish Purdy Holdings Corp. (Ont. Mar. 23, 2018)
Aug. 24, 2020 – Name changed to Melius Capital Corp. ■

Fisher & Burpe Ltd. (Can. 1924)
1959 – Name changed to Finlayson Enterprises Ltd. ■

Fisher Oil and Gas Corp. (B.C. 1960)
Feb. 1, 1993 – Deemed bankrupt. No distribution for shldrs.

Fission Energy Corp. (Can. July 17, 2007)
Apr. 30, 2013 – Acquired by Denison Mines Ltd. for $0.0001 plus 0.355 Denison shs. per Fission com. sh.

Fission Mines Ltd. (Ont. 1946)
Mar. 16, 1976 – Dissolved.

Fission 3.0 Corp. (Can. Sept. 23, 2013)
Jan. 31, 2023 – Name changed to F3 Uranium Corp. (see FPsurvey - Mines & Energy)

Fission Uranium Corp. (Can. Feb. 13, 2013)
Dec. 27, 2024 – Acquired by Paladin Energy Ltd.; basis 0.1076 Paladin ord. shs. for 1 Fission com. sh.

Fitch Street Capital Corp. (B.C. June 20, 2007)
June 10, 2020 – Name changed to Pure Extraction Corp. pursuant to Qualifying Transaction acquisition of Pure Extraction Inc. and Pure Extraction Ltd. ■

Fiton Technologies Corp. (N.B. Apr. 14, 1999)
Jan. 6, 2005 – Privatized for $0.0683 per sh.

Fittings Ltd. (Can. 1902)
1931 – Name changed to Fittings Limited. ■

Fittings Limited (Can. 1902)
Dec. 31, 1979 – Formed Pedlar Industrial Inc. in Canada on amalgamation with 86269 Canada Limited. ■

Fitzpatrick Uranium Mines Ltd. (Ont. 1954)
Dec. 1960 – Charter cancelled.

540 Capital Corp. (Alta. June 7, 2006)
Nov. 19, 2008 – Name changed to Golden Dory Resources Corp. ■

Five M Mining (B.C. 1980)
May 13, 1980 – Name changed to Five M Resources Inc. ■

Five M Resources Inc. (B.C. 1980)
Nov. 28, 1985 – Name changed to Leaders Equity Corp. ■

Five Star Diamonds Limited (B.C. Nov. 14, 2012)
June 12, 2020 – Name changed to Aranjin Resources Ltd. ■

Five Star Petroleum & Mines Ltd. (Alta. Jan. 18, 1964)
June 22, 1977 – Name changed to Consolidated Five Star Resources Ltd.; basis 1 new for 5 old shs. ■

Five Wheels Limited (Can. 1953)
1969 – Name changed to Canadian Leisure Industries Limited.

5Banc Split Inc. (Ont. Nov. 9, 2001)
Dec. 19, 2016 – Redeemed; basis $10 cash per cal. C pre. shs. and $27.51 cash per cal. B capital shs.

Fiveland Mines Ltd. (Ont. 1953)
1953 – Assets sold to Consolidated Orlac Mines Ltd. Charter surrendered.

Fjordland Minerals Ltd. (B.C. Jan. 30, 1986)
May 3, 2002 – Name changed to Fjordland Exploration Inc.; basis 1 new for 2 old shs. (see FPsurvey - Mines & Energy)

Flag Oils Limited (Alta. Mar. 4, 1953)
June 8, 1981 – Name changed to Flag Resources Limited. ■

Flag Resources Limited (Alta. Mar. 4, 1953)
Feb. 18, 1985 – Name changed to Flag Resources (1985) Limited; basis 1 new for 2 old shs. (see FPsurvey - Mines & Energy)

Flagro Mines Limited (Ont. 1945)
1958 – Charter cancelled.

Flagship Energy Inc. (Alta. Feb. 27, 1997)
Aug. 1, 2006 – Amalgamated in Alberta to continue with same name.
Aug. 8, 2008 – Name changed to Insignia Energy Ltd. following reverse takeover acquisition of Insignia Energy Ltd.; basis 1 com. sh. for 100 cl. A shs. and 1 com. sh. for 10 cl. B shs. ■

Flagship Industries Inc. (Ont. June 30, 1988 amalg.)
Dec. 1, 2009 – Continued into British Columbia.
Sept. 21, 2010 – Name changed to Prima Colombia Hardwood Inc. pursuant to acquisition of REM Forest Products Inc. ■

Flagship Resources Ltd. (Ont. June 30, 1988 amalg.)
Mar. 28, 1991 – Name changed to Flagship Industries Inc. ■

Flagstaff Resource Explorations Inc. (Ont. 1977)
Aug. 13, 1985 – Name changed to Mega-Dial Communications Ltd.; basis 1 new for 1 old sh. Previously changed name to Flagstaff Resource Explorations Consolidated Inc. also on Aug. 13, 1985; basis 1 new for 10 old shs. ■

Flagstone Mines Ltd. (B.C. 1964)
Aug. 30, 1976 – Amalgamated into Grand Prix Resources Ltd.; basis 1 cl. A for 8 Flagstone shs., or 1 new cl. B sh. for 5 shs.

Flaherty & Crumrine Investment Grade Fixed Income Fund (Alta. Oct. 29, 2004)
Sept. 5, 2018 – Name changed to Flaherty & Crumrine Investment Grade Preferred Income Fund. ■

Flaherty & Crumrine Investment Grade Preferred Fund (Ont. Apr. 28, 2004)
Jan. 5, 2009 – Converted into Flaherty & Crumrine Investment Grade Fixed Income Fund; basis 1 Flaherty & Crumrine Investment Grade Fixed Income Fund units for 1.119448 Flaherty & Crumrine Investment Grade Preferred Fund unit. (see Flaherty & Crumrine Investment Grade Fixed Income Fund)

Flaherty & Crumrine Investment Grade Preferred Income Fund (Alta. Oct. 29, 2004)
Nov. 26, 2021 – Converted to a exchange-traded fund under the Brompton Flaherty & Crumrine Enhanced Investment Grade Preferred ETF name.

Flair Explorations Inc. (Ont. 1971)
May 1975 – Amalgamated with Vacation Magazine Holdings Ltd. to form Trav-Com Inc.; basis 1 new for 6 old shs.

Flair Resources Ltd. (B.C. Aug. 24, 1979)
Apr. 7, 1986 – Delisted from the Vancouver Stock Exchange. Subsequently dissolved and struck from register.

Flame-Master Limited (unknown)
Nov. 30, 1967 – All com. shs. acquired by Bow Valley Industries Ltd. subsequent to for a cash consideration of $598,792. Shldrs. received $17 per sh.

Flame Petro-Minerals Corp. (B.C. Feb. 27, 1979)
Mar. 22, 2000 – Name changed to LinuxWizardry Systems, Inc. ■

Flamingo Oils Ltd. (Ont. 1950)
Sept. 4, 1964 – Converted to a private co., early 1966. Payment of 25¢ per sh. made to shldrs.

Flanagan McAdam Resources Inc. (Ont. 1959)
Sept. 30, 1996 – Amalgamated with Muscocho Explorations Ltd. and McNellen Resources, Inc. to form Golden Goose Resources Inc.; basis 1 new for 4 Muscocho shs., 1 new for 22.75 McNellen shs. and 1 new for 18.4 Flanagan shs. (see Golden Goose Resources Inc.)

Flank Petroleums Limited (Alta. Feb. 11, 1937)
Aug. 1953 – Assets acquired by Consolidated East Crest Oil Company Limited; basis 3 new for 10 old shs. (see East Crest Oil Company Limited)

Flare Oils Limited (Alta.)
1959 – Struck off register.

Flash Fasteners of Canada Ltd. (Ont. 1936)
Sept. 1951 – An offer of $5.50 per sh. was made for co.'s com. stk. Co. was later wound up.

Flash Pack Ltd. (B.C. Sept. 19, 1986)
Dec. 7, 1994 – Name changed to Canadian Lynx Petroleum Ltd.; basis 1 new for 5 old shs. ■

Flavex Industries Ltd. (B.C. 1985)
Feb. 28, 1992 – Dissolved and struck off register.

Fleck Resources Ltd. (B.C. Mar. 4, 1981)
June 10, 1998 – Name changed to PolyMet Mining Corp. ■

Fleet Aerospace Corporation (Ont. Aug. 20, 1946)
Oct. 22, 1996 – Name changed to Magellan Aerospace Corporation; basis 1 new for 5 old shs. (see FPsurvey - Industrials)

Fleet Aircraft Limited (Can. 1930)
Aug. 15, 1946 – Following an offer to purchase, shares were acquired for $9.00 per sh. or 2 shs. for in a new company, Fleet Manufacturing and Aircraft Limited.

Fleet Aircraft of Canada, Limited (Can. 1930)
Nov. 17, 1936 – Name changed to Fleet Aircraft Limited. ■

Fleet Manufacturing and Aircraft Limited (Can. Mar. 25, 1930; via Dominion charter)
Aug. 20, 1946 – Continued into Ontario.
Jan. 31, 1948 – Name changed to Fleet Manufacturing Limited. ■

Fleet Manufacturing Limited (Ont. Aug. 20, 1946)
Feb. 1, 1973 – Name changed to Ronyx Corporation Limited. ■

Fleetwood Corporation (Que. 1945)
Jan. 1, 1975 – All o/s com. shs. acquired by GTE Sylvania Canada Ltd. through purch. offer of $4.50 per sh.

Fleetwood Mining and Explorations Ltd. (Ont. 1944)
May 27, 1965 – Dissolved.

Fleetwood Petroleum Corporation (B.C. Mar. 28, 1979)
Sept. 18, 1995 – Name changed to Goldie Enterprises Inc.; basis 1 new for 5 old shs. ■

Fleetwood Resources Ltd. (Alta. 1948)
July 31, 1974 – Struck off register.

Fleetwood Yellowknife Mines Ltd. (Ont. 1944)
Feb. 1957 – Name changed to Fleetwood Mining and Explorations Ltd. ■

Fleming Mines Ltd. (Que. 1944)
Aug. 1973 – Charter cancelled.

Fletcher Challenge Canada II Inc. (Can. 1988)
Sept. 14, 1988 – Name changed to Fletcher Challenge Investments II Inc. ■

Fletcher Challenge Canada Inc. (Ont. 1987)
Sept. 2, 1988 – Name changed to Fletcher Challenge Investments Inc. ■

Fletcher Challenge Canada Limited (B.C. Dec. 30, 1971 amalg.)
Dec. 27, 2000 – Name changed to Norske Skog Canada Ltd. following the July 2000 acquistion of parent Fletcher Challenge Limited's 50.76% interest in the co. by Norske Skogindustrier ASA. ■

Fletcher Challenge Finance Canada Incorporated (Ont. 1965)
1986 – Continued into Canada.
Nov. 30, 1993 – All o/s 8% ser. A pref. shs. redeemed Oct. 1, 1993, at $25 per sh. plus $0.0054 accr. divd.; 7.785% ser. B pref. shs. redeemed at $25 plus $0.3263 accr. divd. per sh.

Fletcher Challenge Investments II Inc. (Can. 1988)
Mar. 18, 1996 – All o/s exch. shs. series B redeemed; basis 7.45 ordinary division shs. and 2.7195 Forest division shs. of Fletcher Challenge Limited for each exch. sh.

Fletcher Challenge Investments Inc. (Ont. 1987)
1990 – Continued into Canada.
Sept. 24, 1993 – All o/s ser. 1 exchangeable shs. redeemed; basis 8.2 new Fletcher Challenge Limited ord. shs. for 1 old exchangeable sh. All o/s ser. 2 exchangeable shs. redeemed on July 16, 1993; basis $26.1352 per sh.

Fletcher Leisure Group Inc. (Can. 1966)
Dec. 1994 – Filed a proposal under the Bankruptcy and Insolvency Act. Ernst & Young of Montreal was appointed trustee.
Mar. 1996 – Obligations under the proposal were fulfilled. Creditors received a nominal distribution, leaving nothing for the shldrs.
Apr. 10, 1997 – Trustee discharged.
Feb. 2, 2004 – Dissolved.

Fletcher's Limited (B.C. 1917)
Dec. 27, 1984 – Name changed to Fletcher's Fine Foods Ltd. and continued into Canada. ■

Fletcher's Fine Foods Ltd. (Can. Dec. 27, 1984)
June 26, 2000 – Name changed to Premium Brands Inc. ■

Fleurmont Placer Developments Ltd. (B.C. 1963)
June 4, 1968 – Name changed to Copper-Can Developments Ltd. ■

Fleury-Bissell Ltd. (Can. 1928)
Oct. 1950 – Name changed to Elora Industries Ltd.; basis 1 new pref. and 1 new com. for each 2 old pref. shs. and 1 new com. for 1 old com. sh. ■

Flexwork Properties Ltd. (Ont. July 11, 2005)
Aug. 3, 2022 – Formed Blockchain Venture Capital Inc. in Ontario pursuant to amalgamation with (old) Blockchain Venture Capital Inc. (deemed acquiror); basis 1 new for 21.25353 old shs. (see FPsurvey - Industrials)

Flicka Mines Ltd. (Ont. 1945)
1960 – Charter cancelled.

Flicka Red Lake Mines Ltd. (Ont. 1945)
July 1956 – Name changed to Flicka Mines Ltd. ■

Flin Flon Gold Mines Ltd. (Man. 1936)
Nov. 1939 – Name changed to Douglas Lake Mines Ltd.; basis 1 new for 2.25 old shs. ■

Flinders Resources Limited (B.C. Oct. 27, 2010)
Aug. 25, 2016 – Name changed to Leading Edge Materials Corp. (see FPsurvey - Mines & Energy)

Flint Creek Gold Limited (Alta. 1981)
1983 – Continued into British Columbia.
Apr. 11, 1984 – Name changed to Calpine Resources Incorporated. ■

Flint Energy Services Ltd. (Alta. Apr. 9, 1998)
May 18, 2012 – Acquired by URS Corporation for Cdn$25 per sh.

Flint Rock Mines Ltd. (Ont. 1959)
Mar. 14, 1978 – Charter cancelled.

Flint Rock Mines Limited (Ont. 1959)
Nov. 8, 1990 – Amalgamated with Kalrock Development Limited (basis 1 new for 1 old sh.) to form a new company known as Kalrock Resources Limited; basis 1 new for 6 old shs. (see Kalrock Developments Limited)

Floating Rate Income Fund (Ont.)
July 22, 2016 – Merged into Canoe Floating Rate Income Fund; basis 0.871058546 Canoe ser. Z unit for 1 Floating Rate trust unit.

Flobec Gold Mines Ltd. (Ont. 1936)
Nov. 9, 1959 – Dissolved.

Flock Gas and Oil Corp. Ltd. (Alta.)
1966 – Sold. Small asset distribution made.

Flock Resources Ltd. (Alta. Aug. 1, 1996 amalg.)
July 11, 2002 – Name changed to Endev Energy Inc. ■

Flomic Chibougamau Mines Ltd. (Que. 1951)
Apr. 1974 – Charter cancelled.

Flomore Resources Ltd. (Alta. 1987)
Mar. 7, 1991 – Name changed to Security Energy Corporation; basis 1 new for 2 old shs. ■

Floorco Ltd. (Ont. Jan. 3, 1969)
June 1995 – Obtained protection under the Bankruptcy and Insolvency Act.
Nov. 1995 – Proposal made to convert all pref. shs. ser. C into com. shs., consolidate com. shs. on a 1-for-8.5 basis and change co.'s name to Salem Floor Co. Inc.
May 1996 – Ontario Court of Justice refused to approve an amended proposal by the co., resulting in its bankruptcy.
Mar. 12, 1997 – RSM Richter Inc. of Toronto was discharged as trustee. No further details were available.

Floranada Mines Ltd. (unknown)
July 1960 – Charter cancelled.

Floregold Red Lake Mines Ltd. (Ont. 1946)
Sept. 21, 1959 – Charter cancelled.

Florena Gold Mines Ltd. (Ont. 1936)
Nov. 30, 1964 – Dissolved.

Florence Mining Co. Ltd. (B.C. 1942)
May 29, 1969 – Struck off register.

Florentine Mineral Resources Ltd. (Ont. Aug. 20, 1986)
Apr. 5, 1995 – Name changed to Triangle Multi-Services Corporation; basis 1 new for 2 old shs. ■

Florida Canyon Gold Inc. (Can. July 8, 2024 amalg.)
Nov. 12, 2024 – Acquired by Integra Resources Corp.; basis 0.467 Integra com. shs. for each com. sh. held.

Florin Resources Inc. (B.C. 1982 amalg.)
June 19, 1991 – Amalgamated with Crimsonstar Resources Ltd. (1 for 2) to form a new co. named Crimsonstar Mining Corporation; basis 1 new for 2.5 old shs. (see Crimsonstar Mining Corporation)

Floron Food Services Limited (Alta. Nov. 1, 1984)
Sept. 2, 2003 – Going private transaction via amalgamation with 1049531 Alberta Ltd.; basis $1.40 per sh.

Flotek Industries Inc. (B.C. May 17, 1985)
Sept. 15, 1995 – Continued into Alberta.

Flourish Mushroom Labs Inc. (B.C. Sept. 18, 2019)
Apr. 30, 2020 – Name changed to NeonMind Biosciences Inc. ■

Flow Beverage Corp. (Ont. Sept. 26, 2014)
July 5, 2021 – Continued into Canada. (see FPsurvey - Industrials)

Flow Energy Ltd. (B.C. July 4, 2006)
July 31, 2008 – Name changed to Zimtu Capital Corp. following Qualifying Transaction reverse takeover acquisition of 755032 B.C. Ltd. (see FPsurvey - Mines & Energy; FPsurvey - Industrials)

Flower Affairs Systems Corp. (Alta. Aug. 7, 1996)
Dec. 12, 2000 – Name changed to Canadian Rocky Mountain Properties Inc. following Qualifying Transaction acquisition of WCP Holdings Ltd.; basis 1 new for 5 old shs. ■

Flower One Holdings Inc. (B.C. Jan. 9, 2007)
Dec. 30, 2022 – Pursuant to the Plan of Compromise and the Cdn. and U.S. restructuring plans, all existing shares of wholly owned Cana Nevada Corp. were cancelled and Cana Nevada issued new shs. to the plan sponsor resulting in the company no longer owning any U.S. operating subsids. Under the plan, (i) public noteholder claimants received a U.S. cash distrib. equal to 10% of the claim amount; (ii) general unsecured creditors received a U.S. cash distrib. equal to 10% of the proven claim amount; and (iii) private noteholder claimants received private debs. notes equal to 10% of the proven noteholder claims, with cash distrib. payable by Jan. 13, 2023. All o/s public and private debs. were deemed to have been cancelled and existing com. shlds. would not receive any distrib. under the plans. Upon implementation of the plans, wholly owned Flower One Corp. and FO Labour Management Ltd. made an assignment into bankruptcy. (see FPsurvey - Industrials)

The Flowerman Group Inc. (Ont. June 16, 1987)
Feb. 12, 1996 – Name changed to Nova Growth Corp.; basis 1 new for 4 old shs. ■

Flowing Energy Corporation (Alta. June 3, 1996)
Apr. 11, 2005 – Plan of Arrangement exchange with Daylight Energy Trust; basis 0.0743 new Daylight trust unit or equivalent new Daylight Energy Ltd series A non-vtg. exch. sh. or a combination thereof for 1 old Flowing Energy com. sh. (see Daylight Energy Trust)

The Flowr Corporation (Alta. June 1, 2016)
Sept. 25, 2018 – Continued into Ontario. (see FPsurvey - Industrials)

Flowtech Energy Corporation (Alta. Nov. 25, 1993)
May 10, 1995 – Formed Canadian Chemical Reclaiming Ltd. in Alberta on amalgamation with Canadian Chemical Reclaiming Limited. ■

Fluid Music Canada, Inc. (Can. June 17, 2008)
July 12, 2010 – Name changed to Mood Media Corporation. ■

Fluid Music, Inc. (Del. Sept. 20, 2004)
May 17, 2007 – Continued into Nevada.
June 17, 2008 – Continued into Canada.
June 19, 2008 – Name changed to Fluid Music Canada, Inc. ■

FluidOil Limited (B.C. Jan. 16, 2006)
May 30, 2022 – Name changed to Anibesa Energy Metals Corp. (see FPsurvey - Mines & Energy)

Flukong Enterprise Inc. (Alta. Nov. 19, 1998)
Jan. 28, 2010 – Name changed to Intensity Company Inc.; basis 1 new for 10 old shs. ■

Fluor Bar Mines Ltd. (Que. 1953)
Sept. 30, 1978 – Charter cancelled.

Fluoroc Mines Ltd. (Ont. 1944)
June 1960 – Charter cancelled.

Flyer Resources Ltd. (B.C. Jan. 31, 1980)
May 14, 1984 – Name changed to International Flyer Resources Ltd.; basis 1 new for 4 old shs. ■

Flying A Petroleum Ltd. (B.C. Apr. 10, 1986)
Sept. 28, 2015 – Dissolved and struck from the register.
Sept. 16, 2016 – Restored to register. (see FPsurvey - Mines & Energy)

Flying Cross Petroleum Corp. (Ont. 1966)
Dec. 4, 1985 – Amalgamated with 5 other cos. to form Flying Cross Resources Ltd.; basis 3 new for 8 old shs.

Flying Cross Resources Ltd. (Ont. 1985 amalg.)
Apr. 11, 1986 – Amalgamated with Larder Resources Inc. to form International Larder Minerals Inc.; sh.-for-sh. basis.

Flying Disc Entertainment Inc. (Ont. July 19, 1974)
Mar. 23, 1998 – Name changed to Software Gaming Corp. ■

Flying Monkey Capital Corp. (B.C. Dec. 15, 2014)
Sept. 27, 2018 – Name changed to Fabled Copper Corp.; basis 1 new for 3 old shs. ■

Flying Nickel Mining Corp. (B.C. Dec. 21, 2020)
Nov. 4, 2024 – Name changed to CleanTech Vanadium Mining Corp. (see FPsurvey - Mines & Energy)

Flynn-Bar Gold Mines Ltd. (Ont. 1945)
Jan. 1951 – Name changed to Flynn-Bar Mines Ltd. ■

Flynn-Bar Mines Ltd. (Ont. 1945)
Oct. 1962 – Dissolved.

Focal Resources Limited (Alta. Aug. 18, 1987)
Mar. 24, 2000 – Name changed to Verdx Minerals Corporation; basis 1 new for 5 old shs. (see FPsurvey - Mines & Energy)

Foccini International Inc. (Can. Nov. 25, 2003)
May 3, 2010 – Name changed to Arch Biopartners Inc. pursuant to reverse takeover acquisition of Arch Biotech Inc. (see FPsurvey - Industrials)

Focus Energy Trust (Alta. July 12, 2002)
Feb. 20, 2008 – Acquired by Enerplus Resources Fund; basis 0.425 Enerplus trust units for 1 Focus trust unit.

Focus Metals Inc. (Can. Apr. 5, 2001)
May 25, 2012 – Name changed to Focus Graphite Inc. (see FPsurvey - Mines & Energy)

Focus National Mortgage Corporation (Ont. 1976)
Oct. 30, 1992 – Acquired by The Mutual Trust Company for $16 per sh.

Focus Resources Ltd. (B.C. 1974)
Dec. 8, 1979 – Merged with Bluesky Oil & Gas Ltd. under the latter name; basis 1.8 new for 1 old sh.

Focus Ventures Ltd. (B.C. Apr. 30, 1993)
Apr. 23, 2018 – Name changed to CROPS Inc. and continued into Yukon; basis 1 new for 4 old shs. ■

Focused 40 Income Fund (Ont. Feb. 25, 2005)
June 27, 2009 – Merged into IA Clarington Diversified Income Fund, an open-ended mutual fund.

Focused Capital II Corp. (Ont. July 13, 2011)
Aug. 16, 2018 – Continued into British Columbia.
Aug. 22, 2018 – Name changed to Fortress Blockchain Corp. following Qualifying Transaction reverse takeover acquisition of (old) Fortress Blockchain Corp.; basis 1 new for 3.25077 old shs. ■

Focused Capital Corp. (Ont. May 17, 2010)
Oct. 27, 2017 – Name changed to Orford Mining Corporation pursuant to Qualifying Transaction three-cornered amalgamation of True North Nickel Inc. (deemed acquiror) with a wholly owned subsidiary of Focused Capital; basis 1 new for 2.34 old shs. ■

Focused Global Trends Fund (Ont. June 28, 2007)
Oct. 5, 2011 – Name changed to Connor, Clark & Lunn Financial Opportunities Fund pursuant to merger with Connor, Clark & Lunn Global Financials Fund II, with Focused Global Trends Fund the deemed acquiror. ■

FogChain Corp. (Ont. Feb. 7, 1984)
Apr. 20, 2021 – Name changed to Avisa Diagnostics Inc. pursuant to the reverse takeover acquisition of Avisa Pharma Inc. and concurrent amalgamation of Avisa with wholly owned FogChain USA Inc. (and continued as Avisa Diagnostics USA Inc.).; basis 1 new for 15 old shs. (see FPsurvey - Industrials)

Foley Silver Mines Ltd. (B.C. 1966)
June 12, 1978 – Dissolved.

Folkestone Resources Ltd. (B.C. Jan. 11, 1984)
Apr. 27, 1987 – Name changed to Schmitt Industries, Inc. ■

Folkstone Capital Corp. (B.C. Jan. 5, 2011)
Jan. 18, 2021 – Name changed to Beretta Ventures Ltd.; basis 1 new for 3 old shs. (see FPsurvey - Industrials)

Follansbee Red Lake Gold Mines Limited (Ont. 1945)
Feb. 28, 1984 – Name changed to The Alton Corporation; basis 1 new for 10 old shs. ■

Fomack Energy Inc. (Alta. May 27, 1994)
Nov. 2, 2014 – Struck from registry and dissolved.

Fond-du-Lac Exploration Co. Ltd. (Ont. 1955)
Oct. 1967 – Charter cancelled.

Fond-du-Lac Uranium Mines Ltd. (Ont. 1955)
1957 – Name changed to Fond-du-Lac Exploration Co. Ltd. ■

La Fonderie de l'Islet Limitée (Que. 1916)
Dec. 5, 1970 – Name changed to Industries L'islet Inc. ■

Fondewa Gold Mines Ltd. (Ont. 1939)
Oct. 1967 – In process of winding up; no assets.

fONOROLA Inc. (Can. Nov. 10, 1988)
July 14, 1998 – All o/s com. and cl. A non-vtg. shs. acquired by Call-Net Enterprises Inc.; basis (a) $60 for 1 com. and/or cl. A non-vtg. sh. or (b) 2.4 cl. B non-vtg. shs. of Call-Net plus $0.02 for 1 com. and/or cl. A non-vtg. sh. of fONOROLA. (see Call-Net Enterprises Inc.)

Font Explorations Ltd. (B.C. 1957)
Oct. 1961 – Name changed to Mount Leyland Collieries Ltd. ■

Font Petroleums Ltd. (B.C. 1957)
1960 – Name changed to Font Explorations Ltd. ■

Fontana Gold Mines Ltd. (Que. 1936)
1945 – Property sold to Fontana Mines (1945) Limited; basis 1 new for 2 old shs.
Jan. 31, 1947 – Charter surrendered.

Fontana Resources Ltd. (B.C. Jan. 20, 1969)
Aug. 28, 1986 – Name changed to Pac Ed Systems Corp. ■

Foodcorp Limited (Ont. 1974 amalg.)
Nov. 13, 1978 – Became a wholly owned unit of Cara Operations Limited, as a result of a purchase offer of $12.50 per com. sh. All remaining minority shs. converted into pref. shs. immediately redeemed at $12.50 per sh.

Foodex Inc. (Can. 1928)
June 30, 1984 – Amalgamated with Hatleigh Corporation, to form Dexleigh Corporation. Each pfce. sh. of Foodex exchanged for 1.3 com. shs. and 1.3 sh. purchase wts. of Dexleigh. Each wt. to purchase one com. sh. at $2.00 until Dec. 31, 1986. All com. and jr. pfce. shs. (held by Hatleigh Corporation) cancelled. (see Dexleigh Corporation)

Foodex Systems Limited (Can. 1927)
June 30, 1978 – Amalgamated with Foodex Investments Limited, to become Foodex Inc. Foodex shs. exchanged for new 9.5% cum. redeem. 1st pref. shs. Shs. held by Hatleigh Corp. were cancelled and replaced with new com. shs. (see Foodex Inc.)

Foodquest Corp. (Ont. Apr. 9, 1973)
Nov. 25, 1994 – Name changed to Foodquest International Corp.; basis 1 new for 2 old shs. ■

Foodquest International Corp. (Ont. Apr. 9, 1973)
Jan. 26, 1999 – Name changed to Dealcheck.com Inc.; basis 1 new for 15 old shs. ■

The Foothills Collieries Ltd. (Can. 1919)
1953 – Acquired by Canadian Collieries (Dunsmuir) Ltd.; consideration, if any, unknown. (see Canadian Collieries (Dunsmuir) Ltd.)

Foothills Newspapers Inc. (Alta. Mar. 31, 1987)
May 1, 1991 – Name changed to Skylink Communications Inc. ■

Foothills Oil & Gas Ltd. (Alta. Sept. 3, 1993)
Feb. 10, 2003 – Name changed to Midnight Oil & Gas Ltd. following reverse takeover acquisition of Midnight Oil & Gas Ltd.; basis 1 new for 18 old shs. ■

Footmaxx Holdings Inc. (Ont. Sept. 23, 1935)
Dec. 7, 2007 – Name changed to FMX Ventures Inc. following acquisition by Footmaxx of Canada ULC, Footmaxx of New Hampshire, Inc. and Footmaxx of Virginia, Inc. ■

FootSource Inc. (Alta. Mar. 23, 1992)
Sept. 2, 2018 – Struck from registry and dissolved.

Footwall Explorations Ltd. (B.C. May 12, 1983)
Apr. 8, 1999 – Name changed to Planet Ventures Inc.; basis 1 new for 10 old shs. ■

Foran Mines Ltd. (Ont. 1951)
Nov. 1962 – Dissolved.

Foran Mining Corporation (B.C. June 21, 1989)
Nov. 13, 2007 – Continued into Saskatchewan. (see FPsurvey - Mines & Energy)

Forano Inc. (Que. 1873)
July 7, 1987 – Dissolved.

Forano Limited (Que. 1873)
1978 – Name changed to Forano Inc. ■

Foratek International Inc. (Que. Jan. 30, 1967)
Apr. 7, 1997 – Name changed to F.K.I. International Inc. ■

Forbes & Manhattan Coal Corp. (Ont. Oct. 17, 2006)
July 21, 2014 – Name changed to Buffalo Coal Corp. ■

Forbes Energy Services Ltd. (Bermuda Apr. 9, 2008)
Aug. 12, 2011 – Continued into Texas.

Forbes Lake Mining Corp. (unknown)
Jan. 1957 – Merged into Westore Mines Ltd.; basis 1 new for 3 old shs.

Forbes Medi-Tech Inc. (B.C. Sept. 17, 1985)
Apr. 11, 2001 – Continued into Canada.
Aug. 26, 2010 – Name changed to FMI Holdings Ltd. ■

Forbes Resources Ltd. (B.C. Sept. 17, 1985)
July 9, 1992 – Name changed to Forbes Medi-Tech Inc. ■

Forbex Mining Resources Inc. (Can. May 29, 1985)
Feb. 13, 1995 – Name changed to Fieldex Exploration Inc.; basis 1 new for 10 old shs. ■

Force Crag Mines Limited. (unknown)
1967 – Continued into Ontario.
Nov. 22, 1974 – Amalgamated with Foxdale Mines Limited (1 for 7.5), Canton Explorations Limited (1.for 5.5), Marquis Explorations Limited (1 for 2.5), Long Point Gas & Oil Incorporated (1 for 3), Darwin Mines Limited (1 for 1.5), Gold Acres Mines Limited (1 for 7) and Home Mining Developments Limited (1 for 7) to form New Force Crag Mines Limited; basis 1 new for 4.5 old shs.

Force Resources Ltd. (B.C. May 26, 1981)
Dec. 5, 1994 – Name changed to Force Technologies Inc.; basis 1 new for 5 old shs. ■

Force Technologies Inc. (B.C. May 26, 1981)
Nov. 4, 1997 – Name changed to Glassmaster Industries Inc.; basis 2 new for 1 old sh. ■

ForceLogix Technologies Inc. (B.C. July 25, 2007)
Mar. 21, 2011 – Name changed to Courtland Capital Inc. ■

Ford Credit Canada Limited (Can. July 23, 1962)
Dec. 12, 2016 – Continued into Nova Scotia.
Jan. 9, 2017 – Name changed to Ford Credit Canada Company.

Ford Motor Company of Canada, Limited (Ont. Aug. 17, 1904)
Dec. 1911 – Continued into Canada.
Oct. 2, 1995 – Acquired by Ford Motor Company for $185 per sh.

Ford Motor Credit Company of Canada Limited (Can. July 23, 1962)
Dec. 1, 1978 – Name changed to Ford Credit Canada Limited. ■

Fording Canadian Coal Trust (Alta. Feb. 28, 2003)
Oct. 31, 2008 – Acquired by Teck Cominco Limited; basis US$82.00 plus 0.245 Teck cl. B subord. vtg. shs. for 1 Fording trust unit.

Fording Inc. (Can. June 20, 2001)
Feb. 28, 2003 – Plan of Arrangement with Teck Cominco Limited, Westshore Terminals Income Fund, Ontario Teachers' Pension Plan Board, Sherritt International Corporation and CONSOL of Canada Inc. to create Fording Canadian Coal Trust; basis either 1 new trust unit, or $35.00, or a combination thereof for 1 com. sh. (see Fording Canadian Coal Trust)

Forefront Industries Inc. (Alta. May 5, 1992)
Apr. 16, 1997 – Formed Augen Capital Corp. in Alberta on amalgamation with Augen Capital Corporation and Forefront Finance Inc. constituting a reverse takeover by Augen; basis 2 new for 1 cl. A Augen sh., 1 new for 2 Forefront Finance shs. and 1 new for 2 Forefront Industries shs. ■

Forefront Uranium Mines Limited (Ont. 1974)
Dec. 2, 1976 – Amalgamated with Daverich Minerals Ltd. and Eldex Minerals Ltd. to form Forefront Consolidated Explorations Ltd.; basis 1 new for 2 old shs.

Forefront Ventures Ltd. (B.C. Mar. 28, 1980)
Feb. 16, 1999 – Name changed to First Echelon Ventures Inc.; basis 1 new for 6.5 old shs. ■

Foreign Currency Exchange Corp. (Fla. Dec. 17, 1987)
Apr. 29, 2003 – Acquired by First Rate Acquisition, Inc.; basis either US$3.50 or Cdn$5.23 per sh.

Foreign Exploration Corp. Ltd. (Ont. 1957)
Nov. 25, 1970 – Dissolved.

Foreign Power Securities Corp. Ltd. (Can. 1927)
Dec. 1967 – Amalgamated to form Warnock Hersey International Ltd.

Foremost Energy Corp. (B.C. 1979)
Nov. 17, 1988 – Name changed to Fifth Avenue Ventures Corp. ■

Foremost Industries Income Fund (Alta. Dec. 27, 2001)
Jan. 3, 2006 – Reorganization of the Fund, the operating limited partnerships and Venture Trust to continue as a new entity named Foremost Income Fund; basis 1 new unit for 1 old unit.

Foremost Industries Inc. (Alta. Aug. 1, 1966)
Dec. 31, 2001 – Converted into Foremost Industries Income Fund; basis $4.00 or 1 trust unit for 1 com. sh. (see Foremost Industries Income Fund)

Foremost International Industries Ltd. (Alta. Aug. 1, 1966)
May 6, 1976 – Name changed to Canadian Foremost Ltd.; basis 1 new for 10 old shs. ■

Foremost Lithium Resource & Technology Ltd. (B.C. July 7, 2005)
Sept. 27, 2024 – Name changed to Foremost Clean Energy Ltd. (see FPsurvey - Mines & Energy)

Foremost Ventures Corp. (B.C. Nov. 28, 2017)
Sept. 22, 2020 – Name changed to KWESST Micro Systems Inc. following Qualifying Transaction reverse takeover acquisition of KWESST Inc. by way of a three-cornered amalgamation.; basis 1 new for 4.67 old shs. ■

Forent Energy Inc. (Alta. May 9, 2006)
Mar. 4, 2009 – Name changed to Forent Energy Ltd. ■

Forent Energy Ltd. (Alta. May 9, 2006)
Apr. 27, 2017 – Placed into receivership by senior lender and Grant Thornton Limited appointed receiver.
May 9, 2017 – Directors resigned and all employees were terminated.
Feb. 6, 2019 – Struck from registry and dissolved.

Foresbec Inc. (Can. 1979)
June 28, 1996 – Acquired by a wholly owned subsid. of Penrod Company for $1.17 per sh.

Foreshore Exploration Partners Corp. (B.C. June 12, 2017)
Mar. 28, 2019 – Name changed to POSaBIT Systems Corporation pursuant to the Qualifying Transaction reverse takeover acquisition of POSaBIT, Inc. and concurrent amalgamation of (old) POSaBIT with wholly owned POSaBIT Merger Sub, Inc. with (old) POSaBIT renamed POSaBIT U.S., Inc. (see FPsurvey - Industrials)

Forest & Marine Investments Ltd. (B.C. Aug. 20, 1990)
Feb. 4, 2013 – Dissolved and struck from register.

Forest Gate Energy Inc. (Can. June 25, 1999)
June 20, 2023 – Dissolved and struck from register.

Forest Gate Resources Inc. (Can. June 25, 1999)
June 30, 2009 – Name changed to Forest Gate Energy Inc.; basis 1 new for 10 old shs. ■

Forest Kerr Mines Ltd. (B.C. 1965)
June 28, 1973 – Dissolved and struck off register.

Forester Resources Inc. (B.C. Jan. 13, 1981)
May 11, 1995 – Name changed to Tullaree Resources Ltd.; basis 1 new for 5 old shs. ■

Foresthill Resources Inc. (B.C. Mar. 9, 1987)
Dec. 12, 1995 – Name changed to Cordex Venture Corporation; basis 1 new for 3 old shs. ■

Forewest Industries Ltd. (Alta. 1986)
Dec. 3, 1993 – Amalgamated with Coexco Petroleum Inc. and Shelter Oil & Gas Ltd. to form Tesco Corporation; basis 1 new for 3.3139652 Coexco Petroleum shs., 1 new for 4 Shelter Oil shs. and 1 new for 9.6526944 Forewest Industries shs. (see Tesco Corporation)

Forge Energy Ltd. (B.C. 1978)
Apr. 8, 1988 – Dissolved.

Forlartic Mines Ltd. (Ont. 1950)
June 1960 – Charter cancelled.

Formaque Gold Mines Ltd. (Que. 1944)
1948 – Acquired by New Formaque Mines Ltd.; basis 1 new for 3 old sh. (see New Formaque Mines Ltd.)

Formation Capital Corporation (B.C. June 13, 1988)
Nov. 13, 2009 – Name changed to Formation Metals Inc.; basis 1 new for 7 old shs. ■

Formation Fluid Management Inc. (B.C. Dec. 15, 2006)
Oct. 17, 2016 – Acquired by Robix Environmental Technologies, Inc. by way of amalgamation with a wholly owned subsid. of Robix to continue as Robix

Environmental Technologies Group, Inc.; basis 0.425 Robix shs. for 1 Formation sh.

Formation Metals Inc. (B.C. June 13, 1988)
Aug. 2, 2016 – Name changed to eCobalt Solutions Inc. ■

FormerXBC Inc. (Can. June 12, 2009 amalg.)
Apr. 13, 2023 – Majority of the U.S. assets were sold. (see FPsurvey - Industrials)

Forrester Metals Inc. (Ont. Dec. 24, 1987)
June 5, 2017 – Acquired by Zinc One Resources Inc.; basis 1 Zinc One com. sh. for 5½ Forrester shs.

Forsys Corporation (Ont. May 13, 1985)
Jan. 31, 2003 – Name changed to Forsys Technologies Inc.; basis 1 new for 9 old shs. ■

Forsys Technologies Inc. (Ont. May 13, 1985)
June 29, 2005 – Name changed to Forsys Metals Corp. (see FPsurvey - Mines & Energy)

Forsyth Mines Limited (Ont. 1956)
July 22, 1982 – Amalgamated with Abino Gold Mines Limited (1 for 12.94), Clicker Red Lake Mines Limited (1 for 18.23), Commander Red Lake Mines Limited (1 for 30.82), Dorion Red Lake Mines Limited (1 for 15.59), Duchesne Red Lake Mines Limited (1 for 10.57), Goldquest Explorations Corp. (1 for 1.26), Inore Gold Mines Limited (1 for 9.9), Laddie Gold Mines Limited (1 for 15.22) and Rowan Gold Mines Limited (1 for 4.91) to form Goldquest Exploration Inc.; basis 1 new for 6.38 old shs.

Fort Chicago Energy Partners L.P. (Alta. Oct. 9, 1997)
Jan. 1, 2011 – Succeeded by Veresen Inc. pursuant to plan of arrangement whereby Veresen Inc. was formed to facilitate the conversion of the limited partnership into a corporation. ■

Fort Chimo Minerals Inc. (Ont. Apr. 15, 1997)
June 15, 2011 – Name changed to Mag Copper Limited; basis 1 new for 5 old shs. ■

Fort Chimo Mines Ltd. (Que. 1946)
June 1958 – Charter cancelled.

Fort Garry Brewing Company Ltd. (Man. Aug. 27, 1992)
May 15, 1993 – Amalgamated in Manitoba to continue with same name. (see Russell Breweries Inc.)
Oct. 23, 2007 – Acquired by Russell Breweries Inc.; basis (i) 1 Russell com. sh. for each sh. held, or (ii) 40¢ per sh., or (iii) a combination of cash and shs. (see Russell Breweries Inc.)

Fort Gary Trust Company (Man. 1964)
Dec. 31, 1980 – Amalgamated with The Fidelity Trust Company (parent co.) to continue under the Fidelity Trust name. Common shldrs. received com. stk of amalg. co. on sh.-for-sh. basis. Pref. shldrs. received 9% 1st pfce. shs. on basis of 1.5 new for 1 old sh.

Fort George Mines Ltd. (Ont. 1966)
1968 – Merged into Jubilant Eagle Holdings and Explorations Ltd.; basis 1 new for 4 old shs.

Fort George Mining & Exploration Ltd. (B.C. 1967)
May 1980 – Charter cancelled.

Fort Hope Explorations Limited (Ont. 1961)
Dec. 1973 – Charter cancelled.

Fort Knox Gold Resources Inc. (Ont. June 26, 1984)
June 24, 2002 – Name changed to FNX Mining Company Inc. ■

Fort Knox Minerals Ltd. (B.C. Apr. 13, 1983)
Sept. 27, 1991 – Dissolved and struck off register.

Ft. Lauderdale Resources Inc. (B.C. Mar. 24, 1966)
June 22, 1990 – Name changed to Amcorp Industries Inc.; basis 1 new for 3 old shs. ■

Fort Norman Explorations Inc. (Que. June 8, 1971)
Nov. 6, 1982 – Name changed to Morgan Hydrocarbons Inc. ■

Fort Point Resources Ltd. (B.C. Nov. 18, 1983)
Sept. 14, 1998 – Name changed to Osprey Energy Ltd.; basis 1 new for 10 old shs. ■

Fort Rae Gold Mines Ltd. (Ont. 1946)
June 3, 1963 – Dissolved. Distributed 0.1396 shs. of Iron Bay Mines and 0.01¢ for each sh. Fort Rae held.

Fort Reliance Minerals Ltd. (Ont. Apr. 9, 1956)
July 1974 – Name changed to Nufort Resources Inc.; basis 2 new for 3 old shs. ■

Fort Rouille Mining Corp. Ltd. (Ont. 1936)
Jan. 1955 – Charter cancelled.

Fort Rupert Resources Ltd. (Ont.)
Sept. 3, 1994 – Dissolved.

Fort St. John Petroleums Ltd. (B.C. 1952)
1980 – Acquired by Inter-City Gas Ltd. for $1.75 per sh.

Fort Steele Gold & Silver Mines Ltd. (unknown)
1958 – Assets acquired by Boreas Mines Ltd. for 800,000 shs.
1962 – Dissolved.

Fortaleza Energy Inc. (Alta. Jan. 15, 2007)
July 2, 2018 – Struck from registry and dissolved.

Forte Resources Inc. (Alta. Jan. 21, 2004)
July 12, 2005 – Plan of Arrangement combination with Thunder Energy Inc. and Mustang Resources Inc. to create a new trust named Thunder Energy Trust plus 3 new exploration cos. - Alberta Clipper Energy Inc., Ember Resources Inc. and Valiant Energy Inc.; basis 0.175 new trust unit, or 0.175 new exch. sh., or a combination thereof, plus 0.3333 new Valiant com. sh. for 1 old Forte com. sh. (see Thunder Energy Trust; Valiant Energy Inc.)

Forte Resources Inc. (B.C. Jan. 24, 2011)
Apr. 16, 2012 – Name changed to Santacruz Silver Mining Ltd. pursuant to Qualifying Transaction reverse takeover acquisition of Santacruz Silver Mining Ltd. (private) and subsequent amalgamation of Santacruz with wholly owned 0931204 B.C. Ltd. (see FPsurvey - Mines & Energy)

Forterra Environmental Corp. (Can. Sept. 29, 2006)
July 23, 2017 – Dissolved and struck from register.

Fortify Resources Inc. (B.C. May 31, 2011)
Mar. 2, 2018 – Name changed to Crop Infrastructure Corp. following reverse takeover acquisition of DV Infrastructure Corp. and concurrent amalgamation of DV Infrastructure with wholly owned 1137129 B.C. Ltd. ■

Fortin Electronics Corp. (Man.)
Aug. 31, 1985 – Dissolved.

Fortis Inc. (Can. June 28, 1977)
Aug. 28, 1987 – Continued into Newfoundland and Labrador. (see FPsurvey - Mines & Energy; FPsurvey - Industrials)

Fortress Base Metals Corp. (B.C. Mar. 28, 1980)
July 21, 2008 – Name changed to Lions Gate Metals Inc. ■

Fortress Blockchain Corp. (B.C. Aug. 16, 2018)
Apr. 12, 2019 – Name changed to Fortress Technologies Inc. ■

Fortress Energy Inc. (Alta. Jan. 15, 2007)
Feb. 28, 2013 – Name changed to Alvopetro Inc. ■

Fortress Financial Corporation (B.C. Aug. 25, 1988)
Aug. 22, 2007 – Name changed to Fortress Petroleum Inc. ■

Fortress IT Corp. (Can. July 31, 2002)
June 28, 2004 – Name changed to Fortress Minerals Corp. following reverse takeover acquisition of International Uranium Corporation (Bermuda II) Ltd. ■

Fortress Minerals Corp. (Can. July 31, 2002)
Dec. 17, 2014 – Name changed to Lundin Gold Inc. following acquisition of Fruta del Norte gold project in southeastern Ecuador. (see FPsurvey - Mines & Energy)

Fortress Mines and Oils Ltd. (Ont. 1950)
1956 – Charter cancelled; shldrs. reported to have received 1 pooled sh. Beaumont Mining Corp. for 1 old sh.

Fortress Paper Ltd. (B.C. May 30, 2006)
Feb. 1, 2018 – Name changed to Fortress Global Enterprises Inc. (see FPsurvey - Industrials)

Fortress Petroleum & Resources Ltd. (B.C. 1980)
July 9, 1982 – Formed Tiburon Petroleum Corporation on amalgamation with Intertex Energy, Ltd.; basis 1.75 new for 1 old sh. ∎

Fortress Petroleum Inc. (B.C. Aug. 25, 1988)
Aug. 8, 2008 – Name changed to Petra Petroleum Inc. ∎

Fortress Resources Inc. (B.C. July 28, 1987 amalg.)
Nov. 3, 1997 – Name changed to Consolidated Fortress Resources Inc.; basis 1 new for 2.7 old shs. ∎

Fortress Technologies Inc. (B.C. Aug. 16, 2018)
Dec. 8, 2021 – Name changed to Cathedra Bitcoin Inc. (see FPsurvey - Industrials)

Fortriu Capital Corp. (B.C. Mar. 28, 2008)
June 15, 2009 – Together with Woodbridge Energy Ltd., Chinook Capital Corp. and Bowram Energy Inc., exchanged their respective net cash for shares of Terrace Resources Inc., all Capital Pool Companies, and each of Woodbridge, Chinook, Bowram and Fortriu, subsequently dissolved; basis 1 Terrace sh. for 0.43 Woodbridge shs., 1 Terrace sh. for 0.56 Chinook shs., 1 Terrace sh. for 0.53 Bowram shs. and 1 Terrace sh. for 0.55 Fortriu shs. (see Terrace Resources Inc.)

Fortsum Business Solutions Inc. (Can. Sept. 11, 2002)
May 25, 2009 – Acquired by GFI Solutions Group Inc. for 82¢ per sh.

Fortuna Silver Mines Inc. (B.C. Sept. 4, 1990)
June 20, 2024 – Name changed to Fortuna Mining Corp. (see FPsurvey - Mines & Energy)

Fortuna Ventures Inc. (B.C. Sept. 4, 1990)
June 28, 2005 – Name changed to Fortuna Silver Mines Inc. ∎

Fortunata Mines Ltd. (Que. 1956)
Nov. 4, 1978 – Charter cancelled.

Fortunate Sun Mining Company Limited (B.C. May 31, 2007)
Aug. 29, 2013 – Name changed to Sonoma Resources Inc.; basis 1 new for 8 old shs. ∎

Fortune Bay Corp. (Can. Dec. 12, 2013)
July 5, 2016 – Name changed to kneat.com, inc. (see FPsurvey - Industrials)

Fortune Bay Resources Ltd. (B.C. Oct. 22, 1987)
May 23, 1989 – Continued into Newfoundland and Labrador.
Sept. 9, 1993 – Name changed to FBA Ventures Ltd.; basis 1 new for 5 old shs. ∎

Fortune Channel Mines Ltd. (B.C. 1969)
Nov. 1972 – Name changed to Consolidated Fortune Channel Mines Ltd.; basis 1 new for 5 old shs. ∎

Fortune Energy Inc. (Alta. Sept. 1, 1993 amalg.)
Dec. 23, 1998 – Amalgamated with 798374 Alberta Ltd., a wholly owned subsid.; basis 1 cl. A pref. sh. for 1 com. sh. immediately redeemed for 80¢ per sh. Co. now private.

Fortune Island Mines Ltd. (B.C. 1966)
July 18, 1986 – Amalgamated with Kerry Mining Ltd. (1 new for 3 old shs.) and Berkley Resources Inc. (1 for 1) to form a new co. also called Berkley Resources Inc.; basis 1 new for 6 old shs.

Fortune Oil and Gas Ltd. (B.C. 1979)
1981 – Continued into Alberta. (see Confederation Energy Corporation Limited)
Jan. 29, 1982 – Amalgamated with Confederation Resources (1980) Ltd. to form Confederation Energy Corporation Limited; basis 1 new for 10 old shs. (see Confederation Energy Corporation Limited)

Fortune Oils Ltd. (Alta. 1949)
1955 – Name changed to Canadian Fortune Oil Ltd. ∎

Fortune 1000 Group Inc. (Can. Sept. 11, 2002)
Jan. 10, 2006 – Name changed to Fortsum Business Solutions Inc. ∎

Fortune River Resource Corp. (B.C. Apr. 24, 1987)
Jan. 7, 2011 – Amalgamated with Bravada Gold Corporation; basis 0.85 Bravada Gold shs. for 1 Fortune River sh.

Fortune Valley Resources Inc. (B.C. Mar. 24, 2006)
Jan. 7, 2010 – Acquired by Orosur Mining Inc. (formerly Uruguay Mineral Exploration Inc.); basis 0.4534 Orosur shs. plus C$0.001 for 1 Fortune Valley sh. (see Orosur Mining Inc.)

Fortune Yellowknife Mines Ltd. (Ont. 1954)
Oct. 1977 – Charter cancelled.

Forty-Four Mines Ltd. (Man. 1934)
1970 – Name changed to New Forty-Four Mines Limited. ∎

49 North Resource Flow-Through Limited Partnership (Sask. July 20, 2005)
Oct. 26, 2006 – Name changed to 49 North Resource Fund Limited Partnership. ∎

49 North Resource Fund Limited Partnership (Sask. July 20, 2005)
Jan. 2, 2008 – Merged and amalgamated with 49 North Resource Fund Inc.; basis 2 49 North Resource Fund Limited Partnership units for 1 49 North Resource Fund Inc. sh.

Forty-Niner Properties Ltd. (B.C. 1978)
Oct. 31, 1985 – Name changed to Caribbean Resources Corp.; basis 1 new for 4 old shs. ∎

Forum Beverages Inc. (B.C. Sept. 15, 1969)
Feb. 7, 1992 – Dissolved and struck off register.

Forum Development Corp. (B.C. Apr. 28, 1986)
June 27, 2006 – Name changed to Forum Uranium Corp. ∎

Forum Energy Corporation (Can. July 19, 1993)
June 7, 2005 – Name changed to FEC Resources, Inc. (see FPsurvey - Mines & Energy)

Forum Resources Inc. (Can. May 13, 1987)
Mar. 6, 1997 – Name changed to Condor Gold Fields Inc. ∎

Forum Resources Ltd. (B.C. Sept. 15, 1969)
Feb. 16, 1989 – Name changed to Forum Beverages Inc. ∎

Forum Uranium Corp. (B.C. Apr. 28, 1986)
Feb. 28, 2018 – Name changed to Forum Energy Metals Corp. (see FPsurvey - Mines & Energy)

Forum Ventures Ltd. (B.C. Apr. 28, 1986)
Oct. 15, 2001 – Name changed to Forum Development Corp.; basis 1 new for 2.5 old shs. ∎

Forward Resources Ltd. (Alta. 1980)
May 23, 1984 – Continued into Canada.
Dec. 5, 1984 – Name changed to Exco Energy Ltd.; basis 1 new for 25 old shs. ∎

Forza Lithium Corp. (B.C. Mar. 3, 2022)
Apr. 8, 2024 – Name changed to Planet Green Metals Inc. pursuant to the acquisition of (old) Planet Green Metals Inc. (see FPsurvey - Mines & Energy)

Forza Petroleum Limited (Can. Dec. 31, 2012)
Feb. 27, 2024 – Acquired by Zeg Oil and Gas Ltd.; basis Cdn$0.15 cash per sh.

The Forzani Group Ltd. (Alta. 1974)
Feb. 1, 1991 – Amalgamated in Alberta to continue with same name.
June 28, 1993 – Amalgamated in Alberta to continue with same name.
Aug. 25, 2011 – Acquired by Canadian Tire Corporation, Limited for $26.50 per sh.
Jan. 1, 2012 – Name changed to FGL Sports Ltd.

Fosco Mining Ltd. (Alta. 1969)
Dec. 1978 – Name changed to Marbaco Resources Ltd.; basis 1 new for 5 old shs. ∎

Foslake Mines Ltd. (Ont. 1953)
Aug. 1961 – Charter cancelled.

La Fosse Platinum Group Inc. (Can. Feb. 29, 1988 amalg.)
May 6, 2004 – Dissolved.

Fossil Bay Resources Ltd. (Yuk. Apr. 10, 2000)
Dec. 30, 2004 – Continued into British Columbia. (see Terra Energy Corp.)
Feb. 1, 2005 – Plan of Arrangement amalgamation with subsid. of Terra Energy Corp.; basis either 1 new Terra sh. or 1 new amalco pfd. sh. immediately redeemed for $1.30 for 1 old Fossil Bay sh. (see Terra Energy Corp.)

Fossil Oil & Gas Limited (Alta. Aug. 13, 1976)
Dec. 31, 1996 – Amalgamated with Elk Point Acquisition Corp., a wholly owned subsid. of Elk Point Resources Inc.; basis (a) 1 special sh. immediately purchased after the amalgamation for $3.76 for 1 com. sh. or (b) 0.5785 of a com. sh. of Elk Point for 1 com. sh. of Fossil or (c) a combination of options (a) and (b). (see Elk Point Resources Inc.)

Foster Lake Mines Ltd. (Ont. 1966)
Aug. 1973 – Reported no longer in existence.

Foster Ledge Gold Mines Ltd. (B.C. 1933)
Jan. 10, 1963 – Dissolved.

Fosters Resources Ltd. (Alta. May 26, 1993)
July 16, 2001 – Name changed to Blue Mountain Resources Ltd.; basis 1 new for 4 old shs. ∎

Fosterville South Exploration Ltd. (B.C. July 22, 2019)
Sept. 20, 2023 – Name changed to Great Pacific Gold Corp. (see FPsurvey - Mines & Energy)

Found Lake Gold Mines Ltd. (Ont. Feb. 27, 1937)
July 27, 1948 – Name changed to Consolidated Found Lake Gold Mines Ltd.; basis 1 new for 5 old shs. ∎

The Foundation Company of Canada Ltd. (Can. 1963)
Dec. 20, 1991 – All o/s pref. shs. redeemed at $20 per sh. plus accrued dividends to the redemption date.

Foundation Consolidated Mines Ltd. (Ont. 1937)
1955 – Name changed to Lithanium Mines Ltd. ∎

Foundation Mines Ltd. (B.C. 1955)
Dec. 11, 1982 – Dissolved.

Foundation Petroleums Limited (Alta. 1936)
1941 – Merged with 8 other companies into Amalgamated Oils Limited; basis 34 new for 500 old shs.

Foundation Resources Inc. (B.C. June 1, 2006)
Oct. 28, 2013 – Name changed to Birch Hill Gold Corp.; basis 1 new for 10 old shs. ∎

Foundation Resources Ltd. (B.C. Feb. 10, 1987)
Aug. 28, 1996 – Continued into Yukon.
Aug. 16, 2002 – Name changed to Fury Explorations Ltd.; basis 1 new for 2 old shs. ∎

Founder Resources Inc. (B.C. Feb. 23, 1990)
Aug. 1, 2005 – Dissolved for failure to file and struck from registry.

Founders Advantage Capital Corp. (Alta. Oct. 1, 1998)
Jan. 1, 2021 – Formed Dominion Lending Centres Inc. in Alberta pursuant to amalgamation with (old) Dominion Lending Centres Inc., following acquistion of remainder of Dominion Lending Centres Limited Partnership. (see FPsurvey - Industrials)

Founders Capital Corp. (Alta. Feb. 27, 1998)
Nov. 21, 2000 – Continued into Ontario.
Jan. 15, 2001 – Name changed to Sentry Select Capital Corp. ■

Founders Energy Ltd. (Alta. Aug. 19, 1993)
Mar. 12, 2001 – Acquired by Provident Energy Ltd. and then com. shs. reclassified into a new security named Provident Energy Trust; basis 1 new Provident trust unit for 3 old Founders com. shs. (see Provident Energy Trust)

Founders Metals Inc. (Can. Apr. 6, 2000)
May 12, 2021 – Continued into British Columbia. (see FPsurvey - Mines & Energy)

Foundry Holdings Corp. (B.C. July 20, 1979)
Sept. 8, 2003 – Name changed to Yangtze Telecom Corp. following reverse takeover acquisition of Intervalue Inc. ■

Fountain House Holdings Corp. (B.C. Apr. 13, 1992)
Sept. 18, 2002 – Name changed to Abbastar Holdings Ltd.; basis 1 new for 15 old shs. ■

Fountainhead Projects Corporation (B.C. May 27, 1999)
Oct. 19, 2000 – Name changed to EMedia Networks International Corporation following reverse takeover acquisition of EMedia Networks Incorporated (formerly B.T.M. Music Network Inc.). ■

4-F Foods Ltd. (B.C. 1968)
Mar. 1982 – Placed into receivership; no distribution to shldrs.

Four Point Mines Ltd. (B.C. 1966)
Feb. 25, 1983 – Struck off register.

Four Points Capital Corp. (B.C. Aug. 19, 2009)
Nov. 17, 2010 – Name changed to Yellowhead Mining Inc. pursuant to Qualifying Transaction reverse takeover acquisition of Yellowhead Mining Inc. and subsequent amalgamation with wholly owned 0887988 B.C. Ltd. ■

Four River Ventures Ltd. (B.C. Feb. 2, 2007)
Nov. 9, 2016 – Name changed to Canabo Medical Inc. following reverse takeover acquisition of Canabo Medical Corporation; basis 1 new for 2 old shs. ■

Four Seasons Hotels Inc. (Ont. Jan. 6, 1978)
Apr. 26, 2007 – Name changed to Four Seasons Holdings Inc. following acquisition by Kingdom Hotels International, Cascade Investment LLC and Isadore Sharp for US$82 per limited vtg. sh.

Four Seasons Hotels Limited (Ont. 1968 amalg.)
Feb. 14, 1978 – Amalgamated with F.S.H. Investments Limited under the Four Seasons Hotels Limited name to become a wholly owned subsid. of Four Seasons Hotels Inc. All minority holdings of com. shs. were exch. for newly created 2nd and 3rd pref. shs., redeem. at $5.62 per sh. (see Four Seasons Hotels Inc.)

Four Seasons Manufacturing Ltd. (B.C. June 23, 1961)
Oct. 29, 1974 – Name changed to Renn Industries Inc. ■

Four Seasons Mining & Resources Ltd. (B.C. June 23, 1961)
Oct. 13, 1971 – Name changed to Four Seasons Manufacturing Ltd. ■

Four Seasons Recreation Ltd. (B.C. June 23, 1961)
June 4, 1970 – Name changed to Four Seasons Mining & Resources Ltd. ■

Four Seasons Resources Ltd. (B.C. Nov. 21, 1983)
Jan. 31, 1991 – Name changed to FSR Industries Inc.; basis 1 new for 3 old shs. ■

Four Star Petroleums Ltd. (Alta. Apr. 20, 1937)
Sept. 13, 1950 – All assets sold to Federated Petroleums Ltd. in 1950 for $300,000. Distribution of 30¢ per sh. made.

4008249 Canada Inc. (Can. 1937)
Sept. 28, 2011 – Dissolved.

4325231 Canada Inc. (B.C. July 10, 2007 amalg.)
Oct. 17, 2007 – Name changed to Global Summit Real Estate Inc. (see Lorus Therapeutics Inc.)

4370422 Canada Inc. (Can. Sept. 12, 2006)
July 2011 – Substantially all the assets required to operate the Levis, Que., shipyard were sold to a consortium consisting of SNC-Lavalin Defence Contractors Inc., Upper Lakes Group Inc. and Daewoo Shipbuilding & Marine Engineering Co. Ltd.
June 19, 2012 – Plan of arrangement submitted to creditors under the CCAA was approved by Quebec court. The arrangement provided distribution of $1 million to creditors, estimated to be ½ cent on the dollar owed.
May 2015 – Deloitte Restructuring as monitor distributed the allocated monies under the plan of arrangement to affected and qualified creditors. No funds were available for shldrs.
July 16, 2018 – Dissolved and struck from register.

4404980 Canada Inc. (Can. Oct. 3, 2005)
Dec. 23, 2011 – Dissolved and struck from register.

4504020 Canada Inc. (Can. June 30, 2001 amalg.)
Mar. 8, 2010 – Placed into bankruptcy. RSM Richter Inc. appointed trustee.
Oct. 29, 2012 – Final distribution made in August 2011. Secured and unsecured creditors suffered a shortfall; no funds available for shldrs. Trustee discharged.

48North Cannabis Corp. (Alta. Oct. 29, 2010)
Sept. 3, 2021 – Acquired by HEXO Corp.; basis 0.02366 HEXO shs. for 1 48North sh.

49 North Resource Fund Inc. (Sask. Jan. 1, 2008 amalg.)
Aug. 25, 2009 – Name changed to 49 North Resources Inc. (see FPsurvey - Mines & Energy; FPsurvey - Industrials)

Fourbar Mines Ltd. (B.C. 1964)
Mar. 1973 – Name changed to Cloverdale Resources Ltd.; basis 1 new for 2 old shs. ■

4Front Ventures Corp. (B.C. July 31, 2019)
June 10, 2025 – Made an assignment into bankruptcy and B.Riley Farber was appointed trustee.

Fox Energy Corporation (Alta. Aug. 23, 1993)
Mar. 8, 2002 – Acquired by EOG Resources Canada Inc. for $0.46 per sh.

Fox Lake Mines Ltd. (Ont. 1955)
Mar. 1976 – Charter cancelled.

Fox Mountain Explorations Ltd. (Ont. Dec. 29, 1997)
May 18, 2006 – Name changed to Migao Corporation pursuant to reverse takeover acquisition of H.K. Migao Industry Limited for 20,400,000 com. shs.; basis 1 new for 17 old shs. ■

Fox Resources Ltd. (B.C. 1981)
Aug. 24, 1988 – Name changed to Foxx Industries Inc. ■

Fox Resources Ltd. (Can. Feb. 3, 2006)
July 6, 2009 – Continued into British Columbia.
Dec. 1, 2011 – Name changed to Big Sky Petroleum Corporation pursuant to reverse takeover acquisition of Big Sky Operating LLC. ■

Foxdale Mines Limited (Ont. 1971)
Nov. 22, 1974 – Amalgamated with Canton Explorations Limited (1 for 5.5), Marquis Explorations Limited (1 for 2.5), Long Point Gas & Oil Incorporated (1 for 3), Darwin Mines Limited (1 for 1.5), Gold Acres Mines Limited (1 for 7), Home Mining Developments Limited (1 for 7) and Force Crag Mines Limited (1 for 4.5) to form New Force Crag Mines Limited; basis 1 new for 7.5 old shs.

Foxgrove Exploration Ltd. (Can. Oct. 15, 1986)
July 12, 2004 – Dissolved.

FoxMeyer Canada Inc. (Ont. June 29, 1994 amalg.)
Oct. 7, 1996 – Name changed to HealthStreams Technology Inc. ■

Foxpoint Capital Corp. (Ont. Dec. 16, 2009)
Apr. 25, 2013 – Name changed to Castle Mountain Mining Company Limited pursuant to Qualifying Transaction reverse takeover acquisition of Telegraph Gold Inc. ■

Foxpoint Resources Ltd. (Can. July 27, 1988)
Oct. 25, 2002 – Name changed to Kirkland Lake Gold Inc. ■

Foxright Mines Ltd. (Ont. 1944)
Name changed to Stonada Mines Ltd. ■

Foxx Industries Inc. (B.C. 1981)
Mar. 20, 1992 – Dissolved and struck off register.

Fracmaster Ltd. (Can. Apr. 5, 1976)
Mar. 1999 – Applied for protection under the Companies' Creditors Arrangement Act in March 1999 and extended to May 14, 1999.
May 17, 1999 – Arthur Andersen Inc. was appointed receiver and manager.
May 21, 1999 – Board of Directors resigned.
May 25, 1999 – Proposal was made by Houston-based BJ Services Company to purchase the company's assets for $80,000,000 (US$55,000,000) which was approved by the Alberta court.
June 29, 1999 – All assets sold to BJ Services, including the Canadian operating assets as well as the U.S. subsidiaries and certain foreign subsidiaries operating in Russia and China. In addition to the purchase price, BJ Services assumed US$3,700,000 in debt owed by subsidiaries included in the purchase and purchased certain assets which had been leased by the company. There were no funds available for shldrs.

Fralex Therapeutics Inc. (Ont. Sept. 16, 1998)
June 3, 2009 – Succeeded by Attwell Capital Inc. pursuant to reorganization whereby all assets excluding technology assets were transferred to newly incorporated Attwell Capital Inc. (formerly 2201861 Ontario Inc.); basis $0.0001 plus 1 Attwell com. sh. for 1 Fralex com. sh. Concurrently, Baylis Medical Company Inc. acquired the technology assets of Fralex from Attwell for $900,000. ■

Franc-Or Resources Corporation (Ont. Oct. 31, 1986 amalg.)
Aug. 25, 1997 – Continued into Yukon.
Nov. 2, 2009 – Name changed to Crocodile Gold Corp. pursuant to reverse takeover acquisition of Crocodile Gold Inc. and subsequent amalgamation of Crocodile Gold Inc. with a wholly owned subsid. of Franc-Or; basis 1 new for 6.3 old shs. ■

Francana Oil & Gas Ltd. (Can. 1952)
May 14, 1982 – Sceptre Resources Limited completed acquisition of the Canadian operations of Francana. Under the reorganization, each com. sh. of Francana exchanged for 2.15 com. shs. of Sceptre. Non-Canadian assets acquired by Hudson Bay Mining and Smelting and Minorco Canada Ltd. (see Hudson Bay Mining and Smelting Co., Limited; Sceptre Resources Limited)

La France Explorations Ltd. (Ont. 1976)
Jan. 23, 1979 – Amalgamated with Glenshire Mines Ltd. (231 for 1,000), Huddersfield Uranium Mines Ltd. (129 for 1,000), Kayak Explorations Ltd. (195 for 1,000), Lunel Management Ltd. (923.5 for 1), Sandhurst Mines Ltd. (1 for 1) and Steppingstone Explorations Ltd. (229 for 1,000) to form Lunel Enterprises Inc.; basis 128 new for 1,000 old shs. (see Lunel Enterprises Inc.)

La France Gold Mines Ltd. (Ont. 1944)
May 1958 – Charter cancelled.

Frances Creek Mines Ltd. (Alta. Oct. 14, 1970)
Aug. 20, 1975 – Name changed to Cal-West Petroleums Ltd.; basis 1 new for 5 old shs. ■

Franchise Bancorp Inc. (Ont. Nov. 2, 1995)
Jan. 23, 2017 – All o/s shs. not already held acquired by WTF Holdings Inc. (owned by Dino Fragaglia, Paul Thomson and James Walker, officers and directors of the company); basis $2.13 cash per sh.

Franchise Global Health Inc. (B.C. Nov. 25, 2019)
Dec. 30, 2022 – Acquired by Flora Growth Corp.; basis 0.29102 Flora com. shs. for each sh. held.

Franchise Services of North America Inc. (Can. Aug. 27, 1998)
May 3, 2013 – Continued into Delaware.

FranchiseMaster Technologies Inc. (Can. July 8, 1991)
Nov. 2, 2005 – Dissolved.

Francisco Gold Corp. (B.C. May 14, 1980)
July 16, 2002 – Plan of Arrangement exchange with Glamis Gold Ltd. and Chesapeake Gold Corporation; basis 1.55 new com. shs. and 1 right of Glamis Gold plus 1 new Chesapeake Gold com. sh. for 1 old Francisco Gold com. sh. (see Glamis Gold Ltd.)

Franco Canadian Mining Co. Ltd. (Ont. 1965)
Sept. 20, 1967 – Name changed to Canuc Mines Ltd. ■

Franco-Nevada Mining Corporation Limited (Can. Oct. 5, 1982)
Apr. 3, 2002 – Name changed to Newmont Mining Corporation of Canada Limited following acquisition by Newmont Mining Corporation (NMC); basis either 0.8 Franco-Nevada exchangeable sh. or 0.8 NMC com. sh. for 1 Franco-Nevada com. sh. ■

Franco Oils Ltd. (Can. 1929)
1955 – Reported as being wound up. Sold all assets, except shs. in Fargo Oils which were distributed to Franco shldrs.; basis 1 Fargo for 5 Franco.

Francoeur Gold Mines Ltd. (Can. 1932)
1956 – Name changed to Francoeur Mines Ltd. ■

Francoeur Mines Ltd. (Can. 1932)
1966 – Assets acquired by Wasamac Mines Ltd.; basis 1 new for 10 old shs.

Franconia Minerals Corporation (Alta. Aug. 7, 1998)
Mar. 10, 2011 – Amalgamated with Duluth Metals Limited; basis either Cdn$0.90 per sh. or 0.328 Duluth shs. plus Cdn$0.001 per sh. or a combination thereof. (see Duluth Metals Limited)

Frandi Mining Corp. (Que. 1958)
Mar. 1976 – Charter cancelled.

Frank Chapple Ltd. (Ont. 1959)
May 1964 – Placed into bankruptcy. Secured creditors expected to get 25¢ on the dollar and unsecured creditors and deb. holders between 5¢ and 8¢. Co. had o/s $145,000 7% conv. s.f. debs. due Nov. 15, 1969. Receiver: S. B. Marks, 134 Wellington St. North, Hamilton, Ont.

Frank W. Horner Limited (Can. 1931)
1961 – Control acquired by Carter-Wallace Inc. through private purch. of all cl. B stk., and offer of $40 per sh. for o/s cl. A stk.

Frankfield Consolidated Corporation (Ont. June 22, 1948)
Apr. 26, 1994 – Name changed to Lagasco Corp. following reverse takeover acquisition of Lakeville Holdings Inc. ■

Frankfield Explorations Ltd. (Ont. June 22, 1948)
Aug. 19, 1992 – Name changed to Frankfield Consolidated Corporation; basis 1 new for 3 old shs. ■

Franklin Gold Mines (1936) Ltd. (Ont. Oct. 8, 1936)
Dec. 1954 – Charter cancelled.

Franklin Gold Mining Co. Ltd. (Ont. 1934)
1936 – Formed to acquire a former gold producer (to 1910). Inactive since presumed dead.

Franklin Mines Ltd. (B.C. 1964)
1966 – Name changed to Tro-Buttle Exploration Limited. ■

Franklin Resources Ltd. (B.C. 1983)
Oct. 16, 1986 – Name changed to European Original New York Seltzer Ltd. ■

Franklin Supply Company Ltd. (Alta. 1975)
Dec. 8, 1995 – Name changed to CE Franklin Ltd. prior to the Jan. 1, 1996, amalgamation with wholly owned Continental Emsco Company Limited, which was acquired on Nov. 3, 1995, constituting a reverse takeover by Continental. ■

Frankly Inc. (Ont. June 7, 2013)
July 11, 2016 – Continued into British Columbia. (see Torque Esports Corp.)
May 15, 2020 – Acquired by Torque Esports Corp.; basis 1 Torque sh. (deemed price of Cdn$1.75 per sh.) for 1 Frankly com.sh. (see Torque Esports Corp.)

Frankport Indin Gold Mines Ltd. (Ont. 1946)
1954 – Charter cancelled.

Frank's Corporation (Alta. Sept. 25, 1985)
Apr. 15, 1999 – Name changed to True North Water Corporation; basis 1 new for 4 old shs. ■

Franksin Mines Ltd. (Que. 1958)
Mar. 1, 1980 – Charter cancelled.

Frankview Oils Ltd. (Ont. 1940)
1945 – Taken over by Apex Consolidated Resources Ltd.; basis 1 new for 10 old shs. (see Apex Consolidated Resources Ltd.)

Franz Capital Corporation (Alta. Mar. 17, 1988)
Sept. 2, 2000 – Struck from registry and dissolved.

Fraser Companies Limited (Can. 1917)
Apr. 11, 1979 – Name changed to Fraser Inc. ■

Fraser Inc. (Can. 1917)
May 30, 1985 – Minority shldrs. approved amalgamation with Noranda Inc. Shldrs. of Fraser received 1 fixed/floating rate convertible retractable ser. B pref. sh. of Noranda for 1 com. sh. (see Noranda Inc.)

Fraser Mackenzie Accelerator Corp. (Ont. Feb. 9, 2022)
Oct. 2, 2024 – Amalgamated with 1000925180 Ontario Limited, a wholly owned subsid. of Forward Water Technologies Corp.; basis 0.95 post-consolidation Forward Water shs.for 1 Fraser Mackenzie sh.

Fraser Papers Inc. (Can. Apr. 19, 2004)
June 23, 2011 – Dissolved.

Fraser River Golds Limited (B.C. Mar. 1934)
Nov. 25, 1943 – Dissolved and struck off register.

FraserFund Financial Corporation (B.C. Oct. 11, 1985)
Feb. 9, 2005 – Name changed to South Pacific Minerals Corp. following reverse takeover acquisition of Island Arc Mining Ltd. ■

FraserFund Venture Capital (V.C.C.) Corporation (B.C. Oct. 11, 1985)
Aug. 12, 1994 – Name changed to FraserFund Financial Corporation. ■

Frebert Mines Ltd. (Ont. 1945)
Oct. 30, 1972 – Dissolved.

Frebert Snow Lake Mines Ltd. (Ont. 1945)
1950 – Name changed to Frebert Mines Ltd. ■

Freckle Ltd. (Ont. June 13, 2019)
May 29, 2020 – Name changed to Killi Ltd. following divestiture of offline attribution and data business. ■

Frecom Communications Company Inc. (B.C. 1986)
May 1, 1990 – Continued into Canada.
July 2, 1992 – Name changed to International Frecom Communications Inc.; basis 1 new for 3 old shs. ■

Fred C. Myers Ltd. (B.C. 1925)
Dec. 23, 1963 – All 5% pref. and jr. pref. shs. redeemed. All com. shs. privately held.

Frederick Mining and Development Ltd. (Ont. 1945)
Aug. 26, 1957 – Merged into Consolidated Frederick Mines Ltd. Latter wound up, and Frederick Mining and Development shs. entitled to equivalent of 86.625¢ per sh. (see Consolidated Frederick Mines Ltd.)

Fredonia Mining Inc. (Alta. Sept. 19, 2012)
Sept. 16, 2022 – Continued into Ontario. (see FPsurvey - Mines & Energy)

Fredonia Oil & Gas Ltd. (B.C. May 21, 1980)
Aug. 20, 1984 – Name changed to Consolidated Fredonia Resources Ltd.; basis 1 new for 4 old shs. ■

Free Energy International Inc. (B.C. Feb. 11, 2005)
Apr. 18, 2016 – Name changed to Darelle Online Solutions Inc. following the acquisition of Darelle Media Inc. (see FPsurvey - Industrials)

Free Nations Mines Ltd. (unknown)
Sept. 1976 – Charter cancelled.

Freedman Wholesale Ltd. (Can. 1949)
June 1966 – M. Loeb, Limited acquired all o/s pref. shs. at $3.25 per sh., and substantially all com. at $11 per sh.

Freedom Battery Metals Inc. (B.C. June 10, 2021)
Oct. 14, 2022 – Name changed to Reflex Advanced Materials Corp. (see FPsurvey - Mines & Energy)

Freedom Energy Inc. (B.C. Apr. 7, 2005)
July 3, 2023 – Dissolved for failure to file and struck from register.

Freedom Marine Ltd. (B.C. 1986 amalg.)
Aug. 29, 1992 – Dissolved and struck off register.

Freedom Resources Ltd. (B.C. 1977)
July 3, 1986 – Name changed to Canadian Trace Minerals Ltd.; basis 1 new for 1.77 old shs. ■

Freeform Capital Partners Inc. (B.C. Nov. 5, 2018)
Dec. 23, 2020 – Name changed to Gold Mountain Mining Corp. pursuant to the Qualifying Transaction reverse takeover acquisition of Bayshore Minerals Incorporated. ■

Freegold Mines Ltd. (Que. 1936)
1946 – Name changed to Freegold Mining Co. Ltd. and continued into Ontario; basis 1 new for 4 old shs. ■

Freegold Mining Co. Ltd. (Ont. 1946)
Nov. 4, 1970 – Dissolved.

FreeGold Recovery Inc. (Alta. July 22, 1985)
Aug. 21, 1991 – Continued into British Columbia.
Nov. 25, 1993 – Name changed to International Freegold Mineral Development Inc.; basis 1 new for 6 old shs. ■

Freehold Gas & Oil Ltd. (B.C. 1956)
Jan. 19, 1979 – Name changed to Westgrowth Petroleums Ltd. ■

Freehold Oil Corp. Ltd. (Can. 1928)
1957 – Sold to Freehold Gas & Oil Ltd.; basis 1 new for 20 old shs.

Freehold Royalty Trust (Alta. Sept. 30, 1996)
Dec. 31, 2010 – Succeeded by Freehold Royalties Ltd. pursuant to plan of arrangement whereby Freehold Royalties Ltd. was formed to facilitate the conversion of the trust into a corporation. (see FPsurvey - Mines & Energy)

Freeholders Oil Co. Ltd. (unknown)
1964 – Acquired by Scurry-Rainbow Oil (Sask.) Ltd.

Freeport Capital Inc. (Alta. Feb. 8, 2005)
Aug. 23, 2013 – Name changed to Hybrid Paytech World Inc. ■

Freeway Resources Ltd. (B.C. 1977)
May 10, 1989 – Name changed to GRD Industries Ltd.; basis 1 new for 2 old shs. ■

Freewest Gold Corp. (Can. Mar. 12, 1984)
Nov. 18, 1986 – Name changed to Freewest Resources Inc. ■

Freewest Resources Canada Inc. (Can. Oct. 21, 1994)
Jan. 29, 2010 – Acquired by 7280831 Canada Inc., a wholly owned subsid. of Cliff Natural Resources Inc.; basis 0.02016 Cliff shs. for 1 Freewest sh.

Freewest Resources Inc. (Can. Mar. 12, 1984)
Dec. 21, 1994 – Amalgamated with a wholly owned subsid. of Hemlo Gold Mines Inc. to form Freewest Resources Canada Inc.; basis 1 new Freewest for 1 old sh. and 1 Hemlo sh. for 4.1 old Freewest shs. (see Freewest Resources Canada Inc.; Hemlo Gold Mines Inc.)

Freewest Resources 1987 & Co. LP (U.S. - unspecified)
Dec. 29, 1988 – Name changed to Freewest Mutual Fund Corp.

Freewheelin' Corp. (Alta. Aug. 7, 1996)
July 11, 2000 – Name changed to FW Omnimedia Corp. ■

Frelor Gold Mines Ltd. (Man. 1947)
Name changed to Burtho Gold Mines Ltd. ■

Fremont Gold Ltd. (B.C. June 6, 2007)
Nov. 5, 2024 – Name changed to Hayasa Metals Inc. (see FPsurvey - Mines & Energy)

French Petroleum Company of Canada Ltd. (Can. Sept. 21, 1956; via Dominion charter)
Sept. 30, 1970 – Name changed to Total Petroleum (North America) Ltd. ■

French Riviera Capital Inc. (Can. Oct. 20, 1998)
Oct. 11, 2002 – Name changed to FRV Media Inc. pursuant to Qualifying Transaction acquisition of Cite-Amerique Inc. ■

French Road Explorations Limited (N.S. 1980)
Nov. 22, 1985 – Merged with Coxheath Gold Holdings Limited; basis 1 new for 1 old sh.

Fresco Developments Ltd. (B.C. Apr. 15, 1979)
Feb. 25, 2002 – Amalgamated with Oromin Explorations Ltd.; basis 1 Oromin sh. for 2 Fresco shs. (see Oromin Explorations Ltd.)

Fresh Ideas Food Corporation (B.C. Mar. 30, 1983)
Sept. 30, 1992 – Name changed to Bobby Cadillac's Food Corporation; basis 1 new for 5 old shs. ■

Freshii Inc. (Ont. July 19, 2007)
Feb. 24, 2023 – Acquired by Foodtastic Inc.; basis $2.30 cash per cl. A subord. vtg. shs.

Freshlocal Solutions Inc. (B.C. Jan. 17, 2018)
May 2023 – Pursuant to a reverse vesting order all the shares of Sustainable Produce Urban Delivery Inc., Organic Express Inc., Mainland Fresh Distribution Inc. and Blush Lane Organic Produce Ltd. (target companies) were acquired for repayment of amounts o/s under the DIP loan amount and an amount required to pay the administration charge, the monthly fee charge and the wind-up amount.
June 26, 2023 – Proceedings under the Companies' Creditors Arrangement Act (CCAA) was terminated and Ernst & Young Inc. as monitor was discharged.
June 30, 2023 – Filed for bankruptcy. Ernst & Young Inc. appointed trustee.

FreshXtend Technologies Corp. (B.C. July 10, 1986)
Dec. 12, 2008 – Amalgamated with 832124 B.C. Ltd., a wholly owned subsid. of FreshXtend International Pty Ltd.; basis 1 cl. A pref. sh. for 1 com. sh. All cl. A pref. shs. immediately redeemed on the following basis: i) shldrs. holding less than 50,000 com. shs. will exchange 1 cl. A pref. for $0.03, ii) shldrs. holding more than 50,000

com. shs. will exchange either 1 cl. A pref. sh. for $0.03 or 50 cl. A pref. shs. for 1 FreshXtend com. sh.

Fresnore Mines Ltd. (Ont. 1945)
Apr. 1958 – Charter cancelled.

Frey Porcupine Gold Mines Ltd. (Ont. 1946)
May 1960 – Charter cancelled.

Freyja Resources Inc. (Can. Feb. 17, 2005)
May 27, 2014 – Name changed to Cyprium Mining Corporation. ■

Friday Capital Inc. (Ont. Feb. 3, 2012)
June 16, 2015 – Name changed to Hit Technologies Inc. following Qualifying Transaction reverse takeover acquisition of (old) Hit Technologies Inc.; basis 1 new for 2.2269 old shs. ■

Friday Mines Ltd. (B.C. Apr. 17, 1957)
1966 – Name changed to Polaris Mines Ltd.; basis 1 new for 3 old shs. ■

Friday Nickel Mines Ltd. (B.C. Apr. 17, 1957)
1959 – Name changed to Friday Mines Ltd. ■

Friday Night Inc. (Alta. Jan. 29, 2008)
Sept. 26, 2018 – Name changed to 1933 Industries Inc. and continued into British Columbia. (see FPsurvey - Industrials)

Friday's Dog Holdings Inc. (B.C. Feb. 27, 1987)
Mar. 12, 2025 – Name changed to Patriot Resources Corp. (see FPsurvey - Mines & Energy; FPsurvey - Industrials)

Friedrich Technologies Inc. (B.C. 1983)
May 13, 1988 – Name changed to International Prime Technologies Inc. ■

Frigistors Ltd. (Can. 1959)
July 1967 – Name changed to Termco, Ltd.

Frisco Bay Industries Ltd. (Can. 1989)
Apr. 9, 2004 – Acquired by The Stanley Works for Cdn$15.25 per sh.

Froberta Minerals Limited (Ont. 1956)
Jan. 17, 1983 – Charter cancelled.

Frobex Limited (Ont. 1940)
Nov. 1977 – Charter cancelled.

Frobisher Exploration Co. Ltd. (Ont. 1940)
Mar. 17, 1947 – Name changed to Frobisher Ltd. ■

Frobisher Ltd. (Ont. 1940)
Oct. 30, 1962 – Name changed to Frobex Limited; basis 1 new for 7 old shs. ■

Frobisher Resources Ltd. (B.C. 1978)
Nov. 21, 1991 – Amalgamated with Aurora Gold Ltd. to form Canadian Frobisher Resources Ltd.; basis 1 new for 6.25 Aurora shs. and 1 new for 1 Frobisher sh. (see Canadian Frobisher Resources Ltd.)

Frodac Consolidated Energy Resources Ltd. (Ont. Apr. 26, 1979 amalg.)
July 25, 1985 – Name changed to Global Aerospace Systems Inc.; basis 1 new for 6 old shs. ■

Frodac Mines Ltd. (Ont. 1974)
Apr. 26, 1979 – Amalgamated with Great Bear Silver Mines Limited and Silver Monarch Mines Limited to form Frodac Consolidated Energy Resources Ltd.; basis 1 new for 6 old shs.

Frokar Gold Mines Ltd. (Ont. 1946)
1955 – Charter cancelled.

Frond Lake Mining Co. Ltd. (Ont. 1943)
Oct. 17, 1979 – Name changed to Solo Resources & Energy Inc. ■

Fronsac Capital Inc. (Can. June 2, 2006)
Mar. 11, 2011 – Continued into Quebec.
July 1, 2011 – Succeeded by Fronsac Real Estate Investment Trust pursuant to plan of arrangement whereby Fronsac Real Estate Investment Trust was formed to facilitate the conversion of the corporation into a trust. ■

Fronsac Real Estate Investment Trust (Que. Mar. 11, 2011)
June 22, 2021 – Name changed to Canadian Net Real Estate Investment Trust. (see FPsurvey - Industrials)

Front Range Resources Ltd. (Alta. Aug. 30, 2010)
Oct. 5, 2018 – Name changed to Arrow Exploration Corp. following reverse takeover of Arrow Exploration Ltd. and amalgamation of (old) Arrow with wholly owned 2118295 Alberta Ltd.; basis 1 new for 8.5 old shs. (see FPsurvey - Mines & Energy)

Front Street Long/Short Income Fund (Ont. Apr. 28, 2005)
Aug. 10, 2007 – Merged with Front Street Rollover Fund Limited to continue as Front Street Opportunity Funds Ltd.; basis 1 cl. B sh. of Front Street Opportunity Funds Ltd. for 1 old unit of Long/Short Income Fund.

Front Street Long/Short Income Fund II (Ont. Sept. 21, 2005)
June 2, 2006 – Merged into Front Street Long/Short Income Fund I; basis 0.959157 new Fund I unit for 1 old Fund II unit. (see Front Street Long/Short Income Fund)

Front Street MLP Income Fund Ltd. (Can. Sept. 28, 2010)
Dec. 17, 2012 – Merged into Front Street U.S. MLP Income Fund Ltd.; basis 0.997946 Front Street U.S. MLP shs. for 1 Front Street MLP sh.

Front Street MLP Income Fund II Ltd. (Can. Mar. 23, 2011)
Dec. 17, 2012 – Name changed to Front Street U.S. MLP Income Fund Ltd. following merger with Front Street MLP Income Fund Ltd.; basis 0.997946 Front Street U.S. MLP shs. for 1 Front Street MLP sh. ■

Front Street Performance Fund (Ont. Apr. 16, 2002)
Sept. 5, 2006 – Merged into Front Street Performance Fund II; basis 2.8353 new Fund II units for 1 old Fund unit. (see Front Street Performance Fund II)

Front Street Performance Fund II (Ont. Sept. 29, 2004)
Mar. 2, 2009 – Merged into Front Street Mutual Funds Limited; basis 1.008616 Front Street Canadian Equity Fund cl. B shs. for 1 Front Street Performance Fund II unit.

Front Street Resource Performance Fund Ltd. (Can. May 28, 2007)
Oct. 28, 2009 – Converted to an open-ended mutual fund.

Front Street Strategic Yield Fund Ltd. (Can. Mar. 26, 2010)
Aug. 13, 2013 – Merged into Front Street U.S. MLP Income Fund Ltd.; basis 0.455535 Front Street U.S. equity ser. C shs. for 1 Front Street Strategic sh. (see Front Street U.S. MLP Income Fund Ltd.)

Front Street U.S. MLP Income Fund Ltd. (Can. Mar. 23, 2011)
Jan. 26, 2016 – Merged into Front Street MLP and Infrastructure Income Class, a class of shares of Front Street Mutual Funds Limited; basis 1 Front Street MLP series MC sh. and 1 Front Street MLP series MU sh. for each Front Street U.S. series C and series U equity shs. held., respectively.

Fronteer Development Group Inc. (Ont. Jan. 11, 1999)
May 13, 2010 – Name changed to Fronteer Gold Inc. ■

Fronteer Gold Inc. (Ont. Jan. 11, 1999)
Apr. 11, 2011 – Acquired by Newmont Mining Corporation; basis $14 plus 0.25 Pilot Gold Inc. com. shs. for 1 Fronteer com. sh.

Frontenac Exploration & Development Co. Ltd. (Can. 1939)
1956 – Name changed to Anaconda Co. (Canada) Ltd.

Frontend International Technologies Inc. (B.C. 1982)
Feb. 26, 1993 – Dissolved and struck off register.

Frontend Resources Ltd. (B.C. 1982)
July 16, 1986 – Name changed to Frontend International Technologies Inc.; basis 3 new for 1 old sh. ■

Frontera Copper Corporation (Can. Mar. 12, 2002)
May 5, 2009 – Acquired by Invecture Group, S.A. de C.V. for 75¢ per sh.
May 12, 2009 – Continued into British Columbia.

Frontier Acquisition Corp. (Alta. Oct. 20, 2011)
Feb. 15, 2013 – Name changed to Northern Frontier Corp.; basis 1 new for 15 old shs. ■

Frontier Copper Mines Limited (Ont. 1968)
Aug. 1973 – Charter cancelled.

Frontier Exploration Ltd. (B.C. 1951)
Sept. 27, 1976 – Name changed to New Frontier Exploration Inc.; basis 1 new for 4 old sh. ■

Frontier Minerals Inc. (B.C. May 27, 1987)
Aug. 22, 2005 – Struck from register and dissolved.

Frontier Oil Corporation (Wyo. 1976)
July 1, 2011 – Merged with North Acquisition, Inc., a wholly owned subsid. of Holly Corporation, and then merged into Holly Corporation (renamed HollyFrontier Corporation); basis 0.4811 HollyFrontier shs. for 1 Frontier sh.

Frontier Pacific Mining Corporation (B.C. Jan. 27, 1981)
July 16, 2008 – Acquired by Eldorado Gold Corporation; basis 0.122 Eldorado shs. plus Cdn$0.0001 for 1 Frontier Pacific sh.

Frontier Rare Earths Limited (British Virgin Islands Dec. 20, 2002)
Oct. 1, 2015 – Voluntarily delisted from TSX; continued to trade on U.S. OTC market.

Frontier Royalties Limited (Alta. 1937)
1941 – Merged with 8 other companies into Amalgamated Oils Limited; basis 85 new for 500 old shs.

Frontline Technologies Inc. (Ont. Nov. 30, 1993)
Jan. 4, 2013 – Assigned into bankruptcy. KSV Advisory Inc. (formerly Duff & Phelps Canada Restructuring Inc.) appointed as trustee. All directors resigned.

Frood Deep Nickel Mines Ltd. (Ont. 1927)
Dec. 3, 1980 – Amalgamated with 3 other companies to form Hoffman Exploration & Minerals Limited; basis 2.91489 old for 1 new sh.

Frozya Industries Inc. (B.C. Sept. 19, 1984)
May 4, 1994 – Delisted from the Vancouver Stock Exchange. Subsequently struck from register and dissolved for failure to file.
Aug. 31, 1994 – Name changed to Canex Resources Corporation.

Fruehauf Canada Inc. (Can. 1928)
Jan. 12, 1988 – Acquired by the Trailmobile Group of Companies Ltd. through a wholly owned subsid. at $39 per sh. The acquisition was completed making Fruehauf a wholly owned subsid.

Fruehauf Trailer Company of Canada Limited (Can. 1928)
Apr. 24, 1979 – Name changed to Fruehauf Canada Inc. ■

Fry Red Lake Mines Ltd. (Ont. 1946)
1953 – Charter cancelled.

Fuego Oil Co. Ltd. (Can. 1923)
Dec. 18, 1935 – Dissolved.

Fuel Cell Technologies Corporation (Ont. May 5, 2000)
Apr. 3, 2006 – Name changed to MP Western Properties Inc. pursuant to reorganization which included a transaction with Madison Pacific Properties Inc. and transfer of assets, business and goodwill to Fuel Cell Technologies Ltd. (FCTL). Following a 1-for-10 consolidation, com. shs. were exchanged for 1 MP Western cl. A sh., 1 MP Western cl. B sh. and 1 FCTL com. sh. ■

FuelCell Energy, Ltd. (Alta. Sept. 11, 2003)
Oct. 29, 2004 – Privatized; basis 1 new FuelCell Energy, Inc. com. sh. for 1 old FuelCell Energy, Ltd. exch. sh.

Fuelcorp International Inc. (B.C. Mar. 7, 1979)
May 27, 1994 – Name changed to Specialty Retail Concepts Inc. ■

Fulbro Red Lake Gold Mines Ltd. (Ont. 1945)
June 3, 1947 – Sold property and assets to Consolidated Fulbro Gold.

Fulcrum Capital I Inc. (Alta. July 30, 2004)
Jan. 30, 2006 – Formed Macro Enterprises Inc. in British Columbia on Qualifying Transaction reverse takeover acquisition of Macro Industries Inc. by wholly owned Macro Acquisitions Inc. and amalgamation of Fulcrum with Macro Acquisitions.; basis 1 new for 5 old shs. ■

Fulcrum Developments Ltd. (B.C. Nov. 21, 1980)
Aug. 15, 1996 – Name changed to Wespac Mining Corp.; basis 1 new for 3 old shs. ■

Fulcrum Resources Inc. (Can. Apr. 20, 2004)
Feb. 7, 2013 – Dissolved and struck from register.

Fulcrum Technologies Inc. (Can. Sept. 1983)
Mar. 31, 1998 – Acquired by PC DOCS Group International Inc.; basis 1 PC DOCS sh. for 4.4 Fulcrum shs. (see PC DOCS Group International Inc.)

Full Metal Zinc Ltd. (B.C. Jan. 27, 2011)
Apr. 7, 2014 – Name changed to Aftermath Silver Ltd. (see FPsurvey - Mines & Energy)

Full Riches Investments Ltd. (B.C. Dec. 1, 1980)
Feb. 24, 2004 – Formed Medoro Resources Ltd. in Yukon on amalgamation with Medoro Resources Ltd., a wholly owned subsid. of Gold Mines of Sardinia plc, with Full Riches the deemed acquiror; basis 0.5 new for 1 old sh. ■

Fuller Capital Corp. (B.C. Oct. 30, 2009)
Jan. 8, 2013 – Name changed to Emerita Gold Corp. pursuant to Qualifying Transaction reverse takeover acquisition of 2244182 Ontario Inc. ■

Fummerton Mining and Development Co. Ltd. (Ont. 1945)
Oct. 1949 – Charter cancelled.

Fun Key Studios Inc. (Can. June 26, 1997)
June 17, 2005 – Dissolved.

Functional Technologies Corp. (B.C. Oct. 18, 1999)
June 12, 2013 – Stay of bankruptcy lifted. Abakhan & Associates Inc. appointed trustee and all officers and directors resigned.

Fundamental Applications Corp. (B.C. July 14, 2014)
Apr. 18, 2017 – Name changed to Global Cannabis Applications Corp. ■

Fundy Bay Copper Mines Ltd. (Ont. 1951)
1966 – Name changed to Fundy Explorations Ltd.; basis 1 new for 5 old shs. ■

Fundy Cable Ltd./Ltée (N.B. Mar. 11, 1965)
Mar. 4, 1994 – Continued into Canada.
Sept. 8, 1997 – Name changed to Fundy Communications Inc. ■

Fundy Chemical International Ltd. (N.B. 1964)
1977 – Wound up voluntarily. Distribution to shldrs $1.42 per sh.

Fundy Communications Inc. (Can. Mar. 4, 1994)
Mar. 4, 1998 – All o/s subord. vtg. shs. redeemed for $10.50 per sh. Co. now private.

Fundy Explorations Ltd. (Ont. 1951)
Mar. 1976 – Charter cancelled.

Fundy Forest Industries Limited (N.B. 1969)
Apr. 1972 – Placed into receivership.
Sept. 14, 1973 – All assets sold to Lake Utopia Paper Ltd in 1973. Principal amts. and accr. int. paid in full to holders of 9.75% 1st mtge. bonds, ser. A and 10% 1st mtge. bonds, ser. B.

Funtime Hospitality Corp. (Ont. Dec. 6, 1995 amalg.)
Feb. 1, 2006 – Placed into receivership. Schwartz, Levitsky, Feldman Inc. appointed receiver.

Fura Emeralds Inc. (Ont. June 14, 2013)
Apr. 11, 2017 – Name changed to Fura Gems Inc. ■

Fura Gems Inc. (Ont. June 14, 2013)
Nov. 2, 2020 – All o/s com. shs. not already held acquired by Lord of Seven Hills Holdings FZE; basis 15¢ cash per sh.

Furlong Plastics Ltd. (Ont. 1958)
Nov. 1970 – All o/s pref. and com. shs. exchanged for pref. and com. shs. of The SteelTree Group Inc. Furlong share purchase warrants assumed by SteelTree.

Fury Explorations Ltd. (B.C. May 3, 1966)
May 31, 1990 – Name changed to Sundance Resources Ltd.; basis 1 new for 3 old shs. ■

Fury Explorations Ltd. (Yuk. Aug. 28, 1996)
Sept. 21, 2006 – Continued into British Columbia.
Aug. 15, 2008 – Acquired by Golden Predator Mines Inc.; basis 1 Golden Predator com. sh. and 1.5 Golden Predator wts. for 3 Fury com. shs.

Fuse Cobalt Inc. (B.C. May 31, 2016)
Feb. 2, 2023 – Name changed to Fuse Battery Metals Inc. (see FPsurvey - Mines & Energy)

Fusion Gold Ltd. (B.C. Apr. 16, 2007)
Feb. 12, 2021 – Name changed to Battery Mineral Resources Corp. pursuant to the Qualifying Transaction reverse takeover acquisition of (old) Battery Mineral Resources Corp. and concurrent amalgamation of (old) Battery Mineral with wholly owned 1234525 B.C. Ltd.; basis 1 new for 2 old shs. (see FPsurvey - Mines & Energy; FPsurvey - Industrials)

Fusion Pharmaceuticals Inc. (Can. Dec. 22, 2014)
June 5, 2024 – Acquired by AstraZeneca AB, a wholly owned subsid. of AstraZenca PLC; basis US$21.00 cash per sh.

Fusion Resources Limited (Australia May 14, 2002)
Feb. 20, 2009 – Acquired by Paladin Energy Ltd.; basis 1 Paladin Energy sh. for 6 Fusion Resources shs.

The Futura Loyalty Group Inc. (Can. June 26, 2000)
Feb. 4, 2013 – Acquired by Pong Marketing and Promotions Inc. for an aggregate $1.00 pursuant to CCAA proceedings.

Future Avenir Corp. (Ont. 1987)
June 27, 1996 – Amalgamated with Consolidated Madison Holdings Ltd. to form a new co. known as Ourominas Minerals Inc.; basis 0.9 new com. sh. of Ourominas for 1 cl. A sub. vtg. sh. and 1 new com. sh. of Ourominas for 1 cl. B multi-vtg. sh. (see Ourominas Minerals Inc.)

Future Beach Corporation (Can. Sept. 30, 1992)
Jan. 2006 – Filed a Notice of Intention To Make a Proposal under the Bankruptcy and Insolvency Act of Canada. In addition, the company transferred its manufacturing facilities in favour of third party manufacturing facilities which were still operational. This was expected to achieve major savings in manufacturing and operating costs. The company received interim financing and was preparing a proposal to creditors. H.H.

Davis & Associates, Inc. of Montreal was appointed trustee.
Apr. 19, 2006 – First creditors meeting was held, however assets totaled $0 and liabs. totaled $9,987,339. It was determined that there were no funds available for shldrs.

Future Farm Technologies Inc. (B.C. May 31, 1984)
May 27, 2024 – Dissolved and struck from the registry.

Future Fuel Corporation (B.C. Mar. 3, 2015)
July 8, 2022 – Name changed to American Future Fuel Corporation. ∎

Future Group Innovations Inc. (B.C. Sept. 17, 1985)
Jan. 15, 1992 – Name changed to Interstat Ventures Inc.; basis 1 new for 3 old shs. ∎

Future Link Systems Inc. (Wyo. Jan. 29, 1999)
Sept. 28, 2001 – Name changed to Cal-Star Inc.; basis 1 new for 2 old shs. ∎

Future Media Technologies Corp. (B.C. Aug. 4, 1986)
Jan. 29, 1999 – Continued into Wyoming.
June 21, 1999 – Name changed to Future Link Systems Inc.; basis 1 new for 10 old shs. ∎

Future Mineral Corporation (Yuk. Apr. 13, 1999)
Jan. 25, 2007 – Dissolved and struck off register.

Future Shop Ltd. (B.C. Dec. 2, 1983)
June 11, 1993 – Continued into Canada.
Nov. 5, 2001 – Acquired by Future Shop Acquisition Inc., a wholly owned subsid. of Minnesota-based Best Buy Co. Inc.; basis $17 per com. sh.
June 17, 2002 – Name changed to Best Buy Canada Ltd.

FutureFund Capital (VCC) Corp. (B.C. Mar. 7, 1994)
Aug. 15, 2003 – Name changed to Pender Growth Fund (VCC) Inc.; basis 1 series 1 cl. A sh. for 50 com. shs. ∎

Futureline Communications Co. Ltd. (Ont. 1986)
Sept. 18, 2003 – Dissolved and struck from register.

Futuremed Healthcare Income Fund (Ont. Nov. 25, 2005)
Jan. 1, 2011 – Succeeded by Futuremed Healthcare Products Corporation pursuant to plan of arrangement whereby Futuremed Healthcare Products Corporation was formed to facilitate the conversion of the fund into a corporation. ∎

Futuremed Healthcare Products Corporation (Ont. Mar. 29, 2010)
Mar. 14, 2012 – Acquired by Cardinal Health, Inc. for $8.15 per sh.

Futureplast Technologies Ltd. (Alta. Sept. 14, 1977)
Mar. 1, 1997 – Struck off register.

Futureview Inc. (Man. July 12, 2000)
Aug. 9, 2004 – Dissolved.

Futurity Drilling & Development Co. Ltd. (unknown)
1952 – In voluntary liquidation.

Futurity Oils Limited (Alta. July 9, 1952)
Nov. 1, 1985 – Formed Canadian Futurity Oils Ltd. in Alberta on amalgamation with Kaskada Resources Ltd. (2 for 13); basis 1 Canadian Futurity cl. A sh. for 4 Futurity Oils shs. ∎

Futurtek Communications Inc. (B.C. Dec. 14, 1979)
Sept. 1988 – Acquired by Com Systems Inc.
May 1, 1992 – Dissolved and struck off register.

G

G & B Automated Equipment Limited (Ont. 1964)
Jan. 1994 – Bankrupt. No distribution to shldrs.
Sept. 17, 1994 – Dissolved.

G & H Steel Industries Limited (Can. 1949)
Apr. 1983 – All o/s shs. acquired at $5.75 per sh. by Harris Steel Group Inc.

G & H Steel Service of Canada, Ltd. (Can. 1949)
Feb. 28, 1973 – Name changed to G & H Steel Industries Limited. ∎

G. Tamblyn Limited (Can. 1928)
Mar. 1, 1975 – All o/s com. shs. acquired by a wholly owned subsid. of Loblaws Limited at $20 per sh.

G2 Resources Inc. (Alta. Apr. 8, 2005)
July 22, 2008 – Acquired by Regal Energy Ltd.; basis 2 Regal com. shs. for 3 G2 com. shs.

G2 Technologies Corp. (B.C. Oct. 9, 2014)
June 9, 2022 – Name changed to G2 Energy Corp. (see FPsurvey - Industrials)

G4G Capital Corp. (B.C. Mar. 26, 1987)
Dec. 19, 2016 – Continued into Ontario.
Dec. 23, 2016 – Name changed to White Gold Corp. (see FPsurvey - Mines & Energy)

GA Capital Corp. (Ont. June 25, 2007)
Apr. 21, 2010 – Dissolved following Qualifying Transaction acquisition of 3,500,000 units of Xtierra; basis 0.4117647 Xtierra units for 1 GA Capital com. sh. Subsequently all purchased Xtierra units were distributed to the shldrs. (see Xtierra Inc.)

GAR Limited (Ont. Feb. 20, 1987)
Aug. 29, 2018 – Name changed to Netcoins Holdings Inc. ∎

GASFRAC Energy Services Inc. (Alta. Aug. 6, 2010 amalg.)
July 7, 2015 – Companies' Creditor Arrangement Act (CCAA) plan of compromise and arrangement implemented under which Calfrac Well Services Ltd. acquired the company as an operating entity pursuant to court order. Unsecured creditors, other than holders of 7% unsecured subordinate debentures, would recover 100% of their allowed claims while holders of the 7% debentures would recover between 37% and 55% of the principal amount of the unsecured claims. All o/s com. shs. were cancelled without any consideration, all officers and directors resigned and was dissolved and struck from register.

GATE Energy Inc. (Alta. Aug. 24, 1999)
Oct. 19, 2000 – Continued into British Columbia.
Dec. 5, 2000 – Name changed to Metahost.net Technologies Inc. following Qualifying Transaction reverse takeover acquisition of Metahost.net Technologies Inc. ∎

GB Minerals Ltd. (B.C. July 24, 2007)
Mar. 1, 2018 – All o/s com. shs. not already held acquired by Itafos; basis (i) 0.035714 Itafos sh. for 1 GB Mineral sh.; or (ii) a combination of Cdn$0.05 cash and 0.077905 Itafos sh. for 1 GB Mineral sh. (see Itafos)

GBC Capital Ltd. (Can. Nov. 4, 1968)
Jan. 25, 1989 – Name changed to GBC North America Fund Inc.

GBLT Corp. (Ont. Dec. 9, 2014)
May 14, 2024 – Voluntarily delisted. (see FPsurvey - Industrials)

GBM Explorations Ltd. (B.C. 1984)
June 27, 1986 – Name changed to American Biodynamics Inc.; basis 2 new for 1 old sh. ∎

GBO Inc (Que. July 7, 1976; via letters patent)
Oct. 14, 2011 – Assignment into bankruptcy. RSM Richter Inc. appointed trustee.

G.B.S. Electrical Controls Ltd. (B.C. 1969)
June 1975 – Name changed to North American Technology Limited. ∎

GBS Gold International Inc. (B.C. Feb. 10, 1988)
Mar. 12, 2009 – Ferrier Hodgson, liquidator of the company's Australian group of companies, advised that

the purchase and sale of substantially all of the group's assets was to be finalized shortly. Sale proceeds would not be sufficient to discharge the company's obligations to its secured creditors, resulting in no proceeds available for distrib. to shldrs. The company has ceased operating and all officers and directors have resigned.
Nov. 14, 2011 – Dissolved and struck from register.

GBX Mines Ltd. (B.C. Aug. 21, 1972)
July 1979 – Name changed to El Paso Energy Corp.; basis 1 new for 3 old shs. ∎

GBX Resource Corporation (B.C. 1987)
Dec. 18, 1992 – Dissolved and struck off register.

GC-Global Capital Corp. (Can. Dec. 31, 2005 amalg.)
Aug. 31, 2015 – Name changed to Fountain Asset Corp. (see FPsurvey - Industrials)

GC Greyhawke Corporation (Alta. June 30, 1988 amalg.)
Dec. 1, 1995 – Dissolved and struck off register.

GCH Capital Partners Inc. (B.C. Nov. 9, 2005)
Sept. 19, 2008 – Name changed to Solarvest BioEnergy Inc. following Qualifying Transaction acquistion of Phycobiologics (Europe) Limited. (see FPsurvey - Industrials)

GCL Graphic Communications Limited (Ont. 1970)
Dec. 15, 1976 – Placed into receivership and all assets sold. Price Waterhouse Ltd., Toronto appointed receiver. No distribution to shldrs.

GCM Mining Corp. (B.C. May 27, 1982)
Sept. 28, 2022 – Name changed to Aris Mining Corporation. (see FPsurvey - Mines & Energy)

GCP Mining Corporation (B.C. Feb. 9, 1983)
Sept. 8, 2003 – Name changed to Kodiak Exploration Limited. ∎

GDG Environment Group Ltd. (Que. Feb. 1, 2005)
Feb. 2, 2011 – Privatized; basis 1 for 400,000 shs. or 6¢ per pre-consol. sh. for fraction of post-consol. shs.

GDV Resources Inc. (Ont. Mar. 25, 1994 amalg.)
Sept. 13, 2013 – Name changed to Cardinal Capital Partners Inc. ∎

GE Credit Equipment Finance Inc. (Can. 1959)
Sept. 17, 1988 – Name changed to General Electric Capital Equipment Finance Inc.

GEA Technologies Ltd. (Alta. May 3, 2011)
Dec. 5, 2017 – Name changed to International Cannabrands Inc. following reverse takeover acquisition of DropLeaf, LLC and concurrent amalgamation of DropLeaf with wholly owned International Cannabrands Ltd. to continue as International Cannabrands Ltd. ∎

G.E.L. Oils Limited (Alta. Oct. 1, 1948)
1958 – Struck off register.

G.E.M. Environmental Management, Inc. (B.C. 1980)
July 1990 – Continued into Delaware.
June 29, 1995 – Acquired by G.E.M. Acquisition Co. Inc. for US$0.22 per sh.

GEN III Oil Corporation (B.C. Sept. 27, 1984)
Dec. 6, 2017 – Continued into Alberta.
May 17, 2021 – Name changed to ReGen III Corp. (see FPsurvey - Mines & Energy; FPsurvey - Industrials)

GENIVAR Income Fund (Que. Mar. 31, 2006)
Jan. 1, 2011 – Succeeded by GENIVAR Inc. pursuant to plan of arrangement whereby GENIVAR Inc. was formed to facilitate the conversion of the fund into a corporation and the fund was subsequently dissolved. ∎

GENIVAR Inc. (Que. Jan. 1, 2011; amalg.)
Jan. 1, 2014 – Succeeded by WSP Global Inc. pursuant to plan of arrangement whereby wholly owned WSP Global Inc. was formed to acquire GENIVAR Inc. (renamed WSP Canada Inc.). (see FPsurvey - Industrials)

GEO Piaja Exploration Corp. (Alta. Sept. 1, 1995)
Mar. 27, 1998 – Name changed to Contact Exploration Inc. ∎

GEOCAN Energy Inc. (Alta. Jan. 12, 1998)
Oct. 16, 2008 – Acquired by Arsenal Energy Inc.; basis 70¢ or 0.81 Arsenal shs. for 1 GEOCAN sh.

G.E.Q. Corporation (Que. 1966)
Aug. 23, 1986 – Charter cancelled.

GFE Capital Corp. (B.C. Jan. 24, 2007)
Oct. 21, 2010 – Name changed to Golden Touch Resources Corp. ∎

GFI Oil & Gas Corporation (Alta. Feb. 22, 2006 amalg.)
Mar. 19, 2008 – Acquired by Salamander Energy plc; basis of either US$0.3129 and 0.1573 Salamander ordinary shs., or 0.218 Salamander ordinary shs. for 1 GFI com. sh.

GFK Resources Inc. (B.C. Aug. 29, 1979)
July 13, 2012 – Continued into Canada.
July 31, 2017 – Name changed to Opus One Resources Inc. ∎

GFL Environmental Corporation (Ont. Sept. 4, 2007)
Nov. 3, 2013 – Name changed to GFL Environmental Inc. (see FPsurvey - Industrials)

GFL Waste and Recycling Solutions Corp. (Ont. Sept. 4, 2007)
Feb. 1, 2011 – Name changed to GFL Environmental Corporation. ∎

GFM Resources Limited (B.C. Sept. 3, 1987)
July 25, 2000 – Continued into Yukon. (see FPsurvey - Mines & Energy)

GFY Resources Inc. (Ont. Dec. 19, 1980)
Jan. 20, 1981 – Name changed to Dasher Resources Ltd. ∎

G4G Resources Ltd. (B.C. Mar. 26, 1987)
Jan. 23, 2015 – Name changed to G4G Capital Corp.; basis 1 new for 10 old shs. ∎

GGD Resources Inc. (Can. Mar. 1, 1978)
June 12, 2009 – Name changed to God's Lake Resources Inc. ∎

GGL Diamond Corp. (B.C. May 25, 1981)
Sept. 8, 2009 – Name changed to GGL Resources Corp. (see FPsurvey - Mines & Energy)

G. H. Wood & Company Limited (Can. 1927)
Sept. 1965 – Public interest in co. terminated on redempt. of all o/s 5.5% pref. shs., $100 par.

GHG Resources Limited (B.C. June 7, 1983)
Mar. 29, 2007 – Name changed to Los Andes Copper Limited. (see FPsurvey - Mines & Energy)

G.H.I. Mortgage Investors (Man. 1974)
Nov. 21, 1985 – Dissolved.

GHJ Capital Inc. (Ont. Apr. 29, 2008)
Oct. 6, 2009 – Name changed to xRM Global Inc. (see FPsurvey - Industrials)

GHK Resources Ltd. (B.C. Feb. 1, 1983)
Aug. 1, 1997 – Name changed to Bainbridge Minerals Ltd. ∎

GHP Exploration Corporation (Ont. Apr. 17, 1997 amalg.)
Apr. 30, 1997 – Continued into Yukon. (see TransAtlantic Petroleum Corp.)
Dec. 7, 1998 – Amalgamated with Profco Resources Ltd. to form TransAtlantic Petroleum Corp.; basis 0.87 new for 1 GHP sh. (see TransAtlantic Petroleum Corp.)

GHP Noetic Science-Psychedelic Pharma Inc. (Ont. Mar. 25, 2020)
Nov. 8, 2023 – Name changed to Xcyte Digital Corp. pursuant to the Qualifying Transaction reverse takeover acquisition of (old) Xcyte Digital Corp.; basis 1 new for 1.25 old shs. (see FPsurvey - Industrials)

GHZ Resource Corporation (B.C. Jan. 18, 1979)
June 10, 1994 – Name changed to Canadian Reserve Gold Corporation. ∎

GIS Global Imaging Solutions Inc. (B.C. July 30, 1970)
Feb. 5, 2001 – Name changed to Segami Images Incorporated. (see FPsurvey - Industrials)

GLC Limited (British Virgin Islands Jan. 16, 1997)
Aug. 30, 1999 – Name changed to GalaxiWorld.com Ltd.

G.L.E. Resources Ltd. (Ont. 1977)
July 8, 1986 – Name changed to Chelsea Resources Ltd.; basis 1 new for 3 old shs. ∎

GLENTEL Inc. (Can. Mar. 9, 1989)
May 22, 2015 – Acquired by BCE Inc.; basis either (i) for $26.50 or (ii) 0.4974 BCE com. shs. for 1 GLENTEL com. sh.

GLF Technologies (1979) Ltd. (B.C. 1979)
Feb. 20, 1986 – Name changed to Blackberry Gold Resources Inc.; basis 1 new for 3 old shs. ∎

GLG Life Tech Limited (B.C. June 5, 1998)
Mar. 14, 2007 – Name changed to GLG Life Tech Corporation; basis 1 new for 3 old shs. (see FPsurvey - Industrials)

GLK Strategies Inc. (Alta. Oct. 22, 1993)
Feb. 18, 2003 – Name changed to Yankee Hat Industries Corp.; basis 1 new for 4 old shs. ∎

GLP NT Corporation (Ont. Apr. 26, 1988)
Oct. 3, 2006 – Amalgamated with Great Lakes Holdings Inc. and GLP Financial Limited; basis $8.68 per sh.

GLR Resources Inc. (Can. Jan. 1, 2001)
June 5, 2009 – Filed for bankruptcy; Paddon + Yorke Inc. appointed trustee.
Trustees are discharged.
Mar. 21, 2011 – Name changed to Mistango River Resources Inc.; basis 1 new for 4 old shs. (see FPsurvey - Mines & Energy)

GLS Global Assets Ltd. (B.C. Apr. 8, 1975)
Feb. 17, 2006 – Continued into Canada.
Feb. 20, 2006 – Name changed to Mobile Lottery Solutions Inc. ∎

GLS Global Listing Service Ltd. (B.C. Apr. 8, 1975)
Aug. 27, 1992 – Name changed to GLS Global Assets Ltd. ∎

GLV Inc. (Can. May 15, 2007)
Dec. 18, 2014 – Name changed to Ovivo Inc. ∎

GM Resources Limited (B.C. June 7, 1950)
Sept. 8, 1982 – Continued into Canada. (see Campbell Resources Inc.)
May 12, 1983 – Amalgamated with United Asbestos Inc. (0.3 com. plus 1 pfce. for 1), Campbell Resources Inc. (1 for 1) and Camchib Resources Inc. (0.6 for 1) to continue as a new company also known as Campbell Resources Inc.; basis 1 new for 5 old shs. (see Campbell Resources Inc.)

GMD Resource Corp. (B.C. Aug. 11, 1980)
Oct. 14, 2004 – Name changed to Chatworth Resources Inc.; basis 1 new for 6 old shs. ∎

GMIncome & Growth Fund (Alta. Sept. 29, 2010)
Dec. 28, 2011 – Merged into COMPASS Income Fund; basis 0.86725467 COMPASS units for 1 GMIncome unit. (see COMPASS Income Fund)

GMN The Gospel Music Network, Ltd. (B.C. Nov. 3, 1986)
May 22, 1990 – Name changed to Your Host Foods Inc. ∎

GMP Capital Corp. (Can. Oct. 20, 2003)
Nov. 30, 2005 – Plan of Arrangement to convert company into an income trust named GMP Capital Trust; basis either 2 new fund units and $1.00, or 2 new cl. B Griffiths McBurney L.P. partner units and $1.00 for 1 old GMP com. sh. (see GMP Capital Trust)

GMP Capital Inc. (Ont. Mar. 16, 2009)
Nov. 20, 2020 – Name changed to RF Capital Group Inc. (see FPsurvey - Industrials)

GMP Capital Trust (Ont. Sept. 20, 2005)
May 20, 2009 – Converted into GMP Capital Inc.; basis 1 GMP Capital Inc. com. sh. for 1 GMP Capital Trust trust unit. (see GMP Capital Inc.)

GNE Energy Resources Corporation (Can. Sept. 4, 1987)
Nov. 7, 1988 – Name changed to Canadian 88 Energy Corp.; basis 2 new for 1 old sh. ∎

GNI Petroleum Inc. (B.C. Apr. 11, 1979)
Oct. 11, 2001 – Name changed to Logix Enterprises Inc.; basis 1 new for 2 old shs. ∎

GOAL Energy Inc. (Alta. Dec. 21, 1993 amalg.)
Oct. 13, 1998 – Acquired by Tappit Resources Ltd.; basis (i) 8¢ and 0.75 Tappit shs. for 1 GOAL sh. or (ii) 1 Tappit sh. for 1 GOAL sh. (see Tappit Resources Ltd.)

GPC Limited (unknown)
1972 – Wound up. Reported that nothing available for distribution to com. shldrs.

G.P.I. Industries Limited (B.C. 1959)
1975 – Jim Pattison Enterprises Ltd. acquired all o/s shs. at $6.75 per sh.

GPJ Ventures Ltd. (B.C. Nov. 13, 2006)
Apr. 4, 2007 – Name changed to Peak Gold Ltd. ∎

GPS Investment Corp. (Alta. July 15, 2011)
Oct. 29, 2013 – Formed Astrix Networks Inc. in Alberta pursuant to Qualifying Transaction reverse takeover amalgamation of (old) Astrix Networks Inc. and 1772400 Alberta Ltd., a wholly owned subsidiary of GPS, and the subsequent amalgamation of GPS and the amalgamated entity. ∎

G.R. Pacific Resource Corp. (Yuk. Dec. 2, 1994)
Feb. 3, 2003 – Name changed to Pacific GeoInfo Corp. ∎

GRD Enterprises Inc. (Alta. Feb. 20, 2003)
Aug. 17, 2004 – Formed Call Genie Inc. in Alberta on Qualifying Transaction reverse takeover acquisition of and amalgamation with Call Genie Inc. ∎

GRD Industries Ltd. (B.C. 1977)
Oct. 14, 1994 – Dissolved and struck off register.

GRF Technology Inc. (Ont. Nov. 13, 1925)
July 15, 1997 – Formed Mustang Gold Corp. in Ontario on amalgamation with Mustang Gold Corp., constituting a reverse takeover by Mustang; basis 1 new for 1 Mustang sh. and 1 new for 5 GRF shs. ∎

GRIID Infrastructure Inc. (Del. Oct. 15, 2020)
Oct. 30, 2024 – Acquired by CleanSpark, Inc.; basis 0.06959 CleanSpark com. shs. for 1 GRIID com. sh.

G. S. Eplett Mining & Development Co. Ltd. (Ont. 1945)
1965 – Charter cancelled.

GSI Group Inc. (N.B. Mar. 22, 1999)
May 11, 2016 – Name changed to Novanta Inc. (see FPsurvey - Industrials)

GSI Lumonics Inc. (N.B. Mar. 22, 1999)
June 30, 2005 – Name changed to GSI Group Inc. ∎

G.S.M. Mining Holdings Ltd. (B.C.)
May 1, 1969 – Struck off register.

GSM Resource Capital Inc. (Ont. Sept. 25, 1959)
Sept. 18, 1995 – Formed HMH China Investments Limited in Ontario on amalgamation with 1124376 Ontario Inc.; basis 1 new for 5 old shs. ∎

GSO Solutions, Inc. (N.S. Apr. 27, 1999)
Aug. 6, 2007 – Dissolved and struck from register.

GSR Goldsearch Resources Inc. (B.C. Sept. 18, 1986)
Sept. 24, 1991 – Name changed to Goldrush Mining Corporation. ∎

GST Global Telecommunications Inc. (Yuk. Nov. 29, 1993)
Oct. 29, 1998 – Name changed to Global Light Telecommunications Inc. ∎

GST Telecommunications, Inc. (Can. Apr. 29, 1987)
May 17, 2000 – Filed for bankruptcy protection under Chapter 11 of the U.S. Bankruptcy Code in the U.S. Bankruptcy Court of the District of Delaware.
Sept. 2000 – Court approved the sale of substantially all of the co.'s assets to Time Warner Telecom, Inc. for US$640,000,000, up to a total purchase price of US$690,000,000. Excluded from the sale were customers and certain assets in Hawaii and certain of the co.'s non-core businesses.
Dec. 15, 2000 – Company stopped providing U.S. domestic local, long-distance data/Internet services and proceeded to find a buyer for its remaining assets.
Jan. 2002 – Hearing was held regarding a plan filed under the Bankruptcy Laws and shldrs were asked to file objections to the plan by Dec. 31, 2001.
May 30, 2002 – Adjudged bankrupt with no funds available for distribution to shldrs.

GSW Inc. (Can. Oct. 17, 1927; via Dominion charter)
Apr. 7, 2006 – Acquired by A. O. Smith Corporation for $115 per cl. A com. sh. and cl. B sub. vtg. sh.

GSW Limited (Can. Oct. 17, 1927; via Dominion charter)
Oct. 1, 1980 – Name changed to GSW Inc. ∎

GT Canada Capital Corporation (Can. Mar. 25, 2008)
Mar. 12, 2010 – Name changed to GT Canada Medical Properties Inc. pursuant to Qualifying Transaction acquisition of Queenston Medical-Dental Centre. ∎

GT Canada Medical Properties Inc. (Can. Mar. 25, 2008)
Dec. 24, 2010 – Succeeded by GT Canada Medical Properties Real Estate Investment Trust pursuant to plan of arrangement whereby GT Canada Medical Properties Real Estate Investment Trust was formed to facilitate the conversion of the corporation into a trust; basis 1 new for 10 old shs. ∎

GT Canada Medical Properties Real Estate Investment Trust (Ont. Oct. 13, 2010)
Nov. 2, 2012 – Name changed to NorthWest International Healthcare Properties Real Estate Investment Trust. ∎

GT Gold Corp. (B.C. Sept. 9, 2013)
May 17, 2021 – All o/s com. shs. not already owned acquired by Newmont Corporation; basis $3.25 cash per sh.

GT Group Telecom Inc. (Can. Apr. 12, 1996)
Dec. 23, 2002 – Placed into receivership. Zwaig Associates Inc. was appointed receiver.
Feb. 4, 2003 – Operating subsids. acquired by 360networks Corporation and secured and unsecured creditors received distributions.

GTA CorpFin Capital Inc. (Ont. Aug. 9, 2006)
July 26, 2010 – Name changed to GTA Resources and Mining Inc. ∎

GTA Financecorp Inc. (Ont. Aug. 9, 2006)
Nov. 9, 2021 – Name changed to Tiidal Gaming Group Corp. pursuant to the reverse takeover acquisition of Tiidal Gaming Group Inc. and concurrent amalgamation of Tiidal with wholly owned 2852773 Ontario Inc. (and continued as Tiidal Gaming Holdings Inc.).; basis 1 new for 11.2678 old shs. ∎

GTA Resources and Mining Inc. (Ont. Aug. 9, 2006)
Mar. 4, 2019 – Name changed to GTA Financecorp Inc. ∎

G.T.C. Transcontinental Group Ltd. (Can. Mar. 3, 1978)
Apr. 1, 2003 – Name changed to Transcontinental Inc.; basis 2 new for 1 old sh. (see FPsurvey - Industrials)

GTEC Holdings Ltd. (B.C. July 28, 2017)
July 9, 2021 – Name changed to Avant Brands Inc. (see FPsurvey - Industrials)

G.T.M. Capital Corporation (Alta. Mar. 31, 2008)
Aug. 18, 2010 – Continued into Ontario.
Sept. 9, 2010 – Name changed to Feronia Inc. pursuant to Qualifying Transaction acquisition of (old) Feronia Inc. (renamed Feronia CI Inc.). ∎

GTO Resources Inc. (B.C. Apr. 26, 1984)
Oct. 20, 2009 – Name changed to Ram Power, Corp. pursuant to acquisition of Polaris Geothermal Inc. (deemed acquiror), Western GeoPower Corp. and Ram Power, Inc.; basis 1 new for 10 old shs. ∎

GTO Resources Inc. (B.C. May 10, 2011)
Aug. 13, 2014 – Name changed to Velocity Data Inc. following the reverse takeover acquisition of ACL Computers & Software, Inc. ∎

GTR Group Inc. (Can. Aug. 25, 1993)
Sept. 11, 2001 – Name changed to Mad Catz Interactive, Inc. ∎

GURU Organic Energy Corp. (Ont. Jan. 15, 2018)
Jan. 11, 2021 – Continued into Canada. (see FPsurvey - Industrials)

GVIC Communications Corp. (Can. Mar. 23, 2003)
Apr. 6, 2021 – All cl.B vtg. and cl.C non-vtg. shs. not already held acquired by Glacier Media Inc.; basis 0.8 Glacier com. shs. for each cl.B or cl.C sh.

GVIC Communications Inc. (Can. May 3, 2001)
Dec. 28, 2006 – Acquired by Glacier Ventures International Corp.; basis 0.0429 Glacier shs. for 1 GVIC cl. A or cl. B sh.

GVIC Publications Ltd. (Can. Mar. 23, 2003)
Mar. 31, 2006 – Plan of Arrangement involving an equity investment by an indirect subsid. of Glacier Ventures International Corp. with assets transferred to wholly owned subsid. which continued as a new company named Stressgen Biotechnologies Corporation; basis 1 new Stressgen com. sh., 0.105263158 new GVIC vtg. shs. and 0.052631579 new GVIC non-vtg. shs. for 1 old GVIC sh. Also 1 new Stressgen warrant and 0.157894738 new GVIC second warrants for 1 old GVIC warrant.
May 18, 2007 – Name changed to GVIC Communications Corp.; basis 1 new for 30 old shs. ∎

GW Utilities Limited (Ont. 1987)
Apr. 1, 1993 – Amalgamated with Home Oil Company Limited; basis 0.4112 Home Oil shs. for 1 GW Utilities sh. (see Home Oil Company Limited)

GWG Inc. (Alta. 1911)
1982 – All o/s shs. held by Levi Strauss & Co., San Francisco.

GWG Limited (Alta. 1911)
1980 – Name changed to GWG Inc. ∎

GWR Global Water Resources Corp. (B.C. Mar. 23, 2010)
May 2, 2016 – Merged into Global Water Resources, Inc.; basis 1 new Global Water com. sh. for 1 GWR com. sh.

GWR Resources Inc. (B.C. Feb. 13, 1987)
May 16, 2016 – Name changed to Engold Mines Ltd. (see FPsurvey - Mines & Energy)

Gabo Mining Ltd. (B.C. Dec. 8, 1989 amalg.)
June 16, 2025 – Name changed to Gamma Resources Ltd. (see FPsurvey - Mines & Energy)

Gabriel Resources Inc. (B.C. 1980)
Sept. 6, 1989 – Amalgamated with Kangeld Resources Ltd. and Lockwood Petroleum Inc. to form Appian Resources Ltd.; basis 0.4209 new for 1 old sh. (see Appian Resources Ltd.)

Gabriella's Kitchen Inc. (Alta. Dec. 3, 2003)
Oct. 22, 2019 – Name changed to GABY Inc. (see FPsurvey - Industrials)

Gachin Holdings Ltd. (Ont. 1937)
1957 – Charter cancelled.

Gaff Mines Ltd. (Ont. 1954)
1962 – Charter cancelled.

Gagan Gold Corp. (B.C. Sept. 19, 1990)
Nov. 16, 1993 – Name changed to Cachet Enterprises Corp.; basis 1 new for 3 old shs. ∎

Gage Growth Corp. (Can. Nov. 22, 2017)
Mar. 11, 2022 – Acquired by TerrAscend Corp.; basis 0.3001 TerrAscend shs. for 1 Gage Growth sh.

Gaia Metals Corp. (B.C. May 10, 2007)
June 10, 2021 – Name changed to Patriot Battery Metals Inc.; basis 1 new for 3 old shs. (see FPsurvey - Mines & Energy)

Gainey Capital Corp. (B.C. Feb. 11, 2011)
Mar. 11, 2021 – Name changed to Masivo Silver Corp. (see FPsurvey - Mines & Energy)

Gair Company Canada Limited (Can. 1934)
Nov. 12, 1952 – Public invest. int. in co. eliminated with redemption of all o/s 4% pref. stk. at $102 plus accr. divd. of 80¢ per sh.

Gaitwin Explorations Limited (Ont. 1944)
1970 – Name changed to Wingait Diversified Limited; basis 1 new for 10 old shs. ∎

Gal-Wood Gold Mines Ltd. (Ont. 1946)
1956 – Name changed to Gal-Wood Mines Ltd. ∎

Gal-Wood Mines Ltd. (Ont. 1946)
Feb. 15, 1960 – Charter cancelled.

Gala-Bari International Inc. (B.C. Mar. 3, 1983)
Aug. 21, 2003 – Dissolved and struck from register.

Gala Resources Ltd. (B.C. June 8, 1987)
June 5, 1997 – Continued into Bermuda.
Mar. 4, 1999 – Name changed to Hydromet Technologies Limited; basis 1 new for 4 old shs. ∎

Galactic Resources Ltd. (B.C. 1979)
Jan. 1993 – Filed for bankruptcy under the laws of Canada; Peat Marwick Thorne of Vancouver appointed trustee.
Oct. 1993 – Declared bankrupt. No funds available for distribution to shldrs.
Jan. 27, 1995 – Dissolved and struck off register.

Galahad Metals Inc. (Ont. Sept. 1, 2000)
July 30, 2014 – Continued into British Columbia.
July 31, 2014 – Name changed to Rosehearty Energy Inc.; basis 1 new for 10 old shs. ∎

Galane Gold Ltd. (Ont. Oct. 24, 2007)
Oct. 21, 2022 – Name changed to Golconda Gold Ltd.; basis 1 new for 5 old shs. (see FPsurvey - Mines & Energy)

Galatea Gold Mines Ltd. (Can. Dec. 2, 1932)
Acquired by Duquesne Mining Co. Ltd.; basis 1 new for 7 old shs. (see Duquesne Mining Co. Ltd.)

Galaxy Capital Corp. (B.C. Dec. 14, 2009)
June 12, 2012 – Name changed to Galaxy Graphite Corp. ∎

Galaxy City Mines Inc (B.C. 1964)
Feb. 19, 1982 – Amalgamated with Moly Mite Mines Inc. to form Moly Mite Resources Inc.; sh. for sh. basis.

Galaxy Copper Ltd. (B.C. 1956)
Dec. 1968 – Merged (2 new for 5 old shs.) with Bata Resources Limited and Stampede Oils Ltd. to form United Bata Resources Ltd.

Galaxy Digital Holdings Ltd. (Cayman Islands Aug. 1, 2018)
Apr. 23, 2021 – Continued into Delaware
May 13, 2025 – Succeeded by Galaxy Digital Inc. (see FPsurvey - Industrials)

Galaxy Energy Corp. (B.C. Apr. 16, 1952)
Aug. 10, 2001 – Name changed to Galaxy Sports Inc.; basis 1 new for 3 old shs. ■

Galaxy Graphite Corp. (B.C. Dec. 14, 2009)
Feb. 26, 2015 – Name changed to Global Copper Group Inc.; basis 1 new for 4 old shs. ■

Galaxy Industries Ltd. (B.C. 1983)
Apr. 30, 1993 – Dissolved and struck off register.

Galaxy Minerals Ltd. (B.C. 1956)
1964 – Name changed to Galaxy Copper Ltd.; basis 1 new for 2 old shs. ■

Galaxy OnLine Inc. (Ont. Aug. 21, 1992)
Jan. 31, 2000 – Continued into Yukon.
July 5, 2003 – Dissolved.

Galaxy Sports Inc. (B.C. Apr. 16, 1952)
May 4, 2009 – Dissolved and struck from register.

Gale Cummings Mines Ltd. (Ont. 1950)
Apr. 9, 1966 – Dissolved.

Gale Force Petroleum Inc. (Can. May 29, 2001)
Sept. 23, 2015 – Acquired by Montana Exploration Corp.; basis (i) 0.465 Montana com. shs. for 1 Gale Force com. sh. and (ii) 0.555 Montana com. shs. for 1 Gale Force pref. sh.

Galena Capital Corp. (B.C. Sept. 26, 2006)
Sept. 26, 2012 – Name changed to Ferro Iron Ore Corp.; basis 1 new for 4 old shs. ■

The Galena Farm Consolidated Mines Ltd. (B.C. Feb. 28, 1929)
Feb. 1953 – Struck off register.

Galena International Resources Ltd. (B.C. Apr. 5, 2007)
Jan. 9, 2017 – Name changed to Aurelius Minerals Inc. (see FPsurvey - Mines & Energy)

Galena-Signal Oil Co. of Canada Ltd. (unknown)
Oct. 1, 1943 – Charter surrendered.

Galex Mines Ltd. (Ont. 1971)
Mar. 1977 – Charter cancelled.

Galico Resources Inc. (B.C. Feb. 25, 1988)
Jan. 25, 1993 – Name changed to Image Data International Corporation following acquisition of Image Data Canada Corp. ■

Galilean Resources Corp. (B.C. 1979)
June 15, 1987 – Name changed to New Fibers International, Ltd.; basis 1 new for 2 old shs. ■

Galileo Exploration Ltd. (B.C. Aug. 14, 2000)
Nov. 25, 2020 – Name changed to Visionary Gold Corp. ■

Galileo Petroleum Ltd. (B.C. Aug. 14, 2000)
Dec. 21, 2016 – Name changed to Galileo Exploration Ltd. ■

Galinee Mattagami Mines Limited (Ont. 1958)
July 4, 1996 – Formed Zenda Gold Corp. in Ontario on amalgamation with Paramount Gold Corporation. ■

Galit Resource Corporation (B.C. 1984)
June 11, 1993 – Dissolved and struck off register.

Galkeno Mines Ltd. (Ont. 1950)
1958 – Name changed to Canadian Northwest Mines & Oils Ltd. ■

Gallagher Explorations Ltd. (B.C. 1984)
Nov. 27, 1986 – Formed Gunnar Gold Inc. in Canada on amalgamation with Gunnar Gold Inc. ■

Gallagher Security Corp. (B.C. June 30, 2005)
July 11, 2023 – Name changed to Genesis AI Corp. (see FPsurvey - Industrials)

Gallahad Petroleum Ltd. (B.C. 1972)
Dec. 30, 1988 – Formed Backer Petroleum Corp. in British Columbia on amalgamation with Backer Resources Ltd.; basis 1 new for 1 Backer sh. and 3 new for 1 Gallahad sh. ■

Gallant Gold Mines Ltd. (B.C. 1979)
Sept. 1, 1989 – Amalgamated with Eastern Mines Ltd., Silver Sceptre Resources Ltd. and Standard Gold Mines Ltd. to form HLX Resources Limited; basis 0.1519 new for 1 Eastern Mines sh., 0.1204 new for 1 Silver Sceptre sh., 0.2735 new for 1 Standard Gold sh. and 0.2266 new for 1 Gallant Gold sh. (see HLX Resources Ltd.)

Galleon Energy Inc. (Alta. Mar. 27, 2003)
Nov. 4, 2011 – Name changed to Guide Exploration Ltd. ■

Galleon Mining Limited (B.C. Feb. 13, 1990)
Aug. 10, 1993 – Name changed to Pacific Galleon Mining Corp.; basis 1 new for 4 old shs. ■

Galleria Opportunities Inc. (Alta. July 30, 1993)
Apr. 10, 2014 – Name changed to Galleria Opportunities Ltd.; basis 1 new for 5 old shs. ■

Galleria Opportunities Ltd. (Alta. July 30, 1993)
Mar. 13, 2017 – Name changed to QYOU Media Inc. pursuant to reverse takeover acquisition of (old) QYOU Media Inc. and amalgamation of wholly owned 2561287 Ontario Ltd. with (old) QYOU Media (deemed acquiror); basis 1 new for 2 old shs. (see FPsurvey - Industrials)

Galleria Resources Inc. (Alta. July 30, 1993)
Nov. 13, 2000 – Name changed to Galleria Opportunities Inc.; basis 1 new for 5 old shs. ■

Gallery Gold Mines Ltd. (Alta. Feb. 6, 1987)
June 4, 1990 – Name changed to Gallery Resources Limited; basis 1 new for 5 old shs. ■

Gallery Resources Limited (Alta. Feb. 6, 1987)
Aug. 2, 2008 – Dissolved and struck from registry.

Galliard Resources Corp. (B.C. Oct. 28, 2009)
June 29, 2011 – Name changed to Novo Resources Corp. (see FPsurvey - Mines & Energy)

Gallic Energy Ltd. (Alta. Aug. 10, 1983)
Jan. 7, 2013 – Acquired by Petromanas Energy Inc.; basis 0.3736 Petromanas shs. for 1 Gallic sh. (see Petromanas Energy Inc.)

Gallion Resources Ltd. (B.C.)
Mar. 27, 1984 – Converted into a non-reporting co. by orders of the Superintendent of Brokers and the Registrar of Companies by orders dated Mar. 14, 1984 and respectively.

Galloway Chibougamau Mines Ltd. (Ont. 1956)
1970 – Dissolved.

Galloway Development Ltd. (B.C. 1960)
Jan. 21, 1983 – Struck off register.

Galloway Gordon Lake Gold Mines Ltd. (Can. 1938)
Dec. 16, 1980 – Dissolved.

Galore Gold Mines Ltd. (Ont. Sept. 24, 1936)
1968 – Merged into Associated Porcupine Mines Ltd.; basis 1 new for 136,426 old shs.

Galt Malleable Iron Ltd. (Ont. June 11, 1956)
June 23, 1977 – Name changed to Galtaco Inc. ■

Galtaco Inc. (Ont. June 11, 1956)
Feb. 24, 1997 – Name changed to Strategic Value Corporation; basis 1 new cl. A for 5 old com. shs. ■

Galvanic Applied Sciences Inc. (Alta. Sept. 27, 1995)
Sept. 23, 2013 – Acquired by 1756349 Alberta Ltd., owned by private equity firms Tuckerman Capital IV L.P. (80%), 2SV Capital, LLC (10%) and Right Lane Capital LLC (10%) for $1.70 per sh.

Galveston Mines Ltd. (B.C. 1971)
May 18, 1978 – Name changed to Galveston Petroleums Ltd. ■

Galveston Petroleums Ltd. (B.C. 1971)
July 22, 1986 – Formed Galveston Resources Ltd. in British Columbia on amalgamation with 2 other cos. ■

Galveston Resources Ltd. (B.C. July 22, 1986 amalg.)
July 1, 1988 – Amalgamated with 7 other cos. to form Corona Corporation; basis 0.43 new cl. A sh. for 1 old Galveston cl. A and 0.43 cl. B sh. for 1 old Galveston cl. B. (see Corona Corporation)

Galway Explorations Ltd. (B.C. 1966)
Oct. 1974 – Charter cancelled.

Galway Gold Inc. (N.B. May 9, 2012)
Aug. 11, 2015 – Continued into Ontario.
July 21, 2023 – Name changed to Montauk Metals Inc. (see FPsurvey - Mines & Energy)

Galway Metals Inc. (N.B. May 9, 2012)
July 21, 2015 – Continued into Ontario. (see FPsurvey - Mines & Energy)

Galway Resources Ltd. (B.C. Aug. 31, 2004)
Dec. 24, 2012 – Acquired by EBX Group Ltd.; basis $2.05 plus 1 Galway Metals Inc. com. sh. and 1 Galway Gold Inc. com. sh. for 1 Galway Resources com. sh.

Gama Explorations Inc. (B.C. Aug. 31, 2018)
Feb. 21, 2024 – Name changed to Blackbird Critical Metals Corp. (see FPsurvey - Mines & Energy)

Gambier Exploration Ltd. (B.C. Oct. 15, 1979)
June 23, 1981 – Name changed to Breakwater Resources Ltd. ■

Gambier Gold Corp. (B.C. Mar. 2, 2006)
Oct. 17, 2022 – Name changed to EGR Exploration Ltd.; basis 1 new for 3 old shs. (see FPsurvey - Mines & Energy)

Gambit Explorations Ltd. (Ont. 1974)
July 6, 1976 – Amalgamated with other cos. to form Gambit Consolidated Explorations Ltd.; basis 1 new for 3 old shs.

The Gambol Group Incorporated (Alta. Feb. 11, 1994)
Aug. 1, 2000 – Struck from registry and dissolved.

Gamecorp Ltd. (Ont. Nov. 22, 2000)
Sept. 7, 2012 – Name changed to DealNet Capital Corp. ■

Gamehost Income Fund (Alta. Apr. 9, 2003)
Dec. 31, 2010 – Succeeded by Gamehost Inc. pursuant to plan of arrangement whereby Gamehost Inc. was formed to facilitate the conversion of the fund into a corporation and the fund was subsequently dissolved. (see FPsurvey - Industrials)

Gamelancer Gaming Corp. (B.C. June 24, 1999)
Sept. 27, 2022 – Name changed to Gamelancer Media Corp. ■

Gamelancer Media Corp. (B.C. June 24, 1999)
Apr. 5, 2023 – Continued into Ontario.
Aug. 2, 2024 – Name changed to Vertiqal Studios Corp. (see FPsurvey - Industrials)

Games Trader Inc. (Can. Aug. 25, 1993)
July 19, 1999 – Name changed to GTR Group Inc. ■

Gamesquare Esports Inc. (Ont. Aug. 21, 2014)
Apr. 12, 2023 – Acquired by Engine Gaming and Media, Inc. (renamed GameSquare Holdings, Inc.); basis 0.08262 Engine Gaming shs. for 1 Gamesquare sh.

GameSquare Holdings, Inc. (B.C. Dec. 18, 2020)
Mar. 7, 2024 – Continued into Delaware.

Gamin Resources Inc. (B.C. Nov. 27, 1979)
May 24, 1989 – Name changed to Mineral Park Mining Corp.; basis 1 new for 5 old shs. ■

Gaming Lottery Corporation (Ont. Feb. 4, 1986)
Jan. 16, 1997 – Continued into British Virgin Islands.
Mar. 15, 1999 – Name changed to GLC Limited. ■

Gaming Nation Inc. (Ont. June 5, 2015)
Nov. 30, 2017 – Acquired by OC Special Opportunities Fund, LP; basis Cdn$0.95 cash per sh.

Gamma Industrial Sciences Ltd. (Alta. 1986)
Feb. 1, 1992 – Struck off register.

Gammon Gold Inc. (Que. Feb. 25, 1986)
June 14, 2011 – Name changed to AuRico Gold Inc. ■

Gammon Lake Resources Inc. (Que. Feb. 25, 1986)
June 7, 2007 – Name changed to Gammon Gold Inc. ■

Gamon Oil & Gas Ltd. (Alta. 1954)
Oct. 1, 1982 – Struck off register.

Gamora Capital Corp. (B.C. July 6, 2018)
Mar. 11, 2021 – Name changed to Poda Lifestyle and Wellness Ltd. pursuant to the reverse takeover acquisition of Poda Technologies Ltd. ■

Gamsan Resources Ltd. (Alta. 1986)
Jan. 1, 1992 – Struck off register.

Gan Copper Mines Ltd. (Ont. 1940)
July 1976 – Charter cancelled.

Ganda Silver Mines Ltd. (Ont. 1963)
Mar. 1976 – Charter cancelled.

Gandalf Technologies Inc. (Ont. Apr. 29, 1971)
Nov. 1997 – Placed into receivership.
Aug. 7, 1998 – All assets liquidated; no distribution made to shldrs.

Gandy Resources Corp. (Ont. Dec. 31, 1986)
May 17, 1989 – Name changed to Heritage Living Canada Corp. ■

Gane Energy Corporation (Alta. Dec. 13, 1979)
July 14, 1986 – Name changed to Northstar Energy Corporation; basis 1 new for 10 old shs. ■

Gane Petroleum Corporation Ltd. (Alta. Dec. 13, 1979)
Aug. 17, 1982 – Name changed to Gane Energy Corporation; basis 1 new for 1 old for both com. and pref. stk. ■

Garbell Holdings Limited (Ont. Aug. 24, 1961)
Dec. 15, 2008 – Redeemed 10.5% cum. redeem. first pref. shs. for $5.2326 per sh.

Garbo Industries Ltd. (B.C. 1986)
Mar. 28, 1989 – Name changed to AISI Research Corp.; basis 2 new for 1 old sh. ■

Garda World Security Corporation (Can. Oct. 3, 1997)
Nov. 16, 2012 – Acquired by Apex Partners for $12 per sh.

Garde, Mining Exploration Company Inc. (Can. Sept. 22, 1989)
Mar. 7, 1996 – Name changed to Orezone Resources Inc.; basis 1 new for 5 old shs. ■

Garden Lake Resources Ltd. (Ont. Feb. 20, 1987)
Dec. 10, 1997 – Name changed to GAR Limited; basis 1 new for 4 old shs. ■

Garden Mines Ltd. (Ont. 1944)
Dec. 10, 1962 – Dissolved.

Gardiner Oil and Gas Limited (Alta. Feb. 11, 1988)
Oct. 28, 1996 – All o/s com. shs. acquired by Poco Petroleums Ltd.; basis $5.00 in cash plus 0.6 of a com.
sh. of Poco for 1 com. sh. of Gardiner. (see Poco Petroleums Ltd.)

Garibaldi Granite Corp. (Alta. Nov. 22, 1993)
Jan. 12, 2006 – Name changed to Garibaldi Resources Corp. (see FPsurvey - Mines & Energy)

Garibaldi Lifts Ltd. (B.C. 1960)
Oct. 28, 1980 – Acquired by Hastings West Resorts Ltd. for $938.50 per sh. Name subsequently changed to Whistler Mountain Ski Corporation. Co. now private.

Garisle Red Lake Gold Mines Ltd. (Ont. June 28, 1943)
1948 – Name changed to Radio Active Minerals Ltd.; basis 1 new for 1 old sh. ■

Garland Mining & Development Co. Ltd. (Que. 1953)
1959 – Merged into Amalgamated Mining Development Corp. Ltd.; basis 1 new for 8 old shs.

Garneau Inc. (Alta. 1970)
July 22, 1987 – Amalgamated in Alberta to continue with same name.
Feb. 1, 1993 – Amalgamated in Alberta to continue with same name.
Nov. 30, 2011 – Voluntarily liquidated for 3¢ per sh. and dissolved.

Garnet Gold Mines Ltd. (Ont. 1946)
Jan. 12, 1970 – Charter cancelled.

Garnet Oils Ltd. (Alta. Feb. 25, 1950)
1951 – Taken over by Calvan Consolidated Oil and Gas Co. Ltd.; basis 1 new for 2 old shs.

Garnet Point Resources Corp. (B.C. Jan. 13, 1981)
Feb. 21, 2008 – Name changed to Hastings Resources Corp. ■

Garney Mines Ltd. (Que. 1959)
June 1979 – Charter cancelled.

Garrison Creek Consolidated Mines Ltd. (Ont. Dec. 9, 1954 amalg.)
Sept. 21, 1993 – Amalgamated with Anglo Dominion Gold Exploration Ltd. (18 new for 100 old shs.), Coniagas Mines, Limited (32 new for 100 old shs.) and Quebec Sturgeon River Mines Limited (18 new for 100 old shs.) to form a new co. known as QSR Limited; basis 7 new for 1,000 old shs. (see QSR Limited)

Garrison Creek Mines Ltd. (Ont. 1954)
1954 – Merged with other mining cos. to form Garrison Creek Consolidated Mines Ltd.; basis 1 new for 4 old shs. (see Garrison Creek Consolidated Mines Ltd.)

Garrison Enterprises Inc. (B.C. Apr. 11, 1979)
Apr. 2, 1998 – Name changed to GNI Petroleum Inc.; basis 1 new for 3 old shs. ■

Garrison Gold Inc. (Ont. Oct. 22, 1984)
Aug. 12, 1991 – Name changed to Garrison International Inc.; basis 1 new for 6 old shs. ■

Garrison-Harbour Gold Mines Ltd. (Ont. 1947)
May 27, 1965 – Dissolved.

Garrison International Inc. (Ont. Oct. 22, 1984)
Sept. 30, 1996 – Formed GalaVu Entertainment Inc. in Ontario on amalgamation with GalaVu Entertainment Inc., constituting a reverse takeover by GalaVu.

Garrison International Ltd. (Ont. July 24, 1996)
Jan. 9, 2012 – Name changed to Desert Eagle Resources Ltd.; basis 1 new for 18 old shs. (see FPsurvey - Mines & Energy)

Garrison Oils Ltd. (Alta. Dec. 10, 1949)
1951 – Taken over by Calvan Consolidated Oil and Gas Co. Ltd.; basis 1 new for 2 old shs.

Garry Syndicate Ltd. (unknown)
In voluntary liquidation. E. Richardson, Calgary, liquidator.

Garrymac Gold Mines Ltd. (Ont. 1944)
Feb. 17, 1964 – Charter cancelled.

Garskie Gold Mines Ltd. (Ont. 1949)
Mar. 1976 – Charter cancelled.

Garson Gold Corp. (B.C. June 28, 2007 amalg.)
May 5, 2010 – Acquired by Alexis Minerals Corporation pursuant to plan of arrangement; basis 0.29 Alexis shs. for 1 Garson sh. (see Alexis Minerals Corporation) Name changed to 0876785 B.C. Ltd. (see Alexis Minerals Corporation)

Garson Resources Ltd. (B.C. Nov. 8, 2005)
June 28, 2007 – Acquired by Piper Capital Inc.; basis 1 new Piper sh. for 1.37931 old Garson sh. (see Garson Gold Corp.)

Garthack Mining Co. Ltd. (Ont. 1945)
Dec. 1949 – Dissolved.

Gary Mines Ltd. (B.C. 1965)
Oct. 2, 1978 – Dissolved.

Gas Exploration Co. of Alberta Ltd. (Alta. 1951)
1955 – Acquired by New Gas Exploration Co. of Alta. Ltd.; basis 1 new for 2 old shs.

Gas Machinery Co. (Canada) Ltd. (unknown)
1968 – Acquired by Bartaco Industries Ltd. (see Bartaco Industries Limited)

Gas Management Income Fund (Ont. Sept. 27, 1996)
Aug. 5, 1999 – All o/s units acquired by OPTUS Natural Gas Distribution Income Fund; basis $4.70 in cash or 0.2 of a new OPTUS unit for 1 old Gas Management unit. (see OPTUS Natural Gas Distribution Income Fund)

Gascome Oils Ltd. (Alta. Dec. 23, 1977)
May 31, 1982 – Name changed to Consolidated Gascome Oils Ltd.; basis 1 new for 5 old shs. ■

Gasfinders & Producers Ltd. (Ont. Feb. 23, 1932)
May 10, 1937 – Name changed to Rossmore Exploration Ltd. ■

Gasfinders & Producers Syndicate (Ont. Feb. 23, 1932)
1936 – Formed Gasfinders & Producers Ltd. following merger with Seneca Drillers Selection Syndicate. ■

Gaslite Minerals Ltd. (unknown)
1980 – All issued shs. purch. by Gaslite Petroleum Ltd. in exchange for 1,400,000 shs. and warrants to purchase 350,000 additional shs. of co.

Gaslite Petroleum Ltd. (B.C. 1979)
1983 – Continued into Alberta.
Apr. 1, 1989 – Struck off register.

Gaspe Metals Ltd. (Que. 1950)
1981 – Name changed to Ressources Hinse Inc. ■

Gaspe Oil Ventures Ltd. (Que. 1944)
1963 – Acquired by New Associated Developments Ltd.; basis 1 new for 23 old shs.

Gaspe Park Mines Ltd. (Ont. 1966)
Mar. 1976 – Charter cancelled.

Gaspé Québec Mines Ltd. (Que. 1966)
Aug. 15, 1975 – Name changed to G.E.Q. Corporation. ■

Gaspésie, Société d'Explorations Pétrolière et Minière Inc. (Que. Aug. 21, 1984)
Mar. 6, 1997 – Name changed to Afcan Mining Corporation. ■

Gaspex Mines Ltd. (Que. 1964)
Mar. 1975 – Charter cancelled.

Gastar Exploration Ltd. (Alta. June 5, 2000)
Nov. 14, 2013 – Name changed to Gastar Exploration, Inc. and continued into Delaware.

Gastem Inc. (Can. Oct. 10, 2002)
Aug. 14, 2016 – Struck from register and dissolved.
July 11, 2017 – Restored to registry. (see FPsurvey - Mines & Energy)

Gateford Mines Limited (Ont. July 30, 1934)
July 11, 1986 – Formed Gateford Resources Inc. in Canada following amalgamation of Gateford with Syntactics Group Ltd. a wholly owned subsid. and Nokomis Resources Inc. ∎

Gateford Resources Inc. (Can. July 11, 1986 amalg.)
Jan. 31, 1992 – Amalgamated with Landmark Corporation to form new co. with same name Landmark Corporation (see Landmark Corporation)

Gateway Capital Corp. (Sask. Sept. 29, 1999)
Feb. 27, 2003 – Name changed to Sweeprite Mfg. Inc. following Qualifying Transaction acquisition of and subsequent vertical amalgamation with Sweeprite Mfg. Inc. ∎

Gateway Casinos Income Fund (B.C. Oct. 10, 2002)
Nov. 20, 2007 – Acquired by New World Gaming Partners Ltd. for $25.26 per trust unit.

Gateway Enterprises Ltd. (B.C. Aug. 14, 2000)
Mar. 15, 2004 – Name changed to Portal de Oro Resources Ltd. following Qualifying Transaction acquisition of Portal de Oro (B.V.I.) Ltd. ∎

Gateway Gold Corp. (B.C. May 1, 2002)
Dec. 24, 2008 – Acquired by Victoria Gold Corp.; basis 0.5 Victoria Gold shs. for 1 Gateway Gold sh.

Gateway Gold Ltd. (Alta. 1945)
Nov. 15, 1978 – Struck off register.

Gateway Oils Ltd. (Alta. 1947)
1965 – Name changed to New Gateway Oils & Minerals Ltd.; basis 1 new for 10 old shs. ∎

Gateway Patricia Gold Mines Ltd. (Ont. 1936)
Aug. 18, 1958 – Dissolved.

Gateway Technologies Corporation (B.C. June 16, 1964)
July 6, 2006 – Name changed to Trevali Resources Corp. ∎

Gateway Uranium Mines Limited (Sask. 1953)
Mar. 29, 1990 – Continued into Ontario.
Nov. 8, 1993 – Formed International Gold Resources Corporation in Ontario on amalgamation with American Gold Resources Corporation; basis 0.2778 new for 1 old sh. ∎

Gateway Ventures Inc. (Alta. Jan. 3, 1997)
Dec. 30, 1998 – Name changed to Chinook Testing Inc. following Major Transaction acquisition of Chinook Radiographic Services Ltd. ∎

Gateway Waste Systems Inc. (B.C. June 16, 1964)
Dec. 4, 1995 – Name changed to Gateway Technologies Corporation. ∎

Gatineau Power Company (Que. 1926)
1963 – Purchased by Hydro-Québec. Com. shldrs. received $35 per sh.; pref. shldrs. equal par value in 10-year bds. guaranteed by the Prov. of Quebec, bearing int. equal to divd. rate; plus $5.00 per sh. Funded debt assumed by Quebec Hydro, with guarantee by Prov. of Quebec.

Gatineau Uranium Mines Ltd. (Que. 1953)
1962 – Charter cancelled.

Gatling Exploration Inc. (B.C. Aug. 2, 2018)
May 25, 2022 – Acquired by MAG Silver Corp.; basis 0.0170627 MAG shs. for 1 Gatling sh.

Gator Resources Corporation (B.C. Feb. 8, 1983)
Dec. 30, 1985 – Name changed to EZ Ventures Ltd.; basis 1 new for 3 old shs. ∎

Gatorz Inc. (Can. Sept. 1, 2005)
June 14, 2013 – Name changed to Pacific Vector Holdings Inc. ∎

Gatos Silver, Inc. (Del. Feb. 2, 2011)
Jan. 20, 2025 – Acquired by First Majestic Silver Corp.; basis 2.25 First Majestic shs. for 1 Gatos Silver sh.

Gatrow Resources Inc. (B.C. 1981)
June 24, 1994 – Dissolved and struck off register.

Gattuso Corporation Ltd. (Can. 1953)
1967 – Wholly owned subsid. of Sogena Inc., acquired 100% int. upon purch. of 75,000 com. shs. of Gattuso for $300,000 in 1967-69.

Gauntlet Energy Corporation (Alta. Oct. 13, 1992)
Dec. 10, 2003 – Acquired by Ketch Resources Ltd. following Plan of Arrangement under Companies' Creditors Arrangement Act - Alberta. This sale results in the compromise and settlement of all 'secured', 'unsecured' and 'other' creditors in accordance with the Plan. There was no provision made for the common shldrs. (see Ketch Resources Ltd.)

Gavan Mines Ltd. (Ont. 1954)
July 1976 – Charter cancelled.

Gavex, A Resource Corporation (B.C. 1974)
Apr. 4, 1985 – Name changed to Dorchester Hotels Inc.; basis 1 new for 15 old shs. ∎

Gavex Gold Mines Ltd. (B.C. 1974)
May 11, 1981 – Name changed to Gavex, A Resource Corporation. ∎

Gavwest Resources Ltd. (B.C. July 30, 2003)
July 21, 2006 – Name changed to Ridgeline Energy Services Inc. following Qualifying Transaction acquisition of SDA Technologies Ltd. ∎

Gay River Lead Mines Ltd. (Ont. 1951)
Apr. 9, 1969 – Charter cancelled.

Gaylord Mines Ltd. (B.C. 1966)
Name changed to Moex Industries Ltd. ∎

Gaymont Mines Ltd. (Ont. 1945)
Oct. 1952 – Acquired by New Lorie Mines Ltd.; basis 1 new for 5 old shs. (see New Lorie Mines Ltd.)

Gaz Métro inc. (Que. June 15, 1955)
Nov. 29, 2017 – Name changed to Énergir Inc.

Gaz Métro Limited Partnership (Que. Oct. 1, 1987)
Sept. 30, 2010 – Succeeded by Valener Inc. pursuant to plan of arrangement whereby all of the partnership's publicly held limited partnership units were acquired by Valener and exchanged for Valener common shares on a one-for-one basis. (see Valener Inc.)
Nov. 29, 2017 – Name changed to Énergir, L.P. (see Valener Inc.)

Gaz Métropolitain and Company, Limited Partnership (Que. Oct. 1, 1987)
Nov. 18, 2003 – Name changed to Gaz Métro Limited Partnership. ∎

Gaz Métropolitain, inc. (Que. June 15, 1955)
Aug. 9, 1991 – All o/s ser. C second pref. shs. redeemed at $25 per sh. plus $0.19553 accrued and unpaid dividends per sh. (see Gaz Métropolitain, inc.)

Gaz Métropolitain, inc. (Que. June 15, 1955)
Nov. 18, 2003 – Name changed to Gaz Métro inc. ∎

Gazelle Resources Limited (B.C. Apr. 15, 1983)
Aug. 29, 1990 – Name changed to Pan Oceanic Ventures Inc. ∎

Gazit America Inc. (Ont. June 19, 2009 amalg.)
Aug. 14, 2012 – Acquired by Gazit-Globe Ltd. and First Capital Realty Inc.; basis $3.31 plus 0.2343 First Capital shs. for 1 Gazit America sh. (see First Capital Realty Inc.)

Geac Computer Corporation Limited (Can. May 11, 1971)
Mar. 15, 2006 – Acquired by Golden Gate Capital for Cdn$11.10 per sh.

Gear Energy Ltd. (Alta. May 1, 2010)
Feb. 10, 2025 – Acquired by Cenovus Energy Inc.; basis (i) $0.607 cash per sh. and (ii) 0.3035 Lotus Creek Exploration Inc. shs., or (iii) a combination thereof for those shldrs. who did not make an election deemed to be 50% of the cash consideration and 50% of the Lotus Creek sh. consideration for 1 Gear Energy sh.

gearunlimited.com Inc. (Can. Nov. 26, 1999)
Mar. 12, 2007 – Dissolved.

Gecamex Technologies Inc. (Can. July 15, 1993)
July 22, 1998 – Following Plan of Arrangement with Versatech Industries, Inc. and The Versatech Group Inc., Gecamex and Versatech Group amalgamated to continue under the Versatech Group name; basis 1.02 new com. shs. of Versatech for 1 com. sh. of Gecamex. (see The Versatech Group Inc.)

Geddes Resources Limited (Ont. June 3, 1981)
Jan. 15, 1996 – Acquired by Royal Oak Mines Inc.; basis 0.3 Royal Oak shs. for 1 Geddes sh. (see Royal Oak Mines Inc.)

Gee-Ten Ventures Inc. (B.C. Apr. 24, 1987)
July 30, 2008 – Continued into Canada.
Oct. 26, 2011 – Formed Cabia Goldhills Inc. in Canada on amalgamation with Cabia Goldhills Inc. constituting a reverse takeover by Cabia Goldhills Inc.; basis 1 new for 1 old sh. (see FPsurvey - Mines & Energy)

Gegs Capital Corp. (Alta. Apr. 11, 2018)
July 11, 2019 – Name changed to UMG Media Ltd. pursuant to Qualifying Transaction reverse takeover acquisition of UMG Media Corp.; basis 1 new for 4 old shs. ∎

Gelco Enterprises Ltd. (Can. 1961)
Dec. 14, 1966 – Converted to a private co. Holders of com. shs. received $3.25 per sh. Shs. originally issued as a stk. divd. to com. shldrs. of Gatineau Power Co., in December 1961 and January 1962. Stk. was consol. on basis of 1 sh. $100 par for 10,000 shs. 1 par in December 1965.

Gelling Industries Ltd. (Ont. 1947)
Apr. 1, 1953 – Name changed to Switson Industries Limited. ∎

Gelum Capital Ltd. (B.C. June 8, 1987)
Sept. 24, 2021 – Name changed to Gelum Resources Ltd. (see FPsurvey - Mines & Energy)

Gem Dome Oil and Gas Ltd. (Alta. 1935)
Jan. 31, 1944 – Struck off register.

Gem Exploration Ltd. (B.C. 1962)
1968 – Name changed to Consolidated Gem Explorations Ltd.; basis 1 new for 4 old shs. ∎

The Gem Gold Mines Ltd. (B.C. 1933)
1956 – Charter cancelled.

Gem International Resources Inc. (B.C. Sept. 25, 1985)
Mar. 2, 2020 – Name changed to Norseman Capital Limited. ∎

Gemcom Software International Inc. (B.C. Aug. 20, 1985)
July 29, 2008 – Acquired by The Carlyle Group and JMI Equity Fund VI, L.P., through Eagle Acquisition Canada Inc., for $3.05 per sh.
July 1, 2012 – Name changed to Dassault Systèmes GEOVIA Inc.

Gemex Minerals Inc. (Ont. 1972)
Sept. 23, 1982 – Amalgamated with MM-G Canada Inc. to form MM-G International Inc. Each 10 shs. Gemex exchanged for 1 sh. of amalgamated co., plus warrant to buy 1 additional sh. at $1.50 to Apr. 21, 1983, and at $2.00 up to and incl. Sept. 20, 1983.

Gemini Acquisitions Inc. (Ont. June 1, 2006)
Mar. 4, 2008 – Name changed to Silver Shield Resources Corp. following the Dec. 14, 2007, Qualifying Transaction

reverse takeover acquisition of Silver Shield Resources Inc. ■

Gemini Corporation (Alta. Oct. 6, 2000 amalg.)
Apr. 19, 2018 – Placed into receivership by senior secured creditor, Alberta Treasury Branches (ATB Financial). FTI Consulting Canada Inc. appointed receiver and all officers and directors resigned.
May 2018 – Assets of Field Solutions division sold at auction for net proceeds of $113,968 and the Field Solutions division was wound-down. The Engineering Solutions division's outstanding contract was transitioned back to IPL and all staff were terminated.
Aug. 2018 – Environmental Services division was shut-down as attempts to sell assets valued at $150,000 was unsuccessful. The receiver intends to liquidate the assets by way of public auction.
Sept. 2018 – Fabrication business assets and certain corporate assets were sold to 2129156 Alberta Ltd. for an undisclosed amount.
Nov. 2018 – Interim distribution to ATB Financial was made in the amount of $8,050,075.

Gemini Energy Corp. (B.C. July 2, 1965)
Mar. 4, 2008 – Acquired by NRG Investments Inc.; basis Cdn$4.00 or 1 NRG sh. for 1 Gemini sh.

Gemini Food Corporation (Ont. 1984 amalg.)
Nov. 25, 1988 – Acquired by Prince Edward Island Development Agency for 50¢ per com. sh. and $9.50 per pref. sh.

Gemini Technology Inc. (B.C. Sept. 23, 1983)
Dec. 6, 1993 – Name changed to International Gemini Technology Inc.; basis 1 new for 5 old shs. ■

Gemoscan Canada, Inc. (Ont. Oct. 8, 2003)
Jan. 12, 2016 – Made an assignment into bankruptcy. Harris and Partners Inc. appointed trustee and all officers and directors resigned.

Gemstar Communications Inc. (Ont. Dec. 1944)
Sept. 6, 2001 – Amalgamated with SIRIT Technologies Inc.; basis 1 SIRIT com. sh. for 5 Gemstar com. shs. (see SIRIT Technologies Inc.)

Gemstar Resources Ltd. (B.C. Mar. 31, 1988)
Oct. 23, 2007 – Name changed to Rouge Resources Ltd.; basis 1 new for 10 old shs. ■

Gen Star Resources Ltd. (B.C. Dec. 21, 1979)
Nov. 28, 1980 – Name changed to Anarchist Mountain Resources Ltd. ■

Genalta Power Inc. (Ont. Mar. 10, 1948)
Dec. 1955 – Charter cancelled.

Genco Industries Inc. (B.C. 1964)
May 8, 1990 – Name changed to Consolidated Genco Industries Inc.; basis 1 new for 4 old shs. ■

Genco Resources Ltd. (B.C. Feb. 29, 1980)
Nov. 16, 2010 – Name changed to Silvermex Resources Inc. pursuant to acquisition of Silvermex Resources Inc.; basis 1.1 new for 1 old sh. ■

Gencona Mines Ltd. (Man. 1944)
1968 – Name changed to Kelly Lake Nickel Mines Ltd.; basis 1 new for 4 old shs. ■

Gendis Inc. (Can. Nov. 19, 1962)
Apr. 18, 2018 – Privatized via 1-for-500,000 consolidation; basis $5.25 cash per pre-consolidated sh.

Gene Screen Corp. (Ont. May 11, 1962)
July 14, 1998 – Name changed to Genevest Inc. ■

Gene Screen Inc. (Ont. May 11, 1962)
July 19, 1996 – Name changed to Gene Screen Corp.; basis 1 new for 2 old shs. ■

Genecan Financial Corporation (Que. Jan. 22, 1964)
Mar. 17, 1998 – Final distribution made and operations closed.

Genelcan Limited (Can. 1963)
Feb. 1, 1988 – Name changed to General Electric Capital Canada, Inc. ■

GenEnergy Resources Ltd. (Alta. 1980)
Apr. 9, 1982 – Acquired by American Eagle Petroleums Ltd.; basis 0.73 American Eagle shs. for 1 GenEnergy sh. (see American Eagle Petroleums Ltd.)

GeneNews Limited (Ont. Feb. 20, 1997)
June 26, 2019 – Name changed to StageZero Life Sciences Ltd. (see FPsurvey - Industrials)

General Allied Oil and Gas Co. (W.Va. Apr. 15, 1979)
Jan. 29, 1999 – Name changed to Allied Resources Inc.; basis 1 new for 5 old shs. ■

General American Properties Ltd. (Ont. 1973)
Jan. 31, 1984 – Name changed to General American Technologies Inc. ■

General American Technologies Inc. (Ont. 1973)
Jan. 12, 1987 – Name changed to Kanata Hotels Inc. ■

General Assembly Holdings Limited (Ont. June 30, 2017)
June 24, 2024 – Name changed to CANPR Technology Ltd. pursuant to the reverse takeover acquisition of CanPR Technology Inc. (see FPsurvey - Industrials)

General Bakeries Limited (Ont. 1946)
Dec. 1, 1980 – Amalgamated with wholly owned subsid. of Dominion Stores under the continuing name of General Bakeries Limited; basis 2 com. shs. Dominion Stores for each 3 General Bakeries shs., or $11.65 and 1 ser. A pref. Dominion Stores sh. redeem. for 10 or 1 ser. B pref. sh., redeem. for $11.75. Both ser. were redeem. on the day following redemption.

General Cybernetics Corporation (B.C. 1982)
Oct. 6, 1989 – Delisted from the Vancouver Stock Exchange. Subsequently dissolved for failure to file.

General Diamond Corporation (B.C. June 11, 1987)
Sept. 25, 1995 – Name changed to Consolidated General Diamond Corporation; basis 1 new for 5 old shs. ■

General Distributors of Canada Ltd. (Can. Nov. 19, 1962)
May 2, 1983 – Name changed to Gendis Inc. ■

General Donlee Canada Inc. (Can. Apr. 14, 2010)
Oct. 10, 2013 – Acquired by Triumph Group, Inc. for $5.50 per sh.

General Donlee Income Fund (Ont. Mar. 14, 2002)
Jan. 1, 2011 – Succeeded by General Donlee Canada Inc. pursuant to plan of arrangement whereby General Donlee Canada Inc. was formed to facilitate the conversion of the fund into a corporation and the fund was subsequently dissolved. ■

General Dynamics Canada Ltd. (Can. 1948)
July 20, 2015 – Name changed to General Dynamics Land Systems - Canada Corporation.

General Electric Canada Inc. (Can. 1892)
June 1989 – Acquired by G.E. Acquisition Corp.

General Electric Capital Canada, Inc. (Can. 1963)
Jan. 1, 2006 – Name changed to General Electric Capital Canada.

General Energy Corp. (B.C. Feb. 1, 1966)
July 10, 2006 – Dissolved for failure to file and struck from register.

General Fasteners Inc. (Alta. Oct. 25, 1985)
Sept. 5, 2007 – Acquired by General Packaging Corporation for 58¢ per sh.

General Foods, Limited (unknown)
1981 – Wholly owned subsid. of General Foods Corp., White Plains, N.Y. as of 1980. Name subsequently changed to General Foods Inc.

General Gold Resources Inc. (B.C. Apr. 29, 1982)
Mar. 28, 2021 – Name changed to General Copper Gold Corp. (see FPsurvey - Mines & Energy)

General Hydrocarbons Limited (Ont. 1950)
June 1989 – Formed Colin Investments Inc. on amalgamation with Colin Investments Inc.

General Leaseholds (Sudbury) Limited (Ont. 1964)
May 26, 1981 – Name changed to General Leaseholds Limited. (see FPsurvey - Industrials)

General Leisure Corporation (Alta. Dec. 19, 1986)
July 24, 1991 – Name changed to Westgroup Corporations Inc. ■

General Merchandise Co. Ltd. (Ont. 1947)
1963 – Charter cancelled; liquidation, approved May 1969, provided for payment in full to ser. A and B deb. holders, and payment of $1.75 per sh. to cl. A shldrs. No distribution made to cl. B shldrs. in view of the $7.00 priority of the cl. A shs.

General Minerals Corp. (Can. Sept. 18, 1981)
Mar. 8, 1990 – Declared bankrupt. There were no funds available for distribution to shldrs. (Not to be confused with General Minerals Corporation incorporated, Canada, Aug. 19, 1994.)

General Minerals Corporation (Can. Aug. 19, 1994)
Aug. 31, 2007 – Name changed to Sprott Resource Corp. ■

General Moly, Inc. (Idaho Nov. 23, 1925)
Oct. 4, 2007 – Amalgamated in Delaware to continue with same name.

General Mortgage Corporation of Canada (Can. 1961)
Dec. 1, 1976 – Name changed to Commerce Capital Mortgage Corporation. ■

General Mortgage Service Corp. of Canada (Can. 1961)
Dec. 1966 – Name changed to General Mortgage Corporation of Canada. ■

General Motors Acceptance Corporation of Canada, Limited (Can. Oct. 15, 1953)
May 7, 2010 – Name changed to Ally Credit Canada Limited.

General Motors Corporation (Del. Oct. 13, 1916)
July 10, 2009 – Name changed to Motors Liquidation Company.

General Motors of Canada Limited (Can. Nov. 8, 1918; via Dominion charter)
Nov. 23, 2015 – Name changed to General Motors of Canada Company and continued into Nova Scotia.

General Oriental Investments Limited (Hong Kong)
Sept. 4, 1997 – All o/s shs., other than those held by Enderbury Limited and DIA Holdings, repurchased for US$9.78 per sh.

General Paint Corporation of Canada Ltd. (Can. 1950)
1966 – Canadian Wallpaper Manufacturers Ltd. purch. all o/s cl. A and B shs. at $35 per sh.

General Petroleums Drilling Co. Ltd. (Alta. 1959)
June 1967 – Name changed to Excel Petroleums Ltd. ■

General Petroleums Drilling Ltd. (Alta. June 1967)
Acquired by Westburne Petroleum & Minerals Ltd.; basis 1 new for 1 old sh. into new pref. and com. shs. (see Westburne Petroleum & Minerals Ltd.)

General Petroleums of Canada Ltd. (Alta. 1941)
1959 – Amalgamated with General Petroleums Drilling Ltd. and Eastwood Oil Co. Ltd.; basis 1 sh. of each new co. for 1 old sh.

General Products Mfg. Corporation Limited (Ont. 1927)
July 1, 1975 – Charter cancelled; distribution of $1.30 per sh. on cl. A and B stk. pay. to holders of record Dec. 27, 1974.

General Properties Ltd. (Alta. July 18, 1997)
Oct. 7, 2008 – Name changed to General Mining Properties Ltd. (see FPsurvey - Mines & Energy)

General Refractory Co. Ltd. (Ont. 1944)
Liquidated; no equity for shldrs.

General Resources Ltd. (B.C. 1969)
Dec. 1979 – Amalgamated with Earlcrest Resources Ltd. to form Amalgamated General Resources Ltd.

General Sea Harvest Corporation (B.C. 1983)
June 12, 1990 – Name changed to Consolidated General Sea Harvest Corporation; basis 1 new for 5 old shs. ■

General Steel Wares Limited (Can. Oct. 17, 1927; via Dominion charter)
Dec. 31, 1969 – Name changed to GSW Limited following amalgamation with Beatty Bros. Ltd.; basis 1 new 5% pref. for 1 old 5% pref. and 1 new cl. A and 2 new cl. B GSW com. shs. for 1 old General Steel Ware com. sh. ■

General Strategies Ltd. (B.C. Sept. 22, 1992)
Mar. 14, 2006 – Name changed to Landdrill International Inc. following reverse takeover acquisition of Landdrill International Inc.; basis 1.5 new for 1 old sh. ■

General Systems Research Inc. (Alta. 1967)
Jan. 1990 – In receivership. Peat Marwick Ltd. (subsequently Peat Marwick Thorne) appointed receiver. There were no assets to liquidate, therefore creditors and shldrs. received no distribution.
May 15, 1993 – Receiver discharged.

General Systems Research Ltd. (Alta. 1967)
Oct. 31, 1985 – Name changed to General Systems Research Inc. ■

General Trustco of Canada Inc. (Que. Jan. 22, 1964)
July 6, 1993 – Began liquidation of assets for repayment of deb. hldrs. Montreal Trust Company appointed as trustee. Debenture hldrs. suffered a shortfall and the com. and pref. shldrs. received nothing.
Jan. 14, 1994 – Name changed to Genecan Financial Corporation. ■

General Western Industries Ltd. (B.C. 1975)
Sept. 16, 1986 – Name changed to Consolidated General Western Industries Ltd.; basis 1 new for 20 old shs. ■

Generation Gold Corp. (B.C. Nov. 21, 2018)
Feb. 5, 2024 – Name changed to Generation Uranium Inc. (see FPsurvey - Industrials)

Gener8 Media Corp. (B.C. Jan. 24, 2011)
Feb. 3, 2015 – Name changed to Eight Solutions Inc. ■

Genesis II Enterprises Ltd. (B.C. Nov. 21, 1980)
Oct. 10, 2017 – Dissolved and struck from register.

Genesis Capital Corp. (Alta. Dec. 2, 1997)
Nov. 19, 1998 – Name changed to Genesis Land Development Corp. (see FPsurvey - Industrials)

Genesis Exploration Ltd. (Alta. Dec. 17, 1992)
May 3, 2001 – Acquired by wholly owned subsid. of U.S.-based Vintage Petroleum, Inc. for $18.25 per sh.

Genesis Metals Corp. (B.C. Apr. 26, 2010)
July 18, 2022 – Acquired by Northern Superior Resources Inc.; basis 0.2304 Northern Superior shs. for 1 Genesis Metals sh.

Genesis Resources Corporation (B.C. May 8, 1981)
May 30, 1988 – Name changed to Golden Exodus Ventures Ltd.; basis 1 new for 2 old shs. ■

Genesis Worldwide Inc. (Can. July 16, 2003)
May 14, 2017 – Struck from register and dissolved.

Genesys Pharma Inc. (B.C. Dec. 10, 1986)
Aug. 25, 1997 – Amalgamated with Novopharm Biotech Inc. to continue under the Novopharm name; basis 1.6 new shs. of Novopharm for 1 old sh. of Genesys. (see Novopharm Biotech Inc.)

GeneTether Therapeutics Inc. (B.C. Oct. 13, 2021)
Jan. 9, 2025 – Name changed to Rize Oncology Inc. ■

Genetic Diagnostics Technologies Corp. (Can. Feb. 20, 2003)
Aug. 1, 2007 – Formed Polar Star Mining Corporation in Canada on reverse takeover acquisition of and amalgamation with Polar Mining Corporation; basis 1 new for 1 Polar sh. and 1 new for 3.36 Genetic Diagnostics shs. ■

Genetron Marine Inc. (B.C. Apr. 3, 1986)
Mar. 22, 1990 – Name changed to Trilogy Entertainment Corp. ■

Genetronics Biomedical Corporation (Del. June 15, 2001)
Apr. 4, 2005 – Name changed to Inovio Biomedical Corporation. ■

Genetronics Biomedical Ltd. (B.C. Aug. 8, 1979)
June 15, 2001 – Continued into Delaware.
June 21, 2001 – Name changed to Genetronics Biomedical Corporation. ■

Geneva Gold Mines Ltd. (Man. 1934)
1947 – Charter cancelled; shldrs received 10.271 shs. Gencona Mines Ltd. for each Geneva Gold sh.

Geneva Lake Minerals Corporation (Ont. 1927)
June 17, 1992 – Name changed to Mt. Kearsarge Minerals Inc. ■

Geneva Lake Mines Ltd. (Ont. 1949)
1956 – Name changed to Genex Mines Ltd.; basis 1 new for 5 old shs. ■

Geneva Metals Inc. (Ont. 1972)
Mar. 14, 1978 – Charter cancelled.

Geneva Resources Ltd. (B.C. 1962)
Dec. 1973 – Amalgamated with New World Jade Ltd. to form Pacific Jade Industries Ltd. (see Pacific Jade Industries Ltd.)

Genève Cosmeceuticals Inc. (B.C. Jan. 8, 1986)
Aug. 30, 1991 – Name changed to Pacific Concord Holding (Canada) Limited; basis 1 new for 5 old shs. ■

Genevest Inc. (Ont. May 11, 1962)
June 1, 2004 – Succeeded by Pinetree Capital Ltd. following reverse takeover acquisition of Genevest Inc. by Pinetree Capital Corp. and name change of Pinetree Capital Corp. to Pinetree Capital Ltd.; basis 1 new sh. for 1.75 old Pinetree shs. and 1 new sh. for 0.7955 Genevest shs. (see FPsurvey - Industrials)

Genex Mines Ltd. (Ont. 1949)
1966 – Name changed to Irvington Mining Co. Ltd.; basis 1 new for 5 old shs. ■

genifi inc. (Can. Feb. 6, 2008)
May 7, 2025 – Voluntarily liquidated and dissolved; basis $0.0116 cash per sh. payable to shldrs. of record Apr. 10, 2025, paid on Apr. 16, 2025.

Genius Metals Inc. (Can. May 25, 2018)
Jan. 25, 2025 – Name changed to Morocco Strategic Minerals Corporation. (see FPsurvey - Mines & Energy)

Genius Properties Ltd. (Can. Jan. 28, 2014)
Oct. 5, 2018 – Name changed to Cerro de Pasco Resources Inc. pursuant to the reverse takeover acquisition of Lima, Peru-based Cerro de Pasco Resources S.A. (see FPsurvey - Mines & Energy)

Genius World Investments Limited (Cayman Islands Aug. 3, 2007)
Aug. 31, 2012 – Name changed to CINS Holding Corp. pursuant to Qualifying Transaction reverse takeover acquisition of CINS Holding Limited and amalgamtion of CINS with wholly owned Stand Capital Limited. ■

Genix Pharmaceutical Corp. (B.C. June 19, 2015)
May 10, 2016 – Name changed to 1040442 B.C. Ltd. ■

Gennum Corporation (Ont. May 28, 1973)
Mar. 23, 2012 – Acquired by Semtech Corporation for Cdn$13.55 per sh.

Genoco Aluminum Ltd. (Ont. 1958)
Nov. 9, 1967 – Dissolved.

Genomics One Corporation (Can. Oct. 6, 1995)
June 29, 2006 – Name changed to Alert B&C Corporation. ■

Genovation Capital Corp. (B.C. Jan. 14, 1981)
Nov. 17, 2016 – Name changed to Valens GroWorks Corp. ■

Genprobe Technologies Ltd. (B.C. Mar. 13, 1987)
Nov. 6, 1989 – Name changed to CBR International Biotechnologies Corp. ■

GenSci Regeneration Sciences Inc. (B.C. Dec. 4, 1980)
Oct. 27, 2003 – Name changed to SMC Ventures Inc. pursuant to plan of arrangement whereby IsoTis S.A. acquired wholly owned GenSci OrthoBiologics, Inc. for issuance of 27,521,930 IsoTis com. shs., which were subsequently distributed to shldrs. on the basis of 0.46 IsoTis com. shs. for each pre-cons. com. sh. held; basis 1 new for 10 old shs. ■

Gensel Biotechnologies Ltd. (Ont. July 9, 1997)
Apr. 30, 2004 – Name changed to Greenfield Commercial Credit (Canada) Inc. pursuant to reverse takeover acquisition of Greenfield Commercial Credit LLC; basis 1 new for 2.8 old shs. ■

Gensource Capital Corporation (Ont. Nov. 19, 2004)
July 1, 2013 – Name changed to Gensource Potash Corporation. ■

Gensource Potash Corporation (Ont. Nov. 19, 2004)
July 8, 2022 – Continued into Saskatchewan. (see FPsurvey - Mines & Energy)

Genstar Corporation (Can. May 9, 1951)
Aug. 1, 1986 – All o/s com. shs. acquired under a $58 per sh. takeover bid which expired Aug. 1, 1986, through a wholly owned subsid. of Imasco Limited. Preferred shs. were redeem. as follows: ser. A and B pref. at $20 per sh. and ser. D pref. at $24 per sh. on June 30, 1986; Second pref. shs. redeem. as follows: ser. B at US$25 on June 30, 1986, ser. C on Mar. 17, 1986 at $33.10 plus $0.496 accr. divid., ser. D at $44.61538 plus $0.1630 accr. divid. and ser. E at $27.10 on Sept. 15, 1986. Second pref. ser. A shs. (privately held) were repurchased and cancelled on June 30, 1986. (see Imasco Limited)

Genstar Financial Corporation (Alta. 1982)
Oct. 31, 1984 – Continued into Canada.
Oct. 23, 1987 – Name changed to Imasco Financial Corporation remaining a wholly owned subsid. of Imasco Limited. ■

Genstar Limited (Can. May 9, 1951)
June 15, 1981 – Name changed to Genstar Corporation. ■

Gentech Capital Corp. (B.C. Apr. 21, 1999)
Aug. 27, 2001 – Name changed to CareerExchange Interactive Corp. pursuant to Qualifying Transaction reverse takeover acquisition of Corpnet InfoHub Ltd. ■

Genterra Capital Corporation (B.C. 1987)
Feb. 28, 1997 – Continued into Ontario.
Aug. 26, 1998 – Name changed to Genterra Capital Incorporated; basis 1 new for 10 old shs. ■

Genterra Capital Corporation (Ont. 1995 amalg.)
May 2, 1997 – Amalgamated with First Corporate Capital Inc. and Mutec Equities Ltd. to form a new co. known as Genterra Capital Corporation; basis 1 cl. A sh. for 1 cl. A sh., 1 new cl. B sh. for 1 cl. B sh.

Genterra Capital Incorporated (Ont. Feb. 28, 1997)
June 8, 1999 – Amalgamated with Unavest Capital Corp. to form Genterra Investment Corporation; basis 1 new for 14 Unavest shs. and 1 new for 1 Genterra Capital sh. (see Genterra Investment Corporation)

Genterra Capital Inc. (Ont. May 10, 2010 amalg.)
Oct. 30, 2015 – Privatized by Fred Litwin and members of his family (Litwin Group). Common shares other than those held by Litwin Group were exchanged for (i) $2.25 for shareholders holding less than 500 shs. or (ii) $1.96 plus 2 Gencan Capital Inc. com. shs. (spun off as new public company) for shareholders holding more than 500 shs. All cl. B pfce. shs. were redeemed for 5¢ per sh.

Genterra Energy Inc. (Ont. Oct. 31, 2013)
Aug. 15, 2015 – Name changed to Gencan Capital Inc. (see FPsurvey - Industrials)

Genterra Inc. (Ont. Dec. 31, 2003)
May 14, 2010 – Amalgamated with Consolidated Mercantile Incorporated to form Genterra Capital Inc., with Consolidated Mercantile the deemed acquiror; basis 1 new for 1 Consolidated Mercantile sh. and 1 new for 3.6 Genterra shs. (see Genterra Capital Inc.)

Genterra Investment Corporation (Can. June 8, 1999)
Mar. 5, 2004 – Amalgamated with Mirtronics Inc. (1.25 cl. A for 1) to form a new co. named Genterra Inc.; basis 1 new Genterra Inc. sh. for 1 old Genterra Investment sh. (see Genterra Inc.)

Gentor Resources Inc. (Fla. Mar. 24, 2005)
Feb. 29, 2012 – Continued into Cayman Islands. (see FPsurvey - Mines & Energy; FPsurvey - Industrials)

Gentra Inc. (Can. Nov. 3, 1978 amalg.)
May 7, 2001 – Name changed to BPO Properties Ltd. ■

Gentry Mines Ltd. (B.C. June 1, 1971)
June 27, 1973 – Name changed to Gentry Oil & Gas Ltd. ■

Gentry Oil & Gas Ltd. (B.C. June 1, 1971)
June 25, 1979 – Name changed to Laredo Petroleums Ltd.; basis 1 new for 2 old shs. ■

Gentry Resources Ltd. (Can. June 29, 1981 amalg.)
Aug. 27, 2008 – Acquired by Crew Energy Inc.; basis 0.22 Crew com. shs for 1 Gentry com. sh.

Genuine Autotronics of Canada Limited (Ont. 1954)
Mar. 1966 – Placed into bankruptcy. Assets liquidated; no equity for shldrs.

Genus Equity Corporation (Ont. May 26, 1964)
Sept. 19, 1995 – Name changed to Golden Hill Mining Corp.; basis 1 new for 10 old shs. ■

Genview Capital Corp. (B.C. Mar. 15, 2007)
Apr. 15, 2016 – Name changed to Hempco Food and Fiber Inc. pursuant to the Qualifying Transaction reverse takeover acquisition of Dharma Distributors Ltd. (concurrently renamed Hempco Canada Superfoods Inc.); basis 1 new for 2 old shs. ■

Genworth MI Canada Inc. (Can. May 25, 2009)
Feb. 5, 2021 – Name changed to Sagen MI Canada Inc. ■

Geo-Data International Ltd. (B.C. Jan. 13, 1983)
July 29, 1994 – Name changed to Trellis Technology Corporation. ■

Geo-Dyne Resources Ltd. (B.C. May 2, 1972)
Sept. 27, 1976 – Name changed to Cube Resources Ltd.; basis 1 new for 5 old shs. ■

Geo. H. Hees Co. Ltd. (Can. 1954)
Aug. 14, 1963 – Name changed to National Hees Industries Limited; basis of exchange was: 50 1st pref. shs., $10 par, for each $500 1st mtge. bd. or cash to extent of 80% of princ. amt. (cash offer open for 180 days only); 30 1st pref. shs. for $500 gen. mtge. bds.; 2.5 1st pref. shs. for one $100 par pref.; 1 new com. for 3 old com. shs. ■

Geo Minerals Ltd. (B.C. June 9, 2005)
Dec. 22, 2011 – Acquired by New Gold Inc. for Cdn$0.16 per sh. for 1 Geo sh. plus 1 sh. of GeoNovus Minerals Corp. (a new subsid. to which Geo transferred all its assets except the West Blackwater property) for 15 Geo shs.

Geo-Pax Mines Ltd. (Ont. 1949)
Mar. 1976 – Charter cancelled.

Geo-Scientific Prospectors Ltd. (Ont. 1952)
1961 – Assets acquired by Goldfields Mining Corp. Ltd.; basis 3 new for 1 old sh.

Geo-Star Resources Ltd. (B.C. Mar. 15, 1965)
May 3, 1977 – Name changed to Northern Energy Corporation; basis 1 new for 5 old shs. ■

Geocan Exploration & Development Limited (Alta. 1966)
1968 – Name changed to Voyager Petroleums Ltd. ■

Geocore Exploration Inc. (B.C. Aug. 19, 1966)
Dec. 31, 2007 – Name changed to Emerick Resources Corp.; basis 1 new for 3 old shs. ■

Geocrude Energy Inc. (Can. 1980)
Nov. 22, 1985 – Became a subsid. of Canada Northwest Energy Limited (CNW) under plan of reorganization as approved by shldrs. Each 1,000 com. shs. of Geocrude exchanged for the following: a) 62.49 com. shs. of CNW; b) 73.65 9% pref. shs. of CNW; c) 23.55 CNW wts. exercisable at $30 for 4 yrs.; d) 83.72 com. shs. of PanCana Minerals Ltd. (representing 75% int.; the remaining 25% int. held by CNW). (see Canada Northwest Energy Limited)

Geodex Minerals Ltd. (B.C. Mar. 23, 1967)
Oct. 30, 2017 – Continued into Ontario.
Nov. 6, 2017 – Name changed to Intercontinental Gold and Metals Ltd. (see FPsurvey - Mines & Energy)

Geodome Petroleum Corporation (B.C. 1966)
May 1, 1978 – Continued into Canada.
Nov. 16, 1983 – Name changed to Geodome Resources Limited. ■

Geodome Resources Limited (Can. May 1, 1978)
May 9, 1989 – Formed CoCa Mines Inc. in Colorado on amalgamation with CoCa Mines Inc.

Geodyne Energy Inc. (Alta. Aug. 21, 1992)
Jan. 16, 2003 – Name changed to Ranchgate Energy Inc. following reverse takeover acquisition of Ranchgate Oil and Gas Limited; basis 1 new for 3 old shs. ■

Geodyne Technologies Inc. (Ont. Oct. 20, 1983)
Aug. 21, 1992 – Continued into Alberta.
Dec. 24, 1999 – Name changed to Geodyne Energy Inc.; basis 1 new for 8 old shs. ■

Geoffrion, Leclerc Inc. (Que. Nov. 1, 1979 amalg.)
May 26, 1989 – Acquired by the National Bank of Canada.

Geoinformatics Exploration Inc. (Yuk. Aug. 29, 1996)
Aug. 6, 2009 – Name changed to Kiska Metals Corp. following acquisition of Rimfire Minerals Corporation; basis 1 new for 3 old shs. ■

Geolex Resources Ltd. (Ont. 1974)
June 3, 1985 – Charter cancelled.

Geologix Explorations Inc. (B.C. July 5, 1996)
June 28, 2018 – Name changed to ValOro Resources Inc.; basis 1 new for 10 old shs. ■

Geomaque Explorations Ltd. (Que. Dec. 5, 1936)
July 2, 2003 – Amalgamated with wholly owned subsid. of Defiance Mining Corporation to continue as a new company also known as Defiance Mining Corporation; basis 0.125 new Defiance sh. for 1 old Geomaque com. sh. (see Defiance Mining Corporation)

Geomark Exploration Ltd. (Alta. Apr. 20, 2010)
Oct. 23, 2012 – Acquired by Pine Cliff Energy Ltd.; basis 1.5 Pine shs. for 1 Geomark sh.

Geometal Mines Ltd. (Ont. 1944)
Apr. 9, 1969 – Charter cancelled.

GéoNova Explorations Inc. (B.C. Mar. 14, 1988)
Jan. 25, 1996 – Continued into Canada. (see Campbell Resources Inc.)
July 6, 2001 – Merged with Campbell Resources Inc. and MSV Resources Inc. (1 for 4.1); basis 1 Campbell sh. for 10 GéoNova shs. (see Campbell Resources Inc.)

GeoNovus Media Corp. (B.C. Oct. 11, 2011)
May 4, 2016 – Name changed to Imagination Park Entertainment Inc. ■

GeoNovus Minerals Corp. (B.C. Oct. 11, 2011)
Apr. 10, 2015 – Name changed to GeoNovus Media Corp. following acquisition of Greenstock Publishing Ltd. ■

GeoPetro Resources Company (Wyo. Aug. 22, 1994)
June 1996 – Continued into California.

Geophysical Micro Computer Applications (International) Ltd. (Alta. May 31, 1982)
Mar. 9, 2000 – Name changed to NetDriven Solutions Inc. ■

Geophysical Prospecting Inc. (Ont. Sept. 19, 1997)
Mar. 18, 2008 – Name changed to Revolution Technologies Inc. (see FPsurvey - Mines & Energy)

Geoquest Resources Ltd. (B.C. 1969)
Dec. 8, 1976 – Name changed to Claytron Energy Corporation; basis 1 new for 4 old shs. ■

Geor Mine & Oil Ltd. (B.C. 1972)
Sept. 17, 1976 – Name changed to Caprice Resources Inc. ■

George Enterprise Mining Co. Ltd. (B.C. 1928)
June 19, 1978 – Dissolved.

George Gold-Copper Mining Co. Ltd. (B.C. 1925)
May 11, 1979 – Charter cancelled.

George Resource Company Ltd. (B.C. Oct. 27, 1986)
May 11, 1998 – Name changed to Rocca Resources Ltd.; basis 1 new for 10 old shs. ■

George Sparling Ltd. (B.C. 1947)
Nov. 30, 1976 – Placed into receivership.
1979 – Wound up. No distribution for creditors or shldrs.

Georgetown Capital Corp. (B.C. June 9, 2008)
Oct. 11, 2013 – Name changed to Auryn Resources Inc. ■

Georgia Investment Corp. (Alta. Sept. 28, 1987)
May 29, 1990 – Name changed to Environmental Technologies Inc. ■

Georgia Lake Lithium Mines Ltd. (Ont. 1955)
1966 – Name changed to Georgia Lake Mines Ltd. ■

Georgia Lake Mines Ltd. (Ont. 1955)
Mar. 1976 – Charter cancelled.

Georgia Strait Resources Ltd. (B.C. 1983)
May 22, 1992 – Dissolved and struck off register.

Georgia Ventures Inc. (B.C. Aug. 5, 1977)
Oct. 19, 2007 – Name changed to Creston Moly Corp. ■

Georgian Bancorp Inc. (Ont. 1960)
Jan. 8, 2007 – Dissolved and struck from register.

Georgian Minerals Industries Ltd. (Can. 1958)
All assets sold.

Georox Resources Inc. (Can. Feb. 14, 2005 amalg.)
July 18, 2018 – Name changed to Prospera Energy Inc. (see FPsurvey - Mines & Energy)

Geosimm Integrated Technologies Corporation (Alta. July 26, 1995)
Jan. 2, 2005 – Dissolved and struck from register.

Geostar Metals Inc. (B.C. Aug. 19, 1979)
Nov. 27, 2006 – Name changed to SKANA Capital Corp. ■

Geostar Mining Corp. (B.C. 1984)
Aug. 22, 1994 – Dissolved and struck off register.

Geotech Capital Corp. (B.C. Sept. 25, 1986)
Dec. 31, 1991 – Name changed to Vector Venture Corp.; basis 1 new for 2.5 old shs. ■

Geotech Resources Inc. (B.C. 1983)
Feb. 11, 1986 – Name changed to Sea-1 Aquafarms Ltd. ■

GeoVenCap Inc. (Alta. Sept. 15, 2009)
Feb. 1, 2014 – Made an assignment into bankruptcy. PricewaterhouseCoopers Inc. appointed trustee.

Geovex Petroleum Corporation (Ont. 1954)
Dec. 4, 1985 – Amalgamated with 5 other cos. to form Flying Cross Resources Ltd.; basis 1 new for 8 old shs. (see Flying Cross Resources Ltd.)

Geovolco Mining Ltd. (Ont. 1938)
May 15, 1974 – Dissolved.

Gerald Red Lake Gold Mines Ltd. (Ont. 1945)
Feb. 16, 1959 – Dissolved.

Geraldton Long Lac Gold Mines Ltd. (Ont. 1935)
Nov. 5, 1956 – Dissolved.

Gerdau Ameristeel Corporation (Ont. Sept. 10, 1970)
May 25, 2006 – Continued into Canada.
Sept. 1, 2010 – Acquired by Gerdau S.A. for US$11 per sh.

GeriatRx Pharmaceutical Corp. (B.C. Feb. 25, 1983)
May 10, 1996 – Name changed to Paladin Labs Inc.; basis 1 new for 10 old shs. ■

Gerin Inc. (Ont. 1954)
May 27, 1985 – Reverted to private co. status upon redemption of 7% pfce. shs. at $10.275 per sh. together with sum of $0.0806 per sh., representing accrued and unpaid divds.

Gerin Limited (Ont. 1954)
July 1981 – Name changed to Gerin Inc. ■

Gerle Gold Ltd. (B.C. May 25, 1981)
June 13, 2000 – Name changed to GGL Diamond Corp. ■

Gerling Canada Insurance Company (Can. - unspecified)
June 30, 2003 – Name changed to GCAN Insurance Company.

Germain Industries Limited (Alta. Apr. 28, 1964)
Nov. 9, 1989 – Name changed to Marquis Resource Corporation. ■

Germansen Mines Ltd. (B.C. 1934)
June 1956 – Charter cancelled.

Germinate Capital Ltd. (B.C. Aug. 14, 2020)
Nov. 2, 2021 – Name changed to BEACN Wizardry & Magic Inc. pursuant to the Qualifying Transaction reverse takeover acquisition of Beacon Hill Innovations Ltd. (see FPsurvey - Industrials)

Gesco Distributing Limited (Ont. Sept. 30, 1968)
Nov. 27, 1981 – Name changed to Gesco Industries Inc. and continued into Canada. ■

Gesco Industries Inc. (Can. Nov. 27, 1981)
May 9, 2000 – Privatized; basis $4.00 per cl. A or com. sh.
Mar. 1, 2013 – Continued into Ontario.

Gespeg Copper Resources Inc. (B.C. May 31, 2006)
June 25, 2019 – Name changed to Gespeg Resources Ltd. ■

Gespeg Resources Ltd. (B.C. May 31, 2006)
Jan. 4, 2021 – Name changed to 1844 Resources Inc. (see FPsurvey - Mines & Energy)

Gestalt International Limited (Can. 1967)
Mar. 1979 – Name changed to Northway-Gestalt Corporation; basis 1 new for 20 old com. shs. and 2 com. for 1 old pref. sh. ■

Getchell Resources Incorporated (B.C. May 6, 1986)
Jan. 31, 2000 – Name changed to Discovery-Corp Enterprises Inc. (see FPsurvey - Mines & Energy)

Getty Copper Corp. (Can. Sept. 23, 1985)
Mar. 7, 2003 – Name changed to Getty Copper Inc.; basis 1 new for 2 old shs. (see FPsurvey - Mines & Energy)

Getty Resources Limited (B.C. Jan. 28, 1974)
Feb. 1986 – Continued into Canada.
Sept. 14, 1988 – Formed TOTAL Energold Corporation in Canada on amalgamation with Total Erickson Resources Ltd. ■

Gexplor Inc. (Que. 1969)
1971 – Name changed to Société Minière d'Exploration Somex Ltée. ■

Geyser Brands Inc. (B.C. Sept. 19, 2016)
Dec. 16, 2022 – Placed into receivership and BDO Canada Limited appointed receiver.

Ghana Goldfields Ltd. (B.C. June 27, 1988)
Nov. 18, 1999 – Name changed to Icon Industries Limited; basis 1 new for 17 old shs. ■

Ghislau Mining Corp. Ltd. (Que. 1957)
1971 – Name changed to Cedarvale Mines Ltd.; basis 1 new for 3 old shs. ■

Ghost Valley Holdings Ltd. (Can. Dec. 4, 1928)
Assets sold to Clinch Petroleums Ltd.

Ghostmount Mines Ltd. (Ont. 1946)
Dec. 19, 1979 – Dissolved.

Giant Bachelor Mines Ltd. (Que. 1956)
Feb. 1974 – Charter cancelled.

Giant Bay Resources Ltd. (B.C. Feb. 17, 1983)
Sept. 15, 1995 – Name changed to The Kafus Capital Corporation; basis 1 new for 12 old shs. ■

Giant Chibougamau Mines Ltd. (Que. 1952)
June 1, 1974 – Dissolved.

Giant Explorations Limited (B.C. 1965)
Oct. 30, 1981 – Amalgamated with Piper Petroleums to form Giant Piper Explorations Inc.; basis 3 new for 10 old shs.

Giant Mascot Mines Ltd. (B.C. June 7, 1950)
Mar. 31, 1977 – Name changed to GM Resources Limited. ■

Giant Metallics Mines Ltd. (B.C. 1964)
June 14, 1973 – Name changed to Consolidated Giant Metallics Mines Ltd.; basis 1 new for 5 old shs. ■

Giant Mines & Metals Ltd. (B.C. 1946)
Oct. 23, 1958 – Struck off register.

Giant Nickel Mines Ltd. (B.C. 1959)
1961 – Absorbed by Giant Mascot Mines Ltd. Wound up. (see Giant Mascot Mines Ltd.)

Giant North Resources Ltd. (B.C. Feb. 16, 1983)
Nov. 27, 1984 – Name changed to Euromin Canada Ltd. ■

Giant Pacific Petroleum Inc. (B.C. Oct. 1981 amalg.)
Dec. 5, 1991 – Name changed to Red Rock Mining Corporation; basis 1 new for 10 old shs. ■

Giant Piper Explorations Inc. (B.C. Oct. 1981 amalg.)
May 12, 1988 – Name changed to Giant Pacific Petroleum Inc. ■

Giant Reef Petroleums Limited (B.C. 1966)
1984 – Continued into Alberta. (see Numac Oil & Gas Ltd.)

Giant Sturgeon Mining Corp. Ltd. (Ont. 1970)
May 1972 – Amalgamated into Bayfor Corp. Inc.; basis 2 new for 9 old shs.

Giant Ventures Development Company Ltd. (B.C. 1963)
June 13, 1977 – Name changed to Nor-Quest Resources Ltd. ■

Giant Yellowknife Gold Mines Ltd. (Ont. Aug. 4, 1937)
June 30, 1960 – Amalgamated with Consolidated Sudbury Mines Ltd. to form Giant Yellowknife Mines Ltd. (see Giant Yellowknife Mines Limited)

Giant Yellowknife Mines Limited (Ont. June 30, 1960 amalg.)
July 25, 1991 – Amalgamated with Royal Oak Resources Ltd. (5 for 6), Pamour Inc. (3 for 4), Pamorex Minerals Inc. (3 for 5) and Akaitcho Yellowknife Gold Mines Limited (3 for 5) to form a new co. named Royal Oak Mines Inc.; basis 13 new Royal Oak shs. for 2 old Giant Yellowknife shs. (see Royal Oak Mines Inc.)

Giantstar Ventures Inc. (B.C. Feb. 22, 2002)
Nov. 19, 2003 – Name changed to Chalk Media Corp. pursuant to Qualifying Transaction reverse takeover acquisition of Chalk Media Corp. ■

Gibbex Mines Ltd. (B.C. 1969)
Aug. 1972 – Amalgamated with International Video Cassettes Ltd. to form T.V.S. Industries Ltd.; basis 1 sh. T.V.S. for 3 shs. Gibbex.

Gibraltar Growth Corporation (Ont. June 11, 2015)
June 9, 2017 – Name changed to LXRandCo, Inc. following reverse takeover acquisition of LXR Produits de Luxe Internationale Inc. ■

Gibraltar Mines Limited (B.C. July 5, 1962)
Dec. 18, 1996 – Acquired by Westmin Resources Limited for $8.80 per sh. (see Westmin Resources Limited)

Gibraltar Springs Capital Corporation (Que. June 20, 1968)
June 4, 2010 – Dissolved.

Gibson Chibougamau Mines Ltd. (Ont. 1956)
1957 – Merged into Gibson Mines Ltd.; basis 1 new for 2 old shs.

Gibson Energy Holding ULC (Alta. Dec. 13, 2008)
June 15, 2011 – Formed Gibson Energy Inc. in Alberta following amalgamation with (old) Gibson Energy Inc. and 1441682 Alberta Ltd. (privately held). (see FPsurvey - Mines & Energy; FPsurvey - Industrials)

Gibson Girl Mines Limited (B.C. June 8, 1951)
Nov. 10, 1988 – Dissolved and struck off register.

Gideon Capital Corp. (Ont. June 15, 2011)
Dec. 31, 2013 – Name changed to Morgan Resources Corp. pursuant to Qualifying Transaction reverse takeover acquisition of Bathurst Resources Corp. ■

Gienow Windows & Doors Income Fund (Alta. Sept. 9, 2004)
Nov. 2, 2007 – Assets sold by H.I.G. Capital, LLC; subsequently unitholders received $4.20 per trust unit.

Giffels Holdings Inc. (Can. - unspecified)
Jan. 1, 2003 – Name changed to Ingenium Group Inc.

Giga Capital Corporation (Alta. Jan. 17, 2007)
July 2, 2014 – Dissolved and struck from register.

Gigi Oil & Gas Ltd. (B.C. 1980)
Sept. 29, 1986 – Name changed to Gigi Resources Ltd. ■

Gigi Resources Ltd. (B.C. 1980)
Oct. 23, 1991 – Name changed to Rocket Resources Ltd.; basis 1 new for 5 old shs. ■

Gignac Gold Mines Ltd. (Que. Jan. 19, 1937)
1944 – Name changed to Commando Gold Mines Ltd. ■

Gilbec Mines Ltd. (Can. 1927)
1941 – Name changed to Pasgil Mines Ltd. and continued into Ontario; basis 1 new for 5 old shs. ■

Gilbert Gold Mines Ltd. (Ont. 1944)
Jan. 4, 1960 – Dissolved.

Gilchrist Vending Ltd. (Ont. 1947)
1968 – Sold its assets to Ven Par Vending Equipment Sales Ltd. for equivalent of $5.64 per sh.

Gilford Resources Ltd. (unknown)
May 24, 1979 – Amalgamated with International Pyramid Mines Inc., and Bute Resources Inc. to form American Pyramid Resources Inc.; basis 1 new for 2 old shs.

Gilgreer Mines, Ltd. (Ont. Oct. 2, 1922)
1953 – Amalgamated with Cobalt Consolidated Mining Corp. Ltd.; basis 1 new for 12 old shs. (see Cobalt Consolidated Mining Corp. Ltd.)

Gill Mining Corp. (Que. 1957)
Nov. 1974 – Charter cancelled.

Gill Uranium Mines Ltd. (Ont. 1954)
Sept. 20, 1960 – Dissolved.

Gillette Pool Products Limited (Ont. 1957)
Jan. 1966 – Name changed to Scapa Products Limited. ■

Gillies Lake Porcupine Gold Mines Ltd. (Ont. 1933)
1953 – Name changed to Consolidated Gillies Lake Mines Ltd.; basis 2 new for 5 old shs. ■

Gilmont Mines Ltd. (Que. 1956)
Oct. 13, 1973 – Dissolved.

Gilmour Gold Explorations Limited (Ont. 1980)
Apr. 2, 1985 – Charter cancelled.

Giltana Copper Corp. Ltd. (B.C. 1969)
Feb. 11, 1975 – Charter cancelled.

Gimbel Vision International Inc. (Alta. June 8, 1994)
Oct. 16, 2002 – Name changed to Aris Canada Ltd. ■

Gimus Resources Inc. (Can. Sept. 6, 2011)
Dec. 20, 2013 – Name changed to Lamêlée Iron Ore Ltd. pursuant to reverse takeover acquisition of Lac Lamêlée South iron project. ■

Gincho International Ventures Inc. (B.C. 1979)
Aug. 9, 1994 – Name changed to Banner Mining Corporation. ■

Ginger Beef Corporation (Alta. Apr. 26, 2000)
Nov. 14, 2022 – Amalgamated with Leung & Son Holdings Inc.; basis 1 redeem. pref. cl. A sh. for 1 com. sh. immediately redeemed for 25¢ cash per sh.

Ginguro Exploration Inc. (Can. Mar. 2, 2005)
May 1, 2015 – Name changed to Inventus Mining Corp. (see FPsurvey - Mines & Energy)

Gioconda Mines Ltd. (Ont. 1967)
1969 – Assets acquired by Reactor Uranium Mines Ltd.; basis 4 new for 5 old shs.
Dec. 19, 1973 – Dissolved.

Gipsy Gold Mines Ltd. (Ont. Mar. 25, 1937)
1946 – Acquired by White Karry Gold Mines Ltd.; basis 3 new for 1 old sh. (see White Karry Gold Mines Ltd.)

Gipsy Oils, Ltd. (unknown)
Assets acquired by Associated Refineries, Ltd., Wainwright, Alta.

Girard Lake Mines Limited (Ont. 1944)
Apr. 1, 1963 – Dissolved.

Gitennes Exploration Inc. (Ont. Dec. 18, 1992)
May 13, 1993 – Amalgamated with Marmora Mineral Products Inc. to form new co. with same name Gitennes Exploration Inc.
Feb. 4, 2017 – Continued into British Columbia.
Jan. 31, 2025 – Name changed to REV Exploration Corp. (see FPsurvey - Mines & Energy)

Givex Corp. (Ont. Nov. 10, 2022)
Nov. 12, 2024 – Acquired by Shift4 Payments, Inc.; basis $1.50 cash per sh.

Givex Information Technology Group Limited (B.C. Oct. 15, 2019)
Nov. 10, 2022 – Name changed to Givex Corp. and continued into Ontario. ■

Giyani Gold Corp. (B.C. Aug. 4, 2010)
July 17, 2017 – Name changed to Giyani Metals Corp. (see FPsurvey - Mines & Energy)

Glacial Mines Ltd. (B.C. 1967)
Feb. 25, 1983 – Struck off register.

Glacier Explorers Ltd. (Ont. 1957)
Oct. 1966 – Name changed to New Glacier Explorers Ltd.; basis 1 new for 2.5 old shs. ■

Glacier Gulch Mining Co. Ltd. (B.C. 1950)
Apr. 1953 – Name changed to Twin Falls Mining Co. Ltd. ■

Glacier Ice Company Ltd. (B.C. Apr. 2, 1985)
Dec. 5, 2003 – Dissolved and struck from register.

Glacier Mining Ltd. (Ont. 1957)
Sept. 25, 1957 – Name changed to Glacier Explorers Ltd. ■

Glacier Resources Ltd. (B.C. Dec. 8, 1986)
May 18, 2001 – Name changed to Bayfield Ventures Corp.; basis 1 new for 3 old shs. ■

Glacier Resources Ltd. (Alta. 1987)
Aug. 1, 1992 – Struck off register.

Glacier Ventures International Corp. (B.C. Mar. 23, 1988)
Sept. 20, 1999 – Continued into Canada. (see Glacier Ventures International Corp.)
Apr. 28, 2000 – Amalgamated with SevenWay Capital Corporation to form new co. with same name Glacier Ventures International Corp.; basis 0.446 new for 1 SevenWay Capital sh. and 1 new for 1 Glacier Ventures sh. (see Glacier Ventures International Corp.)

Glacier Ventures International Corp. (Can. Apr. 28, 2000 amalg.)
July 15, 2008 – Name changed to Glacier Media Inc. (see FPsurvey - Industrials)

Glade Explorations Ltd. (Ont. 1972)
July 27, 1976 – Charter cancelled.

Gladiator Minerals Inc. (Can. Apr. 23, 1997)
Sept. 25, 2002 – Name changed to Hinterland Metals Inc.; basis 1 new for 2 old shs. ■

Gladiator Resources Ltd. (B.C. 1959)
Jan. 10, 1983 – Dissolved.
July 16, 1993 – Struck off register.

Gladstone Resources Ltd. (B.C. 1984)
Mar. 7, 1989 – Name changed to VAALCO Energy, Inc. ■

Glamis Gold Ltd. (B.C. Sept. 14, 1972)
Nov. 8, 2006 – Acquired by Goldcorp Inc.; basis 1.69 new Goldcorp sh. for 1 old Glamis sh. (see Goldcorp Inc.)

Glamis Resources Ltd. (Alta. Oct. 13, 2005)
Nov. 10, 2009 – Name changed to Legacy Oil + Gas Inc. ■

Glance Technologies Inc. (B.C. Oct. 24, 2014)
Feb. 25, 2020 – Name changed to Perk Labs Inc. (see FPsurvey - Industrials)

Glass Earth Gold Limited (B.C. Mar. 23, 1989)
Mar. 24, 2014 – Name changed to Antipodes Gold Limited; basis 1 new for 10 old shs. ■

Glass Earth Limited (B.C. Mar. 23, 1989)
Dec. 28, 2007 – Name changed to Glass Earth Gold Limited. ■

Glassmaster Industries Inc. (B.C. May 26, 1981)
Apr. 24, 1998 – Continued into Wyoming.
Jan. 31, 2000 – Name changed to Interlink Systems Inc.; basis 1 new for 10 old shs. ■

Gleemar Gold Mines Ltd. (Ont. Feb. 25, 1937)
1956 – Charter cancelled.

Gleichen Resources Ltd. (B.C. Nov. 13, 1980)
Apr. 30, 2010 – Name changed to Torex Gold Resources Inc. and continued into Ontario. (see FPsurvey - Mines & Energy)

Glen Auden Resources Limited (Ont. 1984)
Jan. 24, 1990 – Amalgamated with Tarzan Gold Inc. (1 for 1.5) to continue with the same name Glen Auden Resources Limited; basis 1 new for 1 old sh.
July 22, 1996 – Name changed to Maple Minerals Inc.; basis 1 new for 5 old shs.

Glen Copper Mines Ltd. (B.C. Nov. 19, 1965)
Jan. 18, 1974 – Name changed to Cusac Industries Ltd.; basis 1 new for 5 old shs. ■

Glen Echo Mines Ltd. (Ont. 1950)
Apr. 9, 1975 – Dissolved.

Glen Hawk Minerals Ltd. (B.C. Jan. 22, 1987)
Nov. 24, 2009 – Name changed to Oronova Resource Corp.; basis 1 new for 4 old shs. ■

Glen Lake Silver Mines Ltd. (Ont. 1960)
Apr. 9, 1975 – Charter cancelled.

Glen Lyon Mines Ltd. (B.C. 1966)
Mar. 1966 – Name changed to Glenlyon Mines Ltd. ■

Glen Roy Resources Inc. (Ont. Nov. 13, 1981)
Mar. 29, 2000 – Formed RX Neutriceuticals Corp. in Ontario on amalgamation with ANL BioSpray 2000, Ltd. (deemed acquiror); basis 1 new for 6 old shs. ■

Glenarum Mining Explorations Limited (Ont. 1976 amalg.)
Oct. 18, 1978 – Charter cancelled.

Glenavy Investments Corporation (Alta. Aug. 26, 1997)
Apr. 19, 2002 – Name changed to RHN-Recreational Enterprises Ltd. following non-arm's length Qualifying Transaction acquisition of RHN-Recreational Hockey Network Ltd. (see FPsurvey - Industrials)

Glenayre Electronics Ltd. (B.C. Oct. 28, 1963)
Mar. 9, 1989 – Continued into Canada.
Aug. 5, 1993 – Name changed to GLENTEL Inc. ■

Glenbriar Developments Ltd. (Alta. July 15, 1994)
Apr. 2, 2001 – Name changed to Glenbriar Technologies Inc. ■

Glenbriar Technologies Inc. (Alta. July 15, 1994)
Sept. 20, 2021 – Name changed to Love Pharma Inc. and continued into British Columbia pursuant to the reverse takeover acquisition of Kick Pharmaceuticals Inc.; basis 1 new for 2 old shs. ■

Glenburk Mines Ltd. (Ont. 1954)
Apr. 1976 – Amalgamated into Glenarum Mining Explorations Ltd.; basis 1 new for 4 old shs.

Glencairn Explorations Ltd. (Ont. Apr. 22, 1987)
Oct. 15, 2002 – Name changed to Glencairn Gold Corporation. ■

Glencairn Gold Corporation (Ont. Apr. 22, 1987)
Oct. 24, 2003 – Amalgamated with Black Hawk Mining Inc. via reverse takeover to continue as Glencairn Gold Corporation. (see Glencairn Gold Corporation)

Glencairn Gold Corporation (Ont. Apr. 22, 1987)
June 8, 2005 – Continued into Canada.
Dec. 5, 2007 – Name changed to Central Sun Mining Inc.; basis 1 new for 7 old shs. ■

Glencannon Resources Inc. (Ont. 1982)
May 25, 1988 – Name changed to National Quotes Inc. ■

Glencona Exploration Mining Ltd. (Que. 1956)
Sept. 9, 1972 – Dissolved.

Glencona Mining Co. Ltd. (Ont. 1945)
Apr. 1961 – Name changed to Glencona Exploration Mining Ltd.; basis 1 new for 10 old shs. ■

Glendale Corporation (Ont. 1954)
Nov. 30, 1978 – Amalgamated with Firan International Limited to become Firan-Glendale Corporation.

Glendale Homes Limited (Ont. 1954)
June 14, 1973 – Name changed to Glendale Corporation. ■

Glendale International Corp. (Ont. Dec. 1, 1993 amalg.)
Jan. 19, 2010 – Filed for voluntary bankruptcy, and all directors resigned. Ernst & Young Inc. was appointed trustee.

Glendale Mines & Properties Ltd. (Ont. 1943)
1958 – Acquired by Rockdale Mines Ltd. (see Rockdale Mines Ltd.)

Glendale Resources Inc. (B.C. Feb. 8, 1983)
Dec. 16, 1993 – Name changed to International Glendale Resources Inc.; basis 1 new for 4 old shs. ■

Glendora Resources Inc. (B.C. July 9, 1969)
Sept. 26, 1986 – Name changed to Romulus Resources Ltd. ■

Gleneagle Graphite Mines Ltd. (Ont. 1955)
1964 – Name changed to Silverplace Mines Ltd. ■

Gleneagles Petroleum Corp. (B.C. Aug. 5, 1987)
July 29, 1999 – Name changed to ClickHouse.com Online Inc. ■

Glenex Industries Inc. (B.C. May 1, 1984 amalg.)
July 9, 2002 – Amalgamated with Bradstone Equity Partners, Inc., Peruvian Gold Limited and Stockscape.com Technologies Inc. to form Quest Investment Corporation; basis 1 new cl.A sh. for 1 Bradstone sh., 1 new cl.A sh. for 1.7156 Peruvian shs., 1 new cl.A sh. for 4.1387 Stockscape.com shs. and 1 new cl.A sh. for 2.268 Glenex shs. (see Quest Investment Corporation)

Glengair Group Ltd. (Ont. 1962)
June 29, 1973 – Amalgamated with Atlantic Sugar Refineries Co. Limited to form Jannock Corporation Limited; basis 1 new 6% cl. B sh. for 4 old 6% non-cum. conv. non-voting cl. B sh.; 1 new special sh. for 4 com. shs. (see Jannock Corporation Limited)

Glenhaven Minerals Inc. (B.C. Aug. 11, 1997)
Jan. 30, 2001 – Name changed to Glenhaven Ventures Inc.; basis 1 new for 3 old shs. ■

Glenhaven Resources Inc. (B.C. Aug. 11, 1997)
Oct. 6, 1999 – Name changed to Glenhaven Minerals Inc.; basis 1 new for 6 old shs. ■

Glenhaven Ventures Inc. (B.C. Aug. 11, 1997)
July 16, 2002 – Name changed to Red Lake Resources Inc. ■

Glenlivet Gold Mines Ltd. (Ont. 1945)
Mar. 10, 1958 – Charter cancelled.

Glenlyon Mines Ltd. (B.C. 1966)
Jan. 18, 1974 – Name changed to Amca Industries Ltd.; basis 1 new for 5 old shs. ■

Glenmar Lithium Mines Ltd. (Ont. 1955)
Apr. 9, 1969 – Charter cancelled.

Glenmark Capital Corp. (B.C. Apr. 13, 1992)
Aug. 5, 2015 – Name changed to Aldever Resources Inc.; basis 1 new for 2 old shs. ■

Glenmore Highlands Inc. (Alta. Sept. 5, 1986)
July 26, 2000 – Amalgamated with a wholly owned subsid. of Mountain Province Mining Inc.; basis 0.5734 Mountain Province shs. for 1 Glenmore sh. (see Mountain Province Mining Inc.)

Glenn Explorations Ltd. (Ont. June 15, 1933)
Apr. 1969 – Name changed to Camindex Mines Limited; basis 1 new for 5 old shs. ■

Glenn Uranium Mines Ltd. (Ont. June 15, 1933)
Aug. 1964 – Name changed to Glenn Explorations Ltd. ■

Glenora Gold Mines Ltd. (Ont. June 15, 1933)
Apr. 1955 – Name changed to Glenn Uranium Mines Ltd.; basis 1 new for 5 old shs. ■

Glenora Resources Inc. (B.C. July 14, 1983)
Feb. 16, 1990 – Dissolved and struck off register.

Glenray Pershing Mines Ltd. (Ont. 1945)
Jan. 11, 1960 – Charter cancelled.

Glenrock Gold Mines Ltd. (Ont. 1944)
1958 – Acquired by Rockdale Mines Ltd.; basis 1 new for 10 old shs. (see Rockdale Mines Ltd.)

Glenshire Mines Ltd. (Ont. 1975)
Jan. 23, 1979 – Amalgamated with Huddersfield Uranium Mines Ltd. (129 for 1,000), Kayak Explorations Ltd. (195 for 1,000), Lunel Management Ltd. (923.5 for 1), La France Explorations Ltd. (128 for 1,000), Sandhurst Mines Ltd. (1 for 1) and Steppingstone Explorations Ltd. (229 for 1,000) to form Lunel Enterprises Inc.; basis 231 new for 1,000 old shs. (see Lunel Enterprises Inc.)

Glenstar Ventures Inc. (B.C. Nov. 26, 2020)
Apr. 1, 2025 – Name changed to Glenstar Minerals Inc. (see FPsurvey - Mines & Energy)

Glenthorne Enterprises Inc. (B.C. Jan. 31, 2006)
Dec. 9, 2010 – Name changed to Asantae Holdings International Inc. pursuant to Qualifying Transaction reverse takeover acquisition of Asantae, Inc. and amalgamation of Asantae with a wholly owned subsid. ■

Glenvet Resources Ltd. (B.C. Nov. 18, 1983)
Oct. 10, 1991 – Name changed to Fort Point Resources Ltd.; basis 1 new for 3 old shs. ■

Glenwood Ventures Inc. (Alta. Sept. 29, 2000)
Nov. 29, 2001 – Name changed to Toro Energy Inc. following Qualifying Transaction reverse takeover acquisition of Toro Energy Corporation at a deemed price of 30¢ per sh. for 16,427,581 com. shs. and 10,000,000 convert. pfd. shs. ■

Glider Developments Inc. (B.C. Mar. 18, 1986)
Sept. 28, 1992 – Name changed to Venture Pacific Development Corporation; basis 1 new for 6 old shs. ■

Glider Resources Inc. (B.C. Mar. 18, 1986)
Nov. 21, 1988 – Name changed to Glider Developments Inc. ■

Glidmac Mining Company Ltd. (Que. 1944)
1952 – Wound up. Assets distributed on pro-rata basis.

Glimmer Resources Inc. (Ont. Mar. 10, 1986)
Feb. 10, 2004 – Name changed to Baffinland Iron Mines Corporation following reverse takeover acquisition of Baffinland Iron Mines Ltd.; basis 1 new for 3 old shs. ■

Glitter Gold Mines Ltd. (B.C. 1981)
May 8, 1992 – Dissolved and struck off register.

Global Advantaged Telecom & Utilities Income Fund (Ont.)
June 22, 2016 – Name changed to Global Telecom & Utilities Income Fund. ■

Global Aerospace Systems Inc. (Ont. Apr. 26, 1979 amalg.)
Oct. 7, 1987 – Name changed to Venga Aerospace Systems Inc. (see FPsurvey - Mines & Energy; FPsurvey - Industrials)

Global Agribusiness Trust (Ont. Oct. 29, 2007)
Jan. 24, 2011 – Name changed to Aston Hill Global Agribusiness Fund. ■

Global Alert Systems Corp. (B.C. 1985)
Mar. 5, 1990 – Name changed to Delta Star Resources Inc.; basis 1 new for 3 old shs. ■

Global Alpha Worldwide Growth Fund (Ont. July 20, 2015)
Nov. 27, 2018 – Converted into an open-end mutual fund under the BMO Global Water Solutions TACTIC™ Fund name.

Global Alternative Investments Inc. (Alta. Aug. 2, 2006)
Oct. 15, 2010 – Distribution of $0.0528 cash per sh. paid to shldrs. of record Sept. 30, 2010.
Nov. 2, 2010 – Voluntarily dissolved and struck from register.

Global Alumina Corporation (N.B. May 26, 2004)
July 31, 2013 – All o/s shs. redeemed for US$0.169 per sh and co. dissolved.

Global Alumina Products Corporation (Ont. Jan. 29, 1937)
May 26, 2004 – Continued into New Brunswick.
Apr. 29, 2005 – Name changed to Global Alumina Corporation. ■

Global Banks Premium Income Trust (Ont. Jan. 27, 2005)
Nov. 18, 2013 – Converted from a closed end to an open-ended fund.

Global Biotech Corp. (Del. Nov. 2, 1998)
Sept. 30, 2013 – Name changed to Purthanol Resources Limited.

Global Blockchain Mining Corp. (B.C. Nov. 9, 2017)
May 21, 2019 – Name changed to Metaverse Capital Corp. (see FPsurvey - Industrials)

Global Blockchain Technologies Corp. (B.C. Feb. 12, 2010)
Feb. 12, 2019 – Name changed to Global Gaming Technologies Corp. ■

Global CT & T Telecommunications Inc. (B.C. Apr. 9, 1987)
Aug. 15, 2005 – Dissolved and struck from register.

Global Cable Systems Inc. (B.C. 1987)
Dec. 19, 2000 – Name changed to Consolidated Global Cable Systems, Inc.; basis 1 new for 5 old shs. ■

Global Cannabis Applications Corp. (B.C. July 14, 2014)
July 14, 2022 – Name changed to Global Compliance Applications Corp. (see FPsurvey - Industrials)

Global Capital Securities Trust (Ont. Oct. 23, 2009)
Dec. 20, 2017 – Name changed to Redwood Global Financials Income Fund. ■

Global Care Capital Inc. (B.C. May 25, 2004)
Mar. 29, 2023 – Name changed to Polaris Northstar Capital Corp.; basis 1 new for 20 old shs. (see FPsurvey - Industrials)

Global Champions Split Corp. (Ont. Nov. 27, 2012)
Aug. 20, 2018 – Redeemed; basis Cdn$25.25 plus accrued and unpaid dividends of Cdn$0.1374 cash per ser, 1 preferred shs.

Global Cobalt Corporation (B.C. Mar. 9, 2007)
July 23, 2018 – Dissolved for failure to file and struck from registry.

Global Cogenix Industrial Corporation (B.C. June 10, 1983)
July 18, 2006 – Name changed to Highwater Power Corporation; basis 1 new for 5 old shs. ■

Global Commerce Development Inc. (Alta. Dec. 21, 1995)
Nov. 1, 2006 – Going private transaction via amalgamation with 1250656 Alberta Ltd.

Global Communications Limited (Can. 1969)
July 1985 – Acquired by Global Ventures Western Limited for $40 per sh.
1997 – Name changed to Global Television Network, Inc.

Global Consumer Technologies Inc. (Alta. Dec. 1, 1997)
June 2, 2006 – Dissolved and struck from register.

Global Copper Corp. (B.C. Feb. 28, 2005)
Aug. 8, 2008 – Acquired by Teck Cominco Limited and all assets except Relincho project were spun off to newly formed Lumina Copper Corp.; basis either 0.2973 Teck cl. B shs. plus $0.0001 and 1 Lumina Copper com. sh. or 0.0782 Teck cl. B shs. plus $8.84 and 1 Lumina Copper com. sh. for each Global Copper com. sh.

Global Copper Group Inc. (B.C. Dec. 14, 2009)
Oct. 24, 2016 – Name changed to Cobalt Power Group Inc. ■

Global Credit Pref Corp. (Ont. May 11, 2005)
Feb. 25, 2011 – Name changed to Shoreline Energy Corp. ■

Global Crossing Airlines Inc. (B.C. June 23, 2020)
Dec. 22, 2020 – Continued into Delaware.
Dec. 24, 2020 – Name changed to Global Crossing Airlines Group Inc. (see FPsurvey - Industrials)

Global Daily Fantasy Sports Inc. (B.C. Sept. 23, 2005)
July 31, 2020 – Name changed to Playgon Games Inc. (see FPsurvey - Industrials)

Global Data Systems Corp. (B.C. May 23, 1986)
Nov. 22, 1989 – Name changed to Comtron Enterprises Inc.; basis 1 new for 3 old shs. ■

Global Defence Metals Corp. (B.C. Feb. 16, 2022)
Feb. 21, 2025 – Name changed to Global Tactical Metals Corp. (see FPsurvey - Mines & Energy)

Global Development Resources, Inc. (Ont. Mar. 25, 1994 amalg.)
Dec. 21, 2010 – Name changed to GDV Resources Inc.; basis 1 new for 3 old shs. ■

Global DiSCS Trust 2004-1 (Ont. Oct. 28, 2004)
Dec. 20, 2009 – Matured. Unitholders received $25 per trust unit plus accrued interest of $0.286 per trust unit.

Global Diversified Investment Grade Income Trust (Ont. Aug. 30, 2004)
Sept. 9, 2014 – All tr. units redeemed for $9.55 per unit.
Dec. 23, 2014 – Paid final adjustment of 12¢ per unit and was wound up.

Global Diversified Investment Grade Income Trust II (Ont. Feb. 28, 2005)
Feb. 9, 2017 – Redeemed; basis 24¢ per trust unit.

Global Dividend Fund (Ont. Dec. 12, 2006)
June 16, 2016 – Voluntarily delisted from TSX in connection with manager BlackBridge Capital Management Corp. having determined to terminate the fund.
Oct. 25, 2016 – Special distrib. of $4.10 per unit paid to unitholders of record Oct. 21, 2016.
Mar. 31, 2017 – All o/s units other than those held by an affiliate of Tralucent Asset Management Inc. were redeemed. A final special distrib. of $0.405 cash per unit was payable on Apr. 28, 2017, to unitholders of record Mar. 30, 2017.

Global Dividend Growers Income Fund (Alta. Feb. 26, 2013)
Mar. 15, 2022 – Converted into an exchange-traded fund; basis 1 Middlefield Sustainable Global Dividend ETF for 1 Global Dividend Growers fund unit.

Global Election Systems Inc. (B.C. Nov. 22, 1991 amalg.)
Jan. 31, 2002 – Amalgamated with Diebold, Incorporated and Diebold Acquisition Ltd.; basis US$0.227 plus 0.02421 Diebold shs. for 1 Global Election sh.

Global Elsimate Capital Corp. (B.C. Jan. 16, 2015)
Oct. 6, 2020 – Name changed to Extreme Vehicle Battery Technologies Corp.; basis 6 new for 1 old sh. ■

Global Energy Corporation (B.C. Nov. 20, 1968)
Sept. 13, 1985 – Name changed to United Global Petroleum Inc.; basis 1 new for 3 old shs. ■

Global Energy Services Ltd. (Alta. Dec. 23, 1993)
Nov. 2, 2011 – Name changed to Raise Production Inc. ■

Global Equity Corporation (Ont. Sept. 30, 1983)
Dec. 23, 1998 – Acquired by PICO Holdings, Inc.; basis 0.4628 PICO shs. for 1 Global Equity sh.

Global Explorations Corporation (B.C. June 23, 1987)
Oct. 29, 1999 – Acquired by Trincomali Ltd.; basis 1 Trincomali sh. for 1 Global sh.

Global Express Energy Inc. (Alta. Apr. 18, 1997)
Dec. 1, 2005 – Formed Challenger Energy Corp. in Canada on amalgamation with Challenger Energy Corp., constituting a reverse takeover by Challenger. ■

Global Financial Group Inc. (B.C. Dec. 12, 1977)
Apr. 17, 2007 – Name changed to egX Group Inc. ■

Global Focus Resources Ltd. (B.C. 1983)
July 25, 2003 – Dissolved and struck from register.

Global Food and Ingredients Ltd. (Ont. Dec. 21, 2020)
May 30, 2024 – Placed into receivership and FTI Consulting Canada Inc. appointed receiver.

Global Fortress Inc. (Can. May 1, 2000)
Feb. 11, 2004 – Continued into Manitoba.
Apr. 15, 2004 – Name changed to Lakeview Hotel Real Estate Investment Trust following Qualifying Transaction acquisition of hotel property and operations known as Lakeview Inn & Suites plus a percentage of trademarks, systems and goodwill; basis 1 new for 10 old shs. ■

Global 45 Split Corp. (Ont. Mar. 29, 2004)
Oct. 3, 2011 – All o/s shs. redeemed for $10 plus the previously announced quarterly distribution of $0.13125 per pref. sh. and $4.4827 per cl. A sh.

Global (GMPC) Holdings Inc. (Can. June 3, 1977)
Dec. 31, 2009 – Formed GC-Global Capital Corp. in Canada on amalgamation with E & E Capital Funding Inc.; basis 1 new subord. vtg. sh. for 1 E & E com. sh. and 0.3 new multiple vtg. and 0.3 new subord. vtg. sh. for 1 Global (GMPC) multiple vtg. and subord. vtg. sh. ■

Global Gaming Technologies Corp. (B.C. Feb. 12, 2010)
July 24, 2023 – Dissolved for failure to file and struck from registry.

Global Gardens Group Acquisition Corp. (B.C. Nov. 11, 2014)
Oct. 1, 2015 – Name changed to Global Gardens Group Inc. (see FPsurvey - Industrials)

Global Government Plus Fund Limited (Bermuda Nov. 9, 1987)
Aug. 29, 1994 – Wound up. Shldrs. received a cash distribution of US$6.43330 or CDN$8.84206 per sh.

Global Green Matrix Corp. (Alta. Oct. 25, 1995)
Sept. 23, 2013 – Name changed to Intercept Energy Services Inc. ■

Global Healthcare Dividend Fund (Alta. Sept. 24, 2014)
Dec. 20, 2016 – Converted to an open-ended mutual fund trust.

Global Healthcare Income & Growth Fund (Ont. Jan. 1, 2015)
Apr. 3, 2018 – Converted to an exchange traded fund (ETF).

Global Hunter Corp. (B.C. Mar. 30, 1988)
Sept. 13, 2016 – Dissolved and struck from registry.

Global Immune Technologies Inc. (B.C. Sept. 18, 1985)
June 2, 2006 – Dissolved and struck from register.

Global Industries Inc. (Alta. May 2, 1994)
July 8, 1998 – Name changed to American Resource Corporation. ■

Global Infrastructure Dividend Fund (Alta.)
Aug. 17, 2016 – Merged into Middlefield Global Infrastructure Fund, an open-ended mutual fund; basis 0.78634836 new series A units per trust unit.

Global Innovation Dividend Fund (Alta. Feb. 22, 2018)
Mar. 15, 2022 – Converted into an exchange-traded fund; basis 1 Middlefield Innovation Dividend ETF for 1 Global Innovation Dividend fund unit.

Global International Energy Inc. (Ont. 1985)
Dec. 4, 1987 – Amalgamated with Equican Ventures Inc. (25 for 8), Glenrealco Inc. (1,828,519 for 200), Four Fifty Dobbie Inc. (23 for 38) and Southern Eagle Enterprises Inc. (23 for 38) to form a new co. named Equican Venture Corp.; basis 1 new for 1 old sh.

Global Investment Financial Group Inc. (B.C. Dec. 12, 1977)
Mar. 4, 2002 – Name changed to Global Financial Group Inc.; basis 1 new for 20 old shs. ■

Global Investment.com Financial Inc. (B.C. Dec. 12, 1977)
Apr. 4, 2001 – Name changed to Global Investment Financial Group Inc. ■

Global Key Investment Limited (B.C. Oct. 25, 2007)
Apr. 11, 2017 – Dissolved for failure to file and struck from registry.

Global Light Telecommunications Inc. (Yuk. Nov. 29, 1993)
May 19, 2005 – Dissolved and struck off register.

Global Link Data Solutions Ltd. (Alta. Dec. 23, 1993)
Aug. 17, 2005 – Name changed to Global Energy Services Ltd. ■

Global Link International Inc. (Alta. Dec. 23, 1993)
May 10, 2000 – Name changed to Global Link Data Solutions Ltd.; basis 1 new for 4 old shs. ■

Global Met Coal Corporation (B.C. Apr. 7, 2005)
July 15, 2014 – Name changed to Minecorp Energy Ltd. ■

Global Metals Ltd. (B.C. July 23, 1987)
Jan. 9, 1998 – Name changed to Global Petroleum Inc. ■

Global Mineral & Chemical Ltd. (Alta. July 24, 1989)
Jan. 13, 1999 – Name changed to Consolidated Global Minerals Ltd.; basis 1 new for 5 old shs. ■

Global Mineral Corporation Ltd. (B.C. 1959)
Mar. 21, 1983 – Struck off register.

Global Minerals Ltd. (B.C. Mar. 31, 2006)
June 27, 2016 – Name changed to MK2 Ventures Ltd.; basis 1 new for 2 old shs. ∎

Global Net Entertainment Corp. (B.C. Sept. 30, 1967)
Nov. 17, 2006 – Name changed to Guildhall Minerals Ltd.; basis 1 new for 5 old shs. ∎

Global-Pacific Minerals Inc. (B.C. June 2, 1981)
Apr. 19, 2001 – Name changed to UNIREX Technologies, Inc. and continued into Wyoming pursuant to plan of arrangement whereby Global-Pacific transferred its mineral assets and cash to newly incorporated Pacific Minerals, Inc. (spun out to shldrs. on a 1-for-6 basis) and completed the reverse takeover acquisition of UNIREX, Incorporated. ∎

Global Petroleum Inc. (B.C. July 23, 1987)
June 15, 2000 – Name changed to Stellar Pacific Ventures Inc.; basis 1 new for 2 old shs. ∎

Global Plus Income Trust (Ont. Aug. 30, 1999)
Nov. 9, 2009 – Name changed to Premier Canadian Income Fund. ∎

Global Preferred Securities Trust (Ont. May 31, 2004)
July 3, 2007 – Amalgamated with Fairway Investment Grade Income Fund and subsequently merged into Fairway Diversified Income and Growth Trust; basis 0.678498 Fairway Diversified units for 1 Fairway Investment unit and 0.713949 Fairway Diversified units for 1 Global unit. (see Fairway Diversified Income and Growth Trust)

Global Railway Industries Ltd. (Alta. Jan. 30, 1997)
Aug. 13, 2013 – Name changed to Chinook Tyee Industry Limited; basis 1 new for 4 old shs. ∎

Global Real Estate & E-Commerce Dividend Fund (Alta. Sept. 19, 2018)
Feb. 17, 2022 – Merged into Global Innovation Dividend Fund; basis 0.96902767 Global Innovation fund units for 1 Global Real Estate fund unit. (see Global Innovation Dividend Fund)

Global Real Estate Dividend Growers Corp. (Ont. May 27, 2015)
Feb. 12, 2019 – Merged into REIT INDEXPLUS Income Fund; basis 0.63545389 REIT INDEXPLUS units for 1 Global Real Estate equity sh. (see REIT INDEXPLUS Income Fund)

Global Remote Technologies Ltd. (B.C. Jan. 16, 2015)
Mar. 23, 2018 – Name changed to Cryptobloc Technologies Corp. following acquisition of 1Linx Ltd. in January 2018. ∎

Global Resource Champions Split Corp. (Ont. Feb. 9, 2016)
June 14, 2019 – All o/s cl. A pref. shs, ser. 1 redeemed for cash; basis Cdn$25.00 plus Cdn$0.321181 in accrued and unpaid dividends.

Global Resource Split Corp. (Ont. Mar. 1, 2004)
June 25, 2009 – Redeemed all o/s pref. and cl. A shs. for $10 and $19.6204 per sh., respectively.
July 3, 2009 – Dissolved.

Global SeaFarms Corporation (Can. Oct. 20, 1998)
Aug. 13, 2017 – Dissolved and struck from register.

Global Shelter Systems Inc. (Ont. Aug. 1977)
Dec. 15, 1987 – Name changed to Shelling Industries Ltd. ∎

Global SortWeb.com Inc. (B.C. July 30, 1998)
June 12, 2006 – Name changed to Mantra Mining Inc. following agreement with Geodex Minerals Ltd. to acquire a 65% interest in an exploration mineral resource property; basis 2 new for 1 old sh. ∎

Global Stone Corporation (B.C. Jan. 24, 1992)
June 22, 1998 – Acquired by Oglebay Acquisition Limited, a subsid. of Oglebay Norton Company of Cleveland, Ohio, for $7.80 per sh.

Global Strategy Corporation (Can. - unspecified)
July 26, 1990 – Initial distribution to shldrs. of record consisted of capital gains dividend of 0.577 units of Global Strategy Canadian Fund or $5.5565 per sh. or a taxable dividend of 0.023 units of the Canadian Fund or $0.2215 per sh.
Mar. 15, 1991 – Final distribution of assets to cl. A shldrs. of record consisted of units of Global Strategy Canadian Fund (net asset value as of Feb. 15, 1991 was $5.63 per cl. A sh.).

Global Strategy Limited Partnership III (Ont. Apr. 5, 1991)
Feb. 1, 1999 – Merged with Global Strategy Limited Partnership VI and Global Strategy Partners LP V to continue as Global Strategy Master LP (New LP) basis 0.93 of a New LP unit for 1 old unit. (see Global Strategy Master LP)

Global Strategy Master LP (Ont. Jan. 29, 1999 amalg.)
Nov. 6, 2012 – Dissolved for 12¢ per unit.

Global Strategy Partners LP VI (Ont. Mar. 31, 1993)
Feb. 1, 1999 – Merged with Global Strategy Limited Partnership III and Global Strategy Partners LP V to continue as Global Strategy Master LP (New LP); basis 1.13 new New LP units for 1 old unit. (see Global Strategy Master LP)

Global Strategy Partners LP V (Ont. Oct. 19, 1992)
Jan. 29, 1999 – Formed Global Strategy Master LP in Ontario on merger with Global Strategy Limited Partnership 1990, Global Strategy Limited Partnership II, Global Strategy Limited Partnership III, Global Strategy Partners LP IV, Global Strategy Partners LP VI, Global Strategy Partners LP VII and Global Strategy Partners LP VIII. ∎

Global Technologies Inc. (B.C. Jan. 13, 1981)
Dec. 5, 2001 – Name changed to Consolidated Global Technologies Inc.; basis 1 new for 9 old shs. ∎

Global Telecom & Utilities Income Fund (Ont.)
June 15, 2021 – Terminated; basis $7.6607 per unit.

Global Telecom Split Share Corp. (Ont. May 7, 1998)
July 3, 2008 – All o/s pref. shs. & com. shs. redeemed for $12.4838 per pref. shs. and nil per com. sh.

Global Teleworks Corp. (B.C. 1988)
Mar. 3, 1997 – Delisted from the Vancouver Stock Exchange. Subsequently struck from register and dissolved for failure to file.

Global Thermoelectric Inc. (Alta. Mar. 10, 1975)
Nov. 5, 2003 – Merged with Fuel Cell Energy, Inc.; basis either 0.279 Fuel Cell com. shs. or 0.279 FCE Canada Inc. exchangeable shs. for 1 Global com. sh.

Global Tree Technologies Inc. (Alta. Dec. 13, 1994 amalg.)
Feb. 7, 2011 – Name changed to Acadia Resources Corp. and continued into British Columbia; basis 1 new for 20 old shs. ∎

Global Uranium Corporation (B.C. Apr. 7, 2005)
Nov. 1, 2011 – Name changed to Global Met Coal Corporation. ∎

Global Uranium Fund Inc. (Ont. Apr. 19, 2007)
Sept. 12, 2011 – Name changed to Aston Hill Global Uranium Fund Inc. ∎

Global Vanadium Corp. (B.C. Mar. 11, 2016)
Sept. 16, 2020 – Name changed to K9 Gold Corp. (see FPsurvey - Mines & Energy)

Global Water Solutions Fund (Ont. Jan. 29, 2015)
Nov. 27, 2018 – Converted into an open-end mutual fund under the BMO Global Growth TACTIC™ Fund name.

Global Wellness Strategies Inc. (B.C. Jan. 30, 2006)
Sept. 25, 2023 – Name changed to Xtacy Therapeutics Corp. ∎

Globalance Dividend Growers Corp. (Ont. Aug. 28, 2015)
Aug. 29, 2018 – Merged with 2649317 Ontario Inc., a wholly owned subsid. of MBN Corporation; basis 1.11019292 MBN shs. for 1 Globalance com. sh. A special redemption of $9.1248 cash per sh. was paid Aug. 22, 2018. (see MBN Corporation)

GlobalBanc Advantaged 8 Split Corp. (Ont. May 1, 2007)
Dec. 17, 2012 – Redeemed for $4.58589 pfd. sh. and nil per cl.A sh.

Globalive Technology Inc. (Ont. Oct. 11, 2012)
Feb. 10, 2021 – Formed Yooma Wellness Inc. in Ontario pursuant to the reverse takeover acquisition of and amalgamation with Yooma Corp. ∎

Globally Local Technologies Inc. (B.C. Jan. 7, 2015)
July 5, 2021 – Name changed to Odd Burger Corporation. (see FPsurvey - Industrials)

Globalstore.com, Incorporated (N.S. Apr. 27, 1999)
May 31, 2000 – Name changed to GSO Solutions, Inc. ∎

Globaltex Industries Inc. (B.C. Mar. 5, 1993 amalg.)
May 14, 2003 – Name changed to Pine Valley Mining Corporation. (see FPsurvey - Mines & Energy)

Globe Copper Mines Ltd. (Ont. 1946)
Oct. 1957 – Name changed to Globe Exploration & Mining Co. Ltd. ∎

Globe Development Co. Ltd. (unknown)
Liquidated; Prudential Trust Co., liquidator, Calgary, Alta.

Globe Envelopes Limited (Can. 1933)
Aug. 1969 – Name changed to DRG Limited. ∎

Globe Exploration & Mining Co. Ltd. (Ont. 1946)
Apr. 1975 – Charter cancelled.

Globe Oil Co. Ltd. (Alta. Apr. 20, 1944)
Dec. 30, 1950 – Taken over by Trans Empire Oils Ltd.; basis 1 new for 6 old shs.

Globe Oil Co. (1958) Ltd. (Alta. 1951)
Nov. 1, 1982 – Amalgamated with Trans-Canada Resources Ltd. and 2 other cos. to form a new co. also called Trans-Canada Resources Ltd.; basis 1 cl. A sh. for each 18.5 old com. shs.

Globe Realty Corporation, Limited (Can. 1912)
1978 – Name changed to Globe Realty Limited. ∎

Globe Realty Limited (Can. 1912)
Feb. 27, 1981 – All o/s pref. shs. acquired by The Royal Bank of Canada; basis 1 new pref. sh. of The Royal Bank for 1 old pref. sh. of Globe Realty. Name subsequently changed to Royal Bank Realty Inc. effective Sept. 6, 1982.

Globe Resources Inc. (B.C. Feb. 29, 1980)
Mar. 30, 1998 – Name changed to Genco Resources Ltd.; basis 1 new for 3 old shs. ∎

Globe Rouyn Gold Mines Ltd. (Que. 1938)
1949 – Charter cancelled.

Globe Royalties Ltd. (Alta. 1935)
Dec. 2, 1940 – In liquidation. Shldrs. realized 1 sh. of British Dominion Oil & Development Corp. Ltd. for each 4 shs. of Globe held.

Globel Direct, Inc. (Alta. Sept. 25, 1997)
Dec. 12, 2007 – Placed into receivership. Meyers Norris Penny LLP appointed receiver.
June 2, 2009 – Receiver was discharged and struck off register.

Globelle Corporation (Ont. Mar. 9, 1993)
Aug. 9, 1999 – All com. shs. acquired by Tech Data Canada Inc.; basis $2.50 per share.

Globemin Resources Inc. (B.C. June 7, 1990)
Dec. 29, 2004 – Name changed to Sutter Gold Mining Inc. following reverse takeover acquisition of Sutter Gold Mining Company. ■

GlobeNet Resources Inc. (B.C. May 30, 1980)
Jan. 28, 2003 – Name changed to Terra Nova Gold Corp. ■

GlobeStar Mining Corporation (Can. Jan. 11, 2002)
Jan. 18, 2011 – Acquired by Perilya Limited for Cdn$1.65 per sh.

GlobeTel Communications Limited (B.C. Aug. 29, 1980)
Oct. 23, 2006 – Dissolved and struck from register.

Globex Biotechnologies Inc. (Ont. June 9, 1988 amalg.)
Apr. 30, 1996 – Formed MGI Software Corp. in Ontario on non-arms' length amalgamation with MGI Software Corp., which was acquired by reverse takeover; basis 1 new for 15 old shs. ■

GlobeX Data Ltd. (B.C. Mar. 1, 2017)
Apr. 14, 2022 – Name changed to Sekur Private Data Ltd. (see FPsurvey - Industrials)

Globex Financial Inc. (Ont. 1963)
June 9, 1988 – Formed Globex Biotechnologies Inc. in Ontario on amalgamation with Codon Biotechnologies Inc.; basis 1 new for 1 old sh. ■

Globex Resources Ltd. (Alta. Aug. 18, 1997)
June 24, 2005 – Acquired by Innova Exploration Ltd.; basis 0.75 new Innova sh. for 1 old Globex sh. (see Innova Exploration Ltd.)

Glorious Creation Limited (Can. Dec. 24, 2015)
July 16, 2018 – Continued into British Columbia.
May 30, 2024 – Name changed to Mustang Energy Corp. (see FPsurvey - Mines & Energy)

Glory Explorations Ltd. (B.C. Mar. 7, 1979)
July 13, 1987 – Name changed to National Fuelcorp Ltd.; basis 2 new for 7 old shs. ■

Glossy Mines Ltd. (Ont. 1956)
Apr. 9, 1985 – Charter cancelled.

Gloucester Mining Corp. Ltd. (N.B. 1962)
July 3, 1968 – Charter cancelled.

Glow Resources Inc. (B.C. Mar. 3, 1983)
Dec. 17, 1985 – Name changed to Esstra Industries Corp. ■

Gluskin Sheff + Associates Inc. (Ont. Apr. 17, 1984)
June 5, 2019 – Acquired by Onex Corporation; basis $14.25 cash per sh.

GlycoDesign Inc. (Can. Dec. 30, 1993)
June 9, 2003 – Amalgamated with Inflazyme Pharmaceuticals Ltd.; basis 1.8424 new Inflazyme shs. for 1 old GlycoDesign sh. (see Inflazyme Pharmaceuticals Ltd.)

Glyko Biomedical Ltd. (Can. June 26, 1992)
Aug. 22, 2002 – Plan of Arrangement with California-based BioMarin Pharmaceutical Inc.; basis 0.3309 new BioMarin com. sh. for 1 old Glyko com. sh.

Go Cobalt Mining Corp. (B.C. Apr. 27, 2012)
July 8, 2019 – Name changed to Go Metals Corp. (see FPsurvey - Mines & Energy)

Gobi Gold Inc. (Yuk. Jan. 10, 2000)
Sept. 26, 2005 – Continued into British Columbia.
Aug. 29, 2006 – Name changed to East Energy Corp.; basis 2 new for 1 old sh. ■

Gobi Oil & Gas Ltd. (Alta. 1988)
Jan. 9, 1995 – Amalgamated with Dominion Explorers Inc. (1 for 12.5 shs. plus 1 participating rt. in Croinor Inc.) to continue as a new company also known as Dominion Explorers Inc.; basis 1 new for 5.5 old shs. (see Dominion Explorers Inc.)

GobiMin Inc. (Can. Sept. 30, 2005 amalg.)
Mar. 10, 2023 – Privatized via a 1-for-30,000,000 consolidation; basis Cdn$1.84 cash per sh.

Godbeau Porcupine Mines Ltd. (Ont. 1941)
Dec. 7, 1977 – Dissolved.

Godden Porcupine Gold Mines Ltd. (Ont. 1941)
1953 – Name changed to Godbeau Porcupine Mines Ltd.; basis 1 new for 2 old shs. ■

Goderich Elevator and Transit Company Limited (Ont. May 27, 1898)
July 1, 1978 – Name changed to Goderich Elevators Limited. ■

Goderich Elevators Limited (Ont. May 27, 1898)
Jan. 1, 2011 – Name changed to Thirdcoast Limited. ■

Godfrey Lake Copper Mines Ltd. (Ont. 1952)
Dec. 1959 – Charter cancelled.

Godfrey Mines Ltd. (Ont. 1964)
1972 – Dissolved.

God's Lake Gold Mines Ltd. (Man. 1933)
1956 – Acquired by R. J. Jowsey Mining Co. Ltd.; basis 4 new for 9 old shs. (see R. J. Jowsey Mining Co. Ltd.)

God's Lake Resources Inc. (Can. Mar. 1, 1978)
Dec. 17, 2018 – Name changed to FAX Capital Corp.; basis 1 new for 3.7 old shs. ■

Gogama Minerals Ltd. (Ont. 1970)
Feb. 28, 1972 – Amalgamated with 2 other cos. to form Coniston Explorations & Holdings Ltd.; basis 1 new for 3.75 Gogama shs. ■

Golar Mines Ltd. (Ont. 1945)
Charter cancelled; no equity for shldrs.

Golconda Capital Corp. (Alta. Feb. 12, 2007)
Sept. 28, 2010 – Name changed to Angus Mining (Namibia) Inc. pursuant to Qualifying Transaction reverse takeover acquisition of Angus Mining (Namibia) Ltd. and subsequent amalgamation with a wholly owned subsidiary. ■

Golconda Mines Limited (Que. 1938)
July 29, 1978 – Charter cancelled.

Golconda Resources Ltd. (Alta. Oct. 6, 1986)
Apr. 29, 2016 – Voluntarily dissolved; no distrib. available for shldrs.

Gold X Mining Corp. (B.C. Nov. 29, 2019)
June 8, 2021 – All o/s shs. not already held acquired by Gran Colombia Gold Corp.; basis 0.6948 Gran Colombia shs. for 1 Gold X sh. (see GCM Mining Corp.)
Sept. 27, 2022 – Name changed to Aris Mining Guyana Holdings Corp. (see GCM Mining Corp.)

Gold Acres Mines Limited (Ont. 1973)
Nov. 22, 1974 – Amalgamated with Foxdale Mines Limited (1 for 7.5), Canton Explorations Limited (1 for 5.5), Marquis Explorations Limited (1 for 2.5), Long Point Gas & Oil Incorporated (1 for 3), Darwin Mines Limited (1 for 1.5), Home Mining Developments Limited (1 for 7) and Force Crag Mines Limited (1 for 4.5) to form New Force Crag Mines Limited; basis 1 new for 7 old shs.

Gold Angel Resources Inc. (B.C. 1974)
Nov. 15, 1981 – Name changed to Gold-Pan Resources Inc.; basis 1 new for 2 old shs. ■

Gold Bar Resources Inc. (Can. Aug. 29, 1988)
June 28, 2013 – Dissolved and struck from register.

Gold Belle Mines Ltd. (Ont. July 19, 1974)
June 2, 1987 – Name changed to Equus Industries Inc. ■

Gold Belt Mining Co. Ltd. (B.C. Mar. 3, 1933)
Defunct.

Gold-Bln Mines Ltd. (unknown)
Oct. 1960 – Dissolved.

Gold Bridge Development Corporation (B.C. 1979)
May 15, 1989 – Name changed to Bridge River Development Corp.; basis 1 new for 3 old shs. ■

Gold Bull Resources Corp. (B.C. Apr. 13, 1995)
Mar. 17, 2025 – Acquired by Borealis Mining Company Limited; basis 0.93 Borealis shs. for 1 Gold Bull sh.

Gold Bullion Development Corp. (B.C. July 17, 1985)
Jan. 16, 2017 – Name changed to Granada Gold Mine Inc. (see FPsurvey - Mines & Energy)

Gold Butte Energy Inc. (Alta. Sept. 12, 1996)
Oct. 31, 1997 – Formed BelAir Energy Corporation in Alberta on amalgamation with Holdco Resources Ltd. and constituted a pooling of interests. ■

Gold Button Mines Ltd. (Man. 1950)
Oct. 28, 1964 – Dissolved.

Gold Canyon Mines Inc. (B.C. 1980)
July 16, 1984 – Name changed to Island Canyon Mines Inc.; basis 1 new for 3 old shs. ■

Gold Canyon Resources Inc. (B.C. Aug. 20, 1985)
Nov. 19, 2015 – Acquired by First Mining Finance Corp.; basis 1 First Mining com. sh. and 0.0333 Irving Resources Inc. com. shs. for 1 Gold Canyon com. sh. (see First Mining Finance Corp.)

Gold City Industries Ltd. (B.C. Oct. 27, 1994 amalg.)
July 7, 2005 – Amalgamated with San Gold Resources Corporation (1 for 1) to form San Gold Corporation; basis 1 San Gold Corp. sh. for 1.9321346 Gold City shs. (see San Gold Corporation)

Gold City Mining Corporation (B.C. Oct. 27, 1994 amalg.)
Oct. 29, 1997 – Name changed to Consolidated Gold City Mining Corporation; basis 1 new for 3 old shs. ■

Gold City Porcupine Mines Ltd. (Ont. 1945)
Aug. 1968 – Charter cancelled; no record of equity for shldrs.

Gold City Resources Inc. (B.C. 1982)
Mar. 12, 1987 – Continued into Canada. (see Gold City Mining Corporation)
Dec. 7, 1994 – Amalgamated with Providence Industries Inc. and McKinney Mines Corp. to form Gold City Mining Corporation; basis 1 new for 0.8 Providence shs., 1 new for 1.3 McKinney shs. and 1 new for 1 Gold City sh. (see Gold City Mining Corporation)

Gold Coast Mines Ltd. (unknown)
1952 – Liquidated.

Gold Coin Exploration Co. Ltd. (B.C.)
May 1, 1969 – Struck off register.

Gold Coral Resources Inc. (Ont. Dec. 12, 1967)
July 28, 2000 – Name changed to Ca-Network Inc.; basis 5 new for 1 old sh. (see FPsurvey - Mines & Energy; FPsurvey - Industrials)

Gold Creek Mining Ltd. (B.C. 1948)
Mar. 15, 1975 – Struck off register.

Gold Crest Products Limited (Ont. 1965)
June 1974 – Acquired by Reed Decorative Products Ltd., a wholly owned subsid. of Reed Paper Ltd.; basis cl. A shldrs. received new cl. A shs. and com. shldrs. received new cl. B shs.; shs. subsequently redeemed for $10 and $8.50 per sh., respectively.

Gold Cup Resources Ltd. (B.C. 1966)
May 9, 2003 – Dissolved and struck from register.

Gold Digger Resources Inc. (B.C. July 16, 2021)
May 14, 2025 – Name changed to Nuclear Vision Limited. (see FPsurvey - Mines & Energy)

Gold Drop Mines Ltd. (B.C. 1945)
Jan. 1957 – Dissolved.

Gold Eagle Gold Mines Ltd. (Ont. 1934)
1959 – Name changed to Goldray Mines Limited; basis 1 new for 3 old shs. ■

Gold Eagle Mines Ltd. (B.C. 1965)
Dec. 6, 1976 – Dissolved.

Gold Eagle Mines Ltd. (Ont. Dec. 21, 2006 amalg.)
Oct. 1, 2008 – Acquired by Goldcorp Inc.; basis $13.60 or 0.292 Goldcorp shs. plus $0.0001 for 1 Gold Eagle sh.

Gold Finder Explorations Ltd. (B.C. Sept. 12, 1996)
Dec. 21, 2017 – Name changed to Venzee Technologies Inc. following reverse takeover acquisition of and amalgamation of Venzee Inc. with a wholly owned subsid.; basis 1 new for 2 old shs. (see FPsurvey - Industrials)

Gold Flora Corporation (Del. July 7, 2023)
Mar. 27, 2025 – Voluntarily filed for receivership and Stone Capital Blossom, LLC appointed receiver.

Gold Frontier Mines Ltd. (Ont. Nov. 1939)
Nov. 15, 1944 – Shldrs. received 1 sh. of Bayview Red Lake Gold Mines Ltd. for each 2 shs. held at.

Gold Giant Minerals Inc. (B.C. May 5, 1987)
Feb. 20, 2002 – Name changed to Gold Giant Ventures Inc.; basis 1 new for 10 old shs. ■

Gold Giant Ventures Inc. (B.C. May 5, 1987)
Dec. 8, 2003 – Plan of Arrangement amalgamation with Cross Lake Minerals Ltd.; basis 2 new Cross Lake shs. for 1 old Gold Giant sh. (see Cross Lake Minerals Ltd.)

Gold Hawk Exploration Ltd. (Ont. 1945)
Apr. 9, 1975 – Charter cancelled.

Gold Hawk Mines Ltd. (Que. 1971)
Mar. 10, 1980 – Name changed to Gold Hawk Resources (Ontario) Ltd. and continued into Ontario. ■

Gold Hawk Resources Inc. (Can. Sept. 4, 1985)
Aug. 16, 2011 – Name changed to Oracle Mining Corp. ■

Gold Hawk Resources (Ontario) Ltd. (Ont. Mar. 10, 1980)
July 11, 1983 – Name changed to Consolidated Gold Hawk Resources Inc.; basis 1 new for 3 old shs. ■

Gold Hill Resources Inc. (Ont. July 27, 1983)
Sept. 2, 1988 – Name changed to Rave Resources Inc.; basis 1 new for 1.5 old shs. ■

Gold Island Mining Co. Ltd. (Man. Mar. 13, 1936)
Dec. 19, 1962 – Charter cancelled.

Gold Island Porcupine Mines Ltd. (Ont. 1934)
1959 – Name changed to Milmar Island Mines Ltd. ■

Gold Jubilee Capital Corp. (B.C. July 19, 2007)
Sept. 15, 2016 – Name changed to OK2 Minerals Ltd. ■

Gold Key Capital Corp. (B.C. May 24, 2006)
Dec. 30, 2009 – Name changed to Unity Energy Corp. pursuant to Qualifying Transaction mineral property acquisition. ■

Gold Lake Mines Ltd. (Man. 1934)
Nov. 29, 1972 – Name changed to Gold Lake Resources Ltd.; basis 1 new for 10 old shs. ■

Gold Lake Resources Ltd. (Man. 1934)
Dec. 16, 1983 – Acquired by Consolidated Imperial Resources Energy Inc.; basis 50 com. shs. and 40, 10% vtg. conv. pref. shs. of Consolidated Imperial for 100 old com. shs. of Gold Lake. Pref. shs. conv. into com. shs. on a sh.-for-sh. basis for 5 years from issue date.

Gold Leaf Ventures Inc. (B.C. 1988)
June 16, 1992 – Name changed to Tokyo Trading Ltd. (see FPsurvey - Industrials)

Gold Line Resources Ltd. (Can. May 7, 2001)
Feb. 28, 2024 – Acquired by Barsele Minerals Corp.; basis 0.7382 Barsele shs. for 1 Gold Line sh. (see Barsele Minerals Corp.)

Gold Lion Resources Inc. (B.C. Oct. 5, 2018)
July 31, 2023 – Name changed to Lithium Lion Metals Inc. ■

Gold Medal Group Inc. (Ont. 1969)
Dec. 11, 1990 – Defunct. All key assets have been sold and no distribution was anticipated for preferred and unsecured creditors or for shldrs.

Gold-Medal Resources Ltd. (B.C. Oct. 16, 1978)
Nov. 27, 1989 – Name changed to Rare Earth Resources Ltd.; basis 1 new for 2.5 old shs. ■

Gold Miners Split Corp. (Ont. Nov. 8, 2018)
Sept. 25, 2020 – Converted into Evolve Fund Corp., an exchange traded fund; pref. shs. redeemed and cl.A shs. redesignated as exchange traded fund shs. of a new class of shs. called Evolve Gold Miners Fund series.

Gold Mountain Mining Corp. (B.C. June 12, 2008)
Oct. 7, 2016 – Acquired by Lowell Copper Ltd. (renamed JDL Gold Corp.); basis 1.032 Lowell com. shs. for 1 Gold Mountain sh.
Dec. 3, 2020 – Name changed to Elk Gold Mining Corp.

Gold Mountain Mining Corp. (B.C. Nov. 5, 2018)
July 31, 2025 – Placed into receivership by creditor. MNP LLP appointed receiver.

Gold-Ore Resources Ltd. (Alta. Oct. 22, 1996)
May 4, 2012 – Acquired by Elgin Mining Inc.; basis 1 Elgin com. sh. plus 0.5 wts. for 1 Gold-Ore com. sh. Each wt. exercisable for 1 Elgin com. sh. at $1.30 for a 2-year period. (see Elgin Mining Inc.)

Gold Pan Mines Ltd. (unknown)
1945 – Property acquired by Gold Pan Mines (1945) Ltd. Pref. shldrs. received 3.875¢ per sh.; no equity for com. shldrs. (see Gold Pan Mines (1945) Ltd.)

Gold Pan Mines (1945) Ltd. (Ont. 1945)
Dec. 23, 1965 – Charter cancelled.

Gold-Pan Resources Inc. (B.C. 1974)
July 23, 1993 – Dissolved and struck off register.

Gold Parl Resources Ltd. (B.C. July 3, 1987)
Sept. 3, 1993 – Name changed to Canmet Resources Limited; basis 1 new for 2 old shs. ■

Gold Participation and Income Fund (Ont.)
Feb. 1, 2016 – Name changed to U.S. Tactical Allocation Fund pending change in investment objective and investment strategy and conversion to a mutual fund. ■

Gold Plus Mining Inc. (B.C. Feb. 18, 2015)
Mar. 4, 2021 – Name changed to Musk Metals Corp. ■

Gold Point Energy Corp. (B.C. Dec. 6, 1988)
Sept. 18, 2009 – Acquired by San Leon Energy plc; basis 0.1667 San Leon shs. for 1 Gold Point sh.

Gold Point Exploration Ltd. (B.C. Dec. 6, 1988)
June 22, 2005 – Name changed to Gold Point Energy Corp. ■

Gold Point Resources Ltd. (B.C. Feb. 13, 1980)
July 10, 1987 – Dissolved and struck off register.

Gold Port Resources Ltd. (Ont. June 20, 1995)
Oct. 28, 2013 – Name changed to Codrington Resource Corporation; basis 1 new for 10 old shs. ■

Gold Port Resources Ltd. (B.C. Nov. 18, 2016)
Oct. 1, 2018 – Name changed to Corsurex Resource Corp. ■

Gold Power Resources Corp. (B.C. Feb. 15, 1985 amalg.)
Dec. 6, 1991 – Name changed to Triple Force Industries Inc.; basis 1 new for 4.5 old shs. ■

Gold Quartz Mining Corporation Limited (Ont. 1937)
Aug. 1960 – Charter cancelled.

Gold Rapids Mines Ltd. (Ont. 1945)
1957 – Charter cancelled.

Gold Reach Resources Ltd. (B.C. Nov. 29, 1965)
Feb. 21, 2018 – Name changed to Surge Copper Corp. (see FPsurvey - Mines & Energy)

Gold Reef International, Inc. (Ont. Dec. 21, 2000)
Jan. 5, 2011 – Name changed to Montana Gold Mining Company Inc.; basis 1 new for 10 old shs. ■

Gold Reef Resources Limited (B.C. 1980)
Oct. 28, 1986 – Name changed to Venture Gold Corp. ■

Gold Reserve Corporation (Mont. Dec. 5, 1956)
Feb. 19, 1999 – Succeeded by Gold Reserve Inc. pursuant to plan of reorganization with Gold Reserve Inc. (a newly formed Canadian company); basis 1 new cl. A com. sh. for 1 old com. sh. ■

Gold Reserve Inc. (Yuk. Oct. 5, 1998)
Sept. 9, 2014 – Continued into Alberta.
Sept. 30, 2024 – Name changed to Gold Reserve Ltd. and continued into Bermuda. (see FPsurvey - Mines & Energy)

Gold Rex Kirkland Mines Ltd. (Ont. May 30, 1921)
Reported defunct.

Gold Ridge Exploration Corp. (Alta. May 3, 2011)
Aug. 8, 2016 – Name changed to GEA Technologies Ltd.; basis 1 new for 5 old shs. ■

Gold Ridge Resources Inc. (B.C. May 9, 1986)
Dec. 9, 2005 – Name changed to Cariboo Gold Fields Ltd. ■

Gold River Mines & Enterprises Ltd. (B.C. 1970)
May 27, 1983 – Dissolved.

Gold River Mines Ltd. (B.C. 1970)
May 1973 – Name changed to Gold River Mines & Enterprises Ltd. ■

Gold Royalties Corporation (Alta. Nov. 4, 2010)
May 6, 2015 – Acquired by Sandstorm Gold Ltd., basis 0.045 Sandstorm com. shs. for 1 Gold Royalties com. sh.

Gold Rush Cariboo Corp. (Ont. July 7, 1997)
Apr. 1, 2021 – Name changed to Allied Copper Corp.; basis 1 new for 15 old shs. ■

Gold Seeker Resources Ltd. (B.C. 1981)
Mar. 25, 1994 – Dissolved and struck off register.

Gold Shield Exploration and Development Inc. (Alta. 1983)
Feb. 1, 1990 – Struck off register.

Gold Shore Mine Ltd. (Man. 1934)
Nov. 21, 1956 – Dissolved.

Gold Spoke Mines Ltd. (B.C. 1979)
Apr. 19, 1985 – Struck off register.

Gold Standard Resources Inc. (B.C. 1981)
Oct. 9, 1986 – Name changed to Consolidated Gold Standard Resources Inc.; basis 1 new for 5 old shs. ■

Gold Standard Ventures Corp. (B.C. Feb. 6, 2004)
Aug. 16, 2022 – Acquired by Orla Mining Ltd,; basis 0.1193 Orla shs. plus $0.0001 in cash for 1 Gold Standard sh.

Gold Star Energy Inc. (Alta. May 12, 1994)
July 2, 1998 – Name changed to Netherfield Energy Corporation; basis 1 new for 3 old shs. ■

Gold Star Resources Corp. (B.C. Sept. 19, 1990)
Feb. 19, 2010 – Name changed to Simba Energy Inc. ■

Gold Star Resources Ltd. (B.C. Sept. 17, 1979)
May 2, 1990 – Name changed to E.E.C. Marketing Corp.; basis 1 new for 3 old shs. ■

Gold State Resources Inc. (B.C. May 20, 1988)
Oct. 31, 2022 – Name changed to International Metals Mining Corp.; basis 1 new for 10 old shs. (see FPsurvey - Mines & Energy)

Gold Summit Corporation (Ont. Dec. 9, 2002)
Sept. 2, 2003 – Continued into Canada. (see Crown Gold Corporation)
Sept. 3, 2010 – Amalgamated with Crown Minerals Inc. to form Crown Gold Corporation; basis 1 Crown Gold com. sh. for 1 Crown Minerals cl. A sh. and 1.65 Crown Gold com. shs. for 1 Gold Summit com. sh. (see Crown Gold Corporation)

Gold Summit Mines Ltd. (B.C. Aug. 6, 1987)
Dec. 9, 2002 – Continued into Ontario.
July 10, 2003 – Name changed to Gold Summit Corporation following reverse takeover acquisition of Millennium Mining Company; basis 1 new for 5 old shs. ■

Gold Texas Resources Ltd. (B.C. 1980)
Nov. 30, 1989 – Acquired by Crown Resources Corp.; basis 1.43 Crown shs. for 1 Gold Texas sh.

Gold Torch Resources Ltd. (B.C. May 25, 1987)
Sept. 27, 1991 – Name changed to European Ventures Inc.; basis 1 new for 2 old shs. ■

Gold Tree Resources Ltd. (B.C. June 21, 2019)
Mar. 1, 2023 – Name changed to Live Energy Minerals Corp. (see FPsurvey - Mines & Energy)

Gold-Uranium Exploration Limited (Ont. 1947)
May 1957 – Charter cancelled.

Gold Valley Mines Ltd. (B.C. June 1936)
1946 – Acquired by Hedley Monarch Gold Mines Ltd.; basis 1 new for 4 old shs. (see Hedley Monarch Gold Mines Ltd.)

Gold Valley Resource Explorations Ltd. (Ont. Dec. 21, 1978)
Aug. 26, 1983 – Name changed to R.F. Oil Industries Ltd.; basis 1 new for 4 old shs. ■

Gold Valley Resources Ltd. (B.C. 1959)
June 6, 1977 – Name changed to NCA Minerals Corp.; basis 1 new for 5 old shs. ■

Gold Venture Placers Ltd. (Alta. May 27, 1988)
Nov. 13, 1990 – Name changed to White Gold Ventures Ltd. ■

Gold Ventures Limited (B.C. 1984)
Mar. 9, 1989 – Name changed to MBS Software Inc.; basis 1 new for 2.5 old shs. ■

Gold Vessel Resources Inc. (Can. Aug. 26, 1985)
Mar. 21, 1995 – Name changed to Consolidated Gold Vessel Resources Inc.; basis 1 new for 10 old shs. ■

Gold Wheaton Gold Corp. (B.C. Oct. 20, 1999)
Mar. 17, 2011 – Amalgamated with a wholly owned subsid. of Franco-Nevada Corporation to form Franco-Nevada GLW Holdings Corp.; basis either Cdn$5.20 per sh. or 0.1556 Franco-Nevada shs.

Gold Win Ventures Inc. (B.C. Oct. 2, 1984)
June 17, 1998 – Name changed to Consolidated Gold Win Ventures Inc.; basis 1 new for 5 old shs. ■

Gold Wind Exploration Inc. (Que. Nov. 9, 1985)
Nov. 9, 1989 – Formed Exploration Acabit Inc. in Quebec on amalgamation with Ressources Claverny Inc.; basis 0.76438 new for 1 Ressources Claverny sh. and 0.35269 new for 1 Gold Wind sh. ■

Gold World Resources Inc. (B.C. Sept. 28, 1987)
Apr. 18, 2007 – Continued into Ontario. (see FPsurvey - Mines & Energy)

Goldale Investments Limited (Ont. Oct. 12, 1977)
Nov. 14, 1986 – Name changed to E. A. Viner Holdings Limited. ■

Goldale Ltd. (Ont. 1919)
June 1965 – Name changed to Canadian Goldale Corporation Limited; basis 1 new for 10 old shs. ■

Goldale Mines Ltd. (Ont. 1919)
Sept. 1962 – Name changed to Goldale Ltd. ■

Goldbank Ventures Ltd. (Alta. Oct. 21, 1987)
Sept. 15, 2000 – Name changed to Consolidated Goldbank Ventures Ltd.; basis 1 new for 4 old shs. ■

Goldbanks-Kirkland Mines Ltd. (Ont. Mar. 1933)
June 1937 – Name changed to Goldbanks Mines, Ltd. and continued into Ontario; basis 1 new for 2 old shs. ■

Goldbanks Mines, Ltd. (Ont. June 1937)
1961 – Charter cancelled.

Goldbard Capital Corporation (Ont. June 11, 2007)
Nov. 25, 2011 – Name changed to Eco (Atlantic) Oil & Gas Ltd. and continued into British Columbia pursuant to reverse takeover acquisition of Eco Oil & Gas Ltd. and subsequent amalgamation of Eco Oil with wholly owned subsid. Goldbard Resources Inc.; basis 1 new for 2.5 old shs. (see FPsurvey - Mines & Energy)

Goldbeam Mines Ltd. (Ont.)
1972 – Dissolved.

Goldbec Mines Ltd. (Ont. 1944)
1953 – Charter cancelled.

Goldbelt Empires Limited (Hong Kong Aug. 4, 2011)
Oct. 8, 2020 – Name changed to Lifestyle Global Brands Limited.

Goldbelt Mines Inc. (B.C. July 23, 1976 amalg.)
July 15, 1991 – Name changed to Goldbelt Resources Ltd.; basis 1 new for 2 old shs. ■

Goldbelt Resources Ltd. (B.C. July 23, 1976 amalg.)
Aug. 27, 2001 – Continued into Yukon.
Feb. 16, 2006 – Continued into British Columbia.
Apr. 8, 2008 – Acquired by Wega Mining ASA for $1.55 per sh.

Goldblock Capital Inc. (B.C. Jan. 29, 2019)
Feb. 15, 2022 – Name changed to Golden Shield Resources Inc. pursuant to the reverse takeover acquisition of Virgin Gold Corp. and concurrent amalgamation of Virgin with wholly owned 1294320 B.C. Ltd. (and continued as 1348135 B.C. Ltd.); basis 1 new for 2.6667 old shs. (see FPsurvey - Mines & Energy)

Goldbow Mining Co. (Ont. 1945)
Nov. 1950 – Name changed to Bowsinque Mines Ltd. ■

Goldbrae Developments Ltd. (B.C. 1982)
June 19, 1990 – Name changed to New Goldbrae Developments Ltd.; basis 1 new for 5 old shs. ■

Goldbrae Explorations Ltd. (B.C. 1982)
Apr. 13, 1984 – Name changed to Goldbrae Developments Ltd. ■

Goldbrook Explorations Inc. (Ont. May 20, 1983)
July 22, 2002 – Name changed to Goldbrook Ventures Inc.; basis 1 new for 3 old shs. ■

Goldbrook Ventures Inc. (Ont. May 20, 1983)
Apr. 13, 2003 – Continued into British Columbia.
May 29, 2012 – Acquired by 0931017 B.C. Ltd., an indirect wholly owned subsid. of Jilin Jien Nickel Industry Co., Ltd., for 39¢ per sh.

Goldcap Inc. (Alta. Dec. 17, 1985)
Sept. 24, 1987 – Continued into Canada.
Oct. 26, 1994 – Name changed to Durandel Minerals Corporation; basis 1 new for 2 old shs. ■

Goldco Ltd. (Nev. Nov. 29, 1999)
May 18, 2000 – Name changed to Resource Ventures Inc. ■

Goldcore Resources Ltd. (B.C. Jan. 15, 1979)
Mar. 22, 2021 – Name changed to Green Battery Minerals Inc. ■

Goldcore Ventures Ltd. (B.C. Sept. 30, 1982)
Nov. 30, 1982 – Name changed to New Goldcore Ventures Ltd. ■

Goldcorp Inc. (Ont. 1954)
Mar. 31, 1994 – Principal assets of the company were amalgamated with those of Dickenson Mines Limited (1 for 1) and CSA Management Limited (1 for 1) to form a new Goldcorp Inc., a new CSA Management Inc., and a new wholly owned company, Lexam Explorations Inc.; basis 1.4 new Goldcorp cl. A shs., plus a div. from Goldcorp of 0.5 Lexam com. sh. for 1 old Goldcorp cl. A partially vtg. sh. (see Goldcorp Inc.)

Goldcorp Inc. (Ont. Mar. 31, 1994 amalg.)
Nov. 1, 2000 – Amalgamated in Ontario to continue with same name. (see Newmont Goldcorp Corporation)
Apr. 23, 2019 – Acquired by Newmont Mining Corporation (renamed Newmont Goldcorp Corporation); basis 0.3280 Newmont com. shs. plus US$0.02 cash for 1 Goldcorp com. sh. (see Newmont Goldcorp Corporation)

Goldcorp Investments Limited (Ont. 1954)
Aug. 30, 1991 – Name changed to Goldcorp Inc. ■

Goldcrest Mines Ltd. (Ont. 1934)
1958 – Name changed to North Goldcrest Mines Ltd.; basis 1 new for 3 old shs. ■

Goldcrest Resources Ltd. (Ont. Apr. 14, 2000)
Mar. 31, 2008 – Formed Volta Resources Inc. in Ontario on amalgamation with Birim Goldfields Inc. with Goldcrest the deemed acquiror; basis 1 new for 3 old shs. ■

Golden Adit Resources Ltd. (B.C. Jan. 23, 1984)
June 8, 1990 – Name changed to First Northern Developments Inc. ■

Golden Age Mines, Limited (Ont. 1911)
Sept. 10, 1984 – Charter cancelled.

Golden Age Resources Inc. (Ont. May 13, 1985)
Sept. 11, 1991 – Name changed to Ottawa Structural Services Ltd. following acquisition of Ottawa Structural Concrete Services Ltd.; basis 1 new for 2 old shs. ■

Golden Algoma Metals & Holdings Limited (Ont. 1956)
Feb. 20, 1980 – Dissolved.

Golden Algoma Mines Ltd. (Ont. 1956)
Dec. 22, 1970 – Name changed to Golden Algoma Metals & Holdings Limited. ■

Golden Alliance Resources Corp. (B.C. Sept. 22, 2009)
Feb. 13, 2013 – Name changed to Orovero Resources Corp.; basis 1 new for 3 old shs. ■

Golden Arch Resources Ltd. (B.C. Sept. 27, 1978)
Oct. 25, 2009 – Placed into receivership and Abakhan & Associates Inc. appointed receiver.
Sept. 10, 2012 – Dissolved and struck from register.

Golden Ark Explorations Ltd. (B.C. 1973)
Sept. 5, 1975 – Name changed to Golden Ark Industries Ltd. (see FPsurvey - Mines & Energy)

Golden Arrow Mines Ltd. (Ont. Dec. 8, 1938)
1953 – Name changed to Consolidated Golden Arrow Mines Ltd.; basis 1 new for 4 old shs. ■

Golden Arrow Resources Inc. (B.C. 1987)
Mar. 1, 1991 – Amalgamated with Commonwealth Gold Corporation (1 for 1) and Yellow Band Resources Inc. (1 for 2) to form a new co. also named Commonwealth Gold Corporation; basis 1 new for 3 old shs. (see Commonwealth Gold Corporation)

Golden Ashley Explorations Ltd. (Ont. 1961)
Apr. 3, 1968 – Dissolved.

Golden Band Resources Inc. (B.C. Mar. 17, 1983)
July 4, 2006 – Continued into Saskatchewan.
Aug. 19, 2016 – Proposal made under the Bankruptcy and Insolvency Act (BIA) to creditors was approved resulting in all existing equity interests being cancelled and Procon Resources Inc. acquiring 1 cl. A com. of the company. Shares acquired by Procon were in settlement of certain indebtedness owed to Procon which amounted to approx. $19.6 million. No distribution was made to existing shldrs.

Golden Bear Explorations Inc. (Ont. Aug. 11, 1980)
Sept. 1986 – Name changed to Telephony Communications International Incorporated; basis 1 new for 14 old shs. ■

Golden Bear Minerals Inc. (Can. Aug. 26, 1985)
July 4, 1997 – Name changed to Augusta Gold Corporation. ■

Golden Bear Minerals Inc. (B.C. Sept. 26, 1986)
May 21, 1993 – Name changed to West Coast Forest Products Ltd.; basis 1 new for 4 old shs. ■

Golden Belle Consolidated Mines Ltd. (B.C. 1931)
July 1933 – Name changed to Gold Belt Mining Co. Ltd.; basis 5 new for 4 old shs. ■

Golden Birch Resources Inc. (Can. Oct. 4, 2017)
Aug. 12, 2021 – Name changed to PNG Copper Inc. ■

Golden Bounty Mining Co. Ltd. (Ont. 1973)
Mar. 15, 1979 – Amalgamated with Golden Sabre Mines Ltd. (1 for 1.5), Grand Valley Mining Co. Ltd. (1 for 3), Pacesetter Mines Ltd. (1 for 1) and Prestige Mines Ltd. (1 for 3) to form Golden Bounty Mining Co. Ltd.; basis 1 new for 1 old sh.

Golden Bounty Mining Co. Ltd. (Ont. Mar. 15, 1979 amalg.)
May 17, 1984 – Name changed to Falcon Point Resources Ltd.; basis 1 new for 8 old shs. ■

Golden Bridge Development Corporation (Ont. Feb. 18, 2010)
Apr. 29, 2016 – Name changed to CIM International Group Inc. following reverse takeover acquisition of an indirect interest in Mackenzie Creek residential condominium development project in Markham, Ont.; basis 1 new for 5 old shs. ■

Golden Bridge Mining Corporation (Ont. Feb. 18, 2010)
Sept. 23, 2014 – Name changed to Golden Bridge Development Corporation. ■

Golden Cache Mines Ltd. (Ont. 1946)
Dec. 10, 1962 – Dissolved.

Golden Cadillac Resources Ltd. (B.C. June 9, 1983)
July 9, 1985 – Name changed to Seymour-Moss International Limited. ■

Golden Caribou Explorations Inc. (Ont. Mar. 14, 1983)
Dec. 21, 1993 – Name changed to Neotel Inc.; basis 1 new for 3 old shs. ■

Golden Chalice Resources Inc. (B.C. Apr. 20, 1982)
Oct. 13, 2010 – Name changed to Rogue Resources Inc.; basis 1 new for 9 old shs. ■

Golden Chance Resources Inc. (B.C. June 16, 1983)
Oct. 16, 1990 – Name changed to Trimark Resources Ltd.; basis 1 new for 9 old shs. ■

Golden Chief Resources Inc. (B.C. June 15, 1987)
May 24, 2004 – Continued into Ontario.
Nov. 17, 2004 – Name changed to Roscan Minerals Corporation; basis 1 new for 2 old shs. ■

Golden China Resources Corporation (Can. Mar. 17, 2005)
July 1, 2005 – Amalgamated in Canada to continue with same name.
Dec. 20, 2007 – Acquired by Sino Gold Mining Limited; basis 0.2222 Sino Gold shs. for 1 Golden China sh.

Golden Coast Energy Corp. (B.C. May 26, 2006)
Nov. 20, 2017 – Dissolved and struck from register.

Golden Coast Energy Ltd. (B.C. Sept. 14, 1987)
Dec. 4, 1996 – Amalgamated with 704889 Alberta Inc., a wholly owned subsid. of Founders Energy Ltd.; basis 1 com. sh. plus 0.25 wt. of Founders for 1.75 old com. shs. of Golden Coast. Series 1 convert. debs. holders received debs. of Founders convert., as to principal only, into Founder shs. at 60¢ per sh. (see Founders Energy Ltd.)

Golden Coast Minerals Ltd. (B.C. Sept. 14, 1987)
Mar. 16, 1994 – Name changed to Golden Coast Energy Ltd. ■

Golden Coin Resources Ltd. (B.C. Feb. 22, 1978)
Nov. 20, 1986 – Name changed to P.M.C. Technologies Ltd. ■

Golden Concord Mining Corporation (B.C. Dec. 31, 1980)
Apr. 18, 1985 – Name changed to Crossland Industries Corporation; basis 1 new for 3 old shs. ■

Golden Contact Mines Ltd. (B.C. 1947)
Feb. 2, 1967 – Dissolved.

Golden Crescent Resources Corp. (Ont. Dec. 30, 1987 amalg.)
Mar. 26, 1998 – Name changed to Golden Crescent Corporation; basis 1 new for 9 old shs. (see FPsurvey - Mines & Energy)

Golden Croesus Mines Ltd. (Ont. 1955)
Nov. 25, 1970 – Charter cancelled.

Golden Cross Resources Inc. (B.C. June 20, 2006)
May 15, 2013 – Name changed to Blue Gold Water Technologies Ltd.; basis 1 new for 2 old shs. ■

Golden Crown Resources Ltd. (B.C. 1981)
Mar. 3, 1995 – Dissolved and struck off register.

Golden Dawn Explorations Ltd. (B.C. Feb. 22, 1983)
Oct. 8, 1987 – Name changed to Chuan Hup Canada Limited. ■

Golden Dawn Minerals Inc. (B.C. Jan. 9, 2004)
Sept. 22, 2022 – Name changed to CanXGold Mining Corp. ■

Golden Day Mining Exploration Inc. (Que. 1986)
Sept. 19, 1991 – Amalgamated with Gothic Resources Inc.; basis 1 Gothic sh. for 10 Golden Day shs. (see Gothic Resources Inc.)

Golden Dividend Resources Corp. (B.C. Jan. 24, 1983)
Apr. 17, 1996 – Name changed to Caesars Gold Ltd.; basis 1 new for 5 old shs. ■

Golden Dory Resources Corp. (Alta. June 7, 2006)
Oct. 1, 2013 – Name changed to Sokoman Iron Corp.; basis 1 new for 10 old shs. ■

Golden Dragon Resources Ltd. (B.C. Apr. 24, 1981)
June 22, 1990 – Amalgamated with Goldrock Resources Ltd. (1.5 for 1) to continue with the same name Golden Dragon Resources Ltd.; basis 1 new for 1 old sh.
May 16, 1994 – Name changed to Canadian Golden Dragon Resources Ltd.; basis 1 new for 5 old shs. ■

Golden Dragon Resources Ltd. (B.C. Apr. 11, 1983)
Dec. 18, 1985 – Name changed to MDC Financial Inc. (see FPsurvey - Industrials)

Golden Dynasty Resources Ltd. (B.C. June 15, 1987)
Sept. 12, 2008 – Name changed to Columbus Energy Limited; basis 1 new for 6 old shs. (see FPsurvey - Mines & Energy)

Golden Eagle Capital Corp. (Ont. Sept. 10, 1992 amalg.)
Apr. 4, 1996 – Name changed to Points North Digital Technologies, Inc.; basis 1 new for 30 old shs. ■

Golden Eagle Exploration Inc. (Ont. Mar. 9, 1979)
Dec. 5, 1979 – Name changed to Bald Eagle Explorations Inc. ■

Golden Eagle Mines Ltd. (Alta. Apr. 4, 1990)
Nov. 2, 1995 – Name changed to Golden Eagle Ventures Inc.; basis 1 new for 4 old shs. ■

Golden Eagle Resources Inc. (Ont. Aug. 31, 1987)
Sept. 10, 1992 – Formed Golden Eagle Capital Corp. in Ontario on amalgamation with private co.; basis 1 new for 1 old sh. ■

Golden Eagle Ventures Inc. (Alta. Apr. 4, 1990)
July 3, 1998 – Name changed to Alberta Diamondfields Inc.; basis 1 new for 2 old shs. ■

Golden Earth Resources Inc. (Ont. 1984)
May 3, 1989 – Formed Health and Environment Technologies Inc. in Ontario on amalgamation with 732891 Ontario Limited; basis 1 new for 14.9 old shs. ■

Golden Exodus Ventures Ltd. (B.C. May 8, 1981)
Jan. 16, 1990 – Name changed to ILM Resources Ltd.; basis 1 new for 4 old shs. ■

Golden Eye Minerals Ltd. (B.C. Mar. 8, 1983)
Jan. 31, 1991 – Name changed to Annex Exploration Corp.; basis 1 new for 2 old shs. ■

Golden Falcon Explorations Inc. (Ont. 1979)
Dec. 29, 1982 – Amalgamated with 3 other cos. to form Parapet Petroleums Inc.; basis 1 new for 6 old shs.

Golden Falcon Mining Co. Ltd. (B.C. 1964)
Sept. 23, 1974 – Dissolved.

Golden Fame Resources Corp. (B.C. Jan. 14, 2008)
Aug. 2, 2013 – Name changed to Pan American Fertilizer Corp. pursuant to acquisition of (old) Pan American Fertilizer Corp. and subsequent amalgamation of old Pan American Fertilizer with wholly owned 0971771 B.C. Ltd.; basis 1 new for 4 old shs. ■

Golden Gate Explorations Ltd. (B.C. Apr. 7, 1964)
Oct. 24, 1991 – Name changed to Texas Dome Resource Corporation; basis 1 new for 3 old shs. ■

Golden Gate Mining Co. Ltd. (Ont. July 30, 1934)
Nov. 1946 – Name changed to Kirkland Golden Gate Mines Ltd.; basis 1 new for 2 old shs. ■

Golden Gate Resources Ltd. (B.C. Jan. 31, 1983)
Aug. 26, 1998 – Continued into Yukon.
June 30, 2003 – Acquired by Valdera Resources Ltd.; basis 1.6 Valdera shs. for 1 Golden Gate sh.

Golden Glacier Resources Inc. (B.C. Feb. 10, 1984)
Oct. 11, 2002 – Name changed to Exeter Resource Corporation; basis 1 new for 10 old shs. ■

Golden Glory Resources Ltd. (B.C. 1987)
Feb. 21, 1990 – Name changed to Shimoda International Systems Inc. ■

Golden Goose Resources Inc. (Que. Dec. 12, 1962)
Dec. 29, 2010 – Acquired by Kodiak Exploration Limited; basis 1.2 Kodiak com. shs. plus ¼ wts. for 1 Golden Goose com. sh. (see Kodiak Exploration Limited)

Golden Grail Resources Inc. (B.C. 1987)
Apr. 16, 1993 – Dissolved and struck off register.

Golden Gram Capital Inc. (Can. Aug. 11, 1994)
Apr. 25, 2002 – Name changed to Events International Holding Corporation following reverse takeover acquisition

of Events International Meeting Planners Inc.; basis 1 new for 2 old shs. ∎

Golden Gram Resources Inc. (Can. Aug. 11, 1994)
Mar. 9, 1999 – Name changed to Golden Gram Capital Inc. ∎

Golden Granite Mines Ltd. (B.C. 1971)
Sept. 2, 1983 – Dissolved.

Golden Group Explorations Inc. (Que. 1984)
Sept. 19, 1991 – Amalgamated with Brookline Minerals Inc/Mineraux Brookline Inc.; basis 1 new for 2.4 old shs. (see Brookline Minerals Inc.)

Golden Harker Explorations Limited (Ont. Jan. 7, 1924)
Jan. 1, 2010 – Amalgamated with Union Gold Inc., Milestone Exploration Limited, Sheldon-Larder Mines Limited and Wood-Croesus Gold Mines Limited to form Jubilee Gold Inc.; basis 0.393 Jubilee sh. for 1 Golden Harker sh., 0.557 Jubilee sh. for 1 Union Gold sh., 1.749 Jubilee sh. for 1 Milestone sh., 0.269 Jubilee sh. for 1 Sheldon-Larder sh. and 0.367 Jubilee sh. for 1 Wood-Croesus sh. (see Jubilee Gold Inc.)

Golden Hart Exploration Inc. (Ont. July 17, 1998 amalg.)
Sept. 1, 1999 – Name changed to Beaufort Hills Resources Inc.; basis 1 new for 10 old shs. ∎

Golden Hat Resources Inc. (B.C. Jan. 14, 1982)
Mar. 28, 1984 – Continued into Manitoba.
July 16, 2010 – Formed Premier Diagnostic Health Services Inc. in British Columbia pursuant to amalgamation with Premier Diagnostic Health Services Inc. (deemed acquiror); basis 1 new for 12 Golden Hat shares and 1.73 new for 1 Premier share. ∎

Golden Hemlo Resources Inc. (B.C. Feb. 9, 1983)
June 9, 1986 – Name changed to Pan World Ventures Inc. ∎

Golden Hemlock Explorations Ltd. (B.C. Apr. 26, 1985)
Dec. 4, 2001 – Delisted CDNX. Subsequently struck from register and dissolved.

Golden Hill Mining Corp. (Ont. May 26, 1964)
Mar. 9, 1998 – All o/s com. shs. acquired by MacDonald Mines Exploration Ltd.; basis 0.66 of a com. sh. and 0.27 of a sh. purchase wt. of MacDonald for 1 com. of Golden Hill. (see MacDonald Mines Exploration Ltd.)

Golden Hind Ventures Ltd. (B.C. 1983)
July 1988 – Amalgamated with Cuvier Mines Inc., which subsequently amalgamated with Kam Creed Mines Ltd. to continue under the name Kam Creed Mines Ltd.

Golden Hope Mines Limited (Ont. Jan. 19, 1945)
July 18, 2019 – Name changed to Delta Resources Limited. (see FPsurvey - Mines & Energy)

Golden Hope Resources Inc. (B.C. 1979)
July 26, 1991 – Name changed to Brookline Minerals Inc./Minearux Brookline Inc.; basis 1 new for 2 old shs. ∎

Golden Horizon Resource Corporation (B.C. Jan. 18, 1979)
Jan. 2, 1990 – Name changed to GHZ Resource Corporation; basis 1 new for 4 old shs. ∎

Golden Independence Mining Corp. (B.C. May 31, 2017)
Nov. 27, 2023 – Name changed to Nexus Uranium Corp. (see FPsurvey - Mines & Energy)

Golden Iskut Resources Incorporated (B.C. 1983)
Aug. 1, 1990 – Amalgamated with Achilles Resources Ltd. (1 for 4.5), International Phoenix Energy Corporation (1 for 8) and Interstate Energy Corp. (1 for 14) to form a new co. Aegis Resources Ltd.; basis 1 new for 8 old shs. (see Aegis Resources Ltd.)

Golden Key Resources Limited (B.C. May 27, 1983)
Oct. 27, 1988 – Name changed to Trax Petroleums Limited; basis 1 new for 5 old shs. ∎

Golden Knight Resources Inc. (B.C. June 9, 1981)
Apr. 26, 1999 – Acquired by Repadre Capital Corporation; basis (i) 0.125 Repadre shs. plus 33¢ or (ii) 0.20 Repadre shs. plus 10¢ and 0.20 Repadre wts. for 1 Golden Knight sh. (see Repadre Capital Corporation)

Golden Kootenay Resources Inc. (B.C. May 27, 1987)
Apr. 18, 2000 – Name changed to Frontier Minerals Inc.; basis 1 new for 5 old shs. ∎

Golden Kristy Resources Ltd. (B.C. Dec. 4, 1985)
Apr. 24, 1992 – Charter cancelled and co. dissolved.
July 1992 – Charter and company revived.
Sept. 23, 1994 – Name changed to Pan Pacific Gold Corporation. ∎

Golden Lake Resources Ltd. (B.C. Feb. 10, 1984)
June 1, 1993 – Amalgamated with Kestrel Resources Ltd. to form Ella Resources Inc.; basis 0.35 new for 1 Kestrel sh. and 0.5 new for 1 Golden Lake sh. (see Ella Resources Inc.)

Golden Leaf Holdings Ltd. (Ont. Oct. 6, 2015)
May 25, 2021 – Name changed to Chalice Brands Ltd.; basis 1 new for 23 old shs. (see FPsurvey - Industrials)

Golden Lion Resources Ltd. (B.C. May 25, 1983)
Mar. 8, 1989 – Name changed to Consolidated Golden Lion Resources Ltd.; basis 1 new for 10 old shs. ∎

Golden Manitou Mines Ltd. (Ont. 1941)
1957 – Acquired by Manitou-Barvue Mines Limited; basis 1 new for 5 old shs. (see Manitou-Barvue Mines Limited)

Golden Maritime Resources Ltd. (B.C. Sept. 28, 1970)
Dec. 24, 2003 – Dissolved and struck from register.

Golden Marlin Resources Limited (Sask. Nov. 30, 1987)
Dec. 6, 1995 – Continued into Yukon.
Dec. 11, 1995 – Name changed to Indomin Resources Limited; basis 1 com. for 6 cl. A shs. ∎

Golden Miller Mines Ltd. (Ont. 1949)
Aug. 25, 1966 – Dissolved.

Golden Nevada Resources Inc. (B.C. Aug. 19, 1987 amalg.)
June 19, 1989 – Name changed to Goldnev Resources Inc.; basis 1 new for 5 old shs. ∎

Golden News Resources Inc. (B.C. Mar. 29, 1983)
Jan. 17, 1995 – Name changed to Laminco Resources Inc. ∎

Golden North Resource Corporation (B.C. Aug. 30, 1984 amalg.)
Oct. 1, 1986 – Amalgamated with Good Hope Resources Ltd. to form new co. with same name Golden North Resource Corporation. (see Caledonia Mining Corporation)
Feb. 17, 1992 – Amalgamated with Thorco Resources Inc. to form Caledonia Mining Corporation; basis 0.19426 new for 1 Thorco sh. and 0.71672 new for 1 Golden North sh. (see Caledonia Mining Corporation)

Golden Nugget Exploration Inc. (B.C. Aug. 24, 1984)
May 2, 2002 – Name changed to Lucky 1 Enterprises Inc.; basis 1 new for 5 old shs. ∎

Golden Oasis Exploration Corp. (B.C. Nov. 2, 2004)
Feb. 2, 2009 – Amalgamated with American Copper Corporation and Lebon Gold Mines Limited to form American Consolidated Minerals Corp.; basis 1 new for 1 American Copper sh., 1.2 new for 1 Lebon Gold sh. and 1 new for 1 Golden Oasis sh. (see American Consolidated Minerals Corp.)

Golden Odyssey Mining Inc. (Can. Apr. 16, 2004)
Jan. 27, 2011 – Name changed to Deer Horn Metals Inc. ∎

Golden Opportunity Resources Corp. (B.C. Jan. 31, 2018)
June 8, 2020 – Name changed to Silver Sands Resources Corp. (see FPsurvey - Mines & Energy)

Golden Pacific Capital Corporation (B.C. Mar. 17, 2006)
Dec. 12, 2011 – Dissolved and struck from register.

Golden Pacific Corporation (Alta. Feb. 7, 1967)
Dec. 10, 1993 – Name changed to Pinpoint Retail Solutions Inc. ∎

Golden Pacific Resources Inc. (Alta. Feb. 7, 1967)
June 13, 1991 – Name changed to Golden Pacific Corporation. ∎

Golden Palm Resources Ltd. (B.C. Dec. 19, 1986)
Dec. 6, 1996 – Continued into Yukon.
July 5, 2003 – Dissolved.

Golden Patriot Mining Inc. (B.C. May 11, 1999)
Mar. 1, 2007 – Name changed to Hana Mining Ltd. ∎

Golden Peak Minerals Inc. (B.C. Mar. 31, 2011)
Apr. 17, 2018 – Name changed to BlueBird Battery Metals Inc. ∎

Golden Peaks Resources Ltd. (B.C. Oct. 20, 1987)
Jan. 9, 2012 – Name changed to Reliance Resources Limited. ∎

Golden Penguin Resources Ltd. (Ont. Dec. 17, 1987)
Oct. 8, 1997 – Name changed to Partner Jet Corp.; basis 1 new for 3 old shs. ∎

Golden Pheasant Resources Ltd. (B.C. Aug. 16, 1986)
Jan. 22, 1993 – Dissolved and struck off register.

Golden Point Explorations Ltd. (Ont. July 13, 1987)
Oct. 28, 1993 – Name changed to Michael Lombardi Publishing Inc. following reverse takeover by Michael Lombardi Publishing Corporation; basis 1 new for 2 old shs. ∎

Golden Pond Resources Ltd. (B.C. 1983)
Jan. 21, 2013 – Dissolved and struck from register.

Golden Pool Resources Ltd. (Alta. May 2, 1988)
Jan. 11, 1993 – Name changed to 1st Century Healthcare International Inc.; basis 1 new for 2 old shs. ∎

Golden Predator Corp. (B.C. Jan. 6, 2009)
Feb. 19, 2013 – Name changed to Americas Bullion Royalty Corp. ∎

Golden Predator Mines Inc. (B.C. July 17, 2006)
Mar. 11, 2009 – Name changed to EMC Metals Corp. pursuant to plan of arrangement whereby most of the company's precious metals assets were transferred to newly created Golden Predator Royalty & Development Corp. (GPRD) and spun out to shareholders on the basis of 1 GPRD unit (1 sh. plus 0.5 wt.) for each 4 shs. held. ∎

Golden Predator Mining Corp. (Alta. Apr. 29, 2008)
Oct. 21, 2015 – Continued into British Columbia. (see Arizona Gold Corp.)
Sept. 7, 2021 – Acquired by Arizona Gold Corp.; basis 1.65 Arizona Gold shs. for 1 Golden Predator sh. (see Arizona Gold Corp.)

Golden Predator Royalty & Development Corp. (B.C. Jan. 6, 2009)
May 25, 2010 – Name changed to Golden Predator Corp. ∎

Golden Princess Mining Corporation (B.C. Aug. 5, 1977)
Sept. 28, 1992 – Name changed to Pandora Industries Inc.; basis 1 new for 5 old shs. ∎

Golden Pyramid Resources Inc. (B.C. May 18, 1983)
July 6, 1992 – Name changed to Consolidated Golden Pyramid Resources Ltd.; basis 1 new for 5 old shs. ∎

Golden Quail Resources Ltd. (B.C. May 29, 1963)
Jan. 21, 1998 – Name changed to Consolidated Golden Quail Resources Ltd.; basis 1 new for 15 old shs. (see FPsurvey - Mines & Energy)

Golden Queen Mining Co. Ltd. (B.C. Nov. 21, 1985)
July 26, 2019 – Name changed to Golden Queen Mining Consolidated Ltd.; basis 1 new for 10 old shs. ■

Golden Queen Mining Consolidated Ltd. (B.C. Nov. 21, 1985)
Apr. 2, 2020 – Acquired by Falco Resources Ltd.; basis 1.35 Falco com. shs. for 1 Golden Queen sh.

Golden Rainbow Resources Inc. (B.C. July 28, 1987)
Aug. 8, 1994 – Name changed to First Silver Reserve Inc. ■

Golden Range Resources Inc. (Can. Feb. 1, 1983)
Oct. 19, 1999 – Charter cancelled and co. dissolved.

Golden Raven Resources Ltd. (B.C. Mar. 11, 1987)
Oct. 19, 2009 – Dissolved and struck from register.
Sept. 9, 2010 – Restored to register.
June 27, 2017 – Name changed to Xineoh Technologies Inc. (see FPsurvey - Mines & Energy)

Golden Regent Resources Ltd. (Alta. Mar. 12, 1993)
July 26, 1999 – Name changed to Touchstone Petroleum Inc.; basis 1 new for 4 old shs. ■

Golden Reign Resources Ltd. (Yuk. Apr. 1, 2004)
Nov. 14, 2007 – Continued into British Columbia.
Nov. 14, 2018 – Name changed to Mako Mining Corp. following acquisition of Marlin Gold Mining Ltd. (see FPsurvey - Mines & Energy)

Golden Rim Resources Inc. (B.C. 1983)
Jan. 26, 1990 – Name changed to Edge Resources Ltd.; basis 1 new for 2 old shs. ■

Golden Ring Resources Ltd. (B.C. Jan. 31, 1983)
June 6, 1994 – Name changed to Golden Gate Resources Ltd.; basis 1 new for 5 old shs. ■

Golden Rock Explorations Inc. (Que. Feb. 25, 1986)
Apr. 17, 1998 – Name changed to Gammon Lake Resources Inc. following reverse takeover acquisition of (old) Gammon Lake Resources Inc.; basis 1 new for 15 old shs. ■

Golden Rock Resources Ltd. (B.C. May 31, 1984)
Jan. 15, 1993 – Name changed to Bismillah Ventures Inc.; basis 1 new for 2.4 old shs. ■

Golden Rule Resources Ltd. (Alta. Oct. 12, 1979)
Apr. 30, 2002 – Name changed to CDG Investments Inc. ■

Golden Sabre Mines Ltd. (Ont. 1974)
Mar. 15, 1979 – Amalgamated with Golden Bounty Mining Co. Ltd. (1 for 1), Grand Valley Mining Co. Ltd. (1 for 3), Pacesetter Mines Ltd. (1 for 1) and Prestige Mines Ltd. (1 for 3) to form Golden Bounty Mining Co. Ltd.; basis 1 new for 1.5 old shs.

Golden Saturn Oil & Gas Limited (Ont. 1952)
Dec. 10, 1994 – Dissolved.

Golden Sceptre Mines Ltd. (B.C. Mar. 17, 1980)
May 7, 1981 – Name changed to Golden Sceptre Resources Ltd. ■

Golden Sceptre Resources Ltd. (B.C. Mar. 17, 1980)
Feb. 11, 1987 – Amalgamated with Goliath Gold Mines, Noranda Inc. and Hemlo Gold Mines Inc. to form a new Hemlo Gold Mines Inc., New Goliath Gold Minerals Ltd. and New Golden Sceptre Minerals Ltd. Shldrs. of Golden Sceptre received 1 sh. of Hemlo Gold Mines Inc. for each sh. held; plus 1 sh. of New Golden Sceptre Minerals Ltd. and 1 sh. New Goliath Minerals Ltd. for each 2 shs. of Hemlo Gold Mines Inc. held. (see Hemlo Gold Mines Inc.; New Golden Sceptre Minerals Ltd.)

Golden Seal Mining & Exploration Co. Ltd. (Ont. 1947)
1958 – Charter cancelled.

Golden Seal Resources Ltd. (B.C. Apr. 3, 1984)
July 30, 1987 – Name changed to Easton Minerals Ltd. ■

Golden Secret Ventures Ltd. (B.C. Apr. 25, 1969)
Nov. 2, 2018 – Name changed to Thunderbird Entertainment Group Inc. pursuant to reverse takeover acquisition of Thunderbird Entertainment Inc.; basis 1 new for 10 old shs. (see FPsurvey - Industrials)

Golden Seven Industries Inc. (B.C. Mar. 30, 1971)
Mar. 2, 1990 – Delisted from the Vancouver Stock Exchange. Subsequently dissolved for failure to file.

Golden Shadow Resources Inc. (Ont. Mar. 1, 1945)
Jan. 21, 1991 – Name changed to Denroy Manufacturing Corporation following acquisition of Denroy Manufacturing Ltd.; basis 1 new for 9.5 old shs. ■

Golden Shaft Mines Limited (Ont. 1946)
Nov. 15, 1995 – Name changed to Cybermind Group Inc.; basis 1 new for 3 old shs. ■

Golden Shamrock Mines Ltd. (W.A. 1939)
1988 – Continued into Victoria.
Oct. 21, 1996 – All o/s com. shs. and 7.5% conv. unsecured sub. debentures acquired by Ashanti Goldfields Company Limited; basis 1 Ashanti Goldfields ordinary sh. and 1 Ashanti GSM Limited pref. sh., which entitled the holder to receive five annual cash payments of US$0.648 commencing Mar. 31, 1998, for 22.5 Golden Shamrock com. shs. Debentures exchanged on the basis of (i) 1 Ashanti Goldfields ordinary sh. for US$14.19 principal value and (ii) 1 Ashanti GSM pref. sh. for US$16.16 principal value, each of which pref. sh. entitles the holder to receive five annual cash payments of US$0.648 commencing Mar. 31, 1998, and (iii) a cash payment in respect of interest accrued from May 9, 1996, to June 30, 1996.

The Golden Shamrock Resources Corp. (B.C. Mar. 4, 1983)
July 20, 1990 – Dissolved and struck off register.

Golden Shamrock Resources Ltd. (B.C. 1968)
June 10, 1982 – Amalgamated with Marquis Development Corp. Ltd. to form Colt Exploration (Western) Ltd.; basis 1 new for 2 old shs.

Golden Share Mining Corporation (Can. Aug. 7, 2007)
Aug. 9, 2013 – Amalgamated with Silvore Fox Minerals Corp. (deemed acquiror) to form a new co. also named Golden Share Mining Corporation; 1 new Golden sh. for 5 Silvore shs. and 1 new Golden sh. for 5 old Golden shs. (see Golden Share Mining Corporation)

Golden Share Mining Corporation (Can. Aug. 9, 2013 amalg.)
June 28, 2017 – Name changed to Golden Share Resources Corporation. ■

Golden Share Resources Corporation (Can. Aug. 9, 2013 amalg.)
Feb. 3, 2025 – Name changed to Lipari Mining Ltd. ■

Golden Shield Resources Limited (B.C. 1980)
Mar. 28, 1990 – Declared voluntary bankruptcy July 4, 1989. Via a proposal to its creditors a private co. was formed known as GSR Mining Corporation which acquired all assets and liabs. of Golden Shield. All secured and preferred creditors paid off in cash and unsecured creditors received 22% of the shs. of GSR Mining as settlement. No equity for shldrs.

Golden Shore Mines Ltd. (Ont. 1967)
Mar. 1976 – Charter cancelled.

Golden Sitka Resources Inc. (B.C. Mar. 24, 1987)
Aug. 8, 2000 – Name changed to Aurora Platinum Corp. and continued into Yukon; basis 1 new for 4 old shs. ■

Golden Sky Resources Inc. (B.C. Dec. 11, 1986)
June 8, 1994 – Name changed to Golden Sky Ventures International Inc. ■

Golden Sky Ventures International Inc. (B.C. Dec. 11, 1986)
July 26, 2000 – Name changed to iNsu Innovations Group Inc. ■

Golden Slipper Mines Ltd. (Can. 1945)
Believed defunct.

Golden Slipper Resources Inc. (B.C. 1981)
June 30, 1983 – Name changed to Napa Resources Incorporated. ■

Golden Spike Oils Limited (Alta. 1949)
Feb. 28, 1951 – Name changed to Aldina-Leduc Oil Company Limited. ■

Golden Spike Western Petroleums Ltd. (Alta. 1949)
July 1973 – Name changed to Oilex Industries Ltd.; basis 1 new for 10 old shs. ■

Golden Spirit Resources Inc. (Ont. Oct. 20, 1983)
Jan. 28, 1988 – Name changed to LEA Security International Inc. ■

Golden Standard Mines Ltd. (B.C. Jan. 13, 1960)
Feb. 27, 1979 – Name changed to International Standard Resources Ltd.; basis 1 new for 5 old shs. ■

Golden Star Consolidated Mines Ltd. (Ont. Feb. 15, 1934)
Aug. 1, 1936 – Name changed to Orelia Mines Ltd. and continued into Ontario. ■

Golden Star Mines Ltd. (B.C. Sept. 28, 1970)
Mar. 30, 1981 – Name changed to Golden State Resources Ltd. ■

Golden Star Resources Ltd. (Alta. Mar. 7, 1984)
May 20, 1992 – Amalgamated with South American Goldfields Inc. to form same name Golden Star Resources Ltd.; basis 1 new for 2 Golden Star shs. (see Golden Star Resources Ltd.)

Golden Star Resources Ltd. (Can. May 15, 1992 amalg.)
Feb. 1, 2022 – Acquired by Chifeng Jilong Gold Mining Co., Ltd.; basis US$3.91 cash per sh.

Golden State Resources Ltd. (B.C. Sept. 28, 1970)
June 18, 1993 – Charter cancelled.
June 14, 1996 – Charter revived.
May 12, 1997 – Name changed to Golden Maritime Resources Ltd.; basis 1 new for 3 old shs. ■

Golden Summit Mines Ltd. (Ont. 1924)
Jan. 12, 1959 – Dissolved.

Golden Sun Capital Inc. (Alta. July 23, 2008)
Mar. 2, 2017 – Name changed to Voyageur Minerals Ltd. pursuant to Qualifying Transaction reverse takeover acquisition of Voyageur Industrial Minerals Ltd.; basis 1 new for 2 old shs. ■

Golden Sun Mining Corp. (B.C. Mar. 14, 2007)
Aug. 15, 2017 – Dissolved and struck from register.
May 7, 2018 – Restored to register.
July 14, 2022 – Name changed to Pan American Energy Corp. (see FPsurvey - Mines & Energy)

Golden Sunset Trail Inc. (Alta. July 28, 2004)
Jan. 2, 2011 – Struck from registry and dissolved.

Golden Tag Resources Ltd. (B.C. Sept. 22, 1980)
July 20, 1995 – Continued into Canada.
Nov. 7, 2023 – Name changed to Silver Storm Mining Ltd. (see FPsurvey - Mines & Energy)

Golden Tanager Resources Inc. (Can. Apr. 1, 1985)
Jan. 22, 1990 – Dissolved.
Feb. 23, 1990 – Revived.
Feb. 26, 1990 – Name changed to Registry Resources Inc.; basis 1 new for 2 old shs. ■

Golden Tech Resources Ltd. (B.C. Feb. 16, 1984)
May 7, 1987 – Name changed to Golden Tech Systems Inc. ■

Golden Tech Systems Inc. (B.C. Feb. 16, 1984)
1988 – Bankrupt.
July 6, 1990 – Dissolved and struck off register.

Golden Temple Mining Corp. (B.C. Jan. 23, 1984)
Mar. 8, 2002 – Name changed to Amerigo Resources Ltd.; basis 1 new for 4 old shs. (see FPsurvey - Mines & Energy)

Golden Thunder Resources Ltd. (B.C. June 7, 1983)
Dec. 4, 2000 – Name changed to Consolidated Golden Thunder Resources Ltd.; basis 1 new for 3 old shs. ■

Golden Tiger Mining Exploration Company Inc. (Que. 1981)
Aug. 5, 1988 – Name changed to Tiger Resources Incorporated; basis 1 new for 5 old shs. (see FPsurvey - Mines & Energy)

Golden Tiger Resources NL (Vic. 1940)
Sept. 29, 1999 – Name changed to ISP Limited.

Golden Titan Resources Ltd. (B.C. Feb. 26, 1979)
Dec. 28, 1989 – Formed Titan Pacific Resources Ltd. in British Columbia on amalgamation with No. 182 Dynamic Endeavours Inc.; basis 0.2495742 new for 1 No. 182 Dynamic sh. and 0.2 new for 1 Golden Titan sh. ■

Golden-Tonkin Resources Ltd. (B.C. 1981)
June 17, 1994 – Dissolved and struck off register.

Golden Touch Resources Corp. (B.C. Jan. 24, 2007)
Dec. 19, 2012 – Name changed to Arian Resources Corp.; basis 1 new for 5 old shs. ■

Golden Transit Resources Inc. (Ont. 1983)
June 9, 1989 – Name changed to Posters Plus Marketing Corp. (see FPsurvey - Industrials)

Golden Treasure Explorations Ltd. (B.C. July 20, 1979)
June 21, 2001 – Name changed to Foundry Holdings Corp.; basis 1 new for 7 old shs. ■

Golden Trend Energy Ltd. (B.C. Oct. 24, 1980)
Jan. 3, 1991 – Name changed to World Power Bike Inc.; basis 1 new for 3 old shs. ■

Golden Trend Petroleum Ltd. (Alta. Apr. 8, 1994)
Feb. 2000 – After extensive discussions with the primary lender, the company was placed into receivership and all directors and officers resigned. RSM Richter Inc. of Calgary was appointed receiver/manager.
2002 – After all assets had been sold, secured creditors received a distribution of between 80¢ and 85¢ on the dollar. There were no funds available for unsecured or preferred creditors or shldrs.
June 2004 – Administration was ongoing with some issues still to be resolved.
Oct. 7, 2005 – Receiver/manager was discharged.

Golden Triangle Mining Exploration Inc. (Can. Jan. 22, 1986)
May 17, 1989 – Name changed to Spectrum Gold Corporation; basis 1 new for 8 old shs. ■

Golden Trio Minerals Ltd. (Ont. Mar. 1, 1988 amalg.)
Apr. 11, 1994 – Name changed to PCS Wireless, Inc.; basis 1 new for 2 old shs. ■

Golden Trump Resources Ltd. (B.C. Oct. 27, 1971)
Sept. 11, 2002 – Name changed to Golden Triumph Resources Ltd.; basis 1 new for 5 old shs. (see FPsurvey - Mines & Energy)

Golden Unicorn Mining Corporation (B.C. June 25, 1986)
Mar. 29, 1995 – Name changed to Consolidated Golden Unicorn Mining Corporation; basis 1 new for 5 old shs. ■

Golden Vale Explorations Corp. (B.C. 1983)
Oct. 12, 1987 – Name changed to RFC Resource Finance Corporation. ■

Golden Valley Mines and Royalties Ltd. (Can. Aug. 15, 2000)
Nov. 8, 2021 – Acquired by Gold Royalty Corp.; basis 2.1417 Gold Royalty shs. for 1 Golden Valley sh.

Golden Valley Mines Ltd. (Ont. 1944)
Oct. 1, 1956 – Charter cancelled.

Golden Valley Mines Ltd. (Can. Aug. 15, 2000)
July 15, 2021 – Name changed to Golden Valley Mines and Royalties Ltd. ■

Golden Virtue Resources Inc. (B.C. Sept. 1, 2005)
Apr. 23, 2015 – Name changed to Moseda Technologies, Inc. following reverse takeover acquisition of MobSafety, Inc. ■

Golden West Brewing Company, Inc. (Del. Dec. 23, 2003)
Dec. 11, 2009 – Name changed to Athena Silver Corporation. ■

Golden West Mines Ltd. (B.C. Nov. 9, 1966)
July 1969 – Name changed to Golden West Resources Ltd. ■

Golden West Resources Ltd. (B.C. Nov. 9, 1966)
Dec. 5, 1972 – Name changed to Sachem Exploration Inc.; basis 1 new for 4 old shs. ■

Golden Winner Resources Ltd. (Ont. 1985)
Mar. 30, 1990 – Amalgamated with Rainbow Lake Resources Ltd. (1 for 0.915), Mountain Frontier Explorations Ltd. (1 for 1.08), Thunder Valley Resources Ltd. (1 for 1.10) and Premier Lake Resources Inc. (1 for 1.10) to form Castlestar Capital Developments Corp.; basis 1 new Castlestar sh. for 0.97 old Winner shs. (see Castlestar Capital Developments Corp.)

Golden Zone Developments Ltd. (B.C. 1985)
Aug. 18, 1988 – Name changed to Golden Zone Resources Inc. ■

Golden Zone Resources Inc. (B.C. 1985)
Mar. 5, 1993 – Delisted from the Vancouver Stock Exchange. Subsequently struck from register and dissolved.

Goldenbell Resources Incorporated (B.C.)
Mar. 28, 1989 – Acquired by wholly owned subsid. of ABM Gold Corp.; basis 1 cl. A for 3 old shs. (see ABM Gold Corp.)

GoldenGoals.com Ventures Inc. (B.C. Sept. 22, 1992)
Apr. 27, 2001 – Name changed to General Strategies Ltd.; basis 1 new for 10 old shs. ■

Goldenlode Resourses Ltd. (B.C. May 17, 1985)
May 12, 1987 – Name changed to Abbey Woods Developments Ltd. ■

Goldenrod Resources & Technology Inc. (B.C. 1983)
Mar. 5, 1990 – Name changed to Astic Ventures Inc.; basis 1 new for 5 old shs. ■

Goldenville Explorations Limited (Ont. 1982)
June 24, 1985 – Taken over by Northumberland Mines Ltd. shldrs. received 2 shs. Northumberland for each 3 shs. Goldenville.

Golder Ridge Oil and Gas Co. Ltd. (Can. Dec. 10, 1931)
Mar. 6, 1935 – Name changed to Vera Oilfields Ltd. ■

Goldera Resources Inc. (B.C. Jan. 9, 1967)
June 1, 1990 – Dissolved and struck off register.

Goldex Mines Limited (Ont. 1971)
1989 – Continued into Canada. (see Agnico-Eagle Mines Limited)
Dec. 14, 1993 – Acquired by Agnico-Eagle Mines Limited; basis 0.36 Agnico-Eagle shs. for 1 Goldex sh. (see Agnico-Eagle Mines Limited)

Goldex Resources Inc. (B.C. Mar. 21, 1980)
May 10, 1993 – Name changed to Goldmax Resources Inc.; basis 1 new for 2.5 old shs. ■

Goldeye Explorations Limited (Ont. Sept. 24, 1986)
Nov. 28, 2016 – Acquired by Treasury Metals Inc.; basis 0.1 Treasury com. shs. for 1 Goldeye com. sh. (see Treasury Metals Inc.)

The Goldfarb Corporation (Ont. Sept. 22, 1971)
July 19, 2011 – Privatized at $3.02 per sh.

Goldfever Resources Ltd. (B.C. 1980)
July 31, 1992 – Dissolved and struck off register.

Goldfields Mining Corp. Ltd. (Sask. 1949)
1964 – Acquired by Copperfields Mining Corp.; basis 1 new for 3 old shs.

Goldfields Uranium Mines Ltd. (Sask. 1949)
1959 – Name changed to Goldfields Mining Corp. Ltd. ■

Goldgroup Mining Inc. (Que. Nov. 9, 1989 amalg.)
July 28, 2011 – Continued into British Columbia. (see FPsurvey - Mines & Energy)

Goldhaven Resources Ltd. (B.C. Jan. 17, 1983)
June 7, 1985 – Name changed to International Vending Technology Corp.; basis 4 new for 1 old sh. ■

Goldhawk Porcupine Mines Ltd. (Ont. 1944)
Nov. 23, 1955 – Name changed to Greyhawk Uranium Mines Ltd.; basis 1 new for 2 old shs. ■

Goldhill Industries Inc. (B.C. Nov. 13, 1985)
Apr. 23, 2001 – Acquired by private Japanese corporation S.G.M. Co. Ltd. for $0.60 per sh.

Goldhill Resources Inc. (B.C. Nov. 13, 1985)
July 5, 1995 – Name changed to Goldhill Industries Inc. ■

Goldhunter Explorations Inc. (Ont. Sept. 7, 1982)
Jan. 21, 2002 – Name changed to Tribute Minerals Inc. pursuant to reverse takeover acquisition of Tribute Minerals Corporation; basis 1 new for 2 old shs. ■

Goldhurst Resources Inc. (Ont. 1972)
1979 – Continued into British Columbia. (see Société d'Exploration Minière Vior Inc.)
1988 – Continued into Canada. (see Société d'Exploration Minière Vior Inc.)
Aug. 10, 1995 – Acquired by 3145310 Canada Inc., a wholly owned subsid. of Société d'exploration minière Vior Inc.; basis 1 Vior sh. for 2 Goldhurst shs. (see Société d'Exploration Minière Vior Inc.)

Goldie Enterprises Inc. (B.C. Mar. 28, 1979)
May 3, 2001 – Name changed to MagiCorp Entertainment Inc. pursuant to reverse takeover acquisition of MagiCorp Inc. ■

Goldking Mining Ltd. (B.C. June 7, 2004)
July 28, 2007 – Name changed to Wolverine Minerals Corp. ■

Goldknife Mines Ltd. (Ont. 1945)
Nov. 1961 – Charter cancelled.

Goldlist Properties Inc. (Ont. Jan. 23, 1997)
Jan. 31, 2002 – Acquired by Acktion Corporation; basis $14.50 per sh. consisting of $7.25 plus payment of $7.25 on fourth anniversary of 6% promissory note. (see Acktion Corporation)

Goldlund Mines Limited (Ont. 1949)
Dec. 1, 1986 – All o/s shs. and secured debt acquired by Camreco Inc. for $5,376,775 in cash ($246,661) and shs. (1,883,523 common and 200,000 2nd pref. shs.) (see Camreco Inc.)

Goldmac Explorations Inc. (Ont. 1979)
Mar. 2, 1992 – Amalgamated with Concentrated Rare Earth Minerals Ltd., Enertex Developments Inc. (1 for 12.6), Norlode Resources Inc., Offset Natural Resources Ltd. (1 for 11), Preston Resources Ltd., Saranac Resources Ltd. and Uranex Resources Limited (1 for 13.5) to form a new co. named Marvas Developments Ltd.; basis 1 new for 17.5 old shs. (see Marvas Developments Ltd.)

Goldman Sachs U.S. Income Builder Trust (Ont. Jan. 1, 2014)
Feb. 9, 2018 – Merged into Symphony Floating Rate Senior Loan Fund; basis 0.926707 Symphony cl. A units for 1 Goldman cl. A unit and 0.937273 Symphony cl. U units for 1 Goldman cl. U unit.

Goldmaque Mines Ltd. (Ont. 1944)
Dec. 1966 – Charter cancelled.

Goldmarca Limited (Bermuda June 5, 1997)
Oct. 25, 2007 – Name changed to Ecometals Limited.

Goldmark Minerals Ltd. (Alta. Dec. 8, 1977)
Oct. 20, 2009 – Acquired by Tuscany Energy Ltd.; basis 0.6 Tuscany shs. for 1 Goldmark sh. (see Tuscany Energy Ltd.)

Goldmaster Mines Ltd. (Ont. 1946)
Apr. 9, 1975 – Dissolved.

Goldmax Resources Inc. (B.C. Mar. 21, 1980)
Aug. 29, 1996 – Continued into Yukon.
Apr. 26, 1999 – Name changed to Aegean Gold Inc. ■

Goldmember Minerals Inc. (B.C. May 18, 2006)
Mar. 13, 2008 – Name changed to GMV Minerals Inc. (see FPsurvey - Mines & Energy)

Goldminco Consolidated Mining Corp. (Can. Aug. 29, 1994)
Apr. 6, 2000 – Name changed to Goldminco Corporation; basis 1 new for 4 old shs. ■

Goldminco Corporation (Can. Aug. 29, 1994)
Aug. 2, 2011 – Acquired by 7874987 Canada Inc., a wholly owned subsid. of Straits Resources Limited, for 10¢ per sh.

Goldminco Mining Corp. (Can. Aug. 29, 1994)
Dec. 22, 1997 – Name changed to Goldminco Consolidated Mining Corp.; basis 1 new for 4 old shs. ■

Goldmint Explorations Ltd. (Ont. June 11, 1996 amalg.)
Feb. 2, 1999 – Name changed to AXcension Capital Corp.; basis 1 new for 5 old shs. ■

GoldMoney Inc. (Can. Apr. 29, 2015 amalg.)
Oct. 3, 2019 – Continued into British Columbia.
Sept. 20, 2024 – Continued into British Virgin Islands. (see FPsurvey - Industrials)

Goldmont Porcupine Mines Ltd. (Ont. 1947)
1966 – Wound up. Assets distributed on basis of 4 shs. of Jericho Mines Ltd. for 25 of Goldmont.

Gold'n Futures Mineral Corp. (Ont. Feb. 24, 2014 amalg.)
Continued into British Columbia. (see FPsurvey - Mines & Energy)

Goldnev Resources Inc. (B.C. Aug. 19, 1987 amalg.)
May 21, 2007 – Struck from register and dissolved.
Nov. 30, 2007 – Restored to register.
Nov. 20, 2017 – Struck from register and dissolved.

GoldON Resources Ltd. (B.C. June 14, 1977)
Apr. 21, 2025 – Name changed to Gold Finder Resources Ltd. (see FPsurvey - Mines & Energy)

Goldora Mines Ltd. (Ont. 1944)
1956 – Name changed to Burchell Lake Mines Ltd.; basis 1 new for 5 old shs. ■

Goldpac Investments Ltd. (B.C. June 29, 1983)
July 27, 1988 – Continued into Canada.
May 19, 1994 – Name changed to Brimstone Gold Corp.; basis 1 new for 5 old shs. ■

Goldpac Yellowknife Mines Ltd. (Ont. 1945)
Aug. 1965 – Charter cancelled.

Goldpark China Limited (Ont. Aug. 11, 1983)
June 24, 2004 – Continued into British Columbia.
June 25, 2004 – Name changed to Bankers Petroleum Ltd. ■

Goldpark Mines and Investments Ltd. (Ont. Aug. 11, 1983)
Sept. 28, 1994 – Name changed to Goldpark China Limited. ■

Goldpatch Resources Ltd. (Ont. 1987)
Nov. 3, 1992 – Name changed to Brooks Distributors Inc. following acquisition of 986814 Ontario Limited. ■

Goldplay Exploration Ltd. (B.C. Mar. 1, 2018 amalg.)
Jan. 13, 2020 – Name changed to GR Silver Mining Ltd. (see FPsurvey - Mines & Energy)

Goldplay Mining Inc. (B.C. June 16, 2017)
Jan. 6, 2023 – Name changed to Europacific Metals Inc. ■

Goldplex Development Corporation (Can. Aug. 26, 1985)
Mar. 3, 2003 – Dissolved.

Goldpost Resources Inc. (Ont. July 10, 1984)
Sept. 8, 1993 – Formed Antares Mining and Exploration Corporation in Ontario on reverse takeover acquisition of and amalgamation with Antares Mining and Exploration Corporation; basis 1 new for 14 old shs. ■

Goldquest Exploration Inc. (Ont. 1982 amalg.)
Jan. 1, 1985 – Amalgamated with Redcon Gold Mines Ltd. to form new co. with same name Goldquest Exploration Inc.; basis 1 new for 3.5 Redcon shs. and 1 new for 1 Goldquest sh. (see Goldcorp Inc.)
Mar. 31, 1994 – Amalgamated with 1056624 Ontario Inc. wholly owned subsid. of Dickenson Mines Limited to continue as Goldquest Exploration Inc. effective Feb. 1994; basis 1 new Dickenson cl. A sub. vtg. sh. for 20 old Goldquest com. shs. Subsequently assets of Goldquest were amalgamated into Goldcorp Inc. the continuing company formed by the amalgamation of Goldcorp Inc., Dickenson Mines Limited and CSA Management Limited. (see Goldcorp Inc.)

Goldquest Explorations Corp. (Ont. 1979)
July 22, 1982 – Amalgamated with Abino Gold Mines Limited (1 for 12.94), Clicker Red Lake Mines Limited (1 for 18.23), Commander Red Lake Mines Limited (1 for 30.82), Dorion Red Lake Mines Limited (1 for 15.59), Duchesne Red Lake Mines Limited (1 for 10.57), Forsyth Mines Limited (1 for 6.38), Inore Gold Mines Limited (1 for 9.9), Laddie Gold Mines Limited (1 for 15.22) and Rowan Gold Mines Limited (1 for 4.91) to form Goldquest Exploration Inc.; basis 1 new for 1.26 old shs.

GoldQuest Mining Corp. (Ont. July 12, 1989)
2004 – Continued into Canada. (see FPsurvey - Mines & Energy)

Goldray Inc. (Alta. Oct. 28, 1999)
July 2, 2018 – Struck from registry and dissolved.

Goldray Mines Limited (Ont. 1934)
Dec. 1976 – Amalgamated with Canadian Malartic Gold Mines Limited to form Canray Resources Limited; basis 1 new for 2 old shs.

Goldrich Resources Inc. (B.C. 1979)
Oct. 22, 1984 – Amalgamated with Arizako Mines Ltd. to form new co. with same name Goldrich Resources Inc.
Apr. 9, 2018 – Dissolved and struck from register.

Goldrich Resources Ltd. (B.C. 1979)
Jan. 16, 1980 – Name changed to Goldrich Resources Inc. ■

Goldrich Yellowknife Mines Ltd. (Ont. 1944)
Apr. 1958 – Charter cancelled.

Goldrim Mining Co. Ltd. (Ont. 1943)
July 27, 1976 – Dissolved.

Goldrite Mining Corp. (Can. Feb. 17, 1983)
July 28, 1993 – Name changed to Consolidated Goldrite Mining Corp.; basis 1 new for 5 old shs. ■

Goldrock Mines Corp. (B.C. May 9, 1975)
July 29, 2016 – Acquired by Fortuna Silver Mines Inc.; basis 0.1331 Fortuna com. shs. for 1 Goldrock com. sh. (see Fortuna Silver Mines Inc.)

Goldrush Casino & Mining Corporation (B.C. Sept. 18, 1986)
July 6, 1998 – Name changed to Phoenix Leisure Corporation. ■

Goldrush Mining Corporation (B.C. Sept. 18, 1986)
Sept. 10, 1992 – Name changed to Goldrush Casino & Mining Corporation. ■

Goldrush Resources Ltd. (Yuk. Oct. 4, 1999)
Aug. 10, 2006 – Continued into British Columbia. (see First Mining Finance Corp.)
Jan. 12, 2016 – Acquired by First Mining Finance Corp.; basis 0.0714 First Mining com. shs. for 1 Goldrush com. sh. (see First Mining Finance Corp.)

Goldsat Mining Inc. (Can. Mar. 15, 1996)
Sept. 30, 2005 – Formed GobiMin Inc. in Canada on amalgamation with 4209931 Canada Inc. and reverse takeover acquisition of Alexis Resources Limited. ■

Goldsearch Inc. (Ont. 1971)
Mar. 25, 1985 – Name changed to CSA Minerals Corp. following acquisition of CSA Minerals Corp. from CSA Management Ltd. ■

Goldsearch Limited (Ont. 1971)
Oct. 13, 1981 – Name changed to Goldsearch Inc. ■

Goldsec Explorations Ltd. (Ont. 1975)
Dec. 5, 1980 – Amalgamated with Beetz Explorations Ltd. to form Consolidated Goldsec Explorations Limited; basis 1 new for 15 old shs.

Goldseek Resources Inc. (B.C. Sept. 21, 2018)
Oct. 13, 2023 – Name changed to Abitibi Metals Corp. (see FPsurvey - Mines & Energy)

Gold79 Mines Ltd. (B.C. July 28, 2020)
Dec. 19, 2024 – Name changed to West Point Gold Corp. (see FPsurvey - Mines & Energy)

Goldside Mining Co. Ltd. (Ont. 1931)
1949 – Charter cancelled.

Goldsil Resources Ltd. (B.C. 1983)
Dec. 10, 1990 – Amalgamated with International Mahogany Corp. and Magellan Resources Corp. to form a new company also known as International Mahogany Corp.; basis 0.22 new cl. B sub. vtg. sh. for 1 com. sh. (see International Mahogany Corp.)

Goldsmith Minerals Limited (B.C. Feb. 15, 1985)
Nov. 9, 1993 – Name changed to Unitec International Controls Corporation following acquisition of United Nuclear Technologies Inc.; basis 1 new for 2 old shs. ■

Goldsource Mines Inc. (Yuk. Sept. 9, 1997)
Aug. 3, 2005 – Continued into British Columbia.
July 8, 2024 – Acquired by Mako Mining Corp.; basis 0.22 Mako shs. for 1 Goldsource sh.

Goldspike Exploration Inc. (Ont. Sept. 29, 2010)
Mar. 6, 2015 – Name changed to Nevada Zinc Corporation. (see FPsurvey - Mines & Energy; FPsurvey - Industrials)

GoldSpot Discoveries Corp. (Can. May 1, 2017)
Sept. 2, 2022 – Name changed to EarthLabs Inc. (see FPsurvey - Mines & Energy; FPsurvey - Industrials)

Goldstack Resources Ltd. (B.C. Aug. 29, 1979)
July 13, 1994 – Name changed to Consolidated Goldstack International Resources Inc.; basis 1 new for 5 old shs. ■

Goldstalker Resources Ltd. (Ont. May 26, 1974)
1987 – Name changed to Willingdon Resources Limited; basis 2 new for 1 old sh. ■

Goldstar Exploration and Investments Ltd. (Ont. 1964)
Feb. 1980 – Dissolved.

Goldstar Explorations Ltd. (Ont. 1964)
Aug. 15, 1966 – Name changed to Goldstar Exploration and Investments Ltd. ■

Goldstar Minerals Inc. (B.C. May 25, 2010)
Sept. 4, 2014 – Continued into Canada.
Nov. 8, 2023 – Name changed to Green Mining Innovation Inc. (see FPsurvey - Mines & Energy)

Goldstone Exploration Ltd. (B.C. Mar. 19, 1980)
Aug. 25, 1986 – Name changed to INX Insearch Group of Companies Ltd.; basis 2.5 new for 1 old sh. ■

Goldstone Resources Inc. (Ont. Dec. 16, 1998 amalg.)
Aug. 22, 2011 – Acquired by Premier Gold Mines Limited; basis $0.0001 plus 0.16 Premier com. shs for 1 Goldstone com. sh. (see Premier Gold Mines Limited)

Goldstream Minerals Inc. (Can. Aug. 10, 2010)
May 22, 2020 – Name changed to Bluma Wellness Inc. and continued into British Columbia pursuant to reverse takeover acquisition of CannCure Investments Inc.; basis 1 new for 16.07201 old shs. ■

Goldstrike Resources Ltd. (B.C. Oct. 25, 1989)
Mar. 22, 2021 – Name changed to Trailbreaker Resources Ltd. (see FPsurvey - Mines & Energy)

Goldteck Mines Limited (Ont. Aug. 11, 1983)
Oct. 7, 1992 – Name changed to Goldpark Mines and Investments Ltd. ■

Goldtex Resources Ltd. (Alta. Oct. 31, 1994)
Apr. 14, 1998 – Name changed to Cantex Mine Development Corp. following the Apr. 9, 1998, amalgamation of Canadian Mountain Minerals Ltd. and 766002 Alberta Ltd., a wholly owned subsid., constituting a pooling-of-interests. (see FPsurvey - Mines & Energy)

Goldtrail Mines Co. Ltd. (Que. 1945)
Oct. 13, 1973 – Dissolved.

GoldTrain Resources Inc. (Can. Apr. 27, 2009 amalg.)
Aug. 23, 2018 – Name changed to Idaho Champion Gold Mines Canada Inc. prior to reverse takeover acquisition of Idaho Champion Gold Mines Ltd.; basis 1 new for 3 old shs. ■

Goldust Mines Ltd. (Alta. Nov. 28, 1995)
Aug. 19, 1997 – Name changed to Huntington Exploration Inc. ■

Goldvue Mines Ltd. (Ont. Sept. 7, 1944)
1949 – Name changed to New Goldvue Mines Ltd.; basis 1 new for 4 old shs. ■

Goldwater Resources Ltd. (B.C. July 15, 1985)
Dec. 24, 1999 – Name changed to First Goldwater Resources Inc. ■

Goldways Resources Inc. (B.C. Feb. 12, 1985)
Oct. 1, 1993 – Name changed to Inter-Citic Envirotec Inc. ■

Goldwest Resources Ltd. (B.C. Aug. 25, 1980)
Mar. 4, 1988 – Name changed to Consolidated Goldwest Resources Ltd.; basis 1 new for 2.5 old shs. ■

Goldwin Exploration Co. Ltd. (Ont. 1944)
1962 – Merged to form Cessland Corporation Limited; basis 54 new for 100 old shs. (see Cessland Corporation Limited)

Goldwinn Resources Ltd. (B.C. Dec. 12, 1974)
Nov. 2, 1988 – Delisted from the Vancouver Stock Exchange. Subsequently dissolved.

Goldyke Mines Ltd. (Ont. 1946)
Mar. 1976 – Charter cancelled.

Goldzone Exploration Inc. (B.C. Jan. 30, 1981)
Aug. 13, 2001 – Name changed to EnerGulf Resources Inc.; basis 1 new for 3 old shs. ■

Golex Resources Ltd. (Alta. 1979)
Aug. 20, 1982 – Amalgamated with Samson Energy Corporation (1 for 5) to form Kala Exploration Ltd.; basis 1 Kala cl. A com. sh. for either 5 Golex pref. shs. or 5.473 Golex com. shs.

Golf Town Income Fund (Ont. Oct. 1, 2004)
Oct. 2, 2007 – All trust units redeemed by way of special distribution of $17.15 per trust unit following acquisition of Golf Town Canada Inc. which consisted all of the indirect operating assets of the fund by the Ontario Municipal Employees Retirement System through OMERS Capital Partners Inc.'s wholly owned OCPI Golf Inc.

GolfNorth Properties Inc. (Ont. June 28, 1984 amalg.)
July 25, 2002 – Amalgamated with 1458306 Ontario Inc.; basis 1 1458306 Ontario cl. A redeem. pref. sh. for 1 GolfNorth sh. Pref. shs. redeemed immediately for 30¢.

Goliath Gold Mines Ltd. (B.C. 1973)
Feb. 11, 1987 – Amalgamated with Golden Sceptre Resources Ltd., Noranda Inc. and Hemlo Gold Mines Inc. to form a new Hemlo Gold Mines Inc., New Goliath Gold Minerals Ltd. and New Golden Sceptre Minerals Inc. Shldrs. of Goliath received 1.12495 shs. of Hemlo Gold Mines Inc. for each sh. held; plus 1 sh. New Goliath Minerals Ltd. and 1 sh. New Golden Sceptre Minerals Ltd. for each 2 shs. of Hemlo Gold Mines Inc. held. (see Hemlo Gold Mines Inc.)

Golsil Mines Ltd. (Ont. June 15, 1959)
Nov. 8, 1971 – Name changed to Zahavy Mines Limited; basis 1 new for 5 old shs. ■

Gomar Mines Ltd. (Ont. 1963)
1969 – Amalgamated into Summit Exploration & Holdings; basis 1 new for 8 old shs.

Gomara Resources Ltd. (B.C. Feb. 14, 1972)
Aug. 4, 1972 – Name changed to Adar Resources Ltd. ■

Gondwana Gold Inc. (Ont. July 24, 2007)
June 17, 2013 – Name changed to Pan African Oil Ltd. ■

Gondwana Oil Corp. (Ont. Feb. 24, 2014 amalg.)
Sept. 18, 2014 – Name changed to European Metals Corp. ■

Gonzaga Resources Ltd. (B.C. Apr. 8, 2010)
Feb. 27, 2017 – Name changed to Osprey Gold Development Ltd. ■

Gonzales Gold Mines Ltd. (B.C. Sept. 10, 1981)
Oct. 7, 1991 – Name changed to Osito Ventures Ltd.; basis 1 new for 2.6 old shs. ■

The Good Flour Corp. (B.C. Sept. 4, 2014)
July 4, 2025 – Name changed to Intellistake Technologies Corp. (see FPsurvey - Industrials)

Good Hope Resources Ltd. (B.C. 1979)
Oct. 1, 1986 – Amalgamated with Golden North Resource Corporation (1 for 1) to continue as Golden North Resource Ltd.; basis 1 new for 1 old sh. (see Golden North Resource Corporation)

Good Life Networks Inc. (B.C. Jan. 26, 2018 amalg.)
Nov. 29, 2019 – Name changed to Aquarius AI Inc. ■

good natured Products Inc. (B.C. Mar. 26, 2015)
Nov. 26, 2024 – Acquired by HUK 149 Limited pursuant to a reverse vesting order under the Companies' Creditors Arrangement Act (CCAA). All o/s shs. were redeemed and cancelled for no consideration. Non acquired assets and liabilities transferred to 1508538 B.C. Ltd. which was declared bankrupt.

The Good Shroom Co Inc. (Can. Apr. 15, 2021)
Feb. 10, 2025 – Name changed to Mercanto Holdings Inc. (see FPsurvey - Industrials)

Good2Go2 Corp. (Can. Mar. 21, 2019)
Dec. 4, 2020 – Name changed to Leveljump Healthcare Corp. following Qualifying Transaction three-cornered amalgamation with private Canadian Teleradiology

Services, Inc.; basis 1 new for 1.8 old shs. (see FPsurvey - Industrials)

Goodbody Health Inc. (B.C. Feb. 14, 2011)
Aug. 19, 2022 – Continued into Guernsey.

Goodbridge Capital Corp. (B.C. Feb. 7, 2021)
May 29, 2025 – Name changed to IDEX Metals Corp. pursuant to the Qualifying Transaction reverse takeover acquisition of (old) IDEX Metals Corp.; basis 1 new for 3 old shs. (see FPsurvey - Mines & Energy)

Goodco International Ltd. (B.C. 1966)
Feb. 25, 1983 – Struck off register.

Goode Industries Inc. (B.C. Nov. 18, 1986)
Sept. 21, 1994 – Continued into Alberta.
Sept. 28, 1994 – Name changed to Paxton Pacific Resource Products Inc. ■

Goodfellow Resources Ltd. (B.C. Dec. 11, 1996)
Mar. 29, 2005 – Name changed to Standard Uranium Inc. ■

Goodfish Gold Mines Ltd. (Ont. Oct. 17, 1933)
1934 – Name changed to Goodfish Mining Co.; basis 1 new for 2 old shs. ■

Goodfish Mining Co. (Ont. Oct. 17, 1933)
1955 – Name changed to Cusco Mines Ltd.; basis 1 new for 32 old shs. ■

Goodfood Market Corp. (Ont. Mar. 23, 2015)
Sept. 1, 2017 – Amalgamated in Canada to continue with same name. (see FPsurvey - Industrials)

Goodgold Resources Limited (B.C. Feb. 24, 1988)
June 3, 1994 – Name changed to Classic Gold Resources Limited; basis 1 new for 5 old shs. ■

Goodman Gold Trust (Ont. Dec. 20, 2007)
June 24, 2016 – Terminated; basis $3.93858311 per tr. unit.

Goodness Growth Holdings Inc. (Alta. Nov. 23, 2004)
June 25, 2024 – Name changed to Vireo Growth Inc. (see FPsurvey - Industrials)

Goodrock Gold Mines Ltd. (Ont. 1930)
Feb. 1961 – Dissolved.

Good2Go Corp. (Ont. Feb. 28, 2018)
June 28, 2021 – Name changed to NowVertical Group Inc. pursuant to the Qualifying Transaction reverse takeover acquisition of (old) NowVertical Group, Inc. and concurrent amalgamation of (old) NowVertical with wholly owned Good2Go (US) Corp.; basis 1 new for 4.5 old shs. (see FPsurvey - Industrials)

Good2GoRTO Corp. (Can. Dec. 31, 2020)
May 16, 2022 – Name changed to FRX Innovations Inc. pursuant to the Qualifying Transaction reverse takeover acquisition of FRX Polymers, Inc. and concurrent amalgamation of FRX with wholly owned 13448061 Canada Inc.; basis 1 new for 3.5 old shs. (see FPsurvey - Industrials)

Goodyear Canada Inc. (Ont. Mar. 30, 1927)
May 5, 1993 – Acquired by The Goodyear Tire and Rubber Company for $65 per sh.

Goodyear Tire & Rubber Co. of Canada, Ltd. (Ont. Mar. 30, 1927)
Apr. 1, 1975 – Name changed to Goodyear Canada Inc. ■

Goose River Capital Inc. (Alta. May 24, 2000)
Sept. 14, 2001 – Name changed to Goose River Resources Ltd. ■

Goose River Resources Ltd. (Alta. May 24, 2000)
Aug. 15, 2005 – Plan of Arrangement with SignalEnergy Inc. (SEI) and G2 Resources Inc.; basis either 0.83 new SEI com. sh. and $1.00 or, 0.60 new SEI com. sh. and $0.28, plus 0.05 new G2 cl. A com. sh. for 1 old Goose River com. sh. (see G2 Resources Inc.; SignalEnergy Inc.)

Gopher Media Services Corporation (Can. Oct. 31, 1997)
Aug. 19, 2008 – Dissolved.

Gopher Oil & Gas Company Ltd. (B.C. Mar. 25, 1994)
Dec. 30, 1998 – Name changed to Ventus Energy Ltd. following acquisition of Scarlet Exploration Inc.; basis 1 new for 4 old sh. ■

Goran Capital Inc. (Can. Dec. 30, 1985)
Feb. 4, 2022 – Struck from register and dissolved.

Gordon & Belyea Ltd. (B.C. 1941)
Jan. 1, 1958 – Current assets and goodwill acquired by Marshall Wells of Canada Ltd. in 1957. Pref. shs. redeemed at $105 plus accr. int. Co. became private and name subsequently changed to Mark Long Investments Ltd.

Gordon Gas & Oil Co. Ltd. (B.C.)
1958 – Struck off register.

Gordon-Lebel Mines Ltd. (Ont. 1927)
Dec. 3, 1980 – Amalgamated with 3 other cos. to form Hoffman Exploration & Minerals Limited; basis 1 new for 12.4545 old shs. (see Hoffman Exploration & Minerals Ltd.)

Gordon Mackay & Stores Limited (Ont. 1923)
June 25, 1976 – Amalgamated into Walkers Holdings Limited; basis 1 new $8.75 pref. sh. for 1 cl. A sh. Subsequently all $8.75 pref. shs. not already held by Peoples Department Stores redeemed for $8.75 plus accr. divds.

Gordon Resources Limited (B.C. 1975)
July 30, 1985 – Name changed to Shogun Developments Corp.; basis 1 new for 2 old shs. ■

Gordona Mining Corp. Ltd. (Ont. 1948)
1961 – Charter cancelled.

Gorham Gold Mines Ltd. (Ont. 1938)
Aug. 15, 1960 – Dissolved.

Gorilla Minerals Corp. (B.C. Apr. 27, 2012)
June 8, 2018 – Name changed to Go Cobalt Mining Corp. ■

Gorilla Resources Corp. (B.C. Oct. 14, 2011 amalg.)
June 22, 2012 – Name changed to Winston Resources Inc. pursuant to reverse takeover acquisition of CNRP Mining Inc. ■

Gortdrum Mines Ltd. (Ont. 1964)
1970 – Acquired by Northgate Exploration Ltd.; basis 1 new for 3 old shs. (see Northgate Exploration Limited)

Goshawk Mines Limited (Ont. Nov. 13, 1974)
Nov. 18, 1977 – Name changed to Insulite Development Corporation Inc. ■

Gosselin Gold Mines Ltd. (Ont. 1913)
June 6, 1955 – Dissolved.

Gotham Capital Corporation (Alta. Aug. 17, 2000)
Nov. 3, 2004 – Continued into Alberta.
Nov. 11, 2004 – Name changed to Long View Resources Corporation following Qualifying Transaction acquisition of Long View Resources Corporation for $1,046,215. ■

Gotham Resource Corp. (B.C. Oct. 8, 2020)
Feb. 8, 2024 – Name changed to CopperEx Resources Corporation pursuant to the Qualifying Transaction reverse takeover acquisition of (old) CopperEx Resources Corporation and concurrent amagamation of (old) CopperEx with wholly owned 1442695 B.C. Ltd. (and continued as CopperEx Holdings Corporation); basis 1 new for 3 old shs. (see FPsurvey - Mines & Energy)

Gotham Yellowknife Mines Ltd. (Ont. 1944)
1960 – Charter cancelled.

Gothic Gold Mines Ltd. (Ont. Mar. 5, 1945)
1953 – Name changed to Gothic Mines & Oils Limited. ■

Gothic Mines & Oils Limited (Ont. Mar. 5, 1945)
July 1957 – Assets and liabs. sold to Cessford Gas & Oil Corp. Ltd.; basis 1 new sh. of Cessford for 6 old shs. of Gothic.
May 8, 1987 – Name changed to Aurora Corporation. ■

Gothic Resources Inc. (B.C. July 9, 1991)
Feb. 12, 2002 – Succeeded by American Natural Energy Corporation pursuant to plan of arrangement whereby wholly owned American Natural Energy Corporation completed a share exchange to become parent of Gothic.

Goths Resources Inc. (Can. Apr. 11, 1996)
Sept. 26, 2000 – Name changed to Diagnos Inc. (see FPsurvey - Industrials)

Government Strip Bond Trust (Ont. Feb. 15, 2001)
Jan. 2, 2013 – Redeemed for $26.06 per unit.

Governor Gold Mines Ltd. (Ont. 1944)
Apr. 2, 1985 – Charter cancelled.

GoviEx Uranium Inc. (British Virgin Islands June 16, 2006)
Mar. 1, 2011 – Continued into British Columbia. (see FPsurvey - Mines & Energy)

Goward Gold Mines Ltd. (Ont. Feb. 13, 1935)
1956 – Charter cancelled.

Gowest Amalgamated Resources Ltd. (Ont. May 27, 1982)
Apr. 13, 2011 – Name changed to Gowest Gold Ltd. ■

Gowest Gold Ltd. (Ont. May 27, 1982)
Sept. 24, 2024 – Privatized; basis 15¢ cash per sh.

Gowest Gold Resources Ltd. (Ont. 1980)
May 27, 1982 – Name changed to Gowest Amalgamated Resources Ltd. and continued into Ontario following amalgamation with 508813 Ontario Ltd.; basis 1 new for 1 old sh. ■

Gowganda Resources Inc. (Ont. 1968)
Feb. 27, 1985 – Name changed to Calgroup Graphics Corporation Ltd. ■

Gowganda Silver Mines Ltd. (Ont. 1968)
Jan. 18, 1982 – Name changed to Gowganda Resources Inc. ■

Gozlan Brothers Limited (Ont. 1964)
1976 – Placed into receivership mid-; no distribution for shldrs.

Grace Resources Inc. (Alta. May 23, 1996)
Mar. 13, 2001 – Acquired by Cebanx Investments Inc. for $1.00 per sh.

Gracefield Capital Corporation Ltd. (Can. Jan. 13, 1984)
Oct. 24, 1995 – Continued into Ontario.
Aug. 7, 1996 – Formed Southern Reef Ventures Inc. in Ontario on amalgamation with 1181979 Ontario Inc. and 1181980 Ontario Inc.; basis 1 new for 20 old shs. (see FPsurvey - Mines & Energy)

Gracefield Explorations Inc. (Can. Jan. 13, 1984)
May 24, 1989 – Name changed to Gracefield Capital Corporation Ltd. ■

Gracey Resources Inc. (B.C. 1987)
Nov. 6, 1992 – Dissolved and struck off register.

Grad & Walker Energy Corporation (Alta. Feb. 16, 1993)
Aug. 18, 1997 – Acquired by Crestar Energy Inc.; basis $13.50 or 0.509 new Crestar sh. for 1 old Grad & Walker sh. (see Crestar Energy Inc.)

Gradore Mines Ltd. (Ont. 1951)
Oct. 1972 – Charter cancelled.

Graffoto Industries Corporation (B.C. Oct. 16, 1984)
Mar. 3, 1997 – Delisted from the Vancouver Stock Exchange. Subsequently struck from register and dissolved.

Grafton & Co. Ltd. (Ont. 1904)
Jan. 1963 – Formed Grafton's Limited on amalgamation with wholly owned Kilbride Distributors Ltd. ■

Grafton-Fraser Limited (Ont. 1961)
1969 – Acquired by Grafton Group Limited; basis 11 Grafton shs. for 10 Grafton-Fraser shs. (see Grafton Group Limited)
Mar. 1975 – All pref. shs. called for redemption at par plus $1. (see Grafton Group Limited)
1978 – Name changed to Grafton-Fraser Inc. (see Grafton Group Limited)

Grafton Group Limited (Ont. Nov. 3, 1961)
Apr. 7, 1993 – Declared bankrupt, BDO Dunwood Limited in Toronto appointed trustee.
May 1999 – Trustee finalizing the wind-up of the company.
Sept. 1999 – Creditors received a dividend.
May 2, 2000 – Trustee discharged. No funds available for distribution to shldrs.

Grafton's Limited (Ont. 1904)
1974 – Substantially all o/s shs. acquired by Grafton-Fraser Limited; basis 1 Grafton-Fraser 6% pref. sh. for 1 Grafton's cl. A or com. sh. (see Grafton-Fraser Limited)

Graftons 1953 Limited (Ont. 1961)
Nov. 22, 1967 – Name changed to Grafton-Fraser Limited. ■

Graham Bell Ltd. (Ont. 1954)
1959 – Name changed to Cerametal Industries Limited. ■

Graham-Bousquet Gold Mines Ltd. (Ont. May 15, 1934)
1958 – Merged into Cadamet Mines Ltd.; basis 1 new for 4 old shs.

Graham Gold Mining Corporation (B.C. May 25, 1988)
Oct. 27, 1997 – Name changed to Sense Technologies Inc. ■

Gram Minerals Corporation (Can. Sept. 12, 1996)
Dec. 15, 2003 – Charter cancelled.

Gramara Mercantile Corp. Ltd. (B.C. Nov. 19, 1968)
July 11, 1973 – Name changed to Groundstar Resources Limited; basis 1 new for 5 old shs. ■

Gramara Mines Ltd. (B.C. Nov. 19, 1968)
Aug. 24, 1971 – Name changed to Gramara Mercantile Corp. Ltd. ■

Gramercy Holdings Ltd. (unknown)
Name changed to Jordan Valley Wines. ■

Gran Colombia Gold Corp. (B.C. May 27, 1982)
Nov. 2, 2021 – Name changed to GCM Mining Corp. ■

Gran Colombia Resources Inc. (B.C. July 7, 1995 amalg.)
June 21, 1996 – Continued into Yukon.
Nov. 1, 1999 – Name changed to Wavve Telecommunications, Inc. (see FPsurvey - Industrials)

Gran Tierra Energy Inc. (Nev. June 6, 2003)
Oct. 31, 2016 – Continued into Delaware. (see FPsurvey - Mines & Energy)

Gran Tierra Exchangeco Inc. (Alta. July 25, 2008)
July 5, 2018 – Redeemed; basis 1 Gran Tierra Energy Inc. com. sh. plus any declared and unpaid dividends for 1 exchangeable sh.

Granada Exploration Corporation (B.C. 1979)
July 10, 1992 – Dissolved and struck off register.

Granby Consolidated Mining, Smelting & Power Co. Ltd. (B.C. Mar. 1901)
1959 – Name changed to The Granby Mining Co. Ltd. ■

Granby Elastic & Textiles Limited (Can. Feb. 4, 1940)
1969 – Entered bankruptcy.
1971 – First pay. to 1st mtge. bds. & debs. of $65.
Nov. 4, 1975 – Second and final pay. to 1st mtge. bds. & debs. of $281.40.

Granby Elastic Web of Canada Ltd. (Can. Feb. 4, 1940)
1952 – Name changed to Granby Elastic & Textiles Limited. ■

Granby Industries Income Fund (Ont. Dec. 7, 2004)
Mar. 5, 2008 – Acquired by Clarke Inc. for $0.17 per trust unit.

The Granby Mining Co. Ltd. (B.C. Mar. 1901)
Feb. 5, 1975 – Name changed to Granby Mining Corporation. ■

Granby Mining Corporation (B.C. Mar. 1901)
Jan. 1979 – Amalgamated with 2 other cos. to form Zapata Granby Corp. All o/s com. shs. exch. for redeemable pref. shs. of amalg. co.

Granby Resources Limited (B.C. 1982)
Mar. 17, 1995 – Name changed to Consolidated Granby Resources Limited; basis 1 new for 4.6 old shs. ■

Grancour Gold Mines Ltd. (Ont. 1945)
1952 – Charter cancelled.

Grand America Minerals Ltd. (B.C. June 16, 1987)
Apr. 22, 1994 – Name changed to G.D.M. Grand Development Corp. (see FPsurvey - Mines & Energy)

Grand Bahama Industries Ltd. (Ont. 1962)
Mar. 1966 – Name changed to Bahamas-Caribbean Development Corporation Limited. ■

Grand Banks Energy Corporation (Alta. July 25, 2002)
June 20, 2008 – Acquired by Fairborne Energy Ltd. for $2.90 per sh.
Dec. 4, 2009 – Dissolved.

Grand Bay Explorations Limited (Ont. Jan. 10, 1975)
May 31, 1995 – Name changed to Tropika International Limited; basis 1 new for 2 old shs. (see FPsurvey - Industrials)

Grand Canadian Mining Corp. Ltd. (Ont. 1965)
Dec. 1973 – Charter cancelled.

Grand Canyon Resources Inc. (B.C. 1979)
Dec. 20, 1985 – Name changed to T.I. Travel International Inc. (see FPsurvey - Industrials)

Grand Chibougamau Mines Ltd. (Ont. 1945)
Aug. 26, 1957 – Merged into Consolidated Frederick Mines Ltd. Latter wound up and Grand Chibougamau shs. entitled to receive 33¢ per sh. C/o Guaranty Trust Co., Toronto. (see Consolidated Frederick Mines Ltd.)

Grand China Resources Ltd. (B.C. 1982)
June 12, 1989 – Name changed to New China Resources Limited; basis 1 new for 5 old shs. ■

Grand Duchess Mining Ltd. (Alta. 1966)
Feb. 1973 – Charter cancelled.

Grand Empire Explorations Ltd. (Ont. June 3, 1985)
Aug. 15, 1995 – Formed Warp 10 Technologies Inc. in Ontario on amalgamation with (old) Warp 10 Technologies Inc.; basis 1 new for 10 old shs. ■

Grand Forks Mines Ltd. (B.C. July 25, 1977)
June 16, 1989 – Name changed to Attwood Gold Corporation; basis 1 new for 5 old shs. ■

Grand Manitou Mines Ltd. (Que. 1950)
July 1972 – Charter cancelled.

Grand National Resources Inc. (B.C. Nov. 25, 1980)
Mar. 16, 2000 – Name changed to Consolidated Grand National Resources Inc.; basis 1 new for 10 old shs. ■

Grand Oakes Resources Corp. (Ont. Feb. 23, 1988)
June 2, 2004 – Formed Midlands Minerals Corporation in Ontario on amalgamation with Midlands Minerals Corporation, constituting a reverse takeover by Midlands; basis 1 new for 1 Midlands sh. and 1 new for 4.5 Grand Oakes shs. ■

Grand Petroleum Inc. (Alta. Jan. 1, 2004 amalg.)
Aug. 24, 2007 – Acquired by Harvest Grand Inc., a wholly owned subsid. of Harvest Energy Trust; basis $3.84 per sh. (see Harvest Energy Trust)

Grand Power Logistics Group Inc. (Alta. Apr. 1, 2004)
Jan. 9, 2017 – Privatized via amalgamation with 2001123 Alberta Ltd.; basis 1 redeem. pref. cl. A sh. for 1 com. sh., redeemed for Cdn$0.09 cash per cl. A sh.

Grand Prix Resources (B.C. 1972)
Dec. 1979 – Name changed to Omenica Resources Ltd.; basis 1 new for 5 old shs. ■

Grand River Natural Gas Co. Ltd. (unknown)
1936 – Assets sold to R. H. Smith, Low Banks, Ont.

Grand Saguenay Mines and Minerals Limited (Ont. Sept. 25, 1959)
Feb. 1, 1989 – Name changed to GSM Resource Capital Inc. ■

Grand Valley Mining Co. Ltd. (Ont. 1974)
Mar. 15, 1979 – Amalgamated with Golden Bounty Mining Co. Ltd. (1 for 1), Golden Sabre Mines Ltd. (1 for 1.5), Pacesetter Mines Ltd. (1 for 1) and Prestige Mines Ltd. (1 for 3) to form Golden Bounty Mining Co. Ltd.; basis 1 new for 3 old shs.

Grandad Gold Mines Ltd. (Ont. 1923)
June 8, 1977 – Name changed to Grandad Resources Limited. ■

Grandad Resources Limited (Ont. 1923)
Mar. 1, 1978 – Continued into Canada.
July 19, 1988 – Name changed to Great Grandad Resources Limited. ■

Grandcru Resources Corporation (B.C. Jan. 18, 1988)
May 12, 2008 – Acquired by Bell Resources Corporation; basis 0.25 Bell Resources com. sh. for 1 Grandcru com. sh.

Grande Cache Coal Corporation (Alta. July 24, 2000)
Mar. 7, 2012 – Acquired by 1629835 Alberta Ltd., a company jointly owned by Winsway Coking Coal Holdings Limited and Marubeni Corporation, for $10 per sh.

Grande Portage Resources Ltd. (B.C. Oct. 17, 1984)
July 17, 1998 – Continued into Yukon.
May 3, 2007 – Continued into British Columbia. (see FPsurvey - Mines & Energy)

Grande Prairie Petroleums Ltd. (Ont. 1942)
1945 – Taken over by Apex Consolidated Resources Ltd.; basis 1 new for 4 old shs. (see Apex Consolidated Resources Ltd.)

Grande Trunk Resources Inc. (B.C. Sept. 28, 1978)
Jan. 15, 1986 – Name changed to Erient Resources Inc.; basis 1 new for 5 old shs. ■

Grande West Transportation Group Inc. (B.C. Dec. 4, 2012)
Mar. 29, 2021 – Name changed to Vicinity Motor Corp.; basis 1 new for 3 old shs. ■

Granden Gold Mine Ltd. (Ont. 1946)
1959 – Merged into Hydra Explorations Ltd.; basis 2 new for 13 old shs.

GrandeTel Technologies Inc. (B.C. 1984)
Sept. 28, 1995 – Continued into Canada.
Nov. 2, 2005 – Dissolved.

Grandeur Mines Ltd. (B.C. Feb. 20, 1969)
Sept. 14, 1971 – Name changed to China Commercial Corporation Ltd. ■

Grandex Exploration and Investment Co. Ltd. (Ont. 1968)
Mar. 1976 – Charter cancelled.

Grandex Gold Mines Ltd. (Ont. 1968)
Sept. 1968 – Name changed to Grandex Exploration and Investment Co. Ltd. ■

Grandex Resources Ltd. (B.C. 1986)
June 19, 1992 – Dissolved and struck off register.

Grandfield Pacific Inc. (Can. Aug. 30, 1994)
Oct. 21, 2016 – Continued into British Columbia.
Oct. 26, 2016 – Name changed to Radiant Health Care Inc. ■

Grandines Mines Ltd. (Ont. 1951)
1957 – Name changed to Grandroy Mines Ltd.; basis 1 new for 4 old shs. ■

Grandma Lee's Inc. (Que. Aug. 9, 1949)
Jan. 26, 1998 – Name changed to Heritage Concepts International Inc. ■

Grandmaster Technologies Inc. (B.C. May 17, 1983)
Aug. 31, 1998 – Name changed to EM Net Corp.; basis 1 new for 5 old shs. ■

Grand'mere Knitting Co. Ltd. (Que. 1933)
1961 – Placed into liquidation. Paul Rainville of Montreal was appointed liquidator.
June 23, 1987 – Charter cancelled.

Grandora Explorations Ltd. (B.C. 1966)
Mar. 2, 1977 – Name changed to Dora Explorations Ltd.; basis 1 new for 5 old shs. ■

Grandoro Mines Ltd. (B.C. 1934)
1957 – Three distributions reported made, totaling 98¢, including final of 13¢ per sh.

Grandroy Mines Ltd. (Ont. 1951)
June 1973 – Name changed to New Grandroy Resources Inc.; basis 1 new for 5 old shs. ■

Granduc Mines Limited (B.C. Mar. 19, 1953)
Nov. 8, 1993 – Amalgamated with Cazador Explorations Limited to form Granduc Mining Corporation; basis 0.6 new for 1 Cazador sh. and 1 new for 1 Granduc Mines sh. (see Granduc Mining Corporation)

Granduc Mining Corporation (B.C. Nov. 2, 1993 amalg.)
July 19, 1996 – Acquired by Black Hawk Mining Inc.; basis 1 Black Hawk sh. for 1 Granduc sh. (see Black Hawk Mining Inc.)

Grandview Energy Resources Incorporated (Ont. Nov. 23, 1945)
Sept. 22, 1983 – Name changed to Consolidated Grandview Inc.; basis 1 new for 3 old shs. ■

Grandview Gold Inc. (Ont. Nov. 23, 1945)
July 13, 2015 – Name changed to PUDO Inc. following reverse takeover acquisition of My Courier Depot Inc.; basis 1 new for 20 old shs. (see FPsurvey - Industrials)

Grandview Resources Inc. (B.C. 1982)
July 26, 1988 – Amalgamated with WMC Acquisition (B.C.) Corp.; basis 1 new pref. for 1 com.

Granex Mines Ltd. (B.C. 1969)
Apr. 1976 – Name changed to Granex Resources Corporation. ■

Granex Resources Corporation (B.C. 1969)
Nov. 23, 1979 – Continued into Canada.
Oct. 19, 1999 – Charter cancelled and co. dissolved.

Grange Gold Corporation (B.C. Jan. 31, 1980)
Nov. 23, 2005 – Name changed to Lovitt Nutriceutical Corporation. ■

Granger Development Corporation (Can. June 26, 1987)
Sept. 12, 2002 – Dissolved and struck from register.

Granger Energy Corp. (Alta. June 23, 1993)
Nov. 9, 1998 – Merged with 766720 Alberta Inc., a wholly owned subsid. of BelAir Energy Corporation; basis 2.06152 new com. shs. of BelAir for 1 cl. A sh. of Granger; 1.85884 new com. shs. of BelAir for 1 cl. B sh. of Granger and 14.59401 new com. shs. of BelAir for 1 cl. C sh. of Granger. (see BelAir Energy Corporation)

Granger Petroleum Corporation (B.C. 1969)
May 1975 – Name changed to Granger Resources Corporation. ■

Granger Resources Corporation (B.C. 1969)
June 26, 1987 – Continued into Canada.
July 16, 1991 – Name changed to Granger Development Corporation. ■

Granges Exploration Ltd. (B.C. Nov. 28, 1983)
June 9, 1989 – Name changed to Granges Inc. ■

Granges Exploration Ltd. (B.C. Nov. 28, 1983)
June 28, 1985 – Continued into British Columbia.
June 19, 1989 – Name changed to Granges Inc. ■

Granges Inc. (B.C. Nov. 28, 1983)
Nov. 1, 1996 – Formed Vista Gold Corp. in British Columbia on amalgamation with Da Capo Resources Ltd.; basis 1 Vista sh. for 1 Granges sh. and 2 Vista shs. for 1 Da Capo sh. ■

Granges Inc. (B.C. June 28, 1985)
May 15, 1995 – Amalgamated with Hycroft Resources & Development Corporation to form new co. with same name Granges Inc.; basis 0.88 new for 1 Hycroft sh. and 1 new for 1 Granges sh. (see Granges Inc.)

Grango Pershing Mines Ltd. (Ont. 1945)
1952 – Charter cancelled.

Grangold Mines Ltd. (unknown)
Dec. 3, 1962 – Dissolved.

Granisko Resources Inc. (Can. Jan. 23, 1987)
Apr. 7, 2003 – Dissolved.

Granisle Copper Limited (B.C. 1957)
Jan. 1979 – Amalgamated with 2 other cos. to form Zapata Granby Corporation. All o/s com. shs. exch. for redeemable pref. shs. of amalg. co.

Granite Capital Development Corporation (Ont. 1981)
Dec. 17, 1985 – Name changed to Granite Capital Development Corporation (Northern and Eastern). ■

Granite Capital Development Corporation (Northern and Eastern) (Ont. 1981)
Aug. 31, 1989 – Acquired by Granite Tourism Corporation; basis 1 new for 1.119 old sh. (see Granite Tourism Corporation)
May 16, 1994 – Dissolved. (see Granite Tourism Corporation)

Granite City Platinum Ltd. (B.C. 1966)
May 17, 1971 – Charter cancelled.

Granite Creek Copper Ltd. (B.C. June 23, 2010)
Aug. 18, 2025 – Acquired by Cascadia Minerals Ltd.; basis 0.25 Cascadia shs. for 1 Granite Creek sh.

Granite Creek Gold Ltd. (B.C. June 23, 2010)
Oct. 17, 2018 – Name changed to Granite Creek Copper Ltd. ■

Granite Destinations Corporation (Northern and Eastern) (Ont. Oct. 30, 1986)
Jan. 3, 1995 – Delisted from the CDN. Subsequently dissolved and charter cancelled.

Granite Development Corporation (Ont. 1981)
Aug. 31, 1989 – Acquired by Granite Tourism Corporation; basis 1 new for 4.085 old shs. (see Granite Tourism Corporation)

Granite Mountain Mines Ltd. (B.C. 1971)
Apr. 18, 1975 – Name changed to Golden Granite Mines Ltd.; basis 1 new for 5 old shs. ■

Granite Oil Corp. (Alta. Jan. 1, 2010 amalg.)
Mar. 10, 2020 – Acquired by International Petroleum Corporation; basis 95¢ cash per sh.

Granite Real Estate Inc. (Ont. Aug. 29, 2003 amalg.)
Jan. 3, 2013 – Succeeded by Granite Real Estate Investment Trust pursuant to plan of arrangement whereby Granite Real Estate Investment Trust and Granite REIT Inc. were formed to facilitate the conversion to a real estate investment trust. (see FPsurvey - Industrials)

Granite Resorts Inc. (Ont. 1983)
Apr. 3, 1986 – Name changed to Granite Resorts Inc. (Northern and Eastern). ■

Granite Resorts Inc. (Northern and Eastern) (Ont. 1983)
Aug. 31, 1989 – Acquired by Granite Tourism Corporation; basis 1 new for 1.637 old shs. (see Granite Tourism Corporation)

Granite Tourism Corporation (Ont. 1988)
May 16, 1994 – Charter cancelled and co. dissolved.

Granite Tourism Corporation (Northern and Eastern) (Ont. 1985)
Aug. 31, 1989 – Acquired by Granite Tourism Corporation; basis 1 new for 1.236 old shs. (see Granite Tourism Corporation)
May 16, 1994 – Dissolved. (see Granite Tourism Corporation)

Graniz Mondal Inc. (Alta. May 5, 1995)
Aug. 17, 2012 – Continued into Canada.
Aug. 23, 2017 – Name changed to NanoXplore Inc. pursuant to the reverse takeover acquisition of Group NanoXplore Inc.; basis 1 new for 15 old shs. (see FPsurvey - Industrials)

Granja Gold Inc. (Ont. Nov. 1, 2011)
May 1, 2013 – Continued into British Columbia.
Dec. 31, 2013 – Formed PDC Diagnostics Corp. in British Columbia on amalgamation with Eidam Diagnostics Corporaion; basis 1 new for 1 PDC Diagnostics sh.and 1 new for 1 Granja Gold sh. ■

Grant Exploration Ltd. (B.C. 1979)
July 5, 1984 – Name changed to Argo Development Corp.; basis 1 new for 5 old shs. ■

Grantham Resources Inc. (Alta. Apr. 26, 1993)
Oct. 2, 2003 – Dissolved and struck from registry.

Grantland Gold Ltd. (Ont. 1936)
Dec. 1962 – Dissolved.

Granum Oils Ltd. (Alta. 1953)
1964 – Struck off register.

Granville Island Brewing Company Ltd. (B.C. 1981)
Nov. 1989 – Acquired by International Potter Distilling Corporation. (see International Potter Distilling Corporation)

Granville Lake Nickel Mines Ltd. (Ont. 1946)
Jan. 5, 1970 – Charter cancelled.

Granville Mines Corporation Ltd. (B.C. 1950)
1952 – Charter cancelled.

Granville Pacific Capital Corp. (Alta. June 23, 1998)
Apr. 17, 2013 – Acquired by H&H Total Care Services Inc. for 8¢ per sh.

Granville Resources Inc. (B.C. Mar. 23, 1983)
Aug. 9, 1991 – Dissolved and struck off register.

Granwick Mines Ltd. (Ont. 1956)
Charter cancelled.

Graph Blockchain Inc. (B.C. Oct. 6, 1982)
Dec. 22, 2023 – Name changed to New World Solutions Inc. (see FPsurvey - Mines & Energy; FPsurvey - Industrials)

Graph-Com Systems Ltd. (Can. 1970)
Sept. 10, 1979 – Placed into bankruptcy. No distribution made to creditors.

Graph/Max Inc. (Ont. Nov. 13, 1925)
Jan. 30, 1996 – Name changed to GRF Technology Inc.; basis 1 new for 20 old shs. ■

Graphene Manufacturing Group Pty Ltd. (Australia Aug. 10, 2016)
Apr. 2, 2021 – Name changed to Graphene Manufacturing Group Ltd. (see FPsurvey - Industrials)

Graphene 3D Lab Inc. (B.C. Jan. 18, 2011)
Jan. 23, 2020 – Name changed to G6 Materials Corp. (see FPsurvey - Industrials)

The Graphite Corporation of Canada Ltd. (Alta. Nov. 25, 1982)
May 9, 1991 – Name changed to Takla Star Resources Ltd. following reverse takeover acquisition of AOK Explorations Ltd.; basis 1 new for 8 old shs. ■

Graphite Energy Corp. (B.C. Oct. 14, 2016)
Mar. 12, 2021 – Name changed to Australian Goldfields Limited pursuant to the acquisition of Pilbara Gold Group Pty Ltd. ■

Graphite One Resources Inc. (Alta. Mar. 16, 2006)
Mar. 18, 2019 – Name changed to Graphite One Inc.; basis 1 new for 10 old shs. (see FPsurvey - Mines & Energy)

Grasslands Entertainment Inc. (Alta. July 11, 2001)
Dec. 20, 2011 – Name changed to Lakeside Minerals Inc. and continued into Ontario pursuant to reverse takeover acquisition of Lakeside Minerals Corp.; basis 1 new for 5 old shs. ■

Gratiam Resources Inc. (B.C. Sept. 8, 1987)
May 2000 – Struck off register as reported by the company.

Gravis Computer Peripherals Inc. (B.C. 1982)
Nov. 14, 1985 – Name changed to International Gravis Computer Technology Inc.; basis 1 new for 2 old shs. ■

Gravis Energy Corp. (B.C. Aug. 24, 2007)
Nov. 24, 2017 – Name changed to Biocure Technology Inc. following reverse takeover acquisition of BiocurePharm Corporation; basis 1 new for 6.033479 old shs. (see FPsurvey - Industrials)

Gravis Oil Corporation (Alta. Feb. 12, 2008)
Sept. 7, 2012 – Name changed to Petro River Oil Corp. ■

Gravitas II Capital Corp. (B.C. Jan. 18, 2021)
Mar. 3, 2023 – Name changed to Parvis Invest Inc. pursuant to the Qualifying Transaction reverse takeover acquisition of (old) Parvis Invest Inc. and concurrent amalgamation of (old) Parvis with wholly owned 14492528 Canada Inc. (and continued as Parvis Fintech Inc.); basis 1 new for 2.49 old shs. (see FPsurvey - Industrials)

Gravitas III Capital Corp. (B.C. July 6, 2021)
July 12, 2023 – Name changed to Monaghan Capital Fund Ltd. (see FPsurvey - Industrials)

Gravitas Financial Inc. (Can. Nov. 22, 1996)
Oct. 4, 2022 – Name changed to New Frontier Ventures Inc.; basis 1 new for 25 old shs. (see FPsurvey - Industrials)

Gravitas One Capital Corp. (B.C. June 25, 2020)
Nov. 12, 2021 – Name changed to Xybion Digital Inc. pursuant to the reverse takeover acquisition of Xybion Corporation and concurrent amalgamation of Xybion with wholly owned Gravitas US Corp.; basis 1 new for 10.65 old shs. ■

Gravity West Mining Corp. (B.C. June 14, 1996)
Mar. 9, 2009 – Name changed to Rock Tech Resources Inc.; basis 1 new for 10 old shs. ■

Grawmont Mines Ltd. (Que. 1950)
May 18, 1974 – Dissolved.

Gray Rock Mining Company Limited (B.C. May 31, 1950)
Apr. 28, 1986 – Name changed to Gray Rock Resources Ltd. ■

Gray Rock Resources Ltd. (B.C. May 31, 1950)
Oct. 8, 2020 – Name changed to Silver Wolf Exploration Ltd. (see FPsurvey - Mines & Energy)

Gray Wolf Capital Corporation (Ont. July 14, 2004)
Apr. 20, 2015 – Dissolved and struck from register.

Grayd Resource Corporation (B.C. Aug. 1, 1980)
Feb. 10, 2012 – Acquired by Agnico-Eagle Mines Limited; basis either (i) $2.80 or (ii) 5¢ plus 0.04039 Agnico shs for 1 Grayd sh. (see Agnico-Eagle Mines Limited)

Graydel Malartic Gold Mines Ltd. (Ont. 1945)
Aug. 1957 – Charter cancelled.

Graymac Gold Mines Ltd. (Ont. 1943)
Feb. 26, 1953 – Charter cancelled.

Graymar Resources Inc. (Alta. Sept. 17, 1993)
June 13, 1996 – Name changed to Friendly Fuels Group Inc. (see FPsurvey - Industrials)

Graystone Corporation (Alta. Jan. 11, 1978)
Feb. 27, 2006 – Amalgamated with Stonington Capital Corporation (1 for 1) to continue with the new name Pyxis Capital Inc.; basis 1 new Pyxis non-vtg. sh. plus 0.38 new Pyxis dividend sh. for either 1 old sub. vtg. or 1 old junior pfd. sh.; 1 new Pyxis com. sh. plus 0.38 new Pyxis dividend sh. for 1 old multiple vtg. sh.; and 1 new Pyxis dividend sh. for 1 old dividend sh. (see Pyxis Capital Inc.)

Grease Creek Petroleum Corp. Ltd. (B.C. 1937)
1943 – Assets transferred to Grease Creek Petroleums Ltd. in 1938. Charter surrendered.

Grease Creek Petroleums Ltd. (B.C. 1937)
Mar. 25, 1954 – Name changed to Consolidated Grease Creek Petroleum Ltd.; basis 1 new for 3 old shs. ■

Great Alaska Services Ltd. (B.C. Mar. 8, 1951)
Jan. 9, 1980 – Name changed to Vanstates Resources Ltd. ■

Great Basin Gold Ltd. (B.C. Dec. 31, 1997 amalg.)
June 28, 2013 – Placed into receivership. FTI Consulting Canada Inc. appointed receiver and all officers and directors resigned.
Feb. 2016 – FTI Consulting Canada Inc. discharged as receiver. No distrib. available for shldrs.
May 17, 2016 – Dissolved and struck from register.
Oct. 7, 2016 – Restored to registry.
Oct. 7, 2018 – Dissolved and struck from registry.

Great Basin Metal Mines Ltd. (Ont. 1965)
Aug. 22, 1973 – Charter cancelled.

Great Basins Petroleum Limited (B.C.)
1958 – Struck off register.

Great Bear Development Corp. (B.C. 1981)
June 24, 1988 – Dissolved and struck off register.

Great Bear Lake Mines Ltd. (Can. Sept. 12, 1931)
June 4, 1935 – Name changed to Athona Mines.

Great Bear Lake Syndicate Ltd. (Can. Feb. 17, 1931)
1931 – Name changed to Great Bear Lake Mines Ltd. ■

Great Bear Lake Uranium Mines Ltd. (Sask. 1953)
1962 – In liquidation. Assets subsequently acquired by Tri-West Oil & Gas Ltd.

Great Bear Mining Ltd. (Yuk. May 20, 1958)
May 18, 1977 – Name changed to Aries Resources Inc.; basis 1 new for 5 old shs. ■

Great Bear Resources Ltd. (B.C. Dec. 6, 2001)
June 22, 2007 – Name changed to Great Bear Uranium Corp. ■

Great Bear Resources Ltd. (B.C. Dec. 6, 2001)
Feb. 28, 2022 – Acquired by Kinross Gold Corporation; basis (i) Cdn$29.00 in cash or (ii) 3.8564 Kinross shs. for 1 Great Bear sh.

Great Bear Royalties Corp. (B.C. Jan. 31, 2020)
Sept. 12, 2022 – Acquired by Royal Gold, Inc. through wholly owned International Royalty Corporation; basis $6.65 per sh. cash.

Great Bear Silver Mines Limited (Ont. 1976)
Apr. 26, 1979 – Amalgamated with Fodac Mines Ltd. and Silver Monarch Mines Limited to form Frodac Consolidated Energy Resources Ltd.; basis 1 new for 10 old shs.

Great Bear Uranium Corp. (B.C. Dec. 6, 2001)
Jan. 29, 2010 – Name changed to Great Bear Resources Ltd. ■

Great Bend Oils Ltd. (Ont. 1943)
Dec. 1956 – Charter cancelled.

Great Bend Resource Corp. (Can. Sept. 27, 1985)
Apr. 28, 1993 – Name changed to Rockport Energy Corporation; basis 1 new for 2 old shs. ■

Great British Uranium Mines Ltd. (Alta. 1955)
Nov. 1960 – Dissolved.

Great Cameron Lake Resources Inc. (Ont. 1983)
Mar. 5, 1986 – Name changed to Cam-Turf Corporation; basis 1 new for 2 old shs. (see FPsurvey - Industrials)

Great Canadian Cider Exporters Ltd. (B.C. 1986)
Jan. 15, 1993 – Dissolved and struck off register.

Great Canadian Gaming Corporation (B.C. June 13, 1990)
Sept. 22, 2021 – Acquired by Raptor Acquisition Corp., an affiliate of funds managed by affiliates of Apollo Global Management, Inc., for $45 per sh.

Great Central Mines Ltd. (B.C. Aug. 20, 1968)
Mar. 17, 1993 – Name changed to Wedco Development Corp.; basis 1 new for 6 old shs. ■

Great Crow Mines Ltd. (Ont. 1947)
1948 – Name changed to Keelynn Mines Limited. ■

Great Dare Copper Co. Ltd. (Que. 1961)
Dec. 2, 1978 – Charter cancelled.

Great Divide Explorations Ltd. (Ont. 1963)
Mar. 20, 1968 – Charter cancelled.

Great Eagle Explorations and Holdings Limited (Ont. 1969)
Aug. 29, 1978 – Amalgamated with 3 other cos. to form Belle Aire Resource Explorations Limited; basis 10 com. shs. and 27 cl. A pf. shs. of Belle Aire for 100 shs. Great Eagle.

Great Eagle Gold Corp. (B.C. Oct. 7, 2019)
June 19, 2025 – Name changed to NatBridge Resources Ltd. (see FPsurvey - Mines & Energy)

The Great Eastern Corporation Limited (P.E.I. June 5, 1941)
Nov. 4, 2009 – Amalgamated with wholly owned The North Eastern Corporation Limited, whereby all o/s 5.5% first pref. and 4.5% first pref. shs. were redeemed for $10 per sh.

Great Eastern Financial Management of Canada Limited (Can. 1970)
Aug. 17, 1984 – Formed Greatok Group Ltd. following acquisition by Greatok Group Ltd.; basis 1 new for 4 old shs. ■

Great Eastern Oil & Import Co. Limited (N.L. 1926)
June 1984 – Name changed to Great Eastern Oil Limited.

Great Eastern Resources Canada Ltd. (Can. 1970)
Feb. 22, 1977 – Name changed to Great Eastern Financial Management of Canada Limited; basis 1 new for 10 old shs. ■

Great Expectations & Mines Ltd. (B.C. 1971)
Dec. 16, 1977 – Name changed to Great Explorations & Mines Ltd. ■

Great Explorations & Mines Ltd. (B.C. 1971)
Nov. 6, 1978 – Name changed to Shackleton Petroleum Corporation Ltd. ■

Great Falls Mining & Smelting Ltd. (Man. Oct. 27, 1935)
1937 – Assets acquired by Stanmore Mining and Smelting Ltd.

Great Fortress Resources Inc. (Ont. Sept. 22, 1987)
Sept. 15, 1994 – Continued into Canada.
July 7, 1995 – Formed Akrokeri-Ashanti Gold Mines Inc. in Ontario on amalgamation with Akrokeri-Ashanti Gold Mines Inc. ■

Great Grandad Resources Limited (Can. Mar. 1, 1978)
July 4, 2007 – Name changed to GGD Resources Inc.; basis 1 new for 6.8 old shs. ■

Great Hercules Resources Inc. (B.C. Aug. 1, 1969)
Apr. 4, 1979 – Name changed to Pacific Coast Funding & Resources Inc. ■

Great Icelandic Water Corporation (B.C. 1983)
Oct. 28, 1992 – Continued into Canada.
June 10, 2004 – Dissolved.

Great Indian Explorations Ltd. (Ont. 1970)
Aug. 11, 1972 – Amalgamated into Staple Mining Co. Ltd.; basis 1 new for 7 old shs.

Great Lakes Carbon Income Fund (Ont. June 25, 2003)
May 10, 2007 – Acquired indirectly by Oxbow Carbon and Minerals Holdings, Inc. for $14 per unit.

Great Lakes Forest Products Limited (Ont. Apr. 3, 1936)
June 7, 1988 – Name changed to Canadian Pacific Forest Products Limited following amalgamation with CIP Inc., a wholly owned subsid. of Canadian Pacific Limited. ■

Great Lakes Group Inc. (Ont. Oct. 17, 1969)
June 1, 1992 – Name changed to Great Lakes Power Inc. ■

Great Lakes Hydro Income Fund (Que. Sept. 14, 1999)
Sept. 2, 2009 – Name changed to Brookfield Renewable Power Fund. ■

Great Lakes Iron Mines Ltd. (Ont. 1943)
Oct. 1, 1956 – Charter cancelled.

Great Lakes Minerals Inc. (Ont. Nov. 28, 1989)
Feb. 18, 1998 – Name changed to Communicorp Corporation following acquisition of all o/s shs. of Communicorp Multimedia Inc.; basis 1 new for 20 old shs. ■

Great Lakes Minerals Inc. (Ont. Nov. 28, 1989)
Mar. 18, 1998 – Amalgamated with Communicorp Multimedia Inc. to form Communicorp Corporation.

Great Lakes Nickel Corp. Ltd. (Ont. 1955)
1969 – Amalgamated with Thunder Bay Nickel Mining Corp. Ltd. to form Great Lakes Nickel Ltd.

Great Lakes Paper Company, Limited (Ont. Apr. 3, 1936)
Jan. 1, 1979 – Name changed to Great Lakes Forest Products Limited. ■

Great Lakes Power Corporation Limited (Ont. 1949)
1973 – Brascan Ltd. acquired virtually all o/s com. shs. of the co. at $30 or 1 conv. 6% pref. sh. for 1 old sh.

Great Lakes Power Inc. (Ont. Oct. 17, 1969)
Mar. 13, 2001 – Privatized via amalgamation with wholly owned subsid. of Brascan Corporation for $21 per sh.
Dec. 1, 2004 – Name changed to Brascan Power Inc. ■

Great Lakes Pure Aire Smelting Corporation Limited (Can. Nov. 17, 1971)
Apr. 26, 1979 – Name changed to Diepdaume Mines Limited. ■

Great Lakes Silver Holdings Limited (Ont. July 20, 1967)
Mar. 20, 1981 – Continued into Canada.
Dec. 22, 1982 – Name changed to Springlake Resources Limited. ■

Great Lakes Silver Mines Limited (Ont. July 20, 1967)
June 13, 1974 – Name changed to Great Lakes Silver Holdings Limited. ■

Great Larder Gold Mines Ltd. (Ont. 1948)
Nov. 10, 1966 – Dissolved.

Great Laurier Uranium Mines Ltd. (Ont. 1969)
Mar. 1976 – Charter cancelled.

Great Molly Explorations and Enterprises Ltd. (Ont. 1967)
1969 – Merged into Great Eagle Explorations and Holdings Ltd.

Great Molly Explorations Ltd. (Ont. 1967)
1967 – Merged into Great Molly Explorations and Enterprises Ltd.; basis 1 new for 3 old shs.

Great Mountain Iron Corp. (Que. 1948)
May 11, 1974 – Charter cancelled.

Great National Land and Investment Corp. Ltd. (B.C. 1963)
June 16, 1987 – Insolvent. Creditors were disposing of all assets.

Great Northern Capital Company, Ltd. (Can. 1950)
Aug. 7, 1964 – All o/s pref. shs. and debs. redeemed. (see Great Northern Capital Corporation Limited; Lakeland Natural Gas Limited)
Aug. 21, 1964 – Initial distribution of assets, made to shldrs. of record, consisted of 1 new sh. of Great Northern Capital Corporation Limited, 0.26 new sh. of Lakeland Natural Gas and $2.20 for 1 com. sh. of Great Northern Capital Co. (see Great Northern Capital Corporation Limited; Lakeland Natural Gas Limited)
1965 – Final distribution of cash of 15.3666¢ per sh. (see Great Northern Capital Corporation Limited; Lakeland Natural Gas Limited)

Great Northern Capital Corporation Limited (Ont. 1954)
Apr. 29, 1974 – Amalgamated with Western Realty Projects Ltd. to form Abbey Glen Property Corp.; basis 1.5 new for 1 old sh.

Great Northern Energy Metals Inc. (B.C. Oct. 5, 2022)
July 31, 2025 – Name changed to American Atomics Inc. (see FPsurvey - Mines & Energy)

Great Northern Exploration Ltd. (Alta. Mar. 30, 1978)
June 9, 2004 – Acquired by APF Energy Trust; basis either 0.414614 new APF trust unit or, $1.573252 plus 0.285447 new APF trust unit for 1 old Great Northern com. sh. (see APF Energy Trust)

Great Northern Financial Corporation (Ont. 1926)
Aug. 12, 1983 – Amalgamated into Embassy Resources Ltd.; basis 1 new for 1 old sh. (see Embassy Resources Ltd.)

Great Northern Gas Utilities Ltd. (Can. 1950)
1962 – Name changed to Great Northern Capital Company, Ltd. ■

Great Northern Gas Utilities Ltd. (Can. 1962)
Feb. 9, 1979 – Name changed to ICG Utilities Ltd. ■

Great Northern Gold Exploration Corporation (B.C. July 27, 2009)
May 5, 2014 – Name changed to Poydras Gaming Finance Corp. and continued into Ontario following reverse takeover acquisition of Poydras Specialty Finance Corp. ■

Great Northern Gold Inc. (Alta. Dec. 21, 1989 amalg.)
Feb. 6, 1992 – Amalgamated with 499804 Alberta Ltd., a wholly owned subsid. of Ascentex Energy Inc.; basis 1 Ascentex sh. for 16.04 Great Northern shs. (see Ascentex Energy, Inc.)

Great Northern Petroleums & Mines Ltd. (B.C. Jan. 26, 1961)
Mar. 5, 1991 – Name changed to GNP Oil & Gas Ltd.; basis 1 new for 5 old shs. (see FPsurvey - Mines & Energy)

Great Northland Development Ltd. (Sask. 1955)
Oct. 2, 1959 – Struck off register.

Great Northwest Resources Corp. (B.C. July 6, 1983)
Aug. 5, 1993 – Name changed to Quadrant Financial Corporation. ■

Great Oak Enterprises Ltd. (Can. Dec. 27, 2017)
Dec. 23, 2021 – Name changed to Mijem Newcomm Tech Inc. pursuant to the reverse takeover acquisition of Mijem Inc. and concurrent amalgamation of Great Oak with wholly owned 2845964 Ontario Inc. (see FPsurvey - Industrials)

Great Pacific Enterprises Inc. (B.C. May 29, 1992)
July 7, 1997 – Acquired by Jim Pattison Industries Ltd. for $80 per sh.

Great Pacific Industries Inc. (Ont. 1927)
1981 – Continued into British Columbia.

Great Pacific Industries Ltd. (B.C. 1959)
Feb. 12, 1975 – Name changed to G.P.I. Industries Limited; basis 1 new for 4 old shs. ■

Great Pacific International Inc. (Alta. Nov. 4, 1993)
Oct. 4, 2012 – Name changed to WesCan Energy Corp.; basis 1 new for 20 old shs. (see FPsurvey - Mines & Energy)

Great Pacific Resources Inc. (B.C. Mar. 19, 1979)
Nov. 17, 1994 – Name changed to Micro Minerals Resources Inc.; basis 1 new for 6.5 old shs. ■

Great Panther Inc. (Yuk. Apr. 11, 1996)
Oct. 2, 2003 – Name changed to Great Panther Resources Limited; basis 1 new for 10 old shs. ■

Great Panther Mining Limited (B.C. July 9, 2004)
Dec. 16, 2022 – Voluntarily assigned into bankruptcy, terminating proceedings under the Companies' Creditors Arrangement Act (CCAA). Alvarez & Marsal Canada Inc. appointed insolvency trustee.

Great Panther Resources Limited (Yuk. Apr. 11, 1996)
July 9, 2004 – Continued into British Columbia.
Jan. 1, 2010 – Name changed to Great Panther Silver Limited. ■

Great Panther Silver Limited (B.C. July 9, 2004)
Mar. 5, 2019 – Name changed to Great Panther Mining Limited following acquisition of Beadell Resources Limited. ■

Great Pine Mines Ltd. (Ont. 1965)
Mar. 1976 – Charter cancelled.

Great Plains Development Company of Canada (Can. 1950)
Jan. 1, 1975 – Acquired by Burmah Oil Canada Ltd. in 1974. Through purch. offer of $40 per sh., the company was purchased by Canadian Industrial Gas & Oil Ltd. from Burmah for the account of Norcen Energy Resources Ltd.

Great Plains Exploration Inc. (Can. Mar. 4, 2004)
June 17, 2008 – Continued into Alberta. (see Avenir Diversified Income Trust)
Nov. 11, 2010 – Acquired by Avenir Diversified Income Trust; basis 0.088 Avenir trust units or 0.088 Avenir exch. shs. for 1 Great Plains sh. (see Avenir Diversified Income Trust)

Great Plains Waste Management Inc. (Alta. Aug. 27, 1987 amalg.)
Feb. 1, 1992 – Struck off register.

Great Prairie Energy Services Inc. (Alta. Feb. 4, 2011)
Jan. 22, 2016 – Assigned into receivership. Grant Thornton Limited appointed receiver and all officers and directors resigned.
Aug. 2, 2017 – Struck from registry and dissolved.

Great Quest Fertilizer Ltd. (B.C. Mar. 10, 1989)
July 29, 2024 – Name changed to Great Quest Gold Ltd. (see FPsurvey - Mines & Energy)

Great Quest Metals Ltd. (B.C. Mar. 10, 1989)
June 9, 2014 – Name changed to Great Quest Fertilizer Ltd. ■

Great Shield Uranium Mines Ltd. (Ont. 1954)
Dec. 10, 1962 – Dissolved.

Great Slave Mines Ltd. (B.C. 1965)
Apr. 6, 1972 – Name changed to Alaska Kenai Oils Ltd.; basis 1 new for 10 old shs. ■

Great Southern Enterprises Corp. (B.C. Jan. 24, 1983)
Mar. 29, 2010 – Name changed to Balmoral Resources Ltd.; basis 1 new for 15 old shs. ■

Great Sweet Grass Oils Ltd. (Ont. 1943)
1962 – Name changed to Kardar Canadian Oils Ltd.; basis 1 new for 5 old shs. ■

Great Thunder Gold Corp. (B.C. Apr. 12, 1977)
Oct. 1, 2021 – Name changed to Newfoundland Discovery Corp. (see FPsurvey - Mines & Energy)

Great Valley Exploration & Mining Co. Ltd. (Que. 1956)
1967 – Merged into Resource Exploration & Development Co. Ltd.; basis 100 new for 237 old shs.

Great Weighs! Industries Inc. (B.C. Nov. 22, 1983)
Jan. 9, 1989 – Delisted from the Vancouver Stock Exchange. Subsequently struck from register and dissolved for failure to file.

The Great West Coal Company, Limited (Alta. 1911)
May 19, 1954 – Placed into liquidation.
Jan. 24, 1955 – Liquidator's final account filed.
June 15, 1955 – Struck off register.

Great West Coal Co. Ltd. (Can. 1917)
1964 – All o/s cl. B sh. acquired by Loram Coal Ltd. for $5.85 per sh.

The Great-West Life Assurance Company (Can. Aug. 28, 1891)
Dec. 21, 1999 – 97.4% interest in the company was acquired by Great-West Lifeco Inc. on June 12, 1986, under a reorganization. Great-West Lifeco increased interest to 99.5% in 1989 and 1990. The remaining 0.4% was purchased by Great-West Lifeco for $5,200, 233.18 com. shs. of Great-West Lifeco, 208.84 cl. A pref. shs., ser. 1, of Great-West Lifeco, or a combination of cash and shs. based on sh. prices of $22.30 per com. sh. or $24.90 per pref. sh.
Oct. 31, 2010 – All 7.7% pref. ser.A shs. redeemed Sept. 30, 1997, at $25 per sh.; 7.8% pref. ser.B shs. redeemed

Dec. 31, 1992, at $25.50 per sh.; and 5.55% pref. ser.O shs. redeemed Oct. 31, 2010, at $25 per sh.
Jan. 1, 2020 – Amalgamated with wholly owned London Life Insurance Company and The Canada Life Assurance Company plus holding cos. Canada Life Financial Corporation and London Insurance Group Inc. to continue as The Canada Life Assurance Company.

Great West Mining and Smelting Corp. Ltd. (Ont. 1956)
Mar. 1976 – Charter cancelled.

Great West Mining Corp. Ltd. (B.C. June 23, 1961)
Feb. 13, 1970 – Name changed to Four Seasons Recreation Ltd.; basis 1 new for 10 old shs. ∎

Great West Saddlery Ltd. (Can. 1928)
Mar. 18, 1970 – Name changed to Great West International Equities Ltd.

Great West Steel Industries Ltd. (B.C. July 15, 1969)
Apr. 18, 1988 – Name changed to Gwil Industries Inc. ∎

Great West Uranium Mines Ltd. (Sask. 1950)
Sept. 27, 1963 – Struck off register.

Great Western Diamonds Corp. (B.C. July 23, 2002)
Oct. 25, 2006 – Continued into Canada.
Mar. 12, 2008 – Acquired by Vaaldiam Resources Ltd.; basis 0.45 Vaaldiam shs. for 1 Great Western sh.

Great Western Gold Corp. (B.C. Sept. 30, 1983)
Aug. 14, 2002 – Name changed to Great Western Minerals Group Ltd. ∎

Great Western Minerals Group Ltd. (B.C. Sept. 30, 1983)
Dec. 12, 2007 – Continued into Canada.
Dec. 3, 2015 – Assignment in bankruptcy filed under the Bankruptcy and Insolvency Act (BIA). PricewaterhouseCoopers Inc. appointed trustee.

Great Western Oils Limited (Sask.)
1959 – Struck off register.

Great Western Petroleum Corporation (B.C. Apr. 14, 1978)
Aug. 7, 1985 – Name changed to Cassidy Resources Ltd.; basis 1 new for 3 old shs. ∎

Great World Resources Ltd. (B.C. 1968)
July 10, 1992 – Dissolved and struck off register.

Great Yellowknife Mines Ltd. (Ont. 1945)
1952 – Charter cancelled.

Great Yukon Mines Ltd. (Ont. 1966)
1967 – Merged into The Great Molly Explorations and Enterprises Ltd.; basis 1 new for 4 old shs. ∎

Greatbanks Resources Ltd. (B.C. Dec. 20, 1996)
Feb. 19, 2015 – Continued into Ontario.
Apr. 9, 2019 – Continued into British Columbia.
Oct. 24, 2019 – Name changed to Goldhills Holding Ltd. (see FPsurvey - Mines & Energy)

Greater Canada Mines Ltd. (Ont. Feb. 5, 1934)
Dec. 18, 1936 – Merged into Maralgo Mines Limited; basis 1 new for 10 old shs. (see Maralgo Mines Limited)

Greater China Capital Inc. (Ont. Feb. 18, 2010)
July 9, 2012 – Name changed to Golden Bridge Mining Corporation pursuant to Qualifying Transaction acquisition of option to earn 50% interest in Hebecourt gold prospect. ∎

Greater Lenora Resources Corp. (Ont. Dec. 31, 1988 amalg.)
May 3, 2001 – Continued into Canada.
July 24, 2001 – Name changed to GVIC Communications Inc. pursuant to reorganization whereby 3796299 Canada Inc. (wholly owned by Glacier Ventures International Corp.) acquired 45% of the vtg. shs. and 55% of the non-vtg. shs. of Greater Lenora and Greater Lenora's mining assets were spun out in the form of new co. GLR Resources Inc. (formerly 3851419 Canada Inc.); basis 1

cl. A vtg. and 1 cl. B non-vtg. sh. of GVIC plus 1 GLR cl. A vtg. sh. for 1 Greater Lenora com. sh. ∎

The Greater Montreal Central Market Co. Ltd. (Que. 1948)
1983 – Name changed to Marché Central Métropolitain Inc. / Metropolitan Central Market Inc. ∎

Greater Temagami Mines Ltd. (B.C. June 14, 1985)
Jan. 28, 1994 – Name changed to Max Communications Corp. following acquisition of Max Communications Ltd. ∎

Greater Winnipeg Gas Company (Man. 1953)
Jan. 1, 1990 – Name changed to ICG Utilities (Manitoba) Ltd. following acquisition of ICG Utilities (Manitoba) Ltd. and subsequent amalgamation of the 2 companies. ∎

Greatlakes Copper Mines Ltd. (Ont. 1945)
1958 – Merged into Andover Mining & Exploration Ltd.; basis 1 new for 4 old shs. ∎

Greatok Group Ltd. (Can. 1970)
Aug. 27, 1997 – Charter cancelled and dissolved.

Greb Industries Ltd. (Ont. 1930)
May 1, 1974 – All o/s cl. B and C pref. shs. acquired by Warrington Products Ltd. for $16.50 per sh. (see Warrington Products Limited)
1980 – Merged with Warrington Products Ltd and continued under the Warrington Products Ltd. name. (see Warrington Products Limited)

Grecian Specialty Foods Inc. (Alta. Apr. 2, 1993)
Oct. 2, 2001 – Struck from registry and dissolved.

Greek Canadian Mines Limited (Ont. 1955)
Oct. 19, 1994 – Name changed to Biogenetic Technologies Inc.; basis 1 new for 2 old shs. ∎

Green Axis Capital Corp. (B.C. Feb. 25, 1985)
Jan. 10, 2019 – Name changed to Ignite International Brands, Ltd.; basis 1 new for 5 old shs. ∎

Green Battery Minerals Inc. (B.C. Jan. 15, 1979)
June 20, 2025 – Name changed to First Canadian Graphite Inc. (see FPsurvey - Mines & Energy)

Green Bay Mining & Exploration Ltd. (Alta. 1955)
Aug. 1974 – Charter cancelled.

Green Bay Uranium Limited (Alta. 1955)
Oct. 1955 – Name changed to Green Bay Mining & Exploration Ltd. ∎

Green Bluff Copper Mines Ltd. (B.C. Nov. 21, 1972)
Nov. 6, 1987 – Delisted from the Vancouver Stock Exchange. Subsequently struck from register and dissolved.

Green Coast Resources Limited (Que. Feb. 4, 1958)
Sept. 1988 – Name changed to Ridgepoint Resources Ltd. ∎

Green Diamond Oil Corporation (Ont. Dec. 20, 1982)
Nov. 18, 1991 – Name changed to Can-Med Technology Inc.; basis 1 new for 6 old shs. (see FPsurvey - Industrials)

Green Eagle Mines Ltd. (B.C. Mar. 12, 1970)
Mar. 1, 1976 – Name changed to Northern Eagle Mines Ltd. ∎

Green Forest Lumber Corporation (Ont. 1978)
Feb. 7, 1995 – Acquired by MacMillan Bloedel Limited for $12.50 per sh. (see MacMillan Bloedel Limited)

Green Forest Lumber International (Ont. 1978)
Mar. 1987 – Name changed to Green Forest Lumber Corporation. ∎

Green Growth Brands Inc. (Ont. Nov. 24, 1999)
May 20, 2020 – Filed for protection under the Companies' Creditors Arrangement Act and Ernst & Young Inc. was appointed monitor.
Mar. 31, 2021 – Sale transaction between the company, All Js Greenspace LLC and Capital Transfer Agency, ULC, was completed including the vesting in a newly incorporated entity all of the company's right, title and interest in and to all the purchased assets. The sale transaction was structured as a credit bid and no funds were available for distribution to shldrs. The company no longer has any assets or active business and will be wound down.
June 17, 2021 – Assigned into bankruptcy and Ernst & Young Inc. appointed trustee.

Green Hurst Mines Ltd. (Ont. 1966)
1967 – Merged into W.G.N. Explorations & Holdings Ltd.; basis 1 new for 8 old shs. ∎

Green Ice Corporation (B.C. Sept. 28, 1992)
July 21, 1999 – Name changed to International Green Ice Inc.; basis 1 new for 5 old shs. ∎

Green Lake Gold Mines Ltd. (Ont. 1946)
Nov. 6, 1961 – Dissolved.

Green Lake Resources Ltd. (B.C. May 3, 1984)
Mar. 4, 1992 – Delisted from the Vancouver Stock Exchange. Subsequently dissolved for failure to file.
June 18, 1993 – Name changed to Thunderbird Development Corp.; basis 1 new for 4 old shs.

Green Light Metals Inc. (B.C. Apr. 8, 2020)
Apr. 8, 2025 – Name changed to GreenLight Metals Inc. (see FPsurvey - Mines & Energy)

Green Line Business Stores Inc. (Utah 1982)
Jan. 5, 1995 – Name changed to Rico Resources Ltd.

Green Maple Energy Inc. (Alta. June 16, 1993)
Nov. 29, 2001 – Name changed to Overlord Financial Inc. ∎

Green Oil Ltd. (Alta. Apr. 8, 1987)
Sept. 20, 1990 – Name changed to Koval Resources Ltd. ∎

The Green Organic Dutchman Holdings Ltd. (Can. Nov. 16, 2016)
Feb. 23, 2023 – Name changed to BZAM Ltd. (see FPsurvey - Industrials)

Green Park Capital Corp. (B.C. June 4, 2007)
Mar. 25, 2011 – Name changed to Josephine Mining Corp. pursuant to Qualifying Transaction reverse takeover acquisition of (old) Josephine Mining Corp.; basis 1 new for 5 old shs. ∎

Green Point Mines Ltd. (Ont. 1945)
Mar. 1976 – Charter cancelled.

Green Point Resources Inc. (B.C. Dec. 10, 1996)
Oct. 19, 2000 – Name changed to Wildcard Wireless Solutions Inc. pursuant to reverse takeover acquisition of Wildcard Communications Canada Inc.; basis 1 new for 2 old shs. ∎

Green Rise Capital Corporation (Ont. June 9, 2017)
Sept. 2, 2020 – Name changed to Green Rise Foods Inc. (see FPsurvey - Industrials)

Green River Holdings Inc. (Alta. May 21, 1993)
Oct. 3, 2000 – Name changed to Netco Energy Inc.; basis 1 new for 2 old shs. ∎

Green River Petroleum Inc. (Alta. May 21, 1993)
Sept. 13, 1999 – Name changed to Green River Holdings Inc.; basis 1 new for 5 old shs. ∎

Green River Resources Ltd. (B.C. Apr. 7, 1981)
July 3, 1986 – Name changed to Canus Laboratories Ltd. ∎

Green Standard Vanadium Resources Corp. (B.C.)
Apr. 24, 2016 – Dissolved and struck from register.

Green Swan Capital Corp. (Can. Apr. 29, 2008)
Apr. 24, 2017 – Continued into Ontario.
June 12, 2017 – Name changed to CBLT Inc. (see FPsurvey - Mines & Energy)

Green 2 Blue Energy Corp. (B.C. Oct. 9, 2014)
Oct. 26, 2020 – Name changed to G2 Technologies Corp. ■

Green Valley Mine Incorporated (B.C. July 8, 1977)
Sept. 21, 2018 – Name changed to Skychain Technologies Inc. (see FPsurvey - Industrials)

Green Valley Mines Ltd. (Ont. 1966)
1969 – Merged into Alchib Developments Ltd.; basis 29 new for 100 old shs.

GreenAngel Energy Corp. (B.C. Oct. 26, 2007)
Sept. 23, 2015 – Name changed to Timia Capital Corp. ■

Greenbank Ventures Inc. (B.C. May 26, 1969)
Dec. 16, 2024 – Voluntarily delisted. (see FPsurvey - Industrials)

Greenberg Stores Ltd. (Can. 1946)
1967 – Acquired by Metropolitan Stores of Canada Ltd., following purch. offer of $8.00 per sh.

Greenbriar Capital Corp. (B.C. Apr. 2, 2009)
Nov. 14, 2023 – Name changed to Greenbriar Sustainable Living Inc. (see FPsurvey - Industrials)

Greenbridge Gold Mines Ltd. (Can. 1938)
Jan. 1943 – Dissolved.

Greenbrook TMS Inc. (Ont. Feb. 9, 2018)
Dec. 9, 2024 – Acquired by Neuronetics, Inc.; basis 0.01021 Neuronetics shs. for 1 Greenbrook sh.

Greenfield Acquisition Corp. (B.C. Jan. 19, 2021)
Sept. 20, 2022 – Name changed to Inspire Semiconductor Holdings Inc. following Qualifying Transaction three-cornered amalgamation with Inspire Semiconductor, Inc. constituting a reverse takeover acquisition by Inspire. ■

Greenfield Commercial Credit (Canada) Inc. (Ont. July 9, 1997)
Aug. 16, 2005 – Name changed to Greenfield Financial Group Inc. following reorganization. ■

Greenfield Financial Group Inc. (Ont. July 9, 1997)
Jan. 18, 2012 – Name changed to Wheels Group Inc. pursuant to reverse takeover acquisition of Logistics Holdings International Inc., Wheels Holdco Inc. and Bluenose Holdings (Ontario) Inc. ■

Greenfields Development Corp. Ltd. (B.C. 1965)
Nov. 15, 1976 – Dissolved.

Greenfields Industries Inc. (B.C. May 19, 1981)
Dec. 6, 1993 – Name changed to Oracle Minerals Inc.; basis 1 new for 2 old shs. ■

Greenfields Petroleum Corporation (Tex. Nov. 28, 2007)
Feb. 19, 2010 – Continued into Delaware.
Aug. 18, 2011 – Continued into Cayman Islands.

GreenFirst Forest Products Inc. (B.C. Sept. 17, 1979)
Feb. 23, 2022 – Continued into Ontario. (see FPsurvey - Industrials)

Greenflag Ventures Inc. (B.C. Nov. 25, 2009)
Aug. 6, 2015 – Amalgamated in British Columbia to continue with same name.
Mar. 18, 2016 – Name changed to Prosalutis Holdings Inc. ■

Greenhope Resources Inc. (Can. Mar. 31, 1995)
June 27, 2000 – Name changed to Head4 Solutions Inc. following acquisition of 3695336 Canada Inc. (Head4 Solutions). ■

Greening Industries Limited (Can. 1923)
1964 – Acquired by Donald Ropes & Wire Cloth Ltd. for $4.00 per sh.

Greenland Exploration Company Ltd. (Alta. 1971 amalg.)
Feb. 18, 1980 – Name changed to Pac-West Industries Ltd. ■

Greenland Mining Ltd. (B.C. 1970)
Nov. 1976 – Charter cancelled.

Greenlaw Developments Ltd. (Ont. 1972)
Mar. 1973 – Amalgamated with 2 other cos. to form Newore Developments Ltd.; basis 1 new for 2.5 old shs.

Greenlee Mines Ltd. (Ont. 1936)
Nov. 1954 – Assets acquired by New Athona Mines Ltd.; basis 1 new for 8 old shs. (see New Athona Mines Ltd.)

Greenlight Resources Inc. (B.C. Feb. 24, 1997)
June 19, 2012 – Name changed to Great Atlantic Resources Corp. (see FPsurvey - Mines & Energy)

Greenoaks Mines Ltd. (Ont. 1946)
Nov. 28, 1973 – Charter cancelled.

Greenock Resources Inc. (Ont. July 15, 1994)
May 22, 2015 – Continued into British Columbia.
Feb. 3, 2016 – Name changed to BeWhere Holdings, Inc. following reverse takeover acquisition of BeWhere Inc. (see FPsurvey - Industrials)

Greenray Mines Limited (Ont. 1950)
Jan. 1960 – Charter cancelled.

GreenRidez 4.0 Acquisitions Corp. (B.C. Feb. 2, 2021)
June 23, 2021 – Name changed to Birchtree Investments Inc. ■

Greenridez 2.0 Acquisitions Corp. (B.C. Oct. 14, 2020)
Feb. 4, 2022 – Name changed to Lophos Holdings Inc. pursuant to the reverse takeover acquisition of Lophos Pharmaceuticals Corp. (see FPsurvey - Industrials)

Greenscape Capital Group Inc. (B.C. Dec. 6, 2006)
Sept. 11, 2013 – Name changed to Parkit Enterprise Inc.; basis 1 new for 10 old shs. ■

Greenshield Explorations Limited (Ont. Oct. 20, 2002 amalg.)
Oct. 19, 2007 – Continued into British Columbia.
Sept. 24, 2019 – Name changed to PEZM Gold Inc.; basis 1 new for 20 old shs. (see FPsurvey - Mines & Energy)

Greenshield Resources Inc. (Ont. July 7, 1995)
Oct. 20, 2002 – Formed Greenshield Resources Ltd. in Ontario pursuant to plan of arrangement amalgamation with Providence Resources Inc. to form new co. with same name Greenshield Resources Inc. whose shs. were then exchanged for shs. of Greenshield Resources Ltd. which became parent co. ■

Greenshield Resources Ltd. (Ont. Oct. 20, 2002 amalg.)
June 13, 2006 – Name changed to Greenshield Explorations Limited; basis 1 new for 20 old shs. ■

Greenskeeper, Inc. (Ont. 1971)
1978 – Placed into bankruptcy.
Apr. 30, 1979 – All assets of the co. were sold and distribution made to secured creditors. No distribution to shldrs.

GreenSpace Brands Inc. (Ont. June 11, 2013)
Apr. 6, 2023 – Filed for protection under the Companies' Creditors Arrangement Act (CCAA) and PricewaterhouseCoopers Inc. was appointed monitor.
June 2023 – Love Child Organics assets sold to Nature's Path Foods Inc. for monies sufficient to satisfy the term loan from Pivot Financial I Limited Partnership and other incidentals related to the CCAA filing. In addition, certain assets of Central Roast Inc. were sold to The Health and Beauty Distributor Inc. No monies were available for distrib. to shldrs. All directors and majority of the officers resigned.
Sept. 26, 2023 – The CCAA distribution and termination order was issued.
Nov. 22, 2023 – Assigned into bankruptcy. PricewaterhouseCoopers Inc. assigned as trustee.

GreenStar Agricultural Corporation (Ont. Aug. 7, 2007)
May 5, 2015 – Dissolved and struck from register.

GreenStar Biosciences Corp. (B.C. May 13, 2010)
Nov. 16, 2020 – Name changed to Lobe Sciences Ltd. (see FPsurvey - Industrials)

Greenstar Resources Ltd. (Can. Apr. 29, 1987)
Mar. 9, 1993 – Name changed to Greenstar Telecommunications Inc. ■

Greenstar Telecommunications Inc. (Can. Apr. 29, 1987)
Mar. 9, 1995 – Name changed to GST Telecommunications, Inc. ■

Greenstone Capital Corp. (Alta. June 6, 2018)
Sept. 29, 2021 – Name changed to Comprehensive Healthcare Systems Inc. pursuant to the Qualifying Transaction reverse takeover acquisition of (old) Comprehensive Healthcare Systems Inc.; basis 1 new for 3.5322575 old shs. (see FPsurvey - Industrials)

Greenstone Resources Ltd. (B.C. May 3, 1983)
Dec. 30, 1987 – Continued into Canada.
Mar. 9, 2000 – Declared bankrupt. Shimmerman, Penn, Title & Associates Inc. was appointed trustee.

Greenstreet Equities Inc. (Alta. Sept. 29, 1997)
Mar. 2, 2004 – Struck from registry and dissolved.

Greenstrike Gold Corp. (Ont. 1985)
Oct. 13, 1989 – Formed IATCO Industries Inc. in Ontario on amalgamation with 846241 Ontario Limited. ■

Greenswan Ventures Inc. (B.C. Aug. 7, 1986)
Feb. 23, 1995 – Name changed to Canbras Communications Corp. ■

Greentree Energy Inc. (B.C. July 23, 1980)
Dec. 28, 1990 – Name changed to STS Power Pedal Corp.; basis 1 new for 3 old shs. ■

Greenwell Resources Corporation (B.C. Feb. 9, 1982)
Oct. 27, 1987 – Delisted from the Vancouver Stock Exchange. Subsequently dissolved for failure to file.

Greenwich Global Capital Inc. (Ont. Feb. 11, 2005)
Dec. 18, 2009 – Name changed to Xinergy Ltd. pursuant to Qualifying Transaction reverse takeover acquisition of Xinergy Corp.; basis 1 new for 19.92 old shs. ■

Greenwich Lake Exploration Ltd. (Ont. 1977)
Mar. 17, 1983 – Name changed to G.L.E. Resources Ltd. ■

Greenwich Petroleums Ltd. (Alta. 1952)
Jan. 1953 – Acquired by American Petroleum Industries Canada Ltd. In voluntary liquidation. (see American Petroleum Industries Canada Ltd.)

Greenwich Resources Inc. (B.C. 1979)
1985 – Acquired by Greenwich Resources plc of England; basis 1 Greenwich Resources plc sh. for 1 Greenwich Resources Inc. sh.

Greenwich Silver Mines Ltd. (Ont. 1969)
Feb. 1974 – Charter cancelled.

Greenwood Environmental Inc. (Can. May 15, 1987)
Jan. 2, 2003 – Dissolved.

Greenwood Explorations Ltd. (B.C. July 17, 1974)
Jan. 12, 1983 – Name changed to United Greenwood Explorations Ltd.; basis 1 new for 5 old shs. ■

Greenwood Ventures Corporation (Alta. June 16, 1986)
Aug. 30, 1991 – Name changed to Norwich Ventures Ltd.; basis 1 new for 5 old shs. ■

Gregor Goldfields Corp. (Ont. June 17, 1983)
Feb. 16, 1998 – Name changed to Aavdex Corporation; basis 1 new for 8 old shs. ■

Gregory Exploration Ltd. (Alta. July 24, 1989)
Mar. 4, 1992 – Name changed to Global Mineral & Chemical Ltd. ■

Gregory Industries Limited (B.C. May 27, 1963)
Apr. 24, 1986 – Name changed to Primex Forest Industries Ltd. ■

Grenache Inc. (Que. 1963)
1973 – Québec-Lait Inc., a controlled subsid. of Cooperative Agricole de Granby, acquired all o/s com. shs. for $7.97 per sh.

Grenadier Resource Corp. (B.C. June 2, 2014)
Sept. 18, 2015 – Name changed to Laguna Blends Inc. pursuant to the reverse takeover acquisition of (old) Laguna Blends Inc. ■

Grenfell Acquisitions Inc. (Can. May 27, 1987)
Jan. 20, 1994 – Name changed to International Grenfell Acquisitions Inc.; basis 1 new for 5 old shs. ■

Grenfell-Kirkland Gold Mines Ltd. (Ont. 1945)
1946 – Name changed to Grengold Mines Ltd.; basis 1 new for 2 old shs. ■

Grengold Mines Ltd. (Ont. 1945)
Dec. 10, 1962 – Dissolved.

Grenlard Kirkland Mines Ltd. (Ont. 1937)
Oct. 16, 1952 – Charter cancelled.

Grenloch Energy Inc. (B.C. 1979)
Jan. 14, 1994 – Dissolved and struck off register.

Grenmac Silver Mines Ltd. (B.C. 1967)
1971 – Name changed to Buckeye Explorations Ltd.; basis 1 new for 3 old shs. ■

Grenoble Energy Limited (B.C. 1979)
Oct. 30, 1984 – Name changed to Grenloch Energy Inc.; basis 1 new for 5 old shs. ■

Grenview Corp. (Ont. Nov. 17, 1995)
Jan. 9, 1997 – Name changed to LINMOR Inc. ■

Grenville Gold Corporation (Ont. Nov. 17, 1994)
June 19, 2009 – Continued into British Columbia.
Dec. 24, 2010 – Name changed to Grenville Gold Corp.; basis 1 new for 10 old shs. ■

Grenville Gold Corp. (B.C. June 19, 2009)
Mar. 1, 2019 – Name changed to Sierra Growth Corp. ■

Grenville Mining Ltd. (Que. 1957)
Feb. 1976 – Charter cancelled.

Grenville Strategic Royalty Corp. (B.C. Dec. 2, 1935)
June 11, 2018 – Acquired by LOGiQ Asset Management Inc.; basis 6.25 LOGiQ com. shs. for 1 Grenville sh.

Gresham Resources Inc. (B.C. Oct. 5, 1987)
Aug. 15, 2002 – Acquired by True Energy Inc.; basis 1.4 True Energy shs. for 1 Gresham sh. (see True Energy Inc.)

Grew Ventures Inc. (N.B. Aug. 25, 1993)
Feb. 14, 2005 – Dissolved and struck from register.

Grey & Bruce Trust & Savings Co. (unknown)
Nov. 1950 – Amalgamated into Victoria & Grey Trust Co.; basis 5 new for 1 old sh.

Grey Goose Corporation Limited (Ont. 1961)
1979 – Continued into Canada.
Apr. 26, 1985 – Redeemed all o/s 9.75% 1st pfce. shs., ser. A, at $10.30 per sh. on Feb. 28, 1985. On Mar. 1, 1985, co. offered to acquire all of the 172,500 o/s com. shs. not held by the co. or its affils., at $30 per sh. For the purposes of the offer, shs. of Towmart Holdings Limited (a predecessor co.) represented 1 Grey Goose

com. sh. for each Towmart sh. held. More than 90% of shs. were tendered under the offer which expired (as extended), and the balance were obtained under the provisions of the C.B.C.A.

Grey Horse Capital Corporation (Can. Jan. 17, 2005)
June 25, 2007 – Name changed to Grey Horse Corporation. ■

Grey Horse Corporation (Can. Jan. 17, 2005)
Dec. 21, 2010 – Name changed to Equity Financial Holdings Inc. ■

Grey Island Systems International Inc. (Alta. July 18, 1996)
Oct. 28, 2009 – Acquired by WebTech Wireless Inc.; basis 0.35 WebTech shs. for 1 Grey Island sh. (see Webtech Wireless Inc.)

Grey Wolf Exploration Inc. (Alta. Dec. 23, 1986)
Oct. 3, 2001 – Acquired by Abraxas Petroleum Corporation; basis 0.6 Abraxas shs. for 1 Grey Wolf sh.
Dec. 6, 2002 – Name changed to 967173 Alberta Ltd.

Grey Wolf Exploration Inc. (Alta. Dec. 6, 2002)
July 24, 2009 – Amalgamated with Insignia Energy Ltd. to form new co. Insignia Energy Ltd.; basis 0.34 Insignia shs. for 1 Grey Wolf sh. (see Insignia Energy Ltd.)

Greyhawk Oil & Gas Inc. (Alta. Sept. 5, 1996)
Mar. 5, 1999 – Acquired by Braegen Energy Ltd.; basis 0.27548 Braegen shs. for 1 Greyhawk sh. (see Braegan Energy Ltd.)

Greyhawk Resources Ltd. (B.C. Feb. 1, 1983)
Aug. 17, 1992 – Name changed to GHK Resources Ltd.; basis 1 new for 5 old shs. ■

Greyhawk Uranium Mines Ltd. (Ont. 1944)
Mar. 23, 1964 – Unsecured creditors received approx. 38¢ on the dollar. No equity for shldrs. Charter cancelled.

Greyhound Canada Transportation Corp. (Can. Dec. 8, 1995)
Nov. 14, 1997 – Acquired by Laidlaw Inc. for $5.50 per sh.
Name changed to Greyhound Canada Transportation ULC.

Greyhound Communications Ltd. (B.C. 1987)
Jan. 7, 1991 – Name changed to Eastmin Resources Inc. ■

Greyhound Computer of Canada Ltd. (Can. July 19, 1968)
Nov. 1, 1987 – Name changed to Greyvest Financial Services Inc. ■

Greyhound Lines of Canada Ltd. (Can. Sept. 11, 1957; via Dominion charter)
June 5, 1996 – Spun off into a new co. known as Greyhound Canada Transportation Corp. with the old Greyhound Lines being renamed Brewster Tours Inc.; basis 3.1775 Greyhound Canada shs. for 1 Greyhound Lines sh. (see Greyhound Canada Transportation Corp.)

Greymantle Industries Ltd. (Alta. June 2, 1995)
Mar. 17, 1997 – Name changed to Newhaven Media Inc. following reverse takeover acquisition of True Color Media Inc. ■

Greystar Resources Ltd. (Can. Apr. 29, 1987)
Aug. 15, 1997 – Amalgamated with Churchill Resources Ltd. to form new co. with same name Greystar Resources Ltd.; basis 1.3 new for 1 Churchill sh. and 1 new for 1 Greystar sh.
Aug. 19, 2011 – Name changed to Eco Oro Minerals Corp. (see FPsurvey - Mines & Energy)

Greystoke Explorations Ltd. (B.C. 1987)
Aug. 14, 1992 – Dissolved and struck off register.

Greystone Research Corp. (Can. Mar. 14, 2000)
Aug. 4, 2005 – Acquired by Javelin Capital Corp.; basis 0.285 new Javelin sh. for 1 old Greystone sh. (see Javelin Capital Corp.)

Greyvest Capital Inc. (Can. July 19, 1968)
Nov. 2, 2005 – Dissolved.

Greyvest Financial Services Inc. (Can. July 19, 1968)
Dec. 7, 1994 – Name changed to Greyvest Capital Inc. ■

Greywacke Exploration Ltd. (Can. June 5, 2006)
Aug. 25, 2017 – Name changed to Green River Gold Corp. (see FPsurvey - Mines & Energy; FPsurvey - Industrials)

Grid Capital Corporation (Can. July 26, 2000)
Sept. 22, 2008 – Name changed to Lornex Capital Inc.; basis 1 new for 3 old shs. ■

Grid Resources Ltd. (B.C. Sept. 1, 1981)
Mar. 15, 1985 – Name changed to F M Resources Ltd. ■

Gridoil Freehold Leases Ltd. (Alta. 1950)
Feb. 18, 1966 – Merged into Canadian Gridoil Ltd.; basis 1 new for 5 old shs.

GridSense Systems Inc. (B.C. June 18, 1998)
July 17, 2009 – Name changed to Viridis Energy Inc.; basis 1 new for 10 old shs. ■

The Griffin Corporation (Ont. Feb. 23, 1998 amalg.)
Jan. 31, 2008 – Acquired by Zayma Realty Holdings Inc. for 8¢ per sh.

Griffin Skye Corporation (Ont. Dec. 21, 2007)
Sept. 29, 2016 – Voluntarily delisted.
Oct. 1, 2016 – Name changed to ANB Canada Inc. following acquisition of and amalgamation with Associated National Brokerage Inc. (see FPsurvey - Industrials)

Griffon Petroleum Ltd. (Alta. June 2, 1987)
Apr. 8, 1997 – Name changed to High Plains Energy Inc.; basis 1 new for 4 old shs. ■

Grilli Property Group Inc. (Que. Jan. 21, 1965)
Oct. 26, 2004 – Privatized at $3.82 per sh.

Grindlays Bank of Canada (Can. 1982)
Feb. 6, 1986 – Name changed to ANZ Bank Canada. ■

Grissol Foods Limited (Ont. 1960)
Mar. 31, 1973 – Acquired by Imasco Limited for 50¢ per pref. sh. and $11 per com. sh. (see Imasco Limited)

Grit Resources Inc. (B.C. Mar. 22, 1983)
June 11, 1985 – Name changed to Canamera Explorations Inc. ■

Grizzly Creek Resources Ltd. (B.C. Mar. 7, 1987)
July 14, 1993 – Name changed to Luzon Minerals Ltd. ■

Grizzly Diamonds Ltd. (Alta. May 31, 2002)
Jan. 8, 2010 – Name changed to Grizzly Discoveries Inc. (see FPsurvey - Mines & Energy)

The Grocery People Ltd. (Alta. 1960)
Mar. 30, 1992 – Amalgamated into a susid. of Federated Co-operatives Limited; all o/s shs. redeemed on the basis of $500 per cl. A sh. and $15 per cl. B sh.

Grom Resources Inc. (B.C. Mar. 29, 1984)
Mar. 31, 1986 – Name changed to Micro-Phonics Technology International Corporation; basis 1 new for 3 old shs. ■

Grompo Red Lake Mines Ltd. (Ont. 1946)
1952 – Name changed to Deermont Oil & Gas Co. Ltd. ■

gronArctic Energy Inc. (Can. Dec. 13, 1978)
Jan. 19, 1998 – Name changed to gronArctic resources inc.; basis 1 new for 10 old shs. ■

gronArctic resources inc. (Can. Dec. 13, 1978)
July 9, 1999 – Continued into Alberta. (see Kicking Horse Resources Limited)
Oct. 12, 1999 – Amalgamated with Kicking Horse Resources Inc. and Taber Energy Corp. to form Kicking Horse Resources Ltd.; basis 0.0167523 new shs. and

0.5 new wts. for 1 gronArctic cl. A sh. (see Kicking Horse Resources Limited)

Grosmont Resources Ltd. (Alta. 1981)
Jan. 9, 1992 – Acquired by Paramount Resources Ltd.; basis $2.60 or 0.377 Paramount shs. for 1 Grosmont sh.

Gross Athletic Equipment Ltd. (unknown)
1968 – Acquired by Bartaco Industries Ltd. in 1968-69.

Grosse Pointe Exploration Co. Ltd. (Ont. 1945)
Dec. 23, 1965 – Charter cancelled.

Grosvenor International Holdings Limited (B.C. 1973 amalg.)
1978 – Following amalgamation with three of its subsids., co. converted its com. shs. in hands of minority shldrs. to redeem. pfce. shs. and immediately redeemed these new shs. Co. now private.

Groton Minerals Limited (B.C. July 21, 1966)
Nov. 16, 1990 – Delisted from the Vancouver Stock Exchange. Subsequently dissolved for failure to file.

Grounded Clothing Inc. (B.C. Apr. 20, 2020)
June 15, 2021 – Name changed to Grounded People Apparel Inc. (see FPsurvey - Industrials)

Groundhog Gold Mines Ltd. (Ont. 1934)
Nov. 30, 1964 – Charter cancelled.

Groundstar Petroleums Ltd. (B.C. 1973)
July 17, 1973 – Amalgamated with Blackline Resource Corporation Ltd. and Shelter Petroleums Ltd. to form a new company known as August Petroleums Ltd.

Groundstar Resources Limited (B.C. Nov. 19, 1968)
Dec. 5, 2005 – Continued into Alberta.
May 2, 2019 – Struck from registry and dissolved.

Group Ten Metals Inc. (B.C. Apr. 28, 2006)
June 13, 2022 – Name changed to Stillwater Critical Minerals Corp. (see FPsurvey - Mines & Energy)

Group West Systems Ltd. (B.C. July 29, 1982)
Mar. 14, 2001 – Plan of Arrangement to amalgamate with Appareo Software Inc. and to continue as Appareo Software Inc.; basis 0.3 new Appareo com. sh. for 1 old Group West com. sh. (see Appareo Software Inc.)

Le Groupe Alimentaire Vachon Inc. (Que. 1947)
Feb. 16, 1977 – Name changed to Culinar Inc. ∎

Le Groupe Beaugarte Inc. (Que. 1982)
Nov. 20, 1990 – Acquired by Gestion Demago Inc. for 50¢ per sh.

Groupe Cabano d'Anjou Inc. (Que. Apr. 30, 1985)
Jan. 25, 1988 – Name changed to Cabano Expéditex Incorporated. ∎

Groupe Champlain Inc. (Que. 1975)
July 6, 1990 – Acquired by Cadres Groupe Champlain Acquisition Inc. for $2.00 per sh.

Groupe Distinction Inc. (Que. Nov. 23, 2007 amalg.)
Jan. 10, 2012 – Privatized at $4.50 per sh.
Jan. 1, 2013 – Name changed to GDI Integrated Facility Services Inc.

Le Groupe Equipements Denis Inc. (Que. 1976)
May 27, 1991 – All o/s shs. redeemed for $1.75 following privatization of the co. via a takeover bid by themselves and Gestion Danmar.

Groupe Espadon Peterborough Inc. (Can. June 21, 1983)
Nov. 1989 – Filed for bankruptcy. Raymond, Chabot, Farard, Gagon Inc. (Montreal) appointed trustee in bankruptcy.
Aug. 1, 1990 – Most of the assets liquidated. Shortfall to secured creditors and no distribution available for unsecured creditors or shldrs.

Le Groupe Forex Inc. (Que. Mar. 26, 1982)
Nov. 11, 1999 – All o/s cl. A and cl. B shs. acquired by Delaware-based Louisiana-Pacific Corporation; basis (a)

$33 per sh. or (b) $33 payable in five-year instalment notes with interest or combination of (a) and (b).

Groupe Goyette Inc. (Can. July 27, 1979)
Dec. 19, 1997 – Acquired by 3319954 Canada Inc. for $5.00 per sh.

Groupe Harricana Inc. (Que. 1986)
Aug. 1992 – Declared bankruptcy, after its Formtech unit ceased operations, and its Metcoat unit filed for bankruptcy.
Mar. 1994 – All assets seized by the secured creditors, and no distribution to shldrs.
June 1, 1994 – Trustee discharged.

Le Groupe Lacroix (Québec) Inc. (Can. Oct. 22, 1985)
Jan. 26, 1990 – Declared bankrupt.

Le Groupe Opus Communications Inc. (B.C. Apr. 7, 1978)
Aug. 29, 1989 – Dissolved and struck off register.

Groupe Plastique Moderne Inc. (Que. Aug. 12, 1986)
Oct. 12, 1990 – Declared bankrupt.

Le Groupe Ro-Na Dismat Inc. (Que. Jan. 2, 1984 amalg.)
May 14, 1998 – Name changed to RONA Inc. ∎

Le Groupe Ro-Na Inc. (Que. Jan. 2, 1984 amalg.)
Feb. 2, 1989 – Name changed to Le Groupe Ro-Na Dismat Inc. following acquisition of Dismat Inc. ∎

Groupe Sani Mobile inc. (Que. Feb. 1, 1984 amalg.)
Feb. 11, 1999 – Acquired by Vivendi S.A. for $1.50 per sh.

Groupe Soficorp Inc. (Can. Jan. 9, 1987)
Feb. 2, 2004 – Dissolved.

Groupe T.C.G. (Québec) Inc. (Que. Dec. 31, 1983 amalg.)
May 25, 1990 – Name changed to Autostock Inc. ∎

Groupe Tolgeco inc. (Can. June 1, 1987)
Feb. 14, 2003 – Acquired by Mecyva Acquisition Inc. for $2.40 per sh.

Groupe Transat A.T. Inc. (Can. Feb. 13, 1987)
Aug. 3, 1993 – Name changed to Transat A.T. Inc. (see FPsurvey - Industrials)

Groupworks Financial Corp. (Ont. July 5, 2006)
Oct. 1, 2011 – Formed People Corporation in Ontario following amalgamation with wholly owned People Corporation and Advansis Capital Corporation, a wholly owned subsid. of People Corporation. ∎

Grouse Creek Barkerville Gold Ltd. (B.C. 1961)
1963 – Name changed to Grouse Creek Mines Ltd.; basis 1 new for 4 old shs. ∎

Grouse Creek Mines Ltd. (B.C. 1961)
May 27, 1971 – Name changed to New Grouse Creek Mines Ltd.; basis 1 new for 200 old shs. ∎

Grouse Mountain Resorts Ltd. (B.C. 1950)
Mar. 15, 1989 – Privatized. Wholly owned subsid. of Western Delta Lands Inc.

Grove Energy Limited (Yuk. May 15, 1997)
June 2, 2005 – Continued into British Columbia.
Apr. 30, 2007 – Acquired by Stratic Energy Corporation; basis 0.61879 Stratic Energy shs. for 1 Grove Energy sh.

Grove Explorations Ltd. (B.C. 1972)
Aug. 30, 1984 – Formed Golden North Resource Corporation in British Columbia on amalgamation with N.W.P. Resources Ltd. and Rosmac Resources Ltd.; basis 0.3667 new for 1 N.W.P. sh., 0.3 new for 1 Rosmac sh. and 0.3333 new for 1 Grove sh. ∎

Growers' Wine Company Limited (B.C. 1923)
Nov. 1971 – Under an offer made Imasco Limited, which then held a 64% int. in the co., acquired the remaining

o/s cl. A and B shs. of the co.; basis $4.00 per cl. A and $3.75 per cl. B sh. (see Imasco Limited)

GrowMax Resources Corp. (Alta. Aug. 22, 2008 amalg.)
Jan. 27, 2020 – Continued into British Columbia.
Nov. 29, 2021 – Name changed to Coloured Ties Capital Inc.; basis 1 new for 10 old shs. (see FPsurvey - Industrials)

GrowPros Cannabis Ventures Inc. (Can. May 17, 2007)
Sept. 28, 2016 – Name changed to Tetra Bio-Pharma Inc. ∎

Growth Income Properties Limited (Alta. 1964)
1970 – Name changed to Centron Equity Corp. Ltd. ∎

Growth Investment Corporation (Ont. Jan. 31, 1978)
Jan. 17, 1985 – Continued into British Columbia.
Oct. 30, 1992 – KPMG Inc. (formerly Peat Marwick Thorne Inc.), Toronto, Ont., was appointed liquidator by the Supreme Court of British Columbia.
Dec. 29, 1992 – Com. shldrs. received distribution of $11.50 per sh.
Dec. 30, 1993 – Com. shldrs. received distribution of 82¢ per sh.
Oct. 11, 1994 – Dissolved and struck off register.
1994 – Final distribution of $0.0216 per sh. was made.
Dec. 11, 1996 – Trustee was subsequently discharged.

Growthgen Equity II Inc. (Ont. Dec. 6, 2006)
Aug. 1, 2007 – Formed GuestLogix Inc. in Ontario on Qualifying Transaction reverse takeover acquisition of and amalgamation with GuestLogix Inc. ∎

Growthgen Equity Inc. (Ont. July 28, 2004)
Apr. 4, 2007 – Name changed to Tarquin Group Inc. ∎

Grull-Wihksne Gold Mines Ltd. (B.C. 1933)
June 1952 – Dissolved.

Gryphon Gold Corporation (Nev. Apr. 24, 2003)
June 28, 2013 – Voluntarily delisted from TSX.

Gtech International Resources Limited (Yuk. Dec. 17, 1997)
Dec. 3, 2013 – Name changed to Simavita Limited and continued into British Columbia pursuant to reverse takeover acquisition of Simavita Holdings Limited; basis 1 new for 3 old shs. ∎

The Guarantee Company of North America (Can. 1851)
Apr. 1, 2021 – Amalgamated with parent company Intact Insurance Company to continue under the Intact Insurance name.

Guaranty Trust Company of Canada (Can. 1925)
Dec. 31, 1988 – Amalgamated (1 for 1) with Central Trust Company, Yorkshire Trust Company and Nova Scotia Savings and Trust Company (1 for 1) to form Central Guaranty Trust Company. (see Central Guaranty Trust Company)

Guaranty Trustco Limited (Can. May 25, 1966)
Oct. 19, 1984 – Continued into Ontario.
May 10, 1988 – Name changed to Central Guaranty Trustco Limited. ∎

Guardcor Investments Inc. (Que. 1984)
May 24, 1991 – All o/s shs. not already held acquired by Guardian Trustco Inc.; basis $10 per sh. (see Guardian Trustco Inc.)

Guardian Bancorp Ltd. (Alta. July 4, 1996)
Oct. 16, 2000 – Amalgamated with wholly owned subsid. of Infiniti Resources International Ltd.; basis 0.75 Infiniti sh. for 1 Guardian sh. (see Infiniti Resources International Ltd.)

Guardian Communication Industries Inc. (B.C. Oct. 5, 1979)
Feb. 11, 1994 – Name changed to Guardian Enterprises Ltd. ∎

Guardian Enterprises Ltd. (B.C. Oct. 5, 1979)
Dec. 7, 1999 – Name changed to Interactive Enterprises Inc.; basis 1 new for 5 old shs. ∎

Guardian Explorations Ltd. (Ont. 1960)
Aug. 9, 1972 – Dissolved.

Guardian Mines Ltd. (Que. Feb. 4, 1958)
1971 – Name changed to Green Coast Resources Limited; basis 1 new for 10 old shs. ∎

Guardian-Morton Shulman Precious Metals Inc. (Ont. 1966)
1983 – Continued into British Columbia.

Guardian Resource Corporation (B.C. Oct. 5, 1979)
June 28, 1991 – Name changed to Guardian Communication Industries Inc. ∎

Guardian Trust Company (Que. 1929)
July 25, 1980 – All o/s shs. exchanged for a federally incorp. co., Guardian Trustco Inc.; basis 1 new for 1 old sh. Guardian Trust Company became a wholly owned subsid. of new co. (see Guardian Trustco Inc.)

Guardian Trustco Inc. (Can. July 25, 1980)
May 26, 1992 – David Azoulay & Associates Inc. of Montreal was appointed liquidators.
Dec. 1997 – Debentures holders received the following instalments: $5,000,000 or 19¢ on the dollar in November 1992; $8,000,000 in December 1995; $3,800,000 in December 1996; and $368,242 in December 1997 for a cumulative distribution of 65.7% of the total debt.
Apr. 1998 – All assets liquidated and proceeds distributed to creditors only as there were no funds available for distribution to shldrs.
July 23, 1998 – Dissolved.
Apr. 1999 – David Azoulay & Associates Inc. was discharged as liquidator.

Guarnaccio Gold Mines Ltd. (Ont. 1949)
1955 – Name changed to Kent Mines Limited. ∎

Guatemala Sulphur and Resources Corporation Limited (Ont. 1968)
May 1, 1970 – Name changed to Basic Resources International Limited; basis 2 new for 1 old sh. ∎

Guerrero Exploration Inc. (Alta. Mar. 19, 2010)
Sept. 2, 2016 – Struck from registry and dissolved.

Guerrero Ventures Inc. (B.C. Feb. 20, 1961)
Jan. 7, 2020 – Continued into Canada.
May 22, 2020 – Name changed to Nomad Royalty Company Ltd. pursuant to reverse takeover acquisition of precious metals royalty, stream and gold loan assets from Orion Mine Finance Group and Yamana Gold Inc. ∎

Guess Capital Corporation (Alta. Aug. 26, 1996)
May 16, 1997 – Name changed to Helix Hearing Care of America Corp. following Qualifying Transaction acquisition of all the o/s shs. of Helix Hearing Care of America Ltd.; basis 1 new for 1 old sh. ∎

Guest-Tek Interactive Entertainment Ltd. (Alta. May 23, 1997)
Dec. 3, 2009 – Acquired by 1456537 Alberta Inc. for 50¢ per sh.

GuestLogix Inc. (Ont. Aug. 1, 2007 amalg.)
Sept. 21, 2016 – Privatized under restructuring transaction whereby the company emerged from CCAA under a new ownership group. All existing equity was cancelled and unsecured creditors would receive an estimated $0.67 to $0.81 on the dollar.

Gui-Por Gold Mines Ltd. (Ont. 1945)
1953 – Name changed to Gui-Por Uranium Mines & Metals Limited. ∎

Gui-Por Uranium Mines & Metals Limited (Ont. 1945)
Oct. 6, 1976 – Dissolved.

Guichon Mine Ltd. (B.C. 1945)
Aug. 9, 1976 – Charter cancelled.

Guide Exploration Ltd. (Alta. Mar. 27, 2003)
Oct. 29, 2012 – Acquired by WestFire Energy Ltd.; basis 0.4167 WestFire shs. for 1 Guide sh. Subsequently WestFire changed its name to Long Run Exploration Ltd. (see Long Run Exploration Ltd.)

Guildhall Minerals Ltd. (B.C. Sept. 30, 1967)
July 23, 2009 – Continued into Alberta.
July 28, 2009 – Name changed to Edge Resources Inc. ∎

Guilford Acquisitions Inc. (Can. May 13, 1987)
Feb. 1, 1991 – Name changed to Wildcat Acquisitions Inc.; basis 1 new for 6 old shs. ∎

Guillevin International Inc. (Can. Feb. 1, 1980)
May 11, 1995 – Acquired by Consolidated Electrical Distributors Ltd. for $10.25 per sh.
Jan. 2001 – Name changed to Guillevin International Co.

Guilt-Free Goodies Ltd. (B.C. Apr. 21, 1987)
June 6, 1990 – Name changed to Epicure Food Products, Inc. ∎

Guinness Gold Resources Ltd. (Ont. Feb. 13, 1987)
Oct. 28, 1991 – Name changed to Roycefield Resources Ltd.; basis 1 new for 7 old shs. ∎

Guinor Gold Corporation (Yuk. Feb. 12, 2004)
Mar. 3, 2006 – Acquired indirectly by Crew Gold Corporation for $1.50 per sh. (see Crew Gold Corporation)

Gulch Mines Inc. (Ont. 1953)
1977 – Continued into Alberta.
May 31, 1978 – Name changed to Gulch Resources Ltd.; basis 1 new for 4 old shs. ∎

Gulch Mines Ltd. (Ont. 1953)
July 10, 1974 – Name changed to Gulch Mines Inc.; basis 1 new for 5 old shs. ∎

Gulch Resources Ltd. (Alta. 1977)
Oct. 21, 1982 – Acquired by Camel Oil & Gas Ltd. for total consideration of 2,869,184 com. shs. of Camel.

Guld Resources Corp. (B.C. Apr. 11, 1983)
Dec. 15, 1986 – Name changed to Medsource Systems Inc. ∎

Gulf + Western Industries, Inc. (Del. 1967)
June 5, 1986 – Name changed to Paramount Communications Inc.

Gulf Bay Mines Ltd. (Ont. 1964)
1969 – Merged into Alchib Developments Ltd.; basis 22 new for 100 old shs.

Gulf Canada Corporation (Can. June 4, 1909; via Dominion charter)
July 1, 1987 – Name changed to Gulf Canada Resources Limited under terms of a reorganization plan; basis 0.666 Gulf Canada Resources Limited shs., 0.29 shs. of Abitibi-Price Inc., and 0.2 shs. of GW Utilities Limited for 1 old Gulf Canada Corporation sh. ∎

Gulf Canada Limited (Can. June 4, 1909; via Dominion charter)
Feb. 10, 1986 – Name changed to Gulf Canada Corporation. ∎

Gulf Canada Resources Limited (Can. June 4, 1909; via Dominion charter)
July 17, 2001 – All o/s ord. shs. acquired by Conoco Northern Inc., an indirect wholly owned subsid. of Texas-based Conoco Inc., for $12.40 per sh.
Aug. 21, 2001 – Name changed to Conoco Canada Resources Limited. ∎

Gulf International Minerals Ltd. (B.C. May 15, 1969)
Aug. 14, 2002 – Continued into Yukon.
Aug. 11, 2004 – Continued into British Columbia. (see FPsurvey - Mines & Energy)

Gulf Lead Mines Ltd. (Ont. 1942)
Mar. 1976 – Charter cancelled.

Gulf Oil Canada Limited (Can. June 4, 1909; via Dominion charter)
June 1, 1978 – Name changed to Gulf Canada Limited. ∎

Gulf Shores Resources Ltd. (B.C. Dec. 16, 1993)
Aug. 15, 2016 – Name changed to Ashanti Gold Corp. ∎

Gulf Titanium Ltd. (B.C. 1967)
Oct. 28, 1994 – Dissolved and struck off register.

Gulf Uranium Mines Ltd. (Ont. 1967)
July 14, 1969 – Dissolved.

Gulfside Industries Ltd. (B.C. Oct. 14, 1987)
Jan. 14, 1998 – Name changed to Consolidated Gulfside Resources Ltd.; basis 1 new for 5 old shs. ∎

Gulfside Minerals Ltd. (B.C. Oct. 14, 1987)
Mar. 7, 2012 – Name changed to Arrowstar Resources Ltd. ∎

Gulfstream Acquisition 1 Corp. (Ont. June 8, 2012)
Apr. 4, 2019 – Name changed to Liberty Defense Holdings, Ltd. pursuant to the Qualifying Transaction reverse takeover acquisition of Liberty Defense Holdings, Inc. and concurrent amalgamation of Liberty with wholly owned 2675553 Ontario Limited (and continued as LDH GS Amalco Corp.).; basis 1 new for 2.5 old shs. ∎

Gulfstream Resources Canada Limited (Ont. Sept. 29, 1943)
Aug. 14, 2001 – Acquired by Anadarko Petroleum Corporation for $2.65 per sh.

Gull-Kirk Gold Mines Ltd. (unknown)
1926 – Name changed to Gull-Kirkland Mines Ltd. ∎

Gull-Kirkland Mines Ltd. (Ont. June 4, 1926)
1945 – Acquired by Kirkland-Eastern Gold Mines Ltd.; basis 1 new for 7 old shs.

Gull Lake Energy Resources Ltd. (Ont. 1959)
Aug. 18, 1981 – Formed Petroflo Petroleum Corporation in Ontario on amalgamation with Silver Leader Mines Ltd. ∎

Gull Lake Iron Mines Ltd. (Ont. 1959)
Aug. 11, 1977 – Name changed to Gull Lake Energy Resources Ltd. ∎

Gull Rock Mining Corp. Ltd. (Ont. 1965)
Aug. 1972 – Name changed to Maple Film Ltd. ∎

Gullbridge Mines Limited (unknown)
June 17, 1980 – Acquired by Consolidated Rambler; wound up Dec. 31, 1980.

The Gummy Project Inc. (B.C. Jan. 14, 2020)
June 19, 2023 – Name changed to Vice Health and Wellness Inc. (see FPsurvey - Industrials)

Gump Creek Mining Ltd. (unknown)
1967 – Merged into Mamit Lake Mining Ltd.

Gunflint Iron Mines Limited (Ont. 1940)
Oct. 1, 1956 – Charter cancelled.

Gunflint Resources Ltd. (B.C. Feb. 14, 1984)
May 6, 1992 – Name changed to Advent Communications Corp.; basis 1 new for 2 old shs. ∎

Gunn Mines Ltd. (B.C. July 21, 1966)
Jan. 19, 1977 – Name changed to United Gunn Resources Ltd.; basis 1 new for 5 old shs. ∎

Gunnar Gold Inc. (Can. Nov. 27, 1986 amalg.)
Dec. 14, 1988 – Name changed to Gunnar Gold Mining Corp.; basis 1 new for 10 old shs. ∎

Gunnar Gold Mines Ltd. (Ont. 1933)
1954 – Name changed to Gunnar Mines Ltd. ∎

Gunnar Gold Mining Corp. (Can. Nov. 27, 1986 amalg.)
Mar. 4, 1992 – Name changed to AI TN Aveca Entertainment Corporation; basis 1 new for 10 old shs. ∎

Gunnar Mines Ltd. (Ont. 1933)
1960 – Merged into Gunnar Mining Ltd.

Gunnar Mining Ltd. (Ont. 1960 amalg.)
Jan. 28, 1971 – Name changed to Bovis Corporation Limited. ■

Gunpowder Capital Corp. (Ont. June 1, 2006)
Dec. 2, 2019 – Name changed to Bluesky Digital Assets Corp. (see FPsurvey - Industrials)

Gunsteel Resources Incorporated (B.C. July 26, 1985)
Jan. 1, 2018 – Dissolved and struck from registry.

Guodong Capital Corp. (Alta. Oct. 12, 1999)
Dec. 2, 2003 – Name changed to Cosmo Capital Corp. following the Oct. 1, 2003, Qualifying Transaction acquisition of Reco Decorating Group Inc. and Z & Z Holdings Inc. ■

Gurney Foundry Co. Ltd. (unknown 1893)
Dec. 1950 – Com. shldrs. received $260.50 per sh.
1950 – Name changed to Gurney Industries Ltd. ■

Gurney Gold Mines Ltd. (Man. 1935)
1947 – Charter cancelled.

Gurney Industries Ltd. (unknown 1893)
Jan. 1951 – Sold all assets except shs. of wholly owned subsid., Gurney Properties Ltd. (net book value $2,527) and certain mtges. amounting to $112,500, for $1,307,930 and 51,000 com. shs. of Gurney Products Ltd.

Gurney Products Ltd. (Can. 1951)
May 15, 1961 – Name changed to Tappan-Gurney Ltd. ■

Gusto Mines Limited (Ont. 1954)
June 13, 1960 – Charter cancelled.

Guy-Guibord Gold Mines Ltd. (Ont. 1936)
1956 – Charter cancelled.

Guyana Frontier Mining Corp. (B.C. June 24, 1987)
Dec. 18, 2017 – Dissolved and struck from register.
July 20, 2020 – Restored to registry. (see FPsurvey - Mines & Energy)

Guyana Gold Corp. (B.C. May 26, 1986)
Nov. 18, 1996 – Name changed to Beringer Gold Corp. ■

Guyana Goldfields Inc. (Que. Jan. 24, 1953)
May 2, 2003 – Dissolved.
Sept. 5, 2003 – Revived.
Apr. 8, 2005 – Amalgamated with 9152-7598 Quebec Inc. to become a wholly owned subsid. of 6357458 Canada Inc. which changed its name to Guyana Goldfields Inc.
Aug. 27, 2020 – Acquired by Zijin Mining Group Co., Ltd.; basis Cdn$1.85 cash per sh.

Guyana Mines Ltd. (Ont. 1946)
1952 – Name changed to Consolidated Guyana Mines Ltd.; basis 1 new for 2 old shs. ■

Guyana Precious Metals Inc. (Ont. Apr. 23, 2004)
Aug. 27, 2013 – Name changed to GPM Metals Inc. (see FPsurvey - Mines & Energy)

Guyanor Ressources S.A. (France Apr. 20, 1993)
July 19, 2005 – Name changed to EURO Ressources S.A. ■

Guysborough Mines Ltd. (N.S. June 25, 1934)
In liquidation. Liquidator J. A. Walker, Tramway Bldg., Halifax, N.S.

Gwil Industries Inc. (B.C. July 15, 1969)
Dec. 6, 1999 – Acquired by Hugh A. Magee and M. B Schwitzer through Gil Acquisition Corp. for $5.65 per sh. Co. now private.

Gwillim Lake Gold Mines Ltd. (Ont. 1945)
Dec. 1966 – Charter cancelled.

Gwyn Beardmore Gold Mines Ltd. (Ont. 1937)
1956 – Charter cancelled.

Gypsum Lime & Alabastine Canada Ltd. (Can. 1927)
Feb. 1959 – Domtar Limited acquired assets; basis 2 com. shs. Domtar plus $14.50 for each Gypsum Lime sh.
Apr. 27, 1959 – Name changed to Kamic Ltd. to facilitate winding-up procedure.

Gypsy Resources Ltd. (B.C. July 15, 1985)
Feb. 5, 1990 – Name changed to Pacific Century Explorations Ltd. ■

Gyro Energy & Minerals Corp. (B.C. 1979)
Mar. 4, 1987 – Name changed to Dimension House International, Inc. ■

Gyro Mining & Exploration Ltd. (unknown)
1967 – Charter cancelled.

Gyzer Capital Inc. (Can. July 25, 2001)
Dec. 29, 2004 – Name changed to Manicouagan Minerals Inc. following Qualifying Transaction acquisition of Manicouagan Minerals Inc. ■

H

H. & M. Taxsavers Limited (Can. 1968)
1970 – Not formally placed into bankruptcy but withdrew from business. No known assets; no known distributions to shldrs.

H. Corby Distillery Ltd. (Can. Sept. 30, 1924; via letters patent)
Jan. 24, 1969 – Name changed to Corby Distilleries Limited. ■

H. Jager Developments Inc. (Alta. 1986)
Dec. 6, 1999 – Name changed to Westbridge Land Developments Inc. ■

H. Simon & Sons Ltd. (Can. 1928)
1958 – All o/s com. shs. acquired by Consolidated Cigar Corp. at equivalent of US$35 per sh. payable in cash and stk. All o/s 5% pref. shs. red. Feb. 28, 1962, at $105 plus accr. divds.

H2O Innovation Inc. (Can. Aug. 23, 1995 amalg.)
Dec. 12, 2023 – Acquired by Ember Infrastructure Management, LP; basis $4.25 cash per sh.

The H. A. Roberts Group Ltd. (Sask. 1971 amalg.)
May 1986 – In receivership.

H.A.L. Concepts Ltd. (Yuk. June 6, 2000)
Feb. 27, 2007 – Name changed to Halmont Properties Corporation. ■

HARS Systems Inc. (B.C. Sept. 17, 1986)
Sept. 13, 2002 – Acquired indirectly by Trimin Capital Corp. for 62¢ per sh. (see Trimin Capital Corp.)

HAW Capital Corp. (Alta. Nov. 29, 2016)
June 26, 2019 – Name changed to GOLO Mobile Inc. and continued into Canada pursuant to Qualifying Transaction reverse takeover acquisition of GOLO Inc. and amalgamation of GOLO Inc. with a wholly owned subsidiary. (see FPsurvey - Industrials)

HBanc Capital Securities Trust (Ont. Sept. 28, 2010)
Feb. 4, 2016 – Merged into North American Financials Capital Securities Trust to continue as Global Capital Securities Trust; basis 0.949297 and 0.968918 Global Capital cl. A units for 1 HBanc cl. A ser. 1 and ser. 2 unit, respectively. (see Global Capital Securities Trust)

HCI Holdings Ltd. (Can. Sept. 6, 1930)
Dec. 23, 1986 – Name changed to Consolidated HCI Holdings Corporation; basis 1 new for 7 old shs. ■

HCO Energy Company Ltd. (Can. 1987)
May 4, 1989 – Name changed to Consolidated HCO Energy Ltd.; basis 1 new for 10 old shs. ■

HCO Energy Ltd. (Can. 1987)
Nov. 5, 1997 – Acquired by Pinnacle Resources Ltd.; basis $10 or 0.4819 Pinnacle shs. for 1 HCO sh. (see Pinnacle Resources Ltd.)

HCR Realty Limited (Can. 1927)
Apr. 1, 1975 – Name changed to Heitman Canadian Investors Services Ltd. ■

HEARx Canada Inc. (Can. Nov. 7, 2001)
Dec. 30, 2009 – Redeemed exchangeable shs.; basis 1 new HearUSA Inc. com. sh. for 1 old HEARx exch. sh.

HEC Hitech Entertainment Corporation (B.C. Aug. 5, 1987)
Feb. 4, 1997 – Name changed to Gleneagles Petroleum Corp. ■

HEC Investments Ltd. (Alta. June 20, 1984)
Aug. 29, 1994 – Name changed to Humboldt Capital Corporation. ■

HEGCO Canada, Inc. (Alta. July 27, 1995)
Feb. 22, 2002 – Placed into receivership. RSM Richter Inc. was appointed receiver.
June 5, 2005 – Released from receivership. (see FPsurvey - Mines & Energy)

H.E.R.O. Industries Ltd. (B.C. Dec. 23, 1980)
Apr. 10, 1997 – Name changed to Middlefield Bancorp Limited and continued into Ontario. ■

HEXO Corp. (Ont. Oct. 29, 2013)
June 27, 2023 – Acquired by Tilray Brands, Inc.; basis 0.4352 Tilray shs. for 1 HEXO sh.

HF Capital Corp. (Alta. Feb. 19, 2004)
Apr. 28, 2005 – Name changed to MicroPlanet Technology Corp. following Qualifying Transaction reverse takeover acquisition of MicroPlanet, Inc. ■

HFG Holdings Inc. (Alta. Mar. 2, 2007)
Nov. 17, 2009 – Acquired by Cequence Energy Ltd.; basis 0.04 Cequence shs. for 1 HFG sh. (see Cequence Energy Ltd.)

HFI Flooring Inc. (Alta. Feb. 15, 1998)
Mar. 23, 2001 – Acquired indirectly by Domco Tarkett Inc. for consideration of $1.04 million. (see Domco Tarkett Inc.)

H. G. Young Mines International Ltd. (Ont. 1946)
Nov. 1, 1982 – Charter cancelled.

H. G. Young Mines Ltd. (Ont. 1946)
Jan. 18, 1972 – Name changed to H. G. Young Mines International Ltd.; basis 1 new for 20 old shs. ■

HHT Investments Inc. (Ont. Mar. 19, 2013)
Apr. 4, 2014 – Reorganized into a real estate investment trust following Qualifying Transaction reverse takeover of Boulevard Industrial Real Estate Investment Trust; basis 1 new trust unit and/or class B LP unit for 1 old com. shs. (see Boulevard Industrial Real Estate Investment Trust)

HIC Horizon Investments Capital Ltd. (B.C. Nov. 9, 2018)
Mar. 27, 2020 – Name changed to FansUnite Entertainment Inc. pursuant to the reverse takeover acquisition of (old) FansUnite Entertainment Inc. and concurrent amalgamation of (old) FansUnite with wholly owned 1209080 B.C. Ltd. to form FansUnite Holdings Inc. ■

HIL Corporation Limited (Ont. 1982)
Dec. 4, 1995 – Amalgamated with a wholly owned subsid.; basis 1 cl. A sh. converted into 1 redeem. cl. B pref. sh. redeemed for 0.4 com. shs. of Hees International Bancorp Inc. Co. now wholly owned by Edper Investments Limited and The Edper Group Limited. (see Hees International Bancorp Inc.; The Edper Group Limited)

HIP Energy Corporation (B.C. June 22, 1983)
Dec. 8, 2014 – Dissolved and struck from register.

H.I.S.A. Investments Ltd. (B.C. Jan. 26, 1966)
June 11, 1993 – Dissolved and struck off register.

HIVE Blockchain Technologies Ltd. (B.C. June 24, 1987)
July 12, 2023 – Name changed to HIVE Digital Technologies Ltd. (see FPsurvey - Industrials)

H.J. Forest Products Inc. (Alta. Feb. 14, 1992)
Sept. 9, 1997 – Name changed to Bradstone Equity Partners, Inc.; basis 0.5 multiple vtg. and 0.5 subord. vtg. for 1 com. sh. ∎

H. K. Explorations Ltd. (Ont. 1959)
July 27, 1976 – Charter cancelled.

H.L. International Inc. (Alta. Jan. 31, 1989 amalg.)
Apr. 17, 1996 – Name changed to Maple Mark International Inc. ∎

HLE Capital Corp. (Ont. Aug. 3, 1990)
Sept. 29, 1995 – Name changed to Worldtec Sciences Incorporated. (see FPsurvey - Industrials)

HLT Energies Inc. (Can. Jan. 12, 2005)
Dec. 23, 2011 – Dissolved and struck from register.

HLT Energies 2006 Inc. (Can. Jan. 12, 2005)
Feb. 28, 2007 – Name changed to HLT Energies Inc. ∎

HLX Resources Ltd. (B.C. Aug. 31, 1989 amalg.)
Mar. 30, 1992 – Name changed to Emperor Gold Corporation; basis 1 new for 5 old shs. ∎

HMC HealthGuard Marketing Corp. (B.C. Sept. 27, 1979)
Aug. 7, 1996 – Name changed to Reward Mining Corporation; basis 1 new for 5 old shs. ∎

HMD Capital Corp. (Ont. Jan. 1, 1989)
Jan. 1, 1997 – Amalgamated in Ontario to continue with same name.
Apr. 8, 1997 – Name changed to Moneysworth & Best Shoe Care Inc. following the Jan. 1, 1997, amalgamation with wholly owned Moneysworth & Best Shoe Repair Corp. ∎

HMH China Investments Limited (Ont. Sept. 18, 1995 amalg.)
Dec. 21, 1995 – Continued into Bermuda.

HMR World Enterprises Inc. (B.C. 1984)
June 17, 1994 – Dissolved and struck off register.

HMZ Metals Inc. (Can. July 22, 2002)
May 17, 2012 – Dissolved.

HNR Ventures Inc. (Ont. Mar. 2, 1988)
June 6, 2006 – Name changed to RMM Ventures Inc.; basis 1 new for 10 old shs. ∎

HNZ Group Inc. (Can. May 7, 2010)
Jan. 4, 2018 – Privatized; basis $18.70 cash per sh.

H.O. Financial Limited (Ont. Dec. 15, 1971)
Mar. 2, 2007 – Privatized at $1.03 per sh.

HOMEQ Corporation (Ont. Mar. 10, 2009)
Dec. 5, 2012 – Acquired by Birch Hill Equity Partners Management Partners Inc. for $9.50 per sh.

HORIZON Total Return Fund (Ont. Oct. 11, 2006)
Dec. 28, 2006 – Name changed to HTR Total Return Fund. ∎

HOST International Holdings Inc. (B.C. Oct. 11, 1985)
Mar. 31, 2014 – Dissolved and struck from register.

HPB Investments Inc. (Ont. Apr. 18, 1997)
Dec. 30, 2015 – Name changed to Bradstone Capital Corp. following reverse takeover acquisition of Bradstone Financial Corp. ∎

HPIL Resources Ltd. (Alta. Dec. 6, 1972)
June 1, 1993 – Dissolved and struck off register.

HPQ-Silicon Resources Inc. (Can. Dec. 20, 1996)
July 4, 2022 – Name changed to HPQ Silicon Inc. (see FPsurvey - Mines & Energy; FPsurvey - Industrials)

HPVC Inc. (Can. Aug. 5, 2005)
Oct. 3, 2006 – Converted into an income trust named Temple Real Estate Investment Trust following Qualifying Transaction acquisition of property from Temple Gardens Mineral Spa Inc.; basis 1 new Temple unit for 10 old HPVC shs. (see Temple Real Estate Investment Trust)

H.Q. Minerals Ltd. (B.C. 1986)
June 5, 1992 – Dissolved and struck off register.

H. R. MacMillan Export Company Limited (Can. 1930)
Oct. 24, 1951 – Name changed to MacMillan & Bloedel Limited. ∎

HRC Development Corporation (B.C. Mar. 5, 1991)
Nov. 26, 1996 – Amalgamated with Eldorado Gold Corporation to continue as Eldorado Gold Corporation; basis 0.5 of a com. sh. and/or non-vtg. sh. for 1 com. and/or non-vtg. sh. plus 1 new wt. for 1 old wt.

H.R.S. Industries Inc. (B.C. May 5, 1982 amalg.)
May 1, 1984 – Formed International H.R.S. Industries Inc. in British Columbia on amalgamation with Stampede International Resources Inc.; basis 1 com. sh for 1 cl. A sh. and 1 com. sh. for 4 cl. B shs. ∎

HRT Participações em Petróleo S.A. (Brazil Oct. 13, 2008)
June 22, 2015 – Name changed to Petro Rio S.A.

HS GovTech Solutions Inc. (B.C. May 15, 2015)
Nov. 23, 2023 – Acquired by Banneker Partners LLC; basis Cdn$0.54 cash per sh.

HSBC Bank Canada (Can. July 30, 1981)
Mar. 28, 2023 – Acquired by Royal Bank of Canada.

HSBC Canada Asset Trust (B.C. May 26, 2000)
Jan. 3, 2011 – Redeemed all o/s HaTS at $1,000 per HaTS.

HSE Integrated Ltd. (Alta. July 2, 1998)
July 17, 2012 – Acquired by DXP Enterprises, Inc. for $1.80 per sh.

HSF Capital Corporation (B.C. July 26, 2005)
May 5, 2010 – Name changed to China Keli Electric Company Ltd. pursuant to Qualifying Transaction reverse takeover acquisition of Creative Grace Ltd. (see FPsurvey - Industrials)

HSI Hydrosystems International Inc. (B.C. June 8, 1987)
May 3, 1994 – Name changed to R.W. Gas Group Inc.; basis 1 new for 4 old shs. ∎

HSK Minerals Limited (Man. 1950)
1988 – Continued into Canada. (see Queenston Mining Inc.)
Jan. 1, 1990 – Amalgamated with Queenston Gold Mines Ltd. to form Queenston Mining Inc.; basis 0.434 new for 1 old sh. (see Queenston Mining Inc.)

HT Capital Inc. (B.C. Jan. 25, 2010)
July 13, 2011 – Name changed to Asia Packaging Group Inc. ∎

HTC Hydrogen Technologies Corp. (Alta. Nov. 26, 1996)
Feb. 21, 2008 – Name changed to HTC Purenergy Inc. ∎

HTC Purenergy Inc. (Alta. Nov. 26, 1996)
July 14, 2025 – Voluntarily delisted from the NEX. Company intends to cease to be a reporting issuer in B.C., Alberta and Saskatchewan. (see FPsurvey - Industrials)

HTI Ventures Corp. (Can. July 7, 1981)
Aug. 31, 2016 – Name changed to Leagold Mining Corporation and continued into British Columbia. ∎

HTN Inc. (Alta. Sept. 27, 1994)
Apr. 27, 2015 – Name changed to Internet of Things Inc. and continued into Ontario. ∎

H.T.R. Industries Inc. (B.C. 1981)
June 2, 1989 – Name changed to Lazer Maze Industries Inc.; basis 1 new for 4 old sh. ∎

HTR Total Return Fund (Ont. Oct. 11, 2006)
May 27, 2008 – Acquired by INDEXPLUS Income Fund; basis 0.74976784 INDEXPLUS trust units for 1 HTR fund unit.

HTS Company Ltd. (Alta. Apr. 21, 1993)
Feb. 21, 1996 – Name changed to Prism Petroleum Ltd.; basis 1 new for 1 old sh. ∎

HTTL Enterprises Inc. (Ont. Aug. 23, 1928)
Nov. 3, 1989 – Formed Unisphere Satellite Corp. on amalgamation with Unisphere Scientific Inc. (see FPsurvey - Industrials)

H2O Entertainment Corp. (B.C. May 5, 1972)
July 13, 2005 – Name changed to Consolidated H2O Entertainment Corp.; basis 1 new for 10 old shs. ∎

H2O Innovation (2000) Inc. (Can. Aug. 23, 1995 amalg.)
Jan. 21, 2009 – Name changed to H2O Innovation Inc. ∎

HWI Industries Inc. (Ont. 1978)
May 23, 1988 – Dissolved.

HYWY Corp. (Ont. Nov. 29, 1991)
Jan. 19, 2006 – Name changed to Hy Lake Gold Inc. following reorganization to sell software assets and to acquire mineral properties; basis 1 new for 10 old shs. ∎

Habanero Resources Inc. (B.C. Mar. 11, 1983)
Jan. 24, 2014 – Name changed to Sienna Resources Inc.; basis 1 new for 10 old shs. (see FPsurvey - Mines & Energy)

Habibi Resources Corporation (B.C. Nov. 9, 1982 amalg.)
Oct. 7, 2009 – Name changed to One World Investments Inc.; basis 1 new for 8 old shs. ∎

Habitant Gold Mines Ltd. (Ont. 1945)
Feb. 1958 – Charter cancelled.

Habsburg Resources Inc. (Ont. 1981)
Sept. 14, 1994 – Name changed to Dome Mountain Resources Ltd. ∎

Hacker Atompower Mines Ltd. (Ont. 1953)
Apr. 15, 1965 – Dissolved.

Hackett Gold Mining Co. Ltd. (unknown)
1953 – Charter cancelled; assets distributed.

Haddington International Resources Limited (B.C. Feb. 13, 1984)
June 23, 2000 – Continued into Australia.

Haddington Resources Ltd. (B.C. Feb. 13, 1984)
May 20, 1999 – Name changed to Haddington International Resources Limited; basis 1 new for 6 old shs. ∎

Hadley Mining Inc. (Ont. Mar. 26, 2010)
Mar. 26, 2018 – Name changed to Speakeasy Cannabis Club Ltd. following acquisition of 10161233 Canada Ltd. (SpeakEasy). ∎

Haemacure Corporation (Can. Aug. 19, 1991)
Jan. 11, 2010 – Filed a notice of intention to creditors under the Bankruptcy and Insolvency Act (Canada). PricewaterhouseCoopers Inc. appointed monitor.
Apr. 7, 2010 – Angiotech Pharmaceuticals, Inc., the company's secured creditor, purchased substantially all the assets. (see FPsurvey - Industrials)

Hafner Fabrics of Canada Ltd. (Can. 1984 amalg.)
May 25, 1990 – Name changed to Hafner Inc. following privatization.

Hagensborg Resources Ltd. (B.C. Aug. 5, 1983)
Jan. 6, 1995 – Dissolved and struck off register.

Häglund Industries International Incorporated (B.C. Feb. 8, 1983)
Mar. 1, 1999 – Delisted from the Vancouver Stock Exchange. Subsequently dissolved for failure to file and struck from register.

Hahn Brass Co. Ltd. (Ont. 1902)
Oct. 18, 1950 – Name changed to Hahn Brass Limited.

Haitian Copper Mining Corp. Ltd. (Ont. 1953)
Jan. 7, 1965 – Dissolved.

Hajtek Vision Inc. (Can. Apr. 26, 2004)
June 14, 2004 – Name changed to Haivision Systems Inc. (see FPsurvey - Industrials)

Hakken Capital Corp. (B.C. Oct. 11, 2018)
Apr. 11, 2025 – Name changed to Eshbal Functional Food Inc. pursuant to the Qualifying Transaction reverse takeover acquisition of Eshbal Functional Food (Agricultural Cooperative) Ltd. (see FPsurvey - Industrials)

Hal Roach Studios Corp. (B.C. 1951)
May 5, 1982 – Formed H.R.S. Industries Inc. in British Columbia following merger with Mission Financial Corporation; basis 1 new for 1 old preferred, cl. A and cl. B shs. ■

Halbrown Mines Limited (Ont. Jan. 19, 1966)
Jan. 3, 1967 – Name changed to Teco Mines and Oils Limited. ■

Halcro Oil Ltd. (Alta. 1951)
Apr. 1, 1983 – Struck off register.

Halcrow Swayze Mining Co. Ltd. (Ont. Nov. 4, 1932)
Aug. 1952 – Name changed to Landover Oils & Mines Ltd.; basis 1 new for 4 old shs. ■

Halcyon Resources Ltd. (B.C. 1985 amalg.)
June 9, 1995 – Dissolved and struck off register.

Halcyon Ventures Ltd. (B.C. Mar. 7, 2017)
June 11, 2021 – Name changed to Nova Lithium Corp. ■

Haldane Silver Mines Ltd. (unknown)
1974 – Taken over by Paramount Mining Ltd.; basis 5 shs. of Haldane for 1 sh. of Paramount.

Halden Red Lake Mines Ltd. (Ont. 1944)
1958 – Charter cancelled.

Hale Resources Ltd. (B.C. 1980)
July 12, 1993 – Name changed to Consolidated Hale Resources Ltd.; basis 1 new for 3 old shs. ■

Halex Resources Inc. (Que. Mar. 24, 1986)
Apr. 2, 1990 – Formed William Resources Inc. in Quebec on amalgamation with William Resources Inc.; basis 1 new for 1.29 William shs. and 1 new for 4.77 Halex shs. ■

Haley Industries Limited (Ont. Oct. 4, 1962)
Dec. 3, 2002 – Acquired by Magellan Aerospace Limited; basis $2.16 or 0.45 Magellan shs. for 1 Haley sh.

Hali Capital Corporation (Alta. Aug. 18, 2005)
Dec. 31, 2006 – Formed Athabasca Minerals Inc. in Alberta on Qualifying Transaction amalgamation with Athabasca Minerals Inc., constituting a reverse takeover by Athabasca; basis 1 com. sh. for 1 Athabasca cl. A com. sh. and 1 com. sh. for 2.5 Hali shs. ■

Halifax Developments Limited (N.S. Apr. 19, 1965)
Sept. 21, 1993 – Acquired by Empire Company Limited for $1.50 per sh.

Halitec Industries Corporation (B.C. Apr. 11, 1988)
Aug. 9, 1996 – Name changed to Senco Sensors Inc. (see FPsurvey - Industrials)

Halkin Mines Ltd. (Ont. 1951)
Apr. 29, 1965 – Dissolved.

Hall-Pat Mines Limited (Ont. 1950)
Sept. 8, 1958 – Charter cancelled.

Hall Train Entertainment Inc. (Can. Apr. 26, 1995)
Apr. 27, 2009 – Formed GoldTrain Resources Inc. in Canada on amalgamation with Goldwright Exploration Inc., constituting a reverse takeover by Goldwright; basis 1 new for 1 Goldwright sh. and 1 new for 15 Hall Train shs. ■

Halley Resources Ltd. (B.C. Dec. 31, 1985)
Sept. 13, 1991 – Name changed to Rugby Resources Limited; basis 1 new for 9 old shs. ■

The Hallicrafters Communications International Co. Ltd. (B.C. June 22, 1978)
Dec. 1, 1987 – Name changed to Johnston & Frye Securities Ltd. ■

Halliday Mines Ltd. (Ont.)
1968 – Charter cancelled.

Halliwell Gold Mines Ltd. (Que. 1933)
1954 – Name changed to Consolidated Halliwell Ltd.; basis 1 new for 4 old shs. ■

Hallmac Mines Ltd. (B.C. Nov. 21, 1966)
May 23, 1986 – Name changed to Royal Oak Resources Ltd. and continued into Alberta; basis 1 new for 3 old shs. ■

Hallmark Exploration Ltd. (Ont. 1943)
Sept. 22, 1966 – Dissolved.

Hallmark Resources Ltd. (B.C. 1972)
Jan. 13, 1995 – Dissolved and struck off register.

Hallmark Technologies Inc. (unknown 1972)
Oct. 26, 1993 – Continued into Ontario.
Jan. 24, 2001 – Acquired by HTI Acquisition Inc. for $4.00 per sh.

Hallmark Yellowknife Gold Mines Ltd. (Ont. 1946)
Jan. 1957 – Charter cancelled.

Hallnor Mines Ltd. (Ont. 1936)
Apr. 1971 – Assets sold to Pamour Porcupine Mines Ltd. Distributions to Hallnor shldrs. of $3.00 per sh. June 1, 1971; 30¢ per sh. Mar. 1, 1972; 50¢ per sh. June 1, 1972; and final distribution of 32.814¢ per sh. in 1974.
Aug. 6, 1975 – Charter cancelled.

Halmon Mining & Processing Ltd. (Ont. 1946)
Dec. 20, 1978 – Charter cancelled.

Halmont Properties Corporation (Yuk. June 6, 2000)
Feb. 18, 2009 – Continued into Ontario. (see FPsurvey - Industrials)

Halo Gaming Corporation (B.C. Sept. 23, 1965)
May 31, 2001 – Delisted from the CDNX. Subsequently dissolved for failure to file and struck from registry.

Halo Labs Inc. (Ont. Jan. 21, 2005)
Jan. 22, 2021 – Name changed to Halo Collective Inc. (see FPsurvey - Industrials)

Halo Resources Ltd. (Yuk. Dec. 14, 1993)
Nov. 16, 2004 – Continued into British Columbia.
July 10, 2013 – Acquired by Sendero Mining Corp.; basis 0.689553 Sendero shs. plus wts. for 1 Halo sh.

Halo Uranium Mines Ltd. (Ont. 1954)
1957 – Name changed to Consolidated Halo Uranium Mines Ltd.; basis 15 new for 100 old shs. ■

Halogen Software Inc. (Ont. Jan. 9, 1996)
May 4, 2017 – All o/s shs., other than those held by Michael Slaunwhite the company's founder, acquired by Saba Software Inc. and Vector Capital Corporation; basis $12.50 cash per sh.

Halozone Technologies Inc. (Ont. July 28, 1987)
Dec. 15, 2003 – Dissolved and struck from register.

Halport Mines Ltd. (Ont. 1940)
Mar. 1976 – Charter cancelled.

Halren Mines Ltd. (Ont. 1968)
Mar. 1976 – Charter cancelled.

Halterm Income Fund (N.S. Mar. 25, 1997)
Jan. 18, 2007 – Acquired by indirect wholly owned subsid. of Macquarie Infrastructure Partners; basis Cdn$19.08 per unit.

Halton & Peel Trust & Savings Company (Ont. 1955)
Sept. 1968 – Acquired by The Huron & Erie Mortgage Corp. through an offer of 1 sh. of Huron & Erie plus $8.00 for each sh. of Halton & Peel.

Halton Reinsurance Company Limited (Bermuda Nov. 21, 1985)
June 5, 1995 – Name changed to Alexander Touche Insurance Inc.; basis 1 new com. for 1 old ordinary sh. ■

Hamac-Leduc Oils Limited (Alta.)
1960 – Struck off register.

Hamard Mines & Explorations Ltd. (B.C. 1969)
Jan. 1975 – Charter cancelled.

Hamason Mines Ltd. (Ont. 1954)
May 30, 1960 – Charter cancelled.

Hambro Canada Limited (Ont. 1919)
June 30, 1978 – Name changed to Hatleigh Corporation. ■

Hambro Canada (1972) Limited (Ont. 1919)
May 8, 1974 – Name changed to Hambro Canada Limited. ■

Hambro Resources Inc. (B.C. 1978)
Apr. 29, 1987 – Name changed to Richwell Resources Ltd.; basis 1 new for 3 old shs. ■

Hamcon Mines Ltd. (Ont. 1964)
1972 – Dissolved.

Hamil Silver-Lead Mines Ltd. (B.C. 1950)
Jan. 2, 1958 – Name changed to New Hamil Silver-Lead Mines Ltd.; basis 1 new for 5 old shs. ■

Hamilton Bridge Company Limited (Can. 1928)
Jan. 1954 – All assets subject to liabs. were sold to Bridge & Tank Co. of Canada Ltd. for $5,456,500. Prior to acquisition by Bridge & Tank, Gairdner & Co. acquired over 90% of 245,750 o/s shs. under a $22 per sh. offer which expired Jan. 25, 1954.

Hamilton Cotton Company Limited (Can. 1928; via Dominion charter)
May 1970 – Name changed to The Hamilton Group Limited; basis 5 new for 1 old sh. ■

The Hamilton Group Limited (Can. 1928; via Dominion charter)
Sept. 30, 1993 – Acquired by 293887 Canada Limited, a wholly owned subsid. of General Electric Capital Canada Inc., for $13.75 per sh.

The Hamilton Natural Gas & Mining Co. Ltd. (Ont. 1892)
Presumed dead.

Hamilton Thorne Ltd. (Ont. Feb. 19, 2007)
Dec. 3, 2024 – All o/s sh. not already held acquired by Astorg Group S.a.r.l. through Cradle Acquisition ULC; basis Cdn$2.25 cash per sh.

Hamilton Trust and Savings Corporation (Ont. 1963)
Dec. 31, 1977 – Merged with Canada Permanent Trust Company, a subsid. of Canada Permanent Mortgage Corporation. Terms included issuance of 1 ser. B. pref., $25 par, of Canada Permanent Trust Company for each 1.13 com. shs. or each 0.625 pref. sh. of Hamilton Trust.

Hamilton United Theatres Ltd. (Ont. 1922)
Jan. 2, 1944 – Assets sold to Theatre Properties (Hamilton) Ltd. for $711,881. 2,295 pref. holders received

one $100 par 5% bond of Theatre Properties, guaranteed by General Theatre Investment Co. Ltd., plus $25.35 in cash against accr. divds., plus $4.24 of undistributed surplus; 44,875 com. holders received 1 sh. of Theatre Properties new com. stk. Remainder of 2,892 pref. shs. received $100 princ. amt. plus cash shown above; 3,145 com. holders received $1.00 a sh.

Hammarlen Mining Co. Ltd. (Ont. 1940)
1953 – Charter cancelled.

Hammarlen Mining Company Ltd. (Ont. 1946)
Aug. 20, 1953 – Dissolved.

Hammarlen Porcupine Gold Mines Ltd. (Ont. 1940)
1945 – Name changed to Hammarlen Mining Co. Ltd. ■

Hammerhead Energy Inc. (Alta. Sept. 1, 2022 amalg.)
Dec. 28, 2023 – Acquired by Crescent Point Energy Corp.; basis $15.50 cash and 0.5340 Crescent Point com. shs. for 1 Hammerhead cl. A com. sh. (see Crescent Point Energy Corp.)

Hammerson Canada Inc. (Ont. Dec. 31, 1978)
June 29, 1990 – All o/s 9% pref. shs., ser. B redeemed; basis $25 plus all accrued and unpaid divs. All o/s 9.12% pref. shs., ser. A redeemed on Jan. 19, 1990; basis $25 plus $0.1203 in accrued and unpaid divs.

The Hammerson Property Investment and Development Corporation plc (U.K. 1940)
Dec. 6, 1993 – Name changed to Hammerson plc; basis 2 new ord. for 19 old ord. shs.

Hampshire Mines Ltd. (Ont. 1957)
June 1965 – Name changed to Kaiser Mines of Canada Ltd. ■

Hampshire Nickel Mines Ltd. (Ont. 1957)
July 1959 – Name changed to Hampshire Mines Ltd. ■

Hampton Bay Capital Inc. (Can. Aug. 13, 2018)
Apr. 28, 2020 – Name changed to Lendified Holdings Inc. pursuant to Qualifying Transaction reverse takeover acquisition of (old) Lendified Holdings Inc.; basis 1 new for 1.88 old shs. (see FPsurvey - Industrials)

Hampton Financial Corporation (Ont. Sept. 10, 2014)
Oct. 3, 2022 – All o/s cl. A pref. shs. redeemed for cash consisting of $10 plus a div. of 6¢ per sh. (see FPsurvey - Industrials)

Hana Mining Ltd. (B.C. May 11, 1999)
Feb. 22, 2013 – Acquired by Cupric Canyon Capital LP for 82¢ per sh.

Hanbury River Explorations Ltd. (B.C. Feb. 19, 1969)
Feb. 12, 1970 – Name changed to Mid-North Explorations Ltd. ■

Hanco Foods Inc. (Alta. June 1, 1990)
Aug. 31, 1994 – Name changed to Continental Fashion Group Inc. ■

Hand Chemical Industries Limited (Can. Sept. 6, 1930)
Mar. 22, 1977 – Name changed to HCI Holdings Ltd. ■

Handa Copper Corporation (B.C. Nov. 10, 2009)
June 11, 2018 – Name changed to Handa Mining Corporation. (see FPsurvey - Mines & Energy)

Handley-Gerlach Mines Ltd. (Ont. 1931)
Mar. 1960 – Name changed to Kimo Gold Mines Ltd.; basis 1 new for 5 old shs.

Handy Andy Auto-Centres Inc. (Que. 1937)
June 1, 1984 – All o/s com. shs. acquired by UAP Inc. at $8.53 per sh. (see UAP Inc.)

Handy Andy Company (Que. 1937)
July 24, 1978 – Name changed to Handy Andy Inc. ■

Handy Andy Inc. (Que. 1937)
July 12, 1982 – Name changed to Handy Andy Auto-Centres Inc. ■

Handy Andy Merchandising (Eastern) Limited (Ont. 1950)
Dec. 31, 1974 – Dissolved.

Hanfeng Evergreen Inc. (Ont. June 1, 2003 amalg.)
Aug. 20, 2014 – Ernst & Young Inc. of Toronto was appointed receiver and manager. Sale by the company of wholly owned Hanfeng Slow-Release Fertilizer (Heilongjiang) Co., Ltd. to Heilongjiang Pengcheng Fertilizer Co., Ltd. was approved by the Court.

Hank Payments Corp. (Can. Feb. 26, 2015)
Apr. 7, 2025 – Name changed to The FUTR Corporation; basis 1 new for 5.75 old shs. (see FPsurvey - Industrials)

Hankin Atlas Industries Limited (Can. July 20, 1989)
Nov. 29, 2000 – Name changed to Hankin Water Technologies Limited. ■

Hankin Water Technologies Limited (Can. July 20, 1989)
May 20, 2009 – Dissolved.

Hanna Gold Mines Ltd. (B.C. May 25, 1960)
Feb. 14, 1972 – Name changed to Dorchester Resources Ltd. ■

Hanna Pacific Steel Company Ltd. (B.C. Jan. 5, 1988)
Mar. 5, 1993 – Name changed to FOCH Consumer Electronics Corporation; basis 1 new for 5 old shs. ■

Hanover Explorations Limited (Ont. 1967)
Oct. 20, 1976 – Amalgamated with 3 other cos. to form Ameracrude International Inc.; basis 1 new for 10 old shs. (see Ameracrude International Inc.)

Hansa Corporation (Alta. Feb. 25, 1980)
Dec. 1, 2006 – Name changed to Azteca Gold Corp. pursuant to reverse takeover acquisition of Minera Azteca de Oro y Plata S.A. de C.V. (see FPsurvey - Mines & Energy)

Hansa International Resources Ltd. (B.C. 1979)
Jan. 21, 1994 – Dissolved and struck off register.

Hansa Petroleum Corporation (B.C. 1980)
Jan. 19, 1982 – Amalgamated with Orbit Oil & Gas Ltd. (1 for 1) to continue as Orbit Oil & Gas Ltd.; basis 1 new for 8 old shs.

Hansa Resources Limited (B.C. Mar. 19, 1980)
Nov. 2, 2022 – Name changed to Tribeca Resources Corporation; basis 1 new for 5 old shs. (see FPsurvey - Mines & Energy)

Hansa.net Global Commerce, Inc. (Anguilla Dec. 11, 1996)
Sept. 27, 2013 – Name changed to KMT-Hansa Corp. (see FPsurvey - Industrials)

Hanson Mineral Exploration Limited (Ont. 1957)
Mar. 21, 1989 – Formed McNickel Inc. in Ontario on amalgamation with Perch River Mines Limited; basis 1 new for 1 Perch sh. and 1 new for 5 Hanson shs. ■

Hanson Mines Ltd. (Ont. 1957)
Sept. 1980 – Name changed to Hanson Mineral Exploration Limited; basis 1 new for 3 old shs. ■

Hanson's Wholesale Grocers Ltd. (Ont. 1944)
Nov. 1950 – Unsecured creditors received 40.5696¢ on the dollar; nothing available for shldrs. Charter surrendered.

Hanstone Capital Corp. (B.C. Oct. 11, 2018)
Aug. 18, 2020 – Name changed to Hanstone Gold Corp. pursuant to Qualifying Transaction acquisition of Doc property option. (see FPsurvey - Mines & Energy)

Hanwei Energy Services Corp. (B.C. Oct. 26, 2005)
Apr. 20, 2023 – Name changed to Peak Discovery Capital Ltd. (see FPsurvey - Industrials)

Happy Gut Brands Limited (B.C. Aug. 12, 2019)
May 19, 2022 – Name changed to Bettermoo(d) Food Corporation. (see FPsurvey - Industrials)

Happy Resources Ltd. (B.C. 1983)
Jan. 13, 1987 – Name changed to HPY Industries Ltd. (see FPsurvey - Industrials)

Happy Supplements Inc. (B.C. Aug. 12, 2019)
Dec. 6, 2021 – Name changed to Happy Gut Brands Limited. ■

Hapuna Ventures Inc. (B.C. Jan. 31, 2017)
Nov. 23, 2020 – Name changed to ACME Lithium Inc. ■

Harambee Mining Corp. (B.C. May 29, 1984)
Jan. 3, 2002 – Name changed to Neuer Kapital Corp.; basis 1 new for 3 old shs. ■

Harben Industries Ltd. (B.C. Apr. 7, 1981)
July 19, 2000 – Formed Merit Industries Inc. on amalgamation with Merit Health and Beauty Inc., constituiting a reverse takeover by Merit Health. ■

Harbinger Gold Mines Ltd. (Ont. 1946)
Charter cancelled.

Harborside Inc. (Ont. Dec. 20, 2011)
July 25, 2022 – Name changed to StateHouse Holdings Inc. ■

Harbour Ferries Ltd. (unknown)
Dec. 23, 1975 – Amalgamated with A-1 Steel and Iron Foundry (Vancouver) Ltd. (10 for 1), Ardiem Holdings Ltd. (5 for 1), and E. C. Warner Investments Ltd. (1 for 1) to form The Ardiem Industrial Corp.; basis 1 new for 3 old shs.

Harbour Natural Resources Ltd. (Alta. 1957)
Oct. 31, 1968 – Struck off register.

Harbour Pacific Oil & Gas Ltd. (B.C. Mar. 2, 1989)
Aug. 30, 2005 – Name changed to Harbour Pacific Minerals Inc.; basis 1 new for 10 old shs. (see FPsurvey - Mines & Energy)

Harbour Petroleum Company Limited (Alta. Apr. 14, 1977)
Aug. 9, 1999 – Name changed to Boundary Creek Resources Ltd. pursuant to plan of arrangement whereby Harbour sold 65% of its oil and gas assets, fixed assets and certain working capital to Boundary Creek Resources Ltd. and became a wholly owned subsidiary of ENCO Gas, Ltd.; basis 1 new for 5 old shs. ■

Harbour Star Capital Inc. (Alta. Oct. 24, 2014)
Nov. 30, 2018 – Name changed to EastWest Bioscience Inc. (see FPsurvey - Industrials)

Hard Creek Nickel Corporation (B.C. Jan. 17, 1983)
Aug. 28, 2017 – Name changed to Giga Metals Corporation; basis 1 new for 2 old shs. (see FPsurvey - Mines & Energy)

Hard Rock Gold Mines Ltd. (Ont. 1934)
1967 – Merged into MacLeod Mosher Gold Mines Ltd.; basis 1 new for 10 old shs.

Hard Suits Inc. (B.C. July 25, 1986)
July 2, 1997 – Acquired by American Oilfield Divers, Inc. for $1.65 per sh.

Hardee Farms International Ltd. (Can. Feb. 2, 1959; via Dominion charter)
Dec. 16, 1978 – Amalgamated in Ontario to continue with same name.
May 1, 1986 – Formed Cobi Foods Inc. in Ontario on amalgamation with wholly owned subsidiaries The Baxter Canning Company Limited and Cobi Foods Inc. ■

Hardee Farms International Ltd. (Can. 1959)
Dec. 16, 1978 – Amalgamated with Federal Diversiplex Limited to continue as Hardee Farms International Ltd.; basis 1 new for 1 old sh.

Hardiman Bay Mines Ltd. (Ont. 1956)
Mar. 1976 – Charter cancelled.

Hardiman Bay Resources Inc. (Ont. May 21, 1987)
Nov. 21, 1996 – Name changed to Avenza Global Technologies Corp. following acquisition of Intelligraphics Technology Corp.; basis 1 new for 10 old shs. ■

Harding Carpets Ltd. (Ont. July 7, 1927)
Jan. 7, 1987 – Name changed to The New Harding Group Inc. ■

Hardwood Lake Nickel Mines Ltd. (Ont. 1957)
June 17, 1965 – Dissolved.

Hardwoods Distribution Income Fund (B.C. Jan. 30, 2004)
Apr. 5, 2011 – Continued into Canada.
July 1, 2011 – Succeeded by Hardwoods Distribution Inc. pursuant to plan of arrangement whereby Hardwoods Distribution Income Fund was formed to facilitate the conversion of the fund into a corporation. ■

Hardwoods Distribution Inc. (Can. Apr. 5, 2011)
Dec. 2, 2022 – Name changed to ADENTRA Inc. (see FPsurvey - Industrials)

Hardy International Developments Inc. (B.C. Feb. 11, 1981)
Nov. 6, 1986 – Name changed to Unisave Energy Ltd.; basis 1 new for 3.5 old shs. ■

Hargal Oils Ltd. (Can. 1928)
1957 – Acquired by Freehold Gas and Oil Ltd.; basis 1 new for 10 old shs.

Hargor Resources Inc. (B.C. Jan. 18, 1980)
Mar. 10, 1986 – Name changed to Harken Technologies Inc. ■

Harico Mining & Development Co. Ltd. (Ont. 1953)
July 1, 1963 – Dissolved.

Hariston Corporation (Can. Jan. 8, 1952)
Feb. 15, 1999 – Name changed to Midland Holland Inc.; basis 1 new for 5 old shs. (1-for-500 consolidation immediately followed by 100-for-1 split). ■

Harkema Industries Limited (Alta. 1981)
June 14, 1990 – Name changed to Acuma International Inc. ■

Harken Technologies Inc. (B.C. Jan. 18, 1980)
Feb. 2, 1989 – Delisted from the Vancouver Stock Exchange. Subsequently dissolved and struck from registry.

Harker Gold Mines Ltd. (Ont. Jan. 7, 1924)
1965 – Name changed to Golden Harker Explorations Limited; basis 1 new for 5 old shs. ■

Harlake Capital Group Inc. (Que. 1951)
Sept. 28, 1990 – Name changed to Madison Grant Resources Inc. following acquisition of Madison Grant Mining Corp. for $600,000. ■

Harlequin Books Ltd. (Can. 1949)
Mar. 1969 – Name changed to Harlequin Enterprises Limited. ■

Harlequin Enterprises Limited (Can. 1949)
Apr. 21, 1981 – Torstar Corporation offered to purchase all o/s shs. it did not own on basis of $60, one $2.68 1st pfce. sh., 1981 ser. of $25 par value and one wt. to purchase one cl. B sh. of Torstar at $20.50 on or before June 30, 1986, for each 3 cl. A or B shs. of Harlequin. Non-Canadian shldrs. received $90 for each 3 cl. A or B shs. held. Purchase completed by July 31, 1981.
Dec. 9, 1983 – Continued into Ontario.
June 5, 2019 – Name changed to Harlequin Enterprises ULC and continued into British Columbia.

Harley Street Software Ltd. (B.C. Oct. 26, 1989)
Dec. 7, 1998 – Name changed to CardioComm Solutions Inc.; basis 1 new for 3 old shs. ■

Harlight Gold Mines Ltd. (Ont. 1945)
1954 – Charter cancelled.

Harlin Capital Inc. (Alta. 1987)
Oct. 11, 1989 – Continued into Canada.
Dec. 11, 1989 – Formed C.A.T. Computer Assisted Training Software Inc. on amalgamation with C.A.T. Computer Assisted Training Software Inc.; basis 1 new for 1 old sh. ■

Harlin Resources Limited (B.C. 1979)
Mar. 15, 1989 – Name changed to Consolidated Harlin Resources Limited; basis 1 new for 3 old shs. (see FPsurvey - Mines & Energy)

Harlow Resources Inc. (B.C. 1985)
Oct. 14, 1986 – Name changed to American Daleco Technologies Corp.; basis 1 new for 3 old shs. ■

Harlow Ventures Inc. (B.C. Aug. 24, 1990)
July 19, 2007 – Name changed to International LMM Ventures Corp.; basis 1 new for 2 old shs. ■

Harmac Pacific Inc. (B.C. Mar. 7, 1994)
Nov. 15, 1999 – Acquired by Pope & Talbot Ltd., a wholly owned subsid. of Pope & Talbot, Inc.; basis $9.25, 0.4732 Pope shs. or a combination thereof or $4.625 and 0.2366 Pope shs. for 1 Harmac sh.

Harman Oils & Minerals Ltd. (Ont. 1951)
1952 – Acquired by Sapphire Petroleums Ltd.; basis 9 new for 10 old shs.

Harmony Gold Corp. (B.C. June 7, 1999)
Oct. 22, 2012 – Name changed to Pure Energy Minerals Limited. (see FPsurvey - Mines & Energy)

Harmony Gold Mines Ltd. (Ont. 1945)
Nov. 14, 1955 – Dissolved.

Harmony Integrated Solutions, Inc. (Can. Sept. 6, 2000)
Sept. 19, 2005 – Dissolved.

Haro Metals Corp. (B.C. Nov. 9, 2017)
Oct. 25, 2019 – Name changed to Pioneer Media Holdings Inc. ■

Harricana Amalgamated Gold Mines Inc. (Que. 1927)
1939 – Name changed to Harricana Gold Mines Inc. (1939) Ltd.; basis 1 new for 3 old shs. ■

Harricana Gold Mines Inc. (1939) Ltd. (Que. 1927)
1953 – Name changed to New Harricana Mines Ltd.; basis 1 new for 4 old shs. ■

Harrier Capital Corporation (Alta. Nov. 19, 1996)
Jan. 31, 2000 – Name changed to e-Manufacturing Networks Inc. ■

Harrington Financial Inc. (Ont. Mar. 11, 1988)
Apr. 11, 1994 – Charter cancelled and co. dissolved; subsequently revived.
June 19, 1997 – Name changed to TecnoPetrol Inc. and continued into Yukon; basis 1 new for 15 old shs. ■

Harrington Sound Resources Inc. (Ont. Mar. 11, 1988)
Nov. 7, 1989 – Name changed to Harrington Financial Inc.; basis 1 new for 2 old shs. ■

Harris Steel Group Inc. (Ont. May 20, 1953)
Mar. 13, 2007 – Acquired by Nucor Corporation for $46.25 per sh.

Harrisburg-Dayton Resource Corp. (B.C. June 12, 1987)
Nov. 5, 1991 – Name changed to San Fernando Mining Company Ltd.; basis 1 new for 3 old shs. ■

Harrison-Hibbert Mines Ltd. (Ont. 1935)
1955 – Name changed to Harrison Minerals Ltd.; basis 1 new for 5 old shs. ■

Harrison Minerals Ltd. (Ont. 1935)
1964 – Name changed to Cantri Mines Limited; basis 1 new for 4 old shs. ■

Harrowston Corporation (Can. Jan. 2, 1992)
Feb. 10, 1993 – Continued into Ontario.
Apr. 1, 1993 – Name changed to Harrowston Inc. ■

Harrowston Inc. (Ont. Feb. 10, 1993)
July 30, 2001 – Acquired by 1479523 Ontario Inc., a subsid. of TD Capital's Canadian Private Equity Partners Fund, for $7.35 per sh.

Harry Smith & Sons Ltd. (B.C. 1956)
Apr. 3, 1973 – Merged with Canadian Centura Developments to form the amalgamated International Centura Industries Ltd.

Harry Winston Diamond Corporation (Can. July 12, 2002)
Jan. 27, 2013 – Name changed to Dominion Diamond Corporation. ■

Hart Acquisition Corp. (Alta. Feb. 15, 1998)
Jan. 15, 1999 – Name changed to HFI Flooring Inc. following acquisition of all o/s shs. of HFI Hardwood Flooring Inc.; basis 1 new for 1 old sh. ■

Hart Battery Company (1957) Limited (Can. 1957)
1963 – Certain assets of co. reported purch. by Electric Storage Battery Co. of Philadelphia; subsequently stated co. had discontinued business. Trans. agent for stock was Guaranty Trust Co. of Canada; trustee for bonds, Montreal Trust Co.

Hart River Mines Ltd. (B.C. Dec. 1, 1967)
Feb. 18, 1976 – Name changed to North Hart Resources Ltd.; basis 1 new for 5 old shs. ■

Hart Stores Inc. (Can. Oct. 25, 1984)
Feb. 20, 2015 – Acquired by Paul Nassar for 20¢ per sh. by way of amalgamation with 9102221 Canada Inc. (wholly owned by Mr. Nassar).

Hartco Corporation (Can. July 12, 2000 amalg.)
Aug. 31, 2005 – Converted into an income trust named Hartco Income Fund; basis 1 new trust unit for 1 com. sh. (see Hartco Income Fund)

Hartco Enterprises Inc. (Can. Oct. 25, 1984)
July 14, 2000 – Name changed to Hart Stores Inc. pursuant to reorganization whereby wholly owned subsidiaries Multimicro Inc. and Hartco Corporation were amalgamated to form Hartco Corporation and spun out to shareholders on a share-for-share basis. ■

Hartco Income Fund (Ont. June 23, 2005)
Apr. 20, 2009 – Converted into Hartco Inc.; basis 1 Hartco Inc. com. sh. for 1 Hartco Income Fund trust unit. (see Hartco Inc.)

Hartco Inc. (Can. Feb. 17, 2009)
July 6, 2015 – Acquired by 9187669 Canada Inc., a wholly owned subsid. of H&N Family Subco Inc., for $3.40 per Hartco sh.

Harte Gold Corp. (Ont. Jan. 22, 1982)
Feb. 18, 2022 – Assets acquired under CCAA proceedings by a subsid. of Silver Lake Resources Limited for an undisclosed amount which provides for repayment of substantially all of the company's liabilities but no consideration for any existing equity interests. All o/s com. shs. were cancelled without consideration and all officers and directors resigned.

Harte Resources Corporation (Ont. Jan. 22, 1982)
Jan. 8, 2004 – Name changed to Harte Gold Corp. ■

Harte Resources Ltd. (Ont. Jan. 22, 1982)
Nov. 7, 1986 – Name changed to Harte Resources Corporation; basis 1 new for 2.5 old shs. ■

Hartland Mine Ltd. (Que. 1971)
June 1979 – Charter cancelled.

Hartland Pipeline Services Ltd. (Alta. Aug. 29, 1997)
Nov. 25, 1999 – Placed into receivership. PricewaterhouseCoopers Inc. was appointed receiver.

Hartley Oils Ltd. (Alta. 1952)
1963 – Struck off register.

HartWell Petroleums Ltd. (Alta. Jan. 19, 1988)
Mar. 7, 1997 – Acquired by CrownJoule Exploration Ltd. of Calgary, Alta., for $1.667 per sh.

Hartz Equities Inc. (Alta. Dec. 3, 1986)
Feb. 9, 1989 – Name changed to Solid Resources Ltd. ■

Harvard Capital Corporation (B.C. Nov. 12, 1987)
Feb. 16, 1993 – Name changed to Harvard International Technologies Ltd.; basis 1 new for 5 old shs. ■

Harvard Capital Corp. (Alta. Mar. 12, 1998)
Dec. 17, 1999 – Name changed to Nework Corp. ■

Harvard International Technologies Ltd. (B.C. Nov. 12, 1987)
Oct. 21, 1994 – Filed an assignment into bankruptcy and Deloitte & Touche Inc. of Vancouver was appointed trustee.
Apr. 1995 – Most assets had been sold and a deferred payment scheme (over 10 yrs) was set up throughwhich unsecured creditors could receive a distribution.
June 2002 – No deferred payments had been made and it was unlikely funds would be available for distribution.
Oct. 25, 2005 – Trustee discharged

Harvard Mines Ltd. (Ont. 1955)
June 24, 1965 – Dissolved.

Harvard Uranium Mines Ltd. (Ont. 1955)
Name changed to Harvard Mines Ltd. ■

Harvest Acquisition Corp. (Alta. Dec. 13, 1996)
Nov. 25, 1997 – Formed Helin Industries Inc. on amalgamation with Helin Industries Ltd.; basis 1 new for 5 old shs. ■

Harvest Banks & Buildings Income Fund (Ont. Sept. 25, 2009)
Oct. 18, 2011 – Converted into an open-ended mutual fund.

Harvest Canadian Income and Growth Fund (Ont. May 31, 2010)
June 8, 2012 – Converted from a closed-end to an opened-end fund.

Harvest Energy Trust (Alta. July 10, 2002)
Dec. 30, 2009 – Acquired by KNOC Canada Ltd., a wholly owned subsid. of Korea National Oil Corporation, for $10 per trust unit.
May 6, 2010 – Name changed to Harvest Operations Corp.

Harvest Explorations Ltd. (Alta. 1952)
May 5, 1978 – Charter cancelled.

Harvest Health & Recreation Inc. (B.C. Nov. 20, 2007)
Oct. 5, 2021 – Acquired by Trulieve Cannabis Corp.; basis 0.1170 Trulieve sub. vtg. sh. for 1 Harvest Health sub. vtg. sh.

Harvest One Cannabis Inc. (B.C. Aug. 28, 2008)
Sept. 8, 2022 – Name changed to Delivra Health Brands Inc. (see FPsurvey - Industrials)

Harvest One Capital Inc. (B.C. Aug. 28, 2008)
Apr. 26, 2017 – Name changed to Harvest One Cannabis Inc. following Qualifying Transaction acquisition of United Greeneries Holdings Ltd. and Satipharm AG; basis 1 new for 1.79 old shs. ■

Harvest Petroleums Limited (Alta. 1952)
1969 – Name changed to Harvest Explorations Ltd.; basis 1 new for 5 old shs. ■

Harvest-Spring Nutritional Systems (1981) Corporation (B.C. Jan. 7, 1981)
Apr. 7, 1996 – Continued into Canada.
May 28, 1996 – Name changed to Xemac Resources Inc.; basis 1 new for 5 old shs. ■

Harvest Sustainable Income Fund (Ont.)
Nov. 29, 2012 – Converted from a closed-end fund to an open-ended fund.

Harvey Creek Gold Placers Ltd. (B.C. Mar. 11, 1983)
Mar. 23, 1999 – Name changed to New Millennium Metals Corporation. ■

Harvey Woods Limited (Ont. 1911)
Feb. 11, 1985 – Amalgamated with 606937 Ontario Inc., a wholly owned subsid. of Ambramco (1984) Inc. Com. shs. of Harvey Woods exchanged on sh.-for-sh. basis into pref. shs. of amalg. co. and immediately redeemed at $3.30 per sh.

Harvey's Food Ltd. (Ont. 1959)
Jan. 7, 1974 – Amalgamated with Industrial Growth Management Ltd. to form Foodcorp Ltd.

Harwell Mining & Exploration Co. Ltd. (Ont. 1944)
1955 – Charter cancelled.

Harwin Exploration & Development Inc. (B.C. 1984)
June 23, 1995 – Dissolved and struck off register.

Hasaga Gold Mines Ltd. (Ont. Oct. 18, 1938)
Apr. 27, 1967 – Merged into The Little Long Lac Gold Mines Ltd.; basis 1 new for 20 old shs. (see The Little Long Lac Gold Mines Ltd.)

The Hash Corporation (Ont. Mar. 28, 1967)
Nov. 18, 2024 – Name changed to Street Capital Inc. (see FPsurvey - Industrials)

HashChain Technology Inc. (B.C. Feb. 18, 2017)
Feb. 20, 2020 – Name changed to Digihost Technology Inc. pursuant to reverse takeover acquisition of Digihost International, Inc.; basis 1 new for 40 old shs. ■

Hasina Resource Corp. (B.C. Feb. 13, 1980)
Nov. 5, 1987 – Name changed to Bradbury International Equities Ltd.; basis 1 new for 2 old shs. ■

Hastings Mining and Development Co. Ltd. (Que. 1955)
Sept. 1968 – Assets acquired by Sullivan Mines for cash consideration.
Mar. 17, 1969 – Hastings acquired 800,000 shs. of Sullivan, which were distributed with cash; basis 16 Sullivan plus 50¢ cash for each 100 Hastings.

Hastings Resources Corp. (B.C. Jan. 13, 1981)
Sept. 22, 2010 – Name changed to Trigen Resources Inc.; basis 1 new for 5 old shs. ■

Hat Creek Energy Corp. (B.C. Apr. 12, 1977)
Mar. 29, 1984 – Name changed to Fairchild Resources Inc.; basis 1 new for 3 old shs. ■

Hatch Interactive Technologies Corp. (B.C. May 12, 2006)
July 28, 2016 – Name changed to Fandom Sports Media Corp. ■

Hatco Capital Inc. (B.C. Apr. 27, 1982)
Dec. 7, 1992 – Name changed to SoftQuad International Inc. ■

Hathaway Metal Mines Ltd. (Ont. 1964)
Mar. 1976 – Charter cancelled.

Hathor Exploration Limited (Alta. June 28, 1996)
Sept. 26, 1996 – Continued into Canada.
Jan. 13, 2012 – Acquired by Rio Tinto plc for $4.70 per sh.

Hatleigh Corporation (Ont. 1919)
June 30, 1984 – Formed Dexleigh Corporation in Canada on amalgamation with Foodex Inc. Upon amalg., each cl. A sh. of Hatleigh exchanged for 1 com. sh. and 1 wt. of Dexleigh, each Hatleigh 3rd pfce. sh. ser. 1 exchanged for 4 cl. AA ser. a pref. shs. of Dexleigh; and each Hatleigh 3rd pfce. sh. ser. 2 exchanged into 1 com. sh. and 1 wt. of Dexleigh. Each wt. of Dexleigh entitled to purch. one com. sh. at $2 until Dec. 31, 1986. ■

Hatthaway-Matheson Enterprises Inc. (B.C. June 7, 1983)
Oct. 8, 1993 – Name changed to Innovis Corporation. ■

Hatton Capital Corp. (Can. Feb. 9, 2004)
Dec. 29, 2006 – Name changed to Nevgold Resource Corp. ■

Haultain Resources Ltd. (B.C. Apr. 15, 1981)
Aug. 15, 1986 – Name changed to Canasia Industries Corporation. ■

Hav-Info Computers Inc. (B.C. Apr. 12, 1985)
Aug. 14, 1989 – Name changed to National Hav-Info Communications Inc.; basis 1 new for 5 old shs. ■

Havelock Energy Resources Inc. (Ont. Sept. 24, 1937)
Mar. 9, 1994 – Name changed to Municipal Ticket Corporation; basis 1 new for 3 old shs. ■

Havilah Mining Corporation (B.C. May 3, 2018)
June 24, 2019 – Name changed to 1911 Gold Corporation. (see FPsurvey - Mines & Energy)

Hawk Energy Corp. (Alta. Jan. 16, 2003)
May 19, 2006 – Acquired by Flagship Energy Inc.; basis for cl. A shldrs - either $2.85, or 1.5566 new Flagship cl. A shs., or 1.2692 new Flagship cl. B shs., or a combination thereof for 1 old Hawk cl. A sh.; basis for cl. B shldrs - either $10, or 1.8868 new Flagship cl. A shs., or 1.5385 new Flagship cl. B shs., or a combination thereof for 1 old Hawk cl. B sh. (see Flagship Energy Inc.)

Hawk Exploration Ltd. (Alta. Feb. 2, 2009)
July 18, 2016 – Acquired by Kaisen Energy Corp.; basis 8¢ cash per sh. (see Kaisen Energy Corp.)

Hawk-Jen Mining Corp. Ltd. (Sask. 1956)
Oct. 1963 – Struck off register.

Hawk Junction Capital Corp. (Ont. Mar. 17, 1999)
Jan. 1, 2003 – Formed Hawk Precious Minerals Inc. in Ontario on amalgamation with 1541386 Ontario Inc. and 1541387 Ontario Inc. with Hawk Junction Capital Corp. the deemed acquiror; basis 1 new for 2 1541386 Ontario Inc. shs., 1 new for 1 1541387 Ontario Inc. sh. and 1 new for 1 Hawk Junction sh. ■

Hawk Oil Inc. (Alta. Nov. 18, 1996)
Feb. 7, 2003 – Acquired by APF Energy Trust; basis $4.80 or 0.5079365 new APF trust units or a combination thereof for 1 old Hawk cl. A sh. (see APF Energy Trust)

Hawk Precious Minerals Inc. (Ont. Jan. 1, 2003 amalg.)
Mar. 28, 2007 – Name changed to Hawk Uranium Inc. ■

Hawk Resources Inc. (B.C. Apr. 28, 1983)
Aug. 2, 1995 – Name changed to Zicor Mining Inc.; basis 1 new for 4 old shs. ■

Hawk Uranium Inc. (Ont. Jan. 1, 2003 amalg.)
July 28, 2010 – Name changed to Ring of Fire Resources Inc. ■

Hawker Industries Limited (unknown)
Oct. 2, 1978 – Amalgamated with parent, Hawker Siddeley Canada Ltd., and continued under that name. Each com. sh. not held by parent was converted into 2 shs. of amalg. co.

Hawker Resources Inc. (Alta. Feb. 14, 1994)
July 11, 2005 – Name changed to Iteration Energy Ltd. ■

Hawker Siddeley Canada Inc. (Can. Sept. 1, 1945; via letters patent)
Sept. 17, 2001 – Acquired by Glacier Ventures International Corp.; basis 77¢ or 0.63 Glacier Ventures shs. for 1 Hawker Siddeley sh. (see Glacier Ventures International Corp.)
Dec. 22, 2004 – Continued into British Columbia. (see Glacier Ventures International Corp.)

Hawker Siddeley Canada Ltd. (Can. Sept. 1, 1945; via letters patent)
July 1, 1980 – Name changed to Hawker Siddeley Canada Inc. ■

Hawker Uranium Mines (Alta. 1953)
1956 – Assets acquired by Inland Resources Corp., a Delaware co.; basis 1 new for 4 old shs.

Hawkeye Developments Ltd. (B.C. July 15, 1988)
June 22, 1992 – Name changed to Western Garnet Company Ltd. ■

Hawkeye Gold Corporation (B.C. Jan. 5, 1988)
Dec. 17, 1998 – Name changed to Hawkeye Gold International Inc.; basis 1 new for 4 old shs. ■

Hawkeye Gold International Inc. (B.C. Jan. 5, 1988)
May 29, 2003 – Name changed to Hawkeye Gold & Diamond Inc.; basis 1 new for 4 old shs. (see FPsurvey - Mines & Energy)

Hawkeye Ventures Inc. (Alta. Aug. 11, 2000)
July 16, 2003 – Name changed to Puma Exploration Inc. following Qualifying Transaction acquisition of certain Quebec mineral claims. ■

Hawklin Industries Inc. (Ont. 1963)
Apr. 15, 1981 – Name changed to Video Industries Inc.

Hawkmoon Resources Corp. (B.C. Apr. 26, 2019)
Apr. 21, 2023 – Name changed to Earthwise Minerals Corp. (see FPsurvey - Mines & Energy)

Hawkpoint Gold Mines Ltd. (Ont. 1946)
Jan. 16, 1961 – Charter cancelled.

Hawkstone Energy Corp. (B.C. Mar. 1, 2005)
Nov. 17, 2011 – Name changed to Range Energy Resources Inc. ■

Hawkwood Energy Ltd. (Alta. Jan. 22, 1987)
Sept. 21, 1989 – Name changed to Hawkwood Industries Inc. ■

Hawkwood Industries Inc. (Alta. Jan. 22, 1987)
Aug. 24, 1992 – Name changed to Environmental Containment Systems Limited; basis 1 new for 5 old shs. ■

Hawley Group Ltd. (Sweden 1984)
Apr. 21, 1988 – Name changed to ADT Limited.

Hawthorn Publishing Co. Ltd. (Ont. Feb. 6, 1958)
Apr. 1958 – Name changed to Toronto Star Limited. ■

Hawthorn Resources Corp. (B.C. Sept. 8, 2020)
July 11, 2025 – Name changed to Prince Silver Corp.; basis 0.75 new for 1 old sh. (see FPsurvey - Mines & Energy)

Hawthorne Gold Corporation (B.C. 1979)
May 9, 1990 – Amalgamated with Eureka Resources, Inc. to form new co. with same name Eureka Resources, Inc.; basis 0.2 new for 1 Eureka sh. (see Eureka Resources, Inc.)

Hawthorne Gold Corp. (B.C. Jan. 18, 2006)
Apr. 5, 2011 – Name changed to China Minerals Mining Corporation. ■

Hayden Resources Ltd. (B.C. Apr. 17, 1979)
Mar. 14, 2000 – Name changed to Austin Developments Corp.; basis 1 new for 4 old shs. ■

Hayes-Cadillac Mines Ltd. (Ont. 1936)
1953 – Charter cancelled.

Hayes-Dana Inc. (Can. July 10, 1922; via Dominion charter)
Dec. 31, 1987 – Amalgamated in Canada to continue with same name.
May 23, 1995 – Acquired by Dana Canada Acquisition Inc., a wholly owned subsid. of Dana Corporation, for $18.50 per sh.

Hayes-Dana Limited (Can. July 10, 1922; via Dominion charter)
Sept. 1, 1979 – Name changed to Hayes-Dana Inc. ■

Hayes Steel Products Limited (Can. July 10, 1922; via Dominion charter)
Oct. 28, 1966 – Name changed to Hayes-Dana Limited. ■

Hayes Trucks Ltd. (B.C. 1929)
Feb. 1974 – Gearmatic Co. Ltd., a Cdn. subsid. of PACCAR Inc. of Bellevue, Wash., acquired all o/s com. shs. and substantially all o/s pref. shs.

Hayes Wheel & Forgings, Ltd. (Can. July 10, 1922; via Dominion charter)
May 1936 – Name changed to Hayes Steel Products Limited. ■

Hayes Wheel Co. of Canada (Can. July 10, 1922; via Dominion charter)
1927 – Name changed to Hayes Wheel & Forgings, Ltd. ■

Hazelton Sunrise Mines Ltd. (B.C. Feb. 20, 1911)
Mar. 1970 – Name changed to Anoda Nickel Ltd.; basis 1 new for 15 old shs. ■

Hazeur Chibougamau Mines Ltd. (Ont. 1952)
Nov. 30, 1964 – Dissolved.

Head of the Lakes Iron Ltd. (Ont. 1948)
July 25, 1963 – Name changed to Lakehead Mines Ltd.; basis 1 new for 2 old shs. ■

Head4 Solutions Inc. (Can. Mar. 31, 1995)
Jan. 25, 2005 – Name changed to Saratoga Electronic Solutions Inc. following reverse takeover acquisition of Saratoga ATM Corporation Inc.; basis 1 new for 4 old shs. ■

Headley Amalgamated Gold Mines Ltd. (B.C. 1934)
1956 – Charter cancelled.

Headline Media Group Inc. (Can. Nov. 24, 2000)
Mar. 14, 2005 – Name changed to Score Media Inc. ■

Headline Uranium Mines Ltd. (Ont. 1940)
Sept. 26, 1960 – Dissolved.

Headvue Mines Ltd. (Ont. 1951)
Aug. 22, 1979 – Name changed to Phaeton Exploration Ltd.; basis 1 new for 2 old shs. ■

Headwater Mines Ltd. (Ont. 1950)
Dec. 1977 – Charter cancelled.

Headway Builders Ontario Ltd. (Ont. 1967)
1969 – Amalgamated into Headway Corporation Ltd.

Headway Corporation Ltd. (Ont. 1969 amalg.)
Nov. 1980 – Amalgamated with wholly owned subsid. of Nu-West Group Limited following sh. purch. offer; basis 1 cl. A com. sh. Nu-West for each 2 shs. Headway, or option to receive 1.35 Nu-West 9% ser D 1st pref. shs. for each 4 Headway shs.

Headway Hotels Ltd. (Can. Nov. 23, 1972)
May 29, 1984 – Dissolved.

Headway Red Lake Gold Mines Ltd. (Ont. Sept. 7, 1944)
Mar. 3, 1977 – Amalgamated with Coulee Lead and Zinc Mines Ltd. (1 for 10) to form Wayfair Explorations Ltd.; basis 1 new for 20 old shs. (see Wayfair Explorations Inc.)

Healey Capital Corp. (Alta. Nov. 26, 1999)
July 4, 2005 – Name changed to Run of River Power Inc. following Qualifying Transaction acquisition of Rockford Energy Corporation, Jascott Holdings Corp. plus 20% interest in the right to develop five hydroelectric power generating projects in British Columbia. ■

Healing Waters, Inc. (Ont. Aug. 23, 1993 amalg.)
Dec. 9, 2004 – Name changed to Rocky Mountain Brands, Inc.; basis 1 new for 8 old shs. ■

Health and Environment Technologies Inc. (Ont. May 3, 1989 amalg.)
Aug. 30, 1993 – Struck from the registry and dissolved.

The Health Care and Biotechnology Venture Fund (Ont. Jan. 17, 1992)
Feb. 25, 2004 – Return of capital of $1.06 per unit paid to unitholders of record Feb. 20, 2004.
May 3, 2005 – Fund was wound up. Final distribution of $0.3319 per unit paid to unitholders of record Aug. 4, 2004.

Health Care Products Inc. (Ont. July 5, 1985)
Mar. 31, 1994 – Name changed to Celltech Media Inc.; basis 1 new for 10 old shs. ■

Health Development Services Inc. (Can. Sept. 14, 1982)
Oct. 4, 1990 – Continued into Ontario.
Oct. 30, 1990 – Name changed to Spinnaker Development Corporation. (see FPsurvey - Industrials)

HealthCare Capital Corp. (Alta. July 27, 1993)
Feb. 10, 1998 – Name changed to Sonus Corp.; basis 1 new for 5 old shs. ■

Healthcare Leaders Income Fund (Ont. Nov. 19, 2014)
Oct. 24, 2014 – Converted to an exchange-traded fund.

HealthLease Properties Real Estate Investment Trust (Ont. Apr. 17, 2012)
Nov. 25, 2014 – Acquired by U.S.-based Health Care REIT, Inc.; basis Cdn$14.20 cash per trust unit.

HealthPricer Interactive Limited (Can. Feb. 20, 2004)
Mar. 18, 2013 – Name changed to Disani Capital Corp.; basis 1 new for 30 old shs. ■

Healthscreen Solutions Incorporated (B.C. May 13, 1981)
Sept. 8, 2011 – Placed into receivership. Deloitte & Touche Inc. appointed receiver.

HealthSpace Data Systems Ltd. (B.C. May 15, 2015)
Apr. 27, 2022 – Name changed to HS GovTech Solutions Inc. ■

HealthStreams Technology Inc. (Ont. June 29, 1994 amalg.)
Sept. 30, 1997 – Name changed to MediSolution Ltd. ■

Healthtrac, Inc. (Can. Feb. 1, 1991)
Nov. 9, 2012 – Dissolved.

Healthy Eating Inc. (Alta. Oct. 25, 1990)
Sept. 12, 1991 – Name changed to Humpty's Restaurants International Inc. ■

Heaps Engineering (1940) Ltd. (B.C. 1911)
July 1948 – Name changed to Heaps Waterous Ltd. ■

Heaps Waterous Ltd. (B.C. 1911)
1955 – Placed into liquidation.
Jan. 1957 – Assets distributed to shldrs. as follows: $2.25 pd. January 1956; $2.00 pd. April 1956; $1.00 pd. November 1956; $1.0689 pd. January 1957 (final payment).

Hearne Coppermine Explorations Ltd. (B.C. July 20, 1967)
Sept. 1973 – Name changed to United Hearne Resources Ltd.; basis 1 new for 2 old shs. ■

Hearne Yellowknife Mines Ltd. (Ont. 1945)
Nov. 28, 1973 – Charter cancelled.

Hearst Larder Mines Ltd. (Ont. 1950)
Sept. 29, 1966 – Dissolved.

Heart Minerals Ltd. (B.C. Apr. 11, 1983)
June 27, 1984 – Name changed to SRO Entertainment International Inc. ■

Heartfield Mining Corp. (B.C. Mar. 24, 2021)
Nov. 8, 2024 – Name changed to Mercado Minerals Ltd. (see FPsurvey - Mines & Energy)

Heartland Oil & Gas Corporation (B.C. 1979)
Aug. 1, 1982 – Amalgamated with American Energy Corporation (1 for 1) and Canzona Minerals Inc. (1 for 4) to form a new co. also named American Energy Corporation; basis 1 new for 2 old shs.

Heartland Resources Inc. (Ont. Apr. 25, 1975)
Sept. 10, 2007 – Name changed to Ryland Oil Corporation. ■

Heartwood Capital Corporation (Alta. June 24, 2003)
Apr. 10, 2006 – Name changed to Neo Alliance Minerals Inc. following Qualifying Transaction acquisition of Neo Alliance Holdings Limited. ■

Heaston Resources Ltd. (B.C. July 29, 1983)
June 16, 1987 – Name changed to W. M. Helijet Airways Inc. ■

Heath Gold Mines Ltd. (Ont. 1944)
Mar. 1975 – Charter cancelled.

Heatherdale Resources Ltd. (Alta. Nov. 6, 2007)
Nov. 16, 2009 – Continued into British Columbia.
Apr. 20, 2021 – Name changed to Blackwolf Copper and Gold Ltd. ■

Heathridge Mines Ltd. (Ont. 1966)
Apr. 9, 1975 – Charter cancelled.

Heating Oil Partners Income Fund (Ont. Mar. 20, 2002)
June 26, 2006 – Following reorganization of indirectly held Heating Oil Partners, LP and Heating Oil Partners GP, Inc. under an order by the U.S. Bankruptcy Court, wholly owned HOP Holdings, Inc. filed an assignment into bankruptcy under the Bankruptcy and Insolvency Act. There would be no distributions to unitholders and it was anticipated that the fund would be dissolved and all trust units cancelled.

Hecate Gold Corp. (Ont. 1948)
1977 – Continued into British Columbia.
June 28, 1982 – Acquired by Host Ventures Limited; basis 1 Host sh. for 1 Hecate sh.

Hector Resources Inc. (B.C. Oct. 17, 1983)
Mar. 12, 1993 – Name changed to Abacus Minerals Corporation; basis 1 new for 4 old shs. ■

Hedgehog Mines Ltd. (Ont. 1947)
1955 – Charter cancelled.

Hedger Capital Inc. (B.C. Mar. 8, 2006)
Feb. 3, 2010 – Name changed to Pinestar Gold Inc. pursuant to Qualifying Transaction reverse takeover acquisition of Oretech Resources Inc. ■

Hedley Basin Mines Ltd. (B.C. 1946)
1953 – Name changed to Copper Basin Mines Ltd. ■

Hedley Gordon Gold Mines Ltd. (B.C. 1947)
Nov. 1971 – Name changed to Hedley Pacific Mining Corp. Ltd. ■

Hedley Mascot Gold Mines Ltd. (B.C. June 7, 1934)
1951 – Merged into Giant Mascot Mines Ltd.; basis 55 new for 100 old shs.

Hedley Monarch Gold Mines Ltd. (B.C. 1945)
1961 – Acquired by Friday Mines Ltd.; basis 1 new for 10 old shs. (see Friday Mines Ltd.)

Hedley Pacific Mining Corp. Ltd. (B.C. 1947)
Aug. 21, 1992 – Name changed to Hedley Pacific Ventures Ltd. ■

Hedley Pacific Ventures Ltd. (B.C. 1947)
July 16, 1996 – Name changed to Hedley Technologies Inc. ■

Hedley-Sterling Explorations Inc. (Alta. Apr. 28, 1987)
Mar. 5, 1991 – Name changed to Western Envirotech Inc.; basis 1 new for 4 old shs. ■

Hedley Technologies Inc. (B.C. 1947)
May 19, 1999 – Continued into Canada.
June 13, 2006 – Name changed to BioSyent Inc. (see FPsurvey - Industrials)

Hedley Yuniman Gold Mines Ltd. (B.C. 1937)
June 1974 – Charter cancelled.

Hedman Mines Limited (Ont. Aug. 13, 1956)
Sept. 3, 1982 – Name changed to Hedman Resources Limited. ■

Hedman Resources Limited (Ont. Aug. 13, 1956)
June 2, 2016 – Dissolved and certificates of incorporation have been cancelled.

Hedong Energy Inc. (Can. Sept. 25, 1995)
Feb. 9, 2004 – Name changed to Benchmark Energy Corp.; basis 1 new for 3 old shs. ■

Heenan Petroleum Limited (Can. Feb. 14, 1928)
Aug. 1, 1986 – Formed Heenan Senlac Resources Limited in Canada on amalgamation with Senlac Resources Inc.; basis 1 new for 1 Senlac sh. and 3 new for 2 Heenan shs. ■

Heenan Senlac Resources Limited (Can. Aug. 1, 1986 amalg.)
Sept. 17, 1992 – Amalgamated with Mining and Allied Supplies (Canada) Limited to form new co. with same name Mining and Allied Supplies (Canada) Limited; basis 1 Mining and Allied sh. plus 1 wt. for 25 Heenan shs. (see Mining and Allied Supplies (Canada) Limited)

Hees International Bancorp Inc. (Ont. Dec. 11, 1970)
Dec. 31, 1996 – Formed The Edper Group Limited in Ontario on amalgamation with The Edper Group Limited; basis 1 new cl. A limited vtg. sh. for 1 old com. sh. and 1 new cl. A pref. ser. D and/or ser. E sh. for 1 old cl. A pref. ser. D and/or ser. E sh. ■

Hees International Corporation (Ont. Dec. 11, 1970)
May 6, 1988 – Name changed to Hees International Bancorp Inc. ■

Heiberg Sulphur Mines Ltd. (Ont. 1969)
May 1975 – Charter cancelled.

Heitman Canadian Investors Services Ltd. (Can. 1927)
June 30, 1977 – Name changed to Canreit Investors Limited.

Heitman Canadian Realty Investors (Ont. 1973)
June 1977 – Name changed to Canadian Realty Investors. ■

Helena Gold Mines Ltd. (B.C. 1933)
Sept. 30, 1948 – Struck off register.

Helena Resources Limited (Yuk. Feb. 24, 1997)
Mar. 5, 2007 – Name changed to THEMAC Resources Group Limited. (see FPsurvey - Mines & Energy)

Helgena Mines Ltd. (B.C. Jan. 1, 1968)
1972 – Amalgamated in British Columbia to continue with same name.
Dec. 18, 1981 – Amalgamated with Pan Arctic Explorations Ltd. to form new co. with same name Strategic Metals Corporation; basis 1 new for 1 Pan Arctic sh. and 1 new for 4 Strategic Metals shs.
1981 – Name changed to Strategic Metals Corporation. ■

The Helical Corporation Inc. (N.S. Aug. 12, 1998)
Mar. 3, 2007 – Dissolved and struck from register.

Helicopter Exploration Co. Ltd. (Can. 1950)
1958 – Wound up and charter surrendered. Partial distribution made in May 1957, of $1.50 and 2.05 shs. Granduc Mines, Limited per sh. of Helicopter; final distribution of $3.63 and 2.154 shs. Gibson Girl Mines Ltd. per sh. of Helicopter made.

Helijet International Inc. (B.C. July 29, 1983)
July 29, 2019 – Privatized; basis 30¢ cash per sh.

Helin Industries Inc. (Alta. Dec. 13, 1996)
July 25, 2001 – Name changed to Second Chance Corp. (see FPsurvey - Industrials)

Helio Capital Corp. (B.C. Nov. 8, 1998)
Nov. 3, 2004 – Name changed to Helio Resource Corp. following Aug. 30, 2004, Qualifying Transaction reverse takeover acquisition of Bafex Holdings Limited. ■

Helio Resource Corp. (B.C. Nov. 8, 1998)
Jan. 7, 2020 – Name changed to Winshear Gold Corp. (see FPsurvey - Mines & Energy)

HeliosX Lithium & Technologies Corp. (B.C. Jan. 13, 2022 amalg.)
June 21, 2023 – Name changed to D2 Lithium Corp. (see FPsurvey - Mines & Energy)

HeliosX Technologies Corp. (B.C. Jan. 13, 2022 amalg.)
Feb. 1, 2022 – Name changed to HeliosX Lithium & Technologies Corp. ■

Helium Corporation of America (Del. 1961)
1962 – Assets sold to The International Helium Co. Ltd.; basis 1 new for 3 old shs. (see The International Helium Company Limited)

Helius Medical Technologies, Inc. (B.C. Mar. 13, 2014)
June 2, 2014 – Continued into Wyoming.
July 20, 2018 – Continued into Delaware.

Helix Applications Inc. (B.C. Sept. 23, 1991)
July 22, 2021 – Name changed to GlobalBlock Digital Asset Trading Limited. (see FPsurvey - Industrials)

Helix Biotech Corporation (B.C. 1983)
Oct. 22, 1993 – Name changed to International Helix Biotechnologies Inc.; basis 1 new for 2 old shs. ■

Helix Circuits Inc. (Can. Apr. 18, 1983)
Aug. 14, 1995 – Name changed to Circuit World Corporation. ■

Helix Hearing Care of America Corp. (Alta. Aug. 26, 1996)
July 9, 1999 – Continued into Canada. (see HEARx Canada Inc.)
July 15, 2002 – Plan of Arrangement amalgamation with Florida-based HEARx Ltd.; basis either 0.3537 new HEARx Ltd. com. sh., or 0.3537 new HEARx Canada Inc. exchangeable sh. for 1 old Helix com. sh. (see HEARx Canada Inc.)

Helix Systems Limited (B.C. 1983)
Apr. 28, 1989 – Dissolved.

Hellenic Resources Inc. (B.C. 1981)
Sept. 17, 1987 – Name changed to U.S. Grant Gold Mining Co. Ltd.; basis 1 new for 4 old shs. ■

Hellens Mining & Reduction Co. (Ont. 1951)
1953 – Acquired by Cobalt Consolidated Mining Corp. Ltd.; basis 1 new for 3 old shs. (see Cobalt Consolidated Mining Corp. Ltd.)

The Hello Channel Inc. (Alta. May 8, 1985)
Nov. 1, 1992 – Struck off register.

Hemagold Mines Ltd. (Ont. 1964)
1968 – Name changed to Northern Nuclear Mines Ltd. ■

Hemgold Resources Ltd. (B.C. 1983)
Nov. 15, 1985 – Name changed to Hydro Home Appliances Ltd. ■

Hemisphere Development Corp. (B.C. Mar. 6, 1978)
Jan. 14, 2000 – Name changed to Northern Hemisphere Development Corp.; basis 1 new for 5 old shs. ■

Hemisphere GPS Inc. (Alta. July 31, 1990)
May 24, 2013 – Name changed to AgJunction Inc. ■

Hemisphere Mining Co. Ltd. (Man. 1947)
1952 – Charter cancelled.

Hemlo Explorations Ltd. (B.C. 1982)
May 20, 1988 – Name changed to Akiko-Lori Gold Resources Ltd. ∎

Hemlo Explorers Inc. (Ont. July 21, 2008)
Feb. 10, 2025 – Name changed to Rocky Shore Gold Ltd. (see FPsurvey - Mines & Energy)

Hemlo Gold Mines Inc. (Ont. Dec. 31, 1968)
July 25, 1996 – Amalgamated with Battle Mountain Gold Company to form Battle Mountain Canada Ltd.; basis 1.48 new for 1 Hemlo sh. (see Battle Mountain Canada Ltd.)

Hemosol Corp. (Ont. Feb. 24, 2004)
July 6, 2007 – Sale of the operating assets and business of the company to an entity controlled by Catalyst Fund Limited Partnership II, the company's primary creditor, was completed. No distrib. was expected for subordinate creditors or to shldrs.
Aug. 7, 2007 – Name changed to 1608557 Ontario Inc. ∎

Hemosol Inc. (Ont. July 11, 1985)
May 5, 2004 – Name changed to Hemosol Corp. following reorganization whereby MDS Inc. acquired Hemosol Inc. and Hemosol Corp. acquired the business of Hemosol Inc.; basis 1 Hemosol Corp. com. sh. plus 1 LPBP Inc. cl. A com. sh. (successor co. to Hemosol Inc.) for 1 Hemosol Inc. com. sh. ∎

Hemp for Health Inc. (B.C. Oct. 1, 2018)
June 20, 2022 – Name changed to Yellow Stem Tech Inc. ∎

Hempco Food and Fiber Inc. (B.C. Mar. 15, 2007)
Aug. 21, 2019 – All o/s com. shs. not already held acquired by Aurora Cannabis Inc.; basis 0.08659 Aurora com. shs. for 1 Hempco sh.

Hempfusion Wellness Inc. (B.C. July 18, 2019)
June 22, 2023 – Made an assignment in bankruptcy. FTI Consulting Canada Inc. appointed trustee.

Hempsana Holdings Ltd. (B.C. Jan. 31, 1980)
May 27, 2024 – Assigned into bankruptcy. B. Riley Farber Inc. appointed trustee.

Hendershot Paper Products Ltd. (Ont. 1946)
Sept. 1, 1973 – Com. shs. purchased in 1960 by Canadian International Paper Co. at $9.00 per sh. and wts. at $3.00 each. All o/s 6% pref. shs. called for redemption on May 15, 1970, at $105 plus $11.24 divd. per sh. All o/s 6.5% pref. 1st mtge. bds. due 1977 called for redempti at par plus accr. int.

Henderson Oil Holdings Ltd. (unknown)
1959 – Acquired by Medallion Petroleums Ltd.; basis 1 new for 50 old shs.

Henderson Petroleum Ltd. (unknown)
Merged with Stockmen Oils, Ltd. (see Stockmen Oils Ltd.)

Hendricks Minerals Canada Limited (Ont. Mar. 22, 1994 amalg.)
May 6, 1997 – Name changed to MCK Mining Corp.; basis 1 com. for 2.5 cl. A subord. vtg. sh. ∎

Henlys Group Limited (Can. 1961)
Sept. 8, 1989 – Name changed to Sechura Inc. ∎

Hennessy Resource Corporation (B.C. 1983)
May 20, 1992 – Name changed to Fastlane International Enterprises Inc. ∎

Henning-Maloney Gold Mines Ltd. (Ont. Nov. 7, 1933)
Believed defunct.

Henninger Brewery (Ontario) Ltd. (Ont. Dec. 15, 1971)
Aug. 26, 1981 – Name changed to H.O. Financial Limited following sale of assets and undertakings to Amstel Brewery Holdings Ltd. for $5.4 million. ∎

Henrietta Mines Ltd. (B.C. Feb. 15, 1967)
Feb. 22, 1978 – Name changed to Caledonia Resource Ltd.; basis 1 new for 2.5 old shs. ∎

Henrosco-Larder Mines Ltd. (Ont. 1946)
Feb. 1960 – Charter cancelled.

Henry Birks and Sons Inc. (Can. 1879)
Nov. 15, 2005 – Name changed to Birks & Mayors Inc. ∎

Hepburn Transport Ltd. (Can. - unspecified)
1966 – Amalgamated into Laidlaw Motorways Ltd.

Hera Resources Inc. (B.C. Dec. 8, 1989 amalg.)
Feb. 10, 1998 – Name changed to Medallion Resources Ltd.; basis 1 new for 5 old shs. ∎

Herb Lake Mining & Exploration (Ont. 1947)
1957 – Name changed to Big Herb Lake Mining & Exploration Ltd.; basis 1 new for 3 old shs. ∎

Herbal Clone Bank Canada Inc. (B.C. Nov. 12, 2010)
June 18, 2015 – Name changed to High Hampton Holdings Corp. ∎

Herbdix Gold Mines Ltd. (Ont. 1946)
1961 – Charter cancelled.

Herbert Mining Company Limited (Ont. 1947)
May 2, 1960 – Dissolved.

Herblet Hudson Mines Ltd. (Ont. 1945)
Feb. 17, 1972 – Dissolved.

HerbTech Inc. (Alta. Aug. 10, 1992)
July 24, 1998 – Amalgamated with CV Technologies Inc. (1.561 for 1) to continue as CV Technologies Inc.; basis 0.896 new CV com. sh. for 1 old HerbTech cl. A com. sh. (see CV Technologies Inc.)

Hercon Resources Ltd. (Alta. 1952)
1978 – Continued into British Columbia.
Apr. 1980 – Amalgamated with wholly owned subsid. to form Chilco Resources Ltd.

Hercules Silver Corp. (Ont. Jan. 25, 2018)
June 28, 2024 – Name changed to Hercules Metals Corp. (see FPsurvey - Mines & Energy)

Hercules Uranium Mines Ltd. (Ont. 1953)
Mar. 1976 – Charter cancelled.

Hercules Ventures Inc. (B.C. Sept. 21, 1987)
May 7, 1993 – Name changed to Tucan Ventures Inc.; basis 1 new for 2.5 old shs. ∎

Herdis International Canada Inc. (B.C. July 21, 1983)
Feb. 10, 1987 – Name changed to Deep Shaft Technology International Incorporated. ∎

Herdron Capital Corp. (Can. Dec. 10, 2007)
Mar. 9, 2010 – Name changed to El Tigre Silver Corp. following Qualifying Transaction acquisition of Pacemaker Silver Mining, S.A. de C.V. ∎

Here Fault Copper Limited (Ont. 1956)
Aug. 11, 1986 – Name changed to First Toronto Capital Corporation. ∎

Heritage American Resource Corp. (B.C. July 25, 1994 amalg.)
Sept. 17, 2001 – Name changed to Heritage Explorations Ltd.; basis 1 new for 4 old shs. ∎

Heritage Cannabis Holdings Corp. (B.C. Oct. 25, 2007)
Nov. 4, 2019 – Continued into Ontario.
Aug. 29, 2024 – Acquired by HAB Cann Holdings Ltd. pursuant to a reverse vesting order under the Companies' Creditors Arrangement Act (CCAA) and all o/s com. shs. were terminated and cancelled without consideration.

Heritage Concepts International Inc. (Que. Aug. 9, 1949)
Mar. 26, 2001 – Name changed to NEXUS Group International Inc. ∎

Heritage Explorations Ltd. (B.C. July 25, 1994 amalg.)
Aug. 25, 2005 – Plan of Arrangement acquisition by St Andrew Goldfields Ltd.; basis 1.2 new St Andrew shs. for 1 old Heritage sh. (see St Andrew Goldfields Ltd.)

The Heritage Group Inc. (Ont. Dec. 30, 1930)
Apr. 29, 1986 – Name changed to Schneider Corporation. ∎

Heritage Living Canada Corp. (Ont. Dec. 31, 1986)
Oct. 31, 1994 – Dissolved.
June 13, 1997 – Revived.
Jan. 26, 1998 – Name changed to Global Biotech Inc. (see FPsurvey - Industrials)

Heritage Oil Corporation (Alta. Oct. 30, 1996)
May 13, 2014 – All exch. shs. redeemed for parent Heritage Oil plc ord. shs.; basis 1 for 1.

Heritage Petroleums Inc. (B.C. May 9, 1967)
July 25, 1994 – Amalgamated with American Fibre Corporation to form Heritage American Resource Corp.; basis 1 new for 8 American shs. and 1 new for 7 Heritage shs. (see Heritage American Resource Corp.)

Heritage Savings & Trust Company (Alta. 1968)
Mar. 13, 1987 – As of the company merged with North West Trust Company to operate in the name of the latter.

Heritage Ventures Ltd. (Alta. Dec. 23, 1987)
June 2, 2007 – Dissolved and struck from register.

Hermes Acquisition Corp. (B.C. Dec. 17, 2020)
Mar. 3, 2021 – Name changed to Nevada Lithium Resources Inc. (see FPsurvey - Mines & Energy)

Hermes Mines Ltd. (Ont. 1944)
Dec. 1960 – Charter cancelled.

Hermes Ventures Ltd. (B.C. May 14, 1987)
Sept. 26, 1994 – Name changed to Profile Ventures Ltd.; basis 1 new for 3 old shs. ∎

Héron Exploration Inc. (Que. June 4, 1963)
Dec. 16, 2012 – Voluntarily dissolved.

Heron Resources Ltd. (B.C. 1978)
Aug. 18, 1988 – Name changed to Consolidated Heron Resources Ltd.; basis 1 new for 5 old shs. ∎

Heron Resources Limited (Australia Feb. 17, 1995)
Apr. 2, 2018 – Voluntarily delisted.

Héroux-Devtek Inc. (Que. Mar. 17, 1942; via letters patent)
Feb. 14, 2025 – Acquired by Platinum Equity Advisors, LLC; basis $32.50 cash per sh.

Héroux Inc. (Que. Mar. 17, 1942; via letters patent)
Sept. 25, 2000 – Name changed to Héroux-Devtek Inc. ∎

Herron-Elder Gas & Oil Development Co., Ltd. (unknown)
1914 – Acquired by Alberta Petroleum Consolidated Ltd.; basis 3.5 new for 1 old sh. (see Alberta Petroleum Consolidated Ltd.)

Hershey Oil Corporation (Del. 1971)
Sept. 20, 1990 – Merged with American Exploration Acquisition Corp.; basis 1.611 new for 1 old or US$7.00 per sh.

Hertz Industries Limited (B.C. 1967)
May 2, 1986 – Struck off register.

Hertz Lithium Inc. (B.C. Feb. 15, 2019)
Feb. 9, 2024 – Name changed to Hertz Energy Inc. (see FPsurvey - Mines & Energy)

Hespanola Mines Ltd. (Ont. 1956)
1972 – Charter cancelled.

Heva Cadillac Gold Mines Ltd. (Ont. 1936)
1946 – Name changed to Heva Gold Mines Ltd.; basis 1 new for 2 old sh. ∎

Heva Gold Mines Ltd. (Ont. 1936)
1956 – Name changed to Heva Mines Ltd. ■

Heva Mines Ltd. (Ont. 1936)
Sept. 1959 – Merged into Hydra Explorations Ltd.; basis 1 new for 25 old shs.

Hewbet Mines Ltd. (Ont. 1948)
Sept. 1979 – Name changed to Sundance Energy Resources Limited and continued into Canada. ■

Hewfran Gold Mines, Ltd. (Ont. 1947)
Apr. 9, 1975 – Charter cancelled.

The Hewlyn Corporation (Alta. 1987)
Aug. 1, 1992 – Struck off register.

Heximer Oil Company, Limited (Ont. 1928)
1958 – Struck off register.

HeyBryan Media Inc. (B.C. Dec. 3, 2010)
Dec. 9, 2020 – Name changed to Fasttask Technologies Inc.; basis 1 new for 5 old shs. ■

Heyson Red Lake Gold Mines Ltd. (Ont. 1936)
Dec. 23, 1965 – Dissolved.

Hi-Alta Capital Inc. (Alta. Nov. 14, 1995)
June 5, 2002 – Name changed to Western Financial Group Inc. ■

Hi-Cor Resources Ltd. (B.C. 1979)
Dec. 2, 1986 – Name changed to International Burgers Now Ltd.; basis 1 new for 3 old shs. ■

Hi-Core Resources Ltd. (B.C. 1979)
Oct. 24, 1979 – Name changed to Hi-Cor Resources Ltd. ■

Hi-Ho Curb Serv-us Ltd. (Ont. 1947)
Nov. 26, 1994 – Charter cancelled and co. dissolved.

Hi Ho Silver Resources Inc. (Can. Apr. 7, 2005)
Mar. 30, 2018 – Continued into British Columbia. (see FPsurvey - Mines & Energy)

Hi-Lite Mines Ltd. (Ont. 1955)
1968 – Name changed to Hi-Lite Uranium Explorations Ltd. ■

Hi-Lite Uranium Explorations Ltd. (Ont. 1955)
Feb. 28, 1973 – Dissolved.

Hi-Lite Uranium Mines Ltd. (Ont. 1955)
1964 – Name changed to Hi-Lite Mines Ltd. ■

Hi-Lode Mining Co. (B.C. 1969)
July 1973 – Name changed to Starbuck Mines Ltd. ■

Hi-Peg Resources Ltd. (B.C. Jan. 4, 1984)
Jan. 29, 1987 – Name changed to Elegance Business Corporation. ■

Hi Tech Ventures Inc. (B.C. Dec. 14, 1982)
Sept. 7, 1993 – Name changed to Pro-Tech Venture Corp.; basis 1 new for 5 old shs. ■

Hi-Tower Drilling Co., Ltd. (Alta. Feb. 16, 1950)
June 1, 1962 – Name changed to Bow Valley Industries Ltd. ■

Hiawatha Gold Mines Ltd. (Ont. 1936)
Dec. 23, 1965 – Charter cancelled.

Hibernia Mining Co. Ltd. (B.C. 1968)
Oct. 20, 1972 – Name changed to Great World Resources Ltd. ■

Hibernian International Development Corporation Ltd. (B.C. 1969)
June 30, 1980 – Dissolved.

Hibiki Capital Corp. (B.C. Sept. 25, 2018)
Apr. 29, 2021 – Name changed to Sanu Gold Corp. (see FPsurvey - Mines & Energy)

Hibiscus Developments Limited (Can. 1972)
June 2, 1976 – Name changed to Mongowin-Sudbury Explorations Ltd. ■

Hibright Minerals Inc. (B.C. Jan. 27, 1981)
Oct. 25, 1996 – Name changed to Frontier Pacific Mining Corporation. ■

Hiburd Properties Inc. (B.C. 1983)
Jan. 15, 1993 – Dissolved and struck off register.

Hicbar Exploration Co. Ltd. (Ont. 1947)
Apr. 24, 1952 – Charter cancelled.

Hicco Energy Inc. (Alta. 1983)
Oct. 26, 1989 – Name changed to Intersoft Technologies Inc. ■

Hidden Valley Mines Inc. (Alta. June 13, 1986)
Aug. 5, 1993 – Name changed to Blis International Inc.; basis 1 new for 3 old shs. ■

Higginson Gold Mines Ltd. (Que. 1937)
1953 – Charter cancelled.

High American Gold Inc. (Ont. Apr. 25, 1997 amalg.)
July 30, 2008 – Name changed to Antioquia Gold Inc. following reverse takover acquisition of Am-Ves Resources Inc.; basis 1 new for 10 old shs. ■

High Arctic Energy Services Trust (Alta. June 10, 2005)
July 5, 2007 – Converted into High Arctic Energy Services Inc.; basis 1 new for 1 old unit.

High Bullen Resources Ltd. (Alta. Jan. 19, 1995)
Aug. 12, 1996 – Acquired by Highridge Exploration Ltd.; basis 1 Highridge sh. for 28 High Bullen shs. (see Highridge Exploration Ltd.)

High Crest Oils Ltd. (Alta. 1949)
1957 – Name changed to Canadian High Crest Oils Ltd.; basis 1 new for 4 old shs. ■

High Desert Gold Corporation (Can. Apr. 10, 2007)
Dec. 24, 2013 – Acquired by South American Silver Corp.; basis 0.275 South American shs. for 1 High Desert sh. (see South American Silver Corp.)

High Desert Mineral Resources, Inc. (B.C. Aug. 11, 1986)
June 19, 1995 – Continued into Canada.
Sept. 13, 1995 – Continued into Delaware.

High Energy Ventures Inc. (Alta. May 17, 1988)
Nov. 2, 2006 – Dissolved and struck from register.

High Five Oilfield Services Ltd. (Alta. July 2, 1998)
Nov. 2, 2000 – Name changed to Patch Safety Services Ltd. ■

High 5 Ventures Inc. (B.C. Aug. 24, 1984)
July 7, 2014 – Name changed to 37 Capital Inc.; basis 1 new for 6 old shs. (see FPsurvey - Mines & Energy)

High Frontier Resources Ltd. (B.C. Nov. 23, 1981)
Dec. 25, 2006 – Struck from registry and dissolved.

High Fusion Inc. (Can. July 19, 2004)
May 1, 2023 – Continued into British Columbia.
May 8, 2023 – Name changed to Vertical Peak Holdings Inc. ■

High Hampton Holdings Corp. (B.C. Nov. 12, 2010)
June 24, 2019 – Name changed to Mojave Jane Brands Inc. ■

High Income Preferred Shares Corporation (Can. Apr. 26, 2002)
Mar. 15, 2010 – All o/s ser. 1 and ser. 2 pref. shs. redeemed for $27.80 per sh. and $16.46 per sh., respectively, including accrued distributions.
Jan. 20, 2011 – Name changed to Carpincho Capital Corp. ■

High Income Principal And Yield Securities Corporation (Ont. Dec. 7, 2001)
Aug. 1, 2008 – All o/s pref. shs. and equity shs. redeemed for $25 per pref. sh. and $11.49 per equity sh.

High Lake Molybdenum Ltd. (Man. 1953)
Nov. 1967 – Name changed to Laronex Copper Mines Ltd. ■

High Level Design Systems, Inc. (Calif. Apr. 1991)
Dec. 31, 1996 – Merged into Cadence Design Systems Inc., a U.S. based company; basis 0.22 of a sh. of Cadence for 1 old sh. of High Level.

High Level Resources Ltd. (B.C. 1978)
Nov. 23, 1990 – Name changed to Colorfax International Inc.; basis 1 new for 4 old shs. ■

High Mountain Capital Corporation (Alta. Jan. 18, 2018)
Sept. 19, 2019 – Name changed to Facedrive Inc. pursuant to Qualifying Transaction reverse takeover acquisition of (old) Facedrive Inc. and concurrent amalgamation of (old) Facedrive with wholly owned 2696170 Ontario Inc. to continue as 2696170 Ontario Inc.; basis 1 new for 50 old shs. ■

High North Resources Inc. (Ont. Mar. 2, 1988)
July 27, 2000 – Name changed to HNR Ventures Inc.; basis 1 new for 4 old shs. ■

High North Resources Ltd. (B.C. Oct. 5, 2010)
Jan. 28, 2016 – Placed into receivership. PricewaterhouseCoopers Inc. was appointed receiver and all officers and directors resigned.
Dec. 2016 – Sale of the assets was completed. Secured creditors will suffer a shortfall and no funds available for unsecured creditors or shldrs.

High Plains Energy Inc. (Alta. Apr. 8, 1992)
Nov. 27, 2006 – Name changed to Action Energy Inc. pursuant to reverse takeover acquisition of Action Energy Inc.; basis 1 new for 5 old shs. ■

High Plains Uranium, Inc. (N.B. Feb. 8, 2005)
Jan. 19, 2007 – Plan of Arrangement acquisition by Energy Metals Corporation; basis 1 new Energy Metals sh. for 6.2 old High Plains shs. (see Energy Metals Corporation)

High Point Energy Corp. (Alta. Apr. 15, 1994)
June 26, 2002 – Plan of Arrangement with Mesquite Exploration Ltd. to continue under a new name High Point Resources Inc.; basis 1 new High Point Resources sh. for 3 old High Point Energy shs. (see High Point Resources Inc.)

High Point Exploration Inc. (B.C. Sept. 27, 2018)
May 26, 2021 – Name changed to Canamera Energy Metals Corp. (see FPsurvey - Mines & Energy)

High Point Resources Inc. (Alta. Sept. 1, 2000 amalg.)
Aug. 23, 2005 – Acquired by Enterra Energy Trust; basis either 0.105 Enterra units, 0.105 exch. shs. or a combination thereof for 1 High Point com. sh. (see Enterra Energy Trust)

High Reserve Resources Limited (B.C. 1972)
July 9, 1993 – Dissolved and struck off register.

High Rider Capital Inc. (B.C. Oct. 19, 2006)
May 4, 2009 – Name changed to Sirona Biochem Corp. following Qualifying Transaction license agreement with TFChem S.A.R.L. (see FPsurvey - Industrials)

High Ridge Resources Inc. (B.C. June 24, 2004)
Jan. 1, 2010 – Name changed to New High Ridge Resources Inc.; basis 1 new for 4 old shs. ■

High Rise Resources Inc. (B.C. July 30, 1980)
Dec. 28, 1990 – Dissolved and struck off register.

High River Gold Mines Ltd. (Can. Dec. 5, 1988 amalg.)
Feb. 2, 2011 – Continued into Yukon. (see Nord Gold N.V.)
Mar. 15, 2013 – Acquired by Nord Gold N.V.; basis either $1.40 or 0.285 Nord Gold N.V. global depositary receipts

(1 depositary receipt representing 1 ord. sh.) for 1 High River sh. (see Nord Gold N.V.)

High River Oilfields, Ltd. (Can. May 13, 1925)
1931 – Placed into liquidation.

High River Resources Limited (B.C. 1984)
Dec. 5, 1988 – Formed High River Gold Mines Ltd. in Canada on amalgamation with Nor-Acme Gold Mines Limited; basis 1 new for 1.2 Nor-Acme shs. and 1 new for 1 High River sh. ■

High Rock Canadian High Yield Bond Fund (Ont. July 29, 2014)
Dec. 30, 2016 – Terminated: basis $8.11 cash per cl. A unit.

High Tide Ventures Inc. (Alta. Feb. 8, 2018)
Oct. 4, 2018 – Name changed to High Tide Inc. (see FPsurvey - Industrials)

High Yield & Mortgage Plus Trust (Ont. Nov. 28, 2003)
Dec. 31, 2014 – Redeemed; basis $12.3990 per trust unit.

Highbank Metals & Holdings Limited (Ont. 1966)
Feb. 1980 – Charter cancelled.

Highbank Mines Ltd. (Ont. 1966)
Dec. 22, 1970 – Name changed to Highbank Metals & Holdings Limited. ■

Highbank Resources Ltd. (B.C. Mar. 17, 1980)
Apr. 11, 2025 – Filed for bankruptcy and D. Manning & Associates Inc. was appointed trustee.

Highbourne Capital Corporation (Can. Nov. 8, 1979)
Aug. 20, 1996 – Name changed to A & E Capital Funding Inc.; basis 1 new for 10 old shs. ■

Highbourne Explorations Ltd. (Alta. 1978)
Sept. 10, 1987 – Name changed to Universal Genetics Corporation Limited; basis 1 new for 5 old shs. ■

Highbury Projects Inc. (B.C. May 13, 2005)
Feb. 15, 2023 – Name changed to IFS Global Software Inc. pursuant to the reverse takeover acquisition of Interfield Solutions Ltd. ■

Highfield Oil & Gas (unknown)
Nov. 30, 1979 – Amalgamated with Clarion Petroleums Ltd. to continue under the latter name.

Highfield Property Investments Ltd. (Alta. Dec. 6, 1972)
Dec. 5, 1985 – Name changed to HPIL Resources Ltd.; basis 1 new for 10 old shs. ■

HighGold Mining Inc. (B.C. Apr. 16, 2019)
July 12, 2024 – Acquired by Contango ORE, Inc.; basis 0.019 Contango shs. for 1 HighGold sh.

Highgrade Ventures Ltd. (B.C. Aug. 20, 1987)
Mar. 23, 2000 – Name changed to Brasilca Mining Corporation following reverse takeover acquisition of Tapajos Gold Inc. ■

Highground Capital Corp. (Can. Aug. 1, 2007)
Aug. 11, 2008 – Amalgamated with a newly incorporated subsidiary of Algonquin Power Income Fund; basis 0.9749 Algonquin trust units for 1 Highground com. sh.

Highhawk Mines Limited (B.C. Jan. 20, 1948)
Mar. 12, 1979 – Name changed to Newhawk Gold Mines Ltd.; basis 1 new for 5 old shs. ■

Highland-Bell Ltd. (B.C. May 13, 1936)
Apr. 1, 1971 – Acquired by Teck Corporation Limited; basis 2 cl. B Teck shs. for 3 Highland-Bell shs. (see Teck Corporation Limited)

Highland Beverages Limited (Ont. June 2, 1949)
July 27, 1987 – Continued into Canada.
Aug. 5, 1987 – Name changed to T.C.C. Beverages Ltd. ■

Highland Chief Mines Ltd. (B.C. 1966)
July 31, 1973 – Name changed to New Chief Mines Ltd.; basis 1 new for 2.5 old shs. ■

Highland Dairy Ltd. (unknown)
1958 – Business sold to Rutherford's Dairy Ltd. and Valley View Dairy Ltd.

Highland Development Co. Ltd. (B.C. 1949)
1976 – Placed into receivership with Pickerin, Cook & Co., C.A., Kamloops, B.C. Subsequently dissolved and struck off register.

Highland Energy Inc. (Alta. Jan. 27, 1994)
Aug. 3, 2000 – Acquired by Ketch Energy Ltd. (was named Interaction Resources Ltd. at time of offer); basis 0.96 Interaction (now Ketch Energy) shs. for 1 Highland sh. (see Ketch Energy Ltd.)

Highland Lass Ltd. (B.C. Mar. 1928)
May 13, 1936 – Merged into Highland-Bell Ltd.; basis 2 new for 1 old sh. (see Highland-Bell Ltd.)

Highland Lode Mines Ltd. (B.C. Sept. 22, 1967)
Jan. 13, 1977 – Name changed to CDR Resources Inc.; basis 1 new for 3 old shs. ■

Highland Mercury Mines Ltd. (B.C. 1966)
Feb. 22, 1977 – Formed Highland-Crow Resources Ltd. on amalgamation with Pickle Crow Explorations Ltd. (1 for 5), Cariboo-Bell Copper Mines Ltd. (1 for 9), Beacon Mining Co. Ltd. (1 for 40) and Abex Mines Ltd. (1 for 50); basis 1 new for 5 old shs.

Highland Queen Mines Ltd. (B.C. 1965)
Apr. 10, 1992 – Dissolved and struck off register.

Highland Resources Inc. (B.C. June 7, 2006)
Oct. 31, 2012 – Name changed to Highland Copper Company Inc.; basis 1 new for 5 old shs. (see FPsurvey - Mines & Energy)

Highland Resources Ltd. (B.C. 1979)
1988 – Declared bankrupt.

Highland Star Mines Ltd. (B.C. Mar. 24, 1966)
Mar. 9, 1977 – Name changed to Pembroke Star Resources Ltd.; basis 1 new for 2 old shs. ■

Highland Surprise Gold Mines Ltd. (B.C. 1937)
1944 – Placed into bankruptcy. No equity for shldrs. Struck off register.

Highland Valley Mines Ltd. (B.C. 1955)
June 1973 – Name changed to New Highland Valley Mines Ltd.; basis 1 new for 2.5 old shs. ■

Highland Valley Mining Corp. Ltd. (B.C. 1955)
1968 – Name changed to Highland Valley Mines Ltd.; basis 1 new for 20 old shs. ■

Highland Valley Resources Ltd. (B.C. Feb. 4, 1982)
May 20, 1988 – Name changed to Loki Gold Corporation. ■

Highlander Minerals Ltd. (Ont. May 9, 1990)
Sept. 24, 1993 – Name changed to CaribGold Resources Inc.; basis 1 new for 10 old shs. ■

Highmark Marketing Inc. (B.C. Apr. 2, 2014)
June 20, 2016 – Name changed to Lightning Ventures Inc. ■

Highmark Resources Ltd. (B.C. July 31, 1979)
Dec. 28, 1990 – Dissolved and struck off register.

Highmont Mining Corporation (B.C. 1977 amalg.)
Sept. 28, 1979 – Merged with Iso Mines Limited and a specially formed Teck subsid.; basis $8.50 for ea. sh. held or 6 cl. B pref. shs. of Teck Corporation for ea. 10 shs. held. Teck pref. redeem. within 30 days or conv. into Teck B common shs.

Highmont Mining Corp. Ltd. (B.C. 1966)
Apr. 29, 1977 – Amalgamated with Torwest Resources (1962) Ltd. to form Highmont Mining Corporation. (see Highmont Mining Corporation)

Highpine Oil & Gas Limited (Alta. Apr. 2, 1998)
Oct. 16, 2009 – Acquired by Daylight Resources Trust through plan of arrangement; basis either $7.00 or 0.85 Daylight units for 1 Highpine cl. A sh. or a combination thereof. (see Daylight Resources Trust)

Highplain Exploration Ltd. (B.C. 1968)
June 27, 1977 – Dissolved.

Highpoint Capital Corporation (Alta. Feb. 1, 1996)
July 29, 1998 – Continued into Yukon.
July 31, 1998 – Name changed to Highpoint Telecommunications Inc. pursuant to reverse takeover acquisition of GST Global Telecommunications Inc. ■

Highpoint Mines Ltd. (B.C. Jan. 20, 1948)
Apr. 25, 1972 – Name changed to Highhawk Mines Limited; basis 1 new for 3 old shs. ■

Highpoint Telecommunications Inc. (Yuk. July 29, 1998)
May 19, 2005 – Dissolved and struck off register.

Highpointe Exploration Inc. (B.C. Nov. 19, 2009)
Nov. 8, 2013 – Name changed to Oxford Resources Inc.; basis 1 new for 5 old shs. ■

Highridge Exploration Ltd. (Alta. Aug. 3, 1984 amalg.)
Aug. 31, 1999 – Acquired by Talisman Energy Inc.; basis 0.11 Talisman shs. for 1 Highridge sh.

Highridge Mining Co. Ltd. (Ont. Mar. 1, 1939)
1952 – Name changed to New Highridge Mining Co. Ltd.; basis 1 new for 3 old shs. ■

Highvale Copper Mines Ltd. (Ont. 1961)
Oct. 28, 1977 – Wound up.

Highview Resources Ltd. (Alta. July 30, 1993)
July 6, 2007 – Name changed to Paris Energy Inc.; basis 1 new for 10 old shs. ■

Highwater Power Corporation (B.C. June 10, 1983)
Aug. 29, 2007 – Acquired by Taylor NGL Limited Partnership for $1.50 per sh. (see Taylor NGL Limited Partnership)

Highwire Entertainment Group Inc. (Alta. Oct. 22, 1997)
May 21, 2002 – Name changed to Creation Ventures Inc.; basis 1 new for 10 old shs. ■

Highwood Distillers Ltd. (Alta. 1987)
Feb. 16, 2001 – Privatized at 20¢ per sh.

Highwood Oil Company Ltd. (Alta. Jan. 23, 2019 amalg.)
July 19, 2021 – Name changed to Highwood Asset Management Ltd. pursuant to change of focus from oil and gas to asset management. (see FPsurvey - Industrials)

Highwood Petroleum & Natural Gas Co. Ltd. (Can. 1926)
1928 – Taken over by Highwood-Sarcee Oils Ltd.; basis 12 new com. for 1 old pref. sh., and 8 new com. for 1 com. sh.

Highwood Resources Ltd. (Ont. Jan. 1, 1997 amalg.)
Dec. 4, 2002 – Plan of Arrangement with 2016507 Ontario Ltd. (ThorNewco) and 2016964 Ontario Ltd. to privatized the company; basis either $0.145, or 1 new ThorNewco sh. or a combination thereof.

Highwood-Sarcee Oils Ltd. (Can. 1928)
1958 – Acquired by New Chamberlain Petroleums Ltd.; basis 1 new for 4 old shs. (see New Chamberlain Petroleums Ltd.)

Hiku Brands Company Ltd. (B.C. Dec. 20, 2011)
Sept. 7, 2018 – Acquired by Canopy Growth Corporation; basis 0.046 Canopy Growth com. shs. for 1 Hiku Brands sh.

Hildon Mining Explorations Ltd. (B.C. Aug. 27, 1987)
Oct. 23, 2006 – Dissolved and struck from register.

Hill Street Beverage Company Inc. (B.C. Apr. 6, 2016)
Nov. 30, 2018 – Continued into Ontario.
May 30, 2023 – Name changed to Hill Incorporated; basis 1 new for 75 old shs. (see FPsurvey - Industrials)

Hill Top Resources Corp. (B.C. June 29, 2007)
Sept. 7, 2010 – Name changed to Tanzania Minerals Corp. ■

Hillcraft Industries Ltd. (Ont.)
Charter cancelled.

Hillcrest Collieries Ltd. (Can. 1910)
1960 – Acquired by Hillcrest Collieries Ltd. of Nassau, Bahamas. Shldrs. of Cdn. co. received 1 £1 sh. of Bahamas co. for each sh. held.
1961 – Cdn. company wound up and charter surrendered.

Hillcrest Mohawk Collieries, Ltd. (unknown 1939)
1951 – Merged with 2 other cos. to form Coleman Collieries Limited. Final and total distribution for each 1,000 shs. held: $375; $250 par value of shs. and $1,160 par value of 5% 1st mtge. bds. of Coleman.
1961 – Reported wound up.

Hillcrest Petroleum Ltd. (B.C. May 2, 2006)
Apr. 9, 2021 – Name changed to Hillcrest Energy Technologies Ltd. (see FPsurvey - Industrials)

Hillcrest Resources Ltd. (Alta. June 11, 1980)
May 12, 1995 – Acquired by Mark Resources Inc.; basis $4.50 or 0.80 Mark shs. for 1 Hillcrest sh. (see Mark Resources Inc.)

Hillcrest Resources Ltd. (B.C. May 2, 2006)
Mar. 11, 2015 – Name changed to Hillcrest Petroleum Ltd. ■

Hilldale Explorations Corp. (Ont. 1961)
Aug. 26, 1996 – Formed Oro Blanco Resources Corp. in Ontario on amalgamation with Oro Blanco Resources Inc.; basis 1 new for 1 Oro Blanco sh. and 1 new for 5 Hilldale shs. ■

Hilldale Holdings Inc. (Ont. 1961)
Sept. 18, 1995 – Name changed to Hilldale Explorations Corp. ■

Hillestad Pharmaceuticals Inc. (B.C. May 26, 1983)
Oct. 5, 2006 – Continued into Canada. (see FPsurvey - Industrials)

Hillsborough Exploration Ltd. (Ont. 1951)
Mar. 13, 1987 – Name changed to Hillsborough Resources Limited. ■

Hillsborough Resources Limited (Ont. 1951)
Nov. 5, 1997 – Continued into Canada.
Dec. 24, 2009 – Acquired by Vitol Anker International B.V., a wholly owned subsid. of Vitol Holding B.V., for 50¢ per sh.

Hillside Energy Corporation (B.C. Mar. 20, 1978)
Apr. 10, 1989 – Name changed to Charter Minerals Inc.; basis 1 new for 2.5 old shs. ■

Hillstake Mining Co. Ltd. (B.C. 1945)
May 29, 1969 – Struck off register.

Hilltop Cybersecurity Inc. (B.C. June 30, 2005)
June 20, 2019 – Name changed to Gallagher Security Corp.; basis 1 new for 10 old shs. ■

Hilltop Minerals Limited (Ont. Mar. 11, 1976)
Apr. 29, 1985 – Struck from registry and dissolved.

Hilltown Resources Inc. (B.C. Mar. 1, 2006)
June 19, 2013 – Name changed to Anexco Resources Ltd.; basis 1 new for 5 old shs. ■

Hilo Mining Ltd. (B.C. Feb. 2, 2021)
Apr. 25, 2023 – Name changed to European Energy Metals Corp. ■

Hilstar Capital Corporation (Alta. May 21, 1993)
Dec. 13, 1995 – Name changed to KINeSYS Pharmaceutical Inc.; basis 1 new for 3 old shs. ■

Hilton Petroleum Ltd. (B.C. Sept. 7, 1989)
Apr. 1, 1999 – Continued into Yukon.
Mar. 2, 2004 – Name changed to Hilton Resources Ltd. ■

Hilton Resource Corporation (B.C. Apr. 29, 1980)
June 13, 1991 – Name changed to North Slope Minerals Inc.; basis 1 new for 3.5 old shs. ■

Hilton Resources Ltd. (Yuk. Apr. 1, 1999)
Dec. 3, 2004 – Continued into British Columbia.
Aug. 25, 2005 – Name changed to Rochester Resources Ltd.; basis 1 new for 10 old shs. (see FPsurvey - Mines & Energy)

Himac Resources Ltd. (B.C. Aug. 5, 1977)
July 5, 1985 – Name changed to O.T. Industries Inc.; basis 1 new for 2 old shs. ■

Himalayan Capital Corp. (Ont. Mar. 15, 2007)
May 4, 2012 – Name changed to Azul Ventures Inc. ■

Hinde & Dauch Ltd. (Ont. 1924)
Oct. 31, 1978 – Merged into Domtar Inc.; basis $125 per sh. (see Domtar Inc.)

Hinde & Dauch Paper Co. of Canada Ltd. (Ont. 1924)
Apr. 22, 1960 – Name changed to Hinde & Dauch Ltd. ■

Hinterland Metals Inc. (Can. Apr. 23, 1997)
Dec. 17, 2020 – Name changed to Novamind Inc. pursuant to the reverse takeover acquisition of Novamind Ventures Inc. ■

Hip Interactive Corp. (Ont. Dec. 14, 1999 amalg.)
July 5, 2005 – Placed into receivership. Ernst & Young Inc. appointed receiver.

Hiram Walker-Consumers Home Ltd. (Ont. 1954)
June 1, 1981 – Name changed to Hiram Walker Resources Ltd. following reorganization which resulted in its subsid., Hiram Walker Resources Ltd., becoming the parent company. Subsequently, name changed to The Consumers' Gas Company Ltd. All stock exchanged on sh. for sh. basis, except group 1 pref. shs. (37,121 5.5% ser. A; 66,641 5.5% ser. B; and 21,275 5% ser. C at Sept. 30, 1980), which became shs. of the newly incorporated Consumers' Gas Company Ltd. ■

Hiram Walker-Gooderham & Worts Limited (Can. 1926)
Apr. 9, 1980 – Amalgamated with The Consumers' Gas Company; basis 1 3/8 com. sh. Consumers' for each Walker sh.

Hiram Walker Resources Ltd. (Ont. 1954)
Oct. 24, 1986 – Company became a wholly owned subsid. of Gulf Canada Corporation. (see Gulf Canada Corporation)

Hirtz Bros. Construction Ltd. (B.C. 1966)
Sept. 1972 – Name changed to Wasi Enterprises Ltd.

Hisbert Mines Ltd. (Ont. Jan. 16, 1935)
Feb. 1967 – Charter cancelled.

Hiskerr Gold Mines Ltd. (Ont. 1944)
Apr. 11, 1973 – Dissolved.

Hislop Gold Mines Ltd. (Ont. 1927)
1944 – Name changed to Hislop Mines Ltd. and continued into Ontario; basis 1 new for 3 old shs. ■

Hislop Mines Ltd. (Ont. 1944)
Dec. 9, 1960 – Charter cancelled.

Hispyke Explorations Inc. (Ont. Aug. 28, 1922)
Feb. 29, 1988 – Name changed to RJK Mineral Corp. ■

Hisway Resources Corp. (B.C. Sept. 2, 1987)
Oct. 31, 1989 – Amalgamated in British Columbia to continue with same name.
Apr. 26, 1993 – Name changed to International Bioremediation Services Inc.; basis 1 new for 3 old shs. ■

Hit Technologies Inc. (Ont. Feb. 3, 2012)
Sept. 11, 2018 – Continued into British Columbia.
July 2, 2021 – Continued into Alberta.
July 14, 2021 – Name changed to Carbeeza Inc. pursuant to the reverse takeover acquisition of Carbeeza Ltd., and concurrent amalgamation of Carbeeza Ltd. and wholly owned 2330654 Alberta Ltd.; basis 1 new for 2.5 old shs. (see FPsurvey - Industrials)

Hiview Gold Mines Ltd. (Ont. 1974)
Mar. 1, 1978 – Amalgamated with 3 other cos. to form Jaridge Explorations Inc.; basis 1 new for 4 old shs.

Hixon Gold Resources Inc. (Alta. Oct. 10, 1986)
Mar. 15, 2001 – Name changed to Aloak Corp. following reverse takeover acquisition of Aloak Inc. ■

Hobo Creek Coppermines Ltd. (B.C. 1970)
Feb. 1, 1977 – Name changed to Storm Cloud Development Corporation. ■

Hobrough Limited (Can. 1967)
Apr. 10, 1974 – Name changed to Gestalt International Limited. ■

The Hockey Company Holdings Inc. (Can. Feb. 25, 2003)
June 25, 2004 – Acquired by Reebok International Ltd. for Cdn$21.25 per sh.

Hodden Grey Inc. (Ont. 1969)
Nov. 15, 1978 – Name changed to Hodden Grey Oil & Gas Ltd. ■

Hodden Grey Mining & Explorations Ltd. (Ont. 1969)
Aug. 16, 1973 – Name changed to Hodden Grey Inc. ■

Hodden Grey Oil & Gas Ltd. (Ont. 1969)
Jan. 24, 1983 – Name changed to Nelma Information Inc. following acquisition of Nelma Data Corporation. ■

Hodgins Auctioneers Inc. (Alta. July 24, 2004 amalg.)
Jan. 18, 2016 – Privatized; com. shs. converted on a 1-to-1 basis into cl. B redeem. pref. shs. and immediately redeemed for $0.0001 per cl. B sh.

Hoffman Exploration & Minerals Ltd. (Ont. 1980 amalg.)
Dec. 18, 1985 – Amalgamated with Thompson-Lundmark Gold Mines Ltd. (1 for 2.03043) to form Consolidated Thompson-Lundmark Gold Mines Limited; basis 1 new for 3.17918 old shs.

Hogan Mines Ltd. (B.C. July 19, 1965)
Jan. 1972 – Name changed to Bow River Resources Ltd.; basis 1 new for 5 old shs. ■

Hoist Capital Corp. (Alta. Apr. 2, 2018)
June 24, 2022 – Name changed to The Hempshire Group, Inc. pursuant to the Qualifying Transaction reverse takeover acquisition of (old) The Hempshire Group, Inc.; basis 1 new for 4 old shs. (see FPsurvey - Industrials)

Hoko Exploration Ltd. (B.C. 1982)
Feb. 29, 1988 – Name changed to ABDA International Holdings Corp. ■

Hol-Booth Gold Mines Ltd. (Ont. 1938)
Nov. 1973 – Dissolved.

Hol-Lac Gold Mines, Limited (Ont. Jan. 14, 1937)
July 4, 1997 – Name changed to Augusta Resource Corporation. ■

Holberg Mines Ltd. (B.C. Nov. 23, 1959)
Oct. 1978 – Name changed to World Cement Industries Inc. ■

Holborough Investments Limited (Can. July 22, 1963)
May 4, 1972 – Name changed to MICC Investments Limited; basis 2 new for 1 old sh. ■

Holbrook Red Lake Mines Ltd. (Ont. 1936)
1957 – Charter cancelled.

Holcorp Gold Mines Ltd. (Ont. 1940)
June 27, 1991 – Name changed to Holcorp Mines Limited; basis 1 new for 2 old shs.

Holcot Capital Corp. (B.C. May 18, 2006)
Dec. 21, 2007 – Name changed to Goldmember Minerals Inc. following Qualifying Transaction reverse takeover acquisition of Goldmember Ventures Corp. ■

Holden Manufacturing Co. Ltd. (Can. 1911)
1967 – Name changed to S. E. Woods-Holden Ltd. ■

Holdfast Natural Resources Ltd. (B.C. 1959)
Feb. 7, 1973 – Dissolved.

Holdmar Red Lake Gold Mines Ltd. (Ont. 1946)
Aug. 1958 – Charter cancelled.

Holland-Gaspe Mines Ltd. (Ont. 1950)
Nov. 14, 1973 – Charter cancelled.

Holland Global Capital Corporation (Ont. Jan. 15, 2013)
Sept. 9, 2013 – Succeeded by Maplewood International Real Estate Investment Trust pursuant to plan of arrangement whereby Maplewood International Real Estate Investment Trust was formed to facilitate the conversion of the corporation into a trust; basis 1 trust unit or 1 class B LP unit of Maplewood International Limited Partnership for 8 old shs. ■

Holland Lake Silver Mines Ltd. (Ont. 1964)
Oct. 15, 1969 – Charter cancelled.

Hollinger Argus Limited (Ont. 1916)
1984 – Continued into Canada. (see Hollinger Inc.)
Sept. 17, 1985 – Amalgamated with Argcen Holdings Inc. (sh-for-sh) and Labmin Resources Limited (3.5 new for 1 old sh.) to form Hollinger Inc.; basis 2.5 shs. of Hollinger Inc. for each sh. of Hollinger Argus (other than those held by Argcen Holdings Inc.). (see Hollinger Inc.)

Hollinger Canadian Newspapers, Limited Partnership (Ont. Apr. 14, 1999)
Mar. 17, 2006 – Acquired by Glacier Ventures International Corp. for $0.737 per partnership unit.
Dec. 2006 – Name changed to Glacier Publications Limited Partnership.

Hollinger Canadian Publishing Holdings Co. (N.B. Sept. 11, 1996)
Feb. 7, 2002 – Privatized by Hollinger International Inc. Outstanding special shs. redeemed at US$8.88 per sh. effective June 26, 2000; subsequently delisted.

Hollinger Canadian Publishing Holdings Inc. (N.B. Sept. 11, 1996)
Sept. 25, 2001 – Formed Hollinger Canadian Publishing Holdings Co. on amalgamation with 3048512 Nova Scotia Company. ■

Hollinger Consolidated Gold Mines Ltd. (Ont. 1916)
1968 – Name changed to Hollinger Mines Limited. ■

Hollinger Eastern Publishing Inc. (N.B. Sept. 11, 1996)
June 19, 1997 – Formed Hollinger Canadian Publishing Holdings Inc. on amalgamation with Holbidco Inc., a wholly owned subsid. of Hollinger International Inc.; basis 1 new for 1 old sh. ■

Hollinger Gold Mines, Limited (Ont. 1910)
1916 – Merged with 3 other cos. to form Hollinger Consolidated Gold Mines Ltd.; basis 4 new for 1 old sh.

Hollinger Inc. (Can. Sept. 17, 1985 amalg.)
Aug. 1, 2008 – Filed for protection under the Companies' Creditors Arrangement Act (CCAA) in Canada and Chapter 15 of the U.S. Bankruptcy Code. Ernst & Young Inc. was appointed monitor.
June 30, 2015 – Stay of proceedings under the CCAA was extended to Aug. 2, 2017.
Jan. 22, 2018 – Distribution made to Catalyst Capital Fund I amounting to $25,000. (see FPsurvey - Industrials)

Hollinger Mines Limited (Ont. 1916)
Aug. 23, 1979 – Name changed to Hollinger Argus Limited. ■

Hollinger North Shore Exploration Company Limited (Que. 1942)
1980 – Name changed to Hollinger North Shore Exploration Inc. ■

Hollinger North Shore Exploration Inc. (Que. 1942)
July 28, 1983 – As a result of the restructuring of Hollinger Argus, Labrador Mining & Exploration, and Norcen Energy Resources, the co. was merged into Norcen Energy Resources Ltd. Prior to restructuring, co. was 60% owned by Hollinger Argus Ltd. and 40% by Hanna Mining.

Hollingfield Capital Corp. (B.C. Mar. 1, 2000)
Aug. 10, 2001 – Name changed to PKI Innovations (Canada) Inc. pursuant to Qualifying Transaction reverse takeover acquisition of PKI Innovations Inc. ■

Hollingport Venture Inc. (B.C. Dec. 21, 2005)
May 5, 2009 – Name changed to Changyu Medtech Ltd. following Qualifying Transaction reverse takeover acquisition of Asia Oriental Investment Ltd. ■

Hollingsworth Iron Mines Ltd. (Ont. 1970)
Mar. 1976 – Charter cancelled.

Hollister Biosciences Inc. (B.C. Apr. 17, 2019)
Dec. 13, 2021 – Name changed to YourWay Cannabis Brands Inc. (see FPsurvey - Industrials)

HollisWealth Inc. (Ont. Nov. 6, 1998)
Nov. 1, 2017 – Name changed to 1985275 Ontario Inc.

Holloway Capital Corporation (Can. Nov. 17, 2005)
June 8, 2006 – Qualifying Transaction acquisition of a 50 unit Super 8 hotel property in Truro, Nova Scotia with subsequent conversion into an income trust named Holloway Lodging Real Estate Investment Trust; basis 1 new trust unit for 5 com. shs. (see Holloway Lodging Real Estate Investment Trust)

Holloway Lodging Corporation (Ont. Apr. 8, 2010)
Oct. 2, 2019 – Acquired by Clarke Inc.; basis 0.65 Clarke com. shs. for each Holloway com. sh. for an implied acquisition price of $8.46 per sh.

Holloway Lodging Real Estate Investment Trust (Ont. Mar. 28, 2006)
Dec. 31, 2012 – Succeeded by Holloway Lodging Corporation pursuant to plan of arrangement whereby Holloway Lodging Corporation was formed to facilitate the conversion of the trust into a corporation. ■

Holly Street Capital Ltd. (B.C. July 31, 2019)
Apr. 11, 2022 – Name changed to US Critical Metals Corp. pursuant to the Qualifying Transaction reverse takeover acquisition of US Critical Metals Corp. (Old US CMC) and concurrent amalgamation of Old US CMC with wholly owned US Critical Holdings Corp. (USCH) to continue as USCH.; basis 1 new for 1.5 old shs. (see FPsurvey - Mines & Energy)

Hollycroft Resource Corporation (B.C. 1983)
June 14, 1990 – Name changed to Beretta Resource Corp.; basis 1 new for 5 old shs. ■

Hollyhead Resources Inc. (Ont. Oct. 29, 1985)
June 19, 1992 – Name changed to Canadian Maple Leaf Financial Corporation and continued into Canada following merger with Canadian Maple Leaf Fund (Manitoba) Ltd.; basis 1 new for 6 old shs. ■

Hollywood Investment Corporation (B.C. Mar. 6, 1987)
June 7, 1990 – Name changed to Walking Stick Oil & Gas Corp. ■

Holmer Gold Mines Limited (Ont. Jan. 20, 1964)
Dec. 31, 2004 – Acquired by Lake Shore Gold Corp.; basis 1 Lake Shore sh. for 1.5 Holmer shs. (see Lake Shore Gold Corp.)

Holt International Investments Ltd. (B.C. Sept. 3, 1985)
Nov. 4, 1998 – Name changed to Argent Resources Ltd. ■

Holtyrex Gold Mines Ltd. (Ont. 1921)
1955 – Charter cancelled.

Holwood Mines Ltd. (Ont. 1951)
May 6, 1965 – Dissolved.

Holy Cow Foods Inc. (B.C. Mar. 10, 2016)
Jan. 24, 2023 – Name changed to NextGen Food Robotics Corp. (see FPsurvey - Industrials)

Holy Cross Mountain Mines Ltd. (B.C. Aug. 2, 1966)
Jan. 29, 1974 – Name changed to Camero Resource Industries Ltd. ■

Holy Smoke Capital Corp. (Alta. Mar. 22, 2000)
Nov. 1, 2002 – Name changed to Anterra Corporation pursuant to Qualifying Transaction acquisition of Carnico Oil & Gas Ltd. ■

Hombre Capital Inc. (Alta. July 31, 2012)
Mar. 27, 2015 – Name changed to NovaTeqni Corporation. ■

Homburg Canada Real Estate Investment Trust (Que. Mar. 30, 2010)
Oct. 13, 2011 – Name changed to CANMARC Real Estate Investment Trust. ■

Homburg Invest Inc. (Alta. May 8, 1996)
Sept. 9, 2011 – The company and certain subsidiaries were granted protection under the Companies' Creditors Arrangement Act (CCAA) and Deloitte & Touche Inc. was appointed as monitor.
June 30, 2013 – Creditors of the company and Homburg Shareco Inc. approved the second joint amended and restated plan of compromise and reorganization and the amended and restated plan of compromise and reorganization of Homco Realty Fund (61) Limited Partnership. The Quebec court sanctioned the plans.
Mar. 27, 2014 – The fourth amended and restated plan of compromise and reorganization of the company and Homburg Shareco Inc. as well as the restated plan of compromise of Homco Realty Fund (61) Limited Partnership was successfully implemented. The company's core assets have been transferred to Geneba Properties N.V., a closed end property investment company. All of the company's o/s shares, other than the shares issued Geneba under the plans, were cancelled without consideration and certain holders of debt securities issued directly or indirectly by the company and certain trade creditors of the company have received or will receive cash payments and/or shares of Geneba in exchange for compromise of their claims against the company. Additionally, the company, Homburg Shareco, Holland Garden Development Ltd., Homburg Invest USA Limited and Swiss Bondco Inc. were amalgamated effective Mar. 24, 2014, to form 1810040 Alberta Ltd. Amalco will be controlled by Deloitte & Touche Inc., as monitor under the plans, for the purpose of selling any remaining assets in order to repay creditor as set out in the plans.
Apr. 10, 2014 – First distrib. was made to the company's electing creditors of cash and the non-electing creditors received shs. of Geneba Properties N.V. Under the company's and Shareco's plan 3.65 Geneba shs. were distributed for each $100 value in proven claims and 4.82 Geneba shs. were distributed for $100 value of Homco 61 proven claims under the Homco 61 plan.
May 14, 2021 – Final distrib. made to affected creditors.
Nov. 7, 2021 – Deloitte Restructuring (formerly Deloitte & Touche) was terminated as monitor for the CCAA proceedings. The company was subsequently dissolved.

Homco Industries Ltd. (Sask. 1971 amalg.)
Sept. 30, 1977 – Placed into bankruptcy. Henfrey Mason & Co. Ltd. of Vancouver appointed trustee.
Sept. 29, 1978 – Struck off register.

Home Capital Group Inc. (Can. June 21, 1968)
July 18, 1988 – Continued into Ontario.
Sept. 5, 2023 – All o/s shs. not already held acquired by Smith Financial Corporation; basis $44.28 cash per sh.

Home Equity Income Trust (Ont. May 15, 2002)
July 3, 2009 – Converted into newly incorporated HOMEQ Corporation; basis 1 HOMEQ com. sh. for 1 Home Equity trust unit. (see HOMEQ Corporation)

Home Industries Inc. (Alta. 1987)
Mar. 27, 1989 – Formed Highwood Distillers Ltd. on amalgamation with 35046 Alberta Inc. and Highwood Distillers Ltd.; basis 1 new for 1 old sh. ■

Home Lake Resources Ltd. (unknown Apr. 2, 1990)
June 11, 1992 – Formed Dovetec Corporation in Ontario on amalgamation with Dovetec Corporation; basis 1 new for 1 Dovetec sh. and 1 new for 2 Home Lake shs. ■

Home Media Corp. (Alta. Nov. 28, 1996)
Aug. 13, 2003 – Amalgamated with Ivrnet Inc. (1 for 2.361) to continue as Ivrnet Inc.; basis 1 new Ivrnet sh. for 5.028 old Home Media shs. (see Ivrnet Inc.)

Home Mining Developments Limited (Ont. 1969)
Nov. 22, 1974 – Amalgamated with Foxdale Mines Limited (1 for 7.5), Canton Explorations Limited (1 for 5.5), Marquis Explorations Limited (1 for 2.5), Long Point Gas & Oil Incorporated (1 for 3), Darwin Mines Limited (1 for 1.5), Gold Acres Mines Limited (1 for 7), and Force Crag Mines Limited (1 for 4.5) to form New Force Crag Mines Limited; basis 1 new for 7 old shs.

Home Oil Co., Ltd. (Alta. July 10, 1925)
1929 – Formed Home Oil Company Limited on amalgamation with Home Oil Company Limited. ■

Home Oil Company Limited (Alta. July 10, 1925)
Dec. 21, 1979 – Acquired by The Consumers' Gas Company Ltd.; basis 3.8 Consumers' conv. pref. shs. or $95 for 1 Home Oil sh. Subsequently in December 1986, Home Oil was acquired by Interhome Energy Inc. and then on May 1, 1991, Home Oil was spun off as a new public company. (see Anderson Exploration Ltd.)
May 1, 1991 – Continued into Canada. (see Anderson Exploration Ltd.)
Sept. 28, 1995 – Acquired by Anderson Exploration Ltd.; basis 1.38 Anderson shs. for 1 Home Oil sh. (see Anderson Exploration Ltd.)

Home Ticket Network Corporation (Alta. Jan. 28, 1994)
Sept. 20, 2001 – Name changed to Applause Corporation. ■

Home Ventures Ltd. (B.C. Feb. 2, 1981)
Feb. 15, 2000 – Name changed to Buck Lake Ventures Ltd.; basis 1 new for 3 old shs. ■

Homebank Technologies Inc. (Que. Feb. 11, 1998 amalg.)
June 15, 2005 – Name changed to Selient Inc. ■

Homeguard Mines Ltd. (B.C. 1971)
1987 – Charter cancelled.

Homeland Energy Group Ltd. (Can. Oct. 12, 2006)
Mar. 22, 2017 – Name changed to Sixonine Ventures Corp. and continued into British Columbia; basis 1 new for 75 old shs. ■

Homeland Uranium Inc. (Ont. Dec. 29, 2006)
Dec. 15, 2014 – Name changed to Western Uranium Corp. following reverse takeover acquisition of Pinon Ridge Mining LLC. ■

Homeproject.com Inc. (Can. Oct. 2, 1985)
Oct. 4, 2005 – Dissolved.

Homer Exploration Co. Ltd. (B.C. 1969)
Feb. 24, 1975 – Charter cancelled.

Homer Yellowknife Mines Ltd. (Ont. 1944)
1955 – Name changed to Desmont Mining Corp. Ltd.; basis 1 new for 5 old shs. ■

Homeserve Technologies Inc. (Ont. Feb. 27, 1987)
July 29, 2011 – Acquired by Brookfield Asset Management Inc. for $2.75 cash per sh.

Homestake Canada Inc. (Ont. Jan. 1, 1999)
June 27, 2003 – Name changed to Barrick Gold Inc. ■

Homestake Enterprises Ltd. (B.C.)
1958 – Struck off register.

Homestake Explorations Limited (Man. 1950)
Oct. 24, 1986 – Name changed to HSK Minerals Limited. ■

Homestake Mining Company (Del. 1983)
Dec. 14, 2001 – Acquired by wholly owned subsid. of Barrick Gold Corporation; basis 0.53 new Barrick sh. for 1 old Homestake sh. (see Barrick Gold Corporation; Takepoint Ventures Ltd.)

Homestake Resource Corporation (B.C. July 18, 1983)
Sept. 8, 2016 – Acquired by Auryn Resources Inc.; basis 0.0588 Auryn com. shs. for 1 Homestake com. sh. (see Auryn Resources Inc.)

Homestake Silver Ltd. (B.C. Oct. 30, 1964)
June 1971 – Name changed to Northern Homestake Mines Ltd.; basis 1 new for 5 old shs. ■

Homestead Consolidated Oil Co. Ltd. (Alta. Mar. 18, 1947)
Name changed to Consolidated Homestead Oil Co. Ltd.; basis 1 new for 1 old sh. ■

Homestead Oil & Gas Ltd. (Ont. 1930)
1947 – Acquired by Homestead Consolidated Oil Co. Ltd.; basis 1 new for 4 old shs. (see Consolidated Homestead Oil Co. Ltd.)

Homestead Resources Inc. (B.C. Oct. 23, 1980)
May 13, 1993 – Name changed to International Homestead Resources Inc.; basis 1 new for 3 old shs. ■

Homestock Resources Ltd. (B.C. June 9, 1980)
Jan. 31, 1986 – Name changed to International Homestock Resources Ltd.; basis 1 new for 2 old shs. ■

Homeward Mines Ltd. (B.C. 1953)
June 1956 – Struck off register.

The Homewood Corporation (Ont. May 18, 1883)
Dec. 2, 2010 – Acquired by Schlegel Health Care Inc. for $68 per sh.

The Homewood Sanitarium of Guelph, Ontario, Limited (Ont. May 18, 1883)
Aug. 21, 1995 – Name changed to The Homewood Corporation. ■

HomeXpress Limited (Alta. May 26, 1999)
Nov. 2, 2002 – Struck from registry and dissolved.

Honcho Gold Mines Inc. (B.C. Aug. 10, 1981)
July 13, 1988 – Name changed to Takla Gold Mines Ltd. and continued into Canada. ■

Honco Inc. (Que. 1974)
Aug. 8, 1995 – Amalgamated with Gestion L. Inc.; basis 1 cl. A pref. sh. for 1 com. sh. immediately repurchased for 40¢.

Honda Mining Co. Ltd. (B.C. 1967)
Feb. 25, 1983 – Struck off register.

Honey Badger Exploration Inc. (Ont. June 19, 2008)
Nov. 20, 2020 – Name changed to Honey Badger Silver Inc. (see FPsurvey - Mines & Energy)

Honey Bee Gold Mines Ltd. (Ont. 1946)
1951 – Name changed to Peak Oils Ltd. ■

Honey Dew Ltd. (Ont. Mar. 29, 1928)
1943 – Name changed to Canadian Food Products Limited. (see FPsurvey - Industrials)

Honeybee Technology Inc. (Can. Mar. 16, 1999)
Aug. 19, 2008 – Dissolved and struck from register.

Hong Kong Gold Corporation (B.C. Dec. 16, 1983)
Sept. 28, 1993 – Name changed to Inovision Technologies Inc. ■

Hongkong Bank of Canada (Can. July 30, 1981)
June 21, 1999 – Name changed to HSBC Bank Canada. ■

Hoodoo Hydrocarbons Ltd. (Alta. Oct. 9, 1998)
July 28, 2005 – Name changed to Cruiser Oil & Gas Ltd. following reverse takeover acquisition of Terra Rica Resources Ltd. ■

Hoodoo Lake Mines Ltd. (Ont. 1946)
1950 – Name changed to Dunvegan Mines Limited. ■

HookUp Communication Corporation (Ont. Mar. 29, 1993)
July 20, 1999 – Name changed to PC Chips Corporation. (see FPsurvey - Industrials)

HooXi Network Inc. (B.C. Dec. 31, 2016 amalg.)
Apr. 3, 2019 – Continued into British Virgin Islands.
July 23, 2019 – Name changed to Enlighta Inc. (see FPsurvey - Industrials)

Hope Bay Gold Corporation Inc. (Que. Feb. 21, 1993)
May 31, 2002 – Amalgamated with Miramar Mining Corporation; basis 0.263 new Miramar com. sh. plus 0.01 special wts. of Ariane Gold Corp. for 1 old Hope Bay com. sh. (see Miramar Mining Corporation)

Hope Bay Mines Ltd. (B.C. 1973)
May 4, 1984 – Struck off register.

Hope Brook Gold Inc. (Ont. 1981)
1986 – Continued into Canada. (see BP Canada Inc.)
June 26, 1991 – Following capital reorganization plan proposed by BP Canada, co. exchanged com. shs. for redeemable cl. 1 pref. shs.; basis $1.20 per redeemable cl. 1 pref. sh. making Hope Brook a wholly owned subsid. of BP Canada. (see BP Canada Inc.)

Hope Gold Mines Ltd. (Man. Oct. 1936)
1949 – Charter cancelled.

Hope Well Capital Corp. (Ont. Dec. 1, 2016)
Oct. 20, 2021 – Name changed to Forward Water Technologies Corp. pursuant to the Qualifying Transaction reverse takeover acquisition of Forward Water Technologies Inc. (FWT) and concurrent amalgamation of FWT with wholly owned 2644246 Ontario Limited. (see FPsurvey - Industrials)

Hopefield Ventures Inc. (B.C. Apr. 6, 2021)
Apr. 12, 2023 – Name changed to CyberCatch Holdings, Inc. pursuant to the Qualifying Transaction reverse takeover acquisition of (old) CyberCatch Holdings, Inc. (renamed CyberCatch Global, Inc.); basis 1 new for 3.87 old shs. (see FPsurvey - Industrials)

Hopefield Ventures Two Inc. (B.C. Jan. 24, 2022)
Feb. 14, 2025 – Name changed to Carrier Connect Data Solutions Inc. pursuant to the Qualifying Transaction acquisition of Carrier Connect Systems Ltd. (see FPsurvey - Industrials)

Hopes Advance Mines Limited (Ont. 1956)
Feb. 13, 1984 – Charter cancelled.

Horizon Capital Inc. (Alta. Dec. 16, 1996)
Mar. 30, 1999 – Name changed to Altachem Pharma Ltd. following Qualifying Transaction acquisition of Steroidogenesis Inhibitors Canada Inc.; basis 1 new for 1 old sh. ■

Horizon Industries Ltd. (B.C. Feb. 24, 1997)
Feb. 13, 2009 – Name changed to Petro Horizon Energy Corp.; basis 1 new for 8 old shs. ■

Horizon North Logistics Inc. (Alta. May 24, 2006 amalg.)
Nov. 13, 2020 – Name changed to Dexterra Group Inc. (see FPsurvey - Industrials)

Horizon Oil & Refining Ltd. (Can.)
Dec. 9, 1958 – Charter cancelled.

Horizon Petroleum plc (Jersey Sept. 23, 2013)
Apr. 5, 2016 – Name changed to Horizon Petroleum Ltd. and continued into Alberta. (see FPsurvey - Mines & Energy)

Horizon Village Corporation, Canada (Can. June 21, 1988)
Sept. 1, 1993 – Name changed to Roxbury Capital Corp.; basis 1 new for 5 old shs. ■

Horizons Active Advantage Yield ETF (Ont.)
Sept. 17, 2013 – Name changed to Horizons Active Yield Matched Duration ETF. ■

Horizons Active Global Fixed Income ETF (Ont.)
May 1, 2024 – Name changed to Global X Active Global Fixed Income ETF.

Horizons Active Yield Matched Duration ETF (Ont.)
Feb. 2, 2015 – Name changed to Horizons Active Global Fixed Income ETF. ■

Horizons AlphaPro Fiera Tactical Bond ETF (Ont.)
Sept. 27, 2011 – Name changed to Horizons Tactical Bond ETF. ■

Horizons AlphaPro Fiera Tactical Bond Fund (Ont.)
Jan. 4, 2011 – Name changed to Horizons AlphaPro Fiera Tactical Bond ETF following conversion from a closed end fund to an exchange-traded fund. ■

Horizons AlphaPro Gartman ETF (Ont.)
Oct. 25, 2011 – Name changed to Horizons Gartman ETF.

Horizons AlphaPro Gartman Fund (Ont.)
Nov. 19, 2009 – Name changed to Horizons AlphaPro Gartman ETF following conversion from a closed end fund to an exchange-traded fund. ■

Horizons AlphaPro Income Plus ETF (Ont.)
Sept. 27, 2011 – Name changed to Horizons Income Plus ETF. ■

Horizons AlphaPro Income Plus Fund (Ont.)
May 9, 2011 – Converted from a closed end fund to an exchange-traded fund.
Name changed to Horizons AlphaPro Income Plus ETF following conversion from a closed end fund to an exchange-traded fund. ■

Horizons AlphaPro Inflation/Deflation Protection Fund (Ont.)
Name changed to Horizons AlphaPro Income Plus Fund. ■

Horizons Enhanced U.S. Equity Income Fund (Ont. Apr. 29, 2011)
Sept. 2, 2012 – Converted from a closed-end fund into an exchange-traded fund.
Sept. 4, 2012 – Name changed to Horizons Enhanced U.S. Equity Income ETF following conversion from a closed end fund to an exchange-traded fund.

Horizons Gold Yield ETF (Ont. Nov. 26, 2010)
May 1, 2024 – Name changed to Global X Gold Yield ETF.

Horizons Gold Yield Fund (Ont. Nov. 26, 2010)
Feb. 28, 2012 – Converted from a closed-end fund to an exchange-traded fund.
Feb. 28, 2012 – Name changed to Horizons Gold Yield ETF. ■

Horizons Income Plus ETF (Ont.)
Oct. 2, 2012 – Name changed to Horizons Active Income Plus ETF.

Horizons Tactical Bond ETF (Ont.)
Oct. 2, 2012 – Name changed to Horizons Active Advantage Yield ETF. ■

Horizonte Minerals Plc (U.K. Jan. 16, 2006)
May 16, 2024 – Deemed insolvent and FRP Advisory was appointed administrator.

Horlac Mines Ltd. (Ont. 1951)
Apr. 1970 – Dissolved.

Horn Petroleum Corporation (B.C. Sept. 19, 2011)
Mar. 11, 2015 – Name changed to Africa Energy Corp. (see FPsurvey - Mines & Energy)

Horn River Resources Ltd. (Alta. 1970)
Nov. 6, 1981 – Name changed to Dome Resources Limited.

Hornby Bay Exploration Limited (Ont. Oct. 31, 1997 amalg.)
May 1, 2006 – Name changed to Unor Inc. ■

Hornby Bay Mineral Exploration Ltd. (Ont. Oct. 31, 1997 amalg.)
May 17, 2021 – Name changed to Royal Fox Gold Inc. pursuant to the reverse takeover acquisition of 9396-1217 Québec Inc. ■

Hornby Oils Limited (B.C.)
1958 – Struck off register.

Horne & Pitfield Foods Limited (Alta. 1945)
Nov. 4, 1978 – Amalgamated with 88676 Canada Ltd., a wholly owned subsidiary of M. Loeb Ltd. Com. shs. held by M. Loeb's subsid. were cancelled and minority shldrs. received 1 new pref. for each com. sh. held. Pref. shs. were redeemed at $15.50 per sh. on Nov. 26, 1978.

Horne Fault Mines Limited (Que. 1941)
1976 – Name changed to Les Mines de la Faille Horne Limitée/Horne Fault Mines Limited; basis 1 new for 5 old shs. ■

Hornet Energy Ltd. (Can. Apr. 25, 1989)
Aug. 3, 2001 – Acquired by Compton Petroleum Acquisition Corporation, wholly owned subsid. of Compton Petroleum Corporation; basis $2.00 per sh. (see Compton Petroleum Corporation)

Horn's Provisioners Limited (Ont. 1964)
Oct. 1974 – Placed into receivership by deb. holder.
Nov. 1974 – Assets sold to Albert Schneider Food Services Ltd. No distribution made to shldrs.

Horsehoe Mines Ltd. (Ont. Feb. 5, 1929)
Dec. 1957 – Charter cancelled.

Horseshoe Bend Uranium Co. (unknown)
Merger of Ranger Lake Uranium Co. Ltd., Horseshoe Bend Uranium Co. and Century Uranium Corp. to form Century Mining & Development Corp. (see Century Mining & Development Corp)

Horseshoe Gold Mining Inc. (Alta. Dec. 21, 1987)
Apr. 21, 2011 – Name changed to Cosigo Resources Ltd. and continued into British Columbia pursuant to reverse takeover acquisition of Cosigo Resources Inc.; basis 1 new for 3 old shs. (see FPsurvey - Mines & Energy)

The Horsham Corporation (Que. May 23, 1923)
June 19, 1996 – Name changed to Horsham Corporation and continued into Ontario. ■

Horsham Corporation (Ont. June 19, 1996)
Nov. 4, 1996 – Formed TrizecHahn Corporation in Ontario on amalgamation with Trizec Corporation Ltd.; basis 1 TrizecHahn subord. vtg. sh. for 1 Horsham subord. vtg. sh. ■

Horton Hydrocarbons Inc. (B.C. 1982)
Sept. 4, 1985 – Name changed to Pencrude Resources Inc. ■

Horton Technologies Ltd. (B.C. July 2, 1986)
July 7, 1989 – Delisted from the Vancouver Stock Exchange. Subsequently dissolved for failure to file and struck from the registry.

Horwood Exploration Corp. (Can. Apr. 27, 2022)
Oct. 10, 2022 – Name changed to Avventura Resources Ltd. (see FPsurvey - Mines & Energy)

Hosco Gold Mines Ltd. (Ont. 1944)
Nov. 1954 – Name changed to New Hosco Mines Limited; basis 1 new for 4 old shs. ■

Hospital Greetings Corporation (Alta. June 19, 1996)
Apr. 30, 2003 – Name changed to Culane Energy Corp. following reverse takeover acquisition of Culane Energy Ltd.; basis 1 new for 7.25 old shs. ■

Host Ventures Ltd. (B.C. 1982 amalg.)
Apr. 23, 1984 – Name changed to Hot Resources Ltd.; basis 1 new for 5 old shs. ■

Hosted Data Transaction Solutions Inc. (Ont. Oct. 22, 2001)
Oct. 7, 2010 – Name changed to Posera-HDX Inc. ■

Hostee Mines Ltd. (Ont. 1947)
1957 – Charter cancelled.

Hostopia.com Inc. (Del. Dec. 10, 1999)
Aug. 7, 2008 – Acquired by Deluxe Corporation for Cdn$10.55 per com. sh.

Hot House Growers Income Fund (B.C. Nov. 10, 2003)
Nov. 1, 2006 – Name changed to Village Farms Income Fund. ■

Hot Resources Ltd. (B.C. 1982 amalg.)
Apr. 16, 1985 – Name changed to Inter-Globe Resources Ltd. (see FPsurvey - Mines & Energy)

Hôtel des Sept-Iles Ltée (Que. 1950)
Dec. 1954 – Name changed to Lower St. Lawrence Realty Corp. ■

Hotstone Gold Mines Ltd. (Ont. 1946)
1955 – Name changed to Hotstone Minerals Ltd.; basis 3 new for 10 old shs. ■

Hotstone Minerals Ltd. (Ont. 1946)
Feb. 14, 1978 – Dissolved.

Hottah Lake Uraniums Ltd. (B.C. 1953)
1955 – Assets acquired by Hottah Lake Uraniums (1955) Ltd.; basis 1 new for 2 old shs.

Hottah Lake Uraniums (1955) Ltd. (B.C. 1955)
1965 – Struck off register.

House of Braemore Furniture Limited (Ont. 1968)
Dec. 31, 1979 – All o/s shs. acquired at $6.32 per sh. (revised from $5), subsequently amalgamated with subsid. of The Strathearn House Group.

House of Stein Electronics Ltd. (B.C. 1958)
Dec. 7, 1970 – Name changed to Steintron International Electronics Ltd. ■

Household Financial Corporation Limited (Can. 1947)
Apr. 1, 2005 – Name changed to HSBC Financial Corporation Limited.

Houston Lake Mining Inc. (Alta. Mar. 13, 1995)
May 19, 2016 – Name changed to Frontier Lithium Inc. (see FPsurvey - Mines & Energy)

Houston Metals Corporation (B.C. Oct. 27, 1986 amalg.)
Mar. 30, 1989 – Name changed to Pacific Houston Resources, Inc.; basis 1 new for 5 old shs. ■

Houston Oils Ltd. (Alta. 1971)
Sept. 30, 1975 – Name changed to Bridger Petroleum Corporation Ltd.; basis 1 new for 2 old shs. ■

Hovik Medical Corporation (B.C. Aug. 29, 1980)
July 14, 1993 – Name changed to GlobeTel Communications Limited; basis 1 new for 3 old shs. ■

Howe Exploration & Development Co. Limited (Ont. June 1, 1989 amalg.)
Apr. 20, 1993 – Name changed to Howex Enterprises Ltd. ■

Howe Sound Exploration Ltd. (Alta.)
Sept. 30, 1980 – Amalgamated with Zodiac Resources Ltd. under the latter name; basis 1 new for 2.5 old shs. ■

Howex Enterprises Ltd. (Ont. June 1, 1989 amalg.)
Sept. 23, 1994 – Name changed to Diadem Resources Ltd.; basis 1 new for 2.5 old shs. (see FPsurvey - Mines & Energy)

Howey Consolidated Mines Ltd. (Ont. Mar. 12, 1926)
1964 – Liquidated. Distributed 1 sh. Geco Mines for each 20 Howey; 4 shs. Teck Corp. for each 5 Howey; 1 sh. Goldfields Mining Corp. for each 5 Howey shs., plus final divd. of $6.56 per sh.

Howey Gold Mines Ltd. (Ont. Mar. 12, 1926)
Nov. 1949 – Name changed to Consolidated Howey Gold Mines Ltd.; basis 2 new for 5 old shs. ■

Howie Controls (Canada) Limited (Ont. Apr. 20, 1964)
Dec. 9, 1982 – Name changed to Benvan Holdings Inc. ■

Hoyle Mining Co. Ltd. (Ont. 1944)
Mar. 4, 1963 – Following sale of certain assets to Ventures Ltd. in late 1960, co. wound up its affairs by distributing remaining assets on basis of 2/3 sh. Opemiska Copper, 1/15 sh. United Keno Hill, 1 sh. Onaping Mines and 35¢ cash for each com. sh. of Hoyle held. Dissolved.

Hoyle Resources Inc. (B.C. July 2, 1981)
Mar. 27, 1992 – Name changed to Westate Energy Inc.; basis 1 new for 2.5 old shs. ■

Huakan International Mining Inc. (B.C. June 16, 1986)
Apr. 29, 2014 – Amalgamated with 0996059 B.C. Ltd. to form a new co. also known as Huakan International Mining Inc.; basis 1 new Huakan cl. A pref. sh. for 1 old Huakan com. sh., redeemed for 50¢ cash per cl. A pref. sh.

Huaxing Machinery Corp. (B.C. Aug. 1, 2008)
Jan. 16, 2017 – Dissolved and struck from registry. (see FPsurvey - Industrials)

The Hub Group Limited (Ont. Nov. 25, 1998)
Sept. 21, 2000 – Name changed to Hub International Limited. ■

Hub International Limited (Ont. Nov. 25, 1998)
May 18, 2004 – Continued into Canada.
June 15, 2007 – Acquired by Apax Partners and Morgan Stanley through Morgan Stanley Principal Investments; basis US$41.50 per com. sh.
July 27, 2007 – Continued into Nova Scotia.
Aug. 2, 2007 – Name changed to Hub International West Co. ■

Hub International West Co. (N.S. July 27, 2007)
Dec. 22, 2009 – Name changed to Hub International Canada West ULC and continued into British Columbia. ■

Hub Mining & Exploration Ltd. (B.C. 1963)
Aug. 2, 1978 – Name changed to Senator Minerals Corp.; basis 1 new for 4 old shs. (see FPsurvey - Mines & Energy)

Hub Yellowknife Mines Ltd. (Ont. 1945)
Apr. 9, 1956 – Dissolved.

Hubbard Dyers Inc. (Que. Nov. 15, 1984)
July 3, 1991 – Name changed to Hubbard Holding inc. ■

Hubbard Dyers Limited (Can. 1937)
1972 – All o/s com. and pref. shs. acquired for $12.50 per com. and $14 per pref. sh. by Dominion Textile Limited.

Hubbard Felt Co. Ltd. (Can. 1937)
Apr. 1965 – Name changed to Hubbard Dyers Limited. ■

Hubbard Holding inc. (Que. Nov. 15, 1984)
Apr. 18, 2002 – Assigned into bankruptcy and KPMG Ltd. appointed trustee.

Hubble Capital Inc. (Que. Sept. 24, 2004)
June 23, 2005 – Name changed to Bigknowledge Enterprises Inc. following Qualifying Transaction acquisition of Bigknowledge Inc. for total consideration of 24,000,000 com. shs. ■

Hubert Balboa Mines Ltd. (Ont. 1945)
Nov. 1954 – Charter cancelled.

Hubert Lake Ungava Nickel Mines Ltd. (Que. 1957)
Jan. 23, 1990 – Name changed to Superior Financial Holdings Inc. ■

Huclif Porcupine Mines Ltd. (Ont. 1945)
Mar. 1976 – Charter cancelled.

HudBay Minerals Inc. (Ont. Jan. 15, 1996 amalg.)
Oct. 25, 2005 – Continued into Canada.
Jan. 1, 2017 – Name changed to Hudbay Minerals Inc. following amalgamation with wholly owned Hudson Bay Exploration and Development Company Limited and Hudson Bay Mining and Smelting Co., Limited. (see FPsurvey - Mines & Energy)

Huddersfield Uranium Mines Ltd. (Ont. 1974)
Jan. 23, 1979 – Amalgamated with Glenshire Mines Ltd. (231 for 1,000), Kayak Explorations Ltd. (195 for 1,000), La France Explorations Ltd. (128 for 1,000), Lunel Management Ltd. (923.5 for 1), Sandhurst Mines Ltd. (1 for 1) and Steppingstone Explorations Ltd. (229 for 1,000) to form Lunel Enterprises Inc.; basis 129 new for 1,000 old shs. (see Lunel Enterprises Inc.)

Hudon & Orsali Ltée (Can. 1932)
1957 – Name changed to Shop & Save (1957) Ltd. ■

Hudson Bay Diecasting Limited (Ont. 1966)
Sept. 29, 1995 – Declared bankruptcy. PricewaterhouseCoopers Inc. of Toronto appointed trustee. Ventra Doorhandle Systems Inc., a wholly owned subsidiary of Ventra Group Inc., acquired certain assets of the company including land, building, machinery, equipment and inventory. Terms were not disclosed.
Mar. 1996 – Liquidation essentially complete and interim distributions to secured creditors made. There were insufficient funds for distribution to unsecured creditors or shldrs.
June 1, 2004 – Trustee discharged.

The Hudson Bay Mines Limited (Ont. July 16, 1909)
July 18, 1984 – Name changed to T & H Resources Ltd. ■

Hudson Bay Mining and Smelting Co., Limited (Can. Dec. 27, 1927)
July 6, 1993 – All o/s special shs. were automatically exchanged for com. shs. of Terra Industries Inc. Hudson Bay Mining is now a wholly owned subsid. of Minorco (Luxembourg) S.A.

Hudson Bay Mountain Silver Mines Ltd. (B.C. 1963)
Oct. 30, 1978 – Dissolved.

Hudson Hope Mines Ltd. (Alta. 1958)
Feb. 29, 1964 – Struck off register.

Hudson Oil Co. of Canada Ltd. (unknown)
May 31, 1971 – Charter cancelled.

Hudson Patricia Gold Mines Ltd. (Ont. Apr. 1934)
May 1960 – Charter cancelled.

Hudson Petroleum Ltd. (B.C. Apr. 1, 1981)
Sept. 29, 1983 – Name changed to Hudson Resources Ltd. ■

Hudson-Porcupine Gold Mines Ltd. (Ont. 1919)
Sept. 1959 – Charter cancelled.

Hudson Rand Gold Mines Ltd. (Ont. 1944)
1956 – Name changed to Hudson Rand Mines Ltd. ■

Hudson Rand Mines Ltd. (Ont. 1944)
1957 – Name changed to Canorama Explorations Ltd.; basis 1 new for 5 old shs. ■

Hudson Resources Inc. (B.C. Mar. 7, 2000)
Mar. 21, 2024 – Name changed to AnorTech Inc. (see FPsurvey - Mines & Energy)

Hudson Resources Ltd. (B.C. Apr. 1, 1981)
Mar. 22, 1989 – Name changed to United Hudson Resources Inc.; basis 1 new for 8 old shs. ■

Hudson River Minerals Ltd. (Can. May 10, 2010 amalg.)
Mar. 10, 2015 – Dissolved and struck from register.

Hudson-Ungava Nickel Mines Ltd. (Ont. 1957)
Oct. 30, 1961 – Charter cancelled; co. dissolved. Cash of 4.9¢ per sh. placed in hands of Public Trustee for shs. not turned in.

Hudson's Bay Company (U.K. May 2, 1670; via Royal charter)
May 29, 1970 – Continued into Canada.
Mar. 20, 2006 – Acquired by Maple Leaf Heritage Investments Acquisition Corporation; basis $15.25 per com. sh. and $1,020 per $1,000 principal amount of 7.5% debs.
Mar. 3, 2020 – Continued into British Columbia.
Mar. 5, 2020 – Privatized; basis $11 cash per sh.
Mar. 6, 2020 – Name changed to Hudson's Bay Company ULC. ■

Hudson's Bay Company ULC (B.C. Mar. 3, 2020)
Aug. 8, 2025 – Name changed to Rupert Legacy.

Hudson's Bay Oil and Gas Company Limited (Can. 1926)
Dec. 31, 1984 – Acquired by Dome Petroleum Ltd. through wholly owned subsids. Public shldrs. received one 10% retractable pref. sh. of Dome Resources Limited and one wt. to buy one sh. of Dome Petroleum Ltd. at $23.1125 to for each sh. held. Pref. shs. retractable at $57.50 and wts. expire on same date. All o/s pref. shs. redeemed at $57.50 on Mar. 25, 1983. Previously shs. had been purchased at $50 and $55.50 per sh. under tender offers.

Hudvam Mines Ltd. (Man. 1972)
Dec. 1985 – Dissolved.

Huestis Mining Corp. Ltd. (B.C. 1959)
1965 – Assets sold to Bethex Explorations Ltd.; basis 1 new for 2 old shs.

Huestis Molybdenum Corp. Ltd. (B.C. 1959)
1961 – Name changed to Huestis Mining Corp. Ltd. ■

Huffington Capital Corp. (B.C. July 21, 2015)
Nov. 10, 2020 – Name changed to Black Mountain Gold USA Corp. pursuant to Qualifying Transaction acquisition of Mohave Mine gold property option in Arizona. ■

Hugh Malartic Mines Ltd. (Ont. 1935)
July 1950 – Name changed to New Hugh Malartic Mines Ltd.; basis 1 new for 4 old shs. ■

Hugh-Pam Porcupine Mines Ltd. (Ont. 1935)
Apr. 26, 1983 – Amalgamated with Broulan Reef Mines Limited to form Broulan Resources Inc.; basis 1 new for 3 old shs.

Hugh Russel Inc. (Can. 1931)
Feb. 1981 – Name changed to York Russel Inc. ■

Hugh Russel Limited (Can. 1931)
Nov. 1977 – Name changed to Hugh Russel Inc. ■

Hughes Lang Corporation (B.C. July 31, 1989 amalg.)
Feb. 14, 1994 – Amalgamated with Nova-Cogesco Resources Inc., Orofino Resources Limited and Equity Reserve Corp. to form CanGold Resources Inc.; basis 2 new for 5 Nova-Cogesco shs., 1 new for 12 Orofino shs., 3 new for 5 Equity Reserve shs. and 1 new for 1 Hughes Lang cl. A com. or cl. B subord. vtg. sh. (see CanGold Resources Inc.)

Hughes-Owens Limited (Can. 1900)
1985 – Name changed to Hughes-Owens (1985) Inc. ■

Hughes-Owens (1985) Inc. (Can. 1900)
1988 – Name changed to Azon Canada, Inc. following acquisition by Azon Corporation. All o/s were redeemed; basis unknown.

Hughmar Gold Mines Ltd. (Ont. 1939)
Nov. 1960 – Charter cancelled.

Huhill Yellowknife Mines Ltd. (Ont. 1944)
Jan. 1959 – Charter cancelled.

Huldra Silver Inc. (B.C. Mar. 31, 1980)
June 1, 2015 – Name changed to Nicola Mining Inc. (see FPsurvey - Mines & Energy)

Hull Explorations Limited (Ont. 1973)
Aug. 29, 1978 – Amalgamated with 3 other cos. to form Belle Aire Resource Explorations Limited; basis 11 new for 100 old shs.

Hull Iron Mines Ltd. (Que. 1957)
1965 – Acquired by Corgemines Ltd.; basis 13 new for 25 old shs. (see Corgemines Ltd.)

Hull Lake Gold Mines Ltd. (Ont. 1946)
1956 – Charter cancelled.

Human Resources for Growth Inc. (Ont. Sept. 18, 1946)
Dec. 12, 1994 – Name changed to IBI Corporation. (see FPsurvey - Mines & Energy)

Humber Amusement Pier Limited (Ont. 1927)
Dec. 29, 1966 – Distribution of $1.00 per sh. paid to shldrs. of record Dec. 20, 1966.

Humber Capital Corporation (Can. Dec. 14, 2007)
Sept. 21, 2009 – Name changed to Rocky Mountain Liquor Inc. (see FPsurvey - Industrials)

Humber Oils Ltd. (Ont. 1956)
1958 – Acquired by Pacific Petroleums; basis 1 new for 9 old shs.

Humberstone Shoe Co., Ltd. (Can. 1926)
May 1961 – The Almer Shoe Co. Ltd. (majority shldr.) acquired remaining shs. at $17.50 per sh. Name subsequently changed to Sunbeam Shoes Ltd. in June 1964.

Humble & Fume Inc. (Ont. Feb. 15, 2007)
Mar. 11, 2024 – Pursuant to a reverse vesting order with 10000760498 Ontario Inc. (the Purchaser) under which all the secured debt and retained liabilities were assumed by the Purchaser through the purchasing of 100,000,000,000 com. shs. at a price per sh. equal the value of the secured debt. All o/s shs. were then consolidated on a basis determined by the Purchaser and subsequently cancelled and extinguished without any payment or other compensation. The proceedings under the Companies' Creditors Arrangement Act (CCAA) were terminated and Deliotte Restructuring Inc. was discharged as monitor.

Humbleford Exploration & Investment Ltd. (Ont. 1968)
Feb. 20, 1980 – Dissolved.

Humbleford Exploration Ltd. (Ont. 1968)
Nov. 28, 1969 – Name changed to Humbleford Exploration & Investment Ltd. ■

Humboldt Capital Corporation (Alta. June 20, 1984)
June 29, 2016 – Privatized through amalgamation with Lamond Investments Inc. to continue under the Lamond name: basis $1.075 cash plus 1.4074 Tuscany Energy Ltd. com. shs. for 1 Humboldt com. sh.

Humboldt Energy Corporation (B.C. Jan. 16, 1981)
June 20, 1984 – Continued into Alberta.
Aug. 4, 1989 – Name changed to HEC Investments Ltd.; basis 1 new for 10 old shs. ■

Humboldt Flour Mills Inc. (Can. Oct. 21, 1991)
May 28, 1998 – Acquired by 3483142 Canada Inc., a wholly owned subsid. of Saskatchewan Wheat Pool, for $1.20 per sh. (see Saskatchewan Wheat Pool)

Humboldt Grain & Milling Inc. (Can. Oct. 21, 1991)
Mar. 26, 1993 – Name changed to Humboldt Flour Mills Inc. ■

Humboldt Petroleums Ltd. (Sask.)
1958 – Struck off register.

HuMedaTech International Inc. (Can. Aug. 12, 1985)
Nov. 10, 1999 – Name changed to Feathertouch E-Comm Inc.; basis 1 new for 10 old shs. ■

Humlin Red Lake Mines Limited (Ont. 1945)
Feb. 6, 1996 – Formed Pan African Resources Corporation in Yukon on amalgamation with Pan African Resources Corporation, a subsidiary of Golden Star Resources Ltd.; basis 1.001 new for 1 Pan African sh. and 1 new for 5 Humlin shs. ■

Hummingbird Communications Ltd. (Can. Sept. 27, 1984)
Apr. 25, 2000 – Name changed to Hummingbird Ltd. ■

Hummingbird Ltd. (Can. Sept. 27, 1984)
Oct. 2, 2006 – Plan of Arrangement acquisition by Open Text Corporation; basis US$27.85 per share.

Hummingbird Mines Ltd. (B.C. Jan. 31, 1966)
Mar. 1, 1982 – Name changed to Hummingbird Resources Ltd. ■

Hummingbird Resources Ltd. (B.C. Jan. 31, 1966)
June 22, 1990 – Dissolved and struck off register.

Humpty Dumpty Snack Foods Inc. (Ont. Dec. 2, 1994)
May 23, 2006 – Acquired indirectly by Old Dutch Foods Ltd. for Cdn$2.85 per sh.

Humpty's Restaurants International Inc. (Alta. Oct. 25, 1990)
Oct. 13, 2009 – Acquired by 823533 Alberta Ltd. (wholly owned by the Koenig family) for 26¢ per sh.

Hunch Mines Ltd. (Ont. 1944)
Nov. 9, 1976 – Charter cancelled.

Hunt Mining Corp. (Alta. Jan. 10, 2006)
Nov. 5, 2013 – Continued into British Columbia.
July 22, 2019 – Name changed to Patagonia Gold Corp. following reverse takeover acquisition of Patagonia Gold plc. (see FPsurvey - Mines & Energy)

Hunter Basin Mines Ltd. (B.C. 1968)
May 1979 – Charter cancelled.

Hunter Douglas Canada Limited (Man. 1944)
1981 – All o/s pref. shs. called for redemption. Co. is now completely private.

Hunter Financial Group Ltd. (Alta. Mar. 26, 1998 amalg.)
Jan. 2, 2009 – Struck from register and dissolved.

Hunter Oil Corp. (B.C. Feb. 22, 1980)
Nov. 2, 2020 – Name changed to Hunter Technology Corp. (see FPsurvey - Industrials)

Hunter Rose Co. Ltd. (Can. - unspecified)
Apr. 1965 – Amalgamated into Copp Clark Limited.

Hunters Creek Resources Limited (Ont. 1982)
1988 – Name changed to Intercept America Corp. (see FPsurvey - Industrials)

Huntingdon Capital Corp. (B.C. Aug. 16, 2011)
Nov. 10, 2014 – All o/s com. shs. acquired by Slate Capital Corporation, a wholly owned subsid. of Slate Asset Management LP; basis $13.25 cash per sh.

Huntingdon Capital Inc. (Can. Oct. 6, 2004)
July 30, 2007 – Name changed to MetroBridge Networks International Inc. following Qualifying Transaction acquisition of MetroBridge Networks Corporation; basis 0.784 new for 1 old sh. ■

Huntingdon Real Estate Investment Trust (Man. Jan. 10, 2005)
Dec. 31, 2011 – Succeeded by Huntingdon Capital Corp. pursuant to plan of arrangement whereby Huntingdon Capital Corp. was formed to facilitate the conversion of the trust into a corporation. ■

Huntington Exploration Inc. (Alta. Nov. 28, 1995)
May 19, 2022 – Name changed to Angel Wing Metals Inc. (see FPsurvey - Mines & Energy)

Huntington Resources Inc. (B.C. Apr. 11, 1983)
Oct. 20, 1999 – Name changed to Vulcan Ventures Corp.; basis 1 new for 5 old shs. ■

Huntington Rhodes Inc. (Ont. Dec. 27, 1945)
Aug. 10, 2017 – Dissolved and stuck from registry.

The Huntington-Rockford Corporation Limited (Ont. 1967)
June 28, 2004 – Charter cancelled.

Hunt's Limited (Ont. 1919)
1953 – Acquired by Canadian Food Products Ltd. in 1953-54, through offer to purch. cl. A shs. at $10.50 per sh., and cl. B shs. at $11.50 per sh.

Huntsman Resources Ltd. (B.C. 1969)
Mar. 31, 1983 – Struck off register.

Hupon Mining & Exploration Corp. (Que. 1960)
Nov. 25, 1978 – Charter cancelled.

Hurley River Gold Corp. (B.C. Sept. 13, 1985)
Dec. 16, 1997 – Continued into Yukon.
Mar. 20, 1998 – Name changed to Ouro Brasil Ltd.; basis 1 new for 2 old shs. ■

Hurley River Mines Ltd. (B.C. 1959)
1967 – Name changed to Hurley Uranium Ltd.; basis 1 new for 10 old shs. ■

Hurley Uranium Ltd. (B.C. 1959)
1968 – Name changed to New Cinch Uranium Ltd. ■

Huron and Erie Mortgage Corporation (Can. 1864)
Feb. 24, 1976 – Name changed to Canada Trustco Mortgage Company. ■

Huron-Bruce Mines Ltd. (Ont. 1966)
Mar. 1976 – Charter cancelled.
May 19, 1977 – Chart revived.
Dec. 5, 1985 – Amalgamated with Intrex, The International Real Estate Exchange Corporation to continue under the Intrex name.

Huron Star Resources Ltd. (Ont. 1986)
July 7, 1993 – Name changed to Triangle Capital Energy Corp. ■

Huronian Mines Limited (Ont. 1972)
Dec. 15, 1995 – Formed Far East Gold Inc. in Ontario on amalgamation with Far East Gold Inc.; 1 new for 1 Far East sh. and 1 new for 10 Huronian shs. ■

Huronian Mining & Finance Co. Ltd. (Ont. Oct. 25, 1929)
1933 – Merged into Anglo-Huronian Ltd.; basis 1 new for 5 old shs.

Hurricane Hydrocarbons Ltd. (Alta. Sept. 5, 1986)
June 2, 2003 – Name changed to PetroKazakhstan Inc. ■

Hurricane Rescue Craft Inc. (B.C.)
Oct. 2, 1987 – Amalgamated with Zodiac Marine Ltd. to form Zodiac Hurricane Marine Inc.

Husky Energy Inc. (Alta. June 21, 2000)
Jan. 6, 2021 – Acquired by Cenovus Energy Inc.: basis 0.7845 Cenovus com. shs. and 0.0651 Cenovus wts. for 1 Husky com. sh. Preferred shs. exchanged into Cenovus preferred shs. on a 1-for-1 basis.

Husky Injection Molding Systems Ltd. (Ont. June 18, 1953)
Dec. 17, 2007 – Acquired by 2151000 Ontario Inc., an indirect subsid. of Onex Corporation, Onex Partners I, Onex Partners II and Onex management; basis $8.235 per sh.

Husky Oil Canada Ltd. (Can. 1953)
Sept. 1968 – Name changed to Husky Oil Ltd. ■

Husky Oil Ltd. (Can. 1953)
Apr. 30, 1987 – Amalgamated with UFSC Holdings Inc. to continue as Husky Oil Ltd.; basis 1 cl. A pf. sh. for 1 com. sh. immediately redeemable and/or convertible for $6.726 and one com. sh. of Oil Term Investment Ltd., or $11.80 for each cl. A pf. sh. following amalgamation and redemption/conversion of shs, co. became a wholly owned subsid. of Nova Corp. of Alberta and Hong Kong-based Hutchison Whampoa Limited. Subsequently, on Nov. 29, 1991, Nova sold its interests in Husky to the Hong Kong based Li Ka-Shing Group, making it a wholly owned subsid.
Jan. 31, 1998 – Name changed to Husky Oil Limited. ■

Husky Oil Limited (Can. 1953)
Aug. 28, 2000 – Merged with Renaissance Energy Ltd. to form Husky Energy Inc. (see Husky Energy Inc.)

Huston Red Lake Resources Ltd. (Ont. 1941)
Sept. 3, 1994 – Dissolved.

Hut 8 Mining Corp. (B.C. June 9, 2011)
Nov. 30, 2023 – Succeeded by Hut 8 Corp. pursuant to the merger of equals with U.S. Data Mining Group, Inc. (Hut 8 Corp. parent entity); basis 1 new for 5 old shs. (see FPsurvey - Industrials)

Hutch Apparel Limited (B.C. June 22, 1978)
June 29, 1988 – Name changed to Cherry Lane Fashion Group (North America) Ltd. ■

Hutchison Lake Gold Mines Ltd. (Ont. 1935)
July 5, 1946 – Name changed to Maylac Gold Mines Limited and continued into Ontario; basis 1 new for 4 old shs. ■

Hy & Zel's Inc. (Ont. Apr. 1, 1963)
Dec. 19, 2003 – Acquired by 2012413 Ontario Inc. for $2.25 per sh. Co. now private.

Hy-Charger Petroleums Ltd. (Ont. 1950)
1956 – Name changed to Vandoo Consolidated Explorations Ltd.; basis 1 new for 5 old shs. ■

Hy-Drive Technologies Ltd. (Alta. Mar. 29, 2004 amalg.)
May 30, 2011 – Name changed to blutip Power Technologies Ltd. following a corporate rebranding. ■

Hy-Flow Petroleums Ltd. (Ont. Sept. 27, 1950)
1952 – Assets acquired by Ellesmere Oil & Development Ltd.; basis 1 new for 10 old shs. (see Ellesmere Oil & Development Ltd.)

Hy Lake Gold Inc. (Ont. Nov. 29, 1991)
June 21, 2012 – Name changed to West Red Lake Gold Mines Inc. ■

Hyal Pharmaceutical Corporation (Ont. Dec. 31, 1968)
July 27, 2001 – Name changed to Cade Struktur Corporation and continued into Yukon; basis 1 new for 10 old shs. ■

Hyatt Financial Corporation Ltd. (Alta. July 23, 1980)
June 20, 2003 – Delisted from the TSX-Venture Exchange. Subsequently dissolved.

Hyball Explorations Inc. (Ont. Dec. 18, 1984)
Apr. 22, 1986 – Name changed to Findore Minerals Inc. ■

Hyberlab Teknologies Corp. (Ont. June 1, 1994 amalg.)
Mar. 5, 2007 – Dissolved and struck from register.

Hybrid Minerals Inc. (B.C. Nov. 7, 2011)
June 15, 2021 – Name changed to Stallion Gold Corp. ■

Hybrid Paytech World Inc. (Alta. Feb. 8, 2005)
Feb. 13, 2015 – Name changed to Mobi724 Global Solutions Inc. (see FPsurvey - Industrials)

Hybrid Power Solutions Inc. (Ont. Dec. 7, 2015)
June 13, 2022 – Continued into British Columbia. (see FPsurvey - Industrials)

Hycroft Resources & Development Corporation (B.C. Dec. 31, 1980)
May 15, 1995 – Amalgamated with Granges Inc. to form new co. with same name Granges Inc.; basis 0.88 new for 1 old sh. (see Granges Inc.)

Hydaway Ventures Corp. (B.C. Jan. 29, 2021)
May 13, 2025 – Name changed to Hydaway Digital Corp. pursuant to the Qualifying Transaction reverse takeover acquisition of DMT Digital Corp. (see FPsurvey - Industrials)

Hyder Gold Inc. (B.C. Nov. 13, 1980)
Aug. 3, 2006 – Name changed to Gleichen Resources Ltd.; basis 1 new for 2 old shs. ■

Hydra Capital Corp. (Ont. Nov. 16, 1959)
Nov. 12, 1996 – Name changed to Waterford Capital Management Inc. ■

Hydra Corp. (Ont. Jan. 1, 1989)
Dec. 1, 1995 – Name changed to HMD Capital Corp. ■

Hydra Explorations Limited (Ont. Nov. 16, 1959)
Dec. 30, 1992 – Name changed to Hydra Capital Corp. ■

The Hydro-Electric Power Commission of Ontario (Ont. May 14, 1906)
Mar. 4, 1974 – Name changed to Ontario Hydro. ■

Hydro Home Appliances Ltd. (B.C. 1983)
1985 – Continued into Ontario.
Dec. 16, 1987 – Name changed to Santa Marina Gold Ltd. ■

Hydro One Inc. (Ont. Dec. 1, 1998)
Nov. 5, 2015 – Acquired by Hydro One Limited prior to a secondary offering of that company's com. shs. by the Province of Ontario.

Hydro66 Holdings Corp. (B.C. Nov. 15, 2007)
Apr. 13, 2021 – Name changed to Sixty Six Capital Inc. (see FPsurvey - Industrials)

Hydrogenics Corporation (Can. Aug. 1, 1988)
Oct. 27, 2009 – Name changed to Algonquin Power & Utilities Corp. pursuant to a plan of arrangement with Algonquin Power Income Fund to convert the fund into a corp., resulting in the fund becoming a wholly owned subsidiary; basis 1 Algonquin Power sh. for 1 Algonquin Power trust unit. All Hydrogenics assets and liabilities were transferred (except tax assets) to newly formed publicly listed Hydrogenics Corporation. Hydrogenics shldrs. exchanged shs. on a 1-for-1 basis for shs. of new Hydrogenics. (see FPsurvey - Mines & Energy; FPsurvey - Industrials)

Hydrogenics Corporation (Can. June 10, 2009)
Sept. 12, 2019 – Acquired by Atlantic Acquisitionco Canada Corporation, a wholly owned subsid. of Cummins Inc.; basis US$15.00 cash per sh.

Hydrogenics Corporation Incorporated (Can. Aug. 1, 1988)
Jan. 24, 2000 – Name changed to Hydrogenics Corporation. ■

HydroMet Environmental Recovery Ltd. (Alta. July 24, 1986)
Nov. 2, 2005 – Struck from registry and dissolved.

Hydromet Technologies Limited (Bermuda June 5, 1997)
July 10, 2003 – Name changed to Goldmarca Limited. ■

Hyduke Capital Resources Ltd. (Alta. Dec. 8, 1995)
Dec. 13, 1999 – Name changed to Hyduke Resources Ltd. ■

Hyduke Resources Ltd. (Alta. Dec. 8, 1995)
Jan. 22, 2002 – Name changed to Hyduke Energy Services Inc. (see FPsurvey - Mines & Energy; FPsurvey - Industrials)

Hygeia Holdings Inc. (Del. Mar. 3, 1993 amalg.)
July 21, 1995 – Continued into British Columbia.
Aug. 1, 1995 – Name changed to Novopharm Biotech Inc. ■

Hygold Mines Ltd. (Ont. 1960)
Apr. 17, 1968 – Charter cancelled.

Hyland River Industries & Resources Ltd. (B.C. May 4, 1966)
Nov. 12, 1981 – Name changed to Sun-Dar Energy Corp. ■

Hyland River Mines Ltd. (B.C. May 4, 1966)
Aug. 23, 1972 – Name changed to Hyland River Industries & Resources Ltd. ■

Hylands International Holdings Inc. (B.C. Aug. 2, 2007)
Dec. 5, 2022 – Name changed to Ocham's Razor Capital Limited; basis 1 new for 65 old shs. (see FPsurvey - Mines & Energy)

Hylo Gas Producers Ltd. (Alta. 1961)
Jan. 1966 – Acquired by Nith River Petroleums Ltd.

Hymex Diamond Corp. (B.C. Feb. 28, 1986)
Sept. 4, 1996 – Continued into Yukon.
May 31, 2005 – Dissolved and struck off register.

Hypaz Technology Corp. (B.C. Oct. 23, 1986)
Sept. 12, 1994 – Name changed to Calibre Technologies Corporation. ■

HyperBlock Inc. (Ont. July 10, 2018 amalg.)
May 15, 2020 – Filed for bankruptcy and Crowe Soberman Inc. appointed trustee.

Hyperion Exploration Corp. (Alta. Oct. 17, 1995)
Jan. 14, 2015 – Acquired by a wholly owned subsid. of Tri-Win International Investment Group Inc. for 14¢ per sh.

Hyperion Resources Corp. (Yuk. Nov. 12, 1996)
Feb. 21, 2002 – Name changed to Chariot Resources Limited; basis 1 new for 5 old shs. ■

Hyperion Resources Ltd. (B.C. May 11, 1984)
Sept. 20, 1989 – Name changed to First Security Corporation; basis 1 new for 2 old shs. ■

Hy's of Canada Ltd. (B.C. 1968)
1979 – Acquired by Prime Food Systems for $5.50 per sh.

Hystar Aerospace Corporation (B.C. Aug. 14, 1986)
Sept. 12, 2005 – Dissolved and struck from register.

Hytec Electronics Limited (Ont. 1968)
1971 – Placed into bankruptcy in mid-. No distribution made to com. shldrs.

I

---

i-minerals inc. (Can. Jan. 22, 2004)
Dec. 15, 2011 – Name changed to I-Minerals Inc. ■

I-Minerals Inc. (Can. Jan. 22, 2004)
Apr. 5, 2023 – Continued into British Columbia.
Apr. 11, 2023 – Name changed to Highcliff Metals Corp.; basis 1 new for 10 old shs. (see FPsurvey - Mines & Energy)

i3 Interactive Inc. (B.C. May 25, 2007)
Mar. 4, 2021 – Name changed to Interactive Games Technologies Inc. ■

IA Clarington Aston Hill Tactical Yield Fund (Ont. Mar. 29, 2010)
Apr. 30, 2012 – Converted from a closed-end fund to an open-ended fund.

IAC Limited (Can. 1925)
Nov. 1, 1981 – Amalgamated with wholly owned subsidiary, Continental Bank of Canada, to continue under the latter name. Stock of IAC exchanged into equivalent stock of bank on sh. for sh. basis.

IAE Hong Kong Equities Inc. (Can. Mar. 3, 1987)
May 2, 2002 – Dissolved.

IAF Biochem International Inc. (Que. Dec. 14, 1972)
Mar. 6, 1992 – Name changed to BioChem Pharma Inc. ■

IAMGOLD International African Mining Gold Corporation (Can. Mar. 27, 1990)
July 7, 1998 – Name changed to IAMGOLD Corporation. (see FPsurvey - Mines & Energy)

IAT Air Cargo Facilities Income Fund (B.C. Mar. 15, 1997)
Jan. 6, 2010 – Acquired by Huntingdon Real Estate Investment Trust; basis 9.75 Huntingdon trust units for 1 old IAT trust unit. (see Huntingdon Real Estate Investment Trust)

IATCO Industries Inc. (Ont. Oct. 13, 1989 amalg.)
May 4, 1994 – Name changed to AirBoss of America Corp. (see FPsurvey - Industrials)

IBEX Technologies Inc. (Can. Apr. 10, 1972)
Apr. 12, 2024 – Acquired by BBI Solutions OEM Limited; basis $1.45 cash per sh.

IBF 1 Corp. (Can. Sept. 1, 2005)
July 11, 2007 – Name changed to Gatorz Inc. ■

IBI Group Inc. (Can. June 30, 2010)
Sept. 28, 2022 – Continued into Ontario.
Sept. 29, 2022 – Acquired by Arcadis N.V.; basis $19.50 cash for 1 com. or cl. B shs. and $0.000001 cash for 1 non-participating vtg. shs.

IBI Income Fund (Ont. July 23, 2004)
Jan. 1, 2011 – Succeeded by IBI Group Inc. pursuant to plan of arrangement whereby IBI Group Inc. was formed to facilitate the conversion of the fund into a corporation and the fund was subsequently wound up. ■

IBIS Ventures Inc. (B.C. Oct. 31, 1989 amalg.)
Dec. 10, 2001 – Name changed to Tranzcom Security Networks Inc. following reverse takeover acquisition of SafeChina (BVI) Inc. ■

IBL Equities Ltd. (B.C. July 17, 1987)
Jan. 3, 1996 – Name changed to Serena Resources Ltd.; basis 1 new for 5 old shs. ■

I.B.S. Technologies Ltd. (B.C. 1983)
Feb. 26, 1993 – Dissolved and struck off register.

IC Capitalight Corp. (B.C. June 12, 2008)
Dec. 16, 2024 – Name changed to Cupani Metals Corp. (see FPsurvey - Mines & Energy; FPsurvey - Industrials)

IC Potash Corp. (Can. Nov. 8, 2002)
Nov. 21, 2017 – Name changed to Belgravia Capital International Inc. ■

ICC International Cannabis Corp. (B.C. Mar. 1, 2006)
Feb. 12, 2020 – Name changed to Transnational Cannabis Ltd. ■

ICC International Cannabis Corporation (B.C. Oct. 19, 2010)
Dec. 21, 2017 – Name changed to ICC Labs, Inc. ■

ICC Labs, Inc. (B.C. Oct. 19, 2010)
Nov. 27, 2018 – Acquired by Aurora Cannabis Inc.; basis 0.2448 Aurora com. shs. for 1 ICC com. sh.

ICCI Integrated Credit and Commerce Inc. (B.C. May 22, 1986)
Dec. 10, 1996 – Delisted from the Vancouver Stock Exchange. Subsequently dissolved.

ICE Drilling Enterprises Inc. (Alta. Dec. 31, 1992)
June 2, 2003 – Struck from registry and dissolved.

I.C.E. - Ice Factory, Inc. (B.C. 1978)
Apr. 16, 1992 – Dissolved and struck off register.

ICG Utilities Ltd. (Can. 1962)
Oct. 25, 1984 – Name changed to ICG Utilities Investment Ltd.

ICG Utilities (Manitoba) Ltd. (Man. 1953)
Jan. 21, 1991 – Name changed to Centra Gas Manitoba Inc. ■

ICG Utilities (Ontario) Ltd. (Ont. May 6, 1954)
Jan. 21, 1991 – Name changed to Centra Gas Ontario Inc. ■

ICM Ventures Inc. (B.C. Aug. 24, 1986)
Apr. 30, 1996 – Name changed to RMS Medical Systems Inc. ■

ICN Resources Ltd. (B.C. June 27, 1988)
Oct. 19, 2012 – Acquired by 0947474 B.C. Ltd., a wholly owned subsid. of Corazon Gold Corp.; basis 1 Corazon sh. for 1 ICN sh.

ICON Laser Eye Centers, Inc. (Ont. Sept. 1, 1999 amalg.)
June 2001 – Placed into receivership.
Sept. 10, 2007 – Dissolved and charter cancelled.

ICOX Innovations Inc. (Nev. July 20, 2010)
Sept. 3, 2019 – Name changed to CurrencyWorks Inc. ■

ICPEI Holdings Inc. (Ont. Jan. 11, 2005 amalg.)
Mar. 6, 2023 – Privatized by major shldrs.; basis $4 cash per sh.

ICS Copper Systems Ltd. (B.C. Oct. 28, 2004)
Feb. 9, 2011 – Name changed to Nubian Resources Ltd.; basis 1 new for 5 old shs. ■

ICV Integrated Commercial Ventures Inc. (Ont. 1968)
Mar. 5, 1998 – Formed Blue Gold International Inc. following acquisition of all o/s shs. of Blue Gold Holdings Inc. of Massachusetts; basis 2 new for 3 old shs. ■

ID Biomedical Corporation (B.C. Mar. 4, 1991)
Dec. 12, 2005 – Plan of Arrangement indirect acquisition by GlaxoSmithKline plc; basis Cdn$35 per com. sh. and Cdn$9.20 per warrant.

ID Internet Direct Ltd. (B.C. 1985)
Jan. 25, 1999 – Amalgamated in Canada to continue with same name.
Oct. 31, 1999 – Formed Look Communications Inc. in Canada on amalgamation with Look Communications Inc., constituting a reverse takeover by Look. ■

I.D. Investments Inc. (Ont. Sept. 24, 1937)
Mar. 18, 1997 – Formed BioLink Corp. in Ontario on amalgamation with 1149250 Ontario Inc., a wholly owned subsid. of BioLink Corp.; basis 1 new for 4 old shs. ■

ID Watchdog, Inc. (Cayman Islands May 13, 2008)
Aug. 18, 2017 – Merged with a wholly owned subsid. of Equifax Inc.; basis US$0.40 cash per ordinary sh.

IDG Holdings Inc. (Alta. Oct. 20, 1995)
Aug. 30, 2024 – Continued into British Columbia.
Sept. 13, 2024 – Name changed to Bantam Capital Corp; basis 1 new for 10 old shs. (see FPsurvey - Industrials)

IDM Mining Ltd. (B.C. July 14, 2009)
Apr. 3, 2019 – Acquired by Ascot Resources Ltd.; basis 0.0675 Ascot com. shs. for 1 IDM Mining sh.

IDS Intelligent Detection Systems Inc. (Ont. Sept. 30, 1997 amalg.)
Nov. 17, 2008 – Dissolved and struck from register.

IDT Entertainment Canada, Corp. (N.S. July 1, 1996)
Name changed to Starz Media Canada Co. ■

IDYIA Innovations Inc. (Man. May 15, 2000)
June 23, 2006 – Delisted from the TSX-Venture Exchange. Subsequently dissolved.

IEI Energy Inc. (Alta. Apr. 30, 2002)
Feb. 21, 2003 – Formed Rider Resources Ltd. in Alberta on reverse takeover acquisition of Rider Resources Inc., acquisition of 840927 Alberta Ltd. and amalgamation of all 3 cos. ■

I.E.S. Technologies Corp. (B.C. June 23, 1987)
Mar. 4, 1992 – Delisted from the Vancouver Stock Exchange. Subsequently dissolved for failure to file and struck from the register.

IESI-BFC Ltd. (Ont. May 5, 2008)
May 11, 2011 – Name changed to Progressive Waste Solutions Ltd. ■

IFL Investment Foundation (Canada) Ltd. (Can. Mar. 11, 1977)
Mar. 30, 2012 – Assets liquidated and dissolved; shldrs. received $195.10 per sh.
Sept. 26, 2012 – Charter revived.
Jan. 10, 2014 – Dissolved.

IFM Food Management (Canada) Ltd. (Ont. 1975)
Feb. 25, 1992 – Name changed to Air Systems Plus Corp. ■

IFS Global Software Inc. (B.C. May 13, 2005)
May 1, 2023 – Name changed to Interfield Global Software Inc. (see FPsurvey - Industrials)

IGC International Golf Corporation (B.C. 1987)
Mar. 2, 1992 – Name changed to Medilase Industries Inc.; basis 1 new for 2 old shs. (see FPsurvey - Industrials)

IGC Internet Gaming Corporation (B.C. Sept. 15, 1987)
Nov. 20, 1996 – Name changed to IGN Internet Global Network Inc. ■

IGC Resources Inc. (B.C. July 21, 2004)
Dec. 27, 2018 – Name changed to Westleaf Inc. and continued into Alberta pursuant to reverse takeover acquisition of Westleaf Cannabis Inc.; basis 1 new for 2.9233 old shs. ■

IGF Metals Inc. (Can. June 7, 1983)
July 10, 1998 – Name changed to Independent Growth Finders Inc. ■

IGN Internet Global Network Inc. (B.C. Sept. 15, 1987)
Sept. 17, 2003 – Name changed to AssistGlobal Technologies Corp.; basis 1 new for 3 old shs. ■

IGT International Growth Technologies Inc. (B.C. Feb. 22, 1983)
Feb. 27, 1997 – Name changed to IGT Pharma Inc. ■

IGT Pharma Inc. (B.C. Feb. 22, 1983)
Feb. 16, 2001 – Name changed to Prescient NeuroPharma Inc. and continued into Canada folowing acquisition of NTB Neurotrophic Bioscience Inc. ■

IITC Holdings Ltd. (Can. Nov. 1989)
Oct. 26, 2004 – Dissolved following distribution of final assets; basis 0.039 Intermap Technologies Corporation sh. for 1 IITC sh.

ILI Technologies Corp. (Alta. Apr. 1, 1999 amalg.)
Jan. 31, 2003 – Name changed to ILI Technologies (2002) Corp.; basis 1 new for 3 old shs. ■

ILI Technologies Group Inc. (Alta. Oct. 21, 1996)
Apr. 1, 1999 – Formed ILI Technologies Corp. in Alberta on amalgamation with wholly owned ILI Technologies Corp. ■

ILI Technologies (2002) Corp. (Alta. Apr. 1, 1999 amalg.)
Sept. 15, 2011 – Name changed to Cdn Oilfield Technologies & Solutions Corp. ■

ILM Resources Ltd. (B.C. May 8, 1981)
Feb. 11, 1993 – Name changed to Rainier Resources Ltd.; basis 1 new for 3.5 old shs. ■

IM Exploration Inc. (Can. Apr. 19, 2017)
Oct. 7, 2021 – Name changed to Westward Gold Inc. (see FPsurvey - Mines & Energy)

I.M. Technologies Inc. (B.C. 1972)
Jan. 30, 2004 – Dissolved and struck from register.

IMA Exploration Inc. (B.C. Sept. 17, 1979)
Oct. 1, 2009 – Name changed to Kobex Minerals Inc. following acquisition of Kobex Resources Ltd. and International Barytex Resources Ltd.; basis 1 new for 2.4 old shs. ■

IMA Resource Corporation (B.C. Sept. 17, 1979)
July 7, 1998 – Name changed to IMA Exploration Inc.; basis 1 new for 4 old shs. ■

IMARK Corporation (Ont. Jan. 1, 1989 amalg.)
Aug. 19, 2003 – Name changed to Maxim Atlantic Corporation following reverse takeover acquisition of TomaNet Inc.; basis 1 new for 5 old shs. ■

IMAX Corporation (Can. Sept. 11, 1967; via letters patent)
Mar. 1, 1994 – Amalgamated in Canada to continue with same name. (see FPsurvey - Industrials)

IMC Integrated Marketing Communications Inc. (Ont. Jan. 7, 1986)
May 1, 2017 – Struck from registry and dissolved.

IMC International Mining Corp. (B.C. Aug. 30, 2018)
May 31, 2021 – Name changed to Interra Copper Corp. ■

IMC Ventures Inc. (B.C. Sept. 2, 1987)
Jan. 29, 2004 – Continued into Yukon.
Mar. 29, 2004 – Name changed to Triumph Gold Corp. following reverse takeover acquisition of L.B. Mining, LLP. ■

IMC2 Corporation (Alta. Jan. 14, 2004)
Sept. 30, 2005 – Formed Aztek Energy Ltd. in Alberta following the Sept. 12, 2005, Qualifying Transaction acquisition of and subsequent amalgamation with Aztek Energy Ltd. ■

IMI International Medical Innovations Inc. (Can. Nov. 9, 1992)
Sept. 30, 2005 – Name changed to PreMD Inc. ■

I.M.P. Industrial Mineral Park Mining Corp. (B.C. Nov. 27, 1979)
Nov. 6, 2000 – Name changed to Crystal Graphite Corporation. ■

I.M.P.A.C.T. Minerals Inc. (B.C. Dec. 21, 1987)
Aug. 20, 1999 – Name changed to IMPACT Minerals International Inc.; basis 1 new for 5 old shs. ■

IMPACT Minerals International Inc. (B.C. Dec. 21, 1987)
Aug. 17, 2005 – Name changed to IMPACT Silver Corp. (see FPsurvey - Mines & Energy)

IMRIS Inc. (Can. May 18, 2005)
Dec. 31, 2005 – Amalgamated in Canada to continue with same name.
Aug. 2015 – Assets sold on going concern basis to Deerfield Management Company, L.P. under Chapter 11 proceedings for US$9,500,000. No distribution to shldrs.
Oct. 22, 2015 – Name changed to Imaging Canada Liquidating Corporation. ■

IMS Experts-Consultants inc. (Can. Jan. 13, 2004)
Sept. 9, 2008 – Name changed to Investissements TSPL inc. ■

IMS Petroleum Inc. (Alta. May 29, 1996)
Jan. 14, 2005 – Name changed to Pocaterra Energy Inc. following reverse takeover acquisition of Pocaterra Resources Ltd.; basis 1 new for 8 old shs. ■

IMT Mobile Medical Technologies Ltd. (B.C. 1987)
Mar. 26, 1993 – Dissolved and struck off register.

IMUTEC Corporation (Ont. Oct. 28, 1991 amalg.)
Nov. 27, 1996 – Name changed to Imutec Pharma Inc. ■

IMV Inc. (Can. May 18, 2007)
Nov. 29, 2023 – Declared bankrupt and FTI Consulting Canada Inc. was appointed trustee.

IND DairyTech Limited (Cayman Islands Dec. 2, 2008)
Aug. 4, 2011 – Privatized at 50¢ per sh.

INDEXPLUS Dividend Fund (Alta. Jan. 27, 2011)
Dec. 21, 2012 – Merged into INDEXPLUS Income Fund; basis 0.77023960 INDEXPLUS Income units for 1 INDEXPLUS Dividend unit.

INDEXPLUS Income Fund (Ont. July 29, 2003)
June 5, 2017 – Converted into an open-ended mutual fund; basis 1 series F unit for 1 fund unit.

INDEXPLUS 2 Income Fund (Ont. Oct. 30, 2003)
Apr. 26, 2006 – Amalgamated with INDEXPLUS Income Fund; basis 0.8969775 INDEXPLUS units for 1 INDEXPLUS 2 unit. (see INDEXPLUS Income Fund)

INFOR Acquisition Corp. (Ont. Apr. 17, 2015)
May 5, 2017 – All o/s cl. A restricted voting shs. automatically redeemed for $10.04 cash per sh.

ING Canada Inc. (Can. May 21, 1982)
May 13, 2009 – Name changed to Intact Financial Corporation. (see FPsurvey - Industrials)

ING Diversified Floating Rate Senior Loan Fund (Ont.)
Aug. 24, 2015 – Name changed to Voya Diversified Floating Rate Senior Loan Fund. ■

ING Floating Rate Senior Loan Fund (Ont.)
Aug. 24, 2015 – Name changed to Voya Floating Rate Senior Loan Fund. ■

ING High Income Floating Rate Fund (Ont. Sept. 26, 2013)
Aug. 24, 2015 – Name changed to Voya High Income Floating Rate Fund. ■

INN Investment News Network Ltd. (B.C. June 19, 1987)
Mar. 2, 1994 – Name changed to Interactive Telesis, Inc. ■

INS Insurance Network Systems Inc. (B.C. Nov. 17, 1980)
Mar. 11, 1992 – Name changed to World Marketing Corporation; basis 1 new for 5 old shs. (see FPsurvey - Industrials)

INSCAPE Corporation (Ont. Dec. 18, 1989 amalg.)
Dec. 20, 2023 – Filed an assignment into bankruptcy and Albert Gelman Inc. appointed trustee.

INTERCAP eCommerce Inc. (Alta. Mar. 8, 1996)
Oct. 29, 2014 – Name changed to BioNeutra Global Corporation following the reverse takeover acquistion of BioNeutra North America Inc. (deemed acquiror) and

BioNeutra International Limited; basis 1 new for 10 old shs. (see FPsurvey - Industrials)

INTERCAP Enterprises Group Inc. (Alta. Mar. 8, 1996)
Sept. 1, 2000 – Name changed to INTERCAP eCommerce Inc. ■

INV Metals Inc. (Ont. Oct. 20, 2005)
July 28, 2021 – All o/s com. shs. not already held acquired by Dundee Precious Metals Inc.; basis 0.0910 Dundee Precious shs. for 1 INV Metals sh.
July 2021 – Name changed to DPM Ecuador Holdings Inc.

INVESCO Inc. (N.S. June 1, 1997)
Dec. 6, 2007 – All exch. shs. redeemed for parent company com. shs.; basis 1 INVESCO com. sh. for 2 exch. shs.

INX Insearch Group of Companies Ltd. (B.C. Mar. 19, 1980)
Feb. 22, 1988 – Name changed to Nova Marketing Ltd.; basis 1 new for 2 old shs. ■

IOU Financial Inc. (Que. Sept. 1, 1977)
Oct. 10, 2023 – All o/s shs. not already held acquired by 9494-3677 Quebec Inc.; basis 22¢ per sh.

IP Applications Corp. (B.C. Sept. 22, 1989)
Oct. 28, 2009 – Name changed to Monexa Technologies Corp. ■

IPC Financial Network Inc. (Can. May 14, 1998)
May 12, 2004 – Formed Investment Planning Counsel Inc. following acquisition by IGM Financial Inc.; basis either $1.95 per sh. or $0.975 plus 0.02973 new IGM com. sh. for 1 old IPC com. sh. (see Investors Group Inc.)

IPC International Prospector Corp. (B.C. Feb. 27, 1987)
May 17, 1991 – Name changed to Kingston Resources Ltd.; basis 1 new for 2.5 old shs. ■

IPC US Real Estate Investment Trust (Ont. Nov. 8, 2001)
Dec. 14, 2007 – Acquired by Everclear Acquisition Corporation for Cdn$9.75 plus US$0.0237 per sh.

IPC US Income Commercial Real Estate Investment Trust (Ont. Nov. 8, 2001)
June 11, 2004 – Name changed to IPC US Real Estate Investment Trust. ■

IPEC Ltd. (Alta. Aug. 1, 1996)
Nov. 26, 2001 – Merged with Flint Energy Services Ltd. to form a new company also known as Flint Energy Services Ltd.; basis either $2.67 or 0.0297 com. shs. of new company for 1 old IPEC com. sh. (see Flint Energy Services Ltd.)

IPICO Inc. (Ont. Mar. 30, 2006 amalg.)
Apr. 8, 2011 – Acquired by a wholly owned subsid. of Trilon Bancorp Inc., pursuant to completion of its restructuring proposal to its creditors under Bankruptcy and Insolvency Act. No funds were available for shldrs.

IPL Energy Inc. (Can. Apr. 30, 1949; via Special Act of Parliament)
Oct. 7, 1998 – Name changed to Enbridge Inc. (see FPsurvey - Mines & Energy; FPsurvey - Industrials)

IPL Inc. (Que. Mar. 14, 1945)
Oct. 20, 2010 – Amalgamated with certain affiliates of Novacap Investments Inc. and Fonds de solidaritée des travailleurs du Québec (F.T.Q.); basis 1 Amalco pref. sh. for 1 IPL vtg. sh., immediately redeemed for $6.50.

IPL Plastics Inc. (Can. Apr. 20, 2018)
Oct. 19, 2020 – Acquired by Intelligent Packaging Limited Purchaser Inc., an entity controlled by certain funds managed by Madison Dearborn Partners, LLC; basis Cdn$10.00 cash per sh.

IPSCO Inc. (Can. Jan. 28, 1977)
July 18, 2007 – Acquired by SSAB Svenskt Stal AB for US$160 per sh.

IRI Separation Technologies Inc. (B.C. Jan. 15, 2001)
Oct. 8, 2012 – Dissolved and struck from register.

IROC Energy Services Corp. (Can. Dec. 1, 2000)
Apr. 26, 2012 – Acquired by Western Energy Services Corp.; basis either (i) $1.35 and 0.23 Western shs., (ii) 0.4063 Western shs. or (iii) $1.24 and 0.2438 Western shs. for 1 IROC sh.

IROC Systems Corp. (Can. Dec. 1, 2000)
May 22, 2007 – Name changed to IROC Energy Services Corp. ■

ISACSOFT Inc. (Can. Feb. 9, 2000)
July 15, 2008 – All remaining o/s com. shs. not already held acquired by way of an amalgamation with 4468783 Canada Inc.; basis 1 cl. A pfd. sh. for 1 com. sh. immediately redeemed for 33¢ per sh.

ISG Capital Corporation (Can. July 23, 2007)
Nov. 29, 2012 – Succeeded by Firm Capital Property Trust pursuant to plan of arrangement whereby Firm Capital Property Trust was formed to facilitate the conversion of the corporation into a trust. (see FPsurvey - Industrials)

I.S.G. Technologies Inc. (Ont. Jan. 19, 1982)
Jan. 24, 2000 – Name changed to Cedara Software Corp. ■

ISI Ventures Inc. (Alta. July 23, 1996)
Feb. 27, 1998 – Formed Ayotte Music Inc. in Alberta on amalgamation with wholly owned Ayotte Drums Only Inc., acquired on Dec. 4, 1997. ■

ISIS Lab Corporation (B.C. Feb. 9, 2011)
Sept. 19, 2014 – Name changed to Imperus Technologies Corp. ■

I.S.L. Industries Ltd. (B.C. Dec. 21, 1979)
Apr. 1, 1985 – Delisted from the Vancouver Stock Exchange. Subsequently dissolved for failure to file.

ISM Information Systems Management Corporation (Sask. Jan. 21, 1988)
Feb. 3, 1995 – Acquired by 607029 Saskatchewan Ltd. for $14.25 per sh. Co. now private.

ISM Resources Corp. (B.C. Oct. 26, 2021)
Sept. 1, 2023 – Name changed to Discovery Lithium Inc. ■

ISO Ventures Inc. (B.C. 1983)
June 29, 1993 – Name changed to Steadfast Ventures Inc.; basis 1 new for 5 old shs. (see FPsurvey - Industrials)

ISX Resources Inc. (B.C. May 21, 1976)
Dec. 5, 2007 – Continued into Canada.
Dec. 6, 2007 – Name changed to Potash One Inc. ■

IT Staffing Ltd. (Ont. 1994)
Feb. 24, 2000 – Name changed to Thinkpath.com Inc. ■

ITC International Trading Corp. (B.C. 1984)
July 15, 1994 – Dissolved and struck off register.

I.T.C. Microcomponents Inc. (Alta. Aug. 31, 1992)
July 19, 1995 – Continued into British Columbia.
June 16, 1997 – Name changed to Intrinsyc Software, Inc. ■

I.T.D. International Technology Development Inc. (Can. Nov. 18, 1985)
Oct. 19, 1999 – Charter cancelled and co. dissolved.

ITEC-Mineral Inc. (Que. Sept. 23, 1987)
Sept. 25, 2000 – Name changed to Electromed Inc. pursuant to reverse takeover acquisition of Electromed Imaging Inc.; basis 1 new for 7.445704 old shs. ■

ITI Education Corporation (Can. Oct. 31, 1986 amalg.)
Aug. 16, 2001 – Placed into receivership. Ernst & Young Inc. appointed receiver.
Sept. 19, 2005 – Dissolved.

ITI World Investment Group Inc. (Alta. Jan. 12, 1989)
Oct. 1, 2008 – Amalgamated in Alberta to continue with same name.
Jan. 29, 2009 – Name changed to First Choice Products Inc. ■

ITL Capital Corporation (B.C. May 30, 1980)
Dec. 19, 2005 – Name changed to MPH Ventures Corp.; basis 1 new for 5 old shs. ■

I.T.L. Industries Limited (Ont. Dec. 4, 1963)
Dec. 1, 1985 – Amalgamated in Ontario to continue with same name.
Apr. 12, 1989 – Name changed to Ventra Group Inc. ■

ITM Corporation (Ont. Jan. 7, 1986)
June 30, 1987 – Name changed to IMC Integrated Marketing Communications Inc.; basis 1 new for 7.5 old shs. ■

ITN Technologies Inc. (Alta. July 18, 1996)
Apr. 2, 1998 – Formed Softwex Technologies Inc. following acquisition of all o/s shs. of SoftWex International Ltd.; basis 1 new for 1 old sh. (see FPsurvey - Industrials)

ITOK Capital Corp. (Ont. Jan. 21, 2005)
July 18, 2023 – Name changed to Blue Sky Global Energy Corp. pursuant to the Qualifying Transaction reverse takeover acquisition of 2413017 Alberta Ltd. ■

ITP Thermal Packaging Inc. (B.C. Oct. 22, 1980)
Aug. 8, 1996 – Name changed to Stratford Ventures Ltd.; basis 1 new for 9 old shs. ■

ITT Canada Limited (Can. Dec. 12, 1984)
Dec. 22, 1995 – Name changed to ITT Industries Ltd.

ITT Hartford Life Insurance Company of Canada (Ont. 1963)
Oct. 31, 1997 – Name changed to Hartford Life Insurance Company of Canada.

IU International Corporation (Md. 1924)
May 6, 1988 – Became a wholly owned subsid. of NEOAX Inc. of Stamford, Conn., following acceptance of a $22.25 per sh. bid for IU International's shs.

IVG Corporation (Alta. Mar. 19, 1996)
Aug. 1, 2002 – Name changed to IVG Enterprises Ltd.; basis 1 new for 4 old shs. ■

IVG Enterprises Ltd. (Alta. Mar. 19, 1996)
Sept. 2, 2009 – Dissolved and struck from register.

IVI Checkmate Corp. (Del. Jan. 15, 1998)
Aug. 28, 2001 – Acquired by Idaho Acquisition Corp., wholly owned subsid. of Ingenico S.A. of France; basis US$3.30 per com. sh.

IVI Checkmate Ltd. (Can. Oct. 1, 1984)
Aug. 28, 2001 – Acquired by Idaho Acquisition Corp., a wholly owned subsid. of Ingenico S.A., for US$3.30 per exch. sh.

IVS Intelligent Vehicle Systems Inc. (B.C. 1987)
Jan. 30, 2006 – Dissolved and struck from register.

IWC Communications Limited (Ont. 1954)
July 1, 1973 – Amalgamated with Slaight Broadcasting Ltd. to form new co. with same name; basis 3.5 new for 1 Slaight sh. and 1 new for 1 IWC sh.
Apr. 7, 1978 – Name changed to Radio IWC Limited; basis 1 new for 10 old shs. ■

IWC Industries Limited (Ont. 1954)
Sept. 1972 – Name changed to IWC Communications Limited. ■

IWG Technologies Inc. (B.C. Mar. 7, 2011)
Jan. 26, 2017 – WM Capital Management, Inc. and BASE Equity Partners, L.P., through 1096777 B.C. Ltd., acquired all o/s com. shs. for 43¢ cash per sh.

IX Capital Inc. (B.C. June 11, 1998)
July 28, 2000 – Name changed to P.Z. Resort Systems Inc. ■

i3 Energy plc (U.K. 2014)
Nov. 4, 2024 – Acquired by Gran Tierra Energy Inc.; basis (a) 1 new Gran Tierra sh. for 207 old i3 Energy shs.; and (b) 10.43 pence cash per sh.

Iago Mines Ltd. (B.C. 1966)
Feb. 25, 1983 – Struck off register.

Ialta Industries Ltd. (B.C. Apr. 7, 1981)
Nov. 3, 2008 – Dissolved and struck from register.

Ian-Mac Porcupine Gold Mines Ltd. (Ont. 1928)
1957 – Charter cancelled.

Ian Sutherland Limited (Can. May 5, 1987)
July 17, 1987 – Name changed to Northern Stores Inc,. ■

iaNett International Systems Ltd. (B.C. May 13, 1985)
Sept. 3, 2002 – Name changed to Data Fortress Systems Group Ltd. following reverse takeover acquisition of Data Fortress Technologies Group (2002) Inc. ■

IberAmerican Lithium Corp. (B.C. July 27, 2021)
Sept. 18, 2023 – Continued into Ontario. (see FPsurvey - Mines & Energy)

Iberian Minerals Corp. (Can. Oct. 5, 2005)
June 15, 2009 – Continued into Switzerland.
Feb. 7, 2013 – Acquired by Urion Minerals International B.V. for $1.10 per sh.

Iberian Minerals Ltd. (Alta. Dec. 3, 1986)
June 6, 2017 – Name changed to Mineworx Technologies Ltd. ■

Ibes International Limited (B.C. 1969)
Sept. 7, 1973 – Name changed to Accra Industries Ltd. ■

Ibex Oil Ltd. (Can. Apr. 26, 1926; via Dominion charter)
July 12, 1982 – Name changed to Dalier Resources Ltd.; basis 1 new for 3 old shs. ■

Ibsen Cobalt Silver Mines Limited (Ont. 1953)
Oct. 4, 1977 – Amalgamated with Mayfair Mines Limited to form Mayfair Resources & Developments Limited; basis 1 new for 25 old shs.

Ibstone Petroleum Limited (Can. Nov. 14, 1947)
1959 – Name changed to Swiss Oils of Canada (1959) Ltd. ■

Ican Minerals Ltd. (B.C. Dec. 18, 1986 amalg.)
Dec. 2, 1992 – Continued into Alberta.
Dec. 24, 1998 – Name changed to Net Resources Inc.; basis 1 new for 6 old shs. ■

Ican Resources Ltd. (B.C. 1979)
Dec. 18, 1986 – Formed Ican Minerals Ltd. in British Columbia on amalgamation with Canu Resources Limited (1 for 2); basis 1 new for 1 old sh. ■

Icanic Brands Company Inc. (B.C. Sept. 15, 2011)
Dec. 7, 2022 – Name changed to Leef Brands Inc. (see FPsurvey - Industrials)

Ice Station Resources Ltd. (B.C. 1970)
July 23, 1993 – Dissolved and struck off register.

Iceberg Media.com Inc. (Ont. Mar. 8, 1956)
Sept. 1, 2002 – Acquired by Standard Radio Inc., a wholly owned subsid. of privately owned Standard Broadcasting Corporation Limited; basis 1 Standard Radio pref. sh. immediately redeem. for 5¢ for 1 Iceberg sh.

Icefloe Technologies Inc. (Ont. Jan. 1, 1992)
Jan. 31, 2008 – Filed an assignment in bankruptcy under the Bankruptcy and Insolvency Act and BDO Dunwoody appointed trustee.

Icelandic Gold Corporation (N.B. Aug. 25, 1997 amalg.)
Feb. 5, 2001 – Name changed to PGM Ventures Corporation; basis 1 new for 10 old shs. ■

Iciena Ventures Inc. (B.C. Jan. 13, 1981)
Jan. 18, 2013 – Name changed to Barksdale Capital Corp.; basis 1 new for 40 old shs. ■

iCo Therapeutics Inc. (B.C. Apr. 20, 2006)
Aug. 13, 2021 – Succeeded by Satellos Bioscience Inc. pursuant to the reverse takeover acquisition of (old) Satellos Bioscience Inc.; basis 1 new for 20 old shs. (see FPsurvey - Industrials)

Icon Capital Corporation (Alta. Aug. 16, 1996)
Oct. 9, 1997 – Name changed to Extreme Energy Corporation following Major Transaction acquisition of Skipper Petroleums Ltd. for total consideration of 750,000 shs. and $250,000 cash payment; basis 1 new for 1 old sh. ■

Icon Energy Limited (Alta. Dec. 18, 1992)
May 3, 2000 – All o/s com. shs. acquired by Lexxor Energy Inc.; basis 2 cl. A shs. of Lexxor plus 1 Lexxor warrant (exercisable at $0.30 until June 30, 2001) for 8 com. shs. Icon. (see Lexxor Energy Inc.)

Icon Exploration Inc. (B.C. May 20, 2011 amalg.)
Feb. 27, 2019 – Name changed to City View Green Holdings Inc. pursuant to reverse takeover acquisition of 2590672 Ontario Inc. (dba City View Green); basis 1 new for 1.25 old shs. (see FPsurvey - Industrials)

Icon Industries Limited (B.C. June 27, 1988)
Nov. 16, 2009 – Name changed to ICN Resources Ltd. ■

Icon Resources Limited (Alta. Dec. 18, 1992)
Nov. 29, 1994 – Name changed to Icon Energy Limited; basis 1 new for 2.5 old shs. ■

Icor Oil & Gas Company Ltd. (Alta. 1980)
Feb. 7, 1990 – Placed into receivership; Deloitte & Touche Inc., Calgary Alberta, appointed receiver.
May 1992 – All the assets had been liquidated. The creditors suffered a shortfall, and there was no distribution to unsecured creditors or shldrs.
Oct. 1, 1994 – Receiver discharged.

Icron Systems Inc. (Alta. Jan. 11, 1999 amalg.)
Jan. 25, 1999 – Continued into Canada.
July 10, 2001 – Name changed to Icron Technologies Corporation; basis 1 new for 7 old shs. ■

Icron Technologies Corporation (Can. Jan. 25, 1999)
Aug. 30, 2011 – Privatized at 53¢ per sh.

Ida-May Resources Ltd. (B.C. Jan. 22, 1981)
Oct. 9, 1985 – Name changed to Limoges Porcelaines Ltd. ■

Idaho Champion Gold Mines Canada Inc. (Can. Apr. 27, 2009 amalg.)
May 29, 2023 – Name changed to Champion Electric Metals Inc. (see FPsurvey - Mines & Energy)

Idaho Consolidated Metals Corp. (B.C. Sept. 15, 1988)
Aug. 17, 2001 – Continued into Yukon.
July 24, 2002 – Name changed to Beartooth Platinum Corporation. ■

Idaho-Maryland Mining Corporation (B.C. Sept. 27, 1979)
June 23, 1993 – Name changed to HMC HealthGuard Marketing Corp.; basis 1 new for 2 old shs. ■

Idaho Natural Resources Corp. (Alta. July 21, 2006)
Dec. 2012 – Filed for voluntary assignment into bankruptcy pursuant to provisions of the Bankruptcy and Insolvency Act (Canada).
Dec. 2, 2014 – Dissolved and struck from registry. ■

Ideal Bay Explorations Ltd. (Ont. 1969)
July 27, 1976 – Charter cancelled.

The Ideal Group of Companies Inc. (Can. 1982)
June 15, 1989 – All o/s shs. acquired at $10 per sh. by a wholly owned subsid. of Waxman Industries Inc.

Ideal Metal Inc. (Que. Sept. 23, 1985)
Aug. 12, 1998 – Acquired by AAI Acquisition Inc., a wholly owned subsid. of Rio Algom Limited, for $5.75 per sh.

Ideal Plumbing Supplies Canada Inc. (Can. 1982)
May 1987 – Name changed to The Ideal Group of Companies Inc. ■

Idle Lifestyle Inc. (B.C. July 6, 2018)
Feb. 4, 2023 – Name changed to Generative AI Solutions Corp. pursuant to the reverse takeover acquisition of Ultron Capital Corp. and concurrent amalgamation of Ultron with wholly owned 1399318 B.C. Ltd. (and continued as Ultron Capital Inc.). (see FPsurvey - Industrials)

iForum Financial Network Inc. (Can. Apr. 2, 1998)
Mar. 14, 2006 – Declared bankruptcy. Le Group Boudreau, Richard Inc. was appointed trustee.

iFuture Inc. (Ont. Aug. 3, 1999 amalg.)
Sept. 11, 2000 – Name changed to iFuture.com Inc. ■

iFuture.com Inc. (Ont. Aug. 3, 1999 amalg.)
May 20, 2005 – Formed Red Dragon Resources Corporation in Ontario on amalgamation with Red Dragon Gold Corporation, constituting a reverse takeover by Red Dragon; basis 144,629 new for 1 Red Dragon sh. and 1 new for 1 iFuture sh. ■

iGaming Corporation (Ont. Sept. 25, 1995 amalg.)
June 29, 2007 – Name changed to Big Stick Media Corporation. ■

Igloo Vikski Inc. (Can. May 11, 1986)
Feb. 13, 2007 – Acquired by Lanctôt Licensing Inc. for $1.10 per sh.

Ignite International Brands, Ltd. (B.C. Feb. 25, 1985)
Sept. 1, 2022 – Privatized via a 1-for-100,000 sh. consolidation; basis 62¢ cash per pre-consolidated sh.

Ignition Point Technologies Corp. (Can. May 7, 2001)
Aug. 24, 2009 – Name changed to Tilting Capital Corp.; basis 1 new for 3 old shs. ■

Iiyama Mines Ltd. (B.C. 1969)
Aug. 30, 1973 – Charter cancelled.

Ikanik Farms Inc. (B.C. Sept. 4, 1986)
May 25, 2022 – Name changed to Pideak Group Inc. (see FPsurvey - Mines & Energy)

Ikkuma Resources Corp. (Alta. Oct. 27, 2005)
Dec. 20, 2018 – Acquired by Pieridae Energy Limited by way of plan of arrangement; basis 0.1926 Pieridae com. shs. for 1 Ikkuma com. sh. (see Pieridae Energy Limited)

iLOOKABOUT Corp. (Ont. Apr. 1, 2008 amalg.)
Feb. 3, 2021 – Name changed to Voxtur Analytics Corp. pursuant to the acquisition of Voxtur Technologies, Inc. and Bright Line Title, LLC (dba Brightline), as well as certain technology and non-legal assets of James E. Albertelli, P.A. and certain of its affiliates. (see FPsurvey - Industrials)

Îledor Exploration Corporation (Can. July 12, 2010)
Feb. 17, 2023 – Name changed to LSL Pharma Group Inc. pursuant to the reverse takeover acquisition of LSL Laboratory Inc.; basis 1 new for 25 old shs. (see FPsurvey - Industrials)

illumiCell Corporation (Alta. Dec. 8, 2006 amalg.)
Aug. 16, 2007 – Name changed to Multiplied Media Corporation. ■

Illusion Systems Inc. (B.C. Aug. 24, 1979)
Feb. 27, 2001 – Continued into Delaware.

iLoveTV Entertainment Inc. (B.C. Oct. 20, 1982)
Nov. 27, 2006 – Dissolved and struck from register.

Image Data International Corporation (B.C. Feb. 25, 1988)
June 10, 1993 – Continued into Ontario. (see FPsurvey - Industrials)

Image Power, Inc. (B.C. Dec. 4, 1985)
July 4, 2005 – Dissolved and struck from register.

Image Processing Systems Inc. (Ont. Apr. 8, 1988)
Jan. 3, 2001 – Acquired by U.S.-based Photon Dynamics, Inc.; basis 0.0447 Photon exch. shs. for 1 Image sh. The Photon shs. may be exchanged for Photon com. shs. (1-for-1) which trade on NASDAQ.

Image Resources and Systems Ltd. (B.C. Mar. 31, 1981)
Feb. 3, 1984 – Name changed to Big M Petroleum Inc.; basis 1 new for 5 old shs. ■

Image Resources Ltd. (B.C. Aug. 4, 1986)
Name changed to Approach Resources Ltd. ■

Image Sculpting International Inc. (Alta. Mar. 11, 1997)
Sept. 3, 2002 – Struck from registry and dissolved.

Image West Entertainment Corporation (B.C. Dec. 4, 1970)
Feb. 2, 1989 – Delisted from Vancouver Stock Exchange. Subsequently struck from register and dissolved.

ImagicTV Inc. (Can. Dec. 24, 1997)
Apr. 30, 2003 – Plan of Arrangement with France-based Alcatel; basis 0.158517 new Alcatel cl. A American Depository Share (ADS) for 1 old ImagicTV com. sh. The ADSs trade on NYSE.

Imagination Park Entertainment Inc. (B.C. Oct. 11, 2011)
Jan. 21, 2019 – Name changed to Imagination Park Technologies Inc. ■

Imagination Park Technologies Inc. (B.C. Oct. 11, 2011)
Apr. 17, 2019 – Continued into Canada.
Apr. 16, 2020 – Name changed to ImagineAR Inc. (see FPsurvey - Industrials)

Imaging Canada Liquidating Corporation (Can. Dec. 31, 2005 amalg.)
Nov. 9, 2018 – Dissolved and struck from register.

Imaging Dynamics Corporation (Alta. May 25, 1995)
Nov. 2, 2001 – Name changed to Imaging Dynamics Company Ltd.; basis 1 new for 5 old shs. (see FPsurvey - Industrials)

Imagis Technologies Inc. (B.C. Mar. 23, 1998)
July 6, 2005 – Name changed to Visiphor Corporation and continued into Canada. ■

iMarketing Solutions Group Inc. (Alta. Nov. 5, 1998 amalg.)
Apr. 12, 2013 – Filed for protection under the Companies' Creditors Arrangement Act (CCAA) and Duff & Phelps Canada Restructuring Inc. (subsequently KSV Advisory Inc.) was appointed monitor.
Dec. 6, 2013 – Substantially all the company's business and assets were sold to IMKT Direct Solutions Corporation and iMarketing Solutions Acquisition, LLC. Secured creditors suffered a shortfall and there were no funds available for distribution to shldrs.
Feb. 15, 2015 – Duff & Phelps was discharged as monitor.

Imasco Financial Corporation (Can. Oct. 31, 1984)
Oct. 22, 1990 – Final quarterly divd. of $0.5625 per sh. paid and subsequently all $2.25 cum. retract. first pref. ser.A shs. redeemed for $25 per sh.

Imasco Limited (Can. Apr. 3, 1912; via Dominion charter)
Feb. 1, 2000 – Formed Imperial Tobacco Canada Limited following acquisition of all o/s shs. by British American Tobacco (Canada) Limited for $41.60 cash per sh. and the amalgamation with British American Tobacco (Canada).

ImaSight Corp. (Ont. Aug. 8, 2000)
Feb. 24, 2009 – Filed for protection under the Bankruptcy and Insolvency Act (BIA).
Feb. 19, 2010 – Sale of the CRD-5 drug assets was completed with proceeds used to pay creditors. (see FPsurvey - Industrials)

Imbrex Limited (Can. 1965)
1968 – Acquired by Neon Products of Canada Ltd.; basis 0.46 Neon shs. for one Imbrex sh. (see Neon Products of Canada Ltd.)

Imco Resources Ltd. (Que. June 21, 1966)
Sept. 14, 1995 – Name changed to Meridian Peak Resources Corporation; basis 1 new for 3.5 old shs. ∎

iMining Blockchain and Cryptocurrency Inc. (B.C. June 1, 2007)
Aug. 3, 2021 – Name changed to iMining Technologies Inc. (see FPsurvey - Industrials)

Immedia Infomatic Corporation (Can. Dec. 11, 1986)
Feb. 2, 1994 – Name changed to MPACT Immedia Corporation. ∎

Immedia Infomatic International Inc. (Can. Dec. 11, 1986)
Dec. 19, 1991 – Name changed to Immedia Infomatic Corporation; basis 1 com. for 10 cl. A shs. ∎

Immersive Media Corp. (Alta. Feb. 17, 2004)
May 4, 2010 – Name changed to EmberClear Inc. ∎

Immigrant Resources Inc. (Alta. July 12, 1993)
June 25, 1996 – Name changed to Alta Natural Herbs & Supplements Ltd. ∎

Immogroup Lemaire Corporation (Can. Dec. 30, 1983)
Mar. 4, 1997 – Dissolved.

Immunall Science Inc. (Alta. Feb. 26, 1986)
June 30, 2016 – Name changed to AREV Nutrition Sciences Inc. and continued into British Columbia. ∎

Immune Network Ltd. (B.C. Apr. 24, 1996 amalg.)
Oct. 12, 2015 – Dissolved and struck from register.

Immune Network Research Ltd. (B.C. Apr. 24, 1996 amalg.)
Aug. 16, 2000 – Name changed to Immune Network Ltd. ∎

Immuno Research Inc. (B.C. Jan. 15, 2001)
Aug. 14, 2006 – Name changed to IRI Separation Technologies Inc. ∎

Immunotec Inc. (Can. Jan. 24, 2007 amalg.)
May 18, 2017 – Continued into British Columbia.
May 23, 2017 – Acquired by 1111267 B.C. Ltd., a wholly owned subsid. of Immuno Holding, S.A. de C.V.; basis $0.485 cash per sh.

ImmunoVaccine Inc. (Can. May 18, 2007)
May 10, 2018 – Name changed to IMV Inc.; basis 1 new for 3.2 old shs. ∎

ImNat Ltd. (Que. 1971)
Feb. 15, 1986 – All assets and liabs. transferred to National Bank of Canada. Co. subsequently dissolved.

Impact Acquisitions Corp. (B.C. Dec. 5, 2019)
July 4, 2025 – Name changed to Fort Technology Inc. pursuant the Qualifying Transaction reverse takeover acquisition of Fort Product Limited. (see FPsurvey - Industrials)

Impact Analytics Inc. (Alta. Jan. 28, 2020)
Sept. 18, 2024 – Name changed to Credissential Inc. (see FPsurvey - Industrials)

Impact Capital Resources Inc. (Ont. June 3, 1986)
Oct. 15, 1997 – Formed Polar Innovative Capital Corp. in Ontario on reverse takeover acquisition of and amalgamation with Polar Innovative Capital Inc.; basis 1 new for 1 Polar Innovative Capital Inc. sh. and 1 new for 4.9 Impact shs. ∎

Impact Energy Inc. (Alta. Dec. 5, 1996)
May 4, 2004 – Plan of Arrangement acquisition by Thunder Energy Inc.; basis 0.22222 new Thunder sh. for 1 old Impact sh. (see Thunder Energy Inc.)

Impact Resources Inc. (B.C. Apr. 17, 1969)
Oct. 27, 1986 – Name changed to New Impact Resources Inc. ∎

Impact Telemedia International Ltd. (Can. Apr. 5, 1983)
Aug. 26, 1992 – Name changed to UC'NWIN Systems Ltd. ∎

Impact Travel Technology Inc. (B.C. Nov. 25, 1983)
Mar. 12, 1999 – Name changed to MCF Enterprises Inc.; basis 1 new for 2 old shs. ∎

Impala Mines Ltd. (Ont. 1969)
Mar. 24, 1972 – Amalgamated with 2 other cos. to form Nordev Resources Ltd.; basis 1 new for 10 Impala shs.

Impala Resources Ltd. (B.C. May 27, 1982)
Aug. 26, 1987 – Name changed to International Impala Resources Ltd.; basis 1 new for 5 old shs. ∎

impatica.com inc. (Ont. Mar. 30, 1998)
Jan. 11, 2002 – Name changed to Impatica Inc. (see FPsurvey - Industrials)

Impax Energy Services Income Trust (Ont. Mar. 15, 2006)
Dec. 14, 2009 – Filed for protection under the Companies' Creditors Arrangement Act (CCAA) and KPMG Inc. was appointed monitor.
Dec. 23, 2009 – Operating assets of wholly owned McClelland Oilfield Rentals Limited Partnership, EGOC Enviro Group Limited Partnership and Dwayne Hommy Trucking Limited Partnership were sold to 1438961 Alberta Ltd. for $12,500,000. Net proceeds were used to pay down secured debt.
Jan. 20, 2010 – All o/s partnership units of wholly owned Denray Rathole Drilling Limited Partnership and all of the shs. of Denray Rathole Drilling General Partner Ltd. were sold to Gridiron Drilling Services Inc. for $3,700,000. Net proceeds were used to pay down secured debt.
Jan. 27, 2010 – All trustees, directors and officers resigned. As the trust no longer had any remaining operating business units or material assets, a bankruptcy filing was made. Any monies received on realization of the trust's remaining non-material assets would be paid to the secured creditors, who would suffer a shortfall, and no distributions would be available to unitholders.

Imperial Bank of Canada (Can. 1875)
June 1, 1961 – Merged with Canadian Bank of Commerce to form a new co. Canadian Imperial Bank of Commerce; basis 7 new for 6 old shs.

The Imperial Flo-Glaze Paints Limited (Ont. 1899)
May 26, 1964 – Name changed to Morse Paint Manufacturing Limited. ∎

Imperial General Properties Limited (Ont. 1979 amalg.)
June 4, 1982 – Resolution signed to wind up co. voluntarily. Thorne Riddell Inc. of Toronto appointed liquidator.

Imperial Helium Corp. (B.C. Oct. 18, 2018)
July 26, 2022 – Acquired by Royal Helium Ltd.; basis 0.614 Royal shs. for 1 Imperial sh.

Imperial Investment Corp. Ltd. (B.C. 1950)
Aug. 31, 1961 – Name changed to Laurentide Financial Corporation Ltd. ∎

The Imperial Life Assurance Company of Canada (Can. 1896)
1987 – Amalgamated in Canada to continue with same name. (see Desjardins Financial Security Life Assurance Company)
Jan. 1, 1998 – Amalgamated in Canada to continue with same name. (see Desjardins Financial Security Life Assurance Company)
Jan. 28, 2002 – Amalgamated with Desjardins-Laurentian Life Assurance Company Inc. to continue as Desjardins Financial Security Life Assurance Company. (see Desjardins Financial Security Life Assurance Company)

Imperial Marine Industries Ltd. (B.C. 1955)
1975 – Rivtow Straits Ltd. acquired all o/s shs. not already held for 7¢ per sh.

Imperial Metals & Power Ltd. (B.C. Dec. 10, 1959)
Dec. 1, 1981 – Amalgamated with Risby Tungsten Mines Ltd. (1 for 2) and Invex Resources Limited (1 for 1) to continue as a new company named Imperial Metals Corporation; basis 1 new for 2 old shs.

Imperial Minerals Ltd. (Que. 1953)
Dec. 1970 – Name changed to Consolidated Imperial Minerals Ltd.; basis 1 new for 2 old shs. ∎

Imperial Mines & Metals Ltd. (Alta. 1954)
1957 – Name changed to New Imperial Mines Ltd.; basis 1 new for 4 old shs. ∎

Imperial Mining Group Ltd. (Can. Sept. 11, 2017)
Feb. 7, 2024 – Name changed to Scandium Canada Ltd. (see FPsurvey - Mines & Energy)

Imperial Modular Industries Ltd. (B.C. 1963)
Mar. 3, 1978 – Charter cancelled.

Imperial Parking Canada Corporation (B.C. Jan. 9, 1962)
June 26, 1996 – Acquired by Vencap Acquisition Holdings Inc., a wholly owned subsid. of Onex Corporation; basis $5.00 per sh.

Imperial PlasTech Inc. (Ont. Oct. 11, 1984)
Nov. 13, 2006 – Name changed to GPJ Ventures Ltd. and continued into British Columbia. ∎

Imperial Reserve Mines Ltd. (Ont. 1915)
1958 – Dissolved.

Imperial Royalties Co. (Okla. 1920)
1942 – Dissolved; assets sold to Toklan Royalty Corp., Tulsa, Okla.

Imperial Tobacco Company of Canada Limited (Can. Apr. 3, 1912; via Dominion charter)
Sept. 18, 1970 – Name changed to Imasco Limited. ∎

Imperial Varnish and Color Co. Ltd. (Ont. 1899)
Feb. 1955 – Name changed to The Imperial Flo-Glaze Paints Limited. ∎

Impero Copper Mines Ltd. (Ont. 1956)
1960 – Name changed to Impero Minerals Ltd. ∎

Impero Minerals Ltd. (Ont. 1956)
1961 – Name changed to Proteus Minerals Ltd. ∎

Imperus Technologies Corp. (B.C. Feb. 9, 2011)
Oct. 15, 2014 – Continued into Ontario.
June 28, 2016 – Name changed to Tangelo Games Corp. ∎

Imtrex Industries & Recycling Inc. (B.C. 1981)
June 17, 1994 – Dissolved and struck off register.

Imutec Pharma Inc. (Ont. Oct. 28, 1991 amalg.)
Nov. 19, 1998 – Name changed to Lorus Therapeutics Inc. ∎

Imvescor Restaurant Group Inc. (Can. Oct. 10, 2009)
Mar. 6, 2018 – Acquired by MTY Food Group Inc.; basis $0.8259 cash and 0.0626 MTY com. shs. for 1 Imvescor com. sh.

In-Fal Mines Ltd. (Ont. 1943)
1954 – Charter cancelled.

In-Flight Phone Canada Inc. (Ont. Sept. 20, 1984)
Sept. 17, 1996 – Name changed to Normex Technologies Corporation following acquisition of Normex Telecom Inc. ■

In-Place Electronics Limited (Ont. 1968)
May 14, 1975 – Dissolved.

In-Touch Survey Systems Ltd. (Can. Jan. 24, 2002)
July 15, 2016 – Name changed to Intouch Insight Ltd. (see FPsurvey - Industrials)

InBusiness Solutions Inc. (Can. Mar. 7, 2000)
May 6, 2004 – Acquired by TrekLogic Technologies Inc. for $0.15 per sh. (see TrekLogic Technologies Inc.)

Inca Copper Mines Ltd. (B.C. 1952)
1956 – Charter cancelled.

Inca Energy Inc. (B.C. 1980)
Nov. 26, 1980 – Name changed to Mayan Energy Inc. ■

Inca Gold Ltd. (B.C. Mar. 12, 1980)
Dec. 10, 1992 – Name changed to AirPro Industries Inc. following acquisition of all o/s shs. of AirPro Automotive Services Ltd. ■

Inca Mining Corp. (Alta. May 5, 1995)
July 12, 2000 – Name changed to Graniz Mondal Inc.; basis 1 new for 5 old shs. ■

Inca One Gold Corp. (B.C. Sept. 17, 2014)
Oct. 7, 2024 – Placed into receivership by a major secured creditor and FTI Consulting Canada Inc. was appointed receiver.

Inca One Metals Corp. (Can. Nov. 9, 2005)
Oct. 26, 2011 – Name changed to Inca One Resources Corp. ■

Inca One Resources Corp. (Can. Nov. 9, 2005)
Sept. 17, 2014 – Name changed to Inca One Gold Corp. and continued into British Columbia. ■

Inca Pacific Resources Inc. (B.C. Apr. 25, 1983)
Oct. 28, 2011 – Acquired by Compañía Mineral Milpo S.A.A. for 61¢ per sh.

Inca Resources Inc. (B.C. 1980)
Dec. 8, 1989 – All o/s com. shs. acquired by ABM Gold Corp.; basis 1 cl. A sh. of ABM for 15 com. shs. of Inca. (see ABM Gold Corp.)

InCana Investments Inc. (B.C. May 19, 2009)
Feb. 16, 2010 – Name changed to EasyMed Services Inc. pursuant to reverse takeover acquisition of EasyMed Services S.A. ■

The Incentive Design Group Ltd. (B.C. Dec. 28, 1973)
Jan. 22, 1996 – Name changed to Envoy Communications Group Inc.; basis 1 new for 5 old shs. ■

Inco Limited (Can. July 25, 1916; via Dominion charter)
Feb. 9, 2007 – Name changed to CVRD Inco Limited following acquisition by Companhia Vale do Rio Doce (CVRD) for Cdn$86.00 per com. sh. ■

Income & Equity Index Participation Fund (Alta. Dec. 17, 2003)
Feb. 17, 2009 – Amalgamated with CGF Mutual Funds Corporation to continue as CGF Income & Equity Fund.

Income & Growth Split Trust (Ont. Oct. 29, 2004)
Feb. 2, 2007 – Name changed to Faircourt Income & Growth Split Trust following merger with Faircourt Split Seven Trust, Faircourt Split Five Trust and Faircourt Income Split Trust; basis 1 new pfd. sh. and unit for 1 old pfd. sh. and unit. ■

Income Financial Plus Trust (Ont. Jan. 29, 2002)
Mar. 2, 2006 – Merged into Income Financial Trust; basis 0.74373548 new Income Financial Trust trust unit for 1 old Income Financial Plus trust unit.

Income STREAMS III Corporation (Ont. May 18, 2001)
Dec. 4, 2013 – Merged into Dividend 15 Split Corp.; basis 1.22352296 cl A shs. and 1.22352296 pfd shs. of Dividend 15 for 1 Income Streams capital sh.; and 0.37682901 cl A shs. and 0.37682901 pfd shs. of Dividend 15 for 1 Income Streams equity sh.

Income Trustco Corporation (Can. June 20, 1986)
Mar. 1, 1995 – Subsid. Income Trust Company was seized by federal regulators under the Trust and Loan Companies Act and wound up by the Office of the Superintendent of Financial Institutions.
July 1995 – An assignment into bankruptcy filed and Mintz & Partners Limited in Toronto appointed trustee.
Apr. 1996 – All assets liquidated
Sept. 30, 1997 – Trustee discharged and there was no distribution to shldrs.

Incomealta Corporation (Alta. 1988)
July 5, 1995 – Amalgamated with 622305 Alberta Ltd.; basis 1 cl. A redeemable pfd. sh. of the amalgamated co., (immediately redeemed at $6.50 per sh.), for each com. sh. of Incomealta held.

IncomeAlta II Corp. (Alta. Mar. 14, 1989)
July 23, 1996 – Name changed to Pacific Mercantile Company Limited. ■

InContext Systems Inc. (B.C. Apr. 17, 1969)
July 15, 1997 – Merged with EveryWare Development Canada Corp. to form EveryWare Development Inc. (EveryWare); basis 1 new sh. of EveryWare for 28.57 old shs. of InContext and 1 sh. purchase wt. of EveryWare for 20 com. shs. of InContext. (see EveryWare Development Inc.)

Indal Canada Limited (Can. 1964)
Mar. 27, 1975 – Name changed to Indal Limited. ■

Indal Limited (Can. 1964)
Dec. 1, 1988 – Acquired by The RTZ Corp., PLC for $14 per sh.

Indefinitely Capital Corp. (B.C. Sept. 23, 2009)
Feb. 7, 2012 – Name changed to Spearmint Resources Inc. pursuant to Qualifying Transaction acquisition of Otter precious metals prospect. ■

Independence Mining Co. Ltd. (B.C. 1953)
Dec. 7, 1961 – Dissolved.

Independence Petroleums Inc. (B.C. 1979)
Aug. 25, 1997 – Following special resolution, shldrs. approved the winding up of the co. and distributing its assets to Tren Exploration Inc.; basis (a) 1 new cl. B sh. of Tren Exploration for 20 com. shs. of Independence, (b) 1 new cl. B sh. of 3020622 Canada Inc. for 20 com. shs. of Independence, (c) 1 new cl. B sh. of 15626 Yukon Inc. for 20 com. shs. of Independence, (d) 1 new cl. B sh. of 15636 Yukon Inc. for 20 com. shs. of Independence and (e) 1 new cl. B sh. of 5122 Investments Ltd. for 20 com. shs. of Independence.

Independence Resources Inc. (B.C. Oct. 20, 1982)
Jan. 15, 2002 – Name changed to iLoveTV Entertainment Inc. ■

Independent Energy Inc. (Alta. Mar. 1, 1993)
Mar. 20, 1996 – Acquired by Stampeder Exploration Ltd. for $4.00 per sh. (see Stampeder Exploration Ltd.)

Independent Enterprises Inc. (Ont. Nov. 30, 1944)
Jan. 9, 2003 – Name changed to Becker Gold Mines Ltd.; basis 3 new for 1 old sh. ■

Independent Factors Ltd. (Alta. Oct. 1976)
Nov. 9, 2001 – Following amalgamation agreement amalgamated with 95102 Alberta Ltd. and Lewin (Wainwright) Estates Inc., resulting in the shldrs. of Independent Factors (IF) (other than Wainwright Estates and Mr. Lewin) receiving 1 new ser. A 1st pref. sh. immed.

redeem. for $2.10 for 1 cl. A com. sh. and cl. B com. sh. of IF tendered. Co. now private.

Independent Growth Finders Inc. (Can. June 7, 1983)
Mar. 12, 2007 – Dissolved.

Independent Mining Corporation Limited (Ont. Nov. 30, 1944)
Aug. 18, 2000 – Name changed to Independent Enterprises Inc.; basis 1 new for 4 old shs. ■

Independent Nickel Corp. (B.C. Apr. 24, 1972)
Sept. 11, 2007 – Continued into Ontario. (see Victory Nickel Inc.)
Jan. 6, 2009 – Amalgamated with Victory Nickel Inc.; basis 1.1 Victory Nickel shs. for 1 Independent Nickel sh. (see Victory Nickel Inc.)

Indescor Hydrodynamics Inc. (B.C. Oct. 15, 1981)
July 29, 1985 – Name changed to Consolidated Indescor Corp.; basis 1 new for 3 old shs. ■

Index Mines Ltd. (Alta. Mar. 7, 1966)
Feb. 19, 1982 – Name changed to Tiffany Resource Corporation. ■

Indian Chemical & Exploration Co. (Que. 1955)
Oct. 1974 – Charter cancelled.

Indian Chief Copper Mines Ltd. (Ont. 1956)
Jan. 1967 – Charter cancelled.

Indian Gold Resources Ltd. (B.C. 1983)
June 4, 1985 – Name changed to Advanced Aero-Wing Systems Corporation. ■

Indian Head Long Lac Mines Ltd. (Ont. 1936)
Nov. 30, 1964 – Dissolved.

Indian Lake Gold Mines Ltd. (Ont. 1945)
1955 – Name changed to Indian Lake Mines Ltd. ■

Indian Lake Mines Ltd. (Ont. 1945)
1959 – Merged into Hydra Explorations Limited; basis 1 new for 20 old shs.

Indian Mines Corp. Ltd. (B.C. 1923)
1946 – Name changed to Indian Mines (1946) Ltd. and continued into British Columbia; basis 1 new for 4 old shs. ■

Indian Mines (1946) Ltd. (B.C. 1946)
1957 – Name changed to New Indian Mines Ltd.; basis 1 new for 5 old shs. ■

Indian Molybdenum Ltd. (Que. 1943)
1953 – Charter cancelled.

Indian Mountain Metal Mines Ltd. (Ont. 1951)
Dec. 18, 1979 – Amalgamated with Initiative Explorations Ltd. (1 for 1) to form a new co. also known as Initiative Explorations Inc.; basis 1 new for 7.75 old shs.

Indian River Resources Inc. (B.C. 1983)
Mar. 17, 1989 – Name changed to Mainfort Marine International Corporation. ■

Indicator Minerals Inc. (Alta. Nov. 7, 2000)
June 13, 2005 – Continued into British Columbia.
Jan. 11, 2012 – Name changed to Bluestone Resources Inc.; basis 1 new for 20 old shs. ■

Indico Resources Ltd. (Bermuda Apr. 12, 2002)
Oct. 15, 2009 – Continued into British Columbia. (see FPsurvey - Mines & Energy)

Indico Technologies Corporation (Alta. Jan. 18, 1996)
Apr. 12, 2002 – Continued into Bermuda.
May 23, 2002 – Name changed to Indico Technologies Limited. ■

Indico Technologies Limited (Bermuda Apr. 12, 2002)
Apr. 27, 2007 – Name changed to Indico Resources Ltd. ■

Indigo Books & Music Inc. (Ont. Aug. 16, 2001 amalg.)
June 5, 2024 – All o/s shs. not already held acquired by Trilogy Investments L.P.; basis $2.50 cash per sh.

Indigo Consolidated Gold Mines Limited (Ont. 1945)
June 1952 – Assets acquired by Nationwide Minerals Ltd.; basis 1 new for 2 old shs.

Indigo Exploration Inc. (B.C. Feb. 29, 2008)
May 23, 2025 – Name changed to Noble Plains Uranium Corp. (see FPsurvey - Mines & Energy)

Indigo Gold Mines Inc. (Alta. Oct. 8, 1986)
Oct. 5, 1992 – Name changed to New Indigo Resources Inc.; basis 1 new for 5 old shs. ■

Indigo Sky Capital Corp. (B.C. Aug. 26, 2010)
May 28, 2013 – Name changed to Gatekeeper Systems Inc. pursuant to Qualifying Transaction reverse takeover acquisition of (old) Gatekeeper Systems Inc. (subsequently renamed GSI Systems Inc.). (see FPsurvey - Industrials)

Indigo Technologies Inc. (B.C. July 28, 1983)
July 31, 1987 – Name changed to Robop.tek (Canada) Inc. ■

Indio Ventures Inc. (Alta. Dec. 9, 1996)
Aug. 21, 1998 – Name changed to Reliance Services Group Ltd.; basis 1 new for 1 old sh. ■

Indiva Limited (B.C. Sept. 13, 1979)
Dec. 13, 2017 – Continued into Ontario.
Nov. 4, 2024 – Pursuant to a reverse vesting order under the Companies' Creditors Arrangement Act (CCAA) the business and assets were acquired by SNDL in the form of a credit bid equal to the indebtedness owed by the company to SNDL which amounted to $20,700,000. Additional funds of $400,000 was used to repay certain priority indebtedness. SNDL also acquired all o/s shs. which were terminated and cancelled for no consideration.
Dec. 6, 2024 – The CCAA proceedings were terminated and PricewaterhouseCoopers Inc. was discharged as monitor.

Indo Metals Ltd. (B.C. Jan. 29, 1986)
Mar. 14, 2001 – Name changed to Blue Lagoon Ventures Inc.; basis 1 new for 10 old shs. ■

Indo-Pacific Energy Ltd. (B.C. July 31, 1979)
Sept. 25, 1997 – Continued into Yukon.
Jan. 2, 2004 – Name changed to Austral Pacific Energy Ltd. ■

Indo Pacific Resources Ltd. (Alta. July 9, 1986)
Jan. 2, 2022 – Struck from registry and dissolved.

Indochina Goldfields Ltd. (B.C. Jan. 25, 1994)
Feb. 25, 1995 – Continued into Yukon.
July 5, 1999 – Name changed to Ivanhoe Mines Ltd. ■

Indomin Resources Limited (Yuk. Dec. 6, 1995)
June 15, 1998 – Name changed to Battlefield Minerals Corporation. ■

Indostar Gold Corp. (Can. July 26, 1994)
Oct. 28, 1997 – Name changed to Petroflow Energy Ltd. ■

Indus Holdings, Inc. (B.C. Apr. 25, 2019)
Mar. 5, 2021 – Name changed to Lowell Farms Inc. (see FPsurvey - Industrials)

Indusmin Energy Corporation (Yuk. Nov. 7, 2000)
Oct. 7, 2004 – Name changed to Transeuro Energy Corp. ■

Industra Service Corporation (B.C. 1977)
Jan. 24, 1997 – Acquired by a wholly owned subsid. of American Eco Corporation; basis 0.425 American Eco shs. for 1 Industra sh.

Industria Metals Inc. (B.C. June 16, 2017)
Nov. 30, 2020 – Name changed to Goldplay Mining Inc. ■

Industrial Acceptance Corporation (Can. 1925)
Nov. 1970 – Name changed to IAC Limited. ■

Industrial Alliance Insurance and Financial Services Inc. (Que. 1987 amalg.)
Jan. 4, 2019 – All o/s com. shs. exchanged for iA Financial Corporation Inc. com. shs.
Mar. 31, 2023 – All o/s cl. A ser. 1 pref. shs. redeemed for $25 plus div. of $0.3000 per pref. sh. payable to shldrs. of record Feb. 24, 2023.
July 29, 2024 – All o/s non-cumulative cl. A pref. shs., series B redeemed for $25 plus div. of $0.090625.

Industrial-Alliance Life Insurance Company (Que. 1987 amalg.)
June 16, 2003 – Name changed to Industrial Alliance Insurance and Financial Services Inc. ■

Industrial & Environmental Services Ltd. (Bermuda Nov. 25, 1985)
Jan. 10, 1994 – Name changed to Trask Corporation Limited. ■

The Industrial Bank of Japan (Canada) (Can. 1982)
Nov. 1, 2000 – Amalgamated with Dai-Ichi Kangyo Bank (Canada) to form Mizuho Bank (Canada). (see Mizuho Bank (Canada))

Industrial Disposal Limited (unknown)
Nov. 1968 – Amalgamated to form Intermetco Limited. (see Intermetco Limited)

Industrial Disposal (Oshawa) Limited (unknown)
Nov. 1968 – Amalgamated to form Intermetco Limited. (see Intermetco Limited)

Industrial Growth Income Corporation (Can. Sept. 22, 2005)
July 11, 2011 – Formed PyroGenesis Canada Inc. in Canada pursuant to Qualifying Transaction amalgamation with (old) PyroGenesis Canada Inc.; basis 1 new sh. for 1 old PyroGenesis sh. and 0.32298 new shs. for 1 Industrial Growth sh. ■

Industrial Life Insurance Company (Que.)
1969 – Converted into a mutual life co. through purch. of o/s shs. at $35 a share.

Industrial Life Insurance Company (Que. May 20, 1905)
1987 – Formed Industrial-Alliance Life Insurance Company in Quebec following merger with Alliance Mutual Life Insurance Company. ■

Industrial Metals Mining Co. Ltd. (B.C. 1942)
Jan. 1957 – Charter cancelled.

Industrial Minerals of Canada Ltd. (Ont. 1945)
1968 – Merged into Indusmin Ltd.

Industrial Mortgage & Trust Company (Ont. 1889)
1969 – Acquired by The Royal Trust Company; basis $6.00 and 1 Royal Trust sh. for 1 Industrial Mortgage sh.
Dec. 31, 1981 – Amalgamated with Royal Trust Corporation of Canada.

Industrial Phosphate Mines Ltd. (Ont. 1949)
Nov. 5, 1962 – Dissolved.

Industrial Quartzite Ltd. (Alta. Oct. 16, 1961)
Apr. 19, 1971 – Name changed to Inqua Resources Ltd. ■

Industrial Services LLC (Colo. Sept. 23, 1994)
1997 – Name changed to Industrialex Manufacturing LLC. ■

Industrial Wire & Cable Co. Ltd. (Ont. 1954)
Apr. 25, 1969 – Name changed to IWC Industries Limited. ■

Industrialex Manufacturing LLC (Colo. Sept. 23, 1994)
Jan. 19, 2000 – Formed Industrialex Manufacturing Corp. in Colorado.

Industries Cover Inc. (Que. 1987)
June 8, 1990 – Acquired by 2750-7268 Quebec Inc. for $2.91 per com. sh. and 9¢ per wt.

Industries L'islet Inc. (Que. 1916)
Dec. 14, 1985 – Charter cancelled.

Industrionics (Canada) Limited (Ont. 1955)
Oct. 11, 1982 – Dissolved.

Indyke Gold Mines Ltd. (Ont. 1945)
Dec. 30, 1970 – Dissolved.

Inel Resources Ltd. (B.C. 1987)
Apr. 9, 1990 – Amalgamated with Gulf International Minerals Ltd.; basis 1 new for 2.5 old shs. (see Gulf International Minerals Ltd.)

Inex Pharmaceuticals Corporation (B.C. July 28, 1992)
May 11, 2007 – Name changed to 1322256 Alberta Ltd. and continued into Alberta following spin-off of Inex business into a new co. Tekmira Pharmaceuticals Corporation; basis 1 Tekmira com. sh. and 1 cl. A com. sh. of the co. for each 2 com. shs. ■

Inexco Mining Corp. (B.C. May 11, 2011)
Mar. 23, 2015 – Name changed to Worldwide Marijuana Inc. following reverse takeover acquisition of (old) Worldwide Marijuana Inc. ■

Infinite Lithium Corp. (B.C. Dec. 5, 2007)
Mar. 20, 2020 – Name changed to Infinite Ore Corp. ■

Infinite Ore Corp. (B.C. Dec. 5, 2007)
Feb. 1, 2022 – Name changed to Imagine Lithium Inc. (see FPsurvey - Mines & Energy)

Infiniti Resources International Ltd. (Alta. Mar. 15, 2000 amalg.)
Aug. 8, 2005 – Acquired by Welton Energy Corporation; basis 1 Welton com. sh. plus 0.25 Welton wt. for 5 Infiniti com. shs. (see Welton Energy Corporation)

Infinitum Copper Corp. (Alta. Oct. 22, 2003)
Feb. 25, 2022 – Continued into British Columbia. (see FPsurvey - Mines & Energy)

Infinity Alliance Ventures Inc. (B.C. Apr. 26, 2006)
Nov. 18, 2008 – Name changed to CBM Asia Development Corp. pursuant to Qualifying Transaction reverse takeover acquisition of CBM Asia Development Corp. ■

Infinity Income Trust (Ont. Feb. 5, 1998)
Apr. 30, 2013 – Terminated. No liquidation distribution to unitholders.

Infinity Minerals Corp. (B.C. Nov. 12, 2010)
Aug. 29, 2014 – Name changed to Herbal Clone Bank Canada Inc. following reverse takeover acquisition of The Herbal Clone Bank Inc. ■

Inflazyme Pharmaceuticals Ltd. (B.C. Apr. 2, 1980)
Aug. 26, 2008 – Name changed to EACOM Timber Corporation. ■

Info-Group Ventures Inc. (Alta. Feb. 9, 1987)
Aug. 1, 1995 – Dissolved and struck off register.

Info-Stop Communications Inc. (B.C. Feb. 25, 1985)
Sept. 20, 1990 – Name changed to Alpha Gold Corp. ■

Info Touch Technologies Corp. (B.C. June 17, 1997)
Apr. 11, 2006 – Name changed to TIO Networks Corp. ■

InfoInterActive Inc. (Alta. Feb. 14, 1994)
July 19, 2001 – Acquired by wholly owned subsid. of America Online Inc. for Cdn$1.42 per sh.

Infolink Technologies Ltd. (Ont. Nov. 7, 1996)
Dec. 12, 2007 – Privatized via amalgamation with 2153357 Ontario Inc.; basis $0.0472 cash per sh.

Inform Exploration Corp. (B.C. July 5, 2010)
Aug. 25, 2014 – Name changed to OrganiGram Holdings Inc. following reverse takeover acquisition of OrganiGram Inc.; basis 1 new for 0.8836047 old shs. ■

Inform Resources Corp. (B.C. Nov. 4, 2010)
May 26, 2020 – Name changed to Apollo Gold Corp. ■

Informatrix 2000 Inc. (Que. 1970)
Apr. 29, 1991 – Acquired by Softkey Software Products Inc.; basis $2.57 or 0.925 Softkey shs. for 1 Informatrix sh., or 1 Softkey $0.20 cum. pref. ser. A sh. for 1 Informatrix sh. (see SoftKey Software Products Inc.)

Informission Group Inc. (Can. Nov. 19, 1985)
May 29, 2000 – Name changed to Nurun inc. ■

Infotec Industries Inc. (B.C. June 2, 1981)
Nov. 13, 1986 – Name changed to Sellectek Industries Inc.; basis 1 new for 3.5 old shs. ■

The InfoUtility Corporation (Ont. June 15, 2000 amalg.)
Jan. 19, 2005 – Name changed to Lynden Ventures Ltd.; basis 1 new for 4 old shs. ■

Infowave Software, Inc. (B.C. Feb. 21, 1997 amalg.)
Dec. 11, 2011 – Dissolved and struck from register.

Infowave Wireless Messaging Incorporated (B.C. Feb. 21, 1997 amalg.)
Oct. 14, 1999 – Name changed to Infowave Software, Inc. ■

Infrastructure Materials Corp. (Del. June 3, 1999)
Jan. 28, 2016 – Voluntarily delisted from TSX-VEN.

Infrationics Industries Ltd. (Alta. 1954)
July 30, 1977 – Struck off register.

Ingenika Mines Ltd. (B.C. 1928)
1976 – Voluntarily liquidated.

Ingersoll Machine and Tool Company, Limited (Can. 1920)
1970 – Ivaco Industries Ltd. acquired 98% of the o/s shs.

Inglenook Ventures Ltd. (B.C. Jan. 14, 2021)
May 30, 2022 – Name changed to Atha Energy Corp. (see FPsurvey - Mines & Energy)

Inglis Limited (Ont. Nov. 23, 1936)
Feb. 14, 1990 – Amalgamated with Whirlpool Investments Canada Inc., a wholly owned subsid. of the Whirlpool Corp. of Benton Harbour, Mich.; basis $33 per sh.
2001 – Name changed to Whirlpool Canada LP.

Ingot Resources Ltd. (B.C. Feb. 2, 1983)
Feb. 25, 1985 – Formed Candol Developments Ltd. in British Columbia on amalgamation with Candol Developments Ltd.; basis 0.76776 new for 1 old sh. ■

Ingraham Yellowknife Gold Mines Ltd. (Ont. 1944)
July 1957 – Charter cancelled.

Ingram & Bell Ltd. (Ont. 1905)
1963 – International Bronze Powders Limited acquired control through offer in 1959 of $13.50 per com. and $12.50 per pref. sh. The pref. were converted into com. of Int'l Bronze on a sh.-for-sh. basis. remaining com. sh. of Ingram & Bell acquired by Int'l Bronze.
Feb. 14, 1997 – Name changed to MDS Ingram & Bell Inc.

Ingray Yellowknife Mines Ltd. (Ont. 1945)
July 1958 – Charter cancelled.

Initial Capital Inc. (Alta. Nov. 23, 2004)
May 10, 2007 – Name changed to Digifonica International Inc. following Qualifying Transaction acquisition of Digifonica International Corp.; basis 1 new for 5 old shs. ■

Initial Developers Corporation Ltd. (B.C. 1972)
May 2, 1974 – Amalgamated with North Pacific Mines Ltd. to form Initial Developers Limited; basis 1 new for 2 old shs.

Initiative Explorations Inc. (Ont. Dec. 18, 1979 amalg.)
Apr. 26, 1995 – Amalgamated with Canhorn Mining Corporation to form Canhorn Chemical Corporation; basis 0.5 new for 1 Canhorn Mining sh. and 0.45 new for 1 Initiative sh. (see Canhorn Chemical Corporation)

Initiative Explorations Ltd. (Ont. 1959)
Dec. 18, 1979 – Amalgamated with Indian Mountain Metal Mines (1 new for 7.75 old shs.) to form a new co. also known as Initiative Explorations Inc.; basis sh. for sh. (see Initiative Explorations Inc.)

Initiative Mining Co. Ltd. (Ont. 1956)
1959 – Merged into Penelope Explorations Ltd.; basis 3 new for 2 old shs.

Inland Cement Co. Ltd. (Can. 1954)
Oct. 1965 – Formed Lehigh Cement Limited following merger with Sogemines Limited under the latter's name; basis 1.5 new com. for 1 old partic. pref. sh. Ord. shldrs. received 1/10 of distribution made to pref. holders.

Inland Chemicals Canada Limited (Alta. 1954)
1969 – Name changed to Inland Chemicals Ltd. ■

Inland Chemicals Ltd. (Alta. 1954)
1976 – Through purchase offer made in 1973, Canadian Industries Ltd. acquired all o/s shs. at $7.50 per sh. All o/s pref. shs. redeemed.

Inland Copper Ltd. (B.C. 1966)
Feb. 25, 1983 – Struck off register.

Inland Copper Mines Ltd. (B.C. 1956)
1962 – Name changed to Inland Gold Mines Ltd. ■

Inland Gold Mines Ltd. (B.C. 1956)
May 15, 1969 – Struck off register.

Inland Mining Corp. Ltd. (Ont. 1943)
1957 – Charter cancelled.

Inland Natural Gas Co. Ltd. (B.C. June 4, 1952)
July 1, 1989 – Formed BC Gas Inc. on amalgamation with wholly owned subsids. BC Gas Inc., Columbia Natural Gas Ltd. and Fort Nelson Gas Ltd.; subsid. shs. cancelled upon amalgamation. ■

Inland Oils Ltd. (B.C.)
1961 – Struck off register.

Inland Recovery Group Ltd. (B.C. 1980)
May 24, 1988 – Name changed to Consolidated Inland Recovery Group Ltd.; basis 1 new for 7 old shs. ■

Inland Trust and Savings Corporation Limited (Man. 1966)
June 1994 – All o/s ser. A and ser. B pref. shs. redeemed for $5.00 per ser. A sh. and $4.40 per ser. B sh. A total of 92,273 com. shs. were repurchased or cancelled at an average price of $5.03 per sh. with the remainder converted on a 1 new for 4,400 old shs. basis.
Dec. 9, 1994 – Name changed to Inland Mortgage Corporation Ltd.

Inlet Devices Corporation (Alta. Mar. 24, 1995)
Apr. 20, 2000 – Continued into Ontario.
May 1, 2000 – Name changed to Sangoma.com Inc. following acquisition of Sangoma Technologies Inc.; basis 1 new for 2 old shs. ■

Inlet Mining Corp. Ltd. (Ont. 1952)
Apr. 15, 1965 – Dissolved.

Inlet Resources Ltd. (B.C. Feb. 20, 1961)
Aug. 19, 2014 – Name changed to Guerrero Ventures Inc. ■

In.Mark Corporation (Ont. 1928)
1984 – Formed Gemini Food Corporation in Ontario on amalgamation with Gemini Foods Ltd. ■

InMedia Presentations Inc. (B.C. Dec. 1, 1995)
July 14, 1999 – Name changed to Photochannel Networks Inc. ■

Inmet Mining Corporation (Can. June 1, 1987)
Apr. 10, 2013 – Acquired by First Quantum Minerals Ltd.; basis either (i) $72, (ii) 3.2967 First Quantum com. shs.

or (iii) $36 plus 1.6484 First Quantum com. shs. for 1 Inmet sh.
Apr. 23, 2013 – Amalgamated with FQM (Akubra) Inc., a wholly owned subsid. of First Quantum Minerals Ltd., to continue under the FQM (Akubra) Inc. name.
Apr. 23, 2013 – Formed FQM (Akubra) Inc. on amalgamation with FQM (Akubra) Inc., a wholly owned subsid. of First Quantum Minerals Ltd.

Inmont Copper Mines Ltd. (Ont. 1951)
Aug. 9, 1972 – Charter cancelled.

Inn-House Video Ltd. (B.C. Jan. 10, 1986)
June 8, 1988 – Name changed to Sleeping Gold Ltd. ■

Inner Spirit Holdings Ltd. (Alta. Mar. 16, 2017)
July 21, 2021 – Acquired by Sundial Growers Inc.; basis 0.0835 Sundial com. shs. plus 30¢ cash for 1 Inner Spirit sh. (see Sundial Growers Inc.)

Innergex Power Income Fund (Que. Oct. 25, 2002)
Apr. 1, 2010 – Converted into a corporation pursuant to plan of arrangement reverse takeover acquisition of Innergex Renewable Energy Inc.; basis 1 Innergex Renewable sh. for 1.46 Innergex fund unit.

Innergex Renewable Energy Inc. (Can. Oct. 25, 2002)
July 23, 2025 – Acquired by Caisse de dépôt et placement du Québec; basis $13.75 cash per com. sh. and $25 cash plus all accrued and unpaid dividends for each ser. A and ser. C pref. shs.

Innexus Biotechnology Inc. (B.C. Sept. 5, 1997)
Mar. 4, 2013 – Dissolved and struck from register.

Innicor Subsurface Technologies Inc. (Alta. Apr. 7, 1999)
May 30, 2008 – Acquired by BJ Services Company for $2.50 per com. sh.

Innogis Technology Inc. (Can. May 4, 1992)
July 12, 2004 – Dissolved.

InnoMat Solutions Corp. (Ont. Dec. 30, 1985)
Nov. 17, 1999 – Name changed to Carber Capital Corp.; basis 1 new for 40 old shs. ■

Innopac Inc. (Can. June 23, 1983)
May 27, 1991 – Name changed to International Innopac Inc.; basis 1 new for 5 old shs. ■

Innotech Aviation Enterprises Limited (Can. 1984)
Apr. 25, 1989 – Acquired by IMP Aerospace Limited for $3.10 per sh.

Innotech Multimedia Corporation (Ont. Feb. 22, 1988)
Mar. 3, 1999 – Name changed to ASTAware Technologies Inc.; basis 1 new for 2 old shs. ■

Innova Exploration Ltd. (Alta. Apr. 21, 2004)
Nov. 6, 2007 – Merged into Crescent Point Energy Trust for $7.55 per com. sh. (see Crescent Point Energy Trust)

Innova Gaming Group Inc. (Ont. Feb. 25, 2015)
Sept. 19, 2017 – Acquired by Pollard Banknote Limited for Cdn$2.50 cash per share.

Innova LifeSciences Corporation (Ont. Apr. 28, 1998)
Nov. 24, 2004 – Acquired by Sybron Dental Specialties, Inc. for $1.4106 per sh.

Innova Technologies Corp. (B.C. Dec. 22, 1986)
Apr. 28, 1998 – Continued into Ontario.
May 12, 1998 – Name changed to Innova Technologies Corporation. ■

Innova Technologies Corporation (Ont. Apr. 28, 1998)
Aug. 3, 2000 – Name changed to Innova LifeSciences Corporation. ■

Innovadent Technologies Ltd. (Ont. Feb. 18, 1988)
Dec. 1999 – Company's proposal under the Bankruptcy and Insolvency Act was annulled and the company filed

for bankruptcy. Toronto-based Harold Brief and Associates Limited was appointed trustee.
June 1, 2000 – Liquidation of the remaining assets was concluded. Secured creditors suffered a major shortfall and there were no distributions made to unsecured creditors or to shldrs.

Innovation Capital Corporation (Alta. 1988)
May 11, 1989 – Name changed to Capital Markets West Inc. following amalgamation with Capital Markets West Inc. ■

Innovative Capital Inc. (Alta. Sept. 9, 1993)
July 29, 1998 – Name changed to Vertex Properties Inc. ■

Innovative Composites International Inc. (Ont. Sept. 22, 2009 amalg.)
May 25, 2018 – Dissolved and struck from register.

Innovative Environmental Services Ltd. (Alta. Jan. 7, 1988)
Aug. 4, 1995 – Delisted from the Alberta Stock Exchange. Subsequently dissolved.

Innovative Marketing & Technologies Corp. (Ont. Aug. 16, 1985)
Feb. 1, 1990 – Name changed to Dino International Inc.; basis 1 new for 6 old shs. ■

Innovative Product Opportunities Inc. (Del. Apr. 3, 2009)
July 26, 2016 – Name changed to Two Hands Corporation. (see FPsurvey - Industrials)

Innovative Properties Inc. (Can. Oct. 31, 2002 amalg.)
May 29, 2019 – Name changed to Nabis Holdings Inc. and continued into British Columbia. ■

Innovative Waste Technologies Inc. (B.C. Apr. 16, 1980)
June 8, 1995 – Name changed to International Tire Recycling and Manufacturing Corp.; basis 1 new for 10 old shs. ■

Innovative Water & Sewer Systems Inc. (Alta. Jan. 28, 2000)
July 6, 2005 – Name changed to Clearford Industries Inc. and continued into Canada. ■

Innovative Wireline Solutions Inc. (Alta. June 30, 2010 amalg.)
Jan. 2, 2014 – Dissolved and struck from register.

Innovente Inc. (Que. July 1, 2004)
Dec. 18, 2014 – Filed for bankruptcy and PricewaterhouseCoopers Inc. was appointed trustee.

Innoventures International Inc. (Alta. May 1, 2001)
July 24, 2004 – Formed Hodgins Auctioneers Inc. in Alberta on Qualifying Transaction reverse takeover amalgamation with Hodgins' Auctioneers (Alberta) Inc.; basis 1 new for 2 old shs. ■

Innovis Corporation (B.C. June 7, 1983)
Oct. 15, 1993 – Continued into Wyoming.

Innovium Capital Corp. (Can. Dec. 15, 1992 amalg.)
Oct. 10, 2007 – Name changed to Innovium Media Properties Corp. (see FPsurvey - Industrials)

InnVest Real Estate Investment Trust (Ont. Jan. 1, 2002)
Aug. 18, 2016 – Acquired by Bluesky Hotels and Resorts Inc., a private Canadian company backed by Hong Kong investors, for $7.25 cash per unit.

Inocan Technologies Ltd. (B.C. 1985)
June 21, 1993 – Name changed to Arling Resources Ltd.; basis 1 new for 3 old shs. ■

Inore Gold Mines Limited (Ont. 1945)
July 22, 1982 – Amalgamated with Abino Gold Mines Limited (1 for 12.94), Clicker Red Lake Mines Limited (1 for 18.23), Commander Red Lake Mines Limited (1 for 30.82), Dorion Red Lake Mines Limited (1 for 15.59),

Duchesne Red Lake Mines Limited (1 for 10.57), Forsyth Mines Limited (1 for 6.38), Goldquest Explorations Corp. (1 for 1.26), Laddie Gold Mines Limited (1 for 15.22) and Rowan Gold Mines Limited (1 for 4.91) to form Goldquest Exploration Inc.; basis 1 new for 9.9 shs.

Inouye Technologies (Canada) Inc. (Can. Apr. 26, 1926; via Dominion charter)
Oct. 4, 2005 – Dissolved.

Inova Optics Inc. (Can. 1984)
Jan. 4, 1989 – Placed into bankruptcy and assets sold. Nothing for shldrs.

Inova Resources Limited (Australia Jan. 20, 2004)
Nov. 28, 2013 – Acquired by Shanxi Donghui Coal Coking & Chemicals Group Co., Ltd. for A$0.22 per sh.

Inovent Capital Inc. (B.C. Aug. 23, 2012)
Feb. 1, 2017 – Name changed to Inomin Mines Inc. pursuant to the acquisition of the King's Point property which constituted the company's Qualifying Transaction. (see FPsurvey - Mines & Energy)

Inovio Biomedical Corporation (Del. June 15, 2001)
May 17, 2010 – Name changed to Inovio Pharmaceuticals, Inc.

Inovision Solutions Inc. (B.C. Dec. 16, 1983)
May 16, 2006 – Name changed to Sierra Geothermal Power Corp. ■

Inovision Technologies Inc. (B.C. Dec. 16, 1983)
May 15, 2001 – Name changed to Inovision Solutions Inc.; basis 1 new for 8 old shs. ■

Input Capital Corp. (Ont. Feb. 13, 2012)
Aug. 8, 2013 – Continued into Saskatchewan.
Oct. 1, 2021 – Name changed to SSC Security Services Corp.; basis 1 new for 3 old shs. (see FPsurvey - Industrials)

Inqua Resources Ltd. (Alta. Oct. 16, 1961)
Apr. 1, 1984 – Charter cancelled.
Sept. 9, 1987 – Charter revived.
Sept. 30, 1987 – Name changed to Locator Systems Inc. ■

Insco Mines Ltd. (Que. 1938)
1953 – Name changed to New Insco Mines Ltd.; basis 1 new for 2 old shs. ■

Insecta Research Corp. (1986) Inc. (Can. May 12, 1986)
Nov. 3, 1995 – Dissolved.

Inside Holdings Inc. (B.C. July 7, 1992)
Oct. 6, 2000 – Continued into Yukon.
Sept. 17, 2002 – Name changed to SHEP Technologies Inc. following reverse takeover acquisition of SHEP Limited, an Isle of Man co.; basis 2 new for 1 old sh. ■

Insignia Energy Ltd. (Alta. Aug. 1, 2006 amalg.)
July 24, 2009 – Amalgamated in Alberta to continue with same name. (see Brookfield Asset Management Inc.)
July 25, 2013 – Acquired by Brookfield Capital Partners II L.P., a wholly own subsid. of Brookfield Asset Management Inc., for $1.35 per sh. (see Brookfield Asset Management Inc.)

Inspan Investments Limited (Alta. May 15, 1987)
June 12, 1998 – Name changed to Slade Energy Inc.; basis 1 new for 4 old shs. ■

Inspira Financial Inc. (B.C. July 7, 2010)
Jan. 15, 2020 – Name changed to Brattle Street Investment Corp. ■

Inspiration Ltd. (Que. Oct. 3, 1934)
Jan. 1974 – Placed into bankruptcy. Payment of 20¢ per dollar made to unsecured creditors.
1980 – Final distribution of 54% made to unsecured creditors.

Inspiration Mining & Development Co. Ltd. (Que. Oct. 3, 1934)
Aug. 30, 1962 – Name changed to Inspiration Ltd. ■

Inspiration Mining Corporation (B.C. Nov. 15, 1972 amalg.)
Aug. 18, 2008 – Continued into Ontario.
July 4, 2019 – Name changed to Silk Energy Limited; basis 1 new for 3 old shs. (see FPsurvey - Mines & Energy)

Inspiration Resources Corporation (Md. 1983)
May 6, 1992 – Name changed to Terra Industries Inc.

Inspire Semiconductor Holdings Inc. (B.C. Jan. 19, 2021)
Jan. 2, 2025 – Voluntarily delisted from the TSX-Venture Exchange. (see FPsurvey - Industrials)

Insta-Rent Inc. (Ont. Oct. 30, 2007)
Nov. 10, 2008 – Acquired by Easyhome Ltd. for 50¢ per sh.

Instaglide Transportation Corporation (Can. Apr. 10, 1989)
Jan. 27, 1994 – Name changed to Skygame Corporation; basis 10 new for 1 old sh. ■

The Instant Publisher Inc. (Ont. Dec. 8, 1993 amalg.)
Feb. 5, 1997 – Name changed to Diversinet Corp. ■

Instar Energy Corp. (B.C. 1979)
Aug. 22, 1994 – Dissolved and struck off register.

Instep Mobile Communications Inc. (B.C. May 1, 1991)
Nov. 20, 1998 – Name changed to eDispatch.com Wireless Data Inc. ■

InStorage Real Estate Investment Trust (Ont. June 20, 2006)
Mar. 20, 2009 – Acquired by Canadian Storage Partners, ULC for $4.00 per unit.

iNsu Innovations Group Inc. (B.C. Dec. 11, 1986)
July 8, 2003 – Name changed to MTY Food Group Inc. (see FPsurvey - Industrials)

Insular Explorations Ltd. (B.C. July 7, 1981)
Sept. 1, 1999 – Name changed to Masuparia Gold Corporation. ■

Insulblock Systems Inc. (Ont. 1943)
Sept. 3, 1994 – Dissolved and struck off register.

Insulite Development Corporation Inc. (Ont. Nov. 13, 1974)
Feb. 10, 1982 – Name changed to Insulite Explorations Inc. ■

Insulite Explorations Inc. (Ont. Nov. 13, 1974)
Apr. 11, 1994 – Name changed to Northampton Group Inc. following reverse takeover acquisition of Shihasi Investment Corporation; basis 1 new for 4 old shs. ■

InsulPro Industries Inc. (Can. Oct. 18, 1990)
Jan. 8, 1999 – Acquired by Builder Products of Canada Inc., an indirect wholly owned subsid. of BSI Holdings, Inc. of California, for $1.20 per sh.

Insurcom Financial Corporation (Alta. Jan. 29, 1993)
July 2, 2005 – Dissolved and struck from register.
Aug. 16, 2007 – Restored to register. (see FPsurvey - Industrials)

In.Sync Industries Inc. (B.C. Apr. 24, 1987)
May 27, 2003 – Name changed to Jet Gold Corp. ■

Intasys Corporation (Ont. July 5, 1985)
Jan. 12, 2004 – Name changed to Mamma.com Inc. ■

Integra Gold Corp. (B.C. July 2, 1986)
July 18, 2017 – All o/s com. shs. not already held acquired by Eldorado Gold Corporation; basis (i) 0.24250 Eldorado shs. plus $0.001 cash; or (ii) $1.21250 cash; or (iii) 0.18188 Eldorado shs. for 1 Integra com. sh.

Integra Resources Corp. (Ont. Apr. 15, 1997)
June 29, 2020 – Continued into British Columbia. (see FPsurvey - Mines & Energy)

Integra Systems Inc. (B.C. 1983)
Oct. 29, 1993 – Dissolved and struck off register.

Integrated Asset Management Corp. (Ont. Dec. 23, 1996)
July 5, 2019 – Acquired by Fiera Capital Corporation; basis (i) $2.576 in cash; or (ii) 0.2247936192 Fiera cl. A subord. vtg. shs.; or (iii) $1.932 in cash plus 0.0561984048 Fiera cl. A subord. vtg. shs. for 1 Integrated Asset sh.

Integrated Cannabis Company Inc. (B.C. Sept. 15, 2011)
Feb. 18, 2020 – Name changed to Icanic Brands Company Inc. ■

Integrated Card Technologies Inc. (B.C. Sept. 3, 1987)
July 29, 1997 – Name changed to Rizona Ventures Ltd.; basis 1 new for 5 old shs. ■

Integrated Communications Industries Inc. (B.C. Jan. 22, 1985)
Oct. 17, 2005 – Dissolved and struck from register.

Integrated Energy Storage Corp. (Can. Dec. 2, 2016)
May 17, 2019 – Name changed to Medcolcanna Organics Inc. and continued into British Columbia pursuaunt to reverse takeover acquisition of Medcolcanna (BVI) Inc. (see FPsurvey - Industrials)

Integrated Enviro-Capital Inc. (Alta. May 3, 2000)
Dec. 13, 2002 – Formed Canadian Stevia Corporation in Alberta on Qualifying Transaction amalgamation with Canadian Stevia Corporation, constituting a reverse takeover by Canadian Stevia; basis 1.5 new for 1 Canadian Stevia sh. and 1 new for 1 Integrated Enviro-Capital sh. ■

Integrated Flight Systems Inc. (Alta. Apr. 20, 1994)
Oct. 2, 2001 – Struck from registry and dissolved.

Integrated Growth Fund Inc. (Can. Jan. 11, 1993)
Dec. 6, 1993 – Name changed to UFC Canadian Growth Fund Inc. ■

Integrated Media Communications Inc. (B.C. Sept. 2, 1987)
Sept. 29, 1998 – Name changed to IMC Ventures Inc.; basis 1 new for 10 old shs. ■

Integrated Network Services Inc. (B.C. Feb. 4, 1988)
Dec. 8, 1994 – Acquired by Call-Net Enterprises Inc.; basis 0.9664 Call-Net cl. B non-vtg. shs. for 1 Integrated Network sh. (see Call-Net Enterprises Inc.)

Integrated Oil NT Corp. (Ont. Mar. 9, 1998)
Apr. 9, 2003 – Redeemed in full. Capital shs. redeemed for the amount that unit value exceeds $10 ($36.456064). Preferred shs. redeemed for the lesser of $10 and the unit value ($10).

Integrated Paving Concepts Inc. (B.C. Aug. 15, 1991)
Aug. 24, 2006 – Privatized; basis $1.30 per sh.

Integrated Production Services Ltd. (Alta. Apr. 5, 2000 amalg.)
July 5, 2002 – Acquired by Texas-based SCF-IV, L.P. for $3.05 per sh.

Integrated Resources Ltd. (Alta. Apr. 24, 1986)
Oct. 1, 1993 – Dissolved and struck off register.

Integrated Travel Systems, Inc. (Tex. 1985)
Sept. 25, 1992 – Acquired by Lifeco Services Corporation, a wholly owned subsid. of American Express Travel Related Services Company, for 40¢ per sh.

Integrated Wood Products Ltd. (B.C. 1968)
1977 – Acquired by Balco Industries Ltd. for $2.50 per sh. (see Balco Industries Ltd.)

Integrity Gaming Corp. (Ont. May 5, 2014)
Feb. 14, 2019 – Acquired by PlayAGS Canada ULC a wholly owned subsid. of PlayAGS, Inc.; basis Cdn$0.46 cash per sh.

IntelCom Group Inc. (B.C. June 5, 1981)
Oct. 30, 1995 – Continued into Canada.
Aug. 6, 1996 – Name changed to ICG Holdings (Canada), Inc. following restructuring of the co. as a publicly traded U.S.-domiciled corporation; basis 1 com. sh. of ICG Communications, Inc. (a Delaware corporation) for 1 com. sh. Shldrs. who elected to hold onto their com. shs. could exchange them on a 1-for-1 basis for cl. A shs. exchangeable at any time for com. shs. of ICG Communications, Inc. Subsequently, the cl. A shs. delisted from the Vancouver Stock Exchange at the company's request as ICG Communications, Inc. then held 98% of the o/s cl. A shs. effective Mar. 12, 1997.

Intelect Communications, Inc. (Del. Dec. 5, 1997)
Jan. 31, 2001 – Name changed to TeraForce Technology Corporation.

Intelect Communications Systems Limited (Bermuda 1980)
Dec. 5, 1997 – Name changed to Intelect Communications, Inc. and continued into Delaware. ■

IntelGenx Technologies Corp. (Del. June 15, 2003)
Oct. 2, 2024 – Pursuant to a reverse vesting order under the Companies' Creditors Arrangement Act all o/s shs. were acquired by atai Life Sciences AG for no consideration resulting in shldrs. not receiving any payments or distrib.

Intelimax Media Inc. (B.C. May 28, 2009)
Jan. 31, 2014 – Name changed to DraftTeam Fantasy Sports Inc.; basis 1 new for 5 old shs. ■

IntellaEquity Inc. (Del. Oct. 13, 1999)
Oct. 11, 2019 – Name changed to Media Central Corporation Inc. and continued into Ontario pursuant to the reverse takeover acquisition of CannCentral Inc. and concurrent amalgamation of CannCentral with wholly owned Paragon Blockchain Inc. ■

Intelligent Content Enterprises Inc. (Ont. Nov. 30, 2009 amalg.)
May 26, 2017 – Name changed to Novicius Corp.; basis 1 new for 10 old shs. ■

IntelliPharmaCeutics International Inc. (Can. Oct. 22, 2009 amalg.)
Oct. 31, 2024 – Filed an assignment in bankruptcy and KPMG Inc. was appointed trustee.

Intelpro Media Group Inc. (Alta. July 10, 1997)
June 21, 2006 – Formed Jite Technologies Inc. in Ontario on amalgamation with Jite Connectors Inc., constituting a reverse takeover by Jite; basis 1 new for 2 old shs. ■

Intema Solutions Inc. (Can. Sept. 1, 2003)
Apr. 12, 2022 – Name changed to React Gaming Group Inc. (see FPsurvey - Industrials)

Intensity Company Inc. (Alta. Nov. 19, 1998)
Dec. 7, 2012 – Name changed to LX Ventures Inc. ■

Intensity Resources Ltd. (Alta. July 19, 1984 amalg.)
May 12, 1997 – Amalgamated with Renata Resources Inc.; basis $2.30 or 1.916667 Renata shs. for 1 Intensity sh., subject to maximum cash limit not to exceed $115,000,000 and maximum Renata com. shs. issuable not to exceed 21,500,000 shs. (see Renata Resources Inc.)

IntePac Corporation (Alta. Mar. 9, 1988)
Jan. 15, 1999 – Name changed to IntePac Inc.; basis 1 new for 10 old shs. ■

IntePac Inc. (Alta. Mar. 9, 1988)
Oct. 2, 2003 – All business assets acquired by California-based Airflopac Corp. for total consideration of US$150,000.

Intequest Corporation (Alta. Jan. 8, 1996)
Feb. 7, 2008 – Acquired by 1364289 Alberta Ltd. for $1.70 per sh.

Inter-Asia Equities Inc. (B.C. 1984)
Dec. 15, 2008 – Dissolved and struck from register.

Inter Cable Communications Inc. (B.C. Sept. 12, 1980)
July 26, 1991 – Delisted from the Vancouver Stock Exchange. Subsequently dissolved for failure to file.

Inter Canadian Development Corp. (B.C. Jan. 21, 1980)
Mar. 3, 1997 – Delisted from the Vancouver Stock Exchange. Subsequently dissolved for failure to file.

Inter-Citic Envirotec Inc. (B.C. Feb. 12, 1985)
Oct. 4, 1999 – Name changed to Inter-Citic Mineral Technologies Inc. ■

Inter-Citic Mineral Technologies Inc. (B.C. Feb. 12, 1985)
Dec. 19, 2003 – Name changed to Inter-Citic Minerals Inc. ■

Inter-Citic Minerals Inc. (B.C. Feb. 12, 1985)
Nov. 23, 2012 – Acquired by Western Mining Group Co., Ltd. for $2.05 per sh.

Inter City Baking Co. Ltd. (Can. 1907)
Dec. 1955 – Com. stk. purch. by Lake of the Woods Milling Co. Ltd. at $20 per sh.

Inter-City Gas Corporation (Man. Oct. 29, 1954)
Sept. 1, 1988 – Amalgamated in Manitoba to continue with same name.
Apr. 18, 1990 – Name changed to Inter-City Products Corporation following reorganization whereby the co.'s interest in its utilities and propane businesses were sold to Westcoast Energy Inc.; basis $2,100 in cash divds. plus 25 new ord. shs. and 25 new wts. to purchase 8% cl. C convert. pref. shs. of MICC Investments Limited for 100 old com. shs. ■

Inter-City Gas Limited (Man. 1954)
Apr. 14, 1980 – Amalgamated with Canadian Homestead Oils Limited to form Inter-City Gas Corporation; basis sh. for sh.

Inter-City Manufacturing Limited (Man. 1946)
Apr. 1972 – All o/s cl. A shs. not already held acquired by Inter-City Gas Limited; basis $8.00 per sh. (see Inter-City Gas Limited)

Inter-City Products Corporation (Man. Sept. 1, 1988 amalg.)
Aug. 14, 1992 – Continued into Canada.
July 9, 1997 – Name changed to International Comfort Products Corporation. ■

Inter-City Western Bakeries, Ltd. (Can. 1930)
1938 – Acquired by George Weston Ltd. for $629,988. First mtge. bdhldrs. received $41 for each $100 princ. amt.; pref. shldrs. $0.5125 per sh.; com. shldrs. $0.1025 per sh.

Inter-Commonwealth Mines (Canada) Ltd. (Ont. 1966)
Feb. 14, 1973 – Charter cancelled.

Inter-Continental Energy Corp. (B.C. 1980)
Aug. 10, 1984 – Name changed to Tajee Resources Ltd.; basis 1 new for 3 old shs. ■

Inter Energy Corp. (Alta. Nov. 12, 2001)
July 16, 2004 – Name changed to Entech Investments Inc. following Qualifying Transaction acquisition of Sentry Select Focused Technologies Fund and Sentry Select Focused Alternative Energy Fund. ■

Inter-Leduc Oil Co. Ltd. (Ont. 1948)
1952 – Assets sold to Inter-Rock Oil of Canada Ltd.; basis 1 new for 2.5 old shs.

Inter-Link Communications Inc. (Alta. May 14, 1987)
Aug. 3, 1993 – Name changed to International Inter-Link Inc.; basis 1 new for 5 old shs. ■

Inter-Med Technologies Inc. (B.C. Apr. 11, 1983)
Aug. 7, 1998 – Name changed to Botex Industries Corp.; basis 1 new for 3 old shs. ∎

Inter-Oceanic Oil & Gas Corp. (B.C. Sept. 24, 1979)
Feb. 1, 1985 – Name changed to Inter-Oceanic Resources Ltd. ∎

Inter-Oceanic Resources Ltd. (B.C. Sept. 24, 1979)
Feb. 11, 1987 – Name changed to Odin Industries Ltd.; basis 1 new for 3 old shs. ∎

Inter-Pacific Resource Corp. (B.C. 1984)
Apr. 2, 1990 – All o/s shs. not already held acquired by Brookfield Infrastructure Partners L.P.; basis (i) Cdn$20 cash; or (ii) 0.250 Brookfield Infrastructure cl. A exch. shs; or (iii) 0.250 Brookfield Infrastructure Corporation Exchange Limited Partnership cl. B limited partnership unit; or (iv) any combination thereof for 1 Inter Pipeline com. sh.

Inter Pipeline Fund (Alta. Oct. 9, 1997)
Sept. 2, 2013 – Succeeded by Inter Pipeline Ltd. pursuant to plan of arrangement whereby Inter Pipeline Ltd. was formed to facilitate the conversion of the limited partnership into a corporation. ∎

Inter Pipeline Ltd. (Alta. Sept. 2, 2013; amalg.)
Nov. 2, 2021 – All o/s shs. not already acquired by Brookfield Infrastructure Partners L.P.; basis (i) Cdn$20 cash; or (ii) 0.250 Brookfield Infrastructure cl. A exch. shs; or (iii) 0.250 Brookfield Infrastructure Corporation Exchange Limited Partnership cl. B limited partnership unit; or (iv) any combination thereof for 1 Inter Pipeline com. sh.

Inter-Provincial Commercial Discount Corp. Ltd. (Ont. 1956)
Mar. 1969 – Name changed to Inter-Provincial Diversified Holdings Limited. ∎

Inter-Provincial Diversified Holdings Limited (Ont. 1956)
Nov. 29, 1999 – Acquired by major shareholder for $6.47 per sh.

Inter-Rock Gold Inc. (Can. Oct. 5, 1978)
Feb. 3, 1999 – Name changed to Inter-Rock Minerals Inc. ∎

Inter-Rock Minerals Inc. (Can. Oct. 5, 1978)
Nov. 20, 2000 – Continued into Barbados.
Dec. 29, 2017 – Continued into Ontario. (see FPsurvey - Mines & Energy; FPsurvey - Industrials)

Inter-Rock Oil Co. Of Canada Limited (Ont. June 13, 1952)
Oct. 5, 1978 – Continued into Canada.
Dec. 7, 1992 – Name changed to Inter-Rock Gold Inc. ∎

Inter-Tech Development and Resources Ltd. (B.C. 1933)
1971 – Name changed to Inter-Tech Resources Ltd.; basis 1 new for 1 old sh. (see FPsurvey - Mines & Energy)

Inter-Tech Drilling Solutions Ltd. (Alta. Nov. 20, 1990)
July 13, 1998 – Acquired by Precision Drilling Corporation for $2.10 per sh. (see Precision Drilling Corporation)

Inter-United Foods Corp. (Ont. Jan. 10, 1980)
Sept. 14, 1988 – Name changed to Mueller Medical International Inc. ∎

Inter West Energy Corporation (B.C. Nov. 9, 1993)
Nov. 5, 1997 – Acquired by New Cache Petroleums Ltd.; basis 0.08 New Cache shs. for 1 Inter West sh. (see New Cache Petroleums Ltd.)

Intera Information Technologies Corporation (Barbados Jan. 1987)
Nov. 1989 – Continued into Canada.
Dec. 28, 1995 – Name changed to IITC Holdings Ltd. ∎

Interaction Resources Ltd. (B.C. Dec. 22, 1982 amalg.)
Apr. 20, 1994 – Continued into Alberta.
June 13, 2000 – Name changed to Ketch Energy Ltd.; basis 1 new for 5 old shs. ∎

Interactive Capital Partners Corporation (Ont. Apr. 30, 2008)
Sept. 29, 2023 – Name changed to Medicus Pharma Ltd. pursuant the reverse takeover acquisition of Medicus Pharma Ltd. (see FPsurvey - Industrials)

Interactive Communications Corporation (B.C. Aug. 24, 1986)
Dec. 13, 1993 – Name changed to ICM Ventures Inc.; basis 1 new for 4 old shs. ∎

Interactive Digital Systems Corporation (Ont. Aug. 14, 1989)
June 5, 1996 – Name changed to CRM Capital Inc.; basis 1 new for 10 old shs. ∎

Interactive Enterprises Inc. (B.C. Oct. 5, 1979)
Feb. 16, 2004 – Name changed to Interactive Exploration Inc. ∎

Interactive Entertainment Limited (Bermuda Feb. 22, 1995)
Sept. 19, 2000 – Name changed to Creator Capital Limited.

Interactive Exploration Inc. (B.C. Oct. 5, 1979)
Aug. 22, 2005 – Name changed to Anglo-Canadian Uranium Corp. ∎

Interactive Games Technologies Inc. (B.C. May 25, 2007)
May 18, 2021 – Name changed to I3 Interactive Inc. (see FPsurvey - Industrials)

Interactive Telesis, Inc. (B.C. June 19, 1987)
Sept. 23, 1996 – Continued into Delaware.

Interactive Video Systems Inc. (B.C. Sept. 22, 1983)
Aug. 31, 1994 – Name changed to Interactive VideoSystems Inc. ∎

Interactive VideoSystems Inc. (B.C. Sept. 22, 1983)
Aug. 16, 1995 – Name changed to NCC Mining Corporation. ∎

Interamerican Industries Ltd. (Alta. 1954)
Dec. 15, 1969 – Struck off register.

Interbev Packaging Corp. (B.C. 1976)
Dec. 14, 1987 – Amalgamated with The Jolt Beverage Co., Ltd.

Interbit Ltd. (Alta. Mar. 28, 2011)
June 24, 2020 – Name changed to North Peak Resources Ltd.; basis 1 new for 2 old shs. (see FPsurvey - Mines & Energy)

Intercan Leasing Inc. (Can. Apr. 1, 1967)
Jan. 3, 1989 – Amalgamated in Canada to continue with same name.
Nov. 9, 1994 – Declared bankrupt. Further information was not available.
May 1, 2006 – Dissolved.

Intercap Resource Management Corp. (B.C. Apr. 19, 1985)
Apr. 7, 1999 – Name changed to Pine Resources Corporation; basis 1 new for 3.5 old shs. ∎

Intercedent Ventures Ltd. (Can. Jan. 26, 2000)
June 30, 2003 – Formed ARISE Technologies Corporation in Canada on Qualifying Transaction amalgamation with (old) ARISE Technologies Corporation (deemed acquiror); basis 1 ARISE com. sh. plus 0.5 ARISE wt. for 4.875 Intercedent com. shs. ∎

Intercep Industries Ltd. (B.C. 1973 amalg.)
Oct. 22, 1982 – Formed Intercep Resources Ltd. in British Columbia on amalgamation with BMC Oil & Gas Inc.; basis 1 new for 1 BMC sh. and 3 new for 2 Intercep shs. ∎

Intercep Resources Ltd. (B.C. Oct. 22, 1982 amalg.)
Mar. 18, 1988 – Dissolved and struck off register.

Intercept Energy Services Inc. (Alta. Oct. 25, 1995)
Aug. 31, 2020 – Struck from registry and dissolved.

Intercoast Resources Corp. (B.C. 1969)
Oct. 4, 1985 – Struck off register.

Intercolonial Coal Co. Ltd. (N.S. 1923)
1962 – Reported wound up following distribution (amount unknown) to holders of com. stk.

Intercon Petroleum Inc. (B.C. 1966)
Apr. 10, 1992 – Dissolved and struck off register.

Intercontinental Data Control Corporation Ltd. (Can. 1978)
Apr. 3, 1987 – In receivership and substantially all assets were sold to Canadian Marconi Company.

Intercontinental Environmental Industries Ltd. (B.C. 1966)
July 6, 1972 – Name changed to Mexxon Mines Ltd. ∎

Intercontinental Mining Corporation (B.C. Sept. 25, 1985)
Feb. 24, 2005 – Formed Maple Leaf Reforestation Inc. in British Columbia on amalgamation with Maple Leaf Reforestation Inc., constituting a reverse takeover by Maple Leaf. ∎

Interex Development Corp. (Alta. Feb. 14, 1986)
Jan. 20, 1989 – Name changed to Interex Minerals Ltd.; basis 1 new for 5 old shs. (see FPsurvey - Mines & Energy; FPsurvey - Industrials)

Interfirst Resources Inc. (Ont. Sept. 29, 1987)
Oct. 6, 1998 – Name changed to Miltec Technology Inc. following reverse takeover acqisition of Miltec Technology Solutions Inc.; basis 1 new for 6 old shs. ∎

Intergold Ltd. (Alta. Sept. 21, 1989)
Apr. 27, 2010 – Acquired by Intergold Acquisition Corp., an indirect subsid. of Visant Corporation, for 16¢ per sh.

Intergold Resources Inc. (B.C. Feb. 15, 1965)
Apr. 17, 1979 – Name changed to Internetwork Realty Corp. ∎

Intergulf Resources Corp. (B.C. July 21, 1999)
Dec. 12, 2003 – Acquired by Result Energy Inc.; basis 0.4372 new Result sh. for 1 old Intergulf sh. (see Result Energy Inc.)

Interhome Energy Inc. (Can. Apr. 30, 1949; via Special Act of Parliament)
May 1, 1991 – Name changed to Interprovincial Pipe Line Inc. following spin-off of wholly owned Home Oil Company Limited. ∎

Interhome Energy Inc. (Can. June 2, 1980)
May 1, 1991 – Name changed to Interprovincial Pipe Line Inc. ∎

Interim Capital Corp. (B.C. July 6, 2005)
July 28, 2008 – Name changed to ERA Carbon Offsets Ltd. following Qualifying Transaction reverse takeover acquisition of ERA Ecosystem Restoration Associates, Inc.; basis 1 new for 2.5 old shs. ∎

Interior Breweries Ltd. (B.C. 1950)
Mar. 23, 1972 – Name changed to Columbia Brewing Company Ltd. ∎

Interior Mines Corporation Ltd. (B.C. 1951)
Nov. 16, 1961 – Dissolved.

Interlake Development Corp. (B.C. 1977)
Dec. 31, 1986 – Formed International Interlake Industries Inc. in British Columbia on amalgamation with 3 other cos.; basis 1 new for 5 old shs. ∎

Interlapse Technologies Corp. (B.C. Sept. 22, 2004)
June 9, 2021 – Name changed to LQwD FinTech Corp. pursuant to the acquisition of LQwD Financial Corp.

Interlearn Holdings Ltd. (B.C. 1987)
Feb. 20, 2004 – Dissolved and struck from register.

Interlink Systems Inc. (Wyo. Apr. 24, 1998)
Aug. 14, 2000 – Name changed to iQuest Networks Inc.; basis 1 new for 2 old shs. ■

Interlude Capital Corp. (B.C. July 18, 2005)
Oct. 24, 2006 – Name changed to OneMove Technologies Inc. following Qualifying Transaction acquisition of Remotelaw Online Systems Corp. ■

Intermap Technologies Ltd. (Alta. Feb. 25, 1997 amalg.)
June 10, 1999 – Name changed to Intermap Technologies Corporation; basis 1 new for 12.5 old shs. (see FPsurvey - Industrials)

Intermedia Capital Corp. (Alta. June 28, 1999)
Aug. 21, 2003 – Name changed to Savanna Energy Services Corp. following Qualifying Transaction reverse takeover acquisition of Savanna Energy Services Corp.; basis 1 new for 45 old shs. ■

Intermet Resources Ltd. (B.C. Nov. 27, 1979)
Dec. 22, 1982 – Formed Interaction Resources Ltd. in British Columbia on amalgamation with Action Resources Ltd. and Gryphon Petroleum Corporation; basis 1 new for 1.5 Intermet shs. ■

Intermetco Limited (Ont. Nov. 1, 1968 amalg.)
Sept. 3, 1997 – Acquired by Philip Services Corp. for $16.75 per sh. (see Philip Services Corp.)

Intermont Exploration Inc. (Can. Jan. 6, 1987)
Apr. 25, 1994 – Name changed to Intermont inc. ■

Intermont inc. (Can. Jan. 6, 1987)
Aug. 23, 1996 – Name changed to Pebercan Inc.; basis 1 new for 10 old shs. ■

InterMune Life Sciences Inc. (Ont. Mar. 9, 1992)
Nov. 30, 1993 – Continued into Canada.
July 12, 2004 – Dissolved.

International X-Chequer Resources Inc. (Que. Aug. 11, 1987)
Oct. 18, 2007 – Name changed to Passport Metals Inc.; basis 3 new for 1 old sh. ■

International Absorbents Inc. (B.C. May 13, 1983)
May 28, 2010 – Privatized at US$4.75 per sh.

International AcuVision Systems, Inc. (B.C. Aug. 26, 1983)
Sept. 15, 1993 – Continued into Delaware.
Apr. 1, 1999 – Name changed to AcuBid.com Inc.; basis 1 new for 2 old shs.

International Airborne Systems Corp. (B.C. June 16, 1964)
June 10, 1994 – Name changed to Gateway Waste Systems Inc.; basis 1 new for 4 old shs. ■

International Akash Ventures Inc. (B.C. May 13, 1981)
Jan. 18, 2001 – Name changed to Healthscreen Solutions Incorporated prior to reverse takeover acquisition of 1161166 Ontario Limited. ■

International Albany Resources Ltd. (Yuk. Dec. 14, 1993)
Mar. 21, 1997 – Name changed to Brazilian Goldfields Ltd. and continued into Bahamas. ■

International All-North Resources Ltd. (B.C. Aug. 8, 1988 amalg.)
Apr. 14, 1999 – Name changed to Kaieteur Resource Corporation; basis 1 new for 14 old shs. ■

International Alliance Resources Inc. (Que. Mar. 11, 1986)
Sept. 21, 1993 – Name changed to Covitec Group Inc. ■

International Alliance Resources Inc. (Yuk. June 12, 1997)
July 25, 2012 – Name changed to Bluenose Gold Corp. ■

International Amco Corporation (Ont. 1954)
Nov. 10, 1989 – Name changed to Amco Corporation Plc and continued into United Kingdom.

International Amera Industries Corp. (B.C. Sept. 17, 1979)
Feb. 21, 1996 – Name changed to IMA Resource Corporation; basis 1 new for 3 old shs. ■

International American Minerals Ltd. (N.S. 1956)
Reported to be out of business.

International Annax Ventures Inc. (B.C. Feb. 10, 1987)
Sept. 3, 2002 – Acquired by Australia-based Herald Resources Limited; basis 1 new Herald sh. for 1 old International Annax sh.

International Antam Resources Ltd. (Yuk. Sept. 9, 1997)
Jan. 23, 2004 – Name changed to Goldsource Mines Inc. ■

International Antarex Metals Ltd. (Alta. Sept. 3, 1997)
Sept. 2, 2003 – Struck from registry and dissolved.

International Anthracite Mines Ltd. (Ont. 1919)
Sept. 22, 1934 – Charter cancelled.

International Aqua Foods Ltd. (B.C. 1984)
Jan. 27, 2000 – Acquired by Stolt-Neilsen S.A. for Cdn$1.70 per sh.

International Arimex Resources Inc. (B.C. May 30, 1986)
Sept. 10, 2007 – Name changed to WestCan Uranium Corp. ■

International Arlo Resources Ltd. (Yuk. Jan. 27, 1995)
Dec. 31, 2004 – Dissolved.
Feb. 14, 2007 – Revived. (see FPsurvey - Mines & Energy)

International Asbestos Co. Ltd. (Que. 1943)
May 1974 – Charter cancelled.

International Atlantis Resources Ltd. (Alta. 1980)
Nov. 3, 1986 – Name changed to Atlantis International Ltd. ■

International Atlas Development & Exploration Limited (Que. 1951)
Feb. 9, 1980 – Charter cancelled.

International Avalon Aircraft Inc. (B.C. June 1, 1983)
Jan. 10, 1992 – Dissolved and struck off register.

International Avanti Productions Inc. (B.C. Mar. 18, 1983)
Aug. 6, 1993 – Dissolved and struck off register.

International Avino Mines Ltd. (B.C. May 15, 1969)
Aug. 29, 1997 – Name changed to Avino Silver & Gold Mines Ltd. (see FPsurvey - Mines & Energy)

International Azora Minerals Inc. (B.C. Jan. 1, 1980)
Mar. 5, 1991 – Name changed to Power Battery Holdings Corporation following acquisition of Power Battery Corporation of Washington state. ■

International Balfour Resources Ltd. (B.C. 1969)
July 15, 1980 – Name changed to Quartet Energy Resources Ltd. ■

International Ballater Resources Inc. (B.C. June 16, 1987)
Dec. 11, 1997 – Amalgamated with First Quantum Minerals Yukon Ltd., a wholly owned subsid. of First Quantum Minerals Ltd.; 1 new for 2.75 International Ballater shs. (see First Quantum Minerals Ltd.)

International Baron Resources Ltd. (B.C. Aug. 20, 1981)
Feb. 20, 1992 – Name changed to Azco Mining, Inc.; basis 1 new for 6 old shs. ■

International Barrier Technology Inc. (B.C. July 10, 1986)
Oct. 16, 2017 – Acquired by Louisiana-Pacific Canada Ltd., wholly owned subsid.of Louisiana-Pacific Corporation; basis US$0.41 cash per sh.

International Barytex Resources Ltd. (B.C. July 12, 1965)
Oct. 1, 2009 – Acquired by IMA Exploration Inc.; basis 0.221 IMA shs. for 1 Barytex sh. (see Kobex Minerals Inc.)

International Base Metals Ltd. (Man. 1956)
Mar. 1, 1969 – Dissolved.

International Bellevue Ventures Ltd. (B.C. Oct. 3, 1984 amalg.)
Feb. 1989 – Dissolved.

International Beryllium Corporation (B.C. Dec. 11, 2002)
Mar. 6, 2009 – Name changed to IBC Advanced Alloys Corp. (see FPsurvey - Industrials)

International Beryllium Corporation Ltd. (B.C. 1960)
Dec. 18, 1969 – Struck off register.

The International Beverage Corporation (B.C. Mar. 18, 1981)
May 14, 1990 – Name changed to Clearly Canadian Beverage Corporation; basis 1 new for 3.5 old shs. ■

International Bibis Tin Mines Ltd. (Ont. Dec. 18, 1950 amalg.)
Nov. 1, 1973 – Name changed to Laurasia Resources Limited; basis 1 new for 4 old shs. ■

International BigSky Resources Corp. (Yuk. Nov. 27, 1996)
Dec. 3, 2004 – Dissolved.

International Bio Recovery Corporation (B.C. Aug. 17, 1993)
Jan. 21, 2011 – Name changed to Terrabiogen Technologies Inc. ■

International Bio Waste Systems Inc. (B.C. May 4, 1987)
Apr. 22, 1994 – Name changed to Bioflow Environmental Technologies Inc.; basis 1 new for 5 old shs. ■

International BioAnalogics Systems, Inc. (Ore. Nov. 5, 1992)
Sept. 29, 2006 – Continued into Canada.
May 14, 2007 – Name changed to reWORKS Environmental Corp. pursuant to amalgamation of reWORKS Inc. with a wholly owned subsidiary, constituting a reverse takeover by reWORKS; basis 1 new for 1 reWORKS sh. and 1 new for 2.9543557 International BioAnalogics shs. ■

International Bioremediation Services Inc. (B.C. Oct. 31, 1989 amalg.)
Feb. 23, 2000 – Name changed to IBIS Ventures Inc.; basis 1 new for 10 old shs. ■

International Biotechnology Corporation (Ont. Sept. 22, 1987)
Mar. 9, 2001 – Name changed to Veris Biotechnology Corporation; basis 1 new for 2 old shs. ■

International Blue Gold Corp. (B.C. Apr. 7, 1986)
Jan. 16, 1998 – Name changed to Buddha Resources Inc.; basis 1 new for 2 old shs. ■

International Blue Sun Resource Corporation (B.C. 1983)
May 26, 1994 – Name changed to Dalton Enterprises Ltd. ■

International Bond & Equity Corp. Ltd. (Ont. 1963)
June 1973 – Amalgamated with 2 other cos. to form Life Investors International Ltd.; basis 5 cl. A and 1 new com. for 5 cl. A shs.; 1 new com. for 2 com. shs.

International Bornite Mines Ltd. (B.C. 1964)
Dec. 1976 – Charter cancelled.

International Brace Resources Inc. (B.C. May 17, 1966)
Apr. 4, 1997 – Name changed to Prescott Resources Inc.; basis 1 new for 5 old shs. ■

International Bravo Resource Corporation (B.C. July 18, 1983)
Mar. 15, 2002 – Name changed to Bravo Venture Group Inc.; basis 1 new for 7 old shs. ■

International Brenmac Development Corp. (B.C. 1965)
Nov. 1, 1985 – Name changed to Oberg Industries Ltd.; basis 1 new for 3 old shs. ■

International Brican Resources Ltd. (B.C. Apr. 6, 1976)
Feb. 6, 1992 – Name changed to C & E Furniture Industries Inc. following acquisition of C & E German Furniture Limited. ■

International Broadcasting Centre Ltd. (Alta. July 31, 1987 amalg.)
Sept. 28, 1992 – Name changed to Ensel Corporation; basis 1 new for 3.4 old shs. ■

International Broadlands Resources Ltd. (B.C. Apr. 6, 1995 amalg.)
Mar. 15, 1999 – Name changed to Broadlands Resources Ltd.; basis 1 new for 4 old shs. ■

International Bronze Powders Limited (Can. 1934)
1959 – Approx. 94.6% o/s com. sh. and 98.7% o/s pref. sh. acquired by Warnock Hersey International Ltd.; basis 1 ser. A pref. sh. and 1 com. sh. of Warnock, or $30, for each com. or pref. sh. of International.

International Brooks Petroleum Ltd. (B.C. Apr. 10, 1986)
Aug. 14, 2003 – Name changed to Flying A Petroleum Ltd.; basis 1 new for 10 old shs. ■

International Burgers Now Ltd. (B.C. 1979)
Jan. 19, 1990 – Dissolved.

International Business Schools Inc. (Can. May 18, 1989)
Aug. 9, 1999 – Name changed to Educor International Inc. ■

International Butec Industries Corp. (B.C. Nov. 29, 1965)
Oct. 17, 2000 – Name changed to WebSmart.com Communications Inc. following acquisition of WebSmart Communications Inc.; basis 1 new for 5 old shs. ■

International CHS Resource Corporation (Ont. 1988)
Dec. 16, 2010 – Name changed to CHS Resources Inc. (see FPsurvey - Mines & Energy)

International Cablecasting Technologies Inc. (B.C. Apr. 25, 1977)
May 1990 – Continued into Delaware.

International Calneva Gold Corp. (B.C. Jan. 19, 1987)
Sept. 30, 1999 – Name changed to Tenacity Resources Corp.; basis 1 new for 7 old shs. (see FPsurvey - Mines & Energy)

International Camero Resources Ltd. (B.C. Aug. 2, 1966)
Jan. 24, 1985 – Name changed to International Pharmadyne Ltd. ■

International CanAlaska Resources Ltd. (B.C. May 22, 1985)
Dec. 3, 1999 – Name changed to CanAlaska Ventures Ltd.; basis 1 new for 5 old shs. ■

International Cannabrands Inc. (Alta. May 3, 2011)
July 24, 2020 – Name changed to Radiko Holdings Corp. (see FPsurvey - Industrials)

International Canstat Petroleum Corporation (B.C. Sept. 14, 1979)
Sept. 16, 1993 – Name changed to Blackwater Gold Corporation; basis 1 new for 2.5 old shs. ■

International Capri Resources Ltd. (B.C. June 20, 1980)
June 30, 2000 – Name changed to Apiva.com Web Corporation. ■

International Captain Industries Corp. (Ont. 1945)
Apr. 12, 1993 – Name changed to Rocklite International Inc.; basis 1 new for 3 old shs. ■

International Cardero Resources Inc. (B.C. 1976)
Feb. 23, 1990 – Dissolved.

International Cargocare Incorporated (B.C. Dec. 3, 1980)
Dec. 14, 1993 – Name changed to CVAC Industries, Inc.; basis 1 new for 5 old shs. ■

International Catalyst Ventures Inc. (B.C. July 14, 1987)
Sept. 8, 2000 – Continued into Yukon.
Nov. 23, 2001 – Name changed to Aberdeen International Inc.; basis 1 new for 3 old shs. ■

International CDIS Software Inc. (B.C. June 22, 1973)
July 24, 1990 – Name changed to A.T.H. Fund Inc. ■

International Centura Industries Ltd. (B.C. 1973 amalg.)
Dec. 28, 1977 – Name changed to Intercep Industries Ltd.; basis 1 new for 5 old shs. ■

International Ceramic Mining Ltd. (Ont. 1945)
Sept. 26, 1973 – Charter cancelled.

International Cetec Investments Inc. (B.C. Nov. 10, 1982)
Nov. 1, 2005 – Amalgamated with 0731537 B.C. Inc.; basis 1 0731537 B.C. cl. A. pfd. sh. for 1 Cetec com. sh. Pref. shs. were immediately redeemed for $1.65 per sh.

International Chalice Resources Inc. (B.C. Apr. 20, 1982)
Aug. 15, 2003 – Name changed to Golden Chalice Resources Inc.; basis 1 new for 4 old shs. ■

International Chargold Resources Ltd. (B.C. Feb. 10, 1988)
May 23, 2002 – Name changed to Odessa Gold Corp.; basis 1 new for 3 old shs. ■

International Chemalloy Corporation (Ont. Jan. 15, 1952; via letters patent)
Sept. 20, 1985 – Name changed to Denbridge Capital Corporation; basis 1 new for 100 old shs. ■

International Cherokee Developments Ltd. (B.C. Apr. 8, 1975)
Nov. 30, 1989 – Name changed to GLS Global Listing Service Ltd.; basis 1 new for 5 old shs. ■

International Chess Enterprises Inc. (B.C. May 17, 1983)
June 22, 1994 – Name changed to Grandmaster Technologies Inc.; basis 1 new for 5 old shs. ■

International Choice Ventures Inc. (B.C. Sept. 19, 1977)
Nov. 1, 2002 – Continued into Alberta.
Mar. 21, 2003 – Name changed to Rhodes Resources Corp. pursuant to reverse takeover acquisition of Terra Capital Corp.; basis 1 new for 2 old shs. ■

International Clean Power Dividend Fund (Alta.)
May 8, 2024 – Merged into Infrastructure Dividend Split Corp.; basis 0.46707742 Infrastructure cl. A shs. for 1 Clean Power fund unit.

International Coal & Coke Co. Ltd. (Can. 1919)
Nov. 1951 – Merged with 2 other cos. to form Coleman Collieries Ltd. Final and total distribution for each 1,000 shs. held: $375; $250 p.v. of shs. and $1,160 p.v. of 5% first mtge. bds. of Coleman.

International Coast Minerals Corporation (B.C. 1984)
Sept. 2, 1994 – Dissolved and struck off register.

The International Cobalt & Silver Mining Co. Ltd. (Ont. 1906)
1958 – Assets acquired by International Copper & Cobalt Mines Ltd.

International Cobalt Corp. (B.C. Nov. 17, 2014)
Apr. 25, 2024 – Name changed to Musk Ventures Ltd. (see FPsurvey - Mines & Energy)

International Colby Resources Corp. (B.C. Feb. 15, 1967)
Mar. 15, 2000 – Name changed to Canplats Resources Corporation. ■

International Colin Energy Corporation (Alta. Aug. 10, 1973 amalg.)
July 4, 1996 – Acquired by Morgan Hydrocarbons Inc.; basis 1.975 Morgan Hydrocarbons shs. for 1 International Colin sh. (see Morgan Hydrocarbons Inc.)

International Comfort Products Corporation (Can. Aug. 14, 1992)
Aug. 31, 1999 – All o/s ord. shs. acquired by Titan Acquisitions Ltd. (a wholly owned subsidiary of U.S.-based United Technologies Corporation); basis US$11.75 per sh.

International Commercial Television Inc. (Nev. June 25, 1998)
Aug. 22, 2014 – Name changed to ICTV Brands Inc.

International Comstock Exploration Ltd. (B.C. Sept. 18, 1985)
Oct. 2, 2001 – Name changed to Secureview Systems Inc.; basis 1 new for 5 old shs. ■

International Conquest Exploration Ltd. (B.C. Apr. 8, 1980)
Feb. 7, 2000 – Name changed to Conquest Ventures Inc.; basis 1 new for 3 old shs. ■

International Consolidated Uranium Inc. (B.C. Apr. 26, 2004)
July 23, 2021 – Continued into Ontario.
July 26, 2021 – Name changed to Consolidated Uranium Inc. ■

International Consort Industries Inc. (B.C. Feb. 13, 1981)
Nov. 12, 1993 – Name changed to Cryopak Industries Inc. ■

International Contour Technology Inc. (B.C. Sept. 22, 1987)
Nov. 3, 1995 – Name changed to TSI TelSys Corporation. ■

International Controlled Investments Inc. (B.C. 1965)
Aug. 23, 1991 – Name changed to New Age Ventures Inc.; basis 1 new for 5 old shs. ■

International Copper & Cobalt Mines Ltd. (Ont. 1957)
1965 – Charter cancelled.

International Copper Corp. Ltd. (B.C. 1964)
Sept. 3, 1974 – Dissolved and struck off register.

International Coromandel Resources Ltd. (B.C. Nov. 8, 1984)
Aug. 17, 2004 – Name changed to Sonora Gold Corp. ■

International Corona Capital Corp. (B.C. June 12, 2008)
Oct. 2, 2019 – Name changed to IC Capitalight Corp. pursuant to the completion of a change of business transaction to an investment company through the acquisition of Murenbeeld & Co. Inc. and certain fixed income debentures of Stone Investment Group Limited.; basis 1 new for 2 old shs. ■

International Corona Corporation (Ont. July 1, 1988 amalg.)
Aug. 17, 1992 – Acquired by Homestake Mining Company; basis 0.54 of Homestake com. sh. and $0.50 for each Corona ser. A pfd. sh.; 1.08 of Homestake com. sh. for each Corona ser. C pfd. sh.; and 0.35 of Homestake com. sh. for each Corona com. sh. (see Homestake Mining Company)

International Corona Resources Ltd. (B.C. 1979)
1985 – Continued into Canada. (see Corona Corporation)
July 1, 1988 – Amalgamated with 7 other cos. to form Corona Corporation; basis 1 cl. A for 1 old International Corona cl. A. sh. (see Corona Corporation)

International Croesus Ventures Corp. (B.C. Mar. 14, 1983)
Jan. 29, 2007 – Name changed to Zinco Mining Corporation. (see FPsurvey - Mines & Energy)

International Cruiseshipcenters Corp. (B.C. Oct. 15, 1986)
June 24, 1991 – Name changed to Riley Resources Ltd.; basis 1 new for 8 old shs. ■

International Curator Resources Ltd. (B.C. Feb. 3, 1983)
Dec. 30, 2003 – Name changed to Canadian Gold Hunter Corp.; basis 1 new for 5 old shs. ■

International Damascus Resources Ltd. (B.C. Apr. 5, 1968)
July 13, 1998 – Name changed to Ravenhead Recovery Corporation; basis 1 new for 3 old shs. ■

International Data Service Corporation (B.C. 1967)
Jan. 15, 1993 – Dissolved and struck off register.

International Datacasting Corporation (Can. Mar. 21, 1958)
Aug. 31, 2001 – Amalgamated in Canada to continue with same name.
Feb. 1, 2003 – Amalgamated in Canada to continue with same name.
June 21, 2016 – Amalgamated with 9711350 Canada Inc., a wholly owned subsid. of Novra Technologies Inc.; basis 1 Novra com. sh. for 10 International Datacasting com. shs. and 1 redeem. Novra pref. sh. for 1 International Datacasting com. sh. immediately redeemed for $0.01 cash.

International Datashare Corporation (Alta. May 31, 1968 amalg.)
Sept. 23, 2003 – Amalgamated with Divestco.com Inc. and 1059778 Alberta Ltd. to form Divestco Inc.; basis 0.501225 Divestco shs. for 1 International Datashare sh. (see Divestco Inc.)

International Delta Resources Limited (Can. July 7, 1981)
Nov. 13, 1992 – Name changed to Delpet Resources Ltd.; basis 1 new for 3 old shs. ■

International Destron Technologies Inc. (Can. 1984)
June 3, 1988 – Name changed to Destron/IDI Inc.; basis 1 new for 5 old shs. ■

International Domesticated Furs Limited (B.C. Dec. 18, 1984 amalg.)
May 11, 1990 – Dissolved and struck off register.

International Dorado Resources Ltd. (B.C. Mar. 8, 1978)
Dec. 14, 1990 – Name changed to Calco Resources Inc.; basis 1 new for 4 old shs. ■

International Dunlap Minerals Corporation (Yuk. Feb. 11, 1997)
Aug. 26, 1999 – All com. shs. acquired by Iriana Resources Corporation; basis 0.825 Iriana shs. for 1 International Dunlap Minerals sh. (see Iriana Resources Corporation)

International Dunraine Limited (Can. July 6, 1942)
July 18, 1996 – Name changed to World Point Terminals Inc. ■

International Dusty Mac Enterprises Ltd. (B.C. Aug. 6, 1968)
May 10, 1994 – Name changed to Dusty Mac Oil and Gas Ltd. ■

International Dynasty Resources Inc. (B.C. Mar. 30, 1983)
Oct. 23, 1985 – Name changed to Commander Resources Ltd. ■

International Eagle Tool Inc. (Ont. Sept. 22, 1987)
Sept. 29, 1995 – Name changed to Lignex Inc.; basis 1 new for 9 old shs. ■

International En-R-Tech Inc. (B.C. Aug. 7, 1991)
Oct. 16, 2000 – Name changed to National Telcom Solutions Inc.; basis 1 new for 10 old shs. ■

International Enexco Limited (B.C. Apr. 24, 1967)
June 6, 2014 – Amalgamated with 0999256 B.C. Ltd., a wholly owned subsid. of Denison Mines Corp., to form Denison AB Holdings Corp. Each com. sh. was exchanged for 0.26 Denison com. sh. and 1 sh. of 0999279 B.C. Ltd., formed to hold the company's Contact copper property in Nevada. Each 0999279 B.C. share would subsequently be exchanged for 8.8 com. shs. of Choice Gold Corp. plus 4.4 Choice wts.

International Engineering Services Limited (N.S. July 13, 1984)
Aug. 10, 1992 – Name changed to Nova Scotia Power Incorporated. ■

International Epitek Inc. (Can. Dec. 9, 1981 amalg.)
June 15, 1993 – Formed CompAS Electronics Inc. in Canada on amalgamation with wholly owned Computer Assembly Systems Limited. ■

International Equity Ltd. (Bermuda Nov. 25, 1985)
Feb. 19, 1992 – Name changed to Industrial & Environmental Services Ltd. ■

International Eros Holdings Ltd. (B.C. 1987)
Apr. 12, 1996 – Name changed to Global Cable Systems Inc. ■

International Euromin Corporation (Can. Apr. 28, 1989)
June 30, 1995 – Name changed to Eurogas Corporation; basis 1 new for 2 old shs. ■

International Europrime Capital Corporation (B.C. Sept. 15, 1986)
Mar. 6, 1998 – Dissolved and struck off register.

International Exotic Motors Corp. (B.C. 1987)
1991 – Continued into Wyoming.
Oct. 5, 1993 – Name changed to North American Advanced Materials Corp.

International Exploration Corp. (Que. 1956)
Mar. 2, 1974 – Dissolved.

International Fairhaven Resources Ltd. (B.C. Sept. 27, 1962)
Sept. 19, 2005 – Struck from registry and dissolved.
July 9, 2007 – Restored to registry.
July 10, 2009 – Struck from registry and dissolved.

International Falcon Resources Inc. (B.C. Feb. 1980)
July 10, 2006 – Dissolved and struck from register.

International Financial Income and Growth Trust (Ont. July 15, 2005)
Dec. 15, 2009 – Terminated; basis unknown.

International Fitness Unlimited Centres Inc. (Ont. Sept. 6, 1983 amalg.)
Feb. 2, 1989 – Delisted from Alberta Stock Exchange. Subsequently dissolved.

International Flyer Resources Ltd. (B.C. Jan. 31, 1980)
July 31, 1987 – Name changed to Spectair Industries Inc. ■

International Focus Resources Inc. (B.C. May 29, 1984)
Dec. 28, 1995 – Name changed to Continental Copper Corporation; basis 1 new for 5 old shs. ■

International Forest Products Limited (B.C. Dec. 1, 1979 amalg.)
May 6, 2014 – Name changed to Interfor Corporation. (see FPsurvey - Industrials)

International Frecom Communications Inc. (Can. May 1, 1990)
Sept. 27, 2002 – Struck from registry for failure to file.

International Freegold Mineral Development Inc. (B.C. Aug. 21, 1991)
Sept. 4, 2002 – Name changed to Freegold Ventures Limited; basis 1 new for 4 old shs. (see FPsurvey - Mines & Energy)

International Gemini Technology Inc. (B.C. Sept. 23, 1983)
July 12, 2006 – Name changed to Widescope Resources Inc. ■

International Geographics Ltd. (B.C. 1973)
July 29, 1991 – Acquired by its wholly owned subsid. Geographics, Inc.; basis 6 new for 5 old shs.

International Giant Mining Corporation (B.C. 1979)
Aug. 31, 1982 – Formed International Phasor Telecom Ltd. in British Columbia on amalgamation with International Phasor Telecom Ltd.; basis 1 new for 1 old sh. (see FPsurvey - Industrials)

International Glendale Resources Inc. (B.C. Feb. 8, 1983)
Mar. 10, 1997 – Name changed to Odessa Petroleum Corporation. ■

International Gold Mining Limited (Australia Feb. 21, 1996)
Jan. 18, 2010 – Name changed to Central Iron Ore Limited; basis 1 new for 10 old shs. (see FPsurvey - Mines & Energy)

International Gold Resources Corporation (Ont. Nov. 8, 1993 amalg.)
June 26, 1996 – Acquired by Ashanti Goldfields Company Limited; basis 0.175 Ashanti shs. plus 90¢ for 1 International Gold sh.

International Gravis Computer Technology Inc. (B.C. 1982)
Apr. 30, 1987 – Formed Advanced Gravis Computer Technology Ltd. in British Columbia on amalgamation with Abaton Resources Ltd. (1 for 1); basis 1 new for 3 old shs. ■

International Green Ice Inc. (B.C. Sept. 28, 1992)
Mar. 3, 2000 – Continued into Yukon.
July 21, 2004 – Name changed to IGC Resources Inc. and continued into British Columbia. ■

International Grenfell Acquisitions Inc. (Can. May 27, 1987)
July 21, 1995 – Name changed to Worldwide Ginseng Corporation. ■

International Gryphon Resources Inc. (Alta. Oct. 1, 1993)
Apr. 27, 1995 – Amalgamated with Pilgrim Resources Corp. (1 for 1) to form a new co. also named International Gryphon Resources Inc.; basis 1 new for 1 old sh. (see International Gryphon Resources Inc.)

International Gryphon Resources Inc. (Alta. Feb. 28, 1995 amalg.)
Dec. 5, 2000 – Name changed to Wirbac Resources Inc.; basis 1 new for 5 old shs. ■

International Halliwell Mines Ltd. (Que. 1933)
Nov. 28, 1981 – Charter cancelled.

International Hard Suits Inc. (B.C. July 25, 1986)
Nov. 29, 1993 – Name changed to Hard Suits Inc.; basis 1 new for 3 old shs. ■

International Harvester Canada Limited (Ont. 1903)
Feb. 26, 1986 – Name changed to Navistar International Corporation Canada. ■

International Harvester Company of Canada, Limited (Ont. 1903)
Nov. 1, 1979 – Name changed to International Harvester Canada Limited. ■

International Harvester Credit Corporation of Canada Limited (Can. 1959)
Feb. 28, 1986 – Name changed to Navistar Financial Corporation Canada Inc. ■

International Health Partners Inc. (Alta. Mar. 5, 1997)
June 2, 2010 – Name changed to Patient Home Monitoring Corp. pursuant to Qualifying Transaction reverse takeover acquisition of PHM DME Healthcare, Inc. and Stancap Holdings I Limited. ■

The International Helium Company Limited (Ont. May 26, 1960)
Oct. 3, 1970 – Name changed to Mineral Resources International Limited; basis 1 new for 10 old shs. ■

International Helium Corporation Limited (Ont. May 26, 1960)
Sept. 8, 1961 – Name changed to The International Helium Company Limited. ■

International Helix Biotechnologies Inc. (B.C. 1983)
July 31, 1995 – Formed Helix BioPharma Corp. in Canada on amalgamation with Intercon Pharma Inc.; basis 1 new for 2 old shs. (see FPsurvey - Industrials)

International Hi-Tech Industries Inc. (B.C. Feb. 16, 1987)
May 31, 1996 – Continued into Canada.
Mar. 2, 2010 – Dissolved and struck from register.
June 7, 2010 – Revived. (see FPsurvey - Industrials)

International Homestead Resources Inc. (B.C. Oct. 23, 1980)
Sept. 11, 1996 – Name changed to NovaWest Resources Inc. ■

International Homestock Resources Ltd. (B.C. June 9, 1980)
Feb. 15, 1989 – Name changed to Coscient Group Inc. and continued into Canada. ■

International Hospitality Inc. (Ont. July 7, 1993 amalg.)
July 18, 1996 – Receiver Grant Thornton Limited of Toronto, called a meeting of creditors. There were no funds available for creditors or shldrs.
Dec. 5, 1996 – Amalgamated with Casino Financing Corporation to form new co. with same name International Hospitality Inc.; basis 1 new for 250 old shs.
Aug. 27, 2001 – Receiver discharged.

International H.R.S. Industries Inc. (B.C. May 1, 1984 amalg.)
May 25, 1987 – Name changed to Glenex Industries Inc. ■

International Hydro Electric System (Mass. 1929)
1949 – Liquidated. Deb. holders received 39 com. shs. of Gatineau Power Company for each deb. held; remaining U.S. and all Cdn. deb. holders received final cash payments ($400 pd. previously) of $60 princ. plus $12 int.
1953 – Pref. shs. exchanged; basis 5.5 Gatineau com. shs. plus divd. adjustment of $2.50 per pref. sh. for ea. pref. sh. held.
1956 – Continued under name of Abacus Fund, an American corp.

International Hydrocarbons Corp. (Alta. Mar. 25, 1996)
Jan. 29, 2007 – Amalgamated with Tudor Corporation Ltd. to continue with the Tudor name; basis 1 new Tudor for 4 old Hydrocarbons shs. (see Tudor Corporation Ltd.)

International Hydrocarbons Ltd. (unknown)
Oct. 31, 1967 – All assets and liabs. acquired by Omega Hydrocarbons Ltd.; basis 2 mew Omega shs. for 1 old International sh. (see Omega Natural Gas Co. Ltd.)

International Hydrodynamics Company, Ltd. (B.C. 1964)
Oct. 1978 – H. S. Sigurdson appointed receiver by Royal Bank of Canada. Subsequently assets sold. No distribution made to shldrs.

International Impala Resources Ltd. (B.C. May 27, 1982)
Nov. 13, 1992 – Name changed to Tapestry Ventures Ltd.; basis 1 new for 5 old shs. ■

International Infopet Systems Ltd. (Ont. Mar. 9, 1965)
Feb. 26, 1997 – Name changed to New International Infopet Systems Ltd.; basis 1 new for 2.5 old shs. ■

International Innopac Inc. (Can. June 23, 1983)
May 29, 1992 – Continued into British Columbia.
June 1, 1994 – Name changed to Great Pacific Enterprises Inc. ■

International Inter-Link Inc. (Alta. May 14, 1987)
Nov. 25, 1997 – Name changed to Parton Capital Inc. ■

International Interlake Industries Inc. (B.C. Dec. 31, 1986 amalg.)
July 9, 1993 – Acquired by Newport Petroleum Corporation; basis 77¢ per sh. Subsequently amalgamated Sept. 14, 1993. (see Newport Petroleum Corporation)

International Ionarc Inc. (B.C. 1967)
June 4, 1993 – Dissolved and struck off register.

International Iron & Metal Co., Limited (unknown)
Nov. 1968 – Amalgamated into Intermetco Limited. (see Intermetco Limited)

International Iron Processors Limited (unknown 1958)
Nov. 1968 – Amalgamated into Intermetco Limited. (see Intermetco Limited)

International Jaguar Equities Inc. (B.C. Sept. 22, 1981)
Feb. 7, 2000 – Name changed to Jaguar International Equities Inc.; basis 1 new for 5 old shs. ■

International James Industries Inc. (B.C. June 22, 1973)
July 8, 1988 – Name changed to CDIS Software Inc. ■

International Jazzman Ventures Corp. (B.C. Feb. 13, 1986)
Dec. 15, 1995 – Formed Oro Belle Resources Corporation on amalgamation with Oro Belle Resources Corporation (1 for 1); basis 1 new for 1 old sh. ■

International KRL Resources Corp. (B.C. July 10, 1978)
Dec. 7, 2009 – Name changed to Acme Resources Inc.; basis 1 new for 15 old shs. ■

International Kenergy Resource Corporation (Sask. June 6, 1946)
June 13, 1985 – Formed Interquest Resources Corporation in Ontario on amalgamation with The Alton Corporation. ■

International Kengate Ventures Inc. (B.C. Aug. 9, 1979)
Mar. 31, 1994 – Name changed to Latin American Gold Inc. ■

International Kenville Gold Mines Ltd. (Ont. 1945)
Mar. 1980 – Charter cancelled.

International Keystone Entertainment Inc. (B.C. Mar. 21, 1974)
Nov. 3, 1994 – Continued into Canada.
June 15, 2005 – Continued into British Columbia.
May 25, 2006 – Privatized following acquisition by Keystone Pictures Inc.; basis 1 new participation right (which entitled holders to receive 75% of the revenue from sales and licensing of the distribution rights to the Film Library until Dec. 31, 2008) for 1 com. sh.

International King Jack Resources Ltd. (B.C. Aug. 7, 1985)
Apr. 18, 1996 – Name changed to Petromin Resources Ltd.; basis 1 new for 5 old shs. (see FPsurvey - Mines & Energy)

International Kingdom Mining & Exploration Ltd. (Ont. 1946)
Apr. 15, 1965 – Dissolved.

International Kirby Energy Corp. (B.C. June 29, 1978)
Feb. 23, 1996 – Name changed to Kingsway International Holdings Limited. ■

International Kirkland Minerals Inc. (B.C. Sept. 26, 1997)
Feb. 22, 2010 – Name changed to Legion Resources Corp.; basis 1 new for 7 old shs. ■

International LMM Ventures Corp. (B.C. Aug. 24, 1990)
Apr. 18, 2011 – Name changed to US Oil Sands Inc. pursuant to reverse takeover acquisition of Earth Energy Resources Inc. ■

International Laco Resources Inc. (B.C. 1972)
Jan. 13, 1985 – Amalgamated with 4 other cos. following agreement dated to form Aurex Resources Inc.; basis 1 new for 2.5 old shs.

International Land Corp. Ltd. (B.C. 1959)
Oct. 1978 – All o/s shs. not already held acquired by Hastings West Investment Co. for $12.50 per sh.

International Landmark Environmental Inc. (B.C. Sept. 5, 1975)
Jan. 15, 2003 – Name changed to Shabute Ventures Inc.; basis 1 new for 7 old shs. ■

International Larder Minerals Inc. (Ont. Oct. 27, 1941)
Jan. 29, 2001 – Amalgamated with Prospectors Alliance Corporation, private co. Explorers Alliance Corporation and two numbered companies to continue as a new company also named Explorers Alliance Corporation; basis 1 new Explorers sh. for 0.049 old Larder sh.

International Laser Tech Inc. (B.C. 1983)
Dec. 23, 1988 – Dissolved.

International Lead & Zinc Mines Ltd. (B.C. 1951)
May 1958 – Charter cancelled.

International Legacy Inc. (Ont. Oct. 29, 1979)
Nov. 2, 1995 – Name changed to Complex Minerals Corp.; basis 1 com. for either 1 multiple vtg. or subord. vtg. sh. ■

International Light Aircraft Corporation (B.C. Nov. 3, 1988)
Oct. 16, 1992 – Name changed to Pacific Vista Industries Inc. ■

International Lima Resources Corp. (B.C. Sept. 2, 1966)
Mar. 1, 2004 – Name changed to Crosshair Exploration & Mining Corp. ■

International Lithium Mining Corporation Limited (Ont. 1954)
July 27, 1976 – Charter cancelled.

International Loan Company (Man. 1913)
May 1960 – Name changed to International Savings and Mortgage Corporation. ■

International Loumic Resources Ltd. (Ont. Oct. 2, 1987)
Feb. 27, 2003 – Name changed to Loumic Exploration Inc.; basis 3 new for 1 old sh. ■

International Machinery Company Limited (unknown 1958)
Nov. 1968 – Amalgamated to form Intermetco Limited. (see Intermetco Limited)

International Maggie Mines Ltd. (B.C. Feb. 27, 1978)
Apr. 26, 1995 – Name changed to Hall Train Entertainment Inc. and continued into Canada. ■

International Magnetics Corporation (B.C. 1983)
Nov. 1, 1988 – Name changed to United Southern Minerals Corp. ■

International Mahogany Corp. (B.C. Mar. 17, 1980)
Dec. 1, 1990 – Amalgamated with Magellan Resources Corp. and Goldsil Resources Ltd. to form new co. with same name International Mahogany Corp.; basis 0.22 new cl. B shs. for 1 Magellan com. sh., 0.22 new cl. B shs. for 1 Goldsil com. sh. and 1 new cl. A or B sh. for 1 old cl. A or B sh.
June 2, 2000 – Name changed to Reliant Ventures Ltd.; basis 1 new for 10 old shs. ■

International Mahogany Corp. (B.C. 1987 amalg.)
Dec. 1, 1990 – Amalgamated with Megellan Resources Corp. (0.22 new cl. B sub. vtg. sh. for 1) and Goldsil Resources Limited (0.22 new cl. B sub. vtg. sh. for 1) to form a new company also known as International Mahogany Corp.; basis 1 cl. B com. sh for 1 com. sh. and 1 new cl. B sub. vtg. sh. for 1 cl. B sub. vtg. sh.

International Makaoo Limited (Can. Oct. 22, 1953)
Dec. 16, 1991 – Name changed to Non-Par Developments Ltd.; basis 1 new for 2 old shs. ■

International Maple Leaf Resource Corporation (B.C. Jan. 25, 1980)
Sept. 11, 1989 – Name changed to Maple Resource Corp.; basis 1 new for 2.5 old shs. ■

International Maple Leaf Springs Ltd. (B.C. Aug. 21, 1972)
Jan. 23, 2004 – Dissolved and struck from registry.

International March Resources Ltd. (B.C. 1977)
Apr. 22, 1986 – Name changed to Mode Products Inc. ■

International Mariner Resources Ltd. (B.C. 1972)
Mar. 1978 – Charter cancelled.

International Markatech Corporation (B.C. Dec. 5, 1979)
Nov. 3, 1995 – Name changed to Markatech Industries Corporation; basis 1 new for 3 old shs. ■

International Medical Imaging Specialists Inc. (B.C. 1983)
Aug. 18, 1986 – Struck off register following change of domicile to Wyoming.

International Mega-Dyne Industrial Corp. (B.C. June 11, 1980)
Apr. 5, 1991 – Name changed to ESC Envirotech Systems Corporation following acquisition of Envirotech Alberta Inc. ■

International Megaline Resources Ltd. (B.C. 1979)
July 8, 1986 – Name changed to Dyonix Greentree Technologies Inc. ■

International Membership Marketing Inc. (B.C. 1985)
July 30, 1991 – Name changed to Internova Resources Ltd.; basis 1 new for 3 old shs. ■

International Meridian Resources Ltd. (B.C. 1967)
Mar. 29, 1985 – Amalgamated with 3 other cos. to form Meridor Resources Limited; basis 0.3381 new for 1 old sh.

International Message Centers Inc. (B.C. 1987)
Nov. 13, 1990 – Name changed to Interlearn Holdings Ltd. ■

International Metal and Petroleum Corp. (Que. 1957)
Apr. 13, 1974 – Dissolved.

International Metal Industries Limited (Can. 1922)
Apr. 1957 – Name changed to John Wood Industries Limited. ■

International Micham Resources Inc. (B.C. 1981)
May 22, 1996 – Name changed to Link Mineral Ventures Ltd. and continued into Ontario; basis 1 new for 10 old shs. (see FPsurvey - Mines & Energy)

International Millennium Mining Corp. (B.C. Nov. 19, 1984)
July 13, 2021 – Name changed to Millennium Silver Corp. (see FPsurvey - Mines & Energy)

International Minerals & Chemical Corporation (Canada) Limited (Sask. 1930)
Feb. 22, 1995 – Name changed to International Minerals & Chemical (Canada) Global Limited.

International Minerals Corporation (Yuk. Feb. 14, 1994)
Dec. 30, 2013 – Acquired by HOC Canada Inc., a wholly owned subsid. of Hochschild Mining plc; basis US$2.38 cash plus 1 Chaparral Gold Corp. sh. for 1 International Minerals sh.

International Mining and Development Corp. (Liberia 1955)
Apr. 1970 – Assets distributed in liquidation. Shldrs. received 1 sh. Precious Metals Ltd. for 4 old shs. and 1 sh. plus 1 wt. International Diversified Developers Ltd. for each 10 old shs.

International Mirtone Inc. (Ont. Mar. 20, 1985)
Feb. 21, 1990 – Name changed to Mirtronics Inc. ■

International Mogul Mines Limited (Ont. 1968 amalg.)
Aug. 20, 1982 – Amalgamated with Conwest Exploration Company Limited (1 new cl. A and cl. B for 1 cl. A and cl. B), Central Patricia Limited (1.1 new cl. B for 1 com.), Chimo Gold Mines Limited (either $2.20 or 0.3 new cl. B for 1 com.) and 456128 Ontario Limited (0.88 new cl. A for 1 com.) to form a new co. also named Conwest Exploration Company Limited; basis 2 new Conwest cl. B shs. for 1 old Mogul com. sh. and 1 new ser. A Conwest pref. sh. for 1 old 6% Mogul 1st pref. sh. (see Conwest Exploration Company Limited)

International Mogul Mines (Ontario) Limited (Ont. 1968 amalg.)
Dec. 1, 1978 – Amalgamated with Calmor Iron Bay Mines Ltd. to form Calmor Iron Bay Mines (1978) Limited.

International Molybdenum Mines Ltd. (Ont. 1949)
1962 – Name changed to Pax International Mines Ltd.; basis 1 new for 4 old shs. ■

International Montoro Resources Inc. (B.C. Jan. 30, 1987)
Feb. 24, 2021 – Name changed to Marvel Discovery Corp. (see FPsurvey - Mines & Energy)

International Movie Group, Inc. (Can. 1980)
May 1991 – Continued into Delaware.

International Murex Technologies Corporation (B.C. Oct. 31, 1983)
July 13, 1998 – Acquired by AAC Acquisition Ltd., a wholly owned subsid. of Abbott Industries, for US$13 per sh.

International Musto Explorations Limited (B.C. Mar. 7, 1979)
July 15, 1994 – Continued into Canada.
June 19, 1995 – Acquired by RN Galaxy Inc. (a co. formed by North Limited and Rio Algom Limited) for $14.99 per sh.

International Nesmont Industrial Corporation (B.C. 1986)
Jan. 16, 2006 – Dissolved and struck from register.

International Nickel Company of Canada, Limited (Can. July 25, 1916; via Dominion charter)
Apr. 21, 1976 – Name changed to Inco Limited. ■

International Nickel Ventures Corporation (Ont. Oct. 20, 2005)
June 16, 2010 – Name changed to INV Metals Inc. ■

International Norfolk Acquisition Inc. (Can. Mar. 15, 1985)
Nov. 8, 1996 – Formed Ventures Resource Corporation in Barbados on amalgamation with INA Acquisition Inc., constituting a reverse takeover by INA; basis 1 new for 1 INA sh. and 0.608608 new for 1 International Norfolk sh. ■

International Norsemont Ventures Ltd. (B.C. June 10, 1977)
Sept. 29, 1999 – Name changed to Consolidated Norsemont Ventures Ltd.; basis 1 new for 5 old shs. ■

International North American Resources Inc. (B.C. Jan. 16, 1979)
Jan. 5, 1990 – Name changed to Sonoma Resource Corp.; basis 1 new for 5 old shs. ■

International Northair Mines Ltd. (B.C. Sept. 13, 1966)
Nov. 20, 2014 – Name changed to Northair Silver Corp. ■

International Northland Resources Inc. (Alta. 1949)
Sept. 10, 1997 – Formed Combined Logistics International Ltd. in Bahamas on amalgamation with Concord Logistics Limited, constituting a reverse takeover by Concord; basis 1.8133 new for 1 Concord sh. and 1 new for 10 International Northland shs. ■

International Norvalie Mines Ltd. (Ont. Apr. 10, 1937)
Aug. 31, 1992 – Delisted from CDN. Subsequently struck from register.

International Nutrition Technologies Inc. (B.C. 1985)
Aug. 14, 1992 – Dissolved and struck off register.

International Obaska Mines Ltd. (Can. Dec. 16, 1942)
Dec. 16, 1980 – Dissolved.

International Oil & Gas Co. Ltd. (Alta. 1914)
1920 – Struck off register.

International Oiltex Ltd. (Alta. Oct. 18, 1989)
Sept. 12, 1994 – Amalgamated with Aztec Resources Ltd. to form new co. with same name Aztec Resources Ltd.; basis 1 new for 4.8 International Oiltex shs. (see Aztec Resources Ltd.)

International Onword Learning Systems Inc. (B.C. July 14, 1987)
Apr. 2, 1996 – Name changed to Catalyst Ventures Corporation; basis 1 new for 4 old shs. ■

International Oregon Resources Corp. (B.C. Apr. 2, 1980)
Mar. 16, 1993 – Name changed to Dalphine Enterprises Ltd.; basis 1 new for 2 old shs. ■

International PBX Ventures Ltd. (B.C. Aug. 19, 1987)
Feb. 28, 2014 – Name changed to Chilean Metals Inc.; basis 1 new for 10 old shs. ■

International Pacific Cypress Minerals Ltd. (B.C. 1957)
Jan. 22, 1993 – Dissolved and struck off register.

The International Pagurian Corporation Limited (Ont. Apr. 18, 1978)
Mar. 30, 1988 – Amalgamated in Ontario to continue with same name.
May 9, 1988 – Name changed to Canadian Express Limited. ■

International Paints (Canada) Limited (Can. 1928)
Dec. 1985 – International Paints Holdings (Canada), a wholly owned subsid. of International Paint PLC of Britain, acquired 90% of o/s shs. of company, and used the provisions of the C.B.C.A. to acquire the balance of the o/s shs. at $180 per sh. for each common or pref. sh. not held, making the company a wholly owned subsid.

International Panorama Resource Corp. (B.C. Feb. 19, 1980)
Sept. 27, 2002 – Name changed to Kakanda Development Corp.; basis 1 new for 15 old shs. ■

International Park West Financial Corporation (B.C. 1978)
Nov. 28, 1986 – Struck off register.

International Pastel Food Corporation (B.C. 1986)
May 29, 1991 – Control of the company acquired by Comac Food Group Inc. for a deemed value of $770,095; basis 1 cl. B Comac com. sh., 0.5 cl. A wts. and 0.5 cl. B wts. for each sh. of Pastel. (see Comac Food Group Inc.)
Mar. 1, 1995 – All assets and liabs. sold to Comac Food Group Inc. (see Comac Food Group Inc.)
Mar. 31, 1995 – Wound up. (see Comac Food Group Inc.)

International Pathfinder Inc. (Ont. Nov. 5, 1986 amalg.)
Sept. 1, 1988 – Acquired by Pepsi-Cola/Seven-Up Bottling of Toronto for $3.75 per sh.

International Pathfinder Resources Ltd. (B.C. 1968)
Aug. 3, 1983 – Name changed to Pathfinder Financial Corp. ■

International PCBX Systems Inc. (B.C. July 7, 1989)
Nov. 1, 1994 – Name changed to Extreme Technologies Inc.; basis 1 new for 1 old sh. ■

International Pedco Energy Corporation (Alta. Nov. 15, 1993 amalg.)
Mar. 13, 1996 – Amalgamated with Lateral Vector Acquisitions Inc., a wholly owned subsid. of Lateral Vector Resources Inc.; basis either 0.6959 Lateral Vector com. sh. plus 1 amalco special sh. redeemed for $0.418 per sh., or 0.994 new Lateral Vector sh. for 1 old International Pedco com. sh.

International Petroleum Co. Ltd. (Can. 1920)
1960 – Esso Standard (Inter-America) Inc. purch. 99.65% of o/s shs. for US$45 per sh., subject to adjustment of 30¢ for each divd. declared. Minority shldrs., through courts, retained remaining int.

International Petroleum Corporation (B.C. June 1, 1985 amalg.)
May 3, 1994 – Continued into Canada. (see Sands Petroleum AB)
Feb. 4, 1998 – All o/s com. shs. acquired by Sands Petroleum AB of Sweden; basis 1 Sands global depository security for 1.15 International Petroleum com. shs. (see Sands Petroleum AB)

International Petroleum Ltd. (B.C. 1980)
June 1, 1985 – Formed Consolidated International Petroleum Corporation in British Columbia on amalgamation with North South Resources Ltd. and Peninsula Petroleum Corp.; basis 1 new for 3.05 old shs. ■

International PetroReal Oil Corporation (B.C. July 27, 1987)
May 8, 2007 – Continued into Alberta.
Sept. 17, 2008 – Name changed to PetroReal Energy Inc. ■

International Pharmadyne Ltd. (B.C. Aug. 2, 1966)
Mar. 5, 1993 – Delisted Vancouver Stock Exchange. Subsequently struck from register and dissolved.

International Phoenix Energy Corporation (B.C. 1968)
Aug. 1, 1990 – Amalgamated with Achilles Resources Ltd. (1 for 4.5), Golden Iskut Resources Incorporated (1 for 8) and Interstate Energy Corp. (1 for 14) to form a new co. Aegis Resources Ltd.; basis 1 new for 8 old shs. (see Aegis Resources Ltd.)

International Platinum Corporation (Ont. July 22, 1980)
Oct. 23, 1995 – Name changed to International Precious Metals Corporation; basis 1 new for 10 old shs. (see FPsurvey - Mines & Energy)

International Player Enterprises Inc. (B.C. Oct. 25, 1985)
Apr. 24, 2003 – Dissolved and struck from register.

International Polaris Energy Corp. (B.C. 1979)
Jan. 7, 1991 – Acquired by O'Shanter Development Company Limited for $0.40 per sh. consisting of $0.20 cash and $0.20 in a promissory note maturing in 1992.

International Potential Explorations Inc. (B.C. Dec. 28, 1973)
Apr. 12, 1991 – Name changed to Banyan Industries International Inc. ■

International Potter Distilling Corporation (Can. Jan. 30, 1978)
Apr. 27, 1995 – Name changed to Cascadia Brands Inc. ■

International Powerhouse Energy Corp. (B.C. Jan. 18, 1979)
July 30, 2003 – Name changed to Sea Breeze Power Corp. ■

International Powertech Systems Inc. (B.C. Feb. 10, 1984)
Jan. 20, 1992 – Name changed to Powertech Industries Inc.; basis 1 new for 5 old shs. ■

International Praxis Resource Corp. (B.C. Aug. 22, 1984)
May 3, 1996 – Dissolved and struck off register.

International Prime Technologies Inc. (B.C. 1983)
June 20, 2000 – Reported to be deregistered during.

International Prism Exploration Ltd. (B.C. Oct. 31, 1969)
Mar. 15, 1995 – Name changed to Prism Resources Inc.; basis 1 new for 3 old shs. (see FPsurvey - Mines & Energy)

International Properties Group Ltd. (Alta. Jan. 10, 1997)
Mar. 20, 2009 – Name changed to Acorn Income Corp. ■

International Pursuit Corporation (Ont. June 30, 1936)
July 3, 2002 – Amalgamated with Nevoro Gold Corporation to form Apollo Gold Corporation; basis 1 new for 43.57 International Pursuit shs.

International Pyramid Mines Inc. (B.C. 1964)
Continued into Canada.
May 24, 1979 – Amalgamated with Bute Resources Inc. and Gilford Resources Ltd. to form American Pyramid Resources Inc.; basis 1 new for 5 old shs.

International Ranwick Ltd. (Ont. 1949)
1959 – Name changed to International Molybdenum Mines Ltd. ■

International Reef Resources Ltd. (Alta. Dec. 23, 1977)
Aug. 5, 1998 – Amalgamated with 784308 Alberta Inc., a wholly owned subsid. of UTS Energy Corporation (formerly United Tri-Star Resources Ltd.); basis 1 new for 1.75 old shs. (see UTS Energy Corporation)

International Republic Aircraft Manufacturing Corporation (B.C. Dec. 23, 1986)
May 27, 1993 – Name changed to Urban Juice and Soda Company Ltd. ■

International Retail Systems Inc. (B.C. 1986)
Sept. 11, 1992 – Continued into Wyoming.
Feb. 2, 1995 – Name changed to Canmax Inc. ■

International Rex Ventures Inc. (B.C. 1984)
Sept. 17, 1990 – Name changed to Prosperex Minerals Corp.; basis 1 new for 2 old shs. ■

International Rhodes Resources Ltd. (B.C. Sept. 27, 1962)
Feb. 6, 1989 – Name changed to Consolidated Rhodes Resources Inc.; basis 1 new for 5 old shs. ■

International Rice Bran Industries Ltd. (B.C. 1983)
Mar. 13, 1990 – Name changed to Blue Star Investment Limited; basis 1 new for 3 old shs. ■

International Richey Pacific Cablevision, Ltd. (B.C. July 16, 1987)
Feb. 13, 1995 – Name changed to Richey Communications, Ltd. ■

International Riley Resources Ltd. (B.C. Oct. 15, 1986)
Nov. 22, 2001 – Name changed to Wind River Resources Ltd.; basis 1 new for 5 old shs. ■

International Road Dynamics Inc. (Sask. Dec. 4, 1980)
Aug. 28, 1997 – Continued into Canada.
June 6, 2017 – Acquired by Wi-LAN Inc. (renamed Quarterhill Inc.); basis $4.25 cash per sh.

International Rochester Energy Corp. (B.C. Oct. 3, 1983)
Mar. 5, 1999 – Continued into Alberta.
June 16, 2004 – Name changed to Rochester Energy Corp.; basis 1 new for 9 old shs. ■

International Roraima Gold Corporation (B.C. Feb. 5, 1988 amalg.)
Jan. 17, 2003 – Dissolved and struck from register.
Feb. 5, 2010 – Restored to registry.
Feb. 4, 2014 – Dissolved and struck from registry.

International Royalon Minerals Inc. (B.C. Dec. 5, 1979)
July 20, 1987 – Name changed to International Markatech Corporation; basis 1 new for 3 old shs. ■

International Royalty Corporation (Yuk. May 7, 2003)
Nov. 12, 2004 – Continued into Canada. (see Royal Gold, Inc.)
Feb. 26, 2010 – Acquired by Royal Gold Inc. pursuant to plan of arrangement; basis either for Cdn$4.20 plus 0.0593 Royal Gold shs. or 0.0593 exch. shs. for 1 sh. or 0.1385 Royal Gold shs. or 0.1385 exch. shs for 1 sh. or a combination thereof. (see Royal Gold, Inc.)

International R.S.V. Resources Corporation (B.C. May 29, 1984)
May 5, 1997 – Name changed to Harambee Mining Corp.; basis 1 new for 5 old shs. ■

International Safety-Ject Industries Inc. (B.C. Jan. 22, 1987)
Sept. 30, 1993 – Name changed to Specialty Medical Products Inc.; basis 1 new for 4 old shs. ■

International Sales Information Systems Inc. (B.C. Sept. 28, 1955)
Sept. 18, 2000 – Name changed to Versatile Mobile Systems (Canada) Inc. ■

International Samuel Exploration Corp. (B.C. June 14, 1985)
Aug. 27, 2020 – Name changed to CopAur Minerals Inc. (see FPsurvey - Mines & Energy)

International Santana Resources Inc. (B.C. Dec. 4, 1970)
Aug. 21, 1986 – Name changed to Image West Entertainment Corporation. ■

International Sargon Resources Ltd. (B.C. Mar. 5, 1981)
July 28, 1999 – Name changed to Canoil Exploration Corporation. ■

International Sasha Corp. (Alta. June 7, 2000)
June 28, 2004 – Name changed to PanWestern Energy Inc. ■

International Savannah Ventures Ltd. (B.C. Mar. 30, 1981)
June 10, 1999 – Name changed to Softcare EC.Com, Inc. following reverse takeover acquisition of SoftCare Electronic Commerce Inc. ■

International Savings and Mortgage Corporation (Man. 1913)
1966 – Acquired by and became a subsidiary of York Trust & Savings Company. York Trust was acquired by The Metropolitan Trust Company in 1967.
Oct. 1979 – Name changed to Victoria and Grey Mortgage Corporation following amalgamation of The Metropolitan Trust Company and Victoria and Grey Trustco Ltd. ■

International Secondary Materials Limited (unknown 1958)
Nov. 1968 – Amalgamated to form Intermetco Limited. (see Intermetco Limited)

International Semi-Tech Microelectronics Inc. (Ont. Dec. 9, 1965)
Sept. 22, 1994 – Name changed to Semi-Tech Corporation. ■

International Seniors Housing Corporation (Alta. 1988)
Sept. 12, 1990 – Name changed to Redux Energy Corporation. ■

International Shasta Resources Ltd. (B.C. Sept. 2, 1966)
May 20, 1994 – Name changed to Consolidated Shasta Resources Inc.; basis 1 new for 10 old shs. ■

International Sigma Security Inc. (B.C. 1982)
Apr. 28, 1989 – Dissolved.

International Silver Ridge Resources Inc. (B.C. Sept. 27, 1984)
June 13, 2011 – Name changed to PNG Gold Corporation pursuant to reverse takeover acquisition of NMC Mining Corp. ■

International Sinabarb Industries Ltd. (B.C. Mar. 31, 1978)
Oct. 15, 1990 – Name changed to Primero Industries Ltd.; basis 1 new for 3 old shs. ■

International Skyline Gold Corporation (B.C. Sept. 1, 1992)
Dec. 18, 1996 – Name changed to Iriana Resources Corporation pursuant to acqusitions of Supreme Resources Inc. and Jeraldo Investments Ltd. and spin-off of 507675 B.C. Ltd. (renamed International Skyline Gold Corporation) to shldrs. on a sh.-for-sh. basis. ■

International Skyline Gold Corporation (B.C. Dec. 18, 1996)
Apr. 4, 2000 – Following Plan of Arrangement all o/s com. shs. exchanged for shs. of Skyline Gold Corp. (1 sh. Skyline Gold for 1 sh. Int'l Skyline) and Copper Mountain Mines Ltd. (1 sh. Copper Mountain for 8 shs. Int'l Skyline). (see Copper Mountain Mines Ltd.; Skyline Gold Corporation)

International Slocan Developments Ltd. (B.C. Apr. 16, 1952)
Aug. 15, 1995 – Name changed to Slocan Holdings Ltd.; basis 1 new for 3.5 old shs. ■

International Sovereign Energy Corp. (Alta. Aug. 12, 1992)
Dec. 27, 2012 – Continued into Canada.
Jan. 25, 2013 – Formed Wi2Wi Corporation in Canada pursuant to reverse takeover acquisition of and amalgamation with (old) Wi2Wi Corporation. (see FPsurvey - Industrials)

International Space Modules Ltd. (B.C. 1928)
July 8, 1976 – Charter cancelled.

International Spectair Resources Inc. (B.C. Jan. 31, 1980)
Nov. 5, 1991 – Name changed to Camden Oil Corporation. ■

International Standard Resources Ltd. (B.C. Jan. 13, 1960)
Mar. 15, 1988 – Name changed to First Standard Mining Ltd. ■

International StarTeck Industries Ltd. (B.C. Apr. 27, 1987)
Apr. 8, 2013 – Dissolved and struck from register. ■

International Sterling Holdings Inc. (Ont. 1980)
June 1994 – Dissolved. No funds available for distribution to shldrs.

International Submarine Safaris (Canada) Ltd. (B.C. Apr. 19, 1983)
Jan. 31, 1990 – Delisted from the Vancouver Stock Exchange. Subsequently struck from register and dissolved.
June 18, 1990 – Continued into Canada.
Dec. 21, 1990 – Continued into British Columbia.

International Sunatco Industries Ltd. (B.C. Jan. 11, 1991 amalg.)
May 30, 2003 – Dissolved and struck from register.

International Suneva Resources Ltd. (B.C. July 19, 1965)
Dec. 19, 1991 – Name changed to Nevsun Resources Ltd.; basis 1 new for 4 old shs. ■

International Sunstate Ventures Ltd. (B.C. Sept. 13, 1982)
May 23, 2002 – Name changed to Thelon Ventures Ltd.; basis 1 new for 3 old shs. ■

International Systcoms Limited (Can. Dec. 19, 1958)
Sept. 13, 1979 – Name changed to International Systcoms Ltd. ■

International Systcoms Ltd. (Can. Dec. 19, 1958)
Feb. 7, 1983 – Name changed to Memotec Data Inc. ■

International TME Resources Inc. (B.C. 1983)
Oct. 1, 2013 – Amalgamated with Australian-Canadian Oil Royalties Ltd. to form Chelsea Oil and Gas Ltd.; basis 0.5431 Chelsea com. sh. for 1 International TME sh. ■

International Tako Industries Inc. (B.C. Sept. 18, 1972)
Nov. 26, 2002 – Continued into Alberta.
May 14, 2004 – Name changed to Ironhorse Oil & Gas Inc. ■

International Taurus Resources Inc. (B.C. May 25, 1960)
Mar. 30, 2005 – Amalgamated with American Bonanza Gold Mining Corp. to form American Bonanza Gold Corp.; basis 1 new for 4 American Bonanza shs. and 1 new for 5 International Taurus shs. (see American Bonanza Gold Corp.)

International Technologies Corporation (Can. Jan. 25, 2002 amalg.)
Sept. 26, 2011 – Dissolved and struck from register.

International Technologies Inc. (Alta. Oct. 24, 1983)
May 31, 1993 – Name changed to Canadian Crude Separators Inc.; basis 1 new for 4 old shs. ■

International Telepool Corp. (B.C. 1983)
Aug. 8, 1986 – Name changed to U.S. Pay-Tel Inc. ■

International Telepresence (Canada) Inc. (Can. Feb. 9, 1981)
June 22, 1999 – Name changed to Isee3D, Inc. ■

International Telesis Industries Corp. (B.C. July 12, 1982 amalg.)
Feb. 6, 1989 – Name changed to Madonna Educational Group of Canada Ltd. ■

International Tessa Capital Corporation (B.C. Feb. 22, 1984)
Oct. 5, 1993 – Name changed to Apex Resorts Corporation. ■

International Texcan Technology Corp. (B.C. June 20, 1983)
Mar. 7, 1990 – Delisted from the Vancouver Stock Exchange. Subsequently dissolved for failure to file and struck from register.

International Texoro Resources Ltd. (B.C. Sept. 30, 1983)
July 24, 1991 – Name changed to Great Western Gold Corp.; basis 1 new for 2 old shs. ■

International Thomson Organization Limited (Ont. Dec. 28, 1977)
June 5, 1989 – Formed The Thomson Corporation on amalgamation with Thomson Newspapers Limited; basis 1.67 new for 1 Thomson sh. and 1 new for 1 International Thomson sh. ■

International Thunderbird Gaming Corporation (B.C. Sept. 4, 1987)
Feb. 5, 1999 – Continued into Yukon.
Sept. 30, 2005 – Name changed to Thunderbird Resorts, Inc. ■

International Thunderwood Explorations Ltd. (B.C. Oct. 30, 1964)
Apr. 27, 1987 – Continued into Canada.
June 1, 1989 – Formed Thunderwood Resources Inc. in Ontario on amalgamation with Syngold Exploration Inc.; basis 1 new for 1.4 Syngold shs. and 1 new for 1 International Thunderwood sh. ■

International Ticker Tape Resources Ltd. (B.C. 1984)
Oct. 25, 1993 – Name changed to Econogreen Environmental Systems Ltd. ■

International Tika Resources Ltd. (B.C. 1972)
Mar. 31, 1977 – Continued into Alberta.
Sept. 1, 1991 – Charter cancelled; subsequently revived, date unknown; charter cancelled again Sept. 2, 1999.

International Tillex Enterprises Ltd. (B.C. Feb. 11, 1983)
July 5, 1991 – Dissolved and struck off register.

International Tire Recycling and Manufacturing Corp. (B.C. Apr. 16, 1980)
Dec. 5, 1997 – Name changed to Intirmac Industrial Corporation; basis 1 new for 4 old shs. ■

International Topaz Business Development Corp. (B.C. Oct. 4, 1984)
Aug. 9, 1996 – Name changed to Leopardus Resources Limited. ■

International Tournigan Corporation (B.C. Nov. 10, 1966)
Mar. 26, 2001 – Name changed to Tournigan Ventures Corporation; basis 1 new for 10 old shs. ■

International Training Rinks Corp. (Alta. Mar. 8, 1996)
Dec. 2, 1999 – Name changed to National Training Rinks Corp.; basis 1 new for 10 old shs. (see FPsurvey - Industrials)

International Trans Asia Trading Corp. (B.C. 1984)
July 20, 1989 – Name changed to ITC International Trading Corp.; basis 1 new for 5 old shs. ■

International Trimark Resources Ltd. (Yuk. Dec. 14, 1993)
June 17, 1997 – Name changed to Trimark Oil & Gas Ltd.; basis 1 new for 2 old shs. ■

International Trojan Development Corporation (B.C. Aug. 25, 1967)
June 20, 1991 – Name changed to Trojan Ventures Inc.; basis 1 new for 2 old shs. ■

International Trojan Explorations Inc. (unknown)
Dec. 23, 1982 – Amalgamated (1 new for 1.5 old shs.) with other cos. to form Centurion Exploration Inc. (see Centurion Exploration Inc.)

International Truck and Engine Corporation Canada (Ont. 1903)
Continued into Canada.
Name changed to Navistar Canada Inc.

International Tungsten Inc. (B.C. Feb. 7, 1992)
June 15, 2018 – Name changed to Arbutus Brands Inc.

International Tungsten Mines Ltd. (Ont. 1942)
July 1958 – Charter cancelled.

International Turbine Technologies Inc. (B.C. 1980)
Aug. 17, 1990 – Dissolved and struck off register.

International Turbomist Inc. (B.C. 1988)
June 10, 1994 – Dissolved and struck off register.

International UNP Holdings Ltd. (B.C. Mar. 15, 1965)
Aug. 4, 1993 – Continued into Canada.
Feb. 14, 2000 – Acquired by CHP Investors N.V. for US$0.17 per sh.

International Union Resources Inc. (B.C. Apr. 19, 1983)
Nov. 19, 1986 – Name changed to Tropical Submarine Safaris Ltd. ■

International Uranium Corporation (Ont. May 9, 1997 amalg.)
Dec. 1, 2006 – Name changed to Denison Mines Corp. pursuant to plan of arrangement acquisition of Denison Mines Inc. on the basis of 2.88 International Uranium shs. for 1 Denison sh. (see FPsurvey - Mines & Energy)

International Uranium Mining Co. Ltd. (Ont. 1942)
Dec. 1949 – Name changed to Acadia Uranium Mines Limited; basis 1 new for 4 old shs. ■

International Utilities Corp. (Md. 1924)
Apr. 27, 1973 – Name changed to IU International Corporation. ■

International Utility Structures Inc. (B.C. Feb. 1, 1994)
Apr. 1, 2005 – Wound up following sale of assets and interim distributions to secured creditors. There were no funds available for shldrs.

International Vending Technology Corp. (B.C. Jan. 17, 1983)
Nov. 12, 1985 – Name changed to Universal Movie Butler Inc.; basis 1 new for 4 old shs. ■

International Verifact Inc. (B.C. Apr. 15, 1983)
Oct. 1, 1984 – Continued into Canada.
July 3, 1998 – Name changed to IVI Checkmate Ltd. pursuant to plan of arrangement with Checkmate Electronic, Inc. Prior to name change, com. shs. exchanged for either exch. shs. of IVI Checkmate Ltd. or com. shs. of IVI Checkmate Corp., both on a one-for-one basis. ■

International Verifact Inc. (B.C. 1983)
Oct. 1, 1984 – Continued into Canada.
Jan. 5, 1995 – Amalgamated with Soricon Corporation and North Acquisition Corp. (a wholly owned subsid.) to continue under the International Verifact Inc. name; basis 1 new for 10 old shs.

International Veronex Resources Ltd. (B.C. Mar. 8, 1974)
Dec. 4, 1997 – Name changed to Veronex Technologies, Inc. ■

International Vestor Resources Ltd. (B.C. 1980)
Apr. 21, 1999 – Amalgamated with Auspex Minerals Ltd. to form EuroZinc Mining Corporation; basis 0.75 new for 1 Auspex sh. and 1 new for 1 International Vestor sh. (see EuroZinc Mining Corporation)

International Viking Resources Inc. (B.C. May 14, 1985)
Nov. 13, 1992 – Name changed to Saxony Explorations Ltd.; basis 1 new for 4 old shs. ■

International Visual Systems Ltd. (B.C. 1969)
1976 – Liquidated.

International Wallcoverings Ltd. (Can. July 13, 1972)
June 29, 1999 – Placed into receivership. KPMG Inc. was appointed receiver.

International Wastewater Systems Inc. (B.C. Feb. 4, 2011)
Sept. 11, 2017 – Name changed to Sharc International Systems Inc.; basis 1 new for 3.5 old shs. (see FPsurvey - Industrials)

International Water-Guard Industries Inc. (B.C. Sept. 22, 1989)
May 16, 2011 – Succeeded by IWG Technologies Inc. pursuant to an internal reorganization whereby International Water-Guard became a wholly owned subsid. of IWG Technologies. ■

International Waterways Navigation Ltd. (Can. 1922)
Dec. 31, 1941 – Ceased operations. Charter surrendered.

International Wayside Gold Mines Ltd. (B.C. Feb. 12, 1970)
Jan. 21, 2010 – Name changed to Barkerville Gold Mines Ltd. ■

International Wellington Resources Ltd. (B.C. June 20, 1953)
Aug. 2, 1983 – Name changed to Consolidated Wellington Resources Ltd.; basis 1 new for 5 old shs. ■

International Werner Technologies Inc. (B.C. 1981)
Aug. 5, 1994 – Dissolved and struck off register.

International Westward Development Corporation (B.C. June 9, 1978)
Apr. 23, 1986 – Name changed to J.R. Energy Ltd.; basis 1 new for 5 old shs. ■

International Wex Technologies Inc. (Can. June 3, 1987)
Oct. 27, 2004 – Name changed to Wex Pharmaceuticals Inc. ■

International Wildcat Resources Ltd. (B.C. Mar. 5, 1979)
Oct. 2, 1991 – Name changed to Wildcat Trading Corp.; basis 1 new for 3 old shs. ■

International Wildrose Resources Ltd. (B.C. 1979)
Dec. 8, 1987 – Amalgamated with Brigade Resources Inc. (1 for 3), Consolidated Dakota Resources Ltd. (1 for 1) and Mac-Am Resources Corp. (1 for 1) to continue as Colossus Resource Equities Inc.; basis 1 new for 1 old sh.

International Zimtu Technologies Inc. (B.C. Oct. 27, 1986)
Sept. 19, 2006 – Name changed to Petrol One Corp. and continued into Canada; basis 1 new for 1 old sh. ■

Internet Card Security Inc. (Que. Feb. 26, 1996)
June 4, 2010 – Dissolved.

Internet Identity Presence Company Inc. (Ont. Sept. 19, 1997)
Nov. 16, 2005 – Name changed to Geophysical Prospecting Inc. ■

Internet Liquidators International Inc. (Ont. Nov. 28, 1983)
July 17, 1998 – Name changed to Bid.Com International Inc. ■

Internet of Things Inc. (Ont. Apr. 27, 2015)
Sept. 1, 2020 – Name changed to Predictiv AI Inc.; basis 1 new for 5.5 old shs. (see FPsurvey - Industrials)

Internetwork Realty Corp. (B.C. Feb. 15, 1965)
Oct. 20, 1980 – Name changed to Skalbania Enterprises Ltd.; basis 1 new for 2 old shs. ■

InterNorth, Inc. (Del. 1930)
Apr. 10, 1986 – Name changed to Enron Corp.

Internova Resources Ltd. (B.C. 1985)
Jan. 22, 1996 – Name changed to Parisco Foods Limited; basis 1 new for 5 old shs. ■

InterOil Corporation (N.B. May 29, 1997 amalg.)
Aug. 24, 2007 – Continued into Yukon.
Feb. 23, 2017 – Acquired by Exxon Mobil Corporation; basis 0.5459 Exxon com. shs. and contingent resource payment (CRP) of up to US$33.94 per sh. for 1 InterOil sh.

Interplex Mining & Industrial Ltd. (B.C. 1937)
June 1972 – Name changed to Interplex Spa Industries Ltd. ■

Interplex Spa Industries Ltd. (B.C. 1937)
Jan. 27, 1978 – Name changed to Interplex Industries Ltd.

Interpool International Ltd. (Ont. 1960)
Nov. 30, 1971 – Assets transferred to Steadman Containers Ltd. and shs. exchanged on a 1 for 1 basis for shs. of Interpool Limited.

Interpool Limited (Bahamas 1968)
Sept. 18, 1978 – Acquired by Thyssen-Bornemisza N.V. for US$40 per sh.

Interprovincial Building Credits, Ltd. (Can. 1950)
Jan. 2, 1969 – Most com. shs. acquired early 1963 by Traders Finance Corp. Ltd. for $9.75 per sh. Name subsequently changed to Traders Homeplan Ltd.

Interprovincial Cold Storages Ltd. (Can. 1954)
Mar. 14, 1955 – Name changed to Trans Canada Freezers Limited.

Interprovincial Dredging & Mining Co. Ltd. (Ont. 1945)
1971 – Name changed to Interprovincial Allied Enterprises Ltd.

Interprovincial Metals Ltd. (B.C. Feb. 1, 1966)
1968 – Name changed to Interprovincial Silver Mines Ltd. ■

Interprovincial Mining Corp. Ltd. (Que. 1945)
Apr. 13, 1974 – Charter cancelled.

Interprovincial Pipe Line Inc. (Can. Apr. 30, 1949; via Special Act of Parliament)
July 2, 1992 – Formed Interprovincial Pipe Line System Inc. following reorganization with substantially all of Interprovincial's assets and liabilities acquired by Interprovincial Pipe Line System Inc. making Pipe Line System Inc. the parent company; basis 1 new com. sh. and 1 new instalment receipt of Pipe Line System Inc. for 1 old com. sh. and 1 old instalment receipt. ■

Interprovincial Pipe Line Inc. (Can. June 2, 1980)
Oct. 13, 1998 – Name changed to Enbridge Pipelines Inc.

Interprovincial Pipe Line Ltd. (Can. Apr. 30, 1949; via Special Act of Parliament)
May 5, 1988 – Name changed to Interhome Energy Inc. ■

Interprovincial Pipe Line Limited (Can. June 2, 1980)
May 5, 1988 – Name changed to Interhome Energy Inc. ■

Interprovincial Pipe Line System Inc. (Can. Apr. 30, 1949; via Special Act of Parliament)
May 5, 1994 – Name changed to IPL Energy Inc. ■

Interprovincial Satellite Services Ltd. (Alta. May 24, 1991)
Nov. 9, 1995 – Continued into Canada.
Apr. 29, 1996 – Amalgamated in Canada to continue with same name.
May 10, 2000 – Name changed to Wireless Matrix Corporation. ■

Interprovincial Silver Mines Ltd. (B.C. Feb. 1, 1966)
Oct. 1977 – Name changed to Turismo Industries Ltd. ■

Interprovincial Steel and Pipe Corporation Ltd. (Sask. July 13, 1956)
Jan. 28, 1977 – Continued into Canada.
Apr. 2, 1984 – Name changed to IPSCO Inc. ∎

Interprovincial Utilities Ltd. (Can. 1950)
May 1957 – The Consumers' Gas Co. acquired all property, assets and rights for $19.25 per sh.

Interpublishing (Canada) Limited (Que. 1926)
1979 – Acquisition of all o/s shs. by The Pagurian Corporation Limited; basis 14 cl. A Pagurian spec. shs. for 10 com. shs.
1980 – Wound up.

Interpublishing Limited (Ont. Oct. 28, 1975)
Oct. 17, 1977 – Name changed to The Pagurian Corporation Limited. ∎

Interquest Incorporated (Ont. June 13, 1985 amalg.)
Dec. 13, 2007 – Placed into receivership. RSM Richter Inc. appointed receiver.

Interquest Resources Corporation (Ont. June 13, 1985 amalg.)
Dec. 2, 1992 – Name changed to Interquest Technologies Inc. ∎

Interquest Technologies Inc. (Ont. June 13, 1985 amalg.)
Oct. 5, 1995 – Name changed to Interquest Incorporated; basis 1 new for 4 old shs. plus 1 wt. for 20 old shs. ∎

Interra Copper Corp. (B.C. Aug. 30, 2018)
Mar. 3, 2025 – Name changed to Copper Quest Exploration Inc. (see FPsurvey - Mines & Energy)

Interra Exploration Inc. (B.C. Apr. 30, 2008)
Mar. 10, 2011 – Name changed to Simba Gold Corp. pursuant to Qualifying Transaction reverse takeover acquisition of Rogi Mining Limited. ∎

InterRent International Properties Inc. (Ont. July 17, 1998 amalg.)
Dec. 7, 2006 – Converted into an income trust named InterRent Real Estate Investment Trust following acquisition of 3 private property companies; basis 1 trust unit for 10 com. shs.

InterRent Properties Ltd. (Ont. July 17, 1998 amalg.)
Feb. 28, 2001 – Name changed to InterRent International Properties Inc.; basis 1 new for 4 old shs. ∎

Intersoft Technologies Inc. (Alta. 1983)
Feb. 1, 1997 – Dissolved and struck from register.

InterStar Group Inc. (Can. Aug. 22, 1989)
Nov. 2, 2004 – Name changed to Theralase Technologies Inc. (see FPsurvey - Industrials)

InterStar Mining Group Inc. (Can. Aug. 22, 1989)
Nov. 12, 2003 – Name changed to InterStar Group Inc. ∎

Interstat Ventures Inc. (B.C. Sept. 17, 1985)
Apr. 23, 1996 – Name changed to Consolidated Interstat Ventures Inc.; basis 1 new for 3 old shs. ∎

Interstate Energy Corp. (B.C. 1981)
Aug. 1, 1990 – Amalgamated with Achilles Resources Ltd. (1 for 4.5), Golden Iskut Resources Incorporated (1 for 8) and International Phoenix Energy Corporation (1 for 8) to form a new co. Aegis Resources Ltd.; basis 1 new for 14 old shs. (see Aegis Resources Ltd.)

Interstate Royalty Corp. Ltd. (Can. 1932)
1955 – Name changed to Lochaber Oil Corporation Ltd. ∎

Interstrat Resources Inc. (B.C. 1979)
June 12, 1992 – Dissolved and struck off register.

InterTAN, Inc. (Del. June 1986)
May 20, 2004 – Acquired indirectly by Circuit World Stores, Inc. for Cdn$14 per sh.

The Intertain Group Limited (Ont. Nov. 26, 2010)
Jan. 25, 2017 – All o/s com. shs. exchanged on a 1-for-1 basis for: a) 1 ordinary sh. of Jackpotjoy plc (new parent company); or b) 1 Intertain exchangeable sh. (eligible Cdn. residents only).
Jan. 13, 2020 – All o/s exch. shs. not already held acquired by Intertain CallCo ULC; basis £6.83389 cash per exch. sh.

Intertainment Media Inc. (Alta. Aug. 22, 2000)
Oct. 2, 2019 – Struck from registry and dissolved.

Inter.tain.net Inc. (Ont. Mar. 7, 1996 amalg.)
Aug. 12, 1996 – Name changed to CryptoLogic Inc. ∎

Intertape Polymer Group Inc. (Can. Dec. 22, 1989)
July 4, 2022 – Acquired by Clearlake Capital Group, L.P.; basis Cdn$40.50 cash per sh.
July 4, 2022 – Continued into British Columbia.

Intertech Minerals Corp. (B.C. Feb. 10, 1988)
Apr. 25, 2002 – Name changed to Mantle Minerals Inc.; basis 1 new for 8 old shs. ∎

Intertel Communications Inc. (B.C. June 5, 1981)
Sept. 1, 1993 – Name changed to IntelCom Group Inc. ∎

IntesaBci Canada (Can. Oct. 8, 1981)
May 1, 2003 – Name changed to Intesa Bank Canada.

Intex Mining Company Limited (Ont. May 14, 1969)
Apr. 25, 1997 – Formed High American Gold Inc. in Ontario on amalgamation with Stromatalite Resource Corp., constituting a reverse takeover by Stromatalite; basis 1 new for 1 Stromatalite sh. and 1 new for 3 Intex shs. ∎

Inti Gas Engineering Ltd. (Can. - unspecified)
1968 – Assets and franchises acquired by James United Steel.

Intier Automotive Inc. (Ont. Jan. 2, 2000)
Apr. 4, 2005 – Privatized by major shldr. Magna International Inc.; basis either 0.41 new Magna cl. A sh. or cash equivalent for 1 old Intier cl. A sh.

Intigold Mines Ltd. (B.C. Apr. 18, 2008)
Oct. 26, 2020 – Voluntarily delisted.
Apr. 19, 2021 – Name changed to Calibri Resources Inc. (see FPsurvey - Mines & Energy)

Intimate Apparel Inc. (unknown)
Oct. 1964 – Acquired by Montex Holdings Ltd. (see Montex Holdings Ltd.)

Intirmac Industrial Corporation (B.C. Apr. 16, 1980)
Dec. 7, 1998 – Name changed to Sniper Enterprises Inc. ∎

IntraCoastal System Engineering Corporation (B.C. Dec. 10, 1992)
Oct. 10, 2005 – Dissolved and struck from register.

Intracorp Resources Corporation (Alta. Mar. 4, 1993)
Mar. 29, 1996 – Name changed to Proteus Environmental Inc. ∎

Intrawest Corporation (B.C. Nov. 23, 1979)
Jan. 14, 2002 – Continued into Canada.
Oct. 26, 2006 – Name changed to Intrawest ULC pursuant to Plan of Arrangement acquisition by Fortress Investment Group LLC for US$35 per sh.

Intrawest Development Corporation (B.C. Nov. 23, 1979)
Mar. 10, 1993 – Name changed to Intrawest Corporation. ∎

Intrepid Minerals Corporation (Can. Aug. 11, 1995)
July 4, 2006 – Plan of Arrangement amalgamation with Australian co. NuStar Mining Corporation Limited to continue as NuStar (which subsequently changed its name to Intrepid Mines Limited); basis either 1 new Intrepid NuStar Exchange Corporation exch. sh., or 1 new Intrepid Mines ordinary sh. for 1 old Intrepid Minerals sh.
Name changed to Troy Resources Argentina Ltd.

Intrepid NuStar Exchange Corporation (Can. 2006)
May 1, 2009 – All o/s exch. shs. redeemed by 6554636 Canada Ltd.; basis 1 Intrepid Mines Limited ord. sh. for 1 Intrepid NuStar exch. sh.

Intrex, The International Real Estate Exchange Corporation (B.C. May 17, 1979)
Aug. 1, 1984 – Name changed to 2018 Investments Ltd. ∎

Intrinsic Capital Inc. (B.C. Nov. 10, 1999)
Jan. 30, 2004 – Transaction with Stealth Ventures Ltd. to acquire ($0.25 per unit) and distribute 700,000 Stealth units to shldrs. Subsequent wind-up represents company's Qualifying Transaction. (see Stealth Ventures Ltd.)

Intrinsic4D Inc. (Ont. Sept. 7, 2010)
Jan. 29, 2019 – Name changed to Must Capital Inc.; basis 1 new for 25 old shs. (see FPsurvey - Industrials)

Intrinsyc Software, Inc. (B.C. July 19, 1995)
May 1, 2003 – Continued into Canada.
May 9, 2003 – Name changed to Intrinsyc Software International, Inc. ∎

Intrinsyc Software International, Inc. (Can. May 1, 2003)
June 19, 2014 – Name changed to Intrinsyc Technologies Corporation. ∎

Intrinsyc Technologies Corporation (Can. May 1, 2003)
Jan. 21, 2020 – Acquired by Lantronix. Inc.; basis US$0.55 cash and 0.2135 Lantronix com. shs for 1 Intrinsyc sh.

Intuitivo Capital Corporation (Ont. Apr. 3, 2007)
Dec. 30, 2009 – Name changed to Argonaut Gold Ltd. pursuant to Qualifying Transaction reverse takeover acquisition of Argonaut Gold Inc. and subsequent amalgamation of Argonaut with wholly owned 1813214 Ontario Inc. to continue as Argonaut Gold Inc.; basis 1 new for 30 old shs. ∎

Invaday Mining & Exploration Ltd. (Ont. 1944)
Nov. 5, 1962 – Dissolved.

Invader Exploration Inc. (Alta. May 8, 1996)
Apr. 21, 2004 – Plan of Arrangement acquisition by Troutline Investments Inc. which was subsequently acquired by Innova Exploration Ltd.; basis 0.86 new Troutline sh. for 1 old Invader sh. (see Troutline Investments Inc.)

Invader Resources Ltd. (B.C. 1983)
Feb. 4, 1985 – Name changed to Chapel Resources Inc. ∎

Invenio Resources Corp. (B.C. Dec. 20, 1996)
Feb. 12, 2015 – Name changed to Greatbanks Resources Ltd. ∎

Inventronics Limited (Man. Feb. 10, 1970)
Nov. 2, 2000 – Continued into Alberta. (see FPsurvey - Industrials)

Invermere Resources Ltd. (Can. Jan. 26, 1981)
Feb. 28, 1983 – Name changed to Canalands Resources Corporation prior to amalgamation with Canalands Energy Corporation; basis 1 new for 1 old sh. ∎

Inverness Petroleum Ltd. (Can. Nov. 16, 1987)
Mar. 26, 1996 – Amalgamated with 3220206 Canada Ltd., a wholly owned subsid. of Rigel Energy Corporation; basis 0.625 Rigel shs. for 1 Inverness sh. (see Rigel Energy Corporation)

Inverpower Controls Ltd. (Ont. Aug. 8, 1980)
July 17, 2001 – Substantially all assets and a portion of liabilities acquired by Cambridge, Mass.-based SatCon Technology Corporation for US$100,000 and 400,000 com. shs. paid to creditors. Name subsequently changed to 1080854 Ontario Limited and delisted May 31, 2002.

Invesprint Corporation (Ont. Mar. 19, 1956)
May 20, 2005 – Acquired indirectly by Metro Label Group Inc. for $1.20 per sh.

Les Investissements Embrygènes ltée (Que. Apr. 24, 1987)
Apr. 24, 1992 – Acquired by J.S. Finance Canada Inc.; basis 1 J.S. Finance pref. sh. for 10 Embrygenes shs. (see J.S. Finance Canada Inc.)

Investissements St-Pierre inc. (Que. July 17, 2006)
June 7, 2007 – Name changed to Cartier Resources Inc. (see FPsurvey - Mines & Energy)

Investment Foundation Ltd. (Que. Mar. 2, 1929)
Mar. 11, 1977 – Continued into Canada.
Dec. 2, 1982 – Name changed to IFL Investment Foundation (Canada) Ltd. ∎

Investment Grade Infrastructure Bond Fund (Ont. Jan. 26, 2015)
Sept. 20, 2019 – Terminated. Net assets of the fund were distributed to the unithldrs. on a pro rata basis and the fund was dissolved.

Investment Grade Managed Duration Income Fund (Ont. July 3, 2015)
Jan. 31, 2022 – Terminated. Class T units redeemed for an amount equal to the net asset value per unit.

Investment Grade Trust (Ont. Jan. 28, 2003)
Jan. 2, 2013 – Redeemed for $9.78 per unit.

Investment Properties International, Limited (Ont. 1965)
Oct. 22, 1973 – Placed into liquidation. PricewaterhouseCoopers Inc. was appointed liquidator.

InvestorLinks.com Inc. (Ont. May 14, 1985)
Sept. 7, 2001 – Name changed to API Electronics Group Inc. following reverse takeover acquisition of Delaware-based API Electronics, Inc.; basis 1 new for 3 old shs. ∎

The Investors Group (Man. 1940)
Sept. 22, 1986 – Name changed to 280 Broadway Holding Corp. ∎

Investors Group Inc. (Can. Aug. 3, 1978)
May 17, 2004 – Name changed to IGM Financial Inc. (see FPsurvey - Industrials)

Investors Syndicate of Canada Ltd. (Man. 1940)
Sept. 1964 – Name changed to The Investors Group. ∎

Investus Real Estate Inc. (Can. Feb. 27, 2007)
July 6, 2011 – Acquired by a wholly owned subsid. of Société de Développement Alpha by way of amalg.; basis 1 redeemable pref. cl. A sh. for 1 Investus com. sh. immediately redeemed for 20¢ per pref. sh.

Invex Resources Limited (B.C. Sept. 29, 1980 amalg.)
Dec. 1, 1981 – Amalgamated with Imperial Metals & Power Ltd. (1 for 2) and Risby Tungsten Mines Ltd. (1 for 2) to form Imperial Metals Corporation; basis 1 new Imperial Metals sh. for 1 old Invex sh.

Invicta Energy Corp. (Alta. Nov. 12, 2009)
May 6, 2013 – Acquired by Whitecap Resources Inc.; basis either $0.51911 or 0.05891 Whitecap shs. for 1 Invicta sh.

Invicta Explorations Ltd. (Ont. 1968)
Oct. 18, 1976 – Dissolved. Distributed $1.19 per sh. to shldrs., Dec. 31, 1975.

Invicta Oil & Gas Ltd. (B.C. Feb. 24, 2000)
Mar. 28, 2008 – Name changed to LNG Energy Ltd. ∎

Invictus Financial Inc. (Colo. Dec. 6, 1994)
Dec. 22, 2022 – Name changed to Mapath Capital Corp. and continued into British Columbia. (see FPsurvey - Industrials)

Invictus MD Strategies Corp. (B.C. Feb. 11, 2014)
Mar. 1, 2023 – Privatized via an amalgamation with wholly owned Gene-Etics Strains Co.; basis 0.005 Amalco shs. for 1 Invictus sh., redeemed for $1.60 cash per sh.

Invictus Mines & Oils Ltd. (Alta. 1973)
May 1976 – Name changed to Invictus Petro Minerals Ltd.; basis 1 new for 2 old shs. ∎

Invictus Oil & Minerals Ltd. (Que. 1971)
Nov. 1975 – All assets and undertakings sold to Invictus Mines & Oils Ltd. Charter surrendered.

Invictus Petro Minerals Ltd. (Alta. 1973)
Dec. 22, 1977 – Amalgamated with Sackville Oils & Minerals Ltd. (1 for 4) to form Seagull Resources Ltd.; basis 1 new for 10 old shs. ∎

Inwest Resources Ltd. (Can. Apr. 16, 1987)
May 2, 2002 – Dissolved.

Inzeco Holdings Inc. (Alta. May 30, 1997)
Apr. 9, 2001 – Name changed to RTICA Corporation. ∎

IoGold Systems Canada Incorporated (N.S. Mar. 5, 1997)
Mar. 29, 1999 – Continued into Ontario.
July 27, 2001 – Name changed to Candor Ventures Corp.; basis 1 new for 5 old shs. ∎

Ion Energy Ltd. (Alta. June 5, 2017)
Sept. 1, 2023 – Name changed to Lithium ION Energy Ltd. (see FPsurvey - Mines & Energy)

Iona Appliances Inc. (Ont. May 12, 1986)
May 6, 1997 – Name changed to Fantom Technologies Inc. ∎

Iona Energy Inc. (Alta. May 27, 2011 amalg.)
Nov. 2, 2017 – Dissolved and struck from registry.

Iona Industries Inc. (B.C. 1976)
Dec. 10, 1986 – Name changed to Aigner Holdings Ltd.; basis 1 new for 8 old shs. ∎

Ionarc Smelters Ltd. (B.C. 1967)
Jan. 30, 1978 – Name changed to International Ionarc Inc. ∎

Ionic Energy Inc. (Alta. Jan. 1, 1998 amalg.)
Apr. 17, 2001 – Acquired by Shiningbank Energy Income Fund; basis 0.306 Shiningbank trust units or $5.10 for 1 Ionic sh. (see Shiningbank Energy Income Fund)

Ionic Ventures Inc. (Alta. Jan. 16, 1995)
Jan. 1, 1998 – Formed Ionic Energy Inc. in Alberta on Major Transaction reverse takeover acquisition of and amalgamation with Ionic Energy Inc. ∎

Iori Enterprises Inc. (B.C. Mar. 17, 1983)
Feb. 16, 1987 – Name changed to Golden Band Resources Inc. ∎

Iori International Oil Royalties Inc. (B.C. Mar. 17, 1983)
Apr. 14, 1986 – Name changed to Iori Enterprises Inc. ∎

Iota Explorations Ltd. (B.C. Sept. 4, 1986)
Feb. 10, 1992 – Name changed to Mekong International Development Corp. ∎

iPerceptions Inc. (Can. July 3, 2007 amalg.)
Mar. 28, 2012 – Privatized at 8¢ per sh.

iPerform Strategic Partners Hedge Fund (Ont. Apr. 29, 2002)
Mar. 24, 2003 – Name changed to BluMont Strategic Partners Hedge Fund. ∎

iPerformance Fund Inc. (Alta. Dec. 17, 1999)
June 30, 2003 – Name changed to BluMont Capital Inc. and continued into Ontario. ∎

Iplayco Corporation Ltd. (Alta. July 27, 1999)
Jan. 3, 2020 – Acquired by TSL888 Investments, Inc.; basis Cdn$0.50 cash per com. sh.

iQuest Networks Inc. (Wyo. Apr. 24, 1998)
Oct. 28, 2003 – Name changed to Quest Ventures Inc.; basis 1 new for 4 old shs. ∎

Irex Iron Mines Ltd. (Ont. 1958)
1962 – Amalgamated with Kelsey Lake Development Co. Ltd. to form Choiceland Iron Mines Ltd.; basis 1 new for 2 old shs.

Iriana Resources Corporation (B.C. Sept. 1, 1992)
Dec. 19, 1996 – Continued into Yukon.
June 21, 2004 – Formed Polaris Geothermal Inc. in Yukon on amalgamation with Polaris Geothermal Inc., constituting a reverse takeover by Polaris; basis 1 new cl. A vtg. sh. for 1 Polaris sh. and 1 new cl. B non-vtg. sh. for 40 Iriana shs. ∎

Iris Gold Mines Ltd. (Ont. Mar. 7, 1929)
Apr. 1, 1963 – Dissolved.

Iris Resources Inc. (B.C. 1984)
Sept. 26, 1986 – Name changed to Madison Holdings Ltd. ∎

Irish Copper Mines Ltd. (Ont. 1955)
July 11, 1978 – Name changed to Irish International Energy Resources Inc.; basis 1 new for 10 old shs. ∎

Irish Energy, Oil and Minerals Inc. (Ont. 1955)
Feb. 27, 1981 – Name changed to Lumax Oil & Gas Inc. ∎

Irish International Energy Resources Inc. (Ont. 1955)
Feb. 1980 – Name changed to Irish Energy, Oil and Minerals Inc. ∎

Iron Bay Mines Ltd. (Ont. 1954)
Dec. 19, 1966 – Name changed to Calmor Iron Bay Mines Limited; basis 1 new for 1 old sh. ∎

Iron Bridge Resources Inc. (Alta. Dec. 3, 2004)
Nov. 9, 2018 – Remaining 12.27% interest not previously acquired by Velvet Energy Ltd.; basis 1 redeem. pref. sh. for 1 Iron Bridge com. sh., immediately redeemed for $0.845 cash.

Iron City Mines Limited (Ont. Nov. 23, 1965)
Oct. 9, 1980 – Name changed to Petrolantic Resources Inc. ∎

Iron Cliff Mines Ltd. (Ont. 1957)
Jan. 28, 1976 – Amalgamated to form Gerrard Realty Incorporated; basis 1 new for 50 old shs.

Iron Creek Capital Corp. (Alta. Sept. 14, 2006)
June 25, 2008 – Continued into British Columbia.
Dec. 16, 2014 – Name changed to Revelo Resources Corp. following acquisition of Polar Star Mining Corporation. ∎

Iron Horse Resources Corp. (B.C. 1983)
June 5, 1992 – Dissolved and struck off register.

Iron King Mines Inc. (B.C. Feb. 16, 1983)
Apr. 23, 1992 – Name changed to Corriente Resources Inc.; basis 1 new for 3 old shs. ∎

Iron Lady Resources Inc. (B.C. July 7, 1987 amalg.)
Aug. 3, 1994 – Name changed to Takepoint Ventures Ltd.; basis 1 new for 3.4 old shs. ∎

Iron Lake Minerals Inc. (Alta. Aug. 10, 1996)
Apr. 10, 2006 – Formed Alturas Minerals Corp. in Canada pursuant to reverse takeover acquisition of and amalgamation with Alturas Minerals Corp.; basis 1 new for 3 old shs. (see FPsurvey - Mines & Energy)

Iron River Resources Ltd. (B.C. Dec. 5, 1983)
July 9, 1996 – Name changed to South Duval Gold Corp.; basis 1 new for 5 old shs. ∎

Iron South Mining Corp. (B.C. Apr. 11, 2000)
Sept. 21, 2016 – Name changed to Argentina Lithium & Energy Corp. (see FPsurvey - Mines & Energy)

Iron Springs Capital Corp. (Alta. Mar. 15, 2005)
Nov. 28, 2005 – Formed Kaboose Inc. in Canada following Qualifying Transaction acquisition of Kaboose Inc. (previously named Kaboose.com Inc.) for total consideration of 43,923,412 com. shs. at a deemed price of $0.70 per sh. ■

Iron Tank Resources Corp. (B.C. July 6, 2007)
Feb. 19, 2016 – Name changed to Spriza Media Inc. following reverse takeover acquisition of the assets of Spriza, Inc. ■

Ironclad Systems Inc. (Alta. Jan. 19, 1996)
July 2, 1998 – Name changed to Bikestar Inc. following Qualifying Transaction acquisition of Good Times Roll Bicycle Rentals Inc. ■

Ironco Mining & Smelting Ltd. (Ont. Nov. 7, 1961)
Jan. 1992 – Charter revived.
July 9, 1994 – Dissolved.

Ironhorse Oil & Gas Inc. (Alta. Nov. 26, 2002)
Feb. 6, 2018 – Name changed to Pond Technologies Holdings Inc. pursuant to reverse takeover acquisition of Pond Technologies Inc.; basis 1 new for 6.9 old shs. (see FPsurvey - Industrials)

Ironside Resources Inc. (B.C. Sept. 29, 2010 amalg.)
Nov. 30, 2018 – Name changed to Shine Minerals Corp. (see FPsurvey - Mines & Energy)

Ironwood Capital Corp. (B.C. Aug. 28, 2017)
Nov. 2, 2020 – Name changed to West Mining Corp. pursuant to Qualifying Transaction acquisition of property option. (see FPsurvey - Mines & Energy)

Ironwood Petroleum Ltd. (Alta. Apr. 8, 1987)
Nov. 24, 1998 – Acquired by 80045 Alberta Inc., a wholly owned subsid. of Big Horn Resources Ltd., for 76¢ per sh. (see Big Horn Resources Ltd.)

Ironwood Resources Inc. (Alta. Dec. 19, 1986)
Jan. 15, 1990 – Name changed to Wise Card Holdings Inc. ■

Iroquois Glass Limited (Can. 1958)
Oct. 1965 – Merged with Sogemines Limited; basis 0.75 new com. for each pref. and 0.075 new com. for each ord. sh.

Iroquois-Kirkland Mines Corp., Ltd. (Ont. 1920)
Sept. 17, 1956 – Dissolved.

Iroquois Mines Ltd. (B.C. 1967)
1968 – Name changed to Hertz Industries Limited. ■

Iroquois Petroleum Company (Que. 1963)
Mar. 22, 1975 – Dissolved.

Irvco Resources Corporation (Alta. May 30, 1979)
June 14, 1979 – Name changed to Irvco Resources Ltd. ■

Irvco Resources Ltd. (Alta. May 30, 1979)
Nov. 1, 1995 – Dissolved and struck off register.

Irvin Porcupine Gold Mines Ltd. (Ont. 1939)
Mar. 1960 – Charter cancelled.

Irving Bank Canada (Can. 1981)
Oct. 7, 1989 – Amalgamated with The Bank of New York Company, Inc.

Irvington Mining Co. Ltd. (Ont. 1949)
Dec. 6, 1972 – Dissolved.

Irwin Toy Limited (Ont. Mar. 26, 1969 amalg.)
May 29, 2001 – Acquired by IT Acquisition Ltd. for $6.25 per sh.

iSCOPE INC. (Alta. May 12, 1998)
Nov. 2, 2009 – Dissolved and struck from register.

Isaacs Harbour Gold Explorations Inc. (Ont. 1983)
1986 – Name changed to Sabra-Dent Dental Supplies Ltd. (see FPsurvey - Industrials)

Isec Canada Ltd. (Can. 1967)
Dec. 16, 1980 – Dissolved.

iseemedia inc. (Can. Oct. 31, 2003)
Jan. 11, 2010 – Acquired by Synchornia plc; basis 4.03 ordinary shs. for 1 old sh.
June 7, 2011 – Name changed to Synchronia Inc.

Isee3D, Inc. (Can. Feb. 9, 1981)
Aug. 17, 2014 – Dissolved.

iShares Equal Weight Banc & Lifeco Fund (Ont. Apr. 5, 2007)
Oct. 18, 2013 – Name changed to iShares Equal Weight Banc & Lifeco ETF.

iShares Gold Bullion Fund (Ont. May 19, 2009)
Oct. 30, 2013 – Name changed to iShares Gold Bullion ETF.

iShares Silver Bullion Fund (Ont.)
Oct. 30, 2013 – Name changed to iShares Silver Bullion ETF.

Ishtar Investments Inc. (Alta. Nov. 5, 1996)
Dec. 1, 1998 – Name changed to Ishtar Seniors Communities Inc. ■

Ishtar Seniors Communities Inc. (Alta. Nov. 5, 1996)
Dec. 7, 1998 – Continued into Canada.
Aug. 16, 2000 – Name changed to Amica Mature Lifestyles Inc. ■

Iskut Gold Corp. (B.C. July 13, 1987)
May 2, 1994 – Name changed to A&B Geoscience Corporation. ■

Iskut River Mines Ltd. (Ont. 1943)
Apr. 15, 1965 – Dissolved.

Iskut Silver Mines Ltd. (B.C. 1965)
Mar. 1978 – Name changed to Commonwealth Minerals Ltd.; basis 1 new for 4 old shs. ■

Island Arc Exploration Corporation (B.C. Aug. 29, 1986)
May 17, 2011 – Name changed to Solace Resources Corp.; basis 1 new for 5 old shs. ■

Island Arc Exploration Inc. (B.C. Aug. 29, 1986)
Apr. 30, 2003 – Name changed to Island Arc Mining Corporation; basis 1 new for 4 old shs. ■

Island Arc Mining Corporation (B.C. Aug. 29, 1986)
May 10, 2004 – Name changed to Island Arc Exploration Corporation; basis 1 new for 2 old shs. ■

Island-Arc Resources Corporation (B.C. Aug. 29, 1986)
Nov. 12, 2001 – Name changed to Island Arc Exploration Inc.; basis 1 new for 2 old shs. ■

Island Canyon Mines Inc. (B.C. 1980)
June 26, 1987 – Name changed to Access Technologies Inc. ■

Island Copper Mines Ltd. (B.C. 1952)
Aug. 8, 1963 – Name changed to Arlington Silver Mines Ltd. ■

Island Lake Mines Ltd. (Man. 1932)
Mar. 11, 1959 – Charter cancelled.

Island Mining and Explorations Co. Ltd. (B.C. Mar. 29, 1962)
May 28, 1991 – Delisted from the Vancouver Stock Exchange. Subsequently struck from register and dissolved for failure to file.

Island Mountain Gold Mines Ltd. (B.C. Feb. 4, 1981)
Feb. 1, 2006 – Name changed to Lions Gate Energy Inc.; basis 1 new for 4 old shs. ■

Island Mountain Mines Co. Ltd. (B.C. 1933)
Nov. 1957 – Liquidated.
1959 – Dissolved. Total distribution of 92.6¢ per sh.

Island Oil & Gas Co. Ltd. (Ont. 1907)
Feb. 15, 1960 – Dissolved.

Island Oils Ltd. (unknown)
Sept. 20, 1941 – Placed into voluntary liquidation.

Island Technology Corporation (B.C. 1983)
Feb. 11, 1987 – Name changed to Hiburd Properties Inc. ■

Island Telecom Inc. (P.E.I. 1929)
June 1, 1999 – Amalgamated with Bruncor Inc., Maritime Telegraph and Telephone Company, Limited and NewTel Enterprises Limited to form Aliant Inc.; basis 1 new Aliant com. sh. for 1 old Island Telecom com. sh. (see Aliant Inc.)

The Island Telephone Company Limited (P.E.I. 1929)
May 22, 1998 – Name changed to Island Telecom Inc. ■

Island Tug & Barge Ltd. (B.C. 1943)
1968 – Wholly owned subsid. of Genstar Ltd. Publicly held 5% 1st pref. shs. redeemed at $12.50 per sh.

Isle Dieu Mattagami Mines Ltd. (Ont. 1958)
May 10, 1989 – Amalgamated with Noranda Inc. (see Noranda Inc.)

Isle of Pines Mining Co. Ltd. (Ont. 1947)
1953 – Name changed to Caribbean Gold Mines Ltd.; basis 1 new for 7 old shs. ■

Isleshaven Capital Corporation (B.C. 1979)
June 17, 1991 – Name changed to Nortel Communications Inc. ■

Iso Mines Ltd. (Ont. 1952)
Sept. 1979 – Merged with Highmont Mining Corporation; basis $3.00 for ea. sh. held or 1 cl. B Teck Corporation pref. sh. for ea. 5 shs. held. Teck pref. redeem. within 30 days or conv. into Teck B com.

Iso Uranium Mines Ltd. (Ont. 1952)
1959 – Name changed to Iso Mines Ltd. ■

IsoEnergy Ltd. (B.C. Feb. 2, 2016)
June 20, 2024 – Continued into Ontario. (see FPsurvey - Mines & Energy)

Isotechnika Inc. (Alta. June 16, 1993)
June 18, 2009 – Succeeded by Isotechnika Pharma Inc. pursuant to plan of arrangement with Paladin Labs Inc. whereby Paladin acquired Isotechnika Inc. and spun off the business to Isotechnika Pharma Inc. ■

Isotechnika Pharma Inc. (Alta. Apr. 27, 2009)
Oct. 23, 2013 – Name changed to Aurinia Pharmaceuticals Inc. following acquisition of (old) Aurinia Pharmaceuticals Inc.; basis 1 new for 50 old shs. (see FPsurvey - Industrials)

IsoTis S.A. (Switzerland June 27, 1996)
July 30, 2007 – Acquired by IsoTis, Inc.; basis 1 new IsoTis, Inc. sh. for 10 old IsoTis S.A. shs.

Isotope Products Limited (Ont. 1951)
Nov. 1957 – Merged with Curtiss-Wright of Canada Ltd. to form Canadian Curtiss-Wright Ltd.

Israel Capital Canada Corp. (B.C. Aug. 15, 2019)
Feb. 2, 2022 – Name changed to Frequency Exchange Corp. pursuant to the Qualifying Transaction reverse takeover acquisition of FREmedica Technologies Inc. (see FPsurvey - Industrials)

Israel Continental Oil Company Limited (Ont. 1952)
July 11, 1980 – Name changed to Wimberley Resources Ltd. (see FPsurvey - Mines & Energy)

Israel Discount Bank of Canada (Can. Jan. 21, 1982)
Jan. 1, 1997 – Amalgamated with Republic National Bank of New York (Canada).

iSTAR internet inc. (Can. Aug. 10, 1995)
June 8, 1998 – Privatized for 75¢ per sh. prior to consolidation, all o/s com. shs. consolidated on a 1-for-8,500,000 basis.

Itafos (Cayman Islands Oct. 27, 2016)
July 1, 2021 – Name changed to Itafos Inc. and continued into Delaware pursuant to change of jurisdiction from Cayman Islands to Delaware. (see FPsurvey - Mines & Energy; FPsurvey - Industrials)

Italia Copper Ltd. (Que. 1956)
Sept. 9, 1972 – Dissolved.

Itasca Capital Ltd. (B.C. Sept. 17, 1979)
Jan. 13, 2021 – Name changed to GreenFirst Forest Products Inc. ■

iTech Capital Corp. (Yuk. July 27, 1998)
May 15, 2003 – Name changed to Sirit Inc. ■

itemus inc. (Can. May 13, 1994)
July 31, 2001 – Declared bankruptcy. A. Farber & Partners Inc. was appointed trustee.
Sept. 19, 2005 – Dissolved.

Iteration Energy Ltd. (Alta. Feb. 14, 1994)
June 29, 2010 – Formed Chinook Energy Inc. in Alberta following acquisition by and subsequent amalgamation with Storm Ventures International Inc.; basis $1.05 plus 0.24 Storm Ventures shs. for 1 Iteration Energy sh. ■

Ithaca Energy Inc. (Alta. Apr. 27, 2004)
June 8, 2017 – All o/s shs. not already held acquired by Delek Group Ltd.; basis Cdn$1.95 cash per sh. Continued into Jersey.

Ituna Capital Corporation (B.C. Aug. 26, 2011)
Aug. 26, 2014 – Name changed to Tarku Resources Ltd. following Qualifying Transaction reverse takeover acquisition of Clear Creek Resources Ltd. (see FPsurvey - Mines & Energy)

Ivaco Inc. (Can. Aug. 22, 1969)
Sept. 13, 2004 – Applied for protection under the Companies' Creditors Arrangement Act. Ernst & Young Inc. was appointed monitor.
Dec. 2004 – Sales of assets closed for approximately $275,000,000.
June 2008 – In December 2004, distribution of $12,000,000 made to National Bank of Canada, the company's secured lender and on Oct. 31, 2007, an additional distribution of $8,000,000 was made to the Bank. By June 2008, the Bank's claim had been paid in full.
Apr. 5, 2012 – Filed an assignment in bankruptcy and Ernst & Young Inc. was appointed trustee.
Oct. 12, 2013 – Trustee in bankruptcy, Ernst & Young Inc., was discharged. Unsecured creditors suffered a shortfall and there were no distrib. to shldrs.

Ivaco Industries Limited (Can. Aug. 22, 1969)
Nov. 15, 1978 – Name changed to Ivaco Ltd. ■

Ivaco Ltd. (Can. Aug. 22, 1969)
June 2, 1980 – Name changed to Ivaco Inc. ■

Ivan-Larder Mines Ltd. (Ont. 1937)
June 4, 1969 – Charter cancelled.

Ivana Capital Corporation (Can. May 17, 1984)
Feb. 3, 1993 – Name changed to First Ivana Technologies Ltd.; basis 1 new for 5 old shs. ■

Ivana Ventures Inc. (Alta. May 10, 1996)
Nov. 2, 2005 – Continued into British Columbia.
July 4, 2008 – Name changed to Ely Gold & Minerals Inc. ■

Ivanhoe Australia Limited (Australia Jan. 20, 2004)
July 8, 2013 – Name changed to Inova Resources Limited. ■

Ivanhoe Corporation (Que. 1953)
Oct. 1977 – Name changed to Ivanhoe Inc.

Ivanhoe Energy Inc. (Yuk. Feb. 21, 1995)
June 1, 2015 – Deemed bankrupt. Ernst & Young appointed trustee. All officers and directors resigned.
June 16, 2015 – Placed into receivership. KPMG Inc. court appointed receiver.
Oct. 2015 – Suncor Energy Inc. purchased the Tamarack property for an undisclosed amount.
Dec. 18, 2015 – Court-ordered distributions made and creditors suffered a shortfall; there were no distributions made to shldrs.
Jan. 20, 2016 – KPMG Inc. discharged as receiver and the director and officer funds amounting to $200,000 was turned over to Ernst & Young Inc. as bankruptcy trustee.
May 16, 2017 – Dissolved.

Ivanhoe Mines Ltd. (Yuk. Feb. 25, 1995)
Aug. 8, 2012 – Name changed to Turquoise Hill Resources Ltd. ■

Ivanplats Limited (B.C. Apr. 29, 1993)
May 5, 1995 – Continued into Yukon.
Sept. 11, 2012 – Continued into British Columbia.
Aug. 28, 2013 – Name changed to Ivanhoe Mines Ltd. (see FPsurvey - Mines & Energy)

Ivernia Inc. (N.B. June 16, 2000)
July 23, 2008 – Continued into Canada.
Nov. 18, 2015 – Name changed to LeadFX Inc.; basis 1 new for 75 old shs. ■

Ivernia West Inc. (N.B. June 16, 2000)
July 8, 2004 – Name changed to Ivernia Inc.; basis 1 new for 5 old shs. ■

Ivey Medical Systems Ltd (Can. 1968)
Dec. 16, 1980 – Dissolved.

Ivor Exploration Inc. (Can. July 4, 2011)
May 10, 2022 – Name changed to Kraken Energy Corp. ■

Ivory Energy Inc. (B.C. June 29, 1981)
June 22, 2007 – Continued into Alberta.
Apr. 1, 2009 – Acquired by Emergo Energy Inc. for $0.03782 per sh. and $226.92 for each $1,000 principal amt. of Ivory 9.5% conv. debs. Subsequently dissolved.

Ivory Oils & Minerals Inc. (B.C. June 29, 1981)
June 27, 2006 – Name changed to Ivory Energy Inc. following reverse takeover acquisition of 1078352 Alberta Ltd. for 25,615,264 shs.; basis 1 new for 2 old shs. ■

Ivrnet Inc. (Alta. Aug. 13, 1999)
July 31, 2003 – Continued into Alberta.
Dec. 1, 2023 – Acquired by N. Harris Computer Corporation, a wholly owned subsid. of Constellation Software Inc. All proceeds paid to creditors and all issued and o/s equity interests were cancelled without consideration.

Ivy Capital Corporation (Alta. Oct. 1, 1993)
Aug. 27, 1996 – Name changed to AdvantEdge International Inc.; basis 1 new sub. vtg. for 1 old com. sh. ■

ivyNET Corporation (Ont. Mar. 5, 1937)
Aug. 25, 2000 – Name changed to Saratoga Capital Corp.; basis 1 new for 10 old shs. ■

Iwasaki Explorations Ltd. (B.C. 1969)
June 27, 1977 – Dissolved.

iWave Information Systems Inc. (B.C. Apr. 20, 1979)
July 21, 2005 – Name changed to First Factor Developments Inc. ■

iWave.com, Inc. (B.C. Apr. 20, 1979)
June 28, 2002 – Name changed to iWave Information Systems Inc.; basis 1 new for 3 old shs. ■

iWeb Group Inc. (Can. Nov. 26, 2002)
June 20, 2011 – Amalgamated with 7807201 Canada Inc. and 7807210 Canada Inc., both controlled by Novacap Technologies III, L.P., Caisse de dépôt et placement du Québec and an investment vehicle affiliated with Bank Street Capital Partners to form a new co. (Amalco); basis for 1 Amalco pref. sh. for 1 iWeb sh., immediately redeemed for $1.50.

Ixora Communication Systems Inc. (B.C. May 13, 1981)
Oct. 4, 1991 – Dissolved and struck off register.

Ixpaco Industries Ltd. (Ont. 1972)
Mar. 1976 – Charter cancelled.

Ixtal International Technology Corporation (B.C. 1987)
Aug. 27, 1992 – Name changed to Job Industries Ltd.; basis 1 new for 3 old shs. (see FPsurvey - Industrials)

J

J5 Acquisition Corp. (Ont. July 15, 2009)
July 19, 2011 – Name changed to Trimel Pharmaceuticals Corporation pursuant to Qualifying Transaction acquisition of Trimel BioPharma Holdings Inc.; basis 1 new for 26.666 old shs. ■

J & L Capital Venture Corp. (Alta. May 6, 1997)
Feb. 18, 1999 – Name changed to Cancoil Integrated Services Inc. following Major Transaction acquisition of Cancoil Technology Corporation. ■

J. Bond Capital Corporation (B.C. Jan. 22, 2007)
Nov. 16, 2018 – Name changed to Bond Resources Inc. (see FPsurvey - Mines & Energy)

J. Harris & Sons, Limited (Ont. May 20, 1953)
Nov. 5, 1979 – Name changed to Harris Steel Group Inc. ■

J-Pacific Gold Inc. (B.C. Feb. 8, 1990)
Jan. 27, 2010 – Name changed to Sona Resources Corp.; basis 1 new for 5 old shs. ■

J55 Capital Corp. (B.C. June 27, 2018)
Sept. 5, 2019 – Name changed to Enthusiast Gaming Holdings Inc. pursuant to Qualifying Transaction acquisition of Aquilini GameCo Inc., and concurrent acquisition of (old) Enthusiast Gaming Holdings Inc.; basis 1 new for 8 old shs. (see FPsurvey - Industrials)

J. A. Vachon & Fils Ltée (Que. 1947)
1961 – Name changed to Vachon Inc. ■

JABA Exploration Inc. (Alta. Nov. 5, 1987)
Sept. 8, 2004 – Continued into British Columbia.
Dec. 17, 2004 – Name changed to Dundarave Resources Inc.; basis 1 new for 6 old shs. ■

JABA Inc. (Alta. Nov. 5, 1987)
Apr. 17, 2000 – Name changed to Consolidated JABA Inc.; basis 1 new for 10 old shs. ■

The J. B. McLean Publishing Company of Toronto (Limited) (Ont. Apr. 30, 1891)
Apr. 24, 1919 – Name changed to The Maclean Publishing Company, Limited. ■

JBZ Capital Inc. (Can. Feb. 7, 2008)
Nov. 8, 2011 – Name changed to Strata Minerals Inc. ■

J.C. International Petroleum Ltd. (Alta. Nov. 30, 1985 amalg.)
June 27, 1988 – Placed into receivership under Touche Ross Limited (later Deloitte & Touche Inc., Calgary).
1989 – All oil and gas properties sold. Creditors suffered a shortfall and shldrs. received no distribution.

The J.C. Smith Marketing Corporation (B.C. Jan. 21, 1987)
Oct. 19, 1998 – Name changed to Devin Energy Corporation. ■

The J.C. Smith Marketing Corporation (B.C. 1987)
Sept. 24, 1991 – Amalgamated with Southern Illinois Energy Corporation to form a new co. also known as The

J.C. Smith Marketing Corporation; basis 1 new for 1 old sh.

J. C. Wilson, Limited (Can. 1920)
June 1959 – Price Co. Ltd. (99.5% owned by Abitibi-Price) offered $16 for each com. sh.

JCI Technologies Inc. (Alta. Jan. 20, 1994)
Dec. 11, 2000 – Name changed to JCITech.com Inc. ■

JCITech.com Inc. (Alta. Jan. 20, 1994)
July 2, 2001 – Dissolved and struck from register.

J C P Marketing Inc. (Alta. 1987)
Mar. 1, 1996 – Dissolved and struck off register.

J. D. Carrier Shoe Co. Limited (Ont. 1944)
1979 – Majority of co. creditors accepted proposal for the creation of a new cl. of pref. stk. to be issued to unsecured creditors. Subsequently, all assets of co. liquidated. No distribution made to unsecured creditors nor any action with respect to proposed issue of pref. shs.

JDF Explorations Inc. (B.C. May 9, 2014)
Sept. 15, 2020 – Name changed to Valorem Resources Inc. ■

JDL Gold Corp. (B.C. Mar. 23, 2007)
Mar. 30, 2017 – Name changed to Trek Mining Inc. following acquisition of Luna Gold Corp. ■

JDS Capital Limited (Ont. 1978)
Sept. 16, 1988 – All o/s $2.21875 First Preferred Shares, Series A were redeemed; basis $25.50 per sh. plus accrued dividends of $0.0911813 per sh.

JDS FITEL Inc. (Can. July 21, 1981)
June 1, 1990 – Amalgamated in Canada to continue with same name. (see JDS Uniphase Canada Limited)
July 6, 1999 – Merged with California-based Uniphase Corporation to form JDS Uniphase Ltd.; basis 0.50855 exchangeable shs. in JDS Uniphase Canada Ltd. (a wholly owned subsid. of JDS Uniphase Ltd.) for 1 JDS FITEL com. sh. (see JDS Uniphase Canada Limited)

J.D.S. Investments Limited (Ont. Feb. 28, 1982 amalg.)
Oct. 30, 1995 – Dissolved.

JDS Uniphase Canada Limited (Can. Jan. 26, 1999)
Apr. 1, 2014 – All exch. shs. redeemed for parent JDS Uniphase Corporation com. shs.; basis 1 for 1. (see JDS Uniphase Corporation)

JDV Capital Corp. (B.C. Feb. 9, 2011)
Mar. 27, 2014 – Name changed to Margaret Lake Diamonds Inc. following Qualifying Transaction acquisition of an option to acquire an interest in the Margaret Lake diamond property; basis 1 new for 2 old shs. (see FPsurvey - Mines & Energy)

JEM Group Productions Inc. (B.C. Nov. 12, 1987)
Aug. 9, 1990 – Name changed to Harvard Capital Corporation; basis 1 new for 2 old shs. ■

JER Envirotech International Corp. (Yuk. May 15, 2000)
Feb. 13, 2006 – Continued into British Columbia.
June 4, 2012 – Dissolved and struck from register.

JG Capital Corp. (Ont. Dec. 14, 2007)
Jan. 12, 2010 – Formed VersaPay Corporation in Canada pursuant to Qualifying Transaction amalgamation with (old) VersaPay Corporation constituting a reverse takeover by VersaPay; basis 1 new for 7.5 old shs. ■

JG Wealth Inc. (B.C. Nov. 29, 2007)
Oct. 16, 2018 – Name changed to Pushfor Investments Inc. ■

JG Wealth Management Corporation (B.C. Nov. 29, 2007)
Nov. 24, 2017 – Name changed to JG Wealth Inc. ■

J. H. Ashdown Hardware Co. Ltd. (Can. 1902)
1968 – Acquired by Acklands Limited; basis one $16 par Acklands 6% cum. redeem. conv. and pref. sh. for each cl. A and B sh. of Ashdown. (see Acklands Limited)

JJR II Acquisitions Inc. (Ont. May 30, 2007)
Sept. 15, 2009 – Name changed to Sino Vanadium Inc. following Qualifying Transaction reverse takeover acquisition of Wellkan Resources Limited. ■

JJR IV Acquisition Inc. (B.C. Nov. 19, 2007)
Feb. 25, 2010 – Continued into Canada.
Mar. 1, 2010 – Formed BIOX Corporation in Canada pursuant to Qualifying Transaction amalgamation with (old) BIOX Corporation (deemed acquiror).; basis 1 new for 24 old shs. ■

JJR VI Acquisition Corp. (Ont. Dec. 21, 2009)
Dec. 30, 2010 – Name changed to Atlas Financial Holdings, Inc. and continued into Cayman Islands pursuant to Qualifying Transaction reverse takeover acquisition of American Insurance Acquisition Inc.; basis 1 new for 10 old shs.

JJR Capital Ventures Inc. (Ont. Oct. 1, 2003)
Aug. 2, 2005 – Name changed to Tonbridge Power Inc. ■

JKS Resources Inc. (B.C. Nov. 9, 2020)
May 30, 2024 – Name changed to Yukon Metals Corp. (see FPsurvey - Mines & Energy)

J. L. Retallack & Co. (unknown)
Oct. 1923 – Formed Whitewater Mines, Ltd. ■

JM Capital Corp. (Ont. June 6, 2006)
Nov. 26, 2008 – Formed Stans Energy Corp. in Ontario on Qualifying Transaction amalgamation of Stans Energy Corp. (deemed acquiror) with JM Amalco Corp., a wholly owned subsid. of JM Capital Corp., which then amalgamated with parent JM Capital. (see FPsurvey - Mines & Energy)

J-M Consolidated Gold Mines Ltd. (Ont. Feb. 18, 1932)
1949 – Name changed to Jaculet Mines Ltd.; basis 1 new for 3 old shs. ■

J.M. Saucier Ltée (Que. 1978)
Dec. 8, 1988 – All o/s com. shs. acquired by Atlantique Video and Sound Inc.; basis 1 cl. A sub. vtg. sh. of Atlantique for 4 com. shs. of Saucier. (see Atlantique Video & Sound Inc.)

J. M. Schneider Inc. (Ont. Dec. 30, 1930)
Apr. 30, 1980 – Name changed to The Heritage Group Inc. ■

J. M. Schneider, Limited (Ont. Dec. 30, 1930)
Oct. 26, 1975 – Name changed to Schneider Corporation. ■

J.M.B. Canadian Explorations Ltd. (Can. 1970)
June 17, 2015 – Dissolved and struck from register.

J.M.G. Manufacturing Ltd. (Can. - unspecified)
1967 – Acquired by Vascan Ltd. for $300,000, $200,000 in 5% notes and 250,000 Vascan shs. (see Vascan Ltd.)

JML Resources Ltd. (Ont. Feb. 12, 1997)
May 2, 2006 – Name changed to Aquila Resources Inc. following reverse takeover acquisition of Aquila Resources Corp.; basis 1 new for 3 old shs. ■

JNB Developments Co. Ltd. (B.C. May 19, 1999)
July 14, 2004 – Name changed to Cooper Minerals Inc. ■

JNC Resources Inc. (B.C. Apr. 1, 2019)
Sept. 16, 2021 – Name changed to RooGold Inc.; basis 1 new for 2 old shs. ■

JNR Resources Inc. (B.C. Sept. 18, 1979)
Feb. 6, 2012 – Acquired by Denison Mines Corp.; basis 0.073 Denison shs. for 1 JNR sh. ■

JPY Holdings Ltd. (Ont. June 29, 1993)
Nov. 14, 2007 – Continued into Canada. (see FPsurvey - Industrials)

J-Q Resources Inc. (Ont. June 30, 1936)
Sept. 21, 1987 – Name changed to International Pursuit Corporation. ■

J.R. Energy Ltd. (B.C. June 9, 1978)
Oct. 26, 1990 – Dissolved and struck off register.

J. R. Moodie Co. Ltd. (Ont. 1928)
1958 – Ceased operations. Machinery and equipment sold. Inventory of merchandise liquidated.

JRTL Capital Corp. (B.C. May 12, 2006)
Dec. 1, 2009 – Name changed to Tosca Mining Corp. pursuant to Qualifying Transaction acquisition of Valterra Resource Corp.'s 60% interest in the Swift Katie property. ■

J.S. Finance Canada Inc. (Que. Apr. 25, 1989)
Oct. 25, 1996 – All o/s pref. shs. redeemed for $2.00 per sh. plus accr. and unpaid divds.

J. S. Mitchell & Company Limited (Que. 1923)
Aug. 1964 – Private co. Shs. previously held by public acquired at $35 per sh. by Canada Permanent Trust Co., as agent.

JSS Resources Inc. (B.C. May 13, 1985)
July 26, 1999 – Name changed to WSi Interactive Corporation. ■

J.S.T. Mining Corporation Ltd. (Ont. 1965)
Oct. 1974 – Charter cancelled.

J.U.M. Capital Inc. (Ont. 1987)
Dec. 1, 2004 – Formed West 49 Inc. in Ontario on reverse takeover acquisition of and amalgamation with West 49 Inc.; basis 1 new for 10 old shs. ■

J. W. Mackenzie Oil & Gas Ltd. (Alta. 1977)
June 17, 1987 – Continued into Canada.
Oct. 30, 1987 – Name changed to MacQuest Resources Ltd. ■

JYW Capital Corp. (B.C. May 23, 2006)
June 11, 2010 – Name changed to China Coal Corporation pursuant to Qualifying Transaction reverse takeover acquisition of Golden Hill International Holdings Limited. ■

Jacaranda Gold Mines Ltd. (Ont. 1945)
Oct. 7, 1957 – Dissolved.

Jacaranda Gold Mining Syndicate Ltd. (Ont. 1945)
1945 – Assets acquired by Jacaranda Gold Mines Ltd.; basis 60 new for 1 old sh.

Jack Criswell Resources Ltd. (B.C. 1980)
Mar. 16, 1990 – Dissolved.

Jack The Gripper Inc. (Alta. Nov. 19, 1985)
May 1, 1993 – Dissolved.
May 20, 1994 – Revived.
Sept. 7, 1995 – Name changed to Standard Mining Inc.; basis 1 new for 8 old shs. ■

Jack Lake Mines Ltd. (Ont. Aug. 14, 1945)
1955 – Name changed to New Jack Lake Uranium Mines Ltd.; basis 1 new for 4 old shs. ■

Jack Pine Mines Ltd. (B.C. 1969)
Apr. 1979 – Charter cancelled.

Jackal Energy Inc. (Alta. Oct. 22, 1996)
Apr. 2, 2010 – Struck from registry and dissolved.

Jackfish Explorations Ltd. (B.C. 1983)
Sept. 24, 1985 – Name changed to Watcor Purification Systems Inc. ■

Jackie Mines Ltd. (Ont. 1945)
Mar. 1957 – Charter cancelled.

Jackmay Lead Mines Ltd. (Ont. 1945)
May 11, 1957 – Charter cancelled.

Jacknife Gold Mines Ltd. (Ont. 1944)
1955 – Name changed to Jacobus Mining Corp. Ltd.; basis 1 new for 4 old shs. ■

Jackpine Mining Co. Inc. (B.C. Dec. 23, 1991)
July 12, 1996 – Name changed to USV Telemanagement Inc. pursuant to reverse takeover acquisition of U.S. Voice Telemanagement, Inc. ■

Jackpot Copper Mines Ltd. (B.C. 1967)
Nov. 24, 1975 – Name changed to Con-Am Resources Ltd.; basis 1 new for 5 old shs. ■

Jackpot Uranium Mines Ltd. (Ont. 1952)
1955 – Name changed to Big Jackpot Mines Ltd. ■

Jackpot Uranium Mines Ltd. (Sask. 1953)
1955 – Name changed to Great Bear Lake Uranium Mines Ltd. and subsequently acquired by Tri-West Oil & Gas Ltd. ■

Jackson Basin Mining Co. Ltd. (B.C. 1951)
1955 – Name changed to Jackson Mines Ltd. and continued into British Columbia; basis 1 new for 3 old shs. ■

Jackson Hole Holdings Corp. (B.C. July 8, 1986)
Mar. 3, 1997 – Delisted from the Vancouver Stock Exchange. Subsequently struck from register and dissolved.

Jackson Mines Ltd. (B.C. 1955)
1956 – Merged into Trojan Consolidated Mines Ltd.; basis 1 new for 4 old shs.

Jackson Resources Ltd. (B.C. 1984)
May 17, 1985 – Name changed to Loadmaster Systems Inc.

Jacmar Explorations Ltd. (Ont. 1956)
Nov. 9, 1976 – Charter cancelled.

Jacob Gold Corporation (B.C. Mar. 5, 1981)
May 31, 1990 – Name changed to Sargon Resources Ltd.; basis 1 new for 5 old shs. ■

Jacobus Mining Corp. Ltd. (Ont. 1944)
Mar. 1976 – Charter cancelled.

Jacola Mines Ltd. (Ont. 1937)
Mar. 1976 – Charter cancelled.

Jacomat Mines Ltd. (Ont. 1945)
Aug. 1960 – Distribution of 0.4¢ per sh. made.

Jacomo Mines Limited (Ont. 1974)
Mar. 1, 1978 – Amalgamated with 3 other cos. to form Jaridge Explorations Inc.; basis 1 new for 4 old shs.

Jacqueline Gold Corporation (B.C. Aug. 19, 1979)
May 12, 1995 – Name changed to Stellar Gold Corp.; basis 1 new for 7 old shs. ■

Jacquet River Mines Ltd. (Ont. 1953)
1957 – Acquired by Grandroy Mines Ltd. (see Grandroy Mines Ltd.)

Jaculet Mines Ltd. (Ont. Feb. 18, 1932)
Sept. 1955 – Name changed to New Jaculet Mines Ltd.; basis sh. for sh. plus 1 Copper Cliff Consolidated Mining Corp. for each 6 Jaculet shs. ■

Jade Capital Corp. (Alta. June 9, 1997)
June 1, 2007 – Distribution of $0.0488 cash per sh. paid to shldrs. of record May 9, 2007.
Dec. 2, 2008 – Dissolved and struck from register.

Jade Energy Services Inc. (Alta. Apr. 8, 2004)
Mar. 17, 2006 – Name changed to Canyon Services Group Inc. ■

Jade Exploration and Development Ltd. (Alta.)
1960 – Struck off register.

Jadela Disposal Well Corp. (Alta. Feb. 26, 2009)
Jan. 12, 2021 – Name changed to Waskahigan Oil & Gas Corp. (see FPsurvey - Mines & Energy)

Jadela Oil Corp. (Alta. June 29, 2006 amalg.)
May 19, 2015 – Name changed to Tenth Avenue Petroleum Corp.; basis 1 new for 5 old shs. (see FPsurvey - Mines & Energy)

Jadestone Energy Inc. (B.C. Aug. 25, 1988)
Mar. 17, 2020 – Voluntarily delisted. Will continue to trade on the AIM market of the London Stock Exchange.

Jaeger Resources Ltd. (Ont. Nov. 8, 1985)
May 1, 1987 – Name changed to Edwards Steel Fabricators Inc. ■

Jafta International Inc. (B.C. 1967)
Oct. 5, 1987 – Name changed to Dornoch International Inc.; basis 6 new for 10 old shs. ■

Jaftek Ventures Inc. (Alta. 1986)
Apr. 1, 1991 – Struck off register.

Jager Metal Corp. (B.C. June 8, 1987)
Jan. 24, 2014 – Name changed to Jagercor Energy Corp.; basis 4 new for 1 old sh. ■

Jager Resources Inc. (B.C. Jan. 27, 2009)
Feb. 20, 2014 – Name changed to Sora Capital Corp.; basis 1 new for 10 old shs. ■

Jagercor Energy Corp. (B.C. June 8, 1987)
July 30, 2018 – Name changed to Gelum Capital Ltd.; basis 1 new for 20 old shs. ■

Jagor Resources Ltd. (Can. 1934)
Sept. 3, 1985 – Acquired by Normandie Resource Corporation; basis 1.6 Normandie shs. for 1 Jagor sh. (see Normandie Resource Corporation)

Jaguar Equities Inc. (B.C. Sept. 22, 1981)
June 11, 1993 – Name changed to International Jaguar Equities Inc.; basis 1 new for 5 old shs. ■

Jaguar Financial Corporation (Ont. July 2, 2008 amalg.)
Apr. 1, 2022 – Name changed to Maritime Launch Services Inc. pursuant to the reverse takeover acquisition of Maritime Launch Services Ltd. and concurrent amalgamation of Maritime Launch with wholly owned 4374344 Nova Scotia Limited (and continued as Maritime Launch Services (Nova Scotia) Ltd.). (see FPsurvey - Industrials)

Jaguar Financial Inc. (Que. Apr. 5, 1956)
July 2, 2008 – Formed Jaguar Financial Corporation in Ontario on amalgamation with new entity Jaguar Financial Corporation. ■

Jaguar International Equities Inc. (B.C. Sept. 22, 1981)
Mar. 18, 2002 – Name changed to Advectus Life Sciences Inc. ■

Jaguar Nickel Inc. (Que. Apr. 5, 1956)
July 11, 2007 – Name changed to Jaguar Financial Inc. ■

Jaguar Petroleum Corporation (Can. 1981)
June 17, 1997 – Acquired by Probe Exploration Inc.; basis 60¢ plus 0.34 Probe shs. for 1 Jaguar sh. (see Probe Exploration Inc.)

Jaguar Resources Corporation (B.C. Mar. 12, 1986)
Sept. 8, 2004 – Name changed to Brazauro Resources Corporation. ■

Jahala Lake Mines Ltd. (Ont. 1952)
Nov. 9, 1976 – Charter cancelled.

Jahala Lake Uranium Mines Ltd. (Ont. 1952)
1956 – Name changed to Jahala Lake Mines Ltd. ■

Jakarta Development Corp. (B.C. Sept. 25, 1985)
July 10, 1998 – Name changed to P P M Development Corp. ■

Jakland Capital Inc. (Alta. June 7, 1987)
Dec. 12, 1988 – Name changed to U-Pak Shipping Systems Inc. ■

Jalna Minerals Ltd. (B.C. June 27, 1974)
Sept. 29, 2010 – Formed Papuan Precious Metals Corp. in British Columbia following reverse takeover acquisition of and amalgamation with (old) Papuan Precious Metals Corp.; basis 1 new for 4 old shs. ■

Jalna Mining Corp. (B.C. June 27, 1974)
July 27, 1998 – Name changed to Kolyma Goldfields Ltd. following reverse takeover acquisition of Bahamas-incorporated Boston Management Corp.; basis 1 new for 2 old shs. ■

Jalna Resources Limited (B.C. June 27, 1974)
Feb. 17, 1988 – Name changed to Consolidated Jalna Resources Limited. ■

Jalna Resources Limited (B.C. June 27, 1974)
June 1, 2006 – Name changed to Jalna Minerals Ltd.; basis 2 new for 1 old sh. ■

Jamaica Hotel Enterprises Ltd. (Ont. 1957)
Dec. 28, 1964 – Dissolved.

Jamaica Public Service Ltd. (Can. 1928)
1969 – Charter cancelled; following distribution of 20 ordinary shs. of Jamaica Public Service Co. Ltd. plus a taxable cash distribution of $3.50 Cdn for ea. sh. Jamaica Public Service Ltd.

Jamaican Mining Ltd. (Ont. 1956)
Nov. 9, 1976 – Charter cancelled.

Jameland Mines Limited (Ont. May 10, 1961)
Sept. 10, 1981 – Name changed to Cotton Valley Resources Inc.; basis 1 new for 2.5 old shs. ■

James B. Carter Limited (Man. 1920)
Feb. 1972 – More than 99% of the o/s cl. A and B shs. acquired by The Budd Automotive Company of Canada Limited for $2,795,656 pay. to shldrs.

James Bay Mining Corp. Ltd. (Que. 1964)
Oct. 1973 – Charter cancelled.

James E. Wagner Cultivation Corporation (Ont. Mar. 30, 2017)
Feb. 15, 2022 – Filed an assignment in bankruptcy. KSV Restructuring Inc. was appointed trustee.

James Industries Inc. (B.C. June 22, 1973)
Apr. 28, 1987 – Name changed to International James Industries Inc. ■

James Kirkland Mines Ltd. (Ont. 1937)
1961 – Charter cancelled.

James River Mines Ltd. (Ont. 1965)
Mar. 6, 1979 – Charter cancelled.

James Robertson Co. Ltd. (Can. 1892)
1962 – Acquired by Crane Canada Ltd., a subsid. of Crane Co., through an offer of $16 per sh.

James United Industries Limited (Can. 1933)
July 1970 – In voluntary liquidation.
Mar. 1977 – Secured noteholders were pd. in full; 23¢ on the dollar was pd. to unsecured noteholders. No further payment likely.

Jamestown Explorations Inc. (Ont. 1949)
Oct. 1981 – Name changed to Jamestown Resources Inc.; basis 1 new for 4 old shs. (see FPsurvey - Mines & Energy)

Jamex Resources Limited (Que. 1970)
Aug. 9, 1989 – Amalgamated with Dungannon Explorations Ltd. to form Claddagh Gold Limited. (see Claddagh Gold Limited)

Jamie Frontier Resources Inc. (Ont. 1965)
Feb. 15, 1984 – Continued into Canada.
May 6, 2004 – Dissolved.

Jamieson Exploration and Development Ltd. (Ont. 1927)
Mar. 1959 – Charter cancelled.

Jamieson Wellness Inc. (B.C. Jan. 24, 2014)
June 28, 2017 – Continued into Ontario. (see FPsurvey - Industrials)

Jamob Corp. Ltd. (Can. - unspecified Oct. 1965)
Nov. 3, 1965 – Formed in October 1965 to hold and distribute funds from sale of assets and liabs. of James Morrison Brass Manufacturing Co. Ltd. Assets and liabs. of this co. were taken over by Lunkenheimer Co. of Cincinnati for Cdn$931,250 which in turn was paid to Jamob. Shldrs. of Jamob received 50¢ per sh.

Jan Ken Mine Ltd. (Man. 1968)
Mar. 9, 1972 – Dissolved.

Jan Resources Ltd. (B.C. Oct. 18, 1979)
May 11, 1983 – Name changed to Lode Resource Corporation; basis 1 new for 5 old shs. ■

Jandon Mines Ltd. (Ont. 1966)
Dec. 19, 1973 – Dissolved.

Janet Red Lake Mines Ltd. (Ont. 1945)
Apr. 16, 1953 – Charter cancelled.

Jani International Inc. (Alta. 1986)
Oct. 11, 1989 – Name changed to Altech Resource Services Ltd.; basis 1 new for 10 old shs. ■

Janina Resources Limited (B.C. Dec. 11, 2002)
Nov. 23, 2007 – Name changed to International Beryllium Corporation following reverse takeover acquisition of Horn Rare Metals Ltd. and amalgamation of Horn Rare with a wholly owned subsidiary of Janina Resources. ■

Janlee Explorations Ltd. (Ont. 1962)
1965 – Merged into Great Molly Explorations Ltd.; basis 1 new for 3 old shs.

Janna Systems Inc. (Ont. Oct. 19, 1990)
Nov. 20, 2000 – Plan of Arrangement with Siebel Systems Inc. to create Siebel Janna Arrangement, Inc. (exchangeable shs.); basis either 1 new exchangeable sh. or 1 new Siebel sh. for 0.497 old Janna shs.

Jannock Corporation Limited (Ont. June 29, 1973 amalg.)
July 5, 1977 – Name changed to Jannock Limited. ■

Jannock Limited (Ont. June 29, 1973 amalg.)
Jan. 1, 1994 – Amalgamated in Ontario to continue with same name. (see Vicwest Corporation)
Mar. 10, 2000 – Plan of Arrangement with two subsids. of US-based MAGNATRAX Corporation; basis $16 and $2.50 principal amount of senior sub. notes of amalco. (Vicwest Corporation) for each com. sh. held. Also received 1 com. sh. of Jannock Properties Limited as dividend-in-kind for each Jannock com. sh. held. All second pfce. shs. redeemed at $17 plus accrued dividends. (see Vicwest Corporation)

Jannock Properties Limited (Ont. Dec. 14, 1999)
Jan. 28, 2011 – Dissolved. Final distribution $0.056 per unit (1 cl. B com. sh. and 65 cl. A special shs.)

Jantar Resources Corporation (B.C. Oct. 22, 1980)
June 6, 1991 – Name changed to ITP Thermal Packaging Inc. following acquisition of International Thermal Packaging, Inc. ■

Jantar Resources Ltd. (B.C. Nov. 27, 2004)
Sept. 4, 2009 – Name changed to Ultra Lithium Inc. ■

Jantri Resources Inc. (B.C. June 16, 1986)
Dec. 20, 2004 – Name changed to Merit Mining Corp. ■

Janus Explorations Ltd. (Ont. 1968)
Mar. 1979 – Charter cancelled.

Jarbren Exploration Ltd. (Ont. 1946)
Mar. 30, 1959 – Dissolved.

Jardin Financial Group Inc. (Alta. Jan. 28, 1987)
Oct. 4, 1996 – Delisted from the Alberta Stock Exchange. Subsequently dissolved.

Jardincap Inc. (Alta. May 23, 2006)
May 31, 2008 – Formed Tawsho Mining Inc. in Ontario on amalgamation with Tawsho Mining Inc. (deemed acquiror); basis 1 new for 3 old shs. ■

Jardun Mines Ltd. (Ont. 1951)
June 8, 1964 – Charter cancelled.

Jarex Mines Ltd. (Ont. 1972)
Nov. 26, 1975 – Amalgamated into Spar Holdings & Explorations Ltd.; basis 1 new for 2 old shs.

Jaridge Explorations Inc. (Ont. Mar. 1, 1978 amalg.)
Nov. 9, 1978 – Amalgamated with Edgewood Explorations Inc. to continue as Jaridge Explorations Inc.; basis 1 new for 1.5 old shs. (see FPsurvey - Mines & Energy)

Jarl Energy Inc. (Ont. 1978)
Oct. 26, 1989 – Name changed to ALBA Petroleum Corporation. ■

Jarmack Mining Co. Ltd. (Ont. 1946)
Mar. 30, 1959 – Dissolved.

Jarrow Mines Ltd. (Ont. 1965)
Mar. 14, 1973 – Charter cancelled.

Jarvis Resources Ltd. (B.C. May 16, 1980)
June 11, 1999 – Name changed to Consolidated Stone Industries Inc.; basis 1 new for 10 old shs. ■

Jarviston Mines Ltd. (Ont. 1952)
1960 – Charter cancelled.

Jascan Resources Inc. (Ont. Jan. 11, 1978)
Nov. 16, 2000 – Amalgamated with wholly owned subsid. of Breakwater Resources Ltd.; basis $1.15 per sh. or 0.55 Breakwater shs. for 1 Jascan sh. (see Breakwater Resources Ltd.)

Jasmine Mining Corp. Ltd. (Can. 1972)
Feb. 1974 – Name changed to Rencan Resource Investments Ltd. ■

Jason Mines Ltd. (Ont. Nov. 9, 1938)
1948 – Name changed to New Jason Mines Ltd.; basis 1 new for 3 old shs. ■

Jasper Mining Corporation (Alta. Nov. 28, 1994)
Oct. 19, 2022 – Name changed to Tuktu Resources Ltd. (see FPsurvey - Mines & Energy)

Jasper Oil Corporation (Que. 1952)
Aug. 17, 1955 – Sold to Okalta Oils Ltd.

Jasper Porcupine Mines Ltd. (Ont. 1940)
1969 – Charter cancelled.

Java Capital, Inc. (Alta. May 13, 2008)
Apr. 4, 2011 – Continued into Canada.
July 13, 2011 – Name changed to Peak Positioning Technologies Inc. ■

Java Gold Corporation (Ont. June 1, 1996 amalg.)
Jan. 19, 2001 – Charter cancelled and co. dissolved.

Java Joe's International Corporation (Que. Feb. 28, 1967)
May 7, 2004 – Struck off register.

Javelin Capital Corp. (B.C. Mar. 14, 2000)
Sept. 2004 – Continued into Alberta.
Apr. 7, 2006 – Name changed to Javelin Energy Inc.; basis 1 new for 4 old shs. ■

Javelin Energy Inc. (Alta. Sept. 2004)
Dec. 10, 2009 – Placed into receivership, Alger & Associates Inc. appointed receiver.

Javelin Enterprises Ltd. (B.C. 1959)
May 1971 – Name changed to Canterra Development Corp. Ltd. ■

Javelin International Limited (Can. June 28, 1951; via letters patent)
Aug. 22, 1987 – Name changed to Nalcap Holdings Inc.; basis 1 new for 5 old shs. ■

Javelin Mines Ltd. (B.C. 1959)
Mar. 1971 – Name changed to Javelin Enterprises Ltd. ■

Javelina Resources Ltd. (B.C. Apr. 15, 2010)
May 1, 2013 – Name changed to Midpoint Holdings Ltd. pursuant to Qualifying Transaction reverse takeover acquisition of BuyFX Ltd. ■

Javelle Capital Corp. (B.C. Nov. 2, 2010)
Mar. 28, 2017 – Name changed to Kenadyr Mining (Holdings) Corp. pursuant to Qualifiying Transaction reverse takeover acquisition of Kenadyr Mining Corporation; basis 1 new for 2 old shs. ■

Jaxon Minerals Inc. (B.C. Nov. 6, 2006)
Aug. 30, 2017 – Name changed to Jaxon Mining Inc.; basis 1.25 new for 1 old sh. (see FPsurvey - Mines & Energy)

Jay Chibougamau Mines Ltd. (Ont. 1956)
Nov. 1956 – Name changed to Copperstream Mines Ltd.; basis 1 new for 1 old sh. ■

Jayco Mines Ltd. (Ont. 1964)
June 24, 1966 – Name changed to Jayco Mines (1966) Ltd.; basis 1 new for 2 old shs. ■

Jayco Mines (1966) Ltd. (Ont. 1964)
June 27, 1966 – Amalgamated with Consolidated Silver Belle Mines Ltd. to form Silver Belle Mines (1966) Ltd. (see Silver Belle Mines (1966) Ltd.)

Jayden Resources Inc. (B.C. Apr. 6, 1995 amalg.)
Aug. 8, 2012 – Continued into Cayman Islands.
Sept. 24, 2021 – Continued into British Columbia. (see FPsurvey - Mines & Energy)

Jaye Explorations Ltd. (Ont. 1951)
Mar. 1976 – Charter cancelled.

Jayhawk Energy Resources Inc. (Ont. Feb. 16, 1982)
Mar. 25, 1987 – Name changed to Microbe Corporation. ■

Jaylac Mines Ltd. (Ont. 1956)
May 13, 1965 – Dissolved.

Jazz Air Income Fund (Ont. Nov. 25, 2005)
Dec. 31, 2010 – Succeeded by Chorus Aviation Inc. pursuant to plan of arrangement whereby Chorus Aviation Inc. was formed to facilitate the conversion of the fund into a corporation and the fund was subsequently dissolved. (see FPsurvey - Industrials)

Jazz Golf Equipment Inc. (Can. Dec. 3, 1993)
Nov. 24, 2006 – Name changed to 2980304 Canada Inc. (see FPsurvey - Industrials)

Jazz Resources Inc. (B.C. May 22, 1947)
Jan. 19, 2001 – Charter cancelled for failure to file.
Dec. 20, 2002 – Charter revived.
Oct. 19, 2022 – Name changed to JZR Gold Inc. (see FPsurvey - Mines & Energy)

Jazzman Resources Inc. (B.C. Feb. 13, 1986)
Nov. 16, 1995 – Name changed to International Jazzman Ventures Corp.; basis 1 new for 4 old shs. ■

Jean Lake Lithium Mines Ltd. (Ont. Oct. 7, 1955)
July 28, 1975 – CTO issued. Subsequently struck from register and dissolved.

Jean Pierre Cosmetiques Inc. (Can. Dec. 21, 1983)
Oct. 4, 1993 – Dissolved.

Jean R. Beauchemin Mining Corp. (Que. 1964)
Mar. 14, 1981 – Charter cancelled.

Jeanette Minerals Ltd. (Ont. 1948)
Oct. 10, 1961 – Dissolved.

Jed Mines Ltd. (Can. 1946)
Nov. 1959 – Liquidated.

Jeda Petroleum Ltd. (B.C. Apr. 21, 1986)
Feb. 28, 2000 – Amalgamated with Roseland Resources
Ltd. to form new co. with same name Roseland
Resources Ltd.; basis 1 Roseland sh. for 2 Jeda shs.
(see Roseland Resources Ltd.)

Jedburgh Resources Limited (Can. July 9, 1982)
1984 – Amalgamated with Metalgam Ferrous Applications
Inc. to form new co. with same name Jedburgh Resources
Limited; basis 1 new for 4 Metalgam shs. and 1 new for
1 Jedburgh sh.
Dec. 9, 1986 – Formed OTI Technologies Inc. in Canada
on amalgamation with 141884 Canada Inc.; basis 1 new
for 1 141884 Canada sh. and 1 new for 6 Jedburgh shs. ■

Jeep Gold Mine Ltd. (Man. 1946)
1969 – Name changed to Transtide Industries Ltd. (see
FPsurvey - Industrials)

Jefferson Lake Petrochemicals of Canada Ltd (Can.
1957)
July 12, 1957 – Amalgamated into Canadian Occidental
Petroleum Ltd.; sh. for sh. basis.

Jefjen Capital Corporation (B.C. Oct. 28, 1985)
Mar. 5, 1993 – Delisted from the Vancouver Stock
Exchange. Subsequently dissolved for failure to file.

Jelex Mines Ltd. (Ont. Apr. 3, 1939)
June 21, 1978 – Name changed to Key Lake Explorations
Limited; basis 1 new for 5 old shs. (see FPsurvey - Mines
& Energy)

Jellicoe Consolidated Gold Mines Ltd. (Ont. Jan. 15,
1936)
Apr. 3, 1939 – Shares exchanged for shs. of Jellicoe
Mines (1939) Ltd.; basis 1 new for 3 old shs. (see Jellicoe
Mines (1939) Ltd.)

Jellicoe Gold Mining Co. Ltd. (Ont. May 17, 1934)
1936 – Assets acquired by Jellicoe Consolidated Gold
Mines Ltd.; basis 3 new for 5 old shs. (see Jellicoe
Consolidated Gold Mines Ltd.)
Apr. 30, 1937 – Charter surrendered. (see Jellicoe
Consolidated Gold Mines Ltd.)

Jellicoe Mines (1939) Ltd. (Ont. Apr. 3, 1939)
1963 – Name changed to Jelex Mines Ltd.; basis 1 new
for 5 old shs. ■

Jem Exploration Corp. Ltd. (Ont. 1954)
Sept. 21, 1959 – Dissolved.

Jemi Fibre Corp. (B.C. Aug. 16, 1996)
May 17, 2016 – Acquired by CanWel Building Materials
Group Ltd.; basis 1 CanWel com. sh. for 31.13 Jemi com.
shs. (see CanWel Building Materials Group Ltd.)
May 2017 – Name changed to CanWel Fibre Corp. (see
CanWel Building Materials Group Ltd.)

The Jenex Corporation (Alta. Mar. 5, 2001)
Feb. 8, 2018 – Name changed to Therma Bright Inc. and
continued into British Columbia. (see FPsurvey -
Industrials)

Jenkins Bros. Limited. (Can. May 1, 1906)
1979 – Name changed to Jenkins Canada Inc. ■

Jenkins Canada Inc. (Can. May 1, 1906)
Feb. 1992 – Declared bankruptcy and Raymond Chabot
Inc. of Montreal was appointed trustee.
Mar. 1996 – All assets liquidated.
July 28, 2003 – Trustee discharged. No funds available
for distribution to unsecured creditors or shldrs.

Jenkins Groceteria Ltd. (Can. 1928)
Sept. 1959 – Acquired by Westfair Foods Ltd. (see
Western Grocers Ltd.)

Jennifer Petroleums Ltd. (Alta. 1979)
Mar. 13, 1999 – Struck from registry and dissolved.

Jenny Long Gold Mines Ltd. (B.C. Aug. 1935)
1964 – Dissolved by B.C. government.

Jenosys Enterprises Inc. (B.C. Dec. 16, 1965)
Dec. 10, 2004 – Name changed to Fintry Enterprises Inc.;
basis 1 new for 10 old shs. ■

Jensen Yellowknife Gold Mines Ltd. (Ont. 1944)
1953 – Charter cancelled.

Jentech Ventures Corp. (B.C. Nov. 25, 1983)
Apr. 26, 1993 – Name changed to Impact Travel
Technology Inc.; basis 1 new for 10 old shs. ■

Jeotex Inc. (Can. Apr. 16, 2014)
June 10, 2021 – Adjudged bankrupt. Albert Gelman Inc.
appointed trustee.
May 10, 2023 – Dissolved for non-compliance.

Jeph Yellowknife Gold Mines Ltd. (Ont. 1944)
Sept. 1957 – Charter cancelled.

Jerez Energy International Inc. (Alta. Jan. 4, 1995)
Mar. 2, 2005 – Struck from registry and dissolved.

Jerez Investment Corp. (Can. Sept. 1, 1987)
Jan. 4, 1995 – Continued into Alberta.
Aug. 27, 1996 – Name changed to Jerez Energy
International Inc. ■

Jericho Mines Ltd. (N.P.L.) (B.C. Mar. 26, 1956)
Apr. 13, 1973 – Name changed to New Jericho
Development Corporation Ltd.; basis 1 new for 5 old
shs. ■

Jericho Oil Corporation (B.C. Oct. 21, 2010)
Mar. 3, 2021 – Name changed to Jericho Energy Ventures
Inc. (see FPsurvey - Mines & Energy; FPsurvey -
Industrials)

Jericho Resources Ltd. (B.C. Mar. 26, 1956)
Apr. 18, 1995 – Name changed to Regia Resources Ltd. ■

Jerico Explorations Inc. (Can. Feb. 2, 2004)
Dec. 14, 2014 – Dissolved.
Oct. 15, 2020 – Restored to corporate registry.
Feb. 16, 2022 – Continued into British Columbia.
Dec. 16, 2022 – Name changed to Cumberland
Resources Nickel Corp. pursuant to the reverse takeover
acquisition of Cumberland Resources Corp. ■

Jeroco Gold Mines Ltd. (Ont. 1944)
1953 – Charter cancelled.

Jerome Explorations Limited (B.C. 1971)
June 16, 1982 – Continued into Ontario.
May 20, 1983 – Name changed to Dore Explorations
Inc. ■

Jerome Gold Mines Corporation (Alta. 1981)
May 7, 1991 – Formed Pacific Metals Inc. in Ontario on
amalgamation with International Platinum Mining Limited;
basis 1 new for 6.667 old shs. ■

Jerome Gold Mines Ltd. (Ont. 1939)
1969 – Charter cancelled.

Jersey Consolidated Mines Ltd. (Ont. 1951)
July 1976 – Name changed to Holofile Technology Inc.

Jersey Goldfields Corporation (B.C. Sept. 19, 1977)
Mar. 4, 1998 – Name changed to Jersey Petroleum Inc. ■

Jersey Petroleum Inc. (B.C. Sept. 19, 1977)
Aug. 17, 2000 – Name changed to International Choice
Ventures Inc.; basis 1 new for 7 old shs. ■

Jersey Yukon Mines Ltd. (Ont. 1951)
Oct. 1963 – Shs consol.; basis 1 new for 5 old shs.
May 1964 – Name changed to Jersey Consolidated Mines
Ltd. ■

Jervis Exploration & Mining Co. Ltd. (B.C. 1967)
Aug. 29, 1972 – Name changed to Buckhorn Mines Ltd. ■

Jervis Mines Ltd. (Que. 1948)
Charter cancelled.

Jervois Global Limited (Australia Oct. 25, 1962)
May 9, 2025 – Implementation of a Deed of Company
Arrangement (DOCA) under the Chapter 11 plan of
reorganization under which the company's principal
assets and businesses were transferred to JRV Topco
Holdings LLC and its relevant subsids. including the
entities that hold the Idaho Cobalt Operations, the São
Miguel Paulista refinery and the Finland operations, and
other company assets, including but not limited to certain
receivables and intellectual property. As part of the
DOCA, all o/s shs. were cancelled and shldrs. would not
receive a distrib. On implementation of the DOCA, the
company was placed into liquidation and the liquidators
believed that there is no likelihood of shldrs. receiving
any distrib. following the completion of the liquidation.

Jervois Mining Limited (Australia Oct. 25, 1962)
Aug. 6, 2021 – Name changed to Jervois Global
Limited. ■

Jesko Uranium Mines Ltd. (Ont. 1953)
Nov. 18, 1970 – Charter cancelled.

Jespersen-Kay Systems Limited (Ont. 1968)
June 13, 1972 – Substantially all assets transferred to
wholly owned U.S. subsid. Jespersen-Kay Modular
Construction Limited.
June 15, 1972 – Signed agreement with National Kinney
Corp. (NKC) of New York whereby NKC would purchase
all assets of the co. Shldrs. of record July 19, 1972,
received 0.0269 NKC com. shs. plus a notice of
contingent right to receive 0.1345 NKC shs. for each com.
sh. held.

Jess-Mac Gold Mines Ltd. (Ont. 1947)
Aug. 9, 1972 – Charter cancelled.

Jessian Capital Corp. (Alta. Oct. 25, 1999)
Mar. 1, 2002 – Name changed to Savaria Corporation
following Qualifying Transaction acquisition of Services
Industriels Savaria Inc. (see FPsurvey - Industrials)

Jessie James Mines Ltd. (Ont. 1965)
Nov. 29, 1972 – Dissolved.

Jessop Mines Ltd. (Ont. 1964)
Aug. 1968 – Assets reported distributed.

Jessy Ventures Corp. (B.C. Nov. 21, 2018)
Dec. 13, 2022 – Name changed to Generation Gold Corp.
pursuant to the Qualifying Transaction acquisition of an
option on the Arlington copper-silver prospect in British
Columbia. ■

Jet Drill Canada Inc. (Que. Feb. 4, 1958)
Aug. 5, 2003 – Dissolved following shldrs. meeting.

Jet Energy Corp. (B.C. May 30, 1983)
Dec. 10, 1999 – Acquired by Cabre Exploration Ltd.; basis
$1.55 or 0.1 Cabre shs. plus $0.01 for 1 Jet sh. (see
Cabre Exploration Ltd.)

Jet Gold Corp. (B.C. Apr. 24, 1987)
Nov. 2, 2016 – Name changed to Deep-South Resources
Inc. pursuant to the reverse takeover acquisition of
1054137 B.C. Ltd. completed on Aug. 30, 2016; basis 1
new for 2 old shs. ■

Jet Metal Corp. (B.C. Sept. 2, 1966)
Feb. 28, 2017 – Continued into Canada.
Mar. 7, 2017 – Name changed to Canada Jetlines Ltd.
following reverse takeover acquisition of and
amalgamation of wholly owned Jet Metal Acquisition Corp.
with (old) Canada Jetlines Ltd.; basis 1 new for 1.5 old
shs. ■

Jet Oils Ltd. (Can. July 16, 1948)
1954 – Taken over by Pathfinder Petroleums Ltd.; basis
1 new for 4.71 old shs.

Jet Pacific Investments Ltd. (Alta. Aug. 29, 1986)
Feb. 2, 2005 – Dissolved and struck from registry.

Jet Star Resources Ltd. (B.C. 1977)
Apr. 30, 1982 – Name changed to Radian Petroleum Corporation. (see FPsurvey - Mines & Energy)

Jet Uranium Ltd. (Que. 1958)
Mar. 23, 1974 – Charter cancelled.

Jetcan Limited (Ont. 1945)
Dissolved.

Jetex Resources Ltd. (B.C. 1969)
Mar. 1980 – Name changed to California Silver Ltd. ■

JetForm Corporation (Can. June 10, 1982)
Sept. 17, 2001 – Name changed to Accelio Corporation. ■

Jett Investment Corporation (Alta. July 18, 1996)
Apr. 30, 1998 – Name changed to Jettstar Resource Services Inc. following acquisition of all the o/s shs. of Red Hawk Well Servicing Ltd.; basis 1 new for 1 old sh. ■

Jetta Resources Ltd. (B.C. 1983)
Nov. 5, 1986 – Name changed to Security Environmental Systems Inc. and continued into Delaware; basis 1 new for 2 old shs.

Jetta Resources Ltd. (B.C. June 13, 1990)
Sept. 27, 1991 – Name changed to Jettra Resources Ltd. ■

Jettra Resources Ltd. (B.C. June 13, 1990)
Mar. 12, 1997 – Name changed to Great Canadian Gaming Corporation. ■

Jettstar Resource Services Inc. (Alta. July 18, 1996)
June 14, 1999 – Acquired by Petro Well Energy Services Inc.; basis 1 Petro Well sh. for 2.4 Jettstar shs. (see Petro Well Energy Services Inc.)

Jewel Resources Inc. (B.C. July 4, 1978)
June 1, 1988 – Name changed to Wkay Resources Inc. ■

Jibilie Mining Co. Ltd. (Ont. 1957)
Mar. 1976 – Charter cancelled.

Jilbey Enterprises Ltd. (Can. Sept. 9, 1993)
June 24, 2003 – Name changed to Jilbey Gold Exploration Ltd. ■

Jilbey Exploration Ltd. (B.C. Mar. 14, 1983)
Sept. 9, 1993 – Continued into Canada.
Apr. 30, 1999 – Name changed to Jilbey Enterprises Ltd.; basis 1 new for 5 old shs. ■

Jilbey Gold Exploration Ltd. (Can. Sept. 9, 1993)
Sept. 6, 2005 – Acquired by High River Gold Mines Ltd.; basis 0.75 High River shs. for 1 Jilbey sh. (see High River Gold Mines Ltd.)

Jilbey Industries Ltd. (B.C. Mar. 14, 1983)
Mar. 16, 1990 – Name changed to Jilbey Exploration Ltd. ■

Jimjon Gold Mines Ltd. (Ont. 1945)
1952 – Charter cancelled.

Jimrock Mines Ltd. (B.C. 1968)
May 22, 1974 – Name changed to Orion Mines Ltd. ■

Jinhua Capital Corporation (Alta. Oct. 19, 2009)
Jan. 12, 2018 – Continued into British Columbia. (see FPsurvey - Mines & Energy)

Jinshan Gold Mines Inc. (B.C. May 31, 2000)
July 19, 2010 – Name changed to China Gold International Resources Corp. Ltd. (see FPsurvey - Mines & Energy)

Jite Technologies Inc. (Ont. June 21, 2006 amalg.)
June 5, 2012 – Amalgamated with 1872706 Ontario Limited, a wholly owned subsid. of McVicar Industries Inc.; basis 1 McVicar pref. sh. redeem. at 60¢ for 1 Jite Technologies sh. (see McVicar Industries Inc.)

Jitec Inc. (Can. Feb. 17, 1995)
July 30, 2001 – Name changed to Avantage Link inc. ■

Jiulian Resources Inc. (B.C. Oct. 17, 2006)
Nov. 19, 2020 – Name changed to South Atlantic Gold Inc. (see FPsurvey - Mines & Energy)

Jo-Ami Gold Mines Ltd. (Ont. 1951)
Sept. 22, 1966 – Dissolved.

Jo-Jay Mines Ltd. (unknown)
Mar. 1967 – Name changed to Force Crag Mines Limited. ■

Joannes-Davidson Mines Ltd. (Que. Feb. 16, 1937)
July 22, 1978 – Charter cancelled.

Joannes Gold Mines Ltd. (Ont. 1935)
Mar. 18, 1965 – Dissolved.

Joannes Goldfields Ltd. (Que. 1947)
1952 – Name changed to Titanium Development Corporation. ■

Joannes Mine Corporation Ltd. (Que. Apr. 4, 1928)
Name changed to Joannes-Davidson Mines Ltd. ■

Joburke Gold Mines Ltd. (Ont. 1945)
1969 – Name changed to New Joburke Explorations Ltd.; basis 1 new for 14 old shs. ■

Jocor Mines Ltd. (Que. 1943)
Apr. 1954 – Charter cancelled.

Jodee Explorations Ltd. (Ont. 1952)
Aug. 1972 – Charter cancelled.

Jodelo Gold Mines Ltd. (Ont. July 17, 1936)
1944 – Name changed to Mintrock Mines Ltd.; basis 1 new for 2 old shs. ■

Joe Indian Mountain Metal Mines Ltd. (Ont. 1951)
1953 – Name changed to Indian Mountain Metal Mines Ltd. ■

Joffre Resources Ltd. (Alta. 1980)
Jan. 13, 1984 – Placed into receivership on Jan. 13, and all assets sold. Nothing left for shldrs.

Jogran Mines Ltd. (Ont. 1964)
Mar. 1976 – Charter cancelled.

John A. Lang & Sons Ltd. (Can. 1930)
1956 – Mailman Corporation Ltd. purchased all shs. at $25 per sh.

John Cabot Explorations Ltd. (B.C. 1978)
Nov. 1979 – Name changed to Antrim Resources Ltd. ■

The John Forsyth Company Inc. (Ont. Dec. 14, 1960)
Dec. 6, 1996 – Acquired by Forsyth Acquisition Limited for $1.91 per sh.

John Inglis Co. Limited (Ont. Nov. 23, 1936)
Apr. 1973 – Name changed to Inglis Limited. ■

John Labatt Limited (Can. Dec. 20, 1930)
July 31, 1995 – Acquired by 3150216 Canada Inc., a wholly owned subsid. of Interbrew S.A., for $28.50 per sh.

John Lewis Corporation (Que. 1959)
Sept. 1964 – Merged with subsid. to form John Lewis Inc.

John Northway and Son Limited (Ont. 1900)
June 13, 1966 – Liquidation of assets completed. Secured creditors pd. in full; unsecured received 5.145% of amts. owed; no equity for com. shldrs.

John Wood Company (U.S. - unspecified 1962)
1964 – Anthes Imperial Ltd. acquired 44% of com. stk. from U.S. ints. and remaining stk. on basis of one Anthes 5.25% cum. first pref. sh. ser. C $100 par, and 5 cl. A com. sh. (before 2-for-1 split) of Anthes for each 15 com. shs. of John Wood. Further offer of $14 U.S. per sh. expired Nov. 6.

John Wood Industries Limited (Can. 1922)
1962 – Acquired by John Wood Company; basis 4 com. shs. for each sh. of John Wood Industries.

Johnston & Frye Securities Ltd. (B.C. June 22, 1978)
July 7, 1989 – Delisted from the Vancouver Stock Exchange. Subsequently struck from register and dissolved.

Joliet-Quebec Mines, Limited (Ont. June 30, 1936)
Aug. 14, 1978 – Name changed to J-Q Resources Inc.; basis 1 new for 5 old shs. ■

Jolin Bourlamaque Gold Mines Ltd. (Que. 1945)
June 1, 1976 – Merged into Brominco Inc.; basis 1 Brominco sh. for 5,000 Jolin shs. ■

La Jolla Capital Inc. (Can. June 19, 1997)
Apr. 19, 2022 – Name changed to Web3 Ventures Inc.; basis 1 new for 10 old shs. ■

Jolloco Explorations Ltd. (Ont. 1969)
Mar. 1976 – Charter cancelled.

Jolly Jumper Products of America Limited (Ont. Apr. 24, 1967)
Nov. 1, 1982 – Dissolved.
Sept. 25, 1987 – Name changed to Sun Valley Ranch Inc. following revival of charter on the same date. ■

The Jolt Beverage Company, Ltd. (B.C. Mar. 18, 1981)
May 13, 1988 – Name changed to The International Beverage Corporation. ■

Jomac Gold Syndicate Ltd. (Ont. June 6, 1934)
Charter cancelled; assets taken over by Terimac Mining Dev. Ltd.; basis 97.5¢ plus 1 sh. Terimac Mining Dev. Ltd. plus 3.8 shs. Madsen Red Lake Gold Mines per Jomac sh. (see Terimac Mining Developments Ltd.)

Jomac Mines Ltd. (Ont. 1959)
1961 – Merged into Jorsco Explorations Ltd.

Jomar Capital Corp. (Alta. Oct. 20, 2009)
Mar. 1, 2011 – Name changed to Online Energy Inc. pursuant to Qualifying Transaction reverse takeover acquisition of (old) Online Energy Inc. and subsequent amalgamation of Online Energy with a wholly owned subsid.; basis 1 new for 6 old shs. ■

Jones Bros. of Canada Ltd. (Can. 1929)
Oct. 1, 1946 – Assets and undertakings sold to Jones Industries Ltd. Holders of the 6% 1st mtge. 20-year s.f. bds. due 1956, received $130 princ. amt. of 4% bds. of Jones Industries for each $100 6% bds. of old co.

Jones Industries Ltd. (Can. 1946)
1958 – Wound up. Receiver and manager, E. J. Howson, Toronto.
Aug. 17, 1961 – Holders of 4% (closed) 20-yr. s.f. bds. due 1966, received 40¢ on the $1; final distribution of 8.8¢ on the $1; nothing available for shldrs.

Jonlab Investments Ltd. (Ont. 1966)
1975 – Acquired by Brascan Limited during for total cash consideration of $13,209,000.

Jonpol Explorations Limited (Ont. Mar. 25, 1980 amalg.)
Aug. 31, 1989 – Amalgamated with Newfield Mines Ltd. to form new co. with same name Jonpol Explorations Limited; basis 2 new for 1 Newfield sh. and 1 new for 1 Jonpol sh.
Apr. 28, 2005 – Amalgamated with Elgin Resources Inc. to form Eastern Platinum Limited; basis 1 Eastern Platinum sh. for 4 Jonpol shs.

Jonsmith Gold Mines Ltd. (Ont. 1947)
1952 – Name changed to Jonsmith Mines Ltd. ■

Jonsmith Mines Ltd. (Ont. 1947)
1976 – Name changed to New Jonsmith Exploration Ltd. and continued into Alberta; basis 1 new for 200 old shs. ■

Jopec Resources Ltd. (B.C. Sept. 4, 1990)
Feb. 3, 1999 – Name changed to Fortuna Ventures Inc.; basis 1 new for 7 old shs. ∎

Jorace Petroleums Ltd. (Alta. May 19, 1965)
Apr. 26, 1972 – Name changed to Canadian Obas Oil Limited. ∎

Jordan Petroleum Ltd. (Alta. Aug. 14, 1986)
June 26, 1987 – Continued into Canada.
Dec. 7, 1987 – Amalgamated with Lariat Oil & Gas Ltd. to form new co. also called Jordan Petroleum.; basis 1 cl. A sh. for 1 com. sh.
June 1, 1990 – Formed New Jordan Petroleum Ltd. on amalgamation with Passburg Petroleums Ltd. (1 cl. A and 0.6 cl. B. for 1 old sh. or 1 new cl. D for 1 old sh. redeemable for $3.00 per sh.); basis 1 cl. A sh. and 0.2 of 1 cl. B of new co. for 5 old shs. ∎

Jordan Petroleum Ltd. (Can. June 26, 1987)
Jan. 14, 1998 – Acquired by Reserve Royalty Corporation for $9.80 per sh. (see Reserve Royalty Corporation)

Jordan River Mines Ltd. (B.C. 1971)
Sept. 16, 1983 – Placed into receivership in 1974. Trustee since discharged. Charter cancelled.

Jordan Valley Wines (unknown)
Acquired by Carling O'Keefe.

Jordesco Resources Ltd. (B.C. 1947)
Aug. 1976 – Charter cancelled.

Jordex Resources Inc. (B.C. Jan. 15, 1987)
July 27, 1998 – Continued into Yukon.
Mar. 15, 2000 – Name changed to iTech Capital Corp. ∎

Jorex Limited (Ont. Feb. 28, 1968)
July 27, 1984 – Name changed to Canadian Jorex Limited; basis 1 new for 10 old shs. ∎

Jorsco Explorations Ltd. (Ont. 1961)
Apr. 1970 – Charter cancelled.

Josemaria Resources Inc. (Can. Aug. 20, 2004)
May 3, 2022 – Acquired by Lundin Mining Corporation; basis (i) Cdn$1.60 cash per sh.; or (ii) 0.1487 Lundin com. shs. plus for each whole Lundin shs, Cdn$0.11 cash per sh.; or (iii) any combination thereof for 1 Josemaria sh.

Josephine Mining Corp. (B.C. June 4, 2007)
July 18, 2019 – Name changed to Wolfpack Brands Corporation. ∎

Joss Energy Ltd. (Alta. Aug. 31, 1983)
July 6, 1994 – Amalgamated with Startech Energy Ltd. to form Startech Energy Inc.; basis 1 new for 8.58 Startech shs. and 1 new for 3 Joss shs. (see Startech Energy Inc.)

Jot-It! Software Corp. (B.C. Apr. 11, 1983)
Feb. 18, 1998 – Name changed to Sideware Systems Inc. ∎

Joubi Mining Corporation Limited (Que. 1950)
Feb. 1977 – Charter cancelled.

Jourdan Resources Inc. (Can. Dec. 14, 1994)
June 28, 2023 – Name changed to Consolidated Lithium Metals Inc. (see FPsurvey - Mines & Energy)

Journal Publishing Co. of Ottawa, Ltd. (Ont. 1917)
1959 – Victor Sifton and Associates of Winnipeg acquired over 99% of o/s shs. at $30 per sh. Converted to a private co.

Journey Resources Corp. (B.C. Mar. 29, 2000)
Dec. 17, 2010 – Name changed to Musgrove Minerals Corp.; basis 1 new for 8 old shs. ∎

Journey Unlimited Omni Brand Corporation (B.C. Mar. 29, 2000)
Nov. 29, 2005 – Name changed to Journey Resources Corp. ∎

Journey's End Corporation (Ont. Nov. 19, 1962)
Dec. 4, 1997 – Name changed to UniHost Corporation. ∎

Journey's End Motel Corporation (Ont. Nov. 19, 1962)
Feb. 28, 1989 – Name changed to Journey's End Corporation. ∎

Joutel Resources Limited (Que. 1961)
Nov. 9, 1998 – Amalgamated with Thunderwood Resources Inc. to form Thundermin Resources Inc.; basis 1 Thundermin sh. for 6 Joutel shs. (see Thundermin Resources Inc.)

Jovian Capital Corporation (Can. Sept. 29, 2003)
Oct. 4, 2013 – Acquired by Industrial Alliance Insurance and Financial Services Inc.; basis either (i) $10.23, (ii) 0.2386 Industrial com. shs. or (iii) combination thereof for 1 Jovian com. sh.
Dec. 31, 2015 – Name changed to 8689784 Canada Inc.

Jowsey Denton Gold Mines Limited (Ont. 1935)
Aug. 6, 1981 – Name changed to Eden Roc Mineral Corp.; basis 1 new for 10 old shs.

Jowsey Island Gold Mines Ltd. (Man. 1934)
Apr. 1949 – Dissolved.

Joy Industries Limited (B.C. 1966)
Nov. 10, 1988 – Dissolved.

Joy Mining Ltd. (B.C. 1966)
June 28, 1973 – Name changed to Joy Industries Limited. ∎

Juan de Fuca Mining Co. Ltd. (B.C. 1957)
Apr. 1962 – Name changed to Belle Tahsis Mines Ltd. ∎

Jubilant Creek Mines Ltd. (Ont. 1965)
1968 – Merged into Jubilant Eagle Holdings and Explorations Ltd.; basis 1 new for 3 old shs.

Jubilant Eagle Holdings and Explorations Ltd. (Ont. 1968 amalg.)
Feb. 26, 1980 – Dissolved.

Jubilee Explorations Inc. (B.C. 1965)
June 6, 1986 – Struck off register.

Jubilee Gold Inc. (Ont. Jan. 1, 2010 amalg.)
Jan. 1, 2013 – Formed Jubilee Gold Exploration Ltd. in Ontario pursuant to amalgamation with Ansil Resources Ltd. and Micon Gold Inc.; basis 0.212 new com. shs. for 1 old Jubilee com. sh., 0.551 new com. shs. for 1 Ansil com. sh. and 1.035 new com. shs. for 1 Micon com. sh. (see FPsurvey - Mines & Energy)

Jubilee Iron Corp. (Que. 1957)
Apr. 2, 1969 – Continued into Canada.
1969 – Name changed to Dominion Jubilee Corporation Limited. ∎

Jubilee Long Lac Gold Mines Ltd. (Ont. 1935)
Jan. 1955 – Charter cancelled.

Jubilee Resources Inc. (Alta. Sept. 8, 1987)
May 8, 2003 – Amalgamated with wholly owned subsid. of CanScot Resources Ltd.; basis $0.11 per sh. (see CanScot Resources Ltd.)

Judella Uranium Mines Ltd. (Sask. 1954)
Oct. 24, 1958 – Struck off register.

Julia Resources Corporation (B.C. 1974)
Nov. 1, 1991 – Amalgamated with MacNeill International Industries Inc. to form Spokane Resources Ltd.; basis 1 new for 4 MacNeill shs. and 1 new for 4 Julia shs. (see Spokane Resources Ltd.)

July Resources Corp. (Ont. Feb. 23, 1988)
Jan. 13, 2004 – Formed ONE Signature Financial Corporation in Ontario on amalgamation with ONE Signature Financial Corporation, newly incorporated to acquire U.K.-based Simplex Consulting Limited; basis 1 new for 1 ONE sh. and 0.1 new for 1 July sh. ∎

July Silver Mines Ltd. (B.C. 1960)
1971 – Struck off register.

Juma Mining and Exploration Ltd. (Ont. 1957)
Mar. 1976 – Charter cancelled.

Jumbo Development Corporation (Alta. May 17, 1996)
June 23, 2006 – Name changed to Jumbo Petroleum Corporation. (see FPsurvey - Mines & Energy)

Jumbo Entertainment Inc. (Ont. 1987)
July 15, 2004 – Name changed to J.U.M. Capital Inc. ∎

Jumbo Mines Ltd. (B.C. 1968)
Apr. 4, 1977 – Dissolved.

Jumping Pound Petroleums Ltd. (Alta. 1945)
1962 – Assets acquired by United Oils Ltd.; basis 1 new for 7 old shs., plus equivalent of 1 cl. A sh. and 3 cl. B shs. of Cygnus Corp. Ltd. for 70 old Jumping Pound shs.

JumpTV Inc. (Can. Jan. 14, 2000)
July 13, 2009 – Name changed to NeuLion, Inc. ∎

Junction Explorations Ltd. (Ont. Dec. 12, 1978 amalg.)
June 11, 1984 – Dissolved.

June Resources Inc. (B.C. Sept. 18, 1979)
July 25, 1995 – Name changed to JNR Resources Inc. ∎

June 2020 Corporate Bond Trust (Ont. Sept. 26, 2016)
June 30, 2020 – Terminated; net assets distributed to unitholders on a pro rata basis.

June 2021 Investment Grade Bond Pool (Ont. Jan. 31, 2017)
June 30, 2021 – Terminated; basis

Junex Inc. (Que. Mar. 26, 1999)
Aug. 14, 2018 – Name changed to Cuda Oil and Gas Inc. following acquisition of Cuda Energy Inc.; basis 1 new for 10 old shs. ∎

Junex Mines Ltd. (B.C. 1969)
June 1, 1973 – Name changed to Junex Resources Ltd. ∎

Junex Resources Ltd. (B.C. 1969)
Mar. 25, 1976 – Name changed to C.T. Exploranda Ltd.; basis 1 new for 4 old shs. ∎

Junior Frood Mines Ltd. (Ont. 1927)
1967 – Name changed to Frood Deep Nickel Mines Ltd.; basis 5 new for 1 old sh. ∎

Juniper Mines Ltd. (B.C. June 27, 1966)
Aug. 9, 1978 – Name changed to Tally Resources Inc.; basis 1 new for 2 old shs. ∎

Juno Capital Corp. (Alta. Apr. 10, 2003)
Feb. 6, 2007 – Formed North Peace Energy Corp. in Alberta pursuant to reverse takeover acquisition of and amalgamation with North Peace Energy Inc.; basis 1 new for 5 old shs. ∎

Juno Metals Corp. (Que. 1952)
Oct. 30, 1982 – Charter cancelled.

Jupiter Development Corporation Ltd. (Alta. 1971)
Oct. 1, 1992 – Struck off register.

Jupiter Explorations Ltd. (B.C. 1967)
Nov. 1974 – Charter cancelled.

Jupiter Explorations Ltd. (B.C. Oct. 23, 1986)
June 29, 1993 – Name changed to Hypaz Technology Corp. ∎

Jupiter International Resources Inc. (Alta. July 9, 1993)
Sept. 2, 1999 – Name changed to Jupiter Power International Inc. ∎

Jupiter Oils Limited (Alta. 1948)
1961 – Shares exch. for shs. of Jupiter Corp., a U.S. co.

Jupiter Petroleum Inc. (Alta. July 9, 1993)
Mar. 18, 1997 – Name changed to Jupiter International Resources Inc. ■

Jupiter Power International Inc. (Alta. July 9, 1993)
Feb. 19, 2001 – Name changed to Maxim Power Corp. following reverse takeover acquisition of Maxim Energy Group Ltd. ■

Jupiter Resource Explorations Limited (Ont. Mar. 30, 1978)
July 18, 1985 – Name changed to Video Premiere International Corporation. ■

Jupitor Mines Limited (B.C. May 26, 1978)
Oct. 29, 1981 – Name changed to Jupitor Resources Limited. ■

Jupitor Resources Limited (B.C. May 26, 1978)
Mar. 7, 1990 – Name changed to Pacific Western Capital Corporation; basis 1 new for 5 old shs. ■

Juritel Systems Inc. (Ont. Dec. 27, 1945)
Oct. 27, 1993 – Name changed to Huntington Rhodes Inc.; basis 1 new for 1 old sh. ■

Just Energy Exchange Corp. (Can. Apr. 17, 2009)
Jan. 4, 2011 – Redeemed exchangeable shs.; basis 1 Just Energy Group Inc. sh. for 1 Just Energy exch. sh.

Just Energy Group Inc. (Can. Jan. 1, 2011; amalg.)
Dec. 19, 2022 – Pursuant to a purchase agreement, wholly owned Just Energy (U.S.) Corp., was sold to affiliates of PIMCO. Under the articles of reorganization, the com. shs. of the company were redeemed for no consideration and cancelled.

Just Energy Income Fund (Ont. Feb. 14, 2001)
Jan. 1, 2011 – Succeeded by Just Energy Group Inc. pursuant to plan of arrangement whereby Just Energy Group Inc. was formed to facilitate the conversion of the fund into a corporation and the fund was subsequently dissolved. ■

Just Kitchen Holdings Corp. (B.C. Dec. 5, 2019)
Jan. 31, 2024 – Privatized via acquisition by JF Investment Co., Ltd. jointly owned by officers and directors of the company; basis 9¢ cash per sh.

Justen Resources Ltd. (B.C. 1979)
Nov. 1, 1982 – Amalgamated with New Penn Energy Corporation, Armor Resources Ltd. and Prospect Energy Corporation to form new co. under continuing name of New Penn Energy Corporation; basis 1 new for 5.07 shs. of Justen Resources. ■

Justice Electronic Monitoring Systems Inc. (Can. June 1987)
Dec. 10, 1987 – Continued into Ontario.
Apr. 28, 1994 – Name changed to Jemtec Inc.; basis 1 new for 10 old shs. (see FPsurvey - Industrials)

Justice Mining Corp. (B.C. May 3, 1982)
June 9, 1988 – Name changed to Presidential Forest Products Corp. ■

Justify Capital Corp. (B.C. July 28, 2020)
Aug. 31, 2022 – Name changed to Everyday People Financial Corp. and continued into Alberta pursuant to the Qualifying Transaction reverse takeover acquisition of Everyday People Financial Inc. (see FPsurvey - Industrials)

Justinian Explorations Ltd. (Alta. July 3, 1997 amalg.)
Mar. 23, 2001 – Name changed to Connacher Oil and Gas Limited; basis 1 new for 10 old shs. ■

K

K-Bro Linen Income Fund (Alta. Dec. 10, 2004)
Jan. 1, 2011 – Succeeded by K-Bro Linen Inc. pursuant to plan of arrangement whereby K-Bro Linen Inc. was formed to facilitate the conversion of the fund into a corporation and the fund was subsequently dissolved. (see FPsurvey - Industrials)

K-2 Resources Inc. (B.C. May 22, 1947)
Oct. 28, 1994 – Charter cancelled; subsequently revived.
May 29, 1996 – Name changed to Jazz Resources Inc. ■

K-Zone Fault Mines Ltd. (Ont. 1945)
1953 – Charter cancelled.

K+S Windsor Salt Ltd. (Can. 1950)
Apr. 30, 2021 – Name changed to Windsor Salt Ltd.

K2 Energy Corp. (Alta. Feb. 20, 1992)
May 15, 2005 – Name changed to Resilient Resources Ltd.; basis 1 new for 30 old shs. ■

K45 Capital Corporation (Can. Apr. 8, 2002)
Dec. 8, 2004 – Name changed to VisionSky Corporation following Qualifying Transaction acquisition of VisionSky North America Inc. effective Sept. 3, 2004 for total consideration of 6,666,667 shs. ■

KAB Distribution Inc. (Can. Nov. 28, 2005 amalg.)
Sept. 23, 2009 – Voluntarily delisted following sale of assets. Shldrs. received 65¢ distribution per sh. Co. is in process of liquidating.

KABN Systems NA Holdings Corp. (B.C. Sept. 10, 2014)
Mar. 3, 2021 – Name changed to Liquid Avatar Technologies Inc. (see FPsurvey - Industrials)

KACEE Exploration Inc. (Alta. Jan. 24, 1991)
Apr. 9, 1996 – Amalgamated with Quest Resources Corp. to form Questar Exploration Inc.; basis 1 new for 1 old sh. (see Questar Exploration Inc.)

KAM Capital Corp. (Ont. Nov. 28, 2007)
July 28, 2008 – Formed Titan Medical Inc. in Ontario following Qualifying Transaction reverse takeover amalgamation of wholly owned subsid. Titan Medical Inc. (formerly 2174656 Ontario Limited) with Synergist Medical Inc. to continue as Titan Medical Inc., and subsequent amalgamation of KAM Capital with wholly owned subsid. Titan Medical. ■

KAP Resources Ltd. (B.C. Nov. 14, 1990 amalg.)
Jan. 15, 1991 – Continued into Yukon.
May 17, 2005 – Dissolved and struck off register.

KAPA Capital Inc. (B.C. Jan. 29, 2018)
May 19, 2022 – Name changed to KAPA Gold Inc. pursuant to the Qualifying Transaction reverse takeover acquisition of Quantus Resources Corp. (see FPsurvey - Mines & Energy)

KAPPA Energy Company Inc. (Alta. Oct. 11, 1996 amalg.)
Jan. 17, 2000 – Name changed to Vanguard Oil Corporation. ■

K. B. & G. Metal Products Ltd. (Ont. 1960)
Apr. 4, 1975 – Dissolved.

K. B. Mining Co. Ltd. (Ont. 1945)
Nov. 1972 – Dissolved following final distribution of 8.7¢ per sh. Initial pay. of 8¢ per sh. made Dec. 15, 1971.

K.B. Recycling Industries Ltd. (Israel Jan. 22, 2008)
Mar. 29, 2023 – Name changed to Oceansix Future Paths Ltd. ■

KBSH Leaders Trust (Ont. Apr. 26, 2002)
Nov. 25, 2005 – Wound up; basis 1st distribution $14 per unit paid on Dec. 5, 2005 then 2nd and final distribution $0.01 per unit paid on Dec. 12, 2005.

KCC Capital Corporation (B.C. Aug. 2, 2007)
May 29, 2014 – Name changed to New Era Minerals Inc. pursuant to the Qualifying Transaction reverse takeover acquisition of Haijin International Holdings Limited; basis 1 new for 8.41 old shs. ■

KCO Capital Inc. (B.C. July 29, 2011)
Oct. 30, 2014 – Name changed to 3TL Technologies Corp. following Qualifying Transaction reverse takeover acquisition of 3 Tier Logic Inc. ■

KCP Income Fund (Ont. July 9, 2002)
May 28, 2007 – All assets acquired by KCP Investment Holdings Canada ULC, a subsidiary of Caxton-Iseman Capital Inc., effective May 24, 2007. Fund units were redeemed for $10 per unit plus $0.04375 in accr. dists.

KDR Industrials Ltd. (B.C. Feb. 21, 2013)
Jan. 18, 2021 – Name changed to Dispersion Technologies Inc.; basis 1 new for 35 old shs. ■

KEC Environmental Corp. (Alta. June 29, 1988)
Dec. 1, 1999 – Charter cancelled and co. dissolved.

KEWL Corporation (Can. Feb. 19, 1990)
Feb. 7, 2005 – Indirectly acquired by Accolade Group; basis $0.01 per sh. for pre-consolidated shs. for shldrs who held less than 1 consolidated sh. following previously approved 1-for-500,000 consolidation.

KEYreit (Ont. Aug. 23, 2005)
July 2, 2013 – Acquired by Plazacorp Retail Properties Ltd.; basis either (i) $8.35, (ii) 1.7041 Plazacorp com. shs. or (iii) a combination thereof for 1 KEYreit unit. If no election is made, unitholders will receive $4.175 plus 0.85205 Plazacorp com. shs. for 1 KEYriet unit. (see Plazacorp Retail Properties Ltd.)

KFG Resources Ltd. (B.C. Apr. 7, 1994)
May 5, 2021 – Acquired by Cadillac Ventures Inc.; basis 1 Cadillac sh. for 1 KFG sh.

KGHM International Ltd. (B.C. May 15, 2002)
Mar. 8, 2012 – Acquired by KGHM Polska Miedz S.A. for Cdn$15 per sh. plus Cdn$1.68 per wt.

KGIC Inc. (Alta. Sept. 20, 1996)
Jan. 25, 2017 – BDO Canada Limited appointed interim receiver.
Feb. 22, 2017 – BDO Canada was appointed receiver.
Mar. 2017 – All assets sold. Secured lender suffered a shortfall and no monies available for distrib. to shldrs. BDO Canada discharged as receiver.

KHD Humboldt Wedag International Ltd. (B.C. Nov. 3, 2004)
Mar. 30, 2010 – Name changed to Terra Nova Royalty Corporation. ■

KIK Tire Technologies Inc. (Can. Jan. 22, 1987)
June 20, 2006 – Name changed to Kik Polymers Inc.; basis 1 new for 10 old shs. ■

KING Products Inc. (Ont. 1967)
Apr. 3, 2002 – Acquired by Urmet Group; basis unknown. Continued business under name KING Products and Solutions Inc.

K.M. Ontario Exploration Ltd. (Ont. 1965)
1967 – Name changed to Radio Hill Mines Co. Ltd. ■

KMS Power Income Fund (Alta. Feb. 17, 1997)
June 7, 2002 – Acquired by Algonquin Power Income Trust; basis 0.7428 new Algonquin trust units for 1 old KMS Power trust unit, plus 10.34 Algonquin units for each $100 principal of 10% KMS convert. deb. (see Algonquin Power Income Fund)

KOPR Point Ventures Inc. (B.C. Mar. 10, 2017)
Dec. 5, 2019 – Name changed to Bam Bam Resources Corp. ■

KPI International Inc. (Que. Aug. 28, 1944)
May 2, 2003 – Struck off register. ■

KPS Ventures Ltd. (B.C. Apr. 28, 2005)
Mar. 5, 2007 – Name changed to Energentia Resources Inc. following reverse takeover acquisition of Lerida Bay Ltd. for total consideration of 20,000,000 com. shs., US$1,150,000 cash and a 1% gross revenue royalty interest. ■

KR Investment Ltd. (B.C. Aug. 3, 2010)
May 6, 2024 – Name changed to Global Uranium Corp. pursuant to the reverse takeover acquisition of Rare Earth Element Corp. (see FPsurvey - Mines & Energy)

KRG Management Inc. (Ont. Apr. 29, 1987)
July 5, 2000 – Going private transaction via amalgamation with wholly owned subsid. of controlling shldr. 1379114 Ontario Inc.; basis 1 cl. A redeemable pfd. sh. for 1 com. sh. immediately redeemed for $1.32 per sh.

KRG Television Limited (Alta. July 10, 1997)
Apr. 23, 2003 – Name changed to Intelpro Media Group Inc.; basis 1 new for 2 old shs. ■

KRL Resources Corp. (B.C. July 10, 1978)
Mar. 6, 2002 – Name changed to International KRL Resources Corp.; basis 1 new for 5 old shs. ■

KSAT Satellite Networks Inc. (B.C. Oct. 11, 1979)
2000 – Continued into Yukon.
May 13, 2004 – Dissolved.
June 8, 2005 – Proceeds of liquidation, insufficient to meet major shldrs. and secured creditors' requirements, thus other shldrs. received nothing from dissolution.

K.S.F. Chemical Processes Limited (Ont. 1964)
Jan. 21, 1981 – Name changed to K.C.P. Resources Inc. (see FPsurvey - Mines & Energy)

K. T. Mining Limited (Ont. 1917)
Aug. 25, 1980 – Name changed to K. T. Resources Limited. ■

K. T. Resources Limited (Ont. 1917)
Oct. 6, 1981 – Name changed to K.T. Resources (1981) Limited; basis 1 new for 3 old shs. ■

K.T. Resources (1981) Limited (Ont. 1917)
Oct. 29, 1994 – Charter cancelled and dissolved.

KUM Resources Ltd. (B.C. Dec. 14, 1979)
Jan. 16, 1900 – Filed under Chapter 11 of the Federal Bankruptcy code. No equity available for shldrs.
Aug. 16, 1983 – Name changed to Futurtek Communications Inc. ■

K.W. Resources Ltd. (B.C. Sept. 18, 1972)
Feb. 14, 1992 – Name changed to Tako Resources Ltd.; basis 1 new for 4 old shs. ■

KWESST Micro Systems Inc. (B.C. Nov. 28, 2017)
June 30, 2025 – Name changed to DEFSEC Technologies Inc. (see FPsurvey - Industrials)

KWG Resources Inc. (Que. Aug. 21, 1937)
June 15, 2016 – Continued into Canada.
Aug. 2, 2025 – Name changed to The Canadian Chrome Company Inc. (see FPsurvey - Mines & Energy)

KYC Technology Inc. (B.C. June 6, 2017)
Mar. 3, 2020 – Name changed to CanaFarma Hemp Products Corp. pursuant to the reverse takeover acquisition of private New York, N.Y.-based CanaFarma Corp. (see FPsurvey - Industrials)

Kaaba Resources Inc. (B.C. 1962)
Apr. 17, 1990 – Name changed to International Kaaba Gold Corporation; basis 1 new for 6 old shs. (see FPsurvey - Mines & Energy)

Kaboose Inc. (Can. Nov. 28, 2005 amalg.)
June 9, 2009 – Name changed to KAB Distribution Inc. ■

Kabour Mines Ltd. (Ont. 1946)
Aug. 6, 1957 – Charter cancelled.

Kadrey Energy Corporation (B.C. May 19, 1981)
July 10, 1984 – Name changed to Baroque Resources Ltd.; basis 1 new for 10 old shs. ■

Kadywood Capital Corp. (B.C. Oct. 20, 1999)
July 15, 2008 – Name changed to Gold Wheaton Gold Corp. ■

The Kafus Capital Corporation (B.C. Feb. 17, 1983)
Sept. 15, 1997 – Name changed to Kafus Environmental Industries Ltd. ■

Kafus Environmental Industries Ltd. (B.C. Feb. 17, 1983)
June 23, 1999 – Name changed to Kafus Industries Ltd. ■

Kafus Industries Ltd. (B.C. Feb. 17, 1983)
Aug. 22, 2000 – Placed into bankruptcy. PricewaterhouseCoopers Inc. was appointed trustee.

Kaieteur Resource Corporation (B.C. Aug. 8, 1988 amalg.)
Mar. 21, 2005 – Name changed to Samba Gold Inc. ■

Kainantu Resources Ltd. (B.C. July 4, 2018)
Feb. 9, 2024 – Name changed to South Pacific Metals Corp.; basis 1 new for 10 old shs. (see FPsurvey - Mines & Energy)

Kairos Capital Corporation (Alta. Oct. 18, 2010)
Dec. 20, 2017 – Name changed to Lithium Chile Inc. (see FPsurvey - Mines & Energy)

Kaiser Coal Ltd. (B.C. July 31, 1967)
Apr. 10, 1969 – Name changed to Kaiser Resources Ltd. ■

Kaiser Development Corporation Ltd. (Sask. 1956)
Oct. 24, 1958 – Struck off register.

Kaiser Mines of Canada Ltd. (Ont. 1957)
Shldrs. entitled to equivalent of 0.02159 of a sh. Mission Financial Corporation Limited per one sh. Kaiser Mines. (see Mission Financial Corporation Limited)

Kaiser Resources Ltd. (B.C. July 31, 1967)
Jan. 16, 1981 – Name changed to B.C. Coal Ltd. ■

Kaitone Holdings Ltd. (B.C. Apr. 18, 1988)
Sept. 3, 1991 – Name changed to Consolidated Kaitone Holdings Ltd.; basis 1 new for 3 old shs. ■

Kaiyue International Inc. (Alta. Nov. 23, 2009)
Nov. 2, 2017 – Name changed to Benchmark Botanics Inc. pursuant to reverse takeover acquisition of Potanicals Green Growers Inc. ■

Kaizen Capital Corp. (Alta. Jan. 20, 2010)
Apr. 19, 2016 – Continued into British Columbia.
May 11, 2016 – Name changed to Tudor Gold Corp. following Qualifying Transaction acquisition of Mackie mineral property. (see FPsurvey - Mines & Energy)

Kaizen Discovery Inc. (B.C. Mar. 21, 2006 amalg.)
Feb. 8, 2024 – All o/s shs. not already held acquired by Ivanhoe Electric Inc.; basis 1 Ivanhoe Electric sh. for 127 Kaizen Discovery shs.

Kaizen Technologies Inc. (Alta. Jan. 28, 1992)
Nov. 28, 1996 – Name changed to Underbalanced Drilling Systems Corporation following acquisition of Underbalanced Drilling Systems Ltd.; basis 1 new for 5 old shs. ■

Kakanda Development Corp. (B.C. Feb. 19, 1980)
Jan. 19, 2007 – Name changed to Kakanda Resources Corp. following court-approved corporate reorganization whereby assets were transferred to newly incorporated wholly owned Kakanda Resources Corp. and shares exchanged on a 1-for-1 basis and distributed as a stock divd. to shldrs. ■

Kakanda Resources Corp. (B.C. Nov. 16, 2006)
Mar. 28, 2008 – Name changed to Otish Energy Inc. ■

Kal Minerals Corp. (B.C. Feb. 19, 2016)
Apr. 6, 2020 – Name changed to Tarachi Gold Corp.; basis 2 new for 1 old sh. (see FPsurvey - Mines & Energy)

Kal Resources Ltd. (B.C. 1968)
Nov. 1976 – Name changed to National Irron Resources Ltd.; basis 1 new for 2 old shs. ■

Kala Canada Ltd. (Alta. Aug. 22, 1982 amalg.)
Nov. 4, 1991 – Petitioned into bankruptcy and Calgary-based KPMG Inc. was apppointed trustee.
May 1995 – All the assets had been sold and the secured creditors suffered a shortfall. There were no funds available for distribution to unsecured creditors or shldrs.
Mar. 3, 1998 – Trustee discharged.

Kala Exploration Ltd. (Alta. Aug. 22, 1982 amalg.)
Jan. 14, 1987 – Name changed to Kala Feedlots Ltd.; basis 1 new for 5 old shs. ■

Kala Feedlots Ltd. (Alta. Aug. 22, 1982 amalg.)
Mar. 27, 1989 – Name changed to Kala Canada Ltd. ■

Kaladar Iron Mines Ltd. (Ont. 1957)
Apr. 20, 1965 – Name changed to Kaladar Mines Limited. ■

Kaladar Mines Limited (Ont. 1957)
Jan. 3, 1983 – Charter cancelled.

Kalahari Resources Inc. (B.C. July 2, 1986)
Dec. 22, 2010 – Name changed to Integra Gold Corp.; basis 1 new for 10 old shs. ■

Kalamalka Gold Mines Ltd. (B.C. Nov. 26, 1934)
Wound up. First and final distribution made to shldrs. of 3.3¢ per sh.

Kalamalta Mines Ltd. (B.C. 1968)
Mar. 10, 1969 – Name changed to Kalamalta Resources Ltd. ■

Kalamalta Resources Ltd. (B.C. 1968)
Oct. 24, 1969 – Name changed to Kal Resources Ltd. ■

Kalbrook Mining Co. (Ont. 1945)
Mar. 1962 – Charter cancelled; distribution made of 1¢ per sh.

Kalco Valley Mines Ltd. (B.C. May 17, 1966)
July 9, 1975 – Name changed to Consolidated Kalco Valley Mines Ltd.; basis 1 new for 5 old shs. ■

Kaleeda Resource Industries Inc. (Alta. Dec. 12, 1986)
June 30, 1992 – Name changed to Kaleeda Enterprises Inc.; basis 1 new for 4 old shs. (see FPsurvey - Mines & Energy)

Kali Venture Corporation (B.C. 1980)
July 24, 1992 – Dissolved and struck off register.

Kalibak Gold Mines Ltd. (Ont. 1938)
Nov. 1967 – Charter cancelled.

Kaliber Resources Ltd. (B.C. Oct. 13, 1983)
Oct. 4, 1989 – Name changed to Metro Energy Ltd. ■

Kalimantan Gold Corporation (Ont. Oct. 11, 1995)
Oct. 7, 1997 – Name changed to Kalimantan Gold Corporation Limited and continued into Bermuda. ■

Kalimantan Gold Corporation Limited (Bermuda Oct. 7, 1997)
July 27, 2015 – Name changed to Asiamet Resources Limited. ■

Kallio Iron Mines Limited (Ont. 1970)
Oct. 23, 1978 – Amalgamated (1 new for 5 old shs.) with Alchib Developments Ltd. (1 new for 3 old shs.) to form Kalrock Developments Ltd.

Kallisto Energy Corp. (Alta. May 3, 2004 amalg.)
Nov. 20, 2014 – Name changed to Toro Oil & Gas Ltd. ■

Kalo Gold Holdings Corp. (B.C. Mar. 6, 2019)
Aug. 17, 2021 – Name changed to Kalo Gold Corp. (see FPsurvey - Mines & Energy)

Kalrock Developments Limited (Ont. 1978 amalg.)
Dec. 10, 1990 – Amalgamated with Flint Rock Mines Limited to form a new company known as Kalrock Resources Limited; basis 1 new for 1 old sh. (see Kalrock Resources Limited)

Kalrock Resources Limited (Ont. Aug. 8, 1990 amalg.)
June 1, 1993 – Formed Cercal Minerals Corporation in Ontario on amalgamation with 1013721 Ontario Inc. (a wholly owned subsid. of Laurasia Resources Limited). ∎

Kalvak Coppermines Ltd. (B.C. 1968)
Jan. 1971 – Name changed to Wick Mining Co. Ltd. ∎

Kalytera Therapeutics, Inc. (B.C. Dec. 30, 2016)
Apr. 12, 2021 – Name changed to Claritas Pharmaceuticals, Inc. (see FPsurvey - Mines & Energy)

Kam and Ronson Media Group Inc. (Alta. Mar. 18, 2003)
Feb. 26, 2014 – Privatized; basis 2¢ per post-consolidated sh.

Kam-Kotia Mines Limited (Ont. June 7, 1945)
1985 – Amalgamated in Ontario to continue with same name. (see Goldcorp Investments Limited)
June 1, 1989 – Acquired by Goldcorp Investments Limited for $3.00 per sh. (see Goldcorp Investments Limited)

Kam Scientific Inc. (B.C. 1988)
Jan. 15, 1993 – Name changed to Global Teleworks Corp.; basis 1 new for 2 old shs. ∎

Kamad Silver Co. Ltd. (B.C. Mar. 23, 1967)
Jan. 19, 1993 – Name changed to Agate Bay Resources Ltd.; basis 1 new for 5 old shs. ∎

Kamalta Exploration Ltd. (Alta. 1952)
1970 – Placed into bankruptcy. All assets sold and proceeds distributed to creditors.

Kambern International Industries Limited (Ont. 1969)
1971 – Wound up. Assets acquired by Berncam International Industries Ltd. for 612,505 shs. of Berncam, distributed sh.-for-sh. to Kambern shldrs.

Kamcon Mines Limited (Can. 1946)
June 1, 1990 – Amalgamated with 173431 Canada Inc. to become a wholly owned susid. of Nerco Minerals-Canada, Ltd.

Kaminak Gold Corporation (B.C. July 4, 2005)
July 22, 2016 – Acquired by Goldcorp Inc.; basis 0.10896 Goldcorp com. shs. for 1 Kaminak com. sh. (see Goldcorp Inc.)

Kamis Copper Mines Ltd. (Ont. 1953)
June 1955 – Name changed to Kamis Uranium Mines Ltd. ∎

Kamis Uranium Mines Ltd. (Ont. 1953)
Aug. 8, 1960 – Formed Ver-Million Gold Placer Mining Ltd. ∎

Kamisfair Mines Ltd. (Ont. 1967)
Dec. 9, 1985 – Charter cancelled.

Kamlac Gold Mines Ltd. (Ont. Oct. 19, 1937)
1946 – Wound up. Distribution of 1 sh. Kamcon Mines Limited for 3.5 old shs. Kamlac Gold Mines Ltd. (see Kamcon Mines Limited)

Kamlo Gold Mines Limited (Ont. Apr. 9, 1973)
Oct. 29, 1985 – Name changed to NRT Research Technologies Inc.; basis 1 new for 4 old shs. ∎

Kamlode Resources Inc. (B.C. 1981)
May 31, 1988 – Name changed to Symes Resources Inc.; basis 10 new for 25 old shs. ∎

Kamloops Cablenet Limited (B.C. 1974)
Feb. 1, 1988 – Merged with CableNet Limited.

Kamloops Copper Co. (B.C. 1951)
1964 – Name changed to Kamloops Copper Consolidated Ltd.; basis 1 new for 7 old shs. ∎

Kamloops Copper Consolidated Ltd. (B.C. 1951)
Mar. 1972 – Amalgamated with 2 other cos. to form Davenport Oil and Mining Ltd.; basis 1 new for 6 old shs.

Kamorley Oils Ltd. (Can. 1929)
Mar. 1957 – Assets distributed to shldrs. Charter surrendered.

Kamsack Resource Explorations Limited (Ont. Jan. 11, 1978)
Mar. 5, 1985 – Name changed to Jascan Resources Inc.; basis 1 new for 2 old shs. ∎

Kamstar Mines Ltd. (B.C. 1965)
Sept. 1974 – Dissolved.

Kanadario Gold Inc. (B.C. Nov. 23, 2017)
Dec. 17, 2020 – Name changed to G Mining Ventures Corp. and continued into Canada. (see FPsurvey - Mines & Energy)

Kanata Genesis Fund Ltd. (Ont. Oct. 13, 1982)
Dec. 12, 1989 – Formed Kanata Genesis Ltd. on amalgamation with 840009 Ontario Limited.; basis 1 new for 14.5 old shs. ∎

Kanata Genesis Ltd. (Ont. Oct. 13, 1982)
Oct. 17, 1990 – Name changed to SFP International Ltd. ∎

Kanata Hotels Inc. (Ont. 1973)
May 4, 1987 – Name changed to Kanata Hotels International Inc. ∎

Kanata Hotels International Inc. (Ont. 1973)
Mar. 8, 1989 – Amalgamated in Ontario to continue with same name. (see Armbro Enterprises Inc.)
Mar. 8, 1990 – Acquired by 873445 Ontario Limited, a wholly owned subsid. of Armbro Enterprises Inc.; basis 0.1222 Armbro com. shs. or 1 $1.10 redeem. retractable cl. A pref. sh. redeemed at $1.10 for 1 Kanata com. sh. (see Armbro Enterprises Inc.)

Kancana Ventures Limited (Can. July 19, 1956)
Dec. 21, 1994 – Name changed to Walron Minerals Corporation; basis 1 new for 4 old shs. ∎

Kandahar Resources Limited (B.C. 1952)
July 31, 1984 – Name changed to First Allied Resources Corp.; basis 1 new for 7 old shs. (see FPsurvey - Mines & Energy)

Kane Investment Corp. (Alta. Dec. 4, 1986)
June 2, 2005 – Voluntarily delisted from TSX-VEN. (see FPsurvey - Industrials)

Kaneh Bosm Biotechnology Inc. (B.C. Mar. 1, 2006)
Sept. 20, 2018 – Name changed to ICC International Cannabis Corp. ∎

Kangaroo Capital Inc. (Can. Sept. 22, 2003)
Nov. 15, 2004 – Name changed to Kangaroo Media Inc. ∎

Kangaroo Media Inc. (Can. Sept. 22, 2003)
Dec. 31, 2009 – Acquired by Game Day Entertainment, LLC for 42¢ per sh.

Kangeld Resources Ltd. (B.C. 1981)
Sept. 6, 1989 – Amalgamated with Gabriel Resources Inc. and Lockwood Petroleum Inc. to form Appian Resources Ltd.; basis 0.2131 new for 1 old sh. (see Appian Resources Ltd.)

Kanichee Mining Inc. (unknown)
1976 – Private co. Ceased operations indefinitely. All assets and props. sold in 1977-78 to pay creditors. No payback to principals.

Kanosak Capital Venture Corporation (Can. Feb. 23, 2011)
June 28, 2013 – Name changed to Algold Resources Ltd. ∎

Kansai Mining Corporation (B.C. Apr. 2, 1986)
July 9, 2002 – Continued into Yukon.
Jan. 31, 2008 – Continued into British Columbia. (see FPsurvey - Mines & Energy)

Kanstate Resources Ltd. (Alta. 1979)
Nov. 1, 1987 – Struck off register.

Kanzen Capital Corp. (B.C. Sept. 19, 2016)
Dec. 20, 2018 – Name changed to Geyser Brands Inc. following Qualifying Transaction reverse takeover acquisition of Geyser Management Inc.; basis 1 new for 1.5 old shs. ∎

Kaoclay Resources Inc. (Can. June 21, 1996)
June 12, 2006 – Formed Erdene Resources Inc. on amalgamation with wholly owned subsid. of Erdene Gold Inc.; basis 1.65 new Erdene sh. for 1 old Kaoclay sh. plus 0.5 new Erdene wt. for 0.30303 old Kaoclay wt. (see Erdene Gold Inc.)

Kap Resources Ltd. (B.C. Sept. 18, 1986)
Nov. 14, 1990 – Formed KAP Resources Ltd. in British Columbia on amalgamation with Atacama Resources Ltd.; basis 0.75 new for 1 Atacama sh. and 1 new for 1 Kap sh. ∎

Kapalua Gold Mines Ltd. (Alta. Mar. 21, 1983)
Aug. 1988 – Ceased to carry on active business.
Sept. 1, 1993 – Reactivated.
Nov. 16, 1993 – Name changed to Prize Energy Inc.; basis 1 new for 5 old shs. ∎

Kaphearst Resource Corp. (B.C. Dec. 11, 1985)
June 15, 1990 – Name changed to Tri-Alpha Investments Ltd.; basis 1 new for 3 old shs. ∎

Kapkichi Nickel Mines Ltd. (Ont. 1956)
Dec. 3, 1980 – Amalgamated with 3 other cos. to form Hoffman Exploration & Minerals Limited; basis 1 new for 4.21538 old shs.

Kappa Explorations Limited (Ont. 1962)
July 12, 1977 – Name changed to Kappa Investments Limited. ∎

Kappa Investments Limited (Ont. 1962)
Aug. 24, 1987 – Dissolved.
Oct. 4, 1989 – Revived.

Kappa Resource Corporation (B.C. June 10, 1987)
Apr. 23, 1990 – Name changed to Offshore Systems International Ltd. ∎

Kappa Resources Limited (B.C. 1979)
June 1984 – Merged with Aber Resources Ltd.

Kaps Transport Ltd. (Alta. May 23, 1957)
Jan. 2, 1981 – Name changed to Strathcona Resource Industries Ltd. ∎

Kapuskasing Gold Corp. (B.C. Apr. 26, 2010)
Apr. 23, 2019 – Name changed to MinKap Resources Inc.; basis 1 new for 6 old shs. ∎

Kapuskasing Resources Ltd. (Ont. 1980)
Oct. 1987 – Amalgamated with South American Goldfields Inc. to continue as South American Goldfields Inc.; basis 1 new for 6 old shs. (see South American Goldfields Inc.)

Karado Exploration Ltd. (Ont. 1946)
Feb. 28, 1968 – Dissolved.

Karaka Gold Mines Ltd. (Ont. 1948)
Aug. 24, 1959 – Dissolved.

Karam Minerals Inc. (B.C. Dec. 14, 2016)
Jan. 14, 2022 – Name changed to First Uranium Resources Ltd. ∎

Karat Yellowknife Mines Ltd. (Ont. 1945)
1953 – Charter cancelled.

Kardar Canadian Oils Ltd. (Ont. 1943)
Nov. 1976 – Charter cancelled.

Karel Capital Corporation (Alta. Dec. 6, 2007)
Aug. 3, 2010 – Amalgamated with Preo Software Inc. to form new co. with same name Preo Software Inc. constituting Karel's Qualifying Transaction; 0.5 new Preo shs. for 1 old Preo sh. and 0.333 new Preo shs. for 1 Karel sh.

Kari Resource Explorations Ltd. (Ont. June 13, 1978)
Aug. 9, 1983 – Amalgamated with Pan Geologic Resources Inc., a private co., to form San Paulo Explorations Limited; basis 1 new for 3 old shs.

Kariana Resources Inc. (B.C. Sept. 14, 2010)
May 6, 2015 – Name changed to Lifestyle Delivery Systems Inc. following acquisition of Canna Delivery Systems Inc. ■

Kariba Enterprises Limited (B.C. 1972)
Feb. 14, 1977 – Name changed to Poney Explorations Ltd.; basis 1 new for 3 old shs. ■

Kariba Mines Ltd. (B.C. 1972)
June 4, 1974 – Name changed to Kariba Enterprises Limited. ■

Karisma Capital Corp. (Alta. Mar. 28, 2000)
June 16, 2003 – Name changed to EMM Energy Inc. following non-arm's length Qualifying Transaction reverse takeover acquisition of EMM Energy Corporation; basis 1 new for 2 old shs. ■

Karma Capital Corp. (B.C. Sept. 1, 1999)
July 14, 2006 – Formed Biosign Technologies Inc. in Ontario following Qualifying Transaction amalgamation with Biosign Technologies Inc., constituting a reverse takeover by Biosign; basis 0.3 new for 1 Biosign sh. and 1 new for 20 Karma shs. ■

Karma Ventures Incorporated (B.C. Apr. 25, 1966)
Dec. 21, 1982 – Name changed to Donner Resources Ltd. ■

Karmin Exploration Inc. (Alta. June 14, 1999)
Nov. 4, 2019 – Amalgamated with Votoantim Metals Canada Inc., a wholly owned subsid. of Nexa Resources S.A.; basis US$0.770467 cash per sh. for 1 Karmin sh. Additionally, com. shs. of Kar Gold Inc., the private company into which certain assets and liabilities of Karmin were transferred, were distrib. to Karmin shldrs. by way of a dividend on a 1-for-1 basis.

Karoo Exploration Corp. (B.C. Aug. 15, 2013)
Dec. 4, 2017 – Name changed to Bruin Point Helium Corp. following reverse takeover acquisition of Bruin Point Energy Limited; basis 1 new for 13.5 old shs. ■

Karora Resources Inc. (Can. Dec. 13, 2006)
Aug. 6, 2024 – Acquired by Westgold Resources Limited; basis 2.524 Westgold ord. shs., plus Cdn$0.608 cash and 0.30 Culico Metals Inc shs. for 1 Karora Resources sh.

Karpus Gold Mines Ltd. (Can. 1946)
May 1957 – Charter cancelled.

Karsten Energy Corp. (B.C. Nov. 28, 2012)
Apr. 26, 2021 – Voluntarily delisted.
Oct. 27, 2021 – Name changed to Final Bell Holdings International Ltd. (see FPsurvey - Mines & Energy)

Kasba Explorations Ltd. (Ont. 1948)
Dec. 7, 1964 – Dissolved.

Kaskada Resources Ltd. (B.C. June 1, 1967)
Nov. 1, 1985 – Amalgamated with Futurity Oils Limited (1 for 4) to form Canadian Futurity Oils Ltd.; basis 2 cl. A shs. of Canadian Futurity for each 13 shs. of Kaskada.

Kaslo Base Metals Ltd. (B.C. 1951)
Mar. 1964 – Dissolved.

Kassan Resources Inc. (B.C. Apr. 30, 1987)
Jan. 15, 1993 – Name changed to Consolidated Kassan Resources Inc.; basis 1 new for 2.2 old shs. ■

Kast Telecom Inc. (Can. May 13, 1994)
July 5, 2000 – Continued into Luxembourg.
Apr. 25, 2001 – Name changed to Kast Telecom Europe S.A.

Kasten Chase Applied Research Limited (Ont. July 24, 1996 amalg.)
July 24, 2007 – Continued into Alberta.
Mar. 2, 2010 – Name changed to Kasten Energy Inc. (see FPsurvey - Industrials)

Katana Resources Ltd. (Alta. Nov. 27, 1980 amalg.)
May 1, 1992 – Dissolved and struck off register.

Katanga Mines Ltd. (B.C. 1968)
1973 – Acquired by Far East Minerals Ltd. (see Far East Minerals Ltd.)

Katanga Mining Limited (Bermuda Oct. 6, 1996)
Aug. 31, 2011 – Continued into Yukon.
June 8, 2020 – All o/s com. shs. not already held acquired by Glencore International AG; basis Cdn$0.16 cash per sh. Subsequently amalg. with 836074 Yukon Inc.

Kateri Mining Co. Ltd. (Ont. 1958)
Jan. 1971 – Charter cancelled.

Katherine Lead Mines Ltd. (Ont. 1937)
Oct. 4, 1954 – Charter cancelled.

Kathex Mining Co. Ltd. (B.C. 1969)
June 27, 1977 – Dissolved.

Katipult Technology Corp. (B.C. Dec. 12, 2016)
Oct. 2, 2019 – Continued into Alberta.
Feb. 11, 2025 – Placed into receivership and KSV Restructuring Inc. was appointed receiver.

Katlor Environmental Technologies Inc. (B.C. 1983)
June 20, 1995 – Name changed to Barbican Financial Corp.; basis 1 new for 9 old shs. ■

Katlor Explorations Ltd. (B.C. 1983)
May 31, 1993 – Name changed to Katlor Environmental Technologies Inc. ■

Kaufel Group Ltd. (Can. Nov. 19, 1974)
Nov. 30, 1998 – Acquired by Thomas & Betts Canada Inc., a wholly owned subsid. of Thomas & Betts Corporation, for $8.00 per sh.

Kauz Construction Ltd. (Ont. 1958)
1969 – Amalgamated to form Headway Corp. Ltd.

Kavalmedia Services Ltd. (B.C. Oct. 16, 1997)
Aug. 5, 2008 – Name changed to EmerGeo Solutions Worldwide Inc. following reverse takeover acquisition of EmerGeo Solutions, Inc. ■

Kaw-Crow Patricia Gold Mines Ltd. (Ont. 1936)
Mar. 18, 1965 – Dissolved.

Kay-Hays Mines Ltd. (Ont. 1937)
1948 – Charter cancelled.

Kay Lake Mines Limited (Man. Mar. 7, 1951)
Feb. 16, 1968 – Name changed to Scope Resources Limited. ■

Kayak Explorations Ltd. (Ont. 1975)
Jan. 23, 1979 – Amalgamated with Glenshire Mines Ltd. (231 for 1,000), Huddersfield Uranium Mines Ltd. (129 for 1,000), La France Explorations Ltd. (128 for 1,000), Lunel Management Ltd. (923.5 for 1), Sandhurst Mines Ltd. (1 for 1) and Steppingstone Explorations Ltd. (229 for 1,000) to form Lunel Enterprises Inc.; basis 195 new for 1,000 old shs. (see Lunel Enterprises Inc.)

Kayjon Minerals Ltd. (Ont. 1965)
1970 – Name changed to Spartex Oil & Gas Limited. ■

Kaymac Gold Mines Ltd. (Ont. 1944)
June 1972 – Charter cancelled.

Kaymo Minerals Ltd. (Ont. 1965)
Apr. 9, 1975 – Charter cancelled.

Kayo Management Ltd. (Ont. Jan. 4, 1937)
Apr. 30, 2001 – Name changed to TMI-Learnix Inc. pursuant to reverse takeover acquisition of TMI-Education.com Inc.; basis 1.29017 new for 1 old sh. ■

Kayorum Gold Mines, Limited (Ont. Jan. 4, 1937)
Jan. 20, 1999 – Name changed to Kayo Management Ltd. ■

Kayrand Mining & Development Co. Ltd. (Ont. 1937)
1955 – Name changed to Chib-Kayrand Copper Mines Limited; basis 1 new for 5 old shs. ■

Kayty Exploration Ltd. (Alta. Mar. 18, 1981)
Sept. 10, 1987 – Name changed to Kayty Inc.; basis 1 new for 10 old shs. ■

Kayty Inc. (Alta. Mar. 18, 1981)
Sept. 22, 1987 – Continued into Ontario.
Dec. 7, 1994 – Name changed to WLD Inc.; basis 1 new for 3 old shs. ■

Kaza Copper Ltd. (B.C. 1967)
Feb. 25, 1983 – Dissolved.

Kazakhstan Minerals Corporation (Ont. Oct. 13, 1987)
Nov. 1, 1995 – Continued into Yukon.
July 24, 2001 – Name changed to European Minerals Corporation. ■

Kazakstan Goldfields Corporation (Ont. Oct. 9, 1996 amalg.)
Mar. 12, 2007 – Dissolved and struck from register.

KazaX Minerals Inc. (B.C. Sept. 12, 2005)
Dec. 15, 2016 – Privatized by 1069411 B.C. Ltd.'s acquisition of all o/s com. shs. not already held for Cdn$0.01 cash per sh.

Keaton Resources Ltd. (B.C. Sept. 3, 1987)
Nov. 7, 1997 – Name changed to GFM Resources Limited. ■

Kechika Mines Ltd. (B.C. 1965)
Oct. 21, 1974 – Charter cancelled.

Kedar Mines Limited (Ont. 1962)
Dec. 1976 – Name changed to Maverick Uranium Explorations Inc. ■

Keefer Resources Inc. (B.C. 1984)
Nov. 6, 1992 – Dissolved and struck off register.

Keegan Resources Inc. (B.C. Sept. 23, 1999)
Feb. 21, 2013 – Name changed to Asanko Gold Inc. ■

Keek Inc. (Alta. Jan. 10, 2008)
Mar. 3, 2017 – Name changed to Peeks Social Ltd. ■

Keele Industrial Developments Ltd. (Ont. 1960)
Jan. 3, 1962 – Name changed to Keele Industrial Developments of Canada Limited. ■

Keele Industrial Developments of Canada Limited (Ont. 1960)
Aug. 9, 1972 – Dissolved.

Keeley Extension Mines Ltd. (Ont. 1923)
May 24, 1975 – Name changed to Grandad Gold Mines Ltd. ■

Keeley-Frontier Mines Ltd. (Ont. 1959)
1964 – Name changed to Canadian Keeley Mines Ltd.; basis 1 new for 2 old shs. ■

Keeley-Frontier Resources Limited (Ont. 1959)
Feb. 1, 1984 – Amalgamated with Mount Jamie Mines Limited (1 for 4) to form Jamie Frontier Resources Inc.; basis 2 new for 5 old shs. (see Mount Jamie Mines Ltd.)

Keeley Silver Mines Ltd. (Ont. 1922)
1933 – Merged into Anglo-Huronian Ltd.; basis 1 new for 5 old shs.

Keelynn Mines Limited (Ont. 1947)
Aug. 1957 – Charter cancelled.

Keen Industries Limited (B.C. July 4, 1962)
Mar. 13, 1984 – Continued into Alberta.
Oct. 30, 1986 – Name changed to Delta North Transportation Ltd. ■

Keener Technologies Inc. (Can. Jan. 23, 1987)
Aug. 9, 1993 – Name changed to Mindflight Corporation; basis 1 new for 4 old shs. ■

Keeper Resources Inc. (Alta. Oct. 17, 2003)
May 29, 2008 – Acquired by Vietnam Resource Investments (Holdings) Limited for $1.50 per sh.

Keeprite Inc. (Can. Apr. 1979)
May 15, 1987 – Acquired by Inter-City Gas Corporation and is now a private company.

Keeprite Products Limited (Ont. 1945)
Apr. 1979 – Name changed to Keeprite Inc. and continued into Canada. ■

Keezic Resources Limited (Ont. 1981)
July 5, 1985 – Amalgamated with 2 other cos. under agreement dated to form a new co., Tandem Resources Ltd.; basis 1 new for 4 old shs.

Keg Restaurants Ltd. (B.C. Mar. 20, 1972)
Oct. 1, 1987 – Amalgamated with Whitbread Restaurants (B.C.) Inc. to form new co. with same name Keg Restaurants Ltd. Existing Keg shldrs. exchanged their shs. for pref. shs. subsequently redeemed at $2.00 per sh.
Sept. 21, 2000 – Continued into Ontario.

The Keg Royalties Income Fund (Ont. Apr. 12, 2002)
Aug. 13, 2025 – All o/s fund units not already held acquired by Fairfax Financial Holdings Limited; basis $18.60 cash per fund unit.

Kegamo Mines Ltd. (Ont. 1947)
Charter cancelled.

Keho Dome Oils Limited (Alta. Feb. 17, 1938)
1959 – Struck off register.

Keith Copper Ltd. (B.C. Aug. 25, 1970)
Mar. 12, 1983 – Name changed to Tanker Oil & Gas Ltd.; basis 1 new for 4 old shs. ■

Keith Resources Ltd. (B.C. July 24, 1991 amalg.)
Sept. 30, 1994 – Name changed to Avalon Ventures Ltd.; basis 1 new for 5 old shs. ■

Keithgold Mines Ltd. (Ont. 1946)
Dec. 7, 1977 – Dissolved.

Keithwood Mines Ltd. (Ont. 1946)
1950 – Charter cancelled; no equity.

Kekelac Gold Mines Ltd. (Ont. 1947)
1955 – Charter cancelled.

Kel-Glen Mines Ltd. (B.C. 1965)
Dec. 18, 1978 – Dissolved.

Kelan Resources Inc. (B.C. Aug. 20, 1987)
May 29, 1992 – Name changed to Auromar Development Corporation; basis 1 new for 3.5 old shs. ■

Kelbee Rare Metal Corp. (Ont. 1956)
Dec. 28, 1964 – Dissolved.

Keld'Or Resources Inc. (B.C. May 17, 1984)
Sept. 6, 1990 – Name changed to Consolidated Keld'Or Resources Inc.; basis 1 new for 3 old shs. ■

Kelgray Mines Ltd. (Ont. 1946)
June 1974 – Charter cancelled.

Kelkirk Mines Ltd. (Ont. 1959)
Jan. 1971 – Charter cancelled.

Kellcam Exploration Ltd. (B.C. 1965)
Sept. 9, 1974 – Dissolved.

Kellogg Salada Canada Inc. (Can. 1927)
Sept. 10, 1989 – Name changed to Kellogg Canada Inc.

Kellogg Salada Canada Ltd. (Can. 1927)
Dec. 20, 1978 – Name changed to Kellogg Salada Canada Inc. ■

Kelly-Desmond Mining Corporation Ltd. (Ont. 1954)
Apr. 20, 1994 – Name changed to Premium Letney Canada Inc.; basis 1 new for 10 old shs. ■

Kelly-Deyong Sound Corporation Ltd. (B.C. 1969 amalg.)
Aug. 1978 – Steintron International Electronics Ltd., offered to purch. all o/s shs. not already held; basis one 10% 2nd pref. ser. A sh. for 1 com. sh.

Kelly, Douglas & Company, Limited (B.C. 1906)
June 1989 – Acquired by Loblaw Companies Limited; $80 per sh.

Kelly-K Mines Ltd. (Ont. 1966)
1969 – Amalgamated with Summit Explorations & Holdings; basis 3 new for 50 old shs.

Kelly-Kerr Energy Corporation (B.C. 1981)
Oct. 19, 1988 – Formed Sirius Resource Corporation following amalgamation; basis 1 new for 4 old shs. ■

Kelly-Kirkland Mines Ltd. (Ont. Nov. 5, 1935)
1968 – Charter cancelled.

Kelly Lake Nickel Mines Ltd. (Man. 1944)
Mar. 1971 – Name changed to Albany Oil & Gas Ltd. ■

Kelly Petroleum Inc. (B.C. 1967)
Jan. 12, 1982 – Amalgamated with 3 other cos. to form New Frontier Petroleum Corporation; basis 0.27 new for 1 old sh.

Kelmac Mines Ltd. (Ont. 1939)
May 1947 – Acquired by Baldwin Consolidated Mines Ltd. in 1949; basis 1 new for 7 old shs. Charter cancelled.

Kelmac Oils Limited (Alta. 1955)
1964 – Struck off register.

Kelman Technologies Inc. (Can. Feb. 11, 1991 amalg.)
May 18, 2010 – Privatized at $2.00 per sh.

Kelnick Resources Ltd. (Can. Feb. 19, 1990)
Jan. 18, 2001 – Formed The Kewl Corporation on amalgamation with The Excel Apparel Group Ltd. ■

Kelore Mines Ltd. (Ont. May 9, 1945)
Mar. 27, 1953 – Name changed to New Kelore Mines Limited; basis 1 new for 5 old shs. ■

Kelowna Exploration Co. Ltd. (B.C. 1933)
1951 – Name changed to Kelowna Mines Hedley Limited. ■

Kelowna Mines Hedley Limited (B.C. 1933)
May 1958 – Placed into voluntary liquidation. Distribution of assets made June 1, 1959.

Kelrowe Gold Mines Ltd. (Ont. 1938)
1946 – Assets acquired by Kelwren Gold Mines Ltd.; basis 1 new for 2.4 old shs.

Kelsey-Hayes Canada Limited (Ont. 1913)
Jan. 31, 1991 – Amalgamated with Kelsey-Hayes Company a wholly owned subsid. of Varity Corporation; basis $20 per sh. (see Varity Corporation)

Kelsey Lake Development Co. Ltd. (Ont. 1958)
1962 – Merged into Choiceland Iron Mines Ltd.; basis 1 new for 1 old sh.

Kelsey's International Inc. (Alta. July 4, 1972)
Feb. 10, 1994 – Continued into Ontario. (see Cara Operations Limited)
July 9, 1999 – Acquired by Cara Operations Limited for $3.00 per sh. (see Cara Operations Limited)

Kelsina Kirkland Gold Mines Ltd. (Ont. 1946)
Sept. 9, 1958 – Dissolved.

Kelso Energy Inc. (Ont. Oct. 3, 2000 amalg.)
June 19, 2004 – Continued into Alberta.
Apr. 28, 2006 – Name changed to COSTA Energy Inc. following reverse takeover acquisition of COSTA Resources Ltd.; basis 1 new for 8 old shs. ■

Kelso Explorations Ltd. (B.C. 1966)
May 1980 – Charter cancelled.

Kelso Resources Ltd. (B.C. Mar. 16, 1987)
July 21, 1994 – Name changed to Kelso Technologies Inc. (see FPsurvey - Industrials)

Kelt Exploration (LNG) Ltd. (Alta. Jan. 14, 2010 amalg.)
Apr. 22, 2015 – Acquired by Kelt Exploration Ltd.; basis 0.34 Kelt com. shs. for 1 Artek com. sh.

Keltey Energy Limited (Alta. June 9, 1994)
Oct. 11, 1996 – Formed KAPPA Energy Company Inc. in Alberta on amalgamation with Kappa Energy Company Inc.; basis 4.63 new for 1 Kappa sh. and 1 new for 7.27 Keltey shs. ■

Keltic Incorporated (N.S. Aug. 20, 1985)
Aug. 8, 2000 – Name changed to CrossOff Incorporated; basis 5 new for 1 old sh. ■

Keltic Mining Corp. Limited (Ont. 1963)
May 1977 – Charter cancelled.

Kelver Mines Ltd. (B.C. Jan. 26, 1968)
Apr. 26, 1974 – Name changed to New Kelver Resources Ltd.; basis 1 new for 2 old shs. ■

Kelvin Creek Explorations Ltd. (B.C.)
May 1, 1969 – Struck off register.

Kelvin Energy Ltd. (Alta. 1977)
Mar. 1, 1991 – Struck off register.
Jan. 21, 1993 – Bankrupt. No funds available for distribution to shldrs. or debentureholders.

Kelvinator of Canada Limited (Can. 1926)
Sept. 28, 1972 – Name changed to WCI Canada Inc. ■

Kelwren Gold Mines Ltd. (Ont. May 9, 1945)
1948 – Name changed to Kelore Mines Ltd.; basis 1 new for 2 old shs. ■

Kemano Copper Mining Co. Ltd. (B.C. 1953)
1954 – Name changed to Independence Mining Co. Ltd. ■

Kemano Gold Corp. (Alta. Dec. 5, 1986)
Apr. 13, 1993 – Name changed to Kemano Resources Ltd.; basis 1 new for 5 old shs. ■

Kemano Resources Ltd. (Alta. Dec. 5, 1986)
Nov. 18, 1993 – Amalgamated with Canadian Northcor Energy Inc. (1 for 1) to form new co. Purcell Energy Ltd.; basis 0.9 Purcell shs. for 1 Kemano com. sh., plus 1 Purcell ser. 1 conv. pref. sh. for 1 Kemano ser. 1 conv. pref. sh. (see Purcell Energy Ltd.)

Kemgas International Limited (B.C. Nov. 10, 1978)
June 23, 1995 – Continued into Bermuda.
May 29, 1996 – Name changed to Kemgas Limited. ■

Kemgas Limited (Bermuda June 23, 1995)
July 25, 2000 – Name changed to CalciTech Ltd.

Kemgas Sydney Inc. (B.C. Nov. 10, 1978)
Feb. 15, 1995 – Name changed to Kemgas International Limited. ■

Kemp Uranium Mines Limited (Que. 1954)
Dec. 5, 1981 – Charter cancelled.

Kempton Capital Partners Inc. (Ont. July 9, 1997)
Dec. 8, 1997 – Name changed to Gensel Biotechnologies Ltd. following acquisition of Gensel Biotechnologies Inc.; basis 1 new for 1 old sh. ■

Kemptville Creameries Limited (Can. - unspecified)
Jan. 1969 – Acquired by Western Canadian Seed Processors Ltd. (see Western Canadian Seed Processors Ltd.)

Ken Bay Gold Mines Ltd. (Ont. 1945)
1955 – Name changed to K. B. Mining Co. Ltd.; basis 5 K. B. and 1 Big Nama Creek Mines Ltd. (partly escrowed) for 10 Ken Bay shs. ■

Ken-Moore Mines Ltd. (B.C. 1946)
Dec. 28, 1950 – Charter cancelled.

Ken-Rio Copper Mines Ltd. (Ont. 1956)
June 1958 – Name changed to Ken-Rio Explorations Ltd. ■

Ken-Rio Explorations Ltd. (Ont. 1956)
Oct. 1958 – Name changed to Rash-Mac Explorations Ltd. ■

Kenadyr Mining (Holdings) Corp. (B.C. Nov. 2, 2010)
Aug. 10, 2021 – Name changed to Kenadyr Metals Corp.; basis 1 new for 10 old shs. (see FPsurvey - Mines & Energy)

Kenai Resources Ltd. (B.C. Dec. 22, 2004)
July 22, 2013 – Acquired by Serabi Gold plc; basis 0.85 Serabi ord. shs. for 1 Kenai com. sh.

Kenalex Red Lake Mines Ltd. (Ont. 1946)
1955 – Charter cancelled.

Kenar Oils & Mines Ltd. (Ont. 1952)
July 1952 – Name changed to Kenwell Oils & Mines Ltd. ■

Kenar Resources Ltd. (B.C. Jan. 31, 1980)
Jan. 23, 1990 – Name changed to Western Commonwealth Developments Inc. ■

Kenare Petroleum Corporation Ltd. (Alta. Mar. 27, 1952)
May 12, 1964 – Name changed to Maverick Mines & Oils Limited; basis 1 new for 5 old shs. ■

Kenbridge Nickel Mines Ltd. (Ont. 1956)
Apr. 11, 1988 – Acquired by Falconbridge Limited; basis unknown. (see Falconbridge Limited)

Kencour Gold Mines Ltd. (Ont. 1944)
Jan. 4, 1960 – Charter cancelled.

Kenda Pershing Mines Ltd. (Que. 1944)
Nov. 1968 – Charter cancelled.

Kendal Mining and Exploration Co. Ltd. (B.C. Jan. 28, 1966)
May 10, 1978 – Name changed to Velvet Exploration Co. Ltd.; basis 1 new for 5 old shs. ■

Kendon Copper Mines Ltd. (Ont. 1965)
Mar. 1976 – Charter cancelled.

Kendou Porcupine Mines Ltd. (Ont. Nov. 24, 1936)
Charter cancelled.

Kendra Gold Resources Ltd. (B.C. Feb. 1, 1988)
May 13, 1994 – Name changed to Koda Resources Ltd. ■

Kenecho Gold Mines Ltd. (Ont. Nov. 14, 1936)
1953 – Charter cancelled.

Kenergy Resource Corporation (Sask. June 6, 1946)
Sept. 7, 1984 – Name changed to International Kenergy Resource Corporation; basis 1 new for 5 old shs. ■

Kengate Resources Ltd. (B.C. Aug. 9, 1979)
Mar. 2, 1990 – Name changed to International Kengate Ventures Inc.; basis 1 new for 3 old shs. ■

Kenieba Goldfields Ltd. (B.C. Nov. 17, 2006)
Feb. 19, 2015 – Name changed to EA Education Group Inc. following reverse takeover acquisition of (old) EA Education Group Inc. ■

Kenilworth Explorations Ltd. (Ont. 1953)
Jan. 1960 – Charter cancelled.

Kenilworth Mines Ltd. (Ont. 1962)
Mar. 1976 – Charter cancelled.

Kenland Gold Mines Ltd. (Ont. Sept. 3, 1936)
1957 – Charter cancelled.

Kenlew Mines Ltd. (Ont. 1954)
Apr. 30, 1969 – Charter cancelled.

Kenmac Chibougamau Mines Ltd. (Que. 1952)
June 1, 1974 – Dissolved.

Kenmayo Yukon Mines Ltd. (Ont. 1950)
Mar. 1956 – Name changed to Mercedes Exploration Co. Ltd.; basis 1 new for 3 old shs. ■

Kenmore Gold Mines Ltd. (Ont. 1939)
Apr. 30, 1969 – Dissolved.

Kenn Holdings and Mining Ltd. (Ont. 1945)
Nov. 28, 1973 – Charter cancelled.

Kenna Capital Corp. (Sask. Sept. 25, 2009)
June 19, 2012 – Name changed to Kenna Resources Corp. following April 2012 Qualifying Transaction acquisition of mineral property in Saskatchewan. ■

Kenna Resources Corp. (Sask. Sept. 25, 2009)
Sept. 4, 2014 – Continued into British Columbia.
June 28, 2016 – Name changed to LOOPShare Ltd. pursuant to reverse takeover acquisition of Saturna Green Systems Inc.; basis 1 new for 1.4695652 old shs. ■

Kennady Diamonds Inc. (Ont. Feb. 27, 2012)
Apr. 18, 2018 – Acquired by Mountain Province Diamonds Inc.; basis 0.975 Mountain Province shs. for 1 Kennady Diamond sh.

Kennecom Inc. (Ont. Sept. 19, 1958)
May 15, 1995 – Name changed to Deltona Industries Inc.; basis 1 new for 20 old shs. ■

Kennedy Lake Gold Mines Ltd. (B.C. 1934)
1952 – Charter cancelled.

Kennedy Minerals Ltd. (Ont. 1964)
May 14, 1969 – Charter cancelled.

Kennedy Resources Inc. (B.C. Aug. 24, 1979)
Mar. 31, 1988 – Dissolved and struck off register.

Kennedy Silver Mines Ltd. (B.C. 1965)
Feb. 25, 1983 – Struck off register.

Keno Hill Mining Co. Ltd. (Can. Nov. 6, 1945)
1948 – Name changed to United Keno Hill Mines Limited; basis 1 new for 2 old shs. ■

Keno Industries Inc. (Ont. 1950)
June 1, 1996 – Formed Dayak Goldfields Corporation in Ontario on amalgamation with Dayak Goldfields Corporation; basis 1 new for 1 Dayak sh. and 1 new for 3 Keno shs. ■

Keno Oils Ltd. (Alta. 1950)
1961 – Name changed to Monterey Petroleum Corporation Ltd. ■

Kenogamisis Gold Mines Ltd. (Ont. 1934)
1973 – Name changed to Anglo Keno Developments Ltd. ■

Kenopo Mining and Milling Co. Ltd. (Ont. 1938)
1964 – Charter cancelled.

Kenora Gold Occurrences Inc. (Can. Aug. 31, 1987)
Mar. 24, 1997 – Dissolved.

Kenora Nickel Mines Ltd. (Ont. 1937)
1957 – Charter cancelled.

Kenoratomic Mines Ltd. (Ont. 1956)
Feb. 1962 – Charter cancelled.

Kenova Mines Ltd. (Ont. Dec. 9, 1965)
Aug. 15, 1967 – Name changed to Shawnee Petroleums Limited and converted into a public co. ■

Kenpat Mines Ltd. (Ont. 1962)
1967 – Charter cancelled.

Kenrell Resources Inc. (B.C. Mar. 14, 1980)
May 22, 1984 – Name changed to New Kenrell Resources Inc.; basis 1 new for 5 old shs. ■

Kenrich-Eskay Mining Corporation (B.C. Aug. 15, 1994)
Nov. 3, 2009 – Name changed to Eskay Mining Corp. (see FPsurvey - Mines & Energy)

Kenrich Mining Corp. (B.C. Sept. 10, 1980)
Aug. 15, 1994 – Amalgamated with Ambergate Explorations Inc. (1 for) to form a new co. also named Kenrich Mining Corporation; basis 1 new for 1 old sh. (see Kenrich Mining Corporation)

Kenrich Mining Corporation (B.C. Aug. 15, 1994)
Nov. 19, 2001 – Name changed to Kenrich-Eskay Mining Corporation; basis 1 new for 3 old shs. ■

Kenricia Gold Mines Ltd. (Ont. 1936)
Mar. 29, 1951 – Charter cancelled.

Kenridge Investment Corp. (Ont. Nov. 9, 1989)
Jan. 1, 1997 – Continued into British Columbia.
Mar. 6, 1997 – Formed Exploro Minerals Corporation Ltd. following merger of 1209879 Ontario Limited (a wholly owned subsid. of Kenridge) and Exploro Minerals Corporation Ltd. (1 for 1); basis 1 new for 3 old sh. (see FPsurvey - Mines & Energy)

Kenridge Mineral Corporation (B.C. 1978)
Mar. 20, 1987 – Name changed to Pacific Kenridge Ventures Inc.; basis 1 new for 2 old shs. ■

Kenridge Red Lake Mines Ltd. (Ont. 1945)
Feb. 1958 – Charter cancelled.

Kenroy Malartic Mines Ltd. (Ont. 1945)
Nov. 1953 – Wound up.

Kensbrook Development Corporation (Alta. 1987)
July 1, 1997 – Struck from register.

Kensington Court Ventures Inc. (B.C. Apr. 13, 2010)
Mar. 10, 2014 – Name changed to Para Resources Inc.; basis 1 new for 5 old shs. ■

Kensington Energy Ltd. (Alta. Jan. 25, 1995)
Mar. 8, 2005 – Acquired by Viking Energy Royalty Trust for 52¢ per sh. (see Viking Energy Royalty Trust)

Kensington Resources Ltd. (B.C. Nov. 3, 1993 amalg.)
Dec. 6, 1993 – Continued into Yukon. (see Shore Gold Inc.)
Nov. 1, 2005 – Acquired by Shore Gold Inc.; basis 0.64 new Shore sh. for 1 old Kensington sh. and 1 new Shore wt. for 1 old Kensington wt. (see Shore Gold Inc.)

Kensull Gold Mines Ltd. (Ont. 1946)
July 29, 1965 – Dissolved.

Kent Chibougamau Mines Ltd. (Que. 1956)
May 15, 1982 – Charter cancelled.

Kent Energy Corp. (B.C. June 1, 1967)
Oct. 1982 – Name changed to Kerf Petroleums Corp.; basis 1 new for 4 old shs. ■

Kent Exploration Inc. (Can. Apr. 6, 2004)
May 3, 2010 – Continued into British Columbia.
Dec. 16, 2013 – Name changed to Bayhorse Silver Inc. (see FPsurvey - Mines & Energy)

Kent Mines Limited (Ont. 1949)
Mar. 28, 1960 – Charter cancelled.

Kent Trust & Savings Company (Ont. 1963)
June 30, 1969 – Merged with The Metropolitan Trust Co.; basis 1 new Metropolitan sh. for 2 old Kent shs.

Kenting Aviation Ltd. (Can. 1947)
Apr. 22, 1968 – Name changed to Kenting Limited. ■

Kenting Energy Services Inc. (Alta. Feb. 1, 1997)
June 27, 1997 – Acquired by Precision Drilling Corporation; basis either $9.10 per Kenting sh., or 1 new $9.10 cum. redeem. convert. pref. sh. of Precision with a face value of $9.10 for 1 old Kenting sh., or 0.1752 new Precision sh. for 1 old Kenting sh., or a combination thereof which equates to a deemed price of $9.10 per Kenting com. sh. (see Precision Drilling Corporation)

Kenting Limited (Can. 1947)
May 1, 1977 – Acquired by Trimac Limited; basis $21.25 and warr. for 1 Trimac cl. A sh. at $9.00 per sh. until May 17, 1982, for each co. sh. held. Name subsequently changed to Kenting Energy Services Inc. (see Kenting Energy Services Inc.; Trimac Limited)

Kentlake Gold Mines Ltd. (Ont. 1944)
Feb. 1978 – Charter cancelled.

Kenton Natural Resources Corporation (Can. Oct. 26, 1984)
Oct. 1, 1990 – Name changed to Pacalta Resources Ltd.; basis 1 new for 5 old shs. ■

Kentucky Oil and Gas Inc. (B.C. Sept. 3, 1987)
June 3, 1994 – Name changed to Integrated Card Technologies Inc. ■

Kentwell Energy Inc. (Ont. 1982)
May 1, 1988 – Name changed to Auto Group International Ltd. following amalgamation with Auto Group International Ltd.; basis 1 new for 18 old shs. ■

Kenty Gold Mines Ltd. (Ont. Sept. 21, 1932)
1950 – Wound up. Distributed equivalent of 0.75¢ per sh. plus 1 sh. Argosy Gold Mines per each 4 Kenty shs.

Kenty Resources Limited (Ont. 1983)
Dec. 1, 1986 – Name changed to Browning Communications Canada Inc.; basis 1 new for 3 old shs. ■

Kenver Resources Inc. (B.C. 1969)
Oct. 4, 1985 – Struck off register.

Kenville Gold Mines Ltd. (Ont. 1945)
Aug. 1964 – Name changed to International Kenville Gold Mines Ltd.; basis 1 new for 4 old shs. ■

Kenville Gold Mines Ltd. (B.C. 1969)
Mar. 1975 – Charter cancelled.

Kenwell Oils & Mines Ltd. (Ont. 1952)
1954 – Taken over by Sapphire Petroleums Ltd.

Kenwest Gold Mines Ltd. (Ont. 1939)
1944 – Acquired by Kenwest Mines Ltd.; basis 1 new for 4 old shs.

Keora Mines Ltd. (Ont. 1926)
June 24, 1965 – Dissolved.

Kepler Acquisition Corp. (B.C. June 14, 2018)
Aug. 17, 2020 – Name changed to ESE Entertainment Inc. pursuant to reverse takeover of (old) ESE Entertainment Inc.; basis 1.5 new for 1 old sh. (see FPsurvey - Industrials)

Kepler Private Equity Corp. (B.C. Jan. 23, 2019)
Feb. 23, 2024 – Name changed to Super Copper Corp. (see FPsurvey - Mines & Energy)

Kereco Energy Ltd. (Alta. Dec. 14, 2004)
May 22, 2008 – Name changed to Cadence Energy Inc. ■

Kerf Petroleums Corp. (B.C. June 1, 1967)
Sept. 30, 1985 – Name changed to Kaskada Resources Ltd. ■

Kerkhoff Industries Inc. (Can. May 21, 1986)
Dec. 9, 1999 – Charter cancelled and co. dissolved.

Kermac Petroleums Ltd. (B.C. 1936)
Mar. 5, 1943 – Resolved to wind up voluntarily. H. W. R. Moore, Victoria, liquidator.

Kermode Capital Ltd. (B.C. June 25, 2008)
June 28, 2010 – Name changed to NSGold Corporation pursuant to Qualifying Transaction reverse takeover acquisition of and short form vertical amalgamation with (old) NSGold Corporation. ■

Kermode Exploration Ltd. (Ont. Nov. 23, 1972)
June 1, 2010 – Name changed to Rencore Resources Ltd. ■

Kermode Resources Ltd. (Alta. Oct. 4, 1995)
Mar. 23, 1999 – Continued into British Columbia. (see FPsurvey - Mines & Energy)

Kernow Resources & Developments Ltd. (B.C. Oct. 23, 1990)
Mar. 8, 2010 – Amalgamated with Green Bull Energy Inc. to form Green Bull Resources Ltd. which was concurrently acquired by Galena International Resources Ltd. constituting Galena's Qualifying Transaction; basis 1 Galena sh. for 3 Kernow shs. and 1 Galena sh. for 1.864 Green Bull shs. (see Galena International Resources Ltd.)

Kerr-Addison Gold Mines Ltd. (Ont. 1936)
Nov. 18, 1963 – Merged with Anglo-Huronian Ltd. (8 for 5) and Bouzan Mines Ltd. (1 for 10) to form a new co. named Kerr Addison Mines Limited; basis 1 new for 1 old sh. (see Kerr Addison Mines Limited)

Kerr Addison Mines Limited (Ont. Nov. 18, 1963)
Apr. 25, 1996 – Acquired by Noranda Inc.; basis 1 Noranda sh. for 1 Kerr sh. (see Noranda Inc.)

Kerr Lake Mines, Limited (Ont. 1917)
May 20, 1958 – Name changed to United Principal Properties Limited. ■

Kerr Mines Inc. (Can. Nov. 9, 1987)
Dec. 17, 2020 – Name changed to Arizona Gold Corp. ■

Kerrigan Gold Mines Ltd. (Ont. 1946)
Mar. 1972 – Charter cancelled.

Kerrisdale Resources Ltd. (B.C. 1984)
June 5, 1992 – Dissolved and struck off register.

Kerromac Mining Company Ltd. (Ont. 1945)
May 15, 1974 – Dissolved.

Kerry Mining Ltd. (B.C. 1973)
July 18, 1986 – Amalgamated with 2 other cos. to form Berkley Resources Inc.; basis 1 new for 3 old shs.

Kersley Oil & Gas Company Limited (Ont. 1949)
1958 – Stated to be dead.

Kerwall Gold Mines Ltd. (Ont. 1946)
Dec. 31, 1956 – Name changed to Sunbeam Exploration Co. Ltd. ■

Kestrel Resources Ltd. (B.C. Jan. 28, 1986)
June 1, 1993 – Amalgamated with Golden Lake Resources Ltd. (0.5 for 1) to form a new co. named Ella Resources Inc.; basis 0.35 new for 1 old sh. (see Ella Resources Inc.)

KetamineOne Capital Limited (B.C. Mar. 24, 2017)
Jan. 24, 2022 – Name changed to Wellbeing Digital Sciences Inc. (see FPsurvey - Industrials)

Ketch Energy Ltd. (Alta. Apr. 20, 1994)
Oct. 1, 2002 – Name changed to Acclaim Energy Trust following acquisition by Acclaim Energy Trust, constituting a reverse takeover by Ketch Energy; basis 1.15 Acclaim trust units for 1 Ketch Energy sh., plus 1 Ketch Resources Ltd. sh. for 3 Ketch Energy shs. ■

Ketch Resources Ltd. (Alta. Nov. 12, 2001)
Jan. 20, 2005 – Plan of Arrangement with Bear Creek Energy Ltd. to convert to a new income trust named Ketch Resources Trust and 2 new exploration cos. named Kereco Energy Ltd. and Bear Ridge Resources Ltd.; basis 1 new trust unit plus, either 0.4 new Kereco sh. or $1.06 plus, either 0.4 new Bear Ridge sh. or $0.48 for 1 old Ketch com. sh. (see Bear Ridge Resources Ltd.; Kereco Energy Ltd.; Ketch Resources Trust)

Ketch Resources Trust (Alta. Dec. 16, 2004)
June 27, 2006 – Plan of Arrangement acquisition by Advantage Energy Income Fund; basis 0.565 new Advantage sh. for 1 old Ketch unit. Advantage will assume all obligations of the Ketch 6.5% conv. deb. (see Advantage Energy Income Fund)

Ketchum Capital Corporation (Alta. Mar. 28, 2006)
Jan. 22, 2009 – Name changed to Ammonite Energy Ltd. following Qualifying reverse takeover acquisition of Ammonite Energy Ltd. which was subsequently amalgamated; basis 1 new for 5 old shs. ■

Kettle Copper Company Ltd. (B.C. 1950)
Feb. 13, 1958 – Dissolved.

Kettle River Resources Ltd. (B.C. Oct. 17, 1980)
Nov. 9, 2015 – Acquired by New Nadina Explorations Limited; basis 1 New Nadina com. sh. for 1 Kettle com. sh. (see New Nadina Explorations Limited)

Ketza River Mines Limited (Can. 1960)
Dec. 20, 1994 – Dissolved.

Kevin Capital Corporation (Alta. 1988)
Oct. 11, 1989 – Name changed to Terranova Inc. ■

Kevin Sports Toys International Inc. (Alta. 1988)
Dec. 31, 1993 – Name changed to Gobi Oil & Gas Ltd.; basis 1 new for 10 old shs. ■

Kew Media Group Inc. (Ont. Nov. 4, 2015)
Feb. 28, 2020 – Placed into receivership by secured lender. FTI Consulting Canada Inc. was appointed receiver and all directors resigned.

Kewagama Gold Mines (Québec) Ltd. (Que. Aug. 21, 1937)
Oct. 21, 1991 – Name changed to KWG Resources Inc. ■

Kewanee Industries, Inc. (Del. 1937)
Sept. 19, 1977 – Became a wholly owned subsid. of Kewnew Inc. (subsid. of Gulf Oil Corporation of Pittsburgh, Pa.). Kewanee shldrs. received $47.50 for 1 old sh.

Kewannee Oil Company (Del. 1937)
July 1, 1975 – Name changed to Kewanee Industries, Inc. ■

The Kewl Corporation (Can. Feb. 19, 1990)
Aug. 26, 2004 – Name changed to KEWL Corporation; basis 1 new for 20 old shs. ■

Key Anacon Mines Limited (Ont. 1948)
Jan. 11, 1999 – Privatized following amalgamation agreement with its affiliates, Northern Canada Mines, Limited, Atlantic Coast Copper Corporation Limited, First Maritime Mining Corporation Limited and Hunter Brook Minerals Limited; basis $1.65 per sh.

Key Capital Group Inc. (B.C. Oct. 25, 1989)
Oct. 24, 2003 – Name changed to AccelRate Power Systems Inc. ■

Key Gold Holding Inc. (Que. Nov. 14, 1938)
Mar. 4, 2013 – Formed Pangolin Diamonds Corp. in Ontario pursuant to amalgamation with Pangolin Diamonds Corp.; basis 1 new sh. for 2 Key Gold sh. (see FPsurvey - Mines & Energy)

Key Industries Ltd. (B.C. 1967)
Sept. 17, 1976 – Name changed to New Key Industries Ltd.; basis 1 new for 4 old shs. ■

Key Largo Resources Ltd. (B.C. Sept. 14, 1987)
Mar. 16, 1993 – Name changed to World Organics Inc.; basis 1 new for 2 old shs. (see FPsurvey - Mines & Energy)

Key Oil & Gas (1955) Ltd. (B.C. 1955)
July 1968 – Name changed to Consolidated Key Oils Ltd.; basis 1 new for 100 old shs. ■

Key Point Mines Co. Ltd. (B.C. 1970)
Sept. 6, 1977 – Dissolved.

Key Venture Capital Inc. (B.C. Sept. 15, 2010)
Apr. 23, 2014 – Dissolved following Qualifying Transaction private placement subscription of 2,460,000 Boxxer Gold Corp. units (1 com. sh. plus 1 wt.) at 5¢ per unit (with wts. exercisable at 5¢ per wt. for 5 yrs.) and distribution of Boxxer units to shldrs. on a pro rata basis.

Keyboycon Mines Ltd. (Ont. 1945)
1956 – Name changed to Con-Key Mines Ltd.; basis 1 new for 4 old shs. ■

Keycorp Industries Limited (B.C. 1949)
Aug. 16, 1985 – Name changed to Belkin Inc.; basis 4 new for 1 old sh. ■

Keyera Facilities Income Fund (Alta. Apr. 3, 2003)
Jan. 1, 2011 – Succeeded by Keyera Corp. pursuant to plan of arrangement whereby Keyera Corp. was formed to facilitate the conversion of the fund into a corporation and the fund was subsequently dissolved. (see FPsurvey - Mines & Energy; FPsurvey - Industrials)

Keylock Resources Inc. (Alta. June 6, 1984)
May 15, 1997 – Name changed to Eurasia Gold Corp. ■

Keylode Cobalt Silver Mines Ltd. (Ont. 1950)
1962 – Charter cancelled.

Keymark Resources Inc. (B.C. Apr. 13, 2006)
Aug. 28, 2012 – Name changed to Alabama Graphite Corp. ■

Keymet Mines Ltd. (Ont. 1952)
1956 – Acquired by Anacon Lead Mines Ltd.; basis 1 new for 4 old shs. (see Anacon Lead Mines Ltd.)

Keymor Gold Mines Ltd. (Ont. 1944)
Mar. 18, 1965 – Dissolved.

Keynote Resources Inc. (B.C. Nov. 30, 1983)
Apr. 23, 1993 – Dissolved and struck off register under the name U.S. Ammunition Company Ltd., as the previous name change was never acknowledged or approved by the B.C. Registrar of Companies. However, the name change was acknowledged by the Vancouver Stock Exchange.

KeySpan Facilities Income Fund (Alta. Apr. 3, 2003)
Feb. 10, 2005 – Name changed to Keyera Facilities Income Fund. ■

Keystone Business Forms Limited (B.C. 1949)
Apr. 2, 1976 – Name changed to Keycorp Industries Limited. ■

Keystone Entertainment Group Inc. (B.C. Mar. 21, 1974)
Apr. 20, 1994 – Name changed to International Keystone Entertainment Inc.; basis 1 new for 4 old shs. ■

Keystone Explorations Ltd. (B.C. Mar. 21, 1974)
Feb. 27, 1992 – Name changed to Keystone Entertainment Group Inc. ■

Keystone Mines & Oils Ltd. (Man. 1953)
Sept. 2, 1965 – Name changed to High Lake Molybdenum Ltd. ■

Keystone North America Inc. (Ont. Aug. 27, 2004)
Apr. 30, 2010 – Acquired by SCI Alliance Acquisition Corporation, a wholly owned subsid. of Service Corporation International, for $8.07 per sh.

KeyWest Energy Corporation (Can. May 25, 1998)
Feb. 27, 2003 – Amalgamated with Viking Energy Royalty Trust and Luke Energy Ltd.; basis 0.5214 Viking trust unit and 0.10 Luke com. sh. for 1 KeyWest com. sh. (see Luke Energy Ltd.; Viking Energy Royalty Trust)

Khalkos Exploration Inc. (Can. Nov. 28, 2007)
Feb. 15, 2018 – Name changed to Pershimex Resources Corporation. ■

Khan Resources Inc. (Ont. Oct. 1, 2002)
Nov. 2016 – Initial distrib. of 85¢ cash per sh. payable Nov. 29, 2016, to shldrs. of record Nov. 22, 2016.
Feb. 4, 2019 – Name changed to Cypherpunk Holdings Inc. ■

Khayyam Minerals Ltd. (B.C. Feb. 21, 2012)
May 26, 2014 – Qualifying transaction acquisition of 7,740,000 units (1 com. sh. & 1 wt.) of Kincora Copper Limited and subsequent distribution to shldrs. as a return of capital; basis 0.6397 Kincora units for 1 old Khayyam com. sh.
July 8, 2014 – Voluntarily dissolved.

Khot Infrastructure Holdings, Ltd. (British Virgin Islands Dec. 18, 2013)
Apr. 25, 2018 – Name changed to Blockchain Holdings Ltd. ■

Khutze Mines Ltd. (B.C. 1967)
Oct. 1974 – Charter cancelled.

Kick Energy Corporation (Alta. Dec. 19, 1986)
1987 – Charter cancelled.
Sept. 8, 1989 – Charter revived.
Aug. 3, 2006 – Plan of Arrangement acquisition by Highpine Oil & Gas Limited; basis 0.32 new Highpine cl. A sh. for 1 old Kick Energy sh.
Jan. 1, 2007 – Merged into Highpine Oil & Gas Limited.

Kicking Horse Energy Inc. (Alta. Dec. 19, 2014 amalg.)
Dec. 3, 2015 – Acquired by ORLEN Upstream Canada Ltd., an indirect wholly owned subsid. of PKN Orlen S.A.; basis $4.75 cash per sh.
Jan. 1, 2016 – Amalgamated into ORLEN Upstream Canada Ltd.

Kicking Horse Resources Inc. (Alta. Mar. 6, 1998)
Oct. 12, 1999 – Amalgamated with gronArctic resources inc. and Taber Energy Corp. to form Kicking Horse Resources Ltd.; basis 0.3678913 new for 1 old sh. (see Kicking Horse Resources Limited)

Kicking Horse Resources Limited (Alta. Aug. 13, 1999 amalg.)
Mar. 8, 2004 – Name changed to Launch Resources Inc. ■

Kidd Copper Mines Ltd. (Ont. 1964)
Feb. 14, 1978 – Dissolved.

Kidd Mining Co. Ltd. (Ont. 1964)
1965 – Merged into Great Molly Explorations Ltd.; basis 1 new for 2 old shs.

Kidd Resources Ltd. (B.C. 1979)
Dec. 31, 1987 – Acquired by Monte Carlo Gold Mines Ltd.; basis 1 Monte Carlo cl. A com. sh. for 5 Kidd shs.

Kiddo Technologies Inc. (Can. July 24, 1997)
Jan. 6, 2004 – Dissolved.

Kidihawk Mines Limited (Ont. 1949)
1955 – Charter cancelled.

Kidoz Inc. (Anguilla Sept. 30, 2004)
Jan. 1, 2023 – Continued into Canada. (see FPsurvey - Industrials)

KidsFutures Inc. (Can. June 26, 2000)
May 24, 2007 – Name changed to The Futura Loyalty Group Inc. ■

Kiena Gold Mines Limited (Ont. June 12, 1936)
June 17, 1988 – Amalgamated with a wholly owned subsid. of Placer Dome Inc.; basis 0.92 new for 1 old sh. (see Placer Dome Inc.)

Kierland Capital Corporation (Alta. Dec. 17, 2007)
Aug. 6, 2010 – Formed GASFRAC Energy Services Inc. in Alberta pursuant to Qualifying Transaction reverse takeover acquisition of and amalgamation with GASFRAC Energy Services Inc. ■

Kierland Resources Ltd. (Alta. Oct. 27, 2004)
Nov. 30, 2010 – Name changed to PetroSands Resources (Canada) Inc.; basis 1 new for 10 old shs. ■

Kik Polymers Inc. (Can. Jan. 22, 1987)
Feb. 1, 2012 – Name changed to Edgewater Wireless Systems Inc. pursuant to reverse takeover acquisition of Edgewater Wireless Systems, Ltd. (see FPsurvey - Industrials)

Kilbarry Red Lake Gold Mines Ltd. (unknown)
1955 – Charter cancelled.

Kilembe Copper Cobalt Ltd. (Can. 1952)
July 10, 1979 – Name changed to Renabie Mines Limited. ■

Kilembe Resources Ltd. (B.C. Nov. 22, 1983)
July 10, 1991 – Name changed to Liquid Gold Resources Inc.; basis 1 new for 4 old shs. ■

Kilgore Minerals Ltd. (Can. June 21, 2002)
July 24, 2007 – Name changed to Bayswater Uranium Corporation following amalgamation of Bayswater Uranium Corporation with a wholly owned subsid. of Kilgore to form Bayswater Holdings Inc.; basis 1 new for 1 old Bayswater Uranium sh. and 1.25 new for 1 Kilgore sh. (see Bayswater Uranium Corporation)

Kilkenney Resources Ltd. (B.C. June 27, 1988)
Sept. 18, 1995 – Name changed to Ghana Goldfields Ltd. ■

Killala Lake Mines Ltd. (Ont. 1954)
Aug. 24, 1964 – Charter cancelled.

Killam Properties Inc. (Can. May 26, 2000)
Jan. 1, 2016 – Succeeded by Killam Apartment Real Estate Investment Trust pursuant to plan of arrangement whereby Killam Apartment Real Estate Investment Trust was formed to facilitate the conversion of the corporation into a trust. (see FPsurvey - Industrials)

Killarney Oil and Gas Development Company Limited (N.B. 1956)
1979 – Shares exchanged for shs. of Killarney Oil & Resources Ltd.; sh. for sh. basis.

Killbear Acquisition Corp. (Ont. Aug. 22, 2011)
Aug. 28, 2014 – Dissolved following Qualifying Transaction private placement subscription of 1,000,000 Yangaroo Inc. com. shs. at 30¢ per com. sh. and distribution of Yangaroo com. shs. to shareholders.; basis 0.1363995 Yangaroo com. shs. for 1 Killbear com. sh.

Killdeer Minerals Inc. (B.C. May 28, 2008)
Mar. 1, 2017 – Name changed to Glacier Lake Resources Inc. (see FPsurvey - Mines & Energy)

Killi Ltd. (Ont. June 13, 2019)
Nov. 4, 2021 – Name changed to Reklaim Ltd. (see FPsurvey - Industrials)

Killick Capital Corp. (B.C. June 21, 2007)
Aug. 6, 2009 – Name changed to Sila Industrial Group Ltd. ■

Killick Gold Company Ltd. (B.C. 1969)
July 3, 1992 – Dissolved and struck off register.

Killucan Resources Ltd. (Alta. 1981 amalg.)
Aug. 11, 1983 – Amalgamated with Shelter Hydrocarbons Limited to form Skill Resources Ltd.; basis 0.7143 com. sh. of Skill for each cl. A com. sh. of Killucan.

Kilo Gold Mines Ltd. (Alta. Oct. 15, 1984)
Apr. 30, 1998 – Name changed to Newmex Minerals Inc.; basis 1 new for 5 old shs. ∎

Kilo Goldmines Ltd. (Ont. Sept. 12, 2006)
Mar. 16, 2021 – Name changed to KGL Resources Ltd.; basis 1 new for 20 old shs. (see FPsurvey - Mines & Energy)

Kilroy Gold Mines Ltd. (Ont. 1946)
Mar. 1960 – Charter cancelled.

Kiltie Red Lake Mines Ltd. (Ont. 1945)
Apr. 1950 – Charter cancelled.

Kim Explorations Ltd. (unknown)
Jan. 12, 1973 – Merged into Helgena Mines Ltd.

Kimaclo Mines Ltd. (B.C. 1956)
Aug. 1958 – Property sold to Major Mines for sh. int. (see Major Mines Ltd.)

Kimasca Porcupine Gold Mines Ltd. (Ont. 1946)
Dec. 1954 – Charter cancelled.

Kimball Porcupine Gold Mines Ltd. (Ont. 1944)
Nov. 1958 – Charter cancelled.

Kimber Resources Inc. (B.C. Mar. 31, 1995)
Jan. 14, 2014 – Acquired by Invecture Group, S.A. de C.V. for $0.15 per sh.

Kimberley Copper Mines Ltd. (Ont. 1955)
1964 – Dissolved.

Kimberley Copper Mines Ltd. (B.C. 1966)
1971 – Name changed to Nor-West Kim Resources Ltd.; basis 1 new for 3 old shs. ∎

Kimberley Diamond Company NL (W.A. Sept. 29, 1993)
July 9, 1997 – Name changed to Kimberley Resources Limited; basis 1 new for 5 old shs. ∎

Kimberley Resources Limited (W.A. Sept. 29, 1993)
Nov. 17, 1997 – Name changed to Kimberley Resources NL. ∎

Kimberley Resources NL (W.A. Sept. 29, 1993)
Sept. 20, 1999 – Name changed to Kimberley Diamond Company NL.

Kimberlite Mining Corp. Ltd. (Ont. 1967)
Mar. 1976 – Charter cancelled.

Kimberly Yellowknife Gold Mines Ltd. (Ont. 1944)
1953 – Charter cancelled.

Kimdura Mines Ltd. (B.C. 1956)
May 1972 – Charter cancelled.

Kimex Resources Inc. (Que. July 20, 1987)
June 1, 1993 – Name changed to Dianor Resources Inc.; basis 1 new for 10 old shs. ∎

Kimpex International Inc. (Que. June 8, 1993)
Mar. 26, 1999 – Filed a proposal under the Bankruptcy and Insolvency Act.
Mar. 29, 1999 – All directors resigned. Raymond Chabot Inc. of Montreal appointed receiver.
June 15, 1999 – Les Placements Gilles Soucy Inc., through a wholly owned subsid., acquired all assets and wholly owned Kimpex Action Inc. for an undisclosed amount.

Kinai Resources Corp. (B.C. 1980)
Nov. 29, 1985 – Name changed to Kinai Technologies Inc. ∎

Kinai Technologies Inc. (B.C. 1980)
June 12, 1992 – Dissolved and struck off register.

Kinart Gold Mines Ltd. (Ont. 1945)
Mar. 1957 – Charter cancelled.

Kinart Yellowknife Mines Ltd. (Ont. 1945)
1945 – Name changed to Kinart Gold Mines Ltd. and continued into Ontario. ∎

Kinasco Exploration & Mining Co. (Ont. 1955)
1967 – Charter cancelled.

Kinaxis Inc. (Can. June 29, 1984)
Continued into New Brunswick.
July 24, 2012 – Continued into Canada.
Dec. 16, 2013 – Amalgamated in Canada to continue with same name. (see FPsurvey - Industrials)

Kinbauri Gold Corp. (Can. July 19, 1984)
Sept. 28, 2009 – Acquired by Orvana Minerals Corp. for 75¢ per sh.

Kinder Morgan Canada Limited (Alta. Apr. 7, 2017)
Dec. 16, 2019 – Formed PKM Canada Limited. ∎

KINeSYS Pharmaceutical Inc. (Alta. May 21, 1993)
Jan. 30, 1998 – Name changed to Green River Petroleum Inc.; basis 1 new for 1 old sh. ∎

Kinetex Resources Corp. (B.C. Feb. 10, 2005)
Dec. 20, 2010 – Placed into receivership. Ernst & Young Inc. appointed receiver.
July 29, 2013 – Dissolved.

Kinetic Energy Inc. (B.C. June 1, 1993 amalg.)
Feb. 19, 2003 – Name changed to Torque Energy Inc.; basis 1 new for 8 old shs. ∎

Kinetic Ventures Ltd. (Del. Dec. 31, 1993)
Jan. 4, 1999 – Name changed to Suite 101.com Inc.; basis 1 new for 6 old shs.

King Capital Corporation (Alta. Sept. 28, 1993)
July 26, 2001 – Name changed to King Energy Inc. ∎

King Copper Mines Ltd. (Que. 1954)
1957 – Merged into International Metal & Petroleum Corp.; basis 1 new for 4 old shs.

King Crest Mines Ltd. (B.C. 1957)
Apr. 13, 1967 – Dissolved.

King Edward Hotel Company, Ltd. (Ont. 1918)
1932 – Placed into receivership.
Dec. 1942 – First and final distribution of co. assets of $30 per $100 princ. amt. of refunding s.f. mtge. bds. made to holders.

King Energy Inc. (Alta. Sept. 28, 1993)
Apr. 20, 2006 – Acquired by Vanquish Oil & Gas Corporation for $1.25 per sh.

King-Errington Resources Ltd. (B.C. 1982)
Dec. 21, 1987 – Name changed to Daimler Resources Inc. following amalgamation with Daimler Resources Inc. ∎

King George Development Corporation (Can. Oct. 14, 1993)
Oct. 21, 1999 – Amalgamated with Allied Hotel Properties Inc.; basis 1 com. sh. of Allied Hotel Properties Inc. and 1 new com. sh. of King George Financial Corporation for 1 com. sh.

King George Financial Corp. (B.C. July 21, 1999)
Dec. 24, 2021 – Privatized via a 1-for-3,000,000 consolidation; basis $0.375 cash per sh.

King Island Mines Ltd. (Ont. 1967)
Mar. 1976 – Charter cancelled.

King Jack Resources Ltd. (B.C. Aug. 7, 1985)
July 24, 1990 – Name changed to International King Jack Resources Ltd.; basis 1 new for 5 old shs. ∎

King Kirkland Gold Mines Ltd. (Ont. 1920)
Dec. 20, 1982 – Dissolved.

King Midas Mining Co., Ltd. (B.C. Aug. 1933)
Mar. 1959 – Charter cancelled; co. dissolved.

King Solomon Mines Ltd. (Alta. 1955)
1961 – Name changed to Radisson Oil & Gas. ∎

King Solomon Resources Ltd. (Alta. 1955)
1967 – Merged into Acroll Oil & Gas Ltd.

Kingbird Resources Inc. (Alta. Jan. 28, 1980)
Aug. 29, 1988 – Continued into Canada.
Sept. 29, 1988 – Name changed to Gold Bar Resources Inc.; basis 1 new for 5 old shs. ∎

Kingbridge Capital Corporation (Ont. 1970)
Dec. 6, 1993 – Name changed to Blue Mountain Beverages Inc. ∎

Kingbridge Mines Limited (Ont. 1970)
Mar. 1976 – Charter cancelled; revived February 1986.

Kingbridge Mines Limited (Ont. 1970)
Feb. 1986 – Charter revived.
Feb. 1989 – Name changed to Kingbridge Capital Corporation. ∎

Kingdom Minerals Ltd. (Ont. 1972)
Feb. 20, 1980 – Dissolved.

Kingdom Resources Ltd. (B.C. July 10, 1978)
Sept. 27, 1989 – Name changed to KRL Resources Corp.; basis 1 new for 3 old shs. ∎

Kingdon Mining Co. Ltd. (Ont. 1948)
Nov. 7, 1966 – Dissolved.

Kingfisher Mining & Development Co., Ltd. (Man.)
1952 – Charter cancelled.

Kingfisher Ventures Inc. (Yuk. Dec. 10, 1999)
Feb. 25, 2002 – Name changed to ELF Nonventure Capital Holding Inc. following Qualifying Transaction acquisition by EMedia Networks International Corp.; basis 1 EMedia unit (1 com. sh. plus 1 wt.) for 1.1 Kingfisher com. shs. (see EMedia Networks International Corporation)

Kinghorn Energy Corporation (B.C. Mar. 8, 1971)
Apr. 30, 1991 – Name changed to Kinghorn Petroleum Corporation; basis 1 new for 4 old shs. ∎

Kinghorn Petroleum Corporation (B.C. Mar. 8, 1971)
Nov. 12, 1992 – Name changed to Triple "8" Energy Corporation; basis 1 new for 4 old shs. ∎

Kingman Capital Corp. (Alta. Aug. 10, 1994)
Jan. 20, 1999 – Name changed to Enterra Communications Inc. following reverse takeover acquisition of Enterra Communications Corporation; basis 1 new for 2 old shs. ∎

King's Bay Gold Corporation (Can. Mar. 20, 1998)
Aug. 14, 2017 – Name changed to King's Bay Resources Corp. ∎

King's Bay Resources Corp. (Can. Mar. 20, 1998)
Aug. 11, 2020 – Continued into British Columbia.
July 8, 2022 – Name changed to Lion Rock Resources Inc. pursuant to the acquisition of Lion Rock Exploration Inc. (see FPsurvey - Mines & Energy)

Kings Minerals NL (Australia Feb. 27, 1985)
Dec. 10, 2010 – Name changed to Cerro Resources NL. ∎

Kingscross Communities Incorporated (Ont. June 17, 1974)
Mar. 27, 2006 – Certificate of incorporation cancelled and dissolved.

Kingscross Resources Inc. (Ont. 1983)
Feb. 24, 1994 – Formed Laser Quest Corporation on amalgamation with 1057251 Ontario Inc.; basis 1 new for 3.2 old shs. ∎

Kingsfield Capital Corporation (Alta. June 29, 1988)
Oct. 13, 1995 – Name changed to Kingsfield Environmental Corporation. ■

Kingsfield Environmental Corporation (Alta. June 29, 1988)
June 25, 1997 – Name changed to KEC Environmental Corp.; basis 1 new for 5 old shs. ■

Kingsgate Consolidated NL (N.S.W. Oct. 28, 1970)
Oct. 31, 2002 – Name changed to Kingsgate Consolidated Limited.

Kingsman Resources Inc. (B.C. Oct. 14, 1993)
Sept. 19, 2014 – Name changed to Contagious Gaming Inc. following reverse takeover acquisition of Contagious Sports Limited and Telos Entertainment Inc.; basis 1 new for 2 old shs. (see FPsurvey - Industrials)

Kingsmere Capital Inc. (Alta. Aug. 30, 1996)
Feb. 2, 2005 – Dissolved and struck off registry.

Kingsmill Capital Ventures Inc. (Ont. Oct. 28, 2005)
Oct. 20, 2009 – Amalgamated with Kingsmill Capital Ventures II Inc.(KII); basis 0.5165 KII shs. for 1 Kingsmill Capital Ventures Inc. sh. (see Innovative Composites International Inc.)

Kingsmill Capital Ventures II Inc. (Ont. Mar. 27, 2007)
Sept. 22, 2009 – Formed Innovative Composites International Inc. in Ontario pursuant to amalgamation with Kingsmill Capital Ventures Inc. (KCV) and following Qualifying Transaction reverse takeover acquisition of Innovative Composites Inc.; basis 0.5165 new for 1 KCV sh. and 1 new for Kingsmill Capital Ventures II Inc. ■

Kingston Resources Ltd. (B.C. Feb. 27, 1987)
June 29, 2001 – Name changed to Butler Developments Corp.; basis 1 new for 6 old shs. ■

Kingston Silica Mines Ltd. (Can. 1942)
Wound up.

Kingsvale Resources Ltd. (B.C. May 22, 1986)
Nov. 26, 1993 – Name changed to Niche Peripherals, Inc.; basis 1 new for 2.75 old shs. ■

Kingsville Gas Co. Ltd. (Alta. 1952)
1963 – Acquired by Pere Marquette Petroleums Limited.

Kingsway Arms Retirement Residences Inc. (Ont. May 31, 2007)
Apr. 4, 2016 – Name changed to Mainstreet Health Investments Inc. and continued into British Columbia following reverse takeover acquisition of Mainstreet Health Holdings Inc. ■

Kingsway Financial Services Inc. (Ont. Sept. 19, 1989)
Dec. 31, 2018 – Continued into Delaware.

Kingsway International Holdings Limited (B.C. June 29, 1978)
Feb. 28, 1996 – Continued into Bermuda.
Dec. 16, 2010 – Name changed to Sunwah International Limited. ■

Kingsway Linked Return of Capital Trust (Ont. May 12, 2005)
July 2, 2015 – Voluntarily delisted from TSX; all units redeemed for $25 per unit.

Kingsway Lumber Co. Limited (Ont. 1962)
June 25, 1979 – Charter cancelled.

Kingswood Explorations Limited (Can. Sept. 1, 1970)
Aug. 21, 1985 – Name changed to Kingswood Explorations 1985 Limited; basis 1 new for 2 old shs. ■

Kingswood Explorations 1985 Limited (Can. Sept. 1, 1970)
July 20, 1992 – Name changed to Kingswood Resources Inc.; basis 1 new for 5 old shs. ■

Kingswood Resources Inc. (Can. Sept. 1, 1970)
May 5, 1994 – Formed Southern Africa Minerals Corporation in Canada on amalgamation with Botswana Minerals Corporation; basis 1 new for 2.5 old shs. ■

Kingtron International Inc. (Can. Aug. 19, 1987)
Oct. 19, 1999 – Struck off register.

Kinika Gold Mines Ltd. (Ont. 1937)
Dec. 9, 1957 – Dissolved.

Kinloch Resources Inc. (Ont. June 27, 1996)
June 29, 2001 – Continued into Alberta.
Mar. 1, 2005 – Formed Stylus Energy Inc. in Alberta pursuant to reverse takeover acquisition of and amalgamation with Stylus Exploration Inc.; basis 0.333 new for 1 old sh. ■

Kinmount Uranium Mines Limited (Ont. 1954)
Dec. 12, 1960 – Charter cancelled.

Kinojevis Mining Co. (unknown)
Apr. 1, 1936 – Continued into Quebec.
1936 – Name changed to Bowes Gold Mines Ltd.; basis 6 new for 1 old sh. ■

Kinojevis River Mines Ltd. (Ont. 1944)
May 13, 1957 – Dissolved.

Kinova Holdings Corp. (Ont.)
Nov. 18, 1993 – Name changed to Medyx Inc. ■

Kinross Mortgage Corporation (Can.)
Feb. 8, 1982 – Name changed to CIBC Mortgage Corporation.

Kinstar Resources Ltd. (Alta. 1981)
Nov. 14, 1988 – Acquired by Summit Resources Limited; basis 1 Summit sh. for 33 Kinstar shs. (see Summit Resources Limited)

Kintail Energy Inc. (Alta. July 14, 1997)
Jan. 19, 2000 – Acquired by Canadian Hunter Exploration Ltd. for $3.10 per sh. (see Canadian Hunter Exploration Ltd.)

Kintla Explorations Limited (Alta. 1972)
July 1, 1990 – Struck off register.

Kinvara Ventures Inc. (Alta. May 10, 1996)
May 20, 2005 – Name changed to Ivana Ventures Inc.; basis 1 new for 5 old shs. ■

Kipp & Zonen Inc. (Sask. Dec. 3, 1981)
Apr. 7, 2004 – GrowthWorks WV Canadian Fund Inc., holder of the company's debentures, served the company with notice under the Bankruptcy and Insolvency Act.
Apr. 19, 2004 – All the officers and directors resigned.
Apr. 21, 2004 – GrowthWorks obtained an order of the Saskatchewan Court of Queen's Bench appointing Ernst & Young Inc. receiver of all the undertaking, property and assets of the company.
June 1, 2004 – Company's manufacturing and sales subsidiary in Delft, the Netherlands, were not affected by the receivership and GrowthWork's immediate plan was to continue to support the operations of the company. Ernst & Young Corporate Finance Inc. was engaged to sell the company's international business. The trustee was discharged. No further information was available.

Kipper Tashota Gold Mining Co. Ltd. (Ont. 1928)
Name changed to Lincoln Gold Mines Ltd.
1936 – Continued into Ontario. ■

Kipwater Mines Ltd. (Ont. 1956)
Apr. 23, 1969 – Charter cancelled.

Kirana Kirkland Gold Mines (Ont. 1936)
Nov. 1954 – Charter cancelled.

Kirby Energy Inc. (B.C. June 29, 1978)
Aug. 3, 1995 – Name changed to International Kirby Energy Corp.; basis 1 new for 3 old shs. ■

Kirgal Silver Mines Ltd. (B.C. 1967)
Dec. 2, 1974 – Charter cancelled.

Kirgood Gold Mines Ltd. (Ont. 1936)
Apr. 18, 1960 – Charter cancelled.

Kirk Asbestos Mines Ltd. (Ont. 1951)
1952 – Name changed to Donegal Petroleums Limited. ■

Kirk-Hudson Mines Ltd. (Ont. Jan. 7, 1919)
Dec. 5, 1958 – Name changed to Northgate Exploration Limited; basis 1 new for 4 old shs. ■

Kirkcaldy Capital Corp. (B.C. Feb. 21, 2007)
Apr. 20, 2015 – Amalgamated with Royal Road Canada Minerals Limited (Tigris Subco), a wholly owned subsid. of Tigris Resources Limited (TRL), to form a new Royal Road Canada Minerals Limited; basis 0.5 TRL post-consol. shs. for 1 Tigris subco. sh. and 0.5 TRL post-consol. shs. for 1 Kirkcaldy sh. Prior to arrangement TRL changed its name to Royal Road Minerals Limited. The new Royal Road Canada Minerals Limited continues to be a wholly owned subsid. of Royal Road Minerals Limited.

Kirkland Basin Gold Mines, Ltd. (Ont. 1931)
Mar. 15, 1972 – Dissolved.

Kirkland Central Mining Co. Ltd. (Ont. 1923)
Nov. 27, 1961 – Dissolved.

Kirkland Consolidated Gold Mines Ltd. (Ont. 1928)
June 1934 – Name changed to Kirkland Consolidated Mines Ltd. and continued into Ontario. ■

Kirkland Consolidated Mines Ltd. (Ont. June 1934)
Feb. 1949 – Charter cancelled.

Kirkland-Diorite Gold Mines Ltd. (Ont. 1920)
1956 – Acquired by Gordon-Lebel Mines Ltd.; basis 1 new for 10 old shs. (see Gordon-Lebel Mines Ltd.)

Kirkland-Eastern Gold Mines Ltd. (Ont. 1927)
1958 – Charter cancelled.

Kirkland Gateway Gold Mines Ltd. (Ont. 1922)
1964 – Acquired by Upper Kirkland Mines Ltd.; basis 1 new for 5 old shs. (see Upper Kirkland Mines Ltd.)

Kirkland Gold Belt Mines Ltd. (Can. 1927)
1935 – Name changed to Morris-Kirkland Gold Mines Ltd. and continued into Ontario; basis 1 new for 3 old shs. ■

Kirkland Gold Rand Ltd. (Ont. June 26, 1931)
1944 – Acquired by Hudson Rand Gold Mines Ltd.; basis 1 new for 3 old shs. (see Hudson Rand Gold Mines Ltd.)

Kirkland Golden Gate Mines Ltd. (Ont. July 30, 1934)
Aug. 1950 – Name changed to Gateford Mines Limited; basis 1 new for 10 old shs. ■

Kirkland Hudson Bay Gold Mines Ltd. (Ont. Jan. 7, 1919)
May 10, 1956 – Name changed to Kirk-Hudson Mines Ltd. ■

Kirkland Hunton Mines Ltd. (Ont. 1939)
July 15, 1942 – Acquired by Amalgamated Kirkland Mines Ltd.; basis 1 new for 12 old shs. (see Amalgamated Kirkland Mines Ltd.)

Kirkland Lake Gold Inc. (Can. July 27, 1988)
Dec. 6, 2016 – Acquired by Newmarket Gold Inc. (renamed Kirkland Lake Gold Ltd.) in a reverse takeover transaction; basis of 1 new sh. for 1 old Kirkland Lake sh. (following a 0.475-for-1 consolidation of Newmarket shs.).

Kirkland Lake Gold Ltd. (Ont. July 10, 2015 amalg.)
Feb. 10, 2022 – Acquired by Agnico Eagle Limited; basis 0.7935 Agnico com. shs. for 1 Kirkland Lake sh.

Kirkland Lake Gold Mining Co. Ltd. (Ont. 1915)
1956 – Name changed to Kirkland Minerals Corp. Ltd.; basis 1 new for 5 old shs. ■

Kirkland Larder Mines Ltd. (Ont. 1947)
Dec. 23, 1965 – Dissolved.

Kirkland Minerals Corp. Ltd. (Ont. 1915)
Aug. 1973 – Merged with 3 other cos. to form Groundstar Resources Ltd.; basis 1 Groundstar for 10 Kirkland shs.

Kirkland Premier Mines Ltd. (Ont. July 4, 1927)
June 26, 1931 – Continued into Ontario.
1933 – Name changed to Kirkland Gold Rand Ltd.; basis 1 new for 3 old shs. ■

Kirkland-Townsite Gold Mines Ltd. (Ont. 1917)
Dec. 3, 1970 – Name changed to K. T. Mining Limited. ■

Kirklees Capital Inc. (Alta. Dec. 17, 1999)
Mar. 23, 2001 – Name changed to iPerformance Fund Inc. pursuant to reverse takeover acquisition of iPerformance Fund Inc.; basis 3.33 new for 1 old sh. ■

Kirkroyale Gold Mines Ltd. (Ont. Mar. 2, 1937)
Sept. 1959 – Dissolved.

Kirkstone Ventures Ltd. (B.C. June 25, 1986)
July 31, 2000 – Formed Balaton Power Inc. on amalgamation with Bahamas-based Balaton Power Corporation S.A.; basis 3.1 new for 1 old sh. (see FPsurvey - Mines & Energy)

Kirkton Resources Corp. (Ont. June 30, 1989)
Jan. 23, 1995 – Name changed to Constellation Capital Enterprises Inc.; basis 1 new for 12 old shs. ■

Kirktwin Gold Mines Ltd. (Ont. 1946)
1949 – Name changed to Athabaska Goldfields & Uranium Ltd. ■

Kirkwin Gold Mines Ltd. (Ont. Oct. 26, 1936)
1952 – Charter cancelled; no equity.

Kiro Explorations Ltd. (Ont. 1960)
May 6, 1980 – Dissolved.

Kirriemuir Oil & Gas Ltd. (Alta. June 18, 1987)
Dec. 21, 1994 – Name changed to WWB Oil & Gas Ltd. ■

Kirrin Resources Inc. (Alta. Aug. 31, 1996 amalg.)
July 2, 2014 – Struck from registry and dissolved.

Kiryan Gold Mines Ltd. (Ont. 1938)
1952 – Charter cancelled.

Kisco Copper Mines Ltd. (Ont. 1956)
Mar. 1976 – Charter cancelled.

Kiska Gold Mines Ltd. (Ont. 1945)
1957 – Charter cancelled.

Kiska Metals Corp. (Yuk. Aug. 29, 1996)
July 30, 2010 – Continued into British Columbia. (see AuRico Metals Inc.)
Mar. 15, 2017 – All o/s com. shs. not already held acquired by AuRico Metals Inc.; basis 0.0667 AuRico com. shs. plus $0.016 cash for 1 Kiska sh. (see AuRico Metals Inc.)

Kismet Mining Corporation Ltd. (B.C. 1964)
Dec. 17, 1973 – Amalgamated into Panex Resources Ltd.

Kismet Resources Corp. (B.C. Mar. 14, 2018)
Dec. 11, 2020 – Name changed to TDG Gold Corp. pursuant to Qualifying Transaction reverse takeover acquisition of (old) TDG Gold Corp.; basis 1 new for 2 old shs. (see FPsurvey - Mines & Energy)

Kismet Ventures Inc. (B.C. July 24, 1987)
Dec. 16, 1998 – Name changed to Mighty Beaut Minerals Inc. ■

Kit Resources Ltd. (Can. Aug. 13, 1997)
Mar. 3, 2000 – Amalgamated with 1395896 Ontario Inc. to form new co. with same name Kit Resources Ltd. following agreement with Wheaton River Minerals Ltd. under which all assets of the co. were transferred to wholly owned Kit Resources NWT Ltd. which then amalgamated with a subsid. of Wheaton River. Shldrs.

received 0.408 Wheaton River shs. for 1 Kit Resources sh.
Dec. 29, 2006 – Continued into British Columbia.
Feb. 9, 2007 – Name changed to Bayou Bend Petroleum Ltd. ■

Kitrinor Metals Inc. (Ont. Jan. 28, 2005)
Aug. 1, 2017 – Name changed to Scythian Biosciences Corp. following reverse takeover acquisition of Scythian Biosciences Inc.; basis 1 new for 20 old shs. ■

Kitsault Silver Mines Ltd. (unknown)
Dec. 21, 1979 – Amalgamated with Dolly Varden Resources Limited, Yorkshire Resources Limited, Yorkshire Copper Mines Limited and Copper Cliff Mines Ltd. to form Dolly Varden Minerals Inc.; basis 0.0038 new cl. A sh. for 1 old sh.

Kittson Hazelton Gold Mines Ltd. (Ont. 1934)
1952 – Charter cancelled.

Kivalliq Energy Corporation (B.C. Feb. 13, 2008)
June 28, 2018 – Name changed to ValOre Metals Corp.; basis 1 new for 10 old shs. (see FPsurvey - Mines & Energy)

Kiwago Gold Mines Ltd. (Man. 1945)
1947 – Acquired by Valrex Gold Mines Ltd.; basis 1 new for 2 old shs. (see Valrex Gold Mines Ltd.)

Kiwetinohk Resources Corp. (Alta. Feb. 12, 2018)
Aug. 31, 2021 – Continued into Canada.
Sept. 22, 2021 – Name changed to Kiwetinohk Energy Corp. following the acquisition of the remaining 50% interest in Distinction Energy Corp. (see FPsurvey - Mines & Energy; FPsurvey - Industrials)

Klad Enterprises Ltd. (Alta. Feb. 9, 2001)
Feb. 11, 2005 – Formed Diamond Hawk Mining Corp. in Alberta on amalgamation with Slave Lake Diamond Corp. with Klad the deemed acquiror; basis 1.586 new for 1 Slave Lake sh. and 1 new for 1 Klad sh. ■

Klappan Copper Ltd. (B.C. 1969)
1970 – Name changed to Copper Keays Mines Ltd. ■

Kleanza Mines Ltd. (B.C. Jan. 28, 1966)
Mar. 20, 1972 – Name changed to Kendal Mining and Exploration Co. Ltd.; basis 1 new cl. B for 5 old shs. ■

Kleen Hy-DRO-GEN Inc. (B.C. Apr. 21, 2006)
Continued into Ontario. (see FPsurvey - Industrials)

Kleena Kleene Gold Mines Ltd. (Can. Mar. 20, 1968)
Oct. 3, 1994 – Amalgamated with Chromex Nickel Mines Ltd. to form Maiden Creek Mining Company Inc.; basis 1 new for 1 Chromex sh. and 1 new for 1 Kleena sh.

Klimat X Developments Inc. (B.C. Feb. 7, 2018)
Mar. 4, 2024 – Name changed to Carbon Done Right Developments Inc. (see FPsurvey - Industrials)

Klinik Health Ventures Corp. (Ont. Apr. 17, 2019)
June 25, 2020 – Name changed to NeuPath Health Inc. pursuant to Qualifying Transaction reverse takeover acquisition of 2576560 Ontario Inc. (dba NeuPath Health); basis 1 new for 5 old shs. (see FPsurvey - Industrials)

Klintar Oils Ltd. (unknown)
1957 – Acquired by Humber Oil Limited; basis 2 new for 1 old sh. (see Humber Oils Ltd.)

Klondex Mines Ltd. (B.C. Aug. 25, 1971)
July 24, 2018 – Acquired by Hecla Mining Company; basis (A) either (i) US$2.47 cash per sh., (ii) 0.6272 Hecla com. shs. or (iii) US$0.8411 cash per share and 0.4136 Hecla com. shs.; and (B) 0.125 Havilah Mining Corporation com. sh. per Klondex com. sh.

Klondike Capital Corp. (Alta. June 9, 2007)
July 8, 2008 – Formed Pacific Iron Ore Corporation in Alberta on amalgamation with Emerald Fields Resource Corporation (deemed acquiror); basis 1 new for 1.5 old shs. (see FPsurvey - Mines & Energy)

Klondike Destor Gold Mines Ltd. (Ont. 1945)
July 11, 1980 – Dissolved.

Klondike Explorations Ltd. (B.C. 1969)
Nov. 15, 1978 – Name changed to Kenver Resources Inc.; basis 1 new for 3 old shs. ■

Klondike-Keno Mines Ltd. (Ont. 1951)
1955 – Name changed to Jaye Explorations Ltd.; basis 1 new for 4 old shs. ■

Klondike Lode Gold Mines Ltd. (B.C. 1960)
Aug. 12, 1974 – Struck off register.

Klondike Reef Mines Ltd. (B.C. 1969)
Oct. 14, 1974 – Charter cancelled.

Klondyke Destor Gold Mines Ltd. (Ont. 1945)
July 11, 1960 – Dissolved.

Klondyke Yellowknife Mines Ltd. (Ont. 1945)
Apr. 1946 – Name changed to Klondyke Destor Gold Mines Ltd. ■

Knee Hill Energy Canada Ltd. (Can. Feb. 28, 1987 amalg.)
Mar. 10, 1989 – Merged with 15814 Canada Inc., a subsid. of Inuvialuit Petroleum Corporation; basis 47¢ per sh.

Knee Hill Energy Ltd. (N.W.T. 1904)
1905 – Continued into Alberta.
Feb. 28, 1987 – Amalgamated with Madison Oil & Gas Limited to form Knee Hill Energy Canada Ltd.; basis 1 new for 3 old sh. of Knee Hill.

Knee Lake Gold Mines Ltd. (Man. Oct. 1934)
1947 – Acquired by Amalgamated Knee Lake Mines Ltd.; basis 1 new for 5 old shs. (see Amalgamated Knee Lake Mines Ltd.)

Knexa Solutions Inc. (B.C. Nov. 4, 1986)
Feb. 13, 2004 – Name changed to ClearFrame Solutions Inc. ■

Knexa.com Enterprises Inc. (B.C. Nov. 4, 1986)
Feb. 18, 2003 – Name changed to Knexa Solutions Inc. ■

Knie Resources Inc. (B.C. May 13, 1981)
July 17, 1987 – Name changed to Alta Explorations Inc.; basis 1 new for 4 old shs. ■

Knight Metals Ltd. (B.C. Apr. 11, 1983)
Feb. 2, 2012 – Name changed to Africa Hydrocarbons Inc. ■

Knight Mining Corp. (Alta. July 18, 1985)
Sept. 19, 1991 – Name changed to Choice Software Systems Ltd. ■

Knight Petroleum Corp. (B.C. Apr. 11, 1983)
Mar. 7, 2003 – Name changed to Knight Resources Ltd. ■

Knight Resources Ltd. (B.C. Apr. 11, 1983)
May 25, 2011 – Name changed to Knight Metals Ltd.; basis 1 new for 19 old shs. ■

KnightHawk Airlines Inc. (B.C. Dec. 8, 1993)
Sept. 29, 1998 – Continued into Canada.
Apr. 15, 1999 – Name changed to KnightHawk Inc. (see FPsurvey - Industrials)

Knightswood Financial Corp. (B.C. Aug. 24, 1987)
May 8, 2017 – Name changed to Cannabis Wheaton Income Corp. ■

Knobby Lake Mines Limited (Can. July 19, 1956)
June 15, 1984 – Name changed to Consolidated Knobby Lake Mines Limited; basis 1 new for 5 old shs. ■

Knobhill Gold Mines Ltd. (Ont. 1945)
Nov. 5, 1962 – Dissolved.

Knogo Corporation Limited (Ont. Jan. 3, 1969)
July 3, 1974 – Name changed to Plumbing Mart Corporation. ∎

Knol Resources Corp. (Alta. Feb. 24, 2004 amalg.)
June 13, 2019 – Continued into Ontario.
June 19, 2019 – Name changed to Freckle Ltd. pursuant to reverse takeover acquisition of Freckle I.O.T. Ltd.; basis 1 new for 2.2278588 old shs. ∎

Knomex Resources Inc. (Ont. Mar. 9, 1981)
Nov. 10, 1998 – Name changed to Afitex Financial Services Inc.; basis 1 new for 10 old shs. ∎

Knowledge House Publishing Limited (N.S. Mar. 14, 1984)
Nov. 3, 1999 – Name changed to Knowledge House Inc. (see FPsurvey - Industrials)

Knowledge Plus Multimedia Publishing Ltd. (Alta. May 12, 1993)
Nov. 2, 2002 – Dissolved and struck from register.

Knowlton Capital Inc. (Can. July 9, 2004)
Jan. 26, 2007 – Name changed to Buzz Telecommunications Services Inc. ∎

Knowlton Capital Inc. (Can. July 9, 2004)
July 19, 2016 – Name changed to LGC Capital Ltd. pursuant to reverse takeover acquisition of Leni Gas Cuba Limited; basis 1 new for 1.2779553 old shs. ∎

Knox Western Capital Inc. (Can. May 24, 1985)
May 6, 2004 – Dissolved and struck from register.

Knutson Mining Corp. Ltd. (Ont. 1937)
July 1965 – Dissolved.

Koala Beverages Limited (B.C. Nov. 19, 1980)
July 21, 1997 – Name changed to Tribridge Enterprises Corp. ∎

Koala Kreme Inc. (Can. Aug. 2, 1929; via letters patent)
Apr. 4, 1995 – Name changed to Sur American Gold Corporation; basis 1 new for 6 old shs. ∎

Koala Resources Ltd. (B.C. Mar. 30, 1981)
Mar. 30, 1993 – Name changed to Dragon Gem Corp.; basis 1 new for 5 old shs. ∎

Kobex Capital Corp. (B.C. Sept. 17, 1979)
June 23, 2016 – Name changed to Itasca Capital Ltd. ∎

Kobex Minerals Inc. (B.C. Sept. 17, 1979)
Aug. 29, 2014 – Name changed to Kobex Capital Corp. ∎

Kobex Resources Ltd. (B.C. Aug. 30, 1996)
Oct. 1, 2009 – Acquired by IMA Exploration Inc.; basis 1.311 IMA Shs. for 1 Kobex sh. (see Kobex Minerals Inc.)

Kobold Resources Ltd. (B.C. Feb. 6, 1984)
Feb. 1, 1990 – Name changed to Canton Ventures Ltd.; basis 1 new for 2 old shs. ∎

Koch Pipelines Canada, L.P. (Alta. Oct. 9, 1997)
Nov. 12, 2002 – Name changed to Inter Pipeline Fund following sale of general partner Koch Pipelines Canada Ltd. to Pipeline Assets Corp. ∎

Koda Resources Ltd. (B.C. Feb. 1, 1988)
Mar. 10, 2004 – Formed African Gold Group Inc. in Ontario following reverse takeover acquisition of and amalgamation with African Gold Group, Inc.; basis 1 new for 3.5 old shs. ∎

Kodiak Energy Services Ltd. (Alta. July 5, 1999)
Aug. 10, 2005 – Placed into receivership. RSM Richter Inc. was appointed receiver/manager.

Kodiak Exploration Limited (B.C. Feb. 9, 1983)
Dec. 31, 2010 – Name changed to Prodigy Gold Inc. ∎

Kodiak Minerals Ltd. (Man. 1952)
Mar. 9, 1972 – Dissolved.

Kodiak Mines Ltd. (B.C. 1966)
Jan. 31, 1972 – Name changed to Command Resources Ltd. ∎

Kodiak Oil & Gas Corp. (Yuk. Sept. 28, 2001)
Dec. 8, 2014 – Acquired by Whiting Petroleum Corporation; basis 0.177 Whiting com. shs. for 1 Kodiak com. sh.

Kodiak Petroleums Ltd. (Alta. 1958)
Jan. 22, 1970 – Acquired by Manhattan Continental Development Corp. in 1969; basis 4 new for 5 old shs. All 7% secured conv. debs. were called for redemp. at 107.5; they were conv. into Manhattan shs. at $1.75 per sh. to Jan. 21, 1970.

Koffler Stores Limited (Ont. 1968 amalg.)
May 31, 1978 – All o/s cl. A and B shs. acquired by Imasco Limited; basis $55 plus 1 conv. pref. sh. ser. A of Imasco ($35 stated value) for any combination of 10 cl. A or B shs. of Koffler. During second half of 1978, all o/s 2nd pref. shs. of Koffler acquired by Imasco at $9.00 per sh. Koffler's 1st pref. shs. ser. A called for redemp. on Sept. 15, 1978. (see Imasco Limited)

Kokanee Explorations Ltd. (B.C. 1988)
July 27, 1992 – Acquired by Consolidated Ramrod Gold Corporation; basis 1 Consolidated Ramrod sh. for 1 Kokanee sh. (see Consolidated Ramrod Gold Corporation)

Kokanee Minerals Inc. (B.C. Aug. 26, 2005)
Apr. 5, 2012 – Name changed to Declan Resources Inc. ∎

Kokanee Moly Mines Ltd. (B.C. 1966)
Aug. 1970 – Name changed to Remco Financial Corp. Ltd.; basis 1 new for 10 old shs.

Kokanee Resources Ltd. (B.C. 1983)
Mar. 3, 1987 – Name changed to Integra Systems Inc. ∎

Kokko Creek Mining Corp. (Que. 1950)
1955 – Acquired by Quebec Chibougamau Goldfields Ltd.; basis 1 new for 7 old shs. (see Quebec Chibougamau Goldfields Ltd.)

Kokomo Enterprises Inc. (B.C. Aug. 24, 1984)
Aug. 31, 2012 – Name changed to High 5 Ventures Inc.; basis 1 new for 15 old shs. ∎

Kola Mining Corp. (B.C. Nov. 23, 2004)
May 27, 2015 – Name changed to Mitchell Resources Ltd. ∎

Kolak Mines Ltd. (Ont. 1956)
Oct. 21, 1958 – Name changed to Queensland Explorations Ltd. ∎

Kolombo Technologies Ltd. (Can. May 20, 2000)
June 21, 2010 – Name changed to Minerva Venture Technologies Ltd. (see FPsurvey - Industrials)

Kolvox Communications Inc. (Alta. 1987)
July 2, 1996 – Formed WildCard Technologies Inc. in Ontario on amalgamation with Pure Data Ltd., constituting a Pooling of Interests; basis 1 com. for 9.47148 Pure Data cl. A shs. and 1 com. for 8 Kolvox com. shs. (see FPsurvey - Industrials)

Kolyma Goldfields Ltd. (B.C. June 27, 1974)
Feb. 29, 2000 – Name changed to BidCrawler.com Online Inc. following acquisition of BidCrawler.com Online Inc. ∎

Kombat Copper Inc. (Can. Mar. 31, 2004 amalg.)
Dec. 28, 2016 – Name changed to Trigon Metals Inc. (see FPsurvey - Mines & Energy)

Komet Manufacturers Inc. (Que. June 20, 2007 amalg.)
Dec. 19, 2013 – Name changed to Komet Resources Inc. ∎

Komet Resources Inc. (Que. June 20, 2007 amalg.)
Sept. 16, 2020 – Name changed to Brunswick Exploration Inc. (see FPsurvey - Mines & Energy)

Komo Explorations Ltd. (B.C. 1966)
June 25, 1976 – Name changed to Canzona Minerals Inc.; basis 1 new for 5 old shs. ∎

Komunik Corporation (Can. July 25, 2000)
June 12, 2007 – Amalgamated in Canada to continue with same name.
Mar. 30, 2009 – Assets sold for $17,500,000 and operations ceased.
Dec. 7, 2009 – Petitioned into bankruptcy by secured creditor. RSM Richter Inc. appointed trustee.
Mar. 2012 – Distributions to secured and unsecured creditors was completed; there were no funds available for distribution to shldrs.
June 2012 – RSM Richter Inc. was discharged as trustee.

Kona Bay Technologies Inc. (B.C. July 25, 2000)
Name changed to Yerbaé Brands Corp. pursuant to the reverse takeover acquisition of Yerbaé Brands Co. ∎

Kona Capital Ltd. (B.C. Apr. 3, 2018)
May 14, 2019 – Name changed to Wikileaf Technologies Inc. pursuant to the reverse takeover acquisition of One Web Services, Inc. ∎

Kona Industrial Capital Corp. (Alta. Nov. 29, 1994)
July 3, 1996 – Name changed to Mobilift Inc. ∎

Konexus Technologies Limited (Ont. Aug. 25, 1999 amalg.)
Mar. 13, 2006 – Certificate of incorporation cancelled and company dissolved.

Konteko Resources Inc. (Ont. 1981)
Dec. 8, 1988 – Amalgamated with Tashota-Nipigon Mines Limited (1 for 2) and McAdam Resources Inc. (1 for 1) to form a new co. also named McAdam Resources Inc.; basis 1 new for 10 old shs. (see McAdam Resources Inc.)

Kontiki Lead & Zinc Mines Limited (Ont. 1951)
Sept. 11, 1985 – Name changed to The Olympic Victor Corp.; basis 1 new for 3 old shs. ∎

Kontrol Energy Corp. (B.C. Nov. 16, 2006)
Jan. 25, 2021 – Name changed to Kontrol Technologies Corp. and continued into Ontario. (see FPsurvey - Industrials)

Kookaburra Gold Corp. (B.C. July 23, 1987)
Jan. 21, 1993 – Name changed to Kookaburra Resources Ltd. ∎

Kookaburra Resources Ltd. (B.C. July 23, 1987)
June 18, 2001 – Continued into Yukon.
July 16, 2004 – Continued into British Columbia.
Mar. 8, 2006 – Name changed to Consolidated Kookaburra Resources Ltd.; basis 1 new for 2 old shs. ∎

Koone Lake Mines Ltd. (Can. 1945)
Jan. 4, 1975 – Dissolved.

Kootenay Base Metals Ltd. (B.C. 1951)
May 1961 – Name changed to Kootenay Base Metals (Consolidated) Ltd.; basis 1 new for 5 old shs.

Kootenay Belle Gold Mines Ltd. (B.C. Feb. 15, 1932)
June 18, 1959 – Principle payment of 31% made to o/s deb. holders in full satisfaction of claim; no equity for com. shldrs. Co. reported dissolved.

Kootenay Energy Inc. (Alta. Sept. 17, 2003)
Sept. 23, 2008 – Acquired by Golden Oil Canada Corporation, a wholly owned subsid. of Golden Oil Corporation, for 66¢ per sh.

Kootenay Exploration Limited (B.C.)
1958 – Struck off register.

Kootenay Gold Corp. (Alta. Mar. 7, 2003)
Nov. 9, 2006 – Name changed to Kootenay Resources Inc. and continued into British Columbia. (see FPsurvey - Mines & Energy)

Kootenay Gold Inc. (Alta. Aug. 2, 2000)
Nov. 9, 2006 – Continued into British Columbia.
Feb. 21, 2012 – Name changed to Kootenay Silver Inc.
(see FPsurvey - Mines & Energy)

Kootenay King Resources Inc. (B.C. Apr. 19, 1985)
June 13, 1995 – Name changed to Intercap Resource
Management Corp.; basis 1 new for 5 old shs. ■

Kootenay Ore Hill Gold Mines Ltd. (B.C. 1936)
1942 – Wound up.

Kootenay Telephone Co. Ltd. (B.C. 1928)
Oct. 31, 1953 – Kootenay Telephone 5% cum. pref. called
for redemp. at 103.
Nov. 1953 – Wound up. Assets acquired by British
Columbia Telephone Co., Ltd. Kootenay Telephone 5%
cum. pref. called for redemp. on Oct. 31, 1953, at 103.

Kootenay Zinc Corp. (B.C. Mar. 23, 2015)
Sept. 8, 2020 – Name changed to Peakbirch Logic Inc.
prusuant to acquisition of Canndora Delivery Ltd. and
Greeny Collaboration Group (Canada) Ltd., and reverse
takeover acquisition of Lifted Innovations Inc.; basis 1
new for 23 old shs. ■

Kop Beverages Ltd. (unknown 1948)
Mar. 1952 – Went into receivership; no equity for shldrs.
Charter surrendered Mar. 16, 1963.

Kopan Developments Ltd. (B.C. 1947)
Aug. 1972 – Name changed to Jordesco Resources Ltd.;
basis 1 new for 5 old shs. ■

Koporok Mines Ltd. (B.C. 1967)
Nov. 25, 1974 – Charter cancelled.

Korby Gold Mines Ltd. (Ont. 1944)
1955 – Charter cancelled.

Kordol Explorations Ltd. (Ont. 1959)
Dec. 12, 1978 – Amalgamated with 2 other cos. to form
Junction Explorations Limited; basis 1 sh. Junction for 5
shs. Kordol.

Korea Exchange Bank of Canada (Can. 1981)
Name changed to KEB Hana Bank Canada.

Korich Mining Company Limited (Ont. 1958)
Feb. 9, 1991 – Name changed to TPB & T, Ltd.; basis 1
new for 5 old shs. ■

Korola-Larder Mines Ltd. (Ont. 1937)
Apr. 9, 1975 – Charter cancelled.

Kosa Resources Ltd. (B.C. 1986)
July 24, 1992 – Dissolved and struck off register.

Koval Resources Ltd. (Alta. Apr. 8, 1987)
Jan. 17, 1994 – Name changed to Ironwood Petroleum
Ltd.; basis 1 new for 6 old shs. ■

Kovo Healthtech Corporation (B.C. Feb. 20, 2020)
Oct. 28, 2024 – Name changed to Kovo+ Holdings Inc. ■

Kovo+ Holdings Inc. (B.C. Feb. 20, 2020)
May 16, 2025 – Continued into Alberta. (see FPsurvey -
Industrials)

Kowkash Gold Corp. (Alta. 1986)
Mar. 26, 1993 – Dissolved and struck off register.

Kozak Gold Mines Ltd. (Ont. 1934)
Oct. 16, 1952 – Charter cancelled.

Krain Copper Resources Ltd. (unknown)
1964 – Merged into Comet Krain Mining Corp. Ltd.; basis
1 new for 2 old shs.

Kraken Energy Corp. (Can. July 4, 2011)
June 24, 2025 – Acquired by Aero Energy Limited; basis
0.97037 Aero shs. for 1 Kraken sh.

Kraken Sonar Inc. (Can. Feb. 17, 2015)
Sept. 22, 2017 – Name changed to Kraken Robotics Inc.
(see FPsurvey - Industrials)

Kramer Capital Corp. (Alta. Oct. 29, 2010)
June 5, 2018 – Name changed to 48North Cannabis Corp.
pursuant to Qualifying Transaction reverse takeover
acquisition of (old) 48North Cannabis Corp.; basis 1 new
for 2 old shs. ■

Krancor Oil and Gas Ltd. (B.C. Mar. 22, 1972)
Jan. 9, 1976 – Name changed to Sanilogical Industries
Ltd.; basis 1 new for 2 old shs. ■

Kree Tech International Corporation (Can. Dec. 4,
2003)
Oct. 14, 2009 – Dissolved and struck from register.

Krefeld Graphite Gold Mines Ltd. (Ont. 1950)
Nov. 9, 1976 – Charter cancelled.

Kremzar Gold Mines Ltd. (Ont. 1930)
Dec. 28, 1988 – Dissolved following sale of interest in its
gold mine to Canamax Resources Inc. in 1987. (see
Canamax Resources Inc.)

Kria Resources Ltd. (Ont. July 17, 2009 amalg.)
Apr. 18, 2011 – Amalgamated with Trevali Resources
Corp.; basis 0.2 Trevali shs. for 1 Kria sh.

Krieger Data International Corp. (B.C. Aug. 9, 1984)
Nov. 17, 1987 – Name changed to Promark Software
Inc. ■

Krigold Resources Ltd. (Ont. Oct. 16, 1986)
Apr. 20, 1988 – Continued into British Columbia.
Sept. 24, 1993 – Dissolved and struck off register.

Kristiansen Cycle Engines Ltd. (Can. 1974)
1986 – Placed into receivership on Nov. 19, 1983. Co.
dissolved.

Kristina Capital Corp. (Alta. June 6, 2007)
Mar. 22, 2010 – Name changed to Black Marlin Energy
Holdings Limited and continued into British Virgin Islands
pursuant to reverse takeover acquisition of Black Marlin
Energy Ltd.; basis 1 new for 2 old shs. ■

Kristina Copper Mines Ltd. (Ont. 1952)
1956 – Name changed to Coppercrest Mines Ltd.; basis
1 new for 5 old shs. ■

Krno Mines Ltd. (Ont. 1959)
Apr. 30, 1969 – Charter cancelled.

Kroes Energy Inc. (Alta. Dec. 20, 1995)
June 9, 2009 – Name changed to Vecta Energy
Corporation. ■

Kronofusion Technologies Inc. (Yuk. May 15, 2000)
Aug. 13, 2003 – Name changed to Consolidated
Kronofusion Technologies Inc.; basis 1 new for 4 old
shs. ■

Kroy Oils Limited (Alta. 1949)
Oct. 9, 1959 – Name changed to Pamoil Limited. ■

Kruger Capital Corp. (B.C. Feb. 14, 1984)
Nov. 5, 2008 – Name changed to Nextraction Energy
Corp. (see FPsurvey - Mines & Energy)

Kruger Explorations Ltd. (B.C. Feb. 14, 1984)
Sept. 2, 1993 – Name changed to Kruger Capital Corp. ■

Krystal Bond Inc. (Ont. Jan. 21, 1980)
May 26, 2014 – Dissolved and struck from register.

Kualta Resources Ltd. (Alta. Dec. 15, 1986)
Oct. 7, 1993 – Name changed to Capco Resources Ltd.;
basis 1 new for 3 old shs. ■

Kukatush Mining Corporation (1960) Ltd. (Can. 1960)
Aug. 10, 1984 – Dissolved.

Kukatush Mining Corporation Ontario Limited (Ont.
1963)
Nov. 29, 1982 – Charter cancelled.

Kulczyk Oil Ventures Inc. (Alta. Mar. 16, 1987)
June 24, 2013 – Name changed to Serinus Energy Inc.
following acquisition of Winstar Resources Ltd.; basis 1
new for 10 old shs. ■

Kuma Oils Ltd. (Alta. 1965)
Sept. 3, 1971 – Amalgamated with Lassiter Petroleums
Ltd. to form Lassiter Kuma Oils Ltd.; basis 2 new for 1
old sh.

Kuma Resources Ltd. (Alta. 1959)
Mar. 18, 1997 – Name changed to Algonquin Petroleum
Corporation. ■

Kumix Resources Corporation (B.C. 1982)
Dec. 15, 1989 – Dissolved.

Kupfer Mines Ltd. (Ont. 1971)
Jan. 1973 – Name changed to Kupfer Corp.

Kusten Mines Ltd. (Ont. 1961)
1968 – Charter cancelled.

Kuta Ridge Exploration Inc. (Can. June 22, 2018)
July 31, 2020 – Name changed to Pacific Precious Inc. ■

Kwik Products International Corporation (B.C. 1984)
May 20, 1992 – Name changed to Trend Vision
Technologies, Inc.; basis 1 new for 2 old shs. (see
FPsurvey - Industrials)

Kwikstar Communications Ltd. (Alta. Nov. 30, 1993)
May 2, 1996 – Name changed to Digital Courier
International Corporation; basis 1 new for 3 old shs. ■

Kyack Copper Mines Ltd. (Ont. 1946)
Sept. 17, 1956 – Charter cancelled.

Kyber Resources Inc. (B.C. Aug. 23, 1987)
Feb. 20, 1995 – Name changed to Magin Energy Inc.;
basis 1 new for 3 old shs. ■

Kyle Gold Mines Ltd. (Ont. 1945)
Dec. 23, 1965 – Dissolved.

Kyle Resources Inc. (B.C. Oct. 21, 1980)
May 29, 1990 – Name changed to Consolidated Kyle
Resources Inc.; basis 1 new for 5 old shs. ■

Kyrgoil Corporation (Ont. Sept. 28, 1960)
Nov. 20, 2000 – Continued into British Virgin Islands.
Jan. 4, 2001 – Name changed to Kyrgoil Holding
Corporation. ■

Kyrgoil Holding Corporation (British Virgin Islands Nov.
20, 2000)
Jan. 29, 2004 – Formed Serica Energy Corporation in
British Virgin Islands on amalgamation with Petroleum
Development Associates (Oil & Gas) Limited, constituting
a reverse takeover by Petroleum Development; basis 1
new for 1.84 Petroleum Development shs. and 1 new for
10 Kyrgoil shs. ■

L

L & D Property Operations (Canada) Ltd. (B.C. Dec.
1, 1980)
Apr. 12, 1992 – Name changed to Uni-Way Pacific
Holdings Ltd. ■

L. McBrine Co. Limited (Ont. 1902)
June 1970 – Placed into bankruptcy
1971 – Unsecured creditors received an interim divd. of
25¢ on the dollar
June 1977 – Final 2nd divd. of 17¢ paid
1977 – Admin. of bankruptcy fully completed.

L1 Capital Corp. (B.C. Oct. 10, 2017)
Dec. 15, 2020 – Name changed to Sierra Madre Gold
and Silver Ltd. pursuant to the reverse takeover
acquisition of (old) Sierra Madre Gold and Silver Ltd. and

concurrernt amalgamation of (old) Sierra Madre with wholly owned 1262760 B.C. Ltd. (and continued as Sierra Madre Holdings Ltd.). (see FPsurvey - Mines & Energy)

L.A. Varah Ltd. (B.C. 1986 amalg.)
July 30, 1986 – Name changed to Saynor Varah Inc. ■

LAB International Inc. (Can. May 9, 2002)
July 13, 2007 – Name changed to Akela Pharma Inc. ■

LAB Research Inc. (Can. May 24, 2006)
Feb. 21, 2011 – Placed into receivership and Samson Belair Deloitte and Touche appointed receiver. All remaining directors resigned and Belair Deloitte took control of the operations.
Apr. 2011 – Applied Biology Company, holding company for CIT Safety & Health Research Laboratories, purchased substantially all the assets consisting of facilities located in Canada, Denmark and Hungary for undisclosed amount.
June 2011 – Merged with CIT Safety & Health Research Laboratories to form CiToxLAB group.

LAC Minerals Ltd. (Ont. Dec. 31, 1982 amalg.)
July 29, 1985 – Amalgamated with Lake Shore Mines Limited (2.871 for 1), Little Long Lac Gold Mines Limited (2.377 for 1) and Wright-Hargreaves Mines Limited (0.498 for 1) to continue with the same name LAC Minerals Ltd.; basis 1 new for 1 old sh.
Apr. 21, 1992 – Name changed to Lac Minerals Ltd. ■

L. A. P. Mining Co. Ltd. (B.C.)
Jan. 24, 1957 – Struck off register.

LARR Capital Corp. (Ont. Oct. 15, 1986)
Nov. 3, 1994 – Formed Pembridge Inc. in Ontario following acquisition of Pembridge Capital and amalgamation with 1057499 Ontario Limited; basis 1 new for 40 old shs. ■

LASMO Canada Inc. (Alta. Jan. 14, 1988 amalg.)
Nov. 10, 1992 – Name changed to ELAN Energy Inc. ■

LAVA Systems Inc. (Ont. June 14, 1995)
Dec. 1998 – Placed into receivership and Richter & Associates Inc. was appointed receiver. Certain assets and liabilities sold to Open Text Corporation for $2,300,000.

LBL Skysystems Corporation (Can. Sept. 28, 1979)
Dec. 14, 2005 – Dissolved.

LCTI Low Carbon Technologies International Inc. (B.C. Aug. 11, 2008)
Jan. 23, 2017 – Dissolved and struck from register.

LDC Ventures Inc. (Alta. Aug. 22, 1997)
Jan. 21, 2004 – Name changed to Mint Technology Corp. following reverse takeover acquisition of Mint Inc.; basis 1 new for 9.5824654 old shs. ■

L.E. Shaw Investments Limited (N.S. May 6, 1931)
Oct. 22, 1984 – Struck off register.

L.E. Shaw Limited (N.S. May 6, 1931)
June 8, 1978 – Redeemed cl. A and C shs. at $12.28 and $12.24 per sh., respectively. Co. now private.
Jan. 1, 1979 – Name changed to L.E. Shaw Investments Limited. ■

L. E. Waterman Pen Company Limited (Can. 1902)
Jan. 1964 – Receiving order made against the co.

LEA Security International Inc. (Ont. Oct. 20, 1983)
Jan. 19, 1989 – Name changed to Geodyne Technologies Inc. ■

LED Medical Diagnostics Inc. (B.C. Apr. 9, 2010)
Sept. 3, 2019 – Name changed to Apteryx Imaging Inc. ■

LEED NT Corp. (Ont. July 19, 1996)
Sept. 7, 2001 – All o/s cap. shs. and equity dividend shs. redeemed; basis $54.41 per capital sh. and $29.81 per equity dividend sh.

LEF International Inc. (Ont. Jan. 26, 1980)
May 24, 1996 – Formed LEF McLean Brothers International Inc. in Ontario on amalgamation with McLean Brothers (Domestic Great Lakes) Fisheries Ltd., accounted as a Pooling of Interests. ■

LEF McLean Brothers International Inc. (Ont. May 24, 1996 amalg.)
Sept. 9, 2013 – Dissolved and struck from register.

L.E.H. Ventures Ltd. (B.C. July 17, 1981)
Sept. 15, 2005 – Name changed to Discovery PGM Exploration Ltd. ■

LEV Scientific Industries Ltd. (B.C. 1983)
May 13, 1994 – Dissolved and struck off register.

LFNT Capital Corp. (B.C. June 23, 2022)
Feb. 10, 2023 – Name changed to LFNT Resources Corp. (see FPsurvey - Mines & Energy)

LFP Holdings Inc. (Ont. Sept. 18, 1980)
Jan. 1, 1989 – Formed Durkin Hayes Publishing Ltd. in Ontario on amalgamation with Hayes Publishing Limited. ■

LG Technologies Group Inc. (Can. Apr. 10, 1996)
Oct. 4, 1999 – All o/s com. shs. acquired by C-MAC Industries Inc.; basis payable in C-MAC shs. with value of approx. $4.00 per LG sh. based on trading formula of C-MAC shs. (see C-MAC Industries Inc.)

LGC Capital Ltd. (Can. July 9, 2004)
Aug. 6, 2019 – Name changed to Elixxer Ltd. (see FPsurvey - Industrials)

LGC Skyrota Wind Energy Corp. (Can. July 8, 2004)
May 7, 2013 – Dissolved and struck from register.

LGO Net.com Inc. (B.C. Aug. 19, 1985)
Jan. 26, 2001 – Name changed to Prolific Technology Inc. pursuant to reverse takeover acquisition of Prolific Smart Card Software and Systems Inc. ■

L.G.R. Resources Ltd. (B.C. Jan. 11, 2005)
Apr. 9, 2008 – Name changed to Stream Oil & Gas Ltd. following reverse takeover acquisition of (old) Stream Oil & Gas Ltd.; basis 1 Stream Oil sh. for 1 L.G.R. sh. (after a 1-for-4 cons.). ■

LGS Data Processing Consultants Inc. (Can. 1979)
Nov. 24, 1988 – Name changed to LGS Group Inc. ■

LGS Group Inc. (Can. 1979)
May 4, 2000 – Acquired by IBM Corporation for $19 per sh.

LGX Oil + Gas Inc. (Can. Sept. 8, 1994)
June 27, 2013 – Continued into Alberta.
June 7, 2016 – Placed into receivership. Ernst & Young Inc. appointed receiver and all officers and directors resigned.

L.I.F.T. Systems Inc. (Alta. Apr. 11, 1996)
June 25, 1999 – Name changed to Laniuk Industries Inc. ■

LINMOR Inc. (Ont. Nov. 17, 1995)
May 31, 2004 – Plan of Arrangement exchange with NUVO Network Management Inc.; basis 1 NUVO sh. for 115.54 LINMOR shs. (see NUVO Network Management Inc.)

L.K. Ranches Ltd. (Alta. Mar. 31, 1954)
Oct. 4, 1979 – Formed L.K. Resources Ltd. in Alberta pursuant to amalgamation with public company Oilex Industries Ltd. ■

L.K. Resources Ltd. (Alta. Oct. 4, 1979 amalg.)
Mar. 24, 1986 – Name changed to XL Food Systems Ltd. ■

LKP Solutions Inc. (B.C. Jan. 13, 2011)
Nov. 1, 2018 – Name changed to Osoyoos Cannabis Inc. following reverse takeover acquisition of (old) Osoyoos Cannabis Inc., which amalgamated with wholly owned 1160546 B.C. Ltd. and changed its name to 1160546 B.C. Ltd. ■

LL Capital Corp. (Ont. Nov. 28, 2014)
June 29, 2015 – Name changed to Syncordia Technologies and Healthcare Solutions, Corp. following Qualifying Transaction reverse takeover acquisition of Syncordia Technologies and Healthcare Solutions, Inc.; basis 1 new for 20 old shs. ■

LL One Inc. (Ont. Mar. 14, 2018)
Mar. 2, 2021 – Name changed to The Limestone Boat Company Limited pursuant to the Qualifying Transaction revere takeover acquisition of The Limestone Boat Company Inc. (LBCI) and concurrent amalgamation of LBCI with wholly owned 2790889 Ontario Inc. (see FPsurvey - Industrials)

LMC Resources Ltd. (B.C. 1969)
Nov. 14, 1978 – Amalgamated with Nahatlatch Resources Ltd. to form Seadrift Resources Ltd.; basis 1 new for 3 old shs.

LMK Energy Inc. (Alta. Aug. 20, 1993)
Feb. 2, 2003 – Struck from registry and dissolved.

LML Payment Systems Inc. (Yuk. Nov. 10, 1997)
Jan. 11, 2013 – Amalgamated with LML Acquisition Corp., a wholly owned subsid. of Digital River, Inc.; basis US$3.45 cash per sh.

LMS Medical Systems Inc. (Can. Jan. 14, 2003)
Aug. 20, 2012 – Name changed to Maclos Capital Inc. (see FPsurvey - Industrials)

LMX Resources Ltd. (B.C. Nov. 28, 1985)
Sept. 9, 2004 – Name changed to Merrex Resources Inc.; basis 1 new for 10 old shs. ■

LNG Energy Ltd. (B.C. Feb. 24, 2000)
Nov. 15, 2013 – Name changed to Esrey Energy Ltd.; basis 1 new for 20 old shs. ■

LOGiQ Asset Management Inc. (Alta. June 16, 1993)
June 7, 2018 – Name changed to Flow Capital Corp. and continued into British Columbia following the reverse takeover acquisition of and amalgamation with Grenville Strategic Royalty Corp.; basis 1 new for 12 old shs. (see FPsurvey - Industrials)

LOGiQ Advantage Bond Fund (Ont. Jan. 12, 2009)
Dec. 22, 2017 – Voluntarily delisted pursuant to termination of the fund on or about Dec. 29, 2017, following distribution of net assets.

LOGiQ Advantage Oil & Gas Income Fund (Ont. Feb. 24, 2005)
Dec. 20, 2017 – Name changed to Redwood Energy Income Fund. ■

LOGiQ Advantage VIP Income Fund (Ont. Jan. 1, 2006)
Dec. 20, 2017 – Name changed to Redwood Advantage Monthly Income Fund. ■

LOGiQ VIP Income Fund (Ont. Oct. 25, 2001)
Dec. 20, 2017 – Name changed to Redwood Monthly Income Fund. ■

LOM River Gold Corporation (B.C. May 20, 1988)
Oct. 17, 2001 – Name changed to Catalina Energy Corp. ■

LOOPShare Ltd. (B.C. Sept. 4, 2014)
Nov. 1, 2021 – Name changed to The Good Flour Corp. pursuant to the reverse takeover acquisition of VGAN Brands Inc. ■

LOR Capital Inc. (Can. Nov. 18, 2003)
Aug. 4, 2005 – Name changed to Decision Dynamics Technology Ltd. following Qualifying Transaction reverse takeover acquisition of Time Industrial, Inc. and Malibu Engineering & Software Ltd.; basis 1 new for 3.0435 old shs. ■

LOREX Technology Inc. (Ont. Sept. 25, 1979)
Dec. 28, 2012 – Acquired by FLIR Systems, Inc. for $1.30 per sh.
Jan. 1, 2015 – Name changed to FLIR Lorex Inc.

L1 Capital Corp. (Can. Dec. 20, 2007)
Apr. 30, 2010 – Amalgamated in Canada to continue with same name. (see Breaking Point Developments Inc.)
July 23, 2010 – Amalgamated with Breaking Point Developments Inc.; basis 1.333 Breaking Point shs. for 1 L1 Capital sh. (see Breaking Point Developments Inc.)

L.P. Industries Ltd. (B.C. Mar. 5, 1962)
July 25, 1979 – Name changed to May-Ralph Resources Ltd.; basis 1 new for 5 old shs. ∎

LPT Capital Ltd. (B.C. Dec. 15, 2006)
Aug. 17, 2009 – Name changed to Lincoln Mining Corporation pursuant to Qualifying Transaction reverse takeover acquisition of Lincoln Gold Corporation; basis 1 new for 1.5 old shs. ∎

LQwD FinTech Corp. (B.C. Sept. 22, 2004)
July 28, 2023 – Name changed to LQWD Technologies Corp. (see FPsurvey - Industrials)

L. R. Steel Company Inc. (Del.)
May 1923 – Went into bankruptcy. Assets sold; nothing for shldrs. The L. R. Steel Protective Trust Association obtained subscriptions from some shldrs. of the bankrupt companies, and purchased the assets, which were then operated under the name of Steel's Consolidated Inc.
1932 – Operating subsids. of Steel's Consolidated Inc. went into bankruptcy between 1930 and 1932. Their assets were sold and nothing remained for shldrs. of Steel's Consolidated Inc.

L. R. Steel Realty Development Corp. (unknown)
May 1923 – One of the companies of the L. R. Steel group. Shares have no value.

LRG Restaurant Group, Inc. (B.C. Jan. 13, 1960)
June 13, 2003 – Dissolved and struck from register.

LRX Capital Corp. (B.C. Oct. 18, 1979)
May 3, 1996 – Name changed to North American Tungsten Corporation Ltd. and continued into Canada. ∎

LS Laser Systems Ltd. (Alta. 1987)
July 1, 1992 – Struck off register.

LSC Lithium Corporation (B.C. Oct. 30, 2009)
Mar. 21, 2019 – Acquired by Pluspetrol Resources Corporation B.V.; basis US$0.6612 cash per sh.

LSI Logic Corporation of Canada, Inc. (Can. 1985)
Sept. 14, 1995 – Acquired by 3096467 Canada Inc., an indirect wholly owned subsid. of LSI Logic Corporation, for $4.00 per sh.

LTT Capital Corp. (B.C. Oct. 31, 2005)
June 28, 2007 – Formed Arura Pharma Inc. in Canada following Qualifying Transaction amalgamation with Arura Pharma Inc. with Arua the deemed acquiror. ∎

LW Capital Pool Inc. (Can. Aug. 5, 2009)
Mar. 26, 2014 – Name changed to Tweed Marijuana Inc. following Qualifying Transaction reverse takeover acquisition of Tweed Inc.; basis 1 new for 5 old shs. ∎

L W Resources Ltd. (B.C. Oct. 11, 1996)
June 12, 2000 – Name changed to Bancorp Financial Group Inc. following Qualifying Transaction acquisition of Bancorp Financial Services Inc. ∎

LWP Capital Inc. (Can. Apr. 20, 2011)
Dec. 31, 2015 – Commenced voluntary liquidation and dissolution. KSV Advisory Inc. appointed liquidator and all directors resigned.
May 2017 – Interim distrib. of 40¢ cash per sh. payable to shldrs. of record May 5, 2017.
Nov. 2017 – Interim distrib. of 62¢ cash per sh. payable to shldrs. of record Nov. 8, 2017.
Nov. 2018 – Interim distrib. of 10¢ cash per sh. payable to shldrs. of record Nov. 12, 2018.

LX Ventures Inc. (Alta. Nov. 19, 1998)
July 7, 2014 – Name changed to Mobio Technologies Inc. (see FPsurvey - Industrials)

LXRandCo, Inc. (Ont. June 11, 2015)
Nov. 5, 2023 – Filed for bankruptcy and KPMG Inc. appointed trustee.

La Senza Corporation (Can. May 5, 1982)
Jan. 17, 2007 – Acquired indirectly by Limited Brands, Inc. for Cdn$48.25 per sh.

Labarre Explorations Limited (Ont. 1976)
Nov. 9, 1981 – Dissolved.

Labatt Breweries of British Columbia Limited (Can. 1928)
1979 – Amalgamated into Labatt Brewing Company Limited.

Label Depot Corporation (Alta. Aug. 22, 1997)
Sept. 20, 2001 – Name changed to LDC Ventures Inc. ∎

Labine-McCarthy Uranium Mines Ltd. (Ont. 1949)
Nov. 30, 1964 – Dissolved.

Labmin Resources Limited (N.L. July 6, 1983 amalg.)
Sept. 17, 1985 – Amalgamated with Hollinger Argus Limited and Argcen Holdings Inc. to form Hollinger Inc; basis 2.5 new for 1 Hollinger Argus sh., 1 new for 1 Argcen sh. and 3.5 new for 1 Labmin sh. (other than those held by Argcen). (see Hollinger Inc.)

Labopharm Inc. (Que. Oct. 26, 1990)
Oct. 13, 2011 – Acquired by Chimigen Inc., a wholly owned subsid. of Paladin Labs Inc., for $0.2857 per sh. (see Paladin Labs Inc.)

Labrador Acceptance Corporation (Que. 1952)
Jan. 29, 1969 – Declared bankrupt. Secured noteholders received 85¢ per $1.00 of notes held. Trustees: Royal Trust Co. (for Secured Notes); Montreal Trust Co. (for Unsecured Notes).

Labrador International Mining Ltd. (B.C. Aug. 26, 1985)
Mar. 18, 1999 – Name changed to Royal International Venture Corporation; basis 1 new for 5 old shs. ∎

Labrador Iron Ore Royalty Income Fund (Ont. Oct. 5, 1995)
July 1, 2010 – Succeeded by Labrador Iron Ore Royalty Corporation pursuant to plan of arrangement whereby Labrador Iron Ore Royalty Corporation was formed to facilitate the conversion of the fund into a corporation and the fund was subsequently dissolved. (see FPsurvey - Mines & Energy)

Labrador Mining and Exploration Company Limited (N.L. 1936)
July 6, 1983 – Formed Labmin Resources Limited in Newfoundland and Labrador following acquisition by Hollinger Argus Limited. ∎

Labrador Nickel Mining Corp. (Que. 1962)
Apr. 13, 1974 – Charter cancelled.

Labrador Technologies Inc. (Alta. June 11, 1981)
Feb. 3, 2023 – Name changed to Labrador Resources Inc. (see FPsurvey - Mines & Energy)

Labrador Ungava Explorations Ltd. (Ont. 1955)
Aug. 1964 – Name changed to Little Tex Mining Corp. ∎

Labrador Uranium Inc. (Ont. July 13, 2021)
June 29, 2023 – Name changed to Latitude Uranium Inc. ∎

Labyrinth Resources Corp. (B.C. July 4, 1986)
Dec. 20, 1993 – Name changed to El Callao Mining Corp. ∎

Lac de Renzy Nickel Ltd. (Ont. 1955)
1967 – Merged into Delahey Consolidated Nickel Mines Ltd.; basis 10 new for 34 old shs.

Lac du Bonnet Chromium Ltd. (Man. 1946)
Mar. 1, 1969 – Dissolved.

Lac du Bonnet Mines (unknown)
1946 – Assets acquired by Lac du Bonnet Chromium Ltd.; basis 1 new for 2 old shs. (see Lac du Bonnet Chromium Ltd.)

Lac Minerals Ltd. (Ont. July 29, 1985 amalg.)
Oct. 17, 1994 – Acquired by AB Acquisition Inc., a wholly owned subsid. of American Barrick Resources Corporation; basis $5.00 plus 0.325 American Barrick shs., or 0.487 American Barrick shs. for 1 Lac sh. (see American Barrick Resources Corporation)

Lacana Mining Corporation (Ont. 1975 amalg.)
July 1, 1988 – Amalgamated with 7 other cos. to form Corona Corporation; basis 1.32 new Cl. A shs. for 1 old Lacana com. sh. (see Corona Corporation)

Lacanex Mining Co. Ltd. (Ont. 1969)
Sept. 22, 1975 – Merged into Lacana Mining Corporation; basis 30 Lacana shs. for 100 Lacanex shs.

Lachance Mines Ltd. (Que. 1951)
May 20, 1972 – Dissolved.

Lachib Development Corporation (Ont. 1959)
June 25, 1991 – Name changed to Syntech Diamond Films Inc. ∎

Laclothian Mines Ltd. (Ont. 1944)
July 4, 1949 – Charter cancelled; distribution to shldrs. of 9¢ per 100 shs.

Laco Resources Inc. (B.C. 1972)
Aug. 27, 1982 – Name changed to International Laco Resources Inc.; basis 1 new for 5 old shs. ∎

Lacoma Gold Mine Ltd. (Ont. May 28, 1935)
Mar. 1943 – Distribution made; basis 1 New Barber-Larder Mines Ltd. sh. for 20 Lacoma shs. (see New Barber-Larder Mines Ltd.)

Lacorne Lithium Mines Ltd. (Ont. 1947)
May 1957 – Wound up. For each 10 shs. of LaCorne Lithium, distribution made of $14, 3 shs. Quebec Lithium Corp. and 2 shs. LaCorne Mines 1957 Ltd.

Lacorne Mines 1957 Limited (Que. Aug. 10, 1935)
Jan. 18, 1960 – Charter cancelled.

Lacroix & Frères Inc. (Que. 1957)
Mar. 3, 1972 – Name changed to Lacroix Inc. ∎

Lacroix Inc. (Que. 1957)
1976 – Acquired by Hugh Russel Limited for $8.50 per sh.

Lacwin Mining Co. Ltd. (Alta. 1956)
Oct. 31, 1966 – Struck off register.

Lada Development Ltd. (B.C. 1961)
Feb. 4, 1983 – Struck off register.

Laddie Gold Mines Limited (Ont. 1945)
July 22, 1982 – Amalgamated with Abino Gold Mines Limited (1 for 12.94), Clicker Red Lake Mines Limited (1 for 18.23), Commander Red Lake Mines Limited (1 for 30.82), Dorion Red Lake Mines Limited (1 for 15.59), Duchesne Red Lake Mines Limited (1 for 10.57), Forsyth Mines Limited (1 for 6.38), Goldquest Explorations Inc. (1 for 1.26), Inore Gold Mines Limited (1 for 9.9) and Rowan Gold Mines Limited (1 for 4.91) to form Goldquest Exploration Inc. for; basis 1 new for 15.22 old shs.

Ladera Ventures Corp. (B.C. May 21, 1987)
May 28, 2018 – Name changed to MedMen Enterprises Inc. following reverse takeover acquisition of MM Enterprises USA, LLC; basis 1 new for 9.2623 old shs. ∎

Laduboro Enterprises Ltd. (Que. 1954)
June 2, 1987 – Name changed to Laduboro Ltd.; basis 1 new for 5 old shs. ∎

Laduboro Ltd. (Que. 1954)
Dec. 1, 1989 – Name changed to Monterey Capital Inc. ■

Laduboro Oil Ltd. (Que. 1954)
Sept. 1, 1985 – Name changed to Laduboro Enterprises Ltd. ■

Ladulama Gold Mines Ltd. (Ont. Dec. 2, 1944)
Mar. 31, 1953 – Name changed to Nudulama Mines Ltd.; basis 1 new for 2 old shs. ■

Lady Robyn Resources Inc. (B.C. 1982)
Nov. 23, 1987 – Name changed to Sino Business Machines Inc. ■

Lady Rouyn Mines Ltd. (Ont. 1944)
June 1, 1959 – Dissolved.

Ladysmith Exploration Ltd. (Ont. 1959)
1970 – Wound up.

Lafarge Canada Inc. (Can. Oct. 22, 1927; via letters patent)
Aug. 3, 2006 – Acquired by Efalar Canada Inc., a wholly owned subsid. of Lafarge S.A., for US$85.26 per exch. pfce. sh.
Dec. 31, 2022 – Continued into Alberta.
Jan. 1, 2023 – Continued into Canada.
June 20, 2025 – Name changed to Amrize Canada Inc.

Lafarge Canada Ltd. (B.C. 1956)
1970 – Acquired by Canada Cement Lafarge Ltd.; basis 2 Canada Cement com. shs. for 5 com. or 6% pref. shs. of Lafarge. (see Canada Cement Lafarge Ltd.)

Lafarge Corporation (Md. Apr. 25, 1977)
Sept. 4, 2001 – Name changed to Lafarge North America Inc. ■

Lafarge North America Inc. (Md. Apr. 25, 1977)
May 17, 2006 – Acquired by Afalar Inc., a wholly owned subsid. of Lafarge S.A., for Cdn$85.50 per sh.

Lafayette Asbestos Co. Ltd. (Que. June 10, 1950)
June 27, 1955 – Name changed to New Lafayette Asbestos Company Limited; basis 1 new for 4 old shs. ■

Lafayette Long Lac Gold Mines Ltd. (Ont. 1928)
Dec. 7, 1967 – Dissolved.

Laflamme Barraute Mines Ltd. (Ont. 1941)
1956 – Charter cancelled.

Lafontaine Gauthier Shattner Inc. (Can. 1979)
Mar. 31, 1984 – Amalgamated with 1208309 Canada Inc. to form LGS Data Processing Consultants Inc.

Lagasco Corp. (Ont. June 22, 1948)
Aug. 4, 2010 – Name changed to El Condor Minerals Inc. and continued into British Columbia. ■

Lagava Minerals Ltd. (Ont. 1955)
Sept. 1961 – Name changed to Fox Lake Mines Ltd. ■

Lago Dourado Minerals Ltd. (Can. May 21, 2009)
July 21, 2016 – Name changed to Sandy Lake Gold Inc. ■

Lago Gold Mines Ltd. (Que. 1937)
1944 – Sold assets to Renfort Gold Mines for 200,000 shs.

Lago Resources Ltd. (Ont. Aug. 21, 1992)
Jan. 16, 1997 – Name changed to RUX Resources Inc. following reverse takeover acquisition of RUX Resources Ltd.; basis 1 new for 5 old shs. ■

Laguerre Gold Mines Limited (Ont. 1939)
Aug. 31, 1950 – Name changed to New Laguerre Mines Limited; basis 1 new for 2 old shs. ■

Laguna Blends Inc. (B.C. June 2, 2014)
June 9, 2017 – Name changed to Isodiol International Inc. following the May 2017 acquisition of ISO International, LLC. (see FPsurvey - Industrials)

Laguna Gold Mines Ltd. (Ont. 1933)
1939 – Liquidated for 19.2¢ per sh.

Laguna Resources Ltd. (B.C. 1972)
Jan. 1978 – Name changed to Laco Resources Inc.; basis 1 new for 5 old shs. ■

Laidlaw Inc. (Can. Mar. 16, 1979)
June 20, 2003 – Following Plan of Reorganization (Plan) under the United States Bankruptcy Act and the Companies' Creditors Arrangement Act (Canada), shares of Laidlaw International, Inc. (formerly Laidlaw Investments Ltd.) were used to pay off selected Laidlaw Inc.'s creditors. Laidlaw Inc.'s com. shs. were deemed to have no value under the Plan.

Laidlaw International, Inc. (Ont. Sept. 25, 1985)
June 20, 2003 – Continued into Delaware.

Laidlaw Motor Sales Ltd. (Can. - unspecified)
1966 – Amalgamated to form Laidlaw Motorways Ltd.

Laidlaw Motorways Limited (Ont. Apr. 27, 1966 amalg.; via letters patent)
July 30, 1973 – Name changed to Laidlaw Transportation Limited. ■

Laidlaw Transportation Limited (Ont. Apr. 27, 1966 amalg.; via letters patent)
Mar. 16, 1979 – Continued into Canada.
Jan. 2, 1990 – Name changed to Laidlaw Inc. ■

L'Air d'Or Corporation (Ont. Aug. 16, 1961)
July 11, 1996 – Formed Tagalder Incorporated in Ontario on amalgamation with Tagalder Corporation; basis 1 new for 1 Tagalder sh. and 1 new for 10 L'Air shs. ■

The Laird Group Inc. (Can. Jan. 9, 1931)
1988 – Amalgamated in Canada to continue with same name. (see Printera Corporation)
Nov. 29, 1996 – Acquired by a subsid. of Printera Corporation; basis 14¢ or 1 Printera sh. for 18 Laird shs. (see Printera Corporation)

Laiterie Dallaire Ltée (Que. 1954)
1974 – Acquired by Beurrerie Lafreniere Ltée of Laverlochere, Que.

Laiteries Papineau Inc. (Que. 1947)
Aug. 5, 1974 – Dissolved.
June 6, 1978 – Proceeds from sale were used to retire all 5-6% 1st mtge. bonds o/s. Cash surplus was retained by co. No disposition had been reported to creditors, pref. or com. shldrs.

Lake Bearskin Mining Synd. Ltd. (Ont. 1944)
1950 – Charter cancelled.

Lake Beaverhouse Mines Ltd. (Ont. 1935)
Feb. 20, 1980 – Dissolved.

Lake Capital Corp. (Ont. Nov. 9, 1989)
July 14, 1993 – Name changed to Valavaara Environmental Technologies Ltd. ■

Lake Caswell Mines Ltd. (Ont. June 26, 1934)
1957 – Charter cancelled.

Lake Central Mines Ltd. (B.C. 1957)
May 1, 1969 – Struck off register.

Lake Cinch Mines Ltd. (Ont. 1949)
1960 – Acquired by Dickenson Mines Ltd.; basis 1 new for 4.5 old shs. (see Dickenson Mines Ltd.)

Lake City Gaming Corp. (B.C. Sept. 15, 1997)
July 18, 2002 – Acquired by Gateway Casinos Okanagan Ltd., a wholly owned subsid. of Gateway Casinos Inc., for $3.25 per sh.

Lake Dufault Mines Limited (Que. 1937)
Dec. 16, 1971 – Merged with Opemiska Copper Mines (Quebec) Limited and Falconbridge Mines Quebec Limited into Falconbridge Copper Limited; basis 3 new for 2 Lake Dufault shs.

Lake Erie Gas Limited (Ont. 1958)
May 1971 – Merged into Erieshore Industries Inc.; basis 2 new for 5 old shs.

Lake Erie Petroleum Company, Limited (Ont. 1952)
1958 – Wound up.

Lake Expanse Gold Mines Ltd. (Ont. 1935)
July 6, 1972 – Name changed to Lakex Mines Ltd.; basis 1 new for 5 old shs.

Lake Fortune Gold Mines Ltd. (Can. 1934)
Mar. 1952 – Name changed to New Fortune Mines Ltd. and continued into Ontario; basis 1 new for 4 old shs. ■

Lake Geneva Mining Co. Ltd. (Que. 1928)
1949 – Acquired by Geneva Lake Mines Ltd. (see Geneva Lake Mines Ltd.)

Lake George Mines Ltd. (Ont. 1971)
Mar. 1976 – Charter cancelled.

Lake Horwood Gold Mines Limited (Ont. 1949)
Apr. 1958 – Charter cancelled.

Lake Kaginu Mines Ltd. (Ont. 1954)
1956 – Assets acquired by Crowpat Minerals Ltd.; basis 1 new for 2 old shs.

Lake Kingston Mines Ltd. (Ont. 1956)
Apr. 1975 – Charter cancelled.

Lake Kozak Mines Ltd. (Ont. 1965)
Apr. 9, 1975 – Charter cancelled.

Lake Lauzon Mines Ltd. (Ont. 1954)
Apr. 1, 1965 – Dissolved.

Lake Lingman Gold Mining Co. Ltd. (Ont. Feb. 9, 1945)
1964 – Name changed to Lakelyn Mines Ltd.; basis 1 new for 3.5 old shs. ■

Lake Marron Gold Mines, Ltd. (Can. Jan. 14, 1926)
Dec. 18, 1936 – Merged into Maralgo Mines Limited; basis 1 new for 4 old shs. (see Maralgo Mines Limited)

Lake McIvor Mines Ltd. (Ont. 1963)
1975 – Charter cancelled.

Lake Mine Resources Inc. (Ont. Mar. 4, 1983)
June 23, 1987 – Name changed to Delicorp Foodservice Inc. ■

Lake Nordic Uranium Mines Ltd. (Ont. 1954)
1956 – Merged into Northspan Uranium Mines Ltd.; basis 3 new for 4 old shs.

Lake of the Woods Milling Co. Ltd. (Can. 1903)
Apr. 12, 1960 – Wholly owned subsid. of Ogilvie Flour Mills Company, Limited. Com. stk. acquired by Ogilvie in November 1954; basis 1 sh. Ogilvie plus $10 for each Lake of the Woods com. sh. Pref. stk. acquired by Ogilvie at $130 per sh.

Lake Ontario Cement Ltd. (Can. 1956)
Dec. 5, 1986 – Acquired by Ciments Français Canada Limitée, a wholly owned subsid. of Société des Ciments Français, for $36.25 per sh.

Lake Ontario Portland Cement Co. Ltd. (Can. 1956)
Feb. 1965 – Name changed to Lake Ontario Cement Ltd. ■

Lake Opawica Mines Ltd. (Que. 1946)
July 1960 – Charter cancelled.

Lake-Osu Mines Ltd. (Ont. 1945)
Aug. 1976 – Wound up.

Lake Placid Resources Ltd. (Alta. Aug. 6, 1992)
Feb. 22, 1995 – Name changed to Electra Energy Corporation following amalgamation with Electra Petroleum Ltd. (1 new com. sh. for 1 old cl. A sh.); basis 1 new for 10 old shs. ■

Lake Ponask Gold Corp. (Ont. Feb. 23, 1984)
Nov. 25, 1991 – Name changed to Leadley, Gunning & Culp International Corp.; basis 1 new for 8 old shs. ■

Lake Renzy Mines Ltd. (Que. 1955)
Mar. 1965 – Name changed to Renzy Mines Limited; basis 1 new for 4 old shs. (see FPsurvey - Mines & Energy)

Lake-Ridge Mines Ltd. (Ont. 1943)
Aug. 25, 1966 – Dissolved.

Lake Rowan Gold Mines Ltd. (Can. 1943)
1945 – Assets acquired by Lake Rowan (1945) Mines Ltd.; basis 1 new for 3 old shs. (see Lake Rowan (1945) Mines Ltd.)

Lake Rowan (1945) Mines Ltd. (Ont. 1945)
1951 – Name changed to Rowan Consolidated Mines Ltd.; basis 1 new for 4 old shs. ■

Lake Shore Gold Corp. (Yuk. June 25, 2002)
June 4, 2004 – Continued into British Columbia. (see Tahoe Resources Inc.)
July 18, 2008 – Continued into Canada. (see Tahoe Resources Inc.)
Apr. 8, 2016 – Acquired by Tahoe Resources Inc.: basis 0.1467 Tahoe com. shs. for 1 Lake Shore com. sh. (see Tahoe Resources Inc.)

Lake Shore Mines Limited (Ont. 1914)
July 29, 1985 – Amalgamated with Wright-Hargreaves Mines Limited (0.498 for 1), Little Long Lac Gold Mines Limited (2.377 for 1) and LAC Minerals Ltd. (1 for 1) to continue as LAC Minerals Ltd.; basis 2.871 new LAC shs. for 1 old Lake Shore sh. (see LAC Minerals Ltd.)

Lake Superior Iron Ltd. (unknown)
1960 – Merged into St. Lawrence Columbium & Metals Corp.; basis 1 new for 25 old shs. ■

Lake Superior Mining Corp. Ltd. (Ont. 1947)
Feb. 25, 1965 – Dissolved.

Lake Superior Nickel Corp. Ltd. (Ont. 1967)
1979 – Charter cancelled.

Lake Surprise Mine Ltd. (Ont. 1947)
Name changed to Le Prix Explorations Ltd. ■

Lake Ventures Ltd. (B.C. 1983)
Mar. 2, 1990 – Dissolved.

Lake Wasa Mining Corp. (Que. 1946)
Aug. 31, 1960 – Name changed to Wasamac Mines Ltd.; basis 1 new for 3 old shs. ■

Lakefield Marketing Corporation (Ont. Dec. 12, 1989)
Nov. 24, 2014 – Dissolved and struck from registry.
Feb. 2, 2018 – Restored to registry.
Sept. 24, 2019 – Name changed to Class 1 Nickel and Technologies Limited pursuant to the reverse takeover acquisition of Legendary Ore Mining Corporation. (see FPsurvey - Mines & Energy)

Lakefield Minerals Ltd. (Ont. Dec. 12, 1989)
Feb. 19, 2004 – Name changed to Lakefield Marketing Corporation. ■

Lakefield Porcupine Gold Mines Ltd. (Ont. 1933)
1946 – Wound up.

Lakehead Gold Mines Ltd. (Ont. 1936)
Nov. 18, 1958 – Reported dissolved.

Lakehead Mines Ltd. (Ont. 1948)
Jan. 11, 1979 – Amalgamated with Vespar Mines Ltd., to form Parlake Resources Limited; basis 1 new for 8 old shs.

Lakeland Base Metals Ltd. (B.C. 1966)
1968 – Assets acquired by BrenMac Mines Ltd.

Lakeland Gold Mines Ltd. (Ont. 1936)
Nov. 18, 1958 – Reported dissolved.

Lakeland Natural Gas Limited (Ont. 1954)
Jan. 1, 1968 – Amalgamated into Northern and Central Gas Corporation Limited. Each 2.5 5.4% pref. shs. of Lakeland, $20 par, exch. for 1 sh. $2.70 1st pref. stk., 2nd ser. $50 par. of Northern; each 3 com. shs. Lakeland for 2 com. shs. Northern. Lakeland wts. were also exch. for wts. of Northern.

Lakeland Resources Inc. (B.C. Oct. 11, 2007)
Sept. 25, 2015 – Name changed to ALX Uranium Corp.; basis 1 new for 3 old shs. ■

Lakeland Royalty & Petroleum Corporation (B.C. Aug. 23, 1983)
Sept. 23, 1996 – Continued into Yukon. (see FPsurvey - Mines & Energy)

Lakeleaf Silver Mining Co. Ltd. (Ont. 1946)
Oct. 1978 – Charter cancelled.

Lakelyn Mines Inc. (Ont. Feb. 9, 1945)
Sept. 1979 – Name changed to Twin Gold Mines Ltd. ■

Lakelyn Mines Ltd. (Ont. Feb. 9, 1945)
Oct. 5, 1978 – Name changed to Lakelyn Mines Inc. ■

Lakemount Mines Limited (Ont. 1943)
Feb. 22, 1982 – Charter cancelled.

Lakeport Brewing Income Fund (Ont. Apr. 27, 2005)
Mar. 30, 2007 – Acquired by Labatt Brewing Company Limited, a wholly owned subsid. of Interbrew S.A., for $28 per trust unit.

Laker Resources Ltd. (B.C. Sept. 22, 1983)
June 11, 1990 – Name changed to Videogram International Corp. ■

Lakeshore Minerals Inc. (Ont. Mar. 5, 1937)
July 7, 1990 – Name changed to Leggo Holdings Inc. ■

Lakeside Kirkland Gold Mines Ltd. (Ont. Apr. 1934)
1956 – Charter cancelled.

Lakeside Lorrain Silver Mines Ltd. (Ont. 1923)
1927 – Operations closed. Assets sold. Proceeds insufficient to meet liabs.

Lakeside Minerals Inc. (Ont. Dec. 20, 2011)
July 25, 2017 – Name changed to Lineage Grow Company Ltd. ■

Lakeside Oil & Gas Limited (Ont. 1967)
May 1971 – Merged into Erieshore Industries Inc.; basis 2 new for 5 old shs.

Lakeside Steel Inc. (Ont. Oct. 10, 2008)
Apr. 4, 2012 – Acquired by JMC Steel Group, Inc. for $0.2983 per sh.

Lakeview Hotel Investment Corp. (Can. Oct. 11, 2012)
Dec. 22, 2021 – Acquired by 13487369 Canada Inc. a company managed by First Canadian Management Corporation for 2¢ cash per sh.

Lakeview Hotel Real Estate Investment Trust (Man. Feb. 11, 2004)
Dec. 31, 2012 – Succeeded by Lakeview Hotel Investment Corp. pursuant to plan of arrangement whereby Lakeview Hotel Investment Corp. was formed to facilitate the conversion of the trust into a corporation and the trust was subsequently dissolved. ■

Lakeview (Stewart, B.C.) Mines (unknown)
Stock reported exchangeable into Ventures Explorations Ltd.; basis 1 new for 1 old sh. (see Ventex Ltd.)

Lakewood Energy Inc. (Can. Apr. 17, 1990)
Aug. 4, 1994 – Merged into Serenpet Inc.; basis 0.686 Serenpet shs. for 1 Lakewood sh. (see Serenpet Inc.)

Lakewood Exploration Inc. (B.C. May 2, 2017)
Oct. 1, 2021 – Name changed to Silver Hammer Mining Corp. (see FPsurvey - Mines & Energy)

Lakewood Forest Products Ltd. (B.C. 1983)
Sept. 4, 1992 – Dissolved and struck off register.

Lakewood Mining Co. Ltd. (B.C. Apr. 25, 1969)
Nov. 14, 2013 – Name changed to Golden Secret Ventures Ltd.; basis 1 new for 15 old shs. ■

Lakota Resources Inc. (Ont. Mar. 3, 1937)
Sept. 26, 2011 – Name changed to Tembo Gold Corp.; basis 1 new for 18 old shs. ■

Lalani Thompson Holdings Inc. (Ont. June 30, 2017)
Dec. 15, 2020 – Name changed to General Assembly Holdings Limited. ■

Lalo Ventures Ltd. (Yuk. Nov. 1, 2001)
Aug. 5, 2005 – Continued into British Columbia.
Dec. 20, 2005 – Name changed to Sunrise Minerals Inc. ■

Lama Exploration & Mining Co. Ltd. (Ont. 1956)
Dec. 1960 – Charter cancelled.

Lamaque Gold Mines Limited (Can. Dec. 16, 1932)
Sept. 12, 1963 – Merged with The Teck-Hughes Gold Mines Limited and Canadian Devonian Petroleums Limited to form Teck Corporation Limited; basis 4 new for 5 old shs.

Lamaque Mining Company 1964 Limited (B.C. 1964)
Sept. 30, 1981 – Amalgamated into Teck Corporation. (see Teck Corporation)

Lamaska Capital Corp. (B.C. Feb. 6, 2019)
Dec. 24, 2021 – Name changed to TinOne Resources Inc. pursuant to the Qualifying Transaction reverse takeover acquisition of TinOne Resources Corp. (see FPsurvey - Mines & Energy)

Lambda Mercantile Corporation (Ont. Aug. 12, 1940)
Sept. 30, 1987 – Name changed to Consolidated Mercantile Corporation. ■

Lambda Mercantile Corporation Ltd. (Ont. Aug. 12, 1940)
Dec. 7, 1978 – Name changed to Lambda Mercantile Corporation; basis 2 new for 1 old sh. ■

Lambert Somec Inc. (Que. Apr. 29, 1985)
Jan. 3, 1995 – Amalgamated with 9011-5643 Quebec Inc. and 9011-6955 Quebec Inc. to form new co. with same name Lambert Somec Inc.; basis 1 pref. sh. for 1 com. sh. immediately repurchased for $1.65 per sh. Co. now private.

Lambton Copper Mines Ltd. (Ont. 1955)
Apr. 9, 1969 – Charter cancelled.

Lambton Loan and Investment Co. (Ont. 1844)
Oct. 31, 1978 – Merged with parent co. Victoria and Grey Trust Company and The Lambton Trust Co. to form Victoria and Grey Trust Company. Minority shldrs. of Lambton Loan received 2 new com. shs. for 1 old sh.

The Lambton Trust Company, Limited (Ont. 1928)
Oct. 31, 1978 – Merged with 2 other cos. to form Victoria and Grey Trust Company; basis 5 com. shs. for 1 old sh.

Lamêlée Iron Ore Ltd. (Can. Sept. 6, 2011)
July 9, 2018 – Continued into Ontario.
Aug. 16, 2019 – Name changed to Aura Health Inc. pursuant to reverse takeover acquisition of Aura Health Corp. ■

Laminco Resources Inc. (B.C. Mar. 29, 1983)
Oct. 17, 2000 – Continued into Yukon.
Nov. 1, 2000 – Name changed to Zaruma Resources Inc. following acquisition of Zaruma Mining Corporation ASA; basis 1 new for 10 old shs. ■

Lammermoor Gold Mines Limited (Ont. 1937)
Nov. 1973 – Dissolved.

Lamontagne Limitée (Que. 1961)
June 1969 – Acquired by Couvrette & Provost Ltée; basis 5 Couvrette com. shs. for 7 Lamontagne cl. A or cl. B shs.

Lamplighter Energy Ltd. (Alta. May 29, 1996)
Jan. 12, 2006 – Formed Blackdog Resources Ltd. in Alberta on amalgamation with Blackdog Resources Ltd. (deemed acquiror). ∎

Lana Gold Corp. (B.C. Jan. 13, 1981)
Mar. 2, 1995 – Name changed to Global Technologies Inc.; basis 1 new for 3 old shs. ∎

Lanark Silver Mines Ltd. (Ont. 1957)
Nov. 10, 1966 – Dissolved.

Lanark Uranium Mines Ltd. (Ont. 1953)
1956 – Charter cancelled.

Lancaster Capital Corp. (B.C. Apr. 26, 2004)
Nov. 18, 2016 – Name changed to NxGold Ltd. ∎

Lancaster Mining Corp. Ltd. (Ont. 1965)
Nov. 1978 – Charter cancelled.

Lancaster Resource Corporation (B.C. Aug. 13, 1982)
July 8, 1985 – Name changed to Synex International Inc. ∎

Lancaster Sierra Capital Corp. (Ont. Aug. 17, 2004)
May 1, 2006 – Formed EFT Canada Inc. in Ontario on Qualifying Transaction amalgamation with EFT Canada Inc., constituting a reverse takeover by EFT Canada. ∎

Lancer of Canada Limited (B.C. 1969 amalg.)
Aug. 18, 1977 – Acquired by Modern Shirt Industries Ltd. for 60¢ per sh.

Lancer Petroleums Ltd. (Ont. 1950)
1970 – Struck off register.

Lancer Resources Inc. (B.C. Oct. 7, 1986)
Jan. 25, 1991 – Name changed to V-Tech Diagnostics (Canada) Inc.; basis 5 new for 1 old sh. ∎

Lancer Resources Ltd. (Ont. 1965)
Jan. 2, 1979 – Name changed to Mount Jamie Mines Ltd. following acquisition of assets of Mount Jamie Mines (Quebec) Limited in 1978. ∎

Landair Explorations Ltd. (Ont. 1971)
Feb. 28, 1978 – Amalgamated with Powerex Resources Ltd. to form Uranex Resources Ltd.; basis 1 new for 1 Powerex sh. and 0.75 new for 1 Landair sh. (see Uranex Resources Ltd.)

Landdrill International Inc. (B.C. Sept. 22, 1992)
May 30, 2013 – Petitioned into bankruptcy by secured creditor and subsequently declared bankrupt. All officers and directors resigned. Grant Thorton Poirier appointed trustee.

Landen Capital Corp. (B.C. July 11, 2006)
June 22, 2010 – Name changed to Sama Resources Inc. ∎

Lander Energy Corporation (Ont. Oct. 11, 2007)
Apr. 25, 2012 – Name changed to Prosper Gold Corp. and continued into British Columbia. (see FPsurvey - Mines & Energy)

Landhawk Petroleum Corporation (Alta. June 1, 1994)
Dec. 7, 1998 – Name changed to Campion Resources Ltd.; basis 1 new for 4 old shs. ∎

Landis Energy Corporation (Alta. Aug. 16, 1996)
Mar. 30, 2010 – Acquired by AltaGas Income Trust for 80¢ per sh. (see AltaGas Income Trust)

Landis Mining Corporation (Alta. Aug. 16, 1996)
July 1, 2006 – Name changed to Landis Energy Corporation. ∎

Landmark Capital Corp. (Alta. Feb. 21, 2001)
Dec. 10, 2003 – Name changed to Landmark Oil & Gas Corp. following Qualifying Transaction acquisition of Alford Petroleum 2001 Corp. and Alford Petroleum 2001 Inc. ∎

Landmark Corporation (Ont. Mar. 15, 1984 amalg.)
Jan. 31, 1992 – Amalgamated with Gateford Resources Inc. to form new co. with same name Landmark Corporation; basis 11 new for 13 Landmark shs. (see Landmark Corporation)

Landmark Corporation (Ont. Jan. 31, 1992 amalg.)
Aug. 6, 1996 – Name changed to Landmark Global Financial Corporation; basis 1 new for 10 old shs. (see FPsurvey - Industrials)

Landmark Environmental Inc. (B.C. Sept. 5, 1975)
June 12, 1997 – Name changed to International Landmark Environmental Inc.; basis 1 new for 10 old shs. ∎

Landmark Minerals Inc. (B.C. July 14, 2005)
Aug. 20, 2007 – Acquired by Ucore Uranium Inc.; basis 0.68 Ucore sh. for 1 Landmark sh. (see Ucore Uranium Inc.)

Landmark Mines Ltd. (Ont. 1947)
Dec. 1972 – Dissolved.

Landmark Motor Inns of Canada Ltd. (Can. Nov. 23, 1972)
Apr. 26, 1977 – Name changed to Headway Hotels Ltd. ∎

Landmark Oil & Gas Corp. (Alta. Feb. 21, 2001)
Sept. 2010 – Struck from the registry and dissolved.

Landmark Oils Ltd. (Alta.)
May 1961 – Acquired by Pamoil Ltd. for 1,700,000 shs.

Landmark Resources Ltd. (B.C. Sept. 5, 1975)
Oct. 10, 1995 – Name changed to Landmark Environmental Inc. ∎

Landmark Savings and Loan Association (Ont. 1964)
Nov. 1, 1993 – Acquired by Co-Operative Trust Company of Canada in a share purchase agreement with Credit Union Central of Ontario Limited. Subsequently wound up.

Landolac Mines Ltd. (Ont. 1956)
Aug. 3, 1964 – Dissolved.

Landon Resources Ltd. (B.C. Apr. 7, 1981)
Mar. 27, 1995 – Name changed to Adikann Goldfields Ltd. ∎

Landore Resources Inc. (Alta. Mar. 6, 1996)
Apr. 5, 2005 – Plan of Arrangement acquisition by Guernsey, U.K. based Landore Resources Limited; basis 1 new for 1 old sh.

Landover Energy Inc. (Alta. Mar. 25, 1987)
July 5, 2002 – Acquired by Viking Energy Royalty Trust for $0.625 per sh. (see Viking Energy Royalty Trust)

Landover Oils & Mines Ltd. (Ont. Nov. 4, 1932)
1954 – Name changed to Belcher Mining Corporation Ltd.; basis 1 new for 5 old shs. ∎

Landowners Mutual Minerals Ltd. (Sask. 1951)
1964 – Acquired by Scurry Rainbow Oil (Sask.) Ltd.; basis 1 new for 5 old shs.

Landstar Properties Inc. (B.C. Dec. 13, 1978)
June 3, 2013 – Dissolved and struck from register.

Lang Bay Resources Ltd. (B.C. Jan. 27, 1981)
Nov. 6, 1995 – Name changed to Hibright Minerals Inc.; basis 1 new for 5 old shs. ∎

Langford Mines Ltd. (B.C. 1939)
July 1954 – Charter cancelled.

Langham Oils Ltd. (Alta.)
1959 – Struck off register.

Langis Silver & Cobalt Mining Company Limited (Ont. Feb. 18, 1953)
July 27, 2005 – Name changed to Aranka Gold Inc. ∎

Langley Bay Uranium Mines Ltd. (Ont. 1953)
Nov. 30, 1964 – Dissolved.

Langley's Limited (Ont. 1929)
Feb. 23, 1931 – Charter cancelled; dissolved,

Langmuir Longlac Gold Mines Ltd. (Ont. July 9, 1934)
Dec. 18, 1936 – Merged into Maralgo Mines Ltd.; basis 1 new for 5 old shs. (see Maralgo Mines Limited)

Langtec Capital Corp. (B.C. July 7, 1987)
Aug. 25, 1997 – Name changed to VisionQuest Enterprise Group Inc. ∎

Laniuk Industries Inc. (Alta. Apr. 11, 1996)
July 8, 2004 – Plan of Arrangement to convert company into an income trust named TerraVest Income Fund; basis 1 new TerraVest trust unit for 6 old Laniuk com. shs. (see TerraVest Income Fund)

Lanpar Technologies Inc. (Can. 1970)
Mar. 1989 – Placed into receivership.
Apr. 6, 1989 – Assets acquired by Softco Manufacturing Inc. No equity for shldrs.
Jan. 28, 2003 – Dissolved and struck from the register.

Lansco Petroleum Inc. (B.C. 1977)
Dec. 14, 1982 – Formed Lansco Resources Ltd. in British Columbia on amalgamation with Cameo Resources Inc.; basis 1 new for 1 old sh. ∎

Lansco Resources Ltd. (B.C. Dec. 14, 1982 amalg.)
Nov. 22, 1993 – Name changed to Bomax Resource Corp.; basis 1 new for 10 old shs. ∎

Lansdowne Explorations Ltd. (Ont. 1965)
Feb. 20, 1980 – Dissolved.

Lansdowne Minerals Ltd. (Ont. Apr. 21, 1937)
1959 – Charter cancelled.

Lansdowne Minerals Ltd. (B.C. Nov. 3, 1987 amalg.)
Apr. 13, 1995 – Name changed to Conquistador Mines Ltd. ∎

Lansdowne Oil & Minerals Ltd. (B.C. May 27, 1980)
Nov. 3, 1987 – Formed Lansdowne Minerals Ltd. in British Columbia on amalgamation with Beaver Creek Goldfields Inc.; basis 1 new for 1 old sh. ∎

Lansing Enterprises Inc. (B.C. Feb. 23, 1987)
Jan. 19, 1993 – Name changed to White Hawk Ventures Inc.; basis 1 new for 2 old shs. ∎

Lansview Resource Corporation (Ont. July 20, 1977)
May 14, 1984 – Continued into British Columbia.
Aug. 30, 1985 – Name changed to Neumed Systems Corporation and continued into Canada. ∎

Lantern Gas & Oil Ltd. (B.C. 1971)
Sept. 14, 1978 – Amalgamated with 3 other cos. into Stand-Skat Resources Ltd.; basis 0.17728 new for 1 old Lantern sh. (see Stand-Skat Resources Ltd.)

Lapa Cadillac Gold Mines Ltd. (Ont. 1934)
1955 – Name changed to Zulapa Mining Corporation Ltd.; basis 1 new for 4 old shs. ∎

Lapalartic Mines Ltd. (Ont. 1944)
Jan. 6, 1958 – Dissolved.

Lapaska Mines Ltd. (Ont. 1944)
Dec. 20, 1954 – Name changed to Can-Met Explorations Ltd.; basis 1 new for 3 old shs. ∎

Groupe Laperrière & Verreault Inc. (Que. Apr. 1, 1986)
Aug. 13, 2007 – All o/s cl. A and cl. B shs. acquired by FLSmidth & Co. of Denmark for $33 per sh. following spin-off of certain assets to a new co. GLV Inc. whereby shldrs. received 1 GLV cl. A and cl. B sh. for 1 cl. A and cl. B sh. (see GLV Inc.)

Lapexco Gold Mines Ltd. (Ont. 1945)
1958 – Name changed to Regal Mining and Development Ltd. ∎

Laplante Red Lake Gold Mines Ltd. (Ont. 1946)
1947 – Name changed to New Mic Mac Mines Ltd. ∎

Laprairie Company Inc. (Ont. 1935)
1953 – All o/s com. shs. acquired by The Cooksville Company, Limited for $25 per sh. Concurrently, Cooksville was acquired by Domtar Limited.

Lar-Add Mines Ltd. (Ont. 1937)
1981 – Dissolved Dec. 6, 1972; revived 1975; charter cancelled.

Laramide Resources Ltd. (B.C. 1980)
June 27, 1996 – Continued into Canada. (see FPsurvey - Mines & Energy)

Larandona Mines Ltd. (Ont. 1944)
1971 – Acquired by New Insco Mines Ltd.; basis 1 Insco sh. for 50 Larandona shs.
Apr. 1975 – Charter cancelled.

Larbel Gold Mines Ltd. (Ont. 1944)
1947 – Sold assets to Aurlando Consolidated Mining Corp. Ltd.; basis 1 new for 5 old shs. (see Aurlando Consolidated Mining Corp. Ltd.)

Larch Resources Ltd. (B.C. 1969)
Jan. 28, 1987 – Name changed to Manticore Petroleum Corp. ■

Lardeau Lead & Zinc Mines Ltd. (B.C. 1951)
1954 – Name changed to Perlite Industries Ltd.; basis 1 new for 50 old shs.

Lardego Gold Mines (Ont. 1937)
May 1960 – Charter cancelled.

Larder Resources Inc. (Ont. Oct. 27, 1941)
Apr. 11, 1986 – Formed International Larder Minerals Inc. on amalgamation with Flying Cross Resources Ltd.; basis 1 new for 2 old shs. ■

Larder Road Mines Ltd. (Ont. 1944)
Feb. 1954 – Charter cancelled; no equity.

Larder "U" Island Mines Ltd. (Ont. 1943)
Sept. 10, 1952 – Name changed to New Larder "U" Island Mines Ltd.; basis 1 new for 3 old shs. ■

Larderknife Gold Mines Ltd. (Ont. 1946)
Aug. 18, 1958 – Charter cancelled.

Lardershores Mines Ltd. (Ont. 1943)
Oct. 1957 – Charter cancelled.

Lardon Gold Mines Ltd. (Ont. 1944)
Wound up. No equity for shldrs.

Laredo Mines Ltd. (B.C. 1966)
1967 – Name changed to Largo Mines Ltd. ■

Laredo Petroleums Ltd. (B.C. June 1, 1971)
June 26, 1986 – Name changed to Pedco Energy Limited. ■

Lareva Gold Mines Ltd. (Ont. 1946)
Mar. 1958 – Dissolved.

Largo Mines Ltd. (B.C. 1966)
Sept. 15, 1986 – Name changed to Advanced Growth Systems Inc.; basis 1 new for 4 old shs. ■

Largo Resources Ltd. (B.C. Apr. 18, 1988)
June 10, 2004 – Continued into Ontario.
Nov. 8, 2021 – Name changed to Largo Inc. (see FPsurvey - Mines & Energy)

Largold Mines Ltd. (Ont. 1941)
1944 – Acquired by Largold Mining Co. Ltd.; basis 1 new for 2 old shs. (see Largold Mining Co. Ltd.)

Largold Mining Co. Ltd. (Ont. 1944)
1957 – Charter cancelled.

Lariat Capital Inc. (Alta. June 3, 1997)
Dec. 22, 1999 – Formed Medicure Inc. in Alberta on Qualifying Transaction amalgamation with Medicure Inc. constituting a reverse takeover by Medicure. ■

Lariat Energy Ltd. (Yuk. Jan. 5, 1996)
Sept. 23, 2005 – Continued into British Columbia.
June 17, 2016 – Name changed to Global Daily Fantasy Sports Inc. ■

Lariat Exploration and Development Ltd. (Ont. 1951)
1954 – Acquired by Dominion Asbestos Mines Ltd.; basis 1 new for 10 old shs. (see Dominion Asbestos Mines Ltd.)

Lariat Oil & Gas Ltd. (Alta. 1969)
Dec. 7, 1987 – Amalgamated with Jordan Petroleum Ltd. to form a new co. also known as Jordan Petroleum Ltd.; basis 1 cl. A sh., 1 cl. B sh., and 0.25 cl. C sh. of new co. for 1 com. sh.

Lariat Property Corporation (Yuk. Jan. 5, 1996)
June 2, 2003 – Name changed to Lariat Resources Ltd.; basis 1 new for 5 old shs. ■

Lariat Resources Ltd. (Yuk. Jan. 5, 1996)
Sept. 23, 2004 – Name changed to Lariat Energy Ltd.; basis 1 new for 2 old shs. ■

Larkfield Capital Corp. (B.C. May 15, 2000)
Jan. 15, 2002 – Continued into Ontario.
Jan. 17, 2002 – Formed Rentcash Inc. in Ontario on Qualifying Transaction amalgamation with Rentcash Inc. (deemed acquiror); basis 1 new for 1 Rentcash sh. and 1 new for 3 Larkfield shs. ■

Larmont Mines Ltd. (Ont. 1943)
Jan. 1967 – Charter cancelled.

Laroma Midlothian Mines Ltd. (Ont. 1944)
Nov. 1977 – Charter cancelled.

Laronex Copper Mines Ltd. (Man. 1953)
1967 – Name changed to Northern Copper Ltd. ■

Laronex Mining & Exploration Co. Ltd. (Man. 1958)
1967 – Acquired by Laronex Copper Mines Ltd. (see Northern Copper Ltd.)

LaRonge Mining Ltd. (B.C. Nov. 27, 1968)
June 8, 1976 – Name changed to La Teko Resources Ltd.; basis 1 new for 3 old shs. ■

Lartic Mines Ltd. (Can. 1928)
Nov. 3, 1959 – Charter surrendered.

Larum Mines Ltd. (Ont. 1953)
Apr. 1976 – Amalgamated to form Glenarum Mining Explorations Ltd.; basis 1 new for 4 old shs.

Larutan Petroleum Corporation Ltd. (Ont. 1958)
1962 – Merged to form Cessland Corporation Limited; basis 13 new for 100 old shs. (see Cessland Corporation Limited)

Las Maderas Mining & Petroleum Ltd. (B.C. 1949)
Aug. 30, 1976 – Dissolved.

Las Vegas From Home.com Entertainment Inc. (B.C. May 27, 1980)
June 18, 2015 – Name changed to Jackpot Digital Inc. (see FPsurvey - Industrials)

Las Western Entertainment Inc. (Alta. Dec. 31, 1993)
Dec. 13, 1999 – Name changed to mBase.com Inc. ■

LaSalle Exploration Corp. (B.C. Nov. 30, 2011)
Apr. 19, 2022 – Acquired by Harfang Exploration Inc.; basis 0.1813 post-consolidated Harfang shs. for 1 LaSalle Exploration sh.

Lasalle Yellowknife Gold Mines Ltd. (Ont. 1944)
1954 – Name changed to Ormsby Mines Ltd. and continued into Ontario; basis 1 new for 10 old shs. ■

Lasco Gold Mines Ltd. (B.C. 1945)
1950 – Reported out of business.

Laser Blade Systems Inc. (Alta. Aug. 16, 1995)
Sept. 2, 2000 – Struck from registry and dissolved.

Laser Blade Technologies Inc. (Alta. Aug. 16, 1995)
July 18, 1997 – Name changed to Laser Blade Systems Inc. ■

Laser Expressions Inc. (Ont. Nov. 6, 1975)
Dec. 17, 1992 – Name changed to Speer Darrow Management Inc.; basis 1 new for 4 old shs. ■

Laser Friendly Inc. (Ont. Feb. 4, 1986)
Aug. 3, 1995 – Name changed to Gaming Lottery Corporation. ■

Laser Magic International Inc. (Can. Mar. 2, 1983)
May 2, 2002 – Dissolved.

Laser Quest Corporation (Ont. 1983)
Feb. 26, 1998 – Name changed to Versent Corporation; basis 1 new for 5 old shs. ■

Laser Rejuvenation Clinics Inc. (Alta. Aug. 31, 1994)
Oct. 29, 2003 – Going private transaction via amalgamation with 1024386 Alberta Ltd.; basis 1 new amalco redeemable pref. sh. for 1 old Laser sh. immediately redeemed for 22¢ per sh.

Laser Rejuvenation Clinics Ltd. (Alta. Aug. 31, 1994)
Feb. 17, 2003 – Name changed to Laser Rejuvenation Clinics Inc.; basis 1 new for 10 old shs. ■

Lasermedia Communications Corp. (Ont. Apr. 20, 1964)
Aug. 19, 1999 – Name changed to ActFit.com Inc. ■

Lashburn Petroleums Limited (Ont. July 22, 1949)
1952 – Sold assets to Scarlet Oils Ltd.; basis 1 new for 3 old shs.

Lasidon Gold Mines Ltd. (Ont. 1945)
Jan. 1958 – Charter cancelled.

Lasik Vision Corporation (B.C. Apr. 15, 1998)
May 14, 2001 – Acquired by ICON Laser Eye Centers, Inc.; basis 0.5 new ICON sh. for 1 old Lasik sh. (see ICON Laser Eye Centers, Inc.)

Lasir Gold Inc. (B.C. Mar. 19, 1980)
Feb. 13, 1989 – Name changed to Lasir Gold Industries Inc. ■

Lasir Gold Industries Inc. (B.C. Mar. 19, 1980)
Nov. 22, 1995 – Name changed to First Fortune Investments Inc.; basis 1 new for 10 old shs. ■

Lassie Red Lake Gold Mines Limited (Ont. June 22, 1945)
Oct. 15, 1998 – Amalgamated with 1296922 Ontario Limited, a wholly owned subsid. of Placer Dome (CLA) Limited (a wholly owned subsid. of Placer Dome Inc.); basis 1 new redeem. cl. A pref. sh. for 1 com. sh. immediately redeem. for $1.50. (see Placer Dome Inc.)

Lassiter Kuma Oils Ltd. (Alta. 1971 amalg.)
Feb. 14, 1986 – Name changed to Baloil Lassiter Petroleum Ltd.; basis 1 new for 10 old shs. ■

Lassiter Petroleums Ltd. (Alta. 1952)
Sept. 3, 1971 – Amalgamated with Kuma Oils Ltd. to form Lassiter Kuma Oils Ltd.; basis 1 new for 4 old shs.

Last Mile Holdings Ltd. (B.C. Sept. 5, 1980)
Feb. 10, 2021 – Name changed to AZN Capital Corp. (see FPsurvey - Industrials)

Lasthope Lake Gold Mines Ltd. (Man. 1940)
Sept. 1977 – Charter cancelled.

Lateegra Gold Corp. (B.C. Sept. 27, 1979)
Aug. 9, 2011 – Amalgamated with Excellon Resources Inc.; basis 0.54 Excellon shs. for 1 Lateegra sh.

Lateegra Resources Corp. (B.C. Sept. 27, 1979)
Jan. 12, 2006 – Name changed to Lateegra Gold Corp.; basis 1 new for 10 old shs. ■

Lateral Capital Corp. (Alta. Jan. 26, 2012)
July 21, 2014 – Name changed to Jaguar Resources Inc. (see FPsurvey - Mines & Energy)

Lateral Gold Corp. (B.C. Apr. 14, 1999)
Oct. 25, 2016 – Name changed to Trakopolis IoT Corp. following reverse takeover acquisition of CANHaul International Corp.; basis 1 new for 4 old shs. ■

Lateral Vector Resources Inc. (Sask. Aug. 23, 1991)
July 27, 2001 – Acquired by CanArgo Acquisition Corp. wholly owned subsid. of CanArgo Energy Corporation; basis $0.11 per sh.

Lathwell Resources Ltd. (B.C. Apr. 11, 1983)
Feb. 5, 1988 – Name changed to Optima Energy Corporation; basis 1 new for 5 old shs. ■

Latigo Capital Corporation (Alta. Apr. 9, 2007)
Mar. 11, 2010 – Together with Warnic 1 Enterprises Ltd., Valentine Ventures Corp. and Blackwater Capital Corp.(Capital Pool Companies) amalgamated with Cumberland Oil & Gas Ltd. constituting Capital Pool Companies' Qualifying Transaction to form Cumberland Oil & Gas Ltd; basis Latigo (0.3879-for-1), Warnic (0.3032-for-1), Valentine (0.3474-for-1), Blackwater (0.2875-for-1) and Cumberland (1-for-1). (see Cumberland Oil & Gas Ltd.)

Latigo Resources Inc. (B.C. Aug. 19, 1985)
July 22, 1999 – Name changed to LGO Net.com Inc. ■

Latin American Gold Inc. (B.C. Aug. 9, 1979)
Mar. 31, 1995 – Name changed to Latin American Gold Ltd. and continued into Bermuda.

Latin American Minerals Inc. (Can. Dec. 9, 2003)
Nov. 5, 2020 – Name changed to Sterling Metals Corp.; basis 1 new for 10 old shs. (see FPsurvey - Mines & Energy)

Latin American Mines Ltd. (Ont. 1946)
1972 – Charter cancelled.

Latin American Telecommunications Corp. (B.C. Nov. 9, 1988)
Dec. 13, 1993 – Continued into Turks and Caicos Islands.
Oct. 17, 1997 – Name changed to LATelco International, Inc.

LatinGold Inc. (Ont. July 21, 1986)
June 11, 1999 – Name changed to travelbyus.com ltd. ■

Latitude Minerals Corp. (B.C. Mar. 2, 1981)
May 21, 2002 – Name changed to Coal Creek Energy Inc.; basis 1 new for 10 old shs. ■

Latitude Uranium Inc. (Ont. July 13, 2021)
Mar. 8, 2024 – Acquired by ATHA Energy Corp.; basis 0.2769 ATHA shs. for 1 Latitude sh.

Latomic Red Lake Gold Mines Ltd. (Ont. 1945)
Apr. 22, 1965 – Assets sold to Loisan Red Lake Gold Mines Ltd.; basis 1 new for 3 old shs. Dissolved.

Lattice Biologics Ltd. (B.C. June 6, 1985)
May 27, 2024 – Dissolved for failure to file and struck from register. (see FPsurvey - Industrials)

Lattice Capital Corporation (B.C. May 16, 2000)
June 26, 2003 – Plan of Arrangement agreement with Millennium Ventures Ltd. (1 for 2.04) and Verb Exchange Inc. to continue as Verb Exchange Inc.; basis 1 new Verb sh. for 2.789 old Lattice shs. (see Verb Exchange Inc.)

Lauder Red Lake Mines Ltd. (Ont. 1946)
Nov. 1961 – Dissolved.

L'Auditorium Ltée (Can. - unspecified)
Nov. 1968 – Wholly owned subsid. of Famous Players Canadian Corp. In June 1963, bond holders approved sale of its property in Quebec City to Famous Players. Co. remained in existence until 1st mtge. bonds were retired. Responsibility for bds. assumed by Famous Players.

Launay Resources Inc. (Ont. Sept. 11, 1984)
July 14, 1997 – Name changed to Southern Star Resources Inc.; basis 1 new for 2 old shs. ■

Launch Resources Inc. (Alta. Aug. 13, 1999 amalg.)
Feb. 2005 – Placed into receivership. RSM Richter Inc. appointed receiver.

Laura Industries and Resources Ltd. (B.C. 1966)
Sept. 1978 – Name changed to Lorcan Resources Ltd.; basis 1 new for 5 old shs. (see FPsurvey - Mines & Energy)

Laura Mines Ltd. (B.C. 1966)
Sept. 1973 – Name changed to Laura Industries and Resources Ltd. ■

Laura Secord Candy Shops Ltd. (Can. 1926)
Oct. 28, 1974 – All o/s com. shs. not already held acquired by Catelli Ltd., a wholly owned subsidiary of John Labatt Limited, at $7.50 per sh. and Laura Secord and Catelli combined operations, with Laura Secord agreeing to acquire the operating assets of Catelli in exchange for treasury shares. (see John Labatt Limited)

Laurasia Resources Limited (Ont. Dec. 18, 1950 amalg.)
June 30, 1994 – Amalgamated with Boomerang Resources Inc. to form new co. with same name Laurasia Resources Limited; basis 2.8 new for 1 Boomerang sh. and 1 new for 1 Laurasia sh.
Feb. 25, 1998 – Acquired by Startech Energy Inc.; basis 24¢ plus 0.0362 Startech shs. for 1 Laurasia sh.

Laurbec Mining Co. (Que. 1955)
Charter cancelled.

Laurel Explorations Ltd. (B.C. Oct. 29, 1981)
Feb. 22, 1991 – Name changed to Linden Explorations Inc.; basis 1 new for 4 old shs. ■

Laurel Finance Corporation Ltd. (Sask. 1959)
June 1, 1966 – Assets acquired by Sterling Finance Ltd. of Saskatoon; basis 1 Sterling for 7 Laurel shs.

Laurel West Publishing Inc. (Alta. May 26, 1987)
Jan. 22, 1990 – Continued into Canada.
Mar. 22, 1990 – Name changed to Elite Real Estate Canada Inc. ■

Laurence-Lee Gold Mines Ltd. (Ont. 1945)
Oct. 27, 1958 – Charter cancelled.

Laurent Venture Capital Corporation (Can. Jan. 20, 2005)
Oct. 7, 2009 – Name changed to Carbon2Green Corporation pursuant to Qualifying Transaction reverse takeover acquisition of Carbon2Green Developments Ltd. ■

Laurentian Feldspar Corp. Ltd. (Ont. 1946)
Dec. 1966 – Charter cancelled.

Laurentian Goldfields Ltd. (B.C. Nov. 14, 2005)
June 24, 2014 – Name changed to Pure Gold Mining Inc. ■

The Laurentian Group Corporation (Que. 1981)
Feb. 16, 1994 – All o/s cl. A multiple vtg. shs. and cl. B sub. vtg. shs. acquired by Desjardins Laurentian Financial Corporation. At the holder's option shares were exch. under one of four combinations of cash and shs. Holders could choose from $0.56 to $6.22 in cash plus a varied issuance of cl. A and cl. B shs. of Desjardins Laurentian Financial. All o/s cl. III ser. 1 pfd. shs. were redeemed Mar. 18, 1994; basis $25 plus all accrued and unpaid divids. of $0.3955548 per sh. (see Desjardins Laurentian Financial Corporation)

The Laurentian Life and Health Insurance Corporation (Que. 1938)
Jan. 1, 1994 – Merged with Desjardins Laurentian Financial Corporation (DLFC); basis (a) $6.22 for each 50% portion of each Laurentian share deposited and a comb. of 0.0996 cl. A pref. sh. of DLFC having a par value of $25 and 0.1794 cl. A sub. vtg. sh. of DLFC for the other

50% portion of each Laurentian sh. deposited; or, an unsecured prom. note having a par value of $6.22 issued by DLFC for each 50% portion of each Laurentian sh. deposited and a comb. of 0.0996 pref. sh. of DLFC and 0.1794 cl. B sh. of DLFC for the other 50% portion of each Laurentian sh. deposited; or 68¢ in cash, 0.234 of a DLFC pref. sh. and 0.284406 of a cl. B DLFC sh. for each Laurentian sh. deposited; or 56¢ in cash, 0.0972 of a DLFC pref. sh. and 0.45449 of a cl. B DLFC sh. for each Laurentian sh. deposited. (see Desjardins Laurentian Financial Corporation)

The Laurentian Life Insurance Company Inc. (Que. 1938)
Jan. 1, 1991 – Name changed to The Laurentian Life and Health Insurance Corporation. ■

The Laurentian Mutual Insurance (Que. 1938)
Jan. 16, 1989 – Name changed to The Laurentian Life Insurance Company Inc. ■

Laurentian Silk Mills Ltd. (Can. 1937)
Jan. 1949 – Name changed to Wesley Mason Mills Limited. ■

Laurentide Dairy Products Corporation (Que. 1950)
Jan. 1955 – Acquired by Co-Operative Agricole de Granby, Quebec, for about $500,000.

Laurentide Financial Corporation Ltd. (B.C. 1950)
1979 – Continued into Canada.
Oct. 7, 1983 – Name changed to National Bank Leasing Inc.; basis 1 new for 1 old sh.

Laurentide Financial Realty Corporation Ltd. (unknown)
Oct. 31, 1982 – Amalgamated with Laurentide Mortgage Corporation to continue under the latter co.'s name.

Laurier Resources Inc. (B.C. May 14, 1981)
Nov. 8, 1999 – Name changed to Zarcan International Resources Inc. ■

Laurier Resources Ltd. (Que. 1968)
1982 – Acquired by Humboldt Energy Corporation; basis 6 subordinated voting shs. of Humboldt for each 10 com. shs. of Laurier. (see Humboldt Energy Corporation)

Laurion Gold Inc. (Ont. Apr. 17, 1945)
Nov. 3, 2006 – Name changed to Laurion Mineral Exploration Inc. (see FPsurvey - Mines & Energy)

Lauzon Computer Software Ltd. (Alta. Sept. 18, 1980)
Mar. 2, 2001 – Struck from registry and dissolved.

Lava Cap Resources Ltd. (Ont. Sept. 7, 1944)
Sept. 26, 1985 – Name changed to Lava Capital Corporation. ■

Lava Capital Corporation (Ont. Sept. 7, 1944)
Feb. 17, 1988 – Name changed to Samoth Capital Corporation; basis 1 new for 5 old shs. ■

Lava Minerals Limited (Ont. 1970)
Jan. 18, 1972 – Amalgamated with Spar Mines Limited, Polex Mines Limited and Winnebago Mines Limited to form a new co. known as Spar Holdings & Explorations Limited; basis 1 new for 4 old shs.

Laval Acceptance Corporation (Que. 1967)
Mar. 15, 1961 – Placed into bankruptcy.
May 17, 1983 – All assets sold. Approx. $73,000 available for distribution which can not be made prior to 1996 due to certain legal procedures. Trustee - Trust General of Canada, Montreal. Fault on 7% secured notes ser. A, due Sept. 15, 1969. Liquidating. Distribution expected after 1979. Trustee - Trust General du Canada, Montreal.

Laval Resources Ltd. (Alta. 1987)
Dec. 6, 1989 – Amalgamated with Oiltex International Ltd. and Dugite Resources Inc. to form International Oiltex Ltd. (see International Oiltex Ltd.)

Laval Transport Inc. (Que. 1947)
1960 – Assets absorbed by Inter-City Bus Ltd., approx.

Lavalie Mines Ltd. (Ont. Apr. 10, 1937)
1955 – Name changed to Norvalie Mines Ltd.; basis 1 new for 4 old shs. ■

Lavalin Inc. (Que. 1970)
Aug. 1991 – Control seized by a syndicate of Canadian and International banks. Most of the assets were acquired by The SNC-Lavalin Group Inc. (formerly The SNC Group Inc.).
Nov. 1991 – Arthur Andersen Inc. of Montreal appointed trustee.
Apr. 15, 1998 – Distribution made to secured creditors.
June 4, 1998 – Trustee discharged and no distribution made to unsecured creditors and shldrs.

Lavalin Industries Inc. (Can. Jan. 25, 1980)
Aug. 1991 – Control of the parent company, Groupe Lavalin Ltée, was seized by its banks and most of its assets were later acquired by The SNC Group Inc. (now SNC-Lavalin Group Inc.). (see SNC-Lavalin Group Inc.)
Sept. 1991 – Ceased operations of wholly owned Kemtec Petrochemical Corporation and the Montreal East plant was closed. (see SNC-Lavalin Group Inc.)
Oct. 10, 1991 – Interest payments on the convert. subordin. ser. A debs. suspended. (see SNC-Lavalin Group Inc.)
Nov. 8, 1991 – Filed for voluntary bankruptcy and Arthur Andersen Inc.of Montreal appointed trustee. (see SNC-Lavalin Group Inc.)
May 5, 1997 – Trustee discharged and there was no distribution to unsecured creditors and shldrs. (see SNC-Lavalin Group Inc.)
Jan. 28, 2003 – Dissolved. (see SNC-Lavalin Group Inc.)

LavalinTech Inc. (Can. Oct. 10, 1985)
Mar. 13, 1992 – Name changed to Benvest Capital Inc. ■

Lavandin Mining Co. Ltd. (Que. 1956)
1961 – Acquired by Malartic Hygrade Gold Mines Ltd. (see Malartic Hygrade Gold Mines Ltd.)

Lavant Iron Mines Ltd. (Ont. 1956)
July 10, 1959 – Name changed to Lavant Mines Ltd. ■

Lavant Mines Ltd. (Ont. 1956)
July 8, 1965 – Dissolved.

Lavco Inc. (Alta. Mar. 11, 1997)
Nov. 11, 1999 – Name changed to EnterCor Entertainment Corp. following Qualifying Transaction acquisition of Lavco Inc. ■

Laverty Industrial Development Ltd. (Ont. 1982)
Apr. 17, 1997 – Formed GHP Exploration Corporation in Ontario following reverse takeover acquisition of and amalgamation with GHP Corporation; basis 1 new for 15 old shs. ■

Laverty Red Lake Mines Ltd. (Ont. 1936)
May 1958 – Charter cancelled.

Laverty Red Lake Resources Inc. (Ont. 1982)
July 19, 1991 – Name changed to Laverty Industrial Development Ltd.; basis 1 new for 5 old shs. ■

Lavicha Gold Mines Ltd. (Ont. 1946)
1952 – Charter cancelled.

Laviolette Mining & Metallurgical Corp. (Que. 1960)
1976 – Name changed to Société Minéralurgique Laviolette, Inc. (see FPsurvey - Mines & Energy)

Lawless Creek Mines Ltd. (B.C. 1965)
Dec. 6, 1976 – Dissolved.

Lawrence Conservative Payout Ratio Trust (Ont. Feb. 25, 2005)
Dec. 30, 2005 – Merged with Lawrence Payout Ratio Trust (1.193269952 for 1) to continue as Lawrence Payout Ratio Trust II (subsequently renamed Lawrence Payout Ratio Trust); basis 1.014990409 new for 1 old unit. (see Lawrence Payout Ratio Trust II)

Lawrence Mining Corporation (B.C. 1970)
Feb. 4, 1994 – Dissolved and struck off register.

Lawrence Payout Ratio Trust (Ont. Nov. 29, 2004)
Dec. 30, 2005 – Merged with Lawrence Conservative Payout Ratio Trust (1.014990409 for 1) to continue as Lawrence Payout Ratio Trust II (subsequently renamed Lawrence Payout Ratio Trust); basis 1.193269952 new for 1 old unit. (see Lawrence Payout Ratio Trust II)

Lawrence Payout Ratio Trust (Ont. Aug. 30, 2005)
Aug. 24, 2007 – Converted into an open-ended mutual fund.
Aug. 27, 2007 – Name changed to Lawrence Income & Growth Fund following conversion from a closed-end fund to an open-ended fund.

Lawrence Payout Ratio Trust II (Ont. Aug. 30, 2005)
Jan. 3, 2006 – Name changed to Lawrence Payout Ratio Trust following acquisition of net assets of Lawrence Payout Ratio Trust (1.19326 for 1) and Lawrence Conservative Payout Ratio Trust (1.01499 for 1). ■

Lawson & Jones Limited (Can. 1930)
Dec. 31, 1985 – Amalgamated with the Lawson Mardon Group Limited to continue under the same name. (see Lawson Mardon Group Limited)

Lawson Mardon Group Limited (Ont. Dec. 31, 1985)
Feb. 4, 1994 – Acquired by A-L Acquisition Inc. for $14 per cl. A and cl. B sh.

Lawson Mines Ltd. (Ont. Jan. 1937)
May 1939 – Name changed to Melinda Mines Ltd. ■

Layfield Resources Inc. (B.C. Aug. 26, 1988)
Oct. 30, 2000 – Name changed to Playfair Mining Ltd.; basis 1 new for 5 old shs. (see FPsurvey - Mines & Energy)

Lazard Global Convertible Bond Fund (Ont. Nov. 23, 2009)
June 14, 2011 – Name changed to Aston Hill Global Convertible Bond Fund. ■

Lazarus Resources Ltd. (B.C. Oct. 25, 1983)
Oct. 21, 1988 – Name changed to Lazurus Distributing Corp. ■

Lazer Maze Industries Inc. (B.C. 1981)
Sept. 29, 1995 – Dissolved and struck off register.

Lazurus Distributing Corp. (B.C. Oct. 25, 1983)
Apr. 23, 1990 – Name changed to Discovery Distributing Corp.; basis 1 new for 3 old shs. ■

Lea Park Oils Limited (Sask. Apr. 6, 1950)
Struck off register.

Lead Energy Ltd. (Alta. June 8, 1953)
Aug. 31, 1983 – Name changed to Troymin Resources Ltd. ■

Lead Ventures Inc. (B.C. Nov. 13, 2014)
Oct. 25, 2018 – Name changed to Curaleaf Holdings, Inc. following reverse takeover acquisition of Curaleaf, Inc. (see FPsurvey - Industrials)

Leader Capital Corp. (Ont. July 6, 1983 amalg.)
Feb. 24, 2009 – Privatized via a 1-for-500,000 sh. consolidation. Shldrs. holding less than 500,000 com. shs. received 51¢ cash per sh.

Leader Energy Services Ltd. (Alta. Apr. 20, 1998)
Aug. 20, 2015 – Deemed bankrupt; MNP Ltd. was appointed trustee.

Leader Industries Inc. (Que. Feb. 14, 1972)
Dec. 31, 2001 – Filed for an Assignment under the Bankruptcy and Insolvency Act as it was unable to come to an arrrangement with its creditors. Raymond Chabot Inc. of Montreal was appointed trustee.
June 2002 – All assets sold and the principal secured creditor suffered a shortfall of about $4,000,000.
Nov. 6, 2002 – Trustee discharged. No funds available for distribution to unsecured creditors or shldrs.

Leader Manufacturing Inc. (Que. Feb. 14, 1972)
June 26, 1992 – Name changed to Leader Industries Inc.; basis 1 new for 10 old shs. ■

Leader Mining Corporation (Alta. June 22, 1987)
July 29, 1994 – Name changed to Leader Mining International Inc.; basis 1 new for 5 old shs. ■

Leader Mining Corp. Ltd. (B.C. 1961)
1963 – Name changed to Stellako Mining Co. Ltd. ■

Leader Mining International Inc. (Alta. June 22, 1987)
Sept. 2, 2010 – Dissolved and struck from registry.

Leader Oil & Gas Ltd. (Alta. Nov. 24, 1986)
Aug. 29, 1994 – Name changed to Canadian Leader Energy Inc. ■

Leader Resources Inc. (B.C. Apr. 7, 1978)
Nov. 29, 1984 – Name changed to United Leader Resources Inc.; basis 1 new for 5 old shs. ■

Leader Yellowknife Gold Mines Ltd. (Ont. 1945)
Apr. 1958 – Charter cancelled.

Leaders Equity Corp. (B.C. 1980)
July 20, 1990 – Dissolved.

The Leadership Fund Inc. (Can. July 3, 2003)
May 2, 2005 – Name changed to NSP Pharma Corp. following Qualifying Transaction reverse takeover acquisition of Naturale Science Pharma Inc. ■

LeadFX Inc. (Can. July 23, 2008)
May 10, 2019 – Privatized via 1-for-5,000,000 consolidation; basis US$1.00 cash per sh. Major shldrs., InCoR Energy Materials Ltd., Sentient Executive GP II, Limited and Sentient Executive GP IV, Limited hold all the issued and o/s post-consolidated shs. of the company.

Leading Brands, Inc. (B.C. Feb. 4, 1986)
Aug. 10, 2018 – Name changed to Liquid Media Group Ltd. following reverse takeover acquisition of Liquid Media Group Inc. (see FPsurvey - Industrials)

Leadley, Gunning & Culp International Corp. (Ont. Feb. 23, 1984)
Oct. 15, 1994 – Dissolved.

Leadville Silver Mining Corp. (Que. 1956)
Aug. 1972 – Charter cancelled.

Leaf Mobile Inc. (B.C. Nov. 29, 2018)
May 25, 2022 – Name changed to East Side Games Group Inc. (see FPsurvey - Industrials)

Leagold Mining Corporation (B.C. Aug. 31, 2016)
Mar. 13, 2020 – Acquired by Equinox Gold Corp.; basis 0.331 Equinox Gold shs. for 1 Leagold sh.

Leamac Petroleums Limited (Can. 1923)
1961 – Name changed to Embassy Petroleums Ltd.; basis 1 new for 20 old shs. ■

Lear Oil & Gas Corporation (B.C. Jan. 30, 1981)
Mar. 17, 1987 – Name changed to Priority Ventures Ltd.; basis 1 new for 3 old shs. (see FPsurvey - Mines & Energy)

Learnco International Inc. (Alta. Mar. 11, 1996)
Sept. 2, 2009 – Struck from registry and dissolved.

The Learning Library Inc. (Ont. June 25, 2002 amalg.)
Jan. 5, 2005 – Name changed to Street Resources Inc.; basis 1 new for 2.75 old shs. ■

Learningwell Incorporated (Ont. Mar. 30, 1998)
Feb. 7, 2000 – Name changed to impatica.com inc. ■

Learnsoft Corporation (Ont. June 20, 1996)
Jan. 4, 2004 – Continued into British Columbia.
Dec. 13, 2007 – Name changed to Reva Resources Corp.; basis 1 new for 3 old shs. ■

Lease-Rite Corporation Inc. (Ont. Nov. 23, 1972)
June 2, 2006 – Name changed to Kermode Exploration Ltd.; basis 10 new for 1 old sh. ∎

Lease 64 Ltd. (Alta. Nov. 16, 1949)
1951 – Acquired by Triad Oil Co. Ltd.; basis 2.5 new for 1 old sh. (see Triad Oil Co. Ltd.)

Leaseholds Securities Ltd. (Alta. 1951)
Mar. 21, 1956 – Voluntarily liquidated.

Lebel Lode Ltd. (Ont. 1921)
Apr. 8, 1980 – Charter cancelled.

Lebel Oro Mines Ltd. (Ont. Apr. 1920)
1949 – Name changed to Consolidated Lebel Oro Mines Ltd.; basis 1 new for 3 old shs. ∎

Leberta-Redwater Oil Co. Ltd. (Ont. Feb. 16, 1949)
Dec. 12, 1960 – Dissolved.

LeBoldus Capital Inc. (Alta. Jan. 29, 2008)
Oct. 26, 2010 – Name changed to Viper Gold Ltd. pursuant to Qualifying Transaction acquisition of Corongo property in Peru. ∎

Lebon Gold Mines Ltd. (Ont. Apr. 24, 1945)
Mar. 16, 1976 – Charter cancelled. (see American Consolidated Minerals Corp.)
June 29, 1988 – Charter revived. (see American Consolidated Minerals Corp.)
June 24, 2005 – Continued into British Columbia. (see American Consolidated Minerals Corp.)
Feb. 2, 2009 – Amalgamated with American Copper Corporation and Golden Oasis Exploration Corp. to form American Consolidated Minerals Corp.; basis 1 new for 1 American Copper sh., 1 new for 1 Golden Oasis sh. and 2.1 new for 1 Lebon Gold sh. (see American Consolidated Minerals Corp.)

LeChamp Capital Corp. (Alta. Feb. 19, 2002)
Jan. 16, 2004 – Formed HydraLogic Systems Inc. in Ontario pursuant to Qualifying Transaction reverse takeover acquisition of and amalgamation with HydraLogic Systems Inc. (see FPsurvey - Industrials)

Lecopa Mines Ltd. (Ont. 1949)
Mar. 1976 – Charter cancelled.

Lectus Developments Ltd. (B.C. May 30, 1980)
May 15, 1991 – Name changed to Swannell Minerals Corp.; basis 1 new for 5 old shs. ∎

LeddarTech Holdings Inc. (Can. Dec. 21, 2023 amalg.)
June 18, 2025 – Made an assignment into bankruptcy. Raymond Chabot Inc. appointed trustee and all officers and directors resigned.

The Lederic Group Inc. (Que. 1956)
1981 – Placed into liquidation on June 23, 1976. Dissolved; no distribution made.

Lederic Mines Ltd. (Que. 1956)
1972 – Name changed to The Lederic Group Inc.; basis 1 new for 5 old shs. ∎

Ledge Uranium Mines Ltd. (Ont. 1955)
1955 – Name changed to Kimberley Copper Mines Ltd. and continued into Ontario. ∎

Leduc Calmar Oil Co. Ltd. (Alta. Dec. 24, 1947)
Aug. 1970 – Name changed to Liberty Resources Limited; basis 1 new for 20 old shs. ∎

Leduc Consolidated Oils Ltd. (Alta. May 15, 1947)
1953 – Assets acquired by Mill City Petroleums Ltd. (see Mill City Petroleums Limited)

Leduc Leaseholds Ltd. (Alta. 1948)
Apr. 1960 – Assets offered for sale.

Leduc-West Oil Co. Ltd. (Alta. Feb. 24, 1947)
Dec. 30, 1950 – Taken over by Trans-Empire Oils Ltd.; basis 1 new for 3 old shs.

Leduc-Whitemud Oil Syndicate (unknown)
1955 – Inactive; being wound up.

Leduc-Woodbend Oil Syndicate (unknown)
1955 – Inactive; being wound up.

Lee-Carlson Oils Ltd. (Alta. May 19, 1951)
1952 – Assets acquired by Campo United Petroleums Ltd.; basis 1 new for 7 old shs. Lee-Carlson shldrs. also received rts. to purch. 1 Campo sh. at $1.25 for each sh. received through exch.

Lee Gordon Mines Ltd. (Ont. 1949)
1965 – Property acquired by Vamp Lake Mines Ltd. for 350,000 shs.

Leedoro Snow Lake Mines Ltd. (Ont. 1945)
Apr. 1958 – Charter cancelled.

Leeds Construction Ltd. (Can. Mar. 30, 1953)
May 2, 1957 – Name changed to Richard Costain (Canada) Ltd. ∎

Leeds Metals Co. Ltd. (Que. 1953)
Oct. 1974 – Charter cancelled.

Leeds Richardson Co. Ltd. (unknown)
1968 – Acquired by Bartaco Industries Ltd. in 1968-69.

Leemac Mines Ltd. (B.C. 1969)
Apr. 5, 1976 – Name changed to LMC Resources Ltd.; basis 1 new for 5 old shs. ∎

Leemac Red Lake Mines Ltd. (Ont. 1945)
1976 – Dissolved, following sale of min. cls. to Duchesne Red Lake Mines Limited. Shldrs. received 1 sh. Duchesne for each 5 shs. Leemac. (see Duchesne Red Lake Mines Limited)

LeenLife Pharma International Inc. (B.C. Jan. 12, 2014)
Jan. 15, 2018 – Name changed to LeanLife Health Inc. (see FPsurvey - Industrials)

Leesa Explorations Ltd. (Ont. 1964)
1970 – Name changed to Leesa Metals & Holdings Ltd.; basis 1 new for 15 old shs. ∎

Leesa Metals & Holdings Ltd. (Ont. 1964)
Feb. 1980 – Charter cancelled.

Leeta Gold Corp. (B.C. June 24, 1987)
Sept. 18, 2017 – Name changed to HIVE Blockchain Technologies Ltd. ∎

Leeward Capital Corp. (B.C. Sept. 14, 1983)
Aug. 20, 2002 – Continued into Alberta. (see FPsurvey - Mines & Energy)

Leezamax Capital Corp. (Alta. Apr. 9, 2007)
Sept. 13, 2011 – Name changed to iFabric Corp. pursuant to Qualifying Transaction reverse takeover acquisition of Coconut Grove Textiles Inc. (see FPsurvey - Industrials)

Legacy Ability Products and Services, Inc. (B.C. May 11, 1990)
Apr. 23, 1996 – Name changed to Canadian Medical Legacy Corp.; basis 1 new for 6 old shs. ∎

Legacy Explorations Ltd. (Ont. Oct. 1, 1985)
Sept. 16, 1999 – Name changed to TriNexus Holdings Ltd.; basis 1 new for 2 old shs. ∎

Legacy Hotels Real Estate Investment Trust (Alta. Sept. 11, 1997)
Sept. 19, 2007 – Acquired by LGY Acquisition LP; subsequently trust units were redeemed for $12.60 per trust unit.

Legacy Oil + Gas Inc. (Alta. Oct. 13, 2005)
July 7, 2015 – Acquired by Crescent Point Energy Corp.; basis 0.095 Crescent com. sh. for 1 Legacy com. sh. (see Crescent Point Energy Corp.)

Legacy Petroleum Ltd. (Alta. Oct. 14, 1970)
June 2, 2001 – Struck from registry and dissolved.

Legacy Storage Systems International Inc. (Can. Aug. 25, 1993)
Jan. 8, 1997 – Name changed to Tecmar Technologies International Inc. ∎

Legardo Gold Mines Ltd. (Ont. 1939)
May 1958 – Charter cancelled.

Legare Company Limited (Can. 1936)
Sept. 30, 1955 – Wholly owned subsid. of Great Universal Stores of Canada Limited. All o/s 6% pref. shs., $25 par, were redeemed at $22.50 per sh. plus accr. divds. (a total pay. of $27.48 per sh.).

Legend Capital Corp. (Alta. Jan. 31, 2001)
June 12, 2003 – Amalgamated with Arsenal Energy Inc. was considered to be Legend's Qualifying Transaction; basis 1 new Arsenal sh. for 2.63759225 old Legend shs. (see Arsenal Energy Inc.)

Legend Explorations Ltd. (B.C. 1947)
May 1973 – Amalgamated with Lorraine Explorations Ltd. (1 for 5.41) in March 1973 to continue with the same name Legend Explorations Ltd.; basis 1 new Legend sh. for 2.95 old Legend shs. Subsequently amalgamated with 2 other cos. to form a new company named Shelter Petroleum Ltd.

Legend Gold Corp. (Ont. May 8, 1997)
Feb. 2, 2018 – Acquired by Altus Strategic Plc; basis 3 Altus ordinary shs. for 1 Legend com. sh.

Legend Gold Mines Ltd. (Ont. 1946)
Sept. 1960 – Charter cancelled.

Leger Mines (1964) Ltd. (Ont. 1964)
June 20, 1973 – Charter cancelled.

Legg Mason BW Investment Grade Focus Fund (Ont. Aug. 28, 2012)
Mar. 17, 2014 – Merged into Limited Duration Investment Grade Preferred Securities Fund (PFD); basis 0.381662192 PFD cl. A units for 1 Legg Mason trust unit. (see Limited Duration Investment Grade Preferred Securities Fund)

Legg Mason Canada Holdings Ltd. (Ont. May 13, 1998)
May 27, 2010 – All Legg Mason Canada Holdings Ltd. exch. shs. redeemed for parent Legg Mason, Inc. com. shs. on a sh.-for-sh. basis and subsequently acquired by 3040692 Nova Scotia Company.

Leggo Holdings Inc. (Ont. Mar. 5, 1937)
Sept. 29, 1997 – Name changed to Transarctic Petroleum Corp. ∎

Legion Metals Corp. (B.C. Dec. 8, 2016)
Mar. 14, 2019 – Name changed to Nextleaf Solutions Ltd. pursuant to reverse takeover acquisition of private Vancouver, B.C.-based Nextleaf Solutions Ltd. on a share-for-share basis.; basis 1 new for 3.5 old shs. (see FPsurvey - Industrials)

Legion Oils Limited (Alta. 1950)
1959 – Acquired by Medallion Petroleums Ltd.; basis 1 new for 25 old shs.

Legion Resources Corp. (B.C. Sept. 26, 1997)
May 20, 2011 – Formed Samaranta Mining Corporation in British Columbia pursuant to reverse takeover acquisition of and amalgamation with Samaranta Mining Corporation (deemed acquiror): basis 1 new for 6.5 old Samaranta shs. and 1 new for 4 old Legion shs. ∎

Legion Resources Ltd. (B.C. Nov. 21, 1963)
July 17, 1998 – Name changed to Earl Resources Limited and continued into Cayman Islands; basis 1 new for 2 old shs. ∎

Legumex Walker Inc. (Can. Apr. 20, 2011)
Nov. 25, 2015 – Name changed to LWP Capital Inc. ∎

Lehndorff Canadian Properties (Alta. June 22, 1979)
Oct. 1, 1999 – Wound up. Distribution of $0.22 paid to unithldrs.

Lehndorff Corporation (Ont. June 22, 1973)
June 22, 1979 – Name changed to Lehndorff Canadian Properties and continued into Alberta. ■

Leicester Diamond Mines Ltd. (B.C. June 1, 1993)
Apr. 30, 2004 – Name changed to Target Exploration and Mining Corp.; basis 1 new for 10 old shs. ■

Leigh Resource Corporation (B.C. Sept. 23, 1987)
Nov. 6, 2000 – Name changed to Upland Resource Corporation; basis 1 new for 10 old shs. ■

Leis Industries Limited (B.C. May 26, 1969)
Aug. 25, 2020 – Name changed to Greenbank Ventures Inc. ■

Leisure Canada Inc. (Ont. Mar. 1, 1993 amalg.)
Oct. 17, 2011 – Name changed to 360 VOX Corporation pursuant to acquisition of 360 VOX Inc. ■

Leisure Developments Ltd. (B.C. Sept. 15, 1969)
June 28, 1974 – Name changed to Leisure Gold Ltd. ■

Leisure Gold Ltd. (B.C. Sept. 15, 1969)
Mar. 24, 1975 – Name changed to United Leisure Gold Ltd.; basis 1 new for 3 old shs. ■

Leisure World Nursing Homes Limited (Ont. 1964)
1983 – Approx. 80% of o/s com. shs. acquired by 494122 Ontario Ltd. in 1982, through offer of $13.60 per sh. Co. stated to be private.

LeisureTech Sports Corp. (B.C. Aug. 4, 1987)
Feb. 22, 1994 – Name changed to Concept Industries Inc.; basis 1 new for 3 old shs. ■

Leisureways Marketing Ltd. (B.C. Mar. 31, 1992 amalg.)
Nov. 10, 1997 – Continued into Yukon.
Sept. 2, 1998 – Name changed to LML Payment Systems Inc.; basis 1 new for 3 old shs. ■

Leisureworld Senior Care Corporation (Ont. Feb. 10, 2010)
May 1, 2015 – Name changed to Sienna Senior Living Inc. (see FPsurvey - Industrials)

Leitch Gold Mines Ltd. (Ont. July 23, 1935)
Feb. 26, 1970 – Name changed to Leitch Mines Ltd. ■

Leitch Mines Ltd. (Ont. July 23, 1935)
Nov. 1974 – Acquired by Teck Corporation Limited on Apr. 1, 1971; basis 1 Teck cl. B com. for 3 old shs. Dissolved. (see Teck Corporation Limited)

Leitch Technology Corporation (Ont. May 3, 1971)
Oct. 31, 2005 – Name changed to Harris Canada Systems Inc. following acquisition by a wholly owned subsid. of Delaware-based Harris Corporation; basis $14 per sh.

Leith Mines Ltd. (Ont. 1956)
Nov. 1956 – Name changed to Cobalt Leith Mines Ltd. ■

Leitrim Group Inc. (Alta. Aug. 22, 2000)
July 24, 2006 – Name changed to Savers Plus International Inc. ■

Leland Publishing Limited (Ont. 1961)
1964 – Inactive. Co.'s two main subsidiaries, Leland Printing and Lithographing Ltd. and Leland Book Distributors, were Placed into bankruptcy with the Clarkson Co. (Toronto). A first and final payment was made to the unsecured creditors of 2¢ on the $1.00.

Lemans Resources Ltd. (B.C. 1967)
Feb. 25, 1983 – Struck off register.

Lemieux Copper Explorations Ltd. (Que. 1963)
1969 – Assets sold to Lemtex Developments Limited.; basis 1 new for 2 old shs.

Lemming Resources Ltd. (B.C. Apr. 21, 1986)
Oct. 11, 1994 – Name changed to Dimitra Developments Corp.; basis 1 new for 4 old shs. ■

Lemontonic Inc. (Ont. July 18, 2002 amalg.)
Feb. 15, 2006 – Formed Pioneering Technology Inc. in Ontario on amalgamation with Pioneering Technology Inc. which constituted a reverse takeover of Lemontonic by Pioneering Technology; basis 1 new for 5 old shs. ■

Lemtex Developments Limited (Ont. Apr. 1, 1969 amalg.)
July 29, 1982 – Name changed to B.Y.G. Natural Resources Inc. ■

Lencourt Gold Mines Ltd. (Que. 1945)
1965 – Name changed to Canadian Lencourt Mines Limted; basis 1 new for 4 old shs. ■

Lenmac Mines Ltd. (Ont. 1959)
Nov. 28, 1973 – Dissolved.

Lennie Red Lake Gold Mines Limited (Ont. Nov. 23, 1945)
May 29, 1984 – Continued into British Columbia.
May 29, 1985 – Name changed to Sun Valley, Id. and Red Lake Resources Ltd.; basis 1 new for 5 old shs. ■

Lennox Mines Co. Ltd. (Ont. 1936)
Nov. 1961 – Dissolved.

Lenora Explorations Ltd. (Ont. 1979)
Dec. 31, 1988 – Formed Greater Lenora Resources Corp. in Ontario on amalgamation with AXR Resources Ltd. and Mary Ellen Resources Ltd.; basis 1 new for 5 AXR shs., 1 new for 6 Mary Ellen shs. and 1 new for 4 Lenora shs. ■

Lenox Polymers Limited (Ont. Aug. 9, 1988)
Aug. 15, 2005 – Dissolved and struck from register.

Lenwood Mining & Exploration Ltd. (Ont. 1953)
July 8, 1965 – Dissolved.

Leo Acquisitions Corp. (Ont. Oct. 28, 2009)
Feb. 18, 2021 – Continued into British Columbia.
Feb. 25, 2021 – Name changed to PsyBio Therapeutics Corp. pursuant to the Qualifying Transaction reverse takeover acquisition of PsyBio Therapeutics, Inc., and concurrent amalgamation of (old) PsyBio Therapeutics with wholly owned ELUSS, Inc.; basis 1 new for 1.6667 old shs. (see FPsurvey - Industrials)

Leo Resources Inc. (B.C. 1980)
Feb. 28, 1986 – Formed Uni-Globe International Energy Corporation on amalgamation with several wholly owned subsids.; basis 1 new for 1 old sh. ■

Leo Resources Inc. (B.C. Mar. 18, 2013)
Aug. 20, 2018 – Name changed to Global Health Clinics Ltd. following change of business acquisition of Green Life Clinics Ltd. (see FPsurvey - Industrials)

Leocor Gold Inc. (B.C. July 26, 2018)
Jan. 21, 2025 – Name changed to Leocor Mining Inc. (see FPsurvey - Mines & Energy)

Leocor Ventures Inc. (B.C. July 26, 2018)
Aug. 5, 2020 – Name changed to Leocor Gold Inc. ■

Leona Gold Mines Ltd. (B.C. 1937)
1943 – Dissolved.

Leonids Investments Inc. (Can. Nov. 26, 2002)
Sept. 28, 2004 – Name changed to iWeb Group Inc. following Qualifying Transaction acquisition of iWeb Technologies Group Inc. ■

Leopardus Resources Limited (B.C. Oct. 4, 1984)
Feb. 12, 1999 – Acquired by Zarara Oil and Gas Limited; basis 1 Zarara sh. for 1 Leopardus shs.

Lepas Flin Flon Mines Ltd. (Ont. 1949)
Apr. 7, 1958 – Dissolved.

Lépine-Cloutier Ltée (Que. 1974)
Dec. 31, 1988 – Acquired by Montreal Funeral Home Urgel Bourgie Ltée.

Lepine Lake Gold Mines Ltd. (Ont. 1945)
Dec. 1966 – Charter cancelled.

Lequer Mines and Investments Ltd. (Ont. 1968)
Oct. 28, 1970 – Name changed to Mobilex Development Corporation Ltd. ■

Lequer Mines Ltd. (Ont. 1968)
1969 – Name changed to Lequer Mines and Investments Ltd. ■

Leric Mines Ltd. (Ont. 1946)
1952 – Charter cancelled.

Lero Gold Corp. (B.C. Dec. 19, 1994)
June 27, 2008 – Acquired by European Minerals Corporation (EMC), basis 1 EMC com. sh. for 1 Lero Gold com. sh.

Leroy Mining Corp. Ltd. (Que. 1962)
Nov. 24, 1976 – Dissolution commenced. No subsequent report.

Leroy Ventures Inc. (B.C. Oct. 6, 2003)
July 20, 2006 – Name changed to Unbridled Energy Corporation. ■

Leslie Oil & Gas Co. Ltd. (B.C. Jan. 6, 1966)
May 27, 1988 – Dissolved.

Less Mess Storage Inc. (B.C. Sept. 21, 2010)
Dec. 15, 2015 – Acquired by Less Mess Holdings Inc. for $1.415 per sh.

Lessard Beaucage Lemieux Inc. (Can. Sept. 28, 1979)
Nov. 30, 1998 – Name changed to LBL Skysystems Corporation. ■

Lethalta Oils Ltd. (Can. Feb. 1929)
Assets acquired by Chinalta Petroleums Ltd. prior to 1937.

Lethbridge Collieries, Ltd. (Alta. 1935)
Jan. 31, 1976 – Dissolved.

Letho Resources Inc. (B.C. 1972)
Nov. 18, 1983 – Struck off register.

Leucrotta Exploration Inc. (Alta. June 10, 2014)
June 6, 2022 – Acquired by Vermilion Energy Inc.; basis (i) $1.73 cash plus (ii) 1 Coelacanth com. sh. and 0.1917 Coelacanth wt. for 1 Leucrotta sh.

Levack Mines Ltd. (Ont. 1952)
Sept. 5, 1979 – Dissolved.

Levack Nickel Mines Ltd. (Ont. 1952)
Oct. 1963 – Name changed to Levack Mines Ltd. ■

Levega Mines Ltd. (Ont. 1963)
Apr. 9, 1969 – Charter cancelled.

Level 14 Ventures Ltd. (B.C. Nov. 7, 2018)
Dec. 27, 2023 – Name changed to Copper Standard Resources Inc.; basis 1 new for 3 old shs. (see FPsurvey - Mines & Energy)

Levelland Energy and Resources Ltd. (B.C. Mar. 11, 1981)
Aug. 27, 2002 – Name changed to Endeavour Gold Corp.; basis 1 new for 4 old shs. ■

Levengood Oil & Gas Inc. (Can. Sept. 24, 1981)
Jan. 30, 1995 – Continued into British Columbia.
Aug. 8, 1995 – Name changed to Fortune Resources Corporation; basis 1 new for 6 old shs. (see FPsurvey - Mines & Energy)

Lévesque, Beaubien and Company Inc. (Que. 1946)
Nov. 1, 1988 – All o/s cl. A subordinate shs. acquired by The National Bank of Canada; basis 0.30 National Bank shs. and $3.075 for 1 Lévesque sh.

Levi Developments Inc. (B.C. May 28, 1980)
June 9, 1994 – Name changed to R.I.S. Resources International Corp.; basis 1 new for 6 old shs. ■

Leviathan Cannabis Group Inc. (Ont. June 15, 2011)
July 21, 2020 – Name changed to Leviathan Natural Products Inc. ■

Leviathan Natural Products Inc. (Ont. June 15, 2011)
Sept. 6, 2022 – Name changed to 1CM Inc. (see FPsurvey - Industrials)

Levon Resources Ltd. (B.C. Apr. 9, 1965)
July 9, 2015 – Name changed to SciVac Therapeutics Inc. ■

Levon Resources Ltd. (B.C. Feb. 18, 2015)
Aug. 7, 2019 – Acquired by Discovery Metals Corp.; basis 0.55 Discovery com. shs. for 1 Levon sh. (see Discovery Metals Corp.)

Levtech Medical Technologies Ltd. (B.C. 1985)
May 28, 1993 – Dissolved and struck off register.

Levy Auto Parts Co. Ltd. (Ont. 1944)
May 27, 1960 – Name changed to Levy Industries Limited. ■

Levy Industries Limited (Ont. 1944)
Mar. 1987 – Company's banker, CIBC, demanded payment on $20,000,000 in loans of an operating subsidiary before Mar. 31, 1987.
Apr. 2, 1987 – Placed into receivership by CIBC. Peat Marwick Ltd. was appointed the receiver.

Lewes River Mines Ltd. (B.C. 1968)
Oct. 1973 – Name changed to Olympian International Resources Limited; basis 1 new for 6 old shs. ■

Lewis Brook Resources Ltd. (Ont. Feb. 20, 1997)
June 1, 2000 – Name changed to ChondroGene Limited following reverse takeover acquisition of ChondroGene Inc. and amalgamation of ChondroGene with wholly owned Lewis Brook Holdings Limited. ■

Lewis Red Lake Mines Ltd. (Ont. 1960)
June 1, 1973 – Name changed to Arcap Diversified Inc. ■

Lewmul Gold Mines Ltd. (Ont. 1950)
Mar. 10, 1952 – Name changed to Denlake Mining Co. Ltd. ■

Lex Corporation (Alta. Jan. 28, 1994)
Nov. 5, 1996 – Name changed to Home Ticket Network Corporation following Major Transaction reverse takeover acquisition of Home Ticket Network Ltd. ■

Lexcal Investment Corp. (Can. Feb. 11, 1986)
Oct. 26, 2007 – Name changed to New West Energy Services Inc. ■

Lexam Explorations Inc. (Ont. Nov. 12, 1993)
Jan. 3, 2011 – Amalgamated with VG Gold Corp.; basis 2.1 VG Gold shs. for 1 Lexam sh. (see Lexam VG Gold Inc.)

Lexam VG Gold Inc. (Ont. Jan. 1, 2011 amalg.)
May 2, 2017 – Acquired by McEwen Mining Inc.; basis 0.056 McEwen shs. for 1 Lexam sh.

Lexaria Corp. (Nev. Dec. 9, 2004)
Apr. 11, 2016 – Name changed to Lexaria Bioscience Corp.

Lexicon Building Systems Ltd. (B.C. Oct. 19, 1984)
Apr. 5, 2018 – Struck from registry and dissolved.

Lexindin Gold Mines Ltd. (Ont. 1945)
1963 – Name changed to Norlex Mines Ltd.; basis 1 new for 5 old shs. ■

Lexington Biosciences, Inc. (B.C. Apr. 12, 2016)
May 4, 2020 – Name changed to Registered Plan Private Investments Inc. (see FPsurvey - Industrials)

Lexington Mines Ltd. (B.C. June 1, 1967)
Nov. 6, 1975 – Name changed to Kent Energy Corp.; basis 1 new for 5 old shs. ■

Lexington Resources Inc. (Alta. Dec. 19, 1986)
Feb. 12, 1988 – Name changed to Nett-Workk Inc. ■

Lexington Resources Ltd. (B.C. May 30, 1986)
Apr. 27, 1992 – Name changed to Churchill Resources Ltd.; basis 1 new for 5 old shs. ■

Lexoil Incorporated (Alta. Mar. 6, 2001)
Dec. 18, 2003 – Acquired by Aquest Explorations Ltd.; basis 1 Aquest com. sh. plus 0.5 Aquest wts. for 5 Lexoil com. shs. (see Aquest Explorations Ltd.)

Lexston Capital Corp. (B.C. Jan. 3, 2020)
Jan. 18, 2021 – Name changed to Lexston Life Sciences Corp. pursuant to the reverse takeover acquisition of Egret Bioscience Ltd. ■

Lexston Life Sciences Corp. (B.C. Jan. 3, 2020)
Oct. 23, 2023 – Name changed to Lexston Mining Corporation. (see FPsurvey - Mines & Energy)

Lexxor Energy Inc. (Alta. Aug. 8, 1995)
Sept. 18, 2003 – Name changed to Find Energy Ltd. following reverse takeover acquisition of Sine Energy Ltd.; basis 1 new for 2 old shs. ■

Li-Metal Corp. (Ont. July 31, 2008)
Mar. 21, 2025 – Name changed to Skycap Investment Holdings Inc. (see FPsurvey - Industrials)

Li3 Lithium Corp. (Ont. Nov. 8, 1989)
Sept. 13, 2024 – Name changed to Global Copper Corp. (see FPsurvey - Mines & Energy)

Libby K Industries Inc. (B.C. July 5, 2018)
Sept. 17, 2020 – Name changed to Plurilock Security Inc. pursuant to the Qualifying Transaction reverse takeover acquisition of Plurilock Security Solutions Inc. and concurrent amalgamation of Plurilock with wholly owned 1243540 B.C. Ltd.; basis 1 new for 2 old shs. (see FPsurvey - Industrials)

Liberal Petroleums Ltd. (Alta. 1950)
1958 – Acquired by Canadian Husky Oil Ltd.; basis 1 new for 8 old shs. (see Canadian Husky Oil Ltd.)

Liberian Iron Ore Limited (Can. Sept. 8, 1958)
Sept. 6, 1996 – Name changed to LionOre Mining International Ltd. ■

Libero Copper & Gold Corporation (B.C. June 5, 2008)
May 1, 2025 – Name changed to Copper Giant Resources Corp. (see FPsurvey - Mines & Energy)

Libero Copper Corporation (B.C. June 5, 2008)
Sept. 16, 2019 – Name changed to Libero Copper & Gold Corporation. ■

Libero Mining Corporation (B.C. June 5, 2008)
Nov. 1, 2017 – Name changed to Libero Copper Corporation. ■

Liberty-Bell Mines Inc. (B.C. 1983)
May 23, 1990 – Name changed to Canadian Liberty Development Corp.; basis 1 new for 4 old shs. ■

Liberty Biopharma Inc. (B.C. Dec. 31, 2016 amalg.)
Oct. 11, 2018 – Name changed to HooXi Network Inc. ■

Liberty Defense Holdings, Ltd. (Ont. June 8, 2012)
July 27, 2020 – Continued into British Columbia. (see FPsurvey - Industrials)

Liberty Explorations Limited (B.C. 1978)
Feb. 1979 – Name changed to John Cabot Explorations Ltd. ■

Liberty Gold Corp. (B.C. May 18, 1983)
Apr. 2, 1992 – Name changed to Parkside Ventures Inc. ■

Liberty Health Sciences Inc. (B.C. Nov. 9, 2011)
Mar. 1, 2021 – Acquired by Ayr Wellness Inc.; basis 0.03683 Ayr sub. vtg. shs. plus $0.0001 cash for 1 Liberty Health sh.

Liberty Leaf Holdings Ltd. (B.C. Oct. 27, 2004)
June 26, 2020 – Name changed to Nova Mentis Life Science Corp. pursuant to the acquisition of Nova Mentis Biotech Corp.; basis 1 new for 4 old shs. ■

Liberty Mineral Exploration Inc. (Alta. Jan. 6, 1997)
Feb. 14, 2005 – Continued into Ontario.
July 18, 2005 – Name changed to Liberty Mines Inc. ■

Liberty Mines Inc. (Ont. Feb. 14, 2005)
Oct. 21, 2013 – Name changed to Northern Sun Mining Corp. ■

Liberty Mines Ltd. (B.C. 1966)
1972 – Charter cancelled.

Liberty Oil & Gas Ltd. (Can. Sept. 27, 1985)
Aug. 12, 2002 – Acquired by Lexxor Energy Inc.; basis 1 Lexxor sh. plus 1 wt. for 18.1818 Liberty shs. (see Lexxor Energy Inc.)

Liberty One Lithium Corp. (B.C. Sept. 15, 2015)
Aug. 4, 2022 – Name changed to Three Sixty Solar Ltd. pursuant to the reverse takeover acquisition of (old) Three Sixty Solar Ltd. and concurrent amalgamation of (old) Three Sixty with wholly owned 1345100 B.C. Ltd. (and continued as Three Sixty Solar Operations Ltd.).; basis 1 new for 2 old shs. (see FPsurvey - Industrials)

Liberty Petroleums Inc. (B.C. 1950)
May 1982 – Acquired by Corrida Oils Ltd. through offer made; basis 1/4 Corrida com. sh. and 1/6 ser. B Corrida wt. for each Liberty sh. Wts. exercisable at $12 per sh. to Nov. 20, 1982. (see Corrida Oils Ltd.)

Liberty Resources Corp. (Alta. Mar. 20, 2006)
Nov. 14, 2006 – Name changed to Lochaird Capital Corp. ■

Liberty Resources Limited (Alta. Dec. 24, 1947)
July 1971 – Name changed to Turbo Resources Limited. ■

Liberty Silver Corp. (Nev. Feb. 20, 2007)
Nov. 29, 2017 – Name changed to Bunker Hill Mining Corp. (see FPsurvey - Mines & Energy)

Libra Energy Inc. (B.C. May 26, 1981)
Nov. 20, 1985 – Name changed to Libra Industries Inc. ■

Libra Industries Inc. (B.C. May 26, 1981)
Mar. 4, 1991 – Delisted from the Vancouver Stock Exchange. Subsequently struck from register and dissolved.

Library Information Software Corp. (Ont. Nov. 4, 1997 amalg.)
Feb. 5, 1999 – Amalgamated with 1337387 Ontario Inc. to form new co. with same name Library Information Software Corp.
Apr. 28, 2006 – Name changed to Starwood Industries Inc. prior to the May 3, 2006, reverse takeover acquisition of Starwood Manufacturing Inc. ■

Licefa International Inc. (B.C. Apr. 18, 1984)
Dec. 24, 1996 – Name changed to Continuum Arts Inc.; basis 1 new for 8 old shs. ■

Lichen Lake Gold Mines Ltd. (Que. 1961)
June 16, 1973 – Dissolved.

LiCo Energy Metals Inc. (B.C. May 31, 2016)
Mar. 10, 2020 – Name changed to Fuse Cobalt Inc. ■

Lidco Industries Inc. (Alta. 1979)
Oct. 1, 1994 – Struck off register.

Lido Metals & Holdings Ltd. (Ont. 1967)
Feb. 1980 – Charter cancelled.

Lido Minerals Ltd. (Ont. 1967)
Dec. 22, 1970 – Name changed to Lido Metals & Holdings Ltd. ■

Lido Minerals Ltd. (B.C. Oct. 19, 2016)
Aug. 12, 2021 – Name changed to Highlander Silver Corp. pursuant to the reverse takeover acquisition of CAPPEX Mineral Ventures Inc., and concurrent amalgamation of CAPPEX with wholly owned 1303554 B.C. Ltd. (see FPsurvey - Mines & Energy)

Lieberman Brothers Ltd. (unknown)
1967 – Acquired by Montex Apparel Industries Ltd. (see Montex Apparel Industries Ltd.)

Life Aid Products Ltd. (Ont. 1967)
Nov. 12, 1970 – Name changed to Millmore Products Ltd. ■

Life Investors International Limited (Ont. June 6, 1973)
Mar. 1, 1974 – CTO issued. Subsequently struck from register and dissolved.

Life Investors Ltd. (unknown)
June 1973 – Amalgamated with 2 other cos. to form Life Investors International Ltd.; basis 5 cl. A and 1 new com. sh. for 1 com. sh. (see Life Investors International Limited)

Life Medical Corporation (Alta. May 7, 1991)
Nov. 2, 2010 – Struck from registry and dissolved.

Life Sciences Institute Inc. (Alta. Feb. 21, 1997)
Nov. 23, 2011 – Name changed to Quattro Exploration and Production Ltd.; basis 1 new for 3 old shs. ■

Lifebank Corp. (Can. Feb. 14, 2002)
Oct. 4, 2012 – Acquired by Insception Biosciences Inc. for $0.495 per sh.

Lifebank Cryogenics Corp. (B.C. Feb. 21, 1996)
Aug. 19, 1997 – Continued into Delaware.
Feb. 14, 2002 – Continued into Canada.
Jan. 16, 2006 – Name changed to Lifebank Corp. ■

Lifecall of Canada Inc. (Can. Jan. 6, 1989)
Aug. 26, 1993 – Name changed to VOXCOM Incorporated. ■

Lifeco Split Corporation Inc. (Que. June 1, 2000)
Aug. 1, 2012 – All o/s shs. redeemed for $4.4466 per cl. A capital shs. and $36.84 per cl. C pref. shs.

Lifequest International Inc. (Can. 1984)
Sept. 21, 1988 – Name changed to Amswiss Pharmaceuticals Inc.; basis 1 new for 7 old shs. ■

Lifesciences Capital Corp. (Ont. Mar. 16, 2006)
May 9, 2007 – Name changed to Bio-Extraction Inc. on Qualifying Transaction reverse takeover acquisition of Bio-Extraction Ltd. ■

LifeSpace Environmental Walls Inc. (Alta. 1980)
July 3, 1996 – Name changed to SMED International Inc. following amalgamation with private co. SMED Manufacturing Inc. (1 for 1); basis 1 new for 34.2631 old shs. ■

LifeSpeak Inc. (Can. Apr. 1, 2004)
July 2, 2025 – All o/s shs. not already held acquired by 1001180076 Ontario Inc. (succeeded by 17104944 Canada Inc.); basis 32¢ cash per sh.

Lifestart Multimedia Corp. (Alta. Oct. 22, 1993)
Nov. 20, 2000 – Name changed to GLK Strategies Inc.; basis 1 new for 3 old shs. ■

Lifestyle Beverage Corporation (B.C. 1981)
Oct. 23, 1987 – Name changed to Australian Corporate Holdings Limited.

Lifestyle Delivery Systems Inc. (B.C. Sept. 14, 2010)
Sept. 6, 2019 – Name changed to Core One Labs Inc.; basis 1 new for 6 old shs. (see FPsurvey - Industrials)

Lifestyles N.A. Beverage Corp. (B.C. Aug. 4, 1992)
June 6, 1996 – Name changed to Sasha Ventures Ltd.; basis 1 new for 5.3 old shs. ■

LifeTECH Corporation (Ont. July 11, 1994)
Mar. 13, 2002 – Name changed to IATRA Life Sciences Corporation. (see FPsurvey - Industrials)

Lifetime Ventures Ltd. (B.C. Feb. 11, 1980)
Oct. 17, 2005 – Dissolved and struck from register.

Lifetrends Behavioral Systems Inc. (B.C. 1983)
July 28, 1989 – Dissolved.

LifeWorks Inc. (Ont. Oct. 19, 2010)
Sept. 6, 2022 – Acquired by TELUS Corporation; basis (i) $33 cash per sh. or (ii) 1.06420 TELUS shs. for 1 LifeWork sh.

Lift & Co. Corp. (Ont. Feb. 10, 2017)
Sept. 17, 2020 – Voluntarily filed for bankruptcy and all officers and directors resigned. PricewaterhouseCoopers Inc. was appointed trustee.

Lighthouse Resources Inc. (B.C. Nov. 17, 1980)
June 22, 1995 – Name changed to Saxon Capital Corp.; basis 1 new for 3 old shs. ■

Lightning Creek Gold Alluvials Ltd. (B.C. 1947)
Jan. 9, 1964 – Dissolved.

Lightning Creek Mines Ltd. (B.C. 1952)
July 10, 1992 – Dissolved and struck off register.

Lightning Energy Ltd. (Alta. Jan. 23, 1979)
Apr. 26, 2005 – Plan of Arrangement with Argo Energy Ltd. (0.17125 + 0.17125 for 1) to convert company into a new income trust named Sequoia Oil & Gas Trust and a new exploration company named White Fire Energy Ltd.; basis 0.25 new Sequoia trust unit and 0.25 new White Fire com. sh. for 1 old Lightning com. sh. (see Sequoia Oil & Gas Trust; White Fire Energy Ltd.)

Lightning Minerals Inc. (B.C. Aug. 11, 1978)
Aug. 25, 1988 – Name changed to Vangold Resources Inc.; basis 1 new for 4 old shs. ■

Lightning Ventures Inc. (B.C. Apr. 2, 2014)
Sept. 12, 2022 – Dissolved and struck from register.

Lightspeed POS Inc. (Can. Mar. 21, 2005)
Aug. 10, 2021 – Name changed to Lightspeed Commerce Inc. (see FPsurvey - Industrials)

Lightspeed Retail Inc. (Can. Mar. 21, 2005)
Oct. 22, 2014 – Name changed to Lightspeed POS Inc. ■

Lightstream Resources Ltd. (Alta. Dec. 31, 2012 amalg.)
Dec. 29, 2016 – Completed the sale of substantially all of the assets and business of the company to Ridgeback Resources Inc., a new private co. owned by former holders of co.'s 9.875% secured notes. Holders of the secured notes received a pro rata number of com. shs. of Ridgeback resulting in the automatic cancellation of the secured notes. All officers and directors resigned and through FTI Consulting, the court-appointed monitor, the co. will be wound down.
June 2, 2018 – Dissolved and struck from registry.

Ligneris Goldfields Ltd. (Que. 1947)
Aug. 19, 1978 – Charter cancelled.

Ligneris Mining Exploration Limited (Can. May 16, 1985)
Oct. 9, 1992 – Name changed to Andreane Mining Resources Inc.; basis 1 new for 7 old shs. ■

Lignex Inc. (Ont. Sept. 22, 1987)
Sept. 8, 2000 – Name changed to International Biotechnology Corporation following takeover of International Biotech Corporation. ■

Lignol Energy Corporation (B.C. Sept. 14, 1964)
Aug. 29, 2014 – Placed into receivership and The Bowra Group Inc. was appointed receiver.
Mar. 2015 – Wholly owned Lignol Energy Corporation was sold and all proceeds were paid to secured lender, which suffered a significant shortfall.

Liht Cannabis Corp. (B.C. Apr. 24, 2007)
June 12, 2019 – Name changed to Citation Growth Corp.; basis 1 new for 4 old shs. ■

Lilrich Mines Ltd. (Ont. 1968)
July 7, 1980 – Dissolved.

Lima Gold Corporation (B.C. Sept. 2, 1966)
Sept. 21, 1999 – Name changed to International Lima Resources Corp.; basis 1 new for 3 old shs. ■

Lime Hill Capital Corporation (Can. Nov. 2, 2007)
May 13, 2011 – Formed Liquid Nutrition Group Inc. in Canada pursuant to Qualifying Transaction amalgamation with (old) Liquid Nutrition Group Inc. (deemed acquiror); basis 1 new for 8 old shs. ■

Liminal BioSciences Inc. (Can. Oct. 14, 1994)
Sept. 27, 2023 – Remaining 35.97% acquired by Structured Alpha LP; basis US$7.50 cash per sh.

Limited Duration Investment Grade Preferred Securities Fund (Ont. Mar. 27, 2013)
Aug. 27, 2018 – Merged into Purpose U.S. Preferred Share Fund; basis (i) 0.881314 Purpose ETFs for 1 Limited Duration cl. A unit; (ii) 0.963747 Purpose ETFs for 1 Limited Duration cl. F unit; (iii) 1.301973 Purpose ETFs for 1 Limited Duration cl. U. unit; and 1.379099 Purpose ETFs for 1 Limited Duration cl. V unit.

Limoges Porcelaines Ltd. (B.C. Jan. 22, 1981)
Oct. 20, 1988 – Name changed to Boch & Limoges Limited; basis 1 new for 10 old shs. ■

Limtech Lithium Industries Inc. (Que. June 26, 1969; via letters patent)
Mar. 30, 2004 – All assets acquired by QIE North America LLC, the principal secured creditor, which also agreed to discharge debt and assume all other liabs. There was nothing available for shldrs.

Limtech Lithium Métal Technologies Inc. (Que. June 26, 1969; via letters patent)
Jan. 23, 2003 – Name changed to Limtech Lithium Industries Inc.; basis 1 new for 10 old shs. ■

Linamar Machine Limited (Ont. Aug. 17, 1966)
Nov. 26, 1992 – Name changed to Linamar Corporation. (see FPsurvey - Industrials)

Lincoln Acquisitions Corp. (B.C. July 19, 2019)
Mar. 29, 2021 – Formed BYND Cannasoft Enterprises Inc. in British Columbia pursuant to the amalgamation with Israel-based 1232986 B.C. Ltd., and concurrently completed the reverse takeover acquisition of Israel-based BYND - Beyond Solutions Ltd. ■

Lincoln Capital Corporation (Ont. 1987)
Aug. 28, 1996 – Name changed to Jumbo Entertainment Inc. ■

Lincoln Gas Co., Ltd. (Ont. 1925)
1942 – Sold to W. J. Sanderson, Fort Erie, Ont.

Lincoln Gold Mines Ltd. (Ont. 1936)
Apr. 1, 1965 – Dissolved.

Lincoln Mining Corporation (B.C. Dec. 15, 2006)
Sept. 24, 2019 – Name changed to Lincoln Gold Mining Inc.; basis 1 new for 10 old shs. (see FPsurvey - Mines & Energy)

The Lincoln Oil Co. Ltd. (unknown)
July 2, 1942 – In voluntary liquidation. Nothing available for shldrs.

Lincoln Resources Inc. (B.C. 1969)
June 15, 1988 – Name changed to United Lincoln Resources Inc.; basis 1 new for 10 old shs. ■

Lincoln Trust and Savings Co. (Ont. 1964)
Dec. 31, 1976 – Amalgamated with Ontario Trust Co. and Canada Trustco Mortgage Co., to continue as Canada Trustco Mortgage Company.

Lincoln Waste Management Inc. (Ont. Aug. 10, 1990)
July 16, 1991 – Name changed to Philip Environmental Inc. ■

Lincolnberg Capital Corp. (Alta. June 21, 1994)
June 1, 1995 – Formed Mancap Global Ventures Inc. in Alberta on amalgamation with Lincolnberg International Inc.; basis 1 new for 2 Lincolnberg International shs. and 1 new for 1 Lincolnberg Capital sh. ■

Linden Explorations Inc. (B.C. Oct. 29, 1981)
May 23, 1996 – Name changed to Australian Oilfields Pty. Ltd. ■

Lindex Explorations Ltd. (B.C. May 30, 1980)
Feb. 14, 1986 – Name changed to Lectus Developments Ltd. ■

Lindsay Explorations Ltd. (Ont. 1955)
Jan. 31, 1963 – Name changed to Sapawe Gold Mines Limited; basis 1 new for 2 old shs. ■

Lindsay Uranium Mines Ltd. (unknown)
1955 – Name changed to Lindsay Explorations Ltd. and continued into Ontario. ■

Lindsey Morden Group Inc. (Can. Mar. 12, 1987)
Apr. 19, 2006 – Name changed to Cunningham Lindsey Group Inc. ■

Line & Cable Accessories Ltd. (Can. 1929)
July 1964 – Industrial Wire & Cable Co. Ltd. purchased all o/s pref. and com. shs. for $167,015, 199,548 com. shs. Industrial Wire & Cable, and a further $325,700 subject to possible adjustment, pay. in 10 annual installments.

Line Islands Exploration Inc. (Can. Apr. 11, 1996)
Feb. 1, 2000 – Name changed to Dia Bras Exploration Inc. ■

Lineage Grow Company Ltd. (Ont. Dec. 20, 2011)
May 30, 2019 – Name changed to Harborside Inc. pursuant to the reverse takeover acquisition of FLRish Inc. (dba Harborside); basis 1 new for 41.818182 old shs. ■

Linear Gold Corp. (Alta. Jan. 31, 1989 amalg.)
Nov. 10, 2004 – Continued into Canada.
June 25, 2010 – Formed Brigus Gold ULC in Canada. ■

Linear Metals Corporation (Can. Nov. 17, 2004)
May 1, 2012 – Name changed to Stockport Exploration Inc. ■

Linear Resources Inc. (Alta. Jan. 31, 1989 amalg.)
Nov. 24, 2003 – Name changed to Linear Gold Corp. ■

Linear Technology Inc. (Ont. May 28, 1973)
Dec. 3, 1990 – Name changed to Gennum Corporation. ■

Lingkey Gold Mines Ltd. (Ont. 1945)
Apr. 2, 1962 – Dissolved.

Lingman Lake Gold Mines Ltd. (Ont. Feb. 9, 1945)
1948 – Name changed to Lake Lingman Gold Mining Co. Ltd.; basis 1 new for 2 old shs. ■

Lingnora Gold Mines Ltd. (Ont. 1945)
Dec. 1967 – Charter cancelled.

Lingo Media Corporation (Ont. Apr. 22, 1998)
Oct. 17, 2022 – Name changed to Everybody Loves Languages Corp. (see FPsurvey - Industrials)

Lingo Media Inc. (Ont. Apr. 22, 1998)
Oct. 16, 2007 – Name changed to Lingo Media Corporation; basis 1 new for 7 old shs. ■

Lingside Copper Mining Co. Limited (Ont. 1945)
July 5, 1982 – Dissolved.

Lingside Gold Mines Ltd. (Ont. 1945)
1953 – Name changed to Lingside Copper Mining Co. Limited. ■

Lingxian Capital Inc. (B.C. July 16, 2012)
Sept. 14, 2015 – Name changed to Crownia Holdings Ltd. following Qualifying Transaction reverse takeover acquisition of Jinsili International Steel Holdings Co., Limited. ■

Link Global Technologies Inc. (B.C. Jan. 22, 2018)
Mar. 25, 2022 – Name changed to Green Block Mining Corp. (see FPsurvey - Industrials)

Link Resources Inc. (B.C. Feb. 13, 1984)
July 14, 1992 – Name changed to Haddington Resources Ltd.; basis 1 new for 5 old shs. ■

Linland Equipment Sales Limited (Ont. 1965)
1974 – Placed into receivership; no distribution to unsecured creditors or shldrs.

Linlothian Mines Ltd. (Ont. 1944)
Nov. 3, 1958 – Dissolved. No equity for shldrs.

Lintex Minerals Ltd. (B.C. May 31, 1983 amalg.)
Dec. 7, 1987 – Name changed to New Lintex Minerals Ltd.; basis 1 new for 3 old shs. ■

Lintronics International Ltd. (B.C. 1985)
Aug. 9, 1988 – Name changed to Bi-Petro Resources Inc.; basis 1 new for 2 old shs. ■

Linux Gold Corp. (B.C. Feb. 27, 1979)
Aug. 8, 2017 – Struck from registry and dissolved.
Dec. 2, 2021 – Restored to registry.
Feb. 2, 2022 – Name changed to 0187279 B.C. Ltd. (see FPsurvey - Industrials)

LinuxWizardry Systems, Inc. (B.C. Feb. 27, 1979)
Feb. 26, 2003 – Name changed to Linux Gold Corp. ■

Linval Acceptance Corporation Limited (Can. 1960)
Jan. 31, 1973 – First and final payment made on secured notes, as follows: 32.7% on ser. A, 46.4% on ser. B and 84.2% on ser. C. Trustee General Trust Co. of Canada, Montreal. No recent report.

The Lion Electric Company (Que. July 25, 2008)
May 22, 2025 – Reverse vesting order under which 9539-5034 Quebec Inc. was issued a new class of com. shs. and all the o/s com. shs. were cancelled for no consideration. Certain excluded assets and excluded liabilities were vested-out and transferred to entities newly incorporated for that purpose.

Lion Energy Corp. (B.C. Sept. 28, 1979)
June 24, 2011 – Acquired by Africa Oil Corp.; basis 0.2 Africa Oil shs. for 1 Lion Energy sh. (see Africa Oil Corp.)

Lion Mines Ltd. (B.C. 1968)
Sept. 20, 1985 – Struck off register.

Lion Nickel Mines of Canada Ltd. (Ont. 1966)
Aug. 1971 – Assets sold to Indian Mountain Metal Mines Ltd.; basis 1 new for 4.25 old shs.
1975 – Charter cancelled.

Lion Oils Limited (Alta. 1933)
1950 – Reported to be wound up voluntarily. Liquidator, Leon L. Plotkins, Calgary.

Lionheart Capital Corporation (B.C. 1984)
Oct. 6, 1988 – Acquired by 1726 Holdings Ltd. for $3.28 per sh.

Lionheart Energy Corp. (Alta. June 2, 1993)
May 20, 1997 – Acquired by Search Energy Corp.; basis 0.81 new Search sh. for 1 old Lionheart sh. (see Search Energy Corp.)

Lionheart Resource Corporation (B.C. 1984)
July 15, 1987 – Name changed to Lionheart Capital Corporation. ■

LionOre Mining International Ltd. (Can. Sept. 8, 1958)
Aug. 20, 2007 – Acquired by 0789970 B.C. Ltd., a wholly owned subsid. of OJSC MMC Norilsk Nickel; basis $27.50 per com. sh.

Lions Bay Mining Corp. (B.C. Apr. 25, 2018)
Sept. 30, 2020 – Name changed to BioVaxys Technology Corp. pursuant to reverse takeover acquisition of BioVaxys LLC. (see FPsurvey - Industrials)

Lions Gate Energy Inc. (B.C. Feb. 4, 1981)
July 27, 2015 – Name changed to Starr Peak Exploration Ltd.; basis 1 new for 6 old shs. ■

Lions Gate Entertainment Corp. (Can. Apr. 28, 1997)
Sept. 24, 1997 – Continued into British Columbia.
Nov. 13, 1997 – Amalgamated in British Columbia to continue with same name.
May 6, 2025 – Name changed to Starz Entertainment Corp. (see FPsurvey - Industrials)

Lions Gate Metals Inc. (B.C. Mar. 28, 1980)
Jan. 23, 2018 – Name changed to Block X Capital Corp. ■

Lionsgate Mines Ltd. (Ont. 1964)
1968 – Assets sold to Mission Financial Corp. Ltd.; basis 0.03171 Mission shs. for 1 Lionsgate sh.

Lionsgate Studios Corp. (B.C. May 13, 2024)
May 7, 2025 – Reorganized whereby Lionsgate Studio Holdings Corp. (New Lionsgate and renamed Lionsgate Studio Corp.) acquired the businesses of the company and of Lions Gate Entertainment Corp. (renamed Starz Entertainment Corp.), namely the motion picture and television studio operations; basis 0.989632 New Lionsgate shs. for 1 Lionsgate Studio sh. (see Lionsgate Studios Corp.)

Lionsgate Studios Holding Corp. (B.C. Jan. 10, 2025)
May 7, 2025 – Name changed to Lionsgate Studios Corp. (see FPsurvey - Industrials)

Lipari Energy, Inc. (B.C. Mar. 10, 2011)
Nov. 4, 2013 – All o/s com. shs. not already held acquired by Lipari Private Holdings, Inc.; basis $0.48 cash per sh.

Lipari Mining Ltd. (Can. Aug. 9, 2013 amalg.)
July 11, 2025 – Continued into Ontario. (see FPsurvey - Mines & Energy)

Liponex Inc. (Ont. Aug. 8, 2000)
June 24, 2008 – Name changed to ImaSight Corp. following amalgamation of a wholly owned subsidiary with ImaSight Inc., constituting a reverse takeover by ImaSight Inc.; basis 1 new for 5 old shs. ■

Liquest International Marketing Corp. (B.C. Mar. 2, 1983)
Apr. 9, 1992 – Name changed to Massey Mercantile Ltd.; basis 1 new for 2 old shs. ■

Liquid Asphalt Ltd. (unknown)
In liquidation; K. M. Robertson, Imperial Bank Chambers, Weyburn, Sask., liquidator.

Liquid Gold Resources Inc. (B.C. Nov. 22, 1983)
May 7, 1999 – Name changed to West African Venture Exchange Corp. ■

Liquid Nutrition Group Inc. (Can. May 13, 2011 amalg.)
May 23, 2023 – Struck from register and dissolved.

Liquidation World Inc. (Alta. Dec. 4, 1986)
July 22, 2011 – Acquired by Big Lots, Inc. for 6¢ per sh.
July 2011 – Name changed to Big Lots Canada, Inc.

Liquor Barn Income Fund (Alta. Apr. 3, 2006)
June 12, 2007 – Acquired and subsequently merged with Liquor Stores Income Fund; basis 0.57 Liquor Stores new units for 1 Liquor Barn old unit. (see Liquor Stores Income Fund)

Liquor Stores Income Fund (Alta. Aug. 10, 2004)
Dec. 31, 2010 – Succeeded by Liquor Stores N.A. Ltd. pursuant to plan of arrangement whereby Liquor Stores

N.A. Ltd. was formed to facilitate the conversion of the fund into a corporation. ■

Liquor Stores N.A. Ltd. (Can. Nov. 8, 2010)
May 14, 2018 – Name changed to Alcanna Inc. ■

Listed Ventures Incorporated (Alta. Sept. 4, 1985)
May 3, 1993 – Name changed to Listed Ventures International Inc.; basis 1 new for 3 old shs. ■

Listed Ventures International Inc. (Alta. Sept. 4, 1985)
July 5, 1994 – Name changed to Command Performance Network Ltd. ■

Lite Oil Corporation (B.C. Sept. 12, 1980)
Jan. 30, 1984 – Name changed to Wescal Resources Inc.; basis 1 new for 5 old shs. ■

Lite Resources Ltd. (Alta. Dec. 14, 1983)
June 17, 1987 – Amalgamated in Alberta to continue with same name.
Dec. 1, 1993 – Dissolved and struck off register.

LiteLink Technologies Inc. (B.C. June 11, 2010)
Feb. 26, 2021 – Name changed to TechX Technologies Inc. ■

Lithanium Mines Ltd. (Ont. 1937)
Nov. 1979 – Charter cancelled.

Lithia Mine Ltd. (Ont. 1955)
Name changed to Lithia Mines & Chemicals Ltd.

Lithic Resources Ltd. (Can. June 7, 2002)
Feb. 18, 2014 – Name changed to InZinc Mining Ltd. (see FPsurvey - Mines & Energy)

Lithion Energy Corp. (B.C. Jan. 25, 2011)
Jan. 29, 2020 – Continued into Cayman Islands.
Feb. 5, 2020 – Name changed to Queen's Road Capital Investment Ltd. (see FPsurvey - Industrials)

Lithium X Energy Corp. (B.C. May 11, 2011)
Mar. 14, 2018 – Acquired by NNRL Holding Corp., a wholly owned subsid. of NextView New Energy Lion Hong Kong Limited; basis $2.61 cash per sh.

Lithium Americas (Argentina) Corp. (B.C. Nov. 27, 2007)
Jan. 23, 2025 – Name changed to Lithium Argentina AG and continued into Switzerland. (see FPsurvey - Mines & Energy)

Lithium Americas Corp. (B.C. Nov. 27, 2007)
Oct. 3, 2023 – Name changed to Lithium Americas (Argentina) Corp. ■

Lithium Americas Corp. (Ont. Apr. 28, 2009)
Sept. 8, 2015 – Acquired by Western Lithium USA Corporation; basis 0.789 Western com. shs. for 1 Lithium Americas com. sh. (see Western Lithium USA Corporation)

The Lithium Corporation of Canada, Limited (Man. 1934)
Jan. 31, 1993 – Amalgamated with Stockgold Resources Inc. (basis 0.2622851 new for 1 old sh.) to form a new company called Rusty Lake Resources Ltd.; basis 1 new for 1 old sh. (see Rusty Lake Resources Ltd.)

Lithium Energy Products Inc. (Ont. Nov. 20, 2009)
Feb. 13, 2020 – Name changed to Ares Strategic Mining Inc. pursuant to the acquisition of American Strategic Minerals Inc. (see FPsurvey - Mines & Energy)

Lithium Lion Metals Inc. (B.C. Oct. 5, 2018)
Apr. 19, 2024 – Name changed to Panther Minerals Inc. (see FPsurvey - Mines & Energy)

Lithium One Inc. (Ont. Sept. 8, 1993 amalg.)
July 5, 2012 – Acquired by Galaxy Resources Limited; basis 1.96 Galaxy Resources ord. shs. for 1 Lithium One sh.

Lithjean Mines Limited (Ont. 1956)
Mar. 5, 1980 – Charter cancelled.

Lithoquest Diamonds Inc. (B.C. Feb. 25, 1986)
Nov. 24, 2020 – Name changed to Lithoquest Resources Inc. ■

Lithoquest Resources Inc. (B.C. Feb. 25, 1986)
Nov. 9, 2022 – Name changed to Storm Exploration Inc. (see FPsurvey - Mines & Energy)

Lithos Corporation (Que. June 26, 1969; via letters patent)
Apr. 5, 2000 – Name changed to Limtech Lithium Métal Technologies Inc. ■

Lithos Energy Ltd. (B.C. Oct. 22, 2010)
Jan. 24, 2024 – Name changed to Lithos Group Ltd. (see FPsurvey - Mines & Energy)

Little Abitibi River Resources Inc. (Ont. Oct. 15, 1986)
Jan. 15, 1990 – Name changed to LARR Capital Corp. ■

Little Ag Mines Ltd. (Ont. 1963)
Jan. 13, 1971 – Dissolved.

Little Bear Resources Ltd. (B.C. Aug. 20, 1980)
Oct. 11, 1991 – Name changed to Response Biomedical Corp. ■

Little Hatchet Minerals Ltd. (Ont. 1959)
Mar. 1976 – Charter cancelled.

Little Herb Mines Limited (Ont. 1951)
Mar. 1958 – Charter cancelled.

Little Klondyke Oil & Gas Ltd. (Ont. 1939)
1960 – Wound up.

Little Lake Resources Ltd. (B.C. 1978)
May 4, 1987 – Name changed to I.C.E. - Ice Factory, Inc. ■

The Little Long Lac Gold Mines Ltd. (Ont. Jan. 1933)
June 1966 – Amalgamated in Ontario to continue with same name.
Nov. 1970 – Formed Little Long Lac Mines Ltd. in Ontario on amalgamation with Little Long Lac Mines Ltd. ■

Little Long Lac Gold Mines Ltd. (Ont. Nov. 1970 amalg.)
July 29, 1985 – Amalgamated with Lake Shore Mines Limited (2.871 for 1), LAC Minerals Ltd. (1 for 1) and Wright-Hargreaves Mines Limited (0.498 for 1) to continue as LAC Minerals Ltd.; basis 2.377 new LAC shs. for 1 old Little Long Lac sh. (see LAC Minerals Ltd.)

Little Long Lac Mines Ltd. (Ont. Nov. 1970 amalg.)
Apr. 22, 1975 – Name changed to Little Long Lac Gold Mines Ltd. ■

Little Mountain Resources Ltd. (B.C. Feb. 5, 1996)
Aug. 10, 2005 – Name changed to Petrostar Petroleum Corporation. ■

Little Pine Tex Mining Corp. Ltd. (B.C. Mar. 24, 1966)
May 2, 1969 – Name changed to Highland Star Mines Ltd. ■

Little River Mines Ltd. (Ont. 1955)
Nov. 1962 – Dissolved.

Little Rocky Holdings Ltd. (B.C. 1966)
1978 – Charter cancelled.

Little Rocky Mining Co. Ltd. (B.C. 1966)
1970 – Name changed to Little Rocky Holdings Ltd. ■

Little Tex Mining Corp. (Ont. 1955)
1966 – Assets acquired by Little Pine Tex Mining Corp. No record of equity for shldrs.

Liuyang Fireworks Limited (Bermuda Jan. 13, 2006)
Oct. 2, 2015 – Privatized; basis Cdn$0.048 cash per com. sh.

Live Entertainment of Canada Inc. (Ont. Dec. 8, 1989)
June 2, 1995 – Name changed to Livent Inc. ■

Livent Inc. (Ont. Dec. 8, 1989)
Jan. 1, 1997 – Amalgamated in Ontario to continue with same name.
Sept. 29, 1999 – Placed into receivership. Ernst & Young Inc. appointed receiver.

LiveReel Media Corporation (Ont. Mar. 18, 1997 amalg.)
Oct. 20, 2006 – Continued into Canada.
Jan. 3, 2018 – Name changed to CordovaCann Corp. (see FPsurvey - Industrials)

LiveWell Canada Inc. (Can. June 18, 2014)
Apr. 12, 2019 – Name changed to Eureka 93 Inc. pursuant to the reverse takeover acquisition of Vitality CBD Natural Health Products Inc., which occurred immediately following the concurrent completion of Vitality's merger with public Mercal Capital Corp.; basis 1 new for 15 old shs. ■

Livingston Industries Limited (Ont. 1945)
Dec. 1, 1978 – Amalgamated with Allpak Holdings Ltd., a wholly owned subsid. of Allpak Ltd. Minority shldrs. held option to convert their shs. into either first or second pfce. shs. of amalco. First pfce. shs. of amalco. had par value of $36 while second pfce. shs. had par value of $2.14 plus divd. of $33.86. Shldrs. could elect to have their shs. redeemed on Dec. 27, 1978, or Jan. 5, 1979, respectively, at $36 per sh.
1978 – Amalgamated in Ontario to continue with same name.
Aug. 1, 1981 – Name changed to Livingston International Inc.

Livingston International Income Fund (Ont. Jan. 4, 2002)
Jan. 20, 2010 – Acquired by Canada Pension Plan Investment Board and Sterling Partners for $9.50 per unit.

Livingston Wood Manufacturing Ltd. (Ont. 1945)
Apr. 17, 1967 – Name changed to Livingston Industries Limited. ■

Livingstone Mining Co. Inc. (B.C.)
Property sold to Kenville Gold Mines for 583,333 shs.; no record of distribution. (see Kenville Gold Mines Ltd.)

Liza Lanzet Lingerie Ltd. (B.C. Aug. 24, 1987)
Mar. 30, 1995 – Name changed to First Venture Developments Ltd. ■

Lizard Point Oil Co. Ltd. (Man. July 1940)
1959 – Struck off register.

Lloyd Gold Mines (1945) Ltd. (Ont. 1945)
1954 – Charter cancelled.

Lloyd-Leduc Oils Ltd. (Alta.)
1960 – Struck off register.

Lloydaire Ltd. (Can. - unspecified)
May 1969 – Formerly Lloyd Register and Grill Co. Ltd. Acquired by Van Ness Industries Ltd.

Lloydal Petroleums Limited (Ont. 1945)
Aug. 1957 – Acquired by Continental Consolidated Mines and Oils Corp. Ltd.; basis 1 new for 10 old shs. (see Continental Consolidated Mines & Oils Corp. Ltd.)

Lloydbrook Oil Company Limited (Alta. 1947)
Jan. 10, 1984 – Struck off register.

Lloydminster Development Company Limited (Sask. 1946)
1964 – Acquired by Kodiak Petroleums Ltd.; basis 75 new for 1,000 old shs. (see Kodiak Petroleums Ltd.)

The Lloydminster Gas Company Limited (Sask. 1933)
1984 – All o/s voting and nonvoting shs. acquired by Northwestern Utilities Limited for a total consideration of $1,548,000. Payments of $2.00 per sh. (voting and non voting) made to Chieftain Development Company Ltd., and $2.10 per sh. to minority shldrs. (see Chieftain Development Co. Ltd.)

Lloydminster Oil Producers Ltd. (Alta. June 29, 1945)
Reported to be wound up. Struck off register.

Lloydminster Oil Syndicate (unknown)
Reported to be wound up.

Lloydminster Royalties, Ltd. (Alta. 1939)
1950 – Charter cancelled.

Lloyds Bank Canada (Can. 1982)
May 31, 1990 – Acquired by Hongkong Bank of Canada.
(see Hongkong Bank of Canada)

Load Resources Ltd. (B.C. July 30, 1970)
May 29, 2000 – Formed GIS Global Imaging Solutions
Inc. following acquisition of Global Imaging Solutions
Inc. ■

Lobanor Gold Mines Ltd. (Ont. 1944)
Dec. 2, 1965 – Dissolved.

Lobell Mines Ltd. (B.C. 1970)
Jan. 1977 – Name changed to Lobell Oil & Gas Ltd.; basis
1 new for 3 old shs. ■

Lobell Oil & Gas Ltd. (B.C. 1970)
Feb. 26, 1988 – Delisted from the Alberta Stock
Exchange. Subsequently dissolved.

Lobitos Oilfields Canada Ltd. (Alta. 1955)
Nov. 1963 – Acquired by Great Plains Development Co.
of Canada, Ltd. Name subsequently changed to Great
Plains Exploration Ltd.

Loblaw Groceterias Inc. (N.Y. 1939)
May 1950 – Name changed to Loblaw Inc. ■

Loblaw Inc. (N.Y. 1939)
1975 – Became a wholly owned subsid. of Loblaws
Limited following an offer of $6.00 per share.

Loblaw Leased Properties Limited (Ont. 1955)
July 1977 – Name changed to Wittington Leased
Properties Limited.

Loblaws Ltd. (Ont. 1921)
Dec. 1983 – Effective Dec. 23, 1983, all ser. A and B first
pfce. shs. exchanged for first pref., second ser. of Loblaws
Companies Ltd., on the basis of one first pref. sh., second
ser. of Loblaws Companies for each two ser. A first pfce.
shs., and one first pref. sh., second ser. for each two ser.
B first pfce. shs. Also all second pfce. shs. were called
for redemp. at $50 per sh. plus accrued divds.

Lobo Capital Inc. (Ont. July 6, 1983 amalg.)
Apr. 2, 1993 – Name changed to Q & A Communications
Inc. ■

Lobo Gold & Resources Inc. (Ont. July 6, 1983 amalg.)
June 11, 1992 – Name changed to Lobo Capital Inc.;
basis 1 new for 15 old shs. ■

Lobo Mines & Explorations Limited (Ont. 1971)
July 6, 1983 – Amalgamated with 8 other cos. to form
Lobo Gold & Resources Inc.; basis 1 new for 10 old shs.

Locana Corporation Ltd. (Can. 1953)
Feb. 20, 1978 – Dissolved. Final distribution to shldrs.
was $3.976 per sh. and 1,535 shs. of Locana Corporation
(London) Ltd. for 1,000 old shs.

Locana Mineral Holdings Ltd. (Can. 1959)
July 22, 1971 – Name changed to NSI Marketing
Limited. ■

Locarno Copper Mines Ltd. (Can. 1927)
1938 – Name changed to Locarno Gold Mines Ltd. ■

Locarno Gold Mines Ltd. (Can. 1927)
Dec. 16, 1980 – Dissolved.

Locator Explorations Ltd. (B.C. 1986)
July 25, 1988 – Amalgamated with Duration Mines Ltd.;
basis 1.45 new for 1 old sh.

Locator Systems Inc. (Alta. Oct. 16, 1961)
Mar. 18, 1994 – Name changed to Custom Cryogenic
Grinding Corporation. ■

Locators Oils Ltd. (Ont. 1933)
1955 – Reported winding up. Trans. Agent Crown Trust
Co., Toronto.

Loch Alva Mines Ltd. (N.B. 1954)
July 3, 1968 – Charter cancelled.

Loch Lomond Mines Ltd. (Ont. 1953)
Apr. 1, 1965 – Dissolved.

Lochaber Oil Corporation Ltd. (Can. 1932)
Nov. 13, 1974 – Amalgamated with wholly owned
Lochaber Resources Ltd.; basis 1 com. sh. for each
subsid. pref. or com. sh. held.
Dec. 27, 1974 – O/s 8% pref. shs. ($7 par) of the subsid.
were called for redemption at par.
Mar. 12, 1975 – Company distributed 100,000 com. shs.
of wholly owned Frontier Oil and Gas Co. Inc. to shldrs.;
basis 0.14920162 Frontier shs. for each Lochaber sh.
held. Subsequently, The Texas Land & Mortgage Co.,
Inc. (an affiliate of Lochaber) issued 220,340 com. shs.
to Frontier and Lochaber shldrs.; basis 1.02608 shs. for
each Frontier sh. and 0.17565805 shs. for each Lochaber
sh. As a result of this exchange, both Frontier and
Lochaber became wholly owned subsids. of Texas Land.
Mar. 1976 – Acquired by Oakwood Petroleums Ltd. for
$3,463,464.

Lochabie Mines Ltd. (Ont. 1945)
Charter cancelled.

Lochaird Capital Corp. (Alta. Mar. 20, 2006)
May 22, 2008 – Name changed to Lochaird Energy Inc.
following Qualifying Transaction acquisition of Lochaird
Energy Corp. ■

Lochaird Energy Inc. (Alta. Mar. 20, 2006)
Sept. 2, 2011 – Struck from registry and dissolved.

Lochiel Exploration Ltd. (Alta. 1949)
Oct. 20, 1986 – Placed into receivership and
Calgary-based Collins Barrow Limited was appointed
receiver.
1987 – Most assets were sold and secured creditors paid.
Aug. 2000 – Trustee made a final distribution to
unsecured creditors of 15.5¢ on the dollar. There were
no distributions to shldrs.
May 2, 2002 – Dissolved and struck off register.

Lochland Pershing Mines Ltd. (Ont. 1944)
Mar. 1957 – Charter cancelled.

Locke Rich Minerals Ltd. (B.C. Apr. 14, 1987)
Mar. 5, 1996 – Delisted from the Vancouver Stock
Exchange. Subsequently dissolved for failure to file.

Lockerbie & Hole Inc. (Alta. Feb. 29, 2000)
Apr. 7, 2009 – Acquired by Aecon Group Inc.; basis $8.00
or 0.8672 Aecon shs.for 1 Lockerbie sh. or a combination
thereof.

Locksley Capital Partners Inc. (Alta. Aug. 1, 1996)
Mar. 11, 1998 – Name changed to IPEC Ltd. ■

Lockwood Petroleum Inc. (B.C. 1980)
Sept. 6, 1989 – Amalgamated with Gabriel Resources
Inc. and Kangeld Resources Ltd. to form Appian
Resources Ltd.; basis 0.1586 new for 1 old sh. (see
Appian Resources Ltd.)

Lode Metals & Holdings Ltd. (Ont. 1960)
Feb. 1980 – Charter cancelled.

Lode Metals Corp. (B.C. Mar. 3, 2018)
Oct. 17, 2023 – Name changed to Minas Metals Ltd. ■

Lode Mines Ltd. (Ont. 1960)
1970 – Name changed to Lode Metals & Holdings Ltd. ■

Lode Resource Corporation (B.C. Oct. 18, 1979)
June 6, 1990 – Name changed to Lodex Resource
Corporation; basis 1 new for 5 old shs. ■

Lodestar Battery Metals Corp. (B.C. Mar. 21, 2019)
Sept. 3, 2024 – Name changed to Lodestar Metals Corp.
(see FPsurvey - Mines & Energy)

Lodestar Energy Inc. (Alta. Feb. 27, 1996)
Apr. 6, 1998 – Amalgamated with 757090 Alberta Ltd., a
wholly owned subsid. of Torrington Resources Ltd.; basis
(a) 1 new special A sh. or 1 new special C sh. of the
amalgamated company for 1 cl. A sh. of Lodestar
immediately redeemed for $1.15 for each special A sh.
or $0.765 for each special C sh.; (b) 1 new special B sh.
or 0.6 of a com. sh. of Torrington for 1 cl. B sh. of
Lodestar. Special B shs. immediately redeemed for $3.00.
(see Torrington Resources Ltd.)

Lodestar Energy Ltd. (B.C. 1965)
Dec. 20, 1985 – Name changed to Controlled
Environment Farming International Ltd.; basis 1 new for
4 old shs. ■

Lodestar Explorations Inc. (B.C. June 10, 1987)
Oct. 24, 1994 – Name changed to Precision International
Resource Corp.; basis 1 new for 5 old shs. ■

Lodestar Mines Ltd. (B.C. 1965)
Feb. 1, 1980 – Name changed to Lodestar Energy Ltd. ■

Lodestar Yellowknife Gold Mines Ltd. (Ont. 1945)
1956 – Charter cancelled.

Lodex Resource Corporation (B.C. Oct. 18, 1979)
Feb. 1, 1993 – Name changed to LRX Capital Corp.;
basis 1 new for 3 old shs. ■

Lodge Resources Inc. (B.C. Oct. 24, 2018)
May 21, 2020 – Name changed to Freeman Gold Corp.
(see FPsurvey - Mines & Energy)

Lodge Uranium Mines Ltd. (Ont. 1952)
1954 – Assets acquired by St. Michael Uranium Mines
Ltd.; basis 1 sh. St. Michael for 2 shs. Lodge.

Lodi Metals Inc. (B.C. Aug. 11, 1980)
June 26, 1996 – Name changed to Valley High Ventures
Ltd.; basis 1 new for 8 old shs. ■

Loec Minerals Inc. (Del. 1959)
1960 – Name changed to Camerina Petroleum Corp.;
basis 1 new for 4 old shs. ■

Loewen Group Inc. (B.C. 1985)
Jan. 3, 2002 – Name changed to Alderwoods Group Inc.
and continued into Delaware.

Loewen, Ondaatje, McCutcheon Inc. (Ont. Sept. 30,
1983)
Dec. 9, 1992 – Name changed to The Ondaatje
Corporation. ■

Loew's London Theatres, Limited (Can. 1919)
June 8, 1943 – Charter cancelled; distribution of $8.10
per sh. made to pref. shldrs., Apr. 23, 1943. Nothing for
com. shldrs.

Logan International Inc. (Alta. Apr. 7, 1993)
Oct. 26, 2016 – Acquired by Tercel Oilfield Products UK
Ltd. for Cdn$1.58886 per sh.

Logan Mines Ltd. (B.C. July 26, 1978)
July 21, 1992 – Name changed to Consolidated Logan
Mines Ltd.; basis 1 new for 3 old shs. ■

Logan Porcupine Mines Ltd. (Ont. 1948)
1961 – Went bankrupt. Nothing available for unsecured
creditors or shldrs.; charter surrendered.

Logan Resources Ltd. (B.C. July 26, 1978)
May 28, 2019 – Name changed to Voleo Trading Systems
Inc. pursuant to the reverse takeover acquisition of Voleo
Inc.; basis 1 new for 5 old shs. ■

Logan Resources Ltd. (Alta. 1988)
Nov. 1, 1991 – Acquired by Rio Alto Exploration Ltd.;
basis 1.45 Rio Alto shs. for 1 Logan sh. (see Rio Alto
Exploration Ltd.)

Loggie-Miller Oils Ltd. (Alta.)
1958 – Struck off register.

Logibec Groupe Informatique Ltée (Can. Sept. 16, 1982)
Aug. 4, 2010 – Acquired by OPE LGI Inc. for an undisclosed amount.
Dec. 31, 2013 – Name changed to Logibec Inc. ■

Logibec Inc. (Can. Sept. 16, 1982)
Name changed to LGI Healthcare Solutions Inc.

LogicalOptions International Inc. (Can. May 18, 1989)
Aug. 28, 2008 – Dissolved.

Logiciel Systems Limited (Alta. Feb. 9, 1987)
Aug. 1, 1993 – Dissolved and struck off register.

Logicon Products Ltd. (B.C. 1980)
Mar. 26, 1993 – Dissolved and struck off register.

Logicsys Inc. (Alta. Sept. 23, 1992)
Jan. 29, 2001 – Name changed to Wisper Inc. ■

Logistec Corporation (Que. Feb. 29, 1952; via letters patent)
Jan. 11, 2024 – Acquired by 1443373 B.C. Unlimited Liability Company, an entity owned by certain funds managed by Blue Wolf Capital Partners LLC; basis $67 cash for 1 cl. A com. sh. or 1 cl. B subordinate vtg. sh.
June 16, 2024 – Continued into British Columbia.

Logix Enterprises Inc. (B.C. Apr. 11, 1979)
Nov. 27, 2002 – Name changed to Transac Enterprise Corp.; basis 1 new for 8 old shs. ■

Logjam Silver Mines Ltd. (Ont. 1964)
1971 – All assets sold to Fallinger Mining Corp.

Logo Resources Ltd. (B.C. June 25, 1969)
Mar. 1, 1989 – Delisted from the Vancouver Stock Exchange. Subsequently dissolved for failure to file and struck from register.

Logtung Resources Ltd. (B.C. 1977)
May 31, 1982 – Acquired by Regional Resources Ltd.; basis 1 cl. A com. sh. of Regional for 1 com. sh. of Logtung. (see Regional Resources Ltd.)

Loisan Red Lake Mines Limited (Ont. Nov. 23, 1945)
Oct. 1979 – Name changed to Grandview Energy Resources Incorporated. ■

Loki Gold Corporation (B.C. Feb. 4, 1982)
May 31, 1996 – Amalgamated with Baja Gold, Inc. to form VLB Resource Corporation which then was acquired by Viceroy Resource Corporation; basis 0.426 Viceroy shs. for 1 Loki sh.

Loki Mines Ltd. (Ont. 1944)
Feb. 1977 – Charter cancelled.

Loki Resources Inc. (Ont. 1983)
July 6, 1987 – Formed Mill City Gold Inc. in Canada on amalgamation with Mill City Gold Corp.; basis 1 new for 10 old shs. ■

Lollipop Daycare Ltd. (B.C. 1986)
Feb. 25, 1994 – Dissolved and struck off register.

Loma Petroleum Resources Ltd. (Alta. May 27, 1986)
Nov. 20, 1997 – Name changed to Loma Oil & Gas Ltd.; basis 1 new for 2 old shs. (see FPsurvey - Mines & Energy)

Loma Vista Capital Inc. (Ont. June 21, 2012)
Apr. 29, 2015 – Formed BitGold Inc. in Canada on amalgamation with (old) BitGold Inc.; basis 0.060659 new com. shs. for 1 old Loma Vista com. sh. and 1 new com. sh. for 1 old BitGold com. sh. ■

Lombard Consolidated Resources Inc. (Ont. Aug. 31, 1986)
Dec. 8, 1993 – Formed The Instant Publisher Inc. in Ontario on amalgamation with Instant Publisher Inc.,

constituting a reverse takeover by Instant Publisher; basis 1 new for 4 old shs. ■

Lombardi Media Corporation (Ont. July 13, 1987)
Sept. 17, 2007 – Privatized for 22¢ per sh.

Lomega Explorations Ltd. (Ont. 1935)
Jan. 1962 – Charter cancelled.

Lomega Gold Mines Ltd. (Ont. 1935)
1956 – Name changed to Lomega Explorations Ltd. ■

Lomico International Inc. (Alta. Nov. 5, 1987)
Jan. 17, 1996 – Name changed to JABA Inc.; basis 1 new for 3 old shs. ■

Lomiko Enterprises Ltd. (B.C. July 3, 1987)
July 28, 2006 – Name changed to Lomiko Resources Inc.; basis 1 new for 5 old shs. ■

Lomiko Resources Inc. (B.C. July 3, 1987)
Oct. 3, 2008 – Name changed to Lomiko Metals Inc.; basis 4 new for 1 old sh. (see FPsurvey - Mines & Energy; FPsurvey - Industrials)

Loncor Resources Inc. (Ont. Nov. 28, 2008 amalg.)
June 10, 2021 – Name changed to Loncor Gold Inc. (see FPsurvey - Mines & Energy)

Londinium Resources Inc. (B.C. May 14, 1980)
Nov. 22, 1983 – Name changed to Rockmaster Resources Ltd. ■

London Hill Mines Ltd. (B.C. 1950)
May 1957 – Charter cancelled.

London Hosiery Mills Ltd. (Can. 1915)
Jan. 1961 – Almer Co. Ltd., Preston, Ont., offered to purchase all cl. A shs. at $7.70 per sh. and all com. shs. at $3.00 a sh.

London Insurance Group Inc. (Can. May 30, 1990)
Jan. 9, 1998 – All o/s com. shs. acquired by Great-West Lifeco Inc. and The Great-West Life Assurance Company; basis $34 per sh. All o/s ser. A pfd. shs. redeemed Dec. 22, 1997, for $25 plus accr. and unpaid divds. All o/s ser. B pfd. shs. purchased for cancellation effective Dec. 31, 1997; basis $25 per sh. plus accr. and unpaid divds. All o/s ser. D pfd. shs. and ser. E pfd. shs. redeemed Dec. 31, 2002; basis $25 plus accr. and unpaid divds. (see The Great-West Life Assurance Company)
Jan. 1, 2020 – Amalgamated with The Great-West Life Assurance Company, wholly owned subsid. London Life Insurance Company and The Canada Life Assurance Company plus holding co. Canada Life Financial Corporation to continue as The Canada Life Assurance Company. (see The Great-West Life Assurance Company)

London Oil Company, Limited (Ont. 1918)
1958 – Wound up.

London Pride Silver Mines Ltd. (B.C. Mar. 5, 1962)
Aug. 23, 1973 – Name changed to L.P. Industries Ltd.; basis 1 new for 5 old shs. ■

London Strauss Capital Corp. (Ont. Apr. 29, 1980)
Oct. 10, 1996 – Name changed to Viking Gold Corporation. ■

London Union Oil Co. Ltd. (unknown 1914)
Taken over by Royalite Oil Company, Limited; basis 1 new for 232.5 old shs. (see Royalite Oil Company, Limited)

Londonderrie Trail Inc. (Alta. Nov. 6, 2000)
Oct. 2, 2002 – Name changed to Mosaic Mapping Corporation following Qualifying Transaction reverse takeover acquisition of Mosaic Mapping Systems Inc. ■

Lone Creek Mines Ltd. (Alta. 1969)
Dec. 28, 1979 – Amalgamated with Kraus Oil Limited, to form LCM Resources Ltd.; basis 1 new for 10 old shs.

Lone Jack Resources Ltd. (B.C. July 11, 1983)
Feb. 14, 1989 – Name changed to Performance Minerals of Canada Ltd. (see FPsurvey - Mines & Energy)

Lone Mountain Federated Gas & Oil Ltd. (B.C. 1951)
1974 – Reported its registration had lapsed.

Lone Mountain Oil Development Co. Ltd. (B.C.)
1952 – Placed into voluntary liquidation.

Lone Pine Resource Exploration Limited (Ont. 1978)
Sept. 15, 1983 – Name changed to M.S.M. Marketing Ltd.; basis 1 new for 6 old shs. ■

Lone Rock Oils Ltd. (Alta. Jan. 16, 1947)
May 20, 1952 – Assets sold to Inter-Rock Oil Company of Canada Limited; basis 1 new for 5 old shs.

Lone Star Exploration NL (S.A. Aug. 26, 1970)
Aug. 24, 1998 – Name changed to Masmindo Mining Corporation NL; basis 1 new for 10 old shs.

Lone Star Mines Ltd. (B.C. May 26, 1978)
May 13, 1980 – Name changed to Jupitor Mines Limited. ■

Lone Star Petroleum Corporation (B.C. 1980)
Oct. 26, 1983 – Name changed to Lone Star Resource Corporation.

Lone Star Resource Corporation (B.C. 1980)
Aug. 26, 1986 – Name changed to Consolidated Lone Star Resource Corporation. ■

Lonestar Capital Corp. (B.C. Oct. 25, 2007)
May 29, 2009 – Name changed to Acro Energy Technologies Corp. ■

Lonestar West Inc. (Can. June 5, 2008)
July 19, 2017 – Acquired by Clean Harbors, Inc.; basis Cdn$0.72 cash per sh.

Lonetree Resources Ltd. (Alta. May 3, 1984)
Aug. 9, 1993 – Name changed to Columbia Yukon Resources Ltd.; basis 1 new for 3 old shs. ■

Long Bay Gold Mines Ltd. (Ont. 1947)
Apr. 29, 1965 – Dissolved.

Long Harbour Capital Corp. (B.C. Apr. 26, 2004)
June 9, 2011 – Name changed to Long Harbour Exploration Corp. pursuant to acquisition of Madison uranium prospect. ■

Long Harbour Exploration Corp. (B.C. Apr. 26, 2004)
Oct. 16, 2015 – Name changed to Lancaster Capital Corp. ■

Long Island Petroleums Ltd. (Alta. Jan. 10, 1949)
Jan. 26, 1962 – Name changed to Canadian Long Island Petroleums Ltd.; basis 1 new for 5.5 old shs. ■

Long Lac Minerals Ltd. (Que. 1981 amalg.)
Dec. 31, 1982 – Formed LAC Minerals Ltd. in Ontario on amalgamation with Les Terrains Aurifères Malartic (Québec) Ltée, Les Mines-Est Malartic Ltée and Willroy Mines Limited; basis 0.84 new for 1 Les Terrains Aurifères Malartic sh., 0.94 new for 1 Les Mines-Est Malartic sh., 1.24 new for 1 Willroy sh. and 1 new for 1 Long Lac sh. ■

Long Point Gas & Oil Incorporated (Ont. 1973)
Nov. 22, 1974 – Amalgamated with Foxdale Mines Limited (1 for 7.5), Canton Explorations Limited (1 for 5.5), Marquis Explorations Limited (1 for 2.5), Darwin Mines Limited (1 for 1.5), Gold Acres Mines Limited (1 for 7), Home Mining Developments Limited (1 for 7) and Force Crag Mines Limited (1 for 4.5) to form New Force Crag Mines Ltd.; basis 1 new for 3 old shs.

Long Point Gas & Oil Ltd. (Ont. 1957)
1964 – Assets sold to Consolidated West Petroleum Ltd.; basis 1 new for 17.5 old shs.

Long Range Resources Ltd. (Alta. 1988)
Nov. 16, 1992 – Name changed to Sport Specific International Inc. (see FPsurvey - Industrials)

Long Reserve Life Resource Fund (Ont. May 18, 2006)
June 8, 2010 – Name changed to Navina Global Resource Fund. ∎

Long Ridge Uranium Mines Ltd. (Ont. 1955)
Nov. 1979 – Wound up.

Long Run Exploration Ltd. (Alta. Sept. 14, 1999)
July 6, 2016 – Acquired by Calgary Sinoenergy Investment Corp. for 52¢ per sh.

Long View Resources Corporation (Alta. Nov. 3, 2004)
June 18, 2007 – Amalgamated with Reece Energy Exploration Corp.; basis 1 Reece com. sh. for 4 Long View com. shs. (see Reece Energy Exploration Corp.)

Longacre Long Lac Gold Mines Ltd. (Ont. Apr. 4, 1934)
1959 – Wound up.
Apr. 29, 1965 – Charter cancelled.

Longacre Resources Inc. (B.C. Apr. 13, 2011)
Oct. 6, 2015 – Name changed to Golden Leaf Holdings Ltd. and continued into Ontario. ∎

Longboat Capital Corp. (Alta. Oct. 4, 1996)
June 13, 2001 – Name changed to YMG Ventures Inc. following Qualifying Transaction reverse takeover acquisition by YMG Ventures Corp.; basis 1 new for 1.5 old shs. ∎

Longboat Resources Inc. (B.C. Apr. 28, 1983)
Sept. 27, 1991 – Dissolved and struck off register.

LongBow Energy Corp. (Alta. May 30, 2000)
Apr. 11, 2007 – Name changed to LongBow Resources Inc.; basis 1 new for 10 old shs. ∎

LongBow Resources Inc. (Alta. May 30, 2000)
June 20, 2008 – Acquired by TriAxon Resources Ltd. for 70¢ per sh.

Longford Corporation (Ont. Mar. 24, 2004)
Dec. 24, 2007 – Name changed to Longford Energy Inc.; basis 1 new for 10 old shs. ∎

Longford Energy Inc. (Ont. Mar. 24, 2004)
June 24, 2013 – Name changed to UrtheCast Corp. following reverse takeover acquisition of Earth Video Camera Inc.; basis 1 new for 13.4097 old shs. ∎

Longford Equipment International Limited (Ont. 1970)
Mar. 25, 1990 – All o/s com. shs. consolidated on the basis of 1 new for 40,000 old. Shldrs. were subsequently paid $0.82 per sh; co. now private.

Longhorn Exploration Corp. (B.C. Apr. 27, 2021)
Nov. 21, 2024 – Name changed to PureWave Hydrogen Corp. (see FPsurvey - Mines & Energy)

Longold Resources Inc. (B.C. Jan. 26, 1987)
Mar. 9, 1993 – Name changed to Cascadia Technologies Ltd.; basis 1 new for 3.4 old shs. ∎

Longreach Oil and Gas Limited (Jersey Aug. 13, 2010)
July 14, 2014 – Name changed to PetroMaroc Corporation PLC. ∎

Longreach Resources Ltd. (B.C. 1983)
Aug. 14, 1992 – Dissolved and struck off register.

Longrose Gold Mines Ltd. (Ont. 1947)
Nov. 9, 1964 – Charter cancelled.

Longview Capital Partners Incorporated (B.C. May 25, 2004)
Nov. 30, 2009 – Name changed to Resinco Capital Partners Inc. ∎

Longview Oil Corp. (Alta. Mar. 4, 2010)
June 5, 2014 – Acquired by Surge Energy Inc.; basis 0.975 Surge com. shs. for 1 Longview com. sh.

Longview Petroleum Corporation (Alta. Dec. 16, 1999)
Oct. 28, 2002 – Name changed to Rival Energy Inc.; basis 1 new for 6 old shs. ∎

Longview Resources Inc. (Alta. Nov. 13, 1984)
Feb. 15, 1990 – Name changed to Olympia Energy Inc. ∎

Longview Strategies Incorporated (B.C. May 25, 2004)
Oct. 25, 2006 – Name changed to Longview Capital Partners Incorporated. ∎

Lonrho Exploration Ltd. (B.C. 1969)
Jan. 1975 – Charter cancelled.

Lonsdale Public Ventures Inc. (Ont. Sept. 17, 2004)
Mar. 15, 2006 – Formed Cannasat Therapeutics Inc. in Canada on Qualifying Transaction amalgamation with Cannasat Therapeutics Inc., constituting a reverse takeover by Cannasat; basis 1 new for 1.194 old shs. ∎

Lonvest Corporation (Ont. May 20, 1977)
May 30, 1990 – Continued into Canada.
June 18, 1990 – Name changed to London Insurance Group Inc. ∎

Look Communications Inc. (Can. Oct. 31, 1999 amalg.)
July 12, 2013 – Name changed to ONEnergy Inc. ∎

Looking Glass Labs Ltd. (B.C. June 19, 2015)
Feb. 29, 2024 – Name changed to Metasphere Labs Inc. (see FPsurvey - Industrials)

Lookout Mountain Mines Ltd. (Ont. 1952)
Nov. 9, 1964 – Charter cancelled.

Loon Energy Corporation (Alta. Oct. 30, 2008)
Jan. 5, 2022 – Continued into Ontario.
July 27, 2022 – Name changed to Optimind Pharma Corp. pursuant to the reverse takeover acquisition of Optimind Pharma Inc. and concurrent amalgamation of (old) Optimind with wholly owned 1000033135 Ontario Inc.; basis 1 new for 1.713084 old shs. (see FPsurvey - Industrials)

Loon Energy Inc. (Alta. Mar. 16, 1987)
Dec. 10, 2008 – Succeeded by Loon Energy Corporation following plan of arrangement reorganization and transfer of assets in Colombia and Peru and US$3,000,000 to newly incorporated Loon Energy Corporation. Assets held in Brunei, Syria and Slovenia remained with Loon Energy Inc. which changed its name to Kulczyk Oil Ventures Inc. and delisted from the TSX-Venture Exchange. ∎

Loop Energy Inc. (B.C. Aug. 9, 2012)
Nov. 1, 2024 – Pursuant to a reverse vesting order under the Bankruptcy and Insolvency Act the majority of the company's assets acquired by Teralta Hydrogen Solutions Inc. All o/s shs. were cancelled and terminated without consideration.

Loop Insights Inc. (B.C. June 12, 2019 amalg.)
June 4, 2021 – Name changed to Fobi AI Inc. (see FPsurvey - Industrials)

Lorado Uranium Mines Ltd. (Ont. 1952)
1968 – Merged into International Mogul Mines Ltd.; basis 10 new for 89 old shs.

Loranda Uranium Mines Ltd. (Sask. 1955)
Jan. 1957 – Merged into Westore Mines Ltd.; basis 1 new for 3 old shs.

Lord River Gold Mines Limited (B.C. Feb. 15, 1971)
July 2, 1992 – Name changed to Aquamin Resources Inc.; basis 1 new for 4 old shs. ∎

Lord Simcoe Hotel Limited (Ont. 1955)
June 28, 1989 – Final distribution after initial distribution of $1.75 per sh.
Dec. 7, 1989 – Wound up.

Lord's Chemists Limited (Ont. 1960)
Apr. 10, 1974 – Placed into bankruptcy.
Mar. 16, 1977 – Two payments totaling 34.857% of claims o/s were pd. to unsecured creditors and debs. holders.

No further recoveries for creditors. Trustee discharged and bankrupt estate finalized.

Loredi Resources Ltd. (B.C. 1967)
Apr. 23, 1986 – Name changed to Marlin Developments Ltd.; basis 1 new for 5 old shs. ∎

Lorena Mines Ltd. (B.C. 1971)
Sept. 2, 1983 – Struck off register.

Lorex Minerals Inc. (B.C. Mar. 20, 1989)
Dec. 1, 2003 – Name changed to Alinghi Minerals Inc.; basis 1 new for 4 old shs. ∎

Lori Explorations Ltd. (B.C. 1968)
Aug. 1978 – Name changed to O'Lori Holdings Ltd.; basis 1 new for 2 old shs. ∎

Lorian Capital Corp. (Can. July 17, 2006)
Dec. 17, 2007 – Name changed to Medworxx Solutions Inc. following Qualifying Transaction acquisition of Medworxx Inc. ∎

Lorica Resources Ltd. (B.C. May 20, 1988)
Aug. 18, 1999 – Name changed to LOM River Gold Corporation; basis 1 new for 3 old shs. ∎

Lorie Mines Ltd. (Ont. 1945)
Aug. 1950 – Name changed to New Lorie Mines Ltd.; basis 1 new for 1 old sh. ∎

Lorie Resources Inc. (Ont. 1945)
Dec. 18, 1986 – Name changed to Theme Restaurants Incorporated; basis 1 new for 2 old shs. (see FPsurvey - Industrials)

Loring Ward International Ltd. (Can. Nov. 18, 2002)
Jan. 27, 2009 – Acquired by Werba Reinhard, Inc. for US$11.25 per com. sh.

Lormac Explorations Limited (Ont. Oct. 5, 1965)
1986 – Name changed to Canlorm Resources Inc.; basis 1 new for 3 old shs. ∎

Lornco Explorations Ltd. (Ont. 1968)
Feb. 17, 1981 – Charter cancelled.

Lorne Crest Developments Ltd. (Ont. 1955)
1969 – Amalgamated to form Beaver Engineering Ltd.

Lorne Gold Mines Ltd. (B.C. 1928)
1931 – Acquired by Bralorne Mines Ltd.; basis 1 new for 8 old shs.

Lorne Trail Holdings Ltd. (Can. 1987)
Aug. 13, 1990 – Name changed to Brake Check Canada Inc. ∎

Lornex Capital Inc. (Can. July 26, 2000)
Jan. 30, 2016 – Continued into British Columbia.
Feb. 16, 2016 – Name changed to Norsemont Capital Inc. ∎

Lornex Mining Corporation Ltd. (B.C. 1964)
Dec. 30, 1988 – Amalgamated with Rio Algom Limited. (see Rio Algom Limited)

Lorraine Copper Corp. (B.C. Oct. 23, 2007)
Apr. 15, 2019 – Acquired by Sun Metals Corp. and subsequently amalgamated with a wholly owned subsid. of Sun Metals; basis 0.54 Sun Metals com. shs. for 1 Lorraine Copper sh. (see Sun Metals Corp.)

Lorraine Explorations Ltd. (B.C. 1971)
Mar. 1973 – Amalgamated with Legend Explorations Ltd. (1 for 2.95) to continue to be known as Legend Explorations Ltd.; basis 1 new Legend sh. for 5.41 Lorraine shs.

Lorus Therapeutics Inc. (Ont. Oct. 28, 1991 amalg.)
Oct. 1, 2005 – Continued into Canada.
July 10, 2007 – Formed 4325231 Canada Inc. in British Columbia on amalgamation of (old) Lorus Therapeutics Inc. whereby all of its assets, liabs. and shs. of the subsid.

were spun out into a new company Lorus Therapeutics Inc. ■

Lorus Therapeutics Inc. (Can. Nov. 1, 2006)
Aug. 28, 2014 – Name changed to Aptose Biosciences Inc. (see FPsurvey - Industrials)

Lorwells Mines Ltd. (Ont. 1952)
Feb. 4, 1970 – Charter cancelled.

Los Angeles Alberta Petroleum Ltd. (Alta. 1951)
Sept. 15, 1965 – Struck off register.

Los Gauchos Capital Corp. (Alta. Nov. 1, 1996)
Sept. 22, 1997 – Name changed to Service Track Enterprises Inc.; basis 1 new for 1 old sh. (see FPsurvey - Industrials)

Lost Lake Resources Ltd. (B.C. Mar. 19, 1984)
Apr. 29, 1985 – Name changed to Equivest International Financial Corp. ■

Lost River Mining Corporation Limited (Ont. 1970)
1980 – Declared bankrupt.
Feb. 5, 1984 – Settlement agreement made for the sale of assets and distribution of shs. of a new co. to various creditors. No distribution made to existing shldrs.

Lotus Cosmetics International Limited (B.C. 1983)
Mar. 27, 1989 – Name changed to Creative Products Inc.; basis 1 new for 2 old shs. ■

Lotus Resources Limited (N.S. Feb. 13, 1987)
Aug. 2, 1990 – Name changed to Ashgrove Resources Limited. ■

Lotus Ventures Inc. (B.C. Nov. 27, 2014 amalg.)
Aug. 21, 2024 – Pursuant to a reverse-vesting transaction under the Bankruptcy and Insolvency Act (BIA), 1,000 com. shs. were issued to 5008679 Ontario Limited with a deemed value of $2,538,398, resulting in 5008679 Ontario becoming the sole shldr. of the company. All issued and o/s com. shs. were cancelled without consideration.

Lou-Mac Mines Limited (B.C. June 15, 1970)
Feb. 16, 1971 – Name changed to Lou-Mex Mines Limited. ■

Lou-Mex Mines Limited (B.C. June 15, 1970)
Mar. 7, 1977 – Name changed to Continental Minerals Corporation; basis 1 new for 4 old shs. ■

Louada Exploration & Development Co. Ltd. (Ont. 1964)
Feb. 1976 – Charter cancelled.

Louanna Gold Mines Ltd. (Ont. 1963)
Dec. 1972 – Name changed to Consolidated Louanna Gold Mines Ltd.; basis 1 new for 4 old shs. ■

Loubac Top Environmental Inc. (Can. Apr. 20, 1998)
Mar. 20, 2009 – Name changed to Novus Gold Corp. and continued into British Columbia. ■

Loubel Exploration Inc. (Que. Apr. 29, 1953)
Apr. 17, 2006 – Name changed to Lounor Exploration Inc.; basis 1 new for 10 old shs. ■

Louder Financial Group Inc. (Alta. 1986)
Jan. 1, 1991 – Struck off register.

Lougan Investments Inc. (Alta. 1987)
Nov. 20, 1990 – Name changed to Shearhart Corporation; basis 1 new for 2 old shs. ■

Loughborough Gold Mines Ltd. (B.C. 1936)
Feb. 1949 – Dissolved.

Loumic Exploration Inc. (Ont. Oct. 2, 1987)
Nov. 1, 2004 – Name changed to Vast Exploration Inc.; basis 1 new for 10 old shs. ■

Loumic Resources Ltd. (Ont. Oct. 2, 1987)
Apr. 14, 1998 – Name changed to International Loumic Resources Ltd.; basis 1 new for 10 old shs. ■

Lounge Fashion Clothes Ltd. (Can. - unspecified)
Mar. 1969 – Acquired by Fields Stores Limited for $320,000. (see Fields Stores Limited)

Lounor Exploration Inc. (Que. Apr. 29, 1953)
Sept. 26, 2019 – Voluntarily dissolved.

Lourmet Mines Ltd. (Que. 1940)
1950 – Charter cancelled.

Louvem Mines Inc. (Que. Oct. 31, 1969)
July 7, 2010 – Amalgamated with 9222-0383 Québec Inc., a wholly owned subsid. of Richmont Mining Inc.; basis 1 Richmont sh. for 5.4 Louvem shs. (see Richmont Mines Inc.)

Louvibec Mines Ltd. (Ont. 1945)
Mar. 11, 1975 – Charter cancelled.

Louvicourt Goldfield Corp. (Que. 1944)
June 16, 1981 – Name changed to Louvicourt Gold Mines Inc. (see FPsurvey - Mines & Energy)

Louvre Gold Mines Ltd. (Que. 1934)
1945 – Name changed to New Louvre Mines Ltd. and continued into Quebec; basis 1 new for 3 old shs. ■

Love Pharma Inc. (B.C. Sept. 20, 2021)
May 26, 2023 – Name changed to Jolt Health Inc. (see FPsurvey - Industrials)

Lovitt Nutriceutical Corporation (B.C. Jan. 31, 1980)
Sept. 10, 2008 – Name changed to Lovitt Resources Inc. (see FPsurvey - Mines & Energy)

Low Volatility Canadian Equities Income Fund (Ont. Jan. 25, 2012)
Dec. 20, 2017 – Name changed to Redwood Low Volatility High Income Fund. ■

Low Volatility U.S. Equity Income Fund (Ont. Feb. 26, 2013)
Nov. 15, 2019 – Merged into Mulvihill Premium Yield Fund; basis 0.50217 Mulvihill cl. F units for 1 Low Volatility trust unit.

Lowell Copper Ltd. (B.C. Mar. 23, 2007)
Oct. 7, 2016 – Name changed to JDL Gold Corp. following acquisition of Anthem United Inc. (0.774 new for 1 old) and Gold Mountain Mining Corporation (1.032 new for 1 old); basis 1 new for 6.45 old shs. ■

Lowell Petroleum Inc. (Can. Sept. 25, 1995)
Aug. 17, 1998 – Name changed to Hedong Energy Inc.; basis 1 new for 10 old shs. ■

Lowell Porcupine Gold Mines Ltd. (Ont. 1940)
1952 – Charter cancelled.

Lower Canada Gold Mines Ltd. (Ont. 1938)
Nov. 30, 1964 – Dissolved.

Lower St. Lawrence Power Co. (Que. 1922)
1953 – Purch. by Hydro-Québec. Com. shldrs. got $37 per sh.; pref. shldrs. got equal par value in 10-year bds. guaranteed by Prov. of Quebec, bearing int. equal to divd. rate. Funded debt assumed by Quebec Hydro, with guarantee by Prov. of Quebec. Settlement for any remaining pref. shs. may be received from Administration and Trust Co., 10 St. James St. W., Montreal.

Lower St. Lawrence Realty Corp. (Que. 1950)
Apr. 2, 1963 – Placed into bankruptcy. Trustee: P. A. Lawrence, 630 Dorchester Blvd. West, Montreal.

Lower Valley Mines Ltd. (B.C. July 21, 1966)
May 31, 1974 – Name changed to Groton Minerals Limited; basis 1 new for 5 old shs. ■

Lowery Petroleums Ltd. (Can. Mar. 1929)
1950 – Assets sold to Federated Petroleums Ltd. for $750,000. Distribution of 75¢ per sh.

Lowhee Mining Co. Ltd. (B.C. 1929)
Mar. 1975 – Charter cancelled.

Loyalist Group Limited (Alta. Sept. 20, 1996)
Sept. 30, 2015 – Name changed to KGIC Inc. ■

The Loyalist Insurance Group Limited (Alta. Sept. 20, 1996)
June 24, 2010 – Name changed to Loyalist Group Limited. ■

Loyalist Mines Limited (N.B. 1957)
Mar. 1972 – Assets sold to Proto Explorations & Holdings Inc.; basis 1 new for 12 old shs. ■

Loyalist Resources Ltd. (B.C. 1983)
Jan. 2, 1985 – Name changed to I.B.S. Technologies Ltd.; basis 1 new for 1 old sh. ■

Luaaron Metals Ltd. (B.C. Dec. 2, 1965)
July 10, 1981 – Name changed to Lynx Resources Ltd. ■

Lubec Lead Mines Ltd. (Ont. 1959)
Sept. 17, 1994 – Dissolved.

Lubicon Mining Ltd. (B.C. 1967)
Name changed to Lubicon Petroleum & Mining Ltd. in 1972. ■

Lubicon Petroleum & Mining Ltd. (B.C. 1967)
1972 – Acquired by Alberta Petroleum & Resources Ltd.; basis 1 new for 10 old shs.

Lubricon Petroleums Corp. Ltd. (Ont. 1950)
1952 – Acquired by Scarlet Oils Ltd.; basis 1 new for 1.5 old shs. (see Scarlet Oils Limited)

Luca Capital Inc. (Alta. May 4, 2005)
Sept. 18, 2007 – Continued into Canada.
Sept. 26, 2007 – Name changed to VentriPoint Diagnostics Ltd. (see FPsurvey - Industrials)

Lucas Gold Resources Corp. (Ont. 1986)
Dec. 19, 1996 – Formed Altaur Gold Explorations Inc. in Ontario on amalgamation with Seven Gold Explorations Inc. (deemed acquiror); basis 1 new for 1 Seven Gold sh. and 1 new for 6 Lucas shs. ■

Lucayan Beach Hotel Co. Ltd. (Bahamas 1963)
Jan. 18, 1965 – Name changed to Lucayan Beach Hotel and Development, Ltd.

Lucero Energy Corp. (Alta. July 1, 1998 amalg.)
Mar. 11, 2025 – Acquired by Vitesse Energy, Inc.; basis 0.01239 Vitesse com. shs. for 1 Lucero sh.

Lucero Resource Corp. (B.C. Dec. 12, 1985)
July 19, 2001 – Name changed to C Squared Developments Inc.; basis 1 new for 10 old shs. ■

Lucid Entertainment Inc. (B.C. Mar. 28, 1979)
Feb. 4, 2008 – Dissolved and struck from register.

Lucille Yellowknife Mines Ltd. (Ont. 1945)
1952 – Charter cancelled.

Luckridge Phosphate Mines Ltd. (Ont. 1945)
Oct. 1978 – Charter cancelled.
July 1979 – Charter revived.
Nov. 26, 1994 – Dissolved and struck off register.

Lucky Boy Mines Incorporated (B.C. Sept. 17, 1984)
Nov. 29, 1988 – Name changed to Dundarave Resources Incorporated. ■

Lucky Break Gold Inc. (Alta. Mar. 10, 1987)
Mar. 2, 1998 – Delisted the Vancouver Stock Exchange. Subsequently dissolved for failure to file and struck from registry.

Lucky Creek Mining Co. Ltd. (Ont. 1956)
June 21, 1972 – Dissolved.

Lucky Friday Exploration Co. Ltd. (Ont.)
1968 – Charter cancelled.

Lucky Girl Mines Ltd. (Ont. 1947)
Aug. 1958 – Dissolved.

Lucky Kirkland Gold Mines Ltd. (Ont. Apr. 6, 1934)
1946 – Acquired by Baldwin Consolidated Mines Ltd.;
basis 1 Baldwin sh. for 20 Lucky shs. Charter
surrendered.

Lucky Lager Breweries Ltd. (Can. 1928)
1958 – John Labatt Limited offered to purch. all o/s com.
for $5.25 per sh.; 99.75% owned.
1967 – Name changed to Labatt Breweries of British
Columbia Limited. ■

Lucky Lager Breweries (1954) Ltd. (Can. 1928)
Nov. 25, 1957 – Name changed to Lucky Lager Breweries
Ltd. ■

Lucky Lake Mine Ltd. (N.B. 1956)
Nov. 1972 – Charter cancelled.

Lucky 1 Enterprises Inc. (B.C. Aug. 24, 1984)
Jan. 17, 2005 – Name changed to Bronx Ventures Inc.;
basis 1 new for 35 old shs. ■

Lucky 7 Exploration Ltd. (B.C. Sept. 11, 1986)
Jan. 31, 1995 – Name changed to Brett Resources Inc. ■

Lucky Strike Gold Mining Co. Ltd. (B.C. 1936)
1948 – Dissolved.

Lucky Strike Mines Ltd. (B.C. June 26, 1962)
June 23, 1980 – Name changed to Lucky Strike
Resources Ltd. ■

Lucky Strike Resources Ltd. (B.C. June 26, 1962)
Feb. 18, 2015 – Name changed to Rojo Resources Ltd.;
basis 1 new for 8 old shs. ■

Lucky Torrie Mines Ltd. (B.C. 1960)
July 1960 – Name changed to American Pacific
Exploration Ltd. ■

Luckystrike Resources Ltd. (B.C. Jan. 10, 2018)
Feb. 27, 2020 – Name changed to Golden Sky Minerals
Corp. (see FPsurvey - Mines & Energy)

Lucre Ventures Ltd. (B.C. May 15, 1998)
Sept. 5, 2001 – Name changed to Strathclair Ventures
Ltd.; basis 1 new for 6.5 old shs. ■

Lucro Capital Ltd. (Can. Aug. 11, 1995)
Aug. 16, 1996 – Name changed to Intrepid Minerals
Corporation following Major Transaction. ■

Lucrum Capital Corp. (B.C. Mar. 1, 2007)
Dec. 17, 2008 – Name changed to Sheltered Oak
Resources Corp. ■

Luff Enterprises Ltd. (B.C. Aug. 9, 2018 amalg.)
Jan. 20, 2023 – Name changed to Herbal Dispatch Inc.
(see FPsurvey - Industrials)

Lugano Resources Ltd. (B.C. 1981)
Apr. 16, 1986 – Name changed to Ethicorp Resources
Limited and continued into Alberta; basis 1 new for 2 old
shs. ■

Luiri Gold Limited (B.C. Feb. 3, 2004)
Sept. 14, 2012 – Continued into Bermuda.

Luke Energy Ltd. (Can. Jan. 9, 2003)
Mar. 17, 2006 – Plan of Arrangement with 6492894
Canada Inc. and Connacher Oil and Gas Limited; basis
$2.31 and 0.75 new Connacher sh. for 1 old Luke sh.
(see Connacher Oil and Gas Limited)

Luken Resources Ltd. (B.C. 1987)
Oct. 15, 1992 – Formed IVS Intelligent Vehicle Systems
Inc. on amalgamation with IVS Intelligent Vehicle Systems
Inc.; basis 1 new for 1 old sh. ■

Lumax Oil & Gas Inc. (Ont. 1955)
Apr. 28, 1989 – Name changed to First Munich Capital
Ltd.; basis 1 new for 5 old shs. ■

Lumby Resources Corporation (B.C. May 28, 1993)
Oct. 1, 1996 – Name changed to Rock Resources Inc. ■

Lumenpulse Group Inc. (Can. July 1, 2011)
June 23, 2017 – Amalgamated with 1091051 Canada
Inc., a wholly owned subsid. of Power Energy
Corporation: basis $21.25 cash per sh.
July 1, 2019 – Amalgamated in Canada to continue with
same name.
May 3, 2021 – Name changed to LMPG Inc.

Lumenpulse Inc. (Can. July 1, 2011)
June 21, 2017 – Name changed to Lumenpulse Group
Inc. ■

Lumex Capital Corp. (B.C. Jan. 9, 2007)
Nov. 3, 2009 – Amalgamated with Ausex Capital Corp.
and Tasman Metals Ltd. (deemed acquiror) to form new
co. also named Tasman Metals Ltd. constituting a
Qualifying Transaction; basis 1 new for 1 Ausex sh., 1
new for 1 Tasman sh. and 1.0806 new for 1 Lumex sh.
(see Tasman Metals Ltd.)

Lumina Copper Corp. (B.C. Mar. 3, 2000)
May 19, 2005 – Name changed to Regalito Copper Corp.
following reorganization whereby certain assets were
spun out into 3 new companies named Global Copper
Corp. (1 for 1), Lumina Resources Corp. (1 for 1) and
Northern Peru Copper Corp. (1 for 1). ■

Lumina Copper Corp. (B.C. May 12, 2008)
Aug. 22, 2014 – Acquired by First Quantum Minerals Ltd.;
basis a) 0.2174 First Quantum com. shs. and $5 cash;
or b) 0.2724 First Quantum com. shs. and $3.75 cash;
or c) $10 cash per Lumina Copper com. sh.

Lumina Gold Corp. (B.C. Mar. 22, 1988)
June 26, 2025 – Acquired by CMOC Singapore Pte. Ltd.;
basis Cdn$1.27 cash per sh.

Lumina Investment Corp. (B.C. Mar. 2, 1981)
Dec. 2, 1996 – Name changed to Latitude Minerals Corp.;
basis 1 new for 5 old shs. ■

Lumina Resources Corp (B.C. Feb. 28, 2005)
Dec. 5, 2006 – Plan of Arrangement acquisition by
Western Copper Corporation; basis 1 new Western
Copper sh. for 1 old Lumina sh. (see Western Copper
Corporation)

Luminart Inc. (Ont. 1967)
Apr. 28, 1998 – Acquired; details not known.

Luminex Resources Corp. (B.C. Mar. 16, 2018)
Jan. 30, 2024 – Acquired by Adventus Mining
Corporation; basis 0.67 Adventus shs. for 1 Luminex sh.
(see Adventus Mining Corporation)

Luminex Ventures Inc. (B.C. Sept. 27, 1979)
June 12, 2002 – Name changed to Lateegra Resources
Corp.; basis 1 new for 6 old shs. ■

Luminor Medical Technologies Inc. (Can. Nov. 16,
2000)
Mar. 14, 2018 – Name changed to RISE Life Science
Corp. ■

Lumonics Inc. (Ont. Nov. 26, 1970)
Mar. 22, 1999 – Name changed to GSI Lumonics Inc.
and continued into New Brunswick pursuant to merger
of equals with General Scanning Inc. with Lumonics the
deemed acquiror. ■

Lun-Echo Gold Mines Ltd. (Ont. 1950)
Mar. 1971 – Name changed to Lundor Mines Ltd.; basis
1 new for 5 old shs. ■

Lun-Mat Mines Ltd. (Ont. 1959)
Nov. 4, 1970 – Charter cancelled.

Luna d'Or Mines Ltd. (Ont. 1936)
Dec. 9, 1957 – Dissolved.

Luna Gas Ltd. (Alta. July 26, 1947)
Apr. 1953 – Name changed to Propane Credit Corp.
Ltd. ■

Luna Gold Corp. (Wyo. July 14, 1999)
Nov. 24, 2005 – Continued into Canada. (see Trek Mining
Inc.)
Apr. 4, 2017 – Acquired by JDL Gold Corp. (subsequently
renamed Trek Mining Inc.); basis 1.105 JDL com. shs.
for 1 Luna sh. (see Trek Mining Inc.)

Luna Mines Ltd. (B.C. 1969)
Oct. 1974 – Charter cancelled.

Lunco Resources Ltd. (B.C. Aug. 27, 1979)
Dec. 7, 1979 – Name changed to Atlantic Ventures Ltd. ■

Lund Enterprises Corp. (B.C. June 22, 1978)
Aug. 29, 2019 – Name changed to Reconnaissance
Energy Africa Ltd. pursuant to the reverse takeover
acquisition of 1163531 B.C. Ltd.; basis 1 new for 2 old
shs. (see FPsurvey - Mines & Energy)

Lund Gold Ltd. (B.C. June 22, 1978)
Dec. 19, 2013 – Name changed to Lund Enterprises
Corp.; basis 1 new for 10 old shs. ■

Lund Ventures Ltd. (B.C. June 22, 1978)
July 10, 2003 – Name changed to Lund Gold Ltd.; basis
1 new for 2 old shs. ■

Lunday Yellowknife Mines Ltd. (Ont. 1945)
May 29, 1952 – Charter cancelled.

Lundberg Explorations Ltd. (Ont. 1956)
1961 – Liquidated in 1961-62.

Lundin Explorations Ltd. (B.C. 1981)
June 1, 1991 – Wound up. Creditors paid in full and
shldrs. to receive a share of $205,000 in cash, 6,828,556
shs. of International Petroleum Corporation plus 205,000
warrants.

Lundor Mines Ltd. (Ont. 1950)
Placed into liquidation. Liquidator Canada Permanent
Trust Co.

Lundy Petroleums Ltd. (Can. May 25, 1929)
Control acquired by Albertan Federated Oils Ltd. (see
Albertan Federated Oils, Ltd.)

Lunel Enterprises Inc. (Ont. Jan. 23, 1979 amalg.)
July 15, 1989 – Amalgamated with First Ontario Capital
Inc. to form a new co. also known as First Ontario Capital
Inc.; basis 1 cl. C sh. for 2 com. shs. and 1 new cl. D sh.
for 1 cl. A sh. (see First Ontario Capital Inc.)

Lunel Management Ltd. (unknown)
Jan. 23, 1979 – Amalgamated with Glenshire Mines Ltd.
(231 for 1,000), Huddersfield Uranium Mines Ltd. (129
for 1,000), Kayak Explorations Ltd. (195 for 1,000), La
France Explorations Ltd. (128 for 1,000), Sandhurst Mines
Ltd. (1 for 1) and Steppingstone Explorations Ltd. (229
for 1,000) to form Lunel Enterprises Inc.; basis 923.5 new
for 1 old sh. (see Lunel Enterprises Inc.)

Lunenberg Sea Products Ltd. (Can. - unspecified)
Mar. 1, 1967 – Amalgamated to form National Sea
Products Ltd. (see National Sea Products Limited)

Lunward Gold Mines Ltd. (Ont. 1941)
Sept. 1949 – Charter cancelled in 1949. Property taken
over by Newlund Mines Ltd.; basis 1 new for 2 old shs.
Cash and other assets transferred to Warlund Mines Ltd.
on a 1-for-10 basis.

Luscar Coal Income Fund (Alta. Apr. 15, 1996)
June 29, 2001 – Acquired by Sherritt Coal Partnership
and Sherritt International Corporation; basis $4.00, or 1
new Sherritt International restricted voting sh., or a
combination thereof for 1 old Luscar sh.
Apr. 30, 2006 – Name changed to Royal Utilities Income
Fund. ■

Luscar Oil and Gas Ltd. (Alta. Oct. 21, 1993)
Aug. 8, 1994 – Acquired by Encal Energy Ltd.; basis 1 Encal sh. for 2.65 Luscar shs. (see Encal Energy Ltd.)

Lustre Gold Mines Inc. (B.C. 1975)
Mar. 30, 1979 – Name changed to Lustre Resources Inc. ■

Lustre Resources Inc. (B.C. 1975)
Feb. 14, 1986 – Struck off register.

Lustre Yukon Mines Ltd. (Ont. 1949)
Charter cancelled.

Luxell Technologies Inc. (Ont. Dec. 1, 1994 amalg.)
May 14, 2009 – Privatized at 10¢ per sh.

Luxmar Resources Inc. (Ont. 1981)
Sept. 3, 1994 – Dissolved.

Luxmatic Technologies N.V. (Netherlands June 1, 1993)
Nov. 18, 2002 – Name changed to Warrior Energy N.V.; basis 1 new for 10 old shs. ■

Luxor Developments Inc. (Alta. Jan. 26, 1999)
Sept. 20, 2005 – Formed Amorfix Life Sciences Ltd. in Canada on Qualifying Transaction amalgamation with (old) Amorfix Life Sciences Ltd. (deemed acquiror). ■

Luxor Explorations Inc. (Ont. Aug. 27, 1936)
Feb. 2, 2021 – Dissolved.

Luxor Industrial Corporation (B.C. 1979)
Mar. 20, 2017 – Placed into receivership by senior secured lender, HSBC Bank Canada, and Deloitte Restructuring Inc. was appointed receiver. HSBC holds a general security agreement over all the assets of the company.

Luxor Red Lake Mines Limited (Ont. Aug. 27, 1936)
Oct. 1981 – Name changed to Luxor Explorations Inc. ■

Luxor Resources Ltd. (B.C. 1979)
Mar. 30, 1992 – Name changed to Luxor Industrial Corporation. ■

La Luz Mines Limited (Ont. 1938)
July 26, 1985 – Became a wholly owned subsid. of Barrick Resources Corp. through the following exchange: 1 com. sh. of Barrick for each 2 cl. A pfce. or com. shs. held, and 7 Barrick com. shs. for 1 cl. B pfce. sh.

Luzon Minerals Ltd. (B.C. Mar. 7, 1987)
Jan. 14, 2010 – Name changed to Black Isle Resources Corporation; basis 1 new for 10 old shs. ■

Luzon Yellowknife Gold Mines Ltd. (Ont. 1945)
Apr. 28, 1954 – Charter cancelled.

Lydian International Limited (Jersey Dec. 12, 2007)
Aug. 17, 2020 – Applied to the Royal Court of Jersey requesting the company be wound up. Deloitte LLP appointed liquidator.
Mar. 30, 2021 – Liquidation and winding up complete. Asset realizations were insufficient for distrib. to any class of creditor or to shldrs. Certificate of dissolution filed under Jersey Law and the Companies' Creditors Arrangement Act (CCAA) proceedings were terminated. Alverez & Marsal Canada Inc. as court-appointed monitor were discharged.

Lynalda Gold Mines Ltd. (Ont. 1945)
Apr. 29, 1963 – Dissolved.

Lynbar Mines Ltd. (Ont. 1947)
1952 – Charter cancelled.

Lynbar Mining Corp. Ltd. (Ont. 1964)
Mar. 1976 – Charter cancelled.

Lynco Mining Development Inc. (Ont. 1975)
Oct. 1979 – Name changed to Lynco Resources Ltd. ■

Lynco Resources Ltd. (Ont. 1975)
1984 – Name changed to Penn-Lync Resources Ltd. ■

Lynden Energy Corp. (B.C. Feb. 6, 2006)
May 20, 2016 – Acquired by Earthstone Energy, Inc. by way of amalgamation with 1058286 B.C. Ltd. (a wholly owned subsid. of Earthstone); basis 0.02842 Earthstone com. shs for 1 Lynden com. sh.

Lynden Ventures Ltd. (Ont. June 15, 2000 amalg.)
Feb. 6, 2006 – Continued into British Columbia.
Jan. 17, 2008 – Name changed to Lynden Energy Corp. ■

Lyndhurst Mining Company Limited (Que. Oct. 21, 1949)
June 4, 1974 – Name changed to Globex Mining Enterprises Inc.; basis 1 new for 10 old shs. (see FPsurvey - Mines & Energy)

Lyndvue Mines Ltd. (Que. 1956)
Mar. 13, 1959 – Absorbed by Roberval Mining Corp.; basis 1 new for 6 old shs.

Lynn Creek Zinc Mines Ltd. (unknown)
1956 – Acquired by Alscope Explorations Ltd.; basis 1 new for 2 old shs. (see Alscope Explorations Ltd.)

Lynn Valley Copper Co. (B.C. 1914)
Oct. 1974 – Charter cancelled.

Lynn Valley Gas & Oil Co. Ltd. (Ont. 1935)
1939 – Taken over by Domestic Gas & Oil Co. Ltd.

LynnGold Resources Inc. (Ont. 1959)
Dec. 1989 – Made a voluntary assignment of its assets to its creditors under the Bankruptcy Act.
July 6, 1992 – No formal tendering process for sale of the company's assets and no distribution will be made to the shldrs.

Lynnita Consolidated Gold Mines Ltd. (Ont. 1943)
Apr. 1955 – Charter cancelled.

Lynnwood Capital Inc. (B.C. Sept. 28, 2009)
Oct. 21, 2013 – Name changed to Tantalex Resources Corporation pursuant to Qualifying Transaction reverse takeover acquisition of Tantalex Corporation. ■

Lynwatin Nickel Copper Ltd. (Can. 1946)
1967 – Merged into Resource Exploration & Development Co. Ltd.; basis 10 new for 197 old shs.

Lynx-Canada Explorations Limited (Ont. 1964)
Sept. 6, 1989 – Formed CS Resources Limited in Canada on amalgamation with CS Resources Limited; basis 1 new for 1 old sh. following a 1-for-25 consolidation of Lynx-Canada shs. and a 2-for-1 split of CS shs. ■

Lynx Energy Services Corp. (Alta. Apr. 28, 1993)
June 18, 1997 – All o/s cl. A and cl. B shs. acquired by a wholly owned subsid. of Kenting Energy Service Inc.; basis 1.11344 new com. shs. of Kenting Energy for both old cl. A and cl. B shs. of Lynx. (see Kenting Energy Services Inc.)

Lynx Resources Ltd. (B.C. Dec. 2, 1965)
Feb. 9, 1987 – Name changed to Avatar Resource Corporation. ■

Lynx Security Incorporated (B.C. 1987)
Mar. 27, 1992 – Dissolved and struck off register.

Lynx Yellowknife Gold Mines Ltd. (Ont. 1944)
Mar. 1976 – Charter cancelled.

Lyonnaise des Eaux (France)
Nov. 5, 1990 – Formed Lyonnaise des Eaux-Dumez on amalgamation with Dumez S.A.

Lyra Resources Ltd. (B.C. June 10, 1980)
July 2, 2008 – Name changed to Cicada Ventures Ltd. ■

Lysander Gold Corporation (B.C. Dec. 15, 1986)
July 22, 1999 – Name changed to Lysander Minerals Corporation; basis 1 new for 5 old shs. ■

Lysander Minerals Corporation (B.C. Dec. 15, 1986)
Jan. 31, 2011 – Name changed to EastCoal Inc. ■

Lytton Minerals Limited (B.C. May 9, 1963)
July 8, 1983 – Continued into Canada. (see Tahera Corporation)
Mar. 1, 1999 – Amalgamated with New Indigo Resources Inc. to form Tahera Corporation; basis 2.43 new for 1 New Indigo sh. and 1 new for 1 Lytton sh. (see Tahera Corporation)

Lytton Uranium Mines Ltd. (B.C. 1952)
1956 – Name changed to Aztec Exploration Ltd. ■

M

M & M Porcupine Gold Mines Limited (Ont. July 24, 1953)
Sept. 12, 1977 – Continued into British Columbia. (see Diasyn Technologies Limited)
June 28, 1985 – Continued into Canada. (see Diasyn Technologies Limited)
Jan. 15, 1988 – Amalgamated with Diasyn Technologies Limited to form a new co. also known as Diasyn Technologies Limited; basis 1 new for 1 old sh. (see Diasyn Technologies Limited)

M-Corp Inc. (Can. Feb. 28, 1979)
Dec. 14, 1998 – Name changed to Mikes Restaurants Inc. ■

M. Loeb, Limited (Ont. 1928)
June 15, 1979 – Amalgamated with Loebex Limited, a wholly owned subsid. of Provigo Inc.; basis 1 sh. Provigo for 2 shs. M. Loeb. All ser. A pref. shs. redeemed at par. (see Provigo Inc.)

M Pharmaceutical Inc. (Alta. Nov. 26, 2014)
Sept. 20, 2017 – Name changed to Callitas Health Inc.; basis 1 new for 10 old shs. ■

M2 Cobalt Corp. (B.C. Dec. 3, 2007)
June 21, 2019 – Acquired by Jervois Mining Limited; basis 1 new Jervois ordinary sh. for 1 M2 Cobalt com. sh. (see Jervois Mining Limited)

MAAX Inc. (Que. Feb. 16, 1987)
Aug. 1, 1990 – Amalgamated with subsids. Acrylica Inc., Fibre de verre moderne Inc., la Société Immobilière Maax Ltée, Promax Composites Inc. and Multi-Fibres (1989) Inc. to continue with the same name MAAX Inc.
June 7, 2004 – Amalgamated with 9139-4460 Québec Inc. and 9139-7158 Québec Inc. for $22.50 per sh.

MABL Holdings Ltd. (Man. May 16, 1922)
Apr. 30, 2007 – Dissolved following payment of liabs. and sale of assets.

MACCs Sustainable Yield Trust (Ont. Jan. 28, 2005)
Dec. 29, 2008 – Name changed to Crown Hill Fund pursuant to merger with Crown Hill Dividend Fund (deemed acquiror). ■

MAL Holdings Limited (N.S. Feb. 7, 1924)
1980 – Assets sold and the co. became inactive.
Dec. 30, 1990 – Struck off register.

MAS Gold Corp. (B.C. July 7, 1981)
Jan. 28, 2025 – All o/s shs. not already held acquired by Eros Resources Corp.; basis 0.25 Eros shs. for 1 MAS Gold sh. (see Eros Resources Corp.)

MATRIX Income Fund (Alta. Jan. 28, 2005)
May 28, 2007 – Amalgamated with MINT Income Fund; basis 0.68846815 new MINT units fr 1 old MATRIX unit.

MATRRIX Energy Technologies Inc. (Alta. Sept. 15, 2011 amalg.)
June 5, 2019 – Name changed to Stampede Drilling Inc. (see FPsurvey - Mines & Energy; FPsurvey - Industrials)

MAX Minerals Ltd. (Can. July 22, 2008)
Oct. 8, 2010 – Name changed to Standard Exploration Ltd. ■

MAXIN Income Fund (Ont. Mar. 28, 2003)
Oct. 1, 2007 – Merged into YIELDPLUS Income Fund; basis 1.20015552 YIELDPLUS trust unit for 1 MAXIN trust unit. (see YIELDPLUS Income Fund)

MBA Gold Corp. (Can. Nov. 25, 1999)
Oct. 13, 2005 – Name changed to MBA Resources Corp. ■

MBA Resources Corp. (Can. Nov. 25, 1999)
July 27, 2006 – Name changed to Thunderbird Energy Corporation. ■

MBAC Fertilizer Corp. (Can. Dec. 24, 2009)
Oct. 27, 2016 – Continued into Cayman Islands.
Jan. 6, 2017 – Name changed to Itafos. ■

MBMI Resources Inc. (Yuk. Aug. 30, 2000)
Nov. 15, 2005 – Continued into British Columbia.
June 21, 2012 – Continued into Ontario.
Mar. 25, 2020 – Privatized via a 1-for-360,000 sh. consolidation; basis 13¢ cash per pre-consolidated sh.

MBN Corporation (Alta. Mar. 19, 2010)
Apr. 22, 2022 – Terminated. Equity shs. redeemed at $10.5874 cash per sh.

MBS Adjustable Rate Income Fund (Ont. Oct. 28, 2004)
Apr. 9, 2007 – Merged with Mortgage-Backed Securities Trust (0.7021 for 1) to continue as Sentry Select MBS Adjustable Rate Income Fund II; basis 0.978 Sentry Select units for 1 MBS unit. (see Sentry Select MBS Adjustable Rate Income Fund II)

MBS Software Inc. (B.C. 1984)
Aug. 5, 1994 – Dissolved and struck off register.

MC Partners Inc. (B.C. Jan. 28, 2011)
May 22, 2013 – Name changed to bioMmune Technologies Inc. pursuant to Qualifying Transaction acquisition of bioMmune Technologies Inc. ■

MC2 Learning Systems Inc. (B.C. Sept. 28, 1994)
Nov. 21, 1996 – Continued into Canada.
Apr. 12, 2000 – Name changed to Centrinity Inc. ■

MCAP Inc. (Can. Jan. 11, 1991; via Federal Loan Companies Act)
Sept. 15, 2006 – Name changed to MCAN Mortgage Corporation. (see FPsurvey - Industrials)

MCB Investments Corp. (B.C. 1981)
July 11, 2003 – Dissolved and struck from register.

MCF Enterprises Inc. (B.C. Nov. 25, 1983)
Feb. 9, 2001 – Name changed to Online Consortium Corp. ■

MCI Onehealth Technologies Inc. (Ont. July 18, 2012)
Dec. 30, 2020 – Continued into Canada.
Sept. 26, 2023 – Name changed to HealWELL AI Inc. (see FPsurvey - Industrials)

MCK Mining Corp. (Ont. Mar. 22, 1994 amalg.)
July 25, 2006 – Name changed to PhosCan Chemical Corp. ■

MCL Capital Inc. (Ont. Sept. 28, 2004)
Feb. 6, 2006 – Name changed to Feel Good Cars Corporation following Qualifying Transaction acquisition of Feel Good Cars Inc.; basis 1 new for 3 old shs. ■

MCM Capital One Inc. (Ont. Apr. 28, 2010)
Sept. 3, 2014 – Name changed to EnerDynamic Hybrid Technologies Corp. following Qualifying Transaction reverse takeover acquisition of (old) Enerdynamic Hybrid Technologies Inc. ■

MCM Split Share Corp. (Ont. Dec. 5, 1997)
Apr. 1, 2011 – Voluntarily liquidated for $15 per priority equity sh.

MCO Capital Inc. (Que. Sept. 1, 1977)
Feb. 28, 2011 – Name changed to IOU Financial Inc. pursuant to reverse takeover acquisition of IOU Central Inc.; basis 1 new for 4 old shs. ■

MCP Resources Corporation (B.C. Feb. 19, 1969)
June 10, 1981 – Name changed to Petro-American Energy Inc. ■

MCR Capital Inc. (Ont. 1973)
1982 – Amalgamated in Ontario to continue with same name.
Dec. 16, 1993 – Name changed to Covesco Capital Corporation; basis 1 new com. for 15 old com. shs., 1 new cl. A special for 15 old cl. A special shs., 1 new ser. A pfd. for 1 old 1st pfd. ser. A sh., and 1 new ser. Y pfd. for 1 old 2nd pfd. ser. Y. sh. ■

MCS Global Corp. (Alta. Nov. 7, 2000)
May 8, 2006 – Name changed to Newstrike Capital Inc. and continued into British Columbia; basis 1 new for 3 old shs. ■

MCW Energy Group Limited (Ont. Dec. 12, 2012 amalg.)
May 5, 2017 – Name changed to Petroteq Energy Inc.; basis 1 new for 30 old shs. (see FPsurvey - Mines & Energy)

MCW Enterprises Ltd. (B.C. Jan. 4, 2008)
Dec. 12, 2012 – Formed MCW Energy Group Limited in Ontario pursuant to amalgamation with wholly owned MCW Energy Group Limited. ■

McorpCX, Inc. (Calif. Dec. 14, 2001)
Sept. 30, 2020 – Name changed to MCX Technologies Corporation. (see FPsurvey - Industrials)

MD Multimedia Inc. (Can. Apr. 4, 1996)
Sept. 26, 2008 – Dissolved.

MDA Ltd. (Ont. June 2, 2020)
May 9, 2024 – Name changed to MDA Space Ltd. (see FPsurvey - Industrials)

MDC Communications Corporation (Ont. Dec. 19, 1986 amalg.)
May 29, 1999 – Name changed to MDC Corporation Inc. ■

MDC Corporation (Ont. Dec. 19, 1986 amalg.)
May 28, 1996 – Name changed to MDC Communications Corporation; basis 1 new for 6 old shs. ■

MDC Corporation Inc. (Ont. Dec. 19, 1986 amalg.)
Jan. 1, 2004 – Name changed to MDC Partners Inc. ■

MDC Partners Inc. (Ont. Dec. 19, 1986 amalg.)
June 28, 2004 – Continued into Canada.
July 21, 2021 – Continued into Delaware.
Aug. 3, 2021 – Name changed to Stagwell Inc. ■

MDE Explorations Ltd. (B.C. Sept. 27, 1985)
Oct. 27, 1989 – Name changed to Puff Pac Industries Inc. and continued into Delaware. ■

MDI Mobile Data International Inc. (B.C. 1979)
Aug. 12, 1988 – Acquired by Motorola Canada Limited for $13.50 per sh.

MDI Technologies, Inc. (Del. Apr. 27, 1999)
July 14, 2005 – Acquired by Logibec Groupe Informatique Ltée for Cdn$2.60 per sh. (see Logibec Groupe Informatique Ltée)
2007 – Name changed to MDI Achieve, Inc. (see Logibec Groupe Informatique Ltée)

MDN Inc. (Que. Jan. 27, 1954)
Sept. 20, 2016 – Name changed to Niobay Metals Inc.; basis 1 new for 5 old shs. (see FPsurvey - Mines & Energy)

MDP Worldwide Entertainment Inc. (Can. Aug. 16, 1993)
Apr. 14, 2004 – Name changed to M8 Entertainment Inc. ■

MDR Switchview Global Networks Inc. (Can. Jan. 13, 1994)
June 5, 2002 – Name changed to Avotus Corporation. ■

MDS Health Group Limited (Ont. Apr. 17, 1969)
Oct. 10, 1978 – Continued into Canada.
Nov. 26, 1996 – Name changed to MDS Inc.; basis 2 new for 1 old sh. ■

MDS Inc. (Can. Oct. 10, 1978)
Nov. 1, 2010 – Name changed to Nordion Inc. ■

MDSI Mobile Data Solutions Inc. (Can. Dec. 5, 1995 amalg.)
Sept. 23, 2005 – Plan of Arrangement acquisition by Vista Equity Fund and related companies Fortezza Holdings S.A.R.L. and Beech Investment Corp.; basis US$8.00 per sh.

MDX Medical Inc. (B.C. Dec. 3, 1980)
June 21, 2006 – Name changed to Urodynamix Technologies Ltd. ■

M.E. Compu Software Inc. (Can. Feb. 17, 1983)
Mar. 25, 1988 – Name changed to Goldrite Mining Corp. ■

ME Resource Corp. (B.C. Oct. 16, 2009)
Mar. 10, 2022 – Name changed to Albert Labs International Corp. pursuant to the reverse takeover acquisition of private Burnaby, B.C.-based Albert Labs Inc.; basis 1 new for 10 old shs. (see FPsurvey - Industrials)

MEC Holdings (Canada) Inc. (Ont. Mar. 19, 1999)
Dec. 30, 2002 – Called for redemption; basis 1 cl. A sub. vtg. Magna Entertainment Corp. sh. for 1 old MEC exchangeable sh.

MEGA Brands Inc. (Can. May 16, 1983)
May 5, 2014 – Acquired by Mattel, Inc.; basis Cdn$17.75 cash per sh. and Cdn$0.3905 cash per wt.

MENA Hydrocarbons Inc. (Alta. May 25, 2011)
Nov. 2, 2018 – Struck from registry and dissolved.

M.E.P.C. Canadian Properties Limited (Ont. 1954)
Sept. 30, 1977 – Amalgamated into Pensionfund Properties Ltd., a private Ont. corp. Pfce. shs. exch. sh.-for-sh. into 1st pfce. shs. of Pensionfund, with par value of $25.50 and divd. of $1.50 p.a. accr. from Sept. 1, 1977. Com. shs. exch. for 2nd pfce. shs. of Pensionfund with par value of $13.60. Subsequently, in October 1977, all 1st and 2nd pfce. shs. redeemed at par.

M8 Entertainment Inc. (Can. Aug. 16, 1993)
Mar. 19, 2010 – Petitioned into liquidation. RSM Richter Inc. appointed liquidator.
Dec. 2011 – Liquidation complete and RSM Richter discharged as liquidator. No funds available for shldrs.

MF Media Corporation (Alta. May 11, 1987)
Nov. 2, 2002 – Dissolved and struck from registry.

MFC Bancorp Ltd. (Yuk. Aug. 6, 1996)
Nov. 3, 2004 – Continued into British Columbia.
Oct. 28, 2005 – Name changed to KHD Humboldt Wedag International Ltd. ■

MFC Bancorp Ltd. (B.C. Nov. 3, 2004)
July 14, 2017 – Completed plan of arrangement under which com. shs. were exchanged for shs. of Cayman Island incorporated MFC 2017 Ltd. (subsequently renamed MFC Bancorp Ltd.); 1 new MFC 2017 com. sh. plus US$0.0001 cash for 1 MFC Bancorp sh.
July 14, 2017 – Continued into Cayman Islands.
June 4, 2019 – Name changed to Scully Royalty Ltd.

MFC Incorporated (Ont. July 3, 1974)
June 5, 1998 – Name changed to Municipal Bankers Corporation. ■

MFC Industrial Ltd. (B.C. Nov. 3, 2004)
Feb. 16, 2016 – Name changed to MFC Bancorp Ltd. ■

MFC Mining Finance Corporation (B.C. 1972 amalg.)
Aug. 2, 1988 – Formed MinVen Gold Corporation in British Columbia following merger with Brohm Resources Inc.; basis 1 new for 1.5 old shs. ■

MFP Financial Services Ltd. (Ont. Jan. 30, 1984)
Oct. 1, 2004 – Name changed to CLEARLINK Capital Corporation. ■

MFP Technology Services Ltd. (Ont. Jan. 30, 1984)
Sept. 15, 1998 – Name changed to MFP Financial Services Ltd. ■

MG Capital Corporation (Alta. Nov. 9, 2017)
Jan. 6, 2021 – Name changed to DLP Resources (2020) Limited. ■

MG Dividend & Income Fund (Ont. Jan. 30, 2006)
Oct. 1, 2007 – Merged into YIELDPLUS Income Fund; basis 0.64565196 YIELDPLUS trust unit for 1 MG Dividend trust unit. (see YIELDPLUS Income Fund)

MGI Software Corp. (Ont. Apr. 30, 1996 amalg.)
Feb. 6, 2002 – Acquired by Roxio, Inc.; basis 0.0505 Roxio shs. for 1 MGI sh.

MGM Energy Corp. (Alta. Oct. 31, 2006)
June 17, 2014 – Acquired by Paramount Resources Ltd.; basis 1 Paramount cl. A com. sh. for 300 MGM com. shs.

M.G.M. Resource Corporation (B.C. Mar. 11, 1983)
Apr. 6, 1989 – Name changed to Precision Petroleum Services Inc.; basis 1 new for 4 old shs. ■

MGP Asia Capital Inc. (B.C. July 7, 1981)
July 15, 1991 – Name changed to Insular Explorations Ltd.; basis 1 new for 5 old shs. ■

MGX Renewables Inc. (B.C. Dec. 8, 2011)
Mar. 20, 2020 – Name changed to Zinc8 Energy Solutions Inc. ■

MGold Resources Inc. (Que. Feb. 16, 1945)
July 25, 2013 – Continued into Alberta.
Sept. 23, 2013 – Name changed to Tanager Energy Inc. ■

MHB Resources Ltd. (B.C. 1980)
Oct. 1, 1982 – Name changed to Genoveva Resource Inc. (see FPsurvey - Mines & Energy)

MI Developments Inc. (Ont. Aug. 29, 2003 amalg.)
June 13, 2012 – Name changed to Granite Real Estate Inc. ■

MI Software Corporation (B.C. 1983)
June 10, 1994 – Dissolved and struck off register.

MICC Investments Limited (Can. July 22, 1963)
Apr. 8, 2008 – Privatized; basis 1 redeem. pref. sh. for 1 com. sh., redeem. for $2.55 cash per sh.
Dec. 23, 2008 – Continued into Ontario.

MIGENIX Inc. (B.C. Apr. 15, 1991)
Mar. 19, 2010 – Name changed to Metro Vancouver Properties Corp. and privatized pursuant to plan of arrangement with Madison Pacific Properties Inc., which acquired 94.1% of the equity, and a wholly owned subsidiary of BioWest Therapeutics Inc., which acquired the MIGENIX business; basis 0.02 cl B sh. of Metro Vancouver Properties Corp. and 0.1 com. sh. of BioWest Therapeutics Inc.

The MIL Group Inc. (Can. 1937)
Nov. 5, 1996 – Name changed to Davie Industries Inc. ■

MIS International Incorporated (B.C. 1979)
Jan. 26, 1999 – Name changed to Cosmoz.com Inc. (see FPsurvey - Industrials)

MIS Multimedia Interactive Services Inc. (B.C. 1979)
Oct. 22, 1997 – Name changed to MIS International Incorporated. ■

MIST Inc. (Ont. June 14, 2000)
Mar. 17, 2004 – Name changed to NBS Technologies Inc. ■

M.I.T. Ventures Corp. (B.C. Mar. 4, 1983)
Dec. 5, 2011 – Dissolved and struck from register.
July 22, 2016 – Restored to register.
Jan. 22, 2017 – Limited period of restoration to registry expired and dissolved.

MIU Industries Ltd. (B.C. July 18, 1983)
May 8, 1995 – Name changed to Secured Communication Canada 95 Inc.; basis 1 new for 5 old shs. ■

MJ Bioscience Corp. (B.C. Oct. 15, 2014)
Aug. 21, 2020 – Name changed to Penn Capital Inc. ■

MJ Innovation Capital Corp. (Ont. Nov. 13, 2018)
Dec. 29, 2021 – Name changed to SPARQ Corp. pursuant to the Qualifying Transaction reverse takeover acquisition of SPARQ Systems Inc.; basis 1 new for 1.25 old shs. ■

M. J. Mining Co. Ltd. (B.C. 1954)
Feb. 12, 1959 – Dissolved.

MJ Opportunity Corp. (Ont. Feb. 10, 2017)
Sept. 17, 2018 – Name changed to Lift & Co. Corp. pursuant to Qualifying Transaction reverse takeover acquisition of private Toronto, Ont.-based Lift Co. Ltd.; basis 1 new for 2.4 old shs. ■

MJardin Group, Inc. (Ont. Aug. 30, 1978 amalg.)
Mar. 15, 2022 – Placed into receivership and PricewaterhouseCoopers Inc. appointed receiver and manager.

MK2 Ventures Ltd. (B.C. Mar. 31, 2006)
July 17, 2019 – Name changed to District Metals Corp. (see FPsurvey - Mines & Energy)

M.K.L. Textiles Ltd. (Can. - unspecified)
July 1965 – Amalgamated into Montex Apparel Industries Ltd.

MKM Resources Ltd. (B.C. Apr. 11, 2008)
Mar. 9, 2010 – Name changed to Sunward Resources Ltd. pursuant to Qualifying Transaction reverse takeover acquisition of Sunward Investments Ltd. ■

MKS Inc. (Ont. Apr. 24, 1984)
June 2, 2011 – Acquired by PTC NS ULC, an indirect wholly owned subsid. of Parametric Technology Corporation, for $26.20 per sh.

ML Gold Corp. (Can. Feb. 27, 2007)
July 30, 2019 – Name changed to M3 Metals Corp. (see FPsurvey - Mines & Energy)

MLB Industries Inc. (Alta. Jan. 27, 1995)
Aug. 30, 2011 – Succeeded by Blue Horizon Industries Inc. pursuant to reverse takeover acquisition of Blue Horizon Energy Inc.; basis 1 new for 29 old shs. ■

MLI Marble Lending Inc. (B.C. July 7, 2015)
Sept. 15, 2016 – Continued into Canada.
Nov. 8, 2019 – Name changed to Marble Financial Inc. ■

MLK Gold Ltd. (B.C. June 7, 2018)
Apr. 13, 2023 – Name changed to Triple One Metals Inc. (see FPsurvey - Mines & Energy)

MLW-Worthington Limited (Can. June 19, 1902; via letters patent)
June 2, 1975 – In January 1975, Les Entreprises de J. Armand Bombardier Ltée (the principal shldr. in Bombardier Limited) made an offer to acquire all o/s com.

shs. at $21 per sh. which expired June 2, 1975 giving J. Armand Bombardier Ltée controlling interest.
Apr. 1976 – MLW-Worthington acquired all the o/s shs. of Bombardier Limited; basis 1 com. for 5.25 old cl. A or cl. B com. shs.
Aug. 18, 1976 – Name changed to Bombardier-MLW Ltd. ■

MM-G International Inc. (Ont. 1982 amalg.)
Sept. 26, 1983 – Name changed to Stratas Corporation Ltd. (see FPsurvey - Industrials)

MMC Video One Canada Ltd. (B.C. 1981)
Dec. 16, 1988 – Acquired by Standard Broadcasting Corporation Limited for $2.90 per sh.

MMT Resources Ltd. (B.C. 1986)
Apr. 3, 1992 – Dissolved and struck off register.

MMX Ventures Inc. (B.C. Sept. 22, 1989)
June 23, 2000 – Name changed to IP Applications Corp. ■

MNP Petroleum Corporation (Nev. July 9, 1998)
Nov. 6, 2017 – Voluntarily delisted; will continue to trade on the OTC Pink market.

MNT Ltd. (Ont. Feb. 25, 1991 amalg.)
June 30, 1997 – All o/s cap. shs. and equity divd. shs. redeemed for $38.64 per cap. sh. and $16.415 per equity divd. sh.

MOSAID Technologies Incorporated (Ont. May 6, 1975)
Dec. 29, 2011 – Acquired by 7577796 Canada Inc., directly and indirectly controlled by Sterling Partners, for $46 per sh.
Jan. 1, 2014 – Name changed to Conversant Intellectual Property Management, Inc. ■

M-P Petroleum Ltd. (Alta. May 31, 1979 amalg.)
Aug. 16, 1979 – Name changed to Dalco Petroleum Ltd. ■

MP Western Properties Inc. (Ont. May 5, 2000)
June 16, 2006 – Continued into Canada.
July 15, 2011 – Acquired by Madison Pacific Properties Inc. for 6¢ per sh.

MPA Video Inc. (Can. 1982)
July 1986 – Acquired by Astral Bellevue Pathe Inc. for issue of 287,332 com. sh. (see Astral Bellevue Pathe Inc.)

MPAC Industries Corporation (Yuk. May 20, 1994)
July 18, 2006 – Continued into British Columbia.
Aug. 27, 2012 – Dissolved and struck from register.

MPACT Immedia Corporation (Can. Dec. 11, 1986)
Jan. 25, 1999 – Name changed to BCE Emergis Inc. ■

MPG Investment Corporation Limited (Can. Apr. 4, 1928; via Dominion charter)
Aug. 15, 1996 – All o/s com. shs. converted into 1 cl. C convertible redeem. sh.; basis $6.22 per sh. Holders of the cl. C shares also had the option to convert their shs. into cl. D redeem. shs. on a one for one basis which would never be listed or redeemed. The 1964 ser. pref. shs. were called effective Mar. 29, 1996; basis $26.50 per sh. plus dividends accrued up to and including Mar. 29, 1996 of $0.209 per sh.

MPH Ventures Corp. (B.C. May 30, 1980)
Mar. 18, 2016 – Name changed to Cuba Ventures Corp. following acquisition of the remaining interest in Travelucion S.L. ■

MPI Holdings Inc. (B.C. Aug. 6, 1987)
June 24, 1994 – Continued into Wyoming.
Oct. 27, 1995 – Petitioned into bankruptcy.
Jan. 29, 1996 – Filed for bankruptcy.

MPL Communications Inc. (Alta. May 19, 1988)
Nov. 2, 2023 – Struck from register. (see FPsurvey - Industrials)

MPV Exploration Inc. (Can. Apr. 6, 2010)
Nov. 5, 2020 – Name changed to Entheon Biomedical Corp. pursuant to the reverse takeover acquisition of (old)

Entheon Biomedical Corp. and concurrent amalgamation of (old) Entheon with wholly owned 1254912 B.C. Inc. (and continued as Entheon Holdings Corp.).; basis 1 new for 3 old shs. (see FPsurvey - Mines & Energy)

M.P.V. Explorations Inc. (Can. Apr. 6, 2010)
Oct. 30, 2018 – Name changed to MPV Exploration Inc. ■

MPVC Inc. (Can. July 19, 2005)
June 27, 2014 – Name changed to Northern Uranium Corp. (see FPsurvey - Mines & Energy)

MPX Bioceutical Corporation (Ont. Apr. 2, 1974)
Feb. 7, 2019 – Acquired by iAnthus Capital Holdings, Inc.; basis 0.1673 iAnthus com. shs. plus 0.1 com. shs. of newly incorporated MPX International Corporation for 1 MPX Bioceutical com. sh.
Name changed to MPX Bioceutical ULC.

MRC Metall Resources Corp. (B.C. Oct. 22, 1980)
Aug. 24, 1998 – Name changed to Mount Dakota Energy Corp. and continued into Canada. ■

MRC Technologies Inc. (Alta. 1994)
Aug. 19, 1996 – Formed Telkwa Gold Corporation in Alberta on amalgamation with Telkwa Gold Corporation and Limonite Creek Limited Partnership on a share-for-share basis. ■

MRF 2004 Resource Limited Partnership (Ont. Jan. 9, 2004)
Apr. 5, 2006 – Dissolved; net asset value $28.66 per unit.

MRI Medical Technologies Inc. (B.C. July 31, 1979)
Dec. 7, 1992 – Name changed to Tri-National Development Corp.; basis 1 new for 5 old shs. ■

MRP Petroleums Inc. (Ont. Jan. 26, 1987 amalg.)
May 31, 1989 – Name changed to MRP Waste Management Corp. ■

MRP Waste Management Corp. (Ont. Jan. 26, 1987 amalg.)
Sept. 17, 1994 – Dissolved.

MRRM Inc. (Can. July 19, 1929)
Apr. 6, 2015 – Amalgamated with 9135430 Canada Inc. an indirect wholly owned subsid. of Marbour S.A.S., to continue under the MRRM Inc. name; basis $4.45 cash per sh.

MRS Travel Ltd. (Alta. Apr. 2, 1993)
Sept. 27, 1995 – Name changed to ADAM Technologies, Inc. ■

MSA Capital Corp. (Alta. Mar. 16, 1994)
Oct. 29, 2002 – Name changed to Coronation Minerals Inc. ■

MSA Petroleum Limited (B.C. 1984)
Dec. 31, 1988 – Amalgamated with Tygas Energy Inc. (1 new for 4.536 old cl. A com. shs.) to form Tygas Resource Corporation; basis 1 new for 2 old shs. (see Tygas Resource Corporation)

MSI Energy Services Inc. (Alta. Feb. 22, 1993)
Oct. 17, 2001 – Acquired by Willbros Canada Acquisition Corp., a wholly owned subsid. of Panama-based Willbros Group, Inc.; basis $0.95 per com. sh. and $0.05 per cl. C sh.

MSL Management Systems Ltd. (Can. 1967)
Oct. 1968 – Name changed to AGT Data Systems Limited. ■

M.S.M. Marketing Ltd. (Ont. 1978)
June 16, 1986 – Name changed to Sea Hawk Energy Inc.; basis 1 new for 4 old shs. ■

MSN Industries Ltd. (Can. 1942)
Apr. 1, 1974 – Amalgamated with The Resource Service Group Ltd. through purch. offer of $8.83 per sh.

MSP Maxxum Trust (Ont. Nov. 29, 2004)
June 25, 2009 – Merged into Mackenzie Maxxum Dividend Class, an open-ended mutual fund.

MSR Exploration Ltd. (Alta. Apr. 29, 1981)
Oct. 1997 – Continued into Delaware.

MSV Resources Inc. (Que. Nov. 10, 1959)
July 6, 2001 – Amalgamated with GéoNova Explorations Inc. and Campbell Resources Inc.; basis 1 new for 10 GéoNova shs. and 1 new for 4.1 MSV shs. (see Campbell Resources Inc.)

MSZ Resources Ltd. (N.B. 1961)
Jan. 15, 1982 – Name changed to Corrida Oils Ltd. and continued into Alberta; basis 1 new for 3 old shs. ■

MTC Electronic Technologies Co. Ltd. (B.C. 1984)
Sept. 20, 1995 – Name changed to GrandeTel Technologies Inc. ■

MTC Growth Fund-I Inc. (Can. July 21, 1987)
Oct. 28, 2019 – Name changed to Ramm Pharma Corp. pursuant to reverse takeover acquisition of Medic Plast S.A., and Yurelan S.A. (see FPsurvey - Industrials)

MTC Mortgage Investment Corporation (Can. Jan. 11, 1991; via Federal Loan Companies Act)
Jan. 1, 2000 – Name changed to MCAP Inc. concurrent with the acquisition of MCAP Financial Corporation and Interior Capital Corporation. ■

MTI Global Inc. (Ont. Nov. 22, 1995)
June 11, 2010 – Name changed to Zuni Holdings Inc. ■

MTS International Services Incorporated (Ont. Sept. 8, 1971 amalg.)
Sept. 25, 1981 – By agreement dated June 15, 1981 and completed Sept. 25, 1981, co. issued 10,969,887 com. shs. in exchange for all o/s shs. of Epitek Electronics Ltd. Control of combined cos. passed to former shldrs. of Epitek Electronics (reverse takeover).
Dec. 9, 1981 – Formed Epitek International Inc. in Canada. ■

MTS International Services Limited (Ont. 1929)
Sept. 8, 1971 – Formed MTS International Services Incorporated in Ontario on amalgamation with wholly owned MTS Holdings Limited and Miroptic Systems Limited. ■

MTU Investments Inc. (Alta. Oct. 7, 1994)
Dec. 9, 1997 – Name changed to The Prospectus Group Inc. following acquisition of Prospectus Inc.; basis 1 new for 2 old shs. ■

MVE Capital Corp. (B.C. Feb. 16, 2007)
Aug. 6, 2009 – Amalgamated with Range Capital Corp.; basis 1.55 Range Capital shs. for 1 MVE Capital sh. (see Range Capital Corp.)

MVP Capital Corp. (Ont. July 21, 1986)
Nov. 5, 1996 – Name changed to LatinGold Inc.; basis 1 new for 20 old shs. ■

MVS Capital Corp. (B.C. Feb. 3, 2006)
Feb. 26, 2007 – Name changed to CY Oriental Holdings Ltd. following merger of wholly owned CY Oriental Garments Inc. and CY Oriental Holdings Ltd.; basis 1 new for 5 old shs. ■

MVS Modular Vehicle Systems Ltd. (B.C. Sept. 24, 1982)
Mar. 28, 1996 – Name changed to Cobra Pacific Systems, Inc.; basis 1 new for 2.5 old shs. ■

MW Capital Resources Corp. (Ont. Feb. 10, 1944)
July 4, 1996 – Formed Oro Nevada Resources Inc. in Ontario on amalgamation with Oro Nevada Resources Inc. (1 for 1); basis 1.093 new for 1 old sh. ■

MW Resources Limited (Ont. Feb. 10, 1944)
June 28, 1989 – Name changed to MW Capital Resources Corp.; basis 1 new for 20 old shs. ■

MWP Capital Corp. (Alta. May 3, 2005)
June 9, 2006 – Formed Shear Wind Inc. in Alberta pursuant to Qualifying Transaction reverse takeover acquisition of and amalgamation with Shear Wind Inc. ■

MYDAS Fund (Alta. Dec. 18, 2001)
July 20, 2006 – Merged with Citadel Multi-Sector Income Fund and Citadel Income & Growth Fund to continue as a new fund named Citadel Premium Income Fund; basis 1.22 new Citadel Premiun unit plus $0.50 special distribution for 1 old MYDAS unit. (see Citadel Premium Income Fund)

MYM Nutraceuticals Inc. (B.C. June 11, 2014)
July 16, 2021 – Acquired by IM Cannabis Corp.; basis 0.022 IM Cannabis com. shs. for 1 MYM Nutraceuticals sh.

Mabee Minerals Incorporated (B.C. 1976)
Nov. 23, 1984 – Struck off register.

Mac-Am Resources Corp. (B.C. 1979)
Dec. 8, 1987 – Formed Colossus Resource Equities Inc. in British Columbia on amalgamation with International Wildrose Resources Ltd. (1 for 1), Brigade Resources Inc. (1 for 3) and Consolidated Dakota Resources Ltd. (1 for 1); basis 1 new for 1 old sh. ■

Mac-Mel Financial Corporation Inc. (Alta. Feb. 24, 1988)
June 6, 1996 – Name changed to Sparta Capital Ltd. (see FPsurvey - Industrials)

Macamic Resources Inc. (Can. May 8, 1985)
Mar. 6, 1997 – Name changed to Palmer Resources Inc.; basis 1 new for 4 old shs. ■

Macanda Copper Mines Ltd. (Ont. 1965)
Aug. 1979 – Acquired by West Wasa Mines Limited on Jan. 26, 1977, through exchange of 1,056,967 West Wasa shs. for 1,761,612 Macanda shs. Macanda dissolved. (see West Macanda Resources Ltd.)

MacAndrews Red Lake Gold Mines Ltd. (Ont. 1934)
Apr. 21, 2014 – Certificate of incorporation cancelled and dissolved.

Macarthur Diamonds Limited (Yuk. Oct. 1, 2002)
Dec. 2, 2002 – Continued into Australia.
July 7, 2005 – Name changed to Macarthur Minerals Limited; basis 1 new for 10 old shs.

Macassa Gold Mines Ltd. (Ont. 1961)
1970 – Merged into Willroy Mines Ltd.; basis 4 new for 5 old shs.

Macassa Mines Ltd. (Ont. Apr. 12, 1926)
1961 – Merged into Macassa Gold Mines Ltd.

MacBart Mines Ltd. (Ont. 1945)
Jan. 1962 – Charter cancelled.

Maccabi Ventures Inc. (B.C. Nov. 13, 2014)
Mar. 13, 2018 – Name changed to Lead Ventures Inc.; basis 1 new for 10 old shs. ■

MacClare Mines Ltd. (Ont. 1945)
Aug. 1, 1958 – Charter cancelled.

MacDean Mines Ltd. (Ont. 1944)
June 1960 – Charter cancelled.

Macdic Copper Mining & Smelting Co. Ltd. (Man. 1948)
1970 – Charter cancelled.

MacDonald, Dettwiler and Associates Ltd. (Can. Feb. 3, 1969)
Nov. 21, 1995 – All o/s com. shs. exchanged for exchangeable shares of an indirect wholly owned subsid. of Orbital Sciences Corporation; basis 0.3607 exchangeable shs. for 1 MacDonald com. sh.
May 16, 2016 – Continued into British Columbia. ■

MacDonald, Dettwiler and Associates Ltd. (Can. Feb. 3, 1969)
June 16, 2016 – Continued into British Columbia.
Oct. 5, 2017 – Name changed to Maxar Technologies Ltd. ■

MacDonald Mines Exploration Ltd. (Que. Dec. 23, 1936; via letters patent)
Nov. 1, 2011 – Continued into Canada.
May 7, 2025 – Acquired by Canuc Resources Corp.; basis 1.497 Canuc shs. for 1 MacDonald Mines sh.

Macdonald Mines Ltd. (Que. Dec. 23, 1936; via letters patent)
Dec. 22, 1988 – Name changed to MacDonald Mines Exploration Ltd. ■

MacDonald Oil Exploration Ltd. (Bahamas Nov. 22, 1994)
Feb. 21, 1997 – Continued into Ontario. (see FPsurvey - Mines & Energy)

Macdor Quebec Mines Ltd. (Ont. 1945)
1962 – Assets acquired by Tinex Development Exploration Ltd.; basis 1 new for 2 old shs.

MacDougall Development Corp. (B.C. 1986)
Jan. 15, 1993 – Dissolved and struck off register.

MacDougall Porcupine Gold Mines Ltd. (Ont. 1936)
Feb. 14, 1973 – Dissolved.

MacDyke Oil and Mining Industries Ltd. (Ont. 1943)
Mar. 4, 1965 – Dissolved.

Mace Gold Mines Ltd. (Ont. 1937)
Feb. 21, 1949 – Charter cancelled; assets distributed on basis of 8.825¢ per sh.

Mace Technology Inc. (B.C. Oct. 25, 1968)
Mar. 13, 1987 – Dissolved and struck off register.

MacFarlane Consolidated Mines Ltd. (Ont. 1938)
May 8, 1952 – Charter cancelled.

Macfie Explorations Ltd. (Ont. 1945)
Apr. 1963 – Name changed to United Macfie Mines Ltd.; basis 1 new for 5 old shs. ■

Macfie Red Lake Mines Ltd. (Ont. 1945)
June 6, 1952 – Name changed to Macfie Explorations Ltd. ■

Macfie Resources Inc. (B.C. 1979)
Aug. 31, 1992 – Delisted from CDN. Subsequently struck from register and dissolved.

Macfort Gold Mines Ltd. (Ont. 1944)
1960 – Charter cancelled.

Macho River Gold Mines Ltd. (Ont. Aug. 25, 1947)
1953 – Name changed to Aumacho River Mines Ltd.; basis 1 new for 3 old shs. ■

Mack Lake Mining Corp. Ltd. (Can. 1959)
May 6, 1972 – Dissolved.

Mackellar Bay Mines Ltd. (Ont. 1951)
Sept. 1956 – Name changed to Mackellar Bay Mining and Exploration Co. Ltd. ■

Mackellar Bay Mining and Exploration Co. Ltd. (Ont. 1951)
Aug. 1960 – Charter cancelled.

Mackeno Mines Ltd. (Ont. 1950)
1957 – Name changed to Galkeno Mines Ltd.; basis 1 new for 3 old shs. ■

MacKenzie Air Service Ltd. (Can. 1932)
1942 – Controlling interest acquired by Canadian Pacific Railway Co. in 1940-41; entire assets transferred to Canadian Pacific Air Lines, Limited.

MacKenzie Energy Corporation (B.C. 1979)
Mar. 12, 1984 – Name changed to Mac-Am Resources Corp. ■

Mackenzie Financial Corporation (Ont. Feb. 15, 1971)
May 31, 2001 – Acquired by Investors Group Inc.; basis $22.9833 plus 0.280668 Investors Group shs. for 1 Mackenzie sh.

MacKenzie Hill Mines Ltd. (Ont. 1965)
1969 – Merged into Alchib Developments Ltd.; basis 28 new for 100 old shs.

Mackenzie Income Trust (Ont. Mar. 23, 1998)
Dec. 31, 2002 – Trust expired. Final distribution of $1.5048 per preferred A unit to unitholders of record.

Mackenzie Investment Management Inc. (Del. Apr. 18, 1985)
Dec. 17, 2002 – Acquired by Waddell & Reed Financial Inc. for Cdn$4.05 per sh.

MacKenzie Mining Ltd. (B.C. 1968)
Dec. 30, 1974 – Charter cancelled.

Macketta Gold Mines Ltd. (Man. 1936)
1955 – Charter cancelled.

MacKinnon Structural Steel Company, Limited (Can. 1943)
Dec. 31, 1969 – Name changed to QSP Ltd. ■

Mackwa Mines Ltd. (Ont. 1946)
Jan. 1958 – Dissolved.

Mackwick Manganese Mines Ltd. (Ont. 1953)
1957 – Charter cancelled.

Maclan Exploration Inc. (Que. 1952)
June 18, 1986 – Name changed to Can-Mac Exploration Ltd. (see FPsurvey - Mines & Energy)

Maclan Exploration Limited (Que. 1952)
1981 – Name changed to Maclan Exploration Inc. ■

Maclaren Minerals Ltd. (B.C. Feb. 2, 2022)
Mar. 10, 2025 – Name changed to Sankamap Metals Inc. (see FPsurvey - Mines & Energy)

Maclaren Power & Paper Company (Que. 1930)
June 3, 1980 – Acquired by Noranda Mines Ltd.; basis $40 per sh. or 11 Noranda shs. for 6 Maclaren cl. A or B shs. (see Noranda Mines Ltd.)

Maclean-Hunter Cable TV Limited (Ont. 1967)
1978 – Parent co. Maclean-Hunter Limited acquired all remaining o/s shs. in 1977-78 for $14 per sh. (see Maclean-Hunter Limited)

Maclean-Hunter Limited (Ont. Apr. 30, 1891)
Apr. 29, 1981 – Name changed to Maclean Hunter Limited. ■

Maclean Hunter Limited (Ont. Apr. 30, 1891)
May 13, 1994 – Acquired by Rogers Communications Inc. for $17.50 per sh.

Maclean-Hunter Publishing Company, Limited (Ont. Apr. 30, 1891)
Apr. 9, 1968 – Name changed to Maclean-Hunter Limited. ■

The Maclean Publishing Company, Limited (Ont. Apr. 30, 1891)
May 18, 1945 – Name changed to Maclean-Hunter Publishing Company, Limited. ■

MacLeod-Cockshutt Gold Mines Ltd. (Ont. 1933)
1967 – Merged into MacLeod Mosher Gold Mines Ltd.

MacLeod Mosher Gold Mines Ltd. (Ont. 1967)
1968 – Acquired by Lake Shore Mines Ltd.; basis 1 new for 4 old shs.

MacLeod's Limited (Man. 1917)
July 31, 1964 – All o/s 6% pref. shs. ser. A redeemed June 15, 1964, at $21 per sh. plus accr. divd. of 10¢ per sh. All o/s 6% s.f. debs., ser. A, red. at 103.50. No further public interest, as all com. stk. held by Gamble-Skogmo Inc.

MacMillan & Bloedel Limited (Can. 1930)
Dec. 31, 1959 – Merged with Powell River Company Limited to form MacMillan, Bloedel and Powell River Limited; basis 7 new for 3 old shs. (see MacMillan, Bloedel and Powell River Limited)

MacMillan, Bloedel and Powell River Limited (B.C. Dec. 31, 1959 amalg.)
May 10, 1966 – Name changed to MacMillan Bloedel Limited. ■

MacMillan Bloedel Limited (B.C. Dec. 31, 1959 amalg.)
Apr. 27, 1998 – Continued into Canada.
Nov. 1, 1999 – Amalgamated with Weyerhaeuser Company Limited, a wholly owned Cdn. subsid. of Weyerhaeuser Company; basis 0.28 Weyerhaeuser Company Limited exch. shs. or 0.28 Weyerhaeuser Company shs. for 1 MacMillan Bloedel sh.

MacMillan Energy Corp. (Can. Dec. 5, 1979)
Oct. 14, 1988 – Name changed to MacMillan Gold Corp. ■

MacMillan Gold Corp. (Can. Dec. 5, 1979)
Nov. 5, 2008 – Amalgamated with Duran Resources ULC, a wholly owned subsid. of Duran Ventures Inc.; basis 1 Duran Ventures sh. for 2 MacMillan shs. (see Duran Ventures Inc.)

MacMillan Minerals Inc. (Can. Sept. 5, 2008)
July 7, 2016 – Name changed to Maverix Metals Inc. following reverse takeover acquisition of (old) Maverix Metals Inc.; basis 1 new for 2 old shs. ■

MacMillan Rothesay Ltd. (N.B. 1969)
1982 – Name changed to Rothesay Paper Limited , a wholly owned subsid. of Irving Pulp & Paper Ltd. of New Brunswick.

MacNeill Industrial Inc. (B.C. 1987)
Oct. 30, 1989 – Name changed to MacNeill International Industries Inc. ■

MacNeill International Industries Inc. (B.C. 1987)
Nov. 1, 1991 – Amalgamated with Julia Resources Corporation to form Spokane Resources Ltd.; basis 1 new for 4 Julia Resources shs. and 1 new for 4 MacNeill International shs. (see Spokane Resources Ltd.)

Maco Industries Ltd. (B.C. 1945)
Apr. 1983 – Placed into receivership. Thorne Riddell as Trustee in Bankruptcy, liquidated assets. Creditors received 7¢ on the dollar.

Macon Mining Co. Ltd. (Ont. 1959)
Jan. 1973 – Charter cancelled.

Macquarie Emerging Markets Infrastructure Income Fund (Ont.)
Apr. 5, 2017 – Terminated; special distribution of 10¢ per fund unit payable to unithldrs. of record Mar. 31, 2017, plus a final unknown payment based on the NAV per unit.

Macquarie Global Infrastructure Income Fund (Ont. Sept. 27, 2013)
Dec. 20, 2017 – Name changed to Redwood Global Infrastructure Income Fund. ■

Macquarie NexGen Global Infrastructure Corporation (Ont. Jan. 26, 2007)
May 13, 2011 – Merged into NexGen Canadian Balanced Growth Tax Managed Fund (unlisted open-ended fund); basis net asset value of the co. per sh.

Macquarie Power and Infrastructure Corporation (B.C. May 20, 2010)
Apr. 15, 2011 – Name changed to Capstone Infrastructure Corporation pursuant to the internalization of management functions previously provided by Macquarie Power Management Ltd. ■

Macquarie Power & Infrastructure Income Fund (Ont. Mar. 15, 2004)
Jan. 1, 2011 – Succeeded by Macquarie Power and Infrastructure Corporation pursuant to plan of arrangement whereby Macquarie Power and Infrastructure Corporation was formed to facilitate the conversion of the fund into a corporation and the fund was subsequently wound up. ■

Macquarie Power Income Fund (Ont. Mar. 15, 2004)
Feb. 21, 2006 – Name changed to Macquarie Power & Infrastructure Income Fund. ■

MacQuest Resources Ltd. (Can. June 17, 1987)
Sept. 21, 1989 – Name changed to Polo Petroleum Ltd.; basis 1 new for 10 old shs. ■

Macro Enterprises Inc. (B.C. Jan. 30, 2006 amalg.)
Apr. 25, 2022 – Privatized; basis $4 cash per sh. ■

Macrotrends International Ventures Inc. (B.C. Aug. 17, 1988 amalg.)
Nov. 22, 1991 – Formed Global Election Systems Inc. in British Columbia on amalgamation with North American Professional Technologies B.C. Ltd.; basis 1 new for 8 old shs. ■

Macrotrends Ventures Inc. (B.C. 1982 amalg.)
Aug. 17, 1988 – Formed Macrotrends International Ventures Inc. in British Columbia on amalgamation with Racer Resources Ltd. (1 for 1); basis 1 new for 1 old sh. ■

Macu Mines Ltd. (Ont. 1954)
1955 – Acquired by Cusco Mines Ltd. (see Cusco Mines Ltd.)

Macusani Yellowcake Inc. (Ont. Oct. 31, 2007 amalg.)
May 1, 2015 – Name changed to Plateau Uranium Inc.; basis 1 new for 8 old shs. ■

Macvay Red Lake Mines Ltd. (Ont. 1945)
Name changed to Carinor Porcupine Mines Ltd. ■

Macwin Mines Ltd. (Ont. 1961)
1969 – Charter cancelled.

Groupe Macyro Inc. (Can. Nov. 28, 1978)
July 6, 2007 – Acquired by 4418565 Canada Inc., an indirect wholly owned subsid. of RED Holdings Group, Inc.; basis 1 new pref. sh. of 4418565 Canada immediately redeemable for $1.77 per sh. for 1 Macyro com. sh.

Mad Catz Interactive, Inc. (Can. Aug. 25, 1993)
Mar. 31, 2017 – Made a voluntary assignment into bankruptcy. PricewaterhouseCoopers Inc. appointed trustee and all officers and directors resigned.

Mad Jack Holdings Ltd. (B.C. June 14, 1996)
Apr. 26, 2000 – Name changed to Staccato's Inc. following Qualifying Transaction acquisition of 768158 Alberta Ltd. ■

Mad River Resources Inc. (B.C. Jan. 5, 1987)
July 8, 1992 – Name changed to Canadian Educational Courseware, Inc. ■

Madacy Entertainment Income Fund (Que. Mar. 1, 2005)
Mar. 27, 2009 – All fund units redeemed for 39¢ per unit following acquisition of subsid. Madacy Entertainment LP by Clarke Inc. and sr. mgt. of Madacy Entertainment Income Fund.

Madalena Energy Inc. (Alta. Sept. 26, 2006)
Oct. 25, 2019 – Name changed to Centaurus Energy Inc. (see FPsurvey - Mines & Energy)

Madalena Ventures Inc. (B.C. Sept. 14, 2001 amalg.)
Sept. 26, 2006 – Continued into Alberta.
Aug. 2, 2013 – Name changed to Madalena Energy Inc. ■

Madawaska Feldspar Co. Ltd. (Ont. 1948)
Oct. 17, 1960 – Dissolved.

Madeleine Mines Ltd. (Que. Feb. 2, 1968)
Jan. 1992 – Amalgamated with a wholly owned Quebec subsidiary of 2750538 Canada Inc. and wound up into the latter which changed its name to Madeleine Mines Ltd.
June 24, 1993 – Name changed to North American Palladium Ltd. ■

Madenta Communications Inc. (Alta. Nov. 7, 1988)
Apr. 7, 1998 – Name changed to Madenta Inc. ■

Madenta Inc. (Alta. Nov. 7, 1988)
May 2, 2006 – Struck from register and dissolved. ■

Madex Mines Ltd. (Que. 1963)
Aug. 23, 1986 – Charter cancelled.

Madge Mines Ltd. (Ont. Dec. 17, 1946)
June 3, 1947 – Name changed to Consolidated Fulbro Gold Mines Ltd. ■

Madi Minerals Ltd. (B.C. Mar. 4, 2021)
Jan. 27, 2023 – Name changed to Pegmatite One Lithium and Gold Corp. (see FPsurvey - Mines & Energy)

Madison Avenue Partners Inc. (Ont. June 30, 1990 amalg.)
Mar. 27, 1992 – Name changed to Madison Avenue Sports Network Limited; basis 1 new for 5 old shs. ■

Madison Avenue Sports Network Limited (Ont. June 30, 1990 amalg.)
June 3, 1994 – Name changed to Madison Partners Limited. ■

Madison Capital Corporation (Alta. June 13, 2011)
May 22, 2014 – Formed Radient Technologies Inc. in Canada on Qualifying Transaction amalgamation with (old) Radient Technologies Inc. (deemed acquiror); basis 1 new for 10 old shs. (see FPsurvey - Industrials)

Madison Energy Corp. (B.C. Feb. 21, 1974)
Aug. 29, 2003 – Continued into Alberta.
Apr. 16, 2010 – Amalgamated with Clampett Energy Ltd.; basis 1 Clampett cl. B redeem. pref. sh. for 1 Madison com. sh., immediately redeemed for 20¢ per sh. Co. now private.

Madison Enterprises Corp. (B.C. Aug. 20, 1979)
Oct. 29, 2004 – Name changed to Madison Minerals Inc.; basis 1 new for 5 old shs. ■

Madison Grant Resources Inc. (Que. 1951)
June 1, 1994 – Amalgamated with 9003-7136 Quebec Inc., a wholly owned subsid. of Banro International Capital Inc., to continue as Madison Grant Resources Inc. on June 1, 1994; basis 1 new sh. Banro for 6 old shs. of Madison Grant. (see Banro International Capital Inc.)
Mar. 2, 1995 – Voluntarily dissolved. All assets wound up into its parent company, Banro International Capital Inc. (see Banro International Capital Inc.)

Madison Holdings Ltd. (B.C. 1984)
Apr. 10, 1991 – Name changed to Consolidated Madison Holdings Ltd.; basis 1 new for 4 old shs. ■

Madison Holdings Limited (Ont. June 30, 1990 amalg.)
Jan. 13, 1998 – Name changed to Northpoint Corporation. ■

Madison Metals Inc. (B.C. Oct. 11, 2019)
Dec. 16, 2024 – Name changed to Critical One Energy Inc. (see FPsurvey - Mines & Energy)

Madison Minerals Inc. (B.C. Aug. 20, 1979)
May 14, 2014 – Name changed to Battle Mountain Gold Inc. following reverse takeover acquisition of (old) Battle Mountain Gold Inc.; basis 1 new for 4 old shs. ■

Madison Mining Corp. (Que. 1956)
Dec. 1973 – Charter cancelled.

Madison Oil & Gas Limited (Can. 1926)
Feb. 28, 1987 – Formed Knee Hill Energy Canada Ltd. in Canada on amalgamation with Knee Hill Energy Ltd. ■

Madison Oil Company Inc. (Alta. Dec. 20, 1988)
July 12, 2000 – Continued into Delaware. (see Toreador Resources Corporation)
Jan. 7, 2002 – Amalgamated with Toreador Resources Corporation; basis 0.118 Toreador shs. plus 1 rt. for 1 Madison sh. (see Toreador Resources Corporation)

Madison Oils Limited (Can. 1926)
June 26, 1984 – Name changed to Madison Oil & Gas Limited; basis 1 new for 10 old shs. ■

Madison Pacific Properties Inc. (N.S. Apr. 30, 1963)
Nov. 7, 1988 – Continued into British Columbia.
Feb. 26, 1990 – Continued into Canada. (see FPsurvey - Industrials)

Madison Partners Limited (Ont. June 30, 1990 amalg.)
Jan. 2, 1997 – Name changed to Madison Holdings Limited; basis 1 new for 10 old shs. ■

Madoc Mining Company Ltd. (B.C. June 1, 1995)
Jan. 28, 1999 – Name changed to Adobe Ventures Inc.; basis 1 new for 5 old shs. ■

Madonna Educational Group of Canada Ltd. (B.C. July 12, 1982 amalg.)
July 14, 1989 – Delisted from the Vancouver Stock Exchange. Subsequently struck from register and dissolved.

Madonna Mines Ltd. (Ont. 1945)
May 1959 – Name changed to Outlook Explorations Ltd. ■

Madonna Resources Ltd. (B.C. 1980)
July 17, 1984 – Name changed to Aricana Resources Inc. (see FPsurvey - Mines & Energy)

Madre Mining Ltd. (Alta. 1968)
Mar. 20, 1986 – Name changed to Cortez Corporation following amalgamation with Ram Industries, Inc. (a Nevada Corporation); basis 1 new for 5 old shs. ■

Madrona Explorations Co. Ltd. (B.C. 1965)
Feb. 1971 – Merged into International Mariner Resources Ltd.; basis 1 new for 4.75 old shs. plus 1 ser. C sh. purch. wt. of International Mariner for each 2 shs. received on exch.

Madrona Resources Inc. (B.C. 1983)
Jan. 22, 1993 – Dissolved and struck off register.

Madsen Gold Corp. (Ont. June 26, 1987)
June 8, 1998 – Acquired by Claude Resources Inc.; basis 1 Claude sh. for 3.5 Madsen shs. (see Claude Resources Inc.)

Maesa Gaming Management Inc. (B.C. Feb. 16, 1983)
July 17, 1998 – Dissolved and struck off register.

Maesa Petroleum Inc. (B.C. Feb. 16, 1983)
Jan. 13, 1994 – Name changed to Maesa Gaming Management Inc. ■

The Maestral Group Inc. (B.C. 1984)
June 4, 1993 – Dissolved and struck off register.

Maestro Capital Corporation (Alta. Apr. 15, 2014)
Feb. 24, 2017 – Voluntarily dissolved following the distribution of Relevium Technologies Inc.'s units (1 com. sh. & 1 wt.) to shldrs. of record Dec. 21, 2016, on the basis of 0.25 Relevium units for 1 Maestro com. sh. Acquisition of Relevium's units constituted the company's Qualifying Transaction.

Maestro Ventures Ltd. (B.C. Dec. 20, 1996)
Oct. 6, 2010 – Name changed to Invenio Resources Corp.; basis 1 new for 3 old shs. ■

Mafricor Resources Inc. (Que. Aug. 1, 1978 amalg.)
Nov. 5, 1999 – Struck off register.

Mag Copper Limited (Ont. Apr. 15, 1997)
Aug. 22, 2017 – Name changed to Integra Resources Corp.; basis 1 new for 2.5 old shs. ■

Mag-Iron Mining & Milling Ltd. (Ont. 1949)
Dec. 6, 1972 – Dissolved.

Mag One Products Inc. (B.C. June 18, 2007)
Oct. 20, 2020 – Name changed to Cover Technologies Inc.; basis 1 new for 20 old shs. ■

Magadyne Industries Ltd. (Alta. 1965)
1975 – Acquired by Grandview Industries Ltd., a wholly owned subsid. of Noranda Mines, at $1.15 per com. and $1.00 per pref. sh.

Magdalena Red Lake Mines Ltd. (Ont. 1946)
1954 – Merged into Pardee Amalgamated Mines Ltd.; basis 1 new for 20 old shs. (see Pardee Amalgamated Mines Ltd)

Magellan Biotech Inc. (Can. Nov. 16, 2000)
Oct. 11, 2002 – Name changed to Miraculins Inc. following Qualifying Transaction acquisition of Miraculins Inc. ■

Magellan Minerals Ltd. (B.C. Oct. 5, 2004)
May 9, 2016 – Acquired by Anfield Nickel Corp.; basis 0.0863 Anfield com. shs. for 1 Magellan com. sh. (see Anfield Nickel Corp.)

Magellan Resources Corp. (B.C. 1983)
Dec. 10, 1990 – Amalgamated with International Mahogany Corp. and Goldsil Resources Limited to form a new company with the same name International Mahogany Corp.; basis 0.22 cl. B subord. vtg. sh. for 1 com. sh. (see International Mahogany Corp.)

Magen Ventures I Inc. (Ont. Feb. 9, 2021)
Nov. 11, 2022 – Name changed to Grey Wolf Animal Health Corp. pursuant to the Qualifying Transaction reverse takeover acquisition of Grey Wolf Animal Health Inc.; basis 1 new for 16.6667 old shs. (see FPsurvey - Industrials)

Magenta Development Corporation (B.C. 1972)
Oct. 14, 1994 – Dissolved and struck off register.

Maggie Mines Ltd. (B.C. Feb. 27, 1978)
Mar. 29, 1985 – Name changed to International Maggie Mines Ltd.; basis 1 new for 2 old shs. ■

Magi Gold Mines Ltd. (Ont. 1972)
July 6, 1983 – Amalgamated with 8 other cos. to form Lobo Gold & Resources Inc.; basis 1 new for 10 old shs.

Magic Foods Inc. (Ont. May 22, 1973)
May 15, 1998 – Name changed to Lucre Ventures Ltd. and continued into British Columbia; basis 1 new for 2 old shs. ■

Magic Key Petroleums (B.C. Feb. 26, 1937)
In liquidation. H. D. Campbell, 510 W. Hastings St., Vancouver, liquidator.

Magic 3 Industries Ltd. (B.C. Nov. 3, 1982)
Oct. 15, 1986 – Name changed to Rent-A-Wreck Industries Corp. ■

MagiCorp Entertainment Inc. (B.C. Mar. 28, 1979)
July 5, 2004 – Name changed to Lucid Entertainment Inc.; basis 1 new for 10 old shs. ■

Magin Energy Inc. (B.C. Aug. 23, 1987)
Feb. 29, 1996 – Continued into Alberta. (see Magin Energy Inc.)
Oct. 15, 1996 – Amalgamated with Equis Energy Corp. (1 for 11), Denergy Limited (1 for 1) and Magin Finance Corp. to form a new co. also named Magin Energy Inc.; basis 1 new for 1 old sh. (see Magin Energy Inc.)

Magin Energy Inc. (Alta. Sept. 26, 1996)
July 4, 2001 – Acquired by NCE Petrofund Corp., a wholly owned subsid. of NCE Petrofund, for $5.86 or 0.896 NCE trust units, or a combination thereof. (see NCE Petrofund)

MagIndustries Corp. (Ont. Oct. 23, 1997 amalg.)
Jan. 10, 2006 – Continued into Canada. (see FPsurvey - Mines & Energy; FPsurvey - Industrials)

Magino Gold Mines Ltd. (Ont. 1939)
1950 – Wound up. Bondholders received 50¢ on the dollar. Nothing available for shldrs.

Magistral Biotech Inc. (Can. Dec. 18, 1998)
Jan. 24, 2007 – Formed Immunotec Inc. in Canada following reverse takeover acquisition of and amalgamation with Immunotec Research Ltd.; basis 1 new for 40 old shs. ■

Magma Energy Corp. (B.C. Jan. 22, 2008)
May 18, 2011 – Name changed to Alterra Power Corp. pursuant to acquisition of Plutonic Power Corporation. ■

Magma Metals Limited (Australia June 2, 2005)
July 5, 2012 – Acquired by Panoramic Resources Limited; basis 1 Panoramic sh. for 7 Magma Metals shs.

Magna Carta Resources Inc. (Alta. Nov. 19, 1987)
Nov. 5, 1992 – Name changed to Allyn Resources, Inc.; basis 1 new for 2 old shs. ■

Magna Electronics Corporation Limited (Ont. Nov. 16, 1961)
Jan. 2, 1973 – Name changed to Magna International Inc. (see FPsurvey - Industrials)

Magna Minerals International Ltd. (B.C. 1969)
Jan. 27, 1975 – Charter cancelled.

Magna Pipe Line Company Limited (B.C. 1953)
Dec. 1962 – Shldrs. and wt. holders approved sale of assets to Cascade Natural Gas Corp. of Seattle for $5,818,700 in 5 1/4 % conv. subord. Cascade debs., due Sept. 30, 1970. Each sh. of Magna received $5.25 of debs. conv. into 7 Cascade com. shs. for each $100 princ. amt. In addition, Cascade issued a 5-year wt. for each of the 187,500 o/s Magna wts.

Magna Power Corp. (Alta. Mar. 9, 1995)
May 15, 1996 – Name changed to Canyon Creek Food Company Ltd. (see FPsurvey - Industrials)

Magna Resources Ltd. (B.C. June 5, 2006)
Aug. 19, 2014 – Name changed to American Potash Corp. ■

Magna Ventures Ltd. (B.C. Dec. 23, 1983)
Aug. 9, 1990 – Name changed to Consolidated Magna Ventures Ltd.; basis 1 new for 7 old shs. ■

Magnasonic Canada Inc. (Can. 1954)
Feb. 1, 1983 – Under an amended offer dated Dec. 3, 1982, co. acquired more than 90% of its own o/s com. shs. by the expiry date of. Purch. price was $5.70 per sh.; subsequently increased to $7.00 and later to $9.00 per sh. co. acquired the remaining o/s shs. following section 199 of the CBCA.

Magnasonic Canada Ltd. (Can. 1954)
June 30, 1980 – Name changed to Magnasonic Canada Inc. ■

Magnate Ventures Inc. (B.C. Sept. 1, 2006)
Sept. 1, 2009 – Amalgamated with Thor Explorations Ltd. (N.P.L.) to form Thor Explorations Ltd. with Thor the deemed acquiror; basis 0.5 new for 1 old Thor sh. and 0.42 new for 1 old Magnate sh. (see Thor Explorations Ltd.)

Magnatron International Corp. (B.C. July 4, 1978)
Mar. 17, 1994 – Name changed to QI Technologies Corp.; basis 1 new for 5 old shs. ■

Magnesium Alloy Corporation (Ont. Oct. 23, 1997 amalg.)
Feb. 4, 2005 – Name changed to MagIndustries Corp. ■

Magnet Consolidated Mines Ltd. (Ont. Apr. 23, 1936)
1965 – Name changed to Conigo Mines Ltd.; basis 1 new for 5 old shs. ■

Magnet Explorations Ltd. (B.C. 1965)
Sept. 26, 1969 – Formed Ballinderry Explorations Ltd. following merger with Ballinderry Royalties Corporation Ltd.; basis 1 new for 3 old shs. ■

Magnet Forensics Inc. (Ont. Oct. 4, 2010)
Apr. 12, 2023 – Acquired by Thomas Bravo, LLC; basis Cdn$44.25 cash per subordinate vtg. sh.

Magnetics International Ltd. (Que. 1947)
Aug. 31, 1987 – Name changed to Mavtech Holdings Inc. ■

Magnetron Mining Ltd. (B.C. 1968)
Feb. 25, 1983 – Struck off register.

Magni Mining Corp. Ltd. (Ont. 1960)
1962 – Formed Copper Reef Mines Ltd. in Ontario; basis 1 new for 5 old shs. ■

Magnifoam Technology International Inc. (Ont. Nov. 22, 1995)
May 27, 2005 – Name changed to MTI Global Inc. ■

Magnipower Industries Inc. (Ont. 1987 amalg.)
Sept. 16, 1988 – Amalgamated with Battery Technologies Inc. to continue as Battery Technologies Inc.

Magnitude Mining Ltd. (B.C. Feb. 17, 2011)
Sept. 29, 2020 – Name changed to Pucara Gold Ltd. pursuant to Qualifying Transaction reverse takeover acquisition of Pucara Resources Corp.; basis 1 new for 2 old shs. ■

Magnolia Colombia Ltd. (Ont. Aug. 21, 2014)
Sept. 30, 2020 – Name changed to Gamesquare Esports Inc. pursuant to the reverse takeover acquisition of Gamesquare Inc. and concurrent amalgamation of Gamesquare with wholly owned 2631443 Ontario Inc.; basis 1 new for 5.8 old shs. ■

Magnolia Mines Limited (Man. 1950)
1957 – Charter cancelled.

Magnor Mining Corp. Ltd. (Ont. 1966)
Oct. 23, 1974 – Charter cancelled.

Magnotta Winery Corporation (Ont. June 17, 1988)
Jan. 27, 2012 – Privatized at $2.90 per sh.

Magnum Capital Corp. (Alta. Apr. 4, 2011)
Nov. 8, 2013 – Name changed to Magnum Goldcorp Inc. pursuant to Qualifying Transaction acquisition of gold property option in British Columbia. ■

Magnum Consolidated Mining Co. Ltd. (B.C. 1958)
Sept. 7, 1977 – Struck off register.

Magnum Copper Ltd. (B.C. 1958)
Jan. 3, 1962 – Name changed to Magnum Consolidated Mining Co. Ltd.; basis 1 new for 2 old shs. ■

Magnum Energy Inc. (B.C. June 27, 2003)
Feb. 18, 2010 – Continued into Alberta.
May 26, 2016 – Placed into receivership. Grant Thornton Ltd. appointed reciever.
June 24, 2016 – Sale of oil and gas assets was completed. Secured creditors suffered a shortfall, No monies available for unsecured creditors or shldrs.
Dec. 13, 2016 – Receiver was discharged and receivership proceedings terminated. (see FPsurvey - Mines & Energy)

Magnum Fund Limited (Can. 1906)
1978 – Acquired by Copthall (Tillburg) B.V. for US$42.552 per sh.

Magnum Gold Mines Ltd. (Ont. 1945)
1952 – Charter cancelled.

Magnum Goldcorp Inc. (Alta. Apr. 4, 2011)
July 25, 2014 – Continued into British Columbia. (see FPsurvey - Mines & Energy)

Magnum Minerals Corp. (B.C. July 17, 1984)
Oct. 3, 2005 – Name changed to Magnum Uranium Corp. ∎

Magnum Uranium Corp. (B.C. July 17, 1984)
July 3, 2009 – Acquired by Energy Fuels Inc.; basis 0.78 Energy Fuel shs. for 1 Magnum Uranium sh.

Magnus Energy Inc. (Alta. Jan. 25, 2005)
Dec. 24, 2007 – Acquired by Questerre Energy Corp.; basis 0.15316 Questerre sh. for 1 cl. A sh. Previously, each cl. B shs. exchanged for 10 cl. A shs.

Magnus Resources Ltd. (B.C. 1984)
Oct. 24, 1986 – Name changed to Enerteck Energy Technologies Corporation. ∎

Magoma Mines Ltd. (Ont. 1954)
Mar. 1976 – Charter cancelled.

Magra Computer Technologies Corp. (Ont. Aug. 14, 1996 amalg.)
Nov. 20, 2006 – Dissolved and struck from register.

Magusi River Explorations Inc. (Ont. 1972)
Nov. 5, 1976 – Amalgamated with 7 other cos. to form Wolverine Developments Inc.; basis 1 new for 19 old shs.

Magwell Long Lac Gold Mines Ltd. (Ont. 1934)
1957 – Charter cancelled.

Mahalo Energy Ltd. (Alta. Apr. 21, 2004)
Oct. 12, 2010 – All o/s sh. capital cancelled and creditor obligations settled pursuant to Companies' Creditors Arrangement Act (Canada) plan of arrangement.

Maharaja Minerals, Limited (B.C. Nov. 17, 1971)
June 28, 1977 – Name changed to Mecca Minerals Limited. (see FPsurvey - Mines & Energy)

Mahdia Gold Corp. (Alta. Feb. 16, 1987)
Mar. 25, 2013 – Continued into Ontario. (see FPsurvey - Mines & Energy)

Maher Inc. (Ont. 1978 amalg.)
May 1992 – Declared bankrupt.
May 1993 – All assets sold. The secured creditors suffered a significant shortfall, and there was no distribution to unsecured creditors or shldrs.
Aug. 1, 1993 – Trustee, Ernst & Young, discharged.

Maher Shoes Limited (Ont. 1912)
1974 – Grafton Group Limited purchased all o/s com. shs.; basis $41 plus $50 princ. of 7¼% conv. debs. of Grafton Group for each 2 Maher Shoes com. shs. held.
May 6, 1978 – Amalgamated with wholly owned subsid., Copp the Shoe Man Limited, to form Maher Inc.

Maher Shoes Ontario Limited (Ont. 1912)
June 1966 – Name changed to Maher Shoes Limited. ∎

Mahogany Minerals Resources Inc. (B.C. Mar. 17, 1980)
Sept. 8, 1988 – Name changed to International Mahogany Corp.; basis 1 new for 2 old shs. ∎

Mahogany Minerals Resources Inc. (B.C. 1980)
July 7, 1987 – Amalgamated with Canadian Premium Resource Corporation to form a new co. also known as Mahogany Minerals Resources Inc.

Mahogany Mining Co. Ltd. (B.C. 1980)
Nov. 10, 1981 – Name changed to Mahogany Minerals Resources Inc. ∎

Maidstone Oils Ltd. (Ont. Sept. 15, 1948)
1954 – Taken over by Saskalon Uranium & Oils Ltd.; basis 1 new for 5 old shs.

Maiko Resources Ltd. (B.C. 1971)
1978 – Charter cancelled.

Mailman Corp. Ltd. (Que. 1935)
July 1964 – All o/s 5% pref. shs. of $100 par value called Aug. 14, 1964, at $102 plus accr. int. The Mailman family

and associates purchased priority and com. shs. not already owned at $27.50 per sh. Co. now private.

Main Exploration Co. Ltd. (Que. 1959)
Oct. 1974 – Charter cancelled.

Main Malartic Gold Mines Ltd. (Ont. 1944)
May 1958 – Dissolved.

Mainbreak Gold Mines Ltd. (Ont. 1945)
Aug. 25, 1966 – Dissolved.

Mainfort Marine International Corporation (B.C. 1983)
Mar. 4, 1994 – Dissolved and struck off register.

Mainframe Entertainment, Inc. (B.C. June 12, 1995)
June 6, 1997 – Continued into Canada.
Nov. 2, 2006 – Formed Rainmaker Entertainment Inc. on amalgamation with RNK Acquisitions Corp.; basis 1 new redeemable pfd. sh. for 1 old Mainframe com. sh. Preferreds were redeemed immediately at $0.24 cash per sh.

Mainline Cablevision of Kamloops Ltd. (B.C. 1974)
1980 – Name changed to Kamloops Cablenet Limited. ∎

Mainstream Minerals Corporation (Can. July 19, 2006)
Nov. 24, 2021 – Name changed to Radio Fuels Energy Corp. pursuant to the acquisition of Radio Fuels Resources Corp. ∎

Mainstreet Health Investments Inc. (B.C. Apr. 4, 2016)
Jan. 8, 2018 – Name changed to Invesque Inc. (see FPsurvey - Industrials)

Maislin Industries Ltd. (Que. 1970 amalg.)
Oct. 1, 1983 – Main operating subsidiary, Maislin Transport Ltd., was placed into bankruptcy by its creditors. Richter & Partners Inc. of Montreal was appointed trustee. Maislin Transport's U.S. subsids. were subject to Chapter 11 bankruptcy proceedings in Detroit and much of the Cdn. co.'s assets represented advances to U.S. affils. Maislin Transport's assets and operating permits were sold to Consolidated Freightways Corp. of Menlo, Ca., for US$7,300,000.
Mar. 1984 – The 1,160 former employees of Maislin, who held approx. 80% of the dollar value of claims, accepted an offer by Consolidated Freightways for monies owed them in back wages, severance and vacation pay.
May 1984 – Final payment was made to employees, amounting to 32.8¢ on the dollar.

Maisondor Gold Mines Ltd. (Ont. 1949)
1955 – Name changed to Dencroft Mines Ltd. ∎

Maitri Health Technologies Corp. (B.C. Nov. 22, 2011)
Nov. 1, 2021 – Name changed to Bloom Health Partners Inc. ∎

Majescor Resources Inc. (Can. Feb. 23, 1996)
Aug. 1, 2017 – Name changed to Albert Mining Inc. ∎

Majesta Minerals Inc. (Alta. Aug. 6, 2014)
Jan. 27, 2021 – Continued into British Columbia.
Feb. 11, 2021 – Name changed to Verano Holdings Corp. pursuant to reverse takeover acquisition of Verano Holdings, LLC. (see FPsurvey - Industrials)

Majestic Contractors Limited (Ont. Dec. 19, 1977)
Feb. 5, 1993 – Acquired by Banister Pipelines, a division of a wholly owned subsid. of Banister Inc., for $6.65 per sh. (see Banister Inc.)

Majestic Electronic Stores Inc. (Ont. 1981)
July 22, 1994 – Acquired by Adventure Electronics Inc.; basis 0.0092 Adventure Electronics shs. plus 0.021 wts. for 1 Majestic sh. (see Adventure Electronics Inc.)

Majestic Explorations Ltd. (B.C. 1966)
Sept. 25, 1978 – Charter cancelled.

Majestic Mines Ltd. (B.C. 1966)
1969 – Name changed to Majestic Explorations Ltd. ∎

Majestic Pipeline Contractors (Alberta) Limited (Alta.)
May 1974 – Amalgamated with Wiley Oilfield Hauling Ltd. to form Majestic Wiley Contractors Limited.

Majestic Resources Corporation (B.C. 1979)
Dec. 2, 1985 – Name changed to International Majestic Holdings Ltd.; basis 1 new for 5 old shs. (see FPsurvey - Mines & Energy)

Majestic Wiley Contractors Limited (Alta. May 1, 1974 amalg.)
Dec. 19, 1977 – Continued into Ontario.
Aug. 2, 1983 – Name changed to Majestic Contractors Limited. ∎

Major Consolidated Oils Limited (Alta. 1943)
1958 – Struck off register.

Major General Resources Ltd. (B.C. July 23, 1987)
May 6, 2002 – Name changed to Commander Resources Ltd.; basis 1 new for 3 old shs. ∎

Major Holdings & Developments Ltd. (Ont. 1964 amalg.)
1976 – Acquired by Union Gas Ltd.; basis 5/8 of a cl. A com. sh. Union Gas, or $2.00 plus 3/8 of a cl. A sh. Union Gas for each sh. of the co.

Major Laurent Mines Ltd. (Que. 1971)
May 22, 1982 – Charter cancelled.

Major Mines Ltd. (B.C. 1958)
May 15, 1969 – Struck off register.

Major Molybdenite Mines Ltd. (Ont. 1942)
Nov. 5, 1956 – Charter cancelled.

Major Oil Investments Ltd. (unknown)
1963 – Absorbed by parent co. Globe Oil Co. (1958) Ltd.

Major Oil Ltd. (Alta.)
Dec. 1956 – Assets acquired by Majortrans Oil & Mines Ltd.; basis 1 new for 5 old shs. (see Majortrans Oil and Mines Ltd.)

Major Precious Metals Corp. (B.C. June 5, 2006)
May 2, 2024 – Name changed to Intrusion Precious Metals Corp. (see FPsurvey - Mines & Energy)

Major Resources Ltd. (B.C. Aug. 19, 1966)
Dec. 7, 1982 – Name changed to Anvil Resources Ltd. ∎

Majorem Minerals Ltd. (B.C. Feb. 21, 1974)
Feb. 25, 1986 – Name changed to Radcliffe Resources Ltd.; basis 1 new for 5 old shs. ∎

Majorteck Industries Incorporated (B.C. Sept. 29, 1980)
Feb. 15, 1991 – Dissolved and struck off register.

Majortrans Oil and Mines Ltd. (Ont. 1944)
Nov. 9, 1967 – Dissolved.

Majuba Hill Copper Corp. (B.C. Mar. 10, 2017)
Apr. 4, 2024 – Name changed to Giant Mining Corp.; basis 1 new for 20 old shs. (see FPsurvey - Mines & Energy)

Mak Siccar Gold Mines Ltd. (B.C. 1931)
Dec. 28, 1950 – Charter cancelled.

Makaoo Development Company Limited (Can. Oct. 22, 1953)
Jan. 25, 1980 – Name changed to International Makaoo Limited; basis 1 new for 3 old shs. ∎

Makara Mining Corp. (B.C. Sept. 17, 2019)
Dec. 7, 2023 – Name changed to Hardcore Discoveries Ltd. (see FPsurvey - Mines & Energy)

Makena Resources Inc. (B.C. Apr. 15, 1981)
Apr. 15, 2019 – Name changed to Willow Biosciences Inc. pursuant to reverse takeover acquisition of BioCan Technologies Inc., and Epimeron Inc. ∎

Maklyn Ventures Capital Corp. (Alta. Nov. 17, 2003)
Apr. 1, 2005 – Formed QuStream Corporation in Ontario on Qualifying Transaction amalgamation with QuStream Corporation, constituting a reverse takeover by QuStream; basis 1 new for 2 QuStream shs. and 1 new for 2 Maklyn shs. ■

Makus Resources Inc. (B.C. 1986)
June 26, 1992 – Dissolved and struck off register.

Mala Noche Resources Corp. (B.C. Nov. 26, 2007)
Aug. 6, 2010 – Name changed to Primero Mining Corp.; basis 1 new for 20 old shs. ■

Malabar Mines Ltd. (B.C. Feb. 21, 1974)
Aug. 4, 1982 – Name changed to Majorem Minerals Ltd.; basis 1 new for 4 old shs. ■

Malabar Mining Ltd. (unknown)
1970 – Merged into Cosmic Nickel Mines Ltd.

Malabar Silver Mines Ltd. (B.C. Feb. 21, 1974)
July 10, 1978 – Name changed to Malabar Mines Ltd. ■

Malabec Explorations Ltd. (Ont. 1967)
Oct. 1972 – Dissolved.

Malahide Petroleum Corporation (Ont. Jan. 27, 1988)
Dec. 12, 1997 – Formed Stratic Energy Corporation in Ontario on amalgamation with Sahelian Oil Limited (deemed acquiror); basis 1 new for 1 Sahelian sh. and 1 new for 20 Malahide shs. ■

Malartic Gold Fields Ltd. (Que. 1935)
1955 – Merged into Malartic Gold Fields (Quebec) Limited.

Malartic Gold Fields (Quebec) Limited (Que. 1965 amalg.)
Apr. 28, 1979 – Name changed to Les Terrains Aurifères Malartic (Québec) Limitée. ■

Malartic Gold Mines Ltd. (Ont. 1927)
Name changed to Canadian Malartic Gold Mines Limited; basis 1 new for 2 old shs.
May 17, 1933 – Continued into Canada. ■

Malartic Hygrade Gold Mines (Canada) Ltd. (Ont. Feb. 4, 1975)
June 11, 1991 – Name changed to Republic Goldfields Inc. ■

Malartic Hygrade Gold Mines Ltd. (Ont. 1961)
June 1968 – Name changed to Malartic Hygrade Gold Mines (Quebec) Ltd. and continued into Quebec; basis 1 new for 10 old shs., 6% deb. holders received 5 new shs. in exchange for each $1 princ. amt. ■

Malartic Hygrade Gold Mines (Quebec) Ltd. (Que. June 1968)
Mar. 1, 1975 – Name changed to Malartic Hygrade Gold Mines (Canada) Ltd. following acquisition of the company's assets by a newly incorporated Ontario company. ■

Malartic Lakeshore Gold Mines Ltd. (Que. 1945)
Oct. 1973 – Charter cancelled.

Malartic River Mines Ltd. (Que. 1944)
Aug. 18, 1958 – Charter cancelled.

Malaspina Capital Ltd. (Alta. Aug. 2, 1996)
Nov. 21, 2001 – Formed Miranda Mining Corporation in Yukon on Qualifying Transaction amalgamation with Miranda Mining Development Corporation, constituting a reverse takeover by Miranda; basis 1 new for 1 Miranda sh. and 1 new for 4 Malaspina shs. ■

Malbar Goldfields Ltd. (Ont. 1946)
1963 – Charter cancelled.

Malbec Gold Mines Ltd. (Ont. 1945)
Aug. 18, 1958 – Charter cancelled.

Malbex Resources Inc. (Ont. Dec. 8, 2009)
Sept. 6, 2018 – Name changed to COIN HODL INC. ■

Malcolm Resources Ltd. (B.C. June 15, 1987)
Oct. 18, 1988 – Name changed to Pan-Pacific Petroleum Inc. ■

Malette Inc. (Ont. Apr. 14, 1969)
Aug. 15, 1995 – Acquired by Tembec Inc.; basis $16.50 or 1.138 new Tembec cl. A shs. for 1 old Malette sh. The 8-3/4% cv. sub. debs. were converted into sub. vtg. shs. on Jan. 20, 1995. The company continued operating under the name of Malette Inc. as a wholly owned subsidiary of Tembec.
Feb. 18, 1999 – Continued into Canada.
Mar. 1, 1999 – Name changed to Tembec Industries Inc.

Malette Industries Inc. (Can. Apr. 20, 2004)
Oct. 17, 2008 – Dissolved.

Malette Québec Inc. (Can. July 13, 1990)
Feb. 29, 2000 – Acquired by MQI Holdings Inc., an indirect wholly owned subsidiary of Tembec Inc., for $3.20 per sh. (see Tembec Inc.)

Malga Porcupine Gold Mines Ltd. (Ont. 1944)
June 12, 1961 – Dissolved.

Malibu Metals Ltd. (B.C. 1968)
Mar. 31, 1983 – Struck off register.

Malka Resources Ltd. (B.C. 1983)
Jan. 30, 1985 – Name changed to Electra Title Corporation. ■

Mallen Red Lake Gold Mines Ltd. (Ont. 1944)
1960 – Name changed to New Mallen Red Lake Mines Ltd.; basis 1 new for 3 old shs. ■

Mallich Quebec Gold Mines Ltd. (Ont. 1949)
Dec. 10, 1962 – Dissolved.

Malofilm Communications Inc. (Can. Aug. 16, 1993)
Dec. 9, 1997 – Name changed to Behaviour Communications Inc. ■

Malouf Exploration Co. Ltd. (Que. 1956)
Mar. 1976 – Charter cancelled.

Malrobic Mines Ltd. (Ont. 1928)
1952 – Charter cancelled.

Mamainse Mines Ltd. (Ont. Aug. 30, 1951)
1955 – Name changed to Coppercorp Ltd. ■

Mamit Lake Mining Ltd. (B.C. 1964)
1967 – Merged into Mamit Lake Mining Ltd. (see New Copper Mountain Mines Ltd.)
Aug. 9, 1974 – Amalgamated with Rocky Mountain Trench Mines Ltd. (1 for 2.5) to continue as New Copper Mountain Mines Ltd.; basis 1 new for 2.5 old shs. (see New Copper Mountain Mines Ltd.)

Mamma.com Inc. (Ont. July 5, 1985)
June 21, 2007 – Name changed to Copernic Inc. ■

Mammoth Capital Corporation (B.C. Feb. 27, 2007)
Sept. 3, 2009 – Dissolved following completion of Qualifying Transaction acquisition of 10,000,000 com. shs. of Primary Petroleum Corporation. Com. shldrs. received 1.2988 com. shs. of Primary Petroleum Corporation for each sh. held.

Mammoth Capital Corp. (B.C. Jan. 7, 2011)
Dec. 23, 2011 – Name changed to Mammoth Resources Corp. pursuant to Qualifying Transaction acquisition of Urique property option. (see FPsurvey - Mines & Energy)

Mammoth Energy Inc. (B.C. May 3, 1966)
Feb. 26, 1998 – Name changed to Cierra Pacific Ventures Ltd.; basis 1 new for 4 old shs. ■

Mammoth Petroleums Ltd. (Ont. Aug. 3, 1949)
1952 – Assets acquired by Ellesmere Oil & Development Ltd.; basis 1 new for 10 old shs.

Mammoth Resources Ltd. (B.C. 1981)
June 27, 1986 – Name changed to Sicanna Industries Ltd.; basis 1 new for 5 old shs. ■

Mammoth Silver Mines (B.C. 1954)
1975 – Charter cancelled.

Man-Echo Mines Ltd. (Ont. 1954)
1968 – Merged with other cos. to form Milestone Exploration Ltd.; basis 1,000 new for 13,211 old shs.

Man GLG Emerging Markets Income Fund (Ont. Oct. 24, 2011)
June 19, 2014 – Name changed to Next Edge GLG Emerging Markets Income Fund. ■

Man-Lun Mines Ltd. (Ont. 1954)
July 15, 1958 – Name changed to Port Dover Gas & Oil Limited. ■

Man-O-War Mines Ltd. (B.C. 1937)
1951 – Charter cancelled.

Manac Inc. (Que. Apr. 15, 2004)
Oct. 9, 2015 – Privatized; basis $10.20 cash per subordinate vtg. sh.

Manado Gold Corp. (B.C. Aug. 13, 2010)
Jan. 23, 2020 – Name changed to InsuraGuest Technologies Inc. pursuant to the reverse takeover acquisition of InsuraGuest Inc.; basis 1 new for 2 old shs. (see FPsurvey - Industrials)

Manalsab Petroleums Ltd. (Alta. 1952)
1960 – Struck off register.

Manalta Coal Income Trust (Alta.)
Sept. 24, 1998 – All o/s instalment receipts acquired by Luscar Coal Income Fund; basis 0.4 of a trust unit of Luscar for 1 old instalment receipt of Manalta. (see Luscar Coal Income Fund)

Manar Canada Inc. (Alta. 1979)
Jan. 1, 1996 – Dissolved and struck off register.

Manas Petroleum Corporation (Nev. July 9, 1998)
Jan. 20, 2014 – Name changed to MNP Petroleum Corporation. ■

Manasan Mines Limited (Can. 1963)
Jan. 15, 1998 – Dissolved.

Manasseh Silver Cobalt Mines Ltd. (Ont. 1931)
July 1973 – Charter cancelled.

Manataw Gold Mines Ltd. (Ont. 1945)
Mar. 1976 – Charter cancelled.

Manbar Explorations Ltd. (Ont. 1972)
1979 – Charter cancelled.

Mancap Global Ventures Inc. (Alta. June 1, 1995 amalg.)
June 10, 2002 – Privatized; basis 1 pfce. sh. for 1 com. sh. immediately redeemed for 7¢ per sh.

La Mancha Resources Inc. (B.C. Oct. 10, 1996)
Nov. 13, 2012 – Acquired by 0944289 B.C. Ltd., a wholly owned subsid. of Weather Investments II S.A.R.L., for $3.50 per sh.

Manchester Oil Corporation (B.C. 1969)
Jan. 16, 1984 – Name changed to Manchester Resources Corporation. ■

Manchester Resources Corporation (B.C. 1969)
Jan. 26, 1984 – Continued into Alberta.
Sept. 1, 1995 – Formed Danoil Energy Ltd. in Alberta following reverse takeover acquisition of and amalgamation with Danoil Energy Ltd.; basis 1 cl. A subord. vtg. for 1 cl. A vtg. sh. Prior to amalgamation, cl. A vtg. shs. were consolidated on a 1-for-10 basis. ■

Manchica Mining Co. Ltd. (Ont. 1950)
Charter cancelled.

Manco Gold Mines Ltd. (Can. 1924)
Nov. 1938 – Name changed to New Manco Gold Mines Ltd. and continued into Ontario. ■

Mandalay Gold Mines Ltd. (Man. 1934)
1955 – Charter cancelled.

Mandalay Resources Corporation (B.C. Jan. 29, 1997)
Aug. 7, 2025 – Acquired by Alkane Resources Limited; basis 7.875 Alkane ord. shs. for 1 Mandalay com. sh.

Mandarin Capital Corporation (B.C. Jan. 26, 1966)
Dec. 29, 1989 – Name changed to H.I.S.A. Investments Ltd. ■

Mandarin Gold Mines Ltd. (Ont. May 29, 1945)
Feb. 16, 1962 – Name changed to Mandarin Mines Limited; basis 1 new for 1 old sh. ■

Mandarin Industries Ltd. (B.C. July 10, 1987)
Sept. 28, 1997 – Continued into Cayman Islands.
Oct. 9, 1997 – Name changed to Leitak Enterprises Ltd.; basis 1 new for 4 old shs.

Mandarin Mines Limited (Ont. May 29, 1945)
Nov. 15, 1983 – Delisted from the Alberta Stock Exchange. Subsequently dissolved and charter cancelled.

Mandate National Mortgage Corporation (Can. Feb. 7, 1979)
Aug. 7, 1989 – Amalgamated in Canada to continue with same name.
July 4, 2023 – Wound up and dissolved. All o/s com. shs. redeemed for $9.25 cash per sh.

Mandorin Goldfields Inc. (B.C. 1987)
June 11, 1999 – Continued into Yukon.
Nov. 27, 2007 – Name changed to Sphere Resources Inc. (see FPsurvey - Mines & Energy)

Mandusa Resources Ltd. (B.C. 1984)
Aug. 22, 1988 – Name changed to MSA Petroleum Limited; basis 1 new for 5 old shs. ■

Mandy Mines Ltd. (Can. Jan. 1928)
Dec. 15, 1953 – Charter cancelled.

Maneast Uranium Corp. Ltd. (Can. 1928)
Feb. 27, 1973 – Dissolved.

Manele Bay Ventures Inc. (Can. Nov. 25, 1999)
July 15, 2003 – Name changed to MBA Gold Corp.; basis 2 new for 1 old sh. ■

Manera Capital Corp. (B.C. Sept. 9, 2013)
Nov. 22, 2016 – Name changed to GT Gold Corp. following Qualifying Transaction reverse takeover acquisition of New Chris Minerals Ltd. ■

Manfrey Capital Corporation (B.C. Aug. 10, 1995)
July 21, 2004 – Dissolved and struck from register.

Mangava Nickel Mines Ltd. (Ont. 1957)
Feb. 1962 – Charter cancelled.

Mangazeya Mining Ltd. (British Virgin Islands Dec. 10, 2010)
May 25, 2022 – All o/s held by minority shldrs. redeemed for Cdn$0.045 cash per sh.

Mango Resources Ltd. (B.C. Sept. 14, 1987)
Oct. 7, 1999 – Name changed to Consolidated Mango Resources Ltd.; basis 1 new for 5 old shs. ■

Mangrove Bay Resources Inc. (Ont. 1987)
Aug. 23, 1991 – Name changed to Mirror Oilfield Construction Corp.; basis 1 new for 2 old shs. (see FPsurvey - Mines & Energy)

Manhattan Mineral Corp. (B.C. Jan. 22, 1987)
July 12, 1989 – Name changed to Safety-Ject Medical Products Ltd. ■

Manhattan Minerals Corp. (B.C. Nov. 18, 1985)
Feb. 23, 2005 – Name changed to Mediterranean Minerals Corp. ■

Manhattan Oil Ltd. (B.C. June 15, 1979)
Dec. 17, 1981 – Name changed to Tulsa Crude Oil Corporation. ■

Manhattan Resources Ltd. (Alta. Dec. 9, 1999 amalg.)
Jan. 21, 2003 – Formed Pivotal Energy Ltd. on amalgamation with Cigar Oil & Gas Ltd. (0.471429 for 1); basis 1 new for 7 old shs. ■

Manhattan Yellowknife Mines Ltd. (Ont. 1945)
1961 – Charter cancelled.

Manicouagan Minerals Inc. (Can. July 25, 2001)
June 5, 2014 – Name changed to Murchison Minerals Ltd. following reverse takeover acquisition of Flemish Gold Corp. (see FPsurvey - Mines & Energy)

Manilake Mines Ltd. (Ont. 1953)
1956 – Name changed to Lenwood Mining & Exploration Ltd. ■

Manitex Capital Inc. (Ont. Oct. 1, 1986)
Mar. 12, 1998 – Continued into Canada. (see FPsurvey - Industrials)

Manitex Minerals Inc. (Ont. Oct. 1, 1986)
June 16, 1992 – Name changed to Manitex Capital Inc.; basis 1 new for 6 old shs. ■

Manitoba & Eastern Mines Ltd. (Can. 1928)
1954 – Name changed to Maneast Uranium Corp. Ltd.; basis 1 new for 5 old shs. ■

Manitoba Basin Consolidated Mines Ltd. (Ont. 1928)
Mar. 18, 1963 – Dissolved.

Manitoba Basin Mining Co. Ltd. (Ont. 1928)
Aug. 1946 – Name changed to Manitoba Basin Consolidated Mines Ltd.; basis 1 new pooled for 3 old shs. ■

Manitoba Platinum Resources Inc. (Ont. Oct. 1, 1986)
Apr. 11, 1988 – Name changed to Manitex Minerals Inc. ■

Manitoba Properties Inc. (Ont. 1972)
1984 – Continued into Canada.
Aug. 31, 1992 – All o/s 9.25% cum. redeem. retract. pfd. shs. ser. A. redeemed; basis $25.40 plus accr. and unpaid divds. of $0.3896 per sh.

Manitoba Telecom Services Inc. (Man. Apr. 28, 1933; vis special statute)
Aug. 3, 2004 – Amalgamated with wholly owned Qunara Inc. to form new co. with same name Manitoba Telecom Services Inc.
Mar. 17, 2017 – Name changed to Bell MTS Inc. ■

Manitoba Telephone System (Man. Apr. 28, 1933; vis special statute)
Jan. 7, 1997 – Name changed to Manitoba Telecom Services Inc. following the Province of Manitoba's sale of 100% interest in the company to the public. ■

Manitok Energy Inc. (Alta. July 8, 2010 amalg.)
Feb. 21, 2018 – Deemed bankrupt. Alvarez & Marsal Canada Inc. appointed trustee and all directors have resigned.

Manitou-Barvue Mines Limited (Ont. 1950)
May 11, 1983 – Name changed to Terratech Resources Inc. (see FPsurvey - Mines & Energy)

Manitou Capital Corporation (Ont. Oct. 16, 1997)
May 11, 2009 – Acquired by MTF Acquisitionco Ltd. for 23¢ per sh.

Manitou Gold Inc. (Ont. May 8, 2009)
May 25, 2023 – All o/s com. shs. not already held acquired by Alamos Gold Inc.; basis 1 Alamos Gold sh. for 283.68 Manitou Gold shs. (deemed price of 5¢ cash per sh.).

Manitou Lake Gold Mines Inc. (Ont. Oct. 28, 1974)
Dec. 1986 – Name changed to Amercoeur Energy (Canada) Ltd.; basis 1 new for 8 old shs. ■

Manitou Reef Resources Inc. (B.C. May 9, 1983)
July 15, 1988 – Name changed to Consolidated Manitou Resources Inc.; basis 1 new for 3 old shs. ■

Manitouwadge Lake Mining Co. Ltd. (Ont. 1954)
1957 – Name changed to Prudential Mining Co. of Canada. ■

Manix Mines Ltd. (Que. 1971)
Dec. 1972 – Name changed to Ziebart Corp. ■

Manley-O'Reilly Gold Mines Ltd. (Ont. 1921)
1927 – Acquired by Manor Gold Mines Ltd. (see Manor Gold Mines Ltd.)

Mann Oil Resources Inc. (Can. Mar. 3, 1981)
Oct. 26, 1989 – Name changed to Consolidated Mann Oil Inc. ■

Manning Timber Products Ltd. (B.C. 1947)
1957 – All o/s com. shs. acquired by Johnston Terminals and Storage Ltd.; basis 1 2nd pref. Johnston sh. for 1 com. sh.

Mannix Resources Inc. (B.C. Feb. 7, 1992)
July 12, 2000 – Creditor filed an order to have the company declared bankrupt.
July 31, 2000 – Declared bankrupt and Campbell Saunders Ltd. was appointed trustee.
June 2005 – Administration was still ongoing due to a lawsuit under which the trustee was attempting to recoup monies owed under the February 1999 sale of Asia Pacific Energy Company Limited.
Mar. 2006 – Litigation was resolved in the London, England, meetings. Distributions to shldrs. not known.
Dec. 2006 – Emerged from bankruptcy after all creditors had been paid in full with interest from original date of bankruptcy.
Jan. 11, 2007 – Trustee was discharged.
Feb. 27, 2014 – Name changed to International Tungsten Inc. ■

Mannville Oil & Gas Ltd. (Alta. Dec. 31, 1980 amalg.)
Aug. 2, 1995 – Acquired by Gulf Canada Resources Limited for $4.50 per sh. (see Gulf Canada Resources Limited)

Mano River Resources Inc. (Yuk. Mar. 29, 1996)
July 27, 2004 – Continued into British Columbia.
Oct. 14, 2009 – Name changed to African Aura Mining Inc. pursuant to acquisition of African Aura Resources Limited; basis 1 new for 8 old shs. ■

Manoir Industries Ltd. (Can. Sept. 3, 1963)
May 21, 1971 – Name changed to Canadian Manoir Industries Limited. (see FPsurvey - Mines & Energy)

Manoka Mining & Smelting Co. Ltd. (Ont. 1954)
Oct. 18, 1971 – Name changed to Cat Lake Mines Ltd.; basis 1 new for 16 old shs. ■

Manontqueb Exploration Ltd. (Ont. 1946)
Dec. 11, 1952 – Charter cancelled.

Manor Global Inc. (Can. Feb. 1, 2005)
Nov. 30, 2011 – Name changed to Martina Minerals Corp. pursuant to Qualifying Transaction reverse takeover acquisition of Compostela Mining Limited. (see FPsurvey - Mines & Energy)

Manor Gold Mines Ltd. (Ont. 1927)
Aug. 6, 1957 – Charter cancelled.

Manor Mines Ltd. (B.C. 1966)
Jan. 17, 1977 – Dissolved.

Manor Resources Inc. (Can. Dec. 12, 1990 amalg.)
Apr. 7, 1995 – Name changed to American Manor Corp.; basis 1 new for 10 old shs. ■

Manox Petroleum Ltd. (B.C. Mar. 15, 1972)
June 13, 1977 – Name changed to Petrox Petroleum Corporation. ■

Manridge Explorations Limited (Ont. Apr. 24, 1961)
Sept. 16, 1992 – Formed Equisure Financial Network Inc. on amalgamation with Equisure Financial Network Inc. (1.48 for 1); basis 1 new for 25 old shs. ■

Le Mans Explorations Limited (Ont. 1955)
Nov. 28, 1973 – Dissolved.

Mansa Exploration Inc. (B.C. June 10, 2016)
Mar. 11, 2022 – Name changed to Voltage Metals Corp. pursuant to the reverse takeover acquisition of Voltage Metals Inc. (see FPsurvey - Mines & Energy)

Mansa Explorations Ltd. (Ont. 1956)
Mar. 15, 1972 – Dissolved.

Mansfield Minerals Inc. (B.C. May 9, 1975)
Jan. 21, 2013 – Name changed to Goldrock Mines Corp. ■

Manson Creek Resources Ltd. (B.C. Mar. 4, 1983)
May 2, 1995 – Continued into Alberta.
Mar. 21, 2018 – Name changed to Jade Leader Corp. (see FPsurvey - Mines & Energy)

Mantaro Precious Metals Corp. (B.C. Mar. 6, 2008)
Apr. 16, 2024 – Name changed to First Andes Silver Ltd. (see FPsurvey - Mines & Energy)

Mantaro Silver Corp. (B.C. Mar. 6, 2008)
Nov. 4, 2021 – Name changed to Mantaro Precious Metals Corp. ■

Mantaur Goldfields Corp. (Ont. Feb. 2, 1951)
Aug. 11, 1997 – Name changed to Mantaur Petroleum Corporation. ■

Mantaur Petroleum Corporation (Ont. Feb. 2, 1951)
Mar. 23, 1999 – Formed Videoflicks.com Inc. in Ontario on amalgamation with 1318780 Ontario Limited and Videoflicks.com Limited; basis 1 new for 1 1318780 sh., 1 new for 1 Videoflicks.com sh. and 1 new for 5 Mantaur shs. ■

Manticore Petroleum Corp. (B.C. 1969)
May 31, 1988 – Name changed to Dexx Energy Corporation; basis 1 new for 5 old shs. ■

Mantis Mineral Corp. (Ont. May 30, 1997)
Feb. 24, 2014 – Formed Gondwana Oil Corp. in Ontario on amalgamation with Gondwana Energy Corp. (deemed acquiror); basis 1 new for 1 Gondwana Energy sh. and 1 new for 1 Mantis Mineral sh. ■

Mantle Minerals Inc. (B.C. Feb. 10, 1988)
Aug. 9, 2005 – Name changed to Mantle Resources Inc.; basis 1 new for 2 old shs. ■

Mantle Minerals Ltd. (B.C. 1966)
Feb. 25, 1983 – Struck off register.

Mantle Resources Inc. (B.C. Feb. 10, 1988)
Sept. 26, 2008 – Name changed to Canada Zinc Metals Corp. ■

Mantos Copper (Bermuda) Limited (Bermuda Aug. 18, 2015)
Mar. 22, 2022 – Continued into British Columbia.
Mar. 23, 2022 – Name changed to Capstone Copper Corp. pursuant to the reverse takeover acquisition of Capstone Mining Corp. (see FPsurvey - Mines & Energy)

Mantra Capital Inc. (B.C. Apr. 13, 2011)
Sept. 4, 2014 – Name changed to SolidusGold Inc. ■

Mantra Mining Inc. (B.C. July 30, 1998)
Sept. 28, 2009 – Name changed to TintinaGold Resources Inc. ■

Mantra Resources Limited (Australia Sept. 30, 2005)
June 8, 2011 – Acquired by JSC Atomredmetzoloto for A$6.87 plus A$0.15 divd. per sh.
Name changed to Mantra Resources Pty Limited.

Manufacturer Finance Programs Ltd. (Ont. Jan. 30, 1984)
May 27, 1993 – Name changed to MFP Technology Services Ltd. ■

Manufacturers Acceptance Co. Ltd. (Alta. 1960)
1966 – Amalgamated with Foundation Mortgage Corp. Ltd. (privately owned). Shldrs. offered 6.5 % debentures by Foundation.

Manufacturers Hanover Bank of Canada (Can. May 27, 1982)
Dec. 31, 1991 – Amalgamated with Chemical Bank of Canada. (see Chemical Bank of Canada)

Manufacturers Life Capital Corp. Inc. (Ont. 1976)
1984 – Continued into British Columbia.
1985 – Continued into Canada.
Jan. 4, 1993 – All o/s 1st pfd. ser. A shs. redeemed; basis $25 per sh. plus all accr. and unpaid divds. of $0.0149 per sh.

The Manufacturers Life Insurance Company (Can. June 23, 1887; via Special Act of Parliament)
Dec. 30, 2004 – Amalgamated with The Maritime Life Assurance Company and MFC Insurance Company Limited to continue as The Manufacturers Life Insurance Company, wholly owned subsid. of Manulife Financial Corporation.

Manulife Brompton Advantaged Bond Fund (Ont. Jan. 12, 2009)
Sept. 6, 2011 – Name changed to Aston Hill Advantage Bond Fund. ■

Manulife Financial Capital Trust (Ont. Oct. 1, 2001)
July 3, 2012 – All o/s MaCS ser. A shs. redeemed for $1,035 per sh.

Manulife Floating Rate Senior Loan Fund (Ont. Mar. 26, 2013)
Sept. 30, 2020 – Terminated; basis $6.0088 cash per cl. A unit and US$4.5657 cash per cl. U unit payable to unitholders of record Oct. 7. 2020.

Manulife Strategic Income Opportunities Fund (Ont. May 27, 2011)
June 17, 2013 – Converted from a closed-end to an opened-end fund.

Manulife U.S. Regional Bank Trust (Ont. June 25, 2014)
Sept. 30, 2020 – Terminated; basis $6.3800 cash per cl. A unit and US$6.9480 cash per cl. U unit payable to unitholders, of record Oct. 7. 2020.

Manus Industries Inc. (B.C. Sept. 30, 1967)
Nov. 10, 1992 – Name changed to Consolidated Manus Industries Inc.; basis 1 new for 2.6 old shs. ■

Manuweb Software Systems Inc. (B.C. June 11, 2010)
Dec. 21, 2011 – Name changed to VisualVault Corporation; basis 1 new for 7 old shs. ■

Mapan Energy Ltd. (Alta. July 30, 1993)
Aug. 18, 2015 – Acquired by Tourmaline Oil Corp.; basis 0.0379 Tourmaline com. shs. for 1 Mapan sh.

Mapin Gold Mines Ltd. (Ont. 1938)
Sept. 9, 1958 – Charter cancelled.

Maple Bay Copper Mines Ltd. (Ont. 1953)
1970 – Name changed to Consolidated Maple Bay Copper Mines Limited; basis 1 new for 4 old shs. ■

Maple Film Ltd. (Ont. 1965)
Mar. 16, 1976 – Charter cancelled.

Maple Gold Mines Ltd. (Can. June 22, 2011)
Jan. 7, 2021 – Continued into British Columbia. (see FPsurvey - Mines & Energy)

Maple Leaf Aircraft Corp. Limited (Ont. 1940)
Feb. 9, 1945 – Deemed bankrupt. Co. wound up. No equity for shldrs.

Maple Leaf Coal Co. Ltd. (Alta. 1947)
Wound up.

Maple Leaf Foods Inc. (Can. Aug. 13, 1927; via Dominion charter)
Apr. 24, 1995 – Amalgamated with Castlefin Inc. to form new co. with same name Maple Leaf Foods Inc.; basis $15 or 2.143 new for 1 Maple Leaf sh.

Maple Leaf Gardens, Limited (Ont. Feb. 24, 1931)
Aug. 9, 1996 – Amalgamated with MLG Ventures Limited and all o/s com. shs, other than those held by MLG Ventures, exchanged for cl. A or cl. B pref. shs. or any combination thereof. The cl. A (deemed capital) and cl. B (deemed dividend) pref. shs. immediately redeem. for $49.50 per sh. plus an additional payment if certain events occur by Apr. 16, 1999.

Maple Leaf Milling Company, Limited (Ont. 1910)
Apr. 1961 – Amalgamated into Maple Leaf Mills Limited; basis 1 old 5% pref. sh. for 1 new 5.5 % pref. sh., and 1 old com. sh. for 1.4 new com. shs.

Maple Leaf Mills Limited (Ont. 1961)
Feb. 1, 1979 – Amalgamated with Norin Canada Holdings Inc., a wholly owned subsid. of Norin Corp., and Port Colborne & St. Lawrence Navigation Co. Ltd. to continue with the same name Maple Leaf Mills Limited. Minority shldrs. of predecessor co. exch. shs. for 8% pfce. stk. of new co. on a sh.-for-sh. basis. Such pfce. shs. were red. on Mar. 7, 1979. In addition, a divd. of 15¢ per pfce. sh. pd. on Mar. 9, 1979, to shldrs. of record Mar. 6, 1979. (see Canada Packers Inc.)
July 1987 – Acquired by Hillsdown-Holdings plc following sale by Canadian Pacific Limited of 100% interest effective for total consideration of $395,500,000. (see Canada Packers Inc.)
1988 – Amalgamated in Ontario to continue with same name. (see Canada Packers Inc.)
Jan. 1, 1991 – Amalgamated with Canada Packers Limited to form Maple Leaf Foods Limited for $12 per sh. (see Canada Packers Inc.)

Maple Leaf Mines Ltd. (Que. 1970)
Dec. 1975 – Charter cancelled.

The Maple Leaf Oil and Gas Company, Limited (Ont. 1919)
1958 – Wound up.

Maple Leaf Oil Co. Ltd. (Can. Aug. 30, 1928)
Wound up. N. N. Lunn, Vancouver, liquidator.

Maple Leaf Petroleum Ltd. (B.C. Jan. 25, 1980)
Apr. 22, 1986 – Name changed to International Maple Leaf Resource Corporation; basis 1 new for 5 old shs. ■

Maple Leaf Reforestation Inc. (B.C. Feb. 24, 2005 amalg.)
Oct. 5, 2012 – Name changed to Maple Leaf Green World Inc. (see FPsurvey - Industrials)

Maple Leaf Resource Corp. (B.C. Feb. 20, 2012)
Nov. 14, 2014 – Name changed to Maple Leaf Royalties Corp.; basis 1 new for 4 old shs. ■

Maple Leaf Royalties Corp. (B.C. Feb. 20, 2012)
Jan. 27, 2016 – Continued into Alberta. (see Eagle Energy Inc.)
Feb. 1, 2016 – Amalgamated with Eagle Newco Inc., a wholly owned subsid. of Eagle Energy Trust (EET) to form Eagle Energy Inc. (new Eagle) which succeeded EET; basis 1 new Eagle sh. for 1 EET trust unit and 0.0947 new Eagle shs. for 1 Maple Leaf sh. (see Eagle Energy Inc.)

Maple Leaf Springs Water Corporation (B.C. Aug. 21, 1972)
Feb. 24, 1998 – Name changed to International Maple Leaf Springs Ltd.; basis 1 new for 5 old shs. ■

Maple Mark International Inc. (Alta. Jan. 31, 1989 amalg.)
Oct. 15, 1999 – Name changed to Linear Resources Inc.; basis 1 new for 10 old shs. ■

Maple Minerals Corp. (Ont. Jan. 24, 1990 amalg.)
Oct. 18, 2005 – Name changed to Mega Uranium Ltd. (see FPsurvey - Mines & Energy)

Maple Minerals Inc. (Ont. Jan. 24, 1990 amalg.)
Nov. 9, 2001 – Name changed to Maple Minerals Corp.; basis 1 new for 3 old shs. ■

Maple Mountain Resources Ltd. (Ont. Oct. 20, 1983)
Apr. 15, 1987 – Amalgamated with Unicorn Financial Services Inc. to form The Unicorn Corporation; basis unknown.

Maple Partners Investments Inc. (Alta. July 12, 1994)
Jan. 30, 2004 – Privatized following redemption of 2nd pfd. cl. A shs.; basis $0.25 per sh.

Maple Power Capital Corporation (Ont. Sept. 7, 2010)
June 12, 2015 – Name changed to Intrinsic4D Inc. following Qualifying Transaction reverse takeover acquisition of Intrinsic4D LLC; basis 1 new for 4 old shs. ■

Maple Resource Corp. (B.C. Jan. 25, 1980)
Aug. 14, 1992 – Name changed to Birchwood Ventures Ltd.; basis 1 new for 4.4 old shs. ■

Maple Technology Ltd. (B.C. 1981)
Jan. 26, 1987 – Name changed to Peritronics Medical Inc. ■

Maple Valley Explorations Ltd. (B.C. 1981)
June 7, 1985 – Name changed to Maple Technology Ltd. ■

Maplewood International Real Estate Investment Trust (Ont. May 30, 2013)
June 8, 2020 – Terminated; basis 3¢ cash per unit.

Maplex Management & Holdings Limited (Can. 1971)
1987 – Acquired by MER Financial Corp.; basis $21.39 per cl. A or B sh. or $14.26 plus stock divd. of 0.5 cl. A or B shs. per sh.

Mar-Gold Resources Ltd. (B.C. July 26, 1979)
Dec. 19, 1984 – Name changed to West-Mar Resources Ltd.; basis 1 new for 4 old shs. ■

Mar-Jon Oil Co. Ltd. (Can. Nov. 15, 1928)
1943 – Name changed to Arrow-Marjon Oils Ltd and continued into Alberta; basis 1 new for 6 old shs. ■

Mar-West Resources Ltd. (B.C. July 26, 1979)
Oct. 20, 1998 – Acquired by Glamis Gold Ltd.; basis 0.5 Glamis shs. for 1 Mar-West sh. or 0.4 Glamis shs. plus 48¢ for 1 Mar-West sh. (see Glamis Gold Ltd.)

Mara Lake Mines Ltd. (B.C. 1969)
Apr. 1972 – Amalgamated with 2 other cos. to form Action Minerals Ltd.; basis 1 new for 3 old shs.

Mara Minerals & Oils Inc. (B.C. 1977 amalg.)
Sept. 23, 1983 – Formed Cymric Resources Limited in Canada on amalgamation with Cymric Petroleums Ltd.; basis 1 new for 4 old shs. ■

Mara Minerals Limited (B.C. Nov. 19, 1968)
Nov. 23, 1970 – Name changed to Gramara Mines Ltd. ■

Maracambeau Mines Ltd. (Ont. 1965)
Oct. 18, 1978 – Charter cancelled.

Maracote International Resources Inc. (B.C. June 22, 1978)
May 28, 2001 – Name changed to Lund Ventures Ltd.; basis 1 new for 5 old shs. ■

Maradona Resources Inc. (Ont. July 3, 1986)
Apr. 29, 1991 – Name changed to Equashare Management Corp.; basis 4 new for 1 old sh. ■

Maral Gold Mines Ltd. (Ont. 1945)
1956 – Charter cancelled.

Maralgo Mines Limited (Ont. Dec. 18, 1936)
1984 – Continued into British Columbia.
Feb. 5, 1986 – Name changed to Rich Coast Sulphur Ltd.; basis 1 new for 2 old shs. ■

Maramar Ventures Inc. (Alta. May 29, 1996)
Nov. 18, 1999 – Qualifying Transaction acquisition of IMS Petroleum Ltd.
Apr. 4, 2001 – Name changed to IMS Petroleum Inc. ■

Marapharm Ventures Inc. (B.C. Apr. 24, 2007)
Oct. 24, 2018 – Name changed to Liht Cannabis Corp. ■

Marathon Foods Inc. (B.C. Sept. 24, 1982)
Feb. 27, 2004 – Dissolved and struck from register.

Marathon Gold Corporation (Can. Dec. 3, 2009)
Jan. 29, 2024 – Acquired by Calibre Mining Corp.; basis 0.6164 Calibre shs. for 1 Marathon sh. (see Calibre Mining Corp.)

Marathon Minerals Inc. (B.C. 1983)
Aug. 25, 1995 – Dissolved and struck off register.

Marathon Mines Ltd. (Ont. 1965)
1967 – Merged into Trimar Holdings & Explorations Ltd.; basis 1 new for 5 old shs.

Marathon Motor Supplies Limited (Ont. 1963)
1968 – All o/s com. shs. acquired by The Gas Machinery Co. of Canada Ltd. at $4.00 per sh. which then sold in 1969 to McKerlie Automotive Co. Ltd., a subsid. of Sterling Precision Corp. of N.Y.

Marathon Oil Canada Limited (Alta. Oct. 30, 1997)
Aug. 13, 2001 – All o/s exch. shs. called for early redemption by USX Corporation; basis 1 new USX-Marathon Group com. sh. for 1 old Marathon exch. sh. Common shs. of USX-Marathon listed on NYSE.

Marathon PGM Corporation (Can. Sept. 12, 2003)
Dec. 3, 2010 – Acquired by Stillwater Mining Company; basis 0.112 Stillwater shs., Cdn$1.775 and 0.5 of newly incorporated Marathon Gold Corporation shs. for 1 Marathon PGM sh.

Marathon Realty Company Limited (Can. 1963)
Dec. 31, 1990 – Name changed to Marathon Realty Holdings Inc.

Marathon Telecom Corporation (B.C. 1966)
Mar. 3, 1995 – Dissolved and struck off register.

Marauder Resources East Coast Inc. (Alta. Mar. 27, 1997)
Mar. 2, 2016 – Struck from registry and dissolved.

Marbaco Resources Ltd. (Alta. 1969)
Mar. 29, 1985 – Struck off register.

Marbeau Yellowknife Mines Ltd. (Ont. 1938)
Nov. 1958 – Name changed to Norway Lake Iron Mines Ltd. ■

Marbenor Malartic Mines Ltd. (Ont. 1941)
1955 – Name changed to Consolidated Marbenor Mines Limited; basis 1 new for 5 old shs. ■

Marble Bay Mining Co. Ltd. (B.C. 1942)
Feb. 9, 1956 – Dissolved.

Marble Financial Inc. (Can. Sept. 15, 2016)
Jan. 22, 2024 – Name changed to Inverite Insights Inc. (see FPsurvey - Industrials)

Marboy Mines Ltd. (Ont. 1948)
Oct. 1973 – Charter cancelled.

Marcana Petroleum Ltd. (Alta. Aug. 10, 1983)
Nov. 9, 1994 – Name changed to Compact Power Holdings Limited; basis 1 new cl. A for 1 old cl. A sh.

Marcana Resources Ltd. (B.C. 1949)
Apr. 5, 1983 – Continued into Canada.
Apr. 8, 1983 – Name changed to FMG Telecomputer Ltd.; basis 1 new for 5 old shs. ■

March Minerals Ltd. (Ont. 1955)
Mar. 1970 – Charter cancelled.

March Networks Corporation (Ont. Dec. 2, 1986)
Oct. 1, 1996 – Continued into Canada.
May 1, 2012 – Acquired by Infinova (Canada) Ltd., an indirect wholly owned subsid. of Shenzhen Infinova Ltd., for Cdn$5.00 per sh.

March Oils Limited (Sask.)
1958 – Struck off register.

March Resources Corporation (Alta. July 22, 1999)
Aug. 21, 2009 – Name changed to Ranger Energy Ltd.; basis 1 new for 3 old shs. ■

March Resources Inc. (Alta. 1987)
Aug. 1, 1991 – Struck off register.

March Resources Ltd. (B.C. 1977)
Mar. 12, 1985 – Name changed to International March Resources Ltd.; basis 1 new for 3 old shs. ■

Marchant Mining Co. Ltd. (Que. 1957)
Dec. 29, 1971 – Acquired by Wright-Hargreaves Mines, Limited; basis $1.50 plus 7 Wright-Hargreaves shs. for 15 Marchant shs. Charter surrendered.

Marchaud Mines Ltd. (Ont. 1946)
1965 – Merged into Garrison Creek Consolidated Mines Ltd.; basis 1 new for 2 old shs.

Marché Central Métropolitain Inc. (Que. 1948)
Dec. 17, 2012 – Voluntarily dissolved.

Marché Union Inc. (Que. 1958)
Dec. 7, 1977 – Bankrupt.

Marchés d'Aliments Métro Ltée (Que. Dec. 22, 1947; via letters patent)
Sept. 29, 1976 – Name changed to Métro-Richelieu Inc. following merger with Epiceries Richelieu Limitée. ■

Marching Moose Capital Corp. (B.C. Sept. 24, 2013)
Dec. 4, 2017 – Name changed to Avidian Gold Corp. pursuant to Qualifying Transaction reverse takeover acquisition of Avidian Gold Inc. via a three-cornered amalgamation. ■

Marchmont Gold Corp. (Alta. July 18, 1985)
Jan. 19, 2000 – Name changed to Adulis Minerals Corp.; basis 1 new for 2 old shs. ■

Marchwell Capital Corp. (Alta. May 13, 1996)
Dec. 3, 2003 – Name changed to Eurasian Minerals Inc. pursuant to reverse takeover acquisition of Southern European Exploration Ltd.; basis 1 new for 2 old shs. ■

Marchwell Ventures Ltd. (Can. Sept. 4, 2008)
Apr. 11, 2018 – Name changed to Santé Veritas Holdings Inc. pursuant to reverse takeover acquisition of Santé Veritas Therapeutics Inc. (SVT) and concurrent amalgamation of SVT with wholly owned 1148607 B.C. Ltd.; basis 1 new for 3 old shs. ■

Marco Polo Investments Ltd. (Alta. Mar. 30, 2007)
Oct. 1, 2009 – Formed Cobalt Coal Corp. in Alberta pursuant to Qualifying Transaction amalgamation with Cobalt Blue Resources Inc. (deemed acquiror). ■

Marco Resources Limited (B.C. 1964)
Apr. 16, 1993 – Dissolved and struck off register.

Marcoland Mines Ltd. (Que. 1951)
Feb. 7, 1981 – Charter cancelled.

Marcon Mines Ltd. (Ont. 1944)
1966 – Name changed to Conmar Explorations Ltd.; basis 1 new for 4 old shs. ■

Marcourt Nickel Mines Ltd. (Ont. 1948)
Nov. 1957 – Charter cancelled.

Marcus Energy Holdings Inc. (Ont. July 12, 1988 amalg.)
July 21, 2005 – Name changed to Au Martinique Silver Inc. ■

Marcus Energy Inc. (Ont. July 12, 1988 amalg.)
Nov. 27, 2000 – Name changed to Marcus Energy Holdings Inc.; basis 1 new for 10 old shs. ■

Marcus Gold Mines Ltd. (Ont. 1944)
1954 – Acquired by Cochenour Marcus Gold Mines Ltd.; basis 1 new for 3.5 old shs. (see Cochenour Marcus Gold Mines Ltd.)

Le Mare Gold Corp. (B.C. Mar. 9, 2010)
July 14, 2021 – Name changed to Recharge Resources Ltd. ■

Mareast Exploration Ltd. (Ont. Dec. 7, 1962)
Name changed to Cascade Pacific Resources Limited. ■

Maree Uranium Ltd. (Ont. 1953)
Sept. 26, 1960 – Dissolved.

Marengo Exploration Ltd. (Alta. July 3, 1996)
June 15, 2001 – All o/s cl. A and cl. B shs. acquired by True Energy Inc.; basis (a) $2.05 or 1.71 com. shs. of True or a combination thereof for each cl. A sh. Marengo and (b) $9.00 or 7.5 com. shs. of True or a combination thereof for each cl. B sh. of Marengo. (see True Energy Inc.)

Marengo Mining Limited (Australia Feb. 6, 2002)
Nov. 16, 2015 – Name changed to Era Resources Inc.; basis 1 new for 100 old shs. ■

Margaret Red Lake Mines (1940) Ltd. (Ont. 1940)
Mar. 11, 1970 – Dissolved.

Margaux Red Capital Inc. (Can. June 8, 2011)
June 18, 2018 – Name changed to Sigma Lithium Resources Corporation following Qualifying Transaction reverse takeover acquisition of Sigma Lithium Resources Inc.; basis 1 new for 10 old shs. ■

Margaux Resources Ltd. (Alta. Aug. 5, 2009)
Sept. 25, 2020 – Name changed to Cassiar Gold Corp.; basis 1 new for 5 old shs. (see FPsurvey - Mines & Energy)

Marge Enterprises Ltd. (B.C. Dec. 16, 1965)
Sept. 27, 1996 – Name changed to Thunderbird Projects Ltd. ■

Marguerite Lake Mines Ltd. (B.C. 1969)
Dec. 11, 1978 – Dissolved.

Marguerite Mines Ltd. (B.C. 1966)
Apr. 1967 – Name changed to Emperor Mines Ltd. ■

Maria Mining Corp. Ltd. (Ont. 1968)
Mar. 1976 – Charter cancelled.

Mariah Energy Corp. (Alta. Dec. 31, 2002 amalg.)
June 2, 2009 – Dissolved and struck from registry.

Mariah Resources Ltd. (B.C. 1983)
Apr. 3, 1992 – Dissolved and struck off register.

Marian Capital Corp. (Alta. May 7, 1993)
July 27, 1994 – Name changed to Advance Multimedia Corporation. ■

Marian Lake Mines Ltd. (Ont. 1954)
Feb. 18, 1965 – Dissolved.

Marian Lake Uranium Mines Ltd. (Ont. 1954)
1958 – Name changed to Marian Lake Mines Ltd. ■

Marian Minerals Corporation (B.C. Mar. 2, 1981)
Sept. 8, 1992 – Name changed to Lumina Investment Corp.; basis 1 new for 3 old shs. ■

Marian River Uranium Mines Ltd. (Ont. 1953)
1954 – Name changed to Manilake Mines Ltd. ■

Mariana Resources Limited (Guernsey Jan. 31, 2006)
July 6, 2017 – Acquired by Sandstorm Gold Ltd.; basis 0.2573 Sandstorm com. shs. plus £0.2875 cash for 1 Mariana ordinary sh.

Maricana Enterprises Limited (Can. Nov. 25, 1963)
Dec. 16, 1980 – Dissolved.

Maricann Group Inc. (Ont. Dec. 21, 1998)
Jan. 14, 2019 – Name changed to Wayland Group Corp. (see FPsurvey - Industrials)

Maricona Minerals Ltd. (Ont. 1955)
Sept. 18, 1961 – Dissolved.

Marietta Resource Corporation (B.C. Apr. 11, 1979)
Dec. 21, 1993 – Name changed to Garrison Enterprises Inc.; basis 1 new for 3 old shs. ■

Mariette Mines Ltd. (Que. 1952)
May 1974 – Charter cancelled.

Marifil Mines Limited (Yuk. Dec. 2, 2003)
Jan. 21, 2014 – Continued into British Columbia.
Sept. 29, 2021 – Name changed to International Iconic Gold Exploration Corp. (see FPsurvey - Mines & Energy)

Marigold Mining Co. (unknown)
1922 – Name changed to Kirkland Gateway Gold Mines Ltd. and continued into Ontario. ■

Marigold Oils Ltd. (Alta. 1949)
May 1962 – Name changed to Unisphere Explorers Ltd.; basis 1 new for 5 old shs. ■

Marigot Investments Limited (Que. 1964)
Oct. 1972 – Name changed to Mico Enterprises Limited; basis 1 new for 10 old shs. ■

Marillac Rouyn Mines Ltd. (Ont. 1945)
1962 – Charter cancelled.

Marilyn Gold Mines Inc. (B.C. Feb. 26, 1979)
Dec. 22, 1980 – Name changed to Titan Resources Ltd. ■

Marimac Mines Ltd. (Ont. 1950)
1969 – Merged into Alchib Developments Ltd.; basis 6 new for 100 old shs.

Marimba Capital Corp. (Alta. Feb. 8, 2007)
June 25, 2008 – Name changed to Phoenix Coal Inc. prior to Qualifying Transaction reverse takeover acquisition of Phoenix Coal Corporation on June 27, 2008; basis 1 new for 2.35 old shs. ■

Marina Explorations Ltd. (B.C. June 9, 1987)
June 11, 1992 – Name changed to Consolidated Marina Explorations Ltd.; basis 1 new for 3 old shs. ■

Marine BioProducts International Corporation (B.C. Mar. 11, 1983)
May 9, 2006 – Continued into Alberta.
June 6, 2006 – Name changed to Phoenix Oilfield Hauling Inc. following reverse takeover acquisition of Phoenix Oilfield Hauling Ltd. and Alberta Loader Rentals Inc.; basis 1 new for 155 old shs. ■

Marine Industries Limited (Can. 1937)
Jan. 1, 1982 – Merged with certain subsids. to continue operations under name of Marine Industrie Limitée/Marine Industries Limited.

Marine Industries Limited (Can. 1937)
1988 – Name changed to The MIL Group Inc. ■

Marine Oil and Gas Co. Ltd. (Ont. 1959)
Mar. 4, 1965 – Dissolved.

Marine Petroleums Ltd. (Ont. Feb. 5, 1937)
Liquidated. Pref. shldrs. received $4.00 per sh.; com. shldrs., nil.

Mariner Explorations Inc. (B.C. June 5, 1981)
Feb. 15, 1991 – Name changed to Argosy Resources Corporation; basis 1 new for 3.5 old shs. ■

Mariner Mines Ltd. (Ont. 1963)
1971 – Merged into International Mariner Resources Ltd.; basis 1 new for 2.5 old shs.

Mariner Resources Corp. (B.C. May 28, 2018)
Sept. 17, 2020 – Name changed to Exploits Discovery Corp. following acquisition of Exploits Gold Corp. (see FPsurvey - Mines & Energy)

Mariposa Resources Inc. (B.C. Mar. 27, 1984)
July 24, 1989 – Name changed to Adagio Investments Inc.; basis 1 new for 4 old shs. ■

Maris Deloro Gold Mines Ltd. (Ont. 1937)
Aug. 24, 1964 – Dissolved.

Marishell Products Ltd. (B.C. June 3, 1988)
May 12, 1999 – Name changed to Boulevard Capital Ltd.; basis 1 new for 8 old shs. ■

Maritime Accessories, Limited (N.S. Feb. 7, 1924)
Feb. 14, 1980 – Name changed to MAL Holdings Limited. ■

Maritime Barytes Ltd. (Ont. 1948)
May 1960 – Charter cancelled.

Maritime Beverages Limited (N.B. 1944)
Mar. 31, 1977 – All o/s 6 3/4 % 1st pref. shs. redeemed Dec. 30, 1975, and all o/s 6 3/4 % debs. redeemed. Co. now private.

Maritime Electric Company, Limited (Can. June 27, 1917)
Aug. 26, 1994 – Acquired by Fortis Inc.; basis $24.25 or 0.6725 Fortis shs. plus $7.94 for 1 Maritime sh.

The Maritime Life Assurance Company (N.S. Apr. 29, 1922)
Dec. 24, 1999 – Continued into Canada.
Dec. 30, 2004 – Amalgamated with The Manufacturers Life Insurance Company and MFC Insurance Company Limited to continue as The Manufacturers Life Insurance Company, wholly owned subsid. of Manulife Financial Corporation.

Maritime National Fish, Limited (N.S. Apr. 1, 1937)
Sept. 1945 – Assets sold to National Sea Products Ltd.

Maritime National Fish (1937) Limited (N.S. Apr. 1, 1937)
Feb. 12, 1941 – Name changed to Maritime National Fish, Limited. ■

Maritime Rock Products Limited (unknown 1959)
1961 – Went into bankruptcy; assets liquidated.

Maritime Telegraph and Telephone Company, Limited (N.S. Jan. 1, 1910)
May 31, 1999 – Amalgamated with Bruncor Inc., Island Telecom Inc. and NewTel Enterprises Limited to form Aliant Inc.; basis 1.011 new for 1 Bruncor sh., 1 new for 1 Island Telecom sh., 1.567 new for 1 NewTel sh. and 1.667 new for 1 Maritime Telegraph sh. (see Aliant Inc.)

Maritimes Mining Corp. Ltd. (N.B. 1955)
May 16, 1964 – Name changed to First Maritime Mining Corporation Limited; basis 2 new for 5 old shs. ■

Marjas Red Lake Gold Mines Ltd. (Ont. 1945)
Feb. 26, 1953 – Charter cancelled.

Mark-Can Investment Corp. (B.C. July 23, 1980)
Sept. 30, 2003 – Name changed to Yale Resources Ltd. ■

Mark 8 Ventures Inc. (Alta. July 23, 1993)
Nov. 1, 1996 – Formed Pason Systems Inc. in Alberta on reverse takeover acquisition of Pason Systems Corp. and amalgamation with 698367 Alberta Ltd. (see FPsurvey - Mines & Energy; FPsurvey - Industrials)

Mark One Global Industries, Inc. (B.C. June 20, 1980)
Aug. 13, 2012 – Dissolved and struck from register.

Mark Resources Inc. (Alta. Oct. 27, 1980)
Apr. 9, 1996 – Converted into an income trust named EnerMark Income Fund; basis $2.00 plus 1 trust unit for 1 Mark com. sh. and 16 trust units and $2.74 in accr. int. for each $100 principal amount of Mark convert. debs. held. (see EnerMark Income Fund)

Mark V Mines Ltd. (B.C. Jan. 15, 1969)
Mar. 1972 – Name changed to Mark V Petroleums & Mines Ltd. ■

Mark V Petroleums & Mines Ltd. (B.C. Jan. 15, 1969)
Oct. 5, 1994 – Name changed to TLC Ventures Corp.; basis 1 new for 3 old shs. ■

Markatech Industries Corporation (B.C. Dec. 5, 1979)
Feb. 12, 2001 – Name changed to Ameratech Systems Corporation; basis 1 new for 12 old shs. ■

Markay Mining Corporation Ltd. (Ont. 1964)
Apr. 29, 1970 – Charter cancelled.

Markborough Properties Inc. (Ont. Aug. 12, 1965)
Jan. 12, 1984 – Continued into Canada. (see Cambridge Shopping Centres Limited)
June 11, 1997 – All o/s com. and 8% convert. unsecured debs. acquired by Cambridge Shopping Centres Limited; basis (a) 2,500 Markborough com. shs. for each $1,000 deb. tendered, then each converted com. sh. to receive $0.316 plus $0.148 in principal amt. of 6% deb. due June 30, 2007, (b) $0.316 plus $0.148 in principal amt. of 6% convert. subord. debs. of Cambridge for 1 com. sh. The 6% convert. subord. debs. of Markborough exchanged for 6% convert. subord. debs. of Cambridge effective June 12, 1997, on a deb.-for-deb. basis. (see Cambridge Shopping Centres Limited)

Markborough Properties Limited (Ont. 1965 amalg.)
1978 – Acquired by Hudson's Bay Company; basis 1 Hudson's Bay ord. sh. for 1 Markborough com. sh. (see Hudson's Bay Company)

Markbridge Resources Ltd. (Ont. Feb. 18, 1988)
Mar. 3, 1993 – Name changed to Innovadent Technologies Ltd.; basis 0.5762894 new for 1 old sh. ■

Markel Financial Holdings Limited (Can. Mar. 13, 1951)
May 8, 1987 – Name changed to Fairfax Financial Holdings Limited. (see FPsurvey - Industrials)

Marker Petroleums Limited (Ont.)
Dec. 1958 – Charter cancelled.

Marker Resources Co. Ltd. (Alta. 1985)
Dec. 14, 1987 – Formed Varna Gold Inc. in Alberta on amalgamation with Varna Resources Inc. and Varna Gold Inc. ■

Marketfax Infoservices Ltd. (B.C. 1980)
June 30, 1994 – Dissolved and struck off register.

Marketvision Direct, Inc. (Del. July 21, 1998 amalg.)
May 20, 2011 – Name changed to APIC Petroleum Corporation. ■

Markland AGF Precious Metals Corp. (Ont. May 29, 2007)
Dec. 10, 2013 – Voluntarily dissolved. All equity shs. redeemed for $5.941135 per sh.
Mar. 19, 2014 – Dissolved and struck from register.

Marks & Spencer Canada Inc. (Can. 1933)
Aug. 6, 1986 – All o/s shs. not already held acquired by Marks & Spencer plc at $24 per sh.

Mark's Market Corp. (Alta. July 25, 1996)
June 24, 1999 – Name changed to Patchgear.com Inc. ■

Mark's Work Wearhouse Ltd. (Alta. Apr. 12, 1977)
Feb. 7, 2002 – Acquired by CTC Acquisition Limited, a wholly owned subsid. of Canadian Tire Corporation, for $4.10 per sh.

Marksmen Capital Inc. (B.C. Mar. 11, 2008)
Nov. 24, 2010 – Name changed to Brixton Metals Corporation prior to the Dec. 7, 2010, Qualifying Transaction amalgamation of Brixton Metals Corp. and wholly owned Marksmen Acquisition Corp., with Brixton the deemed acquiror. (see FPsurvey - Mines & Energy)

Marksmen Resources Ltd. (Alta. Mar. 14, 1997)
Aug. 23, 2010 – Name changed to Marksmen Energy Inc. (see FPsurvey - Mines & Energy)

Markway Resources Ltd. (B.C. 1977)
July 5, 1984 – Name changed to So-Luminaire Systems Corp. (see FPsurvey - Industrials)

Markwell Gold Mines Ltd. (Ont.)
Sept. 26, 1960 – Dissolved.

Marl Resources Corp. (Alta. Apr. 14, 1997)
May 31, 2000 – Formed Pelangio Mines Inc. pursuant to plan of arrangement with Pelangio-Larder Mines, Limited. ■

Marlat Resources Ltd. (B.C. Apr. 11, 1983)
June 18, 1996 – Name changed to Renco Resources Inc. (see FPsurvey - Mines & Energy)

Marlboro Mines Ltd. (Ont. 1965)
1968 – Merged into Boeing Holdings & Explorations Ltd.; basis 1 new for 2 old shs.

Marlea Oils Limited (Alta.)
1959 – Struck off register.

Marleau, Lemire Inc. (Can. May 4, 1989)
June 26, 1998 – Name changed to Peelbrooke Capital Inc. ■

Marlen Univest Inc. (Can. 1911)
July 1983 – Trustees (Richter & Assoc.) sold all oper. assets to newly-formed Belding Corticelli (1982) Inc. enabling the co. to pay creditors in full (approx. $2.4 million to banks and $1.6 million to other creditors).

Marlex Enviro-Systems & Resources Ltd. (B.C. 1968)
Dec. 29, 1972 – Name changed to Trans Canada Enviro Systems Ltd.

Marlex Mining Corp. Ltd. (B.C. 1968)
Apr. 1971 – Name changed to Marlex Enviro-Systems & Resources Ltd. ■

Marlin Capital Foods Ltd. (Ont. Aug. 20, 1986)
Oct. 4, 1994 – Name changed to Meranto Technology Ltd.; basis 1 new for 10 old shs. ■

Marlin Developments Ltd. (B.C. 1967)
Feb. 4, 2002 – Name changed to Matrix Petroleum Inc. ■

Marlin Gold Mining Ltd. (B.C. June 9, 2000)
Nov. 14, 2018 – Acquired by Golden Reign Resources Ltd. (renamed Mako Mining Corp.); basis 0.5138 Golden Reign shs. for 1 Marlin sh. (see Mako Mining Corp.)

Marlon Rouyn Gold Mines Ltd. (Ont. 1944)
1946 – Name changed to New Marlon Gold Mines Ltd.; basis 1 new for 2 old shs. ■

Marlowe Mines Ltd. (Que. 1953)
June 1974 – Charter cancelled.

Marmac Resources Limited (Ont. 1979)
Dec. 10, 1987 – Formed Star Data Systems Inc. in Ontario on amalgamation with Star Data Systems Inc. ■

Marmal Nickel Mines Limited (Ont. 1961)
Dec. 20, 2000 – Dissolved.

Marmattagami Mines Ltd. (Que. 1960)
1969 – Charter cancelled.

Marmora Minerals Ltd. (Ont. 1937)
1956 – Charter cancelled.

Marmot Lead & Zinc Mines Ltd. (Ont. 1951)
Sept. 1961 – Charter cancelled.

Marosa Mines Ltd. (Ont. 1963)
Dec. 1967 – Charter cancelled.

Marpat Mines Ltd. (Ont. 1965)
Mar. 1972 – Charter cancelled.

Marpic Explorations Ltd. (Ont. 1946)
Mar. 12, 1962 – Dissolved.

Marpoint Gas & Oil Corp. Ltd. (Ont. 1958)
1962 – All assets sold to Dynamic Petroleum Products Ltd. At last report, Marpoint was in liquidation.

Marquee Energy Ltd. (Alta. June 22, 2010 amalg.)
Dec. 8, 2016 – Merged into Alberta Oilsands Inc. (renamed Marquee Energy Ltd.); basis 1.67 Alberta com. shs. for 1 Marquee sh. (see Marquee Energy Ltd.)

Marquee Energy Ltd. (Alta. Dec. 6, 2016 amalg.)
Nov. 30, 2018 – Acquired by Prairie Provident Resources Inc.; basis 0.0886 Prairie com. shs. for 1 Marquee sh.

Marquee Petroleum Ltd. (Alta. Mar. 28, 2006)
Dec. 9, 2011 – Amalgamated with SkyWest Acquisitions Ltd., a wholly owned subsid. of SkyWest Energy Corp.; basis 1.35 SkyWest shs. for 1 Marquee sh. (see Marquee Energy Ltd.)

Marquest Canadian Equity Income Fund (Ont. Apr. 28, 2011)
Jan. 2, 2018 – Terminated; basis $5.32 per unit.

Marquette Capital Corp. (B.C. Sept. 15, 2000)
Jan. 9, 2003 – Name changed to On-Track Learning Systems Ltd. pursuant to Qualifying Transaction reverse takeover acquisition of On-Track Computer Training Ltd. ■

Marquette Long Lac Gold Mines Ltd. (Ont. 1936)
Aug. 18, 1958 – Dissolved.

Marquis Development Corp. Ltd. (B.C. 1965)
June 10, 1982 – Formed Colt Exploration Ltd. in British Columbia on amalgamation with Golden Shamrock Resources Ltd.; basis 1 new for 1.2838 old shs. ■

Marquis Explorations Limited (Ont. 1970)
Nov. 22, 1974 – Amalgamated with Foxdale Mines Limited (1 for 7.5), Canton Explorations Limited (1 for 5.5), Long Point Gas & Oil Incorporated (1 for 3), Darwin Mines Limited (1 for 1.5), Gold Acres Mines Limited (1 for 7), Home Mining Developments Limited (1 for 7) and Force Crag Mines Limited (1 for 4.5) to form New Force Crag Mines Limited; basis 1 new for 2.5 old shs.

Marquis Resource Corporation (Alta. Apr. 28, 1964)
Oct. 22, 1992 – Name changed to Panorama Trading Company Ltd. ■

Marquis Ventures Inc. (B.C. Sept. 29, 2009)
Feb. 8, 2018 – Name changed to PowerBand Solutions Inc. pursuant to Qualifying Transaction reverse takeover of PowerBand Global Dealer Services Inc. ■

Marret High Yield Strategies Fund (Ont.)
Nov. 26, 2024 – Terminated; no funds available for a final distribution.

Marret Investment Grade Bond Fund (Ont. Sept. 29, 2009)
Aug. 22, 2016 – Converted from a closed-end fund into an exchange-traded fund called First Asset Investment Grade Bond ETF on a unit-for-unit basis. (see First Asset Investment Grade Bond ETF)

Marret Multi-Strategy Income Fund (Ont.)
Nov. 26, 2024 – Terminated; no funds available for final distribution.

Marret Resource Corp. (Ont. Aug. 1, 2008 amalg.)
Oct. 19, 2018 – Name changed to Mount Logan Capital Inc. following completion of a plan of arrangement whereby the company changed its investment strategy from a focus on natural resource lending to a broader lending-oriented credit platform. (see FPsurvey - Industrials)

Marsa Energy Inc. (Alta. May 11, 2011)
Mar. 29, 2016 – Acquired by Condor Petroleum Inc.; basis 1.84326 Condor com. shs. for 1 Marsa com. sh. (see Condor Petroleum Inc.)

Marshall-Barwick Inc. (Can. Dec. 30, 1978)
Oct. 30, 2002 – Amalgamated with CEL Marshares Inc.; basis 1 CEL Marshares redeem. pfd. sh. for 1 Marshall-Barwick sh. Immediately redeemed for $4.40 per sh.

Marshall Boston Iron Mines Limited (Ont. Feb. 27, 1964; via letters patent)
Oct. 15, 1981 – Name changed to Marshall Minerals Corp. (see FPsurvey - Mines & Energy)

Marshall Creek Copper Co. Ltd. (B.C. 1963)
Jan. 1973 – Name changed to Shalmar Resources Limited; basis 1 new for 4 old shs. ■

Marshall Drummond McCall Inc. (Can. Dec. 30, 1978)
Feb. 10, 1987 – Name changed to Marshall Steel Limited to reflect sale of the Drummond McCall division operations. ■

Marshall Energy Ltd. (B.C. Dec. 31, 1982)
Aug. 31, 1984 – Continued into Alberta.
Jan. 23, 1991 – Name changed to Stockmen Resources Corp. ■

Marshall Lake Mines Ltd. (Ont. 1963)
Nov. 1967 – Charter cancelled.

Marshall Red Lake Mines Ltd. (Ont. 1945)
1956 – Charter cancelled.

Marshall Steel Limited (Can. Dec. 30, 1978)
June 10, 1996 – Name changed to Marshall-Barwick Inc.; basis 1 new cl. A for 1 old cl. A sh. and 1 new cl. B for 1 old cl. B sh. ■

Marshall Wells Limited (Can. 1957)
Dec. 2, 1985 – Assets sold to Cochrane Dunlop Ltd. to become a wholly owned subsid.

Marshall Wells of Canada Ltd. (Can. 1957)
Nov. 1965 – Merged to form Marshall Wells Limited. Com. shs. exch. sh.-for-sh. for 6.5 % 1st pref. shs. and 6% pref. shs. of old co. for 6% 2nd pref. shs. of merged co.

Marston Minerals Ltd. (Ont. 1943)
Feb. 1959 – Name changed to Hallmark Exploration Ltd.; basis 10 new for 1 old sh. ■

Marsulex Inc. (Can. June 16, 1989 amalg.)
June 29, 2011 – Acquired by a wholly owned subsid. of Chemtrade Logistics Income Fund; basis either (i) $13.80 or (ii) 1 Investis U.S., Inc. sh. plus $10.50 for 1 Marsulex sh.

Mart Resources, Inc. (Alta. Nov. 7, 1994)
Mar. 30, 2016 – Acquired by Midwestern Oil & Gas Company and San Leon Energy plc; basis Cdn$0.25 cash per sh. Co. subsequently dissolved.

Marta Drilling & Development Co. Ltd. (unknown)
Jan. 1953 – Assets acquired by Consolidated Peak Oils Ltd.

Martech Technologies Corporation (Alta. Apr. 22, 1994)
Oct. 5, 1999 – Struck from registry and dissolved.

Martel Mines Ltd. (B.C. Feb. 1, 1972)
Sept. 17, 1979 – Name changed to Martel Oil and Gas Ltd. ■

Martel Oil and Gas Ltd. (B.C. Feb. 1, 1972)
Nov. 27, 1987 – Name changed to Mylan Ventures Ltd.; basis 1 new for 2.7 old shs. ■

Martin-Bird Gold Mines Ltd. (Ont. 1936)
Mar. 14, 1978 – Charter cancelled.

Martin Health Group Inc. (Alta. Mar. 4, 1996)
July 5, 2004 – Placed into bankruptcy. Le Groupe Boudreau, Richard Inc. was appointed trustee.

Martin-Hunt Mining Ltd. (Ont. 1964)
1972 – Charter cancelled.

Martin-McNeely Mines, Limited (Ont. 1927)
Apr. 27, 1978 – Name changed to Neomar Resources Ltd.; basis 1 new for 7 old shs. ■

Martin Pycnogenol Products Inc. (Alta. Mar. 4, 1996)
Feb. 24, 1999 – Formed Martin Health Group Inc. following acquisition of all o/s shs. of Martin Health Care Products Inc.; basis 1 new for 1 old sh. ■

Martlet Venture Management Limited (Ont. July 4, 1996 amalg.)
Oct. 24, 2000 – Amalgamated with German-based Knorr Capital Partner AG; basis 1 Knorr sh. for 35 Martlet shs. Knorr shs. trade on the Frankfurt Stock Exchange.

Maru Uranium Mines Ltd. (B.C.)
June 27, 1977 – Dissolved.

Marum Resources Inc. (Alta. Nov. 5, 1982)
June 26, 2009 – Name changed to StrikePoint Gold Inc. ■

Marun-Pakaraima Diamond Mining Co. Ltd. (Ont.)
1968 – Charter cancelled.

Marvas Developments Ltd. (Ont. Mar. 2, 1992)
Jan. 15, 1996 – Formed Pan American Resources Inc. in Ontario on amalgamation with Pan American Resources Inc. (deemed acquiror); basis 1.2 new for 1 Pan American sh. and 1 new for 1 Marvas sh. ■

Marvel Hemsley Ltd. (Que. 1972)
Feb. 6, 1982 – Charter cancelled.

Marvel Minerals Ltd. (Ont. 1964)
Mar. 1976 – Charter cancelled.

Marvel Mining Co. Ltd. (Que.)
Apr. 20, 1931 – Charter cancelled.

Marvel Oils Ltd. (Can. 1923)
May 11, 1967 – Name changed to New Marvel Oils Ltd.; basis 1 new for 5 old shs. ■

Marvel Rouyn Mines Ltd. (Ont. 1949)
Mar. 1953 – Name changed to Marvel Uranium Mines Ltd. ■

Marvel Uranium Mines Ltd. (Ont. 1949)
June 29, 1964 – Dissolved.

Marven's Limited (N.B. 1936)
July 1978 – Operations ceased. Co. in process of being wound up.

Marvin Investors Limited (unknown)
Nov. 1968 – Amalgamated to form Intermetco Limited. (see Intermetco Limited)

Marvin's Limited (N.B. 1936)
1980 – Acquired by George Weston Limited. Co. subsequently wound up.

Marwayne Oils Ltd. (Ont. Nov. 1944)
1954 – Assets acquired by Consolidated Dragon Oils Ltd.; basis 1 new for 3 old shs.

Marwell Construction Ltd. (B.C. 1962)
Dec. 1968 – Amalgamated into Dillingham Corp. Canada Ltd.

Mary Ann Mines Ltd. (Ont. 1943)
May 15, 1969 – Charter cancelled.

Mary Creek Resource Corp. (B.C. Nov. 7, 1984)
Jan. 28, 1986 – Formed Pundata Gold Corporation on amalgamation with 300347 B.C. Ltd. ■

Mary Ellen Resources Ltd. (B.C. 1982)
Jan. 5, 1989 – Amalgamated with AXR Resources Ltd. (1 for 5) and Lenora Exploration Ltd. (1 for 4) to continue with the new name Greater Lenora Resources Corp.; basis 1 new for 6 old shs. (see Greater Lenora Resources Corp.)

Mary-Jane Copper-Gold Mines Ltd. (Que. 1937)
July 7, 1978 – Charter cancelled.

Maryland Porcupine Gold Mines Ltd. (Ont. 1937)
Feb. 1957 – Charter cancelled.

Maryland Red Lake Gold Mines Ltd. (Ont. 1937)
1939 – Name changed to Maryland Porcupine Gold Mines Ltd. ■

Mascan Corporation (Ont. 1957)
Oct. 1983 – Placed into bankruptcy and Coopers & Lybrand Limited appointed trustee. Certain assets sold by receiver to 128508 Canada Limited. (see The Hammerson Property Investment and Development Corporation plc)
Jan. 1984 – Hammerson Canada Inc., wholly owned by The Hammerson Property Investment and Development Corporation plc, acquired all o/s com. shs. under its offer of $15 plus 1 wt. to purch. 1 com. sh. of 128508 Canada Limited at $4.65 per sh. to Sept. 30, 1984. (see The Hammerson Property Investment and Development Corporation plc)
May 1, 1984 – Mascan redeemed all o/s 1st pref. ser. A shs. at $26.80 plus $5.0625 accr. divds. and all o/s 2nd pref. shs. at $20.40 plus $4.50 accr. divds. (see The Hammerson Property Investment and Development Corporation plc)

Mascot Gold Mines Limited (B.C. 1971)
1984 – Amalgamated in British Columbia to continue with same name. (see Corona Corporation)
July 1, 1988 – Amalgamated with 7 other cos. to form Corona Corporation; basis 1.32 Corona cl. A shs. for 1 Mascot com. sh. (see Corona Corporation)

Mascot Malartic Mines Ltd. (Ont. 1940)
1952 – Charter cancelled.

Mascot Nickel Plate Mines Limited (B.C. 1971)
Aug. 8, 1980 – Name changed to Mascot Gold Mines Limited. ■

Masev Communications International Inc. (B.C. Nov. 6, 1998)
2004 – Dissolved.

Mashiach Capital Inc. (B.C. Sept. 29, 1982)
July 9, 1992 – Continued into Yukon.
Mar. 26, 1993 – Name changed to Animatronix Entertainment Corporation; basis 1 new for 2 old shs. ■

Mask Resources Inc. (B.C. May 12, 1987)
Oct. 1, 2002 – Name changed to American Nevada Gold Corp. ■

Maskal Energy Inc. (Alta. June 16, 2000)
Aug. 13, 2007 – Name changed to Maskal Energy Ltd.; basis 1 new for 4 old shs. ■

Maskal Energy Ltd. (Alta. June 16, 2000)
Dec. 2, 2011 – Struck from registry and dissolved.

Maskwa Mines Ltd. (Man. 1939)
1952 – Charter cancelled.

Mason Graphite Inc. (Ont. Mar. 15, 2011)
Mar. 3, 2016 – Continued into Canada.
Oct. 23, 2023 – Name changed to Mason Resources Inc. (see FPsurvey - Industrials)

Mason Resources Corp. (B.C. Feb. 24, 2017)
Dec. 24, 2018 – Acquired by Hudbay Minerals Inc.; basis Cdn$0.40 cash per sh.

Masonic Temple Corporation Limited (Can. - unspecified)
Jan. 26, 2004 – Dissolved and struck from register.

Masonite International Corporation (Ont. Dec. 31, 1992)
Apr. 6, 2005 – Acquired by Stile Acquisition Corp., an affiliate of Kohlberg Kravis Roberts & Co. L.P., for Cdn$42.25 per sh.
May 27, 2009 – Continued into Canada.
July 7, 2009 – Continued into British Columbia.
May 15, 2024 – Acquired by Owens Corning; basis US$133 cash per sh.
May 29, 2024 – Formed Masonite International ULC.

Massawippi Valley Railway Company (Can. 1862)
Sept. 1999 – PricewaterhouseCoopers Inc. was appointed to begin the voluntary winding-up and liquidation of the company.
May 28, 2001 – Liquidated and wound up and distributions made to shldrs. on the basis of $1,000 per com. sh.

Massberyl Lithium Co. Ltd. (Que. 1954)
1959 – Merged into Massval Mines Ltd.; basis 1 new for 4 old shs.

Massey-Ferguson Limited (Can. July 22, 1891; via Dominion charter)
Jan. 31, 1986 – Name changed to Varity Corporation following major refinancing and restructuring program. ∎

Massey-Harris Company Limited (Can. 1891)
Sept. 1953 – Amalgamated into Massey-Harris-Ferguson Ltd.

Massey-Harris-Ferguson Ltd. (Can. July 22, 1891; via Dominion charter)
1958 – Name changed to Massey-Ferguson Limited. ∎

Massey Mercantile Ltd. (B.C. Mar. 2, 1983)
Jan. 22, 1997 – Name changed to Riosun Resources Corporation. ∎

Massif Minerals Corporation (B.C. Apr. 14, 1978)
June 25, 1991 – Formed World Wide Oil & Gas Inc. in British Columbia on amalgamation with World Wide Oil & Gas Inc.; basis 0.2 new cl. A for 1 old sh. of Massif, 1.178 new cl. A for 1 old cl. A and cl. B com. shs. of World Wide plus 1 new cl. F pfd. sh for 1 old cl. F pfd. sh. of World Wide. ∎

Massive Energy Ltd. (B.C. 1979)
Apr. 30, 1987 – Name changed to Massive Resources Limited. (see FPsurvey - Mines & Energy)

Massive Yellowknife Mines Ltd. (Ont. 1945)
Nov. 28, 1960 – Dissolved.

Massval Mines Ltd. (Que. Nov. 10, 1959)
1979 – Name changed to Massval Resources Inc. ∎

Massval Resources Inc. (Que. Nov. 10, 1959)
Oct. 10, 1986 – Name changed to MSV Resources Inc.; basis 1 new cl. A for 3 old com. shs. ∎

Master Downhole Canada Inc. (Alta. June 9, 1994)
Feb. 25, 1998 – Name changed to Wenzel Downhole Tools Ltd.; basis 1 com. for 1 cl. A sh. ∎

Master Metals (Corporation) Limited (Ont. 1960)
Nov. 9, 1976 – Charter cancelled.

Master-Plan Mineral & Petroleum Developers Corporation (Can. 1986)
Dec. 7, 1995 – Continued into Bermuda.
Jan. 31, 1996 – Name changed to Isleinvest Ltd.; basis 1 new for 35 old shs.

Master Player Home Entertainment Corp. (B.C. Oct. 25, 1985)
Mar. 12, 1997 – Name changed to International Player Enterprises Inc.; basis 1 new for 4 old shs. ∎

Mastermet Cobalt Mines Ltd. (Ont. 1951)
Oct. 16, 1984 – Name changed to Master Resources & Developments Ltd. (see FPsurvey - Mines & Energy)

Masterpiece Games, Inc. (B.C. Dec. 20, 1996)
Aug. 27, 2003 – Name changed to Maestro Ventures Ltd.; basis 1 new for 5 old shs. ∎

Masterpiece Quality Products Inc. (B.C. Jan. 27, 1966)
Mar. 21, 1997 – Name changed to Aruma Ventures Inc.; basis 1 new for 10 old shs. ∎

Masters Energy Inc. (Alta. Feb. 26, 2004 amalg.)
May 6, 2009 – Acquired by Zargon Energy Trust; basis $1.83 or 0.12 Zargon trust units for 1 Masters Energy com. sh. (see Zargon Energy Trust)

Masters Holdings Inc. (B.C. Nov. 17, 1982)
Feb. 15, 1993 – Name changed to Envirotreat Systems Inc. ∎

Masters Oil & Gas Limited (Ont. 1948)
1958 – Wound up.

Masthead Resources Ltd. (Alta. Mar. 29, 2005)
Feb. 8, 2006 – Name changed to C.A. Bancorp Inc. following Qualifying Transaction acquisition of Sentry Select Focused Wealth Management Fund. ∎

Mastodon-Highland Bell Mines Ltd (Ont. 1951)
Jan. 1, 1970 – Former subsid. of Highland-Bell Ltd., co. liquidated following purchase of assets by Leitch Mines Ltd. (see Leitch Gold Mines Ltd.)

Mastodon Zinc Mines Ltd. (Ont. 1951)
1960 – Name changed to Mastodon-Highland Bell Mines Ltd; basis 1 new for 10 old shs. ∎

Mastorak Limited (Can. 1968)
Dec. 4, 1980 – Creditors accepted proposal to receive 25% on all claims as at July 17, 1979, plus 50% of net amounts recovered in connection with a lawsuit instituted by the co. for $3,500,000 against the Department of Supply and Services of Canada (judgement in favour of co.).
Mar. 1982 – Creditors were paid.
Nov. 1, 1982 – Name changed to Matthew Moody Enterprises Inc. ∎

Mastt Resources Inc. (B.C. 1984)
Sept. 29, 1989 – Dissolved.

Masuparia Gold Corporation (B.C. July 7, 1981)
Apr. 9, 2018 – Name changed to MAS Gold Corp. ∎

Matachewan Canadian Gold, Ltd. (Ont. 1923)
July 10, 1932 – Name changed to Matachewan Consolidated Mines, Limited. (see FPsurvey - Mines & Energy; FPsurvey - Industrials)

Matador Capital Inc. (Alta. Jan. 25, 2001)
July 24, 2003 – Name changed to Canadian Public Venture Equities 1 Inc. ∎

Matador Developments Ltd. (B.C. Mar. 16, 1966)
Mar. 1975 – Name changed to Betina Resources Inc.; basis 1 new for 5 old shs. ∎

Matador Exploration Inc. (Alta. Mar. 16, 1994)
Dec. 2, 2005 – Plan of Arrangement acquisition by Committee Bay Resources Ltd.; basis 0.72 new Committee Bay sh. for 1 old Matador sh. (see Committee Bay Resources Ltd.)

Matador Mines Ltd. (Ont. 1967)
Feb. 20, 1980 – Dissolved.

Matador Mining Limited (W.A. June 28, 2016)
May 31, 2024 – Name changed to AuMEGA Metals Ltd. (see FPsurvey - Mines & Energy)

Matamec Explorations Inc. (Que. July 9, 1997)
July 5, 2018 – Acquired by Canada Strategic Metals Inc. (renamed Quebec Precious Metals Corporation); basis 0.267697315 post-consolidated Canada Strategic com. shs. for 1 post-consolidated Matamec sh. (see Quebec Precious Metals Corporation)

Matarrow Lead Mines Ltd. (Ont. 1948)
Mar. 1953 – Name changed to Consolidated Matarrow Mines Ltd.; basis 1 new for 4 old shs. ∎

Matarrow Mines Ltd. (Ont. 1948)
Nov. 1948 – Name changed to Matarrow Lead Mines Ltd. ∎

Match Capital Resources Corporation (Ont. Oct. 26, 1988)
Dec. 28, 2018 – Name changed to Braingrid Limited following reverse takeover acquisition of Braingrid Corporation by way of amalgamation of Braingrid and a wholly owned subsidiary of Match; basis 2 post-consolidated Match common shares for 1 Braingrid share.; basis 1 new for 8 old shs. ∎

Matco Ravary Inc. (Que. Sept. 1, 1977)
Apr. 29, 2005 – Name changed to MCO Capital Inc. ∎

Mate Yellowknife Gold Mines Ltd. (Ont. Aug. 2, 1944)
Dec. 30, 1994 – Delisted from the CDN. Subsequently dissolved and charter cancelled.

Materials Protection Technologies Inc. (Ont. Apr. 22, 1994 amalg.)
Mar. 20, 2006 – Dissolved.

Matériaux Décoren Inc. (Que. July 7, 1976; via letters patent)
Apr. 22, 1987 – Name changed to Groupe Bocenor BF Inc. ∎

Mathan Explorations Inc. (Ont. 1973)
Nov. 5, 1976 – Amalgamated with several other cos. to form Wolverine Developments Inc.; basis 1 new for 6 old shs.

Matiadeka Ventures Inc. (Ont. May 19, 2006)
Apr. 1, 2008 – Name changed to Avante Security Corp. following Qualifying Transaction reverse takeover acquisition of Avante Security Inc. ∎

Matica Enterprises Inc. (B.C. Nov. 13, 2007)
Oct. 20, 2021 – Name changed to West Island Brands Inc.; basis 1 new for 30 old shs. (see FPsurvey - Industrials)

Matica Graphite Inc. (B.C. Nov. 13, 2007)
July 2, 2014 – Name changed to Matica Enterprises Inc. ∎

Matico Mines Ltd. (Ont. 1946)
Sept. 26, 1960 – Dissolved.

Matinenda Uranium Mines Ltd. (Ont. 1954)
Dec. 9, 1959 – Charter cancelled.

Matlo Oils Ltd. (Alta. Sept. 8, 1950)
1952 – Assets acquired by Sweet Grass Oils Ltd.; basis 1 new for 2.5 old shs.

MatNic Resources Inc. (B.C. Jan. 18, 2011)
Aug. 8, 2014 – Name changed to Graphene 3D Lab Inc. following reverse takeover acquisition of Graphene 3D Labs (U.S.) Inc. ∎

Matona Gold Mines Ltd. (Ont. 1929)
1945 – Name changed to Matona Golds Ltd. and continued into Ontario; basis 1 new for 3 old shs. ∎

Matona Golds Ltd. (Ont. 1945)
Nov. 27, 1961 – Dissolved.

Matrikon Inc. (Alta. Mar. 31, 2001 amalg.)
July 2, 2010 – Acquired by Honeywell International Inc. by way of amalg. with 1535758 Alberta Ltd., a wholly owned subsid. of Honeywell, for $4.50 per sh.

Matrix Asset Management Inc. (Can. Oct. 30, 2009)
Jan. 27, 2017 – Dissolved and struck from register.

Matrix Energy Inc. (B.C. Sept. 26, 1980)
Feb. 3, 1999 – Name changed to Promax Energy Inc.; basis 1 new for 5 old shs. ∎

Matrix Exploration Ltd. (Alta. 1969)
Mar. 26, 1986 – Name changed to Matrix Investments Limited. ■

Matrix Investments Limited (Alta. 1969)
Mar. 22, 1993 – Voluntarily dissolved. Final distribution $0.034613 per sh.

Matrix Petroleum Inc. (B.C. 1967)
Dec. 17, 2003 – Amalgamated with Berens Energy Ltd.; basis 0.51 Berens shs. for 1 Matrix sh. (see Berens Energy Ltd.)

Matt Berry Inc. (B.C. 1966)
Jan. 7, 1993 – Continued into Canada.
Dec. 28, 1993 – Name changed to SIRIT Technologies Inc.; basis 1 new for 3 old shs. ■

Matt Berry Mines Limited (B.C. 1966)
Dec. 17, 1992 – Name changed to Matt Berry Inc.; basis 1 new for 2 old shs. ■

Matta-King Mining Corp. Ltd. (Ont. 1969)
May 1972 – Amalgamated into Bayfor Corp. Inc.; basis 1 new for 7 old shs.

Mattabi Mines Limited (Ont. 1970)
Apr. 26, 2000 – Dissolved.

Mattagami Explorers Corporation (Que. 1958)
1979 – Charter cancelled.

Mattagami Lake Mines Limited (Que. 1958)
Jan. 2, 1979 – Merged with Noranda Mines Limited; basis 1 new for 2.25 old shs. (see Noranda Mines Ltd.)

Mattan Corporation (Alta. Feb. 8, 1993)
Aug. 1, 1999 – Dissolved and struck from register.

Mattawin Gold Mines Ltd. (Ont. 1946)
June 3, 1965 – Dissolved.

Matthew Moody Enterprises Inc. (Can. 1968)
June 11, 1984 – Final distribution to creditors made.
Dec. 10, 1984 – Discharged from bankruptcy.
Dec. 31, 1985 – Became private.

Matthews Gold Mines Ltd. (unknown)
Apr. 27, 1967 – Acquired by The Little Long Lac Gold Mines Ltd.; basis 1 new for 20 old shs. (see The Little Long Lac Gold Mines Ltd.)

Maud Creek Explorations Ltd. (B.C. 1969)
Feb. 28, 1975 – Charter cancelled.

Maude Lake Exploration Limited (Ont. Sept. 20, 1996)
Nov. 9, 2004 – Name changed to Maudore Minerals Ltd.; basis 1 new for 6 old shs. ■

Maude Lake Gold Mines Limited (Ont. 1973)
Oct. 1, 1996 – Merged into McWatters Mining Inc.; basis 1 new McWatters sh. for 5 old Maude Lake shs. or 1 new 18 month sh. pur. wt. exercisable for $1.30 a sh. for 10 com. shs. of Maude Lake. (see McWatters Mining Inc.)

Maudore Minerals Ltd. (Ont. Sept. 20, 1996)
May 16, 2016 – Filed assignment in bankruptcy and Deloitte Restructuring Inc. appointed trustee.

Maufort Resources Inc. (Que. Nov. 14, 1983)
Feb. 9, 1994 – Name changed to Dynacor Mines Inc.; basis 1 new for 10 old shs. ■

Maumee Red Lake Gold Mines, Ltd. (Can.)
July 19, 1937 – Name changed to Dalby-Larder Gold Mines Ltd. ■

Maverick Mines & Oils Limited (Alta. Mar. 27, 1952)
Mar. 24, 1972 – Name changed to Peregrine Petroleum Ltd.; basis 1 new for 5 old shs. ■

Maverick Mountain Resources Limited (B.C. 1969)
Sept. 26, 1986 – Merged into Pioneer Metals Corporation; basis 1 new for 2.4 old shs. (see Pioneer Metals Corporation)

Maverick Naturalite Beef Corporation (B.C. 1983)
Sept. 6, 1988 – Name changed to Golden Iskut Resources Incorporated. ■

Maverick Tube (Canada) Inc. (Alta. Sept. 22, 2000)
Sept. 30, 2005 – Redeemed in full; basis 1 com. sh. of Maverick Tube Corporation for 1 old Maverick Tube (Canada) exch. sh.

Maverick Uranium Explorations Inc. (Ont. 1962)
Jan. 5, 1984 – Name changed to Tolken Resource Corporation; basis 1 new for 10 old shs. ■

Maverix Metals Inc. (Can. Sept. 5, 2008)
Jan. 24, 2023 – Acquired by Triple Flag Precious Metals Corp.; basis (i) US$3.92 in cash or (ii) 0.360 Triple Flag shs. for 1 Maverick sh.

Mavrix Balanced Income and Growth Trust (Ont. Sept. 20, 2004)
Oct. 2, 2006 – Merged into Mavrix Canadian Income Trust Fund, a mutual fund; basis 0.9036 new mutual fund unit for 1 old trust unit.

Mavrix Fund Management Inc. (Ont. May 16, 2001)
July 7, 2009 – Acquired by 1796862 Ontario Ltd., a wholly owned subsid. of Growth Works Ltd., for 25¢ per. sh.

Mavtech Holdings Inc. (Que. 1947)
June 6, 1990 – Amalgamated with Ingram & Bell Acquisition Inc., a private co.; basis 1 cl. A pref. sh. for 1 com. sh. redeemable for $0.75 per sh.

Mawson Gold Limited (B.C. Mar. 10, 2004)
Jan. 10, 2025 – Name changed to Southern Cross Gold Consolidated Ltd. (see FPsurvey - Mines & Energy)

Mawson Resources Limited (B.C. Mar. 10, 2004)
Aug. 6, 2020 – Name changed to Mawson Gold Limited. ■

Mawson West Limited (Australia Feb. 12, 1996)
Nov. 20, 2016 – Acquired by Galena Private Equity Resources Fund for Cdn$0.01 cash per ord. sh.

Max Communications Corp. (B.C. June 14, 1985)
Sept. 29, 1995 – Name changed to Speyside Ventures Inc.; basis 1 new for 5 old shs. ■

Max Resource Corp. (Alta. Apr. 25, 1994)
Feb. 5, 2019 – Continued into British Columbia. (see FPsurvey - Mines & Energy)

Maxar Technologies Inc. (Del. Jan. 1, 2019)
May 9, 2023 – Acquired by Advent International Corporation; basis US$53 cash per sh.

Maxar Technologies Ltd. (B.C. June 16, 2016)
Jan. 1, 2019 – Succeeded by Maxar Technologies Inc. pursuant to a plan of arrangement whereby Maxar Technologies Inc., a new Delaware incorporated company, acquired all of the common shares of Maxar Technologies Ltd. on a one-for-one basis, resulting in Maxar Technologies Inc. becoming the parent company. ■

maxill inc. (Ont. Feb. 18, 1988)
May 1, 2011 – Amalgamated with 2277832 Ontario Inc.; basis 8¢ per sh.

Maxim Atlantic Corporation (Ont. Jan. 1, 1989 amalg.)
Nov. 20, 2003 – Voluntarily delisted from TSX.
Dec. 20, 2010 – Dissolved and struck from register.

Maxim Development Ltd. (B.C. Aug. 23, 1983)
Jan. 11, 1991 – Dissolved and struck off register.

Maxim Mining Corporation Limited (Ont. 1951)
Feb. 24, 1958 – Charter cancelled.

Maxim Power Corp. (Alta. July 9, 1993)
Mar. 2, 2010 – Amalgamated with 1494423 Alberta Ltd., a wholly owned subsid. of EarthFirst Canada Inc., and the resulting entity then amalgamated with EarthFirst to continue as Maxim Power Corp. (see FPsurvey - Mines & Energy; FPsurvey - Industrials)

Maxim Resources Inc. (Alta. Jan. 25, 1988)
Jan. 16, 2015 – Continued into Ontario. (see FPsurvey - Mines & Energy)

Maximizer Software Inc. (Can. Oct. 21, 2002)
Dec. 16, 2009 – Privatized at 12¢ per sh.

Maximum Energy Trust (Alta. May 29, 1996)
Nov. 13, 2001 – Name changed to Ultima Energy Trust. ■

Maximum Resources Inc. (B.C. June 24, 1985)
May 31, 1999 – Name changed to Maximum Ventures Inc.; basis 1 new for 7 old shs. ■

Maximum Ventures Inc. (B.C. June 24, 1985)
Oct. 23, 2009 – Name changed to Whistler Gold Exploration Inc.; basis 1 new for 5 old shs. ■

Maximus Resources Inc. (B.C. 1984)
May 27, 1994 – Dissolved and struck off register.

Maximus Ventures Ltd. (B.C. Aug. 25, 1987)
Sept. 18, 2008 – Acquired by NFX Gold Inc. which subsequently changed its name to Bear Lake Gold Ltd.; basis 1 NFX com. sh. for 1 Maximus com. sh.

Maximusic North American Corporation (B.C. Sept. 18, 1984)
Mar. 2, 1995 – Name changed to Trivalence Mining Corporation; basis 1 new for 5 old shs. ■

Maxon Computer Systems Incorporated (Ont. June 30, 1986)
Oct. 31, 1990 – Name changed to The Quartex Corporation. ■

Maxon Energy Inc. (Alta. Mar. 4, 1981)
July 12, 1994 – Amalgamated with Proalta Energy Inc. (1 for 1.6667) to continue with the same name Maxon Energy Inc.; basis 1 new for 1 old sh. (see Maxon Energy Inc.)

Maxon Energy Inc. (Alta. Mar. 4, 1981)
Oct. 19, 1995 – Amalgamated with Neutrino Resources Ltd. (1.81 for 1) and Red Oak Resources Inc. (1 for 10) to form a new co. also name Neutrino Resources Inc.; basis 1 com. sh and 1 wt. for 2 com. shs. Wts. exercisable until Oct. 5, 1997, at $1.00 per sh. (see Neutrino Resources Inc.)

Maxtech Ventures Inc. (B.C. Apr. 19, 2000)
Aug. 19, 2021 – Name changed to St. Anthony Gold Corp. ■

Maxville Mines Ltd. (Alta. 1977)
Aug. 27, 1987 – Formed Great Plains Waste Management Inc. in Alberta on amalgamation with Great Plains Waste Management Inc. ■

Maxwell Energy Corporation (B.C. Jan. 31, 1980)
Sept. 4, 1996 – Continued into Alberta.
Nov. 18, 1996 – Name changed to Maxwell Oil & Gas Ltd.; basis 1 new for 5 old shs. ■

Maxwell Limited (Ont. 1948)
1964 – Wound up. Mindustrial Corporation Limited offered to purch. all o/s $6.00 pref. shs. at $50.25 per sh.; and all o/s com. shs. at $4.00 per sh.

Maxwell Mines Ltd. (B.C. 1971)
1978 – Charter cancelled.

Maxwell Oil & Gas Ltd. (Alta. Sept. 4, 1996)
July 6, 2000 – Acquired by Tethys Energy Inc. for 88¢ per sh. (see Tethys Energy Inc.)

Maxwell Resources Inc. (B.C. Jan. 31, 1980)
May 12, 1993 – Name changed to Maxwell Energy Corporation. ■

Maxx Petroleum Ltd. (Alta. Feb. 11, 1987)
June 4, 2001 – Acquired by Provident Energy Trust; basis $7.00 or 0.63 Provident units for 1 Maxx sh. (see Provident Energy Trust)

MaxxCapp Corporation (Alta. Mar. 15, 1984)
Sept. 2, 2009 – Dissolved and struck from register.

Maxxcom Inc. (Ont. Nov. 2, 1998)
Aug. 5, 2003 – Plan of Arrangement exchange with MDC Corporation Inc.; basis 0.1905 new cl. A MDC sh. for 1 old Maxxcom sh. (see MDC Corporation Inc.)

Maxy Gold Corp. (B.C. Dec. 1, 1986)
Dec. 21, 2008 – Acquired by Lara Exploration Ltd.; basis 0.125 Lara shs. for 1 Maxy sh.

Maxy Oil & Gas Inc. (B.C. Dec. 1, 1986)
Nov. 10, 2003 – Name changed to Maxy Gold Corp.; basis 1 new for 4 old shs. ■

May-Ralph Resources Ltd. (B.C. Mar. 5, 1962)
July 24, 1987 – Dissolved and struck off register.

May-Spiers Gold Mines Ltd. (Ont. June 7, 1934)
Initial and final liquidating divd. of 7¢ per 10 shs.

Maya Gold & Silver Inc. (Can. Dec. 19, 2007)
July 31, 2020 – Name changed to Aya Gold & Silver Inc. (see FPsurvey - Mines & Energy)

Maya Gold Limited (Alta. Oct. 24, 1996)
Apr. 19, 2002 – Name changed to Centram Exploration Ltd.; basis 1 new for 5 old shs. ■

Mayan Energy Inc. (B.C. 1980)
Mar. 1, 1985 – Name changed to Leo Resources Inc.; basis 1 new for 2 old shs. ■

Maybrun Mines Ltd. (Ont. 1953)
July 10, 1978 – Name changed to Consolidated Maybrun Mines Limited. ■

Maycor Mines Ltd. (Ont. 1969)
Mar. 1976 – Charter cancelled.

Maycroft Mines Ltd. (Ont. 1961)
Apr. 29, 1970 – Charter cancelled.

Mayen Minerals Ltd. (B.C. Jan. 14, 1981)
Sept. 25, 2012 – Name changed to Rift Basin Resources Corp.; basis 2 new for 1 old sh. ■

Mayer Mining Co. Ltd. (Ont. 1959)
Dec. 1966 – Charter cancelled.

Mayfair Media Corporation (Alta. May 11, 1987)
Dec. 15, 1998 – Name changed to MF Media Corporation; basis unknown. ■

Mayfair Mines Limited (Ont. 1945)
Oct. 4, 1977 – Amalgamated with Ibsen Cobalt Silver Mines Limited to form Mayfair Resources & Developments Limited; basis 1 new for 5 old shs.

Mayfair Moly Mines Ltd. (B.C. 1966)
Oct. 21, 1974 – Charter cancelled.

Mayfair Oil & Gas Ltd. (Alta. 1957)
1961 – Acquired by Consolidated Mic Mac Oils Ltd.; basis 65 new for 100 old shs. (see Consolidated Mic Mac Oils Ltd.)

Mayfair Resources & Developments Limited (Ont. Oct. 4, 1977)
May 6, 1989 – Struck from register.

Mayfield Explorations & Developments Limited (Que. Mar. 10, 1971)
Dec. 23, 1978 – Charter cancelled.
Feb. 3, 1997 – Charter revived.
Feb. 11, 1998 – Formed Microsolve Computer Capital Inc. in Quebec on amalgamation with 9042-0068 Quebec Inc. and reverse takeover acquisition of Microsolve Computer Solutions Inc.; basis 1 new for 10 old shs. ■

Maygill Petroleum Company Limited (Ont. Aug. 21, 1950; via letters patent)
May 13, 1954 – Name changed to West Maygill Gas & Oil Limited; basis 1 new for 10 old shs. ■

Maylac Gold Mines Limited (Ont. July 5, 1946)
Apr. 17, 1984 – CTO issued. Subsequently dissolved and charter cancelled.

Mayland Oil Co. Ltd. (unknown)
1933 – Liquidated; assets acquired by Royalite Oil Co. Ltd.; basis 1 new for 12 old shs. (see Royalite Oil Company, Limited)

Maymac Explorations Limited (B.C. May 11, 1971)
Aug. 19, 1985 – Name changed to Maymac Petroleum Corporation. ■

Maymac Petroleum Corporation (B.C. May 11, 1971)
May 28, 1999 – Name changed to Consolidated Maymac Petroleum Corporation; basis 1 new for 19 old shs. ■

Maynard Energy Inc. (Can. 1980)
Sept. 9, 1983 – Amalgamated with Zephyr Resources Ltd. to continue as Maynard Energy Inc.; basis 1 new for 1 old sh.
Nov. 15, 1985 – All o/s com. shs. acquired by Tintagel Energy Corporation, a wholly owned subsid. of Avalon Corporation, at $6.00 per sh. under a purchase offer dated.

Mayo Mines Ltd. (Can. 1947)
1953 – Acquired by Maybrun Mines Ltd.; basis 1 new for 3 old shs. (see Maybrun Mines Ltd.)

Mayo Silver Mines Ltd. (B.C. 1962)
Aug. 1974 – Charter cancelled.

Mayou Gold Copper Co. Ltd. (B.C. 1928)
Name changed to Mayou Gold Silver Co. Ltd.

Mazarin Mining Corporation Inc. (Que. Feb. 15, 1985)
Nov. 17, 2000 – Name changed to Mazarin inc. (see FPsurvey - Mines & Energy)

Mazel Petroleums Ltd. (unknown)
1960 – Acquired by Western Decalta Petroleum Ltd.

Mazinaw Base Metals Ltd. (Ont. 1937)
Aug. 7, 1961 – Dissolved.

Mazorro Resources Inc. (Can. May 17, 2007)
Jan. 1, 2015 – Name changed to GrowPros Cannabis Ventures Inc. following acquisition of GrowPros MMP Inc. (deemed acquiror) via amalgamation of GrowPros MMP with wholly owned 9048073 Canada Inc. ■

mBase Commerce Inc. (Alta. Dec. 31, 1993)
Jan. 1, 2007 – Formed Bri-Chem Corp. in Alberta on amalgamation with Gwelan Supply Ltd., constituting a reverse takeover by Gwelan; basis 1 new for 1 Gwelan sh. and 0.2 new for 1 mBase sh. (see FPsurvey - Mines & Energy; FPsurvey - Industrials)

mBase.com Inc. (Alta. Dec. 31, 1993)
July 30, 2002 – Name changed to mBase Commerce Inc. ■

McAdam Mining Corporation Limited (Ont. 1959)
Dec. 2, 1983 – Name changed to Flanagan McAdam Resources Inc.; basis 1 new for 3 old shs. ■

McAdam Resources Inc. (Can. 1984)
Dec. 1, 1988 – Amalgamated with Tashota-Nipigon Mines Limited (1 for 2) and Konteko Resources Inc. (1 for 10) to form a new co. also named McAdam Resources Inc.; basis 1 new for 1 old sh.

McAdam Resources Inc. (Ont. Dec. 1, 1988 amalg.)
May 9, 1995 – Name changed to Boulder Mining Corporation; basis 1 new for 3 old shs. ■

McAllister Towing Ltd. (Can. 1958)
1967 – Taken over by Genstar Limited; basis 9 new for 10 old shs.

McAree Mines Ltd. (Ont. 1958)
Jan. 6, 1971 – Dissolved.

The McArthur Chemical Co. Ltd. (Can. 1947)
1953 – Controlling interest acquired by St. Maurice Chemicals Ltd.
1955 – The operating assets were sold.

McArthur Mills Explorations Ltd. (Ont. 1986)
Dec. 20, 1989 – Name changed to ET 2000 Corp.; basis 1 new for 2 old shs. ■

McBine Porcupine Gold Mines (Ont. 1937)
Nov. 16, 1970 – Charter cancelled.

McCabe Bros. Grain Co., Ltd. (Can. 1928)
Mar. 1946 – Name changed to McCabe Grain Company Ltd. ■

McCabe Grain Company Ltd. (Can. 1928)
Sept. 1968 – National Agri-Services Limited (formerly National Grain Co. Ltd.) acquired all o/s shs. at $11.50 per sh., through an offer made.

McCarthy Milling Company Limited (Ont. 1931)
1972 – George Weston Ltd. acquired 98% int. in co. Under offer dated Jan. 28, 1977, George Weston acquired remaining o/s shs. at $20 per cl. A and $30 per cl. B sh.

McCarthy-Webb-Goudreau Mines Ltd. (Ont. 1926)
May 1934 – Name changed to Algoma Summit Gold Mines Ltd. and continued into Ontario; basis 5 new for 12 old shs. ■

McCarvill Corporation (Ont. Dec. 28, 1995)
July 22, 2002 – Name changed to Rockwater Capital Corporation. ■

McColl-Frontenac Oil Company Limited (Can. 1927)
Feb. 1959 – Name changed to Texaco Canada Limited. ■

McCombe Mining & Exploration Ltd. (Ont. 1952)
Nov. 30, 1964 – Dissolved.

McConnell-Peel Resources Ltd. (B.C. 1957)
July 7, 1992 – Amalgamated with Sheba Copper Mines Limited to form Coast Falcon Resources Ltd.; basis 1 new for 10 Sheba shs. and 1 new for 10 McConnell-Pell shs. (see Coast Falcon Resources Ltd.)

McCool Mines Ltd. (Ont. 1951)
Nov. 1957 – Charter cancelled.

McCord Street Sites Limited (Que. June 26, 1928)
Sept. 22, 2014 – Dissolved and struck from register.

McCorkill Chibougamau Mining Co. (Que. 1956)
Nov. 4, 1978 – Charter cancelled.

McCoy Bros. Inc. (Alta. Feb. 29, 1996)
June 20, 2005 – Name changed to McCoy Corporation. ■

McCoy Corporation (Alta. Feb. 29, 1996)
July 10, 2014 – Name changed to McCoy Global Inc. (see FPsurvey - Mines & Energy; FPsurvey - Industrials)

McCoy Gold Mines Ltd. (Ont. 1937)
1953 – Charter cancelled.

McCoy Lake Mines Ltd. (Que. 1970)
Jan. 25, 1986 – Charter cancelled.

McCuaig Red Lake Gold Mines Ltd. (Ont. Feb. 28, 1934)
Jan. 28, 2008 – Certificate of incorporation cancelled and dissolved.

McCulloch's Canadian Beverages Inc. (B.C. 1981)
Oct. 4, 1994 – Name changed to MCB Investments Corp.; basis 1 new for 5 old shs. ■

McD Resources Ltd. (Alta. 1983)
Sept. 1, 1987 – Name changed to Norpet Resources Limited; basis 1 new for 7 old shs. ■

McDermott Gold Mines Ltd. (Ont. 1922)
Aug. 3, 1949 – Name changed to McDermott Mines Ltd. and continued into Ontario; basis 1 new for 3 old shs.

McDougall-Segur Exploration Co. Ltd. (unknown)
1929 – Taken over by The McDougall-Segur Exploration Co. of Canada Ltd.; basis 10 new for 1 old sh.

The McDougall-Segur Exploration Co. of Canada Ltd. (Can. May 23, 1929)
1954 – Taken over by Pathfinder Petroleums Ltd.; basis 1 new for 4 old shs.

McEnaney Gold Mines Ltd. (Ont. 1931)
Apr. 1962 – Dissolved.

McEwen Mining Inc. (Colo. July 24, 1979)
July 7, 2025 – Name changed to McEwen Inc. (see FPsurvey - Mines & Energy)

McEwen Mining - Minera Andes Acquisition Corp. (Alta. Sept. 19, 2011)
Aug. 23, 2016 – Redeemed; basis 1 McEwan Mining Inc. com. sh. for 1 exch. sh.

McFarlane Lake Mining Limited (B.C. Feb. 3, 2021)
Jan. 26, 2022 – Continued into Ontario. (see FPsurvey - Mines & Energy)

McFarlane Son & Hodgson (Limited) (Can. 1907)
Oct. 19, 1978 – Amalgamated with Domtar Ltd. Pref. shs. were called for redemption at $51.66 per sh.

McFinley Mines Ltd. (Ont. 1944)
July 11, 1984 – Amalgamated (1 for 1) with 575682 Ontario Limited, a wholly owned subsidiary of Sabina Industries Limited which received common and preferred stock in the new company known as McFinley Red Lake Mines Limited.

McFinley Red Lake Gold Mines Ltd. (Ont. 1944)
Jan. 8, 1975 – Name changed to McFinley Mines Ltd.; basis 1 new for 5 old shs. ■

McGarry Minerals Inc. (Ont. Aug. 19, 1985)
May 5, 1989 – Name changed to Whittier Capital Inc.; basis 1 new for 2 old shs. ■

McGillivray Creek Coal & Coke Ltd. (Can. 1909)
Nov. 1951 – Merged with International Coal & Coke and Hillcrest Mohawk Collieries to form a new co. known as Coleman Collieries Ltd. Final and total distribution for each 1,000 shs. held; $185, $29.80 par value of shs. and $690.64 par value of 5% first mtge. bonds of Coleman.

McGinn Gold Mines Ltd. (Ont. 1945)
Dec. 2, 1965 – Dissolved.

McGraw-Hill Ryerson Limited (Ont. Aug. 22, 1944)
June 19, 2014 – Acquired by 2412849 Ontario Inc., a wholly owned subsid. of McGraw-Hill Global Education Holdings, LLC; basis $50 cash per com. sh.

McGregor Capital Corp. (Alta. Apr. 1, 2008)
Nov. 2, 2011 – Formed Canadian Platinum Corp. in Alberta pursuant to Qualifying Transaction reverse takeover acquisition of and amalgamation with (old) Canadian Platinum Corp. ■

McIntyre Mines Limited (Ont. Mar. 16, 1911)
May 1, 1980 – Continued into Canada. (see Falconbridge Limited)
Jan. 24, 1989 – Acquired by Falconbridge Limited; basis $64 or 2.52 Falconbridge shs. for 1 McIntyre sh. (see Falconbridge Limited)

McIntyre Porcupine Mines Ltd. (Ont. Mar. 16, 1911)
Apr. 30, 1974 – Name changed to McIntyre Mines Limited. ■

McIvor Drilling Company Ltd. (Alta. Feb. 16, 1950)
July 9, 1954 – Name changed to Hi-Tower Drilling Co., Ltd. ■

McIvor Gold Mines Ltd. (unknown)
Dec. 1982 – Previously held by Willroy Mines Ltd. Wound up upon amalgamation of Willroy and Lac Minerals Ltd.

McKay-Cormack Holdings Ltd. (B.C. 1963)
1970 – Placed into receivership; assets not sufficient to discharge debenture indebtedness.

McKay Lake Gold Mines Limited (Ont. 1936)
June 23, 1980 – Charter cancelled.

McKay (Quebec) Exploration Ltd. (Que. Apr. 2, 1935)
1948 – Charter cancelled; shldrs. received $13.80 and 60 Scott Chibougamau shs. for 1 old sh.

McKenzie Chibougamau Mines Ltd. (Que. 1956)
Mar. 2, 1974 – Charter cancelled.

McKenzie Northern Mines Ltd. (Que. 1955)
Oct. 1974 – Charter cancelled.

McKenzie Oil & Gas Co. Ltd. (Man. 1948)
1965 – Name changed to Petromines Limited. ■

McKenzie Red Lake Gold Mines Ltd. (Ont. 1933)
June 1966 – Acquired by The Little Long Lac Gold Mines Ltd.; basis 1 new for 20 old shs. (see The Little Long Lac Gold Mines Ltd.)

McKinney Gold Mines Ltd. (B.C. 1959)
1967 – Name changed to Continental McKinney Mines Ltd.; basis 1 new for 5 old shs. ■

McKinney Resources Inc. (B.C. July 11, 1979)
Sept. 3, 1986 – Name changed to Consolidated McKinney Resources Inc.; basis 2 new for 5 old shs. ■

McLaren Minerals Inc. (Ont. 1984)
Dec. 18, 1992 – Amalgamated with Cimatec Engineering Inc. to form Cimatech Environmental Engineering Inc.; basis unknown. Previously continued into Canada effective Dec. 17, 1992. (see Cimatec Environmental Engineering Inc.)

McLaren-Porcupine Gold Mines Ltd. (Ont. 1934)
Aug. 24, 1964 – Dissolved.

McLaren Resources Corp. (Ont. Nov. 29, 1991)
July 29, 1999 – Name changed to Net-Quote.Com Inc. ■

McLaughlin Associates Limited, S.B. (Ont. 1957)
Sept. 30, 1981 – Name changed to Mascan Corporation. ■

McLellan Gold Mines Ltd. (Ont. 1941)
1953 – Name changed to Dyno Mines Ltd.; basis 1 new for 4 old shs. ■

McLellan Long Lac Gold Mines Ltd. (Ont. 1936)
Apr. 1958 – Charter cancelled.

McLennan, McFeeley & Prior Ltd. (B.C. 1929)
Dec. 31, 1966 – Since co. has been a wholly owned subsid. of Acklands Limited.

McLeod Copper Ltd. (B.C. Feb. 19, 1969)
Aug. 31, 1977 – Name changed to MCP Resources Corporation; basis 1 new for 4 old shs. ■

McManus Petroleum Ltd. (Ont. 1938)
1949 – Assets and undertakings sold to Reliance Petroleum Ltd.; basis 18 cl. A shs. for each 19 pref. shs. ($10 par) of McManus, and 5 cl. A shs. for each 13 com. shs. of McManus. (see Reliance Petroleum Ltd.)

McManus Red Lake Gold Mines Ltd. (Ont. 1927)
1977 – Name changed to New McManus Red Lake Gold Mines Ltd.; basis 1 new for 10 old shs. ■

McMarmac Red Lake Gold Mines Ltd. (Ont. 1939)
Mar. 14, 1978 – Charter cancelled.

McMillan Gold Mines Ltd. (Ont. 1928)
Apr. 1979 – Charter cancelled.

McNeely Mines (1937) Ltd. (Ont. June 1937)
1966 – Acquired by Barymin Explorations Ltd.; basis 2 new for 1 old sh.

McNeil, Mantha Inc. (Que. 1930)
Oct. 15, 1991 – Acquired by RBC Dominion Securities Limited for $3.00 per sh.

McNellen Resources, Inc. (B.C. Jan. 17, 1966)
Feb. 27, 1989 – Continued into Canada. (see Golden Goose Resources Inc.)
Sept. 30, 1996 – Amalgamated with Muscocho Explorations Ltd. (1 for 4) and Flanagan McAdam Resources Inc. (1 for 18.4) to form Golden Goose Resources Inc.; basis 1 new for 22.75 old shs. (see Golden Goose Resources Inc.)

McNickel Inc. (Ont. Mar. 21, 1989 amalg.)
Sept. 27, 1996 – Name changed to Sahelian Goldfields Inc.; basis 1 new for 8 old shs. ■

McPhar Instrument Corporation (Ont. 1980 amalg.)
Jan. 31, 1984 – Formed Androck Inc. in Ontario on amalgamation with Androck Inc.; basis 2 new cl. A non-vtg. shs. and 1 new cl. B sh. for 10 McPhar com. shs. ■

McQuillan Gold Ltd. (B.C. 1979)
Oct. 23, 1982 – Formed Nexus Resource Corporation in British Columbia on amalgamation with Christian Petroleum Corporation; basis 1 new for 4 old shs. ■

McSev Exploration Company Ltd. (Alta. Nov. 17, 1977)
July 24, 1990 – Name changed to Eco-Dynamics Industries Inc. ■

McVicar Industries Inc. (Ont. Feb. 19, 2003)
May 1, 2014 – Amalgamated with 1909734 Ontario Limited, wholly owned subsid. of CG Consulting & Investment Corp., to continue as McVicar Industries Inc.; basis 1 new redeem. pref. sh. for 1 old com. sh. immediately redeemed for 50¢ per sh. Co. now private.

McVicar Minerals Ltd. (Can. Dec. 6, 1996)
May 23, 2003 – Continued into Ontario.
June 1, 2003 – Formed Hanfeng Evergreen Inc. in Ontario pursuant to transfer of all resource assets to wholly owned McVicar Resources Inc. and amalgamation with newly created wholly owned Hanfeng Evergreen Inc.; basis 0.5054922 new com. shs. and 1 new special sh. for 1 McVicar sh. Following amalgamation, reverse takeover acquisition of Dalian Hanfeng Evergreen Turf Technologies Co., Ltd. was completed for 26,000,000 com. shs. ■

McVicar Mining Co. Ltd. (B.C. 1948)
Feb. 1962 – Acquired by Western Surf Inlet Mines Ltd.; basis 1 new for 7 old shs. (see Western Surf Inlet Mines Ltd.)

McVicar Resources Inc. (Ont. Feb. 19, 2003)
Sept. 8, 2008 – Name changed to McVicar Industries Inc. ■

McVittie-Graham Mines Ltd. (Ont. Jan. 27, 1928)
1946 – Distributed 1 sh. of McVittie-Graham Mining Company Limited and 2 shs. Conwest Exploration Company Limited for each 10 shs. McVittie-Graham Mines held. Charter surrendered.

McVittie-Graham Mining Company Limited (Ont. 1944)
June 12, 1980 – Amalgamated with Central Patricia Gold Mines Limited to form Central Patricia Limited; basis 1 special pfce. sh. for 1 com. sh.

McVittie-Kirkland Mines Ltd. (Ont. 1928)
1958 – Charter cancelled.

McWatters Gold Mines Ltd. (Can. 1932)
1970 – Acquired by Tontine Mining Ltd.; basis 1 new for 4 old shs. (see Tontine Mining Ltd.)

McWatters Mining Inc. (Que. Nov. 15, 1994)
July 2004 – Placed into receivership. Raymond, Chabot Inc. was appointed receiver.
Feb. 20, 2009 – Released from receivership. (see FPsurvey - Mines & Energy)

McWilliams-Beardmore Mines Ltd. (Ont. 1936)
June 24, 1965 – Dissolved.

mdf commerce inc. (Can. Feb. 16, 1996)
May 23, 2024 – Acquired by Kohlberg Kravis Roberts & Co. L.P.; basis $5.80 cash per sh/

Meacon Bay Resources Inc. (Ont. Aug. 29, 1978 amalg.)
Sept. 16, 1991 – Name changed to Advantex Marketing International Inc. ■

Meadow Bay Capital Corporation (B.C. Mar. 8, 2005)
Apr. 4, 2011 – Name changed to Meadow Bay Gold Corporation. ■

Meadow Bay Gold Corporation (B.C. Mar. 8, 2005)
Feb. 21, 2020 – Name changed to Mountain Valley MD Holdings Inc. pursuant to the reverse takeover acquisition of Mountain Valley MD Inc.; basis 1 new for 8 old shs. (see FPsurvey - Industrials)

Meadow Mountain Resources Ltd. (B.C. June 23, 1987)
Sept. 11, 1989 – Name changed to First Impression Singles Network Ltd. ■

Meadowvale Developments Limited (Ont. 1956)
1966 – Wound up. Assets consisted of 1,659,625 6% pref. and 41,000 com. shs. of Markborough Properties Ltd. Pref. shs. red. for approx. $2.32 per sh., and com. shs. distributed to shldrs., each Meadowvale sh. being exch. for 0.082 sh. Markborough.

Meares Resources Inc. (B.C. Mar. 6, 1980)
Mar. 16, 1982 – Name changed to Templar Mining Corporation. ■

Mecca Medi-Tech Inc. (B.C. Aug. 19, 1998)
Feb. 28, 2000 – Name changed to Pheromone Sciences Corp. following Qualifying Transaction reverse takeover acquisition of Pheromone Sciences Corp. ■

Mechanical Pin Resetter Co. Ltd. (Alta. June 8, 1953)
Feb. 22, 1982 – Name changed to Lead Energy Ltd. ■

Med BioGene Inc. (B.C. Apr. 28, 2006 amalg.)
June 15, 2022 – Name changed to Many Bright Ideas Technologies Inc. (see FPsurvey - Industrials)

Med-Chem Health Care Limited (Ont. Dec. 31, 1981 amalg.)
Dec. 3, 1996 – Amalgamated in Ontario to continue with same name.
Nov. 3, 1998 – Notices of demand and of intention to enforce security from the secured lender and the convertible debentureholder received. Total indebtedness was $40,000,000.
Feb. 1, 1999 – Ontario Court adjudged the co. to be bankrupt and appointed PricewaterhouseCoopers Inc. as trustee and receiver/manager.
Apr. 1999 – Substantially all laboratory assets plus subsid. and related cos. were sold to Canadian Medical Laboratories Limited for approx. $102,750,000.
May 2003 – Secured lender had been paid and a distribution had been made to the unsecured creditors, however no funds were available for shldrs.
July 2005 – Trustee discharged.

Med-Emerg International Inc. (Ont. Dec. 28, 1995)
Jan. 20, 2009 – Acquired by AIM Health Group Inc.; basis 0.78091 AIM shs. for 1 Med-Emerg sh. (see AIM Health Group Inc.)

Med-Tech Systems Inc. (B.C. 1983)
July 15, 1994 – Dissolved and struck off register.

Medallion Books Limited (B.C. 1985)
Jan. 26, 1990 – Dissolved.

Medallion Explorations Ltd. (B.C. Sept. 21, 1966)
July 14, 1987 – Name changed to Compass Resources Ltd.; basis 1 new for 3 old shs. ■

Medallion Mines Ltd. (Ont. 1964)
Mar. 20, 1968 – Dissolved.

Medallion Mortgage Corp. Ltd. (Alta. 1961)
June 1, 1982 – Struck off register.

Medallion Petroleums Limited (Alta. 1952)
1965 – Merged with Canadian Industrial Gas & Oil Ltd.; basis 1 new for 2.1 old shs. (see Canadian Industrial Gas & Oil Ltd.)

Medallion Resources Ltd. (B.C. Dec. 8, 1989 amalg.)
Feb. 14, 2024 – Name changed to Gabo Mining Ltd.; basis 1 new for 7 old shs. ■

Medalta Potteries Ltd. (Can. 1939)
1959 – In bankruptcy.

Medbroadcast Corporation (Can. Jan. 4, 2000)
Feb. 18, 2004 – Continued into Alberta.
Feb. 23, 2004 – Name changed to Rock Energy Inc. following reverse takeover acquisition of Rock Energy Ltd.; basis 1 new for 30 old shs. ■

Medcom Medical Computer Company Limited (Can. 1968)
Jan. 5, 1972 – Name changed to Ivey Medical Systems Ltd. ■

MedcomSoft Inc. (Ont. June 23, 1994)
Jan. 19, 2009 – Filed for bankruptcy. Ira Smith Trustee & Receiver Inc. appointed trustee.

Medcon Resources Ltd. (Alta. 1980)
Nov. 10, 1981 – By agreement dated stock of co. exchanged (1 for 1) for stock of Blake Resources Ltd.

medEra Life Science Corporation (B.C. Feb. 15, 1988)
Jan. 4, 2000 – Name changed to Medbroadcast Corporation and continued into Canada.

Medesto Exploration (Alta. 1952) Ltd. (Alta. 1952)
Name changed to Medesto Oils Ltd. ■

Medesto Exploration Ltd. (Alta. 1952)
1978 – Name changed to Cochrane Oil and Gas Ltd.; basis 1 new for 3 old shs. ■

Medesto Oils Ltd. (Alta. 1952)
Apr. 1967 – Name changed to Medesto Exploration Ltd. ■

Medgold Resources Corp. (B.C. Aug. 19, 1966)
Jan. 18, 2024 – Name changed to Electrum Discovery Corp. pursuant to the reverse takeover acquisition of Balkan Metals Corp.; basis 1 new for 16 old shs. (see FPsurvey - Mines & Energy)

Media Central Corporation Inc. (Ont. Oct. 11, 2019)
Mar. 25, 2022 – Filed for bankruptcy under the Bankruptcy and Insolvency Act. Ira Smith Trustee & Receiver Inc. appointed trustee and all the board of directors resigned.

Media Ventures Corp. (Ont. Feb. 20, 2007)
Aug. 31, 2009 – Name changed to Bassett Media Group Corp. following Qualifying Transaction reverse takeover acquisition of Bassett Media Group Inc. (see FPsurvey - Industrials)

Media Videotex Corp. (B.C. Sept. 2, 1983)
May 9, 1989 – Name changed to New Century Resources Ltd. ■

Mediagrif Interactive Technologies Inc. (Can. Feb. 16, 1996)
Sept. 23, 2020 – Name changed to mdf commerce inc. ■

MediaNet Communications Corp. (Alta. Mar. 11, 1996)
Sept. 2, 2010 – Dissolved and struck from register.

MediaValet Inc. (Alta. Dec. 29, 1993)
Apr. 5, 2024 – Acquired by STG Partners, LLC; basis Cdn$1.71 cash per sh.

Medicago Inc. (Que. July 17, 1997)
Sept. 20, 2013 – Acquired by Mitsubishi Tanabe Pharma Corporation for $1.16 per sh.

Medical Arts Building Limited (Man. May 16, 1922)
Nov. 7, 2006 – Name changed to MABL Holdings Ltd. ■

Medical Data Sciences Limited (Ont. Apr. 17, 1969)
Feb. 26, 1973 – Name changed to MDS Health Group Limited. ■

Medical Facilities Corporation (Ont. Jan. 12, 2004)
May 16, 2005 – Continued into British Columbia. (see FPsurvey - Industrials)

Medical Pathways International Inc. (Can. Oct. 19, 1987)
June 10, 2004 – Dissolved and struck from register.

Medical Polymers Technologies, Inc. (B.C. 1981)
Nov. 17, 1992 – Continued into Delaware.
Dec. 19, 1996 – Name changed to U.S. Medical Systems, Inc.; basis 1 new for 7 old shs. ■

Medical Resorts International Inc. (Ont. June 30, 1988)
Feb. 20, 2001 – Name changed to Medical Services International Inc.; basis 1 new for 15 old shs. ■

Medical Services International Inc. (Ont. June 30, 1988)
June 29, 2015 – Dissolved and struck from register.

Medical Ventures Corp. (B.C. Nov. 2, 2000)
Apr. 19, 2002 – Continued into Canada.
July 2, 2008 – Name changed to Neovasc Inc. following acquisition of Neovasc Medical Ltd. and B-Balloon Ltd.; basis 1 new for 20 old shs. ■

Medican Pharma International Inc. (Ont. Apr. 29, 1983)
Sept. 19, 1995 – Name changed to PrimeNet Communications Inc.; basis 1 new for 2 old shs. ■

Medici Mineral Inc. (Alta. Apr. 14, 1999)
Feb. 14, 2003 – Voluntarily delisted from TSX-VEN and dissolved following Nov. 18, 2002, suspension for failure to complete a Qualifying Transaction within 18 months of listing.

Medicorp Technology Ltd. (Ont. 1968)
Sept. 30, 1980 – Amalgamated with AutoMark International Industries Inc. and 452956 Ontario Inc. to form North American Combustion Technology Corporation; basis sh. for sh. (see North American Combustion Technology Corporation)

Medicure Inc. (Alta. Dec. 22, 1999 amalg.)
Feb. 23, 2000 – Continued into Canada. (see FPsurvey - Industrials)

Medifocus Inc. (Ont. Apr. 25, 2005)
Aug. 22, 2022 – Pursuant to restructuring under the Companies' Creditors Arrangement Act (CCAA) the secured lender, Asset Profits Limited, acquired all o/s com. shs. which were then consolidated on a 1-for-184,984,215 basis resulting in Asset Profits becoming the sole security holder. Monitor for the CCAA was msi Spergel Inc.

Medina Energy Resources Corporation (Ont. Mar. 26, 1973)
Jan. 31, 1984 – Name changed to Meenreco Energy Corporation; basis 1 new for 2 old shs. ■

Medipak Corporation Ltd. (Ont. 1968)
Feb. 10, 1975 – Name changed to Crown-Meakins Inc.; basis 1 new for 3 old shs. ■

The Medipattern Corporation (Ont. Apr. 22, 2005 amalg.)
May 7, 2013 – Placed into receivership. BDO Canada Limited appointed receiver.
July 15, 2013 – Assets sold to Salient Imaging, Inc. for $500,000. Secured creditors suffered a shortfall and no distributions available for unsecured creditors or shldrs. Receiver discharged.

MediSolution Ltd. (Ont. June 29, 1994 amalg.)
May 13, 2009 – Acquired by Brookfield Asset Management Inc.; basis 1 Brookfield Asset pref. sh. for 1 MediSolution com. sh. immediately redeem. at 30¢ per sh. (see Brookfield Asset Management Inc.)

Medisys Health Group Income Fund (Ont. Nov. 19, 2004)
Apr. 1, 2008 – Acquired by Persistence Capital Partners LP for $8.50 per fund unit.

Medisys Health Group Inc. (Can. Mar. 3, 1987)
Jan. 4, 2005 – Converted into an income fund named Medisys Health Group Income Fund; basis 1 trust unit for 2.5 sub. voting shs.

Medisystem Technologies Inc. (Ont. June 18, 1992)
Nov. 10, 2006 – Acquired by Shoppers Drug Mart Corporation; basis either $3.80 or, $0.05 plus 0.0808 new Shoppers sh. for 1 old Medisystem sh. (see Shoppers Drug Mart Corporation)

Mediterranean Minerals Corp. (B.C. Nov. 18, 1985)
Dec. 19, 2005 – Name changed to Mediterranean Resources Ltd.; basis 1 new for 10 old shs. ■

Mediterranean Resources Ltd. (B.C. Nov. 18, 1985)
Nov. 3, 2015 – Acquired by Transeastern Power Trust; basis 0.247 Transeastern units plus Transeastern 0.247 wt. for 1 Mediterranean com. sh. Each wt. is exercisable at $1.00 per unit for a period of 36 months. (see Transeastern Power Trust)

Meditrust Healthcare Inc. (Ont. Feb. 19, 1992)
Jan. 20, 1999 – Inactive.

Medius Communications Inc. (Ont. Aug. 19, 1994)
Jan. 2, 2006 – Dissolved and struck from register.

MedMen Enterprises Inc. (B.C. May 21, 1987)
Apr. 24, 2024 – Filed an assignment in bankruptcy and B. Riley Farber was appointed bankruptcy trustee.

Medmerica Incorporated (Ont. Sept. 18, 1980)
Feb. 22, 1988 – Name changed to Contach Industries Inc. ■

Mednow Inc. (B.C. Jan. 17, 2018)
Nov. 3, 2023 – Placed into receivership. Ernst & Young Inc. was appointed receiver.

Medoro Resources Ltd. (Yuk. Feb. 24, 2004 amalg.)
June 15, 2011 – Amalgamated with a wholly owned subsid. of Gran Colombia Gold Corp. basis 1.2 Gran shs. plus 0.5 com. sh. wts. for 1 Medoro sh. (see Gran Colombia Gold Corp.)

Medpath Petroleums Ltd. (Alta. 1963)
1965 – Merged with Canadian Industrial Gas & Oil Ltd.; basis 1 new for 6.1 old shs.

MedReleaf Corp. (Ont. Feb. 28, 2013)
July 27, 2018 – Acquired by Aurora Cannabis Inc.; basis 3.575 Aurora com. shs. and $0.000001 cash for 1 MedReleaf com. sh.

Medsana Medical Systems Inc. (B.C. Jan. 31, 1983)
Jan. 22, 1996 – Name changed to Connect Inter-Tel Media Inc.; basis 1 new for 4 old shs.

Medsource Systems Inc. (B.C. Apr. 11, 1983)
Oct. 3, 1995 – Name changed to Inter-Med Technologies Inc.; basis 1 new for 5 old shs. ■

Medsurge Medical Products Corp. (B.C. Apr. 12, 2001)
Apr. 28, 2006 – Name changed to CRH Medical Corporation. ■

Medwell Capital Corp. (Alta. July 31, 2001)
May 13, 2015 – Name changed to GDI Integrated Facility Services Inc. and continued into Canada following reverse takeover acquisition of and amalgamation with (old) GDI Integrated Facility Services Inc.; basis 1 new for 10.4 old shs. (see FPsurvey - Industrials)

Medworxx Solutions Inc. (Can. July 17, 2006)
Oct. 19, 2015 – Acquired by Aptean, Inc. for $0.5656 per sh.

MedXtractor Corp. (Alta. Jan. 24, 2018)
Oct. 22, 2021 – Name changed to nDatalyze Corp. (see FPsurvey - Industrials)

Medyx Inc. (Ont.)
June 5, 1996 – Name changed to Alterra Resources Inc.; basis 1 new for 5 old shs. ■

Meenreco Energy Corporation (Ont. Mar. 26, 1973)
Aug. 30, 1984 – Name changed to Millers Cove Resources Inc. ■

Meewood Yellowknife Mines Ltd. (Ont. 1944)
Feb. 14, 1952 – Charter cancelled.

Mega Bloks Inc. (Can. May 16, 1983)
July 27, 2006 – Name changed to MEGA Brands Inc. ■

Mega Capital Investments Inc. (B.C. Apr. 21, 1999)
Apr. 22, 2003 – Name changed to MAG Silver Corp. following Qualifying Transaction acquisition of Minera Los Lagartos, S.A. de C.V. (see FPsurvey - Mines & Energy)

Mega-Dial Communications Ltd. (Ont. 1977)
Sept. 3, 1987 – Name changed to Faleck and Margolies Ltd. ■

Mega-Dyne Industrial Corp. (B.C. June 11, 1980)
Dec. 7, 1989 – Name changed to International Mega-Dyne Industrial Corp.; basis 1 new for 2.5 old shs. ■

Mega Gold Resources Ltd. (B.C. 1981)
Mar. 4, 1994 – Dissolved and struck off register.

Mega Minerals Ltd. (B.C. 1967)
Oct. 24, 1974 – Charter cancelled.

Mega Moly Inc. (B.C. Nov. 21, 2007)
Aug. 23, 2010 – Name changed to Terreno Resources Corp. (see FPsurvey - Mines & Energy)

Mega Precious Metals Inc. (Ont. Sept. 2, 2009)
June 25, 2015 – Acquired by Yamana Gold Inc.; basis 0.02092 Yamana com. shs. plus Cdn$0.001 for 1 Mega sh. (see Yamana Gold Inc.)

Mega Silver Inc. (B.C. Nov. 17, 1982)
Sept. 2, 2009 – Continued into Ontario.
Sept. 14, 2009 – Name changed to Mega Precious Metals Inc. ■

Megacard Technologies Inc. (Ont. Mar. 9, 1979)
Aug. 31, 1992 – Delisted from the CDN. Subsequently dissolved.

Megaflo Mines & Energy Corp. (Ont. 1985)
Dec. 14, 1988 – Name changed to Chocolate Pix Corporation; basis 1 new for 5 old shs. ■

Megal Capital Corporation (B.C. July 8, 2008)
Feb. 14, 2014 – Name changed to Gourmet Ocean Products Inc. pursuant to Qualifying Transaction reverse takeover acquisition of Wen Lian Aquaculture Co., Ltd. (see FPsurvey - Industrials)

Megaline Resources Ltd. (B.C. 1979)
Mar. 27, 1985 – Name changed to International Megaline Resources Ltd.; basis 1 new for 5 old shs. ■

Megalode Resources Inc. (Ont. June 17, 1983)
Jan. 20, 1994 – Name changed to Megalode Corporation. (see FPsurvey - Industrials)

Megantic Mining Corp. (Que. 1957)
Mar. 15, 1986 – Charter cancelled.

Megasol Corporation (Can. Dec. 29, 1982)
June 20, 1997 – Name changed to Clonus Corporation; basis 1 new for 20 old shs. ■

Megastar Development Corp. (B.C. Sept. 24, 1984)
Mar. 29, 2004 – Name changed to Madoro Metals Corp. (see FPsurvey - Mines & Energy)

Megastar Ventures Ltd. (B.C. Sept. 24, 1984)
Nov. 3, 2000 – Name changed to Megastar Development Corp.; basis 1 new for 3 old shs. ■

MegaWest Energy Corp. (B.C. Feb. 8, 2000)
Feb. 12, 2008 – Continued into Alberta.
June 20, 2011 – Name changed to Gravis Oil Corporation; basis 1 new for 10 old shs. ■

Megawheels Inc. (Can. May 27, 1999)
Feb. 28, 2002 – Name changed to Megawheels Technologies Inc.; basis 1 new for 2 old shs. ■

Megawheels Technologies Inc. (Can. May 27, 1999)
Mar. 2, 2010 – Dissolved and struck from register.

Megawheels.com Inc. (Can. May 27, 1999)
July 4, 2001 – Name changed to Megawheels Inc. ■

Megiscane Mines Ltd. (Ont. 1945)
Mar. 15, 1972 – Dissolved.

Mekong International Development Corp. (B.C. Sept. 4, 1986)
Dec. 28, 1995 – Name changed to Everest Mines and Minerals Ltd.; basis 1 new for 8 old shs. ■

Melanesian Minerals Corporation (Ont. Jan. 31, 1997)
July 3, 2006 – Certificate of incorporation cancelled and dissolved.

Melard Mining Ltd. (B.C. Mar. 15, 1965)
Mar. 1972 – Name changed to Geo-Star Resources Ltd. ■

Melba Gold Mine Ltd. (Ont. 1936)
Nov. 5, 1956 – Dissolved.

Melcan Distillers Limited (Can. 1977)
Nov. 1, 1984 – This private co., a consortium of distilling interests, was formed to acquire the assets from the bankrupt Melchers Distilleries Limited amalgamated with a wholly owned subsid. of The Seagram Company Ltd.

Melchers Distillers Limited (Que. 1928)
Mar. 11, 1977 – Filed for bankruptcy.
Nov. 1977 – Assets sold to Melcan Distillers Limited (private co.) for $8,500,000, approx. $5.5 million less than amt. to settle bankrupt account.

Melco China Resorts (Holding) Limited (B.C. May 28, 2008 amalg.)
Oct. 22, 2010 – Name changed to Mountain China Resorts (Holding) Limited. ■

Melcor Real Estate Investment Trust (Alta. Jan. 25, 2013)
Apr. 25, 2025 – All o/s trust units not already held acquired by Melcor Developments Ltd.; basis $5.50 cash per trust unit.

Melinda Mines Ltd. (Ont. Jan. 1937)
1958 – Dissolved.

Melinga Resources Limited (B.C. Feb. 22, 1983)
Dec. 8, 1993 – Name changed to Milagro Minerals Inc.; basis 1 new for 3 old shs. ■

Melior Resources Inc. (B.C. June 1, 1995)
Oct. 7, 2021 – Name changed to Ranchero Gold Corp. prusuant to the reverse takeover acquisition of Ranchero BC Holding Corp. (formerly Ranchero Gold Corp.); basis 1 new for 32.6764 old shs. (see FPsurvey - Mines & Energy)

Melissa Resources Inc. (B.C. 1985)
June 15, 1987 – Name changed to Bauska Manufacturing (B.C.) Ltd. (see FPsurvey - Industrials)

Melita Mining Co. Ltd. (Ont. 1948)
Dec. 1960 – Charter cancelled.

Melius Capital Corp. (Ont. Mar. 23, 2018)
July 8, 2021 – Name changed to Arctic Fox Minerals Corp. ■

Melius Capital 3 Corp. (Ont. Apr. 8, 2021)
July 27, 2021 – Name changed to Melius Metals Corp. ■

Melius Metals Corp. (Ont. Apr. 8, 2021)
Apr. 12, 2022 – Name changed to Canadian Copper Inc. (see FPsurvey - Mines & Energy)

Melkior Resources Inc. (Can. Aug. 31, 1986)
Feb. 20, 2018 – Continued into British Columbia. (see FPsurvey - Mines & Energy)

Melma Lake Mines Ltd. (Alta. 1968)
Dec. 31, 1972 – Struck off register.

Melton Petroleums Ltd. (Alta. 1952)
1962 – Name changed to Trans-Canada Mortgage Corp. (Western) Ltd.; basis 1 new for 10 old shs. ■

Melton Real Estate Ltd. (Alta. Nov. 29, 1968; via memorandum of association)
June 11, 1976 – Name changed to Melcor Developments Ltd. (see FPsurvey - Industrials)

Melville Industries & Holdings (Ont. 1966)
Sept. 1979 – Charter cancelled.

Memotec Communications Inc. (Can. Oct. 7, 1993)
July 4, 2001 – Acquired by Germany-based Kontron Embedded Computers AG; basis 0.03377 new exchangeable shs. Kontron Communications Inc. for 1 old Memotec com. or pfd. sh.

Memotec Data Inc. (Can. Dec. 19, 1958)
Dec. 31, 1985 – Amalgamated in Canada to continue with same name.
Aug. 6, 1991 – Name changed to Teleglobe Inc. ■

Memsog Mining Co. Ltd. (Ont. 1959)
1962 – Charter cancelled.

Mena Resources Inc. (B.C. Feb. 9, 1990)
Mar. 6, 2007 – Acquired by Rusoro Mining Ltd.; basis 1 new Rusoro sh. for 1.7 old Mena shs.

Mendocino Resources Inc. (Alta. Oct. 20, 1987)
Feb. 2, 1995 – Name changed to EMR Microwave Technology Corporation; basis 1 new for 1 old sh. ■

Mendoza Capital Corp. (Alta. Sept. 22, 1997)
Dec. 1, 1998 – Name changed to Clement Systems Inc. following Qualifying Transaction acquisition of Clement Water Diversion Systems Ltd.; basis 1 new for 1 old sh. ■

Mengold Resources Inc. (Que. Feb. 16, 1945)
Sept. 22, 2010 – Name changed to MGold Resources Inc.; basis 1 new for 8 old shs. ■

Menifee Uranium Mines, Limited (Ont. 1953)
Nov. 1962 – Dissolved.

Menika Mining Ltd. (B.C. Feb. 25, 1974)
Apr. 15, 2016 – Name changed to American Lithium Corp. (see FPsurvey - Mines & Energy)

Menika Mining Ltd. (NPL) (B.C. Feb. 25, 1974)
Mar. 29, 2004 – Name changed to Menika Mining Ltd. ■

Meno Resources Ltd. (B.C. Jan. 22, 1982)
May 2, 1983 – Name changed to Preferred Resources Inc. ■

Menora Resources Inc. (Que. Feb. 16, 1945)
Dec. 4, 2003 – Name changed to Mengold Resources Inc.; basis 1 new for 8 old shs. ■

Menorah Mines Ltd. (Que. Feb. 16, 1945)
June 29, 1983 – Name changed to Menora Resources Inc. ■

Mensilvo Mines Ltd. (Ont. 1946)
June 1, 1964 – Dissolved.

Mentor Exploration and Development Co., Limited (Ont. May 1, 1926)
Oct. 22, 2001 – Acquired by Agnico-Eagle Mines Limited; basis 0.21 Agnico-Eagle shs. and 1.2753303 Sudbury Contact Mines Limited shs. for 1 Mentor sh. (see Agnico-Eagle Mines Limited)

Menu Foods Income Fund (Ont. Mar. 25, 2002)
Nov. 4, 2010 – Acquired by Simmons Pet Food for $4.80 per unit.

Meota Resources Corp. (Can. Dec. 28, 1966)
Oct. 4, 2002 – Acquired indirectly by Provident Energy Trust; basis $4.60, or 0.415 Provident trust units, or 0.415 Provident exchangeable shs., or a combination thereof, for 1 Meota com. sh. (see Provident Energy Trust)

Mera Petroleums Inc. (Alta. Apr. 29, 1993)
Oct. 15, 2004 – Name changed to West Isle Energy Inc.; basis 1 new for 4 old shs. ■

Meranto Technology Ltd. (Ont. Aug. 20, 1986)
May 5, 1998 – Formed World Sports Merchandising Inc. following acquisition of World Sports Merchandising Inc.; basis 1 new for 4 old shs. ■

Merbank Capital Corporation (Ont. Oct. 5, 1965)
June 13, 1995 – Continued into British Columbia.
July 7, 1995 – Formed Gran Colombia Resources Inc. in British Columbia on amalgamation with Gran Colombia Resources Inc.; basis 1 new for 1 Gran Colombia sh. and 1 new for 10 Merbank shs. ■

Merc International Minerals Inc. (Ont. Oct. 8, 2004)
Apr. 30, 2012 – Name changed to Nighthawk Gold Corp. ■

Mercal Capital Corp. (Can. Aug. 31, 2015)
July 24, 2019 – Amalgamated with 11293320 Canada Inc., a wholly owned subsidiary of LiveWell Canada Inc. (subsequently renamed Eureka 93 Inc.), which constituted the company's Qualifying Transaction; basis 0.27 post-consolidated LiveWell shs. for 1 Mercal sh. (see Eureka 93 Inc.)

Mercana Industries Ltd. (B.C. 1966)
June 28, 1995 – Continued into Ontario.

The Mercantile Bank of Canada (Can. 1953; via Bank Act)
Feb. 10, 1986 – Amalgamated into National Bank of Canada; basis 1.2 new for 4 com. shs. All o/s series 1 and 2 pref. shs. of Mercantile exchanged (1 for 1) for series 6 and 7 pref. shs. of National.

Mercantile Gold Corp. (B.C. 1986)
Nov. 10, 1994 – Dissolved and struck off register.

Mercantile International Petroleum Inc. (British Virgin Islands Nov. 23, 1994)
Mar. 11, 1996 – Continued into Cayman Islands.

Mercantile Transport and Forwarding, Ltd. (Can. 1938)
Mar. 3, 1942 – Assets transferred to former English subsid., London Forwarding Ltd., London, England. Shldrs. of 6% pref. shs. and com. shs. received 6% pref. shs. and com. shs. of London Forwarding Ltd. Charter surrendered.

Mercari Acquisition Corp. (Ont. Jan. 20, 2010)
Dec. 18, 2013 – Name changed to Concordia Healthcare Corp. pursuant to Qualifying Transaction reverse takeover acquisition of Concordia Healthcare Inc.; basis 1 new for 48.08 old shs. ■

Mercator Minerals Ltd. (Yuk. Apr. 16, 1997)
Apr. 7, 2005 – Continued into British Columbia.
Sept. 5, 2014 – Filed for bankruptcy. Deloitte Restructuring Inc. was appointed trustee and all officers and directors resigned.
Feb. 19, 2015 – All shares of wholly owned Creston Moly Corp. were sold by the trustee to Starcore International Mines Ltd. for Cdn$2,000,000.

Mercator Resource Corporation (Can. Sept. 28, 1984)
Mar. 14, 1990 – Name changed to Arimetco International Inc.; basis 1 new for 3 old shs. ■

Mercator Transport Group Corporation (Can. Jan. 15, 2004)
Nov. 28, 2023 – Dissolved for non-compliance and struck from register.

Mercedes Exploration Co. Ltd. (Ont. 1950)
Sept. 18, 1961 – Charter cancelled.

Mercer International Inc. (Wash. July 1, 1968)
June 12, 2018 – Voluntarily delisted.

Mercer Park Brand Acquisition Corp. (B.C. Apr. 16, 2019)
June 29, 2021 – Name changed to Glass House Brands Inc. pursuant to the Qualifying Acquisition of GH Group, Inc. (dba Glass House Group, Inc.) and concurrent amalgamation of GH Group with wholly owned MPB Mergersub Corp. (see FPsurvey - Industrials)

Merchant Capital Group Incorporated (Ont. July 11, 1985)
Apr. 20, 2004 – Delisted from the TSX-Venture Exchange. Subsequently struck from register and dissolved.

Merchant Private Limited (Ont. 1985)
May 26, 1997 – Name changed to Connor Clark Ltd. ■

Merchant Resources Inc. (Alta. 1987)
Aug. 10, 1990 – Formed Osprey Energy Ltd. in Alberta on amalgamation with Procana Resources Inc. and Osprey Resources Inc.; basis 1 new for 20 old shs. ■

Merchants' Bank of Halifax (N.S. June 22, 1869)
1871 – Continued into Canada; via Bank Act.
1901 – Name changed to The Royal Bank of Canada. ■

Mercier Explorations Limited (Ont. 1979)
Feb. 29, 1984 – Amalgamated with Offset Oil & Gas Resources Ltd. (1 for 1) to form Offset Natural Resources Ltd.; basis 1.1 new Offset sh. for 1 old Mercier sh.

Merco International Ltd. (B.C. 1967)
Feb. 25, 1983 – Struck off register.

Mercuria Industries Limited (B.C. 1945)
May 28, 1979 – Dissolved.

Mercury Acquisitions Corp. (B.C. Nov. 25, 2019)
Mar. 25, 2022 – Name changed to Franchise Global Health Inc. pursuant to the Qualifying Transaction reverse takeover acquisition of Franchise Cannabis Corp. and concurrent amalgamation of Franchise with wholly owned 2868303 Ontario Inc.; basis 1 new for 10 old shs. ■

Mercury Capital II Limited (Ont. Mar. 27, 2012)
Dec. 30, 2013 – Name changed to Revive Therapeutics Ltd. pursuant to Qualifying Transaction reverse takeover acquisition of Revive Therapeutics Inc. (see FPsurvey - Industrials)

Mercury Capital Limited (Ont. July 22, 2010)
Feb. 23, 2012 – Formed Canada Coal Inc. in Ontario following Qualifying Transaction amalgamation with (old) Canada Coal Inc. (deemed acquiror). ■

Mercury-Chipman Knit Limited (Can. 1922)
1956 – Equipment and machinery sold.
Jan. 22, 1957 – Distribution of some $400,000 equal to 50% princ. amt. to 1st mtge. bondholders through National Trust. Still o/s after distribution were $400,000 to 1st mtge. bondholders, $300,000 to 2nd mtge. bondholders and $300,000 to other creditors.

Mercury Explorations Ltd. (B.C. 1968)
Apr. 1977 – Charter cancelled.

Mercury Gold Mines Ltd. (Ont. 1940)
Nov. 4, 1970 – Charter cancelled.

Mercury Mills Limited (Can. 1922)
Aug. 25, 1954 – Name changed to Mercury-Chipman Knit Limited. ■

Mercury Oils Ltd. (Can. 1929)
June 1955 – Acquired by Mill City Petroleums Ltd.; basis 1 new for 3.5 old shs. (see Mill City Petroleums Limited)

Mercury Partners & Company Inc. (Can. Jan. 8, 1952)
Dec. 28, 2001 – Continued into Yukon.
May 2, 2005 – Name changed to Black Mountain Capital Corporation. ■

Mercury Scheduling Systems Inc. (B.C. Nov. 17, 1995)
July 8, 2003 – Name changed to Aventine Ventures Inc. ■

Merendon Canada Inc. (Alta. July 26, 1988)
May 2, 2013 – Struck from register and dissolved.

Merfin Hygienic Products Ltd. (B.C. Aug. 31, 1983)
Aug. 22, 1996 – Name changed to Merfin International Inc. ■

Merfin International Inc. (B.C. Aug. 31, 1983)
July 25, 1997 – Acquired by Buckeye Acquisition Inc., a wholly owned subsid. of Buckeye Cellulose Corporation, for $7.50 per sh.

Merfin Resources Ltd. (B.C. Aug. 31, 1983)
May 25, 1987 – Name changed to Merfin Hygienic Products Ltd. ■

Merge Cedara Exchange Co Limited (Ont. 2005)
Apr. 16, 2009 – All o/s exch. shs. redeemed by parent Merge Technologies Holdings Co.; basis 1 Merge Healthcare Incorporated com. sh. for 1 Merge Cedara exch. sh.

Mergecorp Inc. (Alta. 1986)
Apr. 1, 1990 – Struck off register.

Merged Enterprises Inc. (Ont. Apr. 27, 1943)
Jan. 17, 2005 – Delisted CDN Aug. 31, 1992, and the name was subsequently change to HR Cafe, Ltd. (date unknown). The certificate of incorporation was cancelled and dissolved.

Merged Mining Enterprises Limited (Ont. Apr. 27, 1943)
Dec. 9, 1997 – Name changed to Merged Enterprises Inc.; basis 1 new for 5 old shs. ■

Merican Capital Ventures Inc. (Can. Dec. 11, 1986)
Dec. 30, 1992 – Name changed to Encore Tickets Limited. ■

Merico Explorations Ltd. (Ont. 1955)
Apr. 9, 1975 – Dissolved.

Merida Merger Corp. I (Del. June 20, 2019)
Feb. 7, 2022 – Name changed to Leafly Holdings, Inc. following the reverse takeover Qualifying Acquisition of (old) Leafly Holdings, Inc.

Merida Minerals Holdings Inc. (Ont. Apr. 7, 2022)
Dec. 14, 2022 – Name changed to Hispania Resources Inc. (see FPsurvey - Industrials)

Merida Minerals Inc. (Alta. Oct. 22, 2018)
Apr. 7, 2022 – Continued into Ontario.
Apr. 21, 2022 – Name changed to Merida Minerals Holdings Inc. ■

Meriden Energy Corp. (Alta. Apr. 29, 1976)
Aug. 4, 1994 – Name changed to Triumph Energy Corporation. ■

Meridex Network Corporation (B.C. May 19, 1981)
Feb. 13, 2003 – Name changed to Meridex Software Corporation; basis 1 new for 10 old shs. ■

Meridex Software Corporation (B.C. May 19, 1981)
May 16, 2014 – Name changed to Cannabis Technologies Inc. ■

Meridian Concepts Ltd. (Can. Sept. 29, 1966)
July 22, 1982 – Name changed to Meridian Technologies Inc. ■

Meridian Energy Corporation (B.C. Dec. 18, 1992)
Sept. 9, 1996 – Continued into Alberta. (see True Energy Inc.)
Apr. 5, 2005 – Acquired by True Energy Inc.; basis either $3.85 or 0.91 new True sh. for 1 old Meridian sh. (see True Energy Inc.)

Meridian Gold Inc. (Can. Feb. 28, 1996)
Jan. 3, 2008 – Acquired by Yamana Gold Inc.; basis 2.235 Yamana com. shs. plus Cdn$7.00 per sh.

Meridian Mining and Exploration Co. Ltd. (Can. Sept. 29, 1966)
Nov. 22, 1978 – Name changed to Meridian Concepts Ltd. ■

Meridian Mining Co. Ltd. (B.C. 1932)
June 12, 1952 – Dissolved.

Meridian Mining N.V. (Netherlands Dec. 16, 2013)
Oct. 11, 2016 – Name changed to Meridian Mining S.E. ■

Meridian Mining S.E. (Netherlands Dec. 16, 2013)
Aug. 21, 2017 – Continued into United Kingdom.
Dec. 31, 2020 – Name changed to Meridian Mining UK Societas. (see FPsurvey - Mines & Energy)

Meridian Peak Resources Corporation (Que. June 21, 1966)
May 12, 1997 – Continued into Canada.
Oct. 4, 1999 – Continued into Yukon.
Sept. 26, 2001 – Name changed to Arcata Resources Corp.; basis 1 new for 4 old shs. ■

Meridian Petroleum Corporation (B.C. Dec. 18, 1992)
Mar. 31, 1993 – Name changed to Meridian Energy Corporation. ■

Meridian Resources Ltd. (B.C. 1967)
June 16, 1983 – Name changed to International Meridian Resources Ltd.; basis 1 new for 2 old shs. ■

Meridian Resources Ltd. (Alta. 1979)
July 23, 1979 – Name changed to Silverton Resources Ltd. ■

Meridian Technologies Inc. (Can. Sept. 29, 1966)
Oct. 14, 1998 – Privatized at $11 per sh.
2008 – Name changed to Meridian Lightweight Technologies Inc.

Meridius Resources Limited (B.C. July 10, 2017)
Aug. 31, 2020 – Name changed to BMEX Gold Inc. ■

Meridor Resources Limited (B.C. Mar. 29, 1985 amalg.)
Aug. 1, 1989 – Amalgamated with New Goliath Minerals Ltd. and Hughes Lang Corporation to form Hughes Lang Corporation; basis 0.1623 new cl. B for 1 New Goliath sh., 0.0462 new cl. A for 1 Hughes Lang cl. A sh., 0.0462 new cl. B for 1 Hughes Lang cl. B sh. and 0.1623 new for 1 Meridor sh. (see Hughes Lang Corporation)

Merino Yellowknife Mines Ltd. (Ont. 1945)
Mar. 1957 – Charter cancelled.

Merit Energy Ltd. (Alta. Jan. 25, 1988)
Sept. 22, 2000 – Declared bankrupt. Deloitte & Touche Inc. was appointed trustee.

Merit Industries Inc. (B.C. Apr. 7, 1981)
June 28, 2002 – Name changed to Ialta Industries Ltd.; basis 1 new for 3 old shs. ■

Merit Mining Corp. (B.C. June 16, 1986)
Dec. 23, 2010 – Name changed to Huakan International Mining Inc. ■

Merit Oil Ltd. (Ont. Sept. 23, 1957)
May 1968 – Name changed to Pacific Asbestos Ltd.; basis 1 new for 4 old shs. ■

Merit Resources Ltd. (B.C. Feb. 3, 1983)
July 3, 1986 – Name changed to Merit Technologies Ltd. ■

Merit Technologies Ltd. (B.C. Feb. 3, 1983)
Jan. 16, 1998 – Name changed to Systech Retail Systems Inc. following acquisition of Systech Retail Systems (Canada) Inc., a subsid. of Systech Group Inc. ■

Merland Explorations Limited (Can. 1926)
July 1, 1986 – Amalgamated into North Canadian Oils Limited; basis 1 com. for each 5.75 com. shs. of Merland; 1 cl. B ser. 6 pref. for each ser. A pref. and 1 cl. B ser. 7 for each series B pref. (see North Canadian Oils Limited)

Merland Oil Company of Canada Limited (Can. 1926)
1970 – Name changed to Merland Explorations Limited. ■

Merlin Capital (Canada) Inc. (B.C. 1986)
May 26, 1995 – Dissolved and struck off register.

Merlin Mines Ltd. (Ont. 1959)
Apr. 1970 – Wound up. No equity for shldrs.

Merlin Resources Inc. (B.C. Jan. 9, 1987)
June 12, 1998 – Dissolved and struck off register.

Merlin Resources Limited (B.C. 1986)
Sept. 27, 1989 – Name changed to Merlin Capital (Canada) Inc. ■

Merr Gold Mines Ltd. (Ont. 1945)
Oct. 25, 1954 – Charter cancelled.

Merr Yellowknife Gold Mines Ltd. (Ont. 1945)
1947 – Name changed to Merr Gold Mines Ltd. ■

Merrex Gold Inc. (B.C. Nov. 28, 1985)
Mar. 2, 2017 – All o/s com. sh. not already held acquired by IAMGOLD Corporation; basis 0.0433 IAMGOLD shs. for 1 Merrex sh.

Merrex Resources Inc. (B.C. Nov. 28, 1985)
May 24, 2006 – Name changed to Merrex Gold Inc. following reverse takeover acquisition of Jubilee Minerals Limited. ■

Merrican International Industries Ltd. (B.C. 1961)
Charter cancelled.

Merrican International Mines Ltd. (B.C. 1961)
July 12, 1971 – Name changed to Merrican International Industries Ltd.; basis 1 new for 3 old shs. ■

Merrican Mining Explorations Ltd. (B.C. 1961)
Feb. 1962 – Name changed to Merrican International Mines Ltd. ■

Merrill Island Mining Corporation Ltd. (Que. 1950)
1971 – Name changed to Canadian Merrill Ltd.; basis 1 new for 5 old shs. ■

Merrill Lynch & Co., Canada Ltd. (Can. Dec. 22, 1953)
Dec. 28, 1983 – Continued into Ontario.
Dec. 15, 2008 – All exch. shs. redeemed for Merrill Lynch & Co., Inc. com. shs. on a 1-for-1 basis.

Merrill Lynch Mortgage Loans Inc. (Can. Mar. 13, 1995)
Mar. 20, 2001 – Name changed to Merrill Lynch Financial Assets Inc.

Merrill-Obalski Mines Ltd. (Que. 1964)
Oct. 15, 1976 – Charter cancelled.

Merrill Petroleums Ltd. (Alta. 1951)
1957 – Merged with Pacific Petroleums Ltd.; basis 1 new for 2 old shs.

Merritech Development Corporation (B.C. Sept. 12, 1986)
Aug. 17, 1992 – Name changed to Dencam Development Corporation; basis 1 new for 3 old shs. ■

Merritt Copper Co. Ltd. (B.C. May 19, 1965)
Feb. 21, 1968 – Name changed to National Nickel Ltd. ■

Merritt Mining Explorations Ltd. (B.C. 1961)
1966 – Name changed to Banff Mines Ltd. ■

Mersington Capital Inc. (Can. May 3, 2004)
Feb. 22, 2007 – Formed Prime Meridian Resources Corp. in Canada following Qualifying Transaction reverse takeover acquisition of and amalgamation with Prime Meridian Resources Ltd.; basis 1 new for 2 old shs. ■

Merus Labs International Inc. (B.C. Nov. 2, 2009)
Dec. 19, 2011 – Amalgamated with Envoy Capital Group Inc.; basis 1 Envoy sh. for 4 Merus Labs shs. (see Merus Labs International Inc.)

Merus Labs International Inc. (B.C. Dec. 19, 2011 amalg.)
July 21, 2017 – Acquired by Norgine B.V.; basis Cdn$1.65 cash per sh.

Mervyn Malartic Gold Mines Ltd. (Ont. 1937)
Dec. 16, 1957 – Dissolved.

Meryllion Resources Corporation (B.C. July 25, 2013)
Oct. 27, 2020 – Continued into Canada. (see FPsurvey - Mines & Energy)

Mesa Biomedical Inc. (Alta. Sept. 25, 1987)
Dec. 18, 1996 – Name changed to Meteor Minerals Inc. and continued into Canada. ■

Mesa Exploration Corp. (B.C. Dec. 16, 1965)
Oct. 26, 2021 – Name changed to CoinSmart Financial Inc. pursuant to the reverse takeover acquisition of Simply Digital Technologies Inc. (dba CoinSmart) and concurrent amalgamation of CoinSmart with wholly owned 12553562 Canada Inc.; basis 1 new for 8.6282 old shs. ■

Mesa Resources Inc. (B.C. Apr. 10, 1997)
Mar. 3, 2004 – Amalgamated with LongBow Energy Corp. (1 for 1) to continue as LongBow Energy Corp.; basis 1 new LongBow sh. for 1 old Mesa sh. (see LongBow Energy Corp.)

Mesa Resources Ltd. (B.C. Mar. 29, 1984)
Sept. 25, 1987 – Continued into Alberta.
Sept. 28, 1993 – Name changed to Mesa Biomedical Inc. ■

Mesa Uranium Corp. (B.C. Dec. 16, 1965)
Mar. 30, 2011 – Name changed to Mesa Exploration Corp. ■

Mespi Mines Ltd. (Ont. 1955)
May 17, 1973 – Dissolved.

Mesquite Energy Inc. (Alta. Mar. 13, 1996)
July 7, 2000 – Name changed to Mesquite Exploration Ltd.; basis 1 new for 3 old shs. ■

Mesquite Exploration Ltd. (Alta. Mar. 13, 1996)
Sept. 1, 2000 – Amalgamated with Kispiox Resources Ltd. to form new co. with same name Mesquite Exploration Ltd.
June 26, 2002 – Name changed to High Point Resources Inc. following acquisition by High Point Energy Corp., constituting a reverse takeover by Mesquite. ■

Mesquite Resources Inc. (Alta. Mar. 13, 1996)
June 24, 1999 – Name changed to Mesquite Energy Inc.; basis 1 new for 3 old shs. ■

Messina Diamond Corporation (Ont. Jan. 27, 1988)
Aug. 2, 2000 – Name changed to Minegem Inc. ■

Messina Minerals Inc. (B.C. Oct. 27, 1989 amalg.)
Dec. 23, 2013 – Acquired by Canadian Zinc Corporation; basis 0.16949 Canadian Zinc com. shs. for 1 Messina sh. (see NorZinc Ltd.)
Jan. 2019 – Name changed to NorZinc-Newfoundland Ltd. (see NorZinc Ltd.)

Meston Lake Mines Ltd. (Ont. 1952)
Jan. 5, 1970 – Charter cancelled.

Meta Communications Group Inc. (B.C. 1985)
July 21, 1989 – Acquired by International Movie Group Inc.; basis 1 new for 15 old shs.

Meta Growth Corp. (Alta. June 18, 2015)
Nov. 19, 2020 – Acquired by High Tide Inc.; basis 0.824 High Tide shs. for 1 Meta Growth sh.

Meta Health Services Inc. (Alta. Mar. 23, 1998)
Dec. 21, 2009 – Name changed to Brookwater Ventures Inc. and continued into British Columbia; basis 1 new for 2 old shs. ■

Meta Uranium Mines Limited (Ont. July 4, 1951)
Aug. 24, 1978 – Name changed to Metina Developments Inc. ■

Metahost.net Technologies Inc. (B.C. Oct. 19, 2000)
July 30, 2001 – Name changed to Network Technology Professionals Inc. ■

Metal Closures (Canada) Ltd. (unknown July 1963)
Jan. 1, 1964 – Amalgamated with John Dale (Canada) Ltd. into Metal Closures Canada Ltd.

Metal Mines Ltd. (Que. 1953)
May 4, 1967 – Merged into Consolidated Canadian Faraday Ltd.; basis 1 new for 2 old shs.

MetalCORP Limited (Ont. July 10, 2002 amalg.)
May 10, 2023 – Acquired by Palladium One Mining Inc.; basis 0.30 Palladium shs. for 1 MetalCORP sh. (see Palladium One Mining Inc.)

Metalcoat International Corp. (Ont. Dec. 8, 1945)
July 4, 2003 – Name changed to Wycliffe Resources Inc. following reverse takeover acquisition of 1458216 Ontario Inc.; basis 2 new for 1 old sh. ■

Metalhawk Mining Ltd. (Ont. 1972)
Feb. 20, 1980 – Dissolved.

Metall Mining Corporation (Can. June 1, 1987)
May 24, 1995 – Name changed to Inmet Mining Corporation. ■

Metallgesellschaft Canada Investments Ltd. (Can. 1979)
July 31, 1990 – All o/s cl. B preferred shs., ser. 1 redeemed at $25 per sh. plus accr. divds. Company is now wholly owned subsid. of Metallgesellschaft Canada Limited. (see Metall Mining Corporation)

Metallic Ventures Gold Inc. (Ont. May 11, 1998)
Mar. 3, 2010 – Acquired by International Minerals Corporation for Cdn$3.80 per sh. or US$0.4615 plus 0.1635 International Minerals com. shs. per sh. (see International Minerals Corporation)

Metallic Ventures Inc. (Ont. May 11, 1998)
July 11, 2003 – Name changed to Metallic Ventures Gold Inc. ■

Metallica Metals Corp. (B.C. Mar. 3, 1987)
Nov. 20, 2023 – Name changed to Quebec Rare Earth Elements Corp. (see FPsurvey - Mines & Energy)

Metallica Resources Inc. (Ont. June 23, 1977)
July 16, 2002 – Continued into Canada.
July 7, 2008 – Acquired by New Gold Inc.; basis 0.9 New Gold shs. plus Cdn$0.0001 for 1 Metallica sh.

Metalline Mining Company (Nev. Nov. 8, 1993)
May 2, 2011 – Name changed to Silver Bull Resources, Inc. (see FPsurvey - Mines & Energy)

Metalline Resource Corporation (B.C. Apr. 29, 1987)
Mar. 14, 1995 – Name changed to Direct Choice T.V. Inc. ■

Metalline Resources Inc. (Ont. 1975)
July 6, 1976 – Amalgamated into Gambit Consolidated Explorations Ltd.; basis 1 new for 1.5 old shs.

Metallum Resources Inc. (Ont. Jan. 13, 1932)
Feb. 6, 2017 – Name changed to Torrent Capital Ltd.; basis 1 new for 3 old shs. (see FPsurvey - Industrials)

Metallum Resources Inc. (B.C. Mar. 24, 2021)
May 11, 2023 – Name changed to Waroona Energy Inc. pursuant to the reverse takeover acquisition of Waroona Energy Pty Ltd. ■

Metalore Mining Corp. Ltd. (Que. Nov. 1943)
1950 – Acquired by New Metalore Mining Co. Ltd.; basis 1 new for 3 old shs. (see New Metalore Mining Company Limited)

MetalQuest Minerals Inc. (B.C. Nov. 8, 1984)
Sept. 1, 2009 – Name changed to Canada Gold Corporation; basis 1 new for 3 old shs. ■

Metals Plus Income Corp. (Ont. Dec. 6, 2010)
Feb. 29, 2016 – Terminated; all o/s cl. A shs. redeemed for an undisclosed amount.

Metamaterial Inc. (Ont. July 7, 1987 amalg.)
June 29, 2021 – Acquired by Metamaterial Exchangeco Inc., a wholly owned subsid. of Torchlight Energy Resources, Inc. (renamed Meta Materials Inc.); basis 1.845 Meta Material shs. or 1.845 Meta Exchangeco shs. for 1 Metamaterial sh.

Metamedia Capital Corp. (Alta. Apr. 28, 2003)
Aug. 10, 2010 – Name changed to Brea Resources Corp. and continued into Canada; basis 1 new for 10 old shs. ■

Metanor Resources Inc. (Can. Jan. 10, 2003)
Sept. 26, 2018 – Acquired by BonTerra Resources Inc.; basis 1.6039 BonTerra com. sh. for 1 Metanor com. sh.

Metaxa Resources Ltd. (B.C. 1987)
Oct. 30, 1992 – Dissolved and struck off register.

Metcal Oil Company Limited (Ont. 1959)
July 29, 1965 – Dissolved.

Metco Resources Inc. (Que. Nov. 1, 1999 amalg.)
Apr. 18, 2008 – Acquired by Breakwater Resources Ltd.; basis 1 Breakwater sh. for 18.3 Metco shs.

Meteor Creek Resources Inc. (Ont. Dec. 22, 2000 amalg.)
Dec. 31, 2007 – Certificate of incorporation cancelled and dissolved.

Meteor Minerals Inc. (Can. Dec. 18, 1996)
Nov. 9, 1999 – Name changed to Meteor Technologies Inc. ■

Meteor Mining Co. Ltd. (B.C. June 25, 1962)
Sept. 24, 1979 – Name changed to Tesla Explorations Ltd.

Meteor Technologies Inc. (Can. Dec. 18, 1996)
Nov. 8, 2001 – Formed ThoughtShare Communications Inc. following acquisition of ThoughtShare Communications Inc. ■

Meteorite Capital Inc. (Can. Apr. 27, 2018)
Mar. 29, 2023 – Name changed to Kobo Resources Inc. pursuant to the reverse takeover acquisition of Boko Resources Inc. (formerly (old) Kobo Resources Inc.); basis 1 new for 5 old shs. (see FPsurvey - Mines & Energy)

MethylGene Inc. (Que. Dec. 13, 1995)
May 19, 2010 – Succeeded by (new) MethylGene Inc. under an arrangement whereby the company transferred all its assets and liabilities, including $7,013,500 in related non-dilutive financing, to a new wholly owned subsidiary, 7503547 Canada Inc., and 7503547 Canada amalgamated with 7503466 Canada Inc. to form new MethylGene. Common shares of old MethylGene were exchanged for common shares of new MethylGene on a 1-for-1 basis.
June 28, 2013 – Succeeded by Mirati Therapeutics, Inc. pursuant to plan of arrangement whereby a new Delaware-incorporated holding company was formed to be the ultimate parent of the company and its subsidiaries; basis 1 new for 50 old shs.

Metina Developments Inc. (Ont. July 4, 1951)
Nov. 5, 1992 – Name changed to Olympus Holdings Ltd. and continued into British Columbia; basis 1 new for 4.5 old shs. ■

Metoil Resources Ltd. (B.C. Sept. 15, 1980)
Apr. 1, 1986 – Name changed to Mohave Gold Inc. ■

Metoils Ltd. (Ont. 1945)
1950 – Name changed to Pentagon Oils & Mines Ltd. ■

Metro Automatic Washing Machine Corp. Limited (Ont. 1958)
Oct. 1961 – Name changed to Metro-Matic Services Limited. ■

Metro Drugs Ltd. (Ont. 1945)
Jan. 3, 1983 – Dissolved.

Metro Energy Ltd. (B.C. Oct. 13, 1983)
Mar. 15, 1996 – Dissolved and struck off register.

Metro Gold Mines Ltd. (Ont. 1944)
1946 – Shldrs. received 5 shs. Mogador Mines Ltd., 5 shs. Prahova Mines Ltd., and 4 shs. Barmont Gold Mines Ltd. for 100 old shs. Charter cancelled.

Metro Industrial Corporation (B.C. Nov. 5, 1979)
Apr. 27, 2009 – Dissolved and struck from registry.

Metro-Matic Services Limited (Ont. 1958)
1979 – Acquired by group composed of Moses and Sarah Buksbaum, Morris Kuhnreich and others. Co. now private.

Metro Minerals Ltd. (Ont. 1954)
1957 – Charter cancelled.

Metro Montreal Mutual Loan Company (Que. June 1, 1984)
Sept. 24, 1990 – Name changed to Société d'épargne de la Montérégie inc. ■

Metro Mortgage Corp. Ltd. (Alta. 1961)
Feb. 1967 – Name changed to Medallion Mortgage Corp. Ltd. ■

Metro Oil & Gas Co. Ltd. (Alta. 1949)
June 22, 1983 – Went into liquidation by special resolution of shldrs. Unpaid divds. owing to be paid by Public Trustee of Alberta.
Dec. 1, 1985 – Struck off register.

Metro Realty and Management Ltd. (Can. - unspecified)
1969 – Acquired by Medallion Mortgage Corp. Ltd. for $8.00 per sh. (see Medallion Mortgage Corp. Ltd.)

Metro Resources Company Limited (Yuk. Aug. 23, 1996)
Jan. 25, 1999 – Acquired by Asia Pacific Resources Ltd.; basis 0.44 new Asia Pacific sh. for 1 old Metro sh. (see Asia Pacific Resources Ltd.)

Metro Resources Inc. (B.C. Nov. 5, 1979)
May 12, 1983 – Name changed to Metro Industrial Corporation. ■

Métro-Richelieu Group Inc. (Que. Dec. 22, 1947; via letters patent)
Apr. 30, 1982 – Formed Métro-Richelieu Inc. in Quebec on amalgamation with United Grocers Inc. ■

Métro-Richelieu Inc. (Que. Dec. 22, 1947; via letters patent)
Sept. 29, 1979 – Name changed to Métro-Richelieu Group Inc. ■

Métro-Richelieu Inc. (Que. Apr. 30, 1982 amalg.)
Jan. 25, 2000 – Name changed to METRO Inc. (see FPsurvey - Industrials)

MetroBridge Networks International Inc. (Can. Oct. 6, 2004)
Dec. 5, 2011 – Name changed to Clemson Resources Corp. ■

Metroland Development Corp. Ltd. (Can. 1958)
1961 – Name changed to Oceanic Films and Enterprises Ltd. ■

Metron Capital Corp. (B.C. Mar. 4, 2008)
Jan. 27, 2020 – Name changed to INEO Tech Corp. following reverse takeover acquisition of INEO Solutions Inc.; basis 1 new for 1.6191 old shs. (see FPsurvey - Industrials)

MetroNet Communications Corp. (Alta. Sept. 1995)
July 14, 1997 – Continued into Canada.
June 1, 1999 – Name changed to AT&T Canada Inc. pursuant to plan of arrangement with AT & T Corp.; basis 1 new cl. B deposit receipt for 1 old cl. B non-vtg. sh. ■

Metropolitan Energy Corp. (B.C. July 16, 2007)
Nov. 8, 2018 – Name changed to Cannabis One Holdings Inc. pursuant to the reverse takeover acquisition of Bertram Capital Finance, Inc. (dba Cannabis One). ■

Metropolitan Mining Inc. (B.C. July 16, 2007)
Feb. 2, 2012 – Name changed to Metropolitan Energy Corp. ■

Metropolitan Stores of Canada Limited (Can. 1961)
1977 – General Distributors of Canada Ltd. acquired all remaining o/s cl. A and B shs. of co. not already held on basis of $11 and 1 wt., entitling the holder to buy 1 cl. A sh. of General Distributors at $8.00 for each Metropolitan sh. tendered. (see Gendis Inc.)
Nov. 28, 1983 – Became private upon redemption of all o/s 1961 ser. pref. shs. at $21.46 per sh. and all o/s 1967 ser. pref. shs. at $20.71 per sh. (see Gendis Inc.)
Jan. 13, 1998 – Name changed to Gendis Realty Inc. (see Gendis Inc.)

The Metropolitan Trust Company (Ont. 1969 amalg.)
Nov. 1, 1979 – Amalgamated with Victoria and Grey Trust Company to form Victoria Grey Metro Trust Company; basis 1 new for 2 old shs.

Metrowerks Inc. (Can. Jan. 1, 1990)
Oct. 21, 1999 – Acquired by Motorola Canada Acquisition Corp. for US$6.25 per sh.

Mettrum Health Corp. (Ont. Mar. 29, 2011)
Feb. 3, 2017 – Acquired by Canopy Growth Corporation; basis 0.7132 Canopy com. shs. for 1 Mettrum com. sh.
Sept. 18, 2017 – Name changed to Spectrum Health Corp.

Metx Research Corp. (B.C. Nov. 9, 2021)
Mar. 9, 2023 – Name changed to ME Therapeutics Holdings Inc. pursuant to the reverse takeover acquisition of ME Therapeutics Inc. (see FPsurvey - Industrials)

Mexgold Resources Inc. (Ont. Apr. 30, 2002 amalg.)
Aug. 9, 2006 – Acquired by Gammon Lake Resources Inc.; basis 0.47 new Gammon Lake sh. for 1 old Mexgold sh. (see Gammon Lake Resources Inc.)

Mexican Copper Corp. (Can. Apr. 15, 2021)
May 15, 2024 – Name changed to Axo Copper Corp. (see FPsurvey - Mines & Energy)

Mexican Gold Corp. (Ont. Jan. 14, 2011)
Feb. 10, 2020 – Name changed to Mexican Gold Mining Corp. and continued into British Columbia. (see FPsurvey - Mines & Energy)

The Mexican Light and Power Company, Limited (Can. 1902)
1980 – Continued into Ontario.
Nov. 21, 1991 – Liquidated. Final distribution of $5.00 for each pfd. $1.00 sh. held and $1.00 for each com. sh. held for holders of record Dec. 13, 1989.

Mexican Silver Mines Ltd. (Alta. May 7, 2007)
July 24, 2009 – Acquired by Rio Alto Mining Limited. ■

Mexicana Explorations Ltd. (Ont. 1956)
July 1, 1963 – Dissolved.

Mexicanus Explorations Ltd. (Ont. 1965)
Aug. 1979 – Charter cancelled.

Mexigold Corp. (B.C. Aug. 19, 1998)
Aug. 22, 2016 – Name changed to Savannah Gold Corp.; basis 1 new for 2 old shs. ■

Mexivada Mining Corp. (B.C. Sept. 13, 2004)
Feb. 26, 2018 – Dissolved and struck from register/
July 24, 2019 – Restored to register.
June 15, 2020 – Name changed to Carbon Streaming Corporation; basis 1 new for 100 old shs. (see FPsurvey - Industrials)

Mextor Minerals Ltd. (Ont. 1968)
1985 – Name changed to Commercial Industrial Minerals Limited. ■

Mexuscan Development Corporation Ltd. (B.C. 1956)
June 24, 1974 – Charter cancelled.

Mexxon Mines Ltd. (B.C. 1966)
July 18, 1977 – Name changed to Trans Canadian Equities Corporation. ■

Mezuma Inc. (Alta. Aug. 7, 1996)
Feb. 16, 2001 – Name changed to How to Web TV Inc. (see FPsurvey - Industrials)

Mezzi Holdings Inc. (B.C. Apr. 13, 2006)
Apr. 13, 2018 – Name changed to Omni Commerce Corp. ■

Mezzotin Minerals Inc. (Ont. Oct. 27, 2005)
Apr. 25, 2019 – Continued into British Columbia.
Apr. 30, 2019 – Name changed to Indus Holdings, Inc. pursuant to the reverse takeover acquisition of Salinas, Calif.-based Indus Holding Company; basis 485.3 new for 1 old sh. ■

Mi-Co Meter (Canada) Limited (Can. 1945)
Nov. 1950 – Declared bankrupt. C/o Canada Permanent Trust Co., Montreal, trustee for noteholders.

Mi-Lo Health & Beauty Aids Ltd. (B.C. 1967)
1980 – Acquired by Conventional General Investment Corporation of Ohio. Each co. sh. exchanged into 12%, 15-year bonds of EFW Corporation, with shs. valued at $1.75 each. Subsequently co. liquidated.

Miata II Capital Corp. (B.C. July 12, 2021)
Mar. 7, 2023 – Name changed to Miata Metals Corp. (see FPsurvey - Mines & Energy)

Mic-Mac Mines Ltd. (Ont. 1946)
1947 – Property sold to Mac Mac Mines Ltd.; basis 1 new for 3 old shs., subject to escrow.

Mic Mac Oils Limited (Man. Jan. 26, 1949)
1953 – Merged into Consolidated Mic Mac Oils Ltd.; basis 1 new for 4.5 old shs. (see Consolidated Mic Mac Oils Ltd.)

Mich Resources Ltd. (B.C. Aug. 16, 2018)
Oct. 19, 2023 – Name changed to Green Bridge Metals Corporation. (see FPsurvey - Mines & Energy)

Michael Lombardi Publishing Inc. (Ont. July 13, 1987)
Nov. 19, 1996 – Name changed to Lombardi Media Corporation. ■

Michael Resources Ltd. (B.C. 1971)
Apr. 15, 1994 – Dissolved and struck off register.

Michael Sohl and Associates Limited (Ont. 1964)
1986 – Amalgamated with Central Welders & Fabricators (Rodney) Limited and subsequently dissolved.

Michaely Silver Lead Mines Ltd. (B.C. Apr. 18, 1933)
May 8, 1969 – Struck off register.

Micham Exploration Inc. (B.C. 1981)
Dec. 17, 1990 – Name changed to International Micham Resources Inc.; basis 1 new for 3 old shs. ■

Michaud Porcupine Gold Mines Ltd. (Ont. 1939)
Jan. 23, 1956 – Dissolved.

Michel Oils Ltd. (Man. Jan. 26, 1949)
May 6, 1952 – Assets acquired by Bailey Selburn Oil & Gas Co. Ltd.; basis 1 cl. A sh. for 15 old shs.

Michele Gold Mines Ltd. (B.C. June 18, 1975)
Mar. 4, 1991 – Delisted from the Vancouver Stock Exchange. Subsequently dissolved and struck from registry.

Michelin Capital Limited (Alta. 1972)
1977 – Continued into Canada.
1987 – Continued into Nova Scotia.
June 4, 1997 – All o/s fltg. rate cum. redeem. cl. A pref. shs. redeemed; basis $25 per sh. plus $0.148 in accr. and unpaid divds.

Michelin Mining Corp. (B.C. Aug. 16, 2018)
Dec. 4, 2019 – Name changed to Mich Resources Ltd.; basis 2 new for 1 old sh. ■

Michigan Industries Ltd. (Alta. 1987)
Feb. 25, 1994 – Name changed to Aquatex Corporation; basis 1 new for 10 old shs. ■

Michipicoten Gold Mines Ltd. (Ont. 1934)
1952 – Charter cancelled.

Mico Enterprises Limited (Que. 1964)
1980 – Acquired by National Hees Enterprises Limited; basis 1.5 new National shs. for 1 old Mico com. or cl. A sh. (see National Hees Enterprises Limited)

Micrex International Corp. (Alta. Feb. 16, 1987)
Dec. 13, 1989 – Name changed to Micrex Development Corp.; basis 1 new for 10 old shs. (see FPsurvey - Mines & Energy)

Micro Concepts Inc. (B.C. 1986)
Nov. 26, 1993 – Dissolved and struck off register.

Micro Graphics Limited (B.C. Dec. 1, 1967)
Dec. 1970 – Name changed to Computrex Centres Ltd. ■

Micro Minerals Resources Inc. (B.C. Mar. 19, 1979)
Sept. 4, 2003 – Dissolved and struck from register.

Micro-Phonics Technology International Corporation (B.C. Mar. 29, 1984)
May 24, 1989 – Name changed to VAR Computer Solutions Corporation; basis 1 new for 5 old shs. ■

Micro Tempus Inc. (Can. Dec. 16, 1982)
Feb. 2, 2000 – Name changed to SureFire Commerce Inc. ■

Micro Ventures Ltd. (B.C. 1983)
Dec. 29, 1988 – Name changed to Diversified Entertainment Inc.; basis 1 new for 1 old sh. ■

Microbe Corporation (Ont. Feb. 16, 1982)
Oct. 15, 1994 – Struck from register.

Microcell Telecommunications Inc. (Can. Oct. 16, 1992)
Nov. 16, 2004 – Acquired indirectly by Rogers Wireless Communications Inc.; basis $35 per cl. A sh., $35 per cl. B sh., $15.79 for 2005 warrants and $15.01 for 2008 warrants.
Jan. 19, 2005 – Name changed to Fido Inc. ■

MicroCoal Technologies Inc. (Can. June 19, 1997)
May 21, 2015 – Name changed to La Jolla Capital Inc.; basis 1 new for 50 old shs. ■

Microdyne Electronics Company (B.C. 1975)
1982 – Dissolved.

Microdyne Modular Electronics Systems Ltd. (B.C. 1964)
1974 – Placed into receivership. Assets acquired by Microdyne Electronics Company.

Microforum Inc. (Ont. Feb. 27, 1987)
Sept. 5, 2003 – Name changed to Homeserve Technologies Inc.; basis 1 new for 25 old shs. ■

Microfuel Systems Inc. (B.C. Nov. 23, 1983)
Feb. 17, 1992 – Name changed to Teranet IA Incorporated. ■

Microkey Communication Systems, Inc. (B.C. Apr. 7, 1964)
May 31, 2001 – Delisted from the CDNX. Subsequently struck from register and dissolved for failure to file.

Microlab Online Inc. (Ont. Sept. 25, 1998)
Mar. 18, 2010 – Name changed to Axios Mobile Assets Corp. following reverse takeover acquisition of Axios Mobile Assets Inc. ■

Micrologix Biotech Inc. (B.C. Apr. 15, 1991)
Sept. 21, 2004 – Name changed to MIGENIX Inc. ■

Micron Industries Ltd. (B.C. 1983)
July 28, 1987 – Name changed to Lakewood Forest Products Ltd.; basis 1 new for 2 old shs. ■

Micron Metals Canada Corp. (Alta. Apr. 18, 1986)
Apr. 21, 1992 – Name changed to USA Video Corporation. ■

Micron Resources Ltd. (B.C. 1983)
Feb. 16, 1986 – Name changed to Micron Industries Ltd. ■

Micron Waste Technologies Inc. (B.C. Nov. 29, 2006)
Jan. 12, 2021 – Name changed to Beyond Medical Technologies Inc. ■

MicroPlanet Technology Corp. (Alta. Feb. 19, 2004)
Oct. 3, 2016 – Proposal was filed under the Bankruptcy and Insolvency Act and Deloitte Restructuring Inc. was appointed proposal trustee. (see FPsurvey - Industrials)

Microsolve Computer Capital Inc. (Que. Feb. 11, 1998 amalg.)
Jan. 29, 2001 – Name changed to Homebank Technologies Inc. ■

Microstar Software Ltd. (Can. Feb. 25, 1983)
Oct. 18, 1999 – Acquired by 3557855 Canada Inc., a wholly owned subsid. of Open Text Corporation, for $2.10 per share.

Microstat Development Corporation (B.C. May 17, 1983)
Mar. 30, 1992 – Name changed to International Chess Enterprises Inc. following acquisition of International Chess Enterprises Inc. ■

Microsystems International Ltd. (Can. 1969)
Apr. 9, 1975 – Under a sh. exchange offer which expired Northern Electric Company, Limited acquired all o/s shs. and warrants; basis 1 sh. Northern for each 7 shs. or 15 wts. of Microsystems.

Microtec Enterprises Inc. (Que. June 30, 1996 amalg.)
June 21, 2005 – Converted into an income trust named First National AlarmCap Income Fund; basis 0.2501202 cl. A trust units for 1 com. sh.

Mid-Bachelor Mines Ltd. (Que. 1946)
July 30, 1977 – Dissolved.

Mid-Can Exploration Ltd. (Sask. 1954)
Nov. 12, 1982 – Name changed to St. Johns Petroleum Ltd. ■

Mid-Canada Gold and Copper Mines Limited (Que. 1970)
June 14, 1989 – Amalgamated with Abitibi Resources Ltd. (1 for 5.7903) and Pioneer Resources (Canada) Ltd. (1 for 1) to form a new co. named Consolidated Abitibi Resources Ltd.; basis 1 new for 1 old sh. (see Consolidated Abitibi Resources Ltd.)

Mid-Canada Magnesium Mines Ltd. (Ont. 1944)
1957 – Charter cancelled.

Mid Central Mining Company Ltd. (Ont. 1946)
June 5, 1952 – Charter cancelled.

Mid Chibougamau Mines Ltd. (Que. 1956)
Sept. 29, 1970 – Name changed to Mid Industries Limited. ■

Mid-Continent Energy Corp. (B.C. 1980)
Dec. 31, 1981 – Amalgamated with Eldorado Minerals & Petroleum Corp. to form new co. under the latter name; basis sh. for sh.

Mid Continent Goldfields Ltd. (Can. 1929)
June 17, 1932 – Charter cancelled.
June 1932 – Continued into Ontario.

Mid Continent Oil & Gas Ltd. (Alta. Sept. 17, 1942)
1953 – Name changed to Midcon Oil & Gas Ltd.; basis 1 new for 5 old shs. ■

Mid Continent Oil Corp. Ltd. (Can. 1929)
Wound up and assets distributed prior to 1937.

Mid-Continental Brewing Co. Ltd. (Man. Aug. 27, 1992)
Feb. 26, 1993 – Name changed to Fort Garry Brewing Company Ltd. ■

Mid-East Developments Ltd. (Alta. Oct. 29, 1975)
1981 – Name changed to Promed Technology Inc. and continued into Canada. ■

Mid-Erie Acceptance Corporation Ltd. (Ont. 1953)
Sept. 22, 1966 – Trustee in Bankruptcy: The Clarkson Co. Ltd. Charter cancelled.

Mid Industries and Exploration Limited (Que. 1956)
May 17, 1980 – Name changed to Mid Industries Inc.; basis 1 new com. for 1 old com. sh. Certain shldrs. received pref. shs. of Mid Industries Inc., which were subsequently redeemed for 50¢ per sh. ■

Mid Industries Inc. (Que. 1956)
Dec. 31, 1980 – Formed Mid Transportation Services Ltd. in Ontario on amalgamation with subsids. ■

Mid Industries Limited (Que. 1956)
Sept. 1971 – Name changed to Mid Industries and Exploration Limited. ■

Mid-Kirk Gold Mines Ltd. (Ont. 1936)
Feb. 18, 1965 – Dissolved.

Mid Mountain Mining Ltd. (B.C. Sept. 12, 1969 amalg.)
Feb. 10, 1989 – Dissolved and struck off register.

Mid-Nation Developments Ltd. (Ont. 1959)
Apr. 16, 1969 – Dissolved.

Mid-North Acceptance Limited (Ont. 1962)
Jan. 11, 1979 – Wound up.
Nov. 26, 1994 – Dissolved and struck off register.

Mid-North Explorations Ltd. (B.C. Feb. 19, 1969)
July 23, 1981 – Name changed to Attila Resources Inc. ■

Mid-North Resources Limited (Man. July 25, 1975)
Nov. 1986 – Continued into Alberta.
Dec. 23, 2005 – Formed Bison Gold Exploration Inc. in Ontario on amalgamation with (old) Bison Gold Exploration Inc. (deemed acquiror); basis 1 new for 1 Bison sh. and 1 new for 4 Mid-North shs. ■

Mid-North Uranium Limited (Man. July 25, 1975)
Sept. 24, 1975 – Name changed to Mid-North Resources Limited. ■

Mid-Northern Explorations Ltd. (Ont. 1968)
Mar. 1976 – Charter cancelled.

Mid-Patapedia Mines Ltd. (Ont. 1967)
1978 – Dissolved.

Mid Transportation Services Ltd. (Ont. Dec. 31, 1980 amalg.)
1986 – Remaining public interest, amounting to 215,375 shs., repurchased by co. at 65¢ per sh.

Mid-West Copper & Uranium Mines Ltd. (B.C. 1955)
Oct. 1964 – Name changed to Mid-West Mines Ltd.; basis 1 new for 5 old shs. ■

Mid-West Energy Inc. (B.C. Oct. 22, 1968)
Aug. 22, 1984 – Name changed to Millrock Development Corp.; basis 1 new for 4 old shs. ■

Mid-West Mines Ltd. (B.C. 1955)
May 31, 1972 – Name changed to Cardigan Development Company Ltd.; basis 1 new for 5 old shs. ■

Mid-West Mining Corp. (Sask. 1956)
1958 – Name changed to Viscount Oil and Gas Ltd.; basis 1 new for 9 old shs. ■

Mid-West Oil Co. Ltd. (Alta. Oct. 18, 1917)
1932 – Assets sold to The Midwest Petroleum Corp. Ltd.

Mid West Petroleum Ltd. (B.C. 1977)
May 3, 1979 – Name changed to March Resources Ltd. ■

Mid-Western Industrial Gas Ltd. (Alta. 1952)
1964 – Acquired by Canadian Industrial Gas Ltd. (subsequently Canadian Industrial Gas & Oil Ltd.); basis 1 new for 3 old shs.

Midas Capital Corporation (Ont. Mar. 27, 1987)
Mar. 20, 2006 – Dissolved and struck from register.

Midas Gold Corp. (B.C. Feb. 22, 2011)
Feb. 15, 2021 – Name changed to Perpetua Resources Corp. (see FPsurvey - Mines & Energy)

Midas Minerals Inc. (Ont. Mar. 27, 1987)
Oct. 13, 1994 – Name changed to Midas Capital Corporation. ■

Midas Mining Co. Ltd. (Ont. 1958)
Oct. 16, 1968 – Charter cancelled.

Midas Oils Limited (Sask. 1951)
1960 – Struck off register.

Midas Resources Limited (B.C. 1966)
Mar. 3, 1977 – Name changed to Continental Silver Corp.; basis 1 new for 5 old shs. ■

Midas Resources Ltd. (Alta. Oct. 13, 1992)
July 21, 1998 – Name changed to Scorpion Energy Corporation following reverse takeover acquisition of Scorpion Energy Inc.; basis 1 new for 3 old shs. ■

Midas Yellowknife Gold Mines Ltd. (Ont. 1945)
Sept. 1957 – Charter cancelled.

Midasco Capital Corp. (Ont. May 16, 1991)
Mar. 17, 2008 – Continued into British Columbia.
July 31, 2025 – Name changed to Spartan Metals Corp. (see FPsurvey - Mines & Energy)

Midasco Gold Corp. (Ont. May 16, 1991)
July 17, 2001 – Name changed to Midasco Capital Corp. ■

Midburn Oil Co. Ltd. (unknown)
May 6, 1952 – Assets acquired by Bailey Selburn Oil & Gas Co. Ltd.; basis 1 new for 1.5 old shs.

Midcamp Mines Ltd. (Ont. 1946)
Jan. 1960 – Charter cancelled; assets distributed on the basis of 9 0.75¢ per sh.

Midcon Oil & Gas Ltd. (Alta. Sept. 17, 1942)
Mar. 1, 1987 – Amalgamated with Discovery Mines Limited (1 for 1) and Yellowknife Bear Resources Inc. (1 for 1) to form Discovery West Corp.; basis 9 new Discovery West shs. for 5 old Midcon shs. (see Discovery West Corp.)

Midd Financial Corp. (B.C. Aug. 25, 1970)
Oct. 23, 2006 – Dissolved and struck from register.

Midd-Pershing Gold Mines Ltd. (Ont. 1945)
May 1958 – Charter cancelled.

Middle Bay Mines Ltd. (Ont. 1943)
Feb. 14, 1973 – Dissolved.

Middle Kingdom Paradiso Corp. (Ont. Aug. 2, 2007)
July 20, 2009 – Name changed to Mega View Digital Entertainment Corp. following Qualifying Transaction reverse takeover acquisition of Mega View Management Services Inc. (see FPsurvey - Industrials)

Middle River Mines Limited (Ont. 1974)
June 3, 1985 – Dissolved. No assets available for distribution.

Middlefield Bancorp Limited (Ont. Apr. 10, 1997)
Feb. 23, 2012 – Dissolved following amalgamation with 2311828 Ontario Inc., a wholly owned subsid. of MBN Corporation (formerly Middlefield Tactical Energy Corporation); basis 0.166887541 MBN Corporation equity shs. for 1 Middlefield Bancorp sh. (see Middlefield Tactical Energy Corporation)

Middlefield Can-Global REIT Income Fund (Alta. Oct. 26, 2012)
Feb. 17, 2022 – Merged into Middlefield REIT INDEXPLUS ETF; basis 0.75651920 Middlefield REIT ETFs for 1 Middlefield Can-Global trust unit.

Middlefield Equal Sector Income Fund (Ont. Sept. 28, 2005)
May 27, 2008 – Acquired by INDEXPLUS Income Fund; basis 0.70861783 INDEXPLUS trust units for 1 Middlefield Equal fund unit.

Middlefield Global Real Asset Fund (Alta. Oct. 11, 2019)
Dec. 5, 2024 – Merged with Real Estate Split Corp.; basis 0.36409573 Real Estate Split units (1 pref. sh. & 1 cl.A sh.) for 1 unit held.

Middlefield Healthcare & Life Sciences Dividend Fund (Alta. June 23, 2017)
Feb. 19, 2019 – Converted from a closed-end fund to an exchange-traded fund.

Middlefield Healthcare & Wellness Dividend Fund (Alta. Sept. 20, 2016)
June 11, 2019 – Converted to an exchange-traded fund; basis 1 new ETF unit for 1 old fund unit.

Middlefield High Income Trust (Ont. Feb. 28, 1997)
Aug. 26, 2002 – Name changed to MINT Income Fund. (see FPsurvey - Industrials)

Middlefield Income Plus II Corp. (Ont. Jan. 25, 2012)
Mar. 4, 2014 – Merged into Middlefield Income Plus Class (an open-ended fund); basis 0.70239004 Middlefield Income Plus Class ser. A units for 1 Middlefield Income Plus II Corp. unit.

Middlefield Tactical Energy Corporation (Alta. Mar. 19, 2010)
Feb. 27, 2012 – Name changed to MBN Corporation pursuant to acquisition of Middlefield Bancorp Limited. ■

Middlegate Resources Inc. (B.C. Nov. 24, 1980)
Aug. 22, 1985 – Name changed to Banner Industries Inc.; basis 1 new for 2.5 old shs. ■

Middleground Mining Co. Ltd. (Ont. 1947)
Sept. 9, 1958 – Charter cancelled.

Midepsa Inc. (Can. 1961)
June 20, 1984 – Name changed to Midepsa International Inc.; basis 1 new for 4 old shs. ■

Midepsa Industries Limited (Can. 1961)
1981 – Name changed to Midepsa Inc. ■

Midepsa International Inc. (Can. 1961)
Nov. 5, 1985 – Name changed to Henlys Group Limited. ■

Midland Bank Canada (Can. Oct. 8, 1981)
May 1, 1988 – Acquired by HongKong Bank of Canada. (see Hongkong Bank of Canada)

Midland Doherty Financial Corporation (Can. Feb. 10, 1983)
June 1, 1990 – Amalgamated with Walwyn Inc. to form new co. Midland Walwyn Inc.; basis 1 new for 2.0 old shs. (see Midland Walwyn Inc.)

Midland Energy Corporation (B.C. Mar. 18, 1981)
Feb. 1, 1988 – Name changed to Midland Gold Corporation. ■

Midland Gold Corporation (B.C. Mar. 18, 1981)
Mar. 23, 1989 – Continued into Ontario.
July 19, 1989 – Name changed to Minera Rayrock Inc.; basis 1 new for 4 old shs. ■

Midland Holland Inc. (Can. Jan. 8, 1952)
Jan. 24, 2000 – Name changed to Mercury Partners & Company Inc.; basis unknown. ■

Midland Nickel Corporation Ltd. (unknown)
1966 – Continued into Ontario.
Apr. 22, 1994 – Formed Materials Protection Technologies Inc. in Ontario on amalgamation with Materials Protection Technologies Inc.; basis 1 new for 0.448625 old shs. ■

Midland Petroleums Limited (B.C.)
Feb. 1972 – Merged into Davenport Oil & Mining Ltd.; basis 1 new for 10 old shs. ■

Midland Walwyn Inc. (Can. June 1, 1990 amalg.)
Aug. 31, 1998 – Following Plan of Arrangement, acquired by Merrill Lynch & Co., Inc., of New York, creating a new company known as Merrill Lynch & Co., Canada Ltd.; basis 1 new exch. sh. of Merrill Lynch & Co., Canada Ltd. for 1 old sh. of Midland. (see Merrill Lynch & Co., Canada Ltd.)

Midlands Minerals Corporation (Ont. June 2, 2004 amalg.)
July 28, 2015 – Name changed to Rosita Mining Corporation; basis 1 new for 10 old shs. ■

Midlartic Mines Ltd. (Ont. 1965)
Mar. 1973 – Charter cancelled.

Midnapore (1979) Resources Inc. (B.C. July 11, 1979)
Nov. 30, 1990 – Dissolved and struck off register.

Midnapore Resources Inc. (B.C. July 11, 1979)
Jan. 22, 1986 – Name changed to Midnapore (1979) Resources Inc.; basis 4 new for 1 old sh. ■

Midnight Consolidated Mines Ltd. (B.C. 1956)
June 24, 1974 – Dissolved and struck off register.

Midnight Oil & Gas Ltd. (Alta. Sept. 3, 1993)
Dec. 2, 2004 – Plan of Arrangement to convert company into an income trust named Daylight Energy Trust and an exploration company named Midnight Oil Exploration Ltd.; basis either 1 new trust unit and 0.5 new com. sh., or 1 new Daylight Acquisition Corp. exchangeable sh. and 0.5 new com. sh., or a combination thereof, for 1 old Midnight Oil & Gas com. sh. (see Daylight Energy Trust; Midnight Oil Exploration Ltd.)

Midnight Oil Exploration Ltd. (Alta. Sept. 10, 2004)
June 29, 2010 – Formed Pace Oil and Gas Ltd. in Alberta pursuant to amalgamation with Provident Energy Resources Inc. (deemed acquiror), the upstream oil and natural gas business unit of Provident Energy Trust; basis 1 new for 10 old shs. ■

Midnight Star Ventures Corp. (B.C. Apr. 19, 2013)
Oct. 29, 2018 – Name changed to Canna-V-Cell Sciences Inc. following Qualifying Transaction reverse takeover acquisiton of Dolarin Ltd. ■

Midnight Sun Capital Corp. (B.C. Apr. 11, 2007)
Feb. 7, 2011 – Name changed to Midnight Sun Mining Corp. (see FPsurvey - Mines & Energy)

Midori Carbon Inc. (B.C. Feb. 11, 2020)
May 29, 2025 – Name changed to Standard Strategies Inc. (see FPsurvey - Industrials)

Midpoint Holdings Ltd. (B.C. Apr. 15, 2010)
May 16, 2022 – Name changed to Blockmate Ventures Inc. (see FPsurvey - Industrials)

Midray Minerals Ltd. (Ont. 1964)
July 17, 1973 – Charter cancelled.

Midrim Mining Company Limited (Ont. 1955)
June 5, 1996 – Name changed to Plasma Environmental Technologies Inc. ■

Midswana Diamond Exploration Corp. (Ont. Jan. 28, 1974)
Mar. 31, 1999 – Name changed to Vertex Ventures Inc.; basis 1 new for 5 old shs. ■

Midvale Explorations Ltd. (Ont. 1971)
Aug. 17, 1973 – Merged into Consolidated Midvale Explorations Ltd.; basis 1 new for 3 old shs.

Midvale Petroleums Ltd. (B.C. 1980)
Feb. 28, 1983 – Amalgamated with Reigate Resources Inc. (1 for 1) and Zodiac Resources Ltd. (1 for 4) to form Reigate Resources (Canada) Ltd.; basis 1 new for 3 old shs.

Midwark Mines Ltd. (Ont. 1966)
1972 – Dissolved.

Midway Energy Ltd. (Alta. July 31, 2009 amalg.)
Apr. 27, 2012 – Acquired by Whitecap Resources Inc.; basis either $4.85 or 0.4802 Whitecap com. shs. for 1 Midway com. sh. or a combination thereof.

Midway Gold Corp. (B.C. May 14, 1996)
June 22, 2015 – Filed for protection under Chapter 11 of the U.S. Bankruptcy Code for the District of Colorado and under the Companies' Creditors Arrangement Act (CCAA) in Canada.Ernst & Young Inc. appointed information officer.
Dec. 2015 – Sale of interest in Spring Valley property to Waterton Global Resource Management, Inc. was completed.
May 17, 2016 – Sale of Pan, Gold Rock and Golden Eagle projects to GRP Minerals, LLC (subsequently GRP Minerals Corp.) was completed. Purchase price and terms included: US$5,250,000 cash and assumption of US$16,100,000 of estimated reclamation liabilities.
Apr. 2017 – Sale of Tonopah project to Aintree Resources Inc. for US$25,000 was completed. Plan of liquidation called for the transfer of substantially all remaining assets to the Midway Liquidating Trust. Distributions expected for priority claims, a dividend to general unsecured creditors of an estimated amount of 2% to 3%, with the remaining funds to be distributed to Commonwealth Bank of Australia as secured creditor.
Oct. 19, 2020 – Dissolved and struck from register.

Midway Mines & Energy Corp. (Ont. June 17, 1987)
Sept. 21, 1994 – Name changed to Dimensional Media Inc.; basis 1 new for 3 old shs. (see FPsurvey - Industrials)

Midway Resources Limited (Alta. July 30, 1993)
Jan. 5, 2000 – Struck from registry and dissolved.

Midway Terminals Ltd. (B.C. 1958)
Name changed to National Forest Products Ltd. ■

Midwest Energy Emissions Corp. (Utah July 19, 1983)
Feb. 2007 – Continued into Delaware.
Oct. 17, 2024 – Name changed to Birchtech Corp. (see FPsurvey - Industrials)

Midwest Farmers Oil Ltd. (unknown)
1964 – Acquired by Scurry-Rainbow Oil (Sask.) Ltd.; basis 1 new for 5 old shs.

Midwest Iron Mining Corp. Ltd. (Ont. 1940)
Jan. 1946 – Sold property to Rawn Iron Mines Ltd.; basis 1 new for 5 old shs. (see Rawn Iron Mines Ltd.)

Migao Corporation (Ont. Dec. 29, 1997)
Sept. 12, 2016 – Privatized by 2521416 Ontario Inc. (controlled by Liu Guocai) for 75¢ per sh.

Migent Software Corp. (B.C. 1983)
Mar. 18, 1988 – Continued into Canada.
Apr. 18, 1997 – Dissolved and struck from register.

Mighty Beaut Minerals Inc. (B.C. July 24, 1987)
Aug. 30, 2000 – Continued into Yukon.
Dec. 20, 2002 – Name changed to MBMI Resources Inc.; basis 1 new for 5.5 old shs. ■

Mija Mines Ltd. (Ont. 1965)
Oct. 18, 1978 – Charter cancelled.

Mika Technology Inc. (Alta. Aug. 7, 1996)
Dec. 16, 2002 – Amalgamated with Imaging Dynamics Company Ltd. and Seventh Wave Capital Corp. to continue as Imaging Dynamics Company Ltd. (IDL) considered to be the company's Qualifying Transaction; basis 25.65792 new IDL units (1 IDL sh. and 1 IDL wt.) for 100 old Mika com. shs.

Mikado Resources Ltd. (B.C. 1981)
Dec. 2, 1994 – Name changed to Silver Peak Resources Ltd.; basis 1 new for 3 old shs. ■

Mikanagan Mining Co. Ltd. (Ont. 1951)
Dec. 1966 – Charter cancelled.

Mikes Restaurants Inc. (Can. Feb. 28, 1979)
Jan. 24, 2001 – Acquired by Pizza Delight Corporation for $4.35 per sh.

Mikes Submarines Inc. (Can. Feb. 28, 1979)
Aug. 8, 1985 – Name changed to M-Corp Inc. ■

Mikotel Networks Inc. (Ont. May 9, 2000 amalg.)
Nov. 2, 2004 – Name changed to Wabi Exploration Inc.; basis 1 new for 2 old shs. ■

Milado Mines (1957) Ltd. (Que. 1957)
Oct. 17, 1975 – Charter cancelled.

Milagro Energy Inc. (Alta. Dec. 17, 1998)
July 27, 1999 – Amalgamated in Alberta to continue with same name. (see FPsurvey - Mines & Energy)

Milagro Minerals Inc. (B.C. Feb. 22, 1983)
Oct. 15, 1996 – Continued into Ontario. (see Geomaque Explorations Ltd.)
Jan. 17, 1997 – Acquired by Geomaque (Central America) Ltd., a wholly owned subsid. of Geomaque Explorations Ltd.; basis 1 Geomaque Exploration sh. for 4 Milagro shs. (see Geomaque Explorations Ltd.)

Milan Resources & Explorations Ltd. (B.C. Sept. 26, 1986)
July 9, 1992 – Name changed to Golden Bear Minerals Inc.; basis 1 new for 4 old shs. ■

Mildale Gold Mines Ltd. (Ont. 1945)
Charter cancelled.

Mile 18 Mines Ltd. (Ont. 1959)
Nov. 4, 1970 – Charter cancelled.

Milerlaun Rouyn Gold Mines Ltd. (Ont. 1945)
1952 – Charter cancelled.

Miles Martin Kirkland Mines Ltd. (Ont. 1937)
Nov. 5, 1956 – Dissolved.

Miles (Red Lake) Mines Ltd. (Ont. 1945)
Feb. 28, 1989 – Amalgamated with Antelope Resources Limited to form Antelope Resources Inc.; basis 1 new for 20 old shs. (see Antelope Resources Inc.)

Milestone Apartments Real Estate Investment Trust (Ont. Jan. 17, 2013)
May 1, 2017 – Privatized; basis US$16.30041 per trust and cl. B partnership units including unpaid monthly distrib. of US$0.05041.

Milestone Exploration Limited (Ont. July 23, 1968)
Jan. 1, 2010 – Amalgamated with Union Gold Inc., Golden Harker Explorations Limited, Sheldon-Larder Mines Limited and Wood-Croesus Gold Mines Limited to form Jubilee Gold Inc.; basis 1.749 Jubilee sh. for 1 Milestone

sh., 0.557 Jubilee sh. for 1 Union Gold sh., 0.393 Jubilee sh. for 1 Golden Harker sh., 0.269 Jubilee sh. for 1 Sheldon-Larder sh. and 0.367 Jubilee sh. for 1 Wood-Croesus sh. (see Jubilee Gold Inc.)

Milestone Mines Ltd. (Ont. 1956)
1968 – Merged with other cos. to form Milestone Exploration Ltd.; basis 100 new for 2,596 old shs.

Milestone Mines Ltd. (B.C. 1966)
July 1976 – Wound up and struck off register.

Milestone Pharmaceuticals Inc. (Can. Feb. 20, 2003)
July 14, 2017 – Continued into Quebec. (see FPsurvey - Industrials)

Milgate Mines Ltd. (Ont. 1965)
1969 – Merged into Alchib Developments Ltd.; basis 4 new for 10 old shs.

Milger Development Corporation Ltd. (Ont. 1967)
July 8, 1971 – Formed Milger Investment & Development Corporation Limited in Ontario; basis 1 new for 4 old shs. ■

Milger Investment & Development Corporation Limited (Ont. July 8, 1971 amalg.)
Aug. 31, 1992 – Delisted from the CDN. Subsequently charter cancelled and dissolved.

Military International Limited (Alta. May 23, 1997)
Dec. 2, 2012 – Dissolved and struck from register.

Milk Capital Corp. (B.C. Dec. 21, 2006)
Sept. 3, 2010 – Name changed to Prescient Mining Corp. ■

Milkyway Networks Corporation (Can. May 2, 1994)
Oct. 14, 1998 – Amalgamated with a wholly owned subsid. of SLM Software Inc.; basis 0.07114 of a com. sh. and 1 exch. sh. of SLM for 1 com. sh. of Milkyway. Exchangeable shs. exchangeable for 0.1717 of a SLM com. sh. or 80¢ cash until Nov. 5, 1998. (see SLM Software Inc.)

Mill Bay Ventures Inc. (B.C. Apr. 12, 1977)
Apr. 16, 2013 – Name changed to Great Thunder Gold Corp.; basis 1 new for 3 old shs. ■

Mill City Gold Corp. (B.C. Sept. 1, 2004)
Aug. 21, 2015 – Name changed to FPS Pharma Inc. in anticipation of the acquisition of Florida Pharmacy Solutions, Inc. which subsequently did not proceed. ■

Mill City Gold Inc. (Can. July 6, 1987 amalg.)
Dec. 14, 1988 – Name changed to Mill City Gold Mining Corp.; basis 1 new for 10 old shs. ■

Mill City Gold Mining Corp. (Can. July 6, 1987 amalg.)
May 29, 1991 – Name changed to East West Trade Finance Corp. ■

Mill City Gold Mining Corp. (Can. July 6, 1987 amalg.)
Feb. 16, 1998 – Name changed to Mill City International Inc. ■

Mill City International Corporation (Alta. Aug. 28, 1998)
Sept. 1, 2004 – Name changed to Mill City Gold Corp. and continued into British Columbia. ■

Mill City International Inc. (Can. July 6, 1987 amalg.)
Dec. 17, 2002 – Name changed to E3 Energy Inc. following reverse takeover acquisition of E3 Energy Ltd.; basis 1 new for 12 old shs. ■

Mill City Oils Ltd. (Can. 1924)
1929 – Taken over by Mill City Petroleums, Limited; basis 4 new for 1 old sh. (see Mill City Petroleums Limited)

Mill City Petroleums Limited (Can. Aug. 7, 1929)
Dec. 1971 – Acquired by Pan Ocean Oil Corp.; basis 19.3 new for 100 old shs.

Mill Hill Mines Ltd. (Ont. 1971)
Nov. 9, 1976 – Dissolved.

Mill-Rock Mines Ltd. (Ont. 1934)
Mar. 1976 – Charter cancelled.

Millarville Oils Ltd. (unknown)
Merged with Alberta Pacific Oil Co. Ltd.; basis 15 new for 100 old shs. (see Alberta Pacific Oil Co. Ltd.)

Millbank Minerals Ltd. (Ont. 1966)
Mar. 1976 – Charter cancelled.

Millbank Mining Corp. (B.C. July 27, 2020)
Nov. 13, 2024 – Name changed to Primary Hydrogen Corp. (see FPsurvey - Mines & Energy)

Millbren Copper Mines Ltd. (Ont. 1948)
Oct. 7, 1957 – Charter cancelled.

Milldale Minerals Ltd. (Ont. 1955)
Aug. 1964 – Charter cancelled.

Millenium Biologix Corporation (Can. Apr. 1, 1998)
May 8, 2007 – Placed into receivership. Ernst & Young Inc. appointed receiver and all officers and directors resigned.

MillenMin Ventures Inc. (Can. Aug. 10, 2009)
Jan. 2, 2018 – Continued into Cayman Islands. (see FPsurvey - Mines & Energy)

Millennia Foods Inc. (Alta. June 13, 1986)
Dec. 1, 1995 – Struck off register.

Millennial Esports Corp. (Ont. Apr. 8, 2011)
Oct. 18, 2019 – Name changed to Torque Esports Corp.; basis 1 new for 5 old shs. ∎

Millennial Lithium Corp. (B.C. Mar. 7, 2005)
Jan. 27, 2022 – Acquired by Lithium Americas Corp.; basis 0.1261 Lithium Americas shs. plus $0.001 in cash for 1 Millennial Lithium sh. (see Lithium Americas Corp.)

Millennial Precious Metals Corp. (B.C. Apr. 8, 2020)
May 8, 2023 – Acquired by Integra Resource Corp.; basis 0.23 Integra shs. for 1 Millennial Precious sh.

Millennium Communications Inc. (Alta. Aug. 19, 1993)
Mar. 31, 2000 – Name changed to StrategyWeb Communications Inc.; basis 1 new for 6 old shs. ∎

Millennium Energy Inc. (Alta. Jan. 12, 1995)
July 29, 2003 – Name changed to Bear Creek Energy Ltd. following reverse takeover acquisition of Crossfield Gas Corp.; basis 1 Bear Creek cl. A com. sh. for 15 Millennium com. shs. ∎

Millennium Network Corporation (Alta. Nov. 4, 1997)
Oct. 2000 – Demand letter and notice of intention to enforce security was received from Lyco Logistics Ltd. Co. owed $2,250,000 under a promissory note to Lyco which became due and payable on Oct. 13, 2000. Co. had until Nov. 21, 2000, to repay the o/s balance.
Dec. 2000 – Canadian Advantage, the main creditor, appointed KPMG Inc. of Vancouver as receiver.
Oct. 21, 2001 – Receiver discharged. No information available regarding distributions to creditors or shldrs.

Millennium Resources Inc. (B.C. Dec. 30, 1986)
Mar. 19, 1992 – Name changed to Calais Resources Inc.; basis 1 new for 5 old shs. ∎

Millennium Ventures Ltd. (B.C. Oct. 8, 1999)
June 26, 2003 – Plan of Arrangement agreement with Lattice Capital Corporation (1 for 2.789) and Verb Exchange Inc. to continue as Verb Exchange Inc.; basis 1 new Verb sh. for 2.04 old Millennium shs. (see Verb Exchange Inc.)

Miller Bay Gold Mines Ltd. (Ont. 1930)
Mar. 4, 1957 – Charter cancelled.

Miller Bros. Drilling & Development Ltd. (unknown)
1952 – Assets acquired by Campo United Petroleums Ltd.; basis 1 new for 9 old shs. Shldrs. also received rights to purchase 1 Campo sh. at $1.25 for each sh. received through exch.

Miller Copper Mines Ltd. (Que.)
Sept. 1960 – Shs. exch. for New Miller Pipe Lines & Mining Exploration Ltd.; basis 1 new for 6 old shs. (see North Mattagami Mines Ltd.)

Miller Lake Mines Ltd. (Ont. 1928)
1956 – Name changed to Three Brothers Mining Exploration Ltd.

Miller-Lorrain Mines Ltd. (Ont. 1961)
May 1980 – Charter cancelled.

Miller-Pyrcz Petroleums Ltd. (Alta. Apr. 16, 1951)
1952 – Assets acquired by Campo United Petroleums Ltd.; basis 4 new for 13 old shs. O/s $175,000 5% s.f. debs. of co. assumed by Campo. Co. shldrs. also received rights to purchase 1 Campo sh. at $1.25 for each sh. received through exch.

Millerfields Silver Corp. Ltd. (Ont. 1966)
Aug. 20, 1975 – Charter cancelled.

Millers Cove Resources Inc. (Ont. Mar. 26, 1973)
June 12, 1991 – Delisted from the Alberta Stock Exchange. Subsequently charter cancelled and dissolved.

Milliken Lake Uranium Mines Ltd. (Ont. 1952)
1960 – Merged into Rio Algom Mines Ltd.; basis 14 new for 100 old shs.

Millkirk Chibougamau Mines Ltd. (Ont. 1955)
Apr. 9, 1975 – Charter cancelled.

Millmore Products Ltd. (Ont. 1967)
May 1971 – Placed into bankruptcy. Pd. 100¢ on each $1.00 for secured creditors; 100¢ on each $1.00 for all pref. creditors except for pref. creditors shown under Section 107-1J who received 6.75¢ on every $1.00. No funds pd. to unsecured creditors.

Millrock Development Corp. (B.C. Oct. 22, 1968)
May 27, 1988 – Charter cancelled.
June 15, 1990 – Charter revived.
Sept. 5, 1991 – Name changed to Delta Gold Mining Corporation; basis 1 new for 3 old shs. ∎

Millrock Resources Inc. (B.C. Apr. 20, 1979)
Mar. 22, 2023 – Name changed to Alaska Energy Metals Corporation; basis 1 new for 10 old shs. (see FPsurvey - Mines & Energy)

Mills Red Lake Mines Ltd. (Ont. 1944)
Sept. 1980 – Charter cancelled.

Millsite Mines Ltd. (Ont. 1956)
Dec. 10, 1962 – Dissolved.

Millstreet Development Corp. (Alta. June 16, 1994)
July 3, 2001 – Name changed to Millstreet Industries Inc.; basis 1 new for 10 old shs. ∎

Millstreet Industries Inc. (Alta. June 16, 1994)
Dec. 19, 2011 – Formed Kingsland Energy Corp. in Alberta pursuant to reverse takeover acquisition of and amalgamation with (old) Kingsland Energy Corp. (see FPsurvey - Mines & Energy)

Milltronics Ltd. (Can. Sept. 24, 1993)
Apr. 11, 2000 – Acquired by Siemens Canada Acquisition (2000) Inc., a wholly owned subsid. of Siemens Canada Limited, for $21 per sh.

Milmac Mines Ltd. (Ont. Dec. 29, 1933)
Nov. 1954 – Charter cancelled.

Milmar Island Metals & Holdings Ltd. (Ont. 1934)
Feb. 1980 – Charter cancelled.

Milmar Island Mines Ltd. (Ont. 1934)
Dec. 22, 1970 – Name changed to Milmar Island Metals & Holdings Ltd. ∎

Milnet Mines Limited (Ont. 1951)
Feb. 1957 – Charter cancelled.

Miltec Technology Inc. (Ont. Sept. 29, 1987)
Mar. 20, 2006 – Dissolved and struck from register.

Milton Brick Co. Limited (Ont. 1936)
Dec. 11, 1972 – Name changed to Milton Group Limited. ∎

Milton Group Limited (Ont. 1936)
Mar. 6, 1979 – Creditors approved the following: full payment to 6 creditors according terms of their security; full payment for other pref. claims, without int.; priority to trustees for fees and expenses; ordinary creditors of $200 or less to be paid in full upon court approval; ordinary creditors of more than $200 to receive 10% non-cum. debs. paying int. only from profits of co.
June 21, 1982 – Notice issued of intention to dissolve.

Mimi's Rock Corp. (Ont. Mar. 27, 2017)
Mar. 9, 2023 – Acquired by FitLife Brands, Inc.; basis 17¢ cash per sh.

Mimiska Exploration Inc. (Can. May 6, 1986)
July 29, 1988 – Formed Mimiska Mining Co. Inc. / Société Minière Mimiska Inc. following amalgamation with Minaki Mining Exploration Inc./Exploration Minière Minaki Inc. ∎

Mimiska Mining Co. Inc. (Can. May 6, 1986)
Mar. 3, 2003 – Dissolved.

Min-Ore Mines Limited (Ont. Mar. 15, 1947)
May 1, 1979 – Charter cancelled.
Apr. 29, 1981 – Charter revived.
Oct. 29, 1984 – Charter cancelled and co. dissolved.

Mina-Nova Mines Ltd. (Ont. 1951)
June 24, 1965 – Dissolved.

Mina Resources Ltd. (B.C. Apr. 12, 1994)
Apr. 28, 1997 – Name changed to Anaconda Uranium Corporation following reverse takeover acquisition of U.S.-based Anaconda Resources, Inc. ∎

Minacs Worldwide Inc. (Ont. Apr. 19, 1996)
Sept. 12, 2006 – Acquired indirectly by TransWorks Information Services Ltd. for $5.50 per sh.

Minaean International Corp. (Alta. Nov. 5, 1998)
Aug. 28, 2015 – Name changed to Minaean SP Construction Corp.; basis 1 new for 2 old shs. ∎

Minaean SP Construction Corp. (Alta. Nov. 5, 1998)
Aug. 31, 2015 – Continued into British Columbia. (see FPsurvey - Industrials)

Minaki Gold Mines Limited (Ont. 1972)
July 6, 1983 – Amalgamated with 8 other cos. to form Lobo Gold & Resources Inc.; basis 1 new for 10 old shs.

Minaki Mining Exploration Inc. (Can. Aug. 18, 1986)
July 29, 1988 – Amalgamated with Mimiska Exploration Inc./Exploration Mimiska Inc. to form Mimiska Mining Co. Inc./Société Minière Mimiska Inc. (see Mimiska Mining Co. Inc.)

Minas De Cerro Dorado Ltd. (B.C. Mar. 13, 1972)
Nov. 13, 1979 – Name changed to Windarra Minerals Ltd.; basis 1 new for 5 old shs. ∎

Minas Metals Ltd. (B.C. Mar. 3, 2018)
Apr. 25, 2025 – Name changed to Universal Digital Inc. (see FPsurvey - Industrials)

Minaterra Minerals Ltd. (B.C. Sept. 23, 1987)
Aug. 31, 2000 – Name changed to Golden Cariboo Resources Ltd.; basis 1 new for 3 old shs. (see FPsurvey - Mines & Energy)

Minati Capital Corp. (B.C. Jan. 8, 2008)
June 9, 2011 – Name changed to Strike Gold Corp. ∎

Minbanco Corporation (Del. 1966)
1971 – Assets acquired by Abitibi Asbestos Corp. Ltd. for 1,812,505 shs.

Minco Gold Corporation (B.C. Nov. 5, 1982)
Feb. 27, 2019 – Name changed to Minco Capital Corp. (see FPsurvey - Mines & Energy; FPsurvey - Industrials)

Minco Mining & Metals Corporation (B.C. Nov. 5, 1982)
Feb. 1, 2007 – Name changed to Minco Gold Corporation. ■

Mincom Capital Inc. (Can. May 24, 2011)
June 21, 2018 – Name changed to Braille Energy Systems Inc. pursuant to the reverse takeover acquisition of an 89.95% interest in Braille Holdings Inc. (see FPsurvey - Industrials)

Mincor Resources Inc. (Que. Mar. 27, 1986)
May 6, 2005 – Struck off register.

Mind Cure Health Inc. (B.C. Mar. 6, 2020)
Aug. 17, 2023 – Name changed to LNG Energy Group Corp. and continued into Ontario pursuant to the revere takeover acquisition of LNG Energy Group Inc. (renamed LNG Holdings Inc.); basis 1 new for 6 old shs. (see FPsurvey - Mines & Energy)

Minda-Scotia Mines Ltd. (Ont. 1951)
June 1955 – Name changed to New Minda-Scotia Mines Ltd.; basis 1 new for 4 old shs. ■

Mindalartic Mines Ltd. (Ont. 1949)
Aug. 1956 – Name changed to Athabaska Research Mining Co. Ltd. ■

Mindamar Energy Resources Limited (Ont. 1950)
Apr. 2, 1984 – Charter cancelled.

Mindamar Metals Corp. Ltd. (Ont. 1950)
Sept. 1961 – Name changed to United Mindamar Metals Ltd.; basis 1 new for 3 old shs. ■

MindBeacon Holdings Inc. (Can. June 14, 2018)
Jan. 18, 2022 – Acquired by CloudMD Software & Services Inc.; basis $1.22 cash plus 2.285 CloudMD shs. for 1 MindBeacon sh. (see CloudMD Software & Services Inc.)

Mindeen Minerals Limited (Ont. 1923)
Dec. 30, 1985 – Name changed to Variety Video Enterprises Inc. ■

Mindflight Corporation (Can. Jan. 23, 1987)
June 19, 1998 – Name changed to RDM Corporation. ■

Mindready Solutions Inc. (Can. Sept. 16, 1999)
Apr. 13, 2000 – Continued into Quebec.
Jan. 30, 2008 – Placed into receivership. Demers Beaulne Inc. appointed trustee.

Mindset Pharma Inc. (B.C. June 22, 2020)
Oct. 30, 2023 – Acquired by Otsuka Pharmaceutical Co., Ltd.; basis 75¢ cash per sh.

Mindus Corporation Ltd. (Ont. 1944)
1955 – Sold to Mindustrial Corporation Limited; basis 1 new for 10 old shs.

Mindustrial Corporation Limited (Ont. 1949)
Oct. 4, 1978 – Effective Sept. 21, 1978, merged with Guthrie Canadian Investments Ltd. to continue under the name of Guthrie Canadian Investments Limited. Com. shldrs. received one 1st pfce. or one 2nd pfce. sh. of amalg. co. for each com. sh. held. Both classes of pfce. shs. red. at $10.50 per sh.

Mindy Explorations Ltd. (B.C. 1983)
Sept. 9, 1985 – Name changed to International Telepool Corp. ■

Mine Lake Minerals Inc. (Ont. Oct. 21, 1985)
June 23, 1988 – Name changed to Avanti Capital Corp. ■

Minecorp Energy Ltd. (B.C. Apr. 7, 2005)
May 29, 2017 – Name changed to Freedom Energy Inc. ■

Minedel Mines Ltd. (Ont. Sept. 24, 1937)
May 1, 1980 – Name changed to Havelock Energy Resources Inc. ■

Minefinders Corporation Ltd. (Ont. Feb. 4, 1975)
Apr. 5, 2012 – Acquired by Pan American Silver Corp.; basis either: (i) Cdn$1.84 plus 0.55 Pan American shs.; (ii) Cdn$0.0001 plus 0.6235 Pan American shs.; or (iii) Cdn$2.0306 plus 0.5423 Pan American shs. for 1 Minefinders sh.

Minefund Development Corporation (B.C. Dec. 6, 1978)
July 4, 2005 – Dissolved and struck from register.

Minegem Inc. (Ont. Jan. 27, 1988)
Feb. 5, 2004 – Acquired by European Diamonds plc; basis 1 new European Diamonds ordinary sh. for 10 old Minegem com. shs.

Minemakers Limited (Australia Sept. 19, 2005)
Nov. 19, 2015 – Name changed to Avenira Limited.

Miner River Resources Ltd. (Alta. May 9, 1994)
June 4, 1999 – Amalgamated with Eagle Plains Resources Ltd. (1 for 1) to continue as Eagle Plains Resources Ltd.; basis 1 Eagle Plains sh. for 1.2 Miner shs.

Minera Andes Inc. (Alta. Nov. 6, 1995 amalg.)
Jan. 27, 2012 – Acquired by US Gold Corporation (renamed McEwen Mining Inc.); basis 0.45 exchangeable shs. of McEwen Mining -Minera Andes Acquisition Corp. for 1 Minera Andes sh. (see McEwen Mining Inc.)

Minera Capital Corporation (Yuk. Mar. 1, 1999)
Sept. 22, 2004 – Continued into British Columbia.
Sept. 22, 2005 – Name changed to Coronado Resources Ltd.; basis 1 new for 5 old shs. ■

Minera Cortez Resources Ltd. (B.C. Jan. 5, 1998)
Feb. 18, 2002 – Name changed to Western Wind Energy Corp. ■

Minera Delta Inc. (Can. July 23, 1984)
Apr. 22, 1999 – Name changed to Whitmore Resource Corp.; basis 1 new for 5 old shs. ■

Minera Delta Inc. (Can. July 23, 1984)
Jan. 26, 2005 – Acquired by Vector Wind Energy Inc. through reverse takeover. (see Vector Wind Energy Inc.)

Minera IRL Limited (Cayman Islands Aug. 27, 2003)
Oct. 25, 2006 – Continued into Jersey. (see FPsurvey - Mines & Energy)

Minera Rayrock Inc. (Ont. Mar. 23, 1989)
June 1, 1998 – Amalgamated with a wholly owned subsid. of Rayrock Yellowknife Resources Inc.; basis 30¢ cash for each sub. vtg. sh. and mutiple vtg. sh. (see Rayrock Yellowknife Resources Inc.)

Minera Sierra Madre Inc. (Alta. Mar. 16, 1994)
July 24, 2000 – Name changed to MSA Capital Corp. ■

Minerais Chabela Inc. (Can. July 19, 1984 amalg.)
May 16, 1997 – Name changed to The Amseco Mining Corporation Ltd. ■

Mineral Exploration Corp. Ltd. (Que. 1952)
Aug. 1979 – Charter revived.
Mar. 4, 1983 – Name changed to Temex Resources Ltd. ■

Mineral Hill Mines Ltd. (Alta. 1969)
Aug. 1976 – Charter cancelled.

Mineral Mountain Mining Co. Ltd. (B.C. 1932)
Sept. 12, 1969 – Amalgamated with Valley Forge Mining Ltd. to form new co. with same name Mineral Mountain Mining Co. Ltd.; basis 2 new for 3 Valley Forge shs. and 1 new for 1 Mineral Mountain sh.
Sept. 17, 1975 – Name changed to Mid Mountain Mining Ltd.; basis 1 new for 5 old shs. ■

Mineral Mountain Resources Ltd. (B.C. Sept. 1, 2006)
Dec. 1, 2023 – Name changed to Badlands Resources Inc.; basis 1 new for 10 old shs. (see FPsurvey - Mines & Energy)

Mineral Park Mining Corp. (B.C. Nov. 27, 1979)
Mar. 2, 1994 – Name changed to I.M.P. Industrial Mineral Park Mining Corp.; basis 1 new for 4.5 old shs. ■

Mineral Research Ltd. (B.C.)
1967 – Charter cancelled.

Mineral Resources Corporation (Ont. Sept. 23, 1968)
June 10, 1998 – Name changed to Minroc Mines Inc. ■

Mineral Resources International Limited (Ont. May 26, 1960)
June 1, 1990 – Amalgamated with Conwest Exploration Company Limited (1 for 1) to form a new Conwest Exploration Company Limited; basis 1 cl. B sh. for 2.35 old com. shs. (see Conwest Exploration Company Limited)

Minerals Development Ltd. (Ont. Sept. 20, 1929)
Mar. 1957 – Charter cancelled.

Les Minéraux Laurentiens Limitée (Que. 1957)
Nov. 4, 1978 – Charter cancelled.

Minéraux Manic Inc. (Que. Aug. 27, 1986)
May 2, 2003 – Struck off register.

Minerex Resources Ltd. (B.C. July 7, 1983)
Dec. 1992 – Continued into Ontario. (see Canada Tungsten Inc.)
Jan. 7, 1993 – Amalgamated with Canamax Resources Inc.(1 for 5) and Canada Tungsten Mining Corporation Limited (1 for 1) to form a new co. named Canada Tungsten Inc.; basis 1 new for 0.5 old sh. (see Canada Tungsten Inc.)

Minerva Gold Mines Ltd. (B.C. Jan. 14, 1981)
Feb. 19, 1996 – Name changed to Consolidated Minerva Gold Mines Ltd.; basis 1 new for 3 old shs. ■

Minerva Intelligence Inc. (B.C. Aug. 16, 2017)
Aug. 17, 2023 – Name changed to Aisix Solutions Inc. (see FPsurvey - Industrials)

Minerva Minerals Limited (Can. June 5, 2006)
May 22, 2013 – Name changed to Greywacke Exploration Ltd.; basis 1 new for 2 old shs. ■

Les Mines Cam Limitée (Que. Jan. 25, 1938)
Sept. 7, 1979 – Name changed to Energy & Resources (Cam) Limited; basis 1 new for 4 old shs. ■

Les Mines Chasm Limitée (Que. May 5, 1966)
July 29, 1983 – Name changed to Barexor Minerals Inc. ■

Les Mines C.M. & S. Inc. (Que. 1953)
Oct. 31, 1980 – Name changed to Les Ressources Camchib Inc.; basis 1 new for 5 old shs. ■

Les Mines d'Argent Abcourt Inc. (Que. Jan. 11, 1971 amalg.)
May 16, 1985 – Name changed to Abcourt Mines Inc. (see FPsurvey - Mines & Energy)

Les Mines de la Faille Horne Limitée/Horne Fault Mines Limited (Que. 1941)
Oct. 22, 1992 – Voluntarily liquidated. Distribution of sold asset, shs. in Spider Resources Inc., to shldrs. of record Oct. 8, 1992, on the following basis: 1 new com. sh. of Spider for 4 com. shs. of Horne Fault.
Oct. 30, 1992 – Final distribution of 3 Spider com. shs. for 4 Horne Fault com. shs.

Les Mines d'Or Thompson Bousquet Ltée (Que. 1936)
Nov. 1, 1981 – Amalgamated with Copper Giant Mining Corp. (1 for 4.5) and Silverstack Mines Ltd. (1 for 1) to form Long Lac Resources Limited; basis 5 new for 4 old shs.

Les Mines-Est Malartic Ltée (Que. 1934)
Dec. 31, 1985 – Amalgamated with Les Terrains Aurifères Malartic (Québec) Ltée (0.84 for 1), Long Lac Minerals Ltd. (1 for 1) and Willroy Mines Limited (1.24 for 1) to form LAC Minerals Ltd.; basis 0.94 LAC shs. for 1 Est Malartic sh.

Mines Management (B.C.) Limited (B.C. Mar. 13, 1951)
Aug. 30, 1982 – Name changed to Bitterroot Resources Ltd. (see FPsurvey - Mines & Energy)

Mines Management, Inc. (Idaho Feb. 20, 1947)
Sept. 15, 2016 – Acquired by Hecla Mining Company by way of amalgamation with HL Idaho Corp., a wholly owned subsid. of Helca Mining Company; basis 0.2218 Hecla com. shs. for 1 Mines com. sh.

Les Mines Messeguay Inc. (Can. Aug. 31, 1986)
Feb. 2, 1995 – Name changed to Melkior Resources Inc.; basis 1 new for 10 old shs. ■

Mineta Resources Ltd. (B.C. Aug. 15, 1979)
Feb. 21, 1992 – Name changed to Star of Mineta Ltd.; basis 1 new for 4 old shs. ■

Mineworks Resources Corp. (B.C. Aug. 4, 1988)
July 25, 2005 – Name changed to Tower Energy Ltd. ■

Mineworx Technologies Ltd. (Alta. Dec. 3, 1986)
Oct. 31, 2022 – Name changed to Regenx Tech Corp. (see FPsurvey - Mines & Energy)

Minex Corporation Ltd. (unknown)
Nov. 1, 1955 – Name changed to Caminex Corporation Limited. ■

Minex Development Ltd. (B.C. 1955)
Dec. 14, 1973 – Name changed to New Minex Resources Ltd.; basis 1 new for 5 old shs. ■

Minfocus Exploration Corp. (B.C. May 6, 2010)
Dec. 6, 2021 – Name changed to Queensland Gold Hills Corp. ■

Ming Financial Corporation (Alta. Apr. 7, 1989)
Dec. 23, 1997 – Name changed to Eastern Meridian Mining Corporation. ■

Ming Mines Limited (B.C. 1979)
Aug. 6, 1993 – Dissolved and struck off register.

Mining and Allied Supplies (Canada) Limited (Ont. 1992 amalg.)
Apr. 6, 1994 – Name changed to Bearing Power (Canada) Limited. ■

The Mining Corp. of Canada Ltd. (Can. 1916)
1963 – Acquired by Noranda Mines Ltd.; basis 0.5 new sh. plus $1.00 for 1 old sh. Mining Corp. (see Noranda Mines Ltd.)

Mining Endeavor Co. Ltd. (Ont. 1956)
Nov. 30, 1964 – Dissolved.

Mining Futures and Holdings Ltd. (Ont. 1953)
May 30, 1979 – Dissolved.

Mining Projects of Canada Ltd. (Ont. 1935)
1957 – Charter cancelled.

Ministik Lake Gold Mines Ltd. (Man. Feb. 1937)
1937 – Charter cancelled.

Mink Gold Mines Ltd. (Ont. 1945)
Mar. 7, 1952 – Distributed 1 sh. Joburke Gold Mines for each 5 old shs. Charter surrendered.

Mink International Resources Corp. (B.C. Feb. 10, 1983)
July 10, 2006 – Dissolved and struck from registry.

Mink Mineral Resources Inc. (B.C. Feb. 10, 1983)
Jan. 16, 1997 – Name changed to Mink International Resources Corp. ■

MinKap Resources Inc. (B.C. Apr. 26, 2010)
Oct. 21, 2020 – Name changed to Ophir Gold Corp. ■

Minnesota and Ontario Paper Company (Minn. 1941)
Mar. 3, 1965 – Effective Jan. 29, 1965, merged with Boise Cascade Corp. of Boise, Idaho, through exch. of 1 com. sh. for 1 $1.40 cum. conv. pref. sh. of Boise. Funded debt 3.3% S.F. debents. red. at 102.02% plus accr. int.

Minnissabik Mineral Corp. (Ont. Feb. 22, 1996)
Oct. 26, 1998 – Name changed to e-minerals exploration corp. ■

Minnitaki Iron Range Ltd. (Ont. 1964)
Mar. 1976 – Charter cancelled.

Minnova Inc. (Que. 1917)
May 18, 1993 – Acquired by Metall Mining Corporation; basis $4.00, 1 new Metall sh. and 0.5 Metall sh. purchase wt. for 1 old Minnova sh. (see Metall Mining Corporation)

Minorca Resources Inc. (Can. Jan. 30, 1995 amalg.)
Oct. 27, 1998 – Acquired by McWatters Mining Inc.; basis 0.555 McWatter shs. for 1 Minorca sh. (see McWatters Mining Inc.; Moss Resources Inc.)

Minorca Resources Ltd. (Que. 1988)
Jan. 27, 1995 – Amalgamated with Denyvan Resources Inc. (0.92 for 1) and Orco Resources Inc. (0.38 for 1) to continue as Denyvan Resources Inc.; basis 1 new for 1 old sh. The amalgamated co. subsequently changed its name to Minorca Resources Inc. on Jan. 30, 1995. (see Minorca Resources Inc.)

Minorco Canada Limited (Ont. 1979)
Mar. 2, 1999 – All o/s 150,000 ser. A and 100,000 ser. B first pref. shs. redeemed for $101.5625 per sh. including all accr. and unpaid divds.

Minotaur Explorations Ltd. (B.C. 1987)
Sept. 14, 1994 – Name changed to China Growth Enterprises Corp. ■

Minprotech Mining Ltd. (Bermuda Dec. 21, 1993)
Apr. 2, 1996 – Name changed to Aurient Resources Ltd.; basis 1 new for 2 old shs.

MinRes Resources Inc. (Yuk. Aug. 29, 1996)
Feb. 14, 2005 – Name changed to Geoinformatics Exploration Inc. following reverse takeover acquisition of Geoinformatics Explorations Limited. ■

Minroc Mines Inc. (Ont. Sept. 23, 1968)
June 8, 1999 – Name changed to Cassiar Mines & Metals Inc. ■

Minster Capital Corporation (Can. 1987)
Sept. 22, 1989 – Amalgamated with Capital Markets West Inc. (see Capital Markets West Inc.)

Mint Gold Resources Ltd. (Ont. Sept. 5, 1986)
Oct. 28, 1991 – Formed RML Medical Laboratories Inc. in Ontario on amalgamation with RML Medical. ■

Mint Technology Corp. (Alta. Aug. 22, 1997)
Aug. 12, 2013 – Name changed to The Mint Corporation; basis 1 new for 10 old shs. (see FPsurvey - Industrials)

Mintek Resources Ltd. (B.C. Jan. 1, 1983 amalg.)
Oct. 19, 1992 – Name changed to Coast Diamond Ventures Ltd.; basis 1 new for 3 old shs. ■

Mintel International Development Corp. (B.C. Oct. 27, 1971)
Apr. 5, 1989 – Name changed to Golden Trump Resources Ltd.; basis 1 new for 5 old shs. ■

Minterra Resource Corp. (B.C. Jan. 15, 1979)
Aug. 16, 2011 – Dissolved and struck from register.

Minto Explorations Ltd. (B.C. Apr. 20, 1993)
June 28, 2005 – Acquired by Sherwood Mining Corporation; basis $0.615 and 1 new Sherwood pfd. sh. or, 2.5 new Sherwood com. shs. and 1 new Sherwood pfd. sh. or, combination thereof for 1 old Minto com. sh. (see Sherwood Mining Corporation)

Minto Hill Mines Ltd. (Ont. 1970)
Feb. 20, 1980 – Dissolved.

Minto Industries Ltd. (B.C. 1970)
Apr. 22, 1981 – Name changed to Minto Resources Ltd. ■

Minto Metals Corp. (B.C. Nov. 23, 2021 amalg.)
July 24, 2023 – Placed into receivership and PricewaterhouseCoopers Inc. was appointed receiver.

Minto Mining Ltd. (B.C. 1970)
Feb. 1, 1974 – Name changed to Minto Industries Ltd. ■

Minto Resources Ltd. (B.C. 1970)
1981 – Continued into Ontario.
Mar. 4, 1994 – Delisted from the Vancouver Stock Exchange. Subsequently struck from register and dissolved.

Mintrock Mines Ltd. (Ont. July 17, 1936)
1952 – Charter cancelled.

MinVen Gold Corporation (B.C. Aug. 2, 1988 amalg.)
Dec. 16, 1988 – Continued into Canada.
Sept. 20, 1993 – Name changed to Dakota Mining Corporation; basis 1 unit (1 com. and 0.5 wt.) for 12.43452 old com shs. ■

Minvita Enterprises Ltd. (B.C. June 15, 1980)
Feb. 27, 2006 – Name changed to Silver Grail Resources Ltd. (see FPsurvey - Mines & Energy)

Minwealth Explorations Ltd. (B.C. 1969)
Feb. 26, 1973 – Name changed to Saiwa Resources Ltd. ■

Miocene Metals Limited (Ont. Mar. 29, 2010)
Dec. 11, 2014 – Name changed to Miocene Resources Limited; basis 1 new for 10 old shs. ■

Miocene Resources Limited (Ont. Mar. 29, 2010)
June 18, 2015 – Name changed to Carube Copper Corp. following reverse takeover acquisition of Carube Resources Inc. ■

Mira X Acquisition Corp. (Ont. Jan. 15, 2018)
Oct. 28, 2020 – Name changed to GURU Organic Energy Corp. pursuant to Qualifying Transaction reverse takeover acquisition of 6384269 Canada Inc. (dba GURU Beverage); basis 1 new for 83.846 old shs. ■

Mira II Acquisition Corp. (Ont. Feb. 4, 2011)
Dec. 15, 2011 – Formed Element Financial Corporation in Ontario pursuant to Qualifying Transaction reverse takeover acquisition of and amalgamation with (old) Element Financial Corporation; basis 1 new for 32.3077 old shs. ■

Mira III Acquisition Corp. (B.C. Feb. 14, 2012)
Apr. 22, 2014 – Name changed to Northern Power Systems Corp. following Qualifying Transaction reverse takeover acquisition of Wind Power Holdings Inc.; basis 1 new for 34.7826 old shs. ■

Mira IV Acquisition Corp. (Ont. July 16, 2014)
June 3, 2015 – Name changed to Profound Medical Corp. pursuant to the Qualifying Transaction reverse takeover amalgamation of Profound Medical Inc. with wholly owned Mira IV Subco Inc. (see FPsurvey - Industrials)

Mira VI Acquisition Corp. (Ont. Nov. 5, 2014)
July 9, 2015 – Name changed to Perk.com Inc. following Qualifying Transaction reverse takeover acquisition and amalgamation of (old) Perk.com Inc. with wholly owned Mira VI Subco Inc. to form Perk.com US Inc.; basis 1 new for 41.6667 old shs. ■

Mira VII Acquisition Corp. (Ont. Mar. 23, 2015)
May 30, 2017 – Name changed to Goodfood Market Corp. pursuant to Qualifying Transaction reverse takeover acquisition of Goodfood Market Inc.; basis 1 new for 22.2222 old shs. ■

Mira IX Acquisition Corp. (Ont. July 17, 2015)
Dec. 29, 2017 – Name changed to Nuuvera Inc. following Qualifying Transaction reverse takeover acquisition of Nuuvera Corp. and amalgamation of Nuuvera with a wholly owned subsid.; basis 1 new for 16.6666667 old shs. ■

Mira Properties Ltd. (B.C. Mar. 31, 1980)
Aug. 19, 2003 – Name changed to Resolve Ventures Inc.; basis 1 new for 5 old shs. ∎

Mira Resources Corp. (B.C. Apr. 8, 2008)
June 8, 2015 – Name changed to Serrano Resources Ltd. (see FPsurvey - Mines & Energy)

Mirabeau 88 Limited (Alta. Feb. 4, 1987)
Sept. 9, 1994 – Name changed to Xenotech Inc. ∎

Mirabeau Resources Limited (Alta. Feb. 4, 1987)
Oct. 6, 1988 – Name changed to Mirabeau 88 Limited; basis 1 new for 5 old shs. ∎

Mirabel Resources Inc. (Que. July 18, 2000)
Feb. 10, 2006 – Name changed to Rocmec Mining Inc. ∎

Miracle Yellowknife Mines Ltd. (Ont. 1944)
Aug. 1957 – Charter cancelled.

Miraculins Inc. (Can. Nov. 16, 2000)
Apr. 14, 2016 – Name changed to Luminor Medical Technologies Inc.; basis 1 new for 25 old shs. ∎

Mirado Nickel Mines Limited (Ont. Feb. 15, 1956)
Jan. 1, 2011 – Amalgamated with Brenbar Mines Limited and Concopper Enterprises Inc. to form Micon Gold Inc.; basis 0.0363 Micon Gold cl. A shs. for 1 Brenbar sh.; 1.0200 Micon Gold cl A. shs. for 1 Concopper cl. A sh. and 0.3116 Micon Gold cl. B shs. for 1 Concopper cl. B sh.; and 0.4185 Micon Gold cl. A shs. for 1 Mirado sh.

Mirador Mines Ltd. (Ont. 1955)
Mar. 15, 1976 – Charter cancelled.

Mirage Energy Ltd. (Alta. July 21, 2006 amalg.)
Mar. 31, 2008 – Amalgamated with Sahara Energy Ltd. (deemed acquiror) pursuant to plan of arrangement; basis 0.5 Sahara com. shs. for 1 Mirage com. sh. (see Sahara Energy Ltd.)

Mirage Resource Corporation (B.C. Mar. 25, 1980)
Apr. 12, 2000 – Acquired by Dayton Mining Corporation; basis 0.03335 post-consolidated Dayton com. sh. for 1 Mirage sh. (see Dayton Mining Corporation)

Miralta Energy Corp. (Alta. 1987)
July 9, 1990 – Amalgamated with 2 numbered cos., 414110 Alberta Ltd. (a wholly owned subsid. of CanEuro Resources Ltd.) and 421681 Alberta Ltd. to become a wholly owned subsid. of CanEuro; basis 1.15 shs. of CanEuro for 1 sh. of Miralta. (see CanEuro Resources Ltd.)

Miramar Energy Corporation (B.C. Jan. 11, 1983)
July 17, 1989 – Name changed to Miramar Mining Corporation. ∎

Miramar Mining Corporation (B.C. Jan. 11, 1983)
Mar. 13, 2008 – Acquired by Newmont Mining Corporation for $6.25 per sh.

Miramare Capital Inc. (B.C. Aug. 31, 2006)
July 15, 2013 – Dissolved and struck from register.

Miramichi Mines Ltd. (Ont. 1954)
1967 – In process of winding up. Distributed $0.0063 per sh. C/o F. E. Hall, sec., 1620-101 Richmond St. West, Toronto.

Miramont Resources Corp. (B.C. July 15, 2015)
Oct. 1, 2020 – Name changed to Kuya Silver Corporation; basis 1 new for 10 old shs. (see FPsurvey - Mines & Energy)

Miranda Diamond Corp. (B.C. May 4, 1993)
Mar. 4, 2003 – Name changed to Miranda Gold Corp. ∎

Miranda Gold Corp. (B.C. May 4, 1993)
Feb. 11, 2019 – Name changed to Outcrop Gold Corp.; basis 1 new for 10 old shs. ∎

Miranda Industries Inc. (B.C. May 4, 1993)
Aug. 3, 2001 – Name changed to Thrush Industries Inc.; basis 1 new for 5 old shs. ∎

Miranda Mining Corporation (Yuk. Nov. 21, 2001 amalg.)
Dec. 10, 2003 – Acquired indirectly by Wheaton River Minerals Ltd. for Cdn$0.53637 per sh. (see Wheaton River Minerals Ltd.)

Miranda Technologies Inc. (Que. June 1, 1996)
Aug. 1, 2012 – Acquired by Belden CDT (Canada) Inc., a wholly owned subsid. of Belden Inc., for $17 per sh.

Mirasol Resources Ltd. (Yuk. Oct. 15, 2003)
June 1, 2004 – Continued into British Columbia. (see FPsurvey - Mines & Energy)

Mircan Industries Limited (Ont. 1973)
Mar. 1985 – Amalgamated with 610397 Ontario Ltd. to continue as MCR Capital Inc. Shs. of Mircan exchanged for shs. of MCR Capital as follows: 2 com. shs. plus one 2nd pref. ser. Y sh. for each com. sh. held; 2 special cl. A shs. plus one 2nd pref. ser. Y sh. for each cl. A sh. held; and one 1st pref. sh. for each 4% pref. ser. A sh. for 1 old 4% pref. ser. B sh.

Mirival Gold Mines Ltd. (Ont. 1945)
1953 – Charter cancelled.

Miro Mines Ltd. (Ont. 1964)
Mar. 1976 – Charter cancelled.

Miromit Solar Corp. (B.C. 1970)
May 6, 1983 – Dissolved.

Miron Company Limited (Que. 1961 amalg.)
Sept. 1, 1973 – Acquired by Genstar Limited; basis 1 Genstar $1.20 conv. ser. B pref. sh. for 3.4 Miron cl. A shs. and 11 Genstar $1.10 conv. ser. A pref. shs. for 17 Miron ser. A pref. shs. (see Genstar Limited)

Miron Inc. (Que. 1961 amalg.)
Mar. 31, 1989 – Acquired cement assets and operations from Genstar Limited. All o/s shs. acquired under takeover bid at $10 per cl. A and B sh. by The Ciments Français Group, through Lake Ontario Cement, a wholly owned subsidiary of Société des Ciments Français.

Mirtone International, Inc. (Ont. Mar. 20, 1985)
Feb. 2, 1988 – Name changed to International Mirtone Inc.; basis 1 new com. and 1 new pref. series 1 sh. for 2 old com. or cl. A shs. ∎

Mirtronics Inc. (Ont. Mar. 20, 1985)
Mar. 5, 2004 – Amalgamated with Genterra Investment Corporation to form Genterra Inc.; basis 1 new for 1 Genterra Investment sh. and 1.25 new for 1 Mirtronics sh. (see Genterra Inc.)

Mischief Enterprises Ltd. (B.C. 1979)
July 15, 1985 – Name changed to CV Sportsmark International Inc.; basis 1 new for 1 old sh.

Misema Lake Mining Corporation Limited (Ont. 1959)
Nov. 28, 1973 – Dissolved.

Mises Capital Corporation (Alta. Nov. 19, 2004)
Apr. 1, 2008 – Name changed to Saha Petroleum Ltd. following acquisition of Gotham Resources Inc. ∎

Mishibishu Gold Corporation (B.C. Oct. 27, 1989 amalg.)
Apr. 7, 2003 – Name changed to Messina Minerals Inc.; basis 1 new for 3 old shs. ∎

Mishibishu Resources Ltd. (B.C. 1983)
Oct. 27, 1989 – Amalgamated with Exmar Resources Ltd. (0.5334 for 1), Caribbean Resources Corp. (0.4215 for 1) and Mishi Lake Resources Inc. (1 principal escrow sh. for 1) to form Mishibishu Gold Corporation; basis 0.6278 new Mishibishu Gold sh. for 1 old sh. (see Mishibishu Gold Corporation)

Mispec Resources Inc. (Can. Apr. 23, 1986)
Feb. 26, 2003 – Dissolved.

Missanabie Gold Shore Mines Ltd. (Ont. 1943)
Sept. 3, 1994 – Dissolved.

Missi Energy Limited (Alta. Mar. 7, 1988)
Feb. 9, 1993 – Formed Torino Oil & Gas Limited in Alberta on amalgamation with Torino Oil & Gas Limited. ∎

Missi Island Mines Ltd. (Sask. 1971)
Nov. 23, 1983 – Name changed to Missi Resources Ltd.; basis 1 new for 4 old shs. ∎

Missi Resources Ltd. (Sask. 1971)
Mar. 7, 1988 – Continued into Alberta.
Aug. 11, 1989 – Name changed to Missi Energy Limited. ∎

Missile Metals and Mining Corp. Ltd. (Ont. 1959)
June 24, 1965 – Dissolved.

Missinaibi Clays & Mining Ltd. (Ont. 1940)
1944 – All assets sold to General Refractory Products Ltd.; deb. holders received 3 2/3 shs. for each pric., and shldrs. 1 new for 10 old shs.

Mission Financial Corporation (B.C. 1980)
May 5, 1982 – Merged with Hal Roach Studios Corp. to form H.R.S. Industries, Inc.; basis 2 cl. B shs. of H.R.S. for each sh. of Mission. (see H.R.S. Industries Inc.)

Mission Financial Corporation Limited (Ont. 1962)
1980 – Name changed to Mission Financial Corporation and continued into British Columbia. ∎

Mission Gold Ltd. (B.C. Apr. 20, 2011)
Dec. 24, 2015 – Acquired by Northern Dynasty Minerals Ltd.; basis 0.5467 Northern Dynasty com. shs. for 1 Mission Gold com. sh.
Dec. 24, 2015 – Formed MGL Subco Ltd. on amalgamation with 1055495 B.C. Ltd., a wholly owned subsid. of Northern Dynasty Minerals Ltd.

Mission Mining & Development Ltd. (B.C. 1973)
Sept. 21, 1984 – Struck off register.

Mission Mining Ltd. (B.C. 1973)
Apr. 25, 1975 – Name changed to Mission Mining & Development Ltd. ∎

Mission Oil & Gas Inc. (Alta. Nov. 11, 2004)
Feb. 14, 2007 – Plan of Arrangement amalgamation with Crescent Point Energy Trust; basis 0.695 new Crescent Point unit plus $0.78 for 1 old Mission sh. (see Crescent Point Energy Trust)

Mission Oil Development Ltd. (Alta. 1957)
1970 – Merged with Canadian Reserve Oil and Gas Ltd.

Mission Petroleums Limited (B.C.)
1959 – Struck off register.

Mission Ready Services Inc. (B.C. June 1, 2009)
June 5, 2018 – Name changed to Mission Ready Solutions Inc. (see FPsurvey - Industrials)

Mission River Petroleum Ltd. (Ont. 1981)
Jan. 26, 1987 – Amalgamated (1 for 1) with 651446 Ontario Inc., a private Ont. corporation to form MRP Petroleums Inc. (see MRP Petroleums Inc.)

Mistango Consolidated Resources Limited (Ont. Mar. 1, 1962)
Apr. 30, 1989 – Formed Canadian Black River Petroleum Ltd. in Ontario on amalgamation with Black River Petroleum Ltd.; basis 1 new for 10 old shs. ∎

Mistassini Uranium Mines Ltd. (Que. 1968)
Aug. 23, 1986 – Charter cancelled.

Mr. Build Industries Inc. (B.C. 1986)
Jan. 22, 1990 – Name changed to Canadian Mr. Build Industries Inc.; basis 1 new for 8 old shs. ∎

Mr. Jax Fashions Inc. (B.C. 1979)
Feb. 7, 1995 – Acquired by Koret Canada Inc. for $1.40 per sh.

Mistral Pharma Inc. (Can. Apr. 29, 2005 amalg.)
Oct. 1, 2008 – Declared bankrupt. Demers Beaulne Inc. appointed trustee.

Mistral Resources Ltd. (B.C. Nov. 22, 1983)
Mar. 2, 1989 – Delisted from the Vancouver Stock Exchange. Subsequently dissolved for failure-to-file.

Misty Mountain Gold Limited (B.C. Feb. 7, 1962)
Oct. 16, 2001 – Name changed to Continental Minerals Corporation following reorganization whereby the Harmony gold project was transferred to Gibraltar Mines Ltd. for Gibraltar preferred shares.; basis 10 redeem. pref. shs. and 1 new com. sh. for 10 old com. shs. ■

Mitchell-Hearst Gold Mines Ltd. (Ont. 1944)
Feb. 14, 1973 – Dissolved.

Mitchell Resources Ltd. (B.C. Nov. 23, 2004)
Jan. 10, 2017 – Name changed to Hannan Metals Ltd. (see FPsurvey - Mines & Energy)

Mitec Technologies Inc. (Can. May 1, 1996)
July 21, 2014 – Continued into Ontario.
Oct. 3, 2016 – Liquidated via 1-for-5,200,000 consolidation; holders of fractional shs. received 2¢ cash per pre-consolidated sh.

Mitec Telecom Inc. (Can. May 1, 1996)
Feb. 26, 2013 – Name changed to Mitec Technologies Inc.; basis 1 new for 40 old shs. ■

Mitek Industrial Corporation (B.C. 1981)
Mar. 27, 1987 – Name changed to International Mitek Computer Inc.; basis 1 new for 4 old shs. (see FPsurvey - Industrials)

Mitel Corporation (Can. Mar. 8, 1971)
Sept. 7, 2001 – Name changed to Zarlink Semiconductor Inc. ■

Mitel Networks Corporation (Can. Jan. 12, 2001)
Nov. 30, 2018 – Continued into British Columbia.
Dec. 3, 2018 – Acquired by Searchlight Capital Partners, L.P.; basis US$11.15 cash per sh.

Mithrandir Capital Corp. (Ont. Sept. 25, 2018)
July 8, 2020 – Name changed to PopReach Corporation pursuant to Qualifying Transaction reverse takeover acquisition of PopReach Incorporated; basis 1 new for 8 old shs. ■

Mithril Resources Limited (Australia Apr. 26, 2002)
Sept. 5, 2024 – Name changed to Mithril Silver and Gold Limited. (see FPsurvey - Mines & Energy)

Mitmor Oil & Gas Ltd. (Alta. 1951)
Feb. 1954 – Taken over by Canadian Pipe Lines Producers Ltd.; basis 1 new for 6 old shs. (see Canadian Pipe Lines Producers Ltd.)

Mitnor Gold Mines Ltd. (Ont. 1938)
Nov. 5, 1956 – Dissolved.

Mitra Energy Inc. (B.C. Aug. 25, 1988)
Dec. 7, 2016 – Name changed to Jadestone Energy Inc. ■

Mitron Technologies Inc. (Ont. Aug. 14, 1989)
June 27, 1994 – Name changed to Interactive Digital Systems Corporation; basis 1 new for 10 old shs. ■

Mitsubishi Bank of Canada (Can. 1982)
Apr. 1, 1996 – Amalgamated with The Bank of Tokyo Canada to form Bank of Tokyo-Mitsubishi (Canada). (see Bank of Tokyo-Mitsubishi UFJ (Canada))

The Mitsui Bank of Canada (Can. 1982)
Apr. 1, 1990 – Formed Mitsui Taiyo Kobe Bank (Canada) in Canada on amalgamation with the Taiyo Kobe Bank (Canada). ■

Mitsui Taiyo Kobe Bank (Canada) (Can. Apr. 1, 1990 amalg.)
Apr. 1, 1992 – Name changed to Sakura Bank (Canada). ■

Mittal Canada Contrecoeur-Ouest Inc. (Can. - unspecified)
Nov. 18, 2016 – Dissolved.

Mitto Pershing Mines Ltd. (Ont. 1945)
1957 – Charter cancelled.

Mix Gold Mines Ltd. (B.C. 1933)
1954 – Wound up voluntarily.

Mix Resources Ltd. (B.C. 1980)
Nov. 29, 1984 – Name changed to Rococco Resources Ltd. ■

Miza II Resources Inc. (B.C. Oct. 7, 2019)
July 4, 2023 – Name changed to Great Eagle Gold Corp.; basis 2.5 new for 1 old sh. ■

Miza Enterprises Inc. (B.C. Feb. 4, 2008)
June 21, 2017 – Name changed to BQ Metals Corp. ■

Mizuho Bank (Canada) (Can. Nov. 1, 2000)
Apr. 1, 2002 – Name changed to Mizuho Corporate Bank (Canada).

Moag Copper Gold Resources Inc. (Can. Dec. 1, 2011 amalg.)
Nov. 25, 2024 – Struck from registry and dissolved for non-compliance.

Moberly Yellowknife Gold Mines Ltd. (Ont. Mar. 18, 1937)
1944 – Name changed to Red Colley Gold Mines Ltd. ■

Mobiko Mines Ltd. (Ont. 1966)
Mar. 1976 – Charter cancelled.

Mobil Corporation (Del. Mar. 1976)
Dec. 1, 1999 – Amalgamated with Exxon Corporation to form Exxon Mobil Corporation; basis 1.32015 new for 1 Mobil sh.

Mobile Climate Control Industries Inc. (Alta. Jan. 5, 1996)
Sept. 24, 1997 – Continued into Ontario.
Mar. 24, 2004 – Going private transaction via amalgamation with Gunnar Mannerheim Holdco Inc.; basis 22¢ cash plus 22¢ principal amount of 6% unsecured promissory notes for 1 com. sh.

Mobile Computing Corporation (Ont. June 14, 1988)
Oct. 15, 2003 – Name changed to Canada West Capital Inc. following restructuring transactions with The VenGrowth Investment Fund Inc., The VenGrowth II Investment Fund Inc. and NBC Canada West Capital Inc.; basis 1 new for 27 old shs. ■

Mobile Knowledge Inc. (Can. Apr. 15, 1999)
Mar. 14, 2003 – Acquired by Longitude Fund Limited Partnership.

Mobile Lottery Solutions Inc. (Can. Feb. 17, 2006)
Sept. 27, 2007 – Name changed to NuMedia Games Inc. ■

Mobilex Development Corporation Ltd. (Ont. 1968)
Oct. 11, 1977 – Dissolved.

Mobilift Inc. (Alta. Nov. 29, 1994)
Sept. 2001 – Placed into receivership by major creditor.

Mobirk Beryllium Mining Ltd. (Ont. 1939)
1952 – Charter cancelled.

Mobius Resources Inc. (Alta. Sept. 28, 2010)
Aug. 6, 2015 – Name changed to Sintana Energy Inc. following reverse takeover acquisition of (old) Sintana Energy Inc. (see FPsurvey - Mines & Energy)

Mobrun Copper Inc. (Que. Mar. 7, 1956)
June 16, 2006 – Struck off register.

Mobrun Copper Ltd. (Que. Mar. 7, 1956)
Apr. 1, 1981 – Name changed to Mobrun Copper Inc. ■

Moccasin Mines Ltd. (B.C. 1947)
1950 – Entered liquidation.
Apr. 3, 1952 – Charter cancelled.

Mocena Mines, Ltd. (B.C. 1946)
July 1954 – Dissolved and struck off register.

Moche Resources Inc. (B.C. 1986)
Jan. 22, 1993 – Dissolved and struck off register.

Modatech Systems Inc. (B.C. Feb. 28, 1983)
Oct. 22, 2008 – Amalgamated with 0828688 B.C. Ltd. to form a private co., CHR Investment Corporation; basis (i) 1 CHR cl. A pref. and cl. B pref. shs. for 1 0828688 B.C. cl. A pref. and cl. B pref. shs., respectively. (ii) 1 CHR cl. C pref. sh. for 1 Modatech cl. B pref. sh. (iii) 1.0711 CHR com. shs. for 1 Modatech com. sh.

Mode Products Inc. (B.C. 1977)
Mar. 5, 1993 – Delisted from the Vancouver Stock Exchange. Subsequently dissolved for failure to file.

Mode 6S Biovironmental Inc. (Ont. May 10, 2000)
June 21, 2004 – Name changed to Straight Forward Marketing Corporation following reverse takeover acquisition of Straight Forward Marketing Inc.; basis 1.75 new for 1 old sh. (see FPsurvey - Industrials)

Mode6S Inc. (Ont. May 10, 2000)
Aug. 26, 2002 – Name changed to Mode 6S Biovironmental Inc.; basis 1 new for 10 old shs. ■

Model Oils Limited (Alta. Apr. 3, 1926)
Dec. 30, 1953 – Assets acquired by Canadian Pipe Lines Producers Ltd.; basis 1 new for 2 old shs. (see Canadian Pipe Lines Producers Ltd.)

Modern Containers Limited (Ont. 1939)
May 21, 1963 – Amalgamated with The Metal Closures (Canada) Limited. dated July 15, 1963. Purchase offer of $13 for each cl. A sh. made by John Dale (Canada) Ltd. and Aluminum Goods Ltd. Subsequently, offer made on basis of 15 com. shs. of Metal Closures for each cl. A sh., and 12 com. shs. for each com. sh. held. Exch. made through Canada Permanent Trust Co., Toronto.

Modern Meat Inc. (B.C. July 5, 2017)
Mar. 1, 2021 – Name changed to Modern Plant Based Foods Inc. (see FPsurvey - Industrials)

Modern Metals Exploration Ltd. (Ont. 1959)
1968 – Distribution made of 364 shs. Peerless Canadian Explorations Ltd. for each 1,000 shs. held. Charter cancelled.

Modern Plastic Company Limited (Que. 1957)
Apr. 16, 1977 – Name changed to Modern Plastics Limited. ■

Modern Plastics Limited (Que. 1957)
1980 – Name changed to Coronet Housewares Inc. ■

Modern Tool Works Limited (Ont. 1940)
1950 – Majority of stk. purchased at $8.50 per sh. by A. C. Wickman (Canada) Ltd.
1954 – Shs. of Modern Tool Works Ltd. purchased by The Staveley Coal & Iron Company Ltd.; and subsequently operating assets and liabs. trans. to Standard-Modern Tool Company Ltd.

Modico Industries Ltd. (Que. Jan. 31, 1973)
Nov. 10, 1997 – Name changed to Annabelle Inc. ■

Modoc Oils Ltd. (unknown)
Mar. 1956 – Name changed to Canadian Chieftain Petroleums Ltd.; basis 1 new for 5 old shs. ■

Moducan Building Systems Ltd. (Ont. 1952)
Jan. 3, 1995 – Delisted from the CDN. Subsequently charter cancelled and dissolved.

Module Resources Inc. (B.C. Aug. 26, 1981)
Oct. 18, 2011 – Name changed to New Carolin Gold Corp. ■

Modus Energy Industries Ltd. (Alta. Mar. 17, 1999)
Aug. 1, 2001 – Name changed to AgriTec Systems, Inc. and continued into Delaware pursuant to Qualifying Transaction acquisition of AgriTec, Inc. and enviroLife,

Inc.; constituting a reverse takeover by AgriTec Systems, Inc.

Moex Industries Ltd. (B.C. 1966)
Sept. 20, 1985 – Struck off register.

Moffat Communications Limited (B.C. June 16, 1954)
Aug. 17, 1979 – Continued into Canada. (see Shaw Communications Inc.)
Jan. 29, 2001 – Acquired by Shaw Communications Inc.; basis $35 or 1.0508 Shaw cl. B non-vtg. shs. plus 5¢ for 1 Moffat sh. (see Shaw Communications Inc.)

Moffat Gas & Oil Co. Limited (Ont. 1928)
1958 – Wound up.

Moffat Lake Explorations Inc. (Ont. 1972)
Feb. 15, 1982 – Amalgamated with New Bedford Resources & Developments Limited to form Tipperary Resources Limited; basis 1 convertible pfce. sh. for 5 Moffat Lake shs.

Moffatt-Hall Gold Mines Ltd. (Ont. 1936)
1938 – Name changed to Moffatt-Hall Mines Ltd. ■

Moffatt-Hall Mines Ltd. (Ont. 1936)
1948 – Name changed to Moffatt-Hall Mining Co. Ltd.; basis 1 new for 2 old shs. ■

Moffatt-Hall Mining Co. Ltd. (Ont. 1936)
1958 – Charter cancelled.

Mogador Mines Ltd. (Que. 1946)
1962 – Name changed to Consolidated Mogador Mines Ltd.; basis 1 new for 4 old shs. ■

Mogar Mines Ltd. (Ont. 1959)
Feb. 28, 1973 – Dissolved.

Mogo Finance Technology Inc. (B.C. Aug. 26, 2003)
June 25, 2019 – Amalgamated with wholly owned subsid. of Difference Capital Financial Inc. (renamed Mogo Inc).

Mogul Gold Mines Ltd. (Ont. 1945)
1954 – Name changed to Mogul Mining Corp. Ltd. ■

Mogul Mines Ltd. (Ont. 1945)
1968 – Merged into International Mogul Mines Ltd.; basis 1 new for 4 old shs. ■

Mogul Mining Corp. Ltd. (Ont. 1945)
1958 – Name changed to Consolidated Mogul Mines Ltd.; basis 1 new for 5 old shs. ■

Mohave Exploration and Production Inc. (B.C. Nov. 14, 2006)
Jan. 30, 2010 – Formed Porto Energy Corp. in British Columbia following amalgamation with (old) Porto Energy Corp.; basis 1 new Porto com. sh. for 1 old Porto com. sh., 0.57425 new Porto com. sh. for 1 old Mohave cl. A sh. and 1 new Porto com. sh. for 1 old Mohave cl. B sh. ■

Mohave Gold Inc. (B.C. Sept. 15, 1980)
July 1990 – Continued into Nevada.

Mohawk Canada Limited (Can. Jan. 21, 1980)
Aug. 21, 1998 – All o/s com. shs. acquired by HB Acquisition Inc. of Calgary; basis $7.25 per sh.

Mohawk Industries Limited (B.C. 1962)
Feb. 4, 1983 – Struck off register.

Mohawk Mines Ltd. (Que. 1939)
Aug. 1974 – Charter cancelled.

Mohawk Oil Canada Limited (Alta. May 22, 1970)
Jan. 21, 1980 – Continued into Canada.
June 25, 1996 – Name changed to Mohawk Canada Limited. ■

Mohawk Porcupine Gold Mines Ltd. (Ont. 1936)
Dec. 16, 1957 – Dissolved.

Moher Yellowknife Gold Mines Ltd. (Ont. 1945)
Jan. 1, 1980 – Dissolved.

Moiibus Environmental Corporation (Alta. Nov. 16, 1993)
Feb. 26, 1996 – Name changed to Moiibus Resource Corporation. ■

Moiibus Resource Corporation (Alta. Nov. 16, 1993)
May 18, 1999 – Amalgamated with TransGlobe Energy Corporation; basis 0.615 new TransGlobe com. sh. for 1 old Moiibus com. sh. (see TransGlobe Energy Corporation)

Moimstone Corporation (B.C. Sept. 11, 2013 amalg.)
May 22, 2014 – Name changed to Apivio Systems Inc. ■

Moirs Limited (N.S. 1967)
1967 – Acquired by Standard Brands Limited. (see Standard Brands Limited)

Mojave Brands Inc. (B.C. Nov. 12, 2010)
Dec. 13, 2024 – Name changed to Light AI Inc. pursuant to reverse takeover acquisition of (old) Light AI Inc. (see FPsurvey - Industrials)

Mojave Gold Corp. (B.C. Aug. 21, 2014)
Apr. 26, 2021 – Name changed to Benjamin Hill Mining Corp. ■

Mojave Jane Brands Inc. (B.C. Nov. 12, 2010)
Mar. 30, 2021 – Name changed to Mojave Brands Inc.; basis 1 new for 25 old shs. ■

Molco Industries Limited (Ont. 1965)
Mar. 24, 1981 – Continued into Canada.
Apr. 10, 1997 – Dissolved and struck from register.

Moli Energy Limited (B.C. 1977)
Feb. 27, 1990 – Placed into receivership.
May 1, 1990 – Operations taken over by British Columbia government and are now conducted by Moli Energy (1990) Limited a private company. Nothing left for shldrs.

Molijevis Gold Mines Ltd. (Ont. 1944)
1957 – Charter cancelled.

Mollie Gibson Mines Inc. (B.C. 1987)
Nov. 5, 1993 – Dissolved and struck off register.

Mollie Mac Mines Ltd. (B.C. 1952)
1973 – Name changed to Kandahar Resources Limited; basis 1 new for 7.5 old shs. ■

Mollusca Oils Ltd. (Alta. 1949)
Aug. 1969 – Name changed to Lochiel Exploration Ltd.; basis 1 new for 10 old shs. ■

Molly Gibson Silver Ltd. (Can. June 4, 1929)
Dec. 1974 – Charter cancelled.

Molly River Mines Ltd. (Ont. 1971)
May 1972 – Amalgamated into Bayfor Corp. Inc.; basis 1 new for 4 old shs.

Molnar Capital Corporation (B.C. Feb. 17, 1983)
May 13, 1998 – Name changed to Star Properties Inc. (see FPsurvey - Industrials)

Molori Energy Inc. (B.C. June 5, 2006)
Apr. 6, 2020 – Name changed to TAAT Lifestyle & Wellness Ltd. ■

Molson Breweries Ltd. (B.C. Nov. 27, 2018)
Sept. 5, 1968 – Name changed to Molson Industries Limited. ■

The Molson Companies Limited (B.C. Nov. 27, 2018)
July 5, 1999 – Name changed to Molson Inc. ■

Molson Coors Brewing Company (Del. Aug. 14, 2003)
Jan. 2, 2020 – Name changed to Molson Coors Beverage Company.

Molson Inc (B.C. Nov. 27, 2018)
Feb. 9, 2005 – Acquired by Adolph Coors Company which changed its name to Molson Coors Brewing Company (MC Brewing); basis 0.36 MC Brewing cl. B com. shs., or 0.36 Molson Coors Canada Inc. (MC Canada) cl. B exch. shs., or a combination thereof for each Molson Inc. cl. A sh., and 0.126 MC Brewing cl. A com. shs. and 0.234 MC Brewing cl. B com. shs. or 0.126 MC Canada cl. A exch. shs. and 0.234 MC Canada cl. B exch. shs., or a combination thereof for each Molson Inc. cl. B sh. Floating rate medium-term notes due Sept. 16, 2005, were redeemed on Mar. 2, 2005, at 100.23% of principal amount plus accrued and unpaid interest. (see Molson Coors Brewing Company)
Nov. 27, 2018 – Name changed to Molson ULC and continued into British Columbia. (see Molson Coors Brewing Company)

Molson Industries Limited (B.C. Nov. 27, 2018)
July 16, 1973 – Name changed to The Molson Companies Limited. ■

Molson's Brewery Limited (B.C. Nov. 27, 2018)
Mar. 1, 1962 – Name changed to Molson Breweries Ltd. ■

Moly Hill Mining Corp. Ltd. (Ont. 1964)
1971 – Charter cancelled.

Moly Mines Limited (Australia Jan. 6, 2003)
June 25, 2018 – Name changed to Young Australian Mines Ltd.

Moly Mite Mines Inc. (B.C. 1978)
Feb. 19, 1982 – Amalgamated with Galaxy City Mines Inc. to form Moly Mite Resources Inc.; sh. for sh. basis for each co.

Moly Mite Resources Inc. (B.C. 1982 amalg.)
Apr. 4, 1986 – Name changed to Macrotrends Ventures Inc.; basis 1 new for 4.5 old shs. ■

Moly-Ore Mines Ltd. (Ont. 1965)
Nov. 14, 1978 – Name changed to Molco Industries Limited. ■

Moly-Win Mining Ltd. (B.C. 1966)
Oct. 4, 1974 – Name changed to Goodco International Ltd. ■

Molybdenite Corp. of Canada Ltd. (Que. Aug. 7, 1937)
1974 – Reported in bankruptcy.

Molycor Gold Corporation (B.C. Mar. 24, 1966)
Apr. 17, 2012 – Name changed to Nevada Clean Magnesium Inc. ■

Molymine Explorations Ltd. (B.C. 1965)
Dec. 1, 1972 – Amalgamated with Babine International Resources Ltd. (1 for 6) to form Seneca Developments Ltd.; basis 1 new Seneca for 9 old Molymine shs.

Molystar Resources Inc. (B.C. Nov. 17, 2005)
Nov. 12, 2020 – Name changed to Delic Holdings Inc. pursuant to reverse takeover acquistion of Delic Corp. ■

Momentous Capital Corp. (B.C. July 31, 2020)
Jan. 18, 2022 – Name changed to Astra Exploration Inc. pursuant to the Qualifying Transaction reverse takeover acquisition of Astra Exploration Limited; basis 1 new for 2 old shs. (see FPsurvey - Mines & Energy)

Momentum Advanced Solutions Inc. (Ont. Jan. 8, 1988 amalg.)
May 5, 2009 – Privatized at 22¢ per sh.

Monac Acoustic Monitoring International Corporation (Can. May 21, 1987)
Nov. 28, 1991 – Name changed to Monac International Corporation. ■

Monac International Corporation (Can. May 21, 1987)
Nov. 26, 1993 – Name changed to Sound HealthCare Inc. ■

Monaco Group Inc. (Ont. 1981 amalg.)
Feb. 6, 1989 – Amalgamated with Monaco acquisition Corp., a co. formed by the amalgamation of Sung Holdings Inc., Mimran Holdings Inc. and Marlow Holdings Inc. (all private cos.) to become a private co. The com. shs. were converted into redeemable cl. A pf. shs. valued

at $8.00 per sh. redeemable immediately following amalgamation.

Monaco Mines Ltd. (B.C. 1968)
Jan. 6, 1975 – Charter cancelled.

Monahan Supply Corporation Limited (Can. 1940)
1975 – Acquired by Van Der Hout Associates Ltd. for $3.00 per sh.

Monalta Resources Inc. (B.C. Jan. 30, 1984)
June 21, 1991 – Dissolved and struck off register.

Monarch Development Corporation (Ont. Dec. 21, 1921)
June 15, 2000 – Acquired by Taylor Woodrow plc for $11.25 per sh.

Monarch Energy Limited (B.C. Mar. 26, 1987)
Sept. 8, 2014 – Name changed to ChroMedX Corp. and continued into Ontario following reverse takeover acquisition of ChroMedX Ltd. ■

Monarch Fine Foods Co. Ltd. (Ont. 1950)
June 1968 – Sold business and assets to Lever Brothers Ltd. Shldrs. received $11.50 per sh., of which $5.85 was taxable.
May 23, 1969 – Name changed to M.F.F. Equities Limited after final distribution of $1.2316 per sh. Charter subsequently surrendered.

Monarch Fine Foods Limited (Ont. 1950)
June 28, 1968 – Name changed to Monarch Fine Foods Co. Ltd. ■

Monarch Gold Corporation (Can. Feb. 16, 2011)
Jan. 26, 2021 – All o/s com. shs. not already held acquired by Yamana Gold Inc.; basis (i) 0.0376 Yamana shs.; (ii) $0.192 cash; and (iii) 0.2 Monarch Mining Corporation shs. for 1 Monarch Gold sh. (see Yamana Gold Inc.)
Name changed to Yamana Gold Quebec Inc. (see Yamana Gold Inc.)

Monarch Gold Mines Ltd. (Ont. 1960)
Mar. 1976 – Charter cancelled.

Monarch Investments Limited (Ont. Dec. 21, 1921)
Aug. 18, 1989 – Name changed to Monarch Development Corporation. ■

Monarch Knitting Co. Ltd. (Ont. 1912)
Dec. 1963 – Montex Holdings Ltd. acquired 99.32% of the com. shs. at $8.00 and 1 $8.00 par pref. sh. for 1 com. sh.

Monarch Metal Mines Ltd. (B.C. Feb. 18, 1966)
May 11, 1973 – Name changed to Consolidated Monarch Metal Mines Ltd.; basis 1 new for 3 old shs. ■

Monarch Mortgage and Investments, Limited (Ont. Dec. 21, 1921)
Dec. 7, 1959 – Name changed to Monarch Investments Limited. ■

Monarch Oils Limited (Alta. 1950)
1958 – Assets sold for 460,715 shs. Oregon Natural Gas Reserves Ltd. Liquidated, 1960.

Monarch Royalties Limited (Alta. 1936)
1941 – Merged with 8 other companies into Amalgamated Oils Limited; basis 45 new for 500 old shs.

Monarch Wear Ltd. (Man. 1973 amalg.)
May 1981 – Placed into receivership. All assets sold and distributed to secured creditors. No distribution to shldrs.

Monarques Gold Corporation (Can. Feb. 16, 2011)
Jan. 25, 2019 – Name changed to Monarch Gold Corporation. ■

Monarques Resources Inc. (Can. Feb. 16, 2011)
Jan. 12, 2015 – Name changed to Monarques Gold Corporation. ■

Monax Mining Ltd. (Australia Aug. 3, 2004)
Nov. 8, 2018 – Name changed to AuTECO Minerals Ltd. ■

Monbec Mines Ltd. (Can. 1972)
Dec. 16, 1980 – Dissolved.

Moncoa Corporation (Can. June 21, 2002)
Apr. 10, 2007 – Name changed to Monument Mining Limited following reverse takeover acquisition of Able Return Sdn. Bhd.; basis 1 new for 2 old shs. (see FPsurvey - Mines & Energy)

Moncrieff Uranium Mines Limited (Ont. Sept. 23, 1968)
1980 – Name changed to Tombit Resources Limited. ■

Mond Industries Inc. (Ont. Jan. 23, 1996 amalg.)
July 20, 1999 – Name changed to Trailmobile Canada Limited. ■

Mondana Ventures Inc. (B.C. Apr. 10, 1987)
Aug. 27, 1993 – Dissolved and struck off register.

Mondavi Resources Ltd. (B.C. May 21, 1987)
Dec. 23, 1991 – Name changed to T.M.T. Resources Inc.; basis 1 new for 2 old shs. ■

Mondavi Ventures Ltd. (B.C. Jan. 14, 2021)
Aug. 31, 2023 – Name changed to Allied Gold Corporation and continued into Ontario pursuant to reverse takeover acquisition of Allied Gold Corp Limited. (see FPsurvey - Mines & Energy)

Mondev Senior Living Inc. (Alta. Aug. 3, 1995)
May 20, 2003 – Approval for sale of substantially all assets and then dissolution of corporation sought at Annual and Special Meeting. Results not known.

Mondias Natural Products Inc. (Can. Feb. 6, 2013)
Nov. 5, 2020 – Name changed to Lumiera Health Inc. following acquisition of Lumiera Health Innovation Inc. (see FPsurvey - Industrials)

Moneda Latam Corporate Bond Fund (Ont. Oct. 26, 2011)
Dec. 15, 2020 – Terminated; basis $8.7266 per cl.A unit and US$9.0657 per cl.U unit.

Moneda Latam Fixed Income Fund (Ont. May 30, 2012)
June 21, 2017 – Terminated; basis $10.0688 per cl. A unit and US$10.1271 per cl. U unit.

Moneda LatAm Growth Fund (Ont.)
Nov. 30, 2016 – Terminated; basis $7.06 per cl. A unit.

Moneda Resources Limited (Alta. Apr. 5, 2007)
Jan. 31, 2012 – Name changed to Canada Renewable Bioenergy Corp. pursuant to reverse takeover aquisition of Canada Resurgence New Energy Developments Ltd.; basis 1 new for 1.325 old shs. ■

Monenco Group Ltd. (Alta. Apr. 16, 1963)
July 20, 1992 – Acquired by 174540 Canada Ltd., a wholly owned subsid. of AGRA Industries Ltd.; basis 1 AGRA sh. for 1 Monenco sh.

Monenco Limited (Alta. Apr. 16, 1963)
Oct. 24, 1991 – Name changed to Monenco Group Ltd. ■

Moneta Gold Inc. (Ont. Oct. 14, 1910)
Feb. 6, 2024 – Name changed to STLLR Gold Inc.; basis 1 new for 2 old shs. (see FPsurvey - Mines & Energy)

Moneta Porcupine Mines Inc. (Ont. Oct. 14, 1910)
Aug. 24, 2021 – Name changed to Moneta Gold Inc.; basis 1 new for 6 old shs. ■

Moneta Porcupine Mines Limited (Ont. Oct. 14, 1910)
Aug. 31, 1983 – Name changed to Moneta Porcupine Resources Limited. ■

Moneta Porcupine Resources Limited (Ont. Oct. 14, 1910)
Sept. 22, 1986 – Name changed to Moneta Porcupine Mines Inc. ■

Moneta Resources Inc. (B.C. May 29, 1985)
Aug. 7, 2008 – Name changed to Border Petroleum Inc. ■

Monetary Metals Mining Co. Ltd. (Ont. 1938)
1956 – Charter cancelled.

Monexa Technologies Corp. (B.C. Sept. 22, 1989)
Apr. 3, 2012 – Name changed to Santa Rosa Resources Corp. (see FPsurvey - Mines & Energy)

Monexco Resources Ltd. (Que. 1973)
Aug. 23, 1986 – Charter cancelled.

Money Works Inc. (Alta. 1983)
July 1, 1997 – Name changed to CanArgo Energy Inc. following reverse takeover acquisition of CanArgo Ltd.; basis 1 new for 40 old shs. ■

Moneysworth & Best Shoe Care Inc. (Ont. Jan. 1, 1997 amalg.)
May 2000 – Annual financial statements were unable to be filed on time due to a restructuring of payment obligations and attempts to raise additional working capital.
July 11, 2000 – Made an assignment into bankruptcy and PricewaterhouseCoopers Inc. was appointed trustee.
June 2001 – All tangible assets sold with some intangible assets still left to be sold. There was initial distribution to secured creditors.
May 2003 – All remaining assets sold.
Jan. 1, 2004 – Trustee discharged. No funds available for distribution to unsecured creditors or shldrs.

Moneywise Resources Inc. (B.C. Nov. 17, 1986)
Oct. 1, 1992 – Name changed to Stealth Ventures Inc.; basis 1 new for 3.5 old shs. ■

Mongolia Gold Resources Ltd. (B.C. Mar. 3, 1993)
Aug. 16, 1999 – Name changed to Tyhee Development Corp.; basis 1 new for 20 old shs. ■

Mongowin-Sudbury Explorations Ltd. (Can. 1972)
1978 – Dissolved. Distribution to Cdn. and American shldrs. consisted of 1 sh. Natural Resources Guardian International Inc. for each 3.41 shs. and 3.893 shs. respectively of Mongowin-Sudbury.

Monica Resources Ltd. (B.C. 1980)
Feb. 6, 1990 – Name changed to Fulham Explorations Inc.; basis 1 new for 2 old shs. (see FPsurvey - Mines & Energy)

Monida Mines Ltd. (B.C. 1966)
Oct. 15, 1974 – Charter cancelled.

Monique Exploration Inc. (Que. 1985)
Jan. 2, 1992 – Amalgamated with Bay Ressources and Services Inc., Duverny Exploration Inc. and Ste-Geneviève Explorations (1991) Inc. to form SEG Exploration Inc.; basis 1 new for 5.24 Bay shs., 1 new for 3.71 Duverny shs., 1 new for 3.17 Ste-Geneviève shs. and 1 new for 5.35 Monique shs. (see SEG Exploration Inc.)

Monitor Gold Mines Ltd. (Ont. 1945)
Oct. 1968 – Charter cancelled.

Monitor Resources Ltd. (B.C. 1972)
June 13, 1986 – Struck off register.

Monitor Ventures Inc. (Can. Mar. 2, 2006)
May 16, 2022 – Continued into British Columbia. (see FPsurvey - Mines & Energy)

Monk Gold & Resources Limited (Ont. Mar. 9, 1981)
Oct. 25, 1995 – Name changed to Knomex Resources Inc. ■

Monkman Pass Oil Co. Ltd. (unknown)
1952 – Placed into voluntary liquidation.

Mono Gold Mines Inc. (B.C. Mar. 13, 1981)
Feb. 12, 1991 – Name changed to Canadian Mono Mines Inc.; basis 1 new for 3 old shs. ■

MonoGen, Inc. (Can. Nov. 6, 2006)
Dec. 30, 2008 – Filed an assignment in bankruptcy and all officers and directors resigned. RSM Richter Inc. (now KSV Advisory Inc.) was appointed trustee.

Monogram Developments Ltd. (B.C. Dec. 21, 1972)
Nov. 10, 1981 – Name changed to Monogram Oil & Gas, Inc. ■

Monogram Oil & Gas, Inc. (B.C. Dec. 21, 1972)
June 28, 1991 – Dissolved and struck off register.

Monogram Petroleums Ltd. (Ont. 1950)
Dec. 21, 1959 – Dissolved.

Monor Mining Co. Ltd. (Que. 1957)
Oct. 1974 – Charter cancelled.

Monore Metals Corporation (B.C. 1974)
July 1978 – Name changed to Julia Resources Corporation; basis 1 new for 3 old shs. ■

Monpas Mines Ltd. (Que. 1946)
1956 – Name changed to Consolidated Monpas Mines Limited; basis 1 new for 2 old shs. ■

Monpre Iron Mines Limited (Ont. June 10, 1953)
Aug. 18, 1998 – Formed Techoldmin Limited following acquisition of Techoldmin Corporation; basis 1 new for 3 old shs. ■

Monpre Mining Co. Ltd. (Ont. June 10, 1953)
1967 – Name changed to Monpre Iron Mines Limited; basis 1 new for 5 old shs. ■

Monpre Uranium Exploration Ltd. (Ont. June 10, 1953)
1956 – Name changed to Monpre Mining Co. Ltd. ■

Monroe Minerals Inc. (Alta. Aug. 31, 1996 amalg.)
May 26, 2009 – Name changed to Kirrin Resources Inc.; basis 1 new for 10 old shs. ■

Monster Copper Corporation (Yuk. May 24, 2000)
June 8, 2007 – Acquired by Mega Uranium Ltd.; basis 1 new Mega com. sh. and 0.5 new Mega wt. for 6 old Monster com. shs. Subsequently amalgamated with a wholly owned subsid. of Mega Uranium.

Monster Mining Corp. (B.C. May 3, 2007)
Sept. 12, 2016 – Name changed to Metallic Minerals Corp. (see FPsurvey - Mines & Energy)

Monster Uranium Corp. (B.C. Jan. 29, 1986)
Nov. 15, 2019 – Name changed to Lightspeed Discoveries Inc. (see FPsurvey - Mines & Energy)

Mont Blanc Resources Inc. (B.C. Nov. 23, 1983)
July 17, 2008 – Name changed to Sonora Gold & Silver Corp. ■

Mont Gabriel Lodge Inc. (Que. 1960)
May 1, 1975 – Acquired by group of 11 Montreal businessmen and became a private co.

Mont Laurier Uranium Mines Inc. (Ont. 1969)
Aug. 28, 1970 – Name changed to Great Laurier Uranium Mines Ltd. ■

Mont Saint-Sauveur International Inc. (Can. May 26, 1976)
May 11, 2005 – Privatized for $2.30 per sh.

Mont Ste. Anne Mines Limited (Ont. 1967)
Dec. 26, 1983 – Charter cancelled.

Montan Capital Corp. (B.C. Aug. 16, 2011)
Mar. 6, 2015 – Amalgamated with 1023174 B.C. Ltd., a wholly owned subsid. of Strait Minerals Inc. (renamed Montan Mining Corp.), to form Montan Ventures Corp.; basis 1 Strait com. sh. for 1 Montan com. sh. (see Montan Mining Corp.)
Mar. 6, 2015 – Name changed to Montan Ventures Corp. (see Montan Mining Corp.)

Montan Mining Corp. (Ont. Mar. 7, 2003)
June 7, 2018 – Continued into British Columbia.
Jan. 24, 2019 – Name changed to Fidelity Minerals Corp. (see FPsurvey - Mines & Energy)

Montana Gold Mining Company Inc. (Ont. Dec. 21, 2000)
July 7, 2016 – Name changed to Peloton Minerals Corporation. (see FPsurvey - Mines & Energy)

Montana Mines Ltd. (B.C. 1966)
June 1973 – Name changed to Chatham Resources Ltd.; basis 1 new for 4 old shs. ■

Montario Exploration Ltd. (Ont. 1953)
1960 – Charter cancelled.

Montauban Mines Ltd. (Ont. 1950)
1953 – Merged into United Montauban Mines Ltd.; basis 1 new for 2 old shs. ■

Montclerg Mines Ltd. (Ont. 1939)
1966 – Name changed to Consolidated Montclerg Mines Limited; basis 1 new for 3 old shs. ■

Montclerg Resources Limited (Ont. 1939)
Oct. 4, 1996 – Name changed to Prospectors Alliance Corporation; basis 1 new for 2 old shs. ■

Montco Copper Corp. Ltd. (Ont. 1955)
Dec. 18, 1961 – Charter cancelled.

Montdono Gold Mines Ltd. (Ont. 1945)
1958 – Dissolved.

Monte Carlo Exploration Gold Mines Ltd. (Ont. 1934)
Dec. 9, 1957 – Dissolved.

Monte Carlo Gold Mines Ltd. (Alta. Sept. 12, 1985)
July 12, 1993 – Name changed to Exxadon Technology Corporation; basis 1 new for 10 old shs. ■

Monte Carlo Resources Ltd. (Alta. 1985)
Aug. 12, 1986 – Continued into British Columbia.
May 16, 1989 – Name changed to C.R. Provini Financial Services Corp. ■

Monte Christo Resources Ltd. (B.C. 1973)
Jan. 31, 1986 – Name changed to International Display Corporation. (see FPsurvey - Industrials)

Monte Cristo Mines Ltd. (B.C. 1968)
Dec. 30, 1974 – Charter cancelled.

Monte Grande Exploration Limited (Alta. 1957)
Apr. 16, 1981 – Amalgamated with Mountain States Resources Ltd. to form MSR Exploration Ltd.; basis 2 shs. MSR for each 3 shs. Monte Grande.

Monteagle Explorations Ltd. (Que. 1953)
1978 – Charter cancelled.

Monteagle Minerals Ltd. (Que. 1953)
Sept. 1971 – Name changed to Monteagle Explorations Ltd. ■

Montebello Resources Ltd. (B.C. Jan. 27, 1984)
Oct. 7, 1992 – Name changed to First American Capital Group Inc.; basis 1 new for 5 old shs. ■

Montec Holdings Inc. (Can. May 18, 2004)
Sept. 2, 2009 – Name changed to Datex Technologies Corporation. ■

Montecito Minerals Ltd. (B.C. 1972)
June 28, 1974 – Name changed to Nevex Mines Ltd. ■

Montego Mines Ltd. (Ont. 1968)
Dec. 26, 1973 – Charter cancelled.

Montego Resources Ltd. (B.C. 1968)
June 9, 1975 – Name changed to Phoenix Electric Oil Refiners Canada Ltd. ■

Montego Resources Ltd. (Alta. 1987)
Feb. 25, 1988 – Name changed to Canadian Majestic Resources Ltd.; basis 1 new for 1 old sh. ■

Montello Resources Ltd. (B.C. May 2, 1986)
May 4, 2007 – Continued into Alberta.
Nov. 2, 2021 – Struck from registry and dissolved.

Montemor Resources Inc. (Ont. Sept. 20, 1996 amalg.)
Aug. 11, 1997 – Name changed to European Gold Resources Inc. ■

Monterey Capital Inc. (Que. 1954)
Dec. 18, 1995 – Name changed to Nymox Pharmaceutical Corporation following acquisition by private co. Nymox Pharmaceutical Corporation and subsequent amalgamation with 9022-1334 Québec inc., a wholly owned subsidiary of Nymox; basis 1 new for 2 old shs. ■

Monterey Energy Corp. (Alta. Apr. 3, 1997)
June 4, 1999 – All o/s com. shs. acquired by Constellation Oil & Gas Ltd.; basis 1.1 new cl. A com. shs. of Constellation for 1 com. sh. of Monterey. (see Constellation Oil & Gas Ltd.)

Monterey Exploration Ltd. (Alta. Dec. 28, 2005)
Sept. 22, 2010 – Acquired by Pengrowth Energy Trust; basis either 0.8298 Pengrowth units for 1 Monterey com. sh. or 0.8298 exch. Pengrowth shs. for 1 Monterey com. sh or combination thereof. (see Pengrowth Energy Trust)

Monterey Minerals Inc. (B.C. May 9, 2014)
Apr. 5, 2022 – Name changed to Puranium Energy Ltd. (see FPsurvey - Mines & Energy)

Monterey Petroleum Corporation Ltd. (Alta. 1950)
Sept. 1971 – Name changed to Monterey Petroleum Corporation (1971) Ltd.; basis 1 new cl. A for each 10 old com. shs. ■

Monterey Petroleum Corporation (1971) Ltd. (Alta. 1950)
Apr. 30, 1981 – Charter cancelled.

Montex Apparel Industries Ltd. (Ont. 1965 amalg.)
May 1970 – Placed into receivership.
Dec. 12, 1973 – All assets distributed to secured creditors. No funds available for other creditors or shldrs. Charter cancelled.

Montex Holdings Ltd. (Ont. 1963)
July 1965 – Amalgamated to form Montex Apparel Industries Ltd.

Montgary Explorations Limited (Ont. Jan. 15, 1952; via letters patent)
Dec. 22, 1959 – Name changed to Chemalloy Minerals Limited; basis 2 new for 5 old shs. ■

Montgary Petroleum Corporation Limited (Ont. Jan. 15, 1952; via letters patent)
June 23, 1955 – Name changed to Montgary Explorations Limited. ■

Montgomery Mining Co. Ltd. (Que. 1952)
Oct. 13, 1973 – Dissolved.

Montoco Petroleums Limited (Ont. 1952)
1954 – Name changed to Southern Union Oils Ltd.; basis 1 new for 5 old shs. ■

Montoro Gold Inc. (B.C. 1980)
Aug. 20, 1984 – Amalgamated with Pegasus Gold Ltd. to form Pegasus Gold Inc.; basis 1 new Pegasus sh. for 2.666 Montoro shs. (see Pegasus Gold Inc.)

Montoro Resources Inc. (B.C. Jan. 30, 1987)
Oct. 12, 2005 – Name changed to International Montoro Resources Inc.; basis 1 new for 5 old shs. ■

Montreal Aircraft Industries, Ltd. (Can. 1932)
1942 – Land bought by Dom. Govt. and bldgs. by Canadian Car & Foundry Co., Ltd.
Jan. 1943 – Distribution of $8.00 per sh.
May 1944 – Final payment of 30.6¢ per sh.

Montreal-Alberta Petroleums Ltd. (Can. 1929)
Jan. 31, 1945 – Struck from register.

The Montreal Bank (Can. May 18, 1822)
May 18, 1822 – Name changed to The President, Directors and Company of the Bank of Montreal and continued into Canada. ■

The Montreal City and District Savings Bank (Can. Apr. 27, 1871)
Sept. 28, 1987 – Name changed to Laurentian Bank of Canada. (see FPsurvey - Industrials)

Montréal Exchange Inc. (Que. Sept. 29, 2000)
May 5, 2008 – Acquired by TSX Group Inc.; basis 0.7784 TSX com. shs. for 1 Montreal com. sh. or $39 per com. sh.

Montreal Island Power Co. (Que. 1923)
Apr. 15, 1944 – Properties expropriated by Province of Quebec and control taken over by Quebec Hydro-Electric Commission.
Nov. 1, 1952 – Bonds redeemed.
July 1953 – Arbitration committee rendered a decision whereby pref. shldrs. would have the right to arrears of divds. and accept $100 per sh. in full and final settlement and com. shldrs. receive $5.00 per share.

Montreal Light, Heat & Power Consolidated (Que. 1916)
Apr. 15, 1944 – Electric and gas producing facilities and distributing system expropriated by Quebec Hydro-Electric Commission. Under offer dated Mar. 6, 1947, Quebec Hydro acquired co.'s stk. for $25 per sh. in cash or equivalent in 2%, 10-year government-guaranteed Quebec Hydro debs.

Montreal Locomotive Works, Limited (Can. June 19, 1902; via letters patent)
July 1, 1968 – Name changed to MLW-Worthington Limited. ■

Montreal Oil & Gas Corp. (unknown)
Oct. 8, 1954 – Name changed to Oilmont Petroleums Corporation. ■

Montreal Refrigerating & Storage Ltd. (Can. Nov. 30, 1932)
Dec. 6, 1991 – Dissolved.

The Montreal Telegraph Company (Can. 1947)
Apr. 1954 – Shldrs. approved sale of telegraph system to C.N. Telegraphs.
June 3, 1954 – Distribution of $60 per sh., free of inc. tax.
July 20, 1955 – Final distribution of 88¢ per sh.

Montreal Tramways Company (Que. 1911)
1951 – In accordance with special legislation, the Montreal Transportation Commission offered $60 per sh. Action taken by a former shldr. to have the legislation declared ultra vires dismissed by court.

Montreal Trustco Inc. (Que. 1889; via Special Act of Legislature)
Nov. 18, 1982 – Continued into Canada.
July 30, 1996 – All o/s fltg. rate cum. redeem. ser. A pref. shs. redeemed for $100 per sh. plus $0.138166 accr. and unpaid divds. for a total of $100.138166 and all o/s cum. redeem. ser. B pref. shs. redeemed for $25 per sh. plus $0.34541 accr. and unpaid divds. for a total of $25.03451. All o/s com. shs. previously acquired by The Bank of Nova Scotia from BCE Inc. effective Apr. 11, 1994. The company became a wholly owned subsid. of The Bank of Nova Scotia following this transaction.

Montreal Yellowknife Gold Mine Co. Ltd. (Que. 1948)
Aug. 19, 1978 – Charter cancelled.

Montreux Capital Corp. (B.C. Sept. 24, 2007)
May 15, 2017 – Continued into Nevada.
May 17, 2017 – Name changed to Assure Holdings Corp. following Qualifying Transaction reverse takeover acquisition of Assure Holdings, Inc.; basis 1 new for 3 old shs.

Montrose Energy Ltd. (B.C. 1981)
Oct. 28, 1983 – Name changed to Lunar Resources Ltd.; basis 1 new for 5 old shs. (see FPsurvey - Mines & Energy)

Montrose Gold Resources Inc. (Ont. Oct. 26, 1988)
Feb. 22, 1994 – Name changed to Silver Circle Compact Disc Books Inc.; basis 1 new for 4 old shs. ■

Montrose Mines Ltd. (Ont. 1940)
1958 – Charter cancelled.

Montrusco Associates Inc. (Can. June 20, 1984)
June 21, 1999 – Name changed to Montrusco Bolton Inc. following acquisition of Bolton Tremblay Inc. ■

Montrusco Bolton Income & Growth Fund (Ont. Nov. 29, 2004)
Sept. 20, 2007 – Name changed to First Asset Income & Growth Fund. ■

Montrusco Bolton Inc. (Can. June 20, 1984)
Nov. 13, 2000 – Plan of Arrangement where all o/s shs. were acquired by wholly owned subsid. of First International Asset Management Inc.; basis $14.25 per sh.

Montserat Gold Mines Ltd. (Ont. 1947)
Mar. 4, 1957 – Charter cancelled.

Montval Resources Ltd. (Ont. 1988)
Aug. 16, 1993 – Formed WASTECORP. International Investments Inc. on amalgamation with WASTECORP. International Investments Inc.; basis 0.0179515 new for 1 old sh. (see FPsurvey - Industrials)

Monument Resources Inc. (B.C. May 30, 1986)
Mar. 3, 1992 – Name changed to Westwin Ventures Inc.; basis 1 new for 4 old shs. ■

Monumental Gold Corp. (B.C. June 15, 2020)
Oct. 29, 2021 – Name changed to Monumental Minerals Corp. ■

Monumental Minerals Corp. (B.C. June 15, 2020)
Nov. 21, 2023 – Name changed to Monumental Energy Corp. (see FPsurvey - Mines & Energy)

Mood Media Corporation (Can. June 17, 2008)
June 28, 2017 – Continued into Delaware.
July 4, 2017 – Acquired by affiliates of Apollo Global Management, LLC and funds advised or subadvised by GSO Capital Partners LP or its affiliates; basis Cdn$0.17 cash per sh.

Moon Lake Uranium Mines Ltd. (Ont. 1954)
Aug. 26, 1957 – Merged into Consolidated Frederick Mines Ltd.; basis 38.5¢ per old sh. (see Consolidated Frederick Mines Ltd.)

Moon River Capital Ltd. (Ont. Aug. 6, 2019)
May 17, 2024 – Name changed to Moon River Moly Ltd. (see FPsurvey - Mines & Energy)

Moonbound Mining Ltd. (B.C. July 30, 2021)
Sept. 12, 2024 – Name changed to Cape Lithium Corp. (see FPsurvey - Mines & Energy)

Mooncor Oil & Gas Corp. (Ont. Feb. 10, 2005)
Sept. 6, 2018 – Name changed to Sensor Technologies Corp. following reverse takeover acquisition of FOX-TEK Canada Inc.; basis 1 new for 30 old shs. ■

Moondust Ventures Inc. (B.C. July 23, 1987)
Jan. 26, 1993 – Name changed to Global Metals Ltd.; basis 1 new for 5 old shs. ■

Moongold Resources Inc. (B.C. 1987)
Nov. 6, 1992 – Dissolved and struck off register.

Moonraker Resources Ltd. (B.C. 1979)
Dec. 20, 1979 – Name changed to Goldrich Resources Ltd. ■

Moonshine Productions Ltd. (B.C. June 9, 1983)
Oct. 14, 1986 – Name changed to Vanex Resources Ltd. ■

Moonshine Resources Ltd. (B.C. June 9, 1983)
Apr. 3, 1984 – Name changed to Moonshine Productions Ltd. ■

Moonshoot Capital Corp. (Alta. Mar. 22, 2005)
Apr. 11, 2006 – Name changed to Cematrix Corporation following Qualifying Transaction reverse takeover acquisition of Cematric Corporation. (see FPsurvey - Industrials)

Moore-Albach Gold Mines Ltd. (Ont. 1946)
1947 – Name changed to Sherry Lee Gold Mines. ■

Moore Corporation Limited (Ont. 1882)
Dec. 31, 1938 – Amalgamated in Ontario to continue with same name; via letters patent.
June 3, 2002 – Continued into Canada.
May 27, 2003 – Name changed to Moore Wallace Incorporated. ■

Moore Wallace Incorporated (Can. June 3, 2002)
Mar. 1, 2004 – Indirectly acquired by R.R. Donnelley & Sons Company; basis 0.63 R.R. Donnelley sh. for 1 Moore Wallace sh. ■

Moosewood Gold Mines Ltd. (Ont. 1938)
Aug. 6, 1957 – Charter cancelled.

Mooshla Gold Mines Co. Limited (Ont. May 26, 1936)
Aug. 27, 1984 – Charter cancelled.

Mooshla Gold Mines Ltd. (Ont. May 26, 1936)
Name changed to Mooshla Gold Mines Co. Limited; basis 100 new for 1 old sh. ■

Moraga Resources Ltd. (B.C. Sept. 29, 1986)
Feb. 7, 1992 – Acquired by Jordex Resources Inc.; basis 1 Jordex sh. for 3 Moraga shs. (see Jordex Resources Inc.)

Moran Resources Corporation (B.C. May 22, 1980)
Feb. 28, 1985 – Name changed to Stornaway Resources Corporation; basis 1 new for 2 old shs. ■

Morden & Helwig Group Inc. (Can. Mar. 12, 1987)
Aug. 18, 1995 – Name changed to Lindsey Morden Group Inc. ■

Mordey Copper Mines Ltd. (Ont. 1944)
Mar. 16, 1959 – Dissolved. Shldrs. received 1/3¢ per sh., and 1 sh. Goldfrey Lake Copper Mines Ltd. for each 2.85 old shs.

More Mines Limited (Man. 1968)
May 1974 – Amalgamated with 2 other cos. to form Nufort Resources Inc.; basis 1 new for 3 old shs.

More Resources Inc. (B.C. June 11, 1987)
Aug. 11, 1992 – Name changed to General Diamond Corporation. ■

Moreland-Latchford Productions Limited (Ont. 1964)
Aug. 1977 – Placed into receivership. Subsequently all assets liquidated; no distribution made to shldrs.

Moreland Oil & Gas Ltd. (Alta. 1987)
June 5, 1990 – Amalgamated with Sugar Creek Oil & Gas Inc. (1 for 1) to continue as Sugar Creek Oil & Gas Inc.; basis 0.623 new for 1 old sh. (see Sugar Creek Oil & Gas Inc.)

Morengo Resources Inc. (B.C. 1980)
Feb. 21, 1992 – Dissolved and struck off register.

Moreno Ventures Inc. (B.C. Mar. 30, 1988)
Sept. 25, 2002 – Name changed to Niogold Mining Corp.; basis 1 new for 2.5 old shs. ■

Moresby Mines Limited (B.C. 1965)
Feb. 25, 1983 – Struck off register.

Morfee Wheel Manufacturing Inc. (B.C. Jan. 12, 1987)
Dec. 12, 1991 – Name changed to Transtech Industries Inc.; basis 1 new for 4 old shs. ■

Morgain Minerals Inc. (B.C. May 10, 1983)
Aug. 30, 2007 – Amalgamated with Aurogin Resources Ltd. to form Castle Gold Corporation; basis 1 new for 2 Aurogin shs. and 1 new for 2 Morgain shs. (see Castle Gold Corporation)

Morgan Bank of Canada (Can. 1981)
June 1, 1995 – Name changed to J.P. Morgan Canada.

Morgan Creek Mines Ltd. (Ont. 1946)
1954 – Merged into Garrison Creek Consolidated Mines Ltd.; basis 1 new for 15 old shs.

Morgan Financial Corporation (Ont. 1969)
Jan. 20, 1998 – All assets liquidated to settle all outstanding liabilites, and distribution to shldrs. of record on Jan. 23, 1998 of 8.838¢ per sh.
July 9, 1998 – Dissolved.

Morgan Hydrocarbons Inc. (Que. June 8, 1971)
May 13, 1985 – Continued into Canada. (see Stampeder Exploration Ltd.)
Oct. 17, 1996 – Acquired by Stampeder Exploration Ltd.; basis $4.75 or 0.85 Stampeder shs. for 1 Morgan sh. (see Stampeder Exploration Ltd.)

Morgan Media Capital Corporation (Alta. Dec. 1, 1997)
Dec. 29, 2000 – Name changed to Global Consumer Technologies Inc. ■

Morgan Petroleum Inc. (B.C. Sept. 19, 1983)
May 28, 1993 – Name changed to Mortlock Resource Corporation; basis 1 new for 5 old shs. ■

Morgan Resources Corp. (Ont. June 15, 2011)
Mar. 28, 2018 – Name changed to Leviathan Cannabis Group Inc. ■

Morgan Trustco Inc. (Can. 1983)
Nov. 1986 – Acquired by a wholly owned subsid. of Morgan Financial Corporation in July 1986. Holders of cl. A subord. vtg. shs. (public int.) received non-vtg. pref. shs. (1 new for 3.63 old shs.) redeemable at $2.50 per sh. or convertible into Morgan Financial com. shs. on the basis of 0.71 com. shs. for each pref. sh.

Morguard Corporation (Can. Nov. 30, 1996)
Jan. 1, 2007 – Formed by articles of amalgamation as a result of the amalgamation of Morguard Corporation with wholly owned subsidiaries Morguard Residential Inc., Acktion Capital Corporation, Orange Properties Ltd. and 3391345 Canada Inc. to continue as Morguard Corporation.
Dec. 28, 2008 – Amalgamated in Canada to continue with same name.
Apr. 17, 2012 – Amalgamated in Canada to continue with same name.
Jan. 1, 2024 – Amalgamated in Canada to continue with same name. (see FPsurvey - Industrials)

Morguard Sunstone Real Estate Income Fund (B.C. June 18, 2010)
June 28, 2013 – All class A and F shares redeemed for $11.48 and $12.06 per share, respectively.

Morie Yellowknife Gold Mines Ltd. (Ont. 1944)
Feb. 18, 1954 – Charter cancelled.

Morneau Shepell Inc. (Ont. Oct. 19, 2010)
May 17, 2021 – Name changed to LifeWorks Inc. ■

Morneau Sobeco Income Fund (Ont. Aug. 22, 2005)
Jan. 1, 2011 – Succeeded by Morneau Shepell Inc. pursuant to plan of arrangement whereby Morneau Shepell Inc. was formed to facilitate the conversion of the fund into a corporation and the fund was subsequently dissolved. ■

Morning Star Mines Ltd. (B.C. Aug. 22, 1967)
Apr. 27, 1982 – Name changed to Morning Star Resources Limited. ■

Morning Star Resources Limited (B.C. Aug. 22, 1967)
Feb. 4, 1991 – Name changed to Ballad Enterprises Ltd.; basis 1 new for 3 old shs. ■

Morningdale Mines Ltd. (Ont. 1946)
Jan. 1967 – Charter cancelled.

Morningside Oil & Gas Ltd. (Alta.)
July 1960 – Acquired by Keno Oils for 600,000 shs.
1962 – Struck off register.

Morocco Explorations Inc. (B.C. May 12, 1987)
Sept. 2, 1998 – Name changed to Mask Resources Inc.; basis 1 new for 3 old shs. ■

Morocco Mines Ltd. (B.C. 1968)
Oct. 1972 – Name changed to Remar Resources Ltd.; basis 1 new for 4 old shs. ■

Morono Copper Mines Ltd. (Que. Sept. 12, 1957)
July 30, 1979 – Name changed to Morono Mines Ltd. ■

Morono Mines Ltd. (Que. Sept. 12, 1957)
Feb. 27, 2015 – Dissolved.

Morris-Kirkland Gold Mines Ltd. (Ont. 1935)
Sept. 6, 1972 – Dissolved.

Morris Summit Gold Mines Ltd. (B.C. 1945)
Jan. 29, 1979 – Name changed to Scottie Gold Mines Ltd. ■

Morrison Brass Corporation Limited (Can. 1929)
Apr. 1961 – Name changed to The James Morrison Brass Manufacturing Co. Ltd.; basis 1 unit consisting of 1 sh. of The James Morrison Brass Manufacturing Co. Ltd. and 1 sh. of Fidelitron Corp for 1 old shs.

Morrison Facilities Income Fund (Alta. Jan. 10, 1997)
May 10, 1999 – Name changed to Western Facilities Fund. ■

Morrison-Grey Enterprises Limited (B.C. July 7, 1981)
May 1, 1989 – Name changed to MGP Asia Capital Inc. ■

Morrison-Lamothe Bakery Limited (Can. Jan. 3, 1938)
June 19, 1970 – Name changed to Morrison Lamothe Foods Limited. ■

Morrison Lamothe Foods Limited (Can. Jan. 3, 1938)
July 10, 1978 – Name changed to Morrison Lamothe Inc.

Morrison Middlefield Resources Limited (Can. May 3, 1993)
June 12, 1995 – Continued into Alberta. (see 2M Energy Corp.)
Aug. 4, 1999 – All U.K. assets sold to Roc Oil Company Limited and most of the Canadian assets sold to 2M Energy Corp.; basis 1 2M Energy sh. and $5.50 for 1 Morrison Middlefield sh. (see 2M Energy Corp.)

Morrison Minerals Limited (Ont. 1986)
Nov. 10, 1992 – Amalgamated with OGY Petroleums Ltd.; basis 1 OGY sh. for 2.2 Morrison shs. (see OGY Petroleums Ltd.)

Morrison Mines Limited (Ont. Apr. 1951)
1952 – Name changed to New Morrison Mines Limited; basis 1 new for 3.6 old shs. ■

Morrison Mines Ltd. (B.C. 1971 amalg.)
1976 – Amalgamated with Oro Mines Limited, to form Ronoco Resources Limited.

Morrison Petroleums Ltd. (Ont. Apr. 1951)
Nov. 20, 1989 – Continued into Alberta. (see Northstar Energy Corporation)
Apr. 2, 1997 – Amalgamated with Northstar Acquisition Corporation, a wholly owned subsid. of Northstar Energy Corporation,; basis 0.7 Northstar shs. for 1 Morrison sh. (see Northstar Energy Corporation)

Morrisroe-Mitten Oils Ltd. (unknown)
1955 – Acquired by Canadian Pipe Lines & Petroleums Ltd. for 280,000 shs. (see Canadian Pipe Lines & Petroleums Ltd.)

Morro Bay Capital Ltd. (Alta. Aug. 21, 2012)
Jan. 15, 2014 – Name changed to Morro Bay Resources Ltd. ■

Morro Bay Resources Ltd. (Alta. Aug. 21, 2012)
Sept. 20, 2017 – Name changed to Viridium Pacific Group Ltd. and continued into Canada; basis 1 new for 3.603457 old shs. ■

Morse Paint Manufacturing Limited (Ont. 1899)
Major assets sold to Du Pont of Canada Limited. Co. since liquidated. (see Du Pont of Canada Ltd.)
Dec. 11, 1967 – Distributions totaling $46.43 per sh. made from Aug. 21, 1964 to Dec. 11, 1967, on basis free of income tax in hands of shldrs. (see Du Pont of Canada Ltd.)

Mort Lake Mines Ltd. (B.C.)
May 15, 1969 – Struck off register.

Mortcorp Enterprises Inc. (B.C. Apr. 18, 1984)
Oct. 3, 1994 – Name changed to Licefa International Inc.; basis 1 new for 5 old shs. ■

Mortgage-Backed Securities Trust (Ont. Mar. 28, 2003)
Apr. 9, 2007 – Merged with MBS Adjustable Rate Income Fund (0.978 for 1) to continue as Sentry Select MBS Adjustable Rate Income Fund II; basis 0.7021 new Sentry Select unit for 1 old Mortgage-Backed unit. (see Sentry Select MBS Adjustable Rate Income Fund II)

The Mortgage Insurance Company of Canada (Can. Dec. 21, 1963)
1969 – Holborough Investments Limited acquired all the minority shareholdings of the company; basis 10 new for 1 old sh. The company became a wholly owned subsid. and principal asset of Holborough. On Jan. 1, 1982, amalgamated with Insmor Mortgage Insurance Company to continue as The Mortgage Insurance Company of Canada, while still remaining a subsidiary of Holborough.
Jan. 1, 1982 – Amalgamated in Canada to continue with same name.

Mortice Kern Systems Inc. (Ont. Apr. 24, 1984)
Nov. 15, 2001 – Name changed to MKS Inc. ■

Mortlock Resource Corporation (B.C. Sept. 19, 1983)
Jan. 20, 1995 – Name changed to NovaDx International Inc. ■

Morton Lake Gold Mines Ltd. (Man. 1937)
Feb. 26, 1966 – Dissolved.

Morumbi Oil & Gas Inc. (Alta. Dec. 22, 2009)
Oct. 24, 2011 – Continued into Ontario.
Mar. 27, 2012 – Name changed to Morumbi Resources Inc. ■

Morumbi Resources Inc. (Ont. Oct. 24, 2011)
Dec. 21, 2016 – Name changed to Ascendant Resources Inc. following acquisition of American Pacific Honduras S.A. de C.V.; basis 1 new for 5 old shs. ■

Moruya Gold Mines (1983) NL (Australia 1983)
Apr. 11, 1990 – Acquired by United Coin Mines Limited; basis 1 new for 5.3 old shs. (see United Coin Mines Ltd.)

Mosaic Capital Corporation (Alta. Feb. 11, 2011)
Aug. 6, 2021 – Acquired by 2356430 Alberta Inc.; basis $5.50 cash per com. sh. and $1,000 plus accrued unpaid interest for each $1,000 principal amount of unsecured subordinate debentures.

Mosaic Group Inc. (Ont. June 28, 1995)
Sept. 26, 2003 – Placed into receivership. KPMG Inc. was appointed receiver.
May 16, 2007 – KPMG Inc. discharged as receiver. Secured creditors suffered a substantial shortfall and there were no funds available for unsecured creditors or shldrs.

Mosaic Mapping Corporation (Alta. Nov. 6, 2000)
May 28, 2004 – Agreement acquisition by Pulse Data Inc.; basis 0.1176 new Pulse com. sh. plus $0.05 for 1 old Mosaic com. sh.; 0.0588 new Pulse wt. for 1 old

Mosaic wt. and all Series 1 and 2 pfd. shs cancelled for no consideration. (see Pulse Data Inc.)

Mosaic Recycled Paper Ltd. (B.C. July 19, 1983)
Aug. 11, 1997 – Name changed to Mosaic Technologies Corporation. ■

Mosaic Resources Ltd. (B.C. July 19, 1983)
May 31, 1990 – Name changed to Mosaic Recycled Paper Ltd. ■

Mosaic Technologies Corporation (B.C. July 19, 1983)
Nov. 27, 1997 – Continued into Canada.
Feb. 9, 2006 – Dissolved.

Mosaic Travel and Tours Inc. (Alta. Sept. 25, 1995)
Apr. 27, 2000 – Name changed to bookfortravel.com Inc. ■

Mosam Capital Corp. (B.C. Feb. 1, 2006)
Dec. 21, 2009 – Name changed to Pan Global Resources Inc. following Qualifying Transaction mineral property option acquisition. (see FPsurvey - Mines & Energy)

Moseda Technologies, Inc. (B.C. Sept. 1, 2005)
May 10, 2016 – Name changed to Reliq Health Technologies Inc. (see FPsurvey - Industrials)

Mosher Long Lac Gold Mines Ltd. (Ont. May 2, 1934)
1950 – Acquired by New Mosher Longlac Mines Ltd.; basis 15 shs. of Newlund Mines and 100 shs. of New Mosher per 100 old shs. (see New Mosher Longlac Mines Ltd.)

Mosport Limited (Ont. 1958)
1966 – Assets acquired by Cantrack Motor Racing Corp. Ltd. under court order. Proceeds used to retire o/s 3% income debentures. Nothing available for unsecured creditors or shldrs.

Mosport Park Corporation (Ont. 1958)
May 7, 1971 – Continued into Quebec.
Nov. 3, 1994 – Name changed to The Mosport Park Entertainment Corporation; basis 1 new for 2 old shs. ■

The Mosport Park Entertainment Corporation (Que. May 7, 1971)
May 8, 1998 – Struck off registry.
Oct. 1998 – Mosport Park sold to Panoz Motorsports Group a division of Panoz. LLC.
Aug. 28, 2018 – Revived.
Sept. 24, 2020 – Name changed to Darkhorse Technologies Ltd.; basis 1 new for 200 old shs. (see FPsurvey - Industrials)

Mosquito Consolidated Gold Mines Limited (B.C. 1971)
Jan. 4, 2013 – Name changed to American CuMo Mining Corporation. ■

The Mosquito Creek Gold Mining Company Limited (B.C. 1971)
Dec. 4, 1987 – Name changed to Mosquito Consolidated Gold Mines Limited; basis 1 new for 5 old shs. ■

Moss Lake Development Inc. (Ont. 1974)
Nov. 5, 1976 – Amalgamated with 7 other cos. to form Wolverine Developments Inc.; basis 2 new for 19 old shs.

Moss Lake Gold Mines Ltd. (Ont. Oct. 31, 1994)
Apr. 2, 2014 – Amalgamated with 2404027 Ontario Inc., a wholly owned subsid. of Wesdome Gold Mines Ltd.; basis 1 Wesdome com. sh. for 3.85 Moss Lake com. shs.

Moss-Power Resources Inc. (B.C. Mar. 30, 1990 amalg.)
Feb. 14, 1991 – Name changed to WisCan Resources Inc.; basis 1 new for 7 old shs. ■

Moss Resources Inc. (Ont. Mar. 26, 1992)
May 24, 2000 – Name changed to Asset Management Software Systems Corp. pursuant to reverse takeover acquisition of Asset Management Software Systems Inc. (see FPsurvey - Mines & Energy; FPsurvey - Industrials)

Moss Resources Ltd. (B.C. 1980)
May 15, 1988 – Amalgamated with Van Horne Exploration Inc. (1.1 for 1) to continue with the same name Moss Resources Ltd.; basis 1 new for 1 old sh. (see Moss-Power Resources Inc.)
Mar. 30, 1990 – Amalgamated with Power Explorations Inc. (1 for 1) to form a new co. named Moss-Power Resources Inc.; basis 1.5 new Moss-Power sh. for 1 old Moss sh. (see Moss-Power Resources Inc.)

Mota Ventures Corp. (B.C. July 15, 2010)
Aug. 14, 2020 – Name changed to Thoughtful Brands Inc. (see FPsurvey - Industrials)

Motapa Diamonds Inc. (N.B. Mar. 13, 1998)
Nov. 19, 2008 – Continued into British Columbia.
July 6, 2009 – Acquired by Lucara Diamond Corp.; basis 0.9055 Lucara shs. for 1 Motapa sh.

Mother's Restaurants Limited (Ont. 1982 amalg.)
Oct. 10, 1986 – Following successful takeover offer expiring in September 1986 for the acquisition of all outstanding shares and warrants at $12.25 and 30¢ respectively, remaining shares were acquired effective Oct. 8, 1986, through the amalgamation of Mother's with MFC Acquisition Inc. Each remaining publicly held com. sh. was converted into one redeem. pref. sh. of the amalgamated co. and redeemed for $12.25 per sh.

Motion International Inc. (Can. Feb. 15, 1989)
May 25, 2000 – Acquired by TVA Acquisition Inc. for $5.45 per cl. A sh.

Motion Works Corporation (B.C. June 5, 1981)
Aug. 8, 1995 – Name changed to Motion Works Group Limited. ■

Motion Works Group Limited (B.C. June 5, 1981)
May 31, 2000 – Delisted from the CDNX. Subsequently struck from register and dissolved.

Motionsphere Capital Inc. (Can. Feb. 5, 2004)
Oct. 1, 2010 – Name changed to Colba.Net Telecom Inc. following Qualifying Transaction reverse takeover acquisition of Colba.Net Inc. ■

Motivus Inc. (Ont. Jan. 27, 1986)
June 16, 2004 – Going private transaction via amalgamation with 2043921 Ontario Limited; basis 3¢ per sh.

Moto Goldmines Limited (Ont. Mar. 11, 1988)
May 26, 2005 – Continued into British Columbia.
Oct. 21, 2009 – Acquired by 0858065 B.C. Ltd., an indirectly wholly owned subsid. of Randgold Resources Limited; basis either : (i) US$4.47 per sh., (ii) 0.07061 Randgold ord. shs., or (iii) 0.07061 Randgold ADS for 1 Moto Goldmines sh.

Motor Coach Industries Limited (Man. 1932)
Jan. 28, 1993 – Continued into Canada.
Mar. 10, 1994 – Acquired by Motor Coach Industries International, Inc. and Transportation Manufacturing Operations Inc.; basis $17 per sh.

Motor Products Corporation of Canada Ltd. (Ont. 1956)
1959 – Liquidated. First mtge. bonds red. in full. Holders of 6% s.f. debs. received $148.99 per $1,000 princ. amt. Nothing avail. for pref. and com. shldrs.

Motor Specialty Mfrs. (Ontario) Ltd. (Can. - unspecified)
1968 – Acquired by Magna Electronics Corporation Limited for 3,000 com. shs. (see Magna Electronics Corporation Limited)

Motorcade Stores Limited (Ont. Oct. 29, 1956)
Aug. 10, 1978 – Name changed to Motorcade Industries Limited.

Motrlube Inc. (Can. Dec. 8, 1987)
Sept. 20, 1996 – Name changed to MLB Industries Inc.; basis 1 new for 1 old sh. ■

Mount Agnes Mines Ltd. (B.C. July 21, 1966)
July 1969 – Name changed to Lower Valley Mines Ltd. ■

Mount Allard Resources Ltd. (B.C. Apr. 6, 1987)
July 5, 1991 – Name changed to Protection Technology Inc.; basis 1 new for 3 old shs. ■

Mt. Baker Plywood Ltd. (B.C. 1954)
1962 – Purchased by Canadian Collieries Resources Limited.

Mt. Calvery Resources Ltd. (B.C. Mar. 26, 1956)
Aug. 22, 1989 – Name changed to Triumph Resources Ltd.; basis 1 new for 4 old shs. ■

Mount Cheminis (1945) Mining Co. Ltd. (Ont. 1945)
May 1957 – Charter cancelled.

Mount Costigan Mines Ltd. (Ont. 1962)
1967 – Name changed to New Mount Costigan Mines Ltd.; basis 3 new for 5 old shs. ■

Mount Dakota Energy Corp. (Can. Aug. 24, 1998)
Aug. 7, 2015 – Continued into British Columbia.
Feb. 17, 2022 – Name changed to HYTN Innovations Inc. pursuant to the reverse takeover acquisition of HYTN Beverage Corp. and concurrent acquisition of 1306562 B.C. Ltd. (see FPsurvey - Mines & Energy)

Mt. Emily Exploration Ltd. (B.C. Dec. 17, 1981)
Dec. 2, 1991 – Name changed to Brookings Resources Ltd.; basis 1 new for 2 old shs. ■

Mount Evans Copper Corp. Inc. (Ont. 1972)
Nov. 5, 1976 – Amalgamated with 7 other cos. to form Wolverine Developments Inc.; basis 1 new for 19 old shs.

Mt. Expeditor Resources Ltd. (B.C. Sept. 1, 1983)
Mar. 29, 1990 – Name changed to Envirowaste Industries Inc. ■

Mount Grant Mines Ltd. (Alta. 1967)
June 15, 1978 – Dissolved.

Mt. Grant Mines Ltd. (B.C. Oct. 26, 1983)
Jan. 5, 1993 – Name changed to Venezuelan Goldfields Ltd. ■

Mount Hope Resources Corp. (Alta. Nov. 7, 1996)
Feb. 29, 2000 – Name changed to 3Net Media Corporation. ■

Mt. Hyland Mines Ltd. (N.P.L.) (B.C. Sept. 14, 1964)
Mar. 5, 1975 – Name changed to Consolidated Mt. Hyland Mines & Resources Ltd.; basis 1 new for 5 old shs. ■

Mount Jamie Mines Ltd. (Ont. 1965)
Feb. 3, 1984 – Formed Jamie Frontier Resources Inc. following merger with Keeley-Frontier Resources Limited (2 for 5); basis 1 new for 4 old shs. ■

Mount Jamie Mines (Quebec) Ltd. (Que. 1970)
Aug. 1978 – Assets acquired by Lancer Resources Limited.

Mt. Kearsarge Minerals Inc. (Ont. 1927)
Mar. 14, 1994 – Formed Sino-Forest Corporation in Ontario on amalgamation with 1028412 Ontario Inc.; basis 1 new for 10 old shs. ■

Mount Keno Mines Limited (Ont. 1950)
Apr. 15, 1996 – Name changed to Keno Industries Inc.; basis 1 new for 2 old shs. ■

Mount Leyland Collieries Ltd. (B.C. 1957)
May 4, 1972 – Dissolved.

Mount Nansen Gold Mines Ltd. (B.C. 1963)
1964 – Name changed to Peso Carmacks Gold Mines Ltd. ■

Mt. Ogden Mines Ltd. (B.C. 1967)
Jan. 31, 1977 – Dissolved.

Mount Pleasant Resources Inc. (Ont. 1959)
July 8, 1990 – Name changed to Pleasant Realty & Financial Corp. (see FPsurvey - Industrials)

Mount Real Corporation (Alta. Feb. 12, 1987)
July 10, 1998 – Continued into Canada.

Mount Real Financial Corporation (Alta. Feb. 12, 1987)
Aug. 25, 1995 – Name changed to Mount Real Corporation. ■

The Mount Royal Dairies & Co. Ltd. (Que. 1947)
1966 – In trusteeship.
Name changed to Laiteries Papineau Inc. following sale of assets and trademarks, incl. name, to Québec Lait Inc. by trustee. ■

Mount Royal Hotel Company, Ltd. (Que. 1921)
1947 – Property and assets purchased by Cardy Corp. Ltd. Shldrs. received 1 cl. A sh. of Cardy Corp., $6.00 in conv. 5% debentures, and $2.03 in cash for 1 old sh.

Mount Royal Metal Co. Ltd. (Can. 1923)
June 1952 – Name changed to Mountroy Limited following sale of a substantial part of its assets to Federated Metals Canada Ltd. ■

Mount Royal Rice Mills Limited (Can. July 19, 1929)
July 30, 1979 – Name changed to MRRM Inc. ■

Mount Sicker Mines Ltd. (B.C. 1966)
Jan. 1980 – Name changed to Peppa Resources Ltd. ■

Mt. Tom Minerals Corp. (B.C. Sept. 30, 1967)
Oct. 21, 1999 – Name changed to Global Net Entertainment Corp. ■

Mount Vernon Oil Co. Ltd. (unknown)
1929 – Assets acquired by Turner Basin Oil Co. Ltd. (see Turner Basin Oil Co., Ltd.)

Mount Vernon Porcupine Gold Mines Ltd. (Ont. 1940)
1949 – In bankruptcy. No equity for shldrs.

Mt. Washington Copper Co. Ltd. (B.C. 1956)
1984 – Formed Alawas Gold Corporation in British Columbia on amalgamation with Velocity Development Ltd.; basis 1 new for 5 old shs. ■

Mount Wright Iron Mines Company Limited (Ont. Feb. 2, 1951)
May 15, 1996 – Name changed to Mantaur Goldfields Corp. ■

Mount Zeballos Gold Mines Ltd. (B.C. 1938)
Aug. 1943 – Liquidating divd. of 5¢ per sh. distributed in 1942 and 5.4¢ per sh. after which property taken over by Zeballos Interests, Ltd.; shldrs. received 1 Zeballos sh. for 100 old shs.

Mountain Beaver Resources Ltd. (Ont. Feb. 23, 1988)
May 22, 1996 – Name changed to East Asia Gold Corp.; basis 1 new for 20 old shs. ■

Mountain Boy Minerals Ltd. (B.C. Apr. 26, 1999)
Mar. 30, 2023 – Name changed to MTB Metals Corp. (see FPsurvey - Mines & Energy)

Mountain Capital Inc. (B.C. Sept. 1, 2005)
May 14, 2009 – Name changed to First Lithium Resources Inc. ■

Mountain China Resorts (Holding) Limited (B.C. May 28, 2008 amalg.)
Jan. 20, 2023 – Privatized via amalgamation with Sunski BC Holdings Ltd. to form Mountain China Relax Holdings, Ltd.; basis $0.0026 cash per sh.

Mountain Crest Mines Ltd. (Que. 1945)
1952 – Bankrupt.

Mountain Fertilizer Products Inc. (B.C. May 27, 1980)
Aug. 6, 1980 – Name changed to Titleist Petroleums Ltd. ■

Mountain Frontier Explorations Ltd. (Ont. 1984)
Mar. 30, 1990 – Amalgamated with Golden Winner Resources Ltd., Rainbow Lake Resources Ltd., Thunder Valley Resources Ltd. and Premier Lake Resources Inc.

to form Castlestar Capital Developments Corp.; basis 1 new for 0.97 Golden Winner shs., 1 new for 0.915 Rainbow shs., 1 new for 1.10 Thunder shs., 1 new for 0.95 Premier shs. and 1 new for 1.08 Mountain Frontier shs. (see Castlestar Capital Developments Corp.)

Mountain Lake Minerals Inc. (B.C. May 16, 2012)
Apr. 29, 2020 – Name changed to Pac Roots Cannabis Corp. pursuant to the reverse takeover acquisition of private 1157630 B.C. Ltd. ■

Mountain Lake Minerals Inc. (B.C. June 7, 2018)
May 4, 2021 – Name changed to MLK Gold Ltd. ■

Mountain Lake Resources Inc. (B.C. Mar. 25, 1986)
July 16, 2012 – Acquired by Marathon Gold Corporation pursuant to plan of arrangement under which Mountain Lake's mineral assets, other than its 50% interest in the Valentine Lake gold property, were transferred to newly incorporated Mountain Lake Minerals Inc. (Spinco); basis 0.4 Marathon shs. and 0.4 Spinco shs. for 1 Mountain Lake Resources sh.

Mountain Minerals Co. Ltd. (B.C. 1980)
Aug. 21, 1996 – Acquired by Highwood Resources Ltd.; basis 0.284 Highwood shs. for 1 Mountain sh. (see Highwood Resources Ltd.)

Mountain Pass Mines Ltd. (B.C. 1971)
Apr. 12, 1978 – Name changed to Border Resources Limited.

Mountain Province Diamonds Inc. (B.C. Nov. 1, 1997 amalg.)
Sept. 20, 2005 – Continued into Ontario. (see FPsurvey - Mines & Energy)

Mountain Province Mining Inc. (B.C. Dec. 2, 1986)
Nov. 1, 1997 – Amalgamated with 444965 B.C. Ltd. (wholly owned by Glenmore Highlands Inc.) to form new co. with same name Mountain Province Mining Inc., with old Mountain Province the deemed acquiror; basis 11.69 new for 1 444965 B.C. sh. and 1 new for 1 Mountain Province sh.
Oct. 16, 2000 – Name changed to Mountain Province Diamonds Inc. ■

Mountain States Resources Ltd. (Alta. 1971)
Apr. 16, 1981 – Amalgamated with Monte Grande Resources Ltd. to form MSR Exploration Ltd.; basis 1 sh. MSR for 1 sh. Mountain States.

Mountain View Ventures Inc. (B.C. June 19, 1991 amalg.)
Apr. 8, 1997 – Name changed to Blackrun Ventures Inc.; basis 1 new for 4 old shs. ■

Mountain West Resources Inc. (B.C. Dec. 28, 1971)
Apr. 2, 2012 – Name changed to Mountainstar Gold Inc. (see FPsurvey - Mines & Energy)

Mountain World Entertainment Ltd. (B.C. Dec. 9, 1994)
June 9, 1999 – Placed into bankruptcy and Deloitte & Touche Inc. of Vancouver appointed trustee.
Oct. 21, 2001 – Trustee discharged. No funds available for distribution to creditors or shldrs.

Mountaineer Mines Ltd. (B.C. May 9, 1975)
May 1980 – Name changed to Canadian Mineral Corporation; basis 1 new for 2 old shs. ■

Mountainview Energy Ltd. (B.C. May 31, 2000)
May 22, 2012 – Continued into Alberta.
Nov. 2, 2021 – Struck from registry and dissolved.

Mountainview Explorations Inc. (Ont. Mar. 9, 1965)
Mar. 14, 1978 – Charter cancelled.
Jan. 8, 1979 – Charter cancelled.
Mar. 3, 1988 – Name changed to Banro Capital Group Inc. ■

Mountroy Limited (Can. 1923)
Feb. 1954 – Offer to purchase o/s shs. made through Canada Permanent Trust Co., at a price in excess of $11 per sh. Offer expired Mar. 1, 1954, at which time approx. 97% of the o/s shs. had been sold.

Mountvale Placer Gravels Ltd. (B.C. 1960)
Jan. 26, 1970 – Name changed to Challenger Mines Ltd. ■

Movado Mining Co. Ltd. (Ont. 1967)
June 2, 1969 – Name changed to Milger Development Corporation Ltd. ■

Movarie Capital Ltd. (B.C. Nov. 23, 2010)
June 1, 2017 – Name changed to Wellness Lifestyles Inc. ■

Moveitonline Inc. (Alta. Mar. 30, 2000)
June 4, 2003 – Name changed to Producers Oilfield Services Inc. ■

Movie Distribution Income Fund (Ont. Aug. 28, 2003)
Aug. 17, 2007 – Acquired by EdgeStone Capital Partners, Inc. for $10 per trust unit.

Moving Bytes Inc. (Can. June 20, 2000)
Mar. 23, 2006 – Name changed to China International Enterprises Inc.; basis 1 new for 32 old shs. ■

Movit Media Corp. (B.C. Dec. 11, 2009)
Apr. 17, 2018 – Name changed to Ether Capital Corporation pursuant to reverse takeover acquisition of Ethereum Capital Inc.; basis 1 new for 12.5 old shs. Continued into Ontario. ■

Moxie Exploration Ltd. (Alta. Oct. 19, 1999)
Oct. 20, 2003 – Acquired by Endev Energy Inc.; basis either $0.46 or 0.278788 new Endev sh. or a combination thereof for 1 old Moxie sh.
June 30, 2006 – Name changed to Endev Exploration Ltd.

Moxie Petroleum Ltd. (Alta. Feb. 27, 1997)
Jan. 31, 2000 – Plan of Arrangement with Richland Petroleum Corporation whereby shares exchanged for cash and shares of a new company named Moxie Exploration Ltd.; basis $1.135, 0.18 new Richland com. sh. and 0.7 new Moxie Exploration sh. for 1 old Moxie Petroleum com. sh.

Moydow Mines International Inc. (Ont. Dec. 9, 1998)
Dec. 18, 2006 – Continued into British Columbia.
Jan. 22, 2010 – Amalgamated with FN Subco Inc., a wholly owned subsid. of Franco-Nevada Corporation to continue as FN Subco Inc.; basis 0.02863 Franco-Nevada shs. for 1 Moydow sh.

Le Moyne Explorations Ltd. (Ont. 1954)
1969 – Charter cancelled.

Le Moyne Ungava Mines Ltd. (Que. 1956)
June 1968 – Charter cancelled.

Mozart Gold Mines Ltd. (Ont. 1945)
May 1960 – Charter cancelled.

Mudlac Gold Mines Ltd. (Que. 1944)
Dec. 22, 1979 – Dissolved.

Mueller Medical International Inc. (Ont. Jan. 10, 1980)
Apr. 20, 1994 – Name changed to Vasogen Inc.; basis 1 new for 7 old shs. ■

Muirfield Investment Corporation (B.C. Mar. 23, 1984)
Apr. 5, 1994 – Name changed to First Western Minerals Inc.; basis 1 new for 3 old shs. ■

Muirheads Cafeterias Ltd. (Ont. 1926)
Apr. 30, 1963 – Wound up and charter surrendered. Distribution of property made to registered shldrs. and claims from unregistered shldrs. accepted by co. until Oct. 31, 1963, after which the balance of any undistributed property was trans. to the Public Trustee.

Mukuba Resources Limited (Ont. Feb. 7, 1984)
May 23, 2018 – Name changed to FogChain Corp. following reverse takeover acquisition of FogChain, Inc. and concurrent amalgamation of FogChain, Inc. with wholly owned Mukuba Subco Inc.; basis 1 new for 1.66 old shs. ■

Mullen Group Income Fund (Alta. June 3, 2005)
May 8, 2009 – Converted into Mullen Group Ltd.; basis 1 Mullen Group Ltd. com. sh. for 1 Mullen Group Income trust unit.

Mullen Transportation Inc. (Alta. May 30, 1957)
July 7, 2005 – Converted into an income trust named Mullen Group Income Fund; basis either 3 trust units or, 3 Mullen Co. LP exch. cl. B partnership units or, a combination thereof for 1 Mullen Transportation com. sh. (see Mullen Group Income Fund)

Mullen Trucking Ltd. (Alta. May 30, 1957)
Jan. 1, 1997 – Name changed to Mullen Transportation Inc. ■

Mulligan Capital Corp. (B.C. Nov. 30, 2005)
Feb. 7, 2007 – Name changed to Blue Sky Uranium Corp. following Qualifying Transaction acquisition of option on uranium prospect in Saskatchewan. (see FPsurvey - Mines & Energy)

Multi Choice Communications Inc. (Ont. Apr. 9, 1986)
Jan. 3, 1995 – Delisted from the CDN. Subsequently dissolved and charter cancelled.

Multi-Corp Inc. (Alta. Dec. 4, 1987)
July 4, 1997 – Name changed to Zi Corporation. ■

Multi-Energies Developments Ltd. (Alta. June 15, 1987)
June 20, 1994 – Name changed to Sunalta Energy Inc.; basis 1 new for 2 old shs. ■

Multi-Fund Income Trust (Ont. Oct. 8, 1997)
Feb. 19, 2007 – Acquired by Amalgamated Income Limited Partnership; basis 0.18 new Amalgamated unit for 1 old Multi-Fund unit. (see Amalgamated Income Limited Partnership)

Multi-Glass International Corp. (Alta. Dec. 9, 1996)
June 28, 2006 – Amalgamated with a wholly owned subsid. of 2044278 Ontario Inc.; basis 1 new $0.03 cl. A redeemable pfce. sh. for 1 old Multi-Glass sh. The pfce. shs. were immediately redeemed for $0.03 per sh.

Multi-Glass International Inc. (Alta. Dec. 9, 1996)
Oct. 28, 2002 – Name changed to Multi-Glass International Corp.; basis 1 new for 5 old shs. ■

Multi-Manager Limited Partnership I (Ont. Jan. 15, 1993)
Nov. 6, 2012 – Dissolved for 23¢ per unit.

Multi Metal Mines Ltd. (Ont. 1966)
1967 – Shares acquired by Vista Mines Ltd.

Multi-Screen Corporation (Alta. Aug. 15, 1986)
June 29, 1993 – Name changed to Cephalon Resource Corporation; basis 1 new for 5 old shs. ■

Multi Select Income Trust (Ont. Aug. 30, 2004)
June 3, 2009 – Merged into Sentry Select Canadian Income Fund, an open-ended mutual fund.

Multi-Step Industries Inc. (B.C. May 15, 1984)
Oct. 1, 1990 – Delisted from the Vancouver Stock Exchange. Subsequently struck from register and dissolved.

Multi-Step Products Inc. (Ont. 1983)
Apr. 29, 1987 – Name changed to Tarxien International Incorporated. ■

Multi-Structure Holdings Ltd. (Can. May 21, 1929)
Taken over by Sunshine Oils, Ltd.

Multi-Tek Technologies Inc. (Alta. Oct. 30, 1998)
July 18, 2000 – Formed Tactex Controls Inc. in Alberta on reverse takeover amalgamation with private co. Tactex Controls Inc. (see FPsurvey - Industrials)

Multiactive Software Inc. (Can. May 7, 1999)
Dec. 1, 1999 – Amalgamated with wholly owned Multiactive Software Development and Marketing Inc. to form new co. with same name.
Dec. 11, 2002 – Name changed to Maximizer Software Inc. following exchange of shares with wholly owned Maximizer Software Inc. which became the parent co. ■

Multibanc Financial Corp. (Ont. Jan. 7, 1987)
Mar. 6, 2000 – Called for redemption; basis the lesser of a) $17 plus amt. equal to net profit per pfd. sh. or b) amt. equal to net realizable value of co. assets per pfd. sh.

Multibanc NT Financial Corp. (Ont. Jan. 7, 1987)
Mar. 6, 2000 – All o/s cap. shs. repurchased for $81.14 per sh. Co. now inactive.

Multidev Immobilia Inc. (Can. Aug. 26, 1983)
Jan. 28, 2003 – Dissolved and struck from register.

Multilink Technologies Inc. (Alta. Dec. 10, 1986)
Sept. 17, 2003 – Name changed to Airesurf Networks Holdings Inc. and continued into Ontario following reverse takeover acquisition of Airesurf Networks Inc.; basis 1 new for 4 old shs. ■

Multimatic Investments Ltd. (Can. - unspecified)
Dec. 1968 – Acquired by Magna Electronics Corp. Ltd. for $800,000 and 100,000 com. shs.

MultiMedia Capital Corporation (Ont. Mar. 31, 1986)
June 23, 1992 – Name changed to MultiMedia WTM Corporation; basis 1 cl. A for 2.5 com. shs. ■

Multimedia Nova Corporation (Ont. Mar. 31, 1986)
May 27, 2013 – Placed into receivership. Fuller Landau Group Inc. appointed receiver and all officers and directors resigned.

MultiMedia WTM Corporation (Ont. Mar. 31, 1986)
July 24, 2002 – Name changed to Multimedia Nova Corporation. ■

Multinational Resources Inc. (B.C. Feb. 28, 1980)
June 4, 1996 – Name changed to New Guinea Gold Corporation and continued into Yukon; basis 1 new for 5 old shs. ■

Multiple Access Limited (Can. 1969)
Aug. 31, 1979 – Acquired by and amalgamated with CFCF Inc. for $8.50 per sh. (see CFCF Inc.)

Multiple Mining Development Ltd. (Alta. 1968)
Dec. 20, 1979 – Name changed to Madre Mining Ltd. ■

Multiplex Resources Ltd. (B.C.)
Nov. 6, 1991 – Name changed to Multiplex Technologies Inc. and continued into British Columbia. ■

Multiplex Technologies Inc. (B.C. Nov. 6, 1991)
Aug. 29, 2005 – Dissolved and struck from register.

Multiplied Media Corporation (Alta. Dec. 8, 2006 amalg.)
Oct. 27, 2010 – Name changed to Poynt Corporation. ■

Multireal Properties Inc. (Ont. June 28, 1984 amalg.)
June 9, 1992 – Name changed to XPF Development Inc.; basis 2 new for 3 old shs. ■

Multivision Communications Corp. (B.C. May 14, 1987)
Oct. 2, 2000 – Continued into Yukon.
Dec. 10, 2010 – Continued into British Columbia.
Sept. 30, 2016 – Name changed to ZoomAway Travel Inc. ■

Multiwin Explorations Ltd. (Ont. 1954)
June 3, 1965 – Charter cancelled.

Mulvihill Pro-AMS 100 Plus (Cdn$) Trust (Ont. Oct. 18, 2001)
Sept. 29, 2008 – Dissolved for $20.1673 per unit.

Mulvihill Pro-AMS 100 Plus (US$) Trust (Ont. Oct. 18, 2001)
Sept. 29, 2008 – Dissolved for US$16.9049 per unit.

Mulvihill Pro-AMS RSP Split Share Corp. (Ont. Jan. 8, 2002)
Nov. 1, 2010 – Terminated and cl. A and B shs. were redeemed for $8.4840 and $18.8627 per sh., respectively.

Mundee Mines Ltd. (B.C. Aug. 21, 1969)
June 26, 1992 – Name changed to AGM Capital Corp.; basis 1 new for 3 old shs. ■

Mundoro Mining Inc. (Yuk. Jan. 10, 1997)
June 14, 2005 – Continued into British Columbia.
Apr. 22, 2008 – Succeeded by Mundoro Capital Inc. following reorganization whereby Mundoro Mining became a subsidiary of newly incorporated Mundoro Capital Inc. (see FPsurvey - Mines & Energy)

Municipal Bankers Corporation (Ont. July 3, 1974)
Nov. 1, 2000 – Amalgamated with Newco Bancorp Inc. and Mountbirch Limited to form Newco Bancorp Inc.; basis 55¢ plus 0.8 Newco Bancorp shs. for 1 Municipal Bankers sh. (see Newco Bancorp Inc.)

Municipal Financial Corporation (Ont. July 3, 1974)
Sept. 27, 1996 – Name changed to MFC Incorporated. ■

The Municipal Savings & Loan Corporation (Ont. 1987)
Sept. 23, 1996 – All o/s 9 3/4% cum. redeem. 1st pref. shs., ser. A redeemed as of; basis $10 per sh. plus all accrued and unpaid dividends calculated up to the redemption date.

Municipal Solutions Group Inc. (B.C. Feb. 3, 1988)
July 21, 2008 – Name changed to CloudBench Applications, Inc. ■

Municipal Ticket Corporation (Ont. Sept. 24, 1937)
Nov. 18, 1994 – Name changed to I.D. Investments Inc.; basis 1 new for 4 old shs. ■

Munro Copper Mines Ltd. (Ont. 1953)
1968 – Placed into receivership.
Apr. 1969 – Holders of 7% 1st mtge. bonds, ser. B, received $14.82 per $1,000 bond.

Munro-Croesus Mines Ltd. (Ont. 1931)
May 25, 1964 – Charter cancelled.

Muntz Canada Limited (Can. 1966)
June 1977 – Declared bankrupt. No distribution made to pref. or unsecured creditors.

Murbell Gold Mines Ltd. (Ont. 1944)
Jan. 6, 1958 – Charter cancelled.

Murex Clinical Technologies Corporation (B.C. Oct. 31, 1983)
Dec. 11, 1990 – Name changed to International Murex Technologies Corporation; basis 1 new for 7 old shs. ■

Murgold Resources Inc. (B.C. 1980)
Feb. 1, 1991 – Name changed to Arimathaea Resources Inc.; basis 1 new for 10 old shs. ■

Murgor Explorations Limited (Ont. May 22, 1969)
Apr. 22, 1976 – Name changed to Advance Murgor Explorations Limited; basis 1 new for 5 old shs. ■

Murgor Resources Inc. (Ont. May 22, 1969)
Sept. 22, 1989 – Continued into Canada. (see Alexandria Minerals Corporation)
Mar. 13, 2015 – Acquired by Alexandria Minerals Corporation; basis 0.5 Alexandria com. shs. for 1 Murgor com. sh. (see Alexandria Minerals Corporation)

Murky Fault Metal Mines Ltd. (Ont. 1956)
Aug. 1971 – Assets sold to Indian Mountain Metal Mines Ltd.

Murmac Lake Athabaska Mines Ltd. (Ont. 1935)
Mar. 1976 – Charter cancelled.

Murmont Mining & Exploration Ltd. (Ont. 1962)
Mar. 1967 – Charter cancelled.

Murphy Mines Ltd. (Can. Oct. 15, 1927)
1941 – Acquired by Queenston Gold Mines Ltd.; basis 13.5 new for 100 old shs. (see Queenston Gold Mines Ltd.)

Murphy Oil Company Ltd. (Can. 1960)
Oct. 6, 1987 – Acquired by U.S. parent co. Murphy Oil Corporation. At their option, holders received either C$32 or shs. of Murphy Oil Corporation, based on the average closing price of such shs. and conversion of the $32 to US funds.

Murphy Paint Co. Ltd. (Can. 1908)
1952 – Acquired by Canadian Pittsburgh Industries Ltd., a subsid. of Pittsburgh Plate Glass Co. Ltd., for $32 per sh.

Murray Algoma Mines Limited (Ont. 1938)
1956 – Charter cancelled.

Murray and Donald Davis, Ltd. (Ont. 1953)
Assets taken over by Crest Theatre Foundation, a charitable organization.

Murray Anderson Ltd. (unknown)
1968 – Acquired by Bartaco Industries Limited. (see Bartaco Industries Limited)

Murray Consolidated Mines Ltd. (Can. 1924)
Feb. 6, 1934 – Name changed to Manco Gold Mines Ltd. ■

Murray Mining Corp. Ltd. (Que. 1957)
1964 – Acquired by Asbestos Corporation, Ltd.; basis 1 new for 16 old shs.

Murray River Power & Pulp Co. Ltd. (Que. Mar. 30, 1920; via letters patent)
1921 – Name changed to Donohue Brothers Limited. ■

Murray Watts Explorations Ltd. (Ont. 1968)
Dec. 30, 1977 – Amalgamated with Assembly Mines Limited.

Murrit Business Machines Limited (Ont. 1958)
Dec. 21, 1970 – Name changed to Murritt Photofax Limited. ■

Murritt Photofax Limited (Ont. 1958)
1974 – Substantially all assets sold to Nashua Murritt Ltd., wholly owned subsid. of Nashua Corp. of Nashua, N.H.; basis 0.06 of 1 new for 1 old sh.

Murto Red Lake Mines Ltd. (Ont. 1945)
Apr. 1, 1957 – Charter cancelled.

Murwell Resources Ltd. (Alta. Dec. 29, 1983)
Feb. 2, 1996 – All o/s com. shs. acquired by Icon Energy Limited; basis 2 com. Icon shs. for 1 old Murwell sh. (see Icon Energy Limited)

Muscocho Explorations Ltd. (Que. Dec. 12, 1962)
Sept. 30, 1996 – Name changed to Golden Goose Resources Inc. following amalgamation of McNellen Resources, Inc. (1 for 22.75) and Flanagan McAdam Resources Inc. (1 for 18.4) with wholly owned 1120073 Ontario Inc.; basis 1 new for 4 old shs. ■

Musgrove Minerals Corp. (B.C. Mar. 29, 2000)
July 28, 2016 – Formed RewardStream Solutions Inc. in British Columbia on amalgamation with (old) RewardStream Solutions Inc.; basis 1 new for 2 old shs. ■

Music Fair Limited (Ont. 1957)
Dec. 3, 1962 – Went into bankruptcy in 1959 and assets sold. No distribution avail. for sh. or deb. holders. Charter cancelled.

Musicrypt Inc. (Ont. July 28, 1999)
July 18, 2007 – Name changed to YANGAROO Inc. (see FPsurvey - Industrials)

Musk Metals Corp. (B.C. Feb. 18, 2015)
June 10, 2025 – Name changed to Germanium Mining Corp.; basis 1 new for 8 old shs. (see FPsurvey - Mines & Energy)

Musketeer Mines Ltd. (B.C. 1939)
1965 – Struck off register.

Muskox Minerals Corp. (Alta. Aug. 16, 1996)
Mar. 30, 2005 – Name changed to Prize Mining Corporation; basis 1 new for 5 old shs. ■

Muskox Mines Ltd. (Ont. 1968)
Dec. 20, 1978 – Dissolved.

Muskrat Minerals Incorporated (Alta. Oct. 4, 2000)
Dec. 16, 2015 – Name changed to Metalo Manufacturing Inc. (see FPsurvey - Mines & Energy)

Mussens Canada Ltd. (Can. 1942)
Aug. 1963 – Name changed to Mussens Limited. ■

Mussens Limited (Can. 1942)
Aug. 15, 1969 – Name changed to MSN Industries Ltd. ■

Mustang Exploration Co. Ltd. (B.C. 1964)
1969 – Name changed to Topper Mining Co. Ltd. ■

Mustang Gold Corp. (Ont. July 15, 1997 amalg.)
Mar. 10, 1999 – Name changed to Mustang Minerals Corp.; basis 1 new for 3 old shs. ■

Mustang Minerals Corp. (Ont. July 15, 1997 amalg.)
June 8, 2018 – Name changed to Grid Metals Corp. (see FPsurvey - Mines & Energy)

Mustang Mines Ltd. (Que. 1967)
Apr. 5, 1974 – Amalgamated with Panacan Resources Ltd. to form Panacan Minerals & Oils Ltd.; basis 1 new for 3 old shs.

Mustang Petroleum Ltd. (Alta.)
1958 – Struck off register.

Mustang Resources Inc. (B.C. Jan. 18, 1983)
Dec. 4, 1991 – Name changed to Fairlane Transportation Inc.; basis 1 new for 3 old shs. ■

Mustang Resources Inc. (Alta. Mar. 13, 2002)
July 12, 2005 – Plan of Arrangement combination with Thunder Energy Inc. and Forte Resources Inc. to create a new trust named Thunder Energy Trust plus 3 new explorations cos. - Alberta Clipper Energy Inc., Ember Resources Inc. and Valiant Energy Inc.; basis 0.55 new trust unit, or 0.55 new exch. sh., or a combination thereof, plus 0.3666 new Alberta Clipper com. sh., plus 0.0833 new Ember com. sh. for 1 old Mustang com. sh. (see Alberta Clipper Energy Inc.; Ember Resources Inc.; Thunder Energy Trust)

MustGrow Biologics Corp. (B.C. Dec. 2, 2014)
Aug. 18, 2018 – Continued into Saskatchewan. (see FPsurvey - Industrials)

Musto Explorations Limited (Ont. Jan. 4, 1972)
Mar. 7, 1979 – Continued into British Columbia.
Oct. 21, 1991 – Name changed to International Musto Explorations Limited; basis 1 new for 20 old shs. ■

Mutapa Copper & Cobalt Inc. (B.C. Sept. 9, 1996)
July 4, 2003 – Name changed to Springbank Ventures Inc.; basis 1 new for 4 old shs. ■

Mutapa Gold Corporation (B.C. Sept. 9, 1996)
Dec. 8, 1998 – Name changed to Mutapa Copper & Cobalt Inc. ■

Mutec Equities Ltd. (Can. 1976)
May 2, 1997 – Amalgamated with Genterra Capital Corporation and First Corporate Capital Inc. to form a new co. also known as Genterra Capital; basis 4.677 new cl. A shs. for 1 com. sh. (see Genterra Capital Corporation)

Mutual Holdings Ltd. (unknown)
Taken over by Madison Oils Limited. (see Madison Oils Limited)

The Mutual Life Assurance Company of Canada (Can. 1878)
July 21, 1999 – Name changed to Clarica Life Insurance Company following conversion from a policyholder co. into a publicly listed co. ■

Mutual Mines & Metals Ltd. (Alta. 1956)
Dec. 15, 1961 – Struck off register.

Mutual Oil Co. Ltd. (Alta. 1949)
1960 – Purchased by Flag Oils Ltd.; basis 1 new for 5 old shs.

Mutual Resources Limited (B.C. Mar. 23, 1979)
Oct. 17, 1995 – Acquired by Golden Knight Resources Inc.; basis 1 Golden Knight sh. plus 1 wt. for 6.4 Mutual shs. (see Golden Knight Resources Inc.)

Mux Lab Inc. (Can. Aug. 1, 1988 amalg.)
Apr. 1990 – Filed for bankruptcy. Samson, Belair, Deloitte Touche of Montreal appointed trustee. (see National Hav-Info Communications Inc.)
Nov. 23, 1990 – Amalgamated with 174876 Canada Ltd., a wholly owned subsid. of National Hav-Info Communications Inc.; basis 1 National Hav-Info sh. for 5 Mux Lab shs. (see National Hav-Info Communications Inc.)

My Marijuana Canada Inc. (B.C. June 11, 2014)
Feb. 24, 2016 – Name changed to MYM Nutraceuticals Inc. ■

My-Ritt Red Lake Gold Mines Limited (Ont. Dec. 8, 1945)
May 31, 2002 – Name changed to Metalcoat International Corp. following reverse takeover acquisition of Metalcoat Powder Corp.; basis 1 new for 10 old shs. ■

My Student Rewards Inc. (B.C. Jan. 13, 2010)
Sept. 17, 2013 – Name changed to Victory Square Games Inc. ■

My Venture Inc. (B.C. June 7, 1999)
July 21, 2003 – Name changed to Avantec Technologies Inc. following Qualifying Transaction acquisition of Raytec Technologies, Inc.; basis 4 new for 1 old sh. ■

Myconic Capital Corp. (B.C. Mar. 24, 2017)
June 1, 2021 – Name changed to KetamineOne Capital Limited following the transition from an investment issuer to a single-purpose company focused on holding interests in clinics and research operations for the nutraceutical, cannabis and psychedelic industries. ■

Mylake Mines Ltd. (Ont. 1937)
Nov. 7, 1978 – Dissolved.

Mylamaque Gold Mines Ltd. (Ont. 1936)
1943 – Name changed to Mylamaque Mines Ltd.; basis 1 new for 5 old shs. ■

Mylamaque Mines Ltd. (Ont. Sept. 2, 1943)
1953 – Name changed to New Mylamaque Explorations Ltd.; basis 1 new for 4 old shs. ■

Mylan Ventures Ltd. (B.C. Feb. 1, 1972)
Sept. 10, 1996 – Continued into Wyoming.

Mymar Mining & Reduction Ltd. (Ont. Sept. 2, 1943)
Aug. 8, 1977 – Amalgamated with Dynasearch Exploration Ltd. to form Dynamar Energy Limited.

Myra Falls Mines Ltd. (B.C. 1963)
Jan. 13, 1972 – Dissolved. In 1971, assets merged with those of parent, Western Mines Ltd.

Myriad Metals Corp. (B.C. Oct. 5, 2018)
Dec. 12, 2022 – Name changed to Myriad Uranium Corp. (see FPsurvey - Mines & Energy)

Mystery Lake Mines Ltd. (Ont. 1945)
Dec. 1966 – Charter cancelled.

Mystery Mountain Minerals Ltd. (B.C. July 7, 1983)
Mar. 4, 1991 – Delisted from the Vancouver Stock Exchange. Subsequently dissolved for failure to file.

Mystique Energy, Inc. (Alta. Aug. 31, 1993)
May 18, 2011 – Name changed to Bella Resources Inc.; basis 1 new for 10 old shs. ■

Mytec Technologies Inc. (Can. June 25, 1987)
May 1, 2001 – Name changed to Bioscrypt Inc. ■

Myteque Mines Ltd. (Ont. 1956)
Nov. 1973 – Charter cancelled.

Mytolon Chemicals Inc. (Ont. 1965)
1972 – Merged with private co. to form Elkins Productions of Canada Ltd. Each 25 com. shs. of co. and warrants to purch. 25 com. shs. of co. exch. for 1 com. sh. of Elkins. Each $10 princ. amt. of 7% conv. debs. of co. exch. for 1 special sh. and one com. sh. of Elkins.

N

N. Bawlf Grain Company, Ltd. (Can. 1928)
Dec. 30, 1940 – All assets acquired by Alberta Pacific Grain Co. Ltd. for $1,000,000. Distribution of $50 per sh. made to pref. shldrs. No distribution made to com. shldrs.
Dec. 1941 – Charter surrendered.

N-Tone International Ltd. (B.C. 1983)
Aug. 14, 1986 – Continued into Canada.
Oct. 19, 1999 – Dissolved and struck from register.

NA-Churs International Ltd. (Ont. 1963)
May 2, 1978 – Na-Churs Holdings Inc., completed purch. of all the assets of the co.
May 5, 1978 – Distribution of $7.90 per sh.
Nov. 10, 1978 – Final distribution of 60¢ per com. sh. paid. Of the total $8.50 per sh. distribution, $8.077 per sh. deemed divd. and 42.3¢ per sh. considered proceeds of disposition on dissolution of co. Following final distribution, co. filed Articles of Dissolution.

NAL Energy Corporation (Alta. Nov. 1, 2010)
June 6, 2012 – Acquired by Pengrowth Energy Corporation; basis 0.86 Pengrowth shs. for 1 NAL Energy sh. (see Pengrowth Energy Corporation)

NAL Oil & Gas Trust (Alta. Mar. 8, 1996)
Dec. 31, 2010 – Succeeded by NAL Energy Corporation pursuant to plan of arrangement whereby NAL Energy Corporation was formed to facilitate the conversion of the trust into a corporation and the trust was subsequently dissolved. ■

NAL Petroleum (BEL) Ltd. (Alta. Dec. 11, 2009 amalg.)
Dec. 31, 2009 – Formed NAL Petroleum (ACE) Ltd. in Alberta on amalgamation with NAL Petroleum (ACE) Ltd., a wholly owned subsid. of NAL Oil & Gas Trust. (see NAL Oil & Gas Trust)

NAME Inc. (Ont. Oct. 18, 1993)
June 12, 2001 – Acquired by itemus inc.; basis 0.9155 new itemus com. shs. for 1 old NAME com. sh. (see itemus inc.)

NAP Enterprises Inc. (Ont. Aug. 23, 1928)
Mar. 30, 1989 – Name changed to HTTL Enterprises Inc. ■

NAP Quebec Mines Ltd. (Can. Mar. 6, 2006)
Apr. 15, 2013 – Name changed to Aurbec Mines Inc. (see North American Palladium Ltd.)

NAPEC Inc. (Can. Apr. 20, 2005 amalg.)
Feb. 16, 2018 – Acquired by Oaktree Capital Management, L.P. through 9370-0219 Quebec Inc.; basis $1.95 cash per sh.
Feb. 16, 2018 – Formed Thirau Inc. in Canada following amalgamation with wholly owned Thirau Inc.

NAR Resources Ltd. (Ont. Mar. 10, 1994 amalg.)
July 24, 2001 – Formed Titanium Corporation Inc. in Ontario on amalgamation with Titanium Corporation of Canada Limited, constituting a reverse takeover by Titanium. ■

NAV Energy Trust (Alta. Sept. 25, 2003)
Aug. 15, 2006 – Name changed to Sound Energy Trust following amalgamation with Clear Energy Inc. and spin-out of a new company named Sure Energy Inc.; basis 1 Sound trust unit, 0.3333 Sure sh. and 0.085 Sure wt. for 1 NAV trust unit and either 0.5 Sound trust unit or 0.5 Clear exch. sh. for 1 Clear sh. plus 0.1667 Sure sh. and 0.0425 Sure wt. for 1 Clear sh. ■

NAV Master Technologies Inc. (B.C. 1984)
Feb. 23, 1994 – Name changed to Starpoint Systems Inc.; basis 1 new for 5 old shs. ■

N. B. Cook Corporation Ltd. (B.C. Dec. 15, 1966)
May 7, 1993 – Dissolved and struck off register.

NB Split Corp. (Ont. Dec. 15, 2006)
Feb. 16, 2012 – All o/s cl. A cap. and pref. shs. redeemed for $32.72 per 2 cl. A cap. shs. and $32.72 plus $0.3288 divd. per cl. A pref. sh.

NBD Bank, Canada (Can. 1981)
Mar. 28, 1996 – Name changed to First Chicago NBD Bank, Canada.

NBS Capital Inc. (Can. Mar. 1, 2018)
Apr. 29, 2021 – Name changed to Nevada Silver Corporation pursuant to the Qualifying Transaction reverse takeover acquisition of Electric Metals (USA) Limited; basis 0.73271 new for 1 old sh. ■

NBS Technologies Inc. (Can. 1983)
June 14, 2000 – Continued into Ontario.
Nov. 1, 2000 – Name changed to MIST Inc. ■

NBS Technologies Inc. (Ont. June 14, 2000)
Dec. 28, 2006 – Amalgamated with wholly owned subsid. of Brookfield Asset Management Inc.; basis 1 new pfd. sh. which was immediately redeemed for $1.00 for 1 old NBS sh. (see Brookfield Asset Management Inc.)

NBU Mines Limited (N.B. 1955)
July 19, 1985 – Amalgamated with Dominion Explorers Limited (1 for 1) and Tex-Sol Explorations Limited (1 for 2.5) to continue as Dominion Explorers Inc.; basis 1 new for 0.9 old shs.

NCA Minerals Corp. (B.C. 1959)
June 30, 1995 – Dissolved and struck off register.

NCC Mining Corporation (B.C. Sept. 22, 1983)
July 11, 1997 – Name changed to BMA Mining Corporation; basis 1 new for 7 old shs. ■

NCE Diversified Income Trust (Ont. Jan. 17, 1997)
Mar. 1, 2001 – Name changed to Sentry Select Diversified Income Trust. ■

NCE Energy Trust (Ont. Nov. 5, 1996)
June 5, 2002 – Amalgamated with NCE Petrofund; basis 0.2325 NCE Petrofund trust units for 1 NCE Energy trust unit. (see NCE Petrofund)

NCE Petrofund (Ont. Dec. 16, 1988)
Nov. 3, 2003 – Name changed to Petrofund Energy Trust. ■

NCE Petrofund I (Ont. Dec. 16, 1988)
July 4, 1996 – Name changed to NCE Petrofund. ■

NCE Strategic Energy Fund (Ont. Feb. 14, 2002)
Feb. 14, 2003 – Name changed to Strategic Energy Fund. ■

NCN Exploration & Development Corp. (B.C. 1983)
Jan. 5, 1990 – Dissolved.

NDT Energy Ltd. (B.C. Sept. 11, 1986)
May 25, 2006 – Continued into Alberta.
June 23, 2006 – Name changed to Pegasus Oil & Gas Inc. pursuant to acquisition of Pegasus Oil & Gas Inc. (subsequently renamed Pegasus Resources Ltd. and amalgamated). NDT com. shs. were redesignated cl. A shs. and consolidated on a 1-for-2.8693321 basis. New cl. B shs. were created. Pegasus shldrs. received 20 NDT cl. A shs. for each cl. A sh. held following which the NDT cl. A shs. were again consolidated on a 1-for-20 basis. ■

NDT Ventures Ltd. (B.C. Sept. 11, 1986)
Jan. 11, 2006 – Name changed to NDT Energy Ltd. following reorganization from a metals exploration to an oil and gas exploration co. and formation of New Dimension Resources Ltd. spun off to shldrs. on a 1-for-5 basis; basis 1 new for 20 old shs. ■

NDU Resources Ltd. (B.C. Dec. 2, 1986)
Mar. 20, 1998 – Acquired by United Keno Hill Mines Limited; basis 1.35 United Keno shs. for 1 NDU sh.

NDX Growth & Income Fund (Ont. Nov. 28, 2013)
Nov. 21, 2019 – Merged into Mulvihill Premium Yield Fund. basis 0.812727 Mulvihill cl. F units for 1 NDX Growth cl. A unit and 1.143674 Mulvihill cl. F units for 1 NDX Growth cl. U unit.

NEBEX Resources Ltd. (Alta. June 2, 1987)
Dec. 1, 1999 – Struck off register.

NEMI Northern Energy & Mining Inc. (Alta. Oct. 21, 1987)
Apr. 15, 2010 – Continued into British Columbia.
Aug. 17, 2016 – Privatized via 1-for-400,000 sh. consolidation; fractional shldrs. received 71¢ cash per pre-consolidated sh. and fractional shs. subsequently cancelled.
Sept. 28, 2017 – Continued into Nevada.

NEO Battery Materials Ltd. (B.C. Feb. 10, 2006)
Mar. 23, 2023 – Continued into Ontario. (see FPsurvey - Industrials)

NETFORFUN.COM Inc. (Ont. Apr. 28, 1966)
Sept. 20, 2004 – Certificate of incorporation cancelled and dissolved.

NETI Technologies Inc. (B.C. 1983)
July 9, 1993 – Dissolved and struck off register.

N.E.W. Total Group Inc. (Can. June 3, 1977)
Mar. 8, 1995 – Name changed to Global (GMPC) Holdings Inc. ■

NEXUS Group International Inc. (Que. Aug. 9, 1949)
July 20, 2016 – Struck from registry and dissolved.

NFX Gold Inc. (Ont. July 19, 1996)
Sept. 16, 2008 – Name changed to Bear Lake Gold Ltd. pursuant to reverse takeover acquisition of Maximus Ventures Ltd. ■

N.G. Valiquette Limited (Can. Jan. 4, 1905)
Apr. 24, 1964 – Name changed to N. G. Valiquette Limited. ■

N. G. Valiquette Limited (Can. Jan. 4, 1905)
Jan. 8, 2003 – Dissolved.

NGAS Resources, Inc. (B.C. Jan. 31, 1979)
Apr. 14, 2011 – Acquired by Magnum Hunter Resources Corporation; basis 0.0846 Magnum Hunter shs. for 1 NGAS sh.

NGEx Resources Inc. (Can. Aug. 20, 2004)
July 17, 2019 – Name changed to Josemaria Resources Inc. ■

NGX Energy International Corp. (B.C. June 5, 2017)
Nov. 16, 2020 – Name changed to NG Energy International Corp. (see FPsurvey - Mines & Energy)

NHC Communications Inc. (Can. Aug. 13, 1993)
May 18, 2012 – Dissolved.

NHI Nelson Holdings International Ltd. (Can. Sept. 18, 1987)
June 29, 1993 – Continued into Ontario.
July 21, 1994 – Name changed to JPY Holdings Ltd.; basis 1 new for 5 old shs. ∎

NHP Natural Health Ltd. (Alta. Nov. 4, 1993)
Apr. 22, 1999 – Name changed to Whats-Online.Com Inc. ∎

NHS Industries Ltd. (B.C. May 4, 2001)
Aug. 13, 2014 – Amalgamated in British Columbia to continue with same name.
July 27, 2021 – Name changed to Feel Foods Ltd. ∎

NII Norsat International Inc. (B.C. Oct. 15, 1982)
July 8, 1999 – Name changed to Norsat International Inc. ∎

NIM Petroleum Corp. (B.C. 1976)
Sept. 1, 1992 – Continued into Canada.
Sept. 28, 1992 – Name changed to Petrorep Resources Ltd. ∎

NIR Diagnostics Inc. (Ont. Apr. 27, 1978)
Oct. 20, 2008 – Placed into receivership. Deloitte & Touche Inc. appointed receiver.

NLX Resources Inc. (Ont. 1945)
Feb. 14, 1994 – Charter cancelled and co. dissolved.

NMC Resource Corporation (B.C. Feb. 26, 2010)
Feb. 15, 2015 – Privatized by Dong Won Corporation at 20¢ per share.

NOVA, AN ALBERTA CORPORATION (Alta. 1954)
Sept. 1, 1987 – Name changed to NOVA Corporation of Alberta. ∎

NOVA Chemicals Corporation (Alta. Apr. 8, 1954; via Special Act of Legislature)
Apr. 14, 2004 – Continued into Canada.
July 6, 2009 – Continued into New Brunswick.
July 8, 2009 – Acquired by International Petroleum Investment Company, wholly owned by the Government of the Emirate of Abu Dhabi, for US$6.00 per sh.

NOVA Corporation (Alta. Apr. 8, 1954; via Special Act of Legislature)
Jan. 7, 1999 – Name changed to NOVA Chemicals Corporation. ∎

NOVA Corporation (Alta. 1954)
July 2, 1998 – Following Plan of Arrangement with TransCanada PipeLines Limited, a new NOVA Corporation was spun off; basis 0.52 of a TransCanada com. sh. and 0.104 of a New NOVA com. sh. for 1 com. of Old NOVA; 0.5 of a TransCanada ser. S pref. sh. for 1 old cum. redeem. first pref. sh.

NOVA Corporation of Alberta (Alta. 1954)
May 11, 1994 – Name changed to NOVA Corporation pursuant to plan of arrangement whereby operations were separated into four new subsids. wholly owned by NOVA Corporation. ∎

NOVA Gas Transmission Ltd. (Alta. Apr. 8, 1954)
Apr. 1, 2024 – Name changed to NGTL Limited Partnership.

NPN Investment Group Inc. (Ont. Apr. 26, 2004)
Dec. 5, 2007 – Name changed to Alix Resources Corp. and continued into British Columbia. ∎

NPS Allelix Inc. (N.S. Nov. 12, 1999)
July 4, 2003 – Called for redemption; basis 1 new Newco com. sh. (business combination of NPS Pharmaceuticals Inc. and Enzon Pharmaceuticals, Inc.) for 1 old NPS exchangeable sh.

NQ Exploration Inc. (Can. Oct. 24, 2007)
May 15, 2018 – Name changed to AM Resources Corp.; basis 1 new for 50 old shs. (see FPsurvey - Mines & Energy)

NQL Drilling Tools Inc. (B.C. Apr. 28, 1986)
Mar. 29, 1995 – Continued into Alberta.
July 11, 2005 – Name changed to NQL Energy Services Inc. ∎

NQL Energy Services Inc. (Alta. Mar. 29, 1995)
Jan. 17, 2007 – Acquired by Dreco Acquisition Corporation, a wholly owned subsid. of National Oilwell Varco, Inc., for $7.60 per sh.

NQN Mines Ltd. (Que. 1969)
June 6, 1981 – Charter cancelled.

NR2 Resources Corporation (Alta. Apr. 30, 2004)
June 29, 2006 – Formed Unitech Energy Resources Inc. in Alberta on Qualifying Transaction reverse takeover acquisition of and amalgamation with Unitech Energy Corp.; basis 0.2966111 new for 1 old sh. ∎

NRCI Northern Resource Capital Inc. (Alta. 1987)
Dec. 1, 1993 – Dissolved and struck off register.

NRD Mining Ltd. (B.C. June 26, 1972)
Feb. 25, 1987 – Name changed to Consolidated NRD Resources Ltd.; basis 1 new for 5 old shs. (see FPsurvey - Mines & Energy)

The NRG Group Inc. (Ont. Mar. 10, 2000 amalg.)
Aug. 23, 2003 – Name changed to Welton Energy Corporation following acquisition of Welton Energy Limited. ∎

NRG Investments Inc. (B.C. Apr. 28, 2006)
Mar. 4, 2008 – Name changed to Bucking Horse Energy Inc. following acquisition of Gemini Energy Corp. ∎

NRG Metals Inc. (B.C. Jan. 15, 2007)
Nov. 2, 2020 – Name changed to Lithium South Development Corporation. (see FPsurvey - Mines & Energy)

NRG Resources Inc. (Ont. 1971)
Mar. 14, 1978 – Charter cancelled.

NRG Resources Ltd. (B.C. Sept. 23, 1980)
Apr. 7, 1997 – Name changed to Vigor Resources Ltd.; basis 1 new for 3 old shs. ∎

NRI On-Line Inc. (Alta. July 27, 1994)
Apr. 28, 1999 – Acquired by Geophysical Micro Computer Applications (International) Ltd.; basis 1 Geophyscial sh. for 6 NRI shs. (see Geophysical Micro Computer Applications (International) Ltd.)

NRT Industries Inc. (Ont. Apr. 9, 1973)
Mar. 4, 1991 – Name changed to Cuda Consolidated Inc.; basis 1 new for 15 old shs. ∎

NRT Research Technologies Inc. (Ont. Apr. 9, 1973)
Jan. 20, 1988 – Name changed to NRT Industries Inc.; basis 1 new for 15 old shs. ∎

NS Power Holdings Incorporated (N.S. July 23, 1998)
July 10, 2000 – Name changed to Emera Incorporated. (see FPsurvey - Mines & Energy; FPsurvey - Industrials)

NSGold Corporation (B.C. June 25, 2008)
Mar. 2, 2022 – Amalgamated with 13611647 Canada Inc., a wholly owned subsid. of Atlantic Mining NS Inc.; basis 40¢ cash per sh.

NSI Communications Inc. (Can. Jan. 18, 1996)
Aug. 31, 2001 – Name changed to NSI Global Inc. ∎

NSI Global Inc. (Can. Jan. 18, 1996)
Feb. 9, 2006 – Dissolved.

NSI Marketing Limited (Can. 1959)
Mar. 20, 1978 – Reorganized; creditors pd. 20¢ on the dollar and all o/s com. shs. exch. for 1st pfce shs. on a sh.-for-sh. basis. All iss. and o/s 1st pfce. shs. called for redemption at 15¢ per sh., Dec. 29, 1978.

NSI Strategic Investments Ltd. (B.C. June 17, 1993)
Dec. 22, 2016 – Voluntarily dissolved; basis $0.076 cash per com. sh. payable to shldrs. of record Dec. 8, 2016.

NSP Pharma Corp. (Can. July 3, 2003)
Dec. 19, 2008 – Dissolved and struck from register.

NSR Resources Inc. (Que. Mar. 6, 1937)
Nov. 28, 2019 – All o/s shs. not already held acquired by Tintina Mines Limited; basis 0.729756389 Tintina Mines shs. 1 NSR Resources sh.

NSS Resources Inc. (B.C. Mar. 28, 2012)
Oct. 24, 2017 – Name changed to Upco International Inc. following reverse takeover acquisition of Upco Systems Inc. ∎

NSX Silver Inc. (Can. Aug. 9, 2011)
Sept. 12, 2018 – Name changed to ViveRe Communities Inc. ∎

NT Network Systems Inc. (B.C. Sept. 23, 1991)
Jan. 12, 1996 – Name changed to Network Telemetrics Ltd.; basis 1 new for 5 old shs. ∎

NTC Capital Corporation (B.C. Apr. 7, 1986)
Mar. 1, 1994 – Name changed to Sungold Gaming Inc. ∎

NTG Clarity Networks Inc. (Alta. June 19, 2000)
Mar. 19, 2024 – Continued into Ontario. (see FPsurvey - Industrials)

NTI Newmerical Inc. (Alta. July 29, 1999)
Dec. 18, 2009 – Privatize at 4¢ per sh.

NTI Resources Limited (Bermuda Nov. 18, 1994)
Sept. 2, 1997 – Continued into Alberta.
Oct. 5, 1999 – Struck from registry and dissolved.

NTS Computer Systems Ltd. (B.C. Apr. 21, 1988)
June 21, 2001 – Name changed to Brainium Technologies Inc. ∎

NUCRYST Pharmaceuticals Corp. (Alta. Dec. 18, 1997)
Feb. 10, 2010 – Acquired by 1499642 Alberta Ltd., a wholly owned subsid. of Westaim Corporation; basis US$1.77 for 1 NUCRYST com. sh.

NUVO Network Management Inc. (Alta. July 6, 1954)
Feb. 26, 2008 – Acquired by Versata Enterprises, Inc. for 57¢ per sh.

NW Financial Corporation Ltd. (B.C. 1969)
Dec. 23, 1974 – Name changed to Newco Financial Corporation; basis 1 new for 10 old shs. ∎

NW Growth Investments Ltd. (B.C. May 31, 1969)
Mar. 24, 1983 – Name changed to Citco Growth Investments Ltd. ∎

NWE Capital Corp. (Ont. 1974)
Dec. 24, 1992 – Name changed to Petersburg Long Distance Inc. ∎

NWL Financial Corporation Ltd. (B.C. 1969)
May 11, 1972 – Name changed to NW Financial Corporation Ltd. ∎

NWM Mining Corporation (Ont. Mar. 7, 1949)
Oct. 5, 2015 – Acquired by GFM Minería, S.A.P.I. de C.V for $0.005 per sh..

N.W.P. Developments Ltd. (B.C. 1962)
Nov. 10, 1980 – Name changed to N.W.P. Resources Ltd.; basis 1 new for 6 old shs. ∎

N.W.P. Resources Ltd. (B.C. 1962)
Aug. 30, 1984 – Amalgamated with Grove Explorations Ltd. (0.3333 for 1) and Rosmac Resources Ltd. (0.3 for 1) to continue with the name Golden North Resource Corporation; basis 0.3667 new for 1 old sh. (see Golden North Resource Corporation)

N.W.T. Gold Ltd. (Alta. 1938)
1969 – Charter cancelled.

NWT Uranium Corp. (Ont. Sept. 26, 2003)
June 2, 2017 – Name changed to Captor Capital Corp. (see FPsurvey - Industrials)

NWest Energy Corp. (Can. Mar. 7, 2008)
Dec. 30, 2016 – Name changed to Ceylon Graphite Corp. following reverse takeover acquisition of Plumbago Refining Corp. B.V. (see FPsurvey - Mines & Energy)

NWest Energy Inc. (Can. Mar. 7, 2008)
Nov. 4, 2010 – Name changed to NWest Energy Corp.; basis 1 new for 10 old shs. ■

NX Capital Corp. (Alta. Sept. 11, 1998)
July 31, 2007 – Name changed to Newton Energy Corporation following reverse takeover acquisition of Newton Energy Inc.; basis 1 new for 20 old shs. ■

NX Phase Capital Inc. (Can. July 19, 2000)
June 20, 2025 – Dissolved for non-compliance.

NXA Inc. (Ont. Apr. 1, 1996 amalg.)
Nov. 4, 2015 – Name changed to Ellipsiz Communications Ltd. following reverse takeover acquisition of (old) Ellipsiz Communications Ltd.; basis 1 new for 10 old shs. (see FPsurvey - Industrials)

NY85 Capital Inc. (B.C. Oct. 22, 2010)
Oct. 16, 2012 – Name changed to Alchemist Mining Inc. following Qualifying Transaction acquisition of option on West Timmins gold prospect. ■

NYX Gaming Group Limited (Guernsey Mar. 19, 2010)
Jan. 10, 2018 – Acquired by Scientific Games Corporation; basis Cdn$2.40 cash per sh.

Nabco Manganese Mining Co. Ltd. (Ont. 1940)
1943 – Acquired by Regent Mines and Minerals Ltd.; basis 3 new for 1 old sh. (see Regent Mines and Minerals Ltd.)

Nabis Holdings Inc. (B.C. May 29, 2019)
Jan. 14, 2022 – Name changed to Copland Road Capital Corporation. (see FPsurvey - Industrials)

Nabisco Brands Ltd (Can. 1929)
May 11, 1988 – Major shldr. Nabisco Brands Investments Ltd. purchased 3,955,000 of the 4,000,000 com. shs. that it did not already own for $45 per sh. and subsequently exercised its right to acquire the remainder.
Apr. 19, 1995 – Name changed to Nabisco Ltd.

Nabors Drilling Limited (Alta. 1952)
1977 – Acquired by Anglo Co. Ltd. for $18 per sh.

Nabors Exchangeco (Canada) Inc. (Can. Apr. 30, 2002)
Aug. 4, 2009 – All exch. shs. redeemed; basis 1 Nabors Industries Ltd. com. sh. for 1 Nabors Exchangeco exch. sh.

Nabors Industries Ltd. (Del. May 3, 1978)
June 25, 2002 – Continued into Bermuda.

Nabu Manufacturing Corporation (Can. 1981 amalg.)
Jan. 23, 1984 – Name changed to Computer Innovations Distribution Inc. ■

Nabu Network Corporation (Can. 1983)
Dec. 1986 – Placed into receivership; assets insufficient to repay primary lender. Charter cancelled.

Nacasa Ventures Inc. (B.C. Feb. 17, 1983)
Aug. 16, 1993 – Name changed to Molnar Capital Corporation pursuant to reverse takeover acquisition of the Molnar Group. ■

Naco Ltd. (Alta. 1950)
1955 – Name changed to Western Naco Petroleums Ltd.; basis 1 new for 4 old shs. ■

Nadira Mines Ltd. (B.C. 1955)
May 15, 1969 – Struck off register.

Nadoli Capital Inc. (Que. Sept. 1, 2004)
June 20, 2007 – Formed Komet Manufacturers Inc. in Quebec following Qualifying Transaction reverse takeover acquisition of and amalgamation with Komet Manufacturers Inc. ■

Nafta Trading Inc. (Alta. Nov. 3, 1995)
Sept. 23, 2003 – Name changed to AutoTradeCenter Canada Ltd. ■

Naftex Energy Corporation (Ont. Mar. 19, 1997 amalg.)
Sept. 16, 1998 – Continued into Yukon.
June 12, 2006 – Privatized by sole shldr. Norse Energy Corp. ASA following 1-for-3,366,222 share consolidation and $0.66 per fractional sh. held.
Dec. 28, 2011 – Dissolved.

Naganta Mining & Development Co. Ltd. (Que. 1963)
June 1, 1976 – Merged into Brominco Inc.; basis 1 new for 4 old shs., plus distribution of capital of 10¢ per old sh.

Nahanni Mines Limited (Ont. July 30, 1962)
Feb. 3, 1994 – Name changed to RG Properties Ltd. and continued into British Columbia; basis 1 restricted vtg. for 12.5 com. shs. ■

Nahatlatch Resources Ltd. (B.C. 1973)
Nov. 14, 1978 – Amalgamated with LMC Resources Ltd. to form Seadrift Resources Ltd.; basis 1 new for 3 old shs.

NaiKun Wind Energy Group Inc. (B.C. Dec. 31, 1957)
May 28, 2020 – Name changed to Oceanic Wind Energy Inc. (see FPsurvey - Mines & Energy; FPsurvey - Industrials)

Naina Capital Corp. (B.C. July 20, 2009)
May 17, 2011 – Name changed to Sierra Iron Ore Corporation pursuant to acquisition of the El Creston iron ore property.

The Nakhodas Mining Co. Ltd. (Ont. 1938)
Apr. 9, 1975 – Dissolved.

Nakina Mines Ltd. (Ont. 1967)
Aug. 1976 – Wound up.

Nakina Molybdenite Mines Ltd. (Ont. 1939)
1957 – Charter cancelled.

Nakusp Resources Ltd. (B.C. 1982)
Dec. 18, 1985 – Name changed to Western Canadian Land Corp. ■

Nalcap Holdings Inc. (Can. June 28, 1951; via letters patent)
Mar. 28, 1996 – Name changed to Arbatax International Inc.; basis 1.5 new for 1 old sh. ■

Nalcor Energy (N.L. Oct. 11, 2007)
Jan. 1, 2025 – Merged into Newfoundland and Labrador Hydro.

Nalcus Resources Ltd. (B.C. 1979)
Jan. 5, 1988 – Name changed to Trasco Wind-Force Technologies Inc. ■

Nalgar Nickel Mines Ltd. (Ont. 1956)
Sept. 1960 – Dissolved.

Nalos Mining Corporation (B.C. Mar. 28, 1980)
July 29, 1981 – Name changed to Nalos Resources Corporation. ■

Nalos Resources Corporation (B.C. Mar. 28, 1980)
Nov. 21, 1985 – Name changed to Salon Resources Corp.; basis 1 new for 2.4 old shs. ■

Nam Tai Electronics, Inc. (British Virgin Islands Aug. 1987)
Apr. 22, 2014 – Name changed to Nam Tai Property Inc.

Nama Creek Mines Ltd. (Ont. 1954)
1964 – Name changed to Big Nama Creek Mines Ltd.; basis 1 new for 4 old shs. ■

Namaste Technologies Inc. (B.C. Mar. 3, 2005)
Sept. 8, 2021 – Name changed to Lifeist Wellness Inc. (see FPsurvey - Industrials)

Name Brand Sales Inc. (Ont. Jan. 15, 1997)
Jan. 18, 2002 – Name changed to Tele-Find Technologies Corp. pursuant to amalgamation with wholly owned Tele-Find Technologies Corp. ■

Namex Explorations Inc. (Can. Nov. 4, 1988)
Dec. 6, 2019 – Name changed to Namex Ventures Inc. (see FPsurvey - Mines & Energy)

Namibia Rare Earths Inc. (Can. Apr. 26, 2010)
May 24, 2018 – Name changed to Namibia Critical Metals Inc. (see FPsurvey - Mines & Energy)

Namibian Minerals Corporation (Yuk. Sept. 8, 1993)
May 31, 2005 – Dissolved and struck off register.

Nanabajou Iron Mines Ltd. (Ont. 1951)
Charter cancelled.

Nanaimo-Duncan Utilities Limited (B.C. 1934)
July 31, 1945 – Placed into voluntary liquidation. Electrical properties servicing Duncan, Ladysmith, Nanaimo and district, B.C., expropriated by B.C. Power Commission and all revenue controlled since.
June 30, 1947 – Commission advanced $1,105,000 on account of purchase price, used by co. to redeem bonds, etc., and to redeem. pref. stk.
July 1950 – Final payment of $601,586 under award made available by Commission.

Nanaimo Gas Co. Ltd. (B.C.)
1959 – Struck off register.

Naneco Minerals Ltd. (Alta. Dec. 1, 1983)
Mar. 28, 2002 – Name changed to Southpoint Resources Ltd.; basis 1 new for 6 old shs. ■

Naneco Resources Ltd. (Ont. Feb. 6, 1969)
Dec. 1, 1983 – Continued into Alberta.
June 28, 1991 – Name changed to Naneco Minerals Ltd.; basis 1 new for 3 old shs. ■

Naneek Mines Ltd. (Ont. 1950)
Feb. 1954 – Name changed to Armour Uranium & Copper Mines, Ltd. ■

Nanika Resources Inc. (B.C. Apr. 4, 1997)
July 6, 2012 – Name changed to Goldbar Resources Inc.; basis 1 new for 10 old shs. (see FPsurvey - Mines & Energy)

Nano Capital Corp. (Alta. June 15, 2006)
Mar. 16, 2010 – Name changed to Z-Gold Exploration Inc. pursuant to Qualifying Transaction acquisition of mineral assets from 1527805 Ontario Inc. ■

Nanostruck Technologies Inc. (B.C. June 20, 2006)
Aug. 2, 2016 – Name changed to Fineqia International Inc. (see FPsurvey - Industrials)

Nanotec Canada Incorporated (Can. May 18, 1984)
1987 – Went out of business.

Nanotech Sciences Corp. (Ont. Apr. 27, 2007)
Dec. 14, 2009 – Private placement totaling 2,716,875 units with ForceLogix Technologies Inc. (formerly Courtland Capital Corp.) which constituted Qualifying Transaction. Co. will distribute the ForceLogix units to its shldrs. on a pro rata basis and wind up and dissolve.

Nanotech Security Corp. (B.C. May 4, 1984)
Oct. 6, 2021 – Acquired by Meta Minerals Inc.; basis $1.25 cash per sh.

Nanotek Inc. (B.C. Jan. 15, 1979)
Oct. 25, 2002 – Name changed to Minterra Resource Corp. ■

Nansen Yukon Mines Ltd. (Ont. 1947)
May 1957 – Charter cancelled.

Nanton Nickel Corp. (B.C. Sept. 7, 2011)
June 29, 2015 – Name changed to Eyecarrot Innovations Corp. ■

Napa Resources Incorporated (B.C. 1981)
Dec. 13, 1988 – Name changed to Zurfund International Limited. ■

Napier Environmental Technologies Inc. (B.C. Feb. 14, 1984)
Dec. 31, 2009 – Privatized by way of amalgamation with privately owned I.C.T.C. Holdings Corporation; basis 1¢ per sh.

Napier Explorations Inc. (B.C. Dec. 16, 1987)
Oct. 13, 1988 – Name changed to Brockton Resources Inc. ■

Napier International Technologies Inc. (B.C. Feb. 14, 1984)
Jan. 3, 2001 – Name changed to Napier Environmental Technologies Inc. ■

Napier Ventures Inc. (B.C. Mar. 6, 2007)
Mar. 25, 2024 – Struck from register and dissolved for failure to file.

Naples Capital Corp. (Can. Apr. 29, 2005)
Nov. 19, 2007 – Name changed to Takara Resources Inc. following Qualifying Transaction reverse takeover acquisition of Takara Resources (B.C.) Inc. ■

Napoleon Exploration Limited (B.C. Oct. 14, 1981)
June 28, 1993 – Name changed to Argentina Gold Corp. ■

Napoli Explorations Ltd. (B.C. 1967)
Feb. 1977 – Dissolved.

Nareco Gold Mines Ltd. (Ont. 1945)
1968 – Charter cancelled.

Narrow Lake Gold Mines Ltd. (Ont. 1945)
1952 – Charter cancelled.

Nartico Resources Ltd. (Ont. 1986)
Feb. 23, 1988 – Name changed to Privatel Inc. ■

Nasco Cobalt Silver Mines Limited (Ont. June 22, 1948)
Jan. 14, 1974 – Name changed to Frankfield Explorations Ltd. ■

Nasco Metal Mines Limited (Ont. June 22, 1948)
Mar. 1, 1951 – Name changed to Nasco Cobalt Silver Mines Limited. ■

Nash Yellowknife Gold Mines Ltd. (Ont. 1944)
Mar. 1957 – Charter cancelled.

Nashua Exploration & Mining Ltd. (Ont. 1956)
Apr. 9, 1975 – Charter cancelled.

Nass River Mines Ltd. (Ont. 1966)
Nov. 24, 1971 – Dissolved.

Nastek Explorations Ltd. (Ont. Nov. 7, 1996)
Sept. 3, 1999 – Name changed to Infolink Technologies Ltd. following acquisition of all o/s shs. of Infolink Communications Ltd. ■

Natalma Mines Limited (Can. Jan. 14, 1972)
Mar. 22, 1983 – Name changed to Tonka Resources Inc.; basis 10 new for 1 old sh. ■

Natan Resources Ltd. (B.C. Aug. 18, 2010)
Mar. 2, 2017 – Name changed to Enforcer Gold Corp. ■

Natcore Technology Inc. (B.C. Aug. 9, 2007)
Jan. 21, 2019 – Struck from registry and dissolved.

Nation Wide Resources Inc. (Alta. Mar. 5, 1997)
July 14, 2009 – Voluntarily wound up and liquidated.

National Access Cannabis Corp. (Alta. June 18, 2015)
Mar. 23, 2020 – Name changed to Meta Growth Corp. ■

National Automatic Vending Company Ltd. (Ont. 1949)
July 4, 1969 – Name changed to Navco Food Services Ltd. ■

National Bank of Detroit, Canada (Can. 1981)
May 14, 1990 – Name changed to NBD Bank, Canada. ■

National Biscuit & Confection Co. Ltd. (B.C. 1910)
1943 – Acquired by George Weston Ltd. for cash.

National Bowling Centres Ltd. (Que. 1961)
Apr. 9, 1965 – Declared bankrupt.

National Breweries Ltd. (Can. 1909)
1952 – Name changed to Dow Brewery Limited. ■

National Business Systems Inc. (Ont. 1974)
1983 – Continued into Canada.
Apr. 24, 1990 – Name changed to Consolidated NBS Inc.; basis 1 new for 10 old shs. ■

National Challenge Systems Inc. (B.C. Jan. 4, 1990)
Sept. 30, 2003 – Continued into Canada.
July 1, 2007 – Formed Organic Resource Management Inc. in Canada on amalgamation with wholly owned Organic Resource Management Inc. ■

National Computer Products Inc. (Alta. Jan. 25, 1996)
Oct. 14, 1998 – Formed Cambridge Colleges Ltd. following acquisition of all o/s cl. A shs. of Cambridge Colleges Inc. ■

National Construction Inc. (Ont. Aug. 15, 1995 amalg.)
Mar. 16, 2005 – Name changed to E.G. Capital Inc. ■

National Containers Ltd. (Que. 1946)
Sept. 23, 1969 – Acquired by Plant Industries Inc.; basis unknown.

National Drug and Chemical Company of Canada Limited (Can. 1905)
June 2, 1980 – Name changed to National Drug Limited. ■

National Drug Limited (Can. 1905)
Jan. 31, 1981 – Amalgamated with Nadruco Holdings Ltd., a wholly owned subsid. of Provigo Inc., to continue under National Drug Limited name. Shldrs. of co. received pref. shs. of new co. for their com. and pref. shs. on a sh.-for-sh. basis. The pref. shs. of new co. were then redeemed at $16 per sh., making National Drug Limited a wholly owned subsid. of Provigo Inc. (see Provigo Inc.)

National Explorations Ltd. (B.C. 1950)
1967 – Acquired by First National Uranium Mines Ltd.; basis 1 new for 6 old shs.

National FibreTech Inc. (Ont. July 27, 1990 amalg.)
May 2, 1997 – Sought formal protection from creditors under the Companies' Creditors Arrangement Act due to a demand for payment of its operating bank debt.
May 15, 1997 – All directors resigned and the co. was placed into bankruptcy. Toronto-based RSM Richter (formerly Richter & Partners Inc.) was appointed trustee.
Jan. 22, 2004 – Trustee discharged. No distributions made to shldrs.

National Forest Products Ltd. (B.C. 1958)
July 7, 1960 – Name changed to Yoho Timber Ltd. ■

National Fuelcorp Ltd. (B.C. Mar. 7, 1979)
July 31, 1991 – Name changed to Fuelcorp International Inc.; basis 1 new for 5 old shs. ■

National Gold & Nickel Resources Inc. (B.C. 1979)
Mar. 3, 1995 – Dissolved and struck off register.

National Gold Corporation (Alta. May 24, 1996)
Feb. 21, 2003 – Amalgamated with Alamos Minerals Ltd. (1 for 2) to continue as Alamos Gold Inc.; basis 1 new Alamos Gold for 2.352 old National Gold shs. (see Alamos Gold Inc.)

National Hav-Info Communications Inc. (B.C. Apr. 12, 1985)
Aug. 13, 1993 – Continued into Canada.
Feb. 2, 1995 – Name changed to NHC Communications Inc. ■

National Health Stores Inc. (Alta. May 10, 1996)
Nov. 2, 2001 – Struck from register and dissolved.

National Hees Enterprises Limited (Ont. Dec. 11, 1970)
Apr. 26, 1983 – Name changed to Hees International Corporation. ■

National Hees Industries Limited (Can. 1954)
May 10, 1973 – Acquired by National Hees Enterprises Limited; basis for com. shs.: 1 new for 1 old sh. Also scaled basis for pref. shs.: 1.31 new com. shs. to Feb. 28, 1971, 1.16 new com. shs. to Feb. 28, 1972 and 1.04 new com. shs. to Feb. 28, 1973 for 1 old 1st pref. sh. 1963 ser. (see National Hees Enterprises Limited)

National Hosiery Mills Limited (Ont. 1928)
1961 – Name changed to Phantom Industries Limited. ■

National Hospital Management Services Ltd. (B.C. Dec. 15, 1966)
Apr. 7, 1970 – Name changed to National Nursing Homes Ltd. ■

National Irron Resources Ltd. (B.C. 1968)
1979 – Continued into Ontario. (see FPsurvey - Mines & Energy)

National Lake Mines Ltd. (B.C. 1969)
May 12, 1977 – Name changed to Can-Nation Resources Ltd. ■

National Light & Power Co. Ltd. (Can. 1930)
June 1960 – Assets acquired by Sask. government. The o/s 4.5 % 1st mtge. bds. due Mar. 1, 1961, were redeemed at maturity.

National Malartic Gold Mines Ltd. (Que. 1939)
1970 – All assets acquired by Consolidated Marbenor Mines Limited; basis 9 new for 15 old shs.

National Nickel Corporation Ltd. (Que. 1951)
June 9, 1960 – Dissolved.

National Nickel Ltd. (B.C. May 19, 1965)
Feb. 9, 1973 – Name changed to Aberdeen Minerals Limited; basis 1 new for 3 old shs. ■

National Nova Marketing Inc. (B.C. Mar. 19, 1980)
Oct. 19, 1994 – Delisted from the Vancouver Stock Exchange. Subsequently dissolved.

National Nursing Homes Ltd. (B.C. Dec. 15, 1966)
Sept. 8, 1972 – Name changed to N. B. Cook Corporation Ltd. ■

National Pagette Ltd. (Can. 1986)
Nov. 4, 1987 – All o/s shs. acquired under exchange offer of 1 sh. of BCE Mobile Communications Inc. for 2 shs. of National Pagette Ltd. (see BCE Mobile Communications Inc.)

National Quick Lube Ltd. (B.C. Apr. 28, 1986)
June 14, 1994 – Name changed to NQL Drilling Tools Inc.; basis 1 new for 4 old shs. ■

National Quotes Inc. (Ont. 1982)
Aug. 8, 1997 – Name changed to NatQuote Financial Incorporated. (see FPsurvey - Industrials)

National Research Investments, Ltd. (Can. 1932)
Liquidated. No funds available for shldrs. Charter surrendered.

National Resource Explorations Ltd. (B.C. 1976)
May 31, 1990 – Formed NIM Petroleum Corp. on amalgamation with NIM Petroleum Corp.; basis 1 new for 8.5 old shs. ■

National Sea Products Limited (N.S. Mar. 1, 1967 amalg.)
Dec. 31, 1998 – Name changed to High Liner Foods Incorporated. (see FPsurvey - Industrials)

National Seastar Corporation (B.C. 1980)
Jan. 16, 1990 – Name changed to Pacific National Seafarms Ltd.; basis 1 new for 2 old shs. ■

National Steel Car Corporation, Limited (Can. 1919)
Dec. 1961 – Acquired by Dominion Foundries and Steel, Limited through offer; basis 1 new for 3 old shs. (see Dominion Foundries and Steel, Limited)

National Sugar Company (Que. 1941)
Jan. 26, 1980 – Charter cancelled.

National Telcom Solutions Inc. (B.C. Aug. 7, 1991)
Jan. 9, 2004 – Dissolved and struck from register.

National Trust Company, Limited (Ont. Aug. 12, 1898)
Aug. 31, 1984 – Formed The National Victoria and Grey Trust Company in Ontario on amalgamation with Victoria and Grey Trust Company; basis 1.45 new for 1 National Trust sh. Subsequently, over 99% of the o/s com. shs. of the amalg. co. were exchanged for shs. of Victoria and Grey Trustco Limited on basis of 2.069 shs. for each com. sh. acquired upon amalg. The combined effect of the amalg. and exchange offer was that each National Victoria and Grey Trust Company, Limited com. sh. received 3 com. shs. of Victoria and Grey Trustco Limited. ■

National Trustco Inc. (Ont. May 1, 1959)
Aug. 29, 1997 – Acquired by The Bank of Nova Scotia; basis $26.475 plus 0.125 Scotiabank com. shs. for 1 National Trustco sh.

National Uni/Care Health Systems Ltd. (B.C. 1987)
Oct. 31, 1991 – Name changed to Snaper Patent Technologies Inc. ■

The National Victoria and Grey Trust Company (Ont. Aug. 31, 1984 amalg.)
June 1, 1985 – Name changed to National Trust Company.

The National Victoria and Grey Trustco Limited (Ont. May 1, 1959)
Jan. 24, 1989 – Name changed to National Trustco Inc. ■

National Westminster Bank of Canada (Can. Jan. 21, 1982)
May 1, 1998 – Amalgamated with HongkongBank Loan Corporation to form Hongkong Bank of Canada.

Nationwide Books Ltd. (B.C. 1956)
Dec. 24, 1970 – Name changed to Harry Smith & Sons Ltd. ■

Nationwide Minerals Ltd. (Ont. 1952)
Apr. 15, 1965 – Dissolved.

Nationwide Mining & Exploration Ltd. (B.C. 1972)
Sept. 1, 1978 – Dissolved.

Native Minerals Ltd. (Alta. 1950)
Aug. 31, 1976 – Dissolved.

Native Mines Ltd. (B.C. 1964)
June 18, 1979 – Charter cancelled.

Native Strategic Investments Ltd. (B.C. June 17, 1993)
May 8, 2001 – Name changed to NSI Strategic Investments Ltd.; basis 1 new for 8 old shs. ■

Natjo Gold Mines Ltd. (Ont. 1945)
Nov. 23, 1955 – Charter cancelled.

NatraCeuticals Inc. (Can. Jan. 30, 1990)
Feb. 25, 2000 – Name changed to Nu-Life Corp. ■

Natto Mining Corp. Ltd. (Ont. 1960)
Aug. 19, 1965 – Dissolved.

Natunola AgriTech Inc. (Can. June 30, 2004 amalg.)
Feb. 24, 2014 – All o/s shs. not already held acquired by Avrio Ventures Limited Partnership; basis $0.0068 cash per sh.

Natunola Health Biosciences Inc. (Alta. Oct. 17, 1997)
Oct. 14, 2011 – Acquired by Advitech Inc. by way of amalgamation with wholly owned 7894716 Canada Inc.; basis 1.1875 Advitech post-cons. shs. for 1 Natunola sh. Subsequently Advitech changed its name to Botaneco Corp. (see Botaneco Corp.)

Natural Gas Development Corporation (B.C. 1932)
Jan. 23, 1941 – Charter cancelled.

Natural Springs Canada Inc. (Alta. Oct. 2, 1987)
June 20, 2003 – Debt repayment in default, officers resigned Dec. 5, 2001. Delisted TSX-VEN.

Naturally Advanced Technologies Inc. (B.C. Oct. 6, 1998)
Oct. 31, 2012 – Name changed to Crailar Technologies Inc. ■

Naturally Niagara Incorporated (Ont. Dec. 18, 1990)
Jan. 22, 1996 – Name changed to Northern Gaming Inc.; basis 1 new for 6 old shs. ■

Nature Genetiks Capital Inc. (Can. Jan. 15, 2004)
Jan. 30, 2007 – Name changed to Mercator Transport Group Corporation following Qualifying Transaction reverse takeover acquisition of Mercator Transport Group Corporation. ■

NatureBank Asset Management Inc. (B.C. July 6, 2005)
Dec. 9, 2021 – Name changed to Ostrom Climate Solutions Inc. (see FPsurvey - Industrials)

Nautilus Explorations Ltd. (Ont. 1972)
July 1973 – Merged into Sloane Mining Co. Ltd.; basis 1 new for 4.1 old shs.

Nautilus Group Inc. (Wash. Jan. 28, 1993)
Mar. 14, 2005 – Name changed to Nautilus, Inc. ■

Nautilus, Inc. (Wash. Jan. 28, 1993)
Nov. 1, 2023 – Name changed to BowFlex Inc.

Nautilus Minerals Inc. (B.C. Apr. 27, 2006)
July 25, 2019 – Court approval was received for the restructuring acquisition agreement between the company and Deep Sea Mining Finance Ltd. Upon completion of the restructuring transaction, the company's only assets will be the shares of those subsidiaries that were not acquired under the transaction with Deep Sea Mining.
Aug. 13, 2019 – Court approval was received for the plan of compromise and arrangement under which: (a) each convenience creditor with a proven claim would receive in cash an amount equal to the lesser of (i) $10,000; and (ii) the value of said convenience creditor's proven claim; and (b) each affected creditor that is not a convenience creditor with a proven claim would receive 10¢ on every dollar of that affected creditor's proven claim. Holders of non-transferred intercompany indebtedness will not receive any distributions in respect of their claims nor will shareholders.
Nov. 2019 – Assigned into bankruptcy. PricewaterhouseCoopers Inc. appointed trustee.
Oct. 2, 2023 – Struck from register and dissolved.

Nautilus Plus Inc. (Que. 1986 amalg.)
Aug. 23, 1989 – Acquired by Sugesco Acquisitions Inc. for $1.85 per sh.

Nautilus Resources Ltd. (B.C. 1983)
June 14, 1994 – Name changed to New Leather Corporation; basis 1 new for 3 old shs. ■

Nautilus Uranium Mining Corp. Ltd. (Ont. 1955)
1964 – Name changed to Great Lakes Nickel Corp. Ltd. ■

Nava Industries Inc. (Alta. Oct. 25, 1994)
Apr. 30, 1996 – Name changed to BIT Integration Technology Inc.; basis 1 new for 3 old shs. ■

Navan Capital Corp. (B.C. Feb. 7, 2000)
Mar. 21, 2004 – Formed Western Uranium Corporation in British Columbia on reverse takeover acquisition of and amalgamation with (old) Western Uranium Corporation. ■

Navarre Mines Limited (Ont. 1929)
Sept. 1930 – Name changed to Patricia Birch Lake Mining Corp. Ltd. ■

Navarre Resources Corporation (B.C. July 8, 1987)
Aug. 26, 1998 – Name changed to Ameridex Minerals Corp.; basis 1 new for 13.8 old shs. ■

Navasota Resources Inc. (B.C. Mar. 7, 1980)
June 19, 2018 – Voluntarily delisted.
Oct. 4, 2019 – Name changed to IM Cannabis Corp. pursuant to the reverse takeover acquisition of I.M.C. Holdings Ltd. and concurrent amalgamation of I.M.C. with wholly owned Navasota Acquisition Ltd.; basis 1 new for 2.83 old shs. (see FPsurvey - Industrials)

Navasota Resources Ltd. (B.C. Mar. 7, 1980)
Jan. 26, 2010 – Name changed to Anglo Aluminum Corp. ■

Navco Food Services Ltd. (Ont. 1949)
Jan. 19, 1971 – Name changed to Canvedo Industries Ltd. ■

Navigator Exploration Corp. (Alta. Sept. 3, 1996)
May 4, 2004 – Plan of Arrangement amalgamation with Strongbow Resources Inc. (1 for 2) to continue as Strongbow Exploration Inc.; basis 0.7 new Strongbow Exploration for 1 old Navigator sh.

Navigo Energy Inc. (B.C. Mar. 25, 1994)
Jan. 6, 2004 – Plan of Arrangement to convert company to a new junior oil and gas exploration company named C1 Energy Ltd. and a new income trust named NAV Energy Trust; basis 1 new C1 sh. plus either 1 new NAV trust unit or 1 new NAV exch. sh. for 3 old Navigo Energy shs. (see C1 Energy Ltd.; NAV Energy Trust)

Navina Global Resource Fund (Ont. May 18, 2006)
June 28, 2010 – Converted into an open-ended mutual fund.

Navion Capital Inc. (Alta. Oct. 18, 2017)
Feb. 28, 2023 – Name changed to NOA Lithium Brines Inc. pursuant to the Qualifying Transaction reverse takeover acquisition of NOA Lithium Brines S.A. (see FPsurvey - Mines & Energy)

Navis Resources Corp. (Sask. Jan. 15, 2009)
July 5, 2017 – Continued into British Columbia.
June 26, 2020 – Name changed to Modern Meat Inc. pursuant to reverse takeover acquisition of Modern Meat Holdings Inc.; basis 2 new for 1 old sh. ■

Navistar Financial Corporation Canada Inc. (Can. 1959)
Sept. 17, 1987 – Name changed to GE Credit Equipment Finance Inc. following sale of co. by Navistar International Corporation Canada to General Electric Capital Canada Inc. ■

Navistar International Corporation Canada (Ont. 1903)
Feb. 22, 2000 – Name changed to International Truck and Engine Corporation Canada. ■

Navitrak International Corporation (Ont. Jan. 13, 1994)
Jan. 7, 2008 – Dissolved and struck from register.

Navy Resources Corp. (B.C. May 5, 2011)
Feb. 10, 2021 – Name changed to Eminent Gold Corp. (see FPsurvey - Mines & Energy)

Naxos Resources Ltd. (Can. May 23, 1986)
Jan. 3, 2002 – Name changed to Franklin Lake Resources Inc. and continued into Nevada; basis 1 new for 10 old shs.

Nayarit Gold Inc. (Ont. Nov. 27, 2003)
Aug. 9, 2010 – Amalgamated with a wholly owned subsid. of Capital Gold Corporation; basis 0.134048 Capital Gold shs. for 1 Nayarit sh. (see Capital Gold Corporation)

Naybob Gold Mines, Ltd. (Ont. Jan. 3, 1934)
1943 – Name changed to Naybob Mines Ltd. and continued into Ontario; basis 1 new for 10 old shs. ■

Naybob Mines Ltd. (Ont. 1943)
Jan. 20, 1945 – Name changed to Naylor Mines Ltd.; basis 1 new for 10 old shs. ■

Naybob (1945) Gold Mines Ltd. (Ont. 1945)
1948 – Acquired by Logan Porcupine Mines Ltd.; basis 1 new for 3 old shs. (see Logan Porcupine Mines Ltd.)

Naylor Mines Ltd. (Ont. 1943)
1945 – Name changed to Naybob (1945) Gold Mines Ltd. and continued into Ontario. ■

Nazha Mines Ltd. (Ont. 1965)
1967 – Name changed to Prado Explorations Ltd. ■

Nealon Mines Ltd. (Ont. 1943)
Apr. 1975 – Charter cancelled.

Nearctic Resources Inc. (Ont. 1945)
Jan. 3, 1995 – Delisted from the CDN. Subsequently dissolved and charter cancelled.

Neartic Mines Ltd. (unknown)
Nov. 26, 1975 – Amalgamated into Spar Holdings & Explorations Ltd.; basis 1 new for 2 old shs.

Neary Resources Corporation (B.C. May 14, 1996)
Oct. 8, 1999 – Name changed to Red Emerald Resource Corp.; basis 1 new for 2 old shs. ■

Neatt Corporation (Ont. Aug. 1, 2001 amalg.)
Aug. 1, 2005 – Dissolved and struck from register.

Nebo Capital Corp. (Alta. Aug. 12, 2011)
May 1, 2017 – Continued into British Columbia.
Aug. 8, 2018 – Name changed to Quisitive Technology Solutions, Inc. following Qualifying Transaction reverse takeover acquisition of Fusion Agiletech Partners Inc. ■

Nechi Consolidated Dredging Ltd. (B.C. 1936)
1953 – Merged into Pato Consolidated Gold Dredging Ltd.; basis 1 new for 8 old shs.

Needco Cooling Semiconductors Ltd. (Can. 1959)
May 1962 – Name changed to Needco Frigistors Limited. ■

Needco Frigistors Limited (Can. 1959)
June 1963 – Name changed to Frigistors Ltd. ■

The Needle Capital Corp. (Alta. June 1, 2016)
Sept. 21, 2018 – Name changed to The Flowr Corporation following Qualifying Transaction reverse takeover acquisition of (old) The Flowr Corporation and concurrent amalgamation of (old) Flowr with wholly owned 2652253 Ontario Inc. to form The Flowr Group Inc.; basis 1 new for 13 old shs. ■

Needlepoint Resources Ltd. (B.C. 1983)
Mar. 18, 1986 – Name changed to Asian Canadian Resources Ltd. ■

Needler Group Limited (Can. Apr. 6, 1988)
July 29, 1998 – Acquired by Blue Circle Industries plc of London, England, for $1.90 per sh.

Neeland Flin Flon Mining & Exploration Ltd. (Ont. 1960)
Jan. 24, 1962 – Name changed to Silver Belle Mines Ltd. ■

Neepawa Island Gold Mines Ltd. (Ont. 1950)
1955 – Charter cancelled.

Negas Mining & Exploration Ltd. (B.C. 1966)
Feb. 25, 1984 – Dissolved.

Negor Mines Ltd. (Ont. 1958)
Jan. 23, 1979 – Dissolved.

Negus Mines Ltd. (Ont. 1938)
1955 – Name changed to Consolidated Negus Mines Ltd.; basis 1 new for 3 old shs. ■

Neighbors Resources Inc. (Ont. Apr. 12, 1984)
Mar. 11, 1992 – Formed Baitex Medical Technologies Inc. on amalgamation with Baitex Medical Technologies Inc.; basis 1 new for 3 old shs. ■

Neighbourly Pharmacy Inc. (Can. Mar. 20, 2015)
Mar. 22, 2024 – All o/s shs. not already held acquired by Persistence Capital Partners LP; basis $20.50 cash per sh.

Nellie Lake Metal Mines Ltd. (Ont. 1954)
June 1959 – Charter surrendered and co. dissolved.

Nello Mining Limited (Ont. 1936)
July 6, 1982 – Name changed to Nello Resources Inc. ■

Nello Resources Inc. (Ont. 1936)
Aug. 3, 1984 – Formed Highridge Exploration Ltd. in Alberta on amalgamation with Viking Exploration Ltd. (private co.). ■

Nelma Information Inc. (Ont. 1969)
Oct. 15, 1984 – Amalgamated in Ontario to continue with same name. (see FPsurvey - Industrials)

Nelson Consolidated Mines Ltd. (B.C. 1949)
May 1957 – Struck off register.

Nelson Gold Corporation Limited (Bermuda Mar. 31, 1993)
Oct. 31, 2000 – Name changed to Nelson Resources Limited. ■

Nelson Holdings International Ltd. (B.C. May 13, 1985)
Sept. 18, 1987 – Continued into Canada.
Oct. 27, 1989 – Name changed to NHI Nelson Holdings International Ltd.; basis 1 new for 10 old shs. ■

Nelson Resources Limited (Bermuda Mar. 31, 1993)
Dec. 8, 2005 – Amalgamated indirectly with LUKOIL Overseas Holding Ltd.; basis US$2.19162 per sh.

Nelson Slocan Consolidated Mines, Ltd. (B.C. 1942)
June 1954 – Dissolved.

Nelson Trade & Finance Limited (Bermuda Mar. 31, 1993)
July 17, 1995 – Name changed to Nelson Gold Corporation Limited. ■

Nelson Vending Technology Limited (B.C. Jan. 17, 1983)
July 23, 1987 – Continued into Canada. (see Cinram Ltd.)
Aug. 4, 1993 – Amalgamated with its wholly owned subsid., Nelson Videovend Ltd., and Cinram Ltd. (1 for 1) to continue as Cinram Ltd.; basis 1 Cinram com. sh. for 589 Nelson Vending com. shs. (see Cinram Ltd.)

Nelvana Limited (Ont. July 30, 1971)
Dec. 4, 2000 – All o/s subord. vtg. shs. acquired by Corus Entertainment Inc.; basis $48 per sh., or $0.05 in cash plus 1.147 Corus class B non-vtg. shs.

Nelway Mines Ltd. (B.C. 1965)
Oct. 15, 1974 – Charter cancelled.

Nemaska Exploration Inc. (Can. May 16, 2007)
Dec. 1, 2011 – Name changed to Nemaska Lithium Inc. ■

Nemaska Lithium Inc. (Can. May 16, 2007)
Dec. 23, 2019 – Filed for protection under the Companies' Creditors Arrangement Act (CCAA) and PricewaterhouseCoopers Inc. was appointed monitor.
May 15, 2020 – Sale of 15,849,455 com. shs. of Monarch Gold Corporation was completed for $3,500,000. Proceeds to be used for restructuring under the CCAA.
Oct. 15, 2020 – Court approval was received for a transaction under the CCAA structured as a credit bid from a group consisting of the company's largest secured creditor, Orion Mine Finance, Investissement Quebec and The Pallinghurst Group, through a new entity named Quebec Lithium Partners. Under the transaction, Quebec Lithium will acquire on a 50-50 basis all the o/s shs. of the new entity created from the amalgamation of the company and its subsids. Upon emerging from the CCAA proceedings, the new entity will amalgamate with entities controlled by Orion Mine to form the entity that will operate the business of the company. All o/s com. shs. of the company will be cancelled for no consideration.
Dec. 1, 2020 – Sale of the company to Quebec Lithium Partners was completed under the CCAA. Shldrs. did not receive any payment for, or distrib. on, their shs. in connection with CCAA proceedings.

Nemco Exploration Ltd. (B.C. Apr. 3, 1970)
Nov. 16, 1977 – Continued into Alberta.
July 10, 1980 – Name changed to Seaward Resources Ltd. ■

Nemo Mines Ltd. (Ont. 1945)
Oct. 23, 1979 – Charter cancelled.

Nemrod Mining Co. Ltd. (Que. 1947)
June 1, 1976 – Merged into Brominco Inc.; basis 1 for 5 old shs. plus capital distribution of 10¢ per old sh.

Neo Alliance Minerals Inc. (Alta. June 24, 2003)
Dec. 16, 2010 – Name changed to Synergy Acquisition Corp. ■

Neo Lithium Corp. (Ont. Apr. 30, 2014)
Feb. 1, 2022 – Acquired by Zijin Mining Group Co., Ltd.; basis $6.50 cash per sh.

Neo Material Technologies Inc. (Can. Aug. 8, 1994)
June 14, 2012 – Acquired by MCP Exchangeco Inc., a wholly owned subsid. of Molycorp, Inc.; basis either (i) US$11.30 or (ii) 0.4242 Molycorp shs. or (iii) combination thereof for 1 Neo com. sh.
June 27, 2012 – Name changed to Neo Material Technologies ULC. ■

Neo Material Technologies ULC (Can. Aug. 8, 1994)
July 17, 2012 – Name changed to Molycorp Minerals Canada ULC.

Neodym Technologies Inc. (B.C. Feb. 4, 1986)
Sept. 6, 2012 – Name changed to Neoteck Solutions Inc.; basis 1 new for 2 old shs. ■

Neomar Resources Ltd. (Ont. 1927)
July 3, 1987 – Name changed to Tarragon Oil and Gas Limited. ■

Neon Products of Canada Ltd. (Can. 1929)
Mar. 1969 – Name changed to Neonex International Ltd. ■

Neon Products of Western Canada (Can. 1929)
1956 – Name changed to Neon Products of Canada Ltd. ■

Neonex International Ltd. (Can. 1929)
Nov. 1, 1977 – Amalgamated indirectly with Jim Pattison Ltd. through subsid. Jim Pattison (B.C.) Ltd.; basis $3.00 or 1 new non-voting 5.5% redeemable $3.00 pfce. sh. for 1 com. sh.

NeonMind Biosciences Inc. (B.C. Sept. 18, 2019)
June 7, 2023 – Name changed to Lancaster Resources Inc. pursuant to the reverse takeover acquisition of Lancaster Lithium Inc. (see FPsurvey - Mines & Energy)

Neoteck Solutions Inc. (B.C. Feb. 4, 1986)
May 9, 2016 – Name changed to Hello Pal International Inc. pursuant to the acquisition of certain software assets of Hello Pal International, Inc.; basis 1 new for 1.5 old shs. (see FPsurvey - Industrials)

Neotel Inc. (Ont. Mar. 14, 1983)
Apr. 5, 2005 – Name changed to Neotel International Inc.; basis 1 new for 3 old shs. ■

Neotel International Inc. (Ont. Mar. 14, 1983)
Oct. 1, 2008 – Name changed to Tenth Power Technologies Corp. ■

Neovasc Inc. (Can. Apr. 19, 2002)
Apr. 13, 2023 – Acquired by Shockwave Medical, Inc.; basis US$27.25 cash per sh.

Neptune Acquisition Holdings Inc. (Ont. June 2, 2020)
Mar. 19, 2021 – Name changed to MDA Ltd. ■

Neptune Capital Corp. (Alta. Oct. 17, 2000)
Aug. 21, 2003 – Qualifying Transaction amalgamation with Saturn Ventures Inc. (425,000 units) and wholly owned subsid. of Vanguard Aviation Corp. (VAX); basis

875,000 VAX units for all Neptune com. shs. One VAX unit equals 1 VAX com. sh. plus 1 VAX com. sh. wt. (entitling the holder to purchase 1 VAX sh. at $0.25 for 15 mths.). (see Vanguard Aviation Corp.)

Neptune Dash Technologies Corp. (B.C. amalg.)
Dec. 17, 2020 – Name changed to Neptune Digital Assets Corp. (see FPsurvey - Industrials)

Neptune Gold Mines Ltd. (Ont. 1946)
Oct. 1976 – Charter cancelled.

Neptune Resources Corp. (B.C. 1970)
Dec. 8, 1989 – All o/s com. shs. acquired by ABM Gold Corp.; basis 3 cl. A shs. of ABM for 7 com. shs. of Neptune. (see ABM Gold Corp.)

Neptune Technologies & Bioressources inc. (Que. Oct. 9, 1998)
Sept. 21, 2018 – Name changed to Neptune Wellness Solutions Inc. (see FPsurvey - Industrials)

Nesbitt Burns Inc. (Can. 1969)
Feb. 15, 2000 – Name changed to BMO Nesbitt Burns Inc.

Nesbitt Labine Uranium Mines Ltd. (Ont. 1950)
1960 – Merged into Gunnar Mining Ltd.; basis 1 new for 80 old shs.

Nesbitt Thomson Deacon Inc. (Can. 1969)
Sept. 1987 – Acquired by Bank of Montreal for $22 per sh.
Mar. 31, 1991 – Name changed to Nesbitt Thomson Inc. ■

Nesbitt Thomson Inc. (Can. 1969)
Sept. 1, 1994 – Name changed to Nesbitt Burns Inc. ■

Nesbitt Uranium Mines Ltd. (Ont. 1950)
Jan. 1952 – Charter cancelled.

The Nesmont Industrial Corporation (B.C. 1986)
May 10, 1993 – Name changed to International Nesmont Industrial Corporation; basis 1 new for 3.5 old shs. ■

Nesnah Mining & Exploration Co. Ltd. (Can. 1944)
Jan. 1956 – Dissolved.

Nesscap Energy Inc. (Ont. Aug. 2, 2007)
May 3, 2017 – Undergoing voluntary dissolution. Substantially all assets sold to Maxwell Technologies, Inc. for 4,146,538 shs. valued at US$25,874,397.
July 20, 2017 – Initial distrib. of 1 Maxwell Technologies, Inc. sh. for every 226 Nesscap shs.
Mar. 31, 2019 – Final distrib. of the remaining shs. of Maxwell Technologies, Inc. was made on a pro rata basis.
Dec. 10, 2019 – Dissolved and struck from registry.

Nestor Oil & Gas Ltd. (B.C. 1982)
May 9, 1983 – Name changed to Kumix Resources Corporation. ■

Net Nanny Software International Inc. (B.C. Aug. 15, 1983)
Nov. 15, 2000 – Continued into Yukon.
May 24, 2005 – Dissolved and struck off register.

Net-Quote.Com Inc. (Ont. Nov. 29, 1991)
May 18, 2000 – Name changed to HYWY Corp. following acquisition of HYWY.Com Inc. ■

Net Resources Inc. (Alta. Dec. 2, 1992)
Apr. 5, 2000 – Name changed to BakBone Software Incorporated. ■

Net Shepherd Inc. (Alta. Aug. 1, 1996 amalg.)
May 9, 2002 – Name changed to Flock Resources Ltd.; basis 1 new for 10 old shs. ■

Net Soft Systems Inc. (B.C. May 13, 1996)
Feb. 24, 2011 – Name changed to Rhys Resources Ltd.; basis 1 new for 10 old shs. ■

Net Zero Renewable Energy Inc. (Ont. Apr. 28, 2010)
Feb. 24, 2022 – Placed into receivership. B. Riley Farber Inc. appointed receiver and all officers and directors resigned.

Netalco Corporation (Alta. Nov. 20, 1996)
Jan. 9, 1999 – Name changed to Saddle Resources Inc. following reverse takeover acquisition of Saddle Resources Inc.; basis 1 for 5. ■

Netco Energy Inc. (Alta. May 21, 1993)
July 14, 2011 – Name changed to Netco Silver Inc. ■

Netco Silver Inc. (Alta. May 21, 1993)
Feb. 11, 2014 – Name changed to Brisio Innovations Inc. and continued into British Columbia. ■

Netcoins Holdings Inc. (Ont. Feb. 20, 1987)
Aug. 31, 2018 – Continued into British Columbia.
Apr. 20, 2022 – Name changed to Axcap Ventures Inc. (see FPsurvey - Mines & Energy; FPsurvey - Industrials)

NetDriven Solutions Inc. (Alta. May 31, 1982)
July 15, 2004 – Formed Cervus Financial Group Inc. in Alberta on amalgamation with Cervus Financial Group Inc., constituting a reverse takeover by Cervus; basis 1 new for 20 old shs. ■

Netgraphe Inc. (Que. Dec. 18, 1981)
Sept. 16, 2004 – Plan of Arrangement amalgamation with indirectly-owned subsid. of Québecor Media Inc. to form Amalco; basis 1 new Amalco redeemable pfd. sh. for 1 old Netgraphe sub. vtg. sh. The redeemable shs. were immediately redeemed for $0.63 per sh.

Netherfield Energy Corporation (Alta. May 12, 1994)
Sept. 29, 1999 – Formed Antrim Energy Inc. in Alberta on amalgamation with Antrim International Inc., constituting a reverse takeover by Antrim; basis 0.6140625 new for 1 Antrim sh. and 0.25 new for 1 Netherfield sh. ■

NeTrue Communications Inc. (Alta. Aug. 1, 1997)
Apr. 18, 2000 – Continued into Delaware.

NetScout Capital Corp. (Alta. July 12, 1994)
Nov. 8, 2001 – Name changed to Scout Capital Corp. ■

Netseers Internet International Corporation (B.C. Feb. 8, 1984)
Dec. 2, 2003 – Name changed to 1st Anyox Resources Limited; basis 1 new for 10 old shs. ■

Nett-Workk Inc. (Alta. Dec. 19, 1986)
June 1, 1991 – Dissolved and struck off register.

Nettron.Com, Inc. (Alta. Jan. 19, 1996)
Apr. 19, 2005 – Name changed to Valcent Products Inc.; basis 1 new for 3 old shs. ■

Network Exploration Ltd. (B.C. Sept. 2, 1983)
Jan. 12, 2018 – Name changed to Ynvisible Interactive Inc. pursuant to reverse takeover acquisition of a 94.19% interest in YD Ynvisible S.A. (see FPsurvey - Industrials)

Network Gaming International Corp. (B.C. Sept. 2, 1983)
June 22, 2004 – Name changed to Network Exploration Ltd.; basis 1 new for 3 old shs. ■

Network Life Sciences Inc. (B.C. Sept. 19, 2013)
Oct. 16, 2016 – Name changed to ePlay Digital Inc. (see FPsurvey - Industrials)

Network Oncology Inc. (B.C. Sept. 19, 2013)
June 23, 2015 – Name changed to Network Life Sciences Inc.; basis 1 new for 3 old shs. ■

Network Technology Professionals Inc. (B.C. Oct. 19, 2000)
July 4, 2005 – Dissolved and struck from register.

Network Telemetrics Ltd. (B.C. Sept. 23, 1991)
Oct. 14, 1997 – Name changed to Belvedere Resources Ltd. ■

Neuer Kapital Corp. (B.C. May 29, 1984)
Aug. 3, 2005 – Name changed to Crescent Resources Corp. ■

NeuLion, Inc. (Can. Jan. 14, 2000)
Nov. 30, 2010 – Continued into Delaware.
May 9, 2018 – Acquired by WME Entertainment Parent, LLC; basis US$0.84 cash per sh.

Neumed Systems Corporation (Can. Aug. 30, 1985)
May 25, 1988 – Name changed to Reneaux Capital Inc. ■

Neuro-Biotech Corporation (Ont. Sept. 25, 1995 amalg.)
Nov. 30, 2001 – Name changed to DPC Biosciences Corporation. ■

Neuro Discovery Inc. (B.C. Mar. 24, 1994)
June 28, 2002 – Continued into Canada.
Oct. 1, 2004 – Name changed to Allon Therapeutics Inc. following reverse takeover acquisition of Allon Therapeutics, Inc. ■

Neuro Navigational Corporation (Calif. May 20, 1991)
Dec. 31, 1993 – Continued into Delaware.
Nov. 18, 1997 – Name changed to Kinetic Ventures Ltd. ■

Neurochem Inc. (Can. June 17, 1993)
Apr. 21, 2008 – Name changed to BELLUS Health Inc. ■

Neurogenesis Biotech Corp. (Alta. Mar. 31, 2004)
Oct. 19, 2004 – Name changed to Stem Cell Therapeutics Corp. ■

Neurokine Pharmaceuticals Inc. (B.C. June 10, 2002)
Apr. 7, 2017 – Name changed to Pivot Pharmaceuticals Inc. ■

NeuroMedix Inc. (Can. Feb. 11, 2005)
May 15, 2007 – Acquired by Transition Therapeutics Inc.; basis 1 Transition com. sh. for 5.1429 NeuroMedix Inc. com. sh. (see Transition Therapeutics Inc.)

Neutrino Resources Inc. (Alta. Dec. 31, 1994 amalg.)
July 24, 1998 – Acquired by Southern Mineral Corporation of Houston, Tex., for $1.80 per sh.

Nevada Bob's Canada Inc. (Alta. Feb. 27, 1996)
Oct. 29, 1999 – Name changed to Nevada Bob's Golf Inc. (see FPsurvey - Industrials)

Nevada Bob's International Inc. (Ont. Aug. 24, 1993 amalg.)
Nov. 28, 2008 – Formed Loncor Resources Inc. in Ontario on reverse takeover acquisition of and amalgamation with Loncor Resources Inc. ■

Nevada Clean Magnesium Inc. (B.C. Mar. 24, 1966)
May 14, 2019 – Name changed to Western Magnesium Corporation.
Continued into Delaware.

Nevada Copper Corp. (B.C. Nov. 16, 2006)
Oct. 9, 2024 – Substantially all the assets and subsidiaries acquired by Southwest Critical Materials LLC, an affiliate of Kinterra Capital Corp., pursuant to an asset purchase agreement under the Chapter 11 bankruptcy code for US$128 million cash, payment of cure costs for contracts assumed and assumption of certain liabilities. Monies to be distributed to certain creditors under the company's bankruptcy process and was not sufficient enough to allow for any distribution to com. shldrs.
May 5, 2025 – Plan of liquidation completed, confirmed by Nevada Bankruptcy Court on Apr. 17, 2025, and the Ontario Superior Court of Justice on Apr. 28, 2025. All officer and directors resigned. There were no distrib. made to shldrs.

Nevada Energy Metals Inc. (B.C. June 2, 2011)
Nov. 9, 2020 – Name changed to Nickel Rock Resources Inc. ■

Nevada Exploration Inc. (Can. Apr. 6, 2006)
June 13, 2024 – Name changed to URZ3 Energy Corp. (see FPsurvey - Mines & Energy)

Nevada Explorations Ltd. (Can. 1973)
Nov. 26, 1975 – Amalgamated with Spar Holdings & Explorations Ltd.; basis 1 new for 2.5 old shs.

Nevada Geothermal Power Inc. (B.C. Apr. 13, 1995)
Apr. 2, 2013 – Name changed to Alternative Earth Resources Inc.; basis 1 new for 5 old shs. ■

Nevada Goldfields Corporation (B.C. May 11, 1984)
Apr. 27, 1989 – Continued into Canada.
May 1, 1991 – Name changed to Consolidated Nevada Goldfields Corporation; basis 1 new for 6 old shs. ■

Nevada Iron Ltd. (Australia Jan. 12, 2007)
July 28, 2015 – Voluntarily delisted from TSX; continued to trade on Australian Securities Exchange.

Nevada North Resources Inc. (B.C. Apr. 25, 1983)
Dec. 2, 1994 – Name changed to Inca Pacific Resources Inc. ■

Nevada Pacific Gold Ltd. (B.C. Mar. 11, 1997)
July 9, 2007 – Acquired by US Gold Canadian Acquisition Corporation; basis 0.23 new US Gold sh. for 1 old Nevada sh. (see US Gold Canadian Acquisition Corporation)

Nevada Silver Corporation (Can. Mar. 1, 2018)
May 16, 2023 – Name changed to Electric Metals (USA) Limited. (see FPsurvey - Mines & Energy)

Nevada Star Resource Corp. (B.C. Apr. 29, 1987)
June 23, 1998 – Continued into Yukon.
Mar. 30, 2007 – Name changed to Pure Nickel Inc. following reverse takeover acquisition of Pure Nickel Inc. and amalgamation of Pure Nickel with a wholly owned subsidiary; basis 1 new for 5 old shs. ■

Nevada Sunrise Gold Corporation (B.C. Apr. 3, 2007)
Sept. 23, 2022 – Name changed to Nevada Sunrise Metals Corporation. (see FPsurvey - Mines & Energy)

NevadaBobs.com Inc. (Ont. Aug. 24, 1993 amalg.)
Aug. 27, 2001 – Name changed to Nevada Bob's International Inc. ■

Nevado Resources Corporation (Can. June 9, 2006)
July 5, 2019 – Continued into British Columbia. (see FPsurvey - Mines & Energy)

Nevado Venture Capital Corporation (Can. June 9, 2006)
Aug. 27, 2010 – Name changed to Nevado Resources Corporation. ■

Nevaro Capital Corporation (Can. Nov. 13, 1986)
Jan. 1, 2010 – Name changed to Canadian Energy Services & Technology Corp. pursuant to conversion of Canadian Energy Services L.P. (CESLP) into a corp. and transaction with 7280157 Canada Ltd. (renamed Nevaro Capital Corporation); basis 1 co. sh. for 1 CESLP LP unit and 1 new Nevaro sh. for 1 old Nevaro sh. ■

Nevarro Energy Inc. (Alta. Mar. 11, 1997)
Sept. 20, 2000 – Name changed to Nevarro Energy Ltd.; basis 1 new for 3 old shs. ■

Nevarro Energy Ltd. (Alta. Mar. 11, 1997)
Sept. 28, 2006 – Acquired by Pearl Exploration and Production Ltd.; basis either $1.875, 0.125 new Pearl com. sh., 0.5 new Serrano Energy Ltd. com. sh. and 0.20866 new Serrano warrant, or, 0.5 new Pearl com. sh., 0.5 new Serrano com. sh. and 0.20866 new Serrano warrant for 1 old Nevarro com. sh. (see Pearl Exploration and Production Ltd.)

Nevasco Mines Ltd. (Ont. Mar. 22, 1974)
June 1978 – Name changed to Nevasco Corporation. (see FPsurvey - Industrials)

Nevcal Resources Ltd. (B.C. Mar. 16, 1966)
Dec. 3, 1986 – Name changed to Arapahoe Mining Corp.; basis 1 new for 2 old shs. ■

Nevex Mines Ltd. (B.C. 1972)
June 23, 1980 – Name changed to Wasp International Resources Inc.; basis 1 new for 5 old shs. ■

Nevgold Resource Corp. (Can. Feb. 9, 2004)
Mar. 2, 2012 – Acquired by Silver Predator Corp.; basis 0.5 Silver shs.for 1 Nevgold sh.

Nevis Energy Services Ltd. (Alta. Apr. 4, 1996)
Nov. 1, 2002 – Formed Phoenix Technology Services Inc. in Alberta on amalgamation with 1003053 Alberta Ltd., a wholly owned subsid. of Phoenix Technology Services Ltd., constituting a reverse takeover by Phoenix; basis 1 new for 1 Phoenix sh. and 0.5 new for 1 Nevis sh. ■

Nevis petroleum corporation (Alta. Mar. 5, 1996)
Oct. 16, 2002 – All o/s com. shs. acquired by a subsidiary of AC Energy Inc.; basis 10¢ per share. (see AC Energy Inc.)

Nevoro Inc. (Can. May 16, 2007)
Oct. 14, 2009 – Acquired by Starfield Resources Inc.; basis 0.87 Starfield shs. for 1 Nevoro sh. (see Starfield Resources Inc.)

Nevsun Resources Ltd. (B.C. July 19, 1965)
Mar. 8, 2019 – Acquired by Zijin Mining Group Co., Ltd.; basis Cdn$6.00 cash per share.

New Aegis Resources Ltd. (B.C. Aug. 1, 1990 amalg.)
Aug. 19, 1994 – Amalgamated with Nucore Resources Ltd. (1 for 1.777) to form Norcan Resources Ltd.; basis 1 new for 1.333 old shs. (see Norcan Resources Ltd.)

New Age Brands Inc. (B.C. Sept. 27, 2013)
Apr. 16, 2019 – Name changed to NewLeaf Brands Inc. ■

New Age Farm Inc. (B.C. Sept. 27, 2013)
Nov. 16, 2018 – Name changed to New Age Brands Inc. ■

New Age Ventures Inc. (B.C. 1965)
Apr. 11, 1996 – Continued into Yukon.
Jan. 28, 1998 – Name changed to Great Panther Inc.; basis 1 new for 10 old shs. ■

New Ainsworth Base Metals Ltd. (B.C. 1951)
Name changed to Angus River Mines Ltd.; basis 1 new for 10 old shs. ■

New Alger Mines Ltd. (Ont. 1945)
Nov. 1, 1982 – Dissolved.

New Alster Energy Ltd. (B.C. Dec. 22, 1980)
Mar. 26, 1990 – Name changed to Anacondo Explorations Inc.; basis 1 new for 4 old shs. ■

New Altamira Value Fund (Ont. Dec. 17, 1993)
Dec. 31, 2001 – Merged into Altamira Canadian Value Fund following expiry for cash based on a price per unit equal to the net asset value per unit as at.

New Ambassador Developments Ltd. (Ont. 1960)
Feb. 20, 1980 – Dissolved.

New Arcadia Explorations Ltd. (N.P.L.) (B.C. 1967)
Nov. 10, 1992 – Name changed to New Arcadia Resources Ltd. (see FPsurvey - Mines & Energy)

New Arlington Mines Ltd. (B.C. 1951)
Mar. 12, 1964 – Dissolved.

New Arntfield Mines Ltd. (Que. 1925)
1971 – Dissolved.

New Associated Developments Limited (Que. 1959)
Feb. 1971 – Name changed to Consolidated Developments Limited; basis 1 new for 5 old shs.

New Aston Resources Inc. (B.C. 1969)
Sept. 30, 1981 – Amalgamated with Atlantic Energy Corporation; sh. for sh. basis. (see Atlantic Energy Corporation)

New Astral Mining & Resources Ltd. (Ont. 1947)
Oct. 1968 – Charter cancelled.

New Athona Mines Ltd. (Ont. Mar. 3, 1937)
Jan. 3, 1995 – Name changed to Lakota Resources Inc.; basis 1 new for 3.5 old shs. ■

New Augarita Porcupine Mines Limited (Ont. May 13, 1936)
Nov. 10, 1987 – Name changed to Royal Aerospace Corp. ■

New Bailey Mines Limited (Ont. 1951)
1961 – Charter cancelled.

New Barber-Larder Mines Ltd. (Ont. 1937)
1953 – Assets acquired by Mining Futures and Holdings Ltd.; no equity for shldrs. Charter surrendered. (see Mining Futures and Holdings Ltd.)

New Bedford Explorations Limited (Ont. 1969)
Mar. 15, 1978 – Name changed to New Bedford Resources & Developments Limited. ■

New Bedford Resources & Developments Limited (Ont. 1969)
Feb. 15, 1982 – Amalgamated with Moffat Lake Explorations Inc. to form Tipperary Resources Ltd.; basis 1 new conv. pfce. sh. for each 2 New Bedford shs.

New Bethsaida Mines Limited (B.C. 1956)
Apr. 1964 – Sold assets to Western Beaver Lodge Mines Ltd. for 550,002 shs., which were distributed sh.-for-sh. to Bethsaida shldrs. Latter also understood to have received 3¢ per sh.

New Bidlamaque Enterprises Inc. (Can. 1987)
June 10, 1996 – Name changed to Chivor Emerald Corporation Ltd. and continued into British Virgin Islands; basis 1 new for 4 old shs.

New Bidlamaque Gold Mines Limited (Ont. 1944)
1987 – Continued into Canada.
Nov. 10, 1995 – Name changed to New Bidlamaque Enterprises Inc.; basis 1 new for 10 old shs. ■

New Black Bay Minerals Ltd. (Alta. 1953)
Apr. 1975 – Acquired by Thomson Exploration Ltd. for 33¢ per sh.

New Blondeau Nickel Mines Ltd. (Ont. 1952)
May 15, 1974 – Charter cancelled.

New Blue Ribbon Resources Ltd. (B.C. Oct. 4, 1989)
Jan. 28, 2003 – Name changed to Blue Diamond Mining Corporation; basis 1 new for 15 old shs. ■

New Bobs Lake Gold Mines Ltd. (Ont. 1945)
May 5, 1959 – Dissolved.

New Bristol Oils Limited (Ont. 1948)
1959 – Acquired by Able Land & Minerals Ltd.; basis 1 new for 5 old shs.

New British Dominion Oil Company Limited (Can. 1925)
Jan. 20, 1958 – Name changed to Asamera Oil Corporation Ltd. ■

The New Brunswick Electric Power Commission (N.B. 1920)
June 1, 1991 – Name changed to New Brunswick Power Corporation. ■

New Brunswick Power Corporation (N.B. 1920)
Oct. 1, 2004 – Name changed to New Brunswick Power Holding Corporation following reorganization into holding company with four new subsidiary operating companies. ■

New Brunswick Power Holding Corporation (N.B. 1920)
Oct. 1, 2013 – Succeeded by New Brunswick Power Corporation following reorganization into a single crown corporation. (see FPsurvey - Mines & Energy; FPsurvey - Industrials)

The New Brunswick Telephone Company, Limited (N.B. 1888)
July 1, 1985 – Com. stk. exchanged on sh.-for-sh. basis for com. stk. of parent co., Bruncor Inc. No exchange made on company's pref. stk. The cum. redeem. pfd. $1.37 redeemed July 31, 1992 for $20.20 plus accrued and unpaid div.
Dec. 31, 1998 – Name changed to NBTel Inc.

New Brunswick Uranium Metals & Mining Ltd. (N.B. 1955)
July 20, 1971 – Name changed to NBU Mines Limited. ■

New Bullet Group Inc. (B.C. Nov. 6, 1981)
May 31, 2004 – Name changed to Amerix Precious Metals Corporation and continued into Ontario. ■

New Cache Petroleums Ltd. (Alta. Oct. 28, 1986)
Jan. 15, 1999 – Acquired by Canadian Abraxas Petroleum Limited, an affiliate of Grey Wolf Exploration Inc., for $6.50 per sh. (see Grey Wolf Exploration Inc.)

New Calumet Mines Ltd. (Que. 1942)
July 28, 1975 – Assets sold to Consolidated Professor Mines Ltd.; basis 1 new for 3.108 old shs.

New Campbell Island Mines Limited (Ont. Nov. 21, 1945)
July 23, 1984 – Continued into Canada.
Oct. 17, 1997 – Name changed to Minera Delta Inc.; basis 1 new for 4 old shs. ■

New Canalask Minerals Ltd. (Ont. 1953)
Aug. 1974 – Name changed to Bow Island Drilling Canada Ltd. ■

New Canamin Resources Ltd. (B.C. 1980)
July 6, 1995 – Acquired by Princeton Mining Corporation; basis 1.25 Princeton shs. for 1 Canamin sh.

New Candela Resources Ltd. (B.C. June 11, 1987)
Oct. 20, 1999 – Name changed to Sherwood Petroleum Corporation; basis 1 new for 2 old shs. ■

New Cantech Ventures Inc. (B.C. Apr. 4, 1997)
June 20, 2008 – Name changed to Nanika Resources Inc. ■

New Carolin Gold Corp. (B.C. Aug. 26, 1981)
Sept. 16, 2021 – Acquired by Talisker Resources Ltd.; basis 0.3196 Talisker com. shs. per sh. (implied consideration of $0.095 per sh.)

New Cascade Minerals Ltd. (B.C. 1964)
Acquired by Maloney-Steel Crafts Ltd. for 23¢ per sh.

New Casey Cobalt Silver Mines Ltd. (Ont. 1948)
1956 – Charter cancelled.

New Cayzor Athabaska Mines Ltd. (Ont. 1946)
Mar. 1981 – Charter cancelled.

New Century Resources Ltd. (B.C. Sept. 2, 1983)
May 31, 1990 – Name changed to A.I. Software Inc. ■

New Chamberlain Petroleums Ltd. (Alta. 1951)
1959 – Name changed to Sarcee Petroleums Ltd. ■

New Charter Minerals Inc. (B.C. Mar. 20, 1978)
Apr. 23, 1992 – Name changed to Cambridge BioChemics Inc. ■

New Chemcrude Resources Ltd. (B.C. 1963)
Feb. 4, 1983 – Struck off register.

New Chief Mines Ltd. (B.C. 1966)
Jan. 1978 – Name changed to Sydney Development Corporation; basis 1 new for 2.5 old shs. ■

New China Resources Limited (B.C. 1982)
Feb. 6, 1991 – Name changed to Sino Pac International Investments Inc. ■

New Cinch Uranium Ltd. (B.C. 1959)
July 24, 1992 – Dissolved and struck off register.

New Claymore Resources Ltd. (B.C. July 20, 1970)
Nov. 24, 2004 – Continued into Alberta.
Nov. 26, 2004 – Name changed to BrazAlta Resources Corp. ■

New Colony Energy Corp. (Ont. Aug. 31, 1987)
Dec. 9, 1987 – Formed Interfirst Resources Inc. on amalgamation with Interfirst Oil Corp.; basis 1 new for 4 old shs. ■

New Comet Gold Mines Ltd. (Ont. 1946)
Mar. 28, 1960 – Charter cancelled.

New Concept Technologies International Inc. (Ont. 1952)
Nov. 18, 1994 – Continued into Bermuda.
Dec. 15, 1994 – Name changed to New Concept Technologies International Limited. ■

New Concept Technologies International Limited (Bermuda Nov. 18, 1994)
Aug. 16, 1996 – Name changed to NTI Resources Limited. ■

New Concord Development Corp. Ltd. (Ont. 1951)
1966 – Wound up.

New Congress Resources Ltd. (B.C. Apr. 9, 1965)
Jan. 12, 1983 – Name changed to Levon Resources Ltd.; basis 1 new for 5 old shs. ■

New Continental Oil Company of Canada Limited (Alta. 1936)
Dec. 1971 – Acquired by Pan Ocean Oil Corp.; basis 6.47 new for 100 old shs.

New Copper Mountain Mines Ltd. (B.C. Aug. 9, 1974 amalg.)
Jan. 10, 1992 – Dissolved.

New Cosmic Industries Ltd. (B.C. Feb. 23, 1970 amalg.)
Aug. 8, 1977 – Name changed to Cosmic Industries Ltd. ■

New Cronin Babine Mine Ltd. (Ont. 1948)
Apr. 1973 – Name changed to Sproatt Silver Mines Ltd.; basis 1 new for 4 old shs. ■

New Davies Petroleums Limited (Alta. 1952)
Feb. 24, 1972 – Name changed to Davoil Natural Resources Limited; basis 1 new for 5 old shs. ■

New Dawn Mining Corp. (B.C. Aug. 22, 2006)
Nov. 15, 2007 – Continued into Canada.
Dec. 31, 2013 – Continued into Cayman Islands.

New Delhi Mines Ltd. (Ont. Sept. 5, 1934)
1961 – Name changed to Delhi Pacific Mines Limited; basis 1 new for 4 old shs. ■

New Denver Explorations Ltd. (B.C. 1967)
Feb. 25, 1983 – Struck off register.

New Devil's Elbow Mines Ltd. (Ont. 1965)
June 9, 1978 – Name changed to Lancer Resources Ltd.; basis 1 new for 5 old shs. ■

New Devon Petroleums Ltd. (Alta. 1951)
1954 – Acquired by Nuco Petroleums Ltd.; basis 1 new for 8 old shs. (see Nuco Petroleums Ltd.)

New Dickenson Mines Ltd. (Ont. 1944)
1960 – Merged into Dickenson Mines Ltd.

New Digby Dome Mines Ltd. (Ont. 1910)
Mar. 5, 1975 – Charter cancelled.

New Dimension Resources Ltd. (Ont. 1947)
Sept. 1983 – Continued into Wyoming.
June 23, 1997 – Name changed to Global Disposal Corporation.

New Dimension Resources Ltd. (B.C. Nov. 10, 2005)
Nov. 10, 2020 – Name changed to Capella Minerals Limited. (see FPsurvey - Mines & Energy)

New Dimensions Technologies Limited (B.C. Sept. 11, 1986)
Feb. 20, 1995 – Name changed to NDT Ventures Ltd.; basis 1 new for 5 old shs. ■

New Dolly Varden Minerals Inc. (Ont. Dec. 21, 1979 amalg.)
Sept. 15, 2000 – Name changed to Dolly Varden Resources Inc. ■

New Dolomite White Mining Limited (B.C. Oct. 23, 1969)
July 3, 1987 – Dissolved and struck off register.

New Dominion Minerals Development Ltd. (Alta. 1951)
1963 – Acquired by Bow Valley Industries Ltd.; basis 6.2¢ per sh. (see Bow Valley Industries Ltd.)

New Dominion Nickel Mines Ltd. (Ont. 1943)
Apr. 21, 1978 – Name changed to New Dominion Resources Limited. ■

New Dominion Resources Limited (Ont. 1943)
Nov. 5, 1982 – Name changed to Epping Resources Ltd. ■

New Dynasty Resources Inc. (B.C. Mar. 30, 1983)
June 22, 1984 – Name changed to International Dynasty Resources Inc. ■

New Eagle Mining Corp. Ltd. (B.C. 1963)
Aug. 19, 1974 – Dissolved.

New Electra Porcupine Gold Mines Ltd. (Ont. 1944)
1954 – Merged into Pardee Amalgamated Mines Ltd.; basis 2 new for 35 old shs.

New Emjay Petroleums Ltd. (unknown)
May 1966 – Acquired by Thomson Drilling Ltd. for 7.1¢ per sh.

New Energy West Corporation (Alta. Aug. 12, 1988 amalg.)
Nov. 16, 2001 – Acquired by Gastar Exploration Ltd.; basis 1 Gastar sh. for between 14.36 and 16.66 New Energy shs., depending on the New Energy options exercised. (see Gastar Exploration Ltd.)

New Era Developments Ltd. (B.C. 1980)
Apr. 22, 1994 – Dissolved and struck off register.

New Era Minerals Inc. (B.C. Aug. 2, 2007)
June 11, 2020 – Name changed to Hylands International Holdings Inc. ■

New FSV Corporation (Ont. Oct. 6, 2014)
June 1, 2015 – Name changed to FirstService Corporation. (see FPsurvey - Industrials)

New Falcon Oils Limited (Alta.)
1959 – Struck off register.

New Far North Exploration Ltd. (Alta. 1955)
Nov. 1977 – Charter cancelled.

New Faulkenham Mines Ltd. (Ont. July 14, 1936)
1963 – Acquired by Starratt Nickel Mines Ltd. (see Starratt Nickel Mines Limited)

New Federal Chibougamau Mines Ltd. (Ont. 1959)
July 27, 1976 – Charter cancelled.

New Fenimore Iron Mines Ltd. (Que. 1947)
Aug. 10, 1973 – Name changed to Forage Westburne-G.P. Ltée/Westburne-G.P. Drilling Ltd.

New Fibers International, Ltd. (B.C. 1979)
Feb. 25, 1994 – Dissolved and struck off register.

New Fidelity Minerals Ltd. (Ont. 1958)
1974 – Continued into Alberta. (see Kenting Limited)
May 1975 – Acquired by Kenting Limited. (see Kenting Limited)

New Flyer Industries Inc. (Ont. June 16, 2005)
May 18, 2018 – Name changed to NFI Group Inc. (see FPsurvey - Industrials)

New Force Crag Mines Limited (Ont. 1974 amalg.)
Apr. 10, 1976 – Amalgamated with Beaver Hill Lake Uranium Mines Limited (0.75 for 1) and Crow River Gold Mines Inc. (0.6 for 1) to continue with the same name New Force Crag Mines Limited; basis 1 new for 1 old sh.
July 12, 1982 – Dissolved.

New Formaque Mines Ltd. (Que. 1948)
Nov. 1973 – Name changed to Sobiga Mines Limited; basis 1 new for 10 old shs. (see FPsurvey - Mines & Energy)

New Fortune Mines Ltd. (Ont. Mar. 1952)
June 25, 1958 – Name changed to United New Fortune Mines Ltd.; basis 1 new for 4 old shs. ■

New Forty-Four Mines Limited (Man. 1934)
Jan. 22, 1986 – Formed Canadian Gold Mines Ltd. in Manitoba on amalgamation with Portage Avenue Gold Mines Limited. ■

New Found Gold Corp. (Ont. Jan. 6, 2016)
June 23, 2020 – Continued into British Columbia. (see FPsurvey - Mines & Energy)

New Frontier Exploration Inc. (B.C. 1951)
Jan. 12, 1982 – Amalgamated with 3 other cos. to form New Frontier Petroleum Corporation; basis 1 new for 1 old sh.

New Frontier Petroleum Corporation (B.C. 1982 amalg.)
Aug. 23, 1985 – Name changed to Petromac Energy Inc.; basis 1 new for 5 old shs. ■

New Gas Exploration Co. of Alberta Ltd. (Alta. 1951)
1958 – Acquired by Medallion Petroleums Limited; basis 1 new for 2 old shs. (see Medallion Petroleums Limited)

New Gateway Oils & Minerals Ltd. (Alta. 1947)
Sept. 30, 1981 – Amalgamated with Killucan Resources Ltd. to form new co. also known as Killucan Resources; basis sh. for sh. (see Killucan Resources Ltd.)

New Glacier Explorers Ltd. (Ont. 1957)
Oct. 24, 1973 – Charter cancelled.

New Global Ventures International Ltd. (B.C. Apr. 29, 1987)
Oct. 15, 2010 – Name changed to Auro Resources Corp. ■

New Global Ventures Ltd. (B.C. Apr. 29, 1987)
Mar. 14, 2008 – Name changed to New Global Ventures International Ltd.; basis 1 new for 2 old shs. ■

New Gold Star Mines Ltd. (B.C. 1967)
Aug. 1973 – Name changed to Norwich Resources Ltd.; basis 1 new for 5 old shs. ■

New Goldbrae Developments Ltd. (B.C. 1982)
May 13, 1994 – Dissolved and struck off register.

New Goldcore Ventures Ltd. (B.C. Sept. 30, 1982)
Nov. 4, 1988 – Continued into Canada.
Dec. 8, 1997 – Name changed to Namex Explorations Inc.; basis 1 new for 7 old shs. ■

New Golden Rose Mines Ltd. (Ont. 1935)
1942 – Wound up. No distribution.

New Golden Sceptre Minerals Ltd. (B.C. Dec. 22, 1986)
Aug. 22, 1989 – Continued into Canada.
Nov. 8, 1995 – Dissolved.
Nov. 3, 2003 – Revived. (see FPsurvey - Mines & Energy)

New Goldvue Mines Ltd. (Ont. Sept. 7, 1944)
Feb. 23, 1979 – Name changed to Lava Cap Resources Ltd.; basis 1 new for 5 old shs. ■

New Goliath Minerals Ltd. (B.C. 1986)
July 31, 1989 – Formed Hughes Lang Corporation in British Columbia on amalgamation with Meridor Resources Limited and Hughes Lang Corporation; basis 0.1623 new cl. B shs. for 1 Meridor sh., 0.0462 new cl. A shs. for 1 Hughes cl. A sh. and 0.0462 new cl. B shs. for 1 Hughes cl. B sh., and 0.0812 new cl. B shs. for 1 New Goliath sh. ■

New Grandroy Resources Inc. (Ont. 1951)
June 1976 – Name changed to Hillsborough Exploration Ltd.; basis 1 new for 10 old shs. ■

New Grouse Creek Mines Ltd. (B.C. 1961)
1972 – Name changed to Westburne Drilling (B.C.) Ltd. following acquisition by Westburne Petroleum Services Ltd.

New Growth Explorations Inc. (Ont. 1951)
Nov. 5, 1976 – Amalgamated with 7 other cos. to form Wolverine Developments Inc.; basis 3 new for 32 old shs. ■

New Guinea Gold Corporation (Yuk. June 4, 1996)
Oct. 20, 2005 – Continued into British Columbia. (see FPsurvey - Mines & Energy)

New Hamil Silver-Lead Mines Ltd. (B.C. 1950)
May 4, 1972 – Charter cancelled.

New Hana Copper Mining Ltd. (B.C. Nov. 10, 2009)
Apr. 25, 2014 – Name changed to Handa Copper Corporation. ■

The New Harding Group Inc. (Ont. July 7, 1927)
June 19, 1989 – Name changed to Clarus Corporation. ■

New Harricana Mines Ltd. (Que. 1927)
Aug. 1974 – Charter cancelled.

New Hiawatha Gold Mines Ltd. (Ont. 1973)
May 28, 1976 – Name changed to Hull Explorations Limited. ■

New Hibernian Resources Inc. (B.C. Apr. 16, 1987)
Jan. 18, 1991 – Name changed to E.C. Auto Centres Inc. ■

New High Ridge Resources Inc. (B.C. June 24, 2004)
Feb. 7, 2011 – Name changed to Newton Gold Corp. ■

New Highland Valley Mines Ltd. (B.C. 1955)
Aug. 1975 – Amalgamated into Great Manhattan Gold Corp.

New Highridge Mining Co. Ltd. (Ont. Mar. 1, 1939)
1958 – Name changed to Combined Metal Mines Limited; basis 1 new for 3 old shs. ■

New Holland Gold Mines Ltd. (B.C.)
June 3, 1974 – Dissolved and struck off register.

New Hombre Resources Ltd. (B.C. 1981)
Mar. 20, 1989 – Name changed to X.T.C. Resources Ltd.; basis 1 new for 2.5 old shs. ■

New Hope Porcupine Gold Mines Ltd. (Ont. 1960)
July 27, 1976 – Charter cancelled.

New Hope Resources Corp. (B.C. Dec. 14, 1982)
Jan. 17, 1985 – Name changed to Hi Tech Ventures Inc. ■

New Horizon Uranium Corporation (Can. Sept. 3, 2003)
July 6, 2012 – Dissolved.

New Horizons Capital Corp. (B.C. Oct. 1, 1999)
Nov. 27, 2003 – Acquired by Chalk Media Corp. in agreement which represented company's Qualifying Transaction; basis acquisition of 3,800,000 new Chalk shs. at $0.1447 were distributed to shldrs. who became shldrs. of Chalk Media. (see Chalk Media Corp.)

New Horizons Explorations Ltd. (Ont. 1947)
Shldrs. received equivalent of 4 shs. Goldfields Uranium Mines Ltd. for each New Horizons sh. Co. wound up. (see Goldfields Uranium Mines Ltd.)

New Horizons Resources Inc. (B.C. 1981)
June 5, 1992 – Dissolved and struck off register.

New Hosco Mines Limited (Ont. 1944)
Nov. 7, 1978 – Dissolved.

New Hugh Malartic Mines Ltd. (Ont. 1935)
Aug. 1955 – Name changed to Alba Explorations Ltd.; basis 1 new for 4 old shs. ■

New Impact Resources Inc. (B.C. Apr. 17, 1969)
Aug. 22, 1989 – Name changed to Consolidated Impact Resources Inc.; basis 1 new for 2.5 old shs. ■

New Imperial Mines Ltd. (Alta. 1954)
1971 – Name changed to Whitehorse Copper Mines Ltd.; basis 1 new for 2.5 old shs. ■

New Inca Gold Ltd. (Bermuda Oct. 6, 1996)
July 8, 2004 – Name changed to Balloch Resources Ltd.; basis 1 new for 10 old shs. ■

New Indian Mines Ltd. (B.C. 1946)
Mar. 1972 – Name changed to Azure Resources Ltd.; basis 1 new for 5 old shs. ■

New Indigo Resources Inc. (Alta. Oct. 8, 1986)
Mar. 2, 1999 – Amalgamated with Lytton Minerals Limited to form Tahera Corporation; basis 1 new for 1 Lytton sh. and 2.43 new for 1 New Indigo sh. (see Tahera Corporation)

New Insco Mines Ltd. (Que. 1938)
Jan. 1979 – Assets acquired by Nuinsco Resources Limited; basis 1 new for 3 old shs. ■

New International Infopet Systems Ltd. (Ont. Mar. 9, 1965)
Jan. 8, 2014 – Name changed to SponsorsOne Inc. following the Dec. 19, 2013, reverse takeover acquisition of MXM Nation Inc. ■

New Island Minerals Ltd. (Alta. Dec. 14, 1987 amalg.)
Apr. 22, 1997 – Name changed to New Island Resources Inc.; basis 1 new for 8 old shs. ■

New Island Resources Inc. (Alta. Dec. 14, 1987 amalg.)
June 2, 2014 – Struck from registry and dissolved.

New Jack Lake Uranium Mines Ltd. (Ont. Aug. 14, 1945)
1962 – Name changed to Equity Explorations Ltd. ■

New Jaculet Mines Ltd. (Ont. Feb. 18, 1932)
May 16, 1956 – Name changed to Chibougamau Jaculet Mines Ltd.; basis 1 new for 2 old shs. ■

New Jason Mines Ltd. (Ont. Nov. 9, 1938)
May 1976 – Charter cancelled. Trustee (Armac Securities Ltd., 1601, 100 Adelaide St. W., Toronto, Ont. M5H 1S3) holds 400,000 shs. Grand Bay Explorations Limited for benefit of shldrs.

New Jericho Development Corporation Ltd. (B.C. Mar. 26, 1956)
Mar. 10, 1981 – Name changed to Mt. Calvery Resources Ltd.; basis 1 new for 4 old shs. ■

New Jersey Mining Company (Idaho July 18, 1996)
Dec. 6, 2021 – Name changed to Idaho Strategic Resources, Inc.; basis 1 new for 14 old shs.

New Joburke Explorations Ltd. (Ont. 1945)
Aug. 16, 1977 – Name changed to Cenex Limited; basis 1 new for 1 old sh. ■

New Jonsmith Exploration Ltd. (Alta. 1976)
Sept. 26, 1977 – Acquired by Chal-Bert Drilling Co. Ltd. for 16¢ per sh. Name subsequently changed to Chal-Bert (Drilling) Western Ltd.

New Jordan Petroleum Ltd. (Can. June 26, 1987)
May 7, 1992 – Name changed to Jordan Petroleum Ltd. ■

New Kelore Mines Limited (Ont. May 9, 1945)
Feb. 24, 1992 – Formed Orvana Minerals Corp. in Ontario on amalgamation with Pan Orvana Resources Inc.; basis 1 new for 1 Pan Orvana sh. and 1 new for 3.67 New Kelore shs. (see FPsurvey - Mines & Energy)

New Kelver Resources Ltd. (B.C. Jan. 26, 1968)
Jan. 13, 1977 – Name changed to Access Resources Ltd. ■

New Kenrell Resources Inc. (B.C. Mar. 14, 1980)
July 31, 1987 – Formed International Broadcasting Centre Ltd. in Alberta following amalgamation with two wholly owned subsids. ■

New Key Industries Ltd. (B.C. 1967)
June 1, 1978 – Merged with Key Enterprises Ltd. and Ambassador Development Corp. of Canada Ltd. to form Ambassador Industries Ltd.

New Lafayette Asbestos Company Limited (Que. June 10, 1950)
Mar. 2, 1957 – Name changed to North American Asbestos Company Limited; basis 1 new for 1 old sh. ■

New Laguerre Mines Limited (Ont. 1939)
Mar. 26, 1956 – Name changed to Can-Erin Mines Limited; basis 1 new for 6 old shs. ■

New Larder "U" Island Mines Ltd. (Ont. 1943)
1955 – Acquired by Anacon Lead Mines Ltd.; basis 1 new for 3 old shs. (see Anacon Lead Mines Ltd.)

New Larose Mining & Smelting Ltd. (Ont. 1947)
1953 – Acquired by Silver-Miller Mines Ltd.; basis 2 new for 5 old shs.

New Leather Corporation (B.C. 1983)
Nov. 2, 1995 – Name changed to Global Focus Resources Ltd. ■

New Legend Group Limited (Bermuda Jan. 13, 2006)
June 24, 2009 – Name changed to Liuyang Fireworks Limited pursuant to Qualifying Transaction acquisition of Strive Best Holdings Limited; basis 1 new for 12 old shs. ■

New Lintex Minerals Ltd. (B.C. May 31, 1983 amalg.)
Mar. 5, 1993 – Formed Globaltex Industries Inc. in British Columbia on amalgamation with Willow Creek Coal Limited. ■

New Lith Inc. (Ont. Apr. 29, 1980)
June 1987 – Name changed to Barris Klein Holdings Inc. ■

New Look Eyewear Inc. (Can. Jan. 1, 2002 amalg.)
June 1, 2015 – Name changed to New Look Vision Group Inc. ■

New Look Vision Group Inc. (Can. Jan. 1, 2002 amalg.)
May 31, 2021 – Acquired by NL1AcquireCo Inc., an entity created by a group of funds managed by FFL Partners, LLC, Caisse de depot et placement du Quebec and the Dr. H. Doug Barnes family; basis $50 cash per cl. A com. sh.

New Lorie Mines Ltd. (Ont. 1945)
Mar. 10, 1981 – Name changed to Lorie Resources Inc. ■

New Louvre Mines Ltd. (Que. 1945)
1956 – Name changed to Fano Mining & Exploration Inc. ■

New Malartic Gold Mines Ltd. (Que. 1938)
July 30, 1960 – Dissolved.

New Mallen Red Lake Mines Ltd. (Ont. 1944)
1970 – Charter cancelled.

New Manco Gold Mines Ltd. (Ont. Nov. 1938)
1945 – Name changed to Normanco Gold Mines Ltd. ■

New Manitoba Gold Mines Ltd. (Ont. 1946)
1957 – Name changed to New Manitoba Mining & Smelting Co. Ltd. ■

New Manitoba Mining & Smelting Co. Ltd. (Ont. 1946)
Mar. 15, 1962 – 1st mtge. deb. holders received 800,000 shs. and 95,000 shs. of Border Chemical Co. in full settlement of $1,000,000 funded debt.
Mar. 30, 1962 – Acquired by Manoka Mining & Smelting.
Aug. 13, 1962 – Dissolved.

New Market Ventures Inc. (B.C. Mar. 23, 2000)
Apr. 7, 2005 – Name changed to Russell Breweries Inc. following Qualifying Transaction acquisition of Russell Brewing Company Ltd.; basis 4 new for 1 old sh. ■

New Marlon Gold Mines Ltd. (Ont. 1944)
1956 – Name changed to Marcon Mines Ltd.; basis 1 new for 2 old shs. ■

New Marvel Oils Ltd. (Can. 1923)
Dec. 16, 1980 – Dissolved.

The New McDougall-Segur Oil Co., Ltd. (Can. 1926)
1935 – Taken over by The McDougall-Segur Exploration Co. of Canada Ltd.

New McManus Red Lake Gold Mines Ltd. (Ont. 1927)
Aug. 26, 1987 – Name changed to Milestone Resource Corporation; basis 1 new for 4 old shs. (see FPsurvey - Mines & Energy)

New Media Capital Inc. (Alta. Mar. 7, 2000)
June 22, 2001 – Name changed to CSM Systems Corp. ■

New Media Systems Inc. (B.C. Dec. 8, 1980)
Sept. 30, 2003 – Name changed to Wavefront Energy and Environmental Services Inc. and continued into Canada following reverse takeover acquisition of PE-TECH Inc.; basis 4 new for 5 old shs. ■

New Meg Oils Ltd. (Ont. Aug. 20, 1948)
1954 – Acquired by Lubicon Petroleums Ltd.; basis 1 new for 2 old shs. ■

New Meridian Mining Corp. (Alta. Apr. 7, 1989)
Mar. 25, 2010 – Name changed to Philippine Metals Inc. pursuant to Qualifying Transaction reverse takeover acquisition of Philippine Metals Corp.; basis 1 new for 2 old shs. ■

New Metalore Mining Company Limited (Ont. Jan. 1, 1943)
Oct. 22, 1976 – Name changed to Metalore Resources Limited. (see FPsurvey - Mines & Energy; FPsurvey - Industrials)

New Method Laundry Company Limited (Ont. 1929)
May 1969 – Acquired by Canadian Corporate Management Co. Ltd.

New Mic Mac Mines Ltd. (Ont. 1946)
1949 – Name changed to United Mic Mac Mines Ltd. ■

New Millennium Capital Corp. (Alta. Aug. 8, 2003)
June 15, 2011 – Name changed to New Millennium Iron Corp.; basis 1 new for 5 old shs. ■

New Millennium Iron Corp. (Alta. Aug. 8, 2003)
Dec. 14, 2020 – Name changed to Abaxx Technologies Inc. pursuant to the reverse takeover acquisition of (old) Abaxx Technologies Inc. and concurrent amalgamation of (old) Abaxx with wholly owned 12404206 Canada Inc. (and continued as Abaxx Technologies Holdco Inc.). (see FPsurvey - Mines & Energy; FPsurvey - Industrials)

New Millennium Metals Corporation (B.C. Mar. 11, 1983)
Feb. 18, 2002 – Amalgamated with Platinum Group Metals Ltd.; basis 1.65 new Platinum shs. for 1 old New Millennium sh.

New Millennium Technology Trust (Ont. June 28, 1999)
June 20, 2007 – Name changed to First Asset Opportunity Fund. ■

New Miller Copper Mines Ltd. (Que. 1958)
1963 – Name changed to New Miller Pipe Lines & Mining Exploration Ltd. ■

New Miller Pipe Lines & Mining Exploration Ltd. (Que. 1958)
1981 – Name changed to Consolidated Miller Mining Co. Ltd.

New Minda-Scotia Mines Ltd. (Ont. 1951)
1958 – Merged into Andover Mining & Exploration Ltd.; basis 2 new for 5 old shs.

New Minex Resources Ltd. (B.C. 1955)
Apr. 16, 1992 – Dissolved and struck off register.

New Minoils Exploration Ltd. (unknown)
Acquired by Lubicon Petroleums Ltd.; basis 1 new for 2 old shs. (see Lubicon Mining Ltd.)

New Morrison Mines Limited (Ont. Apr. 1951)
1955 – Name changed to Consolidated Morrison Explorations, Limited; basis 1 new for 2 old shs. ■

New Mosher Longlac Mines Ltd. (Ont. 1950)
1954 – Name changed to Consolidated Mosher Mines Ltd.; basis 1 new for 2 old shs. ■

New Mount Costigan Mines Ltd. (Ont. 1962)
1987 – Name changed to Costigan Gold Corporation; basis 1 new for 2 old shs. ■

New Mylamaque Explorations Ltd. (Ont. Sept. 2, 1943)
Oct. 1960 – Name changed to New Mylamaque Mining and Smelting Ltd. ■

New Mylamaque Mining and Smelting Ltd. (Ont. Sept. 2, 1943)
Jan. 11, 1969 – Name changed to Mymar Mining & Reduction Ltd.; basis 1 new for 9 old shs. ■

New Nadina Explorations Limited (B.C. Apr. 7, 1964)
Sept. 13, 2019 – Name changed to Equity Metals Corporation. (see FPsurvey - Mines & Energy)

New Nexus Petroleum Ltd. (B.C. 1983)
May 8, 1992 – Dissolved and struck off register.

New Nipiron Mines Ltd. (Ont. 1952)
1970 – Acquired by New York Oils Ltd.; basis 1 new for 4 old shs.

New Norque Mines Ltd. (Ont. 1956)
Mar. 1976 – Charter cancelled.

New Norseman Mines Ltd. (Ont. 1943)
Feb. 1953 – Name changed to Norsewick Mines Ltd. ■

New North Resources Ltd. (Alta. May 9, 1994)
Apr. 5, 2004 – Acquired by private co. 1080699 Alberta Inc. for $0.47 per sh.

New Northcal Mines Ltd. (Alta. 1947)
Aug. 1973 – Merged with Venture Properties Ltd., to continue under Venture's name; basis 1 new for 2 old shs.

New Norzone Mines Ltd. (Ont. 1946)
1955 – Name changed to Diadem Mines Ltd.; basis 1 new for 7 old shs. ■

New Oroperu Resources Inc. (Yuk. June 24, 1997)
June 11, 2002 – Continued into British Columbia. (see Anacortes Mining Corp.)
Oct. 12, 2021 – Acquired by First Light Capital Corp. (renamed Anacortes Mining Corp.); basis 5.815 First Light shs. for 1 New Oroperu sh. (see Anacortes Mining Corp.)

New Otisse Long Lac Gold Mines Ltd. (Ont. 1936)
1952 – Charter cancelled.

New Pacalta Oils Co. Ltd. (Ont. 1944)
1955 – Name changed to Wespac Petroleums Limited; basis 1 new for 5 old shs. ■

New Pacific Coal & Oils Ltd. (Ont. 1943)
1960 – Name changed to Consolidated New Pacific Ltd.; basis 1 new for 5 old shs. ■

New Pacific Holding Corp. (B.C. Nov. 5, 2003)
July 20, 2017 – Name changed to New Pacific Metals Corp. (see FPsurvey - Mines & Energy)

New Pacific Metals Corp. (B.C. Nov. 5, 2003)
July 1, 2016 – Name changed to New Pacific Holding Corp. ■

New Pascalis Mines Limited (Can. 1932)
Oct. 5, 1992 – Formed Tiomin Resources Inc. in Canada on amalgamation with Tiomin Resources Inc., constituting a reverse takeover by Tiomin; basis 1 new for 3 old shs. ■

New Peninsular Oil Limited (Que. 1952)
Feb. 23, 1973 – Charter cancelled.

New Penn Energy Corporation (B.C. 1976)
Dec. 31, 1986 – Amalgamated with 3 other cos. to form International Interlake Industries Inc.; basis 1 new for 5.85 old shs.

New Picton Uranium Mines Ltd. (Ont. 1953)
Mar. 1976 – Charter cancelled.

New Pioneer Explorations Ltd. (B.C. Mar. 31, 1980)
Mar. 2, 1989 – Delisted from the Vancouver Stock Exchange. Subsequently struck from register and dissolved.

New Placer Dome Gold Corp. (B.C. Apr. 27, 2018)
May 13, 2022 – Acquired by CopAur Minerals Inc.; basis 0.1182 CopAur shs. for 1 New Placer sh.

New Plymouth Ventures Inc. (B.C. 1974)
Aug. 14, 1992 – Dissolved and struck off register.

New Point Exploration Corp. (B.C. Mar. 10, 2017)
Feb. 21, 2019 – Name changed to KOPR Point Ventures Inc. ■

New Potterdoal Mines Ltd. (Ont. 1927)
Mar. 1976 – Charter cancelled.

New Privateer Mine Limited (B.C. Jan. 11, 1937)
June 6, 1995 – Name changed to Phrygian Mining Corporation; basis 1 new for 5 old shs. ■

The New Providence Development Company Limited (Bahamas Mar. 12, 1962)
Jan. 31, 2000 – Acquired by ENAJ International (Bahamas) Limited for $2.54 per sh.

New Prudential Petroleums Ltd. (B.C. 1958)
Dec. 1965 – Name changed to Consolidated Prudential Mines Ltd. ■

New Pyramid Gold Mines Inc. (B.C. 1964)
Jan. 19, 1977 – Name changed to International Pyramid Mines Inc.; basis 1 new for 5 old shs. ■

New Quebec Raglan Mines Limited (Ont. 1956)
June 1989 – Acquired by major shldr. Falconbridge Limited; basis $5.36 or 1 new Falconbridge sh. for each 5.5 old New Quebec shs. (see Falconbridge Limited)

New Ranchmen's Oil Co. Ltd. (Alta. 1942)
1957 – Name changed to Ranchmen's Oils (1957) Ltd.; basis 1 new for 10 old shs. ■

New Rand-Ore Mines Ltd. (Ont. 1937)
July 1960 – Charter cancelled.

New Range Resources Ltd. (Alta. Mar. 30, 2006 amalg.)
June 11, 2010 – Name changed to Relentless Resources Ltd.; basis 1 new for 2 old shs. ■

New Red Lake Centre Mines Ltd. (Ont. Sept. 1936)
Dec. 1957 – Dissolved.

New Redwood Gold Mines Ltd. (Ont. Aug. 20, 1936)
Aug. 31, 1992 – Delisted from the CDN. Subsequently dissolved and charter cancelled.

New Ribago Mines Ltd. (Ont. 1937)
1957 – Shldrs. entitled to receive 1 sh. Consolidated Ribago Mines Ltd. for each 40 old shs., plus 1 sh.

Continental Copper Mines for each 10 old shs. Charter believed surrendered.

New Rice Lake Gold Mines Ltd. (Can. 1934)
1970 – Name changed to Jagor Resources Ltd.; basis 1 new for 4 old shs. ■

New Richfield Petroleum Limited (Can. Mar. 1, 1929; via Dominion charter)
1969 – Name changed to Twin Richfield Oils Ltd.; basis 1 new for 10 old shs. ■

New Ridge Mines Ltd (B.C. Nov. 6, 1978)
July 21, 1981 – Name changed to New Ridge Resources Ltd. ■

New Ridge Resources Ltd (B.C. Nov. 6, 1978)
May 22, 1987 – Name changed to Destiny Resources Ltd.; basis 1 new for 4 old shs. ■

New Rio Resources Ltd. (B.C. Mar. 6, 1962)
Sept. 23, 1994 – Name changed to Southern Rio Resources Ltd. ■

New Rouillard Gold Mines Ltd. (Ont. 1937)
1958 – Charter cancelled.

New Rouyn Exploration Co. Ltd. (Que. 1955)
June 18, 1977 – Charter cancelled.

New Rouyn Merger Mines Ltd. (Ont. 1943)
June 8, 1965 – Name changed to Goldrim Mining Co. Ltd.; basis 1 new for 5 old shs. ■

New Royran Copper Mines Ltd. (Que. 1945)
1956 – Acquired by Copper Rand Chibougamau Mines Ltd.; basis 21 new for 40 old shs. (see Copper Rand Chibougamau Mines Ltd.)

New Rufus Argenta Mines Ltd. (B.C. 1955)
Feb. 21, 1966 – Name changed to Crest Ventures Ltd. ■

The New Russian Kid Mining Co. Ltd. (Ont. 1945)
1966 – Name changed to Augmitto Explorations Limited. ■

New Ryan Lake Mines Limited (Ont. Mar. 15, 1947)
Oct. 6, 1955 – Name changed to Min-Ore Mines Limited; basis 1 new for 3.5 old shs. ■

New Sabina Resources Ltd. (B.C. June 7, 1966)
Dec. 17, 1987 – Name changed to Sabina Resources Limited; basis 2 new for 1 old sh. ■

New Sage Energy Corp. (Can. Oct. 24, 2003)
Aug. 22, 2014 – Dissolved.

New Sage Resources Ltd. (B.C. Dec. 19, 1980)
Feb. 27, 2002 – Name changed to Consolidated New Sage Resources Ltd.; basis 1 new for 2 old shs. ■

New Santiago Mines Ltd. (B.C. 1935)
Aug. 1970 – Name changed to Santico Mining & Exploration Ltd.; basis 1 new for 10 old shs. ■

New Scope Resources Limited (Man. Mar. 7, 1951)
Sept. 13, 1984 – Name changed to Newscope Resources Limited and continued into Canada. ■

New Senator-Rouyn Limited (Que. Mar. 6, 1937)
Aug. 1980 – Name changed to NSR Resources Inc. ■

New Sepha Mines Limited (Ont. 1941)
June 30, 1980 – Charter cancelled.

New Shoshoni Ventures Ltd. (B.C. Apr. 23, 1985)
May 9, 2012 – Name changed to Shoshoni Gold Ltd.; basis 1 new for 5 old shs. ■

New Signet Resources Inc. (B.C. Nov. 16, 1979)
June 29, 1993 – Name changed to Amir Ventures Corp.; basis 1 new for 5 old shs. ■

New Sleeper Gold Corporation (Can. Mar. 15, 2004)
June 2, 2006 – Name changed to Reunion Gold Corporation. ■

New Spirit Resources and Developments Inc. (B.C. 1987)
Dec. 21, 1988 – Name changed to New Spirit Research & Development Corp. (see FPsurvey - Industrials)

New Spring Coulee Oil and Minerals Ltd. (Alta. 1950)
1960 – Name changed to Native Minerals Ltd.; basis 1 new for 4 old shs. ■

New Stafford Industries Ltd. (B.C. Jan. 18, 1988)
July 10, 2003 – Name changed to Grandcru Resources Corporation. ■

New Strategic Metals Inc. (B.C. 1982)
Nov. 18, 1986 – Name changed to P.S.M. Technologies Inc. (see FPsurvey - Industrials)

New Superior Oils of Canada Ltd. (Alta. 1945)
June 1960 – Acquired by Canadian Petrofina Ltd.; basis 0.055625 6% partic. pref. shs. Petrofina for 1 old sh. (see Canadian Petrofina Ltd.)

New Surpass Petrochemicals Ltd. (Ont. 1954)
May 1968 – Name changed to Surpass Chemicals Limited. ■

New Syrus Capital Corporation (B.C. Apr. 29, 1987)
Feb. 25, 1997 – Name changed to Player Petroleum Corporation. ■

New Taku Mines Limited (Ont. May 27, 1938)
Aug. 1974 – Name changed to Rembrandt Gold Mines Ltd.; basis 1 new for 5 old shs. ■

New Tech Lithium Corp. (B.C. June 5, 2006)
Mar. 4, 2019 – Name changed to New Tech Minerals Corp. ■

New Tech Minerals Corp. (B.C. June 5, 2006)
Aug. 31, 2022 – Name changed to American Potash Corp. ■

New Telluride Gold Mines of Canada Ltd. (Ont. 1944)
June 3, 1965 – Dissolved.

New Territorial Uranium Mines Limited (B.C. Oct. 22, 1968)
Aug. 2, 1977 – Name changed to Mid-West Energy Inc. ■

New Thurbois Mines Limited (Ont. 1943)
Sept. 10, 1956 – Name changed to Canadian Thorium Corporation Limited. ■

New True Fissure Mining & Milling Co. Ltd. (Ont. 1937)
Apr. 15, 1963 – Dissolved.

New Tyee Resources Ltd. (B.C. June 25, 1969)
July 31, 1984 – Name changed to Alban Explorations Ltd.; basis 1 new for 5 old shs. ■

New Ungava Copper Corporation Limited (Que. 1954)
Oct. 29, 1982 – Name changed to Unergie Inc. ■

New Uni-Way Holdings Ltd. (B.C. Dec. 1, 1980)
Feb. 25, 1998 – Name changed to Full Riches Investments Ltd. ■

New Unisphere Resources Ltd. (Alta. 1949)
Sept. 30, 1981 – Struck off register.

New United Salt Mines Ltd. (Ont. 1969)
Mar. 1976 – Charter cancelled.

New University Holdings Corp. (Alta. July 14, 2010)
July 26, 2011 – Name changed to ePals Corporation and continued into Ontario pursuant to Qualifying Transaction reverse takeover acquisition of ePals, Inc. and ePals Finance Corp.; basis 1 new for 2.3877 old shs. ■

New Venoro Gold Corp. (Can. Nov. 13, 1986)
May 1, 2000 – Name changed to Vanteck (VRB) Technology Corp. ■

New-View Industries Inc. (Alta. 1988)
Sept. 30, 1992 – Acquired by Home Products Inc.; basis 1 Home Products sh. for 8 New-View shs.

New View Landscaping Ltd. (Alta. 1987)
Nov. 1, 1989 – Struck off register.

New Vinray Mines Ltd. (Ont. 1944)
1960 – Name changed to Atlas Telefilm Ltd.; basis 1 new for 4 old shs. ■

New Walcoro Mines Ltd. (Ont. 1944)
July 1973 – Charter cancelled.

New Wave Esports Corp. (B.C. May 17, 2006)
May 8, 2020 – Name changed to New Wave Holdings Corp.; basis 1 new for 3 old shs. ■

New Wave Holdings Corp. (B.C. May 17, 2006)
June 25, 2025 – Name changed to Humanoid Global Holdings Corp. (see FPsurvey - Industrials)

New Wellington Mines Ltd. (B.C. June 20, 1953)
Sept. 30, 1970 – Name changed to New Wellington Resources Limited. ■

New Wellington Resources Limited (B.C. June 20, 1953)
Mar. 25, 1976 – Name changed to International Wellington Resources Ltd. ■

New West Amulet Mines Ltd. (Que. Aug. 28, 1944)
1966 – Name changed to Waite Dufault Mines Limited; basis 1 new for 5 old shs. ■

New West Energy Services Inc. (Can. Feb. 11, 1986)
May 28, 2021 – Privatized via a 1-for-27,498,810 consolidation; basis $0.002 cash per sh.

New Westwin Ventures Inc. (B.C. May 30, 1986)
July 29, 1997 – Name changed to Arimex Mining Corp. ■

New World Oil & Uranium Ltd. (Alta. 1952)
July 1956 – Acquired by Sastex Oil & Gas Ltd.; basis 1 new for 10 old shs. (see Sastex Oil & Gas Ltd.)

New World Oil Ltd. (Alta. 1952)
July 1955 – Name changed to New World Oil & Uranium Ltd. ■

New World Resource Corp. (B.C. Sept. 22, 1983)
June 29, 2020 – Formed Perimeter Medical Imaging AI, Inc. in British Columbia on amalgamation with Perimeter Medical Imaging, Inc. (PMI), constituting a reverse takeover by PMI; basis 0.20833 new for 1 PMI sh. and 0.36499 new for 1 New World Resource sh. (see FPsurvey - Industrials)

New World Ventures Inc. (Alta. Dec. 31, 1987)
Dec. 2, 1992 – Name changed to Digital Precision Imagery Corp. pursuant to reverse takeover acquisition of Digitizing & Imaging Services Corp.; basis 1 new for 3 old shs. ■

New Xavier Capital Corp. (B.C. Mar. 16, 2000)
May 25, 2001 – Name changed to RET Internet Services Inc. following Qualifying Transaction acquisition of Transmeridian Communications Inc. ■

New Yarandry Ltd. (Ont. Oct. 5, 1965)
Feb. 23, 1988 – Name changed to Merbank Capital Corporation. ■

New York Alaska Mines Ltd. (B.C. 1956)
May 1, 1969 – Struck off register.

New York Oils Limited (B.C. 1937)
July 19, 1982 – Continued into Alberta. (see Sceptre Resources Limited)
Mar. 21, 1989 – Acquired by a wholly owned subsid. of Sceptre Resources Limited; basis 0.053548 Sceptre shs. for 1 New York Oils sh. (see Sceptre Resources Limited)

Newalta Corporation (Alta. July 15, 1980)
Mar. 6, 2003 – Converted into an income trust named Newalta Income Fund; basis 1 trust unit for 2 com. shs.

Newalta Corporation (Alta. Jan. 1, 2010 amalg.)
July 24, 2018 – Amalgamated with Tervita Corporation to continue under the Tervita (new Tervita) name; basis 0.1437 new Tervita com. shs. and 0.0307 new Tervita wts. for 1 Newalta com. sh. (see Tervita Corporation)

Newalta Income Fund (Alta. Jan. 16, 2003)
Jan. 1, 2009 – Converted into Newalta Inc.; basis 1 Newalta Inc. sh. for 1 trust unit. (see Newalta Corporation)
Jan. 1, 2010 – Dissolved pursuant to internal reorganization of Newalta Inc. (see Newalta Corporation)

Newalta Inc. (Alta. Oct. 29, 2008)
Jan. 1, 2010 – Formed Newalta Corporation in Alberta on amalgamation with wholly owned Newalta Corporation. ■

Newalta Oil & Gas Ltd. (Alta. July 15, 1980)
July 7, 1986 – Name changed to Newalta Corporation. ■

Newalta Petroleums Ltd. (Alta. 1950)
Struck off register.

Newbaska Gold and Copper Mines Ltd. (Que. Nov. 28, 1951)
Jan. 25, 1986 – Charter cancelled.
Sept. 24, 1998 – Revived.

Newbec Mines Ltd. (Can. Feb. 1927)
1946 – Wound up and charter surrendered. Shldrs. received 1 Norbec Copper Mines sh. for 10 old and 2 Lartic Mines shs. for 33 old shs.

Newbridge Capital Inc. (B.C. Sept. 12, 2005)
Mar. 15, 2012 – Name changed to KazaX Minerals Inc. ■

Newbridge Networks Corporation (Can. June 6, 1986)
May 26, 2000 – Via Plan of Arrangement with Alcatel S.A., all o/s shs. exchanged for either 0.81 of an Alcatel Networks Corporation exchangeable sh. or 0.81 of Alcatel American Depository Share (ADS), or any combination thereof. (see Alcatel Networks Corporation)

Newbridge Resources Ltd. (Alta. May 29, 1996)
Nov. 15, 1999 – Name changed to Lamplighter Energy Ltd. ■

Newbrun Development Corporation (Ont. Apr. 5, 1984)
Aug. 8, 1997 – Name changed to Beverly Glen Capital Corp.; basis 1 new for 2 old shs. ■

Newbrun Mines Ltd. (Ont. 1953)
Sept. 1962 – Dissolved.

Newbrun Resources Ltd. (Ont. Apr. 5, 1984)
Feb. 1988 – Name changed to Newbrun Development Corporation; basis 1 new for 2 old shs. ■

Newbury Explorations Ltd. (B.C. 1980)
Dec. 30, 1985 – Name changed to Newbury International Ventures Inc. ■

Newbury International Ventures Inc. (B.C. 1980)
Dec. 4, 1992 – Dissolved and struck off register.

Newcan Minerals Limited (Alta. May 27, 1963)
June 20, 1985 – Name changed to World Aquathemes Limited. ■

Newcastle Energy Corp. (B.C. Apr. 6, 1981)
Sept. 10, 2018 – Continued into Canada.
Sept. 12, 2018 – Name changed to Martello Technologies Group Inc. following reverse takeover acquisition of private Kanata, Ont.-based Martello Technologies Inc. via a three-cornered amalgamation whereby Martello

amalgamated with a wholly owned subsidiary of Newcastle. (see FPsurvey - Industrials)

Newcastle Gold Ltd. (Ont. Dec. 16, 2009)
Dec. 28, 2017 – Acquired by Trek Mining Inc.; basis 0.873 Trek shares for each NewCastle share.

Newcastle Market-Neutral Trust (Ont. July 18, 1997)
Feb. 6, 2002 – Name changed to Northwater Market-Neutral Trust. ■

Newcastle Minerals Ltd. (B.C. June 14, 1977)
Mar. 7, 2013 – Name changed to GoldON Resources Ltd.; basis 1 new for 5 old shs. ■

Newcastle Resources Ltd. (Ont. Apr. 24, 1967)
June 22, 2011 – Name changed to RepliCel Life Sciences Inc. and continued into British Columbia following reverse takeover acquisition of TrichoScience Innovations Inc. ■

Newchild International Inc. (Ont. May 27, 1991)
Mar. 20, 2006 – Dissolved and struck from register.

Newclare Oils Limited (Alta. 1952)
1958 – Acquired by Vulcan Oil Ltd.; basis 1 new for 5 old shs.

Newco Bancorp Inc. (Ont. June 22, 2000)
May 5, 2016 – Amalgamated with Munbancorp Realty Inc.; basis 1 redeemable pref. sh. for 1 Newco sh., immediately redeemed for 39¢ per pref. sh.

Newco Financial Corporation (B.C. 1969)
1977 – Continued into Canada.
Mar. 18, 1983 – Name changed to CITCO Financial Corporation. ■

Newco Silver Mines Ltd. (Ont. 1965)
1965 – Name changed to Great Pine Mines Ltd. and continued into Ontario. ■

Newcoast Silver Mines Ltd. (B.C. Apr. 30, 1963)
July 19, 2004 – Name changed to Southern Silver Exploration Corp.; basis 1 new for 7 old shs. (see FPsurvey - Mines & Energy)

Newconex Holdings Limited (Ont. 1962)
Mar. 31, 1978 – Amalgamated with Newconex Investments Ltd. to form Newconex Holdings Limited. Minority shldrs. received (1 for 1) pref. shs. redeemed on Apr. 12, 1978, at $8.40 per sh.

Newcor Mining & Refining Ltd. (Ont. 1943)
1958 – Charter cancelled.

Newcourt Acquisition Corp (Cayman Islands Feb. 25, 2021)
Jan. 25, 2024 – Name changed to Psyence Biomedical Ltd. pursuant to the Qualifying Acquisition of the Therapeutics business of Psyence Group Inc. conducted through its wholly owned Psyence Biomed Corp. As part of the Qualifying Acquisition, Psyence Group transferred the Therapeuitcs business to newly incorporated wholly owned Psyence Biomed II Corp., following which Psyence Biomed was amalgamated into Psyence Group and Pysence Biomed II became a wholly owned subsidiary of the company. ■

Newcourt Credit Group Inc. (Ont. Jan. 13, 1984)
Nov. 16, 1999 – Formed CIT Exchangeco Inc. in Canada following acquisition of all o/s com. shs. by U.S.-based The CIT Group Inc.; basis 0.7 new for 1 old sh. ■

Newcrest Developments Limited (Ont. 1964)
May 27, 1985 – Charter cancelled.

Newcrest Mining Limited (Australia 1990 amalg.)
Nov. 6, 2023 – Acquired by Newmont Corporation; basis 0.4 Newmont com. shs. for 1 Newcrest ord. sh.

Newen Enterprises Inc. (B.C. Mar. 13, 1987)
Nov. 2, 1998 – Name changed to Consolidated Newen Enterprises Inc.; basis 1 new for 5 old shs. ■

Newera Capital Corporation (B.C. Aug. 29, 1988)
Aug. 12, 1997 – Name changed to ThrillTime Entertainment International, Inc. ■

Newfield Mines Ltd. (Ont. 1946)
Aug. 31, 1989 – Amalgamated with Jonpol Explorations Limited (1 for 1) to continue with the same name Jonpol Explorations Limited; basis 2 new for 1 old sh. (see Jonpol Explorations Limited)

Newfoundland and Labrador Hydro (N.L. 1974)
Jan. 1, 2008 – Succeeded by Nalcor Energy as the Province of Newfoundland and Labrador's Crown energy corporation.

Newfoundland Capital Corporation Limited (N.L. Mar. 8, 1949)
Mar. 4, 1987 – Continued into Canada.
Oct. 30, 2018 – Acquired by Stingray Digital Group Inc.; basis 0.15370862 Stingray subord. vtg. shs. or variable subord. vtg. shs. plus $13.1683383 cash for 1 cl. A subord. vtg.sh. of Newfoundland Capital.
Dec. 15, 2018 – Name changed to Stingray Radio Inc.

Newfoundland Exploration Company Limited (N.L. 1929)
Aug. 17, 1988 – Amalgamated with Overton Energy and Resources Limited (1 for 2) to continue as Newfoundland Exploration Company Limited; basis 1 new for 1 old sh.

Newfoundland Exploration Company Limited (N.L. Aug. 17, 1988 amalg.)
Mar. 22, 1993 – Continued into Canada.
Apr. 2, 1993 – Name changed to Drug Royalty Corporation Inc.; basis 1 new for 10 old shs. ■

Newfoundland Goldbar Resources Inc. (N.L. Dec. 30, 1988)
Feb. 12, 2024 – Continued into Ontario. (see FPsurvey - Mines & Energy)

Newfoundland Light & Power Company, Limited (N.L. 1924)
Sept. 8, 1966 – Acquired by Newfoundland Light & Power Co. Limited; basis sh. for sh. Pref. shs., $100 par, received 10 new shs. of $10 par value. Bonds received equivalent value in new bonds. (see Newfoundland Light & Power Co. Limited)

Newfoundland Light & Power Co. Limited (N.L. Sept. 8, 1966)
Dec. 29, 1987 – Acquired by Fortis Inc., previously a wholly owned subsid. of the co.
Sept. 30, 1998 – Name changed to Newfoundland Power Inc.

Newfoundland Municipal Financing Corporation (N.L.)
Jan. 1, 2004 – Name changed to Newfoundland and Labrador Municipal Financing Corporation.

Newfoundland Telephone Company Limited (N.L. May 31, 1919)
Oct. 15, 1985 – Became a wholly owned subsid. of NewTel Enterprises Limited. Com. shs. of co. recognized as sh. certificates of NewTel. Pref. shldrs. continue to hold pref. shs. of Newfoundland Telephone Company Limited. All o/s pref. shs. redeemed on Jan. 15, 1993, as follows: $20.20 per 7.25% pref. sh. plus 12¢ per sh. in accr. and unpaid divd.; $20.60 per 9.75% pref. sh. plus 17¢ per sh. in accr. and unpaid divd.; and $20.60 per 8.85% pref. sh. plus 15¢ per sh. in accr. and unpaid divd.
Apr. 16, 1996 – Name changed to NewTel Communications Inc.

Newfoundland Zinc Mines Ltd. (Ont. 1963)
Jan. 14, 1975 – Name changed to Tecam Limited.

Newgate Resources Ltd. (B.C. Apr. 22, 1986)
July 2, 1991 – Name changed to Consolidated Newgate Resources Ltd.; basis 1 new for 4 old shs. ■

Newgate Resources Ltd. (Alta. May 26, 1992 amalg.)
Dec. 16, 1996 – Formed Para-Tech Energy Corporation in Alberta on reverse takeover acquisition of and amalgamation with Para-Tech Energy Inc. for 16,988,780

post-cons. shs. and 4,488,750 wts.; basis 1 new for 10 old shs. ■

Newgen Environmental Systems Inc. (Alta. Mar. 29, 1995)
Aug. 2, 2004 – Struck from registry and dissolved.

Newgioco Group, Inc. (Del. Aug. 26, 1998)
Nov. 10, 2020 – Name changed to Elys Game Technology, Corp.

NewGrowth Corp. (Ont. June 27, 1991)
June 26, 2009 – All o/s cl. B pref. shs., ser. 1, redeemed; basis $18.25 cash per sh.
June 26, 2014 – All o/s cl. B pref. shs. ser. 2 redeemed for $13.70 cash per sh.
June 27, 2019 – All o/s cl. A capital shs. and cl. B pref. shs., ser. 3, redeemed; basis $46.1427 cash per cl. A capital sh. and $32.07 cash per cl. B pref. sh., ser. 3.

Newhaven Media Inc. (Alta. June 2, 1995)
Aug. 13, 1998 – Filed a Notice of Intention To Make a Proposal under the Bankruptcy and Insolvency Act.
Sept. 23, 1998 – Placed into bankruptcy by a court order and PricewaterhouseCoopers Inc. of Calgary, Alta., was appointed trustee.
June 2002 – All the assets had been sold and the administration had been completed. The major secured creditor suffered a significant shortfall. There were no distributions made to unsecured creditors or shldrs.
June 10, 2003 – Trustee discharged.

Newhawk Gold Mines Ltd. (B.C. Jan. 20, 1948)
Oct. 12, 1999 – Acquired by Silver Standard Resources Inc.; basis 1 Silver Standard sh. for 6 Newhawk shs. (see Silver Standard Resources Inc.)

Newjay Resources Ltd. (B.C. July 31, 1979)
Aug. 25, 1993 – Name changed to Consolidated Newjay Resources Ltd.; basis 1 new for 3.5 old shs. ■

Newkirk Mining Corp. Ltd. (Ont. 1953)
1956 – Name changed to Continental Mining Exploration Ltd. ■

NewLeaf Brands Inc. (B.C. Sept. 27, 2013)
June 5, 2020 – Name changed to Mydecine Innovations Group Inc. (see FPsurvey - Industrials)

Newline Resources Ltd. (B.C. 1975)
Aug. 20, 1987 – Name changed to Newline Development Corporation. (see FPsurvey - Industrials)

Newlook Capital Corp. (B.C. Oct. 26, 1999)
May 17, 2002 – Name changed to Newlook Industries Corp. pursuant to Qualifying Transaction acquisition of Vision Unlimited Equipment Inc., a wholly owned subsid. of Eiger Technology, Inc.; basis 1 new for 2 old shs. ■

Newlook Industries Corp. (B.C. Oct. 26, 1999)
Feb. 3, 2009 – Continued into Ontario. (see FPsurvey - Industrials)

Newlund Mines Ltd. (Ont. 1949)
May 24, 1973 – Name changed to Goldlund Mines Limited; basis 2 new for 5 old shs. ■

Newmar Explorations Ltd. (B.C. 1969)
Dec. 1971 – Assets acquired by Invictus Oils & Minerals Ltd.

Newmark Resources Limited (Alta. Mar. 1, 1969)
May 6, 1977 – Name changed to Trinity Resources Ltd.; basis 1 new for 3 old shs. ■

Newmarket Gold Inc. (Ont. July 10, 2010)
July 10, 2015 – Amalgamated with Crocodile Gold Corp. (deemed acquiror) to form new Newmarket Gold Inc. pursuant to plan of arrangement; basis Cdn$0.37 or 0.2456 new Newmarket com. shs. or a combination thereof for 1 Crocodile com. sh. and 0.2 new Newmarket com. shs. for 1 old Newmarket com. sh. (see Newmarket Gold Inc.)

Newmarket Gold Inc. (Ont. July 10, 2015 amalg.)
Nov. 30, 2016 – Name changed to Kirkland Lake Gold Ltd. pursuant to the reverse takeover acquisition of Kirkland Lake Gold Inc.; basis 1 new for 2.1053 old shs. ■

Newmex Gold Resources Inc. (Ont. 1975)
Sept. 1987 – Amalgamated with Vista Exploration Ltd. and Field Resources Ltd. to form Golden Trio Minerals Ltd.; basis 1 new for 2 old shs.

Newmex Minerals Inc. (Alta. Oct. 15, 1984)
July 19, 2002 – Continued into Canada.
Feb. 28, 2006 – Name changed to Pearl Exploration and Production Ltd. ■

Newmex Mining Company Ltd. (Ont. Dec. 11, 1996)
Sept. 17, 1997 – Amalgamated with Santa Cruz Gold Inc. to form a new co. also known as Santa Cruz Gold Inc. (Santa); basis 2.2 new shs. of Santa for 1 old sh. of Newmex. (see Santa Cruz Gold Inc.)

Newmine Development Ltd. (B.C. 1969)
1971 – Name changed to Geoquest Resources Ltd. ■

Newmont Goldcorp Corporation (Del. Apr. 1, 1988)
Jan. 6, 2020 – Name changed to Newmont Corporation. (see FPsurvey - Mines & Energy)

Newmont Mines Limited (Del. 1965)
Dec. 1, 1988 – Assets sold to a subsid. of Cassiar Resources Inc.

Newmont Mining Corporation (Del. Apr. 1, 1988)
Apr. 18, 2019 – Name changed to Newmont Goldcorp Corporation pursuant to the acquisition of Goldcorp Inc. ■

Newmont Mining Corporation of Canada Limited (Can. Oct. 5, 1982)
Dec. 5, 2011 – Continued into British Columbia. (see Newmont Mining Corporation)
Feb. 19, 2014 – All exch. shs. redeemed for parent Newmont Mining Corporation com. shs. on sh.for sh. basis. (see Newmont Mining Corporation)

Newnorth Gold Mines Limited (Ont. 1945)
July 13, 1982 – Name changed to Canadian Newnorth Resources Limited; basis 1 new for 4 old shs. ■

NewNorth Projects Ltd. (Alta. May 30, 2002)
Feb. 11, 2020 – Acquired by Bordeaux Properties Inc., basis 13¢ cash per share.

Newnote Financial Corp. (B.C. Aug. 16, 2010)
Apr. 24, 2024 – Struck from register and dissolved.

Newore Developments Ltd. (Ont. 1973 amalg.)
1976 – Dissolved.

NewOrigin Gold Corp. (Ont. June 6, 1989)
Nov. 12, 2024 – Acquired by Harfang Exploration Inc.; basis 0.25694426 Harfang com. shs. for 1 NewOrigin com. sh.

Nework Corp. (Alta. Mar. 12, 1998)
June 27, 2001 – Name changed to Talware Networx Inc. (see FPsurvey - Mines & Energy; FPsurvey - Industrials)

Newpass Resources Ltd. (Alta. 1976)
Nov. 27, 1986 – Name changed to First Class Entertainment and Filmworks Corporation. ■

NewPath Capital Corporation (Ont. Sept. 20, 1995)
Apr. 17, 1997 – Name changed to Cyberplex Inc.; basis 1 new for 1.5 old shs. ■

Newport Acquisitions Inc. (Alta. July 21, 2005)
Aug. 30, 2006 – Name changed to Carrington Acquisition Corp. ■

Newport Gold Mines Ltd. (Ont. 1944)
May 2, 1960 – Charter cancelled.

Newport Inc. (Ont. Feb. 18, 2011)
July 5, 2011 – Name changed to Tuckamore Capital Management Inc. ■

Newport Partners Income Fund (Ont. May 13, 2005)
Apr. 1, 2011 – Succeeded by Newport Inc. pursuant to plan of arrangement whereby Newport Inc. was formed to facilitate the conversion of the fund into a corporation and the fund was subsequently dissolved. ■

Newport Petroleum Corporation (B.C. Dec. 19, 1986)
Aug. 31, 1993 – Continued into Alberta.
Sept. 14, 1993 – Amalgamated with wholly owned International Interlake Industries Inc. and the amalgamated co. subsequently on that same date amalgamated with 566741 Alberta Ltd.
June 27, 2000 – Name changed to Hunt Oil Company of Canada, Inc. following acquisition by Texas-based Hunt Oil Company; basis $5.50 per sh.

Newport Petroleums Ltd. (Alta. 1968)
1983 – All o/s shs. not already held acquired by Stanford Resources Ltd. through purchase offers of $1.20 and $1.32 per sh.

Newquest Energy Inc. (Alta. Sept. 6, 1994)
Sept. 18, 2000 – Name changed to Ranchero Energy Inc.; basis 1 new for 3 old shs. ■

Newquest Ventures Corp. (B.C. Apr. 11, 1983)
May 26, 1999 – Name changed to Aster Ventures Corp.; basis 1 new for 2 old shs. ■

Newrange Gold Corp. (B.C. May 16, 2006)
Apr. 9, 2024 – Name changed to Pinnacle Silver and Gold Corp. (see FPsurvey - Mines & Energy)

Newray Mines Ltd. (Ont. 1915)
1924 – Merged to form the original Coniaurum Mines Ltd.; basis 1 new for 10 old shs.

Newrich Explorations Ltd. (Ont. 1945)
Aug. 29, 1978 – Amalgamated with 3 other cos. to form Belle Aire Resource Explorations Limited; basis 12 new for 100 old shs.

Newroy Gold Mines Ltd. (Can. Mar. 9, 1934)
1944 – Name changed to Newroy Mines Ltd. and continued into Ontario; basis 1 new for 5 old shs. ■

Newroy Mines Ltd. (Ont. 1944)
1967 – Charter cancelled.

Newscope Capital Corporation (B.C. Mar. 20, 2019)
Apr. 7, 2021 – Name changed to PharmaTher Holdings Ltd. (see FPsurvey - Industrials)

Newscope Resources Limited (Can. Sept. 13, 1984)
Dec. 24, 1990 – Name changed to Canadian Newscope Resources Ltd.; basis 1 new for 10 old shs. ■

Newscope Resources Ltd. (Can. Sept. 13, 1984)
Dec. 27, 1995 – Name changed to Denbury Resources Inc. ■

Newstar Energy Inc. (Alta. Sept. 16, 1987)
June 28, 1995 – Name changed to Newstar Resources Inc.; basis 1 new for 7 old shs. (see FPsurvey - Mines & Energy)

Newstrike Brands Ltd. (Ont. Sept. 24, 2004)
May 30, 2019 – Acquired by HEXO Corp.; basis 0.06332 HEXO com. shs. for 1 Newstrike sh. (see HEXO Corp.)

Newstrike Capital Inc. (B.C. May 8, 2006)
May 29, 2015 – Acquired by Timmins Gold Corp.; basis 0.9 Timmins com. shs. plus $0.0001 for 1 Newstrike com. sh.

Newstrike Resources Ltd. (Ont. Sept. 24, 2004)
July 27, 2018 – Name changed to Newstrike Brands Ltd. ■

NewSys Solutions Inc. (Alta. July 18, 1997)
Mar. 7, 2000 – Continued into Canada.
Sept. 22, 2000 – Name changed to InBusiness Solutions Inc. ■

Newtec Industries Limited (B.C. 1982)
Aug. 28, 1992 – Dissolved and struck off register.

NewTel Enterprises Limited (N.L. Nov. 28, 1985)
June 1, 1999 – Amalgamated with Bruncor Inc., Island Telecom Inc. and Maritime Telegraph and Telephone Company, Limited to form Aliant Inc.; basis 1.011 new for 1 Bruncor sh., 1 new for 1 Island Telecom sh., 1.667 new for 1 Maritime Telegraph sh. and 1.567 new for 1 NewTel sh. (see Aliant Inc.)

Newton Energy Corporation (Alta. Sept. 11, 1998)
Sept. 30, 2020 – Name changed to Field Trip Health Ltd. pursuant to the reverse takeover acquisition of Field Trip Psychedelics Inc.; basis 1 new for 8 old shs. ■

Newton Gold Corp. (B.C. June 24, 2004)
Nov. 7, 2013 – Name changed to Chlormet Technologies Inc.; basis 1 new for 5 old shs. ■

Newton Ventures Inc. (B.C. Mar. 1, 2000)
Nov. 6, 2006 – Name changed to Rusoro Mining Ltd. following reverse takeover acquisition of Venezuelan co. Grupo Agapov Corp.; basis 0.6 new for 1 old sh. (see FPsurvey - Mines & Energy)

Newvan Resources Ltd. (B.C. June 10, 1966)
May 26, 1977 – Name changed to Tricor Resources Ltd.; basis 1 new for 4 old shs. ■

NewWest Gold Corporation (B.C. May 3, 2006)
Sept. 27, 2007 – Amalgamated with Fronteer Development Group Inc.; basis 0.26 Fronteer com. sh. for 1 NewWest com. sh. (see Fronteer Development Group Inc.)

NexC Partners Corp. (Ont. Dec. 17, 2012)
Jan. 2, 2018 – Merged into Purpose Enhanced Dividend Fund; basis (i) 1 Purpose ETF sh. for 1 NexC cl. A sh.; (ii) 1 Purpose cl. F sh. for 1 NexC cl. F sh.; and (iii) 1.032987 Purpose cl. F shs. for 1 NexC cl. J sh.

Nexen Energy ULC (Can. July 12, 1971 amalg.)
June 18, 2013 – Continued into British Columbia.
Dec. 31, 2018 – Name changed to CNOOC Petroleum North America ULC.

Nexen Inc. (Can. July 12, 1971 amalg.)
Mar. 1, 2013 – Acquired by China National Offshore Oil Corporation for US$27.50 per sh.
Apr. 1, 2013 – Name changed to Nexen Energy ULC. ■

Nexfor Inc. (Can. Dec. 31, 1998 amalg.)
June 30, 2004 – Name changed to Norbord Inc. following separation of the company's three business units - panel unit retained and paper and timber units assumed by new company Fraser Papers Inc. and distribution of Fraser shs. on basis of 1 Fraser sh. for 5 Nexfor shs. ■

NexGen Financial Corporation (Ont. Sept. 20, 2010)
Dec. 29, 2014 – Acquired by 2438801 Ontario Inc., a wholly owned subsid. of Natixis Global Asset Management, S.A.; basis $7.25 cash per sh.

Nexia Biotechnologies Inc. (Can. July 22, 1992)
Oct. 23, 2006 – Formed Enseco Energy Services Corp. in Alberta on plan of arrangement amalgamation with Enseco Energy Services Corp. and Enseco Management Corp. and creation of new Nexia Biotechnologies Inc. to hold the existing biotech assets; basis 1 amalco com. sh. for 1 Enseco Energy sh., 0.45 amalco com. shs. and 0.55 amalco non-vtg. shs. for 1 Enseco Management sh., and 0.08842 amalco com. shs. and 1 new Nexia sh. for 1 old Nexia sh. ■

Nexia Biotechnologies Ltd. (Can. Mar. 6, 2006)
Sept. 18, 2007 – Continued into Alberta.
Nov. 13, 2009 – Name changed to Symax Lift (Holding) Co. Ltd. prior to reverse takeover acquisition of China Elevator (Group) Ltd.; basis 1 new for 10 old shs. ■

Nexient Learning Inc. (N.S. Aug. 20, 1985)
Feb. 15, 2011 – Filed for bankruptcy. KSV Advisory Inc. (formerly RSM Richter Inc.) appointed trustee.

NexJ Systems Inc. (Can. July 27, 2001)
Nov. 15, 2022 – Acquired by N. Harris Computer Corporation; basis Cdn$0.55 cash per sh.

NexMedia Technologies Inc. (B.C. May 27, 1988)
Jan. 18, 2010 – Dissolved and struck from register.

NexPoint Hospitality Trust (Ont. Dec. 3, 2018)
May 23, 2025 – Acquired by NexPoint Diversified Real Estate Trust (NXDT); basis (i) US$0.36 in cash; or (ii) 1 NHT Hospitality, Inc. com. sh., convertible into the number of com. shs. of NXDT equal to the quotient of US$0.36 dividend by the volume weighted average price of the NXDT com. shs for a 10 day period prior to closing for 1 NexPoint Hospitality trust unit. NexPoint Hospitality was dissolved and the subsid. entities merged with and into entities owned or controlled by NXDT.

NexStar Automation, Inc. (N.L. May 23, 1989)
Sept. 19, 1996 – Acquired by NX acquisition Corp., a wholly owned subsid. of Zygo Corporation; basis 1 Zygo sh. for 21.3 NexStar shs.

Nexstar Energy Ltd. (Alta. June 22, 2005)
Feb. 23, 2010 – Acquired by Result Energy Inc.; basis 1.05 Result com. shs. for 1 Nexstar cl. A sh. (see Result Energy Inc.)

Next Edge GLG Emerging Markets Income Fund (Ont. Oct. 24, 2011)
Dec. 30, 2014 – Merged into open-end mutual fund Next Edge Theta Yield Fund; basis 0.70 Theta cl. A1 units for 1 Next Edge cl. A unit and 0.77 Theta cl. F1 units for 1 Next Edge cl. F unit.

Next Gen Metals Inc. (B.C. Mar. 3, 2005)
Feb. 12, 2016 – Name changed to Namaste Technologies Inc. pursuant to the Feb. 26, 2016, reverse takeover acquisition of the former Namaste Vapes division of Dollinger Enterprises USA Ltd.; basis 1 new for 3 old shs. ■

Next Green Wave Holdings Inc. (B.C. July 6, 2011)
Mar. 3, 2022 – Acquired by Planet 13 Holdings Inc.; basis 0.1145 Plant 13 shs. plus Cdn$0.0001 cash for 1 Next Green Wave sh.

Next Millennium Commercial Corp. (Can. Sept. 8, 1994)
July 17, 2008 – Name changed to Roadrunner Oil & Gas Inc. ■

Nextair Inc. (Ont. Apr. 1, 1996 amalg.)
Feb. 23, 2005 – Name changed to NXA Inc.; basis 1 new for 10 old shs. ■

NexTech AR Solutions Corp. (B.C. Jan. 12, 2018)
Oct. 4, 2023 – Name changed to Nextech3D.AI Corporation. (see FPsurvey - Industrials)

Nexterra Property Group Inc. (Can. Oct. 24, 1997)
Dec. 31, 2002 – Formed Mariah Energy Corp. in Alberta on Qualifying Transaction amalgamation with Mariah Energy Corp., constituting a reverse takeover of Nexterra by Mariah; basis 3.4249 new for 1 Mariah sh. and 1 new for 5 Nexterra shs. ■

NextPoint Acquisition Corp. (B.C. July 16, 2020)
July 2, 2021 – Name changed to NextPoint Financial Inc. pursuant to the Qualifying Acquisition of Liberty Tax and LoanMe, Inc. ■

NextPoint Financial Inc. (B.C. July 16, 2020)
July 25, 2023 – Filed for protection under the Companies' Creditors Arrangement Act and FTI Consulting Canada Inc. was appointed monitor.
Jan. 2, 2024 – Pursuant to a reverse vesting transaction, all o/s equity of the entities that operate the Community Tax and Liberty Tax businesses was transferred to the purchaser. There was no recovery for the unsecured creditors of those entities. Subsidiaries not acquired in the sale, including the LoanMe group of companies, would be wound down, following which the company would no longer be a reporting issuer and its shs. would cease to trade on the OTC. (see FPsurvey - Industrials)

Nextra Technologies Inc. (Alta. July 6, 1954)
June 27, 1997 – Name changed to NUVO Network Management Inc. ■

Nextron Corporation (Alta. Aug. 27, 1996)
Oct. 30, 2007 – Acquired by PowerComm Inc.; basis $0.05 per Nextron sh. plus 1 PowerComm sh. for 15 Nextron shs.

NextSource Materials Inc. (Minn. May 14, 2008)
Dec. 27, 2017 – Continued into Canada. (see FPsurvey - Mines & Energy)

Nexttrip.com Travel Inc. (B.C. Apr. 29, 1987)
May 26, 2003 – Name changed to WorldPlus Ventures Ltd.; basis 1 new for 10 old shs. ■

Nextwave Software Corporation (Can. Sept. 23, 1991 amalg.)
July 21, 1994 – Name changed to Stox Infolink Systems Inc.; basis 1 new for 5 old shs. ■

Nexus Real Estate Investment Trust (Ont. May 10, 2013)
Mar. 7, 2022 – Name changed to Nexus Industrial REIT. (see FPsurvey - Industrials)

Nexus Resource Corporation (B.C. Oct. 23, 1982 amalg.)
May 3, 1988 – Amalgamated with Angle Resources Ltd. and Reward Resources Ltd. to form new co. with same name Nexus Resource Corporation; basis 1 new for 1.12 Angle shs., 1 new for 3 Reward shs. and 1 new for 1 Nexus sh.
July 5, 1990 – Name changed to Pacific Gold Corp.; basis 1 new for 6 old shs. ■

Nexus Resource Corporation (B.C. 1982 amalg.)
May 3, 1988 – Amalgamated with Angle Resources Ltd. (0.89 for 1) and Reward Resources Ltd. (1 for 3) to form a new co. also named Nexus Resource Corporation; basis 1 new for 1 old sh.

Nexxlink Technologies Inc. (Can. Dec. 1, 1993 amalg.)
Apr. 7, 2005 – Amalgamated with 4257049 Canada Inc. (Bell Canada); basis 1 new amalco redeem. pfd. for 1 old Nexxlink sh. The pfd. shs. were redeemed immediately for $6.05 per sh. (see Bell Canada)

Ni-Ag-Co Mines Ltd. (Ont. 1946)
Feb. 1958 – Dissolved.

Ni-Cal Developments Ltd. (B.C. July 17, 1972)
Dec. 28, 1988 – Continued into Wyoming.

Niagadoo Mines Ltd. (Ont. 1956)
1964 – Name changed to Nigadoo River Mines Ltd. ■

Niagara Capital Corporation (B.C. Aug. 14, 1979)
July 7, 1989 – Delisted from the Vancouver Stock Exchange. Subsequently dissolved for failure to file and struck from register.

Niagara Finance Company Limited (Ont. 1930)
Oct. 31, 1981 – Amalgamated with Niagara Realty Limited to continue as Continental Bank Capital Corporation.

Niagara Lower Arch Bridge Company Limited (Can. 1847)
Nov. 15, 1958 – As of all the assets of co. and of the U.S. co. (Niagara Falls International Bridge Co.) sold to The Seagram Corp. of Chicago; subsequently the bridge sold to the Canadian and N.Y. Bridge Authorities. Charter cancelled.

Niagara Mining and Development Corp. Ltd. (B.C. 1959)
Oct. 1971 – Name changed to Tiki Development Corporation Ltd. ■

Niagara Mortgage & Loan Company Limited (Que. 1963)
Oct. 26, 1971 – Name changed to Niagara Realty of Canada Limited. ■

Niagara Peninsula Radio Group Limited Partnership (Ont. Nov. 2, 1995)
Feb. 12, 1996 – Name changed to Authentex Software Limited Partnership following acquisition of Authentex Software Inc. ■

Niagara Realty of Canada Limited (Que. 1963)
Oct. 28, 1981 – Name changed to Continental Bank Realty Corp.

Niagara Structural Steel Company Limited (Ont. 1962)
Dec. 16, 1983 – Name changed to TecSyn International Inc. ■

Niagara Ventures Corporation (Ont. May 25, 2012)
Apr. 25, 2017 – Privatized via a 1-for-2,934,311 basis; each pre-consolidated sh. entitled to received $0.015 cash per sh.

Niagara Wire Weaving Company Limited (Ont. 1929)
Nov. 1, 1979 – Amalgamated with parent co. Ivaco Inc. (see Ivaco Ltd.)

Niaski Environmental Inc. (Alta. Feb. 24, 1997 amalg.)
Nov. 22, 2002 – Name changed to Rimron Resources Inc. ■

Nib Yellowknife Mines Ltd. (Ont. 1944)
Mar. 28, 1956 – Amalgamated into Mining Endeavor Co. Ltd.; basis 1 new for 5 old shs.

Niblack Mineral Development Inc. (Alta. July 19, 2002 amalg.)
Jan. 24, 2012 – Acquired by Heatherdale Resources Ltd.; basis 0.5 Heatherdale shs. for 1 Niblack sh. (see Heatherdale Resources Ltd.)

Niblack Mining Corp. (B.C. Nov. 30, 2004)
Oct. 6, 2008 – Acquired by Committee Bay Resources Ltd.; basis 1 Committee sh. for 1 Niblack sh. and amalgamated with 0830928 B.C. Ltd., a wholly owned subsid. of Committee Bay, to form CBR Alaska Holdings Inc.

Nic-Cop Mines Ltd. (Man. 1954)
Feb. 24, 1971 – Dissolved.

Nic-Nik Resources Ltd. (B.C. Apr. 24, 1987)
Oct. 16, 1989 – Name changed to Transtel Communications Corp. ■

Nicanex Mines Ltd. (B.C. 1968)
Nov. 13, 1973 – Struck off register.

Nicer Canada Corp. (Can. Jan. 31, 2003)
Dec. 18, 2015 – Dissolved.

Niche Peripherals, Inc. (B.C. May 22, 1986)
Oct. 31, 1994 – Name changed to Consolidated Niche Peripherals Inc.; basis 1 new for 1.5 old shs. ■

Nicholas Data Services Ltd. (B.C. July 28, 1986)
Aug. 9, 1993 – Name changed to Nicholas Financial, Inc. ■

Nicholas Financial, Inc. (B.C. July 28, 1986)
Apr. 18, 2024 – Continued into Delaware.

Nicholson Mines Limited (Ont. Nov. 23, 1936)
May 2, 1951 – Name changed to Consolidated Nicholson Mines Limited; basis 2 new for 3 old shs. ■

Nichromet Extraction Inc. (Can. July 22, 1997)
Jan. 8, 2014 – Name changed to Dundee Sustainable Technologies Inc. (see FPsurvey - Mines & Energy)

Nickel Hill Mines Ltd. (B.C. Aug. 2, 1968)
Mar. 30, 1973 – Name changed to Vantreal Resources Ltd.; basis 1 new for 4 old shs. ■

Nickel Industries Limited (Que. Aug. 9, 1949)
Dec. 9, 1949 – Name changed to Nocana Mines Limited. ■

Nickel Lake Mines Ltd. (Man. 1947)
Mar. 5, 1979 – Charter cancelled.

Nickel Mining & Smelting Corp. (Que. 1953)
1963 – Name changed to Metal Mines Ltd.; basis 1 new for 5 old shs. ■

Nickel Mountain Mines Ltd. (B.C. 1967)
Jan. 7, 1976 – Charter cancelled.

Nickel Offsets, Limited (Can. Apr. 20, 1938)
Dec. 30, 1985 – Amalgamated with 3 other companies to form Canhorn Mining Corporation; basis 1 new for 11.82 old shs.

Nickel One Resources Inc. (B.C. Jan. 16, 2007)
May 3, 2019 – Name changed to Palladium One Mining Inc.; basis 1 new for 2 old shs. ■

Nickel Petroleum Resources Ltd. (Can. July 21, 2000)
Dec. 18, 2008 – Dissolved.

Nickel Rock Resources Inc. (B.C. June 2, 2011)
Apr. 5, 2023 – Name changed to Grid Battery Metals Inc. (see FPsurvey - Mines & Energy)

Nickel Valley Copper Mines Ltd. (Ont. 1956)
May 16, 1973 – Charter cancelled.

Nickeldale Resources Inc. (Ont. May 13, 1986)
Dec. 17, 1996 – Formed CLN Ventures Inc. following acquisition of all o/s com. shs. and sh. purchase wts. of CLN Industries Ltd.; basis 1 new for 2 old shs. (see FPsurvey - Industrials)

Nickelex Resource Corporation (B.C. Feb. 22, 2008)
Apr. 10, 2025 – Name changed to Paradigm Gold Corporation; basis 1 new for 10 old shs. (see FPsurvey - Mines & Energy)

Nickelodeon Industries Corp. (B.C. June 28, 1983)
Nov. 24, 1989 – Dissolved and struck off register.

Nickelodeon Minerals Inc. (B.C. Mar. 31, 1981)
Aug. 18, 2000 – Name changed to Strongbow Resources Inc. ■

Nickling Resources Inc. (B.C. 1982 amalg.)
May 9, 1989 – Name changed to Florin Resources Inc.; basis 1 new for 3 old shs. ■

NiCo Mining Limited (Ont. June 17, 2005)
Nov. 11, 2010 – Name changed to Red Crescent Resources Limited pursuant to reverse takeover acquisition of Red Crescent Resources (Barbados) Limited. ■

Nicoba Mines Limited (Can. 1947)
Jan. 23, 1987 – Name changed to Better Business Communications Inc.; basis 1 new for 30 old shs. ■

Nicohal Mines Ltd. (Ont. 1969)
Mar. 1976 – Charter cancelled.

Nicola Copper Mines Ltd. (B.C. 1965)
Feb. 6, 1978 – Name changed to Buccaneer Resources Ltd.; basis 1 new for 5 old shs. ■

Nicola Lake Mining Company Ltd. (B.C. 1966)
Feb. 25, 1983 – Struck off register.

Nicolet Asbestos Mines Ltd. (Que. 1928)
Oct. 1975 – Charter cancelled.

Nictau Copper Mines Ltd. (N.B. 1957)
Jan. 20, 1971 – Dissolved.

Niemetz Base Metal Mines Ltd. (Ont. 1952)
1954 – Charter cancelled.

Nigadoo River Mines Ltd. (Ont. 1956)
Aug. 1978 – Name changed to Sullico Resources Ltd. (99% owned by Sullivan Mining Group Ltd.); basis 1 new for 100 old shs. ■

Night Hawk Peninsular Mines Ltd. (Ont. 1922)
Liquidated, no equity for shldrs.

Nighthawk Gold Corp. (Ont. Oct. 8, 2004)
Feb. 9, 2024 – Acquired by Moneta Gold Inc. (renamed STLLR Gold Inc.); basis 0.21 Moneta shs. for 1 Nighthawk sh.

Nighthawk Gold Mines Ltd. (B.C. Jan. 20, 1948)
1966 – Name changed to Highpoint Mines Ltd.; basis 1 new for 4 old shs. ■

Nighthawk Resources Inc. (Alta. Mar. 13, 1995)
Dec. 1, 1997 – Struck off register.

Nighthawk Resources Ltd. (B.C. 1979)
May 24, 1988 – Formed Stratford American Corp. in Arizona on amalgamation with Stratford Bahamas Corporation (1 for 1); basis 1 new for 1 old sh.

Nightingale Informatix Corporation (Ont. Sept. 1, 2005 amalg.)
Sept. 8, 2016 – Name changed to Nexia Health Technologies Inc. following sale of substantially all of the company's Canadian business (but excluding the V10 (Nexia) EMR platform) to TELUS Corporation. (see FPsurvey - Industrials)

Nightlen Mines Ltd. (Ont. 1959)
Nov. 1973 – Charter cancelled.

Nightwatch Resources Inc. (B.C. 1966)
Feb. 25, 1983 – Struck off register.

Nik Capital Corporation (Alta. 1987)
Jan. 31, 1989 – Formed H.L. International Inc. in Alberta on amalgamation with H.L. International Inc.; basis 1 new for 3 old shs. ■

Nik Ventures Inc. (Alta. Oct. 19, 1984)
Apr. 1, 1995 – Struck off register.

Nikana Capital Inc. (Ont. Dec. 1944)
Feb. 29, 1996 – Name changed to Gemstar Communications Inc.; basis 1 new for 15 old shs. ■

Niki Silver-Cobalt Mines Ltd. (Ont. 1942)
1946 – Assets acquired by Ni-Ag-Co Mines Ltd. for 1,000,000 shs.

Nikos Explorations Ltd. (B.C. Apr. 24, 1987)
Dec. 19, 2017 – Name changed to Labrador Gold Corp. (see FPsurvey - Mines & Energy)

Nile Industries Ltd. (Alta. Sept. 8, 2005)
Mar. 2, 2010 – Dissolved and struck from register.

NiMin Capital Corp. (Alta. May 31, 2007)
Sept. 4, 2009 – Name changed to NiMin Energy Corp. pursuant to Qualifying Transaction reverse takeover acquisition of Legacy Energy, Inc.; basis 1 new for 3 old shs. ■

NiMin Energy Corp. (Alta. May 31, 2007)
Apr. 28, 2014 – Voluntarily liquidated. Initial distribution to shldrs. US$1.01 cash per sh. on Oct. 22, 2012; and final distribution of US$0.07 cash per sh. payable on Apr. 28, 2014.

Nimrod Resources Ltd. (Alta. 1977)
1981 – Acquired by Altas Yellowknife Resources Limited following an offer of 6 shs. and 4 wts. for each sh. and 2 wts. for each wt.

9 Capital Corp. (Ont. Apr. 4, 2017)
June 14, 2021 – Name changed to Churchill Resources Inc. pursuant to the Qualifying Transaction reverse takeover acquisition of Churchill Diamond Corporation (CDC) and concurrent amalgamation of CDC with wholly owned 2811807 Ontario Inc.; basis 1 new for 1.7 old shs. (see FPsurvey - Mines & Energy)

92 Resources Corp. (B.C. May 10, 2007)
Oct. 17, 2019 – Name changed to Gaia Metals Corp.; basis 1 new for 10 old shs. ■

9342-8530 Quebec inc. (Que. Dec. 8, 1994)
Nov. 2, 2017 – Liquidation of the assets and settlement of the company's obligations was complete and there were not sufficient funds for a cash distribution to shldrs.
Aug. 28, 2018 – PricewaterhouseCoopers Inc. was discharged as liquidator.
Jan. 21, 2019 – Dissolved and struck from register.

9819495 Canada Inc. (Can. July 5, 2016)
Sept. 16, 2016 – Name changed to Dialogue Technologies Inc. ■

Ninepoint Energy Opportunities Trust (Ont. Nov. 2, 2016)
Nov. 23, 2018 – Merged into Ninepoint Energy Fund; basis 0.4468 Ninepoint Fund ser. F units for 1 Ninepoint Trust trust unit.

99 Capital Corporation (Can. July 26, 2007)
Aug. 4, 2010 – Continued into British Columbia.
Jan. 25, 2011 – Name changed to Giyani Gold Corp. ■

Niocan Inc. (Que. Aug. 29, 1995)
June 15, 2022 – Name changed to Nio Strategic Metals Inc. (see FPsurvey - Mines & Energy)

Niogold Mining Corp. (B.C. Mar. 30, 1988)
Mar. 14, 2016 – Acquired by Oban Mining Corp.; basis 0.4167 Oban com. shs. for 1 Niogold com. sh. (see Oban Mining Corporation)

Niparea Prospectors Ltd. (Ont. 1937)
Dec. 1952 – Charter cancelled.

Nipiron Mines Ltd. (Ont. 1952)
July 1966 – Name changed to New Nipiron Mines Ltd. ■

Nipissing Mines Co. Ltd. (Ont. 1952)
1962 – Amalgamated with Patino of Canada Ltd. to form The Patino Corp. Ltd.; basis 1 new for 5 old shs.

Nipissing-O'Brien Mines Limited (Ont. 1952)
Nov. 30, 1959 – Assets distributed; charter surrendered and dissolved.

Nipmur Gold Mines Ltd. (Ont. 1937)
Nov. 6, 1976 – Struck off register.

Nippon Dragon Resources Inc. (Que. July 18, 2000)
Dec. 6, 2021 – Name changed to G.E.T.T. Gold Inc. (see FPsurvey - Mines & Energy)

Nippon Investments Corp. (B.C. 1979)
Aug. 12, 1994 – Dissolved and struck off register.

Nirvana Industries Ltd. (B.C. Mar. 7, 1980)
Feb. 22, 1989 – Name changed to Consolidated Nirvana Industries Ltd.; basis 1 new for 4 old shs. ■

Nirvana Oil & Gas Ltd. (B.C. Mar. 7, 1980)
Oct. 6, 1986 – Name changed to Nirvana Industries Ltd. ■

Nisson Mining & Development Ltd. (B.C. 1967)
Mar. 23, 1979 – Charter cancelled.

Nisto Mines Ltd. (Ont. 1948)
1966 – Name changed to Canadian Nisto Mines Limited; basis 1 new for 2 old shs. ■

Nithex Exploration and Development Ltd. (B.C. 1970)
June 8, 1976 – Amalgamated with Deer Lake Mines Ltd. to form Nithex Exploration Ltd.; basis 1 new for 2 old shs.

Nithex Exploration Ltd. (B.C. 1976 amalg.)
May 31, 1983 – Formed Lintex Minerals Ltd. in British Columbia on amalgamation with Indin Gold Ltd. ■

Nitinat Minerals Corporation (Nev. June 1, 2004)
June 20, 2007 – Continued into Alberta.
July 19, 2007 – Continued into Ontario.
Oct. 17, 2019 – Name changed to Hanna Capital Corp. (see FPsurvey - Mines & Energy)

Nitracell Canada Ltd. (Alta. 1951)
Nov. 1974 – Name changed to Magnum Resources Ltd.; basis 1 new for 5 old shs. (see FPsurvey - Mines & Energy; FPsurvey - Industrials)

Nitro Developments Inc. (Ont. 1971)
May 24, 1972 – Amalgamated to form Xtra Developments Inc.; basis 1 new for 13 old shs. (see Xtra Developments Inc.)

Nix-O-Tine Pharmaceuticals Ltd. (B.C. 1987)
Mar. 31, 1993 – Wound up. Assets sold, no distribution to shldrs. Creditors paid out $250,000 in loans.

No Cash Keno Lead & Silver Mines Ltd. (Ont. 1950)
1964 – Name changed to Marimac Mines Ltd. ■

Nobel Real Estate Investment Trust (Que. Aug. 1, 2012)
Apr. 5, 2017 – Acquired by Edgefront Real Estate Investment Trust (subsequently renamed Nexus Real Estate Investment Trust); basis 1.67 Edgefront trust units for 1 Nobel trust unit. (see Nexus Real Estate Investment Trust)

Nobelium Tech Corp. (Can. Feb. 26, 2015)
Oct. 13, 2021 – Name changed to Hank Payments Corp. pursuant to the Qualifying Transaction reverse takeover acquisition of (old) Hank Payments Corp.; basis 1 new for 4 old shs. ■

Nobel29 Resources Corp. (B.C. Nov. 21, 2005)
Continued into Ontario.
July 23, 2021 – Name changed to Nobel Resources Corp. (see FPsurvey - Mines & Energy)

Nobilis Health Corp. (B.C. Mar. 16, 2007)
Aug. 14, 2023 – Dissolved for failure to file.

Nobiscum Oil & Gas Ltd. (unknown)
1967 – Merged into King Solomon Resources Ltd.; basis 1,700 new for 1 old sh.

Noble China Corporation (Ont. Oct. 18, 1979)
Oct. 7, 1993 – Name changed to Noble China Inc.; basis 1 new for 2 old shs. ■

Noble China Inc. (Ont. Oct. 18, 1979)
Nov. 2003 – Plan of compromise and arrangement approved by majority of the company's secured and unsecured creditors and sanctioned by the Ontario court. Ernst & Young Inc. appointed monitor. Under the plan, all assets to be transferred to Mega Gain Investment Co. Ltd. and 20,745,467 newly created cl. A shs. to be issued to Mega Gain.
Oct. 31, 2005 – Wound up pursuant to reorganization under the Companies' Creditors Arrangement Act and dissolved.

Noble Five Mines Ltd. (B.C. 1928)
1949 – Dissolved; basis 1 sh. Nelson Slocan for 10 old shs.

Noble House Communications Inc. (Ont. Mar. 4, 1983)
July 24, 2000 – Name changed to WebEngine Corporation. ■

Noble House Entertainment Inc. (Ont. Mar. 18, 1997 amalg.)
Oct. 12, 2006 – Name changed to LiveReel Media Corporation. ■

Noble Mines & Oils Ltd. (Alta. Mar. 10, 1965)
Oct. 18, 1979 – Continued into Ontario.
July 8, 1993 – Name changed to Noble China Corporation. ■

Noble Oils Ltd. (Alta. Mar. 10, 1965)
1969 – Name changed to Noble Mines & Oils Ltd. ■

Noble Peak Resources Ltd. (B.C. Feb. 28, 1983)
Mar. 4, 1987 – Continued into Canada.
Aug. 21, 1998 – Name changed to Vaaldiam Resources Ltd.; basis 1 new for 10 old shs. ■

Nocana Limited (Que. Aug. 9, 1949)
Feb. 26, 1979 – Name changed to Grandma Lee's Inc. ■

Nocana Mines Limited (Que. Aug. 9, 1949)
Dec. 29, 1975 – Name changed to Nocana Limited. ■

Noel Electronics Ltd. (unknown)
1968 – Acquired by Bartaco Industries Ltd.

Noise Media Inc. (B.C. Aug. 29, 1979)
Jan. 17, 2008 – Name changed to GFK Resources Inc.; basis 1 new for 4 old shs. ■

Noka Resources Inc. (B.C. Dec. 15, 2010)
Apr. 27, 2017 – Name changed to Pacton Gold Inc. ■

Nolan Lake Explorations Inc. (Ont. May 11, 1979)
July 4, 1983 – Name changed to Canolan Resources Ltd. ■

Nolan Resources Ltd. (B.C. 1980)
Aug. 7, 1984 – Name changed to Amble Resources Limited; basis 1 new for 3 old shs. ■

Noland Mines Ltd. (B.C. 1949)
1971 – Name changed to Las Maderas Mining & Petroleum Ltd.; basis 1 new for 10 old shs. ■

Noma Industries Limited (Ont. Oct. 26, 1954)
Apr. 29, 1999 – Acquired by Noma Acquisition Corp., a wholly owned subsid. of General Chemical Group Inc., for $9.25 per sh.

Nomad Energy & Resources Ltd. (B.C. Mar. 25, 1971)
Aug. 14, 1987 – Dissolved and struck off register.

Nomad Mines Ltd. (B.C. Mar. 25, 1971)
Mar. 11, 1981 – Name changed to Nomad Energy & Resources Ltd. ■

Nomad Royalty Company Ltd. (Can. Jan. 7, 2020)
Aug. 17, 2022 – Acquired by Sandstorm Gold Ltd.; basis 1.21 Sandstorm shs. for 1 Nomad Royalty sh.

Nomad Ventures Inc. (B.C. Mar. 27, 2007)
Oct. 12, 2017 – Name changed to Bankers Cobalt Corp. ■

Non-Par Developments Ltd. (Can. Oct. 22, 1953)
July 27, 1992 – Continued into British Columbia.
Aug. 17, 1992 – Name changed to Similkameen Hydro-Power Ltd. following acquisition of a hydro-electric project from Princeton Light and Power Company, Limited. ■

Noorduyn Aviation Ltd. (Can. 1938)
Jan. 8, 1946 – Name changed to Nuclear Enterprises. ■

Nor-Acme Gold Mines Ltd. (Can. 1938)
Dec. 31, 1988 – Amalgamated with High River Resources Ltd. to form High River Gold Mines Ltd.; basis 1 new for 1.2 old sh. (see High River Gold Mines Ltd.)

Nor-Penn Mines Ltd. (Ont. 1949)
Apr. 1970 – Charter cancelled.

Nor-Quest Resources Ltd. (B.C. 1963)
May 27, 1991 – Formed Western and Pacific Resources Corp. in British Columbia on amalgamation with 393497 B.C. Ltd. (53.32 for 1); basis 1 new for 10 old shs. ■

Nor-West Kim Resources Ltd. (B.C. 1966)
July 1978 – Charter cancelled.

Nora Exploration Inc. (Can. Aug. 9, 1984)
Aug. 10, 2000 – Name changed to Afri-Can Marine Minerals Corporation. (see FPsurvey - Mines & Energy)

Norac Industries Inc. (Alta. Sept. 22, 1986)
Dec. 23, 2003 – Formed ViRexx Medical Corp. in Alberta on amalgamation with ViRexx Research Inc., constituting a reverse takeover by ViRexx; basis 1 new for 1.891 ViRexx sh. and 1 new for each 4.455 Norac subord. vtg. and 2.5 Norac multiple vtg. shs. ■

Noradco Mines Limited (B.C. 1964)
June 11, 1993 – Dissolved and struck off register.

Norado Mines Ltd. (Ont. 1959)
Apr. 22, 1965 – Dissolved.

Norah Capital Corporation (Alta. May 7, 1998)
Apr. 7, 1999 – Name changed to Ezenet Corp. following acquisition of all o/s com. and pref. shs. of Ezenet Inc.; basis 1 new cl. A com. sh. for 1 old com. sh. ■

Noralmac Mines Limited (Can. 1951)
Dec. 16, 1980 – Dissolved.

Noram Environmental Solutions Inc. (B.C. July 21, 1983)
Feb. 27, 1997 – Continued into Alberta.
July 8, 1997 – Name changed to Alternative Fuel Systems Inc. ■

Noram Ventures Inc. (B.C. June 15, 2010)
July 27, 2021 – Name changed to Noram Lithium Corp. (see FPsurvey - Mines & Energy)

Norambar Inc. (Can. - unspecified)
Mar. 10, 2006 – Name changed to Mittal Canada Contrecoeur-Ouest Inc. ■

Noramco Mining Corporation (B.C. May 26, 1971)
Jan. 3, 1995 – Name changed to Quest Capital Corporation. ■

Noramex Minerals Inc. (B.C. Feb. 17, 1983)
Dec. 29, 1992 – Name changed to Nacasa Ventures Inc.; basis 1 new for 5 old shs. ■

Noramtec Energy Corp. (Alta. Dec. 4, 1987)
June 1, 1996 – Struck off register.

Norancon Exploration Ltd. (Can. 1946)
Name changed to Dorbrun Mines Ltd. ■

Noranda Forest Inc. (Can. May 1, 1987 amalg.)
Dec. 31, 1998 – Formed Nexfor Inc. in Canada on amalgamation with NFI Forest Holdings Ltd., a wholly owned subsid. of Noranda Inc., pursuant to plan of arrangement that effected the divestiture by Noranda Inc. of its interest in Noranda Forest. ■

Noranda Income Fund (Ont. Apr. 18, 2002)
Mar. 20, 2023 – Acquired by Glencore Canada Corporation; basis Cdn$1.98 cash per priority unit.

Noranda Inc. (Ont. May 1, 1922)
June 30, 2005 – Formed Falconbridge Limited in Ontario on amalgamation with old Falconbridge Limited following acquisition by Noranda of the remaining 41% interest in old Falconbridge; basis 1.77 new Falconbridge (previously Noranda) shs. for 1 old Falconbridge sh. Each Noranda pref. sh. or jr. pfce. sh. and old Falconbridge pref. sh. was converted into an equal number of pref. shs. or jr. pfce. shs. of new Falconbridge having the same attributes as before. ■

Noranda Mines Ltd. (Ont. May 1, 1922)
May 4, 1984 – Name changed to Noranda Inc. ■

Noranda Panelboard (Can. 1969)
June 1, 1989 – Name changed to Norbord Industries Inc.

Noranglo Mines Ltd. (Ont. 1959)
Aug. 1964 – Dissolved.

Norart Minerals Limited (Ont. 1948)
1967 – Assets acquired by Angelus Petroleums (1965) Ltd.; basis 1 new for 10 old shs.

Norart Uranium & Gold Mines Ltd. (Ont. 1948)
Nov. 1958 – Name changed to Norart Minerals Limited. ■

Noravena Capital Corporation (Can. Oct. 26, 2009)
Jan. 30, 2012 – Name changed to 3MV Energy Corp. pursuant to Qualifying Transaction reverse takeover acquisition of 3MV Energy Inc.; basis 1 new for 10 old shs. (see FPsurvey - Mines & Energy)

Norbank Explorations Ltd. (Ont. 1950)
Dec. 16, 1970 – Dissolved.

Norbaska Mines Limited (Sask. May 17, 1949)
Nov. 2, 1987 – Formed Dore Norbaska Resources Inc. in Ontario on amalgamation with Dore Explorations Inc.; basis 1 new for 3.5 old shs. ■

Norbeau Mines Inc. (Ont. 1964)
Apr. 28, 1988 – Following takeover offer made by a wholly owned subsid. of Western Mining Corporation Holdings Limited which expired all outstanding shares were acquired at 22¢ per share.

Norbeau Mines (Quebec) Limited (Que. June 16, 1937)
1970 – Acquired by Lake Shore Mines, Ltd.; basis 1 new for 12 old shs.

Norbec Copper Mines Ltd. (Can. 1942)
Mar. 1955 – Acquired by Lake Dufault Mines Ltd.; basis 1 new for 5 old shs.

Norbenite Malartic Mines Ltd. (Ont. 1943)
1949 – Name changed to Norlartic Mines Ltd.; basis 1 new for 4 old shs. ■

Norbert Silver Mines Ltd. (Ont. 1952)
Apr. 1965 – Charter cancelled.

Norbord Inc. (Can. Dec. 31, 1998 amalg.)
Feb. 3, 2021 – Acquired by West Fraser Timber Co. Ltd.; basis 0.675 West Fraser com. shs. for 1 Norbord sh.

Norcal Resources Ltd. (B.C. Dec. 2, 1935)
June 18, 2002 – Name changed to Troon Ventures Ltd.; basis 1 new for 5 old shs. ■

Norcan Mines Ltd. (B.C. 1966)
Dec. 5, 1972 – Name changed to Accent Resources Ltd.; basis 1 new for 5 old shs. ■

Norcan Oils Ltd. (Alta. 1957)
Feb. 18, 1966 – Name changed to Canadian Gridoil Limited; basis 1 new for 1.8 old shs. ■

Norcan Resources Ltd. (B.C. Aug. 19, 1994 amalg.)
June 7, 2000 – Name changed to Odyssey Exploration Inc.; basis 1 new for 5 old shs. ■

Norcana Resources Limited (Ont. June 26, 1979)
Apr. 25, 1983 – Name changed to Orcana Resources Limited and continued into British Columbia. ■

Norcansil Silver Mines Ltd. (B.C. 1961)
1971 – Struck off register.

Norcast Income Fund (Ont. May 10, 2005)
Mar. 27, 2007 – Acquired indirectly by Pala Investments Holdings Limited for Cdn$9.30 per sh.

Norcen Energy Resources Limited (Alta. Oct. 28, 1975 amalg.)
Apr. 15, 1977 – Continued into Canada.
Mar. 11, 1998 – Acquired by Union Pacific Resources Inc., a wholly owned subsid. of Union Pacific Resources Group Inc. of Texas; basis $19.80 per sh. Subsequently amalgamated with Union Pacific Resources Inc. to continue as Union Pacific Resources Inc. effective Apr. 17, 1998.

Norcen Pipelines Ltd. (Man. 1954)
Feb. 27, 1981 – Amalgamated with 50099 Manitoba Ltd. to form Norcen Pipelines (1981) Ltd. Shldrs. received pfce. shs., which were subsequently purchased or redeemed at $70 per sh.

Norco Capital Inc. (Que. Sept. 30, 2004)
Aug. 31, 2007 – Formed Nuvolt Corporation Inc. in Quebec on amalgamation with Nuvolt Corporation Inc. following Qualifying Transaction reverse takeover acquisition of Nuvolt on July 18, 2007. ■

Norco Resources Ltd. (B.C. Nov. 24, 1961)
June 15, 1990 – Dissolved and struck off register.

Norco Thompson Ltd. (Ont. 1940)
1953 – Charter cancelled.

Norcopper & Metals Corporation (Que. 1955)
Sept. 30, 1978 – Charter cancelled.

Norcourt Gold Mines Ltd. (Que. 1945)
Feb. 7, 1987 – Charter cancelled.

Nord Pacific Limited (Bermuda 1988)
Sept. 30, 1998 – Continued into New Brunswick.
Sept. 20, 2004 – Plan of Arrangement acquisition by Australia-based Allied Gold Limited; basis 1 new Allied sh. for 1 old Nord Pacific sh.

Nordac Mining Corporation (B.C. 1985)
Nov. 6, 1987 – Name changed to Big Creek Resources Ltd.; basis 2 new for 5 old shs. ■

Nordac Resources Ltd. (B.C. Dec. 16, 1994)
June 22, 2001 – Name changed to Strategic Metals Ltd.; basis 1 new for 4 old shs. (see FPsurvey - Mines & Energy)

Nordair Inc. (Can. 1947)
Nov. 1985 – Following public offer ($16.25 and wts. to purchase 3 shs. of CP Air at $7.00 for each sh. held) Canadian Pacific Air Lines, Limited acquired a 65% int. by May 9, 1986. The remaining 35% int. was held by the Quebec Government. In early 1987, Nordair Metro (35% owned by Nordair) acquired Québecair from the Quebec Government for approx. $10,000,000. Subsequently the Quebec Government sold their 35% int. in Nordair to Canadian Pacific Air Lines, Limited for $3,500,000. Nordair Inc. was merged into Canadian Pacific Air Lines, Limited on Jan. 2, 1987.

Nordair Ltd. (Can. 1947)
Dec. 18, 1984 – Controlling interest (held by Air Canada) sold to Innocan Inc. Subsequently amalgamated with 132894 Canada Inc. (a wholly owned subsid. of Innocan) to form Nordair Inc.; basis 1.89 new com. sh. for 1 cl. A or cl. B sh.

Nordarm Longlac Mines, Ltd. (Ont. 1936)
Apr. 1965 – Charter cancelled.

Nordeau Mining Co. Ltd. (Ont. 1955)
1980 – Name changed to Vauquelin Iron Mines Ltd.; basis 1 new for 3 old shs.

Nordel Oil & Gas Co. Ltd. (Ont. 1953)
Wound up.

Norden Crown Metals Corporation (B.C. Dec. 31, 2013)
Apr. 2, 2025 – Name changed to Domestic Metals Corp. (see FPsurvey - Mines & Energy)

Nordev Mines Ltd. (Ont. 1966)
Mar. 24, 1972 – Amalgamated with 2 other cos. to form Nordev Resources Ltd.; basis 1 new for 5 old shs.

Nordev Resources Limited (Ont. Mar. 24, 1972)
Apr. 20, 1979 – Name changed to Vedron Limited; basis 1 new for 3 old shs. ■

Nordex Explosives Ltd. (Que. Aug. 4, 1970)
Aug. 26, 2016 – Privatized by way of amalgamation with 9867244 Canada Ltd. to form new Nordex Explosives Ltd.

Nordic Diamonds Ltd. (B.C. Nov. 23, 2003 amalg.)
June 12, 2009 – Name changed to Western Standard Metals Ltd.; basis 1 new for 10 old shs. ■

Nordic Explorations Ltd. (Ont. 1964)
Mar. 1969 – Name changed to Nordic Mines & Investments Ltd. ■

Nordic Gold Corporation (Alta. Feb. 26, 1988)
May 21, 2008 – Continued into British Columbia.
Oct. 3, 2008 – Name changed to Compass Gold Corporation. (see FPsurvey - Mines & Energy)

Nordic Gold Corp. (Alta. Feb. 14, 1992)
Dec. 10, 2018 – Name changed to Nordic Gold Inc. ■

Nordic Gold Inc. (Alta. Feb. 14, 1992)
Dec. 16, 2019 – Name changed to Otso Gold Corp. ■

Nordic Industries Ltd. (Ont. 1964)
Mar. 14, 1978 – Charter cancelled.

Nordic Lite Inc. (Ont. 1986)
Feb. 12, 2007 – Dissolved and struck from register.

Nordic Mines & Investments Ltd. (Ont. 1964)
July 1969 – Name changed to Nordic Industries Ltd.; basis 1 new for 2 old shs. ■

Nordion Inc. (Can. Oct. 10, 1978)
Aug. 11, 2014 – Acquired by 8832528 Canada Inc., an affiliate of Sterigenics International LLC; basis US$13 cash per sh.

NordTech Aerospace Inc. (Can. June 21, 2004 amalg.)
Apr. 19, 2005 – Name changed to ExelTech Aerospace Inc. following reverse takeover acquisition of 3682986 Canada Inc. (operating as ExelTech). ■

Noreagle Uranium Mines Ltd. (Ont. 1954)
Aug. 3, 1964 – Charter cancelled.

Noreloy Larder Lake Mining Syndicate Ltd. (Ont. 1944)
June 10, 1956 – Charter cancelled.

Norex Exploration Services Inc. (Alta. May 28, 1996)
Apr. 18, 2010 – Formed Tesla Exploration Ltd. in Alberta on amalgamation with Tesla Exploration Ltd., with Tesla the deemed acquiror; basis 1 new sh. for 1.0542 Tesla shs. and 1 new sh. for 8 Norex shs.

Norex Mines Ltd. (Ont. 1939)
Sept. 24, 1956 – Charter cancelled.

Norex Resources Ltd. (B.C. 1967)
Sept. 19, 1983 – Name changed to Consolidated Norex Resources Corp.; basis 1 new for 8 old shs. ■

Norex Uranium Ltd. (B.C. 1967)
1970 – Name changed to Norex Resources Ltd. ■

Norfault Mines Ltd. (Ont. 1965)
1969 – Merged into Alchib Developments Ltd.; basis 13 new for 100 old shs.

Norfin Business Advisors Corporation (Can. Oct. 31, 1997)
May 30, 2003 – Name changed to Gopher Media Services Corporation. ■

Norfolk Petroleum Limited (Can. Mar. 15, 1985)
Mar. 17, 1993 – Name changed to International Norfolk Acquisition Inc.; basis 1 new for 10 old shs. ■

Norford Pershing Mines Ltd. (Ont. 1944)
Charter cancelled.

Norgold Energy & Minerals Ltd. (Can. Mar. 30, 1981)
Apr. 9, 1986 – Name changed to Multi Choice Communications Inc. and continued into Ontario. ■

Norgold Mines, Limited (Ont. June 19, 1933)
1977 – Charter cancelled.
1979 – Charter revived.
Mar. 30, 1981 – Name changed to Norgold Energy & Minerals Ltd. and continued into Canada; basis 1 new for 5 old shs. ■

Norgold Resources Inc. (B.C. 1986)
Aug. 2, 1991 – Acquired by Bema Gold Corporation; basis 1 Bema sh. for 2.7 Norgold shs. prior to Apr. 8, 1991, and 0.4 Bema shs. for 1 Norgold sh. after Apr. 8, 1991. (see Bema Gold Corporation)

Norhack-Rouyn Mines Ltd. (Ont. 1947)
1958 – Charter cancelled.

Nori Aquafood Systems Inc. (B.C. Oct. 31, 1984)
Mar. 16, 1990 – Name changed to Royale Nori Foods Inc.; basis 1 new for 3 old shs. ■

Norianium Minerals Ltd. (Sask. 1953)
Sept. 1968 – Struck off register.

Norin Corp. (Del. 1970 amalg.)
1979 – Continued into Florida.
July 1980 – All o/s com. shs. acquired for US$32 per sh. by Canadian Pacific Enterprises Limited. Subsequently, Norin was dissolved and holders of co.'s pref. shs. received US$6.50 per sh. A Canadian subsid. of

Enterprises received the stock of Maple Leaf Mills, the co.'s principal operating entity, and following such dissolution, assumed co.'s obligations on 11% subord. s.f. debs., due 1998.

Norita Quebec Mines Ltd. (Que. 1966)
June 30, 1980 – Amalgamated (1 for 1) into Pyx Explorations Ltd.

Norite Explorations Ltd. (Ont. 1948)
1969 – Merged into Alchib Developments Ltd.; basis 3 new for 100 old shs.

Norjean Mines Ltd. (Ont. 1966)
Mar. 6, 1979 – Dissolved.

Norlac Explorations Ltd. (Ont. 1971)
July 6, 1983 – Amalgamated with 8 other cos. to form Lobo Gold & Resources Inc.; basis 1 new for 10 old shs.

Norlana Energy Inc. (Alta. June 5, 1986)
Dec. 2, 1997 – Name changed to Norlana Resources Limited; basis 1 new for 10 old shs. ■

Norlana Resources Limited (Alta. June 5, 1986)
Mar. 13, 1999 – Dissolved and struck from registry.

Norlartic Mines Ltd. (Ont. 1943)
1966 – Merged into Willroy Mines Ltd.; basis 1 new for 20 old shs.

Norlee Red Lake Gold Mines Ltd. (Ont. 1945)
Mar. 1958 – Charter cancelled.

Norlex Mines Ltd. (Ont. 1945)
Nov. 16, 1987 – Name changed to NLX Resources Inc.; basis 1 new for 3 old shs. ■

Norlode Resources Inc. (Ont. 1982)
Mar. 2, 1992 – Amalgamated with Concentrated Rare Earth Minerals Ltd., Enertex Developments Inc., Goldmac Explorations Inc., Offset Natural Resources Ltd., Preston Resources Ltd., Saranac Resources Ltd. and Uranex Resources Limited to form Marvas Developments Ltd.; basis 1 new for 7 Concentrated Rare Earth shs., 1 new for 12.6 Enertex shs., 1 new for 17.5 Goldmac shs., 1 new for 11 Offset shs., 1 new for 5.5 Preston shs., 1 new for 6.3 Saranac shs., 1 new for 13.5 Uranex shs. and 1 new for 4.6 Norlode shs. (see Marvas Developments Ltd.)

Normabec Mining Resources Ltd. (Can. May 21, 1986)
Nov. 18, 2009 – Acquired by First Majestic Silver Corp. pursuant to plan of arrangement whereby non-Mexican assets of Normabec, including the Pitt Gold property in Quebec, were transferred to newly formed publicly listed Brionor Resources Inc.; basis 0.060425 First Majestic shs. and 0.25 Brionor shs. for 1 Normabec sh.

Normalloy Explorations and Holdings Ltd. (Ont. 1956)
Feb. 26, 1980 – Charter cancelled.

Normalloy Explorations Ltd. (Ont. 1956)
1963 – Name changed to Normalloy Explorations and Holdings Ltd.; basis 1 new for 1 old sh. ■

Norman Malartic Mines Ltd. (Ont. 1942)
Sept. 1960 – Charter cancelled.

Norman Mines Ltd. (Man. June 12, 1979)
Aug. 31, 1992 – Delisted from the Canadian Dealing Network. Subsequently struck from register and dissolved.

Norman Resources Ltd. (B.C. Jan. 31, 1983)
Apr. 5, 1989 – Name changed to Golden Ring Resources Ltd.; basis 1 new for 5 old shs. ■

Normanco Gold Mines Ltd. (Ont. Nov. 1938)
Dec. 1948 – Licence revoked and registration cancelled.

Normand Mines Ltd. (Que. 1965)
Mar. 1975 – Charter cancelled.

Normandie Resource Corporation (Alta. 1985)
Aug. 16, 1989 – Amalgamated with a wholly owned subsid. of Argyll Energy Corporation. (see Argyll Energy Corporation)

Normandy Gold Mines Ltd. (Man. Aug. 1, 1934)
1947 – Continued into Quebec.
1956 – Name changed to Normandy Chibougamau Mines Ltd.

Normandy Mines Ltd. (unknown)
Aug. 1, 1934 – Name changed to Normandy Gold Mines Ltd. and continued into Manitoba; basis 100 new for 1 old sh. ■

Normandy Mining Limited (Vic. 1953)
June 24, 2002 – Acquired by wholly owned limited liability company of US-based Newmont Mining Corporation; basis 3.85 new Newmont com. shs. for 100 old Normandy ordinary shs. (represented by American Depositary shs./ADS) plus A$0.50 per ADS held.

Normar Gold Mines Ltd. (Ont. 1944)
1980 – Charter cancelled.

Normar Mines Ltd. (Que. 1940)
1944 – Name changed to Normar Gold Mines Ltd. and continued into Ontario. ■

Normeric Exploration Company Ltd. (Ont. 1938)
1957 – Charter cancelled.

Normetal Mining Corporation Ltd. (Can. 1931)
Apr. 1968 – Assets acquired by Kerr Addison Mines Limited; basis 3 new for 10 old shs. (see Kerr Addison Mines Limited)

Normetal Mining Exploration Inc. (Que. Dec. 6, 1985)
May 10, 2002 – Struck off register.

Normex Technologies Corporation (Ont. Sept. 20, 1984)
Apr. 7, 1998 – Name changed to Cygnal Technologies Corporation; basis 1 new for 40 old shs. ■

Normick Perron Inc. (Que. Apr. 30, 1968)
Oct. 27, 1989 – Acquired by wholly owned subsid. of Noranda Forest Inc. for $7.63 or redeem. pref. shs. (see Noranda Forest Inc.)

Norminco Developments Limited (Can. 1972)
May 19, 1983 – Name changed to Sumburgh Developments Limited; basis 1 new for 5 old shs. ■

Normine Resources Ltd. (B.C. Nov. 4, 1982)
Dec. 8, 1988 – Amalgamated with Bema International Resources Inc. (1 for 1) and Amir Mines Ltd. (1 for 1) to form Bema Gold Corporation; basis 1 new for 2 old shs. (see Bema Gold Corporation)

Normingo Mines Ltd. (Ont. 1954)
Aug. 3, 1964 – Charter cancelled.

Normiska Corporation (Ont. Jan. 17, 1997)
May 17, 2007 – Privatized via amalgamated with 2129711 Ontario Limited; basis 1 redeem. pref. sh. for 1 Normiska sh. immediately redeemed for 15¢ per sh.

Normiska Mining and Exploration Ltd. (Que. 1952)
1962 – Sold property to Leroy Mining Corp. for 300,000 shs.

Normont Copper Ltd. (B.C. 1966)
1971 – Name changed to Intercontinental Environmental Industries Ltd.; basis 1 new for 5 old shs. ■

Norocona Gold Mines Ltd. (Ont. 1945)
Nov. 30, 1964 – Dissolved.

Noront Mining Co. Ltd. (Ont. 1958)
Mar. 13, 1979 – Dissolved.

Noront Resources Ltd. (B.C. Nov. 14, 1980)
Nov. 26, 2004 – Continued into Ontario.
Apr. 13, 2022 – Acquired by Wyloo Metals Pty Ltd.; basis $1.10 cash per sh.
Sept. 27, 2022 – Name changed to Ring of Fire Metals.

Norpax Nickel Mines Ltd. (Ont. 1945)
Mar. 1976 – Charter cancelled.

Norpax Oils & Mines Ltd. (Ont. 1945)
1957 – Name changed to Norpax Nickel Mines Ltd. ■

Norpet Resources Limited (Alta. 1983)
May 4, 1989 – Merged with HCO Energy Company Ltd. to form Consolidated HCO Energy Ltd.; basis 1 Norpet sh. for 2.894 HCO shs. (see Consolidated HCO Energy Ltd.)

Norpick Gold Mines Ltd. (Ont. 1945)
1952 – Name changed to Norpax Oils & Mines Ltd.; basis 1 new for 3 old shs. ■

Norpoint Explorations Ltd. (Ont. 1965)
1968 – Assets sold to Mission Financial Corporation Ltd.; basis 0.0184 new for 1 old sh.

Norquay Capital Ltd. (Alta. July 6, 2005)
May 1, 2006 – Formed Xtreme Coil Drilling Corp. in Alberta on Qualifying Transaction amalgamation with Xtreme Coil Drilling Corp., constituting a reverse takeover by Xtreme; basis 1 new for 1 Xtreme sh. and 1 new for 30 Norquay shs. ■

Norque Copper Mines Ltd. (Ont. 1956)
1968 – Name changed to New Norque Mines Ltd.; basis 1 new for 4 old shs. ■

Norra Corporation (Alta. June 30, 1988 amalg.)
Dec. 31, 1992 – Name changed to GC Greyhawke Corporation. ■

Norris Communications Corp. (B.C. Feb. 11, 1988)
Nov. 30, 1994 – Continued into Yukon.
Sept. 17, 1996 – Continued into Delaware.
Jan. 20, 1999 – Name changed to E Digital Corp.

Norris Lake Gold Mines Ltd. (Man. 1946)
Mar. 5, 1979 – Dissolved.

Norris Lithium Inc. (B.C. May 26, 2021)
Sept. 28, 2023 – Acquired by Lithium One Metals Inc.; basis 0.672 Lithium One shs. for 1 Norris Lithium sh.

Norrland Gold Corp. (B.C. Jan. 29, 2019)
Apr. 17, 2025 – Name changed to Great Plains Metals Corp. (see FPsurvey - Mines & Energy)

NorRock Realty Finance Corporation (Ont. Dec. 21, 2007)
Jan. 14, 2015 – Name changed to Griffin Skye Corporation. ■

Norsat International Inc. (B.C. Oct. 15, 1982)
Sept. 27, 1989 – Name changed to NII Norsat International Inc.; basis 1 new for 5 old shs. ■

Norsat International Inc. (B.C. Oct. 15, 1982)
July 25, 2017 – Acquired by Hytera Communications Co., Ltd.; basis US$11.50 cash per sh.

Norsco Mines Ltd. (Ont. 1959)
1961 – Merged into Jorsco Explorations Ltd.

Norse Exploration Ltd. (B.C. 1968)
Jan. 1975 – Charter cancelled.

Norseman Capital Limited (B.C. Sept. 25, 1985)
Sept. 16, 2020 – Name changed to Norseman Silver Inc. ■

Norseman Mines Ltd. (Ont. 1943)
Apr. 1950 – Name changed to New Norseman Mines Ltd.; basis 1 new for 2 old shs. ■

Norseman Mines Limited (Que. 1971)
1981 – Acquired by Grosmont Resources Ltd. during in 1981-82; basis 1 Grosmont sh. for 1.795 Norseman shs.

Norseman Nickel Corp. Ltd. (Ont. 1957)
Aug. 19, 1965 – Dissolved.

Norseman Silver Inc. (B.C. Sept. 25, 1985)
Jan. 26, 2024 – Name changed to Fitzroy Minerals Inc. (see FPsurvey - Mines & Energy)

Norseman (Yellowknife) Explorations Ltd. (unknown)
1943 – Acquired by Norseman Mines Ltd.; basis 28 new for 1 old sh. (see Norseman Mines Ltd.)

Norsemines Explorations Ltd. (unknown)
1969 – Acquired by Bathurst Norsemines Ltd.; basis 7 new for 10 old shs. (see Bathurst Norsemines Ltd.)

Norsemont Capital Inc. (B.C. Jan. 30, 2016)
Feb. 24, 2020 – Name changed to Norsemont Mining Inc. (see FPsurvey - Industrials)

Norsemont Mining Corporation (B.C. June 10, 1977)
Oct. 24, 1994 – Name changed to International Norsemont Ventures Ltd.; basis 1 new for 10 old shs. ■

Norsemont Mining Inc. (B.C. June 10, 1977)
July 6, 2011 – Acquired by HudBay Minerals Inc.; basis $0.001 plus 0.2617 HudBay shs. for 1 Norsemont sh. (see HudBay Minerals Inc.)
Sept. 26, 2011 – Name changed to HudBay Peru Inc. (see HudBay Minerals Inc.)

Norsewick Mines Ltd. (Ont. 1943)
July 1953 – Name changed to Brunsman Mines Ltd. ■

Norske Skog Canada Ltd. (B.C. Dec. 30, 1971 amalg.)
Sept. 1, 2001 – Amalgamated with Pacifica Papers Inc. to form new co. with same name Norske Skog Canada Limited.
Oct. 3, 2005 – Name changed to Catalyst Paper Corporation. ■

Norstar Ventures Corp. (B.C. Feb. 3, 2000)
July 30, 2004 – Formed Zongshen PEM Power Systems Inc. in British Columbia following reverse takeover acquisition of and amalgamation with Pem Technologies Inc. ■

Norsul Oil & Mining Limited (Alta. 1949)
Oct. 5, 1999 – Struck from registry and dissolved.

Norsynco Mining & Exploration Ltd. (Ont. 1953)
1956 – Assets acquired by Norsyncomaque Mining Ltd.

Norsyncomaque Mining Limited (Que. Dec. 5, 1936)
July 4, 1961 – Name changed to Silvermaque Mining Limited; basis 1 new for 4 old shs. ■

Norte Resources Ltd. (B.C. July 27, 1992)
Apr. 6, 1998 – Name changed to Banks Ventures Ltd. and continued into Yukon; basis 1 new for 3 old shs. ■

Nortec Ventures Corp. (B.C. June 1, 1999)
Jan. 7, 2010 – Name changed to Nortec Minerals Corp. (see FPsurvey - Mines & Energy)

Nortech Geomatics International Inc. (Alta. May 24, 1996)
Oct. 2, 2005 – Struck from registry and dissolved.

Nortek Capital Corporation (B.C. Jan. 8, 1973)
Nov. 5, 1991 – Name changed to Brigdon Resources Inc.; basis 1 new for 20 old shs. ■

Nortek Energy Corp. (B.C. Jan. 8, 1973)
Oct. 3, 1988 – Name changed to Nortek Capital Corporation. ■

Nortek Engines Ltd. (B.C. Jan. 8, 1973)
Sept. 24, 1979 – Name changed to Nortek Energy Corp. ■

Nortel Communications Inc. (B.C. 1979)
May 11, 1992 – Name changed to American Nortel Communications Inc.; basis 1 new for 10 old shs. ■

Nortel Networks Corporation (Can. Jan. 5, 1914; via Dominion charter)
Jan. 2009 – Filed for protection under the Companies' Creditor Arrangement Act and under Chapter 11 of the U.S. Bankruptcy code. Ernst & Young Inc. was appointed monitor.
June 2012 – As of June 2012, approximately US$7.803 billion in net proceeds were generated through the sale

of businesses and remaining patents and patent applications.

Oct. 2012 – All officers and directors resigned.

Oct. 2016 – Global settlement and support agreement entered into with Nortel Networks Inc., Nortel Networks UK Limited and other Nortel entities plus the significant creditors of said entities, under which the company, Nortel Networks Limited and certain other Canadian affiliates (Nortel Canada) would receive 57.1065% of the US$7.3 billion sale proceeds held in escrow, or approx. US$4.413 billion as at July 31, 2016. The agreement also provides for the release to Nortel Canada of about US$237,000,000 of other sale proceeds. If the agreement is approved, distributions to creditors was expected to occur in 2017; no distributions to shldrs. of the company or Nortel Networks Limited was expected. (see FPsurvey - Industrials)

Norterre Mines Ltd. (Que. 1946)
1961 – Charter cancelled.

Nortex Petroleum Ltd. (Alta. Apr. 18, 1979)
Mar. 5, 1986 – Name changed to Seba Exploration Ltd.; basis 1 new for 5 old shs. ■

North American Advantaged Convertibles Fund (Ont.)
May 20, 2016 – Name changed to First Asset North American Convertibles Fund. ■

North American Aero Dynamics Ltd. (B.C. 1983)
Jan. 22, 1993 – Dissolved and struck off register.

North American Asbestos Company Limited (Que. June 10, 1950)
Sept. 30, 1993 – Name changed to Bishop Resources International Exploration Inc. ■

North American Business Intelligence Systems Inc. (Alta. Nov. 23, 1993)
May 1, 1996 – Struck off register.

North American Combustion Technology Corporation (Ont. 1980 amalg.)
May 19, 1983 – Charter cancelled.

North American Detectors Inc. (Ont. Nov. 3, 1994)
Jan. 7, 2008 – Dissolved and struck from register.

North-American Elevators Ltd. (Can. 1929)
Capital stock now held privately; no public interest.

North American Energy Partners Inc. (Can. Nov. 28, 2006 amalg.)
Apr. 16, 2018 – Name changed to North American Construction Group Ltd. (see FPsurvey - Mines & Energy; FPsurvey - Industrials)

North American Equity Corporation (B.C. Dec. 17, 1982 amalg.)
May 8, 1992 – Dissolved and struck off register.

North American Financials Capital Securities Trust (Ont. Oct. 23, 2009)
Jan. 29, 2016 – Name changed to Global Capital Securities Trust on merger with Australian Banc Capital Securities Trust (basis 0.413485 Global Capital cl. A units for 1 cl. A unit and 0.391346 cl. F units for 1 cl. F unit), Canadian Banc Capital Securities Trust (basis 0.968751 cl. A units for 1 cl. A unit and 0.970716 cl. F units for 1 cl. F unit), Euro Banc Capital Securities Trust (basis 0.382254 cl. A units for 1 unit) and HBanc Capital Securities Trust (basis 0.949297 cl. A units for 1 cl. A ser. 1 unit and 0.968918 cl. A units for 1 cl. A ser. 2 unit). ■

North American Fire Guardian Technology Inc. (B.C. Feb. 10, 1987)
Mar. 21, 2000 – Name changed to Rival Technologies Inc.; basis 1 new for 10 old shs. ■

North American Gas, Limited (Que. 1961)
Aug. 18, 1973 – Dissolved.

North American Gem Inc. (Alta. Mar. 7, 1996)
Sept. 2, 2004 – Continued into British Columbia.
Aug. 3, 2012 – Name changed to Victory Mountain Ventures Ltd.; basis 1 new for 40 old shs. (see FPsurvey - Mines & Energy)

North American Gold Corporation (Alta. 1983)
Dec. 6, 1991 – Name changed to North American Technologies Inc. ■

North American Gold Inc. (B.C. Mar. 13, 1987)
Sept. 7, 2005 – Name changed to Northland Resources Inc. ■

North American Goldfields Ltd. (B.C. 1941)
1952 – Charter cancelled.

North American Health and Fitness Corp. (Ont. Apr. 12, 1983)
Mar. 23, 1998 – Name changed to 1st Miracle Group, Inc. and continued into Delaware. ■

North American Land & Minerals Ltd. (Ont. Nov. 5, 1935)
1937 – Name changed to Kelly-Kirkland Mines Ltd. ■

North American Lithium Ltd. (B.C.)
June 1964 – Dissolved and struck off register.

North American Medical Services, Inc. (B.C. Nov. 15, 1988)
July 30, 1992 – Continued into Yukon.
Feb. 21, 2013 – Continued into British Columbia.
Feb. 25, 2013 – Name changed to KDR Industrials Ltd. ■

North American Metals Corp. (B.C. June 22, 1983)
Mar. 26, 2004 – Acquired by Wheaton River Minerals Ltd. for 30¢ per sh.

North American Mining & Chemical Corp. (Que. 1953)
Name changed to Fluor Bar Mines Ltd. ■

North American Molybdenum Corp. Ltd. (Ont. 1939)
1959 – Charter cancelled.

North American Nickel Inc. (B.C. Sept. 23, 1983)
July 29, 2022 – Name changed to Premium Nickel Resources Ltd. and continued into Ontario pursuant to the reverse takeover acquisition of the remaining 90.2% interest in Premium Nickel Resources Corporation (PNRC) and concurrent amalgamation of PNRC with wholly owned 1000178269 Ontario Inc.; basis 1 new for 5 old shs. ■

North American Nippon Technologies Corp. (B.C. Oct. 11, 1985)
Oct. 2, 1996 – Name changed to Agro International Holdings Inc. ■

North American Palladium Ltd. (Can. Sept. 12, 1991)
Dec. 17, 2019 – Acquired by Impala Platinum Holdings Limited; basis Cdn$19.74 cash per sh.
Dec. 18, 2019 – Name changed to Impala Canada Ltd.

North American Platinum Corporation Ltd. (B.C. 1966)
Feb. 25, 1983 – Struck off register.

North American Platinum Ltd. (B.C. 1986)
Apr. 24, 1992 – Dissolved and struck off register.

North American Potash Developments Inc. (B.C. June 13, 2006)
Sept. 20, 2018 – Name changed to Barolo Ventures Corp.; basis 1 new for 1.75 old shs. ■

North American Power Petroleums Inc. (B.C. Jan. 16, 1979)
Aug. 28, 1985 – Name changed to International North American Resources Inc.; basis 1 new for 5 old shs. ■

North American Preferred Share Fund (Ont. Feb. 28, 2013)
Sept. 20, 2019 – Terminated. Net assets of the fund distributed to unithlds. on a pro rata basis and the fund was dissolved.

North American REIT Income Fund (Ont. Sept. 27, 2012)
May 29, 2017 – Wound-up and dissolved; basis unknown.

North American Rare Metals Limited (Ont. 1955)
Aug. 3, 1994 – Amalgamated with Sunstate International Ltd. to form new co. with same name Sunstate International Ltd.; basis 1 Sunstate sh. plus 1 NAR Resources Ltd. sh. for 10 North American shs. (see NAR Resources Ltd.; Sunstate International Ltd.)

North American Resource Capital Limited (Ont. 1983)
Sept. 3, 1994 – Dissolved.

North American Rockwell of Canada, Limited (Del. 1928)
1973 – Name changed to Rockwell International of Canada Ltd. ■

North American Scientific, Inc. (B.C. 1987)
May 3, 1994 – Continued into Canada.
Apr. 20, 1995 – Continued into Delaware.

North American Systems Corporation (Alta. 1981)
Mar. 1, 1993 – Struck off register.

North American Technologies Inc. (Alta. 1983)
Nov. 25, 1993 – Acquired by North American Technologies Group, Inc.; basis 1 North American Technologies Group sh. for 2 North American Technologies shs.

North American Technology Limited (B.C. 1969)
Feb. 23, 1981 – Name changed to Yalakum Resources Ltd. ■

North American Tire Recycling Ltd. (B.C. 1988)
Apr. 8, 1993 – Merged with NATRL Acquisition Corp., a wholly owned subsid. of Omnicorp Limited, and incorporation continued into Delaware; basis 1 Omnicorp sh. for 1 North American Tire sh. Co. is now a wholly owned subsid. of Omnicorp.

North American Tungsten Corporation Ltd. (Can. May 3, 1996)
Mar. 17, 2018 – Dissolved and struck from registry.
Nov. 7, 2018 – Revived and restored to registry.
Mar. 7, 2020 – Dissolved and struck from registry.
Mar. 11, 2021 – Revived and restored to registry. (see FPsurvey - Mines & Energy)

North American Vanadium Inc. (B.C. Jan. 12, 1987)
June 26, 2007 – Name changed to Veraz Petroleum Ltd. ■

North American Ventures Ltd. (B.C. Dec. 19, 1986)
May 29, 1992 – Name changed to Newport Petroleum Corporation. ■

North Arrow Minerals Inc. (Can. Feb. 27, 2007)
Jan. 25, 2023 – Continued into British Columbia. (see FPsurvey - Mines & Energy)

North Atlantic Nickel Corp. (Ont. May 8, 1997)
June 11, 2004 – Name changed to North Atlantic Resources Ltd. ■

North Atlantic Resources Ltd. (B.C. Apr. 5, 1968)
June 28, 1978 – Name changed to Damascus Resources Ltd.; basis 1 new for 4 old shs. ■

North Atlantic Resources Ltd. (Ont. May 8, 1997)
Feb. 18, 2011 – Name changed to Legend Gold Corp. ■

North Battleford Gas Co. Ltd. (Sask.)
1958 – Struck off register.

North Bay Mines & Oils Ltd. (B.C. 1969)
Aug. 29, 1977 – Dissolved.

North Belleterre Gold Mines Ltd. (Que. 1944)
May 1974 – Charter cancelled.

North Bluff Capital Corp. (B.C. Oct. 15, 2008)
May 8, 2018 – Name changed to Sun Metals Corp. following reverse takeover acquisition of (old) Sun Metals Corp. ■

North Bordulac Mines Ltd. (Ont. 1945)
1969 – Name changed to Gold Hawk Exploration Ltd.; basis 1 new for 2 old shs. ■

North Briar Mines Ltd. (Ont. 1966)
Mar. 1976 – Charter cancelled.

North Canadian Oils Limited (Alta. July 25, 1947)
June 20, 1983 – Continued into Canada. (see Norcen Energy Resources Limited)
July 1, 1986 – Amalgamated with Merland Explorations Limited to form new co. with same name North Canadian Oils Limited; basis 1 new for 5.75 Merland shs. and 1 new for 1 North Canadian Oils sh. (see Norcen Energy Resources Limited)
Dec. 9, 1994 – Acquired by Norcen Energy Resources Limited; basis $14 per sh. The cl. B pref. shs. ser. 7 were redeemed Dec. 10, 1993 for $25 plus accrued and unpaid div. of 36¢ per sh. Also the cl. B pref. shs. ser. 6 were redeemed Aug. 15, 1994 for $25 plus accrued and unpaid div. of 25¢ per sh. (see Norcen Energy Resources Limited)

North Channel Mining & Development Co. Ltd. (Ont. 1944)
Feb. 18, 1963 – Dissolved.

North Coast Industries Ltd. (B.C. Dec. 19, 1984)
Aug. 14, 1991 – Name changed to Consolidated North Coast Industries Ltd.; basis 1 new for 4 old shs. ■

North Coldstream Mines Ltd. (Ont. 1951)
Dec. 30, 1971 – Amalgamated with Tontine Mining Ltd. to form Coldstream Mines Ltd.; basis 1 new for 4 old shs.

North Continent Capital Ltd. (B.C. 1971)
Nov. 24, 1976 – Name changed to NORCO Financial Services Ltd.

North Continental Oil & Gas Corporation Ltd. (Alta. 1938)
June 30, 1986 – Name changed to North Continental Energy Ltd.; basis 1 new for 4 old shs. (see FPsurvey - Mines & Energy)

North Country Gold Corp. (Alta. Feb. 3, 2010)
Sept. 29, 2015 – Acquired by Auryn Resources Inc.; basis 0.1 Auryn com. sh. for 1 North Country sh.

North Country Uranium & Minerals Ltd. (Alta. 1953)
1956 – Assets acquired by Inland Resources Corp., a Delaware co.; basis 1 new for 4 old shs.

North Crescent Explorations Ltd. (Ont. 1964)
1966 – Name changed to North Crescent Holdings & Explorations Ltd. ■

North Crescent Holdings & Explorations Ltd. (Ont. 1964)
1967 – Merged into W.G.N. Explorations & Holdings Ltd.; basis 1 new for 5 old shs.

North d'Arcy Explorations Ltd. (Ont. 1970)
Oct. 1973 – Amalgamated with 3 other cos. to form Tri-Bridge Consolidated Gold Mines Ltd.; basis 1 new for 10 old shs.

North Denison Mines Ltd. (Ont. 1936)
1954 – Name changed to Consolidated Denison Mines Ltd.; basis 1 new for 3.5 old shs. ■

North Devon Mines Ltd. (Ont. 1964)
1967 – Acquired by Dynacore Enterprises Ltd.; basis 1 new for 11 old shs. (see Dynacore Enterprises Ltd.)

North Eastern Energy Group Ltd. (Alta. Mar. 31, 1987)
Dec. 27, 1990 – Name changed to Ensign Resource Service Group Inc.; basis 1 new for 5 old shs. ■

North Expo Mines Ltd. (Ont. 1965)
Feb. 1972 – Amalgamated into Proto Explorations & Holdings Inc.; basis 1 new for 5 old shs.

North Frontier Explorations Ltd. (Ont. 1964)
1968 – Merged into Sakfield Mines & Investments Ltd.; basis 1 new for 3 old shs.

North Goldcrest Mines Ltd. (Ont. 1934)
1965 – Merged into Crestland Mines Ltd.; basis 1 new for 2 old shs.

North Group Finance Limited (Can. July 8, 2002)
Dec. 23, 2005 – Continued into British Columbia.
Sept. 23, 2016 – Name changed to Peekaboo Beans Inc. following reverse takeover acquisition of (old) Peekaboo Beans Inc.; basis 1 new for 3 old shs. ■

North Group Limited (Can. July 8, 2002)
Dec. 21, 2005 – Name changed to North Group Finance Limited. ■

North Hart Resources Ltd. (B.C. Dec. 1, 1967)
May 2, 1984 – Name changed to Calypso Developments Ltd.; basis 1 new for 3 old shs. ■

North Hatley Capital Inc. (Can. June 2, 2003)
Aug. 31, 2004 – Name changed to ORTHOsoft Holdings Inc. following Qualifying Transaction reverse takeover acquisition of ORTHOsoft Inc.; basis 1 new for 7.142857 old shs. ■

North Hawk Resources Ltd. (Ont. July 9, 1987)
Mar. 25, 1994 – Formed ELI Eco Logic Inc. in Ontario on amalgamation with ELI Eco Logic Inc.; basis 1 new for 1 ELI sh. and 1 new for 30 North Hawk shs. ■

North Huron Gold Mines Ltd. (Ont. 1936)
1955 – Charter cancelled.

North Inca Gold Mines (Ont. 1945)
1957 – Name changed to Canadian North Inca Mines Ltd.; basis 1 new for 7 old shs. ■

North Island Mines Ltd. (B.C. 1966)
May 17, 1979 – Name changed to Carnes Creek Explorations Ltd. ■

North Kirkland Mines Ltd. (Alta. 1980)
Nov. 2, 1987 – Name changed to Seal Cove Corporation; basis 1 new for 4 old shs. ■

North Lake Mines Ltd. (Ont. 1954)
1958 – Charter cancelled.

North Malartic Gold Mines Ltd. (Que. 1939) .
July 29, 1978 – Charter cancelled.

North Mattagami Mines Ltd. (Que. 1958)
1960 – Name changed to New Miller Copper Mines Ltd.; basis 1 new for 2 old shs. ■

North Merritt Mines Ltd. (B.C. 1960)
Jan. 1971 – Name changed to Toronado Development Corp. Ltd. ■

North Pacific GeoPower Corp. (B.C. Jan. 18, 1985)
Oct. 5, 2003 – Name changed to Western GeoPower Corp.; basis 1 new for 10 old shs. ■

North Pacific Industries Corporation (B.C. 1980)
Aug. 6, 1993 – Dissolved and struck off register.

North Pacific Mines Ltd. (B.C. 1964)
May 2, 1974 – Amalgamated with Initial Developers Corporation Ltd. to form Initial Developers Limited; basis 1 new for 5 old shs.

North Peace Energy Corp. (Alta. Feb. 6, 2007 amalg.)
Nov. 29, 2010 – Acquired by Southern Pacific Resource Corp.; basis 0.185 Southern Pacific shs. for 1 North Peace sh. (see Southern Pacific Resource Corp.)

North Range Nickel Mines Ltd. (Ont. 1943)
1951 – Charter cancelled.

North Rankin Nickel Mines Ltd. (Ont. 1951)
1970 – Name changed to Tontine Mining Ltd.; basis 1 new for 6 old shs. ■

North Rock Explorations Limited (Ont. 1934)
Mar. 14, 1978 – Charter cancelled.

North Shore Gold Mines Ltd. (Ont. 1933)
July 2, 1957 – Charter cancelled.

North Shore Mercantile Corporation (Can. July 28, 2000)
May 20, 2009 – Dissolved.

North Shore Mines (1936) Ltd. (Ont. May 18, 1936)
June 1, 1959 – Dissolved.

North Shore Uranium Corp. (unknown)
1968 – Continued into Quebec.
June 1, 1976 – Merged into Brominco Inc.; basis 1 new for 250 old shs.

North Siscoe Mines Ltd. (Que. 1942)
July 15, 1949 – Charter cancelled.

North Slave Explorations Limited (B.C. 1967)
1969 – Name changed to Calcorp Resources Limited. ■

North Slope Minerals Inc. (B.C. Apr. 29, 1980)
Jan. 18, 1995 – Name changed to Sino Pacific Development Ltd.; basis 1 new for 4 old shs. ■

North South Petroleum Corp. (B.C. Mar. 1, 2007)
July 5, 2016 – Name changed to Advantage Lithium Corp. ■

North South Resources Ltd. (B.C. 1978)
June 3, 1985 – Amalgamated with International Petroleum Ltd. and Peninsula Petroleum Corp. to continue under the Consolidated International Petroleum Corporation name; basis 1 new Consolidated International sh. for 6.97 old shs. of North South.

North Star Oil Limited (Can. 1919)
1961 – Minority int. held in cl. A and com. stk. purch. by Shell Canada Ltd. in 1960 at $19 and $34.25 per sh., respectively until Feb. 16, 1960, and thereafter at $18.85 and $34.10 respectively. All $2.50 pref. shs. 1956 ser. red. Aug. 8, at $50 per sh. plus an accr. divd. of 26.03¢ per sh. All o/s warr. of co. and its subsid., Cree Oil of Canada, purch. in May 1960, at $3.50 each. In July co. debs. exch. for like debs. of Shell Canada.

North Sullivan Contact Mines Ltd. (Que. 1937)
Nov. 7, 1975 – Charter cancelled.

North Summit Explorations Ltd. (unknown)
1969 – Merged into Summit Explorations & Holdings Ltd.; basis 1 new for 4 old shs.

North Sur Resources Inc. (Alta. Jan. 12, 2011)
June 22, 2020 – Continued into British Columbia.
Sept. 8, 2020 – Name changed to Mindset Pharma Inc. pursuant to the reverse takeover acquisition of (old) Mindset Pharma Inc. ■

North Tech Exploration Ltd. (Ont. 1956)
Jan. 4, 1965 – Dissolved.

North Trinity Mining Corp. Ltd. (Que. 1951)
June 1956 – Name changed to Trinity Copper Mines Ltd.; basis 1 new for 4 old shs. ■

North West Company Fund (Man. Jan. 31, 1997)
Jan. 1, 2011 – Succeeded by The North West Company Inc. pursuant to plan of arrangement whereby The North West Company Inc. was formed to facilitate the conversion of the fund into a corporation and the fund was subsequently dissolved. (see FPsurvey - Industrials)

The North West Company Inc. (Can. May 5, 1987)
Mar. 27, 1997 – Succeeded by North West Company Fund pursuant to conversion into an income fund; basis 1 trust unit for 1 com. sh. ■

North West Pacific Developments Ltd. (B.C. 1962)
1966 – Name changed to N.W.P. Developments Ltd.; basis 1 new for 5 old shs. ■

North-West Telephone Co. (B.C. 1929)
Jan. 1, 1961 – Merged with British Columbia Telephone Co., Ltd. In anticipation of the merger, all 1st mtge. bonds redeemed on Dec. 1, 1960, at 103, and pref. stk. redeemed at $10.30.

North West Trust Company (Alta. 1911)
Jan. 10, 1995 – Amalgamated with Canadian Western Bank for $1.30935 per cl. A sh. and com. sh. (see Canadian Western Bank)

The North Western Pacific Oil Company Limited (Alta.)
1960 – Struck off register.

North Whitney Gold Syndicate Ltd. (unknown 1934)
Aug. 19, 1965 – Dissolved.

North Whitney Resources Limited (Can. July 24, 1936)
Dec. 13, 1995 – Dissolved.

Northabie Mines Ltd. (Ont. 1952)
Mar. 11, 1970 – Dissolved.

Northair Mines Ltd. (B.C. Sept. 13, 1966)
Aug. 15, 1991 – Name changed to International Northair Mines Ltd.; basis 1 new for 5 old shs. ■

Northair Silver Corp. (B.C. Sept. 13, 1966)
Apr. 22, 2016 – Acquired by Kootenay Silver Inc.; basis 0.35 Kootenay com. shs. plus 0.15 Kootenay wts. for 1 Northair com. sh. Each wt. is exercisable at 55¢ per Kootenay sh. for 5 yrs.

Northampton Group Inc. (Ont. Nov. 13, 1974)
Sept. 30, 2014 – Privatized; basis $1.40 cash per com. sh. and 20¢ cash per preference sh.

Northampton Mining Co. Ltd. (Ont. 1915)
Nov. 1933 – Charter cancelled.

Northaven Resources Corp. (B.C. Oct. 29, 2009)
Nov. 14, 2016 – Dissolved and struck from register.

NorthBase Resources Inc. (B.C. Dec. 28, 2017)
Apr. 23, 2021 – Name changed to Vizsla Copper Corp. (see FPsurvey - Mines & Energy)

Northbreak Gold Mines Ltd. (Ont. 1944)
Nov. 6, 1961 – Charter cancelled.

Northbridge Financial Corporation (Can. Apr. 10, 2003)
Feb. 25, 2009 – Amalgamated with FFHL Financial Corp., a wholly owned subsid. of Fairfax Financial Holdings Limited, for $39.00 per sh.

Northcal Mines Ltd. (Alta. 1947)
Aug. 25, 1971 – Name changed to New Northcal Mines Ltd.; basis 1 new for 10 old shs. ■

Northcal Oils Ltd. (Alta. 1947)
1963 – Name changed to Northcal Mines Ltd. ■

Northcal Resources Ltd. (B.C. Dec. 2, 1935)
May 7, 1985 – Name changed to Calnor Resources Ltd.; basis 1 new for 3 old shs. ■

Northcliffe Gold Mines Ltd. (Ont. 1946)
Nov. 1957 – Charter cancelled.

Northcor Resources Ltd. (Alta. Dec. 5, 1986)
Jan. 10, 1990 – Name changed to Canadian Northcor Energy Inc.; basis 1 new for 4 old shs. ■

Northcore Technologies Inc. (Ont. Nov. 28, 1983)
Mar. 12, 2015 – Dissolved and struck off register.

Northcott Gold Inc. (Ont. Apr. 17, 1945)
Mar. 12, 2004 – Name changed to Laurion Gold Inc. ■

The Northeast Exploration Co. (Que. 1959)
Oct. 18, 1986 – Charter cancelled.

Northeastern Group Inc. (Can. July 11, 1989)
Apr. 1, 2015 – Name changed to Titanium Transportation Group Inc. following reverse takeover acquisition of (old) Titanium Transportation Group Inc. (see FPsurvey - Industrials)

Northeastern Hotel Group Inc. (Can. July 11, 1989)
Dec. 14, 2005 – Dissolved.
Oct. 26, 2006 – Revived.
May 20, 2009 – Dissolved.
June 23, 2009 – Revived.
Sept. 16, 2011 – Name changed to Northeastern Group Inc. ■

Northern Abitibi Mining Corp. (Que. Mar. 15, 1971)
July 14, 2011 – Continued into Alberta.
Apr. 3, 2017 – Name changed to CANEX Metals Inc.; basis 1 new for 5 old shs. (see FPsurvey - Mines & Energy)

Northern Acquisition Corp. (Alta. Sept. 11, 1992)
Mar. 15, 1994 – Name changed to Ultra Pure Water Systems (Canada) Inc. ■

Northern and Central Gas Company Limited (Ont. May 6, 1954)
Jan. 1, 1968 – Name changed to Northern and Central Gas Corporation Limited. ■

Northern and Central Gas Corporation Limited (Ont. May 6, 1954)
Jan. 25, 1985 – Acquired by Inter-City Gas Corp. retroactive to Sept. 30, 1984.
May 5, 1986 – Name changed to ICG Utilities (Ontario) Ltd. ■

Northern Aspect Resources Ltd. (Alta. Mar. 28, 2011)
Nov. 6, 2015 – Name changed to BTL Group Ltd. pursuant to Qualifying Transaction acquisition of Blockchain Tech Ltd. ■

Northern Atlas Explorers Ltd. (Can. May 31, 1971)
Mar. 21, 1991 – Name changed to Northern Atlas Inc.; basis 1 new for 4 old shs. ■

Northern Atlas Inc. (Can. May 31, 1971)
Feb. 21, 1996 – Formed Radiant Energy Corporation in Canada on amalgamation with Radiant Energy Corporation, constituting a reverse takeover by Radiant; basis 2 new for 1 Radiant sh. and 1 new for 4 Northern Atlas shs. ■

Northern B.C. Mining Co. Ltd. (B.C.)
Nov. 23, 1961 – Dissolved and struck off register.

Northern Blizzard Resources Inc. (Alta. Nov. 18, 2009)
July 17, 2017 – Name changed to Cona Resources Ltd. ■

Northern Bullion (Keno) Ltd. (B.C. 1965)
Apr. 23, 1979 – Name changed to Jubilee Explorations Inc.; basis 1 new for 3 old shs. ■

Northern Canada Mines, Limited (Ont. 1938)
Jan. 5, 1999 – Privatized following amalgamation agreement with its affiliates, Atlantic Coast Copper Corporation Limited, Key Anacon Mines Limited, First Maritime Mining Corporation Limited and Hunter Brook Minerals Limited; basis 1 new redeem. pref. sh. for 1 com. sh. immediately redeem. for $1.65 per sh.

Northern Canadian Minerals Inc. (B.C. May 12, 1987)
Apr. 9, 2007 – Name changed to Northern Canadian Uranium Inc. ■

Northern Canadian Uranium Inc. (B.C. May 12, 1987)
Dec. 27, 2007 – Acquired by Bayswater Uranium Corporation and amalgamated with a wholly owned subsid. to form NCU Holdings Inc.; basis 0.65 Bayswater Uranium shs. for 1 Northern Canadian sh. ■

Northern Chemicals Ltd. (Man. 1944)
1954 – Wound up. Distributed 1 sh. Lithium Corp. of America for 40 co. shs.

Northern Coal Mines Ltd. (B.C. Nov. 24, 1961)
Jan. 19, 1976 – Name changed to Norco Resources Ltd.; basis 1 new for 10 old shs. ■

Northern Continental Resources Inc. (B.C. Aug. 20, 1986)
Nov. 25, 2009 – Acquired by Hathor Exploration Limited; basis 0.1389 Hathor shs. for 1 Northern Continental sh. (see Hathor Exploration Limited)

Northern Copper Ltd. (Man. 1953)
Mar. 1, 1981 – Dissolved.

Northern Copper Ridge Mines Ltd. (B.C. Feb. 27, 1951)
July 19, 1982 – Name changed to Ventec Resources Inc. ■

Northern Crown Mines Ltd. (B.C. Feb. 24, 1987)
Aug. 15, 2002 – Name changed to Canadian Empire Exploration Corp. ■

Northern Dancer Resources Ltd. (B.C. 1979)
Apr. 8, 1994 – Dissolved and struck off register.

Northern Diatomite Ltd. (Ont. 1943)
Charter cancelled.

Northern Dynasty Explorations Ltd. (B.C. May 11, 1983)
Dec. 9, 1994 – Name changed to Northern Dynasty Minerals Ltd.; basis 1 new for 3 old shs. (see FPsurvey - Mines & Energy)

Northern Eagle Mines Ltd. (Ont. 1966)
1969 – Merged into Great Eagle Explorations and Holdings Ltd.; basis 4 new for 9 old shs.

Northern Eagle Mines Ltd. (B.C. Mar. 12, 1970)
May 28, 1985 – Name changed to Bentley Resources Ltd.; basis 1 new for 5 old shs. ■

Northern Electric Company, Limited (Can. Jan. 5, 1914; via Dominion charter)
Mar. 1, 1976 – Name changed to Northern Telecom Limited. ■

Northern Empire Minerals Ltd. (B.C. Nov. 16, 1986)
July 22, 2003 – Name changed to Stornoway Diamond Corporation. ■

Northern Empire Mines Co. Ltd. (Ont. 1932)
Oct. 1955 – Charter cancelled.

Northern Empire Resources Corp. (B.C. Apr. 24, 2012; amalg.)
Oct. 4, 2018 – All o/s com. shs. not already held acquired by Coeur Mining, Inc.; basis 0.1850 Coeur com. shs. for 1 Northern Empire com. sh.

Northern Energy Corporation (B.C. Mar. 15, 1965)
Mar. 24, 1986 – Name changed to United Northern Petroleum Corp.; basis 1 new for 2 old shs. ■

Northern Engineered Gold Resources Ltd. (B.C. Feb. 14, 1972)
Aug. 29, 1983 – Name changed to Petrocel Industries Inc. ■

Northern Espina Resources Ltd. (B.C. 1972)
Jan. 29, 1981 – Name changed to Erica Resources Ltd. ■

Northern Exploration Ltd. (Que. 1957)
1969 – Name changed to Consolidated Northern Exploration Ltd.; basis 1 new for 3 old shs.

Northern Extension Limited (Alta. Mar. 11, 1937)
1953 – Assets acquired by Consolidated East Crest Oil Co. Ltd.; basis 1 new for 6 old shs.

Northern Financial Corporation (Ont. Oct. 7, 1988)
July 2, 2014 – Name changed to Added Capital Inc.; basis 1 new for 10 old shs. ■

Northern Freegold Resources Ltd. (Alta. Jan. 13, 2006)
Dec. 19, 2011 – Continued into British Columbia.
Jan. 25, 2017 – Name changed to Triumph Gold Corp. (see FPsurvey - Mines & Energy)

Northern Frontier Corp. (Alta. Oct. 20, 2011)
July 14, 2016 – Placed into receivership. PricewaterhouseCoopers Inc. appointed receiver and all officers and directors resigned.
Oct. 5, 2016 – Assigned into bankruptcy and PricewaterhouseCooper Inc. named as trustee.
Aug. 2, 2018 – Struck from registry and dissolved.
June 2022 – Secured creditors suffered a shortfall and no monies avail. for distrib. to creditor or shldrs. PricewaterhouseCoopers discharged as trustee. .

Northern Frosted Foods and Cold Storage Ltd. (Ont. 1943)
Sept. 2, 1963 – Dissolved.

Northern Gaming Inc. (Ont. Dec. 18, 1990)
Sept. 1, 1999 – Formed ICON Laser Eye Centers, Inc. in Ontario on amalgamation with Icon Laser Centre of London Inc.; basis 4,500 new for 1 Icon Laser sh. and 1 new for 10 Northern Gaming shs. ■

Northern Gas & Gasoline (unknown)
1936 – Acquired by Nottawa Oil & Gas Co. Ltd. (see Nottawa Oil & Gas Co., Ltd.)

Northern Gem Mining Corporation Ltd. (B.C. 1955)
Aug. 11, 1988 – Name changed to Cepeda Minerals Inc. ■

Northern Glacier Resources Inc. (Alta. May 8, 1996)
Dec. 10, 1999 – Formed Basic Realty Investment Corporation on amalgamation with 844717 Alberta Ltd.; basis 0.33333 new for 1 old sh. ■

Northern Gold Mining Inc. (Ont. May 1, 2006)
Dec. 24, 2015 – Acquired by Oban Mining Corporation; basis 0.0127 Oban shs. for 1 Northern Gold sh. (see Oban Mining Corporation)

Northern Helicopters Ltd. (B.C. 1965)
Jan. 21, 1983 – Struck off register.

Northern Hemisphere Development Corp. (B.C. Mar. 6, 1978)
Apr. 27, 2009 – Name changed to Hemisphere Energy Corporation; basis 1 new for 5 old shs. (see FPsurvey - Mines & Energy)

Northern Homestake Mines Ltd. (B.C. Oct. 30, 1964)
Apr. 23, 1976 – Name changed to Thunderwood Explorations Ltd.; basis 1 new for 3 old shs. ■

Northern Horizon Resource Corporation (B.C. Jan. 18, 1979)
Sept. 12, 1985 – Name changed to Golden Horizon Resource Corporation; basis 1 new for 4 old shs. ■

Northern Iron Corp. (Ont. Nov. 20, 2009)
Dec. 6, 2016 – Name changed to Lithium Energy Products Inc. ■

Northern Kyanite Mines Ltd. (Ont. 1955)
Jan. 18, 1965 – Dissolved. Distribution made of .7¢ per sh.

Northern Lead-Zinc, Ltd. (Ont. 1929)
1951 – Distributed 1 sh. Pine Point Mines Limited (Can.) for each 6.331 shs. held. Charter surrendered and cancelled.

Northern Lights Acquisition Corp. (Alta. Aug. 4, 2009)
May 27, 2011 – Formed Iona Energy Inc. in Alberta pursuant to Qualifying Transaction amalgamation with Iona Energy Company Ltd. (deemed acquiror); basis 1 new for 2.916 old shs. ■

Northern Lights Minerals Ltd. (B.C. 1968)
Mar. – Amalgamated with Whitey Wilson Oil & Gas Ltd. (1 for 4.6) to continue with the same name Northern Lights Minerals Ltd.; basis 1 new for 3.8 old shs.
May 1973 – Amalgamated with 2 other cos. to form Shelter Petroleums Ltd.

Northern Lights Resources Ltd. (B.C. 1969)
Oct. 4, 1985 – Name changed to Larch Resources Ltd. ■

Northern Machine Works Ltd. (N.B. 1945)
Nov. 16, 1977 – Charter cancelled.

Northern Minerals Ltd. (Can. Sept. 18, 1985)
Feb. 11, 1991 – Formed Capilano International Inc. in Canada on amalgamation with Capilano International Inc.; basis 1 new for 1 Capilano sh. and 1 new com. sh. plus 1 wt. for 4 Northern shs. ■

Northern Mining Explorations Ltd. (Que. Jan. 27, 1954)
July 13, 2007 – Name changed to MDN Inc. ■

Northern Mountain Helicopters Group Inc. (Alta. 1986)
Aug. 2000 – Together with subsids. Peace Helicopters Ltd., Northern Mountain Helicopters Inc. and Northern Heli Log Inc., filed for bankruptcy protection and PricewaterhouseCoopers Inc. of Vancouver was appointed monitor. Previously, all directors had resigned. Distributions were made to secured creditors but there were no funds available for unsecured creditors or shldrs.
Dec. 23, 2004 – Monitor was discharged.

Northern Natural Gas Company (Del. 1930)
Mar. 31, 1980 – Name changed to InterNorth, Inc. ■

Northern Nuclear Energy Ltd. (Ont. 1964)
1977 – Continued into Alberta.
1979 – Continued into British Columbia.
Jan. 28, 1980 – Name changed to Gaslite Petroleum Ltd.; basis 1 new for 2 old shs. ■

Northern Nuclear Mines Ltd. (Ont. 1964)
Oct. 3, 1977 – Name changed to Northern Nuclear Energy Ltd. ■

Northern Oil Co. Ltd. (unknown)
1955 – Believed wound up.

Northern Ontario Natural Gas Company Limited (Ont. May 6, 1954)
Dec. 10, 1965 – Name changed to Northern and Central Gas Company Limited. ■

Northern Orion Explorations Ltd. (B.C. Apr. 30, 1986)
June 24, 2003 – Name changed to Northern Orion Resources Inc.; basis 1 new for 10 old shs. ■

Northern Orion Resources Inc. (B.C. Apr. 30, 1986)
Oct. 18, 2007 – Acquired by Yamana Gold Inc.; basis 0.543 Yamana shs. plus Cdn$0.001 for 1 Northern Orion sh.

Northern Pearl Gold Mines Ltd. (Ont. 1950)
Oct. 28, 1957 – Dissolved.

Northern Peru Copper Corp. (B.C. Feb. 28, 2005)
Mar. 31, 2008 – Acquired by Copper Bridge Acquisition Corp. for $13.75 per sh.

Northern Pine Lake Mines Ltd. (Ont. 1931)
1951 – Name changed to Manasseh Silver Cobalt Mines Ltd. ■

Northern Pine Ventures Inc. (Alta. July 9, 2002)
July 14, 2005 – Continued into British Columbia.
July 15, 2005 – Name changed to Landmark Minerals Inc. ■

Northern Plains Oil Corporation (B.C. May 30, 1986)
Mar. 25, 1994 – Continued into British Columbia.
Oct. 17, 1996 – Name changed to Gopher Oil & Gas Company Ltd.; basis 1 new for 3 old shs. ■

Northern Platinum Ltd. (B.C. Oct. 17, 1986)
Sept. 23, 2010 – Amalgamated with a wholly owned subsid. of Prophecy Resource Corp.; basis 0.5 Prophecy Resource shs. plus 0.1 wts. for 1 Northern Platinum sh. (see Prophecy Resource Corp.)

Northern Power Systems Corp. (B.C. Feb. 14, 2012)
Aug. 22, 2022 – Dissolved and struck from register.

Northern Property Real Estate Investment Trust (Alta. Jan. 2, 2002)
Oct. 30, 2015 – Name changed to Northview Apartment Real Estate Investment Trust. ■

Northern Quebec Power Co. Ltd. (Can. 1923)
1963 – Purchased by Hydro-Québec at $33 per com. sh.; pref. shldrs. received equal par value in 10-year bonds guaranted by the Prov. of Quebec, bearing int. equal to divd. rate. Funded debt assumed by Hydro-Québec.

Northern Rand Resource Corp. (B.C. Oct. 12, 2006)
June 9, 2011 – Name changed to Suparna Gold Corp. ■

Northern Ranger Oil & Gas Ltd. (Ont. Dec. 17, 1982)
Sept. 14, 1988 – Name changed to Northern Ranger Minerals Inc. (see FPsurvey - Mines & Energy)

Northern Reactor DMB Resources Inc. (Alta. May 11, 1987)
Nov. 1, 1991 – Charter cancelled.
Feb. 18, 1994 – Charter revived.
Feb. 10, 1995 – Name changed to TMN Capital Corp.; basis 1 new for 2 old shs. ■

Northern Reef Exploration Ltd. (Alta. Jan. 3, 1984)
Sept. 12, 1995 – Acquired by Penn West Petroleum Ltd.; basis $1.85 or 2.2 Penn West shs. for 7 Northern Reef shs. (see Penn West Petroleum Ltd.)

Northern Resources Ltd. (B.C.)
Assets distributed to shldrs. by voluntary liquidation.

Northern Resources Ltd. (Alta. 1946)
Sept. 15, 1954 – Struck off register.

Northern Spirit Resources Inc. (Alta. June 8, 2007)
Oct. 16, 2015 – Name changed to Altura Energy Inc.; basis 1 new for 10 old shs. ■

Northern Star Mining Corp. (Yuk. July 7, 2000)
July 17, 2006 – Continued into British Columbia.
Aug. 18, 2010 – Filed for protection under the Bankruptcy and Insolvency Act (Canada). Deloitte & Touche Inc. appointed trustee.
Jan. 24, 2011 – Filed for bankruptcy. Deloitte & Touche Inc. appointed trustee and all officers and directors resigned.
Jan. 26, 2015 – Dissolved and struck from register.

Northern Star Resources Inc. (Alta. Apr. 4, 1990)
Mar. 9, 2000 – Name changed to ODAAT Inc.; basis 1 new for 5 old shs. ■

Northern Stores Inc, (Can. May 5, 1987)
Mar. 16, 1990 – Name changed to The North West Company Inc. ■

Northern Sun Exploration Company Inc. (B.C. Sept. 5, 1975)
Nov. 8, 2013 – Name changed to Reparo Energy Partners Corp.; basis 1 new for 50 old shs. (see FPsurvey - Mines & Energy)

Northern Sun Mining Corp. (Ont. Feb. 14, 2005)
Apr. 28, 2016 – All o/s shs., other than those held by Jien International Investment Ltd., acquired by Regal Silver Investments Inc. for 7¢ per sh.

Northern Tar, Chemical and Wood Limited (Ont. 1964)
Aug. 1973 – All o/s shs. not already held acquired by Jannock Corporation Limited for $12 per sh.
Oct. 1974 – In mid-1974, all com. shs. and assets sold to Abitibi Paper Company Ltd. and a distribution of $25.04 per pref. sh. made. Company wound up.

Northern Telecom Limited (Can. Jan. 5, 1914; via Dominion charter)
May 3, 1999 – Name changed to Nortel Networks Corporation. ■

Northern Telephone Company Ltd. (Ont. 1905)
Jan. 1960 – Amalgamated with Norwesto Enterprises Ltd. to form Northern Telephone Ltd.

Northern Telephone Limited (Ont. Apr. 5, 1905)
June 1, 2001 – Amalgamated with 2001595 Ontario Inc. to facilitate the privatization. All o/s com. shs. exchanged for redeemable pfce. shs. (1 for 1) of new company Northern Telephone Limited and were immediately redeemed for $17.50 per sh.
Apr. 23, 2002 – Name changed to NorthernTel, Limited Partnership.

Northern Tiger Resources Inc. (Alta. Apr. 29, 2008)
Apr. 17, 2014 – Name changed to Golden Predator Mining Corp.; basis 1 new for 7 old shs. ■

Northern Tungsten Ltd. (Man. 1952)
Apr. 1976 – Charter cancelled.

Northern Tungsten Mines Ltd. (B.C. 1972)
June 24, 1983 – Struck off register.

Northern Valley Mines Ltd. (B.C. Aug. 13, 1969)
July 1975 – Name changed to Northern Valley Resources Ltd. ■

Northern Valley Resources Ltd. (B.C. Aug. 13, 1969)
Apr. 16, 1979 – Name changed to Black Thunder Petroleum Corporation. ■

Northern Vertex Capital Inc. (B.C. June 7, 2007)
Feb. 16, 2012 – Name changed to Northern Vertex Mining Corp. ■

Northern Vertex Mining Corp. (B.C. June 7, 2007)
Sept. 24, 2021 – Name changed to Elevation Gold Mining Corporation; basis 1 new for 6 old shs. (see FPsurvey - Mines & Energy)

Northern Zinc & Gold Corporation (B.C. 1974)
Sept. 21, 1984 – Struck off register.

Northern Zinc Exploration Ltd. (B.C. 1974)
Apr. 1974 – Name changed to Northern Zinc & Gold Corporation. ■

Northewan Minerals Corp. (B.C. May 17, 1985)
Dec. 11, 1992 – Name changed to Flotek Industries Inc. ■

Northfield Inc. (Ont. Nov. 1, 1985)
Oct. 13, 2006 – Name changed to Northfield Metals Inc.; basis 1 new for 10 old shs. ■

Northfield Metals Inc. (Ont. Nov. 1, 1985)
Jan. 16, 2013 – Name changed to Cartier Iron Corporation. ■

Northfield Minerals Inc. (Ont. Nov. 1, 1985)
Sept. 7, 1999 – Name changed to Northfield Inc. ■

Northfield Petroleum Corporation (Ont. Nov. 23, 1989)
Aug. 8, 1994 – Name changed to Zamora Gold Corp.; basis 1 new for 6 old shs. ■

Northfork Ventures Ltd. (B.C. Jan. 31, 1983)
Mar. 5, 1993 – Delisted from the Vancouver Stock Exchange. Subsequently dissolved and struck from register.
Apr. 14, 1993 – Name changed to Medsana Medical Systems Inc. ■

Northgane Minerals Ltd. (Can. Sept. 18, 1981)
Oct. 29, 1986 – Name changed to General Minerals Corp. ■

Northgate Exploration Limited (Ont. Jan. 7, 1919)
Jan. 31, 2003 – Continued into British Columbia.
June 10, 2004 – Name changed to Northgate Minerals Corporation. ■

Northgate Holdings Limited (Ont. 1969)
Dec. 1970 – Name changed to Kingsgate Holdings Limited.

Northgate Minerals Corporation (B.C. Jan. 31, 2003)
Oct. 28, 2011 – Acquired by AuRico Gold Inc.; basis 0.365 AuRico shs. for 1 Northgate sh. (see AuRico Gold Inc.)

Northglen Petroleums Limited (Ont. 1972)
1977 – Charter cancelled.

Northill Resources Ltd. (B.C. 1979)
Apr. 19, 1984 – Formed Canadian Continental Oil Corp. in British Columbia on amalgamation with West Trend Resources Ltd.; basis 1 new for 2 old shs. ■

Northlake Mines Ltd. (B.C. 1966)
Oct. 15, 1974 – Charter cancelled.

Northland Bank (Can. 1975; via Special Act of Parliament)
Jan. 20, 1986 – Ordered wound up by the Manitoba Court of Queen's Bench, with Touche Ross Limited appointed sole liquidator.

Northland Gold Mines Ltd. (Ont. 1922)
Mar. 1940 – Name changed to Northland Mines (1940) Ltd. and continued into Ontario; basis 1 new for 5 old shs. ■

Northland Helicopters Ltd. (B.C. 1965)
Sept. 4, 2001 – Struck from registry and dissolved.

Northland Mines (1940) Ltd. (Ont. Mar. 1940)
Nov. 1954 – Name changed to Consolidated Northland Mines Ltd.; basis 1 new for 4.5 old shs. ■

Northland Mining Ltd. (B.C. 1966)
May 14, 1968 – Name changed to Monida Mines Ltd. ■

Northland Oils Limited (Alta. 1949)
Oct. 23, 1989 – Name changed to Consolidated Northland Oils Limited; basis 1 new for 7 old shs. ■

Northland Power Income Fund (Ont. Feb. 17, 1997)
Jan. 1, 2011 – Succeeded by Northland Power Inc. pursuant to plan of arrangement whereby Northland Power Inc. was formed to facilitate the conversion of the fund into a corporation and the fund was subsequently dissolved. (see FPsurvey - Mines & Energy; FPsurvey - Industrials)

Northland Power Preferred Equity Inc. (Ont. Apr. 8, 2010)
Jan. 1, 2011 – Amalgamated with (old) Northland Power Inc., Northland Power Income Fund Management Inc., NPIF Holdings GP Inc. and Northland Power Arrangeco Inc. to form Northland Power Inc.; basis series 1 pref. sh. of Northland Power Inc. for series 1 pref. sh. of Northland Power Preferred Equity Inc. (see Northland Power Inc.)

Northland Resources Inc. (B.C. Mar. 13, 1987)
Jan. 18, 2010 – Continued into Luxembourg.
Jan. 19, 2010 – Name changed to Northland Resources S.A.

Northland Systems Training Inc. (Can. Aug. 8, 1997)
May 6, 2005 – Dissolved.

Northland Trust Company (Ont. 1961)
Dec. 31, 1971 – Amalgamated into Ontario Trust Co.; basis 2 new for 1 old sh.

Northland Utilities Limited (Alta. 1945)
1972 – Gas assets acquired by Northwestern Utilities Limited and the electric generating and distributing assets by Alberta Power Ltd.; co. subsequently wound up.

Northline Energy Services Inc. (Alta. Apr. 3, 1997)
Feb. 14, 2000 – Acquired by Trican Well Service Ltd.; basis $1.05 or 0.1736 Trican shs. for 1 Northline sh.

Northlinks Capital Ltd. (Alta. July 10, 1997)
Mar. 30, 1999 – Name changed to Northlinks Limited. ■

Northlinks Limited (Alta. July 10, 1997)
June 7, 2004 – Name changed to Ausam Energy Corporation prior to the July 30, 2004, reverse takeover acquisition of Ausam Resources Limited; basis 1 new for 30 old shs. ■

Northlode Exploration Ltd. (B.C. 1964)
Oct. 10, 1980 – Name changed to Pure Silver Mines Ltd. ■

Northlodge Copper Mines Limited (Ont. Dec. 20, 1955)
Mar. 27, 2006 – Dissolved.

Northmount Mining Corp. Ltd. (Ont. 1966)
Mar. 1976 – Charter cancelled.

Northolt Mining Corporation Ltd. (Ont. 1965)
Mar. 1972 – Charter cancelled.

Northpoint Corporation (Ont. June 30, 1990 amalg.)
May 8, 2000 – Dissolved.

Northpoint Resources Ltd. (B.C. Dec. 8, 1986)
Nov. 2, 1998 – Name changed to Glacier Resources Ltd.; basis 1 new for 7.5 old shs. ■

Northport Minerals Explorers Ltd. (Ont. 1959)
Feb. 11, 1965 – Dissolved.

Northquest Ltd. (Ont. Mar. 18, 2008)
Oct. 20, 2016 – Acquired by Nord Gold SE for 26¢ per sh. plus 10¢ per wt.

Northquest Ventures Inc. (Ont. Oct. 22, 1976 amalg.)
Dec. 22, 1994 – Ernst & Young Inc. appointed receiver and manager of the asset, property and undertaking of ITN Limited, C.R. Telecommunications Inc. and certain telecommunication assets.
Jan. 18, 1995 – fONOROLA Inc. acquired certain assets for an undisclosed amount.
Sept. 12, 1997 – Receiver and manager discharged. All secured creditors suffered a shortfall and no distribution made to unsecured creditors and shldrs.

Northrich Pacific Ventures Inc. (B.C. Apr. 1, 1981)
Mar. 1, 1999 – Delisted from the Vancouver Stock Exchange. Subsequently dissolved and struck from register.

Northridge Exploration Ltd. (Alta. Mar. 24, 1987)
July 27, 1995 – Acquired by Chancellor Energy Resources Inc.; basis 75¢ or 0.428 Chancellor Energy shs. for 1 Northridge sh. (see Chancellor Energy Resources Inc.)

Northrim Mines Ltd. (Alta. 1955)
Nov. 1981 – Placed into receivership in March 1979. Assets subsequently sold and charter cancelled.

Northrock Resources Inc. (B.C. Mar. 14, 2008)
Dec. 13, 2011 – Name changed to Bama Gold Corp. ■

Northrock Resources Ltd. (Alta. Dec. 19, 1986)
July 20, 2000 – Acquired by Unocal Canada Management Limited, a wholly owned subsid. of Unocal Corporation, for $10.10 per sh.

Northshore Gold Development Co. Ltd. (Ont. 1957)
Dec. 3, 1957 – Name changed to North Shore Gold Fields & Mines Ltd.

Northside Group Inc. (Alta. Feb. 7, 1994)
Jan. 28, 2002 – Name changed to Wittke Inc. ■

Northside Resources Ltd. (Alta. 1987)
May 15, 1995 – Name changed to Northside Minerals International Inc.; basis 1 new for 5 old shs. (see FPsurvey - Mines & Energy; FPsurvey - Industrials)

Northspan Uranium Mines Ltd. (Ont. 1956)
1960 – Merged into Rio Algom Mines Ltd.; basis 13 new for 100 old shs. (see Rio Algom Mines Limited)

Northstar Aerospace Inc. (Ont. Mar. 29, 1984)
Aug. 24, 2012 – Substantially all operating assets were sold to Heligear Acquisition Co. (as U.S. purchaser) and Heligear Canada Acquisition Corporation (as Canadian purchaser), both affiliates of Wynnchurch Capital, Ltd.; proceeds were insufficient to repay secured lenders. No proceeds available for unsecured creditors or shldrs.
Apr. 2014 – Ernst & Young Inc. discharged as court appointed monitor and the proceedings under the Companies' Creditors Arrangement Act were terminated.

Northstar Copper Mines Ltd. (B.C. 1906)
Feb. 25, 1983 – Struck off register.

NorthStar Drilling Systems Inc. (Alta. July 26, 1994)
May 31, 2001 – Acquired by NQL Drilling Tools Inc.; basis 0.2 new NQL cl. A com. sh. for 1 old NorthStar cl. A com. sh. (see NQL Drilling Tools Inc.)

Northstar Energy Corporation (Alta. Dec. 13, 1979)
Apr. 2, 1997 – Merged with Morrison Petroleum Inc. and its wholly owned subsid., Northstar Acquisition Corporation, to form a new Northstar Energy Corporation. (see Northstar Energy Corporation)

Northstar Energy Corporation (Alta. Mar. 14, 1997)
Aug. 27, 2004 – Exchangeable shares redeemed in full by parent Devon Energy Corporation; basis 1 new Devon com. sh. for 1 old Northstar exch. sh.

NorthStar Gaming Holdings Inc. (B.C. Jan. 19, 2020)
Dec. 8, 2023 – Continued into Ontario. (see FPsurvey - Industrials)

Northstar Healthcare Inc. (B.C. Mar. 16, 2007)
Dec. 4, 2014 – Name changed to Nobilis Health Corp. ■

Northstar Resources Ltd. (Alta. Jan. 11, 1978)
Jan. 27, 1986 – Name changed to Canadian Northstar Corporation; basis 1 new for 5 old shs. ■

Northstar Venture Technologies Inc. (B.C. Aug. 21, 2017)
Jan. 29, 2021 – Name changed to Northstar Clean Technologies Inc. (see FPsurvey - Industrials)

Northumberland Mines Ltd. (Ont. 1974)
June 9, 1988 – Acquired by NovaGold Resources Inc.; basis 1 NovaGold sh. for 5.5 Northumberland shs.

Northview Apartment Real Estate Investment Trust (Alta. Jan. 2, 2002)
Nov. 4, 2020 – Acquired by Starlight Group Property Holdings Inc. and KingSett Capital Inc.; basis $36.25 cash per trust unit.

Northview Canadian High Yield Residential Fund (Ont. Apr. 14, 2020)
Feb. 15, 2022 – Name changed to Northview Fund. ■

Northview Fund (Ont. Apr. 14, 2020)
Aug. 21, 2023 – Name changed to Northview Residential REIT pursuant to the acquisition of three portfolios of multi-family properties and concurrent restructuring as an open-ended, real estate investment trust; basis 1 new for 1.75 old shs. (see FPsurvey - Industrials)

Northville Mines Ltd. (Ont. Mar. 28, 1967)
Dec. 1979 – Name changed to Century Energy Corporation; basis 1 new for 3 old shs. ■

Northwater Five-Year Market-Neutral Trust (Ont. June 18, 2004)
Oct. 1, 2009 – In the process of liquidating; basis unknown.

Northwater Market-Neutral Trust (Ont. July 18, 1997)
Dec. 31, 2009 – Voluntary liquidation initiated. Initial termination distribution of $3.14 per trust unit paid July 29, 2009. Subsequent termination distributions were as follows: $1.54 per trust unit paid Feb 3, 2010; 50¢ per trust unit paid Apr. 7, 2010; 17¢ per trust unit paid July 8, 2010; 6¢ per trust unit paid Oct. 7, 2010; 5¢ per trust unit paid Jan. 10, 2011; 7¢ per trust unit paid Apr. 7, 2011; 5¢ per trust unit paid July 8, 2011; 7¢ per trust unit paid Oct. 7, 2011; and 53¢ per trust unit paid Jan. 10, 2012. Final termination distribution pending.

Northwater Top 75 Income Trusts PLUS (Ont. Feb. 15, 2005)
Dec. 31, 2009 – Voluntarily terminated and liquidated. Initial termination distribution of $1.00 paid Jan. 15, 2010, to unitholders of record Dec. 31, 2009. Second distribution of $1.00 paid Jan. 29, 2010, to unitholders of record Jan. 22, 2010.

Northway Explorations Limited (Ont. Jan. 26, 1982)
Sept. 2, 2004 – Name changed to Caspian Energy Inc. followed by the Sept. 21, 2004, amalgamation of private

co. Caspian Energy Ltd. with a wholly owned subsidiary of new Caspian. ■

Northway-Gestalt Corporation (Can. 1967)
1980 – Spar Aerospace Limited acquired all shs. of co. on following basis: $100, 9 com. shs., 20 wts. and 100 jr. pref. shs. of Spar for each 100 com. shs. of Northway. Each wt. entitled holder to purchase one com. sh. of Spar at $12 per sh. for 3 yrs., and $14 per sh. for an additional 2 yrs.

Northway Resources Corp. (B.C. May 29, 2018)
Dec. 31, 2020 – Name changed to Kenorland Minerals Ltd. pursuant to reverse takeover acquisition of (old) Kenorland Minerals Ltd.; basis 1 new for 7 old shs. (see FPsurvey - Mines & Energy)

Northwest Arm Capital Inc. (Can. Mar. 23, 2016)
Jan. 4, 2017 – Name changed to Antler Gold Inc. (see FPsurvey - Mines & Energy)

Northwest Brewing Co. Ltd. (Alta. 1924)
June 13, 1958 – Name changed to Bohemian Maid Brewing Co. Ltd.

Northwest Canalask Nickel Mines Ltd. (Ont. 1953)
Aug. 1973 – Name changed to New Canalask Minerals Ltd.; basis 1 new for 100 old shs. ■

Northwest Digital Ltd. (B.C. 1986)
Jan. 21, 1994 – Acquired by Hartco Enterprises Inc. for 10¢ per sh. (see Hartco Enterprises Inc.)

Northwest Drug Company Limited (Alta. Nov. 19, 1957)
Sept. 27, 1993 – Acquired by 1035210 Ontario Inc., a wholly owned subsid. of Drug Trading Company Limited, for $9.25 per sh.

Northwest Drug Ltd. (Alta. Nov. 19, 1957)
Apr. 13, 1984 – Name changed to Northwest Drug Company Limited. ■

Northwest Explorations Inc. (Ont. Feb. 21, 1994)
Oct. 28, 1998 – Formed CGX Energy Inc. in Ontario following reverse takeover acquisition of and amalgamation with CGX Resources Inc.; basis 1 new for 5 old shs. (see FPsurvey - Mines & Energy)

NorthWest Gold Corp. (Ont. 1989)
June 8, 1993 – Amalgamated with NG Holdings Inc., a wholly owned subsid. of Northgate Exploration Limited; basis 1 Northgate com. sh. for 15 NorthWest cl. A sub. vtg. shs. (see Northgate Exploration Limited)

NorthWest Healthcare Properties Real Estate Investment Trust (Ont. Jan. 1, 2010)
July 21, 2025 – Name changed to Northwest Healthcare Properties Real Estate Investment Trust. (see FPsurvey - Industrials)

Northwest Industries Ltd. (Alta. 1943)
1962 – Acquired by CAE Industries Ltd. under offer of $6.50 per sh. (see Canadian Aviation Electronics Ltd.)

NorthWest International Healthcare Properties Real Estate Investment Trust (Ont. Oct. 13, 2010)
May 20, 2015 – All o/s trust units acquired by NorthWest Healthcare Properties Real Estate Investment Trust (NWH); basis 0.208 NHW trust units for 1 NorthWest International trust unit.

Northwest Mines Ltd. (B.C. 1952)
Jan. 6, 1975 – Dissolved.

Northwest Nitro-Chemicals Ltd. (Alta. 1954)
Mar. 1, 1978 – Amalgamated with parent co.'s subsid., International Minerals & Chemicals Corp. Shldrs. received (1 for 1) pref. shs. redeemable at $2.45 ($2.44 deemed divd.) on or after.

Northwest Pacific Oil Co. Ltd. (Alta. 1913)
1917 – Acquired by Mid-West Oil Co. Ltd.; basis 1 new for 3 old shs. (see Mid-West Oil Co. Ltd.)

Northwest Shroom Industries Ltd. (B.C. Jan. 3, 1986)
Mar. 2, 1990 – Delisted from the Vancouver Stock Exchange. Subsequently dissolved for failure to file.

Northwest Sports Enterprises Ltd. (B.C. Nov. 9, 1965)
Nov. 9, 2000 – Amalgamated with wholly owned subsid. 457774 B.C. Ltd. and Orca Bay Hockey Holdings Inc. to form Northern Sports Enterprises Ltd.; basis 1 old Northwest com. sh. exchanged for 1 new Northern Cl. A pfd. sh. which was immediately redeemed at $14 per sh.

Northwest Zinc Company Ltd. (B.C.)
Dec. 23, 1974 – Dissolved.

Northwestern Explorations Ltd. (unknown)
June 18, 1959 – Name changed to Kennco Explorations (Western) Ltd. a wholly owned subsidiary of Kennecott Copper Corp.

Northwestern Mineral Ventures Inc. (Ont. Sept. 26, 2003)
Aug. 3, 2007 – Name changed to NWT Uranium Corp. ■

Northwestern Uranium Ltd. (Alta. 1953)
July 15, 1961 – Dissolved.

Northwestern Utilities Limited (Can. May 26, 1923; via Dominion charter)
Aug. 2, 1972 – Amalgamated in Canada to continue with same name.
Dec. 30, 1996 – All o/s 4% cum. redeem. 1st pref. shs. redeemed; basis $100 plus a premium of $3.00 plus $0.6466 accrued and unpaid dividends per sh.

Northwestern Utilities, Limited (Can. 1923)
Aug. 2, 1972 – Amalgamated with Northland Gas Utilities Limited (1 new for 1 old sh.) to continue under the Northwestern Utilities, Limited name; basis 1 com. sh. for 1 com. sh. and 1 new pref. sh. for 1 old pref. sh.

Northwind Mines Ltd. (B.C. 1972)
June 1979 – Charter cancelled.

Northwind Ventures Ltd. (B.C. Sept. 13, 1985)
July 10, 1998 – Name changed to Sloane Petroleums Inc.; basis 1 new for 3 old shs. ■

Northwood Golds Ltd. (Ont. 1946)
Nov. 1962 – Dissolved.

Northwood Panelboard Limited (Can. 1969)
Name changed to Noranda Panelboard , a wholly owned subsid. of Noranda Forest Inc. ■

Nortoba Mines Ltd. (Ont. 1957)
Apr. 22, 1965 – Dissolved.

Nortoba Nickel Explorations Ltd. (Ont. 1957)
1958 – Name changed to Nortoba Mines Ltd. ■

Nortran Pharmaceuticals Inc. (B.C. Dec. 12, 1986)
June 26, 2001 – Name changed to Cardiome Pharma Corp. ■

Nortran Resources Ltd. (B.C. Dec. 12, 1986)
June 24, 1992 – Name changed to Nortran Pharmaceuticals Inc. ■

Nortyne Gold Mines Ltd. (Ont. 1944)
Mar. 1957 – Charter cancelled.

Norvado Exploration Co. Ltd. (Ont. 1948)
Nov. 1962 – Charter cancelled.

Norvalie Mines Ltd. (Ont. Apr. 10, 1937)
1965 – Name changed to International Norvalie Mines Ltd.; basis 1 new for 3 old shs. ■

Norvane Explorations Inc. (Ont. Dec. 11, 1995)
Oct. 8, 1998 – Name changed to Coffee Tea or Me Cafe Inc.; basis 1 new for 2 old shs. ■

Norvex Mining Co. Ltd. (Que. 1957)
Nov. 11, 1978 – Charter cancelled.

Norvista Capital Corporation (Can. Sept. 4, 2008)
Dec. 30, 2021 – Name changed to Olive Resource Capital Inc. (see FPsurvey - Industrials)

Norwall Group Inc. (Ont. June 28, 1990)
Dec. 15, 2010 – Privatized at 93¢ per sh.

Norway Lake Iron Mines Ltd. (Ont. 1938)
Nov. 28, 1973 – Charter cancelled.

Norwest Financial Canada Company (Ont. Aug. 27, 1992)
Sept. 7, 2001 – Name changed to Wells Fargo Financial Canada Corporation. ■

Norwesto Enterprises Ltd. (Can. - unspecified)
Jan. 1960 – Amalgamated with Northern Telephone Co. Ltd. to form Northern Telephone Ltd.; basis 2 new for 3 old shs.

Norwich Resources Ltd. (B.C. 1967)
Jan. 1980 – Name changed to Kelly Petroleum Inc.; basis 1 new for 5 old shs. ■

Norwich Ventures Ltd. (Alta. June 16, 1986)
Dec. 1, 1997 – Struck from registry and dissolved.

Norwick Capital Corp. (B.C. Jan. 4, 2018)
Nov. 6, 2018 – Name changed to Converge Technology Solutions Corp. pursuant to the Qualifying Transaction reverse takeover acquisition of Converge Technology Partners Inc. and concurrent amalgamation of Converge with wholly owned Norwick Acquisition Corp.; basis 1 new for 3.2 old shs. ■

Norwin Molybdenite Mines Ltd. (Ont. 1938)
Aug. 19, 1965 – Dissolved.

Norwood Exploration Incorporated (Que. 1986)
Mar. 31, 1989 – Amalgamated with Oz Exploration Inc., Omega Exploration Inc., Onyx Resources Inc. and Farboro Resources Inc. to form Orient Resources Inc.

Norwood Kirkland Gold Mines Ltd. (Ont. 1936)
1953 – Charter cancelled.

Norwood Resources Ltd. (B.C. Jan. 22, 1996)
Jan. 20, 2011 – Placed into bankruptcy. D. Manning & Associates Inc. appointed trustee.

NorZinc Ltd. (B.C. May 7, 2018)
Dec. 15, 2022 – Acquired by Resource Capital Fund VI L.P.; basis $0.0325 per sh.

Norzinc Mines Ltd. (Ont. 1946)
Mar. 10, 1958 – Dissolved.

Norzone Rouyn Mines Ltd. (Ont. 1946)
1947 – Name changed to New Norzone Mines Ltd.; basis 1 new for 2 old shs. ■

Nottawa Oil & Gas Co., Ltd. (unknown 1934)
Dec. 2, 1940 – In liquidation. Small payment to shldrs.

Nou Camp Capital Corp. (B.C. Sept. 25, 2018)
June 18, 2021 – Name changed to Moss Genomics Inc. (see FPsurvey - Industrials)

Nouveau Monde Mining Enterprises Inc. (Can. Dec. 31, 2012 amalg.)
Feb. 6, 2017 – Name changed to Nouveau Monde Graphite Inc. (see FPsurvey - Mines & Energy)

Nouvelle Mining Exploration Ltd. (Que. 1956)
Jan. 25, 1986 – Charter cancelled.

Nova Beaucage Mines Limited (Ont. 1953)
Aug. 14, 1996 – Formed Nova Beaucage Resources Limited in Ontario; basis 1 new for 10 old shs. ■

Nova Beaucage Resources Limited (Ont. Aug. 14, 1996 amalg.)
Jan. 13, 1997 – Amalgamated with Canuc Resources Corporation to form new co. with same name Canuc Resources Corporation; basis 1 new for 1 Canuc sh. and 1 new for 3.65 Nova shs.

Nova Canada Enterprises Ltd. (B.C. June 13, 2000)
July 28, 2003 – Capital Pool amalgamation with Stepstone Enterprises Ltd. (1 for 1) to continue as Stepstone Enterprises Ltd.; basis 1 new Stepstone com. sh. for 1 old Nova Canada com. sh. (see Stepstone Enterprises Ltd.)

Nova Cannabis Inc. (Alta. Jan. 4, 2019)
Oct. 22, 2024 – Acquired by SNDL Inc.; basis 0.58 SNDL com. shs. or $1.75 cash.

Nova-Co Exploration Ltd. (Ont. 1927)
July 17, 1987 – Name changed to Optical Data Corp. ■

Nova-Cogesco Resources Inc. (Can. 1985)
Feb. 14, 1994 – Amalgamated with Equity Reserve Corp., Orofino Resources Limited and Hughes Lang Corporation to form CanGold Resources Inc.; basis 5 new for 3 Equity shs., 1 new for 12 Orofino shs., 1 new for 1 Hughes cl. A sh. and 2 new for 5 Nova-Cogesco shs. (see CanGold Resources Inc.)

Nova Energy Corporation (B.C. 1979)
Sept. 16, 1981 – Name changed to Vior Energy Corporation. ■

Nova Growth Corp. (Ont. June 16, 1987)
Aug. 11, 2008 – Acquired by 2155300 Ontario Inc. for 50¢ per sh.

Nova Lithium Corp. (B.C. Mar. 7, 2017)
July 8, 2024 – Name changed to Nova Pacific Metals Corp. (see FPsurvey - Mines & Energy)

Nova Marketing Ltd. (B.C. Mar. 19, 1980)
July 24, 1992 – Name changed to National Nova Marketing Inc.; basis 1 new for 3 old shs. ■

Nova Mentis Life Science Corp. (B.C. Oct. 27, 2004)
Nov. 7, 2024 – Name changed to Restart Life Sciences Corp.; basis 1 new for 5 old shs. (see FPsurvey - Industrials)

Nova Net Lease REIT (Ont. July 27, 2021)
Feb. 20, 2025 – Final distrib. of US$0.44 cash per trust unit payable to shldrs. of record at Feb. 13, 2025.

Nova-Rich Gold Mines Ltd. (N.S. 1938)
1945 – Name changed to Canso Mining Corp.; basis 1 new for 10 old shs. ■

Nova Royalty Corp. (B.C. July 20, 2018)
Dec. 6, 2023 – Acquired by Metalla Royalty & Streaming Ltd.; basis 0.36 Metalla shs. for 1 Nova Royalty sh.

Nova Scotia Light and Power Company, Limited (N.S. Jan. 1, 1914)
Mar. 30, 1973 – Now wholly owned by Nova Scotia Power Corporation. Ord. shldrs. received $13 per sh.; pref. shldrs. had option of accepting N.S. Power Corp. debs. of equal par value or cash, as follows: 4% pref., a 5.625% deb. or $74.50; 4.5 % pref., a 6.25% deb. or $81; 5% pref., a 7% deb. or $44. Offers expired May 31, 1972. The Corporation subsequently elected to acquire all remaining shs., on same basis, and so notified shldrs. under date of. For any shs. not turned in by Apr. 30, 1973, funds were deposited in trust with the Accountant General of the Supreme Court of Nova Scotia, Halifax. (see Nova Scotia Power Corporation)

Nova Scotia Power Corporation (N.S. 1973)
Aug. 10, 1992 – Transferred all of its existing assets, liabs. and retained earnings except for long-term debt and sinking fund assets to Nova Scotia Power Incorporated. Subsequent to the reorganization and privatization, the business activities of Nova Scotia Power Corporation continued under Nova Scotia Power Incorporated and changed its name to Nova Scotia Power Finance Corporation which continues to hold the long-term debt and sinking fund assets.
Aug. 10, 1992 – Name changed to Nova Scotia Power Finance Corporation.

Nova Scotia Power Incorporated (N.S. July 13, 1984)
Jan. 6, 1999 – Following reorganization, all o/s com. shs. transferred to new parent company named NS Power

Holdings Incorporated; basis 1 new NS Power com. sh. for 1 old Nova Scotia Power com. sh. All o/s pref. shs. remain under the Nova Scotia Power name. (see FPsurvey - Mines & Energy; FPsurvey - Industrials)

Nova Scotia Savings & Loan Company (Can. 1964 amalg.)
Dec. 31, 1988 – Formed Central Guaranty Mortgage Corporation (a wholly owned subsid. of Central Guaranty Trust Company) following acquisition of controlling int. (99.7% by November 1987) by Central Capital Corporation interests and amalgamation with Central and Eastern Mortgage Corp.; basis $28 per sh. (see Central Guaranty Trustco Limited)

Nova Scotia Savings and Trust Company (Can. 1980)
Dec. 31, 1988 – Wholly owned subsid. of Nova Scotia Savings & Loan Company. Under corporate reorganization arrangements, amalgamated (1 for 1) with Guaranty Trust Company of Canada (1 for 1), Yorkshire Trust Company and Central Trust Company to form Central Guaranty Trust Company.

Nova Scotia Savings, Loan & Building Society (unknown 1850)
1964 – Amalgamated into Nova Scotia Savings & Loan Company; basis 1 new for $10 credit of Society members.

Nova Scotia Tramways and Power Company Limited (N.S. Jan. 1, 1914)
Jan. 1, 1928 – Name changed to Nova Scotia Light and Power Company, Limited. ■

Nova Uranium Corporation (B.C. Oct. 22, 2004)
Dec. 18, 2009 – Name changed to Secova Metals Corp. ■

Nova Uranium Mines Ltd. (Sask. 1958)
1971 – Charter cancelled.

NovaCan Mining Resources (I985) Limited (N.S. Dec. 5, 1984)
Mar. 20, 1987 – Name changed to NovaGold Resources Inc. ■

Novack Gold Mines Ltd. (Ont. Apr. 17, 1934)
1947 – Charter cancelled; shldrs. received 42.75 shs. Golden Trinity Mines Ltd. for each 100 old shs.

NovaCopper Inc. (B.C. Apr. 27, 2011)
Sept. 1, 2016 – Name changed to Trilogy Metals Inc. (see FPsurvey - Mines & Energy)

Novacor Chemicals Ltd. (Alta. Jan. 1, 1993)
Apr. 1, 1996 – Name changed to NOVA Chemicals Ltd.

Novacorp Realty Finance Ltd. (Alta. 1985)
Feb. 12, 1996 – All o/s 11.25% first mortgage bonds redeemed for a premium $10 plus accrued and unpaid interest of $13.25 per $1000 principal amount.

Novadaq Technologies Inc. (Can. Apr. 14, 2000)
Sept. 6, 2017 – Acquired by Stryker Corporation; basis US$11.75 cash per sh.
Sept. 26, 2017 – Continued into British Columbia.

NovaDx International Inc. (B.C. Sept. 19, 1983)
Dec. 2, 2004 – Name changed to NovaDx Ventures Corp.; basis 1 new for 30 old shs. ■

NovaDx Ventures Corp. (B.C. Sept. 19, 1983)
Mar. 6, 2017 – Dissolved and struck from register.

NovaGold Resources Inc. (N.S. Dec. 5, 1984)
June 10, 2013 – Continued into British Columbia. (see FPsurvey - Mines & Energy)

NovaGreenPower Inc. (B.C. July 8, 1999)
2008 – Name changed to AltaGas Renewable Energy Inc.

Novamerican Steel Inc. (Can. Apr. 4, 1997)
Nov. 21, 2007 – Acquired by Symmetry Holdings Inc. for US$56 per sh.

Novamin Inc. (Que. 1956)
May 26, 1988 – Amalgamated with Breakwater Resources Ltd.; basis 1 new for 2 old shs. (see Breakwater Resources Ltd.)

Novamind Inc. (Can. Apr. 23, 1997)
June 14, 2022 – Acquired by Numinus Wellness Inc.; basis 0.84 Numinus shs. for 1 Novamind sh.

Novamines Corporation (Que. 1939)
May 18, 1974 – Dissolved.

Novatech Power Corporation (B.C. Feb. 22, 1994)
July 25, 2003 – Dissolved and struck from the register.

NovAtel Inc. (Can. Oct. 17, 1978)
Dec. 21, 2007 – Acquired by Hexagon AB for US$50 per sh.

NovaTeqni Corporation (Alta. July 31, 2012)
June 24, 2019 – Continued into British Columbia.
June 25, 2019 – Name changed to NovaTeqni Technology Corporation; basis 1 new for 10 old shs. ■

NovaTeqni Technology Corporation (B.C. June 24, 2019)
Dec. 11, 2019 – Name changed to Trench Solutions Inc. ■

Novaterra Corp. (Alta. 1987)
Dec. 1, 1992 – Struck off register.

Novatron Information Corporation (Can. 1975)
Oct. 31, 1986 – Amalgamated with IAS Research Corporation to form new co. with same name Novatron Information Corporation.
July 14, 1995 – Name changed to ITI Education Corporation; basis 1 new for 35 old shs. ■

NovaWest Resources Inc. (B.C. Oct. 23, 1980)
Apr. 2, 2008 – Name changed to Apella Resources Inc. ■

Novax Capital Corporation (Alta. 1986)
May 6, 1996 – Name changed to Northern Mountain Helicopters Group Inc.; basis 1 new for 2.63 old shs. ■

Novax Equity Corporation (Alta. 1986)
Feb. 16, 1990 – Name changed to Novax Capital Corporation; basis 1 new for 5 old shs. ■

Novéder Inc. (Can. Sept. 23, 1983)
Oct. 11, 2001 – Name changed to Atlantis Exploration Inc.; basis 1 new for 10 old shs. ■

Noveko Echographs Inc. (Can. Sept. 23, 1983)
Jan. 11, 2006 – Name changed to Noveko International Inc. ■

Noveko International Inc. (Can. Sept. 23, 1983)
Apr. 7, 2015 – Filed an assignment under the Bankruptcy and Insolvency Act and Richter Advisory Group Inc. was appointed trustee.

Novelion Therapeutics Inc. (B.C. Feb. 3, 1981)
Nov. 5, 2019 – Shldrs. approved the voluntary liquidation and dissolution of the company.
Jan. 16, 2020 – Filed a statement of intent with the B.C. registrar to establish the effective date for the commencement of the liquidation. Alvarez & Marsal Canada Inc. appointed liquidator and remaining officers and directors resigned.
Mar. 11, 2021 – Interim distribution made of 1 Amryt Pharma plc ADR for 9 Novelion com. shs. to shldrs. of record Jan. 16, 2020. (see FPsurvey - Industrials)

Novelis Inc. (Can. Sept. 21, 2004)
May 18, 2007 – Acquired by AV Metals Inc., a subsidiary of Hindalco Industries Limited; basis US$44.93 for 1 Novelis com. sh.

Novell Porcupine Gold Mines (Ont. 1940)
1955 – Acquired by Consolidated Novell Mines Ltd.; basis 1 new for 8 old shs. (see Consolidated Novell Mines Ltd.)

Noverco Inc. (Que. Dec. 16, 1974)
Sept. 14, 1990 – Acquired by an acquisition co., jointly owned by Canam Manac Group Inc. (50%), the Caisse de dépôt et placement du Québec (25%) and the Société québécoise d'initiatives pétrolières (25%), for $15.25 per sh.

Novicius Corp. (Ont. Nov. 30, 2009 amalg.)
Nov. 1, 2018 – Name changed to Grown Rogue International Inc. pursuant to reverse takeover acquisition of Grown Rogue Unlimited, LLC.; basis 1 new for 1.4 old shs. (see FPsurvey - Industrials)

Novicourt Inc. (Que. Dec. 8, 1992)
Oct. 20, 2006 – Acquired by Falconbridge Limited for $2.30 per sh. (see Falconbridge Limited)

Novik Inc. (Que. Sept. 20, 2005 amalg.)
Feb. 20, 2014 – Acquired by Clearview Capital Fund III, LP for 85¢ per sh.
Jan. 16, 2017 – Name changed to Derby Building Products Inc.

Novitas Energy Ltd. (Alta. June 15, 2001)
Jan. 7, 2005 – Acquired by Bonterra Energy Income Trust; basis either 0.03636 new trust unit or, $0.176 plus 0.0291 new trust unit for 1 old Novitas sh. (see Bonterra Energy Income Trust)

Novo 19 Capital Corp. (B.C. Nov. 21, 2005)
Apr. 14, 2021 – Name changed to Nobel29 Resources Corp. pursuant to the reverse takeover acquisition of Nobel Resources Corp. and concurrent amalgamation of Nobel Resources with wholly owned 2791419 Ontario Inc.; basis 1 new for 6.6667 old shs. ■

Novoheart Holdings Inc. (B.C. Nov. 7, 2016)
Nov. 23, 2020 – Privatized via acquisition by Novomed Limited (a company affiliated with certain directors of the company); basis 53¢ cash per sh.

Novopharm Biotech Inc. (B.C. July 21, 1995)
Aug. 25, 1997 – Amalgamated with Genesys Pharma Inc. to continue as Novopharm Biotech Inc.; basis 1 new for 1 old sh.
July 9, 1998 – Continued into Ontario.
Oct. 17, 2000 – Name changed to Viventia Biotech Inc. ■

Novus Energy Inc. (Alta. Dec. 31, 2005 amalg.)
Jan. 24, 2014 – Acquired by Yanchang International (Canada) Limited, wholly owned subsid. of Yanchang Petroleum International Limited, for C$1.18 per sh.

Novus Gold Corp. (B.C. Mar. 20, 2009)
Apr. 20, 2012 – Acquired by Pan Terra Gold Limited; basis 0.33 Pan Terra Gold shs. for 1 Novus sh.

Nowsco Well Service Ltd. (Alta. Aug. 1, 1970 amalg.)
July 5, 1996 – Acquired by BJ Services Canada Inc. for $35 per sh.

Noxe Petroleum Corporation (B.C. 1979)
Nov. 3, 1986 – Name changed to Noxe Resource Corporation. (see FPsurvey - Mines & Energy)

Nstein Technologies Inc. (Que. Feb. 8, 2000)
Apr. 1, 2010 – Amalgamated with 9218-8150 Quebec Inc., a wholly owned subsid. of Open Text Corporation; basis Cdn$0.65 per share.

Ntex Incorporated (Ont. Sept. 29, 1975 amalg.)
June 2003 – Made an assignment into bankruptcy.

Nu-Age Uranium Mines Ltd. (Ont. 1953)
1956 – Name changed to Haitian Copper Mining Corp. Ltd. ■

Nu-Apex Energy Corp. (B.C. Feb. 11, 1981)
Dec. 30, 1999 – Name changed to Digital Ventures Inc.; basis 1 new for 5 old shs. ■

Nu-Cycle Uranium Mines Ltd. (Ont. 1955)
Feb. 1967 – Charter cancelled.

Nu-Dawn Resources Inc. (B.C. Oct. 3, 1980)
Sept. 27, 1999 – Name changed to World Ventures Inc. (see FPsurvey - Mines & Energy)

Nu-Energy Development Corp. (B.C. 1974 amalg.)
Dec. 31, 1982 – Merged with Agnes & Jennie Mining Company Ltd.
Feb. 15, 1983 – Name changed to Erickson Gold Mines Ltd. ■

Nu Energy Uranium Corporation (B.C. Jan. 19, 2000)
Aug. 14, 2007 – Amalgamated with a subsidiary of Mega Uranium Ltd.; basis 2 new Mega com. shs. for 3 old Nu Energy com. shs.

Nu-Gord Mines Ltd. (Ont. 1959)
Jan. 27, 1966 – Dissolved.

The Nu-Gro Corporation (Ont. Feb. 27, 1987)
May 4, 2004 – Name changed to United Industries Corporation for $11 per sh.

Nu-Lady Gold Mines Ltd. (B.C. May 16, 1979)
Jan. 10, 1990 – Delisted from the Vancouver Stock Exchange. Subsequently dissolved and struck from registry.

Nu-Life Corp. (Can. Jan. 30, 1990)
Oct. 17, 2008 – Dissolved.

Nu-Lite Industries Ltd. (B.C. Feb. 8, 1984)
May 31, 2000 – Name changed to Netseers Internet International Corporation. ■

Nu-Media Industries International Inc. (B.C. Oct. 20, 1986)
Dec. 15, 1994 – Name changed to Consolidated Nu-Media Industries Inc.; basis 1 new for 7 old shs. ■

Nu Pacific Resources Ltd. (B.C. Oct. 7, 1968)
July 7, 1987 – Formed Iron Lady Resources Inc. in British Columbia on amalgamation with Iron Lady Resources Inc.; basis 1 new for 3 old shs. ■

Nu-Reality Oils Limited (Alta. 1949)
1960 – Acquired by Flag Oils Ltd.

Nu-Ridgeway Petroleums Ltd. (Alta. 1952)
Jan. 1963 – Name changed to Pere Marquette Petroleums Limited.

Nu-Silco Mines Ltd. (Ont. 1948)
Nov. 21, 1978 – Dissolved.

Nu-Sky Energy Inc. (Alta. Feb. 28, 1995)
Aug. 8, 2003 – Amalgamated with Kinloch Resources Inc.; basis either $0.8275, or 0.8275 Kinloch shs., or a combination thereof for 1 Nu-Sky sh. (see Kinloch Resources Inc.)

Nu-Sky Exploration Inc. (B.C. July 15, 1986)
May 22, 1991 – Name changed to Consolidated Nu-Sky Exploration Inc.; basis 1 new for 5 old shs. ■

Nu-Start Resource Corporation (B.C. Mar. 19, 1981)
Aug. 9, 1991 – Dissolved and struck off register.

Nu-Vision Resource Corp. (B.C. Apr. 25, 1984)
Feb. 16, 2004 – Name changed to Vision Coatings Group Limited following reverse takeover acquisition of Hong Kong-based Great Hoover Enterprises Limited. ■

Nu-West Development Corporation Ltd. (Alta. 1945)
Dec. 31, 1979 – Name changed to Nu-West Group Limited. ■

Nu-West Group Limited (Alta. 1945)
Jan. 29, 1988 – Formed N-W Group, Inc. in Delaware on amalgamation with wholly owned N-W Group, Inc.; basis 1 new for 25 old shs.

Nu-West Homes Limited (Alta. 1945)
Mar. 1971 – Name changed to Nu-West Development Corporation Ltd. ■

Nu-World Uranium Mines Ltd. (Ont. 1955)
Jan. 17, 1966 – Dissolved.

Nu XMP Ventures Limited (Bermuda Nov. 6, 1997)
Nov. 5, 2003 – Continued into British Columbia.
Nov. 4, 2004 – Name changed to New Pacific Metals Corp. ■

Nubar Mines Ltd. (Ont. 1946)
1954 – Name changed to Tandem Mines Ltd. ■

Nubell Gold Mines Ltd. (Que. 1929)
Apr. 26, 1980 – Charter cancelled.

Nubian Resources Ltd. (B.C. Oct. 28, 2004)
Dec. 30, 2024 – Name changed to Carlton Precious Inc. (see FPsurvey - Mines & Energy)

Nucal Resources Ltd. (B.C. Jan. 8, 1980)
Jan. 22, 1987 – Continued into Canada.
Sept. 29, 1987 – Name changed to Captive Air International Inc. ■

NuCanolan Resources Ltd. (Ont. May 11, 1979)
Oct. 1, 2003 – Name changed to Westchester Resources Inc. ■

Nuclear Enterprises (Can. 1938)
Feb. 9, 1955 – Assets sold to Allied Enterprises Ltd. for $510,000 in securities and $8,000 in cash in 1954. Co. wound up and charter surrendered.

Nuclear Exploration Ltd. (Alta. 1954)
Sept. 30, 1960 – Dissolved.

Nucleus BioScience Inc. (B.C. Sept. 1, 1999)
June 19, 2003 – Amalgamated with Stratos BioTechnologies Inc. (0.3333 for 1) and Brightwave Ventures Inc. (0.3424 for 1) to continue as SNB Capital Corp. (formerly Brightwave); basis 0.3319 new SNB com. sh. for 1 old Nucleus com. sh. (see SNB Capital Corp.)

Nuco Petroleums Ltd. (Alta. 1953)
1964 – Acquired by Kodiak Petroleums Ltd.; basis 28 new for 1,000 old shs. (see Kodiak Petroleums Ltd.)

Nucontex Corporation (Ont. Jan. 11, 2001)
Feb. 12, 2007 – Dissolved and struck from register.

Nucore Resources Ltd. (B.C. 1988)
Aug. 19, 1994 – Amalgamated with New Aegis Resources Ltd. to form new co. with same name Nucore Resources Ltd.; basis 1 new for 1.333 New Aegis shs. and 1 new for 1.777 Nucore shs. (see Norcan Resources Ltd.)

Nucorr Petroleums Ltd. (B.C. 1950)
1985 – Continued into Canada.
Mar. 13, 1990 – Acquired by 168316 Canada Ltd. for nominal consideration.

Nudulama Mines Ltd. (Ont. Dec. 2, 1944)
Feb. 1, 1979 – Name changed to Anglo Dominion Gold Exploration Limited; basis 1 new for 4 old shs. ■

Nuequus Petroleum Corporation (B.C. Nov. 9, 1982 amalg.)
Nov. 28, 2002 – Name changed to Equus Energy Corporation. ■

Nufcor Uranium Limited (Guernsey June 28, 2006)
Sept. 21, 2009 – Name changed to Uranium Limited. ■

Nufort Resources Inc. (Ont. Apr. 9, 1956)
May 9, 2000 – Formed Mikotel Networks Inc. in Ontario on amalgamation with Mikotel Networks Inc., constituting a reverse takeover by Mikotel. ■

NuGas Limited (Can. Apr. 16, 1987)
Sept. 22, 1997 – Acquired by Tarragon Oil and Gas Limited; basis $3.60 and 1 Q Energy Limited sh. for 1 NuGas sh. (see Tarragon Oil and Gas Limited)

Nugget Resources Inc. (Alta. Feb. 22, 1994)
May 9, 2008 – Name changed to Peninsula Resources Ltd.; basis 1 new for 15 old shs. ■

Nugold Enterprises Corporation (B.C. 1979)
Nov. 19, 1984 – Amalgamated with Tunkwa Copper Mines Ltd. (1 for 5) to form United Gold Corp.; basis 1 new for 5 old shs. (see United Gold Corp.)

Nugold Mines (1939) Ltd. (Ont. 1939)
1955 – Charter cancelled.

Nuinsco Resources Limited (B.C. Oct. 24, 1977)
July 26, 1989 – Continued into Ontario. (see FPsurvey - Mines & Energy)

Nulac Gold Mines Ltd. (Ont. 1946)
1956 – Charter cancelled.

NuLoch Resources Inc. (Alta. May 13, 2005)
May 6, 2011 – Acquired by Magnum Hunter Resources Corporation; basis either 0.3304 Magnum Hunter shs., 0.3304 MHR Exchangeco Corporation shs., a Cdn. subsid. of Magnum Hunter, or a combination thereof.

Numac Energy Inc. (B.C. Sept. 21, 1971)
Dec. 5, 1991 – Continued into Alberta. (see Anderson Exploration Ltd.)
Feb. 15, 2001 – Acquired by AXL Acquisition Corp., a wholly owned subsid. of Anderson Exploration Ltd.; basis $8.00 per sh. (see Anderson Exploration Ltd.)

Numac Oil & Gas Ltd. (Alta. Mar. 15, 1963)
Jan. 1, 1991 – Amalgamated with Giant Reef Petroleums Limited, a wholly owned subsid., to continue with the same name Numac Oil & Gas Ltd. (see Numac Energy Inc.)
Sept. 3, 1993 – Amalgamated with Westcoast Petroleum Ltd. to form Numac Energy Inc.; basis 1 new for 1 Numac Oil sh. (see Numac Energy Inc.)

Numalake Mines Ltd. (Ont. May 27, 1938)
1953 – Name changed to New Taku Mines Limited. ■

Numaque Mining Co. (Que. June 12, 1936)
1945 – Merged into Union Mining Corp.; basis 1 new for 3 old shs.

No. 6 Motel Limited (B.C. Oct. 27, 1971)
Nov. 17, 1982 – Name changed to Economy Inns, Inc. ■

NuMedia Games Inc. (Can. Feb. 17, 2006)
June 4, 2008 – Name changed to Brandgamz Marketing Inc.; basis 1 new for 5 old shs. ■

Numine Resources Ltd. (B.C. Dec. 4, 2007)
Dec. 13, 2010 – Name changed to Sunset Cove Mining Inc. pursuant to Qualifying Transaction reverse takeover acquisition of Sunset Cove Mining Inc. ■

Nunamin Explorations Limited (B.C. June 9, 2000)
Sept. 15, 2004 – Name changed to Oro Gold Resources Ltd. ■

Nunavik Nickel Mines Ltd. (B.C. Feb. 18, 2010)
July 27, 2017 – Name changed to Val-d'Or Mining Corporation. (see FPsurvey - Mines & Energy)

NurExone Biologic Inc. (Alta. June 27, 2011)
Apr. 22, 2025 – Continued into Ontario. (see FPsurvey - Industrials)

Nurosene Health Inc. (B.C. Mar. 26, 2021)
Feb. 1, 2023 – Name changed to NetraMark Holdings Inc. (see FPsurvey - Industrials)

Nurosene Inc. (Ont. May 8, 2019)
Mar. 26, 2021 – Name changed to Nurosene Health Inc. and continued into British Columbia. ■

Nurun inc. (Can. Nov. 19, 1985)
Feb. 28, 2008 – Acquired Quebecor Media Inc., a subsid. of Quebecor Inc. for $4.75 per sh.

Nuspar Resources Limited (B.C. 1967)
Sept. 29, 1995 – Dissolved and struck off register.

NuStar Mining Corporation Limited (W.A. June 9, 1993)
July 4, 2006 – Name changed to Intrepid Mines Limited following merger of the Australian-listed company (basis 1 new for 12 old shs.) and TSX-listed Intrepid Minerals Corporation (basis 1 ord. sh. of Intrepid Mines or 1 exch. sh. of Intrepid NuStar Exchange Corporation for 1 Intrepid Minerals com. sh.).

Nustar Resources Inc. (B.C. June 17, 1981)
Apr. 8, 2005 – Amalgamated with Candor Ventures Corp. to form Canstar Resources Inc.

NutraMed Capital Corp. (Yuk. May 26, 2000)
June 14, 2006 – Name changed to Winwell Ventures Inc. and continued into British Columbia; basis 1 new for 3 old shs. ■

Nutrilawn International Inc. (Alta. 1988)
Feb. 12, 2001 – Formed Plus International Corporation pursuant to reverse takeover acquisition of Plus Computer Solutions Inc.; basis 1 new for 6 old shs. (see FPsurvey - Industrials)

Nutritional High International Inc. (Can. July 19, 2004)
Nov. 11, 2021 – Name changed to High Fusion Inc. ■

Nutrivida Biotech Investments Inc. (B.C. July 13, 2017)
Sept. 14, 2018 – Name changed to BevCanna Enterprises Inc. ■

Nuukfjord Gold Ltd. (B.C. July 14, 2009)
Sept. 8, 2010 – Name changed to Revolution Resources Corp. ■

Nuuvera Inc. (Ont. July 17, 2015)
Mar. 23, 2018 – Name changed to Aphria International Inc. ■

Nuva Pharmaceuticals Inc. (B.C. May 30, 2000)
Aug. 7, 2014 – Name changed to Vanc Pharmaceuticals Inc. ■

Nuveen Senior Floating Rate Income Fund (Ont. Oct. 28, 2004)
Sept. 16, 2008 – Merged into Fairway Diversified Income and Growth Trust; basis 0.6505376836 Fairway units for 1 Nuveen unit. (see Fairway Diversified Income and Growth Trust)

Nuvei Corporation (Can. Sept. 1, 2017)
Nov. 18, 2024 – All subord. vtg. shs., and mult. vtg. shs. not rolled over by Philip Fayer, Novacap Investments Inc. and Caisse de dépôt et placement du Québec, were acquired by Advent International Corporation; basis US$34 per sh.

Nuvo Pharmaceuticals Inc. (Ont. Aug. 22, 1983)
Mar. 17, 2023 – Acquired by Searchlight Pharma Inc.; basis $1.35 cash per sh.

Nuvo Research Inc. (Ont. Aug. 22, 1983)
Mar. 1, 2016 – Name changed to Nuvo Pharmaceuticals Inc. ■

Nuvolt Corporation Inc. (Que. Aug. 31, 2007 amalg.)
Mar. 24, 2016 – Filed for bankruptcy. PricewaterhouseCoopers inc. appointed trustee and all officers and directors resigned.

Nventa Biopharmaceuticals Corporation (B.C. Jan. 27, 2006)
May 28, 2009 – Amalgamated with a wholly owned subsid. of Akela Pharma Inc.; basis 0.0355 Akela shs. for 1 Nventa sh. (see Akela Pharma Inc.)

NxGold Ltd. (B.C. Apr. 26, 2004)
Oct. 5, 2020 – Name changed to International Consolidated Uranium Inc. ■

Nyah Resources Corp. (Ont. Oct. 17, 2006)
Sept. 20, 2010 – Name changed to Forbes & Manhattan Coal Corp. pursuant to amalgamation of wholly owned subsid. of Nyah with Forbes & Manhattan (Coal) Inc. (deemed acquiror); basis 1 new for 39.8 old shs. ■

Nycal (Canada) Inc. (B.C. Jan. 19, 1987)
Apr. 5, 1995 – Continued into Yukon. (see FPsurvey - Mines & Energy)

Nycan Energy Corp. (Alta. Mar. 30, 1993)
Apr. 30, 2003 – Acquired by 1036655 Alberta Ltd. wholly owned subsid. of APF Energy Inc. and APF Energy Trust collectively; basis $2.075 per sh. (see APF Energy Trust)

Nycan Petroleum Corp. (Alta. Mar. 30, 1993)
June 1, 1998 – Name changed to Nycan Energy Corp.; basis 1 new for 4 old shs. ∎

Nyco Yellowknife Gold Mines Ltd. (Ont. 1945)
Oct. 1958 – Dissolved.

Nymox Pharmaceutical Corporation (Can. May 30, 1995)
July 31, 2015 – Continued into Bahamas.

O

O-Tech Ventures Corporation (B.C. Dec. 22, 1980)
June 26, 1996 – Name changed to Bright Star Ventures Ltd.; basis 1 new for 3 old shs. ∎

O3 Mining Inc. (Ont. June 28, 2019)
Mar. 20, 2025 – Amalgamated into Agnico Eagle Abitibi Acquisition Corp., a wholly owned subsid. of Agnico Eagle Mines Limited; basis $1.67 cash per sh.

O A Group Inc. (Alta. Oct. 31, 1996)
July 15, 2002 – OA Group of Companies went into receivership and Edmonton-based PricewaterhouseCoopers Inc. was appointed receiver.
July 19, 2002 – Assets of wholly owned OA Solutions Inc. sold to a consortium of existing OA Solutions staff and management. The new company continued to service all former OA Solutions clients.
Oct. 16, 2002 – Modern Digital Communications Inc. acquired from the receiver all of the assets of OA Internet Inc. for an undisclosed amount.
Feb. 3, 2004 – PricewaterhouseCoopers Inc. was discharged as receiver. There were no funds available for distribution to shldrs.

O&Y Properties Corporation (Ont. Jan. 3, 1978 amalg.)
Feb. 1, 1999 – Amalgamated in Ontario to continue with same name.
Oct. 24, 2005 – Indirectly acquired by BPO Properties Ltd., Canada Pension Plan Investment Board and Arca Investments Inc.; basis $12.72 per sh.

O&Y Real Estate Investment Trust (Ont. Mar. 8, 2001)
Nov. 29, 2005 – Acquired by BPO Properties Ltd., the Canada Pension Plan Investment Board and ARCA Investments Inc.; basis $16.25 per sh.

OCI Communications Inc. (Ont. Feb. 2, 1999)
June 1, 2000 – Name changed to AXXENT Inc. ∎

OCP Credit Strategy Fund (Ont.)
Dec. 31, 2019 – Terminated; basis $5.4602 cash per fund unit.

OCP Senior Credit Fund (Ont.)
Oct. 9, 2020 – Terminated; basis &7.7226 cash per fund unit.

OCS Technologies Corp. (B.C. Aug. 17, 1981)
Jan. 19, 1996 – Placed into bankruptcy. Alexander G. May Inc. was appointed trustee.

ODAAT Inc. (Alta. Apr. 4, 1990)
Jan. 29, 2004 – Name changed to Explor Resources Inc.; basis 1 new for 4 old shs. ∎

OE Inc. (Can. 1906)
Mar. 16, 1990 – Acquired by Canon Canada Inc. for $15.95 per sh.

OFI Income Fund (Ont. Aug. 22, 2005)
Feb. 2, 2009 – Redeemed for $3.17 per fund unit following the sale of operating assets to CertainTeed Insulation Canada Inc.

OGY Petroleums Ltd. (B.C. Nov. 28, 1983)
Nov. 1, 1992 – Amalgamated in Alberta to continue with same name. (see Baytex Energy Ltd.)
May 25, 2001 – Acquired by Baytex Energy Ltd.; basis $2.90, or 0.245 Baytex com. shs., or combination thereof. (see Baytex Energy Ltd.)

O.H.I. Investments Ltd. (Ont. 1958)
Sept. 1963 – Name changed to Frontier Acceptance Corporation Ltd.

OHS Capital Corp. (Alta. May 27, 2004)
Apr. 18, 2007 – Name changed to Pay Linx Financial Corporation following Qualifying Transaction acquisition of Pay Linx Corporation. ∎

O.J. Oil and Gas Corporation (B.C. Dec. 8, 1977)
Aug. 26, 1996 – Name changed to U.S. Oil and Gas Inc. ∎

O.K. Copper Gold Mines Ltd. (B.C. 1940)
1943 – Charter cancelled.

OK Gold Inc. (Ont. Mar. 9, 2020)
June 19, 2020 – Name changed to KO Gold Inc. (see FPsurvey - Mines & Energy)

OK2 Minerals Ltd. (B.C. July 19, 2007)
Feb. 15, 2019 – Name changed to Norra Metals Corp.; basis 1 new for 3 old shs. (see FPsurvey - Mines & Energy)

OLDCO International Inc. (Colo. Mar. 4, 2015)
Dec. 23, 2021 – Winding up and dissolving; basis US$0.07 cash per sh. payable to shldrs. of record July 16, 2021.

OMC Capital Corporation. (Alta. Apr. 20, 2005)
June 4, 2007 – Name changed to ReMac Zinc Corp. and continued into British Columbia; basis 1 new for 2 old shs. ∎

OMG Mineral Exploration Inc. (Ont. Dec. 21, 2000)
May 24, 2006 – Name changed to Gold Reef International, Inc. pursuant to reverse takeover acquisition of Gold Reef of Nevada, Inc. ∎

OMNItech Capital Corp. (B.C. July 26, 2000)
Feb. 20, 2004 – Name changed to One Person Health Sciences Inc. and continued into Canada on Qualifying Transaction reverse takeover acquisition of One Person Health Inc.; basis 1 new for 2 old shs. ∎

OMT Inc. (Man. Oct. 1, 1999)
July 11, 2013 – Name changed to AnalytixInsight Inc. following acquisition of AnalytixInsight Inc.; basis 1 new for 3 old shs. ∎

ONE Signature Financial Corporation (Ont. Jan. 13, 2004 amalg.)
Jan. 23, 2017 – Dissolved and struck from register.

ONEnergy Inc. (Can. Oct. 31, 1999 amalg.)
Aug. 4, 2015 – Continued into Ontario. (see FPsurvey - Mines & Energy)

ONTZINC Corporation (Ont. Jan. 15, 1996 amalg.)
Dec. 21, 2004 – Name changed to HudBay Minerals Inc. on acquisition of Hudson Bay Mining and Smelting Co., Limited; basis 1 new for 30 old shs. ∎

O.P. Industries Ltd. (B.C. Nov. 23, 1987)
Jan. 20, 1989 – Name changed to Tridon Oil & Gas Ltd. ∎

O.P. Resources Ltd. (B.C. July 17, 1981)
Feb. 15, 1994 – Name changed to L.E.H. Ventures Ltd.; basis 1 new for 3.41 old shs. ∎

OPE Holdings Ltd. (Alta. Sept. 9, 1998)
May 21, 2009 – Name changed to SSP Offshore Inc. ∎

OPEL Solar International Inc. (Ont. Nov. 30, 2010)
Aug. 29, 2011 – Name changed to OPEL Technologies Inc. ∎

OPEL Technologies Inc. (Ont. Nov. 30, 2010)
July 23, 2013 – Name changed to POET Technologies Inc. (see FPsurvey - Industrials)

OPI Ltd. (Alta. 1960)
1982 – Continued into Canada.
Aug. 1, 1986 – Name changed to Oil Patch Group Inc. ∎

OPMEDIC Group Inc. (Que. Nov. 6, 2001)
Nov. 11, 2013 – Privatized for $2.90 per sh. by way of amalgamation with Kemourmedic Acquisition Inc., a wholly owned subsid. of Kemourmedic Group Inc., to continue as Opmedic Group Inc.

OPTI Canada Inc. (N.B. Jan. 15, 1999)
May 30, 2002 – Continued into Canada.
Nov. 30, 2011 – Acquired by CNOOC Luxembourg S.à r.l., an indirect wholly owned subsid. of CNOOC Limited, for US$2.1 billion.
Dec. 15, 2011 – Name changed to CNOOC Canada Inc.

OPTUS Natural Gas Distribution Income Fund (Ont. June 6, 1996)
Sept. 1, 1999 – Name changed to Direct Energy. ∎

ORAGIN Foods Inc. (B.C. July 25, 2011)
May 18, 2024 – Deemed to have made an assignment into bankruptcy. KPMG Inc. was appointed trustee.

ORTHOsoft Holdings Inc. (Can. June 2, 2003)
June 2, 2005 – Name changed to ORTHOsoft Inc. ∎

ORTHOsoft Inc. (Can. June 2, 2003)
Nov. 9, 2007 – Acquired by Zimmer Holdings Inc. of Indiana for Cdn$1.10 per sh.

OSE Corp. (Ont. Feb. 2, 1994 amalg.)
Sept. 19, 2011 – Name changed to Petro Basin Energy Corp.; basis 1 new for 2 old shs. ∎

OSF Inc. (Ont. Jan. 14, 1960)
Oct. 19, 1994 – Acquired by OSF Acquisition Inc., a co. owned by management of OSF Inc.; basis $17.25 per sh. Subsequently the company reissued common shares and relisted on the TSE, Dec. 5, 1996.
Mar. 9, 2000 – Acquired by O Acquisition Corp., an indirect subsid. of NY-based Centre Partners Management LLC.; basis $7.25 per sh.

OSF Industries Limited (Ont. 1953)
May 1977 – Placed into receivership. Assets subsequently liquidated. No distribution available for unsecured creditors.

OSI Geospatial Inc. (B.C. June 10, 1987)
July 13, 2012 – Privatized by way of plan of arrangement whereby each class B series 2 pfce. sh. was converted into 156.667 com. shs. (valued at $9.40) and all com. shs. were consolidated on a 1-for-250,000 basis resulting in less than 400 shs. o/s. Com. shldrs. holding less than one post-consolidated com. sh. received 6¢ per pre-consolidated com. sh.

O.T. Industries Inc. (B.C. Aug. 5, 1977)
Jan. 30, 1987 – Name changed to Golden Princess Mining Corporation. ∎

OTATCO Inc. (Alta. Aug. 10, 1994)
Apr. 12, 2000 – Amalgamated with Reliance Services Group Ltd. (2.33518 for 1) to form Integrated Production Services Ltd.; basis 1.45949 new OTATCO shs. for 1 old Integrated Production sh. (see Integrated Production Services Ltd.)

OTI Technologies Inc. (Can. Dec. 9, 1986 amalg.)
Aug. 29, 2003 – Dissolved.

OTL Resources Ltd. (B.C. Sept. 28, 1979)
Apr. 21, 1993 – Name changed to Raytec Capital Corp. ∎

OTM International Development Inc. (B.C. July 8, 1992)
June 14, 1995 – Name changed to Epic Energy Inc. ∎

O2 Capital Inc. (Alta. Feb. 7, 2008)
Nov. 26, 2010 – Name changed to Xianburg Data Systems Canada Corporation pursuant to Qualifying

Transaction acquisition of Xianburg Data Systems (Canada) Inc. (see FPsurvey - Industrials)

OV2 CPC 1 Inc. (Can. Nov. 30, 2016)
June 2, 2017 – Name changed to OV2 Investment 1 Inc. ■

OV2 Investment 1 Inc. (Can. Nov. 30, 2016)
Mar. 11, 2022 – Name changed to Eastower Wireless Inc. and continued into British Columbia pursuant to the Qualifying Transaction reverse takeover acquisition of EasTower Group, Inc., and cocurrent amalgamation of EasTower Group wtih wholly owned EasTower Acquisition Corporation; basis 0.7973091 new for 1 old sh. (see FPsurvey - Industrials)

OZ Exploration Inc. (Que. 1986)
Mar. 31, 1989 – Amalgamated with Onyx Resources Inc., Omega Exploration Inc., Norwood Exploration Inc. and Faboro Resources Inc. to form Orient Resources Inc.

Oak Catalyst Corporation (Alta. Dec. 21, 1987)
June 1, 1997 – Dissolved and struck off register.

Oakham Capital Corp. (B.C. Oct. 30, 2009)
Feb. 22, 2017 – Name changed to LSC Lithium Corporation following Qualifying Transaction reverse takeover acquisition of LSC Lithium Inc.; basis 1 new for 6.5 old shs. ■

Oakhill Communications Inc. (Alta. Feb. 4, 1987)
Aug. 1, 2000 – Struck from registry and dissolved.

Oakley Ventures Inc. (B.C. May 17, 2017)
Apr. 9, 2021 – Name changed to Ameriwest Lithium Inc. (see FPsurvey - Mines & Energy)

Oakmont Capital Corp. (B.C. Mar. 30, 2010)
Sept. 18, 2007 – Continued into British Columbia
July 8, 2013 – Name changed to Oakmont Minerals Corp. pursuant to Qualifying Transaction acquisition of 0939181 B.C. Ltd. ■

Oakmont Minerals Corp. (B.C. Sept. 18, 2007)
Dec. 23, 2014 – Succeeded by GreenPower Motor Company Inc. following reverse takeover acquisition of (old) GreenPower Motor Company Inc.; basis 1 new for 2 old shs. (see FPsurvey - Industrials)

Oakridge Mining Corporation Ltd. (Ont. 1945)
1957 – Charter cancelled.

Oakridge Uranium Mines Ltd. (Ont. 1945)
July 1951 – Name changed to Oakridge Mining Corporation Ltd. ■

Oakville Wood Specialties Limited (Ont. 1949)
Sept. 9, 1994 – Voluntarily dissolved. Initial distribution of $3.471737 per sh. made up of a capital dividend of $3.15 and wind up proceeds of $0.321737 was announced in May 1993. Final distribution of $1.13916 per sh. was made Sept. 9, 1994.

Oakwood International Petroleum N.L. (Australia 1980)
Mar. 12, 1986 – Name changed to Winton Oil NL.

Oakwood Mines Ltd. (Ont. 1955)
Nov. 3, 1967 – Dissolved.

Oakwood Petroleums Ltd. (Can. 1925)
Mar. 21, 1989 – Acquired by Sceptre Resources Ltd. for $275,000,000. (see Sceptre Resources Limited)

Oando Energy Resources Inc. (Can. Aug. 9, 2005)
May 17, 2016 – Acquired (other than those shs. owned or controlled by M1 Petroleum Ltd., West African Investment Ltd. and Southern Star Shipping Company Inc.) by Oando Plc and Oando E&P Holdings Limited for US$1.20 per sh.

Oasis Diamond Exploration Inc. (Can. Oct. 21, 1988)
June 23, 2005 – Name changed to Temoris Resources Inc.; basis 1 new for 6 old shs. ■

Oasis Energy Corporation (Alta. May 11, 1993)
Aug. 22, 1997 – Plan of Arrangement with Zargon Oil & Gas Ltd., Skywest Energy Inc. and Mirage Oil & Gas

Canada Inc., merged into Zargon Oil & Gas Ltd.; basis 1 new Zargon sh. for 80 old Oasis shs. or 3¢ per sh. (see Zargon Oil & Gas Ltd.)

Oasis Resources Inc. (B.C. Mar. 7, 1983)
Oct. 21, 1988 – Continued into Canada.
Sept. 21, 1990 – Name changed to Consolidated Oasis Resources Inc.; basis 1 new for 15 old shs. ■

Oatpoint Capital Corp. (B.C. Aug. 31, 2006)
Nov. 8, 2007 – Formed Richfield Ventures Corp. in British Columbia on amalgamation with Richfield Ventures Corp., constituting a reverse takeover by Richfield. ■

Obabika Mines Ltd. (Ont. 1955)
Nov. 5, 1962 – Charter cancelled.

Obalski Mining Corp. (Que. 1945)
1946 – Name changed to Obalski (1945) Ltd.; basis 1 new for 2 old shs. ■

Obalski (1945) Ltd. (Que. 1945)
1961 – Name changed to United Obalski Mining Co. Ltd.; basis 1 new for 5 old shs. ■

Oban Mining Corporation (Ont. Feb. 26, 2010)
June 14, 2016 – Name changed to Osisko Mining Inc. ■

Oban Petroleums Inc. (Alta. Sept. 18, 1992)
Mar. 29, 1996 – Name changed to Devlan Exploration Company Ltd. ■

Obaska Lake Mines Limited (Can. Dec. 16, 1942)
1970 – Name changed to International Obaska Mines Ltd.; basis 1 new for 5 old shs. ■

Obeatro Mines Co. Ltd. (B.C. 1956)
Dec. 1965 – Struck off register.

Oberg Industries Ltd. (B.C. 1965)
Aug. 21, 1990 – Name changed to Consolidated Oberg Industries Ltd.; basis 1 new for 5 old shs. ■

Obolus Resources Inc. (B.C. June 6, 1987)
May 16, 1990 – Name changed to Cajun Oil & Gas Producers Inc. ■

O'Brien Gold Mines Limited (Que. 1934)
Oct. 1977 – Name changed to O'Brien Energy & Resources Limited. (see FPsurvey - Mines & Energy)

Obsco Corporation Limited (Can. 1934)
Dec. 16, 1980 – Dissolved.

Occatilla Exploration Co. Ltd. (B.C. 1968)
Jan. 6, 1975 – Charter cancelled.

Occidental Petroleum Corporation (unknown 1920)
Apr. 9, 1986 – Continued into Delaware.

OccuLogix, Inc. (Del. June 5, 2002)
May 21, 2010 – Name changed to TearLab Corporation.

Ocean Fisheries Ltd. (N.S. May 26, 1953)
Mar. 1, 1967 – Amalgamated into National Sea Products Ltd. (see National Sea Products Limited)

Ocean Marine Technologies Inc. (B.C. May 23, 1986)
May 17, 1994 – Name changed to AGC Americas Gold Corp.; basis 1 new for 5 old shs. ■

Ocean Park Ventures Corp. (B.C. Jan. 12, 1987)
Aug. 6, 2013 – Name changed to Dunnedin Ventures Inc.; basis 1 new for 10 old shs. ■

Ocean Resources N.L. (Australia July 1, 1970)
Sept. 30, 1999 – Name changed to Bambuu Ltd.; basis 1 new for 20 old shs.

Ocean Ventures Inc. (Alta. Nov. 22, 1996)
July 20, 2004 – Name changed to Digital Youth Network Corp. ■

Oceanex Income Fund (Ont. Oct. 31, 1997)
Nov. 13, 2007 – Acquired by consortium of investors consisting of Captain Sidney J. Hynes, OPTrust Private Markets Group and Terrma Capital Corp. for $19 per unit plus $0.0937 per unit on Nov. 15, 2007, as final distribution.

Oceanic Electronics Corporation (Can. Aug. 7, 1981)
May 2, 2002 – Dissolved.

Oceanic Films and Enterprises Ltd. (Can. 1958)
Oct. 14, 1975 – Dissolved.

Oceanic Iron Ore of Canada Ltd. (Ont. 1954)
Aug. 7, 1981 – Name changed to Oceanic Electronics Corporation and continued into Canada. ■

OceanLake Commerce Inc. (B.C. July 25, 1984)
Jan. 15, 2003 – Continued into Ontario.
Jan. 30, 2017 – Certificate of incorporation cancelled and dissolved.

Oceanside Capital Corp. (B.C. Feb. 5, 2008)
June 5, 2015 – Name changed to Gaming Nation Inc. and continued into Ontario following reverse takeover acquisition of Gaming Nation Acquisition Corp.; basis 1 new for 2 old shs. ■

Oceanside Capital Corp. (B.C. Mar. 23, 2015)
Oct. 4, 2016 – Name changed to Kootenay Zinc Corp.; basis 1 new for 2 old shs. ■

Oceansix Future Paths Ltd. (Israel Jan. 22, 2008)
Jan. 28, 2025 – Pursuant to a debt settlement under the Israeli Insolvency and Financial Rehabilitation Law, all o/s shs. have been cancelled. Debts owned to major shldrs. were not repaid but converted into equity of the company.

Oceanus Industries (Bahamas) Ltd. (Ont. 1962)
Sept. 8, 1983 – Became a private co. through amalgamation with Strean Investments Limited and exchange of all publicly held com. shs. into pref. shs., immediately redeemed at $5.15 per sh.
May 9, 2001 – Struck off register.

Oceanus Resources Corporation (Can. June 14, 2010)
May 20, 2020 – Name changed to Silver Tiger Metals Inc. (see FPsurvey - Mines & Energy)

Oceanview Technologies Inc. (B.C. May 10, 2023)
Nov. 20, 2024 – Name changed to DiagnosTear Technologies Inc. pursuant to the reverse takeover acquisition of DiagnosTear Ltd. (see FPsurvey - Industrials)

Ocelot Energy Inc. (Alta. June 18, 1990)
May 31, 1999 – Name changed to Ocelot International Ltd. and continued into Bermuda. ■

Ocelot Industries Ltd. (Alta. Mar. 11, 1968)
Mar. 5, 1992 – Continued into Canada.
Mar. 23, 1992 – Name changed to Methanex Corporation. (see FPsurvey - Mines & Energy; FPsurvey - Industrials)

Ocelot International Ltd. (Bermuda May 31, 1999)
July 6, 2000 – Name changed to PanAfrican Energy Corporation Ltd. following incorporation of PanAfrican Energy Corporation Ltd. in Jersey and exchange of Ocelot shs. for PanAfrican shs. pursuant to a Scheme of Arrangement in May 2000. ■

Octagon Industries Inc. (B.C. 1987)
Aug. 15, 2003 – Dissolved.

Octan Resources Inc. (Alta. 1987)
Mar. 1, 1992 – Struck off register.

Octane Energy Services Ltd. (Alta. Sept. 11, 1998)
Sept. 12, 2005 – Name changed to NX Capital Corp. ■

Octant Energy Corp. (B.C. Mar. 16, 2006)
Sept. 5, 2017 – Completed corporate reorganization under which: all o/s shs. of wholly owned Octant Energy Ltd. were transferred to newly incorporated Octant Energy plc; a capital reduction in the amount equal to not less

than the value of the ordinary sh. capital of Octant plc; and distribution on the basis of 0.3333 Octant plc ord. shs. for 1 Octant Corp. sh. Octant Ltd. indirectly held all the assets of the company. Subsequent to distrib. the company was voluntarily dissolved.

Oculus Ventures Corporation (Can. May 8, 2007)
Mar. 14, 2011 – Continued into British Columbia.
June 26, 2014 – Name changed to SLYCE Inc. and continued into Alberta following Qualifying Transaction reverse takeover acquisition of (private) Slyce Inc.; basis 1 new for 1.75 old shs. ■

Oculus VisionTech Inc. (Wyo. Feb. 21, 1995)
Jan. 16, 2025 – Name changed to Oculus Inc. (see FPsurvey - Industrials)

Ocutech Canada Inc. (B.C. 1983)
Aug. 20, 1993 – Dissolved and struck off register.

Odeon Limited (Ont. 1944)
1967 – All o/s 6% pref. shs. redeemed in 1963. All o/s 5% general mtge. bonds redeemed.

Odesia Group Inc. (Can. Jan. 19, 2005)
Nov. 19, 2018 – Dissolved for non-compliance.

Odessa Capital Ltd. (Alta. Jan. 18, 2023)
Mar. 14, 2025 – Acquired by Margaux Real Estate Investment Trust; basis 1 new Margaux trust unit for 12 old Odessa com. shs.

Odessa Explorations Inc. (B.C. 1981)
Oct. 12, 1989 – Name changed to Amble Green Ventures Inc.; basis 1 new for 5 old shs. ■

Odessa Gold Corp. (B.C. Feb. 10, 1988)
Apr. 19, 2005 – Name changed to Emerson Exploration Inc.; basis 1 new for 10 old shs. ■

Odessa Industries Inc. (Alta. Mar. 30, 1993)
Sept. 4, 2005 – Struck from registry and dissolved.

Odessa Petroleum Corporation (B.C. Feb. 8, 1983)
May 12, 1999 – Name changed to Aquarius Ventures Inc.; basis 1 new for 10 old shs. ■

Odin Industries Ltd. (B.C. Sept. 24, 1979)
Nov. 30, 1999 – Continued into Alberta.
Mar. 2, 2005 – Struck from registry and dissolved.

Odin Mining and Exploration Ltd. (B.C. Mar. 22, 1988)
Nov. 1, 2016 – Name changed to Lumina Gold Corp. following acquisition of Ecuador Gold and Cooper Corp. ■

O'Donnell Investment Management Corporation (unknown Nov. 25, 1993)
Jan. 13, 1995 – Amalgamated in Ontario to continue with same name. (see Strategic Value Corporation)
June 2, 1999 – Acquired by Strategic Value Corporation for $4.00 per share. (see Strategic Value Corporation)

O'Donnell Mines Ltd. (Ont. 1958)
1968 – Charter cancelled.

Odyno Exploration & Développement Ltée (Que. 1953)
June 1980 – Name changed to Odyno Minière Inc.; basis 5 new for 1 old sh. ■

Odyno Minière Inc. (Que. 1953)
Nov. 22, 1989 – Acquired by a wholly owned subsid. of Cambior Inc. for $5.00 per sh. Subsequently liquidated. (see Cambior Inc.)

Odyssey Energy Corporation (Can. Nov. 17, 2000 amalg.)
May 21, 2008 – Dissolved.

Odyssey Exploration Inc. (B.C. Aug. 19, 1994 amalg.)
Dec. 8, 2000 – Name changed to Consolidated Odyssey Exploration Inc.; basis 1 new for 2 old shs. ■

Odyssey Petroleum Corporation (Can. Aug. 29, 1994)
Oct. 26, 1999 – Privatized by becoming a wholly owned subsid. of Melrose Resources plc; basis US$0.125 per com. sh.
Dec. 29, 2004 – Continued into New Brunswick.

Odyssey Petroleum Corp. (B.C. Aug. 26, 2005 amalg.)
Mar. 3, 2011 – Name changed to Petrichor Energy Inc.; basis 1 new for 20 old shs. (see FPsurvey - Mines & Energy)

Odyssey Re Holdings Corp. (Del. Mar. 21, 2001)
Oct. 28, 2009 – All o/s com. shs. not already held acquired by Fairfax Financial Holdings Limited; basis US$65.00 cash per sh.
Oct. 20, 2010 – All o/s 8.125% non-cumulative ser. A pref. shs. and floating rate non-cumulative ser. B pref. shs, not already held by Fairfax Financial Holdings Limited redeemed for US$25.00 cash per ser. A pref. sh. and US$25.375 cash per ser. B pref. sh.
2018 – Name changed to Odyssey Group Holdings, Inc.

Odyssey Resources Ltd. (B.C. 1981)
Feb. 19, 1993 – Dissolved and struck off register.

Odyssey Resources Limited (Barbados Dec. 20, 1994)
Apr. 2008 – Continued into Ontario. (see FPsurvey - Mines & Energy)

Office Specialty Inc. (Ont. Dec. 18, 1989 amalg.)
Oct. 2, 2000 – Name changed to INSCAPE Corporation. ■

The Office Specialty Manufacturing Co. Ltd. (Can. 1922)
Dec. 31, 1961 – All o/s com. shs. acquired by The Anthes-Imperial Company Limited for $15.05 per sh. (see The Anthes-Imperial Company Limited)

Offset Natural Resources Ltd. (Ont. 1984 amalg.)
Mar. 2, 1992 – Amalgamated with Concentrated Rare Earth Minerals Ltd., Enertex Developments Inc. (1 for 12.6), Goldmac Explorations Inc. (1 for 17.5), Norlode Resources Inc., Preston Resources Ltd., Saranac Resources Ltd. and Uranex Resources Limited (1 for 13.5) to form a new co. named Marvas Developments Ltd.; basis 1 new for 11 old shs. (see Marvas Developments Ltd.)

Offset Oil & Gas Resources Ltd. (Ont. 1979)
Feb. 29, 1984 – Amalgamated with Mercier Explorations Limited (1.1 new for 1 old sh.) to form Offset Natural Resources Ltd.; sh.-for-sh. basis. (see Offset Natural Resources Ltd.)

Offsetters Climate Solutions Inc. (B.C. July 6, 2005)
Oct. 16, 2015 – Name changed to NatureBank Asset Management Inc. ■

Offshore Oil & Gas Corporation Ltd. (B.C. 1965)
Oct. 30, 1992 – Continued into Wyoming.

Offshore Systems International Ltd. (B.C. June 10, 1987)
June 5, 2006 – Name changed to OSI Geospatial Inc. ■

Offsite Data Services Ltd. (Alta. Jan. 10, 1995)
Aug. 9, 2000 – Acquired by Jaws Acquisition Corp., a wholly owned subsid. of Jaws Technologies, Inc.; basis 0.3524 Jaws Acquisition exch. sh. for 1 Offsite com. sh.

Ogama-Rockland Gold Mines Ltd. (Man. 1942)
1959 – Name changed to Realm Mining Corp. Ltd.; basis 1 new for 5 old shs. ■

Ogdensburg Yellowknife Mines Ltd. (Ont. 1947)
May 1957 – Charter cancelled.

The Ogilvie Flour Mills Company, Limited (Can. 1924)
June 4, 1975 – Name changed to Ogilvie Mills Ltd. ■

Ogilvie Mills Ltd. (Can. 1924)
Oct. 23, 1981 – John Labatt Limited acquired 99.8% of o/s com. stk. in 1968; basis 1 convertible pref., ser. A $18 par sh. of Labatt, plus $2.10 for each Ogilvie sh. Remaining com. shs. were acquired at $90 per sh. in July 1981 and the remaining pref. shs. were redeemed.

Ogivar Inc. (Que. 1983)
Apr. 3, 1992 – Assets liquidated. Nothing left for shldrs. Trustee in liquidation, David Azoulay & Associes inc.

Ogy Petroleums Ltd. (B.C. 1983 amalg.)
Nov. 10, 1992 – Amalgamated with Morrison Minerals Limited to form new co. with same name OGY Petroleums Ltd.; basis 1 new or 2.2 Morrison shs. and 1 new for 2 Ogy shs. (see OGY Petroleums Ltd.)

O'Hara Resources Ltd. (B.C. 1984)
June 18, 1993 – Dissolved and struck off register.

Ohio Resources Corporation (B.C. June 14, 1968)
July 9, 1997 – Continued into Alberta.
Nov. 16, 1998 – Name changed to Causeway Energy Corporation. ■

Oil & Gas Offsets Limited (Ont. 1948)
1952 – Acquired by Acme Gas & Oil Co. Ltd. for 775,000 shs.

Oil City Lubricants Limited (B.C. Sept. 13, 1979)
May 3, 1996 – Name changed to Thunder Sword Resources Inc.; basis 1 new for 5 old shs. ■

Oil City Petroleums (Leduc) Ltd. (Alta.)
1960 – Struck off register.

Oil Investors Ltd. (Alta. 1932)
No assets, no liabs.; reported to be struck off the register.

Oil Optimization Inc. (Alta. Nov. 2, 2007)
Mar. 2, 2024 – Struck from registry and dissolved.

Oil Patch Equipment Sales & Rental Ltd. (Alta. 1960)
1973 – Name changed to Oil Patch Industries Ltd. ■

Oil Patch Group Inc. (Can. 1982)
May 1, 2000 – Struck from registry and dissolved.

Oil Patch Industries Ltd. (Alta. 1960)
Feb. 1975 – Name changed to OPI Ltd. ■

Oil Sands and Energy Mega-Projects Trust (Ont. Mar. 29, 2006)
Jan. 31, 2011 – Merged with Sentry Energy Growth and Income Fund, an open-end mutual fund.

Oil Sands Ltd. (Alta. 1943)
1967 – Wound up voluntarily. Shldrs. entitled to receive 1 sh. of Great Canadian Oil Sands Ltd. and 24¢ cash for each 48 co. shs. Co.'s remaining assets acquired by Oil Sands (1967) Ltd. on sh.-for-sh. basis.

Oil Sands (1967) Ltd. (Alta. 1967)
Mar. 15, 1977 – Struck off register.

Oil Sands Sector Fund (Ont. Feb. 24, 2006)
June 29, 2018 – Terminated; basis $4.61378 cash per unit payable on or about July 6, 2018.

Oil Sands Split Trust (Ont. June 13, 2003)
Sept. 15, 2010 – Dissolved; basis $108.304 per Oil Sands Split cap. unit and $17.00 per Oil Sands Split pfd. sh., or $0.601929 plus 4.90415 Canadian Oils Sands Trust units for 1 combined Oil Sands Split unit (1 cap. unit and 1 pfd. sh..)

Oil Selections Limited (Can. 1929)
1957 – Sold to Quonto Petroleums Limited; basis 1 new for 4 old shs.

Oil Springs Energy Corp. (Ont. Feb. 2, 1994 amalg.)
Aug. 7, 2002 – Name changed to OSE Corp.; basis 1 new for 4 old shs. ■

Oilco Resources Ltd. (Alta. July 21, 1987)
Feb. 20, 1991 – Name changed to Canadian Hydro Developers, Inc. ■

Oilcrest Petroleums Ltd. (Ont. 1950)
1958 – Wound up.

Oilex Industries Ltd. (Alta. 1949)
Oct. 4, 1979 – Amalgamated with L.K. Ranches Ltd. (private co.) to form L.K. Resources Ltd. (see L.K. Resources Ltd.)

Oilexco Incorporated (Alta. Feb. 24, 1994)
June 9, 2011 – Name changed to Scotoil Petroleum Limited; basis 1 new for 10 old shs. ∎

Oilmont Petroleums Corporation (unknown)
1957 – Acquired by International Metal and Petroleum Corp.; basis 1 new for 2.5 old shs. (see International Metal and Petroleum Corp.)

OilSands Canada Corporation (Ont. June 1, 2007)
Mar. 19, 2010 – Continued into Alberta.
Nov. 2, 2010 – Name changed to Middlefield Tactical Energy Corporation. ∎

Oiltec Resources Ltd. (Alta. Jan. 10, 1992)
June 25, 2004 – Plan of Arrangement acquisition by Forte Resources Inc.; basis $1.40, or 0.45 new Forte sh. or a combination thereof for 1 old Oiltec sh. (see Forte Resources Inc.)

Oiltex International Ltd. (Ont. 1981)
Oct. 18, 1989 – Name changed to International Oiltex Ltd. and continued into Alberta following amalgamation with Laval Resources Ltd. and Dugite Resources Inc.; basis 1 new for 1.80535 old shs. ∎

Ojibway Nickel Mines Ltd. (Ont. 1955)
1980 – Charter cancelled.

Ojibway Resources Ltd. (Que. Nov. 12, 1985)
June 28, 1991 – Name changed to Consolidated Ojibway Resources Ltd.; basis 1 new for 4 old shs. ∎

OjO Electric Corp. (B.C. Sept. 5, 1980)
Mar. 9, 2020 – Name changed to Last Mile Holdings Ltd. ∎

Oka-Bathurst Mining Corp. (Que. 1955)
Nov. 4, 1978 – Charter cancelled.

Oka Rare Metals Mining Co. Ltd. (Ont. 1954)
1962 – Name changed to Manoka Mining & Smelting Co. Ltd.; basis 1 new for 4 old shs. ∎

Okalla Corp. (Alta. Oct. 10, 1986)
July 9, 2008 – Formed SportsClick Inc. in Alberta on amalgamation with Racing Around Wholesale, Inc., constituting a reverse takeover by Racing Around; basis 1 new for 1 Racing Around sh. and 1 new for 9.7 Okalla shs. ∎

Okalta Oils, Limited (Can. 1925)
June 1970 – Name changed to Oakwood Petroleums Ltd.; basis 1 new for 7 old shs. ∎

Okanagan Air Services Ltd. (B.C. 1947)
1952 – Name changed to Okanagan Helicopters Ltd. ∎

Okanagan Helicopters Ltd. (B.C. 1947)
Mar. 15, 1982 – All o/s shs. acquired following cash offer which expired by The Resource Service Group Ltd. at $15 per ordinary and $9.00 per convert. pref. sh.

Okanagan Holdings Limited (B.C. Mar. 31, 1967)
June 30, 1986 – Formed Okanagan Skeena Group Limited in British Columbia on amalgamation with Skeena Broadcasters Ltd.; basis 1 new com. for 1 Skeena sh. and 2 new com. and 1 new 8% ser. A pfce. for 1 Okanagan sh. ∎

Okanagan Skeena Group Limited (B.C. June 30, 1986 amalg.)
Feb. 23, 1999 – Continued into Canada.
June 17, 1999 – All cl. A subord. vtg. shs., cl. B multiple vtg. shs. and 5% convert. redeem. pref. ser.A shs. acquired by TCI Acquisition Corporation, a wholly owned subsid. of Quebec-based Telemedia Communications Inc.; basis $9.00 per cl. A & B shs. and $11.25 per pref. shs.

Okanagan Telephone Company (B.C. 1907)
Dec. 31, 1978 – Assets and operations merged with British Columbia Telephone Co, Ltd. All o/s pref. shs. redeemed Dec. 27, 1978, at $9.00 per sh. and all o/s com. shs. acquired by British Columbia Telephone through offer of $27.30 per sh.

Okanagan Trust Company (Can. - unspecified)
1959 – Acquired by The Royal Trust Company.

Okanagan Valley Telephone Co. Ltd. (B.C. 1947)
1952 – Wound up. Com. and pref. stks. exch. for com. and pref. of Okanagan Telephone Company; debenture holders received 75 Okanagan Telephone com. shs. for each $500 princ. amt.

O'Keefe Red Lake Mines Ltd. (Ont. 1946)
May 8, 1979 – Dissolved.

Oklahoma Crude Ltd. (B.C. July 12, 1982 amalg.)
Jan. 30, 1986 – Name changed to International Telesis Industries Corp.; basis 1 new for 4 old shs. ∎

Okleco Mines Ltd. (Ont. 1954)
1956 – Absorbed by Oklend Gold Mines Ltd.; basis 1 new for 2 old shs. (see Oklend Gold Mines Ltd.)

Oklend Gold Mines Ltd. (Ont. Aug. 28, 1934)
Nov. 1967 – Charter cancelled.

Okotoks Oil Co. Ltd. (unknown)
1914 – Acquired by Alberta Petroleum Consolidated Ltd.; basis 108 new for 100 old shs. (see Alberta Petroleum Consolidated Ltd.)

Olco Petroleum Group Inc. (Can. June 8, 1981)
Aug. 26, 2005 – Privatized at 50¢ per sh.

Old API Wind-down Ltd. (B.C. Dec. 2, 2015)
Mar. 2019 – Sale of TOPROL-XL® franchise to Toprol Acquisition LLC, a subsid. of secured lender Deerfield Management Company, LP, was completed for US$130,000,000. Net proceeds from the sale of company's assets were not sufficient to fully satisfy the company's secured indebtedness or support a distribution to the company's unsecured creditors or shldrs.
May 7, 2019 – Liquidating Chapter 11 plan was approved by the U.S. bankruptcy court. Under the plan a total of US$3,750,000 will be distributed on a pro rata basis to holders of allowed priority non-tax claims and general unsecured claims. No distrib. will be made to shldrs.
May 17, 2019 – The CCAA proceedings were terminated and the company made an assignment into bankruptcy and Richter Advisory Group Inc. was appointed trustee in bankruptcy. Pursuant to bankruptcy proceedings, all directors resigned effective May 30, 2019.

Old Canada Investment Corporation Limited (Ont. Nov. 30, 1979 amalg.)
Nov. 24, 2000 – Continued into Canada.
Dec. 1, 2000 – Name changed to Headline Media Group Inc.; basis 1 cl. A sh. for 1 com. sh. ∎

Old Comrades Brewery Limited (Can. 1946)
Mar. 1955 – Acquired by Carling Breweries Ltd. through offer of 30¢ per sh.

Old Dominion Manganese Co. (unknown)
1957 – Acquired by Mercedes Exploration Co. Ltd. for 194,355 shs. (see Mercedes Exploration Co. Ltd.)

Old Man River Mines Ltd. (Sask.)
Sept. 1962 – Dissolved.

Old Mill Gold Mines Ltd. (Que. 1946)
Aug. 1973 – Charter cancelled.

Old PSG Wind-down Ltd. (B.C. Dec. 2, 2010)
May 31, 2018 – Holders of 18,722,738 shs. of the company elected to exchange said shs. for beneficial trust interests and the right to receive a pro rata share of any other shldr. distributable assets in accordance to the joint plan.
Dec. 2019 – Ernst & Young resolved all general unsecured claims, with all allowed priority claims and allowed general unsecured claims paid to aggregate amount of US$11,817,000.
Mar. 15, 2023 – Shareholders authorized the voluntary dissolution of the company.
Apr. 3, 2024 – Final distrib. of US$0.10795081 cash per com. sh. payable to shldrs. of record Mar. 18, 2024.
May 21, 2024 – Voluntarily dissolved.

Old Settlers' Oils Limited (Alta. 1952)
1967 – Merged into Acroll Oil & Gas Ltd.; basis 1 new for 6 old shs.

Old Smoky Oil & Gas Ltd. (Ont. Oct. 29, 1951)
1967 – Approx. 98.6% of shs. acquired by General Petroleums Drilling Ltd. (see General Petroleums Drilling Ltd.)
1967 – Name changed to Largo Oils & Mines Ltd.; basis 1 new for 100 old shs. (see General Petroleums Drilling Ltd.)

Old Sun Resources Ltd. (Alta. Oct. 20, 2000)
June 11, 2001 – Name changed to Ripper Oil and Gas Inc. ∎

Olds Development Co. Ltd. (unknown)
Wound up. J. E. McLeod, liquidator, 63 Canada Life Bldg., Calgary.

Olds Industries Inc. (B.C. Mar. 8, 1951)
June 20, 2003 – Struck from register and dissolved for failure to file.

O'Leary Advantaged Tactical Global Corporate Bond Fund (Ont. May 28, 2010)
Aug. 16, 2011 – Converted from a closed-end fund to an open-ended fund.

O'Leary BrIC-Plus Income & Growth Fund (Ont.)
Apr. 2, 2012 – Converted from a closed-end fund to an open-ended fund.

O'Leary Canadian Diversified Income Fund (Ont. Dec. 21, 2011)
Feb. 23, 2016 – Name changed to Canoe Canadian Diversified Income Fund. ∎

O'Leary Canadian Equity Income Fund (Ont. Nov. 25, 2009)
Dec. 2, 2011 – Converted from a closed-end fund to an open-ended fund.

O'Leary Canadian Income Opportunities Fund (Ont. Apr. 29, 2009)
Dec. 2, 2011 – Converted from a closed-end fund to an open-ended fund.

O'Leary Canadian Income Opportunities Fund 2 (Ont. Nov. 26, 2010)
Dec. 17, 2012 – Converted from a closed-end fund to an open-ended fund.

O'Leary Founder's Series Income & Growth Fund (Ont. Sept. 28, 2009)
Nov. 2, 2010 – Converted from a closed end fund to an open-ended fund.

O'Leary Global Equity Income Fund (Ont. May 30, 2008)
Mar. 4, 2011 – Merged into O'Leary Global Equity Yield Fund (unlisted open-ended fund); basis 1.012519 O'Leary Global Equity Yield Fund for 1 O'Leary Global Equity Income Fund.

O'Leary Global Income Opportunities Fund (Ont. Jan. 29, 2009)
Aug. 4, 2010 – Merged with O'Leary Global Yield Opportunities Fund; basis 1.196585 O'Leary Global Yield series X units for 1 O'Leary Global Income unit.

O'Leary Global Infrastructure Fund (Ont. Oct. 29, 2008)
June 1, 2010 – Merged into O'Leary Global Infrastructure Yield Fund; basis 1 O'leary Global Infrastructure Yield Fund unit for 1.098816 O'Leary Global Infrastructure Fund units.

O'Leary Hard Asset Income Fund (Ont. Sept. 28, 2010)
Nov. 1, 2012 – Merged into O'Leary Global Infrastructure Yield Fund (an opened-ended fund); basis net asset value per sh.

O'Leary Malartic Mines Limited (Can. Dec. 10, 1928)
May 7, 1997 – Name changed to O'Leary Resources Inc.; basis 1 new for 4 old shs. ■

O'Leary Resources Inc. (Can. Dec. 10, 1928)
Feb. 11, 2009 – Dissolved.

O'Leary U.S. Strategic Yield Advantaged Fund (Ont. Apr. 28, 2011)
Feb. 23, 2016 – Name changed to Canoe U.S. Strategic Yield Advantaged Fund. ■

Oler Mines Ltd. (Ont. 1946)
1965 – Charter cancelled.

Oliver Gold Corporation (B.C. Nov. 24, 1980)
Feb. 6, 2002 – Name changed to Canico Resource Corp. pursuant to reverse takeover acquisition of Hastings Resource Corp.; basis 1 new for 9.3 old shs. ■

Oliver Resources Ltd. (B.C. 1967)
Jan. 29, 1986 – Name changed to Dyna Gold Resources Inc.; basis 1 new for 6 old shs. ■

Oliver Severn Gold Mines Ltd. (Ont. 1934)
Jan. 1976 – Charter cancelled.

Olivet Gold Mines Ltd. (Ont. 1927)
Aug. 9, 1972 – Dissolved.

Olivine Explorations Co. Ltd. (B.C. 1964)
1973 – Charter cancelled.

Olly Industries Inc. (B.C. June 8, 1988)
June 18, 2004 – Name changed to Aurea Mining Inc. following share exchange with Minera Aurea, S.A. de C.V. ■

O'Lori Holdings Ltd. (B.C. 1968)
Mar. 18, 1983 – Struck off register.

Olympia Energy Inc. (Alta. Nov. 13, 1984)
June 10, 2004 – Amalgamated with Provident Energy Trust; basis 0.345 Provident Energy Trust trust units or 0.345 Provident Energy Inc. exch. shs. plus 0.10 Accrete Energy Inc. shs. for 1 Olympia sh. (see Accrete Energy Inc.; Provident Energy Trust)

Olympia Mining Exploration Ltd. (Que. 1959)
Oct. 1974 – Charter cancelled.

Olympian International Resources Limited (B.C. 1968)
June 17, 1983 – Struck off register.

Olympic Computer Systems Corp. (B.C. Aug. 17, 1981)
May 31, 1991 – Name changed to OCS Technologies Corp. ■

Olympic Gold Mines Ltd. (B.C. 1934)
Dec. 12, 1977 – Charter cancelled.

Olympic Oil & Gas Ltd. (B.C. Sept. 7, 1979)
May 17, 1984 – Name changed to Channel Resources Ltd.; basis 1 new for 4 old shs. ■

Olympic Resources Ltd. (B.C. May 23, 1986)
Jan. 8, 2003 – Continued into Wyoming.

Olympic Resources Ltd. (B.C. Apr. 26, 2010)
Feb. 28, 2014 – Name changed to Kapuskasing Gold Corp. ■

Olympic ROM World Inc. (Ont. Oct. 20, 1994 amalg.)
Nov. 1, 1998 – Formed Century Financial Capital Group Inc. in Ontario on amalgamation with 1305206 Ontario Corporation, 1305207 Ontario Inc., Century Financial Capital Group Inc. and Dunberry Graphic Associates Ltd. (wholly owned by Century Financial) and accounted for as an acquisition of Olympic and 1305207 Ontario by 1305206 Ontario; basis 1 new for 10 old shs. ■

The Olympic Victor Corp. (Ont. 1951)
Sept. 19, 1986 – Name changed to The Olympic Victor Enterprises Inc. ■

The Olympic Victor Enterprises Inc. (Ont. 1951)
Feb. 5, 1993 – Name changed to TCS Energy Systems Ltd. ■

Olympus Holdings Ltd. (B.C. Nov. 5, 1992)
Nov. 29, 1996 – Name changed to Olympus Pacific Minerals Inc.; basis 1 new for 3 old shs. ■

Olympus Mines Ltd. (Ont. 1956)
Jan. 20, 1971 – Dissolved.

Olympus Pacific Minerals Inc. (B.C. Nov. 5, 1992)
Nov. 17, 1997 – Continued into Yukon.
July 13, 2006 – Continued into Canada.
Nov. 16, 2012 – Name changed to Besra Gold Inc. ■

Olympus Stone Inc. (Yuk. Jan. 10, 2000)
Oct. 12, 2004 – Name changed to Gobi Gold Inc.; basis 1 new for 2 old shs. ■

Omab Enterprises Ltd. (B.C. Dec. 17, 1973)
Apr. 10, 1986 – Name changed to Consolidated Omab Enterprises Ltd. ■

Omar Gold Mines Ltd. (Ont. 1944)
Aug. 1957 – Charter cancelled.
Jan. 20, 1971 – Dissolved.

Omar Resources Ltd. (Alta. Jan. 28, 1987)
Feb. 21, 1989 – Name changed to Omar Technologies Inc. ■

Omar Technologies Inc. (Alta. Jan. 28, 1987)
Apr. 14, 1993 – Name changed to Pilgrim Resource Corp.; basis 1 new for 5 old shs. ■

Omax Resources Ltd. (B.C. May 1, 1990)
Aug. 1, 1996 – Continued into Yukon.
Oct. 20, 2000 – Continued into Alberta.
July 6, 2004 – Continued into British Columbia.
July 16, 2004 – Name changed to Euromax Resources Ltd. (see FPsurvey - Mines & Energy)

Omega Advisors U.S. Capital Appreciation Fund (Ont. Feb. 25, 2011)
Jan. 10, 2013 – Name changed to Artemis U.S. Capital Appreciation Fund. ■

Omega Exploration Inc. (Que. 1986)
Mar. 31, 1989 – Amalgamated with Oz Exploration Inc., Norwood Exploration Inc., Onyx Resources Inc. and Farboro Resources Inc. to form Orient Resources Inc.

Omega Gold Corporation (B.C. 1978)
Nov. 9, 1992 – Amalgamated with Akiko-Lori Gold Resources Ltd. (1 for 1) to form a new co. called Akiko Gold Resources Ltd.; basis 1 new for 2.5 old shs. (see Akiko Gold Resources Ltd.)

Omega Gold Mines Ltd. (Ont. 1935)
1950 – Name changed to Lomega Gold Mines Ltd.; basis 2 new for 3 old shs. ■

Omega Hydrocarbons Ltd. (Alta. Sept. 4, 1958)
Mar. 12, 1996 – Acquired by Inuvialuit Energy Inc. for $2.90 per sh.

Omega Mines Ltd. (B.C. May 5, 1966)
Dec. 28, 1978 – Name changed to Black Owl Resources Ltd. ■

Omega Natural Gas Co. Ltd. (Alta. Sept. 4, 1958)
1967 – Name changed to Omega Hydrocarbons Ltd. ■

Omenica Resources Ltd. (B.C. 1972)
Dec. 21, 1983 – Name changed to Marilyn Resources Inc.; basis 1 new for 5 old shs. (see FPsurvey - Mines & Energy)

Omni Commerce Corp. (B.C. Apr. 13, 2006)
Dec. 4, 2020 – Name changed to Ready Set Gold Corp. pursuant to the acquisition of (old) Ready Set Gold Corp. and concurrent amalgamation of (old) Ready Set with wholly owned 1258952 B.C. Ltd. (and continued as Ready Set Gold ON Ltd.). ■

Omni-Lite Industries Corp. (Alta. Jan. 3, 1995)
Sept. 15, 1997 – Formed Omni-Lite Industries Canada Inc. in Alberta on amalgamation with Omni-Lite Industries Inc.; basis 1 new for 3 old shs. (see FPsurvey - Industrials)

Omni Resources Inc. (B.C. May 23, 1978)
Dec. 1, 2000 – Amalgamated with Trumpeter Yukon Gold Inc. to form Tagish Lake Gold Corp.; basis 0.1353 new for 1 Trumpeter sh. and 0.2257 new for 1 Omni sh. (see Tagish Lake Gold Corp.)

Omnibus Computer Graphics Inc. (Ont. 1980)
Apr. 16, 1987 – Company's largest creditor, the Royal Bank of Canada, demanded repayment of $9,800,000 in debt. Subsequently the company suspended all operations and closed its facilities. Since then the company has completely wound up operations.

Omnibus Resources Inc. (B.C. Oct. 17, 1980)
Sept. 10, 1981 – Name changed to Berle Oil Corporation. ■

Omnilynn Mines Ltd. (Ont. 1947)
Apr. 1958 – Charter cancelled.

Omnitech Consultant Group Inc. (Can. May 20, 2003)
Sept. 28, 2007 – Filed for bankruptcy. PricewaterhouseCoopers Inc. appointed trustee.

Omnitex Resources Corp. (Alta. May 31, 1991)
Nov. 1, 1999 – Struck off register.

Omnitrans Exploration Ltd. (Ont. June 6, 1944)
Struck off register.

Omo Mines Corp. (Idaho 1926)
1936 – Name changed to Kaslo Mines Corp.

Omoco Holdings Ltd. (B.C. 1986)
Nov. 5, 1993 – Dissolved and struck off register.

On-Track Learning Systems Ltd. (B.C. Sept. 15, 2000)
May 18, 2004 – Name changed to Torq Media Corporation; basis 1 new for 12 old shs. ■

On Wah Investments Corp. (B.C. May 23, 1986)
June 22, 2009 – Dissolved and struck from register.

Ona Energy Inc. (Alta. Aug. 31, 1998)
June 5, 2002 – Name changed to Ona International Inc. following Qualifying Transaction Assignment Agreement with Consolidated Odyssey Exploration Inc. to acquire a 10% working interest in certain oil and gas leases; basis 1 new for 5 old shs. ■

Ona Energy Inc. (B.C. Jan. 30, 2006)
July 16, 2009 – Name changed to Ona Power Corporation; basis 1 new for 5 old shs. ■

Ona Exploration Inc. (Alta. Aug. 31, 1998)
Jan. 30, 2006 – Continued into British Columbia.
May 25, 2007 – Name changed to Ona Energy Inc. ■

Ona International Inc. (Alta. Aug. 31, 1998)
Aug. 6, 2004 – Name changed to Ona Exploration Inc.; basis 2 new for 1 old sh. ■

Ona Power Corporation (B.C. Jan. 30, 2006)
Apr. 30, 2012 – Name changed to AAN Ventures Inc.; basis 1 new for 3 old shs. ■

Onaca Explorations Limited (B.C. 1974 amalg.)
Nov. 1977 – Name changed to Osec Petroleum Corp. following acquisition of Osec Petroleum Canada Limited. ■

Onaco Petroleums Limited (Ont. 1967)
Oct. 18, 1978 – Charter cancelled.

Onaping Mines Ltd. (Ont. 1960)
Oct. 5, 1978 – Amalgamated with 2 other cos. to form Onaping Resources Limited.

Onaping Resources Limited (Ont. 1978)
Mar. 15, 1984 – Amalgamated with Consolidated Durham Mines & Resources Limited to form Durham Resources Inc.; basis 1 new subord. voting sh. for each com. sh. held, and 1 new cl. C sh. for 1 old 1st pref. sh.

Onassis Mining Corp. (Que. 1956)
Nov. 1966 – Name changed to Albatros Gold Mines Ltd. ■

OnBus Technologies Inc. (Alta. Mar. 10, 1997)
June 22, 2006 – Continued into British Columbia.
July 7, 2006 – Name changed to Royal Monashee Gold Corp.; basis 2 new for 1 old sh. ■

Onco Petroleum Inc. (Ont. Oct. 31, 2002)
Sept. 29, 2006 – Continued into Canada.
Feb. 7, 2011 – Petitioned into receivership and S. Funtig & Associates Inc. appointed receiver.

Oncothyreon Inc. (Del. Sept. 7, 2007)
Oct. 22, 2009 – Delisted TSX; continued to trade on NASDAQ.
June 7, 2016 – Name changed to Cascadian Therapeutics, Inc.

The Ondaatje Corporation (Ont. Sept. 30, 1983)
July 5, 1996 – Name changed to Global Equity Corporation. ■

Ondine Biomedical Inc. (B.C. Sept. 9, 1996)
Sept. 12, 2011 – Privatized at 33¢ per sh.

Ondine Biopharma Corporation (B.C. Sept. 9, 1996)
Oct. 14, 2010 – Name changed to Ondine Biomedical Inc.; basis 1 new for 15 old shs. ■

One Click Ventures Inc. (B.C. Aug. 17, 2000)
July 29, 2003 – Acquired by Lund Gold Ltd. considered to be One Click's Qualifying Transaction; basis 1 new Lund com. sh. for 1 old One Click com. sh. (see Lund Gold Ltd.)

One Exploration Inc. (Ont. Feb. 19, 1999)
Nov. 21, 2006 – Continued into Alberta.
Apr. 7, 2010 – Name changed to TriOil Resources Ltd.; basis 1 new for 20 old shs. ■

One Person Health Sciences Inc. (Can. Feb. 20, 2004)
Oct. 17, 2006 – Name changed to HealthPricer Interactive Limited. ■

One World Investments Inc. (B.C. Nov. 9, 1982 amalg.)
Feb. 27, 2017 – Name changed to One World Minerals Inc. ■

One World Minerals Inc. (B.C. Nov. 9, 1982 amalg.)
Jan. 19, 2018 – Name changed to One World Lithium Inc. (see FPsurvey - Mines & Energy)

10000259749 Ontario Inc. (Ont. July 15, 2022)
Aug. 3, 2022 – Name changed to Arway Corporation. (see FPsurvey - Industrials)

1000268474 Ontario Ltd. (Ont. July 13, 2022)
July 26, 2022 – Formed NiCAN Limited in Ontario pursuant to the amalgamation with (old) NiCAN Limited (deemed acquiror); basis 1 new com. sh. for 1 com. sh. of each of 1000268474 Ontario and (old) NiCAN. (see FPsurvey - Mines & Energy)

1014379 B.C. Ltd. (B.C. Sept. 23, 2014)
June 4, 2021 – Name changed to Spotlite360 Technologies, Inc. pursuant to the acquisition of Captios, LLC. ■

10390461 Canada Inc. (Can. Sept. 1, 2017)
Sept. 21, 2017 – Name changed to Pivotal Development Corporation Inc. pursuant to the acquisition of Pivotal Holdings Ltd. ■

1040426 B.C. Ltd. (B.C. June 19, 2015)
July 12, 2017 – Name changed to BluKnight Aquafarms Inc. ■

1040442 B.C. Ltd. (B.C. June 19, 2015)
Sept. 29, 2017 – Name changed to Zenith Exploration Inc. ■

10557510 Canada Corp. (Can. Dec. 27, 2017)
Mar. 25, 2021 – Name changed to Royal Wins Corporation. (see FPsurvey - Industrials)

10557536 Canada Corp. (Can. Dec. 27, 2017)
Mar. 4, 2021 – Name changed to Xigem Technologies Corporation pursuant to the reverse takeover acquisition of (old) Xigem Technologies Corporation and concurrent amalgamation of (old) Xigem with wholly owned 2792189 Ontario Inc. (and continued as Xigem Technology Solutions Inc.). (see FPsurvey - Industrials)

106627 Mines Ltd. (Alta. 1977)
Sept. 14, 1977 – Name changed to Maxville Mines Ltd. ■

10674419 Canada Corporation (Can. Mar. 9, 2018)
July 19, 2018 – Name changed to Bluewater Acquisition Corp. (see FPsurvey - Mines & Energy)

1111 Acquisition Corp. (B.C. Feb. 21, 2020)
Aug. 3, 2021 – Name changed to 1111 Exploration Corp. ■

1111 Exploration Corp. (B.C. Feb. 21, 2020)
Feb. 17, 2023 – Name changed to Teako Minerals Corp. (see FPsurvey - Mines & Energy)

1151139 B.C. Ltd. (B.C. Jan. 30, 2018)
Feb. 2, 2018 – Name changed to Vanadium 23 Capital Corporation. ■

1166469 B.C. Ltd. (B.C. May 31, 2018)
Mar. 23, 2022 – Name changed to Troy Resources Inc. ■

1167343 B.C. Ltd. (B.C. June 7, 2018)
May 14, 2020 – Name changed to Mountain Lake Minerals Inc. ■

1169082 B.C. Ltd. (B.C. June 21, 2018)
June 15, 2021 – Name changed to Awakn Life Sciences Corp. pursuant to the reverse takeover acquisition of Awakn Life Sciences Inc. and concurrent amalgamation of (old) Awakn with wholly owned 2835517 Ontario Ltd. ■

1181718 B.C. Ltd. (B.C. Oct. 2, 2018)
Oct. 27, 2021 – Name changed to The Fresh Factory B.C. Ltd. pursuant to the reverse takeover acquisition of The Fresh Factory, PBC (dba The Fresh Factory). (see FPsurvey - Industrials)

1199515 B.C. Ltd. (B.C. Mar. 1, 2019)
May 14, 2019 – Name changed to Alpha North Esports & Entertainment Inc. ■

12 Exploration Inc. (Ont. Nov. 27, 2017)
Aug. 19, 2020 – Name changed to 79North Inc. ■

1223423 B.C. Ltd. (B.C. Sept. 16, 2019)
Dec. 23, 2019 – Name changed to SLE Synergy Ltd. ■

1236705 B.C. Ltd. (B.C. Jan. 9, 2020)
Apr. 23, 2021 – Name changed to X1 Esports and Entertainment Ltd. pursuant to the reverse takeover acquisition of Rix.GG Europe Ltd. ■

1242455 B.C. Ltd. (B.C. Feb. 27, 2020)
July 28, 2021 – Name changed to Kings Entertainment Group Inc. (see FPsurvey - Industrials)

1246765 B.C. Ltd. (B.C. Apr. 8, 2020)
Apr. 4, 2022 – Name changed to Lahontan Gold Corp. pursuant to the reverse takeover acquisition of (old) Lahontan Gold Corp. and concurrent amalgamation of (old) Lahontan with wholly owned 2812096 Ontario Ltd. (see FPsurvey - Mines & Energy)

1246768 B.C. Ltd. (B.C. Apr. 8, 2020)
Apr. 26, 2021 – Name changed to Millennial Precious Metals Corp. pursuant to reverse takeover acquisition of Millennial Silver Corp. ■

1246773 B.C. Ltd. (B.C. Apr. 8, 2020)
Aug. 23, 2021 – Name changed to Atacama Copper Corporation pursuant to the reverse takeover acquisition of 2311548 Alberta Ltd. and concurrent amalgamation of 2311548 Alberta with wholly owned 2330281 Alberta Ltd. (and continued as Atacama Cobre Ltd.). ■

1246775 B.C. Ltd. (B.C. Apr. 8, 2020)
May 26, 2021 – Name changed to Green Light Metals Inc. ■

1246778 B.C. Ltd. (B.C. Apr. 8, 2020)
Nov. 23, 2021 – Formed Minto Metals Corp. in British Columbia pursuant to the amalgamation with Minto Explorations Ltd. (deemed acquiror). ■

1246779 B.C. Ltd. (B.C. Apr. 8, 2020)
Nov. 4, 2021 – Name changed to Western Alaska Minerals Corp. pursuant to the reverse takeover acquisition of Western Alaska Copper & Gold Company. ■

1258481 B.C. Ltd. (B.C. July 23, 2020)
Mar. 29, 2021 – Name changed to Zoglo's Incredible Food Corp. pursuant to the reverse takeover acquisition of (old) Zoglo's Incredible Food Corp. ■

1262803 B.C. Ltd. (B.C. Aug. 25, 2020)
May 31, 2021 – Name changed to Sprout AI Inc. pursuant to the reverse takeover acquisition of Sprout AI, S.A. (see FPsurvey - Industrials)

1278700 B.C. Ltd. (B.C. Dec. 9, 2020)
Mar. 2, 2021 – Name changed to Origin Therapeutics Holdings Inc. ■

1279006 B.C. Ltd. (B.C. Dec. 10, 2020)
Mar. 11, 2021 – Name changed to Nabati Foods Global Inc. pursuant to the reverse takeover acquisition of Nabati Foods Inc. (see FPsurvey - Industrials)

1283332 B.C. Ltd. (B.C. Jan. 11, 2021)
Apr. 16, 2021 – Name changed to Swarmio Media Holdings Inc. ■

1284684 B.C. Ltd. (B.C. Jan. 19, 2021)
Oct. 28, 2021 – Name changed to TripSitter Clinic Ltd. pursuant to the reverse takeover acquisition of TripSitter Clinic Corp. and concurrent amalgamation of TripSitter with wholly owned 2821573 Ontario Inc. (see FPsurvey - Industrials)

1284696 B.C. Ltd. (B.C. Jan. 19, 2021)
July 29, 2021 – Name changed to Spirit Blockchain Capital Inc. pursuant to the reverse takeover acquisition of (old) Spirit Blockchain Capital Inc. and concurrent amalgamation of (old) Spirit with wholly owned 1302186 B.C. Ltd. (and continued as Spirit Blockchain Holdings Inc.). (see FPsurvey - Industrials)

1287390 B.C. Ltd. (B.C. Feb. 3, 2021)
July 13, 2022 – Name changed to 1000268474 Ontario Ltd. and continued into Ontario. ■

1287396 B.C. Limited (B.C. Feb. 3, 2021)
June 22, 2021 – Formed Filament Health Corp. in British Columbia pursuant to the reverse takeover acquisition of and amalgamation with Filament Ventures Corp. (deemed acquiror); basis 1 new com. sh. for 1 com. sh. of both 1287396 B.C. and Filament Ventures. ■

1287401 B.C. Ltd. (B.C. Feb. 3, 2021)
Jan. 14, 2022 – Name changed to McFarlane Lake Mining Limited pursuant to the reverse takeover acquisition of McFarlane Lake Mining Incorporated and concurrent amalgamation of McFarlane with wholly owned 1000034047 Ontario Inc. ■

1287406 B.C. Ltd. (B.C. Feb. 3, 2021)
Dec. 22, 2021 – Formed Trees Corporation in Canada pursuant to the reverse takeover acquisition of and

amalgamation with (old) Trees Corporation (deemed acquiror). ■

1287409 B.C. Ltd. (B.C. Feb. 3, 2021)
Mar. 17, 2025 – Name changed to Gold Hart Copper Corp. pursuant to the reverse takeover acquisition of Vicunau Metals Corp. (see FPsurvey - Mines & Energy)

1287411 B.C. Ltd. (B.C. Feb. 3, 2021)
Feb. 22, 2022 – Name changed to Base Carbon Inc. and continued into Ontario pursuant to the reverse takeover acquisition of Base Carbon Corp. and concurrent amalgamation of Base Carbon with wholly owned 1000095223 Ontario Inc. (see FPsurvey - Industrials)

1287412 B.C. Ltd. (B.C. Feb. 3, 2021)
June 28, 2024 – Formed Silver Crown Royalties Inc. in British Columbia pursuant to amalgamation with (old) Silver Crown Royalties Inc. (see FPsurvey - Mines & Energy)

1287413 B.C. Ltd. (B.C. Feb. 3, 2021)
Dec. 17, 2021 – Formed Liquid Meta Capital Holdings Ltd. in British Columbia pursuant to the reverse takeover acquisition of and amalgamation with (old) Liquid Meta Capital Holdings Ltd. (deemed acquiror); basis 1 new com. sh. for 5.5146 1287413 B.C. com. shs. and 2.5858 new com. shs. for 1 (old) Liquid Meta com. sh. (see FPsurvey - Industrials)

1290447 B.C. Ltd. (B.C. Feb. 23, 2021)
Nov. 23, 2021 – Name changed to Wellfield Technologies Inc. pursuant to the reverse takeover acquisition of Seamless Logic Software Limited and MoneyClip Inc. (see FPsurvey - Industrials)

1295908 B.C. Ltd. (B.C. Mar. 23, 2021)
July 2, 2021 – Name changed to Algoma Steel Group Inc. (see FPsurvey - Industrials)

1317198 B.C. Ltd. (B.C. July 27, 2021)
Sept. 1, 2023 – Name changed to IberAmerican Lithium Corp. pursuant to the reverse takeover acquisition of IberAmerican Lithium Inc. and concurrent amalgmation of IberAmercian with wholly owned 1000513020 Ontario Inc. ■

1317223 B.C. Ltd. (B.C. July 27, 2021)
Dec. 28, 2023 – Formed Dryden Gold Corp. in British Columbia pursuant to amalgamation with (old) Dryden Gold Corp. (see FPsurvey - Mines & Energy)

1319275 B.C. Ltd. (B.C. Aug. 11, 2021)
Feb. 13, 2023 – Name changed to Critical Infrastructure Technologies Ltd. pursuant to the acquisition of Critical Infrastructure Technologies Pty Ltd. (see FPsurvey - Industrials)

1319732 B.C. Ltd. (B.C. Aug. 13, 2021)
Sept. 27, 2023 – Name changed to Sendero Resources Corp. pursuant to the reverse takeover acquisition of (old) Sendero Resources Corp. and concurrent amalgamation of (old) Sendero with a wholly owned subsidiary (and continued as Sendero Holdings Ltd.). (see FPsurvey - Mines & Energy)

1319738 B.C. Ltd. (B.C. Aug. 13, 2021)
Nov. 4, 2022 – Name changed to DevvStream Holdings Inc. pursuant to the reverse takeover acquisition of DevvStream Inc. ■

1319743 B.C. Ltd. (B.C. Aug. 13, 2021)
Nov. 14, 2024 – Name changed to Zero Candida Technologies Inc. pursuant to the reverse takeover transaction of Zero Candida Ltd. (see FPsurvey - Industrials)

1322256 Alberta Ltd. (Alta. May 11, 2007)
Aug. 1, 2008 – Amalgamated with Trans America Industries Ltd. to form Primary Corp., constituting a reverse takeover by 1322256 Alberta; basis 1 new for 2 Trans America shs. and 1 new for 20 1322256 Alberta shs. (see Primary Corp.)

1324534 B.C. Ltd. (B.C. Sept. 16, 2021)
Aug. 9, 2022 – Name changed to Aurora Sky Ventures Corp. ■

1329300 B.C. Ltd. (B.C. Oct. 20, 2021)
May 9, 2024 – Name changed to Borealis Mining Company Limited pursuant to reverse takeover of (old) Borealis Mining Company Limited. (see FPsurvey - Mines & Energy)

1329306 B.C. Ltd. (B.C. Oct. 20, 2021)
Jan. 25, 2024 – Name changed to Zodiac Gold Inc. pursuant to the reverse takeover acquisition of (old) Zodiac Gold Inc. (see FPsurvey - Mines & Energy)

1344340 B.C. Ltd. (B.C. Jan. 24, 2022)
July 29, 2024 – Name changed to Metavista3D Inc. pursuant to the reverse takeover acquisition of psHolix AG. (see FPsurvey - Industrials)

1348512 B.C. Ltd. (B.C. Feb. 16, 2022)
Nov. 25, 2024 – Name changed to Cizzle Brands Corporation pursuant to the reverse takeover acquisition of Cizzle Brands Ltd. and concurrent amalgamation of Cizzle with wholly owned 1001070471 Ontario Inc. (see FPsurvey - Industrials)

1348515 B.C. Ltd. (B.C. Feb. 16, 2022)
Apr. 26, 2024 – Name changed to ONGold Resources Ltd. following acquisition of Ontario gold properties from Northern Superior Resources Inc. (see FPsurvey - Mines & Energy)

1397468 B.C. Ltd. (B.C. Jan. 23, 2023)
Oct. 3, 2023 – Name changed to Lithium Americas Corp. pursuant to transfer of Lithium Americas (Argentina) Corp.'s Thacker Pass lithium project to the company. (see FPsurvey - Mines & Energy)

1429798 B.C. Ltd. (B.C. July 25, 2023)
May 24, 2024 – Name changed to BluSky Carbon Inc. pursuant to the reverse takeover acquisition of Bluski Inc. and concurrent amalgamation of Bluski with wholly owned 1448451 B.C. Ltd. (see FPsurvey - Industrials)

14943 Alberta Ltd. (Alta. 1952)
Dec. 15, 1981 – Name changed to Ballard Oil & Gas Limited. ■

1562756 Nova Scotia Limited (N.S. Dec. 5, 1984)
Jan. 14, 1985 – Name changed to NovaCan Mining Resources (1985) Limited. ■

15963982 Canada Inc. (Can. Apr. 19, 2024)
May 10, 2024 – Name changed to Greenheart Gold Inc. (see FPsurvey - Mines & Energy)

1608557 Ontario Inc. (Ont. Feb. 24, 2004)
Aug. 13, 2008 – Placed into receivership. PricewaterhouseCoopers Inc. appointed receiver.

161671 Canada Inc. (Can. July 19, 1982)
Mar. 22, 1996 – Dissolved.

1745491 Ontario Limited (Ont. Sept. 4, 2007)
Dec. 19, 2007 – Name changed to GFL Waste and Recycling Solutions Corp. ■

180 Connect Inc. (Alta. Feb. 1, 1999)
June 12, 2002 – Continued into Canada.
Aug. 27, 2007 – Acquired by Ad. Venture Partners, Inc.(AVP) which subsequently changed its name to 180 Connect Inc.; basis 0.6 AVP sh. or 0.6 AVP exchangeable sh. for 1 180 Connect sh.

OneCap Investment Corporation (Can. Apr. 20, 2012)
July 13, 2018 – Name changed to Origin Gold Corporation. ■

Oneida Energy & Resources Corp. (Ont. 1979)
June 30, 1987 – Formed Consolidated Dixie Resources Inc. in Ontario on amalgamation with Rockmere Lake Explorations Ltd. and Dixie Oil & Gas Corp.; basis 0.6 new for 1 Rockmere sh., 1 new for 1 Dixie sh. and 0.667 new for 1 Oneida sh. ■

Oneida Resources Corporation (Ont. 1979)
Jan. 12, 1982 – Amalgamated with 3 other cos. to form New Frontier Petroleum Corporation; basis 0.20 new for 1 old sh.

O'Neill-Thompson Gold Mines Ltd. (Ont. 1935)
Nov. 1954 – Charter cancelled; distributed equivalent of 1 sh. Rouyn Merger Gold Mines Ltd. for each 4 old shs.

OneMove Technologies Inc. (B.C. July 18, 2005)
June 11, 2013 – Acquired by 0955662 B.C. Ltd. by way of amalgamation for $0.425 per sh. 0955662 B.C. Ltd. is a wholly owned subsid. of Plantro Ltd. and Seastone Investments Limited.
July 1, 2016 – Name changed to Dye & Durham Corporation. ■

Oneonta Pershing Mines Ltd. (Ont. 1944)
Mar. 4, 1957 – Charter cancelled.

OnePak, Inc. (Nev. Mar. 30, 2005)
Jan. 3, 2011 – Voluntarily delisted from CNSX.

OneREIT (Ont. Dec. 15, 2003)
Oct. 6, 2017 – Assets acquired by Strathallen Capital Corp. and Smart Real Estate Investment Trust (SmartREIT). Trust units redeemed on the basis of (i) $4.275 cash; or (ii) 0.1376 SmartREIT variable vtg. units for 1 OneREIT trust unit.

OneSoft Solutions Inc. (Alta. Sept. 6, 1996)
Nov. 8, 2024 – Acquired by irth Solutions LLC; basis 88¢ cash per sh.

Onex Packaging Inc. (Ont. 1984 amalg.)
Dec. 8, 1988 – Amalgamated with a subsid. jointly owned by Onex Corporation and Ball Corporation (a private co.); basis $11 per sh.

Onitap Resources Inc. (Can. Apr. 14, 1984)
Oct. 5, 1992 – Name changed to Red Oak Resources Inc.; basis 1 new for 15.263143 old shs. ■

Online Consortium Corp. (B.C. Nov. 25, 1983)
July 11, 2003 – Name changed to Equicap Financial Corp. ■

Online Direct Inc. (Can. Mar. 31, 1999 amalg.)
Sept. 19, 2009 – Dissolved and struck from register.
July 26, 2010 – Restored to company register.
Feb. 7, 2013 – Dissolved and struck from register.
Aug. 12, 2015 – Restored to company register. (see FPsurvey - Industrials)

Online Energy Inc. (Alta. Oct. 20, 2009)
Nov. 9, 2012 – Acquired by Madalena Ventures Inc. for $0.35 per sh. (see Madalena Ventures Inc.)

OnSat.net Canada Inc. (Alta. Apr. 19, 1996)
Oct. 2, 2005 – Struck from registry and dissolved.

Onsino Capital Corporation (Ont. Mar. 7, 2005)
Dec. 22, 2010 – Name changed to Quia Resources Inc. pursuant to Qualifying Transaction reverse takeover acquisition of Quia Resources Inc. and subsequent amalgamation of Quia with wholly owned 1833688 Ontario Inc.; basis 1 new for 1.5 old shs. ■

Ontarget Capital Inc. (Alta. July 26, 1947)
Oct. 20, 1994 – Name changed to Gene Screen Inc. ■

Ontario and Quebec Railway Company (Can. 1881)
Oct. 13, 1998 – Amalgamated into St. Lawrence & Hudson Railway Company Limited.

Ontario Beauty Supply Co. Ltd. (Can. 1934)
Mar. 1964 – Name changed to Obsco Corporation Limited. ■

Ontario Capital Opportunities Inc. (Ont. Dec. 18, 2003)
Jan. 17, 2005 – Name changed to Biorem Inc. following Qualifying Transaction reverse takeover acquisition of Biorem Technologies Inc.; basis 1 new for 4 old shs. (see FPsurvey - Industrials)

Ontario Hose Specialties Inc. (Ont. Mar. 15, 1979 amalg.)
Mar. 13, 2007 – Name changed to Bordeaux Energy Inc. ∎

Ontario Hydro (Ont. May 14, 1906)
Apr. 1, 1999 – Name changed to Ontario Electricity Financial Corporation.

Ontario Hydro Services Company (Ont. Dec. 1, 1998)
May 1, 2000 – Name changed to Hydro One Inc. ∎

The Ontario Jockey Club (Ont. May 16, 1902)
June 1, 2001 – Name changed to Woodbine Entertainment Group.

Ontario Jockey Club Limited (Ont. 1881)
Mar. 12, 1959 – Name changed to The Jockey Club Limited (not to be confused with The Ontario Jockey Club (formerly The Toronto Driving Club Limited) - Ont. 1902).

Ontario Lands and Oil Company Limited (U.K. 1892)
1961 – In voluntary liquidation; liquidator, G. E. Hedgeman, 48 Copthall Ave., London, Eng.

Ontario Lithium Co. Ltd. (Ont. June 3, 1955)
Mar. 1979 – Name changed to Evergreen Energy Resources Ltd. ∎

Ontario Loan & Debenture Company (Ont. 1870)
1969 – Acquired by The Royal Trust Company following $56 per sh. offer in July 1968; subsequently merged into Royal Trust Co. Mortgage Corp. (see Royal Trust Company)

The Ontario Mutual Life Assurance Company (Ont. 1868)
1878 – Continued into Canada.
1900 – Name changed to The Mutual Life Assurance Company of Canada. ∎

Ontario Nickel Corp. Ltd (Ont. Dec. 1933)
May 1946 – Charter cancelled. Name changed to Ontario Nickel Mines Ltd. in 1943; basis 1 new for 5 old shs.

Ontario Nickel Mines Ltd. (Ont. 1943)
June 1961 – Charter cancelled; distribution equivalent of $8, 35 shs. Trebor Mines Ltd. and 24 shs. Canalask Nickel Mines Ltd. for each 100 shs.

Ontario Phosphate Industries Ltd. (Ont. 1944)
1956 – Charter cancelled.

Ontario Pyrites Co. Ltd. (Ont. 1942)
1954 – Name changed to Consolidated Sudbury Basin Mines Ltd.; basis 1 new for 2 old shs. ∎

Ontario Rare Metal Mines Ltd. (Ont. 1954)
Apr. 1960 – Distributed 9.5¢ per sh. Charter surrendered.

Ontario Steel Products Company Ltd. (Can. 1913)
Jan. 1969 – Acquired by North American Rockwell Corp., through sh. offer of $50 per sh.

Ontario Store Fixtures Co. Limited (Ont. 1953)
Aug. 30, 1968 – Name changed to OSF Industries Limited; basis 3 new for 1 old sh. ∎

Ontario Tobacco Plantations Limited (Ont. 1927)
1948 – Bulk of assets sold to Ontario Tobacco Holdings Ltd. Pref. shldrs. received 12 3% pref. shs., $10 par plus $60 for 1 old pref. sh. held, plus final distribution of 20¢ per sh. Nothing for com. shldrs.

Ontario Trust Co. (Ont. 1971)
Dec. 31, 1976 – Amalgamated with The Lincoln Trust and Savings Co. and Canada Trustco Mortgage Co. to continue as Canada Trustco Mortgage Co.; basis 3 com. shs. (or three 7 3/4 % pfce. shs.) for 5 com. shs.

Ontex Mining Limited (Ont. Aug. 8, 1945)
Mar. 27, 1981 – Name changed to Ontex Resources Limited. ∎

Ontex Resources Limited (Ont. Aug. 8, 1945)
Dec. 16, 1998 – Amalgamated with Faymar Gold Mines Limited to form new co. with same name Ontex Resources Limited; basis 1.4286 new for 1 Faymar sh. and 1 new for 1 Ontex sh.
Dec. 22, 2009 – Name changed to Goldstone Resources Inc. following reverse takeover acquisition of Roxmark Mines Limited; basis 1 new for 3 old shs. ∎

Onward Energy Inc. (Alta. June 8, 1993)
Jan. 16, 2003 – Name changed to Avenir Diversified Income Trust following reverse takeover acquisition of Avenir Acquisition Corp. and subsequent conversion into a trust; basis 1 unit (1 sh. and 1 subord. note) of Avenir Acquisition Corp. for 1 Onward sh. Each note was exchangeable for a maximum of 32¢ with the residual amount (32¢ to 40¢) to be paid in Avenir Acquisition Corp. unit consideration. All units of Avenir Acquisition Corp. were exchanged on a 1-for-1 basis with Avenir Diversified Income Trust. ∎

Onwatin Placer Gold Ltd. (Ont. 1947)
Dec. 2, 1970 – Dissolved.

Onword Learning Systems Inc. (B.C. July 14, 1987)
June 11, 1993 – Name changed to International Onword Learning Systems Inc.; basis 1 new for 4 old shs. ∎

OnX Enterprise Solutions Inc. (Ont. Jan. 8, 1988 amalg.)
Dec. 6, 2006 – Name changed to Momentum Advanced Solutions Inc. ∎

OnX Incorporated (Ont. Jan. 8, 1988 amalg.)
Jan. 14, 2002 – Name changed to OnX Enterprise Solutions Inc. ∎

Onyx Petroleum Exploration Company Ltd. (Alta. Nov. 10, 1976)
Jan. 14, 1988 – Formed LASMO Canada Inc. in Alberta on amalgamation with LASMO Exploration (Canada) Ltd. ∎

Onyx Resources Inc. (Que. Feb. 24, 1984)
Mar. 31, 1989 – Amalgamated with Oz Exploration Inc., Omega Exploration Inc., Norwood Exploration Inc. and Faboro Resources Inc. to form Orient Resources Inc.

Opact Energy Ltd. (Alta. 1974)
Feb. 22, 1984 – Name changed to Opact Energy (1983) Ltd.; basis 1 new for 4 old shs. ∎

Opact Energy (1983) Ltd. (Alta. 1974)
July 19, 1984 – Formed Intensity Resources Ltd. in Alberta on amalgamation with Intensity Resources Ltd.; basis 1 new for 4 old shs. ∎

Opact Resources Ltd. (B.C. Feb. 6, 1986)
July 21, 1999 – Name changed to Blue Lightning Ventures Inc.; basis 1 new for 3 old shs. ∎

Opagold Mines Limited (Que. 1945)
1953 – Under voluntary liquidation distributed 1 sh. of Lingside Copper Mining Co. Ltd. for 1 old sh. (see Lingside Copper Mining Co. Limited)

Opal Energy Corp. (B.C. Jan. 2, 2007)
June 14, 2016 – Name changed to Versus Systems Inc. following acquisition of Versus LLC. (see FPsurvey - Industrials)

Opal Energy Inc. (Can. Mar. 20, 1987)
Jan. 19, 1999 – Acquired by Founders Energy Ltd.; basis 42¢ plus 0.44 Founders shs. for 1 Opal sh. (see Founders Energy Ltd.)

Opasatika Iron Mines Ltd. (Ont. 1948)
1954 – Name changed to Waterways Iron and Uranium Ltd. ∎

Opawica Explorations Inc. (Ont. Sept. 17, 1975)
Sept. 29, 2006 – Continued into British Columbia. (see FPsurvey - Mines & Energy)

Opawica Explorers Ltd. (Que. 1953)
Aug. 1973 – Charter cancelled.

Opawica Gold Mines Ltd. (Ont. 1945)
Oct. 1960 – Charter cancelled.

Opel International Inc. (Ont. Jan. 3, 1997)
Jan. 30, 2007 – Continued into New Brunswick.
Nov. 30, 2010 – Name changed to OPEL Solar International Inc. and continued into Ontario. ∎

Opemisca Explorers Ltd. (Que. 1952)
1969 – Merged into Allied Mining Corp.; basis 1 new for 15 old shs.

Opemiska Copper Mines Ltd. (Que. 1937)
1937 – Name changed to Opemiska Copper Mines (Quebec) Limited and continued into Quebec; basis 1 new for 1 old sh. ∎

Opemiska Copper Mines (Quebec) Limited (Que. 1937)
Dec. 16, 1971 – Merged with Lake Dufault Mines Limited and Falconbridge Mines Quebec Limited into Falconbridge Copper Limited; basis 1 new for 1 old sh.

Open EC Technologies, Inc. (B.C. Mar. 30, 1981)
Oct. 31, 2012 – Acquired by QHR Technologies Inc.; basis (i) 4¢, or (ii) 0.0833, or (iii) combination thereof for 1 Open EC sh. (see QHR Technologies Inc.)

Open End Mines Ltd. (Ont. 1928)
1971 – Assets sold to New York Oils Ltd. in late; basis 1 new for 2 old shs.

Open Gold Corp. (B.C. Aug. 1, 2009 amalg.)
Mar. 3, 2017 – Name changed to betterU Education Corp. pursuant to reverse takeover acquisition of SKILLSdox Inc.; basis 1 new for 9.5 old shs. ∎

Open Range Capital Corp. (Alta. Apr. 7, 2004)
Mar. 30, 2006 – Formed New Range Resources Ltd. in Alberta following non-arm's length Qualifying Transaction acquisition of and amalgamation with Siga Resources Limited. ∎

Open Range Energy Corp. (Alta. Nov. 30, 2005 amalg.)
Nov. 1, 2011 – Name changed to Poseidon Concepts Corp. pursuant to plan of arrangement whereby the tank rental business was retained and the oil and gas assets spun off to newly incorporated Open Range Energy Corp. (formerly 1629318 Alberta Ltd.); basis 1 new Open Range sh. and 0.8839 Poseidon Concepts shs. for 1 old Open Range sh. ∎

Open Range Energy Corp. (Alta. Sept. 14, 2011)
Aug. 20, 2012 – Acquired by Peyto Exploration & Development Corp.; basis 0.0723 Peyto Exploration shs. for 1 Open Range sh.

Open Source Health Inc. (Alta. Mar. 16, 2001)
Oct. 10, 2018 – Formed Weekend Unlimited Inc. in Alberta pursuant to amalgamation with (old) Weekend Unlimited Inc. (deemed acquiror); basis 1 new com. sh. for 2 Open Source com. shs. and 1 new com. shs. for 1 (old) Weekend com. sh. ∎

Open Text Corporation (Ont. June 26, 1991)
Dec. 29, 2005 – Continued into Canada. (see FPsurvey - Industrials)

OpenSky Capital Index Income Fund (Ont. Feb. 16, 2005)
June 3, 2008 – All units redeemed for $7.32 per unit and dissolved.

OpenSky Capital Managed Protection Income Trust Fund (Ont. Feb. 16, 2005)
Feb. 26, 2007 – Name changed to OpenSky Capital Index Income Fund. ∎

Ophir Gold Corp. (B.C. Apr. 26, 2010)
June 14, 2024 – Name changed to Ophir Metals Corp. (see FPsurvey - Mines & Energy)

Ophir Ventures Inc. (Alta. Mar. 28, 2005)
Dec. 2, 2005 – Name changed to Consolidated Ophir Ventures Inc.; basis 1 new for 50 old shs. ■

OphiraVencap Inc. (Can. Jan. 21, 2004)
Feb. 12, 2009 – Name changed to Knick Exploration Inc. following Qualifying Transaction reverse takeover acquisition of Knick Resources Inc. (see FPsurvey - Mines & Energy)

The Opimian California Vineyards Corporation (Can. Sept. 24, 1981)
Mar. 6, 2000 – Dissolved.

Oppenheimer Holdings Inc. (Ont. Oct. 12, 1977)
May 11, 2005 – Continued into Canada.
May 11, 2009 – Continued into Delaware.

Opsens Inc. (Que. Oct. 3, 2006 amalg.)
Dec. 14, 2023 – Acquired by Haemonetics Corporation; basis $2.90 cash per sh.

Opta Minerals Inc. (Can. July 8, 2004)
Apr. 11, 2016 – Acquired by Speyside Equity LLC through its wholly owned Speyside Equity Fund I LP; basis $0.5202 cash or $0.3526 cash plus a promissory note of $0.1676 per share.

Optical Data Corp. (Ont. 1927)
Jan. 27, 1992 – Name changed to AVL Information Systems Inc. pursuant to reverse takeover acquisition of Tyrae Technology Inc.; basis 1 new for 5 old shs. ■

Optical Data Systems, Inc. (Alta. Aug. 22, 1991)
Dec. 19, 1994 – Name changed to Compression Technologies Inc. following reverse takeover acquisition of Compression Technologies Inc. ■

Optima Energy Corporation (B.C. Apr. 11, 1983)
July 9, 1992 – Name changed to Optima Petroleum Corporation; basis 1 new for 2.5 old shs. ■

Optima Medical Innovations Corp. (B.C. July 25, 2007)
Dec. 20, 2023 – Placed into receivership. B. Riley Farber Inc. appointed receiver.

Optima Petroleum Corporation (B.C. Apr. 11, 1983)
June 22, 1994 – Continued into Canada.
Sept. 2, 1998 – Name changed to PetroQuest Energy, Inc. and continued into Delaware.

Optima Strategy Master Limited Partnership (Man. Jan. 9, 1996)
Dec. 31, 2004 – Dissolved; distribution was $0.09305548 per unit.

Optimal Geomatics Inc. (Can. Oct. 9, 2003)
Oct. 1, 2009 – Acquired by Aeroquest International Limited; basis 1 Aeroquest sh. for 21 Optimal shs. (see Aeroquest International Limited)

Optimal Group Inc. (Can. Oct. 21, 1996)
July 20, 2010 – Acquired by 7293411 Canada Inc. by way of amalg. with 7533403 Canada Inc., a wholly owned subsid. of 7293411, for US$2.40 per sh.

Optimal Robotics Corp. (Ont. 1984)
Oct. 21, 1996 – Continued into Canada.
Apr. 7, 2004 – Name changed to Optimal Group Inc. ■

Optimark Data Systems Inc. (B.C. 1983)
May 30, 2005 – Dissolved and struck from register.

Optimum General Inc. (Can. July 31, 1985)
Dec. 24, 2007 – Acquired by Optimum Group Inc. for $5.15 per cl. A sh.
Jan. 26, 2016 – Continued into Quebec.

Optimum Ventures Ltd. (B.C. Nov. 23, 2017)
Sept. 15, 2023 – Acquired by Blackwolf Copper and Gold Ltd.; basis 0.65 Blackwolf shs. for 1 Optimum sh. (see Blackwolf Copper and Gold Ltd.)

Optimus Investments Ltd. (Alta. 1988)
Nov. 3, 1994 – Amalgamated with Veritas Energy Services Inc., Decus Enterprises Limited and 584745

Alberta Ltd. to form Veritas Energy Services Inc.; basis 0.101262 Veritas shs. for 1 Optimus sh. (see Veritas Energy Services Inc.)

Option-NFA Inc. (Alta. July 9, 1999)
Dec. 12, 2000 – Continued into British Columbia.
Sept. 16, 2009 – Name changed to Sandwell Mining Ltd. ■

Optipress Inc. (Can. May 16, 2002)
Jan. 21, 2004 – Acquired by wholly owned subsid. of Transcontinental Inc. for $8.00 per sh.

Optival International Laboratories Inc. (B.C. Dec. 23, 1986)
Mar. 3, 1994 – Name changed to Triad Technologies Ltd.; basis 1 new for 5 old shs. ■

Optrix Radiation Inc. (Can. Dec. 9, 1980)
Sept. 28, 1988 – Name changed to Southern Arizona Mining & Smelting Corp. ■

Opus Minerals Inc. (Ont. May 14, 1985)
Aug. 15, 2000 – Name changed to InvestorLinks.com Inc. ■

Opus One Resources Inc. (Can. July 13, 2012)
Oct. 29, 2020 – Name changed to Opus One Gold Corporation. (see FPsurvey - Mines & Energy)

Ora Resources Inc. (Sask. Apr. 9, 1986)
May 27, 1993 – Continued into Alberta.
June 29, 1993 – Name changed to Calahoo Petroleum Ltd.; basis 1 new for 3 old shs. ■

Oracle Minerals Inc. (B.C. May 19, 1981)
May 2, 1997 – Name changed to Prophet Minerals Corporation; basis 1 new for 5 old shs. ■

Oracle Mining Corp. (Can. Sept. 4, 1985)
Dec. 23, 2015 – Wholly owned Oracle Ridge Mining LLC placed into receivership and Christopher G. Linscott appointed receiver. All officers and directors of the company resigned.
July 9, 2018 – Dissolved and struck from register.

Oracle Resources Ltd. (Alta. 1985)
Nov. 30, 1989 – All o/s com. shs. exchanged for preferred shs. of a wholly owned subsidiary of American Eagle Petroleums Ltd.; basis sh. for sh. (see American Eagle Petroleums Ltd.)

Oracle Yellowknife Mines Ltd. (Ont. 1944)
May 21, 1953 – Charter cancelled.

The Oralife Group, Inc. (Ont. Jan. 28, 1988)
Jan. 25, 2000 – All o/s shs. acquired indirectly by Nordic Capital Corporation; basis $0.163 per sh.

Oramericas Corp. (Ont. Nov. 30, 2004 amalg.)
Feb. 21, 2014 – Continued into British Columbia.
Feb. 9, 2016 – Name changed to Backstageplay Inc. (see FPsurvey - Industrials)

Orange Crush, Ltd. (Ont. 1927)
Oct. 1959 – Name changed to Crush International Limited. ■

Orangeroof Canada Limited (Can. 1968)
1977 – Private co. major shldrs. offered to acquire all o/s cl. B shs. at $1.30 per sh. Shs. not tendered under the offer were exchanged on sh.-for-sh. basis into pref. stk., subsequently redeemed.

Orbex Industries Inc. (B.C. July 18, 1979)
Mar. 7, 1990 – Name changed to Silver Glance Resources Inc.; basis 1 new for 5 old shs. ■

Orbex Minerals Limited (B.C. July 18, 1979)
Feb. 17, 1986 – Name changed to Orbex Industries Inc. ■

Orbit Oil & Gas Ltd. (Alta. Jan. 26, 1977)
Jan. 19, 1982 – Amalgamated with Hansa Petroleum Corporation to form new co. with same name Orbit Oil &

Gas Ltd.; basis 1 new for 8 Hansa shs. and 1 new for 1 Orbit sh.
Feb. 18, 1998 – Acquired by Sunoma Energy Corp. for $1.77 per sh.

Orbit Uranium Developments Ltd. (Ont. 1949)
Nov. 28, 1973 – Charter cancelled.

Orbite Aluminae Inc. (Can. June 17, 1983)
June 12, 2015 – Name changed to Orbite Technologies Inc. ■

Exploration Orbite V.S.P.A. Inc. (Can. June 17, 1983)
Oct. 11, 2011 – Name changed to Orbite Aluminae Inc. ■

Orbite Technologies Inc. (Can. June 17, 1983)
Apr. 3, 2017 – Filed for protection under the Bankruptcy and Insolvency Act (BIA) and subsequently continued the proceedings under the Companies' Creditors Arrangement Act (CCAA). PricewaterhouseCoopers Inc. was appointed as monitor of the business and financial affairs of the company.
Apr. 6, 2020 – Sale of substantially all of the company's assets, including the Cap-Chat plant, free and clear of all encumbrances, was completed in exchange for: (i) a cash payment payable to PricewaterhouseCoopers; (ii) issuance of zero-coupon notes to the company's secured creditors; and (iii) the assumption by the purchaser of various liabilities of the company. Secured creditors recovered a portion of their respective debt. No funds were available to shldrs.
Sept. 2020 – Mining properties were sold for an undisclosed amount. (see FPsurvey - Mines & Energy)

Orca Exploration Group Inc. (British Virgin Islands Apr. 28, 2004)
July 31, 2020 – Name changed to Orca Energy Group Inc. (see FPsurvey - Mines & Energy)

Orca Gold Inc. (Can. Jan. 3, 1987)
May 25, 2022 – Acquired by Perseus Mining Limited; basis 0.56 Perseus shs. for 1 Orca Gold sh.

Orca Petroleum Inc. (Alta. Mar. 27, 2002)
Apr. 27, 2006 – Continued into British Columbia.
May 10, 2006 – Name changed to Nautilus Minerals Inc. following reverse takeover acquisition of Nautilus Minerals Corporation and Nautilus Minerals Oceania Limited; basis 1 new for 6 old shs. ■

Orca Power Corp. (B.C. Dec. 16, 2004)
Oct. 12, 2011 – Formed AFG Flameguard Ltd. in Canada pursuant to amalgamation with AFG Flameguard Ltd. (deemed acquiror) ; basis 1 new AFG sh. for 4 Orca shs. and 1 new AFG sh. for 1 old AFG sh. ■

Orca Touchscreen Technologies Ltd. (Can. Mar. 10, 2014)
Oct. 3, 2018 – Name changed to Biome Grow Inc. following reverse takeover acquisition of Cultivator Catalyst Corp. (CCC) and concurrent amalgamation of CCC with wholly owned 1151856 B.C. Ltd.; basis 1 new for 50 old shs. (see FPsurvey - Industrials)

Orcana Resources Limited (B.C. Apr. 25, 1983)
Sept. 29, 1995 – Amalgamated in British Columbia to continue with same name. (see FPsurvey - Mines & Energy)

Orcatech Inc. (Can. July 22, 1981)
Mar. 8, 1983 – Filed for bankruptcy. Clarke Henning Inc. of Toronto appointed trustee.
Jan. 31, 1988 – Name changed to Tele-Radio Systems Limited following amalgamation with Tele-Radio Systems Ltd.; basis 1 new for 10 old shs. ■

Orcatron Communications Ltd. (B.C. Jan. 22, 1985)
Mar. 15, 2004 – Ceased operations and the secured creditors seized all the assets. No trustee was appointed and there were no funds available for distribution to shldrs. or other creditors.

Orchan Mines Limited (Ont. 1953)
Dec. 31, 1978 – Amalgamated into Noranda Mines Ltd.; basis 1 Noranda sh. for 6 old Orchan shs.

Orchan Uranium Mines Ltd. (Ont. 1953)
1957 – Name changed to Orchan Mines Limited. ■

Orchards West Ltd. (Alta. June 18, 1986)
Feb. 5, 1990 – Filed for bankruptcy.
Dec. 1, 1990 – Struck off register.
Oct. 27, 1994 – Released from bankruptcy following governmental approval and settlement with creditors reviving the company.
June 27, 1996 – Name changed to China Clipper Gold Mines Ltd. and continued into Ontario following acquisition of Orient Gold Mines Ltd.; basis 1 new for 4 old shs. ■

Orco Resources Inc. (Que. 1986)
Jan. 27, 1995 – Amalgamated with Denyvan Resources Inc. (0.92 new for 1 old sh.), and Minorca Resources Ltd. (1 new for 1 old sh.), to continue as Denyvan Resources Inc.; basis 0.38 new for 1 old sh. The amalgamated co. subsequently changed its name to Minorca Resources Inc. effective Jan. 30, 1995. (see Minorca Resources Inc.)

Orcour Gold Mines Ltd. (Ont. Dec. 17, 1936)
1940 – Assets acquired by Orcour Gold Mines (1940) Ltd.; basis 100 new for 1 old sh.

Orcour Gold Mines (1940) Ltd. (Ont. 1940)
1968 – Charter cancelled.

Orcus Resources Ltd. (B.C. Sept. 28, 2020)
Apr. 13, 2022 – Name changed to Western Metallica Resources Corp. pursuant to the Qualifying Transaction reverse takeover acquisition of Western Metallica Corp. (see FPsurvey - Mines & Energy)

Ord Mountain Resources Corp. (Cayman Islands Dec. 24, 2010)
Sept. 1, 2021 – Continued into British Columbia. (see FPsurvey - Industrials)

Ordala Mines Ltd. (Ont. 1944)
Nov. 28, 1973 – Charter cancelled.

Les Ordinateurs Hypocrat Inc. (Can. 1980)
May 31, 1995 – Acquired by FoxMeyer Canada Inc.; basis 1 FoxMeyer Canada sh. for 10 Hypocrat shs. (see FoxMeyer Canada Inc.)

Ordorado Resources Corp. (Can. Mar. 11, 2004)
June 22, 2006 – Name changed to Eagle Star Petroleum Corp. ■

Ore-Leave Capital Inc. (Can. Jan. 17, 2003)
Nov. 20, 2003 – Qualifying Transaction acquisition of Carpathian Gold Limited for total consideration of 21,371,594 com. shs. and 2,362,500 wts.
June 24, 2004 – Name changed to Carpathian Gold Inc. ■

Ore Mont Mines Ltd. (Que. 1937)
May 1974 – Charter cancelled.

Orea Mining Corp. (B.C. Dec. 20, 2004)
Apr. 17, 2024 – Filed an assignment in bankruptcy and Crowe MacKay & Company was appointed trustee.

Orecan Mines Ltd. (B.C. 1964)
Aug. 1968 – Bankrupt; all assets either realized or abandoned.
Sept. 3, 1974 – Dissolved and struck off register.

Orecan Oils Ltd. (Sask. Aug. 24, 1954)
1968 – Name changed to American Eagle Petroleums Ltd. ■

Oreco Mines & Energy Corp. (Ont. Jan. 9, 1987)
Apr. 30, 1993 – Name changed to V.R.D. Entertainment Ltd.; basis 1 new for 5 old shs. ■

Orefield Mining Corp. (Que. 1955)
Sept. 30, 1978 – Charter cancelled.

Orefinders Resources Inc. (B.C. July 26, 2011)
May 18, 2023 – Name changed to Orecap Invest Corp. (see FPsurvey - Mines & Energy)

Oregon Natural Gas Reserves Ltd. (Ont. 1957)
May 1961 – Bankrupt; no equity.

Oregon Quebec Gold Mines Limited (Ont. 1946)
Nov. 1962 – Dissolved.

Oregon Resources Corp. (B.C. Apr. 2, 1980)
Jan. 10, 1992 – Name changed to International Oregon Resources Corp.; basis 1 new for 3 old shs. ■

Oreland Mining Corp. (Que. 1953)
Aug. 1974 – Charter cancelled.

Orelia Mines Ltd. (Ont. Aug. 1, 1936)
Charter cancelled.

Orell Copper Mines Ltd. (B.C. 1969)
Sept. 1980 – Name changed to Orell Resources Ltd. ■

Orell Resources Ltd. (B.C. 1969)
July 25, 1984 – Name changed to Killick Gold Company Ltd.; basis 1 new for 5 old shs. ■

Orelock Explorations Limited (Ont. 1944)
Apr. 2, 1984 – Formed A.H.A. Automotive Technologies Corporation in Ontario on amalgamation with A.H.A. Automotive Technologies Inc. ■

Oremar Gold Mines Ltd. (Que. 1947)
May 18, 1974 – Dissolved.

Oremex Resources Inc. (Can. Mar. 22, 1995)
Sept. 9, 2011 – Name changed to Oremex Silver Inc. ■

Oremex Silver Inc. (Can. Mar. 22, 1995)
Aug. 22, 2016 – Name changed to Monarca Minerals Inc. (see FPsurvey - Mines & Energy)

Oremond Gold Mines Ltd. (Ont. 1936)
Sept. 19, 1960 – Dissolved.

Oremont Mines Ltd. (B.C. 1966)
Jan. 31, 1977 – Dissolved.

Oremonte Mines Inc. (Que. 1937)
1956 – Name changed to Ore Mont Mines Ltd. ■

Orenda Forest Products Ltd. (B.C. Dec. 13, 1982)
Sept. 18, 1996 – Acquired by 9753 Acquisition Corp., a wholly owned subsid. of Repap British Columbia Inc., for $3.00 per sh.

Orenda Gold Mines Ltd. (Que. 1938)
1956 – Name changed to Orenda Mines Ltd. ■

Orenda Mines Ltd. (Que. 1938)
1965 – Name changed to First Orenda Mines Ltd.; basis 1 new for 4 old shs. ■

Orenda Mining Co. Ltd. (Man. 1943)
Dec. 1949 – Charter cancelled.

Orex Exploration Inc. (Que. July 30, 1987)
May 24, 2017 – Acquired by Anaconda Mining Inc.; basis 0.85 Anaconda com. shs. for 1 Orex sh. (see Signal Gold Inc.)
Dec. 31, 2022 – Name changed to Goldboro Gold Mines Inc. (see Signal Gold Inc.)

Orex Resources Ltd. (Ont. Apr. 1973)
Dec. 16, 1988 – Name changed to Carlin Gold Company Inc. ■

Orex Ventures Inc. (B.C. Apr. 25, 1996)
Nov. 1, 2007 – Name changed to Orex Minerals Inc. (see FPsurvey - Mines & Energy)

Orezone Resources Inc. (Can. Sept. 22, 1989)
Feb. 25, 2009 – Acquired by IAMGOLD Corporation; basis 0.08 IAMGOLD shs. plus 0.125 Orezone Gold Corporation shs.

Orford Mining Corporation (Ont. May 17, 2010)
Apr. 9, 2024 – All o/s shs. not already held acquired by Alamos Gold Inc.; basis 0.005588 Alamos shs. for 1 Orford Mining sh.

Orford Resources Ltd. (Ont. 1982)
May 3, 1994 – Name changed to Afton Food Group Ltd. ■

Organic Earth Corp. (Alta. June 11, 1999)
Sept. 5, 2003 – Qualifying Transaction amalgamation with Planet Organic Health Corp.; basis 0.1300654 new Planet Organic sh. for 1 old Organic Earth sh. (see Planet Organic Health Corp.)

Organic Flower Investments Group Inc. (B.C. Dec. 6, 2018)
Nov. 5, 2020 – Name changed to Clean Power Capital Corp. ■

Organic Garage Ltd. (B.C. July 25, 2011)
Feb. 24, 2022 – Name changed to ORAGIN Foods Inc. ■

Organic Resource Management Inc. (Can. July 1, 2007 amalg.)
Dec. 18, 2012 – Acquired by Walker Industries Holdings Inc. for $3.25 per sh.

OrganiGram Holdings Inc. (B.C. July 5, 2010)
Apr. 6, 2016 – Continued into Canada.
Mar. 24, 2025 – Name changed to Organigram Global Inc. (see FPsurvey - Industrials)

OrganiMax Nutrient Corp. (B.C. July 10, 2003)
Aug. 3, 2021 – Name changed to Silver Valley Metals Corp. (see FPsurvey - Mines & Energy)

Oriana Capital Inc. (Alta. Feb. 14, 1991)
Apr. 21, 1992 – Name changed to Strathcona Brewing Investments Inc.; basis 1 new for 1 old sh. ■

Oriana Developments Ltd. (B.C. 1971)
May 30, 1980 – Name changed to Ajax Resources Ltd.; basis 1 new for 5 old shs. ■

Oriana Resources Corporation (B.C. June 9, 2011)
Mar. 2, 2018 – Name changed to Hut 8 Mining Corp. following Qualifying Transaction reverse takeover acquisition of (old) Hut 8 Mining Corp. and concurrent amalgamation of (old) Hut 8 with wholly owned 1149835 B.C. Ltd.; basis 1 new for 52.7777 old shs. ■

Oriel Resources plc (U.K. July 2, 2003)
Sept. 22, 2008 – Acquired by OAO Mechel for US$2.1986 per sh.

Orient Express Enterprises Limited (Alta. May 26, 1987)
July 20, 1993 – Name changed to Priva Inc.; basis 1 new for 2 old shs. ■

Orient Venture Capital Inc. (B.C. Feb. 27, 2007)
Aug. 9, 2012 – Name changed to Nickel North Exploration Corp. pursuant to Qualifying Transaction acquisition of mineral property option agreement. (see FPsurvey - Mines & Energy)

Orient Venture Capital II Inc. (B.C. Sept. 12, 2007)
Apr. 8, 2010 – Name changed to China Select Capital Partners Corp. pursuant to Qualifying Transaction acquisition of securities of China Dongxiang (Group) Co. Ltd., Synodon Inc., RX Exploration Inc. and Board Suite Corp. ■

Oriental Minerals Inc. (Yuk. Apr. 18, 2005)
Nov. 1, 2007 – Continued into British Columbia.
Feb. 25, 2010 – Name changed to Woulfe Mining Corp. ■

Origin Gold Corporation (Can. Apr. 20, 2012)
Jan. 14, 2021 – Name changed to O2Gold Inc. (see FPsurvey - Mines & Energy)

Origin Therapeutics Holdings Inc. (B.C. Dec. 9, 2020)
Sept. 21, 2023 – Name changed to Safe Supply Streaming Co Ltd. and continued into Canada pursuant to the reverse takeover acquisition of (old) Safe Supply Streaming Co. Ltd. (renamed Safe Supply Streaming OpCo Ltd.); basis 1 new for 4 old shs. (see FPsurvey - Industrials)

Original Commerce Split Fund (Ont. Mar. 26, 2010)
Nov. 1, 2012 – All cl. A capital and priority equity shs. redeemed on Nov. 13, 2012, for $0.445 and $9.246, respectively.

Original New York Seltzer of Canada Ltd. (Can. June 21, 1985)
Oct. 4, 1993 – Dissolved.

Orinoco Gold Inc. (B.C. Apr. 30, 1993)
Sept. 17, 1999 – Name changed to Active Assets & Associates Inc. ■

Oriole Communications Inc. (B.C. May 23, 1972)
Sept. 10, 1993 – Name changed to Consolidated Oriole Communications Inc.; basis 1 new for 10 old shs. ■

Oriole Systems Inc. (B.C. May 23, 1972)
Aug. 22, 2005 – Dissolved for failure to file and struck from the register.

Orion Energy Inc. (B.C. 1980)
Mar. 17, 1983 – Struck off register.

Orion Energy Trust (Alta. Apr. 24, 1997)
Mar. 17, 1999 – Acquired by ARC Energy Trust; basis 0.875 ARC trust units and 0.175 ARC wts. for 1 Orion trust unit.

Orion Enterprises Inc. (Alta. 1987)
Jan. 24, 1994 – Name changed to Akademia Enterprises Inc.; basis 1 new cl. A for 4 old cl. A shs.; basis 1 new for 4 old shs. ■

Orion International Minerals Corporation (B.C. May 14, 1981)
May 4, 1998 – Name changed to Laurier Resources Inc.; basis 1 new for 6 old shs. ■

Orion Mines Ltd. (B.C. 1968)
Feb. 25, 1983 – Struck off register.

Orion Nutraceuticals Inc. (B.C. Nov. 7, 2017)
July 31, 2025 – Voluntarily delisted from the Canadian Securities Exchange (CSE). (see FPsurvey - Industrials)

Orion Oil & Gas Corporation (Alta. Sept. 5, 2006)
July 11, 2011 – Acquired by WestFire Energy Ltd.; basis either 0.125 WestFire com. shs. or 0.125 WestFire non-vtg. shs. for 1 Orion com. sh. (see WestFire Energy Ltd.)

Orion Petroleum Ltd. (Sask. 1960)
Nov. 2, 1982 – Dissolved.

Orion Resource Corporation (Alta. Mar. 11, 1996)
Sept. 2, 2003 – Struck from registry and dissolved.

Orion Resources Ltd. (B.C. Mar. 23, 1984)
Dec. 11, 1989 – Name changed to Muirfield Investment Corporation; basis 1 new for 3 old shs. ■

Orior Technologies Inc. (Ont. July 13, 2005)
Sept. 12, 2008 – Name changed to AIM Health Group Inc. ■

Orko Gold Corporation (B.C. Aug. 5, 1983)
Apr. 10, 2006 – Name changed to Orko Silver Corp. ■

Orko Silver Corp. (B.C. Aug. 5, 1983)
Apr. 17, 2013 – Acquired by a wholly owned subsid. of Coeur d'Alene Mines Corporation; basis either (i) 70¢ and 0.0815 Coeur com. shs. plus 0.01118 Coeur wts., (ii) 0.1118 Coeur com. shs. plus 0.01118 Coeur wts. or (iii) 74¢ and 0.0797 Coeur shs. plus 0.01118 Coeur wts. for 1 Orko com. sh. (see Coeur d'Alene Mines Corporation)

Orla Mining Ltd. (Ont. Apr. 21, 2015)
Nov. 30, 2016 – Continued into Canada.
Dec. 6, 2016 – Amalgamated in Canada to continue with same name. (see FPsurvey - Mines & Energy)

Orlac Red Lake Mines Ltd. (Ont. 1944)
May 1953 – Name changed to Consolidated Orlac Mines Ltd.; basis 1 new for 2 old shs. ■

Orlando Corporation (Ont. 1969 amalg.)
1978 – Acquired by Wesbar Holdings Ltd. for $23.50 per sh.

Orlando Realty Corporation Limited (Ont. 1969 amalg.)
June 9, 1975 – Name changed to Orlando Corporation. ■

Orlando Resources Limited (B.C. July 25, 1986)
Dec. 20, 1994 – Name changed to Tornado Resources Ltd.; basis 1 new for 4 old shs. ■

Orleans Energy Ltd. (Alta. Dec. 3, 2004)
May 17, 2011 – Name changed to RMP Energy Inc. pursuant to acquisition of RMP Energy Ltd. ■

Orleans Resources Inc. (Que. May 28, 1987)
Jan. 31, 2005 – Succeeded by Orleans Energy Ltd. pursuant to a plan of arrangement whereby shares of Orleans Resources were exchanged for shares of wholly owned Orleans Energy which concurrently completed reverse takeover acquisition of 1133069 Alberta Ltd. ■

Orletto Capital II Inc. (Can. Feb. 27, 2018)
Apr. 14, 2022 – Name changed to Charbone Hydrogen Corporation pursuant to the Qualifying Transaction reverse takeover acquisition of Charbone Corporation; basis 1 new for 1.079365 old shs. (see FPsurvey - Mines & Energy; FPsurvey - Industrials)

Orletto Capital Inc. (Can. Dec. 18, 2013)
May 12, 2017 – Formed Devonian Health Group Inc. in Canada pursuant to Qualifying Transaction reverse takeover acquisition of and amalgamation with (old) Devonian Health Group Inc.; basis 1 new for 2.75 old shs. (see FPsurvey - Industrials)

Ormico Exploration Ltd. (Can. Feb. 18, 1982)
Nov. 23, 1998 – Name changed to Osisko Exploration Ltd.; basis 1 new for 2 old shs. ■

Ormont Explorations Ltd. (B.C. 1983)
Feb. 20, 1987 – Name changed to C.E.L. Industries Ltd. ■

Ormsby Mines Ltd. (Ont. 1954)
1964 – Merged with Consolidated Discovery Yellowknife Mines Ltd. to form Discovery Mines Limited effective Mar. 5; basis 1 new for 4 old shs.

Ornum Copper Mines Ltd. (Ont. 1952)
Sept. 26, 1973 – Dissolved.

Oro X Mining Corp. (B.C. June 4, 2009)
June 18, 2021 – Name changed to Silver X Mining Corp. (see FPsurvey - Mines & Energy)

Oro Belle Resources Corporation (B.C. Feb. 13, 1986)
June 14, 2000 – Acquired by Viceroy Resource Corporation; basis 1 Viceroy sh. for 8 Oro Belle shs. (see Viceroy Resource Corporation)

Oro Blanco Resources Corp. (Ont. Aug. 26, 1996 amalg.)
Mar. 6, 1998 – Formed Minpro International Ltd. in Ontario on amalgamation with Minpro International Ltd. with Oro Blanco the deemed acquiror; basis 1 new for 2.5 old shs. (see FPsurvey - Mines & Energy; FPsurvey - Industrials)

Oro Bravo Resources Ltd. (B.C. Nov. 14, 1986)
Jan. 21, 2000 – Name changed to Bravo Resource Partners Ltd. and continued into Yukon; basis 1 new for 3 old shs. ■

Oro Gold Resources Ltd. (B.C. June 9, 2000)
Oct. 22, 2010 – Name changed to Oro Mining Ltd. pursuant to acquisition of Oro Silver Resources Ltd. ■

Oro Mines Ltd. (B.C. 1966)
June 30, 1976 – Amalgamated with Morrison Mines Ltd. to form Ronoco Resources Ltd.

Oro Mining Ltd. (B.C. June 9, 2000)
Nov. 19, 2012 – Name changed to Marlin Gold Mining Ltd. ■

Oro Nevada Resources Inc. (Ont. July 4, 1996 amalg.)
Sept. 20, 1999 – Name changed to Martlet Venture Management Limited. ■

Oro Plata Mining Corp. Ltd. (Ont. 1936)
1940 – Acquired by Transcontinental Resources Ltd.

Oro Silver Resources Ltd. (B.C. Sept. 5, 2006)
Oct. 22, 2010 – Acquired by Oro Gold Resources Ltd.; basis 0.25 Oro Gold shs. for 1 Oro Silver sh. (see Oro Mining Ltd.)

Oro Yellowknife Gold Mines Ltd. (Ont. 1946)
1954 – Dissolved. Share distribution to Ormsby Mines Ltd.; basis 1 new for 12 old shs.

OroAndes Resource Corp. (Can. July 12, 1987)
Dec. 2, 2011 – Name changed to Fort St. James Nickel Corp. (see FPsurvey - Mines & Energy)

Orocan Resource Corp. (B.C. Sept. 18, 2006)
Jan. 3, 2012 – Name changed to Standard Graphite Corporation. ■

Orocobre Limited (Australia Jan. 20, 2005)
Dec. 14, 2021 – Name changed to Allkem Limited. ■

Orofino Minerals Inc. (B.C. Oct. 9, 2008)
Dec. 7, 2018 – Name changed to EXMceuticals Inc. pursuant to reverse takeover acquisition of EXM Ceuticals Inc.; basis 1 new for 7 old shs. (see FPsurvey - Industrials)

Orofino Mines Ltd. (Ont. 1945)
Dec. 13, 1979 – Name changed to Consolidated Orofino Resources Limited; basis 1 new for 4 old shs. ■

Orofino Resources Limited (Ont. 1945)
Mar. 19, 1993 – Continued into British Columbia. (see CanGold Resources Inc.)
Feb. 14, 1994 – Amalgamated with Nova-Cogesco Resources Inc., Equity Reserve Corp. and Hughes Lang Corporation to form CanGold Resources Inc.; basis 2 new for 5 Nova-Cogesco shs., 5 new for 3 Equity shs., 1 new for 1 Hughes sh,. and 1 new for 12 Orofino shs. (see CanGold Resources Inc.)

OroGrande Resources Inc. (Alta. June 24, 1987)
July 9, 2001 – Name changed to Volcanic Metals Exploration Inc.; basis 1 new for 10 old shs. ■

Orolea Mines Ltd. (Ont. 1952)
Nov. 1959 – Charter cancelled.

Oromaque Mines Ltd. (Ont. 1944)
July 1, 1963 – Dissolved.

Oromin Explorations Ltd. (B.C. Jan. 25, 1980)
Oct. 9, 2013 – Acquired by Teranga Gold Corporation; basis 0.6 Teranga shs. for 1 Oromin sh. (see Teranga Gold Corporation)

Oromonte Resources Inc. (Can. Feb. 14, 2005 amalg.)
Aug. 26, 2008 – Name changed to Georox Resources Inc. ■

Oronova Resource Corp. (B.C. Jan. 22, 1987)
Dec. 16, 2016 – Name changed to Oronova Energy Inc. (see FPsurvey - Mines & Energy)

Oroperu Resources Inc. (B.C. Aug. 29, 1995 amalg.)
June 24, 1997 – Continued into Yukon.
June 6, 2001 – Name changed to New Oroperu Resources Inc.; basis 1 new for 10 old shs. ■

Oropex Minerals Inc. (Yuk. Feb. 17, 1987)
June 7, 1991 – Name changed to Safe Water Products Ltd. (note: shares never traded under this name as the name change was not recognized by the VSE); basis 1 new for 2 old shs. ■

Orotek Resources Corporation (B.C. Apr. 11, 1983)
Dec. 29, 1992 – Name changed to Doucette Developments Corp.; basis 1 new for 4.7 old shs. ■

Orovero Resources Corp. (B.C. Sept. 22, 2009)
Mar. 10, 2014 – Name changed to Standard Tolling Corp. ■

Orovista Resources Ltd. (Alta. Mar. 5, 1997)
Aug. 24, 1999 – Name changed to Total Image Capital Corp. (see FPsurvey - Industrials)

Orphan Boy Resources Inc. (B.C. Apr. 5, 1995)
July 28, 2006 – Name changed to International Bethlehem Mining Corp. (see FPsurvey - Mines & Energy)

Orphée Resources Inc. (Que. Sept. 23, 1987)
Nov. 24, 1994 – Name changed to ITEC-Mineral Inc.; basis 1 new for 4 old shs. ■

Orpit Mines Ltd. (Ont. 1937)
June 1945 – Name changed to Piccadilly Porcupine Mines Ltd.; basis 1 new for 3 old shs. ■

Orrwell Energy Corporation Ltd. (Alta. 1981)
July 9, 1986 – Name changed to Harkema Industries Limited. ■

Orsa Ventures Corp. (Yuk. Jan. 30, 1998 amalg.)
July 23, 2007 – Continued into British Columbia. (see Alamos Gold Inc.)
Sept. 16, 2013 – Acquired by Alamos Gold Inc. for 10¢ per 1 Orsa sh. (see Alamos Gold Inc.)

Orsina Resources Ltd. (B.C. 1983)
Sept. 4, 1992 – Dissolved and struck off register.

Orsu Metals Corporation (British Virgin Islands Apr. 8, 2005)
June 30, 2020 – Continued into British Columbia. (see FPsurvey - Mines & Energy)

Ortega Minerals Ltd. (B.C. 1966)
Jan. 31, 1977 – Dissolved.

Ortho Regenerative Technologies Inc. (Can. Feb. 5, 2015)
Sept. 12, 2022 – Name changed to ChitogenX Inc. (see FPsurvey - Industrials)

Ortho-Tronics Medical Technologies Ltd. (B.C. 1981)
Oct. 1, 1993 – Name changed to PlenTech Electronics, Inc. ■

Orthogonal Global Group Inc. (Can. June 19, 1997)
July 12, 2024 – Name changed to Cloud3 Ventures Inc. (see FPsurvey - Industrials)

Ortona Gold Mines Ltd. (Ont. 1944)
1963 – Charter cancelled.

Orvalley Gold Mines Ltd. (Ont. 1944)
Mar. 1976 – Charter cancelled.

Orvana Mines Ltd. (Ont. 1963)
Mar. 15, 1972 – Dissolved.

Orwell Resources Ltd. (B.C. 1983)
June 11, 1986 – Name changed to International Rice Bran Industries Ltd. ■

Oryx Petroleum Corporation Limited (Can. Dec. 31, 2012)
Nov. 30, 2020 – Name changed to Forza Petroleum Limited. ■

Osage Oil and Exploration Limited (Que. 1944)
July 21, 1972 – Charter cancelled.

Osborne & Chappel Goldfields Limited (Bermuda Mar. 15, 1985)
May 12, 1994 – Name changed to South American Gold and Copper Company Limited pursuant to reverse takeover acquisition of South American Gold & Copper, Ltd.; basis 1 new for 4 old shs. ■

Oscar Resources Ltd. (B.C. Jan. 13, 1981)
July 20, 1989 – Name changed to Overture Ventures Ltd.; basis 1 new for 2.5 old shs. ■

Osec Petroleum Corp. (B.C. 1974 amalg.)
Dec. 6, 1993 – Name changed to ProAm Explorations Corporation; basis 1 new for 3 old shs. (see FPsurvey - Mines & Energy)

Osgoode Holdings Inc. (Ont. Apr. 20, 1964)
Aug. 14, 1997 – Name changed to Lasermedia Communications Corp. following acquisition of Lasermedia Inc. ■

The Oshawa Group Limited (Ont. June 18, 1957 amalg.)
Jan. 27, 1999 – All o/s cl. A non-vtg. shs. acquired by Sobeys Canada Inc.; basis $26.903805 and 0.508877 of a com. sh. of Sobeys or 2 new Sobeys com. shs. and 25¢ for 1 cl. A sh. of Oshawa. Common shldrs received $116 per sh. (see Sobeys Canada Incorporated)

Oshawa Steam and Gas Fittings Co. Ltd. (Can. 1902)
1910 – Name changed to Fittings Ltd. ■

Oshawa Wholesale Limited (Ont. June 18, 1957 amalg.)
Aug. 12, 1971 – Name changed to The Oshawa Group Limited. ■

Osia Ventures Ltd. (B.C. May 28, 2009)
July 27, 2010 – Name changed to Sunshine Agri-Tech Inc. pursuant to Qualifying Transaction reverse takeover acquisition of Sunscape (Hong Kong) Limited. (see FPsurvey - Industrials)

Osias Resources Canada Ltd. (Can. Apr. 14, 1926)
June 1974 – Name changed to Troy Gold Industries Ltd.; basis 1 new for 3 old shs. ■

Osino Resources Corp. (B.C. Nov. 22, 2005)
Sept. 4, 2024 – Acquired by Shanjin International Gold Co., Ltd. (formerly Yintai Gold Co., Ltd.); basis $1.90 cash per sh.

Osisko Development Corp. (B.C. June 13, 2006)
Nov. 27, 2020 – Continued into Canada. (see FPsurvey - Mines & Energy)

Osisko Exploration Ltd. (Can. Feb. 18, 1982)
June 13, 2008 – Name changed to Osisko Mining Corporation. ■

Osisko Gold Royalties Ltd. (Que. Apr. 29, 2014)
May 8, 2025 – Name changed to OR Royalties Inc. (see FPsurvey - Mines & Energy)

Osisko Green Acquisition Limited (B.C. July 8, 2021)
Sept. 11, 2023 – All o/s cl. A restricted vtg. shs. redeemed for $10.3157 cash per sh.

Osisko Lake Mines Ltd. (Ont. Nov. 13, 1925)
Oct. 18, 1989 – Name changed to Graph/Max Inc. ■

Osisko Metals Incorporated (B.C. May 23, 2017)
June 13, 2025 – Continued into Ontario. (see FPsurvey - Mines & Energy)

Osisko Mining Corporation (Can. Feb. 18, 1982)
June 16, 2014 – Acquired by Agnico Eagle Mines Limited and Yamana Gold Inc.; basis Cdn$2.09 cash, 0.07264 Agnico shs., 0.26471 Yamana shs. plus 0.1 Osisko Gold Royalties Ltd. sh. for 1 Osisko Mining sh. (see Yamana Gold Inc.)

Osisko Mining Inc. (Ont. Feb. 26, 2010)
Oct. 30, 2024 – Acquired by Gold Fields Limited; basis $4.90 cash per sh.

Osito Ventures Ltd. (B.C. Sept. 10, 1981)
Aug. 8, 1997 – Name changed to Sennen Resources Ltd. ■

Osler Resources Inc. (B.C. Mar. 17, 1981)
Nov. 16, 1990 – Delisted from the Vancouver Stock Exchange. Subsequently struck from register and dissolved.
Jan. 20, 1994 – Name changed to Arvida Exploration Ltd.; basis 1 new for 2 old shs. ■

Osoyoos Cannabis Inc. (B.C. Jan. 13, 2011)
Aug. 28, 2020 – Name changed to Aion Therapeutic Inc. (see FPsurvey - Industrials)

Osoyoos Mines of Canada Ltd. (Alta. Aug. 12, 1933)
1947 – Removed from Alta. register.

Osprey Energy Ltd. (B.C. Nov. 18, 1983)
Oct. 3, 2005 – Dissolved and struck from registry.
Apr. 13, 2007 – Restored to registry.
May 11, 2009 – Dissolved and struck from registry.

Osprey Energy Ltd. (Alta. Aug. 10, 1990 amalg.)
Aug. 12, 1994 – Acquired by HCO Energy Ltd.; basis $1.25 or 0.65 HCO shs. for 1 Osprey sh. (see HCO Energy Ltd.)

Osprey Gold Development Ltd. (B.C. Apr. 8, 2010)
Sept. 15, 2020 – Acquired by MegumaGold Corp.; basis 1 MegumaGold com. sh. for 2 Osprey shs.

Osprey Media Income Fund (Ont. Jan. 1, 2004)
Aug. 9, 2007 – Acquired by Quebecor Inc. for $8.45 per trust unit.

Osprey Mines Ltd. (B.C. 1969)
1969 – Shares acquired by Condor Mines Ltd.; basis 1 new for 3 old shs.

Ossa Resources Inc. (B.C. Sept. 25, 1985)
Apr. 13, 1994 – Name changed to Pactech Ventures Ltd.; basis 1 new for 8 old shs. ■

Ossian Gold Mines Ltd. (Ont. 1926)
1947 – Name changed to Minedel Mines Ltd.; basis 1 new for 30 old shs. ■

Ossington Explorations Ltd. (Ont. 1968)
Nov. 6, 1972 – Name changed to Ossington Metals & Holdings Ltd. ■

Ossington Metals & Holdings Ltd. (Ont. 1968)
Feb. 1980 – Charter cancelled.

Osta Biotechnologies Inc. (Can. Jan. 9, 2004)
Nov. 5, 2016 – Dissolved and struck from register.

Osulake Mines Ltd. (Ont. 1945)
1950 – Name changed to Lake-Osu Mines Ltd.; basis 1 new for 2 old shs. ■

Osway Explorations Ltd. (Alta. 1981)
Aug. 24, 1984 – Name changed to Jerome Gold Mines Corporation; basis 1 new for 2.6 old shs. ■

Otis Capital Corp. (B.C. Apr. 24, 2007)
Jan. 14, 2009 – Name changed to Otis Gold Corp. ■

Otis Gold Corp. (B.C. Apr. 24, 2007)
Apr. 27, 2020 – Acquired by Excellon Resources Inc.; basis 0.23 Excellon com. shs. for 1 Otis Gold sh.

Otis J. Exploration Corp. (B.C. Oct. 2, 1980)
Feb. 29, 1996 – Name changed to Sedex Mining Corp. ■

Otish Energy Inc. (B.C. Nov. 16, 2006)
Aug. 11, 2011 – Name changed to Arrowhead Gold Corp. ■

Otish Mountain Exploration Inc. (B.C. May 21, 1976)
July 5, 2005 – Name changed to ISX Resources Inc. ■

O'Tooles Food Corporation (Ont. 1980)
Nov. 5, 1987 – Name changed to O'Toole's Group Inc.; basis 1 new for 3 old shs. ■

O'Toole's Group Inc. (Ont. 1980)
Feb. 1992 – Unsuccessful in restructuring and Coopers & Lybrand Limited appointed to assist in the disposition of assets.
May 1992 – Assets sold to two private corporations. Secured creditors received a percentage of debt owed to them but the sale did not generate sufficient funds for distribution to other creditors nor to shldrs.

Otso Gold Corp. (Alta. Feb. 14, 1992)
Jan. 14, 2022 – Placed into receivership and Deloitte Restructuring Inc. was appointed receiver.
Apr. 2022 – The company's 49% interest in Star prospect in British Columbia for sold a cash payment of $220,000.

Ottawa Car and Aircraft Ltd. (Can. 1913)
1947 – Acquired by A. L. Mailman for $10 per sh.

Ottawa Electric Railway Co. (Can. 1894)
May 1948 – All other property liquidated.
July 1948 – Liquidation payments paid from July 1949 to July 1953 totaled $45.42 per sh.

Ottawa Light, Heat & Power Company, Ltd. (Can. 1906)
1950 – Name changed to Interprovincial Utilities Ltd. and continued into Canada. ■

Ottawa Petroleum Products Ltd. (unknown)
Merged with Alberta Pacific Consolidated Oils, Limited; basis 13 new for 10 old shs. (see Alberta Pacific Consolidated Oils, Limited)

Ottawa Silver Mines Ltd. (B.C. Apr. 16, 1952)
1963 – Name changed to Slocan Ottawa Mines Ltd.; basis 1 new for 8 old shs. ■

Ottawa Structural Services Ltd. (Ont. May 13, 1985)
Nov. 12, 1996 – Name changed to Forsys Corporation following acquisition of Forsys Software Corporation; basis 1 new for 10 old shs. ■

Ottawa Uranium Mines Ltd. (B.C. Apr. 16, 1952)
1961 – Name changed to Ottawa Silver Mines Ltd. ■

Ottawa Valley Sugar Refinery (unknown 1951)
Oct. 17, 1960 – Dissolved.

Ottawan Explorations Ltd. (Ont. 1946)
Aug. 1962 – Charter cancelled.

Otter Lake Gold Mines Ltd. (Ont. 1937)
1961 – Charter cancelled.

Otterburn Mines Ltd. (B.C. 1957)
Oct. 2, 1975 – Dissolved.

Otterburn Resources Corp. (B.C. Mar. 22, 2010)
May 20, 2016 – Name changed to K92 Mining Inc. following reverse takeover acquisition of K92 Holdings International Limited; basis 1 new for 3 old shs. (see FPsurvey - Mines & Energy)

Otterburn Ventures Inc. (B.C. Nov. 29, 2006)
Sept. 26, 2011 – Name changed to Finore Mining Inc. ■

Ouillette Mines Ltd. (Ont. 1945)
1958 – Charter cancelled.

Ourgold Mining Co. Ltd. (Ont. 1946)
Nov. 13, 1974 – Dissolved.

Ouro Brasil Ltd. (Yuk. Dec. 16, 1997)
Feb. 18, 2000 – Name changed to Consolidated Ouro Brasil Ltd.; basis 1 new for 10 old shs. ■

Ourominas Minerals Inc. (Yuk. Apr. 26, 1996)
Apr. 27, 1999 – Name changed to Thistle Mining Inc. following reverse takeover acquisition of Paris-based Compagnie Internationale de Developpement Minier; basis 1 new for 10 old shs. (see FPsurvey - Mines & Energy)

Out West Entertainment Ltd. (Alta. July 24, 1996)
July 30, 1999 – Name changed to SURE Print and Copy Centres, Inc. following acquisition of all o/s shs. of SURE Print and Copy Centres, Inc.; basis 1 new for 1 old sh. ■

Outback Goldfields Corp. (Ont. Mar. 6, 2018)
Sept. 17, 2024 – Name changed to Valkea Resources Corp.; basis 1 new for 10 old shs. (see FPsurvey - Mines & Energy)

Outcrop Gold Corp. (B.C. May 4, 1993)
June 14, 2021 – Name changed to Outcrop Silver & Gold Corporation. (see FPsurvey - Mines & Energy)

OutdoorPartner Media Corporation (Ont. Sept. 28, 2004)
Apr. 17, 2014 – Voluntarily delisted from the TSX-VEN. (see FPsurvey - Industrials)

Outer Edge Holdings Inc. (Ont. 1980)
Dec. 20, 2000 – Formed Vision Global Solutions Inc. in Ontario on amalgamation with Vision Ontario Inc.; basis 1 new for 5 old shs. ■

Outer Edge Inc. (Ont. 1980)
July 15, 1997 – Name changed to Outer Edge International Inc.; basis 1 new for 20 old shs. ■

Outer Edge International Inc. (Ont. 1980)
Apr. 28, 1999 – Name changed to Outer Edge Holdings Inc. ■

Outland Resources Corp. (B.C. Sept. 28, 1979)
July 9, 1992 – Name changed to OTL Resources Ltd.; basis 1 new for 5 old shs. ■

Outlook Explorations Ltd. (Ont. 1945)
Nov. 10, 1966 – Dissolved.

Outrider Energy Corp. (B.C. Dec. 17, 2007)
May 31, 2017 – Name changed to Pinedale Energy Limited following reverse takeover acquisition of 0970831 B.C. Ltd. ■

Outrider Resources Ltd. (Alta. Oct. 8, 1993)
Dec. 30, 1996 – Amalgamated with 712919 Alberta Ltd., a wholly owned subsid. of Northstar Energy Corporation; basis 0.85 new cl. A special shs. or 0.85 new cl. B special shs. for 1 com. sh., both redeemed for $1.00 per sh. on or before Jan. 7, 1997. (see Northstar Energy Corporation)

Ovansull Lake Mines Ltd. (Ont. 1946)
May 4, 1957 – Charter cancelled.

Overbridge Cattle Company Limited (B.C. 1985)
Mar. 17, 1989 – Dissolved.

Overbridge Farms International, Ltd. (Can. June 3, 1987)
June 30, 1992 – Name changed to Wex Technologies Inc. ■

Overland Express Ltd. (Ont. 1945)
Oct. 20, 1971 – Name changed to Overland Western Limited. ■

Overland Industries Ltd. (Alta. 1952)
Struck off register.

Overland Oils & Minerals Ltd. (Ont. 1952)
1957 – Name changed to Sheba Mines Ltd. ■

Overland Realty Limited (Can. Dec. 12, 1990 amalg.)
Mar. 17, 2010 – Acquired by Cominar Real Estate Investment Trust for 82¢ per sh. (see Cominar Real Estate Investment Trust)

Overland Western Limited (Ont. 1945)
Apr. 1, 1974 – Acquired by Alltrans Holdings (Ont.) Ltd.; basis $30 per 1st pref. sh., $6.00 per 2nd pref. sh. and $12 per com. sh.

Overlord Capital Ltd. (B.C. Mar. 7, 2011)
May 13, 2013 – Name changed to Avanti Energy Inc. ■

Overlord Financial Inc. (Alta. June 16, 1993)
June 5, 2007 – Name changed to Aston Hill Financial Inc. ■

Overlord Resources Ltd. (Ont. May 19, 1983)
Dec. 6, 1985 – Continued into British Columbia.
Mar. 14, 1986 – Formed Devran Petroleum Ltd. in Canada on amalgamation with Devran Petroleum Ltd. ■

Overseas Bank (Canada) (Can. 1982)
Mar. 21, 1986 – Merged with Citibank Canada.

Overseas Platinum Corporation (B.C. 1978)
May 28, 1991 – Name changed to Broadlands Resources Ltd.; basis 1 new for 5 old shs. ■

Overton Energy & Resources Inc. (Ont. 1983)
Aug. 17, 1988 – Amalgamated into Newfoundland Exploration and Company Limited (1 for 1); basis 1 new for 2 old shs. (see Newfoundland Exploration Company Limited)

Overture Ventures Ltd. (B.C. Jan. 13, 1981)
Jan. 11, 1994 – Name changed to Xyquest Venture Corp.; basis 1 new for 5 old shs. ■

Ovid Capital Ventures Inc. (Can. July 19, 2012)
Aug. 13, 2015 – Name changed to BIOflex Technologies Inc. following Qualifying Transaction acquisition of all of the assets of BIOflex Medical Magnetics, Inc. ■

Ovivo Inc. (Can. May 15, 2007)
Sept. 20, 2016 – Acquired by SKion GmbH, wholly owned by Susanne Klatten, for $4.00 per cl. A or cl. B sh. with Caisse de dépôt et placement du Québec concurrently acquiring 30% interest in Ovivo from SKion for the same price.

Owen Ventures Ltd. (B.C. Sept. 15, 1982)
Oct. 6, 1989 – Delisted from the Vancouver Stock Exchange. Subsequently struck from register and dissolved for failure to file.

Owenbrook Resources Ltd. (Ont. Jan. 8, 1987)
Jan. 10, 1994 – Name changed to Pacific Energy Systems Ltd. ■

Owenden Oils Limited (Sask.)
1958 – Struck off register.

Owens Acme Gold Mines Limited (Ont. 1923)
July 16, 1972 – Name changed to Mindeen Minerals Limited. ■

Owens-Corning Fiberglas Corporation (Del. 1938)
Jan. 3, 1996 – Name changed to Owens Corning.

Owl Capital Corp. (B.C. Sept. 27, 2017)
Mar. 18, 2020 – Name changed to Southern Empire Resources Corp. pursuant to Qualifying Transaction acquisition of mineral interests. (see FPsurvey - Mines & Energy)

Ownamin Ltd. (Can. 1953)
1954 – Name changed to Rio Canadian Exploration Ltd. ■

Oxbow Enterprises Ltd. (Alta. Mar. 20, 1987)
July 8, 1991 – Name changed to Palliser Energy Inc. following reverse takeover acquisition of Palliser Energy Corporation; basis 1 new for 4 old shs. ■

Oxbow Equities Corp. (Alta. July 28, 1995)
Nov. 6, 2006 – Name changed to MonoGen, Inc. and continued into Canada pursuant to acquisition of remaining interest in MonoGen, Inc. (Nevada). ■

Oxbow Exploration Inc. (Alta. Oct. 5, 1994)
July 10, 1998 – Name changed to Volterra Resources Inc.; basis 1 new for 1 old sh. ■

Oxbow Resources Ltd. (B.C. 1968)
June 3, 1981 – Name changed to Pasadena Energy Corp.; basis 1 new for 4 old shs. ■

Oxbow Silver Mines Ltd. (Ont. 1946)
Apr. 1946 – Name changed to Silver Arrow Mines Ltd. ■

Oxbow Silver Mining Co. Limited (Ont. 1946)
June 23, 1980 – Charter cancelled.

Oxford Cobalt Silver Mines Ltd. (Ont. 1960)
1961 – Charter cancelled.

Oxford Development Group Ltd. (unknown)
1980 – All o/s shs. acquired at $26 per sh. by private co. controlled by G. Donald Love, chm.

Oxford Equity Inc. (Alta. Apr. 18, 1989)
Mar. 31, 1994 – Name changed to Schomburg Industries (Canada) Inc. following a reverse takeover acquisition; basis 1 new for 2 old shs. ■

Oxford Mines Limited (Ont. 1973)
Nov. 1978 – Amalgamated with Babylon Minerals Inc., Solvang Explorations Limited, Firebird Petroleums Limited and Drayton Petroleum Limited to form Bab-Sol Resource Explorations Ltd.; basis 4 new for 100 old shs.

Oxford Properties Canada Limited (Ont. Jan. 29, 1953)
July 25, 1995 – Name changed to Oxford Properties Group Inc.; basis 1.2 new com. for 100 old com. shs. and 1.3 new com. for each $100 principal amt. secured participating deb. ■

Oxford Properties Group Inc. (Ont. Jan. 29, 1953)
Nov. 1, 2001 – Acquired by BPC Properties Ltd., a related company of OMERS for $23.75 per sh.

Oxford Resources Inc. (B.C. Nov. 19, 2009)
May 9, 2017 – Dissolved and struck from the register.

Oxford Resources Limited (B.C. 1979)
Apr. 26, 1985 – Struck off register.

Oxin Industries Ltd. (B.C. Feb. 19, 1986 amalg.)
July 6, 1990 – Dissolved and struck off register.

Oxnard Oil Co., Ltd. (Ont. 1937)
1960 – Wound up.

Oxus Acquisition Corp. (Cayman Islands Feb. 3, 2021)
Feb. 8, 2024 – Name changed to Borealis Foods Inc. and continued into Ontario pursuant to the Qualifying Acquisition of (old) Borealis Foods Inc. and concurrent amalgamation of (old) Borealis with wholly owned 1000397116 Ontario Inc., following which (old) Borealis was amalgamated into the company. (see FPsurvey - Industrials)

Oyama Industries Ltd. (Alta. Oct. 9, 1996)
Jan. 17, 2002 – Name changed to Shaker Petroleum Inc. following Qualifying Transaction acquisition of certain oil and gas assets (no shares were issued) from Mesquite Exploration Ltd. ■

Oyster Oil and Gas Ltd. (B.C. Oct. 22, 2012)
June 19, 2019 – Name changed to ZTR Acquisition Corp. ■

Oz Lithium Corporation (B.C. Oct. 14, 2016)
Aug. 17, 2023 – Name changed to Critical Reagent Processing Corp. (see FPsurvey - Mines & Energy)

Ozcapital Ventures Inc. (Alta. June 18, 2007)
Sept. 26, 2011 – Name changed to Strata-X Ltd. pursuant to Qualifying Transaction reverse takeover acquisition of Strata-X, Inc. ■

P

P & H Aircraft Co. Ltd. (Ont.)
Name changed to Paterson and Hill Aircraft Co. Ltd. ■

P. and M. Exploration & Mining Co. Canada Ltd. (Ont. 1947)
1958 – Charter cancelled.

P Squared Renewables Inc. (Alta. Mar. 10, 2017)
Sept. 15, 2021 – Name changed to Universal Ibogaine Inc. pursuant to the Qualifying Transaction reverse takeover acquisition of (old) Universal Ibogaine Inc. and concurrent amalgamation of (old) Universal Ibogaine with wholly owned 1266855 B.C. Ltd. (and continued as Clear Sky Recovery Solutions Inc.). (see FPsurvey - Industrials)

P2P Info Inc. (B.C. Sept. 29, 2014)
May 10, 2021 – Name changed to Pure to Pure Beauty Inc. ■

PACEpartners Inc. (Alta. June 21, 2011)
July 23, 2013 – Name changed to Vivione Biosciences Inc. (see FPsurvey - Industrials)

P.A.I. Sources Ltd. (Ont. Aug. 26, 1999)
Jan. 31, 2001 – Name changed to Titan Employment Services Ltd.; basis 1 new for 10 old shs. ■

P.A.T. Operators Ltd. (unknown)
Jan. 1967 – Acquired by Royal American Petroleums Ltd. for $810,000; comprising $530,000, 100,000 Royal American shs. and $100,000 note (which could be paid by 66,666 Royal American shs.). (see Royal American Petroleums Ltd.)

PATHFINDER Income Fund (Ont. Sept. 25, 2002)
Oct. 1, 2007 – Merged into YIELDPLUS Income Fund; basis 1.19618902 YIELDPLUS trust unit for 1 PATHFINDER trust unit. (see YIELDPLUS Income Fund)

PAW Industries Ltd. (Alta. Feb. 7, 1994)
Aug. 24, 1995 – Name changed to Northside Group Inc.; basis 1 new for 5 old shs. ■

P&P Ventures Inc. (B.C. May 31, 2007)
Sept. 4, 2020 – Name changed to ManifestSeven Holdings Corporation following reverse takeover acquisition of MJIC, Inc. (dba ManifestSeven) by way of a three-cornered amalgamation; basis 1 new for 1.3333323 old shs. (see FPsurvey - Industrials)

PBA Acquisitions Corp. (B.C. Apr. 10, 2015)
July 23, 2015 – Name changed to Breathtec Biomedical, Inc. pursuant to the reverse takeover acquisition of (old) Breathtec Biomedical, Inc. ■

PBB Global Logistics Income Fund (Ont. Mar. 22, 2002)
Jan. 17, 2006 – Acquired by Livingston International Income Fund; basis 1 new Livingston trust unit for 1 old PBB trust unit. (see Livingston International Income Fund)

PBB Venture Corporation (B.C. Apr. 3, 1984)
May 26, 1997 – Continued into Yukon. (see FPsurvey - Industrials)

PBS Coals Limited (Can. May 31, 2007)
Nov. 17, 2008 – Acquired by 7027940 Canada Limited, an affiliate of Mining Holding Company LLC for $8.30 per sh.

PBX Resources Ltd. (B.C. Aug. 19, 1987)
Oct. 5, 1995 – Name changed to International PBX Ventures Ltd.; basis 1 new for 3 old shs. ■

PC DOCS Group International Inc. (Ont. June 30, 1986)
Sept. 2, 1999 – Acquired by Hummingbird Communications Ltd. for $11 per sh. (see Hummingbird Communications Ltd.)

PC Gold Inc. (Ont. Oct. 17, 2007)
Nov. 19, 2015 – Acquired by First Mining Corp.; basis 0.2571 First Mining com. shs. for 1 PC Gold com. sh. (see First Mining Finance Corp.)

P.C. Ventures Ltd. (Alta. May 27, 1963)
Oct. 2, 2003 – Struck from registry and dissolved.

PCE Explorations Ltd. (Ont. Jan. 24, 1945)
Dec. 21, 1971 – Name changed to Pan Central Explorations Limited; basis 1 new for 6 old shs. ■

PCG Ventures Inc. (Yuk. June 26, 2000)
Mar. 12, 2003 – Business combination with International Health Partners Inc. to continue as International Health Partners Inc. considered to be the company's Qualifying Transaction; basis 1 new for 1 old sh. (see International Health Partners Inc.)

PCH Post Career Habitats Inc. (B.C. 1981)
Mar. 4, 1991 – Delisted from the Vancouver Stock Exchange. Subsequently dissolved.

PCI-1 Capital Corp. (Ont. May 14, 2008)
Jan. 31, 2011 – Continued into British Columbia.
Feb. 2, 2011 – Name changed to Curis Resources Ltd. following Qualifying Transaction reverse takeover acquisition of Curis Resources Ltd. and subsequent amalgamation of Curis with a wholly owned subsid. ■

PCNET International Inc. (Alta. Mar. 22, 2000)
Nov. 21, 2003 – Amalgamated with Technovision Systems Inc. (1 for 1) to continue under a new name Uniserve Communications Corp.; basis 0.7296 new Uniserve sh. for 1 old PCNET.

P.C.R. Industries Ltd. (B.C. Apr. 2, 1980)
May 11, 1986 – Name changed to Consolidated P.C.R. Industries Ltd.; basis 1 new for 3 old shs. ■

PCS Wireless, Inc. (Ont. Mar. 1, 1988 amalg.)
July 6, 1995 – Continued into British Columbia.
June 1, 1998 – Formed Unique Broadband Systems, Inc. in Ontario on amalgamation with wholly owned Unique Systems Inc. ■

PD Mines Ltd. (Can. 1957)
1974 – Dissolved.

PDC Diagnostics Corp. (B.C. Dec. 31, 2013 amalg.)
Jan. 15, 2014 – Name changed to PDC Biological Health Group Corporation. (see FPsurvey - Industrials)

P.D.C. Industrial Coatings Inc. (Can. July 28, 1989)
Oct. 17, 1989 – Continued into Delaware.
Dec. 13, 1993 – Name changed to Advanced Industrial Minerals, Inc.; basis 1 new for 3 old shs. ■

PDM Royalties Income Fund (Ont. May 28, 2004)
Oct. 10, 2009 – Dissolved pursuant to plan of arrangement whereby all fund units were exchanged for shares of wholly owned 7209835 Canada Inc. on a share-for-share basis and 7209835 Canada Inc. amalgamated with ImvescorCo (resulting from the amalgamation of Imvescor Inc., Imvescor Restaurants Inc., Pizza Delight Enterprises Ltd. and 045443 NB Ltd.) to form a new publicly traded company, Imvescor Restaurant Group Inc. (see Imvescor Restaurant Group Inc.)

PDX Resources Inc. (Alta. Apr. 14, 1997)
Apr. 1, 2009 – Amalgamated with Detour Gold Corporation; basis 0.2571 Detour Gold shs. for 1 PDX Resources sh. (see Detour Gold Corporation)

PEC Energy Corp. (B.C. Sept. 16, 1950)
June 26, 1991 – Continued into Canada.
Oct. 18, 1991 – Name changed to Perennial Energy Inc.; basis 1 new for 5 old shs. (see FPsurvey - Industrials)

PESA Corporation (Ont. Apr. 1, 2005 amalg.)
Sept. 18, 2023 – Name changed to ASEP Corporation. (see FPsurvey - Industrials)

PEYTO Exploration & Development Corp. (Alta. Feb. 20, 1997)
July 4, 2003 – Converted into an income trust named Peyto Energy Trust; basis 1 trust unit for 1 com. sh.

PFB Corporation (Alta. Mar. 31, 1989 amalg.)
Dec. 22, 2021 – Acquired by PFB Canada Bidco, Inc. an affiliate of The Riverside Company; basis $24.10 cash per sh.

PGE Resource Corporation (Can. May 2, 1988)
June 14, 2006 – Dissolved.

PGM Ventures Corporation (N.B. Aug. 25, 1997 amalg.)
Oct. 5, 2005 – Continued into Canada.
July 24, 2006 – Name changed to Iberian Minerals Corp. ■

PGNX Capital Corp. (Alta. Aug. 29, 2008 amalg.)
Dec. 2014 – Dissolved.

PHH Group, Inc. (Md. 1953)
Aug. 24, 1988 – Name changed to PHH Corporation.

PHL Pinnacle Holdings Inc. (B.C. June 5, 1984)
Jan. 9, 1997 – Name changed to Citrine Holdings Ltd.; basis 1 new for 5 old shs. ■

PIC Capital Inc. (Can. July 10, 1985)
Oct. 11, 1994 – Name changed to Pioneer Geophysical Services Inc. ■

PIC Pacrim International Corp. (British Virgin Islands June 5, 1990)
Aug. 2, 1994 – Name changed to Pacrim International Capital Inc.

PIC Prospectors International Corporation (B.C. July 18, 1986)
Aug. 22, 1994 – Name changed to Starx Resource Corp.; basis 1 new for 4 old shs. ∎

PICorp. Capital Ltd. (Alta. May 20, 2004)
Oct. 27, 2004 – Continued into Ontario.
Oct. 28, 2004 – Name changed to Aeroquest International Limited pursuant to Qualifying Transaction reverse takeover acquisition of Aeroquest Limited; basis 1 new for 3 old shs. ∎

PIH Pacific International Hardwoods Inc. (B.C. July 27, 1988)
Jan. 2, 2004 – Dissolved and struck from register.

PII Photovision International, Inc. (B.C. 1979)
Mar. 3, 1995 – Dissolved and struck off register.

PIMCO Multi-Sector Income Fund (Ont. Jan. 26, 2022)
Dec. 23, 2024 – Merged into PIMCO Monthly Enhanced Income Fund.

PIMCO Tactical Income Fund (Ont.)
Dec. 23, 2024 – Merged into PIMCO Monthly Enhanced Income Fund.

PIMCO Tactical Income Opportunities Fund (Ont.)
Dec. 23, 2024 – Merged into PIMCO Monthly Enhanced Income Fund.

PJ1 Capital Corp. (B.C. June 25, 2018)
Aug. 31, 2020 – Name changed to Element Nutritional Sciences Inc. pursuant to the reverse takeover acquisition of Element Nutrition Inc. ∎

PJX Resources Inc. (Alta. Apr. 22, 2010)
Mar. 7, 2011 – Continued into Ontario. (see FPsurvey - Mines & Energy)

PKI Innovations (Canada) Inc. (B.C. Mar. 1, 2000)
June 6, 2005 – Name changed to Newton Ventures Inc.; basis 1 new for 7 old shs. ∎

PKM Canada Limited (Alta. Apr. 7, 2017)
Dec. 19, 2019 – Acquired by Pembina Pipeline Corporation; 0.3068 Pembina com. shs. for 1 Kinder Morgan restricted voting sh. and preferred shs. were converted into Pembina preferred shs. on a 1-for-1 basis. Subsequently amalgamated with PKM Canada Limited, a wholly owned subsid. of Pembina, to continue under the PKM Canada name.

PKS Capital Corp. (B.C. Jan. 29, 2019)
July 19, 2021 – Name changed to Norrland Gold Corp. pursuant to the Qualifying Transaction reverse takeover acquisition of Horizon Gold Ltd. ∎

PL Internet Inc. (Ont. Jan. 29, 1937)
May 24, 2004 – Name changed to Global Alumina Products Corporation pursuant to reverse takeover acquisition of Guinea Aluminum Products Corporation; basis 1 new for 1.57 old shs. ∎

P.L. Robertson Manufacturing Co., Ltd. (Ont. 1907)
1968 – Procor Ltd. acquired over 99% of o/s com. shs. at $35 per sh., and over 97% of o/s 3rd pref. shs. at $18.25 per sh.

PLB Capital Corp. (B.C. July 4, 2018)
Nov. 23, 2020 – Name changed to Kainantu Resources Ltd. pursuant to Qualifying Transaction reverse takeover acquisition of Kainantu Resources Limited. ∎

PLC Systems Inc. (B.C. Mar. 3, 1987)
Mar. 1999 – Continued into Yukon.
Sept. 23, 2014 – Name changed to Viveve Medical, Inc. following reverse takeover acquisition and recapitalization of Viveve, Inc. ∎

PLD Telekom Inc. (Ont. 1974)
Feb. 28, 1997 – Continued into Delaware.
Oct. 5, 1999 – Acquired by Metromedia International Group, Inc.; basis 0.6353 Metromedia shs. for 1 PLD sh.

PLM Group Ltd. (Alta. Jan. 24, 1994)
Jan. 1, 2001 – Continued into Ontario.
Nov. 2, 2007 – Acquired by Transcontinental Inc. for $3.50 per sh.

PMA Resources Inc. (B.C. Nov. 26, 1984)
Sept. 13, 1996 – Name changed to Cassidy Gold Corp.; basis 1 new for 4 old shs. ∎

PMC Corporation (Ont. Jan. 3, 1969)
July 29, 1994 – Name changed to Floorco Ltd. ∎

P.M.C. Technologies Ltd. (B.C. Feb. 22, 1978)
July 13, 1990 – Dissolved and struck off register.

PMG Financial Inc. (Ont. Mar. 24, 1980)
Apr. 8, 1996 – Name changed to Printera Corporation. ∎

PMI Gold Corporation (B.C. Mar. 31, 1978)
Feb. 11, 2014 – Acquired by Asanko Gold Inc.; basis 0.21 Asanko shs. for 1 PMI sh.

PMI Resources Ltd. (Alta. Nov. 21, 2011)
June 5, 2017 – Name changed to PentaNova Energy Corp. and continued into British Columbia following Apr. 5, 2017, reverse takeover acquisition of (old) PentaNova Energy Corp., which amalgamated with wholly owned PMI Resources (BVI) Ltd. and continued as PentaNova BVI Ltd. ∎

PMI Ventures Ltd. (B.C. Mar. 31, 1978)
May 23, 2006 – Name changed to PMI Gold Corporation. ∎

PMML Corp. (Ont. Oct. 28, 2016)
Sept. 21, 2021 – Name changed to Rivalry Corp. (see FPsurvey - Industrials)

PNG Copper Inc. (Can. Oct. 4, 2017)
Oct. 19, 2023 – Name changed to Loyalist Exploration Limited. (see FPsurvey - Mines & Energy)

PNG Gold Corporation (B.C. Sept. 27, 1984)
May 11, 2017 – Name changed to GEN III Oil Corporation. ∎

PNI Digital Media Inc. (B.C. Dec. 1, 1995)
July 17, 2014 – Acquired by Staples Inc. for $1.70 per sh.

PNO Resources Ltd. (B.C. Dec. 21, 2007)
Sept. 15, 2015 – Acquired by Sandspring Resources Ltd. by way of amalgamation with 1042573 B.C. Ltd., a wholly owned subsid. of Sandspring; basis 1 Sandspring post-consol. shs. (following a 1-for-3 sh. consol.) for 1 PNO sh. (see Sandspring Resources Ltd.)

PNR Food Industries Ltd. (Ont. 1945)
1989 – Declared bankrupt. Deloitte & Touche appointed receiver.
Dec. 9, 1992 – No funds available for distribution to shldrs.

POCML 1 Inc. (Ont. Mar. 15, 2011)
Oct. 11, 2012 – Name changed to Mason Graphite Inc. pursuant to Qualifying Transaction reverse takeover acquisition of Mason Graphite Corp. ∎

POCML 2 Inc. (Ont. Sept. 11, 2012)
Aug. 25, 2014 – Name changed to Bedrocan Cannabis Corp. following the Qualifiting Transaction reverse takeover acquisition of Bedrican Canada Inc.; basis 1 new for 2 old shs. ∎

POCML 3 Inc. (Ont. Apr. 30, 2014)
July 18, 2016 – Name changed to Neo Lithium Corp. pursuant to Qualifying Transaction reverse takeover acquisition of and amalgamation with (old) Neo Lithium Corp.; basis 0.91 new for 1 old sh. ∎

POCML 4 Inc. (Ont. Jan. 23, 2017)
Oct. 4, 2018 – Name changed to MediPharm Labs Corp. following Qualifying Transaction reverse takeover acquistion of MediPharm Labs Inc. completed by way of an amalgamation of MediPharm Labs and a wholly owned subsidiary of POCML 4; basis 1 new for 2 old shs. (see FPsurvey - Industrials)

POCML 5 INC. (Ont. Feb. 21, 2018)
May 20, 2021 – Name changed to Collective Mining Ltd. pursuant to the reverse takeover acquisition of Collective Mining Inc. (CMI) and concurrent amalgamation of CMI with wholly owned 2810651 Ontario Inc.; basis 1 new for 4 old shs. (see FPsurvey - Mines & Energy)

POCML 6 Inc. (Ont. Dec. 21, 2020)
May 17, 2022 – Name changed to Lithium Ionic Corp. pursuant to the Qualifying Transaction reverse takeover acquisition of Lithium Ionic Inc. and concurrent amalgamation of Lithium Ionic with wholly owned 1000088600 Ontario Inc.; basis 0.614504 new for 1 old sh. (see FPsurvey - Mines & Energy)

PPC Capital Corp. (Alta. Dec. 15, 1986)
June 2, 2005 – Struck from register and dissolved.

PPC Oil & Gas Corp. (Ont. 1987 amalg.)
Jan. 4, 1991 – Amalgamated with Paragon Petroleum Limited (1 for 1) and Alterio Resources Limited (1 for 22) to form a new company named Paragon Petroleum Corporation; basis 1 new for 2 old shs.

PPF International Corporation (Alta. June 21, 1995)
Jan. 9, 2003 – Wound up with no assets for distribution.

P P M Development Corp. (B.C. Sept. 25, 1985)
Apr. 27, 1999 – Name changed to Consolidated P P M Development Corp.; basis 1 new for 3 old shs. ∎

PPZ Platinum Products Inc. (B.C. Oct. 23, 1984)
Jan. 20, 1992 – Name changed to Consolidated Platinum Industries Inc.; basis 1 new for 2 old shs. ∎

PRD Energy Inc. (Alta. June 14, 2006)
Sept. 2, 2016 – Undergoing voluntary liquidation and dissolution with return of capital of $0.082 per share payable Sept. 21, 2016.
Dec. 21, 2020 – Final distrib. of $0.00401838 cash per com. sh. to shldrs, of record Dec. 11, 2020, and dissolved.

PRI Automation (Canada), Inc. (Can. Dec. 12, 1985)
May 28, 2002 – Name changed to Brooks-PRI Automation (Canada), Inc. following acquisition of U.S.-based parent PRI Automation Inc. by Brooks Automation, Inc.; basis 1 exch. sh. for 1 com. sh. ∎

PRO-C.I.R. Industries Inc. (B.C. July 27, 1979)
Sept. 9, 1998 – Name changed to Extant Investments Inc.; basis 1 new for 15 old shs. ∎

P.R.P. Explorations Ltd. (B.C. 1953)
July 17, 1973 – Amalgamated with Groundstar Petroleums Ltd. and Brown Bear Petroleums Limited to form August Petroleums Ltd.

PRT Forest Regeneration Income Fund (B.C. May 14, 1997)
Oct. 1, 2011 – Succeeded by PRT Growing Services Ltd. pursuant to plan of arrangement whereby PRT Growing Services Ltd. was formed to facilitate the conversion of the fund into a corporation and the fund was subsequently dissolved. ∎

PRT Growing Services Ltd. (Can. Oct. 1, 2011)
Dec. 19, 2012 – Acquired by Mill Road Capital, Limited Partnership for $4.45 per sh.
Aug. 9, 2018 – Continued into Alberta.

P. S. & D. Oils Limited (unknown)
Holds no property; dormant.

PTP Resource Corp. (B.C. 1982 amalg.)
Mar. 6, 1992 – Dissolved and struck off register.

P2P Health Systems Inc. (B.C. Apr. 12, 2000)
Nov. 26, 2009 – Name changed to Salares Lithium Inc.; basis 1 new for 2 old shs. ■

PUF Ventures Inc. (B.C. June 24, 2004)
Nov. 16, 2018 – Name changed to AgraFlora Organics International Inc.; basis 5 new for 1 old sh. ■

PWA Corporation (Alta. Feb. 22, 1956)
May 11, 1995 – Name changed to Canadian Airlines Corporation; basis 1 new for 20 old shs. ■

PWC Capital Inc. (Can. Mar. 16, 1987)
Feb. 2, 2017 – Amalgamated with VersaBank to continue under the VersaBank name; basis 1 new VersaBank com. sh. for 54.508758 PWC com. shs. Prior to the amalgamation, all o/s cl. A pref. shs. were redeemed for $3.00 cash plus any accrued and unpaid dividends and all o/s cl. B pref. shs. were exchanged for new VersaBank com. shs. on a 1-for-2.793 basis.

P.Z. Resort Systems Inc. (B.C. June 11, 1998)
Jan. 26, 2005 – Name changed to RSI International Systems Inc. ■

Pac-Coast Petroleums Ltd. (B.C.)
1960 – Struck off register.

Pac Ed Systems Corp. (B.C. Jan. 20, 1969)
Apr. 4, 1991 – Name changed to Autobyte Systems Corporation. ■

Pac Explorations Limited (Ont. 1972)
July 6, 1983 – Amalgamated with 8 other cos. to form Lobo Gold & Resources Inc.; basis 1 new for 10 old shs.

Pac Roots Cannabis Corp. (B.C. May 16, 2012)
Nov. 19, 2021 – Name changed to Lords & Company Worldwide Holdings Inc. (see FPsurvey - Industrials)

Pac-West Industries Ltd. (Alta. 1971 amalg.)
Jan. 1, 1986 – Struck off register.

Pacalta Oils Company Ltd. (Ont. 1944)
Mar. 17, 1948 – Name changed to New Pacalta Oils Co. Ltd.; basis 1 new for 4 old shs. ■

Pacalta Resources Ltd. (Can. Oct. 26, 1984)
June 1, 1999 – Acquired by Alberta Energy Company Ltd.; basis $1.25 plus 0.275 Alberta Energy shs. for 1 Pacalta sh.

Pacaust Inc. (Ont. July 20, 1953)
Nov. 19, 1993 – Continued into Alberta.
Feb. 9, 1994 – Name changed to Titleist Energy Inc. ■

Paccom Ventures Inc. (B.C. Aug. 11, 1978)
Aug. 29, 2003 – Name changed to Vangold Resources Ltd. ■

The Pace Corporation (Ont. Apr. 26, 1966)
Dec. 4, 1998 – Charter cancelled and co. dissolved.

Pace II Industries Ltd. (B.C. Apr. 1, 1981)
May 23, 1986 – Name changed to Consolidated Pace II Industries Ltd.; basis 1 new for 3 old shs. ■

Pace Industries Ltd. (B.C. 1965)
Dec. 15, 1977 – Placed into voluntary liquidation.
1978 – Distribution made to shldrs.
Apr. 28, 1979 – Final distribution still to be made.

Pace Industries Ltd. (B.C. Apr. 1, 1981)
Sept. 12, 1983 – Name changed to Pace II Industries Ltd.; basis 1 new for 1 old sh. ■

Pace Metals Ltd. (B.C. June 19, 2020)
Aug. 18, 2025 – Name changed to Total Metals Corp. pursuant to the reverse takeover acquisition of Compton Mining Corp. and concurrent amalgamation of Compton with and into wholly owned 1532367 B.C. Ltd.; basis 1 new for 2 old shs. (see FPsurvey - Mines & Energy)

Pace Oil and Gas Ltd. (Alta. June 29, 2010 amalg.)
Apr. 4, 2013 – Formed Spyglass Resources Corp. on amalgamation with AvenEx Energy Corp. and Charger Energy Corp. and Pace Oil and Gas Ltd. (deemed acquiror); basis 1 new for 1 AvenEx sh., 0.18 new for 1 Charger sh and 1.3 new for 1 Pace sh. ■

Pacemaker Mines and Oils Ltd. (Ont. Oct. 27, 1948)
Aug. 9, 1972 – Dissolved.

Pacemaker Petroleums Ltd. (Ont. Oct. 27, 1948)
July 1953 – Name changed to Pacemaker Mines and Oils Ltd. ■

Pacesetter Mines Ltd. (Ont. 1974)
Mar. 15, 1979 – Amalgamated with Golden Bounty Mining Co. Ltd. (1 for 1), Golden Sabre Mines Ltd. (1 for 1.5), Grand Valley Mining Co. Ltd. (1 for 3) and Prestige Mines Ltd. (1 for 3) to form Golden Bounty Mining Co. Ltd.; basis 1 new for 1 old sh.

Pacgen Biopharmaceuticals Corporation (B.C. Apr. 23, 2004)
May 1, 2012 – Name changed to Pacgen Life Science Corporation. ■

Pacgen Life Science Corporation (B.C. Apr. 23, 2004)
Oct. 1, 2020 – Acquired by Taiwan-based General Biologicals Corporation for $0.0275 per sh.

Pachamama Resources Ltd. (B.C. Aug. 18, 2008)
May 23, 2012 – Acquired by Regulus Resources Inc.; basis 0.815 Regulus com. shs. for 1 Pachamama com. sh.

Pachena Industries Ltd. (B.C. Oct. 1, 1979)
June 1, 1997 – Amalgamated with CVCC Investments Inc. to form new co. with same name Pachena Industries Ltd. (see AimGlobal Technologies Company Inc.)
July 30, 1999 – Acquired by AimGlobal Technologies Company Inc.; basis 91¢ per sh. plus 1 earn-out right based on Pachena's future sales (up to a max. of 23¢ per sh.) for 1 Pachena sh. (see AimGlobal Technologies Company Inc.)

Pacific AD-Link Corp. (B.C. 1981)
July 15, 1999 – Name changed to Pacific E-Link Corporation. ■

Pacific Adera Financial Corp. (B.C. 1971)
May 31, 1993 – Acquired by Adera Development Corporation for 65¢ per sh.

Pacific Amber Resources Ltd. (B.C. June 25, 1969)
July 25, 2002 – Continued into Alberta.
May 14, 2003 – Name changed to Grand Banks Energy Corporation; basis 1 new for 5 old shs. ■

Pacific & Western Bank of Canada (Can. Aug. 1, 2002)
May 13, 2016 – Name changed to VersaBank. ■

Pacific & Western Credit Corp. (Can. Mar. 16, 1987)
Apr. 25, 2014 – Name changed to PWC Capital Inc. ■

Pacific & Western Trustco Ltd. (Can. Mar. 16, 1987)
June 3, 1994 – Name changed to Pacific & Western Credit Corp. ■

Pacific Aqua Foods Ltd. (B.C. 1984)
Oct. 18, 1993 – Name changed to International Aqua Foods Ltd.; basis 1 new for 10 old shs. ■

Pacific Asbestos Corporation Ltd. (B.C. 1950)
July 2, 1954 – Dissolved.

Pacific Asbestos Ltd. (Ont. Sept. 23, 1957)
June 23, 1972 – Name changed to Woodsreef Minerals Ltd. ■

Pacific Asia China Energy Inc. (B.C. Apr. 28, 1988)
July 14, 2008 – Acquired by Greka China Ltd. for 35¢ per sh.

Pacific Asia Technologies Inc. (B.C. July 10, 1986)
Dec. 8, 1997 – Name changed to The SunBlush Technologies Corporation; basis 1 new for 30 old shs. ■

Pacific Axis Ventures Inc. (B.C. June 16, 1987)
Feb. 3, 1997 – Name changed to Petrolex Energy Corporation following reverse takeover acquisition of Coplex Colombia Holdings Limited. ■

Pacific Base Metal Mines Ltd. (B.C. 1946)
Oct. 1958 – Dissolved.

Pacific Base Metals Ltd. (B.C. 1946)
May 29, 1969 – Struck off register.

Pacific Basin Development Corporation (B.C. Sept. 19, 1977)
July 20, 1994 – Name changed to Jersey Goldfields Corporation; basis 1 new for 4 old shs. ■

Pacific Bay Minerals Ltd. (B.C. Dec. 16, 1983)
Aug. 29, 2000 – Name changed to Consolidated Pacific Bay Minerals Ltd.; basis 1 new for 3 old shs. ■

Pacific Bay Street Systems Inc. (B.C. Dec. 16, 1983)
July 17, 1995 – Name changed to Pacific Bay Minerals Ltd. ■

Pacific Cascade Minerals Inc. (B.C. Jan. 24, 2006)
Aug. 14, 2020 – Name changed to Bathurst Metals Corp.; basis 1 new for 3 old shs. (see FPsurvey - Mines & Energy)

Pacific Cascade Resources Corp. (B.C. May 6, 1996)
Feb. 2, 2001 – Name changed to Pacific Sapphire Company Ltd. ■

Pacific Cassiar Limited (B.C. May 8, 1951)
Apr. 26, 1984 – Continued into Canada. (see NCE Petrofund)
Dec. 6, 2000 – Amalgamated with 3809579 Canada Inc., a wholly owned subsid. of NCE Petrofund, ; basis $6.05 for each cl. A and cl. B Pacific Cassiar sh. (see NCE Petrofund)

Pacific Cassiar Mines Ltd. (B.C. May 8, 1951)
Oct. 1978 – Name changed to Pacific Cassiar Limited. ■

Pacific Centre Limited (B.C. 1966)
Jan. 2, 1973 – Amalgamated with The Fairview Corporation (British Columbia) Limited to continue under the Pacific name.

Pacific Century Explorations Ltd. (B.C. July 15, 1985)
June 10, 1994 – Name changed to Goldwater Resources Ltd.; basis 1 new for 5 old shs. ■

Pacific Coal Resources Ltd. (B.C. Aug. 20, 1990)
Feb. 10, 2016 – Name changed to Caribbean Resources Corporation. ■

Pacific Coast Funding & Resources Inc. (B.C. Aug. 1, 1969)
Apr. 23, 1987 – Name changed to Alliance Resources Ltd. ■

Pacific Coast Nickel Corp. (B.C. Apr. 5, 2006)
June 20, 2011 – Name changed to Prophecy Platinum Corp. pursuant to reverse takeover acquisition of Wellgreen platinum group metals and Lynn Lake nickel projects from Prophecy Resource Corp.; basis 1 new for 10 old shs. ■

Pacific Coast Terminals Co. Ltd. (B.C. 1935)
July 1982 – Acquired by Sultran Ltd. for $18 per sh.

Pacific Comox Resources Ltd. (B.C. Apr. 19, 1983)
May 30, 1989 – Amalgamated with Samurai Resources Inc. to form new co. with same name Pacific Comox Resources Ltd.; basis 1 new for 3 Samurai shs. and 1 new for 1 Pacific Comox sh.
Sept. 18, 2023 – Dissolved for failure to file.

Pacific Concord Holding (Canada) Limited (B.C. Jan. 8, 1986)
June 12, 1998 – Name changed to Pacific Stratus Ventures Ltd. ■

Pacific Concord Resource Corporation (B.C. 1983)
Jan. 11, 1989 – Name changed to Pacific Engineered Materials Inc. ■

Pacific Concorde Capital Inc. (Alta. May 11, 1988)
Dec. 6, 1996 – Delisted from the Alberta Stock Exchange. Subsequently struck from register and dissolved.

Pacific Consolidated Resources Corp. (B.C. Nov. 10, 1986)
Apr. 17, 2003 – Struck from registry and dissolved.

Pacific Continuous Steel Limited (B.C. 1968)
1976 – Liquidated. No distribution made.

Pacific Copper Mines Ltd. (Alta. May 27, 1966)
Dec. 9, 1983 – Name changed to Pacific Trans-Ocean Resources Ltd. ■

Pacific Copperfields Inc. (B.C. June 29, 1981)
Dec. 9, 1993 – Name changed to Botswana Diamondfields Incorporated. ■

Pacific Cypress Minerals Ltd. (B.C. 1957)
Mar. 8, 1985 – Name changed to International Pacific Cypress Minerals Ltd.; basis 1 new for 4 old shs. ■

Pacific E-Link Corporation (B.C. 1981)
June 12, 2006 – Dissolved and struck from register.

Pacific Eastern Gold Ltd. (B.C. 1933)
1945 – Name changed to Pacific (Eastern) Gold Mines Ltd.; basis 1 new for 8 old shs. ■

Pacific (Eastern) Gold Mines Ltd. (Ont. Jan. 24, 1945)
Aug. 1957 – Name changed to PCE Explorations Ltd.; basis 1 new for 3 old shs. ■

Pacific 88 Investment Corp. (Alta. Apr. 5, 1994)
Nov. 4, 1994 – Name changed to Ricochet Industries Inc. ■

Pacific Energy Resources Ltd. (B.C. Nov. 20, 1980)
Feb. 4, 2005 – Continued into Delaware.

Pacific Energy Systems Ltd. (Ont. Jan. 8, 1987)
Dec. 31, 1997 – Delisted from the CDN. Subsequently dissolved and charter cancelled.

Pacific Engineered Materials Inc. (B.C. 1983)
Mar. 19, 1993 – Dissolved and struck off register.

Pacific Enterprises Ltd. (B.C. 1969)
Apr. 17, 1974 – Delisted from the Vancouver Stock Exchange. Subsequently dissolved and struck from register.

Pacific Exploration & Production Corporation (B.C. July 9, 2007)
June 12, 2017 – Name changed to Frontera Energy Corporation. (see FPsurvey - Mines & Energy; FPsurvey - Industrials)

Pacific Falkon Resources Corp. (B.C. Nov. 10, 1986)
June 29, 1998 – Name changed to Pacific Consolidated Resources Corp.; basis 1 new for 5 old shs. ■

Pacific Fashion Retailers Corporation (B.C. July 10, 1987)
Feb. 19, 1993 – Dissolved and struck off register.

Pacific Foam Form Inc. (B.C. Apr. 1, 1966)
Oct. 5, 1981 – CTO issued. Subsequently dissolved and struck from register.

Pacific Forest Products Limited (B.C. Nov. 12, 1992)
Dec. 15, 1997 – Acquired by TimberWest Forest Holdings Ltd., a wholly owned subsid. of TimberWest Timber Trust and Doman Forest Products Limited, for $29 per sh. (see TimberWest Timber Trust)

Pacific Galleon Mining Corp. (B.C. Feb. 13, 1990)
May 29, 1998 – Name changed to Prospector International Resources Inc.; basis 1 new for 12 old shs. ■

Pacific Gas Transmission Company (Calif. 1957)
Mar. 21, 1986 – Became a wholly owned subsid. of Pacific Gas and Electric Company through a sh. exchange; basis 1.5621 new Pacific Gas and Electric sh. for 1 old Pacific Gas Transmission sh.

Pacific Genesis Technologies Inc. (B.C. Aug. 24, 1986)
Oct. 1, 2001 – Name changed to Ware Solutions Corporation and continued into Alberta following reverse takeover acquisition of Ware Solutions Inc. ■

Pacific GeoInfo Corp. (Yuk. Dec. 2, 1994)
Aug. 13, 2004 – Continued into British Columbia. (see FPsurvey - Industrials)

Pacific Giant Steel Ores Ltd. (B.C. 1964)
July 12, 1973 – Charter cancelled.

Pacific Gold & Uranium Mines Ltd. (B.C. 1919)
Apr. 1957 – Dissolved.

Pacific Gold Corp. (B.C. May 3, 1988 amalg.)
May 12, 1994 – Continued into Alberta.
June 27, 1995 – Continued into Ontario.
July 3, 1996 – Name changed to WORLDTEK (Canada) Ltd. ■

Pacific Golden Spike Resources Ltd. (B.C. Feb. 4, 1981)
Apr. 22, 1999 – Name changed to Island Mountain Gold Mines Ltd.; basis 1 new for 6 old shs. ■

Pacific Great Eastern Railway Company (B.C. 1912)
Apr. 1, 1972 – Name changed to British Columbia Railway Company.

Pacific Harbour Capital Ltd. (B.C. Mar. 18, 1986)
Nov. 30, 2010 – Name changed to Oceanic Iron Ore Corp. following acquisition of iron prospects near Ungava Bay, Que. (see FPsurvey - Mines & Energy)

Pacific Houston Resources, Inc. (B.C. Oct. 27, 1986 amalg.)
Mar. 26, 1993 – Dissolved and struck off register.

Pacific Hovercraft Ltd. (B.C. 1967)
1971 – Placed into receivership; assets liquidated; no equity for shldrs.

Pacific Insight Electronics Corp. (B.C. July 30, 1979)
Oct. 5, 2017 – Acquired by Methode Electronics, Inc.; basis Cdn$18.50 cash per sh.

Pacific International Hardwoods Inc. (B.C. July 27, 1988)
Nov. 12, 1996 – Name changed to PIH Pacific International Hardwoods Inc.; basis 1 new for 4 old shs. ■

Pacific Jade Industries Ltd. (B.C. 1962)
Feb. 4, 1983 – Struck off register.

Pacific Kelp Company Limited (B.C. 1968)
Oct. 17, 1968 – Name changed to Sea-Chem Industries Ltd. ■

Pacific Kenridge Ventures Inc. (B.C. 1978)
Mar. 3, 1995 – Dissolved and struck off register.

Pacific Laurentian Capital Corporation (Alta. Aug. 21, 1987)
June 13, 1996 – Name changed to FAS International Limited; basis 1 new for 10 old shs. ■

Pacific-Link Capital Inc. (B.C. Feb. 4, 2008)
Apr. 23, 2015 – Name changed to Miza Enterprises Inc.; basis 1 new for 7 old shs. ■

Pacific Link Mining Corp. (B.C. Oct. 31, 1989 amalg.)
May 2, 2019 – Name changed to HempNova Lifetech Corporation. (see FPsurvey - Industrials)

Pacific Lottery Corporation (Alta. Oct. 13, 1995)
May 4, 2011 – Delisted from the TSX-Venture Exchange. Subsequently dissolved and struck from registry.

Pacific Mariner Explorations Ltd. (B.C. June 16, 1983)
Dec. 14, 1995 – Name changed to Abitibi Mining Corp. ■

Pacific Mercantile Company Limited (Alta. Mar. 14, 1989)
Oct. 4, 2001 – Acquired by Mercury Partners & Company Inc. via amalgamation with wholly owned subsid. 940296 Alberta Ltd.; basis 5 new Mercury com. shs. for 1 old Pacific Mercantile com. sh. (see Mercury Partners & Company Inc.)

Pacific Metals Inc. (Ont. May 7, 1991 amalg.)
June 29, 1995 – Name changed to Crescendo Capital Corp.; basis 1 new for 10 old shs. ■

Pacific Minerals Inc. (B.C. May 31, 2000)
Mar. 17, 2004 – Name changed to Jinshan Gold Mines Inc. ■

Pacific Mines, Petroleum & Development Co. Ltd. (B.C. 1922)
1945 – Struck off register.

Pacific Minesearch Limited (B.C. Oct. 20, 1982)
Apr. 20, 1992 – Delisted from the Vancouver Stock Exchange. Subsequently dissolved and struck from register.

Pacific National Financial Corporation (B.C. 1977)
Mar. 10, 1995 – Struck off register.
July 1995 – Declared bankrupt. There were no funds available for distribution to shldrs.

Pacific National Seafarms Ltd. (B.C. 1980)
Oct. 15, 1992 – Continued into Wyoming.
Oct. 21, 1992 – Name changed to StarBase Corporation following acquisition of Neurostar Corporation; basis 1 new for 2 old shs.

Pacific Nickel Mines Ltd. (B.C. 1929)
July 19, 1962 – Shldrs. received 70¢ per sh. in November 1961, and 35¢ per sh. in March 1962; wound up.

Pacific Nickel Mines Ltd. (Que. 1967)
Mar. 22, 1986 – Charter cancelled.

Pacific North West Capital Corp. (Alta. May 29, 1996)
July 13, 2004 – Continued into British Columbia.
Feb. 1, 2017 – Name changed to New Age Metals Inc.; basis 1 new for 3 old shs. (see FPsurvey - Mines & Energy)

Pacific North West Resources Ltd. (B.C. 1979)
Dec. 31, 1981 – Amalgamated with Electra Resources Corporation to form Electra North West Resources Ltd.; basis 1 new for 1 old sh.

Pacific Northern Gas Ltd. (B.C. Oct. 28, 1965)
Dec. 28, 2011 – Acquired by AltaGas Utility Holdings, a wholly owned subsid. of AltaGas Ltd., for $36.75 per sh.

Pacific Northern Oils & Industries Ltd. (B.C. 1958)
Sept. 7, 1976 – Struck off register.

Pacific Northern Oils Ltd. (B.C. 1958)
1970 – Name changed to Pacific Northern Oils & Industries Ltd. ■

Pacific Northern Ventures Ltd. (B.C. July 27, 1988)
Feb. 25, 1994 – Name changed to Pacific International Hardwoods Inc. ■

Pacific Northwest Equipment Leasing Corporation (B.C. 1977)
July 23, 1986 – Name changed to Pacific National Financial Corporation. ■

Pacific Northwest Partners Limited (B.C. Nov. 17, 1995)
July 24, 2006 – Name changed to Enablence Technologies Inc. and continued into Canada following

reverse takeover acquisition of Enablence Inc. (see FPsurvey - Industrials)

Pacific Oil & Refinery Limited (Ont. 1943)
Mar. 31, 1948 – Name changed to New Pacific Coal & Oils Ltd.; basis 1 new for 4 old shs. ∎

Pacific Paradym Energy Inc. (B.C. Mar. 25, 1981)
Mar. 2, 2012 – Continued into Alberta.
Mar. 3, 2023 – Name changed to Olivier Ventures Inc. and continued into British Columbia; basis 1 new for 3 old shs. (see FPsurvey - Mines & Energy)

Pacific Petroleums Ltd. (B.C. 1939)
1977 – Continued into Canada. (see Petro-Canada)
Sept. 4, 1979 – All o/s shs. not already held acquired by Petro-Canada Inc. for $62.05 per sh. in 1979. All o/s 5% conv. debs. redeemed Jan. 17, 1979, at 104.60% plus accrued int. Debs. were convertible into com. at $38.46 per sh. Co. dissolved voluntarily. All liabs. assumed by Petro-Canada Exploration Inc. (see Petro-Canada)

Pacific Potash Corporation (B.C. Apr. 18, 2006)
June 8, 2018 – Name changed to Pacific Silk Road Resources Group Inc. (see FPsurvey - Mines & Energy)

Pacific Precious Inc. (Can. June 22, 2018)
Dec. 1, 2020 – Name changed to American Eagle Gold Corp. (see FPsurvey - Mines & Energy)

Pacific Ranger Petroleum Inc. (Alta. Oct. 22, 1996)
Jan. 24, 2002 – Name changed to In-Touch Survey Systems Ltd. and continued into Canada following reverse takeover acquisition of In-Touch Survey Systems Inc.; basis 1 new for 10 old shs. ∎

Pacific Resources Development Ltd. (B.C. Oct. 7, 1968)
July 2, 1980 – Name changed to Nu Pacific Resources Ltd. ∎

Pacific Ridge Resources Corp. (B.C. 1980)
Oct. 4, 1988 – Name changed to Ecos Resources Limited; basis 1 new for 3.4 old shs. ∎

Pacific Rim Cobalt Corp. (B.C. May 13, 1996)
Feb. 24, 2020 – Name changed to Bolt Metals Corp. (see FPsurvey - Mines & Energy)

Pacific Rim Container Sales Ltd. (B.C. 1987 amalg.)
Apr. 23, 1993 – Dissolved and struck off register.

Pacific Rim Energy Corporation (B.C. 1980)
Jan. 7, 1987 – Name changed to North Pacific Industries Corporation; basis 1 new for 6 old shs. ∎

Pacific Rim Mining Corp. (B.C. Jan. 7, 1986)
Apr. 15, 2002 – Amalgamated with Dayton Mining Corporation to form new co. with same name Pacific Rim Mining Corp.; basis 1.76 new for 1 Dayton sh. and 1 new for 1 Pacific Rim sh. (see Pacific Rim Mining Corp.)

Pacific Rim Mining Corp. (B.C. Apr. 11, 2002 amalg.)
Dec. 3, 2013 – Acquired by OceanaGold Corporation; basis 0.04006 OceanaGold shs. for 1 Pacific Rim sh.

Pacific Rodera Energy Inc. (B.C. Mar. 1, 1999 amalg.)
June 14, 2006 – Continued into Alberta.
Aug. 12, 2010 – Name changed to PRD Energy Inc. ∎

Pacific Rodera Ventures Inc. (B.C. Mar. 1, 1999 amalg.)
June 21, 2004 – Name changed to Pacific Rodera Energy Inc. ∎

Pacific Royal Ventures Ltd. (B.C. June 15, 1984)
Mar. 1, 1999 – Amalgamated with Rodera Diamond Corporation to form Pacific Rodera Ventures Inc.; basis 1 new for 8 Rodera Diamond shs. and 1 new for 5 Pacific Royal shs. (see Pacific Rodera Ventures Inc.)

Pacific Rubiales Energy Corp. (B.C. July 9, 2007)
Aug. 14, 2015 – Name changed to Pacific Exploration & Production Corporation. ∎

Pacific Safety Products Inc. (B.C. June 30, 1994)
Dec. 31, 2010 – Continued into Canada.
Dec. 28, 2016 – Acquired by Med-Eng Holdings ULC; basis 21¢ cash per com. sh.

Pacific Sapphire Company Ltd. (B.C. May 6, 1996)
Jan. 30, 2003 – Name changed to Radiant Resources Inc.; basis 1 new for 4 old shs. ∎

Pacific Seadrift Resources Ltd. (B.C. 1978)
Oct. 31, 1985 – Name changed to Seadrift International Exploration Ltd.; basis 1 new for 3 old shs. ∎

Pacific Sentinel Gold Corp. (B.C. Mar. 19, 1986)
Dec. 1, 1992 – Amalgamated with Big Creek Resources Ltd. (1 for 1) to form a new co. also named Pacific Sentinel Gold Corp.; basis 1 new for 1 old sh. (see Pacific Sentinel Gold Corp.)

Pacific Sentinel Gold Corp. (B.C. Dec. 1, 1992 amalg.)
Jan. 5, 1998 – Amalgamated with Consolidated North Coast Industries Ltd. to form Great Basin Gold Ltd.; basis 1 new for 1 old sh. Prior to amalgamation, shs. consolidated on 1 new for 5 old shs. (see Great Basin Gold Ltd.)

Pacific Silver Mines & Oils Ltd. (Alta. 1965)
Apr. 15, 1978 – Struck off register.

Pacific Southern Mines Ltd. (B.C. 1960)
Name changed to North Merritt Mines Ltd. ∎

Pacific Star Resources Corp. (Alta. July 11, 1996)
Sept. 5, 2002 – Name changed to Virtual China Travel Services Co., Ltd. following reverse takeover acquisition of Virtual China Travel Service Company Limited. ∎

Pacific Stratus Energy Ltd. (B.C. Jan. 8, 1986)
Jan. 28, 2008 – Acquired by Pacific Rubiales Energy Corp.; basis 9.5 Pacific Rubiales shs. for 1 Pacific Stratus sh.

Pacific Stratus Ventures Ltd. (B.C. Jan. 8, 1986)
June 15, 2005 – Name changed to Pacific Stratus Energy Ltd. ∎

Pacific Summa Capital Corp. (B.C. Mar. 21, 1978)
Oct. 22, 1991 – Name changed to Pacific Summa Environmental Corp. ∎

Pacific Summa Environmental Corp. (B.C. Mar. 21, 1978)
Aug. 9, 2000 – Name changed to Truax Ventures Corp.; basis 1 new for 30 old shs. ∎

Pacific Sun Resource Corporation (B.C. Jan. 27, 1966)
Aug. 16, 1993 – Name changed to Masterpiece Quality Products Inc. ∎

Pacific Talc Ltd. (B.C. Mar. 17, 1972)
Nov. 12, 1998 – Name changed to Columbia Copper Company Ltd.; basis 1 new for 4 old shs. ∎

Pacific Therapeutics Ltd. (B.C. Sept. 12, 2005)
Jan. 12, 2017 – Name changed to Tower One Wireless Corp. following reverse takeover acquisition of Tower Three S.A.S. (see FPsurvey - Industrials)

Pacific Tiger Energy Inc. (Que. Sept. 30, 1994)
Dec. 30, 2004 – Name changed to Tiger Petroleum Inc.; basis 1 new for 3 old shs. ∎

Pacific Titan Resource Corp. (B.C. 1986)
Apr. 8, 1994 – Dissolved and struck off register.

Pacific Topaz Resources Ltd. (B.C. Feb. 21, 1983)
June 15, 2018 – Name changed to Western Atlas Resources Inc. pursuant to reverse takeover acquisition of Western Atlas Resources Inc. and subsequent amalgamation of Western Atlas Resources with wholly owned 1157818 B.C. Ltd. to form Atlas (Nunavut) Holding Inc.; basis 1 new for 2 old shs. ∎

Pacific Trans-Ocean Resources Ltd. (Alta. May 27, 1966)
Sept. 18, 1985 – Continued into Canada.
Aug. 30, 1989 – Name changed to Northern Minerals Ltd.; basis 1 new for 5 old shs. ∎

Pacific Unicorn Resources Ltd. (B.C. Aug. 15, 1980)
Aug. 21, 1992 – Name changed to Biopac Industries Inc.; basis 1 new for 6 old shs. ∎

Pacific Vangold Mines Ltd. (B.C. Aug. 11, 1978)
Apr. 18, 2000 – Name changed to Paccom Ventures Inc.; basis 1 new for 10 old shs. ∎

Pacific Vector Holdings Inc. (Can. Sept. 1, 2005)
July 16, 2014 – Filed for bankruptcy. U.S. subsidiaries filed for Chapter 7 bankruptcy liquidation in California. All officers and directors resigned.

Pacific Vegas Global Strategies Inc. (B.C. Mar. 11, 1987)
Sept. 30, 2004 – Name changed to Cathay Forest Products Corp. and continued into Canada following reverse takeover acquisition of Cathay Forest Products Inc. and 1609060 Ontario Inc.; basis 1 new for 5 old shs. ∎

Pacific Vending Technology Limited (B.C. Jan. 17, 1983)
July 10, 1987 – Name changed to Nelson Vending Technology Limited. ∎

Pacific Ventures Inc. (Alta. June 18, 1986)
Nov. 19, 1996 – Name changed to Weda Bay Minerals Inc. following reverse takeover acquisition of Strand Management Pty. Ltd.; basis 1 new for 3 old shs. ∎

Pacific Video Canada Ltd. (Ont. May 8, 1986)
May 1, 1999 – Formed Command Post and Transfer Corporation in British Columbia on reverse takeover acquisition of and amalgamation with Command Post and Transfer Corporation; basis 2.2 new for 1 Command Post sh. and 1 new for 1 Pacific Video sh. ∎

Pacific Vista Industries Inc. (B.C. Nov. 3, 1988)
May 27, 1993 – Continued into Yukon. (see FPsurvey - Industrials)

Pacific West Realty Trust (Wash. July 1, 1968)
Dec. 6, 1985 – Name changed to Asiamerica Equities Ltd. ∎

Pacific Western Airlines Corporation (Alta. Feb. 22, 1956)
Dec. 28, 1987 – Name changed to PWA Corporation. ∎

Pacific Western Airlines Ltd. (B.C. July 7, 1945)
Dec. 2, 1983 – All o/s com. and pref. shs. acquired by the Alberta Government at $13.37 per com. sh. and $52.87 per pref. sh. and a further offer of $13 per com. and $52 per pref. sh. in 1974. Subsequently, PWA Corporation acquired 99.9% of the o/s shs. from the Province of Alberta for 5,532,616 com. shs. of PWA. (see Pacific Western Airlines Corporation)

Pacific Western Capital Corporation (B.C. May 26, 1978)
Oct. 2, 1996 – Name changed to TelcoPlus Enterprises Inc.; basis 1 new for 10 old shs. ∎

Pacific Western Investments Inc. (B.C. Feb. 3, 1987 amalg.)
Jan. 1, 1992 – Amalgamated with a wholly owned subsid. of Revenue Properties Company Limited; basis 1 unit for 7.5 Pacific Western shs. Each unit consisted of 1 com. sh. and 0.5 wts. with 1 wt. exercisable on or before Dec. 31, 1992, for 1 com. sh. at $5.75 per sh. (see Revenue Properties Company Limited)

Pacific Wildcat Resources Corp. (B.C. Mar. 5, 1979)
Jan. 20, 2025 – Struck from register and dissolved for failure to file.

Pacifica Paper Limited Partnership (B.C. Apr. 20, 1998)
Mar. 12, 1999 – Name changed to Pacifica Papers Inc. following reorganization and dissolution of the limited partnership; basis 1 com. sh. for 1 limited partnership unit. Holders of limited partnership at (i) Sept. 30, 1998, received 29¢ per unit held, (ii) Dec. 31, 1998, received 24¢ per unit held and (iii) Mar. 12, 1999, received 16¢ per unit held. ∎

Pacifica Papers Inc. (B.C. Apr. 20, 1998)
Sept. 4, 2001 – Plan of Arrangement with Norske Skog Canada Limited; basis either 2.1 new Norske Skog com. shs., or $7.50 plus 1 new Norske Skog com. sh. for 1 old Pacifica com. sh. (see Norske Skog Canada Ltd.)

Pacifica Resources Ltd. (B.C. Mar. 9, 2004)
June 7, 2007 – Name changed to Selwyn Resources Ltd. ∎

PacificAmerica Equities Inc. (B.C. Dec. 2, 1985)
Jan. 11, 1995 – Name changed to SGI Capital Corporation. ∎

PacificOre Mining Corp. (B.C. Oct. 23, 1980)
Nov. 22, 2013 – Name changed to Vanadiumcorp Resource Inc. (see FPsurvey - Mines & Energy; FPsurvey - Industrials)

Packard Resources Ltd. (B.C. 1978)
June 4, 1986 – Name changed to ConPac Resources Ltd.; basis 1 new for 5 old shs. ∎

Packeno Yukon Mines Ltd. (Ont. 1951)
Nov. 1964 – Charter cancelled.

Packsack Mines Ltd. (Man. 1934)
June 1957 – Wound up. No equity.

Paco Corporation of Canada Limited (Ont. 1981)
Aug. 1985 – All publicly held shs. were acquired at $6.00 per sh. by the major shldr.

Pacolund Mines Ltd. (Ont. 1950)
1955 – Name changed to Aer Nickel Corp. Ltd.

PacRim Entertainment Group Inc. (B.C. Apr. 11, 1983)
Jan. 9, 1991 – Name changed to Evergreen International Technology Inc. ∎

PacRim Resources Ltd. (Can. Sept. 27, 2002)
July 27, 2014 – Dissolved and struck from register.

Pactech Ventures Ltd. (B.C. Sept. 25, 1985)
Aug. 12, 1996 – Name changed to Intercontinental Mining Corporation. ∎

Pacton Gold Inc. (B.C. Dec. 15, 2010)
June 21, 2023 – Acquired by Trillium Gold Mines Inc.; basis 1.275 Trillium shs. for 1 Pacton sh. (see Trillium Gold Mines Inc.)

Pacvest Capital Inc. (Can. 1980)
Feb. 10, 1989 – Amalgamated with First Toronto Capital Corporation to form First Toronto Mining Corporation; basis 1 new for 7 old shs. (see First Toronto Mining Corporation)

PacWest Ventures Ltd. (Ont. May 21, 1997)
Dec. 31, 2001 – Amalgamated with Pacific & Western Credit Corp. (PWC); basis 0.1 new PWC com. sh. for 1 old PacWest com. sh. Also 1 new PWC pfd. sh. for 1 old PacWest cl. A pfd. sh. and $1,000 new PWC notes for $1,000 old PacWest notes. (see Pacific & Western Credit Corp.)

Padre Resources Ltd. (B.C. Feb. 24, 1981)
July 25, 1984 – Name changed to Repadre Resources Ltd. ∎

Pafco Financial Holdings Ltd. (Can. Dec. 30, 1985)
Jan. 29, 1991 – Name changed to Goran Capital Inc. ∎

Page Petroleum Ltd. (Alta. 1971 amalg.)
Feb. 18, 1988 – Placed into receivership. Assets subsequently sold. No equity for shldrs.

Pageant Mines Ltd. (B.C. 1968)
Apr. 18, 1977 – Dissolved and struck off register.

Pagecorp Inc. (Ont. 1986)
Feb. 26, 1988 – Amalgamated with GYR Properties Ltd.
Oct. 15, 1994 – Dissolved.

Paget Minerals Corp. (B.C. Aug. 18, 2009 amalg.)
Aug. 9, 2018 – Formed Ascent Industries Corp. in British Columbia pursuant to amalgamation with (old) Ascent Industries Corp. (deemed acquiror) ; basis 1 new Ascent sh. for 6 Paget shs. and 1 new Ascent sh. for 1 old Ascent sh.; basis 1 new for 6 old shs. ∎

Paget Mines Ltd. (Ont. 1955)
Nov. 30, 1959 – Charter cancelled.

Paget Resources Ltd. (B.C. Oct. 2, 1984)
July 24, 1990 – Name changed to Peltech Industries Inc. ∎

The Pagurian Corporation Limited (Ont. Oct. 28, 1975)
June 8, 1995 – Name changed to The Edper Group Limited. ∎

Paige Innovations Inc. (Ont. Jan. 31, 1988)
Mar. 13, 2006 – Certificate of incorporation cancelled and company dissolved due to non-compliance under the Corporations Tax Act.

Paige Petroleum Ltd. (Ont. July 31, 1947)
1961 – Acquired by Porcupine Prime Mines Ltd. in 1960. Wound up. (see Porcupine Prime Mines Ltd.)

Painted Pony Energy Ltd. (Alta. Feb. 13, 2007)
Oct. 8, 2020 – Acquired by Canadian Natural Resources Limited; basis 69¢ cash per com. sh.

Painted Pony Petroleum Ltd. (Ont. Aug. 12, 1999)
Feb. 13, 2007 – Continued into Alberta.
May 17, 2017 – Name changed to Painted Pony Energy Ltd. ∎

Pak-Man Resources Inc. (B.C. 1982)
Dec. 3, 1993 – Dissolved and struck off register.

The Pal Oil & Gas Co. Ltd. (Ont. 1955)
Struck off register.

Palace Explorations Inc. (Que. Aug. 11, 1987)
Dec. 2, 1996 – Name changed to X-Chequer Resources Inc.; basis 1 new for 10 old shs. ∎

Palace Resources Inc. (B.C. 1983)
June 13, 1986 – Name changed to N-Tone International Ltd. ∎

Paladin Capital Corporation (Alta. 1987)
Feb. 26, 1993 – Name changed to DRW Environmental Technologies Inc. ∎

Paladin Fuel Technology, Inc. (B.C. Jan. 1, 1984)
Sept. 21, 1993 – Name changed to Prima Developments Ltd.; basis 1 new for 8 old shs. ∎

Paladin Labs Inc. (B.C. Feb. 25, 1983)
July 24, 1998 – Continued into Canada.
Mar. 3, 2014 – Acquired by Endo Health Solutions Inc.; basis $1.16 cash, 1.6331 ordinary shs. of Endo International plc and 1 com. sh. of Knight Therapeutics Inc. for 1 old Paladin Labs sh.

Paladin Petroleum Corporation (B.C. 1981)
Feb. 17, 1983 – Name changed to Fox Resources Ltd. ∎

Paladin Petroleum Corporation (Ont. Nov. 14, 1985)
Nov. 9, 1987 – Merged into PPC Oil & Gas Corp.; basis unknown. (see PPC Oil & Gas Corp.)

Paladin Resources Ltd. (B.C. Jan. 1, 1984)
Sept. 24, 1987 – Name changed to Paladin Fuel Technology, Inc. ∎

Paladin Resources Ltd. (W.A. Sept. 24, 1993)
Nov. 27, 2007 – Name changed to Paladin Energy Ltd. (see FPsurvey - Mines & Energy)

Palamino Gold Mines Ltd. (unknown)
1950 – Assets acquired by Indigo Consolidated Gold Mines; basis 3 new for 1 old sh.

Palatine Capital Corp. (B.C. Dec. 11, 2009)
Dec. 22, 2010 – Name changed to Digital Shelf Space Corp. pursuant to Qualifying Transaction reverse takeover acquisition of Pypeline Health Inc. ∎

Palcan Fuel Cells Ltd. (Yuk. Mar. 30, 1998)
Aug. 10, 2004 – Name changed to Palcan Power Systems Inc. (see FPsurvey - Industrials)

Palco Explorations Ltd. (Ont. 1958)
Dec. 20, 1973 – Charter cancelled.

Paleo Resources, Inc. (B.C. Mar. 6, 2019)
Mar. 7, 2022 – Name changed to EF EnergyFunders Ventures, Inc. (see FPsurvey - Mines & Energy; FPsurvey - Industrials)

Palermo Gold Mines Ltd. (Ont. 1946)
Sept. 17, 1962 – Dissolved.

Palermo Resources Inc. (B.C. 1983)
Feb. 15, 1985 – Name changed to Tarn Pure Technology Corp. ∎

Palestine Economic Corp. of Canada Ltd. (Ont. 1947)
1965 – Wound up.

Palisades Acquisitions Corp. (B.C. Aug. 30, 2019)
Apr. 14, 2020 – Name changed to Palisades Goldcorp Ltd. (see FPsurvey - Mines & Energy; FPsurvey - Industrials)

Palisades Nepheline Mining Co. Ltd. (Ont. 1949)
Apr. 21, 1958 – Dissolved.

Palisades Ventures Inc. (B.C. June 6, 2007)
June 29, 2017 – Name changed to Fremont Gold Ltd. following reverse takeover acquisition of Intermont Exploration, LLC and 1027344 B.C. Ltd.; basis 1 new for 1.3333333 old shs. ∎

Palko Environmental Ltd. (Alta. May 3, 2010)
Dec. 15, 2011 – Acquired by Gibson Energy Inc.; basis $3.05 cash or 0.1717 Gibson com. shs., or a combination thereof per sh.

Pall-Mall Copper Mines Ltd. (Ont. 1964)
Aug. 1971 – Assets sold to Indian Mountain Metal Mines Ltd.; basis 1 new for 8.5 old shs.

Palladium One Mining Inc. (B.C. Jan. 16, 2007)
Mar. 4, 2024 – Name changed to GT Resources Inc. (see FPsurvey - Mines & Energy)

Palladium Resource Corp. (Alta. 1986)
Oct. 22, 1998 – Struck from registry and dissolved.

Palladon Ventures Ltd. (B.C. Aug. 25, 1980)
Feb. 10, 2020 – Struck from registry and dissolved.

Pallaum Minerals Ltd. (Can. July 7, 1988)
May 30, 2005 – Name changed to Canoe Resources Ltd. ∎

Pallet Pallet Inc. (Ont. Mar. 19, 1992)
Aug. 2, 1994 – Amalgamated in Ontario to continue with same name. (see FPsurvey - Industrials)

Palliser Energy Corp. (Alta. Mar. 20, 1987)
Aug. 10, 2000 – Acquired by Search Energy Corp.; basis (i) $1.50, (ii) 0.655 Search shs. or (iii) 75¢ plus 0.3275 Search shs. for 1 Palliser sh.

Palliser Energy Inc. (Alta. Mar. 20, 1987)
Sept. 2, 1997 – Name changed to Palliser Energy Corp. following reorganization into two separate companies; basis 1 Palliser Energy Corp. sh. and 1 Petro Well Energy

Services Inc. sh. for each consol. (1 for 2) Palliser Energy Inc. sh. ■

Palliser International Energy Inc. (B.C. June 1, 1982 amalg.)
Aug. 1, 1986 – Name changed to Elan Industries Inc.; basis 1 new for 5 old shs. ■

Palliser Oil & Gas Corporation (Alta. Nov. 2, 2005)
Feb. 12, 2015 – Placed into receivership and all officers and directors resigned. FTI Consulting Canada Inc. appointed receiver.

Palliser Petroleums Inc. (Can. May 29, 1987)
June 14, 1989 – Name changed to Petrostar Petroleums Inc. ■

Palliser Petroleums Limited (Ont. Aug. 20, 1945)
May 3, 1973 – Name changed to Dundee-Palliser Resources Inc. to reflect the merger with Dundee Mines Ltd. ■

Palliser Resources Inc. (B.C. 1978)
June 1, 1982 – Formed Palliser International Energy Inc. in British Columbia on amalgamation with Tiger Oil Inc. (1 for 2.2) and Custer Resources Inc. (1 for 2.5); basis 1 new for 1 old sh. ■

Palmarejo Gold Corporation (Can. Mar. 21, 2005)
Dec. 19, 2005 – Name changed to Palmarejo Silver and Gold Corporation. ■

Palmarejo Silver and Gold Corporation (Can. Mar. 21, 2005)
Dec. 28, 2007 – Merged with Coeur d'Alene Mines Corporation; basis 2.715 Coeur shs. for 1 Palmarejo sh. plus $0.004 per sh. (see Coeur d'Alene Mines Corporation)

Palmer Industries Ltd. (B.C. Dec. 11, 1970)
Sept. 18, 1996 – Name changed to Palmer Resources Ltd. ■

Palmer McLellan (United) Ltd. (N.B. 1958)
Apr. 30, 1980 – Amalgamated with Industrial Safety Equipment Co. of Mississauga, Ontario to continue as a division. All pref. shs. redeemed.

Palmer Oil Development Ltd. (Ont. 1953)
Aug. 1955 – Merged into Rio Palmer Oils Limited; basis 35 new for 100 old shs. (see Rio Palmer Oils Limited)

Palmer Resources Inc. (Can. May 8, 1985)
July 17, 2003 – Dissolved.

Palmer Resources Ltd. (B.C. Dec. 11, 1970)
Feb. 12, 1999 – Acquired by Lyon Lake Mines Ltd.; basis 1 Lyon Lake sh. for 1 Palmer sh.

Palmetto Resources Ltd. (Alta. Mar. 19, 1996)
Mar. 31, 1998 – Name changed to Corlac Oilfield Leasing Ltd. following acquisition of Corlac Leasing; basis 1 new for 1 old sh. ■

Palmyria Resources Corp. (B.C. 1983)
Sept. 12, 1986 – Name changed to Med-Tech Systems Inc. ■

Palo Duro Energy Inc. (Alta. Apr. 16, 2002)
July 28, 2015 – Name changed to CarbonOne Technologies Inc. pursuant to the reverse takeover acquisition of (old) CarbonOne Technologies Inc. and the acquisition of Tapango Resources Ltd.; basis 1 new for 4 old shs. ■

Palofino Petroleums Ltd. (Alta.)
1960 – Struck off register.

Paloma Petroleum Ltd. (Alta. 1964)
Oct. 1, 1974 – Amalgamated with Pinnacle Petroleums Ltd. to continue with the same name Paloma Petroleums Ltd.; basis 1 new for 36,109.95 old shs.
Mar. 24, 1997 – Acquired by Sunalta Acquisitions 1996 Ltd., a wholly owned subsid. of Sunalta Energy Inc.; basis $2.40 per sh.

Paloma Ventures Inc. (B.C. Sept. 6, 1985)
Feb. 25, 2004 – Name changed to Paloma Resources Inc.; basis 1 new for 5 old shs. (see FPsurvey - Mines & Energy)

Palomar Capital Corp. (B.C. 1982)
July 13, 1990 – Acquired by a group of private individuals and Caithness Resources Inc. of New Jersey through PCC Acquisition Corp. for 41¢ per sh.

Palomar Gold Mines Ltd. (Ont. 1946)
May 1967 – Charter cancelled.

Palomino Explorations Ltd. (Ont. 1966)
Feb. 1972 – Amalgamated to form Proto Explorations & Holdings Inc.; basis 3 new for 25 old shs.

Palomino Resources Inc. (Alta. Mar. 22, 2004)
Nov. 29, 2007 – Voluntarily dissolved. Com. shs. redeemed at $0.1075838 cash per sh.

Palston Mining & Development Co. Ltd. (Ont. 1956)
Mar. 16, 1967 – Dissolved.

Pamax Resources Ltd. (Ont. June 16, 1987)
July 12, 1993 – Name changed to The Flowerman Group Inc.; basis 1 new for 2 old shs. ■

Pambelle Mining Co. Ltd. (Ont. 1946)
1953 – Charter cancelled.

Pamerica Corporation (Can. Feb. 20, 2004)
Oct. 3, 2005 – Name changed to Wanted Technologies Corporation pursuant to Qualifying Transaction reverse takeover acquisition of Wanted Technologies Inc. ■

Pamex Mining Ltd. (B.C. 1975)
May 15, 1978 – Name changed to Quintaine Resources Inc. ■

Pamlico Gold Corp. (B.C. Sept. 15, 1993)
Feb. 2, 1998 – Name changed to Pamlico Resources Ltd. (see FPsurvey - Mines & Energy)

Pamoil Limited (Alta. 1949)
1965 – Merged with Canadian Industrial Gas & Oil Ltd.; basis 1 new for 14.9 old shs.

Pamon Gold Mines Ltd. (Man. 1938)
Feb. 26, 1966 – Dissolved; revived Dec. 15, 1983. C/o A. W. Scarth, Suite 903, 386 Broadway, Winnipeg, Man. R3C 3R6.

Pamorex Minerals Inc. (Can. Sept. 30, 1985 amalg.)
July 25, 1991 – Amalgamated with Royal Oak Resources Ltd. (5 for 6), Pamour Inc. (3 for 4), Giant Yellowknife Mines Limited (13 for 2) and Akaitcho Yellowknife Gold Mines Limited (3 for 5) to form a new co. called Royal Oak Mines Inc.; basis 3 new Royal Oak shs. for 5 old Pamorex shs. (see Royal Oak Mines Inc.)

Pamour Inc. (Can. Mar. 7, 1934)
July 25, 1991 – Amalgamated with Royal Oak Resources Ltd., Pamorex Minerals Inc., Giant Yellowknife Mines Limited and Akaitcho Yellowknife Gold Mines Limited to form Royal Oak Mines Inc.; basis 5 new for 6 Royal Oak shs., 3 new for 5 Pamorex shs., 13 new for 2 Giant Yellowknife shs., 3 new for 5 Akaitcho shs. and 3 new for 4 Pamour shs. (see Royal Oak Mines Inc.)

Pamour Porcupine Mines, Limited (Can. Mar. 7, 1934)
July 11, 1986 – Name changed to Pamour Inc. ■

Pampa Metals Corporation (Alta. June 30, 2005)
Aug. 5, 2025 – Name changed to Andina Copper Corporation. (see FPsurvey - Mines & Energy)

Pan Acheron Resources Ltd. (B.C. 1968)
Sept. 30, 1982 – Formed Acheron Resources Ltd. in British Columbia on amalgamation with Citlec Minerals Ltd. (1 for 2) and Cyclone Developments Ltd. (1 for 3); basis 1 new for 4 old shs. ■

Pan African Mining Corp. (B.C. Oct. 1, 2002)
July 9, 2008 – Acquired by Asia Thai Mining Co., Ltd. for $4.50 per sh.

Pan African Oil Ltd. (Ont. July 24, 2007)
Aug. 5, 2014 – Continued into Alberta.
Jan. 28, 2015 – Formed Eco Atlantic Holdings Ltd. in Alberta on amalgamation with 1864361 Alberta Ltd., a wholly owned subsid. of Eco (Atlantic) Oil & Gas Ltd.; basis 0.323 Eco (Atlantic) com. shs. for 1 Pan African com. sh.

Pan African Resources Corporation (Yuk. Feb. 6, 1996 amalg.)
Apr. 21, 1998 – All o/s shs. not already held acquired by Golden Star Resources Ltd.; basis 1 Golden Star sh. for 50 Pan African shs. (see Golden Star Resources Ltd.)

Pan-Ajax Resources Ltd. (B.C. Jan. 26, 1966)
July 11, 1974 – Name changed to Aleta Resource Industries Ltd.; basis 1 new for 5 old shs. ■

Pan American Energy Corporation (B.C. Mar. 7, 1979)
Aug. 30, 1984 – Name changed to Pan American Minerals Corp. ■

Pan American Fertilizer Corp. (B.C. Jan. 14, 2008)
Apr. 2, 2015 – Petitioned into receivership. Boale, Wood & Company Inc. appointed receiver and all officers and directors resigned.
June 27, 2017 – Struck from registry and dissolved.

Pan American Fertilizer Corp. (B.C. Dec. 4, 2009)
Aug. 6, 2013 – Acquired by Golden Fame Resources Corp. by way of amalgamation with 0971771 B.C. Ltd., a wholly owned subsid. of Golden Fame; basis 0.3936 post-consol. Golden Fame shs. for 1 old Pan American sh. (see Pan American Fertilizer Corp.)

Pan American Gold Corporation (Ont. Apr. 24, 1967)
Nov. 21, 2008 – Name changed to Newcastle Resources Ltd.; basis 1 new for 30 old shs. ■

Pan American Lithium Corp. (B.C. Sept. 18, 2006)
Nov. 26, 2012 – Name changed to First Potash Corp. ■

Pan American Minerals Corp. (B.C. Mar. 7, 1979)
Apr. 21, 1995 – Name changed to Pan American Silver Corp. (see FPsurvey - Mines & Energy)

Pan American Mines Ltd. (Que. 1971)
May 8, 1976 – Dissolved.

Pan American Resources Inc. (Ont. Jan. 15, 1996 amalg.)
July 30, 2002 – Name changed to ONTZINC Corporation following reverse takeover acquisition of ONTZINC Corporation. ■

Pan Andean Minerals Ltd. (B.C. Feb. 10, 2006)
Mar. 8, 2021 – Name changed to NEO Battery Materials Ltd. ■

Pan Arctic Explorations Ltd. (B.C. 1969)
Mar. 29, 1982 – Amalgamated with Strategic Metals Corporation to form Consolidated Strategic Metals Inc.; basis sh. for sh.

Pan Asia Mining Corp. (Yuk. Oct. 8, 1997)
Jan. 2, 2004 – Name changed to China Diamond Corp. ■

Pan-Cana Development Corporation (B.C. Mar. 6, 1978)
May 18, 1978 – Name changed to Hemisphere Development Corp. ■

Pan-Canadian Film Distributors Inc. (unknown 1978)
Jan. 31, 1982 – Amalgamated with Cineplex Corporation and Tiberius Productions Inc. to continue as Cineplex Corporation. Com. shs. of Pan-Canadian exchanged for com. shs. of the new amalg. co.; basis 200 new for 1 old sh.

Pan-Canadian Gold Mines Ltd. (Ont. Aug. 4, 1935)
Charter cancelled; distributed 1 sh. West Malartic Mines Ltd. per 100 shs. (see West Malartic Mines Ltd.)

Pan Central Explorations Limited (Ont. Jan. 24, 1945)
Aug. 31, 1992 – Delisted from the CDN. Subsequently dissolved and charter cancelled.

Pan East Petroleum Corp. (Ont. Feb. 5, 1981)
Dec. 14, 1998 – Acquired by Poco Petroleums Ltd.; basis $2.65 or 0.1797 Poco shs. for 1 Pan East sh. (see Poco Petroleums Ltd.)

Pan East Resources Inc. (Ont. Feb. 5, 1981)
Sept. 15, 1992 – Name changed to Pan East Petroleum Corp.; basis 1 new for 4 old shs. ■

Pan-Global Energy Ltd. (B.C. Jan. 11, 1984)
May 12, 2006 – Acquired by Pearl Exploration and Production Ltd.; basis 0.1666 Pearl shs. for 1 Pan-Global sh. (see Pearl Exploration and Production Ltd.)

Pan-Global Enterprises Inc. (B.C. Jan. 11, 1984)
Mar. 7, 2002 – Name changed to Pan-Global Ventures Ltd.; basis 1 new for 20 old shs. ■

Pan-Global Ventures Ltd. (B.C. Jan. 11, 1984)
Jan. 8, 2004 – Name changed to Pan-Global Energy Ltd. ■

Pan Island Resource Corp. (B.C. 1984)
Jan. 5, 1988 – Name changed to Western Harvest Seafarms Ltd. ■

Pan MacKenzie Petroleums Limited (Ont. Jan. 22, 1973)
Nov. 24, 1986 – Name changed to Seabright Explorations Incorporated. ■

Pan-Nevada Gold Corporation (B.C. Feb. 11, 1981)
Apr. 16, 2007 – Acquired by Midway Gold Corp.; basis 1 Midway sh. for 3.5714 Pan-Nevada shs. (see Midway Gold Corp.)

Pan-Ocean Energy Corporation Limited (Jersey Apr. 25, 2000)
Sept. 8, 2006 – Plan of Arrangement combination with Addax Petroleum Corporation; basis $65.80 per cl. A sh. and $58.50 per cl. B sh. (see Addax Petroleum Corporation)

Pan Ocean Explorations Inc. (B.C. Feb. 28, 1979)
May 9, 2005 – Struck from registry and dissolved.

Pan Ocean Oil Corporation (Del. 1968)
May 28, 1976 – Merged with Marathon Energy, Ltd. to continue as Pan Ocean Oil Corporation, a wholly owned subsid. of Marathon Oil Company, following acquisition by Marathon Energy, Ltd.; basis US$18 per com. sh.

Pan Oceanic Ventures Inc. (B.C. Apr. 15, 1983)
Dec. 3, 1991 – Name changed to Falcon Ventures International Corp.; basis 1 new for 8 old shs. ■

Pan-Ore Mines Limited (Ont. 1973)
July 6, 1983 – Amalgamated with 8 other cos. to form Lobo Gold & Resources Inc.; basis 1 new for 10 old shs.

Pan Orient Energy Corp. (Alta. Aug. 26, 1997)
Aug. 29, 2022 – Acquired by Dialog Systems (Asia) Pte Ltd.; basis US$0.788 cash plus 1 CanAsia Energy Corp. sh. for 1 Pan Orient sh. CanAsia holds Pan Orient's non-Thailand assets.

Pan Pacific Development Corporation (B.C. Feb. 24, 1986)
June 10, 1993 – Acquired by Revenue Properties Company Limited; basis 1 Revenue Properties sh. for 2.7 Pan Pacific shs. and 1 Revenue Properties wt. for 1 Pan Pacific wt. (see Revenue Properties Company Limited)

Pan Pacific Gold Corporation (B.C. Dec. 4, 1985)
Dec. 19, 2005 – Dissolved and struck from register.

Pan-Pacific Petroleum Inc. (B.C. June 15, 1987)
July 29, 1994 – Delisted from the Toronto Stock Exchange. Subsequently dissolved and struck from register.

Pan Terra Industries Inc. (Can. Mar. 31, 2004 amalg.)
Apr. 30, 2012 – Name changed to Kombat Copper Inc. ■

Pan Western Oils Ltd. (Alta. 1948)
1958 – Acquired by United Canso Oil & Gas Ltd.; basis 1 new for 6 old shs.

Pan World Ventures Inc. (B.C. Feb. 9, 1983)
Feb. 3, 1997 – Name changed to Weymin Mining Corporation; basis 1 new for 5 old shs. ■

Panacan Minerals & Oils Ltd. (Que. 1974 amalg.)
1975 – All assets sold to Sackville Oils & Minerals Ltd. in consideration for 1,836,973 Sackville shs. which were distributed to co.'s shldrs. Charter surrendered.

Panacan Resources Ltd. (Que. 1965)
1974 – Amalgamated with Mustang Mines Limited to form Panacan Minerals & Oils Ltd.; basis 1 new for 3 old shs.

Panacea Mining and Exploration Ltd. (Ont. 1968)
Mar. 1976 – Charter cancelled.

Panache Resources Inc. (B.C. June 26, 1986)
July 16, 1991 – Name changed to Caprice-Greystoke Enterprises Ltd.; basis 1 new for 3 old shs. ■

PanAfrican Energy Corporation Ltd. (Jersey Apr. 25, 2000)
Aug. 14, 2001 – Name changed to Pan-Ocean Energy Corporation Limited. ■

Panama Mines Ltd. (B.C. 1964)
June 4, 1980 – Name changed to Panama Resources Ltd. ■

Panama Resources Ltd. (B.C. 1964)
Apr. 7, 1986 – Amalgamated into Freedom Marine Ltd.; basis sh. for sh.

Panamerican Ventures Ltd. (Can. Dec. 1, 1955)
1958 – Name changed to Westfield Minerals Limited. ■

Panamex Resources Inc. (B.C. June 12, 1996)
May 28, 2002 – Name changed to Ross River Minerals Inc. pursuant to reverse takeover acquisition of Ross River Gold Ltd.; basis 1 new for 5 old shs. (see FPsurvey - Mines & Energy)

Panarctic Oils Ltd. (Can. May 27, 1966)
Dec. 15, 2000 – Dissolved.

Panarim Resources Inc. (B.C. July 24, 1987)
Dec. 7, 1994 – Name changed to Kismet Ventures Inc.; basis 1 new for 9 old shs. ■

Panasoni Energy Corp. (B.C. 1979)
Feb. 23, 1990 – Dissolved.

PanAtlas Energy Inc. (Ont. Jan. 4, 1945)
June 1, 1998 – Continued into Alberta. (see Velvet Exploration Inc.)
July 18, 2000 – Acquired by Velvet Exploration Ltd.; basis $3.72 or 0.70857 Velvet shs. for 1 PanAtlas sh. (see Velvet Exploration Ltd.)

Pancake Lake Copper Mines Ltd. (Ont. 1965)
Oct. 1981 – Charter cancelled; revived in October 1981.
1981 – Classified as private.
Nov. 26, 1994 – Dissolved and struck off register.

Pancan Oils Ltd. (Alta.)
1960 – Struck off register.

Pancana Industries Ltd. (Alta. 1949)
July 3, 1975 – Amalgamated with 3 Sons Investments Ltd.

Pancana Industries Ltd. (Alta. 1975 amalg.)
Jan. 31, 1980 – Name changed to PanCana Resources Ltd. ■

Pancana Minerals Ltd. (Can. 1985)
Jan. 16, 1987 – Formed to hold mineral assets of PanCana Resources Ltd. and to retain public company status under the takeover of PanCana by Geocrude. All o/s shs. were acquired by American Barrick Resources Corporation under its takeover offer of $9.50 or 0.476 com. shs. of Barrick for each o/s sh.

PanCana Resources Ltd. (Alta. 1975 amalg.)
July 1982 – Acquired by Geocrude Energy Inc.; basis 1.94 Geocrude shs. for 1 PanCana cl. A or B sh. PanCana pref. shs. were exchanged sh.-for-sh. for Geocrude convertible pref. shs. (1.94 com. for 1 pref.). (see Geocrude Energy Inc.)

PanCanadian Energy Corporation (Can. June 26, 2001)
Apr. 5, 2002 – Name changed to Encana Corporation pursuant to plan of arrangement indirect acquisition of Alberta Energy Company Ltd. ■

PanCanadian Petroleum Limited (Alta. July 11, 1947)
Dec. 31, 1971 – Amalgamated with wholly owned Canadian Pacific Oil and Gas Limited to form new co. with same name PanCanadian Petroleum Limited
Oct. 3, 2001 – Name changed to PanCanadian Energy Corporation pursuant to plan of arrangement reorganization of Canadian Pacific Limited (CPL) whereby public shldrs. of PanCanadian Petroleum (PCP) exchanged their shs. for shs. of PanCanadian Energy Corporation (PCE), incorporated on June 26, 2001, on a 1-for-1 basis and CPL's 85.6% equity ownership in PCP was distributed to CPL shldrs. in the form of PCE shs. on a 0.684-for-1 basis. ■

Panco Poultry Ltd. (B.C. 1965)
Apr. 1969 – Acquired by Federal Grain Ltd.; basis $59 per pref. sh. and $29.50 per com. sh.

Pancontinental Energy Inc. (Alta. Feb. 26, 1986)
July 12, 2007 – Name changed to Immunall Science Inc. pursuant to reverse takeover acquisition of Immunall Scientific Inc. ■

Pancontinental Gold Corporation (Can. Sept. 7, 2007)
July 12, 2018 – Name changed to Pancontinental Resources Corporation. ■

Pancontinental Marketing Corporation (Alta. Apr. 19, 1996)
Dec. 24, 1999 – Name changed to OnSat.net Canada Inc. ■

Pancontinental Oil Ltd. (Alta. Feb. 12, 1979)
Aug. 14, 1991 – Acquired by Inverness Petroleum Ltd.; basis 0.975 Inverness shs. for 1 Pancontinental sh. (see Inverness Petroleum Ltd.)

Pancontinental Resources Corporation (Can. Sept. 7, 2007)
Mar. 2, 2023 – Name changed to Carolina Rush Corporation; basis 1 new for 10 old shs. (see FPsurvey - Mines & Energy)

Pancontinental Uranium Corporation (Can. Sept. 7, 2007)
July 25, 2016 – Name changed to Pancontinental Gold Corporation. ■

Panda Capital Inc. (Can. Apr. 12, 2007)
May 3, 2017 – Name changed to ABcann Global Corporation. ■

Pandora Cadillac Gold Mines Ltd. (Ont. 1936)
Acquired by Belleroche Mines Ltd.; basis 1 new for 20 old shs.

Pandora Industries Inc. (B.C. Aug. 5, 1977)
Mar. 3, 2000 – Name changed to Georgia Ventures Inc.; basis 1 new for 8 old shs. ■

Panel Consolidated Uranium Mines Ltd. (Ont. 1954)
1956 – Merged into Northspan Uranium Mines Ltd.; basis 2 new for 7 old shs.

Panet Metals Corp. Ltd. (Que. 1953)
June 1974 – Charter cancelled.

Panex Resources Ltd. (B.C. 1970)
Dec. 18, 1978 – Dissolved.

Pangea Goldfields Inc. (Ont. June 3, 1985)
Aug. 4, 2000 – Acquired by Barrick Gold Corporation; basis $7.00 per sh. (see Barrick Gold Corporation)

PanGeo Pharma Inc. (Can. Sept. 21, 2000)
Jan. 9, 2006 – Name changed to Silvio Ventures Inc.; basis 1 new for 25 old shs. ■

PanGlobel.com Inc. (Alta. Mar. 8, 2000)
Jan. 31, 2002 – Formed Coyotenet Communications Group Inc. in Alberta on Qualifying Transaction amalgamation with Coyotenet Inc. (deemed acquiror); basis 0.647064 new shs. for 1 Coyotenet Inc. sh. and 1 new sh. for 1 PanGlobel.com sh. ■

Pango Gold Mines Ltd. (Ont. 1959)
Dec. 30, 1985 – Formed Canhorn Mining Corporation in Ontario on amalgamation with 3 other cos.; basis 1 new for 6 old shs. ■

Panhandle Eastern Corporation (Del. 1929)
Apr. 26, 1996 – Name changed to PanEnergy Corp.

Panhandle Resources Corp. (Alta. Aug. 31, 1984)
Jan. 27, 1993 – Name changed to Abacan Resource Corporation. ■

Pannex Industries Inc. (Alta. Mar. 21, 1986)
Sept. 1, 1997 – Struck off register.

Pannonia Ventures Corp. (B.C. Apr. 3, 2007)
Feb. 2, 2012 – Name changed to First Americas Gold Corporation pursuant to Qualifying Transaction acquisition of gold basin prospect in Mohave cty., Ariz. ■

PanOil Resources Ltd. (Alta. Apr. 21, 1993)
Jan. 17, 2000 – Acquired by Caravan Oil & Gas Ltd.; basis 1 com. sh. plus 0.5 wt. of Caravan for 7 old PanOil shs. (see Caravan Oil & Gas Ltd.)

Panorama Petroleum Inc. (B.C. Sept. 18, 1984)
Apr. 6, 2017 – Name changed to Stamper Oil & Gas Corp.; basis 1 new for 5.5 old shs. (see FPsurvey - Mines & Energy)

Panorama Petroleums Ltd. (B.C. Feb. 19, 1980)
Nov. 18, 1987 – Name changed to Panorama Resources Ltd. ■

Panorama Resources Ltd. (B.C. Feb. 19, 1980)
Apr. 14, 1993 – Name changed to International Panorama Resource Corp.; basis 1 new for 5 old shs. ■

Panorama Resources Ltd. (B.C. Dec. 19, 2005)
Mar. 9, 2011 – Formed Ethiopian Potash Corp. in Ontario on amalgamation with Ethiopian Potash Corp., constituting a reverse takeover by Ethiopian. ■

Panorama Resources NL (Australia Apr. 19, 1990)
May 12, 1998 – Merged with Tanganyika Gold NL; basis 3 new Tanganyika shs. for 4 old Panorama shs.

Panorama Trading Company Ltd. (Alta. Apr. 28, 1964)
May 21, 1993 – Name changed to Perfect Fry Corporation. ■

Panoramic Care Manager, Inc. (Colo. Sept. 4, 1990)
Apr. 27, 1999 – Name changed to Panoramic Care Systems, Inc. and continued into Delaware. ■

Panoramic Care Systems, Inc. (Del. Apr. 27, 1999)
Aug. 13, 2001 – Name changed to MDI Technologies, Inc. ■

Panoramic Mirrors Inc. (B.C. June 5, 1998)
June 16, 2005 – Name changed to GLG Life Tech Limited pursuant to reverse takeover acquisition of Grand Leaf International Ltd. ■

Panoray Foods Limited (Ont. 1968)
Oct. 19, 1976 – Dissolved.

Pantan Mines Ltd. (Ont. 1951)
1964 – Absorbed by Medallion Mines Ltd.

Pantan Resources Ltd. (Can. May 15, 1987)
Feb. 6, 1992 – Name changed to Greenwood Environmental Inc. ■

Pantera Drilling Income Trust (Alta. June 9, 2005)
Dec. 24, 2010 – Acquired by Western Energy Services Corp.; basis 21.9048 Western com. shs. for 1 Pantera com. sh.

Pantera Enterprises Inc. (Alta. Aug. 28, 1998)
Nov. 29, 2002 – Name changed to Mill City International Corporation following Qualifying Transaction reverse takeover acquisition of 977877 Alberta Inc. ■

Panterra Energy Inc. (B.C. Jan. 9, 1979)
Feb. 11, 1993 – Name changed to Enrich Ventures Ltd.; basis 1 new for 4.3 old shs. ■

PanTerra Exploration Corp. (B.C. Oct. 18, 1979)
Sept. 1, 2004 – Name changed to PanTerra Resource Corp.; basis 1 new for 2 old shs. ■

Panterra Minerals Inc. (B.C. Feb. 4, 1986)
May 1, 2001 – Name changed to Neodym Technologies Inc. following reverse takeover acquisition of Neodym Systems Inc.; basis 1 new for 4 old shs. ■

PanTerra Resource Corp. (B.C. Oct. 18, 1979)
Oct. 27, 2005 – Continued into Alberta.
Sept. 19, 2014 – Name changed to Ikkuma Resources Corp.; basis 1 new for 10 old shs. ■

Panthco Resources Inc. (Ont. 1960)
July 1, 1996 – Formed ZTEST Electronics Inc. in Ontario on amalgamation with ZTEST Electronics Inc., constituting a reverse takeover by ZTEST; basis 1 new for 1 ZTEST sh. and 1 new com. and 1 new cl. A special for 8 old shs. (see FPsurvey - Industrials)

Pantheon Ventures Ltd. (B.C. Dec. 28, 2006)
June 15, 2016 – Name changed to Moovly Media Inc. pursuant to reverse takeover acquisition of Moovly N.V.; basis 1 new for 1.5 old shs. (see FPsurvey - Industrials)

Panther International Mining Co. Ltd. (Ont. 1958)
1960 – Merged into Consolidated Panther Mines Ltd.; basis 3 new for 4 old shs.

Panther Mines Ltd. (B.C. 1968)
Oct. 23, 2006 – Dissolved and struck from register.

Panthera Exploration Inc. (B.C. Apr. 11, 2000)
Feb. 28, 2012 – Name changed to Iron South Mining Corp. ■

Pantorama Industries Inc. (Can. Mar. 31, 1976)
Mar. 5, 2004 – Privatized at 80¢ per sh.

PanWestern Energy Inc. (Alta. June 7, 2000)
July 6, 2010 – Name changed to Valeura Energy Inc. following reverse takeover acquisition of Northern Hunter Energy Inc.; basis 1 new for 4.5 old shs. (see FPsurvey - Mines & Energy)

Paperboard Industries Corporation Inc. (Ont. 1977)
Nov. 12, 1986 – Amalgamated with wholly owned Paperboard Industries Corporation to continue with the same name Paperboard Industries Corporation Inc.
1987 – Acquired by Kinburn Industrial Corp. for $12 per sh.

Paperboard Industries International Inc. (Can. Dec. 28, 1978)
Jan. 8, 2001 – Amalgamation of Perkins Papers Ltd., Rolland inc. and Cascades Inc.; basis 0.24 new for 1 old sh.
Apr. 15, 2002 – Name changed to Cascades Boxboard Group Inc.

Papineau Mica Mines Ltd. (Que. 1941)
1942 – Assets acquired by A. W. White Mica Ltd. (see A. W. White Mica Ltd.)

Papoose Yellowknife Mines Ltd. (Ont. 1945)
Oct. 21, 1957 – Charter cancelled.

Papuan Precious Metals Corp. (B.C. Sept. 29, 2010 amalg.)
Apr. 20, 2015 – Name changed to Ironside Resources Inc. ■

Paquin Gold Mines Ltd. (Que. 1942)
1961 – Properties reported taken over by Belleterre Quebec Mines as payment for debts. Charter surrendered.

Para Red Lake Mines Ltd. (Ont. 1945)
May 6, 1980 – Charter cancelled.

Para Resources Inc. (B.C. Apr. 13, 2010)
May 8, 2020 – Name changed to Soma Gold Corp.; basis 1 new for 10 old shs. (see FPsurvey - Mines & Energy)

Para-Tech Energy Corporation (Alta. Dec. 16, 1996 amalg.)
Sept. 28, 1998 – Name changed to Para-Tech Energy Services Inc. (see FPsurvey - Mines & Energy)

Para Uranium Ltd. (B.C. 1954)
Feb. 12, 1959 – Dissolved.

Paracomp Technologies Inc. (B.C. 1985)
Feb. 26, 1993 – Dissolved and struck off register.

Paracorp Ltd. (Alta. 1952)
July 1, 1992 – Struck off register.

Paradise Petroleums Inc. (Alta. 1987)
July 19, 1988 – Name changed to Santa Fe Energy Group Inc.; basis 1 new for 4 old shs. ■

Paradym Ventures Inc. (B.C. Mar. 25, 1981)
Oct. 1, 2007 – Name changed to Pacific Paradym Energy Inc.; basis 1 new for 4 old shs. ■

Paragon Entertainment Corporation (Ont. 1985)
Aug. 8, 2005 – Dissolved and struck from register.

Paragon Explorations Limited (Ont. 1927)
Oct. 16, 1983 – Name changed to Sagewood Resources Limited; basis 1 Sagewood pref. for 1 Paragon com. sh. ■

Paragon Minerals Corporation (Can. July 4, 2006)
Sept. 25, 2012 – Acquired by 8209103 Canada Ltd., a wholly owned subsid. of Canadian Zinc Corporation; basis 0.136 Canadian Zinc shs. for 1 Paragon sh. (see Canadian Zinc Corporation)

Paragon Petroleum Corporation (Alta. Jan. 1, 1991 amalg.)
Mar. 27, 1998 – All o/s com. shs. acquired by Northrock Resources Ltd.; basis $4.10 or 0.19 of a com. sh. of Northrock or a combination thereof for 1 com. sh. of Paragon. (see Northrock Resources Ltd.)

Paragon Petroleum Limited (Alta. Aug. 16, 1983)
Jan. 4, 1991 – Amalgamated with PPC Oil & Gas Corp. (1 for 2) and Alterio Resources Limited (1 for 22) to form a new company called Paragon Petroleum Corporation; basis 1 new for 1 old sh. (see Paragon Petroleum Corporation)

Paragon Pharmacies Limited (Alta. Oct. 31, 2006 amalg.)
Aug. 29, 2008 – Amalgamated in Alberta to continue with same name.
Aug. 3, 2012 – Name changed to PGNX Capital Corp. ■

Paragon Properties Ltd. (Alta. 1968)
1974 – Acquired by Daon Development Corp.; basis 678,713 shs. for $3.27 per sh. and 269,229 shs. for $5.22 per sh.

Paragon Resources Ltd. (B.C. Dec. 15, 1967)
Sept. 11, 1995 – Name changed to Samex Mining Corp.; basis 1 new for 5 old shs. ■

Parallel Capital Corp. (B.C. Apr. 18, 2007)
Dec. 17, 2009 – Name changed to Parallel Resources Ltd. following Qualifying Transaction mineral property option acquisition on Sept. 25, 2009. ■

Parallel Energy Trust (Alta. Mar. 10, 2011)
Mar. 3, 2016 – Filed an assignment in bankruptcy. KPMG Inc. was appointed trustee and all officers and directors resigned. Was anticipated that no distributions would be made to unsecured creditors or shldrs. ■

Parallel Resources Ltd. (B.C. Apr. 18, 2007)
Dec. 19, 2011 – Name changed to Parallel Mining Corp.; basis 1 new for 4.5 old shs. (see FPsurvey - Mines & Energy)

Paramaque Mines Ltd. (Ont. 1944)
Nov. 28, 1973 – Charter cancelled.

Paramax Resources Ltd. (Alta. Mar. 17, 1997)
June 17, 1998 – Continued into British Columbia.
June 5, 2013 – Name changed to Sabre Graphite Corp. following amalgamation of MEGA Graphite Inc. with a wholly owned subsidiary of Paramax, with Paramax the deemed acquiror; basis 1 new for 1 Paramax sh. and 1 new for 9.401471 MEGA Graphite shs. ■

Parametric Ventures Inc. (B.C. June 9, 1981)
Nov. 12, 1999 – Name changed to Centura Resources Inc.; basis 1 new for 5 old shs. ■

Paramount Energy Trust (Alta. June 28, 2002)
July 6, 2010 – Succeeded by Perpetual Energy Inc. pursuant to plan of arrangement whereby Perpetual Energy Inc. was formed to facilitate the conversion of the trust into a corporation and the trust was subsequently dissolved. ■

Paramount Funding Corp. (Ont. 1979)
Aug. 31, 1989 – All o/s cl. A vtg. shs. acquired by Trical Resources Inc.; basis 0.75 of a Trical sh. for 1 cl. A vtg. sh. of Paramount. (see Trical Resources Inc.)

Paramount Gold and Silver Corp. (Del. Mar. 29, 2005)
Apr. 15, 2015 – Acquired by Coeur Mining Inc.; basis 0.2016 Coeur shs. plus .05 Paramount Gold Nevada Corp. shs.(spun-off from Paramount Gold and Silver Corp.) for 1 Paramount Gold and Silver Corp. sh.

Paramount Life Insurance Company (Alta. 1973)
1984 – Court order was obtained for the liquidation of the company under trustee, Deloitte & Touche, Calgary.
1986 – All assets and affairs were transferred to Rocky Mountain Life Insurance Company.
Mar. 15, 1995 – By court order, the company was wound up and the trustee discharged. Creditors were paid, but there was no distribution to shldrs.

Paramount Mining Corp. (Que. 1947)
1951 – Charter cancelled; shldrs. received 1 sh. New Formaque Mines for 25.73 old shs.

Paramount Mining Limited (B.C. 1966)
Feb. 25, 1983 – Struck off register.

Paramount Petroleum & Mineral Corp. Ltd. (Sask. 1956)
Aug. 1960 – Acquired by Bison Petroleum & Minerals Ltd.; basis 1 new for 4 old shs.

Paramount Petroleum Co. Ltd. (unknown)
May 1941 – Charter surrendered.

Paramount Resources Inc. (B.C. Dec. 7, 1983)
June 24, 1985 – Name changed to Xanaro Technologies Inc.; basis 2 new for 1 old sh. ■

Paramount Ventures and Finance Inc. (Ont. Aug. 14, 1986)
Aug. 24, 1993 – Continued into British Columbia.
Oct. 23, 2006 – Dissolved and struck from register.

Paramount Ventures Inc. (Ont. 1979)
Jan. 9, 1984 – Name changed to Paramount Funding Corp. ■

Parana Copper Corporation (B.C. Jan. 30, 2006)
Aug. 7, 2018 – Name changed to Redfund Capital Corp.; basis 1.6 new for 1 old sh. ■

Parapet Petroleum Inc. (Ont. 1982 amalg.)
Oct. 5, 1984 – Amalgamated with d'Eldona Gold Mines Limited (1 for 2) to continue with the new name d'Eldona Resources Ltd.; basis 1 new d'Eldona sh. for 13 old Parapet shs.

Parbec Malartic Gold Mines Ltd. (Ont. 1944)
1953 – Name changed to Parbec Mines Ltd. ■

Parbec Mines Ltd. (Ont. 1944)
1959 – Merged into Hydra Explorations Ltd.; basis 1 new for 25 old shs.

ParcelPal Technology Inc. (B.C. June 22, 2006)
June 18, 2021 – Name changed to ParcelPal Logistics Inc. (see FPsurvey - Industrials)

Pardee Amalgamated Mines Ltd (Ont. 1954)
1961 – Assets acquired by Rio Algom Mines Ltd.; basis 1 new for 35 old shs., plus 0.25¢ per Pardee sh.

Parent Lake Mines Ltd. (Ont. Oct. 1944)
1951 – Name changed to Atlas Sulphur & Iron Co. Ltd. and continued into Quebec; basis 1 new for 10 old shs. ■

Pareto Corporation (Ont. Dec. 31, 2001 amalg.)
Mar. 21, 2011 – Acquired by The Riverside Company for $2.72 per sh.
Oct. 2, 2013 – Filed for bankruptcy. KPMG Inc. appointed trustee.

Parfield Oil Ltd. (unknown)
Dec. 1940 – Charter surrendered.

Parflo Mines & Energy Corp. (Ont. 1982)
May 16, 1994 – Name changed to Cyber Digital Video Services Ltd.; basis 1 new for 3 old shs. ■

Pargas Enterprises Ltd. (Alta. Apr. 29, 1999)
Dec. 29, 2003 – Name changed to Silk Road Resources Ltd. ■

Paris Canadian Investment Co. Ltd. (unknown)
Dec. 1967 – Formed La Compagnie Foncière du Manitoba (1967) Ltée in Manitoba on amalgamation with La Compagnie Foncière du Manitoba Ltée. ■

Paris Energy Inc. (Alta. July 30, 1993)
Sept. 8, 2014 – Name changed to Mapan Energy Ltd. following reverse takeover acquisition of (old) Mapan Energy Ltd.; basis 1 new for 12 old shs. ■

Paris Petroleums Ltd. (Ont. 1957)
1965 – Assets and liabs. acquired by Canadian Kewanee Ltd. in 1963. Charter surrendered.

Parisco Foods Limited (B.C. 1985)
Mar. 3, 1997 – Delisted from the Vancouver Stock Exchange. Subsequently dissolved and struck from register.

Park Avenue Investment Corporation (Ont. Nov. 29, 2004)
Oct. 5, 2007 – Name changed to Electric-Spin Ltd. following Qualifying Transaction reverse takeover acquisition of Electric-Spin Corporation for 38,314,654 com. shs. at $0.2088 per sh. (see FPsurvey - Industrials)

Park Lawn Cemetery Company Limited (Ont. Oct. 1, 1915)
Sept. 24, 2001 – Name changed to Park Lawn Company Limited; basis 10 new for 1 old sh. ■

Park Lawn Company Limited (Ont. Oct. 1, 1915)
Feb. 11, 2020 – Privatized via 1-for-3000 consolidation; basis $12.93 cash per pre-consolidated sh.

Park Lawn Corporation (Ont. Oct. 15, 2010)
Aug. 13, 2024 – Acquired by Homesteaders Life Company and Birch Hill Equity Partners Management Inc. through Viridian Acquisition Inc.; basis Cdn$26.50 cash per sh.

Park Lawn Income Trust (Ont. July 12, 2006)
Dec. 31, 2010 – Succeeded by Park Lawn Corporation pursuant to plan of arrangement whereby Park Lawn Corporation was formed to facilitate the conversion of the fund into a corporation and the fund was subsequently dissolved. ■

Park Meditech Inc. (unknown May 8, 1986)
Jan. 3, 1992 – Continued into Ontario.
Feb. 29, 1996 – Continued into Canada.
July 12, 2004 – Dissolved and struck from register.

Park Precious Metals Inc. (unknown)
Mar. 1977 – Charter cancelled.

Parkbridge Lifestyle Communities Inc. (Alta. May 26, 2004)
Jan. 12, 2011 – Acquired by British Columbia Investment Management Corporation for $7.30 per sh.

Parkcrest Explorations Ltd. (B.C. June 4, 1984)
Apr. 10, 2000 – Continued into Yukon.
June 13, 2000 – Name changed to Fossil Bay Resources Ltd. ■

Parkdale Exploration Ltd. (Ont. 1966)
Dec. 22, 1970 – Name changed to Parkdale Metals & Holdings Ltd. ■

Parkdale Metals & Holdings Ltd. (Ont. 1966)
Feb. 1980 – Charter cancelled.

Parkdale Oils & Gas Ltd. (Alta.)
1960 – Struck off register.

Parker Drilling Co. of Canada Limited (Alta. 1952)
1966 – Name changed to Nabors Drilling Limited. ■

Parkit Enterprise Inc. (B.C. Dec. 6, 2006)
July 9, 2021 – Continued into Ontario. (see FPsurvey - Industrials)

Parkland Beef Industries Ltd. (Alta. Mar. 16, 1961)
Dec. 29, 1977 – Name changed to Parkland Industries Ltd. ■

Parkland Energy Services Inc. (Alta. June 29, 2006)
Dec. 2, 2014 – Dissolved and struck from registry.

Parkland Fuel Corporation (Alta. Mar. 9, 2010)
May 15, 2020 – Name changed to Parkland Corporation. (see FPsurvey - Mines & Energy; FPsurvey - Industrials)

Parkland Income Fund (Alta. Apr. 30, 2002)
Dec. 31, 2010 – Succeeded by Parkland Fuel Corporation pursuant to plan of arrangement whereby Parkland Fuel Corporation was formed to facilitate the conversion of the fund into a corporation and the fund was subsequently dissolved. ■

Parkland Industries Ltd. (Alta. Mar. 16, 1961)
July 5, 2002 – Converted into Parkland Income Trust; basis either 2 Parkland Income trust units or 2 Parkland Holdings Limited Partnership units plus $1.00 for 1 Parkland Industries sh.

Parkland Resource Explorations Limited (Ont. Sept. 12, 1978)
Sept. 13, 1985 – Name changed to Winteroad Resources Limited. ■

Parklane Explorations Ltd. (B.C. Aug. 27, 1979)
June 27, 1986 – Name changed to Parklane Technologies Inc. ■

Parklane Mines and Minerals Inc. (Alta. Mar. 9, 1988)
May 1, 1990 – Name changed to Consolidated Parklane Resources Inc.; basis 1 new for 3 old shs. ■

Parklane Technologies Inc. (B.C. Aug. 27, 1979)
Mar. 9, 1988 – Continued into Alberta.
June 26, 1989 – Name changed to Parklane Mines and Minerals Inc. ■

Parkside Petroleum Inc. (B.C. 1982)
Jan. 21, 1988 – Name changed to Bethlehem Resources Corporation. ■

Parkside Resources Corporation (B.C. Nov. 21, 2005)
July 8, 2019 – Name changed to Novo 19 Capital Corp. ■

Parkside 2000 Resources Corporation (B.C. Oct. 24, 1980)
May 16, 2003 – Name changed to Amador Gold Corp. ■

Parkside Ventures Inc. (B.C. May 18, 1983)
Feb. 3, 1995 – Name changed to International Parkside Products Inc.; basis 1 new for 3 old shs. (see FPsurvey - Industrials)

Parkway Mines Ltd. (Ont. 1952)
Mar. 6, 1979 – Dissolved.

Parkway Silver Mines Ltd. (Ont. 1952)
1953 – Name changed to Parkway Mines Ltd. ■

Parlake Resources Limited (Ont. Jan. 11, 1979 amalg.)
July 23, 1991 – Name changed to Concord Capital Corp. ■

Parlane Resource Corp. (B.C. June 1, 2007)
Apr. 20, 2018 – Name changed to iMining Blockchain and Cryptocurrency Inc. ■

Parlar Resources Ltd. (B.C. 1984)
June 17, 1985 – Name changed to Kwik Products International Corporation. ■

Parlay Entertainment Inc. (Ont. Nov. 30, 2004 amalg.)
Dec. 10, 2012 – Name changed to Oramericas Corp.; basis 1 new for 2 old shs. ■

Parliament Mines Ltd. (Ont. 1946)
Mar. 1976 – Charter cancelled.

Parmlee Mining Co. Ltd. (Ont. 1958)
1960 – Merged into Consolidated Panther Mines Ltd.; basis 1 new for 20 old shs.

Parnell Red Lake Gold Mines Ltd. (Ont. 1947)
July 9, 1956 – Dissolved.

Parozan Iron Mines & Exploration Ltd. (Ont. 1957)
Sept. 1964 – Dissolved.

Parquet Mines Ltd. (Ont. 1951)
July 1980 – Name changed to Parquet Resources Inc. ■

Parquet Resources Inc. (Ont. 1951)
Dec. 13, 1993 – Name changed to Plexmar Resources Inc.; basis 1 new for 8 old shs. ■

Parr Mines Ltd. (Ont. 1955)
Nov. 1977 – Charter cancelled.

Parran Capital Inc. (B.C. Oct. 5, 2005)
June 26, 2008 – Name changed to Asia Bio-Chem Group Corp. pursuant to Qualifying Transaction reverse takeover acquisition of Asia Bio-Chem Group Company Ltd. which amalgamated with a wholly owned subsidiary of Parran Capital Inc.; basis 1 new for 7.5 old shs. ■

Pars Resources, Ltd. (B.C. Apr. 7, 1988)
May 28, 1992 – Name changed to WDF Capital Corp.; basis 1 new for 2 old shs. ■

Parta Dialogue Inc. (Can. Nov. 26, 2007)
Dec. 30, 2013 – Name changed to Engagement Labs Inc.; basis 1 new for 10 old shs. ■

Parta Growth Capital I Inc. (Can. Nov. 26, 2007)
May 12, 2009 – Name changed to Parta Sustainable Solutions Inc. following Qualifying Transaction reverse takeover acquisition of EDU-Performance Canada Inc.; basis 1 new for 3 old shs. ■

Parta Sustainable Solutions Inc. (Can. Nov. 26, 2007)
Mar. 10, 2011 – Name changed to Parta Dialogue Inc. ■

Partanen Malartic Gold Mines Ltd. (Ont. 1936)
1954 – Name changed to Nello Mining Limited; basis 1 new for 2 old shs. ■

Parterre Gold Mines Ltd. (Ont. 1944)
Charter cancelled; no equity.

Partner Jet Corp. (Ont. Dec. 17, 1987)
Dec. 22, 2021 – Formed Volatus Aerospace Corp. in Ontario pursuant to reverse takeover acquisition of and amalgamation with (old) Volatus Aerospace Corp.; basis 1 new for 2.95454 old shs. ■

Partners Oil & Minerals Ltd. (B.C. 1986)
Aug. 25, 1995 – Dissolved and struck off register.

Partners Real Estate Investment Trust (Ont. Mar. 27, 2007)
Dec. 16, 2019 – All o/s trust units not already held acquired by McCowan and Associates Ltd.; basis 78¢ cash per trust unit. ■

Partners Value Fund Inc. (Ont. Mar. 30, 1988 amalg.)
May 25, 2015 – Name changed to Partners Value Investments Inc. ■

Partners Value Investments Inc. (Ont. Mar. 30, 1988 amalg.)
June 30, 2016 – Succeeded by Partners Value Investments LP. (see FPsurvey - Industrials)

Parton Capital Inc. (Alta. May 14, 1987)
Aug. 2, 2023 – Struck from registry and dissolved.

Partridge Canadian Explorations Ltd. (Ont. 1945)
1961 – Name changed to Newrich Explorations Ltd.; basis 1 new for 4 old shs. ■

Partridge River Mines Ltd. (Ont. 1967)
Mar. 1976 – Charter cancelled.

Partridge Yellowknife Mines Ltd. (Ont. 1945)
1953 – Name changed to Partridge Canadian Explorations Ltd. ■

Partyco Holdings Ltd. (Ont. Oct. 28, 1996)
Aug. 11, 2003 – Dissolved and struck from register.

Parvus Mines Ltd. (Ont. Sept. 28, 1960)
Oct. 23, 1995 – Name changed to Kyrgoil Corporation. ■

Pasadena Energy Corp. (B.C. 1968)
May 31, 1985 – Name changed to Pasadena Technology Corporation. ■

Pasadena Technology Corporation (B.C. 1968)
May 15, 1986 – Name changed to EMS Systems Ltd. ■

Pascal Biosciences Inc. (B.C. Jan. 28, 2011)
June 12, 2023 – Name changed to Nevis Brands Inc.; basis 1 new for 5 old shs. (see FPsurvey - Industrials)

Pascalis Gold Mines Ltd. (Can. 1932)
1962 – Name changed to New Pascalis Mines Limited; basis 1 new for 5 old shs. ■

Pascar Development Corporation Ltd. (Man. 1950)
Sept. 13, 1982 – Amalgamated into Trapper Resources Ltd.; basis 1 new for 10 old shs.

Pascar Oils Ltd. (Man. 1950)
1969 – Name changed to Pascar Development Corporation Ltd. ■

Pasco Maritimes Gold Ltd. (Que. 1945)
Apr. 1947 – Name changed to Pasco Mining Corp. Ltd.

Pasgil Mines Ltd. (Ont. 1941)
1962 – Charter cancelled.

Pasha Brands Ltd. (B.C. Mar. 7, 2012)
May 19, 2020 – Name changed to BC Craft Supply Co. Ltd. (see FPsurvey - Industrials)

Pass Lake Resources Ltd. (B.C. Apr. 14, 1983)
Nov. 13, 1992 – Name changed to Arlington Ventures Ltd.; basis 1 new for 5 old shs. ■

Passion Media Inc. (Ont. July 18, 2002 amalg.)
Mar. 5, 2004 – Name changed to Lemontonic Inc. ■

Passport Energy Ltd. (B.C. Feb. 23, 2007)
June 23, 2014 – Amalgamated with 1815766 Alberta Inc., a wholly owned subsid. of Amarok Energy Inc. (subsequently renamed Powder Mountain Energy Ltd.): basis 1 Amarok com. sh. for 1 Passport com. sh. (see Powder Mountain Energy Ltd.)

Passport Metals Inc. (Que. Aug. 11, 1987)
Nov. 10, 2009 – Name changed to Passport Potash Inc. ■

Passport Mines Ltd. (B.C. 1971)
July 15, 1983 – Struck off register.

Passport Potash Inc. (Que. Aug. 11, 1987)
Apr. 26, 2011 – Continued into British Columbia.
Oct. 11, 2016 – Dissolved and struck from register.

Pastel Food Corporation (B.C. 1986)
Oct. 25, 1990 – Name changed to International Pastel Food Corporation; basis 1 new for 4 old shs. ■

Pat Gold Mines Ltd. (Ont. Dec. 7, 1940)
Aug. 31, 1992 – Delisted from the CDN. Subsequently voluntarily dissolved and removed from registry.

Patagonia Gold plc (U.K. May 16, 2000)
July 26, 2019 – Name changed to Patagonia Gold Limited.

PatCall Inc. (Alta. Sept. 17, 1996)
Feb. 17, 1999 – Name changed to FaxMate.Com Inc. following Qualifying Transaction reverse takeover acquisition of FaxMate Inc.; basis 1 new for 2.5 old shs. (see FPsurvey - Industrials)

Patch Resources Inc. (B.C. 1983)
June 22, 1983 – Name changed to Westate Resources Inc. ■

Patch Safety Services Ltd. (Alta. July 2, 1998)
Aug. 31, 2004 – Name changed to HSE Integrated Ltd.; basis 1 new for 5 old shs. ■

Patch Ventures Inc. (Can. Aug. 25, 1993)
Sept. 29, 1994 – Name changed to Legacy Storage Systems International Inc. ■

Patchgear.com Inc. (Alta. July 25, 1996)
Oct. 2, 2002 – Struck from registry and dissolved.

Patcor Capital Inc. (Can. May 7, 1987)
July 14, 1992 – Name changed to Dion Entertainment Corp. ■

Patent Enforcement and Royalties Limited (Can. Oct. 2, 1996)
July 1, 1999 – Continued into Ontario.
Apr. 22, 2005 – Name changed to Blue Pearl Mining Ltd. following acquisition of mineral leases and claims. ■

Pater Uranium Mines Ltd. (Ont. 1953)
1959 – Assets sold to Pronto Uranium Mines Ltd.; basis 1 new plus 3 0.75¢ for 15 old shs.
Aug. 1961 – Charter cancelled.

Paterson and Hill Aircraft Co. Ltd. (Ont.)
Name changed to Hillcraft Industries Ltd. ■

Patfind Inc. (Alta. May 14, 1999)
Sept. 18, 2000 – Formed Engineering.com Incorporated in Ontario on Qualifying Transaction amalgamation with Engineering.com Incorporated, constituting a reverse takeover by Engineering.com. ■

Patheon Inc. (Can. Jan. 11, 1993 amalg.)
Mar. 13, 2014 – Acquired by JLL/Delta Patheon Holdings L.P.; basis US$9.32 cash per sh.

Pathfinder Convertible Debenture Fund (Alta.)
Nov. 12, 2014 – Name changed to Pathfinder Income Fund. ■

Pathfinder Copper Mines Ltd. (Ont. 1964)
Apr. 29, 1980 – Dissolved.

Pathfinder Credit Ltd. (Can. - unspecified)
Jan. 1965 – Amalgamated with Charter Credit Corp.; basis 1 Charter sh. for 2.5 Pathfinder shs. and 1 Charter pref. sh. for 1 Pathfinder pref. sh.

Pathfinder Financial Corp. (B.C. 1968)
Nov. 5, 1986 – Formed Pathfinder Industries Inc. in Ontario on amalgamation with L. B. Blair Management Ltd. ■

Pathfinder Income Fund (Alta.)
July 8, 2020 – Merged into INDEXPLUS Income Fund; basis 1 cl. F INDEXPLUS unit for 1 Pathfinder trust unit.

Pathfinder Industries Inc. (Ont. Nov. 5, 1986 amalg.)
Apr. 29, 1987 – Name changed to International Pathfinder Inc. ■

Pathfinder International Recreational Corporation (Alta. 1986)
Apr. 30, 1993 – Name changed to Vision Incorporated following acquisition of Vision R.V. Inc. on Feb. 26, 1993; basis 1 new for 10 old shs. ■

Pathfinder Leaseholds Limited (Alta. 1951)
Mar. 8, 1965 – Taken over by Canadian Industrial Gas & Oil Ltd.

Pathfinder Petroleums Ltd. (Alta. 1952)
1956 – Name changed to Medallion Petroleums Limited; basis 1 new for 2.5 old shs. ■

Pathfinder Resources Ltd. (B.C. 1968)
Mar. 23, 1981 – Name changed to International Pathfinder Resources Ltd.; basis 1 new for 5 old shs. ■

Pathfinder Resources Ltd. (B.C. 1968)
Aug. 16, 2006 – Plan of Arrangement amalgamation with Bayswater Ventures Corp. (1 for 1) to continue as Bayswater Uranium Corporation; basis 0.588 new Bayswater Uranium sh. for 1 old Pathfinder sh. (see Bayswater Uranium Corporation)

Pathfinder Uranium and Nickel Mines Ltd. (B.C. 1968)
1969 – Name changed to Pathfinder Resources Ltd. ■

Pathonic Network Inc. (Can. 1984 amalg.)
1986 – Continued into Quebec. (see Télé-Métropole Inc.)
Sept. 1988 – Acquired by Tele-Metropole for $10 a sh. (see Télé-Métropole Inc.)

Pathway Financial Corp. (Ont. 1969)
Sept. 27, 1994 – Name changed to Asia Media Group Corporation. ■

Pathway Food Industries Limited (Ont. 1969)
Dec. 15, 1986 – Name changed to Pathway Financial Corp. ■

Pathway Health Corp. (Alta. Sept. 4, 2014)
Oct. 2, 2023 – Placed into receivership by secured creditor. KSV Restructuring Inc. appointed receiver.

Patican Co., Ltd. (Can. 1945)
Sept. 1955 – Name changed to Patino of Canada Ltd. ■

Patient Home Monitoring Corp. (Alta. Mar. 5, 1997)
Dec. 30, 2013 – Continued into British Columbia.
May 7, 2018 – Name changed to Protech Home Medical Corp. ■

Patino Enterprises of Canada, Ltd. (Can. 1954)
Oct. 5, 1955 – Assets acquired by Patino of Canada Ltd. in exch. for 525,990 shs.

The Patino Mining Corporation (Ont. 1962)
1971 – Acquired by Patino, N.V. Charter surrendered.

Patino of Canada Ltd. (Can. 1945)
June 1962 – Amalgamated with The Nipissing Mines Co. Ltd. to form The Patino Corp. Ltd.; basis 1 new for 1 old sh. (see The Patino Corp. Ltd.)

Patmar Resources Corp. (B.C. 1978)
Feb. 10, 1984 – Name changed to Draw Resources Corporation; basis 1 new for 3 old shs. ■

Patmore Developments Limited (Ont. 1944)
Dec. 31, 1976 – Name changed to Patmore Group Limited and continued into Canada.

Patnora Gold Mines Ltd. (Ont. 1945)
Dec. 1954 – Charter cancelled.

Pato Consolidated Gold Dredging Limited (B.C. 1934)
1977 – Liquidated following sh.-for-sh. exchange with Pato Consolidated Gold Dredging Limited (Bermuda 1976 incorp.), effectively changing the domicile of the corporation.

Paton Manufacturing Co. Ltd. (Que. 1923)
1965 – All o/s com. and over 90% of o/s pref. shs. held by Cleyn & Tinker Ltd. following an offer made at $22.50 per com. and $27.50 per pref. sh.

Patrice-Destor Gold Mines Limted (Ont. 1946)
Feb. 17, 1964 – Dissolved.

Patricia Birch Lake Gold Mines Ltd. (Ont. 1929)
July 27, 1959 – Dissolved.

Patricia Birch Lake Mining Corp. Ltd. (Ont. 1929)
Mar. 1934 – Name changed to Patricia Birch Lake Gold Mines Ltd. ■

Patricia Dent Gold Mines Ltd. (Ont. 1928)
Sept. 19, 1955 – Dissolved.

Patricia Mines Inc. (B.C. Sept. 10, 1987)
Sept. 13, 1999 – Name changed to Patricia Mining Corp.; basis 1 new for 5 old shs. ■

Patricia Mining Corp. (B.C. Sept. 10, 1987)
Jan. 15, 2003 – Continued into Ontario.
Dec. 17, 2008 – Acquired by Richmont Mines Inc.; basis 15¢ plus 0.055 Richmont Mines shs. for 1 Patricia Mining sh.

Patricia Oils Ltd. (B.C. Apr. 2, 1929)
Struck off register.

Patricia Silver Mines Limited (Ont. 1961)
Mar. 12, 1991 – Name changed to Hilldale Holdings Inc. ■

Patrician Consolidated Gold Mines Ltd. (Ont. Jan. 28, 1994)
May 23, 2002 – Name changed to Patrician Diamonds Inc. ■

Patrician Diamonds Inc. (Ont. Jan. 28, 1994)
Jan. 2, 2009 – Name changed to Diamond Exploration Inc.; basis 1 new for 10 old shs. ■

Patrician Gold Mines Ltd. (Ont. Jan. 28, 1994)
Mar. 8, 2000 – Name changed to Patrician Consolidated Gold Mines Ltd.; basis 1 new for 10 old shs. ■

Patrick Computer Services Inc. (Can. Dec. 9, 1980)
Aug. 16, 1984 – Name changed to Optrix Radiation Inc. ■

Patrick Uranium Mines Ltd. (Ont. 1950)
1967 – Charter surrendered.

Patriot Capital Corp. (B.C. Aug. 14, 1998)
Mar. 5, 2002 – Name changed to Patriot Petroleum Corp. following Qualifying Transaction acquisition of all producing oil and gas assets of Netco Energy Inc. ■

Patriot Energy Company Ltd. (Alta. 1987)
Feb. 1, 1991 – Acquired by Giant Pacific Petroleum Inc.; basis 1 Giant Pacific sh. and warrant for 2 Patriot shs. and 2 warrants and $0.25 for 1 Giant Pacific sh. exercisable from Jan. 8, 1992, to July 8, 1992. (see Giant Pacific Petroleum Inc.)

Patriot Equities Corporation (Alta. July 18, 1997)
Aug. 9, 2002 – Acquired by FSI Acquisition Corporation, wholly owned subsid. of Financial Solutions Inc.; basis $4.2375 per sh.

Patriot Equities Group Inc. (Alta. July 18, 1997)
Aug. 17, 1998 – Name changed to Patriot Equities Group Ltd.; basis 1 new for 2 old shs. ■

Patriot Equities Group Ltd. (Alta. July 18, 1997)
July 30, 1999 – Name changed to Patriot Equities Corporation; basis 1 new for 10 old shs. ■

Patriot Minefinders Inc. (Nev. Feb. 9, 2007)
Jan. 14, 2015 – Name changed to Rise Resources Inc. ■

Patriot One Technologies Inc. (B.C. May 11, 2010)
Nov. 28, 2022 – Name changed to Xtract One Technologies Inc. (see FPsurvey - Industrials)

Patriot Petroleum Corp. (B.C. Aug. 14, 1998)
Dec. 1, 2016 – Continued into Canada.
Dec. 2, 2016 – Name changed to Standard Lithium Ltd.; basis 1 new for 5 old shs. (see FPsurvey - Mines & Energy)

Patriots Venture Group Ltd. (B.C. Oct. 7, 1986)
May 22, 1997 – Name changed to Tearlach Resources Limited; basis 1 new for 5 old shs. (see FPsurvey - Mines & Energy)

Patriotstar Ventures Inc. (B.C. Jan. 16, 2007)
Dec. 11, 2009 – Name changed to TinyMassive Technologies Inc. pursuant to Qualifying Transaction reverse takeover acqusition of TinyMassive Technologies Inc. ■

Patrone Gold Corp. (B.C. July 13, 2011)
Oct. 3, 2013 – Name changed to Aurgent Gold Corp. ■

Patseek Capital Inc. (Can. Apr. 6, 1995)
July 5, 1996 – Name changed to Aastra Technologies Inc. ■

Patshare Capital Inc. (Can. Mar. 6, 1991)
Apr. 26, 1996 – Name changed to EveryWare Development Canada Corp. ■

Pattern Energy Group Inc. (Del. Oct. 17, 2012)
Mar. 18, 2020 – Acquired by Canada Pension Plan Investment Board; basis US$26.75 cash per sh.

Patterson-Bell Oil Co. Ltd. (B.C.)
1959 – Struck off register.

Paudash Lake Uranium Mines Ltd. (Ont. 1955)
1959 – Name changed to Paudash Mines Ltd. ■

Paudash Mines Ltd. (Ont. 1955)
Mar. 1976 – Charter cancelled.

Paul-Liane Explorations Ltd. (Ont. 1954)
Charter cancelled.

Paul Service Stores Ltd. (Que. Nov. 7, 1935)
Mar. 17, 1969 – Name changed to Cantol Diversified Ltd.; basis 5 new for 1 old sh. ■

H. Paulin & Co., Limited (Ont. Sept. 21, 1928)
Feb. 26, 2013 – Acquired by The Hillman Companies Inc. for $27.60 per sh.
Mar. 31, 2013 – Amalgamated with The Hillman Group Canada ULC to continue as The Hillman Group Canada ULC.

Paulore Gold Mines Ltd. (Ont. 1934)
Sept. 24, 1956 – Dissolved.

Paulpic Gold Mines Limited (Ont. 1939)
Mar. 1976 – Charter cancelled.

Paulson Mines Ltd. (B.C. 1967)
Sept. 1979 – Name changed to Samson Energy Corporation; basis 1 new for 5 old shs. ■

Pawnee Kirkland Gold Mines Ltd. (Ont. 1922)
June 30, 1962 – Dissolved.

Pawnee Oil Corporation (B.C. Jan. 15, 1979)
Mar. 15, 1983 – Name changed to Canadian Pawnee Oil Corporation; basis 1 new for 5 old shs. ■

Pax Athabasca Uranium Mines Ltd. (Ont. 1949)
1962 – Acquired by Pax International Mines Ltd. (see Pax International Mines Ltd.)

Pax International Mines Ltd. (Ont. 1949)
1968 – Name changed to Geo-Pax Mines Ltd.; basis 1 new for 4 old shs. ■

Pax Petroleum Ltd. (B.C. 1981)
Sept. 1991 – In receivership. Larsen & Zamuda appointed as receiver-manager to liquidate the assets.
May 1993 – Declared bankrupt and most of the assets had been sold. Secured creditors received approximately $40,000. There was no distribution to shldrs.
Dec. 11, 1995 – Receiver discharged.

Paxton International Resources Ltd. (Alta. Sept. 21, 1994)
Dec. 9, 1998 – Continued into British Columbia.
May 27, 2013 – Dissolved and struck from register.

Paxton Pacific Resource Products Inc. (Alta. Sept. 21, 1994)
Nov. 11, 1998 – Name changed to Paxton International Resources Ltd.; basis 1 new for 3 old shs. ■

Pay Linx Financial Corporation (Alta. May 27, 2004)
Nov. 2, 2015 – Struck from registry and dissolved.

Payco Gold Mines (Ont. July 6, 1945)
1946 – Name changed to Quesabe Mines Limited; basis 1 new for 2 old shs. ■

Payco Mines Ltd. (B.C. 1960)
Sept. 1973 – Name changed to Galloway Development Ltd.; basis 1 new for 5 old shs. ■

Paycore Minerals Inc. (Ont. Jan. 29, 2021)
May 12, 2023 – Acquired by i-80 Gold Corp.; basis 0.68 i-80 shs. for 1 Paycore sh.

Paycorma Yellowknife Gold Mines Ltd. (Ont. 1947)
1957 – Charter cancelled.

Payday Resources Inc. (B.C. Aug. 19, 1983)
Oct. 28, 1986 – Name changed to Perimeter Ventures Ltd. ■

Payette International Resources Ltd. (B.C. 1967)
Sept. 12, 1975 – Name changed to Consolidated Payette International Resources Ltd.; basis 1 new for 5 old shs. ■

Payette River Mines Ltd. (B.C. 1967)
Jan. 1975 – Name changed to Payette International Resources Ltd. ■

Payfair Mines Ltd. (B.C. 1966)
Jan. 1971 – Amalgamated with Lymac Industries Ltd. to form Payfair Industries Ltd.

Payfare Inc. (Ont. June 15, 2012)
Mar. 12, 2021 – Continued into British Columbia.
Mar. 5, 2025 – Acquired by Fiserv, Inc.; basis $4 cash per sh.

Paymaster Consolidated Mines Ltd. (Ont. 1930)
1964 – Name changed to Porcupine Paymaster Ltd.; basis 1 new for 3 old shs. ■

Paymaster Mines Incorporated (B.C. May 31, 1979)
Aug. 7, 1981 – Name changed to Paymaster Resources Inc.; basis 1 new for 2 old shs. ■

Paymaster Resources Inc. (B.C. May 31, 1979)
Nov. 12, 1982 – Name changed to Consolidated Paymaster Resources Ltd.; basis 1 new for 2 old shs. ■

Payment Services Interactive Gateway Corp. (Alta. July 17, 1997)
Oct. 31, 2007 – Acquired by Home Capital Group Inc. for $1.60 per sh. (see Home Capital Group Inc.)

Payne Yellowknife Gold Mines Ltd. (Ont. 1945)
1971 – Charter cancelled.

Payore Consolidated Mines Ltd. (Ont. May 24, 1934)
1944 – Name changed to Formaque Gold Mines Ltd. and continued into Quebec; basis 1 new for 5 old shs. ■

Payore Gold Mines Ltd. (Ont. May 24, 1934)
June 1939 – Name changed to Payore Consolidated Mines Ltd.; basis 1 new for 3 old shs. ■

Payout Performers Income Fund (Ont. Jan. 30, 2006)
Oct. 1, 2007 – Merged into First Asset/BlackRock North American Dividend Achievers Trust; basis 0.9051 First Asset/BlackRock trust unit for 1 Payout Performers trust unit. (see First Asset/BlackRock North American Dividend Achievers Trust)

Payqueen Nickel Mines Ltd. (Ont. 1957)
Oct. 1968 – Charter cancelled.

Payrock Mines Ltd. (Ont. 1955)
Nov. 22, 1972 – Dissolved.

Paysan Yellowknife Gold Mines Ltd. (Ont. 1946)
May 1958 – Charter cancelled.

Paytel Industries Ltd. (B.C. Aug. 9, 1983)
Apr. 19, 1996 – Name changed to Rodera Diamond Corporation. ■

Payton Ventures Inc. (B.C. Oct. 8, 1986)
Feb. 17, 1989 – Name changed to Reimer Overhead Doors Ltd. ■

Pcybin Therapeutics Inc. (B.C. July 25, 2019)
Jan. 28, 2020 – Name changed to Doseology Sciences Inc. (see FPsurvey - Industrials)

Pd&e Resource Services Corp. (Alta. June 19, 2003)
Nov. 4, 2004 – Name changed to Leader Energy Services Ltd. following reverse takeover acquisition of Leader Energy Services Corp.; basis 1 new for 4 old shs. ■

Pe Ben Oilfield Services Ltd. (Alta. May 17, 1967)
Sept. 25, 1981 – Continued into Canada. (see Mullen Group Income Fund)
Jan. 17, 2006 – Acquired indirectly by Mullen Group Income Fund for $18.50 per sh. (see Mullen Group Income Fund)

Pe Ben Transport Ltd. (Alta. May 17, 1967)
Jan. 11, 1973 – Name changed to Pe Ben Oilfield Services Ltd. ■

Peace Arch Entertainment Group Inc. (B.C. Oct. 22, 1986)
Sept. 1, 2004 – Continued into Ontario.
May 16, 2013 – Filed for bankruptcy. Schonfeld Inc. (subsequently Link & Associates Inc.) was appointed trustee.

Peace Pipe Line Ltd. (Alta. 1954)
1983 – All shs. are held directly or indirectly by producing oil companies, including Amerada Minerals Corp. of Canada Ltd., Gulf Canada Resources Ltd., Shell Canada Limited, Husky Oil Operations Ltd., Mobil Canada Ltd., Petro-Canada Inc., Esso Resources (1989) Ltd., Unocal Canada Ltd., and Amoco Petroleum Canada Ltd.

Peace River Capital Corp. (B.C. Sept. 15, 2015)
Dec. 2, 2016 – Name changed to Liberty One Lithium Corp. ■

Peace River Mining & Smelting Ltd. (Alta. 1962)
Dec. 1970 – Placed into receivership. Assets subsequently liquidated with no distribution made to any creditor, debentureholder, or shldr.

Peace River Natural Gas Co. Ltd. (B.C.)
1957 – Merged with Westcoast Transmission Co. Ltd.; basis 1 new for 3 old shs.

Peace River Oil Pipe Line Co. Ltd. (Alta. 1954)
Nov. 22, 1973 – Name changed to Peace Pipe Line Ltd. ■

Peace River Petroleums Ltd. (Ont. 1919)
1922 – Bankrupt.
1968 – Charter cancelled. (No connection with Peace River Petroleums Ltd., incorporated in B.C., 1953.)

Peace River Petroleums Ltd. (B.C. 1953)
Apr. 11, 1973 – Name changed to P.R.P. Explorations Ltd.; basis 1 new for 5 old shs. ■

Peace River Placers Ltd. (Alta. 1954)
Aug. 31, 1974 – Struck off register.

Peace River Power Development Company Ltd. (Can. - unspecified)
Aug. 1, 1961 – Expropriated by the Province of British Columbia. Compensation to shldrs. set at 50¢ per sh. At last report, co. had 12,942,086 shs. o/s, of which 49.88% held by Wenner-Gren ints. Remainder held by a number of British and Canadian cos.

Peach Uranium & Metal Mining Ltd. (Ont. 1952)
May 1960 – Distributed 258 shs. Pronto Uranium Mines, 15 shs. Northspan Uranium Mines, and $196 for each 100 Peach shs. held. Charter surrendered.

Peachland Copper Mines Ltd. (B.C. 1966)
Oct. 1974 – Charter cancelled.

Peachtree Network Inc. (Can. Feb. 5, 1997)
Sept. 19, 2003 – Struck from register and dissolved.

Peak Brewing Group Inc. (Alta. Nov. 25, 1993)
Sept. 2, 2004 – Struck from registry and dissolved.

Peak Energy Services Ltd. (Alta. June 14, 1996 amalg.)
May 5, 2004 – Converted into Peak Energy Services Trust; basis 1 trust unit or 1 Peak Energy Services Ltd. exch. sh. for 2 Peak Energy com. shs.

Peak Energy Services Ltd. (Alta. Dec. 31, 2010; amalg.)
June 15, 2011 – Acquired by Clean Harbors, Inc. for 95¢ per sh.

Peak Energy Services Trust (Alta. Mar. 26, 2004)
Dec. 31, 2010 – Succeeded by Peak Energy Services Ltd. pursuant to plan of arrangement whereby Peak Energy Services Ltd. was formed to facilitate the conversion of the trust into a corporation and the trust was subsequently dissolved. ■

Peak Fintech Group Inc. (Can. Apr. 4, 2011)
Nov. 1, 2021 – Name changed to Tenet Fintech Group Inc. (see FPsurvey - Industrials)

Peak Gold Ltd. (B.C. Nov. 13, 2006)
July 7, 2008 – Acquired by New Gold Inc.; basis 0.1 New Gold sh. plus Cdn$0.0001 for 1 Peak Gold sh.

Peak Minerals Ltd. (B.C. May 12, 2021)
Apr. 7, 2025 – Name changed to Sranan Gold Corp. (see FPsurvey - Mines & Energy)

Peak Oils Ltd. (Ont. 1946)
1953 – Name changed to Consolidated Peak Oils Ltd.; basis 1 new for 4 old shs. ■

Peak Positioning Technologies Inc. (Can. Apr. 4, 2011)
Nov. 18, 2020 – Name changed to Peak Fintech Group Inc. ■

Peak Technologies Inc. (B.C. Aug. 24, 1994)
Aug. 16, 1996 – Continued into Alberta.
Nov. 17, 1997 – Name changed to PeakSoft Corporation; basis 1 new cl. A for 1 old com. sh. ■

Peak Yellowknife Mines Ltd. (Ont. 1946)
Jan. 24, 1952 – Charter cancelled.

Peakbirch Logic Inc. (B.C. Mar. 23, 2015)
Feb. 23, 2022 – Name changed to PeakBirch Commerce Inc.; basis 1 new for 3.3 old shs. (see FPsurvey - Industrials)

PeakSoft Corporation (Alta. Aug. 16, 1996)
Feb. 22, 1999 – Name changed to PeakSoft Multinet Corp.; basis 1 new for 8 old shs. ■

PeakSoft Multinet Corp. (Alta. Aug. 16, 1996)
Feb. 2, 2012 – Struck from registry and dissolved.

Pearl Exploration and Production Ltd. (Can. July 19, 2002)
May 14, 2009 – Name changed to BlackPearl Resources Inc. ∎

Peat Resources Limited (Ont. May 23, 1980)
Mar. 23, 2018 – Name changed to Cobalt Blockchain Inc. ∎

Peat Sorb Incorporated (Alta. Nov. 9, 1987)
Oct. 27, 1997 – Name changed to Redex Co. Ventures Inc.; basis 1 new for 5 old shs. ∎

Peat "T" Inc. (Alta. Nov. 9, 1987)
Oct. 4, 1993 – Name changed to Peat Sorb Incorporated. ∎

Pebble Creek Mining Ltd. (B.C. Dec. 15, 2006 amalg.)
Nov. 17, 2014 – Dissolved and struck from register.
Dec. 23, 2015 – Restored to corporate registry.
Nov. 20, 2017 – Dissolved and struck from registry.
Dec. 16, 2019 – Restored to corporate registry. (see FPsurvey - Mines & Energy)

Pebble Gold Resources Ltd. (B.C. Oct. 16, 1984)
July 19, 1989 – Name changed to Drexel Enterprise Corporation; basis 1 new for 3 old shs. ∎

Pebble Uranium Mines Ltd. (Ont. 1955)
Sept. 1959 – Charter cancelled.

Pebercan Inc. (Can. Jan. 6, 1987)
May 5, 2011 – Dissolved.

Pecos Resources Ltd. (B.C. 1979)
June 18, 1985 – Amalgamated into Granges Exploration Ltd.; basis 1 new for 2.1 old shs.

Pedco Energy Limited (B.C. June 1, 1971)
Nov. 15, 1993 – Formed International Pedco Energy Corporation in Alberta on amalgamation with Pembina Ltd., Smokey Loon Ltd. and 571769 Alberta Ltd.; basis 0.41425 new for 1 old sh. ∎

Pediapharm Inc. (Can. Dec. 10, 2013 amalg.)
Dec. 19, 2018 – Name changed to Medexus Pharmaceuticals Inc.; basis 1 new for 15 old shs. (see FPsurvey - Industrials)

Pediment Exploration Ltd. (B.C. Dec. 23, 1983)
Feb. 26, 2009 – Name changed to Pediment Gold Corp. ∎

Pediment Gold Corp. (B.C. Dec. 23, 1983)
Feb. 2, 2011 – Acquired by Argonaut Gold Inc.; basis 0.625 Argonaut shs. for 1 Pediment sh. (see Argonaut Gold Inc.)

Pedlar Industrial Inc. (Can. Dec. 31, 1979 amalg.)
June 30, 1980 – Clarkson Co. appointed receiver and manager. Assets subsequently liquidated. Proceeds distributed to secured creditors as partial payment. No distributions made to unsecured creditors or shldrs.
Aug. 10, 1984 – Dissolved.

Peekaboo Beans Inc. (B.C. Dec. 23, 2005)
Oct. 21, 2024 – Dissolved for failure to file.

Peeks Social Ltd. (Alta. Jan. 10, 2008)
July 15, 2020 – Name changed to Personas Social Incorporated. (see FPsurvey - Industrials)

Peel-Elder Limited (Ont. 1944)
Dec. 5, 1974 – Amalgamated with Hambro Canada Limited under the continuing name of Hambro. All o/s Peel-Elder shs. not already held by Hambro converted into pfce. shs. of the amalg. co.; basis 3 new for 1 old sh. Shs. of Peel-Elder held by the former Hambro Canada were cancelled.

Peel Plateau Exploration (Consolidated) Ltd. (Can. 1953)
Dec. 1961 – Name changed to Basin Oil Exploration Ltd.

Peel Plateau Exploration Ltd. (Can. 1953)
1959 – Name changed to Peel Plateau Exploration (Consolidated) Ltd.; basis 10 new for 66 old shs. ∎

Peel Resources Ltd. (B.C. 1957)
Aug. 3, 1976 – Name changed to McConnell-Peel Resources Ltd.; basis 1 new for 5 old shs. ∎

Peel River Gas & Oil Co. Ltd. (B.C. 1957)
1958 – Name changed to Peel Resources Ltd. ∎

Peelbrooke Capital Inc. (Can. May 4, 1989)
Dec. 30, 1999 – Acquired by Dundee Wealth Management Inc.; basis 0.2 Dundee Bancorp Inc. cl. A subord. vtg. shs., 0.3 Dundee Wealth com. shs., 0.3 Dundee Wealth wts. and $1.50 for 1 Peelbrooke com. sh. (see Dundee Wealth Management Inc.)

Peer 1 Network Enterprises, Inc. (B.C. May 3, 1996)
Apr. 1, 2013 – Acquired by Cogeco Cable Inc. for $3.85 per sh.

Peerless Canadian Explorations Ltd. (Ont. 1952)
1971 – Charter cancelled.

Peerless Carpet Corporation (Can. Apr. 12, 1966)
Dec. 21, 1998 – Acquired by C&M Holdings Inc. for $3.10 per sh.

Peerless Energy Inc. (Alta. Nov. 26, 2004)
Feb. 4, 2008 – Acquired by Petrobank Energy and Resources Ltd.; basis $1.00 and 0.095 Petrobank com. sh. for 1 Peerless cl. A sh. and $10 for 1 Peerless cl. B sh.

Peerless Rug Limited (Can. Apr. 12, 1966)
Dec. 2, 1983 – Name changed to Peerless Carpet Corporation; basis 2 new for 1 old sh. ∎

Peerless Uranium Mining Corp. Ltd. (Ont. 1953)
Nov. 22, 1972 – Dissolved.

Peg Tantalum Mines Ltd. (Ont. 1944)
Apr. 1948 – Assets acquired by Tantalum Refining & Mining Corp. of America Ltd.; basis 1 new for 1 old shs. (see Tantalum Refining & Mining Corp. of America Ltd.)

Pega Capital Resources Ltd. (Ont. 1980)
Sept. 10, 1987 – Name changed to Pega Capital Corporation. (see FPsurvey - Industrials)

Pegasus Explorations Ltd. (B.C. 1961)
June 2, 1981 – Amalgamated with Argo Gold Mining Inc. (1.1 new for 1 old) to form Pegasus Gold Ltd.; basis sh. for sh. (see Pegasus Gold Ltd.)

Pegasus Gold Inc. (B.C. Aug. 20, 1984 amalg.)
Jan. 15, 1999 – Following joint Liquidating Plan of Reorganization for the company, wholly owned Pegasus Gold Corporation and other non-operating subsidiaries filed on July 31, 1998 and amended Sept. 11, 1998, Harrison J. Goldin of Goldin Associates, L.L.C. was appointed liquidating trustee for both companies resulting in no distributions to shldrs. The effective date of the plan was Jan. 15, 1999.

Pegasus Gold Ltd. (B.C. June 2, 1981 amalg.)
Aug. 20, 1984 – Formed Pegasus Gold Inc. in British Columbia on amalgamation with Montoro Gold Inc. (1 for 2.666); basis 1 new for 1 old sh. ∎

Pegasus Oil & Gas Inc. (Alta. May 25, 2006)
Aug. 18, 2009 – Acquired by Harvest Energy Trust; basis 0.015 Harvest trust units for 1 Pegasus cl. A sh. and 0.15 Harvest trust units for 1 Pegasus cl. B sh. (see Harvest Energy Trust)

Pegasus Petroleum & Mining Corp. Ltd. (Ont. 1950)
1958 – Wound up.

Pegaz Energy Inc. (Can. Feb. 23, 1995)
Nov. 25, 2002 – Name changed to Argo Energy Ltd. following capital reorganization; basis 1 com. for 10 cl. A shs. ∎

Pegmabelle Mining Corporation (Que. 1955)
Dec. 6, 1961 – Dissolved.

Pekisko Hills Co. Ltd. (Alta. 1933)
Struck off register.

Pelangio Exploration Inc. (Alta. Feb. 27, 2008)
June 25, 2009 – Continued into Canada. (see FPsurvey - Mines & Energy)

Pelangio-Larder Mines, Limited (Ont. Jan. 29, 1937)
May 31, 2000 – Name changed to PL Internet Inc. pursuant to plan of arrangement with Marl Resources Corp.; basis 1 new for 10 old shs. ∎

Pelangio Mines Inc. (Alta. Apr. 14, 1997)
Sept. 3, 2008 – Name changed to PDX Resources Inc. ∎

Pele Mountain Holdings Inc. (Ont. Jan. 16, 1996 amalg.)
Oct. 1, 1997 – Formed Pele Mountain Resources Inc. in Ontario on amalgamation with Pele Mountain Resources Inc. ∎

Pele Mountain Resources Inc. (Ont. Oct. 1, 1997 amalg.)
May 24, 2019 – Voluntarily delisted.
May 24, 2019 – Name changed to Bhang Inc. pursuant to reverse takeover acquistion of Bhang Corporation; basis 1 new for 10 old shs. (see FPsurvey - Industrials)

Pelham Gold Mines Ltd. (Ont. Jan. 26, 1948)
Apr. 6, 1988 – Name changed to Pelham Gold 'N' Grain Inc. ∎

Pelham Gold 'N' Grain Inc. (Ont. Jan. 26, 1948)
Nov. 29, 1991 – Delisted from the Alberta Stock Exchange. Subsequently dissolved and charter cancelled.

Pelican Long Lac Gold Mines Ltd. (Ont. 1937)
1952 – Charter cancelled.

Pelican Mines Ltd. (Ont. May 26, 1974)
Sept. 8, 1983 – Name changed to Goldstalker Resources Ltd.; basis 1 new for 2 old shs. ∎

Pellaire Mines Ltd. (Ont. 1945)
1964 – Acquired by Flagstone Mines Ltd.; basis 1 new for 10 old shs. (see Flagstone Mines Ltd.)

Peller Brewing Co. Ltd. (Ont. 1945)
Mar. 1, 1954 – Control purchased by Canadian Breweries Ltd. in November 1953; assets purchased by Brading Breweries Ltd. Cdn. Breweries made offers of $25 per sh. for pref., $4.00 per sh. for com. stk.

Pelletier Lake Gold Mines Ltd. (Ont. 1936)
Dec. 1961 – Distribution made of 15¢ per sh. Charter surrendered.

Pelorus Energy Corp. (Alta. June 8, 1981)
Aug. 1, 2005 – Formed RedStar Oil & Gas Inc. in Alberta on amalgamation with Redstar Oil & Gas Inc.; basis 1 new com. for 25 Pelorus shs. and 0.75 new com. and 0.25 new non-vtg. shs. for 25 old RedStar shs. ∎

Pelorus Navigation Systems Inc. (Alta. June 8, 1981)
Nov. 12, 2004 – Name changed to Pelorus Energy Corp. following reverse takeover acquisition of oil and gas assets in southern Alberta from 818541 Alberta Ltd. plus royalty interests from Elkwater Resources Ltd. ∎

Peltech Industries Inc. (B.C. Oct. 2, 1984)
Apr. 2, 1996 – Name changed to Gold Win Ventures Inc.; basis 1 new for 5 old shs. ∎

Pemberton Energy Ltd. (B.C. June 19, 1980)
Nov. 4, 2010 – Name changed to Brixton Energy Corp.; basis 1 new for 3 old shs. ∎

Pemberton Explorations Ltd. (B.C. June 19, 1980)
Jan. 29, 1992 – Name changed to Consolidated Pemberton Technologies Ltd.; basis 1 new for 3.5 old shs. ∎

Pemberton Houston Willoughby Investment Corporation (B.C. 1970)
Aug. 14, 1989 – Acquired by RBC Dominion Securities Limited for $9.00 per sh.

Pembina Pipe Line Ltd. (Alta. 1954)
May 25, 1982 – Name changed to Pembina Resources Limited. ■

Pembina Pipeline Income Fund (Alta. Sept. 4, 1997)
Mar. 1, 2007 – Amalgamated in Alberta to continue with same name.
Oct. 1, 2010 – Succeeded by Pembina Pipeline Corporation pursuant to plan of arrangement whereby Pembina Pipeline Corporation was formed to facilitate the conversion of the fund into a corporation. (see FPsurvey - Mines & Energy; FPsurvey - Industrials)

Pembina Resources Limited (Alta. 1954)
Feb. 1, 1988 – All o/s shs. not already held acquired by Manoil Ltd. by issue of pref. stock (1 for 1) redeemed at $22 per sh.

Pembridge Inc. (Ont. Nov. 3, 1994 amalg.)
Apr. 16, 1998 – Acquired by Pemco Acquition Inc., wholly owned subsid. of Allstate Corporation, for $20 per sh.

Pembroke Capital Corp. (B.C. May 6, 2010)
Jan. 20, 2012 – Name changed to Minfocus Exploration Corp. pursuant to Qualifying Transaction acquisition of Minfocus International Inc. ■

The Pembroke Electric Light Company, Limited (Can. 1931)
1980 – Amalgamated with private corp., 98072 Canada Inc., under continuing name of Pembroke Electric Light Company. Each com. shldr. received 1 special sh. of new co. for each com. sh. held. Special shs. redeemed at $24 per sh. 14 days after the amalgamation. Now wholly owned division of Tamay Realty Ltd.

Pembroke Star Resources Ltd. (B.C. Mar. 24, 1966)
Jan. 29, 1980 – Name changed to Eskimo Resources Ltd.; basis 1 new for 4 old shs. ■

Pemco Resources Ltd. (Alta. Jan. 7, 1988)
Sept. 23, 1991 – Name changed to Innovative Environmental Services Ltd. ■

Pemmican Mines Ltd. (Ont. 1946)
Oct. 1957 – Charter cancelled.

Pemstar Holdings Ltd. (Ont. 1928)
Apr. 30, 1980 – Dissolved.

Pen-Rey Gold Mines Ltd. (Ont. 1944)
1949 – Name changed to El Pen-Rey Mines Ltd.; basis 1 new for 3 old shs. ■

Penalta Oil Corporation Ltd. (Alta. 1951)
1958 – Name changed to Globe Oil Co. (1958) Ltd. ■

Pencari Mining Corporation (B.C. Feb. 2, 1999)
Feb. 2, 2009 – Name changed to Pencari Resource Corporation; basis 1 new for 5 old shs. ■

Pencari Resource Corporation (B.C. Feb. 2, 1999)
Aug. 27, 2009 – Name changed to Sheen Resources Ltd.; basis 1 new for 3 old shs. ■

Pencrude Resources Inc. (B.C. 1982)
May 19, 1989 – Dissolved.

Pendaries Petroleum Ltd. (Can. Aug. 29, 1996)
Sept. 9, 1996 – Continued into New Brunswick. (see Ultra Petroleum Corp.)
Jan. 18, 2001 – Acquired by Ultra Petroleum Corp.; basis 1.58 Ultra shs. for 1 Pendaries sh. (see Ultra Petroleum Corp.)

Pender Capital Corp. (Alta. Nov. 22, 1993)
Oct. 5, 2001 – Name changed to Garibaldi Granite Corp.; basis 1 new for 6 old shs. ■

Pender Financial Group Corporation (B.C. Nov. 30, 2001)
June 10, 2009 – Privatized at 14¢ per sh.

Pender Growth Fund (VCC) Inc. (B.C. Mar. 7, 1994)
Nov. 1, 2016 – Name changed to Pender Growth Fund Inc. (see FPsurvey - Industrials)

Pendragon Capital Corporation (Alta. May 10, 1993)
Sept. 13, 1995 – Name changed to Upland Global Corporation. ■

Pendragon Corp. Ltd. (unknown)
1959 – Merged into Penelope Explorations Ltd.

Pendragon Resources Limited (Alta. Jan. 28, 1987)
Nov. 2, 1989 – Name changed to Fibre-Klad Industries Ltd.; basis 1 new for 4 old shs. ■

Pendulum Capital Corporation (Alta. Nov. 4, 2009)
Dec. 31, 2010 – Formed PetroFrontier Corp. in Alberta pursuant to Qualifying Transaction reverse takeover acquisition of and amalgamation with Australia Energy Corp.; basis 1 new for 12 old shs. (see FPsurvey - Mines & Energy)

Penelope Explorations Ltd. (Ont. 1959)
1964 – Name changed to Initiative Explorations Ltd. ■

Penfield Uranium Mines Ltd. (Ont. 1955)
Jan. 1961 – Charter cancelled; distribution to shldrs. 13.069¢ per sh.

Penfold Capital Acquisition II Corporation (Can. Nov. 14, 2007)
Oct. 6, 2010 – Amalgamated with Penfold Capital Acquisition III (deemed acquiror; basis 0.5 Penfold Capital Acquisition III shs. for 1 Pendfold Capital Acquisition II sh. (see Penfold Capital Acquisition III Corporation)

Penfold Capital Acquisition III Corporation (Can. June 19, 2008)
Sept. 24, 2010 – Amalgamated in Canada to continue with same name.
Jan. 18, 2011 – Private placement totaling 10,000,000 units and 4,000,000 warrants with Phonetime Inc. which constituted Qualifying Transaction. Co. will distribute the Phonetime units and wts. to shldrs. on a pro rata basis and Co. was subsequently wound up and dissolved.

Penfold Capital Acquisition IV Corporation (Ont. Mar. 31, 2010)
July 9, 2014 – Name changed to SEL Exchange Inc. (see FPsurvey - Industrials)

Penfold Capital Acquisition Corporation (Can. May 31, 2007)
Sept. 24, 2008 – Name changed to PBS Coals Limited; basis 1 new for 10 old shs. ■

Pengelly Mines Ltd. (B.C. 1979)
Oct. 30, 1992 – Dissolved and struck off register.

Pengrowth Energy Corporation (Alta. Dec. 31, 2010; amalg.)
Jan. 8, 2020 – Acquired by Cona Resources Ltd.; basis 5¢ per share cash plus a potential Contingent Value Payment (CVP) which was the potential consideration that shareholders would receive on a pro rata basis of any funds that may be received by Pengrowth as a result of a pending litigation matter with Grand Valley Resources Corp. as a dividend-in-kind.

Pengrowth Energy Trust (Alta. Dec. 2, 1988)
Jan. 1, 2011 – Succeeded by Pengrowth Energy Corporation pursuant to plan of arrangement whereby Pengrowth Energy Corporation was formed to facilitate the conversion of the trust into a corporation and the trust was subsequently dissolved. ■

Pengrowth Gas Income Fund (Alta. Dec. 2, 1988)
May 29, 1996 – Name changed to Pengrowth Energy Trust. ■

Penguin Yellowknife Mines Ltd. (Ont. 1945)
Dec. 9, 1957 – Charter cancelled.

Peninsula Gold Explorations Ltd. (Ont. Dec. 11, 1995)
July 26, 2000 – Formed ACEnetx Inc. in Ontario on amalgamation with Aurora Communication Exchange Ltd. with Aurora the deemed acquiror; basis 1 new for 1 Aurora sh. and 1.503 new for 1 Peninsula sh. (see FPsurvey - Industrials)

Peninsula Metals Corporation (Que. 1957)
Aug. 1, 1978 – Amalgamated with Federal Metals Corp. to form Fedpen Ltée; basis 0.7 new for 1 old sh.

Peninsula Petroleum Corporation (B.C. 1983)
June 3, 1985 – Amalgamated with North South Resources Ltd. and International Petroleum Ltd. to continue under the Consolidated International Petroleum Corporation name; basis 1 new for 5.08 old shs.

Peninsula Resources Ltd. (Alta. Feb. 22, 1994)
May 12, 2008 – Continued into British Columbia.
Sept. 28, 2010 – Name changed to Zodiac Exploration Inc. and continued into Alberta pursuant to amalgamation of Zodiac Exploration Corp. (ZEC) with a wholly owned subsid., constituting a reverse takeover by ZEC. ■

Peninsular Oil Corporation Ltd (Que. Mar. 1945)
1952 – Name changed to New Peninsular Oil Limited and continued into Quebec. ■

Penko Gold Mines Ltd. (Ont. 1944)
Feb. 1964 – Dissolved.

Penmans Limited (Can. 1906)
1973 – All o/s com. shs. not already held acquired by Dominion Textile Limited in 1965. All pref. shs. redeemed.

Penn Capital Inc. (B.C. Oct. 15, 2014)
Mar. 25, 2022 – Name changed to Umdoni Exploration Inc. ■

Penn-Cobalt Silver Mines (Ont. 1950)
1953 – Acquired by Cobalt Consolidated Mining Corp. Ltd.; basis 1 new for 13 old shs. (see Cobalt Consolidated Mining Corp. Ltd.)

Penn Energy Corporation (B.C. 1976)
June 1982 – Name changed to New Penn Energy Corporation; basis 1 new for 3 old shs. ■

Penn-Gold Resources Inc. (B.C. Mar. 30, 1988)
Apr. 7, 1998 – Name changed to Moreno Ventures Inc.; basis 1 new for 13 old shs. ■

Penn Holdings Inc. (Ont. 1975)
Sept. 6, 1989 – Name changed to Raider Ventures Ltd.; basis 1 new for 3 old shs. ■

Penn-Lync Resources Ltd. (Ont. 1975)
Jan. 13, 1988 – Name changed to Penn Holdings Inc.; basis 1 new for 2 old shs. ■

Penn West Energy Trust (Alta. Apr. 22, 2005)
Jan. 1, 2011 – Succeeded by Penn West Petroleum Ltd. pursuant to a plant of arrangement whereby Penn West Petroleum Ltd. was formed to facilitate the conversion of the trust into a corporation and the trust was subsequently dissolved. ■

Penn West Petroleum Ltd. (Alta. Dec. 27, 1979 amalg.)
June 2, 2005 – Converted into an income trust named Penn West Energy Trust; basis 3 trust units for 1 com. sh. (see Penn West Energy Trust)

Penn West Petroleum Ltd. (Alta. Jan. 1, 2011; amalg.)
June 26, 2017 – Name changed to Obsidian Energy Ltd. (see FPsurvey - Mines & Energy)

Pennant Energy Inc. (B.C. Aug. 25, 1987)
Apr. 22, 2014 – Acquired by Blackbird Energy Inc.; basis 0.42857 Blackbird com. shs. for 1 Pennant com. sh. (see Blackbird Energy Inc.)

Pennant Oils Ltd. (Alta.)
June 22, 1973 – Amalgamated with Puma Petroleums Ltd. to form Pennant-Puma Oils Ltd.; basis 1 new for 1 old sh.

Pennant Petroleum Ltd. (Alta. Feb. 10, 1995)
Oct. 8, 1997 – Amalgamated with 735498 Alberta Ltd., a wholly owned subsid. of Cascade Oil & Gas Ltd.; basis 1 com. sh. of Cascade for 2 com. shs. of Pennant. (see Cascade Oil & Gas Ltd.)

Pennant-Puma Oils Ltd. (Alta. 1973)
1976 – Acquired by Algas Mineral Enterprises Ltd.
Jan. 1, 1977 – Went into voluntary liquidation.
May 31, 1978 – Dissolved and struck off register.

Pennant Resources Ltd. (Ont. 1945)
Nov. 23, 1987 – Formed PNR Food Industries Ltd. on amalgamation with The Great Canadian Soup Co. ∎

Pennaque Mining Corp. Ltd. (Ont. Mar. 5, 1937)
May 1980 – Charter cancelled.
Apr. 1, 1982 – Charter revived.
Apr. 30, 1986 – Name changed to Lakeshore Minerals Inc. ∎

Pennask Silver Mines Ltd. (B.C. 1966)
Dec. 22, 1975 – Dissolved.

Pennbec Mining Corporation (Que. 1955)
Dec. 1974 – Charter cancelled.

Pennilane Development Corp. (B.C. July 10, 1987)
Mar. 1, 1994 – Name changed to Mandarin Industries Ltd.; basis 1 new for 1.5 old shs. ∎

Pennine Petroleum Corporation (Alta. Sept. 18, 2001)
June 2, 2022 – Name changed to Pambili Natural Resources Corporation. (see FPsurvey - Mines & Energy)

Pennington's Stores Limited (Ont. Apr. 7, 1969)
Dec. 28, 1992 – Declared bankrupt and Richter & Partners Inc. of Toronto was appointed trustee.
Nov. 1994 – Granted protection under the Companies' Creditors Arrangement Act.
Feb. 1995 – All assets sold and Reitmans (Canada) Limited acquired all the assets of the Wearhouse division, all trade names and an additional 10 retail stores in major malls across Canada.
Mar. 1996 – Unsecured creditors received a distribution of 60¢ on the dollar. No funds were available for shldrs.
Oct. 24, 2000 – Trustee discharged.

Penny Spruce Mills Ltd. (Alta. 1946)
Oct. 14, 1961 – Struck off register.

Pennzoil Company (Del. 1968)
Dec. 31, 1998 – Formed PennzEnergy Company following acquisition of Quaker State Corp.

Penobscot Mining Co. Ltd. (Ont. 1956)
Feb. 5, 1980 – Dissolved.

Penrose Gold Mines Ltd. (Ont. 1945)
Nov. 28, 1973 – Charter cancelled.

Penrose Resource Corporation (B.C. Mar. 14, 1983)
May 28, 1993 – Name changed to Network One Holdings Corp.; basis 1 new for 3 old shs. (see FPsurvey - Industrials)

Pensec Explorations Inc. (Ont. 1973)
Oct. 29, 1980 – Amalgamated with Erieshore Industries Inc. and Portfield Petroleums Limited to form Portfield Industries Inc.; basis 1 new for 4 old shs.

Pensive Yellowknife Mines Ltd. (Ont. 1944)
1967 – Charter cancelled.

Penstar Petroleum Ltd. (Alta. 1975)
May 31, 1984 – Amalgamated with Commercial Oil & Gas Ltd. to form a new co. under the continuing name of Commercial Oil & Gas Ltd. Com. stock of Penstar exch. for com. stock of Commercial on sh.-for-sh. basis; 50% of Penstar pref. stock exch. into com. stock on 1 new for

2 old basis, while other 50% exch. for 2nd pref. stock on sh.-for-sh. basis.

PenStar Wirecom, Ltd. (Ont. Sept. 25, 1995 amalg.)
Dec. 10, 1997 – Name changed to Neuro-Biotech Corporation following reverse takeover acquisition of Neuro-Biotech Inc. (deemed acquiror) and 1246895 Ontario Inc.; basis 1 new for 10 old shs. ∎

Pentagon Mining Corporation (Que. 1954)
Oct. 1974 – Charter cancelled.

Pentagon Oils & Mines Ltd. (Ont. 1945)
1951 – Name changed to Savannah Oils & Mines Ltd. ∎

Pentagon Oils Ltd. (Alta. Aug. 1, 1950)
Apr. 3, 1953 – Shldrs. received 13.6¢ per sh.; co. wound up.

Pentagon Resources Ltd. (B.C. 1966)
June 28, 1983 – Name changed to Quintel Industries Limited; basis 1 new for 5 old shs. ∎

PentaNova Energy Corp. (B.C. June 5, 2017)
Sept. 4, 2018 – Name changed to CruzSur Energy Corp.; basis 1 new for 10 old shs. ∎

Penteco Resources Ltd. (B.C. Aug. 25, 1987)
Apr. 29, 2004 – Name changed to Pennant Energy Inc. ∎

Penthouse Holdings Ltd. (Alta. 1954)
Jan. 8, 1980 – Name changed to Gamon Oil & Gas Ltd. ∎

Pentland Firth Holdings Ltd. (Alta. June 19, 1990)
Aug. 4, 1994 – Name changed to Pentland Firth Ventures Ltd. ∎

Pentland Firth Ventures Ltd. (Alta. June 19, 1990)
Sept. 1, 1995 – Continued into Ontario.
Aug. 1, 2001 – Continued into Alberta.
Aug. 8, 2001 – Name changed to Tesoro Energy Corp. following reverse takeover acquisition of Tesoro Energy Ltd. from Quarry Oil & Gas Ltd. ∎

Penway Explorers Ltd. (Ont. 1981)
Feb. 19, 1991 – Delisted from the Alberta Stock Exchange. Charter subsequently cancelled and dissolved.

Penwood Gold Mines Ltd. (Ont. 1946)
1960 – Charter cancelled.

Penyork Energy Resource Inc. (Ont. 1980)
Apr. 1986 – Name changed to Abagold Resources Inc. ∎

People Corporation (Ont. Oct. 1, 2011 amalg.)
Feb. 19, 2021 – Acquired by Goldman Sachs & Co., LLC; basis $15.22 cash per sh.

People's Communications Inc. (Ont. Apr. 6, 1908)
Jan. 24, 2006 – Acquired by Amtelecom Income Fund for $60 per sh. (see Amtelecom Income Fund)

Peoples Credit Securities Limited (Ont. 1942)
Aug. 20, 1954 – In voluntary liquidation. Holders of each com. sh. received (tax free) $10, $7.50 of a $100 par pref. sh. and 2 com. shs. of Peoples Credit Jewellers Ltd.

Peoples Department Stores Ltd. (Can. 1933)
Jan. 31, 1979 – Amalgamated with several of its subsids. to become Marks & Spencer Canada Ltd.

Peoples Jewellers Limited (Can. Apr. 9, 1930)
Apr. 21, 1993 – Filed proposed debt restructuring Plan of Arrangement.
July 29, 1993 – Plan defeated at shldrs. meeting and Peat Marwick Thorne Inc. appointed receiver and manager of the company.
July 29, 1993 – Continued into Ontario.
Sept. 23, 1993 – All the operating assets of the company sold to a new corporate entity known as Peoples Jewellers Corporation.
June 1, 1997 – Receiver discharged having completed its mandate. Secured creditors suffered a shortfall and there was no distribution to shldrs.

People's Oil & Gas Ltd. (Ont. 1920)
Feb. 19, 1929 – Name changed to American Engineering Co.

Peoples Oil Limited (Alta. Aug. 31, 1979)
Feb. 10, 1997 – Name changed to Sterling Resources Ltd. ∎

The People's Telephone Company of Forest Limited (Ont. Apr. 6, 1908)
June 3, 1998 – Name changed to People's Communications Inc. ∎

Pepcap Ventures Inc. (Alta. Jan. 31, 2012)
May 14, 2015 – Continued into British Columbia.
May 19, 2015 – Name changed to Pepcap Resources Inc. following Qualifying Transaction acquisition of 51% interest in Asia Mining Management, B.V. (see FPsurvey - Mines & Energy)

Pepmont Gold Mines Ltd. (Ont. 1945)
Apr. 1959 – Charter cancelled.

Peppa Resources Ltd. (B.C. 1966)
July 17, 1992 – Dissolved and struck off register.

Pepperess Mines Ltd. (Ont. 1947)
1954 – Assets acquired by Dupel Mines Ltd.

Peragis Inc. (Can. Dec. 12, 1996)
Oct. 4, 2005 – Dissolved.

Peralto Resources Corp. (B.C. 1980)
Sept. 4, 1992 – Dissolved and struck off register.

Perbell Mines Ltd. (B.C. 1966)
Feb. 25, 1983 – Struck off register.

Perch River Mines Limited (Ont. 1971)
Mar. 21, 1989 – Amalgamated with Hanson Mineral Exploration Limited (1 new for 5 old shs.) to form McNickel, Inc.; basis 1 com. sh. amalco. for each com. sh. of Perch River. (see McNickel Inc.)

Percy Street Capital Corporation (Can. June 18, 2014)
June 21, 2018 – Name changed to LiveWell Canada Inc. following Qualifying Transaction reverse takeover acquisition of LiveWell Foods Canada Inc.; basis 1 new for 3 old shs. ∎

Peregrine Diamonds Ltd. (Can. Nov. 19, 2002)
Sept. 13, 2018 – Acquired by De Beers Canada Inc.; basis 24¢ cash per sh.

Peregrine Energy Ltd. (Alta. July 21, 2004 amalg.)
June 5, 2006 – Plan of Arrangement acquisition by Mahalo Energy Ltd.; basis 0.48 new Mahalo sh. for 1 old Peregrine sh. (see Mahalo Energy Ltd.)

Peregrine Exploration Ltd. (B.C. 1969)
May 1972 – Amalgamated with Windermere Explorations Ltd. (1 for 2) to form Barrier Reef Resources Ltd.; basis 6 new Barrier shs. for 1 old Peregrine sh.

Peregrine Metals Ltd. (Can. Sept. 20, 2005)
Oct. 12, 2011 – Acquired by Stillwater Mining Company; basis US$1.35 plus 0.08136 Stillwater shs. for 1 Peregrine sh. (see Stillwater Mining Company)

Peregrine Oil and Gas Ltd. (Alta. Mar. 27, 1952)
July 7, 2000 – Amalgamated with Plexus Energy Ltd. and AEGIS Energy Ltd. to form Surge Petroleum Inc.; basis 1 new for 2.8225 Plexus shs., 1 new for 3.3 AEGIS shs. and 1 new for 3.6474 Peregrine shs. (see Surge Petroleum Inc.)

Peregrine Petroleum Ltd. (Alta. Mar. 27, 1952)
Dec. 8, 1994 – Name changed to Peregrine Oil and Gas Ltd.; basis 1 new for 4 old shs. ∎

Perfect Fry Corporation (Alta. Apr. 28, 1964)
July 14, 2010 – Name changed to Woodrose Corporation following sale of assets of wholly owned Perfect Fry Company Ltd. to The Middleby Corporation. ∎

Performance Plus Fund Ltd. (Can. June 21, 1968)
July 1972 – Name changed to Brafor Capital Corporation Limited. ■

Performance Property Capital Inc. (Can. Oct. 24, 2001)
Oct. 31, 2002 – Formed Innovative Properties Inc. in Canada following non-arm's length Qualifying Transaction amalgamation with Innovative Properties Inc. ■

Performance Sports Group Ltd. (B.C. Dec. 2, 2010)
Mar. 20, 2017 – Name changed to Old PSG Wind-down Ltd. ■

Peribec Gold Mines Ltd. (Ont. 1944)
Nov. 18, 1958 – Dissolved.

Perigee Inc. (Can. Jan. 1, 1998)
May 13, 1998 – Continued into Ontario.
May 26, 2000 – Amalgamated with Legg Mason Canada Holdings Ltd., an indirect wholly owned subsid. of US-based Legg Mason, Inc.; basis 0.387 exch. sh. of Legg Mason for 1 sh. Perigee, exch. anytime at option of holder but each is automatically exch. in 2015 for 1 com. sh. Legg Mason.

Perihelion Capital Ltd. (B.C. Apr. 13, 2018)
Nov. 25, 2022 – Name changed to Hydreight Technologies Inc. pursuant to the Qualfying Transaction reverse takeover acquisition of IV Hydreight Inc., indirectly acquired through the acquisition of Victory Square Technologies Inc.'s newly incorporated wholly owned 1362795 B.C. Ltd. Victory Square was the former parent of IV Hydreight, which was transferred to 1362795 B.C. Ltd. immediately prior to completion of the transaction, with 1362795 B.C. Ltd. having concurrently amalgamated with Perihelion's wholly owned 1203500 B.C. Ltd. upon completion of the transaction; basis 1 new for 6.46805 old shs. (see FPsurvey - Industrials)

Perimeter Ventures Ltd. (B.C. Aug. 19, 1983)
Sept. 9, 1993 – Name changed to Warner Ventures Ltd.; basis 1 new for 4 old shs. ■

Peritronics Medical Inc. (B.C. 1981)
Nov. 6, 1989 – Name changed to Consolidated Peritronics Medical Inc.; basis 1 new for 3 old shs. ■

Peritronics Medical, Ltd. (B.C. 1981)
Aug. 28, 2006 – Struck from registry and dissolved for failure to file.

Perk Inc. (Ont. Nov. 5, 2014)
Jan. 23, 2017 – Acquired by RhythmOne plc; basis 4.5116 RhythmOne ord. shs. for 1 Perk com. sh.

Perk.com Inc. (Ont. Nov. 5, 2014)
June 28, 2016 – Name changed to Perk Inc. ■

Perkins Oil Limited (B.C. June 15, 1979)
Nov. 28, 1988 – Dissolved and struck off register.

Perkins Papers Ltd. (Can. Mar. 6, 1930; via letters patent)
Sept. 30, 1983 – Amalgamated in Canada to continue with same name.
Dec. 31, 2000 – All o/s shs. not already held acquired by Cascades Inc.; basis 0.64 Cascades shs. for 1 Perkins sh.

Perle Systems Limited (Ont. July 20, 1976)
Oct. 29, 2003 – Privatized via 1-for-2,000,000 consolidation (Royal Capital Management Inc held 98.1%).

Perlite Canada Inc. (Que. Aug. 23, 1993)
Mar. 15, 2019 – Privatized via all o/s shs. not already held acquired by 9388-6869 Quebec Inc., owned by Richard Barabé, the president and CEO, and Martin Joyal, the corporate secretary of the company; basis 1 new redeemable sh. for 1 Perlite com. sh. immediately redeemed for 82¢ cash.

Perlite Mining Corp. Ltd. (Ont. 1954)
Mar. 1976 – Charter cancelled.

Perma Gold Mines Ltd. (Ont. 1945)
Aug. 3, 1964 – Charter cancelled.

Permian Resources Ltd. (B.C. Mar. 28, 1983)
Dec. 23, 1988 – Name changed to M.L. Cass Petroleum Corporation; basis 1 new for 4 old shs. ■

Permission Marketing Solutions Inc. (B.C. Apr. 28, 1988)
Jan. 4, 2006 – Name changed to Pacific Asia China Energy Inc. pursuant to reverse takeover acquisition of China Canada Energy Corp. ■

Permo Gas & Oil Limited (Ont. 1956)
Dec. 1971 – Acquired by Pan Ocean Oil Corp.; basis 3.6 new for 100 old shs.

Pero Development Group Inc. (Alta. June 30, 1990 amalg.)
Apr. 30, 1996 – Formed Canadiana Genetics Inc. on amalgamation with Canadiana Genetics Inc. (1 cl. A for 0.711744 cl. A and 1 cl. B for 1 cl. B); basis 1 new for 10 old shs. ■

Perpetual Energy Inc. (Alta. Apr. 26, 2010)
Nov. 5, 2024 – Acquired by Rubellite Energy Inc. (renamed Rubellite Energy Corp.); basis 1 Rubellite sh. for 5 Perpetual shs.

Perron Enterprises Inc. (Que. Apr. 30, 1968)
Apr. 17, 1973 – Name changed to Normick Perron Inc.; basis 12 new for 1 old sh. ■

Perron Gold Mines Ltd. (B.C. 1972)
Aug. 31, 1988 – Succeeded by Aurizon Mines Ltd. following acquisition of all assets of Perron Gold Mines and D'Or Val Mines Ltd. by Aurizon Mines Ltd.; basis 0.5 new for 1 Perron sh. and 0.4167 new for 1 D'Or Val sh. Prior to transfer of assets, Perron and D'Or Val were amalgamated to form Amalgamated D'Or Val Perron Mines Ltd. and subsequently dissolved. ■

Perry Creek Mines Ltd. (B.C. Sept. 12, 1967)
Apr. 29, 1974 – Name changed to Rebel Developments Ltd. ■

Perry Kirkland Mines Ltd. (unknown 1928)
Aug. 1972 – Charter cancelled.

Perry River Nickel Mines Ltd. (B.C. 1972)
1978 – Continued into Alberta.
Nov. 17, 1981 – Amalgamated into American Chromium Limited; basis 1 cl. A voting sh. and 1 cl. B non-voting sh. for 10 old shs.

Perseverance Mining & Development Co. Ltd. (Ont. 1935)
Nov. 9, 1959 – Charter cancelled.

Pershcourt Gold Fields Ltd. (Que. 1945)
1955 – Name changed to Consolidated Pershcourt Mining Ltd.; basis 1 new for 3 old shs. ■

Pershimco Resources Inc. (Can. Apr. 3, 1989)
Dec. 7, 2016 – Merged into Orla Mining Ltd.; basis 0.19 com. sh. plus 0.04 cl. A sh. of Orla for 1 Pershimco sh.

Pershimex Resources Corporation (Can. Nov. 28, 2007)
May 17, 2023 – Acquired and merged into Abcourt Mines Inc.; basis 0.5712 Abcourt shs. for 1 Pershimex sh.

Pershing Amalgamated Mines Ltd. (Que. 1947)
May 1974 – Charter cancelled.

Pershing Gold Corporation (Nev. Aug. 2, 2007)
Apr. 8, 2019 – Acquired by Americas Silver Corporation; basis 0.715 Americas Silver com. shs. for 1 Pershing Gold com. sh. (see Americas Silver Corp.)

Pershland Gold Mines Ltd. (Ont. 1945)
Jan. 8, 1975 – Charter cancelled.

Pershon Gold Mines Limited (Ont. Mar. 1, 1945)
Nov. 5, 1982 – Name changed to Golden Shadow Resources Inc. ■

Persian Petroleum Corporation (B.C. Jan. 25, 1978)
Nov. 9, 1982 – Amalgamated with Diana Explorations Ltd. and Arabian Petroleum Corporation to form Equus Petroleum Corporation; basis 1 new Equus for 2.6956 old Persian shs.

Persona Inc. (Can. Oct. 26, 1984)
Aug. 9, 2004 – Plan of Arrangement acquisition by an investor group including TD Capital Canadian Private Equity Partners and CIBC Capital Partners; basis $6.80 per sh.

Pertacal Energy Inc. (Alta. July 18, 1994)
Jan. 2, 2010 – Struck from registry and dissolved.

Perth Venture Capital Corporation (Can. Mar. 2, 1998)
Apr. 30, 2001 – Name changed to Biolix Corporation. (see FPsurvey - Industrials)

Peru Copper Inc. (Can. Feb. 24, 2004)
Sept. 19, 2007 – Acquired by Aluminum Corporation of China for Cdn$6.60 per sh.

Peruvian Gold Limited (B.C. Feb. 15, 1971)
July 9, 2002 – Amalgamated with Bradstone Equity Partners, Inc., Glenex Industries Inc. and Stockscape.com Technologies Inc. to form Quest Investment Corporation; basis 1 new cl.A sh. for 1 Bradstone sh., 1 new cl.A sh. for 2.268 Glenex shs., 1 new cl.A sh. for 4.1387 Stockscape.com shs. and 1 new cl.A sh. for 1.7156 old Peruvian shs. (see Quest Investment Corporation)

Peruvian International Airways (Peru 1946)
Feb. 26, 1949 – Involuntary petition in bankruptcy filed. Randolph Mason, 19 Rector St., New York, appointed trustee.

Peruvian Oils & Minerals, Limited (Ont. 1952)
June 22, 1973 – Name changed to Pominex Ltd. ■

Peruvian Precious Metals Corp. (Alta. July 28, 1987)
Aug. 4, 2016 – Name changed to PPX Mining Corp. (see FPsurvey - Mines & Energy)

Perwal Petroleums Ltd. (Ont. 1938)
1960 – Struck off register.

Peso Carmacks Gold Mines Ltd. (B.C. 1963)
Sept. 21, 1972 – Dissolved.

Peso Silver Mines Limited (B.C. Mar. 17, 1961)
Mar. 30, 1979 – Name changed to Rex Silver Mines Ltd.; basis 1 new for 5 old shs. ■

Pet Valu Canada Inc. (Ont. May 23, 1993)
Sept. 3, 2009 – Privatized at Cdn$13.68 per exch. sh.

Pet Valu Inc. (Ont. May 23, 1993)
June 5, 1996 – Name changed to Pet Valu Canada Inc.; basis 1 new exch. for 1 old com. sh. ■

Pet Yellowknife Gold Mines Ltd. (Ont. 1946)
Feb. 14, 1952 – Charter cancelled.

Petaquilla Copper Ltd. (B.C. Mar. 15, 2006)
Dec. 3, 2008 – Acquired by 6910360 Canada Inc., a wholly owned subsid. of Inmet Mining Corporation, for $2.20 per sh.

Petawaga Mining Corp. (Que. 1955)
Jan. 24, 1981 – Charter cancelled.

Petcan Resources Ltd. (Alta. 1972)
Mar. 10, 1983 – Amalgamated with Backer Resources Ltd. to form new co. under latter name; basis 2 Petcan shs. for 1 new sh.

Peteque Mines Exploration Ltd. (Ont. 1946)
Charter cancelled.

Peter Island Resources Inc. (Ont. June 19, 1984)
Mar. 19, 1993 – Name changed to Tri-Vision International Ltd./Ltée following reverse takeover acquisition of Tri-Vision Electronics Inc.; basis 1 new for 10 old shs. ■

The Peter Miller Apparel Group Inc. (Ont. Mar. 24, 1980)
June 23, 1989 – Name changed to PMG Financial Inc. ∎

Peter Rabbit Energy Corporation (B.C. Apr. 3, 1984)
Jan. 24, 1994 – Name changed to PBB Venture Corporation. ∎

Peter-Rock Mining Co. Ltd. (Ont. 1954)
May 1974 – Charter cancelled.

Peterborough Capital Corp. (Alta. May 10, 2000)
Aug. 28, 2008 – Name changed to Bowmore Exploration Ltd.; basis 1 new for 4 old shs. ∎

Petersburg Long Distance Inc. (Ont. 1974)
Aug. 20, 1996 – Name changed to PLD Telekom Inc. ∎

Petersfield Oil & Minerals Ltd. (B.C. Aug. 29, 1980)
May 26, 1988 – Name changed to Hovik Medical Corporation. ∎

Peterson Cobalt Mines Ltd. (Ont. 1926)
July 1964 – Charter cancelled; distributed 6 shs. Trinova Cobalt Silver for each pref. sh. and 1 sh. Trinova for 17 com. shs.

Petgo Resources Ltd. (B.C. 1977)
Oct. 6, 1987 – Name changed to Wydmar Development Corp. ∎

Pethealth Inc. (Can. Dec. 19, 2000 amalg.)
Nov. 19, 2014 – Acquired by Fairfax Financial Holdings Limited for Cdn$2.79 per sh.
Oct. 31, 2022 – Continued into British Columbia.

Petitclerc Mines Ltd. (Ont. 1945)
Apr. 29, 1970 – Charter cancelled.

Petra Petroleum Inc. (B.C. Aug. 25, 1988)
Apr. 21, 2015 – Name changed to Mitra Energy Inc. pursuant to reverse takeover acquisition of Mitra Energy Limited.; basis 1 new for 4 old shs. ∎

Petra Resource Corp. (B.C. June 8, 1988)
Nov. 30, 2003 – Name changed to Olly Industries Inc.; basis 1 new for 25 old shs. subsequent to year end. ∎

Petro-American Energy Inc. (B.C. Feb. 19, 1969)
July 11, 1986 – Dissolved and struck off register.

Petro Andina Resources Inc. (Alta. July 10, 2003)
Nov. 12, 2009 – Acquired by 1462627 Alberta Ltd., an indirect wholly owned subsid. of Pluspetrol Resources Corporation N.V. by way of plan of arrangement whereby Petro Andina's Colombia and Trinidad & Tobago exploration assets were transferred to newly formed publicly listed Parex Resources Inc.; basis $7.65 per sh. plus 1 Parex Resources com. sh. and 0.10 Parex wt.

Petro Basin Energy Corp. (Ont. Feb. 2, 1994 amalg.)
Sept. 15, 2015 – Continued into British Columbia.
Sept. 15, 2016 – Name changed to Peace River Capital Corp. ∎

Petro-Canada (Can. July 30, 1975; via Petro-Canada Act)
Aug. 7, 2009 – Amalgamated with Suncor Energy Inc.; basis 1.28 Suncor shs. for 1 Petro-Canada sh.

Petro-Canada Enterprises Inc. (Can. 1953)
Feb. 28, 1983 – Petro-Canada subsid. offered to acquire all o/s com. shs. at $120 per sh.

Petro-Canada Products Inc. (Can. 1982 amalg.)
Jan. 1, 1986 – Petro-Canada Inc. completed takeover by purch. of remaining non-voting shs.

Petro-Chemsol Chemicals, Ltd. (Can. 1952)
1958 – Charter cancelled; nothing available for com. shldrs.

Petro Field Industries Inc. (Alta. Nov. 20, 1995)
May 2, 2007 – Name changed to Tornado Technologies Inc. ∎

Petro-Gaspe (1986) Inc. (Que. Mar. 19, 1986)
June 3, 1996 – Name changed to Azimut Exploration Inc. (see FPsurvey - Mines & Energy)

Petro Horizon Energy Corp. (B.C. Feb. 24, 1997)
Aug. 13, 2010 – Name changed to Greenlight Resources Inc. ∎

Petro Occidente Capital Corp. (Alta. Jan. 12, 2011)
Aug. 14, 2013 – Name changed to North Sur Resources Inc. pursuant to Qualifying Transaction mineral property option agreement. ∎

Petro One Energy Corp. (B.C. Apr. 23, 2010)
Mar. 3, 2016 – Acquired by Goldstrike Resources Ltd.; basis 1 Goldstrike sh. for 4 Petro One shs. held. (see Goldstrike Resources Ltd.)

Petro-Pak Resources Ltd. (B.C. 1979)
Nov. 29, 1985 – Struck off register.

Petro-Plus Inc. (Alta. Apr. 4, 1990)
Jan. 14, 1999 – Name changed to Northern Star Resources Inc.; basis 1 new for 5 old shs. ∎

Petro-Reef Resources Ltd. (Alta. Dec. 12, 1988)
Sept. 9, 2012 – Name changed to Alexander Energy Ltd. ∎

Petro River Oil Corp. (Alta. Feb. 12, 2008)
Sept. 11, 2012 – Continued into Delaware.

Petro Rubiales Energy Corp. (B.C. July 9, 2007)
Jan. 24, 2008 – Name changed to Pacific Rubiales Energy Corp. following acquisition of Pacific Stratus Energy Ltd.; basis 9.5 new for 1 old sh. ∎

Petro-Sun Inc. (Ont. 1979 amalg.)
June 15, 1982 – Name changed to Petro-sun International Inc. ∎

Petro-sun International Inc. (Ont. 1979 amalg.)
Feb. 25, 1993 – Deemed bankrupt. No distribution available for shldrs.

Petro Uno Resources Ltd. (Alta. July 12, 2006)
Apr. 20, 2011 – Acquired by Renegade Petroleum Ltd.; basis 0.20 Renegade shs. for 1 Petro Uno sh. (see Renegade Petroleum Ltd.)

Petro Uranium of Canada Ltd. (Alta. 1953)
Jan. 31, 1967 – Struck off register.

Petro Viking Energy Inc. (Alta. Jan. 13, 2010)
Dec. 3, 2021 – Name changed to Avila Energy Corporation. (see FPsurvey - Mines & Energy)

Petro Vista Energy Corp. (B.C. Apr. 6, 2006)
Jan. 8, 2019 – Name changed to 3 Sixty Risk Solutions Ltd. pursuant to reverse takeover acquisition of 3 Sixty Secure Corp. and amalgamation of 3 Sixty with a wholly owned subsidiary of Petro Vista Energy Corp.; basis 1 new for 2 old shs. ∎

Petro Well Energy Services Inc. (Alta. Aug. 28, 1997)
Dec. 2, 1999 – Formed CenAlta Energy Services Inc. on amalgamation with Aldrilco Ltd. (private co.) and the acquired CenAlta Well Servicing Inc.; basis 1 new for 5 old shs. ∎

Petroamerica Oil Corp. (B.C. Mar. 6, 1986)
Dec. 10, 2010 – Continued into Alberta.
Jan. 18, 2016 – Acquired by Gran Tierra Energy Inc.; basis Cdn $1.33 or 0.4 Gran Tierra com. shs. for 1 Petroamerica com. sh.

PetroBakken Energy Ltd. (Alta. July 30, 2009)
Dec. 31, 2012 – Amalgamated with major shareholder Petrobank Energy and Resources Ltd., following spin-off of Petrobank's assets and liabilities excluding its 56% interest in PetroBakken, to continue as (new) PetroBakken Energy Ltd.; basis 1 new PetroBakken sh. for 1 old PetroBakken sh. and 1.1051 new Petrobakken sh. for 1 old Petrobank sh.

PetroBakken Energy Ltd. (Alta. Dec. 31, 2012 amalg.)
May 22, 2013 – Name changed to Lightstream Resources Ltd. ∎

Petrobank Energy and Resources Ltd. (Alta. Dec. 1, 1983)
Dec. 31, 2012 – Formed PetroBakken Energy Ltd. in Alberta on amalgamation with 56%-owned PetroBakken Energy Ltd. following spin-off of Petrobank's assets and liabilities excluding its interest in PetroBakken; basis 1 new PetroBakken sh. for 1 old PetroBakken sh. and 1.1051 new Petrobakken shs. for 1 old Petrobank sh. ∎

Petrobank Energy and Resources Ltd. (Alta. Oct. 24, 2012)
May 13, 2014 – Name changed to Touchstone Exploration Inc. following reverse takeover acquisition of (old) Touchstone Exploration Inc.; basis 1 new for 2 old shs. (see FPsurvey - Mines & Energy)

Petrobar Explorations Inc. (Ont. 1978)
Dec. 29, 1982 – Amalgamated with Thunderbolt Gas & Oil Explorations Ltd., Sidewinder Explorations Inc., Golden Falcon Explorations Inc. and 514567 Ontario Limited to form Parapet Petroleums Inc.; basis 3 new for 2 old shs.

Petrobotics Ventures Ltd. (B.C. June 22, 1983)
June 10, 1986 – Name changed to North American Metals Corp. ∎

Petrocapita Income Trust (Alta. Jan. 22, 2010)
June 12, 2019 – Hudson and Company Insolvency Trustees Inc. appointed receiver and manager of wholly owned Petrocapita G.P. I Ltd. and Petrocapita Oil and Gas L.P. following application by Seaway Holdings (Alberta) Ltd., a secured creditor of the Petrocapita G.P. and Petrocapita Oil. Net proceeds from sale of assets available for distribution to creditors would be first distributed to the trust and Safeway Holdings as both are secured creditors and thereafter to any unsecured creditors. (see FPsurvey - Mines & Energy)

Petrocel Industries Inc. (B.C. Feb. 14, 1972)
July 5, 1991 – Dissolved and struck off register.

Petrock Ventures Inc. (B.C. Feb. 15, 1985 amalg.)
Jan. 22, 2003 – Name changed to Croydon Mercantile Corp.; basis 1 new for 100 old shs. ∎

Petroco of Texas, Inc. (Tex. 1980)
Sept. 19, 1988 – Name changed to Scotia Prime Minerals, Inc. and continued into Nova Scotia; basis 1 new for 4 old shs. ∎

PetroCorp Group Inc. (Alta. Dec. 31, 2006 amalg.)
June 30, 2022 – Continued into Ontario.
July 27, 2022 – Name changed to First Lithium Minerals Corp. pursuant to the reverse takeover acquisition of First Lithium Minerals Inc.; basis 1 new for 81.9672131 old shs. (see FPsurvey - Mines & Energy)

Petrodorado Energy Ltd. (Can. May 25, 2005)
Nov. 27, 2019 – Name changed to ROK Resources Inc. following reverse takeover acquisition of (old) ROK Resources Inc. (see FPsurvey - Mines & Energy)

PetroFalcon Corporation (Alta. Feb. 28, 1996)
Sept. 10, 2009 – Continued into British Columbia.
Sept. 16, 2009 – Name changed to Etrion Corporation. ∎

Petrofina Canada Inc. (Can. 1953)
May 12, 1981 – Substantially all net assets sold to Petro-Canada.
Sept. 1, 1981 – Name changed to Petro-Canada Enterprises Inc. ∎

Petrofina Canada Ltd. (Can. 1953)
Aug. 9, 1979 – Name changed to Petrofina Canada Inc. ∎

Petroflame International Resources Ltd. (B.C. May 22, 1984)
May 8, 1991 – Name changed to Crystallex International Corporation; basis 1 new for 5 old shs. ∎

Petroflo Petroleum Corporation (Ont. Aug. 18, 1981 amalg.)
Dec. 4, 1985 – Amalgamated with 5 other cos. to form Flying Cross Resources Ltd.; basis 1 new for 5 old shs. (see Flying Cross Resources Ltd.)

Petroflow Energy Ltd. (Can. July 26, 1994)
May 27, 2013 – Dissolved and struck from register.

Petroforte International Ltd. (Alta. Feb. 2, 2007)
Feb. 21, 2014 – Name changed to Canamax Energy Ltd.; basis 1 new for 6 old shs. ■

Petrofund Energy Trust (Ont. Dec. 16, 1988)
July 4, 2006 – Plan of Arrangement combination with Penn West Energy Trust; basis $1.10 (as special distribution) plus 0.60 new Penn West unit for 1 old Petrofund unit. (see Penn West Energy Trust)

PetroGlobe Inc. (Alta. Sept. 14, 1999)
Nov. 5, 2013 – Voluntarily filed for bankruptcy under the BIA. Hudson & Company Insolvency Trustees Inc. appointed trustee. All officers and directors resigned.

Petrogold Financial Corporation (B.C. 1964)
Oct. 11, 1988 – Name changed to Columbia Leisure Corporation. ■

Petrogold Resources Corporation (B.C. 1964)
Feb. 14, 1986 – Name changed to Petrogold Financial Corporation. ■

Petrohawk Energy Corporation (Alta. Dec. 6, 1994)
Jan. 22, 1996 – Formed Petrohawk Energy Ltd. on amalgamation with Petrohawk Amalgamation Corporation; basis 1 new for 1 old sh. ■

Petrohawk Energy Ltd. (Alta. Dec. 6, 1994)
Nov. 23, 1999 – Amalgamated with 840536 Alberta Ltd.; to form Fox Energy Ltd. wholly owned subsid. of Fox Energy Corp.; basis 1 new co. sh. for 4 Petrohawk shs.

Petrohunter Energy Ltd. (Alta. Feb. 10, 1981)
Oct. 1, 1986 – Name changed to KT Capital Corporation; basis 3 new for 5.25 old shs. (see FPsurvey - Industrials)

PetroKamchatka Plc (Jersey Dec. 23, 2008)
Oct. 2, 2012 – Name changed to EastSiberian Plc; basis 1 new for 100 old shs.

PetroKazakhstan Inc. (Alta. Sept. 5, 1986)
Oct. 27, 2005 – Acquired by CNPC International Ltd. for US$55 per sh.

The Petrol Oil & Gas Company, Limited (Ont. 1920)
Nov. 1, 1983 – Amalgamated with Universal Explorations Ltd. to form Universal Explorations (83) Ltd.; sh.-for-sh. basis.

Petrol One Corp. (Can. Sept. 19, 2006)
July 12, 2014 – Dissolved and struck from register.

Petrolantic Ltd. (Ont. Nov. 23, 1965)
Jan. 5, 1994 – Continued into Alberta.
May 4, 1994 – Name changed to Cirque Energy Ltd. ■

Petrolantic Resources Inc. (Ont. Nov. 23, 1965)
Oct. 5, 1987 – Name changed to Petrolantic Ltd. ■

Petroleum Advisors Ltd. (Alta. 1951)
Oct. 1953 – Wound up voluntarily.

Petroleum and Uranium Royalties Ltd. (unknown)
1964 – Acquired by Scurry-Rainbow Oil (Sask.) Ltd.; basis 1 new for 10 old shs.

Petroleum Capital Energy Inc. (Alta. Mar. 2, 1987)
May 28, 1998 – Name changed to Marlboro Petroleum Inc. (see FPsurvey - Mines & Energy)

Petroleum Royalties Limited (Can. 1925)
June 8, 1981 – Continued into Nova Scotia.
Nov. 18, 1983 – Formed East Coast Energy Ltd. following acquisition by East Coast Energy Ltd.; basis 2.15 new for 1 old sh. ■

Petroleum Western, Ltd. (Can. 1929)
Aug. 1941 – Charter surrendered.

Petrolex Energy Corporation (B.C. June 16, 1987)
Feb. 10, 1997 – Continued into Yukon.
May 18, 2005 – Dissolved and struck off register.

Petrolia Inc. (Que. Jan. 22, 2002)
Oct. 24, 2017 – Formed Pieridae Energy Limited in Canada pursuant to amalgamation with (old) Pieridae Energy Limited (deemed acquiror); basis 1 new com. sh. for 12 Petrolia com. shs. and 2.2057526 new com. shs. for 1 (old) Pieridae com. sh. ■

Petrolia Oil & Gas Ltd. (B.C. 1984)
1989 – Continued into Canada. (see Fortune Energy Inc.)
Sept. 17, 1993 – Amalgamated with Devnic Energy Inc. (1 for 1.77) and Canadian Fortune Resources Inc. (1 for 0.51) to form a new co. named Fortune Energy Inc.; basis 1 new for 1 old sh. (see Fortune Energy Inc.)

Petrolian Resources Corporation (Alta. 1987)
Aug. 30, 1991 – Amalgamated with Star Tech Energy Systems Inc. to form Startech Energy Ltd.; basis 1 new for 6.75 Petrolian Resources shs. (see Startech Energy Ltd.)

Petrolifera Petroleum Limited (Can. Nov. 9, 2004)
Mar. 24, 2011 – Amalgamated with Gran Tierra Energy Inc.; basis 0.1241 Gran Tierra shs. for 1 Petrolifera sh.

Petroline Explorers Inc. (Ont. 1952)
Feb. 19, 1988 – Name changed to Moducan Building Systems Ltd. ■

Petrologic Petroleum Ltd. (B.C. 1982 amalg.)
Apr. 19, 1985 – Name changed to PTP Resource Corp. ■

Petromac Energy Inc. (B.C. 1982 amalg.)
Mar. 18, 1994 – Dissolved and struck off register.

PetroMagdalena Energy Corp. (B.C. May 3, 1966)
July 31, 2012 – Acquired by 0942183 B.C. Ltd., a wholly owned subsid. of Pacific Rubiales Energy Corp., for Cdn$1.60 per sh. plus Cdn$0.25 per wt. (see Pacific Rubiales Energy Corp.)

Petromanas Energy Inc. (B.C. July 11, 2007)
Nov. 21, 2011 – Continued into Alberta.
June 13, 2016 – Name changed to PMI Resources Ltd.; basis 1 new for 70 old shs. ■

PetroMaroc Corporation (Can. Aug. 29, 2018)
Feb. 25, 2019 – Acquired by Wolverine Energy and Infrastructure Inc.; basis 0.052942 Wolverine com. shs. for 1 PetroMaroc com. sh. (see Wolverine Energy and Infrastructure Inc.)

PetroMaroc Corporation PLC (Jersey Aug. 13, 2010)
Aug. 29, 2018 – Continued into Canada.
Oct. 12, 2018 – Name changed to PetroMaroc Corporation. ■

Petromet Resources Limited (Ont. 1980)
May 29, 2001 – Acquired by TLM Acquisition Corp., a wholly owned subsid. of Talisman Energy Inc.; basis $13.20 per com. sh. and $1,389.47 per $1,000 of debentures. (see Talisman Energy Inc.)

Petromine Exploration & Finance Co. Ltd. (unknown)
June 1952 – Assets acquired by Nationwide Minerals Ltd.; basis 1 new for 2 old shs.

Petrominerales Ltd. (Bahamas Apr. 20, 2006)
Dec. 31, 2010 – Continued into Alberta. (see Pacific Rubiales Energy Corp.)
Dec. 5, 2013 – Acquired by Pacific Rubiales Energy Corp.; basis $11.00 cash plus 1 Alvopetro Energy Ltd. sh. for 1 Petrominerales sh. (see Pacific Rubiales Energy Corp.)

Petromines Limited (Man. 1948)
1986 – Continued into Alberta.
June 8, 1992 – Acquired by Renaissance Energy Ltd.; basis 60¢ or 0.0462 Renaissance shs. for 1 Petromines sh.

Petromont Oil & Gas Ltd. (Alta. 1980)
Feb. 9, 1982 – Name changed to Pillar Petroleums Ltd. ■

PetroNova Inc. (Alta. Sept. 17, 2009)
July 30, 2015 – Acquired by Petroamerica Oil Corp.; basis 0.85 Petroamerica com. shs. for 1 PetroNova sh. (see Petroamerica Oil Corp.)

PetroPower Energy Inc. (Alta. Oct. 1, 1993)
July 3, 1997 – Formed Justinian Explorations Ltd. in Alberta following reverse takeover acquisition of and amalgamation with Justinian Explorations Ltd.; basis 1 new for 7 old shs. ■

Petroquest Ltd. (Alta. 1953)
Aug. 1977 – Acquired by Decca Resources Ltd. for $8.00 per sh.

Petroquin Resources Ltd. (B.C. Jan. 12, 1979)
Oct. 14, 1988 – Name changed to Consolidated Petroquin Resources Limited; basis 2 new for 2 old shs. ■

PetroReal Energy Inc. (Alta. May 8, 2007)
Jan. 2, 2013 – Dissolved and struck from register.

PetroReal Oil Corporation (B.C. July 27, 1987)
Sept. 13, 2002 – Name changed to International PetroReal Oil Corporation; basis 1 new for 3 old shs. ■

Petrorep Resources Ltd. (Can. Sept. 1, 1992)
May 19, 2000 – Acquired by Taurus Exploration Ltd. for $2.62 per sh. (see Trans Asia Resources Inc.)

PetroSands Resources (Canada) Inc. (Alta. Oct. 27, 2004)
Jan. 1, 2012 – Name changed to CanRock Energy Corp. following vertical amalg. with wholly owned subsids. CanRock Energy Corp. and QMAC Ventures Ltd. on Dec. 31, 2011. ■

PetroShale Inc. (Alta. July 1, 1998 amalg.)
May 26, 2022 – Name changed to Lucero Energy Corp. ■

Petrostar Petroleum Corporation (B.C. Feb. 5, 1996)
Aug. 31, 2015 – Name changed to Cerus Energy Group Ltd. ■

Petrostar Petroleums Inc. (Can. May 29, 1987)
June 11, 1992 – Amalgamated with Sugar Creek Oil & Gas Inc. to form new co. with same name Petrostar Petroleums Inc.; basis 1 new for 4.75 Sugar Creek shs. and 1 new for 1 Petrostar sh. (see Crestar Energy Inc.)
July 18, 1996 – Acquired by Crestar Energy Inc.; basis 1 Crestar sh. for 14.8 Petrostar shs. (see Crestar Energy Inc.)

Petrostates Resource Corporation (B.C. Feb. 12, 1985 amalg.)
July 3, 1992 – Dissolved and struck off register.

Petrotech Inc. (Del. 1969)
Sept. 15, 1989 – Name changed to Great Northern Gas Co. following reorganization.

Petrotex Resources Ltd. (B.C. Nov. 21, 1980)
Jan. 28, 1987 – Name changed to Fulcrum Developments Ltd.; basis 1 new for 5 old shs. ■

Petrowest Corporation (Alta. May 24, 2011)
Aug. 15, 2017 – Placed into receivership by banking syndicate. Ernst & Young appointed receiver and all directors resigned.

Petrowest Energy Services Trust (Alta. July 6, 2006)
July 1, 2011 – Succeeded by Petrowest Corporation pursuant to plan of arrangement whereby Petrowest Corporation was formed to facilitate the conversion of the trust into a corporation and the trust was subsequently dissolved. ■

Petrowest Resources Ltd. (B.C. 1965)
Sept. 20, 1985 – Struck off register.

PetroWorld Corp. (Cayman Islands May 26, 2004)
Oct. 4, 2006 – Name changed to Coastal Energy Company following reverse takeover acquisition of NuCoastal (Thailand) Limited. ∎

PetroWorth Resources Inc. (Ont. Mar. 11, 2003)
July 4, 2013 – Name changed to First Sahara Energy Inc. following acquisition of Giant Exploration Inc.; basis 1 new for 10 old shs. ∎

Petrox Capital Corp. (Alta. Feb. 25, 2011)
Aug. 15, 2012 – Name changed to Petrox Resources Corp. (see FPsurvey - Mines & Energy)

Petrox Energy and Minerals Corporation (B.C. Mar. 15, 1972)
Aug. 12, 1985 – Continued into Canada.
Feb. 4, 1997 – Name changed to HuMedaTech International Inc. ∎

Petrox Petroleum Corporation (B.C. Mar. 15, 1972)
June 27, 1983 – Name changed to Petrox Energy and Minerals Corporation. ∎

Petrus Acquisition Corp. (Alta. Nov. 25, 2015)
Feb. 2, 2016 – Name changed to Petrus Resources Ltd. (see FPsurvey - Mines & Energy)

Petrus Resources Inc. (Can. Oct. 19, 2006)
Feb. 8, 2016 – Acquired by Petrus Acquisition Corp. (renamed Petrus Resources Ltd.); basis 0.0452672 Petrus Resources com. sh. and 0.25 Fox River Resources Corporation com. sh. for 1 PhosCan com. sh.

Peyto Energy Trust (Alta. May 22, 2003)
Dec. 31, 2010 – Succeeded by Peyto Exploration & Development Corp. pursuant to plan of arrangement whereby Peyto Exploration & Development Corp. was formed to facilitate the conversion of the trust into a corporation and the trust was subsequently dissolved. (see FPsurvey - Mines & Energy)

Peyto Oils Ltd. (Alta. 1966)
1980 – Acquired by Westburne International Industries Limited; basis $22.75 per sh. or 4 Westburne shs. for 5 Peyto shs.

Pez Resources Limited (B.C. 1980)
Aug. 26, 1982 – Name changed to Pezamerica Resources Corporation; basis 1 new for 4 old shs. ∎

Pezamerica Resources Corporation (B.C. 1980)
Mar. 8, 1985 – Amalgamated into Royex Gold Mining Corporation; basis 3 new for 4 old shs.

Pezgold Resource Corporation (B.C. Oct. 5, 1987)
Aug. 23, 1988 – Amalgamated with Androne Resources Ltd. to form new co. with same name Pezgold Resource Corporation.
June 15, 1990 – Name changed to Braiden Resources Ltd.; basis 1 new for 7 old shs. ∎

Pezgold Resource Corporation (B.C. 1987)
Aug. 31, 1988 – Amalgamated (1 for 1) with Androne Resources Ltd. to continue as Pezgold Resource Corporation.

Phaeton Exploration Ltd. (Ont. 1951)
Dec. 1, 1987 – Formed Falvo Estates Ltd. in Ontario on amalgamation with a private co. ∎

Phantom Industries Limited (Ont. 1928)
1964 – Went into receivership.
Oct. 21, 1966 – Name changed to Consolidated Phantom Industries Limited. ∎

Pharaoh Capital Inc. (Alta. Jan. 26, 2004)
May 3, 2005 – Succeeded by Fairmount Energy Inc. on Qualifying Transaction amalgamation of Pharaoh Capital with a wholly owned subsidiary of Fairmount Energy Inc., thereafter the amalgamated company was dissolved; basis 1 new for 7 old shs. ∎

Pharaoh Mines Ltd. (B.C. 1966)
Oct. 1971 – Name changed to Tannex Resources Ltd. ∎

Pharick Gold Mines Ltd. (Ont. 1949)
1957 – Charter cancelled.

PharmaCan Capital Corp. (Ont. Aug. 21, 2012)
Mar. 1, 2017 – Name changed to Cronos Group Inc. ∎

PharmaGap Inc. (Can. Apr. 15, 2002)
Feb. 20, 2015 – Dissolved.

PharmaGeneric Inc. (Ont. Jan. 25, 1999)
Aug. 8, 2000 – Name changed to The GemStone X.change Corp.; basis 1 new for 20 old shs.

Pharmala Biotech Holdings Inc. (B.C. Jan. 12, 2021)
Dec. 17, 2024 – Continued into Ontario. (see FPsurvey - Industrials)

PharmEng International Inc. (Ont. Oct. 1, 2003)
Jan. 29, 2010 – Deemed bankrupt. B. Riley Farber Inc. (previously A. Farber & Partners Inc.) appointed trustee. Creditors refused proposal. No funds available for shldrs.
Oct. 24, 2016 – Dissolved.

Pharmex Industries Inc. (B.C. Aug. 17, 1987)
Sept. 21, 2000 – Continued into Canada.
Sept. 25, 2000 – Name changed to PanGeo Pharma Inc. ∎

Pheasant Exploration Ltd. (Alta. 1963)
1970 – Merged with Canadian Reserve Oil and Gas Ltd.

Pheasant Petroleums Ltd. (Alta. 1965)
1970 – Merged with Canadian Reserve Oil and Gas Ltd.

Pheasantback Resources Inc. (Alta. Dec. 9, 1996)
Aug. 31, 1999 – Name changed to Multi-Glass International Inc. ∎

Phelps Gold Mines Ltd. (Ont. 1944)
1958 – Dissolved.

Phenex Refrigeration Inc. (Ont. Sept. 30, 1996)
July 12, 1999 – Name changed to ArborScience Inc. ∎

Pheromone Sciences Corp. (B.C. Aug. 19, 1998)
May 29, 2001 – Continued into Canada.
Sept. 20, 2006 – Name changed to Sernova Corp. ∎

Philco Resources Ltd. (B.C. 1967)
Aug. 28, 1992 – Dissolved and struck off register.

Philex Gold Inc. (Can. June 14, 1996)
May 3, 2010 – Acquired by Philex Mining Corp., a wholly owned subsid. of Philex Gold Holdings Inc., for US$0.75 per sh.

Philip Environmental Inc. (Ont. Aug. 10, 1990)
May 30, 1997 – Name changed to Philip Services Corp. ∎

Philip Environmental Services (B.C.) Inc. (B.C. June 23, 1983)
May 17, 1993 – Name changed to Devco Enterprises Inc.; basis 1 new for 2 old shs. ∎

Philip Services Corp. (Ont. Aug. 10, 1990)
Apr. 14, 2000 – Emerged from Chapter 11 of US Bankruptcy Code and also Companies Creditors' Arrangement Act of Canada as a newly reconstructed company to continue as Philip Services Corporation; basis 1 new Philip sh. for 273 old Philip shs. Also continued into Delaware.

Philippine Metals Inc. (Alta. Apr. 7, 1989)
Apr. 17, 2018 – Continued into British Columbia.
Mar. 7, 2022 – Name changed to ReVolve Renewable Power Corp. pursuant to the reverse takeover acquisition of ReVolve Renewable Power Limited.; basis 1 new for 4 old shs. (see FPsurvey - Mines & Energy; FPsurvey - Industrials)

Phillip Resources Inc. (B.C. June 24, 1983)
Mar. 20, 1989 – Name changed to Austin Mines Inc.; basis 1 new for 3.5 old shs. ∎

Phillips Cables Limited (Can. Mar. 2, 1953; via Dominion charter)
May 25, 1995 – Name changed to BICC Phillips Inc. ∎

Phillips Electrical Company Limited (Can. Mar. 2, 1953; via Dominion charter)
Nov. 12, 1964 – Name changed to Phillips Cables Limited. ∎

Phillips Equity Corporation (B.C. Nov. 14, 1967)
Aug. 24, 1979 – Name changed to Corvette Petroleum Corporation; basis 1 new for 5 old shs. ∎

Phillips Oil Co. Ltd. (Alta. 1950)
1963 – Merged with Plains Petroleums Ltd.; basis 9 new for 5 old shs.

Phillips Petroleum Company (Del. 1917)
Sept. 3, 2002 – Formed ConocoPhillips following merger with Conoco Inc.

Phillips Petroleums Limited (Alta. 1937)
1950 – Acquired by Phillips Oil Co. Ltd.; basis 1 new for 20 old shs. (see Phillips Oil Co. Ltd.)

Philmore Yellowknife Gold Mines Ltd. (Ont. 1945)
May 1957 – Charter cancelled.

Philom Bios Inc. (Sask. Dec. 9, 1980)
Dec. 11, 2007 – Acquired by Novozymes Biologicals Holding A/S for $6.50 per sh.

Phinder Technologies Inc. (Ont. Jan. 16, 1984)
May 30, 2007 – Name changed to Zupintra Corporation, Inc. (see FPsurvey - Industrials)

Phivida Holdings Inc. (B.C. Apr. 24, 2015)
Sept. 21, 2021 – Acquired by Choom Holdings Inc.; basis 0.72566 Choom com. shs. for 1 Phivida sh.

Phoenician Holdings Corp. (Ont. Feb. 17, 2004)
Mar. 6, 2006 – Name changed to Asia Now Resources Corp. following Qualifying Transaction reverse takeover acquisition of Asia Now Resources Limited and amalgamation of Asia Now with a newly incorporated wholly owned subsidiary. ∎

Phoenix Canada Oil Company Limited (Ont. Nov. 25, 1944)
June 9, 2023 – Name changed to ZYUS Life Sciences Corporation pursuant to the reverse takeover acquisition of ZYUS Life Sciences Inc. (see FPsurvey - Industrials)

Phoenix Capital Inc. (Alta. Oct. 30, 1989)
Nov. 30, 1995 – Continued into New Brunswick.
June 17, 2005 – Converted into an income trust named Phoenix Capital Income Trust; basis 0.174 trust units for 1 com. sh.

Phoenix Coal Inc. (Alta. Feb. 8, 2007)
July 11, 2008 – Continued into Ontario.
May 10, 2010 – Name changed to Elgin Mining Inc.; basis 1 new for 3 old shs. ∎

Phoenix Copper Corporation (B.C. Oct. 21, 1980)
Dec. 3, 2013 – Name changed to Phoenix Metals Corporation; basis 1 new for 2 old shs. ∎

Phoenix Electric Oil Refiners Canada Ltd. (B.C. 1968)
Feb. 28, 1979 – Name changed to Phoenix International Energy Corporation. ∎

Phoenix Elevator Co., Ltd. (unknown 1929)
1944 – Charter cancelled; co. turned over all assets to Royal Trust Co., Winnipeg, trustee for bondholders, and was released from covenant to pay bond princ. and int. arrears.
Oct. 1, 1945 – Assets sold for $169,392. After all expenses, $140,954 was distributed to holders of $425,000 o/s bonds of Electric Elevator & Grain Co. Ltd. (previous co.), in ratio of $33.15 for each $100 bond held.

Phoenix Financial Holdings Inc. (Ont. Aug. 7, 1986)
Dec. 5, 1996 – Name changed to Cornerstone Industrial Minerals Corporation; basis 1 com. for 1 cl. A subord. vtg. and 1 cl. B multiple vtg. sh. ∎

Phoenix Global Capital Inc. (B.C. Feb. 26, 1986)
July 12, 1991 – Dissolved and struck off register.

Phoenix Gold Mines Limited (Ont. July 6, 1986 amalg.)
July 6, 1986 – Amalgamated with Satellite Consolidated Metals Limited (1 for 1) to continue with the same name Phoenix Gold Mines Limited; basis 1 new for 4 old shs.
July 24, 1990 – Final distribution of the co.'s assets; basis 2 new St. Andrew Goldfields Ltd. shs. for 39 old Phoenix shs. Co. wound up.

Phoenix Gold Resources Corp. (B.C. May 2, 2011)
Feb. 10, 2022 – Name changed to York Harbour Metals Inc. (see FPsurvey - Mines & Energy)

Phoenix Gold Resources Ltd. (B.C. Aug. 4, 1988)
June 9, 1999 – Name changed to Terrastar Resources Corporation; basis 1 new for 5 old shs. ∎

Phoenix Health Group Inc. (Ont. Jan. 14, 1980)
Oct. 29, 2001 – Dissolved and struck off register.

The Phoenix Hedge Fund Limited Partnership (Ont. May 12, 1997)
May 12, 2000 – Liquidated; distribution of $11 per unit to unitholders of record as of May 10, 2000. The date of distribution of residual net asset value of approximately $1.35 not currently known. Transfer agent is Montreal Trust Co. of Canada, Toronto.

Phoenix International Energy Corporation (B.C. 1968)
Nov. 18, 1983 – Name changed to International Phoenix Energy Corporation; basis 1 new for 5 old shs. ∎

Phoenix International, Inc. (Del. Sept. 21, 2001)
May 20, 2004 – Name changed to PICorp. Capital Ltd. and continued into Alberta. ∎

Phoenix International Life Sciences Inc. (Can. June 7, 1988)
May 19, 2000 – Acquired by MDS Inc. for $16, 0.4 MDS shs. or a combination thereof for 1 Phoenix sh. (see MDS Inc.)

Phoenix Leisure Corporation (B.C. Sept. 18, 1986)
July 8, 1998 – Continued into Canada.
Dec. 19, 2008 – Dissolved.

Phoenix Matachewan Mines Inc. (Ont. Sept. 1, 2000)
Jan. 2, 2009 – Name changed to Galahad Metals Inc.; basis 1 new for 10 old shs. ∎

Phoenix Metals Corporation (B.C. Oct. 21, 1980)
Apr. 27, 2018 – Name changed to Envirotek Remediation Inc. ∎

The Phoenix Molybdenite Corp. Ltd. (Ont. Sept. 1923)
Property acquired by Zenith Molybdenite Corp. Ltd. (see Zenith Molybdenite Corporation Ltd.)

Phoenix Oilfield Hauling Inc. (Alta. May 9, 2006)
June 25, 2012 – Name changed to Aveda Transportation and Energy Services Inc. ∎

Phoenix Oils Ltd. (Alta. 1929)
1963 – Struck off register.

Phoenix Technology Income Fund (Alta. May 19, 2004)
Dec. 31, 2010 – Succeeded by PHX Energy Services Corp. pursuant to plan of arrangement whereby PHX Energy Services Corp. was formed to facilitate the conversion of the fund into a corporation and the fund was subsequently dissolved. (see FPsurvey - Mines & Energy; FPsurvey - Industrials)

Phoenix Technology Services Inc. (Alta. Nov. 1, 2002 amalg.)
July 7, 2004 – Converted into an income trust named Phoenix Technology Income Fund; basis 1 trust unit for 1 com. sh.

Phonetime Inc. (Ont. Apr. 5, 1984)
Oct. 25, 2013 – Name changed to Tellza Communications Inc. ∎

Phonettix Intelecom Ltd. (Alta. Apr. 23, 1987)
Apr. 19, 1996 – Continued into Ontario.
July 20, 1999 – Name changed to Minacs Worldwide Inc. following reverse takeover acquisition of The Minacs Group Inc. ∎

PhosCan Chemical Corp. (Ont. Mar. 22, 1994 amalg.)
Oct. 19, 2006 – Continued into Canada.
Feb. 2, 2016 – Name changed to Petrus Resources Inc. ∎

Photo Engravers & Electrotypers Limited (Can. 1927; via Dominion charter)
July 30, 1993 – Acquired by Quebecor Printing Acquisition Corporation, a wholly owned subsid. of Quebecor Printing Inc., for $37.875 per sh. (see Quebecor Printing Inc.)

Photo-Magic, Inc. (Nev. 1979)
Mar. 15, 1979 – Name changed to P M Industries, Inc.

Photo Mines Ltd. (Ont. 1971)
Nov. 26, 1975 – Amalgamated with Spar Holdings & Explorations Ltd.; basis 1 new for 2 old shs.

Photochannel Networks Inc. (B.C. Dec. 1, 1995)
June 9, 2009 – Name changed to PNI Digital Media Inc. ∎

Photon Control Inc. (B.C. Sept. 6, 1988)
July 19, 2021 – Acquired by MKS Instruments, Inc.; basis $3.60 cash per sh.

Phrygian Mining Corporation (B.C. Jan. 11, 1937)
Aug. 12, 1998 – Name changed to Crowflight Minerals Inc.; basis 1 new for 1.5 old shs. ∎

Physinorth Acquisition Corporation Inc. (Can. July 13, 2017)
Feb. 24, 2020 – Name changed to Premier Health of America Inc. pursuant to reverse takeover acquisition of 6150977 Canada Inc. (dba Groupe Premier Soin). (see FPsurvey - Industrials)

Phyto Extractions Inc. (B.C. Oct. 14, 1987)
Sept. 1, 2021 – Name changed to Adastra Holdings Ltd. (see FPsurvey - Industrials)

Pic Nickel Mines Ltd. (Ont. 1953)
Nov. 1957 – Charter cancelled.

Picamine Copper Gold Mines Ltd. (Ont. 1949)
Mar. 1961 – Charter cancelled.

Picardy Oil Co. Ltd. (Man.)
1958 – Struck off register.

Picarium Mines Ltd. (Ont. 1937)
1951 – Name changed to Draper Lake Frontenac Lead-Zinc Mines Ltd.; basis 3 new for 10 old shs. ∎

Picasso Inc. (Alta. Oct. 11, 2006)
Mar. 5, 2009 – Name changed to BlackLine GPS Corp. following Qualifying Transaction reverse takeover acquisition of BlackLine GPS Inc. and BlackLine GPS Employee Retention Corp. ∎

Piccadilly Petroleums Ltd. (Ont. 1945)
1950 – Acquired by Redwater-Piccadilly Petroleums Ltd.; basis 1 new for 2 old shs.

Piccadilly Porcupine Mines Ltd. (Ont. 1937)
1945 – Continued into Ontario.
Name changed to Piccadilly Petroleums Ltd. ∎

Piccadilly Resources Ltd. (B.C. Apr. 7, 1983)
Sept. 12, 1997 – Name changed to Allied Pacific Properties and Hotels Ltd. ∎

Piccolo Mines Ltd. (B.C. 1966)
Nov. 4, 1974 – Charter cancelled.

Piché Gold Mines Inc. (Ont. 1975)
1977 – Amalgamated with 4 other cos. to form Branly Enterprises Inc.; basis 11 new for 50 old shs.

Pick Mines Ltd. (Ont. 1959)
1971 – Merged into Picktex Mining & Investments Ltd.

Pickering Metal Mines Ltd. (Ont. 1953)
Mar. 1976 – Charter cancelled.

Pickering Uranium Mines Ltd. (Ont. 1953)
1954 – Name changed to Pickering Metal Mines Ltd. ∎

Pickle Crow Explorations Ltd. (Ont. 1968)
Feb. 22, 1977 – Amalgamated with Cariboo-Bell Copper Mines Ltd. (1 for 9), Beacon Mining Co. Ltd. (1 for 40), Abex Mines Ltd. (1 for 50) and Highland Mercury Mines Ltd. (1 for 5) to form Highland-Crow Resources Ltd.; basis 1 new for 5 old shs.

Pickle Crow Gold Mines (Consolidated) Ltd. (Ont. 1934)
Aug. 31, 1968 – Amalgamated with Silverfields Mining Corporation Ltd.; basis 1 Silverfields cl. A sh. for 200 Pickle Crow shs. (see Silverfields Mining Corporation Ltd.)

Pickle Crow Gold Mines Ltd. (Ont. 1934)
June 1968 – Name changed to Pickle Crow Gold Mines (Consolidated) Ltd. following sale of assets to Pickle Crow Explorations Ltd. and distribution of shs. received (sh. for sh.). ∎

Pickle Crow Resources Inc. (Alta. Aug. 1, 1997)
Mar. 29, 2000 – Name changed to NeTrue Communications Inc. ∎

Picktex Mining & Investments Ltd. (Ont. 1971 amalg.)
May 1974 – Reported in receivership
Aug. 1974 – Assets sold, with no distribution for shldrs. Charter cancelled.

Pickwick Gold Mines Ltd. (Ont. 1936)
Aug. 18, 1958 – Dissolved.

Pico Resources Ltd. (B.C. Dec. 28, 1972)
July 31, 1992 – Name changed to Tampico Capital Corporation. (see FPsurvey - Industrials)

Picosec Technology Ltd. (B.C. 1979)
May 22, 1987 – Continued into Alberta.
May 1, 1991 – Struck from registry and dissolved.

Picton Mahoney Tactical Income Fund (Ont.)
Aug. 26, 2024 – Terminated; distrib. from net proceeds to be made on or about Aug. 29, 2024.

Picton Uranium Mines Ltd. (Ont. 1953)
1967 – Name changed to New Picton Uranium Mines Ltd.; basis 1 new for 4 old shs. ∎

Picture Properties Corp. (Alta. Dec. 22, 1987)
Nov. 9, 1993 – Name changed to Solstice Natural Resource Corp.; basis 1 new for 10 old shs. ∎

Piedmont Mines Ltd. (Ont. 1947)
Apr. 1958 – Charter cancelled.

Pier Mac Environment Management Inc. (B.C. Sept. 1, 1981)
Apr. 7, 1995 – Name changed to Ebony Gold & Gas Inc.; basis 1 new for 3 old shs. ∎

Pierce Mountain Resources Ltd. (B.C. Feb. 27, 1987)
Dec. 3, 1991 – Name changed to Portal Resources Ltd.; basis 1 new for 3 old shs. ∎

Pieridae Energy Limited (Can. Oct. 24, 2017 amalg.)
May 9, 2025 – Name changed to Cavvy Energy Ltd. and continued into Alberta. (see FPsurvey - Mines & Energy)

Piermond Mining Co. Ltd. (Que. 1956)
Dec. 27, 1980 – Charter cancelled.

Pierpont Gold Mines Ltd. (Ont. 1945)
Aug. 1957 – Charter cancelled.

Pierre Des Marais Inc. (unknown 1930)
1987 – During the company went private.

Pierre EnTerprises Ltd. (B.C. June 24, 1987)
Feb. 1, 2011 – Name changed to Leeta Gold Corp.; basis 1 new for 2 old shs. ■

Pifher Resources Inc. (Ont. Oct. 17, 1997)
Oct. 18, 2004 – Name changed to Echo Energy Canada Inc. following amalgamation of wholly owned 1593485 Ontario Inc. with Echo Energy Inc., constituting a reverse takeover by Echo Energy; basis 3 new for 1 old sh. ■

Pigboss Follow-up Growth Inc. (Que. June 30, 2008 amalg.)
Aug. 23, 2017 – Struck from register.

Pigeon Lake Petroleums Ltd. (Alta. 1952)
Jan. 1963 – Name changed to Supreme Oil and Gas Ltd. ■

Pigeon River Nickel Mines Ltd. (unknown)
May 1966 – Name changed to Midland Nickel Corporation Ltd. ■

Pike Mountain Minerals Inc. (B.C. July 11, 2018)
Oct. 1, 2020 – Name changed to Carebook Technologies Inc. pursuant to the reverse takeover acquisition of Carebook Technologies Inc. and concurrent amalgamation of (old) Carebook with wholly owned 12235978 Canada Ltd. to continue as Carebook Technologies (2020) Inc.; basis 1 new for 13.187 old shs. ■

Pilagold Inc. (B.C. Mar. 25, 1983)
July 2, 2004 – Amalgamated with Radius Explorations Ltd. to form Radius Gold Inc.; basis 1 Radius sh. for 2.25 Pilagold shs.

Pilgrim Coal Corporation (B.C. 1978)
Sept. 23, 1985 – Name changed to Pilgrim Holdings Ltd. ■

Pilgrim Holdings Ltd. (B.C. 1978)
Feb. 26, 1993 – Dissolved and struck off register.

Pilgrim Petroleum Inc. (B.C. 1978)
Apr. 7, 1981 – Name changed to Pilgrim Coal Corporation. ■

Pilgrim Resource Corp. (Alta. Jan. 28, 1987)
Apr. 27, 1995 – Amalgamated with International Gryphon Resources Inc. to form new co. with same name International Gryphon Resources Inc.; basis 1 new for 1 International Gryphon sh. and 1 new for 1 Pilgrim sh. (see International Gryphon Resources Inc.)

Pillar Petroleums Ltd. (Alta. 1980)
Jan. 31, 1983 – Acquired by Renaissance Energy Ltd.; basis 0.2102 com. sh. of Renaissance for each o/s com. sh. of Pillar. (see Renaissance Energy Ltd.)

Pillar Resources Inc. (B.C. Mar. 25, 1983)
Oct. 21, 2003 – Name changed to Pilagold Inc. ■

Pilley's Island Copper-Pyrite Ltd. (Ont. 1951)
1964 – Charter cancelled.

Pilot Energy Ltd. (Alta. Apr. 23, 2004)
Jan. 25, 2008 – Acquired by Crescent Point Energy Trust; basis 0.1284 Crescent Point trust units for 1 Pilot Energy com. sh. (see Crescent Point Energy Trust)

Pilot Gold Inc. (Can. Nov. 18, 2010)
May 12, 2017 – Name changed to Liberty Gold Corp. (see FPsurvey - Mines & Energy)

Pilot Gold Mines Ltd. (B.C. 1934)
July 1950 – Dissolved by B.C. government.

Pilot Laboratories Corporation (B.C. Oct. 31, 1983)
Feb. 20, 1989 – Name changed to Murex Clinical Technologies Corporation. ■

Pilot Molybdenite Mines Ltd. (Ont. 1940)
1943 – Acquired by Aunite Mining Corp. Ltd. (see Aunite Mining Corp. Ltd.)

Pilot Peak Gold Inc. (B.C. 1983)
Mar. 4, 1994 – Dissolved and struck from register.

Pima Zinc Corp. (Cayman Islands June 15, 2011)
June 25, 2021 – Continued into British Columbia.
Nov. 9, 2022 – Name changed to Cybeats Technologies Corp. pursuant to the reverse takeover acquisition of Cybeats Technologies Inc. and concurrent amalgamation of (old) Cybeats with wholly owned 2635212 Ontario Inc. (see FPsurvey - Industrials)

Pincortez Mines Ltd. (Ont. 1946)
1949 – Name changed to Porcupine Prime Mines Ltd. ■

Pine Bell Mines Limited (Ont. Dec. 7, 1965)
July 23, 1981 – Continued into British Columbia.
Nov. 12, 1992 – Name changed to Bell Coast Capital Corp.; basis 1 new for 4 old shs. ■

Pine Buffalo Mines Ltd. (B.C. 1967)
Nov. 12, 1974 – Charter cancelled.

Pine Channel Gold Corp. (B.C. Mar. 24, 1987)
Feb. 7, 1991 – Name changed to Consolidated Pine Channel Gold Corp.; basis 1 new for 5 old shs. ■

Pine Crest Resources Ltd. (B.C. May 1, 1987)
June 24, 1992 – Name changed to Datinvest International Ltd. ■

Pine Glacier Mines Ltd. (B.C. 1968)
Dec. 30, 1974 – Charter cancelled.

Pine Lake Mining Co. Ltd. (B.C. Dec. 16, 1965)
Sept. 30, 1975 – Name changed to Marge Enterprises Ltd.; basis 1 new for 5 old shs. ■

Pine Pacific Mines Ltd. (B.C. 1966)
Jan. 10, 1977 – Dissolved.

Pine Pass Oil & Gas Ltd. (B.C.)
1972 – Purchased in 1971 by Westcoast Petroleum Ltd.; wound up.

Pine Point Mines Inc. (B.C. Aug. 4, 1988)
Jan. 23, 2004 – Name changed to Mineworks Resources Corp. ■

Pine Point Mines Limited (Can. May 16, 1951)
July 11, 1990 – All o/s shs. not held directly by Cominco Limited were acquired by Nunachiaq Inc. at $50 per sh. under a public offer.

Pine Point Mines Limited (Ont. 1966)
May 11, 1981 – Name changed to Flying Cross Petroleum Corp. (not to be confused with Pine Point Mines Limited - Can. 1951). ■

Pine Point Mining Limited (Ont. Nov. 25, 1993)
Mar. 2, 2018 – Acquired by Osisko Metals Incorporated; basis 0.2710 Osisko com. shs. plus 0.0677 Osisko wts. plus 1 Generation Mining Limited com. sh. for 1 Pine Point com. sh.

Pine Resources Corporation (B.C. Apr. 19, 1985)
Jan. 17, 2002 – Name changed to Trimble Resources Corporation. ■

Pine Ridge Exploration Co. Ltd. (Ont. 1966)
1972 – Name changed to Eden Industries International Ltd. ■

Pine River Mines Ltd. (Ont. Dec. 15, 1936)
1957 – Acquired by Trimar Holdings & Explorations Ltd.; basis 1 new for 5 old shs.

Pine Trail Capital Trust (Alta. Dec. 22, 2017)
Nov. 27, 2018 – Name changed to Pine Trail Real Estate Investment Trust pursuant to Qualifying Transaction acquisition of a medical office building in Picton, Ont. (see FPsurvey - Industrials)

Pine Valley Explorers Ltd. (B.C. 1972)
Nov. 5, 1984 – Name changed to V.I.P. Dynasty International Marketing Corp. ■

Pineapple Financial Inc. (Ont. Oct. 16, 2015)
Feb. 14, 2023 – Continued into Canada. (see FPsurvey - Industrials)

Pinebrayle Gold Mines Ltd. (B.C. 1945)
1952 – Charter cancelled.

PineBridge Investment Grade Preferred Securities Fund (Ont. Apr. 28, 2014)
Nov. 27, 2018 – Amalgamated with DoubleLine Income Solutions Trust to form BMO PineBridge Preferred Securities TACTIC™ Fund, an open-end daily redeemable mutual fund.

Pinecrest Energy Inc. (Alta. May 31, 2009 amalg.)
Apr. 17, 2015 – Acquired by Virginia Hills Oil Corp.; basis 1 Virginia com. sh. for 100 Pinecrest shs. (see Virginia Hills Oil Corp.)

Pinecrest Gold Mines Ltd. (B.C. 1946)
July 5, 1951 – Name changed to Craigmont Mines Limited. ■

Pinecrest Resources Ltd. (B.C. Jan. 18, 2010)
Aug. 10, 2020 – Name changed to Newcore Gold Ltd. (see FPsurvey - Mines & Energy)

Pinedale Energy Limited (B.C. Dec. 17, 2007)
Dec. 23, 2022 – Name changed to MCF Energy Ltd. (see FPsurvey - Mines & Energy)

Pinegrove Resources Ltd. (Alta. June 18, 1986)
Apr. 10, 1995 – Name changed to Pacific Ventures Inc.; basis 1 new for 4 old shs. ■

Pinehurst Capital I Inc. (Ont. July 13, 2018)
Dec. 6, 2021 – Name changed to Silver Bullet Mines Corp. pursuant to the Qualifying Transaction reverse takeover acquisition of Silver Bullet Mines Inc.; basis 1 new for 2.142857 old shs. (see FPsurvey - Industrials)

Pinehurst Capital II Inc. (Ont. July 13, 2018)
Sept. 15, 2022 – Name changed to Halcones Precious Metals Corp. pursuant to the Qualifying Transaction reverse takeover acquisition of Halcones Precious Metals Inc. and concurrent amalgamation of (old) Halcones with wholly owned 1000090101 Ontario Inc.; basis 0.4716981 new for 1 old sh. (see FPsurvey - Mines & Energy)

Pineridge Capital Corporation (B.C. 1987)
Jan. 14, 1991 – Name changed to Pineridge Capital Group Inc.; basis 1 new for 4 old shs. ■

Pineridge Capital Group Inc. (B.C. 1987)
Mar. 6, 1995 – Delisted from the Vancouver Stock Exchange. Subsequently dissolved for failure to file.

Pineridge Resources Limited (B.C. 1987)
Dec. 19, 1988 – Name changed to Pineridge Capital Corporation. ■

Pinestar Gold Inc. (B.C. Mar. 8, 2006)
Jan. 8, 2018 – Dissolved and struck from register.
Dec. 3, 2020 – Restored to registry.
Feb. 15, 2022 – Acquired by Jones Soda Co.; basis 1 Jones Soda sh. for 1 Pinestar Gold sh.

Pinetree Capital Corp. (Ont. May 11, 1962)
June 9, 2004 – Merged (basis 1 new share for 1.75 old common shares) with Genevest Inc. (basis 1.257 new shares for 1 old share). The merger was effected by way of reverse takeover acquisition of Genevest and the company changed its name to Pinetree Capital Ltd.

Pinetree Capital Inc. (Ont. May 11, 1962)
July 16, 1996 – Name changed to Pinetree Capital Corp.; basis 1 new for 3 old shs. ■

Pinetree Explorations Limited (Ont. May 11, 1962)
Mar. 11, 1992 – Name changed to Pinetree Capital Inc.; basis 1 new for 10 old shs. ■

Pinetree Software Canada Ltd. (B.C. 1984)
Dec. 11, 1992 – Dissolved and struck off register.

Pinewest Resources Inc. (Ont. Sept. 21, 1998)
Feb. 12, 2001 – Name changed to Arcamatrix Corporation following reverse takeover acquisition of DWX Canada Inc. for 10,591,750 shs. ■

Pinewood Resources Ltd. (B.C. Oct. 21, 1987)
Nov. 27, 2006 – Dissolved.

Pinex Mines Ltd. (B.C. 1965)
1972 – Assets acquired by Greenland Exploration Co. Ltd.; basis 1 Greenland sh. for 6.924 Pinex shs.
1973 – In liquidation.
July 1978 – Charter cancelled.

Pink Lake Mica Mines Ltd. (Ont. 1945)
July 30, 1962 – Dissolved.

Pink Pages Publications Inc. (B.C. 1986)
July 10, 1992 – Dissolved and struck off register.

Pinnacle Gold Mines Ltd. (Ont. 1945)
Dec. 1, 1958 – Dissolved.

Pinnacle Mines Ltd. (B.C. 1966)
Dec. 1974 – Name changed to Redford Mines Inc.; basis 1 new for 5 old shs. ■

Pinnacle Mines Ltd. (B.C. Apr. 6, 1995 amalg.)
June 29, 2010 – Name changed to Jayden Resources Inc. ■

Pinnacle North Gold Corp. (B.C. Mar. 7, 2018)
May 1, 2020 – Name changed to Summa Silver Corp. ■

Pinnacle Petroleums Ltd. (Alta. 1959)
Oct. 1, 1974 – Amalgamated into Paloma Petroleum Ltd.; basis 1 new for 6.5 old shs. (see Paloma Petroleum Ltd.)

Pinnacle Renewable Energy Inc. (B.C. Dec. 6, 2010)
Apr. 15, 2021 – Acquired by Drax Group plc; basis $11.30 cash per sh.

Pinnacle Renewable Holdings Inc. (B.C. Dec. 6, 2010)
Jan. 4, 2019 – Name changed to Pinnacle Renewable Energy Inc. ■

Pinnacle Resources Ltd. (Alta. Jan. 17, 1986)
Nov. 18, 1988 – Amalgamated with Twin Energy Ltd. to form a new Alberta co. also named Pinnacle Resources Ltd. (see Renaissance Energy Ltd.)
July 16, 1998 – Acquired by Renaissance Energy Ltd.; basis 0.66 new Renaissance sh. for 1 old Pinnacle sh. (see Renaissance Energy Ltd.)

Pinpoint Retail Solutions Inc. (Alta. Feb. 7, 1967)
Mar. 12, 1996 – Delisted from the Alberta Stock Exchange. Subsequently dissolved and struck from register.

Pinta Larder Gold Mines Ltd. (Ont. 1946)
1961 – Charter cancelled.

Pinto Malartic Gold Mines Limited (Ont. June 1, 1965)
Apr. 22, 1987 – Name changed to Continental CareTech Corporation. ■

Pioneer Electric Limited (Man. Jan. 15, 1946)
Jan. 2, 1964 – Name changed to FPE-Pioneer Electric Limited. ■

Pioneer Geophysical Services Inc. (Can. July 10, 1985)
Apr. 22, 1997 – Name changed to Xplore Technologies Corp. following reverse takeover acquisition of Xplore Technologies Inc.; basis 1 com. for 8 cl. A shs. ■

Pioneer Gold Mines of B.C. Limited (B.C. 1928)
1959 – Acquired by Bralorne Mines Limited; basis 1 Bralorne sh. for 5 Pioneer shs. Charter surrendered.

Pioneer LifeCo Inc. (Can. July 31, 1968)
Aug. 7, 1992 – Name changed to Wokingham Capital Corporation. ■

Pioneer Media Holdings Inc. (B.C. Nov. 9, 2017)
Feb. 13, 2025 – Name changed to Pioneer AI Foundry Inc. (see FPsurvey - Industrials)

Pioneer Metals Corporation (B.C. Sept. 26, 1986)
Oct. 3, 1995 – Transferred substantially all assets to Galaxy Resource Corporation (renamed Pioneer Metals Corporation), changed name to Scaffold Connection Corporation and continued into Alberta; basis 0.0041466 Scaffold com. shs. and 1 Galaxy com. sh. for 1 Pioneer com. sh. (see Scaffold Connection Corporation)

Pioneer Metals Corporation (B.C. Apr. 6, 1989)
Mar. 6, 2007 – Acquired by Barrick Gold Corporation for $1.00 per sh. (see Barrick Gold Corporation)

Pioneer Natural Resources Canada Inc. (Alta. Dec. 22, 1997)
Dec. 18, 2002 – Called for redemption; basis 1 new Pioneer Natural Resources Company com. sh. for 1 old Pioneer Canada exchangeable sh.

Pioneer Natural Resources (Canada) Ltd. (Alta. Dec. 22, 1997)
Jan. 4, 1999 – Name changed to Pioneer Natural Resources Canada Inc. ■

Pioneer Oils Ltd. (Alta. Mar. 31, 1978)
Apr. 2, 1979 – Name changed to Canadian Pioneer Oils Ltd. ■

Pioneer Resources (Canada) Ltd. (Que. 1984)
June 14, 1989 – Amalgamated with Abitibi-Resources Ltd. (1 for 5.7903) and Mid-Canada Gold and Copper Mines Limited (1 for 1) to form a new co. named Consolidated Abitibi Resources Ltd.; basis 1 new for 1 old sh. (see Consolidated Abitibi Resources Ltd.)

Pioneering Technology Inc. (Ont. Feb. 15, 2006 amalg.)
Sept. 18, 2008 – Name changed to Pioneering Technology Corp.; basis 1 new for 10 old shs. (see FPsurvey - Industrials)

Pipe NT Corp. (Ont. Nov. 27, 1997)
Mar. 3, 2003 – Redeemed in full; basis capital shs. redeemed for amount that unit value exceeds $25 ($16.692736) and preferred shs. redeemed for the lesser of $25 or the unit value.

Pipedreams Mfg. Inc. (Alta. May 14, 1987)
Feb. 14, 1990 – Name changed to Inter-Link Communications Inc.; basis 1 new for 3 old shs. ■

Piper Capital Inc. (Alta. June 13, 2001)
May 12, 2005 – Continued into British Columbia.
June 28, 2007 – Formed Garson Gold Corp. in British Columbia on amalgamation with Garson Resources Ltd. with Piper the deemed acquiror; basis 0.725 Garson Gold shs. for 1 Garson Resources sh. and 1 Garson Gold sh. for 1 Piper sh. ■

Piper Mattawa Iron Mines Ltd. (Ont. 1956)
1969 – Name changed to Pipawa Explorations Ltd. (see FPsurvey - Mines & Energy)

Piper Petroleums Ltd. (B.C. 1973)
Oct. 30, 1981 – Amalgamated (1 for 1) with Giant Explorations Limited to form Giant Piper Exploration Inc.

Piper Petroleums Ltd. (Alta. Feb. 19, 1993)
Mar. 15, 1996 – Amalgamated with Dalton Resources Ltd. (1 for 1) to form a new company also known as Dalton Resources Ltd.; basis 1 new Dalton com. sh. for 3.5 old Piper cl. A shs. (see Dalton Resources Ltd.)

Pipestone Bay Resources Ltd. (Ont. Jan. 26, 1983)
Nov. 1, 1991 – Name changed to Ultracell Medical Technologies Ltd. following acquisition of Ultracell Technologies Inc.; basis 1 new for 3 old shs. ■

Pipestone Energy Corp. (Alta. Jan. 4, 2019 amalg.)
Oct. 5, 2023 – Merged with Strathcona Resources Ltd. to continue under the Strathcona name; basis 0.067967 Strathcona shs. for 1 Pipestone sh.

Pipestone Narrows Gold Mines Ltd. (Ont. 1944)
Aug. 1957 – Charter cancelled.

Pipestone Petroleums Inc. (B.C. Oct. 17, 1979)
Dec. 2, 1993 – Continued into Alberta. (see Blue Range Resource Corporation)
July 19, 1995 – Acquired by Blue Range Resource Corporation; basis 1 Blue Range sh. for 13 Pipestone shs. (see Blue Range Resource Corporation)
Jan. 1, 1996 – Dissolved and struck off register. (see Blue Range Resource Corporation)

Pipex Pharmaceuticals, Inc. (Wyo. Sept. 30, 1992)
Oct. 16, 2008 – Name changed to Adeona Pharmaceuticals, Inc. ■

Pippin Athabasca Uranium Mines Ltd. (Ont. 1955)
Name changed to Pippin Mining & Uranium Corp. ■

Pippin Mining & Uranium Corp. (Ont. 1955)
1979 – Charter cancelled.

Pisces Capital Corp. (Ont. Jan. 19, 2006)
Dec. 21, 2007 – Name changed to Petrolympic Ltd. pursuant to Qualifying Transaction reverse takeover acquisition of Petrolympic Inc. (see FPsurvey - Mines & Energy)

Pistol Bay Mining Company Ltd. (Alta. 1966)
Nov. 22, 1973 – Name changed to Black Gold Resources (1973) Ltd. ■

Pistol Bay Mining Inc. (B.C. Feb. 20, 1995)
Dec. 23, 2020 – Name changed to Pegasus Resources Inc. (see FPsurvey - Mines & Energy)

Pitch-Ore Uranium Mines Ltd. (Ont. 1949)
1963 – Name changed to Allied Pitch-Ore Mines Ltd.; basis 1 new for 5 old shs. ■

Pitchblack Resources Ltd. (Ont. June 14, 2006)
Dec. 19, 2017 – Name changed to Troilus Gold Corp. following reverse takeover acquisition of 2507868 Ontario Inc.; basis 1 new for 4 old shs. (see FPsurvey - Mines & Energy)

Pitchgoma Mines Ltd. (Ont. 1953)
Aug. 26, 1957 – Merged into Consolidated Frederick Mines Ltd. Pitchgoma shldrs. entitled to receive 38.5¢ per 29 old shs. (see Consolidated Frederick Mines Ltd.)

Pitchstone Exploration Ltd. (B.C. Apr. 24, 2003)
July 10, 2012 – Acquired by Fission Energy Corp.; basis 0.2145 Fission com. shs. for 1 Pitchstone com. sh. (see Fission Energy Corp.)

Pitchvein Mines Ltd. (Ont. 1953)
May 6, 1980 – Charter cancelled.

Pitt Gold Mining Co. Ltd. (Ont. 1945)
June 30, 1980 – Dissolved.

Pitt Petroleums Ltd. (unknown)
Dec. 1955 – Assets acquired by Great Sweet Grass Oils Ltd.; basis 1 new for 4 old shs. (see Great Sweet Grass Oils Ltd.)

Pitt Products Limited (Ont. 1946)
1962 – Acquired by Avnet Electronics Corp. of New York; basis 1 Avnet sh. for 2 Pitt cl. A shs. and 0.43 Avnet shs. for 1 Pitt com. sh.

Pitts Engineering Construction Limited (Ont. 1965 amalg.)
Aug. 31, 1978 – Acquired by Banister Continental Ltd. for $9.75 per sh. on July 31, 1978. Remaining shldrs. received pref. shs. in an amalg. co., subsequently redeemed at $9.75 per sh. (see Banister Continental Ltd.)

Pittsonto Mining Co. Ltd. (Ont. 1948)
Dec. 4, 1972 – Dissolved.

Pivit Exploration Inc. (B.C. July 24, 2017)
July 10, 2019 – Name changed to Red Lake Gold Inc. (see FPsurvey - Mines & Energy)

Pivot Pharmaceuticals Inc. (B.C. June 10, 2002)
Dec. 6, 2019 – Name changed to BetterLife Pharma Inc. (see FPsurvey - Industrials)

Pivot Technology Solutions, Inc. (Ont. Mar. 22, 2013)
Nov. 4, 2020 – Acquired by Computacenter plc; basis Cdn$2.60 cash per sh.

Pivotal Corporation (B.C. Dec. 18, 1990)
Mar. 2, 2004 – Plan of Arrangement acquisition by CDC Software Corporation (CDC), wholly owned subsid. of chinadotcom corporation; basis either US$2.14 comprised of US$1.00 plus US$1.14 of cl. A CDC sh. or, US$2.00 for 1 old Pivotal sh.

Pivotal Development Corporation Inc. (Can. Sept. 1, 2017)
Nov. 27, 2018 – Name changed to Nuvei Corporation. ■

Pivotal Energy Ltd. (Alta. Dec. 9, 1999 amalg.)
July 7, 2003 – Amalgamated with Fairborne Energy Ltd.; basis 0.485 Fairborne com. shs. for 1 Pivotal com. sh. (see Fairborne Energy Ltd.)

Pivotal Financial Corp. (Ont. Dec. 21, 2020)
June 10, 2022 – Name changed to Global Food and Ingredients Ltd. pursuant to the Qualifying Transaction reverse takeover acquisition of Global Food and Ingredients Inc. and concurrent amalgamation of (old) Global Food with wholly owned 13476669 Canada Inc.; basis 1 new for 5 old shs. ■

Pivotree Inc. (Ont. Aug. 13, 1998)
June 22, 2015 – Continued into British Columbia.
Oct. 30, 2020 – Continued into Ontario. (see FPsurvey - Industrials)

Pixman Capital Inc. (Can. Apr. 12, 2006)
Dec. 27, 2006 – Name changed to Pixman Nomadic Media Inc. on Qualifying Transaction reverse takeover acquisition of Pixman Corporation. ■

Pixman Nomadic Media Inc. (Can. Apr. 12, 2006)
Feb. 2010 – Filed for bankruptcy, with PriceWaterhouseCoopers Inc. appointed trustee. All directors resigned.

Pizza Patio Management Ltd. (B.C. Dec. 16, 1965)
Aug. 29, 1991 – Name changed to San Andreas Resources Corporation. ■

Pizza Pizza Royalty Income Fund (Ont. May 26, 2005)
Dec. 31, 2012 – Succeeded by Pizza Pizza Royalty Corp. pursuant to plan of arrangement whereby Pizza Pizza Royalty Corp. was formed to facilitate the conversion of the fund into a corporation and the fund was dissolved. (see FPsurvey - Industrials)

Place Gas & Oil Company Limited (Ont. May 6, 1958)
Sept. 29, 1986 – Name changed to Place Resources Corporation; basis 1 new cl. A for 1 old com. sh. ■

Place Resources Corporation (Ont. May 6, 1958)
Feb. 6, 2001 – Acquired by Star Oil & Gas Acquisition Ltd. for $3.00 per sh.

Placer Development Limited (B.C. Feb. 22, 1971)
Aug. 12, 1987 – Continued into Canada. (see Placer Dome Inc.)
Aug. 13, 1987 – Amalgamated with Campbell Red Lake Mines Limited (1.702 for 1) and Dome Mines Limited (0.851 for 1) to form a new company named Placer Dome Inc.; basis 1 new for 1 old sh. (see Placer Dome Inc.)

Placer Dome Inc. (Can. Aug. 13, 1987 amalg.)
Mar. 15, 2006 – Acquired by Barrick Gold Corporation; basis either US$22.50, or 0.8269 new Barrick sh. plus US$0.05 for 1 old Placer sh. (see Barrick Gold Corporation)
May 3, 2006 – Continued into Ontario. (see Barrick Gold Corporation)

Plaer Petroleums Ltd. (Alta. 1952)
1959 – Struck off register.

Plains Creek Phosphate Corporation (B.C. July 24, 2007)
Mar. 28, 2013 – Name changed to GB Minerals Ltd.; basis 1 new for 20 old shs. ■

Plains Energy Services Ltd. (Alta. Oct. 8, 1996)
July 12, 2000 – Acquired by Precision Drilling Corporation; basis either $10.75 plus 0.0885 com. sh. wt., or 0.18676 new Precision com. sh. plus 0.0885 com. sh. wt. for 1 old Plains Energy sh. Each warrant exercisable at $64 per sh. prior to Dec. 31, 2001. (see Precision Drilling Corporation)

Plains Petroleum Corp. Ltd. (Ont. 1936)
1940 – Liquidated; Guaranty Trust Co., Toronto, liquidator. No distribution to unsecured shldrs.

Plains Petroleums Limited (Alta. 1948)
July 8, 1985 – Amalgamated into Scurry-Rainbow Oil Ltd.; basis 1 new for 22 old shs. or, $1.00 for 1 old sh.

Planet Exploration Inc. (Alta. Jan. 29, 1996)
Apr. 12, 2012 – Name changed to Planet Mining Exploration Inc. and continued into British Columbia. ■

Planet Gold Mines Ltd. (Ont. 1937)
Feb. 1958 – Charter cancelled.

Planet Health Corp. (Alta. June 15, 2000)
July 2, 2020 – Acquired by 2255820 Alberta Ltd.; basis 20¢ cash per sh.

Planet Mining Exploration Inc. (B.C. Apr. 12, 2012)
June 28, 2017 – Name changed to Planet Ventures Inc. (see FPsurvey - Industrials)

Planet 13 Holdings Inc. (Can. Apr. 26, 2002)
June 24, 2019 – Continued into British Columbia.
Sept. 15, 2023 – Continued into Nevada. (see FPsurvey - Industrials)

Planet Organic Health Corp. (Alta. June 15, 2000)
May 15, 2014 – Name changed to Planet Health Corp. ■

Planet Ventures Inc. (B.C. May 12, 1983)
Sept. 24, 2004 – Continued into Alberta.
Nov. 25, 2004 – Name changed to Antares Minerals Inc. ■

Planetsafe Enviro Corporation (Ont. Mar. 2, 1995)
June 6, 2005 – Dissolved and struck from register.
July 20, 2010 – Restored to registry. (see FPsurvey - Industrials)

Planex Ventures Ltd. (B.C. Jan. 11, 2000)
May 27, 2002 – Name changed to Tumi Resources Limited pursuant to Qualifying Transaction acquisition of 70% interest in Los Lomas property from Peru-based Compania Minera Urumalqui S.A. ■

Plannedco Inc. (Can. Mar. 17, 1994)
Apr. 28, 1995 – Name changed to Captech Communication Inc. ■

Plant&Co. Brands Ltd. (B.C. June 23, 2017)
Sept. 1, 2022 – Name changed to Happy Belly Food Group Inc. (see FPsurvey - Industrials)

Plantable Health Inc. (B.C. Feb. 10, 2021)
July 18, 2024 – Name changed to Altus Copper Corp. (see FPsurvey - Industrials)

PlantX Life Inc. (B.C. Oct. 14, 2011 amalg.)
Nov. 6, 2024 – Name changed to JIVA Technologies Inc. (see FPsurvey - Mines & Energy)

PlanVest Capital Corp. (B.C. Jan. 31, 1983)
Apr. 10, 1997 – Name changed to C.M. Oliver Inc. and continued into Canada. ■

Plaser Light Corporation (B.C. 1986)
Dec. 24, 1993 – Dissolved and struck off register.

Plasma Environmental Technologies Inc. (Ont. 1955)
Aug. 17, 2007 – Name changed to Blue Vista Technologies Inc.; basis 1 new for 10 old shs. ■

Plasti-Fab Ltd. (Alta. Mar. 31, 1989 amalg.)
Jan. 12, 1996 – Name changed to PFB Corporation. ■

Plastibec Ltée (Can. 1980)
Dec. 9, 1994 – Acquired by Royal Plastics Group Limited for $7.00 per sh. or 0.6222 Royal Plastics subord. vtg. shs. for 1 Plastibec com. sh. (see Royal Plastics Group Limited)

Plastic Engine Technology Corporation (Ont. 1982 amalg.)
Mar. 1989 – Placed into bankruptcy.
July 31, 1989 – Assets liquidated by the summer. Nothing left for shldrs.

La Plata Gold Corporation (B.C. Aug. 12, 1981)
Oct. 27, 2008 – Name changed to Alphamin Resources Corp. ■

Plata Minerals Corp. (B.C. June 29, 1983)
Oct. 5, 2001 – Name changed to Briyante Software Corp. following reverse takeover acquisition of Benchmark Technologies Inc. ■

Plata Mines Ltd. (Ont. 1926)
Aug. 17, 1931 – Charter cancelled.

Plata-Peru Resources Inc. (Ont. Apr. 2, 1987)
Feb. 5, 2007 – Certificate of incorporation cancelled and dissolved.

Plate Resources Inc. (B.C. Feb. 1, 2011)
Dec. 22, 2016 – Name changed to ArcPacific Resources Corp.; basis 1 new for 2 old shs. ■

Plateau Energy Metals Inc. (Ont. Oct. 31, 2007 amalg.)
May 19, 2021 – Acquired by American Lithium Corp.; basis 0.29 American Lithium com. shs. plus 0.145 American Lithium wts. for 1 Plateau Energy com. sh.

Plateau Metals & Industries Ltd. (B.C. Jan. 20, 1951)
Sept. 30, 1972 – Name changed to Wharf Resources Ltd.; basis 1 new for 4 old shs. ■

Plateau Uranium Inc. (Ont. Oct. 31, 2007 amalg.)
Mar. 12, 2018 – Name changed to Plateau Energy Metals Inc. ■

Platexco Inc. (Yuk. May 7, 1997)
Dec. 27, 2000 – Acquired by Impala Platinum Holdings Ltd. for $9.50 per sh.

Platform Eight Capital Corp. (Ont. Apr. 28, 2017)
Feb. 14, 2020 – Name changed to Blue Thunder Mining Inc. pursuant to Qualifying Transaction reverse takeover acquisition of private Blue Thunder Mining Corporation by way of a three-cornered amalgamation. ■

Platform 9 Capital Corp. (Ont. Feb. 15, 2018)
May 19, 2021 – Name changed to Sol Cuisine Ltd. pursuant to the Qualifying Transaction reverse takeover acquisition of Sol Cuisine Inc. and concurrent amalgamation of Sol Cuisine with wholly owned 12835151 Canada Inc.; basis 1 new for 16.2076 old shs. ■

Platform Resources Inc. (Alta. Dec. 5, 2003)
June 28, 2007 – Name changed to Alberta Oilsands Inc. ■

Platinex Inc. (Ont. Aug. 12, 1998)
Feb. 28, 2024 – Name changed to PTX Metals Inc. (see FPsurvey - Mines & Energy; FPsurvey - Industrials)

Platino Energy Corp. (Alta. Nov. 16, 2012)
July 22, 2015 – Amalgamated with a wholly owned subsid. of 1901558 Alberta Ltd. (deemed acquiror) , a co. controlled by Denham Capital Management LP, to form Colombia Oil and Gas Subsidiary Ltd for Cdn$0.25 per Platino sh.

Platinova A/S (Greenland Dec. 3, 1984)
Oct. 24, 1991 – Continued into Denmark.

Platinova Resources Ltd. (Can. May 13, 1986)
Dec. 30, 1986 – Continued into Ontario.

Platinum and Gold Resources Inc. (Ont. 1986)
Mar. 4, 1992 – Name changed to Platinum Capital Inc.; basis 1 new for 6 old shs. ■

Platinum Capital Inc. (Ont. 1986)
June 15, 1994 – Name changed to SoftCop Corporation; basis 1 new cl. B for 1 old com. sh. ∎

Platinum Communications Corporation (Alta. June 20, 2000)
Dec. 17, 2015 – Acquired by Xplornet Communications Inc.; basis 16¢ cash per com. sh.

Platinum Communications Systems Inc. (B.C. Oct. 23, 1984)
Dec. 12, 1990 – Name changed to PPZ Platinum Products Inc.; basis 1 new for 4 old shs. ∎

Platinum Group Metals Ltd. (B.C. Jan. 10, 2000)
Feb. 18, 2002 – Amalgamated in British Columbia to continue with same name. (see FPsurvey - Mines & Energy)

Platinum Resources of Canada Inc. (Ont. Apr. 22, 1986)
May 31, 1991 – Name changed to Portrait Impressions of Canada Limited; basis 1 new for 5 old shs. ∎

Platmin Limited (Can. May 29, 2003)
Apr. 1, 2009 – Continued into British Columbia.
Dec. 9, 2011 – Continued into Guernsey.
Dec. 28, 2011 – Voluntarily delisted from TSX.
Dec. 6, 2013 – Name changed to Sedibelo Platinum Mines Limited. ∎

Platonia Developments Inc. (B.C. 1986)
Aug. 12, 1988 – Name changed to Sun-Gold Developments International Corporation. ∎

Plator Gralouise Gold Mines Ltd. (Ont. 1939)
Sept. 22, 1966 – Dissolved.

Plator Long Lac Gold Mines Ltd. (Ont. June 28, 1934)
Mar. 1935 – Name changed to White Horse Gold Mines Ltd. ∎

Plator Porcupine Gold Mines Ltd. (Ont. 1939)
1948 – Name changed to Plator Gralouise Gold Mines Ltd.; basis 1 new for 10 old shs. ∎

Platoro West Holdings Inc. (B.C. May 16, 2006)
June 24, 2010 – Name changed to Silver Predator Corp.; basis 1 new for 12 old shs. (see FPsurvey - Mines & Energy)

The Plaunt Mining Co. (Ont. 1943)
Feb. 17, 1944 – Name changed to Culver Gold Mines Ltd. ∎

Playdigm Entertainment Corporation (Can. May 25, 1988)
Oct. 17, 2008 – Dissolved.

Playdium Entertainment Corporation (Ont. Dec. 6, 1991)
Dec. 3, 2001 – Restructured under Companies' Creditors Arrangement Act and completed in Feb. 2001. All assets transferred to newly formed company Playdium Corporation.

Player Petroleum Corporation (B.C. Apr. 29, 1987)
Apr. 29, 1998 – Continued into Alberta.
Aug. 10, 2001 – Acquired by National Fuel Exploration Corp. for $16.25 per sh.

Player Petroleum Inc. (B.C. 1981)
June 15, 1984 – Name changed to Player Resources Inc. ∎

Player Resources Inc. (B.C. 1981)
Jan. 26, 1987 – Name changed to Consolidated Player Resources Inc.; basis 1 new for 2 old shs. ∎

Playmaker Capital Inc. (Ont. Jan. 19, 2018)
Feb. 12, 2024 – Acquired by Better Collective A/S; basis (i) Cdn$0.70 cash, (ii) 0.0206 Better Collective ord. shs. or (iii) a combination of Cdn$0.245 cash and 0.0134 Better Collective ord. shs.

Plaza Resources Ltd. (B.C. 1972)
1973 – Name changed to Tika Resources Ltd. ∎

Plazacorp Retail Properties Ltd. (N.B. Feb. 2, 1999)
Jan. 1, 2014 – Succeeded by Plaza Retail REIT pursuant to plan of arrangement whereby Plaza Retail REIT was formed to facilitate the conversion of the corporation into a trust. (see FPsurvey - Industrials)

Pleno Mines Ltd. (Ont. 1954)
May 28, 1986 – Name changed to CanQuest Resource Corporation. ∎

PlenTech Electronics, Inc. (B.C. 1981)
Sept. 21, 1998 – Name changed to Consolidated PlenTech Electronics Inc.; basis 1 new for 6 old shs. ∎

Plexmar Resources Inc. (Ont. 1951)
Aug. 25, 1994 – Continued into Canada. (see Sierra Metals Inc.)
Nov. 2, 2012 – Continued into Ontario. (see Sierra Metals Inc.)
Nov. 19, 2012 – Acquired by Dia Bras Exploration Inc. for 1¢ per sh. (see Sierra Metals Inc.)
2018 – Name changed to Cautivo Peru Inc. (see Sierra Metals Inc.)

Plexore Rouyn Gold Mines Ltd. (Ont. 1945)
1958 – Dissolved.

Plexterre Mining Corporation Ltd. (Ont. 1950)
1964 – Absorbed by Medallion Mines Ltd.

Plexus Energy Ltd. (Alta. Feb. 14, 1996)
July 7, 2000 – Amalgamated with Peregrine Oil and Gas Ltd. (1 for 3.6474) and AEGIS Energy Ltd. (1 for 3.3) to form Surge Petroleum Inc.; basis 1 new Surge cl. A com. sh. for 2.8225 old Plexus com. shs. (see Surge Petroleum Inc.)

Plexus Resources Corporation (B.C. 1972)
June 3, 1993 – Amalgamated with CMP Resources Ltd. to form Kinross Gold Corporation; basis 1.8 new for 1 old sh.

Plicit Capital Corp. (Can. May 25, 2011)
Sept. 8, 2016 – Name changed to 3D Signatures Inc. pursuant to Qualifying Transaction reverse takeover acquisition of (old) 3D Signatures Inc. ∎

Plum Uranium & Metal Mining Ltd. (Ont. 1953)
Aug. 26, 1957 – Merged into Consolidated Frederick Mines Ltd.; basis 5 new for 8 old shs. (see Consolidated Frederick Mines Ltd.)

Plumbing Mart Corporation (Ont. Jan. 3, 1969)
Dec. 16, 1987 – Name changed to PMC Corporation; basis 1 new for 10 old shs. ∎

Plus Products Inc. (B.C. Mar. 29, 2018)
Sept. 21, 2021 – Voluntarily delisted from CSE following securing of court protection under the Companies' Creditors Arrangement Act. (see FPsurvey - Industrials)

Plus8 Global Ventures, Ltd. (B.C. June 22, 2006)
Mar. 17, 2016 – Name changed to ParcelPal Technology Inc. ∎

Pluton Industries Ltd. (B.C. Sept. 19, 1980)
Dec. 21, 1992 – Name changed to Clarion Environmental Technologies, Inc.; basis 1 new for 4 old shs. ∎

Pluton Resource Corporation (B.C. Sept. 19, 1980)
May 30, 1986 – Name changed to Pluton Industries Ltd. ∎

Pluton Uranium Mines Ltd. (Ont. 1953)
Sept. 28, 1964 – Dissolved.

Plutonic Capital Corp. (B.C. May 18, 1999)
July 31, 2003 – Name changed to Plutonic Capital Inc.; basis 1 new for 2 old shs. ∎

Plutonic Capital Inc. (B.C. May 18, 1999)
May 13, 2004 – Name changed to Plutonic Power Corporation prior to the May 17, 2004, Qualifying Transaction acquisition of Plutonic Hydro Inc. ∎

Plutonic Power Corporation (B.C. May 18, 1999)
May 18, 2011 – Merged into Magma Energy Corp. for $0.0001 plus 2.38 Magma shs. per sh. Subsequently, Magma changed its name to Alterra Power Corp. (see Alterra Power Corp.)

Plydom Corporation Ltd. (Ont. 1964)
Mar. 16, 1976 – Dissolved.

Plymouth Financial Corporation (B.C. 1974)
Aug. 16, 1985 – Name changed to New Plymouth Ventures Inc.; basis 1 new for 3 old shs. ∎

Plymouth Oil & Gas Corp. (B.C. 1974)
Nov. 15, 1983 – Name changed to Plymouth Financial Corporation; basis 2 new for 1 old sh. ∎

Plymouth Realty Capital Corp. (Ont. July 15, 2013)
Mar. 21, 2019 – Continued into British Columbia.
Mar. 5, 2021 – Name changed to Silverton Metals Corp. pursuant to Qualifying Transaction acquisition of KCP Minerals Inc., and concurrent amalgamation of KCP Minerals with wholly owned Silverton Finco Inc. and 1269171 B.C. Ltd. ∎

Plymouth Rock Technologies Inc. (B.C. Oct. 17, 2011)
July 31, 2023 – Name changed to Aether Global Innovations Corp. (see FPsurvey - Industrials)

Plympton Uranium & Metal Mines Ltd. (Ont. 1954)
Aug. 26, 1957 – Merged into Consolidated Frederick Mines Ltd.; basis 2 new for 3 old shs. (see Consolidated Frederick Mines Ltd.)

Pocaterra Energy Inc. (Alta. May 29, 1996)
Nov. 28, 2006 – Plan of Arrangement acquisition by The Buffalo Oil Corporation; basis either $0.575 plus 0.2 new Buffalo sh., or $0.915, or 0.538 new Buffalo sh. for 1 old Pocaterra sh. (see The Buffalo Oil Corporation)

Poco Petroleums Ltd. (Alta. Nov. 1, 1979)
Nov. 23, 1999 – Acquired by Texas-based Burlington Resources Inc.; basis 0.25 new exchangeable Burlington Resources Canada Inc. sh. for 1 old Poco sh. making Poco a wholly owned subsid. of Burlington.
Jan. 1, 2000 – Name changed to Burlington Resources Canada Energy Ltd. ∎

Pocono Capital Inc. (Can. June 11, 2007)
Feb. 24, 2009 – Name changed to Crown Minerals Inc. following Qualifying Transaction reverse takeover acquisition of Rykala Resources Inc. ∎

Poda Holdings, Inc. (B.C. July 6, 2018)
June 24, 2022 – Name changed to Idle Lifestyle Inc. following sale of substantially all of the company's business undertakings. ∎

Poda Lifestyle and Wellness Ltd. (B.C. July 6, 2018)
Sept. 27, 2021 – Name changed to Poda Holdings, Inc. ∎

Podium Capital Corporation (Can. Sept. 26, 2007)
Sept. 1, 2009 – Formed CRS Electronics Inc. in Canada on amalgamation with wholly owned 3542114 Canada Inc. (operating as CRS Electronics). ∎

Point Loma Resources Ltd. (Alta. Feb. 10, 2011)
June 8, 2020 – Placed into receivership by senior secured creditors. BDO Canada Limited was appointed receiver.

Point Resources Ltd. (B.C. 1986)
Feb. 25, 1994 – Dissolved and struck off register.

Point West Explorations Ltd. (unknown)
Nov. 30, 1970 – Amalgamated with Cantri Mining Ltd. (1 for 10), Con-Key Mines Ltd. (1 for 10), St. Anthony Mines Ltd. (1 for 30), Temanda Mines Ltd. (1 for 30) and Tinex Development & Exploration Ltd. (1 for 30) to form Can-Con Enterprises and Explorations Limited; basis 1 new for 10 old shs.

Pointe Claire Shopping Centre Trust (Que. 1962)
1975 – Owned the Pointe Claire Shopping Centre in Pointe Claire, Que. The centre was leased to Realty Equities (1962) Ltd., which subsequently went into bankruptcy. Litigation was adjudicated, resulting in payment to participation certificate holders of full face value of certificates, plus interest at 9% paid from date interest was suspended to date of payment in mid-1975.

Pointer Exploration Corp. (Alta. June 12, 1987)
Dec. 9, 1997 – Acquired by PanAtlas Energy Inc.; basis $1.60 or 1.4 PanAtlas shs. for 1 Pointer sh. (see PanAtlas Energy Inc.)

Points International Ltd. (Ont. Feb. 17, 2000)
Nov. 10, 2004 – Continued into Canada.
Jan. 1, 2022 – Name changed to Points.com Inc. ■

Points North Digital Technologies, Inc. (Ont. Sept. 10, 1992 amalg.)
Dec. 12, 1996 – Continued into Canada.
Jan. 2, 2001 – Name changed to Peragis Inc. ■

Points of Call Airlines Ltd. (Alta. 1984)
Apr. 1, 1991 – Struck off register.

Points.com Inc. (Can. Nov. 10, 2004)
July 5, 2022 – Acquired by Plusgrade Parent L.P.; basis US$25 cash per sh.

Poko Innovations Inc. (Can. Aug. 10, 2021)
Aug. 25, 2024 – Struck from registry and dissolved for non-compliance.

Pol-Invest Holdings Ltd. (B.C. May 13, 1996)
Mar. 19, 2003 – Name changed to Net Soft Systems Inc. following reverse takeover acquisition of Net Soft S.A. ■

Pola Resources Ltd. (B.C. 1980)
June 11, 1993 – Dissolved and struck off register.

Polamet Mines Ltd. (Ont. 1955)
Sept. 28, 1964 – Charter cancelled.

Polar Bear Development Corp. (B.C. 1980)
June 14, 1996 – Dissolved and struck off register.

Polar Bear Ventures Ltd. (B.C. Jan. 13, 1981)
Feb. 24, 1999 – Name changed to Iciena Ventures Inc.; basis 1 new for 8 old shs. ■

Polar Exploration & Mining Co. Ltd. (Ont. 1946)
May 1957 – Charter cancelled.

Polar Hedge Enhanced Income Trust (Ont. Apr. 18, 1997)
Oct. 15, 2003 – Acquired by Genesis Land Development Corp. for $8.62 per trust unit.

Polar Innovative Capital Corp. (Ont. Oct. 15, 1997 amalg.)
Dec. 20, 2004 – Name changed to Simplex Solutions Inc.; basis 1 new for 7 old shs. (see FPsurvey - Industrials)

Polar Resources Corporation (B.C. June 9, 1981)
Nov. 23, 2015 – Dissolved and struck from register.
Apr. 23, 2022 – Restored to registry. (see FPsurvey - Mines & Energy)

Polar Star Mining Corporation (Can. Aug. 1, 2007 amalg.)
Dec. 18, 2014 – Acquired by Iron Creek Capital Corp.; basis 0.26 Iron com. shs. for 1 Polar com. sh.

Polaris Energy Corp. (B.C. 1979)
Mar. 12, 1985 – Name changed to International Polaris Energy Corp. ■

Polaris Geothermal Inc. (Yuk. June 21, 2004 amalg.)
Oct. 20, 2009 – Acquired by GTO Resources Inc.; basis 0.2467 GTO shs. for 1 Polaris cl. A vtg. sh. and 1 Polaris pref. sh. (see Ram Power, Corp.)

Polaris Gold Mines (Canada) Ltd. (unknown)
1946 – Taken over by Apollo Porcupine Mines Ltd.; basis 1 new for 3 old shs. (see Apollo Porcupine Mines Ltd.)

Polaris Infrastructure Inc. (B.C. Apr. 26, 1984)
July 5, 2022 – Name changed to Polaris Renewable Energy Inc. and continued into Ontario. (see FPsurvey - Mines & Energy; FPsurvey - Industrials)

Polaris Materials Corporation (B.C. May 14, 1999)
Nov. 21, 2017 – Acquired by U.S. Concrete, Inc.; basis Cdn$3.40 cash per sh.

Polaris Minerals Corporation (B.C. May 14, 1999)
Jan. 1, 2015 – Name changed to Polaris Materials Corporation. ■

Polaris Mines Ltd. (B.C. Apr. 17, 1957)
May 1973 – Name changed to Titan-Polaris Mines Ltd.; basis 1 new for 2.5 old shs. ■

Polaris Oil Co. Ltd. (Alta. 1949)
1951 – Taken over by Calvan Consolidated Oil & Gas Co. Ltd.

Polaris-Taku Mining Co., Ltd. (B.C. 1936)
1953 – Acquired by New Taku Mines Limited. (see New Taku Mines Limited)

Polcon Corporation (Que. 1967)
Jan. 13, 1983 – Wound up under bankruptcy act.

Pole Star Mines Ltd. (Ont. 1946)
1955 – Acquired by Newkirk Mining Corp. Ltd.; basis 1 new for 12 old shs. (see Newkirk Mining Corp. Ltd.)

Polex Mines Limited (Ont. 1969)
Jan. 18, 1972 – Amalgamated with Spar Mines Limited, Lava Minerals Limited and Winnebago Mines Limited to form a new co. known as Spar Holdings & Explorations Limited; basis 1 new for 4 old shs.

Pollard Banknote Income Fund (Ont. June 29, 2005)
May 14, 2010 – Succeeded by Pollard Banknote Limited following conversion of Pollard Banknote Income Fund into a corporation; basis 1 com. sh. for 1 fund unit and 1 com. sh. for 1 class B or class C limited partnership unit of Pollard Holdings Limited Partnership. (see FPsurvey - Industrials)

Polled Cattle Corporation Ltd. (Alta. July 26, 1947)
July 29, 1988 – Name changed to Target Energy Canada Inc. ■

Polly Pond Mining Co. Ltd. (unknown)
1958 – Assets acquired by Polpond Mining Co. Ltd.

Polo Biology Global Group Corporation (B.C. May 31, 2007)
Nov. 23, 2012 – Name changed to P&P Ventures Inc.; basis 1 new for 10 old shs. ■

Polo Petroleum Ltd. (Can. June 17, 1987)
Feb. 7, 1991 – Amalgamated with CanEuro Resources Ltd. (1 for 5) to form a new co. named Attock Oil Corporation; basis 1 new for 1 old sh. (see Attock Oil Corporation)

Polpond Mining Co. Ltd. (Ont. 1958)
1960 – Merged into Consolidated Panther Mines Ltd.; basis 1 new for 20 old shs.

Poly-Converters Ltd. (Ont. May 23, 1969)
Oct. 1974 – Name changed to PCL Industries Limited. (see FPsurvey - Industrials)

Poly Ores Mining Company Ltd. (Ont. Aug. 24, 1953)
Sept. 26, 1988 – Name changed to Polyore Capital Inc. ■

Poly-Pacific International Inc. (Alta. Oct. 25, 1995)
Feb. 25, 2010 – Name changed to Global Green Matrix Corp.; basis 1 new for 15 old shs. ■

Polyair Inter Pack Inc. (Ont. Dec. 4, 1995)
July 17, 2009 – Privatized for 5¢ per sh.

Polyair Tires Inc. (Alta. Nov. 21, 1986)
June 11, 1998 – Formed Bartizan Capital Corporation in Alberta on amalgamation with Bartizan Capital Corporation, constituting a reverse takeover by Bartizan; basis 1 new for 5 old shs. ■

Polychemical Industries Limited (Alta. 1955)
1970 – All o/s pref. and com. shs. acquired by Dart Industries Inc. of Los Angeles, Calif.

PolyCom Systems Limited (Ont. 1968)
Feb. 29, 1988 – All o/s com. shs. and 56.6% of pref. shs. acquired by Memotec Data Inc. for $4,286,000 in cash. (see Memotec Data Inc.)

Polycorp Inc. (Ont. June 30, 1998 amalg.)
Dec. 19, 2001 – Name changed to Atlas Cromwell Ltd. ■

Polymer Corporation Ltd. (Can. 1942)
Mar. 22, 1973 – Name changed to Polysar Limited. ■

Polymer International (N.S.) Incorporation (N.S. 1987 amalg.)
Jan. 10, 1990 – Acquired by PINS Acquisition Corp., a wholly owned subsid. of Intertape Systems Inc.; basis $12.50 per sh.

Polymer Solutions, Inc. (Nev. Feb. 26, 1997)
Feb. 9, 2004 – Acquired indirectly by North Carolina-based Chemcraft Holdings Corporation for total consideration of US$6,264,250.

PolyMet Mining Corp. (B.C. Mar. 4, 1981)
Nov. 9, 2023 – All o/s shs. not already held acquired by Glencore plc; basis US$2.11 cash per sh.

Polyore Capital Inc. (Ont. Aug. 24, 1953)
Aug. 24, 1993 – Formed Taylor Rand Incorporated in Ontario on amalgamation with Taylor Rand Incorporated. ■

Polypump Limited (Ont. 1968)
June 1980 – Charter cancelled.

Polysar Energy & Chemical Corporation (Can. 1971; via Act of Parliament)
Sept. 7, 1988 – Acquired by NOVA Corporation of Alberta; basis 0.5 NOVA com. shs. and $14.50 for 1 Polysar sh. Preferred shs. were redeemed as follows: 1980 ser. at $20 per sh. on Mar. 14, 1988; 1983 ser. at $28 per sh. on Oct. 12, 1988; and 1988 ser. at $11.75 per sh. on Oct. 12, 1988. (see NOVA Corporation of Alberta)

Polysar Limited (Can. 1942)
July 2, 1986 – All o/s 1st pref. shs. 15.5% cumulative, redeem. non-voting ser. A shs. redeemed at $26.25 as at.

Polysource Industries Ltd. (Bermuda 1988)
Feb. 6, 1990 – Acquired by Polysource Holdings Plc; basis 1 Polysource Holdings sh. for 1 Polysource Industries sh.

Polysteel Building Systems Ltd. (Can. Oct. 19, 1987)
Apr. 19, 1999 – Formed Medical Pathways International Inc. following acquisition of A.R.T. Medical Pathways, Inc. and e-Health Technology Corporation. ■

Pomac Mines Limited (Alta. 1988)
Jan. 27, 1989 – Continued into Ontario.
Feb. 17, 1989 – Name changed to Richmond Gulf Resources Ltd. ■

Pominex Ltd. (Ont. 1952)
Dec. 16, 1985 – Name changed to Canarchon Holdings Limited; basis 1 new for 15 old shs. ■

Ponderay Exploration Company Ltd. (Alta. 1962)
May 15, 1980 – Name changed to Canadian Ponderay Energy Limited; basis 1 new for 5 old shs. ■

Ponderous Panda Capital Corp. (B.C. Mar. 22, 2017)
May 17, 2021 – Name changed to Wildpack Beverage Inc. pursuant to the Qualifying Transaction reverse takeover acquisition of Wildpack Beverage Alberta Inc.

and concurrent amalgamation of Wildpack with wholly owned 2342700 Alberta Ltd.; basis 1 new for 2.578 old shs. (see FPsurvey - Industrials)

Poney Explorations Ltd. (B.C. 1972)
Nov. 14, 1985 – Name changed to Steed Ventures Corporation; basis 1 new for 5 old shs. (see FPsurvey - Industrials)

Pono Capital Three, Inc. (Del. Mar. 11, 2022)
Oct. 14, 2022 – Continued into Cayman Islands.
Jan. 11, 2024 – Continued into British Columbia.
Jan. 16, 2024 – Name changed to New Horizon Aircraft Ltd. pursuant to reverse takeover acquisition of Robinson Aircraft Ltd. (dba Horizon Aircraft). (see FPsurvey - Industrials)

Ponoka Calmar Oils Ltd. (Alta. Sept. 20, 1949)
1952 – Acquired by Calmar West Oils Ltd.; basis 25 new Calmar shs. for 1 old Ponoka sh. (see Calmar West Oils Ltd.)

Pontiac Castle Investments Corporation (Can. Apr. 21, 2004)
May 16, 2007 – Name changed to Prosys Tech Corporation. (see FPsurvey - Industrials)

Pontiac Mining Development Inc. (Que. 1972)
July 1973 – Name changed to Calmet Mining & Exploration Ltd.; basis 3 new for 5 old shs. (see FPsurvey - Mines & Energy)

Pontiac Petroleums Ltd. (Alta. 1953)
1959 – Struck off register.

Pontiac Rouyn Mines (1939) Ltd. (Ont. 1939)
May 3, 1943 – Name changed to Anglo-Rouyn Mines Limited; basis 1 new for 2 old shs. ■

Pontibi Gold Mines Ltd. (Ont. 1945)
Charter cancelled.

Pontiff Mining Ltd. (Ont. 1955)
Mar. 1976 – Charter cancelled.

Pontus Capital Corp. (B.C. Feb. 18, 2017)
Jan. 18, 2018 – Name changed to Cryptobuyer Technologies Corp. ■

Pony Sporting Goods Limited (Ont. 1971)
July 19, 1982 – Continued into Canada.
June 1, 1987 – Name changed to 161671 Canada Inc. ■

Pool Mining Corporation (Que. 1955)
Oct. 1974 – Charter cancelled.

Pool Petrol Investments Canada Ltd. (Alta. 1979)
1980 – Name changed to Pool Petrol Energy Ltd. , a wholly owned subsid. of Pool Petrol Gmbh of Munich, Germany.

PoP Shoppes International Inc. (Ont. 1971)
Mar. 17, 1986 – Dissolved.

Pope Valley Holdings Ltd. (B.C. Mar. 24, 1986)
Feb. 28, 1994 – Name changed to Consolidated Pope Valley Holdings Ltd.; basis 1 new for 5 old shs. ■

POPi Group Inc. (Alta. Feb. 17, 1995)
Oct. 9, 2003 – Name changed to Damian Capital Corp.; basis 1 new for 5 old shs. ■

Poplar Oils Ltd. (Alta. 1952)
1957 – Acquired by New Gas Exploration Co. of Alberta Ltd.; basis 1 new New Gas sh. for 5 old Poplar shs. (see New Gas Exploration Co. of Alberta Ltd.)

Poplar Resources Ltd. (B.C. June 9, 1983)
Nov. 23, 2003 – Formed Nordic Diamonds Ltd. in British Columbia on amalgamation with Earth Star Diamonds Ltd. with Poplar the deemed acquiror; basis 1 new for 3 Earth Star shs. and 1 new for 10 Poplar shs. ■

PopReach Corporation (Ont. Sept. 25, 2018)
Nov. 26, 2024 – Name changed to Ionik Corporation. (see FPsurvey - Industrials)

Popular Industries Limited (Que. 1968)
June 1989 – Privatized.

Porcher Island Gold Corporation (B.C. Aug. 25, 1980)
Jan. 8, 1999 – Name changed to Tetra Metals Ltd.; basis 1 new for 5 old shs. ■

Porcupine Balmoral Resources Ltd. (Ont. Aug. 20, 1986)
July 30, 1990 – Name changed to Marlin Capital Foods Ltd. ■

Porcupine Crown Mines Ltd. (Ont. 1913)
1952 – Charter cancelled.

Porcupine Goldor Mines Ltd. (Ont. 1936)
1944 – Name changed to Porcupine Goldtop Mines Ltd. ■

Porcupine Goldtop Mines Ltd. (Ont. 1936)
Mar. 14, 1978 – Charter cancelled.

Porcupine Lake Gold Mining Co. Ltd. (Can. 1927)
1957 – Shldrs. received 11/8 Gold City Porcupine Mines Ltd. shs. for each 2 shs. held.
June 1961 – Charter cancelled.

Porcupine Paymaster Ltd. (Ont. 1930)
1968 – Merged into Associated Porcupine Mines Ltd.; basis 1 new for 3.57196 old shs.

Porcupine Peninsula Gold Mines Ltd. (Ont. 1951)
1953 – Name changed to Brunhurst Mines Ltd.; basis 1 new for 2 old shs. ■

Porcupine Prime Mines Ltd. (Ont. 1946)
Dec. 1965 – Name changed to Prime Potash Corporation of Canada Ltd. ■

Porcupine Reef Gold Mines Ltd. (Ont. Oct. 5, 1935)
June 1951 – Merged into Broulan Reef Mines Ltd. (see Broulan Reef Mines Limited)

Porcupine Southgate Mines Ltd. (Ont. 1944)
1968 – Merged into Associated Porcupine Mines Ltd.; basis 1 new for 28.8566 old shs.

Porcupine Triumph Gold Mines, Ltd. (Ont. July 17, 1936)
May 1938 – Name changed to Jodelo Gold Mines Ltd.; basis 1 new for 4.5 old shs. ■

Porcupine United Gold Mines Ltd. (unknown)
Voluntary liquidation. No equity for shldrs.

Porcupine Watborn Gold Mines, Ltd. (Ont. Apr. 28, 1934)
Oct. 1949 – Sold property to Porcupine Reef Gold Mines Ltd.; basis 1 new for 7 old shs, 7¢ for fractional shs. Co. winding up. (see Porcupine Reef Gold Mines Ltd.)

Porosity Petroleums Ltd. (Alta. 1952)
1954 – Acquired by Nuco Petroleums Ltd.; basis 1 new for 6 old shs. (see Nuco Petroleums Ltd.)

Porpoise Capital Network Inc. (Alta. Mar. 22, 2000)
Feb. 15, 2001 – Name changed to PCNET International Inc. ■

Port Colwell Mines & Metals Ltd. (Ont. 1942)
1957 – Dissolved.

Port Dover Gas & Oil Limited (Ont. 1954)
Jan. 1, 1980 – Dissolved.

Port Maitland Smelting & Mining Co. Ltd. (Ont. 1957)
Apr. 29, 1965 – Dissolved.

Port O'Call Hotel Inc. (Alta. 1988)
Apr. 23, 1993 – Placed into receivership in May 1992. Deemed bankrupt. No distribution to shldrs.

Port Radium Mines Ltd. (Ont. 1944)
Jan. 1962 – Name changed to Silver Strike Mines Ltd. ■

Porta-Lube Automotives Inc. (Alta. Oct. 9, 1987)
Nov. 20, 1990 – Name changed to Cottonballs Corporation. ■

PortaCom Wireless, Inc. (B.C. July 7, 1989)
Dec. 24, 1996 – Continued into Delaware.

Portage Avenue Gold Mines Ltd. (Man. 1949)
Mar. 24, 1986 – Amalgamated with New Forty Four Mines Limited to form Canadian Gold Mines Limited; basis sh. for sh.

Portage Gold Mines Ltd. (B.C. 1936)
Apr. 14, 1975 – Charter cancelled.

Portage Island (Chibougamau) Mines Ltd. (Que. 1945)
1960 – Acquired by Copper Rand Chibougamau Mines Ltd.; basis 1 new for 3.5 old shs. (see Copper Rand Chibougamau Mines Ltd.)

Portage Longlac Mines Ltd. (Ont. 1936)
Sept. 24, 1956 – Charter cancelled.

Portage Minerals Inc. (Can. June 20, 2006)
Oct. 7, 2013 – Acquired by Tri-Star Resources Plc; basis 1 Tri-Star ord. sh. for 7.159849 Portage shs.
Oct. 8, 2013 – Name changed to Tri-Star Antimony Canada Inc.

Portal de Oro Resources Ltd. (B.C. Aug. 14, 2000)
Dec. 21, 2004 – Name changed to Portal Resources Ltd. ■

Portal Resources Ltd. (B.C. Feb. 27, 1987)
Dec. 7, 1994 – Name changed to Capella Resources Ltd.; basis 1 new for 3.7 old shs. ■

Portal Resources Ltd. (B.C. Aug. 14, 2000)
Apr. 2, 2012 – Name changed to Galileo Petroleum Ltd.; basis 1 new for 5 old shs. ■

Portavideo, The Magic Movie Machine Co. Ltd. (Can. 1982)
Mar. 28, 1985 – Name changed to The Shannock Corporation. ■

Portcomm Communications Corporation Limited (B.C. 1951)
Oct. 3, 1977 – Name changed to Hal Roach Studios Corp. ■

Portfield Industries Inc. (Ont. Oct. 29, 1980 amalg.)
Sept. 27, 1990 – Name changed to Canmine Resources Corporation; basis 1 new for 10 old shs. ■

Portfield Petroleums Ltd. (Ont. 1971)
Oct. 29, 1980 – Amalgamated with Pensec Explorations Inc. and Erieshore Industries Inc. to form Portfield Industries Inc.; basis 3 new for 8 old shs.

Portia Exploration Ltd. (B.C. July 17, 2007)
Jan. 6, 2014 – Dissolved and struck from register.

Portland Yellowknife Gold Mines Ltd. (Ont. 1945)
May 1980 – Charter cancelled.

Portman Explorations Ltd. (B.C. Apr. 30, 1987)
Jan. 18, 1999 – Name changed to Daytona Energy Corp.; basis 1 new for 3 old shs. ■

Portneuf Mineral Corp. (Que. 1952)
Apr. 1974 – Charter cancelled.

Porto Energy Corp. (B.C. Jan. 30, 2010 amalg.)
July 18, 2017 – Dissolved and struck from register.

Portola Resources Inc. (B.C. Feb. 13, 1998)
Mar. 22, 2017 – Name changed to Lithium Energi Exploration Inc. following the acquisition of Lithium Energi Agrentina, S.A, Antofalla North, S.A. and Antofalla South, S.A. (see FPsurvey - Mines & Energy)

Portrait Impressions of Canada Limited (Ont. Apr. 22, 1986)
Oct. 8, 1998 – Name changed to Carriage Automotive Group Inc. ■

Portrush Petroleum Corporation (B.C. June 11, 1996)
Dec. 11, 2009 – Name changed to Westbridge Energy
Corporation; basis 1 new for 10 old shs. ■

Poseidon Capital Corp. (Alta. Aug. 6, 2004)
June 14, 2006 – Name changed to Acceleware Corp. ■

Poseidon Concepts Corp. (Alta. Nov. 30, 2005 amalg.)
Apr. 2013 – Filed for protection under the Companies'
Creditor Arrangement Act (CCAA).
PricewaterhouseCoopers Inc. appointed monitor.
Nov. 30, 2015 – Dissolved and struck from registry.
Oct. 2018 – PricewaterhouseCoopers was discharged
as monitor.

Poseidon Minerals Ltd. (B.C. Oct. 18, 1973)
July 22, 2003 – Name changed to Stingray Resources
Inc.; basis 1 new for 2 old shs. ■

Posera-HDX Inc. (Ont. Oct. 22, 2001)
Oct. 7, 2011 – Succeeded by Posera-HDX Limited
following transfer of assets and liabilities, except Dexit
radio frequency identification device (RFID) business, to
Posera-HDX Limited. ■

Posera-HDX Limited (Ont. Oct. 7, 2011)
Jan. 1, 2016 – Name changed to Posera Ltd. ■

Posera Ltd. (Ont. Oct. 7, 2011)
Feb. 4, 2020 – Acquired by PayFacto Inc.; basis
$0.1126907498 cash per sh.

Position Inc. (Alta. Apr. 18, 1996)
July 2, 2009 – Struck from registry and dissolved.

Positive Energy Products Inc. (B.C. 1979)
June 27, 1995 – Name changed to Dimensions West
Marketing Inc.; basis 1 new for 5 old shs. ■

Positron Fiber Systems Corporation (Can. May 30,
1995)
Oct. 16, 1998 – Acquired by RELTEC Acquisition Inc.,
an indirect wholly owned subsid. of RELTEC Corporation;
basis US$13.625 per sh.

Post Energy Corporation (Alta. June 3, 1993)
Dec. 31, 1994 – Amalgamated in Alberta to continue with
same name. (see Ketch Energy Ltd.)
July 9, 2001 – Plan of Arrangement with Ketch Energy
Ltd. and Kick Energy Corporation; basis either $8.60 or
1.3 new Ketch com. shs. or a combination thereof, plus
1/10 of new Kick com. sh., plus $2.1747 promissory notes
of Kick Energy Partnership for 1 old Post com. sh. (see
Ketch Energy Ltd.)

Post Petroleums Limited (Alta. Sept. 12, 1985)
Aug. 5, 1987 – Name changed to Rockford Technology
Corporation. (see FPsurvey - Mines & Energy; FPsurvey
- Industrials)

Postech Corporation (Can. Dec. 1, 1981)
Feb. 20, 1989 – Placed into receivership; Coopers &
Lybrand appointed receivers.
Apr. 1989 – Certain assets sold.
June 1991 – All assets liquidated; creditors received a
shortfall and no distribution made to shldrs.

Potash Company of America Inc. (Can. 1984)
Dec. 31, 1987 – Amalgamated with Rio Algom Ltd.

Potash Corporation of Saskatchewan Inc. (Sask. June
4, 1953)
May 15, 2002 – Continued into Canada.
Jan. 1, 2018 – Succeeded by Nutrien Ltd. (new parent
company) following merger with Agrium Corp. (2.23
Nutrien shs. for 1 Agrium sh.); basis 0.4 new for 1 old sh.
(see FPsurvey - Mines & Energy; FPsurvey - Industrials)

Potash North Resource Corporation (B.C. Jan. 10,
2000)
Apr. 20, 2009 – Acquired by Potash One Inc.; basis
0.3125 Potash One shs. for 1 Potash North sh. (see
Potash One Inc.)

Potash One Inc. (Can. Dec. 5, 2007)
Mar. 18, 2011 – Acquired by K+S Aktiengesellschaft for
$4.50 per sh.
Mar. 29, 2011 – Continued into British Columbia.

Potash Ridge Corporation (B.C. Feb. 16, 2011)
Oct. 21, 2011 – Continued into Ontario.
Aug. 8, 2018 – Name changed to SOPerior Fertilizer
Corp. (see FPsurvey - Mines & Energy)

Potasse Premiere Corp. Ltd. (Ont. 1965)
May 15, 1974 – Dissolved.

Potent Ventures Inc. (B.C. Jan. 14, 2020)
May 26, 2022 – Name changed to The Gummy Project
Inc. ■

Potential Resources Ltd. (B.C. Dec. 28, 1973)
Apr. 7, 1986 – Name changed to Skybridge International
Inc. ■

Potential Technologies Inc. (Alta. Nov. 1, 1996)
Dec. 30, 1998 – Name changed to Delaney Energy
Services Corporation following reverse takeover
acquisition of Delaney Energy Services Corp.; basis 1
new for 3 old sh. ■

Potlatch Petroleums Inc. (Alta. Apr. 3, 1987)
May 16, 1990 – Name changed to Templar Energy Ltd. ■

Potluck Exploration Ltd. (Can. 1953)
1958 – Charter cancelled.

Pott Falls Gold Mines Ltd. (Ont. 1946)
Nov. 21, 1955 – Charter cancelled.

Potter Distilleries Ltd. (B.C. Oct. 6, 1958)
Jan. 30, 1978 – Continued into Canada.
Dec. 31, 1986 – Formed International Potter Distilling
Corporation on amalgamation with Pacific Western
Brewing Co. Ltd., a wholly owned subsid.; basis 1 new
com. sh. for 3 old cl. A or cl B shs. ■

Potterdoal Mines Ltd. (Ont. 1927)
1955 – Name changed to New Potterdoal Mines Ltd.;
basis 1 new for 10 old shs. ■

Pouce Coupe Oils Ltd. (Alta.)
1960 – Struck off register.

Poulmaque Gold Mines Ltd. (Ont. 1944)
1948 – Name changed to Goldmaque Mines Ltd. ■

Pounce Technologies Inc. (Alta. June 26, 2014)
Oct. 19, 2021 – Voluntarily delisted. (see FPsurvey -
Industrials)

Pounder Venture Capital Corp. (Can. Sept. 17, 2009)
Apr. 24, 2017 – Name changed to Pool Safe Inc. pursuant
to Qualifying Transaction reverse takeover acquisition of
(old) Pool Safe Inc.; basis 1 new for 4 old shs. (see
FPsurvey - Industrials)

Powder Mountain Energy Ltd. (Alta. Aug. 22, 2012
amalg.)
Aug. 5, 2015 – Acquired by Canamax Energy Ltd.; basis
0.954667 Canamax shs. for 1 Powder Mountain sh. (see
Canamax Energy Ltd.)

Powder River Resources Ltd. (B.C. Apr. 7, 1981)
Feb. 19, 1982 – Name changed to Stateside Mines Ltd. ■

Powell River Company Limited (B.C. July 13, 1911)
Dec. 31, 1959 – Merged with MacMillan & Bloedel Limited
to form MacMillan, Bloedel and Powell River Limited. (see
MacMillan, Bloedel and Powell River Limited)

Powell Rouyn Gold Mines Limited (Que. 1937)
1970 – Acquired by Lake Shore Mines, Ltd.; basis 1 new
for 10 old shs.

Power Americas Minerals Corp. (B.C. Nov. 8, 2009)
Sept. 5, 2018 – Name changed to Edison Cobalt Corp. ■

Power Battery Holdings Corporation (B.C. Jan. 1,
1980)
May 1991 – Continued into Wyoming.
Dec. 1992 – Continued into Washington.
July 9, 1998 – Name changed to Consolidated Power
Battery Corporation; basis 1 new for 4 old shs.

Power Corporation of Canada, Limited (Can. Apr. 18,
1925)
May 31, 1980 – Name changed to Power Corporation of
Canada. (see FPsurvey - Industrials)

Power Explorations & Holdings Limited (Ont. Dec.
1972)
June 7, 1982 – Charter cancelled.
Apr. 2, 1984 – Charter revived.
July 25, 1985 – Name changed to Power Explorations
Inc.; basis 1 new for 2 old shs. ■

Power Explorations Inc. (Ont. Dec. 1972)
Feb. 28, 1990 – Amalgamated with Moss Resources Ltd.
(1.5 for 1) to form a new co. Moss-Power Resources Inc.;
basis 1 new for 1 old sh. (see Moss-Power Resources
Inc.)

Power Financial Corporation (Man. Apr. 5, 1940; via
Special Act of Legislature)
Aug. 16, 1979 – Continued into Canada.
Dec. 4, 1986 – Amalgamated in Canada to continue with
same name.
Feb. 19, 2020 – All o/s com. shs. not already held
acquired by Power Corporation of Canada; basis 1.05
Power Corporation sub. vtg. shs. and $0.01 in cash for
1 Power Financial com. sh. (see FPsurvey - Industrials)

Power-Fuel Petroleum Ltd. (unknown)
Dec. 1940 – In voluntary liquidation.

Power Mines Ltd. (Ont. 1971)
1972 – Amalgamated with Active Mines Ltd. (1 for 2) and
Eclipse Metals Limited (1 for 2) to form a new co. Power
Explorations & Holdings Limited in December; basis 1
new for 6 old shs.

Power Nickel Inc. (B.C. Aug. 19, 1987)
Feb. 20, 2025 – Name changed to Power Metallic Mines
Inc. (see FPsurvey - Mines & Energy)

Power Plus Corporation (Alta. Dec. 15, 1986)
Aug. 3, 1999 – Name changed to PPC Capital Corp. ■

Power Uranium Company Ltd. (Que. 1954)
Aug. 1956 – Name changed to Power Mining Corporation.

Poweramic Explorations Limited (Ont. 1955)
Nov. 30, 1959 – Charter cancelled.

PowerBand Solutions Inc. (B.C. Sept. 29, 2009)
Oct. 23, 2024 – Name changed to AmeriTrust Financial
Technologies Inc. (see FPsurvey - Industrials)

PowerComm Inc. (Alta. Dec. 31, 2006 amalg.)
Dec. 23, 2009 – Name changed to PetroCorp Group
Inc. ■

Powerex Resources Ltd. (unknown)
Feb. 28, 1978 – Amalgamated with Landair Explorations
Ltd. (0.75 for 1) to form Uranex Resources Ltd.; basis 1
new Uranex sh. for 1 old Powerex sh. (see Uranex
Resources Ltd.)

Powergem Resource Corporation (B.C. 1980)
May 18, 1989 – Name changed to Consolidated
Powergem Resource Corporation; basis 1 new for 5 old
shs. ■

Powerhouse Energy Corp. (B.C. Jan. 18, 1979)
Sept. 18, 2001 – Name changed to International
Powerhouse Energy Corp.; basis 1 new for 10 old shs. ■

Powermax Energy Inc. (Alta. Feb. 18, 1998)
Oct. 17, 2005 – Acquired by High Plains Energy Inc.;
basis $0.5067 plus 0.333 new High Plains sh. for 1 old
Powermax sh. (see High Plains Energy Inc.)

PowerNova Technologies Corporation (B.C. Oct. 6, 1986)
Mar. 25, 2013 – Struck from register and dissolved.

PowerOre Inc. (B.C. Feb. 1, 2018)
Sept. 28, 2020 – Name changed to QC Copper & Gold Inc. ■

Powerstar International Inc. (Alta. Apr. 19, 2004)
Oct. 31, 2007 – Name changed to Solutrea Corp. (see FPsurvey - Industrials)

Powerstone Metals Corp. (B.C. Dec. 13, 2021)
Name changed to Libra Energy Materials Inc. pursuant to the reverse takeover acquisition of Libra Lithium Corp.; basis 1 new for 2.4966 old shs. (see FPsurvey - Mines & Energy)

Powertech Industries Inc. (B.C. Feb. 10, 1984)
June 5, 2006 – Name changed to Powertech Uranium Corp. ■

Powertech Uranium Corp. (B.C. Feb. 10, 1984)
Oct. 29, 2014 – Name changed to Azarga Uranium Corp. following reverse takeover acquisition of Azarga Resources Limited; basis 1 new for 10 old shs. ■

PowerTel Communications Inc. (Alta. Feb. 6, 1997 amalg.)
Aug. 10, 1998 – Name changed to Equess Communications Inc. ■

Powerworks Canada Inc. (Can. Dec. 6, 1994)
July 12, 2004 – Dissolved.

Poydras Gaming Finance Corp. (Ont. May 5, 2014)
Jan. 2, 2018 – Name changed to Integrity Gaming Corp. ■

Poynt Corporation (Alta. Dec. 8, 2006 amalg.)
Oct. 31, 2012 – Assigned into bankruptcy. Hardie & Kelly Inc. appointed trustee.

Practicar Industries Corp. (B.C. Nov. 3, 1982)
Mar. 18, 1991 – Name changed to Practicar Systems Inc. and continued into Canada; basis unknown. ■

Practicar Systems Inc. (Can. Mar. 18, 1991)
June 17, 1999 – Acquired by Rent-A-Wreck Capital Inc.; basis 6,000,000 shs. at 50¢ per sh.

Prada Holdings Ltd. (B.C. May 12, 1993)
July 26, 1996 – Continued into Yukon.
Oct. 23, 2001 – Amalgamated with 33434 Yukon Inc., a wholly owned subsid. of MFC Bancorp Ltd.; basis 1 new redeem. pref. sh. for 1 com. sh., immediately redeem. for 5¢ per sh. Co. now private.

Prado Explorations Ltd. (Ont. 1965)
Dec. 30, 1985 – Amalgamated with 3 other cos. to form Canhorn Mining Corporation; basis 1 new for 15.01 old shs.

Prado Oil and Gas Company Limited (Ont. 1952)
1953 – Assets acquired by Rio-Prado Consolidated Oils Limited; basis 3 new for 4 old shs. (see Rio-Prado Consolidated Oils Limited)

Prago Resources & Energy Inc. (Ont. 1983)
June 30, 1990 – Formed Madison Avenue Partners Inc. in Ontario on amalgamation with Madison Avenue Partners Inc.; basis 1 new for 1 old sh. ■

Prahova Mines Ltd. (Que. 1946)
May 1974 – Charter cancelled.

Prairie Cache Resources Limited (Alta. June 2, 1987)
Sept. 21, 1990 – Name changed to NEBEX Resources Ltd. ■

Prairie Capital Inc. (Ont. Feb. 16, 1962)
Sept. 12, 2002 – Amalgamated with Coastal Group Inc. to form Continental (CBOC) Corporation; basis 1 new divd., 1 new subord. vtg. and 1 new multiple vtg. sh. for 1 divd., 0.8 subord. vtg. and 0.8 multiple vtg. shs. of Prairie Capital Inc. (see Continental (CBOC) Corporation)

Prairie Fire Oil & Gas Ltd. (Alta. Dec. 5, 1997)
June 29, 2004 – Formed Verenex Energy Inc. in Alberta on Qualifying Transaction reverse takeover acquisition of and amalgamation with Verenex Energy Inc. (wholly owned by Vermilion Energy Trust); basis 1 new for 25 old shs. ■

Prairie Gas & Oil Co. Limited (Ont. 1933)
1966 – Acquired by Angelus Petroleums (1965) Limited; basis 1 new for 5 old shs. (see Angelus Petroleums (1965) Limited)

Prairie Gas Ltd. (unknown)
May 1, 1961 – In 1961, Canadian Industrial Gas Ltd. acquired all o/s shs. and warrants on the basis of 2 Canadian Industrial shs. for each 5 shs. of Prairie, and 1 Canadian Industrial sh. for each 3 Prairie warrants. The 6% secured conv. s.f. debs., series A, were red. at $106. (see Canadian Industrial Gas Ltd.)

Prairie Oil Royalties Company, Ltd. (Sask. July 13, 1951)
May 2, 1995 – Amalgamated with 609764 Saskatchewan Ltd., a wholly owned subsid. of Norcen Energy Resources Limited; basis 1 cl. A pref. sh. or cl. B pref. sh. for 1 com. sh. redeemed at $15 per sh. (see Norcen Energy Resources Limited)

Prairie Pacific Energy Corporation (B.C. June 2, 1969)
Mar. 9, 2006 – Acquired by Northrock Resources Ltd. for $2.69 per sh.

Prairie Pipe Manufacturing Co. Ltd. (Sask. July 13, 1956)
Aug. 1960 – Name changed to Interprovincial Steel and Pipe Corporation Ltd. ■

Prairie Pride Manufacturing Co. Ltd. (Man. 1946)
Aug. 1950 – Name changed to Bulloch's Limited. ■

Prairie Royalties Ltd. (Alta. 1936)
1941 – Merged with 8 other cos. into Amalgamated Oils Limited; basis 84 new for 500 old shs.

Prairie Schooner Petroleum Ltd. (Alta. Dec. 22, 1997)
Sept. 26, 2006 – Plan of Arrangement acquisition by True Energy Trust; basis 1.22 new True Energy units for 1 old Prairie Schooner com. sh. (see True Energy Trust)

Prairie Storm Resources Corp. (B.C. Feb. 1, 2018)
Dec. 2, 2021 – Acquired by and subsequently amalgamated into InPlay Oil Corp.; basis $0.2514 cash and 0.0524 InPlay com. shs. for 1 Prairie Storm sh.

Pratecs Technologies, Inc. (Alta. Mar. 16, 1994)
Nov. 6, 1995 – Name changed to YBM Magnex International, Inc.; basis 1 new for 5 old shs. ■

Praxis Resources Ltd. (B.C. Aug. 22, 1984)
Oct. 20, 1987 – Name changed to International Praxis Resource Corp.; basis 1 new for 2 old shs. ■

Praxis Technologies Corporation (Ont. 1980)
June 30, 1988 – Acquired by Cinram Ltd.; basis 1 pref. sh. immediately redeemed at 40¢ for 1 com. sh. and amalgamated with Praxis Technologies Inc. and Cinram Ltd. to continue under the name Cinram Ltd. (see Cinram Ltd.)

Precambrian Shield Resources Limited (B.C. Apr. 27, 1966)
July 1981 – Continued into Alberta. (see Mark Resources Inc.)
July 9, 1993 – Acquired by 468714 Alberta Inc., a wholly owned subsid. of Mark Resources Inc.; basis 1 cl. A redeemable sh. for 1 com. sh., redeemed immediately for $3.25 per sh. (see Mark Resources Inc.)

Precious Metals Bullion Trust (Ont. Mar. 27, 2009)
Oct. 13, 2017 – Terminated; basis $9.66 cash per trust unit.

Precision Drilling Corporation (Alta. Mar. 25, 1985)
Nov. 4, 2005 – Converted into Precision Drilling Trust; basis 1 trust unit for 1 com. sh.

Precision Drilling (1987) Ltd. (Alta. Mar. 25, 1985)
Oct. 14, 1992 – Name changed to Precision Drilling Corporation. ■

Precision Drilling Trust (Alta. Sept. 22, 2005)
June 1, 2010 – Succeeded by Precision Drilling Corporation pursuant to plan of arrangement whereby Precision Drilling Corporation was formed to facilitate the conversion of the trust into a corporation and Precision Drilling Trust subsequently dissolved. (see FPsurvey - Mines & Energy; FPsurvey - Industrials)

Precision Enterprises Inc. (B.C. June 16, 2006)
Dec. 18, 2013 – Name changed to Allante Resources Ltd.; basis 1 new for 3 old shs. ■

Precision International Resource Corp. (B.C. June 10, 1987)
May 7, 1996 – Name changed to Range Petroleum Corporation; basis 1 new for 2 old shs. ■

Precision Petroleum Services Inc. (B.C. Mar. 11, 1983)
Jan. 23, 1991 – Name changed to American Wellhead Services Inc. ■

Predator Blockchain Capital Corp. (Alta. Jan. 25, 2018)
Jan. 23, 2019 – Formed Highwood Oil Company Ltd. in Alberta pursuant to Qualifying Transaction amalgamation with (old) Highwood Oil Company Ltd. (deemed acquiror); basis 1 new for 53 old shs. ■

Predator Capital Inc. (B.C. Jan. 6, 2000)
June 30, 2003 – Continued into Alberta.
July 23, 2003 – Name changed to Predator Exploration Ltd. following Qualifying Transaction acquisition of 30% working interest in certain petroleum and natural gas rights and associated facilities from Virtus Energy Ltd. for total consideration of $600,000 cash and $750,000 private placement. ■

Predator Exploration Ltd. (Alta. June 30, 2003)
Feb. 21, 2005 – Acquired by SignalEnergy Inc.; basis 0.3846 new SignalEnergy sh. for 1 old Predator sh. (see SignalEnergy Inc.)

Predator Ventures Ltd. (B.C. June 24, 1986)
July 14, 1999 – Continued into Wyoming.
Nov. 18, 1999 – Name changed to wwbroadcast.net inc.; basis 1 new for 2 old shs. ■

Predictmedix Inc. (B.C. Sept. 3, 1987)
July 13, 2023 – Name changed to Predictmedix AI Inc. (see FPsurvey - Industrials)

Prefac Concrete Co. Ltd. (Can. Jan. 14, 1957)
Aug. 27, 1986 – Name changed to Prefac Enterprises Inc. ■

Prefac Enterprises Inc. (Can. Jan. 14, 1957)
Sept. 7, 1988 – Name changed to Armbro Enterprises Inc. ■

Preferred Dental Technologies Inc. (B.C. Dec. 8, 2010)
June 26, 2023 – Struck from register and dissolved.

Preferred Enterprises Ltd. (Alta. Apr. 21, 1998)
Sept. 16, 2003 – Qualifying Transaction acquisition of 350,000 Prefco Enterprises Inc. shs. to be distributed to non-escrowed shldrs.; basis 1 new Prefco sh. for 8.57 old Preferred Enterprises shs.

Preferred Foods Ltd. (B.C. 1981)
Aug. 24, 1988 – Name changed to Diversified Preferred Foods Ltd.; basis 1 new for 5 old shs. ■

Preferred Resources Inc. (B.C. Jan. 22, 1982)
Feb. 4, 1985 – Name changed to Shallow Resources Inc. ■

Preferred Securities Income Fund (Ont. Nov. 28, 2003)
Dec. 17, 2007 – Merged into First Asset Yield Opportunity Trust; basis 1 Preferred Securities unit for 0.7465 First Asset series A unit. (see First Asset Yield Opportunity Trust)

Preferred Securities Limited Duration Fund (Ont. Feb. 26, 2004)
Dec. 17, 2007 – Merged into First Asset Yield Opportunity Trust; basis 1 series A unit and 1 series B unit of Preferred Securities for 0.7451 series A and 1 series B unit of First Asset, respectively. (see First Asset Yield Opportunity Trust)

Preferred Share Investment Trust (Ont. Mar. 11, 2009)
Nov. 2, 2016 – Merged into First Asset Preferred Share ETF; basis 0.29955 First Asset Preferred Share ETF units for 1 Preferred Share Investment Trust unit. (see First Asset Preferred Share ETF)

Preissac Molybdenite Mines Ltd. (Que. 1955)
Aug. 1972 – Charter cancelled.

Prelim Capital Inc. (Can. Jan. 31, 2007)
May 10, 2010 – Formed Hudson River Minerals Ltd. in Canada on Qualifying Transaction amalgamation of a wholly owned subsid. with Hudson River Minerals Ltd. and subsequent vertical amalgamation of the new company with Prelim. ■

Prelude Lake Mines Ltd. (Ont. 1950)
Aug. 19, 1965 – Dissolved.

PreMD Inc. (Can. Nov. 9, 1992)
Dec. 10, 2016 – Dissolved and struck from register.

Premdor Inc. (Ont. Dec. 31, 1992)
Jan. 1, 2002 – Name changed to Masonite International Corporation. ■

Premier Border Gold Mining Co. Ltd. (Can. Feb. 14, 1928)
July 1958 – Name changed to Calvert Gas & Oils Limited; basis 1 new for 5 old shs. ■

Premier Cablevision Limited (B.C. 1964)
Jan. 29, 1980 – Name changed to Premier Communications Limited. ■

Premier Canadian Income Fund (Ont. Aug. 30, 1999)
Jan. 2, 2015 – Redeemed.

Premier CDN Enterprises Ltd. (Can. Dec. 24, 1985)
Jan. 17, 2000 – Name changed to Premier Tech Ltd.; basis 1.1 cl. A subord. vtg. or 1 cl. B multiple vtg. for 1 cl. A com. sh. ■

Premier Choix Networks Inc. (Can. 1984)
Dec. 29, 1997 – Acquired by Astral Communications Inc. for $45 per sh. (see Astral Communications Inc.)

Premier Choix: TVEC Inc. (Can. 1984)
Feb. 23, 1996 – Name changed to Premier Choix Networks Inc. ■

Premier Communications Limited (B.C. 1964)
Dec. 19, 1980 – Acquired by and amalgamated with a wholly owned subsid. of Canadian Cablesystems Limited; basis $25, 1 Canadian Cablesystems preferred sh. immediately redeemed at $25, or 3 Canadian Cablesystems cl. B shs. for 1 Premier sh. (see Canadian Cablesystems Limited)

Premier Diagnostic Health Services Inc. (B.C. July 16, 2010 amalg.)
Apr. 22, 2015 – Name changed to Premier Diversified Holdings Inc. ■

Premier Diamond Corp. (B.C. Apr. 3, 1987)
May 7, 2007 – Name changed to Mexican Silver Mines Ltd. and continued into Alberta following reverse takeover acquisition of Mexican Silver Mines (Guernsey) Limited. ■

Premier Diversified Holdings Inc. (B.C. July 16, 2010 amalg.)
Sept. 17, 2024 – Name changed to AJA Health and Wellness Inc. pursuant to the reverse takeover acquisition of AJA Health and Wellness Ltd. ■

Premier Gaspe Mines Ltd. (Ont. 1966)
Dec. 1974 – Name changed to Python Resources & Investment Corp. ■

Premier Gold Mines Limited (Ont. May 29, 2006)
Apr. 13, 2021 – Acquired by Equinox Gold Corp.; basis 0.1967 Equinox shs. plus 0.4 i-80 Gold shs. for 1 Premier Gold sh.

Premier Gold Mining Company, Limited (B.C. 1919)
Oct. 1947 – Voluntary liquidation completed. Shldrs. received 30 shs. Toburn Gold Mines Ltd., 25 shs. Silbak Premier Mines Ltd., 7 shs. Saudi Arabian Mining Syndicate, 3 shs. Big Bell Mines Ltd. (since defunct), and $24.30 for 100 old Premier shs.

Premier Gold Resources Inc. (B.C. Jan. 26, 1987)
Apr. 8, 1992 – Name changed to Cryptic Ventures Inc.; basis 1 new for 3 old shs. ■

Premier Health Group Inc. (B.C. Sept. 19, 2013)
Feb. 24, 2020 – Name changed to CloudMD Software & Services Inc. ■

Premier Lake Resources Ltd. (Ont. 1987)
Mar. 30, 1990 – Amalgamated with Golden Winner Resources Ltd. (1 for 0.97), Rainbow Lake Resources Ltd. (1 for 0.915), Mountain Frontier Explorations Ltd. (1 for 1.08), and Thunder Valley Resources Ltd. (1 for 1.10) to form Castlestar Capital Developments Corp.; basis 1 new Castlestar sh. for 0.95 old Premier shs. (see Castlestar Capital Developments Corp.)

Premier Minerals Ltd. (B.C. Apr. 3, 1987)
Mar. 5, 2001 – Name changed to Premier Diamond Corp.; basis 1 new for 2 old shs. ■

Premier Mining Corporation Ltd. (B.C. 1968)
1971 – Name changed to Premier Resources Ltd. ■

Premier Resources Ltd. (B.C. 1968)
Feb. 22, 1982 – Name changed to Tyrona Resources Ltd.; basis 1 new for 5 old shs. ■

Premier Royalty Inc. (Ont. May 10, 2007)
Oct. 10, 2013 – All o/s shs. not held acquired by Sandstorm Gold Ltd.; basis 0.145 Sandstorm com. shs. for 1 Premier com. sh.

Premier Steel Mills Ltd. (Can. 1954)
June 22, 1962 – All o/s com. shs. acquired by The Steel Company of Canada, Limited by; basis $16 per sh. All o/s 6% pref. shs. redeemed Oct. 15, 1962, at $105 per sh. plus accr. divds. of 75¢ per sh. All o/s serial and s.f. first mtge. bonds (latter due July 15, 1981) redeemed July 15, 1965; s.f. bonds at 105. Co. distributed to shldrs. of record Apr. 4, 1962, 1 com. sh. Peace River Mining & Smelting Ltd. for 1 com. sh.

Premier Tech Ltd. (Can. Dec. 24, 1985)
Feb. 27, 2007 – Privatized at $3.00 per sh.

The Premier Trust Company (Can. 1913)
Aug. 1983 – All o/s shs. acquired following public offering of $96.50 per sh. which expired by Victoria and Grey Trust Co. Ltd.

Premier United Kingdom NT (CDN) Ltd. (Ont. Nov. 19, 1991)
June 30, 1997 – All o/s sr. divd. pref. shs. redeemed for $25 per sh.

Premier United Kingdom NT (US) Ltd. (Ont. Nov. 21, 1991)
June 30, 1997 – All o/s sr. divd. pref. shs. redeemed for US$25 per sh.

Premier Value Income Trust (Ont. Jan. 27, 2005)
Jan. 31, 2011 – Merge with Sentry Canadian Income Fund, an open-ended mutual fund.

Premium Brands Income Fund (B.C. June 8, 2005)
July 27, 2009 – Converted into a corp. pursuant to plan of arrangement whereby the fund and wholly owned Premium Brands Holdings Limited Partnership (PBHLP) became subsids. of Thallion Pharmaceuticals Inc. (old

Thallion) which then changed its name to Premium Brands Holdings Corporation. All assets and liabilities of old Thallion were transferred to Thallion Pharmaceuticals Inc. (new Thallion) formed by way of amalgamation between 4504003 Canada Inc. and 4504011 Canada Inc. (both old Thallion subsids.). The fund was subsequently wound up. (see Thallion Pharmaceuticals Inc.)

Premium Brands Inc. (Can. Dec. 27, 1984)
July 27, 2005 – Plan of Arrangement to convert company into an income trust named Premium Brands Income Fund; basis 1 new trust unit for 1 com. sh. (see Premium Brands Income Fund)

Premium Iron Ores Limited (Ont. 1942)
Mar. 9, 1984 – Name changed to Premium Equity Corporation.

Premium Letney Canada Inc. (Ont. 1954)
May 23, 2005 – Certificate of incorporation cancelled and dissolved.

Premium Nickel Resources Ltd. (Ont. July 29, 2022)
Nov. 15, 2024 – Name changed to Premium Resources Ltd. ■

Premium Petroleums Ltd. (B.C. 1951)
1959 – Struck off register.

Premium Resources Ltd. (Ont. July 29, 2022)
June 9, 2025 – Name changed to NexMetals Mining Corp. (see FPsurvey - Mines & Energy)

Prenor Financial Ltd. (Can. Jan. 29, 1980)
Feb. 9, 2006 – Dissolved.

Prenor Group Ltd. (Que. Oct. 12, 1961)
Nov. 28, 2016 – Struck from registry.

Prenor Trust Company of Canada (Can. May 11, 1989 amalg.)
Dec. 1993 – Deloitte & Touche Inc. of Toronto was appointed provisional liquidator.
Mar. 1998 – Most of the company's mortgage portfolio had been liquidated and uninsured depositors received 100% of balances due and the subordinate creditors, trade and other unsecured creditors received a partial distribution.
Apr. 1999 – All creditors had been paid except for subordinate debt holders who had received a partial payment and might receive an additional distribution once all the funds had been realized from the liquidation.
Dec. 1, 1999 – Deloitte & Touche was discharged as liquidators and the balance of funds had been paid out.

Preo Software Inc. (Alta. July 24, 2008 amalg.)
July 23, 2010 – Amalgamated in Alberta to continue with same name.
Mar. 26, 2013 – Placed into receivership by AVAC Ltd. and intellectual property assets sold to U.S. company for an undisclosed amount.
Jan. 2, 2014 – Struck from register and dissolved.

Prescient Mining Corp. (B.C. Dec. 21, 2006)
Oct. 2, 2014 – Name changed to Aurora Cannabis Inc. pursuant to reverse takeover acquisition of Aurora Marijuana Inc. (see FPsurvey - Industrials)

Prescient NeuroPharma Inc. (Can. Feb. 16, 2001)
Dec. 21, 2007 – Continued into British Columbia.
Feb. 9, 2012 – Name changed to PNO Resources Ltd. ■

Prescott Development Corp. (B.C. Nov. 30, 1983)
Mar. 22, 1988 – Name changed to U.S. Ammunition Company Ltd. ■

Prescott Porcupine Gold Mines Ltd. (Ont. 1944)
Feb. 1964 – Charter cancelled.

Prescott Resources Inc. (B.C. May 17, 1966)
June 29, 1998 – Name changed to Asia Sapphires Limited and continued into Yukon following reverse takeover acquisition of Asia Sapphires (Barbados) Limited. ■

Prescott Resources Ltd. (B.C. Nov. 30, 1983)
Sept. 25, 1986 – Name changed to Prescott Development Corp.; basis 2 new com. for 1 old cl. A voting sh. ■

Presdor Porcupine Gold Mines Ltd. (Ont. June 16, 1936)
1941 – Name changed to Presdor Porcupine Mines (1941) Ltd.; basis 1 new for 3.5 old shs. ■

Presdor Porcupine Mines (1941) Ltd. (Ont. June 16, 1936)
Nov. 1966 – Charter cancelled.

The President, Directors and Company of the Bank of Montreal (Can. May 18, 1822)
June 1, 1831 – Name changed to Bank of Montreal. ■

President Electric Ltd. (Ont. 1948)
1961 – Name changed to Vector Electric Limited. ■

President Mines Ltd. (B.C. May 21, 1976)
Apr. 26, 2002 – Name changed to Otish Mountain Exploration Inc.; basis 1 new for 12 old shs. ■

Presidential Forest Products Corp. (B.C. May 3, 1982)
Mar. 4, 1991 – Delisted from the Vancouver Stock Exchange. Subsequently dissolved for failure to file and struck from register.

Presidio Developments Ltd. (Alta. 1976)
Feb. 1, 1990 – All accr. and o/s divds. paid to upon redemption of all o/s floating rate cum. retract. redeem. pref. ser. B shs. for $25.00.

Presley Laboratories Inc. (Can. Sept. 8, 1986)
Sept. 22, 1992 – Name changed to Voice-it Technologies Inc. ■

Presmac Copper Mines Ltd. (Ont. 1956)
June 21, 1982 – Charter cancelled.

Prestige Mines Ltd. (Ont. 1973)
Mar. 15, 1979 – Amalgamated with Golden Bounty Mining Co. Ltd. (1 for 1), Golden Sabre Mines Ltd. (1 for 1.5), Grand Valley Mining Co. Ltd. (1 for 3) and Pacesetter Mines Ltd. (1 for 1) to form Golden Bounty Mining Co. Ltd.; basis 1 new for 3 old shs.

Prestige Telecom Inc. (Can. July 30, 2007 amalg.)
Mar. 29, 2012 – Filed for protection on Nov. 23, 2011, under the Bankruptcy and Insolvency Act and Raymond Chabot Inc. appointed receiver. Assets acquired by 7922825 Canada Inc., an affiliate of Thornhill Investments Inc., for $400,000 cash, less professional fees and subject to a minimum cash consideration of $100,000, resulting in 7922825 Canada becoming sole shareholder; com. shs. cancelled for no consideration. Secured creditors suffered a shortfall.
Apr. 9, 2013 – Dissolved.

Preston East Dome Mines Ltd. (Ont. 1911)
1960 – Merged into Preston Mines Limited.

Preston Mines Limited (Ont. 1960 amalg.)
Jan. 30, 1980 – Amalgamated with Rio Algom Limited (1 for 1) to continue as Rio Algom Limited; basis 1 new Rio Algom 2nd pref. and 0.75 com. sh. for 1 old Preston sh.

Preston Resource Corp. (B.C. July 20, 1979)
May 4, 1993 – Name changed to Golden Treasure Explorations Ltd.; basis 1 new for 2 old shs. ■

Preston Resources Ltd. (Ont. 1986)
Mar. 2, 1992 – Amalgamated with Concentrated Rare Earth Minerals Ltd., Enertex Developments Inc., Goldmac Explorations Inc., Offset Natural Resources Ltd., Saranac Resources Ltd., Uranex Resources Limited and Norlode Resources Inc. to form Marvas Developments Ltd.; basis 1 new for 7 Concentrated Rare Earth shs., 1 new for 12.6 Enertex shs., 1 new for 17.5 Goldmac shs., 1 new for 11 Offset shs., 1 new for 6.3 Saranac shs., 1 new for 13.5 Uranex shs., 1 new for 4.6 Norlode shs. and 1 new for 5.5 Preston shs. (see Marvas Developments Ltd.)

Prestwick Capital Corporation Limited (Alta. June 4, 2021)
Sept. 30, 2024 – Name changed to Legacy Gold Mines Ltd. pursuant to Qualifying Transaction acquisition of Banner property option. (see FPsurvey - Mines & Energy)

Pretium Capital Corp. (Alta. Dec. 23, 2005)
Sept. 2, 2008 – Name changed to Sitebrand Inc. following Qualifying Transaction reverse takeover acquisition of Sitebrand.com Inc. ■

Pretium Industries Inc. (Alta. Feb. 28, 1996)
June 30, 2003 – Name changed to PetroFalcon Corporation. ■

Pretium Resources Inc. (B.C. Oct. 22, 2010)
Mar. 15, 2022 – All o/s shs. not already held acquired by Newcrest Mining Limited: basis (i) Cdn$10.81 cash plus 0.3357 Newcrest shs. or (ii) 0.8084 Newcrest shs. for 1 Pretium sh.

Previa Resources Ltd. (B.C. Sept. 26, 1988)
Oct. 17, 2006 – Name changed to Rose Marie Resources Ltd.; basis 1 new for 8 old shs. ■

Pricam Explorations Inc. (B.C. July 3, 1987)
June 17, 1994 – Dissolved and struck off register.

Price Brothers & Company, Ltd. (Que. 1920)
Apr. 1966 – Name changed to The Price Company Limited. ■

The Price Company Limited (Que. 1920)
1979 – Acquired by Abitibi Paper Company Ltd. at prices from $18 to $25 per sh. through a series of offers to major shldrs. and the public 1974, 1975, 1978 and 1979. (see Abitibi-Price Inc.)

Price Creek Mines Ltd. (B.C. 1963)
1971 – Assets merged with those of parent, Western Mines Ltd.
Jan. 13, 1972 – Dissolved and struck off register.

Price Manufacturing Inc. (Ont. Oct. 24, 1984)
July 25, 2000 – Name changed to Remworks Inc.; basis 1 new for 5 old shs. (see FPsurvey - Industrials)

Priceless Piranha Capital Corp. (B.C. June 1, 2009)
Dec. 10, 2013 – Name changed to Mission Ready Services Inc. pursuant to Qualifying Transaction reverse takeover acquisition of (old) Mission Ready Services Inc.; basis 1 new for 2 old shs. ■

Pricemore Resources Inc. (B.C. 1981)
Nov. 16, 1984 – Name changed to First China Investment Corp. ■

Pride Mining Co. Ltd. (Ont. 1959)
1961 – Charter cancelled.

Prima Colombia Hardwood Inc. (B.C. Dec. 1, 2009)
Jan. 12, 2015 – Name changed to Bravern Ventures Ltd.; basis 1 new for 60 old shs. (see FPsurvey - Mines & Energy)

Prima Developments Ltd. (B.C. Jan. 1, 1984)
June 28, 2010 – Name changed to ECL Enviroclean Ventures Ltd. ■

Prima Diamond Corp. (B.C. Oct. 1, 2009)
Apr. 14, 2016 – Name changed to Voltaic Minerals Corp.; basis 1 new for 5 old shs. ■

Prima Fluorspar Corp. (B.C. Oct. 1, 2009)
July 3, 2014 – Name changed to Prima Diamond Corp. ■

Primaria Capital (Canada) Ltd. (B.C. Oct. 11, 2011)
Mar. 30, 2015 – Dissolved and struck from register.
July 3, 2015 – Restored to register. (see FPsurvey - Industrials)

Primaris Retail Real Estate Investment Trust (Ont. Mar. 28, 2003)
Apr. 9, 2013 – Acquired by H&R Real Estate Investment Trust; basis either $28 or 1.166 H&R stapled units.

Primary Cobalt Corp. (B.C. July 15, 2010)
Sept. 4, 2018 – Name changed to Primary Energy Metals Inc. ■

Primary Corp. (Ont. Aug. 1, 2008 amalg.)
July 6, 2012 – Name changed to Marret Resource Corp. ■

Primary Energy Metals Inc. (B.C. July 15, 2010)
Nov. 28, 2019 – Name changed to Mota Ventures Corp. to reflect its activities in the South American cannabis sector following the reverse takeover acquisition of NNZ Consulting Corp. ■

Primary Energy Recycling Corporation (Ont. June 10, 2005)
Aug. 5, 2005 – Continued into British Columbia.
Dec. 19, 2014 – Acquired by PERC Holdings 1 LLC, a new co. formed by a consortium led by Fortistar LLC, for US$5.40 per sh.

Primary Gold Mines Ltd. (Ont. 1956)
Apr. 9, 1975 – Charter cancelled.

Primary Metals Inc. (B.C. May 3, 1999)
Dec. 17, 2007 – Acquired by Sojitz Tungsten Resources Inc. for $3.65 per sh.

Primary Mines Ltd. (Ont. 1946)
Aug. 1957 – Charter cancelled.

Primary Petroleum Corporation (B.C. May 20, 2004)
Jan. 10, 2008 – Continued into Alberta.
Mar. 6, 2014 – Name changed to Keek Inc. following reverse takeover acquisition of (old) Keek Inc. ■

Primax Capital Corp. (Alta. Nov. 15, 2004)
Mar. 21, 2006 – Formed Fair Sky Resources Inc. in Alberta on Qualifying Transaction amalgamation with Fair Sky Resources Inc. (deemed acquiror); basis 1 new for 8 old shs. ■

Prime Blockchain Inc. (Can. Jan. 13, 2004)
Oct. 28, 2020 – Name changed to RYAH Group, Inc. pursuant to pending reverse takeover acquisition of Potbotics Inc. (see FPsurvey - Industrials)

Prime City One Capital Corp. (Ont. Sept. 2, 2004)
Nov. 30, 2021 – Name changed to Champion Gaming Group Inc. pursuant to the reverse takeover acquisition of Champion Gaming Inc.; basis 1 new for 4 old shs. (see FPsurvey - Industrials)

Prime Equities Inc. (B.C. Feb. 15, 1988)
Oct. 28, 1991 – Name changed to Prime Equities International Corporation; basis 1 new for 10 old shs. ■

Prime Equities International Corporation (B.C. Feb. 15, 1988)
Aug. 11, 1998 – Name changed to medEra Life Science Corporation. ■

Prime Line Capital Corp. (Alta. June 18, 1987)
Apr. 2, 1991 – Name changed to Kirriemuir Oil & Gas Ltd.; basis 1 new for 3 old shs. ■

Prime-Link Corp. (Alta. July 31, 1989)
Feb. 1, 1996 – Formed Prime-Link Group Ltd. on amalgamation with Kenbrent Holdings Ltd.; basis 1 new for 2 old shs. ■

Prime-Link Group Ltd. (Alta. July 31, 1989)
July 6, 1998 – Name changed to TCT Logistics Inc. ■

Prime Meridian Resources Corp. (Can. Feb. 22, 2007 amalg.)
Mar. 21, 2023 – Name changed to Sonoran Desert Copper Corporation. ■

Prime Petroleum Corporation (Alta. May 19, 1989 amalg.)
Feb. 26, 1990 – Amalgamated with Senex Corporation to form Senex Petroleum Corporation; basis 1 new for 5 Senex shs. and 1 new for 1 Prime sh. (see Senex Petroleum Corporation)

Prime Potash Corporation of Canada Ltd. (Ont. 1946)
Apr. 9, 1975 – Charter cancelled.

Prime Rate Plus Corp. (Ont. May 25, 2005)
May 7, 2009 – Name changed to Canadian Banc Recovery Corp. ■

Prime Resources Corporation (B.C. Feb. 1, 1989 amalg.)
Jan. 26, 1990 – Name changed to Prime Resources Group Inc.; basis 1 new for 2.25 old shs. ■

Prime Resources Group Inc. (B.C. Feb. 1, 1989 amalg.)
Apr. 12, 1990 – Merged with Calpine Resources Incorporated (1 sh. + 0.5 wt. for 1) to continue with the same name Prime Resources Group Inc.; basis 1 new for 1 old sh. (see Homestake Canada Inc.)
Dec. 8, 1998 – Acquired by Homestake Canada Inc. wholly owned subsid. of Homestake Mining Company; basis either 0.74 new Homestake Mining com. sh., or 0.74 new Homestake Canada exch. sh. for 1 old Prime com.sh. (see Homestake Canada Inc.)

Prime Restaurants Inc. (Ont. Apr. 5, 2010; amalg.)
Jan. 10, 2012 – Acquired by Fairfax Financial Holdings Limited for $7.50 per sh.

Prime Restaurants Royalty Income Fund (Ont. May 28, 2002)
Apr. 5, 2010 – Succeeded by Prime Restaurants Inc. following conversion of Prime Restaurants Royalty Income Fund into a corporation; basis 1 cl. A limited vtg. sh. for 1 fund unit. ■

Prime Spot Media Inc. (B.C. Dec. 8, 1980)
Aug. 11, 2000 – Name changed to New Media Systems Inc.; basis 1 new for 10 old shs. ■

PrimeNet Communications Inc. (Ont. Apr. 29, 1983)
May 21, 2007 – Dissolved and struck from register.

Primer Group Minerals Ltd. (B.C. 1961)
July 25, 1975 – Name changed to Lada Development Ltd.; basis 1 new for 5 old shs. ■

Primera Bioscience Research Inc. (Ont. Feb. 7, 2008)
June 10, 2014 – Name changed to Greenland Resources Inc. (see FPsurvey - Mines & Energy)

Primera Energy Resources Ltd. (Alta. Mar. 31, 2005)
Dec. 6, 2012 – Acquired by Touchstone Exploration Inc.; basis 0.90 Touchstone shs. for 1 Primera sh. (see Touchstone Exploration Inc.)

Primero Industries Ltd. (B.C. Mar. 31, 1978)
Mar. 27, 2001 – Name changed to PMI Ventures Ltd.; basis 1 new for 5 old shs. ■

Primero Mining Corp. (B.C. Nov. 26, 2007)
May 14, 2018 – Acquired by First Majestic Silver Corp.; basis 0.00325 First Majestic shs. for 1 Primero com. sh.

Primetech Electronics Inc. (Can. Sept. 22, 1976)
Aug. 9, 2001 – Acquired by Celestica Inc.; basis 0.22 Celestica sub. vtg. shs. for 1 Primetech sh.

PrimeWest Energy Inc. (Alta. Jan. 1, 2002 amalg.)
Jan. 22, 2008 – Acquired by Abu Dhabi National Energy Company PJSC for $26.75 per trust unit and per exch. sh.

PrimeWest Energy Trust (Alta. Aug. 2, 1996)
Jan. 22, 2008 – Acquired by Abu Dhabi National Energy Company PJSC for $26.75 per trust unit and per exch. sh.

PrimeWest Exploration Inc. (Alta. Sept. 11, 2009)
Mar. 5, 2013 – Name changed to Antler Hill Oil & Gas Ltd. ■

PrimeWest Mortgage Investment Corporation (Sask. Mar. 22, 2005)
Oct. 31, 2019 – Court approval was received for the plan of voluntary liquidation and dissolution previously approved by shldrs. and directors of the company. KPMG Inc. was appointed liquidator. (see FPsurvey - Industrials)

PrimeWest Oil and Gas Corp. (Alta. Feb. 23, 2001 amalg.)
Jan. 1, 2002 – Formed PrimeWest Energy Inc. in Alberta on amalgamation with PrimeWest Royalty Corp. and PrimeWest Resources Ltd. ■

Primex Forest Industries Ltd. (B.C. May 27, 1963)
Jan. 12, 1990 – Name changed to Primex Forest Products Ltd. ■

Primex Forest Products Ltd. (B.C. May 27, 1963)
May 18, 2001 – Acquired by International Forest Products Limited; basis $6.65 or 1.5647 International Forest cl. A shs. for 1 Primex sh. (see International Forest Products Limited)

Primo Gold Ltd. (B.C. Aug. 20, 1990)
Apr. 26, 1994 – Name changed to Primo Resources Ltd. ■

Primo Resources International Inc. (B.C. Aug. 20, 1990)
May 2, 2003 – Name changed to Vega Gold Ltd.; basis 1 new for 2 old shs. ■

Primo Resources Ltd. (B.C. Aug. 20, 1990)
Oct. 15, 1999 – Name changed to Primo Resources International Inc.; basis 1 new for 4 old shs. ■

Primo Water Corporation (Can. July 25, 1955)
July 7, 2021 – Continued into Ontario.
Nov. 12, 2024 – Acquired by a subsidiary of Triton Water Parent, Inc. and amalgamated to become a wholly owned subsidiary of Primo Brands Corporation; basis 1 Primo Brands cl.A com. sh. for 1 Primo Water com. sh.

Primont Resources Ltd. (B.C. 1979)
Dec. 18, 1986 – Name changed to Picosec Technology Ltd.; basis 1 new for 4 old shs. ■

Primrock Capital Corporation (Ont. Mar. 31, 1986)
Dec. 12, 1989 – Name changed to MultiMedia Capital Corporation. ■

Primrock Mining & Exploration Ltd. (Ont. 1965)
Mar. 1976 – Charter cancelled.

Primrose Gold Resources Inc. (Ont. 1987)
Aug. 23, 1993 – Amalgamated with Curran Bay Resource Ltd. (1 for 1) to form a new co. also known as Curran Bay Resource; basis 1 new for 1 old sh. (see Curran Bay Resource Ltd.)

Primrose Mines Ltd. (unknown)
1968 – Assets sold to Mission Financial Corp. Ltd.; basis 0.0259 new for 1 old sh.

Primrose Resources Ltd. (B.C. 1982)
Jan. 19, 1984 – Name changed to Primrose Technology Corporation; basis 2 new for 1 old sh. ■

Primrose Technology Corporation (B.C. 1982)
Apr. 1, 1989 – Struck from registry and dissolved.

Primus Yellowknife Gold Mines Ltd. (Ont. 1945)
Aug. 1957 – Charter cancelled.

Prince Stewart Mines Ltd. (B.C. 1969)
June 20, 1974 – Name changed to Arodien Resources Ltd.; basis 1 new for 5 old shs. ■

Princemount Explorations Inc. (B.C. Apr. 26, 1971)
Jan. 14, 1975 – Name changed to Secretariat Resources Inc.; basis 1 new for 3 old shs. ■

Princess Copper Co. Ltd. (B.C. 1956)
Sept. 19, 1968 – Dissolved.

Princess Petroleums (1950) Ltd. (Alta. Oct. 1, 1944)
1951 – Acquired by Canadian Atlantic Oil Co.; basis 1 new for 4 old shs.

Princess Resources Ltd. (B.C. Mar. 19, 1986)
Oct. 13, 2000 – Delisted from the CDNX. Subsequently struck from register and dissolved.

Princess Royal Gold Mines Ltd. (B.C. May 1933)
Jan. 1935 – Name changed to Surf Inlet Consolidated Gold Mines Ltd. ■

Princess Ventures Ltd. (B.C. 1972)
May 1, 1992 – Dissolved and struck off register.

Princeton Exploration Ltd. (B.C. 1963)
1966 – Name changed to Samson Mines Ltd. ■

Princeton Gold Mines Ltd. (Ont. 1947)
Nov. 12, 1993 – Dissolved.

Princeton Media Group Inc. (Ont. Sept. 3, 1986)
Dec. 4, 1998 – Delisted from NASDAQ. Subsequently charter cancelled and dissolved.

Princeton Mining Corporation (B.C. Nov. 7, 1988)
May 12, 1998 – Reorganized by transferring all mining assets to wholly owned 3396061 Canada Inc. and amalgamating it with a wholly owned subsid. of Imperial Metals Corporation, 109781 Canada Limited, forming HML Mining Inc. Princeton Mining then changed name to Madison Pacific Properties Inc.; basis 0.025 Madison cl. B sh. and 0.073 Imperial com. sh. for 1 Princeton com. sh.

Princeton Resource Corp. (B.C. 1983)
July 27, 1988 – Name changed to Canadian Graphite Ltd.; basis 1 new for 4 old shs. ■

Principal Exploration & Mining Ltd. (B.C. 1964)
May 15, 1969 – Struck off register.

Principal Neo-Tech Inc. (Can. Jan. 9, 1931)
July 15, 1988 – Name changed to The Laird Group Inc. ■

Principle Strategic Minerals Ltd. (Ont. 1946)
Apr. 9, 1975 – Charter cancelled.

Le Print Express International Inc. (Ont. May 17, 1993 amalg.)
July 16, 2007 – Inactive.

Print Three Express International Inc. (Ont. May 17, 1993 amalg.)
Dec. 20, 1993 – Name changed to Le Print Express International Inc.; basis 1 new for 3 old shs. ■

Print Ventures International Inc. (Alta. 1987)
Aug. 1, 1994 – Dissolved and struck off register.

Printera Corporation (Ont. Mar. 24, 1980)
May 23, 2006 – Loss of major customer caused serious financial hardships which caused the co. to be in contravention of its borrowing agreements with its secured lenders.
July 24, 2006 – Served with a Notice of Intention to Enforce Security under the Bankruptcy and Insolvency Act of Canada by Peoples Bank of Stamford, Conn. Disposal of assets would result in a shortfall to the secured creditor. No funds would be available for unsecured creditors or shldrs.

Printlux.com Inc. (Alta. Dec. 4, 1995)
Dec. 10, 2007 – Name changed to Allana Resources Inc. ■

Prior Resources Ltd. (Alta. June 3, 1987)
Apr. 4, 1997 – Continued into British Columbia.
July 14, 1997 – Name changed to Rondal Gold Corporation; basis 1 new for 17 old shs. ■

Prism Equities Inc. (Ont. Feb. 15, 1996)
June 9, 2004 – Name changed to Prism Medical Ltd. ■

Prism Medical Ltd. (Ont. Feb. 15, 1996)
Sept. 6, 2016 – Acquired by Handicare Holdings Ltd., a wholly owned subsid. of Handicare Group AB, for $14 per sh.

Prism Petroleum Inc. (Alta. Sept. 1, 1996 amalg.)
Sept. 27, 2000 – Acquired by Real Resources Inc.; basis $1.85 or 0.5 Real shs. for 1 Prism sh. (see Real Resources Inc.)

Prism Petroleum Ltd. (Alta. Apr. 21, 1993)
Sept. 17, 1996 – Amalgamated with Rollinoil Resources Inc. (1 for 1) to form a new co. also named Prism Petroleum Ltd.; basis 1 new for 1.47 old shs. (see Prism Petroleum Ltd.)

Prism Petroleum Ltd. (Alta. Sept. 1, 1996 amalg.)
June 8, 2000 – Name changed to Prism Petroleum Inc.; basis 1 new for 5 old shs. ∎

Prism Resources Limited (B.C. Oct. 31, 1969)
Mar. 8, 1985 – Name changed to International Prism Exploration Ltd.; basis 1 new for 2 old shs. ∎

Prisma Capital Inc. (B.C. Mar. 21, 2018)
Feb. 11, 2022 – Name changed to Prisma Exploration Inc. (see FPsurvey - Mines & Energy)

Pristina Mines Ltd. (B.C. 1972)
Oct. 1978 – Charter cancelled.

Pristine Power Inc. (Can. Aug. 6, 2004)
Nov. 26, 2010 – Acquired by Fort Chicago Energy Partners L.P.; basis 0.2703 Fort Chicago cl. A limited partnership units for 1 Pristine Power sh. (see Veresen Inc.)
May 17, 2012 – Continued into Alberta. (see Veresen Inc.)

Priszm Canadian Income Fund (Ont. Sept. 23, 2003)
Mar. 14, 2007 – Name changed to Priszm Income Fund. ∎

Priszm Income Fund (Ont. Sept. 23, 2003)
Mar. 31, 2011 – Filed for protection under the Companies' Creditors Arrangement Act (CCAA). FTI Consulting Canada Inc. appointed monitor. All trustees and directors resigned.
May 31, 2011 – Sale of 200 restaurants in Ontario and British Columbia, and four restaurants in Quebec to Soul Restaurants Canada Inc. was completed for $42,800,000.
Sept. 19, 2011 – Sale of majority of restaurants in New Brunswick and Nova Scotia to FMI Atlantic Inc. was completed for $2,500,000.
Sept. 20, 2011 – Petitioned into receivership by company's secured lender. RSM Richter Inc. (subsequently Duff & Phelps Canada Restructuring Inc.) was appointed receiver. FTI Consulting Canada Inc. was discharged as monitor under the CCAA.
Sept. 17, 2012 – By September 2012, the receiver had sold the majority of restaurant locations in Alberta and Manitoba sold to Hi-Flyer Foods (Canada) Inc. and the majority of restaurants in Quebec to Olympus Food (Canada) Inc.
Mar. 2013 – By March 2013, all operating restaurants had either been sold or closed and the receiver had either assigned or was in the process of assigning leases to said restaurants and had disclaimed the leases relating to those restaurant locations closed.
July 2014 – Receiver distributed $2,174,000 to The Prudential Insurance Company of America, Pruco Life Insurance Company and Prudential Retirement Insurance and Annuity Company.

Priva Inc. (Alta. May 26, 1987)
Mar. 10, 2008 – Name changed to AXQP Inc. ∎

Private Brand Drug Limited (Ont. 1940)
1966 – Charter cancelled.

Privateer Mine Limited (B.C. Jan. 11, 1937)
Jan. 29, 1959 – Name changed to New Privateer Mine Limited; basis 1 new for 5 old shs. ∎

Privatel Inc. (Ont. 1986)
June 10, 1991 – Charter cancelled.

Le Prix Explorations Ltd. (Ont. 1947)
Acquired by Mineral Exploration Corp. Ltd.; basis 1 new for 10 old shs. (see Mineral Exploration Corp. Ltd.)

Prize Energy Inc. (Alta. Mar. 21, 1983)
Aug. 28, 2000 – Name changed to Canadian Superior Energy Inc.; basis 1 new for 2 old shs. ∎

Prize Exploration Inc. (Can. Apr. 19, 2017)
Feb. 14, 2019 – Name changed to IM Exploration Inc. ∎

Prize Mining Corporation (Alta. Aug. 16, 1996)
Oct. 16, 2019 – Name changed to Boundary Gold and Copper Mining Ltd. (see FPsurvey - Mines & Energy)

Pro-AMS Trust (Ont. Feb. 15, 2001)
May 29, 2006 – Name changed to Government Strip Bond Trust. ∎

Pro-AMS U.S. Trust (Ont. Sept. 27, 2000)
Jan. 5, 2011 – Redeemed at $25 per unit.

Pro Air Systems (1972) Inc. (Ont. 1972 amalg.)
Mar. 1978 – Ceased operations. Mayfair Mechanical purch. Pro Air's service contracts.

Pro-C.I.R. Property Improvements Ltd. (B.C. July 27, 1979)
May 1, 1995 – Name changed to PRO-C.I.R. Industries Inc. ∎

Pro Minerals Inc. (B.C. Apr. 21, 2006)
Oct. 5, 2015 – Dissolved from register.
Apr. 19, 2022 – Restored to registry.
Apr. 19, 2022 – Name changed to 0775461 B.C. Ltd. ∎

Pro-Optic Inc. (Que. 1969)
May 1, 1988 – Formed Actidev Inc. in Quebec on amalgamation with Actidev Inc.; basis 1 new for 1 Actidev cl. A sh. and 1 new for 1 Pro-Optic sh. ∎

Ressources Minières Pro-Or Inc. (Can. Apr. 22, 1986)
Jan. 6, 2014 – Name changed to NovX21 Inc. (see FPsurvey - Mines & Energy)

Pro-Spect-Or Resources Inc. (Can. Dec. 20, 1996)
July 12, 2007 – Name changed to Uranium Bay Resources Inc. ∎

Pro-Tech Venture Corp. (B.C. Dec. 14, 1982)
Dec. 28, 2001 – Delisted from the CDNX. Subsequently dissolved for failure to file and struck from register.

Pro-Veinor Resources Inc. (Can. Aug. 27, 1996)
Mar. 14, 2006 – Name changed to Affinor Resources Inc.; basis 1 new for 6 old shs. ∎

Pro-Vest Growth & Income Fund (Ont. Jan. 29, 2004)
June 3, 2009 – Merged into Sentry Select Canadian Income Fund, an open-ended mutual fund.

Proalta Energy Inc. (Alta. June 28, 1993)
July 12, 1994 – Amalgamated with Maxon Energy Inc. (1 for 1) to continue as Maxon Energy Inc.; basis 1 new for 1.6667 old shs. (see Maxon Energy Inc.)

Probe Exploration & Development Ltd. (Alta. Aug. 7, 1975)
Mar. 30, 1988 – Name changed to Probe Exploration Inc. ∎

Probe Exploration Inc. (Alta. Aug. 7, 1975)
Mar. 2000 – Placed into receivership. PricewaterhouseCoopers Inc. was appointed receiver/manager.

Probe Metals Inc. (Ont. Jan. 16, 2015)
Jan. 9, 2023 – Name changed to Probe Gold Inc. (see FPsurvey - Mines & Energy)

Probe Mines Limited (Ont. Oct. 17, 1933)
Mar. 14, 2015 – All o/s shs. acquired by Goldcorp Inc. and Probe Mines shareholders were issued with 13,264,133 Goldcorp com. shs. and 31,368,363 Probe Metals Inc. com. shs.

Probe Resources Ltd. (B.C. Nov. 15, 1988)
Apr. 30, 2012 – Formed Rooster Energy Ltd. in British Columbia pursuant to reverse takeover acquisition of and amalgamation with Rooster Probe GOM Oil & Gas Ltd.; basis 1 new for 250 old shs. (see FPsurvey - Mines & Energy)

Probuild Proceeds Limited (Can. 1925)
Oct. 1, 1964 – Initial liquidating payment of $37 per sh. (including $22.92 taxable).
Jan. 12, 1965 – Final distribution of $1,738 paid.

Process Minerals Ltd. (Ont. 1971)
Oct. 1977 – Charter cancelled.

Procoloro Resources Inc. (Can. Apr. 1, 1995 amalg.)
Aug. 21, 1998 – Name changed to Allican Resources Inc. ∎

Procom Emerald Company Incorporated (B.C. 1987)
Oct. 22, 1993 – Dissolved and struck off register.

Procordia Explorations Ltd. (B.C. Mar. 2, 1984)
Sept. 15, 1993 – Name changed to Earthworks Industries Inc.; basis 1 new for 5 old shs. (see FPsurvey - Industrials)

Procorp Developments Inc. (Alta. Mar. 3, 1987)
Nov. 30, 1998 – Name changed to Roadking Travel Centres Inc. ∎

Procyon BioPharma Inc. (Ont. Nov. 27, 1986)
Apr. 2, 2001 – Continued into Canada.
Mar. 3, 2006 – Name changed to Ambrilia Biopharma Inc. ∎

Prodec Inc. (Que. 1968)
Nov. 10, 1973 – Dissolved.

Prodeco Oil & Gas Co. Ltd. (Alta. 1981 amalg.)
July 1985 – Acquired by Bow Valley Industries Ltd.; basis 1 com. sh., 1 class Z series 4 pref. sh. and 0.5 wts. to purchase 1 com. sh. of Bow Valley at $24 to June 30, 1988, for 7 Prodeco shs. (see Bow Valley Industries Ltd.)

Prodigy Gold Inc. (B.C. Feb. 9, 1983)
Dec. 12, 2012 – Acquired by Argonaut Gold Inc. for $0.0001 plus 0.1042 Argonaut com. shs. per Prodigy com. sh. (see Argonaut Gold Inc.)

Prodigy Ventures Inc. (Can. Feb. 6, 2008)
July 1, 2023 – Name changed to genifi inc. ∎

Producers' Crude Corp. Ltd. (Alta. Mar. 8, 1938)
May 1940 – Voluntary liquidation; N. D. McDermid, Calgary, liquidator.

Producers Oilfield Services Inc. (Alta. Mar. 30, 2000)
June 2, 2006 – Plan of Arrangement acquisition by Mullen Group Income Fund; basis either 0.444 new Mullen trust unit, or 0.444 new Mullen LP cl. B LP unit, plus 0.1279 new Horizon North Logisitics Inc. com. sh., plus 0.09 new Horizon warrant for 1 old Producers' com. sh. (see Mullen Group Income Fund)

Producers Pipelines Ltd. (Sask. 1957)
1970 – Purchased for cash by Dome Petroleum Ltd.

ProEx Energy Ltd. (Alta. Apr. 8, 2004)
Jan. 21, 2009 – Name changed to Progress Energy Resources Corp. following reverse takeover acquisition of Progress Energy Trust. ∎

Profco Resources Ltd. (B.C. Oct. 1, 1985)
June 10, 1997 – Continued into Alberta.
Dec. 2, 1998 – Name changed to TransAtlantic Petroleum Corp. following acquisition of GHP Exploration Corporation; basis 0.87 Profco shs. for 1 GHP sh. ∎

Professor Silver Mines Ltd. (Ont. 1949)
1964 – Merged into Consolidated Professor Mines Ltd.; basis 1 new for 5 old shs.

Profile Capital Corporation (Alta. Nov. 16, 1987)
Feb. 10, 1995 – Amalgamated with Abacan Resource Corporation (1 for 1), Canadian Angus Resources Ltd. (0.30 for 1), Canadian Industrial Minerals Corp. (0.51 for 1) and Canstar Ventures Corp. (0.45 for 1) to form a new co. also known as Abacan Resource Corporation; basis 0.23 new for 1 old sh. (see Abacan Resource Corporation)

Profile Resources Inc. (Alta. Nov. 24, 1994)
Sept. 27, 2006 – Name changed to Teras Resources Inc.; basis 1 new for 5 old shs. (see FPsurvey - Mines & Energy)

Profile Ventures Ltd. (B.C. May 14, 1987)
Dec. 22, 1995 – Name changed to Multivision Communications Corp. ■

Profin Inc. (Que. Sept. 1975)
July 17, 1976 – Name changed to Crédit Industriel Desjardins Incorporated. ■

Profit Booking Blue Chip Trust (Ont. May 19, 2004)
June 24, 2005 – Name changed to Crown Hill Dividend Fund. ■

Proflex Limited (Can. Aug. 1967)
Feb. 4, 1980 – Continued into Ontario. (see FPsurvey - Industrials)

Profound Energy Inc. (Alta. Nov. 22, 2007 amalg.)
Aug. 20, 2009 – Acquired by Paramount Energy Trust by way of amalgamation with 1463072 Alberta Ltd., an indirect wholly owned subsid. of Paramount; basis either $1.34 or 0.394 Paramount units for 1 Profound com. sh. or a combination thereof. (see Paramount Energy Trust)

Progas of Canada Inc. (Del. 1952)
1961 – Subsids., Progas Ltd., Progas Pipe Lines Ltd. and Stewart Petroleums Ltd. sold to Canadian Hydrocarbons Ltd.

Proginet Corporation (N.Y. 1986)
Dec. 1994 – Amalgamated in Delaware to continue with same name.

Progold Resources Ltd. (B.C. Jan. 8, 1985)
July 28, 1993 – Name changed to Snowcap Waters Limited pursuant to plan of arrangement whereby shs. were exchanged for shs. of Snowcap Waters Limited on a 1-for-10 basis, resulting in a reverse takeover by Snowcap. ■

Progress Diversified Minerals Ltd. (Ont. 1945)
1949 – Name changed to Indigo Consolidated Gold Mines Limited. ■

Progress Energy Canada Ltd. (Alta. Apr. 8, 2004)
Nov. 22, 2018 – Name changed to PETRONAS Energy Canada Ltd.

Progress Energy Ltd. (Alta. Sept. 2, 1997)
Jan. 21, 2009 – Acquired by ProEx Energy Ltd.; basis 0.8125 ProEx com. shs. multiplied by exch. ratio in effect at close of transaction for 1 Progress Energy Ltd. exch. sh.

Progress Energy Resources Corp. (Alta. Apr. 8, 2004)
Dec. 18, 2012 – Acquired by PETRONAS Carigali Canada Ltd. for $22 per sh.
Dec. 19, 2012 – Name changed to Progress Energy Canada Ltd. ■

Progress Energy Trust (Alta. May 26, 2004)
Jan. 21, 2009 – Acquired by ProEx Energy Ltd. (subsequently renamed Progress Energy Resources Corp.); basis 0.8125 ProEx Energy shs. for 1 Progress Energy Trust unit and 1.3169 ProEx com. shs. for 1 Progress Energy Ltd. exch. sh. Subsequently liquidated and dissolved. (see Progress Energy Resources Corp.)

Progress Mines Ltd. (B.C. 1971)
June 1972 – Name changed to Riverwood Resources Limited. ■

Progressive Applied Technologies Inc. (B.C. Mar. 11, 1987)
June 27, 2002 – Name changed to Pacific Vegas Global Strategies Inc.; basis 1 new for 2 old shs. ■

Progressive Minerals Ltd. (B.C. Feb. 24, 1987)
Feb. 10, 1989 – Name changed to Northern Crown Mines Ltd.; basis 1 new for 2.5 old shs. ■

Progressive Technologies Inc. (B.C. Mar. 11, 1987)
Aug. 12, 1999 – Name changed to Progressive Applied Technologies Inc.; basis 1 new for 10 old shs. ■

Progressive Waste Solutions Ltd. (Ont. May 5, 2008)
June 1, 2016 – Name changed to Waste Connections, Inc. pursuant to reverse takeover acquisition of (old) Waste Connections, Inc.; basis 1 new for 2.076843 old shs. (see FPsurvey - Industrials)

Project Finance Corp. (B.C. Oct. 16, 2006)
Sept. 3, 2010 – Name changed to Alaska Hydro Corporation pursuant to Qualifying Transaction reverse takeover acquisition of Cascade Creek, LLC. (see FPsurvey - Mines & Energy; FPsurvey - Industrials)

Project One Resources Ltd. (B.C. Mar. 22, 2018)
Oct. 28, 2021 – Name changed to Alerio Gold Corp. (see FPsurvey - Mines & Energy)

Prolab Technologies Inc. (Que. June 20, 2000 amalg.)
Dec. 7, 2010 – Privatized at 20¢ per sh.

Prolific Petroleum Ltd. (B.C. Sept. 13, 1979)
Aug. 26, 1987 – Name changed to Prolific Resources Ltd. ■

Prolific Resources Ltd. (B.C. Sept. 13, 1979)
June 5, 1990 – Name changed to Skeena Resources Limited; basis 1 new for 3 old shs. (see FPsurvey - Mines & Energy)

Prolific Technology Inc. (B.C. Aug. 19, 1985)
Feb. 9, 2001 – Continued into Alberta.
Mar. 18, 2002 – Name changed to Klad Enterprises Ltd.; basis 1 new for 2 old shs. ■

ProMIS Neurosciences Inc. (Can. Sept. 20, 2005 amalg.)
July 13, 2023 – Continued into Ontario. (see FPsurvey - Industrials)

Promark Software Inc. (B.C. Aug. 9, 1984)
Aug. 30, 1999 – Name changed to clipclop.com Enterprises Inc. ■

Promatek Industries Ltd. (Can. Oct. 22, 1976)
Nov. 13, 2007 – Acquired by 6809618 Canada Inc.; basis 1 6809618 Canada pref. sh. for 1 Promatek com. sh. Pref. shs. redeemed for $2.00 per sh.

Promax Communications Inc. (B.C. Aug. 20, 1968)
Apr. 4, 1998 – Continued into Yukon.
Sept. 3, 2008 – Dissolved and struck off register.

Promax Energy Inc. (B.C. Sept. 26, 1980)
June 8, 2000 – Continued into Alberta.
Apr. 28, 2004 – Placed into receivership. KPMG Inc. was appointed receiver/manager.

Promed Technology Inc. (Can. 1981)
June 24, 1983 – Name changed to Zavitz Technology Inc. ■

ProMetic Life Sciences Inc. (Can. Oct. 14, 1994)
Oct. 3, 2019 – Name changed to Liminal BioSciences Inc. ■

Prominex Resource Corp. (B.C. Apr. 29, 1980)
Nov. 15, 2021 – Name changed to Green Scientific Labs Holdings Inc. pursuant to the the reverse takeover acquisition of Green Scientific Labs, LLC (GSL) and concurrent amalgamation of GSL with wholly owned PRC Merger Sub, Inc.; basis 1 new for 168.68 old shs. (see FPsurvey - Industrials)

Promis Systems Corporation Ltd. (Can. Dec. 12, 1985)
Mar. 19, 1999 – Name changed to PRI Automation (Canada), Inc. ■

Promistora Gold Mines Ltd. (Ont. 1949)
Mar. 1967 – Charter cancelled.

Promotional Products International, Ltd. (Alta. Dec. 15, 1994)
Nov. 20, 2009 – Name changed to Ava Resources Corp.; basis 1 new for 10 old shs. ■

Prong Industries Corporation Ltd. (B.C. May 8, 1981)
Sept. 3, 1996 – Continued into Bermuda.
Nov. 2, 1998 – Name changed to C & C Industries Corporation Ltd. ■

Pronghorn Petroleum Corporation Limited (Can. 1966)
June 1971 – Acquired by Norco Oil Corp.; basis 1.16 new for 1 old sh.

Pronto Uranium Mines Ltd. (Ont. 1953)
1960 – Merged into Rio Algom Mines Ltd.; basis 35 new for 100 old shs.

ProntoForms Corporation (Ont. May 22, 2007)
Nov. 28, 2023 – Name changed to TrueContext Corporation. ■

Propane Credit Corp. Ltd. (Alta. July 26, 1947)
Jan. 30, 1976 – Name changed to Polled Cattle Corporation Ltd. ■

Propel Multi-Strategy Fund (Ont. Nov. 22, 2010)
May 1, 2014 – All o/s fund units were redeemed and cancelled; basis $7.39 cash per unit.

Prophecy Coal Corp. (B.C. Nov. 6, 1978)
Jan. 5, 2015 – Name changed to Prophecy Development Corp. ■

Prophecy Development Corp. (B.C. Nov. 6, 1978)
Mar. 16, 2020 – Name changed to Silver Elephant Mining Corp. (see FPsurvey - Mines & Energy)

Prophecy Entertainment Inc. (B.C. June 27, 1983)
Aug. 29, 2005 – Dissolved and struck from register.

Prophecy Platinum Corp. (B.C. Apr. 5, 2006)
Dec. 19, 2013 – Name changed to Wellgreen Platinum Ltd. ■

Prophecy Potash Corp. (B.C. Mar. 29, 2018)
Jan. 4, 2022 – Name changed to Alpha Copper Corp. ■

Prophecy Resource Corp. (B.C. Nov. 6, 1978)
June 13, 2011 – Name changed to Prophecy Coal Corp. following spin-out of nickel assets to Pacific Coast Nickel Corp. ■

Prophecy Resource Corp. (B.C. Feb. 9, 2006)
Apr. 16, 2010 – Acquired by Red Hill Energy Inc. by way of amalgamation with a wholly owned subsid. of Red Hill; basis 1 Red Hill cl. A sh. for 1 Prophecy sh. Subsequently, Red Hill changed its name to Prophecy Resource Corp. (see Prophecy Resource Corp.)
Apr. 16, 2010 – Formed Prophecy Holdings Inc. in British Columbia on amalgamation with 0875512 B.C. Ltd., a wholly owned subsid. of Red Hill Energy Inc. (see Prophecy Resource Corp.)

Prophesy Developments Ltd. (B.C. 1983)
Sept. 22, 1989 – Dissolved.

Prophet Minerals Corporation (B.C. May 19, 1981)
Feb. 2, 2000 – Name changed to Meridex Network Corporation. ■

Prophet Resources Ltd. (B.C. 1982)
Jan. 21, 1994 – Dissolved and struck off register.

Prophet River Gas & Oil Co. Ltd. (B.C. 1953)
1957 – Acquired by Cedar Oils Ltd.

Proprietary Energy Industries Inc. (Alta. July 8, 1993)
July 27, 2000 – Name changed to Proprietary Industries Inc. ■

Proprietary Industries Inc. (Alta. July 8, 1993)
June 3, 2002 – Continued into Canada.
June 28, 2006 – Name changed to Jura Energy Corporation. (see FPsurvey - Mines & Energy)

Proprietary Mines Holdings Ltd. (Ont. 1951)
1964 – Name changed to Consolidated Proprietary Mines Holdings Ltd.; basis 1 new for 5 old shs. ■

Prosalutis Holdings Inc. (B.C. Aug. 6, 2015 amalg.)
Aug. 10, 2018 – Name changed to Fast Line Holding Inc. ■

ProSep Inc. (Can. Mar. 25, 1993)
Nov. 15, 2013 – Sale of substantially all of the company's assets to a subsid. of Produced Water Absorbents Inc. was completed. Net proceeds to be distributed to creditors with no distrib. available to shldrs.
Nov. 15, 2013 – Name changed to 2907160 Canada Inc. ■

ProSmart Enterprises Inc. (B.C. Jan. 27, 2009)
Feb. 16, 2021 – Name changed to Alset Capital Inc.; basis 1 new for 10 old shs. ■

Prospector Capital Corp. (Cayman Islands Sept. 18, 2020)
Dec. 21, 2023 – Formed LeddarTech Holdings Inc. in Canada pursuant to amalgamation with (old) LeddarTech Holdings Inc. followed by amalgamation with LeddarTech Inc. (deemed acquiror); basis 2 new for 1 old sh. ■

Prospector Consolidated Resources Inc. (B.C. Feb. 13, 1990)
Jan. 31, 2011 – Name changed to Prospector Resources Corp.; basis 1 new for 30 old shs. ■

Prospector International Resources Inc. (B.C. Feb. 13, 1990)
Sept. 11, 2001 – Name changed to Prospector Consolidated Resources Inc.; basis 1 new for 9 old shs. ■

Prospector Resources Corp. (B.C. Feb. 13, 1990)
Apr. 25, 2017 – Continued into Ontario.
Apr. 27, 2017 – Name changed to Rio2 Limited. ■

Prospectors Airways Company Ltd. (Can. Mar. 1, 1931)
Nov. 1963 – Acquired by Kerr Addison Mines Limited; basis 1 new for 10 old shs. Subsequently dissolved effective Dec. 6, 1976. (see Kerr Addison Mines Limited)

Prospectors Airways Co. Ltd. (B.C. 1984)
Oct. 11, 1994 – Name changed to Prospectors Airways Consolidated Ltd. ■

Prospectors Airways Consolidated Ltd. (B.C. 1984)
Sept. 11, 2006 – Dissolved and struck off register.
Sept. 4, 2008 – Restored to company register.
Mar. 21, 2011 – Dissolved and struck from register.

Prospectors Alliance Corporation (Ont. 1939)
Jan. 29, 2001 – Amalgamated with International Larder Minerals Inc. (0.1965 Prospectors sh. for 1 Larder sh.), private co. Explorers Alliance Corporation (0.7363 Prospectors sh. for 1 Explorers com. sh.), and two numbered companies to continue as a new company also named Explorers Alliance Corporation; basis 1 new Explorers sh. for 4 old Prospectors shs.

The Prospectus Group Inc. (Alta. Oct. 7, 1994)
Oct. 15, 2004 – Continued into Ontario.
Oct. 21, 2004 – Name changed to Route1 Inc. following reverse takeover acquisition of IP Co. Limited. (see FPsurvey - Industrials)

Prosper Gold Mines Ltd. (B.C. 1947)
July 2, 1954 – Struck off register.

Prosper Oils and Mines Ltd. (B.C. Apr. 7, 1952)
1969 – Name changed to Southern Pacific Petroleum Ltd. ■

Prosper Oils Ltd. (B.C. Apr. 7, 1952)
Nov. 1965 – Name changed to Prosper Oils and Mines Ltd. ■

Prosperex Minerals Corp. (B.C. 1984)
Aug. 6, 1991 – Name changed to NAV Master Technologies Inc. ■

Prosperity Exploration Corp. (B.C. Sept. 1, 2020)
Sept. 16, 2022 – Name changed to First American Uranium Inc. (see FPsurvey - Mines & Energy)

Prosperity Goldfields Corp. (Can. Sept. 10, 2010)
Dec. 11, 2014 – Name changed to Northern Empire Resources Corp.; basis 1 new for 5 old shs. ■

Prospero Silver Corp. (B.C. Mar. 31, 2008)
Mar. 19, 2021 – Name changed to Keon Capital Inc. (see FPsurvey - Mines & Energy; FPsurvey - Industrials)

Prosperpine Mines Ltd. (B.C. 1945)
June 10, 1959 – Dissolved and struck off register.

Prospex Mining Inc. (Yuk. July 30, 1997)
June 30, 1999 – Acquired by Semafo Inc.; basis 1 Semafo sh. for 10 Prospex shs. Subsequently dissolved Jan. 12, 2007. (see SEMAFO Inc.)

ProspEx Resources Ltd. (Alta. Aug. 13, 2004)
June 3, 2011 – Acquired by Paramount Resources Ltd.; basis for $2.40 per ProspEx com. sh. or 0.07162 Paramount cl.A shs. for 1 ProspEx com. sh.

Protaal Resources Ltd. (Alta. July 15, 1980)
Apr. 19, 1984 – Name changed to Newalta Oil & Gas Ltd.; basis 1 new for 5 old shs. ■

Protea Developments Ltd. (Can. 1971)
Dec. 16, 1980 – Dissolved.

Protech Home Medical Corp. (B.C. Dec. 30, 2013)
May 13, 2021 – Name changed to Quipt Home Medical Corp.; basis 1 new for 4 old shs. (see FPsurvey - Industrials)

Protection Devices International Inc. (Alta. Mar. 24, 1995)
Jan. 16, 1996 – Name changed to Inlet Devices Corporation following reverse takeover acquisition of Inlet Devices Corporation and subsequent amalgamation of old Inlet with 883746 Ontario Limited and Onyx Communications Inc. ■

Protection Plus Development Corporation (Alta. 1987)
Oct. 1, 1989 – Formed ResoQuest Energy Corp. in Alberta on amalgamation with Resoquest Energy Corp.; basis 2,129,380 new for 1 Resoquest sh. and 1 new for 5 Protection Plus shs. ■

Protection Technology Inc. (B.C. Apr. 6, 1987)
Dec. 5, 2005 – Struck from register and dissolved.

Protector Industries Ltd. (Alta. May 7, 1991)
Apr. 14, 2000 – Formed Life Medical Corporation following acquisition of all o/s shs. of Life Medical Inc. and D.L.P. Health Care Inc.; basis 1 new for 4 old shs. ■

Proteus Environmental Inc. (Alta. Mar. 4, 1993)
Apr. 2, 2002 – Struck from registry and dissolved.

Proteus Minerals Ltd. (Ont. 1956)
1971 – Charter cancelled.

Proteus Resources Inc. (B.C. 1984)
July 20, 1989 – Amalgamated with Silverside Resources Inc. (1 new for 1 old sh.) to form a co. also known as Silverside Resources Inc.; basis 1 new for 2.5 old com. shs., and 1 new for 2.5 old pref. shs. (see Silverside Resources Inc.)

Proto Explorations & Holdings Inc. (Ont. 1972 amalg.)
Mar. 1981 – Name changed to Baxter Resources Corporation following acquisition by a private co. ■

Proto Explorations Ltd. (Ont. 1969)
Feb. 1972 – Amalgamated with certain other cos., to form Proto Explorations & Holdings Inc.; basis 2 new for 15 old shs.

Proton Capital Corp. (Alta. Sept. 1, 2021)
July 22, 2024 – Name changed to PharmaCorp Rx Inc. (see FPsurvey - Industrials)

Protox Therapeutics Inc. (B.C. May 20, 2003 amalg.)
Apr. 5, 2012 – Name changed to Sophiris Bio Inc. (see FPsurvey - Industrials)

Proudearth Explorations Inc. (Ont. 1972)
Feb. 20, 1980 – Dissolved.

Provall Mines Ltd. (Ont. 1946)
Aug. 18, 1958 – Charter cancelled.

Proven Resources Ltd. (B.C. 1984)
May 28, 1987 – Name changed to Shayna International Industries Ltd. (see FPsurvey - Industrials)

Provenor Inc. (Can. Aug. 27, 1996)
Oct. 29, 2003 – Name changed to Pro-Veinor Resources Inc.; basis 1 new for 4 old shs. ■

Proventure Income Fund (Ont. Dec. 31, 2005)
Oct. 5, 2012 – Name changed to Summit Industrial Income REIT. ■

Providence Capital Corp. (B.C. Sept. 15, 2006)
Jan. 24, 2011 – Name changed to Providence Resources Corp. ■

Providence Diamond Corp. (Can. June 20, 2003)
July 25, 2005 – Name changed to CIC Mining Resources Ltd. ■

Providence Industries Inc. (B.C. Apr. 1, 1981)
Dec. 7, 1994 – Amalgamated with Gold City Resources Inc. and McKinney Mines Corp. to form Gold City Mining Corporation; basis 1 new for 1 Gold City Resources sh., 1 new for 1.3 McKinney Mines shs. and 1 new for 0.8 Providence Industries shs. (see Gold City Mining Corporation)

Providence Innovations Inc. (B.C. Apr. 1, 1981)
Oct. 4, 1991 – Name changed to Providence Industries Inc.; basis 1 new for 4 old shs. ■

Providence Resources Corp. (B.C. Sept. 15, 2006)
Apr. 15, 2015 – Amalgamated with (old) Desert Star Resources Ltd. to form (new) Desert Star Resources Ltd. (Amalco); basis 1 Amalco com. sh. for 1 old Desert Star sh. and 0.4 Amalco com. shs. plus 0.4 Amalco wts. for 1 Providence com. sh. with wts. exercisable at 25¢ per sh. for two yrs.

Provident Energy Ltd. (Alta. Jan. 1, 2011; amalg.)
Apr. 9, 2012 – Name changed to Pembina NGL Corporation following acquisition by Pembina Pipeline Corporation and concurrent amalgamation with a wholly owned subsidiary of Pembina; basis 0.425 Pembina com. shs. for 1 Provident com. sh.

Provident Energy Trust (Alta. Jan. 25, 2001)
Jan. 1, 2011 – Succeeded by Provident Energy Ltd. pursuant to plan of arrangement whereby Provident Energy Ltd. was formed to facilitate the conversion of the trust into a corporation and the trust was subsequently dissolved. ■

Provigo Inc. (Que. Nov. 14, 1961)
June 26, 1992 – Name changed to Univa Inc. ■

Provigo Inc. (Que. Nov. 14, 1961)
Jan. 20, 1999 – Acquired by Loblaw Companies Limited; basis $15.62 or 0.27 Loblaw shs. plus $7.25 for 1 Provigo sh.

Provinces X Explorations Ltd. (Can. 1969)
Dec. 28, 1984 – Remaining publicly held shs. acquired by Laduboro Oil Ltd.; basis 1.5 Laduboro shs. for each sh. of Provinces X held.

Provincial Asbestos Co. Ltd. (Que. 1951)
Sept. 2, 1978 – Charter cancelled.

Provincial Mining & Development Co. Ltd. (Ont. 1965)
Oct. 26, 1976 – Dissolved.

Provincial Molybdenum Corp. Ltd. (Que. 1959)
Mar. 20, 1976 – Dissolved.

Provincial Transport Company (Que. 1928)
1969 – Name changed to Voyageur (1969) Inc. ∎

Provincial Transport Enterprises Ltd. (Can. 1948)
Nov. 25, 1977 – Name changed to Voyageur Enterprises Ltd.

Provo Gas Producers Limited (Alta. 1955)
1967 – Acquired by Dome Petroleum Ltd.; basis 1 new for 8 old shs. (see Dome Petroleum Limited)

Provo Industries Inc. (Ont. Mar. 3, 1986)
Mar. 1, 1993 – Amalgamated in Ontario to continue with same name.
Feb. 3, 1995 – Name changed to Leisure Canada Inc.; basis 1 new for 8 old shs. ∎

Prow Yellowknife Gold Mines Ltd. (Ont. 1945)
Mar. 1, 1982 – Dissolved.

Prudential Mining Co. of Canada (Ont. 1954)
1967 – Merged into Resource Exploration & Development Co. Ltd.; basis 10 new for 121 old shs.

The Prudential Oil & Gas Co. Ltd. (N.W.T. 1914)
Struck off register. (see Canada Southern Oil & Refining Co. Ltd.)

Prudential Petroleums Ltd. (B.C. 1958)
Apr. 1965 – Name changed to New Prudential Petroleums Ltd.; basis 1 new for 4 old shs. ∎

Prudential Steel Ltd. (Alta. Apr. 4, 1966)
Sept. 27, 2000 – Merged with U.S.-based Maverick Tube Corporation; basis 0.52 exchangeable shs. of Maverick Tube (Canada) Inc. convertible into Maverick Tube Corporation com. shs. (1-for-1) for 1 Prudential sh.

Prudential Trust Company Limited (Can. 1909)
Dec. 1960 – Guaranty Trust Co. of Canada acquired 87.1% of o/s stk.
Dec. 31, 1963 – Final amalgamation into Guaranty Trust completed.

Pryme Energy Resources Ltd. (B.C. July 31, 1979)
Aug. 23, 1985 – Name changed to Newjay Resources Ltd.; basis 1 new for 2.5 old shs. ∎

Psion Canada Inc. (Can. 2000)
Aug. 22, 2005 – All exch. shs. redeemed ahead of scheduled redemption date. Wholly owned subsid. of British Psion plc.

Psychedelic Science Corp. (Ont. June 2, 2020)
Nov. 8, 2021 – Name changed to Neural Therapeutics Inc. (see FPsurvey - Industrials)

Psyence Biomedical Ltd. (Cayman Islands Feb. 25, 2021)
Jan. 26, 2024 – Continued into Ontario. (see FPsurvey - Industrials)

Public Storage Canadian Properties (Alta. Jan. 20, 1992)
Dec. 2, 1998 – Amalgamated in Ontario to continue with same name.
Sept. 10, 2010 – Acquired by PS Canada Company ULC for $20.00 per unit.

Public Storage Canadian Properties (Alta. 1978)
Feb. 7, 1992 – Amalgamated with Public Storage Canadian Properties II and Public Storage Canadian Properties III to form a new partnership also known as Public Storage Canadian Properties; basis 2.20 new units for 1 old unit. (see Public Storage Canadian Properties)

Public Storage Canadian Properties II (Alta. 1979)
Feb. 7, 1992 – Amalgamated with Public Storage Canadian Properties and Public Storage Canadian Properties III to form a new partnership known as Public Storage Canadian Properties; basis 1.92 new units for 1 old unit. (see Public Storage Canadian Properties)

Public Storage Canadian Properties III (Alta. 1980)
Feb. 7, 1992 – Amalgamated with Public Storage Canadian Properties and Public Storage Canadian

Properties II to form a new partnership known as Public Storage Canadian Properties; basis 1 new unit for 1 old unit. (see Public Storage Canadian Properties)

Public Storage Canadian Properties IV Limited Partnership (B.C. June 20, 1986)
Jan. 5, 1999 – Operations combined with Public Storage Canadian Properties (PSCP) to form a single new public partnership to be known as Public Storage Canadian Properties (New Public); basis 0.4 New Public unit for 1 old unit held. (see Public Storage Canadian Properties)

Publix Oil & Gas Ltd. (Can. 1929)
Nothing paid to ordinary creditors.

Pucara Gold Ltd. (B.C. Feb. 17, 2011)
Nov. 25, 2024 – Acquired by Copper Standard Resources Inc.; basis 0.10 Copper Standard shs. for 1 Pucara Gold sh.

Puff Pac Industries Inc. (Del. Oct. 27, 1989)
Sept. 1, 1992 – Name changed to Air Packaging Technologies, Inc.

Puget Ventures Inc. (B.C. Mar. 9, 2007)
June 4, 2013 – Name changed to Global Cobalt Corporation. ∎

Pulsar Energy & Resources Inc. (B.C. Nov. 13, 1980)
Nov. 30, 1987 – Name changed to Star One Resources Inc.; basis 1 new for 3 old shs. ∎

Pulse Capital Corp. (B.C. Oct. 26, 2006)
Dec. 7, 2011 – Name changed to ACT Aurora Control Technologies Corp. following Nov. 3, 2011, Qualifying Transaction reverse takeover acquisition of Aurora Control Technologies Inc. ∎

Pulse Data Inc. (Can. Aug. 26, 1985)
May 28, 2009 – Name changed to Pulse Seismic Inc. (see FPsurvey - Mines & Energy; FPsurvey - Industrials)

Pulse Resources Ltd. (B.C. Oct. 23, 1986)
June 12, 1992 – Name changed to Jupiter Explorations Ltd.; basis 1 new for 3 old shs. ∎

Puma Exploration Inc. (Alta. Aug. 11, 2000)
Sept. 20, 2005 – Continued into Canada. (see FPsurvey - Mines & Energy)

Puma Minerals Corp. (B.C. Aug. 6, 1981)
July 22, 1999 – Name changed to Consolidated Puma Minerals Corp.; basis 1 new for 10 old shs. ∎

Puma Petroleums Ltd. (Alta. 1969)
June 22, 1973 – Amalgamated with Pennant Oils Ltd. to form Pennant-Puma Oils Ltd.; basis 1 new for 3 old shs.

Punch Petroleums Limited (Ont. 1950)
1953 – Acquired by Rio-Prado Consolidated Oils Limited; basis 1 new for 3 old shs. (see Rio-Prado Consolidated Oils Limited)

Pundata Gold Corporation (B.C. Nov. 7, 1984)
July 24, 1991 – Delisted from the Alberta Stock Exchange. Subsequently dissolved for failure to file and stuck from register.

Purcell Development Co. Ltd. (B.C. 1969)
Mar. 31, 1983 – Struck off register.

Purcell Energy Ltd. (Alta. Oct. 20, 1993 amalg.)
Nov. 7, 2005 – Name changed to Point North Energy Ltd. following reorganization with Tenergy Inc. and Tenergy Finco Ltd.; basis 40¢ cash, 0.2 Tenergy Inc. com. sh. and 0.0556 Prairie Schooner com. sh. for 0.2 Purcell com. sh. (following 1-for-5 cons.). (see FPsurvey - Mines & Energy)

Purdex Minerals Ltd. (Ont. Oct. 1942)
Nov. 18, 1970 – Dissolved.

Purdy Mica Mines Ltd. (Ont. Oct. 1942)
June 1956 – Name changed to Purdex Minerals Ltd.; basis 1 new for 1 old sh. ∎

Pure Copper Explorations Ltd. (Ont. 1966)
1971 – Acquired by Ark Explorations Ltd. (see Ark Explorations Ltd.)

Pure Diamonds Exploration Inc. (Ont. Nov. 13, 1997 amalg.)
Aug. 14, 2009 – Name changed to Burnstone Ventures Inc.; basis 1 new for 10 old shs. (see FPsurvey - Mines & Energy)

Pure Energy Hydrogen Corporation Limited (B.C. Oct. 11, 2012)
July 22, 2021 – Continued into Australia.

Pure Energy Resources Inc. (Ont. July 24, 1980)
Aug. 31, 1992 – Delisted from the CDN. Subsequently struck from registry and dissolved.

Pure Energy Services Ltd. (Alta. May 24, 2001)
Oct. 5, 2012 – Acquired by FMC Technologies, Inc. for $11 per sh.

Pure Extraction Corp. (B.C. June 20, 2007)
Oct. 7, 2021 – Name changed to First Hydrogen Corp. (see FPsurvey - Industrials)

Pure Global Cannabis Inc. (B.C. Mar. 2, 2011)
May 1, 2020 – Placed into receivership and B. Riley Farber Inc. (previously A. Farber & Partners Inc.) appointed receiver.

Pure Gold Minerals Inc. (Ont. Nov. 13, 1997 amalg.)
Dec. 5, 2006 – Name changed to Pure Diamonds Exploration Inc.; basis 1 new for 8 old shs. ∎

Pure Gold Mining Inc. (B.C. Nov. 14, 2005)
June 16, 2023 – Acquired by West Red Lake Gold Mines Ltd. pursuant to the plan of compromise and arrangement under the Companies' Creditors Arrangement Act (CCAA). Under the plan, West Red Lake issued shs. and monies to Sprott Resource Lending Corp., holder of the mortgage on the PureGold mine; no monies were made available to shldrs. and other creditors.
June 27, 2023 – Name changed to Red Lake Madsen Mine Ltd.

Pure Gold Resources Inc. (Ont. May 6, 1986)
Nov. 20, 1997 – Amalgamated with Cayo Resources Inc. to form Pure Gold Minerals Inc.; basis 3 new for 5 Cayo shs. and 1 new for 5 Pure Gold shs. (see Pure Gold Minerals Inc.)

Pure Industrial Real Estate Trust (B.C. June 24, 2007)
May 25, 2018 – Acquired by Blackstone Property Partners and Ivanhoe Cambridge; basis $8.10 cash per cl. A trust unit.

Pure Lean Incorporated (Alta. July 19, 1999)
Jan. 2, 2006 – Struck from the registry and dissolved.

Pure Living Media Inc. (B.C. Jan. 16, 2007)
Aug. 16, 2012 – Name changed to Scavo Resource Corp. ∎

Pure Multi-Family REIT LP (Ont. May 8, 2012)
Sept. 30, 2019 – Acquired by Cortland Partners, LLC; basis US$7.61 per LP unit.

Pure Nickel Inc. (Yuk. June 23, 1998)
Apr. 7, 2009 – Continued into Canada.
Dec. 18, 2019 – Name changed to Galleon Gold Corp. (see FPsurvey - Mines & Energy)

Pure Pioneer Ventures Ltd. (B.C. Aug. 23, 1988 amalg.)
Jan. 2, 2006 – Struck from registry and dissolved.
July 9, 2007 – Restored to registry.
July 10, 2009 – Limited restoration to registry expired and company dissolved.

Pure Silver Mines Ltd. (B.C. 1964)
Oct. 2, 1987 – Dissolved. Not to be confused with Ontario company of similar name.

Pure Silver Mines Limited (Ont. 1966)
Sept. 22, 1975 – Merged into Lacana Mining Corporation; basis 60 new for 100 old shs. Not to be confused with B.C. company of similar name.

Pure Technologies Ltd. (Alta. Dec. 18, 1995)
Feb. 1, 2018 – Acquired by Xylem Inc.; basis Cdn$9.00 cash per sh.

Pure to Pure Beauty Inc. (B.C. Sept. 29, 2014)
July 25, 2024 – Name changed to P2P Group Ltd. (see FPsurvey - Industrials)

Pure Zinc Technologies Inc. (Can. Dec. 29, 1982)
Sept. 7, 1999 – Name changed to Charityville.com International Inc. ■

Purecanna Products Inc. (B.C. May 22, 2018)
Aug. 27, 2020 – Name changed to Quebec Silica Resources Corp. ■

PureK Holdings Corp. (B.C. Mar. 19, 2018)
May 3, 2021 – Name changed to Simply Better Brands Corp. ■

Purichlor Technology Ltd. (B.C. Feb. 16, 1984)
July 7, 1989 – Delisted from the Vancouver Stock Exchange. Subsequently dissolved for failure to file.

Puritan Mines Ltd. (Ont. 1939)
1942 – Property taken over by Ajax Tungsten & Molybdenite Mines Ltd.

Purity Flour Mills Limited (Ont. 1905)
1961 – Merged with Maple Leaf Milling and Toronto Elevators to form Maple Leaf Mills Ltd. The 182,605 Purity shs. owned by Maple Leaf Milling were cancelled, and each of remaining 395 shs. converted into 1 3/4 fully pd. com. shs. of merged co.

Purl Capital Corporation (Alta. July 9, 1998)
Nov. 14, 2000 – Name changed to MailBoxCity Corporation pursuant to Major Transaction reverse takeover acquisition of 132780 Canada Inc. (operating as Micro Centra) for 4,550,000 com. shs. and 3,600,000 ser. A first pref. shs. at 40¢ per sh. (see FPsurvey - Industrials)

Purpose Floating Rate Income Fund (Ont.)
Aug. 7, 2018 – Converted into an exchange-traded fund; basis 1 ETF unit for 1 cl.A unit and 1 ETF non-currency hedge US$ unit for 1 cl.U unit.

Purpose Global Financials Income Fund (Ont.)
July 4, 2018 – Converted to an exchange-traded fund (ETF); basis 1 new ETF unit for 1 old cl. A unit.

Pursides Gold Mines Limited (Ont. Mar. 22, 1962)
July 1980 – Name changed to Citadel Gold Mines Inc.; basis 1 new for 3 old shs. ■

Pursuit Gold Corp. (B.C. Sept. 15, 2020)
May 17, 2024 – Name changed to SALi Lithium Corp. pursuant to the reverse takeover acquisition of 1477445 B.C. Ltd. (formerly South American Lithium Corp.). (see FPsurvey - Mines & Energy)

Pursuit Resources Corp. (Alta. Feb. 25, 1997 amalg.)
May 10, 2000 – Acquired by EnerMark Income Fund; basis $3.00 or 0.8 EnerMark trust units for 1 Pursuit sh. (see EnerMark Income Fund)

Pursuit Resources Inc. (Alta. Feb. 25, 1987)
Feb. 24, 1997 – Amalgamated with Aztec Resources Ltd. to form Pursuit Resources Corp.; basis 1 new for 2.7 Pursuit shs. (see Pursuit Resources Corp.)

Pushfor Investments Inc. (B.C. Nov. 29, 2007)
June 9, 2022 – Name changed to Pushfor Tech Inc.; basis 1 new for 10 old shs. ■

Pushfor Tech Inc. (B.C. Nov. 29, 2007)
Nov. 23, 2023 – Name changed to AAPKI Ventures Inc. (see FPsurvey - Industrials)

Pustikama Gold Mines Ltd. (Ont. 1946)
Jan. 1949 – Name changed to Continental Lead Mines Ltd. ■

Putco Holdings Ltd. (Ont. 1959)
Aug. 10, 1995 – Dissolved and struck off register.

Putt-Putt Golf Courses of Canada Inc. (Ont. Aug. 3, 1990)
Nov. 26, 1993 – Name changed to HLE Capital Corp. ■

Pylon Uranium Mines Ltd. (Ont. 1954)
1955 – Assets acquired by Matinenda Uranium Mines Ltd.; basis 1 new for 2 old shs.

Pyng Medical Corp. (B.C. Oct. 15, 1986)
Apr. 3, 2017 – Acquired by Teleflex Medical Canada Inc., a wholly owned subsidiary of Teleflex Incorporated, for US$0.30203 per com. sh.

Pyng Technologies Corp. (B.C. Oct. 15, 1986)
Oct. 14, 2004 – Name changed to Pyng Medical Corp. ■

Pyprr Inc. (Alta. July 2, 1987)
Mar. 1, 1995 – Name changed to Carlyle Inc.; basis 1 new for 5 old shs. ■

Pyramid Energy Inc. (Alta. Sept. 20, 1996)
May 17, 2001 – Acquired by Fox Energy Corporation; basis $0.2324 plus 0.2112 new Fox Energy sh. for 1 old Pyramid sh. (see Fox Energy Corporation)

Pyramid Mining Co. Ltd. (B.C. 1964)
Apr. 1975 – Name changed to New Pyramid Gold Mines Inc.; basis 1 new for 5 old shs. ■

Pyramid Oils Ltd. (Ont. 1949)
1959 – Struck off register.

Pyramid Oils Ltd. (Ont. 1949)
1970 – Struck off register.

Pyroair Technology, Inc. (B.C. Dec. 4, 1986)
Oct. 26, 1992 – Name changed to AMT Environmental Products Inc.; basis 1 new for 6 old shs. ■

PyroGenesis Canada Inc. (Can. July 11, 2011 amalg.)
Nov. 11, 2024 – Name changed to PyroGenesis Inc. (see FPsurvey - Industrials)

Pyroil Resources Inc. (Alta. May 17, 1996)
Jan. 13, 2000 – Name changed to Jumbo Development Corporation. ■

Pyrotex Mining & Exploration Co. Ltd. (Ont. 1966)
1969 – Name changed to Waferboard Corporation Limited; basis 1 new for 5 old shs. ■

Python Oil & Gas Corporation (B.C. Apr. 16, 1987)
July 4, 2003 – Name changed to Goldex Resources Corporation; basis 1 new for 2 old shs. (see FPsurvey - Mines & Energy)

Python Resources & Investment Corp. (Ont. 1966)
Apr. 29, 1987 – Name changed to Python Corporation. (see FPsurvey - Industrials)

Pyx Explorations Limited (Ont. 1980 amalg.)
Dec. 14, 1981 – Amalgamated with Discovery Mines Limited; basis 3 new for 5 old shs.

Pyxis Capital Inc. (Ont. Feb. 22, 2006 amalg.)
Sept. 26, 2008 – Acquired by 2181885 Ontario Inc., a wholly owned subsid. of 1693062 Ontario Inc., for 34¢ per com. sh., 34¢ per vtg. sh. and $11.25 per divd. sh.

Q

Q & A Capital Inc. (Ont. July 6, 1983 amalg.)
Aug. 17, 1998 – Name changed to Leader Capital Corp.; basis 1 new for 2 old shs. ■

Q & A Communications Inc. (Ont. July 6, 1983 amalg.)
Nov. 5, 1997 – Name changed to Q & A Capital Inc.; basis 1 new for 5 old shs. ■

Q Battery Metals Corp. (B.C. Nov. 18, 2016)
Mar. 22, 2024 – Name changed to Q Precious & Battery Metals Corp. (see FPsurvey - Mines & Energy)

Q Broadcasting Ltd. (B.C. 1959)
June 1, 1978 – Offer to purchase 60,000 cl. A shs. at $12 per sh. made by W. E. Pellman. As a result, became 99% owned by the officers and directors.

Q Energy Limited (Alta. June 10, 1997)
Nov. 20, 2000 – Acquired by EOG Resources Canada Inc. for $0.60 per sh.

Q-Gold Resources Ltd. (Alta. Mar. 25, 1998)
Dec. 30, 2011 – Continued into British Columbia.
Oct. 3, 2018 – Continued into Ontario. (see FPsurvey - Mines & Energy)

Q Investments Ltd. (Bermuda Jan. 19, 2001)
Dec. 6, 2018 – Name changed to Organic Flower Investments Group Inc. and continued into British Columbia. ■

Q/Media Services Corporation (B.C. Sept. 29, 1986)
Dec. 19, 2002 – Vancouver-based Deloitte & Touche Inc. was appointed receiver/manager of the company's assets. The receiver intended to sell the assets with the operations continuing on a normal course basis. The directors and officers of the company resigned.
June 2003 – Administration was almost complete as the assets had been sold and a distribution had been made to secured creditors only; there were no funds available for unsecured creditors or shldrs.
May 6, 2004 – Receiver discharged.

Q-Tel Wireless Inc. (Alta. June 27, 1988)
July 2, 2007 – Dissolved and struck from registry.

Q-Zar Inc. (N.B. May 4, 1995)
Aug. 20, 1997 – Name changed to Q-Entertainment Inc. (see FPsurvey - Industrials)

Q4 Inc. (Ont. May 13, 2016 amalg.)
Feb. 5, 2024 – Acquired by Sumeru Equity Partners LLC; basis Cdn$6.05 cash per sh.

Q4 Web Systems Inc. (Ont. May 13, 2016 amalg.)
Mar. 2, 2016 – Name changed to Q4 Inc. following amalgamation with 1955312 Ontario Inc. ■

Q9 Networks Inc. (Ont. June 28, 1995)
Oct. 29, 2008 – Acquired by CDC Acquisition II Corp. for $17.05 per sh.

QC Copper & Gold Inc. (B.C. Feb. 1, 2018)
Dec. 6, 2024 – Name changed to XXIX Metal Corp. (see FPsurvey - Mines & Energy)

QCC Technologies Inc. (Alta. Apr. 30, 1998)
Sept. 22, 2005 – Name changed to Cordy Oilfield Services Inc. following acquisition of several oil and gas site preparation and clean-up companies. ■

QCI Industries Limited (Ont. 1928)
Dec. 13, 1978 – Formed Fincorp Capital Ltd. in Ontario on amalgamation with 364895 Ontario Ltd.; basis 10 cl. A pfce. and 3 cl. B pfce. for each 10 cl. A pfce. or com shs. ■

QCTV Ltd. (Alta. 1969)
Oct. 1986 – As of became a wholly owned subsid. of Groupe Vidéotron Ltée.

QDM Ventures Ltd. (B.C. Dec. 10, 1999)
Sept. 25, 2001 – Name changed to California Exploration Ltd. and continued into Yukon. ■

QE2 Acquisition Corp. (Alta. Sept. 19, 2012)
Aug. 24, 2015 – Name changed to Distinct Infrastructure Group Inc. following reverse takeover acquisition of DistinctTech Inc. ■

Q.E.X. Resources Inc. (Que. June 11, 1957)
Feb. 18, 2013 – Dissolved and struck from register.

QGX Ltd. (Ont. Aug. 1, 2002 amalg.)
Oct. 20, 2008 – Acquired by Mongolia Holdings Corp., an indirect subsid. of Kerry Holdings Limited, for $5 per sh.

QHR Corporation (Can. July 8, 2013)
Oct. 14, 2016 – Acquired by Loblaw Companies Limited for $3.10 per sh.

QHR Technologies Inc. (B.C. May 20, 1988)
July 8, 2013 – Name changed to QHR Corporation and continued into Canada. ■

QI Systems Inc. (B.C. July 4, 1978)
July 1, 2006 – Continued into Delaware.

QI Technologies Corp. (B.C. July 4, 1978)
May 25, 2001 – Name changed to QI Systems Inc. ■

QIS Ventures Inc. (Alta. May 2, 2000)
Oct. 23, 2001 – Name changed to Quorum Information Technologies Inc. (see FPsurvey - Industrials)

QIT-Fer et Titane Inc. (Que. 1957)
Jan. 1, 2013 – Name changed to Rio Tinto Fer et Titane inc.

QLT Inc. (B.C. Feb. 3, 1981)
Nov. 29, 2016 – Name changed to Novelion Therapeutics Inc. following acquisition of Aegerion Pharmaceuticals, Inc. ■

QLT PhotoTherapeutics Inc. (B.C. Feb. 3, 1981)
May 26, 2000 – Name changed to QLT Inc. ■

Q.M.G. Holdings Inc. (Ont. 1943)
Feb. 19, 1990 – Dissolved.

Q.M.I. Minerals Ltd. (Can. 1945)
1968 – Merged into Indusmin Ltd.; basis 1 new for 5 old shs.

QMI Seismic Inc. (B.C. Oct. 16, 2009)
Sept. 6, 2011 – Name changed to ME Resource Corp. ■

QMX Gold Corporation (Ont. Feb. 16, 2004)
Apr. 7, 2021 – Acquired by Eldorado Gold Corporation for Cdn$0.30 per sh. consisting of Cdn$0.075 cash and 0.01523 Eldorado com. sh.

QPX Minerals Inc. (B.C. 1987)
Oct. 6, 1991 – Acquired by Rea Gold Corporation; basis 1 Rea Gold sh. for 3.4 QPX shs.

QR Canada Capital Inc. (Can. Apr. 16, 1996)
Sept. 10, 2003 – Name changed to Section Rouge Media Inc. following Qualifying Transaction reverse takeover acquisition of Section Rouge Media Inc.; basis 1 new for 2 old shs. ■

QRS Capital Corp. (Ont. Nov. 23, 2007)
July 9, 2013 – Name changed to Sendero Mining Corp. pursuant to acquisition of Halo Resources Ltd.; basis 0.635516 new for 1 old sh. (see FPsurvey - Mines & Energy)

QSP Ltd. (Can. 1943)
Mar. 1977 – Proposal made to pay its unsecured creditors 25¢ on the dollar over 2.5 yr. period. In mid-1977, banks took over certain co. assets.
Sept. 1977 – Sidbec, a provincially owned Crown corp., purchased co.'s smelter in Longueuil, Que., for $27.1 million in a sheriff sale.

QSR Limited (Ont. Sept. 8, 1993 amalg.)
June 25, 1999 – Name changed to Coniagas Resources Limited. ■

QUNO Corporation (Que. 1912)
Mar. 6, 1996 – All o/s com. and non-vtg. shs. acquired by Donohue Acquisition Inc., an indirect wholly owned subsid. of Donohue Inc.; basis (i) $20.31; (ii)0.29 cl. A sub. vtg. shs. of Donohue, and (iii) $5.26 principal amount of sr. unsecured 8% notes of Donohue, consisting of $2.63 principal amount of ser. A notes (payable Mar. 1, 1997) and 42.63 principal amount of ser. B notes (payable Mar. 1, 1998). (see Donohue Inc.)

QWIP Systems Inc. (Alta. May 7, 1987)
Dec. 7, 2006 – Amalgamated with Cantronic Systems Inc.; basis 0.9 Cantronic shs. for 1 QWIP sh. (see Cantronic Systems Inc.)

QX Metals Corp. (B.C. Apr. 13, 1995)
Aug. 25, 2020 – Name changed to Gold Bull Resources Corp. ■

QData Systems Inc. (B.C. July 2, 1985)
Sept. 19, 1991 – Name changed to Consolidated QData Systems Inc.; basis 1 new for 3 old shs. ■

Qeva Group Inc. (Alta. June 9, 1997)
Sept. 6, 2006 – Formed Excelsior Energy Limited in Alberta on amalgamation with Excelsior Energy Limited with Qeva the deemed acquiror; basis 1.115261 new for 1 Excelsior sh. and 1 new for 3 Qeva shs. ■

Q.Media Software Corporation (B.C. Sept. 29, 1986)
Jan. 29, 1998 – Name changed to Q/Media Services Corporation; basis 1 new for 5 old shs. ■

Qnetix Inc. (Alta. Oct. 2, 1995)
Dec. 3, 2002 – Acquired by Charon Systems, Inc.; basis unknown.

Quaco Bay Mining Corp. Ltd. (N.B. 1955)
Dec. 1959 – Charter cancelled.

Quad Energy Development Corporation (Alta. Jan. 28, 1987)
June 5, 1992 – Name changed to Jardin Financial Group Inc. ■

Quadex Resources Ltd. (B.C. 1983)
Dec. 6, 1985 – Name changed to F.C. Financial Corp. ■

Quadra FNX Mining Ltd. (B.C. May 15, 2002)
Mar. 5, 2012 – Name changed to KGHM International Ltd. following acquisition by KGHM Polska Miedz S.A. ■

Quadra Leases Ltd. (Alta. Aug. 31, 1950)
1951 – Acquired by Triad Oil Co. Ltd.; basis 2.3 new for 1 old sh. (see Triad Oil Co. Ltd.)

Quadra Logic Technologies Inc. (B.C. Feb. 3, 1981)
July 28, 1995 – Name changed to QLT PhotoTherapeutics Inc. ■

Quadra Mining Ltd. (B.C. May 15, 2002)
May 28, 2010 – Name changed to Quadra FNX Mining Ltd. pursuant to acquisition of FNX Mining Company Inc. ■

Quadra Properties Corporation (Alta. Aug. 5, 1997)
Dec. 14, 2000 – Formed Digital Artisans Guild Inc. in Alberta on Qualifying Transaction amalgamation with Digital Artisans Guild Inc. for $6,650,000. ■

Quadra Resources Corp. (Alta. July 12, 1994)
Aug. 11, 2005 – Plan of Arrangement acquisition by Arsenal Energy Inc.; basis 0.025 new Arsenal com. sh. for 1 old Quadra com. sh., and 0.025 new Arsenal warrant and broker warrant for 1 old Quadra warrant and broker warrant, respectively. (see Arsenal Energy Inc.)

Quadra Resources Ltd. (B.C. May 15, 2002)
Jan. 9, 2003 – Name changed to Quadra Mining Ltd. ■

Quadrant Capital Corporation (Alta. 1986)
Feb. 1, 1988 – Formed Bridges Energy Inc. in Alberta on reverse takeover acquisition of and amalgamation with Bridges Energy Resources Ltd. and 320642 Alberta Inc. ■

Quadrant Financial Corporation (B.C. July 6, 1983)
Nov. 12, 1999 – Acquired by Walker's Hook International, Ltd., a Delaware co.; basis 1 new Walker sh. for 1 old Quadrant sh.

Quadrate Explorations Ltd. (Ont. 1967)
Mar. 1976 – Charter cancelled.

Quadron Cannatech Corporation (B.C. Nov. 7, 2011)
June 18, 2019 – Acquired by World Class Extractions Inc.; basis 25¢ cash per sh. (see World Class Extractions Inc.)

Quadron Capital Corporation (B.C. Nov. 7, 2011)
May 10, 2017 – Name changed to Quadron Cannatech Corporation. ■

Quadron Resources Ltd. (Alta. June 8, 1993 amalg.)
June 28, 1995 – Acquired by HCO Energy Ltd.; basis 1 HCO ser. B sh. for 1 Quadron pref. sh. and 0.625 HCO com. shs. for 1 Quadron com. sh. (see HCO Energy Ltd.)

Quadroyal Mining Co. Ltd. (Ont. 1969)
May 14, 1975 – Charter cancelled.

Quaich Oil Corp. Ltd. (Ont. 1946)
1970 – Struck off register.

Quail Ridge Capital Corp. (Alta. Sept. 2, 1999)
Nov. 14, 2000 – Formed Performance Optician Software Corporation in Alberta on amalgamation with Performance Optician Software Corporation. (see FPsurvey - Industrials)

Quail Ridge Winery Napa Valley Inc. (B.C. Dec. 4, 1985)
June 13, 1990 – Name changed to Redonda Industries Corporation; basis 1 new for 3 old shs. ■

Quaker Energy Inc. (B.C. Jan. 31, 1961)
Aug. 18, 1983 – Name changed to Quaker Resources Inc. ■

The Quaker Oats Company of Canada Limited (Can. 1943)
1978 – Continued into Ontario.

Quaker Resources Canada Ltd. (B.C. Jan. 31, 1961)
Apr. 28, 1987 – Name changed to SPI Safety Packaging International Ltd. ■

Quaker Resources Inc. (B.C. Jan. 31, 1961)
Sept. 14, 1984 – Name changed to Comco Mining and Smelting Corporation. ■

Quality Dino Entertainment Ltd. (Man. Dec. 6, 1984)
Mar. 30, 1998 – Placed into receivership and Mintz & Partners Limited of Toronto was appointed receiver and manager following an order of the Ontario Court (General Division).
June 16, 1998 – Mintz & Partners were discharged as receiver and manager following an order of the Ontario Court (General Division). Following terms of the June court order, the assets of Quality were vested in the Hunter Group (as defined in the court order), subject to prior ranking claims named in said court order. There were no funds available for unsecured creditors or shldrs.

Quality Learning Systems (International) Inc. (B.C. Mar. 14, 1986)
May 27, 1996 – Name changed to Carta Resources Ltd. ■

Quality Quest Systems Inc. (B.C. 1984)
July 30, 1993 – Dissolved and struck off register.

Quality Steels (Canada) Limited (Ont. 1947)
Nov. 1948 – Operations suspended.
1952 – Plant and equipment sold. After prior claims, $99,584, or $24.89 per $100 par value available through Guaranty Trust Co. of Canada, Toronto, for holders of 5% first mtge. bonds.

Quanta Resources Inc. (B.C. Mar. 6, 2009)
Mar. 4, 2019 – Struck from register and dissolved.

Quantitative Alpha Trading Inc. (B.C. Sept. 15, 1987)
Dec. 9, 2011 – Continued into Ontario. (see FPsurvey - Industrials)

Quantum Blockchain Technologies Ltd. (Alta. Feb. 5, 2018)
Aug. 27, 2021 – Name changed to Ocumetics Technology Corp. pursuant to the Qualifying Transaction reverse takeover acquisition of (old) Ocumetics Technology Corp.

and concurrent amalgamation of (old) Ocumetics with wholly owned 2321205 Alberta Ltd. (and continued as Ocumetics Technology Inc.). (see FPsurvey - Industrials)

Quantum Cobalt Corp. (B.C. Aug. 6, 2010)
Mar. 23, 2021 – Name changed to Quantum Battery Metals Corp. (see FPsurvey - Mines & Energy)

Quantum Energy Corporation (B.C. 1981)
Dec. 9, 1985 – Name changed to Granville Island Brewing Company Ltd. following acquisition of the limited partnership entity called Granville Island Brewery. ■

Quantum International Income Corp. (Ont. Aug. 15, 1995 amalg.)
Feb. 20, 2019 – Name changed to Seven Aces Limited. ■

Quantum Numbers Corp. (Ont. July 19, 2007)
June 14, 2021 – Name changed to Quantum eMotion Corp. (see FPsurvey - Industrials)

Quantum Rare Earth Developments Corp. (B.C. Feb. 27, 1987)
Mar. 4, 2013 – Name changed to Niocorp Developments Ltd. (see FPsurvey - Mines & Energy)

Quantum Resource Corp. (B.C. 1987)
Apr. 25, 1991 – Name changed to International Exotic Motors Corp.; basis 1 new for 2 old shs. ■

Quantus Developments Ltd. (B.C. Aug. 5, 1963)
Apr. 18, 1986 – Name changed to C.T.I. Technologies Corp. ■

Quarry Capital Corp. (Alta. May 18, 1995)
Apr. 24, 2001 – Name changed to Quarry Oil & Gas Ltd. ■

Quarry Oil & Gas Ltd. (Alta. May 18, 1995)
Jan. 12, 2005 – Plan of Arrangement acquisition by Assure Energy, Inc.; basis 0.36 new Assure sh. for 1 old Quarry sh.

Quartet Energy Resources Ltd. (B.C. 1969)
1981 – Continued into Ontario.
Mar. 23, 1984 – Name changed to Oiltex International Ltd. ■

Quartet Resources Limited (Hong Kong Aug. 4, 2011)
Oct. 27, 2015 – Name changed to Goldbelt Empires Limited following Qualifying Transaction acquisition of Goldbelt International Limited. ■

The Quartex Corporation (Ont. June 30, 1986)
June 28, 1994 – Name changed to PC DOCS Group International Inc. ■

Quartz Creek Gold Mines (B.C.) Inc. (B.C. 1983)
Dec. 12, 1989 – Name changed to Pilot Peak Gold Inc.; basis 1 new for 3 old shs. ■

Quartz-Crystals Mining Corp. of Canada Ltd. (Ont. 1944)
Nov. 1954 – Charter cancelled.

Quartz Mountain Gold Corp. (B.C. Aug. 3, 1982)
Nov. 5, 1997 – Name changed to Quartz Mountain Resources Ltd.; basis 1 new for 10 old shs. (see FPsurvey - Mines & Energy)

Quasar Petroleum Ltd. (Alta. 1969)
1982 – Under a takeover offer of $3.00 per share Oakwood Petroleums Ltd. completed the acquisition of all o/s shs. during.

Quaterra Resources Inc. (B.C. May 11, 1993)
Nov. 22, 2021 – Name changed to Lion Copper and Gold Corp. (see FPsurvey - Mines & Energy)

Quatsino Copper-Gold Mines Limited (B.C. 1928)
May 26, 1983 – Struck off register.

Quattro Exploration and Production Ltd. (Alta. Feb. 21, 1997)
Feb. 13, 2017 – Placed into receivership by primary lender, The Business Development Bank of Canada, appointing Hardie & Kelly Inc. as receiver and manager.

Quattro Resources Ltd. (B.C. Sept. 8, 1987)
July 31, 2001 – Name changed to Aldershot Resources Ltd.; basis 1 new for 10 old shs. ■

Que-On Mines Ltd. (Ont. 1936)
May 1967 – Charter cancelled; distributed one free sh. and one escrowed sh. of Western Quebec Mines Co. Ltd. for 4 old shs.

Que West Resources Ltd. (B.C. 1983)
Nov. 7, 1989 – Amalgamated with Channel Resources Ltd.; basis 1 Channel sh. for 6.5 Que West shs. (see Channel Resources Ltd.)

Quebec Antimony Mines Ltd. (Que. 1970)
Dec. 14, 1985 – Charter cancelled.

Quebec Asbestos Corporation (Que. 1924)
Charter cancelled.

Quebec Ascot Copper Corp. Ltd. (Que. 1949)
July 15, 1972 – Charter cancelled.

Quebec Bachelor Mining Corp. (Que. 1957)
Dec. 5, 1981 – Charter cancelled.

Quebec Beryllium Ltd. (Que. 1953)
May 15, 1982 – Charter cancelled.

Quebec Cartier Mining Company (Que. 1957)
2008 – Name changed to ArcelorMittal Mines Canada.

Quebec Chibougamau Goldfields Ltd. (Que. 1950)
Aug. 27, 1969 – Name changed to Allied Mining Corporation; basis 1 new for 5 old shs. ■

Quebec Clay Mining Ltd. (Que. 1959)
Jan. 1974 – Charter cancelled.

Quebec Cobalt & Exploration Ltd. (Que. 1987 amalg.)
July 1, 1989 – Amalgamated into Consolidated Thompson-Lundmark Gold Mines Limited; basis 1 new for 2 old shs. (see Consolidated Thompson-Lundmark Gold Mines Limited)

Quebec Columbium Ltd. (Que. Apr. 25, 1956)
Dec. 21, 2010 – Dissolved and stuck from register.

Quebec Copper Corp. (Que. 1950)
1960 – Name changed to Sullico Mines Ltd.; basis 1 new for 40 old shs. ■

Quebec Developers & Smelters Limited (Que. 1953)
June 1974 – Charter cancelled.

Quebec Explorers Corporation Ltd. (Que. June 11, 1957)
Feb. 1, 1995 – Name changed to Q.E.X. Resources Inc.; basis 1 new for 5 old shs. ■

Quebec Explorers Ltd. (Que. 1937)
1957 – Acquired by Quebec Explorers Corporation Ltd. (see Quebec Explorers Corporation Ltd.)

Quebec Gold Belt Mines Limited (Can. 1932)
Nov. 14, 1983 – Amalgamated with Sigma Mines (Canada) Ltd., a wholly owned subsid. of Sigma Mines (Quebec) Ltd. Each 7 shs. of Quebec Gold exch. for 1 sh. of Sigma (Quebec) Ltd.

Quebec Gold Mining Corp. (Que. 1933)
Jan. 1951 – Name changed to Consolidated Quebec Gold Mining & Metals Corp. ■

Quebec Gold Rocks Exploration Ltd. (Que.)
Apr. 1974 – Charter cancelled.

Quebec Industrial Minerals Corp. (Que. 1956)
Apr. 14, 1973 – Charter cancelled.

Quebec Iron and Titanium Corporation (Que. 1957)
1979 – Name changed to QIT-Fer et Titane Inc. ■

Quebec Labrador Development Co. Ltd. (Que. 1947)
1963 – Name changed to Salem Exploration Ltd.; basis 1 new for 7.5 old shs. ■

Quebec Lithium Corporation (Que. 1952)
1969 – Merged into Sullivan Mining Group Ltd.; basis 1 new for 2 old shs.

Quebec Manitou Mines Limited (Ont. 1936)
Oct. 2, 1979 – Amalgamated with Thermo-Solar Inc. to form Petro-Sun Inc.; basis 1 new for 4 old shs.

Quebec Mattagami Minerals Limited (Ont. 1943)
Aug. 31, 1977 – Name changed to Q.M.G. Holdings Inc. ■

Quebec Metallurgical Industries Ltd. (Can. 1945)
1963 – Name changed to Q.M.I. Minerals Ltd.; basis 1 new for 5 old shs. ■

Quebec Mining Exploration Company (Que. July 15, 1965)
1974 – Name changed to Société québécoise d'exploration minière - SOQUEM. ■

Quebec Mining Explorers Ltd. (Que. 1937)
1957 – Charter cancelled.

Quebec Natural Gas Corporation (Que. June 15, 1955)
Oct. 4, 1969 – Name changed to Gaz Métropolitain, inc. ■

Quebec Nickel Corp. Ltd. (Ont. 1952)
1955 – Merged into Eastern Mining & Smelting Corp. Ltd.; basis 1 new for 3 old shs.

Quebec North Mines Ltd. (Que. 1953)
Aug. 1974 – Charter cancelled.

Quebec Oil Development Ltd. (Que. 1946)
Assets acquired by New Associated Developments Ltd.; basis 1 new for 17 old shs. (see New Associated Developments Limited)

Quebec Ore Zone Limited (Que. 1944)
Apr. 13, 1974 – Charter cancelled.

Quebec Pegmatite Holdings Corp. (B.C. Jan. 27, 2017)
July 2, 2024 – Name changed to LaFleur Minerals Inc. (see FPsurvey - Mines & Energy)

Quebec Power Company (Que. 1915)
1963 – Purchased by Hydro-Quebec. Com. shldrs. received $37 per sh. Funded debt assumed by Quebec Hydro.

Quebec Precious Metals Corporation (B.C. Feb. 1, 1984)
May 1, 2025 – Acquired by Fury Gold Mines Limited; basis 0.0741 Fury shs. for 1 Quebec Precious sh.

Quebec Pulp and Paper Corp. (Que. 1927)
Oct. 1942 – Placed into bankruptcy by Que. Govt.
1949 – Que. Govt. acquired co.'s assets for $1,500,000. Shldrs. received $23 for 1 old pref. sh.

Quebec Silica Mine Ltd. (Que. 1958)
May 22, 1982 – Charter cancelled.

Quebec Silica Resources Corp. (B.C. May 22, 2018)
Jan. 12, 2023 – Name changed to Quebec Innovative Materials Corp. (see FPsurvey - Mines & Energy)

Quebec Smelting & Refining Corp. (Que. 1937)
1947 – Assets acquired by Quebec Smelting & Refining Ltd.; basis 60 new for 1 old sh.

Quebec Smelting & Refining Ltd. (Que. 1947)
1965 – Name changed to Consolidated Quebec Smelting & Refining Ltd.; basis 1 new for 5 old shs. ■

Quebec Sturgeon River Mines Limited (Ont. Aug. 22, 1934)
Sept. 21, 1993 – Amalgamated with The Coniagas Mines, Limited, Garrison Creek Consolidated Mines Ltd. and Anglo Dominion Gold Exploration Limited to form QSR Limited; basis 32 new for 100 Coniagas Mines, shs., 7 new for 1,000 Garrison Creek shs., 18 new for 100 Anglo Dominion shs. and 20 new for 100 Quebec Sturgeon shs. (see QSR Limited)

Quebec Tantalum & Lithium Mining Co. Limited (Que. 1953)
1958 – Distribution of 42¢ per sh.
Aug. 15, 1981 – Charter cancelled.

Québec-Téléphone (Que. June 7, 1927)
May 17, 2001 – Name changed to TELUS Communications (Québec) Inc.

Quebec Telephone & Power Corporation (Que. June 7, 1927)
Aug. 1947 – Name changed to Québec-Téléphone. ■

Quebec Terminals Ltd. (Que. Feb. 29, 1952; via letters patent)
Apr. 3, 1969 – Name changed to Logistec Corporation. ■

Quebec Tungsten Ltd. (Que. 1954)
Sept. 30, 1978 – Charter cancelled.

Quebec Uranium Mining Corporation (Que. 1968)
Jan. 1, 1980 – Amalgamated to form Les Mines Cuvier Inc. - Cuvier Mines Inc.; basis 1 new for 10 old shs.

Quebec Yellowknife Gold Mines Ltd. (Que. 1944)
1955 – Name changed to Consolidated Quebec Yellowknife Mines Ltd.; basis 1 new for 4 old shs. ■

Quebecor Printing Capital Corporation (Can.)
Apr. 28, 2000 – Name changed to Quebecor World Capital Corporation.

Quebecor Printing Inc. (Can. Feb. 23, 1989)
Apr. 28, 2000 – Name changed to Quebecor World Inc. ■

Quebecor World Inc. (Can. Feb. 23, 1989)
Aug. 26, 2009 – Name changed to World Color Press Inc. ■

The QuébecTel Group Inc. (Que. June 7, 1927)
July 30, 1968 – Continued into Quebec.
June 7, 2000 – Acquired by TELUS Corporation effective Jun. 7, 2000 for $23 per sh.
Apr. 2, 2001 – Name changed to TELUS Québec Inc.

Quebelle Mines Ltd. (Que. 1946)
July 1972 – Charter cancelled.

Qued Resources Corporation (B.C. 1979)
Apr. 23, 1986 – Name changed to Arwick International Resources Ltd.; basis 1 new for 3 old shs. ■

Quedon Copper Uranium Corp. (Que. 1954)
Oct. 1974 – Charter cancelled.

Quedor Red Lake Mines Ltd. (Ont. 1943)
Nov. 4, 1947 – Name changed to Lynnita Consolidated Gold Mines Ltd. ■

Queen Charlotte Peat Ltd. (B.C. Apr. 17, 1969)
Aug. 2, 1979 – Name changed to Impact Resources Inc. ■

Queen Lebel Gold Mining Co. (Ont. 1921)
Apr. 1934 – Continued into Ontario.
Aug. 7, 1934 – Name changed to Lakeside Kirkland Gold Mines Ltd. ■

Queen Street Camera Inc. (Ont. 1987 amalg.)
Dec. 1989 – Placed into receivership. Peat Marwick Thorne appointed receiver.
May 1990 – Virtually all assets liquidated either by the closing of stores or selling them as going concerns.
June 1992 – Creditors had suffered a substantial shortfall and there was no distribution to shldrs.
Sept. 17, 1994 – Dissolved.

Queen Street Entertainment Capital Inc. (Ont. Apr. 6, 2004)
Aug. 16, 2007 – Name changed to Knightscove Media Corp. (see FPsurvey - Industrials)

Queensland Acceptance Corp. Ltd. (Ont. 1963 amalg.)
Nov. 25, 1970 – Dissolved.

Queensland Explorations Ltd. (Ont. 1956)
1963 – Merged with Brunette-Porcupine Gold Mines Ltd. to form Queensland Acceptance Corporation Ltd.; basis 1 new for 10 old shs.

Queensland Gold Hills Corp. (B.C. May 6, 2010)
Jan. 9, 2023 – Name changed to Q2 Metals Corp. (see FPsurvey - Mines & Energy)

Queensland Minerals Ltd. (B.C. Feb. 15, 1996)
Jan. 30, 2004 – Continued into Yukon.
Apr. 14, 2004 – Continued into British Columbia.
May 4, 2011 – Name changed to Dunav Resources Ltd. ■

Queenstake Resources Limited (B.C. May 3, 1977)
June 24, 1999 – Continued into Yukon. (see Queenstake Resources Ltd.)
July 23, 1999 – Amalgamated with Santa Cruz Gold Inc. to form Queenstake Resources Ltd.; basis 0.1035 new for 1 Santa Cruz sh. and 0.4993 new for 1 Queenstake Resources sh. (see Queenstake Resources Ltd.)

Queenstake Resources Ltd. (Yuk. July 19, 1999 amalg.)
July 10, 2006 – Continued into British Columbia. (see Yukon-Nevada Gold Corp.)
June 20, 2007 – Acquired by YGC Resources Ltd. which changed its name to Yukon-Nevada Gold Corp.; basis 1 Yukon-Nevada Gold com. sh. for 10 Queenstake com. shs. (see Yukon-Nevada Gold Corp.)

Queenston Gas & Oil Co. Ltd. (Ont. May 1945)
Struck off register.

Queenston Gold Mines Ltd. (Ont. July 18, 1941)
Apr. 23, 1985 – Continued into Canada.
Jan. 1, 1990 – Formed Queenston Mining Inc. in Canada on amalgamation with HSK Minerals Limited; basis 0.434 new for 1 HSK sh. and 1 new for 1 Queenston Gold sh. ■

Queenston Mining Inc. (Can. Jan. 1, 1990 amalg.)
Jan. 3, 2013 – Acquired by Osisko Mining Corporation; basis 0.611 Osisko shs. for 1 Queenston sh. (see Osisko Mining Corporation)
Jan. 16, 2013 – Name changed to Osisko Mining Ltd. (see Osisko Mining Corporation)

Queensway Financial Holdings Limited (Ont. Feb. 9, 1993)
May 18, 2001 – Placed into receivership. Ernst & Young Inc. was appointed receiver.

Queensway Mines Ltd. (Ont. 1961)
1969 – Merged into Alchib Developments Ltd.; basis 6 new for 100 old shs.

Queenswear (Canada) Ltd. (Can. 1969)
Sept. 30, 1975 – Quegroup Investments Ltd. offered to purchase all o/s shs. at $3.50 per sh. To Dec. 5, 1975, Quegroup had acquired approximately 95% of the shs.

Quejo Mines Ltd. (Ont. Mar. 21, 1945)
Apr. 1980 – Name changed to Edomar Resources Inc.; basis 1 new for 10 old shs. ■

Quemaque Explorers Ltd. (Que. 1947)
Nov. 5, 1977 – Dissolved.

Quemont Mining Corporation Ltd. (Can. 1928)
Apr. 1968 – Assets acquired by Kerr Addison Mines Limited; basis 2 new for 3 old shs. (see Kerr Addison Mines Limited)

Quendale Capital Corp. (B.C. Feb. 1, 2018)
Dec. 15, 2020 – Name changed to Prairie Storm Resources Corp. pursuant to Qualifying Transaction reverse takeover acquisition of Prairie Storm Energy Corp., and concurrent amalgamation of Prairie Storm Energy with wholly owned 2291479 Alberta Ltd. ■

Quennada Mines Ltd. (Ont. 1950)
1956 – Charter cancelled.

Quentin Ventures Ltd. (B.C. June 18, 2014)
May 19, 2016 – Name changed to Identillect Technologies Corp. following reverse takeover acquisition of (old) Identillect Technologies Corp. (see FPsurvey - Industrials)

Quesabe Mines Limited (Ont. July 6, 1945)
Apr. 14, 1953 – Name changed to Brunston Mining Co. Ltd.; basis 1 new for 2 old shs. ■

Quesada Resources Limited (Alta. Sept. 11, 1986)
Jan. 5, 1993 – Name changed to Advanced Material Resources Limited. ■

Quesnel Indian Oils Ltd. (B.C.)
1957 – Struck off register.

Quest Capital Corporation (B.C. May 26, 1971)
Oct. 28, 1996 – Amalgamated with Epoch Capital Corporation to form a new co. with the same name Quest Capital Corporation. (see Quest Capital Corporation)

Quest Capital Corporation (B.C. Oct. 27, 1980)
Aug. 22, 2007 – Continued into Canada.
Sept. 8, 2010 – Name changed to Sprott Resource Lending Corp. ■

Quest Capital Corporation (B.C. Oct. 25, 1996 amalg.)
Oct. 31, 1996 – Acquired Cody Energy Canada, Ltd.
Dec. 17, 1996 – Name changed to Quest Oil & Gas Inc. ■

Quest Energy Inc. (Alta. June 25, 1992)
Dec. 2, 2000 – Struck from registry and dissolved.

Quest International Resources Corporation (B.C. Dec. 14, 1989 amalg.)
Feb. 12, 1997 – Continued into Yukon.
June 16, 1999 – Name changed to Standard Mining Corporation; basis 1 new for 5 old shs. ■

Quest Investment Corporation (B.C. July 4, 2002 amalg.)
July 4, 2003 – Merged with Viceroy Resource Corporation (1 new for 3 old shs. plus 1 new ViceroyEx sh. for 10 old shs. and 1 new SpectrumGold sh. for 30 old shs.), Arapaho Capital Corp. (863,857 shs. on sale of subsid.) and Avatar Petroleum Inc. (0.2825 for 1) to continue as Quest Capital Corp. (formerly Viceroy); basis 1.0514 new cl. A or 1.0514 new cl. B Quest Capital shs. for 1 cl. A or 1 old cl. B Quest Investment sh. (see Quest Capital Corporation)

Quest Oil & Gas Inc. (B.C. Oct. 25, 1996 amalg.)
May 7, 1997 – All o/s com. shs. acquired by EnerMark Income Fund; basis $2.35 per com. sh. or 0.347 of a trust unit of EnerMark for 1 com. sh. of Quest; 15¢ per wt. or 0.022 of a trust unit of EnerMark for 1 old wt. of Quest. (see EnerMark Income Fund)

Quest Rare Minerals Ltd. (Can. June 6, 2007)
July 2017 – Filed a notice of intention to make a restructuring proposal under the Bankruptcy and Insolvency Act (BIA) and PricewaterhouseCoopers Inc. was appointed proposal trustee.
Jan. 25, 2018 – Secured and unsecured creditors accepted the proposal. Secured creditors would be paid in full. Unsecured creditors with claims equal to or less than $1,000 would receive payment in full up to $1,000; unsecured creditors with claims exceeding $1,000 would receive an amount equal to $1,000 plus a portion equal to 14% of the amount of the claim that exceeds $1,000 and an amount equal to 50% of the portion of the tax credit receivable which exceeds $1,900,000, to be distributed pro rata amongst said creditors in accordance with the portion of their claim that exceeds $1,000. All existing securities would be cancelled.
Apr. 4, 2018 – Court approval for the reorganization proposal was received. Blarney Mining Consortium Group Corp. acquired all of the company's assets for new shares of the company and all the previously issued and outstanding securities were cancelled. Additionally, the company ceased to be a reporting issuer.

Quest Technologies Inc. (Alta. June 25, 1992)
Feb. 14, 1996 – Name changed to Quest Energy Inc. ■

Quest Uranium Corporation (Can. June 6, 2007)
Apr. 26, 2010 – Name changed to Quest Rare Minerals Ltd. ■

Quest Ventures Inc. (Wyo. Apr. 24, 1998)
Apr. 24, 2006 – Name changed to Dorato Resources Inc.; basis 1 new for 2 old shs. ■

Quest Yellowknife Ltd. (Ont. Jan. 23, 1945)
June 16, 1983 – Name changed to Conquest Yellowknife Resources Limited; basis 1 new for 5 old shs. ■

QuestAir Technologies Inc. (B.C. July 19, 1996)
Nov. 1, 1999 – Continued into Canada.
June 12, 2009 – Formed Xebec Adsorption Inc. in Canada pursuant to reverse takeover acquisition of and amalgamation with Xebec Adsorption Inc. ■

Questar Exploration Inc. (Alta. Jan. 24, 1991)
Dec. 17, 1997 – Amalgamated with 752573 Alberta Ltd., a wholly owned subsid., for $1.16 per sh. Co. now private.

Questar Resources Corp. (Alta. Mar. 29, 1993)
Apr. 9, 1996 – Amalgamated with KACEE Exploration Inc. (1 new for 1 old sh.) to form a new co. called Questar Exploration Inc.; basis 1 new Questar Exploration sh. and 0.0898 of a warrant for 2 old Questar Resources com. shs. (see Questar Exploration Inc.)

QuestCap Inc. (Can. Oct. 9, 2009)
Dec. 29, 2020 – Name changed to Medivolve Inc. (see FPsurvey - Industrials)

QuesTec Imaging Inc. (B.C. 1987)
1998 – Continued into Wyoming.

Quested Mining Corporation Ltd. (B.C. 1970)
Sept. 19, 1977 – Dissolved.

Questerre Energy Corporation (Alta. Oct. 25, 1971)
July 13, 1990 – Continued into British Columbia.
Dec. 5, 2000 – Continued into Alberta. (see FPsurvey - Mines & Energy)

Questex Gold & Copper Ltd. (B.C. Oct. 9, 2009)
June 3, 2022 – Acquired by Skeena Resources Limited; basis 0.0367 Skeena shs. plus Cdn$0.65 cash per sh. for 1 Questex Gold sh.

Questfire Energy Corp. (Alta. Jan. 15, 2010)
Nov. 16, 2017 – Placed into receivership following a demand by lenders for repayment of $34,000,000 in credit facilities. PricewaterhouseCoopers Inc. appointed receiver and all directors resigned.

Questmont Mines Ltd. (B.C. 1972)
Oct. 18, 1985 – Name changed to Centurion Minerals Ltd.; basis 1 new for 2 old shs. ■

Quetario Prospectors Ltd. (Ont. Feb. 14, 1927)
May 1949 – Charter cancelled.

Quetide Mining Co. Ltd. (Ont. 1949)
Dec. 9, 1969 – Charter cancelled.

Quetzal Energy Ltd. (Ont. Oct. 15, 2004)
June 7, 2012 – Name changed to Santa Maria Petroleum Inc.; basis 1 new for 10 old shs. ■

Quetzal Studios Investments Inc. (Can. June 26, 1997)
Dec. 16, 1998 – Name changed to Fun Key Studios Inc. following Major Transaction acquisition of 2742471 Canada Inc. doing business as Fun Key Creative Systems for total consideration of $2,160,000. ■

Quia Resources Inc. (Ont. Mar. 7, 2005)
Oct. 6, 2015 – Name changed to The Tinley Beverage Company Inc.; basis 1 new for 5 old shs. ■

Quick Fire Venture Capital Corporation (Alta. Mar. 11, 1997)
Apr. 7, 1998 – Name changed to AM Technologies Limited following the Feb. 28, 1998, Major Transaction acquisition of Applied Mine Technologies Inc. (AMTI) and amalgamation of AMTI with a wholly owned subsidiary; basis 1 new for 4 old shs. ■

Quick Flame Gas Ltd. (Que. 1947)
1965 – Merged with other cos. to form Quebec Propane Inc.

Quicksilver Ventures Inc. (B.C. Sept. 23, 1999)
Mar. 1, 2005 – Name changed to Keegan Resources Inc. ■

QuikFlo Health Inc. (Alta. Jan. 29, 2008)
June 12, 2017 – Name changed to Friday Night Inc. following acquisition of interest in two cannabis based businesses; basis 1 new for 2 old shs. ■

Quilchena Mining & Development Co. Ltd. (B.C. 1961)
July 22, 1974 – Dissolved.

Quillo Resources Inc. (B.C. 1983)
Jan. 6, 1993 – Name changed to Quillo Technologies Inc. (see FPsurvey - Mines & Energy; FPsurvey - Industrials)

Quinalta Petroleums Ltd. (Alta. 1952)
Sept. 15, 1975 – Struck off register.

Quincy Creek Mines, Ltd. (Ont. 1950)
Mar. 1976 – Charter cancelled.

Quincy Energy Corp. (Nev. May 9, 1999)
July 10, 2006 – Acquired by Energy Metals Corporation; basis 0.2 new Energy Metals sh. for 1 old Quincy sh. (see Energy Metals Corporation)

Quincy Gold Corp. (Nev. May 9, 1999)
May 16, 2005 – Name changed to Quincy Energy Corp. ■

Quinella Exploration Limited (B.C. 1979)
Aug. 31, 1984 – Name changed to American Telecommunications Corporation. ■

Quinn Resources Ltd. (B.C. June 24, 1983)
June 5, 1986 – Name changed to Allanco Iolite Monitor Corporation. ■

Quinsam Opportunities I Inc. (Ont. Jan. 9, 2015)
Nov. 28, 2016 – Name changed to Vitalhub Corp. following Qualifying Transaction reverse takeover acquisition of and vertical amalgamation with (old) Vitalhub Corp. (see FPsurvey - Industrials)

Quinstar Oil Corporation (B.C. 1977)
Sept. 15, 1981 – Name changed to Quinstar Resources Corporation. ■

Quinstar Resources Corporation (B.C. 1977)
Aug. 14, 1984 – Name changed to Epoch Capital Corporation; basis 1 new for 4 old shs. ■

Quinta-Black Exploration Ltd. (Ont. 1956)
1958 – Name changed to Kipwater Mines Ltd. ■

La Quinta Resources Corporation (B.C. Aug. 17, 2004)
Feb. 19, 2016 – Name changed to Black Mammoth Metals Corporation; basis 1 new for 4 old shs. (see FPsurvey - Mines & Energy)

Quintaine Resources Inc. (B.C. 1975)
June 20, 1982 – Formed Quinterra Resources Inc. in British Columbia on amalgamation with Seaforth Mines Ltd.; basis 0.325 new for 1 Seaforth sh. and 0.65 new for 1 Quintaine sh. ■

Quinte & Trent Valley Power Co. Ltd. (Ont. 1925)
July 2, 1940 – Dissolved.

Quinte-Canlin Limited (Ont. 1928)
June 10, 1974 – Name changed to QCI Industries Limited. ■

Quinte Creameries, Ltd. (Ont. 1931)
Oct. 10, 1975 – Dissolved.

Quinte Mall and Niagara Square Shopping Centre (Ont. Mar. 16, 2001)
Mar. 31, 2004 – Name changed to Burlington Mall and Place Bourrassa. ■

Quinte Milk Products, Limited (Ont. 1928)
Aug. 11, 1970 – Name changed to Quinte-Canlin Limited. ■

Quinteko Resources Ltd. (Ont. 1981)
May 26, 1988 – Name changed to Konteko Resources Inc. but not effected for trading purposes; basis 1 new for 4 old shs. ■

Quintel Industries Limited (B.C. 1966)
Sept. 18, 1992 – Dissolved and struck off register.

Quinterra Resources Inc. (B.C. June 20, 1982 amalg.)
Aug. 16, 1993 – Amalgamated with Cabot Resources Corp. and Emtech Group Inc. to form Emtech Technology Corporation; basis 1 new for 1 Cabot sh. and 0.75 new for 1 Quinterra sh. (see Emtech Technology Corporation)

Quintex Energy Ltd. (Alta. 1992)
June 8, 1993 – Formed Quadron Resources Ltd. in Alberta on amalgamation with Quadron Resources Ltd.; basis 1 com sh. of amalco. for ea. com sh. Quintex; and one pfd. sh. of amalco. for ea. pfd. sh. of Quintex. ■

The Quinto Mining Corporation (B.C. Feb. 12, 1976)
Dec. 13, 2000 – Name changed to Quinto Technology Inc. ■

Quinto Mining Corporation (B.C. Feb. 12, 1976)
July 9, 2008 – Acquired by Consolidated Thompson Iron Mines Limited; basis 1 Consolidated Thompson com. sh. plus $0.005 for 5 Quinto shs. (see Consolidated Thompson Iron Mines Limited)

Quinto Real Capital Corporation (Can. Jan. 20, 2010)
Aug. 18, 2017 – Name changed to Quinto Resources Inc. (see FPsurvey - Mines & Energy; FPsurvey - Industrials)

Quinto Technology Inc. (B.C. Feb. 12, 1976)
Jan. 10, 2007 – Name changed to Quinto Mining Corporation. ■

Quisitive Technology Solutions, Inc. (B.C. May 1, 2017)
Mar. 13, 2025 – Acquired by H.I.G. Capital, LLC; basis Cdn$0.57 cash per sh.

Qumana Software Inc. (Can. Dec. 18, 1996)
Oct. 5, 2014 – Dissolved and struck from register.

Quonto Explorations Ltd. (Ont. 1957)
July 26, 1972 – Dissolved.

Quonto Petroleums Ltd. (Ont. 1957)
1962 – Name changed to Quonto Explorations Ltd. ■

Quorum Growth Inc. (Ont. Jan. 30, 1987)
Sept. 16, 1992 – Continued into Canada.
May 28, 1997 – Amalgamated with a wholly owned subsid. of Quorum Growth Partners 1, Limited Partnership and dissolved; basis $8.00 per com. sh.; $8.00 plus $0.1406 in accr. and unpaid divds. per pref. sh. and 15¢ per warrant.

Quorum Resource Corp. (B.C. Mar. 25, 1980)
Apr. 16, 1992 – Name changed to Mirage Resource Corporation; basis 1 new for 3 old shs. ■

Quote Resources Incorporated (B.C. 1987)
Nov. 3, 1995 – Dissolved and struck off register.

QuStream Corporation (Ont. Apr. 1, 2005 amalg.)
Dec. 29, 2010 – Voluntarily delisted from TSX-VEN.
Apr. 10, 2014 – Name changed to PESA Corporation. ■

Quyta Gold Mines Ltd. (Ont. 1945)
Nov. 1954 – Assets acquired by New Athona Mines Ltd.; basis 1 new for 12 old shs. (see New Athona Mines Ltd.)

Quyta Yellowknife Mines Ltd. (Ont. 1945)
July 1950 – Name changed to Quyta Gold Mines Ltd. ■

Qwick Media Inc. (Nev. Oct. 5, 2000)
June 26, 2006 – Continued into Washington.
July 7, 2009 – Continued into Wyoming.
July 28, 2009 – Continued into Cayman Islands.

R

R. & M. Bearings Canada Ltd. (Can. 1928)
1969 – Name changed to RHP Canada Limited. ■

R Split II Corp. (Ont. Mar. 8, 2004)
June 1, 2009 – Redeemed for $30.50 per pfd. sh. and $28.6859 per cap. sh.

R Split III Corp. (Ont. Jan. 30, 2007)
June 1, 2017 – Redeemed; basis $13.60 cash per cl. B pref. sh. and $24.2445 cash per cl. A capital sh.

R Split Corporation (Que. July 29, 1999)
Dec. 13, 2004 – Capital and preferred shares redeemed at $43.7853 and $37.76 per sh., respectively.

R1 Capital Corp. (B.C. Oct. 10, 2017)
Jan. 28, 2021 – Name changed to Reyna Gold Corp. ■

R37 Capital Corporation (Alta. Jan. 18, 2005)
Oct. 6, 2005 – Name changed to Rapid Solutions Corporation following Qualifying Transaction acquisition of Rapid Solutions Corp. ■

R.A.N.K.I.N. Technologies Inc. (Can. Jan. 22, 1997)
Dec. 11, 2000 – Name changed to Boomerang Tracking Inc. ■

RAP Acquisition Corp. (B.C. May 31, 2007)
May 13, 2011 – Continued into Canada.
Nov. 30, 2011 – Formed Ferrum Americas Mining Inc. in Canada pursuant to reverse takeover acquisition of and amalgamation with (old) Ferrum Americas Mining Inc.; basis 1 new for 5 old shs. ■

RB Energy Inc. (Can. Jan. 31, 2014)
May 8, 2015 – Placed into receivership. KSV Advisory Inc. (formerly Duff & Phelps Canada Restructuring Inc.) appointed receiver and all officers and directors resigned.

RB Global, Inc. (Can. Dec. 12, 1997)
Sept. 16, 2024 – Continued into Ontario. (see FPsurvey - Industrials)

RBC Capital Trust (Ont. June 21, 2000)
June 30, 2011 – All trust capital secs. ser. 2011 redeemed for $1,000 per unit.

RBD Enterprises Inc. (B.C. June 4, 1987)
May 11, 2000 – Name changed to Texas Gas & Oil Inc.; basis 1 new for 2 old shs. ■

RBI Ventures Ltd. (B.C. Mar. 23, 2000)
Mar. 15, 2021 – Name changed to Tevano Systems Holdings Inc. pursuant to the reverse takeover acquisition of Tevano Systems Inc. and concurrent amalgamation of Tevano with wholly owned 1251858 B.C. Ltd.; basis 1 new for 3.5 old shs. (see FPsurvey - Mines & Energy)

RBK NT Corporation (Ont. 1980)
Sept. 4, 1991 – All o/s pref. shs. redeemed on Sept. 4, 1990, at $30 per sh. and all o/s capital shs. redeemed at $19.10 per sh.

RCG Capital Inc. (B.C. Sept. 28, 2009)
Sept. 23, 2011 – Name changed to Almonty Industries Inc. pursuant to Qualifying Transaction reverse takeover acquisition of 7887523 Canada Inc.; basis 1 new for 6.67 old shs. ■

RCI Corporation (Netherlands Antilles Mar. 18, 1992)
Aug. 4, 1994 – Continued into Turks and Caicos Islands.

RCI Corporation N.V. (Netherlands Antilles Mar. 18, 1992)
Dec. 24, 1998 – All o/s US Funds ser. A, B, C and D pref. shs. redeemed for US$250,000 per sh. plus accr. and unpaid divds.

R.C.J. Resources Ltd. (B.C. Nov. 21, 1983)
May 5, 1988 – Name changed to Venturex Resources Ltd. ■

RCM Minerals Ltd. (B.C. Sept. 26, 2017)
July 20, 2021 – Name changed to Targa Exploration Corp. (see FPsurvey - Mines & Energy)

RCOM Venture Corp. (B.C. Aug. 26, 1985)
July 21, 2005 – Name changed to Wellstar Energy Corp. ■

RDG Minerals Inc. (Ont. Apr. 28, 1966)
Sept. 19, 2000 – Name changed to NETFORFUN.COM Inc.; basis 1 new for 10 old shs. ■

RDM Corporation (Can. Jan. 23, 1987)
Apr. 6, 2017 – Acquired by Deluxe Corporation: basis US$5.45 cash per sh.
Oct. 24, 2017 – Continued into British Columbia.

RDS Acquisition Corp. (Ont. Jan. 19, 2006)
May 30, 2007 – Name changed to Rapid Brands Inc. pursuant to Qualifying Transaction reverse takeover acquisition of Rapid Refill Ink International Corp. (RRIIC) and amalgamation of RRIIC with wholly owned Rapid Refill Corp. ■

REBgold Corporation (Can. Feb. 13, 1997)
Jan. 23, 2014 – Acquired by Aquila Resources Inc.; basis 1 Aquila sh. for 1 REBgold sh. (see Aquila Resources Inc.)

REC Minerals Corp. (Ont. July 11, 2005)
Mar. 2, 2011 – Name changed to Reliant Gold Corp. ■

REIT INDEXPLUS Income Fund (Alta. Mar. 25, 2011)
Feb. 19, 2019 – Converted from a closed-end fund to an exchange-traded fund.

REMCO Environmental Services Ltd. (B.C. Aug. 12, 1981)
June 30, 1994 – Name changed to La Plata Gold Corporation. ■

RES International Inc. (Ont. Jan. 6, 1987)
Feb. 16, 1995 – Continued into Canada.
Mar. 31, 1999 – Formed Online Direct Inc. in Canada on amalgamation with ComCentral Inc. and Online Direct Inc., constituting a reverse takeover by Online Direct; basis 1 new for 1 ComCentral sh., 1 new for 1 Online Direct sh. and 0.042 new for 1 RES sh. ■

RET Internet Services Inc. (B.C. Mar. 16, 2000)
June 11, 2004 – Name changed to Terra Ventures Inc.; basis 1 new for 18 old shs. ■

R.F. Oil Industries Ltd. (Ont. Dec. 21, 1978)
July 12, 1993 – Struck from registry and dissolved.

RFC Resource Finance Corporation (B.C. 1983)
July 12, 1996 – Acquired by 509833 B.C. Ltd., a wholly owned subsid. of Cominco Ltd., for $1.55 per sh. (see Cominco Ltd.)

RG One Corp. (Ont. Sept. 26, 2014)
June 29, 2021 – Name changed to Flow Beverage Corp. pursuant to the reverse takeover acquisition of Flow Water Inc. (FWI), and concurrent amalgamation of FWI with wholly owned RG One Subco Inc. ■

RG Properties Ltd. (B.C. Feb. 3, 1994)
Dec. 18, 2003 – Acquired by G.A. Lee Management Ltd. for 55¢ per restricted vtg. sh.

RGV Resources Ltd. (B.C. 1984)
Feb. 28, 1992 – Dissolved and struck off register.

RHC Capital Corporation (Ont. Aug. 15, 2008)
May 1, 2019 – Name changed to Royal Helium Ltd. and continued into Saskatchewan. (see FPsurvey - Mines & Energy)

RHP Canada Inc. (Can. 1928)
Jan. 1, 1994 – Formed NSK-RHP Canada Inc. in Canada on amalgamation with NSK Bearing Canada Ltd. and Canadian Pollard Bearings Ltd.

RHP Canada Limited (Can. 1928)
1981 – Name changed to RHP Canada Inc. ■

RIO Nevada Energy Inc. (Can. Aug. 3, 1993)
Sept. 19, 2005 – Dissolved.

RIO Nevada Mines Corporation (Can. Aug. 3, 1993)
Nov. 4, 1998 – Name changed to RIO Nevada Energy Inc. ■

R.I.S. Resources International Corp. (B.C. May 28, 1980)
Mar. 9, 1999 – Name changed to RIS Resources International Corp. ■

RIS Resources International Corp. (B.C. May 28, 1980)
Nov. 9, 1999 – Name changed to Cubix Investments Inc. pursuant to plan of arrangement whereby interest in Ultra Petroleum Corp. plus US$300,000 was transferred to newly incorporated wholly owned Ultra Holdings Corporation and spun out to shldrs.; basis 1 new and 0.25 Ultra Holdings shs. for 1 RIS sh. ■

RISE HealthWare Inc. (Alta. Oct. 30, 2001 amalg.)
Dec. 23, 2008 – Redeemed for 4¢ per sh. other than those held by Med Access Inc.

RISE Life Science Corp. (Can. Nov. 16, 2000)
Nov. 10, 2021 – Name changed to Britannia Life Sciences Inc. pursuant to the reverse takeover acquisition of London, U.K.-based Britannia Bud Canada Holdings Inc. (dba Britannia Life Sciences); basis 1 new for 10 old shs. (see FPsurvey - Industrials)

RIV Capital Inc. (Ont. Oct. 31, 2017)
Dec. 19, 2024 – Acquired by Cansortium Inc.; basis 1.245 Cansortium shs. for 1 RIV Capital sh. (see Cansortium Inc.)

R. J. Jowsey Mining Co. Ltd. (Ont. 1928)
June 30, 1971 – Name changed to Open End Mines Ltd. following surrender of 1,303,922 shs. of R. J. Jowsey. Shldrs. received proportionate sh. of co.'s assets amounting to $589,816 or 45.234¢ a sh. ■

RJK Mineral Corp. (Ont. Aug. 28, 1922)
Jan. 28, 1993 – Name changed to RJK Explorations Ltd.; basis 1 subord. vtg. for 2.5 cl. A subord. vtg. shs., 1 subord. vtg. for 2.5 cl. B subord. vtg. shs., and 1 multiple vtg. for 2.5 cl. C vtg. shs. (see FPsurvey - Mines & Energy)

RJR Holdings Inc. (Alta. Nov. 7, 1994)
Jan. 15, 1997 – Name changed to SIGMACOR, Inc.; basis 1 new for 1 old sh. ■

RJZ Mining Corporation (Alta. Jan. 20, 1997)
June 18, 2007 – Name changed to Vostok Minerals Inc. (see FPsurvey - Mines & Energy)

R. L. Crain Inc. (Can. Feb. 20, 1913; via Dominion charter)
Jan. 4, 1990 – Acquired by Craisec Ltd. for $12 per sh.

R. L. Crain Limited (Can. Feb. 20, 1913; via Dominion charter)
May 1980 – Name changed to R. L. Crain Inc. ■

R. M. Ballantyne Company Ltd. (Ont. 1947)
Feb. 14, 1973 – Dissolved.

R.M. Nickel Mines Ltd. (Que. 1957)
Oct. 1972 – Charter cancelled.

RML Medical Laboratories Inc. (Ont. Oct. 28, 1991 amalg.)
Aug. 25, 1992 – Name changed to IMUTEC Corporation. ■

RMM Ventures Inc. (Ont. Mar. 2, 1988)
Dec. 31, 2006 – Formed PowerComm Inc. in Alberta pursuant to reverse takeover acquisition of and amalgamation with PowerComm Inc.; basis 1 new for 1 Powercom sh. and 5 new for 6 RMM Ventures shs. ■

RMMI Corp. (Alta. Feb. 6, 2018)
Jan. 6, 2021 – Name changed to Discover Wellness Solutions Inc. (see FPsurvey - Industrials)

RMN Technologies Inc. (Alta. Jan. 30, 1997)
Feb. 3, 1999 – Name changed to Global Railway Industries Ltd. following acquisition of Transportation Technologies Inc. ■

R.M.P. Développements Inc. (Que. July 29, 1997)
May 2, 2003 – Certificate surrendered.

RMP Energy Inc. (Alta. Dec. 3, 2004)
Nov. 22, 2017 – Name changed to Iron Bridge Resources Inc. ■

RMR Science Technologies Inc. (B.C. Oct. 17, 2017)
June 16, 2022 – Name changed to Turnium Technology Group Inc. pursuant to the Qualifying Transaction reverse takeover acquisition of Turnium Technology Group, Inc. (old TTGI). and concurrent amalgamation of old TTGI and wholly owned 1333633 B.C. Ltd., to continue as TTGI OpCo Inc.; basis 1 new for 5 old shs. (see FPsurvey - Industrials)

RMS Medical Systems Inc. (B.C. Aug. 24, 1986)
Dec. 22, 1999 – Name changed to Pacific Genesis Technologies Inc.; basis 1 new for 7 old shs. ■

RMS Systems Inc. (Alta. Sept. 29, 2008 amalg.)
Dec. 3, 2013 – Acquired by PHX Energy Services Corp.; basis 0.037209 PHX shs. for 1 RMS sh.

RNC Gold Inc. (Can. May 5, 1994 amalg.)
Mar. 3, 2006 – Amalgamated with Yamana Gold Inc.; basis 0.12 Yamana shs. for 1 RNC sh. (see Yamana Gold Inc.)

ROC Pref Corp. (Ont. Apr. 13, 2004)
Oct. 1, 2009 – Redeemed pref. shs. at $25 per sh.

ROC Pref II Corp. (Ont. Aug. 23, 2004)
Dec. 31, 2009 – Redeemed pref. shs. for $25.3243 per sh.

ROC Pref III Corp. (Ont. Jan. 24, 2005)
Dec. 22, 2009 – Redeemed pref. shs. at $6.5495 per sh.

ROI Canadian High Income Mortgage Fund (Ont. Jan. 3, 2007)
July 9, 2014 – Assets transferred to Dream Hard Asset Alternative Trust; basis 0.8427 Dream trust units plus $0.9364 cash per cl. A unit. Fund subsequently terminated. (see Dream Hard Asset Alternatives Trust)

ROI Canadian Mortgage Income Fund (Ont. Jan. 3, 2007)
July 9, 2014 – Assets transferred to Dream Hard Assets Alternatives Trust; basis 0.8723 Dream trust units plus $0.9693 cash per cl. A unit. Fund subsequently terminated. (see Dream Hard Asset Alternatives Trust)

ROI Canadian Real Estate Fund (Ont. Jan. 3, 2007)
July 9, 2014 – Assets transferred to Dream Hard Asset Alternatives Trust; basis 0.8293 Dream trust units plus $0.9215 cash per cl. A unit. Fund subsequently terminated. (see Dream Hard Asset Alternatives Trust)

RONA Inc. (Que. Jan. 2, 1984 amalg.)
May 25, 2016 – All o/s com. shs. acquired by Lowe's Companies Canada, ULC, a wholly owned subsid. of Lowe's Companies, Inc.; basis $24 cash per sh.
Nov. 23, 2016 – All o/s cl. A pref. ser. 6 and cl. A pref. ser. 7 shs. acquired by a wholly owned subsid. of Lowe's Companies, Inc. for $24 cash per sh.
Feb. 3, 2023 – Amalgamated in Quebec to continue with same name.

ROW Entertainment Income Fund (Ont. Sept. 15, 2003)
July 8, 2005 – Name changed to Entertainment One Income Fund. ■

RPF International Bond Fund (Ont. 1988)
June 28, 1996 – Unitholders of record received the total net asset of their Fund units as the fund was terminated.

R.P.M. Tech Inc. (Que. June 6, 1962)
Apr. 13, 2009 – Amalgamated with 9203-6706 Québec inc. for $1.60 per sh. Co. now private.

RPT Resources Ltd. (B.C. Aug. 25, 1987)
Mar. 18, 2011 – Continued into Alberta.
Apr. 8, 2011 – Name changed to ArPetrol Ltd. pursuant to reverse takeover acquisition of ArPetrol Inc. and subsequent amalgamation of ArPetrol with wholly owned 1584128 Alberta Ltd. ■

RPT Uranium Corp. (B.C. Aug. 25, 1987)
June 5, 2009 – Name changed to RPT Resources Ltd. ■

RPV Industries (Canada) Inc. (Alta. May 20, 1987)
Dec. 1997 – Dissolved and struck from register.

RRD Limited (Bahamas 1963)
In receivership. Sole liquidator: Maldwyn G. Evans, P.O. Box N. 3720, Nassau, Bahamas.

RS Technologies Inc. (Alta. Sept. 17, 1998 amalg.)
Sept. 12, 2013 – Plan of arrangement and compromise completed under which all o/s com. and pref. shs. were retracted and cancelled for no consideration, 9,000,000 new cl. A com. shs. at $1.3445 per sh. were issued to Werklund Capital Corporation and Melbye Skandinavia AS and secured creditors received non-vtg. cl. B com. shs.

RSI International Systems Inc. (B.C. June 11, 1998)
Oct. 20, 2022 – Name changed to ARCpoint Inc. and continued into Canada pursuant to the reverse takeover acquisition of Greenville, S.C.-based ARCpoint Group LLC; basis 1 new for 2.4930814 old shs. (see FPsurvey - Industrials)

RSI Retail Solutions Inc. (B.C. Sept. 16, 1983)
Jan. 30, 1990 – Name changed to Consolidated Retail Solutions Inc.; basis 1 new for 5 old shs. ■

RSX Energy Inc. (Alta. May 6, 1997)
Mar. 18, 2008 – Acquired by Talisman Energy Inc. for $1.70 per sh.

RTICA Corporation (Alta. May 30, 1997)
Apr. 25, 2001 – Continued into Ontario. (see FPsurvey - Industrials)

RTM Holdings Inc. (Alta. Nov. 4, 1996)
Dec. 15, 1999 – Name changed to Sustainable Energy Technologies Ltd. ■

RTN Stealth Software Inc. (B.C. Sept. 15, 1987)
Apr. 5, 2011 – Name changed to Quantitative Alpha Trading Inc. ■

RTO Enterprises Inc. (Ont. July 31, 1993 amalg.)
July 2, 2003 – Name changed to easyhome Ltd. ■

RUX Resources Inc. (Ont. Aug. 21, 1992)
Dec. 15, 1999 – Name changed to Galaxy OnLine Inc. ■

R.W. Gas Group Inc. (B.C. June 8, 1987)
Dec. 14, 1995 – Name changed to Anglo-Canadian Gas Corp.; basis 1 new for 5 old shs. ■

RW Packaging Ltd. (B.C. 1984)
Feb. 17, 1995 – Continued into Canada.
Apr. 17, 2008 – Privatized at 65¢ per sh.

RWMC Productions Limited (Ont. 1959)
Nov. 1976 – Name changed to International Phoenix Capital Corp. Ltd.

RX Exploration Inc. (Ont. Mar. 29, 2000 amalg.)
Jan. 13, 2012 – Name changed to RX Gold & Silver Inc. ■

RX Gold & Silver Inc. (Ont. Mar. 29, 2000 amalg.)
Aug. 15, 2012 – Acquired by U.S. Silver & Gold Inc. pursuant to business combination with U.S. Silver Corporation; basis 0.67 U.S. Silver & Gold shs. for 1 U.S. Silver sh. and 0.109 U.S. Silver & Gold shs. for 1 RX Gold sh. (see U.S. Silver & Gold Inc.)

RX Neutriceuticals Corp. (Ont. Mar. 29, 2000 amalg.)
May 8, 2006 – Name changed to RX Exploration Inc.; basis 1 new for 10 old shs. ■

RXT 110 Inc. (Ont. Aug. 20, 1986)
May 31, 2012 – Name changed to BIOSENTA Inc. (see FPsurvey - Industrials)

RY II Financial Corporation (Can. Oct. 5, 1978)
June 30, 1992 – All o/s partic. redeem. retract. preferred shs. redeemed; basis $25 per sh.

RY Financial Corporation (Ont. 1975)
June 30, 1992 – All o/s pref. shs. redeemed; basis $25 per sh.

RY NT Financial Corp. (Can. 1978)
June 1, 1992 – All o/s cap. shs.; basis 2 com. shs. of the Royal Bank of Canada for 1 capital share plus $25.00.

Rabbit Oil & Gas Ltd. (B.C. 1980)
Jan. 13, 1985 – Amalgamated with 4 other cos. following agreement dated to form Aurex Resources Inc.; basis 1 new for 3.5 old shs.

Racan Photo-Copy Corporation Ltd. (Ont. 1960)
Aug. 1965 – In bankruptcy. Most assets subsequently liquidated and realized funds for a small portion of claims of secured creditors. No assets avail. for other creditors or shldrs.

Race Capital Corp. (B.C. Dec. 21, 2010)
Feb. 28, 2013 – Name changed to Naturally Splendid Enterprises Ltd. pursuant to Qualifying Transaction reverse takeover acquisition of Naturally Splendid Enterprises Ltd. (see FPsurvey - Industrials)

Racer Resources Ltd. (B.C. 1984)
Aug. 17, 1988 – Amalgamated with Macrotrends Ventures Inc. (1 for 1) to form Macrotrends International Ventures Inc.; basis 1 new for 1 old sh. (see Macrotrends International Ventures Inc.)

Rachel Lake Mines Ltd. (Ont. 1960)
Sept. 28, 1964 – Dissolved.

Racing Blood Stables Ltd. (Alta. Sept. 13, 1985)
Oct. 15, 1992 – Name changed to Eagle Energy Corp.; basis 1 new for 6 old shs. ■

Racing River Mines Ltd. (B.C. 1966)
Dec. 28, 1971 – Amalgamated to form Morrison Mines Ltd.; basis 1 new for 10 old shs.

Rackla River Mines Ltd. (B.C. Apr. 5, 1968)
June 24, 1976 – Name changed to North Atlantic Resources Ltd.; basis 1 new for 3 old shs. ■

Radar Acquisitions Corp. (Alta. Oct. 24, 1994)
May 25, 2010 – Name changed to CanAm Coal Corp. ■

Radcliffe Resources Ltd. (B.C. Feb. 21, 1974)
Nov. 1, 1993 – Name changed to Madison Energy Corp.; basis 1 new for 7 old shs. ■

Radco B.M.I. of Canada Ltd. (Que. 1964)
Aug. 10, 1971 – Name changed to Reprox Corporation. ■

Radex Minerals Ltd. (Ont. 1968)
Mar. 1976 – Charter cancelled.

Radial Resources Limited (Alta. 1974)
Feb. 11, 1982 – Name changed to Radial Resources (1982) Ltd.; basis 1 new for 5 old shs. ■

Radial Resources (1982) Ltd. (Alta. 1974)
Sept. 14, 1982 – Name changed to Charterhall Oil Canada Ltd. ■

Radiant Communications Corp. (Can. May 22, 2002 amalg.)
Oct. 18, 2013 – Acquired by Comwave Networks Inc. for $1.43 per sh.

Radiant Energy Corporation (Can. Feb. 21, 1996 amalg.)
Dec. 23, 2014 – Dissolved.

Radiant Health Care Inc. (B.C. Oct. 21, 2016)
Oct. 5, 2018 – Name changed to Teal Valley Health Inc. (see FPsurvey - Industrials)

Radiant Resources Inc. (B.C. May 6, 1996)
Oct. 2, 2008 – Amalgamated with 0832591 B.C. Ltd., a wholly owned subsid. of Tiomin Resources Inc., to form Tiomin China Limited.

Radiation Development Co. Ltd. (B.C. 1969)
June 18, 1979 – Dissolved.

Radical Advanced Technologies Corp. (B.C. Jan. 5, 1989)
Mar. 2, 1998 – Delisted from the Vancouver Stock Exchange. Subsequently dissolved for failure to file.

Radical Elastomers Inc. (B.C. Apr. 11, 1983)
Jan. 19, 2009 – Dissolved and struck from register.

Radio Active Minerals Ltd. (Ont. June 28, 1943)
1952 – Name changed to Westall Petroleums Ltd.; basis 1 new for 1 old sh. ∎

Radio Engineering Products Limited (Can. 1946)
Dec. 16, 1980 – Placed into bankruptcy on Nov. 27, 1975. Dissolved.

Radio Fuels Energy Corp. (Can. July 19, 2006)
Feb. 7, 2025 – Acquired by Palisades Goldcorp Ltd.; basis 0.060538 Palisades shs. for 1 Radio Fuels sh.
Feb. 20, 2025 – Name changed to Palisades Investments Ltd.

Radio Hill Mines Co. Ltd. (Ont. 1965)
Mar. 1976 – Charter cancelled.

Radio IWC Limited (Ont. July 1, 1973 amalg.)
June 26, 1979 – In mid-1979, amalgamated with subsid. CFGM Broadcasting Ltd. and parent Slaight Investments Ltd. Offer made by Slaight Investments to acquire publicly held shs. of co. at $8.50 per sh. expired. Shs. not acquired by offer exchanged for pfce. shs. of amalg. co. and redeemed thereafter at $8.50 per sh.

Radiomutuel Inc. (Can. Sept. 1, 1985)
July 29, 1999 – All o/s cl. A and B shs. acquired by Astral Acquisition Inc., a wholly owned subsid. of Astral Communications Inc.; basis $24 per sh. (see Astral Communications Inc.)

Radiore Uranium Mines Ltd. (Ont. 1951)
July 30, 1976 – Merged with 2 other cos. into Pyx Explorations Ltd.; basis 2 new for 5 old shs.

Radisson Gold Mines Ltd. (Que. 1937)
1958 – Charter cancelled.

Radisson Oil & Gas (Alta. 1955)
Acquired by Acroll Oil & Gas Ltd. (see Acroll Oil & Gas Ltd.)

Radius Explorations Ltd. (B.C. Sept. 9, 1997)
July 1, 2004 – Formed Radius Gold Inc. in British Columbia on amalgamation with Pilagold Inc. with Radius the deemed acquiror; basis 1 new for 2.25 Pilagold shs. (see FPsurvey - Mines & Energy; FPsurvey - Industrials)

Radius Resources Corp. (Alta. June 7, 2005)
May 27, 2010 – Acquired by Argosy Energy Inc. for 748,000 Argosy com. shs. and $2,400,000. (see Argosy Energy Inc.)

Rado Reef Resources Inc. (B.C. 1979)
Mar. 15, 1990 – Name changed to National Gold & Nickel Resources Inc.; basis 1 new for 5 old shs. ∎

Rae-Wallace Mining Company (Idaho June 1916)
June 15, 2011 – Continued into Cayman Islands.
Nov. 14, 2017 – Name changed to Pima Zinc Corp. ∎

Raejac Exploration Ltd. (Ont. 1967)
Name changed to Raejac Holdings & Exploration Ltd.; basis 1 new for 3 old shs. ∎

Raejac Holdings & Exploration Ltd. (Ont. 1967)
Feb. 1970 – Merged into Boeing Holding & Explorations Ltd.

Rafael Resources Ltd. (B.C. Feb. 18, 1966)
Sept. 25, 1986 – Name changed to Biologix (B.C.) Ltd. ∎

Rafale Capital Corporation (Can. Mar. 11, 1998)
Dec. 5, 2000 – Name changed to Bioenvelop Technologies Corporation. ∎

Raffles Financial Group Limited (B.C. Jan. 6, 2011)
Apr. 29, 2020 – Continued into Cayman Islands. (see FPsurvey - Industrials)

Ragged Chute Silver Mines Ltd. (Ont. 1967)
Aug. 20, 1975 – Charter cancelled.

Raging River Exploration Inc. (Alta.)
Aug. 28, 2018 – Acquired by Baytex Energy Corp.; basis 1.36 Baytex com. shs. for 1 Raging River com. sh.

Raglan Nickel Mines Limited (Ont. 1956)
Dec. 14, 1965 – Name changed to New Quebec Raglan Mines Limited; basis 1 new for 2 old shs. ∎

Rahill Red Lake Mining Co. Ltd. (Ont. Apr. 30, 1934)
1959 – Acquired by Goldray Mines Ltd.; basis 1 new for 3 old shs. (see Goldray Mines Limited)

Rahn Lake Mines Corp. Ltd. (Ont. 1934)
Oct. 13, 1958 – Dissolved.

Raider Resources Inc. (Alta. June 3, 1987)
June 24, 1994 – Name changed to Raider Resources Ltd.; basis 1 new for 2 old shs. ∎

Raider Resources Inc. (Alta. 1987)
Nov. 29, 1988 – Amalgamated with Facet Energy Inc. to continue as Raider Resources Inc.

Raider Resources Ltd. (Alta. June 3, 1987)
June 12, 2000 – Acquired by Shiningbank Energy Income Fund; basis 0.831 Shiningbank units, or 0.0582 Shiningbank units plus $0.264, for 1 Raider sh. (see Shiningbank Energy Income Fund)

Raider Ventures Ltd. (Ont. 1975)
Nov. 30, 1990 – Name changed to IFM Food Management (Canada) Ltd. ∎

Railhead Mines Ltd. (Ont. 1958)
June 3, 1963 – Dissolved.

Railhead Resources Inc. (Ont. May 27, 1983)
Sept. 15, 1993 – Name changed to Century Circuits Ltd.; basis 1 new for 3 old shs. ∎

RaiLink Ltd. (Alta. Sept. 22, 1983)
Aug. 20, 1999 – All o/s com. shs. acquired by U.S.-based RailAmerica, Inc.; basis $8.75 per share.

Railpower Technologies Corp. (Can. June 30, 2001 amalg.)
May 29, 2009 – Name changed to 4504020 Canada Inc. ∎

Railtown Capital Corp. (B.C. May 11, 2011)
Aug. 15, 2019 – Name changed to Railtown AI Technologies Inc. (see FPsurvey - Industrials)

Raimount Energy Inc. (Can. June 16, 1987)
Aug. 23, 2016 – Amalgamated with 1977746 Alberta Inc., wholly owned subsid. of Manitok Energy Inc., to form Raimount Oil and Gas Inc.; basis 6 Manitok com. shs. & 1.5 wt. for 1 Raimount com. sh.
Aug. 23, 2016 – Name changed to Raimount Oil and Gas Inc. ∎

Raimount Oil and Gas Inc. (Can. June 16, 1987)
June 6, 2017 – Name changed to Raimount Energy Corp. (see Manitok Energy Inc.)

Rain Resources Inc. (B.C. Mar. 16, 2006)
Mar. 9, 2012 – Name changed to Octant Energy Corp. pursuant to Qualifying Transaction reverse takeover acquistion of Propel Energy Corp. and amalgamation of Propel with a wholly owned subsid. ∎

Rainbow Exploration Corp. (Alta. May 7, 1987)
Sept. 6, 1991 – Amalgamated with Flare King Canada Inc. via reverse takeover to continue with the same name Rainbow Exploration Corp. for total consideration of 2,675,000 shs.
Feb. 7, 1994 – Name changed to Rainbow Petroleum Corp.; basis 1 new for 5 old shs. ∎

Rainbow Gold Ltd. (Ont. Sept. 8, 1993 amalg.)
Oct. 9, 2003 – Formed Jaguar Mining Inc. in Ontario on amalgamation with Jaguar Mining Inc., constituting a reverse takeover by Jaguar; basis 1 new for 1 Jaguar sh. and 1 new for 14 Rainbow shs. (see FPsurvey - Mines & Energy)

Rainbow Group of Companies Inc. (Alta. May 7, 1987)
Oct. 13, 2005 – Name changed to QWIP Systems Inc.; basis 1 new for 5 old shs. ∎

Rainbow Lake Resources Ltd. (unknown)
Mar. 30, 1990 – Amalgamated with Golden Winner Resources Ltd. (1 for 0.97), Mountain Frontier Explorations Ltd. (1 for 1.08), Thunder Valley Resources Inc. (1 for 1.10) and Premier Lake Resources Inc. (1 for 0.95) to form Castlestar Capital Developments Corp.; basis 1 new Castlestar sh. for 0.915 old Rainbow shs.

Rainbow Mines Limited (Que. 1956)
Mar. 1970 – Name changed to Lederic Mines Ltd. ∎

Rainbow Mines Ltd. (B.C. 1965)
1971 – Name changed to Greenfields Development Corp. Ltd.; basis 1 new for 5 old shs. ∎

Rainbow Oil Ltd. (Alta. 1951)
1954 – Assets acquired by Scurry-Rainbow Oil Ltd.; basis 3.8 new for 1 old sh. (see Scurry-Rainbow Oil Limited)

Rainbow Petroleum Corp. (Alta. May 7, 1987)
June 22, 1999 – Name changed to Rainbow Group of Companies Inc. ∎

Rainbow Resources Inc. (Ont. Oct. 13, 2009)
Nov. 26, 2014 – Name changed to Braveheart Resources Inc.; basis 1 new for 10 old shs. ∎

Rainbow Resources Ltd. (B.C. 1973)
June 24, 1982 – Name changed to Rainex Resources Ltd.; basis 1 new for 4 old shs. ∎

Raindor Gold Mines Ltd. (Ont. 1945)
Apr. 1967 – Name changed to Consolidated Raindor Mines Ltd.; basis 1 new for 10 old shs. ∎

Raindrop Resources Ltd. (Alta. May 10, 1996)
Nov. 8, 2000 – Name changed to National Health Stores Inc.; basis 1 new for 10 old shs. ∎

Raindrop Ventures Inc. (B.C. Feb. 14, 2018)
Apr. 28, 2022 – Name changed to Torrent Gold Inc. (see FPsurvey - Mines & Energy)

Rainex Industries Ltd. (B.C. 1973)
Aug. 13, 1993 – Dissolved and struck off register.

Rainex Resources Ltd. (B.C. 1973)
May 5, 1987 – Name changed to Rainex Industries Ltd. ∎

Rainforest Mushrooms Ltd. (B.C. 1985)
Dec. 23, 2003 – Dissolved and struck from register.

Raingold Mines Ltd. (Ont. Feb. 3, 1937)
Charter cancelled.

Rainier Red Lake Gold Mines Ltd. (unknown)
1952 – Charter cancelled.

Rainier Resources Ltd. (B.C. May 8, 1981)
Aug. 27, 1996 – Name changed to Prong Industries Corporation Ltd.; basis 1 new for 2 old shs. ■

Rainmaker Digital Pictures Corp. (Can. Jan. 18, 1995)
Nov. 6, 1997 – Continued into British Columbia.
June 23, 1998 – Name changed to Rainmaker Entertainment Group Ltd. following amalgamation with the co.'s principal Canadian operating subsid. Rainmaker Digital Pictures Grop Ltd. ■

Rainmaker Entertainment Group Ltd. (B.C. Nov. 6, 1997)
June 4, 2002 – Converted into Rainmaker Income Fund; basis 1 trust unit for 1 com. sh. (see Rainmaker Income Fund)

Rainmaker Entertainment Inc. (B.C. Aug. 1, 2008 amalg.)
Dec. 15, 2016 – Name changed to Wow Unlimited Media Inc. following the reverse takeover acquisition of Federator Allied Media, Inc. and Broadway Frederator Networks Inc. and acquisition of Ezrin Hirsh Entertainment Inc.; basis 1 new for 10 old shs. ■

Rainmaker Income Fund (B.C. Apr. 22, 2002)
Aug. 7, 2008 – Converted into Rainmaker Entertainment Inc.; basis 1 com. sh. for 1 trust unit. (see Rainmaker Entertainment Inc.)

Rainmaker Mining Corp. (B.C. Sept. 13, 1979)
May 8, 2014 – Name changed to Rainmaker Resources Ltd. ■

Rainmaker Resources Ltd. (B.C. Sept. 13, 1979)
Dec. 11, 2017 – Name changed to Indiva Limited following reverse takeover acquisition of and amalgamation of INDIVA Corporation with a wholly owned subsidiary; basis 1 new for 10.878 old shs. ■

Rainmaker Ventures Ltd. (Alta. July 29, 2003)
June 24, 2004 – Succeeded by Caribou Resources Corp. following Qualifying Transaction acquisition by Caribou Resources Corp.; basis 1 new for 7.6943 old shs. ■

Rainville Copper Mines Limited (Can. July 6, 1942)
Sept. 22, 1954 – Name changed to Rainville Mines Limited; basis 1 new for 3 old shs. ■

Rainville Mines Limited (Can. July 6, 1942)
Aug. 22, 1961 – Name changed to Dunraine Mines Limited; basis 1 new for 3 old shs. ■

Rainy Hollow Ventures Inc. (B.C. Jan. 17, 2018)
Apr. 21, 2021 – Name changed to Freshlocal Solutions Inc. pursuant to Qualifying Transaction reverse takeover acquisition of Sustainable Produce Urban Delivery Inc.; basis 1 new for 8 old shs. ■

Rainy Lake Mining, Limited (Ont. 1955)
Nov. 9, 1976 – Dissolved.

Rainy Mountain Capital Corp (B.C. June 18, 2007)
Mar. 2, 2010 – Dissolved following Qualifying Transaction private placement subscription of 3,750,000 post-consol. com. shs.of Rainy Mountain Royalty Corp. (formerly East West Resources Corporation)

Rainy River Forest Products Inc. (Ont. Apr. 28, 1941)
Nov. 3, 1995 – Amalgamated with Stone-Consolidated Corporation (1 for 1) to continue as Stone-Consolidated Corporation; basis either 1.04 new com. or 1 new cl. A pfd. sh. for 1 com. sh. The 8% debentures were exchanged for 60.46 new Stone-Consolidated shs. plus $160 for each $1,000 principal amt. held. (see Stone-Consolidated Corporation)

Rainy River Resources Ltd. (B.C. July 14, 1982)
Oct. 17, 2013 – Acquired by New Gold Inc.; basis either Cdn$3.83 or 0.5 New Gold com. shs. per 1 Rainy com. sh.

Raise Production Inc. (Alta. Dec. 23, 1993)
Oct. 29, 2021 – Name changed to Cleantek Industries Inc. pursuant to reverse takeover acquisition of private Calgary, Alta.-based CleanTek Industries Inc.; basis 1 new for 58.3 old shs. (see FPsurvey - Mines & Energy; FPsurvey - Industrials)

Rajah Red Lake Gold Mines Ltd. (Ont. 1936)
1957 – Charter cancelled.

Rajong Resources Ltd. (Alta. Apr. 19, 1996)
Nov. 28, 1997 – Name changed to Deloro Minerals Ltd. following Qualifying Transaction acquisition of 698366 Alberta Ltd.

Ral Marketing Group Inc. (B.C. Feb. 25, 1983)
Apr. 20, 1988 – Name changed to DataTracker International Inc.; basis 1 new for 3 old shs. ■

Raleigh Energy Corp. (B.C. Aug. 7, 1979)
Mar. 9, 1993 – Name changed to Subloo International Resource Corporation; basis 1 new for 5 old shs. ■

Raleigh Minerals Limited (Ont. Jan. 28, 1974)
Aug. 15, 1984 – Name changed to Raleigh Resources Ltd.; basis 1 new for 2.5 old shs. ■

Raleigh Resources Ltd. (Ont. Jan. 28, 1974)
Oct. 5, 1994 – Name changed to Somerset Industries Inc.; basis 1 new for 5 old shs. ■

Rally Energy Corp. (Ont. June 30, 1989)
Oct. 3, 2007 – Acquired by Citadel Capital Company for $7.30 per sh.

Ralph Milrod Metal Products Ltd. (unknown)
Jan. 1969 – Acquired by Aimco Industries Limited for 75,000 shs. and $1,656,250.

Ralston Purina of Canada Ltd. (Can. 1927)
July 26, 1978 – Name changed to Ralston Purina Canada Inc.

Ram Petroleums Limited (Ont. Feb. 14, 1958)
June 22, 2009 – Certificate of incorporation cancelled and dissolved.

Ram Power, Corp. (B.C. Apr. 26, 1984)
May 19, 2015 – Name changed to Polaris Infrastructure Inc.; basis 1 new for 2,000 old shs. ■

Ram River Oils Ltd. (Alta. 1937)
1963 – Struck off register.

Ram Telecom Inc. (Alta. May 9, 2005)
June 24, 2005 – Name changed to Ramtelecom Inc. ■

Ramada Mines Ltd. (B.C. 1965)
1969 – Name changed to Ramada Resources Ltd. ■

Ramada Resources Ltd. (B.C. 1965)
Sept. 1974 – Charter cancelled.

Ramardo Mines Ltd. (Ont. 1946)
June 19, 1980 – Charter cancelled.

Ramarro Resources Inc. (Alta. June 24, 1986)
May 2, 2002 – Acquired by EOG Resources Canada Company wholly owned subsid. of EOG Resources Canada Inc.; basis $1.54 per sh.

Rambler-Cariboo Mines Ltd. (unknown)
1928 – Name changed to Slocan Rambler Mining Co. Ltd. ■

Rambler Exploration Co. Ltd. (Ont. 1959)
Mar. 1976 – Charter cancelled.

Rambler Explorations Ltd. (B.C. Oct. 18, 1979)
Jan. 11, 1985 – Name changed to Ramcor Resources Inc.; basis 1 new for 5 old shs. ■

Rambler Mines Ltd. (Ont. 1959)
1960 – Name changed to Rambler Exploration Co. Ltd. ■

Rambo Explorations Inc. (Que. Jan. 23, 1985)
Sept. 21, 1988 – Name changed to Coleraine Mining Resources Inc. ■

Rambull Gold Mines Ltd. (Ont. 1944)
Mar. 1957 – Charter cancelled.

Ramco Industries Ltd. (B.C. 1948)
Nov. 1979 – Name changed to Black Diamond Resources Ltd.; basis 1 new for 4 old shs. ■

Ramcor Resources Inc. (B.C. Oct. 18, 1979)
June 1, 1993 – Name changed to Rampton Oil Corporation; basis 1 new for 5 old shs. ■

Rameses Mines Ltd. (Ont. 1956)
1958 – Name changed to Jacmar Explorations Ltd. ■

Ramid International Ltd. (B.C. 1968)
Aug. 16, 1976 – Name changed to Ramm Venture Corporation. (see FPsurvey - Industrials)

Ramid Resources Ltd. (B.C. 1968)
Nov. 1969 – Name changed to Ramid International Ltd. ■

Ramore Gold Mining Co. Ltd. (Ont. 1934)
Sept. 24, 1956 – Dissolved.

Rampage Resources Inc. (B.C. 1983)
Feb. 25, 1992 – Name changed to Clyde Resources Inc.; basis 1 new for 3 old shs. ■

Rampart Energy Limited (B.C. Dec. 23, 2004)
June 24, 2013 – Continued into Australia.

Rampart Mercantile Inc. (B.C. Nov. 18, 1968)
Nov. 24, 1999 – Continued into Ontario.
Apr. 14, 2011 – Name changed to Aurquest Resources Inc. ■

Rampart Mines Limited (B.C. Nov. 18, 1968)
May 28, 1984 – Name changed to Rampart Resources Limited. ■

Rampart Resources Limited (B.C. Nov. 18, 1968)
July 24, 1987 – Name changed to Trans Rampart Industries Ltd.; basis 1 new for 3 old shs. ■

Rampart Ventures Ltd. (B.C. Aug. 25, 1987)
Feb. 23, 2007 – Name changed to RPT Uranium Corp. ■

Rampton Oil Corporation (B.C. Oct. 18, 1979)
July 17, 1996 – Name changed to Rampton Resource Corporation. ■

Rampton Resource Corporation (B.C. Oct. 18, 1979)
Aug. 15, 2002 – Name changed to PanTerra Exploration Corp. ■

Ramrod Energy Corporation (B.C. Mar. 1, 1983 amalg.)
Aug. 15, 1986 – Name changed to Consolidated Ramrod Gold Corporation; basis 1 new for 4 old shs. ■

Ramrod Mining Corporation (B.C. May 22, 1979)
Nov. 4, 1981 – Name changed to Ramrod Resources Corporation. ■

Ramrod Resources Corporation (B.C. May 22, 1979)
Mar. 1, 1983 – Formed Ramrod Energy Corporation in British Columbia on amalgamation with Stand Skat Resources Ltd. ■

Ramtelecom Inc. (Alta. May 9, 2005)
June 11, 2009 – Name changed to Avalite Inc. ■

Ramton Mining Corporation Ltd. (B.C. 1970)
Oct. 24, 1977 – Dissolved.

Ran-Lux Mines Ltd. (Que. 1956)
Dec. 1, 1977 – Charter cancelled.

Ran Mar Mines Ltd. (Que. 1957)
June 30, 1971 – Charter cancelled.

Ranald Resources Ltd. (B.C. 1983)
Oct. 30, 1986 – Name changed to Marlborough Productions Ltd. (see FPsurvey - Industrials)

Ranaz Corporation (Can. Oct. 17, 1991)
July 16, 2014 – Privatized for 1¢ per sh. Concurrently, all com. shs. were consol. on a 1 for 17,000,000 basis and issued to Fiducie Vanquish.

Rancheria Mining Co. Ltd. (Ont. 1963)
Dec. 5, 1973 – Charter cancelled.

Ranchero Energy Inc. (Alta. Sept. 6, 1994)
Mar. 27, 2001 – Acquired by Cypress Energy Inc.; basis either $1.68 or 0.1723 cl. A Cypress shs. for 1 Ranchero cl. A sh. (see Cypress Energy Inc.)

Ranchero Oil & Gas Ltd. (Alta. Nov. 18, 1999 amalg.)
Apr. 28, 2000 – Acquired by Newquest Energy Inc.; basis 2.86 Newquest shs. for 1 Ranchero sh. (see Newquest Energy Inc.)

Ranchgate Energy Inc. (Alta. Aug. 21, 1992)
Aug. 23, 2004 – Acquired by Clear Energy Inc.; basis 0.386 Clear shs. for 1 Ranchgate sh. (see Clear Energy Inc.)

Ranchmen's Oil & Gas Company Limited (Alta. 1926)
Sept. 30, 1937 – Assets sold to Ranchmen's Oil Company Limited. No further connection exists between the two cos.
Dec. 3, 1937 – Trusts & Guarantee Co. appointed liquidator. Distribution, if any, not reported.

Ranchmen's Oil Company Limited (Alta. 1942)
May 15, 1946 – Struck off register.

Ranchmen's Oils (1957) Ltd. (Alta. 1942)
1970 – Name changed to Ranchmen's Resources Ltd. ■

Ranchmen's Resources Ltd. (Alta. 1942)
Aug. 8, 1975 – Formed Ranchmen's Resources (1975) Ltd. in Alberta on amalgamation with Cogfac Resources Ltd.; basis 1 new cl. A for 5 old com. shs. ■

Ranchmen's Resources Ltd. (Alta. Jan. 4, 1977 amalg.)
Oct. 24, 1995 – Acquired by Crestar Energy Inc.; basis either $6.125 per sh. or, 0.225 Crestar com. shs. plus $2.81 for 1 Ranchmen's sh. (see Crestar Energy Inc.)

Ranchmen's Resources (1975) Ltd. (Alta. Aug. 8, 1975 amalg.)
Jan. 4, 1977 – Formed Ranchmen's Resources (1976) Ltd. in Alberta on amalgamation with wholly owned Ranchmen's Development Ltd., Ranchmen's Minerals Ltd., Davoil Natural Resources Limited, Bluemount Resources Ltd. and Ark Explorations Limited. ■

Ranchmen's Resources (1976) Ltd. (Alta. Jan. 4, 1977 amalg.)
May 2, 1985 – Name changed to Ranchmen's Resources Ltd. ■

Rancho Oil Co. Ltd. (Ont. 1940)
Struck off register.

Rand A Technology Corporation (Ont. Jan. 27, 1986)
Nov. 6, 2007 – Acquired by Ampersand Venture for $2.10 per sh.

Rand Malartic Mines Ltd. (Que. Mar. 25, 1937)
Dec. 31, 2018 – Dissolved.

Rand Reef Mines Limited (Ont. Apr. 17, 1974)
Oct. 31, 1997 – Formed Hornby Bay Exploration Limited in Ontario on amalgamation with Hornby Bay Exploration Limited (deemed acquiror); basis 1 new for 1 Hornby sh. and 1 new for 2 Rand Reef shs. ■

Rand Resources Ltd. (B.C. 1962)
Apr. 13, 1982 – Dissolved.

Rand Service Stores (Canada) Ltd. (Can. 1946)
1948 – Acquired by Burnett Ltd.

Rand Ventures Inc. (B.C. May 4, 1984)
Dec. 2, 1986 – Name changed to Formosa Resources Corporation. (see FPsurvey - Mines & Energy)

Randall Yellowknife Mines Ltd. (Ont. 1945)
1957 – Charter cancelled.

The Randers Group Incorporated (Del. June 19, 1987)
Feb. 1, 1999 – Name changed to The Randers Killam Group Inc.; basis 1 new for 5 old shs.

Randona Quebec Gold Mines Ltd. (Ont. 1944)
1953 – Name changed to Larandona Mines Ltd.; basis 1 new for 3 old shs. ■

Randsburg Gold Corporation (B.C. July 6, 1990)
Dec. 30, 1997 – Name changed to Randsburg International Gold Corp.; basis 1 new for 5 old shs. ■

Randsburg International Gold Corp. (B.C. July 6, 1990)
Nov. 30, 2018 – Name changed to Cresco Labs Inc. following reverse takeover acquisition of Cresco Labs, LLC.; basis 1 new for 812.63 old shs. (see FPsurvey - Industrials)

Randstrom Manufacturing Corp. (B.C. May 14, 1980)
Jan. 18, 1994 – Name changed to Francisco Gold Corp. ■

Range Capital Corp. (B.C. Mar. 21, 2007)
Aug. 1, 2009 – Amalgamated with MVE Capital Corp. to form new co. with same name Range Capital Corp.; basis 1.55 new for 1 MVE sh. and 0.72 new for 1 old sh.
Nov. 5, 2010 – Name changed to Open Gold Corp. pursuant to Qualifying Transaction acquisition of Knob Hill Silver Inc. ■

Range Energy Inc. (B.C. June 10, 1987)
Dec. 5, 2005 – Dissolved and struck from register.

Range Energy Resources Inc. (B.C. Mar. 1, 2005)
Aug. 31, 2011 – Name changed to Hawkstone Energy Corp. ■

Range Energy Resources Inc. (B.C. Mar. 1, 2005)
July 14, 2021 – Name changed to EnviroGold Global Limited pursuant to the reverse takeover acquisition of EnviroGold Global (Can) Ltd. and concurrent amalgamation of EnviroGold with wholly owned 2826847 Ontario Inc. (and continued as EnviroGold Private Limited). (see FPsurvey - Mines & Energy)

Range Gold Corp. (B.C. Nov. 15, 2006)
Sept. 24, 2012 – Dissolved and struck from register.

Range Industries Ltd. (B.C. 1966)
Feb. 1976 – Declared bankruptcy.

Range Metals Inc. (B.C. Mar. 1, 2005)
Jan. 12, 2010 – Name changed to Range Energy Resources Inc. ■

Range Petroleum Corporation (B.C. June 10, 1987)
May 15, 2002 – Name changed to Range Energy Inc.; basis 1 new for 6 old shs. ■

Rangeco Oil & Gas Ltd. (Alta. Nov. 10, 1976)
Nov. 30, 1979 – Name changed to Onyx Petroleum Exploration Company Ltd. ■

Rangeland Resources Ltd. (Alta. Aug. 18, 1987)
Mar. 14, 1997 – Acquired by 716176 Alberta Ltd., a wholly owned subsid. of Deena Energy Inc., for $1.60 per sh. (see Deena Energy Inc.)

Ranger Brewing Company Ltd. (Can. 1927)
Aug. 31, 1953 – Acquired by Canadian Breweries Limited for $37 per sh. Co. later sold to Dow Brewery Limited. (see Canadian Breweries Limited; Dow Brewery Limited)

Ranger Energy Ltd. (Alta. July 22, 1999)
Oct. 7, 2011 – Continued into Ontario.
Oct. 13, 2011 – Name changed to North Sea Energy Inc. pursuant to reverse takeover acquisition of North Sea Energy Inc. and subsequent amalgamation of North Sea with wholly owned 2294409 Ontario Ltd.; basis 1 new for 10 old shs. (see FPsurvey - Mines & Energy)

Ranger Lake Uranium Co. Ltd. (unknown)
Merger of Ranger Lake Uranium Co. Ltd., Horseshoe Bend Uranium Co. and Century Uranium Corp. to form Century Mining & Development Corp. (see Century Mining & Development Corp)

Ranger Oil (Canada) Limited (Ont. Aug. 21, 1950; via letters patent)
June 12, 1980 – Name changed to Ranger Oil Limited and continued into Canada. ■

Ranger Oil Limited (Can. June 12, 1980)
July 28, 2000 – Acquired by Canadian Natural Resources Limited; basis either $8.25 or 0.175 Canadian Natural Resources shs. for 1 Ranger Oil sh.

Ranger Red Lake Mines Ltd. (Ont. 1945)
1953 – Charter cancelled.

Ranger Ridge Resources Ltd. (B.C. Dec. 30, 2006)
July 20, 2009 – Dissolved and struck from register.

RangeStar Telecommunications Ltd. (B.C. Feb. 24, 1987)
Mar. 24, 1999 – Delisted from the Vancouver Stock Exchange. Subsequently struck from register and dissolved for failure to file.

The Rank Organisation Ltd. (U.K. 1937)
Mar. 17, 1982 – Name changed to The Rank Organisation Public Limited Company.

Rankin Inlet Nickel Mines Ltd. (Ont. 1951)
1954 – Name changed to North Rankin Nickel Mines Ltd.; basis 1 new for 2 old shs. ■

Rankin Resources Inc. (B.C. Mar. 6, 1987)
Mar. 12, 1999 – Name changed to Delta International Industries Corp.; basis 1 new for 4 old shs. ■

Ranney Consolidated Gold Mines Limited (Ont. July 28, 1944)
Aug. 31, 1992 – Delisted from the CDN. Subsequently dissolved and charter cancelled.

Ranney Gold Mines Limited (Ont. July 28, 1944)
June 30, 1988 – Name changed to Ranney Consolidated Gold Mines Limited. ■

Ranrouyn Mines Ltd. (Ont. 1945)
Sept. 28, 1964 – Dissolved.

Ransom Resources Ltd. (B.C. Oct. 15, 1981)
Feb. 15, 1984 – Name changed to Indescor Hydrodynamics Inc. ■

Ranson Mines Ltd. (Ont. 1938)
1957 – Charter cancelled.

Ranwick Uranium Mines Ltd. (Ont. 1949)
1953 – Name changed to Consolidated Ranwick Uranium Mines Ltd.; basis 1 new for 5 old shs. ■

Rapid Brands Inc. (Ont. Jan. 19, 2006)
May 31, 2007 – Continued into British Columbia.
Aug. 19, 2010 – Name changed to RAP Acquisition Corp. ■

Rapid Canadian Resource Corporation (B.C. Jan. 11, 1984)
Jan. 15, 1993 – Name changed to Pan-Global Enterprises Inc. ■

Rapid Data Systems & Equipment Ltd. (Can. 1962)
1974 – All assets sold; partial payment made to secured creditors.

Rapid Grip and Batten, Limited (Can. Jan. 9, 1931)
May 1, 1972 – Name changed to Bomac Batten Limited. ■

Rapid Resource Corporation (Alta. 1986)
Mar. 1, 1996 – Dissolved and struck off register.

Rapid River Resources Ltd. (Alta. 1966)
May 1975 – Name changed to Consolidated Rapid River Resources Ltd.; basis 1 new for 3 old shs. ■

Rapid Solutions Corporation (Alta. Jan. 18, 2005)
Mar. 2, 2011 – Struck from registry and dissolved.

Rapidfire Resources Ltd. (Alta. Dec. 11, 1995)
July 22, 2003 – KPMG Inc. was appointed receiver/manager by the Alberta court.
Feb. 2004 – Receiver began soliciting offers for the purchase of the right, title and interest in certain assets of the company.
June 8, 2004 – 591536 Alberta Inc. acquired selected assets for $1,310,018.
June 10, 2005 – In June the receiver/manager confirmed that distributions had been made to secured creditors. There were no funds available for unsecured creditors or shldrs. The receiver/manager was discharged.

Rapier Gold Inc. (B.C. May 4, 2012)
Mar. 1, 2018 – Acquired by GFG Resources Inc.; basis 0.15 GFG Resources com. shs. for 1 Rapier com. sh.

Rapparee Resources Ltd. (Alta. Oct. 25, 1985)
Aug. 10, 1990 – Name changed to General Fasteners Inc. ■

Raptor Capital Corporation (Alta. Feb. 27, 1987)
Feb. 26, 2009 – Name changed to Valparaiso Energy Inc.; basis 1 new for 20 old shs. ■

Rara Terra Capital Corp. (B.C. Dec. 17, 2009)
May 6, 2011 – Name changed to Rara Terra Minerals Corp. pursuant to Qualifying Transaction acquisition of option on Lonnie niobium-rare earth prospect. ■

Rara Terra Minerals Corp. (B.C. Dec. 17, 2009)
May 8, 2013 – Name changed to Echelon Petroleum Corp. ■

Rare Earth Industries Ltd. (Can. May 16, 2000)
Oct. 1, 2012 – Name changed to Ackroo Inc. following reverse takeover acquisition of MoneyBar Rewards Inc.; basis 1 new for 2.5 old shs. ■

Rare Earth Metals Corp. (B.C. Aug. 8, 1996)
Jan. 18, 2007 – Name changed to VMS Ventures Inc. ■

Rare Earth Metals Inc. (B.C. Sept. 26, 2005)
Feb. 7, 2013 – Name changed to Canada Rare Earth Corp. (see FPsurvey - Mines & Energy)

Rare Earth Mining Co. Ltd. (Ont. 1952)
1957 – Merged into Amalgamated Rare Earth Mines Ltd.; basis 1 new for 4 old shs.

Rare Earth Mining Corporation of Canada Ltd. (Ont. 1948)
1956 – Acquired by Rare Earth Mining Co. Ltd. (see Rare Earth Mining Co. Ltd.)

Rare Earth Resources Limited (Ont. 1957)
May 22, 1984 – Amalgamated (1 for 1) with Aurcan Ltd.(1 for 1) to form Golden Earth Resources Inc.

Rare Earth Resources Ltd. (B.C. Oct. 16, 1978)
Feb. 14, 1995 – Continued into Bermuda.
July 17, 1997 – Name changed to Resource Finance & Investment Ltd.

Rare Method Interactive Corp. (Alta. Sept. 7, 1999)
May 2, 2015 – Dissolved and struck from registry.

RareMethod Capital Corp. (Alta. Sept. 7, 1999)
Dec. 12, 2006 – Name changed to Rare Method Interactive Corp. ■

RareMethod Capital Inc. (Alta. Sept. 7, 1999)
Jan. 15, 2002 – Name changed to RareMethod Capital Corp. following Qualifying Transaction acquisition of Pik E.com Inc. ■

Rasa Investments Inc. (Can. Sept. 11, 2002)
Aug. 16, 2004 – Name changed to Fortune 1000 Group Inc. following Qualifying Transaction acquisition of Fortune 1000 Group Inc. ■

Rash-Mac Explorations Ltd. (Ont. 1956)
June 24, 1965 – Dissolved.

Rat International (Marketing) Ltd. (B.C. 1983)
Nov. 21, 2005 – Dissolved and struck from register.
Dec. 22, 2006 – Restored to registry.
Nov. 17, 2008 – Dissolved and struck from registry.

Rat Resources Ltd. (B.C. 1983)
Apr. 24, 1990 – Name changed to Rat International (Marketing) Ltd.; basis 2 new for 1 old sh. ■

Ratel Gold Limited (British Virgin Islands Jan. 27, 2010)
Jan. 7, 2011 – Name changed to St. Augustine Gold and Copper Limited pursuant to reverse takeover acquisition of St. Augustine Mining, Inc. (see FPsurvey - Mines & Energy)

Ratel Group Limited (British Virgin Islands Oct. 18, 2010)
Apr. 15, 2013 – Succeeded by RTG Mining Inc. following merger of Ratel Group and Ratel Merger Ltd., a wholly owned subsidiary of RTG. (see FPsurvey - Mines & Energy)

Rattler Resource Ltd. (B.C. July 14, 1986)
Nov. 3, 1993 – Amalgamated with Reimer Resources Ltd. to form Kensington Resources Ltd.; basis 1 new for 2 Reimer shs. and 1 new for 1 Rattler sh. (see Kensington Resources Ltd.)

Rattlesnake Ventures Inc. (Ont. Oct. 11, 2007)
May 25, 2011 – Name changed to Minsud Resources Corp. pursuant to Qualifying Transaction reverse takeover acquisition of Minsud Resources Inc. and subsequent amalgamation of Minsud with wholly owned 1830835 Ontario Inc. to form Minsud Argentina Inc.; basis 1 new for 2 old shs. (see FPsurvey - Mines & Energy)

Raudin Exploration Inc. (Can. Sept. 1, 1993)
July 6, 2012 – Dissolved.

Rave Industries Inc. (Ont. July 27, 1983)
Feb. 2, 1994 – Formed Wild River Resources Inc. in Ontario on amalgamation with Diversa Vencap Corp. ■

Rave Resources Inc. (Ont. July 27, 1983)
Mar. 16, 1993 – Name changed to Rave Industries Inc.; basis 1 new for 5 old shs. ■

Raven Energy Ltd. (Alta. June 15, 1998)
June 8, 2006 – Plan of Arrangement acquisition by TriStar Oil & Gas Ltd.; basis either $2.25, or 0.32 new TriStar sh., or $0.6525 plus 0.22 new TriStar sh. for 1 old Raven sh. (see TriStar Oil & Gas Ltd.)

Raven Oils Ltd. (Ont. Apr. 26, 1929)
Struck off register prior to 1944.

Raven Rock Strategic Income Fund (Ont. Oct. 29, 2012)
Mar. 17, 2016 – Converted into an open-ended mutual fund.

Ravencrest Resources Inc. (B.C. Aug. 25, 1987)
Mar. 4, 1999 – Continued into Wyoming.
Oct. 25, 2004 – Continued into British Columbia.
Sept. 26, 2017 – Name changed to Ravenquest BioMed Inc. ■

Ravenhead Recovery Corporation (B.C. Apr. 5, 1968)
Mar. 10, 2008 – Dissolved and struck from register.

Ravenquest BioMed Inc. (B.C. Oct. 25, 2004)
Jan. 29, 2024 – Dissolved for failure to file.

Ravenroc Resources Ltd. (B.C. Feb. 11, 1980)
June 5, 1990 – Name changed to Rocraven Resources Ltd.; basis 1 new for 5 old shs. ■

Ravenstar Ventures Inc. (B.C. Mar. 5, 2010)
Oct. 17, 2011 – Name changed to Cancen Oil Canada Inc. pursuant to Qualifying Transaction acquisition of oil battery facility near Edmonton, Alta. ■

Ravenwood Resources Inc. (Alta. Feb. 28, 2001 amalg.)
Aug. 5, 2003 – Acquired by Compass Petroleum Ltd. for $1.05 per sh.

Raw Creek Resources Inc. (Ont. June 30, 1989)
Mar. 25, 1996 – Name changed to Rally Energy Corp.; basis 1 new for 2.5 old shs. ■

Rawdon Resources Ltd. (B.C. 1979)
May 23, 1989 – Name changed to Advanced Ecology Systems Corp. ■

Rawhide International Investment Ltd. (Alta. Mar. 18, 1988)
Apr. 24, 1992 – Name changed to STN Incorporated. ■

Rawhide Resources Ltd. (Ont. Mar. 29, 1968)
Sept. 2, 1975 – Name changed to Restaurant Holdings of Canada Limited; basis 1 new for 10 old shs. ■

Rawhide "U" Mines Ltd. (Ont. Mar. 29, 1968)
1972 – Name changed to Rawhide Resources Ltd. ■

Rawlins Industries Inc. (Alta. Mar. 27, 1987)
June 12, 1989 – Name changed to Vertimac Development Inc. ■

Rawn Iron Mines Ltd. (Ont. 1945)
Feb. 14, 1973 – Dissolved.

Ray-Lac Gold Mines Ltd. (Ont. 1945)
Apr. 1951 – Charter cancelled.

Ray-Net Communication Systems Inc. (B.C. May 13, 1981)
Dec. 21, 1988 – Name changed to Ixora Communication Systems Inc. ■

Raydan Manufacturing Inc. (Alta. Mar. 27, 1992)
Feb. 22, 2012 – Acquired by Link Suspensions of Canada, Limited Partnership and Link Manufacturing, Ltd. for $5,850,000. Concurrently, Raydan changed its name to 523976 Alberta. Inc. for the purpose of winding down.

Rayfield Mining Co. (B.C. 1965)
Jan. 10, 1977 – Dissolved.

Raylartic Consolidated Mines Ltd. (Que. 1943)
Apr. 1974 – Charter cancelled.

Raylloyd Mines & Exploration Limited (Ont. Apr. 28, 1966)
Apr. 19, 1983 – Name changed to Raylloyd Resources Limited; basis 1 new for 3 old shs. ■

Raylloyd Resources Limited (Ont. Apr. 28, 1966)
Mar. 2, 1989 – Name changed to Consolidated Royalgroup Inc.; basis 1 new for 7 old shs. ■

Raymac Oil Corporation (B.C. 1980)
Mar. 15, 1985 – Continued into Canada.
May 3, 1985 – Formed Norfolk Petroleum Limited on amalgamation with Norfolk Petroleum Limited. ■

Raymond Tiblemont Gold Mines Ltd. (Ont. 1934)
Apr. 9, 1975 – Charter cancelled.

Raymor Industries Inc. (Alta. June 12, 1980)
Jan. 21, 2009 – Petitioned into bankruptcy. KPMG Inc. appointed trustee.
Feb. 10, 2010 – Acquired by investor group led by Georges Durst and Rolland Veilleux, whereby all issued and o/s shs. were cancelled. No funds available for shldrs.

Raymor Resources Ltd. (Alta. June 12, 1980)
Nov. 22, 1999 – Name changed to Raymor Industries Inc. ■

Rayno Mining Corp. Ltd. (Ont. 1955)
Dec. 12, 1960 – Dissolved.

Raynor Mines Limited (Ont. 1927)
Sept. 1975 – Charter cancelled.

Rayon d'Or Mines Ltd. (Ont. 1944)
1955 – Charter cancelled.

Rayore Enterprises Ltd. (B.C. May 2, 1966)
July 16, 1974 – Name changed to United Rayore Gas Ltd.; basis 1 new for 5 old shs. ■

Rayore Mines Ltd. (B.C. May 2, 1966)
Jan. 13, 1972 – Name changed to Rayore Enterprises Ltd.; basis unknown. ■

Raypath Resources Ltd. (B.C. Nov. 5, 1973)
Oct. 28, 1999 – Name changed to Goldray Inc. and continued into Alberta following reverse takeover acquisition of Goldray Corporation, a wholly owned subsid. of Goldray Inc.; basis 1 new for 2.3 old shs. ■

Rayrock Mines Limited (Ont. Feb. 5, 1945)
June 1, 1970 – Amalgamated with Elgin Petroleum Corporation to form new co. with same name Rayrock Mines Ltd.
May 18, 1978 – Name changed to Rayrock Resources Limited. ■

Rayrock Resources Inc. (Ont. June 1, 1970 amalg.)
Mar. 8, 1999 – Acquired by Glamis Gold Ltd.; basis 2.4 Glamis shs. for 1 Rayrock sh. (see Glamis Gold Ltd.)

Rayrock Resources Limited (Ont. June 1, 1970 amalg.)
Feb. 1, 1986 – Name changed to Rayrock Yellowknife Resources Inc. following acquisition of Yellowknife Bear Resources Inc. ■

Rayrock Yellowknife Resources Inc. (Ont. June 1, 1970 amalg.)
Nov. 27, 1998 – Name changed to Rayrock Resources Inc. ■

Raystar Capital Ltd. (B.C. May 27, 1998)
July 10, 2010 – Continued into Ontario.
Sept. 26, 2013 – Name changed to Newmarket Gold Inc. ■

Raystar Enterprises Ltd. (B.C. May 27, 1998)
Oct. 19, 2007 – Name changed to Raystar Capital Ltd.; basis 1 new for 3 old shs. ■

Raytec Capital Corp. (B.C. Sept. 28, 1979)
June 4, 2001 – Name changed to Raytec Development Corp.; basis 1 new for 5 old shs. ■

Raytec Development Corp. (B.C. Sept. 28, 1979)
Nov. 19, 2007 – Name changed to Raytec Metals Corp. ■

Raytec Metals Corp. (B.C. Sept. 28, 1979)
Sept. 16, 2009 – Name changed to Lion Energy Corp. ■

Raytomic Uranium Mines Limited (Ont. 1955)
1961 – Charter cancelled.

Rayville Matheson Asbestos Ltd. (Ont. 1949)
Nov. 9, 1976 – Dissolved.

Razor Energy Corp. (Ont. Mar. 5, 2010)
Feb. 3, 2017 – Continued into Alberta.
Dec. 12, 2024 – Acquired by Texcal Energy Canada Inc.; basis $0.00001 cash per sh.

Razore Rock Resources Inc. (Ont. Apr. 12, 1983)
June 14, 2018 – Continued into British Columbia.
Sept. 23, 2022 – Name changed to American Critical Elements Inc. (see FPsurvey - Mines & Energy)

Re-Con Building Products Inc. (B.C. Aug. 27, 1992)
Mar. 15, 2004 – Name changed to Stone Mountain Holdings Inc. pursuant to plan of arrangement reorganization with Stone Mountain Holdings Inc.; basis 1 new for 1 old sh. ■

Rea Gold Corporation (B.C. July 5, 1979)
Dec. 15, 1997 – Company and wholly owned Bissett Gold Mining Company Ltd. filed assignments in bankruptcy

under the Bankruptcy & Insolvency Act (Canada) and Vancouver-based Arthur Andersen was appointed trustee.
Mar. 18, 2002 – Arthur Andersen (Deloitte & Touche) was discharged as trustee. There were no distributions made to unsecured creditors and shldrs.

Rea Petro Corporation (B.C. July 5, 1979)
Apr. 5, 1983 – Name changed to Rea Gold Corporation. ■

Reach Ventures Inc. (B.C. Sept. 26, 1988)
Nov. 13, 1992 – Name changed to Unique Tire Recycling Inc. ■

Reactor Industries Ltd. (Ont. 1968)
1974 – Amalgamated in Ontario to continue with same name.
Sept. 13, 1978 – Name changed to Consolidated Reactor Uranium Mines Ltd.; basis 3 new for 10 old shs. ■

Reactor Uranium Mines Ltd. (Ont. 1968)
Dec. 1971 – Name changed to Reactor Industries Ltd. ■

Read-Authier Mines Ltd. (Que. Nov. 6, 1926)
1938 – Wound up. Distribution of 0.38 sh. Lamaque Gold Mines, 0.20 sh. Sigma Mines (Quebec), and 1 sh. Union Mining Corp. per old sh.

The Reader's Digest Association (Canada) Ltd. (Can. 1943)
Jan. 6, 1983 – Acquired by parent company The Reader's Digest Association, Inc. for $12.50 per sh.
Dec. 2006 – Name changed to The Reader's Digest Association (Canada) ULC. ■

The Reader's Digest Association (Canada) ULC (Can. 1943)
Apr. 2007 – Continued into Alberta.

Ready Set Gold Corp. (B.C. Apr. 13, 2006)
Dec. 8, 2022 – Name changed to Newpath Resources Inc. (see FPsurvey - Mines & Energy)

Readyfoods Limited (Ont. 1980 amalg.)
Feb. 8, 1985 – Amalgamated with Marilona Management Services Ltd. Shldrs. of each co. sh. received $0.60 and one special sh. of amalg. ReadyFoods Ltd., which was subsequently redeemed for $0.45.

Reako Explorations Ltd. (B.C. July 30, 1971)
June 25, 1993 – Name changed to Redell Mining Corp.; basis 1 new for 5 old shs. ■

Real Asset Income and Growth Fund (Ont.)
Mar. 22, 2019 – Terminated; basis $8.03 cash per cl. A unit.

Real De Minas Mining Inc. (B.C. Nov. 4, 1986)
Mar. 4, 1993 – Name changed to Demand Technologies Ltd. ■

Real del Monte Mining Corporation (Can. Apr. 27, 1989)
June 10, 2004 – Dissolved.

Real Estate & E-Commerce Split Corp. (Ont. Oct. 7, 2020)
Jan. 1, 2022 – Name changed to Real Estate Split Corp. (see FPsurvey - Industrials)

Real Par Inc. (Alta. Jan. 16, 1992)
May 11, 1993 – Name changed to Tundra Environmental Corporation Limited. ■

The Real Property Trust of Canada (Ont. 1977)
Apr. 17, 1990 – Trust wound up. Cash payouts to unitholders as follows: $2.50 per unit March 1989; $6.00 per unit Aug. 1, 1989; $1.50 per A unit and $1.80 per B unit to holders of record at Aug. 1, 1989.

Real Resources Inc. (Alta. Oct. 31, 1978)
Aug. 20, 2007 – Amalgamated with TriStar Oil and Gas Ltd. and continued as TriStar Oil and Gas Ltd.; basis 0.4762 new TriStar sh. for 1 old TriStar sh. and 1 new TriStar sh. for 1 old Real sh. (see TriStar Oil & Gas Ltd.)

Real Time Datapro Ltd. (Ont. 1962)
Dec. 31, 1985 – Acquired by and merged with Memotec Data Inc. (see Memotec Data Inc.)

Realex Properties Corp. (Alta. Sept. 29, 2006 amalg.)
Feb. 8, 2011 – Acquired by Dundee Real Estate Investment Trust for $8.25 per sh. (see Dundee Real Estate Investment Trust)

RealFund (Ont. Nov. 12, 1982)
June 2, 1999 – All o/s trust units acquired by RioCan Real Estate Investment Trust; basis 1.45 new RioCan trust units for 1 old RealFund trust unit.

Reality Commerce Corporation (Alta. Dec. 16, 1997)
Aug. 23, 2004 – Amalgamated with RightsMarket Ltd. to form new co. with same name Reality Commerce Corporation, with old Reality Commerce the deemed acquiror; basis 1 new for 8.33 RightsMarket shs. and 1 new for 5 old Reality Commerce shs.
Nov. 11, 2005 – Name changed to Crossfire Holdings Inc.; basis 1 new for 5 old shs. ■

Realm Energy International Corporation (B.C. Oct. 9, 2009)
Nov. 11, 2011 – Acquired by San Leon Energy plc for $1.30, 3.3 San Leon shs. or a combination thereof for 1 Realm Energy sh.

Realm Mining Corp. Ltd. (Man. 1942)
1967 – Charter cancelled.

Realm Resources Inc. (Ont. 1981)
Aug. 14, 1987 – Name changed to Direct Equity Corporation. ■

Realmont Red Lake Gold Mines Ltd. (Ont. 1946)
Apr. 25, 1978 – Dissolved.

Realore Gold Mines Ltd. (Ont. 1945)
Oct. 10, 1961 – Dissolved.

Realsearch International Systems Corporation (B.C. Nov. 20, 1978)
Mar. 9, 1989 – Name changed to Allmed International Investments Corp. ■

Realty Capital Corp., Limited (Ont. Apr. 3, 1962)
May 16, 1979 – Name changed to Federal Trustco Inc. ■

Reatta Resources Ltd. (B.C. July 25, 1977)
Oct. 18, 1983 – Name changed to Grand Forks Mines Ltd.; basis 1 new for 5 old shs. ■

Rebecca Capital Inc. (Ont. May 30, 2007)
Feb. 24, 2010 – Name changed to Arius3D Corp. pursuant to Qualifying Transaction reverse takeover acquisition of Arius3D Inc. ■

Rebel Capital Inc. (B.C. Sept. 16, 2016)
June 29, 2020 – Name changed to Electric Royalties Ltd. pursuant to Qualifying Transaction reverse takeover acquisition of (old) Electric Royalties Ltd. and concurrent amalgamation of (old) Electric Royalties with wholly owned 1238383 B.C. Ltd.; basis 1 new for 2 old shs. (see FPsurvey - Mines & Energy)

Rebel Capital 2.0 Corp. (B.C. Oct. 19, 2017)
Dec. 20, 2022 – Name changed to Arya Resources Ltd. pursuant to the Qualifying Transaction acquisition of Wedge Lake property option. (see FPsurvey - Mines & Energy)

Rebel Developments Ltd. (B.C. Sept. 12, 1967)
Apr. 11, 1986 – Dissolved and struck off register.

Rebus Oil Company Limited (Alta. 1948)
Feb. 16, 1993 – Name changed to Rebus Corporation.

Recap Energy Inc. (Alta. Nov. 30, 2004)
Sept. 29, 2006 – Formed Realex Properties Corp. in Alberta following amalgamation with a wholly owned subsid. of Realex Properties Corp. and Qualifying Transaction acquisition of several commercial real esate properties; basis 1 new for 10 old shs. ■

Recco Research Corporation (B.C. 1986)
Oct. 30, 1992 – Dissolved and struck off register.

Receptagen Ltd. (Can. May 17, 1984)
Oct. 30, 2001 – Name changed to Spantel Communications Inc. and continued into Florida following reverse takeover; basis 1 new for 20 old shs.

Recharge Resources Ltd. (B.C. Mar. 9, 2010)
Mar. 7, 2025 – Name changed to Vanguard Mining Corp. (see FPsurvey - Mines & Energy)

Recipe Unlimited Corporation (Ont. Dec. 31, 2014 amalg.)
Nov. 2, 2022 – All o/s shs. not already held acquired by Fairfax Financial Holdings Limited; basis $20.73 cash per multiple vtg. and subordinate vtg. shs.

Reclamation Management Limited (Ont. Dec. 5, 1986)
Aug. 17, 1999 – Name changed to Euro-Net Investments Ltd. (see FPsurvey - Industrials)

Reco Mining & Milling Co. Ltd. (B.C. 1896)
1971 – Struck off register.

Reco Mountain Base Metal Mines Ltd. (Ont. 1942)
June 1948 – Charter cancelled.

Reco Northern Alberta Inc. (Alta. Nov. 28, 2013)
Apr. 15, 2019 – Name changed to TrustBIX Inc. pursuant to reverse takeover acquisition of ViewTrak Technologies Inc. (see FPsurvey - Industrials)

Reco Silver Mines Limited (B.C. 1964)
May 1980 – Name changed to Silvex Resources Corporation. (see FPsurvey - Mines & Energy)

Record Oil Co. (unknown)
1924 – Acquired by Mill City Oils Ltd.; basis 1 new for 23.5 old shs. (see Mill City Oils Ltd.)

Record Rouyn Mines Ltd. (Ont. 1945)
1955 – Charter cancelled.

Recycled Solutions for Industry Inc. (Alta. Sept. 17, 1998 amalg.)
May 8, 2000 – Name changed to Resin Systems Inc. ■

Red Area Gold Mines Ltd. (Ont. 1944)
Aug. 18, 1956 – Dissolved.

Red Back Mining Inc. (Can. Apr. 23, 2004)
Sept. 22, 2010 – Acquired by Kinross Gold Corporation; basis 1.778 Kinross com. shs. plus 0.11 wts. for 1 Red Back com. sh.

Red Bark Gold Mines Ltd. (Ont. 1946)
May 1953 – Name changed to Red Bark Mines Ltd. ■

Red Bark Mines Ltd. (Ont. 1946)
May 6, 1965 – Dissolved.

Red Cedar Lake Gold Mines Ltd. (Ont. 1938)
1945 – Name changed to Marbeau Yellowknife Mines Ltd. ■

Red Chip Inc. (Can. Oct. 6, 2000)
May 3, 2004 – Formed Arrow Energy Ltd. in Alberta on Qualifying Transaction amalgamation with Arrow Energy Ltd. (deemed acquiror) and a wholly owned subsidiary of Red Chip Inc.; basis 1 new for 8 old shs. ■

Red Cliff Energy Inc. (Alta. 1987)
June 30, 1990 – Amalgamated with York Resources Limited (1 for 10) to form Aviva Petroleum Canada Inc.; basis 1.8247 new for 10 old shs. (see Aviva Petroleum Canada Inc.)

Red Cloud Mining & Smelting Ltd. (Man. 1936)
Feb. 24, 1968 – Dissolved.

Red Colley Gold Mines Ltd. (Ont. Mar. 18, 1937)
Jan. 1962 – Dissolved.

Red Crescent Resources Limited (Ont. June 17, 2005)
Nov. 27, 2014 – Dissolved and struck from register.

Red Crest Gold Mines Ltd. (Can. 1934)
Nov. 1959 – Dissolved.

Red Deer Brewing Co. Ltd. (Alta.)
1953 – Name changed to Carling Breweries (Alberta) Limited. ■

Red Deer Mineral Holdings Ltd. (unknown)
Apr. 1954 – Assets acquired by Canadian Pipe Lines Producers Ltd.; basis 1 new for 5.5 old shs. (see Canadian Pipe Lines Producers Ltd.)

Red Deer Minerals Ltd. (unknown)
1973 – Remaining o/s shs. acquired by Canada Northwest Land Ltd.; basis 1 new for 4 old shs.

Red Desert Uranium Ltd. (B.C. 1968)
Mar. 27, 1981 – Dissolved.

Red Diamond Mines Ltd. (B.C. 1982)
Mar. 24, 1986 – Name changed to Continental Datanet Inc.; basis 1 new for 2 old shs. ■

Red Dragon Resources Corporation (Ont. May 20, 2005 amalg.)
Aug. 23, 2007 – Continued into British Columbia.
Jan. 6, 2010 – Name changed to Brazilian Gold Corporation. ■

Red Eagle Exploration Limited (B.C. Oct. 28, 2010 amalg.)
Apr. 26, 2018 – All o/s com. shs. not already held acquired by Red Eagle Mining Corporation; basis 1 Red Eagle Mining com. sh. for 1 Red Eagle Exploration sh. (see Red Eagle Mining Corporation)

Red Eagle Mining Corporation (B.C. Jan. 4, 2010)
Nov. 21, 2018 – Placed into receivership by secured lenders and FTI Consulting Canada, Inc. appointed receiver.
June 18, 2022 – Dissolved.

Red Earth Energy Ltd. (Sask. Dec. 20, 1982)
Mar. 2, 1988 – Delisted from the Vancouver Stock Exchange. Subsequently dissolved.

Red Emerald Resource Corp. (B.C. May 14, 1996)
July 10, 2002 – Name changed to Midway Gold Corp. ■

Red Engine Exploration Ltd. (B.C. July 30, 1986)
Dec. 1, 1998 – Acquired by Canmine Resources Corporation; basis 0.75 Canmine shs. for 1 Red Engine sh. (see Canmine Resources Corporation)

Red Engine Resources Corporation (B.C. July 30, 1986)
Feb. 26, 1997 – Name changed to Red Engine Exploration Ltd.; basis 2 new for 1 old sh. ■

Red Fault Mining & Oil Corp. Ltd. (unknown)
1957 – Acquired by Share Oils Ltd.; basis 1 new for 2 old shs. (see Share Oils Ltd.)

Red Fox Minerals Ltd. (B.C. Dec. 20, 1983)
Sept. 6, 1996 – Name changed to Earth King Resources Inc.; basis 1 new for 3 old shs. ■

Red Fox Resources Inc. (Ont. Dec. 22, 1987)
Nov. 4, 1997 – Formed Library Information Software Corp. in Ontario on amalgamation with 1177695 Ontario Corporation, constituting a reverse takeover by 1177695 Ontario; basis 1 new for 1.9 old shs. ■

Red Gold Mining Co. Ltd. (Can. Jan. 27, 1928)
1942 – Property sold to Stadacona Rouyn Mines Ltd.; no equity for shldrs. (see Stadacona Rouyn Mines Limited)

Red Hawk Gold Mines Ltd. (B.C. 1932)
1961 – Name changed to Mineral Mountain Mining Co. Ltd.; basis 1 new for 10 old shs. ■

Red Hill Energy Inc. (B.C. Nov. 6, 1978)
Apr. 16, 2010 – Name changed to Prophecy Resource Corp. on acquisition of Prophecy Resource Corp. by way of amalgamation between its wholly owned subsid. and Prophecy; basis 1 cl. A sh. for 1 Prophecy sh. and 0.92

cl. A shs. plus 0.25 Elissa Resources com. shs. for 1 Red Hill sh. Elissa was spun off to hold non-Mongolian mineral properties. ■

Red Hill Marketing Group Ltd. (B.C. 1981)
Mar. 2, 1990 – Delisted from the Vancouver Stock Exchange. Subsequently dissolved.

Red Hill Resources Ltd. (B.C. 1981)
Feb. 18, 1985 – Name changed to Red Hill Marketing Group Ltd. ■

Red Hut Metals Inc. (B.C. Feb. 16, 2010)
July 12, 2017 – Name changed to Providence Gold Mines Inc. (see FPsurvey - Mines & Energy)

Red Lake and Sun Valley Resources Ltd. (B.C. May 29, 1984)
Dec. 27, 1989 – Name changed to International R.S.V. Resources Corporation; basis 1 new for 10 old shs. ■

Red Lake Buffalo Resources Ltd. (Ont. June 26, 1987)
Mar. 7, 1991 – Name changed to Madsen Gold Corp. ■

Red Lake Exploration, Inc. (Nev. Jan. 10, 2005)
Aug. 27, 2008 – Name changed to Red Metal Resources Ltd. ■

Red Lake Gold Shore Mines Ltd. (Ont. Nov. 16, 1927)
1938 – Acquired by Hasaga Gold Mines Ltd.; basis 1 new for 18 old shs. (see Hasaga Gold Mines Ltd.)

Red Lake Resources Inc. (B.C. Aug. 11, 1997)
June 19, 2006 – Name changed to Silver Fields Resources Inc. ■

Red Lantern Corporation (Alta. Jan. 14, 2000)
June 21, 2002 – Continued into Ontario.
July 23, 2002 – Name changed to TrekLogic Technologies Inc. following Qualifying Transaction reverse takeover acquisition of TrekLogic Inc. ■

Red Leaf Oil Ltd. (Alta. 1976)
Apr. 30, 1981 – Amalgamated with Southern Tier Gas Producers Ltd. to continue as Southern Tier Gas Producers Ltd.; basis 1 new for 5 old shs.

Red-Man Oils Ltd. (Man.)
1959 – Struck off register.

Red Metal Mines Ltd. (B.C. 1967)
Feb. 25, 1983 – Struck off register.

Red Metal Resources Ltd. (Nev. Jan. 10, 2005)
Feb. 10, 2021 – Continued into British Columbia. (see FPsurvey - Mines & Energy)

Red Mile Capital Corp. (Alta. May 31, 2007)
Feb. 18, 2010 – Name changed to Red Mile Minerals Corp. ■

Red Mile Minerals Corp. (Alta. May 31, 2007)
June 3, 2010 – Continued into British Columbia.
Apr. 21, 2015 – Continued into Ontario.
June 12, 2015 – Name changed to Orla Mining Ltd. ■

Red Moon Potash Inc. (Alta. June 15, 2011)
Dec. 20, 2016 – Name changed to Red Moon Resources Inc. ■

Red Moon Resources Inc. (Alta. June 15, 2011)
Aug. 10, 2021 – Continued into British Columbia.
Aug. 31, 2021 – Name changed to Atlas Salt Inc. (see FPsurvey - Mines & Energy)

Red Mountain Mines Ltd. (B.C. 1965)
Feb. 19, 1979 – Charter cancelled.

Red Oak Mining Corp. (B.C. Apr. 17, 1979)
Mar. 11, 2021 – Name changed to Pantera Silver Corp. (see FPsurvey - Mines & Energy)

Red Oak Resources Inc. (Can. Apr. 14, 1984)
Oct. 19, 1995 – Amalgamated with Neutrino Resources Ltd. and Maxon Energy Inc. to form Neutrino Resources

Inc.; basis 1.81 new for 1 Neutrino sh., 1 new sh. plus 1 wt. for 1 Maxon sh. and 1 new for 10 Red Oak shs. (see Neutrino Resources Inc.)

Red Oak Trail Corp. (Alta. Jan. 28, 2000)
Sept. 5, 2001 – Name changed to Innovative Water & Sewer Systems Inc. following Qualifying Transaction acquisition of Innovative Sewage Systems Inc. and R.W. Connelly Associates Inc. ■

Red Ore Gold Inc. (B.C. Jan. 13, 2011)
Nov. 17, 2016 – Name changed to LKP Solutions Inc. ■

Red Pine Investment Ltd. (B.C. July 30, 2008)
Jan. 21, 2014 – Name changed to Red Pine Petroleum Ltd. pursuant to Qualifying Transaction farm-in agreement with Golden Coast Energy Corp. ■

Red Pine Petroleum Ltd. (B.C. July 30, 2008)
Sept. 7, 2021 – Name changed to Alpine Summit Energy Partners, Inc. pursuant to reverse takeover acquisition of Nashville, Tenn.-based HB2 Origination, LLC; basis 1 new for 625.5882 old shs. (see FPsurvey - Mines & Energy)

Red Poplar Gold Mines Ltd. (Ont. 1947)
1955 – Name changed to Consolidated Red Poplar Minerals Ltd.; basis 1 new for 3.5 old shs. ■

Red Raven Resources Inc. (Alta. Sept. 13, 1996)
Aug. 17, 2001 – Formed Rise Energy Ltd. in Alberta on amalgamation with Rise Resources Ltd.; basis 1 new for 3 old shs. ■

Red River Capital Corp. (Alta. Dec. 20, 2017)
June 11, 2021 – Name changed to Bitcoin Well Inc. pursuant to the Qualifying Transaction reverse takeover acquisition of 1739001 Alberta Ltd. (dba Bitcoin Well) and concurrent amalgamation of Bitcoin Well with wholly owned 2283971 Alberta Ltd. (and continued as Bitcoin Well Holdings Inc.). (see FPsurvey - Industrials)

Red River Mining & Exploration Ltd. (Ont. 1959)
May 1961 – Acquired by Sudbay Beryllium Mines Ltd.

Red Rock Capital Corp. (Can. July 10, 2007)
May 18, 2011 – Name changed to Century Iron Mines Corporation pursuant to Qualifying Transaction reverse takeover acquisition of Century Iron Ore Holdings Inc. and subsequent amalgamation of Century Iron One with a wholly owned subsid.; basis 1 new for 10 old shs. ■

Red Rock Capital Corp. (B.C. Feb. 9, 2012)
Feb. 27, 2024 – Name changed to Auric Resources Corp. (see FPsurvey - Mines & Energy)

Red Rock Energy Inc. (Alta. Apr. 12, 2005)
Aug. 15, 2017 – Name changed to New Stratus Energy Inc. (see FPsurvey - Mines & Energy)

Red Rock Mines Ltd. (N.B. 1956)
Name changed to Fusion Technologies Limited. (see FPsurvey - Industrials)

Red Rock Mines Ltd. (B.C. 1959)
Oct. 6, 1970 – Name changed to Alakon Metals Ltd.; basis 1 new for 2.5 old shs. ■

Red Rock Mining Corporation (B.C. Oct. 1981 amalg.)
June 10, 1994 – Name changed to American Pacific Minerals Ltd. ■

Red Rocket Explorations Inc. (Ont. 1981)
Dec. 6, 1995 – Formed W.I.N. Gaming Corp. in Ontario on amalgamation with Kimbridge Group Inc.; basis 1 new for 15 old shs. ■

Red Sea Oil Corporation (Can. Nov. 30, 1994)
June 6, 2000 – Plan of Arrangement with International Petroleum Corporation, a wholly owned subsid. of Lundin Oil AB; basis 0.47 cl. B Lundin shs. for 1 Red Sea sh. Lundin shs. trade on the OM Stockholm Exchange.

Red Sea Technologies Ltd. (Alta. Dec. 1, 1997)
May 1, 2000 – Name changed to G.I.E. Environment Technologies Ltd. (see FPsurvey - Industrials)

Red Shirt Larder Gold Mines Ltd. (Ont. 1946)
May 5, 1959 – Dissolved.

Red Star Capital Ventures Inc. (Can. Feb. 17, 2011)
Dec. 9, 2014 – Qualifying Transaction distribution of 3,400,000 Electra Gold Ltd. units (1 com. sh. & 1 wt.) to shldrs. on a pro rata basis. Co. subsequently dissolved. (see Electra Gold Ltd.)

Red Star Petroleum Ltd. (B.C. May 18, 1939)
June 20, 1989 – Dissolved and struck off register.

Red-Tail Infotech Inc. (Alta. Feb. 21, 1997)
Mar. 27, 2003 – Name changed to Life Sciences Institute Inc. ■

Redaurum Limited (Ont. Feb. 7, 1984)
Apr. 14, 2004 – Name changed to BF Minerals Ltd.; basis 1 new for 40 old shs. ■

Redaurum Red Lake Gold Mines Ltd. (Ont. 1944)
July 4, 1977 – Name changed to Orelock Explorations Limited. ■

Redaurum Red Lake Mines Limited (Ont. Feb. 7, 1984)
May 18, 1994 – Name changed to Redaurum Limited. ■

Redbank Gold Mines Ltd. (Ont. 1943)
Apr. 15, 1963 – Dissolved.

Redbird Gold Corp. (B.C. Mar. 25, 1986)
Oct. 18, 1991 – Continued into British Columbia.
July 10, 2002 – Formed MetalCORP Limited in Ontario on amalgamation with 1349563 Ontario Limited, constituting a reverse takeover by 1349563 Ontario; basis 50 new for 1 1349563 Ontario sh. and 1 new for 20 Redbird shs. ■

redCity Search Company Inc. (Ont. Aug. 22, 2005 amalg.)
Mar. 26, 2007 – Name changed to ZipLocal Inc.; basis 1 new for 5 old shs. ■

Redcliffe Exploration Inc. (Alta. Feb. 27, 2007 amalg.)
June 3, 2010 – Amalgamated with 1534586 Alberta Ltd., a wholly owned indirect subsid. of Paramount Resources Ltd., for 42¢ per sh.

Redcliffe Exploration Ltd. (Alta. May 4, 2006)
Feb. 27, 2007 – Formed Redcliffe Exploration Inc. in Alberta on reverse takeover acquisition of and amalgamation with Stallion Energy Ltd. ■

Redcoat Mines Ltd. (N.B. 1967)
July 16, 1980 – Charter cancelled.

Redcon Gold Mines Limited (Ont. 1947)
Jan. 1, 1985 – Amalgamated with Goldquest Exploration Inc. (1 for 1) to continue as Goldquest Exploration Inc.; basis 1 new for 3.5 old shs.

Redcorp Ventures Ltd. (Can. Mar. 20, 2000)
May 29, 2009 – Placed into receivership. McIntosh & Morawetz Inc. (subsequently Alvarez & Marsal Canada Inc.) appointed receiver.
June 26, 2009 – Partial repayment was made to holders of the 13% senior secured redeemable ser. D notes.
June 29, 2009 – Assigned into bankruptcy and Abakhan & Associates Inc. was appointed trustee.
Sept. 22, 2010 – Sale of mineral properties to Chieftain Metals Inc. (subsequently placed into receivership) was completed with proceeds to be distrib. to construction lien claimants and as partial repayment to the secured noteholders.
Nov. 17, 2016 – Secured noteholders suffered a shortfall of approx. $110,000,000. No funds available for shldrs. Alvarez & Marsal Canada Inc. discharged as receiver.

Redding Gold Corporation (B.C. July 18, 1983)
Apr. 6, 1993 – Name changed to Consolidated Redding Explorations Corporation; basis 1 new for 3.5 old shs. ■

Rede-Pak Fine Foods Ltd. (Man. July 31, 1986)
Apr. 4, 1990 – Continued into Alberta.
Oct. 11, 1990 – Name changed to Petro-Plus Inc. ■

Redeco Energy Inc. (Alta. Nov. 9, 1987)
Nov. 2, 2009 – Dissolved and struck from register.

Redekop Properties Inc. (B.C. Nov. 2, 1987)
Mar. 2, 2001 – Majority of the directors resigned and Vancouver-based PricewaterhouseCoopers Inc. was appointed receiver.
Mar. 5, 2001 – Sun Life Assurance Company of Canada issued foreclosure proceedings against 535401 B.C. Ltd. (20% owned) and Montreal Trust Company of Canada filed a notice of intention to enforce security against the company under Bankruptcy and Insolvency Act.
Sept. 1, 2001 – Mall went into foreclosure.
Sept. 2001 – Van City Savings acquired a court order allowing it to sell the Middlegate Mall in Burnaby, B.C. Subsequently the court order was transferred to Sun Life Assurance as co-plaintiff.
Dec. 2002 – Sale of a rental apartment building in Surrey, B.C., was completed for $3,600,000. In December 2002, Bosa Development Corporation expected to close the purchase of the Middlegate Mall early in 2003, for an undisclosed amount.
Apr. 29, 2003 – PricewaterhouseCoopers Inc. was appointed trustee in bankruptcy.
May 21, 2004 – Trustee discharged. No funds available for distribution to shldrs.

Redell Mining Corp. (B.C. July 30, 1971)
Apr. 16, 1998 – Name changed to FM Resources Corp.; basis 1 new for 20 old shs. ■

Redex Co. Ventures Inc. (Alta. Nov. 9, 1987)
Dec. 31, 1997 – Formed Redeco Energy Inc. following acquisition of Redex Co. Ventures Ltd.; basis 1 new for 2 old shs. ■

Redex Gold Inc. (B.C. July 18, 1983)
July 31, 1997 – Name changed to Bravo Gold Inc. ■

Redex Inc. (Alta. Jan. 21, 2000)
Oct. 21, 2004 – Continued into Canada.
June 19, 2011 – Dissolved and struck from register.

Redfern Resources Ltd. (B.C. Jan. 30, 1979)
July 5, 2000 – Name changed to Redcorp Ventures Ltd. pursuant to plan of arrangement reorganization whereby newly incorporated Redcorp Ventures Ltd. completed a sh.-for-sh. exchange to become parent of Redfern. ■

Redford Mines Inc. (B.C. 1966)
Aug. 25, 1981 – Name changed to Redford Resources, Inc. ■

Redford Resources, Inc. (B.C. 1966)
Sept. 24, 1984 – Name changed to United Redford Resources Inc.; basis 1 new for 5 old shs. ■

Redfork Resources, Inc. (B.C. Sept. 26, 1980)
Mar. 31, 1981 – Name changed to Tamara Resources Inc. ■

Redfund Capital Corp. (B.C. Jan. 30, 2006)
Jan. 22, 2021 – Name changed to Global Wellness Strategies Inc.; basis 1 new for 4 old shs. ■

Redhawk Resources, Inc. (B.C. Mar. 8, 1983)
Sept. 15, 2018 – Acquired by Copperbank Resources Corp.; basis 0.929 Copperbank com. shs. for 1 Redhawk com. sh. (see Copperbank Resources Corp.)

Redhill Resources Corp. (B.C. Mar. 7, 2005)
June 24, 2016 – Name changed to Millennial Lithium Corp.; basis 1 new for 2 old shs. ■

RediShred Capital Corp. (Can. Oct. 18, 2006)
Feb. 7, 2025 – Continued into British Columbia.
Feb. 11, 2025 – Acquired by VRC Companies, LLC (dba Vital Records Control®); basis $5 cash per sh.
Feb. 14, 2025 – Name changed to RediShred Capital ULC.

Redknee Solutions Inc. (Can. Nov. 1, 2006)
Mar. 28, 2018 – Name changed to Optiva Inc.; basis 1 new for 50 old shs. (see FPsurvey - Industrials)

Redland Resources Ltd. (B.C. 1978)
Nov. 24, 1981 – Name changed to Forge Energy Ltd. ■

Redline Communications Group Inc. (Can. Sept. 14, 2007)
July 7, 2022 – Acquired by Aviat Networks, Inc.; basis Cdn$0.90 cash per sh.

Redline Resources Inc. (B.C. Jan. 16, 2007)
Feb. 11, 2016 – Name changed to Nickel One Resources Inc. ■

Redmex Resources Inc. (Alta. Sept. 14, 1992)
Dec. 21, 1993 – Formed GOAL Energy Inc. in Alberta on amalgamation with GOAL Energy Inc. ■

Redmond Ventures Corp. (B.C. Mar. 16, 1966)
Mar. 12, 2002 – Name changed to Crown Point Ventures Ltd.; basis 1 new for 6 old shs. ■

Redonda Industries Corporation (B.C. Dec. 4, 1985)
Jan. 24, 1997 – Name changed to Image Power, Inc. ■

Redore Mining Co. Ltd. (Ont. 1938)
Apr. 1958 – Dissolved.

Redpath Industries Limited (Can. Dec. 24, 1930; via Dominion charter)
May 11, 1989 – Acquired by Tate and Lyle Holdings Ltd. of London, England, for $20.375 per sh.

RedPic Petroleums Ltd. (Ont. July 21, 1950)
May 12, 1952 – Name changed to Stanwell Oil & Gas Ltd.; basis 1 new for 3 old shs. ■

Redpoint Resources Inc. (Can. 1987)
July 5, 1988 – Name changed to Rentown Enterprises Inc. ■

Redpointe Gold Mines Ltd. (Ont. 1945)
Nov. 12, 1957 – Charter cancelled.

RedQuest Capital Corp. (B.C. Mar. 30, 2010)
June 22, 2017 – Continued into Quebec.
June 30, 2017 – Name changed to Harfang Exploration Inc.; basis 1 new for 4 old shs. (see FPsurvey - Mines & Energy)

Redruth Gold Mines Limited (Ont. Dec. 1944)
Oct. 27, 1995 – Name changed to Nikana Capital Inc. ■

Redstar Gold Corp. (B.C. Apr. 29, 1983)
Oct. 21, 2020 – Name changed to Heliostar Metals Ltd.; basis 1 new for 15 old shs. (see FPsurvey - Mines & Energy)

RedStar Oil & Gas Inc. (Alta. Aug. 1, 2005 amalg.)
May 20, 2008 – Acquired by Great Plains Exploration Inc.; basis 0.9 Great Plains com. shs. for 1 RedStar com. sh.

Redstar Resources Corporation (B.C. Apr. 29, 1983)
Apr. 26, 2002 – Name changed to Redstar Gold Corp.; basis 1 new for 6 old shs. ■

Redstone Capital Corp. (Alta. June 30, 2005)
Aug. 21, 2006 – Name changed to Fireswirl Technologies Inc. ■

Redstone Mining Corporation (Can. Dec. 3, 1985)
Aug. 20, 2008 – Continued into British Columbia.

Redstone Porcupine Gold Mines Ltd. (Ont. 1944)
1954 – Charter cancelled.

Redstone Resources Inc. (Ont. 1961)
Mar. 8, 1996 – Acquired by Franco-Nevada Mining Corporation; basis 0.05 Franco-Nevada shs. for 1 Redstone sh. (see Franco-Nevada Mining Corporation Limited)

Redtail Metals Corp. (B.C. Aug. 19, 1983)
Apr. 23, 2014 – Acquired by Northern Tiger Resources Inc.; basis 1 Northern Tigers sh. for 7 Redtail com. shs. Subsequently, Northern Tiger Resources Inc. changed its name to Golden Predator Mining Corp. (see Golden Predator Mining Corp.)

Redux Energy Corporation (Alta. 1988)
Oct. 1, 1997 – Formed Thermal Control Technologies Corp. in Alberta on amalgamation with (old) Thermal Control Technologies Corp. ■

Redwater Consolidated Oils Ltd. (Alta. Nov. 22, 1948)
Struck off register.

Redwater Devonian Ltd. (Alta.)
1960 – Struck off register.

RedWater Energy Corp. (Alta. Sept. 18, 2008)
May 12, 2015 – Placed into receivership. Grant Thornton Limited was appointed receiver and all officers and directors resigned.

Redwater Petroleums Ltd. (Ont. Oct. 13, 1948)
1950 – Acquired by Redwater-Piccadilly Petroleum Ltd.; basis 1 new for 2 old shs. (see Redwater-Piccadilly Petroleum Ltd.)

Redwater-Piccadilly Petroleum Ltd. (Ont. July 21, 1950)
Oct. 22, 1951 – Name changed to RedPic Petroleums Ltd. ■

Redwater Utilities Holdings Oil & Gas Limited (Alta. 1952)
1954 – Taken over by Calvan Consolidated Oil & Gas Co. Ltd.; basis 1 new for 6 old shs.

Redwing Resources Inc. (B.C. 1968)
June 30, 1994 – Dissolved and struck off register.

Redwolf Gold Mines Ltd. (Ont. 1945)
Dec. 1977 – Charter cancelled.

Redwood Advantage Monthly Income Fund (Ont. Jan. 1, 2006)
May 7, 2018 – Merged into Purpose Multi-Asset Income Fund; 0.518786 Purpose units for 1 Redwood Advantage trust unit.

Redwood Energy Income Fund (Ont. Feb. 24, 2005)
May 7, 2018 – Merged into Purpose Global Resource Fund; basis 1.216414 Purpose cl. F units for 1 Redwood Energy trust unit.

Redwood Energy, Ltd. (B.C. Apr. 19, 1994)
May 20, 2004 – Acquired by Compton Petroleum Corporation for $0.20 per sh. (see Compton Petroleum Corporation)

Redwood Floating Rate Bond Fund (Ont.)
May 7, 2018 – Merged into Redwood Floating Rate Income Fund; basis 0.867267 Redwood Income units for 1 Redwood Bond cl. A units.

Redwood Floating Rate Income Fund (Ont.)
June 18, 2018 – Name changed to Purpose Floating Rate Income Fund. ■

Redwood Global Financials Income Fund (Ont. Oct. 23, 2009)
May 7, 2018 – Merged into Purpose US Preferred Share Fund; basis 0.882263 Purpose US units for 1 Redwood Global cl. A unit.

Redwood Global Infrastructure Income Fund (Ont. Sept. 27, 2013)
Aug. 27, 2018 – Merged into Purpose Diversified Real Asset Fund; basis 0.497073 Purpose ETFs for 1 Redwood trust unit and final distrib. of $0.1300 cash per unit payable to unitholders of record on Aug. 23, 2018.

Redwood Gold Mines Ltd. (Ont. Aug. 20, 1936)
1949 – Name changed to New Redwood Gold Mines Ltd.; basis 1 new for 3 old shs. ■

Redwood Low Volatility High Income Fund (Ont. Jan. 25, 2012)
Mar. 29, 2018 – Terminated; basis $9.31 cash per fund unit.

Redwood Monthly Income Fund (Ont. Oct. 25, 2001)
May 7, 2018 – Merged into Purpose Multi-Asset Income Fund; basis 0.490446 Purpose units for 1 Redwood Monthly trust unit.

Redwood Resources Inc. (B.C. Mar. 28, 1979)
June 1, 1992 – Name changed to Trooper Explorations Ltd.; basis 1 new for 3 old shs. ■

Redwood Resources Ltd. (Alta. Apr. 26, 1993)
Nov. 20, 2000 – Formed TRI Communication Solutions, Inc. in Delaware on amalgamation with Telemarket Resources, Inc.

Redzone Resources Ltd. (Alta. Dec. 23, 2005)
Mar. 2, 2011 – Continued into Ontario.
Mar. 20, 2019 – Name changed to Global Battery Metals Ltd. (see FPsurvey - Mines & Energy)

Reece Energy Exploration Corp. (Alta. Apr. 13, 2004)
May 15, 2007 – Amalgamated in Alberta to continue with same name. (see Penn West Energy Trust)
May 5, 2009 – Acquired by Penn West Energy Trust; basis 0.125 Penn West trust units for 1 Reece Energy sh. (see Penn West Energy Trust)

Reece Energy Inc. (Alta. Apr. 13, 2004)
May 18, 2005 – Name changed to Reece Energy Exploration Corp. following Qualifying Transaction acquisition of Ganze-Reece Operations Ltd., Blue Denim Exploration Inc. and Render Resources Ltd.; basis 1 new for 4 old shs. ■

Reed Lake Exploration Ltd. (Ont. June 20, 1986)
Nov. 27, 1996 – Formed Westhope Capital Corp. in Ontario on amalgamation with 1198691 Ontario Inc. (deemed acquiror); basis 1 new for 1 1198691 Ontario sh. and 1 new for 7 Reed Lake shs. ■

Reed Paper Group Canada Limited (Can. 1961)
May 22, 1974 – Name changed to Reed Paper Ltd. ■

Reed Paper Ltd. (Can. 1961)
Oct. 6, 1980 – All conv. pref. shs. redeemed at $12.50 per sh.
Oct. 11, 1980 – Amalgamated with subsids. Reed Ltd. and Reed Anglo Ltd. under the name of Reed Paper Ltd. All com. shs. exchanged for redeemable spec. shs., which were redeemed within 14 days at $12.50 per sh., making the co. private.
Mar. 1981 – Name changed to Reed Inc.

Reed Shaw Osler Limited (Can. 1968)
Feb. 10, 1978 – Name changed to Reed Stenhouse Companies Limited. ■

Reed Stenhouse Companies Limited (Can. 1968)
Feb. 17, 1997 – All o/s cl. 1 special shs. redeemed; basis 1 com. sh. and pref. stk. purchase rt. of Alexander & Alexander Services Inc. (A&A) for 1 old special sh. of Reed plus any dividends payable. Following redemption date, A&A will merge with a subsid. of Aon Corporation resulting in each A&A sh. converted to the right to receive US$17.50 per sh. Previously Reed merged with A&A in September 1985; each old Cl. A and C sh. of Reed was exchangeable for 0.576 of a newly issued A&A Cl. A or C sh. Each A&A Cl. A sh. was accompanied by a newly issued Reed Stenhouse Cl. 1 special sh.
Dec. 22, 1997 – Name changed to Aon Canada Inc.

Reef Explorations Ltd. (Ont. Feb. 9, 1948)
1961 – Name changed to United Reef Petroleums Limited; basis 1 new for 4 old shs. ■

Reef Hydrocarbons Ltd. (Alta. Dec. 23, 1977)
Sept. 29, 1988 – Name changed to International Reef Resources Ltd.; basis 1 new for 5 old shs. ■

Reef Petroleums Ltd. (Ont. Feb. 9, 1948)
1956 – Name changed to Reef Explorations Ltd. ■

Reef Point Mines Ltd. (Ont. 1966)
Aug. 1972 – Charter cancelled.

Reef Resources Corporation (B.C. 1979)
Nov. 25, 1981 – Amalgamated with Westland Resources (1 for 2) to form United Westland Resources Ltd.; basis 1 new for 2 old shs.

Reeflex Petroleum Technologies Inc. (Alta. Dec. 3, 1992)
June 2, 2003 – Struck from registry and dissolved.

Reem Capital Corp. (B.C. Mar. 29, 2021)
Aug. 21, 2025 – Continued into Alberta. (see FPsurvey - Industrials)

Reese River Resource Corporation (B.C. Sept. 13, 1985)
Mar. 18, 1994 – Name changed to Hurley River Gold Corp.; basis 1 new for 5 old shs. ■

Reeta Explorations Ltd. (Ont. 1970)
May 14, 1975 – Charter cancelled.

Reff Incorporated (Ont. 1964)
Jan. 30, 1990 – All o/s shs. acquired at $12.75 per sh. by a wholly owned subsid. of Westinghouse Canada Inc.

Refined Metals Corp. (B.C. Apr. 26, 2013)
Mar. 15, 2024 – Name changed to Refined Energy Corp. (see FPsurvey - Mines & Energy)

Reflection Resources Ltd. (Alta. Oct. 31, 1985 amalg.)
July 14, 1989 – Name changed to Corsair Petroleum Inc.; basis 1 new for 10 old shs. ■

Reflex Exploration Inc. (B.C. June 10, 2021)
Apr. 14, 2022 – Name changed to Freedom Battery Metals Inc. ■

Reflow Oil Ltd. (Ont. 1945)
1958 – Struck off register.

Reford Mines Ltd. (Ont. 1958)
July 27, 1976 – Charter cancelled.

Reg Resources Corp. (B.C. Oct. 6, 1982)
Feb. 23, 1993 – Name changed to Reg Technologies Inc. ■

Reg Technologies Inc. (B.C. Oct. 6, 1982)
Feb. 22, 2017 – Assets sold to Regi U.S., Inc.; basis 1.1 Regi U.S. com. shs. for 1 Reg com. sh.
Nov. 6, 2018 – Name changed to Graph Blockchain Inc. following reverse takeover acquisition of Graph Blockchain Limited.; basis 1 new for 10 old shs. ■

Regal Consolidated Ventures Limited (Ont. Mar. 1, 1962)
Dec. 1, 2008 – Struck from register and dissolved.

Regal Energy Corp. (Alta. Feb. 24, 2004)
Dec. 31, 2005 – Formed Regal Energy Ltd. in Alberta on reverse takeover acquisition of and amalgamation with Azeri Capital Inc.; basis 7.37 new for 1 Azeri sh. and 1 new for 5 Regal shs. ■

Regal Energy Ltd. (Alta. Dec. 31, 2005 amalg.)
Aug. 5, 2009 – Name changed to Novus Energy Inc.; basis 1 new for 10 old shs. ■

Regal Gold Corporation (B.C. Sept. 4, 1987)
June 23, 1994 – Name changed to International Thunderbird Gaming Corporation. ■

Regal Goldfields Limited (Ont. Mar. 1, 1962)
Oct. 19, 2000 – Name changed to Regal Consolidated Ventures Limited; basis 1 new for 10 old shs. ■

Regal Greetings & Gifts Inc. (Can. Oct. 11, 1984)
Oct. 17, 1994 – Acquired by RGG Acquisition Corporation, a wholly owned subsid. of MDC Corporation; basis $10.75 ($11.40 less $0.65 special div. paid Sept. 30, 1994) per sh. (see MDC Corporation)

Regal Investment Ventures Ltd. (Alta. 1960)
Aug. 15, 1970 – Charter cancelled.

Regal Lifestyle Communities Inc. (Ont. Apr. 11, 2012)
Oct. 28, 2015 – Acquired by HCN-Revera Joint Venture ULC, a joint investment vehicle of Revera and Welltower, for $12.00 per sh.

Regal Minerals Ltd. (unknown)
1959 – Assets acquired by Westore Mines Ltd.; basis 1 new for 4 old shs.

Regal Mining and Development Ltd. (Ont. 1945)
1967 – Merged into Resource Exploration & Development Co. Ltd.; basis 100 new for 269 old shs.

Regal Mining Co. Ltd. (B.C. 1958)
May 15, 1969 – Dissolved and struck off register.

Regal Petroleum Ltd. (B.C. Apr. 15, 1979)
Feb. 3, 1988 – Name changed to Consolidated Regal Resources Ltd.; basis 1 new for 5 old shs. ■

Regalito Copper Corp. (B.C. Mar. 3, 2000)
July 17, 2006 – Acquired by PPC Canada Enterprise Corp. wholly owned subsid. of Pan Pacific Copper Co. Ltd.; basis US$6.00 per sh.

Regcourt Gold Mines Ltd. (Que. 1944)
1956 – Name changed to Consolidated Regcourt Mines Ltd.; basis 1 new for 5 old shs. ■

Regeena Resources Inc. (B.C. Apr. 18, 1988)
June 9, 2000 – Name changed to Ameridian Ventures Inc. ■

Regency Gold Corp. (Can. Sept. 21, 2000)
Apr. 1, 2020 – Name changed to Clean Air Metals Inc. (see FPsurvey - Mines & Energy)

Regency Oils Limited (Alta. 1951)
Apr. 30, 1977 – Struck off register.

Regency Resources Ltd. (B.C. Nov. 5, 1973)
Mar. 29, 1985 – Name changed to Raypath Resources Ltd.; basis 1 new for 5 old shs. ■

Regent Mines and Minerals Ltd. (Ont. 1943)
June 12, 1952 – Charter cancelled.

Regent Oil Co. Ltd. (Can. 1927)
Acquired prior to 1937 by Mid Continent Oil Corp. Ltd. (see Mid Continent Oil Corp. Ltd.)

Regent Refining (Canada) Ltd. (Ont. 1933)
Feb. 1957 – Acquired by McColl-Frontenac Oil Co. Ltd.; basis 6 McColl-Frontenac shs. for 19 Regent shs.

Regent Resources Ltd. (Ont. 1984)
Nov. 14, 1985 – Amalgamated with 6 other cos. to form Paladin Petroleum Corporation; basis 1.25 new for 1 old sh.

Regent Rock Development Inc. (Ont. Aug. 25, 1987)
May 30, 1995 – Name changed to Pan Pacific Strategies Corp.; basis 1 new for 2 old shs. (see FPsurvey - Industrials)

Regent Rock Resources Inc. (Ont. Aug. 25, 1987)
Feb. 26, 1990 – Name changed to Regent Rock Development Inc. ■

Regent Ventures Ltd. (B.C. Sept. 8, 1986)
Aug. 17, 2020 – Dissolved and struck from register.

Regia Resources Ltd. (B.C. Mar. 26, 1956)
July 7, 1995 – Continued into Canada.
June 10, 2004 – Dissolved.

Regina Resources Inc. (B.C. July 30, 1979)
Oct. 2, 1984 – Name changed to Shanell International Energy Corporation; basis 1 new for 2 old shs. ■

Regina Royalties Ltd. (unknown)
1964 – Acquired by Scurry-Rainbow Oil (Sask.) Ltd.; basis 1 new for 5 old shs.

Regina Yellowknife Gold Mines Ltd. (Ont. 1944)
Apr. 1, 1954 – Charter cancelled.

Regional Cablesystems Inc. (Can. Oct. 26, 1984)
Sept. 10, 2001 – Name changed to Persona Inc. pursuant to plan of arrangement reorganization. ■

Regional Resources Ltd. (B.C. Nov. 27, 1979)
May 25, 1983 – Continued into Canada.
June 9, 1988 – Amalgamated in Canada to continue with same name.
Dec. 6, 1996 – Amalgamated with a wholly owned subsid. of Imperial Metals Corporation; basis $1.00 or 0.8 Imperial Metals shs. for 1 Regional sh.

Regis Development Corporation (B.C. Sept. 30, 1967)
Jan. 10, 1992 – Name changed to Manus Industries Inc.; basis 1 new for 4.5 old shs. ■

Registry Resources Inc. (Can. Apr. 1, 1985)
Apr. 1, 1995 – Formed Procoloro Resources Inc. in Canada on amalgamation with Procoloro Resources Inc. (deemed acquiror); basis 1 new for 1 Procoloro sh. and 1 new for 5 Registry shs. ■

Regulus Resources Inc. (B.C. July 30, 1980)
Dec. 18, 1985 – Name changed to High Rise Resources Inc.; basis 4 new for 1 old sh. ■

Regulus Resources Inc. (Alta. Oct. 15, 2010)
Sept. 30, 2014 – Amalgamated in Alberta to continue with same name. (see FPsurvey - Mines & Energy) (see Southern Legacy Minerals Inc.)

Reichhold Chemicals Limited (Ont. 1949)
Oct. 1, 1977 – Name changed to Reichhold Limited. ■

Reichhold Limited (Ont. 1949)
Mar. 15, 1985 – Acquired by RCI Acquisitions Inc., a subsid. of Reichhold Chemicals Inc., for $15 per sh. Subsequently, amalgamated with other Reichhold subsids. to continue as Reichhold Ltd.

David S. Reid Limited (Ont. July 10, 1997)
Oct. 24, 2016 – Struck from register.

Reid Lithographing Company Limited (Ont. 1961)
1973 – Acquired by Moore Corp. Ltd. for $19.50 per sh.

Reigate Inc. (Alta. Feb. 28, 1983 amalg.)
Feb. 1, 1999 – Dissolved and struck off register.

Reigate Resources (Canada) Ltd. (Alta. Feb. 28, 1983 amalg.)
Sept. 28, 1995 – Name changed to Reigate Inc. ■

Reigate Resources Inc. (Mont. 1979)
Feb. 28, 1983 – Formed Reigate Resources (Canada) Ltd. in Alberta on amalgamation with Midvale Petroleums Ltd. and Zodiac Resources; basis 1 new cl. A sh. for 1 old com. sh. ■

Reimer Overhead Doors Ltd. (B.C. Oct. 8, 1986)
Mar. 31, 1993 – Name changed to Reimer Resources Ltd. ■

Reimer Resources Ltd. (B.C. Oct. 8, 1986)
Nov. 3, 1993 – Amalgamated with Rattler Resource Ltd. to form Kensington Resources Ltd.; basis 1 new for 1 Rattler sh. and 1 new for 2 Reimer shs. (see Kensington Resources Ltd.)

La Reine Metal Mines Ltd. (Que. 1960)
May 5, 1973 – Dissolved.

Du Reine Mines Ltd. (Ont. 1945)
Nov. 25, 1970 – Dissolved.

Relay Creek Resources Ltd. (B.C. Aug. 6, 1985)
Oct. 20, 1987 – Name changed to Aabbax International Financial Corp. ■

Relay Medical Corp. (Ont. Sept. 8, 2014)
Dec. 8, 2021 – Name changed to Scryb Inc. (see FPsurvey - Industrials)

Relentless Dip Fund 1 Lp Corp. (Alta. Feb. 26, 2009)
May 22, 2012 – Name changed to Jadela Disposal Well Corp. ∎

Relentless Resources Ltd. (Alta. Mar. 30, 2006 amalg.)
Oct. 26, 2018 – Name changed to SugarBud Craft Growers Corp. following acquisition of cannabis comapny Grunewahl Organics Inc. ∎

Relevium Technologies Inc. (Can. July 19, 2012)
Aug. 10, 2024 – Dissolved for non-compliance and struck from register.

Reliable Energy Ltd. (Alta. June 5, 2006)
May 4, 2012 – Acquired by Crescent Point Energy Corp.; basis 0.00794 Crescent Point shs. for 1 Reliable Energy sh. (see Crescent Point Energy Corp.)

Reliance Energy Inc. (Alta. May 28, 1996)
Feb. 1, 2002 – Name changed to Norex Exploration Services Inc. following reverse takeover acquisitions of Norex Exploration Inc. and Eclipse Seismic Processors Inc.; basis 1 new for 10 old shs. ∎

Reliance Grain Co. Ltd. (Can. 1927)
1948 – Com. shldrs. offered $50 per sh. by private ints.
1949 – Sold terminal elevator at Thunder Bay, Ont. Former subsids., Alliance Grain Co. and Province Elevator Co. distributed assets and charters surrendered.

Reliance Petroleum Ltd. (Ont. 1928)
1959 – All assets acquired by Supertest Petroleum Corporation, Limited early. (see Supertest Petroleum Corporation, Limited)

Reliance Resources Limited (B.C. Oct. 20, 1987)
Feb. 26, 2016 – Name changed to Resource Capital Gold Corp.; basis 1 new for 5 old shs. ∎

Reliance Services Group Ltd. (Alta. Dec. 9, 1996)
Apr. 12, 2000 – Amalgamated with OTATCO Inc. (1.45949 for 1) to form Integrated Production Services Ltd.; basis 2.33518 new Reliance sh. for 1 old Integrated Production sh. (see Integrated Production Services Ltd.)

Reliance Shoe Company (Ont. 1912)
1957 – Name changed to Maher Shoes Ontario Limited. ∎

Reliant Gold Corp. (Ont. July 11, 2005)
Sept. 17, 2018 – Name changed to Flexwork Properties Ltd. ∎

Reliant Resources Limited (B.C. May 4, 1984)
Dec. 9, 1993 – Name changed to Soranzo International Spirits Inc. ∎

Reliant Ventures Ltd. (B.C. Dec. 1, 1990 amalg.)
May 29, 2003 – Name changed to Esperanza Silver Corporation. ∎

Relief-Arlington Mines Ltd. (B.C. 1905)
1945 – Wound up.

ReMac Zinc Corp. (B.C. June 4, 2007)
Jan. 19, 2011 – Name changed to Corazon Gold Corp. pursuant to reverse takeover acquisition of 0887398 B.C. Ltd. ∎

Remac Resources Ltd. (Alta. 1965)
Apr. 29, 1978 – Charter cancelled Feb. 29, 1972; revived Oct. 1, 1973; cancelled again.

Remar Resources Ltd. (B.C. 1968)
July 15, 1975 – Name changed to Golden Shamrock Resources Ltd.; basis 2 new for 5 old shs. ∎

Rembrandt Gold Mines Ltd. (Ont. May 27, 1938)
1992 – Continued into Canada.
May 16, 1996 – Continued into Cayman Islands.

Rembrandt Jewelry Limited (Ont. 1973 amalg.)
Oct. 1978 – All o/s shs. acquired either for $5.75 or for cl. A special shs. immediately redeemed at $5.75 under an offer by Sagehill Investments Limited, a co. owned by Rembrandt's controlling shldrs.

Remida Ventures Inc. (B.C. May 8, 1987)
Sept. 16, 1993 – Name changed to Caymus Ventures Corp.; basis 1 new for 2.5 old shs. ∎

Remington Creek Resources Inc. (B.C. Aug. 1, 1980)
Feb. 26, 1996 – Name changed to Grayd Resource Corporation; basis 1 new for 3 old shs. ∎

Remington Energy Ltd. (Alta. Sept. 11, 1984)
Apr. 16, 1999 – Acquired by DEI Canada Holding Company Inc., a wholly owned subsid. of Dominion Resources, Inc. of Virginia, for $1.90 per sh.

Remo Resources Inc. (B.C. May 2, 2011)
Jan. 29, 2018 – Name changed to Chakana Copper Corp. following reverse takeover acquisition of (old) Chakana Copper Corp.; basis 1 new for 6.865385 old shs. (see FPsurvey - Mines & Energy)

Remstar Resources Ltd. (B.C. Nov. 3, 1993)
Feb. 3, 2014 – Name changed to Avarone Metals Inc. (see FPsurvey - Mines & Energy)

Renabie Gold Mines Limited (Can. 1974)
Dec. 23, 1988 – Private company. Became a wholly owned subsid. of Corona Corporation, with the acquisition of the 9% int. held by American Barrick Resources Corporation. Originally known as Renabie Mines (1981) Limited, the co. was a jointly owned (50%/50%) subsid. of Cullaton Lake Gold Mines Ltd. (subsequently Corona Corporation) and Barrick Resources Corporation (subsequently American Barrick Resources Corporation) formed to facilitate refinancing and expansion of the Renabie mine. Name was changed October 1984 and in 1986, Barrick reduced its interest to 9% in exch. for a direct 45% int. in the mine.

The Renabie Gold Trust (Ont. 1984)
Aug. 17, 1993 – Wound up. Unitholders received a final cash settlement of $0.05018 for ea. unit surrendered.

Renabie Mines Ltd. (Ont. 1941)
1970 – Merged into Willroy Mines Ltd.; basis 1 new for 3 old shs.

Renabie Mines Limited (Can. 1952)
Nov. 1980 – Name changed to Sungate Resources Ltd. ∎

Renaissance Energy Ltd. (Alta. Jan. 28, 1982)
Aug. 28, 2000 – Acquired by Husky Oil Limited to form Husky Energy Inc.; basis $20.50 or 1 Husky Energy sh. plus $2.50 for 1 Renaissance sh. (see Husky Energy Inc.)

Renaissance Gold Inc. (B.C. May 25, 2010)
Sept. 20, 2020 – Acquired by Evrim Resources Corp., renamed Orogen Royalties Inc.; basis 1.2448 Evrim shs. for 1 Renaissance Gold. sh.

Renaissance Golf (Canada) Inc. (Can. July 8, 1991)
Sept. 12, 2000 – Name changed to FranchiseMaster Technologies Inc.; basis 1 new for 20 old shs. ∎

Renaissance Industrial Corp. (Ont. Apr. 26, 1966)
Mar. 10, 1988 – Name changed to D.A.S. Electronics Industries Inc. ∎

Renaissance Oil Corp. (B.C. June 9, 2010)
July 30, 2021 – Acquired by Reconnaissance Energy Africa Ltd. (ReconAfrica); basis 0.046 ReconAfrica shs. for 1 Renaissance Oil sh.

Renasant Financial Partners Ltd. (Ont. Jan. 30, 1984)
Jan. 19, 2009 – Acquired by Paros Enterprises Limited and Capital Tachane Inc. for $1.75 per sh. Co. now private.

Renata Resources Inc. (Alta. Dec. 31, 1996 amalg.)
June 21, 2000 – Acquired by Rio Alto Exploration Ltd.; basis 77¢, 0.0283 Rio Alto shs. or a combination thereof for 1 Renata sh. (see Rio Alto Exploration Ltd.)

Rencan Resource Investments Ltd. (Can. 1972)
June 9, 1977 – Name changed to Norminco Developments Limited; basis 1 new for 5 old shs. ∎

Rencore Resources Ltd. (Ont. Nov. 23, 1972)
Feb. 14, 2012 – Amalgamated with Bold Ventures Inc.

Rendez Vous Gold Mining Corp. (B.C. July 2, 1980)
Mar. 4, 1987 – Name changed to American Canadian Systems Inc. ∎

Reneaux Capital Inc. (Can. Aug. 30, 1985)
Dec. 18, 1990 – Continued into Ontario.
July 2, 1993 – Name changed to Naturally Niagara Incorporated. ∎

Renegade Mines Ltd. (Ont. 1968)
Apr. 9, 1990 – Dissolved.

Renegade Petroleum Ltd. (Alta. June 22, 1998)
Apr. 9, 2014 – Acquired by Spartan Energy Corp. (formerly Alexander Energy Ltd.); basis 0.5625 Spartan com. shs. for 1 Renegade com. sh. (see Spartan Energy Corp.)

Renewable Energy Developers Inc. (Can. Jan. 31, 2011)
Oct. 8, 2013 – Acquired by Capstone Infrastructure Corporation; basis 0.26 Capstone com. shs. plus $0.001 cash for 1 com. sh. held. (see Capstone Infrastructure Corporation)
Feb. 15, 2014 – Formed Capstone Power Corp. in British Columbia on amalgamation with (old) Capstone Power Corp., a wholly owned subsidiary of Capstone Infrastructure Corporation. (see Capstone Infrastructure Corporation)

Renex Minerals Ltd. (Ont. 1969)
Oct. 30, 1979 – Charter cancelled.

Renfield Enterprises Inc. (Alta. Oct. 24, 1989)
Mar. 19, 1998 – Continued into Yukon. (see FPsurvey - Industrials)

Renfort Gold Mines Ltd. (Ont. 1944)
Oct. 1960 – Dissolved.

Renfrew Aircraft & Engineering Co. Ltd. (unknown)
1968 – Acquired by Bartaco Industries Ltd. (see Bartaco Industries Limited)

Renfrew Minerals Ltd. (Ont. 1933)
1969 – Charter cancelled.

Renfrew Petroleums Ltd. (unknown)
1960 – Acquired by Western Decalta Petroleums Ltd.; basis 1 new for 15 old shs.

Renfrew Textiles Limited (Can. 1919)
Jan. 1954 – Filed an assignment into bankruptcy. No funds available to holders of cl. A pref. shs. and cl. B shs.

Rengold Mines Limited (Can. 1973)
1979 – Payment in full received by secured and pref. creditors and of ordinary creditors of $250 or less. Other creditors received 15¢ per $1.00 claim and right to recover full claim pro-rata from 5% net profits int. in Renabie gold mine sold to Sungate Resources Ltd. Com. shldrs. received 1 sh. Kilembe Copper Cobalt Ltd. (see Renabie Mines Limited)

Renmark Explorations Limited. (Ont. 1969)
May 13, 1980 – Dissolved.

Renn Industries Inc. (B.C. June 23, 1961)
Mar. 26, 1981 – Continued into Canada.
Apr. 30, 1981 – Name changed to Anthes Industries Inc. ∎

Renn Mining & Exploration Ltd. (Alta. 1958)
Sept. 30, 1970 – Charter cancelled.

Renniks Resources Ltd. (B.C. Sept. 14, 1972)
Dec. 12, 1977 – Name changed to Glamis Gold Ltd.; basis 1 new for 3 old shs. ∎

Réno-Dépôt Inc. (Can. Nov. 1, 1986 amalg.)
Apr. 30, 1997 – Acquired by Castorama Canada Inc. for $35.50 per sh.

Reno Gold Mines Limited (B.C. 1920)
1952 – Charter cancelled.

Renoir Water Inc. (Alta. Sept. 25, 1985)
Aug. 20, 1996 – Name changed to Frank's Corporation. ∎

Renold Chains Canada Ltd. (Can. 1932)
July 28, 1992 – Dissolved. shldrs. received $1.12 plus an accrued div. of $0.5997 for 1 cl. A sh.

Renold Coventry Ltd. (Can. 1932)
Apr. 25, 1955 – Name changed to Renold Chains Canada Ltd. ∎

Renox Creek Petroleum Inc. (B.C. 1980)
Nov. 15, 1982 – Name changed to Renox Creek Resources Inc. ∎

Renox Creek Resources Inc. (B.C. 1980)
Jan. 23, 1987 – Name changed to Equinox Entertainment Corp. ∎

Renprior Zinc Mines Ltd. (Ont. 1951)
Dec. 16, 1957 – Dissolved.

Rent-A-Wreck Capital Inc. (Can. Aug. 27, 1998)
Nov. 30, 2006 – Name changed to Franchise Services of North America Inc. pursuant to reverse takeover acquisition of U-Save Auto Rental of America, Inc.; basis 1 new for 4.0785967 old shs. ∎

Rent-A-Wreck Industries Corp. (B.C. Nov. 3, 1982)
Sept. 7, 1988 – Name changed to Practicar Industries Corp.; basis 1 new for 5 old shs. ∎

Rentcash Inc. (Ont. Jan. 17, 2002 amalg.)
Mar. 31, 2008 – Name changed to The Cash Store Financial Services Inc. following spin-off of its rental division to Insta-Rent Inc. ∎

Rentown Enterprises Inc. (Can. 1987)
Jan. 31, 1991 – Entered bankruptcy, Arthur Andersen appointed trustee.
June 1991 – All operating assets were sold. Secured creditors suffered a substantial shortfall and unsecured creditors and shldrs. received no distribution.

Renwick Explorations Ltd. (B.C. Mar. 17, 1983)
July 15, 1985 – Name changed to Iori International Oil Royalties Inc. ∎

Reoplata Mines Ltd. (Ont. 1949)
Dec. 1962 – Charter cancelled.

Repadre Capital Corporation (Ont. Mar. 7, 1990)
Jan. 13, 2003 – Acquired by IAMGold Corporation; basis 1.6 IAMGold shs. for 1 Repadre sh.

Repadre Resources Ltd. (B.C. Feb. 24, 1981)
Mar. 7, 1990 – Name changed to Repadre Capital Corporation and continued into Ontario. ∎

Repap Enterprises Corporation Inc. (Can. Jan. 9, 1963)
Apr. 25, 1989 – Name changed to Repap Enterprises Inc. ∎

Repap Enterprises Inc. (Can. Jan. 9, 1963)
Oct. 19, 2000 – Acquired by UPM-Kymmene Corporation for 20¢ per sh.

RepeatSeat Ltd. (Alta. July 14, 2005 amalg.)
Sept. 22, 2009 – Placed into receivership. David Bromwich of Bromwich and Smith, Inc. has been appointed as trustee.

RepliCel Life Sciences Inc. (B.C. June 22, 2011)
Mar. 3, 2025 – Voluntarily delisted from the TSX-Venture Exchange.
Mar. 3, 2025 – Name changed to 0913693 B.C. Ltd. (see FPsurvey - Industrials)

Reprox Corporation (Que. 1964)
Oct. 1974 – Operations of co. terminated, as it was declared insolvent. Nothing available for shldrs.

Republic Aircraft Manufacturing Corporation (B.C. Dec. 23, 1986)
June 10, 1992 – Name changed to International Republic Aircraft Manufacturing Corporation; basis 1 new for 5 old shs. ∎

Republic Goldfields Inc. (Ont. Feb. 4, 1975)
Apr. 1, 2013 – Certificate of incorporation cancelled for default in complying with the provisions of the Corporations Tax Act resulting in dissolution of the company and being struck from register.

Republic Industries, Inc. (Del. May 31, 1991)
Apr. 6, 1999 – Name changed to AutoNation, Inc.

Republic Lead Mines Ltd. (Ont. 1948)
May 12, 1959 – Name changed to Republic Oils & Mines Ltd. ∎

Republic Oils & Mines Ltd. (Ont. 1948)
Feb. 4, 1960 – Name changed to Republic Ores & Mining Corp. Ltd. ∎

Republic Ores & Mining Corp. Ltd. (Ont. 1948)
June 5, 1981 – Name changed to Sumach Resources Inc.; basis 2 new for 1 old sh. ∎

Republic Resources Limited (Alta.)
1977 – Private co., 100692 Holdings Ltd., acquired o/s shs. of co. at $1.50 per sh.

Republic Tungsten Mines Ltd. (Ont. 1942)
Nov. 1959 – Charter cancelled.

Republic Waste Industries Inc. (unknown Nov. 1980)
May 31, 1991 – Continued into Delaware.
Dec. 7, 1995 – Name changed to Republic Industries, Inc. ∎

ReQuest Income Trust (Alta. Feb. 5, 2001)
Feb. 4, 2002 – Acquired by Pulse Data Inc.; basis 2.1 new Pulse shs. for 1 old ReQuest trust unit. (see Pulse Data Inc.)

ReQuest Seismic Surveys Ltd. (Alta. Dec. 1, 1989)
Aug. 1, 1997 – Amalgamated in Alberta to continue with same name. (see ReQuest Income Trust)
Mar. 20, 2001 – Converted into an income trust named ReQuest Income Trust; basis 1 new trust unit for 2 com. shs. (see ReQuest Income Trust)

Research In Motion Limited (Ont. Mar. 7, 1984)
July 9, 2013 – Name changed to BlackBerry Limited. (see FPsurvey - Industrials)

Resenor Gold Mines Ltd. (Ont. 1945)
1969 – Charter cancelled.

Reserve Mining Co. Ltd. (Ont. 1924)
Wound up and charter surrendered.

Reserve Natural Gas Co., Ltd. (Ont. 1931)
1960 – Struck off register.

Reserve Royalty Corporation (Can. Mar. 14, 1986 amalg.)
Jan. 1, 1996 – Amalgamated in Canada to continue with same name. (see PrimeWest Energy Trust)
July 28, 2000 – Acquired by PrimeWest Royalty Corp.; basis 0.065 PrimeWest Energy Trust units for 1 Reserve com. sh. (see PrimeWest Energy Trust)

Reservoir Capital Corp. (Alta. Mar. 23, 2006)
Nov. 15, 2007 – Continued into British Columbia. (see FPsurvey - Industrials)

Reservoir Minerals Inc. (B.C. Jan. 25, 2011)
June 27, 2016 – Acquired by Nevsun Resources Ltd.; basis 2 Nevsun com. sh. plus $2 for 1 Reservoir com. sh. (see Nevsun Resources Ltd.)

Residential Equities Real Estate Investment Trust (Ont. Oct. 24, 1997)
June 3, 2004 – Acquired by Canadian Apartment Properties Real Estate Investment Trust; basis $18.60 or 1.216 new Canadian Apartment units for 1 old Residential unit.

Resilient Resources Ltd. (Alta. Feb. 20, 1992)
Apr. 21, 2006 – Formed Guardian Exploration Inc. in Alberta on amalgamation with (old) Guardian Exploration Inc. (deemed acquiror); basis 0.489758 new for 1 Guardian sh. and 0.154376 new for 1 Resilient sh. (see FPsurvey - Mines & Energy)

Resin Systems Inc. (Alta. Sept. 17, 1998 amalg.)
June 23, 2010 – Name changed to RS Technologies Inc. ∎

Resinco Capital Partners Inc. (B.C. May 25, 2004)
Apr. 15, 2020 – Name changed to Global Care Capital Inc. ∎

The Resolute Corporation (Ont. 1949)
May 25, 1993 – Declared bankrupt and Deloitte & Touche Inc. of Toronto, Ont. was appointed trustee.
Sept. 1, 2002 – Deloitte & Touche was discharged. There were no distributions to creditors or shldrs.

Resolute Energy Inc. (Alta. June 10, 1997)
May 2, 2005 – Acquired by Esprit Energy Trust; basis either a) 0.338 Esprit cl. B trust units plus 0.2857 Cordero Energy Inc. com. shs. plus 0.0269 Cordero wts., or b) 0.338 Esprit cl. A trust units plus 0.2857 Cordero com. shs. plus 0.0269 Cordero wts. for 1 Resolute com. sh. (see Cordero Energy Inc.; Esprit Energy Trust)

Resolute Forest Products Inc. (Del. Jan. 25, 2007)
Mar. 3, 2023 – Acquired by Paper Excellence Canada Holdings Corporation, through wholly owned Domtar Corporation; basis US$20.50 cash per sh.

Resolute Oil & Gas Co. Ltd. (Ont. 1949)
1965 – Name changed to Resolute Petroleums Limited; basis 1 new for 5 old shs. ∎

Resolute Petroleums Limited (Ont. 1949)
July 26, 1988 – Name changed to The Resolute Corporation; basis 1 new for 10 old shs. ∎

Resolute Resources Ltd. (B.C. Jan. 29, 1986)
Jan. 4, 1994 – Name changed to European Garnet Ltd. ∎

Resolution Energy Inc. (Alta. June 3, 1993)
Nov. 19, 2001 – Name changed to Resolution Resources Ltd.; basis 1 new for 3 old shs. ∎

Resolution Resources Ltd. (Alta. June 3, 1993)
Jan. 1, 2003 – Amalgamated with Voltorb Resources Ltd. and Devinsharpe Resources Ltd. to form new co. with same name Berens Energy Ltd.
Nov. 19, 2003 – Formed Berens Energy Ltd. in Alberta pursuant to acquisition by and amalgamation with Berens Energy Ltd.; basis $0.34 cash plus 0.465 Berens shs. for 1 Resolution sh. ∎

Resolve Business Outsourcing Income Fund (Ont. Feb. 12, 2006)
July 31, 2009 – Acquired by Davis + Henderson Income Fund; basis 0.285 Davis + Henderson trust units for 1 Resolve Business trust unit. (see Davis + Henderson Income Fund)
Aug. 31, 2009 – Dissolved. (see Davis + Henderson Income Fund)

Resolve Energy Inc. (Alta. Nov. 2, 2005)
May 8, 2007 – Amalgamated with Anterra Corporation which continued as Anterra Energy Inc.; basis 1 cl. A and 1 cl. B sh. of Anterra Energy for 1 old Resolve com. sh. (see Anterra Energy Inc.)

Resolve Ventures Inc. (B.C. Mar. 31, 1980)
Nov. 26, 2021 – Name changed to Atomic Minerals Corporation. (see FPsurvey - Mines & Energy)

ResoQuest Energy Corp. (Alta. Oct. 1, 1989 amalg.)
June 12, 1992 – Name changed to ResoQuest Resources Ltd.; basis 1 new for 8 old shs. ∎

ResoQuest Resources Ltd. (Alta. Oct. 1, 1989 amalg.)
July 21, 1994 – Acquired by Pinnacle Resources Ltd.; basis $7.25 or 0.357 Pinnacle shs. for 1 ResoQuest sh. (see Pinnacle Resources Ltd.)

Resorts Unlimited Management Inc. (Can. Aug. 9, 1989 amalg.)
Mar. 6, 2006 – Dissolved.

Resource Capital Gold Corp. (B.C. Oct. 20, 1987)
Jan. 28, 2019 – Filed a notice of intent to make a proposal under the Bankruptcy and Insolvency Act (BIA). PricewaterhouseCoopers Inc. was appointed proposal trustee.
July 11, 2019 – The sales process was completed and the company accepted an offer to sell substantially all of its assets to 2672403 Ontario Inc., a nominee company of Sprott Private Resource Lending (Collector) LP, via a credit bid which resulted in the forgiveness of the interim financing facility provided by Sprott Private.
July 13, 2019 – Deemed bankrupt as the proceeds from the sale of the assets to Sprott Private was not sufficient to satisfy the secured debts owed by the company. PricewaterhouseCoopers was appointed trustee.

Resource Capital International Ltd. (Bermuda Nov. 25, 1985)
Aug. 16, 1989 – Name changed to International Equity Ltd. ■

Resource Equity Ltd. (Alta. Aug. 27, 1984)
Nov. 8, 2001 – Continued into Ontario.
Nov. 21, 2006 – Continued into Delaware.
Dec. 4, 2006 – Name changed to Geovic Mining Corp. following reverse takeover acquisition of Geovic Finance Corp. and 45 shs. of Geovic Cameroon plc; basis 1 new for 2.2344 old shs.

Resource Exploration & Development Co. Ltd. (Ont. 1967)
May 1980 – Charter cancelled.

Resource Hunter Capital Corp. (B.C. July 24, 2007)
May 16, 2011 – Name changed to Plains Creek Phosphate Corporation pursuant to Qualifying Transaction reverse takeover acquisition of Plains Creek Mining Limited and subsequent amalgamation of Plains Creek with wholly owned 0890110 B.C. Ltd. ■

The Resource Service Group Ltd. (Alta. 1972)
1977 – Continued into Canada.
May 13, 1985 – Amalgamated with 139435 Canada Inc. Subord. voting shldrs. received on sh.-for-sh. basis pref. shs. of amalgamated company, which were subsequently redeemed at $3.00 per sh. Warrant holders offered 25¢ per wt.

Resource Ventures Inc. (unknown)
Sept. 1970 – Liquidated and assets distributed to Ranger Oil (Canada) Ltd.

Resource Ventures Inc. (Nev. Nov. 29, 1999)
Aug. 22, 2006 – Name changed to New Dawn Mining Corp. and continued into British Columbia. ■

ResourceCan Limited (N.L. Oct. 10, 1980)
May 28, 1996 – Continued into Canada.
Mar. 6, 1997 – Name changed to Stratos Global Corporation. ■

Resourcexplorer Inc. (Alta. Feb. 19, 2001)
July 24, 2002 – Name changed to Exchequer Resource Corp.; basis 1 new for 10 old shs. ■

Resouro Gold Inc. (B.C. Aug. 4, 1992)
Oct. 17, 2023 – Name changed to Resouro Strategic Metals Inc. (see FPsurvey - Mines & Energy)

Respect Your Universe, Inc. (Nev. Nov. 21, 2008)
Feb. 20, 2015 – Succeeded by RYU Apparel Inc. pursuant to a plan of arrangement with Respect Your Universe continuing as a wholly owned subsid. of RYU Apparel. (see FPsurvey - Industrials)

Response Biomedical Corp. (B.C. Aug. 20, 1980)
Dec. 5, 2016 – Acquired by 1077801 B.C. Ltd.; basis $1.12 cash per sh.

Les Ressources Camchib Inc. (Que. 1953)
May 12, 1983 – Amalgamated with Campbell Resources Inc. (1 for 1), United Asbestos Inc. (0.3 com. plus 1 pfce. for 1) and GM Resources Limited (1 for 5) to continue as a new company also known as Campbell Resources Inc.; basis 0.6 sh. for 1 old sh. (see Campbell Resources Inc.)

Les Ressources du Lac Meston Inc. (Que. 1972)
Dec. 8, 1987 – Amalgamated with a wholly owned subsid. of Campbell Resources Inc.; basis one $6.75 redeemable pref. sh. or 2.35 com. shs. Campbell Resources for 1 old sh.

Ressources Hebron Fjord Inc. (Can. Aug. 23, 1995 amalg.)
June 7, 2001 – Name changed to H2O Innovation (2000) Inc. ■

Ressources Hinse Inc. (Que. 1950)
Feb. 13, 1991 – Dissolved.

Ressources Minières Aabarock Inc. (Can. Nov. 23, 1984)
Dec. 31, 1987 – Name changed to Finor Exploration Inc. ■

Ressources Minières Eider Inc. (Can. Sept. 23, 1983)
June 6, 1988 – Name changed to Novéder Inc.; basis 1 new for 10 old shs. ■

Ressources La Pause Inc. (Que. June 5, 1985)
Nov. 17, 1987 – Name changed to Société Minière Ecudor inc.; basis 1 new for 10 old shs. ■

Restaurant Brands International Inc. (B.C. Aug. 25, 2014)
Oct. 23, 2014 – Continued into Canada. (see FPsurvey - Industrials)

Restaurant Holdings of Canada Limited (Ont. Mar. 29, 1968)
Feb. 28, 1979 – Name changed to Mikes Submarines Inc. and continued into Canada. ■

Result Energy Inc. (Alta. May 19, 2000)
Apr. 8, 2010 – Acquired by PetroBakken Energy Ltd.; basis 42¢, 0.013023 PetroBakken cl. A shs. or a combination thereof for 1 Result sh. (see PetroBakken Energy Ltd.)

Retallack Mines Ltd. (B.C. 1953)
Jan. 1957 – Charter cancelled.

Retirement Residences Real Estate Investment Trust (Ont. Dec. 28, 2000)
Feb. 2, 2007 – Acquired by Public Sector Pension Investment Board for $8.35 per unit.
Name changed to Revera Inc.

Retlaw Resources Inc. (B.C. 1982)
Feb. 4, 1985 – Name changed to Tamavack Resources Ltd. ■

Retrieve Resources Ltd. (B.C. July 6, 1981)
Jan. 16, 1996 – Continued into Wyoming.
Nov. 1, 1998 – Privatized; basis 1-for-1 sh. of Alamo Natural Resources, Inc. distributed to Retrieve shldrs. as a dividend-in-specie.

Retrocom Mid-Market Real Estate Investment Trust (Ont. Dec. 15, 2003)
June 17, 2013 – Name changed to Retrocom Real Estate Investment Trust. ■

Retrocom Real Estate Investment Trust (Ont. Dec. 15, 2003)
July 31, 2015 – Name changed to OneREIT. ■

Return Energy Inc (Alta. Mar. 20, 2006)
June 1, 2020 – Name changed to Spartan Delta Corp.; basis 1 new for 100 old shs. (see FPsurvey - Mines & Energy)

Reunion 56 Oil & Gas Inc. (Alta. Nov. 26, 1987)
June 24, 1993 – Name changed to Call 900 Inc. ■

Reunion Gold Corporation (Can. Mar. 15, 2004)
July 17, 2024 – Business combination with G Mining Ventures Corp. (renamed G Mining TZ Corp.) to create a new company also known as G Mining Ventures Corp. (new); basis 0.07125 new G Mining shs. and 0.05 Greenheart Gold Inc. shs. for 1 Reunion sh.

Reunion Neuroscience Inc. (Can. Oct. 1, 2020)
Aug. 1, 2023 – Acquired by affiliates of MPM BioImpact, Inc., a biotechnology investment firm; basis US$1.12 per sh.

Reva Resources Corp. (B.C. Jan. 4, 2004)
Aug. 3, 2016 – Name changed to Grosvenor Resource Corporation; basis 1 new for 4 old shs. (see FPsurvey - Mines & Energy)

Revelartic Mines Ltd. (Ont. 1944)
Nov. 1954 – Charter cancelled.

Revelation Ventures Inc. (Alta. Oct. 17, 2006)
Mar. 3, 2010 – Dissolved following Qualifying Transaction private placement purchase of units (1 common share & ¾ warrant) of ForceLogix Technologies Inc. and distribution of ForceLogix units to Revelation shareholders on a pro rata basis.

Revelo Resources Corp. (B.C. June 25, 2008)
Feb. 9, 2021 – Acquired by Austral Gold Limited; basis 0.9184 Austral Gold ordinary shs. plus $0.03045715 in cash for 1 Revelo com. sh.

Revelstoke Building Materials Ltd. (Alta. 1928)
June 1972 – Name changed to Revelstoke Companies Ltd. ■

Revelstoke Companies Ltd. (Alta. 1928)
Oct. 17, 1988 – Acquired by West Fraser Timber Co. Ltd. effective for $3.75 for 1 cl. A sh. or cl. B sh.

Revelstoke Equity Inc. (Ont. Nov. 14, 2014)
Nov. 8, 2018 – Name changed to Zonetail Inc. pursuant to Qualifying Transaction reverse takeover acquisition of (old) Zonetail Inc. by way amalgamation of (old) Zonetail with a wholly owned subsidiary of Revelstoke Equity Inc. which was then vertically amalgamated into the company. (see FPsurvey - Industrials)

Trustco Prêt et Revenu Inc. (Que. 1973)
June 3, 1996 – Acquired by Laurentian Bank of Canada for $12,900,000.

Revenue Properties Company Limited (Ont. Aug. 24, 1961)
Dec. 2, 2008 – Remaining 14.6% interest acquired by way of amalgamation with 2187675 Ontario Inc., an indirect wholly owned subsid. of Morguard Corporation, to form new co. with same name; basis $12 or 0.33 Morguard shs. for 1 Revenue Properties sh.

Revere Communications Inc. (Alta. Dec. 21, 1995)
Sept. 3, 2002 – Dissolved and struck from registry.

Revere Mining Corp. Ltd. (Ont. 1960)
Mar. 1976 – Charter cancelled.

Revere Resources Ltd. (B.C. Apr. 10, 1986)
Nov. 5, 1993 – Dissolved and struck off register.

Revett Minerals Inc. (Can. Aug. 25, 2004)
Feb. 18, 2014 – Name changed to Revett Mining Company, Inc. and continued into Delaware. ■

Revett Mining Company, Inc. (Del. Feb. 18, 2014)
June 18, 2015 – Acquired by Hecla Mining Company; basis 0.1622 Hecla com. shs. for 1 Revett sh.

Reviso Energy Ltd. (Alta. Nov. 5, 2009)
Nov. 18, 2010 – Name changed to Avatar Energy Ltd. pursuant to Qualifying Transaction reverse takeover acquisition Rustler Petroleum Inc. and subsequent vertical amalgamation of Rustler into the company. ■

Revolution Resources Corp. (B.C. July 14, 2009)
June 6, 2014 – Name changed to IDM Mining Ltd. ■

Revolve Capital Corp. (Alta. May 29, 2000)
Feb. 26, 2002 – Name changed to True North Corporation following Qualifying Transaction reverse takeover acquisition of TNAG True North Advertising Group Inc. ■

Revolver Resources Inc. (B.C. May 10, 2007)
Oct. 7, 2016 – Name changed to GGX Gold Corp. (see FPsurvey - Mines & Energy)

reWORKS Environmental Corp. (Can. Sept. 29, 2006)
Feb. 22, 2008 – Name changed to Forterra Environmental Corp. ■

Reward Mining Corporation (B.C. Sept. 27, 1979)
Mar. 11, 1998 – Name changed to Riverdance Resources Corp. ■

Reward Mining Corp., Ltd. (Alta. 1954)
June 21, 1974 – Name changed to Penthouse Holdings Ltd. ■

Reward Oils Ltd. (B.C. 1936)
1955 – In voluntary liquidation. Hugh H. Adair, 1818 Marine Bldg., Vancouver, liquidator.

Reward Resources Ltd. (B.C. 1981)
May 5, 1988 – Amalgamated with Angle Resources Ltd. (0.89 for 1) and Nexus Resources Corporation (1 for 1) to form a new co. also named Nexus Resources Corporation; basis 1 new for 3 old shs.

Reward Uranium Ltd. (Alta. 1954)
Mar. 24, 1965 – Name changed to Reward Mining Corp., Ltd. ■

RewardStream Solutions Inc. (B.C. July 28, 2016 amalg.)
Oct. 8, 2020 – Name changed to Balsam Technologies Corp. ■

Rex Diamond Mining Corporation (Ont. Sept. 14, 1995 amalg.)
July 31, 2000 – Continued into Yukon.
Sept. 29, 2011 – Continued into Ontario.
Nov. 9, 2011 – Name changed to Rex Opportunity Corp.; basis 1 new for 20 old shs. (see FPsurvey - Mines & Energy)

Rex Silver Mines Ltd. (B.C. Mar. 17, 1961)
Aug. 3, 1990 – Dissolved and struck off register.

Rexdale Mines Ltd. (Ont. 1964)
Mar. 1976 – Charter cancelled.

Rexford Minerals Ltd. (B.C. Nov. 21, 1983)
Aug. 22, 1991 – Name changed to Derrick Petroleum Corp.; basis 1 new for 4 old shs. ■

Rexora Mining Corp. Ltd. (Ont. 1947)
Apr. 1970 – Charter cancelled.

Rexplore Resources International Limited (B.C. Nov. 10, 1978)
Dec. 29, 1987 – Name changed to Kemgas Sydney Inc. ■

Rexspar Minerals & Chemicals Ltd. (Ont. 1951)
1967 – Name changed to Consolidated Rexspar Minerals & Chemicals Limited; basis 1 new for 5 old shs. ■

Rexspar Uranium & Metals Mining Co. Ltd. (Ont. 1951)
Aug. 14, 1959 – Name changed to Rexspar Minerals & Chemicals Ltd. ■

Rexterra Gold Mines Ltd. (Ont. 1945)
1957 – Charter cancelled.

Rey-Indin Yellowknife Mines Ltd. (Ont. 1945)
Sept. 19, 1960 – Dissolved.

Reymont Gold Mines Ltd. (Can. July 7, 1988)
Dec. 13, 1991 – Name changed to Pallaum Minerals Ltd.; basis 1 new for 10 old shs. ■

Reyna Gold Corp. (B.C. Oct. 10, 2017)
Nov. 4, 2024 – Acquired by Reyna Silver Corp.; basis 1 new Reyna Silver sh. for 3 old Reyna Gold shs. (see Reyna Silver Corp.)

Reyna Silver Corp. (B.C. Aug. 24, 2017)
Aug. 22, 2025 – Acquired by Torex Gold Resources Inc.; basis 13¢ cash per sh.

Reynolds Aluminum Company of Canada Ltd. (Can. 1955)
1986 – Privatized.

Rheba Uranium Mining Corp. Ltd. (Ont. 1953)
1957 – Charter cancelled.

Rheingold Exploration Corp. (B.C. July 29, 2010)
Aug. 29, 2017 – Name changed to International Battery Metals Ltd. (see FPsurvey - Mines & Energy)

Rhino Exploration Inc. (B.C. Dec. 16, 2010)
Mar. 4, 2013 – Name changed to Walker River Resources Corp. (see FPsurvey - Mines & Energy)

Rhino Resources Inc. (B.C. May 7, 1987)
Apr. 19, 1996 – Name changed to DSI DatoTech Systems Inc. ■

Rhino Resources Inc. (Can. May 18, 2007)
Oct. 5, 2009 – Name changed to ImmunoVaccine Inc. pursuant to Qualifying Transaction reverse takeover acquisition of ImmunoVaccine Technologies Inc.; basis 1 new for 5 old shs. ■

Rhodes Energy Corporation (Alta. 1976)
Sept. 1, 1989 – Formed Accord Capital Corporation in Alberta on amalgamation with Accord Capital Corporation; basis 0.6 new for 1 Accord cl. A or B sh. and 1 new for 5 Rhodes shs. ■

Rhodes Resources Corp. (Alta. Nov. 1, 2002)
Jan. 30, 2004 – Formed Terra Energy Corp. in Alberta on amalgamation with Terrapet Energy Corp. and Terra Energy Corp., constituting a reverse takeover by Terrapet; basis 1 new for 5 old shs. ■

Rhodes Resources Inc. (B.C. Sept. 27, 1962)
Sept. 24, 1982 – Name changed to International Rhodes Resources Ltd.; basis 1 new for 2 old shs. ■

Rhona Online.Com Inc. (B.C. May 9, 1983)
Apr. 16, 2004 – Name changed to Winchester Minerals and Gold Exploration Ltd.; basis 1 new for 2 old shs. ■

Rhonda Mining Corporation (Alta. Jan. 26, 1977 amalg.)
Jan. 1, 1992 – Amalgamated in Alberta to continue with same name.
Aug. 22, 2000 – Name changed to Rhonda Corporation. (see FPsurvey - Mines & Energy)

Rhyme Industries Inc. (B.C. June 6, 1987)
Apr. 28, 1999 – Name changed to Viacorp Technologies Inc.; basis 1 new for 4 old shs. ■

Rhynus Ramore Mines Ltd. (Ont. 1945)
1953 – Distributed 1 pref. sh. Mining Futures & Holdings Ltd. for each 310 shs. Rhynus. Charter surrendered.

Rhyolite-Rouyn Mines, Limited (Ont. 1927)
Dec. 1977 – Charter cancelled.
Mar. 21, 1985 – Charter revived.
July 31, 1985 – Name changed to Deerfoot Resources Inc. ■

Rhys Industries Ltd. (B.C. July 22, 1986)
Aug. 30, 1996 – Dissolved and struck off register.

Rhys Resources Ltd. (B.C. May 13, 1996)
Oct. 24, 2017 – Name changed to Pacific Rim Cobalt Corp.; basis 1 new for 4 old shs. ■

Rhys Ventures Limited (B.C. July 22, 1986)
Oct. 6, 1988 – Name changed to Rhys Industries Ltd. ■

Ria Resources Corp. (B.C. June 17, 1998 amalg.)
June 11, 2013 – Acquired by Qwest Diversified Capital Corp.; basis 0.014 Qwest ser. 1 special shs. for 1 Ria sh.

Riata Resources Corp. (Alta. Feb. 2, 2007)
Nov. 2, 2011 – Name changed to Petroforte International Ltd. ■

Riata Resources Ltd. (Alta. Mar. 10, 1995 amalg.)
Oct. 8, 1997 – Acquired by Calahoo Petroleum Ltd.; basis 45¢ or 0.5 Calahoo units for 1 Riata sh. Each Calahoo unit consisted of (i) 1 ser. 1 cl. C pref. sh.; (ii) 0.5 wts., each wt. entitling holder to purchase 1 Calahoo flow-through com. sh. for 90¢ on or before 20 business days after the effective date of arrangement; and (iii) 0.5 wts., each wt. entitling holder to purchase 1 Calahoo flow-through com. sh. for $1.05 on or before Dec. 15, 1998. (see Calahoo Petroleum Ltd.)

Ribago Rouyn Mines Ltd. (Ont. 1944)
1957 – Name changed to Consolidated Ribago Mines Ltd.; basis 1 new for 4 old shs. ■

Ribbon Capital Corp. (Ont. Feb. 23, 2004)
Jan. 18, 2007 – Name changed to Selectcore Ltd. ■

Ribrock Oils Ltd. (unknown)
1965 – Control acquired by Royal American Petroleums Ltd.; basis 5 new for 1 old sh.

Ricafuerte Mining Corp. (B.C. Apr. 24, 1987)
Sept. 16, 1994 – Name changed to Gee-Ten Ventures Inc.; basis 1 new for 3.5 old shs. ■

Ricana Mines Ltd. (Ont. 1946)
Mar. 11, 1957 – Charter cancelled.

Ricanaw Mines Ltd. (Que. 1937)
1949 – Name changed to North Sullivan Contact Mines Ltd. ■

Ricban Mines Ltd. (Ont. 1956)
Feb. 14, 1973 – Dissolved.

Rice Capital Management Plus Inc. (Alta. Mar. 25, 1998)
Sept. 29, 2003 – Name changed to Jovian Capital Corporation and continued into Canada. ■

Rice Lake Gold Mines Ltd. (Can. 1934)
1967 – Name changed to New Rice Lake Gold Mines Ltd.; basis 1 new for 4 old shs. ■

Ricenor Gold Mines Ltd. (Ont. 1945)
1946 – Name changed to Cross Fault Gold Mines Ltd. ■

Rich Capital Corporation (B.C. 1983)
Nov. 26, 1996 – Name changed to Consolidated Rich Capital Corporation; basis 1 new for 10 old shs. ■

Rich Coast Resources Ltd. (B.C. Jan. 25, 1993 amalg.)
Sept. 18, 1996 – Name changed to Rich Coast, Inc. and continued into Delaware.

Rich Coast Sulphur Ltd. (B.C. 1984)
June 19, 1991 – Name changed to Consolidated Rich Coast Sulphur Ltd.; basis 1 new for 5 old shs. ■

Rich Find Mines Ltd. (Alta. 1955)
Sept. 15, 1959 – Struck off register.

Rich Group Yellowknife Mines Limited (Ont. 1945)
June 30, 1986 – Became a wholly owned subsid. of Discovery Mines Limited. Shldrs. received 3 shs. Discovery for each 4 co. shs.

Rich Hill Mines Ltd. (B.C. May 23, 1972)
Mar. 3, 1980 – Name changed to Blackmist Resources Inc. ■

Rich Hill Resources Ltd. (B.C. June 28, 1983)
June 5, 1986 – Name changed to Nickelodeon Industries Corp.; basis 1 new for 2.75 old shs. ■

Rich Lode Gold Corporation (B.C. 1981)
May 28, 1985 – Name changed to Enstar Development
Corporation. ■

Rich Minerals Corporation (Alta. Mar. 25, 1986)
May 12, 2009 – Name changed to Blackhawk Resource
Corp. ■

Rich Resources Ltd. (B.C. 1983)
Mar. 25, 1988 – Name changed to Rich Capital
Corporation. ■

Rich Rock Gold Mines Ltd. (Ont. 1928)
1938 – Acquired by Addington Mines Ltd.; basis 41 new
shs. and 6¢ for 100 old shs. (see Addington Mines Ltd.)

Richan Explorations Ltd. (Ont. 1970)
July 1973 – Merged into Sloane Mining Co. Ltd.; basis 1
new for 5.2 old shs.

Richard Copper Corp. Ltd. (Ont. 1948)
Feb. 1969 – Dissolved.

Richard Costain (Canada) Ltd (Can. Mar. 30, 1953)
May 2, 1978 – Name changed to Costain Limited. ■

Richard Piche Inc. (Que. June 6, 1962)
Dec. 1, 1987 – Name changed to R.P.M. Tech Inc. ■

Richards Oil & Gas Limited (Alta. May 18, 2004)
Jan. 2011 – Completed restructuring under the
Bankruptcy and Insolvency Act resulting in the cancelling
of existing sh. capital and issuance of new sh. capital to
new investors and certain creditors.

Richco Investors Inc. (B.C. 1980)
Aug. 16, 1994 – Continued into Ontario. (see FPsurvey
- Industrials)

Richcor Resources Ltd. (Can. July 13, 1995)
July 31, 2001 – Name changed to Bioxel Pharma Inc.
following reverse takeover acquisition of Bioxel Pharma
Inc.; basis 1 new for 1.322 old shs. ■

Richcour Gold Mines Ltd. (Ont. 1945)
1956 – Charter cancelled.

Richdale Petroleums Limited (B.C. 1968)
June 12, 1978 – Dissolved.

Richey Communications, Ltd. (B.C. July 16, 1987)
Oct. 13, 2000 – Delisted from the CDNX. Subsequently
dissolved and struck from register.

Richey Pacific Cablevision, Ltd. (B.C. July 16, 1987)
Dec. 1991 – Name changed to International Richey
Pacific Cablevision, Ltd.; basis 1 new for 3 old shs. ■

Richfault Explorations Ltd. (Ont. 1969)
1971 – Assets sold to Avilla International Explorations
Ltd.; basis 1 new for 4 old shs.

Richfield Petroleum Limited (Can. Mar. 1, 1929; via
Dominion charter)
1952 – Name changed to New Richfield Petroleum
Limited; basis 1 new for 4 old shs. ■

Richfield Ventures Corp. (B.C. Nov. 8, 2007 amalg.)
June 2, 2011 – Acquired by New Gold Inc. for $0.0001
plus 0.9217 New Gold shs for 1 Richfield sh.

Richglen Mines Ltd. (Ont. 1949)
Mar. 1976 – Charter cancelled.

Richhill Resources Ltd. (B.C. June 28, 1983)
May 31, 1984 – Name changed to Rich Hill Resources
Ltd. ■

Richland Gold Mines Ltd. (Ont. 1934)
1944 – Name changed to Hiskerr Gold Mines Ltd. and
continued into Ontario. ■

Richland Mines Inc. (B.C. May 25, 1987)
Jan. 28, 1998 – Name changed to Consolidated Richland
Mines Inc.; basis 1 new for 9 old shs. ■

Richland Oil & Gas Ltd. (Alta. 1951)
Jan. 4, 1971 – Merged into Todola Drilling Ltd.

Richland Oil Development of Canada Ltd. (Alta. 1951)
Sept. 12, 1955 – Name changed to Richland Oil & Gas
Ltd. ■

Richland Oils Ltd. (Alta. Dec. 1936)
1947 – Wound up. Distributed 4¢ per sh.

Richland Petroleum Corporation (Alta. Jan. 21, 1991)
Jan. 21, 2002 – Plan of Arrangement with Provident
Energy Trust and Terraquest Energy Corporation; basis
0.4 new Provident trust unit plus 1 new Terraquest com.
sh. for 1 old Richland com. sh. (see Provident Energy
Trust; Terraquest Energy Corporation)

Richland Resources Ltd. (unknown)
1970 – Merged with Highland Valley Mines Ltd.; basis 1
new for 2 old shs.

Richlode Investments Corp. (B.C. Mar. 22, 1983)
July 30, 1998 – Name changed to Thundelarra
Exploration Ltd.; basis 1 new for 10 old shs. ■

Richmac Gold Mines Ltd. (Ont. June 1, 1933)
June 2, 1936 – Formed Richmac Gold Mines (1936) Ltd.
in Ontario; basis 5 new for 1 old sh. ■

Richmac Gold Mines (1936) Ltd. (Ont. June 2, 1936
amalg.)
1948 – Acquired by Boymar Gold Mines (1936) Ltd.; basis
1 new for 3 old shs.

Richmark Resources Ltd. (B.C. Mar. 18, 1987)
Aug. 8, 2005 – Dissolved for failure to file.

Richmond Energy Corp. (Ont. July 11, 2005)
Sept. 24, 2009 – Name changed to REC Minerals Corp. ■

Richmond Gulf Resources Ltd. (Ont. Jan. 27, 1989)
Dec. 18, 1992 – Name changed to Richwest Holdings
Inc.; basis 1 com. for 10 subord. vtg. shs. ■

Richmond Hill Mining Co. Ltd. (B.C. 1947)
1952 – Charter cancelled.

Richmond Natural Gas & Oil Co. Ltd. (B.C.)
1960 – Struck off register.

Richmond Road Capital Corp. (Alta. Sept. 19, 2012)
June 22, 2021 – Name changed to Fredonia Mining Inc.
pursuant to the Qualifying Transaction reverse takeover
acquisition of Fredonia Management Ltd., and concurrent
amalgamation of Fredonia Management with wholly
owned Fredonia Mining Corp.; basis 1 new for 1.36 old
shs. ■

Richmond Row Capital Corp. (Alta. Nov. 4, 2010)
Aug. 27, 2012 – Name changed to Gold Royalties
Corporation following Qualifying Transaction
amalgamation of (old) Gold Royalties Corporation with
8229554 Canada Inc., a wholly owned subsid. of
Richmond Row Capital Corp., constituting a reverse
takeover by (old) Gold Royalties; basis 1 new for 5 old
shs. ■

Richmond Street Capital Corp. (B.C. May 31, 2019)
July 14, 2021 – Name changed to LithiumBank Resources
Corp. pursuant to the reverse takeover acquisition of (old)
LithiumBank Resources Corp. (see FPsurvey - Mines &
Energy)

Richmont Mines Inc. (Que. Feb. 12, 1981)
Nov. 27, 2017 – Acquired by Alamos Gold Inc.; basis
1.385 Alamos cl. A com. sh. for 1 Richmont com. sh.

Richore Gold Mines Ltd. (Ont. 1948)
1971 – Assets sold to Avilla International Explorations
Ltd.; basis 2 new for 11 old shs.

Richpine Mines Ltd. (Ont. 1946)
Apr. 29, 1970 – Charter cancelled.

Richport Resources Ltd. (B.C. 1979)
Sept. 2, 1988 – Acquired by Veronex Resources Ltd.;
basis 1 new for 2 old shs. (see Veronex Resources Ltd.)

Richrock Mines Ltd. (B.C. 1955)
Sept. 20, 1985 – Struck off register.

Richtree Inc. (Ont. Nov. 13, 1996 amalg.)
Oct. 18, 2004 – Filed for receivership, and
PricewaterhouseCoopers Inc. was appointed interim
receiver.
Jan. 2005 – Operations ceased in the U.S. and subsidiary
Richtree Markets Inc. ceased restaurant operations at
Place Ville Marie in Montreal, Que., and Caffe-Bar
Masquerade in Toronto, Ont.
May 18, 2005 – Ontario Court ordered the receiver to
complete the purchase of the operating assets of Richtree
Markets Inc. by Richtree Market Restaurant Inc. which
would operate eight market concept restaurants in Ontario
under the newly established Richtree Market Restaurant
brand. The new corporation was controlled by Catalyst
Fund Limited Partnership I.
June 30, 2005 – First meeting of creditors.
Apr. 27, 2006 – Receiver discharged; there were no
funds available for creditors or shldrs.

Richview Gold Mines Ltd. (Ont. 1946)
July 1957 – Charter cancelled.

Richview Resources Inc. (Ont. Apr. 22, 1997)
Nov. 15, 2004 – Amalgamated in Ontario to continue with
same name.
Jan. 19, 2010 – Acquired by Cadillac Ventures Inc. by
way of amalgamation with 2220403 Ontario Inc., a wholly
owned subsid. of Cadillac to continue under the Richview
name; basis 0.1111 Cadillac shs. for 1 Richview sh.

Richwell Petroleums Ltd. (Ont. 1950)
Sept. 29, 1966 – Dissolved. Previously, shs. exchanged
for those of North West Pacific Developments Ltd. on
sh.-for-sh. basis, and debentures similarly exchanged.

Richwell Resources Ltd. (B.C. 1978)
Apr. 15, 1994 – Dissolved and struck off register.

Richwest Holdings Inc. (Ont. Jan. 27, 1989)
Mar. 13, 2006 – Certificate of incorporation cancelled.

Richwood Industries Ltd. (B.C. 1967)
June 25, 1979 – Dissolved.

Richwood Silver Mines Ltd. (B.C. 1967)
Nov. 4, 1969 – Name changed to Richwood Industries
Ltd. ■

Rickaby Mines Limited (Ont. 1972)
Apr. 9, 1985 – Charter cancelled.

Rico Copper Mines Ltd. (unknown)
1968 – In voluntary liquidation. Distributed 1 sh. Rico
Copper (1966) Ltd. for each 20 old shs.

Rico Copper (1966) Limited (B.C. Jan. 17, 1966)
Oct. 9, 1981 – Name changed to McNellen Resources,
Inc.; basis 1 new for 1 old sh. ■

Rico Rouyn Mines Ltd. (Ont. 1946)
May 13, 1957 – Charter cancelled.

Ricochet Industries Inc. (Alta. Apr. 5, 1994)
July 21, 1997 – Name changed to Delicious Alternative
Desserts Ltd. following reverse takeover acquisition of
Delicious Alternative Desserts Inc.; basis 1 new for 5 old
shs. ■

Riczone Mines Ltd. (Ont. 1946)
Aug. 19, 1965 – Dissolved.

Rideau Base Metals Ltd. (unknown)
Dec. 1972 – Charter cancelled.

Rideau Carleton Raceway Investments Limited (Can.
1926)
1972 – Wound up. Unsecured creditors received first and
final payment of 20% on Nov. 24, 1971. Secured creditors
and shldrs. received the following: each $1,000 of 6 3/4

% 1st. mtge. bonds, Ser. A, exch. for $900 of 12% 1st mtge. bonds, $100 and 200 new com. shs. of Rideau Carleton Raceway Holdings; each $1,000 of 6.5 % debentures, Ser. A, exch. for 500 new com. shs. of Rideau Holdings; pref. shs. exch. sh. for sh. for new com. shs. of Rideau Holdings; each 10 com. shs. exch. for 1 new com. sh. of Rideau Holdings.

Rideau Resources Corp. (B.C. May 16, 1979)
June 12, 1989 – Name changed to Consolidated Rideau Resources Corp.; basis 1 new for 3 old shs. ■

Rideau Trust Company (Ont. 1964)
Aug. 1970 – Name changed to United Trust Company. ■

Ridel Resources Ltd. (B.C. Feb. 7, 1992)
Aug. 12, 1999 – Name changed to Mannix Resources Inc.; basis 1 new for 5 old shs. ■

Rider Investment Capital Corp. (Alta. Jan. 30, 2018)
June 3, 2020 – Name changed to Baselode Energy Corp. and continued into Ontario pursuant to Qualifying Transaction acquisition of mineral property. (see FPsurvey - Mines & Energy)

Rider Resources Inc. (Alta. Mar. 23, 1993)
June 8, 2001 – Acquired by Roberts Bay Resources Ltd. (subsequently renamed Rider Resources Inc.); basis 1 new Rider sh. for 3 old Roberts Bay shs. (see Rider Resources Inc.)

Rider Resources Inc. (Alta. Apr. 27, 1993)
Feb. 28, 2003 – Plan of Arrangement acquisition by IEI Energy Inc. (subsequently renamed Rider Resources Ltd.); basis 0.9448 new IEI com. sh. for 1 old Rider com. sh. (see Rider Resources Ltd.)

Rider Resources Ltd. (Alta. Feb. 21, 2003 amalg.)
Mar. 10, 2008 – Acquired by NuVista Energy Ltd.; basis 0.3540 NuVista com. shs. for 1 Rider com. sh.
Jan. 1, 2009 – Amalgamated with NuVista Energy Ltd.

Rider 2 Investment Capital Corp. (Alta. Feb. 1, 2021)
Nov. 17, 2021 – Name changed to Metal Energy Corp. and continued into Ontario pursuant to the Qualifying Transaction reverse takeover acquisition of D Block Discoveries Inc. (see FPsurvey - Mines & Energy)

Ridgecrest Resources Ltd. (B.C. June 22, 1978)
Dec. 31, 1985 – Name changed to The Hallicrafters Communications International Co. Ltd. ■

Ridgefield Development Limited (Can. Apr. 5, 1954)
Apr. 27, 1979 – Name changed to Blake Mineral Resources Ltd. ■

Ridgefield Explorations Ltd. (Ont. 1955)
Feb. 10, 1972 – Name changed to Pontiff Mining Ltd. ■

Ridgegold Porcupine Mines Ltd. (Ont. 1938)
1955 – Charter cancelled.

Ridgeline Energy Services Inc. (B.C. July 30, 2003)
Oct. 4, 2006 – Continued into Alberta.
Aug. 21, 2013 – Name changed to RDX Technologies Corporation. (see FPsurvey - Mines & Energy; FPsurvey - Industrials)

Ridgemar Explorations and Development Company Limited (Ont. 1975)
Mar. 1, 1978 – Amalgamated with 3 other cos. to form Jaridge Exploration Inc.; basis 1 new for 2 old shs.

Ridgemont Capital Corp. (B.C. July 31, 2008)
Nov. 23, 2010 – Name changed to Ridgemont Iron Ore Corp. pursuant to Qualifying Transaction acquisition of Redford property option from Logan Resources Ltd. ■

Ridgemont Iron Ore Corp. (B.C. July 31, 2008)
July 2, 2013 – Acquired by Castillian Resources Corp.; basis 0.593 Castillian shs. for 1 Ridgemont sh. Subsequently, Castillian Resources Corp. changed its name to Coastal Gold Corp. (see Coastal Gold Corp.)

Ridgepoint Mineral Corporation (Que. Feb. 4, 1958)
Sept. 15, 2000 – Name changed to Jet Drill Canada Inc. ■

Ridgepoint Resources Ltd. (Que. Feb. 4, 1958)
Apr. 25, 1997 – Name changed to Ridgepoint Mineral Corporation; basis 1 new for 3 old shs. ■

Ridgeway Corp. (Mich. 1927)
June 27, 1957 – Dissolved. Initial distribution of $35 per sh. made in 1957; interim payments of US$1.40 made in 1960 and 1961; $1.80 in 1962; and $1.00 in 1963.

Ridgeway Petroleum Corp. (B.C. Feb. 22, 1980)
June 11, 2007 – Name changed to Enhanced Oil Resources Inc. ■

Ridgeway Petroleums Ltd. (Alta. 1952)
1957 – Name changed to Nu-Ridgeway Petroleums Ltd.; basis 1 new for 10 old shs. ■

Ridgewood Canadian Investment Grade Bond Fund (Ont. Nov. 27, 2009)
Mar. 25, 2024 – Converted to an open-ended alternative mutual fund from a non-redeemable investment fund.

Ridgley Mining Co., Ltd. (Ont. 1936)
Nov. 1959 – Distribution of 6.825¢ per sh. made in 1958. Dissolved.

Ridley Canada Limited (Man. Jan. 2, 1976 amalg.)
June 1, 1994 – Amalgamated in Manitoba to continue with same name.
Nov. 10, 1998 – Name changed to Ridley Inc. ■

Ridley Inc. (Man. June 1, 1994 amalg.)
June 24, 2015 – Acquired by Alltech, Inc. for Cdn$40.75 per sh.

Ridley Uranium Mines (Canada) Ltd. (Ont. 1954)
1966 – Charter cancelled.

Rifco Inc. (Alta. Dec. 1, 2000)
Jan. 17, 2022 – Acquired by Chesswood Group Limited; basis (i) $1.28 cash per sh.

Rift Basin Resources Corp. (B.C. Jan. 14, 1981)
Aug. 25, 2014 – Name changed to Asean Energy Corp. ■

Rift Resources Ltd. (B.C. 1981)
Sept. 5, 1995 – Continued into Ontario. (see FPsurvey - Mines & Energy)

Rigby Kirkland Mines Ltd. (Ont. 1950)
Sept. 1959 – Charter cancelled.

Rigel Energy Corporation (Can. Apr. 4, 1991)
Oct. 8, 1999 – Acquired by Talisman Energy Inc. for $1.00 plus 0.30 Talisman shs. for 1 Rigel sh. (see Talisman Energy Inc.)

Rigelyn Security Systems Inc. (B.C. Apr. 29, 1986)
Oct. 6, 1989 – Delisted from the Vancouver Stock Exchange. Subsequently dissolved and struck from register.

Riggins Resources Ltd. (B.C. Nov. 18, 1985)
June 1, 1990 – Name changed to Manhattan Minerals Corp.; basis 1 new for 2 old shs. ■

RightsMarket Inc. (Alta. July 30, 1999)
Jan. 1, 2004 – Formed Grand Petroleum Inc. in Alberta on reverse takeover acquisition of and amalgamation with Grand Petroleum Ltd. The company then acquired and amalgamated with Grand Petroleum Limited Partnership; basis 1 new for 40 old shs. ■

RightsMarket.com Inc. (Alta. July 30, 1999)
June 9, 2001 – Name changed to RightsMarket Inc. ■

Rikon Technologies, Inc. (Alta. May 27, 1994)
Mar. 26, 1998 – Formed Hunter Financial Group Ltd. in Alberta on Major Transaction acquisition of and amalgamation with Asgard Investments Ltd. ■

Riley Resources Corp. (B.C. June 3, 2011)
Sept. 29, 2020 – Name changed to Riley Gold Corp. (see FPsurvey - Mines & Energy)

Riley Resources Ltd. (B.C. Oct. 15, 1986)
Jan. 23, 1998 – Name changed to International Riley Resources Ltd.; basis 1 new for 8 old shs. ■

Riley's Datashare International Ltd. (Alta. May 31, 1968 amalg.)
Jan. 9, 1997 – Name changed to International Datashare Corporation; basis 10 new for 1 old sh. ■

Rimfire Minerals Corporation (B.C. May 7, 1991)
Aug. 6, 2009 – Acquired by Geoinformatics Exploration Inc.; basis 2.6 Geoinformatics shs. for 1 Rimfire sh. Concurrently, Geoinformatics Exploration Inc. changed its name to Kiska Metals Corporation and consolidated its shs. on a 1-for-3 basis. (see Kiska Metals Corp.)

The Rimoil Corporation (Can. Sept. 23, 1983 amalg.)
Oct. 6, 1995 – Acquired by Barrington Petroleum Ltd.; basis 85¢ per sh. or 0.190476 Barrington com. shs. for 1 Rimoil cl. A sh. (see Barrington Petroleum Ltd.)

Rimpac Industries Inc. (B.C. June 6, 1987)
July 10, 1991 – Name changed to Rhyme Industries Inc.; basis 1 new for 3 old shs. ■

Rimrock Mining Corp. Ltd. (B.C. 1956)
July 20, 1981 – Name changed to Triton Resources Inc.; basis 1 new for 5 old shs. ■

Rimrock Oils Ltd. (Que. 1962)
1965 – Merged into Delta Mining Corp.

Rimron Resources Inc. (Alta. Feb. 24, 1997 amalg.)
Jan. 22, 2004 – Name changed to Caribou Resources Corp. ■

Ring of Fire Resources Inc. (Ont. Jan. 1, 2003 amalg.)
Mar. 7, 2012 – Name changed to Noble Mineral Exploration Inc. (see FPsurvey - Mines & Energy)

Ring Sights Worldwide Inc. (Ont. Apr. 30, 1974)
Dec. 9, 1991 – Charter cancelled and co. dissolved.

Ring the Bell Capital Corp. (Can. June 28, 2017)
July 31, 2019 – Name changed to Arizona Metals Corp. pursuant to the Qualifying Transaction reverse takeover acquisition of Croesus Gold Corp. and concurrent amalgamation of Croesus with wholly owned 11459040 Canada Inc.; basis 1 new for 2.5 old shs. (see FPsurvey - Mines & Energy)

Ringbolt Ventures Ltd. (B.C. June 13, 2006)
Nov. 4, 2011 – Name changed to North American Potash Developments Inc. ■

Rinoa Enterprises Ltd. (Alta. July 6, 2004)
Oct. 31, 2006 – Formed Paragon Pharmacies Limited in Alberta following Qualifying Transaction amalgamation with Paragon Pharmacies Ltd., constituting a reverse takeover by Paragon. ■

Rio Algom Limited (Ont. June 30, 1960 amalg.)
Jan. 30, 1980 – Amalgamated with Preston Mines Limited to form new co. with same name Rio Algom Limited; basis 1 new pfd. and 0.75 new com. for 1 Preston sh. and 1 new com. for 1 Rio Algom sh.
Nov. 28, 2000 – Acquired by Billiton Copper Holdings Inc., a wholly owned subsid. of England-based Billiton plc; basis $27 per sh.

Rio Algom Mines Limited (Ont. June 30, 1960 amalg.)
Apr. 30, 1975 – Name changed to Rio Algom Limited. ■

Rio Alto Exploration Ltd. (Alta. May 13, 1969)
Dec. 31, 1991 – Amalgamated in Alberta to continue with same name.
July 5, 2002 – Merged with Canadian Natural Resources Limited (CNRL) and Rio Alto Resources International Inc.; basis 1 Rio Alto Resources com. sh. plus either 0.3468 CNRL com. shs. or $18.10, or a combination thereof, for 1 Rio Alto Exploration com. sh.

Rio Alto Mining Limited (Alta. May 7, 2007)
Apr. 8, 2015 – Acquired by Tahoe Resources Inc.; basis 0.227 Tahoe com. shs. and $0.001 cash for 1 Rio Alto sh. (see Tahoe Resources Inc.)

Rio Alto Resources International Inc. (Alta. May 10, 2002)
Oct. 8, 2004 – Formed West Energy Ltd. in Alberta following reverse takeover acquisition of and amalgamation with West Energy Ltd. Prior to the reverse takeover, Rio Alto repurchased 99.41% of its o/s shs. at $1.3200005 per sh. ■

Rio Amarillo Mining Ltd. (B.C. June 7, 1990)
May 20, 1999 – Name changed to Globemin Resources Inc.; basis 1 new for 10 old shs. ■

Rio Blanco Resources Ltd. (B.C. 1981)
Oct. 15, 1985 – Name changed to Studebaker's Resource Development Ltd. (see FPsurvey - Industrials)

Rio Bravo Oil Company, Limited (Can. 1943)
June 9, 1950 – Name changed to Canadian Superior Oil of California Ltd. ■

Rio Canadian Exploration Ltd. (Can. 1953)
1958 – Name changed to Rio Tinto Canadian Exploration Ltd.

Rio Cristal Resources Corporation (B.C. Nov. 24, 2006)
May 11, 2015 – Name changed to Armor Minerals Inc. (see FPsurvey - Mines & Energy)

Rio Cristal Zinc Corporation (B.C. Nov. 24, 2006)
Aug. 10, 2009 – Name changed to Rio Cristal Resources Corporation. ■

Rio Fortuna Exploration Corp. (B.C. Apr. 24, 1987)
Dec. 21, 2005 – Name changed to Fortune River Resource Corp.; basis 1 new for 3 old shs. ■

Rio Grande Mining Corp. (B.C. May 10, 2007)
June 10, 2014 – Name changed to 92 Resources Corp.; basis 1 new for 5 old shs. ■

Rio Grande Ventures Ltd. (B.C. 1984)
Mar. 10, 1989 – Name changed to RGV Resources Ltd.; basis 5 new for 12 old shs. ■

Rio Narcea Gold Mines, Ltd. (Can. Feb. 22, 1994)
Oct. 1, 2007 – Acquired by Lundin Mining Corporation for Cdn$5.50 per sh.

Rio Novo Gold Inc. (British Virgin Islands Jan. 4, 2008)
Mar. 7, 2018 – Merged into Aura Minerals Inc.; basis 0.053 Aura com. shs. for 1 Rio Novo ordinary sh.

Rio Palmer Oils Limited (Ont. 1953)
Oct. 30, 1956 – Acquired by Devon-Leduc Oils Ltd.; basis 1.25 new for 1 old sh. (see Devon-Palmer Oils Ltd.)

Rio Plata Silver Mines Ltd. (B.C. Mar. 6, 1962)
May 25, 1983 – Name changed to Consolidated Rio Plata Resources Ltd.; basis 1 new for 2 old shs. ■

Rio-Prado Consolidated Oils Limited (Ont. 1953)
Aug. 1955 – Formed Rio Palmer Oils Limited following merger with Palmer Oil Development Ltd.; basis 1 new for 4 old shs. ■

Rio Resources Ltd. (B.C. 1968)
Dec. 2, 1974 – Charter cancelled.

Rio Rupununi Mines Ltd. (Ont. 1945)
Feb. 14, 1973 – Dissolved.

Rio Sierra Developments Ltd. (B.C. Aug. 28, 1969)
May 11, 1977 – Name changed to River Mountain Resources Ltd.; basis 1 new for 3 old shs. ■

Rio Sierra Silver Corp. (B.C. Aug. 28, 1969)
Mar. 9, 1989 – Delisted from the Vancouver Stock Exchange. Subsequently dissolved.

Rio-Tinto Alberta Oils Limited (Ont. 1950)
1953 – Assets acquired by Rio-Prado Consolidated Oils Limited; basis 5 new for 4 old shs. (see Rio-Prado Consolidated Oils Limited)

Rio Tinto Mining Co. of Canada Ltd. (Ont. 1955)
Nov. 1961 – Sold major assets to Rio Algom Mines Limited. Distributed $161.50, 8 shs. Rio Algom and 35 shs. Preston Mines Limited for 500 old Rio Tinto shs.

Rio Tundra Mining and Development Co. Ltd. (B.C. 1970)
Oct. 24, 1977 – Dissolved.

Rio Verde Developments Ltd. (B.C. Mar. 22, 1977)
Apr. 5, 1978 – Formed Westfort Petroleums Ltd. following amalgamation with Prosper Petroleums Ltd. ■

Rio Verde Minerals Development Corp. (British Virgin Islands July 15, 2011)
Mar. 26, 2013 – Acquired by B&A Fertilizers Limited, a wholly owned subsidiary of B&A Mineração S.A., for 40¢ per sh.

Riobec Mines Ltd. (Ont. 1956)
June 29, 1964 – Dissolved.

Riosun Resources Corporation (B.C. Mar. 2, 1983)
May 31, 2001 – Delisted from the CDNX. Subsequently dissolved and struck from register.

Rio2 Limited (Ont. Apr. 25, 2017)
July 23, 2018 – Amalgamated in Ontario to continue with same name. (see FPsurvey - Mines & Energy)

Ripley International Limited (Ont. 1963)
1977 – Private co. All o/s cl. A shs. acquired by co.

Ripped Canada Artists Inc. (Ont. June 19, 1997)
Sept. 20, 2002 – Name changed to Condor Gold Corp. following reverse takeover transaction with Northville Gold Corp. for total consideration of 60,000,000 consolidated shs. to former Northville shldrs.; basis 1 new for 2 old shs. ■

Ripper Oil and Gas Inc. (Alta. Oct. 20, 2000)
May 25, 2012 – Continued into British Columbia.
Jan. 31, 2019 – Name changed to Victory Metals Inc. pursuant to reverse takeover acquisition of Iron Point vanadium property in Nevada; basis 1 new for 1.5 old shs. ■

Ripper Resources Ltd. (B.C. May 28, 2020)
Jan. 13, 2021 – Name changed to Advance United Holdings Inc. pursuant to the reverse takeover acquisition of Talisker Gold Corp. and concurrent amalgamation of Talisker with wholly owned 2796446 Ontario Inc. ■

Ripple Lake Diamonds Inc. (B.C. Feb. 6, 2004)
Oct. 10, 2007 – Name changed to Devonshire Resources Ltd.; basis 1 new for 10 old shs. ■

Ripple Resources Ltd. (B.C. 1981)
June 12, 1987 – Name changed to Consolidated Ripple Resources Ltd. ■

Ripple Resources Ltd. (Alta. May 31, 1994 amalg.)
June 11, 1997 – Amalgamated with 732025 Alberta Ltd., a wholly owned subsid. of Ramarro Resources Inc.; basis 1 new for 7 old shs. (see Ramarro Resources Inc.)

Risby Tungsten Mines Ltd. (B.C. 1969)
Dec. 1, 1981 – Amalgamated with Imperial Metals & Power Ltd. (1 for 2) and Invex Resources Ltd. (1 for 1) to form Imperial Metals Corporation; basis 1 new Imperial Metals sh. for 2 old Risby shs. ■

Rise Capital Corp. (Ont. Mar. 4, 2021)
Dec. 1, 2021 – Name changed to MiniLuxe Holding Corp. pursuant to the Qualifying Transaction reverse takeover acquisition of Boston, Mass.-based MiniLuxe, Inc.; basis 1 new for 4 old shs. (see FPsurvey - Industrials)

Rise Energy Ltd. (Alta. Aug. 17, 2001 amalg.)
June 19, 2003 – Formed Delphi Energy Corp. in Alberta on reverse takeover of and subsequent amalgamation with DT Energy Ltd.; basis 1 new for 4 old shs. ■

Rise Resources Inc. (B.C. June 16, 1983)
Mar. 22, 1993 – Name changed to Pacific Mariner Explorations Ltd.; basis 1 new for 5 old shs. ■

Rise Resources Inc. (Nev. Feb. 9, 2007)
Apr. 7, 2017 – Name changed to Rise Gold Corp. (see FPsurvey - Mines & Energy)

RiseTech Capital Corp. (B.C. Feb. 26, 2018)
Jan. 29, 2021 – Name changed to Tantalus Systems Holding Inc. pursuant to the Qualifying Transaction reverse takeover acquisition of (old) Tantalus Systems Holding Inc., and concurrent amalgamation of (old) Tantalus with wholly owned 12384205 Canada Inc. (and continued as 12384205 Canada Inc.); basis 1 new for 16.4 old shs. (see FPsurvey - Industrials)

Rising Phoenix Development Group Ltd. (B.C. Oct. 30, 1987)
Nov. 15, 1999 – Acquired by 2U Online.com, Inc.; basis unknown.
2003 – Name changed to Golden Spirit Minerals Ltd. and continued into Delaware; basis 1 new for 10 old shs.

Rising Resources Ltd. (Alta. July 22, 1987)
June 5, 1995 – Acquired by Gardiner Oil and Gas Limited for $3.75 per sh. (see Gardiner Oil and Gas Limited)

Rita Capital Corp. (Alta. Nov. 12, 2001)
July 19, 2004 – Name changed to Biotech Medical Sciences Inc. following non-arm's length Qualifying Transaction acquisition of all assets of Sentry Select Focused Biotechnology Fund. ■

Ritchie Bros. Auctioneers Incorporated (Can. Dec. 12, 1997)
May 23, 2023 – Name changed to RB Global, Inc. ■

Ritoria Mines Ltd. (Ont. 1937)
Dec. 8, 1969 – Charter cancelled.

The Ritz Larder Mines Ltd. (Ont. 1943)
July 2, 1957 – Charter cancelled.

Ritz Resources Ltd. (B.C. Dec. 7, 1983)
Apr. 23, 1993 – Name changed to Trinity Control Ltd.; basis 1 new for 3 old shs. ■

Riva Gold Corporation (B.C. Mar. 31, 2010)
May 7, 2013 – Amalgamated with a wholly owned subsidiary of Wildcat Silver Corporation; basis 1 Wildcat sh. for 4.7 Riva shs. (see Wildcat Silver Corporation)

Riva Petroleum Inc. (B.C. Dec. 6, 1988)
July 28, 1997 – Name changed to Rivera Explorations Inc.; basis 1 new for 5 old shs. ■

Rival Energy Inc. (Alta. Dec. 16, 1999)
July 10, 2003 – Amalgamated with Roseland Resources Ltd. (1 for 5) to continue as Rival Energy Ltd. (formerly Roseland); basis 1 new Rival Energy Ltd. sh. for 1 old Rival Energy Inc. sh. (see Rival Energy Ltd.)

Rival Energy Ltd. (Alta. Feb. 24, 1995)
Jan. 28, 2008 – Acquired by Zargon Energy Tust; basis either 0.0562 Zargon trust units or $1.35 for 1 Rival com. sh.

Rival Minerals Ltd. (B.C. Sept. 15, 1986)
Jan. 18, 1988 – Name changed to Europrime Capital Corporation. ■

Rival Technologies Inc. (B.C. Feb. 10, 1987)
Oct. 28, 2005 – Amalgamated in Nevada to continue with same name.
June 2, 2022 – Continued into British Columbia.

River Gold Mines Ltd. (Ont. July 2, 1991)
Feb. 6, 2006 – Acquired by Wesdome Gold Mines Inc.; basis 1 Wesdome sh. and for 1.538461538 River shs.

River Mountain Resources Ltd. (B.C. Aug. 28, 1969)
Feb. 16, 1983 – Name changed to Rio Sierra Silver Corp.; basis 1 new for 4 old shs. ■

River Valley Energy Services Corporation (Alta. May 17, 1994 amalg.)
Dec. 18, 2002 – Name changed to River Valley Energy Services Ltd.; basis 1 new for 5 old shs. ■

River Valley Energy Services Ltd. (Alta. May 17, 1994 amalg.)
Oct. 5, 2004 – Converted into River Valley Income Fund following arrangement with River Valley Income Trust, River Valley Holdings Partnership, River Valley Operating Limited Partnership and River Valley Acquisitionco Ltd.; basis 1 trust unit for 1 com. sh.

River Valley Income Fund (Alta. Aug. 18, 2004)
Mar. 31, 2005 – Name changed to Eveready Income Fund following reverse takeover acquisition of Eveready Industrial Group Ltd. ■

River Wild Exploration Inc. (B.C. Apr. 28, 2010)
Sept. 26, 2012 – Amalgamated in British Columbia to continue with same name.
Apr. 1, 2019 – Name changed to CENTR Brands Corp. pursuant to the reverse takeover acquisition of CBD Lifestyle Corp. (see FPsurvey - Industrials)

Rivera Capital Corp. (B.C. Dec. 15, 2006)
Apr. 15, 2009 – Formed Canada Fluorspar Inc. in Alberta on Qualifying Transaction amalgamation with Burin Fluorspar Ltd. (deemed acquiror); basis 1 new for 1.8 Burin shs. and 1 new for 1 Rivera sh. ■

Rivera Explorations Inc. (B.C. Dec. 6, 1988)
Aug. 6, 1998 – Name changed to Silverarrow Explorations Inc.; basis 1 new for 6 old shs. ■

Riverdance Resources Corp. (B.C. Sept. 27, 1979)
May 26, 1999 – Name changed to Luminex Ventures Inc.; basis 1 new for 8 old shs. ■

Riverhead Oil & Gas Co. Ltd. (Alta.)
1958 – Struck off register.

Riverridge Mines Ltd. (Ont. 1955)
Apr. 7, 1971 – Charter cancelled.

Riverside-Chibougamau Mines Ltd. (Que. 1953)
July 7, 1979 – Charter cancelled.

Riverside Forest Products Limited (B.C. June 1, 1978)
Oct. 1, 1998 – Amalgamated in British Columbia to continue with same name.
Dec. 3, 2004 – Acquired by Tolko Industries Ltd. for $40 per sh.

Riverside Silk Mills Ltd. (Ont. 1915)
June 17, 1960 – Name changed to Riverside Yarns Limited. ■

Riverside Yarns Limited (Ont. 1915)
Aug. 1982 – Ceased operations.
Feb. 18, 1986 – All fixed assets sold and final distribution of 86¢ per sh.

Riverstone Resources Inc. (B.C. Oct. 2, 1987)
Feb. 25, 2013 – Name changed to True Gold Mining Inc. ■

Riverton Resources Corp. (B.C. 1983)
May 14, 1993 – Dissolved and struck off register.

Riverwood Resources Limited (B.C. 1971)
Sept. 2, 1983 – Struck off register.

Riviera Explorations Ltd. (B.C. Sept. 3, 1987)
July 20, 1993 – Name changed to Kentucky Oil and Gas Inc.; basis 1 new for 3.69 old shs. ■

Riviera Industries & Resources Ltd. (B.C. Jan. 6, 1966)
Oct. 23, 1981 – Name changed to Leslie Oil & Gas Co. Ltd. ■

Riviera Mines Limited (B.C. Jan. 6, 1966)
May 17, 1971 – Name changed to Riviera Industries & Resources Ltd. ■

Rivtow Straits Limited (B.C. 1975 amalg.)
1978 – Offer of $4.10 per sh. for o/s com. stk. by RivTow Holdings Ltd. made and substantially all shs. purchased. By late 1981, remaining shs. acquired on same basis.

Rix-Athabasca Uranium Mines Ltd. (Ont. 1950)
1970 – Acquired by New York Oils Ltd.; basis 1 new for 4 old shs.

Rize Oncology Inc. (B.C. Oct. 13, 2021)
May 26, 2025 – Voluntarily delisted from the CSE. (see FPsurvey - Industrials)

Rizona Ventures Ltd. (B.C. Sept. 3, 1987)
Aug. 31, 1998 – Name changed to Admiral Bay Resources Inc. ■

Road New Media Corporation (Alta. Sept. 20, 1999)
Dec. 15, 2004 – Continued into Canada.
Nov. 27, 2012 – Name changed to Perisson Petroleum Corporation; basis 1 new for 7 old shs. (see FPsurvey - Mines & Energy)

Roadking Travel Centres Inc. (Alta. Mar. 3, 1987)
Nov. 18, 2014 – Initial distribution of $0.0395 cash per sh. to shldrs. of record Nov. 18, 2015, payable on or about Nov. 25, 2014.
Mar. 19, 2015 – Final distribution of $0.00629 cash per sh. to shldrs. of record Mar. 19. 2015, payable on or about Apr. 2, 2015.
Apr. 7, 2015 – Voluntarily dissolved.

Roadman Investments Corp. (B.C. Sept. 12, 2007)
Jan. 3, 2023 – Name changed to Right Season Investments Corp. (see FPsurvey - Industrials)

Roadrunner Capital Corporation (Ont. Nov. 18, 2004)
Mar. 27, 2006 – Name changed to Brighter Minds Media Inc. following Qualifying Transaction acquisition of Brighter Child Interactive, LLC. (see FPsurvey - Industrials)

Roadrunner Oil & Gas Inc. (Can. Sept. 8, 1994)
June 21, 2010 – Name changed to Bowood Energy Inc. ■

Roain Development Corp. Ltd. (Ont. 1966)
1971 – Merged into Milger Investment & Development Corp. Ltd.; basis 1 new for 4 old shs.

Roanoke Explorations Ltd. (B.C. Jan. 30, 1978)
Apr. 1, 1985 – Delisted from the Vancouver Stock Exchange. Subsequently dissolved for failure to file and struck from registry.

Roaring River Mines Ltd. (Ont. 1957)
July 26, 1972 – Dissolved.

Robb-Montbray Mines Ltd. (Ont. 1927)
Nov. 1977 – Name changed to Paragon Explorations Limited; basis 1 new for 10 old shs. ■

Robb-Murmac Uranium Mines Ltd. (Ont. 1949)
Feb. 1958 – Dissolved.

Robert Mines Ltd. (B.C. 1969)
May 15, 1989 – Formed Edinov Technologies Inc. in Canada on amalgamation with Edinov Technologies Inc.; basis 1 new for 4 old shs. ■

Robert Mitchell Co., Limited (Can. Dec. 4, 1924)
Apr. 12, 1979 – Name changed to Robert Mitchell Inc. ■

Robert Mitchell Inc. (Can. Dec. 4, 1924)
Jan. 9, 2001 – Acquired by Marshall-Barwick Properties Inc., a wholly owned subsid. of Marshall-Barwick Inc., for $11 per sh.

Robert Morse Corp. Ltd. (Can. 1905)
Aug. 4, 1975 – Following an offer to purch. all cl. A and cl. B shs. for $18.50 per sh. in February 1974, Aerojet-General Corp. acquired 98.9% of the cl. A shs. and 99.1% of the cl. B shs., and subsequently the remainder. all 5.5 % ser. A and ser. B pref. shs. red. at $50 per sh. plus 50¢ in accr. divds.

Roberta Oils Ltd. (Can. 1926)
Acquired by Teapot Dome Oils, Ltd. (see Teapot Dome Oils Ltd.)

Roberto Resources Inc. (B.C. Mar. 19, 2019)
July 18, 2025 – Name changed to Pacifica Silver Corp. (see FPsurvey - Mines & Energy)

Roberts Bay Resources Ltd. (Alta. Apr. 27, 1993)
June 8, 2001 – Name changed to Rider Resources Inc. following reverse takeover acquisition of publicly listed Rider Resources Inc.; basis 1 new for 3 old shs. ■

Roberval Mining Corp. (Que. 1957)
Oct. 1973 – Charter cancelled.

Robin Hood Multifoods Inc. (Can. 1912)
Aug. 31, 2003 – Name changed to Smucker Foods of Canada Corp.

Robin Hood Multifoods Limited (Can. 1912)
Aug. 28, 1980 – Name changed to Robin Hood Multifoods Inc. ■

Robin International Inc. (Can. 1946)
Aug. 19, 1988 – Acquired by Algo Group Inc. (see Algo Group Inc.)

Robin, Jones & Whitman Limited (Can. 1910)
1959 – All o/s 6% pref. stk. redeemed Jan. 15, 1965, at $25 per sh. plus accr. divd. of 60¢ per sh. Original 6% pref. eliminated when holders received 1 new pref. sh. $25 par plus cash pay. of $25 for 1 old pref. sh.

Robin Nodwell Manufacturing Ltd. (Alta. 1940)
Jan. 1969 – Name changed to Van Ness Industries Ltd. ■

Robin Red Lake Mines Limited (Ont. 1945)
June 30, 1978 – Amalgamated with Dickenson Mines Ltd. to continue with the same name Dickenson Mines Ltd.; basis 1 new for 2.5 old shs.

Robina Explorations Ltd. (B.C. 1969)
Sept. 14, 1978 – Amalgamated with 3 other cos. into Stand-Skat Resources Ltd.; basis 0.12505 new for 1 old sh. (see Stand-Skat Resources Ltd.)

Robinson Cotton Mills Limited (Ont. 1923)
Oct. 29, 1973 – Placed into liquidation by shldrs. resolution.
July 10, 1975 – Distribution of $2.39 per sh. made to com. shldrs. of record Sept. 4, 1973. Subsequent payments of $4.00 and 80¢ per com. sh. made on Nov. 19, 1973 and Sept. 27, 1974, respectively. Final pay. of 14.5¢ per com. sh. made to shldrs. of record July 10, 1975.

Robinson, Little & Company, Limited (Can. 1913)
Jan. 2, 1985 – Declared bankrupt. Assets sold, secured and preferred creditors paid in full. Unsecured creditors received 10¢ on the dollar. No equity for common shldrs.

Robix Alternative Fuels, Inc. (Alta. June 9, 2011)
Mar. 1, 2016 – Name changed to Robix Environmental Technologies, Inc. (see FPsurvey - Industrials)

Robop.tek (Canada) Inc. (B.C. July 28, 1983)
Mar. 2, 1989 – Delisted from the Vancouver Stock Exchange. Subsequently dissolved.

Robson Petroleum Ltd. (Alta. 1980)
Dec. 1991 – Dissolved. Shldrs. to receive 1 Robson Petroleum Company com. sh. for 1 sh. held.

Roca Mines Inc. (B.C. July 19, 2001)
June 9, 2021 – Name changed to Aardvark Ventures Inc. ■

Rocamsa Mines Ltd. (Ont. 1944)
1962 – Charter cancelled; no equity for shldrs.

Rocca Resources Ltd. (B.C. Oct. 27, 1986)
Mar. 27, 2000 – Name changed to Siegesoft Internet Solutions Inc. ■

Roche Long Lac Gold Mines Ltd. (Ont. 1934)
1957 – Name changed to Roche Mines Ltd. ■

Roche Mines Ltd. (Ont. 1934)
1963 – Name changed to North Rock Explorations
Limited; basis 1 new for 5 old shs. ■

Rocher de Boule Mountain Mines Ltd. (B.C. 1951)
1955 – In voluntary liquidation. Guaranty Trust Co.,
liquidator, 562 Howe St., Vancouver. Distribution was
1.375¢ per sh.

Rocher Deboule Minerals Corp. (B.C. July 8, 1987)
Jan. 19, 2010 – Name changed to American Manganese
Inc. ■

Rochester Energy Corp. (B.C. Oct. 3, 1983)
Sept. 8, 1997 – Name changed to International Rochester
Energy Corp.; basis 1 new for 3 old shs. ■

Rochester Energy Corp. (Alta. Mar. 5, 1999)
Mar. 4, 2009 – Acquired by Southern Pacific Resource
Corp.; basis 0.1977 Southern Pacific shs. for 1 Rochester
sh. Subsequently amalgamated with Rochester. (see
Southern Pacific Resource Corp.)

Rochester Minerals Inc. (B.C. Oct. 3, 1983)
Apr. 28, 1997 – Name changed to Rochester Energy
Corp. ■

Rochette Gold Mines Ltd. (Que. 1936)
May 1950 – Name changed to Consolidated Rochette
Mines Ltd.; basis 1 new for 2 old shs. ■

Rock Capital Corporation (Alta. Nov. 28, 1995)
June 18, 1999 – Name changed to Terraco Energy
Corporation. ■

Rock Creek Resources Ltd. (B.C. Mar. 22, 1988)
Jan. 6, 1993 – Name changed to Altra Ventures Inc.;
basis 1 new for 2 old shs. ■

Rock Creek Resources Ltd. (Alta. Jan. 17, 2002)
Aug. 5, 2005 – Plan of Arrangement acquisition by Great
Plains Exploration Inc. (GPE); basis for cl. A shs. - either
$0.846 plus 0.6616 new GPE sh. or, 1 new GPE sh. for
1 old Rock Creek cl. A sh. and basis for cl. B shs. - either
$3.38 plus 2.648 new GPE shs. or, 4 new GPE shs. for
1 old Rock Creek cl. B sh. (see Great Plains Exploration
Inc.)

Rock-Echo Mines Ltd. (Ont. 1954)
Dec. 12, 1960 – Dissolved.

Rock Edge Resources Ltd. (B.C. Jan. 10, 2020)
Feb. 27, 2024 – Name changed to Inspiration Energy
Corp. (see FPsurvey - Mines & Energy)

Rock Energy Inc. (Alta. Feb. 18, 2004)
July 21, 2016 – Acquired by Raging River Exploration
Inc.; basis 0.082 Raging River com. shs. for each Rock
com. sh. (see Raging River Exploration Inc.)

Rock Hill Uranium Ltd. (B.C. 1953)
1955 – Acquired by Imperial Mines and Metals Ltd.

Rock-Lite Development Corp. Ltd. (Ont. 1968)
1971 – Merged into Milger Investment & Development
Corp. Ltd.; basis 1 new for 9 old shs.

Rock-Lite Uranium Mining Co. Ltd. (Ont. 1968)
1969 – Name changed to Rock-Lite Development Corp.
Ltd. ■

La Rock Mining Corp. (B.C. Jan. 15, 1980)
July 19, 2001 – Name changed to Avola Industries Inc.;
basis 1 new for 10 old shs. ■

Rock Ore Exploration & Development Ltd. (Man. 1971)
Dec. 30, 1985 – Amalgamated with several other cos. to
form Canhorn Mining Corporation; basis 1 new Canhorn
for 17.19 old Rock Ore shs.

Rock Resources Inc. (B.C. May 28, 1993)
Feb. 10, 2004 – Name changed to Adroit Resources Inc.;
basis 1 new for 10 old shs. ■

Rock Tech Resources Inc. (B.C. June 14, 1996)
May 12, 2010 – Name changed to Rock Tech Lithium
Inc. (see FPsurvey - Mines & Energy)

Rockabee Investments Inc. (Ont. Mar. 8, 1957)
Dec. 31, 1993 – Formed Root Industries Inc. in Ontario
on amalgamation with Root Chemical Company Inc.;
basis 1 new for 3 old shs. ■

Rockbound Resources Inc. (Alta. Oct. 8, 1993)
Oct. 27, 1997 – Name changed to Del Mar Energy Inc.;
basis 1 new for 1 old sh. ■

RockBridge Energy Inc. (B.C. Nov. 20, 2007)
Mar. 31, 2010 – Name changed to RockBridge Resources
Inc. ■

RockBridge Resources Inc. (B.C. Nov. 20, 2007)
Nov. 14, 2018 – Name changed to Harvest Health &
Recreation Inc. pursuant to reverse takeover acquisition
of Harvest Enterprises, Inc.; basis 1 new for 29.41125
old shs. ■

Rockcliff Copper Corporation (Ont. Apr. 27, 2011
amalg.)
Nov. 2, 2017 – Name changed to Rockcliff Metals
Corporation. ■

Rockcliff Metals Corporation (Ont. Apr. 27, 2011
amalg.)
Sept. 15, 2023 – Acquired by Hudbay Minerals Inc.; basis
0.006776 Hudbay shs. for 1 Rockcliff sh. ■

Rockcliff Resources Inc. (Ont. Jan. 20, 2006)
June 25, 2015 – Acquired by Solvista Gold Corporation;
basis 0.9 Solvista com. shs. for 1 Rockcliff sh. (see
Solvista Gold Corporation)

Rockcroft Explorations Ltd. (Ont. 1956)
Feb. 18, 1965 – Dissolved.

Rockdale Mines Ltd. (Ont. 1953)
July 30, 1976 – Merged with 2 other cos. into Pyx
Explorations Ltd.; basis 1 new for 50 old shs.

Rockefeller Hughes Corporation (Ont. Aug. 15, 2008)
Feb. 24, 2017 – Name changed to RHC Capital
Corporation. ■

Rockel Mines Ltd. (B.C. Mar. 8, 1974)
May 1, 1978 – Name changed to Veronex Resources
Ltd.; basis 1 new for 5 old shs. ■

Rocket Energy Resources Ltd. (B.C. July 31, 1979)
Apr. 28, 1989 – Name changed to MRI Medical
Technologies Inc. ■

Rocket Indin Mining Co. Ltd. (Ont. 1945)
1949 – Formed Transvaal Explorations Ltd. in Ontario
following merger with West Lloyd Prospecting Syndicate
(1 for 50); basis 1 new for 1 old sh. ■

Rocket Mines Ltd. (B.C. 1966)
Aug. 1973 – Name changed to Vieco Resources Limited;
basis 1 new for 5 old shs. ■

Rocket Resources Ltd. (B.C. 1980)
Dec. 11, 1997 – Name changed to Exeter Oil & Gas
Limited. ■

Rockex Mining Corporation (Alta. May 29, 1996)
Jan. 24, 2011 – Continued into Ontario. (see FPsurvey -
Mines & Energy)

Rockford Minerals Inc. (Ont. Dec. 5, 1986)
Apr. 30, 1992 – Name changed to Reclamation
Management Limited following reverse takeover
acquisition of Reclamation Management Corporation;
basis 1 new for 10 old shs. ■

Rockgate Capital Corp. (B.C. Nov. 23, 2004)
Jan. 21, 2014 – Acquired by Denison Mines Corp.; basis
0.192 Denison shs. for 1 Rockgate sh.

Rockhaven Resources Ltd. (Alta. July 20, 2005)
Sept. 9, 2009 – Continued into British Columbia. (see
FPsurvey - Mines & Energy)

Rockies Financial Corporation (Can. Mar. 17, 2004)
Oct. 9, 2007 – Name changed to Sprylogics International
Corp. following Qualifying Transaction reverse takeover
acquisition of Sprylogics International Inc. ■

Rockingham Resources Inc. (B.C. 1984)
Oct. 30, 1992 – Dissolved and struck off register.

Rockland Minerals Corp. (B.C. June 12, 2008)
Jan. 27, 2017 – Name changed to International Corona
Capital Corp. ■

Rockland Mining Ltd. (B.C. May 9, 1967)
Apr. 3, 1974 – Name changed to Calivada Resources
Limited; basis 1 new for 4 old shs. ■

Rocklite International Inc. (Ont. 1945)
Jan. 3, 1995 – Delisted from the CDN. Subsequently
dissolved and charter cancelled.

Rockmaster Resources Ltd. (B.C. May 14, 1980)
Oct. 14, 1987 – Name changed to Randstrom
Manufacturing Corp. ■

Rockmere Lake Exploration Ltd. (Ont. 1983)
Aug. 31, 1987 – Amalgamated with Oneida Energy &
Resources Corp. (0.667 for 1) and Dixie Oil & Gas Corp.
(1 for 1) to form Consolidated Dixie Resources Inc.; basis
0.6 new for 1 old sh.

Rockminster Exploration Co. (Ont. 1947)
Struck off register.

Rockower of Canada Ltd. (Ont. 1961)
Nov. 1968 – Approx. all o/s com. shs. acquired by
Oshawa Wholesale Limited through exchange of 35
Oshawa cl. A shs. and 400 sh. purch. warrants for 100
old Rockower com. shs.

Rockport Energy Corporation (Can. Sept. 27, 1985)
Dec. 15, 1998 – Formed Liberty Oil & Gas Ltd. following
reverse takeover acquisition of Liberty Oil & Gas Ltd. and
subsequent amalgamation with a wholly owned subsid.;
basis 1 new for 6 old shs. ■

Rockport Resources Ltd. (Alta. 1983)
Sept. 12, 1985 – Name changed to Skywest Resources
Corp.; basis 1 new for 5 old shs. ■

Rockridge Capital Corp. (B.C. Jan. 12, 2007)
Jan. 24, 2017 – Name changed to Zinc One Resources
Inc.; basis 1.5 new for 1 old sh. (see FPsurvey - Mines
& Energy)

Rockridge Gold Ltd. (B.C. Nov. 10, 2015)
Mar. 19, 2018 – Name changed to Rockridge Resources
Ltd. ■

Rockridge Gold Mines Ltd. (Ont. 1945)
1954 – Charter cancelled.

Rockridge Mining Corp. (B.C. May 31, 1984)
July 24, 1991 – Formed Keith Resources Ltd. in British
Columbia on amalgamation with Meadfield Mining Corp.;
basis 1 new for 9 Meadfield shs. and 1 new for 5
Rockridge shs. ■

Rockridge Resources Ltd. (B.C. Nov. 10, 2015)
Jan. 28, 2025 – All o/s shs. not already held acquired by
Eros Resources Corp.; basis 0.375 Eros shs. for 1
Rockridge sh. (see Eros Resources Corp.)

Rockshield Capital Corp. (B.C. Oct. 23, 2007)
Sept. 2, 2021 – Name changed to Eat Well Investment
Group Inc. (see FPsurvey - Industrials)

Rockspan Resources Ltd. (B.C. June 18, 1982)
Nov. 1, 1989 – Name changed to Boswell International Technologies Ltd.; basis 1 new for 2 old shs. ■

Rockstar Capital Corp. (Ont. Mar. 7, 2011)
Nov. 19, 2012 – Name changed to First Global Data Limited pursuant to Qualifying Transaction amalgamation of First Global Data Corp. (deemed acquiror) with wholly owned Rockstar Acquisition Corp.; basis 1 new for 3 old shs. (see FPsurvey - Industrials)

Rockvale Resources Limited (Alta. Mar. 12, 1997)
Sept. 2, 2003 – Struck from registry and dissolved.

Rockwater Capital Corporation (Ont. Dec. 28, 1995)
May 15, 2007 – Acquired by CI Financial Income Fund for $7.62 per sh. (see CI Financial Income Fund)

Rockwealth International Resource Corp. (B.C. May 5, 1993)
Aug. 7, 1996 – Name changed to Strathmore Resources Ltd. ■

Rockwealth Resources Corp. (B.C. May 8, 2007)
Dec. 7, 2021 – Name changed to Strathmore Plus Energy Corp. ■

Rockwell Diamonds Inc. (B.C. Nov. 10, 1988)
Mar. 17, 2021 – Privatized via amalgamated with 1274787 B.C. Ltd., continuing under the Rockwell Diamond name; basis 1 redeem. pref. sh. for 1 com. sh., immediately redeemed for $0.005 cash per sh. ■

Rockwell International Corp. (Del. 1928)
Feb. 26, 2002 – Name changed to Rockwell Automation, Inc.

Rockwell International of Canada Ltd. (Del. 1928)
1979 – Continued into Canada.

Rockwell Mining Corporation (B.C. 1979)
July 24, 1984 – Name changed to Kidd Resources Ltd. following amalgamation with 7 private cos.; basis 1 new for 5 old shs. ■

Rockwell Resources Ltd. (B.C. 1970)
Oct. 1977 – Charter cancelled.

Rockwell Ventures Inc. (B.C. Nov. 10, 1988)
May 17, 2007 – Name changed to Rockwell Diamonds Inc. ■

Rockwin Mines Ltd. (Ont. 1945)
1966 – Merged into Roman Corporation Limited; basis 1 new for 12.5 old shs.

Rocky Brook Mines Ltd. (Ont. 1966)
1967 – Acquired by Trimar Holdings & Explorations Ltd.; basis 1 new for 5 old shs.

Rocky Mountain Brands, Inc. (Ont. Aug. 23, 1993 amalg.)
Dec. 14, 2004 – Continued into Nevada.

Rocky Mountain Dealerships Inc. (Alta. Sept. 17, 2007)
Dec. 29, 2020 – Going private transaction with 2223890 Alberta Ltd. via plan of arrangement; basis $7.41 cash per com. sh.
Dec. 31, 2020 – Succeeded by Rocky Mountain Equipment L.P.

Rocky Mountain Energy Corp. (B.C. Jan. 10, 1979)
Oct. 1, 2004 – Acquired by Enterra Energy Commercial Trust and Rocky Mountain Acquisition Corp.; basis $6.10, or 0.35078 Enterra Energy Trust trust units, or 0.35078 Rocky Mountain Acquisition exch. shs. for 1 Rocky Mountain sh. (see Enterra Energy Trust)

Rocky Mountain Industries Inc. (Alta. 1987)
Feb. 1, 1999 – Struck from registry.

Rocky Mountain Oil & Mines Ltd. (Ont. 1943)
Struck off register.

Rocky Mountain Resources Corp. (Can. Mar. 2, 2006)
Jan. 5, 2011 – Name changed to American Vanadium Corp. ■

Rocky Mountain Trench Mines Ltd. (B.C. Sept. 17, 1973 amalg.)
Aug. 9, 1974 – Formed New Copper Mountain Mines Ltd. in British Columbia on amalgamation with Mamit Lake Mining Ltd. (1 for 2.5); basis 1 new for 2.5 old shs. ■

Rocky Petroleums Limited (Ont. 1952)
Mar. 16, 1976 – Dissolved.

Rocky Valley Resources Ltd. (Alta. 1986)
Jan. 1, 1991 – Struck off register.

Rockyview Energy Inc. (Alta. Apr. 12, 2005)
Feb. 5, 2008 – Acquired by Direct Energy Marketing Limited, a subsid. of Centrica plc, for $3.16 per com. sh.

Rockzone Mines Ltd. (Ont. 1960)
Dec. 1977 – Dissolved.

Rocmec Mining Inc. (Que. July 18, 2000)
Apr. 16, 2014 – Name changed to Nippon Dragon Resources Inc. ■

Rococco Resources Ltd. (B.C. 1980)
May 28, 1993 – Dissolved and struck off register.

Rocraven Resources Ltd. (B.C. Feb. 11, 1980)
Oct. 22, 2002 – Name changed to Lifetime Ventures Ltd.; basis 1 new for 5 old shs. ■

Roctest Ltée (Que. May 11, 1967)
Dec. 15, 2010 – Acquired by Nova Metrix LLC for $4.01 per sh.

Roddy Resources Inc. (B.C. 1980)
July 17, 1989 – Continued into Canada.
June 10, 2004 – Dissolved.

Rodell Corp. (1967) Ltd. (Can. - unspecified 1967)
1969 – Acquired by Great Northern Capital Corp. Ltd. for $2,000,000.

Rodeo Capital II Corp. (Alta. Nov. 23, 2010)
Sept. 27, 2011 – Formed Shona Energy Company, Inc. in British Columbia following Qualifying Transaction amalgamation with Shona Energy Company, Inc. (deemed acquiror), 0910803 B.C. Ltd. (a wholly owned subsid. of Shona) and 091073 B.C. Ltd. (a wholly owned subsid. of Rodeo); basis 1 new sh. for 2.5 Rodeo shs. ■

Rodeo Capital III Corp. (Alta. June 17, 2014)
Mar. 26, 2015 – Name changed to Solegear Bioplastic Technologies Inc. and continued into British Columbia following Qualifying Transaction reverse takeover acquisition of Solegear Bioplastics Inc.; basis 1 new for 1.75 old shs. ■

Rodeo Capital Corp. (Alta. July 15, 2008)
July 29, 2010 – Continued into British Columbia.
July 30, 2010 – Name changed to Avala Resources Ltd. pursuant to Qualifying Transaction acquisition of Dundee Plemeniti Metali d.o.o., a wholly owned subsid. of Dundee Precious Metals Inc., by PJV Resources Inc. and subsequent reverse takeover acquisition of PJV by and amalgamation with a wholly owned subsidiary of Rodeo. ■

Rodeo Resources Ltd. (B.C. Feb. 14, 1980)
Sept. 1, 1988 – Delisted from the Vancouver Stock Exchange. Subsequently dissolved for failure to file.

Rodera Diamond Corporation (B.C. Aug. 9, 1983)
Mar. 1, 1999 – Amalgamated with Pacific Royal Ventures Ltd. to form Pacific Rodera Ventures Inc.; basis 1 new for 5 Pacific Royal shs. and 1 new for 8 Rodera Diamond shs. (see Pacific Rodera Ventures Inc.)

Rodinia Lithium Inc. (Ont. Nov. 3, 2009)
Aug. 16, 2016 – Name changed to Routemaster Capital Inc.; basis 1 new for 10 old shs. ■

Rodinia Minerals Inc. (B.C. Apr. 17, 1986)
Nov. 3, 2009 – Continued into Ontario.
June 30, 2010 – Name changed to Rodinia Lithium Inc. ■

Rodney Gold Mines Ltd. (Ont. 1946)
Nov. 9, 1976 – Charter cancelled.

Rodocanachi Capital Inc. (Que. Mar. 5, 2008)
Jan. 8, 2015 – Name changed to AlliancePharma Inc. following Qualifying Transaction reverse takeover acquisition of (old) AlliancePharma Inc.; basis 1 new for 3 old shs. ■

Rodstrom Yellowknife Mines Ltd. (B.C. 1963)
Feb. 15, 1972 – Name changed to Imperial Modular Industries Ltd.; basis 1 new for 4 old shs. ■

Roford Mines Ltd. (Ont. 1952)
Aug. 20, 1962 – Charter cancelled.

Rogard Red Lake Mines Ltd. (Ont. 1944)
1950 – Charter cancelled.

Roger Lake Mines Ltd. (Ont. 1955)
Wound up.

Roger Red Lake Gold Mines Ltd. (Ont. Feb. 12, 1937)
Dec. 1954 – Charter cancelled.

Roger Williams Music Corporation Ltd. (Ont. 1959)
Aug. 8, 1974 – Name changed to RWMC Productions Limited and capital reorganized as follows: com. shldrs. received one wt. for 1 new sh. at $1.00 for each 50 shs. held, and all issued shs. cancelled; debenture holders received 1 new sh. and 1 wt. for each $10 princ. and accr. int. held, and creditors to the extent of $11,454 received 1 sh. for each $1 held. ■

Rogers Associate Financial Partners Inc. (Alta. Apr. 4, 2002)
Oct. 2, 2013 – Dissolved and struck from register.

Rogers Cablesystems Inc. (Can. Jan. 23, 1920)
Apr. 2, 1986 – Name changed to Rogers Communications Inc. ■

Rogers Cablesystems Ltd. (Ont.)
Jan. 1, 2001 – Name changed to Rogers Cable Inc.

Rogers Cantel Inc. (Can.)
Aug. 21, 2000 – Name changed to Rogers Wireless Inc. ■

Rogers Cantel Mobile Communications Inc. (Can. May 6, 1984)
Aug. 21, 2000 – Name changed to Rogers Wireless Communications Inc. ■

Rogers Communications Inc. (Can. Jan. 23, 1920)
Oct. 20, 1987 – Continued into British Columbia.
Apr. 6, 1990 – Amalgamated with Rogers Canadian Holdings Inc. to continue with the same name Rogers Communications Inc.; basis 7 new for 1 cl. A or B sh. (see FPsurvey - Industrials)

Rogers Inter Design Inc. (B.C. Sept. 29, 1980)
June 4, 1984 – Name changed to Majorteck Industries Incorporated. ■

Rogers-Majestic Corp. Ltd. (Can. 1925)
1941 – Name changed to Standard Radio Ltd.; basis 1 new and $3 for each cl. A and cl. B sh. ■

Rogers Sugar Income Fund (Ont. Sept. 30, 1997)
Jan. 1, 2011 – Succeeded by Rogers Sugar Inc. pursuant to plan of arrangement whereby Rogers Suger Inc. was formed to facilitate the conversion of the fund into a corporation and the fund was subsequently dissolved. (see FPsurvey - Industrials)

Rogers Wireless Communications Inc. (Can. May 6, 1984)
Jan. 6, 2005 – Acquired by Rogers Communications Inc.; basis 1.75 new Rogers Communications cl. B shs. for 1 old Rogers Wireless cl. B sh.

Rogers Wireless Inc. (Can.)
July 1, 2007 – Amalgamated into Rogers Communications Inc.

Rogi Explorations Inc. (Que. Mar. 11, 1986)
Oct. 30, 1991 – Name changed to International Alliance Resources Inc.; basis 1 new for 5 old shs. ■

Rogue Iron Ore Corp. (B.C. Apr. 20, 1982)
Dec. 24, 2013 – Name changed to Rogue Resources Inc.; basis 1 new for 5 old shs. ■

Rogue Point Mines Ltd. (B.C. 1966)
Oct. 15, 1974 – Charter cancelled.

Rogue Resources Inc. (B.C. Apr. 20, 1982)
Jan. 23, 2012 – Name changed to Rogue Iron Ore Corp. ■

Rogue Resources Inc. (B.C. Apr. 20, 1982)
May 29, 2024 – Name changed to Clean Energy Transition Inc. (see FPsurvey - Mines & Energy)

Rohault Mines Ltd. (Que. 1952)
Oct. 29, 1971 – Charter cancelled.

Rojo Resources Ltd. (B.C. June 26, 1962)
May 14, 2020 – Name changed to Numinus Wellness Inc. pursuant to reverse takeover acquisition of Salvation Botanicals Ltd.; basis 1 new for 2 old shs. (see FPsurvey - Industrials)

Rojoll Explorations Ltd. (B.C. July 7, 1981)
Sept. 7, 1988 – Name changed to Morrison-Grey Enterprises Limited. ■

Rokon Mines Ltd. (B.C. 1970)
Oct. 3, 1977 – Dissolved.

Rolac Mines Ltd. (Ont. 1938)
1953 – Charter cancelled.

Roland Gold & Copper Mines Ltd. (Que. 1946)
May 1974 – Charter cancelled.

Roll-Up Capital Corp. (Alta. May 7, 2015)
Mar. 17, 2017 – Continued into British Columbia.
Mar. 21, 2017 – Name changed to VR Resources Ltd. following Qualifying Transaction reverse takeover acquisition of Renntiger Resources Limited; basis 1 new for 3 old shs. (see FPsurvey - Mines & Energy)

Rolland Energy Inc. (Can. May 29, 2001)
June 4, 2008 – Name changed to Gale Force Petroleum Inc.; basis 1 new for 8 old shs. ■

Rolland inc. (Can. June 16, 1928; via Dominion charter)
Jan. 8, 2001 – Amalgamated with Paperboard Industries International Inc., Perkins Papers Ltd. and Cascades Inc.; basis 0.24 new for 1 Paperboard sh., 0.6 new for 1 Perkins sh. and 0.73 new for 1 Rolland sh.

Rolland Mines Ltd. (Ont. 1945)
1956 – Charter cancelled.

Rolland Paper Company, Limited (Can. June 16, 1928; via Dominion charter)
Aug. 27, 1979 – Name changed to Rolland inc. ■

Rolland Virtual Business Systems Ltd. (B.C. May 25, 1983)
May 29, 2001 – Continued into Canada.
Feb. 16, 2007 – Name changed to Rolland Energy Inc. ■

Roller Resources Inc. (B.C. 1983)
Nov. 29, 1985 – Name changed to Transmedica Enterprises Inc.; basis 3 new for 1 old sh. (see FPsurvey - Industrials)

Rollet Uranium Mines Ltd. (Que. 1954)
1963 – Name changed to Rolartic Mines Ltd.

Rollex Mines Ltd. (Ont. 1956)
Nov. 9, 1976 – Dissolved.

Rolling Hills Copper Mines Ltd. (B.C. 1964)
Dec. 1973 – Name changed to Western Rolling Hills Mines & Oils Limited; basis 1 new for 4 old shs. ■

Rolling Rock Resources Corporation (B.C. Mar. 15, 2005)
Dec. 17, 2010 – Amalgamated with 0893573 B.C. Ltd., a wholly owned subsid. of Mega Precious Metals Inc.; basis 0.4 Mega Precious shs. for 1 Rolling Rock sh. (see Mega Precious Metals Inc.)

Rolling Thunder Exploration Ltd. (Alta. Mar. 24, 2005)
Sept. 10, 2007 – Acquired by Action Energy Inc.; basis 0.333 Action Energy com. sh. or $1.15 for 1 Rolling Thunder cl. A sh. and 2.899 Action Energy com. shs. or $10 for 1 Rolling Thunder cl. B sh. (see Action Energy Inc.)

Rollinoil Resources Inc. (Alta. May 21, 1993)
Sept. 18, 1996 – Amalgamated with Prism Petroleum Ltd. (1 for 1.47) to form a new co. also named Prism Petroleum Ltd.; basis 1 new for 1 old sh. (see Prism Petroleum Ltd.)

Roma Lake Gold Mines Ltd. (Ont. 1937)
Mar. 1981 – Charter cancelled.

Romac Mines Ltd. (Que. 1952)
Sept. 2, 1978 – Charter cancelled.

Romac Oils Ltd. (unknown)
In voluntary liquidation. Liquidator - Sylvan H. Pirot, Edmonton.

Roman Corporation Limited (Ont. Aug. 10, 1956)
May 10, 2006 – Acquired by CANAMPAC ULC, a subsid. of US-based Forest Resources LLC, following purchase of substantially all assets sold under a CCAA order. There were no funds available for shldrs.

Romanet Lake Mines Ltd. (Ont. 1962)
July 27, 1976 – Charter cancelled.

Romar Mines Limited (Ont. 1956)
Feb. 28, 1973 – Charter cancelled Jan. 24, 1973; co. dissolved.

Romarco Minerals Inc. (Ont. July 11, 1995 amalg.)
Oct. 6, 2015 – Acquired by OceanaGold Corporation; basis 0.241 OceanaGold com. shs. for 1 Romarco sh.

Rome Resources Ltd. (B.C. Apr. 11, 1990)
Aug. 27, 2001 – Continued into Yukon.
Aug. 25, 2005 – Continued into British Columbia.
July 30, 2024 – Acquired by Pathfinder Minerals Plc (renamed Rome Resources Plc); basis 19.54 Pathfinder ord. shs. for 1 Rome Resources com. sh.

Romex Mines & Explorations Ltd. (Ont. 1966)
May 9, 1977 – Dissolved.

Romex Resources Inc. (B.C. 1978)
Aug. 8, 1991 – Name changed to DRT Resources Ltd.; basis 1 new for 4 old shs. (see FPsurvey - Industrials)

Romfield Building Corporation Limited (Ont. Oct. 5, 1932)
1967 – Secured creditors paid in full and unsecured creditors received 10¢ on the dollar, pay. in com. shs. valued at 30¢; holders of the 7% debs. due Nov. 30, 1968, received same compensation. Trustee since discharged.
Sept. 30, 1996 – Formed Dolphin Quest Inc. in Ontario on amalgamation with 1192778 Ontario Ltd.; basis 1 new for 10 old sh. ■

Romney Gas & Oil Co. Ltd. (Ont. 1933)
1960 – Assets sold.

Romulus Resources Ltd. (B.C. July 9, 1969)
Nov. 10, 1995 – Acquired by Misty Mountain Gold Limited; basis 0.425 new Misty Mountain shs. for 1 old Romulus sh. (see Misty Mountain Gold Limited)

Romulus Resources Ltd. (B.C. Nov. 22, 2005)
June 26, 2018 – Name changed to Osino Resources Corp. following reverse takeover acquisition of private British Columbia-based Osino Resources Corp.; basis 1 new for 10 old shs. ■

Ron-Roy Uranium Mines Ltd. (Ont. 1955)
July 29, 1980 – Amalgamated with Expo Ungava Mines Ltd. (1 for 8) to form Exroy Resources Ltd.; basis 1 new for 5 old shs. (see Exroy Resources Ltd.)

Ronal Red Lake Gold Mines Ltd. (Ont. 1945)
Jan. 23, 1961 – Charter cancelled.

Ronalds-Federated Limited (Can. 1931)
Apr. 1, 1984 – Controlling int. acquired by Tele-Direct Ltd. (a subsid. of Bell Canada Enterprises) through a purch. offer of $40 per sh., dated September 1980. effective remaining publicly-held shs. acquired at $70 per sh.

Ronayne Explorations Ltd. (Ont. 1945)
Mar. 4, 1957 – Charter cancelled.

La Ronciere Gold Mines Ltd. (Ont. 1948)
Nov. 9, 1964 – Charter cancelled.

Ronda Copper Mines Limited (Ont. 1966)
Aug. 4, 1980 – Dissolved.

Rondal Gold Corporation (B.C. Apr. 4, 1997)
Feb. 28, 2000 – Name changed to Cantech Ventures Inc.; basis 1 new for 5 old shs. ■

La Ronge Gold Corp. (B.C. July 31, 2006)
Nov. 13, 2014 – Name changed to Select Sands Corp. (see FPsurvey - Mines & Energy)

La Ronge Resources Inc. (Can. Mar. 3, 1987)
Jan. 4, 1991 – Name changed to IAE Hong Kong Equities Inc. ■

La Ronge Uranium Mines Ltd. (Ont. 1947)
Dec. 1970 – Charter cancelled.

Ronin Resource Corp. (Ont. Oct. 29, 1979)
June 21, 2002 – Delisted from the TSX-Venture Exchange. Subsequently struck from register and dissolved.

Ronnoco Gold Mines Limited (Ont. Feb. 24, 1928)
Aug. 31, 1992 – Delisted from the CDN. Subsequently dissolved and charter cancelled.

Ronson Mines Ltd. (Ont. 1965)
1968 – Assets sold to Mission Financial Corp. Ltd.; basis 0.1606 new for 1 old sh.

Ronyx Corporation Limited (Ont. Aug. 20, 1946)
Mar. 8, 1984 – Name changed to Fleet Aerospace Corporation. ■

RooGold Inc. (B.C. Apr. 1, 2019)
Mar. 27, 2023 – Name changed to Metalite Resources Inc. (see FPsurvey - Mines & Energy)

Roosevelt Capital Group Inc. (Alta. Feb. 22, 2019)
Name changed to Cloud DX Inc. pursuant to reverse takeover acquisition of (old) Cloud DX, inc., which completed a share exchange with its wholly owned subsidiary 12632926 Canada Ltd. (Cloud Canada), and concurrent amalgamation of Cloud Canada and wholly owned 12686163 Canada Inc. (continued as 12632926 Canada Inc.); basis 1 new for 4.8123 old shs. (see FPsurvey - Industrials)

Roosevelt Mines Ltd. (Alta. 1967)
May 31, 1978 – Dissolved and struck off register.

Root Industries Inc. (Ont. Dec. 31, 1993 amalg.)
Jan. 26, 1999 – Formed Armstrong Corporation in Ontario on amalgamation with Ross Armstrong Manufacturing Limited. ■

Ropec Industries Inc. (B.C. 1980)
Sept. 30, 1994 – Dissolved and struck off register.

Roper Resources Inc. (Alta. Mar. 10, 1987)
Nov. 19, 1998 – Name changed to Safe Environment Engineering Canada Inc. ■

Roraima Gold Corporation (B.C. Feb. 5, 1988 amalg.)
June 13, 1996 – Name changed to International Roraima Gold Corporation; basis 1 new for 3 old shs. ■

Rosa Capital Inc. (Alta. Feb. 3, 2011)
Dec. 18, 2015 – Acquired by Raimount Energy Inc. by way of amalgamation with 1929281 Alberta Ltd., a wholly owned subsid. of Raimount, to constitute Rosa's Qualifying Transaction; basis 1 Raimount sh. for 10 Rosa shs. (see Raimount Energy Inc.)

Roscan Minerals Corporation (Ont. May 24, 2004)
Oct. 1, 2018 – Name changed to Roscan Gold Corporation. (see FPsurvey - Mines & Energy)

The Rose Corporation (Can. Dec. 28, 1978)
May 4, 2000 – Privatized at $1.75 per sh.

The Rose Gold and Silver Mining Co. Ltd. (unknown)
1908 – Name changed to Rose Gold Mining Company, Limited and continued into Ontario. ■

Rose Gold Mining Company, Limited (Ont. 1908)
Aug. 25, 1994 – Name changed to AFM Hospitality Corporation; basis 1 new for 5 old shs. ■

Rose Marie Resources Ltd. (B.C. Sept. 26, 1988)
July 17, 2008 – Name changed to Cheetah Ventures Ltd.; basis 1 new for 2 old shs. ■

Rose Mountain Mines Ltd. (Ont. 1966)
June 1969 – Name changed to Roain Development Corp. Ltd. ■

Rose Resource Corporation (B.C. 1982)
Feb. 12, 1985 – Formed Petrostates Resource Corporation in British Columbia on amalgamation with Petrostates Resource Corporation (1 for 1); basis 1 new for 1 old sh. ■

La Rose-Rouyn Mines Ltd. (Ont. 1926)
1952 – Charter cancelled; shareholdings distributed on basis of 1 sh. New La Rose Mining and 1 sh. Mastermet Cobalt Mines Ltd. for co. sh.

Rose Spit Resources Inc. (B.C. 1987)
Nov. 17, 1995 – Dissolved and struck off register.

Rosea Copper Mines Ltd. (B.C. 1954)
Nov. 14, 1963 – Dissolved.

Rosebay Resources Inc. (Alta. Feb. 14, 1994)
Feb. 3, 1997 – Acquired by Oiltec Resources Ltd.; basis 0.333 new Oiltec sh. or 65¢ cash for 1 old Rosebay sh. (see Oiltec Resources Ltd.)

Rosedale Resources Ltd. (B.C. Oct. 21, 2011)
June 13, 2022 – Name changed to Sandbox Royalties Corp. ■

Rosehearty Energy Inc. (B.C. July 30, 2014)
May 14, 2020 – Formed Eden Empire Inc. in British Columbia pursuant to the reverse takeover acquisition of and amalgamation with (old) Eden Empire Inc. (deemed acquiror); basis 1 new com. sh. for 6 Rosehearty com. shs. and 1 new com. sh. for 1 (old) Eden com. sh. (see FPsurvey - Industrials)

Roseland Resources Ltd. (Alta. Feb. 24, 1995)
July 10, 2003 – Name changed to Rival Energy Ltd. following acquisition of Rival Energy Inc.; basis 1 new for 5 old shs. ■

Rosetta Exploration Inc. (Alta. Feb. 22, 1993)
Dec. 11, 2006 – Name changed to Berkana Energy Corp. following reverse takeover acquisition of Mach Resources Ltd.; basis 1 new for 5 old shs. ■

Rosetta Technologies Inc. (B.C. Jan. 27, 1984)
June 30, 1993 – Continued into Wyoming.
July 11, 1994 – Name changed to Tanisys Technology, Inc.

Rosita Mining Corporation (Ont. June 2, 2004 amalg.)
Nov. 14, 2018 – Continued into British Columbia.
Sept. 25, 2019 – Name changed to the name King Global Ventures Inc. (see FPsurvey - Mines & Energy)

Rosmac Mines Ltd. (B.C. 1966)
July 1979 – Name changed to Rosmac Resources Ltd. ■

Rosmac Resources Ltd. (B.C. 1966)
Aug. 30, 1984 – Amalgamated with Grove Explorations Ltd. (0.3333 for 1) and N.W.P. Resources Ltd. (0.3667 for 1) to continue with the name Golden North Resource Corporation; basis 0.3 new for 1 old sh. (see Golden North Resource Corporation)

Ross Island Resources Inc. (Ont. June 3, 1986)
Jan. 12, 1994 – Name changed to Impact Capital Resources Inc. ■

Ross Oils of Alberta Ltd. (Alta.)
1960 – Struck off register.

Ross Petroleums Ltd. (unknown)
1961 – Wound up. Acquired by Sage Oil Co. Ltd.

Rossal Resources Ltd. (B.C. 1987)
Mar. 26, 1993 – Dissolved and struck off register.

Rossland Mines Ltd. (B.C. 1946)
1952 – Name changed to Rossland Mining Co. Ltd.; basis 1 new for 2 old shs. ■

Rossland Mining Co. Ltd. (B.C. 1946)
June 1972 – Name changed to Ross Island Mines Ltd.; basis 1 new for 5 old shs.

Rossmore Exploration Ltd. (Ont. Feb. 23, 1932)
1949 – Inactive, no property held.

Rotary Mines Ltd. (Ont. 1939)
July 1960 – Charter cancelled.

Rotation Minerals Ltd. (B.C. Nov. 24, 2009)
Jan. 14, 2019 – Name changed to Scottie Resources Corp. (see FPsurvey - Mines & Energy)

Rothmans Inc. (Can. May 8, 1956)
Feb. 11, 2000 – Amalgamated in Canada to continue with same name.
Oct. 21, 2008 – Acquired by Philip Morris International Inc. for $30 per sh.

Rothmans of Pall Mall Canada Limited (Can. May 8, 1956)
Sept. 30, 1985 – Name changed to Rothmans Inc. ■

Rothsay Mines Ltd. (Ont. 1958)
1967 – Merged into Resource Exploration & Development Co. Ltd.; basis 10 new for 32 old shs.

Rothwell Industries Ltd. (Ont. 1963)
July 19, 1991 – Name changed to Rothwell Corporation; basis 1 new cl. A and cl. B for 4 old cl. A and cl. B shs. (see FPsurvey - Industrials)

Rotondo Rouyn Mines Ltd. (Ont. 1955)
1956 – Name changed to Cleranda Copper Mines Ltd.; basis 1 new for 3 old shs. ■

Rouandah Gold and Metals Ltd. (Ont. 1948)
1952 – Name changed to Rouandah Oils and Mines Limited. ■

Rouandah Oils and Mines Limited (Ont. 1948)
1965 – Charter cancelled.

Rouge d'Or Mines Ltd. (unknown)
1926 – Acquired by Edena Mines Ltd.; basis 1 new for 10 old shs. (see Edena Mines Ltd.)

Rouge Resources Ltd. (B.C. Mar. 31, 1988)
Aug. 8, 2016 – Name changed to Fiore Exploration Ltd. following acquisition of Pampas El Peñon gold-silver property in Chile. ■

Roughrider Exploration Limited (B.C. Dec. 7, 2011)
Sept. 28, 2021 – Name changed to Coast Copper Corp. (see FPsurvey - Mines & Energy)

Roulette Gold Mines Ltd. (Ont. 1945)
Feb. 1957 – Charter cancelled.

Round Lake Mines Ltd. (Ont. 1966)
May 1980 – Charter cancelled.

Round Valley Oil Co. Ltd. (Alta. 1958)
Nov. 1963 – Acquired by Great Plains Development Co. of Canada, Ltd.

Routemaster Capital Inc. (Ont. Nov. 3, 2009)
Feb. 26, 2021 – Name changed to DeFi Technologies Inc. in conjunction with the transition from an investment issuer to a single purposed company focused on building and managing assets in the decentralized finance (DeFi) sector. ■

Rouyn Merger Gold Mines Ltd. (Ont. 1943)
Nov. 24, 1947 – Name changed to New Rouyn Merger Mines Ltd.; basis 1 new for 2 old shs. ■

Rouyn Mining Resources Inc. (Que. Feb. 12, 1981)
July 30, 1991 – Name changed to Richmont Mines Inc. ■

Rouyn Reward Gold Mines Ltd. (Ont. 1934)
1958 – Dissolved.

Rouyn Swayze Gold Mines Ltd. (unknown)
May 8, 1934 – Acquired by Rouyn Reward Gold Mines Ltd.; basis 10 new for 1 old sh. (see Rouyn Reward Gold Mines Ltd.)

Rouzone Mining Corp. Ltd. (Ont. 1946)
1953 – Charter cancelled.

Rover Critical Minerals Corp. (B.C. June 26, 2018 amalg.)
Aug. 5, 2025 – Name changed to Stockworks Gold Inc. (see FPsurvey - Mines & Energy)

Rover Metals Corp. (B.C. June 26, 2018 amalg.)
Feb. 5, 2024 – Name changed to Rover Critical Minerals Corp. ■

Rover Oil & Gas Ltd. (B.C. 1980)
Oct. 1982 – General Allied Oil and Gas Co. acquired 97.376% of the co.'s o/s shs. as follows: 1 sh. and and 1 wt. of Allied for each 4 shs. of Rover.

Rowan Consolidated Mines Ltd. (Ont. 1945)
Mar. 1974 – Name changed to Rowan Gold Mines Limited; basis 1 new for 10 old shs. ■

Rowan Gold Mines Limited (Ont. 1945)
July 22, 1982 – Amalgamated with Abino Gold Mines Limited (1 for 12.94), Clicker Red Lake Mines Limited (1 for 18.23), Commander Red Lake Mines Limited (1 for 30.82), Dorion Red Lake Mines Limited (1 for 15.59), Duchesne Red Lake Mines Limited (1 for 10.57), Forsyth Mines Limited (1 for 6.38), Goldquest Explorations Corp. (1 for 1.26), Inore Gold Mines Limited (1 for 9.9) and Laddie Gold Mines Limited (1 for 15.22) to form Goldquest Exploration Inc.; basis 1 new for 4.91 old shs.

Roxana Oils Company Limited (Alta. 1936)
Nov. 1957 – Name changed to Allied Roxana Minerals Ltd.; basis 1 new for 4 old shs. ■

Roxana Resources Limited (B.C. 1985)
May 26, 1993 – Name changed to Canadian Roxana Resources Limited; basis 1 new for 2 old shs. ■

Roxbury Capital Corp. (Can. June 21, 1988)
Sept. 19, 1995 – Amalgamated with Optima Petroleum Corporation; basis 1 Optima sh. plus 1 wt. for 7 Roxbury shs. (see Optima Petroleum Corporation)

Roxford Mining Corp. (Que. 1960)
Aug. 1973 – Charter cancelled.

Roxgold Inc. (B.C. Nov. 22, 1983)
July 6, 2021 – Acquired by Fortuna Silver Mines Inc.;
basis 0.283 Fortuna com. shs. plus Cdn$0.001 cash for
1 Roxgold sh. (see Fortuna Silver Mines Inc.)

Roxi Capital Corp. (Alta. Sept. 12, 1997)
Nov. 29, 2002 – Name changed to Advantage
Wallsystems Inc. ■

Roxmark Mines Limited (Ont. Jan. 7, 1969)
Dec. 22, 2009 – Acquired by Goldstone Resources Inc.
(formerly Ontex Resources Limited) by way of
amalgamation with 2223951 Ontario Inc., a wholly owned
subsid. of Goldstone; basis 1 Goldstone sh. for 3.75
Roxmark shs. (see Goldstone Resources Inc.)

Roxton Mining & Development Co. Ltd. (Ont. 1955)
Jan. 1967 – Charter cancelled.

Roxwell Gold Mines Ltd. (N.W.T. 1979)
June 25, 1981 – Continued into British Columbia.
Oct. 27, 2008 – Dissolved and struck from registry.

Roxy Gold Mines Ltd. (Man. 1947)
Dec. 19, 1962 – Charter cancelled.

Roxy Petroleum Ltd. (Alta. Mar. 25, 1980)
June 10, 1985 – Name changed to Canadian Roxy
Petroleum Ltd. ■

Roy-L Merchant Group Inc. (Ont. Feb. 13, 1987)
Dec. 4, 1991 – Name changed to Clairvest Group Inc.
(see FPsurvey - Industrials)

Le Roy Mines Ltd. (Que. 1929)
July 1943 – In bankruptcy. Shldrs. received 18 shs.
Roybell Mines Ltd. for each 100 shs. Le Roy.

Roy Silver Mines Ltd. (Ont. 1949)
1955 – Name changed to Tiara Mines Ltd.; basis 1 new
for 6 old shs. ■

Royal Acquisition Corp. (Alta. Nov. 12, 2009)
Nov. 26, 2010 – Name changed to Invicta Energy Corp.
pursuant to Qualifying Transaction reverse takeover
acquistion of Invicta Energy Ltd. and subsequent
amalgamation of 1547285 Alberta Ltd., a wholly owned
subsid. of Royal, and Invicta Energy Ltd. ■

Royal Aerospace Corp. (Ont. May 13, 1936)
Mar. 11, 1997 – Name changed to Royal Group Capital
Corporation; basis 1 new for 20 old shs. ■

Royal Agassiz Mines Ltd. (Man. Apr. 29, 1955)
Nov. 1977 – Name changed to Agassiz Resources Ltd.;
basis 1 new for 5 old shs. ■

Royal American Oil Company Limited (Alta. 1953)
1963 – Name changed to Royal American Petroleums
Ltd.; basis 1 cl. B for 2 old com. shs. ■

Royal American Petroleums Ltd. (Alta. 1953)
1969 – Acquired by Manhattan Continental Development
Corp.; basis 64.68 new for 100 old shs.

Royal Aviation Inc. (Can. Aug. 3, 1979)
May 10, 2001 – Acquired by Canada 3000 Inc.; basis 0.4
new Canada 3000 sh. for 1 old Royal Aviation sh. (see
Canada 3000 Inc.)

The Royal Bank of Canada (Can. 1871; via Bank Act)
Nov. 1, 1990 – Name changed to Royal Bank of Canada.
(see FPsurvey - Industrials)

Royal Bay Gold Corporation (B.C. June 14, 1977)
July 8, 1998 – Name changed to Featherstone Resources
Ltd.; basis 1 new for 3 old shs. ■

Royal Canadian Oils Limited (Alta. 1936)
1956 – Taken over by Royal Canadian Ventures Ltd.;
basis 1 new for 10 old shs.

Royal Canadian Ventures Ltd. (Alta. 1954)
Dec. 1971 – Acquired by Pan Ocean Oil Corp.; basis 9.67
new for 100 old shs.

Royal Capital Corp. (Alta. Nov. 22, 2007)
June 26, 2009 – Name changed to DeeThree Exploration
Inc. following Qualifying Transaction amalgamation of
wholly owned 1467218 Alberta Ltd. with DeeThree
Exploration Ltd.; basis 1 new for 12 old shs. ■

Royal Coal Corp. (Ont. Aug. 10, 2010)
Dec. 13, 2022 – Name changed to EV Minerals
Corporation. (see FPsurvey - Mines & Energy)

Royal Concorde Capital Inc. (Alta. May 11, 1988)
Nov. 28, 1994 – Name changed to Pacific Concorde
Capital Inc.; basis 1 new for 3 old shs. ■

Royal County Minerals Corp. (B.C. Nov. 21, 1983)
Nov. 24, 2003 – Acquired by International Curator
Resources Ltd.; basis 1 Curator sh. for 4 Royal County
shs. (see International Curator Resources Ltd.)

Royal Crest Petroleums Ltd. (Alta. Jan. 28, 1937)
1950 – Assets sold to Federated Petroleums Ltd. for
$95,000; 10¢ per sh. distributed.

Royal Crest Resources Ltd. (Ont. 1987)
Sept. 19, 1996 – Formed Interprovincial Venture Capital
Corporation in Ontario on amalgamation with 1149284
Ontario Inc. (deemed acquiror); basis 100 new for 1
1149284 Ontario sh. and 1 new for 1.3 Royal Crest shs.
(see FPsurvey - Mines & Energy; FPsurvey - Industrials)

Royal Crystal Resources Ltd. (B.C. Aug. 26, 1985)
Dec. 10, 1991 – Name changed to Eracon Industries Inc.;
basis 1 new for 4 old shs. ■

Royal Ecoproducts Limited (Ont. May 1, 1997 amalg.)
Aug. 27, 1998 – Amalgamated with 1299240 Ontario
Limited, a wholly owned subsid. of Royal Group
Technologies Limited; basis 1 Royal Group subord. vtg.
sh. for 10 Royal Ecoproducts subord. vtg. shs. (see Royal
Group Technologies Limited)

Royal Fox Gold Inc. (Ont. Oct. 31, 1997 amalg.)
Nov. 9, 2022 – Acquired by Northern Superior Resources
Inc.; basis 0.12 Northern Superior shs. for 1 Royal Fox
sh.

Royal Gold & Silver Corporation (Ont. 1983)
June 16, 1988 – Name changed to Royal Gold
Enterprises Inc. ■

Royal Gold Enterprises Inc. (Ont. 1983)
Feb. 11, 1993 – Name changed to Trenton Industries
Inc. ■

Royal Gold, Inc. (Del. Jan. 5, 1981)
July 11, 2016 – Voluntarily delisted from TSX; continued
to trade on NASDAQ.

Royal Gold Mining Inc. (B.C. Apr. 23, 1985)
Nov. 4, 2020 – Name changed to AUQ Gold Mining Inc.
(see FPsurvey - Mines & Energy)

Royal Group Capital Corporation (Ont. May 13, 1936)
Sept. 23, 1997 – Name changed to Copper Hill
Corporation. ■

Royal Group Technologies Limited (Can. Sept. 26,
1994)
Oct. 3, 2006 – Acquired by wholly owned subsid. of
Georgia Gulf Corporation; basis Cdn$13 per sh.
Feb. 5, 2007 – Name changed to Royal Group, Inc.

Royal Host Inc. (Can. Nov. 3, 2010)
July 8, 2014 – Acquired by Holloway Lodging Corporation;
basis for $1.00 plus 0.1 Holloway com. shs. for 1 Royal
com. sh.

Royal Host Real Estate Investment Trust (Alta. Aug.
27, 1997)
Jan. 1, 2011 – Succeeded by Royal Host Inc. pursuant
to plan of arrangement whereby Royal Host Inc. was

formed to facilitate the conversion of the trust into a
corporation and the fund was subsequently dissolved. ■

Royal International Venture Corporation (B.C. Aug.
26, 1985)
July 28, 2000 – Name changed to RCOM Venture Corp.;
basis 1 new for 5 old shs. ■

Royal Laser Corp. (Alta. Feb. 12, 2004)
June 16, 2010 – Acquired by Triple M Metal L.P. for 47¢
per sh.

Royal Laser Tech Corporation (Ont. Feb. 10, 1987)
May 1, 1998 – Amalgamated in Ontario to continue with
same name.
June 27, 2002 – Name changed to Martinrea International
Inc. (see FPsurvey - Industrials)

Royal LePage Capital Properties (Ont. 1982)
Apr. 1, 1988 – All assets sold and subsequently
liquidated.

Royal LePage Franchise Services Fund (Ont. Jan. 3,
2003)
Oct. 31, 2007 – Name changed to Brookfield Real Estate
Services Fund. ■

Royal LePage Limited (Ont. 1984)
May 4, 1999 – Acquired by Trilon Financial Corporation;
basis $4.75 plus 0.5 Trilon wts. to acquire 1 Trilon cl. A
sh. at $11.25 until Feb. 28, 2002. (see Trilon Financial
Corporation)

Royal Lifescience Corp. (B.C. Feb. 23, 2011)
June 26, 2018 – Formed Rover Metals Corp. in British
Columbia on amalgamation with (old) Rover Metals Corp.
constituting the Qualifying Transaction reverse takeover
acquisition of (old) Rover. ■

Royal Mining Corp. (Que. 1970)
Feb. 1976 – Charter cancelled.

Royal Monashee Gold Corp. (B.C. June 22, 2006)
Nov. 7, 2012 – Name changed to Plus8 Global Ventures,
Ltd. ■

Royal Nickel Corporation (Can. Dec. 13, 2006)
June 15, 2020 – Name changed to Karora Resources
Inc. ■

Royal Oak Dairy, Limited (Ont. 1927)
Oct. 5, 1978 – Under an offer dated all o/s shs. of co.
acquired by Execsil Corporation at the following purchase
prices: $24 per cl. A, $4.00 per cl. B and $10 per com.
sh. Subsequently, Royal Oak, Execsil Corp. and
Silverwood Investors Ltd. merged to form amalg. co.
under name Execsil Corporation.

Royal Oak Mines Inc. (Ont. July 23, 1991 amalg.)
Feb. 11, 2000 – Name changed to Royal Oak Ventures
Inc.; basis 1 new for 100 old shs. ■

Royal Oak Resources Ltd. (Alta. May 23, 1986)
July 25, 1991 – Amalgamated with Pamour Inc. (3 for 4),
Giant Yellowknife Mines Limited (13 for 2), Pamorex
Minerals Inc. (3 for 5) and Akaitcho Yellowknife Gold
Mines Limited (3 for 5) to form a new co. called Royal
Oak Mines Inc.; basis 5 new Royal Oak Mines shs. for 6
old Royal Oak Resources shs. (see Royal Oak Mines
Inc.)

Royal Oak Ventures Inc. (Ont. July 23, 1991 amalg.)
Jan. 3, 2014 – All o/s com. shs. and non-vtg. shs. not
already held acquired by Brookfield Asset Management
Inc. for 15¢ per sh. (see Brookfield Asset Management
Inc.)

Royal Pacific Sea Farms Ltd. (B.C. 1979)
Oct. 27, 1989 – Placed into receivership.
Apr. 24, 1992 – Dissolved and struck off register.

Royal Plastics Group Limited (Can. Sept. 26, 1994)
Feb. 14, 1997 – Name changed to Royal Group
Technologies Limited. ■

Royal Resources Ltd. (Alta. Dec. 12, 1969)
July 12, 1987 – Continued into Canada.
May 26, 1988 – Name changed to Royaledge Industries Inc. ■

Royal Roads Corp. (Alta. Mar. 24, 1995)
Apr. 1, 2002 – Amalgamated in Alberta to continue with same name.
July 5, 2010 – Name changed to Buchans Minerals Corporation. ■

Royal Rock Ventures Inc. (B.C. May 31, 1984)
Apr. 6, 2001 – Name changed to Bi-Optic Ventures Inc.; basis 1 new for 2 old shs. ■

Royal Sapphire Corp. (B.C. Mar. 2, 2011)
July 6, 2018 – Name changed to Pure Global Cannabis Inc. pursuant to the reverse takeover acquisition of PureSinse Inc. and concurrent amalgamation of PureSinse with a wholly owned subsid.; basis 1 new for 2 old shs. ■

Royal Scot Resources Ltd. (B.C. 1945)
Aug. 1, 1991 – Amalgamated with Tenajon Resources Corp. (1 for 1) to continue as Tenajon Resources Corp.; basis 1 new for 2 old shs. (see Tenajon Resources Corp.)

Royal Sovereign Exploration Inc. (Alta. May 6, 1997)
July 8, 2002 – Name changed to RSX Energy Inc. ■

Royal Standard Minerals Inc. (Can. Feb. 22, 1988)
Jan. 4, 2002 – Continued into New Brunswick.
July 23, 2007 – Continued into Canada. (see FPsurvey - Mines & Energy)

Royal Stratus Ventures Inc. (B.C. Aug. 6, 1987)
June 1, 1994 – Name changed to MPI Holdings Inc. ■

Royal Trust Company (Que. June 24, 1892)
Nov. 1, 1978 – Cl. A and B shldrs. received a stock dividend of one Royal Trustco Holdings (1978) Ltd. for each sh. held. On Nov. 3, 1978 Royal Trustco Holdings (1978) Ltd. and Royal Trustco Ltd. amalgamated to form a new Royal Trustco Ltd. On Dec.1, 1978 Royal Trust Company exchanged each sh. held for 3 new Royal Trustco Ltd. shs. The Royal Trust Company continues as an operating subsid. of Royal Trustco Limited.

The Royal Trust Company Mortgage Corporation (Que. Mar. 21, 1912)
Aug. 26, 1994 – Wound up. Pfd. shldrs. received $20 plus $0.16 in accrued and unpaid div. per sh.

Royal Trust Energy Income Fund I (Alta. Dec. 1, 1987)
Nov. 26, 1993 – Name changed to Westrock Energy Income Fund I. ■

Royal Trust Energy Income Fund II (Alta. 1987)
Nov. 26, 1993 – Name changed to Westrock Energy Income Fund II. ■

Royal Trust Real Estate Limited Partnership (Ont. Oct. 28, 1988)
Sept. 29, 2003 – Final distribution of $0.06 per unit.
Oct. 8, 2003 – Dissolved following winding up of last real estate investment.

Royal Trustco Limited (Can. Nov. 3, 1978 amalg.)
June 25, 1993 – Name changed to Gentra Inc. ■

Royal Utilities Income Fund (Alta. Apr. 15, 1996)
June 27, 2006 – Re-established as a public company.
May 6, 2008 – Acquired by Sherritt International Corporation, for $12.68 per trust unit or 0.8315 Sherrit com. sh.for 1 Royal Utilities trust unit or any combination thereof.

Royal Valley Copper Mines Limited (Ont. 1969)
Nov. 1969 – Name changed to Systems-Air Corporation Limited. ■

Royal Victoria Minerals Ltd. (Can. Apr. 29, 1987)
Mar. 7, 2002 – Continued into Yukon. (see St Andrew Goldfields Ltd.)
June 25, 2003 – Amalgamated with St Andrew Goldfields Ltd. and United Tex-Sol Mines Inc. (1 for 1); basis 2 St Andrew shs. for 1 Royal Victoria sh. (see St Andrew Goldfields Ltd.)

Royale Nori Foods Inc. (B.C. Oct. 31, 1984)
Nov. 5, 1997 – Name changed to Agrotech Greenhouses Inc. ■

Royaledge Industries Inc. (Can. July 12, 1987)
Feb. 1, 1996 – Name changed to Royaledge Resources Inc. ■

Royaledge Resources Inc. (Can. July 12, 1987)
Sept. 21, 2000 – Name changed to Avalanche Networks Corporation on reverse takeover acquisition of ShopDome.com Inc.; basis 1 new for 10 old shs. ■

Royalite Oil Company, Limited (Can. Jan. 18, 1921)
Apr. 1969 – Acquired by Gulf Oil Canada Limited; basis 1.2 new for 1 old sh. (see Gulf Oil Canada Limited)

Royalon Petroleum Corporation (B.C. Dec. 5, 1979)
Aug. 16, 1984 – Name changed to International Royalon Minerals Inc. ■

Royalstar Resources Limited (Can. Apr. 29, 1987)
Mar. 7, 2000 – Name changed to Royal Victoria Minerals Ltd.; basis 1 new for 10 old shs. ■

Royalty North Partners Ltd. (B.C. Mar. 17, 2011)
Aug. 31, 2022 – Name changed to Horizon Copper Corp. pursuant to reverse takeover transaction with Sandstorm Gold Ltd. (see FPsurvey - Mines & Energy)

Roybar Chibougamau Mines Ltd. (Ont. 1946)
Apr. 1949 – Name changed to Roybar Uranium & Gold Mines Ltd. ■

Roybar Uranium & Gold Mines Ltd. (Ont. 1946)
July 1950 – Name changed to Nubar Mines Ltd.; basis 1 new for 3 old shs. ■

Roybell Mines Ltd. (Que. 1937)
July 22, 1978 – Charter cancelled.

Roycam Copper Mines Limited (Ont. Mar. 7, 1956)
Jan. 21, 1983 – Name changed to Bitech Energy Resources Limited. ■

Royce Copper Mines Limited (Ont. 1956)
1961 – Charter cancelled.

Royce Industries Inc. (B.C. May 26, 1989)
Apr. 22, 1992 – Name changed to BioSource Industries Inc. following reverse takeover acquisition of Biosource International, Inc.; basis 1 new for 2.6 old shs. ■

Royce Resources Corp. (Alta. Aug. 28, 1997)
May 11, 2011 – Continued into British Columbia.
Nov. 25, 2015 – Name changed to Lithium X Energy Corp. ■

Royce Ventures Ltd. (B.C. 1983)
Oct. 3, 1984 – Amalgamated with Bellevue Oil & Minerals Ltd. to form Bellevue Ventures Ltd.; basis 1 new for 1old sh.

Roycefield Resources Ltd. (Ont. Feb. 13, 1987)
June 30, 2014 – Certificate of incorporation cancelled and dissolved.

Royex Gold Mining Corporation (Ont. 1974 amalg.)
July 1, 1988 – Amalgamated with 7 other cos. to form Corona Corporation basis as follows: 0.61 new cl. A sh. for 1 old Royex com. sh.; 1 new 1st pref. ser. A sh. for 1 old Royex ser. A pref. sh.; 1 new convert. 1st pref. sh. ser. B for 1 old Royex ser. B pref. sh.; and 1 new convert. 1st pref. sh. ser. C for 1 old Royex ser. C pref. sh. (see Corona Corporation)

Royex Mining Ltd. (Ont. 1969)
July 31, 1974 – Amalgamated with Sturgex Mines Ltd., to form Royex Sturgex Mining Limited; basis 1 new for 2 old shs.

Royex Sturgex Mining Limited (Ont. 1974 amalg.)
May 25, 1984 – Name changed to Royex Gold Mining Corporation. ■

Roymor Ltd. (Que. 1968)
Dec. 31, 1978 – Assets and liabs. assumed by RoyMor Mortgage Corporation.

RoyMor Mortgage Corporation (Alta. 1969)
1978 – Continued into Canada.
May 1, 1982 – Name changed to Royal Bank Mortgage Corporation.

RoyNat Inc. (Can. 1973 amalg.)
July 1988 – Acquired by Montreal Trustco Inc. for $98,000,000. Prior to the acquisition, Montreal Trustco held 13.5% interest in RoyNat while the remainder was owned 41.5% by the Royal Bank of Canada, 34% by National Bank of Canada, 10% by Canada Trust Co. and 1% by Trust General du Canada.

Royop Properties Corporation (Can. Feb. 10, 1997)
Sept. 5, 2000 – All o/s com. shs. acquired by H & R Real Estate Investment Trust; basis 0.0938 H & R trust unit for 1 Royop com. sh. tendered.

RoyShel Properties Ltd. (Can. Feb. 13, 1981)
Dec. 23, 1996 – Continued into British Columbia.
May 30, 1997 – Name changed to ATC Technologies Corporation following reverse takeover acquisition of AutoSoft Tool Corporation; basis 1 new for 20 old shs. ■

Royster-Clark Ltd. (Ont. Jan. 24, 2005)
Mar. 6, 2006 – Plan of Arrangement acquisition by Agrium Inc.; basis $11.90 per income deposit securities. (see Agrium Inc.)

Royston Oils, Ltd. (Can. 1929)
Mar. 4, 1929 – Name changed to Cartier Oils, Ltd.

Rozak Porcupine Mines Ltd. (Ont. 1945)
Oct. 28, 1957 – Charter cancelled.

Rozdil Capital Corporation (Ont. May 3, 2018)
Mar. 22, 2022 – Name changed to Thiogenesis Therapeutics, Corp. pursuant to the Qualifying Transaction reverse takeover acquisition of Thiogenesis Therapeutics, Inc. (see FPsurvey - Industrials)

Rritual Superfoods Inc. (B.C. May 6, 2019)
Nov. 25, 2022 – Name changed to Aretto Wellness Inc.; basis 1 new for 20 old shs. (see FPsurvey - Industrials)

Rual Porcupine Mines (Ont. 1945)
1959 – Acquired by Wengrace Explorations Ltd.; basis 1 new for 48 old shs. (see Wengrace Explorations Ltd.)

Rubellite Energy Inc. (Alta. July 12, 2021)
Oct. 31, 2024 – Succeeded by Rubellite Energy Corp. (see FPsurvey - Mines & Energy)

Rubicon Minerals Corporation (B.C. Mar. 4, 1996)
July 7, 2020 – Name changed to Battle North Gold Corporation. ■

Rubicon Resources Ltd. (B.C. May 31, 1979)
Oct. 19, 1979 – Name changed to Dentonia Resources Ltd. ■

Rubicon Technologies Inc. (Alta. Dec. 22, 1994)
Mar. 14, 1996 – Name changed to Burnt Sand Solutions Inc. ■

Ruby Foo's Enterprises Ltd. (Que. 1960)
1965 – Acquired by Bedford Construction Co. Ltd. (subsidiary of CDRH) for $4.50 per com. sh. and 35¢ for each wt. Long term debt of Ruby Foo's assumed by Bedford.

Ruby Mountain Mines Inc. (B.C. Apr. 29, 1987)
Mar. 17, 1994 – Name changed to Syrus Capital Corporation; basis 1 new for 3 old shs. ■

Ruby Red Resources Inc. (Alta. Dec. 19, 2006 amalg.)
Oct. 20, 2010 – Name changed to SG Spirit Gold Inc.; basis 1 new for 10 old shs. ■

Ruby Resources Ltd. (B.C. 1980)
Dec. 18, 1984 – Formed International Domesticated Furs Limited in British Columbia on amalgamation with wholly owned International Domesticated Furs Limited. ■

Ruby Silver Mines Ltd. (B.C. 1961)
1966 – Name changed to Silver-Lee Mines Ltd.; basis 1 new for 2 old shs. ■

Ruffo Lake Mines Ltd. (Ont. 1961)
Mar. 26, 1969 – Charter cancelled.

Rufus-Argenta Mines Ltd. (B.C. 1928)
1955 – Name changed to New Rufus Argenta Mines Ltd. and continued into British Columbia; basis 1 new for 10 old shs. ■

Rugby Mining Limited (B.C. Jan. 24, 2007)
Aug. 29, 2022 – Name changed to Rugby Resources Ltd. ■

Rugby Red Lake Gold Mines Ltd. (Ont. 1945)
July 25, 1960 – Dissolved.

Rugby Resources Limited (B.C. Dec. 31, 1985)
Apr. 30, 1993 – Name changed to Euro-Ad Systems Inc. ■

Rugby Resources Ltd. (B.C. Jan. 24, 2007)
July 29, 2025 – Acquired by Pampa Metals Corporation; basis 1 Pampa sh. for every 6.4 Rugby shs. Additionally, shldrs. received 1 Aegis Resources Ltd. sh. for every 10 Rugby shs. (see Pampa Metals Corporation)

Rugged Red Lake Mines Ltd. (Ont. 1945)
May 14, 1975 – Charter cancelled.

RuggedCom Inc. (Ont. Feb. 22, 2001)
Apr. 16, 2012 – Acquired by Siemens Canada Limited, a wholly owned subsid. of Siemens AG, for Cdn$33 per sh.

Rule Resources Ltd. (B.C. Feb. 29, 1980)
Mar. 9, 1990 – Name changed to Globe Resources Inc.; basis 1 new for 5 old shs. ■

Rumson Rare Metals Corp. Ltd. (Ont. 1956)
Feb. 1957 – Name changed to Rockcroft Explorations Ltd. ■

Run of River Power Inc. (Alta. Nov. 26, 1999)
Sept. 23, 2006 – Continued into British Columbia.
Aug. 19, 2014 – Amalgamated with ROR Acquisition Ltd., wholly owned subsid. of Concord Green Energy Inc., to form ROR Power Inc.; basis $0.0026 cash per sh.

Runaway Resources Ltd. (B.C. Apr. 10, 1986)
Mar. 16, 1988 – Name changed to Revere Resources Ltd. ■

Rundle Oils Ltd. (Alta. Apr. 2, 1951)
1954 – Taken over by Pathfinder Petroleums Ltd.; basis 1 new for 5 old shs.

Running Foxes Petroleum Corp. (B.C. Sept. 1, 1981)
Oct. 17, 2000 – Name changed to Running Fox Resource Corp.; basis 1 new for 2 old shs. (see FPsurvey - Mines & Energy)

Rupert's Land Mines Limited (Man. 1928)
1940 – Reported to be in process of winding up.

Rupertsland Resources Co. Ltd. (Alta. May 19, 1965)
Aug. 30, 1985 – Name changed to Bracknell Resources Ltd. following conversion of all o/s 2,400,000 first pfce. shs. into 59,330,000 com. shs. and subsequently all com. shs. consol.; basis 1 new for 10 old shs. ■

The Rupununi Gold Mining Co. (Canada) Ltd. (Ont. 1945)
1955 – Name changed to Rio Rupununi Mines Ltd.; basis 1 new for 3 old shs. ■

Ruscana Mines Ltd. (Ont. 1945)
Charter cancelled; no equity for shldrs.

Rush Energy Corporation (B.C. June 25, 1981)
Aug. 11, 1986 – Name changed to Rush Ventures Inc. ■

Rush Lake Explorations Ltd. (Ont. 1971)
July 1973 – Merged into Sloane Mining Co. Ltd.; basis 1 new for 5.9 old shs.

Rush Lake Gold Mines Ltd. (Ont. 1945)
1947 – Name changed to Joburke Gold Mines Ltd.; basis 1 new for 2 old shs. ■

Rush Uranium Corp. (B.C. Oct. 28, 2021)
Mar. 16, 2023 – Name changed to Rush Rare Metals Corp. (see FPsurvey - Mines & Energy)

Rush Ventures Inc. (B.C. June 25, 1981)
Aug. 1, 1991 – Name changed to Rushmore Energy Corporation; basis 1 new for 4.5 old shs. ■

Rushmore Energy Corporation (B.C. June 25, 1981)
Sept. 30, 1993 – Name changed to Seacorp Properties Inc. ■

Rushriv Gold Mines Ltd. (Ont. 1945)
1956 – Charter cancelled.

Rusk Porcupine Mines Ltd. (Ont. 1941)
July 1960 – Assets distributed to creditors. Charter surrendered.

Ruskin Developments Ltd. (B.C. 1974)
Dec. 3, 1990 – Name changed to Consolidated Ruskin Developments Ltd.; basis 1 new for 4 old shs. ■

Russ-Rae Chibougamau Mines Ltd. (Ont. 1946)
1957 – Charter cancelled.

Russ-Rae Yellowknife Mines Ltd. (Ont. 1946)
1950 – Name changed to Russ-Rae Chibougamau Mines Ltd. ■

Russel Metals Inc. (Can. Aug. 1, 1967 amalg.)
Jan. 1, 2002 – Amalgamated in Canada to continue with same name. (see FPsurvey - Industrials)

Russell Breweries Inc. (B.C. Mar. 23, 2000)
Dec. 5, 2018 – Name changed to RBI Ventures Ltd.; basis 1 new for 25 old shs. ■

Russell Holdings Limited (Que. 1971)
Apr. 26, 1989 – Through a wholly owned subsid. Treats Inc. acquired all o/s shs.; basis 1 new for 2.5 old shs.

Russell Ventures Mining Co. Ltd. (B.C. 1934)
1956 – Charter cancelled.

Russet Red Lake Gold Mines Ltd. (Ont. 1943)
1965 – Merged into Aiken-Russet Red Lake Mines Ltd.; basis 1 new for 3 old shs.

Russian Kid Mining Co. Ltd. (Ont. 1945)
1964 – Name changed to The New Russian Kid Mining Co. Ltd.; basis 1 new for 10 old shs. ■

Rustex Mining Corp. (Que. 1959)
Dec. 1973 – Charter cancelled.

Rusty Creek Mining Co. Ltd. (B.C. 1956)
Sept. 19, 1968 – Dissolved.

Rusty Lake Mining Corp. (Que. 1959)
1968 – Name changed to Rustex Mining Corp.; basis 1 new for 3 old shs. ■

Rusty Lake Resources Ltd. (Ont. Jan. 31, 1993 amalg.)
June 29, 1995 – Formed Seven Seas Petroleum Inc. in British Columbia on amalgamation with Seven Seas Petroleum Inc., with Seven Seas the deemed acquiror; basis 1 new for 35 old shs. ■

Rutel Corporation (Can. June 23, 1998)
Nov. 25, 2003 – Name changed to Rutel Networks Corporation pursuant to reverse takeover acquisition of Phontel Telecom Inc.; basis 1 new for 15 old shs. (see FPsurvey - Industrials)

Ruth Hope Mining Company Limited (B.C. 1924)
Apr. 13, 1983 – Struck off register.

Ruth Vermont Mine Ltd. (N.P.L.) (B.C. 1963)
Apr. 21, 1995 – Dissolved and struck off register.

Rutherford Ventures Corp. (B.C. Feb. 13, 1987)
Apr. 6, 1993 – Name changed to Diamond Fields Resources Inc. ■

Rutland Biotech Limited (B.C. 1984)
Apr. 24, 1992 – Dissolved and struck off register.

Ruttan Lake Explorations Limited (Ont. 1970)
Feb. 20, 1980 – Dissolved.

Rutter Inc. (Can. Mar. 26, 2004 amalg.)
May 5, 2014 – Amalgamated with 8758875 Canada Inc. to continue under the Rutter Inc. name; basis 1 8758875 Canada redeem. pref. sh. for 1 Rutter com. sh. immediately redeemed for $0.061 cash per sh. Co. now private.

Rutter Technologies Inc. (Que. Feb. 1, 1937)
Mar. 26, 2004 – Formed Rutter Inc. in Canada on amalgamation with 9129-5303 Quebec Inc. ■

Rx Drug Mart Inc. (Can. Mar. 20, 2015)
Apr. 30, 2021 – Name changed to Neighbourly Pharmacy Inc. ■

Ryan Energy Corp. (B.C. Mar. 31, 1980)
Feb. 14, 1986 – Name changed to Ryan Resources Ltd. ■

Ryan Energy Technologies Inc. (Alta. Jan. 22, 1993)
Oct. 11, 2002 – Plan of Arrangement with Nabors Exchangeco (Canada) Inc. and Nabors Industries Ltd.; basis Cdn$1.85, or 0.0362 new Nabors Exchangeco exchangeable shs., or a combination thereof for 1 old Ryan com. sh. (see Nabors Exchangeco (Canada) Inc.)

Ryan Gold Corp. (Ont. Aug. 2, 1990)
Aug. 27, 2015 – Acquired by Oban Mining Corporation; basis 0.094 (post consol.) Oban com. shs. for 1 Ryan com. sh. (see Oban Mining Corporation)

Ryan Gold Mines Limited (Alta. Feb. 9, 1937)
Oct. 2, 1990 – Continued into Ontario. (see FPsurvey - Mines & Energy)

Ryan Lake Mines Limited (Ont. Mar. 15, 1947)
Oct. 5, 1951 – Name changed to New Ryan Lake Mines Limited; basis 1 new for 2 old shs. ■

Ryan Petroleums Ltd. (Alta. 1979)
Oct. 31, 1979 – Name changed to Jennifer Petroleums Ltd. ■

Ryan Resources Ltd. (B.C. Mar. 31, 1980)
Dec. 30, 1987 – Name changed to Canadian Crew Energy Corporation; basis 1 new for 5 old shs. ■

Ryanor Mining Co. Ltd. (Ont. 1945)
Mar. 1, 1982 – Dissolved.

Rycon Mines Limited (Can. Jan. 25, 1938)
Nov. 29, 1990 – Continued into Ontario.

Rydal Resources Inc. (Ont. 1963)
May 11, 1989 – Name changed to The Federal Group Inc. following reverse takeover acquisition of Kingstar Developments Inc.; basis 1 new for 1 old sh. ■

Ryde Energy Inc. (Alta. July 27, 1987)
July 17, 1995 – Name changed to Caswan Environmental Services Inc.; basis 1 new cl. A for 4 old cl. A shs.

Ryde Industries Inc. (Alta. July 27, 1987)
June 1, 1994 – Name changed to Ryde Energy Inc. ∎

Rye Patch Gold Corp. (B.C. Apr. 13, 2006)
May 30, 2018 – Acquired by Alio Gold Inc.; basis 0.48 Alio Gold shs. plus $0.001 cash for 1 Rye Patch sh. (see Alio Gold Inc.)

Ryjencap Inc. (Alta. Jan. 18, 2005)
July 10, 2006 – Name changed to Empire Industries Ltd. following Qualifying Transaction acquisition of Empire Iron Works Ltd.; basis 1 new for 4 old shs. ∎

Ryker Resources Ltd. (B.C. 1967)
Feb. 25, 1983 – Struck off register.

Ryland Oil Corporation (Ont. Apr. 25, 1975)
Aug. 24, 2010 – Acquired by Crescent Point Energy Corp.; basis 0.0117 Crescent Point shs. for 1 Ryland sh. (see Crescent Point Energy Corp.)

Rynco Resources Ltd. (Alta. May 22, 1979)
Nov. 1, 1995 – Dissolved and struck off register.

Ryslo Silver Mines Ltd. (B.C. Aug. 19, 1966)
May 2, 1977 – Name changed to Major Resources Ltd. ∎

Rystar Communications Ltd. (Can. Mar. 31, 1998)
Aug. 15, 2006 – Dissolved.

Rystar Development Ltd. (B.C. June 24, 1986)
Mar. 31, 1998 – Name changed to Rystar Communications Ltd. and continued into Canada. ∎

S

S & K Petroleum Ltd. (Alta. 1980)
1983 – Over 98% of o/s shs. acquired by co. from shldrs. at US$1.65 per sh. Subsequently remaining shs. exchanged for shs. of High Plains Oil Corporation; basis 1 sh. High Plains for each 5 shs. S & K.

S & L Diversified Corp. Ltd. (Can. 1928)
Apr. 20, 1975 – Name changed to Publigest Ltd.

S & M Photolabels Inc. (Can. Oct. 10, 1985)
May 6, 2003 – Dissolved.

S. Nord Chemical Co. Ltd. (Can. 1952)
1955 – Name changed to Petro-Chemsol Chemicals, Ltd. ∎

S Split Corp. (Ont. Jan. 26, 2007)
Sept. 17, 2024 – Merged into Premium Gold Income Split Corp.; basis 0.373815 Premium Global cl. A shs. for 1 S Split cl. A sh. Holders of pref. shs. received 0.743873 Premium Global pref. shs and 0.330689 Premium Global cl. A shs. for 1 S Split pref. sh.

SACO SmartVision Inc. (Can. May 30, 1985)
Mar. 15, 2001 – Granted protection under the CCAA and Ernst & Young Inc. was appointed monitor.
Apr. 3, 2001 – All directors but one had resigned and a private placement of 50,000,000 common shares at 10¢ per share was announced. Ernst & Young received $1,000,000 as a downpayment for the private placement.
Apr. 17, 2001 – Protection was extended to July 17, 2001.
Apr. 26, 2001 – U.S. subsidiary, Saco Smartvision Corp., filed a voluntary petition under Chapter 7 of the U.S. Bankruptcy Code to liquidate its assets.
July 6, 2001 – Quebec Superior Court approved the settlement of inter-company receivables from wholly owned Saco Smartvision S.A.
Sept. 4, 2001 – Proposed plan of reorganization to restructure a $15,000,000 loan with the Canadian Imperial Bank of Commerce was denied by the Québec Superior Court. RSM Richter Inc. was appointed trustee in bankruptcy.
June 2004 – Assets sold. Secured creditors suffered a shortfall and there were no funds available for unsecured creditors or shldrs.
Mar. 11, 2005 – Trustee discharged.

SAGE Income Fund (Ont. Oct. 17, 1997)
Apr. 19, 2005 – Amalgamated with MINT Income Fund; basis 1.79391453 new MINT unit for 1 old SAGE unit.

S.A.M. Explorations Ltd. (Sask. 1956)
1959 – Assets sold to Tombill Mines Ltd. for 500,000 shs. No record of distribution. (see Tombill Mines Limited)

SAM Sports Systems Inc. (Alta. Sept. 23, 1997)
Dec. 24, 1999 – Name changed to SAMsports.com Inc. (see FPsurvey - Industrials)

SAMAX Gold Inc. (Can. May 27, 1996)
Nov. 18, 1998 – Acquired by Ashanti Goldfields (Canada) Inc., wholly owned indirect subsid. of Ashanti Goldfields Company Limited; basis $7.94 per sh.

SAMSys Technologies Inc. (Ont. Sept. 24, 1973)
May 13, 2002 – Continued into Canada. (see Sirit Inc.)
Apr. 13, 2004 – Acquired by SIRIT Inc. out of court-appointed receivership proceedings for total consideration of $4,000,000 (exclusive of deal costs) for the assets which included $2,500,000 in cash resources. (see Sirit Inc.)

S.B. Vancouver Studios Inc. (B.C. Oct. 23, 1987)
Aug. 18, 1999 – Name changed to Algorithm Media Inc.; basis 1 new for 6 old shs. ∎

SBI Skin Biology Incorporated (B.C. June 23, 1983)
Aug. 22, 1996 – Continued into Yukon.
Oct. 9, 2009 – Name changed to Realm Energy International Corporation and continued into British Columbia pursuant to reverse takeover acquisition of Realm Energy International Corporation (subsequently renamed Realm Energy Operations Corp.); basis 1 new for 4 old shs. ∎

SBN Systems Inc. (Can. 1983)
May 26, 1994 – Name changed to NBS Technologies Inc. ∎

SCC Resource Corporation Limited (Alta. Mar. 23, 1987)
Dec. 6, 1990 – Name changed to SCC Resources Inc.; basis 1 new for 5 old shs. ∎

SCC Resources Inc. (Alta. Mar. 23, 1987)
Oct. 25, 1995 – Name changed to Turbo Genset Inc. ∎

SCI Income Trust (Ont. Aug. 22, 1997)
Nov. 15, 2006 – Acquired indirectly by Simmons Bedding Company for $16.25 per sh.

SCI Satellite Conferencing International Corporation (B.C. Feb. 15, 1984)
July 8, 1988 – Dissolved and struck off register.

SCI-TEC Instruments Inc. (Sask. Dec. 3, 1981)
Oct. 10, 2000 – Name changed to Kipp & Zonen Inc. ∎

SCITI ROCS Trust (Ont. Apr. 28, 2005)
May 19, 2015 – All units redeemed for $5.471 per unit.

SCITI Total Return Trust (Ont. Apr. 27, 2006)
May 17, 2011 – All o/s trust units redeemed at $14.0966 per unit.

SCITI Trust (Ont. Apr. 24, 2003)
Apr. 27, 2018 – Terminated; basis $7.6977 cash per trust unit payable on Apr. 30, 2018.

SCITI Trust II (Ont. Oct. 16, 2003)
Nov. 4, 2009 – Amalgamated with SCITI Trust; basis 0.9662 SCITI trust units for 1 SCITI II trust unit. (see SCITI Trust)

S.C.O. Medallion Healthy Homes Ltd. (B.C. Aug. 6, 1999)
Mar. 12, 2012 – Struck from register and dissolved.

SCOSS Capital Corp. (Can. Jan. 12, 2006)
Aug. 11, 2006 – Converted into an investment trust named InStorage Real Estate Investment Trust; basis 1 trust unit for 1 com. sh.

SCS Solars Computing Systems Inc. (B.C. Mar. 30, 1983)
Sept. 15, 2014 – Dissolved and struck from register.

SCU Industries Limited (Ont. 1969)
Aug. 27, 1976 – Placed into receivership.
Mar. 30, 1977 – Liquidated by The Clarkson Co. Ltd. No distribution to unsecured creditors.

SDC Sydney Development Corporation (B.C. 1966)
May 23, 1989 – Filed for bankruptcy. Peat Marwick Thorne appointed trustee. No funds available for distribution to unsecured creditors or shldrs.

SDX Energy Inc. (Can. Mar. 28, 2006)
May 27, 2019 – Plan of arrangement whereby wholly owned SDX Energy plc (SDX UK) acquired all the o/s com. shs. of the company, resulting in the company becoming a wholly owned subsid. of SDX UK; basis 1 new SDX UK ordinary sh. for 1 SDX Energy com. shs.

S. E. Storage Express (International) Limited (B.C. 1984)
Aug. 28, 1992 – Dissolved and struck off register.

S. E. Woods-Holden Ltd. (Can. 1911)
June 1968 – Name changed to Cantrend Industries Limited. ∎

SEAMARK Asset Management Ltd. (Can. Nov. 4, 1982)
Jan. 15, 2010 – Acquired by wholly owned subsid. Matrix Asset Management Inc. pursuant to business combination resulting in reverse takeover by Growth Works Ltd (see Matrix Asset Management Inc.)

SEG Exploration Inc. (Que. Jan. 31, 1994 amalg.)
July 17, 1995 – Name changed to West Africa Mining Exploration Corporation Inc. ∎

SEMAFO Inc. (Que. Jan. 31, 1994 amalg.)
July 7, 2020 – Acquired by Endeavour Mining Corporation; basis 0.1422 Endeavour ordinary shs. for 1 SEMFO com. sh. (see Endeavour Mining Corporation)

SENSIO Technologies Inc. (Que. Dec. 19, 2005; amalg.)
Apr. 22, 2016 – Made an assignment in bankruptcy pursuant to the Bankruptcy and Insolvency Act. Deloitte Restructuring Inc. appointed trustee and all officers and directors resigned.

SEP Capital Corporation (Can. Sept. 1, 2006)
Dec. 30, 2009 – Voluntarily dissolved following Qualifying Transaction acquisition of units of Med Biogene Inc. and pro rata distribution to shareholders; basis 0.638 Med Biogene units for 1 old SEP Capital sh.

S.E.R.E.M. Ltd. (Can. Dec. 28, 1966)
Jan. 24, 1980 – Name changed to Serem Ltd. ∎

SFK Pulp Fund (Que. May 21, 2002)
May 25, 2010 – Succeeded by Fibrek Inc. pursuant to plan of arrangement whereby Fibrek Inc. was formed to facilitate the conversion of the fund into a corporation. ∎

SFP Communications Group Inc. (Ont. Jan. 27, 1986)
July 5, 2001 – Name changed to Motivus Inc. ∎

SFP International Ltd. (Ont. Oct. 13, 1982)
May 20, 1995 – Inactive. Struck from registry.

SFR Energy Ltd. (Alta. Nov. 2, 2012)
Jan. 5, 2015 – Name changed to International SoftRock Oil Company Limited following Qualifying Transaction reverse takeover acquisition of SoftRock Resources (Bahamas) Limited. (see FPsurvey - Mines & Energy)

SG Spirit Gold Inc. (Alta. Dec. 19, 2006 amalg.)
Dec. 20, 2011 – Continued into British Columbia.
Aug. 3, 2017 – Name changed to DOJA Cannabis Company Limited following reverse takeover acquisition of Northern Lights Marijuana Company Limited (DOJA) and concurrent amalgamation of DOJA with SG Spirit's wholly owned NLMCO Acquisition Corp. to form DOJA Cannabis Ltd. ∎

SGI Capital Corporation (B.C. Dec. 2, 1985)
Jan. 5, 1996 – Continued into Yukon.
Dec. 10, 1997 – Name changed to Lariat Property Corporation; basis 1 new for 2 old shs. ■

SGI Super Grass Inc. (Alta. 1986)
May 24, 1989 – Name changed to Canadian-Star Industries Inc. ■

S.G.M. Corporation (Que. 1931)
Nov. 7, 1981 – Charter cancelled.

SGX Resources Inc. (Can. Dec. 5, 2008)
June 15, 2018 – Name changed to 55 North Mining Inc.; basis 1 new for 3 old shs. (see FPsurvey - Mines & Energy)

SHEP Technologies Inc. (Yuk. Oct. 6, 2000)
Apr. 17, 2008 – Dissolved.

SHL Systemhouse Inc. (Can. July 26, 1974)
Nov. 20, 1995 – Acquired by SHL Systemhouse Acquisition Corp., an indirect wholly owned subsid. of MCI Communications Corporation, for US$13 per sh.

SID Energy Inc. (B.C. May 21, 1987)
Oct. 28, 1994 – Dissolved and struck off register.

SIGMACOR, Inc. (Alta. Nov. 7, 1994)
May 2, 2008 – Dissolved and struck from registry.

SIMSMART Inc. (Can. July 12, 2001)
June 15, 2016 – Dissolved by the company.

SIRIT Technologies Inc. (Can. Jan. 7, 1993)
Nov. 1, 2002 – Amalgamated with iTech Capital Corp.; basis 0.1132618 iTech shs. for 1 SIRIT sh. (see iTech Capital Corp.)

S.I.S. Explorations Corporation (Ont. Apr. 2, 1974)
July 13, 1987 – Name changed to Allegiance Equity Corporation; basis 1 new for 4 old shs. ■

S.I.S. Resources Corporation (Ont. Apr. 2, 1974)
1980 – Name changed to S.I.S. Explorations Corporation. ■

SJ Resources Ltd. (B.C. Dec. 13, 1978)
June 26, 1984 – Name changed to Ark La Tex Industries Ltd. ■

SKANA Capital Corp. (B.C. Aug. 19, 1979)
May 25, 2011 – Name changed to MENA Hydrocarbons Inc. and continued into Alberta pursuant to reverse takeover acquisition of MENA Hydrocarbons Inc. and subsequent amalgamation of MENA with wholly owned subsid. 1570046 Alberta Ltd. ■

S.K.D. Manufacturing Co. Limited (unknown)
Dec. 1969 – Continental Can Co. of Canada Ltd. acquired 1st pref. and com. shs. on basis of $10.15 plus accr. divds. for each pref. and $9.50 for each com. sh. All o/s 2nd. pref. shs. redeemed.

SKN Resources Ltd. (B.C. Oct. 31, 1991 amalg.)
May 2, 2005 – Name changed to Silvercorp Metals Inc. (see FPsurvey - Mines & Energy)

SL Resources Inc. (Ont. Apr. 8, 2005)
Dec. 10, 2010 – Name changed to White Tiger Gold Ltd. and continued into British Virgin Islands. ■

SL Split Corp. (Ont. Sept. 20, 2007)
Feb. 1, 2013 – All o/s shs. redeemed for $1.55 per cap. sh. and $25.78 per pfd. sh.

SLANG Worldwide Inc. (Can. May 29, 2017)
Nov. 26, 2024 – Filed an assignment into bankruptcy. B. Riley Farber Inc. appointed trustee and all the directors resigned.

SLC Capital Inc. (Can. Sept. 26, 2003)
June 23, 2005 – Formed Conporec Inc. in Canada on Qualifying Transaction amalgamation with Conporec Inc., constituting a reverse takeover by Conporec. ■

SLE Synergy Ltd. (B.C. Sept. 16, 2019)
Jan. 27, 2021 – Name changed to BYT Holdings Ltd. (see FPsurvey - Industrials)

SLM Software Inc. (Ont. Feb. 13, 1986)
June 23, 1999 – Name changed to SLMsoft.com Inc.; basis 0.5 variable multiple vtg. and 0.5 limited vtg. for 1 com. sh. ■

SLMsoft Inc. (Ont. Feb. 13, 1986)
Oct. 31, 2003 – Placed into receivership. RSM Richter Inc. was appointed receiver.

SLMsoft.com Inc. (Ont. Feb. 13, 1986)
Aug. 2, 2002 – Name changed to SLMsoft Inc. ■

SLN Ventures Corporation (B.C. Feb. 28, 1979)
Apr. 1, 1997 – Name changed to Pan Ocean Explorations Inc.; basis 1 new for 6 old shs. ■

SLYCE Inc. (Alta. June 26, 2014)
Jan. 10, 2017 – Name changed to Pounce Technologies Inc. following the sale of all operating assets, which included the transfer of the SLYCE name; basis 1 new for 20 old shs. ■

SM Industries Limited (B.C. 1963)
Aug. 9, 1976 – Dissolved.

S.M.A. Resources Ltd. (B.C. Aug. 17, 1987)
Feb. 15, 1994 – Name changed to Biomin Therapeutic Corporation. ■

S.M.A. (Société de Mathématiques Appliquées) Inc. (Que. 1964)
July 31, 1977 – Sold substantially all its assets and transferred all liabs. except those owing to Power Corp. of Canada Ltd. to The Industrial Life Insurance Co. and L'Industrielle Services Techniques Inc. (IST).
Oct. 1, 1977 – Sold to Power Corp. its invest. in TMS Management Services Ltd.
1978 – Repaid $7,500,000 of $8,000,000 in income debs. owing to Power Corp.
1980 – Charter surrendered.

SMART Technologies Inc. (Alta. June 11, 2007)
Sept. 20, 2016 – Acquired by Hon Hai Precision Industry Co., Ltd. (operating as Foxconn Technology Group) for US$4.50 per sh.

SMC Ventures Inc. (B.C. Dec. 4, 1980)
Feb. 19, 2019 – Name changed to Blockmint Technologies Inc. pursuant to reverse takeover acquisition of (old) Blockmint Technologies Inc. (renamed Blockmint (Canada) Technologies Inc.); basis 1 new for 2 old shs. (see FPsurvey - Industrials)

SMED International Inc. (Alta. 1980)
Mar. 20, 2000 – Acquired by wholly owned subsid. of Haworth Inc. for $24 per sh.

SMG Capital Corporation (Sask. 1987)
July 12, 1990 – Formed CAPA Software Publishing Corporation in Saskatchewan on amalgamation with CAPA Software Publishing Corporation; basis 0.6 CAPA cl. A com. shs. for 1 SMG com. sh. ■

SMI Oil & Gas Inc. (Can. Jan. 22, 1986)
Nov. 7, 1995 – Acquired by wholly owned subsid. of Canadian Leader Energy Inc.; basis 1 new Leader sh. for 2.2 old SMI shs. (see Canadian Leader Energy Inc.)

SMK Speedy International Inc. (Ont. Dec. 1, 1988)
Jan. 13, 2004 – Plan of Arrangement with subsid. of private company Minute Muffler & Brake; basis Cdn$3.53, plus Cdn$1.73 principal amount of Acquisition Notes, plus US$0.65 principal amount of T-Notes.

S.M.M. Enterprises Ltd. (B.C. Aug. 26, 1983)
Oct. 3, 1986 – Name changed to AcuVision Systems Inc. ■

SMTC Manufacturing Corporation of Canada (Can. Aug. 8, 1985)
Aug. 10, 1994 – Continued into Ontario.
June 4, 2012 – Redeemed all o/s exch. shs.; basis 1 SMTC Corporation sh. for 1 SMTC Manufacturing exch. sh.

SNA Resources Ltd. (B.C. 1972)
Oct. 29, 1979 – Name changed to Enterprise Development Corporation; basis 1 new for 5 old shs. ■

SNB Capital Corp. (B.C. May 20, 2003 amalg.)
July 14, 2004 – Name changed to Protox Therapeutics Inc. following Qualifying Transaction acquisition of Protox Pharmaceuticals Inc. ■

SNC Equity Inc. (Alta. June 15, 2000)
Aug. 31, 2002 – Formed RenoWorks Software Inc. in Alberta on Qualifying Transaction amalgamation with RenoWorks Software Inc. which constituted a reverse takeover by RenoWorks; basis 0.35 new for 1 old sh. (see FPsurvey - Industrials)

The SNC Group Inc. (Can. May 18, 1967)
June 7, 1993 – Name changed to SNC-Lavalin Group Inc. ■

SNC-Lavalin Group Inc. (Can. May 18, 1967)
May 16, 2024 – Name changed to AtkinsRéalis Group Inc. (see FPsurvey - Industrials)

SND Energy Ltd. (Can. May 4, 2007)
Feb. 20, 2009 – Name changed to Boyuan Construction Group, Inc. ■

SNG Telecom Inc. (Alta. Apr. 26, 1996)
Sept. 2, 2004 – Struck from registry and dissolved.

SNL Enterprises Ltd. (B.C. Nov. 4, 1999)
Feb. 19, 2010 – Name changed to Logan Copper Inc. (see FPsurvey - Mines & Energy)

SNP Health Split Corp. (Ont. Nov. 29, 2001)
Feb. 12, 2009 – Redeemed pref. shs. and capital shs. for US$25 per pref. sh. and US$2.6507 per capital sh.

SNP Split Corp. (Ont. Apr. 23, 2001)
June 6, 2011 – All o/s shs. redeemed for US$10.25 per pref. sh. and US$3.9418 per capital sh.

S.N.S. Mines Ltd. (Que. 1972)
1976 – Acquired by Graphex Mines Inc. Shs. reported exchanged on basis of 1 sh. Graphex for 4.5 shs. S.N.S.

SNS Precious Metals Inc. (B.C. Sept. 12, 1996)
Oct. 8, 2010 – Name changed to Gold Finder Explorations Ltd.; basis 1 new for 10 old shs. ■

SNS Silver Corp. (B.C. Sept. 12, 1996)
May 17, 2010 – Name changed to SNS Precious Metals Inc. ■

SNT Ltd. (Ont. 1989)
Feb. 8, 1996 – All o/s capital and equity dividend shs. redeemed; basis $19.1775 per capital sh. and $12.6067 per equity dividend sh.

SNV Group Ltd. (Alta. July 17, 1998)
May 17, 1999 – Continued into Canada.
Oct. 18, 2001 – Company and wholly owned SNV International Ltd. applied for and received protection under CCAA.
Dec. 2001 – All directors resigned and Ernst & Young Inc. was appointed trustee.
June 2003 – All assets sold and creditors would receive a distribution pending settlement of a lawsuit to recover an outstanding receivable.
June 2005 – Lawsuit settled and a distribution paid to creditors but no funds were available for shldrs.
Jan. 18, 2006 – Trustee discharged on SNV Group Ltd.
Feb. 2, 2006 – Trustee discharged on SNV International Ltd.

S.O. Resources Inc. (B.C. Dec. 23, 1980)
June 4, 1985 – Name changed to Crimson Tide Resources Ltd. ■

SOFTIMAGE Inc. (Que. 1986)
July 19, 1994 – Acquired by Microsoft Corporation; basis 0.458 Microsoft shs. for 1 SOFTIMAGE sh.

SOK Properties Ltd. (Can. Apr. 5, 1983)
Apr. 8, 1991 – Name changed to Impact Telemedia International Ltd. ■

SPARQ Corp. (Ont. Nov. 13, 2018)
Jan. 1, 2023 – Name changed to SPARQ Systems Inc. (see FPsurvey - Industrials)

SPC International Investments Limited (Ont. 1961)
Aug. 31, 1990 – Acquired by wholly owned subsid. of Eighty-eight Corporation for $29.25 per sh.

SPI Safety Packaging International Ltd. (B.C. Jan. 31, 1961)
June 21, 1991 – Dissolved and struck off register.

SPS Industries Ltd. (Alta. Mar. 25, 1987)
July 7, 1999 – Name changed to Landover Energy Inc.; basis 1 new for 4 old shs. ■

SPT Sulphur Polymer Technologies Inc. (B.C. Jan. 12, 2014)
Dec. 2, 2015 – Name changed to LeenLife Pharma International Inc. following acquisition of 90% interest in LeenLife Pharma S.A. ■

SR Telecom Inc. (Can. Feb. 17, 1981)
June 18, 2008 – Name changed to SRX Post Holdings Inc. ■

SRG Graphite Inc. (Can. Apr. 16, 1996)
July 4, 2019 – Name changed to SRG Mining Inc. ■

SRG Mining Inc. (Can. Apr. 16, 1996)
June 27, 2024 – Name changed to Falcon Energy Materials plc and continued into United Arab Emirates. (see FPsurvey - Mines & Energy)

SRHI Inc. (Can. May 21, 2002)
June 21, 2021 – Name changed to Three Valley Copper Corp. (see FPsurvey - Mines & Energy; FPsurvey - Industrials)

S.R.I. Oil & Gas Inc. (Can. Apr. 25, 1989)
July 29, 1999 – Name changed to Hornet Energy Ltd. ■

SRO Entertainment International Inc. (B.C. Apr. 11, 1983)
Jan. 30, 1990 – Name changed to PacRim Entertainment Group Inc.; basis 1 new for 2.5 old shs. ■

SRR Mercantile Inc. (B.C. Sept. 17, 1984)
Feb. 21, 2003 – Struck from registry and dissolved.

SRS Capital Corp. (Alta. Oct. 6, 1992)
Aug. 20, 1996 – Name changed to Postec Systems Inc.; basis 1 new for 1 old sh. (see FPsurvey - Industrials)

SRX Post Holdings Inc. (Can. Feb. 17, 1981)
Nov. 18, 2008 – Name changed to Bonterra Oil & Gas Ltd. following reverse takeover acquisition of Bonterra Energy Income Trust. ■

S. S. Holden Ltd. (Can. 1911)
Feb. 10, 1947 – Name changed to Holden Manufacturing Co. Ltd. ■

SSP Offshore Inc. (Alta. Sept. 9, 1998)
Dec. 18, 2014 – Dissolved.

SSQ II Acquisitions Inc. (Ont. May 30, 2007)
July 6, 2007 – Name changed to JJR II Acquisitions Inc. ■

SSQ Acquisitions Inc. (Ont. Feb. 2, 2007)
Sept. 1, 2007 – Formed Craig Wireless Systems Ltd. in Canada on Qualifying Transaction reverse takeover acquisition of and amalgamation with Craig Wireless Systems Ltd. and 6809278 Canada Inc., a wholly owned subsidiary of SSQ; basis 1 new for 6 old shs.

ST Systems Corp. (B.C. Mar. 22, 1972)
Dec. 24, 2007 – Name changed to Sky Ridge Resources Ltd.; basis 1 new for 7 old shs. ■

S.T.A. Resources Corporation (B.C. Dec. 6, 1978)
Oct. 3, 1996 – Name changed to T.T.A. Resources Corporation; basis 1 new for 2 old shs. ■

S.T.I. Industries Inc. (Ont. Mar. 30, 1978)
Jan. 3, 1995 – Delisted from the CDN. Subsequently struck from register and dissolved.

STN Incorporated (Alta. Mar. 18, 1988)
July 4, 1995 – KPMG Inc. of Toronto was appointed receiver following resignation of the directors and senior officers.
Aug. 1995 – Sprint Canada Inc. purchased most of the assets of STN, including accounts receivable, for $19,000,000. Creditors suffered a shortfall and there were no funds available for shldrs.
Feb. 1, 2000 – Receiver discharged.

STN Shop Television Network, Ltd. (B.C. Mar. 1982)
May 27, 1987 – Continued into Delaware.
Dec. 21, 1987 – Name changed to Shop Television Network, Inc.

STRATA Income Fund (Ont. Jan. 29, 2004)
Dec. 1, 2009 – Terminated. STRATA Income trust units exchanged for COMPASS Income Fund trust units. Pref. security redeemed for $10.0994565 per security. (see COMPASS Income Fund)

STS Power Pedal Corp. (B.C. July 23, 1980)
Jan. 31, 2001 – Name changed to Mark-Can Investment Corp.; basis 1 new for 7 old shs. ■

STT Enviro Corp. (Can. Jan. 30, 2007)
July 4, 2017 – All o/s com. shs. not already held acquired by Carmeuse Lime (Canada) Limited via compulsory acquisition; basis $0.315 cash per sh.
June 4, 2019 – Name changed to Storage & Transfer Technologies, Inc.

STaRS Income Fund (Ont. Nov. 27, 2001)
Sept. 28, 2009 – Merged into MINT Income Fund; basis 1.34864982 MINT trust units for 1 STaRS trust unit.

SUB Capital Inc. (Can. Nov. 9, 2005)
May 11, 2011 – Name changed to Inca One Metals Corp. ■

SURE Print and Copy Centres, Inc. (Alta. July 24, 1996)
June 2, 2006 – Struck from registry and dissolved.

SVC Second Venture Capital Corp. (B.C. Nov. 6, 1998)
Feb. 24, 2003 – Name changed to Masev Communications International Inc. following Qualifying Transaction acquisition of Masev Communications Inc. for consideration of 17,853,198 shs. ■

SVT Capital Corp. (B.C. May 16, 2001)
Oct. 31, 2017 – Name changed to Delta 9 Cannabis Inc. following reverse takeover acquisition and amalgamation of Delta 9 Bio-Tech Inc. (deemed acquiror) with wholly owned 10240907 Canada Corp. (see FPsurvey - Industrials)

SWI Steelworks Inc. (B.C. June 11, 1980)
Nov. 19, 2007 – Dissolved.

SXC Health Solutions Corp. (Yuk. June 27, 2007)
July 11, 2012 – Name changed to Catamaran Corporation. ■

SXT Resources Ltd. (B.C. 1983)
Oct. 23, 1992 – Dissolved and struck off register.

SYH Corporation (Ont. 1961)
Aug. 20, 1990 – Name changed to Consolidated SYH Corporation; basis 1 new for 10 old shs. ■

SYMC Resources Limited (B.C. Mar. 26, 1987)
Oct. 15, 2007 – Name changed to G4G Resources Ltd.; basis 1 new for 2 old shs. ■

SYNER-SEIS Technologies Inc. (Alta. Jan. 8, 1996)
June 25, 2004 – Name changed to Intequest Corporation; basis 1 new for 8 old shs. ■

SYNSORB Biotech Inc. (Alta. Feb. 14, 1994)
Apr. 11, 2003 – Name changed to Hawker Resources Inc. ■

SZL Sportsight Inc. (B.C. 1987)
Apr. 29, 1996 – Name changed to QuesTec Imaging Inc. ■

SaaSquatch Capital Corp. (B.C. Mar. 22, 2021)
Feb. 16, 2022 – Name changed to Jasper Commerce Inc. pursuant to the Qualifying Transaction reverse takeover acquisition of Jasper Interactive Studios Inc. and concurrent amalgamation of Jasper with wholly owned 2869943 Ontario Inc.; basis 1 new for 2 old shs. (see FPsurvey - Industrials)

Saber Capital Corp. (B.C. Feb. 25, 2008)
Dec. 5, 2016 – Continued into Canada.
Dec. 12, 2016 – Name changed to Emblem Corp. following Qualifying Transaction reverse takeover acquisition of (old) Emblem Corp.; basis 1 new for 4 old shs. ■

Sabertooth Holdings, Inc. (B.C. Jan. 24, 1997)
Sept. 6, 2000 – Name changed to Harmony Integrated Solutions, Inc. and continued into Canada following Qualifying Transaction reverse takeover acquisition of nVector Network Corporation. ■

Sabina Gold & Silver Corp. (B.C. June 7, 1966)
Apr. 19, 2023 – Name changed to B2Gold Back River Corp. ■

Sabina Industries Limited (B.C. June 7, 1966)
Feb. 15, 1984 – Name changed to New Sabina Resources Ltd.; basis 1 new for 2 old shs. ■

Sabina Mines Ltd. (B.C. June 7, 1966)
1971 – Name changed to Sabina Industries Limited. ■

Sabina Resources Limited (B.C. June 7, 1966)
Oct. 17, 2005 – Name changed to Sabina Silver Corporation. ■

Sabina Silver Corporation (B.C. June 7, 1966)
Oct. 28, 2009 – Name changed to Sabina Gold & Silver Corp. ■

Sabine Uranium Mines Ltd. (Ont. 1954)
June 12, 1961 – Dissolved.

Sable Technologies Ltd. (Alta. Mar. 9, 1988)
May 15, 1991 – Name changed to IntePac Corporation. ■

Sables Gold Mines Ltd. (Ont. 1944)
Dec. 1957 – Dissolved.

Sabourin Creek Mines Ltd. (Ont. 1945)
1968 – Charter cancelled.

Sabre Gold Mines Corp. (Can. Nov. 9, 1987)
Feb. 7, 2025 – Acquired by Minera Alamos Inc.; basis 0.693 Minera Alamos shs. for 1 Sabre Gold sh.

Sabre Graphite Corp. (B.C. June 17, 1998)
Mar. 12, 2015 – Name changed to DraftTeam Daily Fantasy Sports Corp. following acquisition of DraftTeam Fantasy Sports Inc. ■

Sabre Marketing Corporation (B.C. Aug. 22, 1986)
Aug. 10, 1994 – Name changed to Sabre Pacific Equities Limited; basis 1 new for 3 old shs. ■

Sabre Pacific Equities Limited (B.C. Aug. 22, 1986)
Dec. 12, 2005 – Dissolved and struck from register.

Sabretooth Energy Ltd. (Ont. Apr. 4, 2000)
Sept. 29, 2005 – Continued into Alberta.
Aug. 17, 2009 – Name changed to Cequence Energy Ltd. ■

Sabrich Capital Corporation (Alta. Aug. 11, 2006)
May 15, 2008 – Formed Sentinel Rock Oil Corporation in Alberta on Qualifying Transaction amalgamation with Sentinel Rock Oilsands Corporation (deemed acquiror); basis 1 new for 4.25 old shs. ■

Saccharum Energy Corp. (Alta. May 15, 2007)
June 27, 2016 – Name changed to SynStream Energy Corp. (see FPsurvey - Mines & Energy)

Sachem Exploration Inc. (B.C. Nov. 9, 1966)
July 10, 1984 – Name changed to Brower Exploration Inc.; basis 1 new for 5 old shs. ■

Sackville Oils & Minerals Ltd. (Alta.)
Dec. 22, 1977 – Amalgamated with Invictus Petro Minerals Ltd. (1 for 10) to form Seagull Resources Ltd.; basis 1 new for 4 old shs.

Saco Industries & Realty Ltd. (Alta. Dec. 12, 1969)
Jan. 31, 1986 – Name changed to Royal Resources Ltd.; basis 1 new for 5 old shs. ■

Saco Mining Corporation Limited (Alta. Dec. 12, 1969)
July 11, 1977 – Name changed to Saco Industries & Realty Ltd. ■

Saco Resources Ltd. (Alta. 1979)
June 24, 1991 – Name changed to Manar Canada Inc. following acquisition of Manar Technology Inc.; basis 1 new for 3 old shs. ■

Sacre-Coeur Minerals, Ltd. (Can. Mar. 9, 2004)
Jan. 8, 2017 – Dissolved and struck from register.

Saddle Mines Ltd. (B.C.)
May 8, 1969 – Struck off register.

Saddle Mountain Mining Corporation (B.C. Apr. 27, 1987)
July 26, 1994 – Continued into Alberta.
Dec. 13, 1994 – Formed Saddle Mountain Timber Corporation in Alberta on amalgamation with (private) Saddle Mountain Timber Corporation. ■

Saddle Mountain Timber Corporation (Alta. Dec. 13, 1994 amalg.)
Mar. 7, 1997 – Name changed to Global Tree Technologies Inc. ■

Saddle Resources Inc. (Alta. Nov. 20, 1996)
June 27, 2002 – Acquired by Devlan Production Company Ltd. wholly owned subsid. of Devlan Exploration Inc.; basis $0.52 per sh. (see Devlan Exploration Inc.)

Saddlerock Resources, Inc. (B.C. Dec. 3, 1980)
July 7, 2000 – Name changed to MDX Medical Inc. ■

Sadie Red Lake Gold Mines Ltd. (Ont. 1946)
1958 – Charter cancelled.

Safari Explorations Ltd. (Ont. 1970)
Feb. 25, 1974 – Amalgamated into Cavalier Energy Inc.; basis 1 new for 25 old shs.

Safari International Resources Ltd. (B.C. Jan. 10, 1986)
June 17, 1998 – Amalgamated with Epic Resources (B.C.) Ltd. to form Epic Oil and Gas Ltd.; basis 1 new for 1 Epic Resources (B.C.) sh. and 0.9 new for 1 Safari International sh. (see Epic Oil and Gas Ltd.)

Safe Environment Engineering Canada Inc. (Alta. Mar. 10, 1987)
Sept. 2, 2010 – Struck from registry and dissolved.

Safe Harbour Capital Ltd. (Alta. Aug. 30, 1996)
Aug. 12, 2002 – Name changed to Kingsmere Capital Inc. ■

The Safe Oil & Gas Co., Ltd. (Ont. 1907)
1960 – Struck off register.

Safe Water Products Ltd. (Yuk. Feb. 17, 1987)
Aug. 7, 1991 – Continued into British Columbia.
June 26, 1992 – Name changed to En-R-Tech International Inc. (shs. never traded under the Safe Water

Products name as the VSE did not recognize the name change); basis 1 new for 2 old shs. ■

Safeguard Biometric Corp. (Wyo. Nov. 10, 1998)
Nov. 30, 2001 – Continued into British Columbia.
Feb. 11, 2002 – Name changed to Devon Ventures Corporation. ■

Safeguard Ventures Inc. (B.C. Sept. 15, 1987)
Jan. 14, 1994 – Name changed to Amar Ventures Inc.; basis 1 new for 5 old shs. ■

Safety-Ject Medical Products Ltd. (B.C. Jan. 22, 1987)
Sept. 23, 1991 – Name changed to International Safety-Ject Industries Inc.; basis 1 new for 4 old shs. ■

Saga Resources Ltd. (B.C. Dec. 2, 1985)
July 24, 1989 – Name changed to PacificAmerica Equities Inc. ■

Sage Gold Inc. (Ont. Oct. 1, 1997 amalg.)
Aug. 29, 2018 – Placed into receivership by secured creditor, CRH Funding II PTE Ltd. and Deloitte Restructuring Inc. appointed receiver.
Jan. 29, 2019 – Court approval was received for the sale of the Onaman claims to RZJ Capital Management LLC and the sale of the Clavos claims to Eric Quint for approx. $3,800,000.
Dec. 18, 2020 – Deloitte Restructuring discharged as receiver. Funds received on sale of assets insufficient for any distrib. to secured creditor or shldrs. (see FPsurvey - Mines & Energy)

Sage High Yield Debt Trust (Ont. Oct. 17, 1997)
Aug. 26, 2002 – Name changed to SAGE Income Fund. ■

Sage Oil Company Limited (Alta. 1951)
Jan. 1967 – Merged with Syracuse Oils Ltd.

Sage Resources Ltd. (B.C. Dec. 19, 1980)
Aug. 6, 1996 – Name changed to New Sage Resources Ltd.; basis 1 new for 5 old shs. ■

Sage Ventures Inc. (Alta. May 14, 1993)
Nov. 14, 1995 – Name changed to Software Control Systems International Inc.; basis 1 new for 1 old sh. (see FPsurvey - Industrials)

Sagen MI Canada Inc. (Can. May 25, 2009)
Apr. 6, 2021 – All o/s com. shs. not already held acquired by Brookfield Business Partners L.P.; basis $43.50 cash per com. sh. Pref. A ser. 1 shs. remain listed. (see FPsurvey - Industrials)

Sagewood Resources Limited (Ont. Dec. 12, 1977)
Apr. 8, 2008 – Dissolved and struck from register.

Sagittarius Capital Corporation (Ont. Apr. 20, 2007)
Mar. 6, 2019 – Name changed to Water Ways Technologies Inc. following Qualifying Transaction reverse takeover acquisition of Irri-Al-Tal Ltd.; basis 1 new for 1.4964285 old shs. (see FPsurvey - Industrials)

Saguenay Electric Company (Que. 1927)
Dec. 28, 1962 – Under offer of Quebec Hydro-Electric Commission acquired all o/s com. stk. at $43 per sh. Funded debt of the co. was assumed by Quebec Hydro and guaranteed by the Province of Quebec.

Saguenay Exploration & Mining Inc. (Que. 1957)
Oct. 1974 – Charter cancelled.

Saguenay Mining and Smelting Co. Ltd. (Que. 1946)
Jan. 29, 1977 – Charter cancelled.

Saguenay Oil & Natural Gas Co. Ltd. (unknown)
1949 – Wound up.

Saguenay Pulp and Power Company (Que.)
1927 – Placed into voluntary liquidation. Ernest Trudel, Quebec, liquidator.
1930 – First and final divd. of 25¢ per sh. paid on $5.00 par pref. stk. Nothing available for com. stk.

Saha Petroleum Ltd. (Alta. Nov. 19, 2004)
Aug. 26, 2009 – Name changed to Western Plains Petroleum Ltd. ■

Sahali Resources Inc. (B.C. 1981)
Oct. 1, 1984 – Name changed to H.T.R. Industries Inc.; basis 2 new for 1 old sh. ■

Sahara Energy Ltd. (Alta. Nov. 18, 2005 amalg.)
Mar. 31, 2008 – Amalgamated in Alberta to continue with same name.
Dec. 22, 2021 – Name changed to Capitan Investment Ltd. (see FPsurvey - Mines & Energy; FPsurvey - Industrials)

Sahelian Goldfields Inc. (Ont. Mar. 21, 1989 amalg.)
Oct. 1, 1997 – Amalgamated in Ontario to continue with same name.
Mar. 3, 2005 – Name changed to Sage Gold Inc.; basis 1 new for 25 old shs. ■

Sahqua Minerals Ltd. (B.C. 1979)
Mar. 29, 1985 – Struck off register.

St Andrew Goldfields Ltd. (Ont. Jan. 11, 1983)
Feb. 1, 2016 – Acquired by Kirkland Lake Gold Inc.; basis of 0.0906 Kirkland Lake shs. for 1 St Andrew sh. (see Kirkland Lake Gold Inc.)

St. Anthony Gold Corp. (B.C. Apr. 19, 2000)
Dec. 23, 2022 – Name changed to Spark Energy Minerals Inc. (see FPsurvey - Mines & Energy)

St. Anthony Gold Mines Ltd. (Ont. 1921)
1944 – Name changed to St. Anthony Mines Ltd.; basis 1 new for 3 old shs. ■

St. Anthony Mines Ltd. (Ont. 1921)
Nov. 30, 1970 – Amalgamated with Cantri Mining Ltd. (1 for 10), Con-Key Mines Ltd. (1 for 10), Point West Explorations Ltd. (1 for 10), Temanda Mines Ltd. (1 for 30) and Tinex Development & Exploration Ltd. (1 for 30) to form Can-Con Enterprises and Explorations Limited; basis 1 new for 30 old shs.

St. Clair Paint & Wallpaper Corporation (Ont. Oct. 27, 1986)
Nov. 1996 – Company and ICI Paints, a business unit of Imperial Chemical Industries plc, signed an agreement in principle which would see ICI Paints acquire substantially all of the assets and business of St. Clair for about $66,800,000.
Jan. 1997 – Declared bankruptcy in order to facilitate the transaction. PricwaterhouseCoopers Inc. of Toronto, Ont. was appointed trustee.
June 1, 2002 – All distributions had been completed with preferred and secured creditors receiving full repayment and unsecured creditors receiving about 15¢ on the dollar. There were no distributions to shldrs. The trustee was discharged.

St. Clair Resources Ltd. (B.C. 1979)
Sept. 19, 1986 – Struck off register.

St. Edwards Minerals Limited (B.C. May 15, 1984)
Nov. 22, 1988 – Name changed to Multi-Step Industries Inc. ■

St. Elias Exploration (B.C. Aug. 1, 1969)
Oct. 1972 – Name changed to Cutlass Explorations Ltd. ■

St. Elias Exploration Corporation (B.C. May 17, 1966)
Dec. 20, 1983 – Name changed to Bigstone Minerals Ltd. ■

St. Eugene Mining Corporation Limited (B.C. Mar. 25, 1939)
Feb. 2, 2012 – Acquired by Claude Resources Inc.; basis 0.0789 Claude shs. plus 0.25 shs. of newly incorporated Satori Resources Inc. for 1 St. Eugene sh. (see Claude Resources Inc.)

St. Fabien Copper Mines Ltd. (Que. 1967)
Oct. 24, 1980 – Name changed to St. Fabien Explorations Inc. ■

St. Fabien Explorations Inc. (Que. 1967)
July 22, 1983 – Name changed to Fabien Explorations Inc.; basis 1 new for 4 old shs. (see FPsurvey - Mines & Energy)

St. Francis Mining Company Ltd. (Que. 1944)
1970 – Wound up.

St. Geneviève Resources Ltd. (Can. Dec. 3, 1985)
Mar. 28, 2008 – Acquired by Ascendant Copper Corporation; basis 1 Ascendant com. sh. for 6.5394054 St. Genevieve com. shs.
Aug. 14, 2008 – Name changed to Redstone Mining Corporation. ■

St. George Minerals Inc. (B.C. July 27, 1979)
Dec. 31, 1990 – Liquidated.
Feb. 7, 1991 – Shares of St. George Metals, Inc. distributed to shldrs.; basis 1 new for 1 old sh.

St. George Red Lake Gold Mines Ltd. (Ont. 1945)
Nov. 5, 1962 – Dissolved.

St. Helen Mining Exploration Ltd. (Que. 1958)
1967 – Merged into Resource Exploration and Development Co. Ltd.; basis 1 new for 2.47 old shs.

St. James Land Company, Limited (Que. 1923)
Sept. 29, 1972 – Name changed to BM-RT Ltd. ■

The St. James Land Co. 1972 Limited (unknown)
Jan. 20, 1983 – Name changed to Bank of Montreal Realty Developments Inc.

St. James Resources Ltd. (Que. 1971)
Aug. 7, 1982 – Dissolved.

Saint Jean Carbon Inc. (Alta. Mar. 26, 2004 amalg.)
Feb. 16, 2022 – Name changed to Volt Carbon Technologies Inc. (see FPsurvey - Mines & Energy; FPsurvey - Industrials)

Saint John Dry Dock Co. Ltd. (Can. 1947)
1959 – Name changed to Saint John Shipbuilding & Dry Dock Co. Ltd.

St. Johns Petroleum Ltd. (Sask. 1954)
June 1, 1985 – Amalgamated with a subsid. of Westgrowth Petroleums Ltd. Shldrs. of St. John's received 3 shs. of Westgrowth for 5 old shs.

St. Joseph-Kirkland Gold Mines Ltd. (Ont. 1923)
Dec. 28, 1978 – Dissolved.

Saint-Jude Gold Mines Ltd. (Que. 1936)
July 22, 1978 – Charter cancelled.

St. Jude Resources Ltd. (Can. May 31, 1985)
Jan. 6, 2006 – Plan of Arrangement acquisition by Golden Star Resources Ltd.; basis 0.72 new Golden Star sh. for 1 old St. Jude sh. (see Golden Star Resources Ltd.)

St. Laurent Paperboard Inc. (Can. Mar. 19, 1993)
June 2, 2000 – Following Plan of Arrangement with US-based Smurfit-Stone Container Corporation; basis 1 com. sh. of St. Laurent exchanged for US$12.50 (equivalent CDN$18.50) plus 0.5 com. shs. of Smurfit-Stone.

St. Lawrence Cement Co. (Que. Mar. 13, 1951)
June 1980 – Name changed to St. Lawrence Cement Inc. ■

St. Lawrence Cement Group Inc. (Can. Mar. 5, 1998)
Aug. 14, 2007 – Acquired by Holcim Ltd. for $43.50 per sh.

St. Lawrence Cement Inc. (Que. Mar. 13, 1951)
Jan. 1, 2000 – Name changed to St. Lawrence Cement Group Inc. pursuant to corporate reorganization whereby shs. of the co. were converted into an equiv. no. of shs. of St. Lawrence Cement Group Inc. effected through an amalgamation to become the parent co. of St. Lawrence Cement Inc. ■

St. Lawrence Columbium and Metals Corporation (Que. 1960)
July 2, 1976 – Placed into bankruptcy; nothing for shldrs.

St. Lawrence Corporation Ltd. (Can. 1930)
Oct. 31, 1978 – Effective Oct. 19, 1978, amalgamated with Domtar (ASL) Inc., continued as St. Lawrence Corp. Ltd. amalgamated with Domtar Inc., to continue as one operation under the name Domtar Inc. All o/s com. shs. of the predecessor co. converted to $0.08 redeem. pref. shs. on a 1-for-34 basis. All shs. called for redemption Nov. 6, 1978. All 5% Pref. shs., ser. A of the predecessor co. redeemed Sept. 18, 1978. The 6 3/4 % S.F. Debs., Ser. A were redeemed on Dec. 1, 1978.

St. Lawrence Diversified Company (Que. Oct. 12, 1961)
May 3, 1973 – Name changed to Prenor Group Ltd. ■

St. Lawrence Flour Mills Co. Ltd. (Can. 1910)
June 25, 1956 – Plan for liquidation approved.
June 30, 1956 – Assets sold to Robin Hood Flour Mills Ltd. at price equal to book value of assets at June 30, 1956. Offer made by International Milling Co. to purchase o/s pref. shs. at $107 per sh., expired July 31, 1956. Following liquidation, o/s pref. shldrs. entitled to par value plus accrued divds.

St. Lawrence Gas Corp. (Que. 1958)
1965 – Purchased by Pacific Petroleums Ltd. in 1964, and with certain other cos., merged to form Quebec Propane Inc., a wholly owned subsid. of Pacific.

St. Lawrence Mining Corp. Ltd. (Que. 1937)
May 1974 – Charter cancelled.

St. Lawrence River Mines Ltd. (Que. 1954)
1960 – Merged into St. Lawrence Columbium & Metals Corp.

St. Mary's Explorations Limited (Ont. 1958)
Nov. 1977 – Charter cancelled.

St. Mary's Mines Ltd. (B.C. 1965)
1971 – Name changed to Can-Base Industries Ltd. ■

St. Mary's Uranium Mines Ltd. (Ont. 1952)
1958 – Name changed to St. Mary's Explorations Limited and continued into Ontario; basis 1 new for 2 old shs. plus 14 shs. Milliken Lake Uranium Mines for each 100 old shs. ■

St. Maurice Capital Corporation Limited (Can. 1970)
June 8, 1973 – Name changed to Commerce Capital Corp. Ltd.; basis 1 new for 4 old shs. ■

St. Maurice Exploration Inc. (Que. 1956)
May 24, 1957 – Name changed to St. Maurice Gas Inc. ■

St. Maurice Gas Inc. (Que. 1956)
Jan. 1, 1971 – St. Maurice Capital Corp. purchased all assets in consideration for assumption of all liabs. and 2,015,150 com. shs. of St. Maurice Capital (1 for 1).
1971 – Charter surrendered.

St. Maurice Gold Mines Ltd. (Ont. 1944)
1954 – Charter cancelled.

St. Michael Uranium Mines Ltd. (Ont. 1953)
1958 – Merged into Cadamet Mines Ltd.; basis 1 new for 4 old shs.

St-Moritz Capital Inc. (Can. Mar. 11, 2004)
July 18, 2005 – Name changed to Medical Intelligence Technologies Inc. following Qualifying Transaction acquisition of Medical Intelligence inc.; basis 1 new for 1 old sh. (see FPsurvey - Industrials)

St. Philips Resources Inc. (B.C. Oct. 3, 1980)
Jan. 15, 1996 – All o/s com. shs. acquired by Royal Oak Mines Inc.; basis $3.40 per sh. Subsequently dissolved effective Dec. 16, 1997. (see Royal Oak Mines Inc.)

St. Pierre Uranium Mines Limited (Ont. 1967)
Oct. 15, 1994 – Dissolved.

St. Regis Lead Mines Ltd. (Ont. 1949)
1956 – Charter cancelled.

St. Roberts Metals Corp. (Que. 1951)
Oct. 1974 – Charter cancelled.

St. Simeon Uranium Corp. (Que. 1950)
July 1956 – Name changed to Consolidated St. Simeon Mines Ltd.; basis 1 new for 4 old shs. ■

St. Stephen Nickel Mines Ltd. (N.B. 1957)
1968 – Charter cancelled.

Saintstar Ventures Inc. (B.C. Mar. 28, 2003)
Oct. 7, 2005 – Acquired by Petrostar Petroleum Corporation via private placement of 2,500,000 units; basis 0.676 new Petrostar units for 1 old Saintstar com. sh. (see Petrostar Petroleum Corporation)

Saiwa Resources Ltd. (B.C. 1969)
Jan. 11, 1974 – Name changed to Granger Petroleum Corporation. ■

Sakami Lake Explorations Ltd. (Ont. 1965)
1968 – Merged into Sakfield Mines & Investments Ltd.; basis 1 new for 3 old shs.

Sakfield Mines & Investments Ltd. (Ont. 1968)
July 27, 1976 – Charter cancelled.

Sakinaw Lake Copper & Iron Mining Ltd. (Ont. 1950)
Feb. 1958 – Charter cancelled.

Sakura Bank (Canada) (Can. Apr. 1, 1990 amalg.)
June 25, 2001 – Name changed to Sumitomo Mitsui Banking Corporation of Canada; basis 6 new for 1 old sh.

Salada Foods Ltd. (Can. 1927)
1974 – Name changed to Kellogg Salada Canada Ltd. ■

Salada-Shirriff-Horsey Ltd. (Can. 1927)
Jan. 1962 – Name changed to Salada Foods Ltd. ■

Salal Molybdenum Mines Limited (Ont. 1965)
July 12, 1982 – Charter cancelled.

Salamet Mines Ltd. (Ont. 1955)
Feb. 5, 1980 – Dissolved.

Salares Lithium Inc. (B.C. Apr. 12, 2000)
Sept. 23, 2010 – Acquired by Talison Lithium Limited; basis 0.35587 Talison ord. shs. for 1 Salares Lithium com. sh. (see Talison Lithium Limited)

Salem Exploration Ltd. (Que. 1947)
1966 – Acquired by Agena Mining Co. Ltd. (see Agena Mining Co. Ltd.)

Salem Mines Ltd. (B.C. 1969)
May 18, 1972 – Amalgamated with Bright Star Trio Mining Ltd. to form a new co. also named Salem Mines Ltd.

Salem Mines Ltd. (B.C. 1972 amalg.)
Sept. 1973 – Name changed to Salem Resources Ltd. ■

Salem Resources Ltd. (B.C. 1972 amalg.)
Nov. 1979 – Charter cancelled.

Sales Initiatives International Inc. (Ont. 1975)
June 15, 1994 – Name changed to Greenlight Communications Inc. (see FPsurvey - Industrials)

Salida Wealth Preservation (Listed) Fund (Ont. Mar. 30, 2011)
Apr. 30, 2013 – Terminated; final distribution was $6.596 per unit.

Salish Ventures Inc. (B.C. May 3, 1999)
Apr. 9, 2003 – Name changed to Primary Metals Inc. pursuant to Qualifying Transaction reverse takeover acquisition of Avocet Mining Canada Inc. together with certain loans from Avocet Mining plc. ■

Salix Holdings, Ltd. (British Virgin Islands Dec. 24, 1993)
Mar. 25, 1998 – Name changed to Salix Pharmaceuticals, Ltd. ■

Salix Pharmaceuticals, Ltd. (British Virgin Islands Dec. 24, 1993)
Dec. 31, 2001 – Continued into Delaware.

Sally Mines Ltd. (B.C. 1925)
1946 – Acquired by Highland-Bell Ltd.; basis 1 new for 4 old shs. (see Highland-Bell Ltd.)

Salmita Consolidated Mines Ltd. (Ont. 1945)
1954 – Assets acquired by Mack Lake Mining Corp. Ltd.; basis 1 new Mack pref. sh. for 1 old Salmita pref. sh. and 1 new Mack com. sh. for 5 old Salmita com. shs. (see Mack Lake Mining Corp. Ltd.)

Salmita Northwest Mines Ltd. (Ont. 1945)
Dec. 30, 1949 – Name changed to Salmita Consolidated Mines Ltd.; basis 1 new for 5 old shs. ■

Salmo Malartic Mines Ltd. (Ont. 1927)
May 1969 – Charter cancelled.

Salmo Prince Mines Ltd. (B.C. 1951)
May 15, 1969 – Struck off register.

Salmon Gold Mines Ltd. (B.C. June 27, 1933)
1945 – Acquired by Morris Summit Gold Mines Ltd.; basis 1 new for 3 old shs. (see Morris Summit Gold Mines Ltd.)

Salmon River Resources Ltd. (B.C. June 29, 2005)
Dec. 14, 2015 – Dissolved and struck from register.

Salon Resources Corp. (B.C. Mar. 28, 1980)
Sept. 23, 1987 – Name changed to Corptech Industries Inc. pursuant to reverse takeover acquisition of Life Force International Inc. ■

Salona Global Medical Device Corporation (B.C. July 7, 2010)
Jan. 22, 2024 – Name changed to Evome Medical Technologies Inc. (see FPsurvey - Industrials)

Salter Street Films Limited (N.S. Mar. 15, 1983)
Apr. 23, 2001 – Acquired by Alliance Atlantis Communications Inc.; basis either $3.33 plus 0.310 new Alliance cl. B shs., or 0.465 new Alliance cl. B shs for 1 old Salter Street sh. (see Alliance Atlantis Communications Inc.)

Salus Resource Corp. (B.C. Mar. 16, 1966)
Dec. 4, 1996 – Name changed to Brandon Gold Corporation. ■

Salvex Resources Ltd. (B.C. July 25, 1984)
Dec. 23, 1988 – Name changed to Brasil Gold Resources Ltd. ■

Sama Graphite Inc. (Can. Apr. 16, 1996)
June 30, 2017 – Name changed to SRG Graphite Inc. ■

Sama Resources Inc. (B.C. July 11, 2006)
May 13, 2013 – Continued into Canada. (see FPsurvey - Mines & Energy)

Samar Yellowknife Gold Mines Ltd. (Ont. 1945)
Dec. 1950 – Name changed to Oakridge Uranium Mines Ltd. ■

Samaranta Mining Corporation (B.C. May 20, 2011 amalg.)
Oct. 28, 2013 – Name changed to Icon Exploration Inc.; basis 1 new for 5 old shs. ■

Samarkand Resources Inc. (B.C. Apr. 11, 1986)
Apr. 5, 1990 – Name changed to Consolidated Samarkand Resources Inc.; basis 1 new for 2 old shs. ■

Samba Gold Inc. (B.C. Aug. 8, 1988 amalg.)
Feb. 26, 2009 – Name changed to Caerus Resource Corporation; basis 1 new for 6 old shs. ■

Samena Resources Corp. (Alta. Jan. 21, 1997)
July 2, 2014 – Dissolved and struck from register.

Samex Mining Corp. (B.C. Dec. 15, 1967)
July 27, 2015 – Dissolved and struck from register.

Samia Ventures Inc. (B.C. Apr. 9, 1980)
Mar. 2, 1998 – Delisted from the Vancouver Stock Exchange. Subsequently dissolved for failure to file and struck from register.

Samos Resources Ltd. (B.C. 1984)
Sept. 7, 1990 – Name changed to Dimples Group Inc. (see FPsurvey - Industrials)

Samoth Capital Corporation (Ont. Sept. 7, 1944)
June 14, 2000 – Name changed to Sterling Financial Corporation. ■

Samoth Oilfield Inc. (Alta. May 8, 2006)
Dec. 12, 2022 – Name changed to Lycos Energy Inc. pursuant to the reverse takeover acquisition of Chronos Resources Ltd.; basis 1 new for 8 old shs. (see FPsurvey - Mines & Energy)

Sams Online Inc. (Ont. Oct. 3, 2000 amalg.)
Jan. 28, 2002 – Name changed to Thistletown Capital Inc.; basis 1 new for 7 old shs. ■

Samson Energy Corporation (B.C. 1967)
Aug. 22, 1982 – Formed Kala Exploration Ltd. in Alberta on amalgamation with Golex Resources Ltd. (1 cl. A com. for either 5 pref. shs. or 5.743 com. shs.) effective Aug. 22, 1982; basis 1 new cl. A for 5 old com. shs. ■

Samson Gold Corporation (B.C. Mar. 8, 1971)
Sept. 21, 1989 – Name changed to Kinghorn Energy Corporation. ■

Samson Healthcare Corp. (Alta. Jan. 21, 1997)
Sept. 28, 2007 – Name changed to Samena Resources Corp. ■

Samson Mines Ltd. (B.C. 1963)
Oct. 30, 1972 – Name changed to Anglo-Pacific Explorations Ltd.; basis 1 new for 5 old shs. ■

Samson Mining Corp. (Alta. 1953)
1954 – Name changed to Elrock Mining Corp. ■

Samson Technologies Inc. (Alta. Jan. 21, 1997)
Jan. 14, 1998 – Name changed to Samson Healthcare Corp. pursuant to Major Transaction acquisition and subsequent amalgamation with Samson Wheelchair Manufacturing Ltd. ■

Samteit Store Fixtures and Refrigeration Limited (unknown)
May 1969 – Acquired by Intermetco Limited. (see Intermetco Limited)

Samuel Manu-Tech Inc. (Ont. Aug. 30, 1985 amalg.)
Sept. 14, 2010 – Privatized at $7.50 per sh.

Samurai Capital Corp. (B.C. Aug. 1, 2008)
Jan. 21, 2011 – Name changed to Huaxing Machinery Corp. pursuant to Qualifying Transaction reverse takeover acquisition of Gold Rhino Limited. ■

San Andreas Resources Corporation (B.C. Dec. 16, 1965)
June 2, 1999 – Name changed to Canadian Zinc Corporation. ■

San Angelo Oil Limited (B.C. Feb. 11, 2014)
Nov. 2, 2017 – Name changed to Cabral Gold Inc. pursuant to reverse takeover amalgamation of wholly owned 1116669 B.C. Ltd. with Cabral Gold Ltd. (deemed acquiror); basis 1 new for 5 old shs. (see FPsurvey - Mines & Energy)

San Anton Capital Inc. (Can. Apr. 1, 2005)
May 14, 2010 – Name changed to Edleun Group, Inc. pursuant to Qualifying Transaction amalgamation of Edleun, Inc. (the deemed acquiror) with a wholly owned subsidiary of San Anton; basis 1 new for 2 old shs. ■

San Anton Resource Corporation (Can. Dec. 6, 2006 amalg.)
Sept. 29, 2010 – Acquired by Kings Minerals NL by way of amalgamation with a wholly owned subsid. of Kings Minerals Inc.; basis 2.5 Kings com. shs. for 1 San Anton com. sh. (see Kings Minerals NL)

San Antonio Explorations Ltd. (B.C. 1977)
1987 – Acquired by Wellore Resources Ltd. for 7,413,006 Wellore shs.

San Antonio Gold Mines Ltd. (Man. 1931)
1971 – Dissolved.

San Antonio Ventures Inc. (B.C. June 9, 2010)
Sept. 12, 2014 – Name changed to Renaissance Oil Corp. following reverse takeover acquisition of R2 Energy Ltd.; basis 1 new for 2 old shs. ■

San Doh Mines Ltd. (B.C. 1964)
Oct. 16, 1970 – Name changed to Fourbar Mines Ltd.; basis 1 new for 4 old shs. ■

San Fernando Mining Company Ltd. (B.C. June 12, 1987)
May 25, 1998 – Continued into Canada.
June 25, 1998 – Name changed to KeyWest Energy Corporation. ■

Les Boutiques San Francisco Incorporées (Can. July 24, 1978)
Aug. 5, 2004 – Name changed to Groupe Les Ailes de la Mode Inc. following emergence from Companies' Creditors Arrangement Act protection and redesignation of cl. B subord. vtg. shs. as com. shs.; basis 1 new for 4 old shs. ■

San Gold Corporation (Man. June 30, 2005 amalg.)
June 22, 2015 – Made an assignment into bankruptcy. All officers and directors resigned. MNP Ltd. appointed trustee.

San Gold Resources Corporation (Man. Jan. 7, 1997)
June 30, 2005 – Formed San Gold Corporation in Manitoba on amalgamation with Gold City Industries Ltd. with San Gold the deemed acquiror; basis 1 new for 1.9321346 Gold City shs. and 1 new for 1 San Gold sh. ■

San Jacinto Explorations Ltd. (B.C. 1965)
Mar. 1980 – Name changed to Canbec Resources Ltd.; basis 1 new for 5 old shs. (see FPsurvey - Mines & Energy)

San Judas Molybdenum Corp. Ltd. (Ont. 1967)
July 9, 1982 – Name changed to Jedburgh Resources Limited and continued into Canada; basis 1 new for 2 old shs. ■

San-Mar Environmental Corp. (Can. Dec. 29, 1982)
Oct. 2, 1998 – Name changed to Pure Zinc Technologies Inc.; basis 1 new for 3 old shs. ■

San Marco Resources Inc. (B.C. Sept. 27, 2005)
Nov. 2, 2020 – Name changed to Sun Summit Minerals Corp. (see FPsurvey - Mines & Energy)

San Oro Mines Ltd. (Man. 1946)
1951 – Charter cancelled.

San Paulo Explorations Inc. (Ont. Aug. 9, 1983)
Jan. 4, 1999 – Name changed to AdvanteXCEL.com Communications Corp. following reverse takeover acquisition of XCEL Communications (USA) Corporation; basis 1 new for 8 old shs. ■

San Pedro Mining Corp. Ltd. (Ont. 1944)
1955 – Charter cancelled.

San Rafael Resources Ltd. (B.C. Feb. 18, 1966)
June 28, 1984 – Name changed to Rafael Resources Ltd.; basis 1 new for 5 old shs. ■

San-Rive Mines Ltd. (Ont. 1946)
Apr. 10, 1955 – Dissolved.

San Telmo Energy Ltd. (B.C. Oct. 7, 1996)
Jan. 16, 2006 – Plan of Arrangement amalgamation with Rolling Thunder Exploration Ltd. (1 for 1) to continue as Rolling Thunder Exploration Ltd.; basis either $0.60, or 0.5 new Rolling Thunder cl. A sh., or a combination thereof for 1 old San Telmo com. sh. (see Rolling Thunder Exploration Ltd.)

San Telmo Resources Ltd. (B.C. Oct. 7, 1996)
Aug. 15, 2002 – Name changed to San Telmo Energy Ltd.; basis 1 new for 7 old shs. ■

Sanatana Diamonds Inc. (B.C. June 25, 2004)
May 2, 2011 – Name changed to Sanatana Resources Inc. (see FPsurvey - Mines & Energy)

Sancono Ventures Inc. (B.C. Oct. 20, 1986)
Feb. 1, 1989 – Name changed to Nu-Media Industries International Inc. ■

Sanction Capital Corp. (Alta. May 11, 2011)
Sept. 24, 2014 – Name changed to Marsa Energy Inc. following Qualifying Transaction reverse takeover of and amalgamation with (old) Marsa Energy Inc. (deemed acquiror). ■

Sanctuary Woods Multimedia Corporation (B.C. Apr. 15, 1991)
Apr. 15, 1997 – Continued into Delaware.

Sand Lake Gold Mines Ltd. (Ont. 1944)
June 23, 1952 – Charter surrendered.

Sand River Gold Mining Co. Ltd. (Ont. 1935)
1964 – Name changed to Sarimco Mines Ltd.; basis 1 new for 5 old shs. ■

Sand River Resources Ltd. (B.C. Apr. 24, 1987)
Dec. 1, 1999 – Name changed to Rio Fortuna Exploration Corp.; basis 1 new for 7 old shs. ■

Sand Technology Inc. (Can. Dec. 10, 1982)
Nov. 15, 2013 – Acquired by N. Harris Computer Corporation, a wholly owned subsid. of Constellation Software Inc.; basis $0.066 cash per sh. ■

Sand Technology Systems International Inc. (Can. Dec. 10, 1982)
Jan. 1, 2000 – Name changed to Sand Technology Inc. ■

Sandbox Royalties Corp. (B.C. Oct. 21, 2011)
June 30, 2022 – Continued into British Columbia.
June 5, 2024 – Name changed to Versamet Royalties Corporation. (see FPsurvey - Mines & Energy)

Sandcherry Mines Limited (Ont. 1961)
Jan. 18, 1995 – Dissolved.

Sandenise Gold Mines Ltd. (Ont. 1944)
Nov. 19, 1956 – Dissolved.

Sanderson Technologies Inc. (B.C. May 28, 1980)
Feb. 15, 1990 – Name changed to Levi Developments Inc.; basis 1 new for 4 old shs. ■

Sandhurst Mines Ltd. (Ont. 1975 amalg.)
Jan. 23, 1979 – Amalgamated with Glenshire Mines Ltd. (231 for 1,000), Huddersfield Uranium Mines Ltd. (129 for 1,000), Kayak Explorations Ltd. (195 for 1,000), La France Explorations Ltd. (128 for 1,000), Lunel Management Ltd. (923.5 for 1) and Steppingstone Explorations Ltd. (229 for 1,000) to form Lunel Enterprises Inc.; basis 1 new for 1 old sh. (see Lunel Enterprises Inc.)

Sandhurst Resources Limited (B.C. Sept. 21, 1987)
Mar. 5, 2003 – Dissolved and subsequently restored to register. (see FPsurvey - Mines & Energy)

Sandoil Recovery Corporation (Alta. July 3, 1998)
Jan. 2, 2004 – Struck from registry and dissolved.

Sandon Silver Lead Mining Co. Ltd. (Wash. 1925)
Nov. 1949 – Struck off register.

Sandpiper Oil & Gas Limited (B.C. 1981)
Sept. 11, 1990 – Name changed to Pax Petroleum Ltd.; basis 1 new for 10 old shs. ■

Sandpoint Capital Inc. (B.C. Sept. 6, 2006)
Oct. 22, 2008 – Formed Swift Power Corp. in British Columbia on Qualifying Transaction amalgamation with Swift Power Corp., with Swift Power the deemed acquiror. ■

Sands Minerals Corporation (B.C. June 18, 1975)
Jan. 25, 1988 – Name changed to Michele Gold Mines Ltd. ■

Sands Petroleum AB (Sweden June 16, 1987)
Apr. 3, 1998 – Name changed to Lundin Oil AB.

Sands Petroleum Inc. (B.C. 1979)
July 15, 1980 – Name changed to Oxford Resources Limited. ■

Sandspring Resources Ltd. (Alta. Sept. 20, 2006)
Mar. 31, 2010 – Continued into Ontario.
Nov. 29, 2019 – Continued into British Columbia.
Dec. 2, 2019 – Name changed to Gold X Mining Corp.; basis 1 new for 8 old shs. ■

Sandstorm Metals & Energy Ltd. (B.C. Jan. 4, 2010)
June 2, 2014 – Acquired by Sandstorm Gold Ltd.; basis 35¢ cash plus 0.178 Sandstorm Gold sh. for 1 old Sandstorm Metals sh.

Sandstorm Resources Ltd. (B.C. Mar. 23, 2007)
Feb. 17, 2011 – Name changed to Sandstorm Gold Ltd. (see FPsurvey - Mines & Energy)

Sandvine Corporation (Ont. Feb. 16, 2006)
Sept. 25, 2017 – Acquired by PNI Canada Acquireco Corp., an affiliate of Francisco Partners LP and Procera Networks, Inc.; basis Cdn$4.40 cash per sh.

Sandwell and Company Limited (B.C. Aug. 20, 1958)
May 8, 1986 – Name changed to Sandwell Swan Wooster Inc. ■

Sandwell Mining Ltd. (B.C. Dec. 12, 2000)
Dec. 24, 2009 – Name changed to MBAC Fertilizer Corp. and continued into Canada pursuant to reverse takeover amalgamation of wholly owned 7272511 Canada Inc. with MBAC Opportunities & Financing Inc.; basis 1 new for 15 old shs. ■

Sandwell Swan Wooster Inc. (B.C. Aug. 20, 1958)
Dec. 5, 1989 – Formed Sandwell Inc. following acquisition of all o/s shs. by Electrowatt Ltd.; basis $40 per sh.

Sandy Cay Resources Inc. (Ont. Nov. 28, 1983)
July 2, 1987 – Name changed to Advance Environmental International Inc. ■

Sandy Lake Explorations Ltd. (Ont. Nov. 9, 1989)
June 4, 1993 – Name changed to Lake Capital Corp.; basis 1 new for 5 old shs. ■

Sandy Lake Gold Inc. (Can. May 21, 2009)
Apr. 8, 2019 – Name changed to G2 Goldfields Inc.; basis 1 new for 2 old shs. (see FPsurvey - Mines & Energy)

Sanelli Contracting Co. Ltd. (Ont. 1957)
Apr. 1969 – Name changed to Sanelli Pools Ltd. ■

Sanelli Pools Ltd. (Ont. 1957)
Dec. 1982 – Dissolved.

Sanfred Resources Ltd. (B.C. Jan. 18, 1980)
Dec. 21, 1999 – Name changed to Falcon Oil & Gas Ltd.; basis 1 new for 5 old shs. (see FPsurvey - Mines & Energy)

Sangamo Company Limited (Can. 1913)
1977 – Acquired by Schlumberger Canada Ltd. for $68 per sh.

Sangold Mines Ltd. (Ont. 1943)
1957 – Charter cancelled.

Sangoma.com Inc. (Ont. Apr. 20, 2000)
Oct. 18, 2001 – Name changed to Sangoma Technologies Corporation. (see FPsurvey - Industrials)

Sanhill Explorations & Development Ltd. (Ont. 1972)
Aug. 17, 1973 – Merged into Consolidated Midvale Explorations Ltd.; basis 1 new for 12 old shs.

Sani-Gestion Inc. (Que. July 20, 1973)
June 10, 1999 – Acquired by 9069-8903 Quebec inc., an indirect subsid. of Vivendi S.A., for $9.84 per sh.

Sanilogical Industries Ltd. (B.C. Mar. 22, 1972)
Nov. 25, 1983 – Charter cancelled.
Apr. 28, 1986 – Charter revived.
July 5, 1988 – Name changed to Encom Environmental & Communications Systems Ltd.; basis 1 new for 2 old shs. ■

Sanita Goldmines Ltd. (Ont. 1944)
Sept. 9, 1958 – Charter cancelled.

Sanivan Group Inc. (Can. 1976)
Dec. 20, 1990 – Acquired by CET Acquisitions Inc. for $4.75 per sh.

Sannorm Mines Ltd. (Ont. 1944)
1952 – Name changed to Consolidated Sannorm Mines Ltd.; basis 1 new for 2 old shs. ■

Sanreta Oil & Gas Resources Ltd. (Ont. 1981)
Nov. 14, 1985 – Amalgamated with 6 other cos. to form Paladin Petroleum Corporation; basis 4 new for 10 old shs.

Sanshaw Mines Ltd. (Ont. 1936)
1944 – Assets acquired by Orlac Red Lake Mines; basis 1 new for 4 old shs.

Santa Barbara Resources Limited (B.C. Mar. 20, 2007)
Dec. 23, 2015 – Voluntarily dissolved.

Santa Barbara Ventures Ltd. (B.C. June 15, 1984)
June 9, 1994 – Name changed to Voodoo Ventures Ltd. ■

Santa Catalina Mining Corp. (Can. Oct. 25, 1994)
Apr. 25, 2002 – Name changed to Valkyries Petroleum Corp.; basis 1 new for 15 old shs. ■

Santa Cruz Gold Inc. (Ont. Mar. 26, 1990)
Sept. 17, 1997 – Amalgamated with Newmex Mining Company Ltd. to form a new co. also known as Santa Cruz Gold Inc.; basis 1 new for 1 old sh. (see Santa Cruz Gold Inc.)

Santa Cruz Gold Inc. (Ont. Sept. 18, 1997 amalg.)
July 23, 1999 – Amalgamated with Queenstake Resources Limited (0.4993 for 1) to form a new company also named Queenstake Resources Ltd.; basis 0.1035 new Queenstake sh. for 1 old Santa Cruz sh. (see Queenstake Resources Ltd.)

Santa Cruz Ventures Inc. (B.C. Sept. 14, 1964)
Jan. 23, 2007 – Name changed to Lignol Energy Corporation following amalgamation of Lignol Innovations Corporation with a wholly owned subsid. of Santa Cruz to form Lignol Innovations Ltd. ■

Santa Elina Gold Corporation (British Virgin Islands Apr. 17, 1990)
July 19, 1996 – Merged with a subsid. of Echo Bay Mines Ltd.; basis 1 new Echo Bay sh. for 6.67 old Santa Elina shs. (see Echo Bay Mines Ltd.)

Santa Fe Energy Group Inc. (Alta. 1987)
June 29, 1992 – Name changed to European Technologies International Inc. ■

Santa Fe Gold Mines Ltd. (Ont. Nov. 4, 1936)
Apr. 1968 – Charter cancelled.

Santa Fe Metals Corporation (B.C. Apr. 27, 2006)
Feb. 16, 2021 – Name changed to Wintertide Ventures Inc. ■

Santa Helena Mining Ltd. (Que. 1970)
May 25, 1985 – Charter cancelled.

Santa Maria Mines Limited (Ont. Nov. 23, 1945)
June 13, 1980 – Name changed to Santa Maria
Resources Limited. ■

Santa Maria Petroleum Inc. (Ont. Oct. 15, 2004)
Dec. 30, 2016 – Name changed to Kalytera Therapeutics,
Inc. and continued into British Columbia following reverse
takeover acquisition of (old) Kalytera Therapeutics, Inc.;
basis 1 new for 2.3 old shs. ■

Santa Maria Resources Limited (Ont. Nov. 23, 1945)
June 4, 1990 – Name changed to Simax Oil & Gas Inc.;
basis 1 new for 10 old shs. ■

Santa Marina Gold Ltd. (Ont. 1985)
Jan. 16, 1991 – Amalgamated with Akiko-Lori Gold
Resources Ltd. (1 for 1) to form a new company also
named Akiko-Lori Resources Ltd.; basis 1 new for 9 old
shs. (see Akiko-Lori Gold Resources Ltd.)

Santa Rita Explorations Ltd. (Ont. 1972)
Apr. 1978 – Amalgamated with Lumsden Building Corp.
Inc. and others under the Lumsden name; basis 1 new
for 21 old shs.

Santa Sarita Mining Company Limited (B.C. 1972)
Aug. 28, 1989 – Name changed to Solid Gold Capital
Corp.; basis 1 new for 4 old shs. ■

Santana International Resources Ltd. (N.P.L.) (B.C.
1970)
Nov. 15, 1972 – Amalgamated with The Taylor-Windfall
Gold Mining Company Limited to form Taywin Resources
Ltd. (N.P.L.).

Santana Petroleum Corp. (B.C. Dec. 4, 1970)
Oct. 21, 1985 – Name changed to International Santana
Resources Inc.; basis 1 new for 4 old shs. ■

Santana Resources Corporation (Alta. 1986)
Jan. 31, 1989 – Name changed to Santana Technology
Corporation. ■

Santana Technology Corporation (Alta. 1986)
Oct. 27, 1993 – Formed Beta Brands Incorporated on
amalgamation with 1041695 Ontario Inc.; basis 1 new
for 5 old shs. ■

Santander Consumer Inc. (Alta. Sept. 28, 2011)
June 11, 2024 – Continued into Canada.
Mar. 5, 2025 – Name changed to Santander Consumer
Bank, Canada.

Santa's Village Limited (Ont. Jan. 1, 1954)
Apr. 28, 2004 – Name changed to SVL Holdings Inc. (see
FPsurvey - Industrials)

Santé Veritas Holdings Inc. (Can. Sept. 4, 2008)
Nov. 5, 2018 – Continued into British Columbia.
Dec. 6, 2018 – Acquired by TILT Holdings Inc.; basis
0.1399 TILT com. shs. for 1 Sante Veritas sh.

Santiago Capital Corp. (B.C. Mar. 30, 1983)
Apr. 4, 1990 – Name changed to Fresh Ideas Food
Corporation; basis 1 new for 2 old shs. ■

Santiago Mines Ltd. (B.C. 1935)
Feb. 1951 – Name changed to New Santiago Mines Ltd.;
basis 1 new for 4 old shs. ■

Santico Mining & Exploration Ltd. (B.C. 1935)
Dec. 18, 1978 – Dissolved.

De Santis Porcupine Mines Ltd. (Ont. May 21, 1928)
Sept. 1961 – Acquired by New Hope Porcupine Gold
Mines Ltd.; basis 1 new for 5 old shs.

Santonia Energy Inc. (Alta. Dec. 19, 2007 amalg.)
Apr. 30, 2014 – Acquired by Tourmaline Oil Corp.; basis
0.03012 Tourmaline com. shs. for 1 Santonia com. sh.

Santos Silver Mines Ltd. (Ont. 1954)
1964 – Acquired by Utica Mines Ltd.; basis 1 new for 6
od shs. (see Utica Mines Ltd.)

Santoy Resources Ltd. (Alta. May 25, 1993)
Apr. 25, 2003 – Amalgamated with Troymin Resources
Ltd. (1.65 for 1) to continue as Santoy Resources Ltd.;
basis 1 new for 1 old Santoy sh. (see Santoy Resources
Ltd.)

Santoy Resources Ltd. (Alta. Apr. 24, 2003 amalg.)
May 21, 2009 – Continued into British Columbia.
July 24, 2009 – Name changed to Virginia Energy
Resources Inc.; basis 1 new for 5 old shs. ■

Sanu Resources Ltd. (Can. Mar. 5, 2004)
Aug. 28, 2009 – Acquired by Canadian Gold Hunter Corp.;
0.5725 Canadian Gold Hunter shares for 1 share.

Sanwa Bank Canada (Can. 1983)
Nov. 30, 2001 – Formed UFJ Bank Canada on
amalgamation with Tokai Bank Canada.

Sanymac Mining & Development Co. Ltd. (Ont. 1937)
Apr. 29, 1954 – Charter cancelled.

Sapawe Gold Mines Limited (Ont. 1955)
Oct. 1, 1994 – Dissolved and struck off register.

Sapphire Petroleums Limited (Ont. 1951)
1962 – Name changed to Cabol Enterprises Ltd.; basis
1 new for 10 old shs. ■

Saputo Group Inc. (Can. July 1, 1992 amalg.)
Oct. 19, 2000 – Name changed to Saputo Inc. (see
FPsurvey - Industrials)

Sarabat Gold Corporation (B.C. Apr. 28, 1988)
Dec. 3, 1996 – Name changed to Consolidated Sarabat
Gold Corporation; basis 1 new for 5 old shs. ■

Sarafand Developments Ltd. (B.C. 1972)
June 14, 1978 – Name changed to Val d'Or Explorations
Ltd.; basis 1 new for 4 old shs. ■

Saranac Resources Ltd. (Can. - unspecified)
Mar. 2, 1992 – Amalgamated with Concentrated Rare
Earth Minerals Ltd., Enertex Developments Inc. (1 for
12.6), Goldmac Explorations Inc. (1 for 17.5), Norlode
Resources Inc., Offset Natural Resources Ltd. (1 for 11),
Preston Resources Ltd. and Uranex Resources Limited
(1 for 13.5) to form a new co. named Marvas
Developments Ltd.

Saranac Uranium Mines Ltd. (Ont. 1955)
Sept. 28, 1964 – Charter cancelled.

Saratoga Capital Corp. (Ont. Mar. 5, 1937)
Oct. 13, 2000 – Delisted from the Canadian Dealing
Network. Subsequently struck from register and dissolved.

Saratoga Electronic Solutions Inc. (Can. Mar. 31, 1995)
May 4, 2015 – Name changed to Abba Medix Group Inc.
following reverse takeover acquisition of Abba Medix
Corp. ■

Saratoga Exploration Co. (Ont. 1947)
May 1956 – Name changed to Landmark Mines Ltd.;
basis 1 new (pooled) for 10 old shs. ■

Saratoga Processing Company Limited (Alta. 1960)
Sept. 30, 1993 – Acquired by 172173 Canada Inc., a
wholly owned subsid. of Morrison Petroleum Ltd., for $23
per cl. A and cl. B shs.

Sarcee Oil & Development Co. Ltd. (Alta. May 9, 1928)
1936 – Taken over by Highwood-Sarcee Oils Ltd.; basis
1 new for 2 old shs. (see Highwood-Sarcee Oils Ltd.)

Sarcee Petroleums Ltd. (Alta. 1951)
1964 – Acquired by Husky Oil Ltd. for $2.30 per sh. (see
Husky Oil Canada Ltd.)

Sargasso Capital Corporation (Ont. July 30, 2008)
May 18, 2011 – Name changed to C2C Industrial
Properties Inc. pursuant to Qualifying Transaction
acquisition of C2C Industrial Properties Ltd. ■

Sargold Resource Corporation (B.C. May 25, 1998)
Oct. 31, 2007 – Acquired by Buffalo Gold Ltd.; basis 1
Buffalo sh. for 3.5 Sargold shs. (see Buffalo Gold Ltd.)

Sargon Resources Ltd. (B.C. Mar. 5, 1981)
July 10, 1996 – Name changed to International Sargon
Resources Ltd.; basis 1 new for 5 old shs. ■

Sarimco Mines Ltd. (Ont. 1935)
Mar. 1976 – Charter cancelled.

Sarment Holding Limited (Singapore Jan. 24, 2018)
Sept. 26, 2019 – Name changed to SAIS Limited.

Sarnia Bridge Company, Limited (Can. 1928)
1958 – Acquired by The Anthes-Imperial Company
Limited; basis $11 and 0.3 new Anthes sh. for 1 old Sarnia
Bridge sh. (see The Anthes-Imperial Company Limited)

Sarnia Oil & Gas Co. Ltd. (Ont. Nov. 11, 1920)
Struck off register.

Sarnoil Limited (Ont. 1960)
Aug. 9, 1972 – Charter cancelled July 5, 1972; co.
dissolved.

Sarpedon Iron Mines (Ont. 1943)
Dec. 1952 – Wound up. Distributed equivalent of 2 shs.
Head of the Lakes Iron Ltd. plus 5¢ cash for 1 old
Sarpedon sh. (see Head of the Lakes Iron Ltd.)

Sartigan Granite Corporation (Can. Oct. 27, 1986)
Aug. 10, 1993 – Name changed to Startigan Corporation;
basis 1 new for 5 old shs. ■

Sartis Medical Systems Canada Inc. (B.C. July 29,
1981)
Dec. 5, 1995 – Name changed to United Sartis
Enterprises Inc.; basis 1 new for 5 old shs. ■

Sasamat Capital Corporation (Can. Feb. 26, 1990)
May 29, 2007 – Acquired by KHD Humboldt Wedag
International Ltd. for issuance of 645,188 common shares.

Sasha Technologies Ltd. (Can. Mar. 9, 1987)
July 26, 1988 – Name changed to Sasha Technology
Systems Ltd.; basis 1 new for 3 old shs. ■

Sasha Technology Systems Ltd. (Can. Mar. 9, 1987)
Sept. 15, 1993 – Name changed to Consolidated Sasha
Technology Ltd. ■

Sasha Ventures Ltd. (B.C. Aug. 4, 1992)
Oct. 24, 2000 – Name changed to eShippers.com
Management Ltd. following acquisition of eShippers.com
Inc.; basis 1 new for 2.2 old shs. ■

Saskalon Uranium & Oils Limited (Ont. 1945)
Nov. 6, 1961 – Dissolved.

The Saskatchewan Loan and Investment Co. Ltd.
(Sask. 1912)
July 1, 1970 – Name changed to Saskatchewan Trust
and Loan Co. ■

Saskatchewan Mining Development Corporation
(Sask. 1974)
Oct. 5, 1988 – Amalgamated with Eldorado Nuclear
Limited to form Cameco - A Canadian Mining & Energy
Corporation. (see Cameco - A Canadian Mining & Energy
Corporation)

Saskatchewan Oil and Gas Corporation (Sask. Jan.
28, 1973)
Nov. 26, 1993 – Name changed to Wascana Energy
Inc. ■

Saskatchewan Trust and Loan Co. (Sask. 1912)
1980 – Name changed to Saskatchewan Trust Company;
basis 10 new cl. A and 40 new cl. B for 1 old com. sh. ■

Saskatchewan Trust Company (Sask. 1912)
Oct. 31, 1991 – Petitioned into liquidation. Deloitte & Touche Inc. was appointed liquidator.

Saskatchewan Wheat Pool (Sask. Mar. 25, 1924)
Mar. 28, 2005 – Name changed to Saskatchewan Wheat Pool Inc.; basis 1 new for 20 old shs. ■

Saskatchewan Wheat Pool Inc. (Sask. Mar. 25, 1924)
Mar. 31, 2005 – Continued into Canada.
Mar. 13, 2008 – Name changed to Viterra Inc. ■

Sasko Holdings Ltd. (Alta. 1952)
1960 – Struck off register.

Sasko Oil & Gas Limited (Can. June 29, 1981 amalg.)
Oct. 29, 1990 – Name changed to Gentry Resources Ltd.; basis 1 new for 5 old shs. ■

Sasko-Wainwright Oil and Gas Limited (B.C. 1926)
1978 – Continued into Canada.
June 29, 1981 – Amalgamated with Marlea Exploration Company Limited, Yandel-Alta Resources Ltd. and 98947 Canada Inc. to form Sasko Oil and Gas Limited; basis 1 new for 1 old sh.

Saskoba Mines Inc. (Ont. 1971)
Mar. 1976 – Charter cancelled.

Saskoil Equipment Leasing (1988) Limited Partnership (Sask. Nov. 7, 1988)
Dec. 31, 1993 – All o/s units redeemed; basis $100 per unit.

Saskuram Explorations Inc. (Ont. Sept. 30, 1919)
Nov. 5, 1980 – Name changed to Team Energy and Minerals Inc. ■

Sassy Resources Corporation (B.C. June 3, 2019)
July 20, 2022 – Name changed to Sassy Gold Corp. (see FPsurvey - Mines & Energy)

Sastex Oil & Gas Ltd. (Alta. 1953)
Apr. 27, 1966 – Name changed to Sastex Petro-Minerals Ltd.; basis 1 new for 7 old shs. ■

Sastex Petro-Minerals Ltd. (Alta. 1953)
July 1, 1992 – Struck off register.

Sat-Tel Corporation (Alta. May 26, 1999 amalg.)
Mar. 18, 2003 – Amalgamated with IROC Systems Corp. (1 for 1) to continue as IROC Systems Corp.; basis 1 new IROC for 6 old Sat-Tel com. shs. (see IROC Systems Corp.)

Satellite Consolidated Metals Ltd. (Ont. 1953)
Aug. 15, 1986 – Amalgamated with Phoenix Gold Mines Limited to form new co. with same name Phoenix Gold Mines Limited; basis 1 new for 4 Phoenix shs. and 1 new for 1 Satellite sh. (see Phoenix Gold Mines Limited)

Satellite Metal Mines Limited (Ont. 1953)
June 23, 1983 – Name changed to Satellite Consolidated Metals Ltd.; basis 1 new for 5 old shs. ■

Satin River Mining Co. Ltd. (Ont. 1972)
July 1973 – Merged into Sloane Mining Co. Ltd.; basis 1 new for 4.9 old shs.

Satinco Mining Corporation (Ont. 1973)
May 18, 1976 – Charter cancelled.

Sativa Wellness Group Inc. (B.C. Feb. 14, 2011)
Jan. 12, 2022 – Name changed to Goodbody Health Inc. ■

Sato Stevia International Inc. (B.C. Feb. 19, 1980)
July 5, 1991 – Dissolved and struck off register.

Sator Capital Inc. (Alta. July 17, 1996)
July 22, 1998 – Name changed to LWT Services Inc. following acquisition of LWT Western Inc.; basis 1 new for 1 old sh. (see FPsurvey - Mines & Energy)

Satori Resources Inc. (B.C. Oct. 24, 2011)
May 5, 2023 – Name changed to Canadian Gold Corp. pursuant to the acquisition of Apollo Exploration Inc. (see FPsurvey - Mines & Energy)

Saturn Disq Inc. (Can. July 19, 1983)
Sept. 1, 1992 – Name changed to Saturn (Solutions) Inc. ■

Saturn Energy & Resources Ltd. (B.C. 1969)
Aug. 21, 1992 – Dissolved and struck off register.

Saturn Minerals Inc. (B.C. Aug. 16, 2001)
Jan. 17, 2017 – Name changed to Saturn Oil & Gas Inc. ■

Saturn Oil & Gas Inc. (B.C. Aug. 16, 2001)
Dec. 17, 2018 – Continued into Saskatchewan.
Jan. 3, 2025 – Continued into Alberta. (see FPsurvey - Mines & Energy)

Saturn (Solutions) Inc. (Can. July 19, 1983)
Apr. 4, 2004 – Deemed bankrupt. RSM Richter Inc. was appointed trustee.

Saturn Ventures Inc. (Alta. Mar. 9, 2000)
Aug. 21, 2003 – Qualifying Transaction amalgamation with Neptune Capital Corp. (875,000 units) and wholly owned subsid. of Vanguard Aviation Corp. (VAX); basis 425,000 VAX units for all Saturn com. shs. One VAX unit equals 1 VAX com. sh. plus 1 VAX com. sh. wt. (entitling the holder to purchase 1 VAX sh. at $0.25 for 15 mths.). (see Vanguard Aviation Corp.)

Saturnyte Gold Mines Ltd. (unknown)
Charter cancelled.

Saucon Development Corp. (Que. 1956)
1963 – Name changed to Quebec Industrial Minerals Corp. ■

The Saucy Bread Company Inc. (Alta. June 15, 1990)
Apr. 2000 – Unable to complete reverse takeover with URC Hospitality Group and the directors assigned the co. into bankruptcy. Some directors continued to provide interim working capital to fund the co. until May 15, 2000.
May 5, 2000 – Sought bankruptcy protection and RSM Richter Inc. of Calgary appointed trustee. Previously, the stores in Richmond, B.C., and in the Edmonton Centre were closed.
June 2003 – All assets sold.
June 2005 – Trustee confirmed that there were no funds available for creditors or shldrs.
Apr. 26, 2006 – Trustee discharged.

Saudi Petroleum Corp. (B.C. 1979)
Dec. 16, 1980 – Name changed to Greenwich Resources Inc. ■

Sault Meadows Resources Inc. (Ont. Sept. 6, 1983 amalg.)
Sept. 6, 1986 – Name changed to International Fitness Unlimited Centres Inc.; basis 1 new for 5 old shs. ■

Sava Yellowknife Gold Mines Ltd. (Ont.)
1953 – Charter cancelled.

Savanette Mines Ltd. (Ont. 1965)
1969 – Merged into Alchib Developments Ltd.; basis 29 new for 100 old shs.

Savanna Creek Gas & Oil Ltd. (Ont. Mar. 26, 1957)
Sept. 19, 1973 – Name changed to Savanna Resources Ltd.; basis 1 new for 10 old shs. ■

Savanna Creek Oil & Gas Ltd. (Ont. 1957)
1957 – Acquired by Savanna Creek Gas & Oil Ltd.

Savanna Energy Services Corp. (Alta. June 28, 1999)
June 26, 2017 – All o/s com. shs. not already held acquired by Total Energy Services Inc.; basis 0.1300 Total Energy shs. and 20¢ cash per sh. for 1 Savanna Energy sh.

Savanna Resources Ltd. (Ont. Mar. 26, 1957)
Feb. 25, 1980 – Continued into Alberta.
Feb. 9, 2001 – Name changed to Hansa Corporation; basis 1 new for 25 old shs. ■

Savannah Gold Corp. (B.C. Aug. 19, 1998)
May 19, 2017 – Name changed to E3 Metals Corp. pursuant to acquisition of 1975293 Alberta Ltd. (operating as E3 Metals). ■

Savannah Oils & Mines Ltd. (Ont. 1945)
1954 – Name changed to Saskalon Uranium & Oils Limited; basis 1 new for 5 old shs. ■

Savannah Ventures Ltd. (B.C. Mar. 30, 1981)
Dec. 2, 1998 – Name changed to International Savannah Ventures Ltd.; basis 1 new for 6 old shs. ■

Savanor Resources Inc. (Que. 1985)
Feb. 16, 1993 – Bankrupt; no distribution to shldrs.

Savant Explorations Ltd. (B.C. Jan. 15, 2007)
July 5, 2017 – Name changed to Blue Moon Zinc Corp. ■

Savant Mines Ltd. (Ont. 1926)
Dec. 31, 1934 – Charter cancelled.

Savard Mines Ltd. (Can. 1929)
Jan. 1941 – Dissolved.

Savary Capital Corp. (Alta. Feb. 15, 2008)
Sept. 12, 2012 – Name changed to Savary Gold Corp. and continued into British Columbia pursuant to Qualifying Transaction acquistion of Burkina Gold Corporation and amalgamation of Burkina with a wholly owned subsidiary. ■

Savary Gold Corp. (B.C. Sept. 12, 2012)
May 3, 2019 – Acquired by SEMAFO Inc.; basis 0.0336 SEMAFO com. shs. for 1 Savary com. sh. (see SEMAFO Inc.)

Save-On Automotive Industries Corporation (B.C. 1979)
Sept. 8, 1993 – Name changed to MIS Multimedia Interactive Services Inc. ■

SaveCann Solutions Inc. (B.C. Mar. 19, 2019)
Aug. 11, 2020 – Name changed to Starmet Ventures Inc. (see FPsurvey - Mines & Energy)

Savers Plus International Inc. (Alta. Aug. 22, 2000)
Apr. 30, 2007 – Name changed to Intertainment Media Inc. ■

Saville Resources Inc. (B.C. July 21, 1987)
Nov. 7, 2024 – Name changed to Future Fuels Inc. (see FPsurvey - Mines & Energy)

Savings and Investment Corporation (Que. 1960)
Jan. 1968 – Name changed to Savings and Investment Group.

Savoy Copper Mines Ltd. (Ont. 1955)
May 20, 1966 – Dissolved.

Savoy Minerals Limited (Can. Mar. 20, 1981)
June 29, 1990 – Entered bankruptcy and Arthur Anderson, Inc. of Calgary appointed receiver.
Feb. 27, 1992 – All assets sold to United Pioneer Ltd. Secured and pfd. creditors were paid but there was no distribution to shldrs.

Savoy Ventures Inc. (B.C. Nov. 7, 2011)
Jan. 15, 2018 – Name changed to Hybrid Minerals Inc. ■

Sawbill Lake Mines, Ltd. (Ont. 1943)
Oct. 1953 – Charter cancelled.

Sawhill Capital Ltd. (Alta. Oct. 21, 2005)
Sept. 22, 2008 – Name changed to Virtutone Networks Inc. ■

Sawtooth Equities Inc. (Alta. Oct. 12, 1994)
June 6, 1997 – Name changed to Sawtooth International Resources Inc.; basis 1 new for 1 old sh. ■

Sawtooth International Resources Inc. (Alta. Oct. 12, 1994)
Mar. 17, 2006 – Plan of Arrangement acquisition by TriStar Oil & Gas Ltd.; basis either $2.25, or 0.2903 new TriStar sh., or a combination of $1.125 plus 0.1452 new TriStar sh. for 1 old Sawtooth sh. (see TriStar Oil & Gas Ltd.)

Sawyer-Massey, Limited (Can. 1927)
1955 – All assets, less liabs. purchased by Bridge & Tank Co. of Canada Ltd. Company wound up and charter surrendered.

Saxon Capital Corp. (B.C. Nov. 17, 1980)
May 16, 1997 – Name changed to Saxon Gold Corp. ■

Saxon Diversified Value Trust (Ont. Oct. 30, 2002)
Jan. 4, 2005 – Name changed to Signature Diversified Value Trust. ■

Saxon Energy Services Inc. (Alta. Dec. 5, 1995)
Nov. 26, 2004 – Amalgamated in Alberta to continue with same name.
Sept. 2, 2008 – Acquired by Sword Canada Acquisition Corporation for $7.00 per sh.

Saxon Financial Inc. (Ont. Sept. 1, 1985)
Oct. 27, 2008 – Acquired by IGM Financial Inc. for $21 per sh.

Saxon Gold Corp. (B.C. Nov. 17, 1980)
Dec. 18, 2000 – Name changed to Avatar Petroleum Inc. ■

Saxon Mining Co. Ltd. (Ont. 1954)
Aug. 19, 1965 – Charter cancelled.

Saxon Oil Company Ltd. (B.C. Aug. 12, 1987)
June 6, 2014 – Liquidated for US$0.0253 per sh.

Saxon Petroleum Inc. (Alta. Aug. 10, 1988)
Aug. 12, 1998 – Acquired by Forest Oil Corporation; basis 1 Forest Oil sh. for 47 Saxon Petroleum shs.

Saxon Uranium Mines Ltd. (Ont. 1954)
July 1956 – Name changed to Saxon Mining Co. Ltd. ■

Saxony Explorations Ltd. (B.C. May 14, 1985)
Sept. 24, 2003 – Name changed to Century Mining Corporation and continued into Yukon; basis 1 new for 3 old shs. ■

Saxony Mines Ltd. (Ont. 1973)
Jan. 2, 1975 – Merged into Sandhurst Mines Ltd.; basis 1 new for 9 old shs.

Saxton Industries Ltd. (B.C. Apr. 17, 1957)
Oct. 6, 1987 – Name changed to Delbancor Industries Inc. ■

Saynor Varah Inc. (B.C. 1986 amalg.)
Jan. 18, 1991 – Amalgamated with a no. company, 172745 Canada Inc., a wholly owned subsid. of Anglo York Industries Limited; basis $0.160 per sh.

Sayvette Ltd. (Can. 1960)
Mar. 1975 – Acquired by subsid. of Loblaws Limited for $2.50 per sh.

Scaddore Gold Mines Ltd. (Ont. 1940)
1955 – Name changed to Headline Uranium Mines Ltd. ■

Scaffold Connection Corporation (B.C. Sept. 26, 1986)
1995 – Continued into Alberta.
Dec. 23, 1999 – Granted protection under the Companies' Creditors Arrangement Act.
Nov. 16, 2001 – Placed into bankruptcy. KPMG Inc. of Edmonton was appointed trustee.
June 26, 2006 – Trustee discharged. No funds available for distribution.

Scaling Capital 1 Corp. (Alta. Nov. 1, 2021)
Dec. 9, 2024 – Name changed to Matador Technologies Inc. pursuant to the Qualifying Transaction reverse takeover acquisition of Matador Gold Technologies Inc.; basis 1 new for 2.2727 old shs. (see FPsurvey - Industrials)

Scandia Mining & Exploration Ltd. (Que. June 16, 1958)
Oct. 26, 1985 – Charter cancelled. (see Comnetix Capital Corporation)

Scandinavian Gold Limited (Can. June 27, 2003)
Feb. 10, 2006 – Name changed to Scandinavian Minerals Limited. ■

Scandinavian Minerals Limited (Can. June 27, 2003)
June 24, 2008 – Acquired by FQML Scandinavia Inc., a wholly owned subsid. of First Quantum Minerals Ltd., for $9.00 plus 0.01 First Quantum com. shs. for 1 Scandinavian Minerals com. sh.

Scapa Products Limited (Ont. 1957)
Apr. 9, 1975 – Dissolved.

Scarab Resource Corporation (B.C. Oct. 31, 1983)
Nov. 29, 1985 – Name changed to Pilot Laboratories Corporation. ■

Scarboro Resources Ltd. (B.C. May 30, 1966)
June 11, 1980 – Continued into Alberta.
Sept. 30, 1987 – Name changed to Hillcrest Resources Ltd. following acquisition of Hillcrest Resources Ltd. (a private co.); basis 1 new for 20 old shs. ■

Scarfe & Co. Limited (Can. 1919)
Dec. 22, 1961 – Rinshed-Mason Co. of Canada Ltd. acquired all cl. A and B shs. at $15 per sh. under an offer which expired.

Scarlet Energy Inc. (B.C. 1981)
May 18, 1984 – Name changed to Nanotec Canada Incorporated and continued into Canada. ■

Scarlet Exploration Inc. (Alta. July 5, 1993)
Jan. 18, 1999 – Acquired by Gopher Oil & Gas Company Ltd.; basis 0.50 Gopher com. shs. for 1 Scarlet com. sh. and special wt.

Scarlet Oils Limited (Ont. 1952)
1953 – Assets acquired by Oil Selections Ltd.

Scarlet Resources Ltd. (B.C. Nov. 6, 2007)
May 10, 2010 – Name changed to United Mining Group, Inc. pursuant to reverse takeover acquisition of United Mines Services Inc. for 50¢ per sh. ■

Scarlett Minerals Inc. (Can. Jan. 22, 1986)
Sept. 20, 1994 – Name changed to SMI Oil & Gas Inc. ■

Scavo Resource Corp. (B.C. Jan. 16, 2007)
Aug. 19, 2015 – Name changed to Brabeia Inc. following the reverse takeover acquisition of (old) Brabeia Inc. ■

Scenc Resources Corp. (B.C. Sept. 9, 2021)
May 3, 2022 – Name changed to Sasquatch Resources Corp. (see FPsurvey - Mines & Energy)

Scenic Oils Limited (Alta. 1944)
1970 – Formed Canadian Scenic Oils Ltd. in Alberta; basis approx. $1.25 cash and 1 new for 1 old sh., plus one $2 cum. pref. sh., $20 par, of Ashland Oil, Inc. for each 6.42 old shs. ■

Sceptre Income & Growth Trust (Ont. Mar. 30, 2004)
Sept. 10, 2007 – Merged into Sceptre Income & High Growth Trust (SIHGT); basis 1.08505 series C-7 units of SIHGT for 1 Sceptre Income & Growth Trust unit. Subsequently, SIHGT converted from a closed end fund to an open-ended fund on the same date. (see Sceptre Income & High Growth Trust)

Sceptre Income & High Growth Trust (Ont. Dec. 16, 2004)
Sept. 10, 2007 – Sceptre Income & Growth Trust (SIGT) was merged into Sceptre Income & High Growth Trust (SIHGT); basis 1.08505 series C-7 units of SIHGT for 1 SIGT unit. Subsequently, SIHGT converted from a closed end fund to an open-ended fund on the same date; basis 1.17413 new series C-7 units for 1 old trust unit.

Sceptre Investment Counsel Limited (Ont. Nov. 22, 1955)
Sept. 1, 2010 – Name changed to Fiera Sceptre Inc. pursuant to reverse takeover acquisition of the operating assets and liabilities of Fiera Capital Inc. ■

Sceptre Resources Limited (B.C. Feb. 18, 1965)
Oct. 31, 1979 – Continued into Canada.
Aug. 19, 1996 – Acquired by Canadian Natural Resources Limited; basis either 0.38 new Canadian Natural com. sh. or, $2.00 plus 0.3025 new Canadian Natural com. sh. for 1 old Sceptre com. sh.

Scheelaur Mines Ltd. (Ont. 1951)
Oct. 5, 1959 – Dissolved.

Scheer Energy Development Corporation (B.C. Jan. 9, 1979)
July 19, 1989 – Name changed to Panterra Energy Inc.; basis 1 new for 3 old shs. ■

Schell Industries Ltd. (Ont. 1945)
Feb. 26, 1969 – Authorization by shldrs. of sale of all assets. Co. controlled by Rosedale Securities Ltd.
Oct. 30, 1969 – Charter surrendered.

Schellex Gold Corp. (B.C. Sept. 14, 1987)
July 23, 1992 – Name changed to Golden Coast Minerals Ltd.; basis 1 new for 4 old shs. ■

Schmitt Industries, Inc. (B.C. Jan. 11, 1984)
Feb. 16, 1996 – Merged with Schmitt Industries, Inc. (Oregon), its wholly owned subsid.
Feb. 16, 1996 – Continued into Wyoming.

Schneider Corporation (Ont. Dec. 30, 1930)
Oct. 28, 1978 – Formed J. M. Schneider Inc. on amalgamation with wholly owned. subsid. J. M. Schneider Inc. ■

Schneider Corporation (Ont. Dec. 30, 1930)
Oct. 3, 2001 – Acquired by 2004171 Ontario Inc., a wholly owned subsid. of Smithfield Foods, Inc.; basis 0.5415 Smithfield shs. for 1 Schneider sh.

Schneider Power Inc. (Ont. Aug. 21, 2008 amalg.)
Apr. 21, 2010 – Acquired by Quantum Fuel Systems Technologies Worldwide, Inc.; basis 0.236 Quantum fuel shs. for 1 Schneider Power sh.

Schomburg Industries (Canada) Inc. (Alta. Apr. 18, 1989)
Aug. 1, 1994 – Amalgamated in Alberta to continue with same name.
Feb. 1, 2000 – Dissolved and struck from registry.

Schooner Capital Corp. (B.C. Dec. 7, 2017)
Dec. 24, 2020 – Name changed to Au Gold Corp. (see FPsurvey - Mines & Energy)

Schott Lake Mines Ltd. (Man. 1960)
1969 – Name changed to Triumph Resources Ltd. ■

Schreiber Pyramid Gold Mines (Ont. Dec. 8, 1934)
1952 – Charter cancelled.

Schreiber Resources Ltd. (Alta. Dec. 23, 1982)
Dec. 22, 1986 – Continued into British Columbia.
Dec. 9, 1992 – Name changed to Briar Glen Developments Corporation; basis 1 new for 5 old shs. ■

Schwanberg International Incorporated (Alta. Aug. 31, 1993)
Feb. 2, 2004 – Name changed to Mystique Energy, Inc. ■

Schyan Exploration Inc. (Ont. Sept. 17, 1940)
Sept. 19, 2018 – Continued into British Columbia.
Sept. 21, 2018 – Name changed to Trulieve Cannabis Corp. following reverse takeover acquisition of Trulieve, Inc. (see FPsurvey - Industrials)

Scienex Mining Co. Ltd. (Que. 1956)
Feb. 7, 1987 – Charter cancelled.

Scientific Metals Corp. (B.C. Oct. 12, 2006)
May 25, 2017 – Name changed to US Cobalt Inc. ■

Sciminex Ltd. (Ont. 1966)
Mar. 1976 – Charter cancelled.

Scimitar Hydrocarbons Corporation (Alta. June 24, 1986)
Aug. 8, 2002 – Amalgamated with Rally Energy Corp.; basis 1 Rally com. sh. for 2.2 Scimitar com. shs. (see Rally Energy Corp.)

Scimitar Resources Ltd. (Alta. 1979)
Nov. 1, 1986 – Struck off register.

Scintilore Mines Limited (Ont. 1953)
Oct. 20, 1975 – Name changed to Scintilore Explorations Limited. (see FPsurvey - Mines & Energy)

Scintrex Limited (Ont. June 22, 1960)
July 29, 1998 – Acquired by IDS Intelligent Detection Systems Inc.; basis $6.00 plus 1.1615 IDS shs., or 1.935 IDS shs. for 1 Scintrex sh. (see IDS Intelligent Detection Systems Inc.)

SciVac Therapeutics Inc. (B.C. Apr. 9, 1965)
May 6, 2016 – Name changed to VBI Vaccines Inc. pursuant to the to acquisition of (old) VBI Vaccines Inc. ■

Scollard Capital Corporation (Alta. Aug. 22, 1997)
Oct. 21, 1998 – Name changed to Label Depot Corporation. ■

Scope AI Corp. (B.C. June 20, 2018)
Sept. 5, 2024 – Name changed to Scope Technologies Corp. (see FPsurvey - Industrials)

Scope Carbon Corp. (B.C. June 20, 2018)
Apr. 1, 2024 – Name changed to Scope AI Corp. ■

Scope Resources Limited (Man. Mar. 7, 1951)
Dec. 7, 1977 – Name changed to New Scope Resources Limited; basis 1 new for 5 old shs. ■

Scope Uranium Mines Ltd. (Alta. Sept. 27, 1954)
July 10, 1956 – Name changed to Alscope Explorations Ltd.; basis 1 new for 2 old shs. ■

ScorCorp Industries Inc. (B.C. 1987)
Oct. 11, 1990 – Name changed to Ixtal International Technology Corporation. ■

Score Media and Gaming Inc. (B.C. Aug. 29, 2019)
Oct. 21, 2021 – Acquired by Penn National Gaming, Inc.; basis US$17.00 cash per sh. plus either (i) 0.2398 Penn National com. sh. or (ii) 0.2398 1317774 B.C. Ltd. exchangeable shs. for 1 Score Media cl. A sh.

Score Media Inc. (Can. Nov. 24, 2000)
Oct. 24, 2012 – All o/s shs. acquired by Rogers Media Inc., a wholly owned subsid. of Rogers Communications Inc., and digital media business was spun off to newly formed theScore, Inc.; basis $1.62 plus 1 theScore cl. A subord. vtg. sh. for 1 Score Media cl. A sh.

Score Resources Ltd. (B.C. 1981)
Feb. 14, 1992 – Dissolved and struck off register.

Scorpio Capital Corp. (Ont. Sept. 2, 2004)
Aug. 28, 2007 – Name changed to Prime City One Capital Corp. on Qualifying Transaction reverse takeover acquisiton of BDE Equities Inc. ■

Scorpio Mining Corporation (Can. May 12, 1998)
May 19, 2015 – Name changed to Americas Silver Corp. ■

Scorpion Energy Corporation (Alta. Oct. 13, 1992)
Oct. 5, 1999 – Name changed to Gauntlet Energy Corporation. ■

Scorpion Minerals Inc. (Ont. Apr. 1, 1996 amalg.)
Mar. 1, 2001 – Name changed to Nextair Inc. following reverse takeover acquisition of Nextair Corporation. ■

Scorpion Resources Inc. (B.C. Sept. 13, 1985)
July 14, 1989 – Name changed to Reese River Resource Corporation. ■

Scorpion Resources Inc. (B.C. Oct. 19, 2011)
May 17, 2018 – Name changed to Blockstrain Technology Corp. following Qualifying Transaction reverse takeover acquisition of (old) BlockStrain Technology Corp. (concurrently renamed Blockstrain Technology Group Inc.). ■

Scotia Covenants Corporation (Can. 1963)
Dec. 31, 1980 – Amalgamated with BNS Mortgage Corporation to form Scotia Mortgage Corporation.

Scotia Mines Ltd. (Ont. 1966)
Sept. 1973 – Charter cancelled.

Scotia Mortgage Investment Corporation (Can. Oct. 17, 1997)
Nov. 1, 2007 – Redeemed all o/s non-cum. pref. cl. A shs. (BOOMS); basis $1,000 plus divd. of $3.285 per pref. sh.

Scotia Prime Minerals, Inc. (N.S. Sept. 19, 1988)
Nov. 6, 1995 – Formed Minera Andes Inc. in Alberta on amalgamation with Minera Andes Inc., constituting a reverse takeover by Minera Andes; basis 1 new for 1 Minera Andes sh. and 1 new for 15 Scotia Prime shs. ■

Scotia Resources Ltd. (B.C. 1980)
Feb. 26, 1986 – Name changed to Senior Savers Guide Publishing Inc. ■

Scotia Split Corp. (Ont. Feb. 5, 1996)
May 1, 2003 – Redeemed in full. Preferred shs. redeemed for $18.85 and Capital shs. redeemed for $90.5282 per sh.

Scotoil Petroleum Limited (Alta. Feb. 24, 1994)
July 28, 2011 – Name changed to 0915998 B.C. Ltd. ■

Scotsman Gold Inc. (Can. Nov. 21, 1983)
Oct. 4, 1993 – Dissolved.

Scott-Chibougamau Mines Ltd. (Que. 1936)
May 8, 1982 – Charter cancelled.

Scott-Lasalle Ltd. (Can. 1936)
Dec. 1, 1979 – Company and subsid., LaSalle Factories Ltd., reported to be in bankruptcy; assets and undertakings taken over by Prudential Insurance Co. of America.

Scott Misener Steamships Limited (Can. 1933)
1976 – Lochiel Investments (1975) Limited offered to acquire all o/s 1st pref. shs. at $15 per sh. to Jan. 7, 1977. However, shldrs. who tendered their shs. by Jan. 5 received a divd. of 27.5¢ per sh. pd. Jan. 15, 1977.
Feb. 9, 1977 – All o/s pref. shs. called for redemp. at $20.27 per sh. All o/s com. shs. were held by Misener Enterprises Ltd.

Scott Paper Limited (B.C. July 24, 1926)
June 10, 1997 – Acquired by Kruger Inc. for $23 per sh.
Oct. 10, 2006 – Name changed to Kruger Products Limited.

Scott Red Lake Gold Mines Ltd. (Ont. 1945)
May 13, 1965 – Dissolved.

Scottie Gold Mines Ltd. (B.C. 1945)
June 2, 1987 – Name changed to Royal Scot Resources Ltd.; basis 1 new for 7 old shs. ■

Scottish & York Holdings Limited (Ont. 1961)
Dec. 20, 1989 – Name changed to SYH Corporation. ■

Scott's Hospitality Inc. (Ont. May 21, 1968 amalg.)
Sept. 13, 1996 – All o/s com. sub. vtg. and cl. C shs. acquired by Laidlaw Inc.; basis $6.25 per sh. plus 0.314831722 of a cl. B non vtg. sh. of Laidlaw for 1 com. sub. vtg. and/or cl. C sh. of Scott's Hospitality (Scott's). Prior to the merger, Scott's shldrs. of record on Aug. 6, 1996, entitled to a dividend-in-kind of 1 cl. C sh. of Scott's Restaurants Inc. for 2 cl. C shs. and 1 sub. vtg. sh. of Scott's Restaurants Inc. for 2 old old sub. vtg. shs. of Scott's. (see Laidlaw Inc.; Scott's Restaurants Inc.)

Scott's Real Estate Investment Trust (Ont. Aug. 23, 2005)
July 9, 2012 – Name changed to KEYreit. ■

Scott's Restaurants Co. Limited (Ont. May 21, 1968 amalg.)
Oct. 6, 1980 – Name changed to Scott's Hospitality Inc. ■

Scott's Restaurants Inc. (Ont. July 22, 1996)
Nov. 2, 1999 – All o/s sub. vtg. com. and cl. C shs. acquired by SR Acquisition Corporation; basis $7.25 per sh.

Scout Capital Corp. (Alta. July 12, 1994)
Jan. 18, 2005 – Formed Birchcliff Energy Ltd. in Alberta on amalgamation with Birchcliff Energy Ltd., constituting a reverse takeover by Birchcliff; basis 1 new for 11.651 old shs. ■

Scout Minerals Corp. (B.C. Oct. 26, 2021)
June 1, 2023 – Name changed to Eureka Lithium Corp. (see FPsurvey - Mines & Energy)

Scout Pershing Mines Ltd. (Ont. 1944)
Mar. 1, 1957 – Charter cancelled.

ScoZinc Mining Ltd. (B.C. Mar. 9, 2004)
Jan. 12, 2022 – Name changed to EDM Resources Inc. (see FPsurvey - Mines & Energy)

Scranton Consolidated Mining Co. (Ore.)
June 1952 – Name changed to Scranton Mines Ltd. ■

Scranton Mines Ltd. (B.C. 1951)
Apr. 22, 1971 – Wound up; basis 1 sh. Silver Star Mines Ltd. for 6 old shs.

Screaming Eagle Acquisition Corp. (Cayman Islands Nov. 3, 2021)
May 13, 2024 – Continued into British Columbia.
May 14, 2024 – Name changed to Lionsgate Studios Corp. following the combination and spin-off of Lions Gate Entertainment Corp.'s Studio business, consisting of the Motion Picture and Television Production segments, into the company. ■

ScreenPro Security Inc. (Ont. Dec. 20, 1945)
May 17, 2023 – Name changed to Justera Health Ltd. (see FPsurvey - Industrials)

Scurry Oils Ltd. (Alta. 1950)
1954 – Assets acquired by Scurry-Rainbow Oil Ltd.

Scurry-Rainbow Oil Limited (Alta. Feb. 5, 1954)
Nov. 10, 1993 – Acquired by Home Oil Company Limited; basis 1.289 Home Oil shs. for 1 Scurry-Rainbow sh. (see Home Oil Company Limited)

Scyther Corporation (Alta. July 22, 1999)
July 24, 2000 – Name changed to Fifth Era Knowledge Inc. ■

Scythes & Company Limited (Can. 1978 amalg.)
July 7, 1978 – Amalgamated with Coloratus Holdings Ltd. to continue under the name Scythes & Co. Ltd. on May 31, 1978. Cl. A or B pfce. shs. of the amalg. co. were issued to com. shldrs. of the predecessor Scythes co. All o/s pfce. shs. were called for redempt. at $4.62 per sh.

Scythian Biosciences Corp. (Ont. Jan. 28, 2005)
Oct. 25, 2018 – Name changed to SOL Global Investments Corp. (see FPsurvey - Industrials)

Sea Band International Inc. (Ont. 1980)
Sept. 20, 1988 – Name changed to Consumer General Inc. ■

Sea Breeze Power Corp. (B.C. Jan. 18, 1979)
Jan. 2017 – Filed a proposal for restructuring purposes under the Bankruptcy and Insolvency Act (BIA). Alvarez & Marsal Canada Inc. was appointed proposal trustee.
May 9, 2017 – The court approved proposal entailed: the transfer by the secured lender group of all the com. shs. of the company to Tu-Can Energy LLC, a limited liability company controlled by the secured lenders; issuance by the company of 1 billion com. shs. to TuCan, following which the company's com. shs. would be consolidated on a 25 million-to-1 basis; and all fractional shs. and other securities of the company, excluding the com. shs. held by TuCan, would be cancelled for no consideration.
Jan. 4, 2021 – Acquired by Synex International Inc. for a nominal amount.

Sea-Chem Industries Ltd. (B.C. 1968)
Jan. 12, 1978 – Name changed to Astra Resources Ltd.; basis 1 new for 4 old shs.

Sea Dragon Energy Inc. (Can. Mar. 28, 2006)
Sept. 30, 2015 – Name changed to SDX Energy Inc.; basis 1 new for 35 old shs. ■

Sea Gold Oil Corp. (B.C. July 26, 1979)
Mar. 7, 1985 – Name changed to Consolidated Sea Gold Corp.; basis 1 new for 5 old shs. ■

Sea Gold Resources Inc. (B.C. July 26, 1979)
June 3, 1994 – Name changed to Fairchild Investments Inc.; basis 1 new for 3 old shs. ■

Sea Green Capital Corp. (Ont. July 7, 1997)
July 23, 2012 – Name changed to Cava Resources Inc.; basis 1 new for 5 old shs. ■

Sea Hawk Energy Inc. (Ont. 1978)
Aug. 5, 1987 – Name changed to Jarl Energy Inc. ■

Sea-1 Aquafarms Ltd. (B.C. 1983)
Nov. 24, 1987 – Name changed to General Sea Harvest Corporation. ■

Seaboard Oil & Mines Limited (Ont. 1947)
1956 – Acquired by Landmark Mines Ltd.; basis 1 new for 5 old shs. (see Landmark Mines Ltd.)

Seaboard Power Corporation Ltd. (Can. - unspecified)
1966 – Sold to Nova Scotia Power Commission. Bonds are now guaranteed as to principal, premium and interest by the Province of Nova Scotia.

Seabridge Gold Inc. (B.C. Sept. 14, 1979)
Oct. 31, 2002 – Continued into Canada. (see FPsurvey - Mines & Energy)

Seabridge Resources Inc. (B.C. Sept. 14, 1979)
June 20, 2002 – Name changed to Seabridge Gold Inc. ■

Seabright Explorations Incorporated (Ont. Jan. 22, 1973)
Apr. 22, 1991 – Formed Corner Bay Minerals Inc. in Ontario following merger of Corner Bay Resources Inc. and wholly owned subsid. of Seabright; basis 1 new for 5 old shs. ■

Seabright Resources Inc. (Can. 1980)
Feb. 24, 1988 – Acquired by subsid. of Western Mining Corp. Holdings Ltd.; basis $8.50 per cl. A sh. and $3.00 per wt.

Seacliff Construction Corp. (B.C. Jan. 23, 2008)
July 20, 2010 – Acquired by The Churchill Corporation for $17.14 per sh. (see The Churchill Corporation)

Seacorp Capital Corporation (B.C. Feb. 6, 1984)
Apr. 7, 1995 – Name changed to Seacorp Communications Inc.; basis 1 new for 5 old shs. ■

Seacorp Communications Inc. (B.C. Feb. 6, 1984)
Mar. 2, 1998 – Delisted from the Vancouver Stock Exchange. Subsequently struck from register and dissolved.

Seacorp Properties Inc. (B.C. June 25, 1981)
Mar. 2, 1998 – Delisted from the Vancouver Stock Exchange. Subsequently struck from register and dissolved.

Seacrest Development Corporation (B.C. Jan. 8, 1985)
Mar. 18, 2004 – Name changed to Norzan Enterprises Ltd.; basis 1 new for 10 old shs. (see FPsurvey - Mines & Energy; FPsurvey - Industrials)

Seadrift International Exploration Ltd. (B.C. 1978)
Jan. 12, 1989 – Amalgamated with Wilco Mining Company Limited (2 for 25) and Deak Ariadne Limited (1 for 1) to form Deak International Resources Corporation; basis 1 new for 2 old shs. (see Wilco Mining Company Ltd.)

Seadrift Resources Ltd. (B.C. 1978)
June 1980 – Name changed to Pacific Seadrift Resources Ltd.; basis 1 new for 2 old shs. ■

Seafield Resources Ltd. (Ont. Apr. 15, 1957)
Sept. 9, 2014 – Petitioned into receivership by secured creditor and KPMG Inc. was appointed receiver.
Aug. 24, 2015 – KPMG Inc. appointed trustee for the general benefit of the creditors on assignment of the company into bankruptcy.
Mar. 2016 – RMB Australia Holding's Ltd., the company's secured creditor, acquired wholly owned Minera Seafield S.A.S. for $19,000,000, consisting of $2,376,697 plus the release of $16,623,303 being the material portion of the indebtedness owned to RMB by the company. There were no funds available for payment to unsecured creditors or shldrs.
July 8, 2016 – Certificate of incorporation cancelled for cause and the company dissolved.
Aug. 23, 2019 – KPMG Inc. was discharged as trustee.
Jan. 15, 2020 – KMPG Inc. discharged as receiver.

Seaforth Mines Ltd. (Que. 1945)
May 1974 – Charter cancelled.

Seaforth Mines Ltd. (B.C. 1972)
June 20, 1982 – Amalgamated with Quinterra Resources Inc. to form a new co. known as Quinterra Resources Inc.; basis 0.325 new for 1 old sh.

The Seagram Company Ltd. (Can. Mar. 2, 1928; via Dominion charter)
Dec. 11, 2000 – Plan of Arrangement with French-based Vivendi Universal; basis 0.80 Vivendi Universal Exchangeco exchangeable shs. or 0.80 Vivendi Universal ADSs for 1 old Seagram com. sh.

Seagull Resources Limited (Alta. 1971)
Oct. 31, 1980 – Amalgamated with Seatu Explorations Ltd. to form a new co. also known as Seagull Resources Limited; basis 1 new for 1 old sh.
Apr. 1, 1991 – Struck off register.

Seahawk Gold Corp. (B.C. Jan. 16, 2007)
Apr. 11, 2025 – Name changed to Seahawk Ventures Inc. (see FPsurvey - Mines & Energy)

Seahawk Minerals Ltd. (Yuk. Nov. 8, 1996)
Feb. 15, 2005 – Dissolved.

Seahawk Oil Corporation (unknown)
May 1979 – All issued shs. purch. by Gaslite Petroleum Ltd.

Seahawk Ventures Inc. (B.C. Jan. 16, 2007)
Sept. 2, 2020 – Name changed to Seahawk Gold Corp. ■

Seair Inc. (Alta. Apr. 12, 2001)
June 30, 2017 – Pursuant to the proposal for the restructuring of the company filed under the Bankruptcy and Insolvency Act by proposal trustee FTI Consulting Canada Inc., all o/s secured debentures were converted into series 2 pref. shs. on the basis of 1 new pref. sh. for every dollar of claim; all existing equity of the company,

including all o/s series 1 pref. and com. shs. have been cancelled for no consideration; the holder of the company's senior debt has converted all of the debt claims against the company into cl. A pref. shs.; and the o/s new series 1 pref. shs. were converted into com. shs. on a 1-for- basis. All equity of the company is now held by holders of the senior debt and secured debentures.
July 6, 2017 – Voluntarily delisted.

Seal Cove Corporation (Alta. 1980)
Jan. 1, 1993 – Struck off register.

Seal Harbour Gold Mines Ltd. (Ont. 1934)
1960 – Went into bankruptcy and charter surrendered.

Seal-O-Sac (Canada) Ltd. (Can. 1932)
Sept. 1951 – Wound up.

SeaMiles Limited (Ont. June 19, 1962)
Apr. 3, 2012 – Name changed to Intellectual Capital Group Ltd. (see FPsurvey - Industrials)

Seaness Capital Corporation (B.C. Apr. 18, 2008)
Nov. 4, 2010 – Name changed to Intigold Mines Ltd. pursuant to Qualifying Transaction reverse takeover acquisition of (old) Intigold Mines Ltd. ■

Seaquest Energy Ltd. (Alta. Nov. 16, 1977)
Jan. 13, 1987 – Name changed to Alta Petroleum Ltd.; basis 1 new for 10 old shs. ■

Searay Oils Ltd. (B.C. June 11, 1980)
Aug. 21, 1986 – Name changed to Mega-Dyne Industrial Corp.; basis 1 new for 4 old shs. ■

Search Capital Inc. (B.C. June 7, 2006)
Oct. 21, 2008 – Name changed to Search Minerals Inc. following Qualifying Transaction acquisition of Alterra Resources Inc. (see FPsurvey - Mines & Energy)

Search Energy Corp. (Alta. Aug. 29, 1979)
Dec. 6, 1994 – Amalgamated in Alberta to continue with same name.
May 29, 2001 – Acquired by and amalgamated with a subsidiary of Advantage Energy Income Fund; basis 1 Advantage trust unit for 4 Search com. shs.
June 26, 2002 – Name changed to Advantage Oil & Gas Ltd. ■

Search Energy Inc. (N.S. Feb. 13, 1987)
Jan. 9, 1997 – Amalgamated with Westrex Energy Corp. (1 for 5) to form a new co. named Search Energy Corp.; basis 1 new for 1 old sh. (see Search Energy Corp.)

SearchGold Resources Inc. (Can. Nov. 22, 1996)
July 8, 2013 – Name changed to Gravitas Financial Inc. following reverse takeover acquisition of Ubika Corp. ■

Searchlight Capital Corp. (B.C. Apr. 9, 2010)
Nov. 24, 2011 – Name changed to LED Medical Diagnostics Inc. pursuant to Qualifying Transaction reverse takeover acquisition of LED Medical Diagnostics Inc. ■

Searchlight Venture Corp. (B.C. Feb. 11, 1999)
Oct. 15, 2003 – Acquisition and distribution of 442,860 units (1 com. sh. and 1 wt.) of Medical Ventures Corp. represented the company's Qualifying Transaction; basis $0.70 per unit. (see Medical Ventures Corp.)

Searchmont Valley Ski Resorts Ltd. (Ont. 1958)
Aug. 28, 1989 – Dissolved.

Searchtech Ventures Inc. (Ont. Aug. 21, 2012)
Dec. 10, 2014 – Name changed to PharmaCan Capital Corp. following Qualifying Transaction reverse takeover acquisition of Hortican Inc.; basis 1 new for 7 old shs. ■

Searle Grain Company, Limited (Can. - unspecified)
Sept. 28, 1966 – Merged with Federal Grain, Limited.

Sears Acceptance Company Inc. (Can. Dec. 23, 1952)
Dec. 15, 2003 – Formed Sears Financial Services Limited.

Sears Canada Inc. (Can. Sept. 17, 1952; via Dominion charter)
June 22, 2017 – Application was made under the Companies' Creditors Arrangement Act (CCAA) and FTI Consulting Canada Inc. appointed monitor.
July 18, 2017 – Court approval attained for the commencement of liquidation of the company.
Jan. 3, 2019 – FTI Consulting Canada Inc. appointed receiver.

Sears Canada Receivables Trust - 1992 (Can. - unspecified)
Feb. 27, 2004 – Name changed to SCRT-1992.

Seashore Organic Marijuana Corp. (B.C. May 14, 2014)
Sept. 2, 2014 – Name changed to Seashore Organic Medicine Inc. ■

Seashore Organic Medicine Inc. (B.C. May 14, 2014)
Dec. 29, 2015 – Name changed to Veritas Pharma Inc. ■

Seashore Resource Partners Corp. (B.C. Sept. 7, 2017)
Mar. 11, 2021 – Name changed to Kingfisher Metals Corp. pursuant to the Qualifying Transaction reverse takeover acquisition of Kingfisher Resources Ltd. and concurrent amalgamation of Kingfisher with wholly owned 1262227 B.C. Ltd. (see FPsurvey - Mines & Energy)

Seaside Exploration Partners Corp. (B.C. Oct. 21, 2016)
Apr. 25, 2018 – Name changed to DelphX Capital Markets Inc. following Qualifying Transaction reverse takeover acquisition of DelphX Corporation. (see FPsurvey - Industrials)

Seastar Resource Corporation (B.C. 1980)
June 30, 1988 – Name changed to National Seastar Corporation; basis 1 new for 5 old shs. ■

Seatac Resources Inc. (B.C. 1976)
Sept. 30, 1986 – Name changed to Interbev Packaging Corp. ■

Seatu Explorations Ltd. (B.C. 1977)
Oct. 31, 1980 – Amalgamated with Seagull Resources Ltd. to form a new co. also known as Seagull Resources Limited; basis 1 new for 5 old shs.

Seaview Energy Inc. (Alta. Dec. 13, 2006)
Mar. 6, 2012 – Name changed to Charger Energy Corp. pursuant to reverse takeover acquisition of Charger Energy Corporation (deemed acquiror), Silverback Energy Ltd. and Sirius Energy Inc.; basis 3.6364 Seaview cl. A shs. for 1 Charger sh., 5.8182 Seaview cl. A shs. for 1 Silverback sh. and 0.8 Seaview cl. A shs. for 1 Sirius sh. Concurrently, cl. A shs. of Seaview were consolidated on a 1-for-5 basis. ■

Seaview Resources Ltd. (B.C. 1988)
Oct. 6, 1995 – Dissolved and struck off register.

Seaward Resources Ltd. (Alta. Nov. 16, 1977)
Sept. 10, 1982 – Name changed to Seaquest Energy Ltd.; basis 1 new for 10 old shs. ■

Seaway Base Metals Limited (Ont. June 21, 1968)
Dec. 18, 1995 – Name changed to Jetcom Inc.; basis 1 new for 20 old shs. (see FPsurvey - Mines & Energy; FPsurvey - Industrials)

Seaway Copper Mines Limited (Ont. June 21, 1968)
May 10, 1972 – Name changed to Seaway Base Metals Limited. ■

Seaway Energy Services Inc. (Alta. Feb. 28, 2005)
Aug. 15, 2014 – Continued into British Columbia.
May 19, 2020 – Name changed to Sweet Earth Holdings Corporation pursuant to reverse takeover acquisition of (old) Sweet Earth Holdings Corporation; basis 1 new for 2.5 old shs. (see FPsurvey - Industrials)

Seaway Mortgage Corporation (Can. 1961)
Mar. 29, 1985 – Charter cancelled.

Seaway Trust Company (Ont. Aug. 23, 1978)
Jan. 22, 2007 – Stuck from register and dissolved.

Seawest Resources Limited (B.C. Nov. 14, 1986)
May 2, 1996 – Name changed to Starfire Minerals Inc.; basis 1 new for 3.5 old shs. (see FPsurvey - Mines & Energy)

Seawind Resources Inc. (B.C. Nov. 6, 1980)
Apr. 7, 1986 – Delisted from the Vancouver Stock Exchange. Subsequently dissolved.

Seba Exploration Ltd. (Alta. Apr. 18, 1979)
Jan. 22, 1991 – Name changed to Camrex Resources Ltd. ■

Sebastiani Ventures Corp. (B.C. Apr. 25, 2017)
Apr. 11, 2023 – Name changed to EvokAI Creative Labs Inc. pursuant to the reverse takeover acquisition of Switzerland-based (old) EvokAI Creative Labs Inc. and concurrent amalgamation of (old) EvokAI with wholly owned Sebastiani Mergerco Inc. (and continued as EvokAI Innovation Corp.); basis 1 new for 2.6628503 old shs. (see FPsurvey - Industrials)

Sebring Resources Ltd. (Alta. Feb. 4, 1997)
Apr. 15, 2002 – Continued into Canada.
Apr. 18, 2002 – Name changed to PharmaGap Inc. following Mar. 28, 2002, Qualifying Transaction acquisition of PharmaGap Inc. and subsequent vertical amalgamation with wholly owned PharmaGap Inc. ■

Sechura Inc. (Can. 1961)
Sept. 5, 1996 – Name changed to Aaxis Limited and continued into Bermuda.

Seco-Cemp Limited (Can. 1950)
Nov. 15, 1988 – Privatized with redemption of publicly held US$3.22 pref. ser.D shs. at US$26.25 per sh.

Seco Investments Ltd. (Can. 1950)
Oct. 27, 1971 – Name changed to Seco-Cemp Limited. ■

Second Canadian General Investments Limited (Ont. Jan. 15, 1930)
Aug. 17, 1931 – Name changed to Canadian General Investments, Limited. (see FPsurvey - Industrials)

Second Canadian International Investment Co. Ltd. (Que. 1937)
Nov. 16, 1954 – Name changed to Pacific Atlantic Canadian Investment Co. Ltd.

Second Century Genetics Ltd. (Ont. July 19, 1994)
Feb. 7, 1995 – Name changed to Stef International Corporation; basis 1 new for 2 old shs. ■

Second Cup Income Fund (Ont. Oct. 22, 2004)
Jan. 1, 2011 – Succeeded by The Second Cup Ltd. pursuant to plan of arrangement whereby The Second Cup Ltd. was formed to facilitate the conversion of the fund into a corporation and the fund was dissolved. ■

The Second Cup Ltd. (Ont. Nov. 7, 1988)
Mar. 4, 2002 – Acquired by Cara Operations Limited for $8.00 per sh. (see Cara Operations Limited)

The Second Cup Ltd. (Ont. Jan. 1, 2011; amalg.)
Sept. 24, 2020 – Name changed to Aegis Brands Inc. (see FPsurvey - Industrials)

Second Cup Royalty Income Fund (Ont. Oct. 22, 2004)
Aug. 21, 2009 – Name changed to Second Cup Income Fund. ■

Second Relief Mining Co. (B.C. 1905)
1929 – Name changed to Relief-Arlington Mines Ltd. ■

Second Wave Petroleum Inc. (Alta. Dec. 19, 2003)
July 4, 2013 – Acquired by Brookfield Bridge Lending Fund Inc. for $0.30 per sh.

Second Wave Petroleum Ltd. (Alta. Dec. 19, 2003)
June 27, 2008 – Name changed to Second Wave Petroleum Inc.; basis 1 new for 10 old shs. ■

Secondo Mining Ltd. (B.C. 1966)
Jan. 31, 1977 – Dissolved.

Secova Metals Corp. (B.C. Oct. 22, 2004)
Feb. 14, 2014 – Continued into Canada.
July 14, 2022 – Name changed to ESGold Corp. (see FPsurvey - Mines & Energy)

Secret Pass Minerals Corp. (B.C. 1987)
Feb. 19, 1993 – Dissolved and struck off register.

Secretariat Resources Inc. (B.C. Apr. 26, 1971)
Aug. 3, 1978 – Name changed to Cosmos Resources Inc.; basis 1 new for 3 old shs. ■

Section Rouge Media Inc. (Can. Apr. 16, 1996)
Jan. 4, 2017 – Name changed to Sama Graphite Inc. following reverse takeover acquisition of Sama Resources Guinée S.A.R.L. ■

Secure Energy Services Inc. (Alta. Apr. 24, 2007 amalg.)
Jan. 1, 2025 – Name changed to Secure Waste Infrastructure Corp. (see FPsurvey - Mines & Energy; FPsurvey - Industrials)

Secure One, Inc. (Alta. Nov. 18, 1993)
Nov. 24, 2005 – Name changed to United Protection Security Group Inc. ■

SecureCom Mobile Inc. (B.C. Nov. 9, 2011)
July 21, 2017 – Name changed to Liberty Health Sciences Inc. following reverse takeover acquisition of DFMMJ Investments Ltd. and concurrent amalgamation of DFMMJ with wholly owned 1006397 B.C. Ltd. to form Liberty Heath Sciences USA Ltd.; basis 1 new for 3 old shs. ■

Secured Communication Canada 95 Inc. (B.C. July 18, 1983)
July 7, 1998 – Delisted from the Vancouver Stock Exchange. Subsequently dissolved.

Secureview Systems Inc. (B.C. Sept. 18, 1985)
May 2, 2005 – Name changed to Global Immune Technologies Inc. ■

Securities Holding Corp. Ltd. (Ont. 1932)
Oct. 1943 – In liquidation.
Dec. 22, 1943 – O/s 6% noncum. pref. stock, $25 par value, called for redemp. at $25 per sh.
1944 – Distribution made to com. shldrs. of $4.21 per sh.

Security Capital Corporation Ltd. (Ont. 1962)
Oct. 30, 1975 – Name changed to Sentinel Holdings Limited. ■

Security Devices International Inc. (Del. Mar. 1, 2005)
Mar. 4, 2020 – Name changed to Byrna Technologies Inc.

Security Energy Corporation (Alta. 1987)
Apr. 12, 1995 – Acquired by Clarinet Resources Ltd.; basis 0.86 new Clarinet sh. for 1 old Security sh. (see Clarinet Resources Ltd.)

Security Freehold Petroleums Limited (Can. 1928)
1963 – Acquired by Hudson's Bay Oil & Gas Co. Ltd.; basis 1 new for 2 old shs.

Security Home Mortgage Corporation (Can. Dec. 31, 1973)
Dec. 12, 1996 – Petitioned into liquidation. RSM Richter Inc. was appointed liquidator.

Security Home Mortgage Investment Corporation (Can. Dec. 31, 1973)
Nov. 1, 1994 – Name changed to Security Home Mortgage Corporation. ■

Sedalia Mining Co. Ltd. (Ont. 1944)
1955 – Charter cancelled.

Seder Capital Corp. (Ont. Apr. 28, 2004)
Dec. 24, 2004 – Name changed to Covalon Technologies Ltd. following Qualifying Transaction reverse takeover acquisition of Covalon Technologies Inc. (see FPsurvey - Industrials)

Sedex Mining Corp. (B.C. Oct. 2, 1980)
Mar. 21, 2017 – Dissolved and struck from register.

Sedibelo Platinum Mines Limited (Guernsey Dec. 9, 2011)
June 9, 2022 – Name changed to Sedibelo Resources Limited.

Sedna Geotech Inc. (Yuk. Dec. 17, 1996 amalg.)
Apr. 17, 2008 – Dissolved.

Sedona Industries Ltd. (B.C. 1986)
July 19, 1994 – Acquired by Harvard International Technologies Ltd.; basis 1 Harvard sh. for 6.78 Sedona shs., 1 Harvard wt. for 24.56 Sedona shs. and 1 Soranzo International Spirits Ltd. sh. for 4.30 Sedona she. for non-U.S. shldrs.; basis 1 Harvard sh. for 5.27 Sedona shs. and 1 Harvard wt. for 24.56 Sedona shs. for U.S. shldrs. (see Harvard International Technologies Ltd.)

Seeber Lake Gold Mines Ltd. (Ont. 1946)
1954 – Charter cancelled.

Seek Resources Ltd. (Ont. 1945)
Mar. 3, 1989 – Name changed to Argor Resources Ltd.; basis 1 new for 2.5 old shs. (see FPsurvey - Mines & Energy)

Seel Mortgage Investment Corporation (Can. Oct. 22, 1974)
June 26, 1992 – Acquired by The Mutual Trust Company for $7.00 per sh.

Seeley Lake Resources Ltd. (Ont. May 29, 1987)
June 4, 1991 – Name changed to Falcon Super Fax Graphics Inc.; basis 1 new for 4 old shs. ■

Seeley Mining Corp. Ltd. (Ont. 1965)
1969 – Merged into Great Eagle Explorations and Holdings Ltd.; basis 1 new for 7 old shs.

Seelite Plastic Enterprises Ltd. (Ont. 1944)
May 7, 1948 – Made an assignment under the Bankruptcy Act. Nothing available for com. shldrs.

Seemar Explorations Inc. (Ont. July 2, 1965)
Aug. 1986 – Name changed to Goldstake Explorations Inc. (see FPsurvey - Mines & Energy)

Seemar Mines Ltd. (Ont. July 2, 1965)
1985 – Name changed to Seemar Explorations Inc.; basis 1 new for 5 old shs. ■

Seguin Consolidated Mines Ltd. (Que. 1937)
May 4, 1974 – Dissolved.

Seguro Resources Ltd. (B.C. Jan. 19, 1987)
Feb. 9, 1990 – Name changed to Aura Industries Inc. ■

Seiberling Rubber Co. of Canada Ltd. (Can. 1927)
May 1, 1964 – Acquired by Goodyear Tire & Rubber Co. of Canada Ltd.

Seigel Associates Ltd. (Can. - unspecified)
Apr. 1967 – Acquired by Scintrex Limited for 327,000 6% cum. pref. shs. (see Sharpe Instruments of Canada Limited)

Seine River Resources Inc. (B.C. Mar. 9, 1987)
Apr. 4, 2002 – Name changed to Trinity Plumas Capital Corp.; basis 1 new for 20 old shs. ■

Selburn Oil Co. Ltd. (Can. Feb. 7, 1950)
1952 – Assets acquired by Bailey Selburn Oil & Gas Ltd.; basis 1 cl. A sh. for 2 old shs.

Selby Green International Ltd. (Ont. Sept. 28, 1987)
Nov. 2, 1995 – Name changed to Berkshire Griffin Inc.; basis 1 new for 10 old shs. ■

Selby Mining Exploration Co. Ltd. (Que. 1954)
1959 – Merged into Amalgamated Mining Development Corp. Ltd.; basis 1 new for 7 old shs.

Selco Exploration Co. Ltd. (Can. 1953)
1971 – Assets acquired by Selco Mining Corporation Limited.

Selco Mining & Development Ltd. (Can. 1968)
1971 – Assets acquired by Selco Mining Corporation Limited.

Selco Mining Corporation Limited (Ont. 1968)
Dec. 23, 1980 – Name changed to Selco Inc.

Seldore Mining Co. Ltd. (Ont. 1969)
1977 – Amalgamated with 4 other cos. to form Branly Enterprises Inc.; basis 7 new for 25 old shs.

Select-Alix Oils Ltd. (Alta.)
1959 – Struck off register.

Select 50 S-1 Income Trust (Ont. July 30, 2003)
June 3, 2009 – Merged into Sentry Select Canadian Income Fund, an open-ended mutual fund.

Select 50 S-1 Income Trust II (Ont. Oct. 30, 2003)
July 7, 2008 – Amalgamated with Select 50 S-1 Income Trust; basis 1.01233 Select 50 S-1 Income trust units for 1 Select 50 S-1 Income Trust II trust unit.

Select Financial Industries Ltd. (Can. 1959)
July 1971 – Name changed to Deltan Corporation Limited. ■

Select Leased Property Finance Ltd. (Ont. 1956)
July 1969 – Merged with Baystate Developments Ltd. to form Select Properties Ltd.

Select Oils Ltd. (Alta. June 4, 1949)
1959 – Assets sold to Medallion Petroleums Ltd.; basis 1 new for 100 old shs.

Select Properties Limited (Ont. 1969 amalg.)
1975 – Acquired by Orlando Realty Corp. for $3.50 per sh.

Select Ventures Inc. (B.C. Oct. 30, 1986)
Dec. 3, 1996 – Name changed to Majestic Gold Corp.; basis 1 new for 2 old shs. (see FPsurvey - Mines & Energy)

Selectcore Ltd. (Ont. Feb. 23, 2004)
Aug. 25, 2017 – Name changed to Fintech Select Ltd. (see FPsurvey - Industrials)

Selected Natural Gas Synd. (unknown)
Assets acquired by Consolidated Natural Gas Co. Ltd.; basis 30 new for 1 unit.

Selena Research Corporation (B.C. Feb. 28, 1979)
Mar. 1, 1994 – Name changed to SLN Ventures Corporation; basis 1 new for 9 old shs. ■

Selient Inc. (Que. Feb. 11, 1998 amalg.)
Dec. 20, 2007 – Acquired by CRI Canada Inc. for $0.1725 per sh.

Selkirk Communications Limited (Ont. May 2, 1979)
1983 – Amalgamated in Ontario to continue with same name. (see Maclean Hunter Limited)
Mar. 15, 1989 – Acquired by MH Acquisition Inc., a wholly owned subsid. of Maclean Hunter Limited; basis $49.50 per cl. A non-vtg. sh. Cl. B vtg. shs. subsequently acquired in September 1989 at $5.00 per sh. (see Maclean Hunter Limited)

Selkirk Holdings Limited (Alta. 1959)
May 2, 1979 – Name changed to Selkirk Communications Limited and continued into Ontario. ■

Selkirk Metals Corp. (B.C. Apr. 13, 2005)
Nov. 6, 2009 – Amalgamated with subsid. of Imperial Metals Corporation to form new co. also named Selkirk Metals Corp. pursuant to plan of arrangement; basis 12¢ for 1 Selkirk sh. or 1 Imperial sh. for 30 Selkirk shs.

Selkirk Springs International Corporation (B.C. Mar. 23, 1988)
Oct. 24, 1995 – Name changed to Canadian Glacier Beverage Corporation. ■

Selkirk Tungs-Tin Mines Limited (Can. Dec. 21, 1942)
Dec. 15, 2009 – Dissolved.

Sellectek Industries Inc. (B.C. June 2, 1981)
Aug. 29, 1989 – Name changed to Global-Pacific Minerals Inc. ■

Selwyn Explorations Ltd. (B.C. 1967)
Mar. 18, 1977 – Dissolved.

Selwyn Resources Ltd. (B.C. Mar. 9, 2004)
Oct. 1, 2015 – Name changed to ScoZinc Mining Ltd. ■

SemBioSys Genetics Inc. (Can. Apr. 25, 1994)
Dec. 18, 2009 – Name changed to Cathedral Energy Services Ltd. pursuant conversion of Cathedral Energy Services Income Trust into a corporation whereby all SemBioSys assets and liabilities were transferred to 1491265 Alberta Ltd. which subsequently amalgamated with 1491277 Alberta Ltd. to form a new co. also named SemBioSys Genetics Ltd.; basis 1 Cathedral sh. for 1 Cathedral trust unit and 1 new SemBioSys sh. for 1 old SemBioSys sh. ■

SemBioSys Genetics Inc. (Can. Dec. 18, 2009)
June 22, 2012 – Placed into receivership; MNP Ltd. appointed receiver. Operations ceased and all officers and directors resigned on May 1, 2012.

Semcan Inc. (Can. Jan. 30, 2007)
Feb. 20, 2013 – Name changed to STT Enviro Corp. ■

Semco Technologies Inc. (Alta. Aug. 25, 2000)
Jan. 30, 2007 – Continued into Canada.
Feb. 9, 2007 – Name changed to Semcan Inc. ■

Semi-Tech Corporation (Ont. Dec. 9, 1965)
Sept. 22, 2000 – Delisted from the Toronto Stock Exchange. Subsequently voluntarily dissolved.

Semi-Tech Microelectronics Inc (Ont. Dec. 9, 1965)
July 20, 1987 – Name changed to International Semi-Tech Microelectronics Inc.; basis 1 new for 10 old shs. ■

Seminole Resources Inc. (B.C. Oct. 2, 1979)
Oct. 28, 1987 – Name changed to Canadian Giant Exploration Limited. ■

Semper Energy Ltd. (Alta. Feb. 5, 2001)
Aug. 21, 2003 – Name changed to Val Vista Energy Ltd. following reverse takeover acquisition of Val Vista Energy Inc. ■

Semper Resources Inc. (B.C. 1967)
Sept. 30, 1981 – Amalgamated with David Minerals Ltd.; basis 1 new for 1 old sh.

Senate Mining and Exploration Limited (B.C. 1968)
Mar. 18, 1983 – Struck off register.

Senator Minerals Inc. (Ont. Jan. 13, 1972)
Sept. 22, 2014 – Continued into British Columbia.
Nov. 15, 2018 – Name changed to Tisdale Resources Corp.; basis 1 new for 4 old shs. ■

Senator Mines Ltd. (B.C.)
May 15, 1969 – Struck off register.

Senator-Rouyn Ltd. (Que. Mar. 6, 1937)
1952 – Name changed to New Senator-Rouyn Limited; basis 2 new for 5 old shs. ■

Sencon Gold Mines Ltd. (Ont. 1945)
1956 – Charter cancelled.

Seneca Developments Ltd. (B.C. Dec. 1, 1972)
Aug. 4, 1981 – Name changed to Award Resources Ltd.; basis 1 new for 4 old shs. ■

Seneca Drillers Selections Syndicate (unknown)
1936 – Merged with Gasfinders & Producers Syndicate to form Gasfinders & Producers Ltd. (see Gasfinders & Producers Ltd.)

Seneca Equities Corp. (Alta. Oct. 17, 2000)
Mar. 9, 2004 – Transaction with MedMira Inc. to acquire and distribute 293,626 com. shs. and 293,626 com. sh. rights ($0.96 for 1 com. sh.) of MedMira to Seneca shldrs. Subsequent wind-up represented company's Qualifying Transaction.

Seneca Explorations Ltd. (Ont. 1962)
May 1967 – Charter cancelled.

Seneca Metal Products Ltd. (Alta. Oct. 28, 1985)
May 18, 1994 – Name changed to Cedar Corporation; basis 1 new for 10 old shs. ■

Seneca Oils (unknown)
July 1928 – Acquired by Calmont Oils Limited; basis 1 new for 15 old shs. (see Calmont Oils Limited)

Seneca Resources Ltd. (Alta. 1970)
Apr. 25, 1973 – Name changed to United Western Oil & Gas Ltd.; basis 1 new for 1 old sh. ■

Senercorp Ventures Inc. (Can. Sept. 29, 1987)
May 17, 1995 – Formed United Kiev Resources Inc. in Alberta on amalgamation with United Kiev Resources Inc. ■

Senet Copper Mines Ltd. (Ont. 1955)
Apr. 11, 1965 – Dissolved.

Senex Corporation (Alta. 1987)
Feb. 26, 1990 – Amalgamated with Prime Petroleum Corporation to form Senex Petroleum Corporation; basis 1 new for 5 old shs. (see Senex Petroleum Corporation)

Senex Petroleum Corporation (B.C. Feb. 26, 1990 amalg.)
Mar. 4, 1993 – Amalgamated with Devran Petroleum Ltd.; basis 1 Devran sh. for 10 Senex shs. (see Devran Petroleum Ltd.)

Senior Gas and Oil Limited (Ont. 1967)
May 1971 – Merged into Erieshore Industries Inc.; basis 2 new for 9 old shs.

Senior Gold Producers Income Corp. (Ont. Dec. 9, 2010)
Sept. 16, 2011 – Name changed to Aston Hill Senior Gold Producers Income Corp. ■

Senior Savers Guide Publishing Inc. (B.C. 1980)
Oct. 20, 1987 – Name changed to Kali Venture Corporation. ■

Senior Secured Floating Rate Loan Fund (Ont. July 22, 2013)
May 28, 2021 – Terminated; net asset distrib. to unitholders. on a pro rata basis.

Senitinel Mines Ltd. (Can. June 28, 1938)
Wound up. Distributed 5.1¢ per sh.

Senlac Resources Inc. (Ont. 1945)
Aug. 1, 1986 – Amalgamated with Heenan Petroleum Limited to form Heenan Senlac Resources Limited; basis 1 new for 1 old sh.

Senmar Capital Corp. (Alta. Oct. 17, 2011)
Oct. 11, 2012 – Succeeded by Toscana Energy Income Corporation following Qualifying Transaction amalgamation with 1668236 Alberta Ltd., a wholly owned subsid. of Toscana Energy, to form Lucca Energy Ltd. ■

Senn d'Or Inc. (Can. Nov. 13, 1986)
Oct. 19, 1993 – Name changed to Venoro Gold Corp.; basis 3 new for 1 old sh. ■

Sennen Resources Ltd. (B.C. Sept. 10, 1981)
Apr. 15, 2013 – Name changed to Sennen Potash Corporation. (see FPsurvey - Mines & Energy)

Sennepas Gold Mines Ltd. (Ont. 1946)
1955 – Charter cancelled.

Senneterre Metals, Gas & Oil Ltd. (Que. 1954)
Apr. 1974 – Charter cancelled.

Senneterre Metals Mines Ltd. (Que. 1954)
1961 – Name changed to Senneterre Metals, Gas & Oil Ltd. ■

Senore Gold Mines Ltd. (Que. June 7, 1937)
Distribution made of 1 sh. Coulville Mines for each 20 shs. Senore.

Sense Technologies Inc. (B.C. May 25, 1988)
Dec. 14, 2001 – Continued into Yukon.
Nov. 29, 2007 – Continued into British Columbia. (see FPsurvey - Industrials)

Sensor Technologies Corp. (Ont. Feb. 10, 2005)
Dec. 8, 2023 – Name changed to Blue Horizon Global Capital Corp. (see FPsurvey - Mines & Energy; FPsurvey - Industrials)

Sensormatic Canada Limited (Can. Nov. 20, 1968)
May 21, 1991 – Name changed to Senvest Capital Inc. (see FPsurvey - Industrials)

Sensormatic Electronics Canada Limited (Can. Nov. 20, 1968)
July 23, 1979 – Name changed to Sensormatic Canada Limited. ■

Senternet Phi Gamma Inc. (Ont. Mar. 28, 1967)
July 8, 2019 – Name changed to The Hash Corporation; basis 1 new for 20 old shs. ■

Senternet Technologies Inc. (Ont. Mar. 28, 1967)
Jan. 22, 2014 – Name changed to Senternet Phi Gamma Inc. ■

Sentex Systems Ltd. (Alta. Oct. 17, 1997)
July 8, 2008 – Name changed to Natunola Health Biosciences Inc. ■

Sentinel Holdings Limited (Ont. 1962)
Dec. 31, 1979 – Amalgamated with Unicorp Financial Corporation (under name Unicorp); basis 1 cl. A & cl. B share Unicorp for 4.8 cl. A shs. of Sentinel, and 1 cl. A & 1 cl. B sh. Unicorp for 24 cl. B shs. Sentinel.

Sentinel Resources Corp. (B.C. Aug. 3, 2018)
Nov. 22, 2021 – Name changed to EMP Metals Corp. (see FPsurvey - Mines & Energy)

Sentinel Resources Ltd. (B.C. July 2, 1986)
Aug. 30, 1995 – Name changed to Ulysses International Resources Ltd. ■

Sentinel Rock Oil Corporation (Alta. May 15, 2008 amalg.)
Nov. 17, 2010 – Name changed to Sentinel Rock Oil Inc.; basis 1 new for 10 old shs. ■

Sentinel Rock Oil Inc. (Alta. May 15, 2008 amalg.)
Apr. 8, 2011 – Formed Sundance Energy Corporation in Alberta pursuant to reverse takeover acquisition of Sundance Energy Corporation and subsequent amalgamation of Sundance with a wholly owned subsid. of Sentinel which in turn vertically amalgamated with Sentinel. ■

Sentinel Self-Storage Corporation (Alta. 1986)
July 9, 1990 – Amalgamated with 2 numbered companies, 418685 Alberta Ltd. and 396870 Alberta Ltd.; basis $3.625 per sh. Amalgamated co. will be equally owned by Cambridge Shopping Centres Limited and Sentinel Investments Inc.

Sentra Resources Corporation (Alta. Sept. 29, 2000)
Oct. 4, 2004 – Amalgamated with Blue Mountain Energy Ltd.; basis 1 Blue Mountain sh. for 5 Sentra shs. (see Blue Mountain Energy Ltd.)

Sentry Oil and Gas Corp. (B.C. Dec. 1, 1980)
Mar. 11, 1987 – Name changed to Sentry Resources Corporation. ■

Sentry Petroleums Limited (Ont. 1951)
Mar. 1976 – Charter cancelled.

Sentry Resources Corporation (B.C. Dec. 1, 1980)
May 20, 2019 – Struck from registry and dissolved.

Sentry Select Blue-Chip Income Trust (Ont. Feb. 27, 2001)
Mar. 31, 2011 – Terminated. Unithldrs. received $25.54 per trust unit.

Sentry Select Capital Corp. (Ont. Nov. 21, 2000)
Jan. 7, 2004 – Going private transaction via amalgamation with Sentry Select Holdings Inc.; basis 1 redeemable pref. sh. for 1 com. sh. immediately redeemed for $1.00 per sh.

Sentry Select China Fund (Ont. Apr. 4, 2007)
Apr. 23, 2009 – Converted into open-ended mutual fund.

Sentry Select Commodities Income Trust (Ont. June 29, 2005)
Jan. 31, 2011 – Merge with Sentry Energy Growth and Income Fund, an open-end mutual fund.

Sentry Select Diversified Income Fund (Ont. Jan. 17, 1997)
Aug. 5, 2009 – Converted into an open-ended mutual fund.

Sentry Select Diversified Income Trust (Ont. Jan. 17, 1997)
Jan. 8, 2009 – Name changed to Sentry Select Diversified Income Fund. ■

Sentry Select FIDAC U.S. Mortgage Trust (Ont. Aug. 30, 2005)
Mar. 11, 2008 – Acquired by Sentry Select MBS Adjustable Rate Income Fund II (ARIF II); basis 1.1315 ARIF II trust units for 1 Sentry Select FIDAC U.S. trust unit.

Sentry Select Focused Growth & Income Trust (Ont. Dec. 20, 2001)
June 3, 2009 – Merged into Sentry Select Canadian Income Fund, an open-ended mutual fund.

Sentry Select 40 Split Income Trust (Ont. Dec. 13, 2006)
June 12, 2009 – Merged into Sentry Select Canadian Income Fund, an open-ended mutual fund; basis 0.3689 Sentry Select Canadian units for 1 Sentry Select 40 unit.

Sentry Select Global Index Income Trust (Ont. Aug. 24, 2001)
June 22, 2012 – Terminated; trust units redeemed for $25.06 per unit.

Sentry Select Global Real Estate Fund (Ont. Nov. 29, 2007)
Feb. 1, 2010 – Merged with Sentry Select REIT Fund, converting from a closed end fund to an open-ended mutual fund. Each series A and series F unit of Sentry Select Global Real Estate Fund was exchanged for 0.6993 series A units and 0.6942 series F units of Sentry Select REIT.

Sentry Select Lazard Global Listed Infrastructure Fund (Ont. Jan. 30, 2007)
Mar. 26, 2009 – Converted from a closed end to an open-ended fund.

Sentry Select MBS Adjustable Rate Income Fund II (Ont. Mar. 29, 2005)
Mar. 17, 2011 – Converted into an open-ended mutual fund.
Mar. 31, 2011 – Name changed to Sentry U.S. Growth and Income Fund converted into an open-ended mutual fund.

Sentry Select Total Strategy Fund (Ont. July 27, 2006)
Mar. 30, 2009 – Terminated. Final distribution of $3.83 per unit paid.

Senvil Mines Ltd. (Ont. 1946)
Sept. 1963 – Dissolved.

Sepha Mines Ltd. (Ont. 1941)
1951 – Name changed to New Sepha Mines Limited; basis 1 new for 3 old shs. ■

Sepik Gold Corporation (Yuk. Nov. 27, 1996)
Oct. 8, 2002 – Struck from registry and dissolved.

Sepp's Gourmet Foods Ltd. (B.C. Apr. 30, 1995)
June 25, 2010 – Acquired by Ralcorp Holdings Inc. for an undisclosed amount.

Seprotech Systems Incorporated (Can. Sept. 6, 1985)
Nov. 6, 2012 – Name changed to BluMetric Environmental Inc. pursuant to reverse takeover acquisition of WESA Group Inc.; basis 1 new for 10 old shs. (see FPsurvey - Industrials)

September Mt. Copper Mines Ltd. (Ont. 1968)
Mar. 1976 – Charter cancelled.

September Resources Ltd. (B.C. 1984)
Dec. 21, 1987 – Name changed to Uranium Resources, Inc. ■

September Resources Ltd. (Can. 1986)
Mar. 6, 1987 – Continued into British Columbia.
Feb. 9, 1998 – Name changed to Aquest Minerals Corporation. ■

Sequoia Minerals Inc. (Que. Dec. 29, 2003)
July 7, 2004 – Amalgamated with wholly owned subsid. of Cambior Inc.; basis either 0.15873 new Cambior com. sh. or 1 pfd. sh. immediately redeemed for $0.60 for 1 old Sequoia com. sh. (see Cambior Inc.)

Sequoia Oil & Gas Trust (Alta. Mar. 14, 2005)
Sept. 26, 2006 – Plan of Arrangement amalgamation with Daylight Resources Trust (formerly Daylight Energy Trust); basis 0.825 new Daylight Resources unit, 0.0517 new Trafalgar Energy Ltd. com. sh. plus 0.0144 new Trafalgar Arrangement warrant for 1 old Sequoia unit. (see Daylight Resources Trust; Trafalgar Energy Ltd.)

Sequoia Resources Inc. (B.C. June 27, 1966)
Aug. 7, 1985 – Name changed to American Technology & Information Inc. ■

Serabi Mining plc (U.K. May 18, 2004)
Oct. 18, 2011 – Name changed to Serabi Gold plc. (see FPsurvey - Mines & Energy)

Serac Sports Ltd. (Alta. Dec. 7, 1995)
May 10, 2000 – Acquired by silverzipper.com, Inc.; basis US$0.2346 or 1 silverzipper sh. for 17.82 Serac shs.

Serebra Learning Corporation (Alta. Feb. 9, 1987)
Jan. 26, 2012 – Name changed to Bluedrop Performance Learning Inc. and continued into Newfoundland and Labrador pursuant to reverse takeover acquisition of Blue Drop Inc. and subsequent vertical amalgamation of Blue Drop into the company; basis 1 new for 4 old shs. ■

Serem Ltd. (Can. Dec. 28, 1966)
Mar. 25, 1987 – Name changed to Cheni Gold Mines Inc. ■

Serena Resources Ltd. (B.C. July 17, 1987)
May 17, 2001 – Name changed to Consolidated Serena Resources Ltd.; basis 1 new for 5 old shs. ■

Serengeti Diamonds Ltd. (B.C. Mar. 5, 1973)
Apr. 26, 1999 – Name changed to Serengeti Minerals Ltd. ■

Serengeti Minerals Ltd. (B.C. Mar. 5, 1973)
Mar. 22, 2001 – Name changed to Serengeti Resources Inc.; basis 1 new for 15 old shs. ■

Serengeti Resources Inc. (B.C. Mar. 5, 1973)
Mar. 5, 2021 – Name changed to Northwest Copper Corp.; basis 1 new for 2 old shs. (see FPsurvey - Mines & Energy)

Serenic Corporation (Alta. Sept. 6, 1996)
Aug. 1, 2014 – Name changed to OneSoft Solutions Inc. ■

Sereno Capital Corporation (Ont. Mar. 19, 2007)
Dec. 30, 2013 – Name changed to Delavaco Residential Properties Corp. pursuant to Qualifying Transaction reverse takeover acquisition of Delavaco Properties Inc.; basis 1 new for 7.36 old shs. ■

Serenpet Energy Inc. (Alta. June 11, 1987)
Apr. 1, 1992 – Formed Serenpet Inc. in Alberta on amalgamation with Manna Resources Inc.; basis 0.81667 new for 1 Manna sh. and 1 new for 3 Serenpet shs. ■

Serenpet Inc. (Alta. Apr. 1, 1992 amalg.)
Jan. 14, 1997 – Acquired by Pembina Resources Limited for $4.80 per sh.

Seriatim Ventures Inc. (Alta. May 9, 2006)
Dec. 30, 2008 – Name changed to Forent Energy Inc. following Qualifying Transaction acquisition of Forent Energy Ltd.; basis 1 new for 2.7 old shs. ■

Serica Energy Corporation (British Virgin Islands Jan. 29, 2004 amalg.)
Sept. 1, 2005 – Succeeded by Serica Energy plc pursuant to plan of arrangement whereby com. shs. were exchanged for ord. shs. of newly incorporated Serica Energy plc on a sh.-for-sh. basis, constituting a reverse takeover by Serica Energy Corporation which became a wholly owned subsidiary.

Series S-1 Income Fund (Alta. Apr. 17, 2003)
Dec. 31, 2009 – Merged into Blue Ribbon Income Fund (formerly Citadel Diversified Investment Trust); basis 0.770898 Blue Ribbon trust units for 1 Series S-1 trust unit.

Serinus Energy Inc. (Alta. Mar. 16, 1987)
May 15, 2018 – Name changed to Serinus Energy plc. Continued into Jersey.

Sernova Corp. (Can. May 29, 2001)
Feb. 4, 2025 – Name changed to Sernova Biotherapeutics Inc. and continued into British Columbia. (see FPsurvey - Industrials)

Serval Growth Fund (Alta. July 25, 1996)
Aug. 27, 1998 – Name changed to Serval Integrated Energy Services. ■

Serval Integrated Energy Services (Alta. July 25, 1996)
June 2, 2001 – Dissolved and struck from registry.

Service Corporation International (Canada) Limited (Can. 1968)
Sept. 5, 1995 – Amalgamated with a wholly owned subsid. effective Aug. 31, 1995, whereby each com. sh. was converted into one cl. A pfd. sh. redeemable for $22.75.

Service Petroleum Ltd. (Ont. Apr. 18, 1978)
Apr. 19, 1984 – Name changed to Cape Resources Inc. ■

Service Plus Hospitality Ltd. (Alta. Sept. 18, 1997)
May 23, 2003 – Plan of Arrangement to convert company to new income trust named Gamehost Income Fund; basis 0.328 new Gamehost units for 1 old Service Plus com. sh. (see Gamehost Income Fund)

Services Techniques Informatiques S.T.I. Inc. (Que. 1976)
Sept. 3, 1996 – Acquired by a subsid. of Foxmeyer Canada Inc.; basis 0.117 Foxmeyer Canada shs. for 1 Services Techniques sh.

Setanta Ventures Inc. (B.C. Apr. 3, 1987)
Nov. 5, 2001 – Delisted from the CDNX. Subsequently struck from register and dissolved.

Setec Security Inc. (B.C. 1982)
Feb. 1983 – Name changed to Sigma Security Inc. ■

Seton Lake Mines Ltd. (B.C. 1969)
June 27, 1977 – Dissolved.

Sevcoeur Gold Mines Ltd. (Ont. 1945)
Charter cancelled; no equity for shldrs.

Seven Aces Limited (Ont. Aug. 15, 1995 amalg.)
Aug. 17, 2020 – Acquired by Trive Capital Management LLC; basis Cdn$2.77 cash per sh.

Seven Arts Productions Ltd. (Ont. 1919)
July 1967 – Name changed to Warner Bros.-Seven Arts Productions Ltd. ■

Seven Clans Resources Ltd. (Alta. Apr. 28, 1993)
Apr. 30, 2002 – Amalgamated in Ontario to continue with same name.
Sept. 18, 2003 – Name changed to Mexgold Resources Inc. following reverse takeover arrangement with Gammon Lake Resources Inc. to acquire Mexgold Resources Inc.; basis 1 new for 2 old shs. ■

7 Crowns Corporation (Alta. Nov. 2, 1987)
Apr. 5, 2004 – Going private transaction by way of consolidation; basis 1 new for 1,000,000 old shs.

Seven Generations Energy Ltd. (Can. Jan. 8, 2001)
Apr. 8, 2021 – Acquired by ARC Resources Ltd.; basis 1.08 ARC com. shs for 1 Seven Generations cl. A com. sh.

Seven Island Mining & Exploration Corp. Ltd. (Que. 1952)
Aug. 1972 – Charter cancelled.

Seven Mile High Group Inc. (B.C. Oct. 29, 1984)
Nov. 20, 1992 – Name changed to Sevex Energy Inc. ■

Seven Mile High Resources Inc. (B.C. Oct. 29, 1984)
Oct. 13, 1989 – Name changed to Seven Mile High Group Inc. ■

Seven Seas Petroleum Inc. (B.C. June 29, 1995 amalg.)
Aug. 12, 1996 – Continued into Yukon.
Mar. 1, 2001 – Continued into Cayman Islands.

701.Com Corp. (Ont. Aug. 13, 1999)
Aug. 15, 2001 – Name changed to 701 Media Group Inc. ■

7188501 Canada Inc. (Can. June 10, 2009)
Oct. 27, 2009 – Name changed to Hydrogenics Corporation. ■

763997 Alberta Ltd. (Alta.)
May 23, 2024 – Name changed to Westgate Energy Inc. pursuant to the reverse takeover acquisition of Grafton Ventures Energy Holdings Corp.; basis 1 new for 40 old shs. (see FPsurvey - Mines & Energy; FPsurvey - Industrials)

79 Resources Ltd. (B.C. Apr. 17, 2019)
Dec. 23, 2024 – Name changed to Rottenstone Gold Inc. (see FPsurvey - Mines & Energy)

7936567 Canada Inc. (Can. Oct. 28, 2011)
Nov. 6, 2019 – The monitor, Deloitte Restructuring Inc., was discharged as monitor of the CCAA proceedings.
Nov. 7, 2019 – Filed an assignment into bankruptcy and Deloitte Restructuring Inc. was appointed trustee.

79North Inc. (Ont. Nov. 27, 2017)
Oct. 18, 2024 – Acquired by Miata Metals Corp. and then merged with a wholly owned subsid. of Miata; basis 0.079 Miata shs. for 1 79North sh.

Seventh Energy Ltd. (Alta. Feb. 27, 1996)
Aug. 11, 1997 – Amalgamated with Westward Energy Ltd. (0.6 for 1) to continue with the same name Seventh Energy Ltd.; basis 1 cl. A sh. for 1 cl. A sh.
Apr. 16, 2004 – Acquired by PrimeWest Gas Corp., a private co. for $1.00 per sh.

Seventh Malartic Mines Ltd. (Ont. 1940)
Feb. 1961 – Charter cancelled.

Seventh Wave Capital Corp. (Alta. Jan. 25, 2000)
Dec. 16, 2002 – Amalgamated with Imaging Dynamics Company Ltd. and Mika Technology Inc. to continue as Imaging Dynamics Company Ltd. (IDL) considered to be the company's Qualifying Transaction; basis 12.69384 new IDL units (1 IDL sh. and 1 IDL wt.) for 100 old Seventh Wave com. shs.

724 Solutions Inc. (Ont. July 28, 1997)
Aug. 18, 2006 – Plan of Arrangement with 724 Holdings, Inc. to privatize company; basis US$3.34 per sh.

71 Capital Corp. (Can. Feb. 6, 2008)
Sept. 4, 2015 – Name changed to Prodigy Ventures Inc. following Qualifying Transaction reverse takeover acquisition of TCB Corporation (dba Prodigy Ventures); basis 1 new for 2 old shs. ■

SevenWay Capital Corporation (Alta. Oct. 4, 1979 amalg.)
Apr. 28, 2000 – Amalgamated with Glacier Ventures International Corp. to form new co. with same name Glacier Ventures International Corp.; basis 1 new for 1 Glacier sh. and 0.446 new for 1 SevenWay sh. (see Glacier Ventures International Corp.)

701 Media Group Inc. (Ont. Aug. 13, 1999)
Dec. 17, 2003 – Name changed to YSV Ventures Inc. (see FPsurvey - Mines & Energy)

Severide Resources Inc. (B.C. 1984)
Feb. 1, 1994 – Name changed to Severide Environmental Industries Inc. (see FPsurvey - Industrials)

Severn Mines Limited (Ont. 1928)
Apr. 25, 1996 – Amalgamated with Mercantile International Petroleum B.V.I. Inc. to form Mercantile International Petroleum Inc. and continued into Cayman Islands; basis 1 new for 5 old shs.

Sevex Energy Inc. (B.C. Oct. 29, 1984)
Nov. 29, 1995 – Name changed to Colony Energy Ltd.; basis 1 new for 8 old shs. ■

Sextant Enterprise Corp. (Alta. Dec. 18, 1995)
June 17, 1998 – Name changed to Pure Technologies Ltd. ■

Sextant Entertainment Group Inc. (Can. Nov. 22, 1994)
June 5, 2002 – Filed for protection under the Companies' Creditors Arrangement Act (CCAA).
June 20, 2002 – Unable to file a formal plan of compromise or arrangement with its creditors following CCAA. The Royal Bank of Canada subsequently appointed Vancouver-based Deloitte & Touche Inc. as interim receiver and applied to the courts and successfully set aside the stay of proceedings granted to the co. and its subsids. under the CCAA.
Mar. 2, 2004 – Receiver discharged. No information was available regarding distributions to creditors or shldrs.

Seymour Exploration Corp. (B.C. Apr. 24, 1972)
June 21, 2006 – Name changed to Independent Nickel Corp. ■

Seymour-Moss International Limited (B.C. June 9, 1983)
Nov. 10, 1988 – Dissolved and struck off register.

Seymour Resources Inc. (B.C. 1978)
June 13, 1985 – Name changed to Crowder Communication Corporation. ■

Seymour Ventures Corp. (Can. May 16, 2000)
July 13, 2011 – Name changed to Rare Earth Industries Ltd. ■

Shabu Gold Mines Ltd. (Can. Aug. 6, 1986)
Apr. 19, 1988 – Name changed to Canadian Eagle Exploration Inc. ■

Shabute Ventures Inc. (B.C. Sept. 5, 1975)
Aug. 18, 2004 – Name changed to Northern Sun Exploration Company Inc. ■

Shackleton Petroleum Corporation Ltd. (B.C. 1977)
1981 – Continued into Alberta.
Sept. 30, 1982 – Name changed to Europa Petroleum Ltd.; basis 1 new for 10 old shs. ■

Shadow Technologies Inc. (Can. Aug. 12, 1994)
July 11, 1997 – Name changed to Sofame Technologies Inc. (see FPsurvey - Industrials)

Shadowfax Resources Ltd. (Can. Feb. 9, 1981)
Apr. 6, 1990 – Name changed to Docu-Fax International Inc. ■

Shadrack Mining Limited (Ont. 1973)
Feb. 20, 1980 – Dissolved.

Shafer Resources Corp. (B.C. Sept. 28, 2018)
Oct. 10, 2023 – Name changed to Kubera Gold Corp. (see FPsurvey - Mines & Energy)

Shaft-Ore Porcupine Mines Ltd. (Ont. 1946)
Aug. 19, 1965 – Dissolved.

Shaker Petroleum Inc. (Alta. Oct. 9, 1996)
June 28, 2002 – Name changed to Shaker Resources Inc.; basis 1 new for 5 old shs. ■

Shaker Resources Inc. (Alta. Oct. 9, 1996)
Sept. 30, 2004 – Plan of Arrangement exchange with Caribou Resources Corp.; basis 0.4224 new Caribou sh. for 1 old Shaker sh. (see Caribou Resources Corp.)

Shakespeare Uranium Mines Ltd. (Ont. 1954)
Nov. 30, 1964 – Dissolved.

Shakwak Exploration Company Limited (B.C. Sept. 5, 1980)
Nov. 10, 1995 – Name changed to Arcturus Resources Ltd.; basis 1 new for 8 old shs. ■

Shallow Resources Inc. (B.C. Jan. 22, 1982)
Mar. 2, 1989 – Delisted from the Vancouver Stock Exchange. Subsequently dissolved.

Shalmar Resources Limited (B.C. 1963)
May 6, 1983 – Struck off register.

Shamrock Enterprises Inc. (B.C. Apr. 17, 2008)
Jan. 8, 2020 – Name changed to Aurwest Resources Corporation; basis 1 new for 4 old shs. (see FPsurvey - Mines & Energy)

Shamrock Gold Mines Ltd. (B.C.)
May 8, 1969 – Struck off register.

Shamrock Petroleum Ltd. (Alta. 1937)
Nov. 1956 – Name changed to Alaska-Yukon Refiners & Distributors Ltd. ■

Shamrock Resources Inc. (B.C. Nov. 20, 1980)
Aug. 22, 2003 – Name changed to Pacific Energy Resources Ltd. ■

Shandon Resources Inc. (B.C. 1981)
Dec. 24, 1993 – Dissolved and struck off register.

Shane Resources Ltd. (Sask. June 15, 1981)
June 20, 2014 – Voluntarily liquidated and dissolved distribution to shldrs. unknown.
Dec. 21, 2018 – Revived and restored to registry.
Nov. 23, 2021 – Continued into British Columbia.
Dec. 3, 2021 – Name changed to Empatho Holdings Inc. pursuant to the reverse takeover acquisition of Empatho Corp. and subsequent amalgamation of Empatho with wholly owned 13348776 Canada Inc. (see FPsurvey - Industrials)

Shanell International Energy Corporation (B.C. July 30, 1979)
June 14, 1989 – Name changed to Pacific Insight Electronics Corp.; basis 1 new for 4 old shs. ■

Shanell Petrochemical Corporation (Alta. 1987)
Dec. 1, 1993 – Struck off register.

The Shannock Corporation (Can. 1982)
Feb. 26, 1988 – Name changed to TSC Shannock Corporation; basis 1 new for 3 old shs. ■

Shannon Energy Ltd. (Alta. 1974)
Mar. 2, 1993 – Name changed to Shannon Environmental Ltd.; basis 1 new for 5 old shs. ■

Shannon Environmental Ltd. (Alta. 1974)
Apr. 1, 1996 – Dissolved and struck off register.

Shanwell Porcupine Gold Mines Ltd. (Ont. 1940)
May 1960 – Charter cancelled.

Sharbot Lake Mines Ltd. (Que. 1956)
Nov. 4, 1978 – Charter cancelled.

Share Mines & Oils Ltd. (Alta. Sept. 21, 1936)
Nov. 20, 1979 – Continued into Ontario.
Oct. 29, 1996 – Name changed to Share Resources Inc.; basis 1 new for 4 old shs. (see FPsurvey - Mines & Energy)

Share Oils Ltd. (Alta. Sept. 21, 1936)
1965 – Name changed to Share Mines & Oils Ltd. ■

Shareco Capital Corp. (Alta. Jan. 13, 1987)
Feb. 19, 1993 – Name changed to Binoptic International Corporation. ■

Sharlake Mines Ltd. (Que. 1958)
Nov. 11, 1978 – Charter cancelled.

Sharon Copper Mines Ltd. (B.C.)
May 15, 1969 – Struck off register.

Sharon Energy Ltd. (B.C. Feb. 15, 1980)
Sept. 24, 2003 – Continued into Alberta. (see Tuscany Energy Ltd.)
June 24, 2011 – Amalgamated with Tuscany Energy Ltd.; basis 0.84 Tuscany shs. for 1 Sharon sh. (see Tuscany Energy Ltd.)

Sharpe Energy & Resources Limited (Ont. Apr. 10, 1980)
June 30, 1996 – Name changed to Sharpe Resources Corporation. ■

Sharpe Instruments of Canada Limited (Ont. June 22, 1960)
May 25, 1967 – Name changed to Scintrex Limited; basis 1 new for 4 old shs. ■

Sharpe Resources Corporation (Ont. Apr. 10, 1980)
2001 – Continued into New Brunswick. (see FPsurvey - Mines & Energy)

Shasper Industries Ltd. (unknown 1971)
Apr. 14, 1980 – Continued into Canada.
Nov. 8, 1991 – Acquired by Shasper Investments Inc. for $1.60 per sh.

Shasta Mines & Oil Ltd. (B.C. Sept. 2, 1966)
Feb. 4, 1975 – Name changed to International Shasta Resources Ltd.; basis 1 new for 5 old shs. ■

Shatheena Capital Corp. (Ont. Jan. 29, 2003)
May 30, 2005 – Formed Plato Gold Corp. in Ontario on Qualifying Transaction reverse takeover acquisition of and amalgamation with Plato Gold Corp. (see FPsurvey - Mines & Energy)

Shaw Cablesystems Ltd. (Alta. Dec. 9, 1966)
May 26, 1993 – Name changed to Shaw Communications Inc. ■

Shaw Communications Inc. (Alta. Dec. 9, 1966)
Apr. 5, 2023 – Amalgamated into Rogers Communications Inc.; basis $40.50 cash per cl. A participating sh. and cl. B non-participating sh.

Shaw Industries Ltd. (Can. Aug. 23, 1968; via Dominion charter)
May 4, 2001 – Name changed to ShawCor Ltd. ■

Shaw-Manson Ltd. (unknown 1948)
Charter cancelled.

Shaw Petroleum Corp. of Canada Ltd. (Ont. Nov. 18, 1948)
Dec. 1956 – Announced intention to wind up voluntarily.

Shaw Petroleums Co. Ltd. (Alta.)
1960 – Struck off register.

Shaw Pipe Industries Ltd. (Can. Aug. 23, 1968; via Dominion charter)
May 12, 1980 – Name changed to Shaw Industries Ltd.; basis 2 new for 1 old sh. ■

Shaw Porcupine Gold Mines Ltd. (Ont. 1936)
1945 – Absorbed by Carshaw Porcupine Gold Mines Ltd.; basis 1 new for 3 old shs. (see Carshaw Porcupine Gold Mines Ltd.)

Shawano Iron Mines Ltd. (B.C. 1956)
Dec. 20, 1982 – Dissolved.

ShawCor Ltd. (Can. Aug. 23, 1968; via Dominion charter)
Mar. 20, 2013 – Amalgamated with 8404810 Canada Inc. to form (new) ShawCor Ltd. pursuant to a capital reorganization.
Feb. 1, 2016 – Name changed to Shawcor Ltd. ■

Shawcor Ltd. (Can. Mar. 20, 2013 amalg.)
Jan. 8, 2024 – Name changed to Mattr Corp. (see FPsurvey - Mines & Energy; FPsurvey - Industrials)

Shawinigan Industries Limited (Can. - unspecified 1963)
1963 – Acquired by Power Corp. of Canada Ltd., through purchase offer of $5.116 per sh.

Shawinigan Mining & Smelting Co. Ltd. (Que. 1929)
July 1974 – Charter cancelled.

Shawinigan Nickel Corp. (Que. 1954)
Oct. 1974 – Charter cancelled.

Shawinigan Water & Power Co. (Que. 1898)
1963 – Purchased by Hydro-Québec. Com. shldrs. got $30 per sh.; cl. A com. shldrs. got $30.25 per sh. In addition, com. and cl. A com. holders of record Apr. 29, received the right (not exercisable by U.S. residents) to acquire shs., at $5.00 each, in Shawinigan Industries Ltd. on a sh.-for-sh. basis. Pref. shldrs. received equal par value in 10-year bonds guaranteed by the Prov. of Quebec, bearing int. equal to divd. rate. Funded debt assumed by Quebec Hydro.

Shawkey Gold Mining Co. Ltd. (Ont. Mar. 6, 1934)
1945 – Acquired by Shawkey (1945) Mines Ltd.; basis 1 new for 3 old shs. (see Shawkey (1945) Mines Ltd.)

Shawkey (1945) Mines Ltd. (Ont. 1945)
1956 – Name changed to Ultra-Shawkey Mines Ltd.; basis 1 new for 4 old shs. ■

Shawmin Consolidated Ltd. (Ont. 1964)
Sept. 5, 1979 – Charter cancelled.

Shawmin Explorations Ltd. (Ont. 1964)
1975 – Name changed to Shawmin Consolidated Ltd.; basis 1 new for 2 old shs. ■

Shawnee Petroleums Limited (Ont. Dec. 9, 1965)
Nov. 17, 1986 – Name changed to Semi-Tech Microelectronics Inc. ■

Shawnex Mines Ltd. (B.C. 1967)
Apr. 4, 1977 – Dissolved and struck off register.

Shaw's Industrial Corporation (Alta. Aug. 16, 1996)
Mar. 26, 2003 – Going private transaction; basis 1 new for 100,000 old shs.

Shaynee Consolidated Metals & Holdings Ltd. (Ont. 1960)
Feb. 1980 – Charter cancelled.

Shaynee Consolidated Mines Ltd. (Ont. 1960)
Dec. 22, 1970 – Name changed to Shaynee Consolidated Metals & Holdings Ltd. ■

Sheadore Gold Mines Ltd. (Ont. 1936)
Mar. 19, 1969 – Charter cancelled.

Shear Diamonds Ltd. (Alta. Nov. 16, 1995)
June 2, 2015 – Dissolved and struck from register.

Shear Minerals Ltd. (Alta. Nov. 16, 1995)
Dec. 30, 2010 – Name changed to Shear Diamonds Ltd.; basis 1 new for 10 old shs. ■

Shear Wind Inc. (Alta. June 9, 2006 amalg.)
Mar. 1, 2010 – Continued into Canada. (see Sprott Power Corp.)
Nov. 27, 2012 – Acquired by Sprott Power Corp. for $0.2213 per sh. (see Sprott Power Corp.)

Shearhart Corporation (Alta. 1987)
May 30, 2000 – Acquired by Midnorthern Appliance Inc. for $1.58 per sh.

Shearzona Mines Ltd. (Ont. 1947)
Nov. 5, 1962 – Dissolved.

Shea's Winnipeg Brewery Ltd. (Can. 1926)
1953 – John Labatt Limited purchased all o/s shs.; basis 1 Labatt com. sh. plus $17.50 for each 2 cl. A shs. or each cl. B sh.
Oct. 1958 – Name changed to Labatt's Manitoba Brewery Ltd.

Sheba Copper Mines Limited (B.C. 1956)
July 7, 1992 – Amalgamated with McConnell-Peel Resources Ltd. to form Coast Falcon Resources Ltd.; basis 1 new for 10 McConnell-Peel shs. and 1 new for 10 Coast Falcon shs. (see Coast Falcon Resources Ltd.)

Sheba Mines Ltd. (Ont. 1952)
Mar. 1976 – Charter cancelled.

Shebandowan Resources Ltd. (B.C. 1983)
Jan. 28, 1987 – Name changed to Videtics International Corp. ■

Shebnor Mines Ltd. (Ont. 1959)
Apr. 16, 1969 – Charter cancelled.

Shediac Bay Resources Inc. (Ont. May 14, 1985)
Feb. 14, 1992 – Name changed to Dally Development Corp.; basis 1 new for 4 old shs. ■

Sheen Minerals Inc. (B.C. Aug. 26, 1983)
Feb. 19, 1986 – Name changed to S.M.M. Enterprises Ltd. ■

Sheen Resources Ltd. (B.C. Feb. 2, 1999)
Oct. 22, 2012 – Dissolved and struck from register.

Sheep Creek Gold Mines Ltd. (B.C. 1933)
1956 – Name changed to Sheep Creek Mines Ltd. ■

Sheep Creek Mines Ltd. (B.C. 1933)
1965 – Name changed to Aetna Investment Corporation Ltd. ■

Sheer Energy Inc. (Alta. Apr. 12, 1996)
Oct. 11, 2005 – Name changed to CYGAM Energy Inc. following reverse takeover acquisitions of Rigo Oil Company Limited and Vega Oil S.r.l. and purchase of $6,000,000 in units of Peyto Energy Trust. ■

Sheer Silk Hosiery Mills Ltd. (Que. 1937)
July 15, 1972 – Charter cancelled.

Sheffield Iron Mines Ltd. (Ont. 1948)
Nov. 9, 1976 – Charter cancelled.

Sheffield Medical Technologies Inc. (Can. 1986)
Sept. 30, 1992 – Continued into Wyoming.
July 3, 1997 – Name changed to Sheffield Pharmaceuticals Inc. ■

Sheffield Pharmaceuticals Inc. (Wyo. Sept. 30, 1992)
June 26, 2007 – Name changed to Pipex Pharmaceuticals, Inc. ■

Sheffield Resources Inc. (B.C. Dec. 7, 1965)
Apr. 27, 1999 – Name changed to Globalstore.com, Incorporated and continued into Nova Scotia pursuant to acquisition of Global eComm Ltd. ■

Sheffield Resources Ltd. (Alta. Oct. 15, 1998)
Aug. 1, 2008 – Acquired by Nevoro Inc.; basis 0.8 Nevoro com. shs. for 1 Sheffield com. sh.

Sheffield Strategic Metals Inc. (Can. 1986)
Apr. 22, 1992 – Name changed to Sheffield Medical Technologies Inc.; basis 1 new for 1 old sh. ■

Shelby Ventures Inc. (B.C. Feb. 27, 2007)
June 22, 2018 – Name changed to Solution Financial Inc. pursuant to Qualifying Transaction reverse takeover acquisition of (old) Solution Financial Inc.; basis 1 new for 2.451 old shs. (see FPsurvey - Industrials)

Sheldon-Larder Mines Limited (Ont. Mar. 20, 1937)
Jan. 1, 2010 – Amalgamated with Union Gold Inc., Golden Harker Explorations Limited, Milestone Exploration Limited, and Wood-Croesus Gold Mines Limited to form Jubilee Gold Inc.; basis 0.269 Jubilee sh. for 1 Sheldon-Larder sh., 0.557 Jubilee sh. for 1 Union Gold sh., 0.393 Jubilee sh. for 1 Golden Harker sh., 1.749 Jubilee shs. for 1 Milestone sh. and 0.367 Jubilee sh. for 1 Wood-Croesus sh. (see Jubilee Gold Inc.)

Shell Canada Limited (Can. Aug. 7, 1925; via Dominion charter)
Apr. 25, 2007 – Acquired by Royal Dutch Shell plc for $45 per sh.

The Shell Oil Company of Canada, Limited (Ont. Mar. 21, 1911)
Aug. 7, 1925 – Continued into Canada; via Dominion charter.
July 1963 – Name changed to Shell Canada Limited. ■

Shellbridge Oil & Gas, Inc. (Alta. July 7, 2005)
June 27, 2006 – Plan of Arrangement acquisition by True Energy Trust; basis 0.14 new True Energy unit for 1 old Shellbridge sh. (see True Energy Trust)

Shelling Industries Ltd. (Ont. Aug. 1977)
Oct. 27, 1992 – Name changed to The CanFibre Group Ltd.; basis 1 new for 2 old shs. ■

Shelter Bay Mining Corp. (Que. 1960)
Name changed to Shelter Bay Mining Corporation Ltd. ■

Shelter Bay Mining Corporation Ltd. (Que. 1960)
1984 – Name changed to Bay Ressources et Services Inc. / Bay Resources and Services Inc. ■

Shelter Gold Ltd. (B.C. Oct. 21, 1966)
Dec. 17, 1976 – Name changed to Shelter Oil & Gas Ltd. ■

Shelter Hydrocarbonds Limited (Alta. 1978)
Aug. 9, 1983 – Amalgamated with Killucan Resources Ltd. to form Skill Resources Ltd.; basis 1 com. sh. of Shelter for 1 com. sh. of Skill, and 1 cl. A sh. of Shelter for 1 cl. B pref. sh. of Skill.

Shelter Oil & Gas Ltd. (B.C. Oct. 21, 1966)
1985 – Continued into Alberta. (see Tesco Corporation)
Dec. 3, 1993 – Amalgamated with Coexco Petroleum Inc. and Forewest Industries Ltd. to form Tesco Corporation; basis 1 new for 3.3139652 Coexco shs., 1 new for 9.6526944 Forewest shs. and 1 new for 4 Shelter shs. (see Tesco Corporation)

Shelter Petroleums Ltd. (B.C. May 1973)
July 1973 – Amalgamated with Blackline Resource Corporation Ltd. to form Groundstar Petroleums Ltd.

Sheltered Oak Resources Corp. (B.C. Mar. 1, 2007)
Apr. 11, 2013 – Acquired by Foundation Resources Inc.;
basis 1 Foundation com. sh. for 6 Sheltered com. shs.
(see Foundation Resources Inc.)

Shelton Canada Corp. (Alta. Dec. 19, 1994)
Dec. 31, 2009 – Acquired by Petrosibir Canada Inc., a
wholly owned subsid. of Petrosibir AB; basis 2.708
Petrosibir ser. B sh. for 1 Shelton sh.

Shenandoah Mines Inc. (Ont. 1972)
1975 – Name changed to Consumers Equity Corporation.

Shenandoah Resources Ltd. (Alta. Aug. 27, 1997)
Sept. 17, 2002 – Placed into receivership. RSM Richter
Inc. was appointed receiver.

Shenango Mining Co. Ltd. (Ont. 1941)
1955 – Charter cancelled.

Shenul Capital Inc. (B.C. Mar. 6, 2007)
Aug. 9, 2011 – Continued into British Virgin Islands.
Aug. 17, 2011 – Name changed to Underground Energy
Corporation pursuant to reverse takeover acquisition of
Underground Energy Inc.

Shephard Insurance Group Limited (B.C. July 14, 1982)
Mar. 11, 1999 – Name changed to Collingwood Capital
Corporation; basis 1 new for 5 old shs. ■

Shepherd Casters Canada Limited (Ont. May 8, 1957)
Nov. 1, 1972 – Name changed to Shepherd Products
Limited. ■

Shepherd Products Limited (Ont. May 8, 1957)
Dec. 29, 1989 – Acquired by Apex Acquisition Corporation
for $33 per sh.

Sheraton Limited (Can. 1947)
All shs. privately held.

Sheraton Uranium Mines Ltd. (Ont. 1952)
Dec. 1959 – Charter cancelled.

Sherbrook SBK Sport Corp. (Can. Apr. 16, 2010)
Feb. 10, 2014 – Dissolved and struck from registry.
Apr. 23, 2021 – Charter revived. (see FPsurvey -
Industrials)

Sherbrooke Trust Company (Que. 1874)
July 22, 1993 – Assets acquired by the National Bank of
Canada.

Sheridan Copper Mines Ltd. (B.C. 1969)
1971 – Amalgamated into Granite Mountain Mines Ltd.
on sh.-for-sh. basis, except for vendor shs., which were
exch. on 1 new for 2 old shs. basis.

Sheridan Reserve Incorporated (Ont. Aug. 24, 1993
amalg.)
Aug. 4, 2000 – Name changed to NevadaBobs.com Inc. ■

Sheritt-Lee Mines Ltd. (B.C. 1958)
Jan. 17, 1972 – Name changed to Vanalta Resources
Ltd. ■

Sherlynn Mines Limited (Ont. 1955)
Oct. 15, 1994 – Dissolved and struck off register.

Shermag Inc. (Que. Jan. 28, 1977)
Apr. 23, 2010 – Privatized at 3¢ per sh.

Sheroomac Mining Corp. Ltd. (Ont. 1953)
May 9, 1977 – Dissolved.

Sherpa Holdings Corp. (B.C. Feb. 3, 2017)
Mar. 1, 2018 – Name changed to Nubeva Technologies
Ltd. pursuant to Qualifying Transaction reverse takeover
acquisition of Nubeva, Inc. and merger of Nubeva with
wholly owned Sherpa USA Ltd.; basis 1 new for 5 old
shs. (see FPsurvey - Industrials)

Sherrgold Inc. (Ont. 1959)
Aug. 2, 1988 – Name changed to LynnGold Resources
Inc. ■

Sherritt Gordon Limited (Ont. July 5, 1927)
July 5, 1993 – Name changed to Sherritt Inc. ■

Sherritt Gordon Mines Limited (Ont. July 5, 1927)
June 1, 1988 – Name changed to Sherritt Gordon
Limited. ■

Sherritt Inc. (Ont. July 5, 1927)
Apr. 25, 1996 – Name changed to Viridian Inc. ■

Sherritt International Corporation (N.B. Oct. 4, 1995)
Aug. 1, 2007 – Continued into Ontario.
June 3, 2016 – Continued into Canada. (see FPsurvey -
Mines & Energy; FPsurvey - Industrials)

Sherritt Power Corporation (N.B. Apr. 14, 1997)
Mar. 31, 2003 – Amalgamated with 605447 N.B. Ltd.
wholly owned subsid. of Sherritt International Corporation;
basis 1.45 new Sherritt Int'l rest. voting shs. for 1 old
Sherritt Power com. sh. Also old 12.125% Sherritt Power
note deb. due 31/03/07 exchanged for new 9.875%
Sherritt Int'l note deb. due 31/03/10. (see Sherritt
International Corporation)

Sherry Lee Gold Mines (Ont. 1946)
1952 – Charter cancelled.

Sherwin Minerals Ltd. (Can. 1973)
Nov. 26, 1975 – Amalgamated with Spar Holdings &
Explorations Ltd.; basis 1 sh. Spar for 2 shs. Sherwin.

Sherwin-Williams Canada Inc. (Can. 1911)
Oct. 15, 1986 – As of 58% of the 7% voting prfce shs.
were acquired at $45 per sh. following an offer by a wholly
owned subsidiary of The Sherwin-Williams Company.
Subsequently, the remaining 42% of the prfce shs. were
redeemed July 31, 1992 at a rate of $100 plus accrued
and unpaid div. of $58.50 per sh. (from Apr. 1, 1984 to
July 30, 1992) for a total of $158.50. Since all the com.
shs. are held by The Sherwin-Williams Company of
Cleveland, Ohio, the redemption of the remaining 7%
preference shs. relinquishes any public interest in the
company.

The Sherwin-Williams Company of Canada Limited
(Can. 1911)
Dec. 12, 1980 – Name changed to Sherwin-Williams
Canada Inc. ■

Sherwood Copper Corporation (Alta. July 20, 2000)
July 11, 2007 – Continued into Canada.
Nov. 24, 2008 – Name changed to Capstone Mining North
Ltd. ■

Sherwood Mining Corporation (Alta. July 20, 2000)
Sept. 12, 2005 – Name changed to Sherwood Copper
Corporation; basis 1 new for 4 old shs. ■

Sherwood Petroleum Corporation (B.C. June 11, 1987)
July 20, 2000 – Continued into Alberta.
Oct. 30, 2001 – Name changed to Sherwood Mining
Corporation. ■

Sheslay Mining Inc. (B.C. June 19, 2014)
June 1, 2015 – Name changed to Alliance Growers Corp.
pursuant to the reverse takeover acquisition of (old)
Alliance Growers Corp. (see FPsurvey - Industrials)

Shewan Copper Mining Corp. Ltd. (Ont. 1943)
Mar. 1976 – Charter cancelled.

Shiega Resources Corporation (Yuk. Nov. 19, 1997)
Jan. 17, 2000 – Name changed to African Metals
Corporation; basis 1 new for 2 old shs. ■

The Shield Development Company Limited (Can. Mar.
17, 1926)
Nov. 14, 1995 – Dissolved.

Shield Gold Inc. (Ont. Feb. 4, 2004)
May 15, 2014 – Name changed to Great Lakes Graphite
Inc. (see FPsurvey - Mines & Energy; FPsurvey -
Industrials)

Shield Petroleum Corporation (unknown)
Dec. 17, 1982 – Amalgamated with Tyrona Resources
Ltd. to form Signal Hill Energy Corporation; basis 1 new
for 2 old shs.

Shield Resources Limited (B.C. Apr. 27, 1966)
Mar. 1974 – Name changed to Precambrian Shield
Resources Limited. ■

Shift Networks Inc. (Alta. Sept. 25, 2002 amalg.)
May 11, 2007 – Filed for protection under the Companies'
Creditors Arrangement Act and PricewaterhouseCoopers
Inc. was appointed monitor.
Oct. 10, 2007 – All realizable assets sold to 1352741
Alberta Ltd. and due to no remaining assets available for
distribution, there will not be any distributions to secured
debenture holders, unsecured creditors or shldrs.
Oct. 19, 2007 – The stay order under the CCAA was
terminated and PricewaterhouseCoopers Inc. was
discharged as monitor. (see FPsurvey - Industrials)

Shilling Resources Inc. (Alta. Sept. 5, 1986)
Mar. 2, 1992 – Dissolved and struck off register.

Shilo Mines Limited (Ont. 1972)
July 6, 1983 – Amalgamated with 8 other cos. to form
Lobo Gold & Resources Inc.; basis 1 new for 10 old shs.

Shiloh Resources Ltd. (B.C. 1983)
Jan. 27, 1995 – Dissolved and struck off register.

Shimoda International Systems Inc. (B.C. 1987)
Dec. 17, 1993 – Dissolved and struck off register.

Shine Factory Systems Limited (Alta. Dec. 7, 1987)
Aug. 15, 1994 – Name changed to Aspen Resources
Corp. ■

Shinell Gold Mines Ltd. (Ont. 1946)
Oct. 26, 1959 – Charter cancelled.

Shiningbank Energy Income Fund (Alta. May 16, 1996)
July 13, 2007 – Acquired by PrimeWest Energy Trust;
basis 0.62 new PrimeWest trust unit for 1 old Shiningbank
trust unit. (see PrimeWest Energy Trust)

Shiningtree Gold Resources Inc. (Ont. Dec. 23, 1980)
Mar. 2, 1987 – Name changed to Shiningtree Resources
Inc.; basis 1 new for 5 old shs. ■

Shiningtree Resources Inc. (Ont. Dec. 23, 1980)
Mar. 13, 2006 – Certificate of incorporation cancelled
and the company was dissolved.

Shiny Health & Wellness Corp. (B.C. Feb. 2, 2021)
Aug. 16, 2022 – Continued into Canada.
Nov. 25, 2024 – Made an assignment into bankruptcy. B
Riley Farber Inc. appointed trustee.

ShinyBud Corp. (B.C. Feb. 2, 2021)
Aug. 15, 2022 – Name changed to Shiny Health &
Wellness Corp. ■

Shipman Boxboards Ltd. (unknown)
1941 – All assets sold; divd. of 8.125% paid to all
creditors, incl. deb. holders.

The Shipping Corp. of New Zealand (Canada) Ltd.
(Can. 1980)
July 17, 1987 – All o/s ser. A preference shs. originally
issued in 1980 at $25 in Cdn. market redeemed at $25.

Shire Acquisition Inc. (Can. Nov. 9, 2000)
Feb. 13, 2008 – Acquired by Shire plc; basis 3 Shire plc
ord. shs. or 1 depository sh. for 1 Shire Acquisition exch.
sh.

Shirex Enterprises Ltd. (Ont. 1968)
May 24, 1972 – Amalgamated into Xtra Developments
Inc.; basis 1 new for 4 old shs. (see Xtra Developments
Inc.)

Shirex Explorations Ltd. (Ont. 1968)
1970 – Name changed to Shirex Enterprises Ltd. ■

Shirma Mines Ltd. (Ont. 1965)
Apr. 9, 1975 – Charter cancelled.

Shirmax Fashions Ltd. (Can. July 25, 1983)
June 13, 2002 – Acquired by Reitmans Acquisition Inc., wholly owned subsid. of Reitmans (Canada) Limited; basis $7.00 per sh.

Shirriff-Horsey Corporation Ltd. (Can. 1927)
June 1957 – Name changed to Salada-Shirriff-Horsey Ltd. ■

Shirriff's Limited (Can. 1927)
1955 – Merged with J. William Horsey Corp. to form Shirriff-Horsey Corp. Ltd.

Shirson Ventures Inc. (Alta. June 28, 1988)
Dec. 7, 1992 – Name changed to Sports Active Inc. ■

Shiva Ventures Inc. (B.C. Aug. 6, 1987)
Sept. 11, 1992 – Name changed to Royal Stratus Ventures Inc.; basis 1 new for 2 old shs. ■

ShivaSoft Inc. (Alta. May 25, 1987)
Apr. 12, 1999 – Name changed to TigrSoft Inc. ■

Shoal Games Ltd. (Anguilla Sept. 30, 2004)
Apr. 9, 2019 – Name changed to Kidoz Inc. ■

Shoal Petroleum Ltd. (B.C. Apr. 24, 1981)
Feb. 11, 1988 – Name changed to Golden Dragon Resources Ltd.; basis 1 new for 2.5 old shs. ■

Shock Energy Metals Corp. (B.C. Oct. 7, 2022)
May 2, 2023 – Name changed to Aspen Resources Corp. ■

Shogun Capital Corp. (B.C. Oct. 19, 2010)
Nov. 29, 2016 – Name changed to ICC International Cannabis Corporation pursuant to Qualifying Transaction reverse takeover acquisition of International Cannabis Corp. ■

Shogun Developments Corp. (B.C. 1975)
May 11, 1988 – Name changed to ESTec Systems Corp. ■

Shogun Properties Corp. (B.C. May 27, 1988)
Nov. 14, 1995 – Name changed to Cyberion Networking Corp. ■

Sholia Resources Ltd. (B.C. 1980)
July 4, 1988 – Amalgamated with Argentex Resource Exploration Corp. to form AXR Resources Ltd.; basis 1 new for 5 Sholia shs. (see AXR Resources Ltd.)

Shona Energy Company, Inc. (B.C. Sept. 27, 2011 amalg.)
Dec. 27, 2012 – Acquired by Canacol Energy Ltd. for Cdn$0.0896 plus 0.10573 Canacol com. shs. for 1 Shona com. sh.

Shooting Star Technologies Inc. (Alta. June 8, 1994)
July 2, 1997 – Name changed to Gimbel Vision International Inc. ■

Shop & Save (1957) Ltd. (Can. 1932)
Nov. 1968 – Oshawa Wholesale Limited acquired all o/s com. shs. and 6.5% conv. debs. ser. A on basis of 2 Oshawa cl. A shs. and 1 cl. A sh. purchase wt. for each 4 Shop & Save com. shs. held, and 32.5 cl. A shs. and 16.25 cl. A sh. purchase wts. for each $1,000 deb.

Shoppers City Ltd. (Can. 1960)
1968 – Acquired by M. Loeb Ltd. through offer of $5.50 per sh.

Shoppers Drug Mart Corporation (Ont. Nov. 16, 1999)
Jan. 31, 2000 – Amalgamated in New Brunswick to continue with same name.
May 30, 2002 – Continued into Canada.
Apr. 1, 2014 – Acquired by Loblaw Companies Limited; $61.54 or $0.01 plus 1.29417 Loblaw com. shs. for 1 Shoppers com. sh.

Shore Gold Fund Inc. (Can. Apr. 29, 1985)
Dec. 5, 1994 – Name changed to Shore Gold Inc. ■

Shore Gold Inc. (Can. Apr. 29, 1985)
Feb. 12, 2018 – Name changed to Star Diamond Corporation. (see FPsurvey - Mines & Energy)

Shore Resources Ltd. (Alta. Nov. 17, 1970)
Mar. 16, 1987 – Name changed to Pacific & Western Trustco Ltd. and continued into Canada. ■

Shore To Shore Corporation Limited (Ont. 1968)
Dec. 1, 1975 – Amalgamated with District Trust Co. (2 for 1) to continue with the new name District Trust Company; basis 1 cl. A or new cl. B District sh. for 1 old Shore To Shore sh.

Shorecrest Mining Ltd. (Ont. 1972)
July 1973 – Merged into Sloane Mining Company Ltd.; basis 1 new for 3 old shs.

Shoreham Resources Ltd. (B.C. June 24, 1987)
Jan. 31, 2011 – Name changed to Guyana Frontier Mining Corp. ■

Shoreland Mines Ltd. (Ont. 1946)
Oct. 10, 1961 – Dissolved.

Shoreline Energy Corp. (Ont. May 11, 2005)
July 6, 2011 – Continued into Alberta.
Dec. 23, 2015 – Filed for bankruptcy under the Bankruptcy and Insolvency Act (BIA). Grant Thornton Limited appointed trustee and all officers and directors resigned.
Aug. 2016 – Sale of oil and gas assets was completed. Claims classified as senior indebtedness would received distrib. amounting to approx. 51% of the amount claimed; and those claims classified as non-senior indebtedness would receive distrib. amounting to approx. 4% of the amount claimed. No distrib. were expected for shldrs. or debenture holders.
July 22, 2021 – Grant Thornton was discharged as trustee. (see FPsurvey - Mines & Energy)

Shorewest Mining Co. Ltd. (unknown)
Mar. 1970 – All o/s 760,000 shs. acquired by Texacal Resources Ltd. for 760,000 shs. (of which 650,000 escrowed).

Shorewest Mining Co. Ltd. (unknown)
June 1976 – Charter cancelled.

Shorewood Explorations Ltd. (B.C. 1981)
Apr. 6, 1995 – Amalgamated with Broadlands Resources Ltd. to form International Broadlands Resources Ltd.; basis 1 new for 1 Shorewood sh. (see International Broadlands Resources Ltd.)

Shoshoni Gold Inc. (B.C. Apr. 23, 1985)
Jan. 23, 1992 – Name changed to Consolidated Shoshoni Gold Inc.; basis 1 new for 3 old shs. ■

Shoshoni Gold Ltd. (B.C. Apr. 23, 1985)
Aug. 1, 2019 – Name changed to Royal Gold Mining Inc.; basis 1 new for 4 old shs. ■

Show-Mart Investment (Que. 1950)
Jan. 1956 – Reported to have been wound up. All o/s shs. due 1957-61 redeemed.

Shully's Industries Limited (Ont. 1962)
1975 – Final liquidation of assets in progress in early; no distribution to be made.

Shunsby Gold Mines Ltd. (Ont. Feb. 10, 1944)
1955 – Name changed to Shunsby Mines Ltd. ■

Shunsby Mines Ltd. (Ont. Feb. 10, 1944)
1965 – Name changed to Consolidated Shunsby Mines Limited; basis 1 new for 5 old shs. ■

Shuswap Mines Limited (B.C. 1950)
July 18, 1957 – Struck off register.

Siam Trading Ltd. (Alta. Sept. 19, 1986)
Feb. 14, 1996 – Formed McCarthy Corporation plc following sh. exchange with McCarthy Corporation plc; basis 1 new for 1 old sh.

Siberian Pacific Resources Inc. (Alta. Aug. 12, 1986)
Apr. 4, 1996 – Delisted from the Alberta Stock Exchange. Subsequently dissolved and struck from register.

Sicamous Resources Ltd. (B.C. July 17, 1972)
Nov. 16, 1976 – Name changed to Ni-Cal Developments Ltd. ■

Sican Ventures Inc. (B.C. June 30, 1997)
July 6, 2009 – Name changed to Abattis Biologix Corporation. ■

Sicanna Industries Ltd. (B.C. 1981)
Mar. 25, 1988 – Name changed to DecorStone Industries Inc. (see FPsurvey - Industrials)

Sicard Inc. (Que. 1929)
June 30, 1971 – All com. shs. acquired by Pacific Car & Foundry Co. of Renton, Washington in 1967 at $8.00 per sh. All pref. shs. redeemed at $21 per sh.

Sicintine Mines Ltd. (B.C. 1967)
May 11, 1979 – Name changed to Mi-Lo Health & Beauty Aids Ltd.; basis 1 new for 5 old shs. ■

Sick's Breweries Limited (Can. 1928)
1958 – Acquired by Molson's Brewery, Ltd. in 1958-59 on basis of 2 cl. A, 2 cl. B and one 5.5%, $40 par pref. sh. of Molson's for each 4 com. shs. or voting trust certificates of Sick's.

Sico Inc. (Que. Jan. 28, 1941)
July 10, 2006 – Acquired by indirect wholly owned subsid. of Akzo Nobel N.V. for $20 per com. sh. and $1.375 per pfd. sh.

Sico Mining Corp. Ltd. (Ont. 1955)
Jan. 6, 1964 – Charter cancelled.

Siconor Mines Ltd. (Ont. 1959)
Dec. 7, 1967 – Dissolved.

Sidar Gold Mines Ltd. (Ont. 1899)
1932 – Charter cancelled.

Sidbec (Que. 1964)
Nov. 22, 1987 – Following restructuring, all manufacturing assets and corresponding liabs. transferred to subsid., Sidbec-Dosco Inc.

Sidbec-Dosco Inc. (Que. Nov. 18, 1964)
Aug. 17, 1994 – The ISPAT Group, through wholly owned ISPAT Mexicana S.A. de C.V. of Mexico, acquired 100% of the share capital of Sidbec-Dosco for $45,000,000 and the assumption of $280,000,000 in debt.

Sideware Systems Inc. (B.C. Apr. 11, 1983)
Jan. 11, 2002 – Continued into Yukon.
June 5, 2002 – Merged with U.S.-based KnowledgeMax, Inc.
June 19, 2002 – Name changed to KnowledgeMax, Inc. and continued into Delaware.

Sidewinder Conversions International Inc. (B.C. June 16, 1987)
Nov. 28, 1995 – Name changed to Pacific Axis Ventures Inc.; basis 1 new for 6 old shs. ■

Sidewinder Explorations Inc. (Ont. 1980)
Dec. 29, 1982 – Amalgamated with Thunderbolt Gas & Oil Explorations Ltd., Petrobar Explorations Inc., Golden Falcon Explorations Inc. and 514567 Ontario Ltd. to form Parapet Petroleums Inc.; basis 2 new for 15 old shs.

Sidney Roofing & Paper Co. Ltd. (B.C. 1927)
Sept. 1962 – Name changed to Burnaby Paperboard Ltd. ■

Sidon International Resources Corporation (B.C. Mar. 3, 1987)
Feb. 14, 2012 – Name changed to Cameo Resources Corp.; basis 1 new for 30 old shs. ■

Sidus Systems Inc. (Ont. Jan. 29, 1981)
Apr. 8, 1999 – Amalgamated with EMJ Data Systems Ltd.; basis 1 EMJ sh. for 50 Sidus Systems shs.

Siebel Janna Arrangement, Inc. (Ont. Sept. 7, 2000)
Dec. 7, 2005 – Acquired by Janna Nova Scotia Sub Company, an affiliate; 1 new Siebel Systems, Inc. com. sh. for 1 old Siebel Janna exch. sh.

Siebens Oil & Gas Ltd. (Alta. 1970 amalg.)
Jan. 3, 1979 – Acquired by subsid. of Canadian National Pension Fund for $38.50 per sh.

Sieger Capital Management Ltd. (B.C. Oct. 12, 2006)
Apr. 16, 2010 – Continued into Canada.
May 5, 2017 – Name changed to Sherbrook SBK Sport Corp. pursuant to Qualifying Transaction reverse takeover acquisition of Sherbrook SBK Hockey Inc. ■

Siegesoft Internet Solutions Inc. (B.C. Oct. 27, 1986)
Oct. 26, 2000 – Name changed to Zimtu Technologies Inc. ■

Siemont Resources Ltd. (B.C. July 17, 1984)
July 24, 1990 – Name changed to Eskay Gold Corp.; basis 1 new for 4 old shs. ■

Sienna Development Corporation (B.C. 1978)
Oct. 6, 1980 – Name changed to Sienna Resources Limited. ■

Sienna Gold Inc. (Alta. July 28, 1987)
July 2, 2013 – Name changed to Peruvian Precious Metals Corp. ■

Sienna Resources Limited (B.C. 1978)
June 30, 1989 – Acquired by Orbit Oil and Gas Ltd.; basis 1 new Orbit sh. for 2.25 old Sienna shs. (see Orbit Oil & Gas Ltd.)

Sierra Capital Corp. (Alta. Oct. 4, 1968)
Oct. 22, 1998 – Dissolved and struck from registry.

Sierra Empire Mines Ltd. (B.C. 1968)
Dec. 18, 1978 – Dissolved.

Sierra Geothermal Power Corp. (B.C. Dec. 16, 1983)
Sept. 2, 2010 – Acquired by Ram Power, Corp.; basis 0.0833333 Ram Power shs. for 1 Sierra Geothermal sh. (see Ram Power, Corp.)

Sierra Growth Corp. (B.C. June 19, 2009)
July 7, 2021 – Name changed to Sierra Grande Minerals Inc. (see FPsurvey - Mines & Energy)

Sierra Iron Ore Corporation (B.C. July 20, 2009)
July 14, 2016 – Name changed to Crystal Lake Mining Corporation. ■

Sierra Madre Developments Inc. (B.C. Apr. 30, 2009)
May 31, 2021 – Name changed to Goldshore Resources Inc. pursuant to the reverse takeover acquisition of (old) Goldshore Resources Inc., and concurrent amalgmation of (old) Goldshore with wholly owned 1284403 B.C. Ltd.; basis 1 new for 6 old shs. (see FPsurvey - Mines & Energy)

Sierra Madre Resources Inc. (B.C. May 9, 1986)
Feb. 19, 1993 – Name changed to Camphor Ventures Inc.; basis 1 new for 2.5 old shs. ■

Sierra Metals Inc. (Can. Apr. 11, 1996)
Aug. 7, 2025 – All o/s shs. not already held acquired by Alpayana Canada Ltd.; basis 1 ser. A pref. sh. redeemed for Cdn.$1.15 cash per sh.

Sierra Minerals Inc. (Que. Nov. 9, 1989 amalg.)
May 7, 2010 – Name changed to Goldgroup Mining Inc. pursuant to amalgamation of its wholly owned subsid.

with Goldgroup Resources Inc., constituting a reverse takeover by Goldgroup; basis 1 new for 2.85 old shs. ■

Sierra Nevada Gold Ltd. (B.C. Jan. 31, 1980)
July 25, 2005 – Dissolved for failure to file and struck from register.

Sierra Resources Ltd. (Can. 1969)
Jan. 1973 – Name changed to Skye Resources Ltd. ■

Sierra Systems Group Inc. (B.C. Oct. 1, 1966)
Jan. 9, 2007 – Plan of Arrangement acquisition by an affiliate of Golden Gate Capital; basis $9.25 per sh.

Sierra Vista Energy Ltd. (Alta. June 7, 2005)
May 23, 2008 – Name changed to Radius Resources Corp. basis 1 com. sh. for 10 cl. A shs. Prior to consolidation, all cl. B shs. converted into cl. A shs. on a 10-for-1 basis. ■

Sierra Wireless, Inc. (Can. May 31, 1993)
Jan. 17, 2023 – Acquired by Semtech Corporation; basis US$31 cash per sh.

Sifton Properties Limited (Ont. 1950)
June 27, 1995 – Privatized at $75 per sh. Whereas, approx. 99.1% of the o/s com. shs. were repurchased for $12 per sh. on Mar. 31, 1978.

Siga Resources Limited (Alta. Apr. 22, 1994)
Apr. 11, 2006 – Plan of Arrangement acquisition by Open Range Resources Ltd. (subsequently named New Range Resources Ltd.) which constitutes Open Range's Qualifying Transaction; basis $0.20 per sh. (see New Range Resources Ltd.)

SiGEM Inc. (Can. Apr. 15, 1999)
Mar. 27, 2002 – Name changed to Mobile Knowledge Inc. ■

Sightus Inc. (Can. Dec. 12, 2003)
Mar. 6, 2007 – Placed into receivership and RSM Richter Inc. appointed interim receiver.
July 2007 – Proposal to creditors was defeated resulting in RSM Richter being named trustee in the bankruptcy of the company.
Mar. 2008 – Sale of the assets was completed. There were no monies available for distrib. to shldrs.
Dec. 5, 2011 – The engagement was transferred to Ernst & Young Inc.
Nov. 2014 – Ernst & Young was discharged as interim receiver.
Aug. 10, 2016 – The bankruptcy was transferred to Deloitte Restructuring Inc.
Oct. 16, 2017 – Deloitte Restructuring was discharged as trustee.

Sigma Industries Inc. (Alta. Sept. 5, 2001)
Feb. 26, 2008 – Continued into Canada.
Oct. 1, 2018 – Acquired by NanoXplore Inc.; basis 0.390625 NanoXplore shs. for 1 Sigma com. sh.

Sigma Lithium Corporation (Can. June 8, 2011)
Oct. 15, 2024 – Continued into Ontario. (see FPsurvey - Mines & Energy)

Sigma Lithium Resources Corporation (Can. June 8, 2011)
July 5, 2021 – Name changed to Sigma Lithium Corporation. ■

Sigma Mines Ltd. (Can. Apr. 21, 1934)
July 26, 1937 – Name changed to Sigma Mines (Quebec) Limited and continued into Quebec; basis 1 new for 3 old shs. ■

Sigma Mines (Quebec) Limited (Que. July 26, 1937)
June 17, 1988 – Amalgamated with a wholly owned subsid. of Placer Dome Inc.; basis 0.97 new for 1 old sh. (see Placer Dome Inc.)

Sigma Science Limited (B.C. May 26, 1986)
July 29, 1994 – Name changed to Guyana Gold Corp. following acquisition of Guyana Goldfields Corp.; basis 1 new for 2.7 old shs. ■

Sigma Security Inc. (B.C. 1982)
June 28, 1985 – Name changed to International Sigma Security Inc.; basis 4 new for 1 old sh. ■

Sigma Ventures Inc. (Alta. Sept. 5, 2001)
Feb. 21, 2008 – Name changed to Sigma Industries Inc. ■

Sigmacom Systems Incorporated (B.C. 1978)
Dec. 3, 1993 – Dissolved and struck off register.

Signal Energy Ltd. (Alta. Aug. 3, 1989)
July 8, 1996 – All o/s com. shs. acquired by Richland Petroleum Corporation; basis 73¢ per sh. (see Richland Petroleum Corporation)

Signal Exploration Inc. (B.C. Mar. 9, 2010)
Nov. 2, 2016 – Name changed to Southern Lithium Corp. ■

Signal Gold Inc. (Ont. July 22, 2002)
Dec. 17, 2024 – Acquired by NexGold Mining Corp.; basis 0.1244 NexGold shs. for 1 Signal Gold sh.

Signal Hill Energy Corporation (B.C. Dec. 17, 1982 amalg.)
June 13, 1985 – Name changed to Texas Petroleum Corporation; basis 1 new for 5 old shs. ■

Signal Hill Oil Co. Ltd. (Can. Dec. 1925)
Acquired by Graystone Consolidated Petroleums Ltd.; basis 1 new for 3 old shs.

Signal Mines Ltd. (Ont. 1951)
Mar. 1962 – Dissolved.

Signal Oils & Metals Co. Ltd. (Que. 1951)
1956 – Name changed to Signal Chibougamau Mining Corp.

SignalEnergy Inc. (Que. May 1, 1996 amalg.)
Feb. 20, 2007 – Succeeded by Fortress Energy Inc. pursuant to reorganization, transfer of all the assets to newly incorporated Fortress Energy Inc. and subsequent dissolution of SignalEnergy Inc.; basis $1.30 per sh. or 1 Fortress sh. for 5 SignalEnergy shs. ■

SignalGene Inc. (Que. May 1, 1996 amalg.)
Mar. 11, 2004 – Name changed to SignalEnergy Inc.; basis 1 new for 10 old shs. ■

Signature Brands Limited (Ont. Jan. 27, 1986)
Aug. 19, 1999 – Name changed to CD Plus.com Ltd. pursuant to reverse takeover acquisition of CD Plus.com Ltd.; basis 1 new for 5 old shs. ■

Signature Diversified Value Trust (Ont. Oct. 30, 2002)
Dec. 14, 2012 – Terminated. Redeemed for $6.0173 per trust unit.

Signature Energy Corp. (Alta. Oct. 6, 1992)
Aug. 19, 1999 – Name changed to Signature Resources Ltd.; basis 1 new for 5 old shs. ■

Signature Resources Ltd. (B.C. Mar. 31, 1988)
Nov. 8, 2005 – Name changed to UrAsia Energy Ltd. following reverse takeover acquisition of UrAsia Energy (BVI) Ltd.; basis 1 new for 2 old shs. ■

Signature Resources Ltd. (Alta. Oct. 6, 1992)
Apr. 5, 2001 – Continued into Canada.
Apr. 20, 2001 – Name changed to 3D Visit Inc. pursuant to reverse takeover acquisition of 3D Visit Inc. ■

Signet Distilleries Limited (Sask. 1956)
Formed to operate a distillery and carry out related activities. No report that operations commenced.

Signet Industries Ltd. (Alta. Nov. 23, 1993)
May 2, 2004 – Struck from registry and dissolved.

Signet Minerals Inc. (Alta. May 9, 2005)
Aug. 16, 2007 – Acquired by Cash Minerals Ltd. following Plan of Arrangement; basis 1 new Cash Minerals unit for 1 old Signet com. sh. with each unit consisting of 0.67 com. sh. plus ½ warrant redeemable for $1.75. Following

spin-out of non-uranium assets of Signet to Troymet Exploration Corp., Signet shldrs. received 0.25 new Troymet com. sh. for 1 old sh. (see Cash Minerals Ltd.)

Signet Oils Ltd. (Ont. 1954)
1960 – Struck off register.

Signet Petroleums Limited (Ont. 1945)
1953 – Acquired by Consolidated Peak Oils Ltd.; basis 1 new for 3 old shs. (see Consolidated Peak Oils Ltd.)

Signet Resources Inc. (B.C. Nov. 16, 1979)
Mar. 11, 1987 – Name changed to New Signet Resources Inc.; basis 1 new for 4 old shs. ■

Signtech Inc. (Ont. 1978)
Mar. 9, 1994 – Petitioned into bankruptcy by its banker, NBD Bank, Canada. Doane Raymond Limited of Toronto was appointed trustee. The administration of the co. was complete. The secured creditors suffered a significant shortfall and there was no distribution to unsecured creditors or shldrs.
June 1, 1994 – Trustee was subsequently discharged in mid-1994.

Sikaman Gold Resources Ltd. (B.C. Sept. 25, 1985)
Apr. 19, 1988 – Continued into Ontario.
July 12, 1999 – Continued into Canada.
Nov. 29, 2000 – Name changed to SKG Interactive Inc. (see FPsurvey - Mines & Energy; FPsurvey - Industrials)

Sikanni Services Ltd. (Alta. Dec. 31, 2006 amalg.)
Apr. 29, 2008 – Formed EnQuest Energy Services Corp. in Alberta on amalgamation with Irontree Oilfield Services Corp., constituting a reverse takeover by Irontree; basis 1 new for 1 Irontree sh. and 1 new for 0.033333 Sikanni shs. ■

Sil-Van Consolidated Mining & Milling Co. Ltd. (B.C. 1950)
May 1957 – Name changed to Sil-Van Mines Ltd.; basis 1 new for 5 old shs. ■

Sil-Van Mines Ltd. (B.C. 1950)
Apr. 1969 – Name changed to Dorita Silver Mines Ltd.; basis 1 new for 10 old com. shs. and 1 new for 1 old pref. sh. ■

Sila Industrial Group Ltd. (B.C. June 21, 2007)
July 8, 2011 – Name changed to West Cirque Resources Ltd. ■

Silanco Mining & Refining Co. Ltd. (Ont. Nov. 26, 1945)
1957 – Name changed to Ansil Mines Ltd.; basis 1 new for 7 old shs. ■

Silanco Mining & Smelting Corp. Ltd. (Ont. Nov. 26, 1945)
1945 – Name changed to Silanco Mining & Refining Co. Ltd. ■

Silba Silver Mines Ltd. (Ont. 1946)
1950 – Acquired by Consolidated Silver Banner Mines Ltd.; basis 1 new for 6 old shs. (see Consolidated Silver Banner Mines Ltd.)

Silbak Premier Mines Ltd. (B.C. 1935)
Sept. 28, 1976 – Name changed to British Silbak Premier Mines Ltd.; basis 1 new for 5 old shs. ■

Silbak Premier Mines Ltd (B.C. 1935)
May 10, 1988 – Amalgamated with Pioneer Metals Corporation on the basis 1 new for 3.5 old shs. (see Pioneer Metals Corporation)

Silco Development Co. Ltd. (B.C. 1961)
Sept. 3, 1974 – Dissolved and struck off register.

Silco Mines Ltd. (Ont. 1943)
Charter cancelled.

Silcorp Limited (Ont. June 14, 1928)
June 1, 1999 – Acquired by Alimentation Couche-Tard Inc.; basis $23 or 1.2 Alimentation Couche-Tard cl. B shs. plus 20¢ for 1 Silcorp sh.

Silcross Copper Mines Ltd. (Ont. 1950)
Dec. 21, 1959 – Charter cancelled.

Silent Canyon Resources Ltd. (B.C. Jan. 23, 1984)
Apr. 27, 1988 – Name changed to Golden Adit Resources Ltd.; basis 1 new for 2 old shs. ■

Silent Witness Enterprises Ltd. (B.C. July 31, 1986)
Feb. 16, 2004 – Acquired indirectly by Honeywell International Inc. for $11.27 per sh.

Sileurian Chieftain Mining Co. Ltd. (B.C. 1953)
Sept. 1972 – Name changed to United Chieftain Resources Ltd.; basis 1 new for 10 old shs. ■

Silex Ventures Ltd. (B.C. Mar. 21, 2007)
Feb. 22, 2011 – Name changed to Argentum Silver Corp. pursuant to Qualifying Transaction acquisition of Lachiguiri property from Arco Resources Corp. (see FPsurvey - Mines & Energy)

Silicon Acquisition Inc. (Alta. Jan. 5, 2000)
July 5, 2002 – Continued into Ontario.
July 18, 2002 – Formed Passion Media Inc. in Ontario pursuant to Qualifying Transaction reverse takeover acquisition of and amalgamation with Passion Media Inc. ■

Silicon Slopes Capital Corp. (B.C. Oct. 14, 1998)
Jan. 1, 2008 – Continued into Delaware.
Feb. 26, 2008 – Name changed to Cyberlink Technologies, Inc.; basis 1 new for 8 old shs.

Silicon Valley Scout Ventures Ltd. (B.C. Jan. 19, 2000)
May 3, 2001 – Name changed to Canadian Resources House Limited. ■

Silicon Vision International Corporation (Que. Oct. 20, 1995)
July 29, 1997 – Name changed to S-VISION Corporation. (see FPsurvey - Industrials)

Silk Road Energy Inc. (Alta. Nov. 9, 2010)
Mar. 21, 2023 – Name changed to Record Resources Inc. (see FPsurvey - Mines & Energy)

Silk Road Finance Inc. (B.C. May 15, 2012)
June 18, 2015 – Continued into Cayman Islands.
Jan. 23, 2017 – Voluntarily delisted.

Silk Road Resources Ltd. (Alta. Apr. 29, 1999)
July 1, 2009 – Amalgamated with 7167911 Canada Ltd., a wholly owned subsid. of Euromax Resources Ltd.; basis 2.2535 Euromax. shs. for 1 Silk Road sh.

Silk Road Ventures Ltd. (B.C. May 15, 2012)
Nov. 28, 2014 – Name changed to Silk Road Finance Inc.; basis 1 new for 10 old shs. ■

Silknit Limited (Can. 1928)
Apr. 1985 – Placed into bankruptcy; assets sold.

Silkridge Resources Ltd. (B.C. 1986)
Sept. 19, 1989 – Name changed to Aquatech Systems Inc. ■

Silmil Explorations Inc. (Ont. 1946)
Aug. 29, 1978 – Amalgamated with 3 other cos. to form Belle Aire Resource Explorations Limited; basis 25 com. shs. Belle Aire for 100 shs. Silmil.

Silmonac Mines Limited (B.C. 1963)
Sept. 8, 1977 – Name changed to Silvana Mines Inc.; basis 1 new for 4 old shs. ■

Silmont Mining Co. Ltd. (Ont. 1956)
Nov. 27, 1961 – Dissolved.

Siloro Gold Mines Ltd. (Ont. 1946)
1946 – Name changed to Siloro Mines Ltd. and continued into Ontario. ■

Siloro Mines Ltd. (Ont. 1946)
1954 – Reported as defunct.

Siloro Mines Ltd. (Ont. 1946)
Oct. 1956 – Name changed to Globe Copper Mines Ltd. ■

Silruca Mines Ltd. (Ont. 1946)
Apr. 1952 – Name changed to Zinc Lake Mines Ltd. ■

Silvana Mines Inc. (B.C. 1963)
Oct. 1980 – Amalgamated into Dickenson Mines Ltd.; basis 1 cl. A and 1 cl. B sh. of Dickenson for each 3 shs. Silvana.

Silver Acorn Developments Ltd. (B.C. 1977)
Dec. 5, 1984 – Name changed to Petgo Resources Ltd.; basis 1 new for 2 old shs. ■

Silver Arrow Explorations Ltd. (B.C. 1963)
1970 – Merged into Stampede International Resources Ltd.; basis 1 new for 2 old shs.

Silver Arrow Mines Ltd. (Ont. 1946)
July 30, 1962 – Dissolved.

Silver Arrow Mines Ltd. (B.C. 1963)
1966 – Name changed to Silver Arrow Explorations Ltd. ■

Silver Banner Mines Ltd. (Ont. 1947)
1950 – Acquired by Consolidated Silver Banner Mines Ltd.; basis 1 new for 3 old shs. (see Consolidated Silver Banner Mines Ltd.)
Dec. 1954 – Charter cancelled. (see Consolidated Silver Banner Mines Ltd.)

Silver Basin Yukon Mines Ltd. (Ont. 1946)
1949 – Merged into Consolidated Yukeno Mines Ltd.; basis 1 new for 3 old shs. (see Consolidated Yukeno Mines Ltd.)

Silver Bay Mines Ltd. (B.C. 1968)
Apr. 1977 – Charter cancelled.

Silver Bear Resources Inc. (Ont. Apr. 8, 2004)
Aug. 30, 2004 – Continued into Yukon.
Feb. 1, 2005 – Continued into Ontario.
Mar. 20, 2017 – Succeeded by Silver Bear Resources Plc following redomiciliation transaction under which com. shs. of Silver Bear Inc. were exchanged for Silver Bear UK on the basis of 1 new ordinary sh. for 1 old com. sh. (see FPsurvey - Mines & Energy)

Silver Belle Mines Ltd. (Ont. 1960)
June 24, 1966 – Name changed to Consolidated Silver Belle Mines Ltd.; basis 1 new for 2 old shs. ■

Silver Belle Mines (1966) Ltd. (Ont. June 27, 1966 amalg.)
1969 – Merged into Alchib Developments Ltd.; basis 25 shs. Alchib for 100 Silver Belle shs.

Silver Benn Mines Ltd. (B.C. 1967)
Feb. 25, 1983 – Struck off register.

Silver Bounty Mines Ltd. (B.C. 1947)
July 1971 – Name changed to Copper Bounty Mines Ltd.; basis 1 new for 5 old shs. ■

Silver Box Resources Ltd. (B.C. 1983)
Dec. 2, 1994 – Dissolved and struck off register.

Silver Bullion Trust (Ont. June 8, 2009)
May 26, 2016 – Converted into exchange traded fund.

Silver Butte Mines Ltd. (B.C. Dec. 31, 1957)
May 1972 – Name changed to Consolidated Silver Butte Mines Ltd.; basis 1 new for 4 old shs. ■

Silver Butte Resources Ltd. (B.C. Dec. 31, 1957)
Aug. 17, 1995 – Name changed to Uniterre Resources Ltd.; basis 1 new for 3 old shs. ■

Silver Century Explorations Ltd. (Ont. Mar. 7, 1980)
Feb. 11, 1999 – Acquired by Sudbury Contact Mines, Limited; basis 1 Sudbury sh. for 1 Silver Century sh. (see Sudbury Contact Mines, Limited)

Silver Chest Mines Ltd. (Ont. 1946)
Sept. 9, 1958 – Charter cancelled.

Silver Chief Minerals Ltd. (Alta. 1966)
1981 – Amalgamated into Quinstar Resources Ltd.; basis 1 new Quinstar sh. for 2 old Silver Chief shs.

Silver Chief Mines Ltd. (Ont. 1945)
Oct. 26, 1959 – Charter cancelled.

Silver Christal Mines Ltd. (B.C. 1968)
1970 – Name changed to Silver Christal Natural Gas & Minerals Ltd. ■

Silver Christal Natural Gas & Minerals Ltd. (B.C. 1968)
1979 – Name changed to Dominion Energy Corporation. ■

Silver Circle Compact Disc Books Inc. (Ont. Oct. 26, 1988)
Oct. 30, 1996 – Formed World Wide Interactive Discs Inc. in Ontario on amalgamation with 1194137 Ontario Inc.; basis 1 new for 1 1194137 Ontario sh. and 1 new for 6 Silver Circle shs. ■

Silver Circle Mines Ltd. (Ont. 1951)
Aug. 1954 – Charter cancelled.

Silver City Mines Ltd. (B.C. 1964)
Jan. 27, 1977 – Name changed to Galaxy City Mines Inc; basis 1 new for 5 old shs. ■

Silver City Petroleums Ltd. (Alta. 1952)
Aug. 12, 1969 – Name changed to Barclay Resources Ltd. ■

Silver Cloud Mines Ltd. (B.C. 1975)
Jan. 1, 1988 – Amalgamated with Angle Resources Ltd. (1 for 1) to form a new co. also named Angle Resources Ltd.; basis 1 new for 3 old sh. ■

Silver Contact Mines Ltd. (Ont. 1946)
1961 – Assets acquired by Silvermaque Mining Ltd.; basis 1 new for 1.75 old shs.

Silver Crater Mines Ltd. (Ont. 1951)
Aug. 19, 1965 – Dissolved.

Silver Cup Mines Ltd. (B.C. 1965)
Feb. 25, 1983 – Struck off register.

Silver Cup Resources Ltd. (B.C. 1983)
Apr. 23, 1987 – Name changed to Supertech Industries Inc. ■

Silver Dollar Mines Ltd. (Ont. 1946)
July 16, 1973 – Name changed to Gold Ridge Mines Inc. (see FPsurvey - Mines & Energy)

Silver Dolly Resources Ltd. (B.C. 1960)
Oct. 26, 1976 – Name changed to Dolly Resources Ltd.; basis 1 new for 5 old shs. ■

Silver Dome Mines Ltd. (B.C. 1962)
Aug. 1974 – Charter cancelled.

Silver Drake Resources Ltd. (B.C. Aug. 5, 1987)
Feb. 24, 1992 – Name changed to BioAnalogics Systems, Inc. ■

Silver Duke Mines Ltd. (B.C. Dec. 15, 1967)
Feb. 3, 1976 – Name changed to Totem Resources Ltd.; basis 1 new for 4 old shs. ■

Silver Eagle Mines Inc. (Ont. June 4, 2003)
June 5, 2009 – Acquired by Excellon Resources Inc.; basis 0.2704 Excellon shs. for 1 Silver Eagle sh.

Silver Eagle Mines Inc. (B.C. May 28, 2018)
May 3, 2023 – Name changed to Nevada Organic Phosphate Inc. (see FPsurvey - Mines & Energy)

Silver Eagle Resources Ltd. (B.C. Mar. 5, 1984)
Apr. 16, 1997 – Continued into Yukon.
Mar. 13, 2001 – Name changed to Mercator Minerals Ltd.; basis 1 new for 5 old shs. ■

Silver Falls Resources Ltd. (B.C. 1972)
Aug. 25, 1994 – Name changed to I.M. Technologies Inc. ■

Silver Fern Financial Ltd. (Alta. Jan. 10, 2005)
June 1, 2007 – Amalgamated with 1313943 Alberta Ltd., a subsidiary of EMedia Networks International Corporation; basis 1 new EMedia sh. for 1 old Silver sh. (see EMedia Networks International Corporation)

Silver Fields Resources Inc. (B.C. Aug. 11, 1997)
Jan. 21, 2019 – Struck from register and dissolved.

Silver Flint Mines Ltd. (B.C. 1951)
1955 – Name changed to Cinnibar Mercury Mines Ltd. and converted to a private co.

Silver George Mines Ltd. (Ont. 1950)
1953 – Acquired by Consolidated Matarrow Mines Ltd.; basis 18 new for 1,000 old shs. (see Consolidated Matarrow Mines Ltd.)

Silver Giant Mines Ltd. (B.C. 1947)
1951 – Merged into Giant Mascot Mines; basis 104 new for 100 old shs.

Silver Giant Mines Ltd. (Que. 1971)
May 25, 1985 – Charter cancelled.

Silver Glance Resources Inc. (B.C. July 18, 1979)
June 17, 1992 – Name changed to Silverspar Minerals Inc. ■

Silver Gulf Mining and Development Ltd. (Ont. 1965)
July 25, 1968 – Name changed to Mija Mines Ltd. ■

Silver Hart Mines Ltd. (Alta. 1982)
June 2, 2009 – Dissolved and struck from registry.

Silver Heart Mines Ltd. (Ont. 1952)
1965 – Charter cancelled.

Silver Hill Mines Ltd. (B.C. 1951)
Feb. 1961 – Dissolved.

Silver Hill Mines Ltd. (B.C. Jan. 15, 1980)
Sept. 30, 1991 – Name changed to La Rock Mining Corp.; basis 1 new for 3 old shs. ■

Silver Hoard Mines Ltd. (Ont. 1951)
Mar. 1976 – Charter cancelled.

Silver Hoarde Resources Inc. (B.C. 1980)
Apr. 21, 1986 – Name changed to American Platinum Inc. ■

Silver Jackpot Mines Ltd. (Ont. 1952)
1953 – Name changed to Jackpot Uranium Mines Ltd. ■

Silver Key Mines Ltd. (Ont. 1964)
Mar. 24, 1972 – Amalgamated with Impala Mines Ltd. and Nordev Mines Ltd. to form Nordev Resources Ltd.; basis 1 new for 10 old shs.

Silver Lady Resources Inc. (B.C. 1983)
Mar. 4, 1994 – Dissolved and struck off register.

Silver Lake Mines Ltd. (Ont. 1946)
Mar. 1976 – Charter cancelled.

Silver Lake Resources Inc. (Ont. July 22, 1980)
Aug. 25, 1986 – Name changed to International Platinum Corporation. ■

Silver Lake Resources Inc. (B.C. Apr. 18, 2006)
June 27, 2011 – Name changed to Pacific Potash Corporation following acquisition of Pacific Canada Potash Ltd. ■

Silver Leader Mines Ltd. (Ont. 1967)
Aug. 18, 1980 – Amalgamated with Gull Lake Energy Resources Ltd. to form Petroflo Petroleum Corporation.

Silver Leaf Mining Co. Ltd. (Ont. 1906)
1946 – Name changed to Lakeleaf Silver Mining Co. Ltd. and continued into Ontario; basis 1 new for 10 old shs. ■

Silver-Lee Mines Ltd. (B.C. 1961)
Mar. 25, 1971 – Name changed to Bear International Industries Ltd. ■

Silver Lode Mining Co. Ltd. (Ont. 1963)
Oct. 10, 1963 – Name changed to Louanna Gold Mines Ltd. ■

Silver Mark Mines Ltd. (Can. Mar. 12, 1929)
Dec. 16, 1980 – Dissolved.

Silver-Men Mines Ltd. (Ont. 1963)
Aug. 20, 1975 – Charter cancelled.

Silver Miller Mines Ltd. (Ont. 1946)
Sept. 1972 – Name changed to Silmil Explorations Inc.; basis 1 new for 6 old shs. ■

Silver Monarch Mines Limited (Ont. 1965)
Apr. 26, 1979 – Amalgamated with Frodac Mines Ltd. and Great Bear Silver Mines Limited to form Frodac Consolidated Energy Resources Ltd.; basis 1 new for 5 old shs.

Silver Mountain Mines Inc. (Alta. May 12, 2008)
Name changed to Nevgold Corp. pursuant to reverse takeover acquisition of (old) Nevgold Corp., and concurrent amalgamation of (old) Nevgold and wholly owned to 1288412 B.C. Ltd. to continue as Nevgold B.C. Holding Inc. (see FPsurvey - Mines & Energy)

Silver Net Equities Corp. (Alta. Jan. 6, 2006)
Oct. 31, 2007 – Formed Macusani Yellowcake Inc. in Ontario on Qualifying Transaction amalgamation with Macusani Yellowcake Inc., constituting a reverse takeover by Macusani; basis 1 new for 1 Macusani sh. and 0.55 new for 1 Silver Net sh. ■

Silver Ore Zone Mines Limited (Ont. 1963)
July 27, 1976 – Charter cancelled.

Silver Peak Resources Ltd. (B.C. 1981)
Nov. 23, 1999 – Deemed bankrupt. Willis Associates Insolvency Services Ltd. was appointed trustee.

Silver Phoenix Resources Inc. (B.C. Feb. 14, 2003)
Dec. 30, 2022 – Name changed to Atlas Global Brands Inc. pursuant to the reverse takeover acquisition of Atlas Biotechnologies Inc., AgMedica Bioscience Inc. and Cambrosia Ltd. and concurrent amalgamation of Atlas Biotechnologies and AgMedica with wholly owned 2432998 Alberta Ltd. and 14060407 Canada Inc., respectively; basis 1 new for 5 old shs. (see FPsurvey - Industrials)

Silver Prince Mines Ltd. (B.C. 1952)
1956 – Dissolved.

Silver Princess Resources Inc. (B.C. Dec. 20, 1978)
Mar. 29, 1996 – Delisted from the Vancouver Stock Exchange. Subsequently struck from register and dissolved.

Silver Pursuit Resources Ltd. (B.C. Sept. 19, 2006)
June 14, 2018 – Name changed to Golden Pursuit Resources Ltd. (see FPsurvey - Mines & Energy)

Silver Quest Resources Ltd. (B.C. Mar. 6, 1962)
Dec. 23, 2011 – Acquired by New Gold Inc. for 0.09 New Gold shs. plus $0.0001 cash for 1 Silver Quest sh., and 1 sh. of Independence Gold Corp. (a subsid. to which Silver Quest transferred all its assets and liabilities except the Davidson and Capoose properties) for 3 Silver Quest shs.

The Silver Recycling Company Inc. (Can. Dec. 4, 2003)
Dec. 16, 2011 – Dissolved and struck from register.

Silver Regent Mines Ltd. (Ont. 1962)
1968 – Acquired by Consolidated Skeena Mines Ltd.; basis 1 new for 2 old shs. (see Consolidated Skeena Mines Ltd.)

Silver Ridge Mining Co. Ltd. (B.C. Dec. 2, 1935)
Oct. 11, 1977 – Name changed to Consolidated Silver Ridge Mines Ltd.; basis 1 new for 5 old shs. ■

Silver Ridge Resources Inc. (B.C. Sept. 27, 1984)
May 7, 1993 – Name changed to International Silver Ridge Resources Inc.; basis 1 new for 3 old shs. ■

Silver Sceptre Mines Ltd. (B.C. Mar. 10, 1980)
July 5, 1982 – Name changed to Silver Sceptre Resources Ltd. ■

Silver Sceptre Resources Ltd. (B.C. Mar. 10, 1980)
Aug. 31, 1989 – Formed HLX Resources Ltd. in British Columbia on amalgamation with Eastern Mines Ltd., Gallant Gold Mines Ltd., Standard Gold Mines Ltd. and HLX Resources Ltd.; basis 0.1519 new for 1 Eastern Mines sh., 0.2266 new for 1 Gallant sh., 0.2735 new for 1 Standard Gold sh., 1 new for 1 HLX sh. and 0.1204 new for 1 Silver Sceptre sh. ■

Silver Shield Mines Inc. (Ont. 1971)
Dissolved.

Silver Shield Resources Corp. (Ont. June 1, 2006)
May 16, 2016 – Name changed to Gunpowder Capital Corp. ■

Silver Spike III Acquisition Corp. (B.C. Mar. 22, 2021)
May 30, 2023 – All o/s cl. A restricted vtg. shs. redeemed for US$10.3080 cash.

Silver Spirit Mines Ltd. (Ont. 1964)
Apr. 9, 1975 – Dissolved.

Silver Spring Mines Ltd. (B.C. 1967)
Apr. 15, 1994 – Dissolved and struck off register.

Silver Spur Resources Inc. (B.C. Aug. 25, 1987)
June 8, 1992 – Name changed to BWI Resources Limited; basis 1 new for 10 old shs. ■

Silver Standard Mines Limited (B.C. Dec. 11, 1946)
July 27, 1984 – Name changed to Consolidated Silver Standard Mines Limited; basis 1 new for 5 old shs. ■

Silver Standard Mining Co., Ltd. (B.C.)
1952 – Liquidation effected. No equity for shldrs.

Silver Standard Resources Inc. (B.C. Dec. 11, 1946)
Aug. 3, 2017 – Name changed to SSR Mining Inc. (see FPsurvey - Mines & Energy)

Silver Star Mines Ltd. (B.C. 1967)
Aug. 1979 – Name changed to Semper Resources Inc. ■

Silver Star Resources Inc. (Que. Aug. 23, 1993)
Nov. 22, 1994 – Name changed to Perlite Canada Inc. ■

Silver Strike Mines Ltd. (Ont. 1944)
1962 – Received 500,000 shs. (80% pooled) of Fontana Mines (1945) Limited for its assets, which were distributed pro rata. Charter surrendered.

Silver Strike Mining Syndicate Ltd. (B.C. 1976)
Nov. 28, 1980 – Name changed to Silver Strike Resources Ltd. ■

Silver Strike Resources Ltd. (B.C. 1976)
Jan. 1, 1985 – Amalgamated into United Mining Corporation; basis 1 new for 3 shs. of Silver Strike.

Silver Summit Mines Ltd. (Ont. 1962)
Feb. 2, 1973 – Name changed to Consolidated Summit Mines Limited; basis 1 new for 4 old shs. ■

Silver Sun Resource Corp. (B.C. Mar. 14, 2007)
Jan. 31, 2013 – Name changed to Golden Sun Mining Corp. ■

Silver Talon Mines Ltd. (B.C. 1983)
June 1, 1993 – Name changed to Score Athletic Products Inc. (see FPsurvey - Industrials)

Silver Tip Gold Mines Ltd. (B.C. 1925)
June 3, 1974 – Charter cancelled.

Silver Tip Mining & Development Co. Ltd. (B.C. 1925)
1946 – Name changed to Silver Tip Gold Mines Ltd. ■

Silver Titan Mines Ltd. (B.C. 1962)
1967 – Acquired by Atlas Explorations Ltd.; basis 1 new for 2 old shs.

Silver Tower Mines Ltd. (Ont. 1963)
Mar. 1976 – Charter cancelled.

Silver Town Mines Ltd. (Ont. 1963)
1968 – Merged into Glen Lake Silver Mines Ltd.; basis 1 new for 3 old shs. (see Glen Lake Silver Mines Ltd.)

Silver Tusk Mines Ltd. (B.C. 1976 amalg.)
Mar. 7, 1994 – Name changed to Consolidated Silver Tusk Mines Ltd.; basis 1 new for 5 old shs. ■

Silver Valley Mines Ltd. (Ont. June 14, 1933)
1940 – Acquired by Zagabelt Mining Corp. Ltd.; basis 1 new for 4 old shs. (see Zagabelt Mining Corp. Ltd.)
1941 – Charter surrendered. (see Zagabelt Mining Corp. Ltd.)

Silver Wheaton Corp. (Alta. Aug. 23, 1994)
Dec. 17, 2004 – Continued into Ontario.
May 10, 2017 – Name changed to Wheaton Precious Metals Corp. (see FPsurvey - Mines & Energy)

Silver-X International Mines Ltd. (B.C. 1967)
Dec. 1974 – Charter cancelled.

Silvera Resources Inc. (Alta. 1985)
Feb. 1, 1999 – Dissolved and struck from register.

Silverado Mines Ltd. (B.C. June 25, 1963)
May 23, 1997 – Name changed to Silverado Gold Mines Ltd.; basis 14 new for 13 old shs. (see FPsurvey - Mines & Energy)

Silverarrow Explorations Inc. (B.C. Dec. 6, 1988)
July 5, 2001 – Name changed to Aladdin Resources Corp.; basis 1 new for 8 old shs. ■

SilverBirch Energy Corporation (Can. June 25, 2010)
Apr. 5, 2012 – Acquired by Teck Resources Limited; basis $8.50 plus 1 sh. of newly incorporated SilverWillow Energy Corporation for 1 SilverBirch sh. (see SilverWillow Energy Corporation)

Silverbucke Mines Ltd. (Ont. 1948)
1953 – Charter cancelled.

SilverCrest Metals Inc. (B.C. June 23, 2015)
Feb. 19, 2025 – Acquired by Coeur Mining, Inc.; basis 1.6022 Coeur shs. for 1 SilverCrest sh.

SilverCrest Mines Inc. (B.C. May 15, 1998)
Oct. 8, 2015 – Acquired by First Majestic Silver Corp.; basis 0.2769 First Majestic com. shs. plus $0.0001 in cash and 0.1667 com. shs. of newly incorporated SilverCrest Metals Inc. for 1 SilverCrest Mines sh.

Silverdale Oils Ltd. (Sask.)
1958 – Struck off register.

Silverfields Mining Corporation Ltd. (Ont. 1968 amalg.)
Apr. 1, 1971 – Acquired by Teck Corporation Limited; basis 2 cl. B. Teck shs. for each 5 com. shs. Silverfields. (see Teck Corporation Limited)

Silverfish Resources Inc. (B.C. Aug. 18, 2020)
Jan. 29, 2024 – Name changed to Metalsource Mining Inc. (see FPsurvey - Mines & Energy)

Silverfish Surfer Mining Corp. (B.C. Aug. 18, 2020)
Jan. 5, 2021 – Name changed to Silverfish Resources Inc. ■

Silverhawk Resources Ltd. (B.C. 1983)
Dec. 8, 1989 – Name changed to Special Waste Management Inc. ■

Silverknife Mines Ltd. (B.C. 1966)
Nov. 4, 1974 – Charter cancelled.

Silverland Capital Corp. (B.C. Jan. 7, 2009)
Dec. 24, 2010 – Continued into Cayman Islands.
July 13, 2011 – Name changed to Sino Environ-Energy Tech Corp. ■

Silverleaf Resources Ltd. (B.C. 1983)
Feb. 28, 1985 – Name changed to Pacific Concord Resource Corporation. ■

Silvermaque Mining Limited (Que. Dec. 5, 1936)
Sept. 19, 1986 – Name changed to Geomaque Explorations Ltd.; basis 1 new for 4 old shs. ■

Silvermet Inc. (Ont. May 27, 1994)
Dec. 27, 2017 – Name changed to Global Atomic Corporation pursuant to acquisition of Global Atomic Fuels Corporation by way of amalgamation of Global Atomic Fuels with a wholly owned subsidiary of Silvermet.; basis 1 new for 2.75 old shs. (see FPsurvey - Mines & Energy)

Silvermex Resources Inc. (B.C. Feb. 29, 1980)
July 9, 2012 – Acquired by First Majestic Silver Corp.; basis 0.0355 First Majestic shs. plus $0.0001 for 1 Silvermex sh.

Silvermex Resources Ltd. (B.C. Apr. 7, 2005)
Nov. 16, 2010 – Name changed to Silver One Mining Corporation following acquisition by Genco Resources Ltd. (subsequently renamed Silvermex Resources Inc.); basis 1.1 new for 1 old sh.

Silverny Gold Mines Ltd. (Ont. 1945)
1958 – Charter cancelled.

Silverplace Mines Ltd. (Ont. 1955)
Nov. 28, 1973 – Charter cancelled.

Silverquest Resources Ltd. (B.C. Oct. 15, 1985)
Dec. 11, 1991 – Name changed to Cash Resources Ltd.; basis 1 new for 5 old shs. ■

Silverquick Development Co. (B.C. 1963)
Dec. 18, 1978 – Name changed to Silverquick Resources Ltd. (see FPsurvey - Mines & Energy)

Silverside Mines Ltd. (Ont. Apr. 22, 1949)
Aug. 31, 1979 – Name changed to Silverside Resources Inc. ■

Silverside Mines Ltd. (Ont. 1949)
Aug. 31, 1979 – Name changed to Silverside Resources Inc. ■

Silverside Resources Inc. (Ont. Apr. 22, 1949)
July 20, 1989 – Amalgamated with Proteus Resources Inc. to form new co. with same name Silverside Resources Inc.; basis 1 new for 2.5 Proteus shs. and 1 new for 1 Silverside sh.
June 17, 1991 – Name changed to Starmin Mining Inc.; basis 1 new for 4 old shs. ■

Silverside Resources Inc. (Ont. 1949)
July 20, 1989 – Amalgamated with Proteus Resources Inc. (1 new for 2.5 old com. shs., and 1 new for 2.5 old pfd. shs.), to continue as Silverside Resources Inc.; basis 1 new for 1 old sh.

Silversmith Mines Ltd. (B.C. 1918)
1953 – Liquidation completed and co. wound up.

Silverspar Minerals Inc. (B.C. July 18, 1979)
Sept. 19, 1997 – Continued into Ontario.
Jan. 22, 2001 – Name changed to Internet Identity Presence Company Inc. ■

Silverstack Mines Ltd. (Que. 1969)
Nov. 1, 1981 – Amalgamated with Les Mines d'Or Thompson Bousquet Ltée (5 for 4) and Copper Giant Mining Corp. Ltd. (1 for 4.5) to form Long Lac Minerals Ltd.; basis 1 new for 1 old sh.

Silverstone Oil Company Ltd. (Ont. 1956)
Dec. 10, 1962 – Dissolved.

Silverstone Resources Corp. (B.C. Apr. 26, 2005)
May 26, 2009 – Acquired by Silver Wheaton Corp.; basis 0.185 Silver Wheaton shs. for 1 Silverstone Resources sh. (see Silver Wheaton Corp.)

Silverstone Resources Ltd. (B.C. May 14, 1969)
Oct. 19, 2001 – Name changed to Sorel Ventures Ltd.; basis 1 new for 5 old shs. ■

Silversword Corporation (Ont. 1965)
Nov. 17, 2008 – Dissolved and struck from register.

Silverton Metals Corp. (B.C. Mar. 21, 2019)
Nov. 7, 2022 – Name changed to Lodestar Battery Metals Corp. ■

Silverton Resources Ltd. (Alta. 1979)
1980 – Continued into Ontario.
Nov. 27, 1987 – Amalgamated (1 new for 2 old shs.) with 61% owned Inverness Petroleum Ltd. to continue as Inverness Petroleum Ltd.

SilverWillow Energy Corporation (Can. Jan. 5, 2012)
Aug. 27, 2015 – Acquired by Value Creation Inc. by way of amalgamation with 9341102 Canada Inc., a wholly own subsid. of Value Creation Inc. for 3¢ per sh.

Silverwing Energy Inc. (Alta. May 28, 2002)
Nov. 18, 2008 – Amalgamated with Bonterra Energy Corp., a wholly owned subsid. of Bonterra Energy Income Trust; basis $0.073, 0.002166 Bonterra trust units, or a combination thereof for 1 Silverwing sh.

Silverwood Dairies, Limited (Ont. June 14, 1928)
July 1, 1970 – Name changed to Silverwood Industries Limited. ■

Silverwood Industries Limited (Ont. June 14, 1928)
May 1, 1984 – Name changed to Silcorp Limited. ■

Silverwood Western Dairies Limited (Ont. 1929)
May 31, 1952 – All the business, undertaking and assets acquired by Silverwood Dairies, Limited.

Silvio Ventures Inc. (Can. Sept. 21, 2000)
July 17, 2008 – Name changed to Regency Gold Corp. ■

Silvor Foxx Capital Corp. (Alta. Mar. 23, 2005)
Oct. 3, 2008 – Name changed to Silvore Fox Minerals Corp. ■

Silvore Fox Minerals Corp. (Alta. Mar. 23, 2005)
Dec. 11, 2008 – Amalgamated in Alberta to continue with same name.
Aug. 9, 2013 – Formed Golden Share Mining Corporation in Canada on amalgamation with (old) Golden Share Mining Corporation, with Silvore Fox the deemed acquiror; basis 1 new for 5 old Golden Share shs. and 1 new for 5 Silvore Fox shs. ■

Sim-Tek Enterprises & Exploration Inc. (Ont. 1931)
Sept. 14, 1983 – Name changed to Bonaventure Technologies Inc. ■

Simard-Beaudry Construction Inc. (Que. 1964)
Nov. 2, 1977 – Merged with Corporation D'Expansion Financière to form Corpex (1977) Inc. (see Corpex (1977) Inc.)

Simard-Beaudry Inc. (Que. 1950)
Oct. 25, 1999 – Acquired by Louisbergy Pipelines Inc. for $5.75 per sh.

Simavita Limited (B.C. Dec. 3, 2013)
Dec. 14, 2021 – Acquired by Smartz Operations Limited, a wholly owned subsid. of Smartz A.G.: basis (i) 1 Smartz sh. for 200 Simavita shs. or (ii) A$0.0271 cash for each Simavita sh. up to a maximum of 36,900 shs.

Simax Oil & Gas Inc. (Ont. Nov. 23, 1945)
Mar. 20, 2006 – Dissolved and struck from register.

Simba Energy Inc. (B.C. Sept. 19, 1990)
Apr. 24, 2017 – Name changed to Simba Essel Energy Inc. (see FPsurvey - Mines & Energy)

Simba Gold Corp. (B.C. Apr. 30, 2008)
Oct. 3, 2022 – Struck from registry and dissolved.

Simba Mines Ltd. (Ont. 1966)
Dec. 1973 – Charter cancelled.

Simba Oils Ltd. (Alta. Mar. 9, 1989)
Nov. 30, 1989 – Amalgamated with Petromines Limited; basis unknown. (see Apex Energy Corp.; Petromines Limited)

Simba Resources Inc. (B.C. Sept. 14, 1983)
Sept. 18, 1987 – Name changed to Leeward Capital Corp. ■

Simberi Gold Corporation (Ont. July 15, 1994)
Aug. 9, 2006 – Name changed to Simberi Mining Corporation. ■

Simberi Mining Corporation (Ont. July 15, 1994)
Sept. 29, 2009 – Name changed to Greenock Resources Inc.; basis 1 new for 10 old shs. ■

Simbud Capital Corp. (Alta. May 27, 1997)
Dec. 17, 1998 – Name changed to CanaDream Corporation. ■

Simcoe Erie Investors Limited (Ont. July 26, 1966)
Mar. 3, 1994 – Acquired by SEIL Acquisition Corporation, a wholly owned subsid. of GAN International, for $7.625 per sh.

Similkameen Hydro-Power Ltd. (B.C. July 27, 1992)
July 25, 1996 – Name changed to Norte Resources Ltd.; basis 1 new for 3 old shs. ■

Simla Red Lake Mines Ltd. (Ont. 1946)
Mar. 1953 – Charter cancelled.

Simmonds Communications Ltd. (B.C. 1980)
Oct. 17, 1995 – Name changed to Simmonds Capital Limited; basis 1 new for 5 old shs. (see FPsurvey - Industrials)

Simms Brushes Ltd. (N.B. 1866)
Nov. 1949 – Name changed to T. S. Simms & Co. Ltd. ■

Simon Cigar Company Limited (Can. 1928)
1958 – All o/s com. shs. acquired by Consolidated Cigar Corp. at the equivalent of US$35 per sh., payable in cash and stk.

Simon Fraser Resources Ltd. (B.C. June 4, 1987)
Mar. 4, 1992 – Delisted from the Vancouver Stock Exchange. Subsequently struck from registry and dissolved.

Simon Lake Mines Ltd. (Ont. 1945)
Wound up.

Simon Lemaire Incorporated (Que. May 31, 1960)
1991 – In bankruptcy. Arthur Anderson Inc. of Montreal appointed trustee.
May 1993 – All assets realized.
Mar. 1996 – Administration complete. No distribution to creditors or shldrs.
Oct. 9, 1996 – Trustee discharged.

Simpatico Wines Ltd. (B.C. Mar. 2, 1983)
Jan. 6, 1989 – Name changed to Liquest International Marketing Corp.; basis 1 new for 5 old shs. ■

Simplon Resources Ltd. (B.C. May 29, 1985)
July 22, 1993 – Name changed to Templar Resources Corporation; basis 1 new for 5 old shs. ■

Simply Better Brands Corp. (B.C. Mar. 19, 2018)
May 21, 2025 – Name changed to TRUBAR Inc. (see FPsurvey - Industrials)

Simpson Chibougamau Mines Ltd. (Que. 1955)
Sept. 9, 1972 – Dissolved.

The Simpson Oil Company Ltd. (Can. 1926)
Jan. 1949 – Dissolved.

Simpsons Acceptance Company Limited (Can. Dec. 12, 1952)
Aug. 1, 1992 – Amalgamated with Hudson's Bay Company. (see Hudson's Bay Company)

Simpsons Limited (Can. 1929)
Sept. 30, 1991 – Hudson's Bay Company offered to purch. all o/s shs. not held by US citizens or residents; basis 1 Hudson's Bay ord. sh. and option of 2 Hudson's Bay pref. or 1 pref. sh. and $22.50 for each 8 Simpsons shs. Subsequently, Simpsons distributed its 41% equity int. in Simpsons-Sears Limited to shldrs. of record Dec. 14, 1978 as a dividend comprising 0.655 cl. B sh. Simpsons-Sears Limited for each Simpsons sh. held. The offer by The Bay was then revised to include a proportionate no. of shs. of Simpsons-Sears given as a stk. dividend. Effective July 31, 1979, Simpsons, Limited amalgamated with Bayhud Inc., a wholly owned subsid. of Hudson's Bay Company. Simpsons shldrs. (other than US citizens or residents) had the option of receiving either 1 ord. sh. of Hudson's Bay or $28.50 made up of $28.40 plus 1 Hudson's Bay pref. ser. B sh., immediately redeem. at 10¢ a sh., for each 8 Simpsons shs. held; fractions in cash at $3.56 per sh. The amalgamated co. continued to operate as Simpsons, Limited, a wholly owned subsid. of Hudson's Bay. Sold all remaining assets to the Hudson's Bay Company on Sept. 30, 1991. All o/s long term debt redeemed: ser. I - 9.125% redeem. Dec. 2, 1991 at par plus $10 and unpaid int. of $27.25 per $1,000 of deb., ser. H - 8.375% redeem. Dec. 2, 1991 at par plus $2.50 and accr. and unpaid int. of $0.2295 per $1,000 of deb. (see Hudson's Bay Company)

Simpsons-Sears Acceptance Company Limited (Can. Dec. 23, 1952)
May 31, 1984 – Name changed to Sears Acceptance Company Inc. ■

Simpsons-Sears Limited (Can. Sept. 17, 1952; via Dominion charter)
May 31, 1984 – Name changed to Sears Canada Inc. ■

Simware Inc. (Can. Oct. 1, 1995)
Nov. 30, 1999 – Acquired by Delaware-based NetManage, Inc. for US$3.75 per sh.

Sin-Mac Lines Ltd. (Can. 1928)
Jan. 1935 – All assets sold. Distribution of $15 and 1 sh. of Sincennes-McNaughton Tugs Ltd. per $100 bond.
Dec. 9, 1940 – Second and final distribution of $9.44 per $100 bond.

Sinchao Metals Corp. (B.C. Dec. 15, 2006 amalg.)
June 28, 2012 – Name changed to Southern Legacy Minerals Inc. pursuant to reverse takeover acquisition of (old) Southern Legacy Minerals Inc.; basis 1 new for 6 old shs. ■

Sinclair Miller Mines Ltd. (Ont. 1961)
May 1, 1974 – Charter cancelled.

Sindor Resources Inc. (Ont. May 18, 1955)
Dec. 31, 1993 – Formed ClubLink Corporation in Ontario on amalgamation with Cherry Downs Development Corporation; basis 1 new for 0.55 Cherry Downs shs. and 1 new for 5 Sindor shs. ■

Sinmax Mines Ltd. (B.C. Oct. 21, 1966)
Apr. 1973 – Name changed to Shelter Gold Ltd.; basis 1 new for 2 old shs. ■

Sino Business Machines Inc. (B.C. 1982)
Nov. 26, 1993 – Dissolved and struck off register.

Sino Environ-Energy Tech Corp. (Cayman Islands Dec. 24, 2010)
Feb. 15, 2012 – Name changed to Ord Mountain Resources Corp. ■

Sino Foods Corp. (Yuk. Dec. 2, 1994)
Sept. 26, 1996 – Name changed to G.R. Pacific Resource Corp.; basis 1 new for 4 old shs. ■

Sino-Forest Corporation (Ont. Mar. 14, 1994 amalg.)
June 25, 2002 – Continued into Canada.
Jan. 30, 2013 – Transferred substantially all its assets including wholly owned Sino-Capital Global Inc. which holds 495,519,012 shs. of Greenheart Group Limited to Emerald Plantation Group Limited, a co. owned by Sino-Forest creditors. Certain excluded assets consisting of litigation claims were transferred to a litigation trust to pursue claims on behalf of affected creditors.
Mar. 4, 2013 – All com. shs. were cancelled and no consideration for shldrs.
June 17, 2015 – Dissolved and struck from register.

Sino Pac International Investments Inc. (B.C. 1982)
Dec. 16, 1996 – Name changed to Paron Resources Inc.; basis 1 new for 5 old shs. (see FPsurvey - Mines & Energy; FPsurvey - Industrials)

Sino Pacific Development Ltd. (B.C. Apr. 29, 1980)
Nov. 17, 2005 – Name changed to Prominex Resource Corp. ■

Sino Vanadium Inc. (Ont. May 30, 2007)
Dec. 12, 2011 – Privatized at 27¢ per sh.

SinoGas West Inc. (Alta. Dec. 21, 2007)
May 9, 2012 – Name changed to Bulldog Explorations Ltd. pursuant to Qualifying Transaction acquisition of an option to earn a 60% interest in the Eagle Lake Property from Eagle Plains Resources Ltd. ■

Sinomar Capital Corp. (Alta. Jan. 10, 2006)
Feb. 5, 2010 – Name changed to Hunt Mining Corp. pursuant to Qualifying Transaction reverse takeover acquisition of Argentina-based Cerro Cazador S.A., a wholly owned subsidary of HuntMountain Resources Ltd. (deemed acquiror). ■

Sinopec Daylight Energy Ltd. (Alta. Dec. 23, 2011 amalg.)
Dec. 30, 2011 – Acquired by Sinopec International Petroleum Exploration and Production Corporation for $10.08 per com. sh.
Jan. 1, 2024 – Name changed to Sinopec Canada Energy Ltd.

Sinotec Ventures Corp. (B.C. Feb. 11, 2000)
Apr. 30, 2003 – Name changed to Can-Chin Entertainment Group Co. Ltd. following Qualifying Transaction reverse takeover acquisition of Sun Bridge Entertainment Co. Ltd. ■

Sintana Energy Inc. (Ont. Sept. 7, 2006)
Aug. 6, 2015 – Formed Sintana Energy Corp. in Ontario on amalgamation with 1935370 Ontario Inc., a wholly owned subsid. of Mobius Resources Inc.; basis 0.26316 Mobius com. shs. for 1 Sintana Energy sh.

Sintra Ltd. (Can. Jan. 29, 1962)
Mar. 15, 2001 – Privatized via amalgamation with wholly owned subsid. of Colas, S.A.

Siocta Ventures Inc. (Can. Aug. 24, 1978)
July 11, 1994 – Name changed to TradeRef Software Corp. ■

Sion Resources Ltd. (Ont. 1969)
Sept. 6, 1979 – Name changed to Argus Resources Ltd. ■

Sioux Mountain Mines Ltd. (B.C. 1975)
June 17, 1978 – Name changed to The Ascot Petroleum Corporation; basis 1 new for 2 old shs. ■

Sioux Petroleums Ltd. (Ont. 1945)
1965 – Struck off register.

Sipald Resources Ltd. (B.C. 1979)
May 19, 1987 – Name changed to Rawdon Resources Ltd.; basis 1 new for 2 old shs. ■

Sire Bioscience Inc. (B.C. Apr. 4, 2014)
Apr. 30, 2021 – Name changed to PlantFuel Life Inc. (see FPsurvey - Industrials)

Sirit Inc. (Yuk. July 27, 1998)
Mar. 10, 2010 – Acquired by Federal Signal Corporation for 46¢ per sh.

Sirius Resource Corporation (B.C. 1981)
May 28, 1993 – Dissolved and struck off register.

Sirius Resources Ltd. (B.C. June 10, 1980)
Oct. 14, 1999 – Name changed to Lyra Resources Ltd.; basis 1 new for 2.9 old shs. ■

Sirius XM Canada Holdings Inc. (Ont. July 31, 2002)
May 29, 2017 – Acquired by 2517835 Ontario Inc., owned by Slaight Communications Inc., Obelysk Media Inc. and Sirius XM Radio Inc.; basis (i) $4.50 cash; (ii) 0.898 Sirius XM Holdings com. shs.; or (iii) a combination thereof per Sirius Canada cl. A sh. Class B shs. exchangeable for (i) $1.50 cash; (ii) 0.299 Sirius Holdings; or (iii) a combination thereof.

Sirmac Mines Ltd. (Ont. 1960)
Mar. 1976 – Charter cancelled.

Sirocco Mining Inc. (Can. Aug. 8, 1997)
Feb. 5, 2014 – Acquired by and amalgamated into Canada Lithium Corp. (renamed RB Energy Inc.); basis 0.3916 RB Energy shs. for 1 Sirocco sh.

Sirola Gold Mines Ltd. (Ont. 1944)
Feb. 15, 1959 – Dissolved.

Siscalta Oils Limited (Alta. 1925)
1963 – Purchased by Siscoe Mines Ltd. for 90¢ per sh.

Siscoe Callahan Mining Corporation (B.C. Apr. 7, 1978)
Sept. 15, 1995 – Dissolved and struck off register.

Siscoe Extension Gold Limited (Ont. Oct. 14, 1936)
1942 – Assets taken over by North Siscoe Mines Ltd. (see North Siscoe Mines Ltd.)

Siscoe Gold Mines Ltd. (Que. May 23, 1923)
1956 – Name changed to Siscoe Mines Ltd. ■

Siscoe Mines Ltd. (Que. May 23, 1923)
1971 – Name changed to United Siscoe Mines Limited; basis 1 new for 2 old shs. ■

Siskon Gold Corporation (B.C. Aug. 23, 1991)
Oct. 1991 – Continued into Delaware.

Sitebrand Inc. (Alta. Dec. 23, 2005)
Sept. 4, 2008 – Continued into Canada.
Oct. 26, 2011 – Name changed to Marchwell Ventures Ltd.; basis 1 new for 5 old shs. ■

Sitec Ventures Corp. (B.C. May 12, 1999)
Dec. 17, 2007 – Name changed to Tulox Resources Inc. ■

6550568 Canada Inc. (Can. May 23, 2006)
July 31, 2008 – Name changed to Alaris Royalty Corp. ■

66 Resources Corp. (B.C. May 31, 2017)
Sept. 8, 2020 – Name changed to Golden Independence Mining Corp. ■

Sixonine Ventures Corp. (B.C. Mar. 22, 2017)
Nov. 26, 2018 – Name changed to DionyMed Brands Inc. following reverse takeover acquisition of DionyMed Holdings Inc.; basis 1 new for 8.4329518 old shs. ■

Sixty Plus Income Trust (Ont. Jan. 27, 1999)
Jan. 2, 2009 – Liquidated for $11.4598 per trust unit.

Sixty Split Corp. (Ont. Jan. 30, 2001)
Mar. 16, 2011 – All o/s shs. redeemed for $25 per pref. sh. and $21.4703 per capital sh.

Skaist Mines Ltd. (B.C. 1969)
Mar. 30, 1977 – Name changed to Intercoast Resources Corp.; basis 1 new for 3 old shs. ■

Skalbania Enterprises Ltd. (B.C. Feb. 15, 1965)
Mar. 3, 1988 – Name changed to Selco International Properties, Inc. (see FPsurvey - Industrials)

Skarb Exploration Corp. (Ont. Mar. 6, 2018)
Dec. 9, 2020 – Name changed to Outback Goldfields Corp.; basis 1 new for 3 old shs. ■

Skat Resources Ltd. (B.C. 1970)
Sept. 14, 1978 – Amalgamated with 3 other cos. into Stand-Skat Resources Ltd.; basis 0.6489 new for 1 old sh. (see Stand-Skat Resources Ltd.)

Skeena Resources Ltd. (B.C. 1979)
Aug. 19, 1987 – Formed Golden Nevada Resources Inc. in British Columbia on amalgamation with Tenore Resources Ltd. ■

Skeena Silver Mines Ltd. (B.C. 1951)
1965 – Name changed to Consolidated Skeena Mines Ltd.; basis 1 new for 5 old shs. ■

Skelly Resources Ltd. (B.C. 1983)
Aug. 31, 1987 – Name changed to Bel Pac Industries Ltd. ■

Ski-Free Marine Inc. (Alta. 1985)
Sept. 1, 1992 – Struck off register.

Skidagate Exploration Ltd. (B.C. 1979)
June 2, 1981 – Name changed to Granada Exploration Corporation. ■

Skill Resources Ltd. (Alta. 1983 amalg.)
June 7, 1984 – Name changed to Unicorp Resources Ltd.; basis 1.25 new com. for 1 old cl. B pref. sh.; and 0.5 cl. A and 0.5 cl. B for 1 old com. sh. ■

Skillcraft Metal Products Ltd. (Ont. 1945)
Wound up. Holders of 5.5% cum. pref. shs., $100 par, received $7.89 per sh.

Skinny Technologies Inc. (B.C. Dec. 23, 1983)
Sept. 21, 2004 – Name changed to Pediment Exploration Ltd.; basis 1 new for 15 old shs. ■

Sklar Manufacturing Limited (Ont. 1965)
Sept. 30, 1982 – Amalgamated into PCL Industries Limited. Each shldr. of Sklar received 1 cl. A pfce. sh. ser. 2; 1 cl. B pfce. sh., which was immediately redeemed at $1.70 per sh.; and 1.25 com. shs. Sklar com. shs. owned by PCL which were cancelled without payment of capital.

Skoobins Resources Inc. (Alta. May 27, 2002)
Apr. 22, 2005 – Formed The Medipattern Corporation in Ontario on Qualifying Transaction amalgamation with The Medipattern Corporation, constituting a reverse takeover by Medipattern; basis 1.617899 new for 1 Medipattern sh. and 0.5325 new for 1 Skoobins sh. ■

Skookum Gold Mines Ltd. (Ont. Dec. 19, 1935)
1939 – Acquired by Bounty Consolidated Mines Ltd.; basis 1 new for 3 old shs. (see Bounty Consolidated Mines, Limited)

Skope Energy Inc. (Alta. June 23, 2010)
Feb. 19, 2013 – All assets and o/s of Skope Energy Inc. and its wholly owned subsidiary Skope International acquired by Pine Cliff Energy Inc. pursuant to the implementation of a Companies' Creditors Arrangement Act plan of reorganization. No consideration for the shareholders and subsequently, Skope Energy Inc. became a wholly owned subsid. of Pine Cliff.

The Skor Food Group Inc. (Ont. Jan. 26, 1983)
June 24, 2011 – Acquired by 2278988 Ontario Inc., a wholly owned subsid. of Colabor Group Inc., for $1.33 per sh.

Skukum Gold Inc. (B.C. 1986)
Apr. 29, 1994 – Dissolved and struck off register.

Skukum Ventures Inc. (B.C. 1986)
Mar. 30, 1988 – Name changed to Skukum Gold Inc. ■

Sky Games International Ltd. (B.C. Jan. 28, 1981)
Feb. 22, 1995 – Continued into Bermuda.
July 8, 1997 – Name changed to Interactive Entertainment Limited. ■

Sky Ridge Resources Ltd. (B.C. Mar. 22, 1972)
Sept. 15, 2016 – Name changed to Japan Gold Corp. following acquisition of Southern Arc Minerals Japan KK; basis 1 new for 2 old shs. (see FPsurvey - Mines & Energy)

Skyberry Capital Corp. (Alta. Jan. 21, 2010)
Mar. 10, 2011 – Continued into British Columbia.
Mar. 11, 2011 – Name changed to Lipari Energy, Inc. pursuant to Qualifying Transaction reverse takeover acquisition of Lipari Coal Holdings, Inc.; basis 1 new for 27.1028 old shs. ■

Skybridge Development Corp. (B.C. Jan. 30, 2007)
Oct. 28, 2008 – Continued into Ontario. (see Mega Silver Inc.)
June 12, 2009 – Acquired by Mega Silver Inc.; basis 1 Mega com. sh. for 2.5 Skybridge com. shs. (see Mega Silver Inc.)

Skybridge International Inc. (B.C. Dec. 28, 1973)
Apr. 30, 1987 – Name changed to International Potential Explorations Inc. ■

Skycreek Minerals Inc. (B.C. Aug. 28, 1968)
Dec. 16, 1993 – Name changed to The Spectra Group of Great Restaurants Inc.; basis 1 new for 100 old shs. ■

Skye PharmaTech Inc. (Ont. Mar. 11, 1997)
May 1, 2000 – Name changed to SynX Pharma Inc. ■

Skye Resources Inc. (B.C. Mar. 20, 1964)
Aug. 28, 2008 – Acquired by HudBay Minerals Inc.; basis 0.61 HudBay com. shs. and Cdn$0.001 per com. sh.
Oct. 6, 2008 – Name changed to HMI Nickel Inc.

Skye Resources Ltd. (Can. 1969)
1978 – Continued into Alberta. (see Campbell Resources Inc.)
Feb. 1, 1982 – Shldrs. received 1.125 shs. of Campbell Resources Inc. for each Skye sh. held under amalgamation. (see Campbell Resources Inc.)

Skygame Corporation (Can. Apr. 10, 1989)
Apr. 13, 1994 – Name changed to Skygame Inc. ■

Skygame Inc. (Can. Apr. 10, 1989)
Apr. 20, 1994 – Continued into Ontario.
June 9, 1997 – Name changed to Alpha Group Industries Inc.; basis 1 new for 4 old shs. (see FPsurvey - Industrials)

Skygold Resources Ltd. (B.C. July 27, 1987)
Jan. 13, 1992 – Name changed to Canadian Water Corporation. ■

Skygold Ventures Ltd. (Alta. Feb. 22, 1996)
Aug. 13, 2004 – Continued into British Columbia.
Jan. 14, 2010 – Name changed to Spanish Mountain Gold Ltd. (see FPsurvey - Mines & Energy)

Skyharbour Developments Ltd. (B.C. Mar. 20, 1981 amalg.)
Oct. 25, 2002 – Name changed to Skyharbour Resources Ltd. (see FPsurvey - Mines & Energy)

Skyhawk Resources Inc. (B.C. 1986)
Dec. 3, 1993 – Dissolved and struck off register.

Skyhigh Resources Ltd. (B.C. July 18, 1983)
Aug. 17, 1989 – Name changed to MIU Industries Ltd. ■

Skyjack Inc. (Ont. 1981)
Apr. 1, 1996 – Amalgamated in Ontario to continue with same name.
Oct. 10, 2002 – Acquired by Linamar Corporation for $2.13 per sh.

Skylark Resources Ltd. (B.C. Aug. 11, 1980)
July 27, 1992 – Name changed to GMD Resource Corp.; basis 1 new for 7 old shs. ■

Skyledger Tech Corp. (B.C. Nov. 29, 2017)
Feb. 25, 2021 – Name changed to Snowline Gold Corp. pursuant to the acquisition of Senoa Gold Corp. (see FPsurvey - Mines & Energy)

Skylight Health Group Inc. (Can. Dec. 27, 2017)
Dec. 5, 2023 – Assigned into bankruptcy and Deloitte Restructuring Inc. was appointed trustee.

Skyline Explorations Ltd. (B.C. Aug. 28, 1968)
Feb. 6, 1989 – Name changed to Skyline Gold Corporation. ■

Skyline Gold Corporation (B.C. Aug. 28, 1968)
July 20, 1993 – Name changed to Skycreek Minerals Inc.; basis 1 new International Skyline Gold Corporation sh. for 1 old Skyline Gold Corp. sh. ■

Skyline Gold Corporation (B.C. June 30, 1999)
May 24, 2012 – Name changed to SnipGold Corp.; basis 1 new for 10 old shs. ■

Skyline Hotels Limited (Ont. 1953)
May 16, 1980 – Amalgamated with 421386 Ontario Ltd. (a wholly owned subsid. of York-Hannover Ltd.) Com. shs. exchanged for either cl. A or B pfce. stk. of the amalg. co. on a sh.-for-sh. basis. Such pfce. stk. called for redemption at $5.50 per sh.

Skyline Natural Resources Ltd. (Alta. Aug. 21, 1978)
Sept. 6, 1996 – Name changed to Stellarton Energy Corporation following acquisition of and subsequent amalgamation with Stellarton Resources Limited and Secure Oil Tools Ltd.; basis 1 new for 12.4 old shs. ■

Skyline Oils Limited (Alta. 1952)
1953 – Merged into Consolidated Mic Mac Oils Ltd.; basis 1 new for 6 old shs.

Skyline Uranium and Minerals Corp. Ltd. (Ont. 1953)
Nov. 27, 1961 – Charter cancelled.

Skylink Communications Inc. (Alta. Mar. 31, 1987)
Sept. 1, 1996 – Struck off register.

Skylon All Asset Trust (Ont. Sept. 30, 2004)
Jan. 5, 2015 – Redeemed for $18.5927 per trust unit pursuant to termination of trust.

Skylon Capital Yield Trust (Ont. Mar. 27, 2002)
Apr. 30, 2007 – Merged into High Yield & Mortgage Plus Trust; basis 0.699308 of High Yield trust unit for 1 old Skylon Capital trust unit. (see High Yield & Mortgage Plus Trust)

Skylon Global Capital Yield Trust (Ont. June 26, 2002)
Aug. 1, 2012 – Terminated. Redeemed for $25.0492 per trust unit.

Skylon Global Capital Yield Trust II (Ont. Feb. 14, 2003)
Aug. 1, 2012 – All tr. units redeemed on July 31, 2012, for $20.3555 per unit.

Skylon Growth & Income Trust (Ont. Jan. 30, 2004)
Aug. 12, 2019 – Merged into CI First Asset Global Asset Association ETF; basis 0.354181 ETF units for 1 Skylon trust units.

Skylon International Advantage Yield Trust (Ont. June 27, 2003)
Dec. 31, 2013 – Redeemed. Net asset value Cdn$23.5746 per ser. A unit and US$9.8165 per ser. B unit.

Skymore Resources Inc. (Alta. Apr. 28, 1993)
Jan. 29, 2002 – Name changed to Seven Clans Resources Corp. following reverse takeover acquisition of Seven Clans Resources Inc.; basis 1 new for 3 old shs. ■

Skynner Lake Gold Mines Ltd. (Ont. 1937)
1968 – Charter cancelled.

Skyscape Capital Inc. (Ont. Jan. 9, 2018)
Feb. 7, 2022 – Name changed to PesoRama Inc. pursuant to the Qualifying Transaction reverse takeover acquisition of (old) PesoRama Inc. (see FPsurvey - Industrials)

Skyway Resources Ltd. (B.C. 1981)
July 24, 1989 – Name changed to Burrard Ventures Inc.; basis 1 new for 2 old shs. ■

SkyWest Energy Corp. (Alta. June 22, 2010 amalg.)
Dec. 5, 2011 – Name changed to Marquee Energy Ltd. pursuant to reverse takeover acquisition of Marquee Petroleum Ltd.; basis 1 new for 8 old shs. ■

Skywest Resources Corp. (Alta. 1983)
June 30, 1987 – Acquired by Summit Resources Limited; basis 1 new for 17.5 old shs. (see Summit Resources Limited)

Skyworld Resources & Development Ltd. (B.C. Aug. 28, 1985)
Mar. 20, 1990 – Name changed to Whitewater Resources Ltd.; basis 1 new for 3.3 old shs. ■

Slade Energy Inc. (Alta. May 15, 1987)
May 16, 2000 – Name changed to Westpoint Energy Inc.; basis 1 new for 4 old shs. ■

Sladen Explorations Ltd. (Ont. Dec. 20, 1927)
1930 – Name changed to Sladen Malartic Mines Ltd. ■

Sladen Malartic Mines Ltd. (Ont. Dec. 20, 1927)
1952 – Assets distributed. Shldrs. received 50 shs. Barnat Mines, 50 Barnat Mines 5% debs. (since redeemed), and 10 shs. Sladen (Quebec) Ltd. for 100 old Sladen Malartic shs.

Sladen (Quebec) Ltd. (Que. 1937)
Nov. 1974 – Charter cancelled.

Slate Bay Gold Mines Limited (Ont. Sept. 23, 1944)
Jan. 3, 1995 – Delisted from the CDN. Subsequently dissolved and charter cancelled.

Slate Office Real Estate Investment Trust (Ont. Aug. 27, 2012)
Dec. 31, 2024 – Name changed to Ravelin Properties REIT. (see FPsurvey - Industrials)

Slate Retail REIT (Ont. Jan. 18, 2012)
Aug. 21, 2020 – Name changed to Slate Grocery REIT. (see FPsurvey - Industrials)

Slater Industries Inc. (Ont. Apr. 1, 1980 amalg.)
Sept. 17, 1986 – All 5.5% pfce. ser. $1.10 redesignated as 7% pfce., 1st ser.; 5.5% pfce. $1.10 2nd ser. redesignated as 7% pfce. 2nd ser.; 6% pfce. $1.20 ser. redesignated as 7.5% pfce. 1st ser. The cl. A and B shs. continued trading under new co. name Slater Industries Inc.
June 25, 1996 – Name changed to Slater Steel Inc. ■

Slater Industries Ltd. (Ont. Oct. 1960)
1962 – Amalgamated to form Slater Steel Industries Ltd.; basis 2 com. shs. for 1 com. sh. and one 6.25% pref. sh. for each pref. sh. (see Slater Steel Industries Ltd.)

Slater Mining Corporation (B.C. June 5, 2008)
Feb. 4, 2016 – Name changed to Libero Mining Corporation; basis 1 new for 2 old shs. ■

Slater Steel Inc. (Ont. Apr. 1, 1980 amalg.)
June 2, 2003 – Filed for creditor protection under the Companies' Creditors Arrangement Act (CCAA) and under Chapter 11 of the U.S. Bankruptcy Code. PricewaterhouseCoopers Inc. was appointed monitor.
Aug. 30, 2004 – CCAA proceedings were terminated and the co. was placed into receivership under the Bankruptcy and Insolvency Act. All officers and directors resigned. PriceWaterhouseCoopers Inc. was subsequently appointed by the Court as receiver and manager. No distributions were available for shldrs.

Slater Steel Industries Ltd. (Ont. Feb. 22, 1962 amalg.)
Apr. 1, 1980 – Amalgamated in Ontario to continue with same name.
July 27, 1984 – Name changed to Slater Steels Corporation. ■

Slater Steels Corporation (Ont. Apr. 1, 1980 amalg.)
Aug. 20, 1986 – Name changed to Slater Industries Inc. ■

Slater, Walker of Canada Limited (Can. Mar. 12, 1931; via Dominion charter)
Feb. 25, 1976 – Name changed to Talcorp Associates Limited. ■

Slater, Walker of Canada Limited (Can. 1931)
June 30, 1972 – Retaining same name, amalgamated with UNAS Investments Limited on the basis of 2 com. shs. of amalg. co. for 1 com. sh. of Slater, Walker and 8 com. shs. of the amalg. co. for each 3 shs. of UNAS not held by Slater, Walker. The 576,599 UNAS com. shs. held by Slater, Walker were cancelled.

Slave Lake Gold Mines Ltd. (Ont. Jan. 4, 1935)
1944 – Charter cancelled; assets acquired in 1942 by International Tungsten Mines Ltd.

Slave Point Consolidated Mines Ltd. (B.C. 1965)
Jan. 24, 1977 – Name changed to Amparo Development Corp. ■

Slave Point Mines Ltd. (B.C. 1965)
Mar. 7, 1972 – Name changed to Slave Point Consolidated Mines Ltd. ■

Slayton Capital Corp. (Alta. 1987)
Apr. 24, 1989 – Continued into Canada.
Sept. 1, 1994 – Formed Earthwhile Developments Inc. in Alberta on amalgamation with Earthwhile Developments Inc.; basis 1 new for 5 old shs. ■

Sleeman Breweries Ltd. (B.C. Oct. 23, 1984)
June 18, 1997 – Continued into Canada.
Oct. 24, 2006 – Acquired by Sapporo Breweries Ltd. for $17.50 per sh.

Sleep Country Canada Holdings Inc. (Can. May 27, 2015)
Oct. 3, 2024 – Acquired by Fairfax Financial Holdings Limited; basis $35 cash per sh.

Sleep Country Canada Income Fund (Ont. Mar. 5, 2003)
Sept. 26, 2008 – Acquired by 7019416 Canada Inc. for $22.00 per unit.

Sleeping Gold Ltd. (B.C. Jan. 10, 1986)
Sept. 14, 1992 – Name changed to Achieva Development Corp.; basis 1 new for 3.5 old shs. ■

Sleepy Giant Mines Ltd. (Que. 1946)
July 1974 – Charter cancelled.

Slemon Yellowknife Mines Ltd. (Ont. 1945)
1954 – Merged into Pardee Amalgamated Mines Ltd.; basis 1 new for 20 old shs.

Sloane Mining Company Ltd. (Ont. 1973 amalg.)
Jan. 28, 1976 – Amalgamated with Gerrard Realty Incorporated to form Gerrard Realty Incorporated; basis 2 new for 17 old shs.

Sloane Petroleums Inc. (B.C. Sept. 13, 1985)
Mar. 9, 2001 – Amalgamated with Gentry Resources Ltd. to continue as Gentry Resources Ltd.; basis 1 new Gentry sh. for 10 old Sloane shs. plus cash component of $0.72 per sh. (see Gentry Resources Ltd.)

Slocan Base Metals Ltd. (B.C. 1950)
Jan. 1964 – Dissolved.

Slocan Development Corporation Limited (B.C. Apr. 16, 1952)
Oct. 7, 1992 – Name changed to International Slocan Developments Inc.; basis 1 new for 3 old shs. ■

Slocan Forest Products Ltd. (B.C. May 2, 1978)
Apr. 2, 2004 – Acquired by Canfor Corporation; basis 1.3147 Canfor shs. for 1 Slocan sh.

Slocan Holdings Ltd. (B.C. Apr. 16, 1952)
Oct. 26, 1999 – Name changed to Galaxy Energy Corp.; basis 1 new for 2 old shs. ■

Slocan-Hughes Mines Ltd. (B.C. 1963)
1966 – Name changed to New Eagle Mining Corp. Ltd. ■

Slocan Lode Mines Ltd. (B.C. 1952)
Sept. 1968 – Struck off register.

Slocan Monitor Mines Ltd. (B.C. Apr. 16, 1935)
1970 – Reported out of business.

Slocan Ottawa Mines Ltd. (B.C. Apr. 16, 1952)
Feb. 4, 1972 – Name changed to Slocan Development Corporation Limited. ■

Slocan-Rambler Mines (1947) Ltd. (Ont. Dec. 20, 1945)
July 30, 2008 – Name changed to Compel Capital Inc. ■

Slocan Rambler Mining Co. Ltd. (B.C. Jan. 28, 1928)
1941 – Dissolved.

Slocan United Mines Ltd. (B.C. Apr. 16, 1952)
1955 – Name changed to Ottawa Uranium Mines Ltd. ■

Slocan Van Roi Mines Ltd. (B.C. 1947)
May 1960 – Name changed to Kopan Developments Ltd.; basis 1 new for 4 old shs. ■

Slovakian Gram Minerals Corp. (Can. Sept. 12, 1996)
Oct. 16, 2000 – Name changed to Gram Minerals Corporation. ■

Slumber Lodge Development Corporation Ltd. (B.C. 1963)
July 17, 1991 – Name changed to Western Dominion Investment Company Ltd. ■

Slumber-Magic Adjustable Bed Co. Ltd. (B.C. Dec. 12, 1977)
May 7, 1996 – Name changed to Victory Ventures Inc. ■

Smackover Mining Corp. Ltd. (B.C. 1969)
Aug. 29, 1977 – Charter cancelled.

Small Fry Snack Foods Limited (Ont. Dec. 2, 1994)
Oct. 23, 2000 – Name changed to Humpty Dumpty Snack Foods Inc. ■

Small Pharma Inc. (B.C. Jan. 23, 2018)
Oct. 26, 2023 – Acquired by Cybin Inc.; basis 0.2409 Cybin shs. for 1 Small Pharma sh.

Smart Api Venture Capital Corporation (Can. Aug. 25, 1998)
Feb. 3, 2003 – Name changed to Vigil Locating Systems Corporation following Qualifying Transaction reverse takeover acquisition of Vigil Technology Locating Systems Inc. for 9,285,714 cl. A shs. valued at $0,35 per sh. ■

Smart Employee Benefits Inc. (Ont. Dec. 23, 2010)
Mar. 6, 2023 – Acquired by Co-operators Financial Services Limited; basis 30¢ cash per sh.

Smart Real Estate Investment Trust (Alta. Dec. 4, 2001)
Oct. 20, 2017 – Name changed to SmartCentres Real Estate Investment Trust. (see FPsurvey - Industrials)

SmartCardeSolutions.Com Ltd. (Alta. Oct. 25, 1994)
Apr. 2, 2022 – Struck from registry and dissolved.

Smartel Communications Corporation (Ont. July 5, 1985)
Aug. 5, 1996 – Name changed to Intasys Corporation. ■

SmarTire Systems Inc. (B.C. Sept. 8, 1987)
Feb. 6, 2003 – Continued into Yukon.
Dec. 20, 2006 – Continued into British Columbia.
Aug. 13, 2009 – Name changed to TTC Technology Corp. ■

SmartSales Inc. (Ont. May 9, 1995)
Nov. 12, 2002 – Declared bankrupt. Perry Krieger & Associates Inc. was appointed trustee.

Smartset Services Inc. (Alta. May 9, 2013)
Feb. 2, 2018 – Continued into British Columbia. (see FPsurvey - Industrials)

Smash Minerals Corp. (B.C. June 4, 2010)
Apr. 24, 2012 – Amalgamated with Prosperity Goldfields Corp. (deemed acquiror), to form a new co. also named Prosperity Goldfields Corp. (amalco), basis 0.625 amalco com. shs. for 1 Smash com. sh. and 1 amalco com. sh. for 1 (old) Prosperity com. sh.

Smelter Gold Mines Ltd. (Can. 1933)
1953 – Charter cancelled.

Smith Cobalt Mines Ltd. (Ont. 1928)
Mar. 1976 – Property sold to Rockzone Mines for 300,000 shs.; no record of distribution. Smith Cobalt charter cancelled.

Smith-Tiblemont Ltd. (Can. 1934)
July 1937 – Name changed to Smith-Tiblemont Mines Ltd. and continued into Quebec; basis 1 new for 1 old sh. ■

Smith-Tiblemont Mines Ltd. (Que. July 1937)
July 1972 – Charter cancelled.

Smithe Resources Corp. (B.C. Feb. 17, 2021)
June 26, 2025 – Name changed to TooGood Gold Corp. pursuant to the Qualifying Transaction reverse takeover acquisition of TGC Gold Corp. (see FPsurvey - Mines & Energy)

Smithfield Canada Limited (Ont. Jan. 19, 1998)
Apr. 6, 2004 – Acquired by Smithfield Foods, Inc.; basis 1 new Smithfield Foods com. sh. plus Cdn$3.35 for 1 old exch. sh.

Smokey Resources Ltd. (Alta. Dec. 19, 1986)
Apr. 5, 1989 – Name changed to General Leisure Corporation. ■

Snackie Jack's Ltd. (Ont. Aug. 23, 1993 amalg.)
Nov. 26, 2004 – Name changed to Healing Waters, Inc.; basis 1 new for 8 old shs. ■

Snaper Patent Technologies Inc. (B.C. 1987)
May 19, 1992 – Name changed to Emerging Growth Technologies Inc.; basis 1 new for 5 old shs. ■

Snare River Mines Ltd. (Ont. 1945)
1955 – Property sold to Tarbell Mines Ltd.; basis 1 new for 2 old shs. Charter surrendered. (see Tarbell Mines Ltd.)

Snif Security Inc. (B.C. Dec. 8, 1986)
May 31, 2000 – Acquired by Acme's Acquisition Company Limited, a wholly owned subsid. of Acme Protection Systems Limited, for 9¢ per sh.

Sniper Enterprises Inc. (B.C. Apr. 16, 1980)
Aug. 16, 2005 – Name changed to TransAmerican Energy Inc. ■

Sniper Resources Ltd. (B.C. July 6, 2006)
May 16, 2022 – Name changed to Metaville Labs Inc. (see FPsurvey - Industrials)

SnipGold Corp. (B.C. June 30, 1999)
June 22, 2016 – Acquired by Seabridge Gold Inc.; basis 0.015873 Seabridge com. shs. for 1 SnipGold com. sh.

Snobro Enterprises Inc. (B.C. May 16, 2016)
Oct. 3, 2017 – Name changed to SIQ Mountain Industries Inc. following Qualifying Transaction acquisition of snow-bike technology. (see FPsurvey - Industrials)

Snow Eagle Resources Ltd. (B.C. Oct. 19, 2010)
May 24, 2018 – Formed FluroTech Ltd. in Alberta pursuant to Qualifying Transaction amalgamation with CannaTest Photonics Ltd. (deemed acquiror); basis 1 new for 4.5 old shs. (see FPsurvey - Industrials)

Snow Goose Mines Ltd. (Ont. 1964)
Apr. 1972 – Charter cancelled.

Snow Lake Gold Mines Ltd. (Ont. Nov. 25, 1944)
Sept. 10, 1956 – Name changed to Snow Lake Mines Ltd. ■

Snow Lake Mines Ltd. (Ont. Nov. 25, 1944)
Mar. 8, 1960 – Name changed to Phoenix Canada Oil Company Limited; basis 1 new for 15 old shs. ■

Snow Lake Mines Ltd. (Alta. 1986)
Sept. 2, 2003 – Struck from the registry and dissolved.

Snowbird Investments Ltd. (Alta. Apr. 28, 1987)
Oct. 1, 1995 – Dissolved and struck off register.

Snowcap Waters Limited (B.C. Jan. 8, 1985)
Apr. 30, 1998 – Name changed to Seacrest Development Corporation; basis 1 new for 10 old shs. ■

Snowden Yellowknife Mines Ltd. (Ont. 1945)
Mar. 30, 1959 – Dissolved.

Snowdon Mining & Explorations Ltd. (Que. 1957)
Charter cancelled.

Snowdrift Base Metal Mines Ltd. (Ont. 1956)
1971 – Assets sold to Indian Mountain Metal Mines Ltd.; basis 1 new for 8.5 old shs.

Snowfield Development Corp. (B.C. July 9, 1987)
Dec. 12, 2016 – Dissolved and struck from register.

Snowfield Resources Ltd. (B.C. July 9, 1987)
Apr. 28, 2000 – Name changed to Snowfield Development Corp.; basis 1 new for 4 old shs. ■

Snowshoe Gold Mines Ltd. (Que. July 1937)
Distributed 1 sh. Western Quebec Mines Co. Ltd. for 4 shs. Snowshoe. Charter surrendered.

Snowy Owl Gold Corp. (B.C. Nov. 9, 2018)
Apr. 22, 2024 – Name changed to Boba Mint Holdings Ltd. pursuant to the reverse takeover acquisition of Bluecorp Capital Corp. (dba Boba Mint) and concurrent amalgamation of Boba Mint with wholly owned 1381603 B.C. Ltd. (see FPsurvey - Industrials)

Sobeys Canada Incorporated (N.S. Oct. 27, 1998)
June 1, 1999 – Name changed to Sobeys Inc. ■

Sobeys Incorporated (N.S. Apr. 18, 1946)
Dec. 9, 1998 – Name changed to Sobeys Group Inc.

Sobeys Inc. (N.S. Oct. 27, 1998)
June 18, 2007 – Acquired by Empire Company Limited for $58 per sh.

Sobeys Stores Limited (N.S. Apr. 18, 1946)
May 17, 1987 – Became a wholly owned subsid. of Empire Company Limited under the name Sobeys Inc. Holders of shs. other than Empire Co. had the option of receiving 1.6 cl. A nonvoting shs. of Empire or 1 cl. A and 0.5 of one 8% pref. sh., series 3 for each sh. held. The pref. shs. are retractable at the holders' option at $25 (par) on May 1, 1994.
Sept. 17, 1987 – Name changed to Sobeys Incorporated. ■

SoCal Capital Corp. (B.C. 1986)
Aug. 5, 1993 – Name changed to Empyrean Diagnostics Ltd. ■

Socanav Inc. (Que. Dec. 28, 1977)
May 8, 1998 – Struck from registry and dissolved.

La Société de Prêts et Placement de Québec (Que. 1922)
June 1957 – Placed into bankruptcy, with Gingras Normandeau Coté & Bisson of Quebec City appointed trustee.
1967 – Proposal made to form new co. to assume co.'s liabs. and to make settlement with creditors. No further report.

Société d'Entraide Economique Métropolitaine de Montréal Inc . (Que. 1984)
Mar. 7, 1989 – Name changed to La Société d'Epargne Métropolitaine de Montréal Inc.

Société d'épargne de la Montérégie inc. (Que. June 1, 1984)
Dec. 4, 1991 – Amalgamated with Société Nationale de Fiducie. All o/s shs. (other than those held by Société Nationale de Fiducie) converted into redeem. cl. A pref. shs. of the amalgamated co. redeemable immediately at $1.50.

La Société d'exploration minière Mazarin inc. (Que. Feb. 15, 1985)
Nov. 30, 1993 – Name changed to Mazarin Mining Corporation Inc. ■

Société d'Exploration Minière La Sarre Incorporated (Que. Aug. 27, 1986)
Oct. 4, 1991 – Name changed to Minéraux Manic Inc.; basis 1 new for 4 old shs. ■

Société Financière pour le Commerce et l'Industrie S.F.C.I. Ltd. (Que. 1961)
1974 – Name changed to BNP Canada Inc. ■

Société Générale (Canada) (Can. 1982)
July 1, 1990 – Amalgamated with Crédit Commercial de France (Canada) to continue as Société Générale (Canada).

Société générale de financement du Québec (Que. 1962)
Apr. 1, 2011 – Amalgamated with Investissement Québec to form (new) Investissement Québec.

La Société Industrielle et Minière du Nord-Ouest Québécois (SIMOQ) Limitée (Que. 1970)
Mar. 14, 1981 – Charter cancelled.

Société Minière d'Exploration Somex Ltée (Que. 1969)
1976 – Acquired by Graphex Mines Inc. Shs. reported exchanged on basis of 1 sh. Graphex for 4 shs. Somex.

Société Minière Ecudor inc. (Que. June 5, 1985)
Sept. 7, 1999 – Name changed to ECU Silver Mining Inc. ■

Société Minière Pershing-Manitou Ltée (Que. 1937)
June 30, 1993 – Amalgamated with Big Town Copper Mines Ltd./Société Minière Grande Ville Ltée (1 for 2) and Eastville Gold Mines Ltd./Société Minière Esteville Ltée (1 for 5) to form Société Minière Pershing Manitou Ltée; basis 1 new for 1 old sh.

Société québécoise d'exploration minière - SOQUEM (Que. July 15, 1965)
July 2, 1998 – Formed SOQUEM INC. following combination of REXFOR, SOQUIP and SOQUIPA and integration into Société générale de financement du Québec (SFG); now a wholly owned subsid. of SGF Minéral Inc., itself a subsid. of SFG du Québec.

Société québécoise d'initiatives pétrolières (SOQUIP) (Que. 1969)
July 2, 1998 – Formed SOQUIP INC. in Quebec on amalgamation with SOQUEM, REXFOR and SOQUIA, and integration into Société générale de financement du Québec (SGF). Now a wholly owned subsid. of SGF.

Sock Fiberglass (Canada) Ltd. (Ont. Aug. 16, 1961)
Sept. 22, 1987 – Name changed to L'Air d'Or Corporation. ■

Sodarcan inc. (Can. 1972)
Aug. 19, 1997 – Acquired by Aon Reed Stenhouse Acquisition Corp. for $3.85 per sh.

Sodisco-Howden Group Inc. (Que. Dec. 7, 1966)
Feb. 16, 2005 – Acquired by CanWel Building Materials Ltd. for $3.25 per sh. (see CanWel Building Materials Ltd.)

Sodisco Inc. (Que. Oct. 11, 1972)
July 10, 1989 – Acquired by Unigesco Inc. for $10.75 per sh. (see Unigesco Inc.)

Soficap Acquisitions Inc. (Alta. July 10, 2001)
Jan. 2, 2012 – Dissolved and struck from the registry.

Softcan Distributing Ltd. (B.C. Feb. 29, 1984)
Feb. 19, 1986 – Name changed to Sona Systems Canada Ltd. ■

Softcare EC Inc. (B.C. Mar. 30, 1981)
June 23, 2003 – Name changed to Open EC Technologies, Inc.; basis 1 new for 10 old shs. ■

Softcare EC.Com, Inc. (B.C. Mar. 30, 1981)
Nov. 9, 2001 – Name changed to Softcare EC Inc. ■

Softchoice Corporation (Can. May 15, 2002 amalg.)
June 21, 2013 – Acquired by Birch Hill Equity Partners Management Inc. for $20 per sh.
Dec. 31, 2019 – Continued into Canada.
Mar. 17, 2025 – Acquired by World Wide Technology Holding Co. LLC; basis Cdn$24.50 cash per sh.
Mar. 19, 2025 – Continued into Nova Scotia.

SoftCop Corporation (Ont. 1986)
Mar. 27, 2006 – Certificate of incorporation cancelled and dissolved.

Softfund Capital Partners Inc. (B.C. Apr. 24, 1987)
June 30, 1994 – Name changed to Sand River Resources Ltd.; basis 1 new for 4 old shs. ■

SoftKey Software Products Inc. (Ont. Jan. 18, 1984)
Jan. 7, 2003 – Early redeemed by parent Mattel, Inc.; basis 1.2 Mattel com. shs. for 1 SoftKey exch. sh.

Softlab9 Software Solutions Inc. (B.C. Oct. 30, 2014)
July 20, 2020 – Name changed to Softlab9 Technologies Inc. ■

Softlab9 Technologies Inc. (B.C. Oct. 30, 2014)
Sept. 8, 2021 – Name changed to CleanGo Innovations Inc. pursuant to the reverse takeover acquisition of CleanGo GreenGo Inc. (see FPsurvey - Mines & Energy; FPsurvey - Industrials)

SoftQuad International Inc. (B.C. Apr. 27, 1982)
Sept. 6, 1994 – Continued into Ontario.
Sept. 18, 1998 – Continued into New Brunswick.
Feb. 9, 1999 – Name changed to NewKidCo International Inc. (see FPsurvey - Industrials)

Softrock Minerals Ltd. (Alta. Apr. 26, 1993)
Sept. 26, 2022 – Name changed to Criterium Energy Ltd. (see FPsurvey - Mines & Energy)

Softrock Petroleums Ltd. (Alta. Apr. 26, 1993)
Aug. 22, 1997 – Name changed to Softrock Minerals Ltd. ■

Software Gaming Corp. (Ont. July 19, 1974)
Nov. 9, 2001 – Name changed to XPeria Corp.; basis 1 new for 6 old shs. ■

Software Growth Inc. (Ont. Feb. 20, 2006)
Feb. 17, 2010 – Dissolved following completion of Qualifying Transaction acquisition of 1,500,000 units (1 com. sh. & 1 wt.) of Enssolutions Group Inc. Com. shldrs. received 0.38 units of Enssolutions Group Inc. for each sh. held.

Sogemines Limited (Can. May 9, 1951)
Feb. 25, 1969 – Name changed to Genstar Limited. ■

Sogena Inc. (Que. 1962)
1987 – Operations dissolved, assets distributed and co. wound up.

Sogepet Limited (Ont. Aug. 16, 1962)
Jan. 19, 1995 – Continued into Alberta.
Feb. 2, 1995 – Name changed to High Bullen Resources Ltd. following amalgamation with High Bullen Energy Ltd.; basis 1 new for 1 old sh. ■

Sogo Capital Inc. (Alta. Feb. 28, 1995)
Aug. 1, 1999 – Struck off register.

Sohio Exploration Corporation (B.C. Feb. 15, 1980)
Dec. 16, 1985 – Name changed to Sensat Technologies Ltd.; basis 1 new for 3 old shs. (see FPsurvey - Industrials)

Soho Resources Corp. (B.C. Apr. 11, 1986)
Jan. 17, 2013 – Name changed to Telson Resources Inc.; basis 1 new for 8 old shs. ■

Sojourn Exploration Inc. (B.C. Dec. 23, 2010)
Feb. 28, 2019 – Name changed to ArcWest Exploration Inc. (see FPsurvey - Mines & Energy)

Sojourn Ventures Inc. (B.C. Dec. 23, 2010)
Aug. 24, 2017 – Name changed to Sojourn Exploration Inc.; basis 1 new for 3 old shs. ■

Sokoman Iron Corp. (Alta. June 7, 2006)
Feb. 13, 2019 – Name changed to Sokoman Minerals Corp. (see FPsurvey - Mines & Energy)

Sol Cuisine Ltd. (Ont. Feb. 15, 2018)
Jan. 25, 2022 – Acquired by PlantPlus Foods Canada Inc., a wholly owned subsid. of PlantPlus Foods, LLC; basis $2.06 cash per sh.

Sola Resource Corp. (Alta. Feb. 13, 1980)
Jan. 24, 2011 – Name changed to Cancana Resources Corp.; basis 1 new for 10 old shs. ■

Solace Resources Corp. (B.C. Aug. 29, 1986)
Mar. 27, 2012 – Name changed to First Graphite Corp. ■

Solaia Ventures Inc. (B.C. Sept. 1, 1994)
Jan. 22, 2003 – Name changed to Trivello Ventures Inc.; basis 1 new for 12 old shs. ■

Solana Petroleum Corp. (Alta. Mar. 25, 1998)
Jan. 21, 2004 – Name changed to Q-Gold Resources Ltd. following reverse takeover acquisition of mineral assets from Hexagon Gold (Ontario) Ltd.; basis 1 new for 9 old shs. ■

Solana Resources Limited (Alta. July 18, 1985)
Nov. 18, 2008 – Acquired by Gran Tierra Energy Inc.; basis 0.9527918 Gran Tierra shs. or 0.9527918 Gran Tierra exch. shs. for 1 Solana sh.

Solar Explorations Ltd. (Ont. 1969)
Mar. 1976 – Charter cancelled.

Solar Reef Petroleums Ltd. (unknown)
Mar. 1973 – Amalgamated with Armada Explorations Ltd., and Copper Plate Mines Ltd. under the name Armada Explorations Ltd.; basis 1 new for 4.58 old shs.

Solar Trust (Ont. July 5, 2000)
Nov. 17, 2003 – Name changed to Schooner Trust.

Solara Exploration Ltd. (Alta. Aug. 8, 2002)
Dec. 19, 2012 – All directors resigned, FTI Consulting Canada Inc. appointed receiver.

SolarBank Corporation (Ont. Sept. 23, 2013)
July 28, 2025 – Name changed to PowerBank Corporation. (see FPsurvey - Mines & Energy; FPsurvey - Industrials)

Solaris Copper Inc. (B.C. June 18, 2018)
Nov. 26, 2019 – Name changed to Solaris Resources Inc. (see FPsurvey - Mines & Energy)

Soldera Mining Corp. (B.C. Dec. 3, 2019)
Apr. 23, 2021 – Name changed to AmmPower Corp. (see FPsurvey - Mines & Energy; FPsurvey - Industrials)

Soldi Ventures Inc. (B.C. Nov. 21, 2007)
Nov. 25, 2013 – Name changed to Vega Mining Inc.; basis 1 new for 10 old shs. ■

Solectron Global Services Canada Inc. (Can. Nov. 9, 2001)
Oct. 2, 2007 – All exch. shs. redeemed for parent Solectron Corporation com. shs. on a sh.-for-sh. basis following amalgamation of Solectron Corp. with Flextronics International Ltd. and Saturn Merger Corp., a wholly owned subsid. of Flextronics; basis 0.345 Flextronics sh. for 1 Solectron Corp. sh. or US$3.89 per sh.

Solegear Bioplastic Technologies Inc. (B.C. Mar. 26, 2015)
Oct. 31, 2017 – Name changed to good natured Products Inc. ■

Soleil Capital Corp. (B.C. Oct. 19, 2016)
Mar. 1, 2018 – Formed Goldplay Exploration Ltd. in British Columbia following Qualifying Transaction reverse takeover of and amalgamation with (old) Goldplay Exploration Ltd.; basis 1 new com. sh. for 2 old Soleil com. shs. and 0.677747234 new com. shs. for 1 (old) Goldplay com. sh. ■

Solex Capital Inc. (Ont. Dec. 23, 1964)
Sept. 13, 1996 – Name changed to The Farini Group Inc. ■

Solex Oil Sands Corporation (Ont. Dec. 23, 1964)
Oct. 23, 1992 – Name changed to Solex Capital Inc. ■

Solex Resources Corp. (Can. July 4, 2003)
May 17, 2010 – Name changed to Southern Andes Energy Inc.; basis 1 new for 3 old shs. ■

SolGold plc (U.K. May 11, 2005)
June 19, 2025 – Voluntarily delisted from the Toronto Stock Exchange; will continue to trade on the main market of the London Stock Exchange.

Solid Gold Capital Corp. (B.C. 1972)
Mar. 31, 1992 – Amalgamated with Consolidated Ruskin Developments Ltd. to form new co. with same name Consolidated Ruskin Developments Ltd.; basis 1 new for 1.2 old shs. (see Consolidated Ruskin Developments Ltd.)

Solid Resources Ltd. (Alta. Dec. 3, 1986)
June 13, 2014 – Name changed to Iberian Minerals Ltd. ■

Solid Silver Metals & Holdings Ltd. (Ont. 1963)
Feb. 20, 1980 – Dissolved.

Solid Silver Mines Ltd. (Ont. 1963)
1970 – Name changed to Solid Silver Metals & Holdings Ltd. ■

Solid State Geophysical Inc. (Alta. Jan. 7, 1985)
Jan. 8, 1998 – Acquired by SSGI Acquisition Corp., a wholly owned subsid. of Grant Geophysical, Inc., for $3.50 per sh.

Solidago Mining Co. Ltd. (Ont. June 9, 1936)
Sept. 9, 1958 – Dissolved.

Solidor Resources Inc. (B.C. Dec. 7, 1965)
Mar. 12, 1997 – Name changed to Sheffield Resources Inc.; basis 1 new for 5 old shs. ■

SolidusGold Inc. (B.C. Apr. 13, 2011)
Sept. 16, 2022 – Name changed to Valhalla Metals Inc. pursuant to the reverse takeover acquisition of (old) Valhalla Metals, Inc.; basis 1 new for 5 old shs. (see FPsurvey - Mines & Energy)

Solis Minerals Ltd. (B.C. Dec. 1, 2005)
June 24, 2025 – Voluntarily delisted from the TSX-V; will continue to trade on the Australian Securities Exchange. (see FPsurvey - Mines & Energy)

Solitaire Minerals Corp. (B.C. Feb. 20, 1995)
Nov. 2, 2012 – Name changed to Pistol Bay Mining Inc.; basis 1 new for 20 old shs. ■

Solitario Exploration & Royalty Corp. (Colo. Nov. 15, 1984)
July 18, 2017 – Name changed to Solitario Zinc Corp. following acquisition of Zazu Metals Corporation. ■

Solitario Resources Corporation (Colo. Nov. 15, 1984)
June 17, 2008 – Name changed to Solitario Exploration & Royalty Corp. ■

Solitario Zinc Corp. (Colo. Nov. 15, 1984)
July 18, 2023 – Name changed to Solitario Resources Corp. (see FPsurvey - Mines & Energy)

Solium Capital Inc. (Alta. Sept. 16, 1999)
May 2, 2019 – Acquired by Morgan Stanley; basis Cdn$19.15 cash per sh.

Solo Growth Corp. (Alta. Jan. 4, 2019)
June 4, 2019 – Name changed to YSS Corp. ■

Solo International Resources Ltd. (B.C. Sept. 8, 1986)
Feb. 1, 1991 – Name changed to Regent Ventures Ltd.; basis 1 new for 2 old shs. ■

Solo Petroleums Ltd. (Alta. Sept. 5, 1986)
Apr. 26, 1996 – Name changed to ETC Transaction Corporation; basis 1 new for 5 old shs. ■

Solo Resources & Energy Inc. (Ont. 1943)
Dec. 4, 1985 – Amalgamated with 5 other cos. to form Flying Cross Resources Ltd.; basis 1 new for 6 old shs. (see Flying Cross Resources Ltd.)

Soloman Gold Corp. (Alta. 1987)
Aug. 1, 1989 – Formed Solomon Resources Limited in British Columbia on amalgamation with The Valhalla Gold Group Corporation; basis 1 new for 1.5 old shs. ■

Solomino Gold Mines Ltd. (Ont. 1962)
Sept. 8, 1966 – Dissolved.

Solomon Development Ltd. (B.C. 1968)
June 27, 1977 – Dissolved.

Solomon Equities Corp. (Alta. Oct. 22, 1993)
Oct. 22, 1998 – Struck off register.

Solomon Mines Ltd. (B.C. 1968)
1971 – Name changed to Solomon Development Ltd. ■

Solomon Resources Limited (B.C. Aug. 1, 1989 amalg.)
Oct. 1, 2014 – Name changed to Damara Gold Corp.; basis 1 new for 10 old shs. ■

Solomon's Pillars Mines Limited (Ont. 1964)
Mar. 16, 1976 – Charter cancelled.

Solstice Natural Resource Corp. (Alta. Dec. 22, 1987)
Apr. 2, 1996 – Name changed to Cayo Resources Inc. ■

Soltoro Ltd. (Can. Sept. 8, 2006 amalg.)
June 11, 2015 – Acquired by Agnico Eagle Mines Limited; basis 0.00793 Agnico Eagle com. shs., $0.01 cash and 1 Palamina Corp. com. sh. (valued at $0.02 per sh.) for 1 Soltoro com. sh.

SolutionInc Technologies Limited (B.C. Feb. 13, 1980)
May 14, 2004 – Continued into Nova Scotia. (see FPsurvey - Industrials)

Solutions4CO2 Inc. (Ont. Sept. 17, 2010)
June 5, 2014 – Name changed to BlueOcean NutraSciences Inc. ■

Solvang Explorations Ltd. (Ont. 1976)
Nov. 1978 – Amalgamated with Oxford Mines Limited, Babylon Minerals Inc., Firebird Petroleums Limited, and Drayton Petroleum Limited to form Bab-Sol Resource Exploration Ltd.; basis 32 new for 10 old shs.

Solvista Gold Corporation (Ont. Apr. 27, 2011 amalg.)
Oct. 21, 2015 – Name changed to Rockcliff Copper Corporation. ■

Soma-Duvernay Gold Mines Ltd. (Que. 1937)
1957 – Name changed to Dolsan Mines Ltd.; basis 1 new for 4 old shs. ■

Sombrero Resources Inc. (B.C. July 23, 2020)
Dec. 16, 2021 – Name changed to Coppernico Metals Inc. (see FPsurvey - Mines & Energy)

Somed Mines Ltd. (Que. 1971)
June 29, 1985 – Charter cancelled.

SoMedia Networks Inc. (Can. Feb. 10, 2006)
Sept. 9, 2015 – Name changed to VidWRX Inc. ■

Somerset Entertainment Income Fund (Ont. Feb. 8, 2005)
Nov. 30, 2009 – Acquired by Fluid Music Canada, Inc.; basis (i) $2.12, (ii) 1.1 Fluid Music com. shs., or (iii) 0.003 of a $1,000 principal amount Fluid Music 8% conv. subord. debs. for 1 Somerset Entertainment Income unit or 1 Somerset Entertainment LP cl. B exch. unit. (see Fluid Music Canada, Inc.)

Somerset Industries Inc. (Ont. Jan. 28, 1974)
Nov. 15, 1994 – Name changed to Midswana Diamond Exploration Corp. ■

Somerville Belkin Industries Limited (Can. 1921)
Aug. 4, 1987 – Private company following redemption of all publicly-held $2.80 pref. shs. at $51 plus 26¢ accr. int., completed. Subsequently amalgamated into Belkin Inc.

Somerville Capital Inc. (Alta. June 23, 1997)
Sept. 22, 1999 – Formed Book4golf.com Corporation in Canada on amalgamation with Book 4 Corporation, constituting a reverse takeover by Book 4 Corporation. ■

Somerville Industries Limited (Can. 1921)
June 23, 1977 – Name changed to Somerville Belkin Industries Limited. ■

Somerville Limited (Can. 1921)
May 16, 1961 – Name changed to Somerville Industries Limited. ■

Sona Resources Corp. (B.C. Feb. 8, 1990)
Sept. 19, 2016 – Acquired by Skeena Resources Limited; basis 0.5111 Skeena com. shs. for 1 Sona com. sh.
Jan. 26, 2021 – Name changed to Tempus Resources (Canada) Ltd.

Sona Systems Canada Ltd. (B.C. Feb. 29, 1984)
May 13, 1988 – Name changed to Startec Marketing Corporation; basis 1 new for 4 old shs. ■

Sonar Energy Corporation (B.C. June 12, 1979)
Mar. 12, 1981 – Name changed to Strata Energy Corporation. ■

Sonartec North American Inc. (Ont. 1968)
Dec. 24, 1987 – Name changed to Sonatel Telecommunications Corp. ■

Sonatel Telecommunications Corp. (Ont. 1968)
Feb. 20, 1992 – Name changed to Cycomm International Inc. ■

Sonco Steel Tube Ltd. (Ont. 1969 amalg.)
Nov. 1970 – Acquired by Atlantic Sugar Refineries Co. Ltd. for $8,750,000 in cash and notes.

Sonde Resources Corp. (Alta. Mar. 21, 1983)
Jan. 30, 2015 – Filed for voluntary assignment in bankruptcy. FTI Consulting Canada Inc. appointed trustee.

Sonesta Resources Ltd. (B.C. 1972)
July 5, 1976 – Name changed to SNA Resources Ltd.; basis 1 new for 5 old shs. ■

The Song Corporation (Ont. Nov. 9, 1999 amalg.)
May 4, 2001 – Declared bankrupt. Mintz & Partners Limited appointed trustee.

Sonic Drying Systems Ltd. (B.C. 1967)
July 27, 1982 – Dissolved.

Sonic Environmental Solutions Inc. (B.C. Feb. 4, 2000)
June 27, 2007 – Name changed to Sonic Technology Solutions Inc. ■

Sonic Ray Resources Ltd. (B.C. Apr. 7, 1952)
Dec. 1978 – Name changed to Stryker Resources Ltd.; basis 1 new for 4 old shs. ■

Sonic Technology Solutions Inc. (B.C. Feb. 4, 2000)
July 7, 2010 – Name changed to Sonoro Energy Ltd. (see FPsurvey - Mines & Energy)

Sonoma Capital Inc. (Can. July 19, 2004)
June 27, 2014 – Name changed to Nutritional High International Inc. ■

Sonoma Resource Corp. (B.C. Jan. 16, 1979)
Nov. 10, 1998 – Name changed to Biometric Security Corp. and continued into Wyoming. ■

Sonoma Resources Inc. (B.C. May 31, 2007)
Dec. 2, 2015 – Name changed to Element Lifestyle Retirement Inc. (see FPsurvey - Industrials)

Sonomax Hearing Healthcare Inc. (Can. Nov. 19, 1999)
Jan. 1, 2002 – Amalgamated in Canada to continue with same name.
Mar. 2, 2010 – Name changed to New Look Eyewear Inc. pursuant to conversion of Benvest New Look Income Fund into a corporation whereby all Sonomax Hearing assets and liabilities were transferred to Sonomax Technologies Inc.; basis 1 New Look sh. for 1 Benvest fund unit and 1 Sonomax Technologies sh. for 1 Sonomax Hearing sh. ■

Sonomed Inc. (Que. July 14, 1997)
Dec. 3, 2007 – Acquired by SND Energy Ltd.; basis 1 SND sh. plus $0.102595 for 1 Sonomed sh. (see SND Energy Ltd.)
Nov. 30, 2008 – Wound up into 4499034 Canada Inc., a wholly owned subsid. of SND Energy Ltd. (see SND Energy Ltd.)

Sonor Petroleum Corporation (Can. June 21, 1968)
Apr. 17, 1986 – Name changed to Sonor Resources Corporation. ■

Sonor Resources Corporation (Can. June 21, 1968)
Dec. 15, 1986 – Name changed to Home Capital Group Inc. ■

Sonora Diamond Corp. (Ont. May 29, 1989)
Jan. 25, 1999 – Continued into Bermuda.
Feb. 26, 1999 – Name changed to Sonora Diamond Corp. Ltd.

Sonora Gold & Silver Corp. (B.C. Nov. 23, 1983)
Feb. 17, 2023 – Name changed to BTQ Technologies Corp. pursuant to the reverse takeover acquisition of BTQ AG; basis 1 new for 10 old shs. (see FPsurvey - Industrials)

Sonora Gold Corp. (B.C. 1983)
May 29, 1989 – Continued into Ontario.
June 3, 1997 – Name changed to Sonora Diamond Corp. ■

Sonora Gold Corp. (B.C. Nov. 8, 1984)
Oct. 17, 2007 – Name changed to MetalQuest Minerals Inc.; basis 1 new for 3 old shs. ■

Sonoran Desert Copper Corporation (Can. Feb. 22, 2007 amalg.)
Aug. 5, 2025 – Name changed to Brasnova Energy Materials Inc. (see FPsurvey - Mines & Energy)

Sonoro Metals Corp. (B.C. Jan. 15, 2007)
Sept. 9, 2020 – Name changed to Sonoro Gold Corp. (see FPsurvey - Mines & Energy)

Sonus Corp. (Alta. July 27, 1993)
Dec. 15, 1998 – Continued into Yukon.
Oct. 25, 2002 – Acquired by Amplifon (USA), Inc. wholly owned subsid. of Milan-based Amplifon S.p.A.; basis US$1.00 per com. sh.

Sonus Venture Capital Corporation (Can. Sept. 28, 1998)
May 25, 2004 – Name changed to ACE/Security Laminates Corporation following Qualifying Transaction reverse takeover acquisition of ACE/Security Laminates Inc. and ACE/Security Laminates (Ottawa) Inc.; basis 1 new for 2.5 old shs. ■

Sony Corporation (Japan May 7, 1946)
Apr. 1, 2021 – Name changed to Sony Group Corporation.

Soo-Tomic Uranium Mines Ltd. (Ont. 1949)
Sept. 21, 1959 – Charter cancelled.

Soocana Explorations Ltd. (Ont. Apr. 2, 1987)
Sept. 15, 1997 – Name changed to Plata-Peru Resources Inc.; basis 1 new for 2 old shs. ■

Sooner Energy Corp. (B.C. Mar. 12, 1980)
July 7, 1994 – Continued into Wyoming.
Oct. 7, 1994 – Name changed to Tatonka Energy, Inc. ■

Sooner Petroleums Ltd. (unknown)
1955 – In bankruptcy.

Sooneyaw Gold Mines Ltd. (Ont. 1945)
Dec. 1954 – Charter cancelled.

Sopha Miller Gold Mines Ltd. (Ont. 1949)
Apr. 22, 1965 – Dissolved.

Sophia Capital Corp. (B.C. July 21, 2010)
Sept. 11, 2013 – Amalgamated with Folkstone Capital Corp.; basis 1.09 Folkstone shs. for 1 Sophia sh. (see Folkstone Capital Corp.)

Sora Capital Corp. (B.C. Jan. 27, 2009)
July 12, 2017 – Name changed to ProSmart Enterprises Inc. following acquisition of ProSmart Sports Development Inc. ■

Soranzo International Spirits Inc. (B.C. May 4, 1984)
Nov. 21, 1997 – Name changed to Firstline Ventures Ltd.; basis 1 new for 5 old shs. ■

Sorel Ventures Ltd. (B.C. May 14, 1969)
Aug. 22, 2005 – Dissolved and struck from register.

Sorrel Resources Ltd. (Alta. Sept. 28, 1979)
Mar. 1, 1994 – Dissolved and struck off register.

Sothman Mines Limited (Ont. 1968)
Nov. 14, 1994 – Dissolved.

Sound Capital Inc. (Ont. 1967)
May 3, 1994 – Name changed to Luminart Inc.; basis 1 new for 10 old shs. ■

Sound Communication Corp. (Alta. 1987)
Dec. 1, 1993 – Dissolved and struck off register.

Sound Energy Trust (Alta. Sept. 25, 2003)
Sept. 11, 2007 – Amalgamated with Advantage Energy Income Fund; basis 0.30 Advantage trust unit, or $0.66 and 0.2557 Advantage trust unit for 1 Sound Energy trust unit. (see Advantage Energy Income Fund)

Sound HealthCare Inc. (Can. May 21, 1987)
June 10, 2004 – Dissolved.

Sound Ideas Inc. (B.C. May 21, 1987)
July 3, 1990 – Name changed to SID Energy Inc. ■

Sound Insight Enterprises Limited (Can. Dec. 1978 amalg.)
Sept. 30, 1992 – Amalgamated with Vector Inc., Vector No. 2 Acquisition Corp., 816831 Ontario Inc., Mid-Continental Property Service Limited and AMJ Campbell Van Lines Inc. to form CamVec Corporation;

basis 93 CamVec shs. for 1,000 Sound Insight shs. (see CamVec Corporation)

Soundvest Equity Fund (Ont. Sept. 28, 2005)
June 15, 2018 – Terminated; basis $4.5612 cash per unit.

Soundvest Split Trust (Ont. Feb. 25, 2005)
July 3, 2019 – All o/s pref. securities redeemed for cash of $10 plus $0.02958 in accrued and unpaid interest and all o/s capital units, other than those held by Bristol Gate Capital Partners Inc., redeemed for 67¢ cash per unit for a combined NAV of $10.67.

Source Capital & Investment Corporation (Alta. May 18, 1988)
Apr. 24, 1998 – Name changed to Berwick Retirement Communities Ltd. ■

Source Capital Corp. (Alta. May 18, 1988)
Oct. 15, 1992 – Name changed to Source Capital & Investment Corporation; basis 1 new for 10 old shs. ■

Source Exploration Corp. (Alta. Oct. 5, 2006)
Jan. 14, 2011 – Continued into Ontario.
Apr. 20, 2017 – Name changed to Mexican Gold Corp. ■

Source Life Sciences Inc. (Can. Jan. 6, 2004)
Nov. 4, 2012 – Struck from registry and dissolved.

Source Resources Ltd. (B.C. Apr. 28, 1967)
Feb. 28, 1977 – Charter cancelled.
May 8, 1978 – Charter revived.
Sept. 8, 1993 – Continued into Yukon.
Oct. 12, 1993 – Name changed to Namibian Minerals Corporation pursuant to reverse takeover acquisition of Namibian Minerals Corp. Ltd.; basis 1 new for 1.5 old shs. ■

Souris Valley Oil Co. Ltd. (Man. 1948)
1959 – Acquired by Landa Oil Co.; basis 1 new for 25 old shs.

South American Gold and Copper Company Limited (Bermuda Mar. 15, 1985)
Oct. 3, 1996 – Continued into Nova Scotia.
May 3, 2007 – Continued into Canada.
Apr. 14, 2011 – Name changed to Cerro Grande Mining Corporation; basis 1 new for 10 old shs. (see FPsurvey - Mines & Energy)

South American Goldfields Inc. (Can. 1987)
May 20, 1992 – Amalgamated with Golden Star Resources Ltd. to form a new co. also known as Golden Star Resources Ltd.; basis 1 new for 6.5 old shs. (see Golden Star Resources Ltd.)

South American Mining Ltd. (Ont. 1956)
1959 – Merged into Able Land & Minerals Ltd.; basis 4 new for 5 old shs.

South American Silver Corp. (Can. Sept. 28, 2006)
Dec. 20, 2013 – Continued into British Columbia.
Mar. 19, 2014 – Name changed to TriMetals Mining Inc. ■

South Atlantic Diamonds Corp. (Can. Sept. 9, 1994)
July 30, 1996 – Name changed to South Atlantic Resources Ltd. ■

South Atlantic Resources Ltd. (Can. Sept. 9, 1994)
Apr. 2, 2002 – Name changed to South Atlantic Ventures Ltd.; basis 1 new for 6 old shs. ■

South Atlantic Ventures Ltd. (B.C. Aug. 27, 1979)
June 15, 1993 – Name changed to Southern Copper Corp. ■

South Atlantic Ventures Ltd. (Can. Sept. 9, 1994)
Aug. 12, 2004 – Name changed to Lundin Mining Corporation. (see FPsurvey - Mines & Energy)

South Bachelor Mining Co. Ltd. (Que. 1952)
Oct. 28, 1978 – Charter cancelled.

South Centremaque Gold Mines Ltd. (Que. 1945)
1950 – Assets sold to Centremaque Gold Mines Ltd.; basis 1 new for 4 old shs.

South Chibougamau Mining Ltd. (Que. 1951)
June 1, 1974 – Dissolved.

South China Industries (Canada) Inc. (Can. Jan. 14, 1972)
July 7, 1999 – Name changed to TriNorth Capital Inc.; basis 1 com. for 1 multiple vtg. sh. and 1 com. for 1 subord. vtg. sh. ■

South Crofty Holdings Ltd. (B.C. Jan. 18, 1985)
Dec. 5, 2001 – Name changed to North Pacific GeoPower Corp. following reverse takeover acquisition of Meager Creek Development Corporation. ■

South Dome Lake Mines Ltd. (Ont. 1923)
Apr. 1, 1957 – Charter cancelled.

South Duquesne Mines Ltd. (Ont. 1946)
Charter cancelled.

South Duval Gold Corp. (B.C. Dec. 5, 1983)
May 31, 2000 – Delisted from the CDNX. Subsequently dissolved for failure to file.

South Eastern Gas and Oil Company Limited (Ont. 1974)
Mar. 14, 1978 – Charter cancelled.

South End Petroleums Ltd. (Can. June 1, 1929)
Struck off register.

South Giroux Mines Ltd. (Ont. 1949)
Feb. 1960 – Name changed to Professor Silver Mines Ltd.; basis 1 new for 3 old shs. ■

South Keora Mines Ltd. (Ont. 1921)
Aug. 19, 1965 – Dissolved.

South Leduc Oil and Gas Co. Ltd. (Alta.)
1959 – Struck off register.

South-Malartic Exploration Inc. (Que. Dec. 12, 1995)
May 4, 2007 – Name changed to X-Ore Resources Inc. ■

South McKenzie Island Mines Ltd. (Ont. 1934)
Aug. 9, 1972 – Dissolved.

South Nelson Forest Products Corp. (N.B. 1961)
June 1966 – Name changed to Acadia Pulp and Paper Ltd.

South Pacific Gold Corporation (B.C. 1987)
Feb. 9, 1989 – Name changed to Western Carlyle Concepts Inc. ■

South Pacific Minerals Corp. (B.C. Oct. 11, 1985)
July 28, 2006 – Name changed to Tribune Resources Corp.; basis 1 new for 8 old shs. ■

South Pacific Mines Ltd. (B.C. 1959)
Apr. 7, 1983 – Struck off register.

South Pacific Resources Corp. (Can. Feb. 11, 1986)
July 24, 1998 – Name changed to Lexacal Investment Corp.; basis 1 new for 4 old shs. ■

South Seas Mining Ltd. (Ont. 1959)
Mar. 1976 – Charter cancelled.

South Shore Gold Mines Ltd. (Ont. 1945)
Mar. 1976 – Charter cancelled.

South Star Mining Corp. (B.C. Nov. 8, 1984)
May 26, 2021 – Name changed to South Star Battery Metals Corp. (see FPsurvey - Mines & Energy)

South State Uranium Mines Ltd. (Ont. 1949)
Nov. 30, 1964 – Dissolved.

South Tiblemont Gold Mines Ltd. (Ont. Feb. 7, 1935)
Dec. 1957 – Charter cancelled.

South Tiblemont Mines, Limited (unknown)
Feb. 7, 1935 – Name changed to South Tiblemont Gold Mines Ltd. and continued into Ontario; basis 1 new for 5 old shs. ■

South Unuk Gold Corporation (B.C. Mar. 30, 1988)
July 26, 1994 – Name changed to Unuk Gold Corporation; basis 1 new for 4 old shs. ■

South Valley Corp., Ltd. (Can. 1926)
Assets taken over by Mar-Jon Oil Co. Ltd.

South Vermillion Gold Mines Ltd. (Ont. 1934)
1956 – Charter cancelled.

South-West Gold Corp. (B.C. 1983)
Sept. 28, 1987 – Name changed to Helix Biotech Corporation. ■

South Winnipeg Limited (Man. 1923)
Feb. 1978 – Duraps Ltd. acquired 96.8% of co.'s shs. at $1.35 per sh. Funds to acquire remaining shs. at same price on deposit with the Montreal Trust Co. in Winnipeg.

The Southam Company Ltd. (Can. Dec. 7, 1927; via letters patent)
Apr. 1964 – Name changed to Southam Press Limited. ■

Southam Inc. (Can. Dec. 7, 1927; via letters patent)
Jan. 22, 1999 – Acquired by Hollinger Canadian Publishing Holdings Inc. for $25.25 per sh. (see Hollinger Canadian Publishing Holdings Inc.)

Southam Press Limited (Can. Dec. 7, 1927; via letters patent)
Dec. 21, 1978 – Name changed to Southam Inc. ■

Southampton Ventures Inc. (Ont. Oct. 15, 2004)
Apr. 21, 2009 – Name changed to Quetzal Energy Ltd. following reverse takeover acquisition of Quetzal Energy Inc. and amalgamation of Quetzal with a wholly owned subsidiary; basis 1 new for 2 old shs. ■

Southbar Mines Ltd. (Ont. 1952)
Dec. 1960 – Charter cancelled.

Southbridge Resources Corp. (B.C. Oct. 31, 2011)
July 28, 2014 – Name changed to Vodis Pharmaceuticals Inc. following reverse takeover acquisition of Vodis Innovative Pharmaceuticals Inc. ■

Southcan Mining Limited (B.C. July 6, 1973)
July 10, 1981 – Name changed to Capella Resources Limited. ■

Southeast Asia Mining Corp. (Can. Aug. 18, 2006)
June 8, 2018 – Name changed to Veta Resources Inc. ■

Southern Africa Minerals Corporation (Can. May 5, 1994 amalg.)
July 2, 2002 – Name changed to Tango Mineral Resources Inc. ■

Southern Alberta Coal Co. Ltd. (Alta. 1946)
1951 – Wound up voluntarily.

Southern Alberta Oil Co., Ltd. (unknown)
1921 – Acquired by Southern Alberta Oils, Ltd.; basis 1 pref. sh. and 15 com. shs. for 1 old sh. (see Southern Alberta Oils Ltd.)

Southern Alberta Oils Ltd. (unknown)
1925 – Acquired by Dalhousie Oil Co., Ltd.; basis 1 com. sh. for 1 old pref. sh., and 49.5 new com. for 100 com. shs.

Southern Alberta Refineries, Ltd. (unknown)
1921 – Acquired by Southern Alberta Oils, Ltd.; basis 3 new for 1 old sh. (see Southern Alberta Oils Ltd.)

Southern Andes Energy Inc. (Can. July 4, 2003)
Apr. 23, 2012 – Acquired by Macusani Yellowcake Inc. by way of amalgamation with 8156956 Canada, a wholly owned subsid. of Macusani, to continue as Peru Uranium Inc.; basis 0.8 Macusani com. shs. for 1 Southern Andes com. sh. (see Macusani Yellowcake Inc.)

Southern Arizona Mining & Smelting Corp. (Can. Dec. 9, 1980)
June 24, 1997 – Name changed to Unirom Technologies Inc. following reverse takeover acquisition of Unirom Inc. ■

Southern Asbestos Co. (Que. 1955)
Oct. 28, 1978 – Charter cancelled.

Southern Bar Minerals Corporation (Ont. Feb. 9, 1956)
Jan. 26, 1996 – Name changed to Texas Gulf Petroleum Corporation. ■

Southern Canada Power Co. Ltd. (Can. 1913)
1963 – Purchased by Hydro-Québec. Com. shldrs. got $56.75 per sh. Pref. shldrs. got equal par value in 10-yr. bonds guaranteed by Prov. of Quebec, bearing int. equal to divd. rate; plus $15 per sh. to compensate for participating feature. Funded debt assumed by Hydro-Québec.

Southern Copper Corp. (B.C. Aug. 27, 1979)
Oct. 25, 1994 – Continued into Canada.
Nov. 1, 1994 – Name changed to Santa Catalina Mining Corp. pursuant to plan of arrangement whereby diamond assets were spun off into a new publicly traded co. South Atlantic Diamonds Corp.; basis 2 South Atlantic shs. and 3 Santa Catalina shs. for 5 Southern Copper shs. ■

Southern Cross Gold Inc. (B.C. 1987)
Dec. 9, 1994 – Dissolved and struck off register.

Southern Cross Resources Inc. (Ont. Jan. 2, 1997)
Mar. 17, 2005 – Continued into Canada.
Dec. 6, 2005 – Name changed to sxr Uranium One Inc. following reverse takeover acquisition of Aflease Gold and Uranium Resources Ltd.; basis 1 new for 5 old shs. ■

Southern Eagle Enterprises Inc. (Ont. Sept. 29, 1987 amalg.)
Dec. 4, 1987 – Amalgamated with Global International Energy Inc. (1 new for 1 old sh.), Equican Ventures Inc. (25 new for 8 old shs.), Glenrealco Inc. (1,828,519 new for 200 old shs.) and Four Fifty Dobbie Inc. to form a new co. called Equican Venture Corp.; basis 23 new for 38 old shs.

Southern Eagle Petroleum Corp. (Ont. Mar. 31, 1986 amalg.)
Sept. 29, 1987 – Amalgamated with Dewey Oil & Gas Inc. to form Southern Eagle Enterprises Inc.; basis 1 com. sh. for 1 com. sh. and new cl. A. non-voting sh. for 1 cl. A. non-voting sh. (see Southern Eagle Enterprises Inc.)

Southern Eagle Petroleum Inc. (Ont. 1984)
Mar. 31, 1986 – Amalgamated with Blazedale Resources Inc. and Alpha Energy Holdings Ltd. to form Southern Eagle Petroleum Corp. Each 100 com. shs. of co. converted into 47 com. shs., 47 cl. A non-voting shs. and 94 pfce. ser. Y shs. of new co. (see Southern Eagle Petroleum Corp.)

Southern Energy Corp. (Can. July 22, 2008)
Jan. 7, 2020 – Continued into Alberta. (see FPsurvey - Mines & Energy)

Southern Exploration & Development Corporation (Que. 1954)
Feb. 1972 – Name changed to Calvin Exploration & Development Corporation. ■

Southern Frontier Resources Inc. (Ont. 1990 amalg.)
Mar. 2, 1995 – Continued into Ontario.
Apr. 18, 1995 – Formed Planetsafe Enviro Corporation on amalgamation with First Organic Garden Company Limited (25 for 1), Planetsafe Enviro Corporation (25 for 1) and 1108161 Ontario Inc. (54.5 for $1 in principal amt. of conv. notes held); basis 1 new for 1.5 old shs. plus 1 com. sh. of Inland National Capital Ltd. for 1 old sh. of Frontier. ■

Southern Gold Resources Ltd. (B.C. 1981)
June 14, 1991 – Private co. following substantial issuer bid by the co. for its shs. ending. The co. acquired 33.52% of the o/s shs. at $0.35 per sh. This did not include the 66.48% of the shs. privately held by the president of the co.

Southern Hemisphere Mining Limited (B.C. Dec. 23, 2005)
Apr. 23, 2013 – Continued into Australia.

Southern Legacy Minerals Inc. (B.C. Dec. 15, 2006 amalg.)
Oct. 3, 2014 – Amalgamated with Regulus Resources Inc. (deemed acquiror) to form (new) Regulus Resources Inc.; basis 0.3333 (new) Regulus com. shs. for 1 (old) Regulus com. sh. and 0.1833 (new) Regulus com. shs. for 1 Southern Legacy com. sh.

Southern Lights Resources Ltd. (B.C. Jan. 15, 1979)
Mar. 27, 1987 – Name changed to Balsam Resources Inc.; basis 1 new for 3 old shs. ■

Southern Lithium Corp. (B.C. Mar. 9, 2010)
Feb. 2, 2018 – Name changed to Le Mare Gold Corp. ■

Southern Lowery Oils Ltd. (unknown)
1932 – Acquired by Royalite Oil Co.

Southern Metals Corporation (Yuk. Nov. 15, 1996)
Nov. 21, 2000 – Name changed to EPICentrix Technologies, Inc. ■

Southern Nites Petroleum Corp. (B.C. Oct. 2, 1985)
July 11, 2000 – Name changed to Oracle Energy Corp. (see FPsurvey - Mines & Energy)

Southern Pacific Development Corporation (B.C. June 20, 1953)
Mar. 3, 2006 – Name changed to Southern Pacific Resource Corp.; basis 1 new for 3 old shs. ■

Southern Pacific Petroleum Ltd. (B.C. Apr. 7, 1952)
July 12, 1971 – Capital stock was consolidated on basis of 1 new for 10 old shs.
Aug. 16, 1971 – Name changed to Sonic Ray Resources Ltd.; basis 1 new for 10 old shs. ■

Southern Pacific Resource Corp. (B.C. June 20, 1953)
Nov. 17, 2006 – Continued into Alberta.
June 1, 2015 – Placed into receivership. PricewaterhouseCoopers Inc. appointed receiver and all officers and directors resigned.
Feb. 2018 – Sale of the oilsands assets was completed. Proceeds were not sufficient to repay the secured creditor resulting in no distrib. to unsecured creditors or shldrs.
May 2022 – PricewaterhouseCoopers was discharged as receiver.

Southern Petro Corp. (B.C. 1979)
Aug. 11, 1987 – Name changed to Can Am Industries Corporation. ■

Southern Platinum Corp. (Can. June 24, 2004)
July 27, 2005 – Acquired by England-based Lonmin Investments Canada Inc.; basis $2.66 for 1 old Southern Platinum pfd. sh. (which had just been exchanged 1 new pfd. sh. for 1 com. sh.).

Southern Rio Resources Ltd. (B.C. Mar. 6, 1962)
Dec. 15, 2005 – Name changed to Silver Quest Resources Ltd.; basis 1 new for 5 old shs. ■

Southern Star Resources Inc. (Ont. Sept. 11, 1984)
Dec. 27, 2006 – Amalgamated with Exall Resources Limited to form Gold Eagle Mines Ltd.; basis 1 Gold Eagle sh. for 1 Southern Star sh. (see Gold Eagle Mines Ltd.)

Southern Star Resources Ltd. (B.C. Nov. 23, 1983)
Oct. 6, 1988 – Name changed to Cheers International Telemarketing Limited. ■

Southern Sun Minerals Inc. (B.C. June 2, 2011)
Feb. 2, 2016 – Name changed to Nevada Energy Metals Inc. ■

Southern Tier Gas Producers Ltd. (Alta. Apr. 30, 1981 amalg.)
Oct. 1, 1993 – Dissolved and struck off register.

Southern Union Oils Ltd. (Ont. 1952)
1975 – Charter cancelled.

Southern Union Resources Inc. (B.C. 1979)
Sept. 14, 1984 – Name changed to Skeena Resources Ltd.; basis 1 new for 3 old shs. ■

SouthernEra Diamonds Inc. (Can. June 6, 2002)
Dec. 27, 2007 – Acquired by Mwana Africa plc; basis 1 Mwana ordinary sh. for 2.28 SouthernEra com.shs. and 1 new warrant for 1 old warrant excercisable for 0.4386 Mwana ordinary sh.

SouthernEra Resources Limited (Ont. Apr. 24, 1987)
June 6, 2002 – Continued into Canada.
Aug. 30, 2004 – Name changed to SouthernEra Diamonds Inc. following reorganization; basis 1 SouthernEra Diamonds com. sh. plus 1 Southern Platinum Corp. com. sh. for 1 SouthernEra Resources com. sh. ■

Southesk Energy Ltd. (Alta. Mar. 8, 1993)
Dec. 3, 2004 – Going private transaction; basis 1 new series A pfd. sh. for 1 com. sh. immediately redeemed for $2.50 per sh.

Southfork Energy Corporation (B.C. 1980)
1981 – Continued into Canada.
July 28, 1982 – Name changed to United Southfork Energy Inc.; basis 1 new for 3 old shs. ■

Southgate Resources Ltd. (B.C. 1983)
July 12, 1985 – Name changed to Consolidated CBA Corporation Ltd. (see FPsurvey - Mines & Energy)

SouthGobi Energy Resources Ltd. (B.C. May 29, 2007)
May 17, 2010 – Name changed to SouthGobi Resources Ltd. (see FPsurvey - Mines & Energy)

Southhampton Enterprises Corp. (B.C. Dec. 9, 1986)
June 16, 1997 – Name changed to Antigua Enterprises Inc.; basis 1 new for 5 old shs. ■

Southlands Mining Corporation (B.C. Sept. 3, 1985)
May 27, 1991 – Name changed to Euro-Pacific Resource Group Inc.; basis 1 new for 5 old shs. ■

Southmark Petroleum Limited (Ont. 1945)
Mar. 16, 1976 – Dissolved.

Southmount Investment Co. Ltd. (Can. 1944)
Feb. 20, 1951 – Charter cancelled; shldrs. received 57.42¢ per sh., of which 14.04¢ deemed to be a divd. Co. had been formed to hold certain assets of Montreal Light, Heat & Power Consolidated, in order to protect MLH&P shldrs. interests.

Southpoint Resources Ltd. (Alta. Dec. 1, 1983)
Aug. 23, 2005 – Name changed to E4 Energy Inc. following acquisition of P3 Energy Ltd. ■

Southport Capital Corp. (B.C. Nov. 18, 1999)
Mar. 28, 2002 – Name changed to VP Group Media Limited pursuant to Qualifying Transaction reverse takeover acquisition of VPG Video Publishing Group Inc. effective Apr. 2, 2002, for 7,947,500 com. shs.; basis 1 new for 2 old shs. ■

Southport Mines Ltd. (Ont. Jan. 29, 1975)
Aug. 22, 1977 – Name changed to Midpines Explorations Inc. (see FPsurvey - Mines & Energy)

Southport Resources Inc. (B.C. Mar. 8, 1951)
June 3, 1992 – Name changed to Olds Industries Inc.; basis 1 new for 2 old shs. ■

SouthTech Capital Corporation (Alta. Apr. 21, 2011)
Sept. 11, 2014 – Formed Vogogo Inc. in Alberta; basis 1 new for 5 old shs. ■

Southview Capital Corp. (Alta. Mar. 31, 1994)
May 22, 1998 – Name changed to Southview Resources Inc.; basis 1 new for 3 old shs. ■

Southview Resources Inc. (Alta. Mar. 31, 1994)
Nov. 28, 2000 – Name changed to Elgin Resources Inc.; basis 1 new for 3 old shs. ■

Southvue Mines Ltd. (Ont. 1945)
Nov. 27, 1968 – Dissolved.

Southward Energy Ltd. (Alta. Apr. 24, 1981)
May 2, 2003 – Acquired by 1022971 Alberta Ltd. wholly owned subsid. of Matco Investments Ltd.; basis $4.77 per sh.

Southward Resources Ltd. (Alta. Apr. 24, 1981)
Mar. 2, 1987 – Name changed to Southward Energy Ltd.; basis 1 new for 4 old shs. ■

Southwest Petroleum Company Limited (Can. 1928)
July 1967 – Merged into Commonwealth Petroleum Services Ltd.

Southwest Technologies Inc. (B.C. Apr. 25, 1983)
May 21, 1991 – Delisted from the Vancouver Stock Exchange. Subsequently dissolved for failure to file.

Southwestern Gold Corporation (B.C. June 18, 1990)
June 5, 2001 – Name changed to Southwestern Resources Corp. ■

Southwestern Resources Corp. (B.C. June 18, 1990)
May 27, 2009 – Acquired by Hochschild Mining plc for 50¢ per sh.

Southwind Resource Explorations Limited (Ont. Sept. 7, 1977)
Oct. 12, 1989 – Delisted from the Alberta Stock Exchange. Subsequently dissolved.

Sovereign Chief Ventures Ltd. (B.C. Aug. 12, 1987)
Apr. 1, 2006 – Name changed to Saxon Oil Company Ltd. following acquisition of Saxon Oil Company by wholly owned Sovereign Resources, Inc. (SRI) and amalgamation of Saxon with SRI. ■

Sovereign Metals Corporation Ltd. (B.C. July 12, 1965)
Mar. 7, 1986 – Name changed to Barytex Resources Corp.; basis 1 new for 3 old shs. ■

Sovereign Royalties Ltd. (Alta. 1936)
Taken over by British American Oil Co. Ltd. (see The British American Oil Company Limited)

Sovereign Yellowknife Mines Ltd. (Ont. 1945)
Charter cancelled.

Soyers Capital Limited (Ont. Apr. 6, 2004)
Dec. 4, 2007 – Name changed to BlueRush Media Group Corp. ■

Spa Mines Limited (B.C. 1966)
Sept. 24, 1973 – Name changed to Copperust Mines Ltd.; basis 1 new for 3 old shs. ■

Spa Oils Ltd. (Can.)
1929 – Taken over by Alberta Superior Oils Ltd.

Space Age Metals Corp. Ltd. (Que. 1962)
1965 – Merged with Delta Mining Corporation Ltd. on a sh.-for-sh. basis.

Space Age Mines Ltd. (Ont. 1959)
1962 – Merged into Aldage Mines Ltd.

Space-Pak International Limited (Ont. 1963)
1971 – Entered bankruptcy in early; no distribution made to equity holders.

Spacemaster Minerals Ltd. (Can. Aug. 2, 1929; via letters patent)
Sept. 30, 1974 – Name changed to Spacemaster Resources Limited. ■

Spacemaster Resources Limited (Can. Aug. 2, 1929; via letters patent)
Sept. 30, 1988 – Name changed to Exmoor Oil & Gas Corporation. ■

Spada Gold Ltd. (B.C. June 23, 2015)
Dec. 29, 2017 – Name changed to Awale Resources Limited following Qualifying Transaction acquisition of an 80% interest in Awale Holdings Limited and a 100% interest in Aforo (Ivory Coast) Holdings Pty Ltd. (see FPsurvey - Mines & Energy)

Span-North Mining Claims Ltd. (Ont. 1956)
Apr. 6, 1967 – Charter cancelled.

Spanallen Mining Ltd. (B.C. 1969)
June 20, 1979 – Name changed to Capilano Resources Inc.; basis 1 new for 5 old shs. (see FPsurvey - Mines & Energy)

Spanex Capital Inc. (Ont. Sept. 24, 1973)
May 20, 1985 – Charter cancelled.
Aug. 26, 1986 – Charter revived.
May 2, 1997 – Name changed to SAMSys Technologies Inc.; basis 1 new for 3 old shs. ■

Spanish American Mines Ltd. (Ont. 1954)
1956 – Merged into Northspan Uranium Mines Ltd.; basis 1 new for 2 old shs.

Spanish River Mines Ltd. (Ont. 1967)
Apr. 9, 1975 – Charter cancelled.

Spantek Industries Inc. (Alta. 1987)
Aug. 31, 1989 – Name changed to Shanell Petrochemical Corporation; basis 1 new for 3 old shs. ■

Spar Aerospace Limited (Can. Oct. 27, 1967)
Jan. 25, 2002 – Acquired by US-based L-3 Communications Corporation for $15.50 per sh.

Spar Aerospace Products Ltd. (Can. Oct. 27, 1967)
Sept. 1, 1978 – Name changed to Spar Aerospace Limited. ■

Spar Holdings and Explorations Limited (Ont. Jan. 18, 1972)
July 12, 1994 – Name changed to Spartec International Corporation; basis 1 new for 5 old shs. (see FPsurvey - Industrials)

Spar Holdings and Explorations Limited (Ont. 1972 amalg.)
Nov. 1, 1972 – Amalgamated with Viva Explorations Limited to continue on as Spar Holdings and Explorations Limited. (see Spar Holdings and Explorations Limited)

Spar Mines Limited (Ont. 1969)
Jan. 18, 1972 – Amalgamated with Lava Minerals Limited, Polex Mines Limited and Winnebago Mines Limited to form a new co. known as Spar Holdings and Explorations Ltd.; basis 1 new for 5 old shs. (see Spar Holdings and Explorations Limited)

Spara Acquisition One Corp. (Can. Mar. 10, 2011)
July 10, 2013 – Dissolved following Qualifying Transaction private placement subscription of 9,199,991 Digital Shelf Space Corp. com. shs. at 5¢ per sh. plus wts. exercisable to acquire Digital com. sh. at 10¢ per sh. for a 3-year period and distribution of Digital shs. to shldrs. (see Digital Shelf Space Corp.)

Sparcap One Ltd. (Ont. May 6, 2008)
Feb. 28, 2014 – Distrib. made of $0.0492 cash per sh.
Apr. 29, 2014 – Voluntarily dissolved.

Spark Power Group Inc. (Ont. June 28, 2017)
Dec. 8, 2023 – Acquired by Generator-Spark Canada Buyer Inc., an affiliate of American Pacific Group, LP; basis $0.825 cash per sh.

Sparky Oils Ltd. (unknown)
1952 – In liquidation.

Sparling Capital Corporation (Alta. Feb. 21, 1997)
Sept. 29, 2000 – Name changed to Red-Tail Infotech Inc. ■

Sparmac Petroleums Limited (Alta. 1952)
1958 – Acquired by Tidal Petroleum Corp. Ltd.; basis 1 new for 4 old shs.

Sparrow Resources Ltd. (B.C. 1972)
Oct. 26, 1984 – Dissolved.

Sparrow Ventures Corp. (B.C. July 4, 2006)
Sept. 14, 2017 – Name changed to Westcot Ventures Corp.; basis 1 new for 10 old shs. ■

Sparta Water Corp. (Alta. Sept. 16, 1998)
Nov. 10, 2003 – Delisted from the TSX-Venture Exchange. Subsequently struck from the register and dissolved.
Jan. 27, 2006 – Name changed to Base of the Bridge Technology Ltd.

Spartacus Capital Inc. (B.C. June 3, 1999)
July 17, 2003 – Name changed to Rare Element Resources Ltd. following Qualifying Transaction acquisition of Paso Rico Resources Ltd. (see FPsurvey - Mines & Energy)

Spartan Acquisition Corp. (B.C. Nov. 18, 2019)
Dec. 16, 2021 – Formed Forbidden Spirits Distilling Corp. in British Columbia pursuant to the Qualifying Transaction reverse takeover acquisition of and amalgamation with Forbidden Distillery Inc. (deemed acquiror). (see FPsurvey - Industrials)

Spartan Air Services Limited (Can. Aug. 30, 1946)
Jan. 29, 1973 – Name changed to Spartan Capital Corp. Ltd. ■

Spartan Capital Corp. Ltd. (Can. Aug. 30, 1946)
July 9, 1986 – Name changed to Akers Medical Technology Ltd. ■

Spartan Energy Corp. (Alta. Dec. 12, 1988)
May 31, 2018 – Acquired by Vermilion Energy Inc.; basis 0.1476 Vermilion shs. for 1 Spartan com. sh.

Spartan Exploration Ltd. (Alta. Jan. 18, 2010 amalg.)
June 6, 2011 – Acquired by Penn West Petroleum Ltd.; basis $4.00, 1 sh. and 0.1667 wts. of newly incorporated Spartan Oil Corp. for 1 Spartan Exploration sh. (see Penn West Petroleum Ltd.)

Spartan Explorations Ltd. (NPL) (B.C. 1967)
Aug. 26, 1974 – Name changed to Nuspar Resources Limited; basis 1 new for 5 old shs. ■

Spartan Oil Corp. (Alta. Mar. 31, 2011)
Jan. 30, 2013 – Acquired by Bonterra Energy Corp.; basis 0.1169 Bonterra com. shs for 1 Spartan com. sh.

Spartan Petroleums Limited (Can. 1929)
Aug. 2, 1929 – Name changed to Brock Petroleums Limited. ■

Spartex Oil & Gas Limited (Ont. 1965)
Mar. 19, 1973 – Amalgamated with Broad Scope Developments Ltd. and Greenlaw Developments Ltd. to form Newore Developments Ltd.; basis 1 new for 3.5 old shs.

Sparton Asbestos Mines Ltd. (Ont. 1952)
Feb. 1974 – Name changed to Sparton Mining and Development Limited. ■

Sparton Mining and Development Limited (Ont. 1952)
Nov. 1982 – Amalgamated with Crackingstone Mines Limited to form Sparton Resources Inc.

Sparx Energy Corp. (B.C. Oct. 5, 2012)
Jan. 16, 2017 – Name changed to Provenance Gold Corp. following acquisition of (old) Provenance Gold Corp. (concurrently renamed 1084160 B.C. Ltd.). (see FPsurvey - Mines & Energy)

Sparx Technology Inc. (B.C. Jan. 14, 2021)
July 18, 2024 – Name changed to Tablas Ventures Corp.; basis 1 new for 13 old shs. (see FPsurvey - Industrials)

Spatializer Audio Laboratories, Inc. (Yuk. Apr. 3, 1992)
July 27, 1994 – Continued into Delaware.
May 26, 2015 – Name changed to AMERI Holdings, Inc. ■

Speakeasy Cannabis Club Ltd. (Ont. Mar. 26, 2010)
Oct. 9, 2018 – Continued into British Columbia. (see FPsurvey - Industrials)

Spearhead Exploration Ltd. (Ont. 1938)
Apr. 1, 1965 – Dissolved.

Spearhead Resources Inc. (Alta. May 24, 1996)
Oct. 4, 2004 – Amalgamated with Camflo International Inc. (3 for 4) to continue with a new name Arctos Petroleum Corp.; basis 1 new Arctos sh. for 1 old Spearhead sh. (see Arctos Petroleum Corp.)

Spearmint Resources Inc. (B.C. Sept. 23, 2009)
June 30, 2025 – Name changed to Adelayde Exploration Inc.; basis 1 new for 10 old shs. (see FPsurvey - Mines & Energy; FPsurvey - Industrials)

Special Resources Inc. (B.C. 1983)
Feb. 13, 1984 – Name changed to Trigon Technologies Inc. ■

Special Waste Management Inc. (B.C. 1983)
July 10, 1992 – Dissolved and struck off register.

Specialty Foods Group Income Fund (Ont. Nov. 5, 2002)
Mar. 2017 – Pursuant to reorganization, subsidiaries Specialty Food Group Holdings, Inc., SFG Parent, Inc., Specialty Foods Group, Inc., Mickelberry's Inc., SMG, Inc., Fischer Packing Company, LLC and Field Packing Company, LLC, merged with and into International Fish & Meat U.S.A., L.L.C. forming Specialty Foods Group, LLC (SFG). The reorganization facilitated the distrib. by SFG an aggregate of US$55,000,000 to stakeholders. Unitholders of the fund would receive a distrib. of approx. Cdn$0.886887 cash per trust unit.
Oct. 2, 2018 – Specialty Foods Group, LLC was sold to Indiana Packers Corporation netting the fund with cash proceeds of approx. US$28,300,000 which will be distrib. to unitholders in accordance with the plan arrangement completed in February 2017.
Jan. 29, 2020 – Distribution to unitholders of Cdn$1.74 cash per unit.
July 20, 2021 – Final distrib. of Cdn$0.16 per unit made to unitholders of record July 12, 2021. (see FPsurvey - Industrials)

Specialty Liquid Transportation Corp. (B.C. Apr. 11, 2017)
Sept. 19, 2022 – Struck from registry and dissolved.

Specialty Medical Products Inc. (B.C. Jan. 22, 1987)
Oct. 20, 1997 – Name changed to Fedora Industries Inc.; basis 1 new for 5 old shs. ■

Specialty Retail Concepts Inc. (B.C. Mar. 7, 1979)
Jan. 9, 1997 – Name changed to Altoro Gold Corp.; basis 1 new for 5 old shs. ■

Specialty Woods Inc. (Alta. Oct. 15, 1998)
Jan. 12, 2005 – Name changed to Sheffield Resources Ltd.; basis 1 new for 2 old shs. ■

Spectair Industries Inc. (B.C. Jan. 31, 1980)
Dec. 1, 1989 – Name changed to International Spectair Resources Inc.; basis 1 new for 3 old shs. ■

Spectra Energy Canada Exchangeco Inc. (Can. Sept. 14, 2001)
Mar. 19, 2010 – All Spectra Energy exch. B shs. and Duke Energy exch. A shs. redeemed for parent Spectra Energy Corp. com. shs. and Duke Energy Corporation com. shs., respectively, on a sh.-for-sh. basis.

Spectra Energy Income Fund (Alta. Nov. 2, 2005)
May 7, 2008 – Privatized whereby Spectra Energy Corp. acquired all o/s trust units for $11.25 per trust unit.

The Spectra Group of Great Restaurants Inc. (B.C. Aug. 28, 1968)
Sept. 14, 1998 – Continued into Canada.
June 25, 2007 – Name changed to 3530639 Canada Inc. ■

Spectra Inc. (Alta. Oct. 4, 1994)
Jan. 1, 2020 – Name changed to Spectra Products Inc. following vertical amalgamation of wholly owned Spectra Products Inc. into the company. (see FPsurvey - Industrials)

Spectra Premium Industries Inc. (Can. Feb. 1, 1993)
Jan. 18, 2007 – Amalgamated with 6651399 Canada Inc.; basis 1 new amalco redeemable pfd. sh. for 1 old Spectra sh. Preferreds immediately redeemed for $2.85 per sh.

Spectra Ventures Ltd. (B.C. Oct. 16, 1984)
Jan. 12, 1994 – Name changed to Consolidated Spectra Ventures Ltd.; basis 1 new for 3 old shs. ■

Spectral Capital Corporation (Alta. Feb. 12, 1987)
May 4, 1994 – Name changed to Mount Real Financial Corporation. ■

Spectral Diagnostics Inc. (Ont. July 29, 1991)
Dec. 31, 2014 – Name changed to Spectral Medical Inc. (see FPsurvey - Industrials)

Spectral Technologies Inc. (Alta. Feb. 12, 1987)
Sept. 28, 1989 – Name changed to Spectral Capital Corporation. ■

Spectran International Limited (Que. 1971)
May 24, 1980 – Charter cancelled.

Spectra7 Microsystems Inc. (Can. Oct. 12, 2010)
July 16, 2021 – Continued into Ontario.
Apr. 29, 2025 – Voluntarily delisted.
May 13, 2025 – Distrib. of US$0.0039 in cash and 1 non-interest bearing contingent value right (CVR) made to shldrs. of record Apr. 28, 2025. (see FPsurvey - Industrials)

Spectroair Explorations Ltd. (B.C. May 17, 1966)
Aug. 18, 1975 – Name changed to Channel Gold Resources Corp.; basis 1 new for 5 old shs. ■

Spectrum Games Corporation (Can. May 25, 1988)
Feb. 23, 2001 – Name changed to Playdigm Entertainment Corporation. ■

Spectrum Gold Corporation (Can. Jan. 22, 1986)
Dec. 30, 1991 – Name changed to Scarlett Minerals Inc.; basis 1 new for 2 old shs. ■

Spectrum Industrial Resources Ltd. (B.C. 1967)
Nov. 26, 1987 – Name changed to International Data Service Corporation following acquisition of Data Support Corp.; basis 1 new for 3 old shs. ■

Spectrum Resources Ltd. (B.C. 1967)
Apr. 1970 – Name changed to Consolidated Spectrum Resources Ltd.; basis 1 new for 2 old shs. ■

Spectrum Signal Processing Inc. (B.C. July 31, 1987)
May 4, 2007 – Acquired by Vecima Networks Inc.; basis $0.8939 per sh. or 0.0889 new Vecima sh. for 1 old Spectrum Signal sh.

SpectrumGold Inc. (B.C. Mar. 31, 2003)
July 19, 2004 – Plan of Arrangement acquisition by NovaGold Resources Inc.; basis 1 new NovaGold com. sh. for 1.35 old SpectrumGold com. shs.

Speculators Fund Limited (Alta. Mar. 1, 1969)
Dec. 7, 1973 – Name changed to Newmark Resources Limited. ■

Speedware Corporation Inc. (Can. Sept. 21, 1983)
Apr. 26, 2005 – Acquired indirectly by Activant Solutions Inc. for $3.91 per sh.

Speedy Muffler King Inc. (Ont. Dec. 1, 1988)
July 23, 1998 – Name changed to SMK Speedy International Inc. ■

Speer Darrow Management Inc. (Ont. Nov. 6, 1975)
Sept. 14, 1995 – Formed Rex Diamond Mining Corporation in Ontario on amalgamation with privately held Kimberlex Resources Ltd. ■

Spelna Capital Corporation (Can. July 19, 2000)
Nov. 28, 2007 – Name changed to NX Phase Capital Inc. ■

Spencar Explorations Ltd. (B.C. Sept. 14, 1983)
Mar. 17, 1986 – Name changed to American Fibre Corporation. ■

Spenhoe Mines Ltd. (B.C. 1959)
May 10, 1972 – Name changed to Bonnevier Mines Ltd.; basis 1 new for 3 old shs. ■

Sperry Mining Ltd. (Ont. 1973)
Jan. 2, 1975 – Merged into Sandhurst Mines Ltd.; basis 1 new for 3 old shs.

Spey Resources Corp. (B.C. July 31, 2017)
Nov. 18, 2024 – Name changed to Armory Mining Corp. (see FPsurvey - Mines & Energy)

Speyside Ventures Inc. (B.C. June 14, 1985)
July 19, 1999 – Name changed to TranDirect.com Technologies Inc. ■

Sphere Development Corp. (B.C. 1966)
Jan. 17, 1977 – Dissolved.

Sphinx Exploration Inc. (Que. May 21, 1985)
July 29, 1988 – Name changed to Sphinx Mining Co. Inc. (see FPsurvey - Mines & Energy)

Spider Resources Inc. (Can. July 20, 1992)
Oct. 7, 2010 – Amalgamated with 7557558 Canada Inc., an indirect wholly owned subsid. of Cliffs Natural Resources Inc., for 19¢ per sh. (see Cleveland-Cliffs Resources Inc.)

Spike Redwater Oil Co. Ltd. (Ont. 1949)
1959 – Struck off register.

Spin Master Corp. (Ont. June 9, 2004)
July 29, 2015 – Amalgamated in Ontario to continue with same name. (see FPsurvey - Industrials)

Spina Porcupine Mines Limited (Ont. 1941)
July 6, 1982 – Name changed to Coloma Resources Limited. ■

Spindle Top Energy & Resources Inc. (Ont. 1970)
Dec. 4, 1985 – Amalgamated with 5 other cos. to form Flying Cross Resources Ltd.; basis 1 new for 3 old shs. ■

Spinet Gold Mines Ltd. (Ont. 1946)
June 3, 1963 – Dissolved.

Spinet Mining Co. Ltd. (unknown Jan. 1946)
1946 – Succeeded by Spinet Gold Mines Ltd.; basis 10 new for 1 old sh. (see Spinet Gold Mines Ltd.)
1949 – Charter surrendered. (see Spinet Gold Mines Ltd.)

Spinnaker Recreational Development Corporation (Can. Sept. 14, 1982)
Dec. 5, 1986 – Name changed to Health Development Services Inc. ■

Spinrite Income Fund (Ont. Dec. 8, 2004)
Nov. 22, 2007 – Acquired by Sentinel Capital Partners. All trust units subsequently redeemed for $2.25 per unit.

Spiral Engineering Corp. (B.C. 1985)
Jan. 17, 1989 – Name changed to Spiral Optics Inc. ■

Spiral Optics Inc. (B.C. 1985)
July 24, 1992 – Dissolved and struck off register.

Spire Energy Ltd. (Alta. May 28, 1993)
June 5, 2002 – Acquired by Quintana Minerals Resources Corp. for $2.41 per sh.

Spire Ventures Ltd. (B.C. Jan. 15, 1979)
Jan. 4, 2001 – Name changed to Consolidated Spire Ventures Ltd.; basis 1 new for 2 old shs. ■

Spirit Banner II Capital Corp. (Ont. Sept. 29, 2017)
Name changed to Sabio Holdings Inc. pursuant to the Qualifying Transaction reverse takeover acquisition of

Sabio Mobile, Inc.; basis 1 new for 15.90909 old shs. (see FPsurvey - Industrials)

Spirit Banner Capital Corp. (Alta. June 5, 2017)
Aug. 26, 2020 – Name changed to Ion Energy Ltd. following Qualifying Transaction reverse takeover of (old) Ion Energy Ltd.; basis 1 new for 2 old shs. ■

Spirit Bear Capital Corp. (B.C. Nov. 8, 2011)
July 23, 2019 – Name changed to Gaia Grow Corp. pursuant to the Qualifying Transaction reverse takeover acquisition of (old) Gaia Grow Corp. (see FPsurvey - Industrials)

Spirit Capital Corporation (Alta. Oct. 27, 1980)
Apr. 12, 1993 – Name changed to Spirit Corporation; basis 1 new for 16 old shs. ■

Spirit Corporation (Alta. Oct. 27, 1980)
May 26, 1997 – Acquired by Best Pacific Resources Ltd.; basis 1 Best Pacific Resources sh. plus 0.5 wts. for 6.5 Spirit shs. (see Best Pacific Resources Ltd.)

Spirit Energy Corporation (Alta. Oct. 27, 1980)
Jan. 29, 1987 – Name changed to Spirit Capital Corporation. ■

Spirit Energy Corp. (B.C. Jan. 22, 1987)
June 23, 2004 – Name changed to Canadian Spirit Resources Inc. ■

Spirit Explorations Ltd. (B.C. Mar. 8, 1971)
May 1, 1975 – Name changed to Cannon Resources Ltd.; basis 1 new for 4 old shs. ■

Spirit Lake Explorations Limited (Ont. July 22, 1936)
Feb. 21, 1994 – Name changed to VenCan Gold Corporation. ■

Spirit Lake Gold Mines Ltd. (Ont. July 22, 1936)
Name changed to Spirit Lake Mines Ltd. ■

Spirit Lake Mines Ltd. (Ont. July 22, 1936)
Mar. 1976 – Name changed to Spirit Lake Explorations Limited; basis 1 new for 5 old shs. ■

Spirit Petroleum Corp. (B.C. Feb. 4, 1981)
Dec. 16, 1987 – Name changed to Dryden Resource Corporation; basis 1 new for 3 old shs. ■

Spirit Resources Ltd. (B.C. 1983)
July 31, 1992 – Continued into Wyoming.
Mar. 3, 1993 – Formed Hygeia Holdings Inc. in Delaware following Plan of Reorganization merger with Hygeia Pharmaceuticals, Inc.; basis 1 new for 1 old sh. ■

Spitfire Energy Ltd. (Alta. Aug. 30, 2001)
July 1, 2010 – Name changed to Whitecap Resources Inc. following reverse takeover acquisition of and vertical amalgamation with (old) Whitecap Resources Inc. (see FPsurvey - Mines & Energy)

Spitfyre Capital Inc. (Ont. June 24, 2021)
Dec. 21, 2023 – Continued into Canada.
Dec. 22, 2023 – Name changed to NeoTerrex Minerals Inc. pursuant to the Qualifying Transaction reverse takeover acquisition of NeoTerrex Corporation. (see FPsurvey - Mines & Energy)

Split Lake Gold Mines Limited (Ont. 1934)
Dec. 31, 1952 – Charter cancelled.

Split REIT Opportunity Trust (Ont. June 20, 2006)
Jan. 3, 2012 – Merged into Criterion REIT Income Fund; basis 1.52 cl. A Criterion unit for 1 cap. Split REIT unit and $10.14375 cash for each 5.75% pref. security.

Split Rock Mines Ltd. (Ont. 1955)
Apr. 22, 1965 – Dissolved.

Split Yield Corporation (Ont. Feb. 25, 1998)
Feb. 2, 2012 – All o/s shs. redeemed for $18.6989 per cl. I pref. sh. No distribution to cl. II pref. and capital shldrs.

Spodateenah Mines Ltd. (Ont. 1949)
Dec. 1954 – Name changed to Copa Mining Corporation Ltd. ■

Spokane Resources Ltd. (B.C. Oct. 31, 1991 amalg.)
July 26, 2001 – Name changed to SKN Resources Ltd.; basis 1 new for 10 old shs. ■

SponsorsOne Inc. (Ont. Mar. 9, 1965)
Feb. 27, 2023 – Continued into British Columbia. (see FPsurvey - Industrials)

Spooner Mines and Oils Limited (Can. Mar. 26, 1926)
Jan. 9, 1986 – Name changed to Canadian Spooner Resources Inc.; basis 1 new for 3 old shs. ■

Spooner Oils Ltd. (Can. Mar. 26, 1926)
May 1956 – Name changed to Spooner Mines and Oils Limited. ■

Sporran Mines Ltd. (Ont. 1957)
Mar. 1976 – Charter cancelled.

Sport Active Television Network Inc. (Alta. June 28, 1988)
Dec. 1, 1999 – Struck from registry and dissolved.

Sports Active Inc. (Alta. June 28, 1988)
Mar. 11, 1997 – Name changed to Sport Active Television Network Inc.; basis 1 new for 4 old shs. ■

Sports Technologies Group Inc. (Alta. Jan. 5, 1999)
Feb. 10, 2000 – Name changed to Exclamation International Incorporated following reverse takeover acquisition of Exclamation Inc. ■

Sportscene Group Inc. (Can. Sept. 15, 1983)
Jan. 20, 2022 – Privatized via acquisition by 13401537 Canada Inc. and subsequent amalgamation with two wholly owned subsids. of 13401537 Canada, a company controlled by president and CEO Jean Bédard; basis $7.25 cash per cl. A sh.

Sportscene Restaurants Inc. (Can. Sept. 15, 1983)
Jan. 23, 2006 – Name changed to Sportscene Group Inc. ■

SportsClick Inc. (Alta. July 9, 2008 amalg.)
Oct. 9, 2009 – Placed into receivership under the Bankruptcy and Insolvency Act and Ernst & Young Inc. appointed court-appointed receiver.
Dec. 2, 2011 – Struck from register and dissolved.

SportsMate International Inc. (Alta. 1987)
Nov. 2, 2000 – Struck from registry and dissolved.

Spotlite360 Technologies, Inc. (B.C. Sept. 23, 2014)
Aug. 20, 2021 – Name changed to SpotLite360 IOT Solutions, Inc. (see FPsurvey - Industrials)

Spray-Air International, Inc. (Alta. Jan. 9, 1987)
Dec. 23, 1991 – Name changed to Epicore Networks, Inc. ■

Spray Resorts Corporation (Alta. 1987)
Nov. 5, 1990 – Name changed to Petrolian Resources Corporation; basis 1 new for 4 old shs. ■

Spring & Mercer Capital Corp. (B.C. Mar. 15, 2007)
July 8, 2010 – Name changed to Genview Capital Corp. ■

Spring Coulee Oil Corp. Ltd. (Alta. 1950)
1954 – Name changed to New Spring Coulee Oil and Minerals Ltd.; basis 1 new for 4 old shs. ■

Springbank Petroleums Ltd. (Alta.)
1960 – Struck off register.

Springbank Ventures Inc. (B.C. Sept. 9, 1996)
Apr. 2, 2004 – Name changed to Ondine Biopharma Corporation pursuant to reverse takeover acquisition of Ondine Biopharma Inc. ■

Springboard Resources Ltd. (B.C. Mar. 19, 1984)
Aug. 17, 1993 – Name changed to Summex Mines Ltd.; basis 1 new for 4 old shs. ■

Springer Resources Ltd. (B.C. June 24, 1986)
May 14, 1992 – Name changed to Bristol Explorations Ltd.; basis 1 new for 5 old shs. ■

Springer Sturgeon Gold Mines Ltd. (Ont. 1934)
1949 – Name changed to Barymin Co. Ltd. ■

Springfield Resources Ltd. (B.C. 1982)
Apr. 22, 1994 – Dissolved and struck off register.

Springhurst Copper Mines Ltd. (Ont. 1956)
Aug. 19, 1965 – Dissolved.

Springlake Resources Limited (Can. Mar. 20, 1981)
Dec. 8, 1988 – Name changed to Savoy Minerals Limited; basis 1 new for 12.5 old shs. ■

Springpoint Resources Ltd. (Alta. 1980)
June 24, 1986 – Name changed to Canadian Platinum Refineries Inc.; basis 1 new for 10 old shs. ■

Springpole Lake Resources Ltd. (Ont. Jan. 10, 1980)
Sept. 19, 1985 – Name changed to Inter-United Foods Corp. ■

Springpole Mines Ltd. (Ont. 1945)
1968 – Merged into Milestone Exploration Ltd.; basis 1,000 new for 7,605 old shs.

Springrock Capital Inc. (Ont. June 26, 2012)
Mar. 31, 2014 – Name changed to ThermoCeramix Corporation following Qualifying Transaction reverse takeover acquisition of ThermoCeramix, Inc.; basis 1 new for 2.5 old shs. ■

Springsyde Resources Ltd. (Alta. Apr. 8, 1987)
Sept. 7, 1995 – Amalgamated with Webex Resources Ltd. to form Courage Energy Inc.; basis 1.1 new for 1 Webex sh. and 1 new for 1 Springsyde sh. (see Courage Energy Inc.)

Springtide Capital Acquisitions 7 Inc. (Ont. Aug. 9, 2023)
Jan. 16, 2024 – Name changed to Mawson Finland Limited. (see FPsurvey - Mines & Energy)

Sprint Resources Ltd. (Ont. Aug. 29, 1978 amalg.)
Mar. 9, 1987 – Name changed to Meacon Bay Resources Inc. ■

Spriza Media Inc. (B.C. July 6, 2007)
Mar. 17, 2017 – Name changed to Fanlogic Interactive Inc. following the acquisition of Fanlogic LLC. ■

Sproatt Silver Mines Ltd. (Ont. 1948)
June 30, 1977 – Name changed to Hecate Gold Corp.; basis 1 new for 5 old shs. ■

Sprott Energy Opportunities Trust (Ont. Nov. 2, 2016)
Mar. 29, 2018 – Name changed to Ninepoint Energy Opportunities Trust. ■

Sprott Molybdenum Participation Corporation (Ont. Dec. 6, 2006)
July 9, 2009 – Name changed to Cadomin Capital Corporation. ■

Sprott Power Corp. (Can. Jan. 31, 2011)
July 2, 2013 – Name changed to Renewable Energy Developers Inc. ■

Sprott Resource Corp. (Can. Aug. 19, 1994)
Feb. 13, 2017 – Acquired by Adriana Resources Inc. (subsequently renamed Sprott Resources Holdings Inc.); basis 3 Adriana com. shs. for 1 Sprott com. sh. (see SRHI Inc.)
June 23, 2020 – Name changed to SRHI Resources Corp. (see SRHI Inc.)

Sprott Resource Holdings Inc. (Can. May 21, 2002)
June 23, 2020 – Name changed to SRHI Inc. ■

Sprott Resource Lending Corp. (Can. Aug. 22, 2007)
July 30, 2013 – Acquired by Sprott Inc.; basis 15¢ plus 0.50 Sprott shs. for 1 Sprott Res. sh.

Sprott Strategic Fixed Income Fund (Ont. May 31, 2011)
Apr. 5, 2016 – Funded terminated. Final distribution of $0.3167 per trust unit was paid in late 2015.

Spruce Falls Acquisition Corp. (Ont. Sept. 11, 1991)
June 6, 1997 – All o/s cl. 2 restr. vtg. and cl. 3 restr. vtg. special shs. acquired by Tembec Acquisition Corp., a wholly owned subsid. of Tembec Inc.; basis (a) $7.00 and 0.3 of a cl. A sh. of Tembec or (b) 1 cl. A sh. of Tembec for 1 cl. 2 or cl. 3 Spruce Falls sh. (see Tembec Inc.)

Spruce Falls Power and Paper Company, Limited (Ont. 1926)
Dec. 2, 1991 – Name changed to Spruce Falls Inc. following acquisition of all the o/s shs. by Spruce Falls Acquisition Corp. for the nominal price of $1.00. Co. is now private. (see Spruce Falls Acquisition Corp.)

Spruce Ridge Resources Ltd. (Ont. May 4, 1989)
May 16, 2024 – Name changed to Homeland Nickel Inc. following amalgamation of wholly owned Homeland Nickel Inc. into the company. (see FPsurvey - Mines & Energy)

Sprylogics International Corp. (Can. Mar. 17, 2004)
Sept. 9, 2015 – Name changed to Breaking Data Corp. ■

Spud Arsenault Mines Ltd. (Ont. 1946)
Apr. 27, 1964 – Dissolved.

Spud Valley Gold Mines Ltd. (B.C. 1937)
1957 – Name changed to Valley Explorations Ltd. ■

Spur Ventures Inc. (B.C. July 24, 1986)
Aug. 20, 2014 – Name changed to Atlantic Gold Corporation. ■

Spy Hill Royalties Limited (Alta. 1937)
1941 – Merged with 8 other cos. into Amalgamated Oils Limited; basis 10 new for 500 old shs.

Spyder Cannabis Inc. (Alta. Feb. 20, 2014)
Nov. 17, 2021 – Name changed to Delota Corp. (see FPsurvey - Industrials)

Spyglass Resources Corp. (Alta. Mar. 28, 2013 amalg.)
Nov. 26, 2015 – Placed into receivership. Ernst & Young Inc. appointed receiver and all officers and directors resigned.
Sept. 2, 2017 – Struck from registry and dissolved.
Nov. 13, 2017 – All assets had been sold and distribs. totalling $58,000,000 had been made to secured creditors, resulting in a short-fall as outstanding amount still owing to secured creditors was approximately $120,600,000. No monies available for distrib. to unsecured creditors or shldrs. Ernst & Young was discharged as receiver and manager.
Nov. 14, 2017 – Adjudged bankrupt. Ernst & Young Inc. appointed trustee.
June 24, 2019 – Ernst & Young discharged as trustee.

Squall Lake Gold Mines Ltd. (Man. 1945)
1971 – Dissolved.

Squaw Creek Iron Mines Ltd. (Ont. 1944)
1955 – Charter cancelled.

Squire Mining Ltd. (B.C. Mar. 23, 2011)
Dec. 16, 2019 – Name changed to Taal Distributed Information Technologies Inc.; basis 1 new for 10 old shs. ■

St Charles Resources Inc. (Ont. July 16, 2021)
May 5, 2023 – Name changed to BULGOLD Inc. following the Qualifying Transaction reverse takeover acquisition of Eastern Resources OOD; basis 1 new for 3 old shs. (see FPsurvey - Mines & Energy)

St-Georges Platinum and Base Metals Inc. (Can. June 21, 2002)
Dec. 22, 2017 – Name changed to St-Georges Eco-Mining Corp. (see FPsurvey - Mines & Energy; FPsurvey - Industrials)

Stabell Resources Inc. (B.C. 1980)
July 17, 1987 – Continued into Canada.
June 23, 1997 – Dissolved.

Staccato Gold Resources Ltd. (B.C. Mar. 13, 2000)
June 3, 2010 – Acquired by Timberline Resources Corporation pursuant to plan of arrangement; basis 1 Timberline sh. plus US$0.0001 for 7 Staccato shs. (see Timberline Resources Corporation)

Staccato's Inc. (B.C. June 14, 1996)
Apr. 14, 2005 – Name changed to Gravity West Mining Corp. ■

Stacia Ventures Inc. (B.C. Oct. 6, 1986)
Mar. 25, 1993 – Continued into Canada.
Nov. 9, 1995 – Name changed to Environmental Applied Research Technology House - EARTH (Canada) Corporation. ■

Stackpal International Inc. (Ont. Dec. 30, 1985)
Oct. 17, 1997 – Name changed to InnoMat Solutions Corp. ■

Stackpole Limited (Ont. Nov. 10, 1952)
June 24, 2003 – Acquired by wholly owned subsid. of British-based Tomkins plc for Cdn$33.25 per sh.
Aug. 2, 2011 – Name changed to Stackpole International Inc.

Stackpool Enterprises Ltd. (unknown)
Name changed to Geneva Capital Ventures Inc.

Stackpool Mining and Holding Corp. Ltd. (Ont. 1948)
1971 – All assets sold for shs. of Stackpool Enterprises Ltd.
Mar. 1976 – Charter cancelled.

Stackpool Mining Co. Ltd. (Ont. 1948)
Sept. 19, 1962 – Name changed to Stackpool Mining and Holding Corp. Ltd.; basis 1 new plus 2 cents cash for 20 old shs. ■

Stackpool Resources Ltd. (B.C. July 28, 1982)
Mar. 16, 1990 – Name changed to Britt Resources Ltd.; basis 1 new for 3 old shs. ■

Stadacona Mines (1944) Limited (Can. Nov. 29, 1944)
1970 – Charter cancelled.

Stadacona Rouyn Mines Limited (Can. Dec. 23, 1925)
Nov. 29, 1944 – Name changed to Stadacona Mines (1944) Limited and continued into Canada. ■

Stade Exploration Inc. (Alta. Sept. 13, 1982)
July 14, 1997 – Name changed to Tessex Energy Inc. ■

Stafford Foods Limited (Ont. 1935)
1976 – Canbra Foods Ltd. offered to acquire o/s shs. for $4.25 per sh. (see Canbra Foods Ltd.)
July 1978 – Canbra Foods Ltd. held 98% of o/s shs. (see Canbra Foods Ltd.)

Stafford Industries Ltd. (B.C. Jan. 18, 1988)
July 21, 1997 – Name changed to New Stafford Industries Ltd.; basis 1 new for 4 old shs. ■

Stag Explorations Ltd. (B.C. 1980)
Nov. 30, 1990 – Name changed to Stag Holdings Ltd. ■

Stag Holdings Ltd. (B.C. 1980)
Feb. 8, 1993 – Name changed to Unidex Communications Corp. ■

Stag Oils Ltd. (Alta.)
1960 – Struck off register.

Stag Yellowknife Mines Ltd. (Ont. 1947)
1956 – Charter cancelled.

Stage Capital Inc. (B.C. May 17, 2006)
Feb. 23, 2009 – Name changed to Trueclaim Exploration Inc. pursuant to Qualifying Transaction reverse takeover acquisition of Trueclaim Resources Inc. ■

Stairs Exploration & Mining Co. Ltd. (Ont. Mar. 1, 1962)
Jan. 6, 1981 – Name changed to Regal Goldfields Limited. ■

Stake Technology Ltd. (Can. Nov. 13, 1973)
Oct. 31, 2003 – Name changed to SunOpta Inc. (see FPsurvey - Industrials)

Stall Lake Mines Limited (Man. Feb. 19, 1959)
July 23, 2002 – Concurrent acquisition by The Sheridan Platinum Group Limited and issuer bid by the company; basis $1.868 per sh. Subsequently delisted TSX-VEN July 20, 2003.

Stallion Discoveries Corp. (B.C. Nov. 7, 2011)
Oct. 30, 2023 – Name changed to Stallion Uranium Corp. (see FPsurvey - Mines & Energy)

Stallion Gold Corp. (B.C. Nov. 7, 2011)
Jan. 19, 2023 – Name changed to Stallion Discoveries Corp. ■

Stallion Resources Ltd. (B.C. 1980)
July 16, 1993 – Dissolved and struck off register.

Stamford Bancorp Inc. (Can. 1973)
Oct. 23, 1987 – Continued into Ontario.
May 1, 1996 – Name changed to Stamford International Inc.; basis 1 new for 6 old shs. ■

Stamford International Inc. (Ont. Oct. 23, 1987)
Nov. 20, 2017 – Inactive.

Stampede International Resources Inc. (B.C. 1982 amalg.)
1984 – Amalgamated with H.R.S. Industries Inc. to form International H.R.S. Industries Inc. Holders of each 3 cl. A shs. of Stampede International given 2 new com. shs.

Stampede Oils Inc. (Alta. Nov. 19, 1987)
Aug. 23, 2004 – Placed into receivership. PricewaterhouseCoopers Inc. appointed receiver.
Dec. 9, 2006 – PricewaterhouseCoopers obtained approval from the Alberta court for the sale of all the assets. There would be no distrib. to creditors or shldrs.

Stampede Oils Ltd. (Alta. 1967)
Dec. 1968 – Merged (2 new for 1 old sh.) with Galaxy Copper Ltd. (2 new for 5 old shs.) and Bata Resources Ltd. (1 for 1) to form United Bata Resources Ltd. (see United Bata Resources Limited)

Stampede Petroleums Ltd. (Ont. June 30, 1950)
1954 – Taken over by Saskalon Uranium & Oils; basis 1 new for 5 old shs.

Stampeder Exploration Ltd. (Alta. June 4, 1987)
Sept. 10, 1997 – Acquired by Gulf Canada Resources Limited for $7.50 per sh. (see Gulf Canada Resources Limited)

Stancor Limited (Ont. 1965)
July 1, 1968 – Name changed to Sklar Manufacturing Limited. ■

Stand Petroleum Ltd. (B.C.)
Sept. 14, 1978 – Amalgamated with 3 other cos. into Stand-Skat Resources Ltd.; basis 0.09154 new for 1 old sh. (see Stand-Skat Resources Ltd.)

Stand-Skat Resources Ltd. (B.C. Sept. 14, 1978 amalg.)
Mar. 1, 1983 – Amalgamated (1 new for 3 old shs.) with Ramrod Resources Corporation (1 for 1) to Ramrod Energy Corporation.

Standard Barrels and Drums Inc. (Que. 1946)
Jan. 1962 – Name changed to National Containers Ltd. ■

Standard Brands Limited (Can. 1929)
Apr. 16, 1982 – Name changed to Nabisco Brands Ltd. ■

Standard Broadcasting Corporation Limited (Can. 1925)
June 1985 – Slaight Communications Inc., through wholly owned Slaight Broadcasting Inc., acquired 5,033,647 shs. (84.8% int.) for $22 per sh. following public offer on June 11, 1985.
Nov. 1985 – Remaining 15.2% int. acquired at the same price to make Standard a wholly owned subsid.

Standard Chartered Bank of Canada (Can. Jan. 21, 1982)
Nov. 1, 1995 – Amalgamated with TD Loan Corporation to form The Toronto-Dominion Bank.

Standard Chemical Company Ltd. (Can. 1911)
1951 – Acquired by Dominion Tar & Chemical Co. Ltd. On May 31, o/s $100 par pref. shs. red. at 105. Com. shldrs. received 2 Dominion Tar shs. for each 5 shs. held plus 58.4¢ cash. Not to be confused with Standard Chemical Limited, a new co. organized in 1955.

Standard Clay Products Ltd. (Can. 1912)
1957 – Acquired by Feralco Industries Ltd. through sh. exch. offer. Standard Clay shldrs. received 5 Feralco shs. and 1 sh. of B. J. Coghlin & Co. for 1 old Standard Clay sh.

Standard Etac Corporation (Can. 1980)
July 4, 1988 – Amalgamated with Etac Sales Ltd.; basis 0.3606 Etac com. for 1 Standard Etac com. (see Etac Sales Ltd.)

Standard Exploration Ltd. (Can. July 22, 2008)
Jan. 4, 2019 – Name changed to Southern Energy Corp. following acquisition of Gulf Pine Energy Partners, LP. ∎

Standard Fuel Co. Ltd. (Can. 1928)
Dec. 1973 – Major asset was 100% int. in The Milnes Coal Co. Ltd. and its wholly owned subsid., Milnes Fuel Oil Ltd. Co. was 98% owned by Milnes Holding Co. Ltd., a private corp. The Milnes Coal Co. Ltd. was sold to Laoc Holdings Ltd. for $2.4 million and proceeds distributed as follows to shldrs. of Standard Fuel Co. Ltd.: $53 per pref. sh. and $48.50 per com. sh. Charter surrendered Jan. 21, 1974.

Standard Gold Mines Ltd. (Que. 1931)
Oct. 16, 1975 – Name changed to S.G.M. Corporation (not to be confused with co. of same name - B.C. 1980); basis 1 new for 5 old shs. ∎

Standard Gold Mines Ltd. (B.C. 1980)
Sept. 1, 1989 – Amalgamated with Eastern Mines Ltd. (0.1519 for 1), Gallant Gold Mines Ltd. (0.2266 for 1) and Silver Sceptre Resources Ltd. (0.1204 for 1) to form HLX Resources Limited; basis 0.2735 new for 1 old sh. (see HLX Resources Ltd.)

Standard Graphite Corporation (B.C. Sept. 18, 2006)
Nov. 17, 2017 – Name changed to Choom Holdings Inc. following acquisition of Medi-Can Health Solutions Ltd. ∎

Standard Industries Ltd. (Ont. 1929)
Dec. 21, 1983 – Amalgamated with Canada Cement Lafarge Ltd. Each com. sh. of Standard exchanged for 1.45 exch. pfce. shs. of Canada Cement Lafarge. Pfce. stk. of Standard redeemed on Nov. 20, 1983, at $10 per sh.

Standard Mercantile Acquisition Corp. (Can. Oct. 18, 2012)
Nov. 20, 2023 – Special distrib. of $0.265 cash payable to shldrs. of record Nov. 14, 2023.
Dec. 4, 2023 – Voluntarily dissolved.

Standard Mining Corporation (Yuk. Feb. 12, 1997)
Nov. 6, 2001 – Amalgamated with Doublestar Resources Ltd.; basis 1 Doublestar sh. for 5 Standard Mining shs. (see Doublestar Resources Ltd.)

Standard Mining Inc. (Alta. Nov. 19, 1985)
Feb. 3, 1999 – Acquired by Quest International Resources Corporation; basis 1 Quest sh. for 1 Standard Mining sh. (see Quest International Resources Corporation)

Standard-Modern Technologies Corporation (Can. 1981 amalg.)
1986 – Genus Equity Corporation acquired 82% of the com. shs. and 80% of the cl. A pref. shs. of the co. for 12,080,244 com. shs. and $395,000 out-of-pocket costs.
Oct. 21, 1987 – Standard Modern went into receivership and Genus Equity wrote off its investment. Nothing left for shldrs.
Aug. 31, 1989 – Dissolved and struck from register.

Standard Nickel Mines Limited (Ont. Dec. 23, 1964)
May 26, 1980 – Name changed to Solex Oil Sands Corporation. ∎

Standard Paving & Materials, Ltd. (Ont. 1929)
Jan. 1, 1974 – Name changed to Standard Industries Ltd. ∎

Standard Radio Ltd. (Can. 1925)
July 5, 1968 – Name changed to Standard Broadcasting Corporation Limited. ∎

Standard Structural Steel Ltd. (Que. 1945)
1971 – All o/s com. shs. acquired by International Utilities Corp. for $5.00 per sh.

Standard Tie and Timber Western Ltd. (Alta. 1946)
1952 – Name changed to Penny Spruce Mills Ltd. ∎

Standard Tolling Corp. (B.C. Sept. 22, 2009)
Apr. 24, 2017 – Voluntarily dissolved.

Standard Trust Company (Can. July 22, 1963)
Oct. 20, 1980 – Following an offer made Standard Trustco Limited (Ont. 1971) obtained 99.44% int.; basis 1 new Standard Trustco com. sh. for 1 old Standard Trust com. sh.

Standard Trustco Limited (Ont. July 22, 1971)
Apr. 23, 1991 – Placed into bankruptcy and Toronto-based PricewaterhouseCoopers Inc. appointed trustee.
Mar. 1997 – All assets liquidated and creditors received proceeds of approx. 15¢ on the dollar of admitted claims.
1998 – Final distribution was made to creditors of slightly more than 15¢ on the dollar of ordinary unsecured claims.
Jan. 1, 2002 – PricewaterhouseCoopers was discharged as trustee. There were no distributions made to shldrs.

Standard Uranium Inc. (B.C. Dec. 11, 1996)
Mar. 27, 2006 – Plan of Arrangement acquisition by Energy Metals Corporation; basis 0.64 new Energy Metals sh. for 1 old Standard Uranium sh. (see Energy Metals Corporation)

Standard Wire and Cable Ltd. (Ont. 1954)
1961 – Name changed to Associated Standard Wire and Cable Ltd.; basis 1 new for 5 old shs. ∎

Standard Yellowknife Mines Ltd. (Alta. 1946)
1953 – Reported defunct.

Stanford Energy Corporation (Alta. June 29, 1990)
July 10, 1998 – Name changed to Stanford Oil & Gas Ltd.; basis 1 new for 2 old shs. ∎

Stanford Oil & Gas Ltd. (Alta. June 29, 1990)
Aug. 10, 1998 – Continued into Yukon. (see Hilton Petroleum Ltd.)
Apr. 1, 1999 – Acquired by Hilton Petroleum Ltd.; basis 0.5263 new Hilton com. sh. for 1 old Stanford com. sh. (see Hilton Petroleum Ltd.)

Stanich Gold Mines Ltd. (Que. 1937)
Apr. 1974 – Charter cancelled.

Stanleigh Uranium Mining Corp. Ltd. (unknown 1954)
1960 – Merged into Preston Mines Ltd.; basis 1 new 4% pref. sh. of Preston for 1 Stanleigh sh.

Stanley Brothers Holdings Inc. (B.C. May 18, 2018)
July 13, 2018 – Name changed to Charlotte's Web Holdings, Inc. (see FPsurvey - Industrials)

Stanley Carroll Industries Inc. (Alta. Jan. 25, 1988)
Sept. 30, 1994 – Name changed to Explogas Inc.; basis 1 new for 6 old shs. ∎

Stanley Reef Resources Ltd. (Ont. 1981)
Nov. 14, 1985 – Amalgamated with 6 other cos. to form Paladin Petroleum Corporation; basis 1.5 new for 1 old sh.

Stanley Resource Management Group Ltd. (B.C. 1979)
June 1980 – Name changed to Stanley Resources Ltd. ∎

Stanley Resources Ltd. (B.C. 1979)
Aug. 22, 1986 – Name changed to Equi Ventures Incorporated. (see FPsurvey - Mines & Energy)

Stanley Technology Group Inc. (Can. Mar. 23, 1984)
Nov. 3, 1998 – Name changed to Stantec Inc. (see FPsurvey - Industrials)

Stanmac Ltd. (Ont. 1945)
1957 – Wound up. Final distribution reported to have been 9.5¢ and 1.25 shs. Sourdough Bay Mines Ltd. per sh.

Stanmack Mining Co. Ltd. (B.C. 1957)
May 4, 1972 – Dissolved.

Stanmar Resources Ltd. (B.C. 1979)
July 5, 1985 – Amalgamated with 2 other cos. under agreement dated to form Tandem Resources Ltd.; basis 1 new for 4 old shs.

Stanmore Mining & Smelting Ltd. (Man. 1937)
1957 – Charter cancelled.

Stannex Minerals Ltd. (B.C. 1967)
May 1973 – Name changed to Ryker Resources Ltd.; basis 1 new for 3 old shs. ∎

Stanrock Uranium Mines Limited (Ont. 1956)
Feb. 12, 1973 – Amalgamated into Denison Mines Limited; basis 1 new for 70 old shs.

Stanstead Capital Inc. (Can. Nov. 14, 2001)
Aug. 25, 2004 – Name changed to Blue Tree Wireless Data Inc. following Qualifying Transaction reverse takeover acquisition of Blue Tree Wireless Data Operating Inc. ∎

Stanton Lead Mines Ltd. (Ont. 1946)
May 6, 1957 – Charter cancelled.

Stanwell Oil & Gas Ltd. (Ont. July 21, 1950)
1966 – Name changed to Cordwell International Developments Ltd.; basis 1 new for 5 old shs. ∎

Staple Mines and Minerals Ltd. (Ont. 1948)
Dec. 26, 1955 – Charter cancelled.

Staple Mining Co. Ltd. (Ont. 1972 amalg.)
Jan. 28, 1976 – Amalgamated with Gerrard Realty Incorporated to form Gerrard Realty Incorporated; basis 1 new for 7.8 old shs.

Star Choice Communications Inc. (Can. Dec. 11, 1996)
Sept. 1, 1999 – All o/s com. shs. acquired by Canadian Satellite Communications Inc.; basis 0.2083333 Canadian Satellite com. shs. for 1 Star Choice com. sh. (see Canadian Satellite Communications Inc.)

Star Dance Resources Ltd. (B.C. Apr. 19, 1973)
Jan. 13, 1999 – Name changed to Dancing Star Resources Ltd.; basis 1 new for 8.5 old shs. ∎

Star Data Systems Inc. (Ont. Dec. 10, 1987 amalg.)
Jan. 31, 2001 – Acquired by CGI Group Inc.; basis 0.737 CGI cl. A subord. shs. for 1 Star Data com. sh. (see CGI Group Inc.)

Star Group Newspaper Networks Inc. (Ont. Jan. 8, 1986)
June 8, 1998 – Name changed to TKN Interactive Marketing Systems Inc. ∎

Star Hedge Managers Corp. (Ont. July 2, 2008)
May 14, 2015 – Terminated. Distribution of $5.5833 cash per cl. A sh.

Star Hedge Managers Corp. II (Ont. Feb. 25, 2011)
May 14, 2015 – Terminated. Distribution of $4.6468 cash per cl. A sh.

Star Lake Gold Mines Ltd. (Man. 1915)
Feb. 1974 – Name changed to Winnipeg Gold Mines Ltd.; basis 1 new for 2 old shs. ∎

Star Land & Exploration Ltd. (Alta. 1955)
Dec. 1961 – Name changed to Victoria Land & Minerals Ltd. ∎

Star Minerals Group Ltd. (Sask. Jan. 15, 2009)
Dec. 23, 2015 – Name changed to Navis Resources Corp. ∎

Star of Mineta Ltd. (B.C. Aug. 15, 1979)
Aug. 24, 1995 – Name changed to International Star Resources Ltd.; basis 1 new for 2 old shs. (see FPsurvey - Mines & Energy)

Star One Resources Inc. (B.C. Nov. 13, 1980)
June 26, 1989 – Name changed to Hyder Gold Inc. ∎

Star Portfolio Corp. (Ont. Aug. 31, 2010)
Jan. 15, 2016 – Succeeded by Star Yield Managers Trust pursuant to a reorganization whereby Star Yield Managers Trust was formed to facilitate the conversion of the mutual fund corporation into a mutual fund trust. ∎

Star Resources Corp. (B.C. Mar. 12, 1986)
Sept. 18, 2003 – Name changed to Jaguar Resources Corporation. ∎

Star Uranium Corp. (B.C. Mar. 24, 1987)
Jan. 15, 2009 – Continued into Saskatchewan.
Oct. 10, 2013 – Name changed to Star Minerals Group Ltd. ∎

Star Uranium Ltd. (Alta. 1955)
Nov. 1959 – Name changed to Star Land & Exploration Ltd.; basis 1 new for 20 old shs. ∎

Star Valley Resources Corporation (B.C. Feb. 29, 1988)
Nov. 26, 1996 – Name changed to Western Pinnacle Mining Ltd. following reverse takeover acquisition of Sakha Gold Overseas Limited. ∎

Star Yield Managers Trust (Ont. Sept. 15, 2015)
Sept. 19, 2017 – Terminated by the fund administrator BMO Nesbitt Burns Inc.; basis $11.4206 per trust unit.

Starbec Inc. (Alta. 1986)
Oct. 18, 1996 – Amalgamated with 3284107 Canada Inc.; basis 1 3284107 Canada cl. C sh. for 1 Starbec sh. Immediately redeemed for 10¢ per sh.

Starbird Mines Ltd. (Man. 1957)
Dec. 19, 1962 – Charter cancelled.

Starbird Mines Ltd. (B.C. 1967)
Mar. 17, 1976 – Name changed to Camrelco Resources Group Ltd. ∎

Starbridge Venture Capital Inc. (Alta. June 25, 1996)
Feb. 25, 1997 – Formed Intermap Technologies Ltd. in Alberta on amalgamation with Intermap Technologies Limited, constituting a reverse takeover by Intermap. ∎

Starbuck Mines Ltd. (B.C. 1969)
Aug. 8, 2017 – Dissolved and struck from register.

Starburst Energy Corp. (B.C. 1980)
Sept. 9, 1987 – Name changed to National Scientific Products Corp. (see FPsurvey - Industrials)

StarCast Corporation (Alta. May 18, 1998)
May 26, 1999 – Formed Sat-Tel Corporation in Alberta following Qualifying Transaction acquisition of Sat-Tel Corporation; basis 1 new for 1.75 old shs. ∎

Starcor Energy Royalty Fund (Alta. Mar. 13, 1996)
Mar. 17, 1999 – Merged with ARC Energy Trust; basis 0.965 of a new ARC Trust Unit, 0.193 of a new ARC warrant and $1.50 in cash for 1 old Starcor Trust Unit. (see ARC Energy Trust)

Starcore International Ventures Ltd. (B.C. Oct. 17, 1980)
Feb. 1, 2008 – Name changed to Starcore International Mines Ltd. (see FPsurvey - Mines & Energy)

Starcore Resources Ltd. (B.C. Oct. 17, 1980)
Feb. 2, 2004 – Name changed to Starcore International Ventures Ltd.; basis 1 new for 10 old shs. ∎

Starcourt Gold Mines Ltd. (Ont. 1945)
Aug. 24, 1964 – Dissolved.

Starfield Communications Group Inc. (Alta. Apr. 22, 1994)
Dec. 18, 1997 – Name changed to Starfield Resources Inc. ∎

Starfield Resources Inc. (Alta. Apr. 22, 1994)
Oct. 27, 2006 – Continued into British Columbia.
June 28, 2013 – Deemed bankrupt. PricewaterhouseCoopers Inc. appointed trustee. All officers and directors resigned.

Starfire Resources Ltd. (B.C. 1979)
June 1, 1985 – Name changed to Starfire Industries Limited. (see FPsurvey - Industrials)

Starfire Technologies International Inc. (B.C. Dec. 8, 1998)
May 16, 2003 – Struck from register and dissolved.

Stargazer Resources Ltd. (Alta. 1978)
Dec. 12, 1984 – Name changed to Stockmen Energy Ltd.; basis 1 new for 5 old shs. ∎

Stark Gold Mines Ltd. (Ont. 1946)
Feb. 1962 – Dissolved.

Starletta Mines Ltd. (B.C. Sept. 28, 1970)
Mar. 24, 1977 – Name changed to Golden Star Mines Ltd. ∎

Starlight Energy Corporation (B.C. 1979)
July 23, 1990 – Name changed to Hansa International Resources Ltd.; basis 1 new for 3.5 old shs. ∎

Starlight Hybrid Global Real Assets Trust (Ont.)
Aug. 12, 2021 – Reorganized as Starlight Private Global Real Assets Trust, a private investment trust; basis 0.954903 Private Global ser. C units for 1 Hybrid Global ser. A unit.

Starlight Mines Ltd. (Ont. 1944)
Nov. 12, 1969 – Charter cancelled.

Starlight U.S. Multi-Family Core Fund (Ont. Feb. 12, 2013)
Oct. 18, 2016 – Merged into Starlight U.S. Multi-Family (No. 5) Core Fund; basis 2.4187 Starlight 5 cl. A units for 1 Starlight cl. A unit and 1.8324 Starlight 5 cl. U units for 1 Starlight cl. U unit. (see Starlight U.S. Multi-Family (No. 5) Core Fund)

Starlight U.S. Multi-Family (No. 5) Core Fund (Ont. Aug. 26, 2016)
June 14, 2019 – Acquired by Tricon Capital Group Inc.; basis 0.9669 Tricon com. shs. for 1 Starlight cl. A limited partnership sh,; 0.9820 Tricon com. shs. for 1 Starlight cl. C limited partnership sh.; 0.9697 Tricon com. shs. for 1 Starlight cl. D limited partnership sh.; 1.2737 Tricon com. shs. for 1 Starlight cl. E limited partnership shs.; 0.9713 Tricon com. shs. for 1 Starlight cl. F limited partnership sh.; 1.0563 Tricon com. shs. for 1 Starlight cl. H partnership sh.; and 1.2800 Tricon com. shs. for 1 Starlight cl. U limited partnership sh. (see Tricon Capital Group Inc.)

Starlight U.S. Multi-Family (No. 4) Core Fund (Ont. Dec. 1, 2014)
Oct. 18, 2016 – Merged into Starlight U.S. Multi-Family (No. 5) Core Fund; basis 1.3532 Starlight 5 cl. A units for 1 Starlight 4 cl. A unit and 1.2801 Starlight 5 cl. U units for 1 Starlight 4 cl. U unit. (see Starlight U.S. Multi-Family (No. 5) Core Fund)

Starlight U.S. Multi-Family (No. 1) Core Plus Fund (Ont. Dec. 10, 2019)
Oct. 26, 2021 – Entire U.S. multi-family property portfolio acquired by Sherrin U.S. Multi-Family (No. 1) Holding LP and net proceeds distributed to unitholders; basis Cdn$13.19 per cl.A unit.

Starlight U.S. Multi-Family (No. 1) Value-Add Fund (Ont. Apr. 27, 2017)
Jan. 15, 2020 – Dissolved and all o/s units cancelled; basis (post-U.S. tax) Cdn$11.19 per cl. A and cl. D LP units; Cdn$11.89 per cl. C LP units; US$11.35 per cl. E and cl. U LP units; and Cdn$11.59 per cl. F LPunits.

Starlight U.S. Multi-Family (No. 3) Core Fund (Ont. May 1, 2014)
Oct. 18, 2016 – Merged into Starlight U.S. Multi-Family (No. 5) Core Fund; basis 1.7804 Starlight 5 cl. A units for 1 Starlight 3 cl. A unit and 1.4074 Starlight 5 cl. U units for 1 Starlight 3 cl. U units. (see Starlight U.S. Multi-Family (No. 5) Core Fund)

Starlight U.S. Multi-Family (No. 2) Core Fund (Ont. Sept. 23, 2013)
Oct. 18, 2016 – Merged into Starlight U.S. Multi-Family (No. 5) Core Fund; basis 2.4615 Starlight 5 cl. A units for 1 Starlight 2 cl. A unit and 1.9081 Starlight 5 cl. U units for 1 Starlight 2 cl. U unit. (see Starlight U.S. Multi-Family (No. 5) Core Fund)

Starlink Capital Corp. (Alta. Apr. 4, 1996)
Oct. 2, 2001 – Name changed to Nevis Energy Services Ltd. following reverse takeover acquisition of Nevis Drilling Systems Ltd.; basis 1 new for 10 old shs. ∎

Starlink Communications Corporation (Alta. Apr. 4, 1996)
Dec. 7, 2000 – Name changed to Starlink Capital Corp. ∎

Starmark Resources Ltd. (B.C. Nov. 14, 1979)
Apr. 11, 1984 – Name changed to Transglobe Resources Ltd.; basis 1 new for 3 old shs. ∎

Starmin Mining Inc. (Ont. July 20, 1989 amalg.)
July 1994 – Continued into Canada.
Aug. 11, 1994 – Name changed to First Dynasty Mines Ltd. and continued into Yukon pursuant to plan of arrangement whereby existing mineral assets and related liabilities were transferred to newly incorporated Tequila Copper Corp. spun out to shldrs. and New Millennium Mining Ltd. and Desarrollos Mineros Ivanhoe Holdings Ltd. were acquired; basis 1 new for 3 old shs. ∎

StarPoint Energy Ltd. (Alta. July 22, 2003)
Jan. 14, 2005 – Plan of Arrangement with E3 Energy Inc. to convert into a new income trust named StarPoint Energy Trust and a new exploration co. named Mission Oil & Gas Inc.; basis 0.25 new trust unit plus 0.1111 new Mission com. sh. or, 0.25 new exch. sh. plus 0.1111 new Mission com. sh. or, a combination thereof for 1 old StarPoint com. sh. (see Mission Oil & Gas Inc.; StarPoint Energy Trust)

StarPoint Energy Trust (Alta. Nov. 11, 2004)
Jan. 9, 2006 – Plan of Arrangement amalgamation with Acclaim Energy Trust (0.8333 for 1) subsequently renamed Canetic Resources Trust; basis 1 new Canetic unit, plus 0.1 new com. sh. and 0.021 new wt. of new exploration co. TriStar Oil & Gas Ltd. for 1 old StarPoint unit. (see Canetic Resources Trust; TriStar Oil & Gas Ltd.)

Starpoint Systems Inc. (B.C. 1984)
May 27, 1996 – Name changed to Starpoint Goldfields Inc. (see FPsurvey - Mines & Energy)

Starr Peak Exploration Ltd. (B.C. Feb. 4, 1981)
Mar. 23, 2021 – Name changed to Starr Peak Mining Ltd. (see FPsurvey - Mines & Energy)

Starratt Nickel Mines Limited (Ont. June 8, 1945)
Nov. 22, 1994 – Name changed to Starratt Resources Limited; basis 1 new for 5 old shs. ■

Starratt Olsen Gold Mines Ltd. (Ont. June 8, 1945)
1957 – Name changed to Starratt Nickel Mines Limited. ■

Starratt Resources Limited (Ont. June 8, 1945)
Oct. 13, 2000 – Delisted from the CDN. Subsequently dissolved and charter cancelled.

Starrex Mining Corporation Ltd. (Can. Oct. 12, 1982)
May 1, 2014 – Name changed to Starrex International Ltd. (see FPsurvey - Industrials)

The Stars Group Inc. (Ont. Aug. 1, 2017)
May 7, 2020 – Acquired by Flutter Entertainment plc; basis 0.2253 Flutter ordinary shs. for 1 Stars Group com. sh.

Startec Marketing Corporation (B.C. Feb. 29, 1984)
Feb. 9, 1993 – Name changed to Vitality Products Inc.; basis 1 new for 5 old shs. (see FPsurvey - Industrials)

Startech Energy Inc. (Alta. Aug. 31, 1983)
Jan. 1, 1995 – Amalgamated in Alberta to continue with same name. (see ARC Resources Ltd.)
Feb. 5, 2001 – Merged with ARC Energy Trust; basis either 0.96 trust units of ARC Energy Trust, or 0.96 exchangeable shs. of ARC Resources Ltd., or a combination thereof, for 1 Startech com. sh. (see ARC Resources Ltd.)

Startech Energy Ltd. (Alta. 1991 amalg.)
July 6, 1994 – Amalgamated with Joss Energy Ltd. (1 new for 3 old shs.), to form Startech Energy Inc.; basis 1 new for 8.58 old shs. (see Startech Energy Inc.)

Starteck Industries Ltd. (B.C. Apr. 27, 1987)
Sept. 24, 1999 – Name changed to International StarTeck Industries Ltd.; basis 1 new for 4 old shs. ■

Startigan Corporation (Can. Oct. 27, 1986)
Feb. 14, 1994 – Name changed to Ecuadorian Minerals Corporation and continued into Yukon. ■

Starwood Industries Inc. (Ont. Feb. 5, 1999 amalg.)
Aug. 12, 2013 – Dissolved and struck from register.

Starx Resource Corp. (B.C. July 18, 1986)
Apr. 11, 1997 – Continued into Yukon.
Apr. 16, 1997 – Name changed to Gabriel Resources Ltd. (see FPsurvey - Mines & Energy)

Starz Media Canada Co. (N.S. July 1, 1996)
Jan. 1, 2007 – Continued into Ontario.
2011 – Name changed to Arc Productions Ltd.

State Bank of India (Canada) (Can. Feb. 4, 1982)
Mar. 1, 2016 – Name changed to SBI Canada Bank.

State Vacuum Stores of Canada Ltd. (Ont. 1948)
1955 – Name changed to President Electric Ltd. ■

StateHouse Holdings Inc. (Ont. Dec. 20, 2011)
Oct. 10, 2024 – Filed an assignment into bankruptcy under the Bankruptcy and Insolvency Act (BIA). B. Riley Farber appointed trustee.

States Exploration Ltd. (B.C. 1980)
Oct. 27, 1982 – Continued into Canada.
May 6, 2004 – Dissolved.

Stateside Energy Corporation (B.C. Nov. 21, 1977)
Mar. 10, 1994 – Name changed to Stateside Oil Corporation; basis 1 new for 2 old shs. ■

Stateside Mines Ltd. (B.C. Apr. 7, 1981)
Oct. 30, 1990 – Name changed to Landon Resources Ltd. ■

Stateside Oil Corporation (B.C. Nov. 21, 1977)
Feb. 5, 1997 – Acquired by 528140 B.C. Ltd., a wholly owned subsid. of Reserve Royalty Corporation, for $1.45 per sh. (see Reserve Royalty Corporation)

Statesman Resources Ltd. (B.C. May 4, 1984)
May 2, 2017 – Dissolved and struck from register.

Steadman Industries Ltd. (Ont. 1960)
June 7, 1971 – Name changed to Interpool International Ltd. ■

Steadright Capital Development Incorporated (Ont. Mar. 6, 2019)
Oct. 29, 2021 – Name changed to Steadright Critical Minerals Inc. (see FPsurvey - Mines & Energy)

Stealth Capital Corp. (Alta. Nov. 4, 1993)
Nov. 25, 1996 – Name changed to NHP Natural Health Ltd. following acquisition of NHP Natural Hair Ltd. ■

Stealth Energy Inc. (B.C. Feb. 21, 2006)
May 4, 2012 – Name changed to Blackstream Energy Corporation; basis 1 new for 10 old shs. ■

Stealth Minerals Limited (Alta. Nov. 19, 1993)
Feb. 25, 2005 – Continued into British Columbia.
June 27, 2014 – Filed an assignment in bankruptcy. Boale, Wood & Company Inc. appointed trustee.

Stealth Mining Corporation (Alta. Nov. 19, 1993)
June 1, 2001 – Name changed to Stealth Minerals Limited; basis 2 new for 3 old shs. ■

Stealth Ventures Inc. (B.C. Nov. 17, 1986)
May 12, 1994 – Name changed to Annova International Holdings Corp. ■

Stealth Ventures Inc. (Alta. Nov. 25, 2011)
June 2, 2017 – Dissolved and struck from registry.

Stealth Ventures Ltd. (B.C. Dec. 19, 1996)
Nov. 25, 2011 – Continued into Alberta.
Aug. 23, 2012 – Name changed to Stealth Ventures Inc.; basis 1 new for 15 old shs. ■

Steamsand Capital Corp. (B.C. May 24, 2017)
Nov. 13, 2018 – Name changed to VOTI Detection Inc. following Qualifying Transaction reverse takeover acquisition of VOTI Inc. with concurrent amalgamation of VOTI Inc. with wholly owned 10971260 Canada Inc.; basis 1 new for 18 old shs. ■

Stedman Bros. Limited (Can. 1912)
1962 – Acquired by Gamble-Skogmo Inc. of Minneapolis in 1962-64, through offers of $20 and $25 per sh.

Steeber Malartic Mines Ltd. (Ont. 1944)
1956 – Charter cancelled.

The Steel Company of Canada, Limited (Can. June 8, 1910)
June 27, 1980 – Name changed to Stelco Inc. ■

Steelhead Resources Ltd. (B.C. 1981)
Apr. 23, 2007 – Dissolved and struck from register.

Steelman Gas Ltd. (Sask. 1957)
1964 – Acquired by Provo Gas Producers Limited. (see Provo Gas Producers Limited)

Steeloy Mining Corp. Ltd. (Ont. 1943)
1964 – Name changed to Texore Mines Limited; basis 1 new for 4 old shs. (see FPsurvey - Mines & Energy)

Steely Group Inc. (Alta. 1987)
June 15, 2001 – Ceased operations and Arthur Anderson Inc. was appointed trustee in bankruptcy and wholly owned ETI Technologies Inc. issued to the petitioning creditor 4,000 shares reducing the company's ownership to 2.5% from 100%.
Mar. 19, 2003 – Deloitte & Touche Inc., the successor trustee, in Calgary, was discharged. There were no funds available for distribution to creditors or shldrs.

Steep Rock Iron Mines Limited (Ont. Feb. 24, 1939)
Apr. 27, 1983 – Name changed to Steep Rock Resources Inc. ■

Steep Rock Resources Inc. (Ont. Feb. 24, 1939)
Nov. 15, 1988 – Acquired by subsid. of Pluess-Staufer, AG for $2.55 per sh.

Steeplejack Industrial Group Inc. (Alta. May 15, 1987)
Oct. 2, 2007 – Acquired by Brock Holdings III, Inc., an affiliate of The Brock Group, Inc., for $11.50 per sh.
Apr. 2, 2014 – Name changed to Brock Canada Inc.

Steer Technologies Inc. (Ont. Dec. 31, 2019)
Aug. 1, 2024 – Name changed to Argo Corporation. (see FPsurvey - Industrials)

Steerola Exploration Co. Ltd. (unknown)
Oct. 18, 1939 – Charter cancelled; distribution on basis of 25 shs. of Steep Rock Iron Mines for 1 old sh. (see Steep Rock Iron Mines Limited)

Steetley Industries Limited (Ont. 1951)
Dec. 31, 1978 – Amalgamated with its majority shldr., Steetley of Canada (Holdings) Ltd. Minority shldrs. of Steetley Industries received either a cl. A or B pfce. sh. of amalg. co. for each com. sh. held. Pfce. shs. redeemed at $19 per sh. Co. is now private.

Stef International Corporation (Ont. July 19, 1994)
Jan. 14, 2000 – Delisted from the CDN. Subsequently charter cancelled and the company dissolved.

Stefan Resources Inc. (B.C. May 11, 1981)
Feb. 15, 1985 – Formed Tugold Resources Inc. in British Columbia following amalgamation; basis 1 new for 3 old shs. ■

Steinberg Inc. (Que. Apr. 7, 1930)
Sept. 29, 1989 – All o/s cl. A shs. acquired by Socanav Inc. at $51 per share. All o/s 5 1/4% Cumulative Redeemable Preferred Shares, Ser. A, $1.95 Cumulative Redeemable Second Preferred Shares, Ser. 1 and $2.9375 Cumulative Redeemable Retractable Second Preference Shares, Ser. A, were redeemed Nov. 30, 1990 at the prices of $101.00, $25 and $25.75 per sh. respectively with all accrued and unpaid dividends to the redemption date.

Steinberg's Limited (Que. Apr. 7, 1930)
Dec. 20, 1977 – Name changed to Steinberg Inc. ■

Steinberg's Properties Ltd. (Que. 1955)
1979 – Merged with Ivanhoe Inc.

Steintron International Electronics Ltd. (B.C. 1958)
1979 – Acquired by Omnitron Investments for $8.00 per sh.

Stelcanus Iron Ore Ltd. (unknown)
Dec. 15, 1950 – Name changed to Femco Mines Ltd. and continued into Ontario. ■

Stelco Holdings Inc. (Can. Sept. 25, 2017)
Nov. 5, 2024 – Acquired by Cleveland-Cliffs Inc.; basis 0.454 Cleveland-Cliffs com. sh. and $60 cash for 1 Stelco sh.
Nov. 8, 2024 – Formed Stelco Inc. in Canada on amalgamation with wholly owned (old) Stelco Inc. and 13421422 Canada Inc. (a wholly owned subsidiary of Cleveland-Cliffs Inc.) following acquisition by Cleveland-Cliffs.

Stelco Inc. (Can. June 8, 1910)
Oct. 31, 2007 – Name changed to U. S. Steel Canada Inc. ■

Stelco Inc. (Can. June 8, 1910)
Nov. 8, 2024 – Amalgamated with parent company Stelco Holdings Inc. and 13421422 Canada Inc. (a wholly owned subsidiary of Cleveland-Cliffs Inc.) following acquisition of Stelco Holdings by Cleveland-Cliffs.

Stelco-McMaster Ltée (Can. - unspecified)
Jan. 21, 2004 – Name changed to Norambar Inc. ■

Stellako Mining Co. Ltd. (B.C. 1961)
Apr. 5, 1976 – Name changed to Arizako Mines Ltd.; basis 1 new for 5 old shs. ■

Stellar AfricaGold Inc. (Can. Apr. 24, 2006)
Jan. 28, 2019 – Continued into British Columbia. (see FPsurvey - Mines & Energy)

Stellar Biotechnologies Inc. (B.C. Nov. 25, 2009)
June 7, 2019 – Name changed to Edesa Biotech, Inc. pursuant to reverse takeover acquisition of (old) Edesa Biotech Inc.; basis 1 new for 6 old shs. (see FPsurvey - Industrials)

Stellar Gold Corp. (B.C. Aug. 19, 1979)
Sept. 23, 1996 – Name changed to Stellar Metals Inc. ■

Stellar International Inc. (Ont. Nov. 14, 1994)
Jan. 4, 2005 – Name changed to Stellar Pharmaceuticals Inc. ■

Stellar Metals Inc. (B.C. Aug. 19, 1979)
Oct. 7, 1999 – Name changed to Geostar Metals Inc.; basis 1 new for 9 old shs. ■

Stellar Metals Ltd. (B.C.)
Sept. 27, 1973 – Dissolved.

Stellar Pacific Ventures Inc. (B.C. July 23, 1987)
Apr. 24, 2006 – Continued into Canada.
Apr. 1, 2013 – Name changed to Stellar AfricaGold Inc.; basis 1 new for 10 old shs. ■

Stellar Pharmaceuticals Inc. (Ont. Nov. 14, 1994)
Jan. 1, 2013 – Name changed to Tribute Pharmaceuticals Canada Inc. ■

Stellar Resource Corporation (B.C. Feb. 16, 1983)
Dec. 15, 1989 – Name changed to Maesa Petroleum Inc.; basis 1 new for 8 old shs. ■

Stellarene Petroleums Ltd. (B.C.)
1960 – Struck off register.

Stellarton Energy Corporation (Alta. Aug. 21, 1978)
Jan. 16, 2001 – Acquired by Colorado-based Tom Brown Resources Ltd. for $5.00 per sh.

Stelway Food Services Inc. (B.C. 1986)
July 9, 1993 – Dissolved and struck off register.

Stem Cell Therapeutics Corp. (Alta. Mar. 31, 2004)
Nov. 7, 2013 – Continued into Ontario.
June 6, 2014 – Name changed to Trillium Therapeutics Inc. ■

Stem 7 Capital Inc. (B.C. Nov. 8, 1984)
Dec. 21, 2017 – Name changed to South Star Mining Corp. ■

Step 2 Software Corporation (B.C. Jan. 12, 1987)
Nov. 1, 1999 – Name changed to Emergo Software Corp.; basis 1 new for 5 old shs. ■

Stephenson's Rental Services Income Fund (Ont. Apr. 21, 2005)
July 18, 2007 – Acquired by EdgeStone Capital Partners, L.P. for $6.875 per trust unit.

Steppe Gold Resources Ltd. (Yuk. Aug. 12, 1996)
May 29, 2003 – Struck off register.

Steppingstone Explorations Ltd. (Ont. 1975)
Jan. 23, 1979 – Amalgamated with Glenshire Mines Ltd. (231 for 1,000), Huddersfield Uranium Mines Ltd. (129 for 1,000), Kayak Explorations Ltd. (195 for 1,000), La France Explorations Ltd. (128 for 1,000), Lunel Management Ltd. (923.5 for 1) and Sandhurst Mines Ltd. (1 for 1) to form Lunel Enterprises Inc.; basis 229 new for 1,000 old shs. (see Lunel Enterprises Inc.)

Stepstone Enterprises Ltd. (B.C. July 25, 2000)
Sept. 8, 2004 – Name changed to ACT360 Solutions Ltd. following Qualifying Transaction acquisition of ACT360 Media Ltd. ■

Sterisystems Ltd. (Can. 1967)
Jan. 5, 1982 – Acquired by Sterivest Holdings Inc.; basis 1 Sterivest pref. sh. for 1 Sterisystems com. sh.. Pref. shs. subsequently redeemed at $5.25 per sh.

Sterivet Laboratories Limited (Ont. Dec. 31, 1968)
May 15, 1990 – Name changed to Hyal Pharmaceutical Corporation. ■

Sterling Centrecorp Inc. (Ont. Sept. 7, 1944)
June 21, 2007 – Acquired by SCI Acquisition Inc.; basis $1.26 per com. sh. and redemption of 8.5% debs. for total consideration of $53,000,000.

Sterling Coal Co., Ltd. (Can. 1910)
July 24, 1950 – Name changed to Conger Lehigh Fuels Ltd. ■

Sterling Energy Corp. (Ont. 1980)
June 21, 1985 – Name changed to International Sterling Holdings Inc.; basis 1 new for 5 old shs. ■

Sterling Financial Corporation (Ont. Sept. 7, 1944)
June 29, 2001 – Name changed to Sterling Centrecorp Inc. ■

Sterling Gas Co. Ltd. (Ont. 1933)
1942 – Sold assets to a shldr.

Sterling Pacific Oil Co. Ltd. (Can. 1928)
1934 – Property sold to Royalite Oil Co. Ltd.; basis 1 new for 25 old shs.

Sterling Pacific Resources Inc. (B.C. Nov. 20, 1986)
Jan. 11, 1999 – Name changed to Tres-Or Resources Ltd.; basis 1 new for 5 old shs. (see FPsurvey - Mines & Energy)

Sterling Resources Ltd. (Alta. Aug. 31, 1979)
Dec. 18, 2017 – Amalgamated in Alberta to continue with same name.
June 4, 2018 – Name changed to PetroTal Corp. (see FPsurvey - Mines & Energy)

Sterling Shoes Income Fund (B.C. May 31, 2005)
July 1, 2010 – Succeeded by Sterling Shoes Inc. pursuant to plan of arrangement whereby Sterling Shoes Inc. was formed to facilitate the conversion of the fund into a corporation and the fund was subsequently dissolved. ■

Sterling Shoes Inc. (Can. Apr. 23, 2010)
Feb. 22, 2015 – Dissolved following court-approved asset sale with resulting proceeds distributed to creditors.

Sterling Silver Mines Ltd. (B.C. 1961)
Nov. 1964 – Acquired by Gem Explorations Ltd.; basis 2 new for 3 old shs.

Sterling Software, Inc. (unknown 1981)
Feb. 14, 1983 – Continued into Delaware.

Sterling Trusts Corporation (Can. 1911)
Mar. 15, 1976 – Name changed to Sterling Trust Corporation. (see General Trustco of Canada Inc.)

Sterlingmarc Mining Ltd. (B.C. June 12, 1984)
June 23, 1999 – Name changed to West Oak Resource Corporation; basis 1 new for 6 old shs. ■

Sterlite Gold Ltd. (Yuk. Aug. 11, 1994)
Oct. 19, 2007 – Acquired by GeoProMining Ltd. for US$0.3845 per sh.

Sterne Stackhouse Inc. (Alta. June 11, 1981)
June 17, 2004 – Name changed to Labrador Technologies Inc. ■

Stetson Oil and Gas Ltd. (Alta. Sept. 30, 2004 amalg.)
Aug. 21, 2014 – Continued into Ontario.
June 14, 2017 – Name changed to Magnolia Colombia Ltd. ■

Stetson Petroleums Ltd. (Alta.)
1960 – Struck off register.

Stevens Gold Nevada Inc. (B.C. June 8, 2018)
Jan. 24, 2022 – Name changed to Nine Mile Metals Ltd. (see FPsurvey - Mines & Energy)

Stewart-Abate Gold Mines Ltd. (Ont. 1927)
Dec. 1959 – Dissolved.

Stewart Canal Gold Mines Ltd. (B.C. 1938)
Dec. 1971 – Charter cancelled.

Stewart Lake Iron Mines of Ontario Limited (Ont. May 6, 1959)
Sept. 16, 1986 – Name changed to Stewart Lake Resources Inc.; basis 1 new for 3 old shs. ■

Stewart Lake Resources Inc. (Ont. May 6, 1959)
Feb. 13, 1995 – Struck from register and dissolved.

Stewart Mines Ltd. (B.C. 1969)
1969 – Name changed to Prince Stewart Mines Ltd. and continued into British Columbia. ■

Stikine Energy Corp. (B.C. July 10, 2000)
Mar. 23, 2021 – Name changed to Springbok Ventures Inc. (see FPsurvey - Mines & Energy)

Stikine Explorations Ltd. (B.C. 1965)
Sept. 23, 1974 – Struck off register.

Stikine Gold Corporation (B.C. July 10, 2000)
Aug. 3, 2010 – Name changed to Stikine Energy Corp. ■

Stikine Iron Mines Ltd. (B.C. 1964)
Feb. 1975 – Name changed to Petrogold Resources Corporation. ■

Stikine Resources Ltd. (B.C. 1963)
Dec. 14, 1993 – Acquired by Prime Resources Group Inc.; basis 7.35 Prime shs. for 1 Stikine sh. (see Prime Resources Group Inc.)
Nov. 30, 1994 – Wound up. (see Prime Resources Group Inc.)

Stikine Resources Ltd. (B.C. 1965)
Dec. 1978 – Charter cancelled for this Coquitlam based company. Not to be confused with Stikine Resources Ltd., B.C. 1963 incorp. and based in Vancouver.

Stikine River Mines Ltd. (B.C. 1964)
1969 – Name changed to Canadian Hidrogas Resources Ltd. ■

Stikine Silver Ltd. (B.C. 1963)
Sept. 28, 1984 – Name changed to Consolidated Stikine Silver Ltd.; basis 1 new for 3 old shs. ■

Stikine Tungsten Ltd. (B.C. 1952)
Feb. 12, 1959 – Dissolved.

StillCanna Inc. (B.C. Feb. 14, 2011)
Sept. 30, 2020 – Name changed to Sativa Wellness Group Inc. pursuant to the reverse takeover acquisition of Sativa Group plc. ■

Stillwater Mining Company (Del. Dec. 2, 1992)
May 4, 2017 – Acquired by Sibanye Gold Limited; basis US$18.00 cash per sh.

Stina Resources Ltd. (B.C. Dec. 8, 1986)
May 17, 2018 – Name changed to CellCube Energy Storage Systems Inc. ■

Stingray Copper Inc. (Can. Sept. 30, 2003)
Dec. 31, 2009 – Amalgamated with 7263678 Canada Inc., a wholly owned subsid. of Mercator Minerals Ltd.; basis 0.25 Mercator shs. for 1 Stingray sh. (see Mercator Minerals Ltd.)

Stingray Digital Group Inc. (Can. Dec. 20, 2006)
Dec. 1, 2018 – Name changed to Stingray Group Inc. (see FPsurvey - Industrials)

Stingray Resources Inc. (B.C. Oct. 18, 1973)
Sept. 30, 2003 – Continued into Canada.
July 18, 2007 – Name changed to Stingray Copper Inc. ■

Stinton Exploration Ltd. (Can. Sept. 1, 2010)
Nov. 19, 2015 – Name changed to ICEsoft Technologies Canada Corp. following reverse takeover acquisition of (old) ICEsoft Technologies Canada Corp. (see FPsurvey - Industrials)

Stirling Exploration Ltd. (B.C. Feb. 3, 2004)
June 23, 2006 – Name changed to Luiri Gold Limited following Qualifying Transaction reverse takeover acquisition of LG Holdings Limited. ■

Stirrup Creek Gold Ltd. (B.C. Apr. 21, 1992)
July 28, 2003 – Name changed to Adanac Gold Corp.; basis 1 new for 5 old shs. ■

Stocker & Yale, Inc. (B.C. Nov. 9, 1966)
July 3, 2000 – Name changed to StockerYale, Inc. Continued into Massachusetts.

Stockgold Resources Inc. (Ont. 1986)
Jan. 31, 1993 – Amalgamated with The Lithium Corporation of Canada Ltd. (basis 1 new for 1 old sh.) to form a new company called Rusty Lake Resources Ltd.; basis 0.2622851 new for 1 old sh. (see Rusty Lake Resources Ltd.)

Stockgroup Information Systems Inc. (Colo. Dec. 6, 1994)
July 10, 2008 – Name changed to Stockhouse Inc. ■

Stockguard Corporation (Ont. Apr. 12, 1984)
Jan. 22, 2007 – Struck from registry.

Stockhouse Inc. (Colo. Dec. 6, 1994)
Apr. 1, 2010 – Name changed to Invictus Financial Inc. ■

Stockmen Energy Ltd. (Alta. 1978)
Apr. 20, 1987 – Name changed to Stockmen Oil and Gas Ltd.; basis 1 new for 10 old shs. ■

Stockmen Minerals Ltd. (Alta. Oct. 8, 1986)
Sept. 8, 1988 – Name changed to Indigo Gold Mines Inc. ■

Stockmen Oil and Gas Ltd. (Alta. 1978)
May 19, 1989 – Formed Prime Petroleum Corporation in Alberta on amalgamation with Broadview Resources Inc.; basis 1 new for 3.5 Broadview shs. and 1 new for 2 Stockmen shs. ■

Stockmen Oils Ltd. (Can. 1926)
1929 – Taken over by Turner Basin Oil Co. Ltd.; basis 9 new for 20 old shs. (see Turner Basin Oil Co., Ltd.)

Stockmen Resources Corp. (Alta. Aug. 31, 1984)
Oct. 16, 1992 – Name changed to Panhandle Resources Corp.; basis 1 new for 5 old shs. ■

Stockport Exploration Inc. (Can. Nov. 17, 2004)
Aug. 8, 2018 – Formed Sona Nanotech Inc. in Canada pursuant to the reverse takeover acquisition of and amalgamation with Sona Nanotech Ltd. (deemed acquiror); basis 1 new Sona sh. for 4 Stockport shs. and 1 new Sona sh. for 1.5802 old Sona shs. (see FPsurvey - Mines & Energy; FPsurvey - Industrials)

Stockscape.com Technologies Inc. (B.C. Nov. 14, 1985 amalg.)
July 9, 2002 – Amalgamated with Bradstone Equity Partners, Inc., Glenex Industries Inc. and Peruvian Gold Limited to form Quest Investment Corporation; basis 1 new cl.A sh. for 1 Bradstone sh., 1 new cl.A sh. for 2.268 Glenex shs., 1 new cl.A sh. for 1.7156 Peruvian shs. and 1 new cl.A sh. for 4.1387 Stockscape.com shs. (see Quest Investment Corporation)

Stompy Bot Corporation (B.C. Oct. 30, 2014)
Jan. 31, 2018 – Name changed to Blocplay Entertainment Inc. ■

Stonada Mines Ltd. (Ont. 1944)
1946 – Assets acquired by Argyll Gold Mines Ltd.; basis 5 new for 1 old sh.

Stone Agribusiness Fund (Ont.)
Dec. 22, 2015 – Investment portfolio liquidated and net assets distributed to shldrs. of record as of Dec. 21, 2015; basis $7.95 per unit. Fund terminated on Dec. 23, 2015.

Stone-Consolidated Corporation (Can. June 22, 1993 amalg.)
Nov. 3, 1995 – Amalgamated with Rainy River Forest Products Inc. (1 pfd. or 1.04 com. for 1) to continue with the same name Stone-Consolidated Corporation; basis 1 new for 1 old sh. The 8% debentures were exchanged for 62.11 new Stone-Consolidated shs. plus $160 for each $1,000 principal amt. held. (see Abitibi-Consolidated Inc.)
May 30, 1997 – Amalgamated with Abitibi-Price Inc. (1 for 1) to continue as Abitibi-Consolidated Inc.; basis 1.0062 new for 1 old sh. (see Abitibi-Consolidated Inc.)

Stone Gold Inc. (Ont. Dec. 13, 2002)
Sept. 8, 2022 – Name changed to Copper Road Resources Inc. (see FPsurvey - Mines & Energy)

Stone Mark Capital Inc. (B.C. 1980)
June 21, 1993 – Continued into Yukon. (see FPsurvey - Industrials)

Stone Mountain Holdings Inc. (B.C. Aug. 27, 1992)
Mar. 1, 2010 – Dissolved and struck from register.

Stone Ridge Exploration Corp. (B.C. Jan. 26, 2012)
July 6, 2018 – Name changed to Sproutly Canada, Inc. following reverse takeover acquisition of Sproutly Inc. by way of an amalgamation with a wholly owned subsidiary; basis 1 new for 2 old shs. (see FPsurvey - Industrials)

Stone Total Return Unit Trust (Ont. Mar. 18, 2005)
May 29, 2009 – Liquidated for $2.28 per sh.

Stonecliffe Capital Inc. (Alta. Nov. 15, 2004)
Dec. 19, 2006 – Formed Ruby Red Resources Inc. in Alberta on Qualifying Transaction amalgamation with Ruby Red Resources Inc. (deemed acquiror). ■

Stonefire Energy Corp. (Alta. July 29, 2005)
Jan. 19, 2010 – Acquired by Angle Energy Inc.; basis $2.00 per cl. A sh. and $10.00 per cl. B sh. (see Angle Energy Inc.)

Stonegate Agricom Ltd. (Ont. Aug. 18, 2008 amalg.)
July 24, 2017 – All o/s com. shs. not already held acquired by Itafos; basis 0.008 Itafos ordinary shs. for 1 Stonegate sh. (see Itafos)

Stoneham Drilling Trust (Alta. May 30, 2003)
June 16, 2011 – Acquired by Western Energy Services Corp.; basis either $24 or 61.538 Western shs. for 1 Stoneham unit.

Stonehaven Exploration Ltd. (Alta. Aug. 30, 2010)
Aug. 10, 2016 – Name changed to Front Range Resources Ltd. following acquisition of Deventa Energy Inc. ■

StonePoint Energy Inc. (Alta. Jan. 12, 2006 amalg.)
Sept. 8, 2015 – Acquired by Endurance Energy Ltd. for $0.078125 per sh.

StonePoint Global Brands Inc. (Ont. Jan. 23, 1997)
Nov. 16, 2005 – Continued into British Columbia.
Mar. 20, 2018 – Struck from registry and dissolved.

StonePoint Group Limited (Ont. Jan. 23, 1997)
June 29, 2005 – Name changed to StonePoint Global Brands Inc.; basis 1 new for 10 old shs. ■

Stoneset Equity Development Corp. (Alta. Nov. 20, 2006)
Sept. 4, 2013 – Struck from registry and dissolved.

Stoneshield Capital Corp. (B.C. Apr. 26, 2007)
Apr. 17, 2013 – Name changed to Wolfeye Resource Corp.; basis 1 new for 3 old shs. ■

Stonewall Resources Inc. (B.C. 1987)
Apr. 23, 1992 – Name changed to Terra Health Corporation. ■

Stoney Creek Mines Ltd. (B.C. July 25, 1986)
July 2, 1992 – Name changed to Cyn-Tech Ventures Inc.; basis 1 new for 3 old shs. ■

Stonington Capital Corporation (Can. Aug. 30, 2002 amalg.)
Feb. 22, 2006 – Formed Pyxis Capital Inc. in Ontario on amalgamation with Graystone Corporation with Stonington the deemed acquiror. ■

Stop & Shop, Limited (Ont. 1927)
1950 – Charter cancelled; 1 sh. Thrift Stores Ltd. com. stk. distributed for each 10 shs. Stop & Shop com.; cash distribution of 5.8¢ per sh. made in February. Previously, pref. shs. converted into com. on basis of 7 com. shs. for each pref. sh.

Storage @ccess Technologies Inc. (Yuk. Sept. 14, 1993)
Jan. 31, 2003 – Name changed to BluePoint Data Storage, Inc.; basis 1 new for 6 old shs. ■

Storage One Inc. (Ont. Oct. 18, 1993)
June 2, 1999 – Name changed to EcomPark Inc. ■

StorageFlow Systems Corp. (B.C. July 5, 2000)
July 9, 2002 – Continued into Alberta.
Nov. 21, 2003 – Name changed to Northern Pine Ventures Inc. following Qualifying Transaction acquisition of Washington-based NW Storage Solutions Inc., the data storage and file management subsid. of Integrated Software Solutions Inc.; basis 1 new for 5 old shs. ■

Storimin Exploration Limited (Ont. Jan. 16, 1984)
Apr. 30, 1997 – Name changed to Storimin Resources Limited following reverse takeover acquisition of Old Trafford Capital Corporation for 3,295,189 com. shs.; basis 1 new for 3 old shs. ■

Storimin Resources Limited (Ont. Jan. 16, 1984)
Jan. 25, 2000 – Name changed to Digital Rooster.com Inc. following reverse takeover acquisition of Web Dream Inc. for 27,512,872 com. shs.; basis 1 new for 12 old shs. ■

Storm Cat Energy Corporation (B.C. May 15, 2000)
Nov. 4, 2013 – Struck from register and dissolved for failure to file.

Storm Cloud Development Corporation (B.C. 1970)
1977 – Continued into California.

Storm Energy Inc. (Alta. Apr. 8, 1994)
Aug. 29, 2002 – Plan of Arrangement to convert company into a separate company named Storm Energy Ltd. and an income trust named Focus Energy Trust; basis 1 new Storm com. sh. plus either 1 new trust unit or 1 new exchangeable sh. of FET Resources Ltd. (a wholly owned subsid. of Focus Energy). (see FET Resources Ltd.; Focus Energy Trust; Storm Energy Ltd.)

Storm Energy Ltd. (Alta. July 10, 2002)
July 2, 2004 – Plan of Arrangement with Storm Exploration Inc., Harvest Energy Trust and Harvest Operations Corp.; basis a) 0.053 new Rock Energy Ltd. com. sh. plus b) 1 new Storm Exploration Inc. com. sh. plus c) either $4.15 or 0.281 new Harvest trust unit for 1 old Storm Energy com. sh. (see Rock Energy Inc.; Storm Exploration Inc.)

Storm Exploration Inc. (Can. Oct. 26, 1999)
Aug. 24, 2010 – Acquired by ARC Energy Trust; basis 0.57 ARC trust units or 0.2021 ARC Resources Ltd. exch. shs. for 1 Storm sh. plus 0.3333 shs. of newly formed 1541229 Alberta Ltd. (to be renamed Storm Resources Ltd.) (see ARC Energy Trust)

Storm Resources Ltd. (Alta. June 8, 2010)
Dec. 23, 2021 – Acquired by Canadian Natural Resources Limited; basis $6.25 cash per sh.

Stormcrow Holdings Corp. (Ont. Nov. 6, 2019)
Nov. 5, 2021 – Name changed to Highmark Interactive Inc. following Qualifying Transaction reverse takeover acquisition of private Toronto, Ont.-based Highmark

Innovations Inc.; basis 1 new for 6 old shs. (see FPsurvey - Industrials)

Stormin Resources Inc. (B.C. Dec. 4, 1980)
Dec. 22, 1992 – Name changed to Biocoll Medical Corp. ∎

Stormont Gold Mines Ltd. (Ont. 1945)
Oct. 21, 1957 – Charter cancelled.

Stormy Mines Ltd. (Ont. 1959)
Mar. 1976 – Charter cancelled.

Stornaway Capital Development Corp. (B.C. May 22, 1980)
May 2, 1991 – Delisted from the Vancouver Stock Exchange. Subsequently dissolved for failure to file.

Stornaway Resources Corporation (B.C. May 22, 1980)
Jan. 6, 1988 – Name changed to Stornaway Capital Development Corp. ∎

Stornoway Diamond Corporation (B.C. Nov. 16, 1986)
Oct. 28, 2011 – Continued into Canada.
Sept. 9, 2019 – The company and its subsidiaries filed for protection under the Companies' Creditors Arrangement Act (CCAA) and Deloitte Restructuring Inc. was appointed monitor.
Oct. 7, 2019 – Obtained an approval and vesting order which approved the transactions contemplated under the share purchase agreement entered into by the company and Osisko Gold Royalties Ltd. and certain other secured creditors. Under the terms of the purchase agreement, the participating secured creditors have agreed to acquire, via a newly formed entity (11272420 Canada Inc.) assets and properties of the company and its subsidiaries, assume the debts and liabilities owing to the secured creditors, as well as the ongoing obligations relating to the operation of the Renard mine. Upon closing of the transaction, the company will no longer have any operating assets or active business.
Nov. 1, 2019 – The transaction was completed with the participating secured creditors being the sole shldr. of 11272420 Canada Inc. The company's name was changed to 7936567 Canada Inc. and all of the officers and directors resigned. Additionally, the monitor was empowered and authorized to assign the company into bankruptcy.
Nov. 1, 2019 – Name changed to 7936567 Canada Inc. ∎

Stornoway Ventures Ltd. (B.C. Sept. 20, 1970)
July 18, 2003 – Acquired by Northern Empire Minerals Ltd.; basis 0.8734 Northern Empire shs. for 1 Stornoway sh. (see Northern Empire Minerals Ltd.)

Stovel Advocate Press Limited (Can. 1947)
1960 – Acquired by Lawson & Jones Ltd. through an offer of $11 per pref. sh. and $1.75 per sh.

Stover Gold Mines Ltd. (Ont. 1948)
1968 – Reported wound up.

Stow Resources Ltd. (B.C. Sept. 19, 1986 amalg.)
June 1, 1993 – Amalgamated with Dryden Resources Corporation to form Leicester Diamond Mines Ltd.; basis 1 new for 1.55 Dryden shs. and 1 new for 1 Stow sh. (see Leicester Diamond Mines Ltd.)

Stowe One Investments Corp. (B.C. June 16, 2017)
Feb. 11, 2021 – Name changed to Solvbl Solutions Inc. (see FPsurvey - Industrials)

Stowell Screw Company Limited (Can. 1913)
1956 – All o/s cl. A and 13 shs. acquired by Dominion Steel and Coal Corp. Ltd. through exchange of 1.5 Dosco ord. shs. for each sh. of Stowell cl. A and 1 sh. Dosco for each Stowell cl. B sh.

Stox Infolink Systems Inc. (Can. Sept. 23, 1991 amalg.)
Feb. 24, 1999 – Name changed to stox.com Inc. ∎

stox.com Inc. (Can. Sept. 23, 1991 amalg.)
July 6, 2005 – Dissolved.

Strachan Resources Ltd. (B.C. May 12, 2010)
Nov. 27, 2014 – Formed Lotus Ventures Inc. in British Columbia following Qualifying Transaction acquisition of

and amalgamation with (old) Lotus Ventures Inc. (deemed acquiror). ∎

Strad Energy Services Ltd. (Alta. Sept. 21, 2005)
June 7, 2019 – Name changed to Strad Inc. ∎

Strad Inc. (Alta. Sept. 21, 2005)
Apr. 24, 2020 – Privatized. All o/s cl. A shs. not already held acquired by 2238399 Alberta Ltd.; basis $2.39 cash per cl. A sh.

Straightup Resources Inc. (B.C. Aug. 22, 2017)
July 6, 2023 – Name changed to Battery X Metals Inc.; basis 1 new for 3 old shs. (see FPsurvey - Mines & Energy)

Strait Gold Corporation (Ont. Mar. 7, 2003)
Aug. 1, 2012 – Name changed to Strait Minerals Inc. ∎

Strait Minerals Inc. (Ont. Mar. 7, 2003)
Mar. 6, 2015 – Name changed to Montan Mining Corp. following reverse takeover acquisition of Montan Capital Corp. (deemed acquiror) and subsequent amalgamation of Montan with wholly owned 1023174 B.C. Ltd. to form Montan Ventures Corp.; basis 1 new for 10 old shs. ∎

Straits Towing & Salvage Co. Ltd. (B.C. 1942)
1951 – Name changed to Straits Towing Limited.

Stralak Resources Inc. (B.C. Jan. 31, 1980)
June 25, 2021 – Name changed to Hempsana Holdings Ltd. pursuant to the reverse takeover acquisition of Hempsana Inc. and concurrent amalgamation of Hempsana with wholly owned 12954991 Canada Inc. ∎

Strand Oil & Gas Ltd. (Alta. 1978)
1986 – Continued into Canada.
Jan. 23, 1987 – Name changed to Bowtex Energy (Canada) Corporation; basis 1 new for 5 old shs. ∎

Strand Resources Inc. (B.C. July 17, 1986)
Oct. 24, 1996 – Formed Tri-Star Gold Corp. in Canada on amalgamation with Tri-Star Gold Corp. (5.21 for 1); basis 1 new for 1 old sh. ∎

Strat Nickel Mines Ltd. (Ont. 1956)
1959 – Name changed to West Range Iron Mines Ltd. ∎

Strata Energy Corporation (B.C. June 12, 1979)
July 20, 1987 – Name changed to U.S. Platinum Inc. ∎

Strata Minerals Inc. (Can. Feb. 7, 2008)
July 10, 2017 – Name changed to Revival Gold Inc. (see FPsurvey - Mines & Energy)

Strata-X Energy Ltd. (B.C. Oct. 11, 2012)
Feb. 25, 2021 – Name changed to Pure Energy Hydrogen Corporation Limited pursuant to the reverse takeover acquisition of Australia-based Real Energy Corporation Limited. ∎

Strata-X Ltd. (Alta. June 18, 2007)
Oct. 11, 2012 – Continued into British Columbia.
Oct. 12, 2012 – Name changed to Strata-X Energy Ltd. ∎

Stratabound Minerals Corp. (Alta. Mar. 5, 1986)
Jan. 23, 2024 – Name changed to Lode Gold Resources Inc. (see FPsurvey - Mines & Energy)

Stratacom Technology Inc. (B.C. Dec. 30, 1987)
Mar. 30, 2005 – Name changed to Strategic Oil & Gas Ltd. following reverse takeover, via a farm-out agreement, of two joint venture oil and gas companies. ∎

StrataGold Corporation (B.C. Apr. 15, 2003)
June 9, 2009 – Acquired by Victoria Gold Corp.; basis 0.1249 Victoria Gold shs. for 1 StrataGold sh. (see Victoria Gold Corp.)
Name changed to Victoria Gold (Yukon) Corp. (see Victoria Gold Corp.)

Strataprop Investments Ltd. (Alta. June 3, 1987)
Oct. 28, 1991 – Name changed to Allied Equities Ltd.; basis 1 new for 3 old shs. ∎

Stratcomm Media, Ltd. (B.C. Feb. 24, 1984)
Nov. 12, 1997 – Continued into Yukon.
July 5, 2003 – Dissolved.

Strateco Resources Inc. (Can. Apr. 13, 2000)
June 9, 2015 – Filed for protection under the Companies' Creditors Arrangement Act (CCAA) and Ernst & Young Inc. appointed monitor.
Apr. 30, 2021 – CCAA proceedings terminated and Ernst & Young Inc. discharged as monitor. All remaining officers and directors resigned.
May 10, 2021 – Filed an assignment under the Bankruptcy and Insolvency Act (BIA). Ernst & Young Inc. was appointed trustee.

Strategic Communications Ltd. (B.C. Feb. 24, 1984)
July 5, 1991 – Name changed to Stratcomm Media, Ltd.; basis 1 new for 5 old shs. ∎

Strategic Data Inc. (Alta. Apr. 8, 1994)
Jan. 17, 1997 – Name changed to Strategic Data Ltd.; basis 1 new for 4 old shs. (see FPsurvey - Industrials)

Strategic Energy Fund (Ont. Feb. 14, 2002)
Feb. 24, 2009 – Converted from a closed end fund to an open-ended fund.

Strategic Exploration (Strex) Inc. (Can. Sept. 12, 1986)
July 23, 2009 – Dissolved.

Strategic Income Allocation Fund (Ont. Jan. 27, 2012)
Mar. 24, 2017 – Voluntarily wound-up and dissolved. Net assets distributed to unitholders; basis unknown.

Strategic Merchant Bancorp Ltd. (B.C. Sept. 12, 1996)
Aug. 2, 2006 – Name changed to Strategic Nevada Resources Corp. ∎

Strategic Metals Corporation (B.C. Dec. 18, 1981 amalg.)
Mar. 29, 1982 – Amalgamated with Pan Arctic Explorations Ltd. to form Consolidated Strategic Metals; basis 3 new for 4 old shs.

Strategic Nevada Resources Corp. (B.C. Sept. 12, 1996)
Feb. 26, 2007 – Name changed to SNS Silver Corp. ∎

Strategic Oil & Gas Ltd. (B.C. Dec. 30, 1987)
Sept. 9, 2010 – Continued into Alberta.
Jan. 28, 2020 – Placed into receivership by secured creditor. KPMG Inc. appointed receiver of the Alberta assets and Alvarez and Marsal Canada Inc. was appointed receiver over the Northwest Territory assets. All officers and directors resigned.

Strategic Resource Acquisition Corporation (Ont. Sept. 25, 2006)
Apr. 21, 2011 – Name changed to Portex Minerals Inc. (see FPsurvey - Industrials)

Strategic Resources Inc. (Ont. Oct. 25, 2004)
June 7, 2016 – Continued into British Columbia. (see FPsurvey - Mines & Energy)

Strategic Technologies Inc. (B.C. May 4, 1984)
Oct. 24, 2006 – Name changed to Wireless2 Technologies Inc. ∎

Strategic Value Corporation (Ont. June 11, 1956)
June 13, 2000 – Acquired by Nova Bancorp Group (Canada) Ltd. for $3.25 per sh.

Strategic Vista International Inc. (Ont. Sept. 25, 1979)
Mar. 20, 2006 – Name changed to LOREX Technology Inc. ∎

StrategyWeb Communications Inc. (Alta. Aug. 19, 1993)
Feb. 2, 2007 – Struck from registry and dissolved.

Stratford Metals Limited (Que. 1951)
May 25, 1974 – Dissolved.

Stratford Software Corporation (B.C. Oct. 2, 1983)
Sept. 1991 – Entered voluntary bankruptcy.
Jan. 24, 1992 – Following realization of certain estate assets the trustee made an interim distribution of 100% to preferred creditors and 95% to unsecured creditors.
Jan. 28, 1993 – Name changed to Bow Flex, Inc. and continued into Washington following amalgamation with Bow Flex of America, Inc.; basis 1 new for 3.5 old shs. ∎

Stratford Ventures Ltd. (B.C. Oct. 22, 1980)
Aug. 29, 1997 – Name changed to MRC Metall Resources Corp. ∎

Strathagami Mines Inc. (Ohio 1960)
Dec. 1965 – Dissolved. Assets acquired by Cliffs of Canada Ltd.

Strathclair Ventures Ltd. (B.C. May 15, 1998)
May 28, 2003 – Name changed to SilverCrest Mines Inc. pursuant to reverse takeover acquisition of 4023307 Canada Inc. ∎

Strathcona Brewing Investments Inc. (Alta. Feb. 14, 1991)
Aug. 1, 1994 – Dissolved and struck off register.

Strathcona Mines Ltd. (Ont. 1959)
Sept. 8, 1966 – Dissolved.

Strathcona Resource Industries Ltd. (Alta. May 23, 1957)
May 24, 1988 – Name changed to Clarepine Industries Inc. ∎

Strathfield Oil & Gas Ltd. (Alta. Jan. 26, 1983)
Jan. 7, 1992 – Acquired by Inverness Petroleum Ltd.; basis 0.925 Inverness com. shs. for 1 Strathfield com. sh. and 1.48 Inverness com. shs. or ser. 3 pref. shs. or $10 for 1 Strathfield 7% cl. C pref. sh. (see Inverness Petroleum Ltd.)

Strathmore Gold Mines Ltd. (Ont. 1938)
1947 – Name changed to Strathmore Mines Ltd. and continued into Ontario. ∎

Strathmore Minerals Corp. (B.C. May 5, 1993)
Sept. 9, 2013 – Acquired by Energy Fuels Inc.; basis 1.47 Energy com. shs. for 1 Strathmore com. sh.

Strathmore Mines Ltd. (Ont. 1947)
Sept. 28, 1964 – Dissolved.

Strathmore Plus Energy Corp. (B.C. May 8, 2007)
Sept. 26, 2022 – Name changed to Strathmore Plus Uranium Corp. (see FPsurvey - Mines & Energy)

Strathmore Resources Ltd. (B.C. May 5, 1993)
Sept. 19, 2000 – Name changed to Strathmore Minerals Corp.; basis 1 new for 5 old shs. ∎

Strathy Basin Mines Ltd. (Ont. 1934)
Sept. 2, 1963 – Dissolved.

Stratic Energy Corporation (Ont. Dec. 12, 1997 amalg.)
Sept. 17, 1998 – Continued into Yukon.
Jan. 1, 2007 – Amalgamated in Yukon to continue with same name.
Nov. 9, 2010 – Acquired by EnQuest plc; basis 0.089626 EnQuest shs. for 1 Stratic sh.

Stratmin Inc. (Can. Sept. 12, 1986)
June 27, 1996 – Name changed to Strategic Exploration (Strex) Inc. ∎

Stratos BioTechnologies Inc. (B.C. July 2, 1999)
June 19, 2003 – Amalgamated with Brightwave Ventures Inc. (0.3424 for 1) and Nucleus BioScience Inc. (0.3319 for 1) to continue as SNB Capital Corp. (formerly Brightwave); basis 0.3333 new SNB com. sh. for 1 old Stratos com. sh. (see SNB Capital Corp.)

Stratos Global Corporation (Can. May 28, 1996)
Dec. 14, 2007 – Acquired by CIP Canada Investment Inc. for $7.00 per sh.

Stratton Capital Corp. (Ont. Apr. 8, 2011)
Oct. 19, 2016 – Name changed to Millennial Esports Corp. pursuant to Qualifying Transaction reverse takeover acquisition of Pro Gaming League Inc.; basis 1 new for 4 old shs. ∎

Stratton Resources Inc. (B.C. Oct. 11, 1985)
Mar. 15, 2017 – Name changed to Torq Resources Inc. (see FPsurvey - Mines & Energy)

Stratum Resources Ltd. (Alta. Jan. 7, 1966)
July 1, 1993 – Dissolved and struck off register.

Straw Lake Beach Gold Mines Ltd. (Ont. Aug. 21, 1934)
Placed into liquidation; no record of equity for shldrs.

Stray Horse Resources Inc. (B.C. May 23, 1972)
July 28, 1987 – Name changed to Oriole Communications Inc. ∎

Stream Communications Network and Media Inc. (B.C. Mar. 28, 1979)
Dec. 22, 2011 – Dissolved and struck from register. ∎

Stream Communications Network, Inc. (B.C. Mar. 28, 1979)
Aug. 17, 2004 – Name changed to Stream Communications Network and Media Inc. ∎

Stream Oil & Gas Ltd. (B.C. Jan. 11, 2005)
Nov. 21, 2014 – Acquired by TransAtlantic Petroleum Ltd.; basis 0.05657 TransAtlantic com. shs. for 1 Stream Oil sh. (see TransAtlantic Petroleum Ltd.)

Stream Ventures Inc. (Ont. Jan. 31, 2000)
Dec. 15, 2015 – Name changed to Beleave Inc. following reverse takeover acquisition of First Access Medical Inc.; basis 1 new for 10 old shs. ∎

Streamline Web Broadcasting Inc. (B.C. Oct. 16, 1997)
May 17, 2005 – Name changed to Kavalmedia Services Ltd.; basis 1 new for 3 old shs. ∎

Streamside Resources Inc. (Ont. Apr. 30, 1974)
Aug. 16, 1982 – Charter cancelled.
June 23, 1983 – Charter revived.
Oct. 14, 1987 – Name changed to Ring Sights Worldwide Inc.; basis 1 new for 5 old shs. ∎

Street Capital Group Inc. (Ont. Dec. 31, 1988 amalg.)
Oct. 22, 2019 – Acquired by RFA Capital Holdings Inc.; basis 68¢ cash per sh.

Street Resources Inc. (Ont. June 25, 2002 amalg.)
July 14, 2005 – Continued into British Columbia.
July 18, 2005 – Name changed to EXMIN Resources Inc. ∎

Streetlight Intelligence Inc. (Alta. Mar. 25, 2003)
Sept. 2, 2015 – Struck from registry and dissolved.

The Streetwear Corporation (Ont. Jan. 21, 1999 amalg.)
Aug. 25, 2015 – Name changed to BitRush Corp. following reverse takeover acquisition of MezzaCap GmbH. (see FPsurvey - Industrials)

Stressgen Biotechnologies Corporation (B.C. Apr. 5, 1990)
June 9, 2001 – Continued into Yukon.
Mar. 23, 2003 – Continued into Canada.
Mar. 23, 2006 – Name changed to GVIC Publications Ltd. ∎

Stressgen Biotechnologies Corporation (B.C. Jan. 27, 2006)
June 7, 2006 – Name changed to Nventa Biopharmaceuticals Corporation. ∎

Stria Capital Inc. (Can. May 24, 2011)
May 9, 2014 – Name changed to Stria Lithium Inc. (see FPsurvey - Mines & Energy; FPsurvey - Industrials)

Stride Exploration and Development Co. Ltd. (Alta. 1956)
Oct. 15, 1960 – Struck off register.

Strike Capital Corp. (Alta. July 28, 2003)
Dec. 13, 2004 – Name changed to Strike Petroleum Ltd. following Qualifying Transaction acquisition of 591536 Alberta Ltd. ∎

Strike Diamond Corp. (B.C. Jan. 8, 2008)
Mar. 15, 2016 – Name changed to Sunvest Minerals Corp.; basis 1 new for 10 old shs. ∎

Strike Energy Inc. (Can. Aug. 3, 1988)
July 6, 1994 – Amalgamated with Battle Creek Developments Ltd. to form new co. with same name Strike Energy Inc.; basis 1.2 new for 1 Battle Creek sh. and 1 new for 1 Strike Energy sh. (see Strike Energy Inc.)

Strike Energy Inc. (Alta. July 1, 1994 amalg.)
May 24, 1996 – Acquired by Tarragon Oil and Gas Limited; basis 1 Tarragon sh. for 3.68 Strike shs. (see Tarragon Oil and Gas Limited)

Strike Gold Corp. (B.C. Jan. 8, 2008)
Jan. 26, 2012 – Name changed to Strike Graphite Corp. ∎

Strike Graphite Corp. (B.C. Jan. 8, 2008)
Nov. 21, 2014 – Name changed to Strike Diamond Corp. ∎

Strike Minerals Inc. (Ont. May 21, 1987)
Nov. 29, 2016 – Filed a notice of intention to make a proposal under the Bankruptcy and Insolvency Act (BIA) and A. Farber & Partners Inc. appointed proposal trustee.
May 10, 2017 – Majority of assets sold to 2549304 Ontario Inc., a wholly owned subsid. of Waterton Global Value L.P., for an undisclosed amount. (see FPsurvey - Mines & Energy)

Strike Petroleum Ltd. (Alta. July 28, 2003)
May 30, 2007 – Acquired by FairWest Energy Corp.; basis 0.5562 new FairWest shs. for 1 old Strike sh. (see FairWest Energy Corporation)

Strike Resources Ltd. (B.C. June 2, 2004)
Sept. 20, 2006 – Name changed to Cleanfield Alternative Energy Inc. following Qualifying Transaction reverse takeover acquisition of Cleanfield Energy Corp. ∎

Strike Uranium Mines Ltd. (Ont. 1952)
Nov. 9, 1959 – Dissolved.

StrikePoint Gold Inc. (Alta. Nov. 5, 1982)
Aug. 12, 2015 – Continued into British Columbia. (see FPsurvey - Mines & Energy)

Striker Exploration Corp. (Alta. Mar. 29, 2000)
July 29, 2017 – Acquired by Gear Energy Ltd.; basis 2.325 Gear com. shs. for 1 Striker com. sh. (see Gear Energy Ltd.)

Strikezone Minerals (Canada) Ltd. (B.C. Sept. 28, 1987)
Jan. 31, 2006 – Name changed to Gold World Resources Inc.; basis 1 new for 5.5 old shs. ∎

Strom Resources Ltd. (Alta. 1979)
1981 – Acquired by Penn West Petroleum Ltd.; basis 2 Penn West com. shs., 8 cl. A shs. and 1 wt. for each 6 Strom shs. (see Penn West Petroleum Ltd.)

Strong Equipment Corporation (Ont. July 26, 1946)
Dec. 31, 1997 – Name changed to Strongco Inc. ∎

Strong Global Entertainment, Inc. (B.C. Nov. 9, 2021)
Sept. 30, 2024 – Merged into Fundamental Global Inc.; basis 1.5 Fundamental Global shs. for 1 Strong Global cl. A com. vtg. sh.

Strongbow Exploration Inc. (Can. May 4, 2004 amalg.)
July 27, 2020 – Name changed to Cornish Metals Inc. (see FPsurvey - Mines & Energy)

Strongbow Resources Inc. (B.C. Mar. 31, 1981)
May 4, 2004 – Formed Strongbow Exploration Inc. in Canada on amalgamation with Navigator Exploration Corp. with Strongbow Resources the deemed acquiror; basis 0.7 new for 1 Navigator sh. and 1 new for 2 Strongbow Resources shs. ∎

Strongco Corporation (Ont. Mar. 23, 2010)
Mar. 20, 2020 – Acquired by a wholly owned subsid. of Nors S.A.; basis $3.15 cash per sh.

Strongco Income Fund (Ont. Mar. 21, 2005)
July 1, 2010 – Succeeded by Strongco Corporation pursuant to plan of arrangement whereby Strongco Corporation was formed to facilitate the conversion of the fund into a corporation and the fund was subsequently dissolved. ■

Strongco Inc. (Ont. July 26, 1946)
May 10, 2005 – Plan of Arrangement to convert company to an income fund named Strongco Income Fund; basis 1 new unit for 1 com. sh. (see Strongco Income Fund)

Strongford Asbestos Mines Limited (Ont. 1951)
June 1962 – Charter cancelled.

Stronghold Metals Inc. (B.C. Oct. 16, 2003)
July 26, 2012 – Name changed to Eagle Mountain Gold Corp.; basis 1 new for 5 old shs. ■

Structure Oil & Gas Co. Ltd. (Can. 1929)
Mar. 1931 – Went into liquidation; nothing available for shldrs.

Structured Biologicals Inc. (Can. May 7, 1993 amalg.)
Dec. 19, 1996 – Formed Ben-Abraham Technologies Inc. in Wyoming on amalgamation with Ben-Abraham Technologies Inc., constituting a reverse takeover of Structured Biologicals by Ben-Abraham; basis 1 subord. vtg. sh. for 3.5 com. shs. ■

Stryker Resources Ltd. (B.C. Apr. 7, 1952)
Sept. 12, 1997 – Name changed to Stryker Ventures Corp.; basis 1 new for 10 old shs. ■

Stryker Ventures Corp. (B.C. Apr. 7, 1952)
Nov. 30, 2021 – Name changed to Global Carbon Credit Corp. (see FPsurvey - Mines & Energy)

Stuart Energy Systems Corporation (Can. June 25, 1948)
Aug. 12, 1986 – Continued into Ontario. (see Hydrogenics Corporation)
July 28, 2000 – Continued into Canada. (see Hydrogenics Corporation)
Feb. 17, 2005 – Acquired by Hydrogenics Corporation; basis 0.74 new Hydrogenics sh. for 1 old Stuart sh. (see Hydrogenics Corporation)

Stuart House International Limited (Can. 1946)
Dec. 1984 – Reverted to status of private co. following an offer of $5.00 per sh. to minority shldrs. Name subsequently changed to Stuart House Canada Ltd.

Stuart Olson Inc. (Alta. Dec. 31, 1987 amalg.)
Sept. 25, 2020 – Acquired by Bird Construction Inc.; basis 0.02006051 Bird com. sh. for 1 sh. held.

Student Transportation Inc. (Ont. Sept. 22, 2004)
May 2, 2018 – All o/s com. shs. not already held acquired by Spinner Can Acquireco Inc., an affiliate of Caisse de dépôt et placement du Québec and Ullico Inc.; basis US$7.50 cash per com. sh.
Oct. 31, 2018 – Dissolved and struck from register.

Student Transportation of America Ltd. (Ont. Sept. 22, 2004)
Nov. 19, 2009 – Name changed to Student Transportation Inc. ■

Studer Gold Mines Ltd. (Sask. 1949)
Feb. 1957 – Name changed to Studer Mines Ltd.; basis 1 new for 1 old sh.

Studio Andre Perry Inc. (Que. 1974)
Nov. 20, 1987 – Name changed to Groupe André Perry Incorporated. (see FPsurvey - Industrials)

Stump Lake Metal Mines Ltd. (B.C. 1953)
Mar. 3, 1971 – Struck off register.

Sturdy Mines Ltd. (Ont. 1955)
Mar. 14, 1978 – Charter cancelled.

Sturgeon Aurora Mines Ltd. (Ont. Oct. 19, 1934)
1951 – Sold property to Don Malartic Gold Mines in 1938; basis 5 new escrowed shs. for 1 old sh. Charter cancelled.

Sturgeon Goldfields, Ltd. (Que. 1934)
Oct. 13, 1973 – Dissolved.

Sturgeon King Mining Corp. Ltd. (Ont. 1970)
May 1972 – Amalgamated into Bayfor Corp. Inc.; basis 2 new for 11 old shs.

Sturgeon Petroleums Ltd. (Alta. Sept. 16, 1950)
Sept. 27, 1994 – Dissolved and struck off register.

Sturgeon River Gold Mines Ltd. (Ont. Aug. 22, 1934)
1955 – Name changed to Sturgeon River Mines Ltd. ■

Sturgeon River Mines Ltd. (Ont. Aug. 22, 1934)
1964 – Name changed to Quebec Sturgeon River Mines Limited; basis 1 new for 4 old shs. ■

Sturgex Mines Limited (Ont. 1970)
July 31, 1974 – Amalgamated with Royex Mining Ltd. to form Royex Sturgex Mining Limited; basis 1 new for 1.7 old shs.

Stylus Energy Inc. (Alta. Mar. 1, 2005 amalg.)
Aug. 30, 2007 – Acquired by Compton Petroleum Corporation for $2.70 per sh.
Mar. 26, 2009 – Dissolved.

Stynro Development Ltd. (B.C. 1972)
Oct. 8, 1976 – Name changed to Syn-Trac Industries Ltd.

Subeo (Ont. 1966)
Mar. 1976 – Charter cancelled.

Subloo International Resource Corporation (B.C. Aug. 7, 1979)
Aug. 29, 1994 – Continued into Canada.
Oct. 7, 1996 – Name changed to Goldminco Mining Corp. ■

Submarine Oil and Gas Ltd. (Ont. 1955)
1960 – Acquired by Camerina Petroleum Corp.; basis 4 new for 10 old shs. (see Camerina Petroleum Corp.)

Subscribe Technologies Inc. (Ont. Sept. 13, 2010)
Mar. 21, 2018 – Continued into British Columbia.
Feb. 28, 2020 – Name changed to VPN Technologies Inc. ■

Suburban Realty Trust (Que. 1961)
Dec. 1976 – Proceeds from sale of assets have been distributed to certificate holders. Approx. 91% of face value was pd. with final payment made.

Subversive Acquisition LP (Ont. Nov. 12, 2019)
Apr. 26, 2021 – Acquired by InterCure Ltd. constituting Subversive's Qualifying Transaction; basis 1 ord. sh. for each lp unit.

Subversive Capital Acquisition Corp. (B.C. June 17, 2019)
Jan. 15, 2021 – Name changed to TPCO Holding Corp. pursuant to the Qualifying Acquisition of CMG Partners, Inc. (Caliva) and Left Coast Ventures, Inc. ■

Subversive Real Estate Acquisition REIT LP (Ont. Nov. 12, 2019)
Feb. 22, 2021 – Name changed to Subversive Acquisition LP. ■

Success Mines Ltd. (Ont. 1960)
Sept. 8, 1966 – Dissolved.

Sudamet Ventures Inc. (Can. June 19, 1997)
May 5, 2005 – Name changed to Avigo Resources Corp.; basis 1 new for 2 old shs. ■

Sudbay Berylium Mines Ltd. (Ont. 1952)
Aug. 19, 1965 – Dissolved.

Sudbay Exploration & Mining Ltd. (Ont. 1952)
Apr. 1960 – Name changed to Sudbay Berylium Mines Ltd. ■

Sudbury Basin Mines Ltd. (Ont. 1928)
1943 – Wound up. Distribution equivalent to 1 sh. Ventures Ltd. and 3 shs. Ontario Pyrites Ltd. for 3 old shs.

Sudbury Capital Corporation (Ont. June 17, 2005)
Mar. 18, 2008 – Name changed to NiCo Mining Limited following Qualifying Transaction reverse takeover acquisition of NiCo Mining Corp.; basis 1 new for 10 old shs. ■

Sudbury Contact Mines, Limited (Ont. Oct. 11, 1927)
Feb. 11, 1999 – Amalgamated in Ontario to continue with same name.
Sept. 3, 2004 – Name changed to Contact Diamond Corporation. ■

Sudbury Midzone Mines Ltd. (Ont. 1952)
1955 – Merged into Midrim Mining Co. Ltd.; basis 1 new for 2 old shs.

Sudbury Northrim Exploration Co. Ltd. (Ont. 1952)
1955 – Merged into Midrim Mining Co. Ltd.; basis 1 new for 3 old shs.

Sudbury Offsets Ltd. (unknown)
1938 – Assets acquired by Nickel Offsets Ltd.; basis 1 new for 5 old shs. (see Nickel Offsets, Limited)

Sudbury Onoman Pyrites Ltd. (Ont. 1952)
Mar. 10, 1958 – Dissolved.

Sudbury Platinum Corporation (B.C. Sept. 9, 2013)
Nov. 23, 2020 – Name changed to SPC Nickel Corp. (see FPsurvey - Mines & Energy)

Sudbury Shepherd Nickel Co. Ltd. (Ont. 1948)
Assets distributed and charter surrendered.

Sudnor Mining Co. Ltd. (Ont. 1964)
Mar. 7, 1977 – Charter cancelled.

Sudonta Gold Mines Ltd. (Ont. 1945)
May 26, 1958 – Dissolved.

Sudore Gold Mines Ltd. (Ont. 1946)
Nov. 10, 1966 – Dissolved.

Suez Petroleum Corporation (B.C. 1978)
Apr. 29, 1987 – Name changed to Overseas Platinum Corporation. ■

Sugar Creek Oil & Gas Inc. (Alta. July 6, 1987)
June 5, 1990 – Amalgamated with Moreland Oil & Gas Ltd. (0.632 for 1) to continue with the same name Sugar Creek Oil & Gas Inc.; basis 1 new for 1 old sh.
June 19, 1992 – Amalgamated with Petrostar Petroleums Inc. to form new co. with same name Petrostar Petroleums Inc.; basis 1 new for 1 Petrostar sh. and 1 new for 4.75 Sugar Creek shs.

SugarBud Craft Growers Corp. (Alta. Mar. 30, 2006 amalg.)
May 30, 2023 – Assets acquired by Connect First Credit Union Ltd. via proceedings under the Companies' Creditors Arrangement Act for an undisclosed amount. The transaction provided release from the secured indebtedness owed to Connect First plus cash to satisfy certain priority payables. There were no funds available for any other creditors or shdlrs.

Sugarloaf Mineral Resources Ltd. (Ont. Sept. 22, 1989)
Oct. 18, 1993 – Name changed to Weaver Lake Explorations Ltd. ■

Sujuron Ltd. (unknown)
1967 – Acquired by Montex Apparel Industries Ltd. (see Montex Apparel Industries Ltd.)

Sukari Ventures Corp. (B.C. Aug. 24, 2007)
Mar. 31, 2010 – Name changed to Gravis Energy Corp. pursuant to acquisition of Gravis Capital Corporation. ■

Sukuma Explorations Ltd. (B.C. Aug. 17, 1987)
Aug. 29, 1991 – Name changed to S.M.A. Resources Ltd.; basis 1 new for 3 old shs. ■

Sulgas Properties Ltd. (B.C. 1951)
Mar. 1957 – Name changed to Ecstall Mining Co. Ltd. ■

Sullico Mines Ltd. (Que. 1950)
1969 – Merged into Sullivan Mining Group Ltd.

Sullico Resources Ltd. (Ont. 1956)
June 23, 1982 – Name changed to Sullivan Resources Ltd.

Sulliden Exploration Inc. (Que. Nov. 20, 1985)
Oct. 15, 2009 – Name changed to Sulliden Gold Corporation Ltd. ■

Sulliden Gold Corporation Ltd. (Que. Nov. 20, 1985)
Aug. 11, 2014 – Acquired by Rio Alto Mining Limited; basis 0.525 Rio Alto com. shs. and 0.10 Sulliden Mining com. shs. for 1 Sulliden Gold com. sh. (see Rio Alto Mining Limited)

Sullimaque Goldfields Ltd. (Ont. 1946)
July 9, 1969 – Charter cancelled.

Sullivan-Bourlamaque Gold Mines Ltd. (Que. 1937)
Aug. 1973 – Charter cancelled.

Sullivan Consolidated Mines Ltd. (Que. Mar. 5, 1932)
Nov. 1968 – Name changed to Sullivan Mines Ltd. ■

Sullivan Mines Inc. (Que. 1969 amalg.)
Oct. 1987 – Amalgamated with a wholly owned subsid. of Cambior Inc. Public shldrs. received one pref. sh. subsequently redeemed at $7.50 per sh. for 1 old Sullivan sh. (see Cambior Inc.)

Sullivan Mines Ltd. (Que. Mar. 5, 1932)
Sept. 2, 1969 – Merged into Sullivan Mining Group Ltd.; basis 1 new for 1 old sh. (see Sullivan Mining Group Ltd.)

Sullivan Mining Group Ltd. (Que. 1969 amalg.)
July 1, 1983 – Amalgamated with East Sullivan Mines Limited to form Sullivan Mines Inc.; sh.-for-sh. basis for both cos. (see Sullivan Mines Inc.)

Sulpetro Limited (Alta. 1966)
Oct. 31, 1981 – Amalgamated with CanDel Oil Ltd. ($44.50 per sh.) to form new co. with same name Sulpetro Limited.
July 5, 1988 – Assets sold to Esso Resources Canada Limited. Nothing left for shldrs.

Sulpetro of Canada Ltd. (Alta. 1966)
Dec. 8, 1978 – Name changed to Sulpetro Limited. ■

Sulphurets Gold Corporation (B.C. 1986)
Dec. 14, 1989 – Acquired by PDI Acquisition Corp., a wholly owned subsid. of Placer Dome Inc., for 95¢ per sh. (see Placer Dome Inc.)

Sulphurok Mines Ltd. (B.C. 1968)
Jan. 1975 – Charter cancelled.

Sultan Minerals Inc. (B.C. Sept. 6, 1989 amalg.)
July 18, 2016 – Name changed to Apex Resources Inc.; basis 1 new for 10 old shs. (see FPsurvey - Mines & Energy)

Sultana Silver Mines Ltd. (B.C. 1968)
Jan. 31, 1977 – Dissolved.

Sumac Explorations Ltd. (Ont. 1959)
1960 – Name changed to Dayjon Explorers Ltd. ■

Sumac Ventures Inc. (B.C. 1983)
Apr. 16, 1993 – Dissolved and struck off register.

Sumach Resources Inc. (Ont. 1948)
Aug. 28, 1989 – Dissolved.

Sumburgh Developments Limited (Can. 1972)
Oct. 2, 1984 – Formed Access Banking Network Inc. in Canada on amalgamation with Access Banking Network Inc. (1 for 1); basis 1 new for 2 old shs. ■

Summa Silver Corp. (B.C. Mar. 7, 2018)
Aug. 6, 2025 – Acquired by Silver47 Exploration Corp.; basis 0.452 Silver47 shs. for 1 Summa Silver sh.

Summerwood Industries Inc. (Alta. June 11, 1996)
Sept. 17, 1998 – Formed Recycled Solutions for Industry Inc. in Alberta on amalgamation with Recycled Solutions for Industry Inc., constituting a reverse takeover by Recycled Solutions. ■

Summex Mines Ltd. (B.C. Mar. 19, 1984)
Oct. 15, 1997 – Continued into Yukon. (see FPsurvey - Mines & Energy)

Summit Diversified Ltd. (Ont. 1969 amalg.)
Aug. 30, 1978 – Amalgamated with Xtra Developments Ltd. into Sumtra Diversified Inc.; basis 2 new for 3 old shs.

Summit Explorations & Holdings Ltd. (Ont. 1969 amalg.)
Mar. 3, 1972 – Name changed to Summit Diversified Ltd. ■

Summit Gold Mines Inc. (Ont. 1973)
June 7, 1993 – Amalgamated with Paragon Entertainment Corporation (1 new for 1 old sh.), to continue as Paragon Entertainment Corp.; basis 1 new for 5 old shs. (see Paragon Entertainment Corporation)

Summit Industrial Income REIT (Ont. Dec. 31, 2005)
Feb. 22, 2023 – Acquired by Dream Summit Industrial LP; basis $23.50 cash per trust unit.

Summit Mine Ltd. (B.C. 1947)
Apr. 2, 1952 – Struck off register.

Summit Oils Ltd. (unknown)
Oct. 2, 1972 – Amalgamated with Western Homes Ltd. to form Summit Resources Ltd.; basis 1 new for 4 old shs.

Summit Pass Resources Corp. (B.C. 1979)
July 12, 1982 – Formed Oklahoma Crude Ltd. in British Columbia on amalgamation with Kansas Petroleum Energy Inc. and Oklahoma Crude Ltd.; basis 1 new for 3 old shs. ■

Summit Real Estate Investment Trust (Ont. Jan. 1, 1996)
Jan. 26, 2007 – Formed ING Summit Industrial Fund LP following acquisition by ING Real Estate Canada Trust following redemption by Summit of outstanding trust and debenture securities; basis Cdn$30.00 cash per unit and Cdn$30.00 cash per debenture.

Summit Resources Limited (Alta. Oct. 2, 1972)
Aug. 1, 2002 – Acquired by Paramount Resources Ltd. for $7.40 per sh.

Summit Ventures Inc. (B.C. 1983)
Aug. 22, 1986 – Name changed to Sumac Ventures Inc. ■

Summo Minerals Corporation (B.C. July 23, 1987)
June 21, 2002 – Continued into Canada.
July 19, 2002 – Name changed to Constellation Copper Corporation. ■

Summus Capital Corp. (Alta. Dec. 17, 2007)
Feb. 4, 2011 – Name changed to Mongolia Growth Group Ltd.; basis 1 new for 2 old shs. (see FPsurvey - Industrials)

Sumner Sports Inc. (Que. 1979)
Nov. 21, 1994 – Declared bankrupt, PricewaterhouseCoopers Inc. (formerly Price Waterhouse Limited) in Quebec City was appointed trustee and receiver.
May 1995 – All assets sold, there were no funds available for distribution to shldrs.
Jan. 21, 2000 – PricewaterhouseCoopers discharged as trustee and receiver and there was no distributions made to creditors.

Sumtra Diversified Inc. (Ont. Aug. 30, 1978 amalg.)
Nov. 15, 2018 – Name changed to MJardin Group, Inc. following reverse takeover acquisition of MJAR Holdings Corp. ■

Sun Bear Mines Ltd. (Ont. 1932)
Mar. 1976 – Charter cancelled.

Sun City Ventures Inc. (Alta. Sept. 18, 1987)
May 4, 1995 – Name changed to Conor Pacific Environmental Technologies Inc.; basis 1 new for 10 old shs. ■

Sun Company, Inc. (unknown 1901)
1971 – Continued into Pennsylvania.
Nov. 9, 1998 – Name changed to Sunoco, Inc.

Sun-Dar Energy Corp. (B.C. May 4, 1966)
Sept. 25, 1990 – Dissolved and struck off register.

Sun Devil Gold Corp. (B.C. Dec. 31, 1985)
May 13, 1999 – Name changed to Cardero Resource Corp. ■

Sun Entertainment Holding Corporation (B.C. Apr. 2, 1986)
Dec. 8, 2014 – Privatized. All o/s com. shs. held by minority shareholders redeemed for 10¢ per sh.

Sun Free Enterprises Ltd. (B.C. Aug. 25, 1987)
Feb. 20, 2004 – Dissolved for failure to file and struck from register.

Sun God Resources Ltd. (B.C. June 2, 1981)
Apr. 14, 1986 – Name changed to Infotec Industries Inc. ■

Sun-Gold Developments International Corporation (B.C. 1986)
Jan. 15, 1993 – Charter cancelled.
Nov. 1, 1993 – Charter revived.
Jan. 26, 1994 – Name changed to Gridiron Resources Ltd.; basis 1 new for 3 old shs. (see FPsurvey - Mines & Energy)

Sun Gro Horticulture Income Fund (B.C. Feb. 12, 2002)
Dec. 31, 2010 – Succeeded by Sun Gro Horticulture Inc. pursuant to plan of arrangement whereby Sun Gro Horticulture Inc. was formed to facilitate the conversion of the fund into a corporation and the fund was subsequently dissolved. ■

Sun Gro Horticulture Inc. (Can. Mar. 13, 2010)
Mar. 10, 2011 – Acquired by IKO Enterprises Ltd. for $6.60 per sh.

Sun Ice Limited (Alta. June 6, 1976)
Feb. 6, 2004 – Name changed to Sylre Ltd. ■

Sun Life Capital Trust (Ont. Aug. 9, 2001)
Jan. 3, 2012 – Redeemed all ser.A cap. secs. for $34.325 per sec.

Sun Life Financial Services of Canada Inc. (Can. Aug. 5, 1999)
July 4, 2003 – Name changed to Sun Life Financial Inc. (see FPsurvey - Industrials)

Sun Media Corporation (Ont. Oct. 3, 1996 amalg.)
Dec. 15, 1997 – New public offering made at $13.50 per sh.
Jan. 15, 1999 – Acquired by Quebecor Inc. for $21 per sh.

Sun Metals Corp. (B.C. Oct. 15, 2008)
Mar. 9, 2021 – Acquired by NorthWest Copper Corp. (formerly Serengeti Resources Inc.); basis 0.215 NorthWest shs. for 1 Sun Metal sh.
Mar. 31, 2023 – Name changed to Tsayta Resources Corp.

Sun Publishing Company Limited (B.C. 1915)
July 27, 1978 – Amalgamated with its wholly owned subsid., F.P. Publications Ltd., to form F.P. Publications (Western) Limited. Cl. A and B shs. of Sun Publishing exchanged for pref. shs. of the new co. on a sh.-for-sh. basis. Such pref. shs. red. Aug. 15, 1978, at $69 per sh.

Sun Red Capital Corporation (Alta. Sept. 23, 2005)
May 31, 2010 – Amalgamated with Compass Acquisition Corp., a wholly owned subsid. of Compass Petroleum Ltd., constituting Sun Red's Qualifying Transaction; basis 1 Compass sh. for 40 Sun Red shs. (see Compass Petroleum Ltd.)

Sun River Gold Corp. (B.C. May 21, 1980)
Mar. 11, 1991 – Name changed to Yellow Point Mining Corp.; basis 1 new for 6 old shs. ■

Sun-Rype Products Ltd. (B.C. May 13, 1946)
Oct. 4, 2013 – Acquired by Great Pacific Industries Inc. for $7.50 per sh.

Sun Steamships Ltd. (Can. 1953)
Dec. 16, 1980 – Dissolved.

Sun Valley Gold Mines Ltd. (B.C. May 13, 1980)
Nov. 1, 1991 – Dissolved and struck off register.

Sun Valley, Id. and Red Lake Resources Ltd. (B.C. May 29, 1984)
Sept. 1, 1987 – Name changed to Red Lake and Sun Valley Resources Ltd. ■

Sun Valley Ranch Inc. (Ont. Apr. 24, 1967)
Mar. 25, 1991 – Name changed to Tri-Lateral Free Trade Inc. ■

Sun-West Minerals Ltd. (B.C. 1962)
July 8, 1974 – Charter cancelled.

Sunalta Energy Inc. (Alta. June 15, 1987)
July 26, 1996 – Acquired by 644073 Alberta Ltd. for 94¢ per sh.

Sunatco Development Corporation (B.C. 1959)
Jan. 11, 1991 – Formed International Sunatco Industries Ltd. in British Columbia on amalgamation with Burmah Mineral Corporation; basis 1 new for 3 old shs. ■

Sunbeam Exploration Co. Ltd. (Ont. 1946)
Dec. 30, 1970 – Dissolved.

Sunbelt Development Corp. (B.C. 1986)
Apr. 8, 1988 – Name changed to Plaser Light Corporation. ■

The SunBlush Technologies Corporation (B.C. July 10, 1986)
Dec. 31, 2003 – Name changed to FreshXtend Technologies Corp.; basis 1 new for 5 old shs. ■

Sunburst Exploration Limited (Ont. July 6, 1945)
Dec. 3, 1991 – Name changed to Sunburst Resources (1991) Inc.; basis 1 new for 10 old shs. ■

Sunburst M.C. Ltd. (Ont. July 6, 1945)
Jan. 10, 1997 – Name changed to Channel i Canada Inc. ■

Sunburst Oil & Gas Inc. (Alta. Mar. 18, 1994)
Mar. 1991 – Proposal made under the Bankruptcy and Insolvency Act which was rejected by its creditors.
May 6, 1999 – Company and wholly owned Western Canada Energy (1996) Ltd. were placed into bankruptcy and Edmonton-based Deloitte and Touche Inc. were appointed trustee.
2000 – Most of the assets had been sold.
Aug. 21, 2001 – Deloitte and Touche were discharged as trustee and unsecured creditors received a distribution of less than 10¢ on the dollar. There were no funds available for distribution to shldrs.

Sunburst Oil Co. Ltd. (Can. 1929)
1951 – Acquired by Newalta Petroleums Ltd.; basis 1 new for 4 old shs. (see Newalta Petroleums Ltd.)

Sunburst Petroleums Ltd. (B.C. Mar. 13, 1979)
Apr. 2, 1984 – Delisted from the Vancouver Stock Exchange. Subsequently dissolved for failure to file and struck from register.

Sunburst Resources (1991) Inc. (Ont. July 6, 1945)
Apr. 28, 1994 – Name changed to Sunburst M.C. Ltd. ■

Suncoast Petroleum Corp. (B.C. Mar. 14, 1980)
Aug. 29, 2017 – Dissolved for failure to file and struck from register.

Suncom Telecommunications Inc. (Can. Feb. 1, 1991)
June 11, 1999 – Name changed to VirtualSellers.com, Inc. ■

Suncor Energy Inc. (Can. Jan. 1, 1989 amalg.)
Aug. 1, 2009 – Amalgamated in Canada to continue with same name. (see FPsurvey - Mines & Energy; FPsurvey - Industrials)

Suncor Inc. (Can. Aug. 22, 1979 amalg.)
Jan. 1, 1989 – Amalgamated in Canada to continue with same name.
Apr. 18, 1997 – Name changed to Suncor Energy Inc. ■

Suncrest Capital Corporation (Alta. July 6, 1954)
July 6, 1993 – Name changed to Suncrest Energy Inc.; basis 1 new for 2 old shs. ■

Suncrest Energy Inc. (Alta. July 6, 1954)
Oct. 18, 1994 – Name changed to Nextra Technologies Inc.; basis 1 new for 3 old shs. ■

Sundance Energy Corporation (Alta. Apr. 8, 2011 amalg.)
June 18, 2014 – Formed Ceno Energy Ltd. in Alberta on amalgamation with (private) Ceno Energy Limited (deemed acquiror). ■

Sundance Energy Resources Limited (Can. Sept. 1979)
Mar. 1980 – Name changed to Sunmist Energy Resources Limited. ■

Sundance Gold Mining and Exploration Ltd. (B.C. 1979)
Nov. 6, 1985 – Name changed to Argrel Resources Ltd.; basis 1 new for 5 old shs. ■

Sundance Resources Inc. (Alta. Feb. 9, 1996)
Aug. 31, 2000 – Formed True Energy Inc. in Alberta on amalgamation with 887733 Alberta Ltd. and 851431 Alberta Ltd. with Sundance the deemed acquiror; basis 0.44 new for 1 old sh. ■

Sundance Resources Ltd. (B.C. May 3, 1966)
Aug. 23, 1995 – Name changed to Mammoth Energy Inc.; basis 1 new for 10 old shs. ■

Sundance Royalties Ltd. (Alta. 1937)
1941 – Merged with 8 other companies into Amalgamated Oils Limited; basis 85 new for 500 old shs.

Sundial Growers Inc. (Alta. Aug. 19, 2006)
July 26, 2022 – Name changed to SNDL Inc.; basis 1 new for 10 old shs. (see FPsurvey - Industrials)

Sundust Resources Inc. (Que. June 9, 1987)
Dec. 16, 2013 – Dissolved and struck from register.

Suneva Resources Limited (B.C. July 19, 1965)
Jan. 20, 1989 – Name changed to International Suneva Resources Ltd.; basis 1 new for 3.5 old shs. ■

Sunex International Resources Ltd. (B.C. 1969)
Mar. 31, 1983 – Struck off register.

Sunexco Energy Corporation (B.C. Feb. 28, 1979)
Jan. 16, 1986 – Name changed to Selena Research Corporation; basis 1 new for 4 old shs. ■

Sunfire Energy Corporation (Alta. Oct. 18, 1984)
July 14, 2003 – Acquired by TUSK Energy Inc. for $3.41 per sh. (see TUSK Energy Inc.)

Sungate Resources Ltd. (Can. 1952)
Oct. 14, 1983 – Amalgamated with Barrick Resources Corporation to form a new co. under the Barrick name. Each com. sh. of Sungate exch. for 0.1897397 1st pref. sh., ser. A, and 0.3890525 2nd pref. sh., ser. A.

Sungold Entertainment Corp. (B.C. Apr. 7, 1986)
Dec. 12, 2003 – Name changed to Sungold International Holdings Corp. and continued into Canada. ■

Sungold Gaming Inc. (B.C. Apr. 7, 1986)
May 26, 1997 – Name changed to Sungold Gaming International Ltd.; basis 3 new for 1 old sh. ■

Sungold Gaming International Ltd. (B.C. Apr. 7, 1986)
Apr. 5, 2000 – Name changed to Sungold Entertainment Corp. ■

Sungold International Holdings Corp. (Can. Dec. 12, 2003)
Nov. 7, 2022 – Dissolved and struck from register.

Sungold Resources Inc. (Ont. Aug. 17, 1987)
Oct. 20, 1994 – Formed Olympic ROM World Inc. in Ontario on amalgamation with 1091181 Ontario Limited; basis 1 new for 1.75 old shs. ■

Sunlight Oils Ltd. (unknown)
Nov. 1929 – Acquired by Mercury Oils Ltd. (see Mercury Oils Ltd.)

Sunlite Oil Company Limited (Alta. 1945)
1982 – Acquired by Sunlite Oil Company of Delaware; sh.-for-sh. basis.

Sunmakers Travel Group Inc. (B.C. Apr. 3, 1987)
Jan. 24, 1996 – Name changed to Setanta Ventures Inc. ■

Sunmist Energy '84 Inc. (Can. Sept. 1979)
Mar. 5, 1987 – Formed Sunmist Energy '86 Inc. in Alberta on amalgamation with 1411835 Canada Limited. ■

Sunmist Energy '86 Inc. (Alta. Mar. 5, 1987 amalg.)
Aug. 1, 1992 – Struck off register.

Sunmist Energy Resources Limited (Can. Sept. 1979)
June 4, 1984 – Name changed to Sunmist Energy '84 Inc.; basis 1 new for 3 old shs. ■

Sunningdale Oils Limited (Alta. 1969)
1976 – All o/s shs. acquired at $17 Cdn. per sh. by Kerr-McGee Corporation.

Sunora Foods Inc. (Ont. Mar. 8, 2011)
Feb. 11, 2022 – Acquired by Folspire Inc.; basis 17¢ cash per sh.

Sunorca Development Corp. (B.C. May 18, 1983)
June 16, 2014 – Name changed to Wildflower Marijuana Inc. ■

Sunport Medical Corporation (B.C. Jan. 29, 1988)
Feb. 27, 1998 – Name changed to Argent Capital Corporation and continued into Wyoming following vertical amalgamation with wholly owned Argent Capital Corporation (a Nevada incorporation); basis 1 new for 30 old shs.

Sunport Metals Corporation (B.C. Jan. 29, 1988)
June 29, 1992 – Name changed to Sunport Medical Corporation following acquisition of Medinvest Holdings Inc. ■

Sunray Mines Ltd. (B.C. 1957)
1979 – Liquidated.

Sunray Resources Inc. (Alta. 1987)
May 11, 1990 – All o/s com. shs. acquired by Pipestone Petroleums Inc.; basis 1 new for 1 old sh. (see Pipestone Petroleums Inc.)

Sunridge Energy Corp. (B.C. May 26, 2006)
July 30, 2013 – Name changed to Golden Coast Energy Corp.; basis 1 new for 4 old shs. ■

Sunridge Gold Corp. (B.C. Dec. 7, 1983)
May 25, 2016 – First distribution of 36¢ per sh. made to shldrs. of record May 18, 2016, following sale of co.'s 60% interest in Asmara Mining Share Company.
Dec. 8, 2016 – Final distrib. of 3¢ cash per sh. made to shldrs. of record Dec. 5, 2016.
Dec. 9, 2016 – Voluntarily dissolved.

Sunridge Investments Corp. (B.C. May 26, 2006)
Mar. 16, 2011 – Name changed to Sunridge Energy Corp. pursuant to Qualifying Transaction acquisition of oil and gas interests in Alberta from Silver Peak Industries Ltd. ■

Sunrise Investment Holding (Canada) Corporation (Alta. May 30, 1988)
July 24, 1995 – Name changed to Amerpro Industries Inc.; basis 1 new for 5 old shs. ■

Sunrise Metals Corporation (B.C. Jan. 27, 1966)
Jan. 24, 1990 – Name changed to Pacific Sun Resource Corporation; basis 1 new for 4 old shs. ■

Sunrise Minerals Inc. (B.C. Aug. 5, 2005)
Mar. 10, 2008 – Name changed to Cronus Resources Ltd.; basis 1 new for 4 old shs. ■

Sunrise Senior Living Real Estate Investment Trust (Ont. Aug. 13, 2004)
Apr. 26, 2007 – Acquired by Ventas, Inc.; basis Cdn$16.50 per unit. Subsequently on May 3, 2007, the 6.40% conv. sub. debs. and the 7.0% conv. sub. debs. both due on Dec. 31, 2011, were delisted.

Sunrise Silver Mines Ltd. (B.C. Jan. 27, 1966)
Jan. 21, 1977 – Name changed to Sunrise Metals Corporation; basis 1 new for 4 old shs. ■

Sunset Company Limited (B.C.)
May 25, 1933 – Charter cancelled.

Sunset Cove Mining Inc. (B.C. Dec. 4, 2007)
Dec. 2, 2016 – Name changed to Manganese X Energy Corp. (see FPsurvey - Mines & Energy; FPsurvey - Industrials)

Sunset Mining Corp. Ltd. (B.C. 1969)
Jan. 27, 1975 – Charter cancelled.

Sunset Oil & Gas Co., Ltd. (unknown)
Struck off register.

Sunset Oils Ltd. (B.C. 1929)
Feb. 6, 1937 – Continued into Alberta.
Mar. 1955 – Acquired by Alberta Pacific Consolidated Oils Ltd.

Sunset Yellowknife Mines Ltd. (Ont. 1945)
Jan. 28, 1972 – Charter cancelled.

Sunshine Capital Corporation (Alta. Mar. 16, 2001)
Jan. 31, 2014 – Name changed to Open Source Health Inc. pursuant to Qualifying Transaction reverse takeover acquisition of Open Source Health Corporation; basis 1 new for 6 old shs. ■

Sunshine Columbia Resources Limited (B.C. May 22, 1947)
Feb. 20, 1987 – Name changed to K-2 Resources Inc.; basis 1 new for 2 old shs. ■

Sunshine Comstock Mines Limited (B.C. May 22, 1947)
Dec. 10, 1974 – Name changed to Sunshine Columbia Resources Limited. ■

Sunshine Lardeau Mines Limited (B.C. May 22, 1947)
Oct. 8, 1965 – Name changed to Sunshine Comstock Mines Limited. ■

Sunshine Oilsands Ltd. (Alta. Feb. 22, 2007)
Oct. 1, 2015 – Voluntarily delisted from TSX; continued to trade on Stock Exchange of Hong Kong Limited. (see FPsurvey - Mines & Energy)

Sunshine Silver Mines Corporation (Del. Feb. 2, 2011)
Sept. 23, 2014 – Name changed to Sunshine Silver Mining & Refining Corporation. ■

Sunshine Silver Mining & Refining Corporation (Del. Feb. 2, 2011)
Oct. 30, 2020 – Name changed to Gatos Silver, Inc. ■

Sunstar Continental Petroleum Corp. (B.C. Feb. 2, 1981)
Oct. 26, 1983 – Name changed to Arch Development Corporation. ■

Sunstar Resources Ltd. (Alta. Sept. 13, 1982)
July 17, 1991 – Name changed to Stade Exploration Inc.; basis 1 new for 4 old shs. ■

Sunstate International Ltd. (Ont. June 1, 1994 amalg.)
Dec. 12, 1997 – Name changed to Hyberlab Teknologies Corp.; basis 1 new for 10 old shs. ■

Sunstate Resources Ltd. (B.C. Sept. 13, 1982)
Dec. 6, 1999 – Name changed to International Sunstate Ventures Ltd.; basis 1 new for 6 old shs. ■

Suntac Minerals Corporation (B.C. Oct. 6, 1987)
Aug. 4, 1992 – Continued into Canada.
July 6, 1993 – Acquired by Canarc Resources Corp.; basis 1 Canarc sh. for 3.5 Suntac shs.

Suntec Capital Inc. (Alta. Oct. 30, 2003)
July 6, 2004 – Name changed to Suntec Pure Water Technologies Inc. following Qualifying Transaction reverse takeover acquisition of Western Symbiotics Ltd. ■

Suntec Pure Water Technologies Inc. (Alta. Oct. 30, 2003)
Apr. 8, 2008 – Name changed to Mira Resources Corp. and continued into British Columbia; basis 1 new for 2.8 old shs. ■

Suntec Ventures Limited (B.C. Aug. 29, 1979)
Jan. 27, 1986 – Amalgamated with Surinam Resources Ltd. to form new co. with same name Suntec Ventures Limited.
May 19, 1987 – Name changed to Consolidated Suntec Ventures Limited; basis 1 new for 4 old shs. ■

Suntree Investments International Corp. (Alta. 1987)
Jan. 1, 1996 – Dissolved and struck off register.

Sunventures Corporation (Alta. June 24, 1986)
Mar. 25, 1994 – Name changed to Sunventures Resources Inc.; basis 1 new for 1 old sh. ■

Sunventures Resources Inc. (Alta. June 24, 1986)
Jan. 31, 1995 – Name changed to Commonwealth Energy Inc.; basis 1 new for 5 old shs. ■

Sunvest Minerals Corp. (B.C. Jan. 8, 2008)
Apr. 17, 2019 – Name changed to Sky Gold Corp. (see FPsurvey - Mines & Energy)

Sunwah International Limited (Bermuda Feb. 28, 1996)
June 15, 2021 – Privatized via a 1-for-36,000,000 consolidation; basis Cdn$0.30 cash per sh.

Sunward Resources Ltd. (B.C. Apr. 11, 2008)
June 25, 2015 – Acquired by NovaCopper Inc.; basis 0.3 NovaCopper com. shs. for 1 Sunward com sh.

Suparna Gold Corp. (B.C. Oct. 12, 2006)
May 6, 2016 – Name changed to Scientific Metals Corp. ■

Super Nova Minerals Corp. (B.C. Sept. 28, 2012 amalg.)
Apr. 3, 2014 – Name changed to Super Nova Petroleum Corp. ■

Super Nova Petroleum Corp. (B.C. Sept. 28, 2012 amalg.)
Apr. 13, 2018 – Name changed to Koios Beverage Corp. following reverse takeover acquisition of Koios, LLC. (see FPsurvey - Industrials)

Super Scoop Ice-Cream Corporation (B.C. Aug. 25, 1967)
Feb. 16, 1982 – Name changed to Trojan Energy Corporation. ■

Super Twins Resources Ltd. (B.C. Jan. 22, 1987)
Feb. 13, 1997 – Name changed to Whitegold Resource Corp. ■

Superburn Systems Ltd. (B.C. 1980)
Feb. 28, 1990 – Acquired by 295692 B.C. Ltd. for 70¢ per sh.

Supercrest Copper Mines Limited (Ont. 1956)
Sept. 2, 1964 – Name changed to Supercrest Mines Ltd. ■

Supercrest Mines Ltd. (Ont. 1956)
Jan. 28, 1992 – Amalgamated with Royal Oak Mines Inc. (see Royal Oak Mines Inc.)

Supercrete Ltd. (Man. 1946)
Nov. 1978 – Became a private co. through co. purchase of shs. held by minority shldrs.

Superior Acceptance Corporation Limited (Ont. 1960)
May 15, 1987 – Acquired by The Great Universal Stores plc; basis $14.513 or 2 Great Universal pref. shs. at $14.503 plus 10¢ (total $14.513) for 1 Superior sh.

Superior Acid & Chemicals Ltd. (Ont. 1968)
Mar. 1976 – Charter cancelled.

Superior Acid & Iron Ltd. (Ont. 1968)
Oct. 1971 – Name changed to Superior Acid & Chemicals Ltd.; basis 1 new for 4 old shs. ■

Superior Canadian Resources Inc. (Yuk. June 12, 2000)
Nov. 30, 2004 – Continued into Alberta. (see FPsurvey - Mines & Energy)

Superior Capital Inc. (Que. 1957)
June 27, 1996 – Name changed to Emerging Africa Gold (EAG) Inc. ■

Superior Copper Corporation (Ont. July 7, 2004)
May 31, 2016 – Acquired by Nighthawk Gold Corp., by way of amalgamation with 2504106 Ontario Inc., a wholly owned subsid. of Nighthawk Gold Corp., basis 0.32493545 Nighthawk com. shs. for 1 Superior com. sh. (see Nighthawk Gold Corp.)

Superior Copper Mines Ltd. (Ont. Mar. 9, 1965)
Mar. 6, 1978 – Name changed to Mountainview Explorations Inc. ■

Superior Diamonds Inc. (Yuk. Dec. 16, 1997)
June 4, 2004 – Continued into British Columbia.
Apr. 15, 2008 – Name changed to Northern Superior Resources Inc. (see FPsurvey - Mines & Energy)

Superior Electronics Industries Ltd. (Can. 1969)
June 1979 – Placed into receivership and Thorne-Riddell of Montreal appointed receiver. No distribution to unithldrs.

Superior Financial Holdings Inc. (Que. 1957)
Apr. 18, 1994 – Name changed to Superior Capital Inc.; basis 1 new for 3 old shs. ■

Superior Gold Inc. (Ont. July 4, 2016)
July 4, 2023 – Acquired by Catalyst Metals Limited; basis 0.3571 Catalyst ordinary shs. for 1 Superior Gold com. sh.

Superior Mining Corporation (Yuk. Dec. 2, 1997)
May 10, 2006 – Name changed to Superior Mining International Corporation; basis 1 new for 5 old shs. ■

Superior Mining International Corporation (Yuk. Dec. 2, 1997)
Feb. 15, 2008 – Continued into British Columbia. (see FPsurvey - Mines & Energy)

Superior Pipeline Corporation (B.C. May 29, 1986)
Dec. 2, 1997 – Continued into Yukon.
Feb. 10, 1998 – Name changed to Superior Mining Corporation. ■

Superior Plus Income Fund (Alta. Aug. 2, 1996)
Jan. 7, 2009 – Converted into Superior Plus Corp. following reorganization with Ballard Power Systems Inc. whereby Ballard acquired Superior Plus Corp. to form Ballard Power Systems Inc. (New Ballard).

Superior Propane Income Fund (Alta. Aug. 2, 1996)
Feb. 19, 2003 – Name changed to Superior Plus Income Fund. ■

Superior Propane Limited (Can. July 24, 1951)
June 30, 1964 – Acquired by Gulf Oil Canada Ltd. by purchase of o/s com. shs. at $18.22 per sh. to Sept. 7, 1962, and thereafter at $18 per sh. All o/s $1.40 pref. shs. called for redemp. at $25.50 plus accr. divd. of 35¢ per sh. Long-term debt assumed by Gulf.

Superior Window Company Ltd. (Que. 1953)
1962 – Name changed to Superseal Corporation.

Supernova Capital Corporation (B.C. Apr. 19, 2002)
June 6, 2003 – Formed Panoro Minerals Ltd. in British Columbia following Qualifying Transaction reverse takeover acquisition of and amalgamation with Panoro Resources Ltd. (see FPsurvey - Mines & Energy)

Superpack Corporation Limited (Ont. 1961)
July 17, 1989 – Name changed to SPC International Investments Limited. ■

Superpack Vending Ltd. (Ont. 1961)
Mar. 14, 1963 – Name changed to Superpack Corporation Limited. ■

Supersilk Hosiery Mills, Ltd. (Ont. 1927)
1944 – Name changed to General Products Mfg. Corporation Limited. ■

Superstar Petroleums Ltd. (Ont. 1969)
Nov. 9, 1976 – Charter cancelled.

Superstition Gold Mines Ltd. (Ont. 1946)
1953 – Charter cancelled.

Supertech Industries Inc. (B.C. 1983)
Oct. 11, 1989 – Name changed to Encore Products Inc.; basis 1 new for 5 old shs. ■

Supertest Petroleum Corporation, Limited (Ont. Dec. 17, 1925)
Dec. 23, 1971 – Merged with BP Canada (1969) Ltd. into BP Canada Limited; basis 1 com. sh. for each 2 old com. shs., and 5 new com. shs. and of a newly created cl. A sh. for 1 old ord. sh.

The Supreme Cannabis Company, Inc. (Can. Dec. 18, 2015)
June 24, 2021 – Acquired by Canopy Growth Corporation; basis 0.01165872 Canopy shs. plus $0.0001 cash for 1 Supreme sh.

Supreme Gas and Oil Ltd. (Alta. 1952)
Nov. 15, 1978 – Struck off register.

Supreme Metals Corp. (B.C. Sept. 19, 2013)
Aug. 13, 2020 – Name changed to Canadian GoldCamps Corp. (see FPsurvey - Mines & Energy)

Supreme Mines Ltd. (Que. 1963)
June 1973 – Charter cancelled.

Supreme Oil and Gas Ltd. (Alta. 1952)
1969 – Name changed to Supreme Gas and Oil Ltd.; basis 2 new for 3 old shs. ■

Supreme Pharmaceuticals Inc. (B.C. June 12, 1979)
Dec. 18, 2015 – Continued into Canada.
Dec. 29, 2017 – Name changed to The Supreme Cannabis Company, Inc. ■

Supreme Resources Inc. (B.C. 1983)
Oct. 28, 1994 – Dissolved and struck off register.

Supreme Resources Ltd. (B.C. June 12, 1979)
Mar. 14, 2014 – Name changed to Supreme Pharmaceuticals Inc. ■

Supremex Income Fund (Que. Feb. 10, 2006)
Jan. 1, 2011 – Succeeded by Supremex Inc. pursuant to plan of arrangement whereby the fund was converted into a corporation and subsequently dissolved. (see FPsurvey - Industrials)

Suquash Collieries Ltd. (B.C. 1952)
Jan. 19, 1961 – Dissolved and struck off register.

Sur American Gold Corporation (Can. Aug. 2, 1929; via letters patent)
Aug. 28, 2007 – Name changed to Cadan Resources Corporation and continued into British Columbia. ■

Suramina Resources Inc. (Can. Apr. 5, 2007)
Apr. 22, 2009 – Acquired by Canadian Gold Hunter Corp.; basis 0.7541 Canadian Gold shs. for 1 Suramina sh. (see Canadian Gold Hunter Corp.)

Sure Energy Inc. (Alta. June 7, 2006)
Jan. 15, 2008 – Amalgamated in Alberta to continue with same name.
Oct. 16, 2013 – Acquired by Tamarack Valley Energy Ltd.; basis 0.105 Tamarack shs. for 1 Sure Energy sh.

SureFire Commerce Inc. (Can. Dec. 16, 1982)
Oct. 3, 2003 – Name changed to Terra Payments Inc. following acquisition in April 2003 of ebs Electronic Billing Systems AG. ■

Surety Oils & Minerals Ltd. (Ont. 1948)
1956 – Name changed to Woodgreen Copper Mines Ltd. ■

Surewin Resources Corp. (B.C. 1969)
Oct. 30, 1992 – Dissolved and struck off register.

Surf Inlet Consolidated Gold Mines Ltd. (B.C. May 1933)
Dec. 1954 – Name changed to Surf Inlet Consolidated Mines Ltd.; basis 1 new for 4 old shs. ■

Surf Inlet Consolidated Mines Ltd. (B.C. May 1933)
Apr. 13, 1959 – Name changed to Western Surf Inlet Mines Ltd.; basis 1 new for 4 old shs. ■

Surf Inlet Mines Ltd. (B.C. Mar. 19, 1986)
Mar. 2, 1993 – Name changed to Princess Resources Ltd.; basis 1 new for 10 old shs. ■

Surf Oils Ltd. (Alta. 1974)
Sept. 10, 1985 – Name changed to Shannon Energy Ltd.; basis 1 new for 10 old shs. ■

Surge Exploration Inc. (B.C. Nov. 6, 2017)
Mar. 15, 2021 – Name changed to Surge Battery Metals Inc. (see FPsurvey - Mines & Energy)

Surge Mines Ltd. (Ont. 1971)
Feb. 1980 – Charter cancelled.

Surge Petroleum Inc. (Alta. July 1, 2000 amalg.)
Apr. 21, 2004 – Plan of Arrangement acquisition by Troutline Investments Inc. which was subsequently acquired by Innova Exploration Ltd.; basis 1.9738 new Troutline shs. for 1 old Surge sh. (see Troutline Investments Inc.)

Surge Resources Inc. (Alta. July 31, 1987 amalg.)
Oct. 30, 2007 – Name changed to Eaglewood Energy Inc. ■

Surimau Minerals Ltd. (Que. 1958)
Nov. 11, 1978 – Charter cancelled.

Surinam Resources Ltd. (B.C. Oct. 17, 1979)
Jan. 27, 1986 – Amalgamated with Suntec Ventures Limited to form a new co. under the continuing name of Suntec Ventures Limited; sh.-for-sh. basis.

Surluga Gold Mines Limited (Ont. Mar. 22, 1962)
May 1973 – Name changed to Pursides Gold Mines Limited; basis 1 new for 10 old shs. ■

Suroco Energy Inc. (Alta. Jan. 31, 2005)
July 21, 2014 – Acquired by Petroamerica Oil Corp.; basis Cdn$0.2079 cash and 1.6401 Petroamerica com. shs. or Cdn$0.80 cash per Suroco Energy sh. (see Petroamerica Oil Corp.)

Surpass Chemicals Limited (Ont. 1954)
1979 – Amalgamated in Ontario to continue with same name.
June 29, 1989 – All com. shs. held by Witco Chemical Corporation of New York. Cl. B convert. shs. exchanged for com. shs. of Witco on basis of 1.5 new for 1 old, or convertible into cl. C shs. of Witco on sh.-for-sh. basis until June 29, 1989. Cl. C special shs. of co. redeem. at $1.00 per sh. any time.

Surpass Petrochemicals Ltd. (Ont. 1954)
1958 – Name changed to New Surpass Petrochemicals Ltd. ■

Surrey Capital Corp. (Ont. Sept. 13, 2010)
Jan. 3, 2017 – Name changed to Subscribe Technologies Inc. ■

Surrey Credit Union (B.C. May 5, 1947)
Aug. 1, 1991 – Name changed to Surrey Metro Savings Credit Union. ■

Surrey Metro Savings Credit Union (B.C. May 5, 1947)
July 2, 2002 – Acquired by Coast Capital Savings Credit Union for $21 per sh. (see Consolidated Takepoint Ventures Ltd.)

Susie Gold Mines Ltd. (B.C. Mar. 18, 1975)
June 6, 1978 – Name changed to Suzie Mining Explorations Ltd. ■

Sussex Explorations Ltd. (Ont. Feb. 14, 1985)
May 17, 1993 – Formed Print Three Express International Inc. in Ontario on amalgamation with Print Three Express International Inc.; basis 1 new for 1 Print Three sh. and 1 new for 4 Sussex shs. ■

Sussex Ginger Ale Ltd. (N.B. 1944)
Apr. 1961 – Name changed to Seven-Up Sussex Ltd.

Sussman Realty Corp. Ltd. (Ont. 1962)
1968 – Name changed to The Sussman Properties Limited.

Sustainable Agriculture & Wellness Dividend Fund (Alta.)
May 17, 2023 – Merged into Middlefield Healthcare Dividend ETF; basis 0.69780078 Middlefield Healthcare ETF units for 1 Sustainable Agriculture fund units.

Sustainable Energy Technologies Ltd. (Alta. Nov. 4, 1996)
Nov. 1, 2013 – Name changed to Eguana Technologies Inc. (see FPsurvey - Industrials)

Sustainable Infrastructure Dividend Fund (Alta.)
Mar. 15, 2022 – Converted into an exchange-traded fund; basis 1 Middlefield Sustainable Infrastructure Dividend ETF for 1 Sustainable Infrastructure Dividend fund unit.

Sustainable Opportunities Acquisition Corp. (Cayman Islands Dec. 18, 2019)
Sept. 9, 2021 – Name changed to TMC the metals company Inc. and continued into British Columbia pursuant to the reverse takeover acquisition of DeepGreen Metals Inc. (see FPsurvey - Mines & Energy)

Sustainable Production Energy Trust (Ont. Aug. 29, 2005)
Oct. 4, 2010 – Name changed to Energy Income Fund pursuant to merger with Energy Plus Income Trust and CGF Resource 2008 Flow Through LP, with Sustainable Production Energy Trust the deemed acquiror. (see FPsurvey - Mines & Energy)

Sustainable Real Estate Dividend Fund (Ont. Feb. 25, 2022)
May 16, 2024 – Merged into Middlefield Real Estate Dividend ETF; basis 0.62971496 Middlefield units for 1 Sustainable fund unit.

Sustainco Inc. (Can. Aug. 22, 2008)
Nov. 25, 2020 – Name changed to Universal PropTech Inc. ■

Sutcliffe Resources Ltd. (B.C. Feb. 6, 1996)
June 3, 1996 – Continued into Ontario.
Nov. 4, 1996 – Continued into Alberta.
July 5, 2007 – Name changed to Zoloto Resources Ltd. (see FPsurvey - Mines & Energy)

Sutherland Resources Ltd. (B.C. Aug. 29, 1979)
Sept. 4, 1985 – Name changed to Suntec Ventures Limited; basis 1 new for 4 old shs. ■

Sutter Gold Mining Inc. (B.C. June 7, 1990)
May 17, 2019 – Placed into receivership by secured lender RMB Australia Holdings Inc. The Bowra Group Inc. was appointed receiver and all officers and directors resigned.

Sutton Group Financial Services Ltd. (Can. June 22, 1987)
Feb. 27, 2004 – Acquired by SGFS Acquisition Inc. for 15¢ per sh. Co. now private.

Sutton Group Realty Services Ltd. (Can. June 22, 1987)
Jan. 24, 1992 – Name changed to Sutton Group Financial Services Ltd.; basis 2 new for 1 old sh. ■

Sutton-Horsley Co. Limited (Ont. 1940)
Apr. 1944 – Shldrs. auth. sale of co. to Cdn. govt. for $160,000. Offer was accepted by govt. and co. wound up and assets distributed on basis of $1.04 per sh.

Sutton Resources Ltd. (B.C. Dec. 4, 1979)
Apr. 8, 1999 – Acquired by Barrick Gold Corporation; basis 0.463 Barrick shs. for 1 Sutton sh.

Suzannah Uraniums Ltd. (B.C. 1954)
Aug. 2, 1962 – Dissolved.

Suzie Mining Explorations Ltd. (B.C. Mar. 18, 1975)
Nov. 7, 1988 – Delisted from the Vancouver Stock Exchange. Subsequently dissolved and struck from registry.

Suzy Shier Limited (Can. May 5, 1982)
July 20, 2001 – Name changed to La Senza Corporation. ■

Svit Gold Corp. (B.C. Sept. 16, 1983)
Feb. 2, 2010 – Name changed to Catalyst Copper Corp. ■

Swan Hills Energy Limited Partnership (Alta. Aug. 18, 2003)
June 4, 2008 – Liquidated for $1.80 per unit.

Swannell Minerals Corp. (B.C. May 30, 1980)
Apr. 1, 1997 – Name changed to GlobeNet Resources Inc.; basis 1 new for 10 old shs. ■

Swansea Gold Mines Inc. (Ont. Apr. 16, 1975)
Jan. 3, 1995 – Delisted from the CDN. Subsequently dissolved and charter cancelled.

Swanson Mines Ltd. (Que. 1955)
1957 – Acquired by Gibson Mines Ltd.; basis 1 new for 2 old shs.

Swarmio Media Holdings Inc. (B.C. Jan. 11, 2021)
Oct. 20, 2023 – Assigned into bankruptcy and Grant Thornton Limited appointed trustee.

Sway Resources Inc. (B.C. May 14, 1981)
Jan. 26, 1996 – Name changed to Orion International Minerals Corporation. ■

Sweepco Industries Inc. (Can. 1972)
Nov. 1977 – Peat, Marwick, Toronto appointed receiver
Dec. 1977 – Operating assets sold.
1979 – Sale of subsids. etc. completed. No cash distributions to unsecured creditors or shldrs.

Sweeprite Mfg. Inc. (Sask. Sept. 29, 1999)
Sept. 6, 2005 – Placed into receivership. Sullivan & Associates Inc. was appointed receiver.

Sweepstake Mines Ltd. (B.C. 1968)
Apr. 14, 1975 – Charter cancelled.

Sweet Grass Oils Limited (Ont. 1943)
Mar. 5, 1954 – Name changed to Great Sweet Grass Oils Ltd.; basis 1 new for 5 old shs. ■

Sweet Poison Spirits Inc. (B.C. Oct. 1, 2018)
Apr. 8, 2025 – Name changed to Hyper Bit Technologies Ltd. (see FPsurvey - Industrials)

Sweetwater Petroleum Corporation (B.C. 1976)
Feb. 8, 1982 – Amalgamated with Canalta Resources Ltd. (0.3 for 1) and The Ascot Petroleum Corporation (0.85 for 1) to form a new company named Consolidated Ascot Petroleum Corporation; basis 0.65 new for 1 Sweetwater sh. (see Consolidated Ascot Petroleum Corporation)

SwiDent Inc. (Ont. May 30, 1997)
July 2, 1999 – Name changed to SwissLink Financial Corporation. ■

Swift Copper Mines Ltd. (Ont. 1954)
Aug. 19, 1965 – Dissolved.

Swift Minerals Ltd. (B.C. Oct. 23, 1986)
Dec. 15, 1992 – Formed Agritek Bio Ingredients Corporation in Canada on amalgamation with Agritek Bio Ingredients Corporation; basis 1 new for 2 old shs. ■

Swift Power Corp. (B.C. Oct. 22, 2008 amalg.)
Aug. 27, 2010 – Acquired by Fort Chicago Pipelines (Canada) Ltd., an indirect wholly owned subsid. of Fort Chicago Energy Partners L.P., for 35¢ per sh.

Swift Resources Inc. (B.C. Sept. 21, 2006)
Mar. 3, 2017 – Name changed to Guyana Goldstrike Inc. following acquisition of Romanex Guyana Exploration Ltd. (see FPsurvey - Mines & Energy)

Swim King Pools Limited (Ont. 1971)
Jan. 8, 1980 – Dissolved.

Swim Lake Mines Ltd. (B.C. Apr. 25, 1966)
Oct. 30, 1978 – Name changed to Karma Ventures Incorporated; basis 1 new for 5 old shs. ■

Swim Pool Supply of Canada Ltd. (Ont. 1957)
Apr. 14, 1961 – Name changed to Gillette Pool Products Limited. ■

Swiss Aluminium Mining Co. of Canada Ltd. (Que. 1970)
Jan. 9, 1985 – Charter cancelled.

Swiss Bank Corporation (Canada) (Can. 1981)
June 29, 1998 – Amalgamated with Union Bank of Switzerland (Canada) to form UBS Bank (Canada).

Swiss Canadian Resources Inc. (Alta. May 26, 1987)
Aug. 20, 1992 – Name changed to Western Star Energy Corporation. ■

Swiss Oils of Canada (1959) Ltd. (Can. Nov. 14, 1947)
Aug. 21, 2003 – Dissolved.

Swiss Water Decaffeinated Coffee Income Fund (B.C. Apr. 3, 2002)
Jan. 1, 2011 – Succeeded by Ten Peaks Coffee Company Inc. pursuant to plan of arrangement whereby Ten Peaks Coffee Company Inc. was formed to facilitate the conversion of the fund into a corporation and the fund was subsequently dissolved. ■

SwissLink Financial Corporation (Ont. May 30, 1997)
Aug. 28, 2001 – Share exchange resulted in 2 new classes of shares, cl. A com. shs. and preference shs. (which were redeemed immed. for $0.10 per pref. sh.).
May 2, 2003 – Outstanding cease trade order partially revoked to permit conclusion of reorganization. Status of cl. A shs. unknown.

Switson Industries Limited (Ont. 1947)
Dec. 1964 – Acquired by General Signal Corp. for $2.75 per sh.

Sword Energy Inc. (Alta. June 26, 2007)
July 1, 2012 – Name changed to Journey Energy Inc. (see FPsurvey - Mines & Energy)

sxr Uranium One Inc. (Can. Mar. 17, 2005)
June 8, 2007 – Name changed to Uranium One Inc. following reverse takeover acquisiton of UrAsia Energy Ltd. ■

Sycee Cobalt Silver Mines Ltd. (Ont. 1936)
1967 – Charter cancelled.

Sycon Corporation (Ont. Dec. 17, 1946)
Jan. 3, 1995 – Delisted from the CDN. Subsequently dissolved and charter cancelled.

Sycon Energy Corporation (Ont. Dec. 17, 1946)
Nov. 1987 – Name changed to Sycon Corporation. ■

Syd Financial Inc. (B.C. Feb. 18, 2015)
Mar. 4, 2020 – Name changed to Gold Plus Mining Inc. ■

Sydenham Capital Inc. (Alta. Feb. 8, 2001)
July 5, 2002 – Amalgamated with E-Amigos.com Inc. (0.66667 for 1) and The Learning Library Inc. to form a new company also named The Learning Library Inc.; basis 1 new Learning Library sh. for 1 old Sydenham sh. (see The Learning Library Inc.)

Sydney Development Corporation (B.C. 1966)
Sept. 17, 1986 – Formed SDC Sydney Development Corporation on amalgamation with Sydney Acquisition Corporation; basis 1 new for 5 old shs. ■

Sydney Resource Corporation (B.C. July 27, 1979)
Sept. 13, 2006 – Formed West Timmins Mining Inc. in British Columbia on amalgamation with Band-Ore Resources Ltd. with Sydney Resources the deemed acquiror; basis 0.9 new for 1 Band-Ore sh. and 1 new for 1 Sydney Resources sh. ■

Sylogist Inc. (Alta. Mar. 1, 1993)
Dec. 4, 2002 – Name changed to Sylogist Ltd.; basis 1 new for 7 old shs. (see FPsurvey - Industrials)

Sylre Ltd. (Alta. June 6, 1976)
Apr. 28, 2005 – Continued into British Columbia.
May 3, 2005 – Name changed to KPS Ventures Ltd. ■

Sylvan Industries Ltd. (B.C. Nov. 22, 1955)
Feb. 16, 1956 – Name changed to Crestbrook Timber Limited. ■

Sylvanite Gold Mines Ltd. (Ont. 1913)
May 20, 1964 – Charter cancelled; in 1960 made distribution of 61 shs. Delnite Mines Ltd., 20 shs. Alminex Ltd. and $16.70 per 100 shs. of Sylvanite. In April 1962, distributed 30¢ per sh.; on Dec. 15, 1962, 9¢ cash; and final distribution of 1.8¢ cash in November 1963.

Sylverite Mines, Ltd. (B.C. 1946)
Wound up.

Sylvestre Gold Mines Ltd. (Ont. 1946)
May 6, 1957 – Charter cancelled.

Symax Lift (Holding) Co. Ltd. (Alta. Sept. 18, 2007)
Apr. 6, 2016 – Privatized by amalgamation with 1060719 B.C. Ltd., a co. owned by Symax's major shldrs., to form Symax Lift (Holding) Inc.; basis 1 cl. A pref. sh. for 1 com. sh., immediately redeemed for 25¢ per sh.

Symbility Solutions Inc. (Alta. July 15, 1999)
Dec. 21, 2018 – All o/s com. shs not already held acquired by 21546328 Alberta Ltd., an indirect wholly owned subsid. of CoreLogic, Inc.; basis $0.615 cash per sh.

Symbio Capital Corp. (B.C. Feb. 14, 2011)
Aug. 7, 2014 – Name changed to Blackeagle Development Corp. ∎

Symbionics Systems Limited (Can. 1969)
1973 – Sold assets and distributed $245 per $1,000 princ. amt. to deb. holders.
1976 – Admin. of estate completed, funds turned over to Royal Trust Co.

Symes Resources Inc. (B.C. 1981)
Oct. 2, 1992 – Dissolved and struck off register.

Symmetry Resources Inc. (Alta. July 29, 1987)
Feb. 7, 2000 – Acquired by Berkley Petroleum Ltd.; basis 0.081 new Berkley sh. for 1 old Symmetry sh. (see Berkley Petroleum Corp.)

Symphony Capital Corporation (Alta. 1987)
Sept. 23, 1991 – Name changed to Kensbrook Development Corporation; basis 1 new for 3 old shs. ∎

Synchronica plc (U.K. Dec. 1, 1994)
May 16, 2012 – Acquired by Myriad Group AG; basis 4.83 Myriad shs. for 100 Synchronica shs.

Syncom Image Display Systems Inc. (Can. Dec. 22, 1995)
Oct. 8, 1998 – Name changed to Syncom Imaging Systems Inc.; basis 1 new for 5 old shs. ∎

Syncom Imaging Systems Inc. (Can. Dec. 22, 1995)
Mar. 9, 1999 – In early March, the company's principal creditor rejected the company's restructuring plan. The company made an assignment under the Bankruptcy and Insolvency Act and Raymond Chabot Inc. of Montreal, Que., was appointed trustee.
June 1, 2002 – All the assets had been sold, a final distribution of $200 had been made to the principal secured creditor, and the receiver had been discharged. There were no funds available for distribution to unsecured creditors or shldrs.

Syncordia Technologies and Healthcare Solutions, Corp. (Ont. Nov. 28, 2014)
Apr. 4, 2018 – Placed into receivership by secured lender. Grant Thornton Ltd. appointed reciever and all directors resigned.

Syncrete Technologies Inc. (Alta. 1986)
Dec. 1, 1994 – Dissolved and struck off register.

Syndicat d'Oeuvres Sociales Limitée (Can. 1912)
Mar. 25, 1970 – Name changed to Le Droit Ltée.

Syndicated Film Services Ltd. (unknown)
1969 – Acquired by Manoir Industries Ltd.; basis 10 com. shs. Manoir for each sh. Syndicated. (see Manoir Industries Ltd.)

Synenco Energy Inc. (Alta. Oct. 22, 1999)
Aug. 12, 2008 – Acquired by Total E&P Canada Ltd. for $10.25 per cl.A com. sh.

Synergex Corporation (Ont. Mar. 16, 2005 amalg.)
Mar. 16, 2016 – Inactive.

Synergistics Industries Limited (Ont. Feb. 18, 1949)
Nov. 25, 1997 – Acquired by The Geon Company for $22 per sh.

Synergy Acquisition Corp. (Alta. June 24, 2003)
Jan. 28, 2014 – Name changed to Genius Properties Ltd. and continued into Canada. ∎

Synergy International Ltd. (B.C. Dec. 20, 1971)
Apr. 1, 1985 – Delisted from the Vancouver Stock Exchange. Subsequently struck from register and dissolved for failure to file.

Synergy Renewable Resources Inc. (B.C. May 27, 1991 amalg.)
Mar. 5, 2018 – Dissolved and struck from register.

Synergy Resource Technologies Inc. (B.C. May 27, 1991 amalg.)
Jan. 9, 1997 – Name changed to Synergy Renewable Resources Inc.; basis 1 new for 5 old shs. ∎

Synergy Resources Ltd. (B.C. Dec. 20, 1971)
Mar. 1, 1976 – Name changed to Synergy International Ltd. ∎

Synex International Inc. (B.C. Aug. 13, 1982)
Jan. 31, 2022 – Name changed to Synex Renewable Energy Corporation; basis 1 new for 10 old shs. ∎

Synex Renewable Energy Corporation (B.C. Aug. 13, 1982)
Aug. 7, 2025 – Acquired by Sitka Power Inc.; basis $2.40 cash per sh.

Syngold Exploration Inc. (Ont. Oct. 16, 1963)
June 21, 1989 – Amalgamated with International Thunderwood Explorations Ltd. (1 for 1) to form a new co. Thunderwood Resources Inc.; basis 1 new for 1.4 old shs. (see Thunderwood Resources Inc.)

Synodon Inc. (Alta. Aug. 14, 2000)
Dec. 1, 2016 – Placed into receivership and The Bowra Group Inc. appointed receiver. All officers and directors resigned.

Syntax Systems Ltd. (Que. June 24, 1972)
Mar. 20, 2013 – Continued into Canada.

Syntech Diamond Films Inc. (Ont. 1959)
July 27, 1993 – Amalgamated with Diasyn Technologies Limited to form Structured Biologicals Inc.; basis 1 new for 5 Diasyn shs. and 1 com. sh. for 5 Syntech com. shs. and 1 new pref. sh. for 5 Syntech pref. shs. (see Structured Biologicals Inc.)

Syntegra Investment Corp. (B.C. June 4, 1999)
Apr. 26, 2002 – Qualifying Transaction Plan of Arrangement with Emercap Ventures Inc. (1 for 2.7173) and Chinacom Technologies Inc. (1 for 2) to continue as VendTek Systems Inc.; basis 1 new VendTek for 4.2953 old Syntegra shs. (see VendTek Systems Inc.)

Synthetic Biologics, Inc. (Nev. Oct. 15, 2009)
Oct. 13, 2022 – Name changed to Theriva Biologics, Inc.

SynX Pharma Inc. (Ont. Mar. 11, 1997)
Apr. 26, 2004 – Plan of Arrangement acquisition by Nanogen, Inc., a Nasdaq traded company; basis 0.123 new Nanogen com. sh. ($1.423 per sh.) for 1 old SynX com. sh.

Sypher Resources Ltd. (Alta. Jan. 21, 2010)
July 16, 2014 – Name changed to Atlas Cloud Enterprises Inc. following acquisition of Atlas Cloud Enterprises (2013) Ltd. ∎

Syracuse Capital Corp. (B.C. Aug. 9, 2007)
May 19, 2009 – Name changed to Natcore Technology Inc. on Qualifying Transaction reverse takeover acquisition of Natcore Technology, Inc. ∎

Syracuse Oils Limited (Alta. 1967)
Apr. 30, 1971 – Merged with Bow Valley Industries Ltd.; basis 1 new for 5 old shs.

Syrus Capital Corporation (B.C. Apr. 29, 1987)
Nov. 19, 1996 – Name changed to New Syrus Capital Corporation; basis 1 new for 2 old shs. ∎

Syscan International Inc. (Can. May 21, 1996)
Dec. 15, 2008 – Declared bankrupt. H.H. Davis & Assoc. Inc. of Montreal appointed Trustee.

Syspower Multimedia Industries Inc. (B.C. Nov. 21, 1983)
Feb. 15, 1995 – Continued into British Virgin Islands.

Systech Retail Systems Corp. (B.C. Feb. 3, 1983)
Nov. 8, 2005 – Acquired by Torex Retail Canada Corp. for $0.0032 per sh.

Systech Retail Systems Inc. (B.C. Feb. 3, 1983)
Sept. 24, 2002 – Name changed to Systech Retail Systems Corp. ∎

Systemhouse Ltd. (Can. July 26, 1974)
Jan. 31, 1985 – Name changed to SHL Systemhouse Inc. ∎

Systems-Air Corporation Limited (Ont. 1969)
Mar. 16, 1976 – Charter cancelled.

Systems Dimensions Ltd. (Can. 1968)
Feb. 14, 1979 – Amalgamated with Niagnat Holdings Ltd., owner of Datacrown Ltd., to become Datacrown Inc. Exchange on basis of 3 com. shs. of amalg. co. for each 4 shs. of Systems Dimensions. Ser. A conv. debs. holders received 65.35 com. shs. of amalg. co. for each $1,000 prin. amt. of Ser. A debs. to be converted. Date for conversion rights expiry extended to Mar. 16, 1979 from Feb. 15, 1979.

Systems West Consultants Ltd. (Can. Aug. 24, 1978)
Mar. 20, 1991 – Name changed to Siocta Ventures Inc.; basis 1 new for 3 old shs. ∎

Systems Xcellence Inc. (Ont. 1983)
Aug. 1, 1995 – Amalgamated in Canada to continue with same name.
June 27, 2007 – Name changed to SXC Health Solutions Corp. and continued into Yukon. ∎

Systerm Inc. (Can. 1987)
Apr. 1, 1990 – Wound up. No distribution to shldrs.

Szyds Ventures Inc. (Alta. Dec. 14, 1987)
Oct. 1, 1997 – Formed Commonwealth Energy Corp. following acquisition of all the o/s shs. of Blue Mountain Resources Inc. and Commonwealth Energy (U.S.A.) Inc. ∎

T

T & E Theatre.com Inc. (Can. Nov. 25, 1999)
Feb. 28, 2002 – Name changed to Manele Bay Ventures Inc.; basis 1 new for 3 old shs. ∎

T & H Resources Ltd. (Ont. July 16, 1909)
Nov. 15, 1988 – Amalgamated with Coastoro Resources Ltd. to form new co. with same name T & H Resources Ltd.
May 9, 2002 – Name changed to LAB International Inc. and continued into Canada following reverse takeover acquisition of LAB International Holdings Inc.; basis 1 new for 20 old shs. ∎

T-Bird Pharma Inc. (B.C. July 31, 2007)
June 18, 2015 – Name changed to Emerald Health Therapeutics, Inc. ∎

T. Boone Pickens Energy Fund (Ont. Dec. 14, 2009)
Mar. 18, 2013 – In voluntarily liquidation. Proceed will be distributed on or about Mar. 20, 2013.

T-Cap Inc. (Alta. Mar. 8, 1988)
June 16, 1992 – Name changed to Eastern Stone Products Ltd.; basis 1 new for 3 old shs. ∎

The T. Eaton Company Limited (Ont. Apr. 21, 1891)
Jan. 7, 2000 – Following Plan of Compromise and Arrangement, all com. shs. became participating units with pro rata interest in a promissory note issued by Sears Canada Inc.; basis 1 Eaton com. for 1 part. unit. Court appointed liquidator Richter & Partners Inc., Toronto.
Nov. 5, 2003 – Dissolved.

The T. Eaton Realty Company, Limited (Can. 1929)
June 11, 1993 – Amalgamated with Eaton Properties Limited; basis unknown.

T-Ray Science Inc. (Ont. Mar. 7, 2006)
Aug. 25, 2009 – Continued into British Columbia.
Jan. 18, 2011 – Name changed to Verisante Technology, Inc. (see FPsurvey - Industrials)

TAAT Lifestyle & Wellness Ltd. (B.C. June 5, 2006)
Apr. 28, 2021 – Name changed to TAAT Global Alternatives Inc. (see FPsurvey - Mines & Energy)

TAC Capital Corporation (B.C. Sept. 14, 2005)
Dec. 21, 2009 – Name changed to TAC Gold Corporation. ■

TAC Gold Corporation (B.C. Sept. 14, 2005)
Feb. 29, 2016 – Dissolved and struck from register.

TAD Capital Corp. (B.C. Apr. 23, 2007)
Mar. 10, 2010 – Name changed to TAD Mineral Exploration Inc. ■

TAD Mineral Exploration Inc. (B.C. Apr. 23, 2007)
Jan. 19, 2016 – Name changed to Everest Ventures Inc.; basis 1 new for 10 old shs. ■

TAG Oil Ltd. (Yuk. Oct. 24, 1997)
Oct. 12, 2006 – Continued into British Columbia. (see FPsurvey - Mines & Energy)

TAL Acquisition Ltd. (B.C. Jan. 31, 1997)
June 9, 1997 – Name changed to TimberWest Forest Holdings Ltd. ■

TALON International Energy Ltd. (Yuk. Oct. 10, 1996)
Jan. 1, 2010 – Formed Canadian Energy Exploration Inc. in Alberta pursuant to reverse takeover amalgamation with Fifth Avenue Diversified Inc. (deemed acquiror); basis 1 new for 3 old shs. ■

TB Advisors Inc. (Alta. Nov. 12, 1996)
Mar. 16, 1999 – Continued into Canada.
Mar. 30, 1999 – Name changed to Honeybee Technology Inc. ■

T.B. Mining Ventures Inc. (Ont. May 2, 2007)
Dec. 21, 2012 – Name changed to Sphere 3D Corporation following Qualifying Transaction amalgamation of Sphere 3D Inc. with wholly owned 8283729 Canada Inc., constituting a reverse takeover by Sphere 3D; basis 1 new for 4 old shs. (see FPsurvey - Industrials)

TBC Investments Inc. (Alta. Feb. 27, 1996)
Nov. 11, 1997 – Name changed to Warwick Communications Inc. following acquisition of Warwick Publishing Inc. ■

TBM NT Corporation (B.C. 1980)
Oct. 1, 1991 – Redeemed at $27.25 per pref. sh. and $13.13 per capital sh.

T. C. Explorations Ltd. (B.C. Feb. 18, 1965)
Oct. 19, 1970 – Name changed to Decca Resources Limited; basis 1 new for 5 old shs. ■

T.C.C. Beverages Ltd. (Can. July 27, 1987)
Aug. 20, 1990 – Stock name changed to Coca-Cola Beverages on the TSE.
Apr. 27, 1992 – Name changed to Coca-Cola Beverages Ltd. ■

TCEnet Inc. (Alta. Jan. 1, 2000 amalg.)
Oct. 9, 2003 – Acquired by WNS Emergent Inc.; basis 1 WNS sh. for 3.061 TCEnet shs. (see WNS Emergent Inc.)

TCF Energy Inc. (Que. 1942)
June 26, 1996 – Amalgamated with a wholly owned subsid. of TriGas Exploration Inc.; basis 1 TriGas com. sh. or $1.00 for 1 TCF com. sh. (see TriGas Exploration Inc.)

TCG International Inc. (Can. Jan. 1990)
May 9, 1996 – Amalgamated with a wholly owned subsid. All o/s cl. A multiple vtg. shs. and cl. B subord. vtg. shs. exchanged for $3.48 per sh. Co. now private.

TCS Energy Systems Ltd. (Ont. 1951)
Oct. 8, 1993 – Name changed to Advanced Pultrusion Technologies Inc. ■

TCT Logistics Inc. (Alta. July 31, 1989)
Jan. 24, 2002 – Placed into receivership. KPMG Inc. appointed receiver.
Feb. 25, 2002 – KMPG Inc. as receiver assigned the company into bankruptcy and was appointed trustee.
Mar. 27, 2008 – KPMG Inc. discharged as receiver. Secured creditors suffered a shortfall and there were no funds avail. for shldrs.

TD Capital Trust (Ont. Feb. 14, 2000)
Dec. 31, 2009 – Terminated. Trust units redeemed at $1,000 per unit.

TD Mortgage Investment Corp. (Can. Oct. 27, 1997)
Nov. 1, 2007 – Redeemed all o/s pref. ser.A shs. (HYBRIDS); basis $1,000 plus divd. of $32.30 per pref. sh.

TD Realty Investments (Ont. 1971)
Aug. 1981 – Assets acquired by The Toronto-Dominion Bank. Distribution of $24 per unit given to unitholders. Operations ceased Sept. 20, 1981.

TD Split Inc. (Ont. July 31, 2000)
Nov. 16, 2015 – All o/s capital and pref. shs. redeemed; basis $28.7964 plus final divd. of $0.4779 per capital sh. and $10 plus final divd. of $0.11875 per pref. sh.

TD Waterhouse Group, Inc. (Del.)
Nov. 27, 2001 – Acquired by and merged with TD Waterhouse Holdings, Inc., a wholly owned subsid. of The Toronto-Dominion Bank, for US$9.50 per sh.

TDI Venture Equities Ltd. (Ont. Sept. 29, 1975 amalg.)
May 4, 1983 – Name changed to VTL Venture Equities Ltd. following reclassification of cl. A pfce. as com. shs.; basis 2 new for 1 old sh. ■

TDRI Limited (Ont. 1963)
Dec. 1981 – Remaining 50% interest not already owned by The Toronto-Dominion Bank was acquired and name subsequently changed to Toronto-Dominion Export Finance Company Limited effective Mar. 11, 1982.

TDZ Holdings Inc. (Ont. Apr. 28, 1999)
Oct. 8, 2013 – Voluntarily dissolved; distribution of $0.097 cash per com. sh. payable to shldrs. at Aug. 27, 2013.

TEAL Exploration & Mining Incorporated (Yuk. June 1, 2005)
Mar. 27, 2009 – Acquired by African Rainbow Minerals Limited for $3.00 per sh.

TEC Technolog Enterprises Corporation (B.C. 1986)
Mar. 26, 1993 – Dissolved and struck off register.

TEGL Systems Corporation (B.C. 1983)
Sept. 2, 1994 – Dissolved and struck off register.

TEL NT Ltd. (Alta. July 15, 1992 amalg.)
July 31, 1998 – All o/s cap. and equity divd. shs. redeemed for $22.0113 per cap. sh. and $13.4362 per equity divd. sh.

TELUS Communications (BC) Inc. (Can. Apr. 12, 1916; via Special Act of Parliament)
Jan. 1, 2000 – Amalgamated with Canadian Telephone and Supplies Ltd., TELUS Systems Support Inc. and MPR Extensys Inc. to form new co. with same name TELUS Communications (BC) Inc.
Jan. 1, 2001 – Formed TELUS Communications Inc. in Canada on amalgamation with TELUS Communications Inc., TELUS Mobility Cellular Inc. and 3759070 Canada Inc. ■

TELUS Communications Inc. (Can. Jan. 1, 2001 amalg.)
Sept. 1, 2001 – Amalgamated with Clearnet PCS Inc. to form new co. with same name TELUS Communications Inc.
Aug. 3, 2004 – All publicly issued pfce. and pref. shs. redeemed on the following dates: July 1, 2004 - $6.00 cum. redeem. pref. shs., $4.50 cum. redeem. pref. shs., $5.75 cum. redeem. pref. shs. and $1.21 cum. redeem. pref. shs.; July 15, 2004 - $4.75 cum. redeem. pref. shs., $4.75 cum. redeem. pref. shs. (ser. 1956) and $5.15 cum. redeem. pref. shs.; and - $6.00 cum. redeem. pref. shs. and $4.375 cum. redeem. pref. shs.

TELUS Corporation (Alta. Jan. 6, 1984)
Feb. 1, 1999 – Merged with BC TELECOM Inc. to form BCT.TELUS Communications Inc.; basis 1 BCT.TELUS sh. for 1 BC TELECOM sh. and 0.7773 BCT.TELUS sh. for 1 TELUS sh. (see BCT.TELUS Communications Inc.)

T.E.N. Private Cable Systems Inc. (Can. Dec. 27, 1985)
July 27, 1999 – Name changed to Cinema Internet Networks Inc.; basis 1 new for 5 old shs. ■

TER Thermal Retrieval Systems Ltd. (Alta. Oct. 23, 1996)
Apr. 2, 2005 – Struck off the registry and dissolved.

TFH International Inc. (Can. Nov. 8, 1979)
Aug. 17, 1995 – Name changed to Highbourne Capital Corporation. ■

T.G. Bright & Co., Limited (Ont. July 11, 1933)
Sept. 1, 1993 – Formed Wine Acquisition Inc. on amalgamation with wholly owned Wine Acquisition Inc.; basis $20 cash for either 1 new T.G. Bright cl. A conv. sh. or cl. B conv. sh. ■

T.G. Bright & Co., Limited (Can. Sept. 7, 1993 amalg.)
Aug. 11, 1994 – Name changed to Vincor International Inc. ■

TG Residential Value Properties Ltd. (B.C. Feb. 8, 2011)
Aug. 22, 2022 – Dissolved and struck from register.

TG World Energy Corp. (Alta. July 10, 2001 amalg.)
Mar. 15, 2011 – Acquired by TVI Pacific Inc.; basis 0.458 TVI shs. for 1 TG sh.

TGS North American Real Estate Investment Trust (Alta. July 31, 2002)
June 16, 2006 – Acquired following agreement with Red Mile Acquisitions Inc. and The Great-West Life Assurance Company; basis Cdn$9.15 per unit. Also paid final distribution of US$0.020835 per unit. (see The Great-West Life Assurance Company)

TGS Properties Inc. (Alta. Sept. 17, 2002)
Apr. 14, 2003 – Privatized via plan of arrangement; basis $1.20 per com. sh. and $1,021.70 per $1,000 conv. deb. (includes unpaid interest).

TGS Properties Ltd. (Alta. Nov. 6, 1997)
Dec. 9, 2002 – Name changed to TGS Properties Inc.; basis 1 new for 1 old com. sh. and 1 new deb. for 1 old deb., however the related deb. conversion price has been reduced to $1.589 per sh. ■

TGW Corp. Inc. (Que. May 25, 1981)
Dec. 6, 2002 – Succeeded by GlobeStar Mining Corporation pursuant to plan of arrangement whereby TGW shs. were exchanged for newly incorporated Globestar Mining Corporation shs. on a sh.-for-sh. basis, resulting in TGW becoming a wholly owned subsid. of Globestar. ■

T. H. Estabrooks Co. Ltd. (Can. 1911)
Apr. 30, 1959 – Name changed to Brooke Bond Canada Ltd. ■

T.H.C. Medical Inc. (B.C. 1987)
Apr. 11, 2003 – Dissolved and struck from the register.

TIE/telecommunications Canada Limited (Can. Dec. 4, 1980)
June 17, 1994 – All o/s com. shs. repurchased for $1.50 per sh.

TIEX Inc. (Alta. Mar. 30, 2005)
Feb. 1, 2006 – Continued into British Columbia.
Oct. 26, 2012 – Name changed to Bullion Gold Resources Corp.; basis 1 new for 3 old shs. (see FPsurvey - Mines & Energy)

TILT Holdings Inc. (Nev. June 22, 2018)
Nov. 14, 2018 – Continued into British Columbia. (see FPsurvey - Industrials)

TIO Networks Corp. (B.C. June 17, 1997)
July 19, 2017 – Acquired by Tahoe Acquisition ULC, a wholly owned subsid. of PayPal Inc.; basis Cdn$3.35 cash per sh.

TIR Systems Ltd. (B.C. Sept. 14, 1982)
June 13, 2007 – Acquired by Royal Philips Electronics Ltd. for $1.60 per sh. (see Koninklijke Philips Electronics N.V.)

TIW Industries Ltd. (Can. 1977)
June 4, 1985 – All assets liquidated. No distribution made to unsecured creditors or shldrs.

TJN Gold Exploration Inc. (Ont. 1983)
Nov. 16, 1987 – Name changed to TJN Industries Ltd. (see FPsurvey - Mines & Energy)

TJR Coatings Inc. (Ont. Dec. 11, 1998)
May 25, 2018 – Name changed to DigiCrypts Blockchain Solutions Inc. ■

TKE Energy Trust (Alta. Sept. 27, 2004)
Nov. 2, 2005 – Name changed to True Energy Trust pursuant to reverse takeover acquisiton of True Energy Inc.; basis 1 new for 2 old trust units. Concurrently, True Energy Inc. spun out its exploration assets in the form of a new co., Vero Energy Inc., and amalgamated with TKE Energy Inc. (wholly owned by TKE Energy Trust) to form new wholly owned subsid. with same name True Energy Inc. True Energy shldrs. received 0.5 pre-consolidated TKE trust units, 0.1 Vero shs. and 1 Vero wt. ■

TKN Interactive Marketing Systems Inc. (Ont. Jan. 8, 1986)
Apr. 21, 1999 – Name changed to eStation.com Inc. ■

T.K.O. Resources Inc. (B.C. Sept. 4, 1986)
June 2, 1999 – Name changed to Canadian Imperial Venture Corp. pursuant to reverse takeover acquisition of Imperial Venture Corp. ■

TLC The Laser Center Inc. (Ont. May 28, 1993)
Nov. 29, 1999 – Name changed to TLC Laser Eye Centers Inc. ■

TLC Laser Eye Centers Inc. (Ont. May 28, 1993)
May 17, 2002 – Name changed to TLC Vision Corporation and continued into New Brunswick following acquisition of Missouri-based Laser Vision Centers, Inc.; basis 1 new for 0.95 old shs. ■

TLC Ventures Corp. (B.C. Jan. 15, 1969)
June 18, 2007 – Name changed to Calibre Mining Corp. ■

TLC Vision Corporation (N.B. May 17, 2002)
May 26, 2010 – Filed for bankruptcy and all officers and directors resigned. Alvarez & Marsal Canada Inc. appointed trustee.

TLO Capital Corp. (B.C. Mar. 21, 2012)
Mar. 18, 2015 – Dissolved following Qualifying Transaction private placement subscription of 1,500,000 units at 10¢ per Eagle unit plus 1/2 wts. of Eagle Graphite Incorporated and distribution of Eagle units to shldrs. Each wts. is exercisable to purchase Eagle unit at 15¢ per unit for a 5 yrs. period. (see Eagle Graphite Incorporated)

TM Capital Corp. (Alta. Oct. 28, 1999)
Oct. 23, 2000 – Name changed to TravellersMall.com Ltd. ■

TMAC Resources Inc. (Ont. Oct. 30, 2012)
Feb. 4, 2021 – Acquired by Agnico Eagle Mines Limited; basis $2.20 cash per sh.

TME Resources Inc. (B.C. 1983)
July 19, 1994 – Name changed to International TME Resources Inc.; basis 1 new for 3 old shs. ■

TMI-Learnix Inc. (Ont. Jan. 4, 1937)
Jan. 10, 2002 – Continued into Canada.
Nov. 2, 2005 – Dissolved.

TML Foods Inc. (Sask. June 28, 1993)
Sept. 12, 2001 – Name changed to TML Ventures Inc. and continued into British Columbia; basis 1 new for 20 old shs. ■

TML Ventures Inc. (B.C. Sept. 12, 2001)
July 8, 2005 – All shs. exchanged by way of plan of arrangement whereby TML Ventures became a wholly owned subsid. of Range Metals Inc.; basis 1 Range sh. for 10 TML shs. ■

TMN Capital Corp. (Alta. May 11, 1987)
Sept. 6, 1995 – Name changed to Mayfair Media Corporation; basis 1 new for 2 old shs. ■

T.M.P. Investments Limited (Ont. 1961)
May 1, 1972 – Name changed to Grey Goose Corporation Limited. ■

T.M.T. Resources Inc. (B.C. May 21, 1987)
Aug. 28, 2017 – Name changed to Ladera Ventures Corp.; basis 1 new for 10 old shs. ■

TMX Group Inc. (Ont. Aug. 23, 2002)
Sept. 14, 2012 – Succeeded by TMX Group Limited pursuant to plan of arrangement resulting in acquisition of the remaining 20% interest in TMX Group Inc. by TMX Group Limited (formerly Maple Group Acquisition Corporation) on a sh.-for-sh. basis. Maple Group acquired an initial 80% interest in TMX Group Inc. on Aug. 10, 2012, for $50 per share. (see FPsurvey - Industrials)

TNK Resources Inc. (Ont. May 14, 1985)
June 4, 1999 – Name changed to Opus Minerals Inc.; basis 1 new for 10 old shs. ■

TNR Resources Ltd. (B.C. Jan. 14, 1988)
June 25, 2003 – Name changed to TNR Gold Corp.; basis 1 new for 4 old shs. (see FPsurvey - Mines & Energy)

TNT Financial Ltd. (Ont. 1989)
Aug. 10, 1995 – All o/s cap. shs. and equity divd. shs. redeemed. Cap. sh. basis: (i) more than $24 - $12.70 plus 75% of the amt. by which the market value of the capital share property (defined as 1.0067 TransAlta Corporation com. shs.) exceeds $24; (ii) more than $11.30 but not more than $24 - the amt. by which the market value of the capital share property exceeds $24; and (iii) less than or equal to $11.30 - 1.0067 TransAlta shs. or $11.30 per cap. sh. Equity divd. shs. basis: (i) the amt. determined by dividing the net asset value of the co. by the number of equity divd. shs. o/s and (ii) the cap. sh. redemption amount.

TORC Oil & Gas Ltd. (Alta. Nov. 19, 2012 amalg.)
Mar. 1, 2021 – Acquired by Whitecap Resources Inc.; basis 0.57 Whitecap shs. for 1 TORC sh.

TORR Canada Inc. (Can. Mar. 25, 1993)
May 23, 2008 – Name changed to ProSep Inc. ■

TOTAL Energold Corporation (Can. Sept. 14, 1988 amalg.)
Mar. 16, 1992 – Acquired by TOTAL Resources (Canada) Ltd., a subsidiary of TOTAL S.A., for $1.55 per sh.

TP Resources Ltd. (B.C. Jan. 18, 1985)
Sept. 28, 1988 – Name changed to Crew Natural Resources Limited. ■

TPB & T, Ltd. (Ont. 1958)
Sept. 3, 1994 – Dissolved.

TPCO Holding Corp. (B.C. June 17, 2019)
July 7, 2023 – Succeeded by Gold Flora Corporation pursuant to the amalgamation of TPCO Holding Corp., Stately Capital Corporation and newly formed Gold Flora Corporation to form (new) Gold Flora Corporation, which concurrently acquired Costa Mesa, Calif.-based Gold Flora, LLC by reverse takeover and domesticated in the U.S. as a Delaware corporation. ■

TR Minerals Ltd. (Ont. June 3, 1985)
Jan. 7, 1994 – Name changed to Pangea Goldfields Inc. following the acquisitions of Normina Mineral Development Corporation (concurrently renamed Pangea Fenn-Gib Limited) and 1051694 Ontario Inc.; basis 1 new for 4.5 old shs. ■

TRAFINA Energy Ltd. (Alta. Dec. 24, 1991)
June 13, 2012 – All directors resigned. FTI Consulting Canada Inc. appointed receiver.
July 2012 – Assets in southwestern Saskatchewan were sold for $1,000,000.
Oct. 2012 – Remaining assets sold for $3,075,000. Secured and unsecured creditors paid in full. No funds available for distribution to shldrs.

TRIAM Automotive Inc. (Ont. Feb. 9, 1994)
June 26, 1998 – Acquired by Magna International Inc.; basis $1.50 and 0.0943 Magna cl. A subord. vtg. shs. for 1 TRIAM sh.

TRL Realty Inc. (Alta. May 29, 1997)
Dec. 11, 1997 – Formed Torode Realty Limited in Alberta on amalgamation with Torode Capital Inc. following Major Transaction acquisition of Torode Capital. ■

TRP NT Corp. (Ont. June 15, 1998)
Aug. 19, 2003 – Pref. shs. redeemed at $16 per sh. and cap. shs. redeemed at $8.76 per sh.

TR3 Trust (Ont. Sept. 26, 2001)
Dec. 1, 2004 – Redeemed at $4.63 per unit (NAV). Unitholders could select the cash offer or acquire units (based on the NAV price) of Montrusco Bolton Income & Growth Fund at $10 per unit.

TRU Precious Metals Corp. (Alta. Dec. 3, 1996)
Aug. 12, 2021 – Continued into Ontario. (see FPsurvey - Mines & Energy)

T.R.V. Minerals Corporation (B.C. 1972)
Oct. 30, 1992 – Dissolved and struck off register.

TRX Gold Corporation (Alta. July 5, 1990)
Mar. 27, 2025 – Continued into British Columbia. (see FPsurvey - Mines & Energy)

TRYP Therapeutics Inc. (B.C. Sept. 24, 2019)
May 2, 2024 – Acquired by Exopharm Limited (renamed Tryptamine Therapeutics Limited); basis 3.616 Exopharm ord. shs. for 1 TRYP Therapeutics sh.

T. S. Simms & Co. Ltd. (N.B. 1866)
Aug. 1, 1980 – Merged with Simms Investments Ltd. to form T. S. Simms & Co. Limited.

TS Telecom Ltd. (B.C. 1987)
Feb. 1996 – Continued into Ontario.
Mar. 6, 2009 – Continued into British Columbia.
Mar. 9, 2009 – Name changed to Quanta Resources Inc.; basis 1 new for 5 old shs. ■

TSA Explorations Ltd. (B.C. June 10, 1987)
July 6, 1992 – Name changed to Boron Chemicals International Ltd. ■

TSB International Inc. (Ont. Nov. 3, 1981)
Apr. 24, 1985 – Continued into Canada.
Oct. 20, 1999 – Name changed to Telco Research Corporation Limited. ■

TSC Shannock Corporation (Can. 1982)
Dec. 4, 1998 – Acquired by Video One Canada Ltd., a wholly owned subsid. of Standard Broadcasting Corporation Limited, for $1.10 per sh.

TSI TelSys Corporation (B.C. Sept. 22, 1987)
Apr. 1996 – Continued into New Brunswick.
Oct. 29, 2003 – Continued into Delaware.

TSO3 Inc. (Que. June 10, 1998)
Oct. 2, 2019 – Acquired by Stryker Corporation; basis Cdn$0.43 cash per sh.

Investissements TSPL inc. (Can. Jan. 13, 2004)
Feb. 15, 2018 – Name changed to Prime Blockchain Inc. ■

TSX Group Inc. (Ont. Aug. 23, 2002)
June 18, 2008 – Name changed to TMX Group Inc. ■

T.T.A. Resources Corporation (B.C. Dec. 6, 1978)
Aug. 26, 1999 – Name changed to Minefund Development Corporation. ■

TTC Technology Corp. (B.C. Dec. 20, 2006)
Sept. 30, 2013 – Struck from registry and dissolved.

TTC/Truck Tech. Corp. (B.C. Sept. 8, 1987)
Apr. 13, 1994 – Name changed to UniComm Signal Inc. ■

TTI Telephone Technologies Inc. (B.C.)
Aug. 13, 1993 – Dissolved and struck off register.

TUSK Energy Corporation (Alta. Sept. 24, 2004)
Apr. 16, 2009 – Acquired by Polar Star Canadian Oil and Gas, Inc., indirectly owned by the Teachers Insurance and Annuity Association of America, for $2.15 per sh.

TUSK Energy Inc. (Alta. Nov. 14, 1986)
Nov. 5, 2004 – Converted into TKE Energy Trust; basis 0.50 TKE trust units plus 0.50 TUSK Energy Corporation shs. for 1 TUSK Energy Inc. sh. (see TKE Energy Trust; TUSK Energy Corporation)

TUSK Minerals Inc. (Alta. Nov. 14, 1986)
Nov. 13, 1991 – Name changed to TUSK Resources Inc.; basis 1 new for 5 old shs. ■

TUSK Resources Inc. (Alta. Nov. 14, 1986)
Sept. 7, 1995 – Name changed to TUSK Energy Inc.; basis 1 new for 10 old shs. ■

TVI Copper Inc. (Alta. Jan. 12, 1987)
July 11, 1994 – Name changed to TVI Pacific Inc. (see FPsurvey - Mines & Energy)

TVS Industries Ltd. (B.C. Aug. 21, 1972)
Feb. 1974 – Name changed to GBX Mines Ltd. ■

TVX Gold Inc. (Ont. Jan. 7, 1991)
Feb. 6, 2003 – Business combination with Kinross Gold Corporation and Echo Bay Mines Ltd. by way of plan of arrangement whereby TVX amalgamated with a wholly owned subsid. of Kinross; basis 2.1667 Kinross com. shs. (following 1-for-3 consolidation) for 1 TVX com. sh.

TVX Mining Corporation (Ont. Oct. 31, 1984)
Nov. 6, 1986 – Name changed to Consolidated TVX Mining Corporation; basis 1 new for 3 old shs. ■

T. W. Hand Fireworks Co. Ltd. (Can. Sept. 6, 1930)
Jan. 1963 – Name changed to Hand Chemical Industries Limited. ■

Taal Distributed Information Technologies Inc. (B.C. Mar. 23, 2011)
July 8, 2021 – Continued into Canada.
Dec. 23, 2022 – Privatized via the acquisition by Calvin Ayre of all o/s com. shs. not already held for $1.07 cash per sh.

Tab Ventures Corp. (B.C. July 15, 1986)
June 22, 1989 – Name changed to Nu-Sky Exploration Inc. ■

Taber-Kamorley Oils Ltd. (B.C. Jan. 28, 1938)
1941 – Name changed to Tagore-Zeballos Mines Ltd. ■

Taber Petroleums Ltd. (Alta.)
1959 – Struck off register.

Tabor Lake Gold Mines Ltd. (Ont. 1942)
Nov. 9, 1976 – Charter cancelled.

Taché Lake Mines Limited (Que. 1951)
Nov. 24, 1971 – Name changed to Consolidated Taché Mines & Investments Ltd.; basis 1 new for 10 old shs. ■

Taché Resources Inc. (Que. 1951)
Feb. 15, 1985 – Name changed to United North American Resources, Inc.; basis 1 new for 6 old shs. ■

Tacoma Resources Ltd. (B.C. 1974)
Nov. 29, 1985 – Struck off register.

Tael Capital Inc. (Alta. Oct. 16, 1998)
Mar. 26, 2004 – Formed Torch River Resources Ltd. in Alberta on Qualifying Transaction amalgamation with Torch River Mines Limited (deemed acquiror). ■

Tag-Alder Mines Ltd. (Ont. 1945)
Apr. 1, 1965 – Dissolved.

Tagalder Incorporated (Ont. July 11, 1996 amalg.)
Jan. 19, 2001 – Name changed to Tagalder (2000) Inc.; basis 1 new for 10 old shs. (see FPsurvey - Industrials)

Tagami Capital Corporation (Que. Aug. 19, 1963 amalg.)
Oct. 25, 1999 – Acquired by CDA International Inc.; basis 1 CDA sh. for 10 Tagami shs. (see CDA International Inc.)

Tagami Mines Ltd. (Que. Aug. 19, 1963 amalg.)
Aug. 29, 1992 – Dissolved.
Oct. 7, 1996 – Revived.
Feb. 25, 1999 – Name changed to Tagami Capital Corporation following amalgamation with 9050-9548 Quebec Inc.; basis 1 new for 10 old shs. ■

Taggart Capital Corp. (Ont. Mar. 26, 2010)
Mar. 11, 2013 – Succeeded by PRO Real Estate Investment Trust pursuant to plan of arrangement whereby PRO Real Estate Investment Trust was formed to facilitate the conversion of the corporation into a trust. (see FPsurvey - Industrials)

Tagish Lake Gold Corp. (B.C. Nov. 30, 2000 amalg.)
Dec. 24, 2010 – Acquired by New Pacific Metals Corp. either for 10¢ per sh. or 0.137 New Pacific com. shs. for 1 Tagish com.sh. or a combination of 5¢ per sh. plus 0.0685 New Pacific com. shs.
Dec. 31, 2021 – Name changed to Whitehorse Gold (Yukon) Corp.

Tagore-Zeballos Mines Ltd. (B.C. Jan. 28, 1938)
1946 – Dissolved.

Tagus Resources Ltd. (B.C. 1972)
Feb. 23, 1984 – Name changed to High Reserve Resources Limited; basis 1 new for 3 old shs. ■

Tahera Corporation (Can. Feb. 28, 1999)
June 29, 2004 – Name changed to Tahera Diamond Corporation. ■

Tahera Diamond Corporation (Can. Feb. 28, 1999)
Jan. 16, 2008 – Filed for protection under the Companies' Creditors Arrangement Act (CCAA). PricewaterhouseCoopers Inc. appointed monitor.
Dec. 15, 2008 – A. Farber and Partners Inc. was appointed CCAA monitor in place of PricewaterhouseCoopers.
Aug. 27, 2010 – Assets consisting of the Jericho diamond mine, processing facilities and supporting exploration assets were sold to Shear Minerals Ltd. for a combination of cash and com. shares and a $500,000 note payable and 2% royalty on all diamonds and minerals paid to Caz Petroleum Inc., the company's secured creditor. No distributions made to shldrs.
Jan. 8, 2012 – Dissolved.

Tahoe Resources Inc. (B.C. Nov. 10, 2009)
Feb. 22, 2019 – Formed 0799714 B.C. Ltd. in British Columbia. ■

Tahtsa Mines Ltd. (B.C. 1979)
Feb. 10, 1982 – Name changed to Tatsa Resources Ltd. ■

Tai Energy Corporation (B.C. June 30, 1993 amalg.)
Mar. 17, 1995 – Acquired by Maxx Petroleum Ltd.; basis 0.334 Maxx shs. plus 18¢ for 1 Tai sh. (see Maxx Petroleum Ltd.)

Tai Energy Resources Corporation (B.C. Nov. 8, 1984 amalg.)
July 6, 1993 – Amalgamated with First Guardian Petroleum Corporation to form Tai Energy Corporation; basis 0.157968 new for 1 First Guardian sh. and 0.489112 new for 1 Tai Energy sh. (see Tai Energy Corporation)

Tai Fan Ventures Inc. (Can. Mar. 3, 1987)
July 19, 1988 – Name changed to La Ronge Resources Inc. ■

Taiga Forest Products Ltd. (B.C. Oct. 1, 1984)
Sept. 1, 2005 – Converted by way of plan of arrangement into an income fund-like structure with stapled units (1 new com. sh. plus 1 new 14% subord. note) named Taiga Building Products Ltd.; basis 4 stapled units for 1 com. sh.

Taiga Gold Corp. (Alta. Sept. 28, 2017)
Apr. 19, 2022 – Acquired by SSR Mining Inc.; basis $0.265 cash per sh.

Taiga Mines Ltd. (B.C. 1954)
Aug. 6, 1974 – Struck off register.

Taiga Motors Corporation (B.C. Mar. 13, 2019)
Oct. 16, 2024 – Acquired by U.K. entrepreneur Stewart Wilkinson pursuant to a reverse vesting order under the Companies' Creditor Arrangement Act (CCAA). Consideration was not disclosed. All o/s shs. were cancelled for no consideration.

Taiga Resources Ltd. (unknown)
Feb. 13, 1968 – Acquired by Coseka Resources Ltd. on a sh.-for-sh. basis. (see Coseka Resources Ltd.)

Tailwind Capital Corporation (Alta. Mar. 24, 2017)
Dec. 16, 2020 – Formed San Lorenzo Gold Corp. in Alberta pursuant to Qualifying Transaction amalgamation with Kairos Metals Corp. (deemed acquiror); basis 1 new for 1.5 old shs. (see FPsurvey - Mines & Energy)

Taina Developments Corporation (B.C. 1980)
Jan. 6, 1994 – Name changed to Double Eagle Entertainment Corp. ■

Taina Gold Inc. (B.C. 1983)
Feb. 19, 1986 – Formed Oxin Industries Ltd. in British Columbia on amalgamation with Oxin Industries Ltd.; basis 1 new for 1 old sh. ■

Taipan Capital Corp. (B.C. June 5, 2006)
Nov. 3, 2009 – Name changed to Taipan Resources Inc. ■

Taipan Resources Inc. (B.C. June 5, 2006)
Jan. 6, 2017 – Name changed to Molori Energy Inc. ■

Tajee Resources Ltd. (B.C. 1980)
June 16, 1995 – Dissolved and struck off register.

Tajen Resources Corporation (Alta. 1986)
Aug. 24, 1988 – Name changed to Syncrete Technologies Inc. ■

Tajiri Ventures Corp. (B.C. Jan. 21, 2008)
Apr. 26, 2011 – Name changed to Tajiri Resources Corp. pursuant to Qualifying Transaction acquisition of Gateau property option. (see FPsurvey - Mines & Energy)

Tajzha Ventures Ltd. (Alta. Apr. 9, 1997)
Sept. 4, 2009 – In bankruptcy. No funds available for shldrs.

Takara Resources Inc. (Can. Apr. 29, 2005)
Nov. 28, 2016 – Name changed to Castle Silver Resources Inc. ■

Takepoint Ventures Ltd. (B.C. July 7, 1987 amalg.)
June 25, 2002 – Name changed to Consolidated Takepoint Ventures Ltd. and continued into Yukon; basis 1 new for 3 old shs. ■

Takla Gold Mines Ltd. (Can. July 13, 1988)
May 18, 1994 – Name changed to Canard Resources Ltd.; basis 1 new for 8 old shs. ■

Takla Silver Mines Ltd. (B.C. 1964)
Oct. 28, 1974 – Charter cancelled.

Takla Star Resources Ltd. (Alta. Nov. 25, 1982)
July 8, 2002 – Name changed to North Group Limited and continued into Canada. ■

Tako Resources Ltd. (B.C. Sept. 18, 1972)
Mar. 27, 1998 – Name changed to Consolidated Tako Resources Ltd.; basis 1 new for 7 old shs. ■

Takoo Mineral Corporation Ltd. (B.C. 1964)
Sept. 21, 1972 – Dissolved.

Taku Gold Corp. (B.C. July 19, 1999)
Dec. 2, 2020 – Name changed to C2C Gold Corp. ■

Taku River Gold Mines Ltd. (B.C. 1945)
1953 – Acquired by New Taku Mines Limited; basis 1 new for 4 old shs. (see New Taku Mines Limited)

Takura Minerals Inc. (B.C. June 13, 1983)
Aug. 28, 1997 – Name changed to Consolidated African Mining Corporation; basis 1 new for 2 old shs. ■

Talborne Capital Corporation (Can. July 30, 1986)
Apr. 1994 – Placed into receivership. Coopers & Lybrand appointed receiver.
May 11, 1994 – All assets liquidated. Secured creditors suffered a significant shortfall and there were no funds available for distribution to unsecured creditors or shldrs.
Apr. 1, 1995 – Receiver discharged.

Talcorp Associates Limited (Can. Mar. 12, 1931; via Dominion charter)
Dec. 1978 – Amalgamated with Toronto and London Investment Company Ltd. to form new co. with same name Talcorp Associates Limited.
Aug. 1, 1982 – Name changed to Talcorp Limited. ■

Talcorp Limited (Can. Dec. 1978 amalg.)
July 24, 1986 – Name changed to Consolidated Talcorp Limited; basis 4 new com. for 1 old $3 convert. pfce sh., 1 new com. for 1 old non-vtg. sh., and 1 new com. for 10 old com. shs. ■

Talemon Investments Ltd. (B.C. 1982)
Mar. 11, 1994 – Dissolved and struck off register.

Talent Infinity Capital Fund Corporation (B.C. June 25, 2020)
Jan. 14, 2022 – Name changed to Talent Infinity Resource Developments Inc. (see FPsurvey - Mines & Energy)

Talent Silver Mines Ltd. (Ont. 1946)
Aug. 24, 1964 – Dissolved.

Talisman Energy Inc. (Can. Dec. 14, 1982)
May 11, 2015 – Acquired by Repsol Energy Resources Canada Inc., an indirect wholly owned subsid. of Repsol S.A.; basis US$8.00 cash per Talisman com. sh. and Cdn$25 cash plus Cdn$0.1093 in accrued divds. for each Talisman 1st pref. sh.
Jan. 1, 2016 – Name changed to Repsol Oil & Gas Canada Inc.

Talison Lithium Limited (Australia Oct. 22, 2009)
Mar. 14, 2013 – Acquired by Windfield Holdings Pty Ltd. for $7.50 per sh.

Tallgrass Energy Corp. (Alta. Dec. 31, 2012 amalg.)
June 2, 2015 – Struck from registry and dissolved.

Talltree Resources Ltd. (B.C. May 3, 1996)
July 23, 2002 – Name changed to Peer 1 Network Enterprises, Inc. ■

Tally-Ho Exploration Ltd. (B.C. June 27, 1983)
Nov. 23, 1990 – Dissolved and struck off register.

Tally Resources Inc. (B.C. June 27, 1966)
July 10, 1984 – Name changed to Sequoia Resources Inc.; basis 1 new for 3 old shs. ■

Talmora Resources Inc. (Alta. May 7, 1996)
Jan. 23, 2007 – Formed Talmora Diamond Inc. in Ontario on Qualifying Transaction amalgamation with Canadian Diamind Limited, constituting a reverse takeover by Canadian Diamind; basis 1 new for 5 Canadian Diamind shs. and 1 new for 1 Talmora Resources sh. (see FPsurvey - Mines & Energy)

Talon Metals Corp. (British Virgin Islands Apr. 5, 2005 amalg.)
Mar. 24, 2010 – Amalgamated with Saber Energy Corp. to form new co. with same name Talon Metals Corp.; basis 0.17685 new Talon shs. for 1 Saber sh. and 1 new Talon sh. for 1 old Talon sh. (see FPsurvey - Mines & Energy)

Talon Petroleums Ltd. (Alta. Mar. 5, 1996)
Sept. 21, 1999 – Acquired by Ventus Energy Ltd.; basis 60¢ or 0.0857 Ventus shs. for 1 Talon sh. (see Ventus Energy Ltd.)

Talos Industries Inc. (B.C. 1980)
Apr. 16, 1992 – Dissolved and struck off register.

Taltal Gold Corp. (Ont. July 7, 1997)
June 13, 2000 – Name changed to Capture.Net Technologies Inc. ■

Talus Ventures Corp. (B.C. Feb. 13, 1980)
June 26, 2002 – Name changed to SolutionInc Technologies Limited following reverse takeover acquisition of SolutionInc Limited. ■

Talvest Growth Fund Inc. (P.E.I. 1947)
Dec. 23, 1996 – Charter cancelled; dissolved.

Talvey Metal Mines Ltd. (Ont. 1954)
Nov. 30, 1964 – Dissolved.

Taman Corporation (Ont. 1953)
Jan. 20, 1989 – Placed into receivership. Assets liquidated, secured creditors suffered a shortfall and shldrs. received nothing.
Oct. 1, 1990 – Released from receivership.

Taman Resources Limited (Ont. 1953)
Nov. 10, 1986 – Name changed to Taman Corporation; basis 1 new com. and 1 cl. A for 5 old com. shs. ■

Taman Uranium Mines Ltd. (Ont. 1953)
1970 – Name changed to Taman Resources Limited. ■

Tamara Mining Ltd. (Que. 1957)
June 1, 1974 – Charter cancelled.

Tamara Resources Inc. (B.C. Sept. 26, 1980)
Feb. 18, 1994 – Name changed to Matrix Energy Inc.; basis 1 new for 2.5 old shs. ■

Tamarac Mines Ltd. (B.C. 1959)
Aug. 25, 1972 – Struck off register.

Tamarind Holding Corp. (B.C. 1978)
Jan. 25, 1983 – Name changed to Canarctic Ventures Ltd. ■

Tamavack Resources Ltd. (B.C. 1982)
May 1, 1990 – Amalgamated with Consolidated Powergem Resource Corporation and Calvada Resources Inc. to form Eurus Resource Corp.; basis 1 new for 2.5 old shs. (see Eurus Resource Corp.)

Tamerlane Ventures Inc. (B.C. May 16, 2000)
July 26, 2010 – Continued into Canada.
Aug. 23, 2013 – Filed for protection under the Companies' Creditors Arrangement Act and Duff & Phelps Canada Restructuring Inc. was appointed monitor.
Jan. 30, 2014 – Placed into receivership. KSV Advisory Inc. (formerly Duff & Phelps Canada Restructuring Inc.) was appointed receiver.
2014 – By April 2014, certain assets had been sold for US$506,900; proceeds were used to pay down debtor-in-possession financing.

Tamicon Iron Mines Ltd. (Ont. 1958)
Oct. 22, 1962 – Dissolved.

Tampico Developments Ltd. (B.C. Dec. 28, 1972)
Dec. 1979 – Name changed to Pico Resources Ltd.; basis 1 new for 4 old shs. ■

Tan Range Exploration Corporation (Alta. July 5, 1990)
Mar. 8, 2006 – Name changed to Tanzanian Royalty Exploration Corporation. ■

Tanager Energy Inc. (Alta. July 25, 2013)
Mar. 6, 2019 – Continued into British Columbia.
Apr. 11, 2019 – Name changed to Paleo Resources, Inc. ■

Tanager Reources Limited (Ont. May 1, 1987)
Jan. 19, 1993 – Name changed to Consolidated Tanager Limited; basis 1 new for 5 old shs. (see FPsurvey - Mines & Energy)

Tanaur Yellowknife Mines Ltd. (Ont. 1940)
Sept. 1958 – Charter cancelled.

The Tanbridge Corporation (Can. Apr. 30, 1999 amalg.)
July 25, 2003 – Petitioned into bankruptcy by CIBC. Remaining directors resigned. A wind-down of operations of the Winnipeg plant and Toronto cutting facility was anticipated. Subsidiaries Wickett & Craig of America, Inc., Freeze-Dry Foods Limited and Freeze-Dry Foods Inc., would not be placed into bankruptcy and were expected to continue to operate. Deloitte & Touche Inc. was appointed trustee.
June 2005 – All assets had been liquidated, the last being the Winnipeg plant in December 2004. Proceeds resulted in a significant shortfall for the major secured creditor and there were no funds available for unsecured creditors or shldrs.
Aug. 29, 2006 – Trustee discharged

Tancord Industries Ltd. (Can. 1931)
1973 – Wholly owned subsid. of Jannock Corporation Limited. Remaining int. acquired.
Mar. 30, 1974 – Wound up.

Tandem Mines Ltd. (Ont. 1946)
1958 – Name changed to Halmon Mining & Processing Ltd.; basis 1 new for 5 old shs. ■

Tandem Resources Ltd. (B.C. Feb. 9, 1972)
Jan. 3, 1997 – Continued into Ontario.
Sept. 25, 2006 – Name changed to Opel International Inc. pursuant to reverse takeover acquisition of Opel.; basis 1 new for 20 old shs. ■

Taneloy Mines Ltd. (B.C. 1968)
Apr. 4, 1977 – Dissolved.

Tanganyika Oil Company Ltd. (Can. Sept. 19, 1995)
Dec. 24, 2008 – Acquired by Sinopec International Petroleum Exploration and Production Corporation, through wholly owned Mirror Lake Oil and Gas Company Limited, for Cdn$31.50 per sh.

Tangarine Payment Solutions Corp. (Can. July 26, 2006)
Mar. 23, 2009 – Acquired by and amalgamated with 4491157 Canada Inc., an affiliate of Pivotal Payments Corporation, for 22¢ per sh..

Tangelo Games Corp. (Ont. Oct. 15, 2014)
Sept. 18, 2018 – Acquired by GoGel Holdings Inc.; basis $0.02565 cash per sh.

Tangent Oil & Gas Ltd. (Del. Feb. 5, 1981)
Apr. 7, 1987 – Name changed to Pacific Star Communications Corporation.

Tanglewood Consolidated Resources Inc. (Ont. 1981)
Dec. 9, 1986 – Name changed to FCMI Financial Corporation; basis 1 new for 12.5 old shs. ■

Tanglewood Petroleum Corporation (Ont. 1981)
Nov. 1982 – Name changed to Tanglewood Consolidated Resources Inc.; basis 1 new for 2 old shs. ■

Tango Energy Inc. (Alta. Mar. 6, 2002)
June 17, 2010 – Name changed to Tamarack Valley Energy Ltd. following acquisition of (old) Tamarack Valley Energy Ltd. (see FPsurvey - Mines & Energy)

Tango Gold Mines Incorporated (B.C. Apr. 10, 2007)
Nov. 21, 2014 – Name changed to Tango Mining Limited. ■

Tango Mineral Resources Inc. (Can. May 5, 1994 amalg.)
Dec. 4, 2003 – Name changed to RNC Gold Inc. following reverse takeover acquisition of RNC Gold Ontario Inc.; basis 1 new for 25 old shs. ■

Tango Mining Limited (B.C. Apr. 10, 2007)
Oct. 28, 2019 – Name changed to Southstone Minerals Limited; basis 1 new for 10 old shs. (see FPsurvey - Mines & Energy)

Tangram Resources Ltd. (unknown)
Dec. 31, 1988 – Acquired by American Eagle Petroleums Ltd.; basis 1.67 American Eagle shs. for 1 Tangram sh. (see American Eagle Petroleums Ltd.)

Tanjo Industries Ltd. (B.C. Mar. 31, 1969)
Jan. 29, 1981 – Name changed to Amerex Development Corp. ■

Tanjo Mines Ltd. (N.P.L.) (B.C. Mar. 31, 1969)
Apr. 26, 1974 – Name changed to Tanjo Industries Ltd. ■

Tanker Oil & Gas Ltd. (B.C. Aug. 25, 1970)
May 23, 1990 – Name changed to Tyson Financial Corp.; basis 1 new for 3 old shs. ■

Tanmount Larder Gold Mines Ltd. (Ont. 1945)
1966 – Charter cancelled.

Tanner Arctic Enterprises Ltd. (Alta. 1959)
Aug. 11, 1993 – Name changed to Kuma Resources Ltd. following reverse takeover acquisition of Zama Production Limited and Baloil Resources Ltd. ■

Tanner Arctic Oil Ltd. (Alta. 1959)
Oct. 23, 1991 – Name changed to Tanner Arctic Enterprises Ltd.; basis 1 new for 10 old shs. ■

Tannex Resources Ltd. (B.C. 1966)
June 24, 1974 – Name changed to Caron Resources Inc.; basis 1 new for 5 old shs.

Tanos Petroleum Corporation (Alta. Feb. 13, 1980)
Nov. 10, 1992 – Name changed to Cypango Ventures Ltd.; basis 1 new for 5 old shs. ■

Tanq Capital Corporation (Ont. July 13, 2012)
Dec. 19, 2012 – Succeeded by True North Commercial Real Estate Investment Trust pursuant to plan of arrangement whereby True North Commercial Real Estate Investment Trust was formed to facilitate the conversion of the corporation into a trust; basis 1 new for 8 old shs. (see FPsurvey - Industrials)

Tanqueray Exploration Ltd. (Alta. Oct. 7, 1986 amalg.)
Sept. 2, 2016 – Continued into British Columbia.
Dec. 29, 2016 – Name changed to ImmunoPrecise Antibodies Ltd. following acquisition of (old) ImmunoPrecise Antibodies Ltd. (see FPsurvey - Industrials)

Tanqueray Resources Ltd. (Alta. Oct. 7, 1986 amalg.)
Sept. 13, 2011 – Name changed to Tanqueray Exploration Ltd.; basis 1 new for 10 old shs. ■

Tansy Resources Inc. (B.C. 1986)
Mar. 22, 1990 – Name changed to Cabot Resources Corp. ■

Tantalex Resources Corporation (B.C. Sept. 28, 2009)
May 11, 2022 – Name changed to Tantalex Lithium Resources Corporation. (see FPsurvey - Mines & Energy)

Tantalum Mining Corporation of Canada Limited (Ont. 1967)
Oct. 13, 1994 – Continued into Canada.

Tantalum Refining & Mining Corp. of America Ltd. (Ont. 1946)
June 1952 – Assets acquired by Nationwide Minerals Ltd.; basis 1 new for 5 old shs. (see Nationwide Minerals Ltd.)

Tantalus Resources Ltd. (B.C. May 28, 1980)
Nov. 22, 1996 – Name changed to Tapango Resources Ltd.; basis 1 new for 3 old shs. ■

Tantato Resources Inc. (B.C. Aug. 24, 1986)
July 25, 1989 – Name changed to Interactive Communications Corporation. ■

Tanzania Minerals Corp. (B.C. June 29, 2007)
June 5, 2019 – Name changed to Jushi Holdings Inc. pursuant to reverse takeover acquisition of Jushi Inc.; basis 1 new for 22.75711 old shs. (see FPsurvey - Industrials)

Tanzanian Gold Corporation (Alta. July 5, 1990)
May 27, 2022 – Name changed to TRX Gold Corporation. ■

Tanzanian Royalty Exploration Corporation (Alta. July 5, 1990)
Apr. 17, 2019 – Name changed to Tanzanian Gold Corporation. ■

Tanzilla Explorations Ltd. (B.C. Sept. 30, 1967)
June 28, 1974 – Name changed to Regis Development Corporation. ■

Taos Capital Inc. (Can. Nov. 1, 2004)
Nov. 25, 2005 – Name changed to TransGaming Inc. following Qualifying Transaction reverse takeover acquisition of TransGaming Technologies Inc. ■

Tapajos Gold Inc. (B.C. Sept. 15, 1986)
Apr. 3, 2000 – Acquired by Highgrade Ventures Ltd.; basis 1 Highgrade sh. for 1 Tapajos sh. (see Brasilca Mining Corporation)

Tapango Resources Ltd. (B.C. May 28, 1980)
July 27, 2015 – Acquired by Palo Duro Energy Inc. (renamed CarbonOne Technologies Inc.); basis 1.071 Palo Duro com. shs. for 1 Tapango sh. (see Palo Duro Energy Inc.)

Taparko Capital Corp. (Can. Feb. 4, 1997)
Nov. 17, 2000 – Formed Odyssey Energy Corporation in Canada on amalgamation with Odyssey Energy Corporation and following reverse takeover acquisition of Charpet Resources Ltd. ■

Tapestry Resource Corp. (B.C. May 27, 1982)
Aug. 24, 2010 – Name changed to Gran Colombia Gold Corp. pursuant to reverse takeover acquisition of Gran Colombia Gold, S.A. which was amalgamated with wholly owned Panamanian subsidiary Masteri Inc. ■

Tapestry Ventures Ltd. (B.C. May 27, 1982)
Dec. 23, 2004 – Name changed to Tapestry Resource Corp.; basis 1 new for 4 old shs. ■

Tapin Copper Mines Ltd. (B.C. 1966)
Feb. 25, 1983 – Struck off register.

Tappan-Gurney Ltd. (Can. 1951)
Dec. 1968 – Control formerly held by Tappan Co. of Mansfield, Ohio, until when Corpex (1977) Inc. acquired 92% of the o/s shs. Subsequently merged with Findbel Inc. to form Belanger-Tappan Inc.

Tappit Resources Ltd. (Can. June 5, 1980)
Sept. 10, 2003 – Business combination with Crescent Point Energy Ltd. to form Crescent Point Energy Trust and StarPoint Energy Ltd.; basis 36¢ plus 0.10 StarPoint com. shs. plus either (i) 0.19 Crescent Point trust units, (ii) 0.19 Crescent Point Acquisition Ltd. ser.A exch. sh. or (iii) a combination thereof for 1 Tappit com. sh. (see StarPoint Energy Ltd.)

Tar Point Oil Co. (unknown)
1963 – Assets acquired by New Associated Developments Ltd.; basis 1 new for 49 old shs.

Tara Exploration And Development Company Limited (Ont. 1953)
May 2, 1986 – Acquired by Outokumpu Oy of Finland for $19 per sh.

Tarasol Ventures Inc. (Alta. Aug. 19, 1993)
Jan. 18, 1995 – Name changed to Founders Energy Ltd.; basis 1 new for 2 old shs. ■

Tarbell Mines Ltd. (Ont. 1954)
Dec. 10, 1962 – Dissolved.

Tarbutt Mines Ltd. (Ont. 1955)
Mar. 3, 1966 – Charter cancelled.

Targa Resource Corporation (Alta. 1987)
Sept. 1, 1993 – Struck off register.

Targas Resources Inc. (B.C. 1986)
Oct. 22, 1993 – Dissolved and struck off register.

Target Capital Inc. (Alta.)
Jan. 31, 2024 – Name changed to 763997 Alberta Ltd. ■

Target Carbons Ltd. (Alta. Dec. 5, 1986)
Feb. 5, 1997 – Acquired by Blue Range Resource Corporation; basis 22¢ per Target sh. or 1 Blue Range cl. A com. sh. for 33 Target com. shs. (see Blue Range Resource Corporation)

Target Energy Canada Inc. (Alta. July 26, 1947)
Feb. 22, 1993 – Name changed to Ontarget Capital Inc.

Target Energy Inc. (Alta. July 12, 1994)
Jan. 24, 2002 – Name changed to Olympia Financial Group Inc.; basis 1 new for 250 old shs. (see FPsurvey - Industrials)

Target Exploration and Mining Corp. (B.C. June 1, 1993)
Apr. 6, 2009 – Acquired by Crosshair Exploration & Mining Corp.; basis 1.2 Crosshair Exploration shs. for 1 Target Exploration sh.
2021 – Name changed to GlobalX A320 Aircraft Acquisition Corp.

Target Petroleums Limited (Ont. Mar. 8, 1951)
1957 – Acquired by Savanna Creek Gas & Oil Ltd.; basis 1 new for 6 old shs.

Target Resources Ltd. (B.C. 1982)
Nov. 6, 1985 – Name changed to Grand China Resources Ltd. ■

Target Ten Inc. (Alta. 1987)
June 1, 1995 – Dissolved and struck off register.

Target Vanguard Capital Inc. (Can. Oct. 15, 1986)
Feb. 22, 1995 – Name changed to Coretek Vencap Inc.; basis 1 new for 2 old shs. ■

Tarn Pure Technology Corp. (B.C. 1983)
Mar. 10, 1995 – Acquired by TP Technology Limited PLC; basis 1 TP Technology sh. for 10 Tarn Pure shs.
July 21, 1995 – Dissolved and struck off register.

Taro Industries Limited (Alta. Dec. 11, 1978 amalg.)
Jan. 20, 1998 – Acquired by EVI, Inc.; basis 0.123 EVI shs. for 1 Taro sh.

Taronga Resources Ltd. (B.C. 1966)
Feb. 25, 1983 – Struck off register.

Tarquin Group Inc. (Ont. July 28, 2004)
June 15, 2009 – Certificate of incorporation cancelled and dissolved.

Tarragon Oil and Gas Limited (Ont. 1927)
Aug. 14, 1998 – Amalgamated with Marathon Oil Canada Limited, an indirect wholly owned subsid. of Marathon Oil Company of Houston, Tex., by way of plan of arrangement; basis $14.25 or 1 Marathon Oil Canada Limited exch. sh. for 1 Tarragon Oil sh. (see Marathon Oil Canada Limited)

Tarron Industries Ltd. (B.C. Aug. 5, 1983)
July 3, 1997 – Name changed to Orko Gold Corporation. ■

Tarron Resources Ltd. (B.C. Aug. 5, 1983)
June 29, 1988 – Name changed to Tarron Industries Ltd. ■

Tarsis Capital Corp. (Alta. Oct. 21, 2005)
Apr. 25, 2008 – Continued into British Columbia.
June 18, 2009 – Name changed to Tarsis Resources Ltd. ■

Tarsis Resources Ltd. (B.C. Apr. 25, 2008)
Apr. 30, 2015 – Name changed to Alianza Minerals Ltd.; basis 1 new for 10 old shs. ■

Tartan Energy Inc. (B.C. Sept. 21, 1966)
Feb. 6, 2006 – Acquired indirectly by Nations Energy Company Ltd.; basis 1 Nations redeem. pfd. sh. for 1 Tartan com. sh. The pfd. shs. were redeemed immediately for 63¢ per sh.

Tartan Lake Gold Mines Ltd. (Ont. 1945)
1947 – Charter cancelled.

Tartan Petroleums Ltd. (Alta. Aug. 1949)
1962 – Struck off register.

Tartisan Resources Corp. (Ont. Mar. 18, 2008)
Mar. 23, 2018 – Name changed to Tartisan Nickel Corp. (see FPsurvey - Mines & Energy)

The Tarxien Corporation (Ont. 1983)
Dec. 23, 1996 – Acquired by Gecamex Acquisitions Corporation, a wholly owned subsid. of Gecamex Technologies, Inc., for $15.40 per sh.

Tarxien International Incorporated (Ont. 1983)
Jan. 31, 1989 – Name changed to The Tarxien Corporation; basis 1 new for 20 old shs. ■

Tarzan Gold Inc. (Ont. 1987)
Jan. 24, 1990 – Amalgamated with Glen Auden Resources Limited to form new co. with same name Glen Auden Resources Limited; basis 1 new for 1 Glen Auden sh. and 1 new for 1.5 Tarzan shs. (see Glen Auden Resources Limited)

Tasca Resources Ltd. (B.C. Oct. 5, 2011)
Mar. 13, 2019 – Name changed to Universal Copper Ltd.; basis 1 new for 2 old shs. ■

Tasex Capital Limited (B.C. Oct. 27, 2010)
Feb. 22, 2012 – Name changed to Flinders Resources Limited pursuant to Qualifying Transaction reverse takeover acquisition of Burke Resources Ltd. ■

Tashota Goldfields Ltd. (Ont. 1932)
1960 – Charter cancelled.

Tashota-Nipigon Mines Limited (Ont. 1939)
Dec. 1, 1988 – Amalgamated with McAdam Resources Inc. and Konteko Resources Inc. to form new co. with same name McAdam Resources Inc.; basis 1 new for 1 McAdam sh., 1 new for 10 Konteko shs. and 1 new for 2 Tashota-Nipigon shs. (see McAdam Resources Inc.)

Tashteck Mines Ltd. (Ont. 1955)
Nov. 5, 1969 – Charter cancelled.

Tasman Metals Ltd. (B.C. Aug. 27, 2007)
Oct. 22, 2009 – Amalgamated in British Columbia to continue with same name.
Aug. 26, 2016 – Acquired by Leading Edge Materials Corp. (formerly Flinders Resources Limited); basis 0.5 Leading Edge com. shs. for 1 Tasman com. sh.

Tasmaque Gold Mines Ltd. (Ont. 1944)
Nov. 22, 1972 – Charter cancelled.

Tasmijopen Mining Co. Ltd. (Ont. 1934)
Jan. 27, 1966 – Dissolved.

Tasu Resources Ltd. (B.C. 1981)
Oct. 15, 1990 – Name changed to Imtrex Industries & Recycling Inc. ■

Tatara Gold Mines Ltd. (Que. 1946)
Oct. 1973 – Charter cancelled.

Tathacus Resources Ltd. (Can. Dec. 11, 1997)
Mar. 31, 2004 – Formed Pan Terra Industries Inc. in Canada pursuant to acquisition of and amalgamation with Pan Terra Industries 2003 Inc. (following Pan Terra's acquisition of Bluebird Excavating and Demolition Ltd. and Bluebird Contracting Ltd.). ■

Tatlar Resources Ltd. (B.C. Feb. 6, 1986)
July 22, 1991 – Name changed to Opact Resources Ltd.; basis 1 new for 4 old shs. ■

Tatmar Ventures Inc. (B.C. June 9, 2004)
July 29, 2011 – Name changed to Highway 50 Gold Corp. (see FPsurvey - Mines & Energy)

Tatonka Energy, Inc. (Wyo. July 7, 1994)
Apr. 20, 1999 – Name changed to Phymed Inc.; basis 1 new for 10 old shs.

Tatrass International Ltd. (Alta. 1987)
Oct. 29, 1992 – Formed Vitreous Environmental Group Inc. in Alberta on amalgamation with Vitreous Enviromental Group Inc.; basis 10 new for 1 Vitreous cl. A, cl. B and cl. C sh. and 1 new for 1 Tatrass sh. ■

Tats Mines Ltd. (B.C. 1970)
Oct. 3, 1977 – Dissolved.

Tatsa Resources Ltd. (B.C. 1979)
July 19, 1983 – Name changed to Acorn Resources Ltd. ■

Taurcanis Mines Ltd. (Ont. 1947)
1963 – Name changed to Tundra Gold Mines Ltd.; basis 1 new pref. for 1 old pref. sh. and 1 new com. for 4 old com. shs. ■

Taurus Exploration Ltd. (B.C. Feb. 3, 1988)
Nov. 26, 1997 – Name changed to Trans Asia Resources Inc. ■

Taurus Footwear Inc. (Can. May 16, 1985)
Nov. 2, 2005 – Dissolved.

Taurus Resources Limited (B.C. May 25, 1960)
Nov. 24, 1988 – Name changed to International Taurus Resources Inc.; basis 1 new for 10 old shs. ■

Tavane Exploration Ltd. (Ont. 1959)
Apr. 1980 – Charter cancelled.

Tawsho Mining Inc. (Ont. May 31, 2008 amalg.)
Mar. 2, 2016 – Acquired by Entourage Metals Ltd.; basis 0.344 Entourage com. shs. for 1 Tawsho com. sh. (see Genesis Metals Corp.)

Tax Optimized Return Oriented Securities Trust (Ont. Sept. 29, 2003)
Jan. 24, 2011 – Name changed to Aston Hill Capital Growth Fund. ■

Tay River Mines Ltd. (B.C. Nov. 29, 1965)
June 24, 1980 – Name changed to Tay River Petroleum Ltd. ■

Tay River Petroleum Ltd. (B.C. Nov. 29, 1965)
Jan. 30, 1981 – Amalgamated with Vicor Resources Ltd. to continue as Tay River Petroleum Ltd.

Tay River Petroleum Ltd. (B.C. Nov. 29, 1965)
Apr. 29, 1985 – Name changed to Butec International Chemical Corp. ■

TayCon Capital Corporation (Ont. May 3, 2006)
Apr. 8, 2010 – Dissolved following Qualifying Transaction private placement subscription of 2,500,000 com. shs. plus 1,250,000 wts. of Xtierra Inc. and distribution of Xtierra units to shldrs. (see Xtierra Inc.)

Taylor (Bridge River) Mines Ltd. (B.C. 1933)
May 26, 1969 – Name changed to Inter-Tech Development and Resources Ltd. ■

Taylor Chemical Foam Industries Ltd. (Can. 1961)
June 22, 1968 – Charter cancelled.

Taylor Creek Mining Co. Ltd. (B.C. 1949)
1950 – Name changed to Zenda Gold Mining (Canada) Ltd. ■

Taylor Gas Liquids Fund (Alta. May 16, 1996)
July 31, 2000 – Continued into Ontario.
Aug. 16, 2000 – Name changed to Taylor NGL Limited Partnership. ■

Taylor Gold Mines Ltd. (Ont. 1965)
Apr. 9, 1975 – Charter cancelled.

Taylor NGL Limited Partnership (Ont. July 31, 2000)
Jan. 16, 2008 – Acquired by AltaGas Income Trust for $11.20 per AltaGas unit or 0.42 AltaGas trust units for 1 Taylor unit. (see AltaGas Ltd.)
July 1, 2010 – Name changed to AltaGas Holding Partnership. (see AltaGas Ltd.)

Taylor North American Equity Opportunities Fund (Ont. Jan. 1, 2012)
Jan. 30, 2019 – Merged into Brompton Global Dividend Growth ETF; basis 0.495198 Brompton Global ETF units for 1 Taylor North America trust unit.

Taylor, Pearson & Carson (Canada) Limited (Can. 1946)
July 1959 – Acquired by Prairie Pacific Distributors Ltd., a subsid. of Booker Brothers, McConnell & Co. of London, England, at $21 per sh. All 5% pref. shs. redeemed Mar. 27, 1961, at $11 per sh. plus accr. divds.

Taylor Rand Incorporated (Ont. Aug. 24, 1993 amalg.)
June 27, 1996 – Name changed to Sheridan Reserve Incorporated; basis 1 new for 10 old shs. ■

The Taylor-Windfall Gold Mining Company Limited (B.C. 1928)
Nov. 15, 1972 – Amalgamated with Santana International Resources Ltd. to form Taywin Resources Ltd. (N.P.L.)

Taywin Resources Limited (B.C. Nov. 15, 1972 amalg.)
Aug. 26, 1994 – Name changed to Consolidated Taywin Resources Ltd.; basis 1 new for 5 old shs. ■

Taywin Resources Ltd. (N.P.L.) (B.C. Nov. 15, 1972 amalg.)
Nov. 5, 1985 – Name changed to Taywin Resources Limited. ■

Tazin Mines Limited (Can. 1934)
1969 – Name changed to Zinat Mines Ltd.; basis 1 new for 4 old shs. ■

Tazin Uranium Mines Limited (B.C. 1955)
Aug. 1962 – Struck off register.

Tchaikazan Enterprises Inc. (B.C. Mar. 12, 1965)
Aug. 2, 1991 – Dissolved and struck off register.

Tchentlo Lake Mines Ltd. (B.C. 1969)
Apr. 23, 1971 – Name changed to National Lake Mines Ltd. ■

Teal Exploration Limited (Ont. 1945)
Dec. 27, 1967 – Dissolved.

Teal Industries Ltd. (B.C. 1983)
1992 – Ceased flooring and truss operations and manufacturing complex in Surrey, B.C., sold following court order.
Mar. 1993 – Petitioned into bankruptcy and Deloitte & Touche of Vancouver appointed receiver.
July 9, 1993 – Bankrupt.
May 1995 – Administration of the company was complete. Secured creditors suffered a shortfall and there were no distributions made to shldrs.
Sept. 15, 1995 – Dissolved and struck off register.
Oct. 11, 2000 – Receiver discharged.

Teal Minerals Ltd. (B.C. 1983)
May 5, 1986 – Name changed to Teal Industries Ltd. ■

Team Energy and Minerals Inc. (Ont. Sept. 30, 1919)
Aug. 31, 1992 – Delisted from the CDN. Subsequently dissolved and charter cancelled.

Team Resources Corp. (B.C. May 20, 1988)
Mar. 7, 1994 – Name changed to Consolidated Team Resources Corp.; basis 1 new for 3 old shs. ■

Teapot Dome Oils Ltd. (Can. Apr. 2, 1929)
Amalgamated with Atlantic Keystone Petroleums, Ltd.

Tech Achievers Growth & Income Fund (Ont.)
June 22, 2017 – Converted to an exchange-traded fund.

Tech Leaders Income Fund (Ont. Jan. 1, 2011)
Apr. 3, 2018 – Converted into an exchange traded fund (ETF).

Tech Solutions Capital Corp. (B.C. Jan. 10, 2005)
Feb. 7, 2008 – Name changed to Upper Canyon Minerals Corp. ■

Techbyte Inc. (Can. Nov. 1, 1984)
June 11, 1990 – Name changed to Techbyte International Inc. ■

Techbyte International Inc. (Can. Nov. 1, 1984)
Aug. 30, 1995 – Declared bankrupt.

Techcana Capital Inc. (Can. Mar. 30, 1998)
Mar. 21, 2001 – Name changed to TechCana Inc. ■

TechCana Inc. (Can. Mar. 30, 1998)
Aug. 19, 2008 – Dissolved.

Techcorp Industries Inc. (Alta. Oct. 6, 1995)
Nov. 9, 1999 – Acquired by Alpine Oil Services Corporation; basis 0.333 new Alpine sh. for 1 old Techcorp sh. (see Alpine Oil Services Corporation)

Techcorp Rentals Inc. (Alta. Oct. 6, 1995)
June 22, 1998 – Name changed to Techcorp Industries Inc. ■

Techgroup Ventures Inc. (B.C. June 17, 1998)
Nov. 17, 2000 – Name changed to eReservation Systems Corp. ■

Techmin Canada Ltd. (Alta. 1986)
Dec. 1, 1993 – Dissolved and struck off register.

Techmire Ltd. (Can. July 3, 1973)
Jan. 15, 2001 – Acquired by Exco Technologies Limited for $3.85 per sh.

Technical Ventures RX Corp. (Alta. Mar. 26, 2012)
Nov. 10, 2014 – Formed Hemostemix Inc. in Alberta following Qualifying Transaction reverse takeover of and amalgamation with TheraVite Inc. (deemed acquiror); basis 1 new for 5 old shs. (see FPsurvey - Industrials)

Technicoil Corporation (Alta. May 6, 1997)
June 7, 2011 – Amalgamated with Essential Energy Services Ltd.; basis 0.80¢ plus 0.7111 Essential shs. for 1 Technicoil sh. (see Essential Energy Services Ltd.)

Technigen Corporation (Can. July 28, 1982)
June 10, 2004 – Dissolved.

Technigen Platinum Corporation (Can. July 28, 1982)
June 8, 1987 – Name changed to Technigen Corporation. ■

Technilab Pharma Inc. (Can. Feb. 20, 1997 amalg.)
Aug. 8, 2000 – Acquired by Ratiopharm Canada Inc. for $6.10 per sh.

Technipure Inc. (Alta. May 24, 1996)
Nov. 14, 1997 – Formed Terra Mannix Incorporated following acquisition of 678101 Alberta Inc. and 678102 Alberta Inc.; basis 1 new for 1 old sh. ■

Technologia Systems Corp. (B.C. Oct. 25, 1985)
Feb. 11, 1994 – Name changed to Master Player Home Entertainment Corp.; basis 1 new for 4 old shs. ■

Technologies of Sterilization with Ozone TSO3 inc. (Que. June 10, 1998)
Dec. 16, 2002 – Name changed to TSO3 Inc. ■

Technology and Resource Capital Corp. (B.C. Apr. 12, 2000)
Oct. 10, 2003 – Name changed to P2P Health Systems Inc. following Qualifying Transaction reverse takeover acquisition of Person to Person Health Systems Inc. ■

Technology Flavors & Fragrances, Inc. (N.Y. Jan. 3, 1989)
Nov. 24, 1993 – Continued into Delaware.

Technology Growth Partners Corp. (B.C. Oct. 22, 1999)
Aug. 21, 2001 – Name changed to VantagePoint Systems, Inc. following reverse takeover acquisition of VantagePoint Group, Inc. ■

Technovision Systems, Inc. (B.C. Jan. 19, 1988)
Dec. 1, 2002 – Amalgamated with Axion Communications Inc. to form new co. with same name Technovision Systems, Inc.; basis 1 new for 0.603 Axion shs. and 1 new for 1 Technovision sh.
Nov. 20, 2003 – Formed Uniserve Communications Corp. in British Columbia on amalgamation with PCNet International Inc. with Technovision the deemed acquiror; basis 0.7296 new for 1 PCNet sh. and 1 new for 1 Technovision sh. (see FPsurvey - Industrials)

Techoldmin Limited (Ont. June 10, 1953)
Feb. 24, 2000 – Formed Enviro Waste Technologies Inc. on amalgamation with Enviro Waste Technologies Inc. ■

Techsite Strategies Corp. (Alta. Feb. 13, 1980)
July 17, 2003 – Name changed to Sola Resource Corp. ■

TechTana Capital Ltd. (B.C. Apr. 28, 1986)
Dec. 21, 1995 – Name changed to Forum Ventures Ltd.; basis 1 new for 7 old shs. ■

TechX Technologies Inc. (B.C. June 11, 2010)
July 20, 2021 – Name changed to Mobilum Technologies Inc. (see FPsurvey - Industrials)

Teck Cominco Limited (Can. Aug. 7, 1978)
Apr. 23, 2009 – Name changed to Teck Resources Limited. (see FPsurvey - Mines & Energy)

Teck Cominco Metals Ltd. (Can. Jan. 9, 1906)
June 1, 2009 – Name changed to Teck Metals Ltd.

Teck Corporation (Can. Aug. 7, 1978)
Sept. 12, 2001 – Name changed to Teck Cominco Limited. ■

Teck Corporation Limited (Ont. Sept. 12, 1963 amalg.)
Aug. 7, 1978 – Name changed to Teck Corporation and continued into Canada. ■

The Teck-Hughes Gold Mines Ltd. (Ont. 1913)
Sept. 12, 1963 – Merged with Canadian Devonian Petroleums Limited and Lamaque Gold Mines Ltd. to form Teck Corporation Limited; basis 2 new for 5 old shs.

Teck Investments Limited (Ont. 1954)
Nov. 28, 1973 – Charter cancelled.

Teck-World Industries Inc. (Alta. June 19, 1986)
Dec. 1, 1997 – Struck off register.

Teckora Mines Limited (Ont. 1971)
July 6, 1983 – Amalgamated with 8 other cos. to form Lobo Gold & Resources Inc.; basis 1 new for 10 old shs.

Teckron Mines & Energy Corp. (Ont. Sept. 24, 1985)
May 1, 1989 – Name changed to Vision Pharmaceuticals Inc.; basis 1 new for 6 old shs. ■

Tecmar Technologies International Inc. (Can. Aug. 25, 1993)
Mar. 31, 1998 – Name changed to Xencet Investments Inc. ■

Tecnecon Gold Industries Inc. (Alta. July 25, 1990)
Jan. 1, 1996 – Dissolved and struck off register.

TecnoPetrol Inc. (Yuk. June 19, 1997)
Jan. 24, 2003 – Name changed to Bolivar Gold Corp. ■

Teco Mines and Oils Limited (Ont. Jan. 19, 1966)
Dec. 11, 1990 – Name changed to Castle Capital Inc. ■

Tecrad Inc. (Que. 1982)
July 1, 1990 – All assets seized and resold by the Royal Bank of Canada, Quebec City. Peat Marwick, Thorne acted for bank. Monies received not sufficient to cover debt. No distribution to shldrs.

TecSyn International Inc. (Ont. 1962)
Sept. 1, 2000 – Privatized at $2.70 per sh.

Tectonic Capital Corp. (B.C. Dec. 13, 2007)
Apr. 24, 2009 – Name changed to Tectonic Minerals Corporation. ■

Tectonic Energy Corporation (Del. 1980)
Apr. 27, 1984 – Name changed to Enertec Corporation; basis 1 new for 10 old shs.

Tectonic Minerals Corporation (B.C. Dec. 13, 2007)
Aug. 10, 2011 – Name changed to Comstock Metals Ltd. pursuant to Qualifying Transaction reverse takeover acquisiton of Comstock Metals Ltd. and subsequent amalgamation with wholly owned 0906032 B.C. Ltd. (see FPsurvey - Mines & Energy)

Tecumseh Developments Ltd. (unknown)
1955 – Acquired by Trans-Canada Explorations Ltd.; basis 1 new for 5 old shs.

Tecumseh Resources Ltd. (B.C. Mar. 25, 1983)
Feb. 11, 1985 – Name changed to Thrust Resources Inc. ■

Teddy Bear Valley Mines Limited (Ont. 1929)
Jan. 1980 – Charter cancelled; revived in same year.

Teddy Glacier Mines Limited (B.C. 1964)
Feb. 4, 1983 – Struck off register.

Tee-Comm Electronics Inc. (Can. 1985)
Apr. 1997 – All assets sold.
May 21, 1997 – In May, The Bank of Montreal demanded immediate repayment of its existing credit facility. Toronto-based Ernst & Young Inc. was appointed interim receiver with respect to the property and assets of the company and certain of its subsidiaries. The board of directors resigned.
June 2002 – All distributions had been made. Secured creditors suffered a shortfall and there were no funds available for distribution to unsecured creditors or shldrs.
June 2003 – All matters had been resolved and administration complete.
Feb. 16, 2004 – Receiver discharged.

Teegana Mines Ltd. (Ont. 1957)
Jan. 1962 – Dissolved.

Teeshin Resources Ltd. (Ont. 1981)
May 8, 1991 – Name changed to Habsburg Resources Inc.; basis 1 new for 8 old shs. ■

Tego Silver Cobalt Mines Ltd. (Ont. 1949)
Apr. 1965 – Dissolved.

Tegra Enterprises Inc. (B.C. 1982)
May 8, 1986 – Continued into Ontario.
Aug. 21, 1989 – Name changed to Pacific Video Canada Ltd.; basis 1 new for 5 old shs. ■

Tejas Petroleum Resources Ltd. (Ont. July 31, 1981)
Jan. 21, 1998 – Name changed to Continental Conquest Capital Corp.; basis 1 new for 2.5 old shs. ■

Tekerra Gas Inc. (Alta. June 16, 1995)
Nov. 5, 1998 – Amalgamated with Del Roca Energy Inc. to form Del Roca Energy Ltd.; basis 0.29875 new for 1 Del Roca sh. and 0.6 new for 1 Tekerra sh. (see Del Roca Energy Ltd.)

Teklogix International Inc. (Ont. Mar. 21, 1983)
Sept. 22, 2000 – Plan of Arrangement with British-based Psion plc; basis either $35.00, or 1 Ordinary Psion plc sh., or 2.021 exchangeable Psion Canada Inc. shs for 1 Teklogix com. sh., or a combination thereof.

Tekmira Pharmaceuticals Corporation (B.C. Oct. 6, 2005)
Aug. 3, 2015 – Name changed to Arbutus Biopharma Corporation. (see FPsurvey - Industrials)

TekModo Industries Inc. (Alta. Apr. 16, 2002)
July 13, 2018 – Name changed to Lincoln Ventures Ltd.; basis 1 new for 10 old shs. (see FPsurvey - Industrials)

Teknion Corporation (Ont. Apr. 14, 1998)
Feb. 29, 2008 – Acquired by A-Tean Holdings Limited for $3.15 per sub. vtg. sh.

Teknol Mining Co. Ltd. (B.C. 1964)
Aug. 29, 1975 – Name changed to Marco Resources Limited; basis 1 new for 2 old shs. ■

Teknor Industrial Computers Inc. (Can. May 30, 1985)
Sept. 2, 1999 – Name changed to SACO SmartVision Inc. ■

La Teko Resources Ltd. (B.C. Nov. 27, 1968)
June 1, 1977 – Amalgamated with Aegean Explorations Inc. to form new co. with same name La Teko Resources Ltd.; basis unknown.
Mar. 4, 1999 – Acquired by Kinross Gold Corporation; basis 1 Kinross sh. for 2.65 La Teko shs.

TekWerks Solutions Inc. (B.C. Mar. 7, 2000)
Dec. 6, 2002 – Name changed to Hudson Resources Inc. following Qualifying Transaction acquisition of a mineral claim covering 851 sq. km in western Greenland. ■

Tel Aviv Resources Ltd. (B.C. May 22, 1980)
Oct. 2, 1981 – Name changed to Moran Resources Corporation. ■

Tel Gold Mines Ltd. (Ont. 1946)
1955 – Charter cancelled.

Telco Research Corporation Limited (Can. Apr. 24, 1985)
Apr. 10, 2000 – Acquired and amalgamated with Peregrine Systems, Inc.; basis 0.165017 Peregrine shs. for 1 Telco sh.

Telco Split Corp. (Ont. June 27, 1997)
Aug. 30, 2002 – Redeemed by company in full; basis Capital shs. redeemed for $4.28 (amount that unit value exceeds $25.00) and Preferred shs. redeemed for $25 (lesser of $25 and unit value per sh).

TelcoPlus Enterprises Inc. (B.C. May 26, 1978)
Dec. 5, 2005 – Name changed to Yamiri Gold and Energy Inc. following reverse takeover acquisition of Yacimientos Mineros Riojanos S.A. ■

Tele-Capital Inc. (Can. 1984 amalg.)
Aug. 28, 1986 – Name changed to Pathonic Network Inc. ■

Tele-Capital Ltd. (Can. 1953)
June 11, 1981 – Amalgamated with Tele-Capital Holdings Inc., a wholly owned subsid. of La Verendrye Management Corporation; each o/s cl. A sh. held by minority shldrs. became a cl. A sh. of the amalg. co., which were subsequently redeemed on June 30, 1982, at $35 per sh. (see La Vérendrye Management Corporation)

Tele-Find Technologies Corp. (Ont. Jan. 15, 1997)
Mar. 13, 2018 – Name changed to Rigel Technologies Inc.; basis 1 new for 10 old shs. (see FPsurvey - Mines & Energy)

Télé-Métropole Corporation (Que. Mar. 29, 1960)
Mar. 1, 1974 – Name changed to Télé-Métropole Inc. ■

Télé-Métropole Inc. (Que. Mar. 29, 1960)
Feb. 17, 1998 – Name changed to TVA Group Inc. (see FPsurvey - Industrials)

Tele Pacific International Communications Corp. (B.C. 1981)
Jan. 16, 1998 – Name changed to Pacific AD-Link Corp. ■

Tele-Radio Systems Limited (Can. July 22, 1981)
Apr. 1998 – Minimal dividend paid to the Winchester Group Inc., the company's secure creditor and major shldr., and administration of the bankrupt estate complete.
June 4, 1998 – Trustee discharged and no distribution made to unsecured creditors and shldrs.
May 6, 2004 – Dissolved.

TeleBackup Exchangeco Inc. (Alta. May 5, 1995)
Mar. 2, 2006 – Redeemed; basis 5.0589 new Symantec Corporation shs. for 1 old TeleBackup sh.

Telebackup Systems Inc. (Alta. May 5, 1995)
May 28, 1999 – Following Plan of Arrangement, merged with US based VERITAS Software Corporation, to form TeleBackup Exchangeco Inc. (Exchangeco); basis 1 new exchangeable cl. A non-vtg. sh. of Exchangeco for 1 com. sh. of Telebackup which in turn will be exchanged for either (i) 0.13233 of an exchang. sh. of Exchangeco exchg. for 1 com. sh. of Veritas Holding Corporation, or (ii) 0.13233 of a com. sh. of Veritas for 1 com. sh. of Telebackup. (see TeleBackup Exchangeco Inc.)

Télébec ltée (Que. June 1, 1976)
June 30, 1999 – Redeemed ser. 6 first pref. shs.; basis $25 plus all accrued and unpaid div. of $0.453125 per sh.
Aug. 7, 2002 – Name changed to Bell Nordiq Group Inc. ■

The Telecommerce Corporation (Ont. July 3, 1986)
Oct. 1, 1994 – Charter cancelled and co. dissolved.
Feb. 3, 1999 – Charter and company revived.
Feb. 25, 1999 – Name changed to E-Ventures Inc.; basis 1 new for 10 old shs. ■

Teledata Ventures Corp. (B.C. Nov. 24, 1980)
Apr. 3, 1998 – Name changed to CTF Technologies Inc. and continued into Yukon pursuant to reverse takeover acquisition of Brazil-based Polinet Engenharia e Sistemas em Telemática S.A. ■

Teledyne Canada, Limited (Ont. Feb. 10, 1948)
Nov. 25, 1993 – Acquired by Teledyne Newco Inc., a wholly owned subsid. of Teledyne Inc., for $18.875 per sh.

Teleflex Ltd. (Can. 1938)
1961 – Charter surrendered after shldrs. exchanged their holdings for stk. in Teleflex Inc.

Teleglobe Inc. (Can. Dec. 31, 1985 amalg.)
July 3, 2014 – Dissolved.

Teleguard Systems International, Inc. (B.C. 1983)
May 1, 1992 – Dissolved and struck off register.

Telehop Communications Inc. (Ont. May 11, 1993)
Feb. 10, 2017 – Name changed to Adya Inc. (see FPsurvey - Industrials)

Telekom Advanced Systems Corporation (Que. May 1, 1996)
May 2, 2003 – Struck from register and dissolved for failure to file.

TeleLink Communications Corporation (B.C. May 11, 1984)
May 7, 2001 – Name changed to Ignition Point Technologies Corp. and continued into Canada; basis 1 new for 3 old shs. ■

Telemac Cellular International Inc. (B.C. 1985)
Dec. 7, 1994 – Name changed to Cancall Cellular Communications Inc. ■

Télémédia Inc. (Can. Sept. 1, 1986 amalg.)
Nov. 11, 1997 – All o/s cl. A shs. acquired by Telemedia Acquisition Inc. and amalgamated with Telemedia Acquisition); basis $7.50 per cl. A sh. Co. now private.
Aug. 31, 1998 – Formed Télémédia Communications Inc. on amalgamation with Télémédia Communications Inc. and two other companies.

Telepanel Inc. (Can. June 9, 1982)
July 12, 1989 – Name changed to Telepanel Systems Inc.; basis 1 new for 47 old shs. ■

Telepanel Systems Inc. (Can. June 9, 1982)
Nov. 17, 2005 – Filed a proposal under the Bankruptcy and Insolvency Act on Nov. 17, 2005, for the reorganization of the co. which included the cancellation of all the issued and o/s com. shs. and the issuance of a new class of shs. which would be acquired by NRT Technology Corporation for $1,000,000. Under the proposal, shldrs. would not receive any consideration for their shs. Mintz & Partners Limited of Toronto were appointed trustee.
Jan. 17, 2006 – NRT Technology completed the acquisition of the co., taking it private.
Jan. 17, 2006 – Continued into Ontario.

Téléphone d'Harricana & Gatineau Limitée (Que. 1934)
1961 – Northern Telephone purchased all com. stk. at $103 per sh.

Telephony Communications International Incorporated (Ont. Aug. 11, 1980)
June 18, 1994 – Struck from register and dissolved.

Telepost Communications Inc. (B.C. Aug. 18, 1986)
Apr. 20, 2004 – Delisted from the TSX-Venture Exchange. Subsequently dissolved for failure to file.

Telescan Electronics & Communications Inc. (Ont. Apr. 28, 1980)
1983 – Name changed to Telescan Technologies Inc. ■

Telescan Industries Inc. (Ont. Apr. 28, 1980)
Aug. 7, 1991 – Struck from registry and dissolved.

Telescan Technologies Inc. (Ont. Apr. 28, 1980)
July 11, 1988 – Name changed to Telescan Industries Inc.; basis 1 new for 5 old shs. ■

Telescene Film Group Inc. (Can. Mar. 17, 1989)
Aug. 2, 2001 – Acquired by CinéGroupe Images; basis unknown.

Telesis Computer Networking Inc. (B.C. Sept. 23, 1991)
Aug. 9, 1993 – Name changed to NT Network Systems Inc.; basis 1 new for 4 old shs. ■

Telesis Corporation Inc. (Alta. May 27, 1963)
Mar. 10, 1989 – Name changed to P.C. Ventures Ltd.; basis 1 new for 10 old shs. ■

Telesis Industrial Group Inc. (Alta. July 26, 1988)
Oct. 9, 1998 – Name changed to Merendon Canada Inc. ■

Telesis North Communications Inc. (B.C. June 12, 1984)
Sept. 25, 2006 – Dissolved and struck from register.

Telesta Therapeutics Inc. (Can. Sept. 1, 1999 amalg.)
Nov. 2, 2016 – Acquired by ProMetic Life Sciences Inc.; basis 0.04698 ProMetic com. sh. for 1 Telesta com. sh. (see ProMetic Life Sciences Inc.)

Telesystem International Wireless Inc. (Can. Sept. 9, 1996)
Dec. 19, 2005 – Plan of Arrangement concluded after court-appointed monitor KPMG Inc. wound up and liquidated business; basis $18.80 per sh. paid Sept. 27, 2005 and $1.1614 per sh. paid Jan. 27, 2006.

Telesystem Telecom Ltd. (Que. Mar. 11, 1992)
Oct. 5, 1998 – All o/s cum. ser. 1 pref. shs. redeemed for $25 per sh. plus $0.02655 accr. and unpaid divds.

Teletec Development Inc. (B.C. Nov. 22, 1983)
Feb. 20, 1987 – Name changed to Great Weighs! Industries Inc.; basis 1 new for 1 old sh. ■

Telferscot Resources Inc. (Can. May 31, 2010)
Apr. 9, 2018 – Name changed to Canntab Therapeutics Limited following reverse takeover acquisition of (old) Canntab Therapeutics Limited and concurrent amalgamation of (old) Canntab with wholly owned 2611780 Ontario Inc. to form Canntab Therapeutics Subsidiary Limited; basis 1 new for 200 old shs. (see FPsurvey - Industrials)

Telford Resources Ltd. (Alta. May 14, 1996)
Sept. 4, 2001 – Name changed to Telford Services Group, Inc. ■

Telford Services Group, Inc. (Alta. May 14, 1996)
Aug. 11, 2009 – Acquired by Aviation Acquisitions Inc. for 10¢ per sh.

Telkwa Gold Corporation (Alta. Aug. 19, 1996 amalg.)
June 19, 2008 – Name changed to Honey Badger Exploration Inc. and continued into Ontario. ■

Telkwa Mountain Mines Ltd. (B.C. 1968)
Dec. 1974 – Charter cancelled.

Tellerian Capital Corp. (Ont. Apr. 29, 1983)
Feb. 28, 2001 – Name changed to Cogient Corp. pursuant to reverse takeover acquisition of TetraConnect Inc. ■

Tellis Gold Mining Company, Inc. (Colo. July 31, 1981)
Mar. 22, 2002 – Name changed to Bannockburn Resources Inc.; basis 1 new for 3 old shs. ■

Telluride Gold Producers Ltd. (Ont. 1931)
1934 – Name changed to Northern Pine Lake Mines Ltd. ■

Tellza Communications Inc. (Ont. Apr. 5, 1984)
Dec. 13, 2017 – Name changed to Tellza Inc. (see FPsurvey - Industrials)

TelSoft Mobile Data Inc. (B.C. 1988)
Dec. 5, 1995 – Formed MDSI Mobile Data Solutions Inc. in Canada on amalgamation with 3181910 Canada Inc. and MDSI Mobile Data Solutions Inc.; basis 1 new com. sh. for 6.233500 old com. shs. or 1 new sh. for 5.9867517 old pref. shs. ■

Telson Mining Corporation (B.C. Apr. 11, 1986)
June 11, 2021 – Name changed to Altaley Mining Corporation. ■

Telson Resources Inc. (B.C. Apr. 11, 1986)
Feb. 21, 2018 – Name changed to Telson Mining Corporation. ■

Telstar Petroleum & Minerals Inc. (B.C. 1980)
Nov. 16, 1982 – Name changed to Telstar Resource Corporation; basis 1 new for 4 old shs. ■

Telstar Resource Corporation (B.C. 1980)
Mar. 20, 1992 – Dissolved and struck off register.

Telstar Resources Ltd. (Alta. June 28, 1971)
Apr. 28, 2006 – Privatized; basis 1 series 1 pref. sh. for 1 com. sh., immediately redeemed for 11¢ per sh.

Telular Canada Inc. (Ont. Apr. 14, 1989)
Dec. 16, 1998 – Name changed to GDI Global Data Inc. (see FPsurvey - Industrials)

Telum International Corporation (Ont. Apr. 20, 1964)
Dec. 1, 2008 – Certificate of incorporation cancelled and dissolved.

Temagami Mining Co. Ltd. (Ont. 1954)
1964 – Name changed to Copperfields Mining Corporation. ■

Temagami Oil & Gas Ltd. (Alta. Feb. 25, 1992)
Jan. 2, 2001 – All o/s com. shs. acquired for $0.041 per sh.

Temanda Mines Ltd. (Ont. 1956)
Nov. 30, 1970 – Amalgamated with Cantri Mines Ltd. (1 for 10), Con-Key Mines Ltd. (1 for 10), Point West Explorations Ltd. (1 for 10), St. Anthony Mines Ltd. (1 for 30) and Tinex Development & Exploration Ltd. (1 for 30) to form Can-Con Enterprises and Explorations Limited; basis 1 new for 30 old shs.

Temba Resources Ltd. (Alta. July 31, 1996)
Sept. 8, 1998 – Amalgamated with Ablevest Holdings Ltd. (1 for 31.25) to form a new co. Westlinks Resources Ltd.; basis 1 new for 5 old shs. (see Westlinks Resources Ltd.)

Tembec Inc. (Que. July 12, 1972)
Nov. 22, 2017 – Acquired by Rayonier Advanced Materials Inc.; basis Cdn$4.75 cash or 0.2542 Rayonier com. shs. for 1 Tembec com. sh.

Tembo Gold Corp. (Ont. Mar. 3, 1937)
Dec. 21, 2023 – Name changed to Lake Victoria Gold Ltd. (see FPsurvey - Mines & Energy)

Temex Mines Ltd. (Ont. 1956)
May 13, 1965 – Dissolved.

Temex Resources Corp. (Ont. Apr. 7, 2000 amalg.)
Sept. 22, 2015 – Acquired by Lake Shore Gold Corp.; basis 0.105 Lake Shore com. shs. for 1 Temex sh. (see Lake Shore Gold Corp.)

Temex Resources Ltd. (Que. 1952)
Apr. 7, 2000 – As a private company, amalgamated with Transgold Explorations & Investments Inc. to continue with the new name Temex Resources Corp. (see Temex Resources Corp.)

Temisca Resources Inc. (Can. Feb. 12, 1990 amalg.)
Oct. 21, 1996 – Name changed to Tom Exploration Inc.; basis 1 new for 10 old shs. ■

The Temiskaming Mining Co., Ltd. (Ont. 1906)
1952 – Distribution made of 13.07¢ per sh. Co. wound up and charter surrendered.

Temoris Resources Inc. (Can. Oct. 21, 1988)
Sept. 10, 2008 – Name changed to Glen Eagle Resources Inc. (see FPsurvey - Mines & Energy)

Tempest Energy Corp. (Alta. June 15, 2000)
Dec. 1, 2005 – Plan of Arrangement acquisition by Daylight Energy Trust; basis 0.4225 new trust unit, plus 0.1344 new Open Range Energy Corp. com. sh., plus 0.02688 new Open Range wt. for 1 old Tempest cl. A sh. (see Daylight Energy Trust; Open Range Energy Corp.)

Tempest Petroleums Ltd. (unknown)
1961 – Acquired by Quinalta Petroleums Ltd. for 350,000 shs. (see Quinalta Petroleums Ltd.)

Templar Energy Ltd. (Alta. Apr. 3, 1987)
Sept. 2, 1999 – Struck from registry and dissolved.

Templar Mining Corporation (B.C. Mar. 6, 1980)
Oct. 19, 1990 – Dissolved and struck off register.

Templar Resources Corporation (B.C. May 29, 1985)
June 7, 2007 – Name changed to Moneta Resources Inc.; basis 1 new for 2 old shs. ■

Temple Explorations Inc. (Ont. June 23, 1977)
1987 – Name changed to Burgess Point Resources Inc.; basis 1 new for 5 old shs. ■

Temple Gold Mines Ltd. (Ont. 1944)
Aug. 24, 1964 – Charter cancelled.

Temple Hotels Inc. (Can. Aug. 27, 2012)
Feb. 21, 2020 – Acquired by Morguard Corporation; basis $2.10 cash per sh.

Temple Real Estate Investment Trust (Man. July 12, 2006)
Dec. 31, 2012 – Succeeded by Temple Hotels Inc. pursuant to plan of arrangement whereby Temple Hotels Inc. was formed to facilitate the conversion of the trust into a corporation and the trust was dissolved. ■

Templeton Emerging Markets Appreciation Fund (Ont. Apr. 11, 1994)
Sept. 25, 2001 – Merged into U.S.-based Templeton Emerging Markets Fund; basis either $0.483381 per Appreciation unit or 1.8787993120 of a Templeton Emerging Markets Fund unit.

Templor Mines Ltd. (Ont. 1945)
Nov. 1962 – Charter cancelled.

Tempo Resources Ltd. (B.C. Aug. 14, 1986)
Sept. 26, 1989 – Name changed to Hystar Aerospace Corporation. ■

Tempus Corp. (Man. May 5, 2000)
Mar. 14, 2003 – Continued into Canada.
Mar. 20, 2003 – Name changed to Acadian Gold Corporation following Qualifying Transaction acquisition of six gold properties in Nova Scotia. ■

Ten Peaks Coffee Company Inc. (Can. Sept. 30, 2010)
Sept. 28, 2018 – Name changed to Swiss Water Decaffeinated Coffee Inc. upon the concurrent amalgamation of wholly owned Swiss Water Decaffeinated Coffee Company Inc. into the company. (see FPsurvey - Industrials)

Tenajon Resources Corp. (B.C. 1972)
Aug. 1, 1991 – Amalgamated with Royal Scot Resources Ltd. (1 for 2) to continue with the same name Tenajon Resources Corp.; basis 1 new for 1 old sh.
Sept. 1, 2009 – Acquired by Creston Moly Corp.; 0.84 Creston Moly shs. for 1 Tenajon cl. A sh.

Tenajon Silver Corp. (B.C. 1972)
Sept. 15, 1988 – Name changed to Tenajon Resources Corp. ■

Tenby Developments Ltd. (B.C. Aug. 25, 1980)
Oct. 18, 1996 – Name changed to Porcher Island Gold Corporation. ■

Tenendo Mining Corp. Ltd. (Ont. 1951)
Feb. 1958 – Dissolved.

Tenergy Ltd. (Alta. Sept. 16, 2005)
Mar. 30, 2006 – Acquired by FRQ Acquisition Corp. as nominee of Quintana Canada Corp. for $6.30 per sh.

Tenex Mines Ltd. (B.C. 1965)
Feb. 17, 1971 – Name changed to Marquis Development Corp. Ltd. ■

Tenga Laboratories Inc. (Alta. Jan. 30, 1992)
Dec. 1, 1998 – Formed Buffalo Diamonds Ltd. in Alberta on amalgamation with Buffalo Diamonds Ltd., constituting a reverse takeover by Buffalo Diamonds, following name change by Tenga Laboratories to TLT Resources Ltd. (not recognized by Alberta Stock Exchange) and 1-for-10 share consolidation effective Aug. 6, 1998. ■

Tenke Mining Corp. (Can. Apr. 19, 1994)
July 4, 2007 – Acquired by Lundin Mining Corporation; basis 1.73 new Lundin com. shs. plus Cdn$0.001 for 1 old Tenke com. sh. Following spin-off of South American assets to Suramina Resources Inc., Tenke shldrs. received 1 new Suramina sh. for 1 old sh. (see Suramina Resources Inc.)
July 31, 2007 – Amalgamated with Lundin Mining Corporation. (see Suramina Resources Inc.)

Tenneco Inc. (Del. 1983)
Dec. 11, 1996 – Reorganized and restructed the operating divisions by spining off Newport News Shipbuilding, merging Tenneco Energy with El Paso Energy Corporation, and leaving the Automotive/Packaging business to continue under the Tenneco Inc. name; basis (1) 1 new sh. of new Tenneco Inc. for 1 old sh. of Tenneco (2) 1 new sh. of Newport News Shipbuilding for 5 old Tenneco shs. and (3) 1 new sh. of El Paso Energy for 10 old Tenneco shs.

Teno-Boston Gold Mines Ltd. (Ont. 1945)
1955 – Charter cancelled.

Tenore Oil & Gas Ltd. (B.C. 1980)
Dec. 10, 1986 – Name changed to Tenore Resource Corporation. ■

Tenore Resource Corporation (B.C. 1980)
Aug. 18, 1987 – Amalgamated with Skeena Resources Ltd. (1 for 1) to form Golden Nevada Resources Inc.; basis sh. for sh.

Tenquille Copper Mines Ltd. (B.C.)
May 1, 1969 – Struck off register.

Tenquille Resources Ltd. (B.C. 1981)
July 3, 1992 – Dissolved and struck off register.

Tenth Power Technologies Corp. (Ont. Mar. 14, 1983)
May 16, 2013 – Privatized at 1¢ per sh.

Tequila Minerals Corp. (B.C. Apr. 27, 2006)
Mar. 6, 2008 – Name changed to Santa Fe Metals Corporation. ■

Teranet IA Incorporated (B.C. Nov. 23, 1983)
May 6, 1996 – Name changed to Triant Technologies Inc. ■

Teranet Income Fund (Ont. May 8, 2006)
Nov. 17, 2008 – Acquired by OMERS for $10.25 per sh.

Teranet Land Information Services Inc. (Ont. 1991)
Feb. 21, 2002 – Name changed to Teranet Inc.

Teranga Gold Corporation (Can. Oct. 1, 2010)
Feb. 17, 2021 – Acquired by Endeavour Mining Corporation; basis 0.47 Endeavour ordinary sh. for 1 Teranga com. sh. (see Endeavour Mining Corporation)

Terasen Gas Inc. (B.C. July 1, 1989 amalg.)
Mar. 1, 2011 – Name changed to FortisBC Energy Inc.

Terasen Inc. (B.C. Aug. 15, 1985)
Nov. 30, 2005 – Acquired by Kinder Morgan, Inc.; basis either Cdn$35.75, or 0.3331 Kinder com. sh., or Cdn$23.25 and 0.1165 Kinder com. sh. for 1 Terasen com. sh.
Mar. 1, 2011 – Name changed to FortisBC Holdings Inc.

Terato Resources Ltd. (Alta. 1977)
July 1, 1989 – Struck off register.

Terex Resources Inc. (Alta. Aug. 12, 1986)
Apr. 6, 1994 – Name changed to United Terrex Corporation; basis 1 new for 4 old shs. ■

Terex Resources Inc. (Ont. July 4, 1996 amalg.)
Nov. 7, 2006 – Name changed to Trelawney Resources Inc. ■

Terimac Mining Developments Ltd. (Ont. 1938)
Distributed 3 shs. of Cobalt Mining Products for each 10 shs. Terimac plus cash payment of 41¢ per sh.

Teriton Resources Ltd. (B.C. Sept. 29, 1982)
Feb. 11, 1992 – Name changed to Mashiach Capital Inc.; basis 1 new for 4 old shs. ■

Termex Resources Inc. (B.C. 1983)
Dec. 31, 1986 – Name changed to TME Resources Inc. ■

Terminal City Capital Inc. (B.C. Sept. 17, 2007)
June 11, 2010 – Dissolved following Qualifying Transaction private placement subscription of 2,666,667 com. shs. at 9¢ per sh. plus wts exercisable at 14¢ per sh. for a two year period of Meridex Software Corporation and distribution of Meridex shs. to shldrs. (see Meridex Software Corporation)

Terminus Mines Ltd. (B.C.)
Oct. 16, 1969 – Struck off register.

Tern Lake Mines Ltd. (Ont. 1948)
Apr. 9, 1975 – Charter cancelled.

Terra Energy Corp. (Alta. Jan. 30, 2004 amalg.)
Nov. 22, 2016 – Adjudged bankrupt and Ernst & Young Inc. appointed trustee.
Nov. 2016 – Sale of assets to Pavilion Energy Corp. and Crew Energy Inc. was approved by the court.

Terra Firma Capital Corporation (Ont. July 26, 2007)
Nov. 1, 2023 – All o/s shs. not already held acquired by GM Capital Corp., a company controlled by executive chair Y. Dov Meyer and managing director Seth Greenspan; basis Cdn$7.30 cash per sh. Company now private.

Terra Firma Resources Inc. (B.C. Apr. 16, 2007)
Nov. 25, 2014 – Name changed to Apple Capital Inc.; basis 1 new for 10 old shs. ■

Terra Health Corporation (B.C. 1987)
Dec. 9, 1993 – Name changed to T.H.C. Medical Inc.; basis 1 new for 3 old shs. ■

Terra Mannix Incorporated (Alta. May 24, 1996)
Mar. 2, 2002 – Dissolved and struck from registry.

Terra Mines Ltd. (B.C. 1965)
Feb. 9, 1994 – Bankrupt. No funds available for distribution to shldrs.

Terra Mining and Exploration Limited (B.C. 1965)
Aug. 12, 1982 – Name changed to Terra Mines Ltd. ■

Terra Nova Energy Inc. (B.C. Feb. 19, 1980)
Dec. 8, 1987 – Name changed to Sato Stevia International Inc.; basis 1 new for 3 old shs. ■

Terra Nova Energy Ltd. (Alta. Aug. 12, 2012)
Oct. 31, 2016 – Continued into British Columbia.
Nov. 10, 2016 – Name changed to Claren Energy Corp.; basis 1 new for 4 old shs. (see FPsurvey - Mines & Energy)

Terra Nova Gold Corp. (B.C. May 30, 1980)
Feb. 19, 2008 – Name changed to Terra Nova Minerals Inc. ■

Terra Nova Minerals Inc. (B.C. May 30, 1980)
Aug. 12, 2012 – Continued into Alberta.
Aug. 20, 2012 – Name changed to Terra Nova Energy Ltd. ■

Terra-Nova Mines Ltd. (unknown)
1971 – Stated it intended to dissolve voluntarily.

Terra Nova Resources Inc. (Alta. Apr. 9, 2012)
Sept. 27, 2017 – Continued into British Columbia.
Mar. 5, 2021 – Name changed to WellteQ Digital Health Inc. pursuant to reverse takeover acquisition of WellteQ Limited and concurrent amalgamation of CBDS Health Inc., and wholly owned 1259724 B.C. Ltd.; basis 0.3 new for 1 old sh. ■

Terra Nova Royalty Corporation (B.C. Nov. 3, 2004)
Sept. 30, 2011 – Name changed to MFC Industrial Ltd. ■

Terra Payments Inc. (Can. Dec. 16, 1982)
Apr. 12, 2004 – Acquired by Optimal Robotics Corp.; basis 0.4532 Optimal Robotics shs. for 1 Terra Payments sh. (see Optimal Group Inc.)

Terra Riche Mines Ltd. (Ont. 1967)
Mar. 1976 – Charter cancelled.

Terra Ventures Inc. (B.C. Mar. 16, 2000)
Aug. 8, 2011 – Acquired by Hathor Exploration Limited; basis 0.20 Hathor shs. for 1 Terra sh. (see Hathor Exploration Limited)

Terrabiogen Technologies Inc. (B.C. Aug. 17, 1993)
June 12, 2012 – Voluntarily delisted from TSX-VEN. (see FPsurvey - Industrials)

Terracamp Developments Ltd. (B.C. 1986)
July 10, 1992 – Dissolved and struck off register.

Terrace Bay Industries Ltd. (B.C. Jan. 31, 1983)
Jan. 11, 1991 – Name changed to PlanVest Capital Corp. ■

Terrace Bay Resources Ltd. (B.C. Jan. 31, 1983)
Apr. 14, 1989 – Name changed to Terrace Bay Industries Ltd. ■

Terrace Global Inc. (Ont. Dec. 15, 2017)
Jan. 7, 2021 – Acquired by Flowr Corporation; basis 0.4973 Flowr com. shs. for 1 Terrace sh.

Terrace Resources Inc. (B.C. July 6, 2006)
June 15, 2011 – Name changed to Terrace Energy Corp. following Qualifying Transaction acquisition of oil and gas interests in Texas. (see FPsurvey - Mines & Energy)

Terraco Energy Corporation (Alta. Nov. 28, 1995)
May 12, 2003 – Name changed to Terraco Gold Corp. ■

Terraco Gold Corp. (Alta. Nov. 28, 1995)
June 8, 2011 – Continued into British Columbia.
Aug. 21, 2019 – Acquired by Sailfish Royalty Corp.; basis 0.12 Sailfish com. shs. for 1 Terraco Gold sh.

Terradyne Energy Corporation (Alta. Apr. 11, 2000)
Feb. 13, 2002 – Company's secured creditors appointed Calgary-based Ernst & Young Inc. to act as receiver in the liquidation of the company's assets. The company was in default under the security agreement with its secured creditor who demanded full payment of the entire principal amount plus interest owing.
May 2003 – All assets sold and there would be a nominial distribution to unsecured creditors.
July 30, 2003 – Receiver discharged. There were no funds available for distribution to shldrs.

Terragold Explorations Inc. (B.C. Nov. 29, 1995)
Jan. 9, 1998 – Name changed to Terramin Resources Inc. and continued into Canada. ■

Terragold Resources Inc. (N.L. Dec. 9, 1988)
Nov. 29, 1995 – Name changed to Terragold Explorations Inc. and continued into British Columbia. ■

Les Terrains Aurifères Malartic (Québec) Limitée (Que. 1965 amalg.)
Dec. 31, 1962 – Amalgamated with Les Mines-Est Malartic Ltée (0.94 for 1), Willroy Mines Limited (1.24 for 1) and Long Lac Minerals Ltd. (1 for 1) to continue as LAC Minerals Ltd.; basis 0.84 new LAC sh. for 1 old Terrains sh.

Terramar Resource Corporation (B.C. 1979)
Sept. 23, 1994 – Dissolved and struck off register.

Terramin Mining Inc. (Can. Jan. 9, 1998)
Feb. 9, 2006 – Dissolved.

Terramin Resources Inc. (Can. Jan. 9, 1998)
Aug. 12, 1999 – Name changed to Terramin Mining Inc.; basis 1 new for 4 old shs. ■

Terrane Metals Corp. (B.C. May 2, 2006)
Oct. 21, 2010 – Acquired by Thompson Creek Metals Company Inc.; basis 90¢ and 0.052 Thompson Creek

shs. for 1 Terrane sh. (see Thompson Creek Metals Company Inc.)

Terranova Inc. (Alta. 1988)
June 19, 1990 – Name changed to Kevin Sports Toys International Inc. ■

Terraquest Energy Corporation (Alta. Nov. 22, 2001)
Feb. 26, 2004 – Formed Masters Energy Inc. in Alberta following reverse takeover acquisition of and amalgamation with Masters Energy Inc.; basis 1 new for 12 Terraquest shs. and 1 new for 2 Masters shs.; basis 1 new for 12 old shs. ■

Terrastar Development Corporation (B.C. Feb. 25, 1985 amalg.)
Aug. 23, 1996 – Dissolved and struck off register.

Terrastar Resources Corporation (B.C. Aug. 4, 1988)
Mar. 7, 2002 – Name changed to Pine Point Mines Inc. ■

TerraVest Capital Inc. (Alta. Oct. 31, 2012)
Feb. 28, 2018 – Name changed to TerraVest Industries Inc. (see FPsurvey - Mines & Energy; FPsurvey - Industrials)

TerraVest Income Fund (Alta. May 3, 2004)
Oct. 31, 2012 – Succeeded by TerraVest Capital Inc. pursuant to plan of arrangement whereby TerraVest Capital Inc. was formed to facilitate the conversion of the fund into a corporation and the fund was subsequently dissolved. ■

Terrawest Industries Inc. (B.C. Sept. 10, 1986)
May 31, 2000 – Delisted from the CDNX. Subsequently dissolved for failure to file.

TerraX Minerals Inc. (B.C. Aug. 1, 2007)
Feb. 19, 2020 – Name changed to Gold Terra Resource Corp. (see FPsurvey - Mines & Energy)

Terrebonne Mines Ltd. (Ont. 1944)
1952 – Charter cancelled.

Terrenex Acquisition Corporation (Alta. Sept. 11, 1991 amalg.)
Nov. 27, 2007 – Formed Terrenex Ltd. in Alberta on amalgamation with 1288942 Alberta Ltd. and 1289166 Alberta Ltd. pursuant to a corporate reorganization whereby all assets and liabilities, excluding a contingent tax liability and $750,000 in cash and cash equivalents, were transferred to the new company to facilitate settlement of a contingent liability arising from reassessments of the company's 1995 corporate reorganization. ■

Terrenex Ltd. (Alta. Nov. 27, 2007 amalg.)
Apr. 30, 2008 – Acquired by Questerre Energy Corporation; basis 4.70 Questerre com. shs. for 1 Terrenex cl. A sh. and $0.001 for 1 Terrenex cl. B sh.

Terrenex Ventures Inc. (Alta. Sept. 11, 1991 amalg.)
Nov. 14, 1995 – Name changed to Terrenex Acquisition Corporation following acquisition by and subsequent amalgamation with Terrenex Acquisition Corporation; basis 1 new com sh. or 1 exch. note or 1 unit (0.4676 new com. sh. and 1 exch. mixed note) for 1 old com. sh. ■

Terrex Energy Inc. (Alta. Jan. 19, 2010)
Mar. 26, 2013 – Amalgamated with Anterra Energy Inc.; basis 0.307 Anterra shs. for 1 Terrex sh.

Terrex Mining Co. Ltd. (Ont. 1958)
Mar. 1976 – Charter cancelled.

Territorial Gold Placers Limited (B.C. 1974)
Sept. 21, 1984 – Dissolved.

Territorial Petroleum Ventures Ltd. (B.C. 1973)
Oct. 16, 1987 – Name changed to First Medical Management Ltd. following acquisition of First Medical Management Ltd. and Med-Stop Medical Management Ltd. ■

Territorial Uranium Mines Ltd. (Ont. 1966)
Oct. 22, 1968 – Continued into British Columbia.
1968 – Name changed to New Territorial Uranium Mines Limited. ■

Territory Mining Co. Ltd. (Que. 1951)
1967 – Merged into St. Fabien Copper Mines Ltd.

Territory Mining Ltd. (B.C. 1966)
Jan. 17, 1977 – Dissolved.

Terry Gold Explorations Inc. (Ont. Apr. 29, 1980)
Sept. 1986 – Name changed to New Lith Inc.; basis 1 new for 10 old shs. ■

Tertiary Mines Ltd. (Alta. Feb. 7, 1997)
Nov. 8, 1999 – Continued into Ontario.
Nov. 9, 1999 – Formed The Song Corporation in Ontario on amalgamation with The Song Corporation, constituting a reverse takeover by Song; basis 1 new for 2.75 old shs. ■

Tervita Corporation (Alta. Apr. 17, 2002)
Sept. 7, 2016 – Continued into Canada. (see Secure Energy Services Inc.)
May 3, 2018 – Amalgamated in Alberta to continue with same name. (see Secure Energy Services Inc.)
July 7, 2021 – Acquired by and amalgamated into Secure Energy Services Inc.; basis 1.2757 Secure com. shs. for 1 Tervita sh. (see Secure Energy Services Inc.)

Teryl Resources Corp. (B.C. July 16, 1985)
Oct. 31, 2017 – Struck from registry and dissolved.
Jan. 25, 2022 – Restored to registry. (see FPsurvey - Mines & Energy)

Tesco Corporation (Alta. Dec. 1, 1993 amalg.)
Dec. 15, 2017 – Acquired by Nabors Industries Ltd.; basis 0.68 Nabors com. shs. for 1 Tesco sh.

Tesla Exploration Ltd. (Alta. Apr. 18, 2010 amalg.)
July 25, 2016 – Placed into receivership. Ernst & Young Inc. was appointed receiver and all officers and directors resigned.
Nov. 2016 – Debt owed to secured creditor was assigned to Echo Seismic Ltd. No distrib. available to unsecured creditors or shldrs.
Aug. 2018 – Ernst & Young was discharged as receiver and manager.

Teslin River Resources Corp. (B.C. Oct. 15, 1986)
July 24, 2015 – Name changed to Siyata Mobile Inc. following reverse takeover acquisition of (old) Siyata Mobile Inc.; basis 1 new for 2.2 old shs. (see FPsurvey - Industrials)

Tesma International Inc. (Ont. June 27, 1989)
Feb. 7, 2005 – Plan of Arrangement acquisition by Magna International Inc.; basis 0.44 new Magna cl. A sub. vtg. sh. or cash equivalent for 1 old Tesma cl. A sub. vtg. sh.

Tesoro Energy Corp. (Alta. Aug. 1, 2001)
July 21, 2004 – Formed Peregrine Energy Ltd. in Alberta on amalgamation with Peregrine Energy Ltd., with Tesoro the deemed acquiror; basis 1 new for 20 Peregrine shs. and 1 new for 20 Tesoro shs. ■

Tessa Ventures Ltd. (B.C. Feb. 22, 1984)
Feb. 23, 1993 – Name changed to International Tessa Capital Corporation; basis 1 new for 2 old shs. ■

Tessex Energy Inc. (Alta. Sept. 13, 1982)
May 19, 1998 – Formed Encounter Energy Inc. in Alberta on acquisition of and amalgamation with Encounter Energy Inc. Tessex cl. A shs. were reclassified as com. shs. and consolidated on a 1-for-3 basis. Encounter was acquired on the basis of 0.5566 new for 1 Encounter sh. ■

Testudo Oil & Gas Exploration Ltd. (Alta. Mar. 24, 2006)
May 31, 2009 – Formed Antler Creek Energy Corp. in Alberta pursuant to Qualifying Transaction acquisition of and amalgamation with Batoche Energy Corp.; basis 1 new for 3.125 old shs. ■

Tethyan Resources Corp. (B.C. May 7, 2019)
Oct. 9, 2020 – Acquired by Adriatic Metals plc; basis 0.166 Adriatic ord. sh. for 1 Tethyan com. sh.

Tethyan Resources Plc (U.K. June 2, 1999)
July 18, 2019 – Succeeded by Tethyan Resources Corp. following redomiciliation transaction under which ord. shs. of Tethyan Resources Plc were exchanged for Tethyan Resources Corp. com. shs. on the basis of 1 new com. sh. for 1 old ord. sh. ■

Tethys Energy Inc. (Alta. Oct. 24, 1991)
July 18, 2001 – Acquired by Northrock Resources Ltd. for $4.25 per sh.

Tethys Petroleum Limited (Guernsey Aug. 12, 2003)
July 17, 2008 – Continued into Cayman Islands. (see FPsurvey - Mines & Energy)

Teton Industries Inc. (B.C. June 14, 1983)
Feb. 4, 1986 – Name changed to Grand Teton Industries Inc.; basis 1 new for 2 old shs. (see FPsurvey - Mines & Energy)

Teton Petroleum Company (Del. Nov. 23, 1998 amalg.)
Jan. 9, 2002 – Voluntarily delisted from CDNX; continued to trade on OTC and Frankfurt Stock Exchange.
July 1, 2005 – Name changed to Teton Energy Corporation.

Tetonka Drilling Inc. (Alta. Apr. 10, 1997)
Nov. 3, 2000 – Acquired by Bonus Resource Services Corp.; basis 1.507 Bonus Resource shs. for 1 Tetonka sh. (see Bonus Resource Services Corp.)

Tetra Bio-Pharma Inc. (Can. May 17, 2007)
Aug. 1, 2023 – Made a voluntary assignment into bankruptcy. HOULE ROY S.A. appointed trustee.

Tetra Metals Ltd. (B.C. Aug. 25, 1980)
Nov. 2, 2000 – Name changed to Palladon Ventures Ltd.; basis 1 new for 4 old shs. ■

Tetra Uranium Mines Ltd. (Ont. 1953)
Aug. 1957 – Acquired by Continental Consolidated Mines & Oils Corp. Ltd.; basis 1 new for 10 old shs. (see Continental Consolidated Mines & Oils Corp. Ltd.)

Tetratel Inc. (Ont. Jan. 29, 1997)
Aug. 14, 2000 – Continued into Alberta.
July 2, 2003 – Struck from registry and dissolved.

Tex-Can Mines Ltd. (unknown)
1971 – Merged with Bright Star Trio Ltd. under latter name.

Tex Gold Resources Ltd. (B.C. Dec. 10, 1986)
Nov. 12, 1992 – Name changed to Genesys Pharma Inc. ■

Tex-Sol Explorations Limited (Ont. 1946)
July 19, 1985 – Amalgamated with Dominion Explorers Limited (1 for 1) and NBU Mines Limited (1 for 0.9) to continue as Dominion Explorers Inc. basis 1 new for 2.5 old shs.

Tex-Tor Oil Corporation (unknown Dec. 9, 1936)
Dec. 28, 1945 – Distribution of assets and surrender of charter approved by shldrs.
1946 – Shldrs. received small payment.

Tex-U.S. Oil & Gas Inc. (Ont. Apr. 1973)
Dec. 29, 1986 – Name changed to Orex Resources Ltd.; basis 1 new for 5 old shs. ■

Texacal Resources Ltd. (B.C. 1967)
May 1974 – Name changed to Rainier Energy Resources Inc.; basis 1 new for 5 old shs. (see FPsurvey - Mines & Energy)

Texaco Canada Inc. (Can. 1978)
May 3, 1989 – Acquired by Imperial Oil Limited for US$34.36 per sh. Name changed to McColl-Frontenac Inc. on Aug. 23, 1989.

Texaco Canada Limited (Can. 1927)
1978 – Name changed to Texaco Canada Inc. and continued into Canada. ∎

Texaco Canada Petroleum Inc. (Can. Sept. 1988)
May 25, 1995 – Acquired by Texaco Acquisition Inc. wholly owned subsid. of Texaco Inc. for $1.48 per sh.

Texaco Capital LLC (Turks and Caicos Oct. 7, 1993)
Apr. 9, 2001 – Non-reporting issuer.

Texada Capital Corp. (B.C. Apr. 6, 2006)
Apr. 11, 2008 – Name changed to Petro Vista Energy Corp. following Qualifying Transaction acquisition of Petro Vista Energy Petroleo do Brasil Ltda. ∎

Texada Resources Ltd. (Alta. June 24, 1986)
Nov. 11, 1987 – Name changed to Ramarro Resources Inc. ∎

Texada Software Inc. (B.C. Mar. 21, 2000)
Nov. 5, 2008 – Continued into Ontario.
July 23, 2012 – Name changed to Noble Iron Inc.; basis 1 new for 5 old shs. (see FPsurvey - Industrials)

Texal Development Ltd. (B.C. 1969)
Apr. 16, 1974 – Name changed to Texal Developments Ltd. ∎

Texal Developments Ltd. (B.C. 1969)
May 1976 – Name changed to TX Resources Ltd.; basis 1 new for 2 old shs. (see FPsurvey - Mines & Energy)

Texalta Petroleum Corp. Ltd. (Alta. 1941)
Struck off register.

Texalta Petroleum Ltd. (Alta. Sept. 16, 1987)
June 6, 2011 – Amalgamated with PetroFrontier Corp.; basis either $1.58, 0.45 PetroFrontier shs. or a combination thereof for 1 Texalta Petroleum sh.

Texas Commonwealth Resources Corporation (B.C. 1983)
Sept. 25, 1984 – Name changed to Black Jade Resources Ltd.; basis 1 new for 3 old shs. ∎

Texas Creek Mines Ltd. (unknown)
Mar. 1971 – Name changed to Tex-Can Mines Ltd.; basis 1 new for 3 old shs. ∎

Texas Dome Resource Corporation (B.C. Apr. 7, 1964)
June 6, 1994 – Name changed to Microkey Communication Systems, Inc. ∎

Texas Eastern Corporation (Del.)
Apr. 27, 1989 – Acquired by a wholly owned subsid. of Panhandle Eastern Corporation for US$53 per sh. (see Panhandle Eastern Corporation)

Texas Gas & Oil Inc. (B.C. June 4, 1987)
July 3, 2008 – Name changed to Legend Power Systems Inc. following reverse takeover acquisition of Legend Power Systems Inc. (see FPsurvey - Industrials)

Texas Gold Quartz (N.P.L.) (B.C. 1965)
Feb. 17, 1971 – Name changed to Marquis Development Corp. Ltd. (see Marquis Development Corp. Ltd.)

Texas Gulf, Inc. (Tex. 1909)
Apr. 1973 – Name changed to Texasgulf Inc. ∎

Texas Gulf Petroleum Corporation (Ont. Feb. 9, 1956)
June 11, 1996 – Continued into British Columbia.
Mar. 15, 2000 – Name changed to Portrush Petroleum Corporation; basis 1 new for 5 old shs. ∎

Texas Gulf Sulphur Co. Inc. (Tex. 1909)
Apr. 1972 – Name changed to Texas Gulf, Inc. ∎

Texas International Company (Del. 1930)
Apr. 9, 1990 – Name changed to The Phoenix Resource Companies, Inc. as a result of bankruptcy proceedings and reorganization of the co.

Texas Kidd Mining Corp. Ltd. (Que. 1964)
June 1973 – Charter cancelled.

Texas Northern Minerals Limited (B.C. Dec. 23, 1980)
Mar. 23, 1992 – Name changed to Consolidated Texas Northern Minerals Limited; basis 1 new for 5 old shs. ∎

Texas Northern Oil & Gas Inc. (B.C. Dec. 23, 1980)
Nov. 18, 1987 – Name changed to Texas Northern Minerals Limited. ∎

Texas Petroleum Corporation (B.C. Dec. 17, 1982 amalg.)
Mar. 7, 1989 – Name changed to North American Equity Corporation; basis 1 new for 3 old shs. ∎

Texas Sevens Resources Inc. (B.C. Jan. 20, 1981)
July 19, 1988 – Name changed to Canadian Eagle Explorations Ltd.; basis 1 new for 5 old shs. ∎

Texas Sidewinder Oil Corporation (B.C. July 31, 1985)
May 29, 1995 – Name changed to Archon Minerals Limited. (see FPsurvey - Mines & Energy)

Texas Star Resources Corporation (B.C. Mar. 12, 1986)
Nov. 4, 1996 – Name changed to Star Resources Corp. ∎

Texas T Minerals Inc. (Alta. Aug. 23, 2001)
May 1, 2006 – Continued into British Columbia. (see Grandcru Resources Corporation)
May 19, 2006 – Acquired by Grandcru Resources Corporation. (see Grandcru Resources Corporation)

Texas T Resources Inc. (B.C. July 20, 1981)
Aug. 23, 2001 – Continued into Alberta.
Feb. 6, 2004 – Name changed to Texas T Minerals Inc.; basis 1 new for 10 old shs. ∎

Texasgulf Inc. (Tex. 1909)
Sept. 25, 1981 – Acquired by E. A. Development Inc., a U.S. subsid. of Société Nationale Elf, Aquitaine of France, for US$178.49 per pref. and US$56 per com. sh. Canada Development Corporation exchanged its 34% int. in Texasgulf and $534,000,000 to acquire the Canadian mining assets of Texasgulf.

Texbeau Industries Inc. (Alta. 1986)
Dec. 21, 1987 – Name changed to SGI Super Grass Inc.; basis 2 new for 1 old sh. ∎

Texcan Energy & Resources Inc. (Ont. 1954)
Oct. 29, 1981 – Name changed to Geovex Petroleum Corporation. ∎

Texcan Technology Corp. (B.C. June 20, 1983)
Nov. 6, 1986 – Name changed to International Texcan Technology Corp.; basis 1 new for 3 old shs. ∎

Texmont Mines Ltd. (Ont. 1956)
Jan. 30, 1979 – Name changed to New Texmont Explorations Ltd.; basis 1 new for 4 old shs. (see FPsurvey - Mines & Energy)

Texoro Resources Ltd. (B.C. Sept. 30, 1983)
Dec. 8, 1989 – Name changed to International Texoro Resources Ltd.; basis 1 new for 5 old shs. ∎

Texpack Limited (Ont. 1935)
Acquired by American Hospital Supply Corp., for 0.317 of a sh. of American Hospital com. or $12.35 (Cdn. funds) for each com. sh. of Texpack. Co. applied to be converted to a private co.

Texpez Oil & Gas Corporation (B.C. 1981)
Dec. 8, 1986 – Name changed to CCW System Ltd. ∎

Texron Explorations Ltd. (Ont. 1965)
1971 – Merged into Picktex Mining & Investments Ltd.; basis 1 new for 5 old shs.

Textiles Dionne Inc. (Que. 1963)
May 11, 1990 – Acquired by Dominion Textile Inc.; basis $4.75 or 0.3125 Dominion Textile shs. for 1 Textiles Dionne sh. (see Dominion Textile Inc.)

Textiles Warwick Inc. (Que. 1947)
Jan. 22, 1982 – Declared bankrupt.

Thaddeus Gold Mines Ltd. (Ont. 1946)
1955 – Charter cancelled.

Thailaska Explorations Ltd. (B.C. June 22, 1973)
Sept. 16, 1976 – Name changed to James Industries Inc. ∎

Thallion Pharmaceuticals Inc. (Can. Mar. 14, 2007 amalg.)
July 22, 2009 – Name changed to Premium Brands Holdings Corporation pursuant to plan of arrangement to convert Premium Brands Income Fund (PBIF) to a corp. resulting in PBIF and wholly owned Premium Brands Holdings Limited Partnership (PBHLP) becoming wholly owned subsids. of Premium Brands Holdings Corporation (PBHC). All assets and liabilities of Thallion Pharmaceuticals Inc. (old Thallion) were transferred to Thallion Pharmaceuticals Inc. (new Thallion) formed by way of amalgamation between 4504003 Canada Inc. and 4504011 Canada Inc. (both old Thallion subsids.). (see FPsurvey - Industrials)

Thallion Pharmaceuticals Inc. (Can. July 22, 2009 amalg.)
Aug. 21, 2013 – Acquired by BELLUS Health Inc. for $0.1889 per sh. (see BELLUS Health Inc.)

Thames Resources Limited (Ont. 1981)
Nov. 14, 1985 – Amalgamated with 6 other cos. to form Paladin Petroleum Corporation; basis 1 new for 7 old shs.

Thayers Limited (unknown)
1949 – Assets and undertakings sold to Reliance Petroleum Ltd. and charter surrendered. Thayers shldrs. received $16.875 and 1 Reliance 4.5 % pref. sh. for each $3.50 cum. pref. sh. and 1 cl. A Reliance sh. for 3 n.p.v. com. shs.

The Hydropothecary Corporation (Ont. Oct. 29, 2013)
Sept. 5, 2018 – Name changed to HEXO Corp. ∎

The Patino Corp. Ltd. (Can. 1962)
Nov. 1962 – Acquired by The Patino Mining Corp. (see Copper Rand Chibougamau Mines Ltd.)

Theia Resources Ltd. (B.C. Jan. 9, 2007)
Sept. 21, 2018 – Name changed to Flower One Holdings Inc. following reverse takeover acquisition of CNX Holdings Inc. and concurrent amalgamation of CNX with and into wholly owned Flower One Corp.; basis 1 new for 10 old shs. ∎

Thelon Capital Ltd. (B.C. Sept. 13, 1982)
Mar. 23, 2015 – Name changed to THC BioMed Intl Ltd. (see FPsurvey - Industrials)

Thelon Ventures Ltd. (B.C. Sept. 13, 1982)
Feb. 4, 2010 – Name changed to Thelon Capital Ltd.; basis 1 new for 10 old shs. ∎

TheraMed Capital Corp. (B.C. Jan. 10, 2000)
Apr. 8, 2003 – Name changed to Vigil Health Solutions Inc. following Qualifying Transaction reverse takeover acquisition of Vigil Health Management Incorporated. ∎

Theramed Health Corporation (B.C. Nov. 9, 2011)
Oct. 24, 2019 – Name changed to EGF Theramed Health Corp.; basis 1 new for 100 old shs. (see FPsurvey - Industrials)

Theresa Gold Mines Ltd. (Ont. 1938)
July 15, 1963 – Dissolved.

Thermal Control Technologies Corp. (Alta. Oct. 1, 1997 amalg.)
May 31, 2000 – Delisted from the CDNX. Subsequently dissolved.

Thermal Exploration Company (Calif. Feb. 18, 1972)
Oct. 7, 1996 – Acquired by Western Copper Holdings Limited; basis 1 Western Copper sh. for 5 Thermal Exploration shs. (see Western Copper Holdings Limited)

Thermatron Corporation Limited (Ont. 1965)
Sept. 1971 – Name changed to Mytolon Chemicals Inc. following amalgamation with Neoteric Chemical Systems Ltd., acquisition of all o/s shs. of Mytolon Chemicals Ltd. and assignment by co. of its wholly owned subsid., Standard Oxygen Ltd., to Mytolon. ■

Thermax International Corp. (Alta. Dec. 15, 1995)
Sept. 25, 2013 – Dissolved and struck from registry.

ThermicEdge Corporation (Alta. Apr. 3, 1997)
May 5, 2000 – Continued into Ontario.
May 19, 2000 – Formed Fuel Cell Technologies Corporation on amalgamation with Fuel Cell Technologies Ltd.; basis 1 new for 1 old sh. ■

Thermo-Plex Industries Ltd. (B.C. 1961)
Oct. 30, 1978 – Dissolved.

Thermo-Solar Inc. (unknown)
Oct. 2, 1979 – Amalgamated with Quebec Manitou Mines Ltd. to form Petro-Sun Inc.

Thermo Tech International Inc. (B.C. 1983)
Sept. 8, 1989 – Name changed to Consolidated Thermo Tech International Inc.; basis 1 new for 5 old shs. ■

Thermo Tech Technologies Inc. (B.C. 1983)
Dec. 2, 1997 – Continued into Canada.
July 25, 2000 – Continued into Yukon.
May 20, 2005 – Dissolved and struck off register.

ThermoCeramix Corporation (Ont. June 26, 2012)
Apr. 28, 2016 – Filed voluntary assignment in bankruptcy under the Bankruptcy and Insolvency Act. PricewaterhouseCoopers Inc. appointed trustee and all officers and directors resigned.

Thermovolt Limited (Ont. 1953)
Dec. 28, 1962 – Name changed to National Controls (Canada) Ltd.

Thesaurus Gold Mines Ltd. (Ont. 1920)
1955 – Charter cancelled.

theScore, Inc. (Ont. Aug. 30, 2012)
Aug. 29, 2019 – Continued into British Columbia.
Sept. 6, 2019 – Name changed to Score Media and Gaming Inc. ■

Theseus Capital Inc. (Que. Feb. 1, 2005)
July 15, 2008 – Name changed to GDG Environment Group Ltd. following Qualifying Transaction reverse takeover acquisition of GDG Environnement Ltée. ■

Thesis Gold (Holdings) Inc. (B.C. June 14, 2013)
Aug. 25, 2023 – Acquired by Benchmark Metals Inc. (renamed Thesis Gold Inc.); basis 2.5584 Benchmark shs. for 1 Thesis Gold sh.

Thesis Gold Inc. (B.C. June 14, 2013)
Aug. 17, 2023 – Name changed to Thesis Gold (Holdings) Inc. ■

Thessalon Copper Mines Ltd. (Man. 1957)
1958 – Name changed to Starbird Mines Ltd. ■

Thib Gold Mines Ltd. (Ont. 1937)
1943 – Name changed to Larmont Mines Ltd. and continued into Ontario; basis 1 new for 3 old shs. ■

Think Research Corporation (Ont. Nov. 29, 2018)
Apr. 23, 2024 – Acquired by Beedie Investments Ltd.; basis 32¢ cash per sh.

Thinkpath.com Inc. (Ont. 1994)
July 31, 2001 – Name changed to Thinkpath Inc.

Thios Resources Inc. (B.C. Jan. 30, 1986)
Sept. 17, 1993 – Name changed to Ellios Resources Ltd.; basis 1 new for 10 old shs. ■

Third Canadian General Investment Trust Limited (Can. Feb. 3, 1928)
Oct. 11, 2011 – Privatized at $41.07 per sh.

Third Dimension Industries Ltd. (Ont. 1970)
Sept. 29, 1975 – Amalgamated with Tesari Holdings (Metro) Ltd. to form Third Dimension Industries Ltd. Basis cl. A pfce. and com. shs. of old co. were exchanged for 1.5 new cl. A pfce. and/or com. shs. of new co.

Third Dimension Industries Ltd. (Ont. Sept. 29, 1975 amalg.)
Aug. 22, 1979 – Name changed to TDI Venture Equities Ltd. ■

Third Wave Commerce Corp. (Alta. Apr. 6, 1987)
July 7, 1993 – Formed International Hospitality Inc. in Ontario on amalgamation with International Hospitality Inc.; basis 6.03 new for 1 International Hospitality sh. and 1 new for 5 Third Wave shs. ■

Thirdcoast Limited (Ont. May 27, 1898)
July 19, 2012 – All o/s shs. not already held by Parrish & Heimbecker, Limited acquired for $155 cash per sh.

Thirteen Coins Restaurants Ltd. (B.C. 1984)
Dec. 18, 1987 – Name changed to M. C. Beverages, Ltd. (see FPsurvey - Industrials)

Thirteen Mile Gold Ltd. (Alta. Oct. 8, 1986)
Apr. 18, 1995 – Name changed to Bow River Exploration Ltd. ■

Thirteen Mile Resources Ltd. (Alta. Oct. 8, 1986)
May 28, 1990 – Name changed to Thirteen Mile Gold Ltd.; basis 1 new for 5 old shs. ■

Thirty-Five Split Corp. (Ont. May 7, 1998)
Apr. 2, 2008 – Dissolved; all o/s pref. shs. and capital shs. redeemed for $25 and $58.9432 per sh., respectively.

Thistle Explorations Ltd. (Alta. June 28, 1988)
July 17, 1991 – Name changed to Shirson Ventures Inc. ■

Thistletown Capital Inc. (Ont. Oct. 3, 2000 amalg.)
June 11, 2003 – Name changed to Kelso Energy Inc. ■

Thitec Recovery Systems Limited (B.C. 1984)
Dec. 30, 1994 – Dissolved and struck off register.

Thomaque Gold Mines Ltd. (Que. 1944)
Name changed to Osage Oil and Exploration Limited. ■

Thomas Nationwide Transport Limited (Australia 1961)
Dec. 16, 1985 – Name changed to TNT Limited.

Thomas O'Sullivan Mines Ltd. (Ont. 1946)
1955 – Charter cancelled.

Thompson & Sutherland, Limited (N.S. Jan. 1, 1902)
1981 – Placed into receivership. No distribution to unsecured creditors.
Nov. 18, 1991 – Struck off register.

Thompson Bousquet Gold Mines Ltd. (Que. 1936)
Apr. 24, 1979 – Name changed to Les Mines d'Or Thompson Bousquet Ltée. ■

Thompson Cadillac Mining Corp. (Que. 1935)
1935 – Took over mine and assets of Thompson-Cadillac Mines, Ltd. and its subsid., Thompson-Cadillac Mining Co. Ltd. from trustee in bankruptcy; basis 1 new Thompson Cadillac Mining Corp. sh. for 5 Thompson-Cadillac Mines shs. and unsecured creditors of Thompson-Cadillac Mining Co. Ltd. received 2.5 shs. of new Thompson Cadillac Mining for each $1.00 of claims.
June 1939 – Made a voluntary assignment into bankruptcy. D.L. Ross, 275 St. James St. West, Montreal appointed joint trustee.
Apr. 1943 – Assets sold to P.A. Lavalle, Montreal for $35,000. Ordinary creditors received 36%. No equity for shldrs.

Thompson Creek Metals Company Inc. (Ont. July 1, 1999)
July 29, 2008 – Continued into British Columbia.
Oct. 24, 2016 – Acquired by Centerra Gold Inc.; basis 0.0988 Centerra com. shs. for 1 Thompson Creek sh.

Thompson Diversacorp Ltd. (Ont. 1956)
Mar. 1, 1977 – During 1976, all o/s com. shs. acquired by Trinity Managed Investments Ltd. at $7.00 per com. sh. all 6% pref. shs. were called for redemp. at $52.50 per sh., plus final divd.

Thompson Joanne Gold Ltd. (Que. 1934)
1947 – Assets acquired by New Rouyn Merger Mines Ltd.; basis 29 new for 1 old sh. (see New Rouyn Merger Mines Ltd.)

Thompson-Lundmark Gold Mines Ltd. (Can. Aug. 31, 1938)
Dec. 18, 1985 – Formed Consolidated Thompson-Lundmark Gold Mines Limited in Canada on amalgamation with Hoffman Exploration and Minerals Limited; basis 1 new for 3.17918 Hoffman shs. and 1 new for 2.03043 Thompson-Lundmark shs. ■

Thompson Paper Box Co. Ltd. (Ont. 1956)
Sept. 1974 – Name changed to Thompson Diversacorp Ltd. ■

Thompson's Service Stations Ltd. (Ont. 1934)
May 1987 – Voluntarily dissolved.

Thomson Co. Ltd. (Ont. 1947)
1958 – Name changed to Thomson Newspapers Limited. ■

The Thomson Corporation (Ont. Dec. 28, 1977)
Apr. 17, 2008 – Name changed to Thomson Reuters Corporation following acquisition of Reuters Group PLC to form a dual listed company structure. (see FPsurvey - Industrials)

Thomson Drilling Company Limited (Ont. 1970)
1973 – Name changed to Thomson Industries Limited. ■

Thomson Gold Co. Ltd. (B.C. 1985)
Oct. 9, 1992 – Dissolved and struck off register.

Thomson Industries Limited (Ont. 1970)
Mar. 3, 1978 – Acquired by ATCO Industries Ltd. for US$20 per sh. (see ATCO Industries Ltd.)

Thomson Newspapers Limited (Ont. 1947)
June 5, 1989 – Amalgamated with International Thomson Organisation Limited to form The Thomson Corporation; basis 1 new for 1 cl. A and cl. B old sh. (see The Thomson Corporation)

Thor Explorations Ltd. (N.P.L.) (B.C. Sept. 11, 1968)
Sept. 1, 2009 – Formed Thor Explorations Ltd. in British Columbia on amalgamation with Magnate Ventures Inc. with Thor the deemed acquiror; basis 0.5 new for 1 old Thor sh. and 0.42 new for 1 Magnate sh. (see FPsurvey - Mines & Energy)

Thor Gold Corporation (Alta. 1987)
Nov. 14, 1988 – Name changed to Soloman Gold Corp. ■

Thor Uranium Mines Ltd. (Ont. 1953)
1955 – Acquired by Consolidated Thor Mines Ltd.; basis 1 new for 1 old sh. (see Consolidated Thor Mines Ltd.)

Thorco Gold Finders Inc. (Ont. 1983)
May 26, 1987 – Name changed to Thorco Resources Inc. ■

Thorco Resources Inc. (Ont. 1983)
Feb. 17, 1992 – Amalgamated with Golden North Resource Corporation (0.71672 for 1) to form a new company named Caledonia Mining Corporation; basis 0.19426 new for 1 old sh. (see Caledonia Mining Corporation)

Thorium Exploration & Gold Ltd. (Ont. 1948)
1952 – Charter cancelled.

Thorlit Exploration Ltd. (Ont. 1959)
Dec. 2, 1965 – Charter cancelled.

Thormac Porcupine Mines Ltd. (Ont. 1945)
July 1960 – Charter cancelled.

Thormoor Copper Mines Ltd. (Ont. 1927)
1927 – Shares issued to holders of shs. in Boischatel-Rouyn Development Co. Ltd.
1929 – Placed into bankruptcy

Thorn Hill Gold Mines (Ont. 1945)
1956 – Merged into Landmark Mines Ltd.; basis 1 new (pooled) sh. for 10 old shs.

Thornapple Capital, Inc. (Cayman Islands Dec. 6, 2010)
Sept. 27, 2013 – Name changed to Agility Health, Inc. Pursuant to Qualifying Transaction reverse takeover acquisition of Agility Health Holdings, Inc.; basis 1 new for 2 old shs. ■

Thornbury Capital Corporation (Ont. Sept. 29, 1950; via letters patent)
May 9, 1997 – Formed International Uranium Corporation in Ontario on amalgamation with International Uranium Corporation (deemed acquiror); basis 1 new for 1 International Uranium sh. and 1 new for 5 Thornbury shs. ■

Thorncliffe Mines Ltd. (Ont. 1958)
Jan. 1967 – Charter cancelled.

Thorncliffe Park Limited (Ont. 1955)
Jan. 1, 1962 – Name changed to Canadianwide Properties Limited. ■

Thorncrest Explorations Limited (Ont. 1952)
Mar. 10, 1994 – Name changed to New Concept Technologies International Inc. ■

Thorne Explorations Ltd. (Ont. 1936)
1940 – Charter cancelled.

Thornecliff Ventures Limited (Can. Sept. 27, 1993)
Mar. 22, 2001 – Name changed to eMobile Data Corporation and continued into Yukon following reverse takeover acquisition of eMoblie Data Inc.; basis 1 new for 2 old shs. ■

Thornloe Porcupine Gold Mines Ltd. (Ont. 1937)
May 13, 1957 – Charter cancelled.

Thornmark Equities Inc. (Ont. Oct. 16, 1987)
Dec. 23, 1996 – All o/s 8% exch. debs. redeemed; basis the principal amt. at par plus accrued interest of $31.52 per $1,000 deb. Holders had right to exchange debs. for Dofasco Inc. com. shs. at $29 per sh. until Dec. 19, 1996.
May 10, 2001 – Struck off register.

Thoroughbred Capital Inc. (Ont. Mar. 8, 2011)
Dec. 20, 2013 – Name changed to Sunora Foods Inc. pursuant to Qualifying Transaction acquisition of (old) Sunora Foods Ltd. ■

Thorpe Bay Explorations Ltd. (Ont. 1966)
Oct. 1973 – Amalgamated with 3 other cos. to form Tri-Bridge Consolidated Gold Mines Ltd. on; basis 1 new for 10 old shs.

ThoughtShare Communications Inc. (Can. Dec. 18, 1996)
Dec. 6, 2004 – Name changed to Qumana Software Inc.; basis 1 new for 20 old shs. ■

Three Arrows Mining Explorations Ltd. (Alta. 1953)
Mar. 14, 1959 – Dissolved and struck off register.

Three Bear Ventures Ltd. (Alta. Nov. 7, 1997)
Apr. 10, 2000 – Name changed to The Art Vault International Limited and continued into Ontario pursuant to Major Transaction reverse takeover acquisition of The Art Vault Limited. ■

Three County Recycling & Composting Inc. (Ont. Oct. 23, 1991)
Dec. 5, 1997 – Name changed to TCR Environmental Corp. (see FPsurvey - Industrials)

3-D Systems Inc. (B.C. 1986)
Aug. 1993 – Amalgamated with Avenue Hall Holding Corporation (its wholly owned subsid.) to form 3D Systems (Canada) Inc. which became a private wholly owned subsid. of 3D Systems Corporation (the new Delaware-incorporated parent company) effective; basis 1 new for 1 old sh.

Three Point Petroleums Ltd. (Alta. Feb. 11, 1937)
Sept. 13, 1950 – Assets sold to Federated Petroleums for $68,250. Distribution of 7¢ per sh.

3 Sixty Risk Solutions Ltd. (B.C. Apr. 6, 2006)
Sept. 13, 2021 – Placed into receivership and Baigel Corp. appointed receiver.

3530639 Canada Inc. (Can. Sept. 14, 1998)
June 28, 2007 – Acquired by Madison Pacific Properties Inc. for $2.60 per sh.

360 Blockchain Inc. (B.C. Sept. 10, 2013)
Feb. 19, 2019 – Name changed to Codebase Ventures Inc. ■

360 Capital Financial Services Group Inc. (B.C. Sept. 10, 2013)
Sept. 29, 2017 – Name changed to 360 Blockchain Inc. ■

360 VOX Corporation (Ont. Mar. 1, 1993 amalg.)
July 4, 2014 – Acquired by Dundee Corporation; basis 0.01221 Dundee cl.A S.V. shs. for 1 360 VOX cl.A sh.
July 4, 2014 – Name changed to Dundee 360 Real Estate Corporation.

3D Signatures Inc. (Can. May 25, 2011)
Apr. 8, 2019 – Name changed to Telo Genomics Corp. (see FPsurvey - Industrials)

3D Visit Inc. (Can. Apr. 5, 2001)
Dec. 9, 2008 – Name changed to Focus Metals Inc.; basis 1 new for 4 old shs. ■

Threegold Resources Inc. (Que. Mar. 19, 2002)
Sept. 22, 2021 – Struck from register and dissolved.

3Net Media Corporation (Alta. Nov. 7, 1996)
Nov. 6, 2002 – Name changed to Everton Resources Inc.; basis 1 new for 4 old shs. ■

3P International Energy Corp. (Ont. Apr. 3, 2008)
Jan. 26, 2012 – Name changed to Cub Energy Inc. pursuant to Mar. 29, 2012, reverse takeover acquisition of Gastek LLC. ■

360networks inc. (Can. Aug. 17, 1999)
Apr. 18, 2000 – Continued into Nova Scotia.
Jan. 9, 2007 – Bankrupt. KPMG Inc. of Vancouver, B.C., appointed trustee.

3TL Technologies Corp. (B.C. July 29, 2011)
May 18, 2018 – Name changed to Datable Technology Corporation. (see FPsurvey - Industrials)

Thrift Stores, Limited (Can. 1939)
May 1955 – Wholly owned by Dominion Stores Limited, following successful offer to purchase shs. at $40 per sh.

ThrillTime Entertainment International, Inc. (B.C. Aug. 29, 1988)
Oct. 25, 2006 – Succeeded by Advanced Proteome Therapeutics Corporation pursuant to plan of arrangement whereby newly incorporated wholly owned subsidiary Advanced Proteome Therapeutics Corporation acquired 56% interest in Advanced Proteome Therapeutics, Inc. and completed a share exchange to become parent of ThrillTime. (see FPsurvey - Industrials)

Thrush Industries Inc. (B.C. May 4, 1993)
Apr. 15, 2002 – Name changed to Miranda Diamond Corp. ■

Thrust Capital Corp. (Alta. Jan. 9, 2001)
Feb. 20, 2004 – Formed Zaio Corporation in Alberta on Qualifying Transaction amalgamation with Xceleron Inc., Advent Energy Capital Inc. and Zaio Canada Inc., constituting a reverse takeover by Zaio Canada; basis 0.6 new for 1 Xceleron sh., 0.45 new for 1 Advent sh., 1 new for 1 Zaio Canada sh. and 1 new for 1 Thrust sh. Thrust Capital, Xceleron and Advent Energy were all Capital Pool Companies. ■

Thrust Resources Inc. (B.C. Mar. 25, 1983)
July 6, 1993 – Name changed to Balaclava Industries Ltd.; basis 1 new for 4.6 old shs. ■

Thumper Resources Corp. (B.C. Feb. 13, 1984)
Sept. 8, 1993 – Name changed to Arequipa Resources Ltd.; basis 1 new for 3 old shs. ■

Thundelarra Exploration Ltd. (B.C. Mar. 22, 1983)
Jan. 23, 2001 – Continued into Yukon.
Sept. 8, 2003 – Continued into Western Australia.

Thunder Bay Amethyst Mining Co. Ltd. (Ont. 1965)
1981 – Operations sold; co. subsequently wound up.

Thunder Bay Capital Corporation (Alta. 1988)
Apr. 1, 1996 – Dissolved and struck off register.

Thunder Bay Gold Mines Ltd. (Ont. 1934)
1943 – Name changed to Gold Island Porcupine Mines Ltd. ■

Thunder Bay Nickel Mining Corp. Ltd. (Ont. 1965)
1969 – Amalgamated with Great Lakes Nickel Corp. Ltd. to form Great Lakes Nickel Ltd.; basis 1 new for 2 old shs.

Thunder Bay Silver Mines Ltd. (Ont. 1928)
1958 – Charter cancelled.

Thunder Bumpers Corporation (Ont. 1983)
Nov. 12, 1994 – Charter cancelled and co. dissolved.

Thunder Creek Mines Ltd. (B.C. 1969)
May 28, 1979 – Name changed to Excalibur Development Ltd. ■

Thunder Creek Mining Co. Ltd. (Ont. 1946)
1955 – Charter cancelled.

Thunder Energy Inc. (Alta. Oct. 17, 1995)
July 12, 2005 – Plan of Arrangement combination with Forte Resources Inc. and Mustang Resources Inc. to create a new trust named Thunder Energy Trust plus 3 new exploration cos. - Alberta Clipper Energy Inc., Ember Resources Inc. and Valiant Energy Inc.; basis 0.5 new trust unit, or 0.5 new exch. sh., or a combination thereof, plus 0.3333 new Alberta Clipper com. sh., plus 0.3333 new Ember com. sh. for 1 old Thunder Energy Inc. com. sh. (see Alberta Clipper Energy Inc.; Ember Resources Inc.; Thunder Energy Trust)

Thunder Energy Trust (Alta. July 7, 2005 amalg.)
June 29, 2007 – Acquired by Aston Hill Financial Inc.; basis $4.00 per trust unit and $1,010 per $1,000 principal amt. for all 7.25% deb. plus a cash amt. equal to accrued and unpaid int. (see Aston Hill Financial Inc.)

Thunder Engines Corporation (B.C. June 7, 1983)
May 2, 1996 – Name changed to Golden Thunder Resources Ltd.; basis 1 new for 5 old shs. ■

Thunder Explorations Ltd. (B.C. Jan. 29, 1982)
Apr. 22, 1985 – Name changed to Cam-Net Communications Network Inc. ■

Thunder Mountain Gold, Inc. (Idaho Nov. 9, 1935)
Jan. 25, 2008 – Continued into Nevada. (see FPsurvey - Mines & Energy)

Thunder Sword Resources Inc. (B.C. Sept. 13, 1979)
Nov. 23, 2009 – Name changed to Rainmaker Mining Corp.; basis 1 new for 10 old shs. ■

Thunder Valley Mines Ltd. (B.C. 1970)
Jan. 9, 1978 – Dissolved and struck off register.

Thunder Valley Resources Ltd. (Ont. 1986)
Mar. 30, 1990 – Amalgamated with Golden Winner Resources Ltd. (1 for 0.97), Rainbow Lake Resources Ltd. (1 for 0.915), Mountain Frontier Explorations Ltd. (1 for 1.08) and Premier Lake Resources Inc. (1 for 0.95) to form Castlestar Capital Developments Corp.; basis 1 new Castlestar for 1.10 old Thunder shs. (see Castlestar Capital Developments Corp.)

Thunderbird Energy Corporation (Can. Nov. 25, 1999)
Oct. 24, 2013 – Name changed to Gordon Creek Energy Inc.; basis 1 new for 15 old shs. (see FPsurvey - Mines & Energy)

Thunderbird Explorations Inc. (Ont. 1976)
Nov. 25, 1977 – Name changed to Thunderbolt Gas & Oil Explorations Ltd. ■

Thunderbird Petroleum Corporation (B.C. Dec. 5, 1979)
Jan. 10, 1980 – Name changed to Royalon Petroleum Corporation. ■

Thunderbird Projects Ltd. (B.C. Dec. 16, 1965)
Dec. 17, 1998 – Name changed to Consolidated Thunderbird Projects Ltd.; basis 1 new for 5 old shs. ■

Thunderbird Resorts, Inc. (Yuk. Feb. 5, 1999)
Oct. 6, 2006 – Continued into British Virgin Islands.

Thunderbolt Gas & Oil Explorations Ltd. (Ont. 1976)
Dec. 29, 1982 – Amalgamated with 4 other cos. to form Parapet Petroleums Inc.l; basis sh. for sh.

Thunderbolt Resources Limited (Ont. 1977)
Jan. 1978 – Name changed to Whirlwind Resource Explorations Ltd. ■

Thunderbolt Resources Ltd. (B.C. 1977)
Aug. 21, 1981 – Name changed to Warwick Petroleum Limited. ■

Thunderhead Gold Mines Limited (Ont. Dec. 27, 1945)
Mar. 31, 1990 – Name changed to Caratel Limited following acquisition of Caratel Inc. ■

Thunderhead Gold Mines Ltd. (Ont. 1945)
Mar. 14, 1978 – Charter cancelled.

Thundermin Resources Inc. (B.C. Oct. 30, 1964)
June 1, 1989 – Continued into Ontario.
Nov. 1, 1998 – Amalgamated in Ontario to continue with same name.
Jan. 13, 2016 – Acquired by Rambler Metals and Mining plc by way of amalgamation with 2496825 Ontario Inc., a wholly owned subsid. of Rambler; basis 0.061261 Rambler ord. shs. for 1 Thundermin com. sh.

Thunderspike Resources Ltd. (Alta. July 9, 1993)
Jan. 1, 1997 – Struck off register.

Thunderwood Explorations Ltd. (B.C. Oct. 30, 1964)
July 18, 1983 – Name changed to International Thunderwood Explorations Ltd.; basis 1 new for 5 old shs. ■

Thunderwood Resources Inc. (Ont. June 1, 1989 amalg.)
Nov. 9, 1998 – Amalgamated with Joutel Resources Limited to form Thundermin Resources Inc.; basis 1 new for 6 Joutel shs. and 1 new for 6 Thunderwood shs. (see Thundermin Resources Inc.)

Thurbois Mines Limited (Ont. 1943)
Oct. 16, 1948 – Name changed to New Thurbois Mines Limited; basis 1 new for 4 old shs. ■

Thyssen Mining Exploration Inc. (B.C. Apr. 3, 1986)
Dec. 8, 2000 – Name changed to Trilogy Metals Inc. ■

ThyssenKrupp Budd Canada Inc. (Ont. Oct. 8, 1965)
May 3, 2005 – Acquired by Budcan Holdings Inc., a wholly owned subsid. of ThyssenKrupp Budd Company, for $9.00 per sh. Co. now private.

Tiara Enterprises Ltd. (B.C. Feb. 15, 1982)
July 7, 1989 – Dissolved and struck off register.

Tiara Mines Ltd. (Ont. 1949)
1961 – Name changed to Tormont Mines Ltd.; basis 1 new for 3 old shs. ■

Tiara Resources Corp. (B.C. Feb. 15, 1982)
Feb. 28, 1986 – Name changed to Tiara Enterprises Ltd.; basis 2 new for 1 old sh. ■

Tib Exploration Ltd. (Ont. 1945)
May 15, 1974 – Charter cancelled.

Tibbett Lake Gold Mines Ltd. (Ont. 1949)
June 13, 1960 – Charter cancelled.

Tiber Energy Corporation (Alta. 1982)
May 23, 1989 – All o/s shs. acquired under public offering of $5.25 per sh. subsequently amalgamated with a wholly owned subsidiary of LASMO Canada Inc.

Tiber Resources Ltd. (Alta. 1978)
1982 – Under reorganization, shldrs. received 1 sh. and 1/3 wt. of Tiber Energy Corporation for 3 old shs.

Tiberius Productions Inc. (unknown)
Jan. 31, 1982 – Amalgamated with Cineplex Corporation and Pan-Canadian Film Distributers Inc., to continue under the Cineplex Corporation name; basis 8 com. shs. for 1 com. sh.; 2 new 6% pfce. shs., $10 par for 1 old non-voting special sh., $20 par.

Tiberon Minerals Ltd. (Alta. Sept. 29, 1995)
Oct. 21, 2002 – Continued into Canada.
Mar. 30, 2007 – Acquired by Dragon Capital Management Limited for $3.65 per sh.

Tiblemaco Gold Mines Ltd. (Ont. 1945)
Mar. 11, 1957 – Charter cancelled.

Tiblemont Goldfields Ltd. (Ont. 1945)
1965 – Name changed to Tib Exploration Ltd. ■

Tiburon Petroleum Corporation (B.C. 1980)
May 12, 1987 – Name changed to Bristol Trading Company.

Ticino Resources Corp. (B.C. Mar. 24, 1994)
Dec. 31, 2001 – Name changed to Neuro Discovery Inc. following reverse takeover acquisition of Neuro Discovery Inc.; basis 1 new for 2 old shs. ■

Ticker Tape Resources Ltd. (B.C. 1984)
Dec. 13, 1991 – Name changed to International Ticker Tape Resources Ltd.; basis 1 new for 3.7 old shs. ■

Ticonda Gold Mines Ltd. (Ont. 1945)
Dec. 10, 1962 – Dissolved.

Tidal Petroleum Corporation Ltd. (Alta. 1957)
1962 – Acquired by British Canadian Holding Corp. for $1.725 per sh.

Tidal Resources Inc. (Alta. Jan. 8, 1993)
Jan. 21, 1997 – All o/s com. shs. acquired by 711841 Alberta Ltd., an indirect wholly owned subsid. of Chauvco Resources Ltd.; basis $2.05 per sh. (see Chauvco Resources Ltd.)

Tidal Royalty Corp. (B.C. Mar. 12, 1980)
Apr. 24, 2020 – Name changed to Red White & Bloom Brands Inc. pursuant to reverse takeover acquisition of MichiCann Medical Inc. (dba Red White & Bloom); basis 1 new for 16 old shs. (see FPsurvey - Industrials)

Tide Lake Lithium Mines Ltd. (Ont. 1954)
Sept. 1964 – Charter cancelled.

Tidelands Copper Mines Ltd. (Ont. 1953)
Sept. 15, 1964 – Dissolved.

Tier One Energy Corp. (Alta. July 31, 1996)
Dec. 15, 1999 – All cl. A and B shs acquired by Northrock Resources Ltd.; basis $4.50 for each cl. A sh. and $10 for each cl. B sh. (see Northrock Resources Ltd.)

Tier One Metals Inc. (B.C. July 23, 2020)
Jan. 14, 2021 – Name changed to Tier One Silver Inc. (see FPsurvey - Mines & Energy)

Tiffany Oil & Gas Corp. (B.C. Feb. 5, 1981)
Apr. 12, 1983 – Name changed to Tiffany Resources Inc. ■

Tiffany Resource Corporation (Alta. Mar. 7, 1966)
Mar. 19, 1984 – Name changed to First Tiffany Resource Corporation. ■

Tiffany Resources Inc. (B.C. Feb. 5, 1981)
May 2, 1991 – Delisted from the Vancouver Stock Exchange. Subsequently struck from register and dissolved.

Tiffany Yellowknife Mines Ltd. (Ont. 1944)
1957 – Charter cancelled.

Tiger-Cat Energy Ltd. (Alta. July 10, 2003)
Sept. 29, 2008 – Formed RMS Systems Inc. in Alberta on amalgamation with C-Data Communications Inc., constituting a reverse takeover by C-Data; basis 1 new for 1 C-Data sh. and 1 new for 2.98 Tiger-Cat shs. ■

Tiger Oil Inc. (B.C. 1979)
June 1, 1982 – Amalgamated with Custer Resources Inc. (1 for 2.5) and Palliser Resources Inc. (1 for 1) to form Palliser International Energy Inc.; basis 1 new for 2.2 old Tiger shs.

Tiger Pacific Mining Corp. (Alta. Dec. 31, 1993 amalg.)
July 29, 2004 – Continued into British Columbia.
Aug. 31, 2010 – Name changed to Chantrell Ventures Corp.; basis 1 new for 2.5 old shs. ■

Tiger Petroleum Inc. (Que. Sept. 30, 1994)
Dec. 8, 2005 – Acquired by Pan Orient Energy Corp.; basis 1 new Pan Orient sh. for 4.25 old Tiger shs. Also debentureholders received either principal plus accrued and unpaid int., or 870 new Pan Orient shs. for $1,000 principal amt., or a combination thereof. (see Pan Orient Energy Corp.)

Tiger River Mines Ltd. (Ont. 1947)
1951 – Charter cancelled.

Tiger Silver Mines Ltd. (B.C. 1968)
Apr. 4, 1977 – Dissolved.

TigerTel Communications Inc. (B.C. Nov. 26, 2001)
Oct. 26, 2009 – All o/s shs. not held acquired by newly formed co. by way of amalgamation with 7212747 Canada Inc. and subsequently privatized; basis 1 pref. sh. for 1 com. sh. immediately redeemed for 25¢.

TigerTel Inc. (Can. May 17, 1996)
Jan. 6, 2000 – Acquired by AT & T Canada Corp. for $9.25 per sh.

Tigertel Telecommunications Corp. (B.C. Nov. 26, 2001)
May 3, 2002 – Name changed to TigerTel Communications Inc. following amalgamation with wholly owned TigerTel Communications Inc. ■

Tignanello Ventures Corp. (B.C. Mar. 11, 1994)
Jan. 10, 1997 – Name changed to Bushman Resources Inc. ■

Tigray Resources Inc. (Can. Sept. 23, 2010)
May 8, 2014 – Acquired by East Africa Metals Inc.; basis 0.55 East Africa com. sh. plus 0.40 East Africa wt. for 1 old Tigray com. sh.

Tigris Minerals Corporation (B.C. Jan. 6, 1987)
Jan. 9, 1996 – Name changed to Vantex Oil, Gas & Minerals Ltd.; basis 1 new for 5 old shs. ■

Tigris Uranium Corp. (B.C. Oct. 30, 2009)
May 21, 2013 – Name changed to Wolfpack Gold Corp. following reverse takeover acquisition of (old) Wolfpack Gold Corp. and amalgamation of (old) Wolfpack with wholly owned 0960926 B.C. Ltd.; basis 1 new for 3 old shs. ■

TigrSoft Inc. (Alta. May 25, 1987)
Mar. 31, 2001 – Formed Matrikon Inc. in Alberta following reverse takeover acquisition of and amalgamation with privately held Matrikin Inc.; basis 1 new for 5 old shs. ■

Tiidal Gaming Group Corp. (Ont. Aug. 9, 2006)
June 4, 2024 – Continued into British Columbia.
June 10, 2024 – Voluntarily delisted from the CSE.
July 10, 2024 – Name changed to WBM Capital Corp. (see FPsurvey - Industrials)

Tijana Mines Ltd. (B.C. 1969)
1969 – Name changed to Marguerite Lake Mines Ltd. and continued into British Columbia. ■

Tika Resources Ltd. (B.C. 1972)
Aug. 1974 – Name changed to International Tika Resources Ltd.; basis 1 new for 2 old shs. ■

Tikal Resources Corp. (Alta. Jan. 5, 1994)
Dec. 21, 2001 – Amalgamated with BelAir Energy Corporation; basis 0.4 BelAir sh. for 1 Tikal sh. (see BelAir Energy Corporation)

Tikal Resources Inc. (B.C. Jan. 8, 1973)
June 3, 1999 – Acquired by Cirque Energy Corp.; basis 1 Cirque sh. for 3.6 Tikal shs. (see Tikal Resources Corp.)

Tiki Development Corporation Ltd. (B.C. 1959)
Aug. 13, 1973 – Name changed to Beermaster Distributors Ltd. ■

Till Capital Corporation (B.C. Nov. 22, 2019)
July 22, 2025 – Acquired by Silver Storm Mining Ltd.; basis 16.360 Silver Storm units (1 com. sh. & ¼ wt. & 1 contingent value right) for 1 Till Capital com. sh. ■

Till Capital Ltd. (Bermuda Aug. 20, 2012)
Nov. 22, 2019 – Name changed to Till Capital Corporation and continued into British Columbia. ■

Tiller Resources Ltd. (B.C. Feb. 12, 2008)
Apr. 25, 2018 – Name changed to Blockchain Foundry Inc. pursuant to reverse takeover acquistion of (old) Blockchain Foundry Inc. ■

Tillex Mineral Corp. (B.C. Feb. 11, 1983)
Sept. 20, 1984 – Name changed to International Tillex Enterprises Ltd. ■

Tillicum Gold Mines Ltd. (B.C. 1982)
Dec. 30, 1986 – Name changed to Tillicum Industries Ltd. ■

Tillicum Industries Ltd. (B.C. 1982)
May 6, 1994 – Dissolved and struck off register.

Tillsonburg Oil & Gas Co. Ltd. (Ont. 1930)
1937 – Taken over by New Tillsonburg Oil & Gas Co. Ltd.

Tilray, Inc. (Del. Jan. 25, 2018)
Jan. 10, 2022 – Name changed to Tilray Brands, Inc. (see FPsurvey - Industrials)

Tilting Capital Corp. (Can. May 7, 2001)
Nov. 4, 2020 – Name changed to Gold Line Resources Ltd. pursuant to reverse takeover acquisition of (old) Gold Line Resources Ltd. (renamed Gold Line Resources Holdings Ltd.). ■

Tim Hortons Inc. (Del. Dec. 4, 1995)
Sept. 28, 2009 – Corporate structure reorganized whereby shares of the Delaware-incorporated company were exchanged for shares of a new company incorporated in Canada on June 23, 2009.
Dec. 12, 2014 – All o/s com. shs. acquired by Burger King Worldwide, Inc.; basis (i) Cdn$65.50 cash and 0.8025 Restaurant Brands International Inc. com. shs.; or (ii) Cdn$88.50 cash (subject to pro ration); or (iii) 3.0879 Restaurant Brands com. shs. for 1 Tim Horton sh.
Jan. 19, 2015 – Continued into British Columbia.
Jan. 21, 2015 – Name changed to Tim Hortons ULC. ■

Tim Hortons ULC (B.C. Jan. 19, 2015)
Mar. 2, 2015 – Formed The TDL Group Corp. in British Columbia on amalgamation with wholly owned Barhav Developments Limited, Fruition Manufacturing Limited, The TDL Group Co. ULC, The TDL Group Corp. ULC, The TDL Marks Corporation, 1024666 B.C. ULC, 1024672 B.C. Ltd., 1025222 B.C. ULC and 1027670 B.C. ULC.

Timagami Gold Mines Ltd. (Ont. May 1934)
1952 – Charter cancelled.

Timal Mining Corp. Ltd. (Ont. 1959)
Dec. 2, 1965 – Charter cancelled.

Timbercreek Global Real Estate Fund (Ont. Aug. 5, 2010)
Jan. 15, 2018 – Voluntarily delisted.
Jan. 23, 2018 – Merged into Timbercreek Global Real Estate Income Fund; basis 1.32 ser. A Income Fund units for 1 cl. A fund unit; and 1.44 ser. F Income Fund units for 1 cl. B fund unit.

Timbercreek Mortgage Investment Corporation (Ont. Apr. 30, 2008)
June 30, 2016 – Formed Timbercreek Financial Corp. in Ontario pursuant to amalgamation with Timbercreek Senior Mortgage Investment Corporation; basis 1 new TF sh. for 1 old TMIC sh. and 1.035 new TF shs. for 1 old TSMIC sh. (see FPsurvey - Industrials)

Timbercreek Senior Mortgage Investment Corporation (Can. Dec. 1, 2011)
June 24, 2016 – Continued into Ontario.
July 5, 2016 – Amalgamated with Timbercreek Mortgage Investment Corporation to form Timbercreek Financial Corp.; basis 1.035 Timbercreek Financial com. shs. for 1 Timbercreek Senior com. sh.

Timberland Properties Limited (Ont. 1956)
1969 – Assets acquired by Timberjack Machines Ltd. in 1967; charter surrendered.

Timberline Resources Corporation (Idaho Aug. 28, 1968)
Aug. 27, 2008 – Continued into Delaware. (see McEwen Mining Inc.)
Aug. 22, 2024 – Acquired by McEwen Mining Inc.; basis 0.01 McEwen shs. for 1 Timberline sh. (see McEwen Mining Inc.)

TimberWest Forest Corp. (B.C. Jan. 31, 1997)
June 14, 2011 – Continued into Canada.
June 30, 2011 – Acquired by British Columbia Investment Management Corporation and the Public Sector Pension Investment Board for $6.16 per unit.

TimberWest Forest Holdings Ltd. (B.C. Jan. 31, 1997)
Jan. 30, 1998 – Name changed to TimberWest Forest Management Limited. ■

TimberWest Forest Limited (B.C. Jan. 8, 1987)
June 25, 1997 – All o/s shs. acquired following Plan of Arrangement with TAL Acquisition Ltd., Fletcher Challenge Canada Limited, 325724 B.C. Ltd. and Fletcher Challenge Securities Canada Inc.; basis $22 per com. sh. (see Fletcher Challenge Canada Limited)

TimberWest Forest Management Limited (B.C. Jan. 31, 1997)
Sept. 30, 1998 – Name changed to TimberWest Forest Corp. following reorganization. ■

TimberWest Timber Trust (B.C. Feb. 17, 1997)
Nov. 12, 1998 – Following reorganization with TimberWest Forest Corp. (TimberWest), trust units exchanged for stapled units (1 com. sh., 100 pref. shs. plus 1 sub. note receipt) of TimberWest; basis 1 new stapled unit for 1 old trust unit. (see TimberWest Forest Corp.)

Timbuktu Gold Corp. (Alta. July 18, 1985)
May 6, 1997 – Name changed to Marchmont Gold Corp. ■

Time Air Corporation (Alta. 1978)
Jan. 4, 1991 – Amalgamated with a wholly owned subsid. of PWA Corporation; basis 1.5191 new for 1 old sh. (see PWA Corporation)

Time Resources Corporation (B.C. 1982)
Nov. 30, 1985 – Formed J.C. International Petroleum Ltd. in Alberta on amalgamation with J.C. International Petroleum Ltd. ■

Timebeat.com Enterprises Inc. (Yuk. Sept. 1999)
Oct. 16, 2001 – Continued into Nevada.

Timer Explorations Inc. (B.C. Jan. 10, 2000)
May 30, 2008 – Name changed to Potash North Resource Corporation; basis 2 new for 1 old sh. ■

Times Square Energy Resources Ltd. (B.C. 1981)
May 21, 1986 – Name changed to New Hombre Resources Ltd.; basis 1 new for 2 old shs. ■

Times Telecom Inc. (B.C. June 25, 2002)
Nov. 21, 2016 – Dissolved and struck from register.

Times Three Wireless Inc. (Alta. Nov. 30, 2011; amalg.)
June 23, 2015 – Adjudged bankrupt. Hardie & Kelly Inc. appointed trustee.

Timia Capital Corp. (B.C. Oct. 26, 2007)
June 15, 2022 – Name changed to Montfort Capital Corp. (see FPsurvey - Mines & Energy; FPsurvey - Industrials)

Timmax Resource Corporation (B.C. Apr. 29, 1987)
June 8, 1994 – Name changed to Metalline Resource Corporation; basis 1 new for 3 old shs. ■

Timminco Limited (Can. July 23, 1980)
Jan. 3, 2012 – Filed for protection under the Companies' Credit Arrangement Act (CCAA) and FTI Consulting Canada Inc. appointed monitor.
June 15, 2012 – Substantially all of the silicon metal business and assets of Becancour Silicon, including the 51% interest in Quebec Silicon Limited Partnership, were sold to QSI Partners Ltd., a subsid. of Globe Specialty Metals, Inc. for approximately $32,000,000. In addition, substantially all the assets relating to the solar grade silicon business formerly conducted by Timminco Solar were sold to Grupo FerroAtlantica S.A. for undisclosed amount.
Aug. 17, 2012 – Russell Hill Advisory Services Inc. was appointed chief restructuring officer (CRO) and the officers and directors resigned.
Aug. 2012 – Interim distrib. of $26,600,000 was made to secured creditor Investissement Quebec.
Mar. 2013 – Court approval was given for the transfer of the Haley property and the Silica Fumes property to subsidiaries of the company with those subsidiaries being assigned into bankruptcy. The Haley property was abandoned by the trustee on or about Mar. 13, 2013.
Oct. 2013 – The Silica fumes property was not transferred due to statutory restrictions on the transfer of agricultural designated land and the property was abandoned.
May 16, 2016 – Dissolved and struck from register.
May 20, 2016 – CCAA terminated and the monitor, FTI Consulting, discharged.

Timmins Gold Corp. (B.C. Mar. 17, 2005)
May 16, 2017 – Name changed to Alio Gold Inc.; basis 1 new for 10 old shs. ■

Timpete Mining Corporation (B.C. July 19, 1995)
Feb. 5, 2001 – Name changed to Entrée Resources Inc.; basis 4 new for 1 old sh. ■

Timrod Mining Co. Ltd. (Que. 1964)
June 1, 1976 – Merged into Brominco Inc.; basis 1 Brominco sh. for 6 Timrod shs., plus capital distribution of 10¢ per Timrod sh.

Timvest Growth Fund Inc. (P.E.I. 1947)
Mar. 23, 1988 – Name changed to Talvest Growth Fund Inc. ■

Tinex Development & Exploration Ltd. (Ont. 1950)
Nov. 30, 1970 – Amalgamated with Cantri Mining Ltd. (1 for 10), Con-Key Mines Ltd. (1 for 10), Point West Explorations Ltd. (1 for 10), St. Anthony Mines Ltd. (1 for 30) and Temanda Mines Ltd. (1 for 30) to form Can-Con Enterprises and Explorations Limited; basis 1 new for 30 old shs.

Tinhorn Resources Ltd. (Alta. June 4, 1999)
Apr. 5, 2002 – Acquired by Redwood Energy, Ltd.; basis 0.9 new Redwood cl. A com. sh. for 1 old Tinhorn com. sh. (see Redwood Energy, Ltd.)

The Tinley Beverage Company Inc. (Ont. Mar. 7, 2005)
Mar. 12, 2025 – Name changed to Beckett's Inc. (see FPsurvey - Industrials)

Tinta Hill Mines Ltd. (B.C. June 25, 1969)
Jan. 1980 – Name changed to Anchor Petroleum Corp. ■

Tintina Mines Limited (Can. Dec. 6, 1961)
Sept. 9, 2024 – Continued into British Columbia. (see FPsurvey - Mines & Energy)

Tintina Resources Inc. (B.C. July 30, 1998)
Feb. 2, 2018 – Name changed to Sandfire Resources America Inc. (see FPsurvey - Mines & Energy)

Tintina Silver Mines Ltd. (Can. Dec. 6, 1961)
July 9, 1980 – Name changed to Tintina Mines Limited. ■

TintinaGold Resources Inc. (B.C. July 30, 1998)
May 26, 2011 – Name changed to Tintina Resources Inc. ■

Tinto Gold Corporation (B.C. 1981)
Nov. 4, 1988 – Name changed to Ortho-Tronics Medical Technologies Ltd. ■

Tinto Iron Mines Ltd. (Ont. 1960)
Aug. 24, 1962 – Name changed to Eagle Rock Iron Mines Ltd.

Tiny Ltd. (B.C. Mar. 4, 2019)
Continued into Canada. (see FPsurvey - Industrials)

TinyMassive Technologies Inc. (B.C. Jan. 16, 2007)
Feb. 28, 2011 – Name changed to Pure Living Media Inc. ■

Tiomin Resources Inc. (Can. Oct. 5, 1992 amalg.)
Mar. 26, 2010 – Name changed to Vaaldiam Mining Inc. pursuant to acquisition of Vaaldiam Resources Ltd.; basis 1 new for 10 old shs. ■

Tip Top Tailors Ltd. (Can. 1928; via Dominion charter)
Aug. 1, 1967 – Name changed to Dylex Diversified (1967) Ltd. ■

Tipperary Resources Limited (Ont. 1982 amalg.)
Nov. 14, 1985 – Amalgamated with 6 other cos. to form Paladin Petroleum Corporation; basis 1.75 new for 1 old sh.

Tipuani Gold Mines Ltd. (Ont. 1973)
May 18, 1976 – Charter cancelled.

Tirex Resources Ltd. (B.C. Sept. 29, 2006)
Jan. 25, 2018 – Name changed to European Electric Metals Inc.; basis 1 new for 10 old shs. (see FPsurvey - Mines & Energy)

Tisdale Clean Energy Corp. (B.C. Sept. 22, 2014)
Oct. 2, 2024 – Name changed to Terra Clean Energy Corp. (see FPsurvey - Mines & Energy)

Tisdale Resources Corp. (B.C. Sept. 22, 2014)
June 8, 2022 – Name changed to Tisdale Clean Energy Corp. ■

Titan Digital Corporation (Alta. Jan. 1, 2003 amalg.)
July 2, 2010 – Struck from registry and dissolved.

Titan Diversified Holdings Ltd. (Alta. Mar. 16, 1987)
Aug. 2, 1991 – Name changed to Titan Diversified Ventures Ltd.; basis 1 new for 6 old shs. ■

Titan Diversified Ventures Ltd. (Alta. Mar. 16, 1987)
Aug. 3, 1993 – Name changed to Trident Systems Inc. following reverse takeover acquisition of Trident Creative Technology Inc. ■

Titan Empire Inc. (Ont. July 13, 1936)
Nov. 2, 1994 – Name changed to AWG American-WestJava Gold Corp.; basis 1 new com. for either 1 old cl. A sub. vtg. sh. or 1 old cl. B multi vtg. sh. ■

Titan Employment Services Ltd. (Ont. Aug. 26, 1999)
Nov. 14, 2008 – Formed Essex Oil Ltd. in Ontario on amalgamation with Adelaide Global Corp. (deemed acquiror); basis 1 Essex sh. for 1 Adelaide sh. and 0.25 Essex shs. for 1 Titan sh. (see FPsurvey - Mines & Energy)

Titan Exploration Ltd. (Alta. Jan. 6, 2004)
Jan. 17, 2008 – Acquired by Canetic Resources Trust; basis 0.1917 Canetic trust units for 1 Titan cl. A sh. and 0.6609 Canetic trust units for 1 Titan cl. B sh.

Titan Goldworx Resources Inc. (B.C. Feb. 4, 2011)
Sept. 10, 2013 – Name changed to Amana Copper Ltd. ■

Titan Iron Mines Ltd. (Ont. 1942)
Mar. 14, 1978 – Charter cancelled.

Titan Medical Inc. (Ont. July 28, 2008 amalg.)
Oct. 11, 2024 – Name changed to Conavi Medical Corp pursuant to the reverse takeover acquisition of Conavi Medical Inc.; basis 1 new for 25 old shs. (see FPsurvey - Industrials)

Titan Oil Co. (Can. 1926)
1929 – Taken over by Anaconda Oil Co. Ltd.; basis 1 new for 2.5 old shs.

Titan Pacific Resources Ltd. (B.C. Dec. 28, 1989 amalg.)
July 2, 2002 – Name changed to Titan Logix Corp. (see FPsurvey - Industrials)

Titan Petroleum Corp. Ltd. (Alta. 1951)
May 14, 1977 – Struck off register.

Titan-Polaris Mines Ltd. (B.C. Apr. 17, 1957)
July 17, 1975 – Name changed to Saxton Industries Ltd.; basis 1 new for 4 old shs. ■

Titan Resources Ltd. (B.C. Feb. 26, 1979)
Sept. 8, 1987 – Name changed to Golden Titan Resources Ltd.; basis 1 new for 2 old shs. ■

Titan Trading Analytics Inc. (B.C. Nov. 30, 1993)
May 2, 2005 – Continued into Alberta. (see FPsurvey - Industrials)

Titan Uranium Exploration Inc. (B.C. Apr. 8, 2005)
June 24, 2005 – Name changed to Titan Uranium Inc.; basis 1 new for 2 old shs. ■

Titan Uranium Inc. (B.C. Apr. 8, 2005)
Mar. 2, 2012 – Acquired by Energy Fuels Inc.; basis 0.68 Energy shs. for 1 Titan sh.

Titanic Mine Holdings Ltd. (Can. 1945)
1957 – Charter cancelled; shldrs. received 1 sh. New Royran Copper for each 8 shs. Titanic, and 1 escrowed sh. Swanson Mines for each 2 shs. Titanic.

Titanium Corporation Inc. (Ont. July 24, 2001 amalg.)
Mar. 19, 2009 – Continued into Canada. ■
Mar. 21, 2022 – Name changed to CVW Cleantech Inc. ■

Titanium Development Corporation (Que. 1947)
June 3, 1966 – Declared bankrupt.

TitanStar Properties Inc. (Can. June 3, 2008)
Oct. 22, 2019 – Name changed to Realia Properties Inc. (see FPsurvey - Industrials)

Title Technologies Inc. (B.C. Dec. 1, 1986)
Oct. 15, 1998 – Name changed to Maxy Oil & Gas Inc. following reverse takeover acquisition of Seafield Gas Pipeline Ltd.; basis 1 new for 5 old shs. ■

Titleist Energy Inc. (Alta. Nov. 19, 1993)
June 25, 1997 – Name changed to TomaNet Inc. ■

Titleist Petroleums Ltd. (B.C. May 27, 1980)
Sept. 5, 1986 – Name changed to Comp-Data International Inc.; basis 1 new for 5 old shs. ■

Titus Capital Corp. (B.C. Feb. 17, 2010)
July 8, 2013 – Name changed to Titus Energy Corp. ■

Titus Energy Corp. (B.C. Feb. 17, 2010)
Dec. 8, 2014 – Voluntarily delisted.
Aug. 2, 2016 – Dissolved and stuck from the registry.
July 31, 2017 – Restored to registry.
Aug. 29, 2017 – Distrib. made to shldrs. of record Aug. 29, 2017, of 1 cl. A Term Oil Inc. sh. for 4 Titus com. shs.
June 8, 2023 – Name changed to Free Battery Metal Limited pursuant to the reverse takeover acquisition of Rift Lithium Inc. (see FPsurvey - Mines & Energy)

Titus Mining & Explorations Ltd. (Ont. 1966)
Mar. 1976 – Charter cancelled.

Tiverton Petroleums Ltd. (Alta. Apr. 19, 1975)
May 13, 1980 – Amalgamated in Alberta to continue with same name. (see Arsenal Energy Inc.)
Oct. 1, 2000 – Amalgamated in Alberta to continue with same name. (see Arsenal Energy Inc.)
Mar. 22, 2006 – Acquired by Arsenal Energy Inc.; basis 0.23 Arsenal shs. for 1 Tiverton sh. (see Arsenal Energy Inc.)

Tm Bioscience Corporation (Ont. Dec. 19, 1980)
Mar. 5, 2007 – Acquired by Luminex Corporation; basis 0.6 Luminex shs. for 1 Tm Bioscience sh.

Tm Technologies Corp. (Ont. Dec. 19, 1980)
July 11, 1997 – Name changed to Tm Bioscience Corporation. ■

Toachi Mining Inc. (Can. Nov. 30, 2011 amalg.)
Sept. 13, 2019 – Acquired by Atico Mining Corporation; basis 0.24897 Atico com. shs. for 1 Toachi com. sh.

Toba Gold Resources Ltd. (B.C. Dec. 31, 1986)
Oct. 15, 1996 – Name changed to Toba Industries Ltd. ■

Toba Industries Ltd. (B.C. Dec. 31, 1986)
Nov. 7, 2008 – Name changed to Beijing Marvel Cleansing Supplies Co. Ltd. following reverse takeover acquisition of Peking Marvel Cleansing Supplies Co., Ltd. ■

Toba Nickel and Copper Mines Ltd. (Ont. 1948)
1949 – Name changed to Transnorthern Nickel & Copper Mines Ltd. and continued into Ontario. ■

Tobe Mines Ltd. (Alta. Jan. 7, 1966)
July 13, 1984 – Name changed to Stratum Resources Ltd. ■

Tobex Resources Ltd. (B.C. July 7, 1987)
May 21, 1992 – Name changed to Langtec Capital Corp. ■

Tobico Consolidated Gold Mines Ltd. (Ont. 1949)
Dec. 19, 1979 – Charter cancelled.

Tobico Gold Mines Ltd. (Ont. 1932)
1949 – Name changed to Tobico Consolidated Gold Mines Ltd. and continued into Ontario; basis 1 new escrowed for 2 old shs. ■

Tobruc Clericy Mines Ltd. (Ont. 1946)
1952 – Charter cancelled.

Toburn-Alberta Ltd. (Can. Mar. 4, 1987)
July 12, 2004 – Dissolved.

Toburn Gold Mines Ltd. (Ont. 1931)
June 1954 – Voluntarily liquidated. Total distribution made of 44.92¢ per sh. (35¢, August 1953; 9.92¢, June 1954).

Toburn Gold Mines Ltd. (Can. Nov. 4, 1980)
Jan. 19, 1996 – Dissolved. Subsequently revived, May 25, 2000.

Toby Creek Resources Ltd. (B.C. July 17, 1984)
Oct. 29, 1993 – Name changed to Banff Resources Ltd.; basis 1 new for 3 old shs. ■

Toby Ventures Inc. (B.C. May 15, 2000)
Jan. 30, 2004 – Name changed to Storm Cat Energy Corporation. ■

Todd Explorations Ltd. (B.C. 1967)
Nov. 25, 1974 – Charter cancelled.

Todwind Development Corporation (B.C. 1972 amalg.)
Dec. 7, 1984 – Placed into receivership. No distribution to shldrs.

Toff Uranium Mines Ltd. (Ont. 1954)
Sept. 16, 1965 – Charter cancelled.

Tofino Gold Mines (B.C.) Ltd. (B.C. 1953)
Mar. 1956 – Name changed to Atlas Mining Corp. Ltd.; basis 1 new for 1 old sh. ■

Tofino Gold Mining Co. Ltd. (B.C. 1947)
1958 – Wound up; basis 1 sh. Tofino Mines Ltd. for 3 old shs.

Tofino Mines Ltd. (B.C. 1953)
Jan. 16, 1978 – Name changed to Banqwest Resources Ltd. ■

Tokar Limited (Que. 1926)
Aug. 20, 1974 – Name changed to Canadian Tokar Limited following reduction in paid-up capital from $8,367,546 to $2,090,109, shldrs. received $6,277,437 (equivalent to $1.90 per share) out of paid-up capital; basis 1 new for 2 old shs. ■

Tokenhouse Yard Holdings Inc. (Alta. Jan. 16, 1987)
July 22, 1992 – Amalgamated with Zoa Petroleum Ltd. to form Newgate Resources Ltd.; basis 1 new for 1.38 Zoa shs. and 1 new for 0.78 Tokenhouse shs. (see Newgate Resources Ltd.)

Tokens.com Corp. (Ont. Dec. 8, 2009)
July 15, 2024 – Name changed to Realbotix Corp. (see FPsurvey - Industrials)

Tolima Gold Inc. (Ont. Sept. 23, 1935)
Jan. 23, 2019 – Name changed to Amilot Capital Inc.; basis 1 new for 10 old shs. (see FPsurvey - Mines & Energy)

Tolken Resource Corporation (Ont. 1962)
Apr. 1987 – Name changed to Equity Standard Corporation; basis 2 new cl. A and 2 new cl. B for 1 old com. sh. ■

Toltec Mines Ltd. (unknown)
Aug. 1974 – Charter cancelled.

Toltec Resources Ltd. (B.C. Mar. 14, 1988)
Nov. 13, 1992 – Name changed to Canso Explorations Ltd.; basis 1 new for 5 old shs. ■

Toluma Mining and Development Co. Ltd. (B.C. 1960)
Jan. 21, 1983 – Struck off register.

Tom Exploration Inc. (Can. Feb. 12, 1990 amalg.)
Apr. 22, 2008 – Name changed to Excel Gold Mining Inc. ■

Tomahawk Iron Mines Ltd. (Ont. Feb. 26, 1938)
1949 – Assets taken over by Mag-Iron Mining & Milling Ltd.; basis 1 new for 20 old shs., with those who paid cash for Tomahawk shs. receiving additional 19 Mag-Iron shs. per old sh. (see Mag-Iron Mining & Milling Ltd.)

Tomahawk Resources Ltd. (B.C. July 29, 1981)
Aug. 23, 1993 – Name changed to Sartis Medical Systems Canada Inc. ■

TomaNet Inc. (Alta. Nov. 19, 1993)
Aug. 19, 2003 – Plan of Arrangement acquisition by IMARK Corporation (subsequently named Maxim Atlantic Corporation); basis 0.13 new IMARK com. sh. for 1 old TomaNet com. sh. and 0.12 new IMARK com. sh. for 1 old TomaNet cl. A sh. (see Maxim Atlantic Corporation)

Tombac Exploration Ltd. (B.C. 1959)
1962 – Acquired by Magnum Consolidated Mining Co. Ltd.; basis 2 new for 7 old shs. (see Magnum Consolidated Mining Co. Ltd.)

Tombill Gold Mines Ltd. (Ont. Oct. 7, 1935)
1959 – Name changed to Tombill Mines Limited. ■

Tombill Mines Limited (Ont. Oct. 7, 1935)
1983 – Continued into Canada.
Jan. 15, 1998 – Amalgamated with 3385701 Canada Inc. and shares called for redemption; basis $7.69 per new cl. A preference sh. into which all o/s cl. A and cl. B shs. of Tombill were exchanged on a one for one basis. Now private.
Oct. 9, 2018 – Continued into British Columbia.
Dec. 9, 2020 – Formed Tombill Exploration Ltd.

Tombill Mines Limited (B.C. Feb. 3, 2011)
Sept. 9, 2021 – Continued into Ontario. (see FPsurvey - Mines & Energy)

Tombit Resources Limited (Ont. Sept. 23, 1968)
1983 – Name changed to Cliff Creek Resources Ltd. ■

Tombstone Explorations Co. Ltd. (B.C. Feb. 9, 1990)
Apr. 17, 2002 – Name changed to Mena Resources Inc.; basis 1 new for 10 old shs. ■

Tomcar Mines Ltd. (Ont. 1953)
Feb. 1962 – Dissolved.

Tomco Developments Inc. (B.C. Dec. 1, 1972)
June 8, 2009 – Dissolved and struck from register.

Tomiska Copper Mines Ltd. (Que. 1951)
Dec. 23, 1976 – Dissolved.

Tommel Oil Ltd. (Alta.)
1959 – Struck off register.

Tomrock Copper Mines Ltd. (Ont. 1955)
Feb. 18, 1963 – Dissolved.

Tonalite Gold Mines Ltd. (Ont. 1948)
1950 – Assets distributed and charter surrendered.

Tonawanda Mines Ltd. (Que. 1929)
June 3, 1978 – Charter cancelled.

Tonbridge Power Inc. (Ont. Oct. 1, 2003)
Oct. 18, 2011 – Acquired by Enbridge Inc. for 54¢ per sh.

Tone Resources Limited (Yuk. Oct. 31, 2001)
Mar. 1, 2005 – Continued into British Columbia. (see US Gold Canadian Acquisition Corporation)
July 9, 2007 – Acquired by US Gold Canadian Acquisition Corporation; basis 0.26 new US Gold sh. for 1 old Tone sh. (see US Gold Canadian Acquisition Corporation)

Tonecraft Limited (Ont. 1955)
Jan. 1, 1980 – Name changed to Color Your World, Inc. ■

Tonecraft Paints Limited (Ont. 1955)
May 1971 – Name changed to Tonecraft Limited. ■

Tonecraft Realty Inc. (Ont. 1979)
Apr. 30, 1986 – Acquired by D. R. Strongman & Son Ltd., W. M. Strongman & Son Ltd. and Bruce Strongman Holdings Ltd. for $8.00 per sh.

Tongue Creek Oil Co. (unknown)
1924 – Taken over by Mill City Oils Ltd.; basis 1 new for 4.7 old shs. (see Mill City Oils Ltd.)

Tonka Resources Inc. (Can. Jan. 14, 1972)
Mar. 3, 1988 – Name changed to Consolidated Tonka Resources Inc.; basis 1 new for 20 old shs. ■

Tonko Development Corp. (Alta. Mar. 9, 1995)
Mar. 21, 2002 – Acquired by 970385 Alberta Ltd. wholly owned subsid. of Pyxis Real Estate Equities Inc.; basis $4.10 per sh.

Tonopah Resources Inc. (B.C. Jan. 30, 1981)
Nov. 6, 1996 – Name changed to Goldzone Exploration Inc.; basis 1 new for 5 old shs. ■

Tontine Mining Ltd. (Ont. 1951)
Dec. 30, 1971 – Amalgamated with North Coldstream Mines Ltd. to form Coldstream Mines Ltd.; basis 1 new for 3 old shs.

Tonto Petroleum Corporation Limited (Ont. 1946)
Jan. 28, 1957 – Dissolved.

Tonto Yellowknife Mines Ltd. (Ont. 1946)
1952 – Name changed to Tonto Petroleum Corporation Limited. ■

Tony G Co-Investment Holdings Ltd. (Ont. Oct. 26, 1988)
June 19, 2025 – Name changed to HYLQ Strategy Corp. (see FPsurvey - Industrials)

Toodoggone Gold Inc. (B.C. Sept. 15, 1986)
June 6, 1995 – Name changed to Tapajos Gold Inc.; basis 1 new for 4 old shs. ■

Tooke Bros. Ltd. (Can. 1911)
1974 – Reported out of business, following bankruptcy and sale of all assets of parent co., Canadian Converters Co. Ltd., to Val Royal Sportswear Mfg. Ltd., a wholly owned subsid. of Queenswear (Canada) Ltd.

Top Environmental Capital Venture Inc. (Can. Apr. 20, 1998)
June 11, 2001 – Name changed to Loubac Top Environmental Inc. ■

Top Exploration Inc. (B.C. Sept. 27, 2018)
Oct. 21, 2020 – Name changed to E79 Resources Corp. ■

Top Gun Capital Corp. (Alta. Feb. 27, 1998)
July 19, 2002 – Name changed to Western Warrior Resources Inc. following Qualifying Transaction reverse takeover acquisition of Western Warrior Resources Ltd.; basis 1 new for 2.5 old shs. ■

Top Gun Explorations Inc. (B.C. Nov. 20, 1986)
Apr. 13, 1992 – Name changed to Consolidated Top Gun Explorations Inc.; basis 1 new for 2.19 old shs. ■

Top Strike Resources Corp. (Alta. Dec. 13, 2012)
Feb. 23, 2024 – Name changed to Vencanna Ventures Inc. (see FPsurvey - Industrials)

Top 10 Canadian Financial Trust (Ont. Feb. 15, 2000)
July 6, 2021 – Merged into Mulvihill Premium Yield Field; basis 0.842468 Mulvihill cl. A units for 1 Top 10 trust unit.

Top 10 Split Trust (Ont. Jan. 22, 1997)
Sept. 11, 2024 – Merged into Premium Global Income Split Corp.; 0.453607 Premium Global cl. A shs. for 1 Top 10 capital unit. Holders of the pref. securities received 0.948049 Premium Global pref. shs. and 0.415545 Premium Global cl. A shs. for 1 Top 10 pref. security,

Top 20 Dividend Trust (Ont. May 29, 2012)
June 1, 2017 – Redeemed; basis $8.7232 cash per trust unit.

Top 20 Europe Dividend Trust (Ont. Nov. 27, 2012)
Jan. 31, 2018 – Terminated; basis $8.83 cash per trust unit.

Top 20 U.S. Dividend Trust (Ont. Sept. 12, 2012)
Dec. 31, 2020 – Terminated; basis Cdn$11.1288 cash per cl. A unit and US$11.4411 cash per cl. U unit.

Topal Mining Co. Ltd. (B.C. 1969)
July 11, 1977 – Dissolved.

Topaz Exploration Ltd. (B.C. Feb. 21, 1983)
Aug. 1, 1989 – Name changed to Consolidated Topaz Exploration Ltd.; basis 1 new for 3 old shs. ■

Topaz Resources International Inc. (B.C. Feb. 21, 1983)
July 21, 1997 – Name changed to Pacific Topaz Resources Ltd.; basis 1 new for 2 old shs. ■

Topkapi Resources Ltd. (B.C. Sept. 15, 1982)
June 13, 1986 – Name changed to Owen Ventures Ltd.; basis 1 new for 2.5 old shs. ■

Topley Copper Corp. Ltd. (Alta. 1969)
1970 – Assets acquired by Criss Creek Mines Ltd.

Topley Criss Mines Ltd. (B.C. 1968)
June 13, 1977 – Dissolved.

Topley-Richfield Mining Company Limited (B.C. Oct. 14, 1927)
1938 – Dissolved.

Topper Gold Corporation (B.C. Nov. 23, 1959)
Apr. 13, 2000 – Name changed to Consolidated Topper Gold Corporation; basis 1 new for 10 old shs. ■

Topper Mining Co. Ltd. (B.C. 1964)
Nov. 1979 – Charter cancelled.

Topper Resources Inc. (B.C. Nov. 23, 1959)
May 3, 2006 – Continued into Alberta.
May 19, 2006 – Name changed to Century Energy Ltd. ■

Topspar Fluorite Mines Ltd. (Ont. 1946)
Jan. 1960 – Charter cancelled.

Toptent inc. (Can. Aug. 1, 2007)
Dec. 3, 2009 – Filed notice of intention under the Bankruptcy and Insolvency Act. PricewaterhouseCoopers Inc. appointed trustee for the proposal.
May 20, 2010 – Creditors accepted the proposal filed under the BIA.
Aug. 3, 2010 – The proposal was completed and PricewaterhouseCoopers discharged as trustee for the proposal. (see FPsurvey - Industrials)

Tor American Oil Limited (Que. Aug. 15, 1950)
1953 – Acquired by Tri-Tor Oils Ltd.; basis 2 new for 4 old shs. (see Tri-Tor Oils Ltd.)

Tor-Branto Exploration Ltd. (Ont. 1928)
1930 – Name changed to Premier Oils, Ltd.

Tor-Cal Resources Limited (Alta. 1979)
Feb. 23, 1988 – Name changed to Lidco Industries Inc. ■

Torbec Mines Ltd. (Ont. 1944)
Feb. 17, 1964 – Dissolved.

Torbrit Silver Mines Ltd. (B.C. 1946)
Acquired by New York Oils Ltd.; basis 3 new for 4 old shs. (see New York Oils Limited)

Torbrook Iron Ore Mines Ltd. (N.S. 1956)
Wound up. Nominal distribution.

Torbruc Clericy Mines Ltd. (Ont. 1945)
1952 – Charter cancelled.

Torc Financial Corp. (Alta. Apr. 10, 1997)
May 5, 1999 – Name changed to Vanguard Aviation Corp. following acquisition of Vanguard Aviation Inc.; basis 1 new for 1 old sh. ■

Torcan Explorations Ltd. (Ont. 1956)
1967 – Charter cancelled.

Torcan Explorations Ltd. (Que. 1962)
Aug. 17, 1985 – Charter cancelled.

Torch River Resources Ltd. (Alta. Mar. 26, 2004 amalg.)
Oct. 30, 2013 – Name changed to Saint Jean Carbon Inc. ■

Toreador Resources Corporation (Del. July 13, 1951)
Feb. 22, 2012 – Name changed to Zaza Energy Corporation.

Torene Gold Exploration Ltd. (Ont. Sept. 16, 1985)
Apr. 5, 1988 – Name changed to AquaGold Resources Incorporated. ■

Torex Minerals Ltd. (B.C. June 1, 1983)
Jan. 27, 1987 – Name changed to Corniche Resources Ltd.; basis 1 new for 4 old shs. ■

Torex Resources Inc. (Can. Sept. 8, 1995)
Sept. 8, 2000 – All o/s com. shs. acquired by Summit Resources Acquisitions Limited, wholly owned subsid. of Summit Resources Limited; basis $1.25 per sh. (see Summit Resources Limited)

Torhsen Energy Corporation (B.C. Aug. 14, 1979)
Nov. 28, 1986 – Name changed to Niagara Capital Corporation. ■

Toric Mines Co. Ltd. (B.C. 1921)
Liquidated.

Torino Oil & Gas Limited (Alta. Feb. 9, 1993 amalg.)
Oct. 2002 – Placed into receivership. RSM Richter Inc. was appointed receiver/manager.

Torino Power Solutions Inc. (B.C. Sept. 10, 2014)
June 3, 2020 – Name changed to KABN Systems NA Holdings Corp. pursuant to reverse takeover acquisition of KABN Systems North America Inc.; basis 1 new for 10 old shs. ■

Tormac Mines Ltd. (Ont. 1966)
1968 – Assets sold to Mission Financial Corp. Ltd.; basis 0.01616 new for 1 old sh.

Tormex Mining Developers Ltd. (Ont. 1966)
Sept. 22, 1975 – Merged into Lacana Mining Corporation; basis 50 new for 100 old shs.

Tormex Resources Ltd. (B.C. 1972)
Dec. 30, 1983 – Dissolved.

Tormont Mines Ltd. (Ont. 1949)
Mar. 14, 1978 – Charter cancelled.

Tornado Global Hydrovacs Ltd. (Alta. Apr. 27, 2016)
Dec. 18, 2024 – Name changed to Tornado Infrastructure Equipment Ltd. (see FPsurvey - Mines & Energy; FPsurvey - Industrials)

Tornado Resources Ltd. (B.C. July 25, 1986)
May 13, 1999 – Continued into Alberta. (see KeyWest Energy Corporation)
Aug. 3, 2001 – Acquired by KeyWest Energy Corporation for $0.0725 per sh. (see KeyWest Energy Corporation)

Tornado Technologies Inc. (Alta. Nov. 20, 1995)
Dec. 10, 2007 – Amalgamated in Alberta to continue with same name. (see Empire Industries Ltd.)
Dec. 12, 2007 – Acquired by Empire Industries Ltd.; basis 1 Empire sh. for 2.09 Tornado shs. (see Empire Industries Ltd.)
Oct. 5, 2009 – Name changed to Petrofield Industries Inc. (see Empire Industries Ltd.)

Toro Energy Inc. (Alta. Sept. 29, 2000)
Sept. 18, 2003 – Name changed to Sentra Resources Corporation following reverse takeover acquisition of Sentra Resources Corporation; basis 1 new for 4 old shs. ■

Toro Oil & Gas Ltd. (Alta. May 3, 2004 amalg.)
Feb. 3, 2017 – Acquired by Steelhead Petroleum Ltd.; basis 37¢ cash per com. sh. and 1¢ cash per wt.

Toro Resources Corp. (B.C. June 30, 2005)
June 15, 2015 – Name changed to Big Wind Capital Inc.; basis 1 new for 5 old shs. ■

Toro Resources Limited (B.C. Aug. 25, 1982)
May 2, 1988 – Name changed to British Medical Services Limited. ■

Torode Realty Limited (Alta. Dec. 11, 1997 amalg.)
Jan. 29, 2004 – Formed CMQ Resources Inc. in Alberta following reverse takeover acquisition of and amalgamation with CMQ Resources Inc. ■

Torogold Resources Inc. (Ont. June 13, 1986)
Dec. 20, 1994 – Name changed to XISS Capital Corporation; basis 1 new for 10 old shs. ■

Toromont Industrial Holdings Ltd. (Can. Jan. 31, 1961)
Apr. 10, 1974 – Name changed to Toromont Industries Ltd. (see FPsurvey - Industrials)

Toronado Development Corp. Ltd. (B.C. 1960)
Apr. 21, 1977 – Name changed to Cyclone Developments Ltd.; basis 1 new for 4 old shs. ■

Toronado Mines Limited (Que. 1970)
Nov. 7, 1981 – Charter cancelled.

Toronto Brick Co. Limited (Ont. 1951)
June 1965 – Took over on Jan. 2, 1952, assets of Toronto Brick Company Limited. Shldrs. of old co. received: 20 first pref., 7 second pref., 6 com. shs. of new co. and $1.50 for 1 old 7% pref. sh. of $100 par (arrears of $126 per sh. at Dec. 15, 1951, reduced prior to Dec. 31, 1951, by payment of $34.50); 7 second pref. shs. and 10 com. shs. for 1 com. sh. held. co. merged with Frontenac Floor and Wall Tile Ltd. to form United Ceramics Limited.

Toronto Cleantech Capital Inc. (B.C. Apr. 14, 2021)
Apr. 25, 2024 – Name changed to THS Maple Holdings Ltd. following Qualifying Transaction amalgamation of THS L.P. with 1000836250 Ontario Inc., a wholly owned subsidiary of Toronto Cleantech Capital, constituting a reverse takeover by THS. (see FPsurvey - Industrials)

Toronto (Community) Baseball Limited (Ont. 1964)
June 1968 – Wound up, liquidated.

Toronto-Dominion Tower Limited (Ont. 1964)
May 1, 1967 – Amalgamated with Toronto-Dominion Centre Ltd. under latter name.

Toronto Driving Club Limited (Ont. May 16, 1902)
Dec. 22, 1971 – Name changed to The Ontario Jockey Club. ■

Toronto Elevators, Limited (Ont. 1928)
Apr. 1, 1961 – Merged (1 for 1) with Maple Leaf Milling Co. Ltd. and Purity Flour Mills Ltd. to form Maple Leaf Mills Ltd.

Toronto General Trusts Corporation (Ont. 1872)
Dec. 1, 1961 – Amalgamated with The Canada Permanent Trust Company (101 for 25) to continue with a new name Canada Permanent Toronto General Trust Company; basis unknown. Name subsequently changed to Canada Permanent Trust Company.

Toronto Harker Mines Ltd. (Ont. 1938)
Apr. 21, 1958 – Dissolved.

Toronto Iron Works Holdings Limited (Ont. 1907)
Jan. 1, 1978 – Amalgamated with its subsids., Warnock Hersey International Ltd. and International Bronze Powders Ltd. to form TIW Industries Ltd.

Toronto Mortgage Co. (Ont. 1899)
Dec. 31, 1958 – All assets acquired by Canada Permanent Mortgage Corp. Shldrs. received $152.03 per sh.

Toronto Star Limited (Ont. Feb. 6, 1958)
Apr. 1, 1967 – Amalgamated in Ontario to continue with same name.
Jan. 19, 1977 – Name changed to Torstar Corporation. ■

The Toronto Sun Publishing Corporation (Ont. Oct. 21, 1971)
Feb. 4, 1978 – Amalgamated in Ontario to continue with same name.
Oct. 3, 1996 – Formed Sun Media Corporation in Ontario pursuant to acquisition of all o/s shs. from Rogers Communications Inc. resulting in privatization and

amalgamation with Sun Media Corporation; basis $16 per sh. ■

The Toronto Sun Publishing Limited (Ont. Oct. 21, 1971)
Feb. 4, 1978 – Amalgamated with Toronto Sun Holdings Limited to form The Toronto Sun Publishing Corporation.

Torq Media Corporation (B.C. Sept. 15, 2000)
May 18, 2005 – Name changed to Quizam Media Corporation; basis 1 new for 4 old shs. (see FPsurvey - Industrials)

Torquay Oil Corp. (Alta. Aug. 25, 2009)
Jan. 2, 2013 – Acquired by CanEra Energy Corp. for 16¢ per cl.A sh. and $1.60 per cl.B sh.

Torque Energy Inc. (B.C. June 1, 1993 amalg.)
Aug. 8, 2011 – Amalgamated with a wholly owned subsid. of Dundee Energy Limited; basis either 50¢ or 0.5 Dundee Energy shs. for 1 Torque sh. (see Dundee Energy Limited)

Torque Esports Corp. (Ont. Apr. 8, 2011)
Aug. 13, 2020 – Name changed to Engine Media Holdings, Inc.; basis 1 new for 15 old shs. ■

Torque Industries Inc. (Alta. July 12, 1993)
Mar. 31, 1994 – Name changed to BCB Holdings Inc. ■

Torrent Capital Corp. (B.C. Feb. 2, 2021)
May 3, 2021 – Name changed to Cranstown Capital Corp. ■

Torrent Resources Ltd. (B.C. 1968)
July 22, 1986 – Amalgamated with 2 other cos. to form Galveston Resources Ltd.; basis 1 new for 1.75 old shs. ■

Torrential Energy Ltd. (Alta. Mar. 28, 2006)
Oct. 21, 2009 – Name changed to Base Oil & Gas Ltd.; basis 1 new for 3 old shs. ■

Torrez Resources Ltd. (B.C. Mar. 27, 1987)
May 11, 1990 – Name changed to WFI Industries Ltd. ■

Torrington Resources Ltd. (Can. July 9, 1992)
Aug. 21, 1998 – Acquired by Magin Energy Inc.; basis 1 Magin sh. and 0.5 Magin wts. for 2.25 Torrington shs. (see Magin Energy Inc.)

Torstar Corporation (Ont. Apr. 1, 1967 amalg.)
Aug. 7, 2020 – Privatized. All o/s cl. A voting shs. and cl. B non-voting shs. acquired by NordStar Capital L.P. for 74¢ cash per cl. A and cl. B shs.

Torvan Mines Ltd. (B.C. 1957)
Jan. 1958 – Name changed to Torwest Resources Ltd. ■

Torwest Resources Ltd. (B.C. 1957)
Jan. 1962 – Name changed to Torwest Resources (1962) Ltd.; basis 1 new for 5 old shs. ■

Torwest Resources (1962) Ltd. (B.C. 1957)
Apr. 29, 1977 – Amalgamated with Highmont Mining Corp. Ltd., to form Highmont Mining Corporation; basis 1 new for 8 old shs.

Tory Hill Mines Ltd. (Ont. 1943)
1956 – Charter cancelled.

Tosca Mining Corp. (B.C. May 12, 2006)
Oct. 9, 2014 – Name changed to Tosca Resources Corp.; basis 1 new for 4 old shs. ■

Tosca Resources Corp. (B.C. May 12, 2006)
Sept. 8, 2015 – Name changed to Hatch Interactive Technologies Corp. pursuant to reverse takeover acquisition of (old) Hatch Interactive Technologies Corp. ■

Toscana Energy Income Corporation (Alta. Mar. 2, 2010)
Nov. 5, 2020 – Acquired by i3 Energy plc; basis 0.03031261 ord. shs. for each com. sh. (see i3 Energy plc)

Toscana Resources Ltd. (B.C. Jan. 14, 1988)
Apr. 15, 1998 – Name changed to TNR Resources Ltd.; basis 1 new for 5 old shs. ■

Total Canada Oil & Gas Ltd. (Alta. Feb. 10, 1984)
Apr. 4, 1991 – Continued into Canada.
June 14, 1993 – Name changed to Rigel Energy Corporation. ■

Total Energy Services Ltd. (Alta. Nov. 4, 1996)
May 3, 2005 – Converted into an income trust named Total Energy Services Trust; basis either 1 trust unit or 1 exch. sh. of the company or a combination thereof for 1 com. sh.

Total Energy Services Trust (Alta. Mar. 23, 2005)
May 27, 2009 – Converted into a corp. pursuant to plan of arrangement with Biomerge Industries Ltd. whereby assets of Total Energy Services Trust (TEST) were distributed to Biomerge and Biomerge changed its name to Total Energy Services Inc. (TESI); basis $0.00282 plus 0.000237 TESI com. shs. for 1 Biomerge vtg. sh., $0.00389 for 1 Biomerge non-vtg. sh. and 1 TESI com. sh. for 1 TEST trust unit. Trust was wound up and terminated. (see Total Energy Services Inc.)

Total Erickson Resources Ltd. (B.C. 1974 amalg.)
Sept. 29, 1988 – Amalgamated with 121359 Canada Inc., a wholly owned subsid. of Getty Resources Limited; basis 0.357 Getty sh. for 1 Total. (see TOTAL Energold Corporation)

Total Global Ventures Inc. (B.C. May 19, 1999)
Oct. 3, 2001 – Name changed to JNB Developments Co. Ltd.; basis 1 new for 10 old shs. ■

Total Helium Ltd. (B.C. Apr. 27, 2006)
May 12, 2025 – Name changed to Altura Energy Corp.; basis 1 new for 10 old shs. (see FPsurvey - Mines & Energy)

Total Petroleum (North America) Ltd. (Can. Sept. 21, 1956; via Dominion charter)
Sept. 29, 1997 – Acquired by Ultramar Diamond Shamrock Corporation; basis 0.322 Ultramar shs. for 1 Total Petroleum sh.

Total Resources Inc. (B.C. 1979)
Dec. 22, 1980 – Name changed to Extotal Resources Inc. ■

Total Restoration Inc. (Can. June 3, 1977)
Apr. 20, 1989 – Name changed to N.E.W. Total Group Inc. ■

Totally Hip Inc. (B.C. Mar. 18, 1999)
Dec. 23, 2003 – Name changed to Totally Hip Technologies Inc.; basis 1 new for 4 old shs. (see FPsurvey - Industrials)

Totally Hip Software Inc. (Alta. Mar. 8, 1995)
Mar. 18, 1999 – Continued into British Columbia.
June 5, 2002 – Name changed to Totally Hip Inc.; basis 1 new for 10 old shs. ■

Totec Group Inc. (Can. May 25, 1976)
Oct. 1990 – Company's bankers seized and liquidated the company's assets.
May 2, 2002 – Dissolved.

Totem Capital Corp. (Can. July 6, 1988)
Dec. 18, 1989 – Name changed to Totem Health Sciences Inc. ■

Totem Health Sciences Inc. (Can. July 6, 1988)
Apr. 13, 1994 – Name changed to Totem Sciences Inc. ■

Totem Industries Ltd. (B.C. Jan. 20, 1975)
July 6, 1988 – Continued into Canada.
July 8, 1988 – Name changed to Totem Capital Corp.; basis 1 new for 2.5 old shs. ■

Totem Minerals Inc. (B.C. Oct. 5, 2005)
Dec. 21, 2010 – Name changed to Abzu Gold Ltd. (see FPsurvey - Mines & Energy)

Totem Mining Corporation (Can. July 6, 1988)
Aug. 20, 1998 – Continued into British Columbia.
July 6, 2001 – Name changed to Comcorp Ventures Inc.; basis 1 new for 16.9 old shs. ■

Totem Oils Ltd. (Alta. 1966)
1967 – Name changed to Abidonne Oils Ltd. ■

Totem Resources Ltd. (B.C. Dec. 15, 1967)
June 9, 1978 – Name changed to Paragon Resources Ltd. ■

Totem Sciences Inc. (Can. July 6, 1988)
Mar. 3, 1997 – Name changed to Totem Mining Corporation. ■

Toubani Resources Inc. (Ont. Mar. 10, 2004 amalg.)
Jan. 8, 2024 – Name changed to Toubani Resources Limited and continued into Australia.

Touchdown Capital Inc. (B.C. July 25, 2005)
Mar. 4, 2010 – Name changed to Touchdown Resources Inc. ■

Touchdown Resources Inc. (B.C. July 25, 2005)
Mar. 3, 2014 – Name changed to Letho Resources Corp.; basis 1 new for 7 old shs. (see FPsurvey - Mines & Energy)

Touchstone Exploration Inc. (B.C. Oct. 5, 1982)
May 21, 2014 – Acquired by Petrobank Energy and Resources Ltd.; basis 0.471 Petrobank shs. for 1 old Touchstone sh. Subsequently, Petrobank changed its name to Touchstone Exploration Inc.

Touchstone Gold Limited (British Virgin Islands July 29, 2009)
Sept. 7, 2012 – Continued into Ontario.

Touchstone Petroleum Inc. (Alta. Mar. 12, 1993)
May 23, 2001 – Name changed to Case Resources Inc. ■

Touchstone Resources Ltd. (B.C. Oct. 5, 1982)
July 6, 2010 – Name changed to Touchstone Exploration Inc.; basis 1 new for 10 old shs. ■

Tournigan Energy Ltd. (B.C. Mar. 27, 2008)
Mar. 1, 2012 – Name changed to European Uranium Resources Ltd.; basis 1 new for 5 old shs. ■

Tournigan Gold Corporation (Yuk. Dec. 3, 2002)
Mar. 27, 2008 – Continued into British Columbia.
May 6, 2008 – Name changed to Tournigan Energy Ltd. ■

Tournigan Mining Explorations Ltd. (B.C. Nov. 10, 1966)
Apr. 22, 1992 – Name changed to International Tournigan Corporation; basis 1 new for 5 old shs. ■

Tournigan Ventures Corporation (B.C. Nov. 10, 1966)
Dec. 3, 2002 – Name changed to Tournigan Gold Corporation and continued into Yukon. ■

Tova Ventures II Inc. (Ont. Feb. 27, 2017)
Sept. 21, 2018 – Name changed to Enthusiast Gaming Holdings Inc. following Qualifying Transaction reverse takeover acquisition of Enthusiast Gaming Inc. and concurrent amalgamation of Enthusiast with wholly owned 2637306 Ontario Inc.; basis 1 new for 4.2 old shs. ■

Tova Ventures Inc. (B.C. Oct. 11, 2007)
June 25, 2010 – Name changed to Auryx Gold Corp. pursuant to Qualifying Transaction reverse takeover acquisition of 0824239 B.C. Ltd.; basis 1 new for 5 old shs. ■

Tovarich-Larder Gold Mines Ltd. (Ont. 1938)
1954 – Mineral properties acquired by Mining Futures and Holdings Ltd. in 1953 in exchange for 1 right for 1 sh. held with each right to purchase 1 Mining Futures sh. at 10¢. Charter surrendered.

Tove Gold Mines Ltd. (Ont. 1951)
Nov. 1961 – Charter cancelled.

Towagmac Exploration Co. Ltd. (Que. 1926)
Dec. 9, 1969 – Name changed to Tokar Ltd.; basis 1 new for 10 old shs.

Tower Energy Ltd. (B.C. Aug. 4, 1988)
Sept. 20, 2011 – Name changed to Tower Resources Ltd.; basis 1 new for 4 old shs. (see FPsurvey - Mines & Energy)

Tower Hill Mines Ltd. (B.C. May 26, 1978)
Mar. 15, 1991 – Name changed to International Tower Hill Mines Ltd.; basis 1 new for 5 old shs. (see FPsurvey - Mines & Energy)

Tower Mines Co. Ltd. (Que. 1955)
Sept. 30, 1978 – Charter cancelled.

Tower Mines Ltd. (B.C. 1961)
Apr. 1970 – Name changed to Tower Resources Ltd. ∎

Tower Petroleums Ltd. (Ont. Aug. 18, 1947)
1952 – Assets acquired by Banff Oil Ltd.; basis 1 new for 5 old shs. (see Banff Oil Ltd.)

Tower Resources Ltd. (B.C. 1961)
Name changed to Consolidated Tower Resources Ltd.; basis 1 new for 5 old shs. ∎

Towers Marts and Properties Ltd. (Ont. 1961)
Mar. 1969 – Name changed to Towmart Holdings Limited. ∎

Towmart Holdings Limited (Ont. 1961)
Mar. 17, 1972 – Name changed to T.M.P. Investments Limited. ∎

Townsend Oil and Gas Limited (Ont. 1967)
1970 – Name changed to Onaco Petroleums Limited. ∎

Trac Industries Inc. (B.C. 1979)
June 30, 1988 – Continued into Ontario.
Jan. 13, 1997 – Name changed to Medical Resorts International Inc.; basis 1 new for 12 old shs. ∎

Trac Resources Inc. (B.C. 1979)
June 10, 1987 – Name changed to Trac Industries Inc. ∎

Tracan Oil & Gas Ltd. (B.C. 1981)
Aug. 22, 1994 – Dissolved and struck off register.

Trace Oil & Gas Ltd. (B.C. 1981)
Apr. 2, 1981 – Name changed to Tracan Oil & Gas Ltd. ∎

Tracer Petroleum Corporation (B.C. Feb. 8, 1982)
July 19, 1993 – Continued into Canada.
July 21, 2003 – Name changed to Forum Energy Corporation following acquisition of Forum Exploration Inc. ∎

Tracer Resources Corporation (B.C. Nov. 27, 1973)
Apr. 15, 1988 – Dissolved and struck off register.

TraceSafe Inc. (British Virgin Islands Dec. 18, 2013)
Dec. 20, 2022 – Name changed to ShiftCarbon Inc.

Tracker Explorations Ltd. (B.C. Nov. 25, 1983)
Sept. 14, 1987 – Name changed to Jentech Ventures Corp.; basis 2 new for 1 old sh. ∎

Tracker Software International Inc. (B.C. July 15, 1993)
Jan. 12, 1996 – Continued into Yukon. (see FPsurvey - Industrials)

Tracker Ventures Corp. (B.C. July 10, 2007)
July 13, 2021 – Name changed to Contakt World Technologies Corp. pursuant to the reverse takover acquisition of (old) Contakt World Technologies Corp. (Contakt Parentco) and concurrent amalgamation of Contakt Parentco with wholly owned 1276313 B.C. Ltd. to form 1315006 B.C. Ltd. ∎

Trackloop Analytics Corp. (B.C. July 10, 2007)
Oct. 25, 2019 – Name changed to Tracker Ventures Corp.; basis 1 new for 20 old shs. ∎

Traction Exploration Inc. (B.C. July 20, 2020)
Nov. 5, 2021 – Name changed to Traction Uranium Corp. (see FPsurvey - Mines & Energy)

Trade Wind Explorations Ltd. (Ont. 1969)
Feb. 22, 1980 – Dissolved.

Trade Winds Resources Ltd. (B.C. Nov. 28, 1986)
July 5, 2002 – Name changed to Trade Winds Ventures Inc.; basis 1 new for 10 old shs. ∎

Trade Winds Ventures Inc. (B.C. Nov. 28, 1986)
Dec. 2, 2011 – Acquired by Detour Gold Corporation; basis Cdn$0.0001 plus 0.0142 Detour shs. for 1 Trade Winds sh. (see Detour Gold Corporation)

Trader Resource Corp. (B.C. 1980)
Jan. 3, 1995 – Name changed to Mountain Minerals Co. Ltd. ∎

TradeRadius Online Inc. (B.C. June 27, 1974)
Apr. 10, 2003 – Name changed to Jalna Resources Limited; basis 1 new for 10 old shs. ∎

TradeRef Software Corp. (Can. Aug. 24, 1978)
Dec. 11, 1996 – Continued into Anguilla.
Feb. 20, 1997 – Name changed to Hansa.net Global Commerce, Inc. ∎

The Traders' Building Association, Limited (Man. 1908)
June 29, 1990 – Dissolved by the company.

Traders Finance Corp. Ltd. (Can. 1926)
1966 – Name changed to Traders Group Limited. ∎

Traders Group Limited (Can. 1926)
Jan. 31, 1995 – All o/s pref. shs. redeemed; basis: (1) 4.5% cum. red. pref. shs. for $104.00 plus $1.50 in accrued and unpaid dividends, (2) 5% pref. shs. for $40.50 plus $6.667 in accrued and unpaid dividends, (3) $30 ser. A pref. shs. for $30 plus $5.00 in accrued and unpaid dividends, (4) $30 ser. B pref. shs. for $30.30 plus $7.20 in accrued and unpaid dividends, (5) 10 1/4% pref. shs., ser. B for $10 plus $3.146 in accrued and unpaid dividends, (6) 7.5% pref. shs. for $50 plus $12.501 in accrued and unpaid dividends. Transferred by the Montreal Trust Company of Canada in Toronto and Vancouver.

Traders International Franchise Systems Inc. (B.C. Apr. 11, 1983)
May 21, 1998 – Name changed to Newquest Ventures Corp.; basis 1 new for 3 old shs. ∎

Tradewinds Exploration, Inc. (Alta.)
1961 – Struck off register.

Traduction MILITECH Translation Inc. (Can. Aug. 1, 1988)
Aug. 20, 1990 – Name changed to Hydrogenics Corporation Incorporated. ∎

Trafalgar Energy Ltd. (Alta. June 6, 2006 amalg.)
July 31, 2009 – Formed Midway Energy Ltd. in Alberta following acquisition of and amalgamation with EET Management Corp. and Energy Investment Limited Partnership pursuant to plan of arrangement recapitalization; basis 0.545454 Midway shs. plus 1 Midway series B wt. for 1 EET sh., 1 Midway sh. for 1 Energy Investment unit and 1 Midway sh. for either 1 Trafalgar com. sh. or 1 non-vtg. sh. plus 1 Midway series A wt. for 3 Trafalgar shs. ∎

Trafalgar Long Lac Gold Mines Ltd. (Ont. May 10, 1934)
May 1942 – Name changed to Trafalgar Mines & Oil Ltd. Continued into Ontario. ∎

Trafalgar Mines & Oil Ltd. (Ont.)
Mar. 19, 1969 – Charter cancelled.

Trafalgar Resources Inc. (B.C. 1983)
May 27, 1987 – Name changed to WCN Investment Corp. ∎

TragoeS Inc. (Ont. May 7, 1991 amalg.)
July 30, 1999 – Name changed to RightsMarket.com Inc. and continued into Alberta. ∎

The Trail Blazer Oil & Gas Co. Ltd. (Sask. 1934)
1935 – Owned one well which was taken over by Senator Oil & Gas Development Co.

Trail Blazing Ventures Ltd. (Alta. Aug. 30, 2021)
Mar. 19, 2024 – Name changed to Hempalta Corp. pursuant to the Qualifying Transaction reverse takeover acquisition of Hempalta Inc. and concurrent amalgamation of Hempalta with wholly owned 2562764 Alberta Inc. (see FPsurvey - Industrials)

Trail Oil Ltd. (Ont. 1930)
1960 – Struck off register.

Trailmobile Canada Limited (Ont. Jan. 23, 1996 amalg.)
May 13, 2002 – Privatized by parent Chicago-based Trailmobile Corporation via wholly owned subsid. 1314385 Ontario Limited; basis $0.10 per sh.

Trakopolis IoT Corp. (B.C. Apr. 14, 1999)
Oct. 27, 2016 – Continued into Alberta.
Jan. 27, 2020 – Filed for bankruptcy. Alvarez & Marsal Canada Inc. appointed trustee and all directors resigned.

Tralea Gold Mines Limited (Ont. 1946)
Apr. 3, 1961 – Dissolved.

TranDirect.com Technologies Inc. (B.C. June 14, 1985)
Aug. 14, 2000 – Name changed to Consolidated TranDirect.com Technologies Inc.; basis 1 new for 4 old shs. ∎

Trans America Industries Ltd. (B.C. Sept. 25, 1963)
Aug. 1, 2008 – Formed Primary Corp. in Ontario on amalgamation with 1322256 Alberta Ltd., constituting a reverse takeover by 1322256 Alberta; basis 1 new for 20 1322256 Alberta shs. and 1 new for 2 Trans America shs. ∎

Trans-America Petroleums Ltd. (Que. 1951)
Sept. 2, 1978 – Charter cancelled.

Trans-American Mining Corp. Ltd. (Ont. 1944)
Oct. 1978 – Charter cancelled.

Trans Asia Resources Inc. (B.C. Feb. 3, 1988)
Jan. 14, 2002 – Name changed to Municipal Solutions Group Inc. ∎

Trans Asian Resources Ltd. (B.C. Nov. 10, 1986)
Sept. 22, 1994 – Name changed to Pacific Falkon Resources Corp.; basis 1 new for 3 old shs. ∎

Trans Atlantic Resources Inc. (B.C. Aug. 28, 1984)
July 12, 1991 – Name changed to Trans Atlantic Enterprises Inc.; basis 1 new for 4 old shs. (see FPsurvey - Mines & Energy)

Trans Border Energy Corp. (B.C. July 31, 1987)
Oct. 1, 1992 – Name changed to Brownstone Investment Inc.; basis 1 new for 2 old shs. ∎

Trans-Border Oil Co. Ltd. (Man. 1952)
Feb. 26, 1966 – Dissolved.

Trans Canada Copper Mines Limited (Que. 1970)
Nov. 30, 1979 – Name changed to Mid-Canada Gold and Copper Mines Limited. ∎

Trans-Canada Corporation Fund (Que. 1954)
1968 – All com. shs. acquired by Power Corp. of Canada Ltd., through exch. of 1 com. sh. of co. for 1 5% cum. redeem. convert. second pref. sh., Ser. A, $12 p.v. of Power Corp.

Trans-Canada Explorations Limited (Ont. 1955)
Nov. 1964 – Merged with Roman Corporation Limited; basis 1 new for 2 old shs.

Trans Canada Glass Ltd. (B.C. Mar. 26, 1969)
Jan. 1990 – Continued into Canada.
Feb. 23, 1990 – Name changed to TCG International Inc. ■

Trans-Canada Mines Ltd. (Ont. 1944)
May 1958 – Dissolved.

Trans-Canada Mortgage Corp. (Western) Ltd. (Alta. 1952)
1968 – Merged to form Melton Real Estate Ltd.

Trans-Canada Oils Ltd. (B.C. 1966)
Jan. 6, 1969 – Name changed to Trans-Canada Resources Ltd. ■

Trans-Canada Petroleums Ltd. (Que. 1951)
1955 – Acquired by Trans-Canada Explorations Ltd.; basis 1 new for 3 old shs.

Trans-Canada Pipe Lines Limited (Can. Mar. 21, 1951; via Special Act of Parliament)
Apr. 19, 1972 – Name changed to TransCanada PipeLines Limited. ■

Trans-Canada Resources Ltd. (B.C. 1966)
Nov. 1, 1982 – Amalgamated with Acroll Petroleums Ltd., Globe Oil Co. (1958) Ltd., and United Western Oil & Gas Ltd. to form new co. known as Trans-Canada Resources Ltd.; basis 1 ser. A pref. sh. of new co. for 1 old ser. A pref. sh. held, and 1 cl. A sh. of new co. for 1 com. sh.

Trans-Canada Resources Ltd. (B.C. 1966)
1984 – Amalgamated in Alberta to continue with same name.
Sept. 12, 1988 – Name changed to Consolidated Trans-Canada Resources Ltd.; basis 1 new for 10 old shs. ■

Trans-Canada Savings and Trust Corporation (unknown)
Feb. 1969 – All o/s shs. acquired at $75 per sh. by Farmers & Merchants Trust Co. Ltd.

Trans-Canada World Security Corporation (Can. Oct. 3, 1997)
Aug. 21, 2000 – Name changed to Garda World Security Corporation. ■

Trans Canadian Equities Corporation (B.C. 1966)
Mar. 31, 1978 – Name changed to Geodome Petroleum Corporation; basis 1 new for 3 old shs. ■

Trans-Ches Mines Ltd. (Ont. 1947)
1948 – Name changed to La Ronge Uranium Mines Ltd. ■

Trans Coastal Industries Inc. (B.C. June 29, 1987)
Mar. 13, 1998 – Name changed to Trans Coastal Resources Corp. ■

Trans Coastal Resources Corp. (B.C. June 29, 1987)
Oct. 15, 1999 – Name changed to Transco Resources Corp.; basis 1 new for 4 old shs. ■

Trans Columbia Explorations Ltd. (B.C. 1967)
May 1973 – Name changed to Consolidated Trans Columbia Industries Ltd.; basis 1 new for 2 old shs. (see FPsurvey - Mines & Energy)

Trans-Dominion Energy Corporation (B.C. June 22, 1950)
Dec. 20, 1988 – Continued into Alberta.
May 30, 2000 – Name changed to Madison Oil Company Inc. pursuant to reverse takeover acquisition of Texas-based Madison Oil Company; basis 1 new for 50 old shs. ■

Trans-Dominion Mining and Oils Corp. (unknown)
1955 – Assets acquired by International Mining and Development Corp.; basis 1 new for 5 old shs. (see International Mining and Development Corp.)

Trans Eastern Oil & Gas Limited (Ont. 1967)
1971 – Merged with Erieshore Industries Inc.; basis 2 new for 9 old shs.

Trans Empire Oils Ltd. (Can. 1950)
1957 – Name changed to West Canadian Oil & Gas Ltd. ■

Trans-Era Oil Limited (Ont. 1952)
Nov. 1956 – Name changed to Rocky Petroleums Limited; basis 0.166666 new for 1 old sh. ■

Trans-Global Resources N.L. (W.A. Sept. 25, 1970)
June 15, 1999 – Name changed to Trans-Global Interactive Limited; basis 1 new for 4 old shs.

Trans Hex International Ltd. (Ont. Feb. 16, 1996 amalg.)
May 2002 – Name changed to Tsodilo Resources Limited and continued into Yukon. (see FPsurvey - Mines & Energy)

Trans International Gold Corporation (B.C. Sept. 3, 1987)
Oct. 16, 1991 – Name changed to Keaton Resources Ltd.; basis 1 new for 2 old shs. ■

Trans-Leduc Oils Ltd. (Ont. 1948)
1964 – Struck off register.

Trans Mountain Pipe Line Company Ltd. (Can. Mar. 21, 1951; via Special Act of Parliament)
Nov. 14, 1994 – Acquired by BC Gas Inc.; basis $24.50 or 1.633 BC Gas shs. for 1 Trans Mountain sh. (see BC Gas Inc.)
Dec. 31, 2002 – Name changed to Terasen Pipelines (Trans Mountain) Inc. (see BC Gas Inc.)

Trans-Nation Incorporated (Ont. 1964)
1979 – Reverted to private co. status following acquisition of minority shldrs. shs. at $4.00 per sh.

Trans-Nation Land Corporation (Toronto) Limited (Ont. 1964)
1974 – Name changed to Trans-Nation Incorporated. ■

Trans Nation Minerals Ltd. (N.B. 1959)
Charter surrendered.

Trans National Minerals Inc. (B.C. Jan. 8, 2008)
Sept. 7, 2010 – Name changed to IEMR Resources Inc. (see FPsurvey - Mines & Energy)

Trans Northern Resources Ltd. (unknown)
1968 – Acquired by Bata Resources Ltd. for 93,796 shs. (see Bata Resources Ltd.)

Trans Ocean Oil, Inc. (Del. 1968)
1979 – Shs. of co., other than those held by Vichers Energy Corp., exch. for shs. of Esmork Inc.; basis 0.9 of a sh. of Esmork for each sh. of Trans Ocean.

Trans-Ore Mines Ltd. (B.C. 1952)
Sept. 1968 – Struck off register.

Trans-Orient Petroleum Ltd. (B.C. July 25, 1986)
Sept. 26, 1997 – Continued into Yukon.
Jan. 16, 2006 – Continued into British Columbia.
Dec. 16, 2009 – Acquired by TAG Oil Ltd.; basis 1 TAG Oil sh. for 2.8 Trans-Orient shs.

Trans Pacific Explorations Ltd. (B.C. 1969)
Mar. 1969 – Name changed to Minwealth Explorations Ltd. ■

Trans Pacific Ventures Ltd. (B.C. Feb. 20, 1911)
Apr. 1, 1985 – Delisted from the Vancouver Stock Exchange. Subsequently dissolved and struck from register.

Trans Rampart Industries Ltd. (B.C. Nov. 18, 1968)
May 28, 1993 – Name changed to Rampart Mercantile Inc. ■

Trans Valley Gas & Oil Corp. Ltd. (Ont. 1957)
Struck off register.

Trans-Western Oils Ltd. (B.C. 1947)
1967 – All assets acquired by Acroll Oil & Gas Ltd. for 1,500,000 shs., equivalent to approx. 1 Acroll sh. for 2.08 co. shs.

TransAKT Corp. (Alta. June 30, 2001)
July 12, 2006 – Name changed to TransAKT Ltd.; basis 1 new for 2 old shs. ■

TransAKT Ltd. (Alta. June 30, 2001)
Dec. 2, 2011 – Continued into Nevada.

Transac Enterprise Corp. (B.C. Apr. 11, 1979)
Oct. 26, 2006 – Name changed to Evergreen Gaming Corporation following reverse takeover acquisition of Washington Gaming Inc. ■

Transair Limited (Can. 1947)
Nov. 29, 1979 – Acquired by Pacific Western (Alberta) Ltd., a wholly owned subsid. of Pacific Western Airlines Ltd.; basis $3.02 per sh. Liquidation and distribution of Transair completed in 1980.

TransAlta Energy Corporation (Can. Jan. 28, 1981)
Jan. 1, 2009 – Amalgamated with parent co. TransAlta Corporation and TransAlta Utilities Corporation and Keephills 3 GP Ltd. (both wholly owned subsids. of TransAlta Corporation) to continue as TransAlta Corporation.

Transalta Explorations Ltd. (Alta. 1966)
Jan. 1973 – Acquired by Dome Petroleum Limited. (see Dome Petroleum Limited)

TransAlta Power, L.P. (Ont. Dec. 16, 1997)
Dec. 11, 2007 – Acquired by Cheung Kong Infrastructure Holdings Limited for $8.38 per unit.

TransAlta Renewables Inc. (Can. May 28, 2013)
Oct. 11, 2023 – All o/s shs. not already held acquired by TransAlta Corporation; basis (i) 1.0337 TransAlta Corporation shs.; or (ii) $13 in cash for 1 TransAlta Renewable sh.

TransAlta Resources Corporation (Alta. May 1, 1963)
Jan. 28, 1981 – Continued into Canada.
Dec. 31, 1992 – Name changed to TransAlta Energy Corporation following redemption of all o/s ser. C pref. shs. on Jan. 1, 1989 and all o/s ser. B pref. shs. on Feb. 1, 1989; basis $25.50 plus accrued and unpaid divds. ■

TransAlta Utilities Corporation (Can. May 12, 1947)
Sept. 10, 2001 – All o/s com. shs. exchanged for shares of TransAlta Corporation making TransAlta Utilities a wholly owned subsid. of TransAlta Corporation effective Dec. 31, 1992; basis 1 new for 1 old sh. All o/s first pref. shs. called for redemption; basis (i) 7.44%, ser. K redeem. for $100 plus accrued and unpaid div. of $1.447 per sh.; (ii) 7.30%, ser. L redeem. for $100 plus accrued and unpaid div. of $1.419 per sh.; (iii) 7.44%, ser. M redeem. for $100 plus accrued and unpaid div. of $1.447 per sh.; (iv) 7.70%, ser. N redeem. for $100 plus accrued and unpaid div. of $1.497 per sh.; (v) 4.00%, ser. C redeem. for $103 plus accrued and unpaid div. of $0.778 per sh.; (vi) 4.50%, ser. D redeem. for $103 plus accrued and unpaid div. of $0.875 per sh.; (vii) 5.00%, ser. E redeem. for $100 plus accrued and unpaid div. of $0.972; (viii) 5.40%, ser. F redeem. for $100 plus accrued and unpaid div. of $1.05 per sh.; (ix) 7.00%, ser. G redeem. for $102 plus accrued and unpaid div. of $1.361 per sh.; (x) 7.50%, ser. H redeem. for $102 plus accrued and unpaid div. of $1.458 per sh.; (xi) 7.20%, ser. V redeem. for $25 plus accrued and unpaid div. of $0.35 per sh.; (xii) 7.08%, ser. W redeem. for $25 plus accrued and unpaid div. of $0.344 per sh.; and (xiii) 7.10%, ser. X redeem. for $25 plus accrued and unpaid div. of $0.345 per sh.
Jan. 1, 2009 – Amalgamated with parent co. TransAlta Corporation and TransAlta Energy Corporation and Keephills 3 GP Ltd. (both wholly owned subsids. of TransAlta Corporation) to continue as TransAlta Corporation.

TransAmerican Energy Inc. (B.C. Apr. 16, 1980)
Sept. 12, 2018 – Name changed to American Biofuels Inc.; basis 1 new for 10 old shs. (see FPsurvey - Industrials)

Transarctic Petroleum Corp. (Ont. Mar. 5, 1937)
Mar. 26, 1999 – Name changed to ivyNET Corporation. ■

TransAtlantic Petroleum Corp. (Alta. June 10, 1997)
Jan. 1, 1999 – Amalgamated with wholly owned GHP Exploration Corporation to form new co. with same name TransAtlantic Petroleum Corp.
Oct. 1, 2009 – Continued into Bermuda.
Oct. 19, 2009 – Name changed to TransAtlantic Petroleum Ltd. ■

TransAtlantic Petroleum Ltd. (Bermuda Oct. 1, 2009)
Dec. 22, 2020 – Amalgamated with TAT Merger Sub LLC, a wholly owned subsid. of TAT Holdco LLC, to continue under the TAT Merger name; basis US$0.13 cash per com. sh.

Transator Explorations Ltd. (Ont. 1957)
Mar. 19, 1969 – Charter cancelled.

Transaurum Mines Ltd. (Ont. 1946)
1954 – Merged into Garrison Creek Consolidated Mines Ltd.; basis 1 new for 15 old shs.

Transbec Mining Co. Ltd. (Ont. 1945)
June 1958 – Dissolved.

Transborder Capital Inc. (Alta. Mar. 4, 2002)
Feb. 1, 2006 – Name changed to Eagle Rock Exploration Ltd. following vertical amalgamation with wholly owned Eagle Rock Exploration Ltd., acquired on Dec. 30, 2005, which constituted Transborder's Qualifying Transaction reverse takeover acquisition of Eagle Rock and amalgamation of Eagle Rock with a wholly owned subsidiary of Transborder. ■

TransCanada Corporation (Can. Feb. 25, 2003)
May 9, 2019 – Name changed to TC Energy Corporation. (see FPsurvey - Mines & Energy; FPsurvey - Industrials)

Transcanada Enviro-Systems Limited (B.C. 1968)
Feb. 25, 1983 – Struck off register.

TransCanada Gas Processing, L.P. (Can. 1951)
Apr. 19, 2000 – All o/s partnership units acquired by ANG Gathering & Processing Ltd., a wholly owned subsid. of TransCanada PipeLines Limited; basis $20.70 per unit.

TransCanada PipeLines Limited (Can. Mar. 21, 1951; via Special Act of Parliament)
May 15, 2003 – Pursuant a Plan of Arrangement completed on May 15, 2003, all com. shs. were acquired by TransCanada Corporation; com. shs. of the co. were exchanged for com. shs. of TransCanada Corporation on a 1-for-1 basis. All debt securities and pref. shs. issued by the co. continued to be obligations and securities of the co.
Mar. 5, 2014 – All o/s 5.60% cum. redeem. 1st pref. shs. ser. Y redeemed for $50 plus $0.0455 in accrued and unpaid div.

TransCanada Power, L.P. (Ont. Mar. 27, 1997)
Sept. 6, 2005 – Name changed to EPCOR Power L.P. ■

Transcend Capital Corporation (Alta. Sept. 20, 1999)
May 24, 2002 – Name changed to Road New Media Corporation pursuant to Qualifying Transaction reverse takeover acquisition of RoadCompanion.ca Inc. ■

Transco Resources Corp. (B.C. June 29, 1987)
July 21, 2006 – Continued into Alberta.
Sept. 8, 2006 – Name changed to Bridge Resources Corp. pursuant to acquisition of Bridge North Sea Ltd. ■

Transco Storage & Transportation Services Ltd. (Can. 1929)
1979 – Acquired remaining 40 com. shs. held by public and became a private co.

TransColt Resources Corporation (B.C. 1972)
Jan. 12, 1982 – Amalgamated with New Frontier Petroleum Inc. and others to form New Frontier Petroleum Corporation; basis 0.83 new for 1 old sh.

Transcon Electronics Ltd. (B.C. 1968)
May 24, 1979 – Dissolved and struck off register.

Transcona Explorations Ltd. (Ont. 1964)
Mar. 1976 – Charter cancelled.

Transcontinent Oil Co. Ltd. (Ont. June 6, 1944)
Sept. 1945 – Name changed to Omnitrans Exploration Ltd. ■

Transcontinental Resources Limited (Ont. 1940)
Oct. 19, 1990 – Amalgamated with subsid. Atkins & Durbrow Ltd. to form a private company known as Tantramar Holdings Ltd.; basis $1.80 per sh.

Transcontinental Storage & Distributing Co. Ltd. (Can. 1929)
1959 – Name changed to Transco Storage & Transportation Services Ltd. ■

Transeastern Power Trust (Ont. Feb. 3, 2014)
Jan. 4, 2018 – Name changed to Blockchain Power Trust. ■

Transeuro Energy Corp. (Yuk. Nov. 7, 2000)
Nov. 9, 2005 – Continued into British Columbia.
Oct. 12, 2020 – Struck from registry and dissolved.

Transfield Petroleums Ltd. (Alta. 1951)
1964 – Struck off register.

TransForce Income Fund (Que. July 30, 2002)
May 20, 2008 – Converted into TransForce Inc.; basis 1 TransForce com. sh. for 1 TransForce Income trust unit or 1 TFI Holdings Inc. tracking sh. unit. (see TransForce Inc.)

TransForce Inc. (Que. Apr. 30, 1985)
Sept. 30, 2002 – Converted into TransForce Income Fund; basis 1 TransForce Income trust unit for 1 TransForce Inc. sh. (see TransForce Income Fund)

TransForce Inc. (Can. Mar. 28, 2008)
Dec. 23, 2016 – Name changed to TFI International Inc. (see FPsurvey - Industrials)

Transformative Ventures Ltd. (B.C. Nov. 1, 2007)
Apr. 19, 2010 – Amalgamated with Decourcy Capital Corp. and Auricle Biomedical Corporation to form Aztech Innovations Inc. which then acquired Aztech Associates Inc. by reverse takeover constituting the Qualifying Transaction for each of Decourcy, Auricle and Transformative; basis 1 Aztech sh. for 1 Decourcy sh., 0.667 Aztech shs. for 1 Auricle sh. and 0.667 Aztech shs. for 1 Transformative sh.

TransGaming Inc. (Can. Nov. 1, 2004)
Sept. 16, 2016 – Name changed to Findev Inc.; basis 1 new for 35 old shs. (see FPsurvey - Industrials)

Transglobal Business News Network Inc. (Can. Dec. 29, 1982)
Apr. 5, 1993 – Name changed to Megasol Corporation; basis 1 new for 5 old shs. ■

TransGlobe Apartment Real Estate Investment Trust (Ont. Apr. 8, 2010)
July 2, 2012 – Acquired by PD Kanco LP and Starlight Investments Ltd. and subsequently privatized for $14.25 per unit.

TransGlobe Energy Corporation (B.C. Aug. 6, 1968)
June 9, 2004 – Continued into Alberta.
Oct. 17, 2022 – Acquired by VAALCO Energy, Inc.; basis 0.6727 VAALCO com. shs. for 1 TransGlobe sh.

TransGlobe Internet and Telecom Co., Ltd. (B.C. June 24, 1999)
Apr. 30, 2021 – Name changed to Wondr Gaming Corp. reverse takeover acquisition of Wondr Gaming Corporation and concurrent amalgamation of (old) Wondr and wholly owned 2778533 Ontario Inc.; basis 1 new for 30 old shs. ■

Transglobe Real Estate Corp. (B.C. Nov. 14, 1979)
Oct. 21, 1993 – Name changed to Ultra Petroleum Corp. ■

Transglobe Resources Ltd. (B.C. Nov. 14, 1979)
June 19, 1990 – Name changed to Transglobe Real Estate Corp. following acquisition of 169476 Canada Inc.; basis 1 new for 3 old shs. ■

Transgold Explorations & Investments Inc. (Ont.)
Apr. 7, 2000 – Formed Temex Resources Corp. in Ontario on reverse takeover acquisition of and amalgamation with Temex Resources Ltd.; basis 1 new for 1 Temex sh. and 1 new for 3 Transgold shs. ■

Transit Financial Holdings Inc. (Can. Nov. 8, 1979)
June 21, 1993 – Name changed to TFH International Inc. ■

Transit Truck Bodies Inc. (Que. 1978)
June 26, 1990 – Acquired by Acquisitions Leclair Inc. for $3.00 per sh.

Transition Therapeutics Inc. (Ont. July 6, 1998)
Sept. 1, 2016 – Acquired by OPKO Health, Inc. of Miami, Fla., by way of plan of arrangement for 0.1657 OPKO com. shs. for each Transition com. sh., valued at US$1.55 per sh.

Transland Uranium Mines Ltd. (Ont. 1952)
Nov. 1961 – Charter cancelled.

Transnational Cannabis Ltd. (B.C. Mar. 1, 2006)
Mar. 25, 2024 – Dissolved for failure to file and struck from register.

Transnorthern Nickel & Copper Mines Ltd. (Ont. 1949)
Mar. 11, 1970 – Charter cancelled.

Transpacific Asbestos Inc. (Ont. Sept. 23, 1957)
June 29, 1984 – Name changed to Transpacific Resources Inc. (see FPsurvey - Mines & Energy)

Transpacific Minerals Inc. (Alta. Feb. 28, 1996)
June 26, 1998 – Name changed to YFMC Healthcare Inc. following acquisition of all o/s shs. of 1189543 Ontario Ltd.; basis 1 new for 1 old sh. ■

Transtech Industries Inc. (B.C. Jan. 12, 1987)
Sept. 23, 1999 – Name changed to International Transtech Inc.; basis 1 new for 5 old shs. (see FPsurvey - Industrials)

Transtel Communications Corp. (B.C. Apr. 24, 1987)
July 23, 1990 – Name changed to Consolidated T.C. Resources Ltd.; basis 1 new for 3 old shs. ■

Transterra Mines Ltd. (Ont. 1945)
1957 – Charter cancelled.

Transterre Explorations Ltd. (Que. 1962)
Sept. 1973 – Name changed to Bayard Resources Limited. (see FPsurvey - Mines & Energy)

Transvaal Explorations Ltd. (Ont. 1949 amalg.)
1968 – Charter cancelled.

Transvision-Television (Canada) Ltd. (Ont. 1937)
July 1953 – Name changed to Arcan Corp. Ltd. ■

Transway Capital Inc. (Ont. Aug. 19, 1983)
Feb. 25, 1997 – Name changed to Dura Products International Inc. ■

Transway Explorations Inc. (Ont. Aug. 19, 1983)
July 16, 1993 – Name changed to Transway Capital Inc.; basis 1 new for 7 old shs. ■

Transwest Energy Inc. (Alta. Oct. 16, 1952)
Feb. 28, 1997 – All o/s com. shs. acquired by Jordan Petroleum Ltd.; basis $1.15 per sh. or 0.14375 of a com. sh. of Jordan for 1 com. sh. of Transwest. All the o/s 9.25% pref. shs., ser. A redeemed as of Apr. 7, 1997; basis $20 per sh. plus accrued and unpaid dividends of $0.498 per sh. (see Jordan Petroleum Ltd.)

Transworld Trading Corporation (Alta. Aug. 3, 1995)
July 30, 1999 – Name changed to Cylinder Enterprises Limited; basis 1 new for 3 old shs. ■

Tranzcom China Security Networks Inc. (B.C. Oct. 31, 1989 amalg.)
Sept. 7, 2007 – Name changed to Pacific Link Mining Corp.; basis 1 new for 3 old shs. ■

Tranzcom Security Networks Inc. (B.C. Oct. 31, 1989 amalg.)
June 25, 2004 – Name changed to Tranzcom China Security Networks Inc. ■

Tranzeo Wireless Technologies Inc. (B.C. Dec. 6, 2000)
Apr. 1, 2004 – Continued into Canada. (see Charlotte Resources Ltd.)
July 7, 2014 – Acquired by Charlotte Resources Ltd. by way of amalgamation with 8865523 Canada Ltd., a wholly owned subsid. of Charlotte Resources Ltd.; basis 1 Charlotte com. sh. for 7.5 Tranzeo com. shs. (see Charlotte Resources Ltd.)

Trapper Resources Ltd. (Alta. 1978)
Mar. 1, 1992 – Struck off register.

Trasco Wind-Force Technologies Inc. (B.C. 1979)
Aug. 25, 1995 – Dissolved and struck off register.

Trask Corporation Limited (Bermuda Nov. 25, 1985)
Jan. 29, 1996 – Name changed to Med Net International Ltd.

Travel Plaza Developments Inc. (Alta. June 2, 1994)
Dec. 2, 2000 – Struck from the registry and dissolved.

Travel Ventures Inc. (Alta. Jan. 12, 1987)
Oct. 20, 1992 – Name changed to TVI Copper Inc. ■

travelbyus.com ltd. (Ont. July 21, 1986)
Jan. 1, 2003 – Plan of Arrangement acquisition by Texas-based Aviation Group, Inc. and Travelbyus Canada Holdings Ltd. whereby co. became an indirect subsid. of Aviation Group (now named travelbyus Inc.) in Jan. 2001; basis 1 new exch. sh. for 1 com. sh. exch. shs. automatically converted to travelbyus Inc. com. shs.

Travelers Group Inc. (Del. Aug. 8, 1968)
Oct. 8, 1998 – Formed Citigroup Inc. on amalgamation with Citicorp; basis 1 new for 1 old sh.

The Travelers Inc. (Del. Aug. 8, 1968)
May 1, 1995 – Name changed to Travelers Group Inc. ■

TravellersMall.com Ltd. (Alta. Oct. 28, 1999)
Feb. 14, 2005 – Formed Oromonte Resources Inc. in Canada pursuant to reverse takeover acquisition of and amalgamation with Oromonte Resources Inc.; basis 1 new for 10 old shs. ■

Travelways Ltd. (Ont. 1972)
May 16, 1979 – Laidlaw Transportation Limited and its subsid. Grey Goose Corp. Ltd. acquired 74% of the o/s shs. for $12,593,046, consisting of the issuance of 366,389 Laidlaw ser. D pref. shs. valued at $9,159,725, Grey Goose pref. shs. valued at $2,100,260 and long-term financing of $1,333,062. Subsequent to fiscal 1979, Laidlaw and Grey Goose acquired the remaining shs. as follows: $19 for the first and every fourth sh. tendered, paid by Grey Goose, and 8% first pfce. ser. E shs. of Laidlaw having stated value of $10 per sh. on the basis of 1.9 series E shs. for 1 Travelways com. sh., for the balance of shs. tendered. Acquired by February 1980.

Traverse Energy Ltd. (Alta. Aug. 25, 1995)
Dec. 6, 2019 – Placed into receivership by ATB Financial, the company's secured lender. Ernst & Young Inc. was appointed receiver and all officers and directors resigned.

Traverse Longlac Mines Ltd. (Ont. 1936)
Apr. 1956 – Assets acquired by Consolidated Beta Gamma Mines Ltd.; basis 1 new for 2 old shs. (see Beta Gamma Mines Ltd.)

Trawler Petroleum Explorations Ltd. (Ont. June 10, 1981)
Aug. 9, 1983 – Continued into British Columbia.
Dec. 5, 1985 – Name changed to Fibrequest International Ltd. ■

Trax Petroleums Limited (B.C. May 27, 1983)
July 12, 1993 – Continued into Alberta.
Feb. 9, 1996 – Amalgamated with Northern Arch Resources Ltd., a wholly owned subsid. of Arch Petroleum Inc., for 71¢ per sh.

Traxion Energy Inc. (Alta. July 14, 2008 amalg.)
Apr. 7, 2010 – Name changed to Anglo Canadian Oil Corp. ■

Traymore Restaurants & Catering Ltd. (Can.)
Mar. 1938 – Placed into liquidation. On realization of assets, total amt. paid to Montreal Trust Co., trustee for holders of $300,000 5% bonds, was $1,030. Nothing available for ordinary creditors or shldrs.

Treasure Island Resources Corporation (B.C. 1979)
Aug. 6, 1993 – Dissolved and struck off register.

Treasure Mountain Copper Ltd. (Ont. 1965)
Nov. 29, 1972 – Dissolved.

Treasure Rouyn Mines Ltd. (Ont. 1949)
1951 – Name changed to Centrefield Petroleums Ltd. ■

Treasure Valley Explorations Ltd. (B.C. Feb. 18, 1980)
Oct. 31, 1984 – Continued into Ontario.
June 12, 1986 – Name changed to TVX Mining Corporation. ■

Treasury Metals Inc. (Ont. Dec. 31, 1997)
Continued into British Columbia.
July 9, 2024 – Name changed to NeXGold Mining Corp.; basis 1 new for 4 old shs. (see FPsurvey - Mines & Energy)

Treat Systems Inc. (B.C. Nov. 17, 1982)
Dec. 18, 2007 – Name changed to Mega Silver Inc. ■

Treatment.com AI Inc. (Can. Feb. 2, 2018)
Aug. 21, 2025 – Name changed to Rocket Doctor AI Inc. (see FPsurvey - Industrials)

Treatment.com International Inc. (Can. Feb. 2, 2018)
Nov. 9, 2023 – Name changed to Treatment.com AI Inc. ■

Treats Inc. (Can. 1979)
Sept. 13, 1990 – All o/s shs. not held by Chocolate Gourmet Treats Limited acquired by Triadon Capital Corporation; basis $2.00 per sh. Company wholly owned by Triadon and Chocolate Gourmet.

Treaty Resources Ltd. (Alta. 1987)
Oct. 4, 1990 – Acquired by ALBA Petroleum Corporation; basis 0.412678 ALBA shs. for 1 Treaty sh. (see ALBA Petroleum Corporation)

Trebor Mines Ltd. (Ont. 1947)
1961 – Name changed to Ajax Minerals Limited; basis 1 new for 4 old shs. ■

Treco Inc. (Que. 1972 amalg.)
Sept. 1980 – All com. shs. acquired by Canam Manac Inc., through offer of $5.00 per sh.

Tredway Gold Mines Ltd. (Ont. 1945)
1959 – Dissolved.

Tree Brewing Company Ltd. (B.C. Mar. 15, 1995)
Aug. 15, 2003 – Dissolved and struck from register.

Tree Island Industries Ltd. (B.C. Oct. 8, 1987 amalg.)
Apr. 21, 1989 – All o/s com. shs. and 8.5% convertible subordin. debentures acquired by TX Acquisition, Inc., an indirect wholly owned subsid. of Georgetown Industries Inc., Charlotte N.C.; basis $14.92 per com. sh. and $1,243.33 per $1,000 principal amt. of debentures in cash.

Tree Island Steel Co. Ltd. (B.C. Sept. 17, 1964)
Oct. 8, 1987 – Formed Tree Island Industries Ltd. in British Columbia on amalgamation with two wholly owned subsids., Tree Island Investments Ltd. and 1687 Holdings Ltd. ■

Tree Island Wire Income Fund (B.C. Sept. 30, 2002)
Oct. 3, 2012 – Succeeded by Tree Island Steel Ltd. pursuant to plan of arrangement whereby Tree Island Steel Ltd. was formed to facilitate the conversion of the fund into a corporation and the fund was subsequently dissolved. (see FPsurvey - Industrials)

Tree of Knowledge International Corp. (B.C. July 25, 2007)
Nov. 18, 2021 – Name changed to Optima Medical Innovations Corp.; basis 1 new for 5 old shs. ■

Trees Corporation (Can. Dec. 22, 2021 amalg.)
May 24, 2024 – Pursuant to a reverse vesting order issued under the Companies' Creditor Arrangement Act (CCAA) the company was acquired by One Plant (Retail) Corp. under which One Plant acquired all o/s com. shs. of the company and provided funds for partial repayment of secured creditors. The com. shs. were then cancelled for no consideration and all excluded assets and liabilities were invested in 15892929 Canada Inc. which filed on May 31 an assignment into bankruptcy and FTI Consulting Canada Inc. was appointed trustee.

Trego Energy Inc. (Alta. May 13, 1991)
Feb. 12, 1998 – All o/s com. shs. acquired by Calibre Energy Inc.; basis $1.20 plus 1/5 of a com. sh. of Calibre for 1 com. sh. of Trego. (see Calibre Energy Inc.)

Trego International Inc. (Alta. Aug. 20, 1996)
July 10, 2001 – Formed TG World Energy Corp. in Alberta on amalgamation with TG World Energy Inc.; basis 1 new for 0.34268 old shs. ■

Trek Energy Inc. (Alta. July 16, 1986)
Jan. 2, 2017 – Dissolved and struck from registry.

Trek Mining Inc. (B.C. Mar. 23, 2007)
Dec. 22, 2017 – Name changed to Equinox Gold Corp. following acquisition of NewCastle Gold Ltd. (0.873 Trek shares for each NewCastle share) and Anfield Gold Corp. (0.407 Trek shares for each Anfield share). (see FPsurvey - Mines & Energy)

TrekLogic Technologies Inc. (Ont. June 21, 2002)
June 22, 2004 – Name changed to Brainhunter Inc. ■

Trelawney Mining and Exploration Inc. (Ont. July 4, 1996 amalg.)
June 25, 2012 – Acquired by IAMGOLD Corporation for $3.30 per sh.

Trelawney Resources Inc. (Ont. July 4, 1996 amalg.)
Apr. 17, 2009 – Name changed to Trelawney Mining and Exploration Inc.; basis 1 new for 5 old shs. ■

Trellis Technology Corporation (B.C. Jan. 13, 1983)
Feb. 12, 1996 – Delisted from the Vancouver Stock Exchange. Subsequently dissolved.

Tremar Minerals Ltd. (B.C. 1965)
1971 – Name changed to Gary Mines Ltd.; basis 1 new for 2 old shs. ■

Treminco Resources Ltd. (B.C. Mar. 12, 1980)
Feb. 24, 1999 – Name changed to Elkhorn Gold Mining Corporation. ■

Tremont Capital Opportunity Trust (Ont. Mar. 28, 2003)
Aug. 21, 2007 – Dissolved; all units redeemed for $10.8702 per unit.

Tren Exploration Inc. (Can. Sept. 23, 1996)
July 31, 1998 – Continued into Wyoming.
Aug. 3, 1998 – Name changed to A Little Reminder (ALR) Inc. ■

Trench Metals Corp. (B.C. June 24, 2019)
Sept. 24, 2024 – Name changed to Patterson Metals Corp.; basis 1 new for 10 old shs. (see FPsurvey - Industrials)

Trench Solutions Inc. (B.C. June 24, 2019)
Nov. 3, 2020 – Name changed to Trench Metals Corp.; basis 3 new for 1 old sh. ■

Trenchant Capital Corp. (B.C. Dec. 17, 2009)
May 17, 2024 – Name changed to Trenchant Technologies Capital Corp. (see FPsurvey - Industrials)

Trenchant Life Sciences Investment Corp. (B.C. Jan. 20, 2021)
Nov. 9, 2021 – Name changed to ASEP Medical Holdings Inc. pursuant to the reverse takeover acquisition of ASEP Medical Inc. and concurrent amalgamation of ASEP with wholly owned 1295277 B.C. Ltd. (see FPsurvey - Industrials)

Trend Capital Corporation (Alta. Apr. 8, 1994)
May 9, 1995 – Name changed to Strategic Data Inc. ■

Trend Exploration and Development Ltd. (Ont. 1962)
May 1970 – Charter cancelled.

Trend Petroleums Ltd. (Ont. 1942)
Sept. 13, 1956 – Name changed to Wayne Petroleums Limited; basis 1 new for 5 old shs. ■

Trend-Set Industries International Inc. (B.C. Jan. 9, 1987)
Sept. 16, 1993 – Name changed to E.P.A. Enterprises Inc.; basis 1 new for 1 old sh. ■

Trent Cotton Company, Limited (Ont. 1929)
Dec. 1970 – Charter cancelled.

Trent-Severn Watershed Ltd. (Alta. Feb. 5, 1998)
Nov. 14, 2002 – Name changed to Fall River Resources Ltd. following Qualifying Transaction acquisition of an oil and gas lease in Kansas. ■

Trenton Energy Inc. (Alta. Apr. 24, 1998)
Apr. 10, 2001 – Acquired by 906727 Alberta Inc. via an insider bid for $0.40 per sh. ■

Trenton Gas and Oil Limited (Ont. 1962)
May 29, 1971 – Dissolved.

Trenton Industries Inc. (Ont. 1983)
Mar. 2, 1995 – Filed a Notice of Intention To Make a Proposal under the Bankruptcy and Insolvency Act. PricewaterhouseCoopers Inc. was appointed monitor.
Nov. 1995 – Court refused to approve the proposals.
Dec. 1, 1995 – Deemed bankrupt.
June 2001 – Trustee expected secured creditors would suffer a shortfall and there would be no funds available for shldrs.
Jan. 3, 2002 – Trustee discharged.

Trenton Mines Ltd. (Sask. 1957)
1958 – Name changed to Trenton Petroleum & Mineral Corp. Ltd. ■

Trenton Petroleum & Mineral Corp. Ltd. (Sask. 1957)
1959 – Acquired by Paramount Petroleum & Mineral Corp. Ltd.; basis 1 new for 4 old shs.

Tresdor Larder Mines Ltd. (Ont. 1946)
May 18, 1976 – Charter cancelled.

Trev Corp. (Alta. June 24, 1987)
Nov. 8, 1994 – Name changed to OroGrande Resources Inc. ■

Trevali Resources Corp. (B.C. June 16, 1964)
Apr. 11, 2011 – Name changed to Trevali Mining Corporation. (see FPsurvey - Mines & Energy)

Trevco Oil and Gas Ltd. (Alta. June 24, 1987)
Sept. 18, 1990 – Name changed to Trev Corp. ■

Trevista Estates Limited (Can. 1968)
1980 – Dissolved.

Trez Capital Mortgage Investment Corporation (Can. Apr. 18, 2012)
June 2016 – Shareholders approved an orderly wind-up of the company's assets and the return of capital to shareholders.
May 22, 2019 – Special distribution of 47¢ cash per cl. A sh. payable to shldrs. of record May 9, 2019.
Apr. 20, 2020 – Special distrib. of 11¢ cash per cl. A sh. payable to shldrs. of record Apt. 13, 2020.
July 14, 2023 – Voluntarily dissolved after final distrib. of $0.04638220 cash per cl. A sh. was paid on July 7, 2023, to shldrs. of record June 29. 2023.

Trez Capital Senior Mortgage Investment Corporation (Can. Oct. 18, 2012)
June 10, 2021 – Name changed to Standard Mercantile Acquisition Corp. ■

Tri-Alpha Investments Ltd. (B.C. Dec. 11, 1985)
Dec. 20, 2004 – Name changed to Tri-Gold Resources Corp. ■

Tri-Basin Resources Ltd. (B.C. Jan. 8, 1980)
Dec. 21, 1987 – Name changed to Trian Equities Ltd. ■

Tri-Bridge Consolidated Gold Mines Limited (Ont. 1973 amalg.)
July 6, 1983 – Amalgamated with 8 other cos. to form Lobo Gold & Resources Inc.; basis 1 new for 10 old shs.

Tri-Bridge Mines Ltd. (Ont. 1970)
Oct. 1973 – Amalgamated with 3 cos. to form Tri-Bridge Consolidated Gold Mines Limited; basis 1 new for 10 old shs.

Tri Capital Opportunities Corp. (B.C. Feb. 20, 2018)
July 29, 2021 – Name changed to Apogee Minerals Ltd. pursuant to Qualifying Transaction acquisition of Pine Channel property option. (see FPsurvey - Mines & Energy)

Tri-Coast Resource Corporation (Ont. 1969)
Dec. 7, 1984 – Name changed to Gold Medal Group Inc.; basis 2.5 new for 1 old sh. ■

Tri-Cor Mining Co. Ltd. (Ont. 1957)
May 1968 – Charter cancelled.

Tri-D Automotive Limited (Ont. 1943)
Apr. 20, 1990 – All assets of U.S. subsid., Tri-D Automotive, Inc., sold, company left without any assets and charter subsequently cancelled.

Tri-Ex Mines Ltd. (Ont. 1965)
1967 – Merged into Trimar Holdings & Explorations Ltd.; basis 1 new for 4 old shs.

Tri-Ex Oil & Gas Ltd. (Alta. Feb. 3, 1994)
Mar. 10, 1998 – Acquired by Real Resources Inc.; basis 0.87 new Real sh. for 1 old Tri-Ex sh. (see Real Resources Inc.)

Tri Gold Industries Inc. (B.C. Mar. 21, 1986)
Mar. 3, 1989 – Name changed to Trimin Resources Inc. ■

Tri-Gold Resources Corp. (B.C. Dec. 11, 1985)
May 4, 2009 – Name changed to Quadro Resources Ltd.; basis 1 new for 7 old shs. (see FPsurvey - Mines & Energy)

Tri-Lateral Free Trade Inc. (Ont. Apr. 24, 1967)
July 17, 1995 – Name changed to Tri-Lateral Investments Corporation; basis 1 new for 10 old shs. ■

Tri-Lateral Investments Corporation (Ont. Apr. 24, 1967)
Nov. 11, 1998 – Name changed to Tri-Lateral Venture Corporation; basis 1 new for 10 old shs. ■

Tri-Lateral Venture Corporation (Ont. Apr. 24, 1967)
May 6, 2004 – Name changed to Pan American Gold Corporation following acquisition of Pan American Gold Corporation; basis 7 new for 1 old sh. ■

Tri-Line Expressways Ltd. (Alta. 1986)
Aug. 14, 1989 – Acquired by a wholly owned subid. of Federal Industries Ltd. for $5.50 per sh. (see Federal Industries Ltd.)

Tri Link Resources Ltd. (Alta. Jan. 18, 1974)
June 20, 2000 – Acquired by National Fuels Corp., a wholly owned subsid. of Seneca Resources Corporation, for $7.05 per sh.

Tri-National Development Corp. (B.C. July 31, 1979)
Feb. 25, 1997 – Continued into Wyoming.

Tri Origin Exploration Ltd. (Ont. June 6, 1989)
Apr. 28, 2021 – Name changed to NewOrigin Gold Corp. ■

Tri Origin Minerals Ltd. (Australia Oct. 21, 1993)
Aug. 6, 2010 – Name changed to TriAusMin Limited. ■

Tri-Pacific Resources Ltd. (B.C. Mar. 13, 1980)
May 1, 1989 – Name changed to International Membership Marketing Inc. ■

Tri-Power Minerals Corporation (B.C. May 3, 1976)
Nov. 20, 1978 – Name changed to Tri-Power Petroleum Corporation. ■

Tri-Power Petroleum Corporation (B.C. May 3, 1976)
Apr. 28, 1983 – Continued into Alberta.
Feb. 14, 1989 – Name changed to Trical Resources Inc.; basis 1 new for 10 old shs. ■

Tri-Side Mining Corp. Ltd. (unknown)
1956 – Merged into Trojan Consolidated Mines Ltd.; basis 1 new for 4 old shs.

Tri-Star Gold Corp. (Can. Oct. 24, 1996 amalg.)
June 17, 2005 – Dissolved.

Tri-Star Resources Ltd. (B.C. Jan. 26, 1977)
Dec. 31, 1986 – Formed United Tri-Star Resources Ltd. in British Columbia on amalgamation with Battle Energy Corp.; basis 1 new for 21.35 Battle Energy shs. and 1 new for 5 Tri-Star shs. ■

Tri-Tor Oils Ltd. (Que. 1951)
Mar. 1955 – Taken over by Bonnyville Oil and Refining; basis 1 new for 3 old shs.

Tri-Vision International Ltd./Ltée (Ont. June 19, 1984)
July 6, 2007 – Acquired by Wi-LAN Inc.; basis 0.2920 Wi-LAN shs. for 1 Tri-Vision sh. (see Wi-LAN Inc.)

Tri-West Petroleums Ltd. (Can. Mar. 22, 1948)
1952 – Assets acquired by Peak Oils for 435,350 Peak shs. Peak shares distributed among pfce. shldrs. of Tri-West; com. shldrs. did not rank in distribution.

Tri-West Resources Ltd. (B.C. Mar. 13, 1980)
Mar. 18, 1985 – Name changed to Tri-Pacific Resources Ltd.; basis 1 new for 5 old shs. ■

Tri-White Corporation (Can. Oct. 22, 1997)
July 22, 2009 – Name changed to ClubLink Enterprises Limited pursuant to acquisition of the remaining interest in ClubLink Corporation by way of an amalgamation of ClubLink with a wholly owned subsid. ■

Triad Leases Ltd. (Alta. Feb. 25, 1950)
1951 – Taken over by Triad Oil Co. Ltd.; basis 6.25 new for 1 old sh.

Triad Oil Co. Ltd. (Alta. 1951)
1970 – Name changed to BP Oil & Gas Ltd. ■

Triad Technologies Ltd. (B.C. Dec. 23, 1986)
May 20, 1994 – Continued into Yukon.
Dec. 16, 1999 – Name changed to MPAC Industries Corporation; basis 1 new for 10 old shs. ■

Trian Equities Ltd. (B.C. Jan. 8, 1980)
Jan. 31, 2003 – Amalgamated with privately held AMT Investments Ltd.; basis 1 cl. A pref. sh. for 1 old Trian com. sh. redeemed for $4.20 per cl. A pref. sh.

Triangle Capital Energy Corp. (Ont. 1986)
May 7, 1997 – Formed Black Mountain Minerals Inc. in Ontario pursuant to reverse takeover acquisition of and amalgamation with Per-X Minerals Inc.; basis 1 new for 4 Triangle shs. and 1 new for 1 Per-X sh. ■

Triangle Explorations Ltd. (Ont. Nov. 6, 1975)
Mar. 24, 1988 – Name changed to Laser Expressions Inc.; basis 1 new for 10 old shs. ■

Triangle Gas and Oil Ltd. (Sask. Aug. 10, 1936)
1958 – Struck off register.

Triangle Growth Capital 1 Inc. (Can. Aug. 2, 2004)
June 7, 2007 – Voluntarily delisted from TSX-VEN and dissolved; shldrs. received 1 Ranaz Corporation unit (1 com. sh. & ½ wt.) for each 3.63 shs. held, with wts. exercisable at 60¢ per Ranaz com. sh. until Dec. 29, 2008.

Triangle Industries Ltd. (B.C. Nov. 16, 1983)
July 28, 2021 – Name changed to CULT Food Science Corp. (see FPsurvey - Industrials)

Triangle Multi-Services Corporation (Ont. Aug. 20, 1986)
Apr. 15, 2011 – Name changed to RXT 110 Inc. ■

Triangle Resources Inc. (B.C. Apr. 18, 1984)
Oct. 19, 1990 – Name changed to Mortcorp Enterprises Inc.; basis 1 new for 3 old shs. ■

Triangulum Corporation (Alta. Mar. 22, 1996)
Feb. 2002 – Ceased discussions regarding sale of subsidiary AVL Automatic Vehicle Location Systems Ltd.
May 2002 – All directors resigned and Smith Cageorge Bailey Inc. of Calgary appointed receiver manager.
June 2004 – All assets sold and there were no funds available for creditors or shldrs.
Nov. 30, 2004 – Receiver manager was discharged.

Triant Holdings Inc. (B.C. Nov. 28, 2005)
Apr. 28, 2009 – Liquidated for 20¢ per sh.

Triant Technologies Inc. (B.C. Nov. 23, 1983)
Dec. 12, 2005 – Name changed to Triant Holdings Inc. following reorganization whereby Triant Technologies became a wholly owned subsid. of Triant Holdings with the existing business and assets of Triant Technologies divided between Triant Technologies Inc. and Triant Technologies (2005) Inc.; basis 0.1 new for 1 old sh. ■

Triarx Gold Corporation (Ont. Feb. 18, 1976)
Feb. 26, 2007 – Struck from register and dissolved.

TriAusMin Limited (Australia Oct. 21, 1993)
Aug. 5, 2014 – Acquired by Heron Resources Limited; basis 1 Heron ord. sh. for 2.33 TriAusMin ord. shs. (see Heron Resources Limited)

Triax CaRTS Trust (Ont. May 23, 2000)
Nov. 6, 2006 – Name changed to First Asset PowerGen Trust I. ■

Triax CaRTS III Trust (Ont. Apr. 25, 2001)
Nov. 6, 2006 – Name changed to First Asset PowerGen Trust III. ■

Triax CaRTS Technology Trust (Ont. Oct. 30, 2000)
Feb. 22, 2007 – Name changed to First Asset Diversified Convertible Debenture Fund. ■

Triax Diversified High-Yield Trust (Ont. Feb. 6, 1997)
Jan. 3, 2017 – Terminated; basis $7.81612 cash per trust unit.

Triax Resource Limited Partnership (Ont. Aug. 9, 1996)
Aug. 3, 2006 – Name changed to First Asset Energy & Resource Fund. ■

Triax Resource Limited Partnership II (Ont. Nov. 12, 1997)
Aug. 3, 2006 – Name changed to First Asset Energy & Resource Income & Growth Fund. ■

Tribag Mining Co., Ltd. (Ont. 1926)
July 7, 1975 – Name changed to Great Northern Financial Corporation; basis 1 new for 5 old shs. ■

Triband Capital Corp. (Alta. Oct. 7, 1994)
Feb. 14, 1997 – Name changed to Triband Resource Corporation. ■

Triband Enterprise Corp. (Alta. Oct. 7, 1994)
Jan. 15, 2004 – Name changed to Wealth Minerals Ltd.; basis 1 new for 4 old shs. ■

Triband Resource Corporation (Alta. Oct. 7, 1994)
Aug. 22, 2001 – Name changed to Triband Enterprise Corp.; basis 1 new for 5 old shs. ■

Tribridge Enterprises Corp. (B.C. Nov. 19, 1980)
Mar. 16, 1999 – Name changed to Vision Gate Ventures Limited; basis 1 new for 2 old shs. ■

Tribune Minerals Corp. (B.C. Oct. 11, 1985)
Sept. 13, 2011 – Name changed to Stratton Resources Inc. pursuant to reverse takeover acquisition of AZ Copper Corp.; basis 2 new for 1 old sh. ■

Tribune Resources Corp. (B.C. Oct. 11, 1985)
June 13, 2007 – Name changed to Tribune Uranium Corp. ■

Tribune Uranium Corp. (B.C. Oct. 11, 1985)
July 18, 2008 – Name changed to Tribune Minerals Corp. ■

Tribute Minerals Inc. (Ont. Sept. 7, 1982)
Dec. 3, 2010 – Name changed to AurCrest Gold Inc.; basis 1 new for 5 old shs. ■

Tribute Pharmaceuticals Canada Inc. (Ont. Nov. 14, 1994)
Feb. 9, 2016 – Amalgamated with a wholly owned subsid. of newly formed British Columbia incorporated Aralez Pharmaceuticals Inc. pursuant to plan of arrangement whereby U.S.-listed POZEN Inc. acquired the company for US$146,000,000. Tribute shareholders received 0.1455 Aralez com. shs for each Tribute com. sh. Concurrently, POZEN Inc. amalgamated with another wholly owned subsid. of Aralez Pharmaceuticals Inc. on a share-for-share basis. Upon completion, POZEN shareholders held 66% of Aralez shares. (see Aralez Pharmaceuticals Inc.)
Feb. 9, 2016 – Name changed to Aralez Pharmaceuticals Canada Inc. (see Aralez Pharmaceuticals Inc.)

Trical Resources Inc. (Alta. Apr. 28, 1983)
Feb. 20, 1990 – Name changed to Voyager Energy Inc. following reverse takeover acquisition of and amalgamation with Voyager Energy Inc.; basis 1 new for 4 old shs. ■

Trican Oilwell Service Co. Ltd. (Alta. Apr. 11, 1979)
June 11, 1997 – Name changed to Trican Well Service Ltd. (see FPsurvey - Mines & Energy; FPsurvey - Industrials)

Trican Petro-Chemical Corporation (Que. 1953)
Mar. 1955 – Taken over by Bonnyville Oil and Refining; basis 1 new for 3 old shs.

Tricentrol Limited (U.K. 1917)
Feb. 1, 1982 – Name changed to Tricentrol plc. ■

Tricentrol plc (U.K. 1917)
Aug. 9, 1988 – Acquired by ARCO UK Ltd.

Trichome Financial Corp. (Ont. Oct. 10, 2019 amalg.)
Mar. 19, 2021 – Acquired by IM Cannabis Corp.: basis 0.24525 IMC shs for 1 Trichome sh.

Tricom Equities Inc. (Alta. Feb. 26, 1997)
Jan. 1, 2000 – Formed TCEnet Inc. in Alberta on amalgamation with Datap Systems Inc. and Technology Capital Group Inc.; basis 11.817 new for 1 Datap sh., 2.78 new for 1 Technology Capital sh. and 1 new for 4 Tricom shs. ■

Tricon Capital Group Inc. (Ont. June 16, 1997)
July 7, 2020 – Name changed to Tricon Residential Inc. ■

Tricon Residential Inc. (Ont. June 16, 1997)
May 3, 2024 – Acquired by Blackstone Inc.; basis US$11.25 cash per sh.

Tricor Resources Ltd. (B.C. June 10, 1966)
Apr. 7, 1986 – Delisted from the Vancouver Stock Exchange. Subsequently struck from register and dissolved for failure to file.

Tridel Enterprises Inc. (Ont. May 25, 1981)
Apr. 28, 1999 – Continued into Ontario.
May 20, 1999 – Name changed to TDZ Holdings Inc.; basis 1 new com. of TDZ and 1 contingent rt. for 1 old Tridel sh. Holders of contingent right entitled to receive up to $0.1418 in cash. ■

Trident Gold Corp. (Ont. Jan. 4, 2011)
Apr. 25, 2017 – Name changed to Sebastiani Ventures Corp. and continued into British Columbia; basis 1 new for 4.75 old shs. ■

Trident Performance Corp. (Ont. Dec. 20, 2007)
Aug. 31, 2016 – Voluntarily dissolved; distribution $9.6541 per cl.A sh. and $10.2248 per cl. F sh.

Trident Performance Corp. II (Ont. Feb. 24, 2009)
Aug. 31, 2016 – Voluntarily dissolved; distribution $7.5441 per cl. A sh.

Trident Porcupine Gold Mines Ltd. (Ont. 1945)
Feb. 1962 – Dissolved.

Trident Resources Inc. (B.C. Oct. 18, 1973)
June 24, 1986 – Name changed to Universal Trident Industries Ltd.; basis 1 new for 5 old shs. ■

Trident Systems Inc. (Alta. Mar. 16, 1987)
Aug. 18, 1997 – Name changed to Loon Energy Inc.; basis 1 new for 4 old shs. ■

Tridon Oil & Gas Ltd. (B.C. Nov. 23, 1987)
July 24, 1992 – Name changed to Energas Resources Inc. ■

Tridont Health Care Inc. (Ont. Jan. 14, 1980)
Feb. 14, 1997 – Name changed to Phoenix Health Group Inc. ■

Triex Minerals Corporation (B.C. June 21, 1994)
Dec. 15, 2009 – Acquired by Canterra Minerals Corporation (formerly Diamondex Resources Ltd.); basis 0.85 Canterra com. shs. for 1 Triex sh.

Triex Resources Ltd. (B.C. June 13, 1972)
Mar. 30, 1988 – Name changed to First Chartered Development Corporation; basis 1 new for 2 old shs. ■

Triex Resources Ltd. (B.C. June 21, 1994)
July 16, 2002 – Name changed to Triex Minerals Corporation; basis 1 new for 3 old shs. ■

Trifield Petroleum Ltd. (Ont. 1947)
1960 – Struck off register.

Triform Explorations (B.C.) Ltd. (B.C. June 26, 1962)
1964 – Name changed to Triform Mining Ltd.; basis 1 new for 5 old shs. ■

Triform Explorations Ltd. (Ont. 1960)
1962 – Acquired by Triform Explorations (B.C.) Ltd. (see Triform Explorations (B.C.) Ltd.)

Triform Mining Ltd. (B.C. June 26, 1962)
1968 – Name changed to Lucky Strike Mines Ltd. ■

TriGas Exploration Inc. (Alta. Mar. 1, 1994)
Nov. 28, 2000 – All o/s com. shs. acquired by 899340 Alberta Ltd., an indirect wholly owned subsid. of California-based Calpine Corporation; basis $3.20 per sh.

Trigas Exploration Ltd. (Alta. 1987)
Dec. 1, 1989 – Acquired by Pinnacle Resources Ltd.; basis 1 Pinnacle sh. for 1.9 Trigas shs. (see Pinnacle Resources Ltd.)

Trigen Resources Inc. (B.C. Jan. 13, 1981)
Feb. 23, 2018 – Name changed to BlissCo Cannabis Corp. following reverse takeover acquisition of Bliss Co Holdings Ltd. ■

Trigold Resources Inc. (B.C. Nov. 9, 2010)
Oct. 14, 2015 – Name changed to Crystal Exploration Inc. ■

Trigon Exploration Canada Ltd. (Can. Nov. 8, 2002)
Dec. 13, 2006 – Name changed to Trigon Uranium Corp. ■

Trigon Technologies Inc. (B.C. 1983)
Oct. 6, 1989 – Dissolved.

Trigon Uranium Corp. (Can. Nov. 8, 2002)
Nov. 30, 2009 – Name changed to IC Potash Corp. pursuant to reverse takeover acquisition of Intercontinental Potash Corp. ■

Trihope Mining & Exploration Ltd. (Can. Jan. 12, 1967)
1968 – Name changed to Trihope Resources Limited. ■

Trihope Resources Limited (Can. Jan. 12, 1967)
Aug. 10, 1984 – Dissolved.

Trijet Mining Corp. (B.C. Oct. 25, 2007)
Mar. 8, 2013 – Name changed to Umbral Energy Corp.; basis 1 new for 2 old shs. ■

Triller Explorations Ltd. (Ont. 1967)
1970 – Name changed to Triller Metals & Holdings Ltd.; basis 1 new for 15 old shs. ■

Triller Metals & Holdings Ltd. (Ont. 1967)
Feb. 1980 – Charter cancelled.

Trillion Energy International Inc. (Del. June 19, 2015)
Jan. 20, 2022 – Amalgamated in British Columbia to continue with same name. (see FPsurvey – Mines & Energy)

Trillion Resources Ltd. (Alta. July 24, 1987)
Jan. 15, 1999 – Name changed to Consolidated Trillion Resources Ltd.; basis 1 new for 6 old shs. ■

Trillium Gold Mines Inc. (B.C. Nov. 3, 2005)
July 17, 2023 – Name changed to Renegade Gold Inc.; basis 1 new for 10 old shs. (see FPsurvey – Mines & Energy)

Trillium North Minerals Ltd. (B.C. June 22, 1990 amalg.)
June 4, 2014 – Name changed to White Metal Resources Corp.; basis 1 new for 10 old shs. ■

Trillium Petroleums Ltd. (Ont. 1951)
1953 – Consolidated Matarrow Lead Mines Ltd. acquired assets for 1,000,000 shs. (see Consolidated Matarrow Mines Ltd.)

Trillium Telephone Systems Inc. (Can. 1983)
Sept. 22, 1988 – Amalgamated with Mitel Corporation. (see Mitel Corporation)

Trillium Therapeutics Inc. (Ont. Nov. 7, 2013)
Nov. 22, 2021 – All o/s com. shs not already held acquired by Pfizer Inc.; basis US$18.50 cash per sh.

TriLoch Resources Inc. (Alta. Mar. 13, 2001)
July 11, 2005 – Plan of Arrangement with EnerMark Inc., Enerplus Resources Fund and NuLock Resources Inc.; basis 0.07151 new Enerplus trust unit for 1 old TriLoch cl. A sh., plus 1 new NuLoch cl. A sh. for 10 old TriLoch cl. A shs., plus 0.23923 new Enerplus trust unit for 1 old TriLoch cl. B sh. (see Enerplus Resources Fund; NuLoch Resources Inc.)

Trilogy AI Corp. (B.C. June 20, 2019)
Aug. 1, 2025 – Name changed to Tokenwell Platforms Inc. (see FPsurvey – Industrials)

Trilogy Energy Corp. (Alta. Dec. 22, 2009)
Sept. 12, 2017 – Name changed to Paramount Resources (TEC) Ltd. following acquisition by Paramount Resources Ltd.; basis 1 Paramount com. sh. for 3.75 Trilogy com. and non-vtg. com. shs.

Trilogy Energy Trust (Alta. Feb. 25, 2005)
Feb. 10, 2010 – Converted into Trilogy Energy Corp. and subsequently dissolved (see Trilogy Energy Corp.)

Trilogy Entertainment Corp. (B.C. Apr. 3, 1986)
Sept. 29, 1993 – Name changed to Consolidated Trilogy Ventures Ltd.; basis 1 new for 5 old shs. ■

Trilogy International Partners Inc. (B.C.)
Apr. 2, 2024 – All o/s shs. not already held acquired by SG Enterprises II, LLC; basis US$0.07 cash per sh.

Trilogy Metals Inc. (B.C. Apr. 3, 1986)
Mar. 7, 2008 – Name changed to NWest Energy Inc. and continued into Canada. ■

Trilogy Resource Corporation (Can. Nov. 4, 1981)
Oct. 12, 1993 – All o/s com. shs., special shs., and special warrants acquired by Mannville Oil & Gas Ltd.; basis 0.60 new com. sh. for 1 com. sh. and/or 1 old special warrant and $4.20 for each special share. (see Mannville Oil & Gas Ltd.)

Trilon Financial Corporation (Can. Dec. 29, 1975)
Feb. 8, 1994 – Continued into Ontario.
May 30, 2002 – Name changed to Brascan Financial Corporation. ■

Trimac Corporation (Alta. Dec. 4, 1970)
Nov. 27, 2000 – Privatized at $9.50 per sh.

Trimac Income Fund (Alta. Jan. 7, 2005)
Jan. 1, 2011 – Succeeded by Trimac Transportation Ltd. pursuant to plan of arrangement whereby Trimac Transportation Ltd. was formed to facilitate the conversion of the fund into a corporation. ■

Trimac Limited (Alta. Dec. 4, 1970)
Feb. 7, 1997 – Name changed to Trimac Corporation following separation of the company into 2 public companies, Trimac Corporation and Kenting Energy Services Inc.; basis 1 Trimac Corp. com. sh. and 1 Kenting Energy com. sh. for 1 Trimac Limited com. sh. ■

Trimac Porcupine Gold Mines Ltd. (Ont. 1945)
1954 – Charter cancelled.

Trimac Transportation Ltd. (Alta. Oct. 19, 2010)
July 7, 2016 – Privatized via amalgamation with a wholly owned subsid. of Trimac Holdings Ltd., owned by Jeffrey J. McCaig; basis $6.25 per cl. A sh.

Trimar Holdings & Explorations Ltd. (Ont. 1967)
Feb. 20, 1980 – Dissolved.

Trimark Energy Ltd. (Yuk. Dec. 14, 1993)
Feb. 23, 2004 – Name changed to Halo Resources Ltd. ■

Trimark Financial Corporation (Ont. Nov. 16, 1978)
Aug. 3, 2000 – Amalgamated with AMVESCAP plc; basis either a) $27 or b) $0.02554 princ. amt. of equity debs. plus 0.05655 AMVESCAP exch. shs. plus $0.08471 or c) 1.05082 AMVESCAP ord. shs. plus $1.57405 or d) 1.05082 AMVESCAP exch. shs. plus $1.57405, or a combination thereof for 1 Trimark com. sh. (see AMVESCAP Inc.)

Trimark Oil & Gas Ltd. (Yuk. Dec. 14, 1993)
Mar. 21, 2002 – Name changed to Trimark Energy Ltd.; basis 1 new for 7 old shs. ■

Trimark Resources Ltd. (B.C. June 16, 1983)
Dec. 14, 1993 – Continued into Yukon.
Dec. 16, 1996 – Name changed to International Trimark Resources Ltd.; basis 1 new for 3 old shs. ■

Trimble Resources Corporation (B.C. Apr. 19, 1985)
July 30, 2002 – Acquired by MFC Bancorp. Ltd.; basis 22¢ or 0.0139 MFC shs. for 1 Trimble sh. (see MFC Bancorp Ltd.)

Trimble Resources Ltd. (Alta. June 24, 1987)
Oct. 3, 1995 – Amalgamated with 662286 Alberta Ltd., a wholly owned subsid. of Grad & Walker Energy Corporation; basis 1 Grad & Walker sh. for 35 Trimble shs. (see Grad & Walker Energy Corporation)

Trimel Corporation (Ont. Mar. 30, 1983)
Mar. 29, 1994 – Formed Biovail Corporation International in Ontario on amalgamation with Biovail Corporation International; basis 1 new for 1 Biovail sh. and 1 new for either 1 Trimel com. sh. or 5.35 Trimel cl. A special shs. ■

Trimel Pharmaceuticals Corporation (Ont. July 15, 2009)
Sept. 8, 2015 – Name changed to Acerus Pharmaceuticals Corporation. ■

TriMetals Mining Inc. (B.C. Dec. 20, 2013)
Nov. 1, 2019 – Name changed to Gold Springs Resource Corp. (see FPsurvey – Mines & Energy)

Trimin Capital Corp. (Can. May 5, 1998)
Jan. 4, 2007 – Plan of Arrangement acquisition by JDM Capital Limited; basis $3.25 per sh.

Trimin Enterprises Inc. (B.C. Mar. 21, 1986)
Apr. 5, 2000 – Acquired by Castings Acquisition Corp. for $7.35 per sh.

Trimin Resources Inc. (B.C. Mar. 21, 1986)
Nov. 1, 1991 – Name changed to Trimin Enterprises Inc. ■

Trimox Energy Inc. (Alta. Sept. 13, 2004)
June 25, 2007 – Amalgamated with Canext Energy Ltd. and Tasman Exploration Ltd. to form a new company named Canext Energy Ltd.; basis 1.0825 Tasman cl. A com. sh. for 1 Trimox cl. A sh. and 10.8247 Tasman cl. A com. sh. for 1 Trimox cl. B sh. and 1.0309 Tasman cl. A com. sh. for 1 Canext sh., following which all Tasman cl. A com. shs. became com. shs. of new Canext on a share-for-share basis. (see Canext Energy Ltd.)

TrinCan Capital Corp. (Alta. Aug. 24, 2007)
Feb. 2, 2018 – Struck from registry and dissolved.

Trincana Resources Ltd. (B.C. July 9, 1985)
July 11, 2000 – Name changed to Bevo Agro Inc. following reverse takeover acquisition of Bevo Farms Ltd. ■

TriNexus Holdings Ltd. (Ont. Oct. 1, 1985)
June 5, 2002 – Delisted from the TSX-Venture Exchange. Subsequently struck from register and dissolved.

Trinidad Drilling Ltd. (Sask. Feb. 23, 1996)
June 29, 1999 – Continued into Alberta.
June 30, 1999 – Amalgamated in Alberta to continue with same name.
Sept. 24, 2002 – Converted into an income trust named Trinidad Energy Services Income Trust; basis 1 trust unit for 1 com. sh.
Feb. 15, 2019 – Amalgamated in Alberta to continue with same name.
Feb. 20, 2019 – Amalgamated with Ensign Holdings Inc., a wholly owned subsid. of Ensign Energy Services Inc., to continue under the Trinidad name; basis 1 new Trinidad redeem. pref. sh. for 1 old Trinidad com. sh., immediately redeem. for $1.68 cash per sh.

Trinidad Energy Services Income Trust (Alta. Sept. 17, 2002)
Mar. 17, 2008 – Reorganization of the business of subsidiaries into a public oil and gas service company under the name of Trinidad Drilling Ltd.; basis 1 Trinidad Drilling com. sh. for 1 Trinidad Energy trust unit. (see Trinidad Drilling Ltd.)

Trinidad Leaseholds (Canada) Ltd. (Ont. 1933)
Aug. 23, 1955 – Name changed to Regent Refining (Canada) Ltd. ■

Trinidad Mines, Gas & Oils, Ltd. (N.S. 1927)
June 1937 – In bankruptcy; no distribution for shldrs.

Trinity Chibougamau Mines Ltd. (Que. 1951)
Mar. 26, 1982 – Name changed to Trinity Mines Inc. ■

Trinity Control Ltd. (B.C. Dec. 7, 1983)
May 23, 2002 – Name changed to Sunridge Gold Corp. ■

Trinity Copper Mines Ltd. (Que. 1951)
Oct. 1956 – Name changed to Trinity Chibougamau Mines Ltd. ■

Trinity Mines Inc. (Que. 1951)
Jan. 11, 1990 – Name changed to Harlake Capital Group Inc.; basis 1 new for 20 old shs. ■

Trinity Plumas Capital Corp. (B.C. Mar. 9, 1987)
May 16, 2005 – Name changed to TrueStar Petroleum Corporation. ■

Trinity Resources Ltd. (Alta. Mar. 1, 1969)
July 23, 1986 – Continued into Canada. (see Enscor Inc.)
July 31, 1991 – Amalgamated with a wholly owned subsid. of Enscor Inc.; basis 1 Enscor sh. for 3.75 Trinity shs. (see Enscor Inc.)

Trinity Valley Energy Corp. (B.C. May 17, 1966)
Nov. 15, 2017 – Name changed to Smooth Rock Ventures Corp.; basis 1 new for 4 old shs. (see FPsurvey - Mines & Energy)

Trinity Ventures Ltd. (B.C. May 13, 1999)
Nov. 5, 2002 – Acquired by Banks Ventures Ltd. was considered to be Trinity's Qualifying Transaction; basis 1 new Banks sh. for 2 old Trinity shs. (see Banks Ventures Ltd.)

TriNorth Capital Inc. (Can. Jan. 14, 1972)
May 28, 2012 – Name changed to Difference Capital Funding Inc.; basis 1 new for 10 old shs. ■

Trinova Cobalt Silver Mines Limited (Ont. 1935)
Sept. 5, 1978 – Name changed to Trinova Resource Explorations Ltd. ■

Trinova Resource Explorations Ltd. (Ont. 1935)
Dec. 4, 1985 – Amalgamated with 5 other cos. to form Flying Cross Resources Ltd.; basis 1 new for 5 old shs.

Trio-Archean Developments Inc. (Can. 1980)
May 27, 1987 – Name changed to International Movie Group, Inc. ■

Trio Mining Exploration Ltd. (Ont. 1952)
Aug. 22, 1973 – Charter cancelled.

Trio Petroleum Corp. Ltd. (Ont. 1952)
Apr. 1954 – Name changed to Trio Uranium Mines Ltd. ■

Trio Resources Ltd. (B.C. 1979)
Oct. 1980 – Acquired by Trio-Archean Resources; basis 4 Trio-Archean cl. B shs. for 3 Trio Resources shs.

Trio Uranium Mines Ltd. (Ont. 1952)
Nov. 28, 1956 – Name changed to Trio Mining Exploration Ltd. ■

TriOil Ltd. (Alta. July 30, 2002)
Aug. 13, 2004 – Amalgamated in Alberta to continue with same name.
Nov. 14, 2005 – Amalgamated with Yangarra Resources Inc. (0.95 for 1) to continue with the new name Yangarra Resources Ltd.; basis 1 new Yangarra sh. for 1 old TriOil sh.

TriOil Resources Ltd. (Alta. Nov. 21, 2006)
Nov. 18, 2013 – Acquired by Polski Koncern Naftowy ORLEN S.A. for $2.85 per sh. (see Polski Koncern Naftowy ORLEN S.A.)
Apr. 2, 2015 – Name changed to ORLEN Upstream Canada Ltd. (see Polski Koncern Naftowy ORLEN S.A.)

Trionics Industries Ltd. (B.C. Jan. 22, 1985)
Sept. 23, 1996 – Name changed to Comptec Industries Ltd. ■

Trionics Technology Ltd. (B.C. Jan. 22, 1985)
Aug. 17, 1994 – Name changed to Trionics Industries Ltd.; basis 1 new for 2 old shs. ■

Trioptimum Capital Corp. (B.C. Apr. 14, 2000)
Aug. 1, 2002 – Name changed to Contec Innovations Inc. following Qualifying Transaction reverse takeover acquisition of Contec Innovations Services Inc. ■

Triox Limited (Hong Kong Aug. 4, 2011)
Oct. 30, 2014 – Name changed to eQube Gaming Limited following Qualifying Transaction reverse takeover acquisition of eQube Technology and Software Inc.; basis 1 new for 3 old shs. ■

Tripet Resources Limited (Alta. 1987)
May 1, 1992 – Acquired by Chauvco Resources Ltd.; basis $12.75 or 0.5624 Chauvco shs. for 1 Tripet sh. (see Chauvco Resources Ltd.)

Triple Crown Electronics Inc. (Ont. Sept. 25, 1973)
Sept. 25, 2000 – Amalgamated with CableServ Electronics Ltd. to form CableServ Inc.; basis 0.029598 CableServ Inc. shs. for 1 Triple Crown sh.

Triple Crown Petroleum Ltd. (Alta. Feb. 10, 2011)
Dec. 22, 2011 – Name changed to First Mountain Exploration Ltd. pursuant to Qualifying Transaction reverse takeover acquisition of (old) First Mountain Exploration Ltd. ■

Triple Crown Resources Inc. (Alta. Aug. 18, 1987)
Oct. 5, 1989 – Name changed to Rangeland Resources Ltd.; basis 1 new for 5 old shs. ■

Triple-Crown Resources Ltd. (B.C. 1976)
Jan. 13, 1985 – Amalgamated with 4 other cos. to form Aurex Resources Inc.; basis 1 new for 5 old shs.

Triple Dragon Resources Inc. (B.C. Feb. 21, 2006)
Aug. 4, 2006 – Continued into British Virgin Islands.
July 10, 2008 – Continued into British Columbia.
Mar. 30, 2012 – Name changed to Pasinex Resources Limited. (see FPsurvey - Mines & Energy)

Triple "8" Energy Corporation (B.C. Mar. 8, 1971)
Feb. 24, 1994 – Continued into Alberta.
Mar. 1, 1994 – Name changed to Oilexco Incorporated. ■

Triple 8 Energy Ltd. (Alta. Oct. 17, 1995)
Nov. 24, 2010 – Name changed to Hyperion Exploration Corp.; basis 1 new for 20 old shs. ■

Triple 8 Ventures Ltd. (Alta. Oct. 17, 1995)
Oct. 30, 2002 – Name changed to Triple 8 Energy Ltd.; basis 1 new for 8 old shs. ■

Triple Force Industries Inc. (B.C. Feb. 15, 1985 amalg.)
Sept. 27, 1996 – Name changed to Petrock Ventures Inc.; basis 1 new for 4 old shs. ■

Triple G Systems Group, Inc. (Ont. Jan. 1, 1998)
Aug. 21, 2003 – Acquired by GE Canada Enterprises Company (related company to US-based General Electric Company); basis $3.30 per sh.

Triple Lake Porcupine Gold Ltd. (Ont. 1937)
1945 – Acquired by Trimac Porcupine Gold Mines Ltd.; basis 1 new for 5 old shs. (see Trimac Porcupine Gold Mines Ltd.)

Triple M Mining Corporation (B.C. 1984)
June 30, 1988 – Name changed to S. E. Storage Express (International) Limited following acquisition of Storage Express Inc. ■

Triple Ridge Mines Ltd. (Ont. 1956)
Dec. 1959 – Dissolved.

Triple Star Resource Corp. (B.C. May 30, 1986)
Aug. 6, 1991 – Name changed to Northern Plains Oil Corporation; basis 1 new for 3 old shs. ■

Triple Strike Mines Ltd. (Man. 1957)
Feb. 26, 1966 – Charter cancelled.

Tripleplay Sports Group Inc. (Ont. Aug. 19, 1985)
Oct. 12, 2000 – Name changed to Bonanza Blue Corp.; basis 1 new for 10 old shs. ■

Tripoint Mines Ltd. (Ont. 1966)
July 1969 – Assets distributed; charter surrendered and dissolved.

Triquanta Investments Limited (Alta. July 23, 1991)
Jan. 5, 2000 – Charter cancelled and co. dissolved.

TriQuest Energy Corp. (Alta. Nov. 1, 1996)
Mar. 12, 2004 – Acquired by Bonavista Petroleum Ltd. a subsid. of Bonavista Energy Trust; basis $3.10 per sh. (see Bonavista Energy Trust)

TriStar Oil & Gas Ltd. (Alta. Sept. 30, 2005)
Aug. 16, 2007 – Merged with Real Resources Inc. by way of reverse takeover of Real to become a wholly owned subsidiary renamed TriStar Resources Ltd. and Real changing its name to TriStar Oil & Gas Ltd. (new); basis 0.4762 new TriStar shs. for 1 old TriStar sh. and 1 new TriStar sh. for 1 Real sh. (see PetroBakken Energy Ltd.)
Oct. 6, 2009 – Acquired by PetroBakken Energy Ltd.; basis $14.75 per sh. or 0.5350 PetroBakken shs., or a combination thereof for 1 TriStar sh. (see PetroBakken Energy Ltd.)

Tritech Investments Inc. (Alta. Feb. 14, 1994)
Feb. 19, 1996 – Name changed to InfoInterActive Inc. ■

Tritech Precision Inc. (Ont. Dec. 30, 1993)
Apr. 5, 2000 – All o/s shs. exchanged via Certificate of Arrangement whereby Castings Acquisition Corp. took co. private; basis $33 per sh.

Tritex Petroleum Corp. (Ont. 1956)
Feb. 5, 1988 – Amalgamated with Justice Electronic Monitoring Sytems Limited to form Peregrine Instruments & Monitoring Inc.; basis unknown. (see Justice Electronic Monitoring Systems Inc.)

Triton Canada Resources Ltd. (Alta. Oct. 16, 1952)
Nov. 22, 1993 – Name changed to Transwest Energy Inc. ■

Triton Capital Corporation (Alta. July 22, 1999)
Nov. 9, 2004 – Name changed to March Resources Corporation following reverse takeover acquisition of March Resources Ltd. ■

Triton Energy Corporation (Tex. 1962)
Mar. 25, 1996 – Name changed to Triton Energy Ltd. ■

Triton Energy Corp. (Alta. Feb. 4, 2004)
June 14, 2010 – Name changed to Waldron Energy Corporation; basis 1 new for 10 old shs. ■

Triton Energy Ltd. (Tex. 1962)
1996 – Continued into Cayman Islands.

Triton Explorations Ltd. (unknown)
Feb. 6, 1979 – Dissolved.

Triton International Industries Ltd. (B.C. 1971)
1973 – Went into receivership and is now defunct.

Triton Mines & Metals Corp. Ltd. (Ont. 1954)
Aug. 1957 – Merged into Continental Consolidated Mines & Oils Corp. Ltd.; basis 1 new for 5 old shs. (see Continental Consolidated Mines & Oils Corp. Ltd.)

Triton Mining Corporation (B.C. Aug. 29, 1991)
July 6, 1994 – Continued into Ontario. (see Black Hawk Mining Inc.)
June 10, 1998 – Amalgamated with Trihawk Mining Inc., a wholly owned subsid. of Black Hawk Mining Inc.; basis 1 Black Hawk sh. for 1 Triton sh. (see Black Hawk Mining Inc.)

Triton Resources Inc. (B.C. 1956)
Sept. 20, 1985 – Struck off register.

Triton Uranium Mines Ltd. (Ont. 1954)
1955 – Name changed to Triton Mines & Metals Corp. Ltd. ■

Triumph Acquisition Corporation Inc. (Can. Aug. 19, 2003)
Aug. 4, 2005 – Formed Chemaphor Inc. in Canada on Qualifying Transaction amalgamation with Occell Inc., a privately held National Research Council of Canada biotechnology spin-off, constituting a reverse takeover by Occell. ■

Triumph Energy Corporation (Alta. Apr. 29, 1976)
June 5, 2001 – Acquired by Baytex Energy Ltd.; basis $4.70 or 0.3475 Baytex shs. for 1 Triumph sh.

Triumph Gold Corp. (Yuk. Jan. 29, 2004)
Dec. 22, 2004 – Continued into British Columbia.
May 1, 2007 – Name changed to Kenai Resources Ltd.;
basis 1 new for 6 old shs. ■

Triumph Mines Ltd. (B.C. 1953)
June 14, 1962 – Dissolved.

Triumph Oil Corporation Limited (Ont. 1952)
1953 – Assets acquired by Rio-Prado Consolidated Oils
Limited; basis 9 new for 20 old shs. (see Rio-Prado
Consolidated Oils Limited)

Triumph Petroleums Ltd. (B.C. May 30, 1980)
Aug. 4, 1988 – Name changed to Arrowfield Resources
Ltd.; basis 1 new for 4 old shs. ■

Triumph Resources Ltd. (B.C. Mar. 26, 1956)
Oct. 2, 1992 – Name changed to Jericho Resources Ltd.;
basis 1 new for 4 old shs. ■

Triumph Resources Ltd. (Man. 1960)
Mar. 31, 1976 – Dissolved.

Triumph Ventures II Corporation (Ont. Jan. 19, 2011)
Aug. 28, 2015 – Pro rata distribution of remaining assets
to shldrs. of record, Aug. 18, 2015, payable Aug. 28,
2015.
Sept. 8, 2015 – Voluntarily dissolved.

Triumph Ventures III Corporation (Ont. Jan. 19, 2011)
Dec. 28, 2012 – Name changed to Altitude Resources
Inc. pursuant to Qualifying Transaction reverse takeover
acquisition of Altitude Resources Ltd.; basis 1 new for 2
old shs. ■

Triumph Ventures Corp. (Ont. Nov. 19, 2009)
Oct. 6, 2011 – Name changed to Highvista Gold Inc.
pursuant to Qualifying Transaction reverse takeover
acquisition of Highvista Gold Corp. and subsequent
amalgamation with a wholly owned subsid.; basis 1 new
for 2 old shs. (see FPsurvey - Mines & Energy)

Trius Investments Inc. (Alta. Dec. 3, 1996)
Oct. 18, 2006 – Name changed to eCycling Technologies
Inc. ■

Trius Investments Inc. (Alta. Dec. 3, 1996)
Oct. 19, 2020 – Name changed to TRU Precious Metals
Corp. ■

Trivalence Mining Corporation (B.C. Sept. 18, 1984)
Mar. 26, 2008 – Name changed to Azure Resources
Corporation. ■

Trivello Energy Corp. (B.C. Sept. 1, 1994)
Oct. 19, 2010 – Name changed to Equitas Resources
Corp. ■

Trivello Ventures Inc. (B.C. Sept. 1, 1994)
May 4, 2006 – Name changed to Trivello Energy Corp. ■

Triwood Capital Corp. (Alta. Jan. 3, 2008)
Apr. 15, 2011 – Name changed to Algae Biosciences
Corporation pursuant to Qualifying Transaction reverse
takeover acquisition of (old) Algae Biosciences
Corporation which was subsequently amalgamated with
a wholly owned subsid. ■

Trizec Canada Inc. (Can. Jan. 29, 2002)
Oct. 5, 2006 – Acquired by Brookfield Properties
Corporation for US$30.9809 per multiple and subord. vtg.
sh. (see Brookfield Properties Corporation)

Trizec Corporation Ltd. (Can. Oct. 5, 1960)
Nov. 4, 1996 – Amalgamated with Horsham Corporation
to form TrizecHahn Corporation; basis 1 TrizecHahn for
1 Horsham sh., 0.58 TrizecHahn subord. vtg. shs. for 1
Trizec com. sh. and 1 TrizecHahn cl. A wt. for 1 Trizec
cl. A wt. (see TrizecHahn Corporation)

Trizec Development Ltd. (B.C. 1970)
Aug. 31, 1971 – Name changed to Wavecom
Development Ltd. ■

TrizecHahn Corporation (Ont. Nov. 4, 1996 amalg.)
Jan. 29, 2002 – Continued into Canada.
May 8, 2002 – Name changed to Trizec Canada Inc.
pursuant to reorganization into two separate companies,
Trizec Properties, Inc. and Trizec Canada Inc. Shldrs.
exchanged their subord. vtg. shs. for either subord. vtg.
shs. of Trizec Canada, com. shs. of Trizec Properties or
a combination of both. ■

Tro-Buttle Exploration Limited (B.C. 1964)
Feb. 25, 1983 – Struck off register.

Troilus Explorations Limited (Que. 1966)
Apr. 1977 – Shs. exchanged for Muscocho Explorations
Ltd. shs.; basis 1 new for 10 old shs. Charter surrendered.

Troilus Mines Ltd. (Que. 1966)
July 1976 – Name changed to Troilus Explorations
Limited. ■

Trojan Consolidated Mines Ltd. (B.C. 1956)
May 1972 – Name changed to B.X. Development Ltd.;
basis 1 new for 5 old shs. ■

Trojan Energy Corporation (B.C. Aug. 25, 1967)
Mar. 27, 1985 – Name changed to International Trojan
Development Corporation; basis 1 new for 5 old shs. ■

Trojan Exploration Ltd. (B.C. 1954)
1956 – Merged into Trojan Consolidated Mines Ltd.; basis
2 new for 3 old shs.

Trojan Gold Inc. (Alta. Oct. 24, 2012)
Aug. 21, 2020 – Continued into Ontario. (see FPsurvey
- Mines & Energy)

Trojan Gold Mines Ltd. (Ont. 1944)
Feb. 18, 1963 – Dissolved.

Trojan Technologies Inc. (Ont. Aug. 25, 1981)
Nov. 18, 2004 – Acquired by wholly owned subsid. of
US-based Danaher Corporation for Cdn$10.65 per sh.

Trojan Ventures Inc. (B.C. Aug. 25, 1967)
Mar. 26, 1999 – Name changed to Alcanta International
Education Ltd. and continued into Cayman Islands; basis
1 new for 5 old shs. ■

Tromac Mines Ltd. (Ont. 1945)
Apr. 9, 1975 – Charter cancelled.

Troon Ventures Ltd. (B.C. Dec. 2, 1935)
Feb. 19, 2014 – Name changed to Grenville Strategic
Royalty Corp. pursuant to reverse takeover acquisition
of (old) Grenville Strategic Royalty Corp.; basis 0.6896
new for 1 old sh. ■

Trooper Explorations Ltd. (B.C. Mar. 28, 1979)
May 4, 1995 – Name changed to Trooper Technologies
Inc. ■

Trooper Technologies Inc. (B.C. Mar. 28, 1979)
Oct. 19, 2001 – Name changed to Stream
Communications Network, Inc. ■

Trophy Capital Inc. (Can. Jan. 14, 2003)
Apr. 15, 2004 – Name changed to LMS Medical Systems
Inc. following Qualifying Transaction reverse takeover
acquisition of LMS Medical Systems Ltd.; basis 1 new
for 20 old shs. ■

Trophy Resources Ltd. (Alta. May 6, 1987)
Nov. 30, 1993 – Name changed to Williston Wildcatters
Oil Corporation. ■

Tropic Trading Company Limited (Alta. Dec. 17, 1991)
June 1, 1997 – Struck off register.

Tropical Submarine Safaris Ltd. (B.C. Apr. 19, 1983)
Aug. 2, 1989 – Name changed to International Submarine
Safaris (Canada) Ltd.; basis 1 new for 5 old shs. ■

Tropicana Development Corporation (B.C. June 15,
1984)
Sept. 8, 1992 – Name changed to Santa Barbara
Ventures Ltd.; basis 1 new for 8 old shs. ■

Tropicana Resources Ltd. (B.C. June 15, 1984)
Oct. 19, 1987 – Name changed to Tropicana
Development Corporation. ■

Troudor Resources Incorporated (B.C. Aug. 1, 1980)
Mar. 14, 1989 – Name changed to Remington Creek
Resources Inc.; basis 1 new for 3 old shs. ■

Troup Porcupine Mines Ltd. (Ont. Aug. 19, 1938)
May 1958 – Charter cancelled.

Trout Lake Mines Ltd. (Alta. 1950)
Nov. 15, 1958 – Struck off register.

Trout Lake Mining Co. Ltd. (unknown)
Aug. 31, 1950 – Assets acquired by Trout Lake Mines
Ltd. for 1,300,000 shs.

Troutline Investments Inc. (Ont. Sept. 23, 1968)
Apr. 22, 2004 – Acquired by Innova Exploration Ltd.; basis
1 Innova sh. for 8.8235 Troutline shs. (see Innova
Exploration Ltd.)

Trove Investment Corporation (B.C. Aug. 15, 1983)
Jan. 29, 1997 – Name changed to Net Nanny Software
International Inc. ■

Trove Resources Ltd. (B.C. Aug. 15, 1983)
Feb. 11, 1991 – Name changed to Trove Investment
Corporation. ■

Troy Consolidated Gold Mines Ltd. (Ont. 1938)
Jan. 1955 – Charter cancelled.

Troy Energy Corp. (B.C. Nov. 18, 2004)
Feb. 24, 2011 – Continued into Alberta.
June 12, 2020 – Name changed to Norse Gold Corp.
(see FPsurvey - Mines & Energy)

Troy Gold Industries Ltd. (Can. Apr. 14, 1926)
Mar. 7, 1978 – Continued into Alberta.
June 30, 1981 – Struck off register.

Troy Minerals & Technology Corp. (B.C. 1983)
Sept. 18, 1992 – Dissolved and struck off register.

Troy Resources Inc. (B.C. May 31, 2018)
Apr. 20, 2022 – Name changed to Troy Minerals Inc. (see
FPsurvey - Mines & Energy)

Troy Resources NL (Australia Feb. 28, 1984)
Jan. 6, 2012 – Name changed to Troy Resources Limited.

Troy Silver Mines Ltd. (B.C.)
June 27, 1977 – Dissolved.

Troymet Exploration Corp. (Alta. June 4, 2007)
Apr. 11, 2019 – Name changed to Bessor Minerals Inc.;
basis 1 new for 10 old shs. (see FPsurvey - Mines &
Energy)

Troymin Resources Ltd. (Alta. June 8, 1953)
Apr. 24, 2003 – Formed Santoy Resources Ltd. in Alberta
on amalgamation with Santoy Resources Ltd. with
Troymin the deemed acquiror; basis 1 new for 1 Santoy
sh. and 1 new for 1.65 Troymin shs. ■

Troysco Mines Ltd. (Que. 1952)
Feb. 15, 1971 – Charter cancelled.

Tru-Wall Concrete Forming Limited (Ont. 1956)
Jan. 22, 1976 – Name changed to Tru-Wall Group
Limited. (see FPsurvey - Industrials)

Truax Resources Corporation (Alta. June 3, 1987)
June 16, 1997 – Acquired by Elk Point Resources Inc.;
basis $2.23 or 0.314 Elk shs. for 1 Truax sh. (see Elk
Point Resources Inc.)

Truax Ventures Corp. (B.C. Mar. 21, 1978)
Sept. 1, 2004 – Name changed to Aries Resource Corp.; basis 1 new for 4 old shs. ■

Trudeau Gold Inc. (B.C. Aug. 24, 2017)
Apr. 30, 2018 – Name changed to Century Metals Inc. ■

Trudev Mining & Exploration Ltd. (Ont. 1949)
May 13, 1965 – Dissolved.

True Energy Inc. (Alta. Aug. 31, 2000 amalg.)
Nov. 2, 2005 – Acquired by TKE Energy Trust (renamed True Energy Trust) with True Energy Inc. the deemed acquiror. Concurrently, True Energy's exploration assets were spun out in the form of a new co., Vero Energy Inc., and True Energy amalgamated with TKE Energy Inc. (wholly owned by TKE Energy Trust) to form a new wholly owned co. with same name True Energy Inc. True Energy shldrs. received 0.5 pre-consolidated TKE trust units, 0.1 Vero Energy shs. and 1 Vero Energy wt. for 1 True Energy sh. held. (see True Energy Trust; Vero Energy Inc.)

True Energy Trust (Alta. Sept. 27, 2004)
Nov. 5, 2009 – Converted into a corp. by way of plan of arrangement whereby all assets and liabilities were transferred to newly formed publicly listed Bellatrix Exploration Ltd.; basis 1 Bellatrix sh. for 1 True Energy trust unit. Wholly owned subsid. True Energy Inc. exch. shldrs. received 1.06272 Bellatrix shs. for 1 True Energy exch. sh. Subsequently, trust dissolved. (see Bellatrix Exploration Ltd.)

True Exploration Corporation (B.C. Apr. 12, 1996)
Oct. 1, 1998 – Formed CompuSoft Canada Inc. in Alberta pursuant to Qualifying Transaction reverse takeover acquisition of and amalgamation with CompuSoft (Canada) Inc.; basis 1.6666664 new for 1 CompuSoft sh. and 1 new for 1 True sh. ■

True Gold Mining Inc. (B.C. Oct. 2, 1987)
Apr. 28, 2016 – Acquired by Endeavour Mining Corporation; basis 0.044 Endeavour com. shs. for 1 True com. sh. (see Endeavour Mining Corporation)

True Grit Resources Ltd. (B.C. May 20, 1988)
Sept. 18, 2020 – Name changed to Cyon Exploration Ltd.; basis 1 new for 6 old shs. ■

True Leaf Brands Inc. (B.C. June 9, 2014)
Oct. 29, 2021 – Name changed to Maven Brands Inc. (see FPsurvey - Industrials)

True Leaf Medicine International Ltd. (B.C. June 9, 2014)
May 27, 2019 – Name changed to True Leaf Brands Inc. ■

True North Apartment Real Estate Investment Trust (Ont. May 1, 2012)
Nov. 5, 2015 – Acquired by Northview Apartment Real Estate Investment Trust (formerly Northern Property Real Estate Investment Trust); basis 0.3908 Northview tr. units for 1 True North tr. unit. (see Northview Apartment Real Estate Investment Trust)

True North Corporation (Alta. May 29, 2000)
Nov. 30, 2007 – Name changed to Empirical Inc. ■

True North Film and Video Productions Inc. (B.C. June 12, 1985)
Nov. 15, 1996 – Dissolved and struck off register.

True North Gems Inc. (Yuk. May 25, 2001)
Feb. 8, 2019 – Continued into British Columbia.
Aug. 16, 2024 – Name changed to TGX Energy & Resources Inc. (see FPsurvey - Mines & Energy)

True North Water Corporation (Alta. Sept. 25, 1985)
Dec. 12, 2003 – Continued into Canada.
Mar. 19, 2004 – Name changed to Watertowne International Inc. following acquisition of Watertowne Bottling Co. Ltd. ■

True-Test Oil and Gas Company Limited (Ont. 1953)
Apr. 1, 1965 – Dissolved.

True Zone Resources Inc. (B.C. Apr. 26, 2007)
Oct. 11, 2016 – Dissolved and struck from register.

Trueborn Gold Mines Ltd. (Ont. 1945)
1960 – Charter cancelled.

Trueclaim Exploration Inc. (B.C. May 17, 2006)
Oct. 24, 2019 – Name changed to New Wave Esports Corp. pursuant to the reverse takeover acquisition of (old) New Wave Esports Corp. (renamed New Wave (BC) Holdings Corp.) and concurrent amalgamation of (old) New Wave with wholly owned 1205619 B.C. Ltd.; basis 1 new for 1.5 old shs. ■

TrueContext Corporation (Ont. May 22, 2007)
May 17, 2024 – Acquired by Battery Ventures L.P.; basis Cdn$1.07 cash per sh. ■

TrueContext Mobile Solutions Corporation (Ont. May 22, 2007)
June 19, 2013 – Name changed to ProntoForms Corporation. ■

TrueStar Petroleum Corporation (B.C. Mar. 9, 1987)
Oct. 19, 2009 – Dissolved and struck from register.
Mar. 5, 2010 – Restored to register.
Aug. 23, 2016 – Dissolved and struck from register.

Trumark Resource Corp. (B.C. Feb. 22, 1984)
Aug. 27, 1991 – Name changed to Tessa Ventures Ltd.; basis 1 new for 4 old shs. ■

Trump Reserve Minerals Ltd. (Ont. June 3, 1985)
Feb. 16, 1993 – Name changed to TR Minerals Ltd.; basis 1 new for 4 old shs. ■

Trumpeter Mines Ltd. (B.C. 1967)
Sept. 28, 1977 – Name changed to Loredi Resources Ltd. ■

Trumpeter Yukon Gold Inc. (Yuk. Apr. 12, 1996)
Dec. 1, 2000 – Amalgamated with Omni Resources Inc. (0.2257 for 1) to form a new company known as Tagish Lake Gold Corp.; basis 0.1353 new Tagish com. sh. for either 1 old cl. A sub. vtg. sh. or 1 old cl. B mult. vtg. sh. (see Tagish Lake Gold Corp.)

Truscan Realty Limited (Can. May 29, 1972)
June 30, 1995 – All o/s 7.75% cum. redeem. retract. pref. ser. I shs. redeemed for $26.45 per sh. plus accr. and unpaid divds.

Trust Général du Canada (Que. Dec. 16, 1970 amalg.)
1986 – Com. stk. exchanged for com. stk. of General Trustco of Canada Inc. on sh.-for-sh. basis.

Trust générale du Canada (Que. 1909)
Dec. 16, 1970 – Formed Trust Général du Canada in Quebec on amalgamation with Administration and Trust Co.; basis 5 new com. shs. for 3 old pref. shs., old com. shs. redeemed at par and cancelled. ■

Trusted Brand 2016 Inc. (Alta. Mar. 4, 2016)
Nov. 20, 2020 – Name changed to Yorkton Equity Group Inc. pursuant to Qualifying Transaction reverse takeover acquisition of 1421526 Alberta Ltd. (see FPsurvey - Industrials)

TrustMark Auto Group, Inc. (B.C. Apr. 13, 2006)
June 23, 2011 – Name changed to Keymark Resources Inc.; basis 1 new for 10 old shs. ■

Try-Mac Golds, Ltd. (Ont. 1936)
1957 – Charter cancelled.

Trylox Environmental Corporation (B.C. June 1, 1982 amalg.)
Sept. 14, 1990 – Continued into Wyoming.

Tu-Tahl Inc. (B.C. Jan. 28, 1981)
Mar. 26, 1984 – Name changed to Tu-Tahl Petro Inc. ■

Tu-Tahl Petro Inc. (B.C. Jan. 28, 1981)
May 10, 1990 – Name changed to Creator Capital Incorporated. ■

Tuc Metals Mines Ltd. (Ont. 1954)
Dec. 1959 – Dissolved.

Tucan Ventures Inc. (B.C. Sept. 21, 1987)
Oct. 15, 1996 – Name changed to Sandhurst Resources Limited. ■

Tuckahoe Financial Corporation (Ont. 1985)
Oct. 6, 1992 – Name changed to Merchant Private Limited. ■

Tuckahoe Gold Mines Ltd. (Ont. 1945)
Feb. 1958 – Charter cancelled.

Tuckamore Capital Management Inc. (Ont. Feb. 18, 2011)
Oct. 13, 2016 – Name changed to ClearStream Energy Services Inc. ■

Tuckett Tobacco Company, Ltd. (Can. 1912)
Nov. 1956 – All pref. stock acquired by Imperial Tobacco Company of Canada Limited at $155 per sh., under an offer made. Imperial previously acquired all the o/s com. shs. in May 1930; basis 30 new Imperial shs. for 1 old Tuckett sh.

Tuco Energy Corporation (B.C. June 3, 1988)
Jan. 7, 1994 – Dissolved and struck off register.

Tucson Acquisition Corporation (Alta. Dec. 20, 2011)
Dec. 31, 2012 – Formed Nouveau Monde Mining Enterprises Inc. in Canada pursuant to Qualifying Transaction reverse takeover acquisition of and amalgamation with Enterprises minières du Nouveau-Monde Inc. ■

Tucson Capital Corp. (Alta. Mar. 23, 1992)
Aug. 12, 1997 – Name changed to First Step Incorporated following amalgamation with First Step International Ltd.; basis 1 new for 1 old sh. ■

Tud Cobalt Mines Ltd. (Ont. 1952)
Aug. 26, 1965 – Dissolved.

Tudex Petroleums Ltd. (Alta. 1980)
July 20, 1983 – Amalgamated with Tudor Hydrocarbons Ltd. to form Tudor Energy Corporation Ltd.

Tudor Corporation Ltd. (Alta. July 20, 1983 amalg.)
July 2, 2018 – Struck from registry and dissolved.

Tudor Energy Corporation Ltd. (Alta. July 20, 1983 amalg.)
May 9, 1986 – Name changed to Tudor Corporation Ltd. ■

Tudor Hydrocarbons Ltd. (Alta. 1980)
July 20, 1983 – Formed Tudor Energy Corporation Ltd. in Alberta on amalgamation with Tudex Petroleums Ltd. ■

Tudor Mining Corporation Ltd. (Ont. 1964)
1967 – Acquired by Dynacore Enterprises Ltd.; basis 1 new for 25 old shs. (see Dynacore Enterprises Ltd.)

Tugold Resources Inc. (B.C. Feb. 15, 1985 amalg.)
Dec. 28, 1988 – Name changed to Gold Power Resources Corp.; basis 1 new for 3 old shs. ■

Tulane Capital Corp. (B.C. Feb. 20, 2002)
May 22, 2003 – Formed Fibre-Crown Manufacturing Inc. in British Columbia following Qualifying Transaction reverse takeover acquisition of and amalgamation with Fibre-Crown Manufacturing Inc. and was considered a recapitalization of Tulane. (see FPsurvey - Industrials)

Tullaree Capital Inc. (B.C. Jan. 13, 1981)
Nov. 21, 2000 – Continued into Yukon.
Dec. 2, 2003 – Name changed to Valucap Investments Inc.; basis 1 new for 15 old shs. ■

Tullaree Resources Ltd. (B.C. Jan. 13, 1981)
Nov. 9, 2000 – Name changed to Tullaree Capital Inc. ■

Tulloch Resources Inc. (B.C. 1984)
Oct. 1, 1992 – Name changed to Eyetel Technologies, Inc. ■

Tulloch Resources Ltd. (B.C. Mar. 12, 1980)
July 18, 2017 – Name changed to Tidal Royalty Corp. ■

Tulox Resources Inc. (B.C. May 12, 1999)
Aug. 11, 2011 – Formed Argentium Resources Inc. in Canada on amalgamation with (old) Argentium Resources Inc. constituting a reverse takeover acquisition of Argentium; basis 1 new for 6 old shs. ■

Tulsa Crude Oil Corporation (B.C. June 15, 1979)
Jan. 28, 1982 – Name changed to Perkins Oil Limited. ■

Tumac Mining & Development Co. (Ont. 1957)
Sept. 16, 1965 – Charter cancelled.

Tumi Resources Limited (B.C. Jan. 11, 2000)
July 6, 2015 – Name changed to Kingsmen Resources Ltd. (see FPsurvey - Mines & Energy)

Tundra Environmental Corporation Limited (Alta. Jan. 16, 1992)
Dec. 16, 1994 – Continued into Ontario.
Jan. 22, 2007 – Certificate of incorporation cancelled and dissolved.

Tundra Gold Mines Ltd. (Ont. 1947)
1982 – Continued into British Columbia.
Oct. 22, 2012 – Dissolved and struck from register.

Tundra Mines Ltd. (Ont. 1941)
1956 – Charter cancelled.

Tundra Semiconductor Corporation (Can. Dec. 12, 1995)
July 2, 2009 – Acquired by Integrated Device Technology, Inc. for $6.25 per sh.

Tungco Resources Corporation (B.C. June 14, 1977)
Aug. 29, 1990 – Name changed to Royal Bay Gold Corporation; basis 1 new for 4 old shs. ■

Tungold Mines Ltd. (Ont. 1940)
1956 – Charter cancelled.

Tungsten Corp. of Canada Ltd. (Ont. Feb. 2, 1951)
1955 – Name changed to Consolidated Tungsten Mining Corp. of Canada Ltd.; basis 1 new for 4 old shs. ■

Tungsten of British Columbia Ltd. (B.C. 1952)
Feb. 12, 1959 – Dissolved.

Tunkwa Copper Mines Ltd. (B.C. 1977)
Nov. 19, 1984 – Formed United Gold Corp. in Ontario on amalgamation with Nugold Enterprises Corporation; basis 1 new for 5 old shs. ■

Tunstall Resources Inc. (B.C. May 13, 1981)
Feb. 24, 1986 – Name changed to Ray-Net Communication Systems Inc. ■

Tupco Mines Ltd. (B.C. 1967)
Dec. 31, 1980 – Dissolved.

Turbo Capital Inc. (B.C. Mar. 28, 2007)
Apr. 12, 2016 – Name changed to Cruz Capital Corp.; basis 1 new for 20 old shs. ■

Turbo Genset Inc. (Alta. Mar. 23, 1987)
Nov. 8, 2004 – Continued into Yukon.
June 27, 2006 – Name changed to Turbo Power Systems Inc. (see FPsurvey - Industrials)

Turbo Resources Limited (Alta. Dec. 24, 1947)
Nov. 8, 1990 – Name changed to Canadian Turbo Inc.; basis 1 new for 10 old shs. ■

Turbodyne Technologies Inc. (B.C. May 18, 1983)
Dec. 3, 1996 – Continued into Canada.
July 24, 1998 – Continued into Delaware.

Turismo Industries Ltd. (B.C. Feb. 1, 1966)
June 30, 1978 – Name changed to General Energy Corp.; basis 1 new for 4 old shs. ■

Turmalina Metals Corp. (B.C. Mar. 21, 2017)
Mar. 11, 2025 – Name changed to King Copper Discovery Corp. (see FPsurvey - Mines & Energy)

Turnberry Resources Ltd. (B.C. Jan. 14, 2011)
Apr. 17, 2014 – Name changed to Anthem United Inc. following reverse takeover acquisition of (old) Anthem United Inc. ■

Turnbull Elevator Ltd. (Can. 1945)
June 1968 – Name changed to Combined Engineered Products Ltd. ■

Turner Basin Oil Co., Ltd. (Can. Apr. 2, 1929)
No longer operating.

Turner Energy & Resources Ltd. (B.C. Sept. 27, 1978)
Aug. 16, 1989 – Name changed to Golden Arch Resources Ltd.; basis 1 new for 5 old shs. ■

Turner-Hindmarsh Tungsten Limited (B.C. June 14, 1977)
Apr. 20, 1978 – Name changed to Tungco Resources Corporation. ■

Turner Research Inc. (Can. July 22, 1992)
Sept. 28, 1993 – Name changed to AgroCultures Biotechnologies Inc. ■

Turner-Tungsten Limited (B.C. June 14, 1977)
June 6, 1977 – Name changed to Turner-Hindmarsh Tungsten Limited. ■

Turner Valley Financial Ltd. (Alta. July 10, 1980 amalg.)
July 5, 1983 – Name changed to Financial Trustco Capital Limited; basis 1 new com. for 3 old com. shs., and 1.65 new com. for 1 pfce. sh. ■

Turner Valley Holdings Ltd. (Alta. 1914)
July 10, 1980 – Amalgamated with its parent co., South Hampton Properties Ltd., to continue as Turner Valley Holdings Ltd.; basis 1 com. sh. for 1 com. sh. or 1 new redeem. jr. pref. sh. for 2 com. shs.

Turner Valley Holdings Ltd. (Alta. 1914)
July 10, 1980 – Amalgamated in Alberta to continue with same name.
1981 – Name changed to Turner Valley Financial Ltd. ■

Turner Valley Oil Company Ltd. (Alta. 1914)
1973 – Name changed to Turner Valley Holdings Ltd. following redemption of pref. shs. ■

Turnkey E & P Inc. (Alta. Dec. 10, 2004)
Mar. 28, 2016 – Struck from registry and dissolved.

Turno Cadillac Gold Mines Ltd. (Ont. 1936)
1953 – Charter cancelled.

Turquoise Capital Corp. (B.C. Nov. 14, 2012)
Apr. 13, 2017 – Name changed to Five Star Diamonds Limited pursuant to Qualifying Transaction reverse takeover acquisition of (old) Five Star Diamonds Ltd. ■

Turquoise Hill Resources Ltd. (Yuk. Feb. 25, 1995)
Dec. 20, 2022 – All o/s com. shs not already held acquired by Rio Tinto plc; basis Cdn$43.00 cash per sh.

Turzone Explorations Ltd. (Ont. 1959)
Dec. 12, 1978 – Amalgamated with 2 other cos. to form Junction Explorations Ltd.; basis 1 sh. Junction for 6 shs. Turzone. (see Junction Explorations Ltd.)

Tuscaloosa Oil & Gas Inc. (B.C. 1981)
Jan. 13, 1985 – Amalgamated with 4 other cos. to form Aurex Resources Inc.; basis 1 new for 3.5 old shs.

Tuscany Energy Ltd. (Alta. Nov. 7, 1994)
June 29, 2016 – Filed voluntary assignment into receivership. Grant Thornton Limited was appointed receiver and all officers and directors resigned.
Oct. 2016 – Oil and gas assets were sold. Secured creditors were paid in full. No distrib. to be made to shldrs.
Mar. 2017 – Grant Thornton was discharged as receiver.

Tuscany International Drilling Inc. (Alta. Apr. 6, 2004)
Feb. 2, 2014 – Company and wholly owned Tuscany International Holdings (U.S.A.) Ltd. filed for protection under Chapter 11 of the U.S. Bankruptcy Code.
Feb. 4, 2014 – Proceedings commenced under the Companies' Creditors Arrangement Act.
June 10, 2014 – Reorganization of the company and Tuscany International Holdings (U.S.A.) Ltd. pursuant to Chapter 11 of U.S. bankruptcy code was completed and assets were sold the secured lenders. All officers and directors have resigned and FTI Consulting Canada Inc. was appointed plan administrator. The company has filed articles of amendment to permit it to redeem all issued and o/s com. shs. for nominal value.
July 25, 2014 – All o/s com. shs. redeemed for US$0.00001 cash per sh.
Oct. 2, 2017 – Dissolved and struck from register.

Tuscany Resources Ltd. (Alta. Nov. 7, 1994)
Sept. 24, 1998 – Name changed to Tuscany Energy Ltd.; basis 1 new for 5 old shs. ■

Tustin Mines Ltd. (Ont. 1955)
July 1, 1963 – Dissolved.

Tut Enterprises Inc. (B.C. 1980)
June 3, 1991 – Name changed to Simmonds Communications Ltd.; basis 1 new for 10 old shs. ■

Tut Explorations Inc. (B.C. 1980)
July 8, 1982 – Name changed to Tut Enterprises Inc. ■

Tuxedo Resources Ltd. (B.C. Mar. 31, 1988)
Apr. 21, 2004 – Name changed to Signature Resources Ltd.; basis 1 new for 2 old shs. ■

Tweed Marijuana Inc. (Can. Aug. 5, 2009)
Sept. 17, 2015 – Name changed to Canopy Growth Corporation. (see FPsurvey - Industrials)

20th Century Energy Corp. (B.C. Jan. 30, 1978)
Mar. 4, 1992 – Delisted from the Vancouver Stock Exchange. Subsequently struck from register and dissolved.

Twentieth Century Explorations Inc. (Ont. Feb. 4, 1975)
May 10, 1979 – Name changed to Minefinders Corporation Ltd.; basis 1 new for 5 old shs. ■

Twentieth Century Explorations Ltd. (Ont. 1969)
Feb. 4, 1975 – Name changed to Twentieth Century Explorations Inc. and continued into Ontario; basis 1 new for 1 old sh. ■

Twentieth Century Mining Co. Ltd. (Ont. 1959)
1969 – Assets sold to Twentieth Century Explorations Ltd.; basis 1 new for 5 old shs. ■

Twenty-Seven Capital Corp. (Can. July 22, 2004)
Feb. 22, 2007 – Acquired by Mega Uranium Ltd.; basis 1 new Mega sh. for 3 old Twenty-Seven shs.

26 Broadway Capital Corp. (B.C. July 26, 2007)
June 29, 2009 – Acquired 8,800,000 com. shs. of Nova Uranium Corp. at 5¢ per sh. which constituted 26 Broadway's Qualifying Transaction. Nova shs. were distributed to 26 Broadway's shldrs. on a pro rata basis. Subsequently wound up. (see Nova Uranium Corporation)

20-20 Technologies Inc. (Que. Sept. 30, 1987)
Sept. 18, 2012 – Acquired by Vector Capital Corporation for Cdn$4.00 per sh.

20/20 Financial Corporation (Ont. 1993)
Jan. 12, 1996 – Acquired by AGF Management Limited; basis either $14.25 or $11.25 plus 0.225 AGF cl. B non-vtg. pref. shs. for 1 20/20 com. sh.

Twenty20 Investments Inc. (Alta. June 7, 1996)
Nov. 26, 2021 – Name changed to Legible Inc. pursuant to the reverse takeover acquisition of Legible Media Inc. (see FPsurvey - Industrials)

Twin Basin Nickel Ltd. (Ont. 1956)
Oct. 22, 1962 – Dissolved.

Twin Bay Mining & Exploration Ltd. (Alta. 1953)
Dec. 1961 – Dissolved.

Twin Bay Uranium Ltd. (Alta. 1953)
1956 – Name changed to Twin Bay Mining & Exploration Ltd. ■

Twin Butte Energy Ltd. (Alta. May 31, 1997 amalg.)
Sept. 1, 2016 – Placed into receivership. FTI Consulting Canada Inc. appointed receiver and all officers and directors resigned.
Mar. 30, 2017 – All assets were sold to West Lake Energy Corp.

Twin Buttes Exploration Inc. (Can. Dec. 29, 1982)
June 28, 1988 – Name changed to Transglobal Business News Network Inc. ■

Twin City Gas Company Limited (Ont. 1954)
Jan. 1, 1968 – Amalgamated into Northern and Central Gas Corporation Limited; basis 5 com. shs. Northern for each 4 shs. Twin City.

Twin Eagle Resources Inc. (B.C. Mar. 20, 1981 amalg.)
May 17, 1993 – Name changed to Cordal Resources Ltd.; basis 1 new for 4 old shs. ■

Twin Energy Ltd. (Alta. 1987)
Nov. 17, 1988 – Amalgamated with Pinnacle Resources Ltd.; basis 1 Pinnacle com. sh. for 0.86 Twin shs. and 1 Pinnacle cl. B sh. for 1 Twin pref. sh. (see Pinnacle Resources Ltd.)

Twin Falls Mining Co. Ltd. (B.C. 1950)
Dec. 1960 – Dissolved.

Twin Fault Mines Ltd. (Ont. 1945)
Dec. 20, 1956 – Charter cancelled.

Twin Glacier Resources Ltd. (B.C. Mar. 22, 2010)
Jan. 30, 2012 – Formed Dolly Varden Silver Corporation in British Columbia pursuant to reverse takeover acquisition of and amalgamation with Dolly Varden Silver Ltd. (see FPsurvey - Mines & Energy)

Twin Gold Corporation (B.C. Mar. 6, 1985)
Mar. 15, 2000 – Continued into Ontario.
May 31, 2000 – Name changed to Twin Mining Corporation. ■

Twin Gold Mines Ltd. (Ont. Feb. 9, 1945)
Feb. 28, 1992 – Delisted from the Alberta Stock Exchange. Subsequently dissolved and charter cancelled.

The Twin "J" Mines Ltd. (B.C. 1942)
1948 – Assets sold to Vancouver Island Base Metals Ltd.; basis 1 new for 10 old shs.

Twin Mining Corporation (Ont. Mar. 15, 2000)
Mar. 28, 2007 – Name changed to Atlanta Gold Inc.; basis 1 new for 15 old shs. (see FPsurvey - Mines & Energy)

Twin Mountain Uranium Mines Ltd. (Que. 1954)
Feb. 6, 1982 – Charter cancelled.

Twin Oils Ltd. (Alta. 1966)
1969 – Acquired by Twin Richfield Oils Ltd. for 750,000 shs. (see Twin Richfield Oils Ltd.)

Twin Peak Mines Ltd. (B.C. 1970)
Dec. 11, 1972 – Formed Twin Peak Resources Ltd. in British Columbia on amalgamation with Whitesail Mines Ltd. ■

Twin Peak Resources Ltd. (B.C. Dec. 11, 1972 amalg.)
July 15, 1991 – Charter cancelled Apr. 19, 1984; revived.

Twin Richfield Oils Ltd. (Can. Mar. 1, 1929; via Dominion charter)
May 2, 2002 – Dissolved.

Twin River Petroleums (Alberta) Ltd. (Alta. 1952)
1958 – Struck off register.

Twin River Petroleums Ltd. (B.C. Mar. 1937)
1952 – Continued into Alberta.
Struck off register.

Twin River Resources Ltd. (B.C. 1972)
Aug. 26, 1974 – Name changed to T.R.V. Minerals Corporation; basis 1 new for 3 old shs. ■

Twin Star Energy Corporation (Ont. June 17, 1985)
Nov. 14, 1995 – Name changed to Blue Power Energy Corporation; basis 1 new for 4 old shs. ■

Twin Star Minerals Ltd. (B.C. May 1, 1996)
Aug. 7, 1998 – Name changed to American Copper Corp. and continued into Yukon. ■

Twin Tires Systems Inc. (B.C. 1980)
Nov. 3, 1995 – Dissolved and struck off register.

Twin Valley Oil Co. Ltd. (Alta. 1940)
1941 – Wound up and assets transferred to Twin Valley Oil Royalties; 1% net royalty unit in Nos. 1 & 2 wells for 20,000 shs. Liquidator - Crown Trust Co., Calgary.

Twindyke Mines Ltd. (Ont. 1938)
Feb. 25, 1965 – Charter cancelled.

Two-In-One Gold Mines, Ltd. (Ont. Apr. 7, 1921)
1938 – Name changed to Troup Porcupine Mines Ltd.; basis 3 new for 20 old shs. ■

Two Macks' Long Lac Gold Mines Ltd. (Ont. 1947)
Nov. 30, 1964 – Dissolved.

Two Owls Ventures Corp. (B.C. Aug. 16, 2017)
May 3, 2019 – Name changed to Minerva Intelligence Inc. pursuant to the Qualifying Transaction reverse takeover acquisition of (old) Minerva Intelligence Inc.; basis 1 new for 2 old shs. ■

2001 Resource Industries Ltd. (B.C. 1982)
July 22, 1994 – Dissolved and struck off register.

2018 Investments Ltd. (B.C. May 17, 1979)
Oct. 9, 1987 – Dissolved and struck off register.

213466 Holdings Ltd. (Alta. 1979)
Mar. 19, 1979 – Name changed to Meridian Resources Ltd. ■

21C Metals Inc. (B.C. Aug. 26, 2005)
Jan. 20, 2020 – Name changed to Canadian Palladium Resources Inc. ■

22 Capital Corp. (Ont. Jan. 4, 2017)
Oct. 10, 2019 – Formed Trichome Financial Corp. in Ontario pursuant to the Qualifying Transaction amalgamation with Trichome Financial Corp. constituting a reverse takeover by Trichome.; basis 0.0702 new for 1 old sh. ■

2242749 Ontario Limited (Ont. May 5, 2010)
July 1, 2015 – Filed for bankruptcy and Ernst & Young Inc. was appointed trustee. All officers and directors resigned. No recovery was expected for shldrs. or debenture holders.

228256 Alberta Ltd. (Alta. Dec. 13, 1979)
Mar. 21, 1980 – Name changed to Gane Petroleum Corporation Ltd. ■

232217 Alberta Ltd. (Alta. 1980)
Apr. 8, 1980 – Name changed to GenEnergy Resources Ltd. ■

2560344 Ontario Inc. (Ont. Feb. 8, 2017)
Oct. 25, 2017 – Name changed to Yukoterre Resources Inc. ■

2737469 Canada Inc. (Can. July 25, 1991)
Oct. 25, 2011 – Subsidiary Canwest Media Inc. made an assignment in bankruptcy; FTI Consulting Canada Inc. appointed trustee.
May 27, 2013 – Dissolved and struck from register.
Mar. 10, 2014 – In April 2012, distributions of $28,942,679.75 were made to ordinary creditors and $4,231,910.32 to 271 former employees. In August 2013, distributions of $3,720,632.86 were made to ordinary creditors. In December 2013, distributions of $536,462.80 were made to former employees. In March 2014, final distribution of $65,000 made as part of a union settlement; there will be no further distributions to creditors or shldrs.
Apr. 14, 2014 – CCAA proceedings were terminated and FTI Consulting was discharged as monitor.

2798832 Ontario Inc. (Ont. Dec. 9, 2020)
Feb. 3, 2021 – Name changed to Metamaterial Exchangeco Inc. (see FPsurvey - Industrials)

280 Broadway Holding Corp. (Man. 1940)
Dec. 1986 – Amalgamated into Power Financial Corporation. Cl. A and common shs. exchanged on basis of 6.5 new for 1 cl. A or common sh. held. Each 5% 1969 series pref. sh. exchanged for 1 new 5% 1969 pref. shs. of the amalg. co.

2907160 Canada Inc. (Can. Mar. 25, 1993)
Jan. 14, 2014 – Dissolved by court order.

Twoco Petroleums Ltd. (Alta. Sept. 21, 2000)
Feb. 28, 2013 – Placed into receivership. PricewaterhouseCoopers Inc. appointed receiver.

2M Energy Corp. (Ont. Mar. 29, 1999)
Jan. 30, 2001 – Acquired by Middlefield Bancorp Limited for $1.15 per sh. (see Middlefield Bancorp Limited)

222 Pizza Express Corp. (B.C. Oct. 20, 1999)
May 1, 2008 – Name changed to Kadywood Capital Corp. ■

Tyche Long Lac Gold Mines Ltd. (Can. Sept. 21, 1933)
Nov. 25, 1948 – Charter cancelled; assets distributed to shldrs. at rate of 1¢ for 30 shs., fractions disregarded.

Tycoon Ventures Inc. (B.C. Sept. 6, 1985)
Sept. 5, 1995 – Name changed to Paloma Ventures Inc.; basis 1 new for 3 old shs. ■

Tyee Lake Resources Ltd. (B.C. June 25, 1969)
Mar. 26, 1980 – Name changed to New Tyee Resources Ltd.; basis 1 new for 3 old shs. ■

Tyee Petroleums Ltd. (unknown)
In liquidation.

Tygas Energy Inc. (Alta. 1983)
1988 – Formed Tygas Resource Corporation on amalgamation with MSA Petroleum Ltd. (1 for 2); basis 1 new for 4.536 old cl. A shs. ■

Tygas Industries Ltd. (Alta. 1983)
July 1988 – Name changed to Tygas Energy Inc.; basis 2 new for 5 old shs. ■

Tygas Resource Corporation (Alta. Dec. 31, 1988 amalg.)
Sept. 19, 1990 – Acquired by ALBERTA Oil & Gas Limited; basis 6 new for 1 old sh. (see ALBERTA Oil and Gas Limited)

Tyhee Development Corp. (B.C. Mar. 3, 1993)
Feb. 1, 2011 – Name changed to Tyhee Gold Corp. ■

Tyhee Gold Corp. (B.C. Mar. 3, 1993)
Aug. 1, 2017 – Filed assignment into bankruptcy and The Bowra Group Inc. appointed trustee.

Tyler Resources Inc. (B.C. Aug. 5, 1980)
Apr. 6, 1995 – Continued into Alberta.
Mar. 14, 2008 – Acquired by Canada Jinchuan Resources Ltd. for $1.60 per sh.

Tylox Resource Corporation (B.C. Feb. 8, 1982)
Dec. 2, 1991 – Name changed to Tracer Petroleum Corporation. ■

Tymar Resources Inc. (B.C. Nov. 9, 1989 amalg.)
Jan. 25, 1993 – Name changed to Baja Gold, Inc. following acquisition of Baja Gold, Inc.; basis 1 new for 10 old shs. ■

Tymbal Resources Ltd. (B.C. June 10, 1980)
Apr. 30, 2024 – Name changed to New Tymbal Resources Ltd.; basis 1 new for 3 old shs. (see FPsurvey - Mines & Energy)

Tyme Resources Ltd. (B.C. 1988)
Nov. 4, 1991 – Name changed to North American Tire Recycling Ltd.; basis 1 new for 4 old shs. ■

Tyndall Explorations Ltd. (Ont. 1960)
Mar. 1967 – Charter cancelled.

Tyner Mining Corporation (Alta. Aug. 21, 1985)
Nov. 4, 1987 – Name changed to Delmay Mining Corporation; basis 1 new for 2 old shs. ■

Tyon Gold Mines Ltd. (Ont. 1944)
Nov. 19, 1956 – Charter cancelled.

Typhon Industries Limited (Ont. Apr. 12, 1983)
May 27, 1996 – Name changed to North American Health and Fitness Corp.; basis 1 new for 10 old shs. ■

Typhon Resources Corp. (Ont. Apr. 12, 1983)
Jan. 19, 1990 – Name changed to Typhon Industries Limited. ■

Typhoon Exploration Inc. (Can. Aug. 13, 1998)
Sept. 22, 2021 – Name changed to Goldflare Exploration Inc. (see FPsurvey - Mines & Energy)

Typhoon Venture Capital Corporation (Can. Aug. 13, 1998)
Feb. 6, 2003 – Name changed to Typhoon Exploration Inc. following Qualifying Transaction acquisition of Black Riverside Venture Capital Inc. ■

Typhoon Yellowknife Mines Ltd. (Ont. 1946)
Nov. 1968 – Charter cancelled.

Tyr-Mac Gold Mines Ltd. (Ont. 1936)
1957 – Charter cancelled; assets acquired by Tyr-Mac Golds Ltd. in 1936; basis 5 new for 1 old sh.

Tyrae Resources Inc. (Alta. 1983)
Sept. 4, 1990 – Name changed to North American Gold Corporation. ■

Tyranex Gold Inc. (Ont. Nov. 17, 1986)
Aug. 25, 1999 – Formed Dotcom 2000 Inc. in Ontario on amalgamation with Dotcom 2000 Inc. (deemed acquiror); basis 1 new for 1 Dotcom sh. and 1 new for 5 Tyranex shs. ■

Tyranite Granite & Marble Inc. (Ont. Sept. 23, 1935)
Nov. 17, 1994 – Name changed to Footmaxx Holdings Inc. ■

Tyranite Mines, Limited (Ont. Sept. 23, 1935)
Sept. 17, 1992 – Name changed to Tyranite Granite & Marble Inc.; basis 1 new for 10 old shs. ■

Tyrona Resources Ltd. (B.C. 1968)
Dec. 17, 1982 – Formed Signal Hill Energy Corporation in British Columbia on amalgamation with Shield Petroleum Corp.; basis 1 new for 4 old shs. ■

Tyson Financial Corp. (B.C. Aug. 25, 1970)
June 1, 1992 – Name changed to Midd Financial Corp.; basis 1 new for 5 old shs. ■

U

U-Can-Brew Corporation (Ont. Aug. 21, 1992)
Oct. 21, 1993 – Name changed to Brew Kettle Corporation following Major Transaction acquisition of The Brew Kettle Ltd. ■

U-Pak Shipping Containers Inc. (Alta. June 7, 1987)
Oct. 25, 1996 – Name changed to Citation Resources Inc. and continued into British Columbia following acquisition of Rand Edgar Capital Corp.; basis 1 new for 1 old sh. ■

U-Pak Shipping Systems Inc. (Alta. June 7, 1987)
Apr. 1, 1991 – Name changed to U-Pak Shipping Containers Inc. following amalgamation with wholly owned U-Pak Containers Inc.; basis 1 new for 3 old shs. ■

U. R. Mines Ltd. (Ont. 1951)
Charter cancelled.

U-Save Foods Ltd. (B.C. 1985)
Apr. 25, 1989 – Name changed to USV International Investment Corporation; basis 4 new for 1 old sh. ■

U3O8 Corp. (Ont. Dec. 6, 2005)
Oct. 18, 2022 – Name changed to Green Shift Commodities Ltd. (see FPsurvey - Mines & Energy)

UAP Inc. (Que. Dec. 29, 1961 amalg.)
Dec. 11, 1998 – Acquired by Genuine Parts Acquisition Inc., a wholly owned indirect subsid. of Genuine Parts Company, for $28.50 per sh.

UBI Resources Inc. (Ont. 1945)
Oct. 1, 1994 – Dissolved and struck off register.

UBS Global Allocation Trust (Ont. Feb. 26, 2004)
Feb. 1, 2014 – Converted to an open-ended mutual fund as UBS (Canada) Global Tactical Allocation ETF Fund.

UBS Total Return Trust (Ont. Dec. 7, 2004)
June 11, 2008 – Amalgamated with UBS Global Allocation Trust (GAT); basis 1.0246995 GAT units for 1 UBS Total unit. (see UBS Global Allocation Trust)

UC Resources Ltd. (B.C. Aug. 30, 1990)
Feb. 11, 2019 – Name changed to Voyager Digital (Canada) Ltd. pursuant to the acquisition of Voyager Digital Holdings, Inc. ■

U.C. Valve Corp. (B.C. Feb. 11, 1981)
Dec. 1, 1989 – Name changed to Blackbridge Capital Corporation. ■

UC'NWIN Systems Corporation (Del. Dec. 11, 1995)
Nov. 5, 1999 – Name changed to Winners Edge.com Inc.

UC'NWIN Systems Ltd. (Can. Apr. 5, 1983)
Dec. 11, 1995 – Continued into Delaware.
Apr. 4, 1996 – Name changed to UC'NWIN Systems Corporation. ■

UE Waterheater Income Fund (Ont. Nov. 7, 2003)
June 28, 2007 – All assets acquired by Alinda Capital Partners LLC; basis $23 per unit.

UEX Corporation (Can. Oct. 2, 2001)
Aug. 22, 2022 – Acquired by Uranium Energy Corp.; basis 0.0831 UEC com. shs. for each UEX com. sh. held, which valued UEX at Cdn$0.43 per sh.

UFC Canadian Growth Fund Inc. (Can. Jan. 11, 1993)
Nov. 13, 1996 – Name changed to Canadian Venture Opportunities Fund Ltd. ■

UFM Ventures Ltd. (B.C. Apr. 21, 1999)
Aug. 3, 2006 – Name changed to Uracan Resources Ltd. ■

UGE International Ltd. (Ont. Mar. 18, 2011)
Aug. 20, 2024 – Acquired by 10000896425 Ontario Ltd., an affiliate of NOVA Infrastructure Fund II, LP; basis Cdn$2.00 cash per sh.

UGL Enterprises Ltd. (B.C. Nov. 6, 1978)
May 29, 2006 – Name changed to Red Hill Energy Inc. ■

UI Capital Inc. (Can. Apr. 6, 2011)
Oct. 4, 2012 – Name changed to Urbanimmersive Technologies Inc. pursuant to Qualifying Transaction reverse takeover acquisition of Urbanimmersive Inc. ■

UKT Recycling Technologies Inc. (B.C. Sept. 26, 1988)
Dec. 4, 2003 – Continued into Canada.
Dec. 8, 2003 – Name changed to Cogent Integrated Solutions Corporation pursuant to reverse takeover acquisition of Cogent Integrated Solutions Inc.; basis 1 new for 3 old shs. ■

ULS Capital Corporation (Ont. Oct. 30, 1978)
Jan. 15, 1992 – Redeemed $2.25 first pref. ser. A shs. for $25 per sh.

UMG Media Ltd. (Alta. Apr. 11, 2018)
Jan. 20, 2020 – Acquired by Torque Esports Corp.; basis 0.0643205 Torque com. shs. for 1 UMG Media sh. (see Torque Esports Corp.)

UNIREX Technologies, Inc. (Wyo. Apr. 19, 2001)
July 19, 2001 – Name changed to UNIREX Corporation; basis 1 new for 5 old shs.

UNP Industries Ltd. (B.C. Mar. 15, 1965)
Nov. 29, 1990 – Name changed to International UNP Holdings Ltd.; basis 1 cl. A and 1 cl. B sh. for 6 com. shs. ■

UNX Energy Corp. (Alta. Sept. 14, 2010)
Apr. 29, 2011 – Acquired by HRT Participações em Petróleo S.A.; basis 0.5579 HRT shs. for 1 UNX sh. (see HRT Participações em Petróleo S.A.)
July 7, 2011 – Name changed to HRT Canada Inc. (see HRT Participações em Petróleo S.A.)

U.R. Flowers Corporation (B.C. Apr. 29, 1983)
Apr. 19, 1996 – Name changed to Redstar Resources Corporation; basis 1 new for 3 old shs. ■

UROHEALTH Systems, Inc. (Del. July 27, 1995)
Oct. 1, 1997 – Name changed to Imagyn Medical Technologies Inc.

URZ Energy Corp. (B.C. Jan. 11, 2008)
July 6, 2018 – Acquired by Azarga Uranium Corp.; basis 2 Azaraga shs. for 1 URZ sh. (see Azarga Uranium Corp.)

U.S. Agency Mortgage-Backed REIT Advantaged Fund (Ont.)
July 4, 2016 – Terminated; basis unknown.

U.S. Ammunition Company Ltd. (B.C. Nov. 30, 1983)
Nov. 21, 1990 – Name changed to Keynote Resources Inc.; basis 1 new for 5 old shs. ■

U.S. Banks Income & Growth Fund (Ont. Oct. 27, 2015)
Jan. 31, 2022 – Terminated. Class T units redeemed for an amount equal to the net asset value per unit.

US Buyback Leaders Fund (Ont. Jan. 1, 2015)
Oct. 24, 2014 – Converted to a exchange-traded fund.

U.S.-Canadian Petroleum Ltd. (Alta.)
1958 – Struck off register.

U.S. Cobalt Inc. (Del. Mar. 10, 2000)
Dec. 22, 2003 – Name changed to U.S. Geothermal Inc. following reverse takeover acquisition of U.S. Geothermal Inc.; basis 1 new for 5 old shs.

US Cobalt Inc. (B.C. Oct. 12, 2006)
June 6, 2018 – Acquired by First Cobalt Corp.; basis 1.5 First Cobalt com. shs. for 1 US Cobalt sh. (see First Cobalt Corp.)

U.S. Diamond Corp. (B.C. 1978)
Jan. 23, 2004 – Dissolved and struck from register.

U.S. Dividend Growers Income Corp. (Ont. Jan. 30, 2015)
July 6, 2017 – Merged into Middlefield U.S. Dividend Growers Class (Mutual Fund); basis 0.78975513 Mutual Fund ser. F shs. for 1 U.S. Dividend sh.

U.S. Financials Income Fund (Ont. Jan. 29, 2015)
July 6, 2021 – Merged into Mulvihill Premium Yield Field; basis 0.58935 Mulvihill cl. F units for 1 U.S. Financial cl. A unit and 0.79067 Mulvihill cl. F units for 1 U.S. Financial cl. U unit.

US Gold Canadian Acquisition Corporation (Alta. Apr. 18, 2006)
May 31, 2012 – All exch. shs. redeemed for McEwen Mining Inc. com. shs. on a sh.-for-sh. basis. (see McEwen Mining Inc.)

U.S. Gold Corporation (Colo. July 24, 1979)
June 21, 2007 – Name changed to US Gold Corporation. ■

US Gold Corporation (Colo. July 24, 1979)
Jan. 24, 2012 – Name changed to McEwen Mining Inc. ■

U.S. Grant Gold Mining Co. Ltd. (B.C. 1981)
Aug. 13, 1990 – Name changed to Atrium Resources Ltd.; basis 1 new for 7 old shs. ■

U.S. Housing Recovery Fund (Ont. Oct. 3, 2012)
Oct. 31, 2017 – Terminated; undisclosed distribution on a pro rata basis based on net asset value of cl. A units and cl. F units made to unithldrs. on Nov. 3, 2017.

U.S. Long Distance Corp. (Del. July 31, 1987)
Sept. 12, 1997 – Name changed to USLD Communications Corp.

U.S. Medical Systems, Inc. (Del. Nov. 17, 1992)
May 6, 2009 – Name changed to Sharps Compliance Corp.

U.S. Oil and Gas Inc. (B.C. Dec. 8, 1977)
Nov. 13, 1997 – Amalgamated with Zeus Energy Corp. to form U.S. Oil and Gas Resources Inc. (see U.S. Oil and Gas Resources Inc.)

U.S. Oil and Gas Resources Inc. (B.C. Nov. 12, 1997 amalg.)
Aug. 26, 2005 – Plan of Arrangement acquisition by Consolidated Odyssey Exploration Inc. (renamed Odyssey Petroleum Corp.); basis 1 new Odyssey sh. for 2 old U.S. Oil shs. (see Odyssey Petroleum Corp.)

US Oil Sands Inc. (B.C. Aug. 24, 1990)
May 9, 2011 – Continued into Alberta.
June 30, 2017 – Voluntarily delisted.
Sept. 14, 2017 – Placed into receivership by ACMO S.a.R.L. and FTI Consulting Canada Inc. appointed receiver.

U.S. Pay-Tel Inc. (B.C. 1983)
July 31, 1987 – Name changed to U.S. Long Distance Corp. and continued into Delaware. ■

U.S. Platinum Inc. (B.C. June 12, 1979)
Jan. 10, 2006 – Name changed to Universal Energy Corporation. ■

U.S. Precious Metals, Inc. (B.C. 1979)
Jan. 24, 1985 – Amalgamated with Baker Gold Ltd. to form new co. with same name U.S. Precious Metals, Inc.
Aug. 23, 1991 – Amalgamated with Centurion Gold Ltd. to form Siskon Gold Corporation; basis 1 new for 0.67 Centurion shs. and 1 new for 1 U.S. Precious Metals sh.

U.S. Silver & Gold Inc. (Ont. June 6, 2012)
Jan. 2, 2015 – Acquired by Scorpio Mining Corporation; basis 1.68 Scorpio com. shs. for 1 U.S. Silver com. sh. (see Scorpio Mining Corporation)

U.S. Silver Corporation (Ont. Mar. 23, 2006)
June 25, 2007 – Continued into Canada.
Aug. 13, 2012 – Succeeded by U.S. Silver & Gold Inc. pursuant to business combination with RX Gold & Silver Inc. with U.S. Silver the deemed acquiror; basis 0.67 U.S. Silver & Gold shs. for 1 U.S. Silver sh. and 0.109 U.S. Silver & Gold shs. for 1 RX Gold sh. ■

U. S. Steel Canada Inc. (Can. June 8, 1910)
Nov. 1, 2007 – Acquired by United States Steel Corporation for $38.50 per sh.
June 30, 2017 – Name changed to Stelco Inc. ■

U.S. Steel Canada Inc. (Can. 1979)
Apr. 30, 1990 – All public interest ceased with the redemption of all o/s 9% pref. shs., series 1; basis $25 per sh.

U.S. Tactical Allocation Fund (Ont.)
Mar. 28, 2016 – Converted from a closed-end to an open-ended fund.

USA REIT Fund LLC (Del. Sept. 4, 2003)
Oct. 26, 2004 – Dissolved and wound up; basis Cdn$9.45 per sh.

USA-Teck Gold Mines Ltd. (Ont. 1938)
Aug. 6, 1957 – Charter cancelled.

USA Tough Inc. (Ont. Dec. 18, 1992 amalg.)
Aug. 6, 1993 – Name changed to First Sports International Inc. ■

USA Video Corporation (Alta. Apr. 18, 1986)
Feb. 21, 1995 – Continued into Wyoming.
Feb. 23, 1995 – Name changed to USA Video Interactive Corp.; basis 1 new for 5 old shs. ■

USA Video Interactive Corp. (Wyo. Feb. 21, 1995)
Jan. 25, 2012 – Name changed to Oculus VisionTech Inc.; basis 1 new for 15 old shs. ■

USMX, Inc. (Colo. Oct. 1979)
Dec. 1987 – Continued into Delaware. (see Dakota Mining Corporation)
June 24, 1997 – Merged into Dakota Mining Corporation; basis 1 Dakota com. sh. for 1.1 USMX com. shs. (see Dakota Mining Corporation)

USV International Investment Corporation (B.C. 1985)
Jan. 1990 – In receivership. Touche Ross Limited of Vancouver, Canada, appointed receiver.
1991 – All assets sold. The creditors suffered a significant shortfall and there was no distribution to shldrs.
Jan. 1, 1992 – Receiver discharged.

USV Telemanagement Inc. (B.C. Dec. 23, 1991)
June 20, 2000 – Name changed to E*Comnetrix Inc. and continued into Canada. ■

UTS Energy Corporation (Can. Oct. 27, 1994)
Oct. 7, 2010 – Acquired by Total S.A., a wholly owned subsid. of Total E&P Canada Ltd.; basis $3.08 plus 0.1 SilverBirch Energy Corporation shs. for 1 UTS Energy Corporation. (see SilverBirch Energy Corporation)

Ubique Minerals Limited (Ont. Sept. 26, 2012)
July 11, 2017 – Continued into British Columbia. (see FPsurvey - Mines & Energy)

Ucana-Whitemud Oil Limited (Alta. May 11, 1950)
Nov. 2, 2002 – Struck from register.
May 5, 2004 – Revived. (see FPsurvey - Mines & Energy)

Uchi Gold Mines Ltd. (Ont. 1937)
1947 – Placed into receivership in 1943. Bondholders paid 45%. No equity for shldrs.

Ucore Uranium Inc. (Alta. Aug. 19, 2005)
June 29, 2010 – Name changed to Ucore Rare Metals Inc. (see FPsurvey - Mines & Energy; FPsurvey - Industrials)

Uddlen Mines Ltd. (Ont. 1951)
Apr. 1956 – Name changed to Aull Metal Mines Ltd. ■

Uganda Gold Mining Ltd. (Alta. Mar. 27, 1996)
July 10, 2006 – Name changed to CanAfrican Metals and Mining Ltd. ■

Ukraine Enterprise Corporation (Ont. Nov. 21, 1994)
May 15, 2002 – Formed Softchoice Corporation in Canada pursuant to amalgamation with Softchoice Corporation (deemed acquiror); basis 1 new for 10 old shs. ■

Uldaman Capital Corp. (B.C. Jan. 16, 2006)
Aug. 10, 2010 – Name changed to Dawson Gold Corp.; basis 1 new for 2 old shs. ■

Ulster Petroleums Ltd. (Alta. Mar. 11, 1963)
Jan. 12, 1970 – Amalgamated with Abidonne Oils Ltd. to form new co. with same name Ulster Petroleums Ltd.; basis 2 new for 3 Abidonne shs. and 1 new for 1 Ulster sh. (see Anderson Exploration Ltd.)
May 24, 2000 – Acquired by Anderson Exploration Ltd.; basis $11 plus 0.09655 Anderson shs. for 1 Ulster sh. (see Anderson Exploration Ltd.)

Ultima Energy Trust (Alta. May 29, 1996)
June 21, 2004 – Acquired by Petrofund Energy Trust; basis 0.442 new Petrofund unit for 1 old Ultima unit. (see Petrofund Energy Trust)

Ultra Capital Inc. (Alta. Nov. 7, 1996)
Jan. 30, 1998 – Name changed to Ag Growth Industries Inc. ■

Ultra Glow Cosmetics Ltd. (B.C. 1982)
Sept. 3, 1999 – Name changed to E-International Fund Management Inc.; basis 1 new for 10 old shs. (see FPsurvey - Industrials)

Ultra Holdings Incorporated (B.C. May 26, 1999)
Oct. 24, 2001 – Plan of Arrangement with Cubix Investments Ltd. and Cubix Acquisitionco whereby Ultra Holdings and Cubix Acquisitionco amalgamated to form a new company wholly owned by Cubix Investments; basis $3.00 plus new company note exchangeable into either $4.00 or 0.5 new Ultra Petroleum Corp. sh. (see Cubix Investments Ltd.)

Ultra Lithium Inc. (B.C. Nov. 27, 2004)
Dec. 2, 2019 – Name changed to Ultra Resources Inc. ■

Ultra Mines & Energy Corp. (Ont. Jan. 8, 1986)
Nov. 14, 1991 – Name changed to Star Group Newspaper Networks Inc.; basis 1 new for 3.5 old shs. ■

Ultra Petroleum Corp. (B.C. Nov. 14, 1979)
Mar. 1, 2000 – Continued into Yukon.
May 19, 2020 – Filed for reorganization under Chapter 11 of the U.S. Bankruptcy Code.
Sept. 14, 2020 – Pursuant to a Plan of Reorganization, all assets were deemed to be contributed to reorganized UP Energy Corporation. All o/s com. shs. were cancelled and were no distrib. made to shldrs.
Oct. 15, 2020 – Dissolved.

Ultra Pure Water Systems (Canada) Inc. (Alta. Sept. 11, 1992)
June 20, 1996 – Delisted from the Alberta Stock Exchange. Subsequently dissolved and struck from register.

Ultra Resources Corp. (B.C. Feb. 2, 1981)
Oct. 22, 2015 – Name changed to Empire Rock Minerals Inc.; basis 1 new for 3 old shs. ■

Ultra Resources Inc. (B.C. Nov. 27, 2004)
Jan. 20, 2022 – Name changed to Ultra Lithium Inc. (see FPsurvey - Mines & Energy)

Ultra-Shawkey Mines Ltd. (Ont. 1945)
1962 – Name changed to Con-Shawkey Gold Mines Ltd.; basis 1 new for 3 old shs. ■

Ultra Uranium Corp. (B.C. Feb. 2, 1981)
Nov. 14, 2012 – Name changed to Ultra Resources Corp.; basis 1 new for 3 old shs. ■

Ultracell Medical Technologies Ltd. (Ont. Jan. 26, 1983)
Nov. 6, 1997 – Name changed to AMT Fine Foods Ltd.; basis 1 new for 10 old shs. ■

Ultramar Capital Corporation (Ont. 1979)
Sept. 25, 1990 – All accrued and unpaid dividends of $0.511209 paid as of following redemption of all the o/s First Preferred Shares, Ser. 1 for $25.50 per sh. All 9.50% exchg. debs. redeemed July 26, 1992; basis $1,000 plus all accrued and unpaid interest for each $1,000 deb. retracted.

Ultramar Company Limited (U.K. May 30, 1935)
Jan. 8, 1982 – Name changed to Ultramar PLC. ■

Ultramar Corporation (Del. Apr. 28, 1992)
Dec. 4, 1996 – Merged with Diamond Shamrock, Inc. (1.02 new for 1 old sh.) to form Ultramar Diamond Shamrock Corp.

Ultramar PLC (U.K. May 30, 1935)
Feb. 27, 1992 – Acquired by LASMO plc; basis 23 LASMO shs. for 20 Ultramar shs. or 1 LASMO sh. and 40 pence for 1 Ultramar sh.

Ultrasonic Industrial Sciences Ltd. (Alta. Sept. 4, 1987)
May 15, 1998 – Name changed to United Industrial Services Ltd. (see FPsurvey - Mines & Energy; FPsurvey - Industrials)

Ultrasonic Systems Incorporated (Del. 1986)
July 11, 1990 – Name changed to E.T. Canada Inc.; basis 1 new for 2 old shs.

UltraVision Corporation (Alta. Sept. 23, 1993)
Sept. 12, 2002 – Filed for bankruptcy. PricewaterhouseCoopers Inc. was appointed trustee.

UltraVision, Inc. (Alta. Sept. 23, 1993)
May 12, 1999 – Name changed to UltraVision Corporation; basis 1 new for 4 old shs. ■

Ultravite Laboratories Limited (Ont. 1960)
Dec. 27, 1967 – Dissolved.

Ultrex Petroleum Ltd. (Alta. 1981)
Apr. 21, 1987 – Name changed to Ultrex Limited following amalgamation with 153589 Canada Inc.; basis 1 new for 4 old shs. (see FPsurvey - Mines & Energy)

The Ulysses Group Ltd. (Alta. Feb. 5, 2001)
Oct. 29, 2002 – Name changed to Semper Energy Ltd. following Qualifying Transaction reverse takeover acquisition of Semper Energy Inc. ■

Ulysses International Resources Ltd. (B.C. July 2, 1986)
Oct. 12, 1995 – Continued into Bermuda.
Mar. 5, 1999 – Name changed to Auric Resources Ltd.; basis 1 new for 2 old shs. ■

Umbertino's Restaurants Inc. (B.C. 1983)
May 28, 1993 – Dissolved and struck off register.

Umberto's Pasta Enterprises Inc. (B.C. 1983)
Nov. 10, 1987 – Name changed to Umbertino's Restaurants Inc. ■

Umbral Energy Corp. (B.C. Oct. 25, 2007)
Jan. 10, 2018 – Name changed to Heritage Cannabis Holdings Corp. ■

Umdoni Exploration Inc. (B.C. Oct. 15, 2014)
Mar. 1, 2024 – Name changed to Zeus North America Mining Corp.; basis 2 new for 1 old sh. (see FPsurvey - Mines & Energy)

Umity Valley Gold Mines Ltd. (B.C. 1945)
1954 – Dissolved.

Unas Investments Limited (Can. 1953)
June 30, 1972 – Amalgamated with Slater, Walker of Canada Ltd. continuing as Slater Walker of Canada Ltd. Basis 2 new for 1 old sh. of Slater and 8 new for 3 shs. of UNAS not already held by Slater.

Unavest Capital Corp. (Can. Dec. 22, 1986 amalg.)
June 8, 1999 – Amalgamated with Genterra Capital Incorporated to form Genterra Investment Corporation; basis 1 new for 1 Genterra Capital sh. and 1 new cl. A subord. vtg. sh. for 14 Unavest Capital cl. A shs. (see Genterra Investment Corporation)

Unbridled Energy Corporation (B.C. Oct. 6, 2003)
Feb. 16, 2010 – Acquired by Altima Resources Ltd. pursuant to plan of arrangement; basis 1 Altima sh. for 1 Unbridled sh. (see Altima Resources Ltd.)

Uncle Ben's Industries Ltd. (B.C. 1965)
1976 – Placed into receivership.
1980 – All operating assets sold. Co. presently inactive.

Underbalanced Drilling Systems Corporation (Alta. Jan. 28, 1992)
Jan. 1, 1999 – Formed Underbalanced Drilling Systems Ltd. on amalgamation with wholly owned subsidiary Underbalanced Drilling Systems Ltd. ■

Underbalanced Drilling Systems Ltd. (Alta. Jan. 28, 1992)
Aug. 17, 1999 – All com. shs. acquired by Precision Drilling Corporation; basis 2.308 new Precision Drilling shs. for 100 old Underbalanced Drilling Systems shs. (or 0.02308 new for 1 old sh.) (see Precision Drilling Corporation)

Undersill Gold Mining Co. Ltd. (Ont. 1944)
1956 – Liquidated. Assets taken over by Leitch Gold Mines Ltd.

Underworld Resources Inc. (B.C. Aug. 12, 2005)
July 7, 2010 – Acquired by Kinross Gold Corporation; basis 0.141 Kinross shs. plus Cdn$0.01 for 1 Underworld sh.

Undur Tolgoi Minerals Inc. (B.C. Nov. 14, 2011 amalg.)
Dec. 18, 2013 – Continued into British Virgin Islands.
Jan. 7, 2014 – Name changed to Khot Infrastructure Holdings, Ltd. ■

Unergie Inc. (Que. 1954)
1985 – Amalgamated into Atlas Yellowknife Resources Ltd.; basis 4 shs. and 2 wts. of Atlas for each 11 shs. of Unergie.

Ungava Bay Mines Ltd. (Ont. 1946)
Aug. 24, 1964 – Dissolved.

Ungava Copper Corp. Ltd. (Que. 1954)
June 23, 1971 – Name changed to New Ungava Copper Corporation Limited; basis 1 new for 4 old shs. ■

Ungava Minerals Corp. (Can. Oct. 15, 1986)
Sept. 7, 2007 – Name changed to Nearctic Nickel Mines Inc. (see FPsurvey - Mines & Energy)

Uni-Globe International Energy Corporation (B.C. 1980)
May 18, 1989 – Declared bankrupt. All assets of value liquidated. Creditors suffered a shortfall, and there was nothing available for shrlders.

Uni-Invest Ltd. (Alta. May 8, 1996)
Jan. 12, 2001 – Name changed to Homburg Invest Inc. ■

Uni-Select Inc. (Que. Nov. 22, 1968; via letters patent)
Aug. 1, 2023 – Acquired by LKQ Corporation; basis Cdn$48 per sh,

Uni-Way Pacific Holdings Ltd. (B.C. Dec. 1, 1980)
Sept. 16, 1993 – Name changed to New Uni-Way Holdings Ltd.; basis 1 new for 5 old shs. ■

Unibroue Inc. (Can. Dec. 3, 1990)
July 5, 2004 – Acquired by Sleeman Breweries Ltd. for $5.25 per sh. (see Sleeman Breweries Ltd.)

Unican Security Systems Ltd. (Can. Nov. 13, 1964; via Dominion charter)
Apr. 17, 2001 – Acquired by USSL Acquisitionco Inc. for $36 per cl. A or cl. B sh.

Unicap Commercial Corp. (Can. Dec. 22, 1986 amalg.)
Oct. 1, 1998 – Name changed to Unavest Capital Corp.; basis 1 new cl. A for 7 old cl. A shs. and 1 new cl. B for 7 old cl. B shs. ■

Unicol Collection Agencies Limited (Can. Oct. 24, 1969)
Apr. 26, 1983 – Declared bankrupt.

UniComm Signal Inc. (B.C. Sept. 8, 1987)
Dec. 24, 1997 – Name changed to SmarTire Systems Inc.; basis 1 new for 8 old shs. ■

The Unicorn Corp. (Ont. Apr. 15, 1987)
Nov. 26, 1994 – Struck from registry and dissolved.

Unicorn Resources Ltd. (B.C. Aug. 15, 1980)
Nov. 22, 1988 – Name changed to Pacific Unicorn Resources Ltd.; basis 1 new for 5 old shs. ■

Unicorp Canada Corporation (Ont. Dec. 31, 1979 amalg.)
June 25, 1991 – Name changed to Unicorp Energy Corporation; basis 1 new for 3 old shs. ■

Unicorp Energy Corporation (Ont. Dec. 31, 1979 amalg.)
May 20, 1999 – Name changed to Unicorp Inc. ■

Unicorp Financial Corporation (Ont. Apr. 3, 1964)
Dec. 31, 1979 – Amalgamated in Ontario to continue with same name.
June 7, 1982 – Name changed to Unicorp Canada Corporation. ■

Unicorp Financial Inc. (Ont. 1964)
June 17, 1974 – Amalgamated with Cherish Properties Inc. to form Unicorp Financial Corporation; basis 1 new for 540 old shs.

Unicorp Inc. (Ont. Dec. 31, 1979 amalg.)
Mar. 8, 2002 – Name changed to Wilmington Capital Management Inc. following capital reorganization. Distribution made of 1 $25 preferred hybrid due Dec. 31, 2050, for 4 Unicorp cl. A and/or cl. B shs. (see FPsurvey - Industrials)

Unicorp Resources Ltd. (Alta. 1983 amalg.)
Apr. 3, 1986 – Acquired by Asamera Inc.; basis 1 Asamera 7% ser. D second pref. sh. and 1 wt. for 10 Unicorp cl. A or cl. B shs. (see Asamera Inc.)

Unidex Communications Corp. (B.C. 1980)
Aug. 9, 1996 – Name changed to United Digital Network, Inc.; basis 1 new for 4 old shs. ■

Uniforêt Inc. (Can. Nov. 22, 1993)
May 17, 2005 – Name changed to Arbec Forest Products Inc. ■

Unigesco Inc. (Que. Dec. 7, 1966)
Sept. 29, 1994 – Name changed to Sodisco-Howden Group Inc.; basis 1 new cl. B for 1 old com. sh. ■

Uniglobe Travel Online Inc. (Can. Dec. 29, 1995)
July 2, 1999 – Name changed to Uniglobe.com Inc. (see FPsurvey - Industrials)

Uniglobe Ventures Ltd. (Alta. Nov. 15, 1994)
June 16, 1999 – Amalgamated with Brittany Energy Inc. and 825281 Alberta Ltd., a wholly owned subsid. of Diaz Resources Ltd., to form Diaz Energy Inc. and became a wholly owned subsid. of Diaz; basis 0.85 of a new cl. A sub-vtg. sh. of Diaz Resources for 1 com. sh. of Uniglobe. (see Diaz Resources Ltd.)

Unigo Mines Ltd. (Ont. 1943)
Apr. 9, 1959 – Charter cancelled.

Unigold Resources Inc. (Can. Oct. 3, 1996)
Feb. 11, 2003 – Amalgamated with 6035442 Canada Inc. wholly owned subsid. of CaribGold Resources Inc.; basis 1 new CaribGold (renamed Unigold Inc.) sh. for 2 old Unigold Resources shs.

Unigold Resources Ltd. (Ont. Mar. 3, 1986)
Dec. 17, 1992 – Name changed to Provo Industries Inc.; basis 1 new for 5 old shs. ■

UniHost Corporation (Ont. Nov. 19, 1962)
June 1, 1999 – Acquired by W-Westmont Corp. for $7.00 per sh.

Unilens Optical Corp. (B.C. Dec. 20, 1982)
Mar. 16, 1992 – Name changed to Unilens Vision Inc.; basis 1 new for 10 old shs. ■

Unilens Vision Inc. (B.C. Dec. 20, 1982)
Apr. 1, 2010 – Continued into Delaware.
Oct. 1, 2013 – Voluntarily delisted from TSX-VEN; continued to trade on U.S. OTC QB.

Unilink Tele.com Inc. (B.C. Mar. 2, 1999)
Oct. 24, 2005 – Struck from registry and dissolved.

Unilock Capital Corp. (B.C. Jan. 23, 2018)
Apr. 28, 2021 – Name changed to Small Pharma Inc. pursuant to the Qualifying Transaction reverse takeover acquisition of Small Pharma Ltd.; basis 1 new for 4.6 old shs. ■

Union Acceptance Corporation Limited (Ont. 1944)
Dec. 31, 1977 – Amalgamated with Union Acceptance (Ontario) Corp. to form Union Acceptance Corporation Ltd. Holders of 1st pfce. shs. of Union Acceptance (predecessor co.) received 1st pfce. shs. of amalg. co. on sh.-for-sh. basis, while holders of 2nd pfce. and com. shs. received convert. jr. pfce. shs. of amalg. co. on sh.-for-sh. basis. On Feb. 20, 1978, all o/s convert. pfce. shs. called for redemption at $22 per sh. plus 23¢ per sh. divd.

Union Carbide Canada Limited (Can. 1922)
Apr. 8, 1991 – Acquired by Electric Furnace Company Limited, a unit of Union Carbide Corporation, for $19 per sh.

Union Electric Light and Power Company (Can. - unspecified)
Sept. 8, 1966 – Acquired by Newfoundland Light & Power Co. Limited; basis 34new for 1 old sh.

Union Energy Inc. (Ont. 1961)
Dec. 15, 1992 – Acquired by Westcoast Energy Inc. for $16 per sh. (see Westcoast Energy Inc.)

Union Enterprises Ltd. (Ont. 1961)
July 10, 1990 – Name changed to Union Energy Inc. ■

Union Gas Company of Canada, Limited (Ont. Dec. 19, 1911)
Oct. 1, 1972 – Name changed to Union Gas Limited. ■

Union Gas Limited (Ont. Dec. 19, 1911)
Jan. 1, 1998 – Amalgamated in Ontario to continue with same name.
Nov. 30, 2018 – All o/s 5.5% cumulative redeem. cl. A pref. shs., ser. A, redeemed for $50.50 cash plus $0.449 in accrued and unpaid div. per ser. A sh.; 6% cumulative redeem. cl. A pref. shs., ser. B, redeemed for $55 cash plus $0.487 in accrued and unpaid div. per ser. B. sh.; and 5% cumulative redeem. cl. A pref. shs., ser. C, redeemed for $50.50 cash plus $0.406 in accrued and unpaid div. per ser. C sh.
Jan. 1, 2019 – Amalgamated with Enbridge Gas Distribution Inc. to form Enbridge Gas Inc.

Union Gold Inc. (Alta. Sept. 5, 1991)
Jan. 1, 2010 – Formed Jubilee Gold Inc. in Ontario on amalgamation with Golden Harker Explorations Limited, Milestone Exploration Limited, Sheldon-Larder Mines Limited and Wood-Croesus Gold Mines Limited; basis 0.557 Jubilee sh. for 1 Union Gold sh., 0.393 Jubilee sh. for 1 Golden Harker sh., 1.749 Jubilee shs. for 1 Milestone sh., 0.269 Jubilee sh. for 1 Sheldon-Larder sh. and 0.367 Jubilee sh. for 1 Wood-Croesus sh. ■

Union Mining Corporation (Que. 1938)
Sept. 5, 1991 – Continued into Alberta.
Mar. 19, 1993 – Name changed to Union Gold Inc. ■

The Union Natural Gas Company of Canada, Limited (Ont. Dec. 19, 1911)
Aug. 25, 1931 – Name changed to Union Gas Company of Canada, Limited. ■

Union Steamship Co. of B.C. Ltd. (B.C. 1889)
Jan. 1959 – Floating assets sold; co. no longer in steamship business.

Unique Broadband Systems, Inc. (Ont. June 1, 1998 amalg.)
Mar. 20, 2017 – Name changed to Kure Technologies, Inc.; basis 1 new for 10 old shs. (see FPsurvey - Industrials)

Unique Capital Corporation (Ont. Jan. 16, 1996 amalg.)
Sept. 30, 1997 – Name changed to Pele Mountain Holdings Inc. pursuant to reverse takeover acquisition of Pele Mountain Resources Inc.; basis 1 new for 11.7 old shs. ■

Unique Crests and Athletic Supplies Ltd. (unknown)
June 1964 – Acquired by Montex Holdings Ltd. (see Montex Holdings Ltd.)

Unique Force Ent. Inc. (B.C. Aug. 7, 1986)
Dec. 2, 1993 – Name changed to Greenswan Ventures Inc.; basis 1 new for 4 old shs. ■

Unique Resources Corp. (B.C. May 20, 2011)
June 30, 2015 – Name changed to Bee Vectoring Technologies International Inc. following reverse takeover acquisition of Bee Vectoring Technology Inc.; basis 1 new for 2.4 old shs. (see FPsurvey - Industrials)

Unique Resources Ltd. (B.C. Aug. 7, 1986)
Dec. 13, 1989 – Name changed to Unique Force Ent. Inc. ■

Unique Tire Recycling Inc. (B.C. Sept. 26, 1988)
Jan. 19, 1998 – Name changed to UKT Recycling Technologies Inc.; basis 1 new for 3 old shs. ■

Unirom Technologies Inc. (Can. Dec. 9, 1980)
Oct. 17, 2008 – Dissolved.

Uniroyal (1966) Ltd. (unknown)
1971 – Name changed to Uniroyal Ltd.

Unisave Energy Ltd. (B.C. Feb. 11, 1981)
Apr. 26, 1989 – Name changed to U.C. Valve Corp.; basis 1 new for 5 old shs. ■

Unisphere Explorers Ltd. (Alta. 1949)
1969 – Name changed to New Unisphere Resources Ltd.; basis 1 new for 10 old shs. ■

Unisphere Waste Conversion Ltd. (Ont. June 10, 2002 amalg.)
Feb. 9, 2005 – Declared bankrupt. SF Partners Inc. appointed trustee.

Unite Capital Corp. (Ont. Nov. 26, 2010)
June 27, 2014 – Amalgamated with a wholly owned subsid. of Lakeside Minerals Inc.; basis 0.4884 Lakeside com. shs. plus 0.2442 wts.

Unitec International Controls Corporation (B.C. Feb. 15, 1985)
Aug. 1, 2005 – Dissolved and struck from register.

Unitech Energy Resources Inc. (Alta. June 29, 2006 amalg.)
July 21, 2011 – Name changed to Jadela Oil Corp.; basis 1 new for 10 old shs. ■

United America eHealth Technologies Inc. (B.C. Aug. 17, 1983)
Apr. 25, 2001 – Continued into Yukon.
Nov. 5, 2010 – Dissolved and struck from register.

United America Enterprises Ltd. (B.C. Aug. 17, 1983)
June 1, 2000 – Name changed to United America eHealth Technologies Inc. ■

United Amusement Corporation Limited (Que. 1924)
Oct. 31, 1970 – Name changed to United Theatres Ltd. ■

United Asbestos Corporation Limited (Que. 1948)
June 28, 1973 – Merged with Allied Mining Corp. to form United Asbestos Inc.

United Asbestos Inc. (Que. 1973 amalg.)
May 12, 1983 – Amalgamated with Campbell Resources Inc. (1 for 1), GM Resources Limited (1 for 5) and Camchib Resources Inc. (0.6 for 1) to continue as a new company also known as Campbell Resources Inc.; basis 0.3 com. plus 1 pfce. Campbell sh. for 1 old United Asbestos sh. (see Campbell Resources Inc.)

United Auto Parts Inc. (Que. Dec. 29, 1961 amalg.)
Oct. 26, 1967 – Name changed to UAP Inc. ■

United Bata Resources Limited (B.C. 1968)
1971 – Acquired by Pan Ocean Oil Corporation; basis 1 new for 3 old shs. (see Pan Ocean Oil Corporation)

United Battery Metals Corp. (B.C. Apr. 28, 2017)
Oct. 28, 2020 – Name changed to United Lithium Corp. (see FPsurvey - Mines & Energy)

United Beverages Limited (B.C. 1980)
July 28, 1995 – Dissolved and struck off register.

United Bison Resources Limited (Ont. 1960)
Apr. 25, 1991 – Acquired by a wholly owned subsid. of Nalcap Holdings Inc.; basis 1 Nalcap sh. for 7.7 United Bison shs. (see Nalcap Holdings Inc.)

United Bolero Development Corp. (B.C. Aug. 13, 1985)
Sept. 19, 2007 – Name changed to Bolero Resources Corp. and continued into Ontario. ■

United Brown Petroleums Ltd. (Alta. Dec. 3, 1937)
1938 – Wound up after transferring assets to parent co., Federated Petroleums, Ltd. (see Federated Petroleums Ltd.)

United Buffadison Mines Ltd. (Ont. 1945)
1969 – Assets acquired by Western-Buff Mines & Oils Ltd. (see Western-Buff Mines & Oils Ltd.)

United Cambridge Mines Limited (B.C. June 15, 1966)
Dec. 27, 1989 – Name changed to Consolidated Cambridge Mines Limited; basis 1 new for 5 old shs. ■

United Canadian Shares Limited (Man. Sept. 19, 1951)
Jan. 1, 1980 – Merged with Dominion Tanners Ltd. and associates, into United Canadian Shares Limited (Fed. 1977).

United Canadian Shares Limited (Man. Sept. 19, 1951)
Dec. 31, 1979 – Amalgamated in Canada to continue with same name.
Apr. 30, 1999 – Formed The Tanbridge Corporation in Canada on amalgamation with major shldr. Crecands Limited; basis 2 new for 1 old sh. ■

United Canso Oil & Gas Ltd. (Can. 1954)
June 6, 1980 – Continued into Nova Scotia.
Sept. 20, 1985 – Continued into Canada.
Nov. 15, 1995 – Placed into receivership on Apr. 14, 1988 by its bankers. Company dissolved following liquidation of assets. No distribution for unsecured creditors or shldrs.

United Carina Resources Corp. (Sask. Dec. 14, 1982)
July 25, 2007 – Name changed to United Uranium Corp. ■

United Chibougamau Copper Corp. (Que. 1956)
Sept. 1973 – Charter cancelled.

United Chieftain Resources Ltd. (B.C. 1953)
June 9, 1995 – Dissolved and struck off register.

United China International Enterprises Group Ltd. (Can. Mar. 10, 1995)
Oct. 31, 1995 – Continued into Bermuda.

United Coal Holdings Limited (B.C. May 19, 1999)
Nov. 12, 2018 – Dissolved and struck from register.
July 14, 2022 – Restored to the B.C. registry.
July 14, 2022 – Name changed to 0941527 B.C. Ltd. (see FPsurvey - Mines & Energy)

United Cobalt Mines Ltd. (Ont. 1944)
Mar. 1976 – Charter cancelled; subsequently revived. In mid-1978, received 1,559,488 shs. Langis Silver & Cobalt Mining Co. Ltd., under agreement for sale of assets to Langis.

United Coin Mines Ltd. (Ont. 1936)
June 25, 1993 – Name changed to Winstaff Ventures Ltd. ∎

United Collision Centers of America Inc. (B.C. 1986)
Apr. 29, 1994 – Dissolved and struck off register.

United Compass Resources Ltd. (B.C. Sept. 21, 1966)
Oct. 2, 1998 – Name changed to Tartan Energy Inc.; basis 1 new for 4 old shs. ∎

United Comstock Lode Mines Ltd. (Ont. 1945)
Feb. 1973 – Charter cancelled.

United Continental Energy Corp. (B.C. Apr. 29, 1980)
Nov. 18, 1983 – Name changed to Hilton Resource Corporation. ∎

United Copper and Mining Ltd. (Alta. 1955)
Sept. 30, 1970 – Charter cancelled.

United Copper Corporation Ltd. (B.C. Sept. 21, 1966)
Jan. 14, 1974 – Name changed to Medallion Explorations Ltd.; basis 1 new for 3 old shs. ∎

United Dairies Limited (Can. 1929)
Jan. 1966 – Silverwood Dairies Limited acquired all o/s com. stk. at $50 per sh., payable in cash or through issue of one Silverwood cl. A sh. plus $34.25. All o/s United Dairies cl. A pref. shs. red. Jan. 15, 1967.

United Digital Network, Inc. (B.C. 1980)
May 3, 1999 – Amalgamated with STAR Telecommunications, Inc.; basis 0.146428 STAR shs. for 1 United Digital Network sh.

United Distillers of Canada Ltd. (Can. 1929)
1953 – Major assets sold to Distillers Corporation-Seagrams Limited, for approx. $14,911,762.
June 27, 1960 – Wholly owned subsid., United Distillers Ltd., being wound up; distribution totaling $18 per sh. made.
Sept. 30, 1960 – Balance of the tax paid undistributed income, was $72,656. O/s 428,658 shs. No further report.
1960 – Major assets sold to Distillers Corporation-Seagrams Limited in 1953, for approx. $14,911,762. Wholly owned subsid., United Distillers Ltd., being wound up; distribution totaling $18 per sh. made to June 27, 1960. Balance of the tax paid undistributed income at Sept. 30, 1960, was $72,656. O/s 428,658 shs. No further report.

United Dixie Resources Inc. (Ont. June 30, 1987 amalg.)
Aug. 14, 1998 – Name changed to United Pacific Capital Resources Corp. pursuant to reverse takeover acquisition of United Pacific Capital Resources Corp.; basis 1 new for 5.4 old shs. ∎

United Dominion Industries Limited (Can. July 30, 1912; via Dominion charter)
May 25, 2001 – Acquired by SPX Corporation; basis 0.2353 SPX shs. for 1 United Dominion sh.

United Dominions Corporation (Canada) Limited (Can. 1937)
Sept. 30, 1982 – Name changed to Commerce - UD Inc. ∎

United Duvex Oils & Mines Ltd. (Ont. Nov. 21, 1944)
Aug. 31, 1992 – Delisted from the CDN. Subsequently dissolved and charter cancelled.

United Equities Ltd. (B.C. 1969 amalg.)
May 1974 – All 250,000 o/s com. shs. acquired by M.P.N. Holdings Ltd. and Rosen Foundation Ltd. Subsequently, status of co. changed to a non-reporting co.

United Estella Mines Ltd. (B.C. 1950)
Mar. 1964 – Charter cancelled; dissolved.

United Explorations & Mining Corp. Ltd. (Que. 1965)
1969 – Assets acquired by Reactor Uranium Mines Ltd.

United Falcon Oils Limited (unknown)
1972 – Amalgamated with Brown Bear Petroleums Limited under name of Brown Bear; basis 1 new for 1 old sh.

United Film & Video Holdings Limited (British Virgin Islands May 14, 1993)
June 24, 1998 – Name changed to United Media Holdings Ltd. and continued into Cayman Islands. ∎

United Financial Management Ltd. (Can. 1954)
June 1986 – Acquired by Central Capital Corporation; basis 3.2 Central Capital shs. for 1 United Financial sh. (see Central Capital Corporation)

United Fortune Channel Mines Ltd. (B.C. 1969)
Oct. 23, 1983 – Name changed to Surewin Resources Corp.; basis 1 new for 5 old shs. ∎

United Fuel Investments Limited (Can. 1928)
Nov. 1963 – Placed into liquidation, cl. A shldrs. received liquidation payment of $60 per sh. plus accrued divd. of 44¢ per sh.; cl. B shldrs. of record Nov. 15 received liquidation pay. of $30 per sh.
Apr. 30, 1968 – After protracted litigation, the Supreme Court of Ontario approved an offer by Union Gas Company of Canada, Ltd. to pur. from United Fuel Investments all o/s shs. of United Gas Ltd., on the basis that would result in a distrib. of $500 per sh. on the com. shs. of United Fuel Investments, all but 92 of which were owned by Union Gas.
1969 – Liquidation completed.

United Global Petroleum Inc. (B.C. Nov. 20, 1968)
Apr. 19, 1991 – Dissolved and struck off register.

United Gold Corp. (Ont. Nov. 19, 1984 amalg.)
Dec. 8, 1989 – Acquired by ABM Gold Corp.; basis 1 ABM cl. A sh. for 6 United Gold shs. (see ABM Gold Corp.)

United Gold Equities of Canada, Ltd. (Can. 1933)
June 25, 1947 – Assets sold to Commonwealth International Corp. Ltd. Distribution of shs. on basis of 0.6 shs. Commonwealth for 1 sh. United Gold Equities.

United Grain Growers Limited (Man. July 20, 1906)
May 19, 1911 – Continued into Canada; via Dominion charter.
Dec. 17, 1992 – Continued into Canada; via United Grain Growers Act.
Jan. 14, 2003 – Name changed to Agricore United. ∎

United Greenwood Explorations Ltd. (B.C. July 17, 1974)
Nov. 16, 1984 – Name changed to Elektra Power Inc. ∎

United Gunn Resources Ltd. (B.C. July 21, 1966)
Dec. 2005 – Dissolved and struck from register.

United Hearne Resources Ltd. (B.C. July 20, 1967)
Nov. 17, 1986 – Continued into Canada.
Mar. 25, 1997 – Dissolved for non-compliance.

United Homes Incorporated (B.C. 1983)
May 14, 1992 – Name changed to Great Icelandic Water Corporation pursuant to reverse takeover acquisition of Great Icelandic Water Holdings Inc. ∎

United Hudson Resources Inc. (B.C. Apr. 1, 1981)
Feb. 17, 1993 – Name changed to Northrich Pacific Ventures Inc.; basis 1 new for 3 old shs. ∎

United Hunter Oil & Gas Corp. (Ont. Feb. 22, 2008)
Jan. 23, 2020 – Continued into British Columbia. Formed Bocana Resources Corp. on amalgamation with Bocana Resources Ltd. (BRL), constituting a reverse takeover by BRL; basis 1 new for 1.6877 old shs. (see FPsurvey - Mines & Energy)

United Inc. (Alta. Jan. 7, 1993)
Oct. 30, 2001 – Going private transaction; basis either 1 redeemable non-vtg. A sh. immediately redeemed for $1.50, or 1 redeemable non-vtg. B sh. immediately redeemed for 20¢ plus $1.65 of series A debs. of United Acquisition Corp.

United Keno Hill Mines Limited (Can. Nov. 6, 1945)
Jan. 8, 2004 – Dissolved.

United Kiev Resources Inc. (Alta. May 17, 1995 amalg.)
July 17, 1997 – Name changed to Carpatsky Petroleum Inc. ∎

United Kingdom Energy Inc. (B.C. 1982)
Mar. 20, 1992 – Dissolved and struck off register.

United Kirkland Gold Mines Ltd. (Ont. Apr. 12, 1926)
Oct. 1933 – Name changed to Macassa Mines Ltd.; basis 1 new for 10 old shs. ∎

United Lead & Zinc Mines Ltd. (Que. 1951)
1953 – Merged into United Montauban Mines Ltd.; basis 1 new for 2 old shs.

United Leader Resources Inc. (B.C. Apr. 7, 1978)
Apr. 13, 1987 – Name changed to Vertica Systems Corporation. ∎

United Leisure Gold Ltd. (B.C. Sept. 15, 1969)
Apr. 14, 1978 – Name changed to Forum Resources Ltd.; basis 1 new for 2 old shs. ∎

United Liberty Resources Ltd. (B.C. 1983)
Apr. 28, 1988 – Name changed to United Liberty Financial Corporation. (see FPsurvey - Industrials)

United Lincoln Resources Inc. (B.C. 1969)
Mar. 15, 1989 – Merged with parent co. Continental Gold Corp. (see Continental Gold Corp.)

United Lithium Corp. (Que. 1955)
1956 – Name changed to Hastings Mining and Development Co. Ltd. ∎

United Lithium Corp. (B.C. Apr. 28, 2017)
Aug. 20, 2018 – Name changed to United Battery Metals Corp. ∎

United Loan Corporation (Que. 1949)
1969 – Wound up when creditors received a final payment of 60% of claim plus cert. of participation.

United Macfie Mines Ltd. (Ont. 1945)
1979 – Continued into British Columbia.
June 12, 1980 – Name changed to Macfie Resources Inc. ∎

United Media Holdings Ltd. (Cayman Islands June 24, 1998)
Dec. 20, 1999 – Name changed to United Media Ltd.

United Mic Mac Mines Ltd. (Ont. 1946)
1955 – Assets acquired by Indian Lake Mines Ltd. (see Indian Lake Mines Ltd.)

United Mindamar Metals Ltd. (Ont. 1950)
June 26, 1973 – Name changed to Mindamar Energy Resources Limited. ∎

United Mining Group, Inc. (B.C. Nov. 6, 2007)
June 8, 2011 – Name changed to United Silver Corp. ∎

United Montauban Mines Ltd. (Ont. 1953)
July 30, 1958 – Name changed to Satellite Metal Mines Limited; basis 1 new for 4 old shs. ∎

United New Fortune Mines Ltd. (Ont. Mar. 1952)
June 23, 1980 – Dissolved.

United North American Resources, Inc. (Que. 1951)
Feb. 12, 1991 – Formed Alliance Resources Plc in United Kingdom following reorganization whereby all assets transferred to and all liabilities and obligations assumed by Alliance Resources (U.S.A.) Inc., a wholly owned subsid. of Alliance Resources Plc; basis 1 ord. for 1 com. sh.

United Northern Petroleum Corp. (B.C. Mar. 15, 1965)
Nov. 6, 1989 – Name changed to UNP Industries Ltd. ■

United Obalski Mining Co. Ltd. (Que. 1945)
1969 – Merged into Allied Mining Corp.; basis 1 new for 3.67 old shs.

United Oils Limited (Can. 1918)
1964 – Transferred its holdings of cl. A and B shs. of Home Oil Company Limited to wholly owned Cygnus Corp. and then distributed shs. of Cygnus to its shldrs.; basis 1 cl. A and 3 cl. B shs. of Cygnus for each 10 United Oil shs. held.
1965 – Home Oil Company Limited acquired the majority of shs. for 75¢ per sh.

United Oils of Alberta, Ltd. (Alta. 1914)
Assets sold to United Oils, Limited. (see United Oils Limited)

United Pacific Capital Resources Corp. (Ont. June 30, 1987 amalg.)
Oct. 13, 2000 – Delisted from the CDN. Subsequently dissolved and charter cancelled.

United Pacific Gold Limited (B.C. 1987)
Nov. 12, 1993 – Dissolved and struck off register.

United Porcupine Mines Ltd. (Ont. 1933)
1967 – Acquired by Dynacore Enterprises Ltd.; basis 1 new for 6.25 old shs. (see Dynacore Enterprises Ltd.)

United Principal Properties Limited (Ont. 1917)
Aug. 28, 1963 – Name changed to Canadian Interurban Properties Limited. ■

United Protection Security Group Inc. (Alta. Nov. 18, 1993)
June 11, 2013 – Declared bankrupt. Meyers Norris Penny LLP appointed trustee.

United Provincial Investments Limited (B.C. 1967)
Mar. 23, 1972 – Name changed to Dunhill Development Corporation Ltd. ■

United Rayore Gas Ltd. (B.C. May 2, 1966)
Aug. 8, 1997 – Amalgamated with Startech Energy Inc.; basis 1 Startech for 10 United Rayore shs. (see Startech Energy Inc.)

United Redford Resources Inc. (B.C. 1966)
Dec. 4, 2006 – Dissolved and struck from register.

United Reef Limited (Ont. Feb. 9, 1948)
Aug. 17, 2012 – Name changed to New Klondike Exploration Ltd.; basis 1 new for 8 old shs. (see FPsurvey - Mines & Energy)

United Reef Petroleums Limited (Ont. Feb. 9, 1948)
Sept. 1, 1993 – Name changed to United Reef Limited. ■

United Renzy Nickel Ltd. (Ont. 1956)
1967 – Merged into Delahey Consolidated Nickel Mines Ltd.; basis 1 new for 10 old shs.

United Research & Development Consolidated Ltd. (B.C. 1966)
Nov. 12, 1975 – Name changed to Delta Refining Corporation. ■

United Safety Technology Inc. (B.C. Aug. 8, 1979)
Jan. 3, 1990 – Name changed to Consolidated United Safety Technology Inc.; basis 1 new for 5 old shs. ■

United Sartis Enterprises Inc. (B.C. July 29, 1981)
Feb. 11, 1999 – Name changed to Wellco Energy Services Inc. ■

United Securities Limited (Que. 1924)
Nov. 1957 – Assets liquidated and charter surrendered.

United Silver Corp. (B.C. Nov. 6, 2007)
Jan. 9, 2014 – Placed into receivership by secured creditor, HUSC, LLC. Duff & Phelps Canada Restructuring Inc. appointed receivers. All officers and directors resigned.

United Siscoe Mines Inc. (Que. May 23, 1923)
June 30, 1987 – Name changed to The Horsham Corporation. ■

United Siscoe Mines Limited (Que. May 23, 1923)
July 11, 1980 – Name changed to United Siscoe Mines Inc. ■

United Southern Minerals Corp. (B.C. 1983)
Oct. 30, 1992 – Dissolved and struck off register.

United Southfork Energy Inc. (Can. 1981)
1987 – Dissolved.

United States Exploration Corporation (Alta. Mar. 22, 1996)
Nov. 18, 1999 – Name changed to Triangulum Corporation following Major Transaction reverse takeover acquisition of AVL Automatic Vehicle Location Systems Ltd. ■

United Steel Corporation Limited (Can. 1933)
Jan. 1965 – Placed into receivership. Certain assets transferred to liquidator to meet demands of secured creditors. Funded debt consisted of 3.5 % serial and 4% s.f. 1st. mtge. bonds, due May 1, 1965 and May 1, 1975, respectively.
Nov. 25, 1965 – Arrangements made to pay off bonds in full; interim payment of 25% of principal made, on total of $1,700,000 princ. amt. then o/s, by trustee, National Trust Co. Ltd., Toronto.

United Telefilms Ltd. (Ont. 1919)
Dec. 1959 – Name changed to Creative Telefilms & Artists Ltd. ■

United Terrex Corporation (Alta. Aug. 12, 1986)
Oct. 20, 1994 – Name changed to Siberian Pacific Resources Inc. ■

United Tex-Sol Mines Inc. (Alta. Aug. 31, 1990)
June 25, 2003 – Plan of Arrangement with St Andrew Goldfields Ltd. and Royal Victoria Minerals Ltd. (2 for 1); basis 1 new St Andrew com. sh. for 1 old United Tex-Sol com. sh. (see St Andrew Goldfields Ltd.)

United Theatres Ltd. (Que. 1924)
1979 – Name changed to Cinémas Unis Ltée. ■

United Tire & Rubber Co. Limited (Ont. 1979)
Sept. 12, 1996 – All o/s com. shs. acquired by 3223302 Canada Inc., a subsid. of Pensler Capital Corp.; basis $2.825 per sh. All o/s 1st pref. ser. A conv. 7% shs. redeemed on May 17, 1995; basis $2.5848 per sh. including all accrued and special dividends.

United Towns Electric Co. Ltd. (N.L. 1902)
1966 – Merged with Newfoundland Light & Power Co. Ltd. Com. shldrs. received 1.5 com. shs. Nfld. Light for each sh. United Towns com.; pref. shs. exchanged share-for-share. Bonds exchanged par-for-par for Nfld. Light bonds having same int. rate, maturity date, and other provisions; except 4% income bonds, due Oct. 1, 1981, which were red. and 6 1/4 % conv. debentures, due May 1, 1981, which were called for redemp. on July 21, at 104.5. O/s pref. stock of subsid., The West Coast Power Co. Ltd., exchanged par-for-par for 6% series C pref. of Nfld. Bonds of subsid., The Public Service Electric Co. Ltd., exch. par-for-par for 5% series Q bonds of Nfld. Light.

United Tri-Star Resources Ltd. (B.C. Dec. 31, 1986 amalg.)
Oct. 27, 1994 – Continued into Canada.
July 22, 1998 – Name changed to UTS Energy Corporation. ■

United Trust Company (Ont. 1964)
Sept. 6, 1977 – By Dec. 31, 1976, The Royal Trust Company had acquired 99.7% of the com. shs. of United Trust (3 com. shs. of Royal Trust for 5 com. shs. of United Trust), and subsequently changed the co.'s name to The Royal Trust Co. (Ontario). Total consideration was $18,000 and 1,214,884 A shs. of The Royal Trust Co. In addition, on Sept. 1, 1976, The Royal Trust Co. had purchased 25,000 ser. A and 60,000 ser. B shs., $20 par for $1,700,000 and $800,000 par value of subord. notes, all for cash. the co. was amalg. with The Royal Trust Corporation of Canada.

United Uranium Corp. (Sask. Dec. 14, 1982)
Aug. 15, 2013 – Name changed to Karoo Exploration Corp. and continued into British Columbia following reverse takeover acquisition of (old) Karoo Exploration Corp.; basis 1 new for 5 old shs. ■

United Uranium Corp. Ltd. (Que. 1955)
Oct. 1973 – Charter cancelled.

United Westburne Inc. (Can. 1977)
May 26, 1995 – Name changed to Westburne Inc. ■

United Westburne Industries Ltd. (Alta. May 8, 1951)
1978 – Continued into Canada.
Aug. 18, 1987 – All o/s com. shs. (other than those already held by Westburne International Industries Ltd. and Dumez) acquired by Dumez Investments I Inc. for $25 per sh. O/s pref. shs. redeemed at $51.50 plus $1.21 accr. divds. Subsequently on Sept. 1, 1987, amalgamated with ten wholly owned subsids., Dumez Investments I Inc. and Westburne International Industries Ltd. to form United Westburne Inc.

United Western Oil & Gas Ltd. (Alta. 1970)
Nov. 1, 1982 – Amalgamated with 3 other cos. to form Trans-Canada Resources Ltd.; 1 new cl. A sh. for 2.7 old com. shs.

United Westland Resources Ltd. (B.C. 1966)
1981 – Amalgamated in British Columbia to continue with same name.
Feb. 28, 1986 – Name changed to Daleco Resources Corporation and continued into Ontario; basis 1 new for 5 old shs. ■

United Yellowknife Explorations Ltd. (Alta. 1946)
Sept. 30, 1952 – Dissolved and struck off register.

Uniterre Resources Ltd. (B.C. Dec. 31, 1957)
Nov. 3, 2006 – Name changed to NaiKun Wind Energy Group Inc. ■

Unitrol Data Protection Systems Inc. (B.C. Jan. 5, 1989)
Apr. 12, 1994 – Name changed to Radical Advanced Technologies Corp. ■

Unity Bank of Canada (unknown 1972)
June 16, 1977 – Merged with La Banque Provinciale du Canada to form an amalg. bank under the continuing name of La Banque Provinciale du Canada. Fully pd. shs. of Unity exchanged on the basis of 1 new for 4 old shs. In addition, 1 sh. of the amalg. bank was issued for $37 pd. on account of the partially pd. shs. of Unity.

Unity Energy Corp. (B.C. May 24, 2006)
Dec. 27, 2018 – Name changed to Unity Metals Corp. ■

Unity Metals Corp. (B.C. May 24, 2006)
Aug. 21, 2019 – Name changed to Academy Metals Inc. ■

Unity Porcupine Mines & Exploration Ltd. (Ont. 1940)
1952 – Charter cancelled.

Unity Valley Oil & Gas Co. Ltd. (unknown)
Voluntarily liquidated. Property taken over by Vera Oilfields Ltd. (see Vera Oilfields Ltd)

Univa Inc. (Que. Nov. 14, 1961)
May 25, 1994 – Name changed to Provigo Inc. ■

Univers Info Inc. (Can. Dec. 1, 1993 amalg.)
Jan. 6, 1997 – Name changed to DTM Information Technology Group Inc. ■

Universal Cooler Co. Ltd. (Ont. 1949)
Nov. 1963 – Placed into bankruptcy. Creditors received about 8¢ on the dollar. No equity for shldrs.

Universal Copper Ltd. (B.C. Oct. 5, 2011)
Apr. 22, 2024 – Acquired by Vizsla Copper Corp.; basis 0.23 Vizsla shs. for 1 Universal Copper sh.

Universal Empire Capital Corp. (Alta. Nov. 18, 1994)
Sept. 24, 1996 – Name changed to Bromley.Marr ECOS Inc. following acquisition of Bromley.Marr ECOS Inc.; basis 1 new for 1 old sh. ■

Universal Energy Corporation (B.C. June 12, 1979)
Feb. 9, 2007 – Name changed to Supreme Resources Ltd. ■

Universal Energy Group Ltd. (Can. Nov. 1, 2006)
July 6, 2009 – Acquired by Just Energy Exchange Corp., a wholly owned subsid. of Just Energy Income Fund (previously Ontario Energy Savings Corp.); basis 0.58 Just Energy exch. shs. for 1 Universal Energy com. sh., resulting in 21,271,804 exch. shs. issued of which 4,348,314 were immediately exchanged for a like number of Just Energy Income trust units. (see Just Energy Exchange Corp.)

Universal Exploration Corporation (B.C. Oct. 8, 1987)
Oct. 5, 2007 – Name changed to Universal Power Corp.; basis 3 new for 1 old sh. ■

Universal Explorations (83) Ltd. (Alta. Nov. 1, 1983 amalg.)
Apr. 29, 1986 – Name changed to Universal Explorations Ltd. ■

Universal Explorations Ltd. (Alta. 1971)
Nov. 1, 1983 – Formed Universal Explorations (83) Ltd. in Alberta on amalgamation with The Petrol Oil & Gas Company Ltd.; basis 1 new for 6 old shs. ■

Universal Explorations Ltd. (Alta. Nov. 1, 1983 amalg.)
Apr. 14, 1989 – Following reorganization, shldrs. received shs. in Canadian Conquest Exploration Inc.; basis $6.45 plus 0.224 com. shs. for 1 ser. A pref. sh., 0.8122 com. shs. for 1 ser. B pref. sh., $5.80 plus 0.2987 com. shs. for 1 ser. C pref. sh., and 0.3734 com. shs. for 1 com. sh. (see Canadian Conquest Exploration Inc.)

Universal Genetics Corporation Limited (Alta. 1978)
Nov. 18, 1997 – Amalgamated with Starbright Venture Capital Inc.; basis 1 Starbright sh. for 1 Universal Genetics sh.

Universal Gun-Loc Industries Ltd. (B.C. Nov. 6, 1978)
Apr. 25, 2002 – Name changed to UGL Enterprises Ltd.; basis 1 new for 2 old shs. ■

Universal Infrastructure Corp. (Alta. Aug. 2, 2006)
Oct. 15, 2010 – Distribution of $0.0374 cash per sh. made to shldrs. of record Sept. 30, 2010.
Nov. 2, 2010 – Voluntarily dissolved and struck from register.

Universal mCloud Corp. (B.C. Dec. 21, 2010)
Nov. 6, 2019 – Name changed to mCloud Technologies Corp. (see FPsurvey - Industrials)

Universal Minerals Corp. (Que. 1968)
Mar. 7, 1981 – Name changed to Laurier Resources Ltd. ■

Universal Minerals Ltd. (B.C. 1960)
May 15, 1969 – Struck off register.

Universal Movie Butler Inc. (B.C. Jan. 17, 1983)
Feb. 27, 1986 – Name changed to Pacific Vending Technology Limited. ■

Universal Patent and Development Ltd. (B.C. Sept. 25, 1963)
Mar. 28, 1972 – Name changed to Trans America Industries Ltd.; basis 1 new for 5 old shs. ■

Universal Petroleum Co. of Canada Ltd. (Ont. 1936)
Mar. 28, 1960 – Dissolved. Liquidator: R. M. Stillman.

Universal Power Corp. (B.C. Oct. 8, 1987)
Sept. 14, 2010 – Name changed to UNX Energy Corp. and continued into Alberta. ■

Universal Pre-Vent Inc. (B.C. 1953)
Apr. 16, 1993 – Dissolved and struck off register.

Universal PropTech Inc. (Can. Aug. 22, 2008)
June 21, 2024 – Name changed to BrandPilot AI Inc. pursuant to the reverse takeover acquisition of Xemoto Media Ltd. (see FPsurvey - Industrials)

Universal Sections Limited (Ont. 1965)
May 30, 1979 – Amalgamated with Fagan Investments Ltd. Minority shldrs. received on sh.-for-sh. basis, 90¢ pfce. sh. of new co. Pfce. shs. redeemable in 5 equal instalments, starting Mar. 31, 1980 at $9.00 per sh. Also redeemable for other than s.f. purposes at $9.50 per sh. in the first year after amalg., with the price declining 10¢ per sh. to $9.00 in the fifth year. Minority shldrs. also given option of having their pfce. shs. redeemed for $9.00 per sh. within 30 days of amalg.

Universal Star Ventures Coropration (Alta. Apr. 18, 1997)
June 16, 2005 – Name changed to Global Express Energy Inc.; basis 1 new for 5 old shs. ■

Universal Trident Industries Ltd. (B.C. Oct. 18, 1973)
Aug. 29, 1994 – Name changed to Poseidon Minerals Ltd.; basis 1 new for 3 old shs. ■

Universal Uranium Ltd. (B.C. Feb. 6, 1986)
July 7, 2010 – Name changed to Expedition Mining Inc. ■

Universal Ventures Inc. (B.C. Dec. 21, 2010)
Oct. 13, 2017 – Name changed to Universal mCloud Corp. following reverse takeover acquisition of mCloud Corp.; basis 1 new for 2 old shs. ■

Universal Wing Technologies Inc. (B.C. Apr. 17, 1979)
Mar. 21, 2014 – Name changed to Red Oak Mining Corp.; basis 1 new for 2 old shs. ■

University Avenue Financial Corporation (Ont. May 30, 1997)
Oct. 18, 2001 – Name changed to Blue Heron Financial Corporation. ■

Univest Resources International Inc. (Que.)
Nov. 1976 – Operations ceased.

Univex Mining Corp. Ltd. (B.C. May 10, 1967)
Sept. 18, 1991 – Name changed to Copperstone Resources Corporation; basis 1 new for 4 old shs. ■

Uniwat Capital Corporation (Alta. Sept. 17, 1987)
July 28, 1994 – Name changed to Waterfront Capital Corporation. ■

Unlimited Minerals Ltd. (Ont.)
Mar. 19, 1969 – Charter cancelled.

Unor Inc. (Ont. Oct. 31, 1997 amalg.)
Apr. 12, 2010 – Name changed to Hornby Bay Mineral Exploration Ltd.; basis 1 new for 3 old shs. ■

Unuk Gold Corporation (B.C. Mar. 30, 1988)
Oct. 1, 1998 – Name changed to Auterra Ventures Inc. ■

Unuk River Copper Mines Ltd. (B.C.)
May 15, 1969 – Struck off register.

Upco International Inc. (B.C. Mar. 28, 2012)
May 3, 2022 – Name changed to Adamant Holdings Inc. (see FPsurvey - Industrials)

Upland Global Corporation (Alta. May 10, 1993)
Nov. 2, 2007 – Struck from register and dissolved.

Upland Mining and Exploration Ltd. (Ont. 1945)
May 1950 – Charter cancelled.

Upland Resource Corporation (B.C. Sept. 23, 1987)
Mar. 15, 2004 – Continued into Canada.
Apr. 1, 2004 – Name changed to New Sleeper Gold Corporation following reverse takeover acquisition of (old) New Sleeper Gold Corp. and amalgamation of old New Sleeper with wholly owned 6193251 Canada Ltd. to continue as 4226844 Canada Ltd.; basis 1 new for 2.5 old shs. ■

Upnorth Gold Mines Ltd. (Ont. 1945)
1945 – Name changed to Bambi Mines Ltd. and continued into Ontario. ■

The Upper Canada Brewing Company Limited (Ont. Oct. 27, 1985)
May 26, 1995 – Amalgamated in Ontario to continue with same name. (see Sleeman Breweries Ltd.)
Mar. 16, 1998 – Acquired by Sleeman Breweries Ltd.; basis $2.75 and 0.433 Sleeman shs. for 1 Upper Canada sh. (see Sleeman Breweries Ltd.)

Upper Canada Gaming Corporation (Alta. June 27, 1988)
Sept. 11, 2000 – Name changed to Q-Tel Wireless Inc. ■

Upper Canada Gold Corporation (Alta. Sept. 17, 1998)
Apr. 12, 2013 – Name changed to California Gold Mining Inc. ■

Upper Canada Mines Ltd. (Ont. 1929)
Sept. 1972 – Name changed to Upper Canada Resources Limited. ■

Upper Canada Resources Limited (Ont. 1929)
June 1978 – Name changed to Challenger International Services Ltd. and continued into Alberta; basis 1 new for 1 old sh. cl. A were convert. for 30 days (to Aug. 3, 1978) into 10 cl. B shs. Previously, o/s shs. designated cl. A. and unissued shs. designated cl. B shs.; basis 1 new for 10 old shs. ■

Upper Canyon Minerals Corp. (B.C. Jan. 10, 2005)
Dec. 17, 2020 – Name changed to Savannah Minerals Corp.; basis 1 new for 4 old shs. (see FPsurvey - Mines & Energy)

Upper Kirkland Mines Ltd. (Ont. 1964)
July 30, 1979 – Dissolved.

Upper Lake Oil and Gas Ltd. (Alta. Aug. 1, 2007)
Sept. 4, 2008 – Acquired by Monterey Exploration Ltd.; basis 0.28 Monterey com. shs. for 1 Upper Lake com. sh.

Upper Shebandowan Mines Ltd. (Ont. 1956)
1960 – Name changed to Primary Gold Mines Ltd. ■

Upsala Mines Ltd. (Ont.)
Mar. 19, 1969 – Charter cancelled.

UpSnap Inc. (Alta. Aug. 17, 2004 amalg.)
Jan. 18, 2024 – Filed for bankruptcy under the Bankruptcy and Insolvency Act. B. Riley Farber Inc. appointed trustee and all officers and directors resigned.

Upstream Gold Mines Ltd. (Ont. 1938)
1972 – Charter cancelled.

Upton Copper Ltd. (Que. Sept. 18, 1963)
Jan. 25, 1986 – Charter cancelled.
Feb. 3, 1997 – Charter revived.
Sept. 4, 1998 – Name changed to Central Canada Foods Corporation. ■

Upton Resources Inc. (Sask. June 15, 1987)
Feb. 4, 2004 – Acquired by StarPoint Energy Ltd.; basis 1.1 StarPoint shs. for 1 Upton sh. (see StarPoint Energy Ltd.)

Uptown Industries Corp. (B.C. 1987)
Sept. 5, 1990 – Name changed to North American Scientific, Inc. ■

Ur-Energy Inc. (Ont. Mar. 22, 2004)
Aug. 8, 2006 – Continued into Canada. (see FPsurvey - Mines & Energy)

Uracan Resources Ltd. (B.C. Apr. 21, 1999)
Oct. 5, 2018 – Name changed to Vanadian Energy Corp.; basis 1 new for 4 old shs. (see FPsurvey - Mines & Energy)

Uragold Bay Resources Inc. (Can. Dec. 20, 1996)
July 4, 2016 – Name changed to HPQ-Silicon Resources Inc. pursuant to plan to spin out the Beauce gold property in Quebec into a new company. ■

UraMin Inc. (British Virgin Islands Feb. 25, 2005)
Aug. 21, 2007 – Acquired by CFMM Developpment, a wholly owned subsidiary of Compagnie Francais de Mines et Metaux S.A.; basis US$7.75 per sh.

Uranco Minerals Inc. (Alta. Dec. 1, 1997)
June 18, 1999 – Name changed to Uravan Minerals Inc. following reverse takeover acquisition of Uravan Minerals Inc.; basis 1 new for 3 old shs. ■

Uranerz Energy Corporation (Nev. May 26, 1999)
June 22, 2015 – Amalgamated with wholly subsid. of Energy Fuels Inc.; basis 0.255 Energy Fuels com. shs. for 1 Uranerz com. sh.

Uranex Resources Ltd. (Ont. 1978 amalg.)
Mar. 2, 1992 – Amalgamated with Concentrated Rare Earth Minerals Ltd., Enertex Developments Inc. (1 for 12.6), Goldmac Explorations Inc. (1 for 17.5), Norlode Resources Ltd., Offset Natural Resources Ltd. (1 for 11), Preston Resources Ltd. and Saranac Resources Ltd. to form a new co. named Marvas Developments Ltd.; basis 1 new for 13.5 old shs. (see Marvas Developments Ltd.)

Urania Ltd. (Bermuda June 26, 2007)
Dec. 22, 2010 – Name changed to Urania Resources Ltd. ■

Urania Resources Ltd. (Bermuda June 26, 2007)
Mar. 16, 2012 – Name changed to Aurania Resources Ltd. (see FPsurvey - Mines & Energy)

Uranibec Mining Enterprises Ltd. (Ont. 1949)
1957 – Charter cancelled.

Uranium Bay Resources Inc. (Can. Dec. 20, 1996)
July 15, 2009 – Name changed to Uragold Bay Resources Inc. ■

Uranium City Resources Inc. (Ont. Oct. 25, 2004)
Mar. 9, 2009 – Name changed to Strategic Resources Inc. ■

Uranium Focused Energy Fund (Ont. Feb. 27, 2007)
Aug. 30, 2013 – Merged into MBN Corporation; basis 0.3271222 MBN equity shs. for 1 Uranium unit. (see MBN Corporation)

Uranium King Corporation (Que. 1954)
1955 – Assets acquired by International Mining and Development Corp.; basis 1 new for 5 old shs. (see International Mining and Development Corp.)

Uranium Limited (Guernsey June 28, 2006)
Mar. 31, 2010 – Acquired by Uranium Participation Corporation ; basis 0.5 Uranium Participation shs. for 1 Uranium Limited sh.

Uranium North Resources Corp. (B.C. Mar. 1, 2006)
Feb. 19, 2013 – Formed Adamera Minerals Corp. in British Columbia on amalgamation with Diamonds North Resources Ltd. with Uranium North the deemed acquiror; basis 0.1333 new for 1 Diamonds North share and 0.2

new for 1 Uranium North share. (see FPsurvey - Mines & Energy)

Uranium One Inc. (Can. Mar. 17, 2005)
Oct. 22, 2013 – Acquired by JSC Atomredmetzoloto for Cdn$2.86 per sh.
Nov. 21, 2018 – Continued into British Columbia.

Uranium Participation Corporation (Ont. Mar. 15, 2005)
July 19, 2021 – Plan of arrangement transaction with Sprott Asset Management LP; basis ½ Sprott Physical Uranium Trust trust unit for 1 Uranium Participation com. sh.

Uranium Power Corp. (B.C. July 23, 1981)
Aug. 6, 2009 – Acquired by Titan Uranium Inc.; basis 0.5393 Titan Uranium shs. for 1 Uranium Power sh. (see Titan Uranium Inc.)

Uranium Resources, Inc. (B.C. 1984)
1987 – Continued into Delaware.
Aug. 21, 2017 – Name changed to Westwater Resources, Inc.

Uranium Ridge Mines Ltd. (Ont. 1953)
Jan. 26, 1977 – Dissolved.

Uranium Standard Resources Ltd. (B.C. June 6, 2007)
Nov. 27, 2015 – Name changed to Palisades Ventures Inc.; basis 1 new for 2 old shs. ■

Uranium Valley Mines Ltd. (Ont. 1969)
Nov. 19, 1973 – Name changed to Superstar Petroleums Ltd. ■

Uranium Valley Mines Ltd. (B.C. Feb. 18, 2010)
Oct. 27, 2017 – Name changed to International Prospect Ventures Ltd. (see FPsurvey - Mines & Energy)

UrAsia Energy Ltd. (B.C. Mar. 31, 1988)
Apr. 24, 2007 – Acquired by sxr Uranium One Inc.; basis 0.45 new sxr Uranium sh. for 1 old UrAsia Energy sh. (see sxr Uranium One Inc.)

Urastar Energy Inc. (B.C. Feb. 22, 2007)
Aug. 3, 2011 – Name changed to Urastar Gold Corp. ■

Urastar Gold Corp. (B.C. Feb. 22, 2007)
May 27, 2013 – Acquired by Agnico Eagle Mines Limited for Cdn$0.25 per sh.

Uravan Minerals Inc. (Alta. Dec. 1, 1997)
July 7, 2022 – Continued into British Columbia.
July 7, 2023 – Name changed to Nuclear Fuels Inc. pursuant to the reverse takeover acquisition of (old) Nuclear Fuels Inc.; basis 0.8 new for 1 old sh. (see FPsurvey - Mines & Energy)

Urban Communications Inc. (B.C. June 3, 1988)
Nov. 20, 2017 – Acquired by ACME Communications Canada, Inc. (subsequently Dr Peng Holding Canada, Inc); basis 7¢ cash per sh.

Urban Juice and Soda Company Ltd. (B.C. Dec. 23, 1986)
Dec. 31, 1999 – Continued into Wyoming.
Aug. 3, 2000 – Name changed to Jones Soda Co. and continued into Washington. (see FPsurvey - Industrials)

Urban Quebec Mines Ltd. (Ont. Aug. 25, 1947)
Apr. 15, 1982 – Name changed to Urban Resources Limited. ■

Urban Resource Technologies Inc. (Alta. May 15, 1990)
Nov. 5, 1998 – Dissolved. Assets transferred to newly formed Oklahoma company Urban Resource Technologies, Inc.

Urban Resources Limited (Ont. Aug. 25, 1947)
June 14, 1985 – Name changed to Urbana Corporation; basis 1 new for 5 old shs. (see FPsurvey - Industrials)

Urban Select Capital Corporation (B.C. Sept. 12, 2007)
Apr. 5, 2019 – Name changed to Roadman Investments Corp. ■

Urbanfund Corp. (Alta. Feb. 4, 1997)
2003 – Continued into Ontario. (see FPsurvey - Industrials)

UrbanGold Minerals Inc. (Can. June 21, 2017)
May 25, 2021 – Amalgamated with 12842971 Canada Inc., a wholly owned subsid. of Troilus Gold Corp.; basis 0.3004 Troilus shs. for 1 UrbanGold sh.

Urbanimmersive Technologies Inc. (Can. Apr. 6, 2011)
Oct. 1, 2015 – Name changed to Urbanimmersive Inc. following amalgamation with wholly owned Urbanimmersive Inc. (see FPsurvey - Industrials)

Urbco Inc. (Alta. June 2, 1988)
May 30, 2002 – Land development and construction business spun off into a new company named NewNorth Projects Inc. and real estate rental business converted into an investment trust named Northern Property Real Estate Investment Trust. (see NewNorth Projects Ltd.)

Urco Mines Ltd. (Ont. 1953)
May 13, 1965 – Dissolved.

Urodynamix Technologies Ltd. (B.C. Dec. 3, 1980)
Aug. 29, 2011 – Name changed to Venturi Ventures Inc.; basis 1 new for 20 old shs. ■

Ursa Major International Inc. (Barbados July 19, 1994)
Apr. 21, 2010 – Continued into Ontario.
Apr. 26, 2010 – Name changed to Auriga Gold Corp.; basis 1 new for 4 old shs. ■

Ursa Major Minerals Incorporated (Ont. June 1, 1992)
July 19, 2012 – Acquired by Prophecy Platinum Corp.; basis 1 Prophecy com. sh. for each 25 Ursa com. shs.

UrtheCast Corp. (Ont. Mar. 24, 2004)
Jan. 1, 2014 – Amalgamated in Ontario to continue with same name.
Sept. 4, 2020 – Filed for protection under the Companies' Creditors Arrangement Act and Ernst & Young Inc. appointed monitor.
Jan. 19, 2021 – Assets consisting of the SAR-XL Constellation Project sold for $1,225,000.
Feb. 26, 2021 – Assets consisting of the UrtheDaily Constellation Project and the UrthePipeline Product were sold to Antarctica Infrastruture Partners LLC for $69,300,000 consisting of: $1,000,000 cash; assumption of $20,500,000 owing to Land O'Lakes; 35% of Antarctica non-vtg. equity in exchange for $36,100,000 in secured debt; and assumption of $11,700,000 of secured debt owed to the Strategic Aerospace and Defence Initiative.Assets were transferred to EarthDaily Holdings, LP, EarthDaily Canada Holdings Corp. and EarthDaily Canada Limited Partnership, wholly owned subsids. of Antarctica,
Mar. 5, 2021 – Proceedings under the CCAA were terminated and Ernst & Young were discharged as monitor. (see FPsurvey - Industrials)

Uruguay Goldfields Inc. (Alta. Feb. 13, 1998 amalg.)
Feb. 8, 2002 – Name changed to Uruguay Mineral Exploration Inc. and continued into Yukon. ■

Uruguay Mineral Exploration Inc. (Yuk. Feb. 8, 2002)
Jan. 7, 2010 – Name changed to Orosur Mining Inc. pursuant to acquisition of Fortune Valley Resources Inc. (see FPsurvey - Mines & Energy)

Us-Ca-Mex Explorations Ltd. (Ont. 1969)
May 1, 1984 – Name changed to Tri-Coast Resource Corporation; basis 1 new for 10 old shs. ■

User Friendly Media Inc. (B.C. Apr. 21, 1999)
Mar. 4, 2004 – Name changed to UFM Ventures Ltd. ■

Utah Electronics (Canada) Ltd. (Can. 1944)
Dec. 16, 1980 – Declared bankrupt in May 1951. Company dissolved.

Utah International Inc. (Del. 1956)
1987 – Name changed to BHP-Utah Minerals International Inc.

Utah Larder Gold Mines Ltd. (Ont. Nov. 28, 1945)
Aug. 31, 1992 – Delisted from the CDN. Subsequently dissolved and charter cancelled.

Utah Products Company of Canada Ltd. (Can. 1944)
June 20, 1949 – Name changed to Utah Electronics (Canada) Ltd. ■

Utica Mines Ltd. (B.C. Mar. 24, 1937)
1971 – Name changed to Dankoe Mines Ltd.; basis 1 new for 5 old shs. ■

Utica Mines (1937) Ltd. (B.C. Mar. 24, 1937)
Dec. 1960 – Name changed to Utica Mines Ltd.; basis 1 new for 20 old shs. ■

UtiliCorp Networks Canada (British Columbia) Ltd. (B.C. May 8, 1897)
May 31, 2002 – Name changed to Aquila Networks Canada (British Columbia) Ltd. ■

UtiliCorp United Inc. (Mo. 1950)
Apr. 1, 1987 – Continued into Delaware.
Mar. 18, 2002 – Name changed to Aquila, Inc.

Utilities and Funding Corporation Limited (Ont. 1965)
Feb. 14, 1984 – Name changed to Glenayr "Kitten" Limited.

Utility Corp. (Ont. May 17, 1993)
May 16, 2018 – Terminated; basis $25.4757 cash per cl. C sh. payable to shldrs. on May 22, 2018.

Utility Gas & Oil Reserves Ltd. (B.C.)
1959 – Struck off register.

Utility Split Trust (Ont. Oct. 24, 2006)
Jan. 3, 2017 – Terminated; basis $16.8393 cash per capital unit and $10.1313 cash per cl. B pref. security.

Utopia Gold Mines Ltd. (Ont. 1946)
1968 – Name changed to Utopia Mining and Holdings Corporation Ltd. ■

Utopia Mining and Holdings Corporation Ltd. (Ont. 1946)
Feb. 1980 – Charter cancelled.

V

V-Tech Diagnostics (Canada) Inc. (B.C. Oct. 7, 1986)
Apr. 17, 2003 – Struck from register and dissolved.

VAALCO Energy, Inc. (B.C. 1984)
1989 – Continued into Delaware.

VAR Computer Solutions Corporation (B.C. Mar. 29, 1984)
June 5, 1995 – Name changed to Econ Ventures Ltd. ■

VAR Resources Corp. (B.C. Nov. 21, 1983)
Aug. 22, 2022 – Continued into Alberta.
Aug. 25, 2022 – Name changed to Grounded Lithium Corp. pursuant to the reverse takeover acquisition of (old) Grounded Lithium Corp. (see FPsurvey - Mines & Energy)

VBI Vaccines Inc. (B.C. Apr. 9, 1965)
Jan. 3, 2025 – Acquired by K2 VBI Equity Trust, LLC, an affiliate of K2 Health Ventures LLC, a secured creditor. All o/s com. shs. were redeemed and cancelled for no consideration.

VCom Inc. (Sask. July 7, 1988)
June 30, 2003 – Continued into Canada.
Nov. 29, 2006 – Name changed to Vecima Networks Inc. (see FPsurvey - Industrials)

VECTOR Energy Fund (Ont. Mar. 30, 2005)
Apr. 28, 2006 – Amalgamated with ACTIVEnergy Income Fund; basis 0.9598691 new ACTIVEnergy unit for 1 old VECTOR unit. (see ACTIVEnergy Income Fund)

VERSUS Technologies Inc. (Can. Dec. 20, 1996)
Aug. 30, 2000 – Acquired by California-based E*TRADE Group, Inc. valued at $18 per sh.; basis 0.724757 E*TRADE com. shs. or 0.724757 EGI Canada Corporation exch. shs. for 1 VERSUS sh. (see EGI Canada Corporation)

VF Capital Ltd. (Alta. Mar. 5, 1997)
Aug. 9, 1999 – Name changed to Canadian Dental Partners Inc. ■

VFC Inc. (Can. Dec. 14, 1994)
Apr. 21, 2006 – Acquired by The Toronto-Dominion Bank; basis $19.50, or $0.05 plus 0.306 new Toronto-Dominion sh., or a combination thereof for 1 old VFC sh.

VG Gold Corp. (Ont. Mar. 24, 1972)
Jan. 1, 2011 – Formed Lexam VG Gold Inc. in Ontario following plan of arrangement amalgamation with Lexam Explorations Inc. ■

VGM Trustco Limited (Ont. May 1, 1959)
Jan. 8, 1981 – Name changed to Victoria and Grey Trustco Limited. ■

VGS Seismic Canada Inc. (Can. June 3, 1992)
Sept. 28, 2009 – Acquired by Plainfield Special Situations Master Fund Limited for 6¢ per sh.

VHQ Entertainment Inc. (Alta. Sept. 5, 1997)
July 5, 2005 – Amalgamated with wholly owned subsid. of Movie Gallery; basis $1.15 per sh.

V.I.P. Dynasty International Marketing Corp. (B.C. 1972)
Dec. 11, 1987 – Dissolved and struck off register.

VIVO Cannabis Inc. (Can. Apr. 12, 2007)
Apr. 5, 2023 – Acquired by MediPharm Labs Corp.; basis 0.2910 MediPharm shs. for 1 VIVO sh.

VLCTY Capital Inc. (B.C. Sept. 16, 2019)
Aug. 13, 2021 – Name changed to BuildDirect.com Technologies Inc. pursuant to the Qualifying Transaction reverse takeover acquisition of (old) BuildDirect.com Technologies Inc. and concurrent amalgamation of (old) BuildDirect with wholly owned 9923896 Canada Inc.; basis 1 new for 26.538 old shs. (see FPsurvey - Industrials)

VLM Ventures Ltd. (B.C. Apr. 4, 2008)
Dec. 15, 2011 – Name changed to Altan Nevada Minerals Limited pursuant to Qualifying Transaction reverse takeover acquisition of (old) Altan Nevada Minerals Limited and subsequent amalgamation of Altan with wholly owned 0912570 B.C. Ltd.; basis 1 new for 2.5 old shs. ■

VM Holding S.A. (Luxembourg Feb. 26, 2014)
Sept. 25, 2017 – Name changed to Nexa Resources S.A.

VM Hotel Acquisition Corp. (B.C. Nov. 16, 2020)
Mar. 4, 2024 – All o/s cl. A restricted vtg. shs. redeemed for US$10.8023351359 cash per sh.

VMS Ventures Inc. (B.C. Aug. 8, 1996)
Apr. 29, 2016 – Acquired by Royal Nickel Corporation; basis either (i) $0.064170, (ii) $0.023942 plus 0.245765 Royal shs. or (iii) 0.392032 Royal shs. for 1 VMS sh.

VMX Resources Inc. (B.C. Jan. 29, 1986)
Sept. 7, 2007 – Name changed to Monster Uranium Corp. ■

VNC Video Network Corp. (B.C. Aug. 18, 1986)
Jan. 23, 1990 – Name changed to WestPost Capital Inc. ■

VON Capital Corp. (B.C. Feb. 24, 2017)
Oct. 5, 2020 – Name changed to Xplore Resources Corp. pursuant to Qualifying Transaction reverse takeover acquisition of (old) Xplore Resources Corp. and concurrent amalgamation of (old) Xplore with wholly owned 2717915 Ontario Inc. (see FPsurvey - Mines & Energy)

VOTI Detection Inc. (B.C. May 24, 2017)
Dec. 28, 2022 – Filed an assignment into bankruptcy and PricewaterhouseCoopers Inc. was appointed trustee.

VOXCOM Income Fund (Alta. Apr. 12, 2005)
June 26, 2007 – Acquired by UE Waterheater Income Fund for $13.25 per fund unit. (see UE Waterheater Income Fund)

VOXCOM Incorporated (Can. Jan. 6, 1989)
May 14, 2004 – Going private transaction; basis $1.03 per sh.

VP Group Media Limited (B.C. Nov. 18, 1999)
Feb. 10, 2005 – Continued into Ontario.
Feb. 3, 2006 – Name changed to DVD Investments Limited; basis 1 new for 5 old shs. ■

VPN Technologies Inc. (B.C. Mar. 21, 2018)
June 1, 2023 – Name changed to Energy Plug Technologies Corp. (see FPsurvey - Industrials)

VR Interactive Corporation (Alta. Oct. 4, 2000)
Mar. 29, 2012 – Name changed to Muskrat Minerals Incorporated pursuant to acquisition of an indirect interest in Grand River Ironsands Incorporated; basis 1 new for 8 old shs. ■

VRB Power Systems Inc. (Can. Nov. 13, 1986)
Aug. 24, 2009 – Name changed to Nevaro Capital Corporation. ■

V.R.D. Entertainment Ltd. (Ont. Jan. 9, 1987)
May 31, 1996 – Delisted from the Canadian Dealing Network. Subsequently dissolved.

VRX WorldWide Inc. (Alta. Dec. 29, 1993)
Oct. 2, 2014 – Name changed to MediaValet Inc. following sale of its photography services business VRX Studios. ■

VS Services Ltd. (Can. June 15, 1961; via Dominion charter)
June 25, 1992 – Name changed to Versa Services Ltd. ■

VSC Technology Inc. (B.C. 1981)
May 4, 1994 – Delsited from the Vancouver Stock Exchange. Subsequently dissolved for failure to file.

VSM Exploration Inc. (Que. Nov. 17, 1986)
Jan. 15, 1993 – Acquired by Cambior Inc.; basis 1 Cambior sh. for 16.5 VSM shs. (see Cambior Inc.)

VTEC Capital Corp. (B.C. July 8, 1999)
Dec. 14, 2001 – Name changed to Coast Mountain Power Corp. following Qualifying Transaction reverse takeover acquisition of Coast Mountain Hydro Corp. ■

VTI Industries Inc. (B.C. May 17, 1984)
Nov. 23, 1990 – Name changed to Emerald Ventures Inc.; basis 1 new for 2 old shs. ■

VTL Venture Corp. (Ont. Sept. 29, 1975 amalg.)
Sept. 2, 1994 – Name changed to Allcorp United Inc. ■

VTL Venture Equities Ltd. (Ont. Sept. 29, 1975 amalg.)
July 7, 1986 – Name changed to VTL Venture Corp.; basis 1 new com., 1 new cl. A and 1 new cl. C sh. for 1 old com. sh. ■

V2 Games Inc. (B.C. Jan. 13, 2010)
Jan. 13, 2021 – Name changed to GameOn Entertainment Technologies Inc. (see FPsurvey - Industrials)

VVC Exploration Corporation (B.C. Apr. 11, 1983)
Aug. 27, 2003 – Continued into Canada. (see FPsurvey - Mines & Energy)

Vaaldiam Mining Inc. (Can. Oct. 5, 1992 amalg.)
July 6, 2012 – Acquired by BCKP Limited for $0.2649292 per sh.

Vaaldiam Resources Ltd. (Can. Mar. 4, 1987)
Mar. 26, 2010 – Acquired by Tiomin Resources Inc.; basis 0.08 Tiomin post-consol. shs. (1 for 10) for 1 Vaaldiam Resources sh. (see Vaaldiam Mining Inc.)

Vachon Inc. (Que. 1947)
Aug. 11, 1976 – Name changed to Le Groupe Alimentaire Vachon Inc. ■

The Vacuum Gas & Oil Co., Ltd. (Ont. 1915)
1960 – Struck off register.

Val d'Bell Mines Ltd. (Ont. 1940)
Apr. 1954 – Charter cancelled.

Val d'Or Consolidated Mines Ltd. (Que. 1946)
Oct. 20, 1973 – Charter cancelled.

Val d'Or Explorations Ltd. (B.C. 1972)
Mar. 29, 1985 – Formed Meridor Resources Limited in British Columbia on amalgamation with 3 other cos.; basis 0.333 new for 1 old sh. ■

Val d'Or Mineral Holdings Ltd. (Ont. Sept. 5, 1935)
Apr. 27, 1967 – Merged into The Little Long Lac Gold Mines Ltd.; basis 1 new for 5 old shs. (see The Little Long Lac Gold Mines Ltd.)

Val d'Or Resources Inc. (Que. 1983)
June 6, 1991 – Name changed to Consolidated Val d'Or Resources Inc.; basis 1 new for 15 old shs. (see FPsurvey - Mines & Energy)

Val Jon Explorations Ltd. (Ont. 1955)
Nov. 12, 1969 – Charter cancelled.

Val-Mar Swimming Pools Ltd. (Que. 1962)
1980 – Following acquisition by KLK Inc. of all o/s cl. A shs. held by public at $1.35 per sh., co. became a wholly owned subsid. of KLK.

Val Royal Group Inc. (Can. Nov. 1, 1986 amalg.)
Sept. 1, 1995 – Name changed to Réno-Dépôt Inc. ■

Val Vista Energy Ltd. (Alta. Feb. 5, 2001)
Apr. 18, 2005 – Acquired by Avenir Diversified Income Trust; basis $1.43, or 0.13364 new Avenir unit, or a combination thereof for 1 old Val Vista sh. (see Avenir Diversified Income Trust)

Valar Resources Ltd. (B.C. 1985)
Nov. 12, 1993 – Dissolved and struck off register.

Valavaara Environmental Technologies Ltd. (Ont. Nov. 9, 1989)
Apr. 12, 1996 – Name changed to Kenridge Investment Corp.; basis 1 new for 10 old shs. ■

Valcent Products Inc. (Alta. Jan. 19, 1996)
June 8, 2012 – Name changed to Alterrus Systems Inc. ■

Valclair Resources Ltd. (B.C. Feb. 15, 1984)
Dec. 2, 1985 – Name changed to SCI Satellite Conferencing International Corporation. ■

Valdemaque Mines Ltd. (Ont. 1950)
Mar. 1968 – Charter cancelled.

Valdex Mines Inc. (Que. 1969)
June 1, 1976 – Merged into Brominco Inc.; basis 1 new for 40 old shs.

Valdez Gold Inc. (Ont. Aug. 2, 1990)
Dec. 24, 2010 – Name changed to Ryan Gold Corp. following acquisition of Ryan Gold Inc. by wholly owned Valdez Gold (Yukon) Inc. and subsequent amalgamation, constituting an asset acquisition of Ryan Gold; basis 1 new for 3.5 old shs. ■

Valdez Resource Industries Ltd. (B.C. Jan. 9, 1967)
Jan. 14, 1980 – Name changed to Goldera Resources Inc.; basis 1 new for 3 old shs. ■

Valdina Gold Mines Ltd. (Ont. 1944)
1956 – Charter cancelled.

Valdor Fiber Optics Inc. (B.C. Mar. 19, 1984)
July 21, 2008 – Name changed to Valdor Technology International Inc.; basis 1 new for 6.5 old shs. (see FPsurvey - Industrials)

Valdora Mines Ltd. (Que. 1946)
1962 – Charter cancelled.

Valdy Investments Ltd. (B.C. Aug. 22, 2018)
Jan. 10, 2022 – Name changed to The INX Digital Company, Inc. pursuant to the reverse takeover acquisition of INX Limited; basis 1 new for 2.7266667 old shs. (see FPsurvey - Industrials)

Vale Inco Limited (Can. July 25, 1916; via Dominion charter)
Aug. 31, 2010 – Name changed to Vale Canada Limited.

Valeant Pharmaceuticals International, Inc. (Can. June 29, 2005)
Aug. 9, 2013 – Continued into British Columbia.
July 13, 2018 – Name changed to Bausch Health Companies Inc. (see FPsurvey - Industrials)

Valemont Mining and Development Co. Ltd. (B.C.)
May 15, 1969 – Struck off register.

Valencia Ventures Inc. (Que. Apr. 2, 1990 amalg.)
June 2, 2014 – Continued into Ontario.
Jan. 10, 2019 – Name changed to EarthRenew Inc. pursuant to reverse takeover acquisition of 2292055 Ontario Inc. (dba EarthRenew). ■

Valener Inc. (Can. June 15, 2010)
Sept. 30, 2019 – Acquired indirectly by Noverco Inc.; basis $25 cash per ser.A pref. sh. and $26 cash per com. sh.
Mar. 10, 2022 – Name changed to Energir Development Inc.

The Valens Company Inc. (Can. June 22, 2020)
Jan. 19, 2023 – Acquired by SNDL Inc.; basis 0.3334 SNDL shs. for 1 Valens sh.

Valens GroWorks Corp. (B.C. Jan. 14, 1981)
June 22, 2020 – Continued into Canada.
June 24, 2020 – Name changed to The Valens Company Inc. ■

Valentia Oil Corp. Ltd. (Ont. 1949)
1970 – Struck off register.

Valentine Gold Corporation (B.C. 1986)
Jan. 11, 1990 – Name changed to Point Resources Ltd.; basis 1 new for 10 old shs. ■

Valentine Ventures Corp. (Alta. Nov. 28, 2006)
Mar. 11, 2010 – Together with Blackwater Capital Corp. Latigo Capital Corporation and Warnic 1 Enterprises Ltd.(Capital Pool Companies) amalgamated with Cumberland Oil & Gas Ltd. constituting Capital Pool Companies' Qualifying Transaction to form Cumberland Oil & Gas Ltd; basis Valentine (0.3474-for-1), Blackwater (0.2875-for-1), Latigo (0.3879-for-1) Warnic (0.3032-for-1) and Cumberland (1-for-1). (see Cumberland Oil & Gas Ltd.)

Valeo Pharma Inc. (Can. Mar. 27, 2003)
Feb. 5, 2025 – Pursuant to a reverse vesting transaction all o/s shs. acquired by Xediton Pharmaceuticals Inc.; basis unknown. It was expected that there would be no recovery for existing shldrs.

Valerie Gold Resources Ltd. (B.C. Apr. 14, 1987)
Mar. 27, 2003 – Name changed to ValGold Resources Ltd. ■

ValGold Resources Ltd. (B.C. Apr. 14, 1987)
Aug. 1, 2018 – Acquired by Metalla Royalty & Streaming Ltd.; basis 0.1667 Metalla com. shs. for 1 ValGold sh. valued at 13¢ per share.

Valhalla Energy Corp. (B.C. 1980)
Feb. 26, 1988 – Name changed to The Valhalla Gold Group Corporation. ■

The Valhalla Gold Group Corporation (B.C. 1980)
Aug. 1, 1989 – Amalgamated with Solomon Gold Corp. to form Solomon Resources Limited; basis 1 new for 1.5 old shs. (see Solomon Resources Limited)

Valhalla Minerals Inc. (B.C. 1980)
Jan. 1, 1985 – Name changed to Valhalla Energy Corp. ■

Valhalla Mines Ltd. (Ont. 1961)
Mar. 25, 1970 – Charter cancelled.

Valiant Energy Inc. (Alta. May 31, 2005)
Sept. 19, 2006 – Plan of Arrangement acquisition by Peerless Energy Inc.; basis 1.06 new Peerless cl. sh. for 1 old Valiant com. sh. (see Peerless Energy Inc.)

Valiant Enterprises Ltd. (Alta. Apr. 26, 1993)
Oct. 2, 2003 – Struck from registry and dissolved.

Valiant Gold Mines Ltd. (Man. 1959)
Mar. 1972 – Assets acquired by Commander Nickel Copper Mines Ltd.

Valiant Minerals Ltd. (B.C. Mar. 19, 2007)
Feb. 12, 2015 – Formed Convalo Health Corp. following Qualifying Transaction amalgamation with 0986282 B.C. Ltd., a wholly owned subsid. of Convalo Health International, Corp.; basis 1 Convalo Health International com. sh. for 2 Valiant com. shs. (see Convalo Health International, Corp.)

Valkyries Petroleum Corp. (Can. Oct. 25, 1994)
Aug. 9, 2006 – Acquired by Lundin Petroleum AB (trades on Stockholm Exchange); basis 1 Lundin sh. for 1 Valkyries sh.

Vallee Lithium Mining Corp. Ltd. (Ont. May 18, 1955)
May 1977 – Charter cancelled.
Sept. 15, 1987 – Charter revived.
Oct. 13, 1987 – Name changed to Sindor Resources Inc. ■

Vallex Mines Ltd. (B.C. 1969)
July 1977 – Dissolved.

Valley Copper Mines Limited (B.C. 1964)
July 31, 1981 – Amalgamated with Anchor Investments Inc., a wholly owned subsid. of Cominco Ltd. Minority shldrs. received 1 pref. sh. of amalg. co. (immediately redeemed at $33 per sh.), for 1 old sh.

Valley Explorations Ltd. (B.C. 1937)
July 13, 1961 – Dissolved.

Valley First Credit Union (Can. - unspecified)
Jan. 1, 2010 – Merged with Envision Credit Union to form First West Credit Union.

Valley Forge Mining Ltd. (B.C. 1968)
1969 – Merged into Mineral Mountain Mining Co. Ltd.; basis 2 new for 3 old shs.

Valley High Ventures Ltd. (B.C. Aug. 11, 1980)
Mar. 29, 2011 – Amalgamated with Levon Resources Ltd.; basis 1 Levon sh. plus 0.125 Bearing Resources Ltd. shs. for 1 Valley High sh. (see Levon Resources Ltd.)

Valley Oil & Gas Corp. (B.C. Sept. 19, 1979)
Jan. 25, 1994 – Name changed to Consolidated Valley Ventures Ltd.; basis 1 new for 4 old shs. ■

Valley Petroleums Ltd. (Alta.)
1960 – Struck off register.

Valley Royalties Ltd. (Sask.)
1960 – Struck off register.

Valley View Gold Mines Ltd. (Utah 1977)
June 3, 1988 – Name changed to Jefferson Valley Gold Mines Inc.; basis 1 new for 2.5 old shs.

Valleyview Resources Ltd. (B.C. Oct. 25, 2021)
Mar. 5, 2025 – Name changed to Homeland Uranium Corp. pursuant to the reverse takeover acquisition of Shift Rare Metals Inc. (see FPsurvey - Mines & Energy)

Valloc Gold Mines Ltd. (Ont. 1935)
May 1958 – Charter cancelled.

Valmec Capital Inc. (Que. Dec. 11, 1995)
June 4, 2010 – Dissolved for failure to file.

Valmont Mining Exploration Inc. (Can. Feb. 22, 1984)
June 21, 1989 – Name changed to Abior Exploration Inc.; basis 1 new for 5 old shs. ■

Valmont Mining Exploration Ltd. (Que. 1957)
1967 – Merged into Resource Exploration & Development Co. Ltd.; basis 100 new for 299 old shs.

Valnicla Copper Mine Ltd. (B.C. 1965)
1969 – Acquired by National Nickel Ltd.; basis 1 new for 5 old shs. (see National Nickel Ltd.)

Valor Lithium Mines Ltd. (Que. 1952)
1959 – Merged into Massval Mines Ltd.; basis 1 new for 4 old shs.

Valor Mines Ltd. (Que. 1952)
1955 – Name changed to Valor Lithium Mines Ltd. ■

Valor Ventures Inc. (B.C. Mar. 1, 2007)
May 19, 2015 – Name changed to North South Petroleum Corp. ■

Valora Explorations & Developments Ltd. (Ont. 1970)
May 24, 1972 – Amalgamated to form Xtra Developments Inc.; basis 1 new for 17 old shs. (see Xtra Developments Inc.)

Valorem Resources Inc. (B.C. May 9, 2014)
Apr. 21, 2023 – Name changed to Avanti Gold Corp. (see FPsurvey - Mines & Energy)

ValOro Resources Inc. (B.C. July 5, 1996)
Jan. 11, 2019 – Acquired by Defiance Silver Corp.; basis 0.71 Defiance com. shs. for 1 ValOro com. sh.

Valour Inc. (Ont. Nov. 3, 2009)
July 10, 2023 – Name changed to DeFi Technologies Inc. (see FPsurvey - Industrials)

Valpar Resources Inc. (B.C. Mar. 4, 1987)
Nov. 14, 1995 – Name changed to Carnival Resources Ltd.; basis 1 new for 12 old shs. ■

Valparaiso Energy Inc. (Alta. Feb. 27, 1987)
Feb. 6, 2017 – Name changed to Catalina Gold Corp. and continued into British Columbia. ■

Valray Explorations Ltd. (Ont. 1946)
July 16, 1976 – Charter cancelled.

Valrex Gold Mines Ltd. (Ont. 1947)
Apr. 9, 1975 – Dissolved.

Valrita Mines Ltd. (Ont. 1945)
Sept. 21, 1959 – Dissolved.

Valterra Resource Corporation (Yuk. May 8, 1997)
Feb. 22, 2008 – Continued into British Columbia.
Oct. 4, 2023 – Name changed to Nickelex Resource Corporation. ■

Valterra Wines Ltd. (Yuk. May 8, 1997)
Apr. 20, 2005 – Name changed to Valterra Resource Corporation. ■

Valu Concepts International Corp. (B.C. Jan. 30, 1987)
Sept. 8, 1994 – Name changed to Double Impact Communications Corp. and continued into Canada; basis 1 new for 3 old shs. ■

Valu-net Corporation (Alta. July 29, 1996)
Oct. 14, 1999 – Continued into Ontario.
Oct. 9, 2001 – Name changed to BSM Technologies Inc. ■

Valucap Investments Inc. (Yuk. Nov. 21, 2000)
Nov. 24, 2008 – Continued into Ontario. (see FPsurvey - Industrials)

Value Capital Trust (Alta. Mar. 16, 2017)
Apr. 21, 2022 – Name changed to AIP Realty Trust pursuant to the Qualifying Transaction reverse takeover acquisition of AIP Yield Fund, LP.; basis 1 new for 20 old shs. (see FPsurvey - Industrials)

Value Investment Corporation (Can. 1939)
Jan. 18, 1984 – Continued into British Columbia.
Nov. 1989 – Entered voluntary dissolution. Pref. shs. redeemed for $25 per sh.
Feb. 1990 – Peat Marwick Thorne Inc. of Toronto, was appointed as trustee.
Jan. 6, 1993 – Distributions were made as follows: $5.25 per sh. to com. shldrs. in September 1990; $3.62 per sh. to com. shldrs. in June 1991; taxable dividend of 16.5¢ in December 1991; final capital distribution of $0.0426 per com. sh. Jan. 6, 1993. Co. wound up following final distribution.

Value Line Minerals Ltd. (B.C. 1966)
Sept. 11, 1975 – Dissolved.

Valverde Capital Corp. (B.C. Dec. 20, 2006)
Aug. 22, 2008 – Formed Americas Petrogas Inc. in Alberta following reverse takeover acquisition of and amalgamation with Americas Petrogas Inc.; basis 1 new for 2 old shs. ■

Vamp Lake Mines Ltd. (Ont. 1964)
1973 – Name changed to Casummit Lake Mines Ltd. ■

Van Chester Mines Ltd. (Ont. 1953)
Apr. 20, 1967 – Dissolved.

Van-City Cultured Marble Products Ltd. (B.C. 1987)
Oct. 3, 1995 – Name changed to Consolidated Van-City Marble Ltd.; basis 1 new for 5 old shs. ■

Van Der Hout Associates Limited (Ont. 1946)
Oct. 12, 1987 – All o/s com. shs. not already held acquired by Maremont Corporation of Chicago.

Van Horne Gold Exploration Inc. (Ont. 1980)
May 5, 1988 – Amalgamated with Moss Resources Ltd. to form Moss Resources Inc.; basis 1.1 new for 1 old sh.

Van Houten Gold Mines Ltd. (Ont. 1940)
Dec. 21, 1959 – Charter cancelled.

Van Houtte Inc. (Can. Mar. 25, 1980)
July 23, 2007 – Acquired by Littlejohn & Co., LLC, through affiliate Littlejohn Fund III, LP; basis $25 per sh.

Van Ness Industries Ltd. (Alta. 1940)
July 18, 1975 – Name changed to Claiborne Industries Limited. ■

Van Ollie Exploration Ltd. (Ont. Oct. 5, 1988)
May 13, 1996 – Name changed to Engineering Power Systems Group Inc. following reverse takeover acquisition of 1169402 Ontario Inc.; basis 1 new for 30 old shs. ■

Van Roi Consolidated Mines Ltd. (B.C. 1947)
1955 – Name changed to Slocan Van Roi Mines Ltd.; basis 1 new for 3 old shs. ■

Van Roi (1947) Ltd. (B.C. 1947)
1950 – Name changed to Van Roi Consolidated Mines Ltd. ■

Van-Sea Resources Ltd. (B.C. 1955)
July 28, 1981 – Dissolved.

Van Silver Explorations Ltd. (B.C. 1966)
Nov. 30, 1976 – Amalgamated with Tedi Resources Ltd. to form Van Silver Mines Ltd.; basis 5 new for 6 old shs.

Van Silver Mines Ltd. (B.C. 1976 amalg.)
Apr. 30, 1979 – Name changed to Silver Tusk Mines Ltd. ■

Van-Tor Oils & Explorations Ltd. (B.C. 1948)
1966 – Name changed to Consolidated Van-Tor Resources Ltd.; basis 1 new for 5 old shs. ■

Vanacor Gold Mines Ltd. (Ont. 1945)
Dec. 22, 1958 – Dissolved.

Vanadium-Alloys Steel Canada Ltd. (Ont. Feb. 10, 1948)
Nov. 1966 – Name changed to Vascan Ltd. ■

Vanadium One Energy Corp. (Ont. Feb. 27, 2007)
June 5, 2019 – Name changed to Vanadium One Iron Corp. ■

Vanadium One Iron Corp. (Ont. Feb. 27, 2007)
Oct. 18, 2021 – Name changed to Voyager Metals Inc. ■

Vanadium 23 Capital Corporation (B.C. Jan. 30, 2018)
Dec. 17, 2021 – Name changed to CMP Mining Inc. (see FPsurvey - Mines & Energy)

Vanalta Limited (Can. 1929)
1959 – Acquired by New Chamberlain Petroleums Ltd.; basis 1 new for 3.75 old shs. (see Sarcee Petroleums Ltd.)

Vanalta Resources Ltd. (B.C. 1958)
June 1975 – Canadian Hidrogas Resources Ltd. offered to acquire all shs. not already held by it on basis of 1 sh. Hidrogas for 14 shs. Vanalta.

Vananda Explorations Ltd. (B.C. 1948)
Nov. 23, 1972 – Name changed to Ramco Industries Ltd.; basis 1 new for 5 old shs. ■

Vananda Gold Ltd. (B.C. Apr. 18, 1986)
Feb. 28, 1995 – Name changed to Consolidated Van Anda Gold Ltd.; basis 1 new for 5 old shs. (see FPsurvey - Mines & Energy)

Vananda Mines (1948) Ltd. (B.C. 1948)
Sept. 1962 – Name changed to Vananda Explorations Ltd.; basis 1 new for 3 old shs. ■

Vananda Mining Co. Ltd. (B.C. 1945)
1948 – Name changed to Vananda Mines (1948) Ltd. and continued into British Columbia; basis 1 new for 2 old shs. ■

Vanbar Oils Ltd. (Alta. 1952)
1954 – Assets acquired by Nuco Petroleums Ltd.; basis 1 new for 66 old shs.

Vanbec Resources Corporation (B.C. Aug. 26, 1986)
Oct. 27, 1986 – Continued into Canada.
June 8, 1987 – Name changed to Sartigan Granite Corporation. ■

Vanc Pharmaceuticals Inc. (B.C. May 30, 2000)
Nov. 5, 2018 – Name changed to Avricore Health Inc. (see FPsurvey - Industrials)

Vancan Capital Corp. (Alta. Apr. 25, 1994)
May 14, 2004 – Name changed to Max Resource Corp. ■

Vancouver Cold Storage Ltd. (B.C. 1928)
1975 – Acquired. Prior to purchase, Transco Storage and Transportation Services Ltd. held 75% of o/s shs.

Vancouver Finance Co. Ltd. (B.C. 1947)
June 1955 – Name changed to Credit Acceptance Corp. Ltd. ■

Vancouver Island Base Metals Ltd. (B.C. 1948)
Aug. 6, 1974 – Struck off register.

Vancouver Oil Co. Ltd. (unknown)
Liquidated.

Vancouver Pacific Oils Ltd. (Can. July 2, 1929)
Struck off register.

Vancouver Pacific Paper Co. Ltd. (B.C. 1929)
Oct. 1958 – Business sold to Canadian International Paper Company. Name subsequently changed to Agnew Industries Ltd.

Vancouver Times Publishing Ltd. (B.C. 1962)
Aug. 1965 – Operations ceased.

Vancouver Venture Corp. (B.C. July 8, 1986)
Aug. 23, 1993 – Name changed to Jackson Hole Holdings Corp. ■

Vanda Mines Ltd. (Ont. 1944)
Apr. 1962 – Dissolved.

Vandoo Consolidated Explorations Ltd. (Ont. 1950)
Nov. 9, 1976 – Charter cancelled.

Vandoo Copper Mining Corp. Ltd. (unknown)
1956 – Acquired by Vandoo Consolidated Explorations Ltd. (see Vandoo Consolidated Explorations Ltd.)

Vandorex Energy Corp. (B.C. 1984)
Mar. 7, 1990 – Name changed to Bentech Industries Inc. ■

Vandyke Snow Lake Gold Mines Ltd. (Ont. 1945)
1947 – Taken over by Lynnita Consolidated Gold Mines Ltd.; basis 1 new for 3 old shs. (see Lynnita Consolidated Gold Mines Ltd.)

Vanessa Uranium Mines Limited (Ont. 1969)
Feb. 20, 1980 – Dissolved.

Vanex Minerals Ltd. (B.C. 1958)
1962 – Assets acquired by Alscope Consolidated Ltd.

Vanex Resources Ltd. (B.C. June 9, 1983)
July 15, 1991 – Name changed to Poplar Resources Ltd.; basis 1 new for 4 old shs. ■

Vangold Mining Corp. (B.C. Aug. 11, 1978)
June 10, 2021 – Name changed to Guanajuato Silver Company Ltd. (see FPsurvey - Mines & Energy)

Vangold Resources Inc. (B.C. Aug. 11, 1978)
Mar. 4, 1994 – Name changed to Pacific Vangold Mines Ltd.; basis 1 new for 3 old shs. ■

Vangold Resources Ltd. (B.C. Aug. 11, 1978)
May 10, 2017 – Name changed to Vangold Mining Corp. ■

Vangorda Mines Ltd. (Can. 1955)
1979 – Acquired by Cyprus Anvil Mining Corp. for $1.50 per sh.

Vanguard Aviation Corp. (Alta. Apr. 10, 1997)
June 1, 2004 – Placed into receivership by secured creditor.
Oct. 2, 2005 – Struck of registry and dissolved.

Vanguard Explorations Ltd. (Que. Feb. 4, 1958)
1965 – Name changed to Guardian Mines Ltd.; basis 1 new for 4 old shs. ■

Vanguard Investments Corp. (Alta. Mar. 20, 2001)
May 10, 2011 – Continued into British Columbia.
June 20, 2011 – Name changed to Vinergy Resources Ltd. ■

Vanguard Long Lac Gold Mines Ltd. (Ont. June 26, 1934)
1949 – Charter cancelled.

Vanguard Oil Corporation (Alta. Oct. 11, 1996 amalg.)
May 30, 2001 – Acquired by Bitech Petroleum Corporation; basis either $0.08, or 0.1 Bitech sh., or a combination, for 1 Vanguard sh. (see Bitech Petroleum Corporation)

Vanguard Response Systems Inc. (Ont. Nov. 17, 2003 amalg.)
Mar. 29, 2005 – Name changed to Allen-Vanguard Corporation. ■

Vanguard Technologies Inc. (Can. Oct. 3, 2005)
Dec. 13, 2006 – Name changed to Eloda 2006 Corporation. ■

Vanguard Venture Corporation (B.C. 1987)
Apr. 8, 1994 – Dissolved and struck off register.

Vankath Mines Ltd. (Ont. 1944)
June 26, 1979 – Dissolved.

Vankirk Mines Ltd. (Ont. 1955)
Dec. 23, 1965 – Dissolved.

Vanlos Oil Lands Ltd. (B.C. 1929)
Aug. 20, 1970 – Dissolved.

Vanmetals Exploration Ltd. (B.C. 1962)
1970 – Name changed to Rand Resources Ltd.; basis 1 new for 3 old shs. ■

Vannessa Ventures Ltd. (B.C. Jan. 22, 1981)
May 28, 2008 – Name changed to Infinito Gold Ltd. (see FPsurvey - Mines & Energy)

Vanoil Energy Ltd. (B.C. Sept. 3, 2009)
Feb. 17, 2020 – Dissolved and struck from register.

Vanpeg Royalties Ltd. (unknown)
In voluntary liquidation. Wm. Kemp, Calgary, liquidator.

Vanstar Mining Resources Inc. (Can. May 4, 2007)
Feb. 16, 2024 – Acquired by IAMGOLD Corporation; basis 0.2008 IAMGOLD shs. for 1 Vanstar sh.

Vanstates Resources Ltd. (B.C. Mar. 8, 1951)
July 16, 1990 – Name changed to Southport Resources Inc.; basis 1 new for 3 old shs. ■

Vantage Enterprises Corp. (B.C. July 24, 1987)
July 14, 1998 – Name changed to African Gemstones Limited. ■

Vantage Group Limited (B.C. 1943)
Mar. 14, 1985 – Formed Barron Hunter Hargrave Strategic Resources Inc. in Canada. ■

Vantage Mining Co. Inc. (Ont. 1974)
Oct. 26, 1976 – Name changed to Aspen Explorations Inc. ■

Vantage Resources Ltd. (B.C. Aug. 10, 1976)
Oct. 17, 1979 – Name changed to Vat Petroleum Limited. ■

VantagePoint Systems, Inc. (B.C. Oct. 22, 1999)
Mar. 20, 2008 – Acquired by Solarsoft Business Systems for US$0.70 per sh.

Vantec Ventures Corporation (Alta. July 29, 1986)
Jan. 1, 1997 – Struck off register.

Vanteck (VRB) Technology Corp. (Can. Nov. 13, 1986)
Jan. 17, 2003 – Name changed to VRB Power Systems Inc. ■

Vanterra Resources Ltd. (B.C. 1983)
Mar. 1987 – Placed into receivership. All assets sold. Nothing for shldrs.

Vantex Oil, Gas & Minerals Ltd. (B.C. Jan. 6, 1987)
June 19, 1998 – Continued into Canada.
May 20, 2004 – Name changed to Vantex Resources Ltd. (see FPsurvey - Mines & Energy)

Vantex Resources Inc. (B.C. 1979)
Dec. 23, 1985 – Name changed to General Cybernetics Corporation following acquisition of General Cybernetics Corporation on Oct. 24, 1985 in exchange for the issuance of 7,787,082 shs. ■

Vantreal Resources Ltd. (B.C. Aug. 2, 1968)
Apr. 11, 1978 – Name changed to Caspian Resources Limited; basis 1 new for 5 old shs. (see FPsurvey - Mines & Energy)

Vanvelsor Mines Ltd. (Ont. 1945)
May 1961 – Charter cancelled.

Vanwin Resources Corporation (B.C. Feb. 8, 1983)
Oct. 6, 1989 – Delisted from the Vancouver Stock Exchange. Subsequently dissolved.

Vapen MJ Ventures Corporation (B.C. Dec. 11, 2015)
Nov. 12, 2019 – Name changed to Vext Science, Inc. (see FPsurvey - Industrials)

Vaqcourt Gold Mines Ltd. (Ont. 1945)
1952 – Charter cancelled.

Vaquero Energy Ltd. (Alta. May 5, 1995)
June 3, 2005 – Plan of Arrangement acquisition by Highpine Oil & Gas Limited; basis 0.391 new Highpine cl. A com. sh. for 1 old Vaquero com. sh. (see Highpine Oil & Gas Limited)

Varenna Holdings Ltd. (Alta. 1985)
Dec. 31, 1990 – Accrued and unpaid dividends of $0.4815 were paid per sh. following redemption at $25 per sh. of all o/s 9 1/4% cum. red. pref. shs. at $25 per sh.

Vargas Mines Ltd. (B.C. 1969)
July 26, 1974 – Name changed to Charleston Resources Ltd. ■

Variety Video Enterprises Inc. (Ont. 1923)
July 29, 1991 – Dissolved.

Varitech Investors Corporation (Can. Dec. 8, 1978)
Apr. 26, 1982 – Continued into Ontario.
Dec. 22, 1995 – Formed GLP NT Corporation following acquisition of and amalgamation with GLP NT Corporation; basis 3.33 new retract. cl. A non-vtg. shs. for 1 old fltg. rate redeem. retract. pref. sh. ■

Varitech Resources Ltd. (B.C. Dec. 8, 1980)
Mar. 23, 1993 – Name changed to Prime Spot Media Inc. ■

Varity Corporation (Can. July 22, 1891; via Dominion charter)
July 25, 1991 – Amalgamated with 2708001 Canada Inc., a wholly owned subsid. of the new co. also known as Varity Corporation. Shs. exchanged for shs. of new Varity Corporation; basis 1 new for 10 old shs. and 1 new cl. I pref. sh. for 1 cl. I pref. sh.
July 31, 1991 – Continued into Delaware.

Varmac Uranium Mines Ltd. (Alta. 1955)
Mar. 15, 1968 – Struck off register.

Varna Gold Inc. (Alta. Dec. 14, 1987 amalg.)
Jan. 18, 1993 – Name changed to New Island Minerals Ltd. ■

Vascan Ltd. (Ont. Feb. 10, 1948)
1969 – Name changed to Teledyne Canada, Limited. ■

Vasogen Inc. (Ont. Jan. 10, 1980)
Aug. 9, 1999 – Continued into Canada.
Oct. 27, 2009 – Name changed to Cervus Equipment Corporation pursuant to a plan arrangement with Cervus LP and Cervus GP Ltd. to convert Cervus LP to a corp., resulting in Cervus LP and Cervus GP Ltd. becoming wholly owned subsids. of Cervus Equipment Corp.; basis 3 Cervus Equipment shs. for 2 Cervus LP units. All Vasogen assets and liabilities were transferred (except tax assets) along with $7,500,000 from Cervus, to a new subsid. 7231971 Canada Inc. which amalgamated with a new subsid. of IntelliPharmaCeutics Ltd. to form publicly listed IntelliPharmaCeutics International Inc. (IPC International). Vasogen shldrs. exchanged shs. on 1-for-1 basis with IPC International. ■

Vassan Resources Inc. (Can. Aug. 2, 1983)
1985 – Continued into Quebec.
Dec. 29, 1989 – Name changed to Savanor Resources Inc.; basis 1 new for 10 old shs. ■

Vast Capital Pool Ltd. (B.C. Apr. 21, 1999)
Mar. 26, 2001 – Name changed to User Friendly Media Inc. following acquisition of UF Media Inc. ■

Vast Exploration Inc. (Ont. Oct. 2, 1987)
Oct. 14, 2014 – Name changed to ARHT Media Inc. following reverse takeover acquisition of Delebrity Inc. ■

Vastlode Mining Co. Ltd. (B.C. Mar. 12, 1965)
May 1972 – Name changed to Ashcroft Resources Ltd.; basis 1 new for 5 old shs. ■

Vat Petroleum Limited (B.C. Aug. 10, 1976)
Apr. 3, 1987 – Delisted from the Vancouver Stock Exchange. Subsequently dissolved for failure-to-file.

Vault Energy Trust (Alta. Apr. 25, 2005)
Jan. 15, 2008 – Acquired by Penn West Energy Trust; basis 0.14 Penn West trust unit for 1 Vault Energy trust unit or exch. sh.

Vault Explorations Inc. (B.C. Apr. 2, 1986)
July 7, 1987 – Name changed to Sun Entertainment Holding Corporation. ■

Vault Minerals Inc. (B.C. Sept. 29, 1980)
Jan. 1, 2006 – Continued into Ontario. (see Queenston Mining Inc.)
Apr. 26, 2010 – Acquired by Queenston Mining Inc.; basis 1 Queenston Mining sh. for 10 Vault shs. (see Queenston Mining Inc.)
Jan. 1, 2011 – Amalgamated with Queenston Mining Inc. (see Queenston Mining Inc.)

Vault Systems Inc. (B.C. Sept. 29, 1980)
June 18, 2003 – Name changed to Vault Minerals Inc.; basis 1 new for 6 old shs. ■

Vaumont Mines Ltd. (Ont. 1944)
1950 – Charter cancelled.

Vauquelin Mines Ltd. (Que. May 28, 1962; via letters patent)
Dec. 10, 1999 – Name changed to BridgePoint International inc.; basis 1 new cl. A for 1 old com. sh. ■

Vauze Dufault Mines Ltd. (Ont. 1944)
1956 – Name changed to Consolidated Vauze Mines Ltd.; basis 1 new for 3 old shs. ■

Vauze Mines Ltd. (Que. 1961)
1965 – Name changed to North American Gas, Limited. ■

Vecta Energy Corporation (Alta. Dec. 20, 1995)
Apr. 2, 2018 – Dissolved and struck from register.

Vector Aerospace Corporation (Can. Apr. 23, 1998)
July 7, 2011 – Acquired by European Aeronautic Defence and Space Company N.V. for $13 per sh. ■

Vector Diamond Corporation (Alta. June 2, 1987)
Sept. 30, 1994 – Continued into British Columbia.
Nov. 1, 1994 – Formed Canabrava Diamond Corporation on amalgamation with Signa Technologies Inc.; basis 1 new for 1 old sh. ■

Vector Electric Limited (Ont. 1948)
1970 – Went bankrupt in 1960 and was discharged in 1961. Went bankrupt again.

Vector Industries International Inc. (Alta. June 2, 1987)
June 28, 1994 – Name changed to Vector Diamond Corporation. ■

Vector Intermediaries Inc. (Alta. Aug. 24, 1994)
June 1, 2004 – Placed into receivership. Stern Cohen Shier Inc. was appointed receiver.

Vector Resources Inc. (Ont. Mar. 5, 2010)
Jan. 31, 2017 – Name changed to Razor Energy Corp. following Qualifying Transaction reverse takeover acquisition of (old) Razor Energy Corp.; basis 1 new for 20 old shs. ■

Vector Venture Corp. (B.C. Sept. 25, 1986)
Aug. 29, 1995 – Acquired by Vector Environmental Technologies Inc.; basis 1 Vector Environmental sh. for 1 Vector Venture sh.

Vector Wind Energy Inc. (Can. Oct. 21, 2003)
Jan. 5, 2007 – Plan of Arrangement acquisition by Canadian Hydro Developers, Inc.; basis $0.30 per sh. (see Canadian Hydro Developers, Inc.)

Vedron Gold Inc. (Ont. Mar. 24, 1972)
Aug. 7, 2007 – Name changed to VG Gold Corp. ■

Vedron Limited (Ont. Mar. 24, 1972)
Jan. 16, 1995 – Name changed to Vedron Gold Inc.; basis 1 new for 10 old shs. ■

Vega Explorations Limited (Ont. 1979)
July 1, 1996 – Formed Verena Minerals Corporation in Ontario pursuant to reverse takeover acquisiton of and amalgamation with Verena Minerals Corporation; basis 1 new for 1 Verena sh. and 1 new for 2 Vega shs. ■

Vega Gold Explorations Inc. (Ont. 1979)
Jan. 1987 – Name changed to Vega Explorations Limited; basis 1 new for 5 old shs. ■

Vega Gold Ltd. (B.C. Aug. 20, 1990)
Sept. 10, 2010 – Name changed to Vega Resources Inc.; basis 1 new for 2 old shs. ■

Vega Gold Mines Ltd. (Ont. Sept. 1936)
Feb. 1955 – Charter cancelled.

Vega Mines Ltd. (B.C. 1970)
Mar. 3, 1978 – Dissolved and struck off register.

Vega Mining Inc. (B.C. Nov. 21, 2007)
Apr. 23, 2018 – Dissolved and struck from register.
Aug. 6, 2020 – Restored to registry.
May 3, 2024 – Name changed to Nations Royalty Corp. and continued into Canada pursuant to the reverse takeover acquisition of Nations Acquisitions Corp. and concurrent amalgamation of Nations Acquisitions with wholly owned 1445146 B.C. Ltd. (and continued as Nass Valley Area Royalty Holdings Corp.). (see FPsurvey - Mines & Energy)

Vega Resources Inc. (B.C. Aug. 20, 1990)
Mar. 10, 2011 – Name changed to Pacific Coal Resources Ltd. pursuant to reverse takeover acquisition of Pacific Coal, S.A.; basis 3 new for 5 old shs. ■

Vegan Lithium Mines Ltd. (Ont. 1956)
1970 – Charter cancelled.

Vegaste Technologies Corp. (B.C. Oct. 14, 2011 amalg.)
Sept. 28, 2020 – Name changed to PlantX Life Inc. ■

Vegreville Gas Utilities Ltd. (Alta. 1935)
1935 – Inactive.

Vehicle Recycling Technologies Inc. (Alta. Aug. 28, 1997)
Aug. 11, 1999 – Name changed to AADCO industries.com inc. ■

Vein Ventures Ltd. (B.C. 1984)
Apr. 13, 1987 – Name changed to HMR World Enterprises Inc. ■

Veji Holdings Ltd. (B.C. July 30, 2019)
Aug. 1, 2025 – Name changed to Plaid Technologies Inc. (see FPsurvey - Industrials)

Vejii Holdings Ltd. (B.C. July 30, 2019)
Aug. 26, 2022 – Name changed to Veji Holdings Ltd. ■

Vela Minerals Ltd. (B.C. May 19, 2011)
Sept. 3, 2019 – Name changed to Arbor Metals Corp. (see FPsurvey - Mines & Energy)

Velcro Industries Limited (Can. 1957)
1972 – Liquidated and reincorporated in the Netherland Antilles under the Velcro Industries N.V. name following relocation out of Canada to the Netherland Antilles.

Velo Energy Inc. (Can. July 8, 2004)
Aug. 3, 2010 – Name changed to Canadian Overseas Petroleum Limited. (see FPsurvey - Mines & Energy)

Velocity Computer Solutions, Ltd. (Bermuda Dec. 16, 1997)
June 9, 2000 – Name changed to Voyus Ltd.

Velocity Data Inc. (B.C. May 10, 2011)
Feb. 15, 2020 – Name changed to Emergence Global Enterprises Inc. (see FPsurvey - Industrials)

Velok Ltd. (Can. 1957)
Feb. 1, 1967 – Name changed to Velcro Industries Limited. ■

Velvet Exploration Co. Ltd. (B.C. Jan. 28, 1966)
May 27, 1998 – Name changed to Velvet Exploration Ltd. and continued into Alberta. ■

Velvet Exploration Ltd. (Alta. May 27, 1998)
Aug. 3, 2001 – Acquired by El Paso Corporation for $8.15 per sh.

Velvet Larder Mines Ltd. (Ont. 1945)
Mar. 24, 1958 – Dissolved.

Vena Resources Inc. (Ont. Dec. 24, 1987)
Oct. 5, 2016 – Name changed to Forrester Metals Inc. ■

Venator Petroleum Company Ltd. (Alta. Oct. 21, 1988)
Apr. 24, 2000 – Acquired by PrimeWest Energy Trust; basis 0.657 PrimeWest units or 0.657 PrimeWest exchangeable shs. or a combination thereof. (see PrimeWest Energy Trust)

VenCan Gold Corporation (Ont. July 22, 1936)
Mar. 2, 2009 – Name changed to Red Pine Exploration Inc. (see FPsurvey - Mines & Energy)

Vencap Equities Alberta Ltd. (Alta. 1982)
Jan. 3, 1996 – Acquired by Vencap Acquisition Corporation, a wholly owned subsid. of Onex Corporation; basis $8.50 per sh. and $85 per cl. B pfd. sh.

Vencap Investments Ltd. (Ont. 1963)
Nov. 1975 – Placed into receivership; Clarkson Gordon & Co. appointed receiver-manager. Proceeds from sale of assets were insufficient to pay secured creditors.

Vendin One Capital Corp. (Yuk. June 28, 2000)
Sept. 26, 2003 – Name changed to Dynasty Metals & Mining Inc. following Qualifying Transaction acquisition of Elipe S.A.; basis 1 new for 2 old shs. ■

Vendomatic Services Ltd. (Can. June 15, 1961; via Dominion charter)
May 1964 – Name changed to Versafood Services Limited. ■

Vendome Capital Corp. (Ont. Nov. 1, 2005)
Aug. 27, 2008 – Name changed to Axiotron Corp. following Qualifying Transaction reverse takeover acquisition of Axiotron, Inc.; basis 1 new for 4 old shs. (see FPsurvey - Industrials)

Vendome Capital II Corp. (Ont. Feb. 27, 2007)
May 26, 2010 – Name changed to Vendome Resources Corp. ■

Vendome Mines Ltd. (Que. 1953)
Nov. 1, 1978 – Merged with another co. to form Les Mines Vendome Inc.

Vendome Resources Corp. (Ont. Feb. 27, 2007)
Jan. 16, 2017 – Name changed to Vanadium One Energy Corp. ■

The Vendron Corporation Ltd. (Can. 1948)
1971 – Assets distributed to debenture holders. Trustee - Canada Trust Co., Toronto.

VendTek Systems Inc. (B.C. Nov. 7, 1980)
Nov. 2015 – Assets acquired by Nexu Transaction Technologies Ltd. No distribution available for shldrs.
Sept. 28, 2020 – Dissolved and struck from register.

Venezuelan Goldfields Ltd. (B.C. Oct. 26, 1983)
May 13, 1994 – Name changed to Vengold Inc. and continued into Canada. ■

Venezuelan Power Co. Ltd. (Can. 1959)
Jan. 1969 – Name changed to Venpower Limited; basis 1 new com. for 2 old com. shs.; 2.5 new com. for 1 old 6% pref. sh. (with pref. divd. arrears waived); 1 new com. per $1 princ. amt. of 6% series A debs. o/s (deferred deb. int. waived). ■

Vengold Inc. (Can. May 13, 1994)
May 8, 2000 – Name changed to itemus inc. ■

Venmar Inc. (Que. 1976)
Jan. 14, 1992 – Acquired by Groupe Pentaction Inc. for 64¢ per sh.

Venoro Gold Corp. (Can. Nov. 13, 1986)
Oct. 30, 1997 – Name changed to New Venoro Gold Corp.; basis 1 new for 8 old shs. ■

Venosta Minerals Ltd. (Can. 1965)
Dec. 1968 – Dissolved.

VenPath Investments Inc. (Alta. Sept. 9, 1998)
Oct. 31, 2007 – Name changed to OPE Holdings Ltd. following reverse takeover acquisition of OPE, Inc. and OPE International, L.P. ■

Venpower Limited (Can. 1959)
Sept. 1982 – Acquired by Phi International Inc. for 90¢ per sh.

Venquest Capital Ltd. (Alta. June 21, 2004)
Sept. 1, 2005 – Formed Nightingale Informatix Corporation in Ontario pursuant to Qualifying Transaction reverse takeover acquisition of and amalgamation with Nightingale Informatix Corporation; basis 1 new for 3.076923 old shs. ■

Vensearch Capital Corp. (Can. Feb. 20, 2003)
Aug. 12, 2005 – Name changed to Genetic Diagnostics Technologies Corp. following Qualifying Transaction amalgamation of wholly owned 1140648 Alberta Ltd. with Genetic Diagnostics Inc., constituting a reverse takeover by Genetic Diagnostics. ■

Venstar Inc. (Alta. Mar. 4, 1996)
Oct. 19, 2004 – Placed into receivership. RSM Richter Inc. was appointed receiver/manager.

Venstone One Capital Corp. (B.C. July 2, 1999)
Sept. 25, 2002 – Formed Shift Networks Inc. in Alberta on Qualifying Transaction amalgamation with Shift Networks Inc., constituting a reverse takeover by Shift. ■

Venstone Ventures Corp. (B.C. Apr. 20, 1979)
Mar. 4, 1999 – Name changed to iWave.com, Inc.; basis 1 new for 4 old shs. ■

Ventana Equities Inc. (Alta. May 15, 1987)
Jan. 5, 1993 – Name changed to Steeplejack Industrial Group Inc. ■

Ventana Gold Corp. (B.C. Mar. 2, 2006)
Mar. 28, 2011 – Acquired by EBX Group Ltd. for $13.06 per sh.

Ventaur Capital Corporation (Ont. Apr. 14, 2000)
Oct. 28, 2003 – Name changed to Goldcrest Resources Ltd. pursuant to Qualifying Transaction acquisition of Goldcrest Mines Limited and Australian mineral interests. ■

Ventec Resources Inc. (B.C. Feb. 27, 1951)
July 26, 1991 – Dissolved.

Ventech Capital Corporation (Alta. 1986)
Jan. 28, 1988 – Name changed to Walker's Capital Corporation. ■

VenTech Healthcare Corporation Inc. (Ont. 1974)
Mar. 31, 1992 – Name changed to NWE Capital Corp. ■

VenTech Healthcare Inc. (Ont. 1974)
July 2, 1987 – Name changed to VenTech Healthcare International Inc.; basis 1 new for 2.5 old shs. ■

VenTech Healthcare International Inc. (Ont. 1974)
Sept. 10, 1987 – Name changed to VenTech Healthcare Corporation Inc. ■

Ventech Industrials Ltd. (Alta. Apr. 11, 1996)
June 5, 1998 – Formed Alta Terra Ventures Corp. in Alberta on Qualifying Transaction amalgamation with Alta Terra Ventures Corp. ■

Ventel, Inc. (Can. July 31, 1991)
July 9, 1999 – Name changed to Fifty-Plus.Net International Inc. following acquisition of Fifty-Plus.net Inc.; basis 1 new for 5 old shs. ■

Ventex Energy Ltd. (B.C. 1980)
Oct. 30, 1992 – Dissolved and struck off register.

Ventex Ltd. (B.C.)
July 1961 – Name changed to Copper Town Mines Ltd. ■

Ventex Resources Corporation (Alta. Nov. 27, 1991)
Sept. 10, 1993 – Name changed to Ventex Technologies Corporation. ■

Ventex Technologies Corporation (Alta. Nov. 27, 1991)
July 24, 1996 – Name changed to Ventex Minerals Inc.; basis unknown. (see FPsurvey - Mines & Energy)

Ventir Challenge Enterprises Ltd. (B.C. Sept. 16, 1983)
Feb. 3, 2006 – Name changed to Whistler Gold Corp.; basis 1 new for 5 old shs. ■

Ventora Resources Ltd. (B.C. 1968)
Oct. 3, 1984 – Name changed to Torrent Resources Ltd.; basis 1 new for 5 old shs. ■

Ventra Group Inc. (Ont. Dec. 1, 1985 amalg.)
Oct. 10, 2001 – Acquired by VTA Acquisition Corporation, an indirect wholly owned subsid. of U.S.-based Flex-N-Gate Corporation, for $1.65 per sh.

Ventura Cannabis and Wellness Corp. (B.C. June 7, 2013)
Sept. 2020 – Distrib. of 1 Vive Bioscience Ltd. com. sh. for every 55 Ventura Cannabis shs. and 1 Vibe Bioscience wt. for every 46 Ventura Cannabis shs. payable to shldrs. of record Sept. 21, 2020. Wts. exercisable for 1 Vibe Bioscience sh. at 60¢ per sh. until Sept. 16, 2021.
Oct. 2020 – Distrib. of 1 Vibe Growth Corporation sh. for every 12 Ventura Cannabis sh. and 1 Vibe Growth wt. for every 31 Ventura Cannabis sh. payable to shldrs. of record Oct. 30, 2020. Wts. exercisable for 1 Vibe Growth sh. at 62¢ per sh. until Oct. 30, 2021.
May 27, 2024 – Dissolved and struck from register.

Ventura Gold Corp. (Yuk. Nov. 15, 1996)
Oct. 7, 2004 – Continued into British Columbia. (see International Minerals Corporation)
Jan. 12, 2010 – Acquired by International Minerals Corp.; basis 1 International Minerals sh. for 10 Ventura Gold shs. (see International Minerals Corporation)

Venturbon Enterprises Inc. (Que. Feb. 28, 1967)
Oct. 8, 1997 – Name changed to Java Joe's International Corporation following amalgamation with 9037-3135 Quebec Inc.; basis 1 new for 5 old shs. ■

Venture Gold Corp. (B.C. 1980)
June 19, 1992 – Dissolved and struck off register.

Venture One Capital Corp. (Alta. Apr. 17, 2007)
Feb. 26, 2010 – Name changed to NMC Resource Corporation and continued into British Columbia following Qualifying Transaction reverse takeover acquisition of NMC, Inc. ■

Venture Pacific Development Corporation (B.C. Mar. 18, 1986)
Oct. 21, 2002 – Name changed to Pacific Harbour Capital Ltd.; basis 1 new for 2 old shs. ■

Venture Properties Limited (Alta. Apr. 9, 1974 amalg.)
Sept. 2, 1975 – Name changed to Allied Venture Properties Limited; basis 1 new for 10 old shs. ■

Venture Seismic Ltd. (Alta. Aug. 24, 1984)
Dec. 31, 1998 – Vessel M/V Pacific Titan, used in marine seismic operations conducted by wholly owned Continental Holdings Ltd., was seized on Dec. 29, 1998, under a motion filed by Western Geophysical, a division of Baker Hughes. The motion filed an alleged breach of contract and sought damages of $5,100,000. Western

Geophysical also provided notice to terminate the contract.
Jan. 15, 1999 – Company and Continental filed a court motion denying Western Geophysical's allegations and seeking $20,000,000 in damages. Four of the company's six directors resigned and all but one of Continental's directors resigned.
Feb. 8, 1999 – Company and Continental were granted protection under the Companies' Creditors Arrangement Act and KPMG Inc. was appointed receiver.
June 2002 – All distributions had been completed and the secured creditors suffered a shortfall. There were no funds available for unsecured creditors or shldrs.
June 30, 2005 – Receiver discharged.

Venturecorp Capital Inc. (B.C. Feb. 17, 1999)
Dec. 18, 2000 – Name changed to BioteQ Environmental Technologies Inc. ■

Ventures Explorations Ltd. (B.C.)
Name changed to Ventex Ltd. ■

Ventures Gained Inc. (Alta. Sept. 10, 1986)
June 18, 1993 – Name changed to Tomahawk Corporation; basis 1 new for 2 old shs. (see FPsurvey - Industrials)

Ventures Ltd. (Can. 1928)
Jan. 1962 – Merger of co. into Falconbridge Nickel Mines Limited approved by shldrs. Merger effected through transfer of all net assets of Ventures in exch. for approx. 800,000 shs. Falconbridge, and subsequent distribution by Ventures of all Falconbridge shs. owned by it pro rata to its shldrs.; basis 104 shs. Falconbridge for each 100 shs. Ventures.

Ventures Mining Ltd. (B.C. 1963)
May 1972 – Name changed to Giant Ventures Development Company Ltd.; basis 1 new for 5 old shs. ■

Ventures Resource Corporation (Barbados Nov. 8, 1996 amalg.)
Apr. 5, 2005 – Formed BrazMin Corp. in British Virgin Islands on amalgamation with Resource Holdings & Investments Inc., constituting a reverse takeover by Resource Holdings; basis 1 new for 1 Resource Holdings sh. and 1 new for 50 Ventures Resource shs. ■

Venturetek International Limited (unknown)
Nov. 19, 1982 – Placed into receivership. All equipment distributed to secured creditors. No other distribution made. Trustee - John Pope, Price Waterhouse, Toronto.

Venturex Explorations Inc. (B.C. Nov. 21, 1983)
June 17, 2008 – Name changed to Black Panther Mining Corp.; basis 1 new for 10 old shs. ■

Venturex Resources Ltd. (B.C. Nov. 21, 1983)
Sept. 24, 1992 – Name changed to Consolidated Venturex Holdings Ltd.; basis 1 new for 5 old shs. ■

Venturi Ventures Inc. (B.C. Dec. 3, 1980)
Apr. 29, 2016 – Voluntarily dissolved; distribution of $0.058 cash per com. sh.

Ventus Energy Ltd. (B.C. Mar. 25, 1994)
May 31, 2002 – Name changed to Navigo Energy Inc. ■

Venus Mines Ltd. (B.C. 1966)
Oct. 6, 1980 – Struck off register.

Venus Oils Ltd. (Alta. 1951)
1958 – Struck off register.

Ver-Million Gold Placer Mining Ltd. (Ont. 1953)
Aug. 24, 1964 – Dissolved.

Vera Cruz Minerals Corp. (B.C. June 19, 1987)
Aug. 20, 1996 – Name changed to Copper Creek Ventures Ltd.; basis 1 new for 5 old shs. ■

Vera Oilfields Ltd (Can. Dec. 10, 1931)
Merged with Bata Petroleums Ltd. (see Bata Petroleums Ltd.)

Veraz Petroleum Ltd. (B.C. Jan. 12, 1987)
Jan. 24, 2008 – Continued into Alberta.
Aug. 16, 2016 – Name changed to AlkaLi3 Resources Inc. ∎

Verb Exchange Inc. (Can. May 16, 2000)
July 5, 2010 – Name changed to Seymour Ventures Corp.; basis 1 new for 25 old shs. ∎

Verbina Resources Inc. (Ont. Oct. 4, 2004)
Apr. 19, 2011 – Name changed to Buccaneer Gold Corp. ∎

Vercan Investments Inc. (B.C. Oct. 10, 1986)
Jan. 26, 1998 – Name changed to WaterSave Logic Corporation. ∎

Verchères Ore-Oil Corporation (Que. 1951)
May 1974 – Charter cancelled.

Verdant Financial Partners I Inc. (Can. July 9, 2008)
July 25, 2016 – Name changed to Axis Auto Finance Inc. following Qualifying Transaction reverse takeover acquisition of 8095981 Canada Inc. (operated as Axis Auto Finance); basis 1 new for 6 old shs. ∎

Verdant Valley Ventures Inc. (Alta. Mar. 13, 1967)
Mar. 21, 1994 – Name changed to Biotechna Environmental Limited. ∎

Verde Agritech Plc (U.K. Aug. 14, 2006)
July 29, 2022 – Succeeded by Verde Agritech Ltd. following redomiciliation transaction under which ord. shs. of Verde Agritech Plc were exchanged for Verde Agritech Ltd. ord. shs. on the basis of 1 new ord. sh. for 1 old ord. sh. (see FPsurvey - Mines & Energy)

Verde Potash plc (U.K. Aug. 14, 2006)
June 20, 2016 – Name changed to Verde Agritech Plc. ∎

Verdstone Gold Corporation (B.C. Mar. 2, 1981)
Apr. 17, 2002 – Name changed to Goldrea Resources Corp.; basis 1 new for 10 old shs. (see FPsurvey - Mines & Energy)

Veren Inc. (Alta. Aug. 1, 2006)
May 14, 2025 – Acquired by Whitecap Resources Inc.; basis 1.05 Whitecap shs. for 1 Veren sh.

Verena Minerals Corporation (Ont. July 1, 1996 amalg.)
July 14, 2010 – Name changed to Belo Sun Mining Corp. (see FPsurvey - Mines & Energy)

La Vérendrye Management Corporation (Que. July 4, 1962)
Mar. 25, 1991 – Amalgamated with Milihuit Inc. to become a wholly owned subsid.; basis 1 cl. B pref. sh. for 1 cl. A sub. vtg. sh. redeemable for $1.60 per sh.

Verenex Energy Inc. (Alta. June 29, 2004 amalg.)
Dec. 21, 2009 – Acquired by Area 47 (Canada) Holdings Limited, a subsid. of the Libyan Investment Authority, for $7.2882 per sh.

Veresen Inc. (Alta. Oct. 1, 2010)
Oct. 5, 2017 – Acquired by and amalgamated with Pembina Pipeline Corporation; basis (i) $18.65 cash per sh. or (ii) 0.4287 Pembina com. sh. for 1 Veresen com. sh. All o/s series A, series C and series E pref. shs. exchanged for an equivalent series of pref. shs. of Pembina on a 1-for-1 basis/

Vergene Capital Corporation (Ont. Dec. 31, 1997)
May 17, 2004 – Name changed to Greencastle Resources Ltd. (see FPsurvey - Mines & Energy)

Veris Biotechnology Corporation (Ont. Sept. 22, 1987)
Mar. 18, 2004 – Name changed to Capital Diagnostic Corporation; basis 1 new for 5 old shs. ∎

Veris Gold Corp. (B.C. May 30, 1988)
June 9, 2014 – Filed for protection under the Companies' Creditors Arrangement Act (Canada) CCAA. Ernst & Young Inc. appointed monitor.
June 2015 – Majority of assets sold to Jerritt Canyon Gold LLC.
Nov. 19, 2018 – Dissolved and struck from register.

Veritas Energy Services Inc. (Alta. May 11, 1993)
May 16, 2006 – Privatized by parent Veritas DGC Inc.; basis 1 new Veritas DGC sh. for either 1 old Veritas Energy exch. sh. or 1 old Veritas Energy cl. A sh.

Veritas Pharma Inc. (B.C. May 14, 2014)
Sept. 24, 2021 – Name changed to Indigenous Bloom Hemp Corp. pursuant to the reverse takeover acquisition of (old) Indigenous Bloom Hemp Corporation and concurrent amalgamation of (old) Indigenous Bloom with wholly owned 12302161 Canada Inc.; basis 1 new for 2 old shs. (see FPsurvey - Industrials)

Veritek Technologies Inc. (Alta. Mar. 19, 2002)
Feb. 1, 2007 – Name changed to California Nanotechnologies Corp. following Qualifying Transaction reverse takeover acquisition of California Nanotechnologies, Inc. ∎

Verity Porcupine Gold Mines Ltd. (Ont. 1937)
1957 – Charter cancelled.

Verlac Gold Mines Ltd. (Ont. 1944)
1959 – Dissolved.

Vermilata Oils Ltd. (Ont. 1939)
1945 – Taken over by Apex Consolidated Resources Ltd.; basis 1 new for 2 old shs. (see Apex Consolidated Resources Ltd.)

Vermilion Energy Trust (Alta. Dec. 16, 2002)
Sept. 1, 2010 – Succeeded by Vermilion Energy Inc. following conversion of Vermilion Energy Trust into a corporation and subsequent dissolution of the trust: basis 1 new com. sh. for 1 old trust unit. (see FPsurvey - Mines & Energy)

Vermilion Resources Inc. (B.C. 1983)
Sept. 12, 1985 – Name changed to Island Technology Corporation. ∎

Vermilion Resources Ltd. (Alta. Nov. 23, 1993)
Jan. 24, 2003 – Reorganized into two new companies, Vermilion Energy Trust and Clear Energy Inc.; basis either 1 new trust unit or a combination of trust unit and exchg. sh. for 1 old Vermilion Resources com. sh. plus 1 new Clear Energy com. sh. for 1 old Vermilion Resources com. sh. (see Clear Energy Inc.; Vermilion Energy Trust)

Vermillion Consolidated Oils Limited (Alta. 1941)
Mar. 31, 1977 – In voluntary liquidation in 1977. Full and final payment of 5¢ per sh. pd. to shldrs. of record.

Vermillion Oils Ltd. (Ont. June 8, 1938)
1941 – Absorbed by Vermillion Consolidated Oils, Ltd. for 800,000 shs.

Vermont Mines Ltd. (Ont. 1951)
May 1977 – Charter cancelled.

Vermont Zinc Mines Ltd. (Ont. 1951)
1960 – Name changed to Vermont Mines Ltd.

Verney-Corduroys Limited (Can. 1949)
1954 – Name changed to Canadian Corduroy Limited.

Verney Corporation of Canada Ltd. (Can. 1924)
Aug. 1954 – Declared bankrupt. Assets were acquired by Hafner Fabrics of Canada Ltd., wholly owned subsidiary of Hafner Associates Inc., New York.

Verney Gold Mines Ltd. (Ont. 1945)
1956 – Charter cancelled.

Verney Mills of Canada Ltd. (Can. 1924)
June 1948 – Name changed to Verney Corporation of Canada Ltd. ∎

Vernon Copper Limited (B.C. 1966)
Feb. 25, 1983 – Struck off register.

Vero Energy Inc. (Alta. Sept. 23, 2005)
Nov. 2, 2005 – Amalgamated in Alberta to continue with same name.
Nov. 19, 2012 – Formed TORC Oil & Gas Ltd. in Alberta on amalgamation with (old) TORC Oil & Gas Ltd. with old TORC the deemed acquiror. ∎

Vero Resource Management Ltd. (Alta. 1986)
Nov. 27, 1989 – Name changed to Vero Resources Ltd. ∎

Vero Resources Ltd. (Alta. 1986)
Feb. 1, 1994 – Amalgamated with a wholly owned subsid. of Excel Engery Inc.; basis 1.05263 com. shs. of Excel for 3 com. shs. of Vero; or 1 com. sh. and 3/4 of a com. sh. purch. wt. of Excel for 3 com. shs. of Vero. (see Excel Energy Inc.)

Verona Development Corp. (B.C. May 16, 2001)
Aug. 19, 2016 – Name changed to SVT Capital Corp. ∎

Veronex Resources Ltd. (B.C. Mar. 8, 1974)
Oct. 20, 1992 – Name changed to International Veronex Resources Ltd.; basis 1 new for 7 old shs. ∎

Veronex Technologies, Inc. (B.C. Mar. 8, 1974)
Mar. 5, 2007 – Dissolved and struck from register.

Versa Services Ltd. (Can. June 15, 1961; via Dominion charter)
Nov. 18, 1994 – Acquired by Versa Merger Corporation, a wholly owned subsid. of ARAMARK Corporation, for $11.125 per sh.

VersaBank (Can. Aug. 1, 2002)
Jan. 31, 2017 – Amalgamated in Canada to continue with same name. (see FPsurvey - Industrials)

Versacold Corporation (B.C. Aug. 12, 1986)
Feb. 12, 2002 – Plan of Arrangement to convert company into an income fund trust named Versacold Income Fund; basis 1 new trust unit for 1 com. sh. (see Versacold Income Fund)

Versacold Income Fund (B.C. Dec. 19, 2001)
Aug. 3, 2007 – Acquired by Eimskip Holdings Inc. Fund units redeemed for $12.25 per unit.

Versafood Services Limited (Can. June 15, 1961; via Dominion charter)
July 12, 1972 – Name changed to VS Services Ltd. ∎

VersaPay Corporation (Can. Jan. 12, 2010 amalg.)
Feb. 26, 2020 – Acquired by Great Hills Partners L.P.; basis Cdn$2.70 cash per sh.
July 31, 2020 – Name changed to VersaPay ULC and continued into British Columbia.

The Versatech Group Inc. (Ont. June 1998)
Oct. 31, 2000 – Placed into receivership. PricewaterhouseCoopers Inc. appointed receiver.

Versatile Cornat Corporation (B.C. July 1, 1978 amalg.)
Jan. 30, 1981 – Name changed to Versatile Corporation and continued into Canada. ∎

Versatile Corporation (Can. Jan. 30, 1981)
May 11, 1988 – Name changed to B.C. Pacific Capital Corporation; basis 1 new for 10 old shs. ∎

Versatile Manufacturing Ltd. (Man. 1963)
July 1, 1978 – Amalgamated with Cornat Industries Limited to form a new company named Versatile Cornat Corporation; basis 1 new ser. A pref. sh. for 1 old Versatile sh. (see Versatile Cornat Corporation)

Versatile Mobile Systems (Canada) Inc. (B.C. Sept. 28, 1955)
Feb. 23, 2004 – Continued into Yukon.
Nov. 16, 2005 – Name changed to Versatile Systems Inc. and continued into British Columbia. ∎

Versatile Systems Inc. (B.C. Nov. 16, 2005)
Oct. 15, 2018 – Struck from registry and dissolved.

Versent Corporation (Ont. 1983)
Oct. 17, 2000 – Acquired by Buckingham Technology Acquisition Group Inc. for $1.75 per sh.

Verses Technologies Inc. (B.C. Nov. 19, 2020)
Mar. 31, 2023 – Name changed to Verses AI Inc. (see FPsurvey - Industrials)

Vertech Systems Corporation (B.C. Oct. 10, 1986)
July 12, 1989 – Name changed to Vercan Investments Inc.; basis 1 new for 3 old shs. ■

Vertex Fund Limited Partnership (B.C. Jan. 23, 1998)
Jan. 21, 2002 – Wound up at company request following extraordinary resolution to shorten term to maturity to enable conversion to investment trust; basis 1 for 1.

Vertex Properties Inc. (Alta. Sept. 9, 1993)
Aug. 22, 2001 – Delisted from the CDNX. Subsequently dissolved.

Vertex Resources Ltd. (B.C. Feb. 16, 1981)
July 5, 1991 – Dissolved and struck off register.

Vertex Ventures Inc. (Ont. Jan. 28, 1974)
Mar. 6, 2000 – Name changed to First Strike Diamonds Inc. ■

Vertica Systems Corporation (B.C. Apr. 7, 1978)
Aug. 3, 1988 – Name changed to Siscoe Callahan Mining Corporation; basis 1 new for 2 old shs. ■

Vertical Peak Holdings Inc. (B.C. May 1, 2023)
Nov. 30, 2023 – Placed into receivership and Zeifman Partners Inc. appointed receiver.

Vertigo Software Corp. (Can. July 16, 1996)
June 22, 2004 – Name changed to Even Technologies Inc. (see FPsurvey - Industrials)

Vertigo 3D, Inc. (Ont. 1928)
July 16, 1996 – Continued into Canada.
Oct. 26, 1998 – Name changed to Vertigo Software Corp.; basis 1 new for 7 old shs. ■

Vertimac Development Inc. (Alta. Mar. 27, 1987)
Dec. 15, 1995 – Name changed to Copper States Resources Inc. ■

The Very Good Food Company Inc. (B.C. Dec. 27, 2016)
Jan. 16, 2023 – Placed into receivership by secured lender. BDO Canada Limited appointed receiver.

Vescan Equities Inc. (Can. Apr. 26, 1926; via Dominion charter)
Dec. 24, 1999 – Name changed to Inouye Technologies (Canada) Inc.; basis 1 new for 110 old shs. ■

Vespar Mines Ltd. (Ont. 1951)
Jan. 11, 1979 – Amalgamated with Lakehead Mines Ltd. to form Parlake Resources Limited; basis 1 new for 8 old shs.

Vesta Capital Corp. (Ont. Feb. 22, 2008)
Sept. 16, 2010 – Name changed to United Hunter Oil & Gas Corp. ■

Vesta Yellowknife Gold Mines Ltd. (Ont. 1944)
1957 – Charter cancelled.

Vestgron Mines Ltd (Can. Feb. 18, 1966)
July 28, 1987 – Name changed to VGM Capital Corporation; basis 1 new for 5 old shs.

Vestor Explorations Ltd. (Alta. 1969)
1980 – Continued into British Columbia.
Sept. 30, 1988 – Name changed to International Vestor Resources Ltd.; basis 1 new for 2 old shs. ■

Vestronix Corporation (U.K. Sept. 1986)
Mar. 18, 1988 – Continued into Ontario. (see FPsurvey - Industrials)

Veta Resources Inc. (Can. Aug. 18, 2006)
Sept. 19, 2024 – Name changed to Syntheia Corp. pursuant to the reverse takeover acquisition of Metaworld Corporation. (see FPsurvey - Industrials)

Veteran Resources Inc. (Alta. Dec. 19, 1990)
Jan. 23, 2006 – Plan of Arrangement acquisition by Bear Ridge Resources Ltd.; basis either $1.60, or 0.33686 new Bear Ridge sh. for 1 old Veteran sh., or a combination of $0.48 for 0.3 old Veteran sh. plus 0.2358 new Bear Ridge sh. for 0.7 old Veteran sh. (see Bear Ridge Resources Ltd.)

Vetina Energy Resources Ltd. (Ont. Apr. 28, 1980)
Oct. 25, 1982 – Name changed to Telescan Electronics & Communications Inc.; basis 1 new for 2 old shs. ■

Veto Resources Ltd. (B.C. Apr. 24, 1987)
Jan. 24, 1997 – Name changed to Baron Gold Corp. ■

Vexco Healthcare Inc. (Alta. 1987)
Jan. 1, 1997 – Formed Ceapro Inc. in Alberta on amalgamation with Ceapro Developments Inc., constituting a reverse takeover by Ceapro; basis 1 new for 2 Ceapro shs. and 1 new for 4.5 Vexco shs. ■

Vexco Laboratories Inc. (Alta. 1987)
Apr. 18, 1996 – Name changed to Vexco Healthcare Inc. ■

Veynore Barraute Mines Ltd. (Ont. 1941)
1956 – Charter cancelled.

Via TV Marketing Corporation (Del. July 25, 1995)
July 21, 1998 – Formed Marketvision Direct, Inc. in Delaware following reverse takeover acquisition of and amalgamation with MarkeTVision Direct, Inc.; basis 1 new for 10 old shs. ■

Viacorp Technologies Inc. (B.C. June 6, 1987)
Jan. 30, 2012 – Struck from registry and dissolved.

Viaguard Pharmaceuticals Limited (Ont. Feb. 9, 1983)
Jan. 3, 1995 – Delisted from the CDN. Subsequently dissolved and charter cancelled.

Vianor Malartic Mines Ltd. (Ont. 1944)
Nov. 8, 1977 – Dissolved.

Viau Limited (Que. 1925)
Apr. 30, 1970 – Grissol Foods Ltd. holds 99% of com. shs. and 93% of pref. shs. Basis of exch. was 2 com. shs. of Grissol for 1 com. sh. of Viau, and 1 conv. pref. sh. of $1.00 par of Grissol for 1 pref. sh. of Viau. (see Grissol Foods Limited)

Vibe Bioscience Ltd. (Ont. Jan. 19, 2011)
Oct. 13, 2020 – Continued into British Columbia.
Oct. 15, 2020 – Name changed to Vibe Growth Corporation. (see FPsurvey - Industrials)

Vican Explorations Ltd. (B.C. 1958)
May 15, 1969 – Struck off register.

Vicana Ridge Resources Inc. (Alta. May 19, 1993)
Sept. 28, 1995 – All o/s com. shs. and com. sh. purchase wts. acquired by Startech Energy Inc.; basis 37¢ per com. sh., or at the holder's option, 1 com. sh. Startech for 14.2 com. shs. Vicana; and 1 com. sh. purchase wt. Startech for 14.2 wts. Vicana. (see Startech Energy Inc.)

Viceroy Exploration Ltd. (B.C. Mar. 31, 2003)
Jan. 3, 2007 – Acquired by Yamana Gold Inc.; basis 0.97 new Yamana sh. for 1 old Viceroy sh. (see Yamana Gold Inc.)

Viceroy Gold Mines Ltd. (B.C. 1959)
May 1960 – Name changed to The Big I Mines Ltd. ■

Viceroy Homes Limited (Ont. Jan. 15, 1955)
Mar. 4, 2008 – Acquired by JSC Open Investments for $5.00 per cl. A sh.

Viceroy Manufacturing Company Limited (Can. 1930)
1968 – Converted to a private co. following purchase offer of $8.25 per sh. made in September 1967, by officers and directors to holders of less than 300 shares.

Viceroy Petroleum Corp. Ltd. (B.C. 1959)
Jan. 1960 – Name changed to Viceroy Gold Mines Ltd. ■

Viceroy Petroleum Ltd. (B.C. Oct. 27, 1980)
Apr. 6, 1984 – Formed Viceroy Resource Corporation in British Columbia on amalgamation with B & B Resource Inc. (see Viceroy Resource Corporation)

Viceroy Resource Corporation (B.C. Oct. 27, 1980)
June 30, 2003 – Name changed to Quest Capital Corporation following acquisitions of Quest Investment Corporation (1.0514 for 1), Quest Management Corp. (863,857 shs.) and Avatar Petroleum Inc. (0.2825 for 1), transfer of Argentinian mineral assets to wholly owned Viceroy Exploration Ltd. spun out to shldrs. and transfer of certain B.C. properties to SpectrumGold Inc.; basis 1 Quest Capital cl. A sh. for 3 Viceroy Resource shs. plus 1 Viceroy Exploration Ltd. sh. for 10 Viceroy Resource shs. and 1 SpectrumGold sh. for 30 Viceroy Resource shs. ■

Vicinity Motor Corp. (B.C. Dec. 4, 2012)
Oct. 21, 2024 – Placed into receivership by secured creditor. FTI Consulting Inc. appointed receiver and all officers and directors resigned.

Vickers, Canada Inc. (Can. 1911)
Dec. 14, 1978 – Acquired by Canvick Industries Inc. for Cdn$50 per sh.

Vickers Mines Ltd. (Ont. 1922)
July 1960 – Charter cancelled.

Vico Explorations Ltd. (Ont. 1945)
Dec. 1960 – Charter cancelled.

Vicom Multimedia Inc. (Alta. Jan. 23, 1979)
Jan. 14, 2002 – Name changed to Brooklyn Energy Corporation; basis 1 new for 5 old shs. ■

Vicor Resources Limited (B.C. Aug. 16, 1979)
Jan. 30, 1981 – Amalgamated with Tay River Petroleum Ltd. to continue as Tay River Petroleum Ltd.; basis sh. for sh.

Vicour Mines Ltd. (Ont. 1945)
1956 – Name changed to Vico Explorations Ltd.; basis 1 new for 5 old shs. ■

Victhom Human Bionics Inc. (Can. Jan. 11, 2002)
Apr. 30, 2013 – Acquired by Ergoresearch Ltd. for 8¢ per sh. (see Ergoresearch Ltd.)

Victor Mining Corporation Ltd. (B.C. 1968)
Mar. 23, 1976 – Name changed to Victor Resources Ltd.

Victor Petroleums Ltd. (Ont. 1952)
1955 – Name changed to Jodee Explorations Ltd. ■

Victoria Algoma Mineral Co. Ltd. (Ont. 1954)
Mar. 1976 – Charter cancelled.

Victoria and Grey Mortgage Corporation (Man. 1913)
Apr. 1, 1994 – Amalgamated in Canada to continue with same name.

Victoria and Grey Trust Company (Ont. July 16, 1951)
Nov. 1979 – Formed Victoria Grey Metro Trust Company in Ontario on amalgamation with Metropolitan Trust Company; basis 1 new com. for 1 old com. or pref. sh. ■

Victoria and Grey Trust Co. (Ont. Nov. 1979 amalg.)
Aug. 31, 1984 – Formed The National Victoria and Grey Trust Company following amalgamation with National Trust Company, Limited. Holders of each com. sh. of co. entitled to receive 2.069 com. shs. of Victoria and Grey Trustco Limited or one com. sh. of the amalg. co. Holders of 5.35% ser. A pfce. shs. of co. received on one-for-one basis similar shs. of amalg. co. Subsequently, over 99% of the o/s com. shs. of the amalg. co. were exchanged for com. shs. of Victoria and Grey Trustco Limited on the

basis of 2.069 shs. for each com. sh. acquired upon amalg. (see The National Victoria and Grey Trust Company)

Victoria and Grey Trustco Limited (Ont. May 1, 1959)
Aug. 31, 1984 – Name changed to The National Victoria and Grey Trustco Limited following amalgamation of its subsid., Victoria and Grey Trust Company with National Trust Company, Limited. ∎

Victoria Copper Zinc Mines Ltd. (Que. 1951)
June 1974 – Charter cancelled.

Victoria County Explorations Inc. (Ont. 1984)
July 12, 1991 – Name changed to Optimal Robotics Corp. following acquisition of Optimal Robotics Inc.; basis 1 new for 4 old shs. ∎

Victoria Diego Resource Corp. (B.C. 1981)
Aug. 14, 1992 – Dissolved and struck off register.

Victoria Fruit Packing Co. Ltd. (B.C. 1937)
May 1952 – Liquidated.

Victoria Gold Corp. (B.C. Sept. 21, 1981)
Aug. 14, 2024 – Placed into receivership and PricewaterhouseCoopers Inc. was appointed receiver and manager.

Victoria Graphite Inc. (Can. Sept. 2, 1986)
July 12, 2004 – Dissolved.

Victoria Grey Metro Trust Company (Ont. Nov. 1979 amalg.)
Jan. 23, 1980 – Name changed to Victoria and Grey Trust Co. ∎

Victoria Land & Minerals Ltd. (Alta. 1955)
1966 – Assets sold to Scurry-Rainbow Oil Ltd. distribution made to shldrs. of 2 Plains Petroleums Ltd. shs. for each sh. of co. (see Plains Petroleums Limited)
In voluntary liquidation. Shldrs. entitled to 1 sh. Plains Petroleums Ltd. per 10 old shs. Liquidator: Guaranty Trust Co., Calgary. (see Plains Petroleums Limited)

Victoria Mines Ltd. (Alta. 1952)
Mar. 1957 – Dissolved.

Victoria Resource Corporation (B.C. Sept. 21, 1981)
Aug. 1, 2008 – Name changed to Victoria Gold Corp. ∎

Victoria Trust & Savings Co. (Can. - unspecified)
Nov. 1950 – Amalgamated to form Victoria & Grey Trust Co.; basis 10 new for 1 old sh.

Victorian Enuretic Services Ltd. (B.C. 1983)
Apr. 22, 1994 – Dissolved and struck off register.

Victory Battery Metals Corp. (B.C. Feb. 8, 1984)
Oct. 21, 2024 – Name changed to Supreme Critical Metals Inc.; basis 1 new for 10 old shs. (see FPsurvey - Mines & Energy)

Victory Capital Corporation (Alta. 1987)
Oct. 21, 1998 – Struck from registry and dissolved.

Victory Capital Corp. (Ont. Nov. 6, 2009)
Apr. 27, 2022 – Name changed to Vortex Metals Inc. pursuant to the Qualifying Transaction reverse takeover acquisition of Acapulco Gold Corp. and concurrent amalgamation of Acapulco with wholly owned 1287878 B.C. Inc. (and continued as Acapulco Gold Holdings Ltd.). (see FPsurvey - Mines & Energy)

Victory Gold Mines Inc. (Ont. May 17, 1965)
Feb. 7, 2013 – Amalgamated with a wholly owned subsid. of Northern Gold Mining Inc.; basis 1 Northern Gold sh. for 2 Victory Gold sh. (see Northern Gold Mining Inc.)

Victory Majors Investments Corporation (Can. Aug. 31, 1998)
Dec. 28, 2001 – Privatized for 15¢ per sh.

Victory Metals Inc. (B.C. May 25, 2012)
Apr. 9, 2021 – Name changed to Nevada King Gold Corp. (see FPsurvey - Mines & Energy)

Victory Nickel Inc. (Ont. Feb. 1, 2007)
July 26, 2022 – Deemed bankrupt. B. Riley Farber Inc. (previously A. Farber and Partners Inc.) appointed trustee and all officers and directors resigned.

Victory Resources Corporation (B.C. Feb. 8, 1984)
Dec. 19, 2022 – Name changed to Victory Battery Metals Corp.; basis 1 new for 3 old shs. ∎

Victory Square Games Inc. (B.C. Jan. 13, 2010)
Dec. 10, 2015 – Name changed to V2 Games Inc. ∎

Victory Tungsten Ltd. (B.C. 1952)
Aug. 6, 1974 – Dissolved.

Victory Ventures Inc. (B.C. Dec. 12, 1977)
July 28, 1999 – Name changed to Global Investment.com Financial Inc. ∎

Victory Ventures Inc. (B.C. Nov. 8, 2009)
Feb. 17, 2017 – Name changed to Power Americas Minerals Corp. ∎

Vicwest Corporation (Ont. Mar. 8, 2000)
July 6, 2005 – Converted into an income trust named Vicwest Income Fund; basis 1 trust unit for 1 com. sh.

Vicwest Income Fund (Ont. May 20, 2005)
Jan. 1, 2011 – Succeeded by Vicwest Inc. pursuant to plan of arrangement whereby Vicwest Inc. was formed to facilitate the conversion of the fund into a corporation and the fund was subsequently dissolved. ∎

Vicwest Inc. (Ont. Sept. 16, 2010)
May 27, 2015 – Acquired by Kingspan Group plc for $12.70 per sh.

Vida Ventures Ltd. (B.C. Jan. 25, 2011)
Nov. 18, 2013 – Name changed to First Growth Holdings Ltd. pursuant to Qualifying Transaction acquisition of WineOnline Marketing Company Ltd. ∎

Vidatron Enterprises Ltd. (B.C. Oct. 22, 1986)
Feb. 13, 1992 – Name changed to The Vidatron Group Inc.; basis 1 new for 5 old shs. ∎

Vidatron Entertainment Group Inc. (B.C. Oct. 22, 1986)
July 14, 1999 – Name changed to Peace Arch Entertainment Group Inc.; basis 1 cl. A and 1 cl. B for 5 com shs. ∎

The Vidatron Group Inc. (B.C. Oct. 22, 1986)
Feb. 5, 1997 – Name changed to Vidatron Entertainment Group Inc.; basis 1 new for 4 old shs. ∎

Vidatron Industries Inc. (B.C. May 17, 1984)
Apr. 3, 1987 – Name changed to VTI Industries Inc. ∎

Video Headquarters Inc. (Alta. Sept. 5, 1997)
Dec. 7, 2000 – Name changed to VHQ Entertainment Inc. ∎

Video Premiere International Corporation (Ont. Mar. 30, 1978)
June 8, 1990 – Name changed to S.T.I. Industries Inc.; basis 1 new for 10 old shs. ∎

Video Science Technology Ltd. (Ont. 1977)
Dec. 9, 1991 – Charter cancelled and co. dissolved.

Video-West Distributors Ltd. (B.C. 1984)
Oct. 22, 1993 – Dissolved and struck off register.

Videoflicks.com Inc. (Ont. Mar. 23, 1999 amalg.)
Jan. 12, 2005 – Amalgamated with 2053938 Ontario Limited; basis 1 pfd. sh. for 1 com. sh. immediately redeemed at 2¢ per sh.

Videogram International Corp. (B.C. Sept. 22, 1983)
Oct. 8, 1992 – Name changed to Interactive Video Systems Inc.; basis 1 new for 10 old shs. ∎

Le Groupe Vidéotron Ltée (Que. Dec. 13, 1979)
Dec. 5, 2000 – Acquired by Quebecor Inc. for $45 per sh. and amalgamated with subsidiary Quebecor Media Inc.

Videtics International Corp. (B.C. 1983)
Feb. 21, 1992 – Dissolved and struck off register.

Vidette Gold Mines Ltd. (B.C. 1933)
1940 – Bankrupt; no equity for shldrs.

VidWRX Inc. (Can. Feb. 10, 2006)
Dec. 14, 2018 – Dissolved and struck from registry.
May 14, 2019 – Certificate of revival issued and company restored to registry.
Dec. 13, 2019 – Dissolved for non-compliance and struck from registry.

Vieco Resources Limited (B.C. 1966)
Feb. 25, 1983 – Struck off register.

Vier Capital Corp. (Alta. Sept. 23, 2014)
Oct. 16, 2017 – Formed Vertex Resource Group Ltd. in Alberta following Qualifying Transaction reverse takeover of (old) Vertex Resource Group Ltd. and amalgamation of (old) Vertex with the company and a wholly owned subsid.; basis 1 new for 10 old shs. (see FPsurvey - Industrials)

Viewpoint Explorations Limited (Ont. 1971)
Apr. 1978 – Amalgamated with Lumsden Building Corp. Inc. and others under the Lumsden name; basis 4 new for 29 old shs.

Vigil Health Solutions Inc. (B.C. Jan. 10, 2000)
Apr. 5, 2022 – Acquired by ASSA ABLOT AB; basis 67¢ cash per sh.

Vigil Locating Systems Corporation (Can. Aug. 25, 1998)
June 16, 2009 – Dissolved and struck from register.

Vigor Resources Ltd. (B.C. Sept. 23, 1980)
Mar. 25, 1999 – Formed Biomax Technologies Inc. in British Columbia on amalgamation with Biomax Technologies Inc., constituting a reverse takeover by Biomax; basis 1 new for 1 Biomax sh. and 1 new for 4.31081 Vigor shs. ∎

Viking Energy Royalty Trust (Alta. Nov. 5, 1996)
Feb. 7, 2006 – Plan of Arrangement acquisition by Harvest Energy Trust; basis 0.25 new Harvest trust unit for 1 old Viking trust unit. All Viking debenture obligations assumed by Harvest. (see Harvest Energy Trust)

Viking Gold Corporation (Ont. Apr. 29, 1980)
Dec. 30, 1999 – Acquired by Dragon Mining NL; basis 1 Dragon sh. for 3.3333 Viking shs.

Viking Gold Exploration Inc. (Ont. May 13, 1936)
Aug. 12, 2019 – Continued into British Columbia.
Dec. 11, 2020 – Name changed to Happy Supplements Inc. pursuant to Qualifying Transaction reverse takeover acquisition of (old) Happy Supplements Inc. ∎

Viking-Kinsella Gas Co. Inc. (Alta. 1952)
1959 – Acquired by Westates Petroleum Co.; basis 9 new for 7 old shs.

Viking Mines & Petroleums Ltd. (B.C. 1966)
May 1979 – Charter cancelled.

Viking Mines Ltd. (B.C. 1966)
July 1972 – Name changed to Viking Mines & Petroleums Ltd.; basis 1 new for 3 old shs. ∎

Viking Oil Co., Ltd. (Ont. 1934)
1960 – Struck off register.

Vikka Oils Ltd. (B.C.)
1959 – Struck off register.

Vikon International Resources Inc. (B.C. Mar. 26, 1987)
May 6, 1998 – Name changed to Covik Development Corp.; basis 1 new for 5 old shs. ∎

Vilaroi Gold Mines Ltd. (Ont. 1945)
1958 – Dissolved.

Villa Lead Mining Corp. Ltd. (Ont. 1947)
Nov. 1959 – Distributed 1 sh. Cobalt Badger Silver Mines for each 3 shs. held. Dissolved.

Villacentres Limited (Alta. 1968)
Jan. 10, 1984 – All o/s com. shs. acquired by Crownx Inc. on basis of $3.50, 1/5 cl. A non-voting share of Crownx and 0.5 sh. purchase wt.; each whole wt. entitling holder to buy one cl. A sh. of Crownx at $20 per sh. to Dec. 31, 1986, and thereafter at $22.50 per sh. to Jan. 12, 1989, for each com. sh. of Villacentres under offer, which expired.

Village Farms Income Fund (B.C. Nov. 10, 2003)
Dec. 31, 2009 – Converted into Village Farms International, Inc., following reorganization with wholly owned Village Farms International, Inc. (formerly Village Farms Canada Inc.) and dissolved; basis 1 Village Farms International sh. for 1 Village Farms Income trust unit.

Village Ventures Inc. (Alta. June 24, 1986)
Nov. 30, 1992 – Name changed to Sunventures Corporation pursuant to reverse takeover acquisition of Do-All Building Blocks Inc.; basis 1 new for 2 old shs. ■

The Villager Shoe Shoppes (Canada) Ltd. (Can. 1967)
July 24, 1981 – In mid-1981, all o/s com. shs. acquired by VWV Enterprises Ltd. for a total consideration of $700,000. Shldrs. of record paid 69¢ per sh. in the form of a cash divd.

Villanova Capital Corp. (B.C. Apr. 4, 2007)
Jan. 31, 2008 – Name changed to Africa West Minerals Corp. following Qualifying Transaction reverse takeover acquisition of Africa West Minerals Corp. ■

Villanova Natural Gas Corporation (Alta. 1983 amalg.)
Mar. 29, 1985 – Amalgamated with Evergreen International Corp. (1 for 1) to continue with the name Evergreen International Corp.; basis 1 new for 2 old shs.

Villaret Resources Ltd. (Can. May 13, 1994)
May 18, 2000 – Name changed to Kast Telecom Inc.; basis 1 new for 3 old shs. ■

Villbona Gold Mines Ltd. (Ont. 1945)
Feb. 1953 – Name changed to Avillabona Mines Ltd.; basis 1 new for 2 old shs. ■

Ville Marie Explorations Limited (Ont. Apr. 25, 1975)
Mar. 7, 1995 – Name changed to Heartland Resources Inc.; basis 1 new for 10 old shs. ■

Villebec Gold Mines Ltd. (Ont. 1945)
Jan. 6, 1958 – Charter cancelled.

Villebon Resources Ltd. (B.C. 1981)
Apr. 18, 1985 – Name changed to Victoria Diego Resource Corp.; basis 1 new for 3 old shs. ■

Villemaque Gold Mines Ltd. (Ont. 1930)
Mar. 7, 1977 – Dissolved.

Vimy Explorations Ltd. (B.C. 1959)
May 1974 – Sold off B.C. register.

Vimy Gold Mines Ltd. (Ont. 1934)
Mar. 1976 – Charter cancelled.

Vincent Metal Industries Limited (unknown)
Nov. 1968 – Amalgamated to form Intermetco Limited. (see Intermetco Limited)

Vincent Mining Corp. Ltd. (Ont. 1944)
1948 – Name changed to Mindus Corporation Ltd. ■

Vincent Resources Ltd. (B.C. Nov. 9, 1988)
Sept. 9, 1993 – Name changed to Latin American Telecommunications Corp. ■

Vincero Capital Corp. (B.C. May 6, 2019)
Mar. 25, 2021 – Name changed to Rakovina Therapeutics Inc. pursuant to the Qualifying Transaction reverse takeover acquisition of (old) Rakovina Therapeutics Inc. and concurrent amalgamation of (old) Rakovina with wholly owned 1260541 B.C. Ltd. (and continued as Rakovina Research Ltd.). (see FPsurvey - Industrials)

Vincor International Inc. (Can. Sept. 7, 1993 amalg.)
June 7, 2006 – Acquired by Constellation Brands, Inc. for $36.50 per sh.
June 1, 2012 – Name changed to Constellation Brands Canada, Inc. ■

Vine Pershing Mines Ltd. (Ont. 1944)
Mar. 11, 1957 – Dissolved.

Vinergy Cannabis Capital Inc. (B.C. May 10, 2011)
Mar. 10, 2021 – Name changed to Vinergy Capital Inc. ■

Vinergy Capital Inc. (B.C. May 10, 2011)
Nov. 7, 2023 – Name changed to MedBright AI Investments Inc. (see FPsurvey - Industrials)

Vinergy Resources Ltd. (B.C. May 10, 2011)
July 9, 2019 – Name changed to Vinergy Cannabis Capital Inc. ■

Vinray Malartic Mines Ltd. (Ont. 1944)
Mar. 1954 – Name changed to New Vinray Mines Ltd.; basis 1 new for 2 old shs. ■

Vinson Biotech Inc. (Can. Jan. 29, 2003)
Oct. 1, 2003 – Formed Kane Biotech Inc. following the Sept. 24, 2003, non-arm's length Major Transaction reverse takeover acquisition of and subsequent amalgamation with Kane Biotech Inc. (see FPsurvey - Industrials)

Vinta Explorations Ltd. (B.C. Mar. 11, 1987)
Aug. 11, 1992 – Name changed to Progressive Technologies Inc.; basis 1 new for 4 old shs. ■

Vintage Mines Ltd. (Ont. 1973)
Jan. 2, 1975 – Merged into Sandhurst Mines Ltd.; basis 2 new for 13 old shs.

Vintage Resource Corp. (Alta. Sept. 27, 1991)
July 18, 2001 – Acquired by Acclaim Energy Trust for $0.292 per sh. (see Acclaim Energy Trust)

Vinza Capital Management Inc. (B.C. Sept. 5, 2018)
Oct. 16, 2023 – Name changed to Nu E Power Corp. pursuant to the reverse takeover acquisition of NU E Corp. (see FPsurvey - Mines & Energy; FPsurvey - Industrials)

Vioclone Biologicals Inc. (B.C. Nov. 17, 1986)
Apr. 22, 1994 – Dissolved and struck off register.

Violamac Mines Ltd. (Ont. June 7, 1945)
1966 – Name changed to Kam-Kotia Mines Limited. ■

Vior Energy Corporation (B.C. 1979)
May 31, 1982 – Amalgamated with Zone Petroleum Corporation to form new co. under the Zone Petroleum name; basis 1 new for 3 Vior shs.

Société d'Exploration Minière Vior Inc. (Que. May 16, 1984)
Dec. 24, 2020 – Name changed to Vior Inc. (see FPsurvey - Mines & Energy)

Viper Gold Ltd. (Alta. Jan. 29, 2008)
Nov. 23, 2015 – Name changed to QuikFlo Health Inc. following reverse takeover acquisition of QuikFlo Technologies Inc. ■

Vipond Consolidated Mines Ltd. (Ont. 1922)
1933 – Merged into Anglo-Huronian Ltd.; basis 1 new for 5 old shs.

Viracocha Energy Inc. (Alta. Apr. 19, 2000)
June 7, 2004 – Plan of Arrangement with Provident Energy Trust, Provident Energy Ltd. and Chamaelo Energy Inc.; basis 0.10 new Chamaelo com. sh. plus, either 0.248 new Provident Trust trust unit or, 0.248 new Provident Energy exch. sh. or, a combination thereof. (see Chamaelo Energy Inc.; Provident Energy Trust)

Vireo Health International, Inc. (Alta. Nov. 23, 2004)
June 9, 2021 – Name changed to Goodness Growth Holdings Inc. ■

ViRexx Medical Corp. (Alta. Dec. 23, 2003 amalg.)
Dec. 23, 2008 – Assets sold to Paladin Labs Inc. for $1,446,000 cash. Pursuant to creditors proposal under Bankruptcy and Insolvency Act, no funds were available for shldrs.

Virgin Energy Inc. (Alta. July 29, 1999)
Oct. 26, 2001 – Name changed to NTI Newmerical Inc. pursuant to Qualifying Transaction amalgamation of wholly owned 3794393 Canada Inc. with Newmerical Technologies International Inc. ■

Virgin Metals Inc. (Ont. Feb. 20, 1996)
May 15, 2014 – Name changed to Minera Alamos Inc.; basis 1 new for 10 old shs. (see FPsurvey - Mines & Energy)

Virginia Dare Limited (Ont. 1925)
Oct. 26, 1967 – Placed into bankruptcy
Apr. 1968 – Assets sold. Payments of 50¢ on the dollar were made to ordinary creditors for a total of $200,000.

Virginia Energy Corporation (Alta. Jan. 2, 1996)
Aug. 1, 2000 – Name changed to Winstar Resources Ltd.; basis 1 new for 5 old shs. ■

Virginia Energy Resources Inc. (B.C. May 21, 2009)
Sept. 28, 2012 – Name changed to Anthem Resources Inc. pursuant to spin-out of certain assets to wholly owned Virginia Uranium Ltd. and amalgamation of Virginia Uranium Ltd. with VA Uranium Holdings, Inc. to form (new) Virginia Energy Resources Inc.; basis 0.1 (new) Virginia Energy shs. plus 0.33 Anthem shs. for 1 (old) Virginia Energy sh. and 0.1817 (new) Virginia Energy shs. for 1 VA Uranium Holdings sh. ■

Virginia Energy Resources Inc. (B.C. Sept. 27, 2012 amalg.)
Jan. 26, 2023 – All o/s shs. other than those already held acquired by Consolidated Uranium Inc.; basis 0.26 Consolidated Uranium shs. for 1 Virginia Energy sh. (see Consolidated Uranium Inc.)

Virginia Gold Mines Inc. (Can. Oct. 31, 1986)
June 3, 1996 – Amalgamated with Diabior Explorations Inc. to form new co. with same name Virginia Gold Mines Inc.;basis 1 new for 2 Diabior shs. and 1 new for 1.22 Virginia Gold shs. (see Virginia Gold Mines Inc.)

Virginia Gold Mines Inc. (Can. June 4, 1996 amalg.)
Apr. 5, 2006 – Exchange with Goldcorp Inc. to continue as a new company named Virginia Mines Inc.; basis 0.4 Goldcorp shs. and 0.5 Virginia Mines shs. for 1 Virginia Gold sh. (see Virginia Mines Inc.)

Virginia Hills Oil Corp. (Alta. Nov. 5, 2014)
Feb. 13, 2017 – Placed into receivership. Alvarez & Marsal Canada Inc. appointed receiver and manager.
Mar. 21, 2017 – All realizable property was sold and proceeds were distributed to first secured creditors.
May 3, 2017 – Adjudged bankrupt. Alvarez & Marsal Canada Inc. appointed trustee.

Virginia Mines Inc. (Can. Nov. 30, 2005)
Feb. 17, 2015 – Name changed to Osisko Exploration James Bay Inc. following acquisition by Osisko Gold Royalties Ltd. and concurrent amalgamation with Osisko Gold's wholly owned 9081798 Canada Inc.; basis 0.92 Osisko Gold com. shs. for 1 Virginia com. sh. (see Osisko Gold Royalties Ltd.)

Virginia Mining Corp. (Que. 1947)
1964 – Name changed to Consolidated Virginia Mining Corp.; basis 1 new for 5 old shs. ■

Virginia Petroleums, Ltd. (Can. 1929)
1935 – Name changed to Perry Creek Gold Mines Ltd.

Virginia Red Lake Mines Ltd. (Ont. 1944)
1957 – Charter cancelled.

Virginia Uranium Ltd. (B.C. Jan. 16, 2007)
Sept. 27, 2012 – Formed Virginia Energy Resources Inc. in British Columbia following amalgamation with privately held VA Uranium Holdings, Inc. ■

Virgo Larder Mines Ltd. (Ont. Sept. 9, 1936)
1954 – Merged into Pardee Amalgamated Mines Ltd.; basis 1 new for 40 old shs.

Viridian Inc. (Ont. July 5, 1927)
Dec. 13, 1996 – Acquired by Agrium Inc.; basis 0.975 Agrium shs. for 1 Viridian sh.

Viridis Energy Inc. (B.C. June 18, 1998)
Aug. 14, 2018 – Name changed to Viridis Holdings Corp. (see FPsurvey - Industrials)

Viridium Pacific Group Ltd. (Can. Sept. 20, 2017)
June 10, 2019 – Name changed to Experion Holdings Ltd. ■

Virita Porcupine Gold Mines Ltd. (Ont. 1936)
1953 – Charter cancelled.

Viropean Ventures Inc. (Alta. June 15, 1990)
May 22, 1998 – Name changed to The Saucy Bread Company Inc. following acquisition of The Saucy Pretzel Inc.; basis 1 new for 2 old shs. ■

Virtek Holdings Inc. (Ont. Dec. 30, 1992)
June 20, 1995 – Name changed to Virtek Vision International Inc. ■

Virtek Vision International Inc. (Ont. Dec. 30, 1992)
Nov. 11, 2008 – Acquired by Gerber Scientific, Inc., through wholly owned Gerber Scientific International Ltd., for $1.05 per sh.

Virtual China Travel Services Co., Ltd. (Alta. July 11, 1996)
May 28, 2008 – Formed Melco China Resorts (Holding) Limited in British Columbia following reverse takeover acquisition of and amalgamation with Melco China Resorts (Holding) Limited; basis 1 new for 20 Virtual China shs. and 1 new for 10 Melco China shs. ■

Virtual Dynamics Corp. (Alta. Dec. 31, 1993)
Oct. 28, 1997 – Name changed to Las Western Entertainment Inc.; basis 1 new for 2 old shs. ■

Virtual Prototypes Inc. (Can. Nov. 19, 1980)
Apr. 17, 2001 – Name changed to Engenuity Technologies Inc. ■

Virtual Universe Corporation (Alta. May 11, 1992)
Apr. 25, 2013 – Privatized by way of amalgamation with 1681675 Alberta Ltd.; basis 1 1681675 Alberta Ltd. redeemable sh. for 1 Virtual sh. other than Mr. Lorn Becker and Man Prince Holdings Ltd., immediately redeemed for 2¢ per sh.

VirtualArmor International Inc. (Colo. Mar. 4, 2015)
Oct. 25, 2016 – Name changed to VirtualArmour International Inc. ■

VirtualArmour International Inc. (Colo. Mar. 4, 2015)
Aug. 5, 2021 – Name changed to OLDCO International Inc. ■

VirtualSellers.com, Inc. (Can. Feb. 1, 1991)
Apr. 2, 2002 – Name changed to Healthtrac, Inc. ■

Virtus Energy Ltd. (Alta. Feb. 28, 1995 amalg.)
June 29, 2005 – Acquired by Titan Exploration Ltd.; basis $0.56 or 0.18 new Titan cl. A sh. for 1 old Virtus com. sh. (see Titan Exploration Ltd.)

Virtutone Networks Inc. (Alta. Oct. 21, 2005)
Feb. 24, 2015 – Filed for bankruptcy. All officers and directors resigned and BDO Canada Ltd. appointed trustee.
Sept. 7, 2016 – Struck from registry and dissolved.

Visa Gold Explorations Inc. (Ont. Nov. 30, 1970 amalg.)
Mar. 27, 2006 – Charter cancelled and dissolved.

Viscount Oil and Gas Ltd. (Sask. 1956)
1960 – Acquired by Bison Petroleums & Minerals Ltd.; basis 1 new for 9 old shs.

Viscount Resources Ltd. (B.C. Mar. 9, 1977)
Nov. 5, 1993 – Name changed to Consolidated Viscount Resources Ltd.; basis 1 new for 5 old shs. ■

Vishnu Resources Inc. (B.C. Nov. 19, 1984)
Oct. 25, 1989 – Name changed to Club Mate Holdings Ltd. ■

Visible Genetics Inc. (Ont. Apr. 1993)
Oct. 14, 2002 – Acquired by US-based Bayer Corporation-Diagnostics Division; basis US$1.50 per com. sh. and US$1,000 plus accrued dividends for Series A pfd. shs.

Visible Gold Inc. (B.C. Feb. 23, 1987)
Nov. 9, 1990 – Name changed to Lansing Enterprises Inc.; basis 1 new for 3 old shs. ■

Vision Coatings Group Limited (B.C. Apr. 25, 1984)
Apr. 2, 2007 – Dissolved and struck from register.

Vision Gate Ventures Limited (B.C. Nov. 19, 1980)
July 10, 2003 – Name changed to Northern Lion Gold Corp. (see FPsurvey - Mines & Energy)

Vision Global Solutions Inc. (Ont. Dec. 20, 2000 amalg.)
Nov. 20, 2003 – Continued into Nevada.

Vision HRM Software Inc. (Alta. Sept. 6, 1996)
Jan. 13, 2005 – Name changed to Serenic Corporation. ■

Vision Incorporated (Alta. 1986)
Dec. 2, 2012 – Struck off the registry and dissolved.

Vision Pharmaceuticals Inc. (Ont. Sept. 24, 1985)
Jan. 3, 1995 – Delisted from the CDN. Subsequently dissolved and charter cancelled.

Vision 2000 Exploration Ltd. (Alta. Mar. 27, 1991)
June 9, 2008 – Acquired by Yoho Resources Inc.; basis 65¢ per com. sh. or 0.24 Yoho com. shs. for 1 Vision 2000 com. sh. or a combination thereof.

Visionary Education Technology Holdings Group Inc. (Can. Aug. 10, 2013)
Feb. 9, 2024 – Name changed to Visionary Holdings Inc. (see FPsurvey - Industrials)

Visionary Gold Corp. (B.C. Aug. 14, 2000)
July 10, 2023 – Name changed to Visionary Metals Corp. (see FPsurvey - Mines & Energy)

Visionary Industries Ltd. (B.C. Apr. 25, 1984)
July 25, 1996 – Name changed to Visionary Mining Corporation. ■

Visionary Mining Corporation (B.C. Apr. 25, 1984)
July 11, 2001 – Name changed to Nu-Vision Resource Corp.; basis 1 new for 12 old shs. ■

Visionary Solutions Corp. (B.C. Jan. 3, 1991)
Mar. 9, 1999 – Acquired by Agresso Group ASA of Norway for 85¢ per sh.

VisionQuest Energy Group Inc. (B.C. July 7, 1987)
Jan. 7, 2013 – Struck from registry and dissolved.

VisionQuest Enterprise Group Inc. (B.C. July 7, 1987)
Nov. 3, 2006 – Name changed to VisionQuest Energy Group Inc. ■

VisionSky Corporation (Can. Apr. 8, 2002)
Feb. 16, 2006 – Name changed to VisionSky Corp. and continued into Alberta. ■

VisionSky Corp. (Alta. Feb. 16, 2006)
Mar. 1, 2013 – Acquired by Dixie Energy Trust; basis 0.125 Dixie trust units for 1 VisionSky sh.

Visiontronique Group Inc. (Can. Mar. 23, 1983)
Nov. 3, 1997 – All o/s cl. A shs. repurchased for 43¢ per sh. Co. now private.

Visiphor Corporation (Can. July 6, 2005)
May 15, 2012 – Dissolved and struck from register. (see FPsurvey - Industrials)

Visor Mines Ltd. (Ont. 1946)
1969 – Charter cancelled; voluntarily liquidated.

Vista Exploration Ltd. (Ont. 1975)
Sept. 1987 – Amalgamated with Field Resources Ltd. and Newmex Gold Resources Inc. to form Golden Trio Minerals Ltd.; basis 1 new for 4 old shs.

Vista Gold Corp. (B.C. Nov. 1, 1996 amalg.)
Dec. 17, 1997 – Continued into Yukon.
June 11, 2013 – Continued into British Columbia. (see FPsurvey - Mines & Energy)

Vista International Petroleums Ltd. (Sask. Jan. 13, 1981)
Oct. 16, 1995 – Acquired by Palindrome Energy Ltd. for $2.20 per sh.

Vista Investments Inc. (Alta. Dec. 1, 2000)
Mar. 31, 2003 – Name changed to Rifco Inc. following Qualifying Transaction reverse takeover acquisition of Repair Industry Finance Corporation; basis 1 new for 2 old shs. ■

Vista Resource Company Ltd. (B.C. Apr. 29, 1987)
June 16, 1992 – Name changed to Brenzac Development Corporation. ■

VistaTech Corporation (Alta. Oct. 4, 2000)
Oct. 22, 2001 – Name changed to VR Interactive Corporation following Qualifying Transaction reverse takeover acquisition of VR Interactive International Inc. ■

Vistech Capital Corp. (B.C. Sept. 10, 2008)
Sept. 24, 2010 – Name changed to Cayden Resources Inc. pursuant to Qualifying Transaction acquisition of 100% interest in the Wildcat property from HRS Resources Corp. ■

Vistior Capital Limited (Ont. May 16, 2006)
Nov. 30, 2009 – Dissolved following completion of Qualifying Transaction acquisition of 6,771,429 shs. of Seafield Resources Ltd. and distribution of the Seafield shs. to Vistior shldrs. on the basis of 2.27 Seafield shs. for each sh. held.

VisuaLABS Inc. (Ont. July 27, 1993)
Feb. 28, 1996 – Continued into Alberta.
Dec. 4, 2002 – Name changed to Pretium Industries Inc. ■

VisualVault Corporation (B.C. June 11, 2010)
Oct. 1, 2013 – Name changed to Certive Solutions Inc.; basis 1 new for 2 old shs. (see FPsurvey - Industrials)

Visway Transport Inc. (Can. Nov. 25, 1983)
Apr. 12, 1988 – Acquired by Intercan Leasing Investments Inc., a wholly owned subsid. of Intercan Leasing Inc., for $5.75 per sh.

Vital Battery Metals Inc. (B.C. Oct. 4, 2021)
May 12, 2025 – Name changed to Aventis Energy Inc. (see FPsurvey - Mines & Energy)

Vital Pacific Resources Ltd. (B.C. Sept. 26, 1979)
May 26, 1987 – Continued into Canada.
Aug. 12, 1998 – Continued into Bahamas.
Jan. 2, 2002 – Continued into Yukon.
Jan. 3, 2002 – Name changed to First Majestic Resource Corp.; basis 1 new for 10 old shs. ■

Vital Resources Corp. (Can. Apr. 20, 2004)
Jan. 15, 2009 – Name changed to Fulcrum Resources Inc.; basis 1 new for 10 old shs. ■

Vitamed Biopharmaceuticals Ltd. (Can. May 17, 1984)
July 12, 1993 – Name changed to Receptagen Ltd. ■

Vite Uranium Mines Ltd. (Ont. 1955)
Nov. 6, 1981 – Dissolved.

Viterra Inc. (Can. Mar. 31, 2005)
Dec. 17, 2012 – Acquired by Glencore International plc for $16.25 per sh.
Jan. 1, 2013 – Amalgamated with 8115222 Canada Inc., an indirect wholly owned subsidiary of Glencore International plc, to continue as Viterra Inc.
Oct. 1, 2014 – Continued into Ontario.
Nov. 30, 2020 – Name changed to Viterra Canada Inc.

Vitran Corporation Inc. (Ont. Apr. 29, 1981)
Mar. 31, 2014 – All o/s not held acquired by 2400520 Ontario Inc., a wholly owned subsid. of TransForce Inc., by way of amalgamation for US$6.50 per sh. (see TransForce Inc.)

Vitreous Capital Inc. (Alta. Oct. 29, 1992 amalg.)
Feb. 15, 2007 – Name changed to Vitreous Glass Inc. (see FPsurvey - Industrials)

Vitreous Environmental Group Inc. (Alta. Oct. 29, 1992 amalg.)
Mar. 20, 1998 – Name changed to Vitreous Capital Inc.; basis 1 new for 10 old shs. ■

Vittforge Inc. (Can. 1979)
Oct. 6, 1989 – Placed into bankruptcy. Assets liquidated by May 1990. Nothing for shldrs.

Vittoria Tobacco Plantations Ltd. (Ont. 1928)
Assets distributed and co. wound up, approx. 1949.

Viva Explorations Ltd. (Ont. 1971)
Nov. 1, 1972 – Amalgamated with Spar Holdings & Explorations Limited to continue under the Spar name; basis 1 new for 5 old shs.

Vivant Natural Spring Water, Inc. (Alta. 1988)
May 4, 1994 – Name changed to The Vivant Group Inc. (see FPsurvey - Industrials)

Vive Yellowknife Gold Mines Ltd. (Ont. 1945)
Feb. 10, 1958 – Charter cancelled.

Vivendi Exchangeco Inc. (Can. Apr. 11, 2000)
Nov. 27, 2006 – Redeemed by parent Vivendi Holdings Company; basis 1 new Vivendi S.A. ordinary sh. plus $1.42 for 1 old series A exch. sh.

Vivendi Universal Exchangeco Inc. (Can. Apr. 11, 2000)
May 18, 2006 – Name changed to Vivendi Exchangeco Inc. following change of name of parent co. to Vivendi S.A. from Vivendi Universal. ■

Viventia Biotech Inc. (Ont. July 9, 1998)
Dec. 30, 2005 – Privatized at $2.50 per sh.

ViveRe Communities Inc. (Can. Aug. 9, 2011)
June 1, 2021 – Name changed to NexLiving Communities Inc. (see FPsurvey - Industrials)

Viveve Medical, Inc. (Yuk. Mar. 1999)
May 10, 2016 – Continued into Delaware.

Vivian Petroleums Ltd. (B.C.)
1958 – Struck off register.

Vivid Capital Corp. (Alta. Jan. 25, 1999)
Oct. 20, 2000 – Name changed to Divcom Technologies Inc. ■

ViXS Systems Inc. (Ont. Nov. 28, 2000)
May 26, 2010 – Continued into Canada.
Aug. 3, 2017 – Acquired by Pixelworks, Inc.; basis 0.04836 Pixelworks common shares for each ViXS share held.

Vizsla Resources Corp. (B.C. Sept. 26, 2017)
Feb. 9, 2021 – Name changed to Vizsla Silver Corp. (see FPsurvey - Mines & Energy)

Vodis Pharmaceuticals Inc. (B.C. Oct. 31, 2011)
Dec. 7, 2020 – Name changed to Gnomestar Craft Inc. (see FPsurvey - Industrials)

Voge Gold Mines Ltd. (Ont. 1948)
Sept. 28, 1964 – Dissolved.

Vogogo Inc. (Alta. Sept. 11, 2014 amalg.)
July 31, 2019 – Name changed to Cryptologic Corp. ■

Vogue Fashions Inc. (B.C. Mar. 17, 1978)
Aug. 3, 1983 – Delisted from the Vancouver Stock Exchange. Subsequently dissolved.

Vogue Resources Inc. (Can. June 10, 1994)
Dec. 6, 1999 – Name changed to gearunlimited.com Inc. pursuant to reverse takeover acquisition of gearunlimited.com Inc. ■

Voice-It Solutions, Inc. (Can. Sept. 8, 1986)
July 12, 2004 – Dissolved.

Voice-it Technologies Inc. (Can. Sept. 8, 1986)
Apr. 11, 1996 – Name changed to Voice-It Solutions, Inc.; basis 1 new for 10 old shs. ■

VoiceIQ Inc. (Ont. Oct. 1, 1996)
Dec. 24, 2004 – Continued into Alberta.
Oct. 18, 2005 – Name changed to Yoho Resources Inc. following reverse takeover acquisition of Yoho Resources Investment Partnership. ■

Voisey Bay Resources Inc. (B.C. 1984)
Apr. 8, 1997 – Amalgamated with Atlanta Gold Corporation to form Twin Gold Corporation; basis 1.5 Twin shs. for 1 Voisey sh. (see Twin Gold Corporation)

Vol Mines Limited (Can. Dec. 24, 1964)
Sept. 8, 1980 – Continued into Canada.

Volatus Aerospace Corp. (Ont. Dec. 22, 2021 amalg.)
Sept. 5, 2024 – Acquired by Drone Delivery Canada Corp. (renamed Volatus Aerospace Inc.); basis 1.785 Drone Delivery shs. for 1 Volatus sh.

Volcanic Capital Corp. (B.C. Apr. 25, 2007)
Feb. 19, 2010 – Name changed to Volcanic Metals Corp. following Qualifying Transaction acquisition of Cougar Mining Sh.p.k., a private Albanian company. ■

Volcanic Gas & Oil Co. Ltd. (Ont. 1936)
1960 – Struck off register.

Volcanic Metals Corp. (B.C. Apr. 25, 2007)
Jan. 19, 2017 – Name changed to Volcanic Gold Mines Inc. (see FPsurvey - Mines & Energy)

Volcanic Metals Exploration Inc. (Alta. June 24, 1987)
Sept. 2, 2005 – Continued into Ontario.
June 27, 2006 – Name changed to Energy Fuels Inc. (see FPsurvey - Mines & Energy)

Volcanic Mines Ltd (Ont. 1968)
Mar. 1976 – Charter cancelled.

Volcanic Oil & Gas Co. Ltd. (unknown)
1929 – Acquired by The Union Natural Gas Co. of Canada, Ltd.; basis 1.07 new for 1 old sh.

Voleo Trading Systems Inc. (B.C. July 26, 1978)
Apr. 11, 2022 – Name changed to Intrepid Metals Corp. (see FPsurvey - Mines & Energy)

Volt Energy Corp. (B.C. Dec. 31, 2010)
Sept. 2, 2020 – Name changed to Supernova Metals Corp. (see FPsurvey - Mines & Energy)

Volt Lithium Corp. (Ont. July 7, 1997)
June 8, 2023 – Continued into Alberta.
June 26, 2025 – Name changed to LibertyStream Infrastructure Partners Inc. (see FPsurvey - Mines & Energy)

Volta Resources Inc. (Ont. Mar. 31, 2008 amalg.)
Dec. 30, 2013 – Acquired by B2Gold Corp.; basis 0.15 B2Gold com. shs. for 1 Volta com. sh.

Voltaic Minerals Corp. (B.C. Oct. 1, 2009)
July 8, 2019 – Name changed to Alpha Lithium Corporation. ■

Volterra Resources Inc. (Alta. Oct. 5, 1994)
May 31, 1999 – Acquired by Edge Energy Inc.; basis 0.227 Edge shs. for 1 Volterra sh. (see Edge Energy Inc.)

Volume Services America Holdings, Inc. (Del. Nov. 21, 1995)
Oct. 21, 2004 – Name changed to Centerplate, Inc. ■

Volumetrex Exchange Inc. (B.C. July 6, 2018)
Aug. 11, 2020 – Name changed to Brascan Gold Inc. ■

Voodoo Ventures Ltd. (B.C. June 15, 1984)
Mar. 1, 1996 – Name changed to Pacific Royal Ventures Ltd.; basis 1 new for 3 old shs. ■

VoodooVox Inc. (Alta. Aug. 17, 2004 amalg.)
July 25, 2014 – Name changed to UpSnap Inc. ■

Vortex Energy & Minerals Ltd. (Alta. July 28, 1987)
May 2, 2001 – Name changed to Vortex Integrated Industrial Corporation; basis 1 new for 5 old shs. ■

Vortex Energy Systems Inc. (B.C. Jan. 27, 1986 amalg.)
Sept. 16, 1994 – Name changed to Autumn Industries Inc.; basis 1 new for 5 old shs. ■

Vortex Integrated Industrial Corporation (Alta. July 28, 1987)
Apr. 15, 2005 – Name changed to Sienna Gold Inc. ■

Vox Royalty Corp. (Ont. Feb. 20, 2018)
June 30, 2020 – Continued into Cayman Islands.
July 6, 2021 – Continued into Ontario. (see FPsurvey - Mines & Energy)

Voya Diversified Floating Rate Senior Loan Fund (Ont.)
Dec. 20, 2017 – Name changed to Redwood Floating Rate Bond Fund. ■

Voya Floating Rate Senior Loan Fund (Ont.)
Dec. 20, 2017 – Name changed to Redwood Floating Rate Income Fund. ■

Voya Global Income Solutions Fund (Ont. Sept. 29, 2014)
Dec. 1, 2016 – Terminated; basis $8.872978 per cl. A unit.

Voya High Income Floating Rate Fund (Ont. Sept. 26, 2013)
July 24, 2017 – Merged into Voya Floating Rate Senior Loan Fund; basis 0.85720 Voya Floating cl. A units for 1 Voya High Income cl. A unit and 0.96336 Voya Floating cl. U units for 1 Voya High Income cl. U unit. (see Voya Floating Rate Senior Loan Fund)

Voyager Digital (Canada) Ltd. (B.C. Aug. 30, 1990)
July 16, 2020 – Name changed to Voyager Digital Ltd. (see FPsurvey - Industrials)

Voyager Energy Inc. (Alta. Apr. 28, 1983)
June 10, 1991 – Acquired by Poco Petroleums Ltd.; basis 0.85 Poco shs. for 1 Voyager sh. (see Poco Petroleums Ltd.)

Voyager Explorations Limited (Ont. Apr. 15, 1957)
June 26, 2003 – Name changed to Seafield Resources Ltd.; basis 1 new for 10 old shs. ■

Voyager Metals Inc. (Ont. Feb. 27, 2007)
June 6, 2023 – All o/s shs. not already held acquired by Cerrado Gold Inc.; basis 0.1667 Cerrado shs. for 1 Voyager Metals sh.

Voyager Petroleums Ltd. (Alta. 1966)
June 1979 – All o/s shs. not already held acquired by Nu-West Development Corporation Ltd. for $25 per sh.

Voyageur Film Capital Corp. (Alta. Oct. 22, 1997)
Dec. 6, 2000 – Name changed to Highwire Entertainment Group Inc. ■

Voyageur Minerals Ltd. (Alta. July 23, 2008)
Dec. 13, 2019 – Name changed to Voyageur Pharmaceuticals Ltd. (see FPsurvey - Mines & Energy; FPsurvey - Industrials)

Voyageur (1969) Inc. (Que. 1928)
1973 – Name changed to Voyageur Inc.

Vulcan-Brown Petroleums Ltd. (Alta. June 12, 1937)
Sept. 13, 1950 – Assets sold to Federated Petroleums Ltd. for $206,667. Distribution of 25¢ per sh.

Vulcan Containers (Canada) Limited (Can. Sept. 16, 1958)
July 15, 1970 – Name changed to Vulcan Industrial Packaging Limited. ∎

Vulcan Gold Exploration Inc. (Cayman Islands May 31, 1994)
Jan. 11, 1996 – Name changed to Alamos Minerals Ltd. and continued into British Columbia. ∎

Vulcan Industrial Packaging Limited (Can. Sept. 16, 1958)
May 30, 1986 – Name changed to Vulcan Packaging Inc. ∎

Vulcan Mines Ltd. (Ont. 1953)
Apr. 27, 1967 – Merged into The Little Long Lac Gold Mines Ltd.; basis 1 new for 5 old shs. (see The Little Long Lac Gold Mines Ltd.)

Vulcan Oils Ltd. (Alta. 1925)
1958 – Name changed to Siscalta Oils Limited; basis 1 new for 2 old shs. ∎

Vulcan Packaging Inc. (Can. Sept. 16, 1958)
Nov. 21, 1988 – Acquired by R & M Metal Inc. for $3.70 per sh.

Vulcan Resources Ltd. (B.C. 1981)
July 17, 1984 – Name changed to Overlord Resources Ltd.; basis 1 new for 5 old shs. ∎

Vulcan Ventures Corp. (B.C. Apr. 11, 1983)
Oct. 1, 2001 – Name changed to VVC Exploration Corporation. ∎

W

W 7 Acquisition Corp. (Can. Jan. 27, 2011)
July 15, 2013 – Amalgamated with a wholly owned subsid. of ViXS Systems Inc.; basis 1 ViXS sh. for 38.889 W 7 shs. (see ViXS Systems Inc.)

W3 Solutions Inc. (Alta. Mar. 6, 1998)
Nov. 3, 2006 – Name changed to WWI Resources Ltd. ∎

WAI Capital Investments Corp. (B.C. Dec. 9, 1987)
June 17, 2019 – Struck from register and dissolved.

WAMCO Resources Limited (B.C. Dec. 14, 1995)
Dec. 14, 2000 – Name changed to Wamco Technology Group Ltd. ∎

WB II Acquisition Corp. (Ont. Feb. 13, 2012)
July 22, 2013 – Name changed to Input Capital Corp. pursuant to reverse takeover acquisition of Input Capital Corp. and subsequent amalgamation of Input Capital with a wholly owned subsidiary of WB; basis 1 new for 16 old shs. ∎

WB III Acquisition Corp. (Ont. June 7, 2013)
Dec. 22, 2014 – Name changed to Frankly Inc. following the Qualifying Transaction reverse takeover amalgamation of wholly owned WB III Subco Inc. with TicToc Planet, Inc. (deemed acquiror); basis 1 new for 20.33 old shs. ∎

W.B. Cross Co. Limited (Ont. 1960)
Dec. 31, 1975 – Stk. delisted. Co. returned to private status.

W. B. Holdings Limited (N.B. Dec. 31, 1963)
Aug. 20, 1985 – Name changed to Keltic Incorporated and continued into Nova Scotia. ∎

W. C. Fisher Oil & Minerals Ltd. (Ont. 1953)
Aug. 3, 1964 – Dissolved.

WCB Capital Ltd. (B.C. Mar. 2, 2007)
Apr. 8, 2010 – Name changed to WCB Resources Ltd. pursuant to Qualifying Transaction resource property acquisition. ∎

WCB Resources Ltd. (B.C. Mar. 2, 2007)
Nov. 21, 2017 – Acquired by Kingston Resources Ltd.; basis 4.5 Kingston ordinary shs. for 1 WCB com. sh.

WCC Services Inc. (Alta. Mar. 23, 1999)
June 16, 2004 – Acquisition of 1,395,956 units (1 common share & ½ warrant) of Greenshield Resources Ltd. and distribution of units to shldrs. on the basis of 0.399 Greenshield shares and 0.199 warrants for each WCC share held constituted the company's Qualifying Transaction. Subsequently wound up and dissolved. (see Greenshield Resources Ltd.)

W.C.G. Sports Industries Ltd. (Ont. Aug. 29, 1969)
July 22, 1971 – Name changed to Warrington Products Limited. ∎

WCI Canada Inc. (Can. 1926)
June 28, 1984 – Parent co., White Consolidated Industries Inc., offered to purchase all o/s shs. at US$33.50 (CDN$44.07) per sh.

WCN Investment Corp. (B.C. 1983)
June 24, 1994 – Dissolved and struck off register.

W.C.W. Western Canada Water Enterprises Inc. (B.C. Oct. 2, 1985)
Mar. 31, 1992 – Name changed to Western Canada Beverage Corporation. ∎

WDF Capital Corp. (B.C. Apr. 7, 1988)
Mar. 29, 1993 – Continued into Wyoming.
Apr. 19, 1993 – Name changed to Soligen Technologies, Inc. following reverse takeover acquisition of Soligen, Inc.

WEQ Holdings Inc. (Can. July 1, 2012)
Dec. 13, 2018 – Voluntarily delisted; undergoing liquidation and dissolution. The Bowra Group Inc. appointed liquidator.
July 2019 – Interim distribution of $2 cash per sh. payable to shldrs. of record July 23, 2019.
Sept. 24, 2020 – Interim distribution of 20¢ cash per sh. payable to shldrs, of record Sept. 25, 2020.
Feb. 5, 2021 – Final distrib. of $0.124 cash per sh. payable to shldrs. of record Feb. 3, 2021.
June 26, 2021 – Dissolved and all issued and o/s com. shs cancelled.

WEW Ventures Inc. (B.C. Oct. 20, 1982)
May 11, 1994 – Name changed to Independence Resources Inc. ∎

WFI Industries Ltd. (B.C. Mar. 27, 1987)
Aug. 28, 1997 – Continued into Ontario.
Sept. 13, 2004 – Continued into Canada.
June 16, 2008 – Name changed to WaterFurnace Renewable Energy, Inc. ∎

WGI Heavy Minerals, Incorporated (B.C. July 15, 1988)
Nov. 14, 2012 – Acquired by Opta Minerals Inc. for $0.60 per sh. (see Opta Minerals Inc.)

W.G.N. Explorations and Holdings Ltd. (Ont. 1967)
Nov. 18, 1981 – Charter cancelled.

W.I. Wheels International Ltd. (B.C. June 5, 1984)
June 8, 1990 – Name changed to Annisquam Art Company Ltd.; basis 1 new for 3 old shs. ∎

WIC Western International Communications Ltd. (Can. Oct. 7, 1981)
Apr. 13, 2000 – Acquired by 3706435 Canada Ltd., an indirect wholly owned subsid. of CanWest Global Communications Corp., for $43.50 per sh.

WIN Energy Corporation (Alta. Feb. 9, 2004)
Dec. 28, 2007 – Acquired by Compton Petroleum Corporation for $0.45 per sh.

W.I.N. Gaming Corp. (Ont. Dec. 6, 1995 amalg.)
Feb. 2, 2000 – Name changed to Funtime Hospitality Corp. ∎

W. J. Gage Limited (Ont. 1893)
May 1, 1971 – All o/s 6.25% 1st mtge. s.f. bds. due May 1, 1972, called for redempti at par and accr. int. It is understood that this co. is now private.

WLD Inc. (Ont. Sept. 22, 1987)
July 12, 1995 – Name changed to Astris Energi Inc. ∎

W. M. Helijet Airways Inc. (B.C. July 29, 1983)
Feb. 14, 2000 – Name changed to Helijet International Inc.; basis 2 new for 1 old sh. ∎

WNS Emergent Inc. (Alta. Aug. 20, 1999 amalg.)
June 14, 2004 – Name changed to CriticalControl Solutions Corp. ∎

WNS Inc. (Alta. Aug. 20, 1999 amalg.)
Oct. 31, 2002 – Name changed to WNS Emergent Inc. ∎

WORLDTEK (Canada) Ltd. (Ont. June 27, 1995)
June 13, 2006 – Certificate of incorporation cancelled and company dissolved.

WPC Resources Inc. (B.C. Apr. 13, 2007)
Jan. 18, 2019 – Name changed to Blue Star Gold Corp. (see FPsurvey - Mines & Energy)

WPI Gold Ltd. (Alta. July 18, 1986)
June 29, 2005 – Continued into British Columbia.
July 12, 2005 – Name changed to Salmon River Resources Ltd. ∎

WPN Resources Ltd. (Yuk. May 15, 1997)
June 1, 2004 – Name changed to Grove Energy Limited. ∎

WPT Industrial Real Estate Investment Trust (Ont. Mar. 4, 2013)
Oct. 21, 2021 – Acquired by Blackstone Real Estate Income Trust, Inc.; basis US$22.00 cash per sh.

WPVC Inc. (Can. May 4, 2004)
Feb. 23, 2005 – Succeeded by Huntingdon Real Estate Investment Trust pursuant to Qualifying Transaction plan of arrangement whereby each 5 shares of WPVC were exchanged for one trust unit of Huntingdon Real Estate Investment Trust. ∎

W.R. King Industrial Ltd. (Alta. Dec. 17, 1991)
Aug. 12, 1994 – Name changed to Tropic Trading Company Limited. ∎

W.R. Partners Ltd. (B.C. Nov. 3, 2006)
Mar. 27, 2008 – Name changed to biOasis Technologies Inc. following Qualifying Transaction acquisition of biOasis Technologies Inc. (see FPsurvey - Industrials)

WSG Group Systems Inc. (Alta. Jan. 30, 1997)
Feb. 22, 2006 – Formed GFI Oil & Gas Corporation in Alberta on amalgamation with Duinord Petroleum Inc., constituting a reverse takeover by Duinord. ∎

WSi Interactive Corporation (B.C. May 13, 1985)
May 7, 2001 – Name changed to iaNett International Systems Ltd.; basis 1 new for 10 old shs. ∎

WSR Gold Inc. (Ont. May 11, 1979)
Dec. 18, 2008 – Name changed to White Pine Resources Inc.; basis 1 new for 10 old shs. ∎

WWB Oil & Gas Ltd. (Alta. June 18, 1987)
Feb. 27, 1998 – Name changed to Cigar Oil & Gas Ltd.; basis 1 new for 5 old shs. ■

WWI Resources Ltd. (Alta. Mar. 6, 1998)
July 11, 2007 – Continued into British Columbia.
Feb. 25, 2010 – Name changed to Petromanas Energy Inc. pursuant to Qualifying Transaction reverse takeover acquisition of Manas Adriatic GmbH. ■

WWS Capital Inc. (Alta. Sept. 9, 1998)
Dec. 31, 2002 – Name changed to VenPath Investments Inc. following Qualifying Transaction reverse takeover acquisition of VenPath Investments Inc.; basis 1 new for 1 old sh. ■

Wabasso Cotton Company Limited (Can. 1907)
Dec. 1967 – Name changed to Wabasso Limited. ■

Wabasso Inc. (Can. 1907)
Sold major assets to Dominion Textile Inc. Dominion Textile continued the bedding and towel product lines under the Wabasso name, and made Wabasso Canada Inc. a wholly owned subsid. (see Dominion Textile Inc.)
June 1985 – Name changed to Tratex Textile Inc. (see Dominion Textile Inc.)

Wabasso Limited (Can. 1907)
June 1979 – Name changed to Wabasso Inc. ■

Wabi Exploration Inc. (Ont. May 9, 2000 amalg.)
May 2, 2018 – Name changed to Getchell Gold Corp. (see FPsurvey - Mines & Energy)

Wabico Mines Ltd. (Ont. 1952)
Aug. 1972 – Charter cancelled.

Wabush Mines (Que. 1961)
Apr. 25, 2018 – Struck from registry for non-compliance.

Waco Petroleums Ltd. (Ont. 1956)
Apr. 9, 1975 – Charter cancelled.

Wadasa Gold Mines (Ont. 1944)
Nov. 29, 1972 – Dissolved.

Waddington Mining Corp. Ltd. (Can. 1946)
1968 – Name changed to Cop-Ex Mining Corp. Ltd. ■

Waddy Lake Mines Ltd. (Ont. Oct. 5, 1960)
Feb. 2, 1979 – Name changed to Waddy Lake Resources Inc.; basis 1 new for 10 old shs. ■

Waddy Lake Resources Inc. (Ont. Oct. 5, 1960)
Mar. 14, 1979 – Continued into Canada. (see Golden Rule Resources Ltd.)
Oct. 20, 1995 – Acquired by Golden Rule Resources Ltd.; basis 0.53 Golden Rule shs. for 1 Waddy Lake sh. (see Golden Rule Resources Ltd.)

Wadge Mines Ltd. (Ont. Feb. 11, 1954)
Oct. 24, 1984 – Name changed to Canper Resources Inc. (see FPsurvey - Mines & Energy)

Waferboard Corporation Limited (Ont. Apr. 14, 1969)
Jan. 20, 1989 – Name changed to Malette Inc. ■

Wagner Oils Ltd. (Alta. Apr. 1951)
1952 – Assets acquired by Blue Crown Petroleums Ltd.; basis 3 new for 1 old sh.

Wain-Con Oils Ltd. (Alta. Apr. 1936)
1960 – Acquired by Arawain Producers Limited; basis 1 new for 3 old shs. (see Arawain Producers Limited)

Wainoco Oil and Chemicals Ltd. (Ont. 1949)
Oct. 13, 1971 – Name changed to Wainoco Oil Ltd. ■

Wainoco Oil Corporation (Wyo. 1976)
Apr. 29, 1998 – Name changed to Frontier Oil Corporation. ■

Wainoco Oil Ltd. (Ont. 1949)
1976 – Name changed to Wainoco Oil Corporation and continued into Wyoming. ■

Wainwell Oils Ltd. (Can. Dec. 1927)
Taken over by Peninsular Petroleums Ltd.; basis 1 new for 10 old shs.

Wainwright-Dome Oil Co. Ltd. (Can. 1924)
Charter cancelled. At last report, one suspended well and 50 freehold acres in Wainwright field, Alta., held in trust for shldrs.

Wainwright Petroleums Ltd. (Can. May 1926)
Struck off register.

Wainwright Producers & Refiners Limited (Ont. 1949)
1966 – Name changed to Wainoco Oil and Chemicals Ltd. ■

Wainwright Refineries Limited (Ont. 1949)
1953 – Name changed to Wainwright Producers & Refiners Limited. ■

Wairiri Gold Mines Ltd. (Ont. 1945)
1952 – Charter cancelled.

Waite Dufault Mines Limited (Que. Aug. 28, 1944)
June 17, 1996 – Name changed to KPI International Inc.; basis 1 new for 10 old shs. ■

Waite Lake Mines Ltd. (Que. 1959)
1981 – Name changed to Waite Lake Mines Inc.

Waitsfield Capital Inc. (Que. Jan. 31, 1973)
Oct. 24, 2013 – Certificate of dissolution issued.

Wajax Income Fund (Ont. Apr. 27, 2005)
Jan. 1, 2011 – Succeeded by Wajax Corporation pursuant to plan of arrangement whereby Wajax Corporation was formed to facilitate the conversion of the fund into a corporation and the fund was subsequently dissolved. (see FPsurvey - Industrials)

Wajax Limited (Can. Feb. 17, 1910; via letters patent)
June 15, 2005 – Converted into Wajax Income Fund; basis 1 trust unit for 1 com. sh.

Wakefield Uranium Mines Ltd. (Que. 1954)
Oct. 1974 – Charter cancelled.

Wakeham Bay Mines Limited (Ont. 1957)
Dec. 7, 1977 – Dissolved.

Wakeko Mines, Ltd. (Ont. 1944)
Nov. 30, 1964 – Dissolved.

Wakemac Denton Gold Mines Ltd. (Ont. 1944)
1961 – Charter cancelled.

Wakita Quebec Gold Mines Ltd. (Ont. 1946)
1947 – Acquired by Lynnita Consolidated Gold Mines Ltd.; basis 1 new for 3 old shs. (see Lynnita Consolidated Gold Mines Ltd.)

Wal-Mart Stores, Inc. (Del. Oct. 31, 1969)
Feb. 1, 2018 – Name changed to Walmart Inc.

Walburt Oils Ltd. (Can. 1953)
1960 – Struck off register.

Walcoro Porcupine Mines Ltd. (Ont. 1944)
1951 – Name changed to New Walcoro Mines Ltd.; basis 1 new for 3 old shs. ■

Walcott Resources Ltd. (B.C. Dec. 11, 2017)
Feb. 4, 2021 – Name changed to MegaWatt Lithium and Battery Metals Corp. (see FPsurvey - Mines & Energy)

Waldorf Ventures Inc. (Alta. June 19, 1996)
Nov. 22, 2001 – Name changed to Hospital Greetings Corporation following Qualifying Transaction reverse takeover acquisition of Hospital Greetings Corporation; basis 1 new for 4 old shs. ■

Waldron Energy Corporation (Alta. Feb. 4, 2004)
Aug. 17, 2015 – Placed into receivership and FTI Consulting Canada Inc. appointed receiver and manager. All officers and directors resigned.

Wales Petroleum Ltd. (Can. Mar. 12, 1929)
1969 – Name changed to Silver Mark Mines Ltd. ■

Walhart Gold Mines Ltd. (Ont. 1944)
Sept. 1962 – Dissolved.

Walker Patricia Gold Mines Ltd. (Ont. 1937)
1957 – Charter cancelled.

Walker's Capital Corporation (Alta. 1986)
Feb. 1, 1994 – Dissolved and struck off register.

Walkerville Brewery Limited (Can. 1928)
1944 – All o/s capital acquired by Canadian Breweries Ltd. during; basis 1 pref. sh. Canadian Breweries for 12 com. shs. Walkerville.

Walking Stick Oil & Gas Corp. (B.C. Mar. 6, 1987)
Mar. 31, 1994 – Acquired by Ascentex Energy, Inc.; basis 1 Ascentex sh. for 3.5 Walking Stick shs. (see Ascentex Energy, Inc.)

Wall & Redekop Corp. (B.C. Jan. 31, 1969 amalg.)
Aug. 8, 1988 – Name changed to Wall Financial Corporation; basis 3 new for 1 old sh. (see FPsurvey - Industrials)

Wall & Redekop Corp. Ltd. (B.C. Jan. 31, 1969 amalg.)
May 30, 1974 – Name changed to Wall & Redekop Corp. ■

Wall Street Ventures Inc. (B.C. Feb. 28, 1986)
Mar. 23, 1993 – Name changed to Bionic Enterprises, Inc.; basis 1 new for 4 old shs. ■

Wallac Yellowknife Gold Mines Ltd. (Ont. 1946)
1956 – Name changed to Valray Explorations Ltd. ■

Waller Red Lake Mines Ltd. (Ont. 1945)
Aug. 1972 – Charter cancelled.

Walloper Gold Resources Ltd. (B.C. June 5, 1996)
Apr. 25, 2005 – Name changed to East Asia Minerals Corporation. ■

Walmer Capital Corp. (Alta. June 27, 2011)
Mar. 30, 2017 – Name changed to EnerSpar Corp. following Qualifying Transaction of feldspar prospect from Globex Mining Enterprises Inc. ■

Walmont Precious Metals Corp. (Can. June 7, 1983)
Aug. 1, 1986 – Name changed to IGF Metals Inc.; basis 1 new for 10 old shs. ■

Walmore Petroleums Limited (Alta.)
June 1958 – Acquired by Tidal Petroleum Corp. Ltd. for 115,000 shs.

Walron Minerals Corporation (Can. July 19, 1956)
May 6, 2004 – Dissolved.

Walsh-Katrine Gold Mines Ltd. (Ont. 1924)
1929 – Name changed to Northern Metals Ltd.

Walsh Lake Gold Mines Ltd. (Alta. Feb. 16, 1937)
Wound up. Shares worthless.

Walter Industries, Inc. (Del.)
Apr. 28, 2009 – Name changed to Walter Energy, Inc.

Walter M. Lowney Co. Ltd. (Can. 1924)
May 15, 1968 – Acquired by Standard Brands Limited for $68.22 per sh.

Walterra Gold Mines Ltd. (Ont. 1944)
1952 – Charter cancelled.

Walters Consulting Corporation (Ont. Jan. 1, 1992)
May 13, 2003 – Name changed to YWL Corp. ■

Walton Gold Ltd. (Man. Sept. 24, 1934)
Liquidated voluntarily and assets distributed.

Waltricia Gold Mines Ltd. (Ont. 1946)
Oct. 21, 1957 – Dissolved.

Walwyn Inc. (Can. Oct. 22, 1980)
1983 – Continued into Nova Scotia.
June 1, 1990 – Formed Midland Walwyn Inc. in Canada on amalgamation with Midland Doherty Financial Corporation; basis 1 new for 3.5 old shs. ■

Wamco Technology Group Ltd. (B.C. Dec. 14, 1995)
Sept. 1, 2011 – Continued into Ontario.
Feb. 22, 2018 – Name changed to Generic Gold Corp. following reverse takeover acquisition of (old) Generic Gold Corp. and amalgamation of (old) Generic with wholly owned 2604935 Ontario Inc. to form 1989670 Ontario Limited. (see FPsurvey - Mines & Energy)

Wampum Gold Mines Ltd. (Ont. 1939)
May 1958 – Charter cancelled.

Wanapitei Basin Mines Ltd. (Ont. Aug. 7, 1934)
1946 – Name changed to Sudore Gold Mines Ltd. and continued into Ontario; basis 1 new for 3 old shs. ■

Wand Capital Corporation (Ont. Jan. 12, 2012)
June 5, 2012 – Succeeded by True North Apartment Real Estate Investment Trust pursuant to Qualifying Transaction acquisition of an apartment building in Guelph, Ont.; basis 1 new for 8 old shs. ■

Waneta Gold Mines Ltd. (B.C. Nov. 19, 1934)
1951 – Charter cancelled.

Wangton Capital Corp. (Alta. Dec. 23, 2010)
Mar. 19, 2018 – Continued into British Columbia. (see FPsurvey - Industrials)

Wanted Technologies Corporation (Can. Feb. 20, 2004)
Nov. 9, 2015 – Acquired by CEB Canada Inc, a wholly owned subsid. of CEB Inc., for Cdn$1.79 per sh.

Wapiti Basin Oils Ltd. (unknown)
1957 – Acquired by Cedar Oils Ltd.

War Eagle Mining Company Inc. (B.C. Mar. 6, 1984)
Oct. 1, 2018 – Name changed to Warrior Gold Inc. ■

War Eagle Resources Ltd. (B.C. Mar. 20, 1964)
1966 – Name changed to Admiral Mines Ltd. ■

Waratah Coal Inc. (B.C. Jan. 19, 2006)
Apr. 6, 2009 – Acquired by Mineralogy Pty Ltd. for $1.41 per sh.

Waratah Pharmaceuticals Inc. (Can. Apr. 20, 2000)
Jan. 25, 2002 – Plan of Arrangement with Transition Therapeutics Inc.; basis 0.83333 new Transition com. sh. for 1 old Waratah com. sh. Outstanding wts and options also exercised at 0.83333 for 1. (see Transition Therapeutics Inc.)

Warburton Minerals Ltd. (B.C. 1981)
Feb. 23, 1987 – Name changed to APP Applied Polymer Products Inc. and continued into Canada. ■

Wardair Canada Ltd. (Alta. 1953)
June 10, 1976 – Name changed to Wardair International Ltd.

Wardair Inc. (Alta. 1953)
Apr. 24, 1989 – Acquired by PWA Corporation for $17.25 per sh., of which $10 was paid in cash and $7.25 in cash or com. shs. or a combination thereof, at the option of PWA. (see PWA Corporation)

Wardlee Gold Mines Ltd. (Ont. 1946)
May 26, 1958 – Charter cancelled.

Wardley China Investment Trust (B.C. Feb. 7, 1994)
Nov. 2003 – Wound up following sale of last active investment.
Aug. 26, 2005 – Distribution to unitholders (approx. $0.38 per unit) was originally anticipated in Feb. 2004. However payment was postponed following series of negotiations between the Trustee, Administrator and unitholder. The Trust was dissolved effective Aug. 26, 2005 and final distribution totaled $0.352304749 per unit.

Ware Resources Ltd. (B.C. 1979)
June 20, 1988 – Name changed to World Enzymes Ltd. (see FPsurvey - Industrials)

Ware Solutions Corporation (Alta. Oct. 1, 2001)
Feb. 18, 2004 – Acquired by BCE Emergis Inc. for $0.2848 per sh. (see BCE Emergis Inc.)

Warka Capital Corp. (Alta. Feb. 27, 1996)
Sept. 11, 1997 – Name changed to Nevada Bob's Canada Inc.; basis 1 new for 2.5 old shs. ■

Warlund Mines Ltd. (Ont. 1949)
Apr. 1961 – Distributed 14¢ per sh. Charter cancelled.

Warnaco of Canada Limited (Can. 1973)
Apr. 23, 1985 – Acquired by Warnaco Inc. for $30 per sh.

Warner Bros.-Seven Arts Productions Ltd. (Ont. 1919)
July 8, 1969 – Assets sold to Kinney National Service Inc.; basis of exch. was 1 sh. of co. for 0.81 of a sh. of $1.25 series D conv. pref. stk., and 0.8 of a sh. of 5¢ series C conv. pref. stk. of Kinney.

Warner Oils Ltd. (Can. Mar. 23, 1926)
1954 – Name changed to Western Warner Oils Limited; basis 1 new for 2 old shs. (see FPsurvey - Mines & Energy)

Warner Ventures Ltd. (B.C. Aug. 19, 1983)
Oct. 6, 1998 – Name changed to Copper Ridge Explorations Inc.; basis 1 new for 4 old shs. ■

Warnex Inc. (Can. Jan. 4, 1996)
July 11, 2014 – Amalgamated with a wholly owned subsid. of Diagnos Inc.; basis 1 Diagnos com. sh. (deemed value of 8¢ per sh.) for 1 Warnex com. sh.

Warnex Pharma Inc. (Can. Jan. 4, 1996)
July 24, 2001 – Name changed to Warnex Inc. ■

Warnic 1 Enterprises Ltd. (B.C. Nov. 16, 2007)
Mar. 11, 2010 – Together with Valentine Ventures Corp., Blackwater Capital Corp. and Latigo Capital Corporation (Capital Pool Companies) amalgamated with Cumberland Oil & Gas Ltd. constituting Capital Pool Companies' Qualifying Transaction to form Cumberland Oil & Gas Ltd; basis Warnic (0.3032-for-1), Valentine (0.3474-for-1), Blackwater (0.2875-for-1), Latigo (0.3879-for-1) and Cumberland (1-for-1). (see Cumberland Oil & Gas Ltd.)

Warnock Hersey International Limited (Can. 1927)
Jan. 1, 1978 – Amalgamated with the subsids., International Bronze Powders Ltd. and Toronto Iron Works Holdings Ltd. and its subsids. to form TIW Industries Ltd. Pref. and com. shs. of Warnock Hersey were exchanged sh.-for-sh. for similar pref. and com. shs. of TIW.

Waroona Energy Inc. (B.C. Mar. 24, 2021)
Dec. 18, 2023 – Acquired by Frontier Energy Limited; basis 0.2342 Frontier Energy ord. shs. for 1 Waroona Energy com. sh.

Warp 10 Technologies Inc. (Ont. Aug. 15, 1995 amalg.)
Jan. 12, 2000 – Name changed to BrandEra.Com Inc. ■

Warren Explorations Limited (Ont. 1973)
Aug. 16, 1983 – Continued into Alberta.
June 30, 1988 – Name changed to Paragon Petroleum Limited; basis 1 new for 8 old shs. ■

Warrington Inc. (Can. Mar. 17, 1981)
Sept. 2, 1988 – Name changed to Canstar Sports Inc.; basis 1 new for 20 old shs. ■

Warrington Products Limited (Ont. Aug. 29, 1969)
Mar. 17, 1981 – Name changed to Warrington Inc. and continued into Canada. ■

Warrior Energy N.V. (Netherlands June 1, 1993)
Nov. 16, 2012 – Name changed to Summus Solutions N.V.

Warrior Gold Inc. (B.C. Mar. 6, 1984)
May 10, 2023 – Name changed to Kirkland Lake Discoveries Corp.; basis 1 new for 4 old shs. (see FPsurvey - Mines & Energy)

Warrior Industries Ltd. (B.C. 1978)
Sept. 9, 1994 – Dissolved and struck off register.

Warrior Resources Ltd. (B.C. 1978)
May 14, 1987 – Name changed to Warrior Industries Ltd. ■

Warstar Resources Inc. (B.C. 1978)
May 14, 1992 – Dissolved and struck off register.

Wartime Oils Ltd. (Can. 1943)
Mar. 21, 1945 – Wound up.

Warwick Communications Inc. (Alta. Feb. 27, 1996)
May 2, 2010 – Struck from registry and dissolved.

Warwick Petroleum Limited (B.C. 1977)
1981 – Continued into Alberta.
1982 – Acquired by Humbolt Energy Corporation in exchange for shs.

Warwick Woolen Mills Co. Ltd. (Que. 1947)
1978 – Name changed to Textiles Warwick Inc. ■

Wasa Lake Gold Mines Ltd. (Que. 1937)
Jan. 1, 1947 – Name changed to Lake Wasa Mining Corp.; basis 1 new for 2 old shs. ■

Wasabi Resources Ltd. (B.C. 1980)
May 20, 1986 – Continued into Canada.
Feb. 7, 1996 – Dissolved and struck off register.

Wasaga Capital Corp. (Alta. May 14, 2004)
July 14, 2005 – Formed RepeatSeat Ltd. in Alberta on Qualifying Transaction amalgamation with RepeatSeat Ltd.; basis 1 new for 7.6 old shs. ■

Wasamac Mines Ltd. (Que. 1946)
1968 – Acquired by Wright-Hargreaves Mines Ltd.; basis 1 new for 2 old shs.

Wascana Energy Inc. (Sask. Jan. 28, 1973)
July 3, 1997 – Amalgamated with CXY Investments Ltd., a wholly owned subsid. of Canadian Occidental Petroleum Ltd., for $20.50 per sh. (see Canadian Occidental Petroleum Ltd.)

Wascanna Mines Ltd. (Ont. 1936)
Oct. 7, 1957 – Dissolved.

Waseco Resources Inc. (B.C. Feb. 10, 1988)
May 8, 1996 – Continued into Ontario. (see FPsurvey - Mines & Energy)

Washington Gold Mines Ltd. (Ont. 1936)
Feb. 16, 1959 – Dissolved.

Washmax Corp. (Alta. Sept. 17, 1998)
Feb. 9, 2010 – Name changed to Upper Canada Gold Corporation following acquisition of Dingman gold properties from Opawica Explorations Inc.; basis 1 new for 4 old shs. ■

Wasp International Resources Inc. (B.C. 1972)
Feb. 1, 1982 – Name changed to Plexus Resources Corporation. ■

Wassanor Gold Mines Ltd. (Ont. 1944)
Jan. 26, 1956 – Dissolved.

Waste Management, Inc. (Del. 1968)
May 25, 1993 – Name changed to WMX Technologies, Inc.

Waste Services, Inc. (Ont. May 23, 1997)
2004 – Continued into Delaware.

Wasu Porcupine Mines Ltd. (Ont. 1938)
Apr. 1960 – Charter cancelled.

Watch Resources Ltd. (B.C. Jan. 5, 1987)
Jan. 1, 2007 – Amalgamated with Energy 51 Inc. to form new co. with same name Watch Resources Ltd.; basis 1 new for 5 old shs. (see Pearl Exploration and Production Ltd.)
Oct. 23, 2007 – Acquired by Pearl Exploration and Production Ltd.; basis 0.23 Pearl shs. for 1 Watch sh. (see Pearl Exploration and Production Ltd.)

Watcor Purification Systems Inc. (B.C. 1983)
June 26, 1992 – Dissolved and struck off register.

Water Capital Inc. (Ont. July 8, 2005)
Aug. 21, 2008 – Formed Schneider Power Inc. in Ontario on Qualifying Transaction reverse takeover acquisition of and amalgamation with Schneider Power Inc.; basis 1 new for 2 old shs. ■

Waterford Capital Management Inc. (Ont. Nov. 16, 1959)
Sept. 21, 1998 – Following Plan of Arrangement, all o/s com. shs. exchanged for multiple vtg. and subord. vtg. shs. of CPI Plastics Group Limited; basis (a) 0.1 of a mult. vtg. sh. and 0.1 of a sub. vtg. sh. of CPI for 1 com. sh. of Waterford or (b) 0.205 of a sub. vtg. sh. of CPI for 1 com. sh. of Waterford. (see CPI Plastics Group Limited)

Waterford Resources Inc. (B.C. Apr. 3, 1987)
June 2, 1993 – Name changed to Premier Minerals Ltd.; basis 1 new for 4 old shs. ■

Waterfront Capital Corporation (Alta. Sept. 17, 1987)
Aug. 11, 2000 – Continued into British Columbia.
Apr. 1, 2020 – Name changed to Entheos Capital Corporation; basis 1 new for 10 old shs. ■

WaterFurnace Renewable Energy, Inc. (Can. Sept. 13, 2004)
Aug. 28, 2014 – Acquired by NIBE Industrier AB for Cdn$30.60 per com. sh.

Waterloo Brewing Ltd. (Ont. Feb. 20, 1984)
Mar. 9, 2023 – Acquired by Carlsberg Breweries A/S; basis $4 cash per sh.

The Waterloo Manufacturing Company Limited (Can. 1928)
1985 – In the fall of the co. sold its assets to a group of employees. Co. is no longer active.

Waterloo Resources Inc. (B.C. Mar. 22, 1983)
Feb. 28, 1992 – Name changed to Burcon Developments Ltd.; basis 1 new for 3 old shs. ■

Waterloo Resources Ltd. (B.C. Mar. 23, 2007)
July 15, 2013 – Name changed to Lowell Copper Ltd. following reverse takeover acquisition of Lowell Copper Inc.; basis 1 new for 2 old shs. ■

Waterloo Trust and Savings Company (Ont. 1913)
Aug. 1968 – Acquired by The Huron & Erie Mortgage Corp.; basis 1.5 Huron & Erie shs. plus $10.75, 1.25 Huron & Erie shs. plus $13.50 or $27.25 Waterloo pfce. shs. converted into com. shs. and exchanged under the offer.

Waterous Equipment Limited (Alta. 1953)
May 1967 – Name changed to Waterous GM Diesel Limited. ■

Waterous GM Diesel Limited (Alta. 1953)
Oct. 1968 – O/s com. shs. acquired by Wajax Limited; basis 1 new for 2 old shs.

Waterous Limited (Can. 1874)
Sept. 15, 1953 – Koehring Co. of Milwaukee acquired 99% of the 37,950 cl. A shs. and 99,475 com. shs. o/s and changed the company's name to Koehring-Waterous Ltd., after an offer to purch. stk. at $14 per share.

WaterSave Logic Corporation (B.C. Oct. 10, 1986)
Aug. 15, 2006 – Name changed to Abode Mortgage Holdings Corp. following reverse takeover acquisition of Abode Mortgage Corporation. ■

Watertowne International Inc. (Can. Dec. 12, 2003)
Mar. 15, 2006 – Name changed to Sightus Inc.; basis 1 new for 8 old shs. ■

Waterways Iron and Uranium Ltd. (Ont. 1948)
1961 – Name changed to Norite Explorations Ltd. ■

Watling-Larder Mines Ltd. (Ont. 1950)
Aug. 31, 1951 – Name changed to Hearst Larder Mines Ltd. ■

Watson Bell Communications Inc. (B.C. June 9, 1987)
Nov. 22, 1995 – Name changed to Cosworth Ventures Ltd.; basis 1 new for 5 old shs. ■

Watson International Resources Ltd. (B.C. Mar. 31, 1980)
Oct. 20, 1982 – Name changed to The Watson Resource Corporation; basis 1 new for 4 old shs. ■

Watson, Jack & Company Limited (Can. 1914)
1954 – Controlling int. acquired by B. J. Coghlin Co. Ltd. (now Wajax Ltd.) through exchange of shs. on basis of 9 shs. of Coghlin for 10 shs. of Watson, Jack.

The Watson Resource Corporation (B.C. Mar. 31, 1980)
Aug. 22, 1986 – Dissolved and struck off register.

Watusi Capital Corp. (Alta. Oct. 6, 2011)
May 12, 2016 – Continued into British Columbia.
Apr. 25, 2018 – Name changed to Aethon Minerals Corporation; basis 1 new for 3 old shs. ■

Wavano Explorations Inc. (Ont. 1980)
May 2, 1986 – Name changed to Sea Band International Inc.; basis 1 new for 10 old shs. ■

Wave Exploration Corp. (B.C. Nov. 22, 1983)
Jan. 16, 2007 – Name changed to Roxgold Inc.; basis 1 new for 2 old shs. ■

Wavecom Development Ltd. (B.C. 1970)
June 21, 1979 – Name changed to Neptune Resources Corp.; basis 1 new for 3 old shs. ■

Wavecrest Resources Ltd. (B.C. Aug. 3, 1982)
June 5, 1986 – Name changed to Quartz Mountain Gold Corp.; basis 3 new for 1 old sh. ■

Wavefire.com Inc. (Alta. Feb. 5, 1992)
June 14, 2011 – Name changed to Butte Energy Inc. ■

WaveForm Energy Ltd. (Alta. Dec. 19, 2003)
Oct. 11, 2007 – Name changed to Second Wave Petroleum Ltd. ■

Wavefront Energy and Environmental Services Inc. (Can. Sept. 30, 2003)
Mar. 27, 2009 – Name changed to Wavefront Technology Solutions Inc. (see FPsurvey - Mines & Energy; FPsurvey - Industrials)

WavePOINT Systems Inc. (Alta. May 11, 1998)
May 29, 2002 – Filed an assignment into bankruptcy and Deloitte & Touche Inc. of Edmonton was appointed trustee. All directors had resigned.
June 2004 – All assets sold. The secured creditors suffered a major shortfall and there were no funds available for unsecured creditors or shldrs.
July 19, 2005 – Trustee discharged.

WavePower Systems International Inc. (Ont. Mar. 21, 1988)
May 31, 2007 – Name changed to Delta Uranium Inc. (see FPsurvey - Mines & Energy)

Waverley Biotech Inc. (Can. Feb. 3, 2006)
Aug. 12, 2008 – Name changed to Fox Resources Ltd. ■

Wavo Gold Mines Ltd. (Ont. 1944)
Feb. 1970 – Charter cancelled.

Wawbano Mines Ltd. (Que. 1936)
July 15, 1978 – Charter cancelled.

Way Ventures Inc. (Ont. Mar. 18, 2011)
July 24, 2014 – Name changed to UGE International Ltd. following Qualifying Transaction reverse takeover acquisition of UGE Holdings Limited; basis 1 new for 5 old shs. ■

Waybo Resources Inc. (B.C. 1981)
Aug. 28, 1992 – Dissolved and struck off register.

Wayburn Oil and Natural Gas Corp. (Alta. Apr. 14, 1993)
Mar. 7, 1997 – Name changed to Wayburn Resources Inc. ■

Wayburn Resources Inc. (Alta. Apr. 14, 1993)
Aug. 29, 2000 – Name changed to Hellix Ventures Inc.; basis 1 new for 9 old shs. (see FPsurvey - Mines & Energy)

Wayfair Explorations Inc. (Ont. Mar. 3, 1977)
Aug. 31, 1992 – Delisted from the CDN. Subsequently dissolved.

Waymar Resources Ltd. (B.C. Oct. 26, 1994)
Feb. 22, 2001 – Continued into Yukon.
July 21, 2006 – Continued into British Columbia.
July 11, 2014 – Amalgamated with 1001545 B.C. Ltd., wholly owned subsid. of Orosur Mining Inc.; basis 0.375 Orosur com. shs. for 1 Waymar sh.

Wayne Petroleums Limited (Ont. 1942)
Mar. 19, 1962 – Name changed to Anglo United Development Corporation Limited. ■

Wayside Gold Mines Ltd. (B.C. Feb. 12, 1970)
Feb. 8, 1994 – Name changed to International Wayside Gold Mines Ltd.; basis 1 new for 3.7 old shs. ■

We X.L. Holdings Corporation (Alta. July 6, 1994)
Aug. 30, 1999 – Filed for bankruptcy. Deloitte & Touche Inc. was appointed trustee.

Weaco Resources Ltd. (B.C. Apr. 17, 1979)
Aug. 25, 1993 – Name changed to Hayden Resources Ltd.; basis 1 new for 3 old shs. ■

Wealth Minerals Ltd. (Alta. Oct. 7, 1994)
Jan. 9, 2006 – Continued into British Columbia. (see FPsurvey - Mines & Energy)

Wealth Resources Ltd. (B.C. June 12, 1984)
Feb. 28, 1996 – Name changed to Sterlingmarc Mining Ltd.; basis 1 new for 10 old shs. ■

Weatherford Oil Services, Inc. (Alta. 2000)
Apr. 20, 2001 – All exch. shs. called for early redemption; basis 1 com. sh. of U.S.-based Weatherford International, Inc. for each exch. sh. Weatherford Oil Services.

Weaver Lake Explorations Ltd. (Ont. Sept. 22, 1989)
May 8, 1996 – Name changed to Edifice Explorations Ltd.; basis 1 new for 10 old shs. ■

Web3 Ventures Inc. (Can. June 19, 1997)
Jan. 11, 2024 – Name changed to Orthogonal Global Group Inc. ■

Webb & Knapp (Canada) Limited (Can. Nov. 18, 1955)
Apr. 18, 1989 – All o/s com. shs. not already held by Jaffsons Properties Inc., redeemed by the company for 25¢ per sh. Now private.

Webb Bay Resources Ltd. (Alta. May 24, 1996)
Mar. 15, 2000 – Name changed to National Gold Corporation. ■

Webbwood Exploration Company Ltd. (Ont. 1947)
Aug. 1972 – Charter cancelled.

Webbwood Mining Co. Ltd. (Ont. 1947)
Apr. 1956 – Name changed to Webbwood Exploration Company Ltd. ■

Webbwood Mobile Home Estates Limited (Ont. 1968)
July 11, 1986 – Name changed to Sonartec North American Inc.; basis 3 new for 1 old sh. ∎

WebEngine Corporation (Ont. Mar. 4, 1983)
Nov. 25, 2003 – Name changed to Foccini International Inc. and continued into Canada pursuant to reverse takeover acquisition of Foccini Trade GmbH; basis 1 new for 3 old shs. ∎

Webex Oil & Gas Ltd. (Alta. Feb. 24, 1987)
July 15, 1992 – Name changed to Webex Resources Ltd.; basis 1 new for 10 old shs. ∎

Webex Resources Ltd. (Alta. Feb. 24, 1987)
Sept. 7, 1995 – Amalgamated with Springsyde Resources Ltd. to form Courage Energy Inc.; basis 1 new for 1 Springsyde sh. and 1.1 new for 1 Webex sh. (see Courage Energy Inc.)

WebSmart.com Communications Inc. (B.C. Nov. 29, 1965)
Oct. 13, 2004 – Name changed to Gold Reach Resources Ltd. ∎

Webtech Wireless Inc. (Alta. Mar. 13, 2003 amalg.)
Aug. 1, 2006 – Continued into British Columbia. (see BSM Technologies Inc.)
Oct. 6, 2015 – Acquired by BSM Technologies Inc.; basis 2.136 BSM com. shs. plus 52¢ cash for 1 Webtech sh. (see BSM Technologies Inc.)

Weco Development Corporation (Del. 1971)
June 14, 1977 – Name changed to Worldwide Energy Corporation.

WeCommerce Holdings Ltd. (B.C. Mar. 4, 2019)
Apr. 17, 2023 – Name changed to Tiny Ltd. pursuant to the reverse takeover acquisition of Tiny Capital Ltd. and concurrent amalgamation of Tiny Capital with wholly owned 1396773 B.C. Ltd. ∎

Weda Bay Minerals Inc. (Alta. June 18, 1986)
Sept. 1, 2006 – Acquired by 3132752 Nova Scotia Limited wholly owned subsid. of France-based Eramet S.A.; basis Cdn$2.70 per sh.

Wedco Development Corp. (B.C. Aug. 20, 1968)
June 9, 1997 – Name changed to Promax Communications Inc.; basis 1 new for 50 old shs. ∎

Wedding River Gold Mines Ltd. (Ont. Mar. 31, 1936)
Charter cancelled; no equity for shldrs.

Wedge Energy International Inc. (Ont. July 5, 1996)
Nov. 14, 2011 – Formed Undur Tolgoi Minerals Inc. in British Columbia pursuant to reverse takeover acquisition of and amalgamation with Undur Tolgoi Minerals Inc. ∎

Wedgewood Resources Ltd. (B.C. July 9, 1987)
Dec. 18, 1998 – Name changed to Clan Resources Ltd.; basis 1 new for 10 old shs. ∎

Wedona Capital Inc. (B.C. Feb. 9, 2011)
Nov. 7, 2013 – Name changed to ISIS Lab Corporation pursuant to Qualifying Transaction reverse takeover acquisition of ISIS Lab Inc. ∎

Wedro Leeds Mining Corp. (Que. 1956)
Nov. 4, 1978 – Charter cancelled.

Wee-Gee Uranium Mines Ltd. (Ont. 1967)
Dec. 1973 – Charter cancelled.

Weed Points Loyalty Inc. (Can. Nov. 4, 2014)
June 23, 2017 – Continued into British Columbia.
Dec. 13, 2017 – Name changed to Cannvas MedTech Inc. to reflect increased focus on technology development within the medical marijuana industry. ∎

WeedMD Inc. (Ont. July 16, 2014)
July 13, 2021 – Name changed to Entourage Health Corp. ∎

Weedon Mining Corp. (Que. 1950)
1964 – Name changed to Wisconsin Mining Co. Ltd.; basis 1 new for 4 old shs. ∎

Weedon Pyrite & Copper Corp. Ltd. (Que. 1950)
1959 – Name changed to Weedon Mining Corp. ∎

Weekapaug Lithium Limited (B.C. Oct. 23, 2007)
Oct. 31, 2024 – Name changed to Protium Clean Energy Corp. (see FPsurvey - Mines & Energy)

Weekend Unlimited Inc. (Alta. Oct. 10, 2018 amalg.)
Jan. 14, 2020 – Continued into British Columbia.
Jan. 21, 2020 – Name changed to Weekend Unlimited Industries Inc.; basis 1 new for 10 old shs. ∎

Weekend Unlimited Industries Inc. (B.C. Jan. 14, 2020)
Apr. 28, 2021 – Name changed to Potent Ventures Inc.; basis 4 new for 1 old sh. ∎

Weifei Capital Inc. (B.C. Oct. 16, 2008)
Oct. 13, 2011 – Name changed to Angkor Gold Corp. pursuant to Qualifying Transaction reverse takeover acquisition of Prairie Pacific Mining Corp. (PPMC) and subsequent amalgamation of PPMC with wholly owned 1602343 Alberta Ltd.; basis 1 new for 1.75 old shs. ∎

Wejack Mines Ltd. (Ont. 1946)
Nov. 18, 1970 – Dissolved.

Wekusko Consolidated Ltd. (Man. 1943)
June 1955 – Name changed to Amanda Mines Ltd.; basis 1 new for 5 old shs. ∎

Wekusko Gold Resources Ltd. (Sask. Sept. 19, 1983)
Feb. 28, 1986 – Dissolved and struck off register.

Welcome North Mines Ltd. (B.C. 1964)
June 20, 1990 – Name changed to Welcome North Resources Inc. ∎

Welcome North Resources Inc. (B.C. 1964)
July 7, 1995 – Name changed to Welcome Opportunities Ltd.; basis 1 new for 8 old shs. ∎

Welcome Opportunities Ltd. (B.C. 1964)
Sept. 10, 2002 – Plan of Arrangement with Endeavour Mining Capital Corp. to continue as a new company also named Endeavour Mining Capital Corp.; basis 1 new Endeavour com. sh. plus 1 Contingent Value right for 1 old Welcome com. sh. (see Endeavour Mining Capital Corp.)

Weld-O-Matic Machines Limited (unknown)
Nov. 1968 – Amalgamated to form Intermetco Limited. (see Intermetco Limited)

Weldon Gold Mines Ltd. (Ont. 1940)
1958 – Charter cancelled.

Weldwood of Canada Limited (B.C. Mar. 17, 1964)
July 5, 1996 – Following Plan of Arrangement the company's major shldr., Champion International Corporation, acquired the 16.3% of the o/s com. shs. that it did not own through Weldwood Acquisitions Limited; basis $40.50 per sh.

Welichem Biotech Inc. (B.C. Nov. 1, 2004 amalg.)
July 9, 2014 – Acquired by LJ Resources Co., Ltd.: basis 15¢ cash per sh.

Welland Consolidated Industries Ltd. (B.C. 1965)
Jan. 1979 – Dissolved.

Welland Consolidated Mining Ltd. (B.C. 1965)
Aug. 1, 1974 – Name changed to Welland Consolidated Industries Ltd. ∎

Welland Mining Ltd. (B.C. 1965)
1970 – Name changed to Welland Consolidated Mining Ltd. ∎

Wellco Energy Services Inc. (B.C. July 29, 1981)
Aug. 9, 2002 – Converted into Wellco Energy Services Trust; basis 1 Wellco Energy Services trust unit for 1 Wellco Energy Services Inc. com. sh.

Wellco Energy Services Trust (Alta. May 28, 2002)
Mar. 18, 2008 – Acquired by Peak Energy Services Trust; basis 0.90 Peak Energy trust units for 1 Wellco Energy trust unit.

Wellgreen Platinum Ltd. (B.C. Apr. 5, 2006)
Jan. 11, 2018 – Name changed to Nickel Creek Platinum Corp. (see FPsurvey - Mines & Energy)

Wellington Bank International Limited (Bahamas 1964)
1972 – Name changed to Wellington Corporation Limited. ∎

Wellington Bank of Canada International Limited (Bahamas 1964)
1966 – Name changed to Wellington Bank International Limited. ∎

Wellington Corporation Limited (Bahamas 1964)
Sept. 1975 – Sole remaining assets (cl. B shs. of York Lambton Corporation Limited) were distributed to shldrs.; basis of 1.17 cl. B sh. of York Lambton for each cl. A or B sh. of Wellington.

Wellington Cove Explorations Ltd. (Ont. July 12, 1989)
July 7, 2004 – Name changed to GoldQuest Mining Corp. pursuant to reverse takeover acquisition of Exploration & Discovery Latin America (Panama) Inc. ∎

Wellington Financial Corporation, Limited (Can. 1926)
Dec. 1966 – Name changed to York Lambton Corporation Limited. ∎

Wellington Mines Ltd. (B.C. Nov. 1927)
1953 – Acquired by New Wellington Mines Ltd.; basis 1 new for 10 old shs.
1960 – Dissolved.

Wellington Oil & Gas Co. Ltd. (Can. Apr. 26, 1926; via Dominion charter)
1968 – Name changed to Ibex Oil Ltd. ∎

Wellness Lifestyles Inc. (B.C. Nov. 23, 2010)
July 6, 2018 – Name changed to WELL Health Technologies Corp. (see FPsurvey - Industrials)

Wellore Energy Inc. (Can. 1985)
Sept. 25, 1990 – All o/s cl. A shs. acquired by 167428 Canada Inc., a wholly owned subsid. of Cabre Exploration Ltd.; basis 1 new for 2.469 old cl. A shs. (see Cabre Exploration Ltd.)

Wellore Resources Ltd (Alta.)
1985 – Continued into Canada.
Oct. 14, 1987 – Name changed to Wellore Energy Inc.; basis 1 new for 4 old shs. ∎

WellPoint Systems Inc. (Alta. Aug. 26, 1999)
Feb. 1, 2011 – All directors resigned. Ernst & Young Inc. appointed receiver.

Wells Fargo Financial Canada Corporation (Ont. Aug. 27, 1992)
Jan. 1, 2012 – Name changed to Wells Fargo Canada Corporation.

Wells Gold Ltd. (B.C. 1986)
Nov. 10, 1989 – Name changed to Astridon Development Corp. ∎

Wells Longlac Mines Ltd. (Ont. June 18, 1934)
Shldrs. received $2.70 and 20 shs. Magnet Consolidated Mines Ltd. per 100 shs., plus accumulated divds. of Magnet of 28¢ per sh. (see Magnet Consolidated Mines Ltd.)

Wellstar Energy Corp. (B.C. Aug. 26, 1985)
Mar. 24, 2017 – Placed into receivership by secured lender and Grant Thornton Limited appointed receiver and manager.
Dec. 2017 – Assets sold. Secured creditors suffered a shortfall; no monies available for distrib. to shldrs.
Feb. 10, 2020 – Struck from register and dissolved.
Feb. 3, 2021 – Grant Thornton Limited discharged as receiver.

WellteQ Digital Health Inc. (B.C. Sept. 27, 2017)
Dec. 7, 2022 – Acquired by Advanced Human Imaging Ltd.; basis 1 Advanced Human ordinary sh. for 6 WelleteQ com. shs.

Welsh-Mac Mines Ltd. (Ont. 1945)
Mar. 4, 1957 – Dissolved.

Welton Energy Corporation (Ont. Mar. 10, 2000 amalg.)
Feb. 19, 2009 – Acquired by Churchill Energy Inc.; basis 0.0199255 Churchill com. shs. for 1 Welton sh. Debentureholders received $429.61 for each $1,000 principal amt. of 8% conv. debs.

Welwyn Energy Ltd. (Alta. Aug. 26, 1997)
June 30, 2003 – Name changed to Welwyn Resources Ltd.; basis 1 new for 5 old shs. ∎

Welwyn Resources Ltd. (Alta. Aug. 26, 1997)
June 30, 2005 – Name changed to Pan Orient Energy Corp. following April 2005 reverse takeover acquisition of Pan Orient Energy Ltd. ∎

Wembley Gold Mines Ltd. (Ont. 1945)
Jan. 4, 1960 – Dissolved.

Wenatchee Resources Ltd. (B.C. 1983)
June 13, 1986 – Name changed to Compleat Health Corporation. ∎

Wendell Gold Mines Ltd. (Que. Feb. 16, 1945)
1949 – Name changed to Wendell Mineral Products Ltd. ∎

Wendell Mineral Products Ltd. (Que. Feb. 16, 1945)
Mar. 1962 – Name changed to Black River Mining Ltd.; basis 1 new for 5 old shs. ∎

Wendigo Gold Mines Ltd. (Ont. 1933)
1945 – Charter cancelled.

Wendmar Gold Mines (Ont. 1945)
1959 – Acquired by Wengrace Explorations Ltd.; basis 1 new for 27 old shs. Wengrace to wind up; no equity. (see Wengrace Explorations Ltd.)

Wenga Copper Mines Inc. (Del. 1954)
1965 – Charter cancelled.

Wenga Gold Mines Ltd. (Ont. 1939)
1954 – Name changed to Wenga Copper Mines Inc. and continued into Delaware. ∎

Wengrace Explorations Ltd. (Ont. 1959)
Dec. 12, 1966 – Dissolved.

Wentworth Radio & Auto Supply Co. Ltd. (Can. 1928)
1945 – Assets sold to net shldrs. for approx. $4.00 per sh. Payment made through Bank of Montreal, Main and James Sts., Hamilton, Ont.

Wenzel Downhole Tools Ltd. (Alta. June 9, 1994)
Aug. 8, 2013 – All o/s shs. not held acquired by Basin Tools, L.P. for $2.25 per sh.
Mar. 31, 2018 – Name changed to Wenzel Downhole Tools ULC.

Werner Dahnz Company Limited (Ont. 1962)
1982 – Amalgamated in Ontario to continue with same name.
Sept. 3, 1994 – Dissolved.

Werner Lake Nickel Mines Ltd. (Ont. 1953)
Mar. 1976 – Charter cancelled.

Werner Oil & Gas Corp. (B.C. 1981)
Oct. 14, 1987 – Name changed to International Werner Technologies Inc. ∎

Wesberta Oils Ltd. (Ont. 1948)
1959 – Struck off register.

Wescal Resources Inc. (B.C. Sept. 12, 1980)
Nov. 26, 1987 – Name changed to C.C.C. Coded Communications Corporation. ∎

Wescam Inc. (Ont. Feb. 3, 1987)
Dec. 27, 2002 – Acquired by L-3 Canada Acquisition Inc., a wholly owned subsid. of N.Y.-based L-3 Communications Corporation, for $9.50 per com. sh.

Wescan Energy Ltd. (B.C. 1978)
Aug. 20, 1993 – Dissolved and struck off register.

Wescap Energy Corporation (B.C. 1968)
Nov. 29, 1986 – Name changed to Wescap Enterprises Limited. ∎

Wescap Enterprises Limited (B.C. 1968)
Apr. 13, 1995 – Dissolved and struck off register.

Wescast Industries Inc. (Ont. Nov. 20, 1946)
Apr. 1, 2013 – Acquired by Taixing International Investment Limited, a wholly owned subsidiary of Sichuan Bohong Industry Co., Ltd., for $11 per sh.

Wescorp Industries Ltd. (B.C. 1950)
May 30, 1980 – Reverted to private co. status following co. purchase of all o/s shs. at $32 per sh.

Wesdel Porcupine Gold Mines Ltd. (Ont. 1941)
Feb. 1982 – Name changed to Huston Red Lake Resources Ltd. ∎

Wesdome Gold Mines Inc. (B.C. Oct. 29, 1999)
Feb. 1, 2006 – Succeeded by Wesdome Gold Mines Ltd. following amalgamation with 9162-6812 Québec Inc., a wholly owned subsid. of River Gold Mines Ltd., with Wesdome Gold Mines Inc. the deemed acquiror and River Gold renamed to Wesdome Gold Mines Ltd. (see FPsurvey - Mines & Energy)

Wesgold Minerals Inc. (B.C. Oct. 20, 2009)
Apr. 30, 2012 – Name changed to Cordoba Minerals Corp. (see FPsurvey - Mines & Energy)

Wesgold Resources Inc. (B.C. Feb. 19, 1980)
May 31, 1983 – Name changed to Terra Nova Energy Inc. ∎

Wesko Mines Ltd. (B.C. 1934)
May 1958 – Entered voluntary liquidation.
Dec. 31, 1958 – Shldrs. received 1 sh. Vectoil Investments Ltd. for 10 shs. Wesko; after that date, shldrs. eligible for cash equivalent to 0.7¢ per sh.

Wesley Gold Mines Limited Inc. (Ont. 1935)
1966 – Name changed to Wesley Mines Ltd. ∎

Wesley Mason Mills Limited (Can. 1937)
Jan. 1964 – Compaby solicitors reported that bank obtained title to all of assets of co. under their debenture and sold these assets to recover bank loan of $350,000, plus accrued interest from January 1963; nothing was available for shldrs.

Wesley Mines Ltd. (Ont. 1935)
Mar. 1976 – Charter cancelled.

Wespac Mining Corp. (B.C. Nov. 21, 1980)
Nov. 19, 1998 – Name changed to Genesis II Enterprises Ltd. ∎

Wespac Petroleums Limited (Ont. 1944)
1971 – Name changed to Canada Geothermal Oil Ltd.; basis 1 new for 5 old shs. ∎

Wessex Petroleum Corp. Ltd. (Alta. 1954)
1959 – Struck off register.

Wesson Mines Ltd. (Ont. 1947)
1957 – Charter cancelled.

West Africa Energy Inc. (B.C. June 29, 2006)
Aug. 20, 2007 – Name changed to Centric Energy Corp. ∎

West Africa Mining Exploration Corporation Inc. (Que. Jan. 31, 1994 amalg.)
Aug. 15, 1997 – Name changed to SEMAFO Inc. ∎

West African Gold Corp. (Yuk. Mar. 17, 1997)
Apr. 27, 1999 – Name changed to First Au Strategies Corp.; basis 1 new for 12 old shs. ∎

West African Iron Ore Corp. (B.C. Dec. 9, 1987)
Mar. 31, 2015 – Name changed to WAI Capital Investments Corp.; basis 1 new for 10 old shs. ∎

West African Venture Exchange Corp. (B.C. Nov. 22, 1983)
Sept. 17, 2002 – Name changed to Wave Exploration Corp.; basis 1 new for 10 old shs. ∎

West Amulet Mines Ltd. (Que. Aug. 28, 1944)
1955 – Name changed to New West Amulet Mines Ltd.; basis 1 new for 3 old shs. ∎

West Bay Capital Corp. (Alta. Apr. 29, 1993)
Oct. 2, 2000 – Struck from registry and dissolved.

West-Bay Yellowknife Mines Ltd. (Ont. 1944)
Jan. 1967 – Charter cancelled.

West Canadian Collieries Ltd. (U.K. 1903)
1964 – Assets acquired by West Canadian Mineral Holdings Ltd.; basis 1 new for 1 old sh.

West Canadian Hydro Electric Corp. Ltd. (B.C. 1930)
Dec. 10, 1947 – British Columbia Govt. took over generating and distributing facilities of co. and its subsids., and co. entered voluntary liquidation. Co. received $3,289,700 for its properties. Holders of each of the 53,810 of 80¢ cum. partic. n.p.v. pref., received in exch. 1 sh. 4% cum. pref., $10 par, and 1 com. sh. n.p.v., covered by voting trust certif. of Okanagan Valley Telephone Co. and 1 sh. n.p.v. com. of Elk Creek Waterworks Co. Holders of the 100,000 o/s com. received $9.61 per sh.

West Canadian Mineral Holdings Ltd. (Alta. 1964)
Sept. 1, 1972 – Merged into Resource Service Group Ltd.; basis 1 new sh. (pref. or com.) for 1 old sh.

West Canadian Oil & Gas Ltd. (Can. 1950)
1961 – Merged with Canadian Delhi Oil Ltd.; basis 1 sh. or 1 wt. of Delhi for each 3.75 shs. or warrants of West Cdn. Holders of shs. had option to accept $1.35 per sh. for up to 50% of holdings. Cash offer did not apply to warrants.

West Canadian Petroleums Ltd. (Alta. May 3, 1951)
1957 – Merged with Trans Empire Oils Ltd.; basis 3 new for 5 old shs.

West Cirque Resources Ltd. (B.C. June 21, 2007)
July 8, 2014 – Acquired by Kaizen Discovery Inc.; basis 0.5 Kaizen com. sh. for 1 West Cirque sh. (see Kaizen Discovery Inc.)

West Coast Canteen Ltd. (Can. - unspecified)
1969 – Acquired by Pace Industries Ltd. for $456,000 plus 10,000 Pace shs.

West Coast Forest Products Ltd. (B.C. Sept. 26, 1986)
June 25, 2018 – Struck from register and dissolved.

West Coast Resources Ltd. (B.C. 1959)
May 1976 – Charter cancelled.

West Delta Resources Limited (Can. July 7, 1981)
May 18, 1988 – Name changed to International Delta Resources Limited; basis 1 new for 3 old shs. ∎

West Duverney Gold Mines Ltd. (Que. 1937)
July 22, 1978 – Charter cancelled.

West Dynamic Toll Road Ltd. (B.C. May 8, 1987)
Apr. 4, 1997 – Continued into Bermuda.

West Energy Ltd. (Alta. Oct. 8, 2004 amalg.)
May 18, 2010 – Acquired by Daylight Energy Ltd. (formerly Daylight Resources Trust); basis $5.50 or 0.465 Daylight shs. or a combination thereof for 1 West Energy sh. (see Daylight Energy Ltd.)

West F.C. Finance Corp. (B.C. 1983)
Apr. 4, 1997 – Amalgamated with 501161 B.C. Ltd., a wholly owned subsid. of MFC Bancorp Ltd.; basis 10¢ per sh. (see MFC Bancorp Ltd.)

West Flank Petroleums Ltd. (unknown)
1939 – Name changed to Excelsior Oils, Ltd. ■

West 49 Inc. (Ont. Dec. 1, 2004 amalg.)
Sept. 2, 2010 – Acquired by Billabong International Limited for $1.30 per sh.

West Fourth Capital Inc. (Can. May 17, 2007)
June 3, 2010 – Name changed to Conifex Timber Inc. pursuant to Qualifying Transaction reverse takeover acquisition of DTR Wood Acquisitionco Ltd.; basis 1 new for 27.5 old shs. (see FPsurvey - Mines & Energy; FPsurvey - Industrials)

West Graham Mines Ltd. (Ont. 1960)
Dec. 31, 1982 – Wound up.

West Hawk Development Corp. (B.C. Feb. 22, 1984)
Aug. 2, 2014 – Dissolved for failure to file.

West Hill Copper Mines Limited (Ont. June 17, 1964)
May 12, 1969 – Name changed to West Hill Enterprises & Mining Limited. ■

West Hill Energy Inc. (Ont. June 17, 1964)
Aug. 19, 1996 – Name changed to Consolidated West Hill Energy Inc.; basis 1 new for 5 old shs. ■

West Hill Enterprises & Mining Limited (Ont. June 17, 1964)
Aug. 7, 1981 – Name changed to West Hill Energy Inc. ■

West Indies Plantations Ltd. (Ont. 1961)
1977 – Name changed to Caruscan Corporation. ■

West Isle Energy Inc. (Alta. Apr. 29, 1993)
May 27, 2019 – Delisted from CSE. Subsequently dissolved for failure to file.

West Jay Petroleums Ltd. (B.C. 1978)
1983 – Amalgamated with Carlyle Eagle Petroleum (British Columbia) Ltd., a wholly owned subsidiary of Carlyle Energy Ltd.; basis 1 new special for 1 old sh.

West Kirkland Mining Inc. (B.C. Apr. 3, 2007)
July 2, 2020 – Name changed to West Vault Mining Inc.; basis 1 new for 10 old shs. (see FPsurvey - Mines & Energy)

West Kootenay Power and Light Company, Limited (B.C. May 8, 1897)
Sept. 2, 1987 – Acquired by UtiliCorp United Inc. from Cominco Ltd.
Sept. 1, 1988 – Name changed to West Kootenay Power Ltd. ■

West Kootenay Power Ltd. (B.C. May 8, 1897)
Dec. 1, 1993 – All 7.9% ser. 2 pref. shs. were redeemed at $25 per sh. plus accrued and unpaid div. of $0.005411 per sh.
Dec. 31, 1996 – All 7% cum. vtg. pref. shs. ser. 1 redeemed for $25 per sh.
Oct. 22, 2001 – Name changed to UtiliCorp Networks Canada (British Columbia) Ltd. ■

West Lake Mining Co. Ltd. (Ont. 1945)
Mar. 13, 1979 – Dissolved.

West Macanda Resources Ltd. (Ont. 1945)
Sept. 23, 1981 – Merged into Nuinsco Resources Limited; basis 1 new for 4 old shs.

West Malartic Mines Ltd. (Que. Jan. 14, 1939)
July 1968 – Charter surrendered.

West Manitou Mines Ltd. (Que. 1950)
1962 – Charter cancelled.

West-Mar Resources Ltd. (B.C. July 26, 1979)
June 2, 1993 – Name changed to Mar-West Resources Ltd.; basis 1 new for 3 old shs. ■

West Maygill Gas & Oil Limited (Ont. Aug. 21, 1950; via letters patent)
Aug. 5, 1958 – Name changed to Ranger Oil (Canada) Limited. ■

West Melville Metals Inc. (B.C. May 3, 2011)
Nov. 2, 2016 – Name changed to K2 Gold Corporation. (see FPsurvey - Mines & Energy)

West Mountain Capital Corp. (Alta. Nov. 30, 2005)
July 2, 2014 – Name changed to West Mountain Environmental Corp. ■

West Mountain Environmental Corp. (Alta. Nov. 30, 2005)
July 4, 2017 – Placed into receivership and KPMG Inc. appointed receiver. All officers and directors resigned.
Mar. 2018 – Auction for the truck and trailer generated net proceeds of $74,570.
Oct. 12, 2018 – Due to presence of hazardous waste at the Wolseley, Sask., site, the receiver determined that there was no realistic prospect of any recovery to the estate and was granted court approval to disclaim, abandon and renounce any and all interest held in the Wolseley site. No monies would be available for distribution to creditors, secured and unsecured, nor to shldrs.
Aug. 15, 2019 – KPMG Inc. was discharged as receiver.

West-Norse Resources Ltd. (B.C. May 13, 1983)
May 28, 1986 – Name changed to Absorptive Technology Inc. ■

West Oak Gold Corp. (B.C. Sept. 1, 2020)
Oct. 10, 2024 – Name changed to Silicon Metals Corp. (see FPsurvey - Mines & Energy)

West Oak Resource Corporation (B.C. June 12, 1984)
Mar. 6, 2001 – Name changed to Telesis North Communications Inc. following reverse takeover acquisition of Telesis North Inc. for 16,787,952 com. shs. ■

West Pacific Ventures Inc. (Alta. 1987)
Jan. 1, 1992 – Dissolved and struck off register.

West Park Resources Inc. (B.C. Oct. 6, 1993)
June 19, 2000 – Name changed to DXStorm.com Inc. and continued into Ontario following reverse takeover acquisition of DXStorm Inc. (see FPsurvey - Industrials)

West Plains Oil Resources Ltd. (Ont. 1950)
Struck off register.

West Point Resources Inc. (B.C. Apr. 5, 2011)
Aug. 12, 2014 – Name changed to Cannabix Technologies Inc. (see FPsurvey - Industrials)

West Pride Industries Corp. (Can. Sept. 9, 1982)
Sept. 7, 1993 – Name changed to Big Horn Resources Ltd.; basis 1 new for 7 old shs. ■

West Provident Resources Ltd. (B.C. 1978)
May 14, 1979 – Name changed to Argyll Resources Ltd. ■

West Range Iron Mines Ltd. (Ont. 1956)
1963 – Name changed to Great West Mining and Smelting Corp. Ltd. ■

West Red Lake Gold Mines Inc. (Ont. Nov. 29, 1991)
Jan. 5, 2023 – Acquired by DLV Resources Ltd. subsequently renamed West Red Lake Gold Mines Ltd.; basis 0.1215 DLV shs. for 1 West Red Lake sh.
Feb. 20, 2023 – Name changed to West Red Lake Gold Mines (Ontario) Ltd.

West Red Lake Gold Mines Ltd. (Ont. 1934)
Apr. 9, 1975 – Charter cancelled.

West Riding Copper Mines Ltd. (Can. 1966)
July 1968 – Name changed to Pronghorn Petroleum Corporation Limited. ■

West Rim Resources Inc. (B.C. Sept. 25, 1985)
Aug. 11, 1989 – Name changed to Cimtek Integrated Manufacturing Technologies Inc. ■

West Sea Development Corp. (B.C. Nov. 14, 1986)
Sept. 14, 1992 – Name changed to Seawest Resources Limited; basis 1 new for 4 old shs. ■

West Sea Marketing Corp. (B.C. Nov. 14, 1986)
Aug. 31, 1988 – Name changed to West Sea Development Corp. ■

West Shore Malartic Gold Mines Ltd. (Que. 1936)
July 15, 1978 – Charter cancelled.

West Siscoe Gold Mines Ltd. (Que. 1936)
July 15, 1949 – Charter cancelled.

West Street Capital Corporation (Ont. Apr. 6, 1984)
Nov. 29, 2013 – Amalgamated with 2390567 Ontario Limited, a wholly owned subsid. of Brookfield Asset Management Inc.; basis $0.32 per sh. (see Brookfield Asset Management Inc.)

West Territories Oils Limited (Alta. 1952)
1955 – Acquired by Canadian Homestead Oils Ltd.; basis 1 new for 10 old shs.

West Timmins Mining Inc. (B.C. Sept. 13, 2006 amalg.)
Nov. 12, 2009 – Acquired by Lake Shore Gold Corp.; basis 0.73 Lake Shore shs. for 1 West Timmins sh. (see Lake Shore Gold Corp.)

West Trend Resources Ltd. (B.C. 1977)
Apr. 19, 1984 – Amalgamated with Northill Resources Ltd. to form Canadian Continental Oil Corp.; basis 1 new for 1 old sh.

West Turner Petroleums Ltd. (B.C. Dec. 11, 1936)
Taken over by Pacific Petroleums Ltd.; basis 1 new for 5 old shs. (see Pacific Petroleums Ltd.)

West Wasa Mines Limited (Ont. 1945)
Jan. 26, 1977 – Name changed to West Macanda Resources Ltd.; basis 1 new for 4 old shs. ■

The Westaim Corporation (Alta. May 7, 1996)
Dec. 31, 2024 – Continued into Delaware. (see FPsurvey - Industrials)

Westall Petroleums Ltd. (Ont. June 28, 1943)
1966 – Charter cancelled.

Westam Minerals Inc. (B.C. Mar. 14, 1983)
Aug. 29, 1983 – Name changed to Augustus Resources Ltd. ■

Westar Group Ltd. (B.C. Feb. 22, 1978)
July 4, 1997 – All o/s shs., other than those already owned by Great Pacific Capital Corp. and its affiliate, acquired by Great Pacific and cancelled; basis $70 per sh. or if shldrs. elected not to have their shs. purchased for cancellation by the company will be deemed to have transferred their shs. to Great Pacific for $70 per sh.

Westar Mining Ltd. (B.C. July 31, 1967)
June 10, 1992 – Filed for protection under the Companies' Creditors Arrangement Act (CCAA).
July 25, 1992 – Filed a notice of motion indicating that it was unable to proceed under the CCAA as it had been unable to gain the concurrence of all key stakeholders on the proposed plan of reorganization. All remaining officers and directors resigned.
Aug. 31, 1992 – Placed into bankruptcy and Vancouver-based Arthur Andersen Inc. (subsequently Deloitte & Touche Inc.) was apppointed trustee.
May 1993 – All the assets had been sold; secured and preferred creditors could possibly receive a distribution.

There would be no distributions made to unsecured creditors or shldrs.
Apr. 2000 – Administration was still ongoing due to unresolved litigations.
Feb. 4, 2002 – Arthur Andersen was discharged. There was no information regarding whether distributions were made to the secured and preferred creditors.

Westario Sulphur Mines Ltd. (Ont. 1938)
Nov. 27, 1968 – Dissolved.

Westate Energy Inc. (B.C. July 2, 1981)
Mar. 4, 1994 – Delisted from the Vancouver Stock Exchange. Subsequently dissolved for failure to file.

Westate Resources Inc. (B.C. 1983)
Apr. 25, 1985 – Name changed to Lifetrends Behavioral Systems Inc. ■

Westates Petroleum Co. Inc. (Del. 1959)
Dec. 14, 1959 – Name changed to Westates Petroleum Company; basis (i) com. shs., 2 new for 1 old; (ii) pref. shs., 1 new pref. and 2 new com. for 1 old pref.

Westaurum Copper Corporation (Can. Mar. 20, 1987)
Oct. 19, 1993 – Name changed to Opal Energy Inc. ■

Westaurum Industries Inc. (Can. Mar. 20, 1987)
Sept. 24, 1992 – Name changed to Westaurum Copper Corporation; basis 1 new for 4 old shs. ■

Westbank Resources Inc. (B.C. May 4, 1981)
Mar. 2, 1990 – Delisted from the Vancouver Stock Exchange. Subsequently struck from register and dissolved.

Westbay Ventures Inc. (B.C. June 24, 1986)
Mar. 8, 2018 – Name changed to Cryptanite Blockchain Technologies Corp. following reverse takeover acquisition of ChargaCard, Inc. ■

Westbow Energy Inc. (Alta. Dec. 21, 2005)
Apr. 7, 2008 – Amalgamated with Blackpool Exploration Ltd. to form Western Canada Energy Ltd. (see Western Canada Energy Ltd.)

Westbridge Computer Corporation (Sask. Jan. 21, 1988)
Dec. 19, 1991 – Name changed to ISM Information Systems Management Corporation. ■

Westbridge Energy Corporation (B.C. June 11, 1996)
Sept. 29, 2022 – Name changed to Westbridge Renewable Energy Corp. (see FPsurvey - Mines & Energy; FPsurvey - Industrials)

Westbridge Land Developments Inc. (Alta. 1986)
Aug. 2, 2005 – Struck from registry and dissolved.

Westbridge Resources Ltd. (B.C. 1983)
Oct. 27, 1987 – Name changed to American Pacific Mining Company Inc. ■

Westbrook Energy Corporation (Alta. Aug. 1, 1997)
Dec. 9, 1999 – Formed Manhattan Resources Ltd. in Alberta on amalgamation with Manhattan Resources Ltd.; basis 1 new for 1 old sh. ■

Westburne Inc. (Can. 1977)
Sept. 27, 2000 – Formed Rexel Canada Inc. following acquisition by Paris-based Rexel S.A.; basis $22.75 per sh.

Westburne Industries Ltd. (Alta. May 8, 1951)
Mar. 28, 1967 – Name changed to United Westburne Industries Ltd.; basis 1 new for 3 old shs. ■

Westburne International Industries Ltd. (Alta. 1969)
May 20, 1987 – Acquired by Dumez Investments I Inc. for $22.50 per sh. Westburne International, parent company of United Westburne Industries Limited, became private as a result of the buyout. Subsequently on Sept. 1, 1987, Westburne International amalgamated with United Westburne Industries Limited, ten wholly owned subsids. and Dumez Investments I Inc. to form United Westburne Inc.

Westburne Oil Company Limited (Alta. May 8, 1951)
Dec. 20, 1965 – Name changed to Westburne Industries Ltd. ■

Westburne Oil Development Ltd. (unknown)
Jan. 1965 – Acquired by Great Plains Development Co. of Canada, Ltd.

Westburne Petroleum & Minerals Ltd. (Alta. 1959)
1970 – Merged with Colling Valley Oils Ltd. into Westburne Petroleum & Minerals Ltd. (inc. Alta.). Shldrs. received 1 new ser. B 7% pref. sh. for 1 old sh.

Westcan Property Development Corporation (Alta. 1988)
Feb. 23, 1994 – Name changed to Clay-Tech Industries Inc. ■

WestCan Uranium Corp. (B.C. May 30, 1986)
Nov. 21, 2016 – Dissolved and struck from register.

WestCap Investments Corp. (Ont. Oct. 15, 2013)
Aug. 25, 2014 – Succeeded by R&R Real Estate Investment Trust pursuant to Qualifying Transaction plan of arrangement acquisition of a hotel property in Maryland. (see FPsurvey - Industrials)

WestCastle Energy Trust (Alta. Jan. 20, 1997)
Oct. 19, 1998 – Acquired by OPTUS Natural Gas Distribution Income Fund; basis $5.70 or 0.3088 new OPTUS unit for 1 old WestCastle unit. (see OPTUS Natural Gas Distribution Income Fund)

Westchester Porcupine Gold Mines Ltd. (Ont. 1940)
1952 – Charter cancelled; no equity for shldrs.

Westchester Resources Inc. (Ont. May 11, 1979)
Feb. 16, 2007 – Name changed to WSR Gold Inc. ■

Westcoast Energy Inc. (Can. Apr. 30, 1949; via Dominion charter)
Mar. 14, 2002 – Acquired by North Carolina-based Duke Energy Corporation; basis Cdn$43.80 or 0.7711 Duke com. sh. or 0.7711 Duke exchangeable sh. or a combination thereof for 1 Westcoast com. sh. Subsequently 5% cum. redeem. first pfd. series 9 shs. redeemed at $25 per sh. effective Oct. 15, 2004; 5.5% cum. redeem. first pfd. series 7 shs. redeemed at $25 per sh. effective Mar. 20, 2019; 4.6% cum. redeem. first pfd. series 8 shs. redeemed at $25 per sh. effective Mar. 20, 2019; 5.25% redeem. first pfd. series 10 shs. redeemed at $25 per sh. effective Jan. 15, 2021; and 5.2% redeem. first pfd. series 12 shs. redeemed at $25 per sh. effective Oct. 18, 2021.

Westcoast Petroleum Ltd. (B.C. 1971 amalg.)
July 8, 1982 – Acquired by Westcoast Transmission Company Limited; basis $29 per com. sh. and $58 per pref. sh. Westcoast Transmission (now Westcoast Energy) subsequently sold its 100% ownership to a consortium of overseas investors on May 5, 1993. Westcoast Petroleum then amalgamated with Numac Oil & Gas Ltd. and changed its name to Numac Energy Inc. effective Sept. 3, 1993. (see Westcoast Transmission Company Limited)

Westcoast Production Co. Ltd. (B.C. 1956)
Sept. 21, 1971 – Merged with Western Pacific Products & Crude Oil Pipelines Ltd., to form Westcoast Petroleum Ltd. Shldrs. received 1 new com. sh. for 1 old sh.

Westcoast Transmission Company Limited (Can. Apr. 30, 1949; via Dominion charter)
June 1, 1988 – Name changed to Westcoast Energy Inc. ■

Westcore Energy Ltd. (Alta. Mar. 30, 2007)
Sept. 2, 2023 – Struck from registry and dissolved.

Westcot Ventures Corp. (B.C. July 4, 2006)
Jan. 14, 2020 – Name changed to WPD Pharmaceuticals Inc. pursuant to reverse takeover acquisition of Poland-based WPD Pharmaceuticals Sp.zo.o. (see FPsurvey - Industrials)

Westech Resources Ltd. (B.C. Nov. 9, 1982)
Aug. 19, 1987 – Continued into Canada.
Sept. 14, 1987 – Name changed to Butte Resources Limited. ■

Westeel Products Ltd. (Can. 1928)
Dec. 1965 – Merged to form Westeel-Rosco Ltd.

Westeel-Rosco Limited (Can. 1928)
Aug. 31, 1980 – Became a wholly owned subsid. of Jannock Limited. o/s shs. acquired for $42.50 per sh. (see Jannock Limited)

Westek Communications Inc. (B.C. 1984)
Dec. 9, 1994 – Dissolved and struck off register.

Western Acceptance Corp. Ltd. (B.C. 1950)
Oct. 1968 – Name changed to Wescorp Industries Ltd. ■

Western Adera Ltd. (B.C. 1964)
June 30, 1975 – Formed Western Adera Limited in Colorado following acquisition by Western Adera Limited. ■

Western Adera Limited (Colo. June 30, 1975 amalg.)
Mar. 7, 1984 – Formed AeroLift, Inc. in Colorado on amalgamation with AeroLift, Inc., a Virginia company; basis 1 new for 1 old sh.

Western Alaska Minerals Corp. (B.C. Apr. 8, 2020)
Apr. 25, 2025 – Name changed to Alaska Silver Corp. (see FPsurvey - Mines & Energy)

Western Albermont Petroleums Limited (Ont. 1951)
Aug. 11, 1972 – Dissolved.

Western Allenbee Oil & Gas Company Limited (Can. Jan. 8, 1952)
Apr. 28, 1989 – Name changed to Convoy Capital Corp. ■

Western America Resources Inc. (Alta. Nov. 30, 1993)
Oct. 21, 1998 – Name changed to CFE Industries Inc. ■

Western America Uranium Exploration Corp. Ltd. (unknown)
1956 – Merged into Alscope Explorations Ltd.; basis 1 new for 2 old shs.

Western & Pacific Bank of Canada (Can. 1982)
1988 – Amalgamated with Bank of Alberta to form Canadian Western Bank. Shldrs. received $5.50 per sh. and up to an additional $1.00 per sh. after Oct. 31, 1989 depending on the performance of Western & Pacific's loan assets acquired through the merger.

Western and Pacific Resources Corp. (B.C. May 27, 1991 amalg.)
July 5, 1994 – Name changed to Consolidated Western and Pacific Resources Corp.; basis 1 new for 20 old shs. ■

Western Arlington Resources Ltd. (B.C. 1952)
Dec. 19, 1986 – Name changed to Lightning Creek Mines Ltd. ■

Western Asbestos & Development Ltd. (B.C. 1953)
Jan. 1955 – Assets sold to Castle Oil and Gas Ltd.; basis 1 new for 4 old shs. (see Castle Oil & Gas Limited)

Western Ashley Minerals Limited (Ont. 1931)
Mar. 29, 1956 – Name changed to Consolidated Ashley Minerals Limited; basis 1 new for 4 old shs. ■

Western Atlas Resources Inc. (B.C. Feb. 21, 1983)
June 27, 2024 – Name changed to Seasif Exploration Inc. (see FPsurvey - Mines & Energy)

Western Barite Mines Ltd. (Ont. 1961)
Dec. 31, 1987 – Charter cancelled following sale of all mineral properties.

Western Beaver Lodge Mines Ltd. (B.C. 1951)
Aug. 1, 1969 – Name changed to Portcomm Communications Corporation Limited; basis 1 new cl. A for 5 old com. shs. ∎

Western Broadcasting Company Ltd. (B.C. 1965)
May 31, 1981 – All o/s shs. acquired following purchase offer dated by North Continent Holdings Ltd. in exchange for $20.75 or 1 pfce. sh. redeemed at $20.75 for each Western sh. tendered.

Western-Buff Mines & Oils Ltd. (B.C. 1969)
June 27, 1977 – Dissolved.

Western Canada Beverage Corporation (B.C. Oct. 2, 1985)
Feb. 23, 1993 – Declared bankrupt and Barnes & Kissack Inc. of Vancouver, B.C., was appointed trustee.
Nov. 3, 1993 – Selkirk Springs International Corporation (subsequently Canadian Glacier Beverage Corporation) completed the purchase of the company's secured debentures from Montreal Trust Company, resulting in Selkirk acquiring all of the equipment at the company's Annacis Island plant. Selkirk also concluded an agreement with the trustee regarding the purchase of the company's assets. Unsecured creditors were paid in the form of common shares and series A warrants of Canadian Glacier to a maximum of approximately 3% of the value of their claim; warrants were issued in April 1996 and the common shares were issued in 1998. There was no distribution to shldrs.
Mar. 3, 1995 – Western Canada Beverage was struck from the B.C. Corporate Registry.
Mar. 25, 2003 – Trustee discharged.

Western Canada Breweries Limited (Can. 1923)
1963 – Canadian Breweries Ltd. acquired all o/s shs. for $36 per sh.
May 19, 1964 – All o/s 4.5% first mtge. and collateral trust bonds due Feb. 15, 1965, redeemed at 100.2 plus accrued int.

Western Canada Energy Ltd. (Alta. Apr. 1, 2008 amalg.)
Jan. 2, 2014 – Struck from registry and dissolved.

Western Canada Flour Mills Co. Ltd. (Ont. 1905)
Feb. 12, 1945 – Name changed to Purity Flour Mills Limited following exchange of each old 6% $100 par pref. stk. for 2 new $40 par pref. shs. and 2 new com. shs., $10 par, and arrears of $67.62 per sh. eliminated. Each old com. sh. of no par value was exch. sh.-for-sh. for new $10 par stock. ∎

Western Canada Oils, Ltd. (Ont. 1929)
1960 – Struck off register.

Western Canada Steel Limited (B.C. 1952)
July 1964 – Name changed to Western Canada Steel (1952) Ltd. ∎

Western Canada Steel (1952) Ltd. (B.C. 1952)
1964 – In voluntary liquidation. Under terms of an agreement with Consolidated Mining & Smelting (now Cominco Ltd.), the co. changed its name from Western Canada Steel Ltd. and the wholly owned subsid., Vancouver Rolling Mills Ltd. (which had acquired all operating assets of the parent co.), changed its name to Western Canada Steel Ltd. Cominco then acquired the o/s sh. of the new Western Canada Steel Ltd. for 306,510 Cominco shs. Distribution made of 1 sh. Cominco for each 2.5 shs. Western Canada Steel (1952) Ltd., with an additional distribution of about $1.50 per sh. cash to be made after tax status settled.

The Western Canada Telephone Company (Can. Apr. 12, 1916)
Nov. 29, 1919 – Name changed to British Columbia Telephone Company. ∎

The Western Canada Telephone Company (Can. Apr. 12, 1916; via Special Act of Parliament)
Nov. 29, 1919 – Name changed to British Columbia Telephone Company. ∎

Western Canadian Coal Corp. (B.C. Oct. 2, 1997)
Oct. 7, 2009 – Name changed to Western Coal Corp. ∎

Western Canadian Entertainment Corporation (Alta. May 27, 1994)
Feb. 6, 1997 – Formed PowerTel Communications Inc. in Alberta on amalgamation with PowerTel Communications Inc. (0.731 for 1); basis 1 new for 2 old shs. ∎

Western Canadian Land Corp. (B.C. 1982)
Oct. 14, 1993 – Continued into Canada.
Nov. 29, 1996 – Name changed to King George Development Corporation; basis 1 new for 5 old shs. ∎

Western Canadian Mining Corporation (B.C. Jan. 1, 1987 amalg.)
Apr. 22, 1991 – All o/s shs. not already held acquired by Consolidated Brinco Limited; basis 1 Consolidated Brinco sh. for 4.25 Western Canadian shs. (see Consolidated Brinco Limited)

Western Canadian Seed Processors Ltd. (Alta. Sept. 13, 1957)
May 17, 1974 – Name changed to Canbra Foods Ltd. ∎

Western Carlyle Concepts Inc. (B.C. 1987)
Nov. 20, 1992 – Dissolved and struck off register.

Western Coal Corp. (B.C. Oct. 2, 1997)
Apr. 7, 2010 – Acquired by Walter Energy, Inc.; basis $11.50 or 0.114 Walter shs. for 1 Western Coal sh.

Western Commonwealth Developments Inc. (B.C. Jan. 31, 1980)
Mar. 15, 1991 – Delisted from the Vancouver Stock Exchange. Subsequently dissolved and struck from register.

Western Consolidated Oils Ltd. (Can. 1924)
1936 – Assets acquired by Wain-Con Oils, Ltd.; basis 1 new for 5 old shs.

Western Copper Corporation (B.C. Mar. 17, 2006)
Oct. 20, 2011 – Name changed to Western Copper and Gold Corporation. (see FPsurvey - Mines & Energy)

Western Copper Holdings Limited (B.C. July 11, 1984)
Mar. 25, 2003 – Name changed to Western Silver Corporation. ∎

Western Copper Mills Ltd. (B.C. 1955)
1963 – Acquired by Noranda Mines Ltd. through offer of $81 for each $100 princ. amt. of first mtge. bonds; $40.50 for each $100 deb. and $0.25 for each warrant to buy 1 sh. The com. stk. was acquired through offer of $1.50 per sh. (see Noranda Mines Ltd.)

Western Copperada Mining Corp. (Que. 1956)
Oct. 10, 1958 – Name changed to Anglo-Alaska Oil Explorations Ltd.

Western Corporate Enterprises Inc. (B.C. 1987)
Nov. 1, 1994 – Amalgamated with 477475 British Columbia Ltd. for $7.53 per sh. Co. now private.

Western Corporate Farms Limited (Alta. 1987)
July 12, 1990 – Name changed to Sound Communication Corp.; basis 1 new for 2 old shs. ∎

Western Cryderman Gold Mines Ltd. (Man. 1934)
Oct. 1934 – Name changed to Cryderman Gold Mines Ltd.; basis 3 new for 2 old shs. ∎

Western Decalta Petroleum Limited (Can. 1947)
Sept. 20, 1976 – Under a formal offer Wesdec Petroleum Ltd., a wholly owned subsid. of Loram Co. Ltd., acquired all o/s shs. for Cdn. $8.00 per sh. (see The Petrol Oil & Gas Company, Limited)
Apr. 1977 – Following successful offer, the co. was liquidated. Wesdec assumed the 6% s.f. debs., ser. A and 84.7% in The Petrol Oil & Gas Company, Limited. (see The Petrol Oil & Gas Company, Limited)

Western D'Eldona Resources Limited (Ont. Oct. 5, 1984 amalg.)
Jan. 10, 1992 – Acquired by Paramount Resources Ltd.; basis $3.25 or 0.444 Paramount shs. for 1 Western D'Eldona sh.

Western Dominion Investment Company Ltd. (B.C. 1963)
June 7, 1996 – Amalgamated with 517648 BC Ltd. for $1.50 per sh.

Western e-com Inc. (Man. Oct. 1, 1999)
Oct. 4, 2001 – Name changed to OMT Inc. following reverse takeover acquisition of OMT Technologies Inc. in August 2001. ∎

Western Electronics & Engineering Ltd. (Alta. 1949)
May 1971 – Name changed to Pancana Industries Ltd. ∎

Western Envirotech Inc. (Alta. Apr. 28, 1987)
Oct. 31, 1995 – Name changed to Aquasol International Group Inc. ∎

Western Exploration Company, Limited (B.C. 1924)
Oct. 1974 – Amalgamated into Tacoma Resources Ltd.; basis 1 new for 5 old shs.

Western Facilities Fund (Alta. Jan. 10, 1997)
Apr. 20, 2001 – Name changed to Acclaim Energy Trust pursuant to amalgamation of wholly owned Nevis Ltd. with Danoil Energy Ltd. (deemed acquiror) to form Acclaim Energy Inc., wholly owned by Acclaim Energy Trust; basis 1 new trust unit for 1 Danoil sh. and 1 new trust unit for 14 Western Facilities trust units. Acclaim Energy Trust subsequently amalgamated with wholly owned Acclaim Energy Inc. (see Acclaim Energy Trust)

Western Financial Group Inc. (Alta. Nov. 14, 1995)
July 15, 2011 – Amalgamated with 1610838 Alberta Inc., a direct wholly owned subsid. of Desjardins Financial Corporation Inc., for $4.15 per sh.

Western Flintstone Mines Ltd. (B.C. 1966)
1974 – Charter cancelled.

Western Garnet Company Ltd. (B.C. July 15, 1988)
July 16, 1996 – Name changed to Western Garnet International Ltd. ∎

Western Garnet International Ltd. (B.C. July 15, 1988)
Feb. 3, 2003 – Name changed to WGI Heavy Minerals, Incorporated. ∎

Western GeoPower Corp. (B.C. Jan. 18, 1985)
Oct. 20, 2009 – Acquired by GTO Resources Inc.; basis 0.0622 GTO shs. for 1 Western GeoPower sh. (see Ram Power, Corp.)

Western Goldfields, Inc. (Idaho Jan. 15, 1924)
Mar. 1988 – WMC Acquisition Inc. acquired all o/s shs. at $11.25 per sh.
July 9, 2007 – Name changed to Western Goldfields Inc. ∎

Western Goldfields Inc. (Idaho Jan. 15, 1924)
July 16, 2007 – Continued into Ontario.
June 5, 2009 – Acquired by New Gold Inc.; basis $0.0001 plus 1 New Gold sh. for 1 Western Goldfields sh.

Western Grain Co., Limited (Can. 1928)
Dec. 1952 – Charter cancelled; all o/s 5% first mtge. bonds, series B, redeemed Jan. 2, 1952, at 102 and accr. int. Pref. shldrs. received $100 return of paid-up capital and, $52 per sh. on account of arrears. Nothing remained for com. shldrs.

Western Grocers Ltd. (Can. Dec. 1, 1912; via Dominion charter)
Jan. 1961 – Name changed to Westfair Foods Ltd. ∎

Western Harvest Seafarms Ltd. (B.C. 1984)
Dec. 30, 1994 – Dissolved and struck off register.

Western Helium Ltd. (Ont. 1962)
1965 – Name changed to Western Tin Mines Ltd.; basis 1 new for 1 old sh. ■

Western Heritage Properties Ltd. (Ont. 1960)
Jan. 1, 1971 – Name changed to Home Smith International Ltd.

Western Homes Ltd. (unknown)
Oct. 2, 1972 – Amalgamated with Summit Oils Limited of Calgary to form Summit Resources Limited; basis 32.72 new for 1 old sh.

Western Homestead Oils Ltd. (Alta. Mar. 18, 1947)
1954 – Name changed to Canadian Homestead Oils Limite; basis 1 new for 4 old shs. ■

Western Interprovincial Petroleum Producers Ltd. (B.C.)
1955 – Acquired by Canadian Pipe Lines & Petroleums Ltd. for 100,000 shs.
1961 – Struck off register.

Western Keltic Mines Inc. (B.C. Nov. 7, 1989)
May 29, 2008 – Name changed to Kutcho Copper Corp. following acquisition by Sherwood Copper Corporation and amalgamation with a wholly owned subsid.; basis 0.08 Sherwood shs. for 1 Western Keltic sh.

Western Lakota Energy Services Inc. (Alta. May 16, 2000)
Aug. 29, 2006 – Acquired by Savanna Energy Services Corp.; basis 0.64 new Savanna sh. for 1 old Western Lakota sh. (see Savanna Energy Services Corp.)

Western Leaseholds Ltd. (Alta. Apr. 21, 1944)
1962 – Acquired by Canadian Fina Oils Ltd. Distribution made of $2.75 per sh. to majority shldr. (Canadian Petrofina) and $6.46 to minority holders.

Western Lithium Canada Corporation (B.C. Nov. 27, 2007)
May 31, 2010 – Name changed to Western Lithium USA Corporation. ■

Western Lithium USA Corporation (B.C. Nov. 27, 2007)
Mar. 21, 2016 – Name changed to Lithium Americas Corp. ■

Western Logic Resources Inc. (Alta. Aug. 28, 1996)
Dec. 2, 2001 – Dissolved and struck from registry.

Western Logic Technologies Inc. (B.C. 1981)
Aug. 28, 1996 – Continued into Alberta.
Sept. 18, 1996 – Name changed to Western Logic Resources Inc. ■

Western Naco Petroleums Ltd. (Alta. 1950)
1961 – Acquired by Provo Gas Producers Ltd.; basis 1 new for 6 old shs.

Western Nickel Ltd. (B.C. 1952)
Wound up. Assets distributed to Newmont Mining Corp. and Pacific Nickel Mines. (see Pacific Nickel Mines Ltd.)

Western Oil Sands Inc. (Alta. June 18, 1999)
Oct. 22, 2007 – Acquired by Marathon Oil Corporation; basis $35.50 and/or 0.5932 Marathon com. sh. (or 0.5932 exch. sh. of 1339971 Alberta Ltd., an indirect subsidiary of Marathon) and 1 WesternZagros Resources Ltd. com. sh. for 1 Western Oil Sands com. sh. (see WesternZagros Resources Ltd.)

Western Pacific Energy Corporation (B.C. 1979)
Aug. 18, 1989 – Name changed to Durham Resources Ltd.; basis 1 new for 2 old shs. ■

Western Pacific Gold Inc. (Alta. July 18, 1986)
Mar. 17, 2004 – Name changed to WPI Gold Ltd.; basis 1 new for 5 old shs. ■

Western Pacific Mining Exploration Inc. (Que. Nov. 9, 1989 amalg.)
Oct. 29, 2002 – Name changed to Sierra Minerals Inc.; basis 1 new for 10 old shs. ■

Western Pacific Oils Ltd. (Alta. Mar. 31, 1987)
July 24, 1990 – Delisted from the Alberta Stock Exchange. Subsequently struck from the register and dissolved.

Western Pacific Products & Crude Oil Pipelines Ltd. (B.C. 1961)
Sept. 21, 1971 – Merged with Westcoast Production Co., to form Westcoast Petroleum Ltd. Shldrs. received 1 pref. share of Westcoast Petroleum for 5 com. shs.

Western Pacific Resources Corp. (B.C. June 4, 2009)
Oct. 13, 2020 – Name changed to Oro X Mining Corp. ■

Western Petroleum Operators Ltd. (unknown)
1963 – Absorbed by parent co., Globe Oil Co. (1958) Ltd.

Western Pinnacle Mining Ltd. (B.C. Feb. 29, 1988)
May 15, 1997 – Continued into Yukon.
Jan. 8, 2002 – Name changed to WPN Resources Ltd.; basis 1 new for 4 old shs. ■

Western Plains Petroleum Ltd. (Alta. Nov. 19, 2004)
Feb. 22, 2014 – Assigned into bankruptcy and all officers and directors resigned. Grant Thornton Alger Inc. appointed receiver.

Western Platinum Holdings Ltd. (Yuk. Jan. 30, 1998 amalg.)
July 23, 2002 – Name changed to Orsa Ventures Corp.; basis 1 new for 5 old shs. ■

Western Plywood Co. Ltd. (Can. 1944)
1961 – Acquired by United States Plywood Corp. through exch. of 1 sh. of its com. stk. for each 3.5 cl. B shs. of Western Plywood or, alternately, $13.25 (Cdn.) cash for each cl. B sh. Each cl. A sh. was offered $10 (Cdn.).

Western Potash Corp. (B.C. Apr. 5, 2007)
Apr. 5, 2017 – Succeeded by Western Resources Corp.; basis 1 new for 5 old shs. (see FPsurvey - Mines & Energy; FPsurvey - Industrials)

Western Potash Corp. Ltd. (Ont. 1951)
1955 – Name changed to Continental Potash Corp. Ltd.; basis 5 new for 1 old sh. ■

Western Power Corp. (Alta. 1987)
Nov. 1, 1992 – Dissolved and struck off register.

Western Prairie Exploration Co. Ltd. (Alta. 1949)
1952 – Acquired by Woodley Canadian Oil Co., and wound up.

Western Premium Resource Corp. (B.C. Apr. 17, 1986)
Aug. 29, 1997 – Name changed to Zodiac Exploration Corp. ■

Western Prospector Group Ltd. (B.C. Apr. 8, 1998)
Aug. 19, 2009 – Privatized at 56¢ per sh.

Western Quebec Mines Co. Ltd. (Que. Jan. 3, 1945)
Dec. 16, 1986 – Name changed to Western Québec Mines Inc. ■

Western Québec Mines Inc. (Que. Jan. 3, 1945)
July 18, 2007 – Acquired by Wesdome Gold Mines Ltd.; basis 1.45 new Wesdome shs. for 1 old Western Quebec sh.
Dec. 31, 2009 – Dissolved.

Western Realty Projects Ltd. (Alta. 1969 amalg.)
Apr. 29, 1974 – Amalgamated with Great Northern Capital Corp. Ltd. to form Abbey Glen Property Corp.

Western Resource Technologies Inc. (B.C. 1985)
Oct. 12, 1992 – Voluntarily wound up. Shrlders received 1 unit of WRT Energy Corporation for ea. 5 shs. of Western Resource held. Each unit is comprised of 1 com. sh. and 1 wt. to purchase additional shs. at US$3.00 per sh.

Western Resources Ltd. (B.C. 1963)
1964 – Name changed to Stikine Silver Ltd. ■

Western Resources Minerals Limited (Ont. Feb. 20, 1969)
Feb. 7, 1978 – Continued into Alberta.
Mar. 29, 1990 – Continued into Canada.
July 12, 2004 – Dissolved.

Western Rolling Hills Mines & Oils Limited (B.C. 1964)
Sept. 29, 1980 – Merged with private co. Invex Resources Ltd. to form a new co. known as Invex Resources Limited; basis 1 new Invex sh. for 1.5 old Western Rolling shs. (see Invex Resources Limited)

Western Rolling Mills Ltd. (Alta. 1959)
Mar. 31, 1975 – Struck off register.

Western Silica Products Ltd. (B.C. 1959)
1969 – Name changed to Javelin Mines Ltd. ■

Western Silver Corporation (B.C. July 11, 1984)
May 4, 2006 – Acquired by Glamis Gold Ltd.; basis 0.688 Glamis shs. plus 1 Western Copper Corporation sh. for 1 Western Silver sh.

Western Spirit Investments Ltd. (Alta. July 26, 1988)
June 4, 2004 – Plan of Arrangement acquisition by Avenir Diversified Income Fund; basis 1 performance right (exchangeable into 0.05 new Avenir trust unit) for 1 old Spirit sh. plus aggregate payment of $3,000,000, 4,987,497 new Avenir trust units and the assumption of $12,400,000 in outstanding debt. (see Avenir Diversified Income Trust)

Western Standard Metals Ltd. (B.C. Nov. 23, 2003 amalg.)
Jan. 26, 2011 – Amalgamated with Terraco Gold Corp.; basis 0.75 Terraco shs. for 1 Western Standard sh. (see Terraco Gold Corp.)

Western Standard Silver Mines Ltd. (B.C. 1964)
Oct. 9, 1975 – Name changed to Western Standard Industries Inc.

Western Star Energy Corporation (Alta. May 26, 1987)
Sept. 21, 1994 – Name changed to Western Star Exploration Ltd.; basis 1 new for 10 old shs. ■

Western Star Exploration Ltd. (Alta. May 26, 1987)
Jan. 25, 2000 – Acquired by EnerMark Income Fund; basis $1.80 or 0.48 EnerMark trust units plus 0.75 wts. for 1 Western Star sh. (see EnerMark Income Fund)

Western Star Trucks Holdings Ltd. (B.C. Oct. 22, 1990)
Sept. 27, 2000 – Acquired by 596951 B.C. Ltd., a wholly owned subsid. of Freightliner LLC, for $42 per sh.

Western Steel Products Corp. Ltd. (Can. 1928)
Sept. 1, 1945 – Name changed to Westeel Products Ltd. ■

Western Stockyards Limited (Can. 1920)
Dec. 31, 1982 – Amalgamated with Commercial Financial Corporation. All Western shs. held by Commercial were cancelled; minority shldrs. paid off through issuance of 17,240 cl. A special shs. and 134,557 com. shs. of amalg. co. plus $10,190.

Western Supplies Limited (Alta. 1909)
Apr. 10, 1979 – Shldrs. given option of $18.50 per sh. or one 8% redeem. pref. sh. (sh.-for-sh. basis) of 120841 Holdings Ltd. for each sh. held. Pref. shs. issued under the takeover were redeemed Apr. 10, 1979, at $18.50 per sh.

Western Surf Inlet Mines Ltd. (B.C. May 1933)
Apr. 1966 – Assets acquired by Matachewan Consolidated Mines Ltd.; basis 5 new for 4 old shs.

Western Tin Mines Ltd. (Ont. 1962)
Mar. 1976 – Charter cancelled.

Western Trinity Resource Corp. (B.C. 1981)
May 28, 1993 – Dissolved and struck off register.

Western Troy Capital Resources Inc. (Ont. Nov. 8, 1989)
Aug. 2, 2022 – Name changed to Li3 Lithium Corp. ■

Western Tungsten Copper Mines Ltd. (B.C. 1949)
1955 – Acquired by Farwest Tungsten Copper Mines Ltd.; basis 1 new for 10 old shs. Debenture holders received 200 Farwest shs. for $100 deb. (see Farwest Tungsten Copper Mines Ltd.)

Western Uranium Cobalt Mines Ltd. (B.C. 1949)
Sept. 30, 1952 – Name changed to Western Tungsten Copper Mines Ltd. ■

Western Uranium Corporation (B.C. Mar. 21, 2006 amalg.)
Apr. 5, 2011 – Name changed to Concordia Resource Corp. ■

Western Uranium Corp. (Ont. Dec. 29, 2006)
Oct. 4, 2018 – Name changed to Western Uranium & Vanadium Corp. (see FPsurvey - Mines & Energy)

Western Uranium Explorations Inc. (Ont. July 20, 1977)
Aug. 11, 1983 – Name changed to Cal-Dataline Corporation; basis 1 new for 8 old shs. ■

Western Warrior Resources Inc. (Alta. Feb. 27, 1998)
Oct. 29, 2008 – Name changed to Whetstone Minerals Inc.; basis 1 new for 4 old shs. ■

Western Wind Energy Corp. (B.C. Jan. 5, 1998)
May 27, 2013 – Acquired by WWE Equity Holdings Inc., an indirect wholly owned subsid. of Brookfield Renewable Energy Partners L.P., for $2.60 per sh. (see Brookfield Renewable Energy Partners L.P.)

WesternOne Equity Income Fund (B.C. June 14, 2006)
Dec. 31, 2012 – Succeeded by WesternOne Inc. pursuant to plan of arrangement whereby WesternOne Inc. was formed to facilitate the conversion of the fund into a corporation and the fund was dissolved. ■

WesternOne Inc. (Can. July 1, 2012)
Nov. 30, 2018 – Name changed to WEQ Holdings Inc. ■

WesternZagros Resources Ltd. (Alta. Aug. 22, 2007)
July 28, 2017 – All o/s com. shs. not already held acquired by WZG Acquisition Ltd., an affiliate of Crest Energy International LLC; basis Cdn$0.28 cash per sh. Name changed to WesternZagros Resources ULC. ■

WesternZagros Resources ULC (Alta. Aug. 22, 2007)
July 1, 2018 – Name changed to WZR Development ULC.

Westerra Resources Ltd. (B.C. June 8, 1987)
Jan. 10, 1990 – Name changed to HSI Hydrosystems International Inc.; basis 1 new for 1 old sh. ■

Westfair Foods Ltd. (Can. Dec. 1, 1912; via Dominion charter)
Jan. 19, 2004 – Privatized at $350 per sh.

Westfield Minerals Limited (Can. Dec. 1, 1955)
Mar. 6, 2000 – Acquired by B.C. Pacific Capital Corporation for $2.35 per sh. (see B.C. Pacific Capital Corporation)

Westfield Properties Ltd. (Can. Dec. 18, 2003)
Dec. 22, 2004 – Converted into a new income trust named Westfield Real Estate Investment Trust; basis 1 new trust unit for 1 com. sh. (see Westfield Real Estate Investment Trust)

Westfield Real Estate Investment Trust (Man. Nov. 8, 2004)
Feb. 15, 2007 – Name changed to Artis Real Estate Investment Trust. (see FPsurvey - Industrials)

WestFire Energy Ltd. (Alta. Sept. 14, 1999)
Oct. 23, 2012 – Name changed to Long Run Exploration Ltd. following acquisition of Guide Exploration Ltd. ■

Westflank Oil Co., Ltd. (Alta. 1936)
1941 – Merged with 8 other companies into Amalgamated Oils Limited; basis 39 new for 500 old shs.

Westfort Energy Ltd. (B.C. Mar. 22, 1977)
Nov. 10, 1993 – Continued into Alberta.
Nov. 2, 2005 – Struck from registry and dissolved.

Westfort Petroleums Ltd. (B.C. Mar. 22, 1977)
Nov. 8, 1993 – Name changed to Westfort Energy Ltd.; basis 1 new for 15 old shs. ■

Westgold Resources Limited (Australia July 27, 1987)
Dec. 20, 2012 – Name changed to Westgold Resources Pty Ltd. ■

Westgold Resources NL (Australia July 27, 1987)
Jan. 25, 2008 – Name changed to Westgold Resources Limited. ■

Westgold Resources Pty Ltd. (Australia July 27, 1987)
Oct. 20, 2016 – Name changed to Westgold Resources Limited. (see FPsurvey - Mines & Energy)

Westgroup Corporations Inc. (Alta. Dec. 19, 1986)
Mar. 15, 1995 – Name changed to Beaumont Select Corporations Inc.; basis 1 new for 7 old shs. ■

Westgrowth Industries Limited (Alta. 1974)
Dec. 31, 1979 – Name changed to Almark Resources Ltd. ■

Westgrowth Investments Limited (Sask. 1960)
Oct. 1979 – Name changed to Orion Petroleum Ltd. ■

Westgrowth Petroleums Ltd. (B.C. 1956)
1981 – Continued into Alberta.
Oct. 7, 1986 – Name changed to Canadian Westgrowth Ltd.; basis 1 new for 20 old shs. ■

Westham Oil Ltd. (B.C. Feb. 11, 1981)
Dec. 10, 1981 – Continued into Canada.
Apr. 22, 1987 – Name changed to BayWest Capital Equities Corp. ■

Westham Resources Corp. (B.C. Dec. 7, 2011)
July 16, 2014 – Name changed to Roughrider Exploration Limited. ■

Westhaven Ventures Inc. (B.C. Apr. 17, 1998)
July 10, 2020 – Name changed to Westhaven Gold Corp. (see FPsurvey - Mines & Energy)

Westhill Resources Limited (B.C. Apr. 26, 1984)
Mar. 3, 1992 – Name changed to Breckenridge Resources Ltd.; basis 1 new for 5 old shs. ■

Westhope Capital Corp. (Ont. Nov. 27, 1996 amalg.)
Mar. 12, 2010 – Name changed to EPM Mining Ventures Inc.; basis 1 new for 10 old shs. ■

Westinghouse Canada Inc. (Can. 1903)
1986 – Parent co., Westinghouse Electric Corporation of Pittsburgh, acquired all of the o/s com. shs. of the co. at $105.00 per sh. after a consolidation on the basis of 1 new for 127,660 old com. shs.

Westinghouse Canada Limited (Can. 1903)
Apr. 15, 1980 – Name changed to Westinghouse Canada Inc. ■

WestJet Airlines Ltd. (Alta. June 27, 1994)
Dec. 16, 2019 – Acquired by Onex Corporation; basis $31 cash per sh.

Westlake Capital Ltd. (B.C. Mar. 15, 2011)
Oct. 28, 2013 – Dissolved following Qualifying Transaction private placement subscription of 3,100,000 RockBridge Resources Inc. units (1 com. sh. plus 1 wt.) at 5¢ per unit (with wts. exercisable at 10¢ per wt. for 1 yr.) and distribution of RockBridge units to shldrs. on a pro rata basis.

Westlake Industries Ltd. (B.C. 1980)
Oct. 31, 1990 – Amalgamated with a wholly owned subsid. of Minera Rayrock Inc.; basis 11 new for 20 old shs. (see Minera Rayrock Inc.)

Westlake Resources Inc. (B.C. 1980)
Dec. 31, 1986 – Name changed to Westlake Industries Ltd. ■

Westland Investment Corporation (Alta. 1986)
Nov. 27, 1996 – Continued into Yukon.
Aug. 15, 1997 – Name changed to Sepik Gold Corporation. ■

Westland Mines Ltd. (B.C. 1966)
Aug. 1974 – Name changed to United Westland Resources Ltd.; basis 1 new for 2 old shs. ■

Westland Mining Co. Ltd. (Ont. 1945)
May 14, 1975 – Dissolved.

Westleaf Inc. (Alta. Dec. 27, 2018)
Mar. 1, 2020 – Name changed to Decibel Cannabis Company Inc. (see FPsurvey - Industrials)

Westley Mines International Inc. (B.C. Jan. 16, 1981)
Dec. 9, 1998 – Continued into Ontario.
Dec. 16, 1998 – Name changed to Moydow Mines International Inc. following reverse takeover acquisition of Moydow Limited; basis 1 new for 12 old shs. ■

Westley Mines Limited (Alta. Dec. 12, 1972)
Jan. 16, 1981 – Continued into British Columbia.
Oct. 28, 1992 – Name changed to Westley Technologies Ltd. ■

Westley Technologies Ltd. (B.C. Jan. 16, 1981)
June 20, 1997 – Name changed to Westley Mines International Inc. ■

Westlinks Resources Ltd. (Alta. June 30, 1998)
Dec. 18, 2001 – Name changed to Enterra Energy Corp. ■

Westlock Petroleums Limited (Ont. 1947)
1955 – Sold to Wespac Petroleums Ltd.; basis 1 new for 4.1 old shs.

Westmills Canada Inc. (B.C. 1966)
Feb. 8, 1985 – Placed into receivership; Thorne Ernst Whinney (later Peat Marwick Thorne) were appointed receivers. All the assets were sold and the secured creditors partially paid.
1992 – Declared bankruptcy.
1993 – Wound up. There were no funds available for unsecured creditors or shldrs.
May 19, 1995 – Trustee discharged.

Westmills Carpets Limited (B.C. 1966)
Jan. 1, 1984 – Name changed to Westmills Canada Inc. ■

Westmin Resources Limited (B.C. Sept. 25, 1951)
Mar. 26, 1981 – Continued into Canada. (see Boliden Limited)
May 19, 1998 – All o/s $2.125 cl. B pref. shs., ser. 1 called for redemption; basis $25 per sh. with accrued and unpaid dividends of $0.2802. All o/s com. shs. previously acquired by Boliden Limited effective Mar. 5, 1998; basis $5.40 per sh. (see Boliden Limited)

Westminster Paper Company Limited (B.C. July 24, 1926)
July 1, 1964 – Name changed to Scott Paper Limited. ■

Westminster Resources Ltd. (Alta. May 5, 1995)
June 26, 2002 – Name changed to Vaquero Energy Ltd. ■

Westminster Resources Ltd. (B.C. Dec. 1, 2005)
July 21, 2021 – Name changed to Solis Minerals Ltd. ■

Westmont Capital Resources Limited (B.C. 1968)
Apr. 1979 – Name changed to Wescap Energy Corporation. ■

Westmount Resources Ltd. (B.C. 1966)
Dec. 7, 1990 – Entered into a special resolution to liquidate and dissolve the company in late 1989. Resolution was approved by the shldrs. on Jan. 30, 1990. Sale of all oil and gas properties for approx. $3,325,000 completed Jan. 31, 1990. First distribution of 25¢ made

to shldrs. on Mar. 27, 1990. Final distribution of $0.11978 per sh. paid to shldrs. of record. Co. now dissolved.

Westmount Resources Ltd. (B.C. Sept. 30, 1967)
May 20, 1998 – Name changed to Mt. Tom Minerals Corp.; basis 1 new for 2 old shs. ■

Westone Ventures Inc. (Alta. Nov. 18, 1993)
June 4, 2004 – Name changed to Secure One, Inc. following reverse takeover acquisition of United Protection Services Inc. ■

Westonian Petroleums Ltd. (Alta. 1951)
Jan. 17, 1957 – Name changed to Titan Petroleum Corp. Ltd. ■

Westore Mines Ltd. (Ont. 1957)
1960 – Assets acquired by Bison Petroleum and Minerals Ltd.; basis 1 new for 13 old shs.

Westpine Metals Ltd. (B.C. Mar. 10, 1989)
July 8, 1998 – Name changed to Great Quest Metals Ltd.; basis 1 new for 4 old shs. ■

Westpoint Energy Inc. (Alta. May 15, 1987)
July 5, 2000 – Acquired by Alberta Energy Company Inc. for $8.00 per sh. (see Alberta Energy Company Ltd.)

Westport Innovations Inc. (Alta. Mar. 20, 1995)
June 1, 2016 – Name changed to Westport Fuel Systems Inc. (see FPsurvey - Industrials)

WestPost Capital Inc. (B.C. Aug. 18, 1986)
Dec. 11, 1990 – Name changed to Telepost Communications Inc.; basis 1 new for 4 old shs. ■

Westrange Corp. (Alta. Nov. 26, 1996)
Jan. 24, 2005 – Name changed to HTC Hydrogen Technologies Corp. following reverse takeover acquisition of HTC Hydrogen ThermoChem Corp. ■

Westrend Natural Gas Inc. (B.C. May 27, 1987)
Aug. 12, 1999 – Name changed to Westrend (Oil & Gas) Technologies Corp.; basis 1 new for 15 old shs. ■

Westrend (Oil & Gas) Technologies Corp. (B.C. May 27, 1987)
Mar. 22, 2001 – Delisted from the CDNX. Subsequently dissolved for failure to file.

Westrex Development Corp. (B.C. Aug. 29, 1979)
Feb. 1, 1988 – Name changed to Consolidated Westrex Development Corp.; basis 1 new for 2.7 old shs. ■

Westrex Energy Corp. (B.C. Aug. 29, 1979)
May 12, 1994 – Continued into Alberta. (see Search Energy Corp.)
Jan. 9, 1997 – Amalgamated with Search Energy Inc. to form Search Energy Corp.; basis 1 Search for 5 Westrex shs. (see Search Energy Corp.)

Westridge Resources Inc. (B.C. Apr. 30, 2007)
Oct. 4, 2018 – Name changed to Harrys Manufacturing Inc. pursuant to the acquisition of Harrys International Manufacturing Inc. (see FPsurvey - Industrials)

Westrock Energy Income Fund I (Alta. Dec. 1, 1987)
June 13, 2000 – Amalgamated with Enerplus Resources Fund; basis 0.447 Enerplus units for 1 Westrock unit. (see Enerplus Resources Fund)

Westrock Energy Income Fund II (Alta. 1987)
June 13, 2000 – Amalgamated with Enerplus Resources Fund; basis 0.445 of a new Enerplus unit for 1 old unit. (see Enerplus Resources Fund)

Westrok Capital Inc. (B.C. Apr. 4, 1979)
Jan. 25, 1994 – Continued into Alberta.
Jan. 8, 1996 – Name changed to Merit Energy Ltd.; basis 1 new for 4 old shs. ■

Westron Ventures Ltd. (B.C. Oct. 28, 1985)
June 27, 1988 – Name changed to Jefjen Capital Corporation. ■

Westshire Capital II Corp. (B.C. June 1, 2015)
Apr. 2, 2018 – Name changed to The Wonderfilm Media Corporation following the Qualifying Transaction reverse takeover acquisition of (old) The Wonderfilm Media Corporation; basis 1 new for 4 old shs. ■

Westshire Capital Corp. (Alta. Dec. 21, 2012)
Dec. 13, 2013 – Name changed to Avagenesis Corp. pursuant to Qualifying Transaction reverse takeover acquisition of and vertical amalgamation with (old) Avagenesis Corp. ■

Westshore Terminals Income Fund (B.C. Dec. 2, 1996)
Jan. 1, 2011 – Succeeded by Westshore Terminals Investment Corporation pursuant to plan of arrangement whereby Westshore Terminals Investment Corporation was formed to facilitate the conversion of the fund into a corporation and the fund was subsequently wound up. (see FPsurvey - Industrials)

Weststar Resources Corp. (B.C. Oct. 27, 2004)
Oct. 20, 2016 – Name changed to Liberty Leaf Holdings Ltd. ■

Westsun Petroleums & Minerals Ltd. (Can. June 9, 1982)
Oct. 29, 1986 – Formed Telepanel Inc. on amalgamation with Telepanel Inc. (1 for 1). ■

Westunit Resources Corp. (B.C. Mar. 18, 1983)
Apr. 4, 1986 – Name changed to Avanti Productions Inc. ■

Westview Commercial Inc. (Alta. Apr. 18, 1995)
Nov. 21, 2007 – Continued into British Columbia.
Nov. 28, 2007 – Name changed to Mega Moly Inc. following reverse takeover acquisition of Magura Holdings s.r.o. ■

Westview Investment Corporation Ltd. (B.C. 1965)
Dec. 1, 1978 – Charter cancelled.

Westview Lifecare Centres Inc. (Alta. Apr. 18, 1995)
Jan. 24, 2003 – Name changed to Westview Commercial Inc.; basis 1 new for 10 old shs. ■

Westview Mining Co. Ltd. (B.C. 1967)
1972 – Merged into Charta Mines Ltd.

Westview Multimedia Inc. (Alta. Apr. 29, 1998)
May 27, 1999 – Name changed to Megawheels.com Inc. and continued into Canada pursuant to reverse takeover acquisition of Megawheels Media Inc.; basis 1 new for 2 old shs. ■

Westview Resources Inc. (B.C. Feb. 25, 1986)
Sept. 20, 1996 – Name changed to Consolidated Westview Resource Corp.; basis 1 new for 3 old shs. ■

Westville Mines Ltd. (Ont. 1945)
Nov. 28, 1973 – Name changed to Jetcan Limited. ■

Westward Energy & Resources Corp. (B.C. June 9, 1978)
Nov. 4, 1982 – Name changed to International Westward Development Corporation; basis 1 new for 4 old shs. ■

Westward Energy Ltd. (Alta. Jan. 31, 1992)
Aug. 11, 1997 – Amalgamated with Seventh Energy Ltd. (1 for 1) to continue as Seventh Energy Ltd.; basis 0.6 new Seventh cl. A sh. for 1 old Westward cl. A sh. (see Seventh Energy Ltd.)

Westward Explorations Ltd. (B.C. Dec. 9, 1987)
Mar. 31, 2011 – Name changed to West African Iron Ore Corp. pursuant to reverse takeover acqusition of Sky Alliance Resources Guinee S.A. ■

Westward Leisure Concepts Ltd. (B.C. Mar. 20, 1972)
June 29, 1973 – Name changed to Keg Restaurants Ltd. ■

Westwark Mines Ltd. (Ont. 1964)
Aug. 8, 1972 – Dissolved.

Westwater Industries Ltd. (B.C. July 18, 1980)
Mar. 5, 1993 – Delisted from the Toronto Stock Exchange. Subsequently dissolved for failure to file.

Westwater Resources Ltd. (B.C. 1983)
Oct. 14, 1985 – Name changed to American Westwater Technology Group Ltd.; basis 2 new for 1 old sh. ■

Westwego Resources Ltd. (B.C. Feb. 19, 1988)
Oct. 3, 1995 – Name changed to Corum Resource Corp. ■

Westwin Ventures Inc. (B.C. May 30, 1986)
Jan. 6, 1995 – Name changed to New Westwin Ventures Inc.; basis 1 new for 3 old shs. ■

Westwind Energy Corporation Ltd. (Alta. Jan. 20, 1987)
July 1, 2000 – Struck from register and dissolved.

Westwind Explorations Ltd. (Ont. 1960)
Mar. 14, 1978 – Charter cancelled.

Westwind Mines Ltd. (B.C. 1973)
Jan. 27, 1981 – Name changed to Territorial Petroleum Ventures Ltd. ■

Westwood Cadillac Mines Ltd. (Que. 1936)
Dec. 22, 1973 – Dissolved.

Wex Pharmaceuticals Inc. (Can. June 3, 1987)
May 6, 2011 – Acquired by 7735308 Canada Limited, a wholly owned subsid. of Pharmagesic (Holdings) Inc., for 14¢ per sh.

Wex Technologies Inc. (Can. June 3, 1987)
Aug. 29, 1996 – Name changed to International Wex Technologies Inc.; basis 1 new for 7 old shs. ■

Wexford Mines Ltd. (Ont. 1957)
Feb. 13, 1968 – All assets acquired by Madeleine Mines Ltd. by issue of 3,705,886 shs. on a share-for-share basis.

Weymarn Oils, Ltd. (Can. Jan. 2, 1929)
May 6, 1929 – Formed Weymarn Petroleums, Limited in Canada following acquisition of assets by Weymarn Petroleums, Limited.

Weymin Mining Corporation (B.C. Feb. 9, 1983)
Sept. 10, 2002 – Name changed to GCP Mining Corporation; basis 1 new for 15 old shs. ■

Whalley Industries Ltd. (B.C. 1969)
Placed into bankruptcy. All assets sold with no distribution to shldrs.

Wharf Resources Ltd. (B.C. Jan. 20, 1951)
Apr. 30, 1973 – Amalgamated with French Exploration Ltd. to form new co. with same name Wharf Resources Ltd. (see Goldcorp Inc.)
July 19, 1991 – Continued into Ontario. (see Goldcorp Inc.)
Dec. 31, 1996 – Acquired by Goldcorp Inc. and its wholly owned subsid., Goldcorp Acquisitions Inc.; basis $9.00 or 0.72 Goldcorp cl. A subord. vtg. shs. for 1 Wharf com. sh. All exch. 7% cl. A pfd. shs. redeemed Dec. 30, 1996; basis $25.25 per sh. plus $0.24863 accr. divds. (see Goldcorp Inc.)

Whatcom Capital Corp. (B.C. Sept. 19, 2019)
Dec. 18, 2020 – Name changed to Nexe Innovations Inc. pursuant to the Qualifying Transaction reverse takeover acquisition of (old) NEXE Innovations Inc.; basis 1 new for 2.5 old shs. (see FPsurvey - Industrials)

Whats-Online.Com Inc. (Alta. Nov. 4, 1993)
Oct. 16, 2001 – Name changed to Great Pacific International Inc.; basis 1 new for 10 old shs. ■

Whattozee Networks Inc. (B.C. Mar. 14, 2008)
Aug. 4, 2017 – Name changed to Chemistree Technology Inc. ■

Wheat Hills Resources Inc. (Ont. Nov. 21, 1994)
May 7, 1999 – Name changed to Multiactive Software Inc. and continued into Canada following reverse takeover

acquisition of Multiactive Software Inc.; basis 1 new for 10 old shs. ∎

Wheaton River Minerals Ltd. (Ont. Mar. 30, 1990)
Apr. 15, 2005 – Plan of Arrangement acquisition by Goldcorp Inc.; basis 0.25 new Goldcorp sh. for 1 old Wheaton sh. Outstanding warrants converted on same basis. (see Goldcorp Inc.)

Wheels Group Inc. (Ont. July 9, 1997)
Apr. 8, 2015 – Acquired by Radiant Logistics, Inc.; basis 77¢ cash, payable in cash or Radiant com. shs. for 1 Wheels com. sh.

Whetstone Minerals Inc. (Alta. Feb. 27, 1998)
Nov. 6, 2009 – Continued into Jersey.
Nov. 20, 2009 – Name changed to Whetstone Minerals Ltd. ∎

Whetstone Minerals Ltd. (Jersey Nov. 6, 2009)
Dec. 17, 2013 – Voluntarily delisted from TSX-VEN. Distribution to be determined upon wind-up.
Nov. 21, 2014 – Dissolved.

Whim Creek Consolidated NL (Australia 1964)
Aug. 30, 1989 – Acquired by Dominion Mining Limited; basis either 2 Dominion shs. for 1 Whim sh. or A$1.25 plus 9 Dominion shs. for 5 Whim shs.

Whipsaw Mines Ltd. (B.C. 1965)
June 18, 1974 – Name changed to Whipsaw Resources Ltd.

Whirlwind Resource Explorations Ltd. (Ont. 1977)
Aug. 5, 1983 – Name changed to Video Science Technology Ltd.; basis 1 new for 5 old shs. ∎

Whiskey Creek Resources Inc. (B.C. Aug. 25, 1987)
Mar. 2, 1998 – Name changed to Arc Pacific Metals Ltd.; basis 1 new for 4 old shs. ∎

Whisper Lake Resources Inc. (Ont. Jan. 27, 1988)
Dec. 24, 1996 – Name changed to Messina Diamond Corporation following acquisition of Becksham Corporation of Barbados; basis 1 new for 5 old shs. ∎

Whistler Blackcomb Holdings Inc. (Can. Oct. 4, 2010)
Oct. 29, 2010 – Continued into British Columbia.
Oct. 18, 2016 – Acquired by 1068877 B.C. Ltd. (Exchangeco), a wholly owned subsid. of Vail Resorts Inc.; basis (i) 0.097294 Vail shs. plus $17.50 cash for 1 Whistler sh. or (ii) 0.097294 Exchangeco shs. plus $17.50 cash for 1 Whistler sh.

Whistler Gold Corp. (B.C. Sept. 16, 1983)
Aug. 11, 2008 – Name changed to Svit Gold Corp. ∎

Whistler Gold Exploration Inc. (B.C. June 24, 1985)
May 1, 2019 – Name changed to American Uranium Mining Corporation. ∎

Whistler Petroleums Limited (Alta. 1969)
1976 – Acquired by Ratel Resources Limited for 74¢ per sh.

Whitby Tire Ltd. (Ont. 1899)
1975 – Name changed to Dayton Tire Canada Ltd. ∎

White Bear Resources Inc. (B.C. May 25, 2006)
Apr. 14, 2014 – Name changed to Tinkerine Studios Ltd. following reverse takeover acquisition of Tinkerine Studio Inc. (see FPsurvey - Industrials)

White Bridge Mines Ltd. (Ont. 1966)
Mar. 5, 1975 – Dissolved.

White Canadian Aircraft Ltd. (Ont. 1940)
Mar. 1948 – Liquidated by The Canadian Credit Men's Trust Association Ltd., Toronto.
Mar. 1950 – Wound up. Small surplus available for com. shldrs.

White Canyon Uranium Limited (Australia July 26, 2005)
Aug. 4, 2011 – Acquired by Denison Mines Corp. for A$0.24 per sh.

White Eagle Silver Mines, Limited (Can. June 7, 1933)
Dec. 16, 1980 – Dissolved.

White Electronic Development Corporation Limited (Ont. 1955)
Nov. 3, 1966 – Acquired by Instrument Systems Corp. of New York; basis 0.152426 new Instrument Systems sh. for 1 old White sh.

White Fire Energy Ltd. (Alta. Mar. 14, 2005)
Feb. 23, 2006 – Plan of Arrangement acquisition by Highpine Oil & Gas Limited; basis 0.132 new Highpine cl. A sh. for 1 old White Fire com. sh. (see Highpine Oil & Gas Limited)

White Gold Ventures Ltd. (Alta. May 27, 1988)
Sept. 25, 1992 – Name changed to Cash Canada Pawn Corp. ∎

White Hardware Limited (Ont. 1950)
Feb. 24, 1966 – Name changed to Handy Andy Merchandising (Eastern) Limited. ∎

White Hawk Ventures Inc. (B.C. Feb. 23, 1987)
Jan. 9, 2001 – Name changed to E-Energy Ventures Inc.; basis 1 new for 5 old shs. ∎

White Horse Gold Mines Ltd. (Ont. June 28, 1934)
Apr. 3, 1939 – Shares exchanged, 1 new for 10 old shs. for stock in Jellicoe Mines (1939) Ltd. (see Jellicoe Mines (1939) Ltd.)

White Karry Gold Mines Ltd. (Ont. 1946)
Nov. 27, 1961 – Dissolved.

White Knight Resources Ltd. (B.C. Dec. 18, 1986)
July 9, 2007 – Acquired by US Gold Canadian Acquisition Corporation; basis 0.35 new US Gold sh. for 1 old White sh. (see US Gold Canadian Acquisition Corporation)

White Lake Mines Ltd. (Ont. Feb. 10, 1928)
Charter cancelled.

White Metal Resources Corp. (B.C. June 22, 1990 amalg.)
July 14, 2022 – Name changed to Thunder Gold Corp. (see FPsurvey - Mines & Energy)

The White Pass and Yukon Corporation Limited (Can. 1951)
May 31, 1988 – All o/s 6 3/4% cum. redeem. pref. ser.A shs. redeemed; basis $25.25 plus accr. and unpaid divds. of $0.421875 per sh. Subsequently a wholly owned subsid. of Federal Industries Ltd.

White Petroleums Ltd. (B.C.)
1959 – Struck off register.

White Pine Resources Inc. (Ont. May 11, 1979)
Mar. 3, 2014 – Voluntarily delisted from TSX-VEN.
Sept. 26, 2017 – Name changed to SBD Capital Corp. (see FPsurvey - Industrials)

White Plains Resources Corp. (B.C. Sept. 26, 1988)
July 26, 1994 – Name changed to American Wollastonite Mining Corp.; basis 1 new for 2 old shs. ∎

The White River Exploration Limited (Que. 1966)
Mar. 2, 1974 – Charter cancelled.

White River Mines Ltd. (B.C. 1968)
Oct. 1974 – Name changed to Ventora Resources Ltd.; basis 1 new for 5 old shs. ∎

White Rock Energy Inc. (Alta. June 16, 2008)
Jan. 26, 2010 – Name changed to Darford International Inc. pursuant to Qualifying Transaction reverse takeover acquisition of Darford International Ltd. ∎

White Rock Mines Ltd. (Ont. 1962)
1967 – Merged into Drope Lake Explorations Ltd.; basis 1 new for 10 old shs.

White Rose Crafts and Nursery Sales Limited (Ont. Aug. 20, 1971)
June 20, 2002 – Following review of the company's most recent year end financials, the Board of Directors was advised that its senior lender, The Bank of Nova Scotia (Scotiabank), would not waive the default or commit to further financial support. Based on this information the Board authorized the company to file a voluntary assignment into bankruptcy under the Bankruptcy and Insolvency Act (Canada). PricewaterhouseCoopers Inc. of Toronto was appointed as trustee/manager and all members of the Board resigned.
Aug. 2002 – Newly incorporated White Rose Home and Garden Centres Ltd. agreed to purchase the assets, inventory and fixtures from 24 stores from PricewaterhouseCoopers.
Sept. 2002 – Sale closed on Sept. 9 and the proceeds amounted to approx. $13,100,000. The remaining seven stores of the chain would be closed following liquidation of stock conducted through Century Services Ltd. By mid-September, all assets had been sold and/or liquidated which resulted in total net proceeds of approx. $27,400,000. This resulted in a major shortfall for Scotiabank as the company's secured creditor and there would be no funds available for distribution to shldrs. On Sept. 9, Scotiabank lodged with PricewaterhouseCoopers a proposal under the Bankruptcy and Insolvency Act for a payment to be made to all of White Rose's creditors in return for the full release of all the creditors' claims against White Rose. The bank determined that there may be tax losses which may only be utilized by them as it was the major shldr. of the company and in order to do so, the company must be free and clear of all third party claims. Under the proposal, all unsecured creditors with claims of $1,000 or less would be paid the lesser of $500 or 50% of the amount of their claim; and unsecured creditors with claims higher than $1,000 could elect to either reduce their claim to $1,000 and be paid in accordance with creditors with claims of less than $1,000 or share in the balance of the proposal funds on a pro-rata basis, to a maximum of 10% of the value of their claim. PricewaterhouseCoopers estimated that the proposal would produce a payment to unsecured creditors of approx. 9.7% of the proven amount of their claim. On Sept. 20, the proposal was approved at a meeting of unsecured creditors and was approved by the court on Oct. 7. As of Oct. 16, all of the proposal's conditions had been met.
Oct. 25, 2002 – First and final distribution by the trustee paid to creditors whose proof of claims had been received and admitted by Oct. 21, 2002. There were no distributions made to shldrs.

White Star Copper Mines Limited (Ont. 1963)
Mar. 19, 2012 – Dissolved and struck from register.

White Swan Resources Inc. (Alta. Mar. 25, 1986)
Jan. 15, 1999 – Name changed to Africa Diamond Holdings Ltd.; basis 1 new for 5 old shs. ∎

White Tiger Gold Ltd. (British Virgin Islands Dec. 10, 2010)
July 30, 2013 – Name changed to Mangazeya Mining Ltd. ∎

White Tiger Mining Corp. (B.C. Oct. 17, 1984)
Sept. 24, 2014 – Name changed to Copper Lake Resources Ltd. ∎

Whitecat Energy Ventures Limited (Alta. Mar. 31, 1987)
Nov. 16, 1988 – Name changed to North Eastern Energy Group Ltd. ∎

Whitegate Mining Co. Ltd. (Ont. 1963)
1976 – Charter cancelled.

Whitegold Natural Resource Corp. (B.C. Jan. 22, 1987)
May 24, 2002 – Name changed to Spirit Energy Corp.; basis 1 new for 3 old shs. ∎

Whitegold Resource Corp. (B.C. Jan. 22, 1987)
Apr. 9, 2001 – Name changed to Whitegold Natural Resource Corp.; basis 1 new for 3 old shs. ∎

Whitehall Canadian Oils Ltd. (Can. 1951)
Jan. 21, 1970 – Name changed to Ashland Canadian Oils Ltd. ■

Whitehorse Copper Mines Ltd. (Alta. 1954)
Dec. 31, 1979 – Became a wholly owned subsid. of Hudson Bay Mining and Smelting Co., Ltd.

Whitehorse Gold Corp. (B.C. Nov. 27, 2019)
Feb. 22, 2023 – Name changed to Tincorp Metals Inc. (see FPsurvey - Mines & Energy)

Whitehorse Silver Mines Ltd. (Alta.)
July 31, 1978 – Dissolved.

Whiteknight Acquisitions Inc. (Ont. Dec. 23, 2010)
Aug. 28, 2012 – Name changed to Smart Employee Benefits Inc. pursuant to Qualifying Transaction reverse takeover acquisition of Smart Employee Solutions Inc. ■

WhiteKnight Acquisitions II Inc. (Ont. June 30, 2011)
Sept. 20, 2013 – Name changed to Diamond Estates Wines & Spirits Inc. pursuant to Qualifying Transaction reverse takeover acquisition of Diamond Estates Wines & Spirits Ltd. (see FPsurvey - Industrials)

Whiteknight Acquisitions III Inc. (Ont. Oct. 21, 2013)
Dec. 21, 2015 – Name changed to Delivra Corp. following Qualifying Transaction reverse takeover acquisition of Delivra Inc.; basis 1 new for 3.75 old shs. ■

Whiterock Estates Development Corporation Ltd. (Que. 1971)
Feb. 8, 1972 – Name changed to Whiterock Industries Ltd. (see FPsurvey - Mines & Energy)

Whiterock Real Estate Investment Trust (Man. May 17, 2005)
Mar. 6, 2012 – Acquired by Dundee Real Estate Investment Trust; basis either $16.25 or 0.4729 Dundee trust units for 1 Whiterock trust unit. (see Dundee Real Estate Investment Trust)

Whitesail Mines Ltd. (B.C. 1958)
Dec. 11, 1972 – Amalgamated with Twin Peak Mines Ltd. to form Twin Peak Resources Ltd. (see Twin Peak Resources Ltd.)

Whitewater Capital Corp. (B.C. Dec. 8, 2010)
June 9, 2017 – Name changed to Preferred Dental Technologies Inc. following reverse takeover acquisition of Preferred Dental Implant Corp. ■

Whitewater Gold Mines Limited (Ont. 1972)
1976 – Amalgamated with 3 other cos. to form Berkwater Explorations Ltd.; basis 1.2 new for 1 old sh.

Whitewater Mines, Ltd. (B.C. 1922)
1954 – Dissolved.

Whitewater Resources Ltd. (B.C. Aug. 28, 1985)
Jan. 27, 1995 – Dissolved and struck off register.

Whitey Wilson Oils & Gas Ltd. (B.C. 1967)
Mar. 1973 – Amalgamated with Northern Lights Minerals Ltd. (1 for 3.8) to continue as Northern Lights Minerals Ltd.; basis 1 new Northern Lights sh. for 4.6 old Whitey Wilson shs.

Whitlaur Capital Corp. (Alta. Nov. 20, 1995)
Sept. 15, 1997 – Name changed to Petro Field Industries Inc. ■

Whitmore Resource Corp. (Can. July 23, 1984)
Oct. 15, 2001 – Name changed to Minera Delta Inc. ■

Whitney Bay Resources Inc. (Ont. July 28, 1987)
Feb. 6, 1991 – Name changed to Dover Development Corp. ■

Whitney Porcupine Resources Ltd. (Ont. Mar. 21, 1988)
July 15, 1993 – Name changed to Birch Capital Inc.; basis 1 new for 3 old shs. ■

Whitney Uranium Mines Ltd. (Que. 1954)
Dec. 1972 – Charter cancelled.

Whittier Capital Inc. (Ont. Aug. 19, 1985)
July 10, 1991 – Name changed to Whittier Industries Inc. ■

Whittier Gold Mines Ltd. (Can. 1939)
1946 – Sold property to Ding-How Mines, Ltd. for 325,000 shs.

Whittier Industries Inc. (Ont. Aug. 19, 1985)
Oct. 6, 1991 – Name changed to Tripleplay Sports Group Inc.; basis 1 new for 3 old shs. ■

Whonnock Industries Limited (B.C. May 6, 1963)
Dec. 1, 1979 – Amalgamated in British Columbia to continue with same name.
Jan. 1, 1988 – Name changed to International Forest Products Limited. ■

Wi-LAN Inc. (Alta. May 14, 1992)
Aug. 2, 2007 – Continued into Canada.
June 1, 2017 – Name changed to Quarterhill Inc. (see FPsurvey - Industrials)

Wick Mining Co. Ltd. (B.C. 1968)
Sept. 1973 – Name changed to Carrigan Creek Gold Mines Ltd.

Widescope Resources Inc. (B.C. Sept. 23, 1983)
Apr. 19, 2010 – Name changed to North American Nickel Inc. ■

Widescope Resources Ltd. (B.C. Sept. 23, 1983)
Sept. 17, 1985 – Name changed to Gemini Technology Inc. ■

Widney Oils Ltd. (Alta. 1929)
1939 – Wound up by pay. of final divd.

Wikileaf Technologies Inc. (B.C. Apr. 3, 2018)
Nov. 3, 2021 – Name changed to Cashbox Ventures Ltd. ■

Wilanour Resources Limited (Ont. Apr. 9, 1936)
Jan. 1, 1989 – Amalgamated with Wilmar Mines Ltd. and Annco Mines Ltd. to form new co. with same name Wilanour Resources Limited; basis 1 new for 2.4 Wilmar shs., 1 new for 5.1 Annco shs. and 1 new for 1 Wilanour sh.
Mar. 5, 1998 – Acquired by Goldcorp Inc.; basis 1 Goldcorp cl. A sh. plus 1 cl. A wt. for 6 Wilanour com. shs.

Wilbec Gold Mines Ltd. (Ont. 1945)
May 30, 1960 – Charter cancelled.

Wilcarr Mines Ltd. (Ont. 1944)
1952 – Charter cancelled; no equity for shldrs.

Wilco Mining Company Ltd. (Ont. 1926)
Jan. 13, 1989 – Formed Deak International Resources Corporation in Ontario on amalgamation with Seadrift International Exploration Ltd. (1 for 2) and Deak Ariadne Limited (1 for 1); basis 2 new for 25 old shs. ■

Wild Grizzly Venture Capital Inc. (Can. Oct. 3, 1997)
Aug. 17, 1999 – Name changed to Trans-Canada World Security Corporation on Qualifying Transaction reverse takeover acquisition of Trans-Canada Security Corporation. ■

Wild Horse Industries Inc. (B.C. Feb. 16, 1987)
Dec. 11, 1992 – Name changed to International Hi-Tech Industries Inc.; basis 1 new for 7 old shs. ■

Wild Horse Resources Ltd. (Alta. May 14, 1993)
Apr. 27, 2001 – Name changed to Azure Dynamics Corporation following reverse takeover acquisition of Azure Dynamics Inc.; basis 1 new for 10 old shs. ■

Wild River Resources Inc. (Ont. Feb. 2, 1994 amalg.)
Feb. 19, 1996 – Name changed to Oil Springs Energy Corp.; basis 1 new for 5 old shs. ■

Wild River Resources Ltd. (B.C. Apr. 20, 1994)
Aug. 1, 2006 – Continued into Alberta.
July 2, 2009 – Name changed to Crescent Point Energy Corp. following reverse takeover acquisition of Crescent Point Energy Trust to facilitate the latter's conversion to a corporation. ■

Wild Rose Resources Ltd. (B.C. June 24, 1986)
Dec. 18, 1991 – Name changed to China Cellular Communications Corp. ■

Wild Stream Exploration Inc. (Alta. Mar. 4, 2002)
Mar. 16, 2012 – Acquired by Crescent Point Energy Corp.; basis 0.17 Crescent com. shs. and 1 New Light Oil Focused Junior Exploration Company (newco) com. sh. plus 0.2 newco wts. for 1 Wild Stream com. sh. (see Crescent Point Energy Corp.)

Wildcard Wireless Solutions Inc. (B.C. Dec. 10, 1996)
June 30, 2001 – Continued into Alberta.
June 20, 2003 – Name changed to TransAKT Corp. ■

Wildcat Acquisitions Inc. (Can. May 13, 1987)
Jan. 29, 1996 – Name changed to Forum Resources Inc. ■

Wildcat Exploration Ltd. (Man. Feb. 11, 1998)
May 31, 2016 – Continued into British Columbia.
Oct. 4, 2016 – Name changed to LiCo Energy Metals Inc. ■

Wildcat Petroleum Ltd. (B.C. Mar. 5, 1979)
July 10, 1984 – Name changed to International Wildcat Resources Ltd.; basis 1 new for 3 old shs. ■

Wildcat Silver Corporation (B.C. Aug. 20, 1998)
June 5, 2015 – Name changed to AZ Mining Inc. ■

Wildcat Trading Corp. (B.C. Mar. 5, 1979)
Apr. 21, 1994 – Name changed to Pacific Wildcat Resources Corp. ■

Wildfire Resources Ltd. (B.C. 1981)
Oct. 26, 1989 – Name changed to Crusader Gold Corporation; basis 1 new for 5 old shs. ■

Wildflower Marijuana Inc. (B.C. May 18, 1983)
May 3, 2018 – Name changed to Wildflower Brands Inc. (see FPsurvey - Industrials)

Wildlaw Capital CPC 2 Inc. (Can. June 28, 2011)
July 14, 2014 – Name changed to AcuityAds Holdings Inc. following Qualifying Transaction reverse takeover acquisition of AcuityAds Inc.; basis 1 new for 31.8 old shs. ■

Wildnest Mines Ltd. (Ont. 1954)
June 1961 – Charter cancelled.

Wildor Gold Mines Ltd. (Ont. 1934)
Apr. 9, 1969 – Charter cancelled.

Wildrose Petroleum Ltd. (B.C. 1979)
Sept. 11, 1984 – Name changed to International Wildrose Resources Ltd. ■

Wildrose Resources Ltd. (B.C. May 1, 1997)
July 8, 2008 – Acquired by Skygold Ventures Ltd.; basis 0.82 Skygold com. shs. for 1 Wildrose com. sh.

Wildrose Ventures Inc. (Alta. 1981)
Mar. 13, 1999 – Dissolved and struck from register.

Wildwood Estates Ltd. (B.C. 1964)
Feb. 22, 1971 – Name changed to Gibralter Enterprises Ltd.

Wildwood Petroleum Ltd. (B.C. 1978)
June 16, 1981 – Name changed to Frobisher Resources Ltd. ■

Wiley Oilfield Hauling Ltd. (Alta. 1956)
May 1, 1974 – Amalgamated with Majestic Pipeline Contractors (Alberta) Ltd. to form Majestic Contractors Ltd.

Wilfred Gold Mines Ltd. (Ont. 1947)
Oct. 13, 1958 – Dissolved.

Wilkie Gas Co. Ltd. (Sask.)
1958 – Struck off register.

Wilkie Mines Ltd. (Ont. 1930)
1968 – Charter cancelled.

Willcrest Resources Ltd. (B.C. July 9, 1985)
Nov. 8, 1994 – Name changed to Trincana Resources Ltd.; basis 1 new for 3 old shs. ■

Willecho Mines Ltd. (Ont. 1964)
Dec. 31, 1970 – Former wholly owned subsid. of Willroy Mines Ltd.; absorbed into Willroy and shs. cancelled.

William Leys Mining Corp. Ltd. (Ont. 1947)
1970 – Charter cancelled.

William Multi-Tech Inc. (Que. Apr. 2, 1990 amalg.)
Jan. 27, 2003 – Name changed to Valencia Ventures Inc.; basis 1 new for 100 old shs. ■

William Resources Inc. (Que. Apr. 2, 1990 amalg.)
Aug. 4, 2000 – Name changed to William Multi-Tech Inc. ■

William Stairs, Son & Morrow Limited (N.S. 1926)
June 1975 – Purchased by J.W. Bird & Co. Ltd. Co. now private.
Nov. 15, 1985 – Struck off register.

William Stone Sons, Limited (Ont. 1907)
1956 – Acquired by Canadian Industries Ltd.

Williams Creek Explorations Limited (Ont. June 19, 1946)
July 5, 1990 – Continued into British Columbia.
June 14, 2011 – Name changed to Williams Creek Gold Limited. ■

Williams Creek Gold Limited (B.C. July 5, 1990)
Aug. 17, 2016 – Acquired by Barkerville Gold Mines Ltd.; basis 0.062352572 Barkerville com. shs. for 1 Williams Creek sh.

Williams Creek Gold Quartz Mining Co. Limited (Ont. June 19, 1946)
Mar. 3, 1981 – Dissolved.
Feb. 12, 1987 – Revived.
Aug. 18, 1988 – Name changed to Williams Creek Explorations Limited; basis 1 new for 4 old shs. ■

Williams Creek Placers Ltd. (B.C. 1958)
Nov. 15, 1962 – Dissolved.

Williamson Gold Mines Ltd. (Ont. 1940)
May 1958 – Dissolved.

Williamson Mines Ltd. (Ont. Nov. 5, 1934)
1940 – Assets acquired by Williamson Gold Mines Ltd.; basis 1 new for 4 old shs. (see Williamson Gold Mines Ltd.)

Willingdon Resources Limited (Ont. May 26, 1974)
1988 – Charter revived.
May 26, 1994 – Formed American Telesource International Inc. in Ontario on amalgamation with LatComm International Inc.; basis 1 new for 4 old shs. ■

Williston Wildcatters Oil Corporation (Alta. May 6, 1987)
Nov. 1995 – Petitioned into bankruptcy. Deloitte & Touche Inc. appointed trustee.

Willow Biosciences Inc. (B.C. Apr. 15, 1981)
June 21, 2019 – Continued into Alberta.
June 19, 2025 – Name changed to Atlas Energy Corp.; basis 1 new for 5 old shs. (see FPsurvey - Industrials)

Willow Creek Capital Corp. (B.C. May 15, 2000)
Aug. 24, 2000 – Name changed to Larkfield Capital Corp. ■

Willow Creek Exploration Ltd. (Alta. Dec. 15, 1994)
Jan. 30, 2002 – Name changed to Promotional Products International, Ltd. pursuant to reverse takeover acquisition of Promotional Products International Corporation; basis 2 new for 1 old sh. ■

Willow Lake Mines Ltd. (Ont. 1968)
1977 – Amalgamated with 4 other cos. to form Branly Enterprises Inc.; basis 12 new for 25 old shs.

Willow Resources Ltd. (B.C. July 27, 1983)
July 14, 1992 – Continued into Ontario.
1998 – Continued into Cayman Islands.

Willow Run Mines Inc. (Ont. 1974)
Nov. 5, 1976 – Amalgamated with 7 other cos. to form Wolverine Developments Inc.; basis 4 new for 22 old shs.

Willowcrest Enterprises Ltd. (Alta. June 30, 1987)
Apr. 14, 1993 – Name changed to World Environmental Inc. following reverse takeover acquisition of 542944 Alberta Ltd.; basis 1 new for 4 old shs. ■

Willowstar Capital Inc. (Ont. Aug. 25, 2004)
June 1, 2010 – Name changed to Creso Exploration Inc. pursuant to Qualifying Transaction reverse takeover acquisition of Creso Resources Inc. ■

Willroy Mines Limited (Ont. 1970 amalg.)
Dec. 31, 1982 – Amalgamated with Les Terrains Aurifères Malartic (Québec) Ltée (0.84 for 1), Les Mines-Est Malartic Ltée (0.94 for 1) and Long Lac Minerals Ltd. (1 for 1) to continue as LAC Minerals Ltd.; basis 1.24 new LAC for 1 old Willroy sh. (see LAC Minerals Ltd.)

Willson Stationers & Envelopes Ltd. (Can. 1929)
June 1965 – Controlling shs. purchased by Commodore Business Machines (Canada) Ltd. from Lawson and Jones Ltd. and subsequently sold to Boise Cascade Corp. of Boise, Idaho. In the fall of 1965, control gained by Boise.

Wilmac Mining Corporation Limited (Ont. Aug. 23, 1928)
June 26, 1986 – Name changed to NAP Enterprises Inc. ■

Wilmar Mines Ltd. (Ont. 1958)
Jan. 1, 1989 – Amalgamated with Wilanour Resources Limited and Annco Mines Ltd. to form Wilanour Resources Limited; basis 1 new for 1 Wilanour sh., 1 new for 5.1 Annco shs. and 1 new for 2.4 Wilmar shs. (see Wilanour Resources Limited)

Wilport Gold Mines Ltd. (Ont. 1935)
Nov. 1959 – Charter cancelled.

Wilshire Energy Resources Inc. (Ont. June 20, 1967)
June 16, 1986 – Continued into Alberta. (see FPsurvey - Mines & Energy)

Wilson Red Lake Gold Mines Ltd. (Ont. 1936)
Mar. 1976 – Charter cancelled.

Wiltsey-Coghlan Mines Ltd. (Ont. 1926)
1964 – Name changed to Wilco Mining Company Ltd.; basis 1 new for 5 old shs. ■

Wilwood Gold Mines Ltd. (Ont. 1936)
1970 – Charter cancelled.

Winabie Gold Mines Ltd. (Ont. 1944)
Feb. 14, 1973 – Dissolved.

Winalta Inc. (Alta. Dec. 29, 1986)
Sept. 5, 2014 – Acquired by CERF Incorporated; basis 0.3352 CERF com. shs. for 1 Winalta com. sh. (see CERF Incorporated)

Winalta Shelters Inc. (Alta. Dec. 29, 1986)
June 30, 1999 – Name changed to Winalta Inc. ■

Winchester Diversified Ltd. (Bermuda 1961)
Mar. 1988 – Name changed to Winchester Futures Limited following merger with Winchester Financial Ltd. The new co. created two new ser. of shs.: 1) the Diversified series shs. (iss. to all existing Winchester

Diversified Ltd. shldrs.); and 2) the Orion series shs. (iss. to all existing Winchester Financial Ltd. shldrs.).

Winchester Exploration Ltd. (Ont. 1941)
May 9, 1977 – Dissolved.

Winchester Financial Ltd. (Bermuda 1980)
Mar. 1988 – Through a merger, the company was absorbed into Winchester Diversified Ltd., which subsequently changed its name to Winchester Futures Limited.

The Winchester Group Inc. (Ont. July 22, 1987)
Sept. 7, 2004 – Struck from register and dissolved.

Winchester Larder Mines Ltd. (Ont. 1941)
1964 – Name changed to Winchester Exploration Ltd. ■

Winchester Minerals and Gold Exploration Ltd. (B.C. May 9, 1983)
Oct. 26, 2015 – Dissolved and struck from register.

Winchester Overseas Limited (Bermuda 1980)
Jan. 17, 1984 – Name changed to Winchester Financial Ltd. ■

Winco Mining & Exploration Ltd. (B.C. 1967)
Apr. 4, 1977 – Dissolved and struck off register.

Winco Steak N'Burger Restaurants Limited (Ont. 1969)
1978 – All o/s shs. not acquired by Cara Operations Ltd. in 1976 or subsequently at $9.50 and $7.50 per sh. from controlling shldrs. and the public, respectively, were converted into pfce. stk. and red. at $7.50 per sh.

Wincore Exploration Ltd. (Ont. 1953)
Sept. 21, 1959 – Charter cancelled.

Wind River Energy Corp. (B.C. Oct. 19, 2007)
Apr. 4, 2017 – Dissolved and struck from register.

Wind River Mines Ltd. (B.C. 1970)
Sept. 19, 1977 – Dissolved.

Wind River Resources Ltd. (B.C. Mar. 22, 1983)
May 3, 1993 – Name changed to Richlode Investments Corp.; basis 1 new for 3 old shs. ■

Wind River Resources Ltd. (B.C. Oct. 15, 1986)
Jan. 3, 2008 – Name changed to Teslin River Resources Corp.; basis 1 new for 5 old shs. ■

Windamere Ventures Ltd. (B.C. Aug. 27, 2010)
Feb. 4, 2013 – Name changed to Antofagasta Gold Inc. ■

Windarra Minerals Ltd. (B.C. Mar. 13, 1972)
Oct. 3, 2013 – Acquired by Wesdome Gold Mines Ltd.; basis 0.1 Wesdome shs. for 1 Windarra sh.

Windermere Explorations Ltd. (B.C. 1969)
May 1972 – Amalgamated with Peregrine Explorations Ltd. (6 for 1) to form Barrier Reef Resources Ltd.; basis 1 new Barrier sh. for 2 old Windermere shs.

Windfall Oils & Mines Limited (Ont. 1946)
June 26, 1981 – Name changed to Camreco Inc. ■

Windfire Capital Corp. (Alta. Dec. 10, 2007)
Mar. 11, 2016 – Continued into British Columbia.
Oct. 19, 2018 – Name changed to Global Vanadium Corp. ■

Windflower Mining Ltd. (B.C. Apr. 3, 1973)
Aug. 16, 1994 – Name changed to Energold Mining Ltd.; basis 1 new for 3 old shs. ■

Windigo Pete Explorations Ltd. (Ont. May 9, 1994)
May 7, 1997 – Continued into Yukon.
May 13, 1997 – Name changed to Platexco Inc.; basis 1 new for 10 old shs. ■

Windjammer Power & Gas Ltd. (Alta. Apr. 29, 1976)
Jan. 8, 1988 – Name changed to Meriden Energy Corp.; basis 1 new for 5 old shs. ■

Windmill Enterprises Ltd. (B.C. 1972 amalg.)
July 5, 1984 – Name changed to Todwind Development Corporation; basis 1 new for 10 old shs. ■

Windridge Technology Corp. (B.C. Aug. 5, 1987)
Jan. 19, 2005 – Name changed to Dajin Resources Corp. ■

Windsor-Cobalt Silvers Ltd. (Ont. 1927)
Oct. 21, 1963 – Dissolved.

Windsor Court Apartments Ltd. (unknown)
1971 – Wound up. Distributions made to shldrs. as follows: $11 per sh. on Jan. 7, 1969; $1.25 on May 27, 1969; $0.46 (final) on Jan. 29, 1971.

Windsor Court Holdings Inc. (B.C. Nov. 24, 1980)
Oct. 1, 1996 – Name changed to Teledata Ventures Corp.; basis 1 new for 4.7 old shs. ■

Windsor Energy Corporation (Alta. Aug. 12, 1994)
Oct. 13, 2000 – Delisted from the Canadian Dealing Network. Subsequently dissolved.

Windsor Oils Ltd. (B.C.)
1959 – Struck off register.

Windsor Raceway Inc. (Ont. May 24, 1962)
Sept. 10, 1990 – CTO issued. Subsequently dissolved.

Windsor Resources Inc. (B.C. Aug. 20, 1979)
Jan. 5, 1990 – Dissolved and struck off register.

Windsor Yellowknife Gold Mines Ltd. (Ont. 1944)
1960 – Charter cancelled.

Windstar Energy Ltd. (Alta. Oct. 20, 1995)
Sept. 21, 1998 – Acquired by BelAir Energy Corporation; basis 0.60 new BelAir sh. for 1 old Windstar com. sh. (see BelAir Energy Corporation)

Windstorm Resources Inc. (B.C. July 16, 2009)
July 10, 2012 – Acquired by Blue Sky Uranium Corp.; basis 0.38868 Blue Sky com. shs. for 1 Windstorm com. sh.

Windward Gold Mines Ltd. (Ont. 1946)
1957 – Name changed to Windfall Oils & Mines Limited; basis 1 new for 3 old shs. ■

Windy Arm Mines Ltd. (Ont. 1946)
1961 – Name changed to Utopia Gold Mines Ltd. ■

Windy Hill Mining Corp. Ltd. (Ont. 1958)
Apr. 9, 1975 – Dissolved.

Windy Mountain Explorations Ltd. (Ont. Feb. 23, 1988)
July 3, 2003 – Filed for bankruptcy. Soberman Isenbaum Colomby Tessis Inc. was appointed trustee.

Windy Point Mining Co. Ltd. (Ont. 1956)
Apr. 1961 – Dissolved.

Wine Acquisition Inc. (Ont. July 11, 1933)
Sept. 7, 1993 – Formed T.G. Bright & Co., Limited in Canada. ■

Winex Resources Inc. (B.C. Nov. 19, 1980)
Jan. 8, 1991 – Name changed to Workhorse Manufacturing Inc.; basis 1 new for 2.5 old shs. ■

Winfield Energy Ltd. (Alta. Jan. 22, 1981)
Jan. 13, 1995 – Acquired by Ballistic Energy Corporation; basis 0.235 new Ballistic sh. for 1 old Winfield sh. (see Ballistic Energy Corporation)

Wingait Diversified Limited (Ont. 1944)
July 21, 1971 – Name changed to Aquablast Inc. ■

Wingait Gold Mines Ltd. (Ont. 1944)
1953 – Name changed to Gaitwin Explorations Limited; basis 1 new for 5 old shs. ■

Wingdam & Lightning Creek Mining Co. Ltd. (B.C. 1960)
1969 – In liquidation. Liquidator: A. J. Achtem, 502, 535 W. Georgia St., Vancouver. Assets sold to Consolidated Vigor Mines Ltd.; basis 1 new for 15 old shs. ■

Wingold Mines Limited (Man. 1931)
Wound up.

Wings Ltd. (Can. 1934)
Dec. 1941 – Assets and undertakings acquired by Canadian Pacific Railway Co. Offer of 85¢ per sh. made to shldrs. by CPR.

Winisk River Mines Ltd. (Ont. 1937)
Jan. 1958 – Dissolved.

Winkelmann Countermeasures Inc. (B.C. Sept. 14, 1979)
Feb. 10, 1989 – Dissolved.

Winnebago Mines Limited (Ont. 1970)
Jan. 18, 1972 – Amalgamated with Spar Mines Limited, Lava Minerals Limited and Polex Mines Limited to form a new co. known as Spar Holdings & Explorations Limited; basis 1 new for 3 old shs.

Winnipeg and Central Gas Company (Man. 1953)
Oct. 1958 – Name changed to Greater Winnipeg Gas Company. ■

Winnipeg Electric Co. (Man. 1892)
Oct. 1952 – Manitoba Government took over co. Com. shldrs. received $36.50 in cash for each com. sh. held plus certificate of int. in 1 com. sh. and $1.75 princ. amt. 5% debenture of Greater Winnipeg Transit, plus 1 com. sh. of Winnipeg Central Gas (name of which changed to Greater Winnipeg Gas Co.). All o/s 5% noncum. $100 par pref. shs. red. at $105 on June 30, 1955. First mtge. bds. o/s were not guar. by Man. Govt. but s.f. payments were incr. to ensure retirement of approx. half existing bds. by maturity in 1971.

Winnipeg Gold Mines Ltd. (Man. 1915)
Mar. 31, 1976 – Dissolved.

Winnipeg River Tin Mines Limited (Can. Aug. 2, 1929; via letters patent)
Mar. 28, 1967 – Name changed to Spacemaster Minerals Ltd. ■

Winnipeg Supply & Fuel Company, Limited (Man. 1904)
1975 – 97.31% of o/s shs. acquired by Bakham Holdings Ltd., a subsid. of Hambro Canada Ltd., at $9.00 per sh. under an offer to purchase all com. shs.

Winoga Patricia Gold Mines Ltd. (Ont. 1935)
1958 – Charter cancelled.

Winora Gold Mines Ltd. (Ont. 1945)
May 1955 – Name changed to Rockwin Mines Ltd.; basis 1 new for 3.5 old shs. ■

Winrock Resources Inc. (B.C. Aug. 16, 2010)
Apr. 9, 2014 – Name changed to Newnote Financial Corp. ■

Winslow Consolidated Ltd. (B.C. 1934)
Oct. 23, 1958 – Struck off register.

Winslow Gold Corp. (B.C. Jan. 31, 1978)
Dec. 21, 2000 – Name changed to Winslow Resources Inc.; basis 1 new for 5 old shs. ■

Winslow Resources Inc. (B.C. Jan. 31, 1978)
Sept. 7, 2007 – Acquired by DualEx Energy International Inc.; basis 0.44 DualEx units for 1 Winslow sh. (see DualEx Energy International Inc.)

Winspear Diamonds Inc. (B.C. Jan. 13, 1997)
Sept. 8, 2000 – Acquired by De Beers Canada Holdings Ltd. for $5.00 per sh.

Winspear Resources Ltd. (B.C. Sept. 5, 1984)
Jan. 13, 1997 – Amalgamated with Antler Resources Ltd. (2.5 new for 1 old sh.) to form a new co. also known as Winspear Resources Ltd.; basis 1 new for 1 old sh. (see Winspear Resources Ltd.)

Winspear Resources Ltd. (B.C. Jan. 13, 1997)
June 30, 2000 – Name changed to Winspear Diamonds Inc. ■

Winstaff Ventures Ltd. (Ont. 1936)
July 11, 1995 – Formed Romarco Minerals Inc. in Ontario on amalgamation with Romarco Holdings Inc., constituting a reverse takeover by Romarco; basis 1 new for 1 Romarco sh. and 1 new for 25 Winstaff shs. ■

Winstar Resources Ltd. (Alta. Jan. 2, 1996)
June 27, 2013 – Acquired by Kulczyk Oil Ventures Inc.; either Cdn$2.50, subject to a max. of Cdn$35,000,000 or 7.555 Kulczyk shs. for 1 Winstar sh. Subsequently Kulczuk Oil Ventures Inc. changed its name to Serinus Energy Inc.

Winston Capital Group Inc. (Alta. Oct. 22, 2018)
Mar. 31, 2022 – Name changed to Merida Minerals Inc. pursuant to the Qualifying Transaction reverse takeover acquisition of (old) Merida Minerals Inc. and concurrent amalgamation of (old) Merida with wholly owned 2797200 Ontario Inc. ■

Winston Gold Mining Corp. (Man. Jan. 31, 2013)
Aug. 24, 2017 – Continued into British Columbia.
Sept. 1, 2017 – Name changed to Winston Gold Corp. (see FPsurvey - Mines & Energy)

Winston Mines Ltd. (Ont. 1965)
1968 – Assets sold to Mission Financial Corp. Ltd.; basis 0.02261 Mission shs. for one Winston sh.

Winston Mining Corp. (unknown)
Jan. 1957 – Merged into Westore Mines Ltd.; basis 1 new for 3 old shs.

Winston Resources Inc. (B.C. Oct. 14, 2011 amalg.)
July 17, 2020 – Name changed to Vegaste Technologies Corp. pursuant to the reverse takeover acquisition of PlantX Life Inc.; basis 1 new for 10 old shs. ■

Winston Resources Ltd. (B.C. 1981)
Nov. 19, 1987 – Name changed to Sandpiper Oil & Gas Limited. ■

Winter Soldier Capital Corp. (B.C. July 6, 2018)
Nov. 26, 2020 – Formed MYND Life Sciences Inc. in British Columbia pursuant to the reverse takeover acquisition of and amalgamation with (old) MYND Life Sciences Inc. (deemed acquiror); basis 1 new com. sh. for 1 com. sh. of both Winter Soldier and (old) MYND. (see FPsurvey - Industrials)

Winterburn Oil and Gas Ltd. (Alta. Nov. 16, 1993)
May 2, 2002 – Struck from registry and dissolved.

Wintercrest Resources Ltd. (Alta. Feb. 16, 1987)
Nov. 17, 2009 – Name changed to Mahdia Gold Corp.; basis 1 new for 2 old shs. ■

Winteroad Resources Limited (Ont. Sept. 12, 1978)
Sept. 25, 1995 – Formed PenStar Wirecom, Ltd. in Ontario on amalgamation with PenStar Wirecom, Ltd., constituting a reverse takeover by PenStar; basis 1 new for 1 PenStar sh. and 1 new for 3 Winteroad shs. ■

Winters Gold Hedley Ltd. (B.C. Sept. 4, 1987)
Aug. 26, 1993 – Name changed to Regal Gold Corporation; basis 1 new for 2.5 old shs. ■

Wintertherm Corporation (Alta. Feb. 16, 1987)
Aug. 20, 1997 – Name changed to Wintercrest Resources Ltd.; basis 1 new for 8 old shs. ■

Wintertide Ventures Inc. (B.C. Apr. 27, 2006)
Sept. 30, 2021 – Name changed to Total Helium Ltd. ■

Wintraysan Capital Corp (Alta. Sept. 5, 2006)
Jan. 8, 2010 – Name changed to Orion Oil & Gas Corporation pursuant to Qualifying Transaction reverse takeover acquisition of Orion Oil & Gas Ltd. which amalgamated with wholly owned 1498513 Alberta Ltd. to continue as Orion Oil & Gas Inc., which was subsequently amalgamated into the co.; basis 1 new for 2 old shs. ■

Winwell Ventures Inc. (B.C. June 14, 2006)
June 7, 2017 – Name changed to Contact Gold Corp. and continued into Nevada pursuant to reverse takeover acquisition of Carlin Opportunities Inc.; basis 1 new for 8 old shs. ■

Winwest Oil and Gas Lands Ltd. (Ont. 1952)
Nov. 21, 1958 – Name changed to Winwest Oil & Mining Ltd.

Winzen International Inc. (B.C. Dec. 1, 1986 amalg.)
Jan. 2, 2003 – Name changed to Winzen Properties Inc. (see FPsurvey - Industrials)

Wirbac Resources Inc. (Alta. Feb. 28, 1995 amalg.)
Sept. 12, 2001 – Name changed to Virtus Energy Ltd.; basis 1 new for 4 old shs. ■

Wired City Communications Limited (Can. 1971)
Oct. 31, 1982 – Amalgamated with CableNet Limited to form a new private co. under the CableNet name.

Wireless Capital Corp. (Alta. Mar. 29, 2000)
July 15, 2003 – Name changed to Elkwater Resources Ltd. following Qualifying Transaction non-arm's length acquisition of approximately 35 eastern Alberta gas wells and units. ■

Wireless Matrix Corporation (Can. Apr. 29, 1996 amalg.)
Dec. 18, 2013 – Liquidated for US$0.56 per sh. on the first distribution dated April 9, 2013 and US$0.03723 per sh. on final distribution dated Nov. 27, 2013.

Wireless One Inc. (Can. Apr. 12, 2000)
Sept. 9, 2002 – Wound up following Qualifying Transaction conversion to a new investment trust named Lanesborough Real Estate Investment Trust; basis 1 new Lanesborough trust unit for 10 old Wireless One com. shs.

Wireless2 Technologies Inc. (B.C. May 4, 1984)
Apr. 15, 2010 – Name changed to Nanotech Security Corp. ■

Wirlwind Resources Ltd. (B.C. 1983)
Dec. 13, 1991 – Name changed to Spirit Resources Ltd.; basis 1 new for 3 old shs. ■

WisCan Resources Inc. (B.C. Mar. 30, 1990 amalg.)
Feb. 9, 1995 – Plan of Arrangement amalgamation with private co. Minera Yamana Inc. to form a new company (incorporated in Canada) known as Yamana Resources Inc. WisCan transferred all assets and liabs. to wholly owned subsid. Moss Resources Inc.; basis 1 new Moss com. sh. and 1/15 new Yamana com. sh. for 1 old WisCan com. sh. (see Moss Resources Inc.; Yamana Resources Inc.)

Wisco of Canada Limited (B.C. 1983)
Oct. 20, 1987 – Name changed to Teleguard Systems International, Inc. ■

Wisconsin Mining Co. Ltd. (Que. 1950)
Nov. 1972 – Name changed to Joubi Mining Corporation Limited; basis 1 new for 3.5 old shs. ■

Wise Boy Resources Inc. (B.C. June 7, 1983)
Apr. 20, 1992 – Name changed to Hatthaway-Matheson Enterprises Inc.; basis 1 new for 7 old shs. ■

Wise Card Consolidated Inc. (Alta. Dec. 19, 1986)
June 1, 1993 – Struck off register.

Wise Card Holdings Inc. (Alta. Dec. 19, 1986)
Dec. 31, 1990 – Name changed to Wise Card Consolidated Inc.; basis 1 new for 2 old shs. ■

Wise Oakwood Ventures Inc. (Alta. Jan. 9, 2013)
Apr. 21, 2016 – Name changed to Zomedica Pharmaceuticals Corp. following Qualifying Transaction reverse takeover of ZoMedica Pharmaceuticals Inc.; basis 1 new for 2.5 old shs. ■

Wise Stores Inc. (Que. 1949)
Jan. 1995 – Declared bankrupt. Ernst & Young Inc. was appointed trustee.

Wise Wood Corporation (Alta. June 9, 2000)
Jan. 11, 2005 – Name changed to Diamond Tree Energy Ltd. following reverse takeover acquisition of Diamond Tree Resources Ltd.; basis 1 new for 10 old shs. ■

Wise Wood Energy Ltd. (Alta. June 9, 2000)
July 9, 2003 – Name changed to Wise Wood Corporation. ■

Wisik Gold Mines Ltd. (Ont. June 17, 1936)
Acquired by Kiena Gold Mines Ltd.; basis 1 new for 5 old shs. (see Kiena Gold Mines Limited)

Wisper Inc. (Alta. Sept. 23, 1992)
Apr. 7, 2004 – Name changed to ECLIPS Inc.; basis 1 new for 10 old shs. ■

Wittke Inc. (Alta. Feb. 7, 1994)
Oct. 4, 2002 – Plan of Arrangement with Illinois-based Federal Signal Corporation; basis either $6.25 and 0.2005 Federal com. shs., or 0.4010 Federal com. shs. for 1 old Wittke com. sh.

Witwatersrand Consolidated Gold Resources Limited (South Africa Dec. 11, 2002)
Apr. 15, 2014 – Acquired by Sibanye Gold Limited; basis R11.55 (Cdn$1.20) cash per sh.

Wix Corporation Limited (Ont. 1942)
Dec. 1, 1981 – Name changed to Wix Inc. ■

Wix Inc. (Ont. 1942)
Nov. 28, 1984 – All o/s publicly owned com. shs. acquired by Hayes-Dana Inc. at $10.50 per sh. (see Hayes-Dana Inc.)

Wizan Productions Inc. (B.C. 1984)
1987 – Continued into Delaware.

Wizard Lake Petroleum Corp. (Ont. 1967)
Feb. 9, 1994 – Name changed to KING Products Inc.; basis 1 new for 10 old shs. ■

Wkay Resources Inc. (B.C. July 4, 1978)
Oct. 18, 1990 – Name changed to Magnatron International Corp. ■

Woco Gold Developments Ltd. (Ont. 1937)
1955 – Charter cancelled.

Woden Venture Capital Corporation (Can. Feb. 5, 2010)
Sept. 25, 2020 – Name changed to Geekco Technologies Corporation pursuant to the Qualifying Transaction reverse takeover acquisition of Geekco Technologies Inc.; basis 1 new for 4 old shs. (see FPsurvey - Industrials)

Wokingham Capital Corporation (Can. July 31, 1968)
July 18, 1994 – Name changed to Coniston Capital Corporation. ■

Wolf Acquisition Corp. (Ont. Jan. 25, 2018)
Mar. 16, 2021 – Name changed to Bald Eagle Gold Corp. pursuant to the Qualifying Transaction reverse takeover acquisition of Frontera Gold Corp. and CX One Inc., and concurrent amalgamation of Frontera and CX with wholly owned 12590425 Canada Inc., to continue as Be Gold Canada Inc.; basis 1.2 new for 1 old sh. ■

Wolf Acquisitions 2.0 Corp. (B.C. Apr. 16, 2021)
Dec. 21, 2021 – Name changed to DiagnaMed Holdings Corp. (see FPsurvey - Industrials)

Wolf Capital Corp. (Alta. July 28, 2003)
July 21, 2006 – Formed Mirage Energy Ltd. in Alberta on Qualifying Transaction reverse takeover acquisition of and amalgamation with Mirage Energy Ltd. ■

Wolf Creek Mines Ltd. (B.C. 1967)
July 1971 – Name changed to Bristol Developments Ltd. ■

Wolf Resource Development Corp. (Ont. June 14, 2013)
Mar. 9, 2015 – Name changed to Fura Emeralds Inc. ■

Wolf River Resources Ltd. (B.C. 1984)
June 8, 1989 – Name changed to Interchem (N.A.) Industries Inc. (see FPsurvey - Industrials)

Wolfden Resources Inc. (Ont. Oct. 5, 1995)
June 18, 2007 – Acquired by Zinifex Canadian Enterprises Inc., a wholly owned subsidiary of Zinifex Limited; basis $3.81 for 1 old Wolfden com. sh.

Wolfe Lake Mines Ltd. (Ont. 1939)
Apr. 22, 1965 – Dissolved.

Wolfeye Resource Corp. (B.C. Apr. 26, 2007)
Oct. 12, 2016 – Name changed to LexaGene Holdings Inc. following reverse takeover acquisition of Bionomics Diagnostics Inc. (see FPsurvey - Industrials)

Wolfpack Brands Corporation (B.C. June 4, 2007)
Mar. 6, 2020 – Name changed to Wolf's Den Capital Corp. ■

Wolfpack Capital Corp. (Alta. Sept. 17, 2012)
Dec. 1, 2016 – Name changed to Pulse Oil Corp. in anticipation of Qualifying Transaction reverse takeover acquisition of Hydrate Resources Corp. (see FPsurvey - Mines & Energy)

Wolfpack Gold Corp. (B.C. Oct. 30, 2009)
Aug. 15, 2014 – Name changed to enCore Energy Corp. (see FPsurvey - Mines & Energy)

Wolfpack Yellowknife Mines Ltd. (Ont. 1946)
Dec. 23, 1965 – Dissolved.

Wolf's Den Capital Corp. (B.C. June 4, 2007)
Jan. 6, 2021 – Name changed to Danavation Technologies Corp. pursuant to the reverse takeover acquisition of Danavation Technologies Inc.; basis 1 new for 30 old shs. ■

Wolfsteve Mining and Development Co. Ltd. (Ont. 1942)
Feb. 1947 – Name changed to Amporco Mining and Development Co. Ltd. ■

Wollasco Minerals Inc. (Ont. June 20, 1995)
Dec. 16, 2004 – Name changed to Gold Port Resources Ltd.; basis 1 new for 8 old shs. ■

Wollaston Lake Mines Ltd. (B.C. 1968)
1971 – Name changed to Comaplex Resources International Ltd.; basis 1 new for 4 old shs. ■

Wollaston Porcupine Gold Mines Ltd. (Ont. 1946)
1956 – Charter cancelled.

Wolverine Developments Inc. (Ont. 1976 amalg.)
Apr. 1978 – Amalgamated with Lumsden Building Corp. Inc. and others under the Lumsden name; basis 5 new for 11 old shs.

Wolverine Energy and Infrastructure Inc. (Alta. Dec. 29, 2017)
Dec. 8, 2023 – Placed into receivership and FTI Consulting Canada Inc. was appointed receiver.

Wolverine Energy Corp. (Alta. Mar. 28, 1995)
Nov. 29, 2000 – Formed Atlas Energy Ltd. in Alberta on amalgamation with Atlas Energy Ltd., constituting a

reverse takeover by Atlas; basis 1 new for 1 Atlas sh. and 1 new for 8 Wolverine shs. ■

Wolverine Minerals Corp. (B.C. June 7, 2004)
Feb. 21, 2018 – Name changed to Aloro Mining Corp. (see FPsurvey - Mines & Energy)

Wolverine Partners Corp. (Can. Nov. 22, 2017)
Oct. 8, 2020 – Name changed to Gage Growth Corp. ■

Wolverton Lake Gold Mines Ltd. (Ont. 1945)
Dec. 7, 1977 – Charter cancelled.
Oct. 6, 1980 – Charter revived.
Jan. 13, 1981 – Name changed to Nearctic Resources Inc. ■

Woman Lake Goldfields Development (Ont. 1927)
1947 – Sold properties to Dougron Gold Mines Ltd.; shs. exchanged on 1 new for 5 old basis. (see Dougron Gold Mines Ltd.)

Woman River Gold Mines Ltd. (Ont. Oct. 1934)
1951 – Charter cancelled.

Wonder Marine Resources Ltd. (B.C. July 21, 1983)
Dec. 22, 1995 – Dissolved and struck off register.

The Wonderfilm Media Corporation (B.C. June 1, 2015)
Apr. 1, 2020 – Name changed to Appreciated Media Holdings Inc. ■

Wondr Gaming Corp. (B.C. June 24, 1999)
Apr. 14, 2022 – Name changed to Gamelancer Gaming Corp. pursuant to the acquisition of Gamelancer, Inc. ■

Wood Alexander Limited (Ont. 1950)
1974 – Macleod Steadman Inc., a wholly owned subsid. of Gambles Canada Ltd., incr. its holding in Wood to 93% of com. shs. and offered to acquire remaining com. shs. at $3.50 per sh. By May 1976, Wood was approx. 96% owned by Macleod and operated as a division of Macleod.

Wood Composite Technologies Inc. (Alta. Apr. 4, 1996)
June 4, 2018 – Name changed to Boardwalktech Software Corp. and continued into British Columbia following reverse takeover acquisition of Boardwalktech, Inc.; basis 1 new for 410 old shs. (see FPsurvey - Industrials)

Wood-Croesus Gold Mines Limited (Ont. Nov. 16, 1925)
Jan. 1, 2010 – Amalgamated with Union Gold Inc., Golden Harker Explorations Limited, Milestone Exploration Limited and Sheldon-Larder Mines Limited to form Jubilee Gold Inc.; basis 0.367 Jubilee sh. for 1 Wood-Croesus sh., 0.557 Jubilee sh. for 1 Union Gold sh., 0.393 Jubilee sh. for 1 Golden Harker sh., 1.749 Jubilee shs. for 1 Milestone sh. and 0.269 Jubilee sh. for 1 Sheldon-Larder sh. (see Jubilee Gold Inc.)

Woodbridge Energy Ltd. (B.C. Sept. 14, 2005)
June 15, 2009 – Together with Chinook Capital Corp., Bowram Energy Inc. and Fortriu Capital Corp., exchanged their respective net cash for shares of Terrace Resources Inc., all Capital Pool Companies, and each of Chinook, Bowram, Fortriu and Woodbridge, subsequently dissolved; basis 1 Terrace sh. for 0.56 Chinook shs., 1 Terrace sh. for 0.53 Bowram shs., 1 Terrace sh. for 0.55 Fortriu shs. and 1 Terrace sh. for 0.43 Woodbridge shs. (see Terrace Resources Inc.)

Woodbridge Ventures Inc. (Ont. May 31, 2017)
Sept. 29, 2020 – Name changed to Jack Nathan Medical Corp. pursuant to Qualifying Transaction reverse takeover acquisition of Jack Nathan Medical Inc.; basis 1 new for 3 old shs. (see FPsurvey - Industrials)

Woodbury Mines Ltd. (B.C. 1950)
Dec. 1960 – Dissolved.

Woodco Resources Inc. (Alta. Sept. 20, 1993)
Jan. 14, 1998 – Continued into Yukon.
Jan. 15, 1998 – Name changed to Anatolia Minerals Development Limited pursuant to reverse takeover acquisition of Anatolia Minerals Development Corp. ■

Woodford Investments Ltd. (Can. 1933)
1979 – All o/s cl. B and C shs. acquired by Brameda Resources Ltd.

Woodford Royalty Corporation Ltd. (Can. 1933)
Nov. 1967 – Name changed to Woodford Investments Ltd. ■

Woodgreen Copper Mines Ltd. (Ont. 1948)
1959 – Name changed to Consolidated Woodgreen Mines Ltd.; basis 1 new for 8 old shs. ■

Woodhall Mines Ltd. (Ont. 1943)
1950 – Property sold to Northern Barite Development Co. Ltd. and to Whitby Ore Mills, Ltd.; basis 1 Northern Barite sh. for 2 free Woodhall shs. and 1 Northern Barite sh. for 4 escrowed Woodhall shs.

Woodhouse Gas & Oil Ltd. (Ont. Feb. 23, 1932)
1935 – Name changed to Gasfinders & Producers Syndicate. ■

Woodland Mining & Development Ltd. (Ont. 1965)
1967 – Merged into W. G. N. Explorations Ltd.; basis 1 new for 10 old shs. ■

Woodridge Resources Inc. (B.C. 1985)
Oct. 13, 1993 – Name changed to Telemac Cellular International Inc. ■

Woodrose Corporation (Alta. Apr. 28, 1964)
Nov. 4, 2016 – Name changed to Woodrose Venture Corporation. ■

Woodrose Venture Corporation (Alta. Apr. 28, 1964)
Nov. 7, 2016 – Continued into British Columbia.
Sept. 27, 2017 – Name changed to Novoheart Holdings Inc. following reverse takeover acquisition of Novoheart Holdings Limited; basis 1 new for 3.5687845 old shs. ■

Woodruff Capital Management Inc. (Ont. Dec. 13, 2002)
July 11, 2006 – Name changed to Cogitore Resources Inc. ■

Woods & Walker Ltd. (Ont. 1923)
May 1946 – Name changed to Gordon Mackay & Stores Limited. ■

Woods Manufacturing Co. Ltd. (Can. 1912)
Apr. 17, 1963 – Shldrs. approved winding up of the co. and distribution of its assets. The cl. A 4% pref. shs. were exch. for equal amount of cl. A shs. of Wabasso Cotton Co. Ltd. Distribution to com. shldrs. of Woods consisted of 32 cl. B and 3 com. shs. Wabasso, plus 50 for each com. sh. Woods held.

Woodsreef Minerals Ltd. (Ont. Sept. 23, 1957)
Mar. 11, 1981 – Name changed to Transpacific Asbestos Inc.; basis 1 new for 5 old shs. ■

Woodview Corporation (Ont. 1984)
July 31, 2002 – Privatized for 15¢ per sh.

Woodward Stores Limited (B.C. 1947)
June 13, 1984 – Name changed to Woodward's Limited. ■

Woodward Stores (1947) Ltd. (B.C. 1947)
Apr. 1964 – Name changed to Woodward Stores Limited. ■

Woodward's Limited (B.C. 1947)
June 7, 1993 – Acquired by Zellers Inc. for 35¢ per sh.

Woodway Resources Limited (Ont. Nov. 12, 1981)
July 17, 1987 – Name changed to Bridge Integrated Technologies Inc. ■

Wool Bay Gold Mines Ltd. (Ont. 1945)
Oct. 28, 1957 – Charter cancelled.

Wool Combing Corporation of Canada Ltd. (Can. 1940)
Dec. 21, 1962 – Assets sold and distribution of proceeds to shldrs. on basis of $14.56 per com. sh.

Woolworth Corporation (N.Y. 1911)
June 12, 1998 – Name changed to Venator Group, Inc.

Work Horse Capital & Strategic Acquisitions Ltd. (Ont. Dec. 30, 2008)
Feb. 17, 2011 – Name changed to LeoNovus Inc. (see FPsurvey - Industrials)

Workbrain Corporation (Ont. Nov. 10, 1999)
June 5, 2007 – Amalgamated with 231365 Ontario Ltd., a subsidiary of Infor Global Solutions European Finance S.A.R.L.; basis $12.50 per com. sh.

WorkGroup Designs Ltd. (Alta. Apr. 12, 2000)
Oct. 2, 2008 – Struck from registry and dissolved.

Workhorse Manufacturing Inc. (B.C. Nov. 19, 1980)
Sept. 4, 1992 – Name changed to Koala Beverages Limited; basis 1 new for 3 old shs. ■

Workplace Technology Dividend Fund (Ont.)
May 17, 2023 – Merged into Middlefield Innovation Dividend ETF; basis 0.46876552 Middlefield Innovation ETF units for 1 Workplace Technology fund unit.

World Aquathemes Limited (Alta. May 27, 1963)
Sept. 2, 1986 – Name changed to Telesis Corporation Inc. ■

World Cement Industries Inc. (B.C. Nov. 23, 1959)
July 5, 1989 – Name changed to Topper Gold Corporation; basis 1 new for 4 old shs. ■

World Class Extractions Inc. (B.C. Oct. 24, 2004)
Feb. 27, 2023 – Name changed to Stock Trend Capital Inc. (see FPsurvey - Industrials)

World Color Press Inc. (Can. Feb. 23, 1989)
July 6, 2010 – Acquired by Quad/Graphics, Inc. pursuant to plan of arrangement; basis US$0.56 plus 0.1254 Quad/Graphics cl. A shs. for 1 World com. sh. and US$8.86 for 1 World Pref. sh.

World Environmental Inc. (Alta. June 30, 1987)
Mar. 13, 1999 – Struck from register and dissolved.

World Financial Split Corp. (Ont. Dec. 5, 2003)
July 5, 2024 – Name changed to Premium Global Income Split Corp.; basis 1 new for 4 old shs. (see FPsurvey - Industrials)

World Heart Corporation (Ont. Apr. 1, 1996)
Dec. 14, 2005 – Continued into Canada.
Jan. 1, 2010 – Continued into Delaware.
Aug. 2, 2012 – Acquired by an indirect subsid. of HeartWare International, Inc.

World Mahjong Limited (B.C. Feb. 15, 1985 amalg.)
Mar. 29, 2018 – Name changed to Avalon Blockchain Inc. ■

World Outfitters Corporation Safari Nordik (Can. May 30, 1988)
Mar. 28, 2015 – Dissolved and struck from register.
Dec. 10, 2020 – Restored to registry. (see FPsurvey - Industrials)

World Point Terminals Inc. (Can. July 6, 1942)
June 10, 2010 – Continued into Nova Scotia.
July 6, 2010 – Privatized by way of amalg. with World Point Holdings, Inc. to continue as World Point Inc. for $19.90 per sh.

World Power Bike Inc. (B.C. Oct. 24, 1980)
Mar. 13, 2000 – Name changed to Parkside 2000 Resources Corporation; basis 1 new for 7 old shs. ■

World Sports Merchandising Inc. (Ont. Aug. 20, 1986)
Mar. 9, 2000 – Name changed to World Sales & Merchandising Inc. (see FPsurvey - Industrials)

World Strategic Yield Fund (Ont. Oct. 30, 1997)
Aug. 14, 2002 – Wound up. Distribution to be $13.664 per unit.

World Tec Industries Inc. (B.C. 1987)
Aug. 19, 1994 – Name changed to Solucorp Industries Ltd. (see FPsurvey - Industrials)

World Wide Co-Generation Inc. (Ont. Oct. 30, 1996 amalg.)
July 17, 2007 – Name changed to World Wide Inc.; basis 1 new for 20 old shs. ∎

World Wide Inc. (Ont. Oct. 30, 1996 amalg.)
Jan. 28, 2019 – Name changed to Abacus Health Products, Inc. following reverse takeover acquisition of (old) Abacus Health Products, Inc. and concurrent amalgamation of (old) Abacus with wholly owned World Wide Subco Inc. ∎

World Wide Interactive Discs Inc. (Ont. Oct. 30, 1996 amalg.)
Feb. 13, 2004 – Name changed to World Wide Co-Generation Inc. ∎

World Wide Minerals Limited (B.C. May 13, 1980)
Feb. 22, 1995 – Continued into Ontario. (see FPsurvey - Mines & Energy)

World Wide Oil & Gas Inc. (Alta. Jan. 31, 1962)
Dec. 21, 1990 – Continued into British Columbia. (see World Wide Oil & Gas Inc.)
June 25, 1991 – Amalgamated with Massif Minerals Corporation to continue with the new name World Wide Oil & Gas Inc.; basis 1.178 new cl. A sh. for 1 cl. A and cl. B com. sh. plus 1 new cl. F pfd. sh. for 1 cl. F pfd. sh. (see World Wide Oil & Gas Inc.)

World Wide Oil & Gas Inc. (B.C. June 25, 1991 amalg.)
Mar. 2, 1998 – Delisted from the Vancouver Stock Exchange. Subsequently dissolved and struck from register.

World Wide Oil & Gas (Western) Ltd. (Alta. Jan. 31, 1962)
Feb. 4, 1986 – Name changed to World Wide Oil & Gas Inc. ∎

World Wide Warranty Inc. (Alta. Mar. 6, 1998)
Aug. 30, 2004 – Name changed to W3 Solutions Inc. ∎

World Wise Resources Inc. (B.C. Jan. 26, 1987)
Sept. 27, 1994 – Name changed to World Wise Technologies Inc. ∎

World Wise Technologies Inc. (B.C. Jan. 26, 1987)
Apr. 9, 1998 – Continued into Ontario. (see FPsurvey - Industrials)

WorldPlus Ventures Ltd. (B.C. Apr. 29, 1987)
June 7, 2007 – Name changed to New Global Ventures Ltd.; basis 1 new for 3 old shs. ∎

Worlds Online Inc. (Del. Jan. 25, 2011)
May 11, 2017 – Name changed to MariMed Inc. (see FPsurvey - Industrials)

Worldwide Energy Company Ltd. (Alta. Oct. 16, 1952)
Jan. 7, 1983 – Name changed to Canadian Worldwide Energy Limited; basis 3 new for 1 old sh. ∎

Worldwide Equities Limited (Ont. 1974)
1983 – Continued into British Columbia.
Dec. 20, 1989 – Amalgamated into Global Strategy Financial. All outstanding cl. A shs. redeemed for units of Global Strategy Fund or Global Strategy RRSP Fund, at the shldrs. option.

Worldwide Fiber Inc. (Alta. Feb. 5, 1998)
Aug. 17, 1999 – Continued into Canada.
Mar. 8, 2000 – Name changed to 360networks inc. ∎

Worldwide Ginseng Corporation (Can. May 27, 1987)
June 10, 2004 – Dissolved.

Worldwide Marijuana Inc. (B.C. May 11, 2011)
Aug. 15, 2017 – Name changed to Endocan Solutions Inc. ∎

Worldwide Monitoring Corporation (Del. 1985)
1987 – Continued into British Columbia. (see FPsurvey - Industrials)

Worldwide Promotional Management Inc. (Nev. Oct. 29, 1999)
Jan. 27, 2009 – Continued into British Columbia.
Oct. 19, 2011 – Name changed to Black Smoker Ventures Inc. ∎

Worldwide Technologies Inc. (B.C. Aug. 9, 1984)
Dec. 26, 2005 – Struck from registry and dissolved.

Worthing Industries Inc. (Alta. Aug. 31, 1990)
Nov. 25, 1996 – Name changed to United Tex-Sol Mines Inc. following acquisition of Nighthawk North Exploration Inc.; basis 1 new for 4 old shs. ∎

Worthington Mines Ltd. (Ont. 1955)
Aug. 9, 1972 – Charter cancelled.

Worthington Resources Corporation (B.C. Apr. 6, 1989)
Oct. 18, 1993 – Name changed to Canadian Imperial Ginseng Products Ltd. ∎

Wosk's Ltd. (B.C. 1939)
1980 – In 1970's, purchase offer of $8.00 per sh. made to minority shldrs. by StanKen Investments Ltd. By early 80's, virtually all o/s shs. acquired under the offer and the co. was deemed to be a private non-reporting co.

Wotan Capital Inc. (Can. Aug. 10, 1998)
Jan. 25, 2002 – Formed International Technologies Corporation in Canada following reverse takeover Qualifying Transaction amalgamation with International Technologies Corp.; basis 1 new for 2.5 old shs. ∎

Woulfe Mining Corp. (B.C. Nov. 1, 2007)
Sept. 14, 2015 – Acquired by Almonty Industries Inc.; basis 0.1029 Almonty com. shs. for 1 Woulfe com. sh.

Wow Unlimited Media Inc. (B.C. Aug. 1, 2008 amalg.)
Apr. 11, 2022 – Acquired by Genius Brands International Inc.; basis Cdn$1.169 cash and 0.271 Genius Brands com. shs. for 1 Wow Unlimited sh.

Wrangler West Capital Corp. (Alta. Mar. 17, 2000)
Jan. 20, 2003 – Name changed to Wrangler West Energy Corp. pursuant to reverse takeover acquisition of Kerr Energy Limited; basis 1 new for 7 old shs. ∎

Wrangler West Energy Corp. (Alta. Mar. 17, 2000)
Mar. 17, 2014 – Amalgamated with 981443 Alberta Ltd., a wholly owned subsid. of Trident Exploration Corp., to continue as Trident Exploration (WX) Corp.; basis $0.2552 cash per sh.

Wrapture Limited (Alta. Apr. 24, 1998)
Feb. 28, 2002 – Name changed to Tallagium Corporation following reverse takeover acquisition of MegaDox Corporation. (see FPsurvey - Industrials)

Wren Resources Ltd. (B.C. Mar. 12, 1984)
Oct. 21, 1987 – Name changed to Control Science Corporation and continued into Canada. ∎

Wright-Hargreaves Mines Limited (Ont. 1916)
July 29, 1985 – Amalgamated with Lake Shore Mines Limited (2.871 for 1), LAC Minerals Ltd. (1 for 1) and Little Long Lac Gold Mines Limited (2.377 for 1) to continue as LAC Minerals Ltd.; basis 0.498 LAC shs. for 1 Wright sh. (see LAC Minerals Ltd.)

Wright-Rouyn Gold Ltd. (Ont. 1939)
May 24, 1980 – Charter cancelled.

Wrightbar Mines Ltd. (Que. 1969)
Nov. 3, 1994 – Amalgamated with Charlim Explorations Ltd. and 3063780 Canada Inc., a wholly owned subsid. of Wrightbar, to form Lithos Corporation; basis 1 new for 2.6 Wrightbar shs. plus 1 Puiseaux Resources Inc. sh. for 10 Wrightbar shs. (see Lithos Corporation)

wwbroadcast.net inc. (Wyo. July 14, 1999)
Aug. 12, 2003 – Name changed to Luna Gold Corp. ∎

Wychwood Oil Co. Ltd. (Ont. 1952)
1958 – Struck off register.

Wycliffe Resources Inc. (Ont. Dec. 8, 1945)
July 28, 2006 – Name changed to Renforth Resources Inc. (see FPsurvey - Mines & Energy)

Wydmar Development Corp. (B.C. 1977)
Aug. 20, 1993 – Dissolved and struck off register.

Wyn Developments Inc. (B.C. Feb. 1, 1984)
June 10, 2008 – Name changed to Canada Gas Corp. following transfer of mineral assets to wholly owned Wyn Metals Inc. and the spin-off of Wyn Metals to shldrs.; basis 1 new for 5 old shs. ∎

Wyn Metals Inc. (B.C. Feb. 2, 2007)
May 28, 2010 – Name changed to Auracle Resources Ltd. ∎

Wynn Yellowknife Gold Mines Ltd. (Ont. 1945)
Oct. 4, 1954 – Charter cancelled.

Wynrock Gold Mines Ltd. (Ont. 1945)
Dec. 10, 1962 – Dissolved.

X

X-Cal Resources Ltd. (B.C. Apr. 8, 1981)
Sept. 3, 2010 – Acquired by Paramount Gold and Silver Corp.; basis 0.125 Paramount Gold shs. for 1 X-Cal sh. (see Paramount Gold and Silver Corp.)
Sept. 4, 2013 – Name changed to Paramount Nevada Gold Corp. (see Paramount Gold and Silver Corp.)

X-Chequer Resources Inc. (Que. Aug. 11, 1987)
Sept. 29, 2004 – Name changed to International X-Chequer Resources Inc.; basis 1 new for 12 old shs. ∎

X Corporation (Alta. Apr. 17, 1996)
Oct. 2002 – Charter cancelled.

X-Ore Resources Inc. (Que. Dec. 12, 1995)
Jan. 19, 2010 – Amalgamated with 9216-4706 Québec Inc., a wholly owned subsid. of Blue Note Mining Inc., to continue as X-Ore Resources Inc.; basis 1 Blue Note sh. for 2 X-Ore shs. (see Blue Note Mining Inc.)

X-Tal Minerals Corp. (B.C. Nov. 12, 1996)
Jan. 31, 2011 – Name changed to Lion One Metals Limited pursuant to reverse takeover acquisition of American Eagle Resources, Inc. (see FPsurvey - Mines & Energy)

X-Tech Innovations Inc. (Man. May 15, 2000)
July 26, 2002 – Name changed to IDYIA Innovations Inc. following reverse takeover acquisition of IDYIA Inc. (formerly Cybershare Ltd.). ∎

X-Terra Resources Corporation (B.C. Feb. 24, 1987)
Sept. 4, 2008 – Continued into Canada.
June 4, 2014 – Name changed to Norvista Capital Corporation pursuant to reverse takeover acquisition of and amalgamation with (old) Norvista Capital Corporation. ∎

X-Terra Resources Inc. (Can. Nov. 14, 2013)
June 1, 2023 – Name changed to Comet Lithium Corporation. (see FPsurvey - Mines & Energy)

X1 Entertainment Group Inc. (B.C. Jan. 9, 2020)
Aug. 20, 2024 – Name changed to Military Metals Corp. (see FPsurvey - Mines & Energy)

X1 Esports and Entertainment Ltd. (B.C. Jan. 9, 2020)
Oct. 19, 2022 – Name changed to X1 Entertainment Group Inc. ∎

XBiotech Inc. (Can. Mar. 22, 2005)
Sept. 23, 2005 – Continued into British Columbia. (see FPsurvey - Industrials)

XIB I Capital Corp. (B.C. Mar. 8, 2018)
Feb. 17, 2021 – Name changed to Adyton Resources Corporation pursuant to Qualifying Transaction reverse takeover acquisition of MR Exploration PNG Pte Ltd.; basis 1 new for 2.62 old shs. (see FPsurvey - Mines & Energy)

XISS Capital Corporation (Ont. June 13, 1986)
Aug. 3, 1999 – Formed iFuture Inc. in Ontario on non-arm's length amalgamation with AstroServices Inc. (deemed acquiror) and 1354717 Ontario Corporation; basis 1 new sh. and 0.5 new ser. A wts. for 4 XISS shs. ■

XL Food Systems Ltd. (Alta. Oct. 4, 1979 amalg.)
June 15, 1989 – Name changed to XL Foods Ltd. ■

XL Foods Ltd. (Alta. Oct. 4, 1979 amalg.)
Mar. 9, 1999 – Name changed to SevenWay Capital Corporation. ■

XL-ID Solutions Inc. (N.B. May 22, 2009)
Feb. 21, 2014 – Capital restructuring and corporate reorganization approved by Quebec court on Feb. 13, 2014. All o/s com. shs. cancelled for no consideration.

X-L Refineries Ltd. (Can. 1954)
1957 – All o/s com. shs. acquired by Pacific Petroleums Ltd. in 1956. Pacific offered to acquire all pref. shs. through exchange of 1 Pacific sh. and $2.25 for each 5 pref. shs. of X-L.

XMC Mortgage Corporation (Ont. Feb. 6, 1997)
Apr. 1, 2022 – Name changed to MCAN Home Mortgage Corporation.

XMP Mining Limited (Bermuda Nov. 6, 1997)
Aug. 29, 2003 – Name changed to Nu XMP Ventures Limited; basis 1 new for 4 old shs. ■

XPEL Technologies Corp. (Nev. Oct. 14, 2003)
July 26, 2018 – Name changed to XPEL, Inc.

XPF Development Inc. (Ont. June 28, 1984 amalg.)
Mar. 26, 1998 – Name changed to GolfNorth Properties Inc. following reverse takeover acquisition of A. E. Kavanagh Holdings Inc.; basis 1 new for 10 old shs. ■

XPeria Corp. (Ont. July 19, 1974)
Nov. 26, 2004 – Name changed to Xgen Ventures Inc.; basis 1 new for 6 old shs. (see FPsurvey - Mines & Energy; FPsurvey - Industrials)

XPhyto Therapeutics Corp. (B.C. Dec. 12, 2017)
Nov. 14, 2022 – Name changed to BioNxt Solutions Inc. (see FPsurvey - Industrials)

XRG International, Inc. (N.J. 1977 amalg.)
Nov. 1983 – Under U.S. federal bankruptcy proceedings. No recent information available.

XS Cargo Income Fund (Alta. Apr. 6, 2005)
June 16, 2011 – Acquired by KarpReilly LLC for $0.7263 per sh.

XS Financial Inc. (B.C. Dec. 3, 2009)
Oct. 1, 2024 – Privatized via acquisition by Mavik Capital Management LP and Axar Capital Management LP; basis Cdn$0.05265 cash per subord. vtg. shs. and Cdn$52.65 cash per proportionate vtg. shs.

X.T.C. Resources Ltd. (B.C. 1981)
June 24, 1994 – Dissolved and struck off register.

Xanadu Fund Limited (Ont.)
July 9, 1994 – Charter cancelled.

Xanadu Mines Limited (Australia May 12, 2005)
Aug. 5, 2025 – All o/s ordinary shs. not already held acquired by Bastion Mining Pty Ltd; basis A$0.08 cash per sh.

Xanaro Technologies Inc. (B.C. Dec. 7, 1983)
Sept. 19, 1986 – Name changed to Canadian Industrial Minerals Corp. ■

Xander Resources Inc. (B.C. Dec. 9, 2010)
Aug. 26, 2025 – Name changed to Core Critical Metals Corp. (see FPsurvey - Mines & Energy)

Xanthic Biopharma Inc. (Ont. Nov. 24, 1999)
Jan. 7, 2019 – Name changed to Green Growth Brands Inc. following reverse takeover acquisiton of Green Growth Brands Inc. ■

Xantrex Technology Inc. (B.C. Mar. 11, 1983)
May 9, 1996 – Continued into Canada.
Oct. 1, 2008 – Acquired by Schneider Electric S.A. for Cdn$15 per sh.
Jan. 1, 2010 – Amalgamated into Schneider Electric Canada Inc.

Xavier Mines Limited (Ont. June 15, 1959)
July 24, 1996 – Name changed to Xavier Corporation and continued into Delaware; basis 1 new for 4 old shs. ■

Xceed Mortgage Corporation (Ont. Feb. 6, 1997)
July 8, 2013 – Acquired by MCAN Mortgage Corporation; basis either $1.75 per sh. or 0.118 MCAN shs. for 1 Xceed sh.
Sept. 1, 2017 – Name changed to XMC Mortgage Corporation. ■

Xcel Capital Corporation (Alta. Jan. 21, 1999)
Jan. 18, 2006 – Name changed to Xcel Consolidated Ltd.; basis 1 new for 10 old shs. ■

Xcel Consolidated Ltd. (Alta. Jan. 21, 1999)
July 2, 2015 – Struck from register and dissolved.

Xceleron Inc. (Alta. Nov. 21, 2000)
Apr. 1, 2004 – Amalgamated with Advent Energy Capital Inc., Thrust Capital Corp. and Zaio Canada Inc. to form Zaio Corporation, constituting a reverse takeover by Zaio Canada; basis 0.45 new for 1 Advent sh., 1 new for 1 Thrust sh., 1 new for 1 Zaio Canada sh. and 0.6 new for 1 Xceleron sh. Xceleron, Advent Energy and Thrust Capital were all Capital Pool Companies and the amalgamation constituted their Qualifying Transaction.

Xcite Energy Limited (British Virgin Islands Jan. 5, 2007)
Sept. 30, 2015 – Voluntarily delisted from TSX-VEN; continued to trade on AIM.

Xebec Adsorption Inc. (Can. June 12, 2009 amalg.)
Sept. 29, 2022 – Filed under the Companies' Creditors Arrangement Act (CCAA) and Deloitte Restructuring Inc. appointed monitor.
Mar. 9, 2023 – Name changed to FormerXBC Inc. ■

Xemac Resources Inc. (Can. Apr. 7, 1996)
Mar. 25, 2004 – Name changed to Abitex Resources Inc.; basis 1 new for 10 old shs. ■

Xemplar Energy Corp. (B.C. Jan. 12, 1979)
May 25, 2020 – Dissolved and struck from register.

Xencet Investments Inc. (Can. Aug. 25, 1993)
Nov. 11, 1998 – Name changed to Games Trader Inc. following acquisition of Trader Games Inc.; basis 1 new for 1 old sh. ■

Xenex Industries & Resources Ltd. (B.C. May 6, 1982)
Sept. 22, 1989 – Dissolved.

Xenex Petroleum Ltd. (B.C. May 6, 1982)
May 26, 1983 – Name changed to Xenex Industries & Resources Ltd. ■

Xenium Resources Inc. (B.C. Dec. 21, 1983)
Nov. 29, 1989 – Name changed to Zeal Capital Ltd.; basis 1 new for 2 old shs. ■

Xenon Pharmaceuticals Inc. (B.C.)
May 17, 2000 – Continued into Canada. (see FPsurvey - Industrials)

Xenos Group Inc. (Ont. Oct. 1, 1989)
Mar. 8, 2010 – Acquired by Actuate Corporation for $3.50 per sh.

Xenotech Inc. (Alta. Feb. 4, 1987)
Oct. 15, 1998 – Name changed to Dynamic Digital Depth Inc.; basis 1 new for 5 old shs. ■

Xentel DM Incorporated (Alta. Nov. 5, 1998 amalg.)
Nov. 26, 2010 – Name changed to iMarketing Solutions Group Inc. ■

Xentel Interactive Inc. (Alta. Nov. 26, 1987)
Nov. 5, 1998 – Formed Xentel DM Incorporated in Alberta on amalgamation with GWE Group Inc., constituting a reverse takeover by GWE; basis 1 new cl. A or cl. B sh. for 0.157 GWE shs. and 1 new cl. A sh. for 34.48 Xentel Interactive shs. ■

Xillix Technologies Corp. (B.C. Nov. 2, 1990 amalg.)
Sept. 27, 2007 – Name changed to Biomerge Industries Ltd. ■

Xinergy Ltd. (Ont. Feb. 11, 2005)
Feb. 11, 2016 – Dissolved and struck from register.

Xinex Networks Inc. (Can. Jan. 2, 1996 amalg.)
June 1998 – Placed into receivership.
Feb. 1999 – Adjudged bankrupt.
June 10, 2004 – Dissolved.

Xing Hai Resources Ltd. (B.C. Sept. 16, 1983)
Apr. 25, 1986 – Name changed to RSI Retail Solutions Inc.; basis 2 new for 1 old sh. ■

Xmet Inc. (Ont. Aug. 2, 2006)
June 25, 2018 – Certificate of incorporation cancelled and company dissolved.

Xplore Technologies Corp. (Ont. Aug. 20, 1996)
Mar. 22, 2000 – Continued into Canada.
June 20, 2007 – Continued into Delaware.

Xpres Communications Inc. (B.C. Dec. 30, 1987)
Feb. 14, 2000 – Name changed to Stratacom Technology Inc.; basis 1 new for 4 old shs. ■

Xsilva Systems Inc. (Can. Mar. 21, 2005)
Apr. 20, 2012 – Name changed to Lightspeed Retail Inc. ■

Xstrata Canada Corporation (Ont. June 30, 2005 amalg.)
Mar. 2, 2009 – Redeemed pref. shs. at $25 per sh. plus $0.2863 accr. and unpaid divd.
July 30, 2013 – Name changed to Glencore Canada Corporation.

Xtacy Therapeutics Corp. (B.C. Jan. 30, 2006)
Nov. 4, 2024 – Name changed to Pegasus Mercantile Inc. (see FPsurvey - Mines & Energy)

Xtierra Inc. (B.C. Mar. 28, 2007)
Apr. 27, 2009 – Continued into Ontario.
Feb. 27, 2023 – Name changed to Royalties Inc. (see FPsurvey - Mines & Energy; FPsurvey - Industrials)

Xtra Developments Inc. (Ont. 1972 amalg.)
Aug. 30, 1978 – Amalgamated with Summit Diversified Ltd. to form Sumtra Diversified Inc.; basis 1 new for 3 old shs.

Xtra-Gold Resources Corp. (Nev. Sept. 1, 1998)
Continued into British Virgin Islands. (see FPsurvey - Mines & Energy)

Xtraction Services Holdings Corp. (B.C. Dec. 3, 2009)
June 26, 2020 – Name changed to XS Financial Inc. ■

Xtreme Coil Drilling Corp. (Alta. May 1, 2006 amalg.)
Apr. 24, 2012 – Name changed to Xtreme Drilling and Coil Services Corp. ■

Xtreme Drilling and Coil Services Corp. (Alta. May 1, 2006 amalg.)
July 4, 2016 – Name changed to Xtreme Drilling Corp. ■

Xtreme Drilling Corp. (Alta. May 1, 2006 amalg.)
Sept. 11, 2018 – Acquired by AKITA Drilling Ltd.; basis either (i) $2.65 cash, (ii) 0.3732394 AKITA class A

non-vtg. shs. or (iii) 0.29 AKITA class A non-vtg shs. and 59¢ cash for each sh. held.

Xxpert Rental Tool Inc. (Ont. Oct. 13, 1987)
Sept. 28, 1995 – Name changed to Kazakhstan Minerals Corporation following reverse takeover acquisition of Three K Exploration and Mining Ltd.; basis 1 new for 25 old shs. ■

Xybion Digital Inc. (B.C. June 25, 2020)
June 28, 2024 – Privatized; basis Cdn$0.90 cash per sh.

Xylitol Canada Inc. (Ont. May 9, 2008)
Dec. 12, 2017 – Name changed to Sweet Natural Trading Co. Limited. (see FPsurvey - Industrials)

Xyquest Venture Corp. (B.C. Jan. 13, 1981)
Nov. 25, 1996 – Name changed to Polar Bear Ventures Ltd. ■

Y

Y & O Ventures Corp. (B.C. Oct. 26, 2005)
Dec. 12, 2006 – Name changed to Hanwei Energy Services Corp. following Qualifying Transaction acquisition of an 85% interest in Daqing Harvest Longwall High Pressure FRP Pipe Co. Ltd. ■

Y & R Properties Ltd. (Ont. 1969)
Amalgamated with Oxford Development Group Ltd. and Oxlea Investments Ltd. to form Oxford Development Group Ltd. The o/s com. shs. of co. became $1.75 cum. redeem. & cl. Y pfce. shs. of the amalg. co.

YBM Magnex International, Inc. (Alta. Mar. 16, 1994)
Dec. 8, 1998 – Ernst & Young YBM Inc. was appointed receiver and manager. Directors tendered their resignations following allegations of possible illegal activities in the company's eastern European operations. Also in December, shldr. class action lawsuits were filed in the U.S. alleging that the company, auditors Deloitte & Touche LLP, and others, including certain officers and/or directors of the company, had violated U.S. securities laws.
Apr. 1999 – Pleaded guilty to criminal charges in the U.S. and paid a $3,000,000 fine.
Feb. 7, 2002 – Parties to two Ontario class action lawsuits and two Ontario actions initiated by the estate of the company arising out of the company's demise, reached an agreement in principle for an out-of-court settlement under which YBM shldrs. would receive $85,000,000 and the defendants would release any claims made against the estate of YBM, which would then have approx. an additional $35,000,000 for distribution to shldrs. with proven claims.
May 2002 – Ontario Court certified the actions as class proceedings, appointed representative plaintiffs and defined the classes as follows; (1) the General Class was each and every person, wherever resident, except certain excluded persons, who, during the period of July 1, 1994 to May 14, 1998, traded in YBM shs. but not including shs. purchased or acquired following YBM prospectus dated Nov. 17, 1997; and (2) the Prospectus Class was each and every person who purchased or acquired YBM shs. following YBM prospectus dated Nov, 17, 1997. YBM shs. included all securities of YBM and Pratecs Technologies, Inc. shldrs., members of either class or both of the proposed classes, had until July 15, 2002 to opt out of the settlement of the class action or to participate in the settlement by submitting a claim in accordance with a distribution plan as approved in May 2, 2002 at a court hearing. Amounts available for distribution were as follows: (a) some of the defendants and third parties to be paid the sum of approximately $85,000,000 in full and final settlement of all claims; (b) the class member of the Prospectus Class action would be paid $7,500,000, pro rata, as a priority payment, estimated to be $0.07 for each $1.00 of net loss; (c) the class members of the Prospectus Class action and the General Class action would then share in the balance of the monies after payment of expenses and lawyer fees,

on a pro rata basis, and including the distributions by the receiver of YBM from the remaining assets in the estate of YBM, which was estimated at $0.20 for each $1.00 of net loss; and (d) the amounts in (b) and (c) were only estimates and were made by class counsel without any assumption of liability and actual payments may be substantially different from the estimated amounts depending upon the number of claims received, costs of distribution and the total net losses. Ernst & Young was appointed by the court as administrator of the settlement plan and proof of claims had to be filed by Sept. 6, 2002.
Feb. 11, 2003 – First distribution was made to claimants, with the second and last expected within the year of $0.097 for each dollar of net loss. On Feb. 11, 2003, the first distribution was made to claimants, with the second and last expected within the year.
Nov. 2003 – Ernst & Young calculated the net loss for the General Class members to be $351,074,187, with an estimated distribution of $0.1986 per dollar of net loss and for the Prospectus Class members to be $78,230,115 with an estimated distribution of $0.097 per dollar of net loss.

YDreams Global Interactive Technologies Inc. (B.C. Apr. 16, 2007)
Jan. 17, 2019 – Name changed to YDx Innovation Corp. (see FPsurvey - Industrials)

YEARS Financial Trust (Ont. Jan. 29, 2001)
Jan. 5, 2009 – Converted into Dividend Growth Split Corp.; basis 0.815986 Dividend Growth units for 1 YEARS Financial Trust unit.

YEARS Trust (Ont. Jan. 29, 2001)
Dec. 16, 2005 – Formed YEARS Financial Trust following merger with YEARS U.S. Trust. ■

YEARS U.S. Trust (Ont. Oct. 22, 2001)
Dec. 16, 2005 – Merged with YEARS Trust (renamed Years Financial Trust); basis 1.0537 new YEARS Trust trust units for 1 old YEARS U.S. trust unit. (see YEARS Financial Trust)

YFMC Healthcare Inc. (Alta. Feb. 28, 1996)
Dec. 22, 1999 – Acquired by U.S.-based Med-Emerg International Inc.

YGC Resources Ltd. (B.C. May 30, 1988)
Jan. 25, 2002 – Dissolved and struck off register.
Aug. 1, 2003 – Restored to the register.
June 20, 2007 – Name changed to Yukon-Nevada Gold Corp. pursuant to acquisition of Queenstake Resources Ltd.; basis 1 new for 1 YGC sh. and 1 new for 10 Queenstake shs. ■

YIELDPLUS Income Fund (Ont. Aug. 30, 2004)
Mar. 22, 2017 – Merged into MINT Income Fund; basis 0.89235573 MINT trust units for 1 YIELDPLUS trust unit.

YIN 88 Corporation (Alta. Jan. 14, 1993)
May 15, 2003 – Name changed to Continental Cash Technologies Corporation; basis 1 new for 5 old shs. ■

YIN 88 Gaming Corporation (Alta. Jan. 14, 1993)
Mar. 4, 1996 – Name changed to YIN 88 Corporation. ■

YIN 88 Resources Limited (Alta. Jan. 14, 1993)
May 24, 1994 – Name changed to YIN 88 Gaming Corporation. ■

YKR International Resources Ltd. (Yuk. Dec. 17, 1997)
Jan. 10, 2001 – Name changed to Gtech International Resources Limited; basis 1 new for 2 old shs. ■

YM BioSciences Inc. (Ont. Aug. 17, 1994)
Dec. 11, 2001 – Continued into Nova Scotia.
Feb. 13, 2013 – Acquired by a wholly owned subsid. of Gilead Sciences, Inc. for US$2.95 per sh.
Feb. 28, 2013 – Name changed to GILEAD YM ULC.

YMG Capital Management Inc. (Can. Jan. 1, 1998 amalg.)
Feb. 6, 2006 – Acquired by Fiera Capital Management Inc. for $3.25 per sh. (see Fiera Capital Management Inc.)

YMG Ventures Inc. (Alta. Oct. 4, 1996)
Oct. 1, 2004 – Privatized via capital reorganization; basis all outstanding com. shs. and Series I pfd. shs. converted into Series II pfd. shs. and Series III pfd. shs. to be immediately redeemed for $0.011 per sh.

YOW Capital Corp. (Ont. Feb. 27, 2007)
Sept. 16, 2009 – Name changed to Caribou Copper Resources Ltd. ■

YPG Holdings Inc. (Can. July 28, 2003)
Feb. 11, 2010 – Name changed to Yellow Media Inc. ■

YRI-York Limited (Can. 1931)
Oct. 27, 2013 – Dissolved.

YSS Corp. (Alta. Jan. 4, 2019)
Mar. 22, 2021 – Name changed to Nova Cannabis Inc. following the acquisition of Alcanna Inc.'s wholly owned Alcanna Cannabis Stores GP Inc. and Alcanna Cannabis Stores Limited Partnership, resulting in the reverse takeover acquisition of YSS by Alcanna Inc.; basis 1 new for 18.353 old shs. ■

YTW Weslea Growth Capital Corporation (Can. Oct. 5, 2004)
Dec. 15, 2005 – Name changed to Broadband Learning Corporation pursuant to Qualifying Transaction reverse takeover acquisition of Broadband Learning Corp. and subsequent amalgamation of Broadband Learning Corp. with a wholly owned subsidiary. ■

YWL Corp. (Ont. Jan. 1, 1992)
Apr. 14, 2004 – Formed Icefloe Technologies Inc. on amalgamation with Icefloe Technologies Inc., constituting reverse takeover by Icefloe; basis 0.12067 new for 1 old sh. ■

Yalakum Resources Ltd. (B.C. 1969)
Oct. 25, 1985 – Charter cancelled.

Yale Lead & Zinc Mines Ltd. (Ont. 1948)
1968 – Merged into International Mogul Mines Ltd.; basis 1 new for 84 old shs.

Yale Mining Co. Ltd. (B.C. 1946)
Struck off register.

Yale Resources Ltd. (B.C. July 23, 1980)
May 28, 2013 – Name changed to Alta Vista Ventures Ltd.; basis 1 new for 10 old shs. ■

Yaletown Entertainment Corp. (B.C. June 29, 1994)
Dec. 15, 2014 – Dissolved and struck from register.

Yalian Steel Corporation (B.C. June 28, 2007)
May 15, 2013 – Acquired by 0957703 B.C. Ltd. for 40¢ per sh.

Yalta Gold Mines Ltd. (Ont. 1945)
Oct. 1957 – Charter cancelled.

Yama Gold Mines Ltd. (Ont. Jan. 19, 1937)
1943 – Name changed to Cathroy Larder Mines Ltd. and continued into Ontario; basis 1 new for 3 old shs. ■

Yamana Gold Inc. (Can. Feb. 7, 1995 amalg.)
Apr. 4, 2023 – All o/s com. shs. acquired by Pan American Silver Corp. and Canadian assets acquired by Agnico Eagle Mines Limited; basis US$1.0406 cash (paid by Agnico Eagle), 0.0376 Agnico Eagle shs. and 0.1598 Pan American shs. for 1 Yamana sh.

Yamana Resources Inc. (Can. Feb. 7, 1995 amalg.)
Aug. 19, 2003 – Name changed to Yamana Gold Inc.; basis 1 new for 27.86 old shs. ■

Yamiri Gold and Energy Inc. (B.C. May 26, 1978)
Apr. 27, 2010 – Name changed to Cannon Point Resources Ltd. ■

Yamoto Resources Ltd. (B.C. 1975)
Apr. 8, 1980 – Acquired by Santa Sarita Mining Company Limited; basis 4 Santa Sarita shs. for 10 Yamoto shs. (see Santa Sarita Mining Company Limited)

Yangarra Resources Inc. (Alta. Jan. 22, 1985)
Nov. 9, 2005 – Formed Yangarra Resources Ltd. in Alberta on non-arm's length amalgamation with TriOil Ltd. with Yangarra the deemed acquiror; basis 1 new for 1 TriOil sh. and 0.95 new for 1 Yangarra sh. (see FPsurvey - Mines & Energy)

Yangtze-Kiang Mines Ltd. (Ont. 1947)
1957 – Charter cancelled.

Yangtze Telecom Corp. (B.C. July 20, 1979)
Aug. 20, 2012 – Dissolved and struck from registry.

Yank Yellowknife Gold Mines Ltd. (Ont. 1945)
May 26, 1958 – Charter cancelled.

Yankee Canuck Oil and Mining Corp. Ltd. (Ont. 1949)
1967 – Acquired by Acroll Oil & Gas Ltd.; in 1969, shldrs. received 1 new for 27 old shs.

Yankee Dundee Mines Ltd. (B.C. 1952)
1963 – Name changed to Dundee Mines Ltd.; basis 1 new for 7 old shs. ■

Yankee Hat Industries Corp. (Alta. Oct. 22, 1993)
Feb. 9, 2005 – Name changed to Yankee Hat Minerals Ltd. and continued into British Columbia. ■

Yankee Hat Minerals Ltd. (B.C. Feb. 9, 2005)
Dec. 1, 2014 – Dissolved and struck from registry.
May 29, 2023 – Restored to registry. (see FPsurvey - Mines & Energy)

Yankee Petroleums Ltd. (B.C. Feb. 1980)
June 12, 1987 – Name changed to Yankee Power Inc. ■

Yankee Power Inc. (B.C. Feb. 1980)
July 9, 1993 – Dissolved and struck off register.

Yankee Princess Oils Ltd. (Alta. 1948)
1956 – Acquired by Medallion Petroleums Ltd.; basis 1 new for 3.5 old shs.

Yanks Peak Resources Ltd. (B.C. Oct. 17, 1984)
June 1, 1998 – Name changed to BHR Buffalo Head Resources Ltd.; basis 1 new for 10 old shs. ■

Yarandry Silver Mines Limited (Ont. Oct. 5, 1965)
Apr. 28, 1972 – Name changed to New Yarandry Ltd.; basis 1 new for 5 old shs. ■

Yardley Capital Inc. (B.C. May 11, 1999)
Sept. 12, 2003 – Name changed to Golden Patriot Mining Inc. following Qualifying Transaction acquisition of the right to purchase up to 51% interest in Scheelite Dome gold prospect in Yukon Territory from Copper Ridge Explorations Inc.; basis 4 new for 1 old sh. ■

Yates Uranium Mines Inc. (Del. 1953)
1957 – Assets acquired by Lake Otter Uranium Mines Ltd.; basis 1 new for 5 old shs.

Yellohill Gold Mines Ltd. (Ont. 1944)
1952 – Charter cancelled.

Yellorex Mines Limited (Ont. 1938)
Sept. 21, 1990 – Formed Bras-American Corporation on amalgamation with Bras-American Mining Ltd.; basis 1 new for 10 old shs. (see FPsurvey - Mines & Energy)

Yellow Band Resources Inc. (B.C. 1985)
Mar. 1, 1991 – Amalgamated with Commonwealth Gold Corporation (1 for 1) and Golden Arrow Resource Inc. (1 for 3) to form a new co. also named Commonwealth Gold Corporation; basis 1 new for 2 old shs. (see Commonwealth Gold Corporation)

Yellow Media Inc. (Can. July 28, 2003)
Nov. 1, 2010 – Amalgamated with YPG General Partner Inc., 7341261 Canada Inc. and 7341296 Canada Inc. (all directly or indirectly wholly owned by parent entity Yellow Pages Income Fund) to form Yellow Media Inc. pursuant to the fund's conversion from an income trust to a corporation. (see Yellow Media Inc.)

Yellow Media Inc. (Can. Nov. 1, 2010; amalg.)
Dec. 20, 2012 – Succeeded by Yellow Media Limited pursuant to plan of arrangement and recapitalization of Yellow Media Inc.; basis 0.0050017 Yellow Media Ltd. com. for 1 Yellow Media Inc. com. and 0.0028581 Yellow Media Ltd. wt. for 1 Yellow Media Inc. com. ■

Yellow Media Limited (Can. July 18, 2012; amalg.)
Dec. 31, 2014 – Formed Yellow Pages Limited in Canada on amalgamation with wholly owned Yellow Pages Limited. ■

Yellow Pages Income Fund (Ont. June 25, 2003)
Nov. 1, 2010 – Succeeded by Yellow Media Inc. pursuant to plan of arrangement whereby Yellow Media Inc. was formed to facilitate the conversion of the fund into a corporation and the fund was dissolved. ■

Yellow Pages Limited (Can. Dec. 31, 2014 amalg.)
May 14, 2020 – Continued into British Columbia. (see FPsurvey - Industrials)

Yellow Pan Gold Mines Ltd. (Ont. 1945)
Dec. 10, 1962 – Dissolved.

Yellow Point Mining Corp. (B.C. May 21, 1980)
Aug. 26, 1994 – Name changed to Desert Sun Mining Corp.; basis 1 new for 5 old shs. ■

Yellow Stem Tech Inc. (B.C. Oct. 1, 2018)
June 1, 2023 – Name changed to Sweet Poison Spirits Inc. following the grant of the worldwide distribution rights to the Sweet Poison brand of tequila and mescal products. ■

Yellowhead Mining Inc. (B.C. Aug. 19, 2009)
Feb. 20, 2019 – Acquired by Taseko Mines Limited; basis 1.1484 Taseko com. shs. for 1 Yellowhead sh. ■

Yellowjack Resources Ltd. (B.C. Apr. 16, 1984)
Aug. 11, 1995 – Formed Canoro Resources Ltd. in British Columbia on amalgamation with Golden Mammoth Resources Ltd.; basis 1 new for 10 old shs. ■

Yellowjacket Resources Ltd. (Alta. Aug. 31, 2011)
June 6, 2013 – Name changed to Athabasca Nuclear Corp. ■

Yellowknife Base Metals Ltd. (Man. 1966)
Mar. 1973 – Charter cancelled.

Yellowknife Base Metals Limited (Man. 1966)
Mar. 1973 – Charter cancelled.

Yellowknife Bear Mines Limited (Ont. 1948)
Oct. 12, 1978 – Continued into Canada.
Oct. 28, 1980 – Name changed to Yellowknife Bear Resources Inc. ■

Yellowknife Bear Resources Inc. (Can. Oct. 12, 1978)
Feb. 1, 1986 – Amalgamated with a wholly owned subsid. of Rayrock Resources Limited (which at the same time changed its name to Rayrock Yellowknife Resources Inc.) to form a new co. also known as Yellowknife Bear Resources Inc. Each sh. of Yellowknife Bear Resources Inc. exch. for one subord. voting sh. of Rayrock Yellowknife Resources Inc. Subsequently, on Mar. 1, 1987, Yellowknife Bear Resources Inc. amalgamated with Discovery Mines Limited (1 for 1) and Midcon Oil & Gas Limited (9 for 5) to form Discovery West Corp. (see Discovery Mines Limited)

Yellowknife Gold Mines Ltd. (Ont. Apr. 1934)
1948 – Merged assets with Bear Exploration & Radium Ltd. to form Yellowknife Bear Mines Limited; basis 2,063 new for 1,000 old shs. (see Yellowknife Bear Mines Limited)

Yellowknife Volcanic Gold Mines Ltd. (B.C. 1948)
1965 – Dissolved and struck off register.

Yellowstone Mines Ltd. (Que. 1944)
Aug. 5, 1978 – Charter cancelled.

Yellowstone Mines Ltd. (B.C. July 9, 1969)
Oct. 6, 1981 – Name changed to Glendora Resources Inc. ■

Yellowstone Petroleums Ltd. (Alta. Jan. 28, 1980)
Aug. 18, 1987 – Name changed to Kingbird Resources Inc. ■

Yeoman Gold Mines Ltd. (Ont. 1945)
Feb. 6, 1956 – Dissolved.

Yerbaé Brands Corp. (B.C. July 25, 2000)
July 2, 2025 – Acquired by Safety Shot, Inc.; basis 0.2918 Safety Shot shs. for 1 Yerbae sh. ■

Yes Capital Corp. (B.C. Oct. 20, 1999)
June 24, 2002 – Name changed to 222 Pizza Express Corp. following Qualifying Transaction acquisition of certain assets of a business named Pizza 222 which were owned by Mandair Distributors Ltd. ■

Yes I.C. Technologies Inc. (Alta. Nov. 26, 1999)
Oct. 26, 2000 – Name changed to EarlyRain Inc. ■

Yield Advantage Income Trust (Ont. Dec. 23, 2004)
Dec. 24, 2015 – Terminated on Dec. 31, 2015; trust units redeemed at $7.418687 per unit.

Yield Advantaged Convertible Debentures Fund (Ont. Dec. 29, 2010)
Mar. 5, 2014 – Name changed to Convertible Debentures Income Fund. ■

The Yield Growth Corp. (B.C. Nov. 28, 2014)
Aug. 18, 2020 – Name changed to Better Plant Sciences Inc. (see FPsurvey - Industrials)

Yield Management Group High Income Trust (Ont. Sept. 4, 1997)
Jan. 22, 2008 – Name changed to Fiera High Income Trust. ■

Ymir Yankee Girl Gold Mines Ltd. (B.C. 1934)
1949 – Property acquired by Alana Mines Ltd.; basis 1 new for 4 old shs.

Yogen Fruz World-Wide Incorporated (Ont. Sept. 7, 1994 amalg.)
Mar. 18, 1998 – Continued into Nova Scotia.
Oct. 6, 2000 – Name changed to CoolBrands International Inc. ■

Yoho Resources Inc. (Alta. Dec. 24, 2004)
Sept. 9, 2016 – Acquired by One Stone Energy Partners LP for $0.475 per sh.

Yoho Timber Ltd. (B.C. 1958)
Nov. 21, 1968 – Charter cancelled.

Yonge Street Capital Corp. (Can. July 6, 2005)
Oct. 2, 2009 – Name changed to Ecosse Energy Corp. pursuant to Qualifying Transaction reverse takeover acquisition of Endeavour Energy (Bengkulu) Pty Ltd. ■

Yooma Wellness Inc. (Ont. Feb. 10, 2021 amalg.)
Dec. 7, 2023 – Filed an assignment in bankruptcy and Richter Inc. was appointed trustee.

Yorbeau Mines Inc. (Que. 1965)
Feb. 29, 1984 – Formed Yorbeau Resources Inc. in Quebec on amalgamation with Les Ressources Reford Inc. (see FPsurvey - Mines & Energy)

Yorcan Exploration Ltd. (Ont. 1956)
1958 – Absorbed by Campbell Chibougamau Mines Ltd.; basis 1 new for 4 old shs. (see Campbell Chibougamau Mines Ltd.)

York Asbestos Mines Ltd. (Ont. 1949)
Nov. 1970 – Charter cancelled.

York Bay Capital Corporation (Ont. Jan. 8, 1986)
Jan. 30, 1997 – Name changed to York Bay Capital Group Inc.; basis 1 restricted vtg. for 3 com. shs. ■

York Bay Capital Group Inc. (Ont. Jan. 8, 1986)
July 27, 1999 – Name changed to CDNet Canada Inc. (see FPsurvey - Industrials)

York Bousquet Gold Mines Ltd. (Que. Dec. 21, 1936)
1961 – Charter cancelled.

York Capital Corp. (Ont. Jan. 16, 2004)
Oct. 7, 2005 – Name changed to SilverBirch Inc. following Qualifying Transaction reverse takeover acquisition of SilverBirch Studios Inc. (see FPsurvey - Industrials)

York Centre Corporation (Ont. 1960)
Apr. 12, 1995 – Name changed to Georgian Bancorp Inc. ■

York Consolidated Exploration Limited (Ont. 1954)
May 25, 1983 – Name changed to Amco Industrial Holdings Limited. ■

York Knitting Mills Ltd. (Ont. 1911)
May 1966 – Name changed to Harvey Woods Limited. ■

York Lambton Corporation Limited (Can. 1926)
May 29, 1979 – Name changed to York Lambton Inc. ■

York Lambton Inc. (Can. 1926)
Sept. 21, 1982 – Declared bankrupt.
June 1, 1987 – Trustee does not anticipate any distrib. to any class of creditors. No further information is available.

York Medical Inc. (Ont. Aug. 17, 1994)
Feb. 7, 2001 – Name changed to YM BioSciences Inc. ■

York Oils, Ltd. (Can. June 24, 1929)
Struck off register.

York Oils Limited (B.C. 1937)
July 3, 1958 – Name changed to New York Oils Limited; basis 1 new for 10 old shs. ■

York Petroleum Inc. (B.C. June 4, 1981)
Dec. 1, 1986 – Formed Winzen International Inc. in British Columbia on amalgamation with Winzen Corporation and the Winzen Group. ■

York Resources Limited (Alta. 1986)
June 30, 1990 – Amalgamated with Red Cliff Enery Inc. to form Aviva Petroleum Canada Inc.; basis 1.8247 new for 10 Red Cliff shs. and 1 new for 10 York shs. (see Aviva Petroleum Canada Inc.)

York Ridge Lifetech Inc. (Ont. Mar. 28, 2007)
Mar. 16, 2011 – Name changed to Acadian Energy Inc. pursuant to Qualifying Transaction reverse takeover acquisition of Acadian Energy Holdings Inc. and subsequent amalgamation of Acadian with wholly owned York Ridge Amalco Inc.; basis 1 new for 4 old shs. (see FPsurvey - Mines & Energy; FPsurvey - Industrials)

York River Uranium Mines Ltd. (Ont. 1955)
Charter cancelled; date unknown. There were no funds available for distribution to shldrs.

York Russel Inc. (Can. 1931)
Dec. 31, 1983 – Name changed to YRI-York Limited. ■

York Trust and Savings Corp. (Ont. 1962)
June 30, 1968 – Acquired by The Metropolitan Trust Company; basis 1 new for 9 old shs.

Yorkshire Copper Mines Limited (Ont. 1953)
Dec. 21, 1979 – Amalgamated with Dolly Varden Resources Limited, Yorkshire Resources Limited, Kitsault Silver Mines Ltd. and Copper Cliff Mines Ltd. to form Dolly Varden Minerals Inc.; basis 0.1497 new cl. A sh. for 1 old sh.

Yorkshire Resources Limited (Ont. Nov. 27, 1923)
Dec. 21, 1979 – Amalgamated with Dolly Varden Resources Limited, Yorkshire Copper Mines Limited, Kitsault Silver Mines Ltd. and Copper Cliff Mines Ltd. to form Dolly Varden Minerals Inc.; basis 1.5752 new cl. A sh. for 1 com. or cl. A sh.

Yorkshire Trust Company (B.C. 1966)
Dec. 31, 1988 – Amalgamated with Guaranty Trust Company of Canada (1 for 1), Central Trust Company (1 for 1) and Nova Scotia Savings and Trust Company (1 for 1) to form Central Guaranty Trust Company.

Yorkton Medical Inc. (Ont. Aug. 17, 1994)
Sept. 28, 1995 – Name changed to York Medical Inc. ■

Yorkton Ventures Inc. (B.C. Aug. 30, 2006)
Apr. 20, 2022 – Name changed to Lithium One Metals Inc. (see FPsurvey - Mines & Energy)

Youandi Capital Corp. (B.C. Dec. 23, 2005)
Dec. 17, 2007 – Name changed to Southern Hemisphere Mining Limited following Qualifying Transaction reverse takeover acquisition of Southern Hemisphere Mining Pty Ltd. ■

Young-Chibougamau-Opemiska Mines Ltd. (Que.)
Aug. 1974 – Charter cancelled.

Young-Davidson Mines Limited (Ont. Apr. 8, 1926)
Nov. 2, 2005 – Amalgamated with 2080263 Ontario Limited, a wholly owned subsid. of Northgate Minerals Corporation; basis 0.7212 Northgate shs. for 1 Young-Davidson sh. (see Northgate Minerals Corporation)

Young-Munro Gold Mines Ltd. (Ont. 1929)
1954 – Charter cancelled.

Young-Shannon Gold Mines, Limited (Ont. Jan. 13, 1932)
July 11, 2008 – Name changed to Metallum Resources Inc. ■

Youngman Oil & Gas Ltd. (B.C. 1980)
Jan. 13, 1985 – Amalgamated with 4 other cos. to form Aurex Resources Inc.; basis 1 new for 2 old shs.

Your Host Foods Inc. (B.C. Nov. 3, 1986)
June 1, 1994 – Name changed to Diaz Resources Ltd. ■

Ypres Cadillac Mines Ltd. (Ont. 1936)
Dec. 1, 1958 – Dissolved.

Yreka Mines Ltd. (Ont. 1954)
May 6, 1980 – Dissolved.

Yubba Capital Corp. (Ont. Jan. 8, 2021)
Nov. 30, 2023 – Name changed to Impact Development Group Inc. pursuant to the Qualifying Transaction reverse takeover acquisition of Panama-based Impact Housing Corporation and concurrent amalgamation of Impact with wholly owned 1000469360 Ontario Inc.; basis 1 new for 26.0903 old shs. (see FPsurvey - Industrials)

Yubet Explorations Ltd. (B.C. 1966)
Aug. 1, 1966 – Name changed to Belcarra Explorations Ltd. ■

Yucana Resources Inc. (B.C. Nov. 20, 1980)
Mar. 9, 1987 – Name changed to Shamrock Resources Inc.; basis 1 new for 2.5 old shs. ■

Yucatan Resources Ltd. (B.C. 1966)
May 27, 1983 – Struck off register.

Yukeno Lead & Silver Mines Ltd. (Ont. 1949)
Oct. 1949 – Merged into Consolidated Yukeno Mines Ltd.; basis 1 new for 3 old shs. (see Consolidated Yukeno Mines Ltd.)

Yukeno Mines Ltd. (Ont. 1951)
Mar. 4, 1966 – Name changed to Gradore Mines Ltd.; basis 1 new for 5 old shs. ■

Yukon Antimony Corp. Ltd. (B.C. 1964)
1971 – Merged into International Mariner Resources Ltd.; basis 1 new for 15 old shs.

Yukon Consolidated Gold Corporation Ltd. (Can. Apr. 14, 1923)
Feb. 28, 1979 – Amalgamated with Brameda Resources and a subsid. of Teck Corporation to form Amalgamated

Brameda Yukon Ltd.; basis 1 Teck cl. B sh. for 3 Yukon shs.

Yukon Explorations Ltd. (B.C. 1946)
Wound up. Bondholders received 70% on account of principal; nothing for shldrs.

Yukon Galena Hill Mines Ltd. (Ont. 1948)
1949 – Merged into Consolidated Yukeno Mines Ltd.; basis 1 new for 3 old shs. (see Consolidated Yukeno Mines Ltd.)

Yukon Gold Corporation (Wash. July 23, 1987)
June 12, 1997 – Name changed to Alliance Pacific Gold Corp. and continued into Yukon. ■

Yukon Gold Placers, Limited (Can. Feb. 18, 1946)
Nov. 19, 1985 – Name changed to Carlin Resources Corp.; basis 1 new for 4 old shs. ■

Yukon Gold Placers Ltd. (Can. 1946)
1957 – In liquidation; assets acquired by Nighthawk Gold Mines Ltd.; basis 1 new for 10 old shs. Yukon's 5% prior lien bonds exchanged on basis of 500 shs. Nighthawk per $1,000; unsecured creditors received 250 shs. per $1,000.

Yukon Minerals Corporation (Alta. 1986)
May 30, 1991 – Name changed to Consolidated Yukon Minerals Corporation; basis 1 new for 5 old shs. ■

Yukon-Nevada Gold Corp. (B.C. May 30, 1988)
Oct. 11, 2012 – Name changed to Veris Gold Corp.; basis 1 new for 10 old shs. ■

Yukon North West Explorations Ltd. (Can. 1945)
1947 – Charter cancelled.

Yukon Properties Limited (Yuk. 1968)
Oct. 17, 1977 – Struck off register.

Yukon Ranges Exploration Ltd. (Ont. 1949)
Charter cancelled.

Yukon Revenue Mines Limited (N.P.L.) (B.C. May 28, 1968)
Dec. 17, 1997 – Continued into Yukon.
Dec. 29, 1997 – Name changed to YKR International Resources Ltd.; basis 1 new for 3 old shs. ■

Yukon Spirit Mines Ltd. (B.C. 1984)
Mar. 26, 1998 – Name changed to Gainey Resources Ltd.; basis 1 new for 7.4 old shs. (see FPsurvey - Mines & Energy)

Yukon Zinc Corporation (B.C. May 21, 1993)
July 8, 2008 – Acquired by Northwest Nonferrous Investment Company, Limited and Jinduicheng Molybdenum Group, Ltd. for 22¢ per sh.

Yukonadian Mineral Resources Ltd. (B.C. 1966)
Aug. 24, 1976 – Name changed to Yucatan Resources Ltd.; basis 1 new for 3 old shs. ■

Yukonite Explorations Limited (Ont. July 24, 1953)
Feb. 20, 1964 – Name changed to M & M Porcupine Gold Mines Limited. ■

Yukore Mines Ltd. (Ont. 1945)
Aug. 1957 – Acquired by Continental Consolidated Mines & Oils Corp. Ltd.; basis 1 new for 5 old shs. (see Continental Consolidated Mines & Oils Corp. Ltd.)

Yukoterre Resources Inc. (Ont. Feb. 8, 2017)
Feb. 26, 2021 – Name changed to Silo Wellness Inc. pursuant to reverse takeover acquisition of FlyOverture Equity Inc., and concurrent amalgamation of FlyOverture with wholly owned 1261466 B.C. Inc. (see FPsurvey - Industrials)

Yuma Copper Corp. (B.C. Nov. 21, 1985)
Apr. 27, 2001 – Dissolved.

Yuma Gold Mines Ltd. (B.C. Nov. 21, 1985)
Dec. 11, 1996 – Name changed to Yuma Copper Corp. ■

Yumy Bear Goods Inc. (B.C. Sept. 22, 1997)
Dec. 30, 2021 – Name changed to The Yumy Candy Company Inc. (see FPsurvey - Industrials)

Yuntone Capital Corp. (B.C. Mar. 6, 2008)
May 21, 2021 – Name changed to Mantaro Silver Corp. pursuant to the Qualifying Transaction reverse takeover acquisition of (old) Mantaro Silver Corp.; basis 1 new for 2 old shs. ■

Yuriko Resources Corp. (B.C. Oct. 7, 1986)
Jan. 23, 1992 – Name changed to Candy Express Stores Ltd.; basis 1 new for 5 old shs. ■

Yvanex Developments Limited (Ont. 1971)
June 12, 1985 – Acquired by Financial Trustco Capital Ltd. Shldrs. of Yvanex received one pref. sh. and 1/3 com. sh. purchase wt. of Financial Trustco for each 7.4 com. shs. of Yvanex.

Z

Z-Gold Exploration Inc. (Alta. June 15, 2006)
May 22, 2014 – Name changed to Brunswick Resources Inc. ■

Z28 Capital Corp. (Alta. Sept. 2, 2004)
Dec. 8, 2006 – Formed illumiCell Corporation in Alberta on Qualifying Transaction reverse takeover acquisition of and amalgamation with illumiCell Corporation; basis 1 new for 2.11 Z28 shs. and 5 new for 1 old illumiCell sh. ■

ZAQ Inc. (Can. Feb. 9, 2000)
Mar. 18, 2004 – Name changed to ISACSOFT Inc. ■

ZCL Composites Inc. (Can. Feb. 23, 1988)
Apr. 4, 2019 – Acquired by Shawcor Ltd. and subsequently merged into Shawcor to continue as Shawcor Ltd.; basis $10 cash per sh. (see Shawcor Ltd.)

ZCL Mfg. Canada Inc. (Alta. Sept. 14, 1987)
Feb. 23, 1988 – Continued into Canada.
Aug. 23, 1994 – Name changed to ZCL Composites Inc. ■

ZEN Graphene Solutions Ltd. (Ont. July 29, 2008)
Nov. 1, 2021 – Name changed to Zentek Ltd. (see FPsurvey - Mines & Energy; FPsurvey - Industrials)

ZENN Motor Company Inc. (Ont. Sept. 28, 2004)
Apr. 6, 2015 – Name changed to EEStor Corporation. ■

ZENON Environmental Inc. (Can. Dec. 10, 1957)
Aug. 11, 1992 – Continued into Ontario.
June 2, 2006 – Acquired by General Electric Company for Cdn$24 for either com. or cl. A shs.

ZEOX Corporation (Alta. Mar. 13, 1997)
Jan. 2, 2014 – Struck from registry and dissolved.

ZTR Acquisition Corp. (B.C. Oct. 22, 2012)
Dec. 21, 2020 – Name changed to Angold Resources Ltd. pursuant to the reverse takeover acquisition of Federal Gold Corp. ■

ZYP Capital Corp. (B.C. Sept. 18, 2007)
Apr. 27, 2011 – Name changed to Baikal Forest Corp. pursuant to Qualifying Transaction reverse takeover acquisition of Irkutskvodlepromstroy-Nebelskiy LPH Ltd. ■

ZZZ Capital Corp. (B.C. July 17, 2007)
Jan. 5, 2015 – Dissolved and struck from register.

Zab Resources Inc. (B.C. Aug. 24, 1984)
Apr. 16, 2009 – Name changed to Kokomo Enterprises Inc.; basis 1 new for 25 old shs. ■

Zaba Lee Enterprises Inc. (B.C. Mar. 25, 1981)
Aug. 12, 1991 – Name changed to Eurotech Building Products Inc. ■

Zacapa Resources Ltd. (B.C. Jan. 9, 2017)
Nov. 23, 2023 – Amalgamated with a wholly owned subsid. of Outcrop Silver & Gold Corporation; basis 1 Outcrop sh. for 4 Zacapa shs.

Zacherra Holdings Inc. (Can. Jan. 25, 1928; via Dominion charter)
Aug. 1, 1997 – Continued into Ontario.
Apr. 14, 2000 – Name changed to First Interactive Inc. (see FPsurvey - Industrials)

Zadar Ventures Ltd. (B.C. Aug. 6, 2008)
July 19, 2021 – Name changed to XRApplied Technologies Inc. following the acquisition of immersive technology solutions provider XRApplied S.A.S. (see FPsurvey - Industrials)

Zagabelt Mining Corp. Ltd. (Ont. 1939)
May 26, 1958 – Dissolved.

Zahavy Mines Limited (Ont. June 15, 1959)
Feb. 10, 1993 – Name changed to Xavier Mines Limited; basis 1 new for 5 old shs. ■

Zaio Corporation (Alta. Feb. 20, 2004 amalg.)
Oct. 17, 2016 – Name changed to Clarocity Corporation. ■

Zakor Gold Mines Ltd. (Ont. 1955)
May 1958 – Charter cancelled.

Zambezi Sports Inc. (B.C. Sept. 15, 2015)
July 9, 2021 – Name changed to SWMBRD Sports Inc. (see FPsurvey - Industrials)

Zamora Gold Corp. (Ont. Nov. 23, 1989)
Aug. 13, 1996 – Continued into British Columbia.
June 2, 1998 – Continued into Yukon. (see FPsurvey - Mines & Energy)

Zanzibar Gold Inc. (B.C. Aug. 21, 2014)
Sept. 23, 2020 – Name changed to Mojave Gold Corp. ■

Zapata Capital Inc. (Alta. Jan. 26, 1998)
June 18, 1999 – Formed Zapata Energy Corporation in Alberta on acquisition of and amalgamation with 744997 Alberta Ltd. ■

Zapata Energy Corporation (Alta. June 18, 1999 amalg.)
June 25, 2010 – Name changed to Surge Energy Inc. (see FPsurvey - Mines & Energy)

Zapata Granby Corporation (Can. - unspecified 1979 amalg.)
Nov. 30, 1979 – Mining assets in west central B.C. sold for approx. $37 million to Noranda Mines Ltd. As a result, Zapata Granby operated only a fishing division as a wholly owned subsid. of Zapata Corporation of Houston, Texas.

Zappa Resources Ltd. (B.C. Oct. 21, 1980)
July 2, 2008 – Name changed to AKA Ventures Inc.; basis 1 new for 2 old shs. ■

Zara Resources Inc. (Ont. Oct. 9, 2012)
July 3, 2013 – Continued into British Columbia.
Mar. 22, 2019 – Name changed to Ionic Brands Corp. following reverse takeover acquisition of Blacklist Holdings Inc.; basis 1 new for 35.9389 old shs. (see FPsurvey - Industrials)

Zarcan International Resources Inc. (B.C. May 14, 1981)
Jan. 30, 2006 – Name changed to Bighorn Petroleum Ltd. ■

Zargon Energy Trust (Alta. June 17, 2004)
Dec. 31, 2010 – Succeeded by Zargon Oil & Gas Ltd. pursuant to plan of arrangement whereby Zargon Oil & Gas Ltd. was formed to facilitate the conversion of the trust into a corporation and the trust was subsequently dissolved. ■

Zargon Oil & Gas Ltd. (Alta. Nov. 12, 1987)
July 21, 2004 – Converted into an income trust named Zargon Energy Trust; basis 1 Zargon Energy trust unit or 1 Zargon Oil exch. sh. for 1 Zargon Oil com. sh.

Zargon Oil & Gas Ltd. (Alta. 2004)
Dec. 31, 2010 – Redeemed all o/s exch. shs.; basis 1.87416 com. shs. of new Zargon Oil & Gas Ltd. (successor to Zargon Energy Trust) for 1 exch. shs. of old Zargon Oil.

Zargon Oil & Gas Ltd. (Alta. Dec. 31, 2010; amalg.)
Sept. 8, 2020 – Filed a notice of intention to make a proposal under the Bankruptcy and Insolvency Act (BIA). MNP Ltd. appointed proposal trustee.
Jan. 29, 2021 – Reorganization under the BIA was completed. Pursuant to the reorganization, the company's articles were amended to provide that all previous o/s com. shs. of the company were redesignated as redeemable com. shs., redeemable for nil consideration and subsequently cancelled.

Zarina Explorations Ltd. (Ont. July 19, 1974)
Nov. 23, 1987 – Name changed to Emfax International Ltd. (see FPsurvey - Industrials)

Zarlink Semiconductor Inc. (Can. Mar. 8, 1971)
Oct. 31, 2011 – Acquired by 0916753 B.C. ULC, a wholly owned subsid. of Microsemi Corporation, for Cdn$3.98 per sh. and Cdn$1,624.49 for each Cdn$1,000 principal amount of Zarlink 6% debs.

Zaruma Resources Inc. (Yuk. Oct. 17, 2000)
Nov. 8, 2011 – Name changed to Red Tiger Mining Inc.; basis 1 new for 10 old shs. (see FPsurvey - Mines & Energy)

Zaurak Capital Corp. (Ont. July 6, 1945)
Nov. 13, 2006 – Certificate of incorporation cancelled and dissolved.

Zavitz Petroleum Corporation (Can. 1981)
Nov. 21, 1994 – Name changed to Jaguar Petroleum Corporation. ■

Zavitz Technology Inc. (Can. 1981)
Aug. 31, 1993 – Name changed to Zavitz Petroleum Corporation; basis 1 new for 5 old shs. ■

Zazu Metals Corporation (Can. Nov. 29, 2006)
July 18, 2017 – Acquired by Solitario Exploration & Royalty Corp. (renamed Solitario Zinc Corp.); basis 0.3572 Solitario shs. for 1 Zazu com. sh. (see Solitario Zinc Corp.)

ZComm Industries Inc. (B.C. Aug. 26, 1985)
Aug. 25, 1995 – Name changed to Labrador International Mining Ltd.; basis 1 new for 2 old shs. ■

Zconnexx Corporation (Ont. June 16, 1998)
June 2002 – Declared bankrupt. Pollard & Associates Inc. appointed trustee.

Zeacan Products Ltd. (Alta. June 5, 1987)
June 15, 1993 – Name changed to Canadian Zeolite Ltd.; basis 1 new for 5 old shs. ■

Zeal Capital Ltd. (B.C. Dec. 21, 1983)
June 16, 1993 – Name changed to First Quantum Ventures Ltd.; basis 1 new for 4 old shs. ■

Zeballos Queen Mines Limited (B.C. 1937)
Dec. 19, 1960 – Struck off register.

Zebedee Oil Limited (Can. Apr. 14, 1926)
Apr. 19, 1971 – Name changed to Osias Resources Canada Ltd. ■

Zebellos Interests Ltd. (B.C. 1943)
1971 – Charter cancelled.

Zecotek Medical Systems Inc. (B.C. Nov. 25, 1983)
Nov. 26, 2007 – Name changed to Zecotek Photonics Inc. (see FPsurvey - Industrials)

Zedcor Energy Inc. (Alta. Aug. 10, 2011)
Sept. 21, 2020 – Name changed to Zedcor Inc. (see FPsurvey - Industrials)

Zedi Inc. (Alta. Oct. 19, 1994)
Feb. 24, 2014 – Acquired by 1779958 Alberta Ltd.; basis $1.05 cash per sh.

zed.i solutions inc. (Alta. Oct. 19, 1994)
June 20, 2007 – Name changed to Zedi Inc. ∎

Zelikovitz Bros. Ltd. (Can. 1949)
Mar. 16, 1964 – Name changed to Freedman Wholesale Ltd. ∎

Zeller's Limited (Can. 1931)
Sept. 1, 1978 – Hudson's Bay Company offered to acquire all o/s cl. A and B shs. on basis of 1 Hudson's sh. and $16.50 for each 4 Zeller's shs. Hudson's Bay acquired 57% int. under the offer which expired Oct. 3, 1978. (see Hudson's Bay Company)
Jan. 1981 – Hudson's Bay made a new offer to acquire the remaining cl. A and B shs. at $18 per sh. or, at the option of Zeller shldrs., either 1 ser. D pref. sh. or 100 ser. E pref. shs. for each Zeller's com. sh. (see Hudson's Bay Company)
May 19, 1981 – Hudson's Bay Company acquired all o/s Zeller's shs. (see Hudson's Bay Company)

Zemex Corporation (Ont. Dec. 4, 1997)
June 5, 1998 – Continued into Canada.
May 9, 2003 – Merged with controlled affiliate of Lima Exchange-listed Cementos Pacasmayo S.A.A.; basis US$8.80 per sh.

Zen International Resources Ltd. (Yuk. Nov. 21, 1996)
Mar. 27, 2002 – Continued into Alberta.
Apr. 1, 2002 – Name changed to Orca Petroleum Inc.; basis 1 new for 10 old shs. ∎

Zena Capital Corp. (B.C. Feb. 8, 2000)
June 30, 2009 – Name changed to Zena Mining Corp. (see FPsurvey - Mines & Energy)

Zenabis Global Inc. (B.C. July 9, 1985)
June 3, 2021 – Acquired by HEXO Corp.; basis 0.01772 HEXO com. shs. for 1 Zenabis cl. A com. sh. (see HEXO Corp.)

Zenas Energy Corp. (Alta. June 28, 2005)
Jan. 4, 2007 – Plan of Arrangement acquisition by TUSK Energy Corporation; basis 1.033 new TUSK sh. for 1 old Zenas sh. (see TUSK Energy Corporation)

Zenco Resources Inc. (B.C. Dec. 7, 1965)
May 7, 1988 – Name changed to Solidor Resources Inc.; basis 1 new for 5 old shs. ∎

Zenda Capital Corp. (Ont. July 4, 1996 amalg.)
Mar. 7, 2005 – Name changed to Terex Resources Inc. ∎

Zenda Exploration Co. Ltd. (B.C. 1949)
Apr. 13, 1967 – Charter cancelled.

Zenda Gold Corp. (Ont. July 4, 1996 amalg.)
Nov. 10, 1999 – Name changed to Zenda Capital Corp. ∎

Zenda Gold Mining (Canada) Ltd. (B.C. 1949)
1952 – Name changed to Zenda Exploration Co. Ltd. ∎

Zenith Electric Supply Limited (Ont. 1940)
May 26, 1978 – Winding up of co. approved by shldrs. Previously, a subsid. of Northern Telecom Ltd. had acquired some 99% int. through a purchase offer of $3.25 per sh.
1978 – Funds deposited with public trustee in 1979 for distribution to fewer than 20 shldrs. who had not participated in liquidation by early 1980.
1980 – Charter surrendered for cancellation.

Zenith Energy Corporation (B.C. 1979)
Nov. 29, 1985 – Struck off register.

Zenith Energy Ltd. (B.C. Sept. 20, 2007)
June 1, 2020 – Voluntarily delisted. Will continue to trade on London Stock Exchange and Oslo Stock Exchange (Merkur Market). (see FPsurvey - Mines & Energy)

Zenith Exploration Inc. (B.C. June 19, 2015)
Oct. 23, 2020 – Name changed to Waraba Gold Limited. (see FPsurvey - Mines & Energy)

Zenith Industries Corp. (Can. July 8, 2004)
Aug. 21, 2009 – Name changed to LGC Skyrota Wind Energy Corp. ∎

Zenith Metals Recovery Inc. (B.C. 1986)
Nov. 17, 2004 – Restored to registry on a limited basis. Previously dissolved and struck from register.
Nov. 18, 2005 – Dissolved and struck from register on expiry of limited restoration.

Zenith Mining Corp. Ltd. (B.C. Dec. 7, 1965)
May 17, 1977 – Name changed to Zenore Resources Inc. ∎

Zenith Molybdenite Corporation Ltd. (unknown)
1956 – Charter cancelled.

Zenith Oils Ltd. (Sask. 1953)
1958 – Struck off register.

Zenmac Explorations Limited (Ont. Feb. 14, 1952)
July 12, 1985 – Name changed to Zenmac Zinc Ltd.; basis 3 new for 1 old sh. ∎

Zenmac Metal Mines Ltd. (Ont. Feb. 14, 1952)
May 11, 1979 – Name changed to Zenmac Explorations Limited. ∎

Zenmac Zinc Ltd. (Ont. Feb. 14, 1952)
June 24, 1999 – Charter cancelled.

Zenon Silver Mines Ltd. (B.C. 1968)
Apr. 20, 1972 – Name changed to Montego Resources Ltd. ∎

Zenore Resources Inc. (B.C. Dec. 7, 1965)
Jan. 20, 1982 – Name changed to Zenco Resources Inc.; basis 1 new for 2 old shs. ∎

Zenyatta Ventures Ltd. (Ont. July 29, 2008)
Jan. 16, 2019 – Name changed to ZEN Graphene Solutions Ltd. ∎

Zeo-Tech Enviro Corp. (Alta. June 5, 1987)
Jan. 31, 2007 – Name changed to Canadian Mining Company Inc. ∎

Zep Energy Corporation (B.C. 1980)
July 6, 1984 – Name changed to Achilles Resources Ltd.; basis 1 new for 3 old shs. ∎

Zephyr Resources Ltd. (Alta.)
1978 – Continued into Canada.
Sept. 9, 1983 – Amalgamated with Maynard Energy Inc.; basis 1 Maynard sh. for 4.25 Zephyr shs.

Zermatt Capital Inc. (Can. Apr. 1, 2005)
Dec. 8, 2006 – Name changed to Aptilon Corporation following Qualifying Transaction reverse takeover acquisition of Aptilon Holdings Inc. ∎

007 Precious Metals Inc. (B.C. Oct. 7, 1987)
Oct. 15, 1993 – Name changed to Cansib Energy Inc.; basis 1 new for 3 old shs. ∎

0373849 B.C. Ltd. (B.C. Aug. 17, 1987)
June 24, 2011 – Amalgamated with Procon Acquisitionco Ltd., a wholly owned subsid. of Procon Mining and Tunnelling Ltd., to form Procon Holdings Ltd. All o/s com. shs., other than those held by Procon, were exchange for 1 redeemable preferred sh., immediately redeemed for $0.00000311839 cash per sh.

0755461 B.C. Ltd. (B.C. Apr. 21, 2006)
July 9, 2025 – Name changed to Kleen Hy-DRO-GEN Inc. pursuant the reverse takeover acquisition of (old) Kleen Hy-Dro-Gen Inc. ∎

0775461 B.C. Ltd. (B.C. Apr. 21, 2006)
May 1, 2023 – Name changed to 0755461 B.C. Ltd. ∎

0799714 B.C. Ltd. (B.C. Feb. 22, 2019 amalg.)
Feb. 27, 2019 – Acquired by Pan American Silver Corp.; basis either US$3.40 cash or 0.2403 Pan American sh. for 1 Tahoe sh.

0915998 B.C. Ltd. (Alta. Feb. 24, 1994)
Apr. 16, 2013 – All o/s shs. not already held by MCI Industrial Inc. acquired for 2¢ cash per sh.
Apr. 19, 2013 – Voluntarily wound-up and dissolved.

0944460 B.C. Ltd. (B.C. June 28, 2012)
Sept. 13, 2019 – Privatized; basis $0.00209 cash per sh.

0968998 B.C. Ltd. (B.C. May 1, 2013)
Oct. 26, 2018 – Name changed to Plank Ventures Ltd. (see FPsurvey - Industrials)

Zeron Resources Ltd. (B.C. 1980)
May 5, 1983 – Formed Deex Resources Corp. in British Columbia on amalgamation with Deex Investment Corporation and Halven Oil Ltd.; basis 1 new for 5 old shs. ∎

Zetta Capital Corp. (B.C. Dec. 11, 2015)
Dec. 6, 2021 – Name changed to PanGenomic Health Inc. (see FPsurvey - Industrials)

ZeU Crypto Networks Inc. (Can. Jan. 4, 2018)
Oct. 15, 2020 – Name changed to ZeU Technologies, Inc. (see FPsurvey - Industrials)

Zeus Energy Corp. (B.C. Sept. 22, 1986)
Nov. 13, 1997 – Amalgamated with U.S. Oil & Gas Inc. (1 for 1) to form a new company named U.S. Oil and Gas Resources Inc.; basis 1 new U.S. Oil sh. for 1 old Zeus sh. (see U.S. Oil and Gas Resources Inc.)

Zeus Red Lake Gold Mines Ltd. (Ont. 1946)
1949 – Name changed to Principle Strategic Minerals Ltd. ∎

Zi Corporation (Alta. Dec. 4, 1987)
Apr. 14, 2009 – Acquired by Nuance Communications, Inc.; basis US$0.34 plus 0.03706 Nuance shs. for 1 Zi sh.

Zicor Mining Inc. (B.C. Apr. 28, 1983)
Mar. 29, 1996 – Continued into Yukon.
Sept. 18, 1998 – Name changed to Mano River Resources Inc. ∎

Zicton Gold Limited (B.C. Apr. 27, 1987)
Jan. 27, 1994 – Name changed to Saddle Mountain Mining Corporation. ∎

Ziebart Corp. (Que. 1971)
Nov. 1, 1983 – Remaining 80% int. not previously held acquired by Ziebart International Corporation of Detroit, Mich.
June 30, 1984 – Wound up.

Zigold Resources Inc. (Alta. 1987)
Dec. 1, 1991 – Struck off register.

Zim-Gold Resources Ltd. (B.C. Aug. 29, 1979)
Feb. 5, 2001 – Name changed to Noise Media Inc. ∎

Zimtu Technologies Inc. (B.C. Oct. 27, 1986)
Apr. 4, 2003 – Name changed to International Zimtu Technologies Inc.; basis 1 new for 30 old shs. ∎

Zinat Mines Ltd. (Can. 1934)
Mar. 1973 – Name changed to Newport Mining & Land Development Ltd.

Zinc Lake Mines Ltd. (Ont. 1946)
1961 – Charter cancelled.

Zinc8 Energy Solutions Inc. (B.C. Dec. 8, 2011)
Jan. 31, 2024 – Name changed to Abound Energy Inc. (see FPsurvey - Industrials)

Zinccorp Resources Inc. (B.C. Nov. 8, 2006)
May 24, 2016 – Dissolved.

Zincfields Mining Corp. Ltd. (Ont. 1964)
1975 – Charter cancelled.

Zincore Metals Inc. (B.C. Sept. 21, 2005)
Apr. 15, 2025 – Name changed to Golden Cross Resources Inc.; basis 1 new for 2.5 old shs. (see FPsurvey - Mines & Energy)

Zinnian Technologies Inc. (Alta. Feb. 13, 1998)
June 5, 2002 – Legal corporate status allowed to lapse.

ZipLocal Inc. (Ont. Aug. 22, 2005 amalg.)
Aug. 21, 2017 – All o/s com. shs. not already held acquired by Intercap Inc.; basis $0.0035 cash per sh. or 1 Intercap redeem. pref. shs., immediately redeemable for $0.0035 cash for 1 ZipLocal sh.

Zoa Petroleum Ltd. (B.C. Mar. 31, 1987)
July 22, 1992 – Amalgamated with Tokenhouse Yard Holdings Inc. to form Newgate Resources Ltd.; basis 1 new for 0.78 Tokenhouse shs. and 1 new for 1.38 Zoa shs. (see Newgate Resources Ltd.)

Zodiac Exploration Corp. (B.C. Apr. 17, 1986)
Dec. 18, 1998 – Name changed to Donnybrook Resources Inc.; basis 1 new for 7 old shs. ■

Zodiac Exploration Inc. (Alta. Sept. 28, 2010)
May 1, 2014 – Name changed to Mobius Resources Inc.; basis 1 new for 15 old shs. ■

Zodiac Hurricane Marine (Consolidated) Inc. (B.C. 1987 amalg.)
Mar. 12, 1990 – Formed Zodiac Hurricane Technologies Inc. on amalgamation with Zodiac Hurricane Technologies Inc. All o/s shs. of Zodiac Hurricane Marine were redeemed at $0.34 per sh. ■

Zodiac Hurricane Marine Inc. (B.C. 1987 amalg.)
June 28, 1989 – Name changed to Zodiac Hurricane Marine (Consolidated) Inc.; basis 1 new for 10 old shs. ■

Zodiac Hurricane Technologies Inc. (B.C. 1987 amalg.)
Jan. 12, 1999 – Amalgamated with Zodiac Hurricane Investments Ltd.; basis 1 new redeemable pfce. sh. of amalg. co. for each sh. held, then pfce. shs. redeemed immediately at $0.80 per sh. ■

Zodiac Ltd. (Que. 1964)
Oct. 18, 1978 – Amalgamated with wholly owned Zodiac Realties Inc., Zodiac Industries Ltd. and its subsid. M.S.M. Industries Inc. to form Zodiac Supreme Inc.

Zodiac Oil Co. Ltd. (Alta. Oct. 18, 1949)
1951 – Acquired by Calvan Consolidated Oil & Gas Co. Ltd.; basis 1 new for 3 old shs.

Zodiac Resources Ltd. (Alta. 1978)
Sept. 30, 1980 – Amalgamated with Howe Sound Exploration Ltd. to continue as Zodiac Resources Ltd.; basis 1 new for 1 old sh.
Feb. 28, 1983 – Amalgamated with Reigate Resources, Inc. and Midvale Petroleum Ltd. to form Reigate Resources (Canada) Ltd.; basis 1 new Reigate sh. for 4 old Zodiac shs.

Zoglo's Incredible Food Corp. (B.C. July 23, 2020)
Feb. 28, 2023 – Name changed to Zoglo's Food Corp. (see FPsurvey - Industrials)

Zohini Mines Ltd. (B.C. 1965)
Dec. 1976 – Charter cancelled.

Zolota Yellowknife Mines Ltd. (Ont. 1946)
Oct. 22, 1965 – Dissolved.

Zomedica Pharmaceuticals Corp. (Alta. Jan. 9, 2013)
Oct. 5, 2020 – Name changed to Zomedica Corp. (see FPsurvey - Industrials)

The Zone Entertainment Group, Inc. (Alta. Jan. 30, 1997)
July 2, 2010 – Struck from registry and dissolved.

Zone Explorations Ltd. (B.C. 1969)
June 27, 1977 – Dissolved.

Zone Petroleum Corporation (B.C. 1978)
1982 – Amalgamated in British Columbia to continue with same name.
July 22, 1994 – Dissolved and struck off register.

Zone Resources Inc. (B.C. July 23, 2009)
Nov. 18, 2021 – Name changed to Sombra Capital Corp. (see FPsurvey - Mines & Energy)

Zone Resources Limited (Ont. 1981)
July 30, 1982 – Name changed to Thames Resources Limited. ■

Zoneore Rouyn Mines Ltd. (Ont. 1946)
Sept. 1960 – Charter cancelled.

Zongshen PEM Power Systems Inc. (B.C. July 30, 2004 amalg.)
Dec. 28, 2012 – Acquired by Hong Kong VAS International Development Limited for 60¢ per sh.

Zonne Investment Corp. (Alta. 1987)
Nov. 1, 1994 – Dissolved and struck off register.

Zoolander Corporation (Ont. Oct. 27, 2005)
Sept. 10, 2013 – Name changed to Mezzotin Minerals Inc. ■

Zoom Telephonics Inc. (B.C. 1986)
1993 – Continued into Delaware.
Feb. 13, 2002 – Name changed to Zoom Technologies, Inc.

ZoomAway Travel Inc. (B.C. Dec. 10, 2010)
Apr. 15, 2021 – Name changed to ZoomAway Technologies Inc.; basis 1 new for 9 old shs. (see FPsurvey - Industrials)

ZoomerMedia Limited (Can. July 1, 2008 amalg.)
Dec. 19, 2024 – All o/s shs. not already held by Moses Znaimer and other major shldrs. acquired for Cdn$0.08 cash per sh. Company now private.

Zorah Media Corporation (B.C. Mar. 19, 1980)
Mar. 1, 1999 – Delisted from the Vancouver Stock Exchange. Subsequently dissolved and struck from register.

Zorin Exploration Ltd. (Alta. May 30, 1997)
Apr. 26, 2004 – Acquired by Hawker Resources Inc.; basis for cash offer - $0.097999415 plus 0.05848633 new Hawker sh. or, for share offer - 0.07746383 new Hawker sh. for 1 old Zorin sh. (see Hawker Resources Inc.)

Zorro Capital Inc. (Alta. June 18, 2012)
Mar. 15, 2016 – Dissolved following Qualifying Transaction private placement subscription of 2,000,000 units at 10¢ per Avanti Energy Inc, unit plus 1/2 wt. of Avanti wt. and distribution of Avanti units to shareholders. Each wt. is exercisable to purchase Avanti unit at 15¢ per unit for a 12 months period fr date of issuance. (see Avanti Energy Inc.)

Zroback Gold Mines Ltd. (Ont. 1960)
Mar. 25, 1965 – Dissolved.

Zulapa Mining Corporation Ltd. (Ont. 1934)
Sept. 27, 1982 – Dissolved.

Zungui Haixi Corporation (Ont. Aug. 11, 2009)
Sept. 12, 2012 – Dissolved and struck from register.

Zuni Energy Corp. (B.C. Feb. 2, 1981)
May 24, 1991 – Name changed to Home Ventures Ltd.; basis 1 new for 5 old shs. ■

Zuni Holdings Inc. (Alta. Dec. 5, 1994)
Nov. 22, 1995 – Continued into Ontario.
Dec. 5, 1995 – Name changed to Magnifoam Technology International Inc.; basis 1 new for 2 old shs. ■

Zuni Holdings Inc. (Ont. Nov. 22, 1995)
Jan. 7, 2011 – Acquired by Pacific Safety Products Inc.; basis 1 Pacific Safety sh. for 1 Zuni sh. (see Pacific Safety Products Inc.)

Zurfund International Limited (B.C. 1981)
Feb. 2, 1990 – Name changed to Atacama Resources Ltd.; basis 1 new for 5 old shs. ■

Zuri Capital Corp. (B.C. May 2, 2011)
Apr. 23, 2014 – Name changed to Phoenix Gold Resources Corp. following Qualifying Transaction reverse takeover acquisition of Phoenix Gold Resources Ltd. ■

Zurich Energy Corp. (B.C. 1982)
Jan. 13, 1988 – Delisted from the Vancouver Stock Exchange. Subsequently struck from registry and dissolved.

Zurich Explorations Limited (Ont. 1968)
Feb. 20, 1980 – Dissolved.

Zycom Corporation (Alta. Oct. 14, 1987)
June 7, 1999 – Delisted from the Alberta Stock Exchange. Subsequently wound-up and dissolved.

Zygote Resources Ltd. (B.C. Apr. 21, 1987)
Sept. 4, 1992 – Name changed to Cana Telecommunications Inc. ■

Zymeworks Inc. (Can. Sept. 8, 2003)
May 2, 2017 – Continued into British Columbia.
Oct. 13, 2022 – All o/s com. shs. exchanged for (a) com. shs. of Zymeworks Delaware Inc. (renamed Zymeworks Inc.); or (b) exchangeable shs. of Zymeworks ExchangeCo Ltd.; or (c) a combination of com. shs. and exchangeable shs. for 1 Zymeworks com. sh. Zymeworks Canada (renamed Zymeworks BC Inc.) now a wholly owned subsid. of Zymeworks Delaware.

Zynex Corporation (Ont. Oct. 11, 1984)
Aug. 15, 1997 – Name changed to Imperial PlasTech Inc.; basis 1 new for 11 old shs. ■

Zytec Computers Ltd. (B.C. 1983)
Oct. 7, 1987 – Name changed to Zytec Systems Inc. (see FPsurvey - Industrials)

CANADA'S INFORMATION RESOURCE CENTRE (CIRC)

Access all these great resources online, all the time, at Canada's Information Resource Centre (CIRC)
http://circ.greyhouse.ca

Canada's Information Resource Centre (CIRC) integrates all of Grey House Canada's award-winning reference content into one easy-to-use online resource. With **over 100,000 Canadian organizations** and **over 140,600 contacts**, plus thousands of additional facts and figures, CIRC is the most comprehensive resource for specialized database content in Canada! Access all 20 databases, including the recently revised *Careers & Employment Canada*, with Canada Info Desk Complete - it's the total package!

KEY ADVANTAGES OF CIRC:

- Seamlessly cross-database search content from select databases
- Save search results for future reference
- Link directly to websites or email addresses
- Clear display of your results makes compiling and adding to your research easier than ever before

DESIGN YOUR OWN CUSTOM CONTACT LISTS!

CIRC gives you the option to define and extract your own lists in seconds. Find new business leads, do keyword searches, locate upcoming conference attendees; all the information you want is right at your fingertips.

Brand new Major Canadian Cities data!

CHOOSE BETWEEN KEYWORD AND ADVANCED SEARCH!

With CIRC, you can choose between Keyword and Advanced search to pinpoint information. Designed for both beginner and advanced researchers, you can conduct simple text searches as well as powerful Boolean searches.

PROFILES IN CIRC INCLUDE:

- Phone numbers, email addresses, fax numbers and full addresses for all branches of the organization
- Social media accounts, such as Twitter and Facebook
- Key contacts based on job titles
- Budgets, membership fees, staff sizes and more!

Search CIRC using common or unique fields, customized to your needs!

ONLY GREY HOUSE DIRECTORIES PROVIDE SPECIAL CONTENT YOU WON'T FIND ANYWHERE ELSE!

- **Associations Canada:** finances/funding sources, activities, publications, conferences, membership, awards, member profile
- **Canadian Parliamentary Guide:** private and political careers of elected members, complete list of constituencies and representatives
- **Financial Services:** type of ownership, number of employees, year founded, assets, revenue, ticker symbol
- **Libraries Canada:** staffing, special collections, services, year founded, national library symbol, regional system
- **Governments Canada:** municipal population
- **Canadian Who's Who:** birth city, publications, education (degrees, alma mater), career/occupation and employer
- **Major Canadian Cities:** demographics, ethnicity, immigration, language, education, housing, income, labour and transportation
- **Health Guide Canada:** chronic and mental illnesses, general resources, appendices and statistics
- **Cannabis Canada:** firm type, foreign activity, type of ownership, revenue sources
- **Canadian Environmental Resource Guide:** organization scope, budget, number of employees, activities, regulations, areas of environmental specialty
- **Careers & Employment Canada:** career associations, career employment websites, expanded employers, recruiters, awards and scholarships, and summer jobs
- **FP Directory of Directors:** names, directorships, educational and professional backgrounds and email addresses of top Canadian directors; list of major companies and complete company contact information
- **FPbonds:** bond information in PDF form and with sortable tables
- **FPsurvey:** detailed profiles of current publicly traded companies, as well as past corporate changes

The new CIRC provides easier searching and faster, more pinpointed results of all of our great resources in Canada, from Associations and Government to Major Companies to Zoos and everything in between. Whether you need fully detailed information on your contact or just an email address, you can customize your search query to meet your needs.

Contact us now for a **free trial** subscription or visit http://circ.greyhouse.ca

For more information please contact Grey House Publishing Canada
Tel.: (866) 433-4739 or (416) 644-6479 Fax: (416) 644-1904 | info@greyhouse.ca | www.greyhouse.ca

Canadian Almanac & Directory

The Definitive Resource for Facts & Figures About Canada

The *Canadian Almanac & Directory* has been Canada's most authoritative sourcebook for 178 years. Published annually since 1847, it continues to be widely used by publishers, business professionals, government offices, researchers, information specialists and anyone needing current, accessible information on every imaginable topic relevant to those who live and work in Canada.

A directory and a guide, the *Canadian Almanac & Directory* provides the most comprehensive picture of Canada, from physical attributes to economic and business summaries, leisure and recreation. It combines textual materials, charts, colour photographs and directory listings with detailed profiles, all verified and organized for easy retrieval. The *Canadian Almanac & Directory* is a wealth of general information, displaying national statistics on population, employment, CPI, imports and exports, as well as images of national awards, Canadian symbols, flags, emblems and Canadian parliamentary leaders.

For important contacts throughout Canada, for any number of business projects or for that once-in-a-while critical fact, the *Canadian Almanac & Directory* will help you find the leads you didn't even know existed—quickly and easily!

ALL THE INFORMATION YOU'LL EVER NEED, ORGANIZED INTO 17 DISTINCT CATEGORIES FOR EASY NAVIGATION!

Almanac—a fact-filled snapshot of Canada, including History, Geography, Economics and Vital Statistics.

Arts & Culture—includes 9 topics from Galleries to Zoos.

Associations—thousands of organizations arranged in over 120 different topics, from Accounting to Youth.

Broadcasting—Canada's major Broadcasting Companies, Provincial Radio and Television Stations, Cable Companies, and Specialty Broadcasters.

Business & Finance—Accounting, Banking, Insurance, Canada's Major Companies and Stock Exchanges.

Education—arranged by Province and includes Districts, Government Agencies, Specialized and Independent Schools, Universities and Technical facilities.

Government—spread over three sections, with a Quick Reference Guide, Federal and Provincial listings, County and Municipal Districts and coverage of Courts in Canada.

Health—Government agencies, hospitals, community health centres, retirement care and mental health facilities.

Law Firms—all Major Law Firms, followed by smaller firms organized by Province and listed alphabetically.

Libraries—Canada's main Library/Archive and Government Departments for Libraries, followed by Provincial listings and Regional Systems.

Publishing—Books, Magazines and Newspapers organized by Province, including frequency and circulation figures.

Religion—broad information about religious groups and associations from 37 different denominations.

Sports—Associations in 110 categories, with detailed League and Team listings.

Transportation—complete listings for all major modes.

Utilities—Associations, Government Agencies and Provincial Utility Companies.

GREY HOUSE PUBLISHING CANADA

For more information please contact Grey House Publishing Canada

Tel.: (866)-433-4739 or (416) 644-6479 Fax: (416) 644-1904 | info@greyhouse.ca | www.greyhouse.ca

Répertoire et almanach canadien

La ressource de référence au sujet des données et des faits relatifs au Canada

Le *Répertoire et almanach canadien* constitue le guide canadien le plus rigoureux depuis 178 ans. Publié annuellement depuis 1847, il est toujours grandement utilisé dans le monde des affaires, les bureaux gouvernementaux, par les spécialistes de l'information, les chercheurs, les éditeurs ou quiconque est à la recherche d'information actuelle et accessible sur tous les sujets imaginables à propos des gens qui vivent et travaillent au Canada.

À la fois répertoire et guide, le *Répertoire et almanach canadien* dresse le tableau le plus complet du Canada, des caractéristiques physiques jusqu'aux revues économique et commerciale, en passant par les loisirs et les activités récréatives. Il combine des documents textuels, des représentations graphiques, des photographies en couleurs et des listes de répertoires accompagnées de profils détaillés. Autant d'information pointue et organisée de manière à ce qu'elle soit facile à obtenir. Le *Répertoire et almanach canadien* foisonne de renseignements généraux. Il présente des statistiques nationales sur la population, l'emploi, l'IPC, l'importation et l'exportation ainsi que des images des prix nationaux, des symboles canadiens, des drapeaux, des emblèmes et des leaders parlementaires canadiens.

Si vous cherchez des personnes-ressources essentielles un peu partout au Canada, peu importe qu'il s'agisse de projets d'affaires ou d'une question factuelle anecdotique, le Répertoire et almanach canadien vous fournira les pistes dont vous ignoriez l'existence – rapidement et facilement!

TOUTE L'INFORMATION DONT VOUS AUREZ BESOIN, ORGANISÉE EN 17 CATÉGORIES DISTINCTES POUR UNE CONSULTATION FACILE!

Almanach—un aperçu informatif du Canada, notamment l'histoire, la géographie, l'économie et les statistiques essentielles.

Arts et culture—comprends 9 sujets, des galeries aux zoos.

Associations—des milliers d'organisations classées selon plus de 120 sujets différents, de l'actuariat au jeunesse.

Radiodiffusion—les principales sociétés de radiodiffusion au Canada, les stations radiophoniques et de télévision ainsi que les entreprises de câblodistribution et les diffuseurs thématiques.

Commerce et finance—comptabilité, services bancaires, assurances, principales entreprises et bourses canadiennes.

Éducation—organisé par province et comprend les arrondissements scolaires, les organismes gouvernementaux, les écoles spécialisées et indépendantes, les universités et les établissements techniques.

Gouvernement—s'étend sur trois sections et comprend un guide de référence, des listes fédérales et provinciales, les comtés et arrondissements municipaux ainsi que les cours canadiennes.

Santé—organismes gouvernementaux, hôpitaux, centres de santé communautaires, établissements de soins pour personnes retraitées et de soins de santé mentale.

Sociétés d'avocats—toutes les principales sociétés d'avocats, suivies des sociétés plus petites, classées par province et en ordre alphabétique.

Bibliothèques—la bibliothèque et les archives principales du Canada ainsi que les bibliothèques des ministères, suivis des listes provinciales et des systèmes régionaux.

Édition—livres, magazines et journaux classés par province, y compris leur fréquence et les données relatives à leur diffusion.

Religion—information générale au sujet des groupes religieux et des associations religieuses de 37 dénominations.

Sports—associations de 110 sports distincts; comprend des listes de ligues et d'équipes.

Transport—des listes complètes des principaux modes de transport.

Services publics—associations, organismes gouvernementaux et entreprises de services publics provinciaux.

FORMAT PAPIER OU EN LIGNE— ACCÈS RAPIDE À TOUS LES RENSEIGNEMENTS DONT VOUS AVEZ BESOIN!

Offert sous couverture rigide ou en format électronique grâce au web, le *Répertoire et almanach canadien* offre invariablement un accès instantané aux représentants du gouvernement et aux faits qui font l'objet de vos recherches.

La version imprimée du Répertoire et almanach canadien est vérifiée et mise à jour annuellement. La version en ligne est mise à jour mensuellement. Cette version vous permet de circonscrire la recherche grâce aux champs de l'index comme le nom ou le type d'organisme, le sujet, l'emplacement, le nom ou le titre de la personne-ressource et le code postal.

Les abonnés au service en ligne peuvent générer instantanément leurs propres listes de contacts et les exporter en format feuille de calcul pour une utilisation approfondie – une solution de rechange géniale aux services dispendieux d'un commissionnaire en publipostage.

Pour obtenir plus d'information, veuillez contacter Grey House Publishing Canada
par tél. : 1 866 433-4739 ou 416 644-6479 par téléc. : 416 644-1904 | info@greyhouse.ca | www.greyhouse.ca

Canadian Who's Who

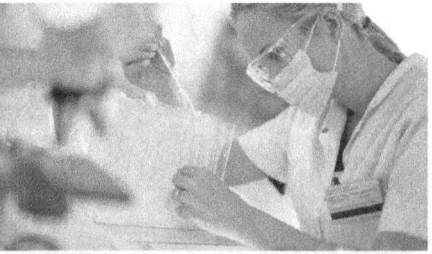
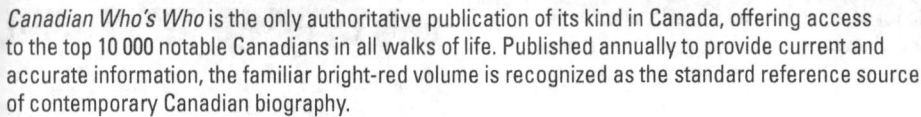

Canadian Who's Who is the only authoritative publication of its kind in Canada, offering access to the top 10 000 notable Canadians in all walks of life. Published annually to provide current and accurate information, the familiar bright-red volume is recognized as the standard reference source of contemporary Canadian biography.

Documenting the achievement of Canadians from a wide variety of occupations and professions, *Canadian Who's Who* records the diversity of culture in Canada. These biographies are organized alphabetically and provide detailed information on the accomplishments of notable Canadians, from coast to coast. All who are interested in the achievements of Canada's most influential citizens and their significant contributions to the country and the world beyond should acquire this reference title.

Detailed entries give date and place of birth, education, family details, career information, memberships, creative works, honours, languages, and awards, together with full addresses. Included are outstanding Canadians from business, academia, politics, sports, the arts and sciences, etc.

Every year the publisher invites new individuals to complete questionnaires from which new biographies are compiled. The publisher also gives those already listed in earlier editions an opportunity to update their biographies. Those listed are selected because of the positions they hold in Canadian society, or because of the contributions they have made to Canada.

AVAILABLE ONLINE!

Canadian Who's Who is also available online, through Canada's Information Resource Centre (CIRC). Readers can access this title's in-depth and vital networking content in the format that best suits their needs—in print, by subscription or online.

The print edition of *Canadian Who's Who 2025* contains 10,000 entries, while the online edition gives users access to over 27,800 biographies, including all current listings and over 16,500 archived biographies dating back to 1999.

GREY HOUSE PUBLISHING CANADA

For more information please contact Grey House Publishing Canada

Tel.: (866)-433-4739 or (416) 644-6479 Fax: (416) 644-1904 | info@greyhouse.ca | www.greyhouse.ca

Canadian Who's Who

  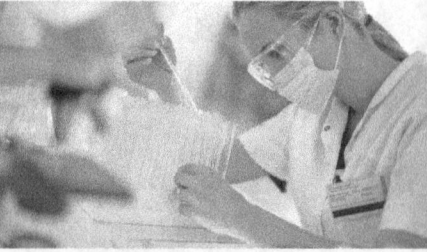

Canadian Who's Who est la seule publication digne de foi de son genre au Canada. Elle donne accès 10 000 dignitaires canadiens de tous les horizons. L'ouvrage annuel rouge vif bien connu, rempli d'information à jour et exacte, est la référence standard en matière de biographies canadiennes contemporaines.

Canadian Who's Who, qui porte sur les réalisations de Canadiens occupant une vaste gamme de postes et de professions, illustre la diversité de la culture canadienne. Ces biographies sont classées en ordre alphabétique et donnent de l'information détaillée sur les réalisations de Canadiens éminents, d'un océan à l'autre. Tous ceux qui s'intéressent aux réalisations des citoyens les plus influents au Canada et à leurs contributions importantes au pays et partout dans le monde doivent se procurer cet ouvrage de référence.

Les entrées détaillées indiquent la date et le lieu de la naissance, traitent de l'éducation, de la famille, de la carrière, des adhésions, des œuvres de création, des distinctions, des langues et des prix - en plus des adresses complètes. Elles comprennent des Canadiens exceptionnels du monde des affaires, des universités, de la politique, des sports, des arts, des sciences et plus encore!

Chaque année, l'éditeur invite de nouvelles personnes à remplir les questionnaires à partir desquels il prépare les nouvelles biographies. Il le remet également aux personnes qui font partie de numéros antérieurs afin de leur permettre d'effectuer une mise à jour. Les personnes retenues le sont en raison des postes qu'elles occupent dans la société canadienne ou de leurs contributions au Canada.

OFFERT EN FORMAT ÉLECTRONIQUE!

Canadian Who's Who est également offert en ligne par l'entremise du Centre de documentation du Canada (CDC). Les lecteurs peuvent accéder au contenu approfondi et essentiel au réseautage de cet ouvrage dans le format qui leur convient le mieux - version imprimée, en ligne ou par abonnement.

L'édition imprimée de *Canadian Who's Who 2025* compte 10 000 entrées tandis qu'en consultant la version en ligne, les utilisateurs ont accès à 27 800 biographies, dont fi ches d'actualité et plus de 16 500 biographies archives qui remontent jusqu'à 1999.

GREY HOUSE PUBLISHING CANADA

Pour obtenir plus d'information, veuillez contacter Grey House Publishing Canada
par tél. : 1 866 433-4739 ou 416 644-6479 par téléc. : 416 644-1904 | info@greyhouse.ca | www.greyhouse.ca

Directory of Directors

Your Best Source for Hard-to-Find Business Information

Since 1931, the *Financial Post Directory of Directors* has been recognizing leading Canadian companies and their execs. Today, this title is one of the most comprehensive resources for hard-to-find Canadian business information, allowing readers to access roughly 16,600 executive contacts from Canada's top 1,400 corporations. This prestigious title offers a definitive list of directorships and offices held by noteworthy Canadian business people. It also provides details on leading Canadian companies—publicly traded and privately-owned, including company name, contact information and the names of their executive officers and directors.

ACCESS THE COMPANIES & DIRECTORS YOU NEED IN NO TIME!

The updated 2025 edition of the *Directory of Directors* is jam-packed with information, including:

- **ALL-NEW front matter**: An infographic drawn from data in the book, a report on diversity disclosure practices, a report on human sustainability, and rankings from the FP500.

- **Personal listings**: First name, last name, gender, birth date, degrees, schools attended, executive positions and directorships, previous positions held, main business address and more.

- **Company listings**: Boards of directors and executive officers, head office address, phone and fax numbers, toll-free number, web and email addresses.

Powerful indexes enabling researchers to target just the information they need include:

- An **industrial classification index**: List of key Canadian companies, sorted by industry type according to the Global Industry Classification Standard (GICS®).

- A **geographic location index** grouping all companies in the Company Listings section according to the city and province/state of the head office; and

- An **alphabetical list of abbreviations** providing definitions of common abbreviations used for terms, titles, organizations, honours/fellowships and degrees throughout the Directory.

AVAILABLE ONLINE!

The Directory is also available online, through Canada's Information Resource Centre. Readers can access this title's in-depth and vital networking content in the format that best suits their needs—in print, by subscription or online.

Create your own contact lists! Online subscribers can instantly generate their own contact lists and export information into spreadsheets for further use. A great alternative to high cost list broker services!

 GREY HOUSE PUBLISHING CANADA — For more information please contact Grey House Publishing Canada

Tel.: (866)-433-4739 or (416) 644-6479 Fax: (416) 644-1904 | info@greyhouse.ca | www.greyhouse.ca

Répertoire des administrateurs

Votre source par excellence de renseignements professionnels difficiles à trouver

Depuis 1931, le Financial Post Directory of Directors (Répertoire des administrateurs du Financial Post) reconnaît les sociétés canadiennes importantes et leur haute direction. De nos jours, cet ouvrage compte parmi certaines des ressources les plus exhaustives lorsqu'il est question des renseignements d'affaires canadiens difficiles à trouver. Il permet aux lecteurs d'accéder à environ 16 600 coordonnées d'administrateurs provenant des 1 400 sociétés les plus importantes au Canada. Ce document prestigieux comprend une liste définitive des postes d'administrateurs et des fonctions que ces gens d'affaires canadiens remarquables occupent. Il offre également des détails sur des sociétés canadiennes importantes – privées ou négociées sur le marché – y compris le nom de l'entreprise, ses coordonnées et le nombre des membres de sa haute direction et de ses administrateurs.

UN ACCÈS RAPIDE ET FACILE À TOUS LES ENTREPRISES ET DIRECTEURS DONT VOUS AVEZ BESOIN!

La version mise à jour de 2025 du Répertoire des administrateurs du Financial Post est remplie d'information, notamment:

- **NOUVELLE section de textes préliminaires** –une infographie inspirée des données de l'ouvrage; un rapport sur les pratiques de divulgation de la diversité; un rapport sur la durabilité humaine; le classement le plus récent au FP500.

- **Données personnelles** – prénom, nom de famille, sexe, date de naissance, diplômes, écoles fréquentées, poste de cadre et d'administrateur, postes occupés préalablement, adresse professionnelle principale et plus encore.

- **Listes de sociétés** – conseils d'administration et cadres supérieurs, adresse du siège social, numéros de téléphone et de télécopieur, numéro sans frais, adresse électronique et site Web.

Des index puissants permettent aux utilisateurs de cibler l'information dont ils ont besoin, notamment:

- **Index de classement industriel** - énumère les sociétés classées par type d'industrie général selon le Global Industry Classification Standard (GICS^{MD}).

- l'**Index des emplacements géographiques** qui comprend toutes les sociétés de la section Liste des sociétés en fonction de la ville et de la province/de l'état où se trouve le siège social;

- une **liste des abréviations en ordre alphabétique** définit les abréviations courantes pour la terminologie, les titres, les organisations, les distinctions/fellowships et les diplômes mentionnés dans le Répertoire.

OFFERT EN FORMAT ÉLECTRONIQUE!

Le Répertoire est également accessible en ligne par l'entremise du Centre de documentation du Canada. Les lecteurs peuvent accéder au contenu approfondi et essentiel au réseautage de cet ouvrage dans le format qui leur convient le mieux - version imprimée, en ligne ou par abonnement.

Créez vos propres listes! Les abonnés au service en ligne peuvent générer instantanément leurs propres listes de contacts et les exporter en format feuille de calcul pour une utilisation approfondie – une solution de rechange géniale aux services dispendieux d'un commissionnaire en publipostage.

Canadian Parliamentary Guide

Your Number One Source for All General Federal Elections Results!

Published annually since before Confederation, the *Canadian Parliamentary Guide* is an indispensable directory, providing biographical information on elected and appointed members in federal and provincial government. Featuring government institutions such as the Governor General's Household, Privy Council and Canadian legislature, this comprehensive collection provides historical and current election results with statistical, provincial and political data.

THE CANADIAN PARLIAMENTARY GUIDE IS BROKEN DOWN INTO FIVE COMPREHENSIVE CATEGORIES

Monarchy—biographical information on His Majesty King Charles III, The Royal Family and the Governor General

Federal Government—a separate chapter for each of the Privy Council, Senate and House of Commons (including a brief description of the institution, its history in both text and chart format and a list of current members), followed by unparalleled biographical sketches*

General Elections

1867–2021

- information is listed alphabetically by province then by riding name

- notes on each riding include: date of establishment, date of abolition, former division and later divisions, followed by election year and successful candidate's name and party

- by-election information follows

2025

- information for the 2025 election is organized in the same manner but also includes information on all the candidates who ran in each riding, their party affiliation and the number of votes won

Provincial and Territorial Governments—Each provincial chapter includes:

- statistical information

- description of Legislative Assembly

- biographical sketch of the Lieutenant Governor or Commissioner

- list of current Cabinet Members

- dates of legislatures since confederation

- current Members and Constituencies

- biographical sketches*

- general election and by-election results, including the most recent provincial and territorial elections.

Courts: Federal—each court chapter includes a description of the court (Supreme, Federal, Federal Court of Appeal, Court Martial Appeal and Tax Court), its history and a list of its judges followed by biographical sketches*

* Biographical sketches follow a concise yet in-depth format:

Personal Data—place of birth, education, family information

Political Career—political career path and services

Private Career—work history, organization memberships, military history

GREY HOUSE PUBLISHING CANADA For more information please contact Grey House Publishing Canada

Tel.: (866)-433-4739 or (416) 644-6479 Fax: (416) 644-1904 | info@greyhouse.ca | www.greyhouse.ca

Guide parlementaire canadien

Votre principale source d'information en matière de résultats d'élections fédérales!

Publié annuellement depuis avant la Confédération, le *Guide parlementaire canadien* est une source fondamentale de notices biographiques des membres élus et nommés aux gouvernements fédéral et provinciaux. Il y est question, notamment, d'établissements gouvernementaux comme la résidence du gouverneur général, le Conseil privé et la législature canadienne. Ce recueil exhaustif présente les résultats historiques et actuels accompagnés de données statistiques, provinciales et politiques.

OFFERT EN FORMAT PAPIER ET DÉSORMAIS ÉLECTRONIQUE!

LE GUIDE PARLEMENTAIRE CANADIEN EST DIVISÉ EN CINQ CATÉGORIES EXHAUSTIVES:

La monarchie—des renseignements biographiques sur Sa Majesté le Roi Charles III, la famille royale et le gouverneur général.

Le gouvernement fédéral—un chapitre distinct pour chacun des sujets suivants: Conseil privé, sénat, Chambre des communes (y compris une brève description de l'institution, son historique sous forme de textes et de graphiques et une liste des membres actuels) suivi de notes biographiques sans pareil.*

Les élections fédérales

1867–2021

- Les renseignements sont présentés en ordre alphabétique par province puis par circonscription.

- Les notes de chaque circonscription comprennent : La date d'établissement, la date d'abolition, l'ancienne circonscription, les circonscriptions ultérieures, etc. puis l'année d'élection ainsi que le nom et le parti des candidats élus.

- Viennent ensuite des renseignements sur l'élection partielle.

2025

- Les renseignements de l'élection 2025 sont organisés de la même manière, mais comprennent également de l'information sur tous les candidats qui se sont présentés dans chaque circonscription, leur appartenance politique et le nombre de voix récoltées.

Gouvernements provinciaux et territoriaux—Chaque chapitre portant sur le gouvernement provincial comprend :

- des renseignements statistiques

- une description de l'Assemblée législative

- des notes biographiques sur le lieutenant-gouverneur ou le commissaire

- une liste des ministres actuels

- les dates de périodes législatives depuis la Confédération

- une liste des membres et des circonscriptions

- des notes biographiques*

- les résultats d'élections générales et partielles, y compris les dernières élections provinciales et territoriales.

Cours : fédérale—chaque chapitre comprend : une description de la cour (suprême, fédérale, cour d'appel fédérale, cour d'appel de la cour martiale et cour de l'impôt), son histoire, une liste des juges qui y siègent ainsi que des notes biographiques.*

* Les notes biographiques respectent un format concis, bien qu'approfondi :

Renseignements personnels—lieu de naissance, formation, renseignements familiaux

Carrière politique—cheminement politique et service public

Carrière privée—antécédents professionnels, membre d'organisations, antécédents militaires

Offert sous couverture rigide ou en format électronique grâce au web, le *Guide parlementaire canadien* donne invariablement un accès instantané aux représentants du gouvernement et aux faits qui font l'objet de vos recherches. Servez-vous de la version en ligne afin de circonscrire vos recherches grâce aux champs spéciaux de l'index comme l'institution, la province et le nom.

Créez vos propres listes! Les abonnés au service en ligne peuvent générer instantanément leurs propres listes de contacts et les exporter en format feuille de calcul pour une utilisation approfondie – une solution de rechange géniale aux services dispendieux d'un commissionnaire en publipostage!

GREY HOUSE PUBLISHING CANADA

Pour obtenir plus d'information, veuillez contacter Grey House Publishing Canada
par tél. : 1 866 433-4739 ou 416 644-6479 par téléc. : 416 644-1904 | info@greyhouse.ca | www.greyhouse.ca

Major Canadian Cities
Compared & Ranked

New edition with 2021 census data!

Major Canadian Cities provides the user with numerous ways to rank and compare 50 major cities across Canada. All statistical information is at your fingertips; you can access details about the cities, each with a population of 100,000 or more. On Canada's Information Resource Centre (CIRC), you can instantly rank cities according to your preferences and make your own analytical tables with the data provided. There are hundreds of questions that these ranking tables will answer: Which cities have the youngest population? Where is the economic growth the strongest? Which cities have the best labour statistics?

A city profile for each location offers additional insights into the city to provide a sense of the location, its history, its recreational and cultural activities. Following the profile are rankings showing its uniqueness in the spectrum of cities across Canada: interesting notes about the city and how it ranks amongst the top 50 in different ways, such as most liveable, wealthiest and coldest! These reports are available only from Grey House Publishing Canada and only with your subscription to this exciting product!

MAJOR CANADIAN CITIES SHOWS YOU THESE STATISTICAL TABLES:

Demographics
- Population Growth
- Age Characteristics
- Male/Female Ratio
- Marital Status

Housing
- Household Type & Size
- Housing Age & Value

Labour
- Labour Force
- Occupation
- Industry
- Place of Work

Ethnicity, Immigration & Language
- Mother Tongue
- Knowledge of Official Languages
- Language Spoken at Home
- Minority Populations
- Education
- Education Attainment

Income
- Median Income
- Median Income After Taxes
- Median Income by Family Type
- Median Income After Taxes by Family Type

Transportation
- Mode of Transportation to Work

AVAILABLE ONLINE!

Major Canadian Cities is available electronically via the Web, providing instant access to the facts you want about each city, as well as some interesting points showing how the city scores compared with others.

Use the online version to search statistics and create your own tables, or view pre-prepared tables in pdf form. This can help with research for academic work, infrastructure development or pure interest, with all the data you need in one, modifiable source.

GREY HOUSE PUBLISHING CANADA

For more information please contact Grey House Publishing Canada

Tel.: (866)-433-4739 or (416) 644-6479 Fax: (416) 644-1904 | info@greyhouse.ca | www.greyhouse.ca

Principales villes canadiennes

Comparaison et classement

Principales villes canadiennes offre à l'utilisateur de nombreuses manières de classer et de comparer 50 villes principales du Canada. Toute l'information statistique se trouve au bout de vos doigts : vous pouvez obtenir des détails sur les villes, chacune comptant 100 000 habitants ou plus. Dans le Centre de documentation du Canada (CDC), vous pouvez classer instantanément les villes selon vos préférences et créer vos propres tableaux analytiques à l'aide des données fournies. Ces tableaux de classement répondent à des centaines de questions, notamment : quelles villes comptent la population la plus jeune? À quel endroit la croissance économique est-elle la plus forte? Quelles villes présentent les meilleures statistiques en matière de main-d'œuvre?

Un profil de ville offre des renseignements supplémentaires afin de vous donner une idée de son emplacement, de son histoire, de ses activités récréatives et culturelles. Suivent des classements qui démontrent l'unicité de la ville dans un spectre de villes qui se trouvent partout au Canada. Vous trouverez également des remarques intéressantes au sujet de la ville et de son classement parmi les 50 principales villes, par exemple selon celle où il fait le mieux vivre, où se trouvent les plus riches et où il fait le plus froid. Ces rapports sont disponibles uniquement auprès de Grey House Publishing Canada et dans le cadre de votre abonnement à ce produit emballant!

PRINCIPALES VILLES CANADIENNES COMPREND CES TABLEAUX STATISTIQUES :

Données démographiques

- Croissance de la population
- Caractéristiques relatives à l'âge
- Ratio homme/femme
- État matrimonial

Logement

- Type et taille du logement
- Âge et valeur du logement

Main-d'œuvre

- Population active
- Emploi
- Industrie
- Lieu de travail

Ethnicité, immigration et langue

- Langue maternelle
- Connaissance des langues officielles
- Langue parlée à la maison
- Populations minoritaires
- Formation
- Niveau scolaire

Revenu

- Revenu médian
- Revenu médian après impôts
- Revenu médian par type de famille
- Revenu médian après impôts par type de famille

Transport

- Moyen de transport vers le travail

OFFERT EN VERSION ÉLECTRONIQUE!

Principales villes canadiennes est offert en version électronique sur le Web. Vous accédez donc instantanément aux faits dont vous avez besoin pour chaque ville, de même que des éléments intéressants qui illustrent la comparaison entre les villes.

Servez-vous de la version en ligne pour effectuer des recherches parmi les statistiques et créer vos propres tableaux, ou consulter les tableaux déjà prêts en format PDF. Elle peut vous aider dans le cadre de recherches pour des travaux universitaires, pour le développement d'infrastructures ou consultez-la par simple curiosité – autant de données réunies en une source modifiable.

GREY HOUSE PUBLISHING CANADA

Pour obtenir plus d'information, veuillez contacter Grey House Publishing Canada
par tél. : 1 866 433-4739 ou 416 644-6479 par téléc. : 416 644-1904 | info@greyhouse.ca | www.greyhouse.ca

Associations Canada

Makes Researching Organizations Quick and Easy

Associations Canada is an easy-to-use compendium, providing detailed indexes, listings and abstracts on over 20,500 local, regional, provincial, national and international organizations (identifying location, budget, founding date, management, scope of activity and funding source—just to name a few).

POWERFUL INDEXES HELP YOU TARGET THE ORGANIZATIONS YOU WANT

There are a number of criteria you can use to target specific organizations. Organized with the user in mind, *Associations Canada* is broken down into a number of indexes to help you find what you're looking for quickly and easily.

- **Subject Index**—listing of Canadian and foreign association headquarters, alphabetically by subject and keyword

- **Acronym Index**—an alphabetical listing of acronyms and corresponding Canadian and foreign associations, in both official languages

- **Budget Index**—Canadian associations, alphabetical within eight budget categories

- **Conferences & Conventions Index**—meetings sponsored by Canadian and foreign associations, listed alphabetically by conference name

- **Executive Name Index**—alphabetical listing of key contacts of Canadian associations, for both headquarters and branches

- **Geographic Index**—listing of headquarters, branch offices, chapters and divisions of Canadian associations, alphabetical within province and city

- **Mailing List Index**—associations that offer mailing lists, alphabetical by subject

- **Registered Charitable Organizations Index**—listing of associations that are registered charities, alphabetical by subject

PRINT OR ONLINE—QUICK AND EASY ACCESS TO ALL THE INFORMATION YOU NEED!

Available in softcover print or electronically via the web, *Associations Canada* provides instant access to the people you need and the facts you want every time. Whereas the print edition is verified and updated annually, ongoing changes are added to the web version on a regular basis. The web version allows you to narrow your search by using index fields such as name or type of organization, subject, location, contact name or title and postal code.

Create your own contact lists! Online subscribers have the option to instantly generate their own contact lists and export them into spreadsheets for further use—a great alternative to high cost list broker services.

ASSOCIATIONS CANADA PROVIDES COMPLETE ACCESS TO THESE HIGHLY LUCRATIVE MARKETS:

Travel & Tourism
- Who's hosting what event...when and where?
- Check on events up to three years in advance

Journalism and Media
- Pure research—What do they do? Who is in charge? What's their budget?
- Check facts and sources in one step

Libraries
- Refer researchers to the most complete Canadian association reference anywhere

Business
- Target your market, research your interests, compile profiles and identify membership lists
- Warm up your cold calls with all the background you need to sell your product or service
- Preview prospects by budget, market interest or geographic location

Association Executives
- Look for strategic alliances with associations of similar interest
- Spot opportunities or conflicts with convention plans

Research & Government
- Scan interest groups or identify charities in your area of concern
- Check websites, publications and speaker availability
- Evaluate mandates, affiliations and scope

GREY HOUSE PUBLISHING CANADA

For more information please contact Grey House Publishing Canada

Tel.: (866)-433-4739 or (416) 644-6479 Fax: (416) 644-1904 | info@greyhouse.ca | www.greyhouse.ca

Associations du Canada

La recherche d'organisations simplifiée

Il s'agit d'un recueil facile d'utilisation qui offre des index, des fiches descriptives et des résumés exhaustifs de plus de 20 500 organismes locaux, régionaux, provinciaux, nationaux et internationaux. Il donne, entre autres, des détails sur leur emplacement, leur budget, leur date de mise sur pied, l'éventail de leurs activités et leurs sources de financement.

En plus d'affecter plus d'un milliard de dollars annuellement aux frais de transport, à la participation à des congrès et à la mise en marché, *Associations du Canada* débourse des millions de dollars dans sa quête pour répondre aux intérêts de ses membres.

DES INDEX PUISSANTS QUI VOUS AIDENT À CIBLER LES ORGANISATIONS VOULUES

Vous pouvez vous servir de plusieurs critères pour cibler des organisations précises. C'est avec l'utilisateur en tête qu'*Associations du Canada* a été divisé en plusieurs index pour vous aider à trouver, rapidement et facilement, ce que vous cherchez.

- **Index des sujets**—liste des sièges sociaux d'associations canadiennes et étrangères; sujets classés en ordre alphabétique et mot-clé.

- **Index des acronymes**—liste alphabétique des acronymes et des associations canadiennes et étrangères équivalentes; présenté dans les deux langues officielles.

- **Index des budgets**—associations canadiennes classées en ordre alphabétique parmi huit catégories de budget.

- **Index des congrès**—rencontres commanditées par des associations canadiennes et étrangères; classées en ordre alphabétique selon le titre de l'événement.

- **Index des directeurs**—liste alphabétique des principales personnes-ressources des associations canadiennes, aux sièges sociaux et aux succursales.

- **Index géographique**—liste des sièges sociaux, des succursales, des sections régionales et des divisions des associations canadiennes; ordre alphabétique au sein des provinces et des villes.

- **Index des listes de distribution**—liste des associations qui offrent des listes de distribution; en ordre alphabétique selon le sujet.

- **Index des œuvres de bienfaisance enregistrées**—liste des associations enregistrées en tant qu'œuvres de bienfaisance; en ordre alphabétique selon le sujet.

OFFERT EN FORMAT PAPIER OU EN LIGNE—UN ACCÈS RAPIDE ET FACILE À TOUS LES RENSEIGNEMENTS DONT VOUS AVEZ BESOIN!

Offert sous couverture souple ou en format électronique grâce au web, *Associations du Canada* donne invariablement un accès instantané aux personnes et aux faits dont vous avez besoin. Si la version imprimée est vérifiée et mise à jour annuellement, des changements continus sont apportés mensuellement à la base de données en ligne. Servez-vous de la version en ligne afin de circonscrire vos recherches grâce à des champs spéciaux de l'index comme le nom de l'organisation ou son type, le sujet, l'emplacement, le nom de la personne-ressource ou son titre et le code postal.

Créez vos propres listes! Les abonnés au service en ligne peuvent générer instantanément leurs propres listes de contacts et les exporter en format feuille de calcul pour une utilisation approfondie – une solution de rechange géniale aux services dispendieux d'un commissionnaire en publipostage.

ASSOCIATIONS DU CANADA OFFRE UN ACCÈS COMPLET À CES MARCHÉS HAUTEMENT LUCRATIFS

Voyage et tourisme
- Renseignez-vous sur les hôtes des événements... sur les dates et les endroits.
- Consultez les évènements trois ans au préalable.

Journalisme et médias
- Recherche authentique—quel est leur centre d'activité? Qui est la personne responsable? Quel est leur budget?
- Vérifiez les faits et sources en une seule étape.

Bibliothèques
- Orientez les chercheurs vers la référence la plus complète en ce qui concerne les associations canadiennes.

Commerce
- Ciblez votre marché, faites une recherche selon vos sujets de prédilection, compilez des profils et recensez des listes des membres.
- Préparez votre sollicitation au hasard en obtenant les renseignements dont vous avez besoin pour offrir votre produit ou service.
- Obtenez un aperçu de vos clients potentiels selon les budgets, les intérêts au marché ou l'emplacement géographique.

Directeurs d'associations
- Recherchez des alliances stratégiques avec des associations partageant vos intérêts.
- Repérez des occasions ou des conflits dans le cadre de la planification des congrès.

Recherche et gouvernement
- Parcourez les groupes d'intérêts ou identifiez les organismes de bienfaisance de votre domaine d'intérêt.
- Consultez les sites Web, les publications et vérifiez la disponibilité des conférenciers.
- Évaluez les mandats, les affiliations et le champ d'application.

Pour obtenir plus d'information, veuillez contacter Grey House Publishing Canada
par tél. : 1 866 433-4739 ou 416 644-6479 par téléc. : 416 644-1904 | info@greyhouse.ca | www.greyhouse.ca

Canadian Environmental Resource Guide

The Only Complete Guide to the Business of Environmental Management

The *Canadian Environmental Resource Guide* provides data on every aspect of the environment industry in unprecedented detail. It's one-stop searching for details on government offices and programs, information sources, product and service firms and trade fairs that pertain to the business of environmental management. All information is fully indexed and cross-referenced for easy use. The directory features current information and key contacts in Canada's environmental industry including:

ENVIRONMENTAL UP-DATE

- Information on prominent environmentalists, environmental abbreviations and a summary of recent environmental events

- Updated articles, rankings, statistics and charts on all aspects of the environmental industry

- Trade shows, conferences and seminars for the current year and beyond

ENVIRONMENTAL INDUSTRY RESOURCES

- Comprehensive listings for companies and firms producing and selling products and services in the environmental sector, including markets served, working language and percentage of revenue sources: public and private

- Environmental law firms, with lawyers' areas of speciality

- Detailed indexes by subject, geography and ISO

ENVIRONMENTAL GOVERNMENT LISTINGS

- Information on important intergovernmental offices and councils, and listings of environmental trade representatives abroad

- In-depth listings of environmental information at the municipal level, including population and number of households, water and waste treatment, landfill statistics and special by-laws and bans, as well as key environmental contacts for each municipality

Available in softcover print or electronically via the web, the *Canadian Environmental Resource Guide* provides instant access to the people you need and the facts you want every time. The *Canadian Environmental Resource Guide* is verified and updated annually. Ongoing changes are added to the web version on a regular basis.

CANADIAN ENVIRONMENTAL RESOURCE GUIDE OFFERS EVEN MORE CONTENT ONLINE!

Environmental Information Resources— Extensive listings of special libraries and thousands of environmental associations, with information on membership, environmental activities, key contacts and more.

Government Listings—Every federal and provincial department and agency influencing environmental initiatives and purchasing policies.

The web version allows you to narrow your search by using index fields such as name or type of organization, subject, location, contact name or title and postal code.

Create your own contact lists! Online subscribers have the option to instantly generate their own contact lists and export them into spreadsheets for further use—a great alternative to high cost list broker services.

GREY HOUSE PUBLISHING CANADA

For more information please contact Grey House Publishing Canada

Tel.: (866)-433-4739 or (416) 644-6479 Fax: (416) 644-1904 | info@greyhouse.ca | www.greyhouse.ca

Guide des ressources environnementales canadiennes

Le seul guide complet dédié à la gestion de l'environnement

Le *Guide des ressources environnementales canadiennes* offre de l'information relative à tous les aspects de l'industrie de l'environnement dans les moindres détails. Il permet d'effectuer une recherche de données complètes sur les bureaux et programmes gouvernementaux, les sources de renseignements, les entreprises de produits et de services et les foires commerciales qui portent sur les activités de la gestion de l'environnement. Toute l'information est entièrement indexée et effectue un double renvoi pour une consultation facile. Le répertoire présente des renseignements actualisés et les personnes-ressources clés de l'industrie de l'environnement au Canada, y compris les suivants.

MISE À JOUR SUR L'INDUSTRIE DE L'ENVIRONNEMENT

- De l'information sur d'éminents environnementalistes, les abréviations utilisées dans le domaine de l'environnement et un résumé des événements environnementaux récents

- Des articles, des classements, des statistiques et des graphiques mis à jour sur tous les aspects de l'industrie verte

- Les salons professionnels, conférences et séminaires qui ont lieu cette année et ceux qui sont prévus

RESSOURCES DE L'INDUSTRIE ENVIRONNEMENTALE

- Des listes exhaustives des entreprises et des cabinets qui fabriquent ou offrent des produits et des services dans le domaine de l'environnement, y compris les marchés desservis, la langue de travail et la ventilation des sources de revenus – publics et privés

- Une liste complète des cabinets spécialisés en droit environnemental

- Des index selon le sujet, la géographie et la certification ISO

LISTES GOUVERNEMENTALES RELATIVES À L'ENVIRONNEMENT

- De l'information sur les bureaux et conseils intergouvernementaux importants ainsi que des listes des représentants de l'éco-commerce à l'extérieur du pays

- Des listes approfondies portant sur de l'information environnementale au palier municipal, notamment la population et le nombre de ménages, le traitement de l'eau et des déchets, des statistiques sur les décharges, des règlements et des interdictions spéciaux ainsi que des personnes-ressources clés en environnement pour chaque municipalité

Offert sous couverture rigide ou en format électronique grâce au Web, le *Guide des ressources environnementales canadiennes* offre invariablement un accès instantané aux représentants du gouvernement et aux faits qui font l'objet de vos recherches. Il est vérifié et mis à jour annuellement. La version en ligne est mise à jour mensuellement.

LE GUIDE DES RESSOURCES ENVIRONNEMENTALES CANADIENNES DONNE ACCÈS À PLUS DE CONTENU EN LIGNE!

Des ressources informationnelles sur l'environnement—Des bibliothèques et des centres de resources spécialisés, et des milliers d'associations environnementales, avec de l'information sur l'adhésion, les activités environnementales, les personnes-ressources principales et plus encore.

Listes gourvenementales—Toutes les agences et tous les services gouvernementaux fédéraux et provinciaux qui exercent une infl uence sur les initiatives en matière d'environnement et de politiques d'achat.

Servez-vous de la version en ligne afin de circonscrire vos recherches grâce à des champs spéciaux de l'index comme le nom de l'organisation ou son type, le sujet, l'emplacement, le nom de la personne-ressource ou son titre et le code postal.

Créez vos propres listes! Les abonnés au service en ligne peuvent générer instantanément leurs propres listes de contacts et les exporter en format feuille de calcul pour une utilisation approfondie—une solution de rechange géniale aux services dispendieux d'un commissionnaire en publipostage.

 GREY HOUSE PUBLISHING CANADA

Pour obtenir plus d'information, veuillez contacter Grey House Publishing Canada

par tél. : 1 866 433-4739 ou 416 644-6479 par téléc. : 416 644-1904 | info@greyhouse.ca | www.greyhouse.ca

Libraries Canada

Gain Access to Complete and Detailed Information on Canadian Libraries

Libraries Canada brings together the most current information from across the entire Canadian library sector, including libraries and branch libraries, educational libraries, regional systems, resource centres, archives, related periodicals, library schools and programs, provincial and governmental agencies and associations.

As the nation's leading library directory for over 35 years, *Libraries Canada* gives you access to almost 10,000 names and addresses of contacts in these institutions. Also included are valuable details such as library symbol, number of staff, operating systems, library type and acquisitions budget, hours of operation—all thoroughly indexed and easy to find.

INSTANT ACCESS TO CANADIAN LIBRARY SECTOR INFORMATION

Developed for publishers, advocacy groups, computer hardware suppliers, internet service providers and other diverse groups which provide products and services to the library community; associations that need to maintain a current list of library resources in Canada; and research departments, students and government agencies which require information about the types of services and programs available at various research institutions, *Libraries Canada* will help you find the information you need—quickly and easily.

EXPERT SEARCH OPTIONS AVAILABLE WITH ONLINE VERSION...

Available in print and online, *Libraries Canada* delivers easily accessible, quality information that has been verified and organized for easy retrieval. Five easy-to-use indexes assist you in navigating the print edition while the online version utilizes multiple index fields that help you get results.

Available on Grey House Publishing Canada's CIRC interface, you can choose between Keyword and Advanced search to pinpoint information. Designed for both novice and advanced researchers, you can conduct simple text searches as well as powerful Boolean searches, plus you can narrow your search by using index fields such as name or type of institution, headquarters, location, area code, contact name or title and postal code. Save your searches to build on at a later date or use the mark record function to view, print, e-mail or export your selected records.

Online subscribers have the option to instantly generate their own contact lists and export them into spreadsheets for further use. A great alternative to high cost list broker services.

LIBRARIES CANADA GIVES YOU ALL THE ESSENTIALS FOR EACH INSTITUTION:

Name, address, contact information, key personnel, number of staff

Collection information, type of library, acquisitions budget, subject area, special collection

User services, number of branches, hours of operation, ILL information, photocopy and microform facilities, for-fee research, Internet access

Systems information, details on electronic access, operating and online systems, Internet and e-mail software, Internet connectivity, access to electronic resources

Additional information including associations, publications and regional systems

With almost 60% of the data changing annually it has never been more important to have the latest version of *Libraries Canada*.

GREY HOUSE PUBLISHING CANADA

For more information please contact Grey House Publishing Canada

Tel.: (866)-433-4739 or (416) 644-6479 Fax: (416) 644-1904 | info@greyhouse.ca | www.greyhouse.ca

Bibliothèques Canada

Accédez aux renseignements complets et détaillés au sujet des bibliothèques canadiennes

Bibliothèques Canada combine les renseignements les plus à jour provenant du secteur des bibliothèques de partout au Canada, y compris les bibliothèques et leurs succursales, les bibliothèques éducatives, les systèmes régionaux, les centres de ressources, les archives, les périodiques pertinents, les écoles de bibliothéconomie et leurs programmes, les organismes provinciaux et gouvernementaux ainsi que les associations.

Principal répertoire des bibliothèques depuis plus de 35 ans, *Bibliothèques Canada* vous donne accès à près de 10 000 noms et adresses de personnes-ressources pour ces établissements. Il comprend également des détails précieux comme le symbole d'identification de bibliothèque, le nombre de membres du personnel, les systèmes d'exploitation, le type de bibliothèque et le budget attribué aux acquisitions, les heures d'ouverture – autant d'information minutieusement indexée et facile à trouver.

Offert en version imprimée et en ligne, *Bibliothèques Canada* offre des renseignements de qualité, facile d'accès, qui ont été vérifiés et organisés afin de les obtenir facilement. Cinq index conviviaux vous aident dans la navigation du numéro imprimé tandis que la version en ligne vous permet de saisir plusieurs champs d'index pour vous aider à découvrir l'information voulue.

ACCÈS INSTANTANÉ AUX RENSEIGNEMENTS DU DOMAINE DES BIBLIOTHÈQUES CANADIENNES

Conçu pour les éditeurs, les groupes de revendication, les fournisseurs de matériel informatique, les fournisseurs de services Internet et autres groupes qui offrent produits et services aux bibliothèques; les associations qui ont besoin de conserver une liste à jour des ressources bibliothécaires au Canada; les services de recherche, les organismes étudiants et gouvernementaux qui ont besoin d'information au sujet des types de services et de programmes offerts par divers établissements de recherche, *Bibliothèques Canada* vous aide à trouver l'information nécessaire – rapidement et simplement.

LA VERSION EN LIGNE COMPREND DES OPTIONS DE RECHERCHE POUSSÉES...

À partir de l'interface du Centre de documentation du Canada de Grey House Publishing Canada, vous pouvez choisir entre la recherche poussée et rapide pour cibler votre information. Vous pouvez effectuer des recherches par texte simple, conçues à la fois pour les chercheurs débutants et chevronnés, ainsi que des recherches booléennes puissantes. Vous pouvez également restreindre votre recherche à l'aide des champs d'index, comme le nom ou le type d'établissement, le siège social, l'emplacement, l'indicatif régional, le nom de la personne-ressource ou son titre et le code postal. Enregistrez vos recherches pour vous en servir plus tard ou utilisez la fonction de marquage pour afficher, imprimer, envoyer par courriel ou exporter les dossiers sélectionnés.

Les abonnés au service en ligne peuvent générer instantanément leurs propres listes de contacts et les exporter en format feuille de calcul pour une utilisation approfondie – une solution de rechange géniale aux services dispendieux d'un commissionnaire en publipostage.

BIBLIOTHÈQUES CANADA VOUS DONNE TOUS LES RENSEIGNEMENTS ESSENTIELS RELATIFS À CHAQUE ÉTABLISSEMENT :

Leurs nom et adresse, les coordonnées de la personne-ressource, les membres clés du personnel, le nombre de membres du personnel

L'information relative aux collections, le type de bibliothèque, le budget attribué aux acquisitions, le domaine, les collections particulières

Les services aux utilisateurs, le nombre de succursales, les heures d'ouverture, les renseignements relatifs au PEB, les services de photocopie et de microforme, la recherche rémunérée, l'accès à Internet

L'information relative aux systèmes, des détails sur l'accès électronique, les systèmes d'exploitation et ceux en ligne, Internet et le logiciel de messagerie électronique, la connectivité à Internet, l'accès aux ressources électroniques

L'information supplémentaire, y compris les associations, les publications et les systèmes régionaux

Alors que près de 60 % des données sont modifiées annuellement, il est plus important que jamais de posséder la plus récente version de *Bibliothèques Canada*.

Financial Services Canada

Unparalleled Coverage of the Canadian Financial Service Industry

With corporate listings for over 30,000 organizations and hard-to-find business information, *Financial Services Canada* is the most up-to-date source for names and contact numbers of industry professionals, senior executives, portfolio managers, financial advisors, agency bureaucrats and elected representatives.

Financial Services Canada is the definitive resource for detailed listings—providing valuable contact information including: name, title, organization, profile, associated companies, telephone and fax numbers, e-mail and website addresses. Use our online database and refine your search by stock symbol, revenue, year founded, assets, ownership type or number of employees.

POWERFUL INDEXES HELP YOU LOCATE THE CRUCIAL FINANCIAL INFORMATION YOU NEED.

Organized with the user in mind, *Financial Services Canada* contains categorized listings and 4 easy-to-use indexes:

Alphabetic—financial organizations listed in alphabetical sequence by company name

Geographic—financial institutions broken down by town or city

Executive Name—all officers, directors and senior personnel in alphabetical order by surname

Insurance class—lists all companies by insurance type

Reduce the time you spend compiling lists, researching company information and searching for e-mail addresses. Whether you are interested in contacting a finance lawyer regarding international and domestic joint ventures, need to generate a list of foreign banks in Canada or want to contact the Toronto Stock Exchange—*Financial Services Canada* gives you the power to find all the data you need.

PRINT OR ONLINE—QUICK AND EASY ACCESS TO ALL THE INFORMATION YOU NEED!

Available in softcover print or electronically via the web, *Financial Services Canada* provides instant access to the people you need and the facts you want every time.

Financial Services Canada print edition is verified and updated annually. Ongoing changes are added to the web version on a regular basis. The web version allows you to narrow your search by using index fields such as name or type of organization, subject, location, contact name or title and postal code.

Create your own contact lists! Online subscribers have the option to instantly generate their own contact lists and export them into spreadsheets for further use—a great alternative to high cost list broker services.

ACCESS TO CURRENT LISTINGS FOR...

Banks and Depository Institutions
- Domestic and savings banks
- Foreign banks and branches
- Foreign bank representative offices
- Trust companies
- Credit unions

Non-Depository Institutions
- Bond rating companies
- Collection agencies
- Credit card companies
- Financing and loan companies
- Trustees in bankruptcy

Investment Management Firms, including securities and commodities
- Financial planning / investment management companies
- Investment dealers
- Investment fund companies
- Pension/money management companies
- Stock exchanges
- Holding companies

Insurance Companies, including federal and provincial
- Reinsurance companies
- Fraternal benefit societies
- Mutual benefit companies
- Reciprocal exchanges

Accounting and Law
- Accountants
- Actuary consulting firms
- Law firms (specializing in finance)

Major Canadian Companies
- Key financial contacts for public, private and Crown corporations

Associations
- Associations and institutes serving the financial services sector

Financial Technology & Services
- Companies involved in financial software and other technical areas.

Access even more content online:
Government and Publications
- Federal, provincial and territorial contacts
- Leading publications serving the financial services industry

 **GREY HOUSE PUBLISHING CANADA** For more information please contact Grey House Publishing Canada

Tel.: (866)-433-4739 or (416) 644-6479 Fax: (416) 644-1904 | info@greyhouse.ca | www.greyhouse.ca

Services financiers au Canada

Une couverture sans pareille de l'industrie des services financiers canadiens

Grâce à plus de 30 000 organisations et renseignements commerciaux rares, *Services financiers du Canada* est la source la plus à jour de noms et de coordonnées de professionnels, de membres de la haute direction, de gestionnaires de portefeuille, de conseillers financiers, de fonctionnaires et de représentants élus de l'industrie.

Services financiers du Canada intègre les plus récentes modifications à l'industrie afin de vous offrir les détails les plus à jour au sujet de chaque entreprise, notamment le nom, le titre, l'organisation, les numéros de téléphone et de télécopieur, le courriel et l'adresse du site Web. Servez-vous de la base de données en ligne et raffinez votre recherche selon le symbole, le revenu, l'année de création, les immobilisations, le type de propriété ou le nombre d'employés.

DES INDEX PUISSANTS VOUS AIDENT À TROUVER LES RENSEIGNEMENTS FINANCIERS ESSENTIELS DONT VOUS AVEZ BESOIN.

C'est avec l'utilisateur en tête que Services financiers au Canada a été conçu; il contient des listes catégorisées et quatre index faciles d'utilisation :

Alphabétique—les organisations financières apparaissent en ordre alphabétique, selon le nom de l'entreprise.

Géographique—les institutions financières sont détaillées par ville.

Nom de directeur—tous les agents, directeurs et cadres supérieurs sont classés en ordre alphabétique, selon leur nom de famille.

Classe d'assurance—toutes les entreprises selon leur type d'assurance.

Passez moins de temps à préparer des listes, à faire des recherches ou à chercher des contacts et des courriels. Que vous soyez intéressé à contacter un avocat en droit des affaires au sujet de projets conjoints internationaux et nationaux, que vous ayez besoin de générer une liste des banques étrangères au Canada ou que vous souhaitiez communiquer avec la Bourse de Toronto, *Services financiers au Canada* vous permet de trouver toutes les données dont vous avez besoin.

OFFERT EN FORMAT PAPIER OU EN LIGNE – UN ACCÈS RAPIDE ET FACILE À TOUS LES RENSEIGNEMENTS DONT VOUS AVEZ BESOIN!

Offert sous couverture rigide ou en format électronique grâce au Web, Services financiers du Canada donne invariablement un accès instantané aux personnes et aux faits dont vous avez besoin. Si la version imprimée est vérifiée et mise à jour annuellement, des changements continus sont apportés mensuellement à la base de données en ligne. Servez-vous de la version en ligne afin de circonscrire vos recherches grâce à des champs spéciaux de l'index comme le nom de l'organisation ou son type, le sujet, l'emplacement, le nom de la personne-ressource ou son titre et le code postal.

Créez vos propres listes! Les abonnés au service en ligne peuvent générer instantanément leurs propres listes de contacts et les exporter en format feuille de calcul pour une utilisation approfondie – une solution de rechange géniale aux services dispendieux d'un commissionnaire en publipostage.

ACCÉDEZ AUX LISTES ACTUELLES...

Banques et institutions de dépôt
- Banques nationales et d'épargne
- Banques étrangères et leurs succursales
- Bureaux des représentants de banques étrangères
- Sociétés de fiducie
- Coopératives d'épargne et de crédit

Établissements financiers
- Entreprises de notation des obligations
- Agences de placement
- Compagnies de carte de crédit
- Sociétés de financement et de prêt
- Syndics de faillite

Sociétés de gestion de placements, y compris les valeurs et marchandises
- Entreprises de planification financière et de gestion des investissements
- Maisons de courtage de valeurs Courtiers en épargne collective
- Entreprises de gestion de la pension/de trésorerie
- Bourses
- Sociétés de portefeuille

Compagnies d'assurance, fédérales et provinciales
- Compagnies de réassurance
- Sociétés fraternelles
- Sociétés de secours mutuel
- Échanges selon la formule de réciprocité

Comptabilité et droit
- Comptables
- Cabinets d'actuaires-conseils
- Cabinets d'avocats (spécialisés en finance)

Principales entreprises canadiennes
- Principaux contacts financiers pour les sociétés de capitaux publiques, privées et de la Couronne

Les associations et Technologie et services financiers

Accès à plus de contenu en ligne: Gouvernement et Publications
- Personnes-ressources aux paliers fédéral, provinciaux et territoriaux
- Principales publications qui desservent l'industrie des services financiers

GREY HOUSE PUBLISHING CANADA Pour obtenir plus d'information, veuillez contacter Grey House Publishing Canada
par tél. : 1 866 433-4739 ou 416 644-6479 par téléc. : 416 644-1904 | info@greyhouse.ca | www.greyhouse.ca

Careers & Employment Canada

Careers & Employment Canada is the go-to resource for job-seekers across Canada, with detailed, current information on everything from industry associations to summer job opportunities. Divided into five helpful sections, this guide contains 10,000 organizations and 20,000 industry contacts to aid in research and jump-start careers in a variety of fields.

ADDITIONAL RESOURCES INCLUDE:

- **Associations**
- **Employers**
    Arts & Culture
    Business & Finance
    Education
    Environmental
    Government
    Healthcare
    Legal
    Major Corporations in Canada
    Telecommunications & Media
    Transportation

- **Recruiters**
- **Summer Jobs**
- **Career & Employment Websites**
    National & Regional
    Industry
    Topic-Specific
    Employment Options
    Clientele
    Where to Get Resources

Rounding off this guide are 70 pages of reports on the current job market in Canada, a list of industry Awards and Honours, as well as Entry, Executive, and Government Contact indexes for even easier reference. Valuable for employment professionals, librarians, teachers, and job-seekers alike, *Careers & Employment Canada* helps take the strain out of job searching by providing a direct link to the organizations and contacts that matter most.

A CLOSER LOOK AT WHAT'S INSIDE:

Reports on the Job Market—A series of articles on the current job market sourced from Statistics Canada—everything from equity in the workplace to the many ways in which the COVID-19 pandemic has affected the labour market.

Associations—Nearly 800 national associations covering an array of industries and professions.

Employers—Need-to-know companies and organizations broken down into 11 master categories such as Arts & Culture, Education, Government, and Telecommunications & Media.

Recruiters—Top recruiting firms across Canada, organized by national and provincial scope.

Summer Jobs—National and regional summer job opportunities—everything from government agencies to summer camps

Career & Employment Websites—Includes hiring and job board platforms broken down by industry, employment tools, and resources by job type and specialized clientele such as Indigenous, New Canadians, People with Disabilities, Women, and Youth.

GREY HOUSE PUBLISHING CANADA For more information please contact Grey House Publishing Canada

Tel.: (866)-433-4739 or (416) 644-6479 Fax: (416) 644-1904 | info@greyhouse.ca | www.greyhouse.ca

Carrières et emploi Canada

Carrières et emploi Canada est la ressource privilégiée pour les personnes en recherche d'emploi partout au Canada. Elle contient de l'information détaillée et actuelle, des associations de l'industrie aux offres d'emploi d'été. Divisé en cinq sections pratiques, ce guide comprend 10 000 contacts d'organisations et 20 000 d'industrie pour aider à la recherche d'emploi et démarrer des carrières dans divers domaines.

LES RESSOURCES SUPPLÉMENTAIRES COMPRENNENT :

- **Associations**
- **Employeurs**
  - Arts et culture
  - Affaires et finances
  - Formation
  - Environnement
  - Gouvernement
  - Soins de santé
  - Domaine juridique
  - Grandes entreprises au Canada
  - Télécommunications et médias
  - Transport

- **Recruteurs**
- **Emplois d'été**
- **Sites sur les carrières et l'emploi**
  - À l'échelle nationale et régionale
  - Industrie
  - Relatif à un sujet précis
  - Possibilités d'emploi
  - Communauté
  - Où trouver les ressources

À la fin de ce guide, vous trouverez 70 pages de rapports sur le marché de l'emploi actuel au Canada, une liste des prix remis par l'industrie ainsi que des index classés par entrée, direction et contact gouvernemental pour en faciliter davantage la consultation. Outil précieux pour les professionnels de l'emploi, bibliothécaires, enseignants et chercheurs d'emploi, *Carrières et emploi Canada* aide à alléger la recherche d'emploi en offrant un lien direct avec les organisations et personnes-ressources plus essentielles que jamais.

UN EXAMEN PLUS APPROFONDI DU CONTENU :

Rapports sur le marché de l'emploi—Une série d'articles sur le marché du travail actuel provenant de Statistiques Canada : de l'équité en milieu de travail aux divers impacts de la pandémie de la COVID-19 sur le marché de l'emploi.

Associations—Près de 800 associations nationales portant sur une gamme d'industries et de professions.

Employeurs—Les entreprises et organisations essentielles, divisées en 11 catégories principales comme les arts et la culture, l'éducation, le gouvernement, les télécommunications et les médias.

Recruteurs—Les principales agences de recrutement partout au Canada, selon leur portée nationale et provinciale.

Emplois d'été—Les occasions d'emploi d'été, à l'échelle nationale et régionale; des agences gouvernementales aux camps d'été.

Sites Web professionnels et d'emplois—Comprend les plateformes d'embauche et d'offres d'emploi, divisées par industrie, outils d'embauche et les ressources par type d'emploi et communautés précises, notamment les Autochtones, nouveaux Canadiens, personnes handicapées, femmes et jeunes.

GREY HOUSE PUBLISHING CANADA

Pour obtenir plus d'information, veuillez contacter Grey House Publishing Canada

par tél. : 1 866 433-4739 ou 416 644-6479 par téléc. : 416 644-1904 | info@greyhouse.ca | www.greyhouse.ca

Health Guide Canada

An Informative Handbook on Health Services in Canada

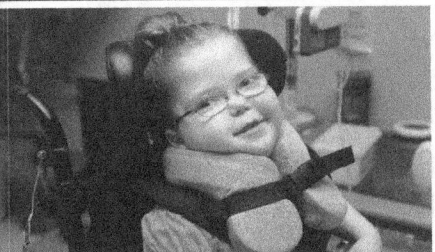  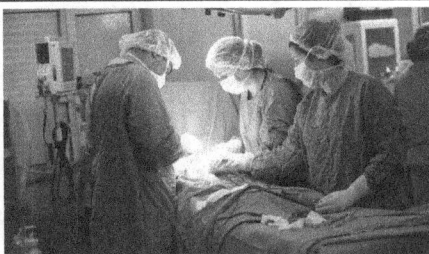

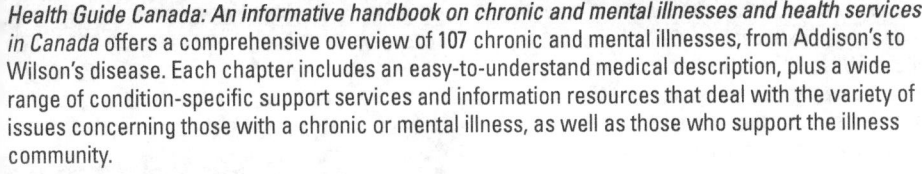

Health Guide Canada: An informative handbook on chronic and mental illnesses and health services in Canada offers a comprehensive overview of 107 chronic and mental illnesses, from Addison's to Wilson's disease. Each chapter includes an easy-to-understand medical description, plus a wide range of condition-specific support services and information resources that deal with the variety of issues concerning those with a chronic or mental illness, as well as those who support the illness community.

Health Guide Canada contains thousands of ways to deal with the many aspects of chronic or mental health disorder. It includes associations, government agencies, libraries and resource centres, educational facilities, hospitals and publications. In addition to chapters dealing with specific chronic or mental conditions, there is a chapter relevant to the health industry in general, as well as others dealing with charitable foundations, death and bereavement groups, homeopathic medicine, indigenous issues and sports for the disabled.

Specific sections include:

- Educational Material
- Section I: Chronic & Mental Illnesses
- Section II: General Resources
- Section III: Appendices
- Section IV: Statistics

Each listing will provide a description, address (including website, email address and social media links, if possible) and executives' names and titles, as well as a number of details specific to that type of organization.

In addition to patients and families, hospital and medical centre personnel can find the support they need in their work or study. *Health Guide Canada* is full of resources crucial for people with chronic illness as they transition from diagnosis to home, home to work, and work to community life.

PRINT OR ONLINE—QUICK AND EASY ACCESS TO ALL THE INFORMATION YOU NEED!

Available in softcover print or electronically via the web, *Health Guide Canada* provides instant access to the people you need and the facts you want every time. Whereas the print edition is verified and updated annually, ongoing changes are added to the web version on a regular basis. The web version allows you to narrow your search by using index fields such as name or type of organization, subject, location, contact name or title and postal code.

HEALTH GUIDE CANADA HELPS YOU FIND WHAT YOU NEED WITH THESE VALUABLE SOURCING TOOLS!

Entry Name Index—An alphabetical list of all entries, providing a quick and easy way to access any listing in this edition.

Tabs—Main sections are tabbed for easy look-up. Headers on each page make it easy to locate the data you need.

Create your own contact lists! Online subscribers have the option to instantly generate their own contact lists and export them into spreadsheets for further use—a great alternative to high cost list broker services.

GREY HOUSE PUBLISHING CANADA

For more information please contact Grey House Publishing Canada

Tel.: (866)-433-4739 or (416) 644-6479 Fax: (416) 644-1904 | info@greyhouse.ca | www.greyhouse.ca

Guide canadien de la santé

Un manuel informatif au sujet des services en santé au Canada

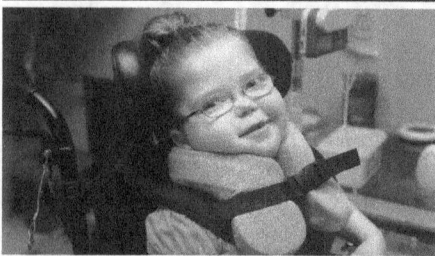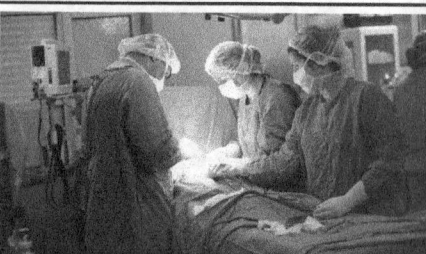

Le *Guide canadien de la santé : un manuel informatif au sujet des maladies chroniques et mentales de même que des services en santé au Canada* donne un aperçu exhaustif de 107 maladies chroniques et mentales, de la maladie d'Addison à celle de Wilson. Chaque chapitre comprend une description médicale facile à comprendre, une vaste gamme de services de soutien particuliers à l'état et des ressources documentaires qui portent sur diverses questions relatives aux personnes qui sont aux prises avec une maladie chronique ou mentale et à ceux qui soutiennent la communauté liée à cette maladie.

Le *Guide canadien de la santé* contient des milliers de moyens pour composer avec divers aspects d'une maladie chronique ou d'un problème de santé mentale. Il comprend des associations, des organismes gouvernementaux, des bibliothèques et des centres de documentation, des services d'éducation, des hôpitaux et des publications. En plus des chapitres qui portent sur des états chroniques ou mentaux, un chapitre traite de l'industrie de la santé en général; d'autres abordent les fondations qui réalisent des rêves, les groupes de soutien axés sur le décès et le deuil, la médecine homéopathique, les questions autochtones et les sports pour les personnes handicapées. Les sections incluent

- Matériel didactique
- Section I : Les maladies chroniques ou mentales
- Section II : Les ressources génériques
- Section III : Les annexes
- Section IV : Les statistiques

Chaque entrée comprend une description, une adresse (y compris le site Web, le courriel et les liens des médias sociaux, lorsque possible), les noms et titres des directeurs de même que plusieurs détails particuliers à ce type d'organisme.

Les membres du personnel des hôpitaux et des centres médicaux peuvent trouver, au même titre que parents et familles, le soutien dont ils ont besoin dans le cadre de leur travail ou de leurs études. Le *Guide canadien de la santé* est rempli de ressources capitales pour les personnes qui souffrent d'une maladie chronique alors qu'elles passent du diagnostic au retour à la maison, de la maison au travail et du travail à la vie au sein de la communauté.

OFFERT EN FORMAT PAPIER OU EN LIGNE—UN ACCÈS RAPIDE ET FACILE À TOUS LES RENSEIGNEMENTS DONT VOUS AVEZ BESOIN!

Offert sous couverture souple ou en format électronique grâce au web, le *Guide canadien de la santé* donne invariablement un accès instantané aux personnes et aux faits dont vous avez besoin. Si la version imprimée est vérifiée et mise à jour annuellement, des changements continus sont apportés mensuellement à la base de données en ligne. Servez-vous de la version en ligne afin de circonscrire vos recherches grâce à des champs spéciaux de l'index comme le nom de l'organisation ou son type, le sujet, l'emplacement, le nom de la personne-ressource ou son titre et le code postal.

LE GUIDE CANADIEN DE LA SANTÉ VOUS AIDERA À TROUVER CE DONT VOUS AVEZ BESOIN GRÂCE À CES OUTILS DE REPÉRAGE PRÉCIEUX!

Répertoire nominatif—une list alphabétique offrant un moyen rapide et facile d'accéder à toute liste de cette edition.

Onglets—les sections principals possèdent un onglet pour une consultation facile. Les notes en tête de chaque page vous aident à trouver les données voulues.

Créez vos propres listes! Les abonnés au service en ligne peuvent générer instantanément leurs propres listes de contacts et les exporter en format feuille de calcul pour une utilisation approfondie – une solution de rechange géniale aux services dispendieux d'un commissionnaire en publipostage.

GREY HOUSE PUBLISHING CANADA

Pour obtenir plus d'information, veuillez contacter Grey House Publishing Canada

par tél. : 1 866 433-4739 ou 416 644-6479 par téléc. : 416 644-1904 | info@greyhouse.ca | www.greyhouse.ca

Cannabis Canada

Cannabis Canada is a one-of-a-kind resource covering all aspects of this growing industry. Featuring a wide-ranging collection of reports and statistics, you'll find everything you need to know about this now-legal marketplace, including need-to-know international information.

This first edition includes the State of the Cannabis Industry 2019, exploring the history of marijuana, current regulations, insightful reports, and listings of upcoming trade shows and conferences.

Readers will also discover the brand new Cannabis Industry Buyer's Guide, featuring everything from Licensed Producers to consulting firms, equipment manufacturers to security firms, and more. All listings include specialized fields that go far beyond name and address, and boast crucial, current key contacts.

ADDITIONAL RESOURCES INCLUDE:

- Industry associations
- Financial and venture capital firms
- Law firms
- Government agencies
- Post-secondary schools
- Healthcare and treatment facilities
- Publications

Rounding out the book are Appendices containing detailed statistics, and multiple Indexes to help you navigate this comprehensive body of work.

A CLOSER LOOK AT WHAT'S INSIDE:

State of the Cannabis Industry 2019—A large, detailed section containing everything from the history of cannabis to current legal regulations. Objective reports on all aspects of the industry are also included, as are listings of Canadian and foreign trade shows and conferences.

Cannabis Industry Buyer's Guide—In-depth company listings covering all essential aspects of the industry. This is your go-to source for crucial contacts you need to expand your business, grow your network, or answer your research questions.

Associations—Everything from professional associations to health organizations, including international bodies essential to the industry.

Finance and Venture Capital—All the information you need on insurance, banking, and industry investment.

Law Firms—Find out which law firms offer services in the cannabis space, right down to specific lawyers' specialties!

Government—Federal and provincial departments and agencies that regulate and oversee the cannabis industry in Canada. This is your source for the best contacts in government.

Education—Colleges, universities and specialized schools that offer or are planning to offer cannabis-related courses.

Health—Locations of specialized health facilities, including mental health and addiction treatment programs across the country.

Publications—Listings of Canadian and foreign magazines, both in print and online, serving members of the cannabis community.

AVAILABLE ONLINE!

The *Canadian Cannabis Guide* is also available online on Canada's Information Resource Centre (CIRC). Thousands of companies and contacts are just a click away! Search by name or type of organization, subject, location, contact name or title and postal code. Export results and create mailing lists with this easy-to-use online database – an essential tool for researchers, students, marketing professionals and industry experts alike.

GREY HOUSE PUBLISHING CANADA

For more information please contact Grey House Publishing Canada

Tel.: (866)-433-4739 or (416) 644-6479 Fax: (416) 644-1904 | info@greyhouse.ca | www.greyhouse.ca

Cannabis au Canada

Cannabis du Canada est une ressource unique qui porte sur tous les aspects de cette industrie en pleine expansion. Il comprend des entrées exhaustives ainsi qu'une vaste gamme de rapports et de statistiques : vous y trouverez tout ce qu'il y a à savoir sur ce marché désormais légal, y compris des renseignements à portée internationale.

La première édition inclut le document l'État de l'industrie du cannabis 2019 sur l'histoire de la marijuana, les réglementations en vigueur ainsi que des rapports éclairants et des annonces de salons commerciaux et de congrès à venir.

Les lecteurs découvriront également le tout nouveau guide de l'acheteur de l'industrie du cannabis qui couvre un vaste éventail de sujets : des producteurs autorisés aux sociétés de conseil en passant par les sociétés de sécurité et plus encore. Toutes les entrées comprennent des champs spécialisés qui vont bien plus loin que le nom et l'adresse : elles regorgent de contacts essentiels et actuels.

PARMI LES RESSOURCES SUPPLÉMENTAIRES, MENTIONNONS :

- Associations de l'industrie
- Sociétés financières et de capital de risque
- Cabinets d'avocats
- Agences gouvernementales
- Établissements de soins de santé et de traitement
- Publications

Des annexes avec des statistiques détaillées et plusieurs index vous aident à parcourir cet ouvrage exhaustif.

UN EXAMEN PLUS APPROFONDI DU CONTENU :

L'état de l'industrie du cannabis en 2019—Une section détaillée volumineuse : de l'histoire du cannabis à la réglementation actuelle. S'y trouvent également des rapports objectifs portant sur tous les aspects de l'industrie, des entrées relatives aux salons professionnels ainsi qu'aux conférences, au Canada et à l'étranger.

Guide de l'acheteur—Industrie du cannabis : entrées commerciales exhaustives sur tous les aspects essentiels de l'industrie. Il constitue votre source d'information par excellence de personnes-ressources essentielles à l'expansion de votre entreprise et de votre réseau ou à la recherche de réponses.

Associations—Des associations professionnelles aux organismes de santé, y compris les organismes internationaux essentiels à l'industrie.

Finances et capital-risque—Toute l'information dont vous avez besoin au sujet de l'assurance, des services banquiers et du secteur des placements.

Cabinets d'avocats—Découvrez les cabinets d'avocats qui offrent des services reliés aux enjeux du cannabis, jusqu'aux domaines de spécialité d'avocats précis!

Gouvernement—Les agences et ministères fédéraux et provinciaux qui réglementent et surveillent l'industrie du cannabis au Canada. Cette source vous offre les meilleurs contacts à l'échelle du gouvernement.

Enseignement—Collèges, universités et écoles spécialisées qui offrent des cours ayant trait au cannabis ou qui comptent le faire.

Santé—L'emplacement d'établissements de santé spécialisés, notamment en santé mentale et en programmes de traitement des dépendances, partout au pays.

Publications—Listes de magazines, canadiens et étrangers, imprimés et en ligne, que peuvent consulter les participants du secteur du cannabis.

OFFERT EN LIGNE!

Le *Guide canadien du cannabis* sera également offert en ligne dans le Centre de documentation du Canada (CIRC). Un seul clic vous donne accès à des milliers d'entreprises et de personnes-ressources! Effectuez une recherche par nom ou par type d'organisation, par sujet, par emplacement, par code postal, par personne-ressource ou par titre. Exportez les résultats pour créer des listes d'envoi grâce à cette base de données en ligne conviviale, un outil essentiel tant pour les chercheurs, étudiants, professionnels du marketing que pour les experts de l'industrie.

GREY HOUSE PUBLISHING CANADA

Pour obtenir plus d'information, veuillez contacter Grey House Publishing Canada par tél. : 1 866 433-4739 ou 416 644-6479 par téléc. : 416 644-1904 | info@greyhouse.ca | www.greyhouse.ca